2018
Harris
Indiana
Industrial Directory

MERGENT

Exclusive Provider of
Dun & Bradstreet Library Solutions

dun & bradstreet

HOOVERS™

First Research

HARRIS INFOSOURCE™

Published November 2018 next update November 2019

Publisher

Mergent Inc.
444 Madison Ave
New York, NY 10022

©Mergent Inc All Rights Reserved
2018 Mergent Business Press
ISSN 1080-2614
ISBN 978-1-68200-776-1

MERGENT
BUSINESS PRESS
by FTSE Russell

TABLE OF CONTENTS

SUMMARY OF CONTENTS

Number of Companies 14,475
Number of Decision Makers 27,218
Minimum Number of Employees 2

EXPLANATORY NOTES

How to Cross-Reference in This Directory

Sequential Entry Numbers. Each establishment in the Geographic Section is numbered sequentially (G-0000). The number assigned to each establishment is referred to as its "entry number." To make cross-referencing easier, each listing in the Geographic, SIC, Alphabetic and Product Sections includes the establishment's entry number. To facilitate locating an entry in the Geographic Section, the entry numbers for the first listing on the left page and the last listing on the right page are printed at the top of the page next to the city name.

Source Suggestions Welcome

Although all known sources were used to compile this directory, it is possible that companies were inadvertently omitted. Your assistance in calling attention to such omissions would be greatly appreciated. A special form on the facing page will help you in the reporting process.

Analysis

Every effort has been made to contact all firms to verify their information. The one exception to this rule is the annual sales figure, which is considered by many companies to be confidential information. Therefore, estimated sales have been calculated by multiplying the nationwide average sales per employee for the firm's major SIC/NAICS code by the firm's number of employees. Nationwide averages for sales per employee by SIC/NAICS codes are provided by the U.S. Department of Commerce and are updated annually. All sales—sales (est)—have been estimated by this method. The exceptions are parent companies (PA), division headquarters (DH) and headquarter locations (HQ) which may include an actual corporate sales figure—sales (corporate-wide) if available.

Types of Companies

Descriptive and statistical data are included for companies in the entire state. These comprise manufacturers, machine shops, fabricators, assemblers and printers. Also identified are corporate offices in the state.

Employment Data

The employment figure shown in the Geographic Section includes male and female employees and embraces all levels of the company: administrative, clerical, sales and maintenance. This figure is for the facility listed and does not include other plants or offices. It should be recognized that these figures represent an approximate year-round average. These employment figures are broken into codes A through G and used in the Product and SIC Sections to further help you in qualifying a company. Be sure to check the footnotes on the bottom of pages for the code breakdowns.

Standard Industrial Classification (SIC)

The Standard Industrial Classification (SIC) system used in this directory was developed by the federal government for use in classifying establishments by the type of activity they are engaged in. The SIC classifications used in this directory are from the 1987 edition published by the U.S. Government's Office of Management and Budget. The SIC system separates all activities into broad industrial divisions (e.g., manufacturing, mining, retail trade). It further subdivides each division. The range of manufacturing industry classes extends from two-digit codes (major industry group) to four-digit codes (product).

For example:

Industry Breakdown	Code	Industry, Product, etc.
*Major industry group	20	Food and kindred products
Industry group	203	Canned and frozen foods
*Industry	2033	Fruits and vegetables, etc.

*Classifications used in this directory

Only two-digit and four-digit codes are used in this directory.

Arrangement

1. The **Geographic Section** contains complete in-depth corporate data. This section is sorted by cities listed in alphabetical order and companies listed alphabetically within each city. A County/City Index for referencing cities within counties precedes this section.

IMPORTANT NOTICE: It is a violation of both federal and state law to transmit an unsolicited advertisement to a facsimile machine. Any user of this product that violates such laws may be subject to civil and criminal penalties, which may exceed $500 for each transmission of an unsolicited facsimile. Mergent Inc. provides fax numbers for lawful purposes only and expressly forbids the use of these numbers in any unlawful manner.

2. The **Standard Industrial Classification (SIC) Section** lists companies under approximately 500 four-digit SIC codes. An alphabetical and a numerical index precedes this section. A company can be listed under several codes. The codes are in numerical order with companies listed alphabetically under each code.

3. The **Alphabetic Section** lists all companies with their full physical or mailing addresses and telephone number.

4. The **Product Section** lists companies under unique Harris categories. An index preceding this section lists all product categories in alphabetical order. Companies can be listed under several categories.

USER'S GUIDE TO LISTINGS

GEOGRAPHIC SECTION

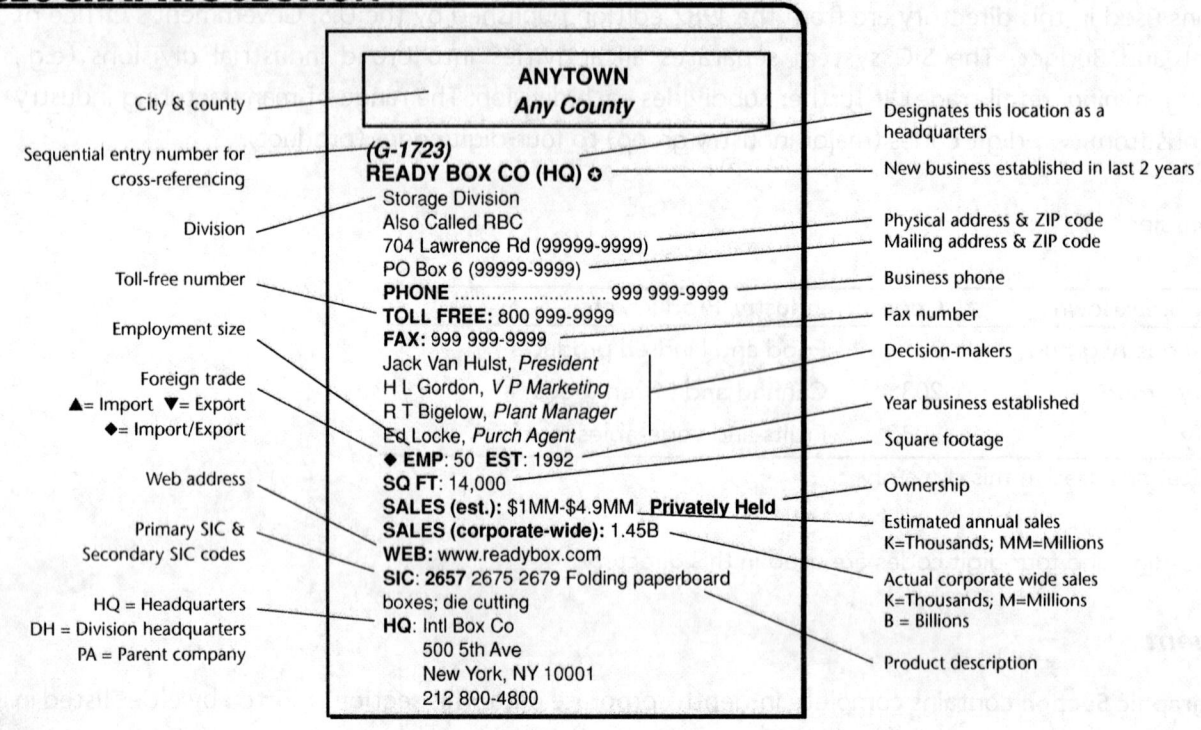

City & county

Sequential entry number for cross-referencing

Division

Toll-free number

Employment size

Foreign trade
▲= Import ▼= Export
◆= Import/Export

Web address

Primary SIC & Secondary SIC codes

HQ = Headquarters
DH = Division headquarters
PA = Parent company

ANYTOWN
Any County

(G-1723)
READY BOX CO (HQ) ✪
Storage Division
Also Called RBC
704 Lawrence Rd (99999-9999)
PO Box 6 (99999-9999)
PHONE 999 999-9999
TOLL FREE: 800 999-9999
FAX: 999 999-9999
Jack Van Hulst, *President*
H L Gordon, *V P Marketing*
R T Bigelow, *Plant Manager*
Ed Locke, *Purch Agent*
◆ **EMP:** 50 **EST:** 1992
SQ FT: 14,000
SALES (est.): $1MM-$4.9MM **Privately Held**
SALES (corporate-wide): 1.45B
WEB: www.readybox.com
SIC: 2657 2675 2679 Folding paperboard boxes; die cutting
HQ: Intl Box Co
    500 5th Ave
    New York, NY 10001
    212 800-4800

Designates this location as a headquarters

New business established in last 2 years

Physical address & ZIP code
Mailing address & ZIP code

Business phone

Fax number

Decision-makers

Year business established

Square footage

Ownership

Estimated annual sales
K=Thousands; MM=Millions

Actual corporate wide sales
K=Thousands; M=Millions
B = Billions

Product description

SIC SECTION

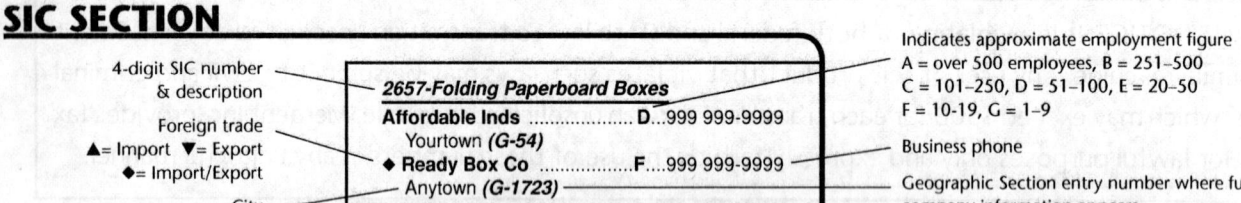

4-digit SIC number & description

Foreign trade
▲= Import ▼= Export
◆= Import/Export

City

2657-Folding Paperboard Boxes
Affordable Inds .... **D**...999 999-9999
  Yourtown *(G-54)*
◆ **Ready Box Co** .... **F**....999 999-9999
  Anytown *(G-1723)*

Indicates approximate employment figure
A = over 500 employees, B = 251–500
C = 101–250, D = 51–100, E = 20–50
F = 10-19, G = 1–9

Business phone

Geographic Section entry number where full company information appears

ALPHABETIC SECTION

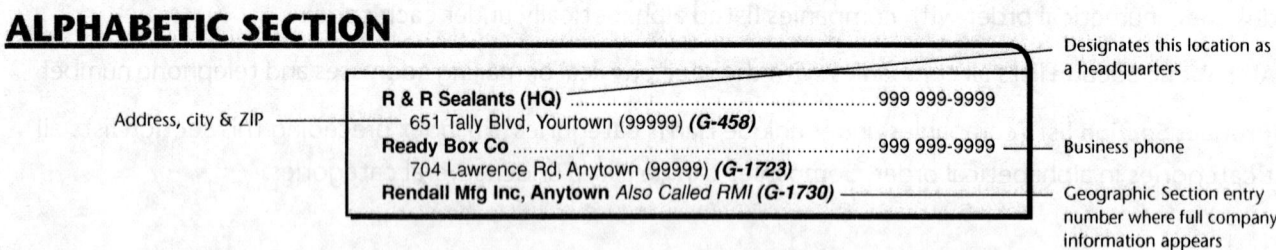

Address, city & ZIP

R & R Sealants (HQ) 999 999-9999
    651 Tally Blvd, Yourtown (99999) *(G-458)*
Ready Box Co 999 999-9999
    704 Lawrence Rd, Anytown (99999) *(G-1723)*
Rendall Mfg Inc, Anytown *Also Called RMI (G-1730)*

Designates this location as a headquarters

Business phone

Geographic Section entry number where full company information appears

PRODUCT SECTION

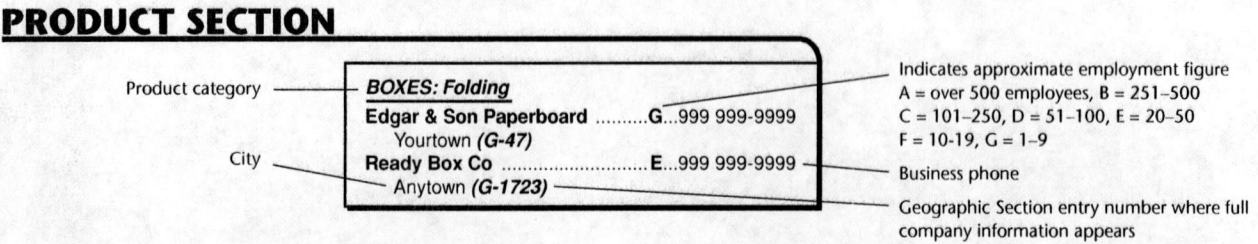

Product category

City

BOXES: Folding
Edgar & Son Paperboard ....**G**...999 999-9999
  Yourtown *(G-47)*
Ready Box Co ....**E**...999 999-9999
  Anytown *(G-1723)*

Indicates approximate employment figure
A = over 500 employees, B = 251–500
C = 101–250, D = 51–100, E = 20–50
F = 10-19, G = 1–9

Business phone

Geographic Section entry number where full company information appears

GEOGRAPHIC SECTION

Companies sorted by city in alphabetical order

In-depth company data listed

STANDARD INDUSTRIAL CLASSIFICATIONS

Alphabetical index of classifcation descriptions

Numerical index of classifcation descriptions

Companies sorted by SIC product groupings

ALPHABETIC SECTION

Company listings in alphabetical order

PRODUCT INDEX

Product categories listed in alphabetical order

PRODUCT SECTION

Companies sorted by product and manufacturing service classifications

GEOGRAPHIC

SIC

ALPHABETIC

PRDT INDEX

PRODUCT

Indiana
County Map

	ENTRY #		ENTRY #		ENTRY #		ENTRY #		ENTRY #

Adams
Berne .... (G-606)
Decatur .... (G-2363)
Geneva .... (G-5133)
Monroe .... (G-10181)
Pleasant Mills .... (G-11658)

Allen
Fort Wayne .... (G-4031)
Grabill .... (G-5358)
Harlan .... (G-5966)
Hoagland .... (G-6062)
Huntertown .... (G-6134)
Leo .... (G-9239)
Monroeville .... (G-10190)
New Haven .... (G-10926)
Spencerville .... (G-13042)
Woodburn .... (G-14380)
Yoder .... (G-14397)
Zanesville .... (G-14413)

Bartholomew
Columbus .... (G-1849)
Elizabethtown .... (G-2651)
Hope .... (G-6110)
Jonesville .... (G-8447)

Benton
Ambia .... (G-55)
Boswell .... (G-939)
Earl Park .... (G-2513)
Fowler .... (G-4794)
Otterbein .... (G-11417)
Oxford .... (G-11431)
Templeton .... (G-13178)

Blackford
Hartford City .... (G-5976)
Montpelier .... (G-10289)

Boone
Jamestown .... (G-8230)
Lebanon .... (G-9166)
Thorntown .... (G-13375)
Whitestown .... (G-14249)
Zionsville .... (G-14414)

Brown
Nashville .... (G-10712)

Carroll
Bringhurst .... (G-1037)
Burlington .... (G-1209)
Camden .... (G-1273)
Cutler .... (G-2328)
Delphi .... (G-2414)
Flora .... (G-3992)

Cass
Galveston .... (G-4993)
Logansport .... (G-9319)
Royal Center .... (G-12212)
Twelve Mile .... (G-13450)
Walton .... (G-13815)

Clark
Borden .... (G-926)
Charlestown .... (G-1556)
Clarksville .... (G-1671)
Henryville .... (G-6031)
Jeffersonville........... (G-8315)

Marysville.............. (G-9649)
Memphis .... (G-9683)
Nabb .... (G-10639)
New Washington ...... (G-11012)
Otisco .... (G-11416)
Sellersburg .... (G-12387)

Clay
Bowling Green .... (G-952)
Brazil .... (G-953)
Carbon .... (G-1292)
Centerpoint .... (G-1538)
Clay City .... (G-1701)
Coalmont .... (G-1745)
Harmony .... (G-5975)
Knightsville .... (G-8561)
Staunton .... (G-13072)

Clinton
Colfax .... (G-1756)
Frankfort .... (G-4818)
Kirklin .... (G-8547)
Michigantown.......... (G-9864)
Mulberry .... (G-10416)
Rossville .... (G-12209)

Crawford
English .... (G-3312)
Leavenworth .... (G-9163)
Marengo .... (G-9504)
Milltown .... (G-9976)

Daviess
Cannelburg .... (G-1283)
Elnora .... (G-3286)
Montgomery........... (G-10213)
Odon .... (G-11319)
Plainville .... (G-11654)
Washington............ (G-13978)

Dearborn
Aurora .... (G-368)
Dillsboro.............. (G-2463)
Greendale .... (G-5482)
Guilford .... (G-5796)
Lawrenceburg.......... (G-9130)
Moores Hill............ (G-10296)
West Harrison .... (G-14039)

Decatur
Burney .... (G-1212)
Greensburg .... (G-5588)
New Point .... (G-11003)
Saint Paul .... (G-12277)
Westport .... (G-14208)

Dekalb
Ashley................. (G-283)
Auburn .... (G-311)
Butler .... (G-1221)
Corunna .... (G-2083)
Garrett .... (G-4995)
Saint Joe .... (G-12252)
Waterloo .... (G-14009)

Delaware
Albany .... (G-10)
Daleville .... (G-2337)
Eaton .... (G-2581)
Gaston .... (G-5129)

Muncie .... (G-10420)
Selma .... (G-12422)
Yorktown .... (G-14400)

Dubois
Birdseye .... (G-634)
Celestine .... (G-1535)
Dubois .... (G-2475)
Ferdinand .... (G-3845)
Holland .... (G-6104)
Huntingburg........... (G-6150)
Ireland .... (G-8229)
Jasper .... (G-8235)
Saint Anthony .... (G-12245)

Elkhart
Bristol .... (G-1040)
Elkhart .... (G-2653)
Goshen .... (G-5162)
Middlebury .... (G-9866)
Millersburg .... (G-9968)
Nappanee .... (G-10644)
New Paris .... (G-10975)
Wakarusa .... (G-13775)

Fayette
Connersville........... (G-2038)

Floyd
Floyds Knobs .... (G-4006)
Georgetown .... (G-5140)
Greenville .... (G-5646)
New Albany .... (G-10740)

Fountain
Attica .... (G-296)
Covington .... (G-2118)
Kingman .... (G-8532)
Veedersburg .... (G-13642)

Franklin
Brookville .... (G-1110)
Cedar Grove .... (G-1522)
Laurel .... (G-9127)
Metamora .... (G-9762)
Oldenburg............. (G-11346)

Fulton
Akron .... (G-1)
Kewanna .... (G-8525)
Rochester .... (G-12113)

Gibson
Fort Branch .... (G-4025)
Francisco .... (G-4816)
Haubstadt .... (G-5997)
Hazleton .... (G-6009)
Oakland City .... (G-11306)
Owensville .... (G-11426)
Patoka .... (G-11465)
Princeton .... (G-11863)

Grant
Fairmount .... (G-3828)
Gas City .... (G-5118)
Jonesboro............ (G-8444)
Marion .... (G-9506)
Matthews .... (G-9652)
Sims .... (G-12683)
Swayzee .... (G-13123)
Upland .... (G-13468)

Van Buren............... (G-13639)

Greene
Bloomfield............. (G-635)
Jasonville .... (G-8234)
Linton .... (G-9306)
Lyons .... (G-9439)
Newberry .... (G-11015)
Owensburg .... (G-11423)
Solsberry .... (G-12684)
Switz City .... (G-13126)
Worthington .... (G-14393)

Hamilton
Arcadia .... (G-261)
Atlanta .... (G-293)
Carmel .... (G-1299)
Cicero .... (G-1661)
Fishers .... (G-3865)
Indianapolis .... (G-6262)
Noblesville .... (G-11059)
Sheridan .... (G-12587)
Westfield .... (G-14131)

Hancock
Fishers .... (G-3987)
Fortville .... (G-4766)
Greenfield .... (G-5497)
Maxwell .... (G-9660)
McCordsville .... (G-9664)
New Palestine......... (G-10965)
Wilkinson .... (G-14279)

Harrison
Central .... (G-1545)
Corydon .... (G-2086)
Crandall .... (G-2124)
Depauw .... (G-2456)
Elizabeth .... (G-2641)
Laconia .... (G-8835)
Lanesville .... (G-9101)
Mauckport .... (G-9653)
New Salisbury......... (G-11007)
Palmyra .... (G-11435)
Ramsey .... (G-11892)

Hendricks
Avon .... (G-423)
Brownsburg .... (G-1133)
Clayton .... (G-1707)
Danville .... (G-2343)
Lizton .... (G-9316)
Pittsboro .... (G-11582)
Plainfield .... (G-11590)

Henry
Kennard .... (G-8516)
Knightstown .... (G-8550)
Lewisville .... (G-9248)
Middletown .... (G-9933)
Mooreland .... (G-10295)
Mount Summit .... (G-10378)
New Castle .... (G-10890)
Shirley .... (G-12661)
Spiceland .... (G-13053)
Springport .... (G-13059)

Howard
Greentown .... (G-5643)
Kokomo .... (G-8589)

Russiaville .... (G-12240)

Huntington
Andrews .... (G-185)
Huntington .... (G-6184)
Roanoke .... (G-12098)
Warren .... (G-13828)

Jackson
Brownstown .... (G-1179)
Crothersville .... (G-2213)
Freetown .... (G-4950)
Medora .... (G-9680)
Norman .... (G-11202)
Seymour .... (G-12426)
Vallonia .... (G-13478)

Jasper
Demotte .... (G-2431)
Fair Oaks .... (G-3817)
Remington .... (G-11904)
Rensselaer .... (G-11911)
Wheatfield .... (G-14222)

Jay
Bryant .... (G-1199)
Dunkirk .... (G-2483)
Pennville .... (G-11513)
Portland .... (G-11807)
Redkey .... (G-11896)

Jefferson
Canaan .... (G-1281)
Deputy .... (G-2458)
Dupont .... (G-2491)
Hanover .... (G-5959)
Madison .... (G-9441)

Jennings
Butlerville .... (G-1247)
Commiskey .... (G-2036)
North Vernon .... (G-11247)
Paris Crossing .... (G-11460)
Vernon .... (G-13651)

Johnson
Bargersville .... (G-478)
Edinburgh .... (G-2593)
Franklin .... (G-4862)
Greenwood .... (G-5657)
New Whiteland .... (G-11013)
Nineveh .... (G-11057)
Trafalgar .... (G-13434)
Whiteland .... (G-14233)

Knox
Bicknell .... (G-631)
Bruceville .... (G-1197)
Monroe City .... (G-10188)
Oaktown .... (G-11317)
Vincennes .... (G-13668)
Wheatland .... (G-14231)

Kosciusko
Atwood .... (G-310)
Burket .... (G-1208)
Claypool .... (G-1706)
Etna Green .... (G-3320)
Leesburg .... (G-9233)
Mentone .... (G-9684)
Milford .... (G-9948)

	ENTRY #
North Webster	(G-11288)
Pierceton	(G-11572)
Sidney	(G-12674)
Silver Lake	(G-12675)
Syracuse	(G-13128)
Warsaw	(G-13834)
Winona Lake	(G-14349)

La Porte

Michigan City	(G-9763)

Lagrange

Howe	(G-6120)
Lagrange	(G-9030)
Shipshewana	(G-12602)
South Milford	(G-12994)
Stroh	(G-13077)
Topeka	(G-13410)
Wolcottville	(G-14368)

Lake

Cedar Lake	(G-1524)
Crown Point	(G-2222)
Dyer	(G-2492)
East Chicago	(G-2514)
Gary	(G-5025)
Griffith	(G-5760)
Hammond	(G-5833)
Highland	(G-6034)
Hobart	(G-6068)
Lake Station	(G-9074)
Leroy	(G-9247)
Lowell	(G-9399)
Merrillville	(G-9690)
Munster	(G-10590)
Saint John	(G-12259)
Schererville	(G-12312)
Schneider	(G-12354)
Shelby	(G-12515)
Whiting	(G-14266)

Laporte

Hanna	(G-5958)
Kingsbury	(G-8535)
Kingsford Heights	(G-8546)
La Crosse	(G-8719)
La Porte	(G-8725)
Long Beach	(G-9376)
Michigan City	(G-9764)
Rolling Prairie	(G-12184)
Trail Creek	(G-13440)
Union Mills	(G-13463)
Wanatah	(G-13819)
Westville	(G-14213)

Lawrence

Bedford	(G-526)
Heltonville	(G-6026)
Mitchell	(G-10154)
Springville	(G-13060)
Williams	(G-14281)

Madison

Alexandria	(G-37)
Anderson	(G-56)
Chesterfield	(G-1586)
Elwood	(G-3293)
Frankton	(G-4943)
Lapel	(G-9119)
Markleville	(G-9585)
Pendleton	(G-11482)
Summitville	(G-13099)

Marion

Beech Grove	(G-591)
Clermont	(G-1711)
Indianapolis	(G-6284)
Speedway	(G-13011)

Marshall

Argos	(G-272)
Bourbon	(G-942)
Bremen	(G-981)
Culver	(G-2324)
Lapaz	(G-9116)
Plymouth	(G-11659)
Tippecanoe	(G-13380)

Martin

Crane	(G-2125)
Loogootee	(G-9380)
Shoals	(G-12664)

Miami

Bunker Hill	(G-1205)
Converse	(G-2079)
Denver	(G-2453)
Macy	(G-9440)
Peru	(G-11514)

Monroe

Bloomington	(G-650)
Ellettsville	(G-3272)
Stinesville	(G-13075)

Montgomery

Crawfordsville	(G-2131)
Darlington	(G-2359)
Ladoga	(G-8838)
Linden	(G-9303)
New Market	(G-10963)
New Richmond	(G-11004)
New Ross	(G-11005)
Waveland	(G-14028)

Morgan

Camby	(G-1264)
Martinsville	(G-9594)
Monrovia	(G-10201)
Mooresville	(G-10300)
Morgantown	(G-10346)
Paragon	(G-11458)

Newton

Brook	(G-1098)
Goodland	(G-5156)
Kentland	(G-8517)
Lake Village	(G-9082)
Morocco	(G-10359)

Noble

Albion	(G-14)
Avilla	(G-400)
Brimfield	(G-1036)
Cromwell	(G-2207)
Kendallville	(G-8450)
Kimmell	(G-8529)
Laotto	(G-9104)
Ligonier	(G-9274)
Rome City	(G-12197)
Wawaka	(G-14029)
Wolflake	(G-14379)

Ohio

Rising Sun	(G-12085)

Orange

French Lick	(G-4983)
Orleans	(G-11361)
Paoli	(G-11442)
West Baden Springs	(G-14034)

Owen

Coal City	(G-1741)
Freedom	(G-4946)
Gosport	(G-5349)
Poland	(G-11743)
Quincy	(G-11890)
Spencer	(G-13017)

Parke

Bloomingdale	(G-647)
Marshall	(G-9590)
Mecca	(G-9678)
Montezuma	(G-10209)
Rockville	(G-12174)
Rosedale	(G-12203)

Perry

Bristow	(G-1094)
Cannelton	(G-1286)
Derby	(G-2462)
Magnet	(G-9502)
Mount Pleasant	(G-10377)
Rome	(G-12196)
Saint Croix	(G-12251)
Tell City	(G-13155)

Pike

Otwell	(G-11422)
Petersburg	(G-11561)
Stendal	(G-13073)
Velpen	(G-13649)
Winslow	(G-14357)

Porter

Beverly Shores	(G-630)
Burns Harbor	(G-1214)
Chesterton	(G-1590)
Hebron	(G-6011)
Kouts	(G-8717)
Portage	(G-11747)
Porter	(G-11803)
Valparaiso	(G-13479)

Posey

Cynthiana	(G-2329)
Mount Vernon	(G-10380)
New Harmony	(G-10924)
Poseyville	(G-11856)
Wadesville	(G-13770)

Pulaski

Francesville	(G-4808)
Medaryville	(G-9679)
Monterey	(G-10207)
Star City	(G-13069)
Winamac	(G-14301)

Putnam

Bainbridge	(G-473)
Cloverdale	(G-1723)
Coatesville	(G-1746)
Greencastle	(G-5453)
Reelsville	(G-11900)
Roachdale	(G-12093)
Russellville	(G-12238)

Randolph

Farmland	(G-3840)
Lynn	(G-9426)
Modoc	(G-10173)
Parker City	(G-11462)

Ridgeville

Ridgeville	(G-12080)
Union City	(G-13452)
Winchester	(G-14324)

Ripley

Batesville	(G-488)
Cross Plains	(G-2212)
Friendship	(G-4991)
Holton	(G-6107)
Milan	(G-9944)
Napoleon	(G-10641)
Osgood	(G-11388)
Sunman	(G-13109)
Versailles	(G-13653)

Rush

Arlington	(G-281)
Carthage	(G-1512)
Falmouth	(G-3836)
Homer	(G-6109)
Manilla	(G-9503)
Mays	(G-9663)
Milroy	(G-9977)
Rushville	(G-12217)

Scott

Austin	(G-394)
Lexington	(G-9249)
Scottsburg	(G-12355)
Underwood	(G-13451)

Shelby

Boggstown	(G-899)
Fairland	(G-3819)
Flat Rock	(G-3991)
Fountaintown	(G-4788)
Gwynneville	(G-5800)
Morristown	(G-10365)
Shelbyville	(G-12517)
Waldron	(G-13798)

Spencer

Chrisney	(G-1641)
Dale	(G-2330)
Evanston	(G-3325)
Fulda	(G-4992)
Grandview	(G-5386)
Lamar	(G-9099)
Richland	(G-11950)
Rockport	(G-12163)
Saint Meinrad	(G-12274)
Troy	(G-13445)

St. Joseph

Granger	(G-5388)
Lakeville	(G-9092)
Mishawaka	(G-9988)
New Carlisle	(G-10878)
North Liberty	(G-11215)
Notre Dame	(G-11303)
Osceola	(G-11370)
South Bend	(G-12688)
Walkerton	(G-13801)
Wyatt	(G-14396)

Starke

Grovertown	(G-5795)
Hamlet	(G-5831)
Knox	(G-8562)
North Judson	(G-11205)
San Pierre	(G-12309)

Steuben

Angola	(G-186)

Fremont / Steuben

Fremont	(G-4951)
Hamilton	(G-5818)
Hudson	(G-6132)
Orland	(G-11347)

Sullivan

Carlisle	(G-1294)
Dugger	(G-2479)
Fairbanks	(G-3818)
Farmersburg	(G-3837)
Shelburn	(G-12508)
Sullivan	(G-13078)

Switzerland

Bennington	(G-605)
Florence	(G-4004)
Patriot	(G-11467)
Vevay	(G-13660)

Tippecanoe

Battle Ground	(G-525)
Clarks Hill	(G-1670)
Colburn	(G-1752)
Dayton	(G-2362)
Lafayette	(G-8844)
Romney	(G-12202)
Stockwell	(G-13076)
West Lafayette	(G-14045)
Westpoint	(G-14204)

Tipton

Sharpsville	(G-12503)
Tipton	(G-13387)
Windfall	(G-14346)

Union

Brownsville	(G-1195)
Liberty	(G-9257)
West College Corner	(G-14037)

Vanderburgh

Evansville	(G-3326)

Vermillion

Cayuga	(G-1518)
Clinton	(G-1713)
Dana	(G-2342)
Hillsdale	(G-6061)
Newport	(G-11056)
Universal	(G-13467)

Vigo

Fontanet	(G-4024)
Pimento	(G-11580)
Riley	(G-12084)
Sandford	(G-12310)
Seelyville	(G-12386)
Terre Haute	(G-13184)
West Terre Haute	(G-14123)

Wabash

La Fontaine	(G-8722)
Lagro	(G-9072)
Laketon	(G-9090)
North Manchester	(G-11224)
Roann	(G-12097)
Urbana	(G-13476)
Wabash	(G-13719)

Warren

Pine Village	(G-11581)
State Line	(G-13071)
West Lebanon	(G-14119)
Williamsport	(G-14286)

Warrick

	ENTRY #
Boonville	(G-904)
Chandler	(G-1548)
Elberfeld	(G-2633)
Lynnville	(G-9434)
Newburgh	(G-11016)
Tennyson	(G-13179)

Washington

	ENTRY #
Campbellsburg	(G-1276)

	ENTRY #
Fredericksburg	(G-4945)
Hardinsburg	(G-5964)
Pekin	(G-11470)
Salem	(G-12281)

Wayne

	ENTRY #
Cambridge City	(G-1252)
Centerville	(G-1541)
Economy	(G-2591)
Fountain City	(G-4784)

	ENTRY #
Greens Fork	(G-5587)
Hagerstown	(G-5801)
Milton	(G-9987)
Richmond	(G-11951)
Williamsburg	(G-14283)

Wells

	ENTRY #
Bluffton	(G-862)
Craigville	(G-2121)
Markle	(G-9575)

	ENTRY #
Ossian	(G-11397)
Poneto	(G-11744)
Uniondale	(G-13466)

White

	ENTRY #
Brookston	(G-1101)
Buffalo	(G-1203)
Chalmers	(G-1546)
Monon	(G-10175)
Monticello	(G-10250)

	ENTRY #
Reynolds	(G-11944)
Wolcott	(G-14362)

Whitley

	ENTRY #
Churubusco	(G-1642)
Columbia City	(G-1757)
Larwill	(G-9121)
South Whitley	(G-12996)

GEOGRAPHIC SECTION

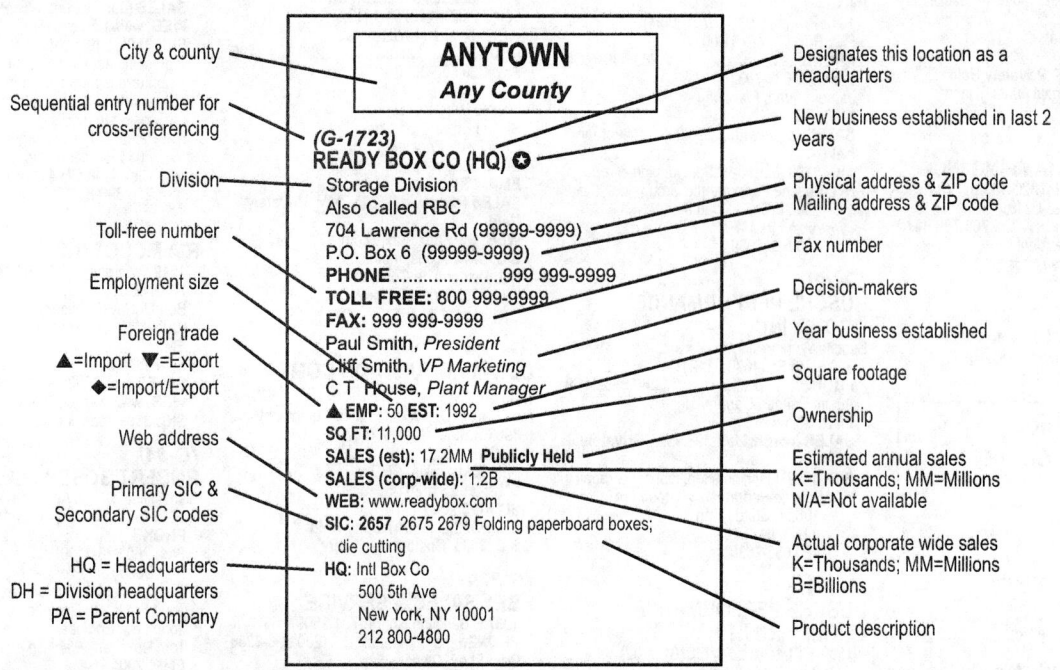

See footnotes for symbols and codes identification.

- This section is in alphabetical order by city.
- Companies are sorted alphabetically under their respective cities.
- To locate cities within a county refer to the County/City Cross Reference Index.

IMPORTANT NOTICE: It is a violation of both federal and state law to transmit an unsolicited advertisement to a facsimile machine. Any user of this product that violates such laws may be subject to civil and criminal penalties which may exceed $500 for each transmission of an unsolicited facsimile. Harris InfoSource provides fax numbers for lawful purposes only and expressly forbids the use of these numbers in any unlawful manner.

Akron
Fulton County

(G-1)
AKRON CONCRETE PRODUCTS INC (PA)
321 N Maple St (46910-9265)
P.O. Box 215 (46910-0215)
PHONE.................................574 893-4841
Fax: 574 893-4159
Pat Walgamuth, *President*
EMP: 10 EST: 1928
SQ FT: 16,234
SALES (est): 1.5MM **Privately Held**
WEB: www.akronconcreteproducts.com
SIC: 3272 Burial vaults, concrete or precast terrazzo; steps, prefabricated concrete; liquid catch basins, tanks & covers: concrete

(G-2)
AKRON FOUNDRY INC
502 E Main St (46910-9164)
PHONE.................................574 893-4548
Fax: 574 893-4549
David Ellenwood, *President*
EMP: 55 EST: 1964
SALES (est): 5MM **Privately Held**
WEB: www.akronfoundry.net
SIC: 3321 Gray iron castings

(G-3)
BUDDY EUGENE PUBLISHING LLC
2031 S 650 E (46910-9757)
PHONE.................................574 223-6048
Roger Bailey, *Principal*

EMP: 2 EST: 2010
SALES (est): 81.6K **Privately Held**
SIC: 2741 Miscellaneous publishing

(G-4)
DRAGON ESP LTD
Also Called: Enviromental Services Pdts Mfg
8857 E State Road 14 (46910-9749)
PHONE.................................574 893-1569
Fax: 574 893-1480
Bobby Satterfield, *President*
▲ EMP: 100 EST: 1999
SQ FT: 60,000
SALES (est): 10.4MM **Privately Held**
SIC: 3443 Dumpsters, garbage; bins, prefabricated metal plate

(G-5)
FRENCH INTERNATIONAL COATINGS ✪
15205 E 200 S (46910-9716)
PHONE.................................574 505-0774
Tyler French, *Principal*
EMP: 2 EST: 2017
SALES (est): 128.2K **Privately Held**
SIC: 3479 Metal coating & allied service

(G-6)
NORTHERN IND INDUS CATINGS LLC
619 E Main St (46910-9509)
PHONE.................................574 893-4621
Andy Martin,
Kim Martin,
EMP: 5
SALES (est): 319.3K **Privately Held**
SIC: 3479 1721 7532 Etching & engraving; industrial painting; aircraft painting; top & body repair & paint shops; truck painting & lettering

(G-7)
SONOCO PRODUCTS COMPANY
1535 S State Road 19 Th (46910-9469)
P.O. Box 338 (46910-0338)
PHONE.................................574 893-4521
Fax: 574 893-4782
Dedra Bockelman, *Branch Mgr*
EMP: 80
SALES (corp-wide): 5B **Publicly Held**
WEB: www.sonoco.com
SIC: 2631 Paperboard mills
PA: Sonoco Products Company
1 N 2nd St
Hartsville SC 29550
843 383-7000

(G-8)
TIC TOC TROPHY SHOP INC
930 E Rochester St (46910-9485)
P.O. Box 308 (46910-0308)
PHONE.................................574 893-4234
Fax: 574 893-7054
Chad Hartzler, *President*
EMP: 2
SALES (est): 246.5K **Privately Held**
SIC: 3499 5999 Trophies, metal, except silver; trophies & plaques

(G-9)
VALLEY SANITATION
8526 Fort Wayne Rd (46910-9179)
PHONE.................................574 893-7070
Robert Rudd, *Owner*
EMP: 6
SALES (est): 502.6K **Privately Held**
SIC: 2842 Sanitation preparations, disinfectants & deodorants

Albany
Delaware County

(G-10)
ALBANY METAL TREATING INC
400 S Gray St (47320-1549)
P.O. Box 65 (47320-0065)
PHONE.................................765 789-6470
Fax: 765 789-6839
Marion Auker, *President*
EMP: 55 EST: 1978
SQ FT: 55,000
SALES (est): 11MM **Privately Held**
WEB: www.albanymetal.com
SIC: 3398 3471 Metal heat treating; plating & polishing

(G-11)
LITTLER DIECAST A BRAHM CORP
500 W Walnut St (47320-1028)
P.O. Box 994, Chesterfield MO (63006-0994)
PHONE.................................765 789-4456
Fax: 765 789-4112
Bhavook Tripathi, *President*
John D Littler, *President*
Mark D Littler, *Vice Pres*
Marie Vaughn, *Vice Pres*
Douglas R Littler, *Treasurer*
▲ EMP: 90 EST: 1954
SQ FT: 85,000
SALES (est): 31.9MM **Privately Held**
WEB: www.littlerdiecast.com
SIC: 3363 5084 Aluminum die-castings; machinists' precision measuring tools

---

(G-12)
PRECISION PRINT LLC
10910 E County Road 500 N (47320-9554)
PHONE..................................765 789-8799
Jon M Kern, *Principal*
EMP: 2 **EST:** 2016
SALES (est): 92.3K **Privately Held**
SIC: 2752 Commercial printing, lithographic

(G-13)
T & T TOOL & STAMPING INC
1090 W Walnut St (47320-1532)
P.O. Box 248 (47320-0248)
PHONE..................................765 789-4670
Archie Thomas, *President*
Tommy Thomas, *Treasurer*
Mena Pence, *Manager*
EMP: 5
SQ FT: 12,000
SALES (est): 628.7K **Privately Held**
SIC: 3544 Special dies, tools, jigs & fixtures

Albion
Noble County

(G-14)
A B C EMBROIDERY INC
Also Called: ABC Embroidery
3008 S 50 W (46701-9660)
PHONE..................................260 636-7311
Vickie L Gaerte, *President*
Steven G Gaerte, *Vice Pres*
EMP: 5
SALES: 25K **Privately Held**
SIC: 2395 Embroidery products, except schiffli machine; embroidery & art needlework

(G-15)
ALL PRINTING AND PUBLICATIONS
Also Called: Albion New ERA
407 S Orange St (46701-1132)
P.O. Box 25 (46701-0025)
PHONE..................................260 636-2727
Fax: 260 636-2042
Robert Allman, *President*
EMP: 25
SQ FT: 4,000
SALES (est): 1.4MM **Privately Held**
SIC: 2711 2752 Newspapers, publishing & printing; commercial printing, lithographic

(G-16)
BCBG MAX AZRIA GROUP LLC
815 Trail Rd (46701)
PHONE..................................574 289-3937
EMP: 2
SALES (corp-wide): 979.1MM **Privately Held**
SIC: 2335 Women's, juniors' & misses' dresses
HQ: Bcbg Max Azria Group, Llc
2761 Fruitland Ave
Vernon CA 90058
323 589-2224

(G-17)
BONAR INC
Also Called: Bonar Well Drilling
307 Woods Dr (46701-1531)
PHONE..................................260 636-7430
Eric L Bonar, *President*
Judy Bonar, *Corp Secy*
Tenel Bonar, *Vice Pres*
▲ **EMP:** 5
SALES (est): 570K **Privately Held**
SIC: 1781 3053 Water well drilling; gaskets, all materials

(G-18)
BURGESS ENTERPRISES LLC
Also Called: Burgess Auction Resale
441 S 400 E (46701-9517)
PHONE..................................260 615-5194
Judi Burgess,
Shannon Burgess,
◆ **EMP:** 4
SQ FT: 3,340
SALES: 85K **Privately Held**
SIC: 3569 Filters

(G-19)
BUSCHE ENTERPRISE DIVISION INC
1612 Progress Dr (46701-1494)
P.O. Box 77 (46701-0077)
PHONE..................................260 636-7030
Fax: 260 636-7031
James Stuart, *Plant Mgr*
EMP: 70
SALES (corp-wide): 398.9MM **Privately Held**
SIC: 3599 Machine shop, jobbing & repair
HQ: Busche Performance Group, Inc.
1563 E State Road 8
Albion IN 46701
260 636-7030

(G-20)
BUSCHE PERFORMANCE GROUP INC
Busche Workholding
600 S 7th St (46701-1421)
PHONE..................................260 636-1069
Austin Pender, *General Mgr*
EMP: 38
SALES (corp-wide): 398.9MM **Privately Held**
SIC: 3599 Machine shop, jobbing & repair
HQ: Busche Performance Group, Inc.
1563 E State Road 8
Albion IN 46701
260 636-7030

(G-21)
BUSCHE PERFORMANCE GROUP INC (HQ)
1563 E State Road 8 (46701-9702)
P.O. Box 77 (46701-0077)
PHONE..................................260 636-7030
Nick Busche, *President*
Jim Stewart, *General Mgr*
Brett Sherwin, *Vice Pres*
Roger Prentice, *Plant Mgr*
Cheryl Smith, *Materials Mgr*
▲ **EMP:** 600
SQ FT: 273,000
SALES (est): 193.2MM
SALES (corp-wide): 398.9MM **Privately Held**
WEB: www.busche-cnc.com
SIC: 3599 Machine shop, jobbing & repair
PA: Shipston Group U.S., Inc.
44 Timber Swamp Rd
Hampton NH 03842
603 929-6825

(G-22)
D & J TOOL CO INC
300 S 7th St (46701-1415)
PHONE..................................260 636-2682
Delbert Smith, *President*
Janet Smith, *Treasurer*
EMP: 8
SQ FT: 2,800
SALES (est): 580K **Privately Held**
SIC: 3544 Forms (molds), for foundry & plastics working machinery; industrial molds

(G-23)
D A MERRIMAN INC
2259 E State Road 8 (46701-9703)
PHONE..................................260 636-3464
Don Merriman, *President*
Sally Merriman, *Vice Pres*
EMP: 2
SALES (est): 127.3K **Privately Held**
SIC: 3999 0782 Lawn ornaments; lawn & garden services

(G-24)
DANA LIGHT AXLE PRODUCTS LLC
401 E Park Dr (46701-1444)
PHONE..................................260 636-4300
Fax: 260 636-4328
Bridget Gaff, *Branch Mgr*
EMP: 50
SQ FT: 100,000 **Publicly Held**
SIC: 3714 Motor vehicle parts & accessories
HQ: Dana Light Axle Products, Llc
2100 W State Blvd
Fort Wayne IN 46808

(G-25)
DEXTER AXLE COMPANY
Also Called: Dexter Axle Division
500 S 7th St (46701-1419)
P.O. Box 108 (46701-0108)
PHONE..................................260 636-2195
Fax: 260 636-3030
Mike Fulton, *Plant Mgr*
Dennis Mort, *Warehouse Mgr*
Shawn Pulver, *QC Mgr*
Greg Reef, *Engineer*
Steve Schermerhorn, *Engineer*
EMP: 150
SALES (corp-wide): 245.3MM **Privately Held**
WEB: www.dexteraxle.com
SIC: 3714 Axles, motor vehicle
HQ: Dexter Axle Company
2900 Industrial Pkwy
Elkhart IN 46516

(G-26)
DIAL-X ACQUISITION COMPANY INC
Also Called: Dial-X Automated Equipment
3903 S State Road 9 (46701-9634)
PHONE..................................260 636-7588
Patrick Mavrakis, *CEO*
EMP: 21 **EST:** 2014
SQ FT: 35,000
SALES: 3.2MM **Privately Held**
SIC: 3599 Custom machinery

(G-27)
EBEY SALES & SERVICE
1037 E Baseline Rd (46701-9509)
PHONE..................................260 636-3286
Brad Ebey, *Owner*
EMP: 2
SALES: 54K **Privately Held**
SIC: 3651 Household audio & video equipment

(G-28)
HAYES ENTERPRISES LLC
2174 N River Rd W (46701-9543)
PHONE..................................260 636-3262
John P Hayes, *Principal*
EMP: 2
SALES (est): 152.8K **Privately Held**
SIC: 3843 Dental hand instruments

(G-29)
KNEPPERS INC (PA)
2359 N 300 E (46701-9745)
PHONE..................................260 636-2180
Greg Knepper, *President*
Kelly Knepper, *Admin Sec*
EMP: 12
SQ FT: 10,000
SALES (est): 1.5MM **Privately Held**
SIC: 3713 Truck bodies & parts

(G-30)
NORTH AMERICAN EXTRUSN & ASSEM
200 E Park Dr (46701-1439)
PHONE..................................260 636-3336
Jack Caudill, *Principal*
▲ **EMP:** 28
SALES (est): 5.9MM **Privately Held**
SIC: 3089 Extruded finished plastic products

(G-31)
OPI INC
Also Called: Orthopedic Precision Instrs
71 E 400 S Ste A (46701-9230)
PHONE..................................260 636-2352
Matthew Minthorn, *President*
Ernie Rice,
EMP: 4
SALES (est): 596.8K **Privately Held**
SIC: 3599 Machine shop, jobbing & repair

(G-32)
PARKER-HANNIFIN CORPORATION
Also Called: Brass Products Division
903 N Orange St (46701-1523)
PHONE..................................260 636-2104
Fax: 260 636-3134
Dan Barrett, *Safety Mgr*
Brenda Elion, *Purch Agent*
Kevin Likes, *Buyer*
Russ Kalis, *Branch Mgr*
Tammy Stewart, *Manager*
EMP: 125
SALES (corp-wide): 12B **Publicly Held**
WEB: www.parker.com
SIC: 3561 3491 3463 3432 Pumps & pumping equipment; industrial valves; nonferrous forgings; plumbing fixture fittings & trim; copper foundries; blast furnaces & steel mills
PA: Parker-Hannifin Corporation
6035 Parkland Blvd
Cleveland OH 44124
216 896-3000

(G-33)
R A MCCOY INC
1512 Progress Dr (46701-1492)
PHONE..................................260 636-2341
Bob McCoy, *President*
Karol McCoy, *Corp Secy*
EMP: 3
SQ FT: 10,000
SALES (est): 293.6K **Privately Held**
WEB: www.ramccoy.com
SIC: 3599 Machine shop, jobbing & repair

(G-34)
ROBERT BOSCH LLC
Also Called: Bosch Automotive
1613 Progress Dr (46701-1495)
PHONE..................................260 636-1005
Fax: 260 636-1106
Kurt Bendixen, *President*
Tim Christopher, *Warehouse Mgr*
Todd Freeman, *Engineer*
John Lew, *Engineer*
Tom Dukehart, *Plant Engr*
EMP: 200
SALES (corp-wide): 261.7MM **Privately Held**
WEB: www.boschservice.com
SIC: 3714 Motor vehicle engines & parts
HQ: Robert Bosch Llc
2800 S 25th Ave
Broadview IL 60155
248 876-1000

(G-35)
SHERMAN ENTERPRISES
4426 S 100 W (46701-9621)
PHONE..................................260 636-6225
Todd Sherman, *Owner*
EMP: 3
SALES (est): 328K **Privately Held**
SIC: 3449 Bars, concrete reinforcing: fabricated steel

(G-36)
TODD L WISE
5440 W 450 S (46701-9483)
PHONE..................................260 799-4828
Todd Wise, *Principal*
EMP: 2 **EST:** 2007
SALES (est): 131.2K **Privately Held**
SIC: 1442 Construction sand & gravel

Alexandria
Madison County

(G-37)
CABINET CRAFTERS CORP
120 S Sheridan St (46001-1944)
PHONE..................................765 724-7074
Tony Collins, *President*
EMP: 7
SALES (est): 886.9K **Privately Held**
SIC: 2434 Wood kitchen cabinets

(G-38)
COTTAGE INDUSTRIES DBA
7633 N 200 E (46001-8727)
PHONE..................................765 617-8360
Brenda W Swinford, *Principal*
EMP: 2
SALES (est): 104.9K **Privately Held**
SIC: 3999 Manufacturing industries

(G-39)
D 1 MOLD & TOOL LLC
8201 N State Road 9 (46001-8649)
PHONE..................................765 378-0693
Fax: 765 378-0991

▲ = Import ▼=Export
◆ =Import/Export

Tami Miller, *Office Mgr*
Anthony Dungan,
Steve Dungan,
EMP: 17
SQ FT: 9,600
SALES (est): 3.6MM **Privately Held**
SIC: 3544 Special dies & tools

(G-40)
ELWOOD PUBLISHING CO INC
Also Called: Alexandria Times-Tribune
1 Harrison Sq (46001-2054)
P.O. Box 330 (46001-0330)
PHONE..................................765 724-4469
Fax: 765 724-4460
Jack Barnes, *CEO*
EMP: 6
SALES (corp-wide): 8.7MM **Privately Held**
WEB: www.dailychiefunion.com
SIC: 2711 Newspapers: publishing only, not printed on site
HQ: Elwood Publishing Co Inc
317 S Anderson St
Elwood IN 46036
765 552-3355

(G-41)
ENERGY INC
Also Called: Airlift Services International
8201 N State Road 9 (46001-8649)
PHONE..................................765 948-3504
Daniel C Roberts, *CEO*
Roy Hawley, *Principal*
Alan Moore, *Principal*
Dr John Marvel, *Chairman*
C David Monroe, *CFO*
EMP: 6
SALES (est): 590K **Privately Held**
WEB: www.nojakpumps.com
SIC: 1381 Drilling oil & gas wells

(G-42)
FIX & SONS MANUFACTURING INC
219 E Washington St (46001-2043)
P.O. Box 256 (46001-0256)
PHONE..................................765 724-4041
Fax: 765 724-7009
Uwe Fix, *President*
Jean Fix, *Admin Sec*
EMP: 11
SQ FT: 15,000
SALES: 1MM **Privately Held**
WEB: www.fixandsonsinc.com
SIC: 3496 0742 3523 Cages, wire; veterinary services, specialties; farm machinery & equipment

(G-43)
GLOVE CORPORATION
Also Called: Dura Bull
301 N Harrison St Ste X (46001-1664)
PHONE..................................501 362-2437
EMP: 78
SALES (corp-wide): 14.7MM **Privately Held**
SIC: 2381 3842 3151 Mfg Fabric Gloves Mfg Surgical Appliances/Supplies Mfg Leather Gloves/Mittens
PA: Glove Corporation
4000 W 106th St Ste 130
Carmel IN
501 362-2437

(G-44)
GLS MACHINING & DESIGN LLC
12516 N 300 W (46001-8694)
PHONE..................................765 754-8248
Gary Glass, *Owner*
Pamela Glass,
EMP: 5
SQ FT: 6,000
SALES: 250K **Privately Held**
SIC: 3569 Filters

(G-45)
J & H TOOL INC
109 S Clinton St (46001-2001)
PHONE..................................765 724-9691
Fax: 765 724-9926
Tommie Jones, *President*
Chris Wyatt, *Corp Secy*
EMP: 5
SQ FT: 5,000

SALES: 400K **Privately Held**
SIC: 3599 Machine shop, jobbing & repair

(G-46)
JAMES W HAGER
5731 N 100 E (46001-8795)
PHONE..................................765 643-0188
James W Hager, *Principal*
EMP: 4
SALES (est): 299.5K **Privately Held**
SIC: 3423 3546 Hand & edge tools; power-driven handtools

(G-47)
PEGGY WILLIAMS
3049 E 1100 N (46001-9045)
PHONE..................................765 724-3862
Peggy Williams, *Principal*
EMP: 2
SALES (est): 96.5K **Privately Held**
SIC: 2512 Upholstered household furniture

(G-48)
RAM GRAPHICS INC
Also Called: Ram Apparel
1509 S Longwood Dr (46001-2819)
P.O. Box 114 (46001-0114)
PHONE..................................765 724-7783
Fax: 765 724-9767
Ronald Ruby, *President*
Larry Mercer, *Vice Pres*
Patricia Mercer, *Treasurer*
Paulette Ruby, *Admin Sec*
EMP: 40
SQ FT: 22,000
SALES (est): 5.6MM **Privately Held**
WEB: www.ramgraphics.com
SIC: 5136 5137 5094 5699 Men's & boys' clothing; women's & children's clothing; trophies; customized clothing & apparel; T-shirts, custom printed; screen printing on fabric articles; pleating & stitching

(G-49)
RED GOLD LP
2595 W State Road 28 (46001-8673)
P.O. Box 83, Elwood (46036-0083)
PHONE..................................765 754-8750
Brian Reichart, *Mng Member*
Maurie Fetting,
EMP: 10
SALES (est): 1.7MM **Privately Held**
SIC: 3411 Food & beverage containers

(G-50)
REMINGTON MACHINE INC
6 Twin Oaks St (46001-1244)
PHONE..................................765 724-3389
David Remington, *Principal*
EMP: 2
SALES (est): 198.9K **Privately Held**
SIC: 3599 Machine shop, jobbing & repair

(G-51)
RESIN PARTNERS INC
Also Called: Home Design Products
602 S Fairview St (46001-2249)
PHONE..................................765 724-7761
Don Eileirt, *Plant Mgr*
Bill Kirsch, *Finance Mgr*
Darleen Vanheirseele, *Human Res Dir*
Jeffery White, *Marketing Staff*
Mary Baber, *Branch Mgr*
EMP: 75
SALES (corp-wide): 74.7K **Privately Held**
SIC: 2519 Fiberglass & plastic furniture
HQ: Resin Partners, Inc.
6435 S Scatterfield Rd
Anderson IN 46013

(G-52)
ROBERT BURKHART
Also Called: Graphics 55
434 W State Road 28 (46001-8466)
PHONE..................................219 448-0365
Robert Burkhart, *Owner*
EMP: 2
SALES (est): 86.2K **Privately Held**
SIC: 2396 2395 Screen printing on fabric articles; fabric printing & stamping; embroidery & art needlework; emblems, embroidered; decorative & novelty stitching, for the trade

(G-53)
S PHILLIPPE LAWN & LANDSCAPE
2806 E 1100 N (46001-8489)
PHONE..................................765 724-2020
Kent Phillippe, *Owner*
EMP: 2
SALES (est): 96K **Privately Held**
SIC: 3524 0781 Lawn & garden equipment; landscape counseling & planning

(G-54)
ULTIMATE ETHANOL LLC
Also Called: Poet Brfnng- Alexandria 21200
13179 N 100 E (46001-7703)
P.O. Box 717 (46001-0717)
PHONE..................................765 724-4384
Doug Berven, *Director*
Blake Hoffman, *Director*
Duane Sather, *Director*
Jeff Broin,
Fred Thurman, *Admin Sec*
EMP: 2
SALES (est): 713.6K **Privately Held**
SIC: 2869 Ethyl alcohol, ethanol
PA: Poet, Llc
4615 N Lewis Ave
Sioux Falls SD 57104

Ambia
Benton County

(G-55)
HELENA AGRI-ENTERPRISES LLC
210 N 1st St (47917-8555)
PHONE..................................765 869-5518
EMP: 2
SALES (corp-wide): 70.7B **Privately Held**
SIC: 5191 2819 Farm supplies; industrial inorganic chemicals
HQ: Helena Agri-Enterprises, Llc
255 Schilling Blvd # 300
Collierville TN 38017
901 761-0050

Anderson
Madison County

(G-56)
3D PARTS MFG LLC
3248 Dr Mar L King Jr Blv Martin (46013)
PHONE..................................317 860-6941
Josh Barber, *Mng Member*
Adam Brand,
Kim Brand,
Alan Michel,
▲ **EMP:** 5 **EST:** 2013
SQ FT: 3,000
SALES (est): 824.6K **Privately Held**
SIC: 3082 3312 Unsupported plastics profile shapes; stainless steel

(G-57)
A1 PALLET LIQUIDATORS
2700 Indiana Ave (46012-1342)
PHONE..................................765 356-4020
EMP: 4
SALES (est): 235.3K **Privately Held**
SIC: 2448 Pallets, wood & wood with metal

(G-58)
AAA SATELLITE LINK
1529 W 2nd St (46016-2405)
PHONE..................................765 642-7000
Fax: 765 641-7746
Lonnie Short, *Owner*
EMP: 2
SALES (est): 120K **Privately Held**
SIC: 3663 Space satellite communications equipment

(G-59)
ADVANCED MAGNESIUM ALLOYS CORP
Also Called: Amacor
1820 E 32nd St (46013-2144)
PHONE..................................765 643-5873
Jan Guy, *CEO*
Charles W Moisan, *CFO*

▲ **EMP:** 35
SQ FT: 340,000
SALES (est): 10.4MM **Privately Held**
WEB: www.amacor.us
SIC: 3341 Secondary nonferrous metals

(G-60)
ALTAIR NANOTECHNOLOGIES INC
3019 Enterprise Dr (46013-8800)
PHONE..................................317 333-7617
Kevin Robinson, *Engineer*
Richard Lee, *Branch Mgr*
Kelly Hiatt, *Manager*
EMP: 541 **Privately Held**
SIC: 2816 Inorganic pigments
PA: Altair Nanotechnologies Inc.
204 Edison Way
Reno NV 89502

(G-61)
AMERICAN METAL COATINGS INC
6501 Production Dr (46013-9407)
PHONE..................................765 608-2100
Rob Wineland, *President*
EMP: 11
SQ FT: 28,500
SALES (est): 950K **Privately Held**
WEB: www.americanmetalcoatings.com
SIC: 3479 Coating of metals & formed products

(G-62)
AMERICAN PLAYGROUND CORP
505 E 31st St Ste X (46016-5375)
PHONE..................................765 642-0288
Fax: 765 649-7162
Rob Wineland, *Principal*
EMP: 4
SALES (est): 415.6K **Privately Held**
SIC: 3949 Playground equipment

(G-63)
AMERICAN PLAYGROUND CORP
2320 Jefferson St (46016-4507)
PHONE..................................765 642-0288
Troy Pickett, *Principal*
EMP: 2
SALES (est): 203K **Privately Held**
SIC: 3949 Playground equipment

(G-64)
AMERICAN PRINTING INDIANA LLC
1047 Broadway St (46012-2526)
PHONE..................................765 825-7600
Fax: 765 825-6150
Ron Smith, *Mng Member*
Randy Smith,
EMP: 25
SALES (est): 2.8MM
SALES (corp-wide): 3.8MM **Privately Held**
SIC: 2759 Commercial printing
PA: American Printing & Lithographing Co Inc
528 S 7th St
Hamilton OH

(G-65)
ANDERSON MEMORIAL PARK
Also Called: Park Developement
6805 Dr Martin Luther (46013)
PHONE..................................765 643-3211
Fax: 765 643-7717
Diane Wiley, *President*
EMP: 15
SALES (est): 1.1MM **Privately Held**
SIC: 6531 3272 6553 Cemetery management service; burial vaults, concrete or precast terrazzo; cemetery subdividers & developers

(G-66)
ANDERSON SIGN PRO
633 Jackson St (46016-1156)
PHONE..................................765 642-0281
Imran Ashiq, *Principal*
EMP: 2
SALES (est): 124.6K **Privately Held**
SIC: 3993 Signs & advertising specialties

GEOGRAPHIC

(G-67)
AP ACQUISITION LLC
Also Called: American Playground
505 E 31st St Ste X (46016-5375)
PHONE..................................765 642-0288
Peadar O'Scanaill,
EMP: 15
SALES (est): 940K **Privately Held**
SIC: 3949 Playground equipment

(G-68)
APPLE BLOSSOM FLORAL
1845 N Scatterfield Rd (46012-1551)
PHONE..................................765 649-2480
Patty Wilder, *Principal*
EMP: 2
SALES (est): 132.8K **Privately Held**
SIC: 3571 Personal computers (microcomputers)

(G-69)
ASCENSION SPACE TECHNOLOGY LLP
7315 Colonial Ct (46013-3844)
PHONE..................................765 623-5164
Daniel Schrader, *Partner*
Austin McGee, *Partner*
EMP: 2
SALES (est): 122.4K **Privately Held**
SIC: 3812 7389 Aircraft/aerospace flight
instruments & guidance systems;

(G-70)
AT T
4711 S Scatterfield Rd (46013-2907)
PHONE..................................765 649-5900
EMP: 4
SALES (est): 264.3K **Privately Held**
SIC: 3663 Mobile communication equipment

(G-71)
AVERY DENNISON CORPORATION
5710 Douglas Way (46013-9625)
PHONE..................................765 221-9277
Avery Dennison, *Manager*
EMP: 2
SALES (corp-wide): 6.6B **Publicly Held**
SIC: 2672 Coated & laminated paper
PA: Avery Dennison Corporation
207 N Goode Ave Ste 500
Glendale CA 91203
626 304-2000

(G-72)
BARBER MANUFACTURING CO INC (PA)
1824 Brown St (46016-1661)
P.O. Box 2454 (46018-2454)
PHONE..................................765 643-6905
Fax: 765 642-7480
John W Barber Jr, *Ch of Bd*
James R Barber, *President*
Jeffery W Barber, *President*
Jack R Barber, *Exec VP*
Jack Barber, *Exec VP*
▲ **EMP:** 93
SQ FT: 80,000
SALES (est): 13.1MM **Privately Held**
WEB: www.barbermfg.com
SIC: 3495 Upholstery springs, unassembled; precision springs

(G-73)
BCW DIVERSIFIED INC
Also Called: Bcw Supplies
514 E 31st St (46016-5329)
P.O. Box 970 (46015-0970)
PHONE..................................765 644-2033
Fax: 765 649-2884
Eric A Brownell, *President*
Ted Litvan, *Marketing Mgr*
Jay M Brownell, *Admin Sec*
Randal L Brownell, *Admin Sec*
▲ **EMP:** 35
SQ FT: 78,000
SALES (est): 7.5MM **Privately Held**
WEB: www.bcwdiv.com
SIC: 5999 3081 Packaging materials:
boxes, padding, etc.; unsupported plastics film & sheet; vinyl film & sheet; plastic
film & sheet; packing materials, plastic
sheet

(G-74)
BEST WELD INC
1315 W 18th St (46016-3800)
PHONE..................................765 641-7720
Fax: 765 641-7784
Terry E Carl, *President*
EMP: 16
SQ FT: 39,000
SALES (est): 974.8K **Privately Held**
WEB: www.bestweldinc.com
SIC: 7539 3315 1799 Automotive repair
shops; steel wire & related products;
welding on site

(G-75)
BORGWARNER INC
6628 Production Dr (46013-9405)
PHONE..................................765 609-3801
James R Verrier, *President*
EMP: 3
SALES (est): 202.2K **Privately Held**
SIC: 3714 Motor vehicle parts & accessories

(G-76)
BORGWARNER PDS ANDERSON LLC
Also Called: Live Engine Test Building
6628 Production Dr (46013-9405)
PHONE..................................765 778-6499
Fax: 765 778-6414
David Stoll, *Principal*
EMP: 175
SALES (corp-wide): 9.8B **Publicly Held**
WEB: www.remy.net
SIC: 3714 8741 3694 3625 Motor vehicle
transmissions, drive assemblies & parts;
management services; engine electrical
equipment; relays & industrial controls;
motors & generators
HQ: Borgwarner Pds (Anderson), L.L.C.
13975 Borgwarner Dr
Noblesville IN 46060

(G-77)
BRIGHT CORP
3040 E 38th St (46013-2673)
P.O. Box 403 (46015-0403)
PHONE..................................765 642-3114
Fax: 765 642-7475
William D Bowser, *President*
Edward L Bowser, *Corp Secy*
Mark Bowser, *Vice Pres*
Steve Bowser, *Vice Pres*
Steven J Bowser, *Vice Pres*
EMP: 20 **EST:** 1946
SQ FT: 13,000
SALES (est): 1.3MM **Privately Held**
SIC: 2741 2731 2752 Miscellaneous publishing; books: publishing only; commercial printing, lithographic

(G-78)
BROADWAY PRESS
2112 Broadway St (46012-1605)
PHONE..................................765 644-8813
Fax: 765 644-8268
Richard L Zarse II, *Owner*
EMP: 5
SQ FT: 3,500
SALES (est): 561.8K **Privately Held**
WEB: www.broadwaypress.com
SIC: 2752 Commercial printing, offset

(G-79)
C & H SIGNS INC
Also Called: C&H Plastic Letters & Signs
805 Morton St (46016-1355)
PHONE..................................765 642-7777
Fax: 765 642-7777
Linda L Laird, *President*
EMP: 2
SQ FT: 800
SALES (est): 50K **Privately Held**
SIC: 3993 Signs & advertising specialties

(G-80)
CABINETS BY GENTRY
3516 Andover Rd (46013-4217)
PHONE..................................765 378-7900
Mike Gentry, *Owner*
EMP: 3
SALES (est): 185.8K **Privately Held**
SIC: 2434 Wood kitchen cabinets

(G-81)
CARRARA INDUSTRIES INC
1619 W 5th St (46016-1071)
PHONE..................................765 643-3430
Jack Henricks, *President*
Richard Hartman, *Vice Pres*
EMP: 6
SQ FT: 6,000
SALES: 300K **Privately Held**
SIC: 3479 Painting of metal products

(G-82)
CENTRAL COCA-COLA BTLG CO INC
3200 E 38th St (46013-2657)
PHONE..................................765 642-9951
Fax: 765 642-9954
Scott Devall, *Manager*
EMP: 70
SQ FT: 10,000
SALES (corp-wide): 35.4B **Publicly Held**
WEB: www.cokecce.com
SIC: 2086 Bottled & canned soft drinks
HQ: Central Coca-Cola Bottling Company,
Inc.
555 Taxter Rd Ste 550
Elmsford NY 10523
914 789-1100

(G-83)
CHAPPYS RENT TO OWN LLC
615 S Scatterfield Rd # 1 (46012-3662)
PHONE..................................765 622-9500
Fax: 765 622-9400
EMP: 3
SALES (est): 250K **Privately Held**
SIC: 3699 7359 Mfg Electrical Equipment/Supplies Equipment Rental/Leasing

(G-84)
CHARM-LITE INC
2448 E 39th St (46013-2606)
PHONE..................................765 644-6876
Mark Young, *CEO*
Jacob Love, *General Mgr*
Teresa Love, *CFO*
Mike Young, *Manager*
EMP: 9
SALES (est): 300.8K **Privately Held**
WEB: www.charm-lite.com
SIC: 3648 1731 Lighting equipment; general electrical contractor

(G-85)
CITY OF ANDERSON
Water Pollution Control
2801 Gene Gustin Way (46011-1900)
PHONE..................................765 648-6560
Fax: 765 648-6570
Nara Manor, *Superintendent*
Ryan Paschal, *CTO*
EMP: 64 **Privately Held**
SIC: 3589 Water treatment equipment, industrial
PA: City Of Anderson
120 E 8th St
Anderson IN 46016
765 648-6034

(G-86)
CITY OF ANDERSON
Also Called: Anderson Parking Authority
1035 Main St (46016-1745)
PHONE..................................765 648-6715
Wayne Wright, *Branch Mgr*
Joseph Newman, *Council Mbr*
EMP: 4 **Privately Held**
SIC: 9121 3559 ; parking facility equipment & supplies
PA: City Of Anderson
120 E 8th St
Anderson IN 46016
765 648-6034

(G-87)
COEUS TECHNOLOGY INC
2701 Entp Dr Ste 230 (46013)
PHONE..................................765 203-2304
Nathan J Richardson, *President*
Nate Richardson, *Managing Prtnr*
David E Parker, *Vice Pres*
EMP: 6
SQ FT: 700
SALES: 256K **Privately Held**
SIC: 2869 Accelerators, rubber processing:
cyclic or acyclic

(G-88)
COMMUNITY HOLDINGS INDIANA INC
Also Called: Herald Bulletin, The
1133 Jackson St (46016-1433)
P.O. Box 1090 (46015-1090)
PHONE..................................765 622-1212
Fax: 765 640-4815
Joann Reed, *Branch Mgr*
Peggy Crabtree, *Manager*
Denver Sullivan, *MIS Dir*
EMP: 10 **Privately Held**
WEB: www.clintonnc.com
SIC: 2711 Newspapers, publishing & printing
HQ: Community Holdings Of Indiana, Inc.
3500 Colonnade Pkwy # 600
Birmingham AL 35243

(G-89)
CONNECTICUT ELECTRIC INC (PA)
1819 W 38th St (46013-1014)
PHONE..................................800 730-2557
Jeff Jensen, *President*
Chuck Whitaker, *Engineer*
Leeann Neel, *Cust Mgr*
Shawna Richardson, *Sales Staff*
Kathleen Sutton, *Sales Staff*
▲ **EMP:** 15 **EST:** 2006
SQ FT: 30,000
SALES: 18.8MM **Privately Held**
WEB: www.compu-tech.com
SIC: 3699 Electrical equipment & supplies

(G-90)
CONTINENTAL MANUFACTURING LLC
Also Called: Solas Ray Lighting
1524 Jackson St (46016-1621)
PHONE..................................765 778-9999
John Leeper, *Engineer*
Jeff Rhodes, *VP Mktg*
Judith Nagengast,
Mary Jane Gonzalez, *Tech Recruiter*
Mary Ann Fultz, *Recruiter*
▲ **EMP:** 50
SALES (est): 12.1MM **Privately Held**
SIC: 3714 Motor vehicle parts & accessories

(G-91)
COWPOKES INC
Also Called: Cowpokes Western Outfitters
1812 E 53rd St (46013-2830)
PHONE..................................765 642-3911
Fax: 765 642-3962
Jeff Boone, *President*
Lynnette Boone, *Treasurer*
EMP: 21
SQ FT: 20,000
SALES: 2MM **Privately Held**
WEB: www.cowpokes.com
SIC: 5699 5932 5947 5941 Western apparel; antiques; gift shop; saddlery &
equestrian equipment; boots; embroidery
products, except schiffli machine

(G-92)
DEER TRACK ARCHERY
648 W 500 S (46013-5412)
PHONE..................................765 643-6847
James Hasty, *President*
Madonna Hasty, *Co-Owner*
EMP: 2
SALES: 90K **Privately Held**
SIC: 5941 3949 Archery supplies; targets,
archery & rifle shooting

(G-93)
DELTA EXCELL INCORPORATED
Also Called: American Playground
505 E 31st St Ste X (46016-5375)
PHONE..................................765 642-0288
Phillip Abookire, *President*
EMP: 35
SQ FT: 40,000
SALES (est): 3.3MM **Privately Held**
SIC: 3949 2514 Playground equipment;
metal household furniture

(G-94)
DERBY INDUSTRIES LLC
4301 W 73rd St (46011-8809)
PHONE..................................765 778-6104

▲ = Import ▼=Export
◆ =Import/Export

Bill Craig,
▲ **EMP:** 3
SALES (est): 265.2K **Privately Held**
SIC: 3999 Atomizers, toiletry

(G-95)
DILLON PATTERN WORKS INC
1010 W 21st St (46016-3907)
P.O. Box 41 (46015-0041)
PHONE.............................765 642-3549
Fax: 765 642-3549
Ronnie E Dillon, *President*
Prudy Dillon, *Admin Sec*
EMP: 12 **EST:** 1970
SALES (est): 1.7MM **Privately Held**
SIC: 3365 3543 Aluminum & aluminum-
based alloy castings; industrial patterns

(G-96)
DISCOUNT POWER EQUIPMENT
2650 E State Road 236 (46017-9757)
PHONE.............................765 642-0040
EMP: 2
SALES (est): 72.6K **Privately Held**
SIC: 3524 1796 3714 3711 Lawn & garden equipment; power generating equipment installation; power transmission
equipment, motor vehicle; snow plows
(motor vehicles), assembly of

(G-97)
DIVERSIFIED QULTY SVCS IND LLC
1315 W 18th St (46016-3800)
PHONE.............................765 644-7712
Will Nichols, *President*
Sharon Montgomery, *Partner*
Frank Shekell, *Partner*
Stacee Nichols, *Corp Secy*
Kelli Perry, *Vice Pres*
EMP: 6
SQ FT: 35,000
SALES (est): 689.5K **Privately Held**
WEB: www.dqsicorp.com
SIC: 3537 Containers (metal), air cargo

(G-98)
DON HARTMAN OIL CO INC
Also Called: His
4193 Alexandria Pike (46012-9792)
PHONE.............................765 643-5026
Fax: 765 649-3747
William Inholt, *President*
Shirley Fox, *Treasurer*
EMP: 3
SQ FT: 1,500
SALES: 1.1MM **Privately Held**
SIC: 2911 5191 Petroleum refining; fertil-
izer & fertilizer materials

(G-99)
DOVEY CORPORATION
3220 W 25th St (46011-4617)
P.O. Box 2249 (46018-2249)
PHONE.............................765 649-2576
Fax: 765 649-1934
Kay Reed, *President*
Craig Smith, *Vice Pres*
▲ **EMP:** 16
SQ FT: 18,000
SALES (est): 3.2MM **Privately Held**
WEB: www.doveyco.com
SIC: 3554 Corrugating machines, paper

(G-100)
DUGOUT
2203 Broadway St (46012-1606)
PHONE.............................765 642-8528
Fax: 765 642-8577
Robert Stecher, *Owner*
EMP: 6
SQ FT: 1,100
SALES (est): 390.7K **Privately Held**
SIC: 5699 2395 Sports apparel; uniforms;
embroidery products, except schiffli ma-
chine

(G-101)
E & B PAVING INC (HQ)
286 W 300 N (46012-1200)
PHONE.............................765 643-5358
Fax: 765 643-0699
Gary Stebbins, *President*
Dave Christman, *Superintendent*
Spencer Coe, *Area Mgr*
Richard Knief, *Corp Secy*

Larry Canterbury, *Vice Pres*
EMP: 25
SQ FT: 6,000
SALES (est): 264.9MM
SALES (corp-wide): 800.6MM **Privately
Held**
SIC: 1611 2951 1794 Highway & street
paving contractor; asphalt & asphaltic
paving mixtures (not from refineries); ex-
cavation work
PA: Irving Materials, Inc.
8032 N State Road 9
Greenfield IN 46140
317 326-3101

(G-102)
E C SCHLEYER PUMP CO INC
501 Sycamore St (46016-1046)
PHONE.............................765 643-3334
Fax: 765 643-3336
J L Henricks III, *President*
EMP: 6 **EST:** 1927
SQ FT: 29,000
SALES: 500K **Privately Held**
SIC: 3561 Pumps & pumping equipment

(G-103)
E H BAARE CORPORATION (PA)
3620 W 73rd St (46011-9608)
PHONE.............................765 778-7895
John R Reynolds, *President*
Richard Parsons, *Treasurer*
Johaannes P Jansen, *Admin Sec*
EMP: 2
SQ FT: 2,000
SALES (est): 23.2MM **Privately Held**
WEB: www.ehbaare.com
SIC: 3315 3444 Wire products,
ferrous/iron; made in wiredrawing plants;
sheet metal specialties, not stamped

(G-104)
EAST SIDE JERSEY DAIRY INC
722 Broadway St (46012-2924)
PHONE.............................765 649-1261
Fax: 765 649-8268
Doug Banning, *Branch Mgr*
EMP: 25
SALES (corp-wide): 1.8B **Privately Held**
SIC: 2026 Milk processing (pasteurizing,
homogenizing, bottling)
HQ: East Side Jersey Dairy Inc
1100 Broadway
Carlinville IL 62626
217 854-2547

(G-105)
ERTL ENTERPRISES INC
2316 Jefferson St (46016-4507)
PHONE.............................765 622-9900
Daniel A Ertl, *President*
Deborah Kramer, *Finance Mgr*
EMP: 10
SQ FT: 12,000
SALES (est): 2.2MM **Privately Held**
WEB: www.ertlenterprises.com
SIC: 3519 Parts & accessories, internal
combustion engines

(G-106)
ERTL FABRICATING INC
2316 Jefferson St (46016-4507)
PHONE.............................765 393-1376
Daniel A Ertl, *President*
EMP: 10
SALES (est): 940K **Privately Held**
SIC: 3449 Curtain wall, metal

(G-107)
FRANKS WOODWORKING
3314 E 500 N (46012-9238)
PHONE.............................765 378-0424
EMP: 2 **EST:** 2008
SALES (est): 110K **Privately Held**
SIC: 2431 Mfg Millwork

(G-108)
GENERAL CAGE LLC
1106 Meridian St Ste 325 (46016-1776)
PHONE.............................765 552-5039
Fax: 765 552-6962
Bruce Cook,
▲ **EMP:** 40
SQ FT: 108,000

SALES (est): 5.6MM **Privately Held**
WEB: www.generalcage.com
SIC: 3496 Cages, wire; fencing, made from
purchased wire

(G-109)
GENTRYS CABINET INC
415 Main St (46016-1529)
PHONE.............................765 643-6611
Fax: 765 643-1722
Tim Miller, *Principal*
EMP: 4
SALES (est): 367.2K **Privately Held**
SIC: 2434 Wood kitchen cabinets

(G-110)
GET NOTICED PORTABLE SIGNS
1842 Lowell Ave (46011-2126)
PHONE.............................765 649-6645
Alvin Renschler, *Owner*
EMP: 2
SALES (est): 143.6K **Privately Held**
SIC: 3993 Signs & advertising specialties

(G-111)
GO ELECTRIC INC
1920 Purdue Pkwy Ste 400 (46016-5564)
PHONE.............................765 400-1347
Lisa M Laughner, *CEO*
EMP: 17
SQ FT: 30,000
SALES (est): 2.8MM **Privately Held**
SIC: 3621 3629 Generators for gas-elec-
tric or oil-electric vehicles; storage battery
chargers, motor & engine generator type;
generators for storage battery chargers;
battery chargers, rectifying or nonrotating

(G-112)
GREAT DEALS MAGAZINE
1232 Broadway St Ste 300 (46012-2564)
PHONE.............................765 649-3302
Jim Mougeotte, *Owner*
Jill Omalia, *Marketing Staff*
Sarah Bardwell, *Admin Asst*
EMP: 10
SALES (est): 1.3MM **Privately Held**
SIC: 3661 5192 Modems; magazines

(G-113)
GREENVILLE TECHNOLOGY INC
3511 W 73rd St (46011-9606)
PHONE.............................765 221-7576
EMP: 11
SALES (corp-wide): 1.7B **Privately Held**
SIC: 3089 Injection molded finished plastic
products
HQ: Greenville Technology, Inc.
5755 State Route 571
Greenville OH 45331
937 548-3217

(G-114)
HICKORY FURNITURE DESIGNS INC
415 E 38th St (46013-4651)
PHONE.............................765 642-0700
Brad McQueen, *President*
Myrta McQueen, *Admin Sec*
EMP: 12
SQ FT: 22,000
SALES (est): 1.5MM **Privately Held**
WEB: www.hickoryfurnituredesigns.com
SIC: 2511 Wood household furniture

(G-115)
HOLDER BEDDING INC
1923 W 8th St (46016-2513)
PHONE.............................765 642-1256
Fax: 765 642-1029
Mark Beaman, *Manager*
EMP: 3
SALES (corp-wide): 889.7K **Privately
Held**
SIC: 2515 5712 Mattresses, containing
felt, foam rubber, urethane, etc.; mat-
tresses, innerspring or box spring; box
springs, assembled; mattresses; bedding
& bedsprings
PA: Holder Bedding Inc
230 Farabee Dr N
Lafayette IN 47905
765 447-7907

(G-116)
HOOSIER PRESS INC
1027 Meridian St (46016-1749)
PHONE.............................765 649-3716
Woody Farmer, *President*
Dan Shaw, *Vice Pres*
EMP: 3
SQ FT: 3,100
SALES (est): 290K **Privately Held**
SIC: 2752 Commercial printing, offset

(G-117)
HY-PRO CORPORATION
Also Called: Hy-Pro Filtration
6810 Layton Rd (46011-9494)
PHONE.............................317 849-3535
Fax: 317 849-9201
Larry Hoeg, *President*
Aaron Hoeg, *Treasurer*
▲ **EMP:** 100
SQ FT: 90,000
SALES (est): 34.3MM
SALES (corp-wide): 2.3B **Publicly Held**
WEB: www.filterelement.com
SIC: 3569 Filter elements, fluid, hydraulic
line; lubrication equipment, industrial
PA: Donaldson Company, Inc.
1400 W 94th St
Minneapolis MN 55431
952 887-3131

(G-118)
HY-TECH MACHINING SYSTEMS LLC
2900 S Scatterfield Rd (46013-1817)
PHONE.............................765 649-6852
Fax: 765 649-6874
Stan Lay, *President*
Teresa Lay, *COO*
Joseph Lay, *Mng Member*
EMP: 11
SQ FT: 30,000
SALES (est): 2.1MM **Privately Held**
WEB: www.htmachines.com
SIC: 3549 3569 3541 Assembly ma-
chines, including robotic; assembly ma-
chines, non-metalworking; boring mills

(G-119)
I HSG INC
2902 Enterprise Dr (46013-9667)
PHONE.............................765 778-6499
Kerry A Shiba, *Vice Pres*
Craig J Hart, *Treasurer*
Sheila Cannon, *Admin Sec*
EMP: 4
SALES (est): 214.4K
SALES (corp-wide): 9.8B **Publicly Held**
SIC: 3714 Motor vehicle parts & acces-
sories
HQ: Old Remco Holdings, L.L.C.
600 Corporation Dr
Pendleton IN 46064

(G-120)
I POWER ENERGY SYSTEMS LLC
4640 Dr M L King Jr Blvd Martin (46013)
PHONE.............................765 621-9980
Terry Pahls,
Mike Hudson,
EMP: 23
SQ FT: 66,000
SALES (est): 3.9MM **Privately Held**
WEB: www.ipoweres.com
SIC: 3621 Generator sets: gasoline, diesel
or dual-fuel

(G-121)
IPOWER TECHNOLOGIES INC
Also Called: I Power
4640 Dr Mrtn Lthr Kng Jr (46013-2317)
PHONE.............................317 574-0103
John H Combes, *Vice Ch Bd*
James E Luckman, *President*
EMP: 25
SALES (est): 4.2MM **Privately Held**
SIC: 3621 Power generators

(G-122)
IRVING MATERIALS INC
Also Called: I M I
1601 N Scatterfield Rd (46012-1584)
PHONE.............................765 644-8819
Fax: 765 644-3613

Doug Layman, *Branch Mgr*
EMP: 8
SALES (corp-wide): 800.6MM **Privately Held**
SIC: 3273 Ready-mixed concrete
PA: Irving Materials, Inc.
8032 N State Road 9
Greenfield IN 46140
317 326-3101

(G-123)
IRVING MATERIALS INC
5002 S State Road 67 (46013-9784)
PHONE..................................765 778-4760
Fax: 765 778-3962
Pete Irving, *Branch Mgr*
EMP: 10
SALES (corp-wide): 800.6MM **Privately Held**
SIC: 3273 5032 1442 Ready-mixed concrete; stone, crushed or broken; construction sand & gravel
PA: Irving Materials, Inc.
8032 N State Road 9
Greenfield IN 46140
317 326-3101

(G-124)
J & J PRINTING CO
2107 State St (46012-1743)
PHONE..................................765 642-6642
Fax: 765 644-3998
John D Bagley, *Owner*
EMP: 3
SALES (est): 170K **Privately Held**
SIC: 2752 Commercial printing, offset

(G-125)
JAM PRINTING INC
Also Called: PIP Printing & Marketting Svcs
1200 Meridian St (46016-1715)
PHONE..................................765 649-9292
John Specht, *President*
EMP: 6
SALES (est): 162.8K **Privately Held**
SIC: 7336 2752 8742 Commercial art & graphic design; color lithography; marketing consulting services

(G-126)
KEIHIN NORTH AMERICA INC (HQ)
2701 Enterprise Dr # 100 (46013-6100)
PHONE..................................765 298-6030
Fax: 317 578-5261
Koki Onuma, *President*
Sosuke Sese, *Principal*
Masami Watanabe, *Principal*
Greg York, *Vice Pres*
Gregory S Young, *Vice Pres*
▲ **EMP:** 1768
SALES: 1B
SALES (corp-wide): 3.3B **Privately Held**
WEB: www.kipt-inc.com
SIC: 3714 Fuel systems & parts, motor vehicle; manifolds, motor vehicle; motor vehicle engines & parts
PA: Keihin Corporation
1-26-2, Nishishinjuku
Shinjuku-Ku TKY 160-0
333 453-411

(G-127)
KELLEY ELECTRIC
2905 Enterprise Dr (46013-9667)
PHONE..................................765 778-8203
EMP: 2
SALES (est): 120K **Privately Held**
SIC: 3699 Mfg Electrical Equipment/Supplies

(G-128)
KENNEDY ENTERPRISES INC
2310 Broadway St (46012-1609)
PHONE..................................765 724-2225
Fax: 765 724-2247
Brian S Kennedy, *President*
EMP: 40
SALES (est): 5.1MM **Privately Held**
SIC: 3541 Machine tools, metal cutting type

(G-129)
KETER NORTH AMERICA LLC
6435 S Scatterfield Rd (46013-9619)
PHONE..................................765 298-6800

Orgad Shapiro, *Mng Member*
Andrea Harwell,
EMP: 3
SALES (est): 374.1K **Privately Held**
SIC: 2392 2519 Household furnishings; lawn & garden furniture, except wood & metal
PA: Keter Holdings Ltd
9 Rothschild Blvd.
Tel Aviv-Jaffa
995 912-12

(G-130)
KIRBY RISK CORPORATION
Also Called: Kirby Risk Electrical Supply
633 Broadway St (46012-2921)
PHONE..................................765 643-3384
Fax: 765 643-5309
Bryan Jones, *Principal*
Brian Jones, *Manager*
Charles Stevenson, *Manager*
EMP: 3
SALES (corp-wide): 401.3MM **Privately Held**
WEB: www.kirbyrisk.com
SIC: 5063 7694 Electrical supplies; rewinding stators; electric motor repair
PA: Kirby Risk Corporation
1815 Sagamore Pkwy N
Lafayette IN 47904
765 448-4567

(G-131)
L D BARGER WHOLESALE NEON INC
749 E 500 S (46013-9508)
PHONE..................................765 643-4506
Lawson Barger, *President*
EMP: 2
SQ FT: 1,800
SALES: 80K **Privately Held**
SIC: 3993 3229 Neon signs; novelty glassware

(G-132)
L M PRODUCTS INC
1325 Meridian St (46016-1828)
PHONE..................................765 643-3802
Fax: 765 641-1205
Larry Mechem Jr, *President*
Larry Mechem Sr, *Shareholder*
EMP: 26
SQ FT: 7,000
SALES (est): 3.7MM **Privately Held**
SIC: 3199 3161 Straps, leather; musical instrument cases

(G-133)
LECLANCHE SA
2705 Enterprise Dr (46013-9670)
PHONE..................................765 610-0050
Thom Reddington, *Senior VP*
EMP: 6
SALES (est): 217.1K **Privately Held**
SIC: 3621 Storage battery chargers, motor & engine generator type

(G-134)
MANCOR INDIANA INC
7825 American Way (46013-9669)
PHONE..................................765 779-4800
Art Church, *CEO*
Jeffrey A Abrams, *Principal*
Craig Sloan, *Vice Pres*
▲ **EMP:** 24
SALES (est): 3.1MM
SALES (corp-wide): 66MM **Privately Held**
SIC: 1721 3714 Exterior commercial painting contractor; motor vehicle parts & accessories
PA: Mancor Canada Inc
2485 Speers Rd
Oakville ON L6L 2
905 827-3737

(G-135)
MID AMERICA PROTOTYPING INC
428 E 21st St (46016-4412)
PHONE..................................765 643-3200
Todd Wetz, *President*
Kimberly Wetz, *Vice Pres*
EMP: 3
SQ FT: 6,000

SALES: 150K **Privately Held**
SIC: 3999 Miniatures

(G-136)
MILL STEEL CO
444 E 29th St (46016-5319)
PHONE..................................765 622-4545
EMP: 120
SALES (corp-wide): 319.1MM **Privately Held**
SIC: 5051 3316 Steel; cold-rolled strip or wire
PA: The Mill Steel Co
5116 36th St Se
Grand Rapids MI 49512
616 949-6700

(G-137)
MITCHELL SMITH RACING
Also Called: Mitchell Smith Auto Service
4570 W State Road 32 (46011-1542)
PHONE..................................765 640-0237
Fax: 765 640-0716
Mitchell Smith, *Owner*
Mary Smith, *Co-Owner*
EMP: 9
SALES (est): 1.3MM **Privately Held**
SIC: 3519 7549 7538 Internal combustion engines; high performance auto repair & service; general automotive repair shops

(G-138)
MOFAB INC (PA)
1415 Fairview St (46016-3524)
PHONE..................................765 649-1288
Fax: 765 641-1555
L William Hains, *Ch of Bd*
Max W Hains, *President*
Doug Nagel, *Opers Staff*
Bruce S Hains, *Treasurer*
Bruce Hains, *Treasurer*
EMP: 35
SQ FT: 60,000
SALES (est): 6.8MM **Privately Held**
SIC: 3441 5051 3446 Fabricated structural metal; steel; ornamental metalwork

(G-139)
MOFAB INC
Also Called: Ornamental Division
619 W 14th St (46016-3502)
PHONE..................................765 649-1288
Fax: 765 641-1558
Michelle Howard, *Office Mgr*
Bruce Hains, *Manager*
EMP: 8
SQ FT: 6,000
SALES (corp-wide): 6.8MM **Privately Held**
SIC: 3446 5999 1799 Architectural metalwork; awnings; fence construction
PA: Mofab Inc
1415 Fairview St
Anderson IN 46016
765 649-1288

(G-140)
MUHLEN SOHN INDUSTRIES LP
Also Called: MSI
4640 Martin Lut (46013)
PHONE..................................765 640-9674
Fax: 765 640-0914
Petra Muhlen, *President*
Dick Wohlberg, *General Mgr*
Albert Hagen, *Prdtn Mgr*
Melanie Vincent, *Office Mgr*
Zac Swan, *Manager*
▲ **EMP:** 18
SQ FT: 60,000
SALES (est): 3.7MM **Privately Held**
SIC: 2296 Cord & fabric for reinforcing industrial belting

(G-141)
N-COMPLETE INC
804 Lincoln St (46016-1320)
P.O. Box 2309 (46018-2309)
PHONE..................................765 649-2244
Christopher T Ashby, *Principal*
EMP: 2
SALES (est): 209.4K **Privately Held**
SIC: 3537 Trucks, tractors, loaders, carriers & similar equipment

(G-142)
NATIVE CROSSBOWS LLC
2310 Broadway St (46012-1609)
P.O. Box 712, Frankton (46044-0712)
PHONE..................................765 641-2224
EMP: 2
SALES (est): 109.1K **Privately Held**
SIC: 3949 Crossbows

(G-143)
NATURAL COATING SYSTEMS
3220 W 25th St (46011-4617)
PHONE..................................765 642-2464
Chuck Thomas, *Principal*
EMP: 2
SALES (est): 91K **Privately Held**
SIC: 3479 Coating of metals & formed products

(G-144)
NESTLE USA INC
4301 W 73rd St (46011-8809)
PHONE..................................765 778-6000
Grant Normann, *Branch Mgr*
EMP: 139
SALES (corp-wide): 90.8B **Privately Held**
WEB: www.nestleusa.com
SIC: 2023 2033 2064 2047 Evaporated milk; canned milk, whole; cream substitutes; fruits: packaged in cans, jars, etc.; tomato paste: packaged in cans, jars, etc.; tomato sauce: packaged in cans, jars, etc.; candy & other confectionery products; breakfast bars; dog food; cat food
HQ: Nestle Usa, Inc.
1812 N Moore St
Rosslyn VA 22209
818 549-6000

(G-145)
NEWCO METALS INC
1515 E 22nd St (46016-4613)
PHONE..................................765 644-6649
Chris Rasmussen, *Branch Mgr*
EMP: 3
SALES (est): 132.3K
SALES (corp-wide): 18.8MM **Privately Held**
SIC: 5093 5051 3341 Nonferrous metals scrap; metals service centers & offices; secondary nonferrous metals
PA: Newco Metals, Inc.
7268 S State Road 13
Pendleton IN 46064
317 485-7721

(G-146)
NOTABLES
1325 Meridian St (46016-1828)
PHONE..................................765 649-1648
Connie Eutsler, *Owner*
EMP: 2
SALES (est): 211K **Privately Held**
SIC: 2759 Screen printing

(G-147)
OAK LIEF
3211 Jay Dr (46012-1217)
PHONE..................................765 642-9010
Losie W Wools, *Partner*
Jerry Wools, *Partner*
EMP: 2
SALES (est): 155K **Privately Held**
SIC: 2511 Whatnot shelves: wood

(G-148)
OPEN GATE LLC
Also Called: Open Gate Design & Decor
2834 W 900 W (46011-9128)
PHONE..................................765 734-1314
Eric Scott,
EMP: 6
SALES (est): 945.8K **Privately Held**
SIC: 3446 Fences, gates, posts & flagpoles

(G-149)
PARALLAX GROUP INC
600 Broadway St (46012-2922)
PHONE..................................800 443-4859
Joseph Brandon, *President*
Marty Redd, *Technical Staff*
David Smart, *Services*
EMP: 7

SALES (est): 214.3K **Privately Held**
SIC: 3799 Recreational vehicles

(G-150)
PERFECTO TOOL &
ENGINEERING CO
1124 W 53rd St (46013-1305)
P.O. Box 2039 (46018-2039)
PHONE....................................765 644-2821
Fax: 765 644-2881
Stephen D Skaggs, *President*
Andrew Skaggs, *President*
Chris Sharp, *Vice Pres*
▼ EMP: 40
SQ FT: 37,000
SALES: 4.1MM **Privately Held**
WEB: www.perfecto.com
SIC: 3599 3544 3469 Custom machinery;
dies & die holders for metal cutting, form-
ing, die casting; industrial molds; machine
parts, stamped or pressed metal

(G-151)
PERKINSVILLE POWER SPORTS
2834 N 900 W (46011-9128)
PHONE....................................765 734-1314
G Robert Likens Jr, *Principal*
EMP: 4
SALES (est): 457.5K **Privately Held**
SIC: 3799 All terrain vehicles (ATV)

(G-152)
PIERCE TRACY
4663 State Road 32 E (46017-9511)
PHONE....................................765 748-2361
Tracy Pierce, *Owner*
EMP: 2
SALES (est): 150.4K **Privately Held**
SIC: 3537 Industrial trucks & tractors

(G-153)
PLASTICRAFT-COMPLETE
ACRYLICS
4441 S Scatterfield Rd (46013-2944)
PHONE....................................765 610-9502
Stan Boyd, *Principal*
EMP: 3
SALES (est): 231.6K **Privately Held**
SIC: 3083 Plastic finished products, lami-
nated

(G-154)
PRAIRIE FARMS DAIRY INC
722 Broadway St (46012-2924)
PHONE....................................765 649-1261
Jeffrey Heygen, *Branch Mgr*
EMP: 66
SALES (corp-wide): 1.8B **Privately Held**
SIC: 2026 Milk processing (pasteurizing,
homogenizing, bottling)
PA: Prairie Farms Dairy, Inc.
3744 Staunton Rd
Edwardsville IL 62025
618 659-5700

(G-155)
PRAISE GATHERING MUSIC
GROUP
9 W 10th St (46016-1408)
P.O. Box 350 (46015-0350)
PHONE....................................765 640-4428
Fax: 765 608-5163
Julie Wilson, *President*
Randy Vader, *Owner*
Jay Rouse, *Vice Pres*
Carol Vader, *CFO*
Chrislyn Reed, *Publications*
EMP: 10 EST: 1993
SALES (est): 1.1MM **Privately Held**
WEB: www.praisegathering.com
SIC: 5735 2741 Records; music book &
sheet music publishing

(G-156)
PRINTER ZINK INC
Also Called: Quality Printing
1047 Broadway St (46012-2526)
PHONE....................................765 644-3959
Fax: 765 643-3809
Steve Harney, *President*
John Oblazney, *President*
David Doll, *Business Mgr*
John Thomas, *Business Mgr*
Beth Champe, *Project Mgr*
EMP: 70

SQ FT: 40,000
SALES (est): 16.3MM **Privately Held**
WEB: www.quality-printing.com
SIC: 2752 2789 2053 Commercial print-
ing, offset; bookbinding & related work;
frozen bakery products, except bread

(G-157)
RAINE INC
6401 S Madison Ave (46013-3336)
P.O. Box 2219 (46018-2219)
PHONE....................................765 622-7687
Fax: 765 622-7691
Raine John Jr, *President*
EMP: 12
SQ FT: 13,000
SALES (est): 968K **Privately Held**
WEB: www.raineinc.com
SIC: 2311 5131 2393 3161 Military uni-
forms, men's & youths': purchased mate-
rials; nylon piece goods, woven; textile
bags; luggage; blankbooks & looseleaf
binders; broadwoven fabric mills, man-
made

(G-158)
REBOUND PROJECT LLP
1125 N Madison Ave (46011-1211)
PHONE....................................765 621-5604
Eric Foley, *Partner*
Rob Spaulding, *Partner*
EMP: 2
SALES: 6K **Privately Held**
SIC: 8748 6794 7372 Business consult-
ing; music licensing to radio stations; ap-
plication computer software

(G-159)
RECYCLE DESIGN INC
804 Hazlett St (46016-2324)
PHONE....................................765 374-0316
Edward Boutwell, *President*
Josh Boutwell, *Marketing Staff*
EMP: 4
SQ FT: 1,600
SALES (est): 666.7K **Privately Held**
SIC: 2531 Benches for public buildings;
picnic tables or benches, park

(G-160)
REMY LOGISTICS LLC (DH)
2902 Enterprise Dr (46013-9667)
PHONE....................................765 683-3700
Paul Newport,
Rod English,
Rick Stanley,
EMP: 1
SALES (est): 3.8MM
SALES (corp-wide): 9.8B **Publicly Held**
SIC: 5013 3694 Testing equipment, electri-
cal: automotive; automotive electrical
equipment

(G-161)
RESIN PARTNERS INC (DH)
Also Called: Home Design Products
6435 S Scatterfield Rd (46013-9619)
PHONE....................................765 298-6800
Sami Sagol, *Ch of Bd*
Yossi Sagol, *President*
Jeff Flagg, *VP Finance*
▲ EMP: 130
SQ FT: 500,000
SALES (est): 43.3MM
SALES (corp-wide): 74.7K **Privately Held**
SIC: 3089 Boxes, plastic
HQ: Sunterrace Casual Furniture, Inc.
2369 Chrles Rper Jnas Hwy
Stanley NC 28164
704 263-1967

(G-162)
REYNOLDSRUSSELL ENTPS
LLC
2324 Jefferson St (46016-4507)
PHONE....................................317 431-5886
Alex Russell, *Mng Member*
EMP: 4
SALES: 170K **Privately Held**
SIC: 3559 7539 Automotive related ma-
chinery; machine shop, automotive

(G-163)
RIGDON INCORPORATED
209 S 500 W (46011-9069)
PHONE....................................765 393-2283

Tamra L Rigdon, *President*
EMP: 2
SALES (est): 83.9K **Privately Held**
SIC: 2752 Commercial printing, litho-
graphic

(G-164)
RUBY ENTERPRISES INC
Also Called: Soft Stop
1150 W 29th St (46016-6001)
PHONE....................................765 649-0115
Fax: 765 649-0115
John Ruby, *Owner*
Jill Ruby, *Owner*
EMP: 7
SQ FT: 8,000
SALES (est): 595.3K **Privately Held**
SIC: 2299 5999 Padding & wadding, tex-
tile; awnings

(G-165)
SHORTS MACHINE SHOP
509 E 29th St (46016-5322)
PHONE....................................765 622-6259
David Short, *Owner*
Dave Short, *Owner*
EMP: 7
SALES (est): 507.1K **Privately Held**
SIC: 3599 Machine shop, jobbing & repair

(G-166)
SIGN PROS INC
633 Jackson St (46016-1156)
P.O. Box 233, Chesterfield (46017-0233)
PHONE....................................765 642-1175
Fax: 765 642-1175
Ronald Kinder, *President*
EMP: 3
SALES (est): 310.4K **Privately Held**
SIC: 3993 Signs & advertising specialties

(G-167)
SIRMAX NORTH AMERICA INC
2915 Dr Martin Luther Kin (46016-4848)
PHONE....................................765 639-0300
Massimo Pavin, *President*
Lorenzo Ferro, *Vice Pres*
Roberto Pavin, *Admin Sec*
EMP: 20 EST: 2015
SALES: 18.6MM
SALES (corp-wide): 10.5K **Privately Held**
SIC: 2295 Resin or plastic coated fabrics
HQ: Sirmax Spa
Viale Dell'artigianato 42
Cittadella PD 35013

(G-168)
SPECTRUM MARKETING
1629 Pearl St (46016-2022)
PHONE....................................765 643-5566
Donna Trueblood, *Manager*
EMP: 2
SQ FT: 2,500
SALES: 60K **Privately Held**
SIC: 7389 2396 7641 2262 Embroidering
of advertising on shirts, etc.; screen print-
ing on fabric articles; reupholstery & furni-
ture repair; finishing plants, manmade
fiber & silk fabrics; emblems, embroidered

(G-169)
SPOTLIGHT ON DRAMA
3551 W 8th Street Rd (46011-9170)
PHONE....................................765 643-7170
Stacie Bower, *Owner*
EMP: 2
SALES (est): 88.3K **Privately Held**
SIC: 3648 Spotlights

(G-170)
STANDOUT CREATIONS LLC
1078 E 500 S (46013-9639)
P.O. Box 1412 (46015-1412)
PHONE....................................765 203-9110
William Richardson, *President*
EMP: 2
SALES (est): 164.9K **Privately Held**
SIC: 2759 Commercial printing

(G-171)
STORED ENERGY SOLUTIONS
INC
3619 W 73rd St (46011-9608)
PHONE....................................574 457-2199
Robert Sikorski, *CEO*
Frank Levinson, *Managing Dir*

Alan Tehan, *COO*
Dane Davis, *Chief Engr*
EMP: 3
SALES (est): 560.4K **Privately Held**
SIC: 3714 Transmissions, motor vehicle

(G-172)
T & H SWEEPER CO
4134 S Scatterfield Rd (46013-2627)
PHONE....................................765 641-9800
Tom Hickey, *Branch Mgr*
EMP: 2
SALES (corp-wide): 1.3MM **Privately**
Held
SIC: 3699 Household electrical equipment
PA: T & H Sweeper Co
626 S Walnut St
Muncie IN 47305
765 282-9976

(G-173)
TECHNOLOGY MGT GROUP INC
Also Called: T M G
16 Edgewood Dr (46011-2206)
PHONE....................................765 606-1512
Katherine Tanner, *President*
Brian Tanner, *CTO*
EMP: 12
SQ FT: 1,200
SALES (est): 569.4K **Privately Held**
SIC: 7371 7379 3721 Computer software
systems analysis & design, custom; com-
puter hardware requirements analysis;
aircraft

(G-174)
TECNOPLAST USA LLC
3619 W 73rd St Ste 1 (46011-9608)
PHONE....................................317 769-4929
Gloria Da Ros, *CEO*
Ronnie Da Ros, *Vice Pres*
▲ EMP: 7
SQ FT: 40,000
SALES: 1MM
SALES (corp-wide): 379.8K **Privately**
Held
SIC: 3089 Hardware, plastic
PA: Tecnoplast Srl
Via Del Fangario 22
Cagliari CA
070 208-0026

(G-175)
TERRANCE SMITH
DISTRIBUTING
2215 N Madison Ave (46011-9583)
PHONE....................................765 644-3396
Fax: 765 649-7958
Terrance A Smith, *President*
▲ EMP: 55
SQ FT: 800,000
SALES (est): 12.9MM **Privately Held**
SIC: 5181 2082 Beer & other fermented
malt liquors; malt beverages

(G-176)
TETRASOLV INC
Also Called: Tetrasolv Filtration
1424 Abraham Dr (46013-1184)
PHONE....................................765 643-3941
Eric D Patterson, *President*
◆ EMP: 10
SQ FT: 12,000
SALES: 710K **Privately Held**
WEB: www.tetrasolv.com
SIC: 3677 Filtration devices, electronic

(G-177)
TOP IN SOUND INC
3273 N State Road 9 (46012-1235)
PHONE....................................765 649-8111
Fax: 765 641-7261
Patrick E Topolsky, *President*
EMP: 8
SALES (est): 670K **Privately Held**
WEB: www.topinsound.com
SIC: 3699 5731 7812 Electric sound
equipment; radio, television & electronic
stores; audio-visual program production

(G-178)
TRE PAPER CO INC
5395 S 50 W (46013-9500)
PHONE....................................765 649-2536
Fax: 765 649-4033
Robert T Mier, *President*

EMP: 20
SQ FT: 25,000
SALES (est): 3.8MM Privately Held
SIC: 2653 2675 2657 Corrugated & solid
fiber boxes; die-cut paper & board; folding
paperboard boxes

(G-179)
TRU-CUT INC
3111 S Madison Ave (46016-6011)
PHONE..................................765 683-9920
Fax: 765 683-9921
Kevin Elpers, *President*
Brian Elpers, *VP Mfg*
Eric Norton, *Opers Mgr*
Tony Anderson, *Admin Sec*
▲ **EMP:** 33
SQ FT: 90,000
SALES (est): 6.3MM Privately Held
WEB: www.trucut.com
SIC: 2431 Millwork

(G-180)
UNIQUE GLOBAL SOLUTIONS
LLC
5729 S 200 E (46017-9536)
P.O. Box 36, Chesterfield (46017-0036)
PHONE..................................765 779-5030
Ralph E Gardner,
EMP: 2
SALES (est): 140K Privately Held
SIC: 2522 7389 Office furniture, except
wood;

(G-181)
VEE ENGINEERING INC (PA)
3620 W 73rd St (46011-9608)
PHONE..................................765 778-7895
John Reynolds, *President*
David Lawson Sr, *Vice Pres*
Jay Porter, *Office Mgr*
EMP: 2 **EST:** 1967
SQ FT: 2,000
SALES (est): 11.9MM Privately Held
SIC: 3089 Injection molded finished plastic
products

(G-182)
WANDA HARRINGTON
Also Called: Bush Trophy Case & Embroidery
5215 S 100 W (46013-9404)
PHONE..................................765 642-1628
Wanda Harrington, *Owner*
EMP: 3
SQ FT: 1,200
SALES (est): 218.2K Privately Held
SIC: 5999 2395 Trophies & plaques; em-
broidery products, except schiffli machine

(G-183)
XEROX CORPORATION
2828 Enterprise Dr (46013-9663)
PHONE..................................765 778-6249
Jeremiah Lapole, *Principal*
Matt Weisgerber, *Technology*
EMP: 2
SALES (est): 85.9K Privately Held
SIC: 3577 Computer peripheral equipment

(G-184)
XTREME ADS LIMITED
Also Called: Xtreme Alternative Def Systems
1735 W 53rd St (46013-1105)
PHONE..................................765 644-7323
Peter V Bitar, *President*
Bill Hazelbaker, *Prdtn Mgr*
Sandall Darrel, *Regl Sales Mgr*
Chase Hill, *Technology*
Brad Jamison, *Technician*
EMP: 23
SQ FT: 80,000
SALES: 3.5MM Privately Held
SIC: 3812 8711 Defense systems & equip-
ment; engineering services

Andrews
Huntington County

(G-185)
W & W LOCKER
8896 W 600 N (46702-9507)
PHONE..................................260 344-3400
Gary Lopshire, *Owner*

EMP: 3
SALES (est): 204.8K Privately Held
SIC: 2011 Meat packing plants

Angola
Steuben County

(G-186)
200 EXPRESS
2040 N 200 W (46703-8185)
PHONE..................................260 833-2125
Lynn Garman, *Owner*
EMP: 2
SALES (est): 136.8K Privately Held
SIC: 2741 Miscellaneous publishing

(G-187)
AAA-GPC HOLDINGS LLC (PA)
Also Called: AAA Sales and Engineering
1411 Wohlert St (46703-1062)
PHONE..................................260 668-1468
Bradley Long, *CEO*
EMP: 67
SQ FT: 160,000
SALES (est): 25MM Privately Held
SIC: 3365 3547 3542 Machinery castings,
aluminum; steel rolling machinery; forging
machinery & hammers

(G-188)
AARDVARK VINYL SIGNS
1875 W 275 N (46703-9540)
PHONE..................................260 833-0800
Josh Kugler, *Owner*
EMP: 3
SALES (est): 261.4K Privately Held
SIC: 3993 Signs & advertising specialties

(G-189)
AGGREGATE INDUSTRIES -
MWR INC
1310 W Maumee St (46703-1359)
PHONE..................................260 665-2052
Fax: 260 665-8425
Gary Manley, *Branch Mgr*
Andy Williams, *Manager*
EMP: 21
SALES (corp-wide): 26.4B Privately Held
SIC: 3273 Ready-mixed concrete
HQ: Aggregate Industries - Mwr, Inc.
2815 Dodd Rd
Eagan MN 55121
651 683-0600

(G-190)
AMI INDUSTRIES INC
1501 Wohlert St (46703-1064)
PHONE..................................989 786-3755
Jeff Evans, *Branch Mgr*
EMP: 25
SALES (corp-wide): 39.6MM Privately
Held
SIC: 3559 Automotive related machinery
PA: Ami Industries, Inc.
5093 N Red Oak Rd
Lewiston MI 49756
989 786-3755

(G-191)
ANGOLA CANVAS CO INC
2301 N Wayne St (46703-9110)
PHONE..................................260 665-9913
Fax: 260 665-1051
Richard A Hocker, *President*
Barbara Hocker, *Corp Secy*
EMP: 10
SQ FT: 6,700
SALES: 720K Privately Held
SIC: 2394 3732 Convertible tops, canvas
or boat: from purchased materials; boat
building & repairing

(G-192)
ANGOLA WIRE PRODUCTS INC
(PA)
803 Wohlert St (46703-1079)
PHONE..................................260 665-9447
Fax: 260 665-6182
Michael G Heroy, *CEO*
Kenneth Brine A, *Principal*
Todd Boots, *VP Mfg*
Mike Walters, *Project Mgr*
Mike Golliff, *Maint Spvr*

▲ **EMP:** 170 **EST:** 1960
SALES: 21.4MM Privately Held
WEB: www.angolawire.com
SIC: 3496 3479 Miscellaneous fabricated
wire products; shelving, made from purchased wire; coating of metals & formed
products

(G-193)
ANGOLA WIRE PRODUCTS INC
Also Called: A W Manufacturing
1300 Wohlert St (46703-1059)
PHONE..................................260 665-3061
Fax: 260 665-3849
Todd Boots, *Manager*
EMP: 35
SALES (corp-wide): 21.4MM Privately
Held
WEB: www.angolawire.com
SIC: 3496 5051 3599 Miscellaneous fab-
ricated wire products; metals service cen-
ters & offices; machine shop, jobbing &
repair
PA: Angola Wire Products, Inc.
803 Wohlert St
Angola IN 46703
260 665-9447

(G-194)
ASTBURY WATER
TECHNOLOGY INC
601 W 400 N (46703-9516)
PHONE..................................260 668-8900
Daniel Astbury, *Owner*
Dan Fox, *Sr Project Mgr*
Chelsea Sanders, *Manager*
EMP: 23
SALES (corp-wide): 12.5MM Privately
Held
SIC: 2899 3826 Water treating com-
pounds; water testing apparatus
PA: Astbury Water Technology, Incorpo-
rated
5940 W Raymond St
Indianapolis IN 46241
317 328-7153

(G-195)
AUTOFORM TOOL & MFG LLC
Also Called: Atm
1501 Wohlert St (46703-1064)
PHONE..................................260 624-2014
Fax: 260 495-2724
Douglas Jackson, *General Mgr*
Doug Jackson, *General Mgr*
Jake Christen, *Engineer*
Roger Pressler, *Engineer*
John H Balser, *Treasurer*
EMP: 240
SQ FT: 135,000
SALES: 72.1MM
SALES (corp-wide): 1.4B Publicly Held
WEB: www.autoformtool.com
SIC: 3714 5084 3463 3462 Motor vehicle
parts & accessories; industrial machinery
& equipment; pump, compressor, turbine
& engine forgings, except auto; pump,
compressor & turbine forgings; industrial
pumps & parts; pump jacks & other
pumping equipment
PA: Park-Ohio Holdings Corp.
6065 Parkland Blvd Ste 1
Cleveland OH 44124
440 947-2000

(G-196)
BARIL COATINGS
401 Growth Pkwy (46703-9323)
PHONE..................................260 665-8431
Fax: 260 665-5829
David Harman Sr, *President*
EMP: 10
SQ FT: 12,000
SALES (est): 1.7MM Privately Held
WEB: www.fredainc.com
SIC: 1799 2891 Epoxy application; epoxy
adhesives

(G-197)
BARIL COATINGS USA LLC
401 Growth Pkwy (46703-9323)
PHONE..................................260 665-8431
David P Harmon Sr,
David P Harmon Jr,
EMP: 16
SQ FT: 24,000

SALES (est): 6MM Privately Held
SIC: 2851 Paints & allied products

(G-198)
BSC VNTRES ACQUISITION SUB
LLC
Also Called: Triton Plant
100 Woodhull Dr (46703-9339)
PHONE..................................260 665-7521
Fax: 260 665-7609
John Roberts, *General Mgr*
David McDonald, *Plant Mgr*
Jeannette Wall, *Production*
Lisa Woods, *Buyer*
Steve Stapleton, *Purchasing*
EMP: 65
SQ FT: 90,000
SALES (corp-wide): 11.7MM Privately
Held
SIC: 2677 2791 Envelopes; typesetting
HQ: Bsc Ventures Llc
7702 Plantation Rd
Roanoke VA 24019
540 362-3311

(G-199)
BUDGET INKS LLC
45 S Public Sq (46703-1926)
PHONE..................................877 636-4657
James Schall, *Mng Member*
EMP: 5
SALES (est): 725.9K Privately Held
SIC: 2893 Printing ink

(G-200)
BURKHART MANUFACTURING
INC
6534 N 450 W (46703-9445)
PHONE..................................260 316-0715
Travis Burkhart, *Principal*
EMP: 2
SALES (est): 120.1K Privately Held
SIC: 3999 Manufacturing industries

(G-201)
C & K ENTERPRISES INC
Also Called: C & K Tool
240 Growth Pkwy (46703-9331)
PHONE..................................260 624-3123
Mike Pahl, *President*
Lucy Meeks, *Office Mgr*
Michael Lee Pahl, *Manager*
EMP: 25
SQ FT: 12,000
SALES (est): 4.5MM Privately Held
SIC: 3841 3571 Surgical & medical instru-
ments; electronic computers

(G-202)
CHAPMANS CIDER COMPANY
LLC
300 Industrial Dr (46703-1053)
PHONE..................................260 444-1194
Scott Fergusson, *CEO*
EMP: 7
SALES (est): 853.7K Privately Held
SIC: 2082 Malt beverages

(G-203)
CLARK MILLWORKS
1587 S Old Us Highway 27 (46703-8956)
PHONE..................................260 665-1270
Fax: 260 665-7649
Stephen Clark, *Partner*
Tim Fournier, *Partner*
EMP: 2 **EST:** 1988
SALES: 250K Privately Held
WEB: www.clarkmillworks.com
SIC: 2431 Moldings & baseboards, orna-
mental & trim

(G-204)
CONCEPT CARS INC
1280 N 290 W (46703-9004)
PHONE..................................260 668-7553
Steve Asztalos, *President*
EMP: 7
SQ FT: 10,000
SALES: 250K Privately Held
SIC: 3711 Motor vehicles & car bodies

▲ = Import ▼=Export
◆ =Import/Export

(G-205)
COUNTY OF STEUBEN
Also Called: Steuben County Parks
100 Lane 101 Crooked Lk (46703-9162)
PHONE......................260 833-2401
Eric Ditmars, *Director*
EMP: 3 **Privately Held**
SIC: 2531 Picnic tables or benches, park
PA: County Of Steuben
317 S Wayne St Ste 2j
Angola IN 46703
260 668-1000

(G-206)
CUSTOM POLISH & CHROME
114 Lange Ln (46703-2164)
PHONE......................260 665-7448
Fax: 260 665-7448
Jim Himes, *President*
EMP: 3
SALES (est): 307.1K **Privately Held**
SIC: 3471 Polishing, metals or formed products

(G-207)
CUT-PRO INDEXABLE TOOLING LLC
212 Growth Pkwy (46703-9331)
P.O. Box 657 (46703-0657)
PHONE......................260 668-2400
Scott Traylor,
Marci Traylor,
EMP: 2
SQ FT: 2,500
SALES (est): 151.2K **Privately Held**
SIC: 3541 Machine tools, metal cutting type

(G-208)
E M F CORP (PA)
505 Pokagon Trl (46703-9320)
P.O. Box 389 (46703-0389)
PHONE......................260 665-9541
Fax: 260 665-3040
Steve Daugherty, *CEO*
Howards Sanders, *President*
Jacqueline Poe, *Corp Secy*
Buzz Steele, *Production*
Jeff Sager, *Purch Mgr*
▲ **EMP:** 40
SQ FT: 175,000
SALES (est): 40.4MM **Privately Held**
WEB: www.emfusa.com
SIC: 3643 3699 3694 Connectors, electric cord; electrical equipment & supplies; engine electrical equipment

(G-209)
EJ BROOKS COMPANY (DH)
Also Called: Tydenbrooks
409 Hoosier Dr (46703-9335)
PHONE......................800 348-4777
Robert Logeman, *CEO*
Phil Whitley, *Vice Pres*
Michael Roberson, *Accountant*
Karina Lopez, *Business Anlyst*
Barbara Hanshaw, *Clerk*
◆ **EMP:** 75 **EST:** 1873
SQ FT: 44,000
SALES (est): 332.2MM
SALES (corp-wide): 392.1MM **Privately Held**
WEB: www.ejbrooks.com
SIC: 3679 Hermetic seals for electronic equipment
HQ: Tyden Group Holdings Corp.
409 Hoosier Dr
Angola IN 46703
740 420-6777

(G-210)
EJ BROOKS COMPANY (HQ)
Also Called: Tyden Brooks
409 Hoosier Dr (46703-9335)
PHONE......................260 624-4800
Fax: 260 655-8309
John Spillane, *President*
Ian Morton, *President*
Bruce Heinemann, *Treasurer*
Paul Baldetti, *Admin Sec*
◆ **EMP:** 89
SQ FT: 82,000

SALES (est): 26.8MM
SALES (corp-wide): 392.1MM **Privately Held**
WEB: www.tydenbrammall.com
SIC: 3429 Clamps, metal
PA: Crimson Capital Silicon Valley
601 California St # 1450
San Francisco CA 94108
650 233-6900

(G-211)
ELECTRIC-TEC LLC
Also Called: Electri-Tec Inc.
509 Growth Pkwy (46703-9324)
PHONE......................260 665-1252
Michael Khorshid, *CEO*
Bill Khorshid, *President*
Greg Baker, *CFO*
EMP: 45
SQ FT: 30,000
SALES: 5.5MM
SALES (corp-wide): 52.7MM **Privately Held**
SIC: 3679 Harness assemblies for electronic use: wire or cable
PA: Khorporate Holdings, Inc.
6492 State Road 205
Laotto IN 46763
260 357-3365

(G-212)
ERIE HAVEN INC
1310 W Maumee St (46703-1359)
PHONE......................260 665-2052
EMP: 4
SALES (est): 211.6K **Privately Held**
SIC: 3273 Ready-mixed concrete

(G-213)
FEDDEMA INDUSTRIES INC
Also Called: Special Cutting Tools
1305 Wohlert St (46703-1060)
P.O. Box 246 (46703-0246)
PHONE......................260 665-6463
Fax: 260 665-2665
Leonard Feddema, *President*
EMP: 15 **EST:** 1968
SQ FT: 9,800
SALES (est): 2.4MM **Privately Held**
WEB: www.specialcuttingtools.net
SIC: 3599 3545 Machine shop, jobbing & repair; machine tool accessories

(G-214)
FLEX-N-GATE CORPORATION
3000 Woodhull Dr (46703-9318)
PHONE......................260 665-8288
Matt Tacia, *Branch Mgr*
EMP: 210
SALES (corp-wide): 3.3B **Privately Held**
WEB: www.meridianautosystems.com
SIC: 3465 3714 Automotive stampings; motor vehicle parts & accessories
PA: Flex-N-Gate Corporation
1306 E University Ave
Urbana IL 61802
217 384-6600

(G-215)
G & S SUPER ABRASIVES INC
1601 Wohlert St (46703-1066)
P.O. Box 461 (46703-0461)
PHONE......................260 665-5562
Fax: 260 665-8266
Paul M Jordan, *President*
Lisa Jordan, *Treasurer*
EMP: 23
SQ FT: 8,400
SALES: 3.3MM **Privately Held**
WEB: www.gssuperabrasives.com
SIC: 3291 3541 3545 Hones; abrasive wheels & grindstones, not artificial; grinding, polishing, buffing, lapping & honing machines; machine tool accessories

(G-216)
GENERAL PRODUCTS ANGOLA CORP
1411 Wohlert St (46703-1062)
PHONE......................260 665-8441
Fax: 260 665-6727
Gerald Kyro, *President*
▲ **EMP:** 127
SQ FT: 90,000

SALES (est): 18.4MM
SALES (corp-wide): 50.5MM **Privately Held**
WEB: www.general-products.com
SIC: 3714 Manifolds, motor vehicle; axles, motor vehicle
PA: General Products Corp.
146 Monroe Center St Nw # 701
Grand Rapids MI 49503
260 668-1475

(G-217)
GENERAL PRODUCTS CORPORATION
1411 Wohlert St (46703-1062)
PHONE......................260 668-1440
EMP: 115
SALES (corp-wide): 50.5MM **Privately Held**
SIC: 3599 3462 3369 Machine shop, jobbing & repair; iron & steel forgings; non-ferrous foundries
HQ: General Products Corporation
146 Monroe Center St Nw # 701
Grand Rapids MI 49503
270 726-6126

(G-218)
HI-PRO INC
Also Called: Hpi Wire Assemblies
1410 Wohlert St Ste C (46703-1061)
P.O. Box 480 (46703-0480)
PHONE......................260 665-5038
Wally Stevens, *President*
Stephanie Gaff, *Shareholder*
Robert Hiatt, *Shareholder*
▲ **EMP:** 10
SQ FT: 22,000
SALES (est): 1.7MM **Privately Held**
SIC: 3679 Harness assemblies for electronic use: wire or cable

(G-219)
HIGHLAND COMPUTER FORMS INC
1510 Wohlert St (46703-1063)
PHONE......................260 665-6268
Fax: 260 665-3644
James Reas, *Production*
Tracy Thackston, *Sales Associate*
Robert Jones, *Manager*
EMP: 20
SALES (corp-wide): 28.5MM **Privately Held**
WEB: www.hcf.com
SIC: 2761 Computer forms, manifold or continuous
PA: Highland Computer Forms, Inc.
1025 W Main St
Hillsboro OH 45133
937 393-4215

(G-220)
HUDSON AQUATIC SYSTEMS LLC
1100 Wohlert St (46703-1034)
PHONE......................260 665-1635
George Hunter, *President*
Tom Ellis, *Principal*
EMP: 14
SQ FT: 42,000
SALES: 3MM **Privately Held**
WEB: www.hudsonaquatic.com
SIC: 3949 Water sports equipment

(G-221)
JKR INC
Also Called: Ramco of Indiana
301 Growth Pkwy (46703-9322)
PHONE......................260 665-1067
EMP: 13
SALES (est): 870K **Privately Held**
SIC: 3321 Mfg Manholes & Pipe Guards

(G-222)
JOHNNY LEMAS
2314 N 200 W (46703-9125)
PHONE......................260 833-8850
Fax: 260 833-5288
Johnny Lemas, *Principal*
▲ **EMP:** 3
SALES (est): 422.5K **Privately Held**
SIC: 2899 5961 Fireworks; catalog & mail-order houses

(G-223)
JROWE SIGNS
311 S Superior St (46703-1816)
PHONE......................260 668-7100
Judy Rowe, *Owner*
EMP: 2
SQ FT: 2,000
SALES: 100K **Privately Held**
SIC: 3993 Electric signs

(G-224)
KAS SATELLITE & CABLE INC (PA)
Also Called: King's Antenna Service
60 Lane 165 Jimmerson Lk (46703-9179)
P.O. Box 1027 (46703-5027)
PHONE......................260 833-3941
King D Oberlin, *President*
Lori Oberlin, *Vice Pres*
EMP: 3
SQ FT: 2,000
SALES: 750K **Privately Held**
WEB: www.kas-satellite.com
SIC: 3651 Home entertainment equipment, electronic

(G-225)
KIRK ENTERPRISES
333 Hoosier Dr (46703-9336)
PHONE......................260 665-3670
Fax: 260 665-9432
Jeff Kirk, *Partner*
Mike Kirk, *Partner*
EMP: 5
SQ FT: 5,000
SALES (est): 589.3K **Privately Held**
WEB: www.kirkphoto.com
SIC: 3599 Machine shop, jobbing & repair

(G-226)
KNOX INC
Also Called: Dodge Heating and Coolg Contrs
101 Fox Lake Rd (46703-2162)
PHONE......................260 665-6617
Fax: 260 665-9654
Roger Knox, *President*
Deborah Knox, *Corp Secy*
EMP: 12 **EST:** 1926
SQ FT: 4,800
SALES (est): 800K **Privately Held**
SIC: 1711 3444 Warm air heating & air conditioning contractor; sheet metalwork

(G-227)
KPC MEDIA GROUP INC
45 S Public Sq (46703-1926)
PHONE......................678 645-0000
Lindsay Brown, *Branch Mgr*
EMP: 4
SALES (corp-wide): 28.7MM **Privately Held**
SIC: 2711 Newspapers, publishing & printing
PA: Kpc Media Group Inc.
102 N Main St
Kendallville IN 46755
260 347-0400

(G-228)
LOMONT HOLDINGS CO INC
Also Called: Illuminated Image
1825 W Maumee St (46703-7066)
P.O. Box 537 (46703-0537)
PHONE......................800 545-9023
Barbara Lomont, *President*
Judy Kunce, *Project Mgr*
Connie Wilson, *Project Mgr*
Von Lomont, *Prdtn Mgr*
Marry McKenzie, *Human Res Mgr*
EMP: 35
SQ FT: 37,000
SALES (est): 6.8MM **Privately Held**
WEB: www.illuminatedimage.com
SIC: 2394 3646 3829 2396 Awnings, fabric: made from purchased materials; fluorescent lighting fixtures, commercial; measuring & controlling devices; fabric printing & stamping; adhesives; electric lamps

(G-229)
METAL SPINNERS INC (PA)
914 Wohlert St (46703-1078)
P.O. Box 269 (46703-0269)
PHONE......................260 665-2158
Fax: 260 665-3244

Olin M Wiland, *President*
Craig Wehr, *President*
Eric Van Wagner, *Maint Spvr*
Max Armes, *QC Mgr*
Karyn Meyer, *Accounts Mgr*
EMP: 15 **EST:** 1941
SALES (est): 44.2MM **Privately Held**
WEB: www.metalspinners.com
SIC: 3469 3449 3341 Spinning metal for
the trade; miscellaneous metalwork; sec-
ondary nonferrous metals

(G-230)
METAL SPINNERS INC
800 Growth Pkwy (46703-9328)
PHONE.................................260 665-7741
Fax: 260 665-3244
EMP: 32
SALES (corp-wide): 28MM **Privately
Held**
SIC: 3469 Mfg Metal Stampings
PA: Metal Spinners, Inc.
914 Wohlert St
Angola IN 46703
260 665-2158

(G-231)
MORGAN OLSON LLC
300 Growth Pkwy (46703-9326)
PHONE.................................269 659-0243
Kathy Schumacher, *Branch Mgr*
EMP: 4
SALES (corp-wide): 1B **Privately Held**
SIC: 3713 Truck bodies (motor vehicles)
HQ: Morgan Olson, Llc
1801 S Nottawa St
Sturgis MI 49091
269 659-0200

(G-232)
NDIANA WARM FLOORS INC
Also Called: Shelters Specialty & Supply
935 N 275 W Ste B (46703-7149)
PHONE.................................260 668-8836
Fax: 260 668-8839
Scott Patton, *President*
Brooke Agar, *Manager*
EMP: 3
SQ FT: 6,000
SALES: 900K **Privately Held**
SIC: 3567 Radiant heating systems, indus-
trial process

(G-233)
OWENS CORNING SALES LLC
1211 Wohlert St (46703-1058)
PHONE.................................260 665-7318
Mike Aiello, *Manager*
EMP: 40
SQ FT: 6,000 **Publicly Held**
WEB: www.owenscorning.com
SIC: 3296 Fiberglass insulation
HQ: Owens Corning Sales, Llc
1 Owens Corning Pkwy
Toledo OH 43659
419 248-8000

(G-234)
**PARAGON MANUFACTURING
INC**
700 Wohlert St (46703-1029)
P.O. Box 814 (46703-0814)
PHONE.................................260 665-1492
Fax: 260 665-1397
J Andrew Spears, *President*
Cindy Dehaan, *Manager*
Andy Spears, *Manager*
EMP: 15
SQ FT: 5,000
SALES (est): 1.2MM **Privately Held**
WEB: www.noisedamp.com
SIC: 3446 Partitions & supports/studs, in-
cluding accoustical systems

(G-235)
PATRICK INDUSTRIES INC
Also Called: Indiana Marine Products
409 Growth Pkwy (46703-9323)
PHONE.................................260 665-6112
Todd M Cleveland, *CEO*
EMP: 80
SALES (corp-wide): 1.6B **Publicly Held**
SIC: 3694 3089 Engine electrical equip-
ment; harness wiring sets, internal com-
bustion engines; thermoformed finished
plastic products

PA: Patrick Industries, Inc.
107 W Franklin St
Elkhart IN 46516
574 294-7511

(G-236)
PERRY PRODUCTS INC
959 Growth Pkwy (46703-9338)
PHONE.................................260 668-7860
Matthew Perry, *President*
EMP: 2
SQ FT: 3,000
SALES: 150K **Privately Held**
SIC: 3423 7699 Hand & edge tools; tool
repair services

(G-237)
POLYFUSION LLC
395 Lane 101 (46703)
PHONE.................................260 624-7659
Dennis Springer, *CEO*
EMP: 3 **EST:** 2013
SALES (est): 214.6K **Privately Held**
SIC: 2821 Plastics materials & resins

(G-238)
POLYFUSION LLC
959 Growth Pkwy Ste D (46703-9338)
P.O. Box 629 (46703-0629)
PHONE.................................260 624-7659
EMP: 2 **EST:** 2015
SALES (est): 156.7K **Privately Held**
SIC: 2899 Chemical preparations

(G-239)
**PRINTING PLACE INC-PHOTOS
PLUS**
1500 N Wayne St Ste B (46703-2305)
P.O. Box 688 (46703-0688)
PHONE.................................260 665-8444
Fax: 260 665-9785
Robert Osterholt, *President*
Jane Osterholt, *Treasurer*
EMP: 10
SQ FT: 5,500
SALES: 80K **Privately Held**
SIC: 2752 2791 2789 2759 Commercial
printing, offset; typesetting; bookbinding &
related work; commercial printing

(G-240)
**PROFESSIONAL FABRICATORS
INC**
1103 Redding Ln (46703-2226)
PHONE.................................260 665-2555
David Schlegel, *President*
Teresa Schlegel, *Admin Sec*
EMP: 2
SQ FT: 3,000
SALES (est): 210K **Privately Held**
SIC: 3444 Sheet metal specialties, not
stamped

(G-241)
PULLMAN COMPANY
Also Called: Tenneco
503 Weatherhead St (46703-1057)
PHONE.................................260 667-2200
Steven Hoeper, *Branch Mgr*
EMP: 257
SQ FT: 90,000
SALES (corp-wide): 9.2B **Publicly Held**
WEB: www.tenneco-automotive.com
SIC: 3714 Motor vehicle transmissions,
drive assemblies & parts
HQ: The Pullman Company
1 International Dr
Monroe MI 48161
734 243-8000

(G-242)
**R R DONNELLEY & SONS
COMPANY**
611 W Mill St (46703-1021)
PHONE.................................260 624-2350
Patricia Mc Laughlin, *Vice Pres*
Jack N Curtis, *Branch Mgr*
EMP: 400
SQ FT: 180,000
SALES (corp-wide): 6.9B **Publicly Held**
WEB: www.rrdonnelley.com
SIC: 2761 2672 Manifold business forms;
coated & laminated paper

PA: R. R. Donnelley & Sons Company
35 W Wacker Dr Ste 3650
Chicago IL 60601
312 326-8000

(G-243)
RISE INC
1600 Wohlert St (46703-1065)
PHONE.................................260 665-9408
Fax: 260 665-1012
Dr Donald Mason, *President*
Denise Payton, *Director*
Joyce A Hevel, *Director*
David D Wilson, *Admin Sec*
EMP: 40 **EST:** 1964
SQ FT: 27,000
SALES: 2MM **Privately Held**
SIC: 8331 2789 Sheltered workshop;
bookbinding & related work

(G-244)
SPEEDWAY REDI MIX INC
260 E 300 N (46703-7503)
PHONE.................................260 665-5999
Becki Fredrick, *President*
Micheal Klink, *President*
EMP: 8 **Privately Held**
SIC: 3273 Ready-mixed concrete
PA: Speedway Redi-Mix Inc
4820 Industrial Rd
Fort Wayne IN 46825

(G-245)
SPX CORPORATION
300 Growth Pkwy (46703-9326)
P.O. Box 509 (46703-0509)
PHONE.................................704 752-4400
John Mc Coy, *Branch Mgr*
EMP: 230
SALES (corp-wide): 1.4B **Publicly Held**
WEB: www.spx.com
SIC: 3443 Cooling towers, metal plate
PA: Spx Corporation
13320a Balntyn Corp Pl
Charlotte NC 28277
980 474-3700

(G-246)
STEFFY WOOD PRODUCTS INC
701 W Mill St (46703-1046)
PHONE.................................260 665-8016
Fax: 260 665-5180
John Steffy, *President*
Eva Speaker, *Admin Sec*
Donna Steffy, *Admin Sec*
EMP: 30
SQ FT: 18,000
SALES (est): 4.9MM **Privately Held**
SIC: 2521 Cabinets, office: wood

(G-247)
STEUBEN FABG & ENGRG INC
2797 Woodhull Dr (46703-9348)
PHONE.................................260 665-3001
Jeff Counterman, *President*
Derek Craig, *Vice Pres*
EMP: 4
SQ FT: 7,200
SALES: 1.2MM **Privately Held**
SIC: 3498 3317 Fabricated pipe & fittings;
welded pipe & tubes

(G-248)
**STOFFEL SEALS CORPORATION
(DH)**
409 Hoosier Dr (46703-9335)
PHONE.................................845 353-3800
Ian Morton, *CEO*
Jerome Anderson, *President*
Andrew Rattray, *CFO*
Miguel Companioni, *Controller*
◆ **EMP:** 50 **EST:** 1941
SQ FT: 40,000
SALES (est): 43.8MM
SALES (corp-wide): 392.1MM **Privately
Held**
WEB: www.stoffel.com
SIC: 3089 3993 2759 2671 Identification
cards, plastic; signs & advertising special-
ties; commercial printing; packaging
paper & plastics film, coated & laminated;
pleating & stitching
HQ: Tyden Group Holdings Corp.
409 Hoosier Dr
Angola IN 46703
740 420-6777

(G-249)
T & S EQUIPMENT COMPANY
2999 N Wayne St (46703-9122)
P.O. Box 496 (46703-0496)
PHONE.................................260 665-9521
Fax: 800 526-3133
Ralph D Trine, *President*
▲ **EMP:** 250 **EST:** 1952
SQ FT: 83,000
SALES (est): 29.4MM **Privately Held**
WEB: www.tseq.com
SIC: 3448 3999 Ramps: prefabricated
metal; dock equipment & supplies, indus-
trial

(G-250)
**THRASHER WELDING AND MCH
SP**
2085 S 600 W (46703-9670)
PHONE.................................260 475-5550
Fax: 260 475-1001
Mark Thrasher, *Owner*
EMP: 6
SALES (est): 294K **Privately Held**
WEB: www.thrashercnc.com
SIC: 7692 Welding repair

(G-251)
TITAN METAL SPINNING INC
301 Growth Pkwy (46703-9322)
PHONE.................................260 665-1067
Roy A Meyer, *President*
Cindy Meyer, *Admin Sec*
EMP: 9
SALES: 28MM **Privately Held**
SIC: 3441 Fabricated structural metal

(G-252)
TOPSPEED
319 Pokagon Trl (46703-9357)
PHONE.................................260 665-8889
EMP: 2
SALES (est): 100K **Privately Held**
SIC: 3548 Mfg Welding Apparatus

(G-253)
**TYDEN GROUP HOLDINGS
CORP (HQ)**
409 Hoosier Dr (46703-9335)
PHONE.................................740 420-6777
Steve Oneil, *CEO*
Bruce Heinemann, *CFO*
◆ **EMP:** 19
SALES (est): 365.3MM
SALES (corp-wide): 392.1MM **Privately
Held**
SIC: 3953 2891 Figures (marking de-
vices), metal; sealants
PA: Crimson Capital Silicon Valley
601 California St # 1450
San Francisco CA 94108
650 233-6900

(G-254)
**UNIVERTICAL HOLDINGS INC
(HQ)**
203 Weatherhead St (46703-1024)
PHONE.................................260 665-1500
Eiitsu Masaki, *CEO*
Junichi Kitagaki, *CFO*
EMP: 4 **EST:** 2012
SALES (est): 65.9MM
SALES (corp-wide): 2.3B **Privately Held**
SIC: 5051 3339 Ferrous metals; primary
nonferrous metals
PA: Alconix Corporation
2-11-1, Nagatacho
Chiyoda-Ku TKY 100-0
335 967-400

(G-255)
UNIVERTICAL LLC (DH)
203 Weatherhead St (46703-1024)
PHONE.................................260 665-1500
Fax: 260 665-1400
Kevin Williams, *CEO*
David W Whitehead, *Vice Pres*
Junichi Titagaki, *CFO*
Lyle Halstead, *Controller*
Becky Boyer, *Sales Mgr*
▲ **EMP:** 80 **EST:** 1955
SQ FT: 160,000

SALES (est): 65.9MM
SALES (corp-wide): 2.3B **Privately Held**
WEB: www.univertical.com
SIC: 3331 2899 Refined primary copper
products; chemical preparations
HQ: Univertical Holdings, Inc.
203 Weatherhead St
Angola IN 46703
260 665-1500

(G-256)
UNIVERTICAL LLC
Univertical Semiconductors
203 Weatherhead St (46703-1024)
PHONE...................................260 665-1500
Gena Burch, *Purch Mgr*
Dave Whitehead, *Branch Mgr*
EMP: 50
SALES (corp-wide): 2.3B **Privately Held**
WEB: www.univertical.com
SIC: 3559 Semiconductor manufacturing
machinery
HQ: Univertical Llc
203 Weatherhead St
Angola IN 46703
260 665-1500

(G-257)
**UNIVERTICAL SEMICDTR PDTS
INC**
Also Called: Walker Shores Development Co
203 Weatherhead St (46703-1024)
PHONE...................................260 665-1500
Wayne Walker, *President*
Myrtle Walker, *Admin Sec*
EMP: 3
SQ FT: 160,000
SALES (est): 20.2K
SALES (corp-wide): 2.3B **Privately Held**
WEB: www.univertical.com
SIC: 2899 Metal treating compounds
HQ: Univertical Llc
203 Weatherhead St
Angola IN 46703
260 665-1500

(G-258)
**VESTIL MANUFACTURING CORP
(PA)**
2999 N Wayne St (46703-9122)
P.O. Box 507 (46703-0507)
PHONE...................................260 665-7586
Sheri A Trine, *CEO*
Ralph Trine, *President*
Alec Trine, *COO*
Ken Schneider, *Vice Pres*
Barry Trine, *Vice Pres*
◆ EMP: 350
SQ FT: 140,000
SALES (est): 106.8MM **Privately Held**
WEB: www.vestilmfg.com
SIC: 3999 3535 3069 Dock equipment &
supplies, industrial; conveyors & convey-
ing equipment; molded rubber products

(G-259)
**WORLD CLASS NORTH
AMERICA LLC**
1460 Wohlert St (46703-1061)
P.O. Box 775 (46703-0775)
PHONE...................................260 668-5511
Jack De Vries, *Mng Member*
◆ EMP: 14
SQ FT: 30,000
SALES (est): 950K **Privately Held**
SIC: 3792 Automobile house trailer chassis

(G-260)
YNOT METAL INC
301 Growth Pkwy (46703-9322)
P.O. Box 388 (46703-0388)
PHONE...................................517 617-6039
James Behnke, *President*
EMP: 4
SALES (est): 472K **Privately Held**
SIC: 3541 Plasma process metal cutting
machines

Arcadia
Hamilton County

(G-261)
C & E EXTERIORS INC
517 E S St (46030)
P.O. Box 260 (46030-0260)
PHONE...................................317 984-5463
Fax: 317 984-8898
James Wright, *President*
Nicole Wright, *Vice Pres*
EMP: 6
SALES: 250K **Privately Held**
SIC: 3299 Stucco

(G-262)
CARTER ENTERPRISES INC
119 W Main St (46030)
PHONE...................................317 984-1497
John A Carter, *President*
John Carter, *Principal*
EMP: 8
SALES (est): 1.1MM **Privately Held**
WEB: www.carterent.com
SIC: 3999 Manufacturing industries

(G-263)
DEBRA SCHNEIDER
Also Called: A Lit'le Bit of Heaven Farm
25610 Salem Church Rd (46030-9494)
PHONE...................................317 420-9360
Debra Schneider, *Owner*
Philip Schneider, *Co-Owner*
EMP: 2
SALES (est): 115.7K **Privately Held**
SIC: 2824 Organic fibers, noncellulosic

(G-264)
DURA PRODUCTS INC
504 Demoss Ave (46030)
PHONE...................................855 502-3872
▲ EMP: 13
SALES (est): 738K **Privately Held**
SIC: 3561 Pumps & pumping equipment

(G-265)
**MCKINNEYS EMBROIDERY &
SUP CO**
201 E Broadway Ave (46030-9643)
P.O. Box 39 (46030-0039)
PHONE...................................317 984-9039
Neal McKinney, *CEO*
Neal Rex McKinney, *CEO*
Ronna McKinney, *Corp Secy*
EMP: 4
SQ FT: 1,200
SALES (est): 137.5K **Privately Held**
SIC: 2395 Embroidery & art needlework

(G-266)
**MOORES COUNTRY WOOD
CRAFTING**
507 Demoss Ave (46030)
P.O. Box 389 (46030-0389)
PHONE...................................317 984-3326
Fax: 765 984-2615
Robert David Moore, *President*
Thomas Henson, *Corp Secy*
EMP: 16
SQ FT: 35,000
SALES (est): 2.5MM **Privately Held**
WEB: www.mooreyp.com
SIC: 2511 3231 2499 Wood household
furniture; products of purchased glass;
decorative wood & woodwork

(G-267)
PUMP METER SOLUTIONS
6660 E 266th St Ste 100 (46030-9751)
PHONE...................................317 984-7867
Bob Babbitt, *Office Mgr*
EMP: 5
SALES (est): 755.9K **Privately Held**
SIC: 3561 Industrial pumps & parts

(G-268)
RAM NORTH AMERICA INC
25415 State Road 19 (46030-9522)
PHONE...................................317 984-1971
Leanne Yeary, *President*
EMP: 17 EST: 2010

SALES (est): 3.5MM **Privately Held**
SIC: 3089 3272 Panels, building: plastic;
panels & sections, prefabricated concrete

(G-269)
REHCO PRODUCTS INC
700 S East St (46030)
P.O. Box 430 (46030-0430)
PHONE...................................317 984-3319
Fax: 317 773-7507
John Hawkins, *President*
Robert L Hawkins, *Vice Pres*
Wanda Hawkins, *Admin Sec*
EMP: 10 EST: 1945
SQ FT: 40,000
SALES: 220.5K **Privately Held**
SIC: 3599 Machine shop, jobbing & repair

(G-270)
SYLVIA KAY HARTLEY (PA)
Also Called: Hartley Interiors
103 E Main St (46030)
PHONE...................................317 984-3424
Fax: 317 776-0404
Sylvia Kay Hartley, *Owner*
EMP: 2
SQ FT: 20,000
SALES: 750K **Privately Held**
WEB: www.hartleyinteriors.com
SIC: 2512 5712 Upholstered household
furniture; furniture stores

(G-271)
VIBCON CORP
6660 E 266th St Ste 200 (46030-9751)
P.O. Box 542 (46030-0542)
PHONE...................................317 984-3543
Jeffrey Anderson, *President*
EMP: 12
SQ FT: 20,000
SALES (est): 878.4K **Privately Held**
WEB: www.vibcon.com
SIC: 3559 3535 ; conveyors & conveying
equipment

Argos
Marshall County

(G-272)
**B & G TRUCK CONVERSIONS
INC**
10478 16th Rd (46501-9511)
P.O. Box 918, Plymouth (46563-0918)
PHONE...................................574 892-6666
Fax: 574 892-6664
Kevin Bammerlin, *President*
Arch Grafton, *Vice Pres*
Karen Edwards, *Admin Asst*
EMP: 15
SQ FT: 15,000
SALES: 4MM **Privately Held**
WEB: www.bgtruck.com
SIC: 3713 Truck bodies (motor vehicles)

(G-273)
CLOVER INDUSTRIES LLC
20240 Michigan Rd (46501-9794)
PHONE...................................574 892-5760
Celesta Conover, *Principal*
EMP: 3 EST: 2015
SALES (est): 98.3K **Privately Held**
SIC: 3999 Manufacturing industries

(G-274)
HAPPY HEADGEAR LLC
128 Westview Ct (46501-1031)
PHONE...................................574 892-5792
Christen Ellis, *Principal*
EMP: 2
SALES: 20K **Privately Held**
SIC: 2399 7389 Emblems, badges & in-
signia; personal service agents, brokers &
bureaus

(G-275)
LOEB-LORMAN METALS INC
402 West St (46501-1281)
PHONE...................................574 892-5063
Fax: 574 892-5037
EMP: 2

SALES (corp-wide): 65.3MM **Privately
Held**
SIC: 5093 4953 3341 Whol Scrap/Waste
Material Refuse System Secondary Non-
ferrous Metal Producer
PA: Loeb-Lorman Metals Inc.
1111 S 10th St
Watertown WI 53094
920 261-4920

(G-276)
NORTH CENTRAL PALLETS INC
13990 State Road 10 (46501-9572)
P.O. Box 840, Plymouth (46563-0840)
PHONE...................................574 892-6142
Fax: 574 892-5381
Patrick Hanley, *President*
Cliff Baumgartner, *General Mgr*
Caroline Hanley, *Vice Pres*
J Shawn Hanley, *Vice Pres*
Caroline W Hanley, *Admin Sec*
EMP: 35
SQ FT: 10,000
SALES (est): 6.8MM **Privately Held**
WEB: www.ncpallets.com
SIC: 2448 Pallets, wood

(G-277)
STAMPCRAFTER
324 Weidner Ave (46501-1030)
PHONE...................................574 892-5206
Paul J Phillips, *Owner*
EMP: 2
SALES: 80K **Privately Held**
SIC: 3953 Postmark stamps, hand: rubber
or metal

(G-278)
T I B INC
Also Called: Ameri-Can Engineering
775 N Michigan St (46501-1171)
PHONE...................................574 892-5151
Fax: 574 892-5150
David Harling, *President*
Gladys Bird, *Shareholder*
Ron Bird, *Shareholder*
▼ EMP: 22
SQ FT: 25,000
SALES (est): 4.5MM **Privately Held**
WEB: www.ameri-can.com
SIC: 3799 Boat trailers; trailers & trailer
equipment

(G-279)
TOPPS INDUSTRIES
820 Dewey St (46501-1284)
P.O. Box 420, Rochester (46975-0420)
PHONE...................................574 892-5016
EMP: 2
SALES (est): 152.9K **Privately Held**
SIC: 3999 Manufacturing industries

(G-280)
VAN DER WEELE JON D
Also Called: Mr Trophy
200 W Walnut St (46501-1026)
PHONE...................................574 892-5005
Fax: 574 892-5005
Jon D Van Der Weele, *Owner*
Darleen Van Derweele, *Co-Owner*
EMP: 3
SQ FT: 4,096
SALES (est): 239.9K **Privately Held**
SIC: 5999 3993 5731 Trophies & plaques;
signs & advertising specialties; radio, tele-
vision & electronic stores

Arlington
Rush County

(G-281)
BRIAN J SPILMAN
2443 N 700 W Ste 100 (46104-9771)
PHONE...................................765 663-2860
Brian J Spilman, *CEO*
EMP: 2
SALES (est): 170K **Privately Held**
SIC: 3524 7389 Snowblowers & throwers,
residential;

(G-282)
ORIGINAL TRACTOR CAB CO INC
Also Called: Morgan Francis
6849 W Front St (46104)
PHONE.................................765 663-2214
Fax: 765 662-2101
Wayne D Williams, *President*
Phil Vogelgesang, *Corp Secy*
Robert S Williams, *Vice Pres*
EMP: 40 EST: 1939
SQ FT: 60,000
SALES (est): 2.9MM Privately Held
WEB: www.originalcab.com
SIC: 3524 3446 3523 3713 Snowblowers & throwers, residential; flagpoles, metal; cabs, tractors & agricultural machinery; truck & bus bodies; sheet metalwork

Ashley
Dekalb County

(G-283)
ASHLEY INDUSTRIAL MOLDING INC (PA)
310 S Wabash St (46705-5266)
P.O. Box 398 (46705-0398)
PHONE.................................260 587-9155
Scott Pflughoeft, *CEO*
Rod Schoon, *Ch of Bd*
Mike Morgan, *CFO*
▼ EMP: 187
SALES (est): 41.3MM Privately Held
WEB: www.ashinmold.com
SIC: 3089 Molding primary plastic

(G-284)
COMPLETE FINISH INC
200 S Parker Dr (46705-5250)
P.O. Box 400 (46705-0400)
PHONE.................................260 587-3588
James Clifford, *President*
EMP: 11
SQ FT: 15,000
SALES (est): 1.1MM Privately Held
SIC: 3471 Sand blasting of metal parts

(G-285)
CUSTOM BOTTLING & PACKG INC
101 S Parker Dr (46705-9649)
P.O. Box 9 (46705-0009)
PHONE.................................877 401-7195
Kriss Stackhouse, *President*
EMP: 25
SALES (est): 4.7MM Privately Held
SIC: 2842 7389 Specialty cleaning preparations; drain pipe solvents or cleaners; window cleaning preparations; bleaches, household: dry or liquid; packaging & labeling services

(G-286)
HARTLAND WINERY LLC
2409 County Road 4 (46705-9717)
PHONE.................................260 587-3316
Brenda Lockhart, *Principal*
EMP: 3
SALES (est): 123.1K Privately Held
SIC: 2084 Wines, brandy & brandy spirits

(G-287)
K TECH SPECIALTY COATINGS INC
111 W Garfield St (46705-5232)
P.O. Box 428 (46705-0428)
PHONE.................................260 587-3888
Wayne Klink, *President*
Carol Klink, *Admin Sec*
Tony Winters, *Admin Sec*
EMP: 10
SALES (est): 2.6MM Privately Held
SIC: 2952 Asphalt felts & coatings

(G-288)
MTR MACHINING CONCEPT INC
2878 W 800 S (46705-9625)
P.O. Box 383 (46705-0383)
PHONE.................................260 587-3381
Mervin Topp, *President*
Richard Bowers, *Vice Pres*
EMP: 9

SQ FT: 4,000
SALES (est): 1.6MM Privately Held
SIC: 3462 7699 Gears, forged steel; industrial equipment services

(G-289)
PARKER-HANNIFIN CORPORATION
201 S Parker Dr (46705-5250)
P.O. Box 368 (46705-0368)
PHONE.................................260 587-9102
Fax: 260 587-9104
Kurt Peters, *Plant Mgr*
Cedrick Barber, *Engineer*
Steve Merryman, *Program Mgr*
Kurt Peter, *Manager*
EMP: 27
SALES (corp-wide): 12B Publicly Held
WEB: www.parker.com
SIC: 3599 3592 3498 3312 Tubing, flexible metallic; carburetors, pistons, rings, valves; fabricated pipe & fittings; blast furnaces & steel mills
PA: Parker-Hannifin Corporation
6035 Parkland Blvd
Cleveland OH 44124
216 896-3000

(G-290)
ROYAL ARC WELDING COMPANY
640 County Road 27 (46705-9709)
PHONE.................................260 587-3711
Fax: 260 587-3712
Joe Rosen, *Branch Mgr*
EMP: 25
SALES (corp-wide): 17MM Privately Held
PA: Royal Arc Welding Company
23851 Vreeland Rd
Flat Rock MI 48134
734 789-9099

(G-291)
TI GROUP AUTO SYSTEMS LLC
507 H L Thompson Jr Dr (46705-0050)
P.O. Box 397 (46705-0397)
PHONE.................................260 587-6100
Lori Casiano, *Manager*
Natalie Depew, *Maintence Staff*
EMP: 250
SALES (corp-wide): 4B Privately Held
WEB: www.tiautomotive.com
SIC: 3356 3714 Nonferrous rolling & drawing; motor vehicle parts & accessories
HQ: Ti Group Automotive Systems, Llc
2020 Taylor Rd
Auburn Hills MI 48326
248 296-8000

(G-292)
TRIN INC (DH)
Also Called: Tokai Rika of Indiana
803 H L Thompson Jr Dr (46705-0030)
PHONE.................................260 587-9282
Makato Goto, *President*
Mark Holbrook, *Program Mgr*
Denise Phillips, *Program Mgr*
▲ EMP: 37
SQ FT: 54,000
SALES (est): 15MM
SALES (corp-wide): 4.5B Privately Held
SIC: 3714 Motor vehicle electrical equipment
HQ: Tram, Inc.
47200 Port St
Plymouth MI 48170
734 254-8500

Atlanta
Hamilton County

(G-293)
CUSTOM BLACKSMITH SHOP
Also Called: Custom Blacksmithing
29579 N State Road 19 (46031-9623)
PHONE.................................765 292-2745
Kurt Fehrenbach, *Owner*
Rick Bagby, *Manager*
EMP: 2
SQ FT: 5,400

SALES (est): 120K Privately Held
SIC: 3462 1799 Iron & steel forgings; welding on site

(G-294)
FAULKNERS BINDERY
1596 E 400 S (46031-9555)
PHONE.................................765 292-2285
Chris Faulkner, *Owner*
EMP: 2
SALES (est): 140.4K Privately Held
SIC: 2789 Binding & repair of books, magazines & pamphlets

(G-295)
HOOSIER CRUSH CORP
325 E Michael Dr (46031-9487)
PHONE.................................765 292-6375
Brian Greene, *Principal*
EMP: 2
SALES (est): 77.8K Privately Held
SIC: 2084 Wines, brandy & brandy spirits

Attica
Fountain County

(G-296)
ARCHER-DANIELS-MIDLAND COMPANY
Also Called: ADM
105 E Harrison St (47918)
P.O. Box 209 (47918-0209)
PHONE.................................765 762-6763
Matt Hartman, *Manager*
EMP: 4
SALES (corp-wide): 60.8B Publicly Held
WEB: www.admworld.com
SIC: 2041 Flour & other grain mill products
PA: Archer-Daniels-Midland Company
77 W Wacker Dr Ste 4600
Chicago IL 60601
312 634-8100

(G-297)
ATTICA READY MIXED CONCRETE (PA)
104 W Sycamore St (47918-1833)
PHONE.................................765 762-2424
Fax: 765 764-4966
Steve Wagner, *President*
EMP: 20 EST: 1952
SQ FT: 1,400
SALES (est): 2.3MM Privately Held
WEB: www.irmca.com
SIC: 3273 5251 Ready-mixed concrete; hardware

(G-298)
C&D TECHNOLOGIES INC
200 W Main St (47918-1344)
P.O. Box 279 (47918-0279)
PHONE.................................765 762-2461
Dale Brown, *Manager*
EMP: 240
SALES (corp-wide): 669.8MM Privately Held
WEB: www.cdtechno.com
SIC: 3691 3692 3661 Storage batteries; primary batteries, dry & wet; telephone & telegraph apparatus
PA: C&D Technologies, Inc.
1400 Union Meeting Rd # 110
Blue Bell PA 19422
215 619-2700

(G-299)
COUNTRY CHARM
Also Called: Real Log Homes
2721 E Flint Rd (47918-8235)
PHONE.................................765 572-2588
David L Hatke, *Owner*
EMP: 4
SALES (est): 250K Privately Held
SIC: 2452 Log cabins, prefabricated, wood

(G-300)
FOUNTAIN COUNTY NEIGHBOR
Also Called: Messenger, The
113 S Perry St (47918-1349)
PHONE.................................765 762-2411
Fax: 765 762-1547
Greg Willhite, *Principal*
EMP: 3

SALES (est): 143.5K Privately Held
WEB: www.fountaincountyneighbor.com
SIC: 2711 Newspapers, publishing & printing
HQ: The Times Republic
1492 E Walnut St
Watseka IL 60970
815 432-5227

(G-301)
GECKOS
111 S Perry St (47918-1349)
PHONE.................................765 762-0822
Mark Palmer, *Owner*
EMP: 3
SALES (est): 159.6K Privately Held
SIC: 5699 3993 2396 Uniforms & work clothing; signs & advertising specialties; automotive & apparel trimmings

(G-302)
GLORIA J BURNWORTH
Also Called: B & G Woodworking
2875 N 70 W (47918-8082)
PHONE.................................765 366-3950
Gloria J Burnworth, *Owner*
EMP: 2
SALES (est): 157.7K Privately Held
SIC: 2511 Wood household furniture

(G-303)
HARRISON STEEL CASTINGS CO (PA)
900 S Mound St (47918-1632)
P.O. Box 60 (47918-0060)
PHONE.................................765 762-2481
Fax: 765 762-2487
Edward G Curtis, *Ch of Bd*
Wade C Harrison II, *President*
Timothy Walters, *Asst Supt*
Edward Curtis, *Vice Pres*
Geoffrey H Curtis, *Vice Pres*
▲ EMP: 800 EST: 1906
SALES (est): 118.1MM Privately Held
WEB: www.hscast.com
SIC: 3325 Alloy steel castings, except investment

(G-304)
HILL TOP WELDING LLC
217 N State Road 55 (47918-7769)
PHONE.................................765 585-2549
Chris Reifel, *Owner*
EMP: 2 EST: 2007
SALES (est): 159.9K Privately Held
SIC: 7692 Welding repair

(G-305)
HOME CITY ICE COMPANY
200 S Market St (47918-1371)
PHONE.................................765 762-6096
Chris V Dywater, *Manager*
Chris Van De Water, *Manager*
EMP: 50
SALES (corp-wide): 314.5MM Privately Held
WEB: www.homecityice.com
SIC: 2097 Manufactured ice
PA: The Home City Ice Company
6045 Bridgetown Rd Ste 1
Cincinnati OH 45248
513 574-1800

(G-306)
KERST PALLET
945 N Milligan Hill Rd (47918-7860)
PHONE.................................765 585-3026
Correy Kerst, *Principal*
EMP: 3
SALES (est): 119.9K Privately Held
SIC: 2448 Pallets, wood

(G-307)
MILLENNIUM SUPPLY INC
1111 E Main St (47918-1949)
P.O. Box 127 (47918-0127)
PHONE.................................765 764-7000
Fax: 765 764-6400
L Gene McGowen, *President*
EMP: 9
SQ FT: 78,000
SALES (est): 2MM Privately Held
WEB: www.millenniumsupply.com
SIC: 3568 Joints & couplings

▲ = Import ▼=Export
◆ =Import/Export

(G-308)
NEUMAYR LUMBER CO INC
Also Called: Do It Best
401 S Union St (47918-1496)
P.O. Box 399 (47918-0399)
PHONE.................................765 764-4148
Fax: 765 762-6023
Martha L Neumayr, *President*
Rick Turpin, *Vice Pres*
Kathy Turpin, *Treasurer*
Marti Martigus, *Admin Sec*
EMP: 10
SQ FT: 3,000
SALES (est): 1.4MM **Privately Held**
SIC: 5251 2448 Hardware; pallets, wood

(G-309)
SERIE HARDWOODS INC
2521 E Bethel Rd (47918-8256)
PHONE.................................765 275-2321
Fax: 765 275-2222
Russell Serie, *President*
Richard Serie, *Vice Pres*
Janice Serie, *Admin Sec*
EMP: 2
SQ FT: 25,000
SALES: 500K **Privately Held**
SIC: 5099 5211 2499 5031 Wood & wood by-products; lumber products; decorative wood & woodwork; lumber, plywood & millwork

Atwood
Kosciusko County

(G-310)
SWANSONS SERVICE CENTER
U S 30 County Road 650 W (46502)
PHONE.................................574 858-9406
Tony Swanson, *Principal*
EMP: 3
SALES (est): 280.9K **Privately Held**
SIC: 3599 Machine shop, jobbing & repair

Auburn
Dekalb County

(G-311)
99 NUFAB REBAR LLC
1610 S Grandstaff Dr (46706-2667)
PHONE.................................260 572-1315
Jeff Albert, *General Mgr*
Dale Bernard, *Controller*
EMP: 99
SALES (est): 10.1MM **Privately Held**
SIC: 3441 Fabricated structural metal

(G-312)
ARTISTIC CARTON COMPANY
1201 S Grandstaff Dr (46706-2660)
PHONE.................................260 925-6060
Tina Gil, *Accountant*
Drew Ellerkamp, *Manager*
EMP: 44
SQ FT: 140,000
SALES (est): 11.2MM
SALES (corp-wide): 61.5MM **Privately Held**
WEB: www.artisticcarton.com
SIC: 2631 2652 2657 Folding boxboard; binders' board; setup paperboard boxes; folding paperboard boxes
PA: Artistic Carton Company
    1975 Big Timber Rd
    Elgin IL 60123
    847 741-0247

(G-313)
AUBURN GEAR LLC (PA)
400 E Auburn Dr (46706-3400)
PHONE.................................260 925-3200
Fax: 260 925-4725
George E Callas, *Ch of Bd*
Robert Martin Palmer, *President*
Elizabeth Callas, *Corp Secy*
Tim Bennett, *Opers Staff*
▲ **EMP:** 150
SQ FT: 250,000

(G-314)
AUBURN HARDWOOD MOLDING
1109 W Auburn Dr (46706-3459)
PHONE.................................260 925-5959
Fax: 260 837-7548
Brian Rugsegger, *President*
EMP: 3
SALES (est): 212.8K **Privately Held**
SIC: 3089 Molding primary plastic

(G-315)
AUBURN MANUFACTURING INC
1929 Wayne St (46706-3514)
P.O. Box 6078 (46706-6078)
PHONE.................................260 925-8651
Fax: 260 925-8653
Cris Horton, *President*
Angela Horton, *Vice Pres*
Norm Hartman, *Controller*
Wil Horton, *Sales Dir*
EMP: 15
SQ FT: 12,000
SALES (est): 3.4MM **Privately Held**
WEB: www.auburnmanufacturing.com
SIC: 3714 3451 Motor vehicle parts & accessories; screw machine products

(G-316)
BARON EMBROIDERY CORP
Also Called: Vigred Sports
103 S Main St (46706-2355)
PHONE.................................260 484-8700
Brian Thomas, *President*
EMP: 4
SALES (est): 171.3K **Privately Held**
SIC: 2395 Embroidery & art needlework

(G-317)
BASSETT ELECTRIC MOTOR REPAIR
215 E 11th St (46706-2314)
PHONE.................................260 925-0868
Polly Bassett, *President*
Kevin Bassett, *Vice Pres*
EMP: 2 **EST:** 1960
SALES (est): 251.6K **Privately Held**
SIC: 7694 Electric motor repair

(G-318)
BRALIN LASER SERVICES INC
2233 County Road 72 (46706-2268)
P.O. Box 88, Garrett (46738-0088)
PHONE.................................260 357-6511
Fax: 260 357-5720
Bill Hohler, *President*
EMP: 24
SQ FT: 12,000
SALES (est): 5.8MM **Privately Held**
WEB: www.bralinlaser.com
SIC: 3441 Fabricated structural metal

(G-319)
C & A TOOL ENGINEERING INC
1015 W 15th St (46706-2047)
PHONE.................................260 693-2167
Mark Boling, *Safety Mgr*
Lori Blotkamp, *Facilities Mgr*
Ward Krause, *Branch Mgr*
EMP: 50
SALES (corp-wide): 8.2B **Privately Held**
SIC: 3544 3545 Diamond dies, metalworking; machine tool accessories
HQ: C & A Tool Engineering Inc.
    4100 N Us 33
    Churubusco IN 46723
    260 693-2167

(G-320)
CARLEX GLASS AMERICA LLC
Also Called: Carlex Glass Ind Inc-Auburn
1900 Center St (46706-9685)
PHONE.................................260 925-5656
Fax: 260 927-2685
Jeff Fraelich, *Principal*
Janie Lowe, *Human Res Mgr*
EMP: 400

SALES (corp-wide): 2.1B **Privately Held**
SIC: 3231 3211 Windshields, glass: made from purchased glass; flat glass
HQ: Carlex Glass America, Llc
    7200 Centennial Blvd
    Nashville TN 37209

(G-321)
CLASSIC CITY SIGNS INC
551 N Grandstaff Dr (46706-1682)
PHONE.................................260 927-8438
Fax: 260 927-8441
Daron White, *President*
Carla White, *Vice Pres*
EMP: 3
SALES (est): 50K **Privately Held**
WEB: www.classiccitysigns.com
SIC: 3993 Signs & advertising specialties

(G-322)
COOPER-STANDARD AUTOMOTIVE INC
725 W 15th St (46706-2136)
PHONE.................................260 925-0700
Fax: 260 925-1473
Julie Hess, *Vice Pres*
Richard Meeks, *Branch Mgr*
EMP: 301
SALES (corp-wide): 3.6B **Publicly Held**
SIC: 3061 Mechanical rubber goods
HQ: Cooper-Standard Automotive Inc.
    39550 Orchard Hill Pl
    Novi MI 48375
    248 596-5900

(G-323)
COOPER-STANDARD AUTOMOTIVE INC
725 W 11th St (46706-2022)
PHONE.................................260 637-5824
Connie Lepley, *Manager*
Chet Brown, *Technical Staff*
EMP: 500
SALES (corp-wide): 3.6B **Publicly Held**
SIC: 3714 Motor vehicle parts & accessories
HQ: Cooper-Standard Automotive Inc.
    39550 Orchard Hill Pl
    Novi MI 48375
    248 596-5900

(G-324)
COOPER-STANDARD AUTOMOTIVE INC
207 S West St (46706-2021)
PHONE.................................260 925-0700
Devin Renkenberger, *Production*
Cassy Wallace, *Purchasing*
Geoffrey Braun, *Engineer*
Tom Delaney, *Engineer*
Ricky Dennis, *Engineer*
EMP: 500
SALES (corp-wide): 3.6B **Publicly Held**
WEB: www.cooperstandard.com
SIC: 3061 Mechanical rubber goods
HQ: Cooper-Standard Automotive Inc.
    39550 Orchard Hill Pl
    Novi MI 48375
    248 596-5900

(G-325)
CUSTOM COATING INC
1937 Jacob St (46706-3516)
P.O. Box 143 (46706-0143)
PHONE.................................260 925-0623
Fax: 260 925-5774
Terry Hines, *CEO*
Vincent Hines, *Vice Pres*
EMP: 25
SQ FT: 64,345
SALES: 2.8MM **Privately Held**
WEB: www.customcoatinginc.com
SIC: 3479 Coating of metals & formed products

(G-326)
CUSTOM MFG & FABRICATION LLC
5536 County Road 31 (46706-9656)
PHONE.................................260 908-1088
EMP: 2
SALES (est): 100.1K **Privately Held**
SIC: 3999 Manufacturing industries

(G-327)
DEKALB METAL FINISHING INC
625 W 15th St (46706-2133)
P.O. Box 70 (46706-0070)
PHONE.................................260 925-1820
Fax: 260 925-5258
Dennis Fry, *Ch of Bd*
EMP: 45 **EST:** 1932
SQ FT: 30,000
SALES (est): 6MM **Privately Held**
WEB: www.dekalbmetal.com
SIC: 3471 Plating of metals or formed products

(G-328)
EATON CORPORATION
201 Brandon St (46706-1643)
PHONE.................................260 925-3800
Paul Carper, *Purchasing*
John Cordes, *Engineer*
Dan Faylor, *Engineer*
Jim Hockemeyer, *Engineer*
Mike Hornbrook, *Engineer*
EMP: 200
SQ FT: 350,000 **Privately Held**
WEB: www.eaton.com
SIC: 3714 3713 3568 3537 Clutches, motor vehicle; truck & bus bodies; power transmission equipment; industrial trucks & tractors; metal stampings
HQ: Eaton Corporation
    1000 Eaton Blvd
    Cleveland OH 44122
    440 523-5000

(G-329)
ENVISION GRAPHICS INC
506 Brandon St (46706-1648)
PHONE.................................260 925-2266
Fax: 260 925-5726
Fritz Busch, *President*
Byron Wentworth, *Principal*
EMP: 5
SALES (est): 685.3K **Privately Held**
SIC: 2752 Commercial printing, offset

(G-330)
ERIE-HAVEN INC
1204 S Union St (46706-2934)
PHONE.................................260 478-1674
Duane Ellert, *Plant Mgr*
EMP: 2
SALES (corp-wide): 25.2MM **Privately Held**
WEB: www.eriehaven.com
SIC: 3273 Ready-mixed concrete
PA: Erie-Haven Inc
    3909 Limestone Dr
    Fort Wayne IN 46809
    260 478-1674

(G-331)
FABTRON CORPORATION
1820 Sprott St (46706-3429)
PHONE.................................260 925-9553
Fax: 260 925-9553
Kevin Marquardt, *President*
Cina Marquardt, *Corp Secy*
Wyatt Decker, *Manager*
EMP: 3
SQ FT: 17,000
SALES (est): 526.4K **Privately Held**
WEB: www.fabtroncorp.com
SIC: 3499 Furniture parts, metal

(G-332)
FOLEY PATTERN COMPANY INC
500 W 11th St (46706-2142)
P.O. Box 150 (46706-0150)
PHONE.................................260 925-4113
Fax: 260 925-4115
Ellen E Stahly, *President*
Stephen Foley, *Vice Pres*
EMP: 22 **EST:** 1920
SQ FT: 35,000
SALES (est): 3.7MM **Privately Held**
SIC: 3365 3543 Aluminum & aluminum-based alloy castings; industrial patterns

(G-333)
FXI INC
Also Called: Foamex
2211 Wayne St (46706-3518)
P.O. Box 606 (46706-0606)
PHONE.................................260 925-1073
Fax: 260 925-2410

Steve Setzer, *Branch Mgr*
EMP: 130
SQ FT: 136,000 **Privately Held**
SIC: 3086 Plastics foam products
HQ: Fxi, Inc.
1400 N Providence Rd # 2000
Media PA 19063

(G-334)
HARRIS REBAR NUFAB LLC (PA)
1342 S Grandstaff Dr (46706-2661)
P.O. Box 627 (46706-0627)
PHONE................................260 925-5440
Mike Lewis, *General Mgr*
Ronald Latimer, *Plant Supt*
Dave Worthington, *Treasurer*
Greg Hall, *Manager*
Kevin Thompson, *Manager*
EMP: 55
SALES (est): 98.5MM **Privately Held**
SIC: 3441 Fabricated structural metal

(G-335)
HERMAC INCORPORATED
540 North St (46706-1622)
P.O. Box 129 (46706-0129)
PHONE................................260 925-0312
Fax: 260 925-0313
Kathy Mc Aninch, *President*
EMP: 39
SQ FT: 11,000
SALES: 4MM **Privately Held**
SIC: 3679 Harness assemblies for electronic use: wire or cable

(G-336)
HK MANUFACTURING INC
203 Hunters Rdg (46706-9116)
PHONE................................260 925-1680
Elisa Kruse, *Owner*
EMP: 2
SALES (est): 74.6K **Privately Held**
SIC: 3999 Manufacturing industries

(G-337)
INNOTEK INC
Also Called: Innotek Pet Products
923 Cardinal Ct (46706-2678)
PHONE................................800 826-5527
Richard W Frank, *President*
Patt Kelly Pollet, *Manager*
▲ **EMP:** 150
SQ FT: 72,000
SALES (est): 18.6MM **Privately Held**
SIC: 3699 Electronic training devices

(G-338)
K V S INC
1105 W Auburn Dr (46706-3459)
PHONE................................260 925-0525
Fax: 260 925-1146
EMP: 4
SQ FT: 3,000
SALES (est): 481.4K **Privately Held**
SIC: 2752 Commercial Offset Printer

(G-339)
KPC MEDIA GROUP INC
Evening Star, The
118 W 9th St (46706-2225)
PHONE................................260 925-2611
Terry Housholder, *President*
EMP: 23
SQ FT: 2,000
SALES (corp-wide): 28.7MM **Privately Held**
WEB: www.kpcnews.net
SIC: 2711 Newspapers: publishing only, not printed on site
PA: Kpc Media Group Inc.
102 N Main St
Kendallville IN 46755
260 347-0400

(G-340)
L & D INDUSTRIES INC
201 Fulton St (46706-2024)
PHONE................................260 925-4714
Fax: 260 925-4878
Leonard Vincent, *President*
EMP: 6
SQ FT: 3,500
SALES (est): 646.8K **Privately Held**
SIC: 3599 Machine shop, jobbing & repair

(G-341)
LANE BYLER WINERY
5858 County Road 35 (46706-9652)
PHONE................................260 920-4377
Alvin J R Byler Jr, *President*
EMP: 2
SALES (est): 145.3K **Privately Held**
SIC: 2084 Wines

(G-342)
MARSHALL SIGNS
1270 Rohm Dr (46706-2056)
PHONE................................260 350-1492
Steve Marshall, *Owner*
Tav Marshall, *Admin Sec*
EMP: 2
SALES: 55K **Privately Held**
SIC: 3993 Signs & advertising specialties

(G-343)
MESSENGER LLC
318 E 7th St (46706-1804)
PHONE................................260 925-1700
Fax: 260 925-6281
Kevin Keane, *President*
Robert Hoaglund, *Vice Pres*
Bruce Smith, *CFO*
▲ **EMP:** 46
SALES (est): 39.5MM **Privately Held**
SIC: 2752 Commercial printing, lithographic
PA: Prairie Capital, L.P.
191 N Wacker Dr Ste 800
Chicago IL 60606

(G-344)
METAL TECHNOLOGIES AUBURN LLC
1401 S Grandstaff Dr (46706-2664)
PHONE................................260 925-4717
Matthew Setter, *CEO*
▼ **EMP:** 280
SALES (est): 30.1MM
SALES (corp-wide): 289.7MM **Privately Held**
SIC: 3315 Steel wire & related products
PA: Metal Technologies Of Indiana, Inc.
1401 S Grandstaff Dr
Auburn IN 46706
260 925-4717

(G-345)
METAL TECHNOLOGIES INC ALABAMA (PA)
1401 S Grandstaff Dr (46706-2664)
PHONE................................260 925-4717
Rick James, *CEO*
Matthew J Fetter, *President*
EMP: 60
SALES (est): 37.9MM **Privately Held**
SIC: 8711 3321 Acoustical engineering; gray iron castings

(G-346)
METAL TECHNOLOGIES INDIANA INC (PA)
1401 S Grandstaff Dr (46706-2664)
PHONE................................260 925-4717
Rick James, *CEO*
Mike Payne, *President*
Jeffrey L Turner, *Senior VP*
John Neiger, *Vice Pres*
Gordy Michalec, *Opers Mgr*
◆ **EMP:** 170
SALES (est): 289.7MM **Privately Held**
SIC: 3321 3443 Gray & ductile iron foundries; metal parts

(G-347)
PETROGAS INTERNATIONAL CORP
2444 Woodland Trl (46706-9688)
PHONE................................260 484-0859
Pablo Migros, *CEO*
EMP: 5
SALES (est): 391.1K **Privately Held**
SIC: 2813 Industrial gases

(G-348)
PRECISION GAGE LLC
1401 S Grandstaff Dr (46706-2664)
PHONE................................260 925-4717
EMP: 2
SALES (est): 93.3K **Privately Held**
SIC: 3321 Cooking utensils, cast iron

(G-349)
RIEKE CORPORATION (HQ)
Also Called: Rieke Packaging Systems
500 W 7th St (46706-2095)
PHONE................................260 925-3700
Fax: 260 925-3700
Lynn Brooks, *President*
▲ **EMP:** 310
SQ FT: 195,000
SALES (est): 79.4MM
SALES (corp-wide): 817.7MM **Publicly Held**
WEB: www.riekecorp.com
SIC: 3466 3089 Closures, stamped metal; fittings for pipe, plastic
PA: Trimas Corporation
38505 Woodward Ave # 200
Bloomfield Hills MI 48304
248 631-5450

(G-350)
ROYAL STAMPING INC
530 North St (46706-1622)
PHONE................................260 925-3312
Benjamin Nagel, *President*
Thomas Cape, *Vice Pres*
EMP: 10
SALES (est): 1.4MM **Privately Held**
SIC: 3443 3469 Metal parts; metal stampings

(G-351)
S & R CONCESSIONS LLC
813 E 9th St (46706-2427)
P.O. Box 510 (46706-0510)
PHONE................................260 570-3247
Rhonda K Freed,
Rhonda Freed,
EMP: 10
SALES (est): 826.7K **Privately Held**
SIC: 2599 7389 Food wagons, restaurant;

(G-352)
SCHER MAIHEM PUBLISHING LTD
Also Called: Midwest Film Factory
650 North St (46706-1630)
P.O. Box 313, Avilla (46710-0313)
PHONE................................260 897-2697
Julia Scher, *President*
Claire Tindall, *Vice Pres*
EMP: 3
SALES (est): 162.7K **Privately Held**
SIC: 2741 Miscellaneous publishing

(G-353)
SCOT INDUSTRIES INC
1729 W Auburn Dr (46706-3343)
PHONE................................608 778-2251
EMP: 17
SALES (corp-wide): 172.8MM **Privately Held**
SIC: 3498 Fabricated pipe & fittings
PA: Scot Industries, Inc.
3756 Fm 250 N
Lone Star TX 75668
903 639-2551

(G-354)
SCP HOLDINGS INC
1700 S Indiana Ave (46706-3414)
PHONE................................260 925-2588
James A Buchanan, *CEO*
Ryan Criswell, *Finance*
Paul Schlueter, *VP Sales*
EMP: 8 **EST:** 2016
SALES (est): 340K **Privately Held**
SIC: 2899 Igniter grains, boron potassium nitrate

(G-355)
SEILER EXCAVATING INC
6310 County Road 31 (46706-9682)
PHONE................................260 925-0507
Larry Seiler, *President*
Donna Seiler, *Vice Pres*
EMP: 7
SALES (est): 880K **Privately Held**
SIC: 1794 7692 Excavation work; welding repair

(G-356)
SHILOH INDUSTRIES INC
1200 Power Dr (46706-2671)
PHONE................................260 925-4711

Fax: 260 925-0457
Gerald Craycraft, *Plant Mgr*
EMP: 36
SQ FT: 68,000 **Publicly Held**
SIC: 3363 Aluminum die-castings
PA: Shiloh Industries, Inc.
880 Steel Dr
Valley City OH 44280

(G-357)
SPECILZED CMPNENT PRTS LTD LLC
Also Called: Scp Limited
1700 S Indiana Ave (46706-3414)
P.O. Box 560 (46706-0560)
PHONE................................260 925-2588
Fax: 260 925-6321
James A Buchanan, *President*
▲ **EMP:** 150
SQ FT: 27,000
SALES (est): 8.3MM **Privately Held**
WEB: www.scplimited.com
SIC: 3491 Gas valves & parts, industrial

(G-358)
STAMETS TOOL & ENGINEERING
510 North St (46706-1622)
PHONE................................260 925-1382
Fax: 260 925-1450
Michael S Stamets, *President*
David L Stamets, *Vice Pres*
Robert W Stamets, *Admin Sec*
EMP: 9
SQ FT: 10,000
SALES (est): 710K **Privately Held**
SIC: 3599 3544 Machine shop, jobbing & repair; special dies, tools, jigs & fixtures

(G-359)
SUPERIOR EQUIPMENT & MFG
717 Lakeshore Dr (46706-2615)
P.O. Box 97, Waterloo (46793-0097)
PHONE................................260 925-0152
Fax: 260 925-0640
Brian Ruegsegger, *President*
Sandra Rhaos, *Admin Sec*
EMP: 2 **EST:** 1979
SQ FT: 2,600
SALES (est): 230.4K **Privately Held**
SIC: 3441 Fabricated structural metal

(G-360)
TD CONSULTING LLC
812 Allison Blvd (46706-3102)
PHONE................................260 925-3089
Thomas Dendinger, *Principal*
EMP: 2
SALES (est): 98K **Privately Held**
SIC: 3069 Mittens, rubber

(G-361)
THREE DAUGHTERS CORP
Also Called: Rathbun Tool and Mfg
5005 County Road 29 (46706-9601)
PHONE................................260 925-2128
Fax: 260 925-5158
Richard Allen, *President*
EMP: 20
SQ FT: 20,000
SALES (est): 3.8MM **Privately Held**
WEB: www.rathburntool.com
SIC: 3599 Machine shop, jobbing & repair

(G-362)
TOMS DONUTS OF AUBURN LLC
202 S Dewey St (46706-2512)
PHONE................................260 927-1224
Susan B Davidson, *Mng Member*
EMP: 4
SALES (est): 278.2K **Privately Held**
SIC: 2051 Breads, rolls & buns

(G-363)
TOWER AUTOMOTIVE OPERATIONS
801 W 15th St (46706-2030)
PHONE................................260 925-5113
Fax: 260 925-3648
Tom Vestergaard, *Opers Mgr*
Don Stroud, *Manager*
EMP: 155 **Publicly Held**
SIC: 3465 Automotive stampings

HQ: Tower Automotive Operations Usa Ii,
Llc
17672 N Laurel Park Dr 400e
Livonia MI 48152

(G-364)
TRIMAS CORPORATION
500 W 7th St (46706-2006)
PHONE.................................260 925-3700
EMP: 5
SALES (corp-wide): 817.7MM **Publicly
Held**
SIC: 3799 Trailer hitches
PA: Trimas Corporation
38505 Woodward Ave # 200
Bloomfield Hills MI 48304
248 631-5450

(G-365)
TROPHIES & AWARDS INC
1916 Wayne St (46706-3515)
PHONE.................................260 925-4672
Carol Bavis, *President*
Sandy Griffin, *Manager*
EMP: 6
SQ FT: 600
SALES (est): 625.7K **Privately Held**
SIC: 3499 5999 Trophies, metal, except
silver; trophies & plaques

(G-366)
VANS TV & APPLIANCE INC
Also Called: Van's Home Center
106 Peckhart Ct (46706-9589)
PHONE.................................260 927-8267
Fax: 260 927-0310
Van Dick, *President*
Douglas A Dick, *President*
Mary Lou Dick, *Corp Secy*
Brian Stroh, *Database Admin*
EMP: 10
SQ FT: 40,000
SALES (est): 2.3MM **Privately Held**
SIC: 5722 5731 2515 2512 Electric
household appliances, major; gas house-
hold appliances; television sets; mat-
tresses & foundations; upholstered
household furniture; flooring contractor

(G-367)
WEST ALLIS GRAY IRON
Also Called: Metal Technologies
1401 S Grandstaff Dr (46706-2664)
PHONE.................................260 925-4717
Keith Turner, *Principal*
EMP: 100
SQ FT: 5,000
SALES (est): 8.5MM **Privately Held**
WEB: www.metaltechnologies.com
SIC: 3325 3321 Steel foundries; gray &
ductile iron foundries

Aurora
Dearborn County

(G-368)
AFTER HOURS EMBROIDERY
406 2nd St (47001-1326)
PHONE.................................812 926-9355
Donna Ashley, *Partner*
Charles Ashley, *Partner*
EMP: 2
SALES (est): 107.8K **Privately Held**
SIC: 2395 2759 Embroidery & art needle-
work; screen printing

(G-369)
ALL-RITE READY MIX INC
10513 Morgan Branch Rd (47001-8248)
PHONE.................................812 926-0920
Fax: 812 926-3870
Saron Dillion, *Principal*
Bill Cumming, *Branch Mgr*
EMP: 10
SALES (corp-wide): 10.5MM **Privately
Held**
WEB: www.allriteready mix.com
SIC: 3273 5251 Ready-mixed concrete;
tools
PA: All-Rite Ready Mix, Inc
139 Aristocrat Dr
Florence KY 41042
859 371-3314

(G-370)
**AURORA CASKET COMPANY
LLC (HQ)**
Also Called: Matthews Aurora Fnrl Solutions
10944 Marsh Rd (47001-2328)
P.O. Box 29 (47001-0029)
PHONE.................................800 457-1111
Fax: 812 926-1889
Michael Quinn, *President*
Gary Weber, *President*
Bill Hudson, *Senior VP*
Don Sizemore, *Opers Mgr*
David Titkemeyer, *Opers Staff*
EMP: 450
SQ FT: 309,000
SALES (est): 61.1MM
SALES (corp-wide): 1.5B **Publicly Held**
WEB: www.funeralplan2.com
SIC: 7261 3995 3281 Funeral service &
crematories; burial caskets; urns, cut
stone
PA: Matthews International Corporation
2 N Shore Ctr Ste 200
Pittsburgh PA 15212
412 442-8200

(G-371)
**AURORA CASKET COMPANY
LLC**
50 Factory (47001)
PHONE.................................812 926-1110
Linda Bushman, *Manager*
EMP: 2
SALES (corp-wide): 1.5B **Publicly Held**
WEB: www.funeralplan2.com
SIC: 3995 Burial caskets
HQ: Aurora Casket Company, Llc
10944 Marsh Rd
Aurora IN 47001
800 457-1111

(G-372)
**AURORA CASKET COMPANY
LLC**
202 Conwell St (47001-1112)
P.O. Box 29 (47001-0029)
PHONE.................................812 926-1111
William Barrott, *Manager*
EMP: 100
SALES (corp-wide): 1.5B **Publicly Held**
WEB: www.funeralplan2.com
SIC: 3995 Burial caskets
HQ: Aurora Casket Company, Llc
10944 Marsh Rd
Aurora IN 47001
800 457-1111

(G-373)
BATESVILLE PRODUCTS INC
Also Called: Huber Industries
10367 Randall Ave (47001-9390)
PHONE.................................812 926-4230
Fax: 812 926-2855
Richard Weber, *President*
EMP: 65
SALES (corp-wide): 10.5MM **Privately
Held**
WEB: www.batesvilleproducts.com
SIC: 3369 3365 Nonferrous foundries; alu-
minum foundries
PA: Batesville Products Inc
434 Margaret St
Lawrenceburg IN 47025
513 381-2057

(G-374)
CA STEEL COUNTRY CANDLES
138 W Conwell St Apt 1 (47001-1130)
PHONE.................................812 290-8516
Jennifer Casteel, *Principal*
EMP: 2
SALES (est): 62.5K **Privately Held**
SIC: 3999 Candles

(G-375)
COLOR GLO
5083 Country Hills Dr (47001-1777)
PHONE.................................812 926-2639
Steve Gray, *President*
Laurie Gray, *CFO*
EMP: 2
SALES (est): 85.8K **Privately Held**
SIC: 7389 3111 Interior design services;
leather tanning & finishing

(G-376)
**DIAMOND CONSTRUCTION
SVCS LLC**
6534 Hartford Pike (47001-9204)
PHONE.................................513 314-3609
Richard Strobl, *Co-Owner*
EMP: 2
SALES (est): 209.3K **Privately Held**
SIC: 3536 Hoists, cranes & monorails

(G-377)
GARY W MARTIN
9588 Old State Road 350 (47001-9342)
PHONE.................................812 926-0935
EMP: 2
SALES: 150K **Privately Held**
SIC: 3271 Mfg Concrete Block/Brick

(G-378)
**HESS ELECTRIC MOTOR
SERVICE**
242 Railroad Ave Ste 2 (47001-1036)
P.O. Box 86 (47001-0086)
PHONE.................................812 926-0346
James Hess, *President*
Elaine Hess, *Corp Secy*
EMP: 4
SQ FT: 3,000
SALES: 390K **Privately Held**
SIC: 7694 5063 Electric motor repair; mo-
tors, electric

(G-379)
HOOSIER WALLBEDS INC
8787 State Road 48 (47001-8995)
PHONE.................................812 926-0055
Mike Worthington, *President*
EMP: 6
SALES (est): 512K **Privately Held**
WEB: www.hoosierwallbeds.com
SIC: 2514 Metal bedroom furniture

(G-380)
HOTMIX INC (PA)
110 Forest Ave (47001-1065)
P.O. Box 67 (47001-0067)
PHONE.................................812 926-1471
Randy Wanstrath, *President*
Keith Mosier, *Vice Pres*
EMP: 6
SQ FT: 5,000
SALES (est): 1.5MM **Privately Held**
SIC: 2951 Asphalt & asphaltic paving mix-
tures (not from refineries)

(G-381)
**JOHN PATER DESIGN
FABRICATION**
5298 Hartford Pike (47001-9788)
PHONE.................................812 926-4845
Fax: 812 926-4845
John T Pater, *Owner*
EMP: 10
SQ FT: 10,000
SALES: 773.2K **Privately Held**
SIC: 2431 1751 2434 Doors, wood; cabi-
net building & installation; finish & trim
carpentry; wood kitchen cabinets

(G-382)
KLEEMAN CABINETRY
9814 Hueseman Rd (47001-9175)
PHONE.................................812 926-0428
Thomas E Kleeman, *Owner*
Thomas Kleeman, *Owner*
EMP: 2
SALES (est): 122.5K **Privately Held**
SIC: 2431 Woodwork, interior & ornamen-
tal

(G-383)
MORETON PRINTING CO
511 2nd St (47001-1327)
PHONE.................................812 926-1692
Fax: 812 926-1359
James Pieper, *President*
Andrew Pieper, *Vice Pres*
EMP: 7 EST: 1971
SQ FT: 4,500
SALES: 800K **Privately Held**
WEB: www.solutionsforprint.com
SIC: 2752 5112 Commercial printing, off-
set; business forms

(G-384)
PAUL H ROHE CO INC
110 Forest Ave (47001-1065)
P.O. Box 67 (47001-0067)
PHONE.................................812 926-1471
Mork Richardson, *President*
James P Jurgensen, *Corp Secy*
Gina Davidson, *Executive*
EMP: 13
SQ FT: 10,000
SALES (est): 3MM
SALES (corp-wide): 16.2MM **Privately
Held**
SIC: 2951 1442 1422 Asphalt & asphaltic
paving mixtures (not from refineries); con-
struction sand & gravel; crushed & broken
limestone
PA: Morrow Gravel Company Inc
11641 Mosteller Rd
Cincinnati OH 45241
513 771-0820

(G-385)
PINPOINT PRINTER
541 Green Blvd (47001-1501)
PHONE.................................812 577-0630
EMP: 2
SALES (est): 127K **Privately Held**
SIC: 2752 Commercial printing, litho-
graphic

(G-386)
**ROBERTS PRECISION
MACHINING**
Also Called: Roberts Precission Machining
8007 Us Highway 50 (47001-2282)
PHONE.................................812 926-3233
Jonathon Roberts, *Owner*
EMP: 2
SQ FT: 2,500
SALES (est): 160K **Privately Held**
SIC: 3599 Machine shop, jobbing & repair

(G-387)
**SPECIALTY ADHESIVE FILM CO
(PA)**
Also Called: USA Flap
10510 Randall Ave (47001-9496)
P.O. Box 150 (47001-0150)
PHONE.................................812 926-0156
Fax: 812 926-0634
John Mahn Jr, *President*
Joan Coyle, *Plant Mgr*
Bob Engels, *Controller*
EMP: 35
SQ FT: 25,000
SALES (est): 7.1MM **Privately Held**
WEB: www.specialtyadhesive.com
SIC: 2672 3081 2891 Adhesive backed
films, foams & foils; unsupported plastics
film & sheet; laminating compounds

(G-388)
SPINDLE-TECH INC
14434 Goose Run Rd (47001-9376)
PHONE.................................812 926-1114
Richard Hollin, *President*
EMP: 2
SQ FT: 3,000
SALES: 500K **Privately Held**
SIC: 3541 Machine tools, metal cutting
type

(G-389)
SPORTS SCREEN IMPACT
718 Green Blvd (47001-1506)
PHONE.................................812 926-9355
Casey Roberts, *Owner*
EMP: 3
SALES (est): 220.3K **Privately Held**
SIC: 2759 Screen printing

(G-390)
STEDMAN MACHINE COMPANY
129 Franklin St (47001-1064)
PHONE.................................812 926-0038
Dennis Gilmour, *President*
Scotty Strunk, *Purch Mgr*
Aaron Potter, *Engineer*
Mike Tinkey, *CFO*
Bob Bammann, *Regl Sales Mgr*
EMP: 80

GEOGRAPHIC

SALES (est): 3.3MM **Privately Held**
SIC: 3532 8711 3541 3531 Rock crushing machinery, stationary; engineering services; machine tools, metal cutting type; construction machinery

(G-391)
SUPERIOR VAULT CO INC
Also Called: Individual Mausoleum Co
714 Green Blvd (47001-1506)
PHONE..............................812 539-1830
Fax: 812 926-2612
Chuck Ehlers, *Owner*
EMP: 7
SQ FT: 3,200
SALES (corp-wide): 1.4MM **Privately Held**
SIC: 3272 Burial vaults, concrete or precast terrazzo; septic tanks, concrete
PA: Superior Vault Co Inc
500 Pike St
Charlestown IN 47111
812 256-5545

(G-392)
VALLEY ASPHALT CORPORATION
Also Called: Rohe, Paul H
110 4th St (47001-1202)
P.O. Box 67 (47001-0067)
PHONE..............................812 926-1471
Fax: 812 926-2400
Mark Richardson, *Manager*
EMP: 40
SALES (corp-wide): 84.9MM **Privately Held**
SIC: 2951 Asphalt paving mixtures & blocks
HQ: Valley Asphalt Corporation
11641 Mosteller Rd
Cincinnati OH 45241
513 771-0820

(G-393)
W MARTIN GARY
8467 Lower Dillsboro Rd (47001-2238)
PHONE..............................812 926-0935
Gary W Martin, *Principal*
EMP: 2
SALES (est): 116.9K **Privately Held**
SIC: 3271 Concrete block & brick

Austin
Scott County

(G-394)
AJEM WELDING
261 E State Road 256 (47102-8770)
PHONE..............................812 595-3541
Amy K Youngblood, *Owner*
EMP: 2
SALES (est): 91.2K **Privately Held**
SIC: 3441 Fabricated structural metal

(G-395)
AUSTIN TRI-HAWK AUTOMOTIVE INC
2001 W Just Indus Pkwy (47102)
P.O. Box 40 (47102-0040)
PHONE..............................812 794-0062
Fax: 812 794-0062
Tri Hawk, *CEO*
Tetsuo Kikuchi, *President*
Michael Murry, *President*
Ryuichi Takayama, *President*
Mark E Mueller, *Principal*
▲ **EMP:** 170
SQ FT: 184,000
SALES (est): 70MM
SALES (corp-wide): 2B **Privately Held**
WEB: www.tri-hawk.com
SIC: 3469 Stamping metal for the trade
PA: G-Tekt Corporation
1-9-4, Sakuragicho, Omiya-Ku
Saitama STM 330-0
486 463-400

(G-396)
DEHART PALLET & LUMBER CO
Also Called: De Harts Pallet & Lbr Mfg Co
2737 E State Road 256 (47102-8424)
P.O. Box 118 (47102-0118)
PHONE..............................812 794-2974

Fax: 812 794-2098
Charles W Tutterow, *President*
Joanna Tutterow, *Corp Secy*
EMP: 19
SALES (est): 1.9MM **Privately Held**
SIC: 2421 2448 2426 Sawmills & planing mills, general; pallets, wood; hardwood dimension & flooring mills

(G-397)
GARTECH ENTERPRISES INC
3037 W State Road 256 (47102-8905)
PHONE..............................812 794-4796
Fax: 812 794-2756
Don Hounshell, *President*
Diane Raichel, *Office Mgr*
EMP: 20
SQ FT: 7,000
SALES (est): 3.8MM **Privately Held**
WEB: www.gartechenterprises.com
SIC: 3679 3714 Harness assemblies for electronic use: wire or cable; automotive wiring harness sets

(G-398)
MORGAN FOODS INC
90 W Morgan St (47102-1741)
PHONE..............................812 794-1170
Fax: 812 794-1215
John S Morgan, *Ch of Bd*
Doan Edmundson, *Vice Pres*
Lawrence M Higdon, *Vice Pres*
Stephanie Lloyd, *Manager*
Mark Hartman, *Director*
▲ **EMP:** 550
SQ FT: 1,000,000
SALES (est): 189MM **Privately Held**
WEB: www.morganfoods.com
SIC: 2032 Soups, except seafood: packaged in cans, jars, etc.

(G-399)
P-AMERICAS LLC
Also Called: Pepsico
1402 W State Road 256 (47102-8904)
P.O. Box 69 (47102-0069)
PHONE..............................812 794-4455
Fax: 812 794-5034
Jeff Shutters, *Materials Mgr*
Brad Chastain, *Engineer*
John Johnson, *Engineer*
Rodney Coleman, *Director*
EMP: 195
SALES (corp-wide): 63.5B **Publicly Held**
SIC: 2086 Carbonated soft drinks, bottled & canned
HQ: P-Americas Llc
1 Pepsi Way
Somers NY 10589
336 896-5740

Avilla
Noble County

(G-400)
ACCEL INTERNATIONAL
302 Progress Way (46710-9668)
PHONE..............................260 897-9990
Dan Cole, *Executive*
▲ **EMP:** 15 **EST:** 2009
SALES (est): 3.4MM **Privately Held**
SIC: 3496 3357 3315 Miscellaneous fabricated wire products; nonferrous wire-drawing & insulating; steel wire & related products

(G-401)
BURNS CABINETS AND DISP INC
140 Green Dr (46710-9518)
PHONE..............................260 897-2219
Fax: 260 897-2246
Patrick Burns, *President*
Sue Burns, *Corp Secy*
EMP: 2
SQ FT: 9,000
SALES (est): 201.2K **Privately Held**
SIC: 2542 2434 Partitions & fixtures, except wood; wood kitchen cabinets

(G-402)
BUSCHE PERFORMANCE GROUP INC
100 Progress Way W (46710-9669)
PHONE..............................260 636-7030
EMP: 110
SALES (corp-wide): 398.9MM **Privately Held**
SIC: 3365 Machinery castings, aluminum
HQ: Busche Performance Group, Inc.
1563 E State Road 8
Albion IN 46701
260 636-7030

(G-403)
DIVERSIFIED PATTERN & ENGRG CO
100 Progress Way (46710-9609)
P.O. Box 230 (46710-0230)
PHONE..............................260 897-3771
Fax: 260 897-3687
James Parker, *President*
EMP: 25
SQ FT: 21,000
SALES (est): 4.5MM **Privately Held**
SIC: 3543 Foundry patternmaking

(G-404)
ETA FABRICATION INC
Also Called: Eta Engineering
10605 E Baseline Rd (46710-9646)
PHONE..............................260 897-3711
Samuel Adams, *President*
EMP: 14
SALES (est): 1.4MM **Privately Held**
WEB: www.etaapc.com
SIC: 3444 3564 3441 Sheet metalwork; blowers & fans; blower filter units (furnace blowers); dust or fume collecting equipment, industrial; fabricated structural metal

(G-405)
GREEN THUMB OF INDIANA INC
9999 E Baseline Rd (46710-9800)
PHONE..............................260 897-2319
Fax: 260 897-3967
EMP: 4
SALES (est): 290K **Privately Held**
SIC: 2499 2875 Mulch, wood & bark; potting soil, mixed

(G-406)
INDIANA PHOENIX INC
Also Called: Phoenix Mixers
200 Dekko Dr (46710)
PHONE..............................260 897-4397
Fax: 260 897-4369
Carl Stockberger, *President*
Dane Keener, *General Mgr*
Hartkey Hyder, *Principal*
Wyne Klink, *Corp Secy*
Greg Blevins, *Engineer*
EMP: 90
SQ FT: 58,000
SALES (est): 26.3MM **Privately Held**
WEB: www.indianaphoenix.com
SIC: 3713 Cement mixer bodies

(G-407)
JO MORY INC
Also Called: J O Mory Sheet Metal Division
201 Progress Way (46710-9684)
PHONE..............................260 897-3541
Fax: 260 897-2816
Duane Worman, *Sales Staff*
Thomas Nott, *Manager*
EMP: 50
SALES (corp-wide): 19.5MM **Privately Held**
WEB: www.jomory.com
SIC: 3444 1761 1711 Sheet metalwork; roofing, siding & sheet metal work; plumbing, heating, air-conditioning contractors
PA: J.O. Mory, Inc.
7470 S State Road 3
South Milford IN 46786
260 665-1145

(G-408)
JOHN LEY MONUMENT SALES INC
101 Progress Way (46710-9609)
P.O. Box 5 (46710-0005)
PHONE..............................260 347-7346

Fax: 260 897-3005
Anthony J Ley, *President*
Margaret E Ley, *Corp Secy*
Regina Ley, *Vice Pres*
EMP: 5 **EST:** 1957
SQ FT: 3,200
SALES (est): 553.6K **Privately Held**
SIC: 5999 3281 Monuments, finished to custom order; cut stone & stone products

(G-409)
KAUTEX INC
210 Green Dr (46710-9517)
PHONE..............................937 238-8096
Rob Abfall, *Branch Mgr*
EMP: 300
SALES (corp-wide): 14.2B **Publicly Held**
WEB: www.textronauto.com
SIC: 3089 3714 3498 3429 Injection molding of plastics; motor vehicle parts & accessories; fabricated pipe & fittings; manufactured hardware (general)
HQ: Kautex Inc.
750 Stephenson Hwy # 200
Troy MI 48083
248 616-5100

(G-410)
KAUTEX INC
210 Green Dr (46710-9517)
P.O. Box 795 (46710)
PHONE..............................260 897-3250
Fax: 260 897-3035
Greg Fuller, *Branch Mgr*
EMP: 300
SALES (corp-wide): 14.2B **Publicly Held**
WEB: www.textronautotrim.com
SIC: 3714 Gas tanks, motor vehicle
HQ: Kautex Inc.
750 Stephenson Hwy # 200
Troy MI 48083
248 616-5100

(G-411)
KENDALVILLE MALL
109 N Baum St (46710-5231)
PHONE..............................260 897-2697
EMP: 2
SALES (est): 87.5K **Privately Held**
SIC: 6512 2711 Theater building, ownership & operation; newspapers

(G-412)
KRETLER TOOL & ENGINEERING
104 Well St (46710)
P.O. Box 610 (46710-0610)
PHONE..............................260 897-2662
Fax: 260 897-4162
John Kretler, *President*
Cynthia Kretler, *Vice Pres*
EMP: 7
SQ FT: 10,000
SALES (est): 480K **Privately Held**
SIC: 3312 Tool & die steel & alloys

(G-413)
LAOTTO BREWING LLC
7530 E Swan Rd (46710-9726)
PHONE..............................260 897-3152
David Koepper, *Principal*
EMP: 3
SALES (est): 167.8K **Privately Held**
SIC: 2082 Malt beverages

(G-414)
MAPLE ACRES
535 S 500 E (46710-9618)
PHONE..............................260 636-2073
Kim Owen, *Owner*
Dill Owen, *Co-Owner*
EMP: 2
SALES (est): 86.6K **Privately Held**
SIC: 2099 Maple syrup

(G-415)
MCLAUGHLIN SERVICES LLC (PA)
333 Progress Way (46710-9668)
PHONE..............................260 897-4328
Jeff McLaughlin, *Principal*
EMP: 12
SQ FT: 18,000
SALES (est): 2.8MM **Privately Held**
SIC: 3398 Metal heat treating

(G-416)
NOBLE COUNTY WELDING INC
Also Called: Noble Industrial Fabrications
635 S Van Scoyoc St (46710-9516)
PHONE....................................260 897-4082
Fax: 260 897-4106
Wayne Diehm, *President*
EMP: 11
SQ FT: 16,500
SALES (est): 875K **Privately Held**
WEB: www.indianadata.com
SIC: 7692 3441 Welding repair; fabricated
structural metal

(G-417)
**PEERLESS MANUFACTURING
LLC**
2084 N 800 E (46710-9696)
PHONE....................................260 760-0880
EMP: 3
SALES (est): 171.8K **Privately Held**
SIC: 3999 Manufacturing industries

(G-418)
S & S MACHINE & TOOL INC
731 W Albion St (46710-9310)
P.O. Box 151 (46710-0151)
PHONE....................................260 897-3823
Steve Helmkamp, *President*
Scott Grove, *Vice Pres*
EMP: 5
SQ FT: 800
SALES (est): 541.1K **Privately Held**
SIC: 3599 Machine shop, jobbing & repair

(G-419)
TERNET METAL FINISHING INC
150 Green Dr (46710-9518)
P.O. Box 725 (46710-0725)
PHONE....................................260 897-3903
Fax: 260 897-2908
Jack Ternet, *President*
Neal Ternet, *Vice Pres*
EMP: 6
SQ FT: 20,000
SALES (est): 1.4MM **Privately Held**
SIC: 3471 Plating & polishing

(G-420)
**VICTOR REINZ VALVE SEALS
LLC**
Also Called: Dana Sealing Products
301 Progress Way (46710-9668)
P.O. Box 559 (46710-0559)
PHONE....................................260 897-2827
Roger Gatchell, *Controller*
Tammy McCartney, *Human Res Mgr*
Arthur Lindblom,
Mike Boyersock,
Rich Kozerski,
▲ EMP: 100
SQ FT: 80,000
SALES (est): 26.6MM **Publicly Held**
WEB: www.victorreinz.com
SIC: 3592 Valves, aircraft
HQ: Dana Sealing Products, Llc
3939 Technology Dr
Maumee OH 43537

(G-421)
WICK - FAB INC
Also Called: Wickfab Steel Fabrication
307 E Fourth St (46710-9521)
PHONE....................................260 897-3303
Fax: 260 897-3125
John Wicker, *CEO*
EMP: 23
SALES: 5MM **Privately Held**
SIC: 3531 3444 3441 2542 Aggregate
spreaders; sheet metalwork; fabricated
structural metal; partitions & fixtures, ex-
cept wood

(G-422)
WIRCO INC (PA)
105 Progress Way (46710-9609)
P.O. Box 609 (46710-0609)
PHONE....................................260 897-3768
Fax: 260 897-2525
Dennis L Wright, *CEO*
Chad Wright, *President*
Christopher M Dankert, *Vice Pres*
Aaron Fisher, *Purch Mgr*
Wendy Evans, *CFO*
EMP: 120

SQ FT: 50,000
SALES (est): 42.9MM **Privately Held**
WEB: www.wirco.com
SIC: 3544 3822 3496 3599 Industrial
molds; malleable iron foundries; woven
wire products; machine shop, jobbing &
repair

Avon
Hendricks County

(G-423)
A & A MACHINE SERVICE INC
4830 E Main St (46123-9194)
P.O. Box 388, Danville (46122-0388)
PHONE....................................317 745-7367
Fax: 317 745-5084
Jerry Morgan, *President*
EMP: 9
SQ FT: 8,000
SALES: 550K **Privately Held**
SIC: 3545 7389 Gauges (machine tool ac-
cessories); tools & accessories for ma-
chine tools; grinding, precision:
commercial or industrial

(G-424)
ACME COATINGS INC
240 Production Dr (46123-7030)
PHONE....................................317 272-6202
William Bailey Jr, *President*
EMP: 6
SQ FT: 8,000
SALES: 1.1MM **Privately Held**
SIC: 3479 Painting, coating & hot dipping

(G-425)
ACME MASKING COMPANY INC
240 Production Dr (46123-7030)
PHONE....................................317 272-6202
Fax: 317 272-5314
William H Bailey Jr, *President*
EMP: 30
SQ FT: 25,000
SALES (est): 5.4MM **Privately Held**
WEB: www.acmemasking.com
SIC: 3069 3544 Molded rubber products;
industrial molds

(G-426)
ALLIED BOILER & WELDING CO
1974 N County Road 600 E (46123-9559)
PHONE....................................317 272-4820
Fax: 317 783-3286
Cathryn E Rayball, *President*
EMP: 8
SQ FT: 5,500
SALES (est): 1MM **Privately Held**
SIC: 1711 7692 7629 3443 Boiler main-
tenance contractor; welding repair; electri-
cal repair shops; fabricated plate work
(boiler shop); heating equipment, except
electric

(G-427)
AO INC
Also Called: Newspaper Solutions
9227 E Us Highway 36 (46123-7929)
PHONE....................................317 280-3000
Ronald Musgrave, *President*
Steven Peterka, *Vice Pres*
EMP: 4
SQ FT: 2,500
SALES (est): 299.6K **Privately Held**
SIC: 3648 7389 Stage lighting equipment;
decorative area lighting fixtures; printers'
services: folding, collating

(G-428)
**APOLLO OUTDOOR CSTM
DESIGN INC**
7124 E County Road 150 S B
(46123-2001)
PHONE....................................317 718-2502
Brent Mason, *President*
EMP: 10
SQ FT: 7,500
SALES (est): 1.3MM **Privately Held**
SIC: 2522 Office chairs, benches & stools,
except wood

(G-429)
ASPEN SOLUTIONS GROUP INC
2076 Aspen Dr (46123-7627)
PHONE....................................317 839-9274
James Denson, *President*
EMP: 5
SALES: 650K **Privately Held**
SIC: 7379 7372 Computer related consult-
ing services; prepackaged software

(G-430)
**AVON CARBON CAPTURE RES
ASSOC**
7468 Glensford Dr (46123-7147)
PHONE....................................317 753-8829
David Mullins, *Owner*
EMP: 3
SALES (est): 154.4K **Privately Held**
SIC: 1311 Crude petroleum & natural gas

(G-431)
AVON MOBILE WASH
5518 Muirfield Way (46123-9117)
PHONE....................................317 517-1890
Greg Spencer, *Owner*
EMP: 4 EST: 2008
SALES (est): 442.1K **Privately Held**
SIC: 3589 High pressure cleaning equip-
ment

(G-432)
BATH & BODY WORKS LLC
10343 E Us Highway 36 (46123-7988)
PHONE....................................317 209-1517
Denise Newkirk, *Branch Mgr*
EMP: 20
SALES (corp-wide): 12.6B **Publicly Held**
WEB: www.bath-and-body.com
SIC: 5999 2844 Perfumes & colognes; toi-
let preparations
HQ: Bath & Body Works, Llc
7 Limited Pkwy E
Reynoldsburg OH 43068

(G-433)
BEACON SIGN COMPANY LLC
9305 E Us Highway 36 (46123-7977)
PHONE....................................317 272-2388
Robert Alltop, *Partner*
Linda Alltop, *Partner*
EMP: 2
SALES: 100K **Privately Held**
SIC: 3993 Signs & advertising specialties

(G-434)
BREINER COMPANY INC
259 Production Dr (46123-7030)
PHONE....................................317 272-2521
Fax: 317 272-4503
William T Lucas Sr, *Ch of Bd*
William T Lucas Jr, *President*
Frances Lucas, *Corp Secy*
Janice Parker, *Office Mgr*
Joseph Lucas, *Manager*
EMP: 15
SQ FT: 20,000
SALES: 2MM **Privately Held**
WEB: www.breinerco.com
SIC: 3053 Gaskets, all materials

(G-435)
**CO-ALLIANCE LTD LBLTY
PARTNR (PA)**
5250 E Us Hwy 3 (46123)
P.O. Box 560, Danville (46122-0560)
PHONE....................................317 745-4491
Kevin Still, *Partner*
John Gram, *Partner*
Jen Brown, *Human Res Mgr*
Tim Clark, *Sales Staff*
Colleen OHM, *Med Doctor*
◆ EMP: 55
SALES (est): 483.3MM **Privately Held**
SIC: 5191 5171 5153 2875 Feed; seeds:
field, garden & flower; fertilizer & fertilizer
materials; petroleum bulk stations & ter-
minals; grains; fertilizers, mixing only

(G-436)
**COMMUNITY HOLDINGS
INDIANA INC**
8109 Kingston St Ste 500 (46123-8211)
PHONE....................................317 272-5800
Fax: 317 272-5887
Linna Caldemone, *Sales Executive*

Bev Joyce, *Branch Mgr*
EMP: 10 **Privately Held**
WEB: www.clintonnc.com
SIC: 2711 Newspapers, publishing & print-
ing
HQ: Community Holdings Of Indiana, Inc.
3500 Colonnade Pkwy # 600
Birmingham AL 35243

(G-437)
CONCEPT CABINET SHOP (PA)
7599 E Us Highway 36 (46123-7171)
PHONE....................................317 272-7430
Aaron Albers, *CEO*
EMP: 6
SALES (est): 862.9K **Privately Held**
SIC: 2599 Cabinets, factory

(G-438)
DON MOLINE ELECTRIC
6957 E County Road 100 S (46123-8278)
PHONE....................................317 987-7606
Don R Moline, *Principal*
EMP: 2
SALES (est): 215.4K **Privately Held**
SIC: 3699 Electrical equipment & supplies

(G-439)
**E SQUARED MOTORSPORTS
LLC**
1511 N County Road 600 E (46123-9582)
PHONE....................................317 626-2937
EMP: 3
SALES (est): 162K **Privately Held**
SIC: 3644 Raceways

(G-440)
EJ SCHMIDT INC
Also Called: Sign-A-Rama
8100 E Us Highway 36 # 1 (46123-8284)
PHONE....................................317 290-0491
Edward Schmidt, *President*
EMP: 3
SQ FT: 1,600
SALES: 240K **Privately Held**
SIC: 3993 Signs & advertising specialties

(G-441)
GIGGLICIOUS LLC
1782 Rudgate Dr (46123-8409)
PHONE....................................317 272-4064
Ryan Wolfinbarger, *Managing Dir*
Annette Wolfinbarger,
▲ EMP: 2
SALES: 80K **Privately Held**
WEB: www.gigglicious.com
SIC: 3944 Games, toys & children's vehi-
cles

(G-442)
GINAS CREATIVE JEWELRY INC
8100 E Us Highway 36 # 7 (46123-8284)
PHONE....................................317 272-0032
Fax: 317 272-2933
Gina Fisher, *President*
Bill Fisher, *Vice Pres*
EMP: 6
SQ FT: 1,875
SALES: 400K **Privately Held**
SIC: 5944 3911 7631 Jewelry stores; jew-
elry, precious metal; jewelry repair serv-
ices

(G-443)
HARLAN BAKERIES LLC (PA)
7597 E Us Highway 36 (46123-7171)
PHONE....................................317 272-3600
Fax: 317 272-1110
Hugh Harlan, *President*
Doug Harlan, *Exec VP*
Hal Harlan, *Exec VP*
▲ EMP: 3
SALES (est): 1.1B **Privately Held**
SIC: 5149 2051 2045 Bakery products;
bread, cake & related products; prepared
flour mixes & doughs

(G-444)
HARLAN BAKERIES-AVON LLC
7597 E Us Highway 36 (46123-7171)
PHONE....................................317 272-3600
Fax: 317 894-9458
Hugh Harlan, *Principal*
Doug H Harian, *Exec VP*
Paul G Hayden, *Exec VP*
Chris Taylor, *Controller*

Robert Russell, *Director*
▲ EMP: 375
SQ FT: 225,000
SALES (est): 82MM **Privately Held**
WEB: www.harlanbakeries.com
SIC: 5149 2051 2045 Bakery products; bread, cake & related products; prepared flour mixes & doughs
PA: Harlan Bakeries, Llc
7597 E Us Highway 36
Avon IN 46123

(G-445)
HARRISON MANUFACTURING INC
9973 E Us Highway 36 (46123-7987)
PHONE 812 466-1111
Ron Harrison, *CEO*
Scott Rader, *Info Tech Mgr*
EMP: 7 EST: 2014
SALES (est): 205.8K **Privately Held**
SIC: 3812 Acceleration indicators & systems components, aerospace

(G-446)
HELP HELP LLC
Also Called: Say Help
1935 Acorn Ct (46123-9438)
PHONE 317 910-6631
Javier Casas, *CEO*
EMP: 4
SALES: 500K **Privately Held**
SIC: 7372 7389 Application computer software;

(G-447)
HENDRICKS COUNTY FLYER
8109 Kingston St Ste 500 (46123-8211)
PHONE 317 272-5800
Harold Allen, *Administration*
EMP: 3
SALES (est): 69.2K **Privately Held**
SIC: 2711 Newspapers

(G-448)
INFINITY PRODUCTS INC
Also Called: C-Level
141 Casco Dr (46123-5428)
PHONE 317 272-3435
Fax: 317 272-3445
Linda Scott, *President*
Gregg E Scott, *Treasurer*
EMP: 8
SQ FT: 17,000
SALES: 711.2K **Privately Held**
SIC: 3842 Personal safety equipment

(G-449)
JANI INDUSTRIES INC
2256 N County Road 800 E (46123-8571)
PHONE 317 985-3916
Devendra Jani Jr, *Principal*
EMP: 3
SALES (est): 199.7K **Privately Held**
SIC: 3999 Manufacturing industries

(G-450)
JOHNSONS ORTHOTICS PROSTHETICS
5055 E Us Highway 36 # 200 (46123-6532)
PHONE 317 272-9993
EMP: 2 EST: 2013
SALES (est): 160K **Privately Held**
SIC: 3842 Mfg Surgical Appliances

(G-451)
JT PRINTING LLC
Also Called: Full Circle Printing & Mktg
77 Park Place Blvd (46123-6536)
PHONE 317 271-7700
James Tolley, *President*
Charles Dorton, *General Mgr*
Tamara Tolley,
EMP: 5 EST: 2013
SQ FT: 2,800
SALES: 600K **Privately Held**
SIC: 2759 Commercial printing

(G-452)
KAMREX INC
7367 Business Center Dr (46123-8662)
PHONE 317 204-3779
Fax: 317 227-8808
Rex Doorn, *President*

Pam Elsey, *Admin Sec*
EMP: 20
SQ FT: 8,000
SALES (est): 2MM **Privately Held**
WEB: www.kamrex.com
SIC: 2721 8743 2731 Trade journals: publishing only, not printed on site; public relations & publicity; book publishing

(G-453)
KEYSTONE ENGRG & MFG CORP (PA)
9786 E County Road 200 N (46123-9044)
PHONE 317 271-6192
Chester Latham, *President*
Chris Dugan, *Purch Mgr*
Andrea Latham, *VP Bus Dvlpt*
▲ EMP: 9
SQ FT: 20,000
SALES: 3MM **Privately Held**
WEB: www.keystonecutter.com
SIC: 3531 3532 Construction machinery; mining machinery

(G-454)
LITTLE GREEN APPLE
8100 E Us Highway 36 # 12 (46123-7953)
PHONE 317 272-1168
EMP: 2
SALES (est): 125.8K **Privately Held**
SIC: 3571 Personal computers (microcomputers)

(G-455)
MOODY MEATS
235 N Avon Ave (46123-8476)
PHONE 317 272-4533
Adam Moody, *President*
EMP: 2
SALES (est): 127.3K **Privately Held**
SIC: 2011 5421 Meat packing plants; meat & fish markets

(G-456)
NEW AQUA LLC (PA)
Also Called: Aqua Systems
7785 E Us Highway 36 (46123-7973)
PHONE 317 272-3000
Donald Line, *Mng Member*
Bret Petty,
EMP: 70
SQ FT: 60,000
SALES (est): 18.7MM **Privately Held**
SIC: 3589 7389 5074 5149 Water filters & softeners, household type; water purification equipment, household type; water treatment equipment, industrial; water softener service; water purification equipment; water softeners; water, distilled; water: distilled mineral or spring; water purification equipment

(G-457)
NEW READERS PRESS
6414 Woodhaven Ct (46123-7220)
PHONE 317 514-6515
EMP: 2
SALES (est): 75.1K **Privately Held**
SIC: 2741 Miscellaneous publishing

(G-458)
NOVA MANUFACTURING
1153 S Avon Ave (46123-7662)
PHONE 512 750-5165
Steve Poalson, *Principal*
EMP: 3
SALES (est): 151K **Privately Held**
SIC: 3999 Manufacturing industries

(G-459)
NUMARK INDUSTRIES COMPANY LTD
7124 E County Road 150 S (46123-2000)
PHONE 317 718-2502
Clifton Lee, *Principal*
Tracy Moore, *Exec VP*
▲ EMP: 10
SQ FT: 3,000
SALES: 3MM **Privately Held**
SIC: 2511 Wood lawn & garden furniture

(G-460)
PARSING LASER DESIGNS LLC
365 Austin Dr (46123-9255)
PHONE 317 677-4316

EMP: 2 EST: 2012
SALES (est): 150K **Privately Held**
SIC: 3479 3231 3555 5999 Coating/Engraving Svcs Mfg Prdt-Purchased Glass Mfg Printing Trades Mach Ret Misc Merchandise

(G-461)
PHOENIX FBRCATORS ERECTORS LLC (PA)
182 S County Road 900 E (46123-8973)
PHONE 317 271-7002
Fax: 317 273-1154
Jeffery A Short, *President*
Kurt Fuller, *President*
Charles Lakin, *Vice Pres*
Eugene M Rothgerber Jr, *Vice Pres*
Frank Massey, *QC Mgr*
EMP: 225
SQ FT: 70,000
SALES (est): 95MM **Privately Held**
WEB: www.phoenixtank.com
SIC: 3443 Water tanks, metal plate

(G-462)
PPG INDUSTRIES INC
Also Called: PPG 4366
5201 E Us Highway 36 # 209 (46123-7837)
PHONE 317 745-0427
Jason Ingram, *Manager*
EMP: 24
SALES (corp-wide): 14.2B **Publicly Held**
WEB: www.ppg.com
SIC: 2851 Paints & allied products
PA: Ppg Industries, Inc.
1 Ppg Pl
Pittsburgh PA 15272
412 434-3131

(G-463)
REXNORD INDUSTRIES LLC
Link-Belt Products
1304 Turfway Dr (46123-8385)
PHONE 865 220-7700
Curtis Heatherly, *Branch Mgr*
EMP: 263
SQ FT: 140,000 **Publicly Held**
SIC: 3568 Couplings, shaft: rigid, flexible, universal joint, etc.
HQ: Rexnord Industries, Llc
247 W Freshwater Way # 200
Milwaukee WI 53204
414 643-3000

(G-464)
REXNORD INDUSTRIES LLC
1304 Turfway Dr (46123-8385)
PHONE 317 273-5500
Todd A Adams, *CEO*
Dean Vlasak, *Principal*
Jennifer Polinski, *Principal*
EMP: 100
SQ FT: 470,000 **Publicly Held**
SIC: 3568 Couplings, shaft: rigid, flexible, universal joint, etc.
HQ: Rexnord Industries, Llc
247 W Freshwater Way # 200
Milwaukee WI 53204
414 643-3000

(G-465)
ROGERS MARKETING & PRINTING
Also Called: Sav-or Pack
7588 E County Road 100 S (46123-7536)
PHONE 317 838-7203
Fax: 317 838-5649
Jeff Rogers, *President*
EMP: 4
SQ FT: 9,000
SALES (est): 641.4K **Privately Held**
WEB: www.rogersmp.com
SIC: 8742 2759 Marketing consulting services; commercial printing

(G-466)
SEWING CONNECTION L L C
Also Called: Shirley Adams Publications
786 Cheltenham Way (46123-8258)
PHONE 317 745-1501
Shirley Adams,
John Adams,
EMP: 3
SALES: 75K **Privately Held**
SIC: 2731 Books: publishing only

(G-467)
SPECTRUM PRINT & MARKETING
7546 Corsican Cir (46123-7457)
PHONE 317 908-7471
Rhonda Dorton, *Owner*
EMP: 2
SALES (est): 38K **Privately Held**
SIC: 2711 Newspapers, publishing & printing

(G-468)
SYCAMORE SERVICES INC
Also Called: Sycamore Printing Center
77 Park Place Blvd (46123-6536)
P.O. Box 369, Danville (46122-0369)
PHONE 317 745-5456
Ralph Dunkin, *President*
Paula Winkley, *Coordinator*
EMP: 18
SALES (est): 1.9MM **Privately Held**
SIC: 2752 Color lithography

(G-469)
TMA ENTERPRISES INC
Also Called: Embroidme
7900 E Us Highway 36 C (46123-7871)
PHONE 317 272-0694
Fax: 317 272-0724
Thomas M Albert, *President*
EMP: 4
SQ FT: 1,800
SALES: 300K **Privately Held**
SIC: 5949 2759 Sewing, needlework & piece goods; screen printing

(G-470)
TOMLINSON MANUFACTURING
9165 E Us Highway 36 (46123-7955)
PHONE 317 209-9375
EMP: 2
SALES (est): 76.1K **Privately Held**
SIC: 8711 3999 Mechanical engineering; manufacturing industries

(G-471)
TRANSMED ASSOCIATES INC (PA)
Also Called: Maxcare Bionics
8131 Kingston St Ste 700 (46123-9120)
P.O. Box 225, Danville (46122-0225)
PHONE 317 293-9993
Wilber Haynes, *President*
EMP: 3
SQ FT: 2,000
SALES: 800K **Privately Held**
SIC: 3842 Limbs, artificial

(G-472)
WOODLAND MANUFACTURING & SUP
Also Called: Old Bob's
10896 E Us Highway 36 (46123-7916)
PHONE 317 271-2266
Fax: 317 271-0517
Jonathan Williams, *President*
Shirley Williams, *Admin Sec*
EMP: 11
SQ FT: 10,000
SALES: 1.2MM **Privately Held**
SIC: 2452 5719 5211 5231 Prefabricated buildings, wood; kitchenware; lighting, lamps & accessories; fireplaces & wood burning stoves; window furnishings; lumber & other building materials; paint, glass & wallpaper; prefabricated metal buildings

---

Bainbridge
Putnam County

(G-473)
BROCKS INCORPORATED
6541 N Us Highway 231 (46105-9681)
PHONE 765 721-3068
Fount Brock, *Owner*
EMP: 6
SALES (est): 316.2K **Privately Held**
SIC: 2411 Logging

2018 Harris Indiana
Industrial Directory

▲ = Import ▼=Export
◆ =Import/Export

(G-474)
CENTURY CONCRETE INC
Also Called: Century Memorial
3725 W Us Highway 36 (46105-9650)
PHONE.................................765 739-6210
Martin Evens, *President*
Mary Jane Evens, *Admin Sec*
EMP: 4 **EST:** 1961
SQ FT: 500
SALES: 160K **Privately Held**
WEB: www.centuryconcrete.com
SIC: 3272 Burial vaults, concrete or precast terrazzo

(G-475)
CERTIFIED WELDING CO INC
5355 E County Road 500 N (46105-9590)
PHONE.................................765 522-3238
Phillip Stjohn, *President*
EMP: 3 **EST:** 1964
SQ FT: 800
SALES: 115K **Privately Held**
SIC: 7692 Welding repair

(G-476)
FENWICK MOTOR SPORTS
112 S Washington St (46105-9725)
PHONE.................................765 522-1354
Rooney Fenwick, *Owner*
EMP: 2
SALES (est): 180K **Privately Held**
SIC: 5012 3714 Automobiles & other motor vehicles; motor vehicle parts & accessories

(G-477)
HARRIS STONE SERVICE INC
5588 N County Road 50 E (46105-9634)
PHONE.................................765 522-6241
Fax: 765 522-3595
Gilbert Harris, *President*
William Davis Jr, *President*
Kenneth R Davies, *Corp Secy*
Shirley F Harris, *Vice Pres*
EMP: 10
SALES (est): 643.4K **Privately Held**
SIC: 1422 3274 Crushed & broken limestone; lime

Bargersville
Johnson County

(G-478)
BENNETT TOOL & DIE INC
910 Cherokee Ave (46106)
P.O. Box 55 (46106-0055)
PHONE.................................317 422-5140
Fax: 317 422-8041
Sandra Hilgemeier, *Owner*
William R Million, *General Mgr*
EMP: 8 **EST:** 1949
SQ FT: 3,600
SALES (est): 1MM **Privately Held**
SIC: 3544 Special dies & tools

(G-479)
CSN INDUSTRIES INC
571 Industrial Dr (46106-8200)
PHONE.................................317 697-6549
Carolyn Neff, *President*
EMP: 2
SALES (est): 80.2K **Privately Held**
SIC: 3999 Manufacturing industries

(G-480)
ELEMENT ARMAMENT LLC
5120 N 400 W (46106-9375)
PHONE.................................317 442-7924
Daniel Hill, *Principal*
EMP: 2
SALES (est): 74.4K **Privately Held**
SIC: 2819 Elements

(G-481)
ELIZABETH M GRAHAM
379 W Old South St (46106-8430)
PHONE.................................812 343-1267
Elizabeth M Graham, *Principal*
EMP: 2
SALES (est): 98.4K **Privately Held**
SIC: 3714 Motor vehicle parts & accessories

(G-482)
EMBROIDERY N THINGS INC
3520 W Whiteland Rd (46106-9069)
PHONE.................................317 859-8963
Fax: 317 859-8960
Dan Francis, *President*
EMP: 2
SALES (est): 129.4K **Privately Held**
WEB: www.entr.us
SIC: 2395 Embroidery products, except schiffli machine; embroidery & art needlework

(G-483)
HUCKLEBERRY WINERY
3057 Amber Way (46106-8363)
PHONE.................................317 850-4445
Cheryl Riddle, *Principal*
EMP: 2
SALES (est): 110.2K **Privately Held**
SIC: 2084 Wines

(G-484)
MALLOW RUN LLC
6964 W Whiteland Rd (46106-9199)
PHONE.................................317 422-1556
Bill Richardson, *Managing Prtnr*
Sarah Shadday, *Wholesale*
John Richardson, *President*
Hannah Abraham, *Relations*
EMP: 2
SALES (est): 302.3K **Privately Held**
WEB: www.mallowrun.com
SIC: 2084 Wines

(G-485)
MERRITT MANUFACTURING INC
2146 N 400 W (46106-8436)
PHONE.................................317 422-1167
Barbara Merritt, *Principal*
EMP: 2
SALES (est): 149.9K **Privately Held**
SIC: 3999 Manufacturing industries

(G-486)
ROY UMBARGER AND SONS INC
111 N Baldwin St (46106-9605)
P.O. Box 695 (46106-0695)
PHONE.................................317 422-5195
Fax: 317 422-5196
Roy Martin Umbarger, *President*
Umbarger Jackson, *Admin Sec*
Thomas Umbarger, *Admin Sec*
EMP: 14
SQ FT: 10,000
SALES (est): 13.3MM **Privately Held**
SIC: 5153 5191 2879 2875 Grain elevators; fertilizer & fertilizer materials; animal feeds; agricultural chemicals; fertilizers, mixing only; flour & other grain mill products

(G-487)
SHADY FROG WINERY LLC
3059 Woodhaven Way (46106-8201)
PHONE.................................317 366-3370
Elizabeth Schiefelbusch,
EMP: 2 **EST:** 2016
SALES (est): 62.3K **Privately Held**
SIC: 2084 Wines

Batesville
Ripley County

(G-488)
A & M TOOL INC
23102 Vote Rd (47006-9539)
PHONE.................................812 934-6533
Albert A Rogier, *President*
Mary Rogier, *Vice Pres*
EMP: 8 **EST:** 1991
SALES: 1MM **Privately Held**
SIC: 3599 3542 Machine shop, jobbing & repair; presses: forming, stamping, punching, sizing (machine tools)

(G-489)
ADVANCED NTRDING SOLUTIONS LLC
1688 Lammers Pike (47006-7775)
PHONE.................................812 932-1010
Maryanne Dickman, *Mng Member*
Jeff Scheel, *Director*
▲ **EMP:** 10
SQ FT: 21,000
SALES (est): 780K **Privately Held**
SIC: 3398 Metal heat treating

(G-490)
ALYMAT PUBLISHING LLC
13198 N County Road 400 E (47006-8881)
PHONE.................................812 933-9940
Stephen Stein, *Principal*
EMP: 3
SALES (est): 123.1K **Privately Held**
SIC: 2711 Newspapers

(G-491)
BATESVILLE CASKET COMPANY INC (HQ)
Also Called: Batesville Management Services
1 Batesville Blvd (47006-9229)
PHONE.................................812 934-7500
Fax: 812 934-8618
Kimberly K Ryan, *President*
Bob Pristash, *President*
Joe Raver, *President*
Dan Saller, *General Mgr*
Mitch Lewis, *District Mgr*
◆ **EMP:** 1300 **EST:** 1884
SQ FT: 700,000
SALES (est): 748.1MM **Publicly Held**
SIC: 3995 Burial caskets

(G-492)
BATESVILLE CASKET COMPANY INC
Also Called: Stamping Plant
100 Eastern Ave (47006)
PHONE.................................812 934-8102
Dennis Knigga, *General Mgr*
EMP: 125 **Publicly Held**
SIC: 3995 Burial caskets
HQ: Batesville Casket Company, Inc.
1 Batesville Blvd
Batesville IN 47006
812 934-7500

(G-493)
BATESVILLE SERVICES INC (HQ)
1 Batesville Blvd (47006-7756)
PHONE.................................812 934-7000
Kimberly K Ryan, *President*
Richard S Barnett, *Admin Sec*
EMP: 250
SALES (est): 91.6MM **Publicly Held**
SIC: 3995 Burial caskets

(G-494)
BATESVILLE TOOL & DIE INC (HQ)
177 Six Pine Ranch Rd (47006-9540)
PHONE.................................812 934-5616
Fax: 812 934-5828
Jody Fledderman, *Ch of Bd*
Lance Green, *Vice Pres*
Robert Holtel, *Vice Pres*
Jerry Kretschmann, *Vice Pres*
James Wintz, *Vice Pres*
▲ **EMP:** 164
SQ FT: 217,400
SALES (est): 128.4MM **Privately Held**
WEB: www.btdinc.com
SIC: 3469 3544 Stamping metal for the trade; special dies & tools; jigs & fixtures
PA: Btd Manufacturing, Inc.
177 Six Pine Ranch Rd
Batesville IN 47006
812 934-5616

(G-495)
BTD MANUFACTURING INC (PA)
177 Six Pine Ranch Rd (47006-9248)
PHONE.................................812 934-5616
Ron Fledderman, *Ch of Bd*
Jody Fledderman, *President*
Ronda Green, *Vice Pres*
Gene Lambert, *Vice Pres*
Jay Fledderman, *VP Mfg*
EMP: 8
SALES (est): 128.4MM **Privately Held**
SIC: 3469 3544 Stamping metal for the trade; special dies & tools; jigs & fixtures

(G-496)
CD & R COMPONENTS INC
Also Called: C D & R Components
3247 W State Road 229 (47006-7851)
P.O. Box 166, Napoleon (47034-0166)
PHONE.................................812 852-4864
Fax: 812 852-4865
Regina Benham, *General Mgr*
EMP: 30
SALES (est): 3.7MM **Privately Held**
SIC: 3714 Motor vehicle parts & accessories

(G-497)
COMMUNITY HOLDINGS INDIANA INC
Also Called: Batesville Herald Tribune
475 N Huntersville Rd (47006-9205)
PHONE.................................812 934-4343
Brian Helvey, *Principal*
EMP: 8 **Privately Held**
WEB: www.clintonnc.com
SIC: 2711 Newspapers, publishing & printing
HQ: Community Holdings Of Indiana, Inc.
3500 Colonnade Pkwy # 600
Birmingham AL 35243

(G-498)
ECKSTEIN WELDING & FABRICATION
11385 N Delaware Rd (47006-7995)
PHONE.................................812 934-2059
Maurice Eckstein, *Partner*
Helen Eckstein, *Partner*
EMP: 2
SALES (est): 86.5K **Privately Held**
SIC: 7692 0111 0212 0213 Welding repair; wheat; beef cattle except feedlots; hogs

(G-499)
ENHANCED MFG SOLUTIONS LLC
23 Hillcrest Estates Dr (47006-9590)
PHONE.................................812 932-1101
Mike Femeyer, *Principal*
EMP: 2
SALES (est): 103.4K **Privately Held**
SIC: 3999 Manufacturing industries

(G-500)
ERTEL CELLARS WINERY INC
3794 E County Road 1100 N (47006-8562)
PHONE.................................812 933-1500
Thomas Ertel, *Principal*
EMP: 30
SALES (est): 3.4MM **Privately Held**
SIC: 2084 Wines

(G-501)
GENERAL ELECTRIC COMPANY
1736 Lammers Pike (47006-8635)
PHONE.................................812 933-0700
Fax: 812 933-0404
EMP: 53
SALES (corp-wide): 123.6B **Publicly Held**
SIC: 5063 3511 3641 6211 Whol Electrical Equip Mfg Turbine/Genratr Sets Mfg Electric Lamps
PA: General Electric Company
41 Farnsworth St
Boston MA 02210
617 443-3000

(G-502)
HEADSTAMP FINE BRASS LLC
1120 Delaware Rd (47006-8989)
PHONE.................................812 212-8326
Mark Gardner, *Principal*
EMP: 2 **EST:** 2011
SALES (est): 120.3K **Privately Held**
SIC: 3484 Pistols or pistol parts, 30 mm. & below

(G-503)
HEARTWOOD MANUFACTURING INC
1646 Lammers Pike (47006-7752)
PHONE.................................812 933-0388
Fax: 812 933-0434
Dale F Meyer, *President*
Bernadette S Meyer, *Corp Secy*
▲ **EMP:** 45

SQ FT: 55,000
SALES (est): 7MM **Privately Held**
WEB: www.heartwoodmfg.com
SIC: 2511 Wood household furniture

(G-504)
HILLENBRAND INC (PA)
1 Batesville Blvd (47006-7756)
PHONE..................................812 934-7500
F Joseph Loughrey, *Ch of Bd*
Joe A Raver, *President*
Kimberly K Ryan, *President*
Christopher H Trainor, *President*
Diane R Bohman, *Senior VP*
EMP: 120
SALES: 1.5B **Publicly Held**
SIC: 3535 3995 Conveyors & conveying
equipment; bulk handling conveyor sys-
tems; burial caskets; burial vaults, fiber-
glass

(G-505)
**ITS PERSONAL LASER
ENGRAVING**
3243 County Rd 1150 E (47006)
PHONE..................................812 934-6657
Debbie Rippetoe, *Owner*
EMP: 2
SALES (est): 151.8K **Privately Held**
SIC: 2796 Engraving platemaking services

(G-506)
JOANS T-SHIRT PRINTING LLC
16 E Boehringer St (47006-1235)
PHONE..................................812 934-2616
Joan M Haessig, *Partner*
EMP: 2
SALES (est): 173.2K **Privately Held**
SIC: 2759 Screen printing

(G-507)
KLEIDOSCOPE QUILTING
24 Saratoga Dr (47006-8482)
P.O. Box 74, Oldenburg (47036-0074)
PHONE..................................812 932-3264
EMP: 5 EST: 2005
SALES (est): 160K **Privately Held**
SIC: 2211 Cotton Broadwoven Fabric Mill

(G-508)
LAKER WINERY LLC
1001 Western Ave (47006-1549)
PHONE..................................812 934-4633
Greg Laker, *Owner*
EMP: 2
SALES (est): 53.5K **Privately Held**
SIC: 2084 Wines

(G-509)
LE KEM OF INDIANA INC
1863 Lammers Pike (47006-7774)
PHONE..................................812 932-5536
Esther Feagins, *CEO*
Esther Feagin, *CEO*
Paul Feagin, *President*
Michael Faegins, *Principal*
Alicia Powers, *Admin Sec*
EMP: 4
SQ FT: 25,000
SALES (est): 631.3K **Privately Held**
WEB: www.lekem.com
SIC: 2899 Chemical preparations

(G-510)
LINKEL COMPANY (PA)
1081 Morris Rd (47006-8490)
PHONE..................................812 934-5190
Tom Linkel,
John Linkel,
EMP: 8
SQ FT: 25,000
SALES (est): 2.1MM **Privately Held**
SIC: 3531 Drags, road (construction &
road maintenance equipment)

(G-511)
MOREL COMPANY LLC
100 Progress Dr (47006-7702)
PHONE..................................812 932-6100
William Hillenbrand II, *Principal*
EMP: 14
SQ FT: 10,000
SALES (est): 2.4MM **Privately Held**
SIC: 3845 Electromedical apparatus

(G-512)
NEW POINT STONE CO INC
Also Called: Napolean Quarry
8792 N County Road 300 W (47006-8750)
PHONE..................................812 852-4225
Fax: 812 852-4961
Steve Wanstrath, *Manager*
EMP: 15
SALES (corp-wide): 12.3MM **Privately
Held**
SIC: 1422 Crushed & broken limestone
PA: New Point Stone Co Inc
992 S County Road 800 E
Greensburg IN 47240
812 663-2021

(G-513)
OLDENBURG PALLET INC
19349 Tony Rd (47006-9350)
PHONE..................................812 933-0568
Fax: 812 934-4426
Delma Davidson, *President*
Douglas Davidson, *Vice Pres*
Billie Davidson, *Treasurer*
EMP: 7
SQ FT: 4,580
SALES (est): 985.4K **Privately Held**
SIC: 2448 2421 Pallets, wood; lumber:
rough, sawed or planed

(G-514)
**PAST & PRESENT SOAP & SND
LLC**
10674 N County Road 350 W
(47006-8187)
PHONE..................................812 852-4328
Dorothy Stier,
Gary Stier,
EMP: 3
SALES (est): 20K **Privately Held**
WEB: www.pnpsoap.com
SIC: 2841 5122 5999 Soap: granulated,
liquid, cake, flaked or chip; toiletries; can-
dle shops

(G-515)
PRO PRINTS
394 Northside Dr (47006-7007)
PHONE..................................812 932-3800
John Webber, *CEO*
EMP: 8
SALES (est): 1.1MM **Privately Held**
SIC: 2752 Commercial printing, litho-
graphic

(G-516)
RED FORGE INC
Also Called: Weld & Fabrication Shop
4552 State Road 46 E (47006-7533)
PHONE..................................812 934-9641
Robert Maple, *CEO*
EMP: 3
SQ FT: 4,800
SALES (est): 340K **Privately Held**
WEB: www.redforgeweld.com
SIC: 7692 Welding repair

(G-517)
**RICCA CHEMICAL COMPANY
LLC**
1490 Lammers Pike (47006-8631)
PHONE..................................812 932-1161
Paul Brandon, *Manager*
EMP: 19
SALES (corp-wide): 27.2MM **Privately
Held**
WEB: www.riccachemical.com
SIC: 2899 Chemical preparations
PA: Ricca Chemical Company, Llc
448 W Fork Dr
Arlington TX 76012
817 274-2912

(G-518)
RODNEY SLOAN LOGGING
Also Called: Sloan, Rodney Logging
1324 E Salem Rd (47006-8576)
PHONE..................................812 934-5321
Rodney Sloan, *Owner*
EMP: 6
SALES: 300K **Privately Held**
SIC: 2411 2421 Logging camps & contrac-
tors; sawmills & planing mills, general

(G-519)
THE FINDLAY PUBLISHING CO
Also Called: Radio Station Wrbi
133 S Main St (47006-1344)
P.O. Box 201 (47006-0201)
PHONE..................................812 222-8000
Fax: 812 934-2765
Ron Green, *Manager*
EMP: 8
SALES (corp-wide): 14.3MM **Privately
Held**
WEB: www.thecourier.com
SIC: 4832 2711 Radio broadcasting sta-
tions; newspapers
PA: Findlay Publishing Company, The (Inc)
701 W Sandusky St
Findlay OH
419 422-5151

(G-520)
**THREE POINTS ALPACA FARM
LLC**
944 Locust Ave (47006-9234)
PHONE..................................812 363-3876
Michael J Christin,
EMP: 2 EST: 2014
SALES (est): 145.9K **Privately Held**
SIC: 2281 7389 Animal fiber yarn, spun;

(G-521)
TRINITY GUARDION
4 S Park Ave Ste 204 (47006-1200)
PHONE..................................812 932-2600
Rob King, *Principal*
Joseph Downey,
Bruce Rippe,
EMP: 10
SALES (est): 1.1MM **Privately Held**
SIC: 2211 Sheets, bedding & table cloths:
cotton

(G-522)
TWINCORP INC
2135 N Huntersville Rd (47006-7423)
PHONE..................................812 934-9226
Gary Hawkins, *President*
EMP: 2
SALES: 2MM **Privately Held**
SIC: 3443 Cylinders, pressure: metal plate

(G-523)
VIRTUS INC
1896 Lammers Pike (47006-8637)
PHONE..................................812 932-0131
Fax: 812 933-0749
John Leonard, *President*
▲ EMP: 40
SQ FT: 20,000
SALES (est): 5.2MM **Privately Held**
WEB: www.virtus.com
SIC: 2392 Mattress pads; mattress protec-
tors, except rubber
PA: Dcc Public Limited Company
Dcc House
Dublin

(G-524)
**WEBERDINGS CARVING SHOP
INC**
1230 State Road 46 E (47006-9185)
PHONE..................................812 934-3710
Fax: 812 934-3731
W G Weberding Jr, *President*
Terry Weberding, *President*
William G Weberding Jr, *President*
Timothy Weberding, *Vice Pres*
EMP: 11 EST: 1943
SQ FT: 28,000
SALES (est): 1.3MM **Privately Held**
WEB: www.weberding.com
SIC: 2499 2426 3543 2531 Carved &
turned wood; carvings, furniture: wood; in-
dustrial patterns; public building & related
furniture; wood household furniture; mill-
work

Battle Ground
Tippecanoe County

(G-525)
ZOOK MACHINE INC
100 W 1250 S (47920-8023)
P.O. Box 192, Delphi (46923-0192)
PHONE..................................765 563-6585
Matthew Zook, *President*
EMP: 5
SQ FT: 2,600
SALES (est): 409K **Privately Held**
SIC: 3599 Machine shop, jobbing & repair

Bedford
Lawrence County

(G-526)
37 PIPE & SUPPLY LLC
8987 Hc 37 (47421)
PHONE..................................812 275-5676
Joyce Mounce, *Mng Member*
EMP: 2
SALES (est): 142.5K **Privately Held**
SIC: 3444 3317 3321 Pipe, sheet metal;
seamless pipes & tubes; water pipe, cast
iron

(G-527)
ACHIEVERS INSTITUTE LLC
Also Called: Royalty Publishing Company
1440 Church Camp Rd (47421-7482)
P.O. Box 2125 (47421-7125)
PHONE..................................812 278-8785
Juanita Scoggan, *Mng Member*
EMP: 2 EST: 1982
SALES: 60K **Privately Held**
SIC: 2759 Publication printing

(G-528)
AGGREGATE MFG INTL LLC
Also Called: A M I
309 Oolitic Rd (47421-1618)
PHONE..................................812 278-9670
Fax: 812 278-9678
Joe Hardy, *Purchasing*
Mike Garard,
Bill Dodds,
▼ EMP: 30
SQ FT: 70,000
SALES (est): 12.9MM **Privately Held**
WEB: www.ami-crushers.com
SIC: 3532 Crushing, pulverizing & screen-
ing equipment

(G-529)
**ARCHITECTURAL STONE SALES
INC**
Also Called: Bedford Cut Stone Co
1728 30th St (47421-5450)
PHONE..................................812 279-2421
Fax: 812 279-1691
Gary Evans, *President*
Mary C Evans, *Treasurer*
EMP: 30 EST: 1965
SALES (est): 3.4MM **Privately Held**
WEB: www.architecturalstonesales.com
SIC: 3281 Cut stone & stone products

(G-530)
B & B SAWMILL INC
7142 Leatherwood Rd (47421-8784)
PHONE..................................812 834-5072
Lloyd J Beyers II, *Principal*
EMP: 9
SALES (est): 689.1K **Privately Held**
SIC: 2421 Sawmills & planing mills, gen-
eral

(G-531)
BEDFORD CRANE LLC
957 J St (47421-2630)
P.O. Box 668 (47421-0668)
PHONE..................................812 275-4411
Fax: 812 275-4412
Josoph W Elliott, *President*
Thomas Elliott, *Corp Secy*
Joseph S Elliott, *Vice Pres*
Sherry Elliott, *Manager*
EMP: 30

▲ = Import ▼=Export
◆ =Import/Export

SALES (est): 3.2MM **Privately Held**
SIC: 3441 Bridge sections, prefabricated highway; building components, structural steel

(G-532)
BEDFORD LIMESTONE SUPPLIERS
1319 Breckenridge Rd (47421-1507)
P.O. Box 654 (47421-0654)
PHONE.................................812 279-9120
Fax: 812 275-5387
Robert E Robbins, *President*
Betty Robbins, *Corp Secy*
EMP: 21 **EST:** 1969
SQ FT: 16,900
SALES (est): 2MM **Privately Held**
SIC: 3281 Limestone, cut & shaped

(G-533)
BEDFORD MACHINE & TOOL INC
2103 John Williams Blvd (47421-9800)
PHONE.................................812 275-1948
Fax: 812 275-1991
Paul Douglas Conrad, *President*
Miki Philipps, *Purch Agent*
Arnold Farler, *QC Mgr*
Brian Pemberton, *Controller*
Jim Crane, *Accountant*
EMP: 46
SQ FT: 94,000
SALES: 6.4MM **Privately Held**
WEB: www.bedfordmachine.com
SIC: 3599 Machine shop, jobbing & repair

(G-534)
BEDFORD STONECRAFTERS INC
3160 Mitchell Rd (47421-5432)
PHONE.................................812 275-2646
Kenny Simpson, *President*
Missy Simpson, *Vice Pres*
EMP: 7
SALES (est): 577.8K **Privately Held**
SIC: 3281 Limestone, cut & shaped

(G-535)
COSNER ICE COMPANY INC
2404 U St (47421-4742)
PHONE.................................812 279-8930
Fax: 812 279-8931
Reath Cosner, *President*
Karen Cosner, *Corp Secy*
Jason Cosner, *Vice Pres*
Angie Cosner, *CFO*
Steve Kiernicki, *Human Resources*
EMP: 25
SALES (est): 5.1MM **Privately Held**
SIC: 2097 4215 Manufactured ice; courier services, except by air

(G-536)
CRIDER HOLCOMB PARTNERSHIP LLC
2611 16th St (47421-3503)
PHONE.................................812 279-2200
Dennis Crider,
EMP: 4
SALES (est): 94.8K **Privately Held**
SIC: 7389 2759 Packaging & labeling services; commercial printing

(G-537)
DIAMOND STONE TECHNOLOGIES INC
2237 Industrial Dr (47421-5652)
PHONE.................................812 276-6043
Greg Smoot, *President*
Bryce Bennett, *Vice Pres*
John Slate, *Sales Staff*
EMP: 15
SQ FT: 10,000
SALES: 4MM **Privately Held**
SIC: 3545 Cutting tools for machine tools

(G-538)
E & H BRIDGE & GRATING INC
1 Lavender Ln (47421-7464)
PHONE.................................812 277-8343
Charles Hillenberg, *President*
Debra Emmons, *Principal*
Greg Emmons, *Vice Pres*
Barbara Hillenberg, *Treasurer*
EMP: 9

SALES: 1MM **Privately Held**
SIC: 3499 3446 Fire- or burglary-resistive products; gratings, tread: fabricated metal

(G-539)
E & R FABRICATING INC
8854 State Road 37 (47421-8300)
PHONE.................................812 275-0388
Fax: 812 275-0512
Ernie Mc Cullough, *President*
Sam Bair, *Admin Sec*
EMP: 8
SQ FT: 6,400
SALES: 1MM **Privately Held**
SIC: 3444 1799 Sheet metalwork; welding on site

(G-540)
ELLIOTT STONE CO INC (PA)
7056 State Road 158 (47421-8584)
P.O. Box 756 (47421-0756)
PHONE.................................812 275-5556
Fax: 812 275-7068
Judy T Elliott, *President*
▲ **EMP:** 44 **EST:** 1964
SQ FT: 2,000
SALES (est): 8.2MM **Privately Held**
WEB: www.elliottstone.com
SIC: 3281 1411 Limestone, cut & shaped; limestone, dimension-quarrying

(G-541)
EVANS LIMESTONE CO
1201 Limestone Dr (47421-9155)
P.O. Box 714 (47421-0714)
PHONE.................................812 279-9744
Fax: 812 275-2408
Steve Evans, *President*
Larry Evans, *Corp Secy*
EMP: 50 **EST:** 1973
SQ FT: 18,000
SALES (est): 1.3MM **Privately Held**
SIC: 3281 Stone, quarrying & processing of own stone products

(G-542)
FLINN FARMS BEDFORD SEED INC
917 17th St (47421-4205)
PHONE.................................812 279-4136
David Flinn, *President*
Brad Flinn, *Vice Pres*
Linda Flinn, *Treasurer*
EMP: 6 **EST:** 1968
SALES (est): 660K **Privately Held**
SIC: 0115 0116 2048 5191 Corn; soybeans; livestock feeds; animal feeds; grass seed; garden supplies

(G-543)
FOUR SEASON SPORTS INC
2828 Washington Ave (47421-5311)
P.O. Box 1208 (47421-1208)
PHONE.................................812 279-0384
Fax: 812 279-0388
Rick Vaught, *President*
Georgetta Vaught, *Corp Secy*
EMP: 5
SQ FT: 3,000
SALES (est): 350K **Privately Held**
SIC: 5699 5941 2395 Sports apparel; sporting goods & bicycle shops; embroidery products, except schiffli machine

(G-544)
GARY EARL
Also Called: Gary's Welding and Machining
411 County Complex Rd (47421-7493)
PHONE.................................812 279-6780
Fax: 812 279-6780
Gary Earl, *Owner*
EMP: 3
SQ FT: 2,600
SALES: 85K **Privately Held**
SIC: 7692 3441 Welding repair; fabricated structural metal

(G-545)
GENERAL MOTORS LLC
105 Gm Dr (47421-1558)
PHONE.................................812 379-7360
Nils Crough, *Engineer*
Brent Carmichael, *Design Engr*
Daniel Akerson, *Manager*
Jameson McCracken, *Manager*
Tim Rienks, *Manager*

EMP: 1500 **Publicly Held**
SIC: 3363 Aluminum die-castings
HQ: General Motors Llc
300 Renaissance Ctr L1
Detroit MI 48243

(G-546)
GEO-FLO PRODUCTS CORPORATION
905 Williams Park Dr (47421-6713)
PHONE.................................812 275-8513
Fax: 812 275-8523
Thomas E Miller, *President*
▲ **EMP:** 12
SQ FT: 10,000
SALES (est): 6.1MM **Privately Held**
WEB: www.geo-flo.com
SIC: 3585 1711 Refrigeration & heating equipment; heating & air conditioning contractors

(G-547)
HARRISON CONCRETE
1218 7th St (47421-2328)
PHONE.................................812 275-6682
Travis Harrison, *Principal*
EMP: 2
SALES (est): 155.9K **Privately Held**
SIC: 3273 Ready-mixed concrete

(G-548)
HOOSIER TIMES INC
Rainbow Printing
2139 16th St (47421-3003)
P.O. Box 97 (47421-0097)
PHONE.................................812 275-3372
Tony Strahl, *General Mgr*
EMP: 20
SALES (corp-wide): 882.7MM **Publicly Held**
WEB: www.htinteractive.com
SIC: 2711 2752 Newspapers: publishing only, not printed on site; commercial printing, lithographic
HQ: Hoosier Times, Inc.
1900 S Walnut St
Bloomington IN 47401
812 331-4270

(G-549)
IN-FAB INC
2030 John Williams Blvd (47421-9649)
PHONE.................................812 279-8144
Jay McCollough, *President*
Ay McCollough, *President*
EMP: 6 **EST:** 2012
SALES (est): 1.6MM **Privately Held**
SIC: 3441 Fabricated structural metal

(G-550)
INDIANA CUT STONE INC
616 Guthrie Rd (47421-7900)
P.O. Box 13, Harrodsburg (47434-0013)
PHONE.................................812 275-0264
Fax: 812 275-0266
Kathy Baker Heckard, *President*
Don Baker, *President*
Linda Baker, *Corp Secy*
Ernie Baker, *Vice Pres*
EMP: 18
SALES (est): 2.1MM **Privately Held**
SIC: 3281 Limestone, cut & shaped

(G-551)
INDIANA FABRIC SOLUTIONS INC
1350 9th St (47421-2520)
PHONE.................................812 279-0255
Patricia McCullough, *President*
Angela McCullough, *Vice Pres*
EMP: 29
SALES: 1MM **Privately Held**
SIC: 2399 Automotive covers, except seat & tire covers

(G-552)
INDIANA STEEL & ENGRG INC (PA)
957 J St (47421-2630)
P.O. Box 668 (47421-0668)
PHONE.................................812 275-3363
Joseph W Elliott, *President*
Joseph S Elliott, *President*
Thomas S Elliott, *Corp Secy*
Tom Elliott, *Purch Agent*

Laura Elliott, *CFO*
EMP: 29
SQ FT: 50,000
SALES (est): 5.6MM **Privately Held**
SIC: 3441 3536 3444 Bridge sections, prefabricated highway; building components, structural steel; cranes, overhead traveling; sheet metalwork

(G-553)
INDIANA STONE WORKS
11438 Us Highway 50 W (47421-8336)
PHONE.................................812 279-0448
Fax: 812 279-0461
Donovan D Short, *President*
Theresa Short, *Corp Secy*
▼ **EMP:** 25
SQ FT: 10,000
SALES (est): 4MM **Privately Held**
SIC: 1411 3281 Limestone, dimension-quarrying; cut stone & stone products

(G-554)
IRVING MATERIALS INC
Also Called: I M I
1307 Bundy Ln (47421-9382)
PHONE.................................812 275-7450
Fax: 812 275-8912
Eric Belth, *Branch Mgr*
EMP: 8
SALES (corp-wide): 800.6MM **Privately Held**
SIC: 3273 Ready-mixed concrete
PA: Irving Materials, Inc.
8032 N State Road 9
Greenfield IN 46140
317 326-3101

(G-555)
J & J STABLES
4081 S Leatherwood Rd (47421-8822)
PHONE.................................812 279-2581
EMP: 2 **EST:** 2003
SALES: 10K **Privately Held**
SIC: 3531 Mfg Construction Machinery

(G-556)
KERNS SPEED SHOP
Also Called: Kern's Speed & Racing Products
203 Newton St (47421-1745)
PHONE.................................812 275-4289
Claude Kern, *Owner*
EMP: 2
SALES (est): 118.1K **Privately Held**
SIC: 7538 3599 General automotive repair shops; machine shop, jobbing & repair

(G-557)
KITCHEN KONNECTION INC
227 Eastlake Dr (47421-3426)
PHONE.................................812 277-0393
Russell W Fields, *President*
EMP: 4
SQ FT: 1,000
SALES (est): 250K **Privately Held**
SIC: 2434 2431 Wood kitchen cabinets; vanities, bathroom: wood; millwork

(G-558)
KOPELOV CUT STONE INC
2321 39th St (47421-5605)
P.O. Box 983 (47421-0983)
PHONE.................................812 675-0099
Labe Kopelov, *President*
EMP: 2
SALES (est): 62.6K **Privately Held**
SIC: 3281 Cut stone & stone products

(G-559)
LASERTECH INC
4684 Dixie Hwy (47421-8247)
PHONE.................................812 277-1321
Jay Stout, *President*
EMP: 2
SQ FT: 1,500
SALES (est): 385.8K **Privately Held**
SIC: 3955 7378 Print cartridges for laser & other computer printers; computer maintenance & repair

(G-560)
LONGS LANDING OF BEDFORD
2831 U St (47421-5332)
PHONE.................................812 278-8986
Jack Ragsdale, *Owner*
Brad Ragsdale, *Co-Owner*

EMP: 2
SALES (est): 264.9K **Privately Held**
SIC: 2599 Bar furniture

(G-561)
MANCHESTER TANK & EQUIPMENT CO
905 X St (47421-2451)
PHONE................................812 275-5931
Greg Hammond, *Warehouse Mgr*
Terri Evans, *Human Res Mgr*
Angie Taylor, *Human Res Mgr*
Jane Harker, *Manager*
Carl Tegarden, *Maintence Staff*
EMP: 100
SALES (corp-wide): 1.3B **Privately Held**
WEB: www.mantank.com
SIC: 3443 Tanks, standard or custom fabricated: metal plate
HQ: Manchester Tank & Equipment Co Inc
1000 Corporate Centre Dr # 300
Franklin TN 37067
615 370-6104

(G-562)
MERRIMAN STEEL AND EQUIPMENT
Also Called: Merriman Kiln & Mill Service
10430 Tunnelton Rd (47421-7887)
PHONE................................812 849-2784
Fax: 812 849-6333
Kenneth H Merriman, *President*
EMP: 5
SQ FT: 20,000
SALES: 1MM **Privately Held**
SIC: 3559 Kilns, cement

(G-563)
MICHAEL J MEYER D M D P C
1504 Dental Dr (47421-3574)
PHONE................................812 275-7112
Michael Meyer, *President*
EMP: 8
SALES (est): 615.2K **Privately Held**
SIC: 3843 Enamels, dentists'

(G-564)
MIDWEST AG FLY SERVICES INC
Also Called: Midwest Exterminators
120 S Teddy Bird Ln (47421-6665)
PHONE................................812 275-5579
Tim Huffman, *President*
Cathy Huffman, *Corp Secy*
EMP: 5
SALES: 185K **Privately Held**
SIC: 2879 Insecticides & pesticides

(G-565)
MILLER RAINBOW PRINTING INC
Also Called: Times Mail
813 16th St (47421-3822)
P.O. Box 849 (47421-0849)
PHONE................................812 275-3355
Fax: 812 277-3472
Debbie Turner, *General Mgr*
EMP: 20 **EST:** 1869
SALES (est): 2.6MM **Privately Held**
WEB: www.indianaprinting.com
SIC: 2752 2791 2789 Commercial printing, offset; typesetting; bookbinding & related work

(G-566)
NORLIGHTSPRESSCOM
762 State Road 458 (47421-7545)
PHONE................................812 675-8054
Vorris D Justesen, *CEO*
Sammie L Justesen, *Vice Pres*
Sammie Justesen, *Mktg Dir*
EMP: 5 **EST:** 2009
SALES: 300K **Privately Held**
SIC: 2731 Books: publishing only

(G-567)
PYNCO INC
2605 35th St (47421-5525)
PHONE................................812 275-0900
Fax: 812 275-1934
Bill Ansley, *COO*
Curt Shifflett, *Engineer*
Justin Patton, *Electrical Engi*
Crystal Hays, *Sales Mgr*
Jennifer Ferry, *Office Mgr*

EMP: 24
SQ FT: 1,800
SALES (est): 1.3MM **Privately Held**
WEB: www.pynco.com
SIC: 3728 8731 Aircraft parts & equipment; electronic research

(G-568)
QUALITY CONNECTIONS OF INDIANA
618 H St (47421-2330)
P.O. Box 684 (47421-0684)
PHONE................................812 279-5852
Pamela Jones, *President*
EMP: 3 **EST:** 1999
SALES (est): 176.4K **Privately Held**
SIC: 3462 Anchors, forged

(G-569)
RAINBOW PRINTING LLC
2139 16th St (47421-3003)
P.O. Box 97 (47421-0097)
PHONE................................812 275-3372
Fax: 812 275-3371
Gary Sanders, *General Mgr*
Kevin Robbins, *Mng Member*
Dee Fish, *Manager*
EMP: 10
SQ FT: 10,000
SALES: 1.4MM **Privately Held**
SIC: 2752 Commercial printing, offset

(G-570)
RC ENTERPRISES
2611 16th St 301 (47421-3503)
PHONE................................812 279-2755
Randall Corwin, *Owner*
Cathy Boxx-Corwin, *Co-Owner*
EMP: 2
SALES: 60K **Privately Held**
SIC: 3915 Jewelers' materials & lapidary work

(G-571)
REAL WOOD WORKS
2802 N Poor Farm Rd (47421-9272)
PHONE................................812 277-1462
David Stoops, *Owner*
EMP: 2 **EST:** 1998
SALES (est): 130.9K **Privately Held**
SIC: 2431 5712 Interior & ornamental woodwork & trim; cabinet work, custom

(G-572)
RECYCLING SERVICES INDIANA INC
Also Called: Newco Metals Processing
4635 Peerless Rd (47421-8115)
PHONE................................812 279-8114
Gary Wade, *President*
Paul Boening, *Vice Pres*
Steven Payne, *Controller*
EMP: 37
SQ FT: 18,000
SALES (est): 11.7MM **Privately Held**
WEB: www.nmponline.net
SIC: 3341 Aluminum smelting & refining (secondary)

(G-573)
RED GATE FARMS INC
Also Called: Carousel Winery
8987 State Road 37 (47421-8301)
PHONE................................812 277-9750
Sue Wilson, *President*
EMP: 8
SALES: 175K **Privately Held**
SIC: 2084 5921 Wines; wine

(G-574)
RIVERSIDE PRINTING CO
1407 I St (47421-3389)
PHONE................................812 275-1950
Fax: 812 275-1984
Michael L Chapman, *Owner*
EMP: 3
SALES (est): 310.6K **Privately Held**
WEB: www.riversideprinting.com
SIC: 2752 3953 2759 Commercial printing, offset; marking devices; engraving

(G-575)
ROBERT D MEADOWS
3568 Peerless Rd (47421-8109)
PHONE................................812 797-8294

Robert Meadows, *Owner*
EMP: 2
SALES (est): 156.2K **Privately Held**
SIC: 3441 Fabricated structural metal

(G-576)
SAMCO INC
1000 U St (47421-2704)
P.O. Box 721 (47421-0721)
PHONE................................812 279-8131
Fax: 812 279-8132
Marvin Stahl, *President*
EMP: 20
SQ FT: 20,000
SALES (est): 3.6MM **Privately Held**
SIC: 3469 Stamping metal for the trade

(G-577)
SIDE KICK LURE RETRIEVER
109 Steeple Ridge Ln (47421-9776)
PHONE................................812 329-9068
Tony Peters, *Owner*
EMP: 2
SALES (est): 74.1K **Privately Held**
SIC: 3949 Bags, rosin

(G-578)
SIGMA STEEL INC (PA)
Also Called: Fab Con
1218 5th St (47421-2304)
P.O. Box 1134 (47421-1134)
PHONE................................812 275-4489
Fax: 812 275-0849
Dean Tackett, *President*
Jerry Covey, *Corp Secy*
Brian Faubion, *Dean*
Richard Derrington, *Vice Pres*
EMP: 25
SQ FT: 7,800
SALES (est): 4.3MM **Privately Held**
WEB: www.sigmasteel.com
SIC: 3449 3441 3448 3446 Curtain walls for buildings, steel; building components, structural steel; prefabricated metal buildings; architectural metalwork; sheet metalwork; fabricated plate work (boiler shop)

(G-579)
SPEER RON SAWMILL & LUMBER CO
5667 Leesville Rd (47421-7308)
PHONE................................812 834-5515
Ronald E Speer, *President*
EMP: 3
SALES (est): 330K **Privately Held**
SIC: 2421 Sawmills & planing mills, general

(G-580)
STANDISH STEEL INC
280 Standish Steel Dr (47421-6866)
PHONE................................812 834-5255
Fax: 812 834-5170
James K Standish, *President*
Mike Waggoner, *Foreman/Supr*
Laura Waggoner, *Treasurer*
Robert Brown, *Manager*
EMP: 12
SQ FT: 15,560
SALES: 1.2MM **Privately Held**
WEB: www.regionalwaste.com
SIC: 3599 Machine & other job shop work; custom machinery; machine shop, jobbing & repair

(G-581)
STONE CITY IRONWORKS INC
1771 Us Highway 50 E (47421-8658)
PHONE................................812 279-3023
Brian Slinkard, *President*
EMP: 30
SALES (est): 12MM **Privately Held**
WEB: www.stonecityironworks.com
SIC: 3441 Fabricated structural metal

(G-582)
STONE CITY PRODUCTS INC
1206 7th St (47421-2328)
P.O. Box 369 (47421-0369)
PHONE................................812 275-3373
Fax: 812 275-0649
Stewart D Rariden, *President*
Robert Burgess, *Vice Pres*
Denise Maple, *Treasurer*
Andrew Rariden, *Admin Sec*
EMP: 87

SQ FT: 80,000
SALES (est): 25.8MM **Privately Held**
WEB: www.stonecityproducts.com
SIC: 3469 Stamping metal for the trade

(G-583)
TEK PRINT LLC
812 14th St (47421-3326)
PHONE................................812 336-2525
Fax: 812 279-6183
Elena Hartzell, *Principal*
EMP: 2
SALES (est): 149.9K **Privately Held**
SIC: 2752 Commercial printing, offset

(G-584)
THORNES HOMES INC
3211 State Road 37 S (47421-9105)
PHONE................................812 275-4656
Fax: 812 277-1373
John David Thorne, *President*
Kathy Thorne, *Corp Secy*
EMP: 7
SQ FT: 2,700
SALES (est): 1.1MM **Privately Held**
WEB: www.thorneshomes.com
SIC: 5271 7699 2451 6531 Mobile homes; mobile home repair; mobile homes; broker of manufactured homes, on site

(G-585)
TS2 TCTICAL SPEC-SOLUTIONS INC
11 Hillcrest Cir (47421-5611)
PHONE................................765 437-3650
Bobbi J Benish, *President*
EMP: 5
SALES (est): 428K **Privately Held**
SIC: 2393 Textile bags

(G-586)
TURNER CONTRACTING INC
1044 Old Us Highway 50 E (47421-7360)
PHONE................................812 834-5954
Steve Turner, *President*
EMP: 85
SQ FT: 2,976
SALES: 46.9MM **Privately Held**
SIC: 1081 Metal mining services

(G-587)
UNION OPTICAL EYECARE CTR INC
3250 16th St (47421-3516)
PHONE................................812 279-3466
Nathan McClain, *President*
Brittany McClain, *Principal*
EMP: 5
SALES: 620K **Privately Held**
SIC: 8042 3827 Offices & clinics of optometrists; glasses, field or opera

(G-588)
UPSIDE PRINTS CORPORATION
1011 15th St (47421-3731)
PHONE................................812 205-7374
EMP: 2
SALES (est): 83.9K **Privately Held**
SIC: 2752 Commercial printing, lithographic

(G-589)
W F MEYERS COMPANY INC
1008 13th St (47421-3202)
PHONE................................812 275-4485
Fax: 812 275-4488
Mary Albright Barnes, *Ch of Bd*
Kenneth G Barnes, *President*
John L Keltner Jr, *Treasurer*
Alexander Barnes, *Info Tech Mgr*
Patricia J Hedrick, *Admin Sec*
▲ **EMP:** 50 **EST:** 1888
SQ FT: 10,800
SALES (est): 10.4MM **Privately Held**
SIC: 3545 Diamond cutting tools for turning, boring, burnishing, etc.; drill bushings (drilling jig)

(G-590)
WHITNEY TOOL COMPANY INC
906 R St (47421-2497)
P.O. Box 545 (47421-0545)
PHONE................................812 275-4491
Fax: 812 275-6458

▲ = Import ▼=Export
◆ =Import/Export

Linda Flynn, *President*
Bob O'Callaghan, *General Mgr*
Scott Baker, *Superintendent*
Geri Espy, *Vice Pres*
Euretta Griggs, *Treasurer*
EMP: 30
SQ FT: 17,200
SALES (est): 5.7MM **Privately Held**
WEB: www.whitney-tool.com
SIC: 3545 Cutting tools for machine tools

Beech Grove
Marion County

(G-591)
ADM MILLING CO
854 Bethel Ave (46107-1142)
P.O. Box 610 (46107-0610)
PHONE....................................317 783-3321
Fax: 317 781-0485
Kyle Whistler, *Manager*
EMP: 50
SALES (corp-wide): 60.8B **Publicly Held**
WEB: www.admmilling.com
SIC: 2041 Flour mills, cereal (except rice);
grain mills (except rice)
HQ: Adm Milling Co.
8000 W 110th St Ste 300
Overland Park KS 66210
913 491-9400

(G-592)
ARCHER-DANIELS-MIDLAND COMPANY
Also Called: ADM
854 Bethel Ave (46107-1142)
P.O. Box 610 (46107-0610)
PHONE....................................317 783-3321
Kandi Kaiser, *Branch Mgr*
Garry Strode, *Maintence Staff*
EMP: 5
SALES (corp-wide): 60.8B **Publicly Held**
SIC: 2041 Flour & other grain mill products
PA: Archer-Daniels-Midland Company
77 W Wacker Dr Ste 4600
Chicago IL 60601
312 634-8100

(G-593)
BUSINESS ART & DESIGN INC
402 Main St (46107-1838)
PHONE....................................317 782-9108
Fax: 317 782-9909
Bart Heldman, *President*
EMP: 4
SQ FT: 1,700
SALES (est): 523.4K **Privately Held**
WEB: www.businessart.com
SIC: 7336 3993 2752 Graphic arts & related design; signs & advertising specialties; transfers, decalcomania or dry:
lithographed

(G-594)
FISCHER WOODCRAFT INC
1024 Timber Grove Pl (46107-3002)
PHONE....................................317 627-6035
Glenn D Fischer, *CEO*
EMP: 4
SALES (est): 420K **Privately Held**
WEB: www.fischerwoodcraft.com
SIC: 2431 Woodwork, interior & ornamental

(G-595)
H & H SHEET METAL INC
875 Bethel Ave (46107-1141)
PHONE....................................317 787-0883
Fax: 317 787-5381
Timothy P Harris, *President*
David Harris, *Vice Pres*
EMP: 11 **EST:** 1947
SQ FT: 9,344
SALES: 1.3MM **Privately Held**
WEB: hhheating.info
SIC: 3444 Ducts, sheet metal

(G-596)
HOOSIER TIMES INC
Also Called: Southside Times
301 Main St (46107-1835)
PHONE....................................812 332-4401
Roger Huntzinger, *Manager*

EMP: 10
SALES (corp-wide): 882.7MM **Publicly Held**
WEB: www.htinteractive.com
SIC: 2711 Newspapers
HQ: Hoosier Times, Inc.
1900 S Walnut St
Bloomington IN 47401
812 331-4270

(G-597)
INDY CONTROL CORP
308 Main St (46107-1836)
PHONE....................................317 787-4639
Anthony White, *President*
EMP: 7
SALES (est): 1.4MM **Privately Held**
WEB: www.indycontrol.com
SIC: 3699 Electrical equipment & supplies

(G-598)
J P CORPORATION
227 Main St (46107-1883)
PHONE....................................317 783-1000
Fax: 317 783-1015
James F Petty, *Ch of Bd*
Wanda J Petty, *President*
Charles K Petty, *Vice Pres*
Mark Petty, *Vice Pres*
Tina Matthis, *Admin Sec*
EMP: 9 **EST:** 1964
SQ FT: 3,200
SALES (est): 1.4MM **Privately Held**
WEB: www.jp-corp.net
SIC: 3599 3544 7389 Machine shop, jobbing & repair; special dies & tools; engraving service

(G-599)
JCI JONES CHEMICALS INC
600 Bethel Ave (46107-1356)
PHONE....................................317 787-8382
Fax: 317 787-8384
Tim Beusey, *Manager*
EMP: 15
SALES (corp-wide): 179MM **Privately Held**
WEB: www.jcichem.com
SIC: 2812 2819 Chlorine, compressed or liquefied; industrial inorganic chemicals
PA: Jci Jones Chemicals, Inc.
1765 Ringling Blvd
Sarasota FL 34236
941 330-1537

(G-600)
KRUKEMEIER MACHINE AND TOOL CO
4949 Subway St (46107-1358)
PHONE....................................317 784-7042
Fax: 317 784-7089
Jeff J Krukemieier, *Vice Pres*
EMP: 11 **EST:** 1946
SQ FT: 13,500
SALES (est): 1.7MM **Privately Held**
WEB: www.krukemeier.com
SIC: 3544 3545 3469 Special dies & tools; gauge blocks; metal stampings

(G-601)
L & L ENGINEERING CO INC
4925 Subway St (46107-1358)
PHONE....................................317 786-6886
Fax: 317 786-6895
Jerry Kuner, *President*
EMP: 8
SQ FT: 6,000
SALES (est): 1MM **Privately Held**
SIC: 3599 3544 Machine shop, jobbing & repair; welding repair; special dies, tools, jigs & fixtures

(G-602)
L & R MACHINE COMPANY INC
3136 S Emerson Ave (46107-3337)
P.O. Box 160 (46107-0160)
PHONE....................................317 787-7251
Fax: 317 787-7252
Robert D Litson, *President*
Barbara Litson-Fugate, *Vice Pres*
EMP: 5
SQ FT: 7,000
SALES (est): 543.5K **Privately Held**
SIC: 3599 7692 Machine shop, jobbing & repair; welding repair

(G-603)
RED CASE LLC
1005 Churchman Ave (46107-1709)
PHONE....................................317 250-5538
Dixie Wilson, *Administration*
EMP: 2
SALES (est): 189.7K **Privately Held**
SIC: 3523 Farm machinery & equipment

(G-604)
VAULT
700 Main St (46107-1514)
PHONE....................................317 784-4000
Kim Browning, *Owner*
EMP: 3
SALES (est): 268.9K **Privately Held**
SIC: 3272 Burial vaults, concrete or precast terrazzo

Bennington
Switzerland County

(G-605)
BYLER SAWMILL
9435 State Road 250 (47011-1515)
PHONE....................................812 577-5761
Daniel Byler, *Owner*
EMP: 8
SALES (est): 404.8K **Privately Held**
SIC: 2421 7389 Sawmills & planing mills, general;

Berne
Adams County

(G-606)
AMERICAN GRAPHICS GROUP
269 S Jefferson St (46711-2159)
P.O. Box 213 (46711-0213)
PHONE....................................260 589-3117
Fax: 260 589-4076
Roger Muselman, *Principal*
EMP: 2 **EST:** 1994
SQ FT: 3,000
SALES (est): 223.5K **Privately Held**
SIC: 2721 Magazines: publishing only, not printed on site

(G-607)
AMISH COUNTRY POPCORN INC
5433 S 150 E (46711-9157)
PHONE....................................260 589-8513
Brian Lehman, *CEO*
EMP: 20
SALES (est): 2.3MM **Privately Held**
WEB: www.amishcorn.com
SIC: 2099 5145 Popcorn, packaged: except already popped; popcorn & supplies

(G-608)
BERNE LOCKER STORAGE
524 W Franklin St (46711-2032)
PHONE....................................260 589-2806
Donald Neuenschwand, *Owner*
EMP: 5
SQ FT: 7,500
SALES (est): 244.9K **Privately Held**
SIC: 2011 Meat packing plants

(G-609)
BERNE TRI WEEKLY NEWS INC
153 S Jefferson St (46711-2100)
PHONE....................................260 589-2101
Fax: 260 589-8614
Roger Musselman, *President*
Tom Musselman, *Vice Pres*
EMP: 6
SALES (est): 401K **Privately Held**
WEB: www.bernetriweekly.com
SIC: 2711 Newspapers: publishing only, not printed on site

(G-610)
COPPER SMITH ELECTRIC
992 W 700 S (46711-9403)
PHONE....................................260 849-4299
Travis Smith, *Owner*
EMP: 2

SALES (est): 106.9K **Privately Held**
SIC: 3699 Electrical equipment & supplies

(G-611)
CTS CORPORATION
CTS Resistor/Electrocomponents
406 E Parr Rd (46711-1253)
PHONE....................................574 293-7511
Dave Poole, *Branch Mgr*
EMP: 3
SALES (corp-wide): 422.9MM **Publicly Held**
WEB: www.ctscorp.com
SIC: 3613 Switchgear & switchboard apparatus
PA: Cts Corporation
4925 Indiana Ave
Lisle IL 60532
630 577-8800

(G-612)
DL SCHWARTZ CO LLC
2188 S Us Highway 27 (46711-9778)
PHONE....................................260 692-1464
Roy Schwartz, *Admin Dir*
Marvin Schwartz,
EMP: 8
SQ FT: 9,000
SALES (est): 2.2MM **Privately Held**
SIC: 5072 3441 Hardware; fabricated structural metal

(G-613)
EP GRAPHICS INC (HQ)
Also Called: Mignone Communications
169 S Jefferson St (46711-2157)
PHONE....................................877 589-2145
Tyler N Kitt, *President*
Thomas C Muselman, *Vice Pres*
Roger C Muselman, *Treasurer*
Jan Simmons, *Sales Mgr*
Lisa Brown, *Accounts Mgr*
▲ **EMP:** 155 **EST:** 1926
SQ FT: 200,000
SALES (est): 60.6MM **Privately Held**
WEB: www.epgraphics.com
SIC: 2752 Commercial printing, offset; periodicals, lithographed

(G-614)
FCC (ADAMS) LLC
Also Called: FCC North America
936 E Parr Rd (46711-1267)
PHONE....................................260 589-8555
Hitoshi Yamabe,
▲ **EMP:** 400
SALES: 1.4MM
SALES (corp-wide): 1.6B **Privately Held**
SIC: 3714 Clutches, motor vehicle
PA: F.C.C. Co., Ltd.
7000-36, Nakagawa, Hosoecho, Kita-Ku
Hamamatsu SZO 431-1
535 232-400

(G-615)
GYPSY MOON RAGDOLLS INC
423 Wabash St (46711-2021)
PHONE....................................260 589-2852
Tamela Christian, *President*
EMP: 2
SALES (est): 133.1K **Privately Held**
SIC: 2621 Stationery, envelope & tablet papers

(G-616)
HAINES ENGINEERING
6262 S 550 E (46711-9227)
PHONE....................................260 589-3388
Norman Haines, *Owner*
EMP: 7
SALES (est): 819.6K **Privately Held**
SIC: 3523 3534 Elevators, farm; feed grinders, crushers & mixers; elevators & moving stairways

(G-617)
HITZER INC
269 E Main St (46711-1209)
PHONE....................................260 589-8536
Fax: 260 589-3538
Dean Lehman, *President*
Claren Lehman, *Treasurer*
Jason Lehman, *Gen Mgr*
Cynthia Lehman, *Office Mgr*
Cindy Lehman, *Admin Sec*

GEOGRAPHIC

EMP: 22
SQ FT: 10,200
SALES (est): 3.7MM **Privately Held**
WEB: www.hitzer.com
SIC: 3433 2542 Stoves, wood & coal
burning; racks, merchandise display or
storage: except wood

(G-618)
JL MANFCTURING FABRICATION INC
Also Called: J L Mfg & Fab
3633 E 800 S (46711-9201)
PHONE..................................260 589-3723
Shirley Lehman, *President*
EMP: 2
SALES (est): 257K **Privately Held**
SIC: 3549 3523 Wiredrawing & fabricating
machinery & equipment, ex. die; farm ma-
chinery & equipment

(G-619)
KEY FASTENERS CORP
525 Key Way Dr (46711-1259)
PHONE..................................260 589-2626
Fax: 260 589-8776
Yoshio Jigami, *President*
John Johnston, *Exec VP*
Elaine Twigg, *Vice Pres*
David Bates, *Prdtn Mgr*
Lorie Hancock, *Purch Agent*
▲ EMP: 80
SQ FT: 92,000
SALES (est): 17.5MM
SALES (corp-wide): 67.1MM **Privately
Held**
WEB: www.keyfasteners.com
SIC: 3452 Bolts, metal
PA: Sato Rashi Co., Inc
1-18-10, Minamirokugo
Ota-Ku TKY 144-0
337 323-101

(G-620)
MICRO-PRECISION OPERATIONS
525 Berne St (46711-1246)
PHONE..................................260 589-2136
Fax: 260 589-8966
William Bertke, *Vice Pres*
EMP: 20
SQ FT: 120,000
SALES (est): 3.2MM **Privately Held**
SIC: 3625 3829 3549 3593 Actuators, in-
dustrial; measuring & controlling devices;
assembly machines, including robotic;
fluid power cylinders & actuators; ma-
chine tool accessories; machine tools,
metal cutting type

(G-621)
MICROMATIC LLC (PA)
525 Berne St (46711-1298)
PHONE..................................260 589-2136
Rick Bush, *CEO*
Richard A Bush, *Plant Mgr*
Dave Reinhart, *Engng Exec*
Gregory Myer,
▼ EMP: 85
SQ FT: 100,000
SALES (est): 20.8MM **Privately Held**
WEB: www.micromaticllc.com
SIC: 3599 3593 Custom machinery; fluid
power cylinders & actuators

(G-622)
SCHWARTZ MANUFACTURING INC
Also Called: Schwartz Elmer D Mfg Co
1261 W 200 S (46711-9779)
P.O. Box 124 (46711-0124)
PHONE..................................260 589-3865
Elmer D Schwartz, *President*
Emma Schwartz, *Admin Sec*
▲ EMP: 4
SALES (est): 100K **Privately Held**
SIC: 0191 3999 5941 General farms, pri-
marily crop; candles; bait & tackle

(G-623)
SMITH BROTHERS BERNE INC (PA)
356 Monroe St (46711-1266)
P.O. Box 270 (46711-0270)
PHONE..................................260 589-2131

Fax: 260 589-2934
S W Lehman, *President*
Frederick A Lehman, *Vice Pres*
Jay Hunter, *Plant Supt*
Kevin Nussbaum, *Opers Staff*
Karen Wellman, *Purch Agent*
▲ EMP: 425 EST: 1926
SQ FT: 380,000
SALES (est): 76.2MM **Privately Held**
WEB: www.smithbrosfurn.com
SIC: 2512 Upholstered household furniture

(G-624)
SMOKES - BERNE
428 Wind Ridge Trl (46711-2375)
PHONE..................................260 849-4038
Gwen Muller, *Manager*
EMP: 2
SALES (est): 112.7K **Privately Held**
SIC: 3911 Cigar & cigarette accessories

(G-625)
SPORT FORM INC
151 W Main St (46711-1548)
PHONE..................................260 589-2200
Fax: 260 589-9948
Haidi Fear, *President*
Ladonna Habegger, *President*
EMP: 3
SQ FT: 2,000
SALES (est): 293K **Privately Held**
SIC: 2396 5136 5137 Fabric printing &
stamping; sportswear, men's & boys'; uni-
forms, men's & boys'; sportswear,
women's & children's; uniforms, women's
& children's

(G-626)
ST HENRY TILE CO INC
Berne Ready Mix
155 E Buckeye St (46711-1125)
P.O. Box 29 (46711-0029)
PHONE..................................260 589-2880
Fax: 260 589-3919
Gene Subler, *Opers-Prdtn-Mfg*
EMP: 27
SQ FT: 15,000
SALES (corp-wide): 30MM **Privately
Held**
SIC: 3271 5211 3273 Blocks, concrete or
cinder: standard; cement; tile, ceramic;
ready-mixed concrete
PA: The St Henry Tile Co Inc
281 W Washington St
Saint Henry OH 45883
419 678-4841

(G-627)
SWISS WOODWORKING & SALES
371 W 500 S (46711-9709)
PHONE..................................260 849-9669
Melvin Schwartz, *Principal*
EMP: 2
SALES (est): 128.3K **Privately Held**
SIC: 2431 Millwork

(G-628)
SWISSLAND MILK COMPANY INC
818 Welty St (46711-1263)
PHONE..................................260 589-2761
Fax: 260 589-2761
Kirk Johnson, *President*
Mary Johnson, *Vice Pres*
EMP: 6
SQ FT: 9,000
SALES (est): 363K **Privately Held**
WEB: www.swisslandcheese.com
SIC: 2026 Milk & cream, except fermented,
cultured & flavored

(G-629)
WEAVER LOGGING
2896 West St (46711)
PHONE..................................260 589-9985
Tex Weaver, *Owner*
EMP: 2
SALES (est): 206.8K **Privately Held**
SIC: 2411 Logging

Beverly Shores
Porter County

(G-630)
GLUE + PAPER WORKSHOP LLC
410 E St Clair Ave (46301-0147)
P.O. Box 3 (46301-0003)
PHONE..................................773 275-8935
Amanda Freymann, *Managing Prtnr*
Joan Sommers, *Partner*
EMP: 7
SALES (est): 400K **Privately Held**
SIC: 2731 Book publishing

Bicknell
Knox County

(G-631)
HERMETIC COIL CO INC
Also Called: Herco
12005 E Davis Ln (47512-9681)
P.O. Box 219 (47512-0219)
PHONE..................................812 735-2400
David Barton, *CEO*
Annabell De La Rosa, *General Mgr*
Debra J Barton, *Corp Secy*
Van Davis, *Sales Mgr*
EMP: 27
SQ FT: 15,000
SALES (est): 3.7MM **Privately Held**
WEB: www.hermeticcoil.com
SIC: 3544 3559 3677 Special dies &
tools; plastics working machinery; elec-
tronic coils, transformers & other induc-
tors

(G-632)
HERMETIC COIL CO INC
Also Called: Illinois Precision
12005 E Davis Ln (47512-9681)
PHONE..................................812 735-2401
Fax: 812 735-4218
Dan Davis, *CEO*
Debra Barton, *President*
David Barton, *Vice Pres*
Daniel Davis, *Manager*
EMP: 33
SQ FT: 720
SALES (est): 1.7MM **Privately Held**
SIC: 3544 Dies, plastics forming

(G-633)
SCEPTER INC
6467 N Scepter Rd (47512-8228)
PHONE..................................812 735-2500
John Vulvac, *Manager*
EMP: 100 **Privately Held**
WEB: www.scepterinc.com
SIC: 3341 3334 Secondary nonferrous
metals; primary aluminum
PA: Scepter, Inc
1485 Scepter Ln
Waverly TN 37185

Birdseye
Dubois County

(G-634)
CAMPBELL LOGGING
9100 W State Road 64 (47513-0017)
PHONE..................................812 972-6280
Jerrud Campbell, *Principal*
EMP: 2
SALES (est): 81.7K **Privately Held**
SIC: 2411 Logging

Bloomfield
Greene County

(G-635)
BLOOMFIELD MFG CO INC
Also Called: Kant Slam Door Check Company
46 W Spring St (47424-1473)
P.O. Box 228 (47424-0228)
PHONE..................................812 384-4441

Fax: 812 384-4592
E Austin Harrah, *CEO*
Steve Dowden, *Vice Pres*
Steve Workman, *Vice Pres*
Jared Albright, *Sales Mgr*
Vanessa Harrah, *Shareholder*
▲ EMP: 40 EST: 1895
SQ FT: 55,000
SALES (est): 9.9MM **Privately Held**
WEB: www.hi-lift.com
SIC: 3423 3429 Jacks: lifting, screw or
ratchet (hand tools); door opening & clos-
ing devices, except electrical

(G-636)
CARMICHAEL WELDING INC
9136 E State Road 54 (47424-5900)
PHONE..................................812 825-5156
Ira E Carmichael, *President*
Sheri L Carmichael, *Admin Sec*
EMP: 5
SQ FT: 1,200
SALES (est): 407K **Privately Held**
SIC: 7692 1799 Welding repair; welding
on site

(G-637)
CAVE COMPANY PRINTING INC
5282 S Black Ankle Rd (47424-5519)
PHONE..................................812 863-4333
Don Cave, *Principal*
EMP: 2
SALES (est): 144.1K **Privately Held**
SIC: 2752 Commercial printing, litho-
graphic

(G-638)
GREENE COUNTY PALLET INC
1338 N Harv-Wright Rd (47424-5967)
P.O. Box 344 (47424-0344)
PHONE..................................812 384-8362
Blake Hutchison, *President*
Hanna Hutchinson, *Vice Pres*
EMP: 18
SALES (est): 2.8MM **Privately Held**
SIC: 2448 7389 Pallets, wood;

(G-639)
IMI BLOOMFIELD
9 E Judson St (47424-1651)
PHONE..................................812 384-0045
Fax: 812 384-0046
Norma Bell, *Principal*
EMP: 4
SALES (est): 253.1K **Privately Held**
SIC: 3273 Ready-mixed concrete

(G-640)
JER-MAUR CORPORATION
Also Called: Main Street Sports
119 E Main St (47424-1419)
PHONE..................................812 384-8290
Maureen Workman, *President*
Jerry Workman Jr, *Vice Pres*
EMP: 3
SQ FT: 1,100
SALES (est): 280K **Privately Held**
SIC: 2396 2395 5941 5999 Screen print-
ing on fabric articles; embroidery prod-
ucts, except schiffli machine; sporting
goods & bicycle shops; trophies &
plaques; advertising specialties; screen
printing

(G-641)
MECTRA LABS INC
600 S Us Hwy 231 Blmfield (47424)
P.O. Box 350 (47424-0350)
PHONE..................................812 384-3521
Fax: 812 384-8518
Thomas Clement, *President*
EMP: 24
SQ FT: 40,000
SALES (est): 3.7MM **Privately Held**
WEB: www.mectralabs.com
SIC: 3841 Surgical & medical instruments

(G-642)
METAL TECHNOLOGIES INC
Sr 54 E Rr 1 (47424)
PHONE..................................812 384-9800
Craig Duncan, *Branch Mgr*
EMP: 25 **Privately Held**
SIC: 3441 Fabricated structural metal

PA: Metal Technologies, Inc.
909 E State Road 54
Bloomfield IN 47424

(G-643)
METAL TECHNOLOGIES INC (PA)
909 E State Road 54 (47424-4706)
PHONE..................812 384-9800
Doug Conrad, *President*
Larry Parsons, *Corp Secy*
▲ **EMP:** 65
SQ FT: 219,000
SALES (est): 30MM **Privately Held**
SIC: 3441 3559 Fabricated structural metal; automotive related machinery

(G-644)
MICHAEL AND SONS INCORPORATED (PA)
2606 E Calvertville Rd (47424-4531)
PHONE..................812 876-4736
Fax: 812 876-8391
Edward Michael, *President*
Larry Michael, *Vice Pres*
Jackie Michael, *Admin Sec*
EMP: 18
SQ FT: 7,050
SALES (est): 2.2MM **Privately Held**
WEB: www.michaelandsons.net
SIC: 3281 Granite, cut & shaped

(G-645)
ROLLISON AIRPLANE COMPANY INC
County Road 300 S (47424)
PHONE..................812 384-4972
Rob Rollison, *President*
EMP: 3 **EST:** 1993
SQ FT: 5,000
SALES: 700K **Privately Held**
WEB: www.rlsair.com
SIC: 3721 Aircraft

(G-646)
UNIQUE SIGNS
1650 N Warren Rd (47424-4769)
PHONE..................812 384-4967
Donna A Fields, *Partner*
John R Fields, *Partner*
EMP: 2
SALES (est): 4K **Privately Held**
SIC: 3993 Signs & advertising specialties

Bloomingdale
Parke County

(G-647)
FUTUREX INDUSTRIES INC (PA)
Also Called: Formflex
80 E Smith St (47832)
P.O. Box 158 (47832-0158)
PHONE..................765 498-3900
Fax: 765 498-5200
Richard J Kremer, *President*
Brent Thompson, *Vice Pres*
David Elliott, *VP Opers*
Waldridge Al, *Accounting Mgr*
Tracy Nickle, *Human Res Dir*
▲ **EMP:** 145
SQ FT: 100,000
SALES (est): 89.5MM **Privately Held**
WEB: www.futurexind.com
SIC: 2865 3081 Styrene; plastic film & sheet; polyethylene film

(G-648)
FUTUREX INDUSTRIES INC
Formflex
1 N Main St (47832)
PHONE..................765 498-8900
Brent Thompson, *Manager*
EMP: 50
SALES (corp-wide): 89.5MM **Privately Held**
WEB: www.futurexind.com
SIC: 3089 3081 2782 Molding primary plastic; unsupported plastics film & sheet; blankbooks & looseleaf binders
PA: Futurex Industries, Inc.
80 E Smith St
Bloomingdale IN 47832
765 498-3900

(G-649)
MYERS WOOD PRODUCTS
1287 E 1200 N (47832-8050)
PHONE..................765 597-2147
Duane E Myers, *Partner*
Harold E Myers, *Partner*
EMP: 5
SQ FT: 10,000
SALES: 450K **Privately Held**
SIC: 2448 Wood pallets & skids

Bloomington
Monroe County

(G-650)
39 DEGREES NORTH LLC
908 N Walnut St (47404-3525)
P.O. Box 1937 (47402-1937)
PHONE..................855 447-3939
Randall Smith, *Accounts Mgr*
Chris Walls, *Marketing Staff*
Anthony Chris Walls,
Prem Radhakrishnan,
EMP: 12
SQ FT: 1,600
SALES: 750K **Privately Held**
WEB: www.39degreesnorth.com
SIC: 7371 2741 Computer software development; atlas, map & guide publishing

(G-651)
3D STONE INC
6700 S Victor Pike (47403-9758)
PHONE..................812 824-5805
Fax: 812 825-2039
David Whaley, *President*
Carol Whaley, *Corp Secy*
EMP: 30 **EST:** 1992
SALES (est): 4.7MM **Privately Held**
WEB: www.3dstone.com
SIC: 1422 Limestones, ground

(G-652)
3D STONE PURCHASER INC
6700 S Victor Pike (47403-9758)
PHONE..................812 824-5805
Kurt Michael Sendek, *President*
Chris Puderbaugh, *CFO*
Lily Serena Sendek, *Treasurer*
EMP: 45 **EST:** 2015
SQ FT: 3,000
SALES (est): 6.2MM **Privately Held**
SIC: 3281 Limestone, cut & shaped

(G-653)
A S P PARROTT SIGNS
1820 S Walnut St (47401-7719)
PHONE..................812 325-9102
EMP: 2
SALES (est): 130.5K **Privately Held**
SIC: 3993 Signs & advertising specialties

(G-654)
ABRACADABRA GRAPHICS
5144 E State Road 45 (47408-9672)
PHONE..................812 336-1971
Fax: 812 336-1471
Sally Watkins, *Partner*
James R Watkins, *Partner*
Tracy Steverson, *Officer*
EMP: 4
SQ FT: 2,500
SALES (est): 200K **Privately Held**
SIC: 2759 5199 2395 Screen printing; advertising specialties; embroidery products, except schiffli machine

(G-655)
ACCENT LIMESTONE & CARVING INC
5900 N Maple Grove Rd (47404-9012)
PHONE..................812 876-7040
Michael Donham, *President*
Julie Donham, *Treasurer*
EMP: 3
SALES (est): 150K **Privately Held**
WEB: www.accentlimestone.com
SIC: 3281 1741 Limestone, cut & shaped; stone masonry

(G-656)
ACHAEMENIAN SHAHPUR
Also Called: Honey Pastry
314 W 2nd St (47403-2412)
P.O. Box 6565 (47407-6565)
PHONE..................812 331-1317
Shahpur Achaemenian, *Owner*
EMP: 2
SQ FT: 820
SALES (est): 86.5K **Privately Held**
SIC: 2051 Cakes, bakery: except frozen

(G-657)
ADVANCED DESIGNS CORP (PA)
1169 W 2nd St (47403-2160)
P.O. Box 1907 (47402-1907)
PHONE..................812 333-1922
Fax: 812 333-2030
Martin Riess, *CEO*
Matthew McGrath, *President*
Teri A Riess, *Vice Pres*
EMP: 16 **EST:** 1981
SQ FT: 2,700
SALES (est): 2.8MM **Privately Held**
WEB: www.doprad.com
SIC: 3829 7371 Weather tracking equipment; computer software development

(G-658)
ADVANTEX INC
5981 E State Road 45 (47408-9680)
PHONE..................812 339-6479
Joe Galoupo, *President*
EMP: 3
SALES (est): 210K **Privately Held**
SIC: 2759 Screen printing

(G-659)
AERCHEM LLC
3935 W Roll Ave (47403-3181)
P.O. Box 177, Clear Creek (47426-0177)
PHONE..................812 334-9996
Fax: 812 334-1960
Richard Sikorski,
Judy Sikorski,
▲ **EMP:** 5
SQ FT: 1,000
SALES (est): 350K **Privately Held**
WEB: www.aerchem.com
SIC: 2869 Perfumes, flavorings & food additives

(G-660)
AMERICAN SCHOOL HEALTH ASSN
Also Called: Asha
501 N Morton St Ste 110 (47404-3732)
PHONE..................703 506-7675
Linda Barrett, *President*
Mark Betz, *Director*
EMP: 8 **EST:** 1926
SQ FT: 11,500
SALES: 447.1K **Privately Held**
WEB: www.ashaweb.org
SIC: 2721 8621 Trade journals: publishing only, not printed on site; health association

(G-661)
AMERIFORCE MEDIA LLC
400 W 7th St Ste 233 (47404-3906)
PHONE..................812 961-9478
Peter Rumley, *Accountant*
Tom Aiello,
Dg Elmore,
Todd Taranto,
Ted Wadsworth,
EMP: 4 **EST:** 2015
SALES (est): 173.6K **Privately Held**
SIC: 2721 Magazines: publishing only, not printed on site

(G-662)
APPAREL DESIGN GROUP
671 S Landmark Ave Ste A (47403-2086)
P.O. Box 3321 (47402-3321)
PHONE..................812 339-3355
Dick Huffman, *Owner*
EMP: 5
SALES (est): 320K **Privately Held**
SIC: 2759 2752 Screen printing; commercial printing, lithographic

(G-663)
APPLE CYBER LLC
3307 S Acadia Ct (47401-8118)
PHONE..................812 822-1341
EMP: 2 **EST:** 2012
SALES (est): 83K **Privately Held**
SIC: 3571 Mfg Electronic Computers

(G-664)
ARCTIC ICE EXPRESS INC
2423 W Industrial Park Dr (47404-2601)
PHONE..................812 333-0423
Fax: 812 333-1591
Garnet Don Kinser, *President*
Pamela A Kinser, *Treasurer*
EMP: 20
SQ FT: 10,000
SALES (est): 700K **Privately Held**
SIC: 2097 Manufactured ice

(G-665)
ARGENTUM JEWELRY INC
205 N College Ave Ste 100 (47404-3954)
P.O. Box 1221 (47402-1221)
PHONE..................812 336-3100
Fax: 812 336-3103
Eugene Foltzer, *President*
Sally Walker, *President*
EMP: 5
SALES (est): 540K **Privately Held**
WEB: www.argentum-jewelry.com
SIC: 5944 3911 Jewelry, precious stones & precious metals; jewelry, precious metal

(G-666)
ARSON PRESS
2415 E 4th St (47408-4120)
P.O. Box 26 (47402-0026)
PHONE..................812 345-3527
Jarod Isenbarger, *Principal*
EMP: 2 **EST:** 2009
SALES (est): 86K **Privately Held**
SIC: 2741 Miscellaneous publishing

(G-667)
AUTHOR SOLUTIONS LLC (PA)
Also Called: A S I
1663 S Liberty Dr (47403-5161)
PHONE..................812 339-6000
Mitch Black, *CEO*
Alan Bower, *Publisher*
Joel Pierson, *Editor*
Riley Kacey, *District Mgr*
Keith Ogorek, *Senior VP*
▼ **EMP:** 260
SALES (est): 52.4MM **Privately Held**
WEB: www.authorhouse.com
SIC: 2731 Books: publishing only

(G-668)
AVO CANDLE COMPANY LLC
2406 S Bryan St (47403-3648)
PHONE..................812 822-2302
Julia Smith, *Administration*
EMP: 2
SALES (est): 62K **Privately Held**
SIC: 3999 Candles

(G-669)
B & H ELECTRIC AND SUPPLY INC
4719 W Vernal Pike (47404-9334)
PHONE..................812 333-7303
David Hunt, *Accounts Mgr*
Don Roberts, *Sales Staff*
Greg Hunt, *Branch Mgr*
EMP: 2 **Privately Held**
SIC: 3699 Electrical equipment & supplies
PA: B & H Electric And Supply, Inc.
740 C Ave E
Seymour IN 47274

(G-670)
B & L SHEET METAL & ROOFING
Also Called: B L
1301 N Monroe St (47404-3377)
PHONE..................812 332-4309
Fax: 812 332-8124
David J Lee, *President*
Jay C Lee, *CFO*
Lee I B, *Admin Sec*
EMP: 15
SQ FT: 16,000

GEOGRAPHIC

SALES (est): 3.9MM **Privately Held**
WEB: www.blsmroofing.com
SIC: **1761** 3446 Roofing contractor; sheet metalwork; architectural metalwork

(G-671)
B G HOADLEY QUARRIES INC (PA)
3211 W Arlington Rd (47404-1563)
P.O. Box 1224 (47402-1224)
PHONE............................812 332-1447
Fax: 812 332-6085
Patsy H Fell, *President*
Bert H Fell Jr, *Vice Pres*
David R Fell, *Vice Pres*
James Johnson, *Treasurer*
EMP: 40 EST: 1927
SALES (est): 8.7MM **Privately Held**
SIC: **1411** Limestone, dimension-quarrying

(G-672)
B G HOADLEY QUARRIES INC
2200 W Tapp Rd (47403-3237)
PHONE............................812 332-1447
Bert Fell, *Vice Pres*
EMP: 20
SALES (corp-wide): 8.7MM **Privately Held**
SIC: **1411** Limestone, dimension-quarrying
PA: B G Hoadley Quarries Inc
3211 W Arlington Rd
Bloomington IN 47404
812 332-1447

(G-673)
BARRY COMPANY INC
2037 S Yost Ave (47403-3189)
PHONE............................812 333-1850
Tim Wagner, *Branch Mgr*
Tim J Wagner, *Manager*
EMP: 6
SALES (corp-wide): 21.3MM **Privately Held**
SIC: **3432** 5074 5251 5999 Plumbing fixture fittings & trim; plumbing & hydronic heating supplies; hardware; plumbing & heating supplies
PA: Barry Company Inc
1145 E Maryland St
Indianapolis IN 46202
317 637-5327

(G-674)
BAUGH ENTERPRISES INC
125 S Westplex Ave (47404-5080)
PHONE............................812 334-8189
Fax: 812 332-2479
Loyce B Keough, *President*
Larry Biggerstaff, *Corp Secy*
EMP: 11
SQ FT: 12,000
SALES: 2MM **Privately Held**
WEB: www.baughent.com
SIC: **2752** 7331 5199 7371 Commercial printing, offset; mailing service; advertising specialties; computer software systems analysis & design, custom; signs & advertising specialties

(G-675)
BAXTER HEALTHCARE CORPORATION
927 S Curry Pike (47403-2624)
PHONE............................812 355-7167
Amy Lutes, *Principal*
Trent Cox, *Mfg Dir*
Phillip Mauro, *Opers Mgr*
Kristy Fraizer II, *Mfg Mgr*
Angela Terrell, *Purch Agent*
EMP: 329
SALES (corp-wide): 10.5B **Publicly Held**
SIC: **3841** Surgical & medical instruments
HQ: Baxter Healthcare Corporation
1 Baxter Pkwy
Deerfield IL 60015
224 948-2000

(G-676)
BAXTER HEALTHCARE CORPORATION
2000 N Curry Pike (47404-1434)
PHONE............................812 333-0887
Bob Stoner, *Manager*
EMP: 72

SALES (corp-wide): 10.5B **Publicly Held**
SIC: **3841** Surgical & medical instruments
HQ: Baxter Healthcare Corporation
1 Baxter Pkwy
Deerfield IL 60015
224 948-2000

(G-677)
BAXTER PHRM SOLUTIONS
Also Called: Baxter Biosciences
1801 N Curry Pike (47404)
PHONE............................812 355-5289
David Smith, *Principal*
EMP: 6
SALES (est): 736.7K **Privately Held**
SIC: **2834** Pharmaceutical preparations

(G-678)
BAXTER PHRM SOLUTIONS LLC
927 S Curry Pike (47403-2624)
PHONE............................812 333-0887
Camil Chamoun, *Vice Pres*
Burkhard Wichert, *Vice Pres*
Marc Kelwaski, *Marketing Mgr*
Terry Heilman, *Manager*
Matt Hancock, *Senior Mgr*
▲ EMP: 70
SALES (est): 22.4MM
SALES (corp-wide): 10.5B **Publicly Held**
SIC: **2834** Pharmaceutical preparations
HQ: Baxter Healthcare Corporation
1 Baxter Pkwy
Deerfield IL 60015
224 948-2000

(G-679)
BERRY GLOBAL INC
4100 W Profile Pkwy (47404-2546)
PHONE............................812 334-7090
Pete Lenzen, *Manager*
EMP: 7 **Publicly Held**
SIC: **3089** 3081 Bottle caps, molded plastic; unsupported plastics film & sheet
HQ: Berry Global, Inc.
101 Oakley St
Evansville IN 47710
812 424-2904

(G-680)
BERRY GLOBAL INC
4100 W Profile Pkwy (47404-2546)
PHONE............................812 424-2904
Fax: 812 355-1732
EMP: 222 **Publicly Held**
SIC: **3089** Plastic containers, except foam
HQ: Berry Global, Inc.
101 Oakley St
Evansville IN 47710
812 424-2904

(G-681)
BEST BEERS LLC
1100 S Strong Dr (47403-8742)
PHONE............................812 332-1234
Jamie Per, *Principal*
John Miller, *Principal*
EMP: 9
SALES (est): 777.9K **Privately Held**
SIC: **2082** Beer (alcoholic beverage)

(G-682)
BIBLICAL ENTERPRISES LLC
3428 S Burks Ct (47401-8462)
PHONE............................812 391-0071
EMP: 2
SALES (est): 167.9K **Privately Held**
SIC: **2732** Books: printing & binding

(G-683)
BIG RED LIQUORS INC
Also Called: Karton King
435 S Walnut St (47401-4613)
PHONE............................812 339-9552
Mark Mc Allister, *Owner*
EMP: 4
SALES (corp-wide): 32.5MM **Privately Held**
WEB: www.bigredliquors.com
SIC: **5993** 2111 5963 5921 Tobacco stores & stands; cigarettes; direct selling establishments; liquor stores
PA: Big Red Liquors Inc
5445 S East St
Indianapolis IN 46227
812 339-7345

(G-684)
BLACKWOOD SOLUTIONS INC
205 N College Ave Ste 410 (47404-3952)
P.O. Box 486 (47402-0486)
PHONE............................812 824-6728
Jason M Feagans, *President*
Nathan Broadfoot, *Principal*
Jamie Feagans, *Principal*
EMP: 3 EST: 2015
SALES (est): 627.1K **Privately Held**
SIC: **4214** 2411 5989 4953 Local trucking with storage; fuel wood harvesting; wood (fuel); recycling, waste materials; lumber (log) trucking, local

(G-685)
BLOOM MAGAZINE
414 W 6th St (47404-3914)
P.O. Box 1204 (47402-1204)
PHONE............................812 323-8959
Jaime Sweany, *Publisher*
Malcolm Abrams, *Principal*
Carmen Siering, *Editor*
Rodney Margison, *Assoc Editor*
EMP: 5
SALES (est): 605.7K **Privately Held**
SIC: **2721** Magazines: publishing & printing

(G-686)
BLOOMINGTON CONCRETE SURFACES
615 W Allen St (47403-4703)
PHONE............................812 345-0011
Eric Brown, *Principal*
EMP: 2
SALES (est): 165.4K **Privately Held**
SIC: **2851** Paints & allied products

(G-687)
BLOOMINGTON DESIGN INC
6767 E State Road 46 (47401-9234)
PHONE............................812 332-2033
Gary Anderson, *President*
Linda Anderson, *Vice Pres*
Gary A Anderson, *Manager*
EMP: 3
SALES (est): 198.1K **Privately Held**
SIC: **3993** Signs & advertising specialties

(G-688)
BLOOMINGTON DISCOUNT PRTG INC
1017 S Lincoln St (47401-5845)
PHONE............................812 332-9789
Michael Smith, *President*
Scott Thompson, *Vice Pres*
EMP: 2
SALES (est): 180.7K **Privately Held**
SIC: **2759** 2752 Commercial printing; commercial printing, lithographic

(G-689)
BLUE BURRO INC
8325 W Hinds Rd (47403-8603)
PHONE............................904 825-9900
Erin Martoglio, *Principal*
EMP: 2
SALES (est): 160K **Privately Held**
SIC: **8742** 7371 7372 Management consulting services; custom computer programming services; business oriented computer software; educational computer software

(G-690)
BROWN RIDGE STUDIO
625 N Lwer Brdie Glyan Rd (47408)
PHONE............................812 335-0643
David Beery, *Owner*
EMP: 2
SALES (est): 127.6K **Privately Held**
SIC: **2426** Turnings, furniture: wood

(G-691)
BTR ENGINEERING
2255 W Bolin Ln (47403-9004)
PHONE............................812 360-9415
Brad Freeman, *Principal*
EMP: 4
SALES: 25K **Privately Held**
SIC: **3647** Vehicular lighting equipment

(G-692)
BUTLER VINEYARDS (PA)
Also Called: Butler Winery
6202 E Robinson Rd (47408-9380)
PHONE............................812 332-6660
James Butler, *President*
EMP: 3
SALES (est): 308.5K **Privately Held**
WEB: www.butlerwinery.com
SIC: **2084** Wines

(G-693)
BYERS SCIENTIFIC MFG
2332 W Industrial Park Dr (47404-2689)
PHONE............................812 269-6218
EMP: 3
SALES (est): 193.4K **Privately Held**
SIC: **3999** Manufacturing industries

(G-694)
C & H STONE CO INC
4000 S Rockport Rd (47403-9764)
P.O. Box 147, Clear Creek (47426-0147)
PHONE............................812 336-2560
Fax: 812 331-7292
Lowell Helton, *President*
Jack Chaney, *Vice Pres*
Larry Drake, *Controller*
EMP: 40
SQ FT: 1,000
SALES (est): 3.9MM **Privately Held**
SIC: **3281** Limestone, cut & shaped

(G-695)
CARDINAL SPIRITS LLC
922 S Morton St (47403-2566)
PHONE............................812 202-6789
Adam Christopher Quirk, *Mng Member*
Quirk Adam, *Exec Dir*
Jeff Wuslich,
▲ EMP: 30
SQ FT: 4,500
SALES: 850K **Privately Held**
SIC: **2085** Distilled & blended liquors

(G-696)
CARLISLE INDUSTRIAL BRAKE & FR
1031 E Hillside Dr (47401-6597)
PHONE............................812 336-3811
D Christian Koch, *President*
Kevin Zdimal, *Treasurer*
Steven J Ford, *Admin Sec*
◆ EMP: 283
SALES (est): 58.1MM
SALES (corp-wide): 4B **Publicly Held**
WEB: www.carlislemotion.com
SIC: **3714** Motor vehicle brake systems & parts
PA: Carlisle Companies Incorporated
16430 N Scottsdale Rd # 400
Scottsdale AZ 85254
704 501-1100

(G-697)
CATALENT INDIANA LLC
Also Called: Cook Pharmica LLC
1300 S Patterson Dr (47403-4828)
P.O. Box 970 (47402-0970)
PHONE............................812 355-6746
John Chiminski, *President*
Cory Lewis, *President*
Steven Perry, *President*
Cindy Webster, *Editor*
Ryan Hawkins, *COO*
EMP: 500
SALES (est): 98.4MM **Publicly Held**
WEB: www.cookpharmica.com
SIC: **8731** 2834 Biotechnical research, commercial; pharmaceutical preparations
HQ: Indiana Catalent Holdings Llc
14 Schoolhouse Rd
Somerset NJ 08873
732 537-6200

(G-698)
CENTRAL BRACE & LIMB CO INC
641 S Walker St Ste D (47403-2177)
PHONE............................812 334-2524
Fax: 812 334-0478
Carol Richardson, *Manager*
EMP: 2

SALES (est): 146.3K
SALES (corp-wide): 4MM **Privately Held**
SIC: 3842 Prosthetic appliances
PA: Central Brace & Limb Co Inc
1901 N Capitol Ave
Indianapolis IN 46202
317 925-4296

(G-699)
CENTRAL COCA-COLA BTLG CO INC
1701 S Liberty Dr (47403-5119)
PHONE..................................800 241-2653
EMP: 2
SALES (corp-wide): 35.4B **Publicly Held**
SIC: 5149 2086 8741 Soft drinks; soft drinks: packaged in cans, bottles, etc.; management services
HQ: Central Coca-Cola Bottling Company, Inc.
555 Taxter Rd Ste 550
Elmsford NY 10523
914 789-1100

(G-700)
CIRCLE - PROSCO INC
Also Called: C.P.i
401 N Gates Dr (47404-4824)
PHONE..................................812 339-3653
Douglas K Parker, *President*
Karen Rudicil, *Business Mgr*
Jeff Blain, *Opers Dir*
John Savage, *Maint Spvr*
Bill Morton, *Technical Mgr*
◆ EMP: 70
SQ FT: 38,000
SALES (est): 19.6MM **Privately Held**
WEB: www.circleprosco.com
SIC: 2841 Detergents, synthetic organic or inorganic alkaline

(G-701)
COLLECTIVE PRESS INC
401 W 6th St Ste J (47404-4016)
P.O. Box 3494 (47402-3494)
PHONE..................................812 325-1385
EMP: 2
SALES (est): 124.4K **Privately Held**
SIC: 2741 Miscellaneous publishing

(G-702)
COOK AIRCRAFT LEASING INC
750 N Daniels Way (47404-9120)
PHONE..................................812 339-2044
Carol Seaman, *President*
EMP: 2
SALES (est): 131.8K **Privately Held**
SIC: 3728 Aircraft parts & equipment

(G-703)
COOK BIODEVICE LLC
500 W Simpson Chapel Rd (47404-9426)
PHONE..................................800 265-0945
Rob Lyles, *President*
Michael Cole, *Finance Dir*
EMP: 13
SALES (est): 516.3K **Privately Held**
SIC: 3841 Surgical & medical instruments

(G-704)
COOK GROUP INCORPORATED (PA)
750 N Daniels Way (47404-9120)
P.O. Box 489 (47402-0489)
PHONE..................................812 339-2235
Fax: 812 339-5369
Stephen L Ferguson, *CEO*
William A Cook, *Ch of Bd*
Kem Hawkins, *President*
Christina Anne, *Vice Pres*
Tom Connaughton, *Vice Pres*
EMP: 10
SQ FT: 1,500
SALES (est): 980.1MM **Privately Held**
SIC: 3841 3821 3845 6411 Surgical instruments & apparatus; catheters; holders, surgical needle; hypodermic needles & syringes; pipettes, hemocytometer; pacemaker, cardiac; insurance agents; commercial & industrial building operation; stock brokers & dealers

(G-705)
COOK INCORPORATED (HQ)
Also Called: Cook Endoscopy
750 N Daniels Way (47404-9120)
P.O. Box 489 (47402-0489)
PHONE..................................812 339-2235
Fax: 812 339-7316
M Kem Hawkins, *President*
Phyllis McCullough, *President*
Stefanie Sonier, *General Mgr*
Steve Ferguson, *Chairman*
Leslie Vitelli, *Regional Mgr*
▲ EMP: 1750
SQ FT: 40,000
SALES (est): 593MM
SALES (corp-wide): 980.1MM **Privately Held**
WEB: www.cookgroup.com
SIC: 3841 Catheters
PA: Cook Group Incorporated
750 N Daniels Way
Bloomington IN 47404
812 339-2235

(G-706)
COOK INCORPORATED
750 N Daniels Way (47404-9120)
P.O. Box 489 (47402-0489)
PHONE..................................812 876-7790
Fax: 812 876-7798
Dan Peterson, *Principal*
EMP: 200
SALES (corp-wide): 980.1MM **Privately Held**
WEB: www.cookgroup.com
SIC: 3841 5047 Catheters; medical equipment & supplies
HQ: Cook Incorporated
750 N Daniels Way
Bloomington IN 47404
812 339-2235

(G-707)
COOK MEDICAL LLC
400 N Daniels Way (47404-9155)
PHONE..................................812 339-2235
Phyllis McCullough, *President*
EMP: 5
SALES (corp-wide): 980.1MM **Privately Held**
SIC: 3841 3842 Surgical & medical instruments; surgical appliances & supplies
HQ: Cook Medical Llc
750 N Daniels Way
Bloomington IN 47404
812 339-2235

(G-708)
CRUSHER PARTS DIRECT LLC
3905 W Farmer Ave (47403-5152)
P.O. Box 133, Smithville (47458-0133)
PHONE..................................812 822-1463
Edd Perdue, *Owner*
EMP: 4
SQ FT: 7,900
SALES: 2.9MM **Privately Held**
SIC: 3531 Crushers, grinders & similar equipment

(G-709)
CUSTOM WOODWORKING
732 S Village Dr (47403-1954)
PHONE..................................812 339-6601
Vincent Payne, *Principal*
EMP: 2
SALES (est): 231.7K **Privately Held**
SIC: 2431 Millwork

(G-710)
D X SYSTEMS
317 W 17th St (47404-3453)
PHONE..................................812 332-4699
Dave Burns, *Owner*
EMP: 4
SALES (est): 231.8K **Privately Held**
SIC: 7372 Prepackaged software

(G-711)
DECKER SALES INC
5100 E Four Boys Trl (47408-9299)
PHONE..................................812 330-1580
Chuck Decker, *President*
EMP: 3
SALES: 350K **Privately Held**
SIC: 3714 Motor vehicle body components & frame

(G-712)
DIESEL PUNK CORE ✪
3520 S Mcdougal St (47403-4638)
PHONE..................................812 631-0606
Judder Leinenbach, *President*
EMP: 2 EST: 2018
SALES (est): 87.2K **Privately Held**
SIC: 3714 Motor vehicle parts & accessories

(G-713)
DILLMAN FARM INCORPORATED
4955 W State Road 45 (47403-9362)
PHONE..................................812 825-5525
Fax: 812 825-4650
Cary Dillman, *President*
EMP: 8
SQ FT: 2,160
SALES (est): 1.2MM **Privately Held**
SIC: 2033 2041 2021 Fruit butters: packaged in cans, jars, etc.; preserves, including imitation: in cans, jars, etc.; flour & other grain mill products; creamery butter

(G-714)
DO TECHNOLOGIES LLC
730 N Walnut St Apt 202 (47404-4101)
PHONE..................................812 272-2306
Anthony Quinn Thompson II, *CEO*
EMP: 2
SALES (est): 56.5K **Privately Held**
SIC: 7372 Prepackaged software

(G-715)
DOUBLE E DISTRIBUTING CO INC (PA)
Also Called: Double E Dstrbtng Co
2214 E Rock Creek Dr (47401-6852)
PHONE..................................812 334-2220
Natalie Epstein, *President*
EMP: 3
SQ FT: 900
SALES (est): 150K **Privately Held**
WEB: www.doubleedistributing.com
SIC: 3299 5199 Built-up mica; artists' materials

(G-716)
DR PEPPER BOTTLING COMPANY
214 W 17th St (47404-3536)
PHONE..................................812 332-1200
Thomas Hendrey, *Principal*
EMP: 3
SALES (est): 114.7K **Privately Held**
SIC: 2086 Soft drinks: packaged in cans, bottles, etc.

(G-717)
E-CERTA INCORPORATED
3930 S Walnut St (47401-7393)
PHONE..................................812 323-7824
Joel Deutsch, *President*
EMP: 33
SALES (est): 1.6MM **Privately Held**
SIC: 3674 Semiconductors & related devices

(G-718)
EARTH DROPS HANDCRAFTED SOAPS
3065 N Prow Rd (47404-1605)
PHONE..................................812 336-2491
Cheryl Lehman, *Partner*
David Lehman, *Partner*
EMP: 2
SQ FT: 1,000
SALES: 75K **Privately Held**
SIC: 2841 Soap: granulated, liquid, cake, flaked or chip

(G-719)
ELECTRIC PLUS
1030 W 17th St (47404-3389)
PHONE..................................812 336-4992
EMP: 2
SALES (est): 88.3K **Privately Held**
SIC: 3699 1731 Electrical equipment & supplies; electrical work

(G-720)
ENGRAVING AND STAMP CENTER INC
218 N Madison St (47404-3961)
PHONE..................................812 336-0606
Jan Snoddy, *President*
Ron Snoddy, *Admin Sec*
EMP: 3
SQ FT: 5,000
SALES: 150K **Privately Held**
SIC: 3069 2759 Stationers' rubber sundries; engraving

(G-721)
EVERYWHERE SIGNS LLC
2630 N Walnut St (47404-2008)
PHONE..................................812 323-1471
Fax: 812 323-1472
Gregg Elgar, *President*
Jim Parrott, *Vice Pres*
Lonnie Pratt, *Vice Pres*
Lisa Keough, *Sls & Mktg Exec*
EMP: 5
SQ FT: 1,800
SALES: 300K **Privately Held**
WEB: www.everywheresigns.com
SIC: 3993 Signs & advertising specialties

(G-722)
EXPRESS STUDY LLC
2420 E Rock Creek Dr (47401-6822)
PHONE..................................812 272-2247
Chris Heinrich,
Ye Ji,
EMP: 2
SALES (est): 139.1K **Privately Held**
SIC: 7372 7389 Educational computer software;

(G-723)
FAZTECH LLC
7069 S Leisure Ln (47401-9082)
PHONE..................................812 327-0926
Amed Fazni,
EMP: 5 EST: 2005
SALES (est): 423.8K **Privately Held**
SIC: 3569 8731 3845 Liquid automation machinery & equipment; commercial physical research; commercial physical research; respiratory analysis equipment, electromedical

(G-724)
FERRILL-FISHER INCORPORATED
8768 N Wayport Rd (47404-9463)
PHONE..................................812 935-9000
John L Fisher, *Principal*
EMP: 6 EST: 2015
SALES (est): 102.6K **Privately Held**
SIC: 2295 Metallizing of fabrics

(G-725)
FIBER TECHNOLOGIES LLC
2517 E Caray Ct (47401-8571)
PHONE..................................812 569-4641
James Bennett, *Exec VP*
J Douglas Bennett,
EMP: 2
SQ FT: 200
SALES: 40K **Privately Held**
SIC: 2822 Ethylene-propylene rubbers, EPDM polymers

(G-726)
FOX SMOOTHIES LLC
4000 E Stonegate Dr (47401-9803)
PHONE..................................812 333-3051
John Fox, *Principal*
EMP: 3
SALES (est): 154.8K **Privately Held**
SIC: 2037 Frozen fruits & vegetables

(G-727)
FREIGHT TRNSP RES ASSOC INC
1720 N Kinser Pike # 210 (47404-2210)
PHONE..................................888 988-1699
Eric Starks, *President*
EMP: 15
SALES (est): 1.2MM **Privately Held**
SIC: 2731 Book publishing

G
E
O
G
R
A
P
H
I
C

(G-728)
FROGGY PRINT LLC
1219 E Thornton Dr (47401-6637)
PHONE......................................317 965-7954
Leah Tannen, *Owner*
EMP: 2
SALES (est): 83.9K **Privately Held**
SIC: 2752 Commercial printing, lithographic

(G-729)
FTR TRNSPORTATION INTELLIGENCE
1720 N Kinser Pike (47404-2210)
PHONE......................................888 988-1699
Eric Starks, *CEO*
Ryan Beall, *Business Mgr*
Rhonda Martin, *Office Mgr*
EMP: 5
SALES (est): 115.3K **Privately Held**
SIC: 3441 Railroad car racks, for transporting vehicles: steel

(G-730)
GENERAL MOTORS LLC
3112 E Kensington Park Dr (47401-7117)
PHONE......................................419 576-9472
EMP: 2 **Publicly Held**
SIC: 3711 Motor vehicles & car bodies
HQ: General Motors Llc
300 Renaissance Ctr L1
Detroit MI 48243

(G-731)
GET PUBLISHED INC
Also Called: Iuniverse
1663 S Liberty Dr Ste 200 (47403-5161)
PHONE......................................812 334-5279
Bill Elliot, *President*
EMP: 500
SALES (est): 11.8MM **Privately Held**
SIC: 2731 Book publishing

(G-732)
GOOD EARTH COMPOST LLC
650 E Empire Mill Rd (47401-9273)
PHONE......................................812 824-7928
Fax: 812 824-2068
Aaron Wright,
EMP: 2 EST: 1977
SQ FT: 2,500
SALES: 300K **Privately Held**
SIC: 2493 Reconstituted wood products

(G-733)
GRAPHIC VISIONS
Also Called: Graphic Vsons Screen Prtg Sgns
1314 W Kirkwood Ave (47404-5062)
P.O. Box 1336 (47402-1336)
PHONE......................................812 331-7446
Fax: 812 331-7658
Rob Hudson, *Owner*
EMP: 3
SQ FT: 2,500
SALES (est): 224.3K **Privately Held**
SIC: 7336 2759 3993 Graphic arts & related design; screen printing; signs & advertising specialties

(G-734)
GRINER ENGINEERING INC
2500 N Curry Pike (47404-1431)
PHONE......................................812 332-2220
Fax: 812 332-2229
John Griner, *President*
EMP: 75
SQ FT: 24,000
SALES (est): 19.5MM **Privately Held**
WEB: www.griner.com
SIC: 3599 Machine shop, jobbing & repair

(G-735)
GROWTH PRINCIPALS LLC
1155 E Benson Ct (47401-8828)
PHONE......................................812 320-1574
James Mitchell, *Mng Member*
EMP: 3
SALES: 200K **Privately Held**
SIC: 8742 8732 2522 Marketing consulting services; market analysis, business & economic research; office furniture, except wood

(G-736)
H P PRODUCTS CORPORATION
Also Called: HP Products A Ferguson Entp
502 W 4th St (47404-5128)
PHONE......................................812 331-8793
EMP: 2
SALES (corp-wide): 19.2B **Privately Held**
SIC: 3469 Metal stampings
HQ: H P Products Corporation
4220 Saguaro Trl
Indianapolis IN 46268
317 298-9957

(G-737)
HALL SIGNS INC
4495 W Vernal Pike (47404-9333)
PHONE......................................812 332-9355
Fax: 812 332-9816
Larry Hall, *President*
Chuck Krebbs, *Site Mgr*
Jenni Kalbfleisch, *Buyer*
Janet Wilson, *Sales Executive*
Angi Eads, *Manager*
◆ EMP: 75 EST: 1949
SQ FT: 75,000
SALES (est): 12.8MM **Privately Held**
WEB: www.hallsigns.com
SIC: 3993 Signs, not made in custom sign painting shops

(G-738)
HARTZELLS HOMEMADE ICE CREAM
107 N Dunn St (47408-4047)
PHONE......................................812 332-3502
Hartzell Martel, *Owner*
Hillary Martel, *Owner*
EMP: 16
SALES (est): 976.2K **Privately Held**
SIC: 2052 Cones, ice cream

(G-739)
HEITINK VENEERS INCORPORATED
1141 N Snrise Gretings Ct (47404-2547)
P.O. Box 5176 (47407-5176)
PHONE......................................812 336-6436
Fax: 812 331-7636
Gerrit Heitink, *President*
Jan Berend Heitink, *Vice Pres*
Vera Heitink, *Admin Sec*
▲ EMP: 42
SQ FT: 50,000
SALES (est): 6.5MM **Privately Held**
SIC: 2435 5031 Veneer stock, hardwood; veneer

(G-740)
HI-RISE SIGN & LIGHTING LLC
6524 W Ison Rd (47403-8003)
PHONE......................................812 825-4448
Jeffery A Arbuckle, *Principal*
EMP: 5
SALES (est): 408.1K **Privately Held**
SIC: 3993 Signs & advertising specialties

(G-741)
HOOSIER TIMES INC (DH)
Also Called: Herald Times
1900 S Walnut St (47401-7720)
P.O. Box 909 (47402-0909)
PHONE......................................812 331-4270
Fax: 812 331-4285
Scott C Schurz, *President*
Mayer Malloney, *Vice Pres*
Eric McIntosh, *Treasurer*
Linda Breeden, *Admin Sec*
EMP: 230 EST: 1966
SQ FT: 70,000
SALES (est): 43.4MM
SALES (corp-wide): 882.7MM **Publicly Held**
WEB: www.htinteractive.com
SIC: 2711 4813 2791 2752 Newspapers: publishing only, not printed on site; ; typesetting; commercial printing, lithographic
HQ: Schurz Communications, Inc.
1301 E Douglas Rd Ste 200
Mishawaka IN 46545
574 247-7237

(G-742)
HOOSIER WOOD WORKS
118 E Ridgeview Dr (47401-7316)
PHONE......................................812 325-9823

Roger Kugler, *Owner*
EMP: 2 EST: 2008
SALES (est): 303K **Privately Held**
SIC: 2431 Millwork

(G-743)
INARI INFORMATION SERVICES
Also Called: Iis
804 N College Ave Ste 101 (47404-3599)
PHONE......................................812 331-2298
Michael Kelsey, *President*
Michael O-DEA, *Vice Pres*
EMP: 4
SALES: 330K **Privately Held**
WEB: www.inarionline.com
SIC: 7389 2721 8999 Translation services; magazines: publishing only, not printed on site; technical manual preparation

(G-744)
INDEPENDENT LIMESTONE CO LLC
6001 S Rockport Rd (47403-9152)
P.O. Box 26, Clear Creek (47426-0026)
PHONE......................................812 824-4951
Fax: 812 824-7405
Gordon K Nelson,
EMP: 42 EST: 1927
SQ FT: 1,400
SALES (est): 6.9MM **Privately Held**
SIC: 1411 Limestone, dimension-quarrying

(G-745)
INDIANA LMSTONE ACQSITION LLC
Also Called: Indiana Limestone Company
123 S College Ave (47404-5166)
PHONE......................................812 275-3341
Thomas Quigley, *CEO*
Duffe Elkins, *President*
Benjamin Wojcikiewicz, *Engrg Mgr*
Matthew Howard, *CFO*
Mark Bryant, *Human Res Mgr*
▲ EMP: 99
SALES (est): 10.1MM **Privately Held**
SIC: 3281 1411 Cut stone & stone products; limestone, dimension-quarrying

(G-746)
INDIANA LUMBER INC
8215 S State Road 446 (47401-9742)
PHONE......................................812 837-9493
Fax: 812 837-9468
Dennis Blackwell, *President*
May Blackwell, *Corp Secy*
EMP: 8
SQ FT: 7,000
SALES (est): 850K **Privately Held**
SIC: 2431 5713 Moldings, wood: unfinished & prefinished; trim, wood; doors, wood; staircases, stairs & railings; carpets

(G-747)
INDIANA METAL CRAFT INC
4602 W Innovation Dr (47404-8713)
P.O. Box 546 (47402-0546)
PHONE......................................812 336-2362
Fax: 812 336-1261
Ronald D Davis, *President*
Mark Warner, *Purch Mgr*
Jarod Johnson, *VP Sales*
James Zavala, *Technology*
▲ EMP: 80
SQ FT: 27,000
SALES (est): 11.8MM **Privately Held**
WEB: www.indianaimc.com
SIC: 3993 Advertising novelties

(G-748)
INDIANA UNIVERSITY BLOOMINGTON
Also Called: Journal of American History
1215 E Atwater Ave (47401-3703)
PHONE......................................812 855-2816
Fax: 812 855-9939
James Byrd, *General Mgr*
Edward Linanthal, *Principal*
EMP: 13
SALES (corp-wide): 2.2B **Privately Held**
WEB: www.iupui.edu
SIC: 2711 8221 Newspapers, publishing & printing; university

PA: Trustees Indiana University
Bryan Hall 107 S Ind Ave St Bryan Ha
Bloomington IN 47405
812 855-4848

(G-749)
INNOVTIVE SURGICAL DESIGNS INC
3903 S Walnut St (47401-7394)
PHONE......................................484 584-4230
Mark Bartosh, *CEO*
Wayne Beams,
EMP: 15
SALES (est): 260K **Privately Held**
SIC: 3841 Surgical & medical instruments

(G-750)
INTERNATIONAL A I INC
7909 S Fairfax Rd (47401-8955)
PHONE......................................812 824-2473
Bradley S Blume, *President*
Clem Blume, *Vice Pres*
EMP: 3
SQ FT: 8,600
SALES (est): 485K **Privately Held**
WEB: www.internationalai.com
SIC: 5191 3523 Farm supplies; poultry brooders, feeders & waterers

(G-751)
IRVING MATERIALS INC
Also Called: I M I
1800 N Kinser Pike (47404-1900)
PHONE......................................812 333-8530
Fax: 812 333-8113
Mike La Grange, *Vice Pres*
Mike Lagrange, *Manager*
EMP: 20
SALES (corp-wide): 800.6MM **Privately Held**
SIC: 3273 Ready-mixed concrete
PA: Irving Materials, Inc.
8032 N State Road 9
Greenfield IN 46140
317 326-3101

(G-752)
IUNIVERSE INC
1663 S Liberty Dr (47403-5161)
PHONE......................................812 330-2909
Fax: 812 355-4085
Kevin Weiss, *President*
Joe Steinbach, *Vice Pres*
Tony Arndt, *CFO*
Nikki Chapman, *Marketing Staff*
Jessie Young, *Marketing Staff*
▼ EMP: 65
SALES (est): 6.1MM
SALES (corp-wide): 52.4MM **Privately Held**
WEB: www.iuniverse.com
SIC: 2731 Book publishing
PA: Author Solutions Llc
1663 S Liberty Dr
Bloomington IN 47403
812 339-6000

(G-753)
JEM SOFTWARE DEVELOPMENT LLC
2957 N Ramble Rd E (47408-1063)
PHONE......................................812 339-2970
Gregory S Galbreath, *Principal*
EMP: 2 EST: 2010
SALES (est): 121.2K **Privately Held**
SIC: 7372 Prepackaged software

(G-754)
JERDEN INDUSTRIES INC
1104 S Morton St (47403-4798)
PHONE......................................812 332-1762
Fax: 812 334-7051
William D Jerden, *President*
EMP: 28
SQ FT: 19,000
SALES (est): 5.1MM **Privately Held**
SIC: 3451 Screw machine products

(G-755)
JERICO METAL SPECIALTIES INC
1111 W 17th St Ste 1 (47404-3003)
P.O. Box 7016 (47407-7016)
PHONE......................................812 339-3182
Fax: 812 339-3186

▲ = Import ▼=Export
◆ =Import/Export

Jerry L Curry, *President*
Tyler Curry, *Vice Pres*
Steven Johnson, *Project Mgr*
Joe Townsend, *Project Mgr*
Gene Curry, *Manager*
EMP: 11
SQ FT: 10,000
SALES (est): 1.1MM **Privately Held**
WEB: www.jericometals.com
SIC: 3441 Fabricated structural metal

(G-756)
K W DEER PROCESSING
1715 E Rayletown Rd (47401-9353)
PHONE..................................812 824-2492
Kirby Walerip, *Owner*
EMP: 6
SALES (est): 335.6K **Privately Held**
SIC: 2011 Meat packing plants

(G-757)
KC DESIGNS
Also Called: K C Designs Printing
2801 W Bristol Dr (47404-1207)
PHONE..................................812 876-4020
Karl Clark, *Owner*
EMP: 2
SALES: 180K **Privately Held**
SIC: 2752 Commercial printing, lithographic

(G-758)
KETCH PUBLISHING
4675 N Benton Dr (47408-9503)
PHONE..................................812 327-0072
Allen Ketchersid, *Principal*
EMP: 2
SALES (est): 113.8K **Privately Held**
SIC: 2741 Miscellaneous publishing

(G-759)
KNOWLEDGE DIFFUSION GAMES LLC
1441 S Fnbrook Ln Ste 100 (47401)
PHONE..................................812 361-4424
Margaret Clements, *President*
EMP: 2
SQ FT: 500
SALES (est): 99.3K **Privately Held**
SIC: 7373 7379 7372 Value-added resellers, computer systems; ; application computer software; educational computer software

(G-760)
KP PHARMACEUTICAL TECH INC
1212 W Rappel Ave (47404-1702)
PHONE..................................812 330-8121
Rajinder Matharu, *President*
Joythi Matharu, *Vice Pres*
EMP: 25
SQ FT: 7,000
SALES (est): 6.5MM **Privately Held**
WEB: www.kppt.com
SIC: 2834 8731 Pharmaceutical preparations; commercial physical research

(G-761)
LAKE EFFECT LIGHTING LLC
3635 E Cleve Butcher Rd (47401-9059)
PHONE..................................812 783-9482
EMP: 2
SALES (est): 190.7K **Privately Held**
SIC: 3648 Lighting equipment

(G-762)
LAKOTA LANGUAGE CONSORTIUM
2620 N Walnut St Ste 1280 (47404-2008)
PHONE..................................888 525-6828
Yuliya Manyakina, *Corp Comm Staff*
Meya Wilheim, *Manager*
Wilhelm Meya, *Exec Dir*
Edward Curtis,
Zack Anselm, *Coordinator*
EMP: 15
SALES: 706.6K **Privately Held**
WEB: www.lakhota.org
SIC: 8299 2731 Language school; book publishing

(G-763)
LAMINATED TOPS OF CENTRAL IND
711 E Dillman Rd (47401-9288)
PHONE..................................812 824-6299
Fax: 812 824-6873
Richard Raake, *President*
Robert Raake, *President*
Margaret Raake, *Corp Secy*
Keith Hanson, *Opers Staff*
EMP: 25
SQ FT: 20,000
SALES (est): 2.4MM **Privately Held**
SIC: 5211 2541 Counter tops; wood partitions & fixtures

(G-764)
LEE SUPPLY CORP
1821 W 3rd St (47404-5206)
P.O. Box 757 (47402-0757)
PHONE..................................812 333-4343
David Barnes, *Branch Mgr*
EMP: 2
SALES (corp-wide): 108.4MM **Privately Held**
SIC: 5712 5074 3432 Cabinet work, custom; plumbing & hydronic heating supplies; plumbing fixture fittings & trim
PA: Lee Supply Corp.
   6610 Guion Rd
   Indianapolis IN 46268
   317 290-2500

(G-765)
LENNIES INC
Also Called: Bloomington Brewing Co
1795 E 10th St (47408-3975)
P.O. Box 6955 (47407-6955)
PHONE..................................812 323-2112
Fax: 812 333-3200
Jeffrey Mease, *President*
Lennie Dare, *Treasurer*
EMP: 90
SQ FT: 7,700
SALES (est): 3MM **Privately Held**
WEB: www.bloomington.com
SIC: 5812 2082 Chicken restaurant; beer (alcoholic beverage)

(G-766)
LK TECHNOLOGIES INC
1590 S Liberty Dr Ste A (47403-5167)
PHONE..................................812 332-4449
Fax: 812 332-4493
Larry Kesmodel, *President*
Greg Hepfer, *Director*
EMP: 5
SQ FT: 14,000
SALES (est): 1MM **Privately Held**
WEB: www.lktech.com
SIC: 3826 5049 Spectroscopic & other optical properties measuring equipment; scientific instruments

(G-767)
LONG LEATHER WORKS LLC
203 W Gordon Pike (47403-4520)
PHONE..................................812 336-5309
Fax: 812 336-5509
Michael O Long, *Owner*
EMP: 3
SALES (est): 130K **Privately Held**
SIC: 3172 Personal leather goods

(G-768)
MADDOCK CONSTRUCTION EQP LLC
239 W Grimes Ln (47403-3015)
PHONE..................................812 349-3000
John Goode,
David Maddock,
EMP: 25
SQ FT: 90,000
SALES (est): 4.1MM **Privately Held**
SIC: 3531 Construction machinery; construction machinery attachments

(G-769)
MARCO PLASTICS INC
1616 S Huntington Dr (47401-6619)
P.O. Box 2133 (47402-2133)
PHONE..................................812 333-0062
Fax: 812 331-8723
Martin P Witkiewicz, *President*
Joseph Witkiewicz, *General Mgr*

Donna Witkiewicz, *Corp Secy*
EMP: 12
SQ FT: 12,000
SALES: 2.3MM **Privately Held**
WEB: www.marcoplasticsinc.com
SIC: 3089 Injection molding of plastics

(G-770)
MCD MACHINE INCORPORATED
2345 W Industrial Park Dr (47404-2602)
PHONE..................................812 339-1240
Fax: 812 339-1372
Melinda Davis, *President*
CJ Davis, *Vice Pres*
EMP: 9
SALES (est): 200K **Privately Held**
SIC: 3599 3449 3444 Machine shop, jobbing & repair; miscellaneous metalwork; sheet metalwork

(G-771)
METROPOLITAN PRINTING SVCS LLC
Also Called: Metropolitan Printing, Rrd
720 S Morton St (47403-2498)
PHONE..................................812 332-7279
Fax: 812 331-8209
Mark Leggio, *President*
Wes Menefee, *Vice Pres*
Art Bodkin, *Sales Staff*
Bill French, *Manager*
Pat Mahan, *Technology*
EMP: 34
SQ FT: 23,000
SALES (est): 6.6MM
SALES (corp-wide): 6.9B **Publicly Held**
WEB: www.consolidatedgraphics.com
SIC: 2752 Commercial printing, offset
HQ: Consolidated Graphics, Inc.
   5858 Westheimer Rd # 200
   Houston TX 77057
   713 787-0977

(G-772)
MIDWEST COLOR PRINTING LLC
2458 S Walnut St (47401-7730)
PHONE..................................812 822-2947
Michael Richardson,
EMP: 5
SQ FT: 1,200
SALES (est): 646.8K **Privately Held**
SIC: 2752 Commercial printing, offset

(G-773)
MIRWEC FILM INCORPORATED
601 S Liberty Dr (47403-1925)
P.O. Box 2263 (47402-2263)
PHONE..................................812 331-7194
Fax: 812 331-1119
Yoshinari Yasui, *President*
Albert J Velasquez, *Admin Sec*
▲ **EMP:** 19
SQ FT: 13,000
SALES (est): 3.6MM
SALES (corp-wide): 11MM **Privately Held**
WEB: www.mirwecfilm.com
SIC: 3081 Polypropylene film & sheet
PA: Yasui Seiki Co.,Ltd.
   6-18-30, Kadosawabashi
   Ebina KNG 243-0
   462 380-160

(G-774)
MOLD STOPPERS OF INDIANA
1135 N Logan Rd (47404-2580)
PHONE..................................812 325-1609
Michelle Galloway, *Principal*
EMP: 2
SALES (est): 118.9K **Privately Held**
SIC: 3544 Industrial molds

(G-775)
MONSTER HOUSE PRESS
1608 S Buffstone Ct (47401-6582)
PHONE..................................440 364-4548
Richard Wehrenberg, *Principal*
EMP: 2
SALES (est): 62.9K **Privately Held**
SIC: 2711 Newspapers

(G-776)
MR COPY INC
501 E 10th St (47408-3699)
PHONE..................................812 334-2679
Mary Seeber, *President*

EMP: 4
SALES (est): 535.4K **Privately Held**
SIC: 2752 7334 Commercial printing, offset; photocopying & duplicating services

(G-777)
MSP AVIATION INC
239 W Grimes Ln (47403-3015)
PHONE..................................812 333-6100
John Goode, *President*
Michael Kean, *Opers Mgr*
Jim Edington, *Engineer*
Kevin Kern, *Sales Mgr*
Jennifer Cowden, *Customer Svc Re*
EMP: 30
SQ FT: 20,000
SALES (est): 6.6MM **Privately Held**
WEB: www.msp-aviation.com
SIC: 3728 Aircraft parts & equipment

(G-778)
NEMESIS RACE CARS
6155 S Ison Rd (47403-9322)
PHONE..................................812 361-9743
Anthony Walker, *Principal*
EMP: 2
SALES (est): 103.5K **Privately Held**
SIC: 3711 Automobile assembly, including specialty automobiles

(G-779)
NEUBAU CONTRACTING
1701 E Circle Dr (47401-6027)
PHONE..................................970 406-8084
Piers Peterson, *Principal*
EMP: 2
SALES (est): 86.7K **Privately Held**
SIC: 2452 Prefabricated wood buildings

(G-780)
NEW PHILOSOPHER PRSS
5156 N Brummetts Creek Rd (47408-9616)
PHONE..................................406 992-5791
Fran Weisman, *Owner*
EMP: 2
SALES (est): 79K **Privately Held**
SIC: 2741 Miscellaneous publishing

(G-781)
NSWC CRANE DIVISION
3217 S Rogers St (47403-4351)
PHONE..................................812 854-2865
EMP: 2
SALES (est): 86K **Privately Held**
SIC: 3731 Shipbuilding & repairing

(G-782)
NUAXON BIOSCIENCE INC
899 S College Mall Rd # 161 (47401-6301)
P.O. Box 353, Bloomfield (47424-0353)
PHONE..................................812 762-4400
Jason Edwards, *CEO*
Girish Soman, *Ch of Bd*
EMP: 3
SALES: 7MM **Privately Held**
SIC: 2833 Medicinals & botanicals

(G-783)
ODON VAULT CO
2909 E Kylie Ct (47401-8386)
PHONE..................................812 636-7386
Fax: 812 636-7363
John Sibray, *President*
Susan Sibray, *Corp Secy*
EMP: 16 **EST:** 1922
SALES: 888K **Privately Held**
SIC: 3272 Burial vaults, concrete or precast terrazzo; septic tanks, concrete

(G-784)
OHIO RIVER VENEER LLC
650 E Empire Mill Rd (47401-9273)
P.O. Box 169, Clear Creek (47426-0169)
PHONE..................................812 824-7928
Iamur Wright,
Astar Wright,
Brutus Wright,
EMP: 18
SQ FT: 1,200
SALES (est): 2.2MM **Privately Held**
SIC: 2411 Logging camps & contractors

G E O G R A P H I C

(G-785)
OHM AUTOMOTIVE LLC
Also Called: Custom Manufacturing Solutions
3748 S Claybridge Dr (47401-8565)
PHONE.................................812 879-5455
AMI Shah,
EMP: 8
SALES (est): 286.8K Privately Held
SIC: 7538 7692 General automotive repair shops; welding repair

(G-786)
OLIVE LEAF LLC
879 S College Mall Rd (47401-6301)
PHONE.................................812 323-3073
Troy Kirkman, Mng Member
Marla Kirkman,
EMP: 3 EST: 2010
SALES (est): 202.6K Privately Held
SIC: 2079 Olive oil

(G-787)
OLIVER WINE COMPANY INC (PA)
Also Called: Oliver Winery
200 E Winery Rd (47404-2400)
PHONE.................................812 822-0466
Fax: 812 876-9309
William M Oliver, President
Kathleen Oliver, Corp Secy
▲ EMP: 63 EST: 1972
SQ FT: 30,000
SALES (est): 17.8MM Privately Held
WEB: www.oliverwinery.com
SIC: 5921 2084 Wine; wines

(G-788)
ON THE GO PORTBLE WTR SFTNR LL
3905 W Roll Ave (47403-3181)
PHONE.................................260 482-9614
Benjamin Scherschel,
Bruce Everson,
Benjamin A Scherschel,
EMP: 10
SALES (est): 1.5MM Privately Held
SIC: 3589 7389 Water filters & softeners, household type; water softener service

(G-789)
ONE STOP TRAVEL SHOP INC
317 E Dodds St (47401-4787)
PHONE.................................812 339-9496
Tatiana Moir, President
Marcus Moir, Admin Sec
EMP: 2
SQ FT: 600
SALES (est): 190K Privately Held
WEB: www.1ststoptravelstore.com
SIC: 3161 Traveling bags

(G-790)
OPSYS LTD
2600 S Henderson St # 204 (47401-8439)
PHONE.................................765 236-6331
Chris Haigh, Exec VP
Michael W Baran III, CFO
EMP: 3
SALES (est): 168K Privately Held
SIC: 3841 Surgical & medical instruments

(G-791)
ORGANIZED LIVING INC
1500 S Strong Dr (47403-8741)
PHONE.................................812 334-8839
Fax: 812 349-5701
Marta Holmes, Opers Mgr
Sandra Burchard, Safety Mgr
Roy Hammon, Branch Mgr
EMP: 115
SALES (corp-wide): 33.5MM Privately Held
WEB: www.schultestorage.com
SIC: 3496 2542 5211 Shelving, made from purchased wire; partitions & fixtures, except wood; closets, interiors & accessories
PA: Organized Living Inc.
3100 E Kemper Rd
Cincinnati OH 45241
513 489-9300

(G-792)
ORION GLOBAL SOURCING INC
1516 S Walnut St (47401-7711)
PHONE.................................812 332-3338
Fax: 812 961-0399
Ian Munnoch, President
Alan Carlson, Vice Pres
▲ EMP: 4
SQ FT: 1,500
SALES (est): 625.4K Privately Held
WEB: www.oriongs.com
SIC: 3679 7373 7389 Electronic circuits; computer integrated systems design; printed circuitry graphic layout

(G-793)
OTIS ELEVATOR COMPANY
320 W 8th St Ste 201 (47404-3700)
PHONE.................................812 331-5605
EMP: 2
SALES (corp-wide): 59.8B Publicly Held
SIC: 3534 Automobile elevators
HQ: Otis Elevator Company
1 Carrier Pl
Farmington CT 06032
860 674-3000

(G-794)
P-AMERICAS LLC
Also Called: Pepsico
214 W 17th St (47404-3536)
PHONE.................................812 332-1200
Rick Nicolas, Branch Mgr
EMP: 123
SALES (corp-wide): 63.5B Publicly Held
SIC: 2086 Carbonated soft drinks, bottled & canned
HQ: P-Americas Llc
1 Pepsi Way
Somers NY 10589
336 896-5740

(G-795)
PALIBRIO
1663 S Liberty Dr (47403-5161)
PHONE.................................812 671-9757
Andrew Phillips, CEO
EMP: 2
SALES (est): 79.8K Privately Held
SIC: 2731 Book publishing

(G-796)
PC MAX INC
2534 E 3rd St (47401-5338)
PHONE.................................812 337-0630
Fax: 812 337-0634
Chris Fredrickson, President
Nathan Stohr, Manager
EMP: 9
SQ FT: 3,000
SALES (est): 1.1MM Privately Held
WEB: www.pcmaxinc.com
SIC: 5045 5734 7378 7373 Computers, peripherals & software; computer & software stores; computer maintenance & repair; computer integrated systems design; computer peripheral equipment; electronic computers

(G-797)
PENGUIN ENTERPRISES LLC
Also Called: Chocolate Moose, The
401 S Walnut St (47401-4613)
P.O. Box 1685 (47402-1685)
PHONE.................................812 333-0475
Justin Loveless, Mng Member
EMP: 45
SQ FT: 1,800
SALES: 1.2MM Privately Held
SIC: 2024 Ice cream & frozen desserts

(G-798)
PEPSI-COLA METRO BTLG CO INC
214 W 17th St (47404-3536)
PHONE.................................812 332-1200
Fax: 812 330-4391
Ted Ness, Manager
Jon Adler, Manager
EMP: 35
SALES (corp-wide): 63.5B Publicly Held
WEB: www.joy-of-cola.com
SIC: 2086 5149 Soft drinks: packaged in cans, bottles, etc.; beverages, except coffee & tea

HQ: Pepsi-Cola Metropolitan Bottling Company, Inc.
1111 Westchester Ave
White Plains NY 10604
914 767-6000

(G-799)
PINNACLE TOOL INC
1830 S Walnut St (47401-7719)
PHONE.................................812 336-5000
William Peterson, President
Joe Peterson, Vice Pres
EMP: 3
SQ FT: 5,000
SALES (est): 341.7K Privately Held
SIC: 3544 3599 Industrial molds; electrical discharge machining (EDM)

(G-800)
POLYPHASE MICROWAVE INC
1983 S Liberty Dr (47403-5146)
PHONE.................................812 323-8708
Lowell Hoover, President
Tyson Fish, Electrical Engi
EMP: 3
SALES: 750K Privately Held
WEB: www.polyphasemicrowave.com
SIC: 3679 Microwave components

(G-801)
POWER BRUSHES OF INDIANA INC
2506 S Milton Dr (47403-3642)
P.O. Box 1238 (47402-1238)
PHONE.................................812 336-7395
Deborah A Boling, President
Martin W Boling, Corp Secy
EMP: 5
SALES: 500K Privately Held
WEB: www.powerbrushes.biz
SIC: 3991 Brushes, household or industrial

(G-802)
PRINTPACK INC
2121 N Angelina Ln (47404-8709)
PHONE.................................812 334-5500
EMP: 5
SALES (corp-wide): 1.3B Privately Held
SIC: 2752 Commercial printing, lithographic
HQ: Printpack, Inc.
2800 Overlook Pkwy Ne
Atlanta GA 30339
404 460-7000

(G-803)
QUALITY VAULT COMPANY
Also Called: Sexton
1908 W Allen St (47403-2840)
PHONE.................................812 336-8127
Mark Sexton, President
Tina Sexton, Corp Secy
Michael Sexton, Vice Pres
EMP: 16
SALES (est): 1MM Privately Held
SIC: 3272 5087 Burial vaults, concrete or precast terrazzo; concrete burial vaults & boxes

(G-804)
QUANTUM 7 GROUP LLC
3523 E Harbor Dr (47401-8884)
PHONE.................................812 824-9378
William V West, Owner
EMP: 3 EST: 2013
SALES (est): 184.8K Privately Held
SIC: 3572 Computer storage devices

(G-805)
QUANTUM CREATIVE LLC
6320 E Bender Rd (47401-9217)
PHONE.................................812 381-2586
Kyle Vest, Principal
EMP: 2 EST: 2016
SALES (est): 87.6K Privately Held
SIC: 3572 Computer storage devices

(G-806)
QUANTUM TECH USA ✪
3271 N Obrien Pl (47404-1729)
PHONE.................................360 400-0905
EMP: 2 EST: 2017
SALES (est): 85.9K Privately Held
SIC: 3572 Computer storage devices

(G-807)
RANDY GEHLHAUSEN
2808 E Daniel St (47401-7111)
PHONE.................................812 327-4454
Randy Gehlhausen, Principal
EMP: 3
SALES (est): 274.7K Privately Held
SIC: 2851 Removers & cleaners

(G-808)
RB CONCEPTS
Also Called: RB Apparel
8451 S Marcy Ct (47401-7208)
PHONE.................................317 735-2172
Rick Bomberger, CEO
EMP: 7
SALES (est): 270K Privately Held
SIC: 2231 Apparel & outerwear broadwoven fabrics

(G-809)
REGULATIONS UPDATE SVCS LLC
1819 N Hartstrait Rd (47404-9792)
PHONE.................................812 334-4020
Terry J Bunch, Mng Member
EMP: 4
SALES (est): 240.3K Privately Held
SIC: 2731 Book publishing

(G-810)
REWIND
118 E 6th St (47408-3311)
PHONE.................................812 361-0411
Aaron Chandler, Principal
EMP: 3
SALES (est): 172.5K Privately Held
SIC: 2741 Music book & sheet music publishing

(G-811)
RICHARDSON ENTPS BLMINGTON LLC
Also Called: Fastsigns
2454 S Walnut St (47401-7730)
PHONE.................................812 287-8179
Michael Richardson, Co-Owner
Maranda Richardson, Co-Owner
EMP: 4
SQ FT: 2,000
SALES (est): 286.9K Privately Held
SIC: 3993 5999 Signs & advertising specialties; letters for signs, metal; banners, flags, decals & posters

(G-812)
RIGHTREZ
3010 E David Dr (47401-4470)
PHONE.................................812 219-1893
Michael C Vonforester, CEO
Jim Quinn, President
Huff Templeton, COO
EMP: 3
SALES (est): 250K Privately Held
WEB: www.rightrez.com
SIC: 7372 Prepackaged software

(G-813)
ROGERS GROUP INC
Also Called: Bloomington Crushed Stone
1100 N Oard Rd (47404-9365)
PHONE.................................812 333-8560
Fax: 812 332-2015
Dana Boyd, Manager
EMP: 40
SALES (corp-wide): 1B Privately Held
WEB: www.rogersgroupinc.com
SIC: 1422 5032 Crushed & broken limestone; stone, crushed or broken
PA: Rogers Group, Inc.
421 Great Circle Rd
Nashville TN 37228
615 242-0585

(G-814)
ROGERS GROUP INC
7885 S Victor Pike (47403-9473)
PHONE.................................812 824-8565
EMP: 31
SALES (corp-wide): 1B Privately Held
SIC: 1442 Construction sand & gravel
PA: Rogers Group, Inc.
421 Great Circle Rd
Nashville TN 37228
615 242-0585

▲ = Import ▼ =Export
◆ =Import/Export

(G-815)
ROGERS GROUP INC
2944 E Covenanter Dr (47401-5494)
PHONE...................................812 332-6341
Fax: 812 332-0406
Darin Matson, *President*
Andy Williams, *Vice Pres*
Neil Woldridge, *Manager*
Sara Pearson, *Info Tech Mgr*
EMP: 65
SALES (corp-wide): 1B **Privately Held**
WEB: www.rogersgroupinc.com
SIC: **1221** 5032 Bituminous coal & lignite-surface mining; stone, crushed or broken
PA: Rogers Group, Inc.
421 Great Circle Rd
Nashville TN 37228
615 242-0585

(G-816)
ROGERS GROUP INC
550 S Adams St (47403-2165)
PHONE...................................812 333-6324
Mike Agee, *Vice Pres*
EMP: 35
SALES (corp-wide): 1B **Privately Held**
WEB: www.rogersgroupinc.com
SIC: **5032** 1794 2431 2426 Stone, crushed or broken; concrete mixtures; asphalt mixture; excavation work; millwork; hardwood dimension & flooring mills; construction sand & gravel; coal mining services
PA: Rogers Group, Inc.
421 Great Circle Rd
Nashville TN 37228
615 242-0585

(G-817)
ROGERS GROUP INC
Also Called: Bloomington Asphalt & Cnstr
1110 N Oard Rd (47404-9365)
PHONE...................................812 333-8550
Fax: 812 336-5502
Phil Tews, *Purchasing*
Gary Barrow, *Director*
EMP: 40
SALES (corp-wide): 1B **Privately Held**
WEB: www.rogersgroupinc.com
SIC: **1611** 2951 General contractor, highway & street construction; asphalt paving mixtures & blocks
PA: Rogers Group, Inc.
421 Great Circle Rd
Nashville TN 37228
615 242-0585

(G-818)
ROSMARINO CANDLES LLC
310 S High St (47401-7810)
PHONE...................................970 218-2835
Rachel Whitcomb, *Principal*
EMP: 2
SALES (est): 62.5K **Privately Held**
SIC: **3999** Candles

(G-819)
RUSH HOUR STATION
421 E 3rd St (47401-3630)
PHONE...................................812 323-7874
EMP: 4
SALES (est): 294.9K **Privately Held**
SIC: **3421** Table & food cutlery, including butchers'

(G-820)
SABIN CORPORATION
Also Called: Cook Polymer Technology
3800 W Constitution Ave (47403-3176)
P.O. Box 788 (47402-0788)
PHONE...................................812 323-4500
Fax: 812 339-3395
William A Cook, *President*
Dave Lessard, *Vice Pres*
Scott Lewis, *Opers Mgr*
Mike Davis, *QC Mgr*
Shannon Pilrose, *Research*
▲ EMP: 235
SQ FT: 70,000
SALES (est): 54.6MM
SALES (corp-wide): 980.1MM **Privately Held**
WEB: www.sabincorp.com
SIC: **3082** 3089 3083 Tubes, unsupported plastic; molding primary plastic; laminated plastics plate & sheet

PA: Cook Group Incorporated
750 N Daniels Way
Bloomington IN 47404
812 339-2235

(G-821)
SARAN INDUSTRIES LLC
1425 S Curry Pike (47403-2708)
PHONE...................................317 897-2170
John Warman, *Manager*
EMP: 100
SALES (corp-wide): 44.8MM **Privately Held**
SIC: **3398** 7699 4225 Metal heat treating; industrial equipment services; general warehousing & storage
PA: Saran Industries, Llc
1500 E Murden St
Kokomo IN 46901
317 897-2170

(G-822)
SCHOLARS INN BAKEHOUSE
125 N College Ave (47404-3947)
PHONE...................................812 331-6029
Fax: 812 331-6034
Michael Pollack, *Partner*
Michael Fitzgerald, *Partner*
EMP: 70
SQ FT: 30,000
SALES: 1.2MM **Privately Held**
WEB: www.bakehouse.com
SIC: **2051** 5461 Bakery: wholesale or wholesale/retail combined; bakeries

(G-823)
SELECT EMBROIDERY/TOP IT OFF
1713 N College Ave Ste 3 (47404-2479)
PHONE...................................812 337-8049
Fax: 812 337-8059
Kim Arteel, *Owner*
EMP: 10
SALES (est): 510K **Privately Held**
WEB: www.selectembroidery.com
SIC: **5699** 2395 2396 Customized clothing & apparel; embroidery products, except schiffli machine; automotive & apparel trimmings

(G-824)
SKIRT & SATCHEL ✪
101 W Kirkwood Ave # 107 (47404-6129)
PHONE...................................812 727-0292
EMP: 2 EST: 2017
SALES (est): 77.4K **Privately Held**
SIC: **3161** Satchels

(G-825)
SLEEPY OWL SOFTWARE LLC
3030 E Amy Ln (47408-4223)
PHONE...................................765 299-2862
Christopher Ingerson, *Principal*
EMP: 2 EST: 2016
SALES (est): 68.6K **Privately Held**
SIC: **7372** Prepackaged software

(G-826)
SOAPY SOAP COMPANY
2786 E Bressingham Way (47401-4169)
PHONE...................................812 575-0005
Mohammed Mahdi, *Director*
Anthony Duncan, *Director*
EMP: 2 EST: 2012
SALES (est): 247.5K **Privately Held**
SIC: **2841** 2844 Soap & other detergents; soap: granulated, liquid, cake, flaked or chip; shampoos, rinses, conditioners: hair; shaving preparations

(G-827)
SOCIETY FOR ETHNMUSICOLOGY INC
800 E 3rd St (47405-3657)
PHONE...................................812 855-6672
Fax: 812 855-6673
Anne Rasmussen, *President*
Ellen Koskoff, *Editor*
Stephen Stuempfle, *Director*
EMP: 2
SALES: 501.7K **Privately Held**
SIC: **2721** Periodicals: publishing only

(G-828)
SOLUTION TREE INC (PA)
555 N Morton St (47404-3730)
PHONE...................................812 336-7700
Jeff Jones, *CEO*
David G Elmore, *Ch of Bd*
Ed Ackerman, *President*
Lisa Bacon, *Partner*
Paul Breda, *Partner*
EMP: 110
SQ FT: 28,000
SALES: 45MM **Privately Held**
WEB: www.nationaleducationalservice.com
SIC: **8211** 8748 2731 Specialty education; educational consultant; book publishing

(G-829)
SOUTHFIELD CORPORATION
7100 S Old State Road 37 (47403-9427)
PHONE...................................812 824-1355
Greg Petro, *Manager*
EMP: 25
SALES (corp-wide): 285MM **Privately Held**
WEB: www.prairiegroup.com
SIC: **3273** 3271 1442 Ready-mixed concrete; concrete block & brick; construction sand & gravel
PA: Southfield Corporation
8995 W 95th St
Palos Hills IL 60465
708 344-1000

(G-830)
SPECIALTY CNC INCORPORATED
4900 W State Road 45 (47403-9341)
PHONE...................................812 825-7982
Michael Baker, *President*
Roger Shoufler, *Vice Pres*
EMP: 5
SQ FT: 3,000
SALES: 1MM **Privately Held**
SIC: **3599** Machine shop, jobbing & repair

(G-831)
SPECTRUM PRESS INC
1300 N Loesch Rd (47404-9108)
PHONE...................................812 335-1945
Fax: 812 335-1953
Stan Thomas, *President*
David Thomas, *Corp Secy*
John Garrison, *Vice Pres*
EMP: 30
SALES (est): 4.1MM **Privately Held**
SIC: **2752** 2791 2789 Commercial printing, offset; typesetting; bookbinding & related work

(G-832)
STILLIONS SAW MILL
Also Called: Stillions Sawmill
7208 S Rockport Rd (47403-9157)
PHONE...................................812 824-6542
Dan Stillion, *Owner*
EMP: 4
SALES (est): 260K **Privately Held**
SIC: **2421** Lumber: rough, sawed or planed

(G-833)
STUDIO INDIANA
430 N Sewell Rd (47408-9408)
PHONE...................................812 332-5073
John Bower, *Owner*
EMP: 2
SALES (est): 90.4K **Privately Held**
WEB: www.studioindiana.com
SIC: **2731** Book publishing

(G-834)
TASUS CORPORATION (HQ)
300 N Daniels Way (47404-9139)
PHONE...................................812 333-6500
Fax: 812 333-6521
Melanie Walker, *President*
Yasuyuki O'Hara, *Chairman*
Craig Slater, *Corp Secy*
Shannon Duncan, *COO*
Mike Schab, *Plant Mgr*
▲ EMP: 206
SQ FT: 100,000

SALES: 77.7MM
SALES (corp-wide): 437.5MM **Privately Held**
WEB: www.tasus.com
SIC: **3089** 7389 Injection molding of plastics; trading stamp promotion & redemption
PA: Tsuchiya Co.Ltd.
2-9-29, Kamimaezu, Naka-Ku
Nagoya AIC 460-0
523 315-451

(G-835)
TD INNOVATIONS
515 S Woodscrest Dr # 202 (47401-5303)
PHONE...................................530 477-9780
Thomas K Larsen, *President*
Debbie Williams, *Vice Pres*
▲ EMP: 3
SQ FT: 16,000
SALES (est): 787.4K **Privately Held**
WEB: www.shorelinecases.com
SIC: **5065** 3161 Electronic parts & equipment; traveling bags

(G-836)
TEC PHOTOGRAPHY
Also Called: Beautiful Brides By TEC
1011 W Gourley Pike (47404-2132)
PHONE...................................812 332-9847
Terence E Comstock, *Owner*
Margaret Comstock, *Co-Owner*
EMP: 2
SALES: 50K **Privately Held**
WEB: www.tecphotography.com
SIC: **7221** 2759 Photographer, still or video; letterpress printing

(G-837)
TENDRE PRESS LLC
134 N Overhill Dr (47408-4243)
PHONE...................................812 606-9563
Ann Kreilkamp, *Principal*
EMP: 2
SALES (est): 82.7K **Privately Held**
SIC: **2741** Miscellaneous publishing

(G-838)
TEXACON CUT STONE LLC
4790 Fluck Mill Rd (47403-8900)
PHONE...................................812 824-3211
Darrin Shirley, *Sales Staff*
Marci Bennett, *Office Mgr*
James Pittman, *Shareholder*
EMP: 6
SALES (est): 974.5K **Privately Held**
SIC: **3281** Cut stone & stone products

(G-839)
THE TAP
101 N College Ave (47404-3947)
PHONE...................................812 486-9795
Mallory Korpalski, *Manager*
EMP: 10
SALES (est): 836.2K **Privately Held**
SIC: **2082** 2599 Beer (alcoholic beverage); bar, restaurant & cafeteria furniture

(G-840)
THOMAS CHATEAU WINERY
118 N Walnut St (47404-4911)
PHONE...................................812 339-9463
Charles Thomas, *Principal*
EMP: 3 EST: 2011
SALES (est): 191.5K **Privately Held**
SIC: **5921** 2084 Liquor stores; wines

(G-841)
THORNTONS WELDING
Also Called: Thornton's Welding Serv
4439 W Arlington Rd (47404-1358)
PHONE...................................812 332-8564
Gene Thornton, *Owner*
EMP: 2
SALES (est): 88K **Privately Held**
SIC: **7692** 3792 3471 Welding repair; travel trailers & campers; plating & polishing

(G-842)
TIMOTHY REED CARRY ME MUS PUBG
610 S Washington St Apt D (47401-3626)
PHONE...................................812 322-7187
EMP: 2 EST: 2016

SALES (est): 61.1K **Privately Held**
SIC: 2741 Miscellaneous publishing

(G-843)
TRAFFORD HOLDINGS LTD
Also Called: Trafford Publishing
1663 S Liberty Dr (47403-5161)
PHONE....................................888 232-4444
Kevin G Gregory, *Principal*
Lorna Faye, *Marketing Staff*
Geneva Quinn, *Marketing Staff*
Louella Pace, *Consultant*
Keith Walker, *Consultant*
EMP: 5
SALES (est): 2.5MM
SALES (corp-wide): 52.4MM **Privately Held**
SIC: 2731 Books: publishing only
PA: Author Solutions Llc
   1663 S Liberty Dr
   Bloomington IN 47403
   812 339-6000

(G-844)
TRUFAB STAINLESS
2126 W Industrial Park Dr (47404-2687)
PHONE....................................812 287-8278
Drew Hoffman, *Principal*
EMP: 8
SALES (est): 940.1K **Privately Held**
SIC: 3599 Machine shop, jobbing & repair

(G-845)
TRUSTEES INDIANA UNIVERSITY
Also Called: Slavica Publishers
2611 E 10th St Rm 160 (47408-2603)
PHONE....................................812 856-4186
Vaughn Nuest, *Dept Chairman*
Jennifer Brooks, *Project Mgr*
Carey Beam, *Director*
Amy Cope, *Director*
George Fowler, *Director*
EMP: 4
SALES (corp-wide): 2.2B **Privately Held**
WEB: www.iupui.edu
SIC: 2721 8221 Trade journals: publishing & printing; university
PA: Trustees Indiana University
   Bryan Hall 107 S Ind Ave St Bryan Ha
   Bloomington IN 47405
   812 855-4848

(G-846)
TRUSTEES INDIANA UNIVERSITY
Also Called: Indiana Daily Student
120 Ernie Pyle Hall Ind (47405)
PHONE....................................812 855-0763
Fax: 812 855-8009
Dave Adams, *Principal*
Sara Amanto, *Chief*
Alexandra Mahoney, *Relations*
EMP: 300
SALES (corp-wide): 2.2B **Privately Held**
WEB: www.iupui.edu
SIC: 2711 2731 Newspapers: publishing only, not printed on site; book publishing
PA: Trustees Indiana University
   Bryan Hall 107 S Ind Ave St Bryan Ha
   Bloomington IN 47405
   812 855-4848

(G-847)
TRUSTEES INDIANA UNIVERSITY
Also Called: Indiana Review
465 Ballantine Hall 1020 1020 E (47405)
PHONE....................................812 855-3439
Abdel Shakur, *Principal*
Jenny Burdge, *Assoc Editor*
EMP: 8
SALES (corp-wide): 2.2B **Privately Held**
WEB: www.iupui.edu
SIC: 2721 8221 Magazines: publishing only, not printed on site; university
PA: Trustees Indiana University
   Bryan Hall 107 S Ind Ave St Bryan Ha
   Bloomington IN 47405
   812 855-4848

(G-848)
TRUSTEES INDIANA UNIVERSITY
Also Called: Linguistics Club
900 E 7th St (47405-3905)
PHONE....................................812 855-4848
Robin Gress, *Manager*
EMP: 20
SALES (corp-wide): 2.2B **Privately Held**
WEB: www.iupui.edu
SIC: 2741 8221 Miscellaneous publishing; university
PA: Trustees Indiana University
   Bryan Hall 107 S Ind Ave St Bryan Ha
   Bloomington IN 47405
   812 855-4848

(G-849)
TUSCA 2
3815 N Collins Dr (47404-9344)
PHONE....................................812 876-2857
Joel Milam, *Partner*
EMP: 5 EST: 2016
SALES (est): 178.7K **Privately Held**
SIC: 3499 Fabricated metal products

(G-850)
UGO BARS LLC
1019 W Howe St (47403-2238)
PHONE....................................812 322-3499
Tracy Gates, *Principal*
EMP: 2
SALES (est): 150.9K **Privately Held**
SIC: 2064 Candy & other confectionery products

(G-851)
UPLAND BREWING COMPANY INC
Also Called: Upland Brewing Co.
350 W 11th St (47404-3720)
PHONE....................................812 330-7421
Fax: 812 330-7421
Douglas G Dayhoff, *President*
Mark Sattinger, *Principal*
Tim Spears, *Opers Staff*
Dan Barrett, *Controller*
Sarah Nolan, *Manager*
EMP: 25
SALES (est): 5MM **Privately Held**
WEB: www.uplandbeer.com
SIC: 2082 5813 5812 Beer (alcoholic beverage); drinking places; eating places

(G-852)
VINCENT ALIANO ELC HTG & COOLG
5128 W Vernal Pike (47404-8712)
PHONE....................................812 332-3332
Vincent Aliano, *Owner*
EMP: 2
SALES (est): 140.2K **Privately Held**
SIC: 3699 1711 Electrical equipment & supplies; heating systems repair & maintenance

(G-853)
WASHINGTON 2 MOUNT PUBLI
403 E 3rd St (47401-3601)
PHONE....................................812 332-1600
Fax: 812 333-8299
Ira B Zinman, *Principal*
EMP: 2 EST: 2001
SALES (est): 103.2K **Privately Held**
SIC: 2741 Miscellaneous publishing

(G-854)
WILBERT SEXTON CORPORATION (PA)
Also Called: Sexton Vault Company
1908 W Allen St (47403-2840)
PHONE....................................812 336-6469
Fax: 812 334-0902
Everett J Sexton, *Ch of Bd*
Mark Sexton, *President*
Tina Sexton, *Admin Sec*
EMP: 9 EST: 1946
SQ FT: 5,500
SALES (est): 1.4MM **Privately Held**
WEB: www.meighendemers.com
SIC: 3272 Burial vaults, concrete or precast terrazzo

(G-855)
WILBERT SEXTON CORPORATION
2332 W 3rd St (47404-5219)
PHONE....................................812 334-0883
Mark Sexton, *Branch Mgr*
EMP: 2
SALES (corp-wide): 1.4MM **Privately Held**
SIC: 3281 Burial vaults, stone
PA: Wilbert Sexton Corporation
   1908 W Allen St
   Bloomington IN 47403
   812 336-6469

(G-856)
WILLIAMS BROS HEALTH CARE PHA
Also Called: United Drugs
574 S Landmark Ave (47403-3239)
PHONE....................................812 335-0000
Nathan Jabhart, *Manager*
EMP: 25
SALES (corp-wide): 88.6MM **Privately Held**
SIC: 5912 7352 5999 5169 Drug stores; medical equipment rental; telephone & communication equipment; oxygen; hospital equipment & furniture; wheelchair lifts
PA: Williams Bros. Health Care Pharmacy, Inc.
   10 Williams Brothers Dr
   Washington IN 47501
   812 254-2497

(G-857)
WILSON TOOL & ENGINEERING INC
2460 N Curry Pike (47404-1410)
PHONE....................................812 334-1110
Fax: 812 334-1110
William A Wilson Jr, *President*
William A Wilson Sr, *Admin Sec*
EMP: 8
SQ FT: 7,000
SALES (est): 450K **Privately Held**
SIC: 3599 Machine shop, jobbing & repair

(G-858)
WINTERS ASSOC PRMTNAL PDTS INC (PA)
Also Called: Thadco
1048 W 17th St (47404-3338)
PHONE....................................812 330-7000
Fax: 812 330-7002
Kathy Slinkard, *President*
Kathy A Slinkard, *Corp Secy*
Kelly Slinkard, *Treasurer*
Julie Hamm, *Administration*
EMP: 14
SQ FT: 10,000
SALES (est): 2.6MM **Privately Held**
WEB: www.brentslinkard.com
SIC: 5199 3993 2396 2395 Advertising specialties; signs & advertising specialties; automotive & apparel trimmings; pleating & stitching

(G-859)
WRACO ENTERPRISES INC
Also Called: Fine Print
125 S Westplex Ave (47404-5080)
P.O. Box 1401 (47402-1401)
PHONE....................................812 339-3987
Fax: 812 323-7946
Joe Wray, *President*
EMP: 8 EST: 1977
SQ FT: 8,500
SALES (est): 790K **Privately Held**
WEB: www.fineprint125.com
SIC: 2752 Commercial printing, offset

(G-860)
X PRINTWEAR INC
2121 S Yost Ave (47403-3193)
PHONE....................................812 336-0700
Fax: 812 332-1146
Dax William Collins, *President*
Dax Collins, *President*
EMP: 15
SQ FT: 5,000
SALES (est): 1.2MM **Privately Held**
WEB: www.xprintwear.com
SIC: 2759 Screen printing

(G-861)
XLIBRIS CORPORATION
1663 S Liberty Dr Ste 200 (47403-5161)
PHONE....................................812 671-9162
Joe Steinbach, *President*
Keith Ogorek, *Senior VP*
Bill Becher, *Vice Pres*
Ronald Reese, *Marketing Mgr*
Matthew Martinez, *Marketing Staff*
▲ EMP: 99
SQ FT: 21,000
SALES (est): 8.5MM
SALES (corp-wide): 52.4MM **Privately Held**
WEB: www.xlibris.com
SIC: 2731 7375 Book publishing; information retrieval services
PA: Author Solutions Llc
   1663 S Liberty Dr
   Bloomington IN 47403
   812 339-6000

Bluffton
Wells County

(G-862)
ADVERTISER INC
2917 E State Road 124 C (46714-9388)
P.O. Box 493 (46714-0493)
PHONE....................................260 824-4770
Fax: 260 824-3558
Nidia E Myers, *President*
Nidia Myers, *President*
Arlene Holland, *Vice Pres*
EMP: 2 EST: 1973
SALES (est): 120K **Privately Held**
SIC: 2741 Shopping news: publishing only, not printed on site

(G-863)
ALEXIN LLC
1390 S Adams St (46714-9030)
PHONE....................................260 353-3100
Fax: 260 846-0740
Tom Horter, *President*
▲ EMP: 68
SQ FT: 100
SALES (est): 37.7MM
SALES (corp-wide): 218.8MM **Privately Held**
SIC: 3354 Aluminum extruded products
HQ: Matalco Inc
   850 Intermodal Dr
   Brampton ON L6T 0
   905 790-2511

(G-864)
ARCHER-DANIELS-MIDLAND COMPANY
Also Called: ADM
1800 W Western Ave (46714-9788)
PHONE....................................260 824-0079
Fax: 260 824-9391
Russ Johnson, *Branch Mgr*
EMP: 68
SALES (corp-wide): 60.8B **Publicly Held**
WEB: www.admalliancenutrition.com
SIC: 2041 5191 Flour & other grain mill products; farm supplies
PA: Archer-Daniels-Midland Company
   77 W Wacker Dr Ste 4600
   Chicago IL 60601
   312 634-8100

(G-865)
AT FERRELL COMPANY INC (PA)
1440 S Adams St (46714-9793)
PHONE....................................260 824-3400
Fax: 260 824-5463
B Steven Stuller, *President*
Tom Haines, *Chairman*
Dennis Gerwig, *Sales Staff*
Dale Zeigler, *Admin Sec*
◆ EMP: 42
SQ FT: 58,000
SALES (est): 9.4MM **Privately Held**
WEB: www.atferrell.com
SIC: 3523 Farm machinery & equipment

(G-866)
AUTO & SIGN SPECIALTIES INC
Also Called: Baller Signs
3124 E State Road 124 (46714-9301)
PHONE..............................260 824-1987
Steve B Baller, *Owner*
EMP: 3
SALES (est): 348.6K **Privately Held**
SIC: 3993 Signs & advertising specialties

(G-867)
BLUFFTON MOTOR WORKS LLC (DH)
410 E Spring St (46714-3737)
PHONE..............................800 579-8527
David L Nussear, *CEO*
Christopher R Parke, *CFO*
▲ **EMP:** 194
SALES: 66.4MM **Privately Held**
WEB: www.capitalworks.net
SIC: 3621 Motors, electric

(G-868)
BLUFFTON RUBBER
810 Lancaster St (46714-1700)
P.O. Box 255 (46714-0255)
PHONE..............................260 824-4501
Christina Rouch, *Principal*
EMP: 2
SALES (est): 137.9K **Privately Held**
SIC: 3061 Mechanical rubber goods

(G-869)
BRC RUBBER & PLASTICS INC
810 Lancaster St (46714-1716)
P.O. Box 255 (46714-0255)
PHONE..............................260 827-0871
Guy Broderick, *Manager*
Patricia Decker, *Director*
EMP: 100
SALES (corp-wide): 171.4MM **Privately Held**
SIC: 3061 3053 3069 Automotive rubber goods (mechanical); gaskets, packing & sealing devices; molded rubber products
PA: Brc Rubber & Plastics, Inc.
1029a W State Blvd
Fort Wayne IN 46808
260 693-2171

(G-870)
BUCKHORN INC
785 Decker Dr (46714-9787)
PHONE..............................260 824-0997
Fax: 260 824-5997
Rick Singer, *Branch Mgr*
EMP: 75
SALES (corp-wide): 547MM **Publicly Held**
WEB: www.buckhorninc.com
SIC: 3089 3732 Molding primary plastic; boat building & repairing
HQ: Buckhorn Inc.
55 W Techne Center Dr A
Milford OH 45150
513 831-4402

(G-871)
CROY MACHINE & FABRICATION
2744 Se Mulberry St (46714-9324)
PHONE..............................260 565-3682
Fax: 260 565-3971
Randy Gentis, *President*
Tedd Harter, *Treasurer*
EMP: 3
SQ FT: 5,200
SALES (est): 170K **Privately Held**
SIC: 7699 3443 Farm machinery repair; fabricated plate work (boiler shop)

(G-872)
DEDRICK TOOL & DIE INC
2929 E State Road 124 (46714-9366)
PHONE..............................260 824-3334
Fax: 260 824-9073
Deborah Dedrick, *President*
EMP: 7
SQ FT: 7,000
SALES (est): 962.7K **Privately Held**
WEB: www.dedricktool.com
SIC: 3544 Special dies & tools

(G-873)
EDGE MANUFACTURING INC
1274 S Adams St (46714-9384)
PHONE..............................260 827-0482
Eric Gerber, *President*
Doug Gerber, *Vice Pres*
Lori Gerber, *Admin Sec*
EMP: 30
SQ FT: 20,000
SALES (est): 7.2MM **Privately Held**
WEB: www.edgemanufacturing.net
SIC: 3449 Miscellaneous metalwork

(G-874)
ERIE-HAVEN INC
235 S Adams St (46714-9034)
PHONE..............................260 353-1133
Cherie Moser, *Branch Mgr*
EMP: 39
SALES (corp-wide): 25.2MM **Privately Held**
SIC: 3273 Ready-mixed concrete
PA: Erie-Haven Inc
3909 Limestone Dr
Fort Wayne IN 46809
260 478-1674

(G-875)
GENERAL MANUFACTURING INC
Also Called: Saftlite
1336 W Wiley Ave (46714-2244)
PHONE..............................260 824-3627
Fax: 260 824-3448
Paul J Reiff, *President*
Paul Reiff, *President*
Lu Reiff, *Corp Secy*
Sarah J Meister, *Vice Pres*
Matthew J Reiff, *Vice Pres*
▲ **EMP:** 50
SQ FT: 35,000
SALES (est): 10.6MM **Privately Held**
WEB: www.saftlite.com
SIC: 3648 Lighting equipment

(G-876)
GREEN PLAINS BLUFFTON LLC
1441 S Adams St (46714-9793)
P.O. Box 297 (46714-0297)
PHONE..............................260 846-0011
Todd Becker, *Ch of Bd*
Stephen J Hogan, *President*
Troy D Flowers, *Vice Pres*
EMP: 61
SALES (est): 15.4MM
SALES (corp-wide): 3.6B **Publicly Held**
SIC: 2869 Ethyl alcohol, ethanol
PA: Green Plains Inc.
1811 Aksarben Dr
Omaha NE 68106
402 884-8700

(G-877)
HMS ZOO DIETS INC
1222 Echo Ln (46714-2805)
PHONE..............................260 824-5157
Janis Higginbottom, *President*
A J Higginbottom, *Vice Pres*
EMP: 2
SALES (est): 196.7K **Privately Held**
SIC: 2048 Prepared feeds

(G-878)
IMPRESSIVE STAMPING & MFG CO
1690 E 250 N (46714-9232)
PHONE..............................260 824-2610
Joe Elkins, *President*
Benjamin Nagel, *Vice Pres*
EMP: 4
SQ FT: 21,000
SALES (est): 206.4K **Privately Held**
SIC: 3469 3465 Metal stampings; moldings or trim, automobile: stamped metal; body parts, automobile: stamped metal; tops, automobile: stamped metal; fenders, automobile: stamped or pressed metal

(G-879)
INVENTURE FOODS INC
705 W Dustman Rd (46714-1178)
PHONE..............................260 824-2800
Teri Huffman, *CFO*
Kim Sirinsky, *Supervisor*
EMP: 24

SALES (corp-wide): 644.8MM **Privately Held**
SIC: 2096 Potato chips & similar snacks
HQ: Inventure Foods, Inc.
20860 N Ttum Blvd Ste 300
Phoenix AZ 85050

(G-880)
IRVING MATERIALS INC
Also Called: I M I
2321 E 150 N (46714-9237)
PHONE..............................260 824-3428
Joe Langel, *Branch Mgr*
EMP: 10
SALES (corp-wide): 800.6MM **Privately Held**
SIC: 3273 Ready-mixed concrete
PA: Irving Materials, Inc.
8032 N State Road 9
Greenfield IN 46140
317 326-3101

(G-881)
MCHENRY MANUFACTURING INC
1325 W Wiley Ave (46714-2248)
PHONE..............................260 824-8146
Joseph Milot, *President*
EMP: 10
SQ FT: 6,500
SALES (est): 1.7MM
SALES (corp-wide): 84.8MM **Privately Held**
SIC: 2259 Stockinettes, knit
PA: Protective Industrial Products, Inc.
968 Albany Shaker Rd
Latham NY 12110
518 861-0133

(G-882)
METALDYNE M&A BLUFFTON LLC
Also Called: American Axle
131 W Harvest Rd (46714-9007)
PHONE..............................260 824-2360
Thomas A Amato, *President*
Robert Defauw, *Vice Pres*
Bill Dickey, *Vice Pres*
Christoph Guhe, *Vice Pres*
Ben Schmidt, *Vice Pres*
▲ **EMP:** 90
SQ FT: 190
SALES (est): 38.2MM
SALES (corp-wide): 6.2B **Publicly Held**
WEB: www.metaldyne.com
SIC: 3714 7537 Motor vehicle parts & accessories; motor vehicle engines & parts; automotive transmission repair shops
HQ: Metaldyne Sinterforged Products, Llc
197 West Creek Rd
Saint Marys PA 15857
814 834-1222

(G-883)
NEWS BANNER PUBLICATIONS INC
Also Called: Echo, The
125 N Johnson St (46714-1926)
P.O. Box 436 (46714-0436)
PHONE..............................260 824-0224
Fax: 260 824-0700
Mark Miller, *President*
George B Witwer, *Vice Pres*
Diane Witwer, *Treasurer*
EMP: 50 **EST:** 1892
SQ FT: 6,250
SALES (est): 1.7MM **Privately Held**
WEB: www.news-banner.com
SIC: 2711 8611 2752 2741 Newspapers: publishing only, not printed on site; business associations; commercial printing, lithographic; miscellaneous publishing

(G-884)
PARLOR CITY TROPHY & APPAREL
224 W Market St (46714-1931)
PHONE..............................260 824-0216
Tracy Pace, *Partner*
Elanie Line, *Partner*
EMP: 2
SALES (est): 155.4K **Privately Held**
SIC: 5999 2759 Trophies & plaques; screen printing

(G-885)
POORE BROTHERS - BLUFFTON LLC
Also Called: Wabash Snacks
705 W Dustman Rd (46714-1178)
PHONE..............................260 824-2800
Fax: 219 824-4388
Eric Kufel,
Glen Flook,
Tom Freeze,
EMP: 260
SALES (est): 30.7MM
SALES (corp-wide): 644.8MM **Privately Held**
SIC: 2096 5145 2099 Potato chips & similar snacks; confectionery; food preparations
HQ: Inventure Foods, Inc.
20860 N Ttum Blvd Ste 300
Phoenix AZ 85050

(G-886)
PRETZELS INC (PA)
123 W Harvest Rd (46714-9007)
P.O. Box 503 (46714-0503)
PHONE..............................260 824-4838
Fax: 260 824-2868
Steven R Huggins, *CEO*
William Huggins, *President*
William A Mann II, *President*
Jodi Manning, *Project Mgr*
Tony Mann, *Opers Mgr*
▼ **EMP:** 169
SQ FT: 200,000
SALES (est): 78.3MM **Privately Held**
WEB: www.pretzels-inc.com
SIC: 2052 2099 Pretzels; food preparations

(G-887)
PRINT SOURCE CORPORATION
213 E Perry St (46714-2156)
PHONE..............................260 589-2842
Fax: 260 589-3032
Terry W Steffen, *President*
Gloria J Steffen, *Corp Secy*
EMP: 3 **EST:** 1970
SQ FT: 2,200
SALES (est): 425K **Privately Held**
WEB: www.myprinters.com
SIC: 2752 Commercial printing, offset

(G-888)
PROFESSIONAL PRINT BROKERS
Also Called: Professional Print & Copy
2020 N Main St Ste B (46714-4105)
PHONE..............................260 824-2328
EMP: 3
SQ FT: 6,000
SALES: 135.1K **Privately Held**
SIC: 2759 5943 Copy Center

(G-889)
RITTENHOUSE SQUARE
312 S Main St (46714-2519)
PHONE..............................260 824-4200
George Rittenhouse, *Partner*
Nina Rittenhouse, *Co-Owner*
EMP: 6
SQ FT: 3,000
SALES (est): 416.1K **Privately Held**
SIC: 2369 2389 Girls' & children's outerwear; theatrical costumes

(G-890)
ROCK CREEK STONE LLC
781 N 500 W (46714-9752)
P.O. Box 6 (46714-0006)
PHONE..............................260 694-6880
Darin Johnson, *Branch Mgr*
EMP: 5
SALES (corp-wide): 460.6MM **Privately Held**
SIC: 1422 Cement rock, crushed & broken-quarrying
PA: Rock Creek Stone, Llc
717 Riverview Dr
Bluffton IN 46714
260 249-4446

(G-891)
SILVER PETROLEUM CORP
409 N Main St (46714-1307)
P.O. Box 476 (46714-0476)
PHONE..........................260 824-2220
Gene Moser, *President*
EMP: 3
SALES (est): 298.6K **Privately Held**
SIC: 1382 Oil & gas exploration services

(G-892)
SIMPLY SILVER
1165 Fawncrest Ct (46714-3868)
PHONE..........................260 824-4667
Wayne Barker, *Principal*
EMP: 2
SALES (est): 93K **Privately Held**
SIC: 3914 Silverware

(G-893)
STANDARD PLASTIC CORP
850 Decker Dr (46714-9769)
P.O. Box 355 (46714-0355)
PHONE..........................260 824-0214
Fax: 260 824-3290
Philip E Leonard, *President*
EMP: 13 **EST:** 1955
SQ FT: 36,000
SALES (est): 3MM **Privately Held**
SIC: 3089 Injection molded finished plastic products; thermoformed finished plastic products

(G-894)
STAR ENGINEERING & MCH CO INC
1717 Lancaster St (46714-1512)
PHONE..........................260 824-4825
Fax: 260 824-4845
Keith Steffen, *President*
Paul Simon, *Corp Secy*
Eric Steffen, *Vice Pres*
Tom Steffen, *Controller*
▲ **EMP:** 38 **EST:** 1965
SQ FT: 39,000
SALES: 8.4MM
SALES (corp-wide): 9.5MM **Privately Held**
WEB: www.star-eng.com
SIC: 3599 3568 7692 Machine shop, jobbing & repair; power transmission equipment; welding repair
PA: U. S. Group, Inc.
20580 Hoover St
Detroit MI 48205
313 372-7900

(G-895)
TROYER BROTHERS INC
6691 W State Rd 124 (46714)
PHONE..........................260 565-2244
Mark Troyer, *President*
EMP: 21
SALES (est): 5.5MM **Privately Held**
SIC: 3699 5084 Laser welding, drilling & cutting equipment; hydraulic systems equipment & supplies

(G-896)
W W WILLIAMS COMPANY LLC
Also Called: Midwest Division - Bluffton
610 W Washington St (46714-1851)
PHONE..........................260 827-0553
Fax: 260 827-0644
Alan Gatlin, *CEO*
Dorian Norstrom, *Administration*
EMP: 14
SALES (corp-wide): 2.3B **Privately Held**
SIC: 3621 Motor generator sets; power generators
HQ: The W W Williams Company Llc
5025 Bradenton Ave # 130
Dublin OH 43017
614 228-5000

(G-897)
WEAVER WOODWORKING
7795 E 300 S (46714-9321)
PHONE..........................260 565-3647
Eli Weaver, *Principal*
EMP: 2
SALES (est): 170.6K **Privately Held**
SIC: 2431 Millwork

(G-898)
YODERS QUALITY BARNS
7207 E State Road 124 (46714-9334)
PHONE..........................260 565-4122
John Yoder, *Owner*
EMP: 2
SALES (est): 150K **Privately Held**
SIC: 3448 Prefabricated metal buildings

Boggstown
Shelby County

(G-899)
BIKE-N-TRIKES
6597 W 300 N (46110-9708)
PHONE..........................317 835-4544
Art Bensheimer, *CEO*
EMP: 3
SQ FT: 3,000
SALES: 400K **Privately Held**
SIC: 3751 7699 Motorcycles, bicycles & parts; motorcycle repair service

(G-900)
GREENWOOD LIGHT & SIGN SERVICE
7955 W 400 N (46110-9730)
PHONE..........................317 840-5729
EMP: 2
SALES (est): 183.4K **Privately Held**
SIC: 3993 Signs & advertising specialties

(G-901)
JOHNSONS WELDING SERVICE
7908 W 525 N (46110-9728)
PHONE..........................317 835-2438
Danny Johnson, *Principal*
EMP: 2
SALES (est): 104.3K **Privately Held**
SIC: 7692 Welding repair

(G-902)
RPF INC
6643 W Boggstown Rd (46110-9703)
PHONE..........................317 727-6386
James Townsend, *President*
EMP: 5 **EST:** 2009
SALES: 250K **Privately Held**
SIC: 2499 Food handling & processing products, wood

(G-903)
WITHAM MACHINE
8429 W 525 N (46110-9726)
PHONE..........................317 835-2076
David Witham, *Owner*
EMP: 2 **EST:** 1988
SALES: 125K **Privately Held**
SIC: 2673 Bags: plastic, laminated & coated

Boonville
Warrick County

(G-904)
A-FAB LLC
977 Hyrock Blvd (47601-9571)
P.O. Box 548 (47601-0548)
PHONE..........................812 897-0900
Clay Smith, *Mng Member*
Ted Hemmelgarn,
▲ **EMP:** 83
SALES (est): 14.4MM **Privately Held**
SIC: 3714 5015 Motor vehicle parts & accessories; motor vehicle parts, used

(G-905)
AFCO PERFORMANCE GROUP LLC (PA)
Also Called: Afco Racing Products
977 Hyrock Blvd (47601-9571)
P.O. Box 548 (47601-0548)
PHONE..........................812 897-0900
Fax: 812 897-1757
Jeff Scales, *President*
EMP: 2
SALES (est): 1.8MM **Privately Held**
SIC: 3465 5013 Body parts, automobile: stamped metal; automotive supplies & parts

(G-906)
ALLEGHENY PETROLEUM PDTS CO
422 W Degonia Rd (47601-9765)
PHONE..........................812 897-0760
Bill Fleming, *Branch Mgr*
EMP: 35
SALES (corp-wide): 91.2MM **Privately Held**
SIC: 2992 Lubricating oils & greases
PA: Allegheny Petroleum Products Co
999 Airbrake Ave
Wilmerding PA 15148
412 829-1990

(G-907)
AMERICAN FABRICATING
1302 N Rockport Rd (47601-2346)
P.O. Box 548 (47601-0548)
PHONE..........................812 897-0900
Fax: 812 897-1757
Scott Keyser, *Principal*
EMP: 2
SALES (est): 215.1K **Privately Held**
SIC: 3441 Fabricated structural metal

(G-908)
B-HIVE PRINTING
Also Called: Shipping Plus
804 W Main St (47601-3004)
PHONE..........................812 897-3905
Fax: 812 897-0545
Gail Bailey, *Owner*
EMP: 4
SQ FT: 4,000
SALES (est): 270K **Privately Held**
SIC: 2752 2759 Offset & photolithographic printing; promotional printing

(G-909)
BST CORP
1066 Hunter Blvd (47601-8710)
PHONE..........................812 925-7911
Lawrence Steenberg, *President*
EMP: 2
SALES (est): 174K **Privately Held**
SIC: 1389 Oil field services

(G-910)
BUXTON ENGINEERING INC
1322 S Rockport Rd (47601-7923)
PHONE..........................812 897-3609
Fax: 812 897-4609
Brad Buxton, *President*
EMP: 2
SALES (est): 75K **Privately Held**
WEB: www.buxtonengineering.com
SIC: 3599 Machine shop, jobbing & repair

(G-911)
C A DERR & COMPANY
601 S 3rd St (47601-1903)
P.O. Box 645 (47601-0645)
PHONE..........................812 897-2920
Joseph W Derr Jr, *President*
Barbara Byers, *Corp Secy*
John R Derr, *Vice Pres*
Barb Byers, *Manager*
EMP: 3
SALES (est): 237.7K **Privately Held**
SIC: 2087 Flavoring extracts & syrups

(G-912)
CLIENTS CHOICE LTD
2144 Wildwood Dr (47601-9340)
PHONE..........................812 853-2911
Fax: 812 858-9492
Rosanna Clayton, *President*
EMP: 2
SALES (est): 150K **Privately Held**
WEB: www.clientschoice.com
SIC: 3993 Advertising artwork

(G-913)
COUNTRY ESTATES
6222 Edwards Rd (47601-9542)
PHONE..........................812 925-6443
Virgil Creek, *Principal*
EMP: 2
SALES (est): 151.9K **Privately Held**
SIC: 1442 Common sand mining

(G-914)
INDUSTRIAL WOODKRAFT INC (PA)
811 Hyrock Blvd (47601)
P.O. Box 591 (47601-0591)
PHONE..........................812 897-4893
Fax: 812 897-4969
Stewart Phillips, *President*
Thad Leinenbach, *President*
David Lockhart, *Owner*
Shirley Phillips, *Corp Secy*
▼ **EMP:** 50
SQ FT: 64,000
SALES (est): 10MM **Privately Held**
SIC: 2448 2449 2441 Pallets, wood; skids, wood; wood containers; nailed wood boxes & shook

(G-915)
LINCOLN INDUSTRIES INC
110 W Division St (47601-1919)
P.O. Box 621 (47601-0621)
PHONE..........................812 897-0715
Fax: 812 897-0717
Seyed K Saboohi, *President*
Alan Carr, *Maint Spvr*
Tom Pryor, *Manager*
Gregory A Dueffert, *Admin Sec*
John Zoeller, *Admin Sec*
▲ **EMP:** 50 **EST:** 1981
SQ FT: 19,500
SALES: 5.8MM
SALES (corp-wide): 164.8MM **Privately Held**
WEB: www.lincolnind.com
SIC: 3089 Injection molding of plastics
PA: Zoeller Company
3649 Cane Run Rd
Louisville KY 40211
502 778-2731

(G-916)
LITTLE MFG LLC
2122 N State Route 61 (47601-8341)
PHONE..........................812 453-8137
Alan Elzer, *Principal*
EMP: 2
SALES (est): 152.3K **Privately Held**
SIC: 3999 Manufacturing industries

(G-917)
MILES FARM SUPPLY LLC
Also Called: Miles Farm Service
7187 State Hwy 66 E (47601)
PHONE..........................812 359-4463
Mike Rose, *Manager*
EMP: 11
SALES (corp-wide): 85.6MM **Privately Held**
SIC: 5191 5083 1541 2875 Chemicals, agricultural; fertilizer & fertilizer materials; seeds: field, garden & flower; agricultural machinery & equipment; grain elevator construction; fertilizers, mixing only
PA: Miles Farm Supply, Llc
2760 Keller Rd
Owensboro KY 42301
270 926-2420

(G-918)
MINING MACHINE PARTS INC
420 S 3rd St (47601-1726)
P.O. Box 529 (47601-0529)
PHONE..........................812 897-1256
Wayne Anderson, *President*
Mary Kay Anderson, *Corp Secy*
EMP: 8
SQ FT: 3,600
SALES (est): 2.1MM **Privately Held**
SIC: 5082 3599 Mining machinery & equipment, except petroleum; machine shop, jobbing & repair

(G-919)
NIX SANITARY SERVICE
703 S 2nd St (47601-1961)
PHONE..........................812 475-9774
Toll Free:..........................888 -
Bobbie Nix, *Owner*
Ryan Nix, *Partner*
Robert Nix, *Partner*
EMP: 3
SALES (est): 277.4K **Privately Held**
SIC: 3795 7359 Tanks & tank components; portable toilet rental

▲ = Import ▼=Export
◆ =Import/Export

(G-920)
PARKERS CUSTOM IRONWORKS LLC
1100 Mount Gilead Rd (47601-7831)
PHONE..................................812 897-3007
Mike Choe, *Owner*
EMP: 3 EST: 2001
SALES (est): 233.8K **Privately Held**
SIC: 3446 Architectural metalwork

(G-921)
PERFORMANCE ROD & CUSTOM INC
913 W Main St (47601-1567)
P.O. Box 207 (47601-0207)
PHONE..................................812 897-5805
Duane Davis, *President*
EMP: 8
SQ FT: 2,200
SALES (est): 906.7K **Privately Held**
SIC: 3714 Connecting rods, motor vehicle engine

(G-922)
SONS OF THUNDER
Also Called: Alliance Machine
1233 Mount Gilead Rd (47601-9302)
PHONE..................................812 897-4908
Mike Winge, *Owner*
EMP: 2
SALES (est): 194K **Privately Held**
SIC: 3482 Small arms ammunition

(G-923)
TRUSS SYSTEMS INC
810 Hyrock Blvd (47601)
P.O. Box 191 (47601-0191)
PHONE..................................812 897-3064
Fax: 812 897-3069
Stewart Phillips, *President*
Shirley Phillips, *Corp Secy*
EMP: 15
SALES (est): 2.2MM **Privately Held**
SIC: 2439 Trusses, wooden roof

(G-924)
WARRICK PUBLISHING CO INC (HQ)
204 W Locust St (47601-3005)
PHONE..................................812 897-2330
Fax: 812 897-3703
William J Brehm Sr, *Ch of Bd*
Gary Neal, *Publisher*
▲ EMP: 20
SQ FT: 840
SALES (est): 31.7MM
SALES (corp-wide): 224.9MM **Privately Held**
SIC: 2711 Commercial printing & newspaper publishing combined; job printing & newspaper publishing combined
PA: Brehm Communications, Inc.
    16644 W Bernardo Dr # 300
    San Diego CA 92127
    858 451-6200

(G-925)
WILHITE INDUSTRIES INC
5833 S Yankeetown Rd (47601-8282)
PHONE..................................812 853-8771
Charles F Wilhite, *President*
Jeanne Wilhite, *Corp Secy*
EMP: 7
SQ FT: 6,500
SALES: 300K **Privately Held**
SIC: 3544 Special dies, tools, jigs & fixtures

Borden
Clark County

(G-926)
ABSOLUTE WELDING INC (PA)
130 East St (47106-8947)
PHONE..................................812 923-8001
Ted Wilcox, *President*
EMP: 8
SQ FT: 2,000
SALES: 2MM **Privately Held**
WEB: www.absolutewelding.com
SIC: 7692 Welding repair

(G-927)
ALS WOODCRAFT INC
435 E Main St (47106-8907)
P.O. Box 117 (47106-0117)
PHONE..................................812 967-4458
Fax: 812 967-2028
Jeff Hunt, *President*
Mildred Hunt, *Vice Pres*
Susan Hunt, *Treasurer*
EMP: 10
SQ FT: 9,600
SALES: 1MM **Privately Held**
WEB: www.alswoodcraft.net
SIC: 2426 2511 Dimension, hardwood; wood household furniture

(G-928)
BARR NONE MUSIC PUBLISHERS/LEA
1833 Valley Vista Dr (47106-8502)
PHONE..................................502 413-5443
EMP: 2
SALES (est): 59.2K **Privately Held**
SIC: 2741 Misc Publishing

(G-929)
FASKE WOOD MOULDING INC
10215 Saint Johns Rd (47106-8303)
PHONE..................................812 923-5601
Fax: 812 923-7630
Connie Senn, *President*
Carol J Stephens, *Corp Secy*
Francis C Senn, *Vice Pres*
D Wayne Stephens, *Vice Pres*
EMP: 12
SQ FT: 22,000
SALES (est): 1.5MM **Privately Held**
SIC: 2431 Millwork

(G-930)
HUBER ORCHARDS INC
Also Called: Huber Orchard Winery & Gift
19816 Huber Rd (47106-8309)
PHONE..................................812 923-9463
Fax: 812 923-3013
Greg Huber, *CEO*
Ted Huber, *President*
Ann Jeanette Baker, *Bookkeeper*
▲ EMP: 50
SQ FT: 15,000
SALES (est): 4.8MM **Privately Held**
SIC: 0161 2084 0175 2022 Vegetables & melons; wine cellars, bonded: engaged in blending wines; deciduous tree fruits; natural cheese

(G-931)
INDIANA SOUTHERN TL & ENGRG CO
21718 Martinsburg Rd (47106-7815)
PHONE..................................812 967-2714
Erman E Hurst, *President*
Donna Hurst, *Vice Pres*
EMP: 3
SALES (est): 239.5K **Privately Held**
SIC: 3599 Machine shop, jobbing & repair

(G-932)
KENTUCKY WOOD FLOORS LLC
533 Louis Smith Rd (47106-8100)
PHONE..................................812 256-2164
Shane Koetter, *Plant Mgr*
John P Stern,
John Stern,
EMP: 50
SALES (est): 4.6MM
SALES (corp-wide): 53.9MM **Privately Held**
SIC: 2426 Flooring, hardwood
PA: Koetter Woodworking Inc
    533 Louis Smith Rd
    Borden IN 47106
    812 923-8875

(G-933)
KOETTER WOODWORKING
Also Called: Koetter Sawmill
533 Louis Smith Rd (47106-8107)
PHONE..................................812 923-8875
Tom Koetter, *Owner*
EMP: 10
SALES (est): 420K **Privately Held**
SIC: 2499 2421 Decorative wood & woodwork; sawmills & planing mills, general

(G-934)
KOETTER WOODWORKING INC (PA)
533 Louis Smith Rd (47106-8107)
PHONE..................................812 923-8875
Fax: 812 923-9048
Randall F Koetter, *President*
Randell Eldridge, *General Mgr*
Steve Whitlow, *COO*
Gerald Koetter, *Vice Pres*
Richard A Koetter, *Vice Pres*
▲ EMP: 270
SQ FT: 650,000
SALES (est): 53.9MM **Privately Held**
SIC: 2431 Doors & door parts & trim, wood; moldings, wood: unfinished & pre-finished; staircases & stairs, wood

(G-935)
LM SUGARBUSH LLC
29618 Green Rd (47106-8013)
PHONE..................................812 967-4491
Nicholas Reisenbichler, *Owner*
Michael Georing, *Owner*
Leane Georing, *Manager*
EMP: 2
SALES (est): 85.4K **Privately Held**
SIC: 2099 Maple syrup

(G-936)
NORTHTECH MACHINE LLC
102 Walnut St (47106-8318)
PHONE..................................812 967-7400
Brandon Koetter, *Mng Member*
Richard Koetter,
William Prousa,
EMP: 7
SALES (est): 1MM **Privately Held**
SIC: 3553 Woodworking machinery

(G-937)
PINEAPPLE SOFTWARE INC
707 Lake Shore Dr (47106-8561)
PHONE..................................812 987-8277
Chad Hinton, *Administration*
EMP: 2
SALES (est): 123.2K **Privately Held**
SIC: 7372 Prepackaged software

(G-938)
WRIGHT BROTHERS IMPLEMENTS LLC
17606 State Road 60 (47106-8653)
PHONE..................................812 967-3029
Myra Sue Wright Powell, *Mng Member*
EMP: 9
SQ FT: 217,000
SALES: 800K **Privately Held**
SIC: 3523 5251 Tractors, farm; hardware

Boswell
Benton County

(G-939)
AMERICAN GARDENWORKS INC
205 W Mauzy St (47921-8525)
PHONE..................................765 869-4033
Gary Raines, *Principal*
EMP: 19
SALES (est): 3.9MM **Privately Held**
SIC: 3524 Lawn & garden mowers & accessories

(G-940)
MANTA RUGS
305 N Harrison St (47921-8526)
PHONE..................................765 869-5940
Chris Flynn, *Owner*
EMP: 2
SQ FT: 2,200
SALES: 90K **Privately Held**
SIC: 2273 Carpets & rugs

(G-941)
POWER PLACE PRODUCTS INC
Also Called: Malone Hardwoods
317 N Old Us Highway 41 (47921-8571)
EMP: 2 EST: 2001
SALES: 22K **Privately Held**
SIC: 3829 Mfg Measuring/Controlling Devices

Bourbon
Marshall County

(G-942)
FAULKNER FABRICATING INC
4050 Lincoln Hwy (46504-9610)
P.O. Box 61 (46504-0061)
PHONE..................................574 342-0022
Fax: 574 342-0111
Jerry Faulkner, *President*
EMP: 17
SQ FT: 7,500
SALES (est): 4.2MM **Privately Held**
WEB: www.faulknerfabricating.com
SIC: 7692 Welding repair

(G-943)
HARMONY PRESS INC (PA)
Also Called: Harmony Marketing Group
115 N Main St (46504-1645)
P.O. Box 3 (46504-0003)
PHONE..................................800 525-3742
Fax: 574 342-0409
Timothy J Harman, *President*
Jim Pattison, *COO*
Kevin Heller, *Vice Pres*
Barb Goley, *Purchasing*
Gary Price, *CFO*
EMP: 38 EST: 1941
SQ FT: 30,000
SALES: 5MM **Privately Held**
WEB: www.harmonyink.com
SIC: 2752 2759 Commercial printing, offset; letterpress printing

(G-944)
LEMLER PALLET INC
9200 Apple Rd (46504-9656)
PHONE..................................574 646-2707
Ronald L Lemler, *President*
Ronda Lemler, *Corp Secy*
EMP: 5 EST: 1997
SALES: 750K **Privately Held**
SIC: 2448 Wood pallets & skids

(G-945)
MCKINNEY & SELL INC
Also Called: Bourbon Kitchen and Bath
117 E Center St (46504-1626)
PHONE..................................877 665-3300
Fax: 574 342-2047
EMP: 7
SALES (est): 674.7K **Privately Held**
SIC: 2434 Mfg Wood Kitchen Cabinets

(G-946)
NORTHERN INDIANA MANUFACTURING (PA)
202 S Ecker Ave (46504-1220)
P.O. Box 46 (46504-0046)
PHONE..................................574 342-2105
Fax: 574 342-0120
Robert Dragani Sr, *Principal*
▲ EMP: 45 EST: 1945
SQ FT: 140,000
SALES: 8.5MM **Privately Held**
WEB: www.electroseal.net
SIC: 3451 3599 3398 3229 Screw machine products; machine & other job shop work; metal heat treating; pressed & blown glass

(G-947)
SHELLS INC
502 Old Us Highway 30 E (46504-1644)
PHONE..................................574 342-2673
John Administer, *Manager*
EMP: 75
SALES (est): 6.3MM
SALES (corp-wide): 28.7MM **Privately Held**
WEB: www.shells.com
SIC: 3543 Foundry cores
PA: Shells, Inc.
    1245 S Cleveland Massillo
    Copley OH 44321
    330 808-5558

(G-948)
SLABAUGH METAL FAB LLC
1855 12th Rd (46504-9595)
PHONE..................................574 342-0554
James Slabaugh, *President*

GEOGRAPHIC

EMP: 2
SALES (est): 104K **Privately Held**
SIC: 3444 Sheet metalwork

(G-949)
TEREX CORPORATION
4470 Lincoln Hwy (46504-9610)
PHONE..................................574 342-0086
Fax: 574 342-0117
Michael Charles, *Manager*
EMP: 7
SQ FT: 10,000
SALES (corp-wide): 4.3B **Publicly Held**
WEB: www.dueco.com
SIC: 3531 Construction machinery
PA: Terex Corporation
200 Nyala Farms Rd Ste 2
Westport CT 06880
203 222-7170

(G-950)
TOTSCHLAGER GAME CALLS LLC
4820 8a Rd (46504-9124)
PHONE..................................574 354-1620
Lyndon J Miller, *Administration*
EMP: 2
SALES (est): 123K **Privately Held**
SIC: 3949 Game calls

(G-951)
WTH PUBLICATIONS INC
8690 Apple Rd Bldg 1 (46504-9655)
PHONE..................................574 646-2007
Terry Lemler, *Principal*
EMP: 2
SALES (est): 104.6K **Privately Held**
SIC: 2741 Miscellaneous publishing

Bowling Green
Clay County

(G-952)
BELL PYROTECHNICS INCORPORATED
3201 Mitten Rd (47833-8295)
PHONE..................................812 859-3888
Jeanne Bell, *President*
Carter Bell, *Vice Pres*
▲ **EMP:** 2
SQ FT: 1,500
SALES (est): 176.8K **Privately Held**
SIC: 2899 Pyrotechnic ammunition: flares, signals, rockets, etc.

Brazil
Clay County

(G-953)
ADVANCED DRAINAGE SYSTEMS INC
2340 E Us Highway 40 (47834-7638)
P.O. Box 367 (47834-0367)
PHONE..................................812 443-2080
EMP: 12
SALES (corp-wide): 1.3B **Publicly Held**
SIC: 3084 Plastics pipe
PA: Advanced Drainage Systems, Inc.
4640 Trueman Blvd
Hilliard OH 43026
614 658-0050

(G-954)
BLACKFOOT POWDER COATING
5729 N State Road 59 (47834-7485)
PHONE..................................812 531-9315
Rebecca M Bower, *Owner*
EMP: 2
SALES (est): 51.5K **Privately Held**
SIC: 3479 Metal coating & allied service

(G-955)
BURKES GARDEN WOOD PDTS LLC
Also Called: Classic Baluster
4774 S 1000 E (47834-8469)
PHONE..................................765 344-1724
Joe Glick, *Manager*

EMP: 13
SALES (corp-wide): 2.4MM **Privately Held**
SIC: 2431 Porch work, wood
PA: Burkes' Garden Wood Products Llc
1400 E Polymer Dr
Terre Haute IN

(G-956)
CHRISTOPHER MILLER
Also Called: Timberline Industries
1892 E Us Highway 40 (47834-7637)
P.O. Box 334 (47834-0334)
PHONE..................................812 442-0949
Christopher Miller, *Owner*
EMP: 6
SALES (est): 499.8K **Privately Held**
SIC: 5087 3429 Caskets; casket hardware

(G-957)
CLASSIC BALUSTER LLC
4774 S 1000 E (47834-8469)
PHONE..................................765 344-1619
Samuel Fisher, *CEO*
John Fisher, *Chairman*
John Beiler, *Admin Sec*
EMP: 15
SALES: 7MM **Privately Held**
SIC: 2421 Outdoor wood structural products

(G-958)
CLOVER SIGNS CO
932 W National Ave (47834-2440)
PHONE..................................812 442-7446
Melisa Allender, *President*
Sue Rymer, *Info Tech Mgr*
EMP: 10
SALES (est): 810K **Privately Held**
SIC: 3993 Electric signs

(G-959)
DOVETAIL WOODWORKS
8390 N County Road 500 W (47834-7903)
PHONE..................................812 448-8832
EMP: 2 EST: 2010
SALES (est): 110K **Privately Held**
SIC: 2431 Mfg Millwork

(G-960)
EASTERN BANNER SUPPLY CORP
932 W National Ave (47834-2440)
PHONE..................................812 448-2222
Fax: 317 831-9874
Melissa Allender, *President*
Jacquelyn E Hunt, *President*
Steve Hunt, *Vice Pres*
EMP: 3
SQ FT: 7,200
SALES (est): 130K **Privately Held**
WEB: www.ebsbanners.com
SIC: 2399 Banners, made from fabric

(G-961)
EXACTIFAB
10309 N Industrial Pk Dr (47834-7322)
P.O. Box 315 (47834-0315)
PHONE..................................812 420-2723
Noel Short, *Ch of Bd*
Stephen Short, *President*
Robert Drake, *Vice Pres*
Scott Short, *Vice Pres*
Laura Clark, *Office Mgr*
EMP: 7
SQ FT: 4,560
SALES (est): 481.5K **Privately Held**
SIC: 3451 Screw machine products

(G-962)
GREAT DANE LLC
Also Called: Great Dane Trailers
2664 E Us Highway 40 (47834-7127)
PHONE..................................812 443-4711
Fax: 812 442-1321
Jay Rihey, *Engineer*
Gary Parker, *Manager*
Bruce Thompson, *Manager*
EMP: 900
SALES (corp-wide): 1.5B **Privately Held**
WEB: www.greatdanetrailers.com
SIC: 3715 3537 Truck trailers; industrial trucks & tractors

HQ: Great Dane Llc
222 N Lasalle St Ste 920
Chicago IL 60601

(G-963)
HAMMER TIME FORGE
8969 N 200 W 8969 W N200 (47834)
PHONE..................................812 448-2171
EMP: 3 EST: 2008
SALES (est): 140K **Privately Held**
SIC: 3462 Mfg Iron/Steel Forgings

(G-964)
HANCOR INC
2340 E Us Highway 40 (47834-7638)
P.O. Box 367 (47834-0367)
PHONE..................................812 443-2080
Fax: 812 448-2647
Frank Mitchell, *Branch Mgr*
EMP: 50
SQ FT: 16,000
SALES (corp-wide): 1.3B **Publicly Held**
SIC: 3089 3494 3084 3083 Plastic hardware & building products; valves & pipe fittings; plastics pipe; laminated plastics plate & sheet; pipe & tubing, steel
HQ: Hancor, Inc.
4640 Trueman Blvd
Hilliard OH 43026
614 658-0050

(G-965)
INDIANA OXIDE CORPORATION
Also Called: Corporate Office
10665 N State Road 59 (47834-6961)
P.O. Box 423 (47834-0423)
PHONE..................................812 446-2525
Fax: 812 442-0518
Greg Stevens, *President*
EMP: 15
SALES (est): 4.1MM **Privately Held**
SIC: 2819 Lead compounds or salts, inorganic, not used in pigments

(G-966)
IVC INDUSTRIAL COATINGS INC
2831 E Industrial Park Dr (47834)
PHONE..................................812 442-5080
Michael McCracken, *President*
Kevin S McCracken, *Vice Pres*
Jay Mitchell, *Manager*
Mark A Hewitt, *Shareholder*
Allyn L McCracken, *Shareholder*
◆ **EMP:** 108 **EST:** 1978
SQ FT: 3,000
SALES (est): 2.6MM
SALES (corp-wide): 14.2B **Publicly Held**
WEB: www.teamivc.com
SIC: 2851 Paints & allied products; enamels; varnishes; lacquer: bases, dopes, thinner
PA: Ppg Industries, Inc.
1 Ppg Pl
Pittsburgh PA 15272
412 434-3131

(G-967)
LOVETTS ELECTRONICS
840 E Pinckley St (47834-3334)
PHONE..................................812 446-1093
Fax: 812 448-8742
Henry R Lovett, *Owner*
EMP: 4
SALES (est): 125K **Privately Held**
SIC: 5961 3699 Computer equipment & electronics, mail order; electronic training devices

(G-968)
MAURER CONSTRUCTORS INC
10109 N Harmony Border St (47834-7714)
PHONE..................................812 236-5950
Mitch Maurer, *President*
EMP: 4
SALES: 250K **Privately Held**
SIC: 3448 Prefabricated metal buildings

(G-969)
METALS AND ADDITIVES CORP INC
Indiana Oxide
10665 N State Road 59 (47834-6961)
P.O. Box 423 (47834-0423)
PHONE..................................812 446-2525
Jeff Smith, *Branch Mgr*
EMP: 32

SALES (corp-wide): 17MM **Privately Held**
SIC: 2819 3356 2899 Lead compounds or salts, inorganic, not used in pigments; nonferrous rolling & drawing; chemical preparations
PA: Metals And Additives, Llc
5929 Lakeside Blvd
Indianapolis IN 46278
317 290-5007

(G-970)
MORRIS HOLDING COMPANY LLC (PA)
1015 E Mechanic St (47834-3321)
PHONE..................................812 446-6141
Michael L Morris,
EMP: 125
SQ FT: 42,500
SALES (est): 59.5MM **Privately Held**
SIC: 3714 3599 Motor vehicle transmissions, drive assemblies & parts; machine shop, jobbing & repair

(G-971)
MORRIS MFG & SLS CORP
1015 E Mechanic St (47834-3321)
PHONE..................................812 446-6141
Michael L Morris, *President*
Tina Corbin, *Production*
Russell Walters, *Production*
EMP: 200
SQ FT: 42,500
SALES (est): 57.1MM **Privately Held**
WEB: www.morrismfg.com
SIC: 3714 3599 Motor vehicle transmissions, drive assemblies & parts; machine shop, jobbing & repair
PA: Morris Holding Company, Llc
1015 E Mechanic St
Brazil IN 47834

(G-972)
MS MANUFACTURING LLC
Also Called: Kihm Metal Technologies
301 N Murphy Ave (47834-1552)
PHONE..................................812 442-7468
Fax: 812 835-2086
Brian Deakins, *President*
Buddy Raderstorf, *Vice Pres*
Tim Garrett, *Vice Pres*
EMP: 20
SQ FT: 20,000
SALES: 4MM **Privately Held**
WEB: www.kihmmetaltech.com
SIC: 3499 Machine bases, metal

(G-973)
NP CONVERTERS INC
Also Called: National Printing Converters
18 S Murphy Ave (47834-8297)
PHONE..................................812 448-2555
Fax: 812 669-0329
Brian Buckely, *President*
Kyle McKinney, *Sales Staff*
Walt Strain, *Manager*
EMP: 45
SALES (est): 5.2MM
SALES (corp-wide): 6.5MM **Privately Held**
WEB: www.npclabels.com
SIC: 7374 2761 2672 2671 Data processing & preparation; manifold business forms; coated & laminated paper; packaging paper & plastics film, coated & laminated
PA: Np Converters Inc
16133 Ventura Blvd 741
Encino CA

(G-974)
PAG HOLDINGS INC
10665 N State Road 59 (47834-6961)
PHONE..................................814 446-2525
EMP: 3
SALES (corp-wide): 17MM **Privately Held**
SIC: 2861 Gum & wood chemicals
HQ: Pag Holdings, Inc.
5929 Lakeside Blvd
Indianapolis IN 46278
317 290-5006

▲ = Import ▼=Export
◆ =Import/Export

(G-975)
PROTEQ CUSTOM GEAR LLC
3057 W County Road 1200 N
(47834-6903)
PHONE...............................812 201-6002
Stephen Brannan, *Principal*
EMP: 2
SALES (est): 102.6K **Privately Held**
SIC: 3949 Sporting & athletic goods

(G-976)
PYROTECHNIC PRODUCTIONS INC
2749 E County Road 1200 N (47834-7055)
PHONE...............................812 448-8196
Fax: 812 448-8626
Nathan Kaiser, *President*
Mark Hopkins, *President*
EMP: 2
SALES: 450K **Privately Held**
WEB: www.skymagicpyrotechnics.com
SIC: 7999 2899 Fireworks display service;
fireworks

(G-977)
S-B CAPABLE CONCEPTS LLC
11542 N Murphy Rd (47834-6837)
PHONE...............................812 420-2565
Buddy Raderstorf,
EMP: 2
SQ FT: 1,600
SALES (est): 55.3K **Privately Held**
SIC: 8711 3545 Mechanical engineering;
tools & accessories for machine tools

(G-978)
SOLAR BAT ENTERPRISES INC
Also Called: Outdoor Action Wear Spc
3628 E County Road 600 N (47834-7665)
PHONE...............................812 986-3551
Gary Nesty, *President*
Leesa Nesty, *Vice Pres*
Mendy Shepperd, *Admin Sec*
▲ **EMP:** 3 **EST:** 1994
SQ FT: 5,000
SALES: 1.1MM **Privately Held**
WEB: www.solarbat.com
SIC: 3851 Glasses, sun or glare

(G-979)
TECHNIFAB PRODUCTS INC (PA)
10339 N Industrial Pk Dr (47834-7322)
P.O. Box 315 (47834-0315)
PHONE...............................812 442-0520
Fax: 812 442-0891
Noel Short, *CEO*
Steve Short, *President*
Rob Drake, *Vice Pres*
Phil Redenbarger, *Vice Pres*
Mark May, *Purch Agent*
▲ **EMP:** 80
SQ FT: 43,000
SALES (est): 13.7MM **Privately Held**
WEB: www.technifab.com
SIC: 3559 3498 Cryogenic machinery, in-
dustrial; fabricated pipe & fittings

(G-980)
UNITED MACHINE & DESIGN INC
301 N Murphy Ave (47834-1552)
P.O. Box 404 (47834-0404)
PHONE...............................812 442-7468
Fax: 812 446-2277
Timothy C Callahan, *President*
David Callahan, *Corp Secy*
Grady Don Paddock, *Vice Pres*
Grady Paddock, *Vice Pres*
Lisa Deakins, *Manager*
EMP: 27
SQ FT: 35,000
SALES: 3MM **Privately Held**
WEB: www.umdi-usa.com
SIC: 3312 Tool & die steel

Bremen
Marshall County

(G-981)
ACCRALINE INC
Also Called: ACCRALINE INC-METAL SUR-
GEONS
1420 W Bike St (46506-2199)
PHONE...............................574 546-3484
Fax: 574 546-5094
Richard D Cormican, *President*
Mark Cormican, *Treasurer*
Cris Cormican, *Admin Sec*
▲ **EMP:** 35
SQ FT: 36,000
SALES: 1.9MM **Privately Held**
WEB: www.accraline.com
SIC: 3599 Machine shop, jobbing & repair;
custom machinery

(G-982)
ALMEGA/TRU-FLEX INC
Also Called: Almega Wire Products
3917 State Road 106 (46506-9066)
P.O. Box 67 (46506-0067)
PHONE...............................574 546-2113
Fax: 574 546-5635
Elmo Hurst, *CEO*
Douglas Pomeroy, *President*
Joe E Miller, *Vice Pres*
Dj Pomeroy, *Vice Pres*
John Maurer, *CFO*
◆ **EMP:** 50
SQ FT: 42,000
SALES: 4MM **Privately Held**
WEB: www.almegat.com
SIC: 3679 3643 3694 3357 Harness as-
semblies for electronic use: wire or cable;
power line cable; engine electrical equip-
ment; nonferrous wiredrawing & insulating

(G-983)
BCI DEFENSE LLC
545 N Bowen Ave (46506-2005)
P.O. Box 159 (46506-0159)
PHONE...............................574 546-2411
James Brown, *CEO*
JB Brown, *President*
EMP: 5
SQ FT: 5,000
SALES (est): 577.1K **Privately Held**
SIC: 3484 Small arms

(G-984)
BORKHOLDER WOOD PRODUCTS
2060 5th Rd (46506-9327)
PHONE...............................574 546-2613
Marvin Borkholder, *President*
EMP: 6
SALES (est): 350K **Privately Held**
SIC: 2431 Millwork; moldings, wood: unfin-
ished & prefinished; trellises, wood

(G-985)
BREMEN CASTINGS INC
500 N Baltimore St (46506-1138)
P.O. Box 129 (46506-0129)
PHONE...............................574 546-5016
Fax: 574 546-2411
James E Brown, *CEO*
James L Brown, *President*
Geoffrey Meester, *Vice Pres*
Dan Richard, *Purch Mgr*
Josh Keller, *Senior Engr*
EMP: 220 **EST:** 1939
SQ FT: 129,000
SALES (est): 100.6MM **Privately Held**
WEB: www.bremencastings.com
SIC: 3321 Gray iron castings

(G-986)
BREMEN COMPOSITES LLC
Also Called: Switzer Buildings
425 Industrial Dr (46506-2111)
PHONE...............................574 546-3791
Fax: 574 546-3950
Alvin Hildenbrand, *Vice Pres*
Ken Pearl,
EMP: 70
SALES (est): 21.3MM **Privately Held**
WEB: www.bremencomposites.com
SIC: 3089 Automotive parts, plastic

(G-987)
BREMEN CORPORATION (HQ)
405 Industrial Dr (46506-2100)
PHONE...............................574 546-4238
Fax: 574 546-5093
Wayne Blessing, *President*
James Smith, *Corp Secy*
Conrad D Chapman, *Asst Sec*
▲ **EMP:** 600
SQ FT: 46,000
SALES (est): 49.8MM
SALES (corp-wide): 185.5MM **Privately Held**
SIC: 3086 Packaging & shipping materials,
foamed plastic
PA: Creative Foam Corporation
300 N Alloy Dr
Fenton MI 48430
810 629-4149

(G-988)
BREMTOWN FINE CSTM CBNETRY INC
1456 State Road 331 (46506-8844)
P.O. Box 409 (46506-0409)
PHONE...............................574 546-2781
Fax: 574 546-2453
Timothy Johnson, *President*
Nita R Gerig, *Shareholder*
EMP: 55
SQ FT: 50,000
SALES (est): 5.9MM **Privately Held**
WEB: www.bremtown.com
SIC: 2434 Wood kitchen cabinets; vanities;
bathroom: wood

(G-989)
BROWN ADVANCED MFG LLC
545 N Bowen Ave (46506-2005)
P.O. Box 129 (46506-0129)
PHONE...............................574 209-2003
Lisa Brown,
EMP: 5
SALES (est): 359.2K **Privately Held**
SIC: 3549 Metalworking machinery

(G-990)
COLEMAN CABLE LLC
Also Called: Southwire
1115 W North St (46506-2053)
PHONE...............................574 546-5115
Jacob McLein, *Project Mgr*
Rich Carr, *Manager*
Andy King, *Info Tech Mgr*
EMP: 150
SALES (corp-wide): 2.5B **Privately Held**
WEB: www.copperfieldllc.com
SIC: 3643 Power line cable
HQ: Coleman Cable, Llc
1530 S Shields Dr
Waukegan IL 60085
847 672-2300

(G-991)
COOPER-STANDARD AUTOMOTIVE INC
501 High Rd (46506-1040)
PHONE...............................574 546-5938
Keiji Kyomoto, *Branch Mgr*
EMP: 176
SALES (corp-wide): 3.6B **Publicly Held**
WEB: www.cooperstandard.com
SIC: 3443 Heat exchangers, condensers &
components
HQ: Cooper-Standard Automotive Inc.
39550 Orchard Hill Pl
Novi MI 48375
248 596-5900

(G-992)
CORNERSTONE MOULDING INC
1586 3rd Rd (46506-9608)
PHONE...............................574 546-4249
Eddie Berkholder, *President*
Darrell Yoder, *Vice Pres*
Darryl Yoder, *Vice Pres*
Fred Miller, *Office Mgr*
EMP: 23
SALES: 6MM **Privately Held**
SIC: 2431 Moldings, wood: unfinished &
prefinished

(G-993)
CORNERSTONE WOODS ALPACA LLC
988 Elm Rd (46506-8961)
PHONE...............................574 546-4179
Ted Jones, *Principal*
EMP: 2
SALES (est): 87.6K **Privately Held**
SIC: 2231 Alpacas, mohair: woven

(G-994)
COUNTY LINE WOODWORKING
11594 N 1100 W (46506-9501)
PHONE...............................574 935-7107
EMP: 2
SALES (est): 154.3K **Privately Held**
SIC: 2499 Decorative wood & woodwork

(G-995)
CREATIVE FOAM CORPORATION
405 Industrial Dr (46506-2111)
PHONE...............................574 546-4238
Kent McKesson, *Engineer*
Kent Lutian, *Branch Mgr*
Wes Solmos, *Representative*
EMP: 40
SALES (corp-wide): 185.5MM **Privately Held**
SIC: 3086 Packaging & shipping materials,
foamed plastic
PA: Creative Foam Corporation
300 N Alloy Dr
Fenton MI 48430
810 629-4149

(G-996)
DIGGER SPECIALTIES INC (PA)
3446 Us Highway 6 (46506-9062)
P.O. Box 241 (46506-0241)
PHONE...............................574 546-5999
Fax: 574 546-5099
Loren Graber, *President*
Margaret Borkholder, *Vice Pres*
Everett Hochstetler, *Vice Pres*
Chad Weldy, *Vice Pres*
Larry Burkholder, *Engineer*
▲ **EMP:** 65
SQ FT: 8,800
SALES (est): 19.1MM **Privately Held**
WEB: www.diggerspecialties.com
SIC: 3089 Plastic hardware & building
products; fences, gates & accessories:
plastic

(G-997)
DUTCH KETTLE LLC
6375 Fir Rd (46506-9718)
PHONE...............................574 546-4033
Lyle Bontrager,
EMP: 10
SALES (est): 1.2MM **Privately Held**
SIC: 2033 Jams, including imitation: pack-
aged in cans, jars, etc.

(G-998)
EDGEWOOD METAL FAB LLC
1265 B Rd (46506-9795)
PHONE...............................574 546-5947
Raymond Helmuth, *Principal*
EMP: 2
SALES (est): 225K **Privately Held**
SIC: 3441 Fabricated structural metal

(G-999)
GENY INDUSTRIES LLC
621 E Plymouth St (46506-1269)
PHONE...............................574 536-0297
Carl Borkholder, *Principal*
EMP: 5
SALES (est): 258.9K **Privately Held**
SIC: 3999 Manufacturing industries

(G-1000)
GRAPHIX UNLIMITED INC
3947 State Road 106 (46506-9066)
PHONE...............................574 546-3770
Fax: 574 546-5565
Bernie Erickson, *President*
Brent Murphy, *Purch Mgr*
EMP: 40
SQ FT: 14,000

SALES (est): 4.5MM **Privately Held**
WEB: www.graphixunlimited.com
SIC: 2759 2675 2396 Decals: printing;
screen printing; die-cut paper & board;
automotive & apparel trimmings

(G-1001)
HANWHA MACHINERY AMERICA CORP
Also Called: Universal Bearing
431 N Birkey St (46506-2016)
P.O. Box 38 (46506-0038)
PHONE......................................574 546-2261
Young Tae Kim, *President*
Dave Ketcham, *Vice Pres*
Claude St Hilaire, *Plant Mgr*
EMP: 275
SQ FT: 300,000
SALES (est): 13.5MM
SALES (corp-wide): 4.2B **Privately Held**
SIC: 3714 5085 Bearings, motor vehicle;
bearings
PA: Hanwha Corporation
86 Cheonggyecheon-Ro, Jung-Gu
Seoul 04541
822 729-1114

(G-1002)
HARRINGTONS NOODLES INC
1451 Dogwood Rd (46506-9071)
P.O. Box 93 (46506-0093)
PHONE......................................574 546-3861
Francisco Garza, *President*
Crystal Garza, *Vice Pres*
EMP: 5
SALES (est): 644.2K **Privately Held**
SIC: 2098 Noodles (e.g. egg, plain &
water), dry

(G-1003)
HEADSIGHT INC
4845 3b Rd (46506-9762)
PHONE......................................574 546-5022
Richard Gramm, *President*
▲ EMP: 8
SALES (est): 1MM **Privately Held**
SIC: 3523 Farm machinery & equipment

(G-1004)
INDIANA CARTON COMPANY INC
1721 W Bike St (46506-2123)
PHONE......................................574 546-3848
Fax: 574 546-5953
David L Petty, *CEO*
Kenneth Petty, *President*
James C Petty, *Exec VP*
John Hummer, *Vice Pres*
Matthew Petty, *Vice Pres*
▲ EMP: 95 EST: 1933
SQ FT: 162,000
SALES (est): 50MM **Privately Held**
WEB: www.indianacarton.com
SIC: 2657 Folding paperboard boxes

(G-1005)
INTERNATIONAL WIRE GROUP INC
833 Legner St (46506-1060)
PHONE......................................574 546-4680
Joe Choquette, *Branch Mgr*
EMP: 51
SALES (corp-wide): 432.1MM **Privately Held**
SIC: 3357 3351 Nonferrous wiredrawing &
insulating; wire, copper & copper alloy
HQ: International Wire Group, Inc.
12 Masonic Ave
Camden NY 13316

(G-1006)
JOHNS MANVILLE CORPORATION
1215 W Dewey St (46506-2063)
PHONE......................................574 546-4666
Ray Darmer, *Plant Mgr*
Sandy Hires, *Warehouse Mgr*
Wayne Dill, *Engineer*
Dave Vining, *Engineer*
Dave Mercurio, *Plant Engr*
EMP: 50
SALES (corp-wide): 242.1B **Publicly Held**
WEB: www.jm.com
SIC: 3296 Mineral wool

HQ: Johns Manville Corporation
717 17th St Ste 800
Denver CO 80202
303 978-2000

(G-1007)
KAUFFMAN ENGINEERING INC
Also Called: Bremen Wire Products
510 E 2nd St (46506-1050)
P.O. Box 658, Logansport (46947-0658)
PHONE......................................574 732-2154
Tom Gay, *Branch Mgr*
EMP: 75
SQ FT: 20,500
SALES (corp-wide): 87.5MM **Privately Held**
WEB: www.tmmorrismfg.com
SIC: 3679 Harness assemblies for electronic use: wire or cable; electronic switches
PA: Kauffman Engineering Inc
701 Ransdell Rd
Lebanon IN 46052
765 483-4919

(G-1008)
KEMCO MANUFACTURING LLC
617 E Plymouth St (46506-1269)
PHONE......................................574 546-2025
Ervin Miller, *Principal*
EMP: 3 EST: 2013
SALES (est): 179.4K **Privately Held**
SIC: 3999 Manufacturing industries

(G-1009)
MADISON MANUFACTURING INC
66990 State Road 331 (46506-9478)
PHONE......................................574 633-4433
Daniel Deschepper, *President*
Dale E Deschepper, *Vice Pres*
EMP: 40
SQ FT: 20,000
SALES (est): 8.5MM **Privately Held**
WEB: www.madisonmfg.com
SIC: 3714 3523 Motor vehicle body components & frame; farm machinery & equipment

(G-1010)
MEL RHON INC
Also Called: Mrs T'S Bakery
124 E Plymouth St (46506-1236)
PHONE......................................574 546-4559
Rhonda Triplet, *Partner*
EMP: 4
SALES (est): 374.3K **Privately Held**
SIC: 2051 Bakery: wholesale or wholesale/retail combined

(G-1011)
MJ FINISHING
5311 E County Line Rd (46506-9745)
PHONE......................................574 646-2080
Mathew Schmucker, *Owner*
EMP: 4
SALES: 85K **Privately Held**
SIC: 2499 Decorative wood & woodwork

(G-1012)
NISHIKAWA COOPER LLC
501 High Rd (46506-1040)
PHONE......................................574 546-5938
Fax: 574 546-2878
David Bozell, *Engineer*
Jim Jenney, *Engineer*
Cindy Brown, *Human Res Mgr*
Brad Keller, *Manager*
EMP: 652
SALES (corp-wide): 903.4MM **Privately Held**
SIC: 3069 3714 Weather strip, sponge
rubber; motor vehicle parts & accessories
HQ: Nishikawa Cooper Llc
324 Morrow St
Topeka IN 46571
260 593-2156

(G-1013)
OZINGA BROS INC
524 N Bowen Ave (46506-2006)
PHONE......................................574 546-2550
EMP: 44
SALES (corp-wide): 269.8MM **Privately Held**
SIC: 3273 Ready-mixed concrete

PA: Ozinga Bros., Inc.
19001 Old Lagrange Rd # 30
Mokena IL 60448
708 326-4200

(G-1014)
PATRICK INDUSTRIES INC
Also Called: Charleston
1849 Dogwood Rd (46506-9074)
PHONE......................................574 546-5222
Toni Swiheart, *Branch Mgr*
EMP: 210
SALES (corp-wide): 1.6B **Publicly Held**
SIC: 3089 Gutters (glass fiber reinforced),
fiberglass or plastic
PA: Patrick Industries, Inc.
107 W Franklin St
Elkhart IN 46516
574 294-7511

(G-1015)
PERMALATT PRODUCTS INC
3462 Us Highway 6 (46506-9062)
P.O. Box 405 (46506-0405)
PHONE......................................574 546-6311
Fax: 574 546-6388
Loren Graber, *President*
Everett Hoshstler, *Vice Pres*
Jaren Weldy, *Plant Mgr*
EMP: 5
SALES (est): 752.5K **Privately Held**
WEB: www.permalatt.com
SIC: 3089 Plastic hardware & building
products

(G-1016)
PETROLEUM SOLUTIONS INC
809 Douglas Rd (46506-9602)
P.O. Box 389 (46506-0389)
PHONE......................................574 546-2133
John Kuhns, *CEO*
EMP: 4 EST: 2012
SALES (est): 391.8K **Privately Held**
SIC: 2992 5172 2911 Lubricating oils &
greases; lubricating oils & greases; fuel
additives

(G-1017)
PROGRESSIVE WOODCRAFT LLC
2550 Birch Rd (46506-9043)
PHONE......................................574 546-9010
Henry Hochstetler, *Owner*
EMP: 2
SALES (est): 97K **Privately Held**
SIC: 2511 Wood household furniture

(G-1018)
RADIATOR SPECIALTY COMPANY
Omega Products
860 870 Legner Dr (46506)
PHONE......................................574 546-5606
Scott Sickmiller, *Manager*
EMP: 42
SALES (corp-wide): 81.9MM **Privately Held**
WEB: www.radiatorspecialty.com
SIC: 3052 Rubber hose
PA: Radiator Specialty Company Inc
600 Radiator Rd
Indian Trail NC 28079
704 688-2302

(G-1019)
RBC PRCISION PDTS - BREMEN INC
225 Industrial Dr (46506-2115)
P.O. Box 247 (46506-0247)
PHONE......................................574 546-4455
John Clark, *Vice Pres*
David Ditommaso, *Plant Mgr*
Dean Kruse, *Branch Mgr*
Sue Peto, *Manager*
EMP: 15
SALES (corp-wide): 674.9MM **Publicly Held**
SIC: 3452 Dowel pins, metal
HQ: Rbc Precision Products - Bremen, Inc.
102 Willenbrock Rd
Oxford CT 06478
203 267-7001

(G-1020)
RENTOWN CABINETS
2735 Birch Rd (46506-9042)
PHONE......................................574 546-2569
Dennis Hochstetler, *President*
EMP: 3
SALES: 380K **Privately Held**
SIC: 2511 Wood household furniture

(G-1021)
SCHMUCKER WELDING
3208 Beech Rd (46506-9781)
PHONE......................................574 773-0456
Howard Schmucker, *Owner*
EMP: 6
SALES (est): 423.4K **Privately Held**
SIC: 7692 3548 Welding repair; welding
wire, bare & coated

(G-1022)
SCHWARTZ WHEEL CO
2750 3b Rd (46506-8717)
PHONE......................................574 546-0101
Jerry Schwartz, *Principal*
EMP: 2 EST: 2009
SALES (est): 202.1K **Privately Held**
SIC: 3312 Blast furnaces & steel mills

(G-1023)
SCHWARTZS WHEEL & CLIP C
Also Called: Schwartz's Wheel Repair
4199 Cedar Rd (46506-9755)
PHONE......................................574 546-1302
John Schwartz, *Owner*
EMP: 2
SALES (est): 202.5K **Privately Held**
SIC: 3799 Carriages, horse drawn

(G-1024)
SLABAUGH METAL FAB
2320 4c Rd (46506-8718)
PHONE......................................574 546-2882
Lonnie Slabaugh, *Owner*
EMP: 25
SQ FT: 5,000
SALES (est): 2.7MM **Privately Held**
SIC: 3444 7699 Sheet metalwork; industrial machinery & equipment repair

(G-1025)
STANDARD GLASS AND STAR GLASS
Also Called: Starglas of Bremen
404 N Bowen Ave (46506-2004)
PHONE......................................574 546-5912
James Stone, *President*
Landa Stone, *President*
EMP: 9
SQ FT: 47,000
SALES: 1MM **Privately Held**
SIC: 3714 Motor vehicle parts & accessories

(G-1026)
SUMMIT MFG & MACHINING
723 High Rd (46506-1067)
P.O. Box 9 (46506-0009)
PHONE......................................574 546-4571
Fax: 574 546-4954
John Stoller, *President*
Cory Creighton, *Prdtn Mgr*
Paul Haluda, *Sales Engr*
Joe Ians, *Admin Sec*
EMP: 18
SQ FT: 12,000
SALES (est): 1.8MM **Privately Held**
WEB: www.summitmmi.com
SIC: 3599 Machine shop, jobbing & repair

(G-1027)
SUPERIOR COATINGS INC
1730 W Dewey St (46506-2133)
PHONE......................................574 546-0591
Toby Lakins, *President*
EMP: 9
SQ FT: 10,000
SALES (est): 1.3MM **Privately Held**
SIC: 3449 Plastering accessories, metal

(G-1028)
T J SNUGGLES INC
1851 Dogwood Rd (46506-9074)
P.O. Box 250 (46506-0250)
PHONE......................................574 546-4404
Fax: 574 546-4450

Connie Laudeman, *President*
EMP: 40
SALES (est): 4.7MM **Privately Held**
SIC: 2394 Awnings, fabric: made from purchased materials; tents: made from purchased materials

(G-1029)
TIMOTHY J TROYER
1657 3rd Rd (46506-9608)
PHONE..................................574 546-1115
Timothy Troyer, *Principal*
EMP: 2
SALES (est): 165K **Privately Held**
SIC: 2431 Millwork

(G-1030)
**UNIVERSAL BEARINGS LLC
(DH)**
431 N Birkey St (46506-2016)
P.O. Box 38 (46506-0038)
PHONE..................................574 546-2261
Fax: 574 546-5085
James Sung, *President*
James Wikoff, *Engineer*
Mark Mummert, *Electrical Engi*
David Ketcham, *CFO*
Steve Fackler, *Regl Sales Mgr*
▲ **EMP:** 157 **EST:** 1959
SQ FT: 250,000
SALES: 40.2MM
SALES (corp-wide): 4.2B **Privately Held**
WEB: www.univbrg.com
SIC: 3714 Bearings, motor vehicle

(G-1031)
VERNS WOODWORKING
491 4th Rd (46506-9082)
PHONE..................................574 773-7930
EMP: 2
SALES (est): 76.8K **Privately Held**
SIC: 2431 Millwork

(G-1032)
WALNUT LANE WOODWORKING
12530 Shively Rd (46506-9412)
PHONE..................................574 633-2114
EMP: 4
SALES (est): 363.7K **Privately Held**
SIC: 2431 Millwork

(G-1033)
WILLIAM LEMAN CO (PA)
114 N Center St (46506-1563)
PHONE..................................574 546-2371
Eugene Zimmer, *President*
Verdon Feldman, *Corp Secy*
Brian Shappell, *Exec VP*
Tom Stiles, *Vice Pres*
EMP: 20
SQ FT: 100,000
SALES (est): 1.7MM **Privately Held**
SIC: 2087 Extracts, flavoring

(G-1034)
WOODYS PAINT SPOT LTD
3860 W Shore Dr (46506-9366)
PHONE..................................574 255-0348
Michael E Wood, *President*
EMP: 8
SQ FT: 4,800
SALES: 1MM **Privately Held**
SIC: 2851 Paints & allied products

(G-1035)
YODER WOODWORKING INC
2534 State Road 331 (46506-9051)
PHONE..................................574 546-5100
David Yoder, *President*
Jane Yoder, *Vice Pres*
EMP: 3
SALES: 150K **Privately Held**
WEB: www.yoderwoodworking.com
SIC: 3429 Cabinet hardware

Brimfield
Noble County

(G-1036)
**PLAS-TECH MOLDING & DESIGN
INC**
7037b N Triplett St (46794-9799)
PHONE..................................260 761-3006

Dennis Berkey, *President*
Elaine Berkey, *Vice Pres*
EMP: 15
SQ FT: 30,000
SALES (est): 2.6MM **Privately Held**
SIC: 3089 Injection molding of plastics

Bringhurst
Carroll County

(G-1037)
ADVANTAGE EMBROIDERY INC
1059 E 400 S (46913-9561)
PHONE..................................765 471-0188
Fax: 765 448-3126
Susan Moore, *President*
Renee Dexter, *Admin Sec*
EMP: 2 **EST:** 1996
SQ FT: 1,800
SALES (est): 148K **Privately Held**
SIC: 2395 Embroidery & art needlework

(G-1038)
B & B ENGINEERING INC
7102 E 300 S (46913-9684)
PHONE..................................765 566-3460
William Braden, *President*
Caset W Braden, *Vice Pres*
EMP: 4
SQ FT: 6,000
SALES: 500K **Privately Held**
SIC: 3544 Special dies, tools, jigs & fixtures

(G-1039)
ZINN KITCHENS INC
Also Called: Zinn Cabinets Plus
1211 S Center St (46913-9621)
P.O. Box 7, Flora (46929-0007)
PHONE..................................574 967-4179
Fax: 574 967-4179
Gregg Zinn, *President*
Mary Zinn, *Vice Pres*
Tony Fife, *Treasurer*
Dale Zinn, *Admin Sec*
EMP: 40
SQ FT: 27,000
SALES (est): 4.7MM **Privately Held**
SIC: 2434 5722 Wood kitchen cabinets; household appliance stores

Bristol
Elkhart County

(G-1040)
ADEC INC
19670 State Road 120 (46507-9131)
PHONE..................................574 848-7451
Fax: 574 294-6018
Sally Russell, *Branch Mgr*
Evan Hoover, *Manager*
EMP: 200
SALES (est): 5.1MM
SALES (corp-wide): 18.3MM **Privately Held**
WEB: www.adecinc.com
SIC: 8322 8331 2673 7389 Social services for the handicapped; job training & vocational rehabilitation services; trash bags (plastic film): made from purchased materials; packaging & labeling services
PA: Adec, Inc.
19670 State Road 120
Bristol IN 46507
574 848-7451

(G-1041)
**ADMAR MOLD & ENGINEERING
INC**
21426 Meadowview Ln (46507-9751)
PHONE..................................574 848-7085
Fax: 574 266-4513
Gregory O Pletcher, *President*
EMP: 3
SQ FT: 6,000
SALES (est): 180K **Privately Held**
SIC: 3544 Industrial molds

(G-1042)
ALLIANCE SHEETS LLC
1725 Commerce Ctr Dr (46507)
PHONE..................................574 622-6020
EMP: 21
SALES (est): 6MM **Privately Held**
SIC: 2621 Paper mills

(G-1043)
AMERI-KART CORP
Also Called: Sherwood Plastics
17196 State Road 120 (46507-9593)
PHONE..................................225 642-7874
Eric Gottuso, *President*
EMP: 85
SALES (corp-wide): 547MM **Publicly
Held**
SIC: 2821 3444 3083 Plastics materials & resins; sheet metalwork; laminated plastics plate & sheet
HQ: Ameri-Kart Corp.
17196 State Road 120
Bristol IN 46507
574 848-7462

(G-1044)
AMERI-KART CORP (HQ)
17196 State Road 120 (46507-9593)
P.O. Box 368 (46507-0368)
PHONE..................................574 848-7462
Fax: 574 848-5589
Robin Johnson, *CEO*
Eric Gottuso, *President*
Dennis Roberts, *President*
Robert Wagner, *Plant Mgr*
Angie McCraner, *Purch Agent*
▲ **EMP:** 120
SQ FT: 112,230
SALES (est): 118.1MM
SALES (corp-wide): 547MM **Publicly
Held**
SIC: 3089 3537 2821 5162 Garbage containers, plastic; molding primary plastic; thermoformed finished plastic products; tables, lift: hydraulic; plastics materials & resins; plastics products
PA: Myers Industries, Inc.
1293 S Main St
Akron OH 44301
330 253-5592

(G-1045)
**AMERIMAX FABRICATED
PRODUCTS**
206 Kesco Dr (46507-9497)
PHONE..................................574 389-8960
EMP: 2
SALES (est): 95.2K **Privately Held**
SIC: 3441 Fabricated structural metal

(G-1046)
AR TEE ENTERPRISES INC
19874 County Road 6 (46507-9759)
P.O. Box 562 (46507-0562)
PHONE..................................574 848-5543
Bruce Miller, *President*
EMP: 6
SQ FT: 8,000
SALES (est): 760.3K **Privately Held**
SIC: 3089 3544 Injection molded finished plastic products; industrial molds

(G-1047)
**B D CUSTOM MANUFACTURING
INC**
1100 Bloomingdale Dr (46507-8403)
PHONE..................................574 848-0925
Ronald G Clark, *Ch of Bd*
David Buck, *President*
Jennifer Yoder, *Office Mgr*
Richard Letherman, *Admin Sec*
Dave Dittman, *Maintence Staff*
EMP: 14
SQ FT: 18,000
SALES (est): 2.2MM **Privately Held**
WEB: www.bdcustommfg.com
SIC: 3089 Plastic processing

(G-1048)
**BAY BRIDGE MANUFACTURING
INC**
1301 Commerce Dr (46507-9349)
P.O. Box 215 (46507-0215)
PHONE..................................574 848-7477
Fax: 574 848-5658

Dennis F Mc Carthy, *President*
Merrill M Mc Carthy, *Admin Sec*
EMP: 49
SALES (est): 8.9MM **Privately Held**
WEB: www.baybridgemfg.com
SIC: 3713 Truck bodies (motor vehicles)

(G-1049)
BRAVO TRAILERS LLC
19319 C R 8 (46507)
PHONE..................................574 848-7500
John Bolstetter, *Vice Pres*
Gary Mackelprang, *Vice Pres*
Kate Lockwood, *VP Sales*
Rebacca Hodges, *Sales Mgr*
Mitch Bender, *Mng Member*
EMP: 56
SALES (est): 11.2MM **Privately Held**
SIC: 2448 Cargo containers, wood

(G-1050)
BRISTOL TOOL AND DIE INC
710 Commerce Dr (46507-9354)
PHONE..................................574 848-5354
Fax: 574 848-1934
Brian Price, *President*
EMP: 18
SQ FT: 13,000
SALES: 2MM **Privately Held**
SIC: 3599 3545 3544 Machine & other job shop work; machine tool accessories; special dies, tools, jigs & fixtures

(G-1051)
CHASSIX
51650 County Road 133 (46507-9800)
PHONE..................................574 825-9457
EMP: 4
SALES (est): 515.6K **Privately Held**
SIC: 3599 Machine shop, jobbing & repair

(G-1052)
CHEM TECH INC
501 Bloomingdale Dr (46507-9610)
PHONE..................................574 848-1001
Fax: 574 848-1109
Dennis J Brosh, *President*
EMP: 12
SQ FT: 20,000
SALES (est): 1.2MM **Privately Held**
SIC: 2891 Adhesives

(G-1053)
D & S INDUSTRIES INC
207 W St Joseph St (46507-9169)
P.O. Box 870 (46507-0870)
PHONE..................................574 848-7144
Fax: 574 848-5581
Thomas Sipress, *President*
Derek Sipress, *Vice Pres*
EMP: 13
SQ FT: 23,000
SALES: 500K **Privately Held**
SIC: 3479 Painting of metal products

(G-1054)
DEXTER AXLE COMPANY
Also Called: Ventline
902 S Division St (46507-9187)
PHONE..................................574 295-7888
Fax: 574 848-4825
Rich Roske, *Plant Mgr*
Mike Furfaro, *Purch Mgr*
Tim Grossman, *Engineer*
Adolf Lehner, *Engineer*
Sam Lievore, *Engineer*
EMP: 130
SQ FT: 185,000
SALES (corp-wide): 245.3MM **Privately
Held**
WEB: www.ventline.com
SIC: 3564 3442 3444 Blowers & fans; metal doors, sash & trim; sheet metalwork
HQ: Dexter Axle Company
2900 Industrial Pkwy
Elkhart IN 46516

(G-1055)
DIVERSIFIED MCH BRISTOL LLC
Also Called: Dmi
51650 County Road 133 (46507-9800)
PHONE..................................248 728-8642
Douglas Delgrosso, *CEO*
Michael Beyer, *CFO*
▲ **EMP:** 884

SALES (est): 225.5MM
SALES (corp-wide): 1.3B **Privately Held**
SIC: 3714 Motor vehicle parts & accessories
HQ: Diversified Machine, Inc.
　　300 Galleria Officentre # 501
　　Southfield MI 48034
　　248 728-8642

(G-1056)
DOYLE MANUFACTURING INC
16630 County Road 10 (46507-9573)
P.O. Box 1474 (46507-1474)
PHONE...........................574 848-5624
Fax: 574 848-5624
Myron Miller, *Vice Pres*
Mark E Miller, *Vice Pres*
EMP: 4
SALES: 382K **Privately Held**
SIC: 3825 Test equipment for electronic & electrical circuits

(G-1057)
DYNAMIC PACKG SOLUTIONS INC
406 Kesco Dr (46507-8991)
PHONE...........................574 848-1410
Frank Mass, *President*
Robert P Arbaugh, *COO*
Dan Mackowiak, *CFO*
EMP: 175
SQ FT: 40,000
SALES: 2.5MM **Privately Held**
SIC: 3631 Household cooking equipment

(G-1058)
EARTHWAY PRODUCTS INC
1009 Maple St (46507-8328)
P.O. Box 547 (46507-0547)
PHONE...........................574 848-7491
Cinda McKinney, *Ch of Bd*
Kenneth Pickett, *President*
Sara Barrett, *Owner*
Susan Graff, *Owner*
H Douglas Schrock, *Owner*
◆ **EMP:** 100 **EST:** 1965
SQ FT: 180,000
SALES: 13.8MM **Privately Held**
WEB: www.earthway.com
SIC: 3523 Farm machinery & equipment

(G-1059)
F B C INC (PA)
Also Called: Custom Formulating & Blending
1123 Commerce Dr (46507-9351)
PHONE...........................574 848-5288
Fax: 574 848-5963
John E Ray, *President*
Mike St Amand, *Purchasing*
Cindy Ray, *Office Mgr*
Rich Thatcher, *Manager*
Alma Negrete, *Technology*
▼ **EMP:** 27
SALES (est): 7.9MM **Privately Held**
WEB: www.customformulating.com
SIC: 2842 2992 Cleaning or polishing preparations; lubricating oils & greases

(G-1060)
FOREST RIVER INC
U S Cargo
1280 Commerce Dr (46507-9350)
PHONE...........................574 848-1335
Fax: 574 848-5862
Joseph Greenlee, *Branch Mgr*
EMP: 200
SALES (corp-wide): 242.1B **Publicly Held**
WEB: www.forestriverinc.com
SIC: 3715 3792 Demountable cargo containers; tent-type camping trailers
HQ: Forest River, Inc.
　　900 County Road 1 N
　　Elkhart IN 46514

(G-1061)
FRUIT HILLS WINERY ORCHRD LLC
55535 State Road 15 (46507-9505)
PHONE...........................574 848-9463
David Muir,
EMP: 2 **EST:** 2010
SALES (est): 178.2K **Privately Held**
SIC: 2084 Wines

(G-1062)
HI-TECH HOUSING INC
1103 Maple St (46507-8330)
PHONE...........................574 848-5593
Fax: 574 848-5851
Charles J Fanaro Jr, *CEO*
Doug Mills, *General Mgr*
Lawrence Waco Sr, *Corp Secy*
Kenneth Geljack, *Exec VP*
Amanda Bergen, *Sales Staff*
EMP: 65
SQ FT: 124,000
SALES (est): 13.1MM **Privately Held**
WEB: www.hi-techhousing.com
SIC: 2452 2451 1542 Modular homes, prefabricated, wood; mobile homes, except recreational; commercial & office building contractors

(G-1063)
HINSDALE FARMS LTD
605 Kesco Dr (46507-8980)
P.O. Box 1399 (46507-1399)
PHONE...........................574 848-0344
Milton C Smith, *President*
Philip M Smith, *Vice Pres*
EMP: 2 **EST:** 1997
SALES (est): 355.3K **Privately Held**
SIC: 3556 Dehydrating equipment, food processing

(G-1064)
LAKOTA CORP
4 Stoutco Dr (46507)
P.O. Box 219 (46507-0219)
PHONE...........................574 848-1636
Fax: 574 848-1467
Erik Smith, *President*
George Thomas, *Principal*
Jennifer Lacey, *Accountant*
Andrew Stanfield, *Chief Mktg Ofcr*
Michelle Schmidt, *Office Mgr*
EMP: 35
SQ FT: 1,100
SALES (est): 9.1MM **Privately Held**
SIC: 3715 Truck trailers

(G-1065)
LASALLE BRISTOL CORPORATION
Lasalle Lighting
1203 N Division St (46507-8931)
P.O. Box 98, Elkhart (46515-0098)
PHONE...........................574 295-4400
Dwayne Rosenberry, *Vice Pres*
Brian Sharkey, *Purchasing*
EMP: 20
SQ FT: 88,816
SALES (corp-wide): 356.3MM **Privately Held**
WEB: www.lasallebristol.com
SIC: 5023 3645 Floor coverings; residential lighting fixtures
HQ: Bristol Lasalle Corporation
　　601 County Road 17
　　Elkhart IN 46516
　　574 295-4400

(G-1066)
LAVENDER PATCH FABR QUILTS LLC
20615 Baltimore Oriole Dr (46507-8531)
PHONE...........................574 848-0011
Patricia Harris, *Principal*
EMP: 3
SALES (est): 173.7K **Privately Held**
SIC: 2395 Quilted fabrics or cloth

(G-1067)
LIEVORE CUSTOM MACHINE INC
55265 County Road 14 (46507-9119)
PHONE...........................574 848-0150
Daniel Lievore, *President*
EMP: 3
SQ FT: 2,000
SALES: 180K **Privately Held**
SIC: 3599 7699 7692 Machine shop, jobbing & repair; precision instrument repair; welding repair

(G-1068)
MARK-LINE INDUSTRIES LLC (PA)
51687 County Road 133 (46507-9800)
P.O. Box 277 (46507-0277)
PHONE...........................574 825-5851
Leisa Smith, *Purch Dir*
Trace Cole, *Persnl Dir*
Chris Remke, *Mng Member*
John Peters,
EMP: 125
SQ FT: 100,000
SALES (est): 30.7MM **Privately Held**
WEB: www.marklinein.com
SIC: 2451 Mobile buildings: for commercial use

(G-1069)
MISSION WOODWORKING INC
502 Kesco Dr (46507-9466)
PHONE...........................574 848-5697
Kevin Beck, *President*
Phil Shenk, *Sales Staff*
Gary Horst, *Shareholder*
Patty Beck, *Admin Sec*
EMP: 26 **EST:** 1998
SALES (est): 2.1MM **Privately Held**
WEB: www.missionwoodworking.com
SIC: 2511 2541 Storage chests, household: wood; table or counter tops, plastic laminated

(G-1070)
MOLDED FOAM LLC
Also Called: Molded Foam Products
1203 S Division St (46507-9160)
PHONE...........................574 848-1500
Fax: 574 848-5758
Tim Dugle, *Mng Member*
Cathy Ellsworth, *Manager*
Alan Ferguson, *Maintence Staff*
▼ **EMP:** 95
SALES: 10MM **Privately Held**
SIC: 3086 Plastics foam products

(G-1071)
MONOGRAM COMFORT FOODS LLC
605 Kesco Dr (46507-8980)
PHONE...........................574 848-0344
Wes Jackson, *Ch of Bd*
Karl Schledwitz,
EMP: 100
SQ FT: 35,000
SALES (est): 20.8MM **Privately Held**
SIC: 2096 Corn chips & other corn-based snacks
PA: Monogram Food Solutions, Llc
　　530 Oak Court Dr Ste 400
　　Memphis TN 38117

(G-1072)
MONOGRAM FROZEN FOODS LLC
605 Kesco Dr (46507-8980)
P.O. Box 1399 (46507-1399)
PHONE...........................574 848-0344
Phillip M Smith,
Tiffany Kirkwood, *Executive Asst*
▲ **EMP:** 250
SQ FT: 113,000
SALES (est): 66.6MM **Privately Held**
WEB: www.hinsdalefarms.com
SIC: 2013 Sausages & other prepared meats; sausages & related products, from purchased meat; frozen meats from purchased meat

(G-1073)
MPR CORPORATION
Also Called: Fabric Services
103 Hinsdale Farm Rd (46507-9167)
PHONE...........................574 848-5100
John Wuori, *President*
Don Wade, *Vice Pres*
Steve Kercher, *Admin Sec*
▲ **EMP:** 50
SQ FT: 75,000
SALES (est): 21.8MM **Privately Held**
SIC: 5131 2295 2211 Upholstery fabrics, woven; plastic piece goods, woven; piece goods & other fabrics; laminating of fabrics; broadwoven fabric mills, cotton

(G-1074)
NIBLOCK EXCAVATING INC (PA)
Also Called: Michiana Directional Drilling
906 Maple St (46507-9175)
P.O. Box 211 (46507-0211)
PHONE...........................574 848-4437
Gary Niblock, *President*
Richard Niblock, *Admin Sec*
EMP: 100 **EST:** 1971
SQ FT: 2,500
SALES (est): 16.5MM **Privately Held**
SIC: 2951 1771 1611 1794 Asphalt & asphaltic paving mixtures (not from refineries); foundation & footing contractor; highway & street paving contractor; excavation work; water, sewer & utility lines

(G-1075)
PANDA PRINTS
19647 County Road 8 (46507-9709)
PHONE...........................574 322-1050
Amanda Hatton, *Principal*
EMP: 2
SALES (est): 83.9K **Privately Held**
SIC: 2752 Commercial printing, lithographic

(G-1076)
QUALITY GALVANIZED PDTS INC
Also Called: Galvanized Division
19473 County Road 8 (46507-9708)
PHONE...........................574 848-5151
Fax: 574 848-5502
Louis Chadwick, *President*
Chris Sutterby, *General Mgr*
EMP: 8
SQ FT: 15,000
SALES (est): 1MM **Privately Held**
SIC: 3444 Sheet metalwork

(G-1077)
R S E TOOL AND DIE INC
State Rd 15 N (46507)
P.O. Box 455 (46507-0455)
PHONE...........................574 848-7966
Fax: 574 848-7714
Richard Stutsman, *President*
EMP: 6
SALES (est): 470K **Privately Held**
SIC: 3544 Special dies & tools; die sets for metal stamping (presses); extrusion dies; jigs & fixtures

(G-1078)
RECORD / PLAY TEK INC
Also Called: Rpt
110 E Vistula St (46507)
P.O. Box 790 (46507-0790)
PHONE...........................574 848-5233
Michael H Stoll, *President*
John Haines, *Vice Pres*
EMP: 6 **EST:** 1997
SQ FT: 9,500
SALES (est): 700K **Privately Held**
WEB: www.recordplaytek.com
SIC: 3577 Computer peripheral equipment

(G-1079)
RESCHCOR INC (PA)
Also Called: Omega
2123 Blakesley Pkwy (46507-7000)
PHONE...........................574 295-2413
Fax: 574 522-4696
Tom Reschly, *President*
Kieper David, *Vice Pres*
Jim Reschly, *Vice Pres*
Steve Wise, *Opers Mgr*
Rich Hughey, *Purch Mgr*
EMP: 15
SQ FT: 42,700
SALES (est): 23.6MM **Privately Held**
WEB: www.omegaplasticscorp.com
SIC: 3089 Extruded finished plastic products

(G-1080)
RICHARD SHEETS
15569 State Road 120 (46507-9241)
PHONE...........................574 536-8247
Richard Sheets, *Owner*
Mary Sheets, *Co-Owner*
EMP: 2
SQ FT: 1,092

SALES: 140K **Privately Held**
SIC: 3711 Truck tractors for highway use, assembly of

(G-1081)
ROBERT WEED PLYWOOD CORP
705 Maple St (46507-9103)
P.O. Box 487 (46507-0487)
PHONE.....................................574 848-7631
Fax: 574 848-5679
David Weed, *President*
Matt Ewing, *Superintendent*
Mark Fiquett, *COO*
Matt Bunner, *Vice Pres*
Thomas Longworth, *Vice Pres*
▲ EMP: 350
SQ FT: 616,000
SALES (est): 209.3MM **Privately Held**
WEB: www.robertweedplywood.com
SIC: 5031 2435 2431 Plywood; panels, hardwood plywood; moldings & baseboards, ornamental & trim; moldings, wood: unfinished & prefinished

(G-1082)
RS PALLET INC
19816 County Road 6 (46507-9759)
PHONE.....................................574 596-8777
Sie W Sharp Jr, *Owner*
EMP: 3
SALES (est): 106.9K **Privately Held**
SIC: 2448 Pallets, wood & wood with metal

(G-1083)
RWP WEST LLC
705 Maple St (46507-9103)
P.O. Box 487 (46507-0487)
PHONE.....................................208 549-2410
David Weed, *Principal*
EMP: 8
SALES (est): 1.5MM **Privately Held**
SIC: 2435 Hardwood veneer & plywood

(G-1084)
SATELLITE SHELTERS
Also Called: Satellite Industries
1686 Commerce Dr (46507-9348)
PHONE.....................................574 350-2150
Charlie Senecal, *Principal*
Joshua Carmichael, *Principal*
▲ EMP: 50
SALES (est): 6.8MM **Privately Held**
SIC: 3431 5099 Bathroom fixtures, including sinks; toilets, portable

(G-1085)
SHA-DO CORP
1501 Bloomingdale Dr (46507-9184)
PHONE.....................................574 848-9296
Fax: 574 848-9857
Donald Gingerich, *President*
EMP: 9
SQ FT: 20,000
SALES (est): 1.4MM **Privately Held**
SIC: 3469 Metal stampings

(G-1086)
SIERRA MOTOR CORP
Also Called: Sierra Interiors
19224 County Road 8 (46507-9706)
PHONE.....................................574 848-1300
Michael W Greene, *President*
Kathie Greene, *Vice Pres*
Bryan Greene, *Shareholder*
EMP: 60 EST: 1987
SQ FT: 102,000
SALES (est): 8.7MM **Privately Held**
WEB: www.sierrainteriors.com
SIC: 3799 Horse trailers, except fifth-wheel type

(G-1087)
SKYLINE CORPORATION
Also Called: Bristol Div
State Route 15 (46507)
P.O. Box 217 (46507-0217)
PHONE.....................................574 848-7621
Fax: 574 848-7626
Bill Metzger, *Manager*
EMP: 150
SALES (corp-wide): 236.5MM **Publicly Held**
WEB: www.skylinecorp.com
SIC: 2451 Mobile homes, except recreational

PA: Skyline Champion Corporation
2520 Bypass Rd
Elkhart IN 46514
574 294-6521

(G-1088)
SPARTAN MOTORS USA INC
603 Earthway Blvd (46507-9182)
PHONE.....................................574 848-2000
EMP: 31
SALES (corp-wide): 707.1MM **Publicly Held**
SIC: 3713 Truck & bus bodies
HQ: Spartan Motors Usa, Inc.
1541 Reynolds Rd
Charlotte MI 48813
517 543-6400

(G-1089)
TALON PRODUCTS LLC
1690 Commerce Dr (46507-9348)
PHONE.....................................574 218-0100
EMP: 15
SALES (est): 2.8MM **Privately Held**
SIC: 3229 Glass fiber products

(G-1090)
TRELLBORG SLING PRFILES US INC
1151 Bloomingdale (46507-8403)
PHONE.....................................330 995-5125
Smitty McKee, *President*
EMP: 30
SALES (corp-wide): 3.7B **Privately Held**
SIC: 3053 Gaskets, packing & sealing devices
HQ: Trelleborg Sealing Profiles U.S. Inc.
500 Lena Dr
Aurora OH 44202
330 995-9725

(G-1091)
UNITED TRAILERS INC
19985 County Road 8 (46507-9709)
PHONE.....................................574 848-7088
Terry G Whitesell, *CEO*
Todd M Bontrater, *President*
EMP: 2
SALES (est): 497.5K **Privately Held**
SIC: 3715 Truck trailers; demountable cargo containers; trailer bodies

(G-1092)
UNIVERSAL TRLR CRGO GROUP INC (DH)
14054 C R 4 (46507)
P.O. Box 281 (46507-0281)
PHONE.....................................574 264-9661
Fax: 574 848-0678
Gary Dicamillo, *President*
Jim White, *CFO*
▼ EMP: 400
SQ FT: 44,000
SALES (est): 280.1MM
SALES (corp-wide): 667.9MM **Privately Held**
WEB: www.haulmark.com
SIC: 3715 Demountable cargo containers

(G-1093)
UTILIMASTER HOLDINGS INC
603 Earthway Blvd (46507-9182)
P.O. Box 585, Wakarusa (46573-0585)
PHONE.....................................800 237-7806
Fax: 574 862-4517
Larry Doyle, *CEO*
John Forbes, *President*
◆ EMP: 750
SQ FT: 600,000
SALES (est): 238.7MM
SALES (corp-wide): 707.1MM **Publicly Held**
SIC: 3713 3711 Truck & bus bodies; motor vehicles & car bodies
PA: Spartan Motors, Inc.
1541 Reynolds Rd
Charlotte MI 48813
517 543-6400

Bristow
Perry County

(G-1094)
BRISTOW MILLING CO LLC
4721 Water St (47515-8883)
P.O. Box 51 (47515-0051)
PHONE.....................................812 843-5176
Matt Esarey, *Mng Member*
EMP: 3
SQ FT: 10,000
SALES (est): 368.6K **Privately Held**
SIC: 2048 5191 5261 Prepared feeds; farm supplies; fertilizer & fertilizer materials; fertilizer

(G-1095)
UBELHOR CONSTRUCTION INC
Also Called: Ubelhor Woodworking
26018 State Road 145 (47515-8865)
PHONE.....................................812 357-2220
Fax: 812 357-2614
Zach Ubelhor, *President*
Luke Ubelhor, *Vice Pres*
Joyce Ubelhor, *Treasurer*
Roman Ubelhor, *Admin Sec*
EMP: 12
SQ FT: 33,000
SALES (est): 1.9MM **Privately Held**
SIC: 2431 Moldings, wood: unfinished & prefinished

(G-1096)
WINZERWALD WINERY LLC
26300 N Indian Lake Rd (47515-9117)
PHONE.....................................812 357-7000
Donna Adams,
Daniel Adams,
EMP: 2
SALES: 150K **Privately Held**
WEB: www.winzerwaldwinery.com
SIC: 2084 Wines

(G-1097)
WINZERWALD WINERY LLC
26300 N Indian Lake Rd (47515-9117)
PHONE.....................................812 357-7000
EMP: 4 EST: 2011
SALES (est): 210K **Privately Held**
SIC: 2084 Wines, Brandy, And Brandy Spirits, Nsk

Brook
Newton County

(G-1098)
BROOK LOCKER PLANT
243 W Main St (47922-8723)
P.O. Box 451 (47922-0451)
PHONE.....................................219 275-2611
Jeff Lafflon, *President*
EMP: 4
SQ FT: 2,300
SALES (est): 328.7K **Privately Held**
SIC: 2011 5421 Meat packing plants; meat markets, including freezer provisioners

(G-1099)
PT TOOL MACHINE
5183 E 894 S (47922-8663)
PHONE.....................................219 275-3633
Mike W Wentzel, *Partner*
Wayne Wentzel, *Partner*
EMP: 4
SALES (est): 378.3K **Privately Held**
SIC: 3544 Special dies, tools, jigs & fixtures

(G-1100)
URBAN FOREST PRODUCTS LLC
3126 E 500 S (47922-8738)
PHONE.....................................219 697-2900
Kevin Stangeland, *President*
Donald Meister, *Admin Sec*
▲ EMP: 2
SALES (est): 466.4K **Privately Held**
SIC: 2679 Pressed fiber & molded pulp products except food products

---

Brookston
White County

(G-1101)
BLUME METAL SALES LLC
695 W State Road 18 (47923-8200)
PHONE.....................................765 490-0600
Lee Blume, *Mng Member*
EMP: 4
SALES (est): 320K **Privately Held**
SIC: 3444 Sheet metalwork

(G-1102)
CARTER MANUFACTURING COMPANY
896 E Carter Ct (47923-8297)
PHONE.....................................765 563-3666
Fax: 765 563-3850
A J Batt, *President*
EMP: 3
SQ FT: 6,000
SALES (est): 443.3K **Privately Held**
WEB: www.cartermfgco.com
SIC: 3523 Planting machines, agricultural

(G-1103)
CONAGRA BRANDS INC
Also Called: Orville Redenbacher Popcorn
162 E 900 S (47923-8234)
PHONE.....................................765 563-3182
Kent Korniak, *Branch Mgr*
EMP: 19
SALES (corp-wide): 7.9B **Publicly Held**
WEB: www.conagra.com
SIC: 2033 Tomato products: packaged in cans, jars, etc.
PA: Conagra Brands, Inc.
222 Merchandise Mart Plz
Chicago IL 60654
312 549-5000

(G-1104)
EXCEL COOP INC
11179 S Us Highway 231 (47923)
P.O. Box 25, Flora (46929-0025)
PHONE.....................................574 967-3943
Dan Calvin, *Manager*
EMP: 3
SALES (est): 162.5K **Privately Held**
SIC: 2048 Prepared feeds

(G-1105)
HUNTER NUTRITION INC
Also Called: Hunter Sheep Nutrition
200 Ns St (47923)
PHONE.....................................765 563-1003
Jeffrey A Hunter, *President*
EMP: 7
SALES (est): 1MM **Privately Held**
SIC: 2048 5191 5999 5211 Feed concentrates; feed; feed & farm supply; fencing; building materials, exterior

(G-1106)
LEMAN ENGRG & CONSULTING INC
520 E 1050 S (47923-8362)
PHONE.....................................574 870-7732
Randy Leman, *CEO*
EMP: 6 EST: 2013
SALES: 1MM **Privately Held**
SIC: 3613 8711 Panelboards & distribution boards, electric; consulting engineer

(G-1107)
ROX SOFTWARE INC
1192 E Dollar Ct (47923-8317)
PHONE.....................................765 430-7616
Cortland Sterit, *Owner*
EMP: 5
SALES (est): 354.6K **Privately Held**
WEB: www.roxsoftware.com
SIC: 7372 7371 Prepackaged software; custom computer programming services

(G-1108)
TERRA DRIVE SYSTEMS INC
Also Called: TDS
9098 W 800 S (47923-8048)
PHONE.....................................219 279-2801
Daniel Dickinson, *President*
C Phillip Joy, *President*

GEOGRAPHIC

Mark Hampshire, *Vice Pres*
Jeffrey A Kropfl, *CFO*
◆ **EMP:** 110 **EST:** 1974
SQ FT: 80,000
SALES (est): 35.2MM
SALES (corp-wide): 5.3MM **Privately Held**
WEB: www.tuthill.com
SIC: 3594 5084 Hydrostatic drives (transmissions); hydraulic systems equipment & supplies
PA: Equity Hci Partners L P
　1033 Skokie Blvd Ste 260
　Northbrook IL 60062
　847 291-9259

(G-1109)
TWINROCKER HAND MADE PAPER INC
100 E 3rd St (47923)
P.O. Box 413 (47923-0413)
PHONE......................765 563-3119
Fax: 765 563-8946
Kathryn Clark, *President*
Howard Clark, *Treasurer*
Travis Becker, *Admin Sec*
EMP: 6 **EST:** 1971
SQ FT: 5,000
SALES (est): 919.2K **Privately Held**
WEB: www.twinrocker.com
SIC: 2621 5999 Art paper; newsprint paper; artists' supplies & materials

Brookville
Franklin County

(G-1110)
ADVANCED PRINT SOLUTIONS LLC
10108 State Road 101 (47012-8620)
PHONE......................513 405-3452
Tim Cunningham, *CEO*
EMP: 2 **EST:** 2011
SALES (est): 189.6K **Privately Held**
SIC: 2752 Advertising posters, lithographed

(G-1111)
AMS EMBROIDERY & SIGNS LLC
110 S Main St Unit A (47012-6302)
PHONE......................513 313-1613
Mark Reese, *Administration*
EMP: 2 **EST:** 2015
SALES (est): 98.5K **Privately Held**
SIC: 3993 Signs & advertising specialties

(G-1112)
CHARLES KOLB SONS LOGGING
1135 John St (47012-1041)
PHONE......................765 647-4309
James Kolb, *Owner*
EMP: 2
SALES (est): 81.7K **Privately Held**
SIC: 2411 Logging

(G-1113)
DR PEPPER BOTTLING CO
261 Webers Ln (47012-9642)
PHONE......................765 647-3576
Kelly Joerger, *Manager*
EMP: 3
SALES (est): 112.9K **Privately Held**
SIC: 2086 Soft drinks: packaged in cans, bottles, etc.

(G-1114)
FRANKS INDUSTRIES
9021 State Road 101 (47012-8813)
PHONE......................765 647-2080
EMP: 2
SALES (est): 81.4K **Privately Held**
SIC: 3599 Industrial Machinery, Nec, Nsk

(G-1115)
GREG MINER
Also Called: Brookville Tool Co
10068 Oxford Pike (47012-9285)
PHONE......................765 647-1012
Fax: 765 647-2079
Greg Miner, *Owner*
EMP: 3
SQ FT: 2,428

SALES: 200K **Privately Held**
SIC: 3599 Machine shop, jobbing & repair

(G-1116)
HAUTAU TUBE CUTOFF SYSTEMS LLC
11199 State Road 101 (47012-8817)
PHONE......................765 647-1600
Charles M Hautau Jr,
Fred Hautau,
EMP: 10 **EST:** 2003
SQ FT: 13,000
SALES: 4MM **Privately Held**
WEB: www.hautau.com
SIC: 3541 8711 3354 Deburring machines; designing: ship, boat, machine & product; aluminum extruded products

(G-1117)
HUELSEMAN PRINTING CO
Also Called: Graphic Enterprises
9085 Bath Rd (47012-9769)
PHONE......................765 647-3947
James C Huelseman, *Partner*
Mary Huelseman, *Partner*
EMP: 2
SQ FT: 3,000
SALES (est): 164.1K **Privately Held**
SIC: 2752 Commercial printing, offset

(G-1118)
INLINE SHIRT PRINTING LLC
5062 State Road 252 (47012-9456)
PHONE......................765 647-6356
Dustin Grimmeissen, *Principal*
EMP: 2
SALES (est): 114.8K **Privately Held**
SIC: 2752 Commercial printing, lithographic

(G-1119)
IRVING MATERIALS INC
Also Called: I M I
1352 Fairfield Ave (47012-1030)
PHONE......................765 647-6533
Fax: 765 647-5735
Hans Back, *Branch Mgr*
EMP: 6
SALES (corp-wide): 800.6MM **Privately Held**
SIC: 3273 Ready-mixed concrete
PA: Irving Materials, Inc.
　8032 N State Road 9
　Greenfield IN 46140
　317 326-3101

(G-1120)
JLP MANUFACTURING LLC
6059 Graf Rd (47012-9606)
PHONE......................765 647-2991
James A Pennington, *Owner*
EMP: 2 **EST:** 2016
SALES (est): 117.1K **Privately Held**
SIC: 3999 Manufacturing industries

(G-1121)
NOBBE CONCRETE PRODUCTS INC
11177 Us Highway 52 (47012-9674)
PHONE......................765 647-4017
Paul Nobbe, *President*
Phil Nobbe, *Corp Secy*
Craig Nobbe, *Vice Pres*
EMP: 4
SQ FT: 860
SALES (est): 352.2K **Privately Held**
SIC: 3553 3531 Woodworking machinery; bituminous, cement & concrete related products & equipment

(G-1122)
OWENS CORNING SALES LLC
128 W 8th St (47012-1458)
PHONE......................765 647-4131
Fax: 765 647-3472
Martin Bever, *Manager*
EMP: 110
SQ FT: 50,000 **Publicly Held**
WEB: www.owenscorning.com
SIC: 3296 Mineral wool
HQ: Owens Corning Sales, Llc
　1 Owens Corning Pkwy
　Toledo OH 43659
　419 248-8000

(G-1123)
OWENS CORNING SALES LLC
6102 Holland Rd (47012)
PHONE......................765 647-2857
Fax: 765 647-4131
Dave White, *Branch Mgr*
EMP: 22 **Publicly Held**
WEB: www.owenscorning.com
SIC: 3296 Mineral wool
HQ: Owens Corning Sales, Llc
　1 Owens Corning Pkwy
　Toledo OH 43659
　419 248-8000

(G-1124)
P-AMERICAS LLC
Also Called: Pepsico
261 Webers Ln (47012-9642)
PHONE......................765 647-3576
Fax: 765 647-4062
Erick Lilley, *Sales/Mktg Mgr*
EMP: 30
SALES (corp-wide): 63.5B **Publicly Held**
SIC: 2086 Carbonated soft drinks, bottled & canned
HQ: P-Americas Llc
　1 Pepsi Way
　Somers NY 10589
　336 896-5740

(G-1125)
ROCK GARDEN ENGRAVING
268 Main St (47012-1349)
PHONE......................765 647-3357
Sam Schuck, *Owner*
EMP: 2
SALES (est): 139.3K **Privately Held**
SIC: 2759 Engraving

(G-1126)
SPERRY & RICE LLC (PA)
9146 Us Highway 52 (47012-9657)
PHONE......................765 647-4141
Jerry Tipton, *Marketing Staff*
Jim Gregory,
EMP: 20
SALES (est): 4MM **Privately Held**
SIC: 3069 Medical & laboratory rubber sundries & related products

(G-1127)
TARVER WOLFF LLC
Also Called: Warfytr
1149 Brookhaven Rd (47012)
P.O. Box 112 (47012-0112)
PHONE......................765 265-7416
Douglas Ralph, *President*
Elizabeth Siebert, *Manager*
▲ **EMP:** 5
SQ FT: 2,000
SALES: 100K **Privately Held**
SIC: 3949 Team sports equipment; water sports equipment; winter sports equipment

(G-1128)
TW ENTERPRISES LLC
9021 Meyer Rd (47012-8934)
PHONE......................513 520-8453
Alex Tebbe, *President*
EMP: 2
SALES (est): 123.4K **Privately Held**
SIC: 3842 5047 7389 Personal safety equipment; industrial safety devices: first aid kits & masks;

(G-1129)
VERTEX BUILDING MATERIALS LLC
9111 Whitewater Dr (47012-9412)
PHONE......................765 547-1883
Curtis M Ward, *Principal*
EMP: 5
SALES (est): 270K **Privately Held**
SIC: 3272 Concrete stuctural support & building material

(G-1130)
VOEGELE AUTO SUPPLY LLC
12 Murphy St (47012-1338)
PHONE......................765 647-3541
Robert A Voegele,
EMP: 4

SALES (est): 623.3K **Privately Held**
SIC: 3714 Motor vehicle parts & accessories

(G-1131)
WHITEWATER PUBLICATIONS INC
Also Called: Brookville Democrat
531 Main St (47012-1407)
P.O. Box 38 (47012-0038)
PHONE......................765 647-4221
Fax: 765 647-4811
Donald G Sintz, *President*
Arthur C Feller, *Vice Pres*
Gary Wolf, *Treasurer*
EMP: 25 **EST:** 1943
SQ FT: 2,800
SALES (est): 1.1MM **Privately Held**
WEB: www.thebrookvillenews.com
SIC: 2711 2789 2759 2752 Job printing & newspaper publishing combined; bookbinding & related work; commercial printing; commercial printing, lithographic

(G-1132)
WILLIAM BROWNING
Also Called: Browning, William Logging
7015 Jefferson St (47012-9488)
PHONE......................765 647-6397
William Browning, *Owner*
Viola Browning, *Admin Sec*
EMP: 2
SALES (est): 121.3K **Privately Held**
SIC: 2411 Logging camps & contractors

Brownsburg
Hendricks County

(G-1133)
ANDRESEN GRAPHIC PROCESSORS
10843 E County Road 950 N (46112-9632)
PHONE......................317 291-7071
Jon Andresen, *CEO*
Ann Andresen, *President*
EMP: 10
SQ FT: 5,000
SALES (est): 457.9K **Privately Held**
SIC: 2759 Screen printing

(G-1134)
ANIMALSINK
7489 Windridge Way (46112-8984)
PHONE......................317 496-8467
Sean M Clapp, *Principal*
EMP: 4
SALES (est): 467.3K **Privately Held**
SIC: 2833 Animal based products

(G-1135)
ART OVATION
7615 S State Road 267 (46112-9101)
PHONE......................317 769-4301
Mike Stephens, *Owner*
EMP: 3
SQ FT: 1,600
SALES (est): 195.6K **Privately Held**
SIC: 2399 5999 Banners, pennants & flags; banners, flags, decals & posters

(G-1136)
BC AWARDS INC
Also Called: Promotional Products
480 E Nrthfeld Dr Ste 100 (46112)
P.O. Box 209 (46112-0209)
PHONE......................317 852-3240
Fax: 317 852-6602
Kenneth Crouse, *President*
Randy Crouse, *Vice Pres*
EMP: 4
SALES (est): 589.8K **Privately Held**
SIC: 5999 5199 3993 Trophies & plaques; advertising specialties; signs & advertising specialties

(G-1137)
BIOLOGICS MODULAR LLC
1533 E Northfield Dr # 1000 (46112-2509)
PHONE......................317 456-9191
Clark Byrum Jr, *Principal*
Julian Karras, *Project Mgr*
Charles Hall, *Treasurer*
Clark H Byrum,

EMP: 5
SALES (est): 510K **Privately Held**
SIC: **1541** 3448 Pharmaceutical manufacturing plant construction; prefabricated metal buildings

(G-1138)
BROWNSBURG SIGNS & GRAPHICS
1016 E Main St (46112-1408)
PHONE...............................317 858-1907
Scott Bennett, *Owner*
Scott Benett, *Owner*
EMP: 2
SALES (est): 144.8K **Privately Held**
WEB: www.brownsbursigns.com
SIC: **3993** Signs & advertising specialties

(G-1139)
BUTTONS GALORE INC
110 E College Ave (46112-1207)
PHONE...............................800 626-8168
Joseph V Batic, *President*
EMP: 10
SALES (est): 840K **Privately Held**
SIC: **3993** Signs & advertising specialties

(G-1140)
BUZTRONICS INC
464 Suthpoint Cir Ste 100 (46112)
P.O. Box 415 (46112-0415)
PHONE...............................317 876-3413
Fax: 317 876-3450
Edward D Lewis, *President*
Terry Sanderson, *CFO*
▲ EMP: 85
SQ FT: 70,000
SALES (est): 10.8MM **Privately Held**
WEB: www.buztronics.com
SIC: **3999** Novelties, bric-a-brac & hobby kits; buttons: Red Cross, union, identification

(G-1141)
C F ROARK WLDG ENGRG CO INC
136 N Green St (46112-1238)
P.O. Box 67 (46112-0067)
PHONE...............................317 852-3163
Fax: 317 852-2738
Charles F Roark, *Ch of Bd*
Charles T Roark, *President*
Chris Roark Jones, *Vice Pres*
Connie Kemp, *Vice Pres*
Constance Kemp, *Vice Pres*
EMP: 105 EST: 1949
SQ FT: 60,000
SALES (est): 34MM **Privately Held**
WEB: www.roarkfab.com
SIC: **3728** 3769 Aircraft parts & equipment; casings, missiles & missile components: storage

(G-1142)
CHECKERED PAST RACING PDTS LLC
481 Southpoint Cir Ste 8 (46112-2206)
PHONE...............................317 852-6978
Gregg O Goff, *Mng Member*
Gregg Goff, *Mng Member*
Nathan Overfelt, *Mng Member*
Justin Goff,
Justin Overfelt,
EMP: 4
SALES (est): 550K **Privately Held**
SIC: **3599** Machine & other job shop work; machine shop, jobbing & repair

(G-1143)
CLERMONT NEON SIGN COMPANY
491 Johnson Ln Ste B (46112-9308)
PHONE...............................317 638-4123
Clifford Schrier, *Owner*
EMP: 2
SQ FT: 10,000
SALES (est): 158K **Privately Held**
SIC: **3993** 1799 Electric signs; neon signs; sign installation & maintenance

(G-1144)
COMPOSITE SPECIALTIES
464 Johnson Ln Ste D (46112-7811)
PHONE...............................317 852-1408
Jeff E Burnette, *Owner*

EMP: 2
SALES (est): 240K **Privately Held**
WEB: www.compositespecialties.com
SIC: **3624** Fibers, carbon & graphite

(G-1145)
CORNERSTONE INDUSTRIES CORP (PA)
Also Called: Cornerstone Flooring & Lining
8781 Motorsports Way (46112-2517)
PHONE...............................317 852-6522
Fax: 317 852-6433
Dan Hess, *CEO*
Jim Gray, *COO*
EMP: 60
SALES (est): 23.5MM **Privately Held**
SIC: **1752** 2851 Wood floor installation & refinishing; epoxy coatings

(G-1146)
CRANKSHAFT BREWING CO
1630 E Northfield Dr (46112-2498)
PHONE...............................317 939-0138
EMP: 2
SALES (est): 110.1K **Privately Held**
SIC: **5921** 2082 Liquor stores; malt beverages

(G-1147)
D & E PRINTING COMPANY INC
2 E Main St (46112-1214)
PHONE...............................317 852-9048
Fax: 317 852-0334
Eric Mizell, *President*
Sarah Mizell, *Admin Sec*
EMP: 8
SQ FT: 3,000
SALES (est): 1.6MM **Privately Held**
WEB: www.dandeprinting.com
SIC: **2752** Commercial printing, offset

(G-1148)
DAVIS TOOL AND GAGE COMPANY
5125 E County Road 450 N (46112-8260)
PHONE...............................317 852-5400
Fax: 317 852-5471
Fred Davis, *President*
EMP: 6
SQ FT: 11,000
SALES (est): 300K **Privately Held**
WEB: www.davistoolandgage.com
SIC: **3545** 1796 Precision tools, machinists'; gauges (machine tool accessories); installing building equipment

(G-1149)
FAB2ORDER INC
1145 E Northfield Dr (46112-2425)
P.O. Box 34407, Indianapolis (46234-0407)
PHONE...............................317 975-1056
Fax: 317 388-9536
Jason B Greeson, *President*
E Leroy Williams III, *Vice Pres*
Elizabeth A Greeson, *Admin Sec*
EMP: 32 EST: 2000
SQ FT: 34,000
SALES: 5.2MM **Privately Held**
WEB: www.fab2order.com
SIC: **3599** Amusement park equipment

(G-1150)
FAYETTE WELDING SERVICE INC
7555 S State Road 267 (46112-8992)
PHONE...............................317 852-2929
Don Schooler, *President*
Mary Schooler, *Corp Secy*
EMP: 2
SQ FT: 3,000
SALES (est): 132.4K **Privately Held**
SIC: **7692** 7699 Welding repair; farm machinery repair

(G-1151)
FUEL BLADDER DISTRIBUTORS INC
Also Called: S.B.I.
3800 N State Road 267 B (46112-8166)
PHONE...............................317 852-9156
Keith A Wagoner, *President*
Steve Russel, *Owner*
Louis Billanueba, *Vice Pres*
Alejandra Billanueva, *Shareholder*
Debra F Wagoner, *Shareholder*

EMP: 3
SQ FT: 600
SALES: 700K **Privately Held**
SIC: **3069** Fuel tanks, collapsible: rubberized fabric

(G-1152)
INDY HOLSTERS LLC
1705 Cold Spring Dr (46112-2170)
PHONE...............................317 370-7451
Neil Davis, *Principal*
EMP: 2
SALES (est): 126.4K **Privately Held**
SIC: **3199** Holsters, leather

(G-1153)
INDY METAL FINISHING CO
451 Suthpoint Cir Ste 400 (46112)
PHONE...............................317 858-5353
Carly Lawrence, *President*
EMP: 5
SQ FT: 6,000
SALES (est): 626.8K **Privately Held**
SIC: **3471** Anodizing (plating) of metals or formed products; cleaning, polishing & finishing

(G-1154)
INDY PRFMCE COMPOSITES INC
1185 E Northfield Dr A (46112-2508)
PHONE...............................317 858-7793
Jeffery L West, *President*
Linas A Paskus, *Vice Pres*
EMP: 7
SQ FT: 10,000
SALES (est): 1.4MM **Privately Held**
SIC: **3624** Carbon & graphite products; fibers, carbon & graphite

(G-1155)
INDY WIRING SERVICES LLC
150 Gasoline Aly (46112)
PHONE...............................317 371-7044
Jeremy Gibson,
EMP: 2 EST: 2010
SALES: 600K **Privately Held**
SIC: **3357** Appliance fixture wire, nonferrous

(G-1156)
INTEGRATED ORTHOTIC LAB INC
1630 E Northfield Dr # 400 (46112-2498)
PHONE...............................317 852-4640
Gary Oswald, *President*
EMP: 7
SALES: 1.7MM **Privately Held**
SIC: **5661** 3149 Custom & orthopedic shoes; children's footwear, except athletic

(G-1157)
J GAME VENTURES LLC
2675 Rothchild Pl Apt 207 (46112-9487)
PHONE...............................812 241-7096
Jeffrey McGowan, *President*
EMP: 5
SALES (est): 232.9K **Privately Held**
SIC: **3429** Furniture builders' & other household hardware

(G-1158)
JNS SPORTS
6390 N County Road 550 E (46112-9416)
PHONE...............................317 852-8314
Jason Lewis, *Owner*
EMP: 2 EST: 1995
SALES (est): 146.1K **Privately Held**
SIC: **3949** Sporting & athletic goods

(G-1159)
KASNAK RESTORATIONS INC
Also Called: Kasnak Designs
5505 N County Road 1000 E (46112-8707)
PHONE...............................317 852-9770
Robert Kasnak, *President*
Leslie Kasnak, *Corp Secy*
EMP: 3
SQ FT: 2,700
SALES (est): 286K **Privately Held**
WEB: www.kasnakrestorations.com
SIC: **7641** 2511 Antique furniture repair & restoration; furniture refinishing; wood household furniture

(G-1160)
MAPLEHURST BAKERIES LLC (DH)
50 Maplehurst Dr (46112-9085)
PHONE...............................317 858-9000
Kevin McDonough,
Jonathan Feigen,
Carl Singer,
Kevin Whitlock,
▲ EMP: 244
SQ FT: 188,547
SALES (est): 325.9MM
SALES (corp-wide): 37.8B **Privately Held**
WEB: www.maplehurstbakeries.com
SIC: **2051** Cakes, pies & pastries

(G-1161)
NOVARTIS CORPORATION
30 Lakeshore Pl (46112-1741)
PHONE...............................317 852-3839
Stan Jerrodo, *Manager*
EMP: 3
SALES (corp-wide): 49.1B **Privately Held**
WEB: www.novartis.com
SIC: **2834** Pharmaceutical preparations
HQ: Novartis Corporation
1 S Ridgedale Ave
East Hanover NJ 07936
212 307-1122

(G-1162)
PATRICK CUSTOM CARBON
475 Northpoint Ct Ste 400 (46112-2224)
PHONE...............................815 721-5150
EMP: 4 EST: 2012
SALES (est): 277K **Privately Held**
SIC: **3465** Body parts, automobile: stamped metal

(G-1163)
PNG SPEED AND CUSTOM CTR LLC
454 Johnson Ln Ste A (46112-7873)
PHONE...............................317 858-1919
EMP: 2
SALES (est): 160K **Privately Held**
SIC: **3566** Mfg Speed Changers/Drives

(G-1164)
POPPY CO
10915 N State Road 267 (46112-9297)
PHONE...............................317 442-2491
EMP: 7
SALES (est): 491K **Privately Held**
SIC: **3089** Plastic boats & other marine equipment

(G-1165)
PTG INC
5838 E County Road 800 N (46112-8818)
PHONE...............................317 892-4625
Fax: 317 892-3638
Peter Bloyd, *President*
EMP: 3
SALES (est): 267.2K **Privately Held**
SIC: **2431** Millwork

(G-1166)
ROADHOG INC
464 Southpoint Cir (46112-2203)
P.O. Box 519 (46112-0519)
PHONE...............................317 858-7050
Christopher Zanetis, *President*
EMP: 39
SALES (est): 9.1MM **Privately Held**
WEB: www.zanetispower.com
SIC: **3542** Mechanical (pneumatic or hydraulic) metal forming machines

(G-1167)
ROW PRINTING
7177 Golden Oak (46112-9168)
PHONE...............................317 796-3289
EMP: 2
SALES (est): 83.9K **Privately Held**
SIC: **2752** Commercial printing, lithographic

(G-1168)
SCHINDLER ELECTRIC INC
25 S Green St (46112-1239)
P.O. Box 148 (46112-0148)
PHONE...............................317 858-8215
John W Schindler Sr, *President*
EMP: 4 EST: 1997

SQ FT: 5,000
SALES: 500K **Privately Held**
WEB: www.schindlerelectric.com
SIC: 2899 Heat treating salts

(G-1169)
SCHUMACHER RACING CORPORATION
1681 E Northfield Dr A (46112-2486)
PHONE.............................317 858-0356
Fax: 317 858-3084
Donald A Schumacher, *President*
Mike Lewis, *Vice Pres*
Jeff Wolf, *Pub Rel Mgr*
Kyle Cunningham, *Marketing Staff*
Ted Yerzyk, *Marketing Staff*
◆ **EMP:** 35
SQ FT: 33,000
SALES (est): 11.9MM **Privately Held**
SIC: 3711 Automobile assembly, including specialty automobiles

(G-1170)
SCUTT TOOL & DIE
3245 N State Road 267 (46112-8894)
PHONE.............................317 858-8725
Rusty Scutt, *President*
EMP: 2
SALES (est): 239.2K **Privately Held**
SIC: 3599 Machine shop, jobbing & repair

(G-1171)
SEVIER MANUFACTURING
103 Oak Hill Dr (46112-8361)
PHONE.............................317 892-2784
Larry Lukins, *Owner*
EMP: 2
SALES (est): 400K **Privately Held**
WEB: www.seviermfg.com
SIC: 3949 Buckets, fish & bait

(G-1172)
SG HELMETS
8599 Motorsports Way (46112-2516)
PHONE.............................317 286-3616
John Krise, *Sales Staff*
EMP: 4
SALES (est): 322.5K **Privately Held**
SIC: 3949 Sporting & athletic goods

(G-1173)
TECHNA FIT OF INDIANA
493 Southpoint Cir B (46112-2203)
PHONE.............................317 350-2153
Stuart Trotter, *President*
EMP: 4 **EST:** 2012
SALES (est): 341.3K **Privately Held**
SIC: 3465 Body parts, automobile: stamped metal

(G-1174)
TECHNA-FIT INC
493 Southpoint Cir B (46112-2203)
PHONE.............................317 350-2153
Frederick S Trotter, *President*
Stuart Trotter, *President*
Chris Herman, *Opers Mgr*
Lani Trotter, *Advt Staff*
▲ **EMP:** 5
SALES (est): 880.4K **Privately Held**
SIC: 3714 3492 Motor vehicle brake systems & parts; hose & tube fittings & assemblies, hydraulic/pneumatic

(G-1175)
TONY STEWART RACING ENTPS LLC
438 Southpoint Cir (46112-2203)
PHONE.............................317 858-8620
Anthony Stewart, *Mng Member*
EMP: 7
SALES (est): 548.6K **Privately Held**
SIC: 3711 Automobile assembly, including specialty automobiles

(G-1176)
WESTON FOODS US INC (HQ)
Also Called: Maplehurst Bakeries
50 Maplehurst Dr (46112-9085)
PHONE.............................317 858-9000
Fax: 317 858-9009
Raymond Baxter, *President*
Ed Cassidy, *President*
Donald Niemeyer, *Vice Pres*
Edgar Woodle, *Treasurer*

Diana Bell, *Finance*
EMP: 621
SALES (est): 326.6MM
SALES (corp-wide): 37.8B **Privately Held**
SIC: 2051 2052 Bread, all types (white, wheat, rye, etc); fresh or frozen; rolls, bread type: fresh or frozen; cakes, bakery: except frozen; cookies & crackers
PA: George Weston Limited
22 St Clair Ave E Suite 1901
Toronto ON M4T 2
416 922-2500

(G-1177)
XWIND LLC
1185 E Northfield Dr C (46112-2507)
PHONE.............................317 350-2080
Brad Whitsitt,
EMP: 7 **EST:** 2011
SALES (est): 1MM **Privately Held**
SIC: 3699 Flight simulators (training aids), electronic

(G-1178)
YOUNG & KENADY INCORPORATED
Also Called: Descon
463 Suthpoint Cir Ste 600 (46112)
PHONE.............................317 852-6300
Fax: 317 297-4006
Michael Young, *President*
Jerry Young, *Vice Pres*
EMP: 9
SQ FT: 7,000
SALES (est): 1.2MM **Privately Held**
SIC: 7336 3999 3993 Commercial art & graphic design; education aids, devices & supplies; signs & advertising specialties

---

Brownstown
Jackson County

(G-1179)
AIM MEDIA INDIANA OPER LLC
Jackson Co Banner
116 E Cross St (47220-2011)
PHONE.............................812 358-2111
Melissa Bane, *Branch Mgr*
EMP: 3
SALES (corp-wide): 42.4MM **Privately Held**
SIC: 2711 Commercial printing & newspaper publishing combined
PA: Aim Media Indiana Operating, Llc
2980 N National Rd A
Columbus IN 47201
812 372-7811

(G-1180)
BROWNSTOWN QLTY TL AUTOMTN LLC
Also Called: Brownston Quality Tl & Design
1412 E State Road 250 (47220-9666)
PHONE.............................812 358-9059
Jesse Wheeler, *Mng Member*
Jared Cummings,
EMP: 10
SALES: 14MM **Privately Held**
SIC: 3312 Tool & die steel & alloys

(G-1181)
BROWNSTOWN QULTY TL DESIGN INC
1408 E State Road 250 (47220-9666)
PHONE.............................812 358-4593
Anthony Nehrt, *President*
Sue Nehrt, *Exec VP*
EMP: 10
SQ FT: 7,520
SALES: 1MM **Privately Held**
WEB: www.bqtd.com
SIC: 3544 Dies & die holders for metal cutting, forming, die casting

(G-1182)
BULL MANUFACTURING LLC
1943 E Us Highway 50 (47220-9746)
PHONE.............................812 530-1064
Dillard Whittymore, *Administration*
EMP: 2 **EST:** 2015
SALES (est): 124.9K **Privately Held**
SIC: 3715 Truck trailers

(G-1183)
COCKERHAMS SIGNS & GRAPHICS
1130 S County Road 150 W (47220-9611)
PHONE.............................812 358-3737
Steve Cockerham, *Owner*
EMP: 2
SALES (est): 198.2K **Privately Held**
SIC: 3993 Signs & advertising specialties

(G-1184)
CPC
Also Called: Custom Printing Co
811 Bloomington Rd (47220-1246)
P.O. Box 142 (47220-0142)
PHONE.............................812 358-5010
Tammy Weaver, *Principal*
Steve Weaver, *Principal*
EMP: 3
SALES (est): 227.4K **Privately Held**
SIC: 2752 Commercial printing, offset

(G-1185)
CRAIGS PRINTING CO
811 Bloomington Rd (47220-1246)
P.O. Box 142 (47220-0142)
PHONE.............................812 358-5010
Fax: 812 358-5010
Dennis Craig, *Owner*
EMP: 4
SQ FT: 3,500
SALES (est): 500K **Privately Held**
SIC: 2752 2759 Commercial printing, lithographic; screen printing; letterpress printing

(G-1186)
E & H TUBING INC
848 W Sweet St (47220-9557)
PHONE.............................812 358-3894
EMP: 38
SALES (corp-wide): 8.2MM **Privately Held**
SIC: 3317 Mfg Steel Pipe/Tubes
PA: E & H Tubing, Inc.
4401 W Roosevelt Rd
Chicago IL 60624
773 522-3100

(G-1187)
E & H TUBING INC (HQ)
Also Called: Indiana Steel and Tube
848 W Sweet St (47220-9557)
PHONE.............................812 358-3894
Gary Birnbaum, *President*
Paul Parent, *President*
Michael Cipolla, *Treasurer*
Gary Giles, *VP Sales*
Scott Conrad, *Manager*
EMP: 45
SQ FT: 160
SALES: 75MM
SALES (corp-wide): 66.5MM **Privately Held**
SIC: 3317 Steel pipe & tubes
PA: Charter Steel Trading Co., Inc.
4401 W Roosevelt Rd
Chicago IL 60624
773 522-3100

(G-1188)
GOLDEN AGE AEROPLANE WORK LLC
2375 E State Road 250 (47220-9694)
PHONE.............................812 358-5778
Timothy O'Conner, *Owner*
Gayla O'Connor, *Mng Member*
EMP: 2
SALES (est): 163.3K **Privately Held**
SIC: 3721 Airplanes, fixed or rotary wing

(G-1189)
JACKSON COUNTY BANNER
Also Called: Banner Cablevision, The
116 E Cross St (47220-2011)
P.O. Box G (47220-0307)
PHONE.............................812 358-2111
Fax: 812 358-5606
Larry Puratto, *President*
Larry Morris, *Administration*
EMP: 13
SQ FT: 1,200

SALES (est): 550K **Privately Held**
WEB: www.thebanner.com
SIC: 2711 Newspapers: publishing only, not printed on site

(G-1190)
MARK HACKMAN
Also Called: Hackman Brothers Show Feed
3640 S County Road 400 E (47220-9691)
PHONE.............................812 522-8257
Mark Hackman, *Principal*
EMP: 3
SALES (est): 165.9K **Privately Held**
SIC: 2048 Prepared feeds

(G-1191)
REIDCO INC
Also Called: Marion-Kay Spices
1351 W Us Highway 50 (47220-9530)
PHONE.............................812 358-3000
Fax: 812 358-3400
Kordell Reid, *President*
Tam Warren, *CFO*
Pam Warren, *Admin Sec*
EMP: 20 **EST:** 1986
SQ FT: 50,000
SALES (est): 3.4MM **Privately Held**
WEB: www.reidcogifts.com
SIC: 2099 5149 5499 Seasonings & spices; spices & seasonings; spices & herbs

(G-1192)
WERRCO INC
Also Called: Werrco Tools & Machines
5994 W State Road 58 (47220-9750)
PHONE.............................812 358-8665
Fax: 812 497-3500
James Mann, *President*
April Mann, *Manager*
EMP: 5
SQ FT: 4,000
SALES: 300K **Privately Held**
SIC: 3544 Dies & die holders for metal cutting, forming, die casting; special dies & tools

(G-1193)
WILLIAM S BANE
Also Called: Bane Logging
1414 E Us Highway 50 (47220-9708)
PHONE.............................812 358-5790
William S Bane, *Owner*
EMP: 4
SALES (est): 240K **Privately Held**
SIC: 2411 Timber, cut at logging camp

(G-1194)
WILSONS LOCKER & PROC PLANT
Also Called: Wilsons Slaughtering & Proc
324 N Bolles St (47220-1106)
PHONE.............................812 358-2632
Ed Branum, *Manager*
EMP: 2 **EST:** 1892
SQ FT: 4,000
SALES (est): 80.7K **Privately Held**
SIC: 0751 2013 2011 Slaughtering: custom livestock services; sausages & other prepared meats; meat packing plants

---

Brownsville
Union County

(G-1195)
EAST FORK STUDIO & PRESS INC
104 Ne First St (47325-9731)
PHONE.............................765 458-6103
James Kaufman, *Principal*
EMP: 2
SALES (est): 93.6K **Privately Held**
SIC: 2741 Miscellaneous publishing

(G-1196)
TJ PERFORMANCE LLC
4331 N Jobe Rd (47325-9405)
PHONE.............................765 580-0481
Mike Jobe, *Owner*
EMP: 2
SALES (est): 223.3K **Privately Held**
SIC: 2992 Lubricating oils & greases

▲ = Import ▼=Export
◆ =Import/Export

Bruceville
Knox County

(G-1197)
JFS MILLING INC
5167 N State Road 67 (47516-6279)
PHONE..............................812 324-2022
Theodore Seger, *President*
Kim Weiss, *Controller*
EMP: 24 **EST:** 2003
SALES (est): 550.5K **Privately Held**
SIC: 2048 Prepared feeds

(G-1198)
TRIMAX MACHINE LLC
5852 N Rod And Gun Clb (47516-6005)
PHONE..............................812 887-9281
Traci French, *Co-Owner*
Justin French, *Co-Owner*
EMP: 3
SALES (est): 281.3K **Privately Held**
SIC: 3559 Automotive related machinery

Bryant
Jay County

(G-1199)
BRYANT MACHINING & WELDING LLC
1015 E State Road 67 (47326-9105)
P.O. Box 186 (47326-0186)
PHONE..............................260 997-6059
Fax: 260 997-8317
Larry Stults,
Diana Stults,
EMP: 4
SALES (est): 130K **Privately Held**
SIC: 3599 3548 Machine shop, jobbing & repair; welding apparatus

(G-1200)
HI-TECH TURNING
303 N Hendricks St (47326-9068)
P.O. Box 74 (47326-0074)
PHONE..............................260 997-6668
Fax: 260 997-6698
Steve Billington, *Owner*
Becky Billinton, *Partner*
EMP: 2
SALES: 200K **Privately Held**
SIC: 3599 Machine shop, jobbing & repair

(G-1201)
RICHARDS RESTAURANT INC
Also Called: Bear Creek Farms
8341 N 400 E (47326-9003)
PHONE..............................260 997-6823
Carla Loy, *General Mgr*
Carla Greens, *Manager*
EMP: 10
SALES (corp-wide): 12MM **Privately Held**
SIC: 5812 2035 Restaurant, family: chain; dressings, salad: raw & cooked (except dry mixes)
PA: Richards Restaurant, Inc.
8339 N 400 E
Bryant IN
260 997-6823

(G-1202)
T-FLYERZ PRINTING AND PROM LLC
6073 N Us Highway 27 (47326-8832)
PHONE..............................260 729-7392
EMP: 2
SALES (est): 151.8K **Privately Held**
SIC: 2752 Commercial printing, lithographic

Buffalo
White County

(G-1203)
HITES HARDWOOD LUMBER CORP
309 S East St (47925)
P.O. Box 162 (47925-0162)
PHONE..............................574 278-7783
Lewis Hites, *President*
Cheryl R Hites, *Nurse*
EMP: 12
SALES: 1.5MM **Privately Held**
SIC: 2421 Sawmills & planing mills, general

(G-1204)
LEIS MACHINE SHOP INC
6033 E Hwy 16 (47925)
P.O. Box 227 (47925-0227)
PHONE..............................574 278-6000
Otto Richard Leis, *President*
Patsy Leis, *Treasurer*
EMP: 5
SALES (est): 300K **Privately Held**
SIC: 3599 Machine & other job shop work

Bunker Hill
Miami County

(G-1205)
DOUGS WELDING SHOP
10541 S Strawtown Pike (46914-9573)
PHONE..............................765 689-8396
Doug Le Master, *Owner*
EMP: 3
SALES (est): 220.3K **Privately Held**
SIC: 7692 Welding repair

(G-1206)
GVM INC
8497 S Us Highway 31 (46914-9485)
PHONE..............................765 689-5010
EMP: 2
SALES (corp-wide): 31MM **Privately Held**
SIC: 3523 Fertilizing, spraying, dusting & irrigation machinery
PA: Gvm, Inc.
224 E King St Ste 102
East Berlin PA 17316
717 677-6197

(G-1207)
TIMOTHY WHITE ✪
Also Called: Gold Medal Awards
191 S Elm St (46914-1517)
P.O. Box 214 (46914-0214)
PHONE..............................765 689-8270
Timothy White, *Owner*
EMP: 4 **EST:** 2017
SALES (est): 155.5K **Privately Held**
SIC: 3499 Novelties & giftware, including trophies

Burket
Kosciusko County

(G-1208)
WARSAW BLACK OXIDE INC
310 S Walnut St (46508)
P.O. Box 38 (46508-0038)
PHONE..............................574 491-2975
Fax: 574 491-3305
Craig Doran, *President*
◆ **EMP:** 22
SQ FT: 40,000
SALES: 1.5MM **Privately Held**
SIC: 2899 Plating compounds

Burlington
Carroll County

(G-1209)
ARMSTRONG DRILLING INC
1490 S Michigan St (46915-9492)
P.O. Box 156 (46915-0156)
PHONE..............................765 455-2445
Fax: 765 566-3370
Joseph Armstrong, *President*
EMP: 4
SALES: 400K **Privately Held**
WEB: www.armstrongdrilling.com
SIC: 1781 1381 Water well drilling; drilling oil & gas wells

(G-1210)
BECKS
709 Michigan Rd (46915-1507)
PHONE..............................765 566-3900
Kevin Beck, *President*
EMP: 4 **EST:** 2012
SALES (est): 322K **Privately Held**
SIC: 3421 Table & food cutlery, including butchers'

(G-1211)
KRISTENS HOMEMADE DELIGHT
703 Michigan Rd (46915-1507)
PHONE..............................765 566-2200
EMP: 4
SALES (est): 252.9K **Privately Held**
SIC: 2051 Mfg Bread/Related Products

Burney
Decatur County

(G-1212)
HAUSERS RECLAMATION & REM
811 W Sheridan St (47240-1460)
PHONE..............................812 663-6378
Mary Hausers, *Owner*
EMP: 2
SALES (est): 87.5K **Privately Held**
SIC: 3713 Truck bodies & parts

(G-1213)
RIVERA SCREENPRINTING
1010 E State Road 46 (47240-7723)
PHONE..............................812 663-0816
Jamie Rivera, *Owner*
Beverly Rivera, *Co-Owner*
EMP: 3
SALES: 75K **Privately Held**
SIC: 2759 Screen printing

Burns Harbor
Porter County

(G-1214)
ARCELORMITTAL BURNS HARBOR LLC
250 W Us Highway 12 (46304-9727)
PHONE..............................219 787-2120
Michael Rippey, *CEO*
James Bradley, *Division Mgr*
Dale Heinz, *Division Mgr*
John Battisti, *COO*
John Brett, *Exec VP*
◆ **EMP:** 3100
SALES: 706.4K **Privately Held**
SIC: 3312 Blast furnaces & steel mills
HQ: Arcelormittal Usa Llc
1 S Dearborn St Ste 1800
Chicago IL 60603
312 346-0300

(G-1215)
ISG BURNS HARBOR SERVICES LLC
250 W Us Highway 12 (46304-9727)
PHONE..............................219 787-2120
Michael Pavel, *Foreman/Supr*
Gregory Racich, *Manager*
Carol Snow, *Manager*
EMP: 12
SALES: 523.2K **Privately Held**
SIC: 3312 Blast furnaces & steel mills

(G-1216)
J & F STEEL CORPORATION
310 Tech Dr (46304-8843)
PHONE..............................219 764-3500
Fax: 219 764-0073
J Schoettert, *President*
M Pisacane, *Admin Sec*
EMP: 6
SALES (est): 827.5K **Privately Held**
SIC: 3449 Bars, concrete reinforcing: fabricated steel

(G-1217)
METAL SERVICES LLC
250 W Us Highway 12 (46304-9727)
P.O. Box 619, Chesterton (46304-0619)
PHONE..............................219 787-1514
EMP: 9 **Privately Held**
SIC: 3295 Perlite, aggregate or expanded
HQ: Metal Services Llc
148 W State St Ste 301
Kennett Square PA 19348

(G-1218)
MORTAR NET USA LTD
326 Melton Rd (46304-9719)
PHONE..............................800 664-6638
Fax: 219 787-5088
Gary Johnson, *President*
Tom Sourlis, *Chairman*
Steven Fechino, *Engineer*
Bill Lewis, *Controller*
Michael Stallworth, *Marketing Staff*
▲ **EMP:** 7
SALES (est): 1.3MM **Privately Held**
SIC: 3531 Catch basin cleaners

(G-1219)
RYERSON TULL INC (DH)
310 Tech Dr (46304-8843)
PHONE..............................219 764-3500
Edward J Lehner, *CEO*
Erich Schnaufer, *CFO*
▲ **EMP:** 75
SALES (est): 26.1MM **Publicly Held**
WEB: www.j-fsteel.com
SIC: 5051 3316 3312 Metals service centers & offices; cold finishing of steel shapes; blast furnaces & steel mills
HQ: Joseph T. Ryerson & Son, Inc.
227 W Monroe St Fl 27
Chicago IL 60606
312 292-5000

(G-1220)
SSW INTERNATIONAL INC
1111 State Road 149 (46304-9429)
PHONE..............................219 763-1199
Fax: 219 787-8217
Walter Sieckman, *Principal*
EMP: 23
SALES (corp-wide): 42.4MM **Privately Held**
SIC: 3399 Iron, powdered
HQ: Ssw International, Inc.
661 Andersen Dr Ste 7
Pittsburgh PA 15220
412 922-9100

Butler
Dekalb County

(G-1221)
AIR PRODUCTS AND CHEMICALS INC
4590 County Road 59 (46721-9747)
P.O. Box 413 (46721-0413)
PHONE..............................260 868-9145
Fax: 260 868-9050
Scott Menke, *Branch Mgr*
EMP: 30
SALES (corp-wide): 8.1B **Publicly Held**
WEB: www.airproducts.com
SIC: 2813 Industrial gases
PA: Air Products And Chemicals, Inc.
7201 Hamilton Blvd
Allentown PA 18195
610 481-4911

(G-1222)
AVF MACHINING
5850 County Road 24 (46721-9633)
PHONE...................................260 760-1531
EMP: 2
SALES (est): 164.8K **Privately Held**
SIC: 3599 Machine shop, jobbing & repair

(G-1223)
BUTLER MILL SERVICE COMPANY
4506 County Road 59 (46721-9747)
PHONE...................................260 868-5123
Fax: 260 868-5885
Tim Wozny, *Branch Mgr*
EMP: 32 **Privately Held**
SIC: 3295 Slag, crushed or ground
PA: Butler Mill Service Company
    9300 Dix
    Dearborn MI 48120

(G-1224)
CENTER CONCRETE INC
4225 County Road 79 (46721-9774)
PHONE...................................800 453-4224
Don Pahl, *Branch Mgr*
EMP: 3
SALES (corp-wide): 3.2MM **Privately Held**
SIC: 3273 Ready-mixed concrete
PA: Center Concrete Inc
    8790 Us Highway 6
    Edgerton OH 43517
    419 298-2440

(G-1225)
CJ AUTOMOTIVE INDIANA LLC (PA)
100 Comm St (46721)
P.O. Box 100 (46721-0100)
PHONE...................................260 868-2147
SRI Bramadesam, *President*
Jeff Heller, *Mfg Dir*
Rachel Shupe, *CFO*
▲ EMP: 180
SALES (est): 42.1MM **Privately Held**
SIC: 3441 3423 Fabricated structural metal; jacks: lifting, screw or ratchet (hand tools)

(G-1226)
COLOR MASTER INC (PA)
810 S Broadway St (46721-9514)
P.O. Box 338 (46721-0338)
PHONE...................................260 868-2320
Fax: 260 868-1337
Philip Schlink, *CEO*
Kyle Skaggs, *President*
EMP: 71
SQ FT: 48,000
SALES (est): 17.9MM **Privately Held**
WEB: www.color-master.com
SIC: 3089 3087 Coloring & finishing of plastic products; custom compound purchased resins

(G-1227)
D R PATTERN INC
1835 County Road 61 (46721-9641)
PHONE...................................260 868-5585
Judt A Strock, *Vice Pres*
EMP: 2
SALES (est): 110K **Privately Held**
SIC: 3543 Industrial patterns

(G-1228)
G W ENTERPRISES
7063 County Road 24 (46721-9662)
PHONE...................................260 868-2555
Gloria Wood, *Owner*
EMP: 3
SALES: 250K **Privately Held**
SIC: 3625 Truck controls, industrial battery

(G-1229)
HEIDTMAN STEEL PRODUCTS INC
Also Called: Hs Processing
4400 County Road 59 (46721-9746)
PHONE...................................419 691-4646
Fax: 260 868-0893
Tim Weist, *Facilities Mgr*
Curt McDaniel, *Purchasing*
Sarah Brown, *Branch Mgr*
EMP: 160

SALES (corp-wide): 299.5MM **Privately Held**
WEB: www.heidtman.com
SIC: 3312 3316 3471 3444 Blast furnaces & steel mills; cold finishing of steel shapes; plating & polishing; sheet metalwork; fabricated structural metal
HQ: Heidtman Steel Products, Inc.
    2401 Front St
    Toledo OH 43605
    419 691-4646

(G-1230)
HENDRICKSON INTERNATIONAL CORP
Also Called: Hendrickson Suspension
201 W Cherry St (46721-1441)
PHONE...................................260 868-2131
Fax: 260 868-2850
Dave Cater,
EMP: 4
SQ FT: 44,000
SALES (corp-wide): 1.1B **Privately Held**
SIC: 3714 Motor vehicle parts & accessories
HQ: Hendrickson International Corporation
    500 Park Blvd Ste 450
    Itasca IL 60143
    630 874-9700

(G-1231)
INTERNATIONAL ENGLISH INC
Also Called: National Stock Dog Registry
3597 County Road 75 (46721-9708)
P.O. Box 402 (46721-0402)
PHONE...................................260 868-2670
Rebecca Gorney, *President*
Juanita Russell, *Corp Secy*
David J Gorney, *Vice Pres*
EMP: 3
SALES (est): 81.5K **Privately Held**
SIC: 0752 2721 Animal breeding services; periodicals

(G-1232)
INTERNATIONAL PAPER COMPANY
2626 County Road 71 (46721-9406)
PHONE...................................260 868-2151
Fax: 260 868-2953
John Chambers, *General Mgr*
Bill Haimowitz, *General Mgr*
Dale French, *Sales Associate*
EMP: 150
SQ FT: 132,000
SALES (corp-wide): 21.7B **Publicly Held**
SIC: 2653 Boxes, corrugated: made from purchased materials
PA: International Paper Company
    6400 Poplar Ave
    Memphis TN 38197
    901 419-9000

(G-1233)
MOLD SERVICE INC
2911 County Road 59 (46721-9624)
PHONE...................................260 868-2920
Fax: 260 868-2920
Beverly Martin, *President*
Delbert E Martin, *Admin Sec*
EMP: 7 EST: 1960
SQ FT: 6,000
SALES (est): 972.9K **Privately Held**
SIC: 3544 Special dies & tools

(G-1234)
MULTIMACTIC NEW HAVEN LLC
201 Re Jones Rd (46721-9570)
PHONE...................................260 868-1067
Peter Czapka,
EMP: 96
SALES (corp-wide): 75MM **Privately Held**
SIC: 3465 Body parts, automobile: stamped metal
PA: Multimatic New Haven, Llc
    2808 Adams Center Rd
    Fort Wayne IN 46803
    260 868-1067

(G-1235)
MULTIMATIC INDIANA INC
201 Re Jones Rd (46721-9570)
PHONE...................................260 868-1000
Peter Czapka, *President*
Martin Bressel, *Vice Pres*

Rhys Jones, *Engineer*
Sandie Baker, *Human Res Mgr*
Josh Bowsman, *Admin Asst*
▲ EMP: 200
SQ FT: 25,000
SALES (est): 107.2MM
SALES (corp-wide): 266.7K **Privately Held**
SIC: 3465 Body parts, automobile: stamped metal
HQ: Multimatic Inc
    8688 Woodbine Ave Suite 200
    Markham ON L3R 8
    905 470-9149

(G-1236)
NEW MLLENNIUM BLDG SYSTEMS LLC
6115 County Road 42 (46721-9743)
PHONE...................................260 868-6000
Fax: 260 868-6001
Robbie Deller, *Transptn Dir*
Dan Lewis, *Purchasing*
Jim Fowler, *Sales Mgr*
Damon Hunter, *Sales Mgr*
Bob Bly, *Branch Mgr*
EMP: 101 **Publicly Held**
SIC: 3441 Joists, open web steel: long-span series
HQ: New Millennium Building Systems Llc
    7575 W Jefferson Blvd
    Fort Wayne IN 46804
    260 969-3500

(G-1237)
NEW PROCESS STEEL LP
4258 County Road 61 (46721-9557)
PHONE...................................260 868-1445
Fax: 260 868-0595
Tom Claes, *Manager*
EMP: 50
SALES (corp-wide): 447.2MM **Privately Held**
SIC: 5051 3469 Sheets, metal; steel; sheets, galvanized or other coated; stamping metal for the trade
PA: New Process Steel, L.P.
    1322 N Post Oak Rd
    Houston TX 77055
    713 686-9631

(G-1238)
PETTIGREW
7725 County Road 32 (46721-9704)
PHONE...................................260 868-2032
Dennis Pettigrew, *Owner*
Linda Pettigrew, *Co-Owner*
EMP: 2
SALES (est): 74.2K **Privately Held**
SIC: 3421 Knife blades & blanks

(G-1239)
SERVICE STEEL FRAMING INC
206 Depot St (46721-1312)
P.O. Box 339 (46721-0339)
PHONE...................................260 868-5853
Fax: 260 868-5854
Don B Hollman, *President*
Andy Hollman, *Vice Pres*
Steve Hutton, *Project Mgr*
Brenda Martin, *Project Mgr*
Diane Townsend, *Project Mgr*
EMP: 13
SQ FT: 12,000
SALES (est): 3.9MM **Privately Held**
WEB: www.servicesteelframing.com
SIC: 3441 Building components, structural steel

(G-1240)
SHULL MACHINE SERVICE INC
3877 County Road 49 (46721-9620)
PHONE...................................260 925-4198
Fax: 260 925-6839
Edwin M Shull, *President*
EMP: 2
SALES (est): 246K **Privately Held**
SIC: 3599 Machine & other job shop work

(G-1241)
SRT PROSTHETICS ORTHOTICS LLC
408 E Washington St (46721-1179)
PHONE...................................815 679-6900
Erin Ruxton, *Branch Mgr*
EMP: 3

SALES (corp-wide): 1,000K **Privately Held**
SIC: 3842 Prosthetic appliances; limbs, artificial
PA: Srt Prosthetics & Orthotics, Llc
    408 E Washington St
    Butler IN 46721
    419 633-3961

(G-1242)
SRT PROSTHETICS ORTHOTICS LLC
408 E Washington St (46721-1179)
PHONE...................................847 855-0030
Erin Ruxton, *Branch Mgr*
EMP: 4
SALES (corp-wide): 1,000K **Privately Held**
SIC: 3842 Prosthetic appliances
PA: Srt Prosthetics & Orthotics, Llc
    408 E Washington St
    Butler IN 46721
    419 633-3961

(G-1243)
STAFFORD GRAVEL INC
4225 County Road 79 (46721-9774)
PHONE...................................260 868-2503
Fax: 260 868-2576
Gary Weber, *President*
EMP: 10
SALES (est): 649.8K **Privately Held**
SIC: 1442 Gravel & pebble mining

(G-1244)
STEEL DYNAMICS INC
Flat Roll Division
4500 County Road 59 (46721-9747)
PHONE...................................260 868-8000
Fax: 260 868-8055
Glenn Pushis, *Vice Pres*
Tim Bosserman, *Engineer*
Nick Reinhardt, *Engineer*
Amy Woods, *Engineer*
Brian Butcher, *Project Engr*
EMP: 650 **Publicly Held**
SIC: 3312 Plate, sheet & strip, except coated products
PA: Steel Dynamics, Inc.
    7575 W Jefferson Blvd
    Fort Wayne IN 46804

(G-1245)
THERMA-TRU CORP
601 Re Jones Rd (46721-9571)
PHONE...................................260 868-5811
Fax: 260 868-5058
Michael Moyle, *District Mgr*
Mike Daman, *Vice Pres*
Tara Gutierrez, *QC Mgr*
Dan McBride, *Sales Mgr*
Alma Dietrich, *Cust Mgr*
EMP: 15
SALES (corp-wide): 5.2B **Publicly Held**
SIC: 3089 Garbage containers, plastic
HQ: Therma-Tru Corp.
    1750 Indian Wood Cir # 100
    Maumee OH 43537
    419 891-7400

(G-1246)
THERMA-TRU CORP
601 Re Jones Rd Dock13 (46721-9571)
PHONE...................................260 868-5811
Ken Dearing, *Prdtn Mgr*
Scott Anderson, *Safety Mgr*
Scot Atkinson, *Purch Agent*
Craig Oechsle, *Engineer*
Kassy Davis, *Human Res Mgr*
EMP: 50
SALES (corp-wide): 5.2B **Publicly Held**
WEB: www.thermatru.com
SIC: 3442 Metal doors
HQ: Therma-Tru Corp.
    1750 Indian Wood Cir # 100
    Maumee OH 43537
    419 891-7400

▲ = Import ▼=Export
◆ =Import/Export

Butlerville
Jennings County

(G-1247)
CARGO SKIFF CORPORATION
1280 N County Road 500 E (47223-9685)
PHONE.................................812 873-6349
Daniel L Pohle, President
EMP: 5
SALES: 100K Privately Held
SIC: 3731 Commercial cargo ships, building & repairing

(G-1248)
JENNINGS COUNTY PALLETS INC
5195 E Us Highway 50 (47223-9662)
P.O. Box 307, North Vernon (47265-0307)
PHONE.................................812 458-6288
John Castetter, Manager
EMP: 20 Privately Held
SIC: 2448 Pallets, wood
PA: Jennings County Pallets Inc
5195 E Us Highway 50
Butlerville IN 47223

(G-1249)
JENNINGS COUNTY PALLETS INC (PA)
5195 E Us Highway 50 (47223-9662)
P.O. Box 307, North Vernon (47265-0307)
PHONE.................................812 458-6288
Fax: 812 458-6740
Rolla Millspaugh, President
Steve Millspaugh, Vice Pres
EMP: 20
SALES: 2.5MM Privately Held
SIC: 2448 5031 4213 Pallets, wood; lumber, plywood & millwork; trucking, except local

(G-1250)
KELLER TOOL
Also Called: Keller Tools
1085 N County Road 500 E (47223-9689)
PHONE.................................812 873-7344
Fax: 812 873-7344
Kenneth Keller, Owner
Natalie Keller, Manager
EMP: 2 EST: 1998
SALES: 178K Privately Held
SIC: 3544 Special dies, tools, jigs & fixtures

(G-1251)
STAPLES PIPE & MUFFLER (PA)
1365 S County Road 650 E (47223-9529)
PHONE.................................812 522-3569
Angela Staples, President
EMP: 3
SALES (est): 666.5K Privately Held
SIC: 5013 3498 Automotive supplies & parts; fabricated pipe & fittings

Cambridge City
Wayne County

(G-1252)
ABF WELDING & PIPE LLC
308 N 3rd St (47327-1331)
PHONE.................................765 977-7349
Thomas A Bertsch, Administration
EMP: 2
SALES (est): 185.4K Privately Held
SIC: 7692 Welding repair

(G-1253)
ASTRO CUTTING TOOLS
600 E Church St (47327-1403)
PHONE.................................765 478-3662
Fax: 765 478-5116
Ronald Sheehy, President
EMP: 18
SQ FT: 13,000
SALES (est): 1.8MM Privately Held
SIC: 3545 Cutting tools for machine tools

(G-1254)
CONVERTO MFG CO INC
220 S Green St (47327)
P.O. Box 287 (47327-0287)
PHONE.................................765 478-3205
Fax: 765 478-1223
Clarence France, President
Brenda Chandler, Admin Sec
EMP: 7
SQ FT: 40,000
SALES: 2MM Privately Held
WEB: www.convertomfg.com
SIC: 3537 Truck trailers, used in plants, docks, terminals, etc.

(G-1255)
DESIGN & MFG SOLUTIONS LLC
15421 W Hunnicut Rd (47327-9729)
P.O. Box 336 (47327-0336)
PHONE.................................765 478-9393
Travis Wadle, Mng Member
Julie Wadle,
EMP: 10
SALES (est): 1.3MM Privately Held
SIC: 3544 Special dies & tools

(G-1256)
FAB-TECH INDUSTRIES
14271 W Us Highway 40 (47327-9403)
PHONE.................................765 478-4191
Fax: 765 478-4614
Ken Banning, President
Jill Banning, Admin Sec
EMP: 5
SQ FT: 10,000
SALES (est): 649.2K Privately Held
SIC: 3547 3441 Pipe & tube mills; fabricated structural metal

(G-1257)
IRVING MATERIALS INC
Also Called: I M I
14413 W Us Highway 40 (47327-9403)
PHONE.................................765 478-4914
Fax: 765 478-9088
Steve Lewis, Branch Mgr
EMP: 8
SALES (corp-wide): 800.6MM Privately Held
SIC: 3273 5032 Ready-mixed concrete; concrete & cinder building products
PA: Irving Materials, Inc.
8032 N State Road 9
Greenfield IN 46140
317 326-3101

(G-1258)
JANIS BUHL
Also Called: Wayne Newspapers
26 W Church St (47327-1615)
P.O. Box 337 (47327-0337)
PHONE.................................765 478-5448
Janis Buhl, Owner
EMP: 8
SALES (est): 185K Privately Held
SIC: 2711 Newspapers

(G-1259)
KIDS AT HEART PUBLISHING LLC
215 W Main St (47327-1122)
PHONE.................................765 478-5773
Shelley Davis, Owner
EMP: 2
SALES (est): 50K Privately Held
SIC: 2741 Miscellaneous publishing

(G-1260)
RIHM INC (PA)
Also Called: Rihm Foods
8360 E County Road 950 S (47327-9608)
P.O. Box 148 (47327-0148)
PHONE.................................765 478-3426
Fax: 765 478-4491
James Rihm, President
Donald Rihm, Treasurer
Gerald Rihm, Admin Sec
EMP: 5 EST: 1926
SQ FT: 2,000
SALES (est): 1.6MM Privately Held
WEB: www.rihm.com
SIC: 2011 5411 5921 2013 Meat packing plants; beef products from beef slaughtered on site; grocery stores, independent; liquor stores; sausages & other prepared meats

(G-1261)
ROGERS ENGINEERING AND MFG CO
112 S Center St (47327-1243)
PHONE.................................765 478-5444
Fax: 765 478-3324
William A Rogers, President
Don Marangoni, Vice Pres
Steve Rogers, Vice Pres
William Rogersjr, Vice Pres
Mike Morgan, Plant Mgr
◆ EMP: 45
SQ FT: 100,000
SALES: 7MM Privately Held
SIC: 3567 3444 7692 3398 Industrial furnaces & ovens; sheet metalwork; welding repair; metal heat treating; fabricated plate work (boiler shop)

(G-1262)
WESTERN WAYNE NEWS
Also Called: Mettle Creek
26 W Church St (47327-1615)
P.O. Box 337 (47327-0337)
PHONE.................................765 478-5448
Fax: 765 478-5155
Janis Buhl, Owner
EMP: 7
SALES (est): 204K Privately Held
SIC: 2711 Newspapers: publishing only, not printed on site

(G-1263)
WESTERN WYNE RGONAL SEWAGE DST
200 S Plum St (47327-1231)
PHONE.................................765 478-3788
Darleene Druley, Superintendent
EMP: 3
SALES (est): 260K Privately Held
SIC: 3589 Sewage & water treatment equipment

Camby
Morgan County

(G-1264)
CENTRIFUGE SUPPORT & SUPS LLC
8446 Abbey Dell Dr (46113-8258)
PHONE.................................317 830-6141
Kenneth Sucilla, Mng Member
Janna Caywood, Admin Sec
EMP: 2
SALES (est): 231.1K Privately Held
SIC: 3556 Cream separators (food products machinery)

(G-1265)
CENTURY STEEL FABRICATING INC
4421 E County Line Rd (46113)
PHONE.................................317 834-1295
Fax: 317 834-1579
Greg Sheets, President
Connie R Sheets, Admin Sec
EMP: 14
SQ FT: 7,200
SALES (est): 2.9MM Privately Held
SIC: 3441 Fabricated structural metal

(G-1266)
EUREKA SCIENCE CORP
7631 Reynolds Rd (46113-9270)
P.O. Box 416 (46113-0416)
PHONE.................................317 821-0805
Patricia Andrews, Owner
EMP: 2
SALES (est): 55K Privately Held
SIC: 3944 Science kits: microscopes, chemistry sets, etc.

(G-1267)
GAME FACE GRAPHIX LLC
8903 Squire Boone Ct (46113-8825)
PHONE.................................317 340-0973
Ryan Stokes, President
Heather Stokes, Vice Pres
EMP: 2

SALES (est): 88.6K Privately Held
SIC: 2759 7336 Advertising literature: printing; decals: printing; commercial art & graphic design

(G-1268)
RENK SYSTEMS CORPORATION
8880 Union Mills Dr (46113-9705)
PHONE.................................317 455-1367
Fax: 317 831-2978
Joerg Cordes, President
David Williams Russell, Principal
Kerstin Buchheister, Treasurer
Benjamin Scott, Sales Executive
EMP: 11
SQ FT: 10,000
SALES (est): 2.3MM
SALES (corp-wide): 272B Privately Held
SIC: 3825 Engine electrical test equipment
HQ: Renk Ag
Gogginger Str. 73
Augsburg 86159
821 570-00

(G-1269)
T&T COATINGS INC
8544 E Hadley Rd (46113-8501)
PHONE.................................317 408-3752
David C Thompson, President
EMP: 2
SALES (est): 203.9K Privately Held
SIC: 2851 Polyurethane coatings

(G-1270)
WAX SHIELD
Also Called: John Thrasher
11818 N Bens Ct (46113-8312)
PHONE.................................317 831-1349
John Thrasher, Owner
EMP: 2
SALES (est): 135.4K Privately Held
SIC: 2899 Rifle bore cleaning compounds

(G-1271)
XFMRS HOLDINGS INC (PA)
7570 E Landersdale Rd (46113-8512)
PHONE.................................317 834-1066
Anthony Imburgia, President
Joe Huff, Vice Pres
EMP: 4
SALES (est): 76.3MM Privately Held
SIC: 3699 Electrical equipment & supplies

(G-1272)
XFMRS INC
7570 E Landersdale Rd (46113-8512)
PHONE.................................317 834-1066
Fax: 317 834-1067
Anthony E Imburia, President
Buddy Woods, General Mgr
Cheri Imburgia, Principal
Tony Imburgia, Vice Pres
Randell Barnhorst, Treasurer
▲ EMP: 1100
SQ FT: 7,500
SALES (est): 110.1MM Privately Held
WEB: www.xfmrs.com
SIC: 3677 5065 3612 Electronic transformers; electronic parts & equipment; transformers, except electric

Camden
Carroll County

(G-1273)
DELAPLANE & SON NEON & SIGN
Also Called: Delaplane Son Neon & Sign Svc
7768 E 550 N (46917-9594)
PHONE.................................574 859-3431
Fax: 574 859-3432
Robert K Delaplane, President
Deborah Delaplane, Corp Secy
EMP: 5
SALES: 400K Privately Held
SIC: 3993 5046 Neon signs; neon signs

(G-1274)
HOG SLAT INCORPORATED
200 N Meridian Line Rd (46917)
P.O. Box 26 (46917-0026)
PHONE.................................574 967-4145
Fax: 574 967-4794

Lamont Thornton, *Safety Dir*
Richard Hicks, *Branch Mgr*
EMP: 20
SALES (corp-wide): 635.6MM **Privately Held**
WEB: www.hogslat.com
SIC: 3523 2048 Hog feeding, handling & watering equipment; prepared feeds
PA: Hog Slat, Incorporated
206 Fayetteville St
Newton Grove NC 28366
800 949-4647

(G-1275)
LESH ADVERTISING INC
6938 E State Road 218 (46917-9416)
PHONE....................574 859-2141
Fax: 574 859-2140
Jeffery Lesh, *President*
Cindy Lesh, *Vice Pres*
EMP: 3
SALES (est): 330.2K **Privately Held**
SIC: 3993 1799 Signs, not made in custom sign painting shops; sign installation & maintenance

Campbellsburg
Washington County

(G-1276)
DENNIS MANUFACTURING INC
250 Hwy 56 (47108)
PHONE....................812 755-4891
Fax: 812 755-4891
Gary Dennis, *President*
Aaron Dennis, *Vice Pres*
EMP: 2 **EST:** 1921
SQ FT: 7,200
SALES (est): 247.7K **Privately Held**
SIC: 3443 3599 Drums, knockout (reflux, etc.): metal plate; machine shop, jobbing & repair

(G-1277)
HAWK PRECISION COMPONENTS INC
596 W Oak St (47108-9105)
PHONE....................812 755-4501
Paul Moser, *Principal*
EMP: 3
SALES (est): 223K **Privately Held**
SIC: 3399 Powder, metal

(G-1278)
NETSHAPE TECHNOLOGIES LLC
Also Called: Helsel
596 W Oak St (47108-9105)
PHONE....................812 755-4501
Fax: 812 755-4298
Rhett Luecke, *Branch Mgr*
EMP: 150
SALES (corp-wide): 197.8MM **Privately Held**
SIC: 3399 3566 3561 3545 Powder, metal; speed changers, drives & gears; pumps & pumping equipment; machine tool accessories; iron & steel forgings; copper foundries
HQ: Netshape Technologies Llc
14670 Cumberland Rd
Noblesville IN 46060
812 248-9273

(G-1279)
NST CAMPBELLSBURG INC
596 W Oak St (47108-9105)
PHONE....................812 755-4501
Dax Whitehouse, *CEO*
David Dudding, *CFO*
Don Leonard, *Officer*
EMP: 3 **EST:** 1995
SALES (est): 1.8MM
SALES (corp-wide): 197.8MM **Privately Held**
SIC: 3499 Friction material, made from powdered metal
HQ: Netshape Technologies Llc
14670 Cumberland Rd
Noblesville IN 46060
812 248-9273

(G-1280)
ON SITE WELDING & MAINTENANCE
7632 E County Road 240 N (47108-7922)
PHONE....................812 755-4184
Josh Wallace, *Principal*
EMP: 2
SALES (est): 145K **Privately Held**
SIC: 7692 Welding repair

Canaan
Jefferson County

(G-1281)
THUNDER ROLLS EXPRESS
13449 State Road 129 (47224-9544)
PHONE....................812 667-5111
Joseph Womack, *Owner*
EMP: 2
SALES (est): 131.9K **Privately Held**
SIC: 2741 Miscellaneous publishing

(G-1282)
VEST PALLET CO
8795 N Scotts Ridge Rd (47224-9756)
PHONE....................812 839-6247
Janet Vest, *Owner*
EMP: 2
SALES (est): 90.9K **Privately Held**
SIC: 2448 Pallets, wood & wood with metal

Cannelburg
Daviess County

(G-1283)
CANNELBURG PROCESSING PLANT
204 S Main St (47519-5109)
PHONE....................812 486-3223
Daniel Genrich, *Owner*
EMP: 9
SALES: 500K **Privately Held**
SIC: 2011 Meat packing plants

(G-1284)
DAVIESS COUNTY METAL SALES
9929 E Us Highway 50 (47519-5021)
PHONE....................812 486-4299
Fax: 812 295-4344
John Lengacher, *President*
Kenny Swartzentruber Jr, *Corp Secy*
EMP: 97
SQ FT: 150,000
SALES: 43.2MM **Privately Held**
WEB: www.dcmetal.com
SIC: 3444 2439 Roof deck, sheet metal; siding, sheet metal; trusses, wooden roof

(G-1285)
PEABODY MIDWEST MINING LLC
Also Called: Viking Mine Corning Pit
3066 S 900 E Montgomery (47519)
PHONE....................812 644-7323
EMP: 130
SALES (corp-wide): 5.6B **Publicly Held**
SIC: 1221 Bituminous Coal/Lignite Surface Mining
HQ: Peabody Midwest Mining, Llc
566 Dickeyville Rd
Lynnville IN 47619
812 434-8500

Cannelton
Perry County

(G-1286)
AUSTINS METAL MAFIA INC
8175 Boyd Rd (47520-6841)
PHONE....................812 619-6115
Eddie Austin, *President*
EMP: 2
SALES (est): 62.5K **Privately Held**
SIC: 3999 Manufacturing industries

(G-1287)
BEST CHAIRS INCORPORATED
Highway 66 E (47520)
P.O. Box 158, Ferdinand (47532-0158)
PHONE....................812 367-1761
Don Gill, *Manager*
EMP: 80
SALES (corp-wide): 250MM **Privately Held**
SIC: 2512 2514 2511 Chairs: upholstered on wood frames; metal household furniture; wood household furniture
PA: Best Chairs Incorporated
1 Best Dr
Ferdinand IN 47532
812 367-1761

(G-1288)
CAN-CLAY CORP
402 Washington St (47520-1240)
PHONE....................812 547-3461
Fax: 812 547-6514
Mark H Bruce, *President*
Faith Mattingly, *Manager*
EMP: 24 **EST:** 1982
SQ FT: 7,000
SALES (est): 4.4MM **Privately Held**
SIC: 3255 3259 Clay refractories; sewer pipe or fittings, clay; chimney pipe & tops, clay

(G-1289)
DENNIS ETIENNES LOGGING INC
14370 Ureka Rd (47520-5065)
PHONE....................812 843-4518
Dennis Etienne, *Owner*
EMP: 2
SALES (est): 70.1K **Privately Held**
SIC: 2411 Logging

(G-1290)
EXPRESS MACHINE
6115 Sugar Maple Rd (47520-6768)
PHONE....................812 719-5979
Michele L Kellems, *Owner*
Eddie Kellems, *Principal*
EMP: 2
SALES: 10K **Privately Held**
SIC: 3541 Machine tools, metal cutting type

(G-1291)
RURAL LAND INC
14370 Ureka Rd (47520-5065)
PHONE....................812 843-4518
Dennis Etienne, *Principal*
EMP: 3
SALES (est): 223.1K **Privately Held**
SIC: 2411 Logging

Carbon
Clay County

(G-1292)
CONEQTEC CORP
128 Ne 1st St (47837)
PHONE....................812 446-4055
Fax: 812 446-5038
Gary Cochran, *President*
EMP: 17
SALES (corp-wide): 9.1MM **Privately Held**
SIC: 3531 Construction machinery attachments
PA: Coneqtec Corp.
3348 S Hoover Rd
Wichita KS 67215
316 943-8889

(G-1293)
PIKE LUMBER COMPANY INC
440 W County Rd1450 N (47837)
P.O. Box 255 (47837-0255)
PHONE....................574 893-4511
Jim Steen, *Manager*
EMP: 30

SALES (corp-wide): 36.4MM **Privately Held**
WEB: www.pikelumber.com
SIC: 5211 2426 2421 Planing mill products & lumber; hardwood dimension & flooring mills; sawmills & planing mills, general
PA: Pike Lumber Company, Inc.
719 Front St
Akron IN 46910
574 893-4511

Carlisle
Sullivan County

(G-1294)
5M POULTRY LLC
10977 S County Road 500 E (47838-8084)
PHONE....................812 890-5558
Joseph D McCormick, *Owner*
Joseph McCormick, *Co-Owner*
EMP: 5 **EST:** 2016
SALES (est): 297.5K **Privately Held**
SIC: 3151 Mittens, leather

(G-1295)
AMERICAN PELLET SUPPLY LLC
10228 S Old 41 (47838-8225)
P.O. Box 305 (47838-0305)
PHONE....................812 398-2225
Michael B Myers, *Mng Member*
Richard B Myers,
EMP: 15
SQ FT: 1,500
SALES (est): 1.9MM **Privately Held**
SIC: 2999 Fuel briquettes & waxes

(G-1296)
CARLISLE VENEERS INC
10228 S Old 41 (47838-8225)
P.O. Box 35, Oaktown (47561-0035)
PHONE....................812 398-2225
Fax: 812 398-3206
Herb Manthei, *President*
Pete Rogers, *Treasurer*
EMP: 35
SQ FT: 40,000
SALES (est): 3.2MM **Privately Held**
WEB: www.bloomingtonwebguide.com
SIC: 2435 Hardwood veneer & plywood

(G-1297)
SUNRISE COAL LLC
1466 E State Road 58 (47838-8181)
PHONE....................812 398-2200
J Tony, *Branch Mgr*
EMP: 150
SALES (corp-wide): 57.6MM **Privately Held**
SIC: 1222 Bituminous coal-underground mining
PA: Sunrise Coal, Llc
1183 E Canvasback Dr
Terre Haute IN 47802
812 299-2800

(G-1298)
TRAVIS C AND JAN B PAGE
9606 S County Road 18 Sw (47838-8373)
PHONE....................812 398-5507
Travis Page, *Owner*
EMP: 2
SALES (est): 150K **Privately Held**
SIC: 2452 Farm & agricultural buildings, prefabricated wood

Carmel
Hamilton County

(G-1299)
ABS MFG REP INC
1950 E Greyhound Pass # 18 (46033-7787)
PHONE....................317 407-0406
W Klingensmithmark, *President*
EMP: 2
SALES (est): 67.7K **Privately Held**
SIC: 3999 Manufacturing industries

(G-1300)
ACCENT SOFTWARE INC
12409 Old Meridian St (46032-8713)
PHONE.................................317 846-6025
Benjamin Baxter, *President*
Samuel Baxter, *Admin Sec*
EMP: 2
SALES (est): 237.2K **Privately Held**
SIC: 7372 Business oriented computer software

(G-1301)
ADEC ✪
13085 Hmlton Crssing Blvd (46032-1412)
PHONE.................................503 538-7478
B Urwiller, *Manager*
EMP: 2 **EST:** 2017
SALES (est): 86.6K **Privately Held**
SIC: 3843 Dental equipment & supplies

(G-1302)
ADEPT TOOL AND ENGINEERING ✪
11307 Green St (46033-3738)
PHONE.................................317 896-9250
Neil Anthony Goyer, *Incorporator*
EMP: 2 **EST:** 2017
SALES (est): 115.7K **Privately Held**
SIC: 3599 5084 Machine shop, jobbing & repair; tool & die makers' equipment

(G-1303)
ADVANCED MTLWRKING PRCTCES LLC
4511 W 99th St (46032-7718)
PHONE.................................317 337-0441
Lane Donoho, *General Mgr*
Ken Edwards, *Mng Member*
Dwight Webster, *Technology*
Kishor Kulkarni,
Thomas Lawless,
▲ **EMP:** 5
SALES (est): 596K **Privately Held**
SIC: 3444 Sheet metalwork

(G-1304)
ADVERTISING COMMUNICATIONS GRO
11690 Technology Dr (46032-5600)
P.O. Box 1990 (46082-1990)
PHONE.................................317 843-2523
Fax: 317 816-1000
Charlene Taylor, *Owner*
EMP: 20 **EST:** 2001
SALES (est): 1.5MM **Privately Held**
SIC: 7311 2741 Advertising consultant; miscellaneous publishing

(G-1305)
AGING PARENT SOFTWARE
872 Joann Ct (46032-5295)
PHONE.................................317 848-9548
Maureen Bard, *Owner*
EMP: 2
SALES (est): 119K **Privately Held**
SIC: 7372 Prepackaged software

(G-1306)
AGRI PROCESSING SERVICES LLC
13789 Smokey Ridge Dr (46033-9166)
PHONE.................................765 860-5108
Timothy Ortman,
EMP: 2
SALES (est): 214.7K **Privately Held**
SIC: 2899 Chemical preparations

(G-1307)
ALLEGION PUBLIC LTD COMPANY
11819 N Pennsylvania St (46032-4555)
PHONE.................................317 810-3700
Tim Eckersley, *Vice Pres*
Todd Graves, *Vice Pres*
Donny Minix, *Vice Pres*
Ali Saidi, *Vice Pres*
Mark Vigren, *Vice Pres*
EMP: 12 **Privately Held**
SIC: 6722 5065 3429 5251 ; security control equipment & systems; motor vehicle hardware; door locks & lock sets
PA: Allegion Public Limited Company
Block D, Iveagh Court
Dublin

(G-1308)
ALLEGION S&S HOLDING CO INC (HQ)
11819 N Pennsylvania St (46032-4555)
PHONE.................................317 810-3700
David D Petratis, *CEO*
Nick Watkin, *General Mgr*
Reyn Parsons, *Vice Pres*
Cindy Farrer, *VP Opers*
Donald Dunaway, *Plant Mgr*
EMP: 500 **EST:** 2013
SALES (est): 829.7MM **Privately Held**
SIC: 3429 Locks or lock sets

(G-1309)
ALLEGRO MICROSYSTEMS LLC
11711 N Penn St Ste 240 (46032-4559)
PHONE.................................765 854-2263
Fax: 765 854-2262
Deb Mund, *Branch Mgr*
EMP: 2
SALES (corp-wide): 1.6B **Privately Held**
SIC: 3674 Semiconductors & related devices
HQ: Allegro Microsystems, Llc
115 Ne Cutoff
Worcester MA 01606
508 853-5000

(G-1310)
AMERICAN INTL MFG SLUTIONS LLP
Also Called: Aims
378 Abbedale Ct (46032-7009)
P.O. Box 745, Westfield (46074-0745)
PHONE.................................317 443-5778
Isabel M Smith,
EMP: 2
SALES: 10K **Privately Held**
SIC: 2752 Commercial printing, lithographic

(G-1311)
ANDERSON ENTERPRISES LLC
Also Called: Trinkets & Forget ME Nots
1496 Heathrow Ct (46033-8508)
PHONE.................................317 569-1099
EMP: 2
SALES: 150K **Privately Held**
SIC: 3993 Mfg Signs/Advertising Specialties

(G-1312)
APOLLO NORTH AMERICA INC
301 E Carmel Dr Ste D500 (46032-4812)
PHONE.................................317 573-0777
Charles Cheng, *President*
EMP: 3
SQ FT: 1,500
SALES: 500K **Privately Held**
SIC: 2298 Cable, fiber; twine, cord & cordage

(G-1313)
APPLE III LLC
3928 Kitty Hawk Ct (46033-4801)
PHONE.................................317 691-2869
Tamara A Haubry, *President*
EMP: 2
SALES (est): 85.9K **Privately Held**
SIC: 3571 Personal computers (microcomputers)

(G-1314)
APPLICATION SOFTWARE
13857 Kickapoo Trl (46033-8545)
PHONE.................................317 843-9775
Rober Welter, *Principal*
EMP: 2
SALES (est): 139.4K **Privately Held**
SIC: 7372 Prepackaged software

(G-1315)
ARTICODE INC
12524 Gladecrest Dr (46033-8225)
PHONE.................................317 569-8357
P Roettger, *Principal*
EMP: 2
SALES (est): 180.9K **Privately Held**
SIC: 7372 Prepackaged software

(G-1316)
ASSEMBLY BIOSCIENCES INC (PA)
11711 N Meridian St # 310 (46032-4549)
PHONE.................................317 210-9311
William R Ringo, *Ch of Bd*
Derek Small, *President*
Derek A Small, *President*
David J Barrett, *COO*
Graham Cooper, *COO*
EMP: 57 **EST:** 2005
SALES: 9MM **Publicly Held**
SIC: 2834 Pharmaceutical preparations

(G-1317)
BITTINGER WRITINGS INC
3011 Whispering Trl (46033-3952)
PHONE.................................317 846-9136
Fax: 317 846-2292
Marvin L Bittinger, *President*
Elaine Bittinger, *Corp Secy*
EMP: 2
SALES (est): 100K **Privately Held**
SIC: 2731 Textbooks: publishing only, not printed on site

(G-1318)
BLUSH & BOBBY PINS
600 E Carmel Dr Ste 249 (46032-3064)
PHONE.................................317 789-5166
Stephanie Baker, *Principal*
▲ **EMP:** 5
SALES (est): 308.2K **Privately Held**
SIC: 3452 Pins

(G-1319)
BOB EVANS FARMS INC
931 N Rangeline Rd Ste B (46032-1319)
PHONE.................................317 846-3261
Mike Dorman, *Manager*
EMP: 7 **Publicly Held**
WEB: www.bobevans.com
SIC: 2011 Sausages from meat slaughtered on site
HQ: Bob Evans Farms, Inc.
8111 Smiths Mill Rd
New Albany OH 43054
614 491-2225

(G-1320)
BOLSTRA LLC
12400 N Meridian St # 120 (46032-4600)
PHONE.................................317 660-9131
Haresh Gangwani, *CEO*
David Cochran, *COO*
Steve Ehrlich, *COO*
John Warne, *Vice Pres*
Morgan Cooper, *Marketing Staff*
EMP: 2 **EST:** 2014
SALES (est): 174.6K **Privately Held**
SIC: 7372 Business oriented computer software

(G-1321)
BONNER & ASSOCIATES
12310 Windsor Dr (46033-3144)
PHONE.................................317 571-1911
Edward M Bonner Jr, *Owner*
EMP: 5
SQ FT: 3,000
SALES: 500K **Privately Held**
SIC: 3613 5063 Control panels, electric; light bulbs & related supplies

(G-1322)
BRENT CROXTON INC
12755 Kiawah Dr (46033-8375)
PHONE.................................317 846-7591
Brent Croxton, *Owner*
Micah Cook, *Owner*
EMP: 3
SALES (est): 198.2K **Privately Held**
SIC: 2721 Magazines: publishing & printing

(G-1323)
BUCKINGHAM PALLETS INC
12325 Camberly Ln (46033-3109)
PHONE.................................317 846-8601
Fax: 317 241-4646
Kenneth H Karsh, *President*
Denise Karsh, *Vice Pres*
Kerry Cronin, *Foreman/Supr*
EMP: 15
SQ FT: 14,000
SALES (est): 1MM **Privately Held**
SIC: 2448 5031 Pallets, wood; pallets, wood

(G-1324)
BURKS DOOR & SASH INC
Also Called: Shannon Door
599 3rd Ave Sw (46032-2084)
PHONE.................................317 844-2484
Fax: 317 844-2084
Kent Shively, *President*
Peter B Burks, *Shareholder*
EMP: 13
SQ FT: 17,000
SALES (est): 1.4MM **Privately Held**
WEB: www.iei.net
SIC: 2431 Woodwork, interior & ornamental; doors, wood; staircases & stairs, wood; stair railings, wood

(G-1325)
CAI RAIL
597 Industrial Dr (46032-4207)
PHONE.................................317 669-2555
EMP: 4
SALES (est): 276.8K **Privately Held**
SIC: 3743 Railroad equipment

(G-1326)
CANATURE USA INC (PA)
9760 Mayflower (46032)
PHONE.................................877 771-6789
Jeffrey L Warner, *President*
Michale Fiorante, *Admin Sec*
▲ **EMP:** 8 **EST:** 1986
SALES (est): 4.2MM **Privately Held**
SIC: 3589 Swimming pool filter & water conditioning systems

(G-1327)
CANATURE WATERGROUP USA INC (HQ)
Also Called: Independent Water Tech
9760 Mayflower (46032)
PHONE.................................877 771-6789
Don Fettes, *President*
▲ **EMP:** 4
SALES (est): 1.2MM
SALES (corp-wide): 8.5B **Privately Held**
WEB: www.iwtwater.com/aboutus1.asp
SIC: 3589 Sewage & water treatment equipment
PA: Clayton, Dubilier & Rice, Inc.
375 Park Ave Fl 18
New York NY 10152
212 407-5200

(G-1328)
CAPTIVATED LLC
5483 Kenwood Pl (46033-8848)
PHONE.................................317 554-7400
Bryan Anderson, *President*
EMP: 2
SALES (est): 109.4K **Privately Held**
SIC: 7372 7389 Business oriented computer software;

(G-1329)
CARDINAL PUBLISHERS GROUP
14 Lakeview Ct (46033-3988)
PHONE.................................317 846-8190
Adriane Doherty, *Principal*
EMP: 2
SALES (est): 100K **Privately Held**
SIC: 2741 Miscellaneous publishing

(G-1330)
CARMEL COUNTERTOPS INC
Also Called: Danish Woodworking
904 3rd Ave Sw (46032-2522)
PHONE.................................317 843-0331
Fax: 317 843-0143
Per Laigaare, *President*
EMP: 9
SALES (est): 250K **Privately Held**
WEB: www.carmelcountertops.com
SIC: 2541 1799 Counters or counter display cases, wood; counter top installation

(G-1331)
CARMEL PROCESS SOLUTIONS INC
484 E Carmel Dr Ste 213 (46032-2812)
PHONE.................................317 705-0217

Donald J Audia, *President*
EMP: 4
SALES: 2.8MM **Privately Held**
WEB: www.carmelprocess.com
SIC: 2842 8711 3556 Sanitation preparations; electrical or electronic engineering; food products machinery; meat, poultry & seafood processing machinery

(G-1332)
CARMEL TRAPHIES PLUS
Also Called: Carmel Trophies Plus
411 N Rangeline Rd (46032-1748)
PHONE..........................317 844-3770
Fax: 317 844-3791
Ford Wilson, *Owner*
EMP: 4
SALES (est): 307.7K **Privately Held**
SIC: 5999 3479 Trophies & plaques; etching & engraving

(G-1333)
CARMEL WELDING AND SUPPLY
550 S Rangeline Rd (46032-2183)
PHONE..........................317 846-3493
Fax: 317 848-8760
William K Wiggam Sr, *Owner*
William K Wiggam Jr, *Admin Sec*
EMP: 13
SQ FT: 15,000
SALES (est): 2.3MM **Privately Held**
WEB: www.carmelwelding.com
SIC: 5261 7692 7513 Lawn & garden equipment; welding repair; truck rental & leasing, no drivers

(G-1334)
CASE SHOW HOMES LLC
12965 Old Meridian St (46032-1489)
PHONE..........................317 669-6202
Paul E Estridge Jr, *Administration*
EMP: 3
SALES (est): 423.1K **Privately Held**
SIC: 3523 Farm machinery & equipment

(G-1335)
CHAMPAGNE LIPSTICK
135 Parkview Rd (46032-5125)
PHONE..........................317 691-6045
Beth Jerrels, *Principal*
EMP: 2
SALES (est): 124K **Privately Held**
SIC: 2844 Lipsticks

(G-1336)
CHEERCUSSION LLC
1091 3rd Ave Sw (46032-2523)
PHONE..........................317 762-4009
Patrick Cowherd, *COO*
EMP: 10 **EST:** 2011
SQ FT: 3,500
SALES (est): 100K **Privately Held**
SIC: 3949 Helmets, athletic

(G-1337)
CHERRY HILL VINEYARD LLC
10236 Ditch Rd (46032-9613)
PHONE..........................317 846-5170
Michael P Sweeney, *Principal*
EMP: 5
SALES (est): 405.9K **Privately Held**
SIC: 2084 Wines, brandy & brandy spirits

(G-1338)
CIRCLE CITY MEDICAL INC
10850 Ruby Ct (46032-9303)
PHONE..........................317 228-1144
Todd Katz, *President*
▲ **EMP:** 28
SQ FT: 6,000
SALES (est): 3.3MM **Privately Held**
WEB: www.bell-horn.com
SIC: 3842 Braces, orthopedic; elastic hosiery, orthopedic (support)

(G-1339)
CISCO SYSTEMS INC
11711 N Meridian St # 250 (46032-4534)
PHONE..........................317 816-5200
Fax: 317 816-5216
Nick Traxler, *Partner*
Michael Rieder, *Engineer*
Larry Roberts, *Engineer*
Michael Witzman, *Engineer*
Chris Garrison, *Regl Sales Mgr*
EMP: 30

SALES (corp-wide): 48B **Publicly Held**
WEB: www.cisco.com
SIC: 3577 Data conversion equipment, media-to-media: computer
PA: Cisco Systems, Inc.
170 W Tasman Dr
San Jose CA 95134
408 526-4000

(G-1340)
CLASSIC KITCHEN & GRANITE
9 E City Center Dr (46032-2887)
PHONE..........................317 575-8883
Fred Alvarez, *Owner*
EMP: 4
SALES (est): 401K **Privately Held**
SIC: 5712 3281 Furniture stores; granite, cut & shaped

(G-1341)
CLINICAL ARCHITECTURE LLC
11611 N Meridian St # 450 (46032-4542)
PHONE..........................317 580-8400
Charles E Harp, *CEO*
John Wilkinson, *Exec VP*
Stephanie Broderick, *Vice Pres*
Christopher Cleary, *Software Engr*
Bob Taylor, *Officer*
EMP: 40
SALES (est): 3.3MM **Privately Held**
SIC: 8742 7372 Hospital & health services consultant; application computer software

(G-1342)
CONZER SECURITY INC
231 1st Ave Sw (46032-2010)
PHONE..........................317 580-9460
Dave Conley, *President*
Jeremiah Conley, *COO*
Knapp Julie, *Engineer*
EMP: 4 **EST:** 1999
SALES (est): 705.2K **Privately Held**
WEB: www.conzer.com
SIC: 3699 Security devices

(G-1343)
COOPERATIVE VENTURES IND CORP
Also Called: Mobius Learning
11550 N Meridian St # 180 (46032-6956)
PHONE..........................317 259-7063
Edward J Cross, *CEO*
Jacob B Mansfield, *Co-Founder*
Matthew L Oaldon, *Co-Founder*
EMP: 7
SQ FT: 1,200
SALES: 886.1K **Privately Held**
SIC: 8331 7374 7372 Manpower training; computer graphics service; educational computer software

(G-1344)
CORTEX SAFETY TECHNOLOGIES LLC
Also Called: Millercarlson
421 S Rangeline Rd (46032-2138)
PHONE..........................317 414-5607
S C Curtis, *Mng Member*
Stephanie Carlson Curtis, *Mng Member*
Michael Miller, *Mng Member*
EMP: 2
SQ FT: 1,200 **Privately Held**
SIC: 9229 8734 3586 5015 ; product testing laboratory, safety or performance; measuring & dispensing pumps; automotive supplies, used; personal safety equipment

(G-1345)
COSMOS SUPERIOR FOODS LLC
1020 3rd Ave Sw Bldg A (46032-2524)
PHONE..........................317 975-2747
Sean Litke, *CEO*
EMP: 9
SALES (est): 751.8K **Privately Held**
SIC: 2013 Snack sticks, including jerky: from purchased meat

(G-1346)
COTTOM AUTOMATED BUS SOLUTI
13295 Illinois St Ste 313 (46032-3022)
PHONE..........................317 853-6531
John Cottom, *Managing Prtnr*

EMP: 5 **EST:** 2011
SALES (est): 408.6K **Privately Held**
SIC: 2542 5046 Shelving, office & store: except wood; shelving, commercial & industrial

(G-1347)
CREATIVE PUBLISHING CONCEP
11614 Fairgreen Dr (46032-3450)
PHONE..........................317 844-3549
EMP: 2 **EST:** 2008
SALES (est): 84K **Privately Held**
SIC: 2741 Misc Publishing

(G-1348)
CROSSROADS SOURCING GROUP LTD
737 Edison Way (46032-8223)
PHONE..........................847 940-4123
Michael Kirby, *President*
Marie C Kirby, *Corp Secy*
▲ **EMP:** 11 **EST:** 1998
SALES (est): 1.5MM **Privately Held**
WEB:
www.crossroadsindustrialservices.com
SIC: 2821 Plastics materials & resins

(G-1349)
CROWN PRODUCTS & SERVICES INC (PA)
12821 E New M Ste 100 (46032)
PHONE..........................317 564-4799
Doug Simmons, *President*
EMP: 4
SALES (est): 1.5MM **Privately Held**
SIC: 3585 Refrigeration & heating equipment; air conditioning units, complete: domestic or industrial

(G-1350)
CULTURE MEDIA LLC ✪
5884 Lost Oaks Dr (46033-9574)
PHONE..........................317 966-0847
Jacob Pilkenton, *Principal*
EMP: 2 **EST:** 2017
SALES (est): 74.4K **Privately Held**
SIC: 2836 Culture media

(G-1351)
CURRENT PUBLISHING LLC
30 S Rangeline Rd (46032-2131)
PHONE..........................317 489-4444
Brian Kelly, *Principal*
Steve Greenberg, *Exec VP*
Carmel Westfield, *Sales Executive*
Sophie Pappas, *Director*
Zachary Ross, *Art Dir*
EMP: 5
SALES (est): 28.3K **Privately Held**
SIC: 2741 Miscellaneous publishing

(G-1352)
DATA TECHNOLOGIES INC
231 1st Ave Sw (46032-2010)
PHONE..........................317 580-9161
David Conley, *President*
Jeremiah Conley, *Principal*
EMP: 8
SQ FT: 1,000
SALES: 1.2MM **Privately Held**
WEB: www.datatechnologies.com
SIC: 3699 5045 Security control equipment & systems; computers, peripherals & software

(G-1353)
DAVID TORTORA
Also Called: Accent Bicycles
11700 Oak Tree Way (46032-8269)
PHONE..........................317 506-6902
David Tortora, *Owner*
EMP: 4 **EST:** 2015
SALES (est): 232.1K **Privately Held**
SIC: 3751 7389 Bicycles & related parts;

(G-1354)
DEEP POCKETS FOODS LLC
13283 Aquamarine Dr (46033-2307)
PHONE..........................317 815-4898
David Richman, *Principal*
EMP: 2 **EST:** 2012
SALES (est): 120.9K **Privately Held**
SIC: 2099 Food preparations

(G-1355)
DESIGN MSA INC
Also Called: M S Aronstam Jewelers
200 S Rangeline Rd # 217 (46032-1940)
PHONE..........................317 817-9000
Marc Aronstam, *President*
EMP: 6
SQ FT: 4,000
SALES: 1.8MM **Privately Held**
SIC: 5944 3911 Jewelry, precious stones & precious metals; jewelry apparel

(G-1356)
DETERMINE INC
Also Called: Iasta
12800 N Meridian St # 425 (46032-5405)
PHONE..........................317 594-8600
Jeffrey Davidson, *Info Tech Mgr*
Yoshiaki Tanno, *Analyst*
EMP: 49 **Publicly Held**
SIC: 7372 7373 Prepackaged software; computer integrated systems design
PA: Determine, Inc.
615 W Carmel Dr Ste 100
Carmel IN 46032

(G-1357)
DETERMINE INC (PA)
615 W Carmel Dr Ste 100 (46032-5504)
PHONE..........................650 532-1500
Michael Brodsky, *Ch of Bd*
Alan Howe, *Vice Ch Bd*
Patrick Stakenas, *President*
John Nolan, *CFO*
EMP: 153
SQ FT: 8,795
SALES: 28.1MM **Publicly Held**
WEB: www.selectica.com
SIC: 7372 7373 Prepackaged software; computer integrated systems design

(G-1358)
DETERMINE SOURCING INC
615 W Carmel Dr Ste 100 (46032-5504)
PHONE..........................408 570-9700
Todd Spartz, *Admin Sec*
EMP: 7
SALES (est): 132.8K **Publicly Held**
SIC: 7372 7373 Prepackaged software; computer integrated systems design
PA: Determine, Inc.
615 W Carmel Dr Ste 100
Carmel IN 46032

(G-1359)
DIABCO LIFE SCIENCES LLC
484 E Carmel Dr (46032-2812)
PHONE..........................317 697-9988
EMP: 3
SALES (est): 191.8K **Privately Held**
SIC: 2834 Pharmaceutical preparations

(G-1360)
DIGITAL CMMNTIES INTIATIVE INC
Also Called: DCI
12579 Pembrooke Cir (46032-8340)
PHONE..........................317 580-0111
Steven Zimmerman, *CEO*
EMP: 3
SALES: 200K **Privately Held**
SIC: 3646 7389 Commercial indusl & institutional electric lighting fixtures;

(G-1361)
DIMENSIONS FURNITURE INC
341 Gradle Dr (46032-2533)
P.O. Box 125 (46082-0125)
PHONE..........................317 218-0025
Fax: 317 218-0028
Kenneth J Striebel, *CEO*
Matthew J Striebel, *President*
▲ **EMP:** 18 **EST:** 2000
SQ FT: 2,500
SALES (est): 2.3MM **Privately Held**
SIC: 2519 Wicker & rattan furniture

(G-1362)
DOUGLAS DYE AND ASSOCIATES
Also Called: Dye Woodworks
501 Industrial Dr (46032-4207)
PHONE..........................317 844-1709
Fax: 317 844-1859
Douglas Dye, *President*

Lisa K Dye, *Vice Pres*
EMP: 5
SQ FT: 13,500
SALES (est): 658.7K **Privately Held**
SIC: 2434 2511 2436 7641 Wood kitchen cabinets; vanities, bathroom: wood; wood household furniture; veneer stock, softwood; furniture repair & maintenance; cabinets, kitchen; cabinet & finish carpentry

(G-1363)
DREAMWORK STONES LLC
4161 Kattman Ct (46074-1107)
PHONE....................317 709-2202
Lei Fu, *Principal*
▲ **EMP:** 10
SALES (est): 1.2MM **Privately Held**
SIC: 3281 Cut stone & stone products

(G-1364)
DWYER ENTERPRISES
12075 Waterford Ln (46033-5501)
PHONE....................317 573-9628
William M Dwyer, *President*
EMP: 2
SALES (est): 150K **Privately Held**
SIC: 3714 Motor vehicle body components & frame

(G-1365)
E & H INDUSTRIAL SERVICES LLC
5515 Salem Dr S (46033-8586)
PHONE....................317 569-8819
Phillip Knickrehm,
EMP: 16
SALES (est): 2.4MM **Privately Held**
SIC: 7692 Welding repair

(G-1366)
E&P TECHNOLOGIES LLC
14254 Trailwind Ct (46032-7770)
PHONE....................317 828-8482
Paul Woodling, *Vice Pres*
EMP: 4
SALES (est): 291.1K **Privately Held**
SIC: 3499 7389 Locks, safe & vault: metal;

(G-1367)
ECO PARTNERS INC
515 Twin Oaks Dr (46032-9722)
P.O. Box 496 (46082-0496)
PHONE....................317 450-3346
Elizabeth Roe, *President*
Gary Roe, *Vice Pres*
EMP: 4
SALES (est): 351.1K **Privately Held**
WEB: www.trashtalk.com
SIC: 2721 Periodicals: publishing only

(G-1368)
ECOLAB INC
160 W Carmel Dr Ste 255 (46032-7586)
PHONE....................317 816-0983
Fax: 317 816-0991
Jeffrey Peek, *Manager*
EMP: 34
SALES (corp-wide): 13.8B **Publicly Held**
SIC: 2841 Soap & other detergents
PA: Ecolab Inc.
1 Ecolab Pl
Saint Paul MN 55102
800 232-6522

(G-1369)
EDGEWOOD CORPORATION INDIANA
Also Called: Edgewood Building Supply
430 W Carmel Dr (46032-2530)
PHONE....................317 786-9208
Kathleen Jackman, *General Mgr*
Tony Goben, *Sales Staff*
Kellie Ray, *Sales Staff*
Amy Vaughn, *Sales Staff*
Andy Whiller, *Manager*
EMP: 25
SALES (corp-wide): 10.2MM **Privately Held**
WEB: www.edgewoodbuildingsupply.com
SIC: 5211 5032 3272 Brick; drywall materials; concrete products, precast

PA: Edgewood Corporation Of Indiana
1580 E Epler Ave
Indianapolis IN 46227
317 846-6060

(G-1370)
ELECTRO PAINTERS INC
14712 Alsong Ct (46032-5114)
PHONE....................317 875-8816
Jim De Stefano, *Plt & Fclts Mgr*
Shane Stevens, *Branch Mgr*
EMP: 8
SALES (est): 632.3K
SALES (corp-wide): 8.2MM **Privately Held**
WEB: www.electropainters.com
SIC: 3564 Purification & dust collection equipment
PA: Electro Painters, Inc
8533 Zionsville Rd
Indianapolis IN

(G-1371)
ENERGYPOINT LLC
12400 N Meridian St # 180 (46032-4685)
PHONE....................317 275-7979
Bruce Boyd,
EMP: 6
SALES (est): 228K **Privately Held**
SIC: 3643 Power outlets & sockets

(G-1372)
ENVISTA LLC (PA)
11555 N Meridian St # 300 (46032-1677)
PHONE....................317 208-9100
Jim Barnes, *CEO*
Jim Brownell, *General Mgr*
Mark Sawalha, *Project Dir*
Megan Kuntz, *Transptn Dir*
Eric Berg, *Project Mgr*
EMP: 74
SALES (est): 73.2MM **Privately Held**
SIC: 8742 7372 Banking & finance consultant; general management consultant; application computer software; business oriented computer software; operating systems computer software

(G-1373)
ENVISTA CONCEPTS LLC
11711 N Meridian St # 415 (46032-4534)
PHONE....................317 208-9100
Jim Barnes, *CEO*
Stephen Craig, *Mng Member*
Bruce Eicher, *Mng Member*
Mike Ingardia, *Mng Member*
Mike Kasperski, *Mng Member*
EMP: 36
SALES (est): 2.7MM **Privately Held**
SIC: 7372 4731 Application computer software; business oriented computer software; operating systems computer software; freight transportation arrangement; brokers, shipping
PA: Envista, Llc
11555 N Meridian St # 300
Carmel IN 46032

(G-1374)
ENVISTA ENTP SOLUTIONS LLC
11711 N Meridian St # 415 (46032-4534)
PHONE....................317 208-9100
Jim Barnes, *CEO*
Stephen Craig, *Mng Member*
Bruce Eicher, *Mng Member*
Mike Ingardia, *Mng Member*
Mike Kasperski, *Mng Member*
EMP: 26
SALES (est): 1.2MM **Privately Held**
SIC: 7372 8742 Application computer software; business oriented computer software; operating systems computer software; banking & finance consultant; general management consultant
PA: Envista, Llc
11555 N Meridian St # 300
Carmel IN 46032

(G-1375)
ENVISTA FREIGHT MANAGMENT LLC
11711 N Meridian St # 415 (46032-4534)
PHONE....................317 208-9100
Jim Barnes, *CEO*
Stephen Craig, *Mng Member*
Bruce Eicher, *Mng Member*

Mike Ingardia, *Mng Member*
Mike Kasperski, *Mng Member*
EMP: 18 **EST:** 2008
SALES (est): 3.6MM **Privately Held**
SIC: 7372 4731 Application computer software; business oriented computer software; operating systems computer software; freight transportation arrangement; brokers, shipping
PA: Envista, Llc
11555 N Meridian St # 300
Carmel IN 46032

(G-1376)
EVIA CUSTOM CABINETS LLC
14221 Avian Way (46033-8304)
PHONE....................317 987-5504
EMP: 2
SALES (est): 146.1K **Privately Held**
SIC: 2434 Wood kitchen cabinets

(G-1377)
FAIRCHILD SEMICONDUCTOR CORP
11805 N Pennsylvania St (46032-4555)
PHONE....................317 616-3641
Tom Vertacnik, *Branch Mgr*
EMP: 3
SALES (corp-wide): 5.5B **Publicly Held**
SIC: 3674 Semiconductors & related devices
HQ: Fairchild Semiconductor Corporation
82 Running Hill Rd
South Portland ME 04106
207 775-8100

(G-1378)
FAST TRACK TECHNOLOGIES LLC
484 E Carmel Dr (46032-2812)
PHONE....................317 229-6080
Mike Sherfick,
EMP: 10
SALES (est): 950K **Privately Held**
SIC: 3821 Laboratory apparatus & furniture

(G-1379)
FAVOR IT PROMOTIONS INC
Also Called: Aef Emblem
4250 W 99th St (46032-7775)
PHONE....................317 733-1112
Andrew Falender, *President*
Falender Andy, *Sales Staff*
Marvin Goldstein, *Sales Associate*
EMP: 10
SQ FT: 2,000
SALES (est): 1.4MM **Privately Held**
WEB: www.favor-it.com
SIC: 5961 5199 2395 Clothing, mail order (except women's); women's apparel, mail order; novelty merchandise, mail order; advertising specialties; embroidery & art needlework

(G-1380)
FEDERAL HEATH SIGN COMPANY LLC
Also Called: Federal Sign
160 W Carmel Dr Ste 236 (46032-2588)
PHONE....................317 581-7790
Bill Faul, *Branch Mgr*
William Faul, *Branch Mgr*
EMP: 6 **Privately Held**
WEB: www.zimsign.com
SIC: 3993 1799 7313 Signs, not made in custom sign painting shops; sign installation & maintenance; electronic media advertising representatives
PA: Federal Heath Sign Company, Llc
4602 North Ave
Oceanside CA 92056

(G-1381)
FINVANTAGE LLC
Also Called: Finvantage Solutions
275 Medical Dr Unit 633 (46082-0155)
P.O. Box 633 (46082-0633)
PHONE....................317 500-4949
Daniel Traub, *CEO*
EMP: 10
SALES (est): 108.8K **Privately Held**
SIC: 7372 7389 8742 Prepackaged software; purchasing service; ; ; materials mgmt. (purchasing, handling, inventory) consultant

(G-1382)
FRASCIO INTERNATIONAL LLC
1011 3rd Ave Sw (46032-7568)
PHONE....................317 663-0030
Ruggero Frascio, *President*
Nathan Tobey,
▲ **EMP:** 4
SQ FT: 30,000
SALES: 3.5MM **Privately Held**
WEB: www.frasciointernational.com
SIC: 3429 Keys, locks & related hardware

(G-1383)
G & N FABRICATIONS LLC
1315 Sumac Ct (46033-1952)
PHONE....................317 698-9539
Reed Kendred,
EMP: 5
SALES: 300K **Privately Held**
SIC: 3446 Architectural metalwork

(G-1384)
GENCHEM INTERNATIONAL LLC
484 E Carmel Dr Ste 142 (46032-2812)
PHONE....................317 574-4970
Robert Davis,
Stuart Davis,
EMP: 6
SQ FT: 1,400
SALES (est): 1.1MM **Privately Held**
SIC: 2899 Water treating compounds

(G-1385)
GLIO SOFTWARE INC
14262 Overbrook Dr (46074-7724)
PHONE....................314 856-5855
William Bennett, *Principal*
EMP: 2
SALES (est): 68.4K **Privately Held**
SIC: 7372 Prepackaged software

(G-1386)
GLOBALTECH MANUFACTURING L
14465 Welford Way (46032-7738)
PHONE....................317 571-1910
Lixin Fan, *Administration*
EMP: 4
SALES (est): 301.2K **Privately Held**
SIC: 3559 Sewing machines & attachments, industrial

(G-1387)
GONZALEZ INTERNATIONAL INC
3629 Oak Hollow Ct (46033-6614)
PHONE....................317 558-3700
Adam Gonzalez, *President*
EMP: 1
SALES: 3MM **Privately Held**
SIC: 2099 7389 Tortillas, fresh or refrigerated;

(G-1388)
GOODWILL INDS OF CENTL IND
1122 Keystone Way (46032-3231)
PHONE....................317 587-0281
Alex Wilson, *Manager*
EMP: 20
SALES (corp-wide): 92.8MM **Privately Held**
SIC: 8699 8331 5932 2621 Charitable organization; vocational rehabilitation agency; used merchandise stores; wrapping & packaging papers
PA: Goodwill Of Central And Southern Indiana, Inc
1635 W Michigan St
Indianapolis IN 46222
317 564-4313

(G-1389)
GREEN APPLE ACTIVE LLC
10529 Titan Run (46032-8233)
PHONE....................317 698-1032
Lisa O Berry, *Principal*
EMP: 4
SALES (est): 210K **Privately Held**
SIC: 3571 Personal computers (microcomputers)

(G-1390)
GREEN TEK LLC
4925 Jennings Dr (46033-9786)
PHONE....................317 294-1614

Kimberly Suder,
EMP: 4
SALES (est): 622.4K **Privately Held**
SIC: 5169 2952 Organic chemicals, synthetic; roofing felts, cements or coatings

(G-1391)
GUIDANT INTERCONTINENTAL CORP
11711 N Meridian St # 850 (46032-4534)
PHONE..........................317 218-7012
Todd McKinney, *CFO*
EMP: 45
SALES (est): 2.7MM
SALES (corp-wide): 9B **Publicly Held**
SIC: 3841 3845 Surgical & medical instruments; electromedical equipment
HQ: Guidant Sales Llc
4100 Hamline Ave N
Saint Paul MN 55112

(G-1392)
HAIR ASSOCIATES LLC (PA)
1115 Woodgate Dr (46033-9231)
PHONE..........................317 844-7207
Rick Schack,
John McGullough,
EMP: 13
SQ FT: 10,000
SALES (est): 915.3K **Privately Held**
SIC: 2844 Cosmetic preparations

(G-1393)
HANCO INC
Also Called: Classico Seating
1374 Clay Spring Dr (46032-9754)
PHONE..........................800 968-6655
Fax: 765 473-5442
Kim J Regan, *President*
Hank Richardson, *CFO*
▲ **EMP:** 45
SQ FT: 100,000
SALES (est): 6.2MM
SALES (corp-wide): 14.2MM **Privately Held**
WEB: www.classicoseating.com
SIC: 2599 Restaurant furniture, wood or metal
PA: Facility Concepts, Inc.
4881 S Perry Worth Rd
Whitestown IN 46075
800 915-8890

(G-1394)
HANSA MEDICAL PRODUCTS INC
2000 W 106th St (46032-7918)
PHONE..........................317 815-0708
Eric Blom, *President*
EMP: 2
SALES (est): 119.9K **Privately Held**
SIC: 3841 Surgical & medical instruments

(G-1395)
HARVARD BUSINESS PUBLISHING
1033 3rd Ave Sw Ste 202 (46032-7593)
PHONE..........................317 815-8232
Steve Haigh, *Manager*
EMP: 2
SALES (est): 103.8K **Privately Held**
SIC: 2741 Miscellaneous publishing

(G-1396)
HARVEST FUELS LLC
12716 Norfolk Ln (46032-8655)
PHONE..........................832 895-6621
EMP: 3
SALES (est): 18.3K **Privately Held**
SIC: 2869 Fuels

(G-1397)
HARVEY ADHESIVES INC
10328 E Lakeshore Dr (46033-4127)
PHONE..........................877 547-5558
Harvey Criscuolo, *President*
EMP: 7
SALES (est): 745.4K **Privately Held**
SIC: 2891 Adhesives

(G-1398)
HATFIELD PUBLICATIONS LLC
1401 Olde Briar Ln (46032-7336)
PHONE..........................317 581-9804
Noble C Hatfield, *Principal*

EMP: 2
SALES (est): 89.2K **Privately Held**
SIC: 2741 Miscellaneous publishing

(G-1399)
HAVEN TECHNOLOGIES INC
12202 Hancock St (46032-5805)
PHONE..........................317 490-7197
Peter Murphy, *President*
EMP: 4
SALES (est): 214.4K **Privately Held**
SIC: 3663 3651 3679 Mobile communication equipment; music distribution apparatus; sound reproducing equipment; headphones, radio

(G-1400)
HAWTHORNE PUBLISHING
15601 Oak Rd (46033-9476)
PHONE..........................317 867-5183
Art Baxter, *Owner*
EMP: 2
SALES (est): 155.7K **Privately Held**
SIC: 2731 Books: publishing only

(G-1401)
HEAGY VINEYARDS LLC
10330 Holaday Dr (46032-4049)
PHONE..........................317 752-4484
Raye Heagy, *Principal*
EMP: 4
SALES (est): 186.6K **Privately Held**
SIC: 2084 Wines, brandy & brandy spirits

(G-1402)
HENNESSEY MONTAGE PRINTS
6471 Brauer Ln (46033-8839)
PHONE..........................317 841-7562
John M Hennessey, *Principal*
EMP: 2
SALES (est): 87.9K **Privately Held**
SIC: 2752 Commercial printing, lithographic

(G-1403)
HERON BLUE PUBLICATIONS LLC
11157 Valeside Cres (46032-9159)
PHONE..........................317 696-0674
Mark Guidone, *Vice Pres*
EMP: 2
SALES (est): 100.4K **Privately Held**
SIC: 2741 Miscellaneous publishing

(G-1404)
HICKS MFG
3333 Walnut Creek Dr N (46032-9038)
PHONE..........................317 219-9891
Mark Hicks, *Principal*
EMP: 2
SALES (est): 106.3K **Privately Held**
SIC: 3999 Manufacturing industries

(G-1405)
HINDI PETROLEUM GROUP II INC
993 Deer Lake Dr (46032-7759)
PHONE..........................317 574-0619
Hasan Hindi, *Principal*
EMP: 2
SALES (est): 122.6K **Privately Held**
SIC: 1381 Drilling oil & gas wells

(G-1406)
HOFFMAN SLS & SPECIALTY CO INC
3222 Birch Canyon Dr (46033-3968)
P.O. Box 20398, Indianapolis (46220-0398)
PHONE..........................317 846-6428
Jack Hoffman, *President*
Elinor Hoffman, *Admin Sec*
EMP: 3
SALES (est): 1MM **Privately Held**
WEB: www.hoffmansales.net
SIC: 5074 5084 3491 Steam fittings; industrial machinery & equipment; steam traps

(G-1407)
HOWMEDICA OSTEONICS CORP
Stryker Orthopaedics Division
12348 Hancock St (46032-5807)
PHONE..........................317 587-2008
Michael P Mogul, *Branch Mgr*
EMP: 9

SALES (corp-wide): 12.4B **Publicly Held**
SIC: 3842 Surgical appliances & supplies
HQ: Howmedica Osteonics Corp.
325 Corporate Dr
Mahwah NJ 07430
201 831-5000

(G-1408)
HUB STATES CORPORATION
112 W Carmel Dr (46032-2526)
P.O. Box 1646, Indianapolis (46206-1646)
PHONE..........................317 816-9955
EMP: 2
SQ FT: 3,800
SALES (est): 170K **Privately Held**
SIC: 2879 5191 Mfg & Whol Insecticides

(G-1409)
IBJ BOOK PUBLISHING LLC
11550 N Meridian St # 115 (46032-6900)
PHONE..........................317 564-9924
Michael Maurer, *Principal*
EMP: 2 **EST:** 2015
SALES (est): 62.9K **Privately Held**
SIC: 2711 Newspapers

(G-1410)
IMMINENT SOFTWARE INC
6575 Brauer Ln (46033-8841)
PHONE..........................317 340-4562
Qing Ye, *Principal*
EMP: 2
SALES (est): 159.5K **Privately Held**
SIC: 7372 Prepackaged software

(G-1411)
IN BUSINESS FOR LIFE INC
12400 N Meridian St # 150 (46032-4600)
PHONE..........................317 691-6169
Christopher Mellard Mann, *Director*
EMP: 2 **EST:** 2016
SALES (est): 78.8K **Privately Held**
SIC: 2759 Business forms: printing

(G-1412)
INDIGO BIOAUTOMATION INC
385 W City Center Dr # 200 (46032)
PHONE..........................317 493-2400
Randall K Julian, *CEO*
John Stewart, *CFO*
EMP: 35
SALES (est): 4MM **Privately Held**
SIC: 7372 Prepackaged software

(G-1413)
INDY PALLET COMPANY INC
1017 Indianpipe Cir (46033-1964)
PHONE..........................317 843-0452
EMP: 4 **EST:** 2010
SALES (est): 150K **Privately Held**
SIC: 2448 Mfg Wood Pallets/Skids

(G-1414)
INDYCOAST PARTNERS LLC
2258 Finchley Rd (46032-7347)
PHONE..........................317 454-1050
David W Carfolite, *Principal*
Robert Epstein, *Exec VP*
EMP: 3 **EST:** 2009
SALES (est): 167.4K **Privately Held**
SIC: 2836 Culture media

(G-1415)
INFINITE AI INC
1950 E Greyhound Pass (46033-7787)
PHONE..........................317 965-4850
Nathan Clark, *CEO*
Derek Knutsen, *Director*
EMP: 4
SQ FT: 300
SALES (est): 372.8K **Privately Held**
SIC: 7371 7372 Computer software systems analysis & design, custom; computer software development & applications; computer software development; application computer software; business oriented computer software

(G-1416)
INNOVTIVE NUROLOGICAL DVCS LLC ◆
Also Called: Cervella
13295 Illinois St Ste 312 (46032-3022)
PHONE..........................317 674-2999
Bart Waclawik,

EMP: 3 **EST:** 2018
SALES: 2.5MM **Privately Held**
SIC: 3845 7372 Electromedical apparatus; application computer software

(G-1417)
INTERIOR DESIGN SURFACES INC
5078 Huntington Dr (46033-5934)
PHONE..........................317 829-3970
Trina Tanton, *President*
Jim Tanton, *Vice Pres*
▲ **EMP:** 8
SQ FT: 35,000
SALES: 1MM **Privately Held**
SIC: 2541 3281 Table or counter tops, plastic laminated; curbing, granite or stone

(G-1418)
J PLUS PRODUCTS INC
4000 W 106th St (46032-7720)
PHONE..........................317 660-1003
Joseph T Acklin, *Principal*
EMP: 2
SALES (est): 150K **Privately Held**
SIC: 3089 Plastic hardware & building products

(G-1419)
JB GRAPHICS INC
1422 Keystone Way (46032-3273)
PHONE..........................317 819-0008
Jane Berry, *President*
Kathie Black, *Project Mgr*
Chris Abney, *Graphic Designe*
EMP: 2
SALES (est): 1.3MM **Privately Held**
WEB: www.jbgraphicsinc.com
SIC: 2759 Commercial printing

(G-1420)
JON E GEE ENTERPRISES INC
4000 W 106th St (46032-7720)
PHONE..........................317 291-4522
Jon Gee, *Principal*
EMP: 2
SALES (est): 226.3K **Privately Held**
SIC: 3651 Audio electronic systems

(G-1421)
KENNEY ORTHOPEDICS CARMEL LLC (HQ)
755 W Carmel Dr (46032-5877)
PHONE..........................317 993-3664
John M Kenney, *Mng Member*
Patrick Conley,
William Lester,
Thomas McIntosh,
Timothy C Ruth,
EMP: 4
SALES: 207K
SALES (corp-wide): 15MM **Privately Held**
SIC: 3842 Surgical appliances & supplies
PA: Kenney Ortho Group, Inc.
208 Normandy Ct
Nicholasville KY 40356
859 241-1015

(G-1422)
KERR CONCRETE PIPE CO
Also Called: Old Castle Precast
600 E Carmel Dr Ste 154 (46032-3054)
PHONE..........................317 569-9949
Mark Price, *Office Mgr*
EMP: 3 **EST:** 2011
SALES (est): 352.5K **Privately Held**
SIC: 3272 Concrete products

(G-1423)
KILE ENTERPRISES INC
Also Called: AlphaGraphics
1051 3rd Ave Sw (46032-7568)
PHONE..........................317 844-6629
Michael Kile, *President*
Rhonda Kile, *Principal*
EMP: 15
SALES (est): 2.2MM **Privately Held**
SIC: 2752 Commercial printing, lithographic

(G-1424)
KOKOMO PRESS LLC
5019 Westwood Dr (46033-5974)
P.O. Box 3593 (46082-3593)
PHONE...................................317 575-9903
Bob Schmidt, *Engineer*
EMP: 2
SALES (est): 65.1K **Privately Held**
SIC: 2741 Miscellaneous publishing

(G-1425)
KRISMA DIVERSIFIED
12986 Abraham Run (46033-8615)
PHONE...................................317 413-4788
Mark Stephens, *Owner*
EMP: 2
SALES (est): 120K **Privately Held**
WEB: www.krisma.com
SIC: 3728 Aircraft parts & equipment

(G-1426)
LAPTOP PUBLISHING LLC
3531 Rolling Springs Dr (46033-4452)
P.O. Box 3501 (46082-3501)
PHONE...................................317 379-5716
EMP: 2
SALES (est): 74.7K **Privately Held**
SIC: 2741 Miscellaneous publishing

(G-1427)
LONG ITEM DEVELOPMENT CORP
Also Called: Lid
5753 Turnbull Ct (46033-4814)
PHONE...................................317 844-9491
Gregg H Wood, *President*
▲ **EMP:** 8
SQ FT: 22,000
SALES (est): 3.4MM **Privately Held**
SIC: 3469 5064 Appliance parts, porcelain enameled; electrical appliances, major

(G-1428)
LUCAS OIL PRODUCTS INC
1143 W 116th St (46032-9512)
PHONE...................................317 569-0039
Forrest Lucas, *President*
EMP: 5
SALES (corp-wide): 133.9MM **Privately Held**
SIC: 5172 3999 Crude oil; atomizers, toiletry
PA: Lucas Oil Products, Inc.
302 N Sheridan St
Corona CA 92880
951 270-0154

(G-1429)
LUXLY LLC
Also Called: Barnes Executive Trnsp
14549 Brackney Ln (46032-7743)
PHONE...................................617 415-8031
Sheldon Barnes, *Mng Member*
EMP: 3
SALES: 200K **Privately Held**
SIC: 7363 7372 Chauffeur service; application computer software

(G-1430)
M NELSON & ASSOCIATES INC
4250 W 99th St 140 (46032-7775)
PHONE...................................317 228-1422
Carolina Pimentel-Nelson, *President*
Miles Nelson, *Vice Pres*
▲ **EMP:** 4
SQ FT: 1,000
SALES: 630K **Privately Held**
SIC: 2759 2796 2791 Commercial printing; platemaking services; typesetting

(G-1431)
MAC DESIGNS
1009 3rd Ave Sw (46032-7568)
PHONE...................................317 580-9390
Cathey Brosseau, *President*
EMP: 2
SALES: 500K **Privately Held**
WEB: www.machinedesignsinc.com
SIC: 2396 Screen printing on fabric articles

(G-1432)
MACO PRESS INC
560 3rd Ave Sw (46032-2032)
P.O. Box 329 (46082-0329)
PHONE...................................317 846-5754

Fax: 317 846-5754
Eric Seidensticker, *President*
George Seidensticker, *Treasurer*
Tomeen Seidensticker, *Admin Sec*
EMP: 3
SQ FT: 4,000
SALES (est): 330K **Privately Held**
WEB: www.macopress.com
SIC: 2752 2759 Commercial printing, offset; letterpress printing

(G-1433)
MAGNETIC CONCEPTS CORPORATION
611 3rd Ave Sw (46032-2083)
PHONE...................................317 580-4021
Fax: 317 580-4024
James P Covert, *President*
EMP: 19
SQ FT: 15,000
SALES (est): 2.7MM **Privately Held**
WEB: www.magneticconcepts.com
SIC: 2599 Boards: planning, display, notice

(G-1434)
MAPLE LEAF GRAPHICS INC
Also Called: Skjodt Ink
13540 Kensington Pl (46032-5360)
PHONE...................................317 410-0321
Charles Skjodt, *President*
EMP: 3
SALES (est): 347.4K **Privately Held**
SIC: 2752 Commercial printing, offset

(G-1435)
MCBETH DESIGNS INC
820 W Main St (46032-1430)
PHONE...................................317 848-7313
Beth Porter, *President*
Wade Porter, *Corp Secy*
EMP: 2
SALES (est): 141.5K **Privately Held**
SIC: 2395 Embroidery & art needlework

(G-1436)
MED-REP INC
Also Called: Sentinel Cardio Scan Division
236 John St (46032-1213)
PHONE...................................317 574-0497
Robert Swift, *President*
EMP: 12
SALES (est): 1.1MM **Privately Held**
SIC: 5047 2844 2834 Medical equipment & supplies; shampoos, rinses, conditioners: hair; mouthwashes; toothpastes or powders, dentifrices; powder: baby, face, talcum or toilet; pharmaceutical preparations; druggists' preparations (pharmaceuticals)

(G-1437)
MESH SYSTEMS LLC (PA)
12400 N Meridian St # 175 (46032-4607)
PHONE...................................317 661-4800
Richard V Baxter Jr, *CEO*
Robert Wynne, *Chairman*
Douglas Brune, *COO*
Lisa Landig, *Director*
Rick Fairweather, *Bd of Directors*
EMP: 23
SALES (est): 8MM **Privately Held**
SIC: 4899 8711 7372 Data communication services; electrical or electronic engineering; application computer software

(G-1438)
MESSAGENET SYSTEMS INC
Also Called: Orchid Systems
101 E Carmel Dr Ste 105 (46032-2927)
PHONE...................................317 566-1677
Kevin L Brown, *President*
Sandy Wegner, *Business Mgr*
Jerry Geis, *CTO*
Jerome P Geis, *Admin Sec*
EMP: 6
SALES (est): 1.1MM **Privately Held**
WEB: www.messagenetsystems.com
SIC: 3669 Intercommunication systems, electric

(G-1439)
METEOR MANUFACTURING LLC
3814 Rolling Springs Dr (46033-4459)
PHONE...................................317 587-1414
Karen Najjar, *Owner*

EMP: 2
SALES (est): 103.2K **Privately Held**
SIC: 3999 Manufacturing industries

(G-1440)
MID CENTRAL LAND & EXPLORATION
5825 Dawnwood Dr (46033-8262)
PHONE...................................812 476-9393
Fax: 812 476-9950
Dale Perdue, *Principal*
EMP: 2
SALES (est): 186K **Privately Held**
SIC: 1382 Oil & gas exploration services

(G-1441)
NEBO RIDGE ENTERPRISES LLC
Also Called: Nebo Ridge Bicycles
4335 W 106th St Ste 900 (46032-7754)
PHONE...................................317 471-1089
Timothy T Casady, *Mng Member*
EMP: 4
SALES (est): 408.5K **Privately Held**
SIC: 8748 5941 2389 Business consulting; sporting goods & bicycle shops; apparel for handicapped

(G-1442)
NICKPRINT INC (PA)
484 E Carmel Dr (46032-2812)
PHONE...................................317 489-3033
Nick Bryant, *Principal*
EMP: 2
SALES (est): 210.7K **Privately Held**
SIC: 2759 Screen printing

(G-1443)
NO-LOAD FUND INVESTOR INC
10534 Coppergate (46032-9203)
PHONE...................................317 571-1471
Mark Salzingeo, *President*
EMP: 2
SQ FT: 1,600
SALES (est): 110K **Privately Held**
WEB: www.sheldonjacobs.com
SIC: 2731 Books: publishing & printing

(G-1444)
NORTHWEST ELECTRIC CONNECTION
5894 Hollow Oak Trl (46033-9567)
PHONE...................................219 465-5205
Almarie Johnson, *Principal*
EMP: 2
SALES (est): 150.5K **Privately Held**
SIC: 3699 Electrical equipment & supplies

(G-1445)
OLIVE MILL
Also Called: OLIVE MILL THE
10 S Rangeline Rd (46032-2131)
PHONE...................................317 574-9200
EMP: 5 **Privately Held**
SIC: 2079 Olive oil
PA: Olive Oil Store, Inc
315 James St
Geneva IL 60134

(G-1446)
OPRATO SOFTWARE LLC
14155 Wicksworth Way (46032-9171)
PHONE...................................317 573-0168
Vijay Akella, *Owner*
EMP: 2
SALES (est): 93.1K **Privately Held**
SIC: 7372 Prepackaged software

(G-1447)
ORACLE AMERICA INC
701 Congressional Blvd (46032-5635)
PHONE...................................317 581-0078
Kathryn Sjodin, *Branch Mgr*
EMP: 46
SALES (corp-wide): 39.8B **Publicly Held**
SIC: 3571 Minicomputers
HQ: Oracle America, Inc.
500 Oracle Pkwy
Redwood City CA 94065
650 506-7000

(G-1448)
PARADIGM INDUSTRIES INC
Also Called: Chemstation
12236 Hancock St (46032-5805)
PHONE...................................317 574-8590
Fax: 317 574-8591
Mark O'Connell, *President*
EMP: 9
SQ FT: 3,500
SALES (est): 3.7MM **Privately Held**
SIC: 5169 2841 7349 Chemical additives; soap & other detergents; chemical cleaning services

(G-1449)
PEACE WATER WINERY
37 W Main St (46032-1763)
PHONE...................................317 810-1330
Scott Burton, *Owner*
EMP: 3
SALES (est): 160.7K **Privately Held**
SIC: 2084 Wines

(G-1450)
PICKLE PRINTS LLC
12639 Teaberry Ln (46032-8471)
PHONE...................................317 344-2495
Erica O'Hara, *Principal*
EMP: 2
SALES (est): 83.9K **Privately Held**
SIC: 2752 Commercial printing, lithographic

(G-1451)
PIP PRINTING
11711 N Penn St Ste 107 (46032-4559)
PHONE...................................317 843-5755
Fax: 317 843-5754
Tony Kisstner, *Owner*
Anthony Kistner, *Manager*
EMP: 2
SALES (est): 359.2K **Privately Held**
SIC: 2752 2791 2789 Printers' services: folding, collating; typesetting; bookbinding & related work

(G-1452)
POLICYSTAT LLC
550 Congressional Blvd # 100 (46032-5644)
PHONE...................................317 644-1296
Steven Ehrlich, *President*
Cameron Davis, *Business Mgr*
Dora Grant, *Business Mgr*
Rob Vaughan, *VP Bus Dvlpt*
Tamara Green, *Sales Staff*
EMP: 73 **EST:** 2008
SALES (est): 6.3MM **Privately Held**
SIC: 7371 7372 Computer software development; prepackaged software
PA: Icontracts, Inc.
1011 Rte 22 Ste 104
Bridgewater NJ 08807

(G-1453)
POYSER KELSHAW GROUP LLC
Also Called: Scott Art Castings
4936 Regency Pl (46033-5959)
PHONE...................................317 571-8493
Thomas Dpoyser,
Karen K Poyser,
Thomas D Poyser,
EMP: 6
SQ FT: 15,000
SALES (est): 392.6K **Privately Held**
SIC: 3281 3366 3841 Urns, cut stone; castings (except die); medical instruments & equipment, blood & bone work

(G-1454)
PPG INDUSTRIES INC
Also Called: PPG 4369
10111 N Michigan Rd (46032-7945)
PHONE...................................317 870-0345
Doug Nave, *Branch Mgr*
EMP: 24
SALES (corp-wide): 14.2B **Publicly Held**
WEB: www.ppg.com
SIC: 2851 Paints & allied products
PA: Ppg Industries, Inc.
1 Ppg Pl
Pittsburgh PA 15272
412 434-3131

GEOGRAPHIC

(G-1455)
PRINTING PLUS INC
505 E 116th St (46032-4506)
PHONE..............................317 574-1313
Rex Neal, *President*
EMP: 5
SALES (est): 290K **Privately Held**
WEB: www.printing-plus.net
SIC: 2396 2752 Printing & embossing on plastics fabric articles; commercial printing, lithographic

(G-1456)
PROFESSIONAL LIGHTING SERVICES
1091 3rd Ave Sw (46032-2523)
PHONE..............................317 844-4261
EMP: 13
SALES (est): 1MM **Privately Held**
SIC: 5063 3645 Whol Electrical Equipment Mfg Residential Lighting Fixtures

(G-1457)
PROTOTECH ENTERPRISES INC
1788 Spruce Dr (46033-9025)
PHONE..............................317 250-9644
Larry Hoskins, *President*
EMP: 2
SALES (est): 148.1K **Privately Held**
SIC: 3489 Ordnance & accessories

(G-1458)
PROTOTYPE SYSTEMS INC
481 Gradle Dr (46032-2535)
PHONE..............................317 634-3040
Fax: 317 634-3047
John Caldwell, *President*
EMP: 30
SQ FT: 12,000
SALES (est): 2.6MM **Privately Held**
SIC: 2759 7331 Laser printing; direct mail advertising services

(G-1459)
PRYSM INC
11711 N College Ave # 140 (46032-5601)
PHONE..............................317 324-1222
EMP: 6 **Privately Held**
SIC: 3999 Advertising display products
PA: Prysm, Inc.
180 Baytech Dr Ste 200
San Jose CA 95134

(G-1460)
QUEEN ANN CUSTOM DRAPIES
Also Called: Queen Ann Draperies
4000 W 106th St Ste 125 (46032-7730)
PHONE..............................317 802-6130
Fax: 317 873-3117
EMP: 7
SALES (est): 390K **Privately Held**
SIC: 2391 7299 Mfg Custom Curtains/Draperies And Custom Quilting/Stitching Operation

(G-1461)
R2 PHARMA LLC
11550 N Meridian St # 290 (46032-6956)
PHONE..............................317 810-6205
William Culpepper, *CEO*
Mike Puckett, *CFO*
EMP: 2
SALES (est): 84K **Privately Held**
SIC: 2834 Pharmaceutical preparations

(G-1462)
RACE CARS USA LLC
1530 Woodlake Ct (46032-9596)
PHONE..............................317 508-3500
EMP: 2
SALES (est): 96K **Privately Held**
SIC: 3711 Automobile assembly, including specialty automobiles

(G-1463)
RAU CREATIONS
14617 Strauss Dr Apt 2412 (46032-7013)
PHONE..............................317 774-8789
John Rau, *Owner*
Joan Rau, *Co-Owner*
◆ EMP: 2
SALES: 1MM **Privately Held**
WEB: www.raucreations.com
SIC: 3086 Plastics foam products

(G-1464)
REGAL PRINTING INC
485 Gradle Dr (46032-2535)
PHONE..............................317 844-1723
Fax: 317 844-3621
Mark Frew, *President*
EMP: 5
SQ FT: 3,700
SALES (est): 857.5K **Privately Held**
WEB: www.regalprinting.net
SIC: 2752 7334 2791 Commercial printing, offset; mimeographing; typesetting

(G-1465)
RELEVO INC
5883 William Conner Way (46033-8825)
PHONE..............................317 644-0099
Brian Southard, *President*
Jeffrey Southard, *Principal*
EMP: 3
SALES (est): 205.1K **Privately Held**
SIC: 2834 2844 Pharmaceutical preparations; cosmetic preparations

(G-1466)
RELEVO LABS LLC
5883 William Conner Way (46033-8825)
PHONE..............................317 900-6949
Brian Southard, *President*
Jeff Southard, *Development*
EMP: 5
SQ FT: 1,200
SALES (est): 142K **Privately Held**
SIC: 5999 2842 2844 Toiletries, cosmetics & perfumes; sanitation preparations, disinfectants & deodorants; deodorants, personal

(G-1467)
REMEDIUM SERVICES GROUP LLC
Also Called: Southside Solidification Svcs
11711 N College Ave (46032-5634)
PHONE..............................317 660-6868
Tom McCullough, *Managing Prtnr*
Gary Meyer, *CFO*
EMP: 10
SALES (est): 1.5MM **Privately Held**
SIC: 2819 5093 Inorganic metal compounds or salts; metal scrap & waste materials

(G-1468)
RITRON INC
505 W Carmel Dr (46032-7564)
P.O. Box 1998 (46082-1998)
PHONE..............................317 846-1201
Fax: 317 846-4978
W Stephen Rice, *President*
Elmore W Rice III, *Chairman*
Shirley A Rice, *Corp Secy*
Brian Hipp, *Mfg Staff*
Kevin Matson, *Engineer*
▲ EMP: 90
SQ FT: 40,000
SALES (est): 16.1MM **Privately Held**
WEB: www.ritron.com
SIC: 3663 Transmitter-receivers, radio

(G-1469)
ROLAND INTERNATIONAL CO LLC
1016 3rd Ave Sw Ste 207 (46032-7607)
PHONE..............................319 400-1106
Shaohua Ji, *President*
EMP: 3
SALES (est): 221.9K **Privately Held**
SIC: 3559 3561 Robots, molding & forming plastics; optical lens machinery; plastics working machinery; industrial pumps & parts

(G-1470)
ROUGH NOTES COMPANY INC
11690 Technology Dr (46032-5628)
PHONE..............................800 428-4384
Walter J Gdowski, *Chairman*
Samuel Berman, *COO*
EMP: 29 EST: 1878
SQ FT: 15,000

SALES: 5MM **Privately Held**
WEB: www.roughnotes.com
SIC: 2721 8999 7372 Magazines: publishing only, not printed on site; technical manual preparation; educational computer software
PA: The Rough Notes Company Inc
11690 Technology Dr
Carmel IN 46032

(G-1471)
ROUGH NOTES COMPANY INC (PA)
Also Called: Insurance Publishing Plus
11690 Technology Dr (46032-5628)
P.O. Box 1990 (46082-1990)
PHONE..............................317 582-1600
Fax: 317 816-1000
Walter J Gdowski, *President*
Samuel W Berman, *Exec VP*
Robert Kretzmer, *Exec VP*
Eric Hall, *Vice Pres*
Dick Schoeninger, *Vice Pres*
EMP: 25
SQ FT: 15,000
SALES (est): 5.6MM **Privately Held**
WEB: www.insurancepubplus.com
SIC: 2721 2741 Trade journals: publishing & printing; art copy: publishing & printing

(G-1472)
ROUND WORLD PRODUCTS INC
75 Executive Dr Ste B (46032-2993)
PHONE..............................317 257-7352
Christian M Knoebel, *President*
Lori Gray, *Sales Staff*
▲ EMP: 14
SALES (est): 1.6MM **Privately Held**
SIC: 2741 Globe covers (maps): publishing only, not printed on site

(G-1473)
RS USED OIL SERVICES INC
4501 W 99th St Ste 1000 (46032-7768)
PHONE..............................866 778-7336
Ron Winkle, *President*
EMP: 10
SALES (est): 490.4K **Privately Held**
SIC: 1389 Oil & gas field services

(G-1474)
RYOBI PRESS PARTS
241 N Rangeline Rd (46032-1744)
PHONE..............................800 901-3304
EMP: 2
SALES (est): 77.6K **Privately Held**
SIC: 2741 Miscellaneous publishing

(G-1475)
SCHAFER POWDER COATING INC
4518 W 99th St (46032-7715)
PHONE..............................317 228-9987
Mark P Schafer, *President*
Jared Beeler, *Production*
EMP: 30
SQ FT: 48,000
SALES (est): 4.6MM **Privately Held**
WEB: www.schaferpowdercoating.com
SIC: 3479 Coating of metals & formed products

(G-1476)
SCHOOL DOCTOR NOTES LLC
11555 N Meridian St # 100 (46032-6934)
PHONE..............................317 660-1552
Ryan Murray,
Stan Murray,
EMP: 2
SQ FT: 4,000
SALES (est): 141.9K **Privately Held**
SIC: 7372 Business oriented computer software

(G-1477)
SECURITY PAKS INTL LLC
11405 N Penn St Ste 106 (46032-6905)
PHONE..............................317 536-2662
Fax: 317 587-6785
Andrew Elder, *Mng Member*
EMP: 10
SALES (est): 1.2MM **Privately Held**
WEB: www.securitypaks.com
SIC: 3086 Plastics foam products

(G-1478)
SEPRO CORPORATION (PA)
11550 N Meridian St # 600 (46032-4565)
PHONE..............................317 580-8282
Fax: 317 580-8280
William H Culpepper, *President*
Michael D Puckett, *Treasurer*
▲ EMP: 35
SQ FT: 15,000
SALES (est): 2.9MM **Privately Held**
WEB: www.seapro.net
SIC: 2879 7389 Fungicides, herbicides; mapmaking services

(G-1479)
SHELF TAG SUPPLY CORPORATION
611 3rd Ave Sw (46032-2083)
PHONE..............................317 580-4030
Dixie A Covert, *President*
Pete Blainey, *Mktg Dir*
EMP: 9
SALES (est): 720K **Privately Held**
WEB: www.shelftagsupply.com
SIC: 2679 Tags & labels, paper

(G-1480)
SIGNS OF LIFE LLC
10940 Timber Ln (46032-3544)
PHONE..............................317 575-1049
EMP: 2
SALES (est): 110K **Privately Held**
SIC: 3993 Mfg Signs/Advertising Specialties

(G-1481)
SILK MOUNTAIN CREATION
620 S Rangeline Rd Ste P (46032-2151)
PHONE..............................317 815-1660
David J Malone, *Principal*
EMP: 5 EST: 2007
SALES (est): 396.2K **Privately Held**
SIC: 2391 Draperies, plastic & textile: from purchased materials

(G-1482)
SMART PERGOLA
12958 Brighton Ave (46032-9282)
PHONE..............................317 987-7750
Claudio Bertolini, *Owner*
EMP: 2
SALES (est): 116.8K **Privately Held**
SIC: 3999 Manufacturing industries

(G-1483)
SOUTHEASTERN ALUMINUM PDTS INC
9770 Mayflower Park Dr # 200 (46032-7940)
PHONE..............................904 781-8200
Susan Byers, *Branch Mgr*
EMP: 18
SALES (corp-wide): 25.8MM **Privately Held**
WEB: www.southeasternaluminum.com
SIC: 3442 Sash, door or window: metal
PA: Southeastern Aluminum Products, Inc.
4925 Bulls Bay Hwy
Jacksonville FL 32219
904 781-8200

(G-1484)
SPECIALTY MANUFACTURING
11595 N Meridian St # 705 (46032-6961)
PHONE..............................317 587-4999
Dave Lucas, *Principal*
EMP: 2 EST: 2016
SALES (est): 43.6K **Privately Held**
SIC: 3999 Manufacturing industries

(G-1485)
SPECTACLES OF CARMEL INC
30 1st St Sw (46032-2102)
PHONE..............................317 848-9081
EMP: 2
SALES (est): 85.1K **Privately Held**
SIC: 3851 Spectacles

(G-1486)
SUTTER HOME WINERY
1503 Cool Creek Dr (46033-2318)
PHONE..............................317 848-3003
Rick Jenkins, *Principal*
EMP: 4 EST: 2001

▲ = Import ▼=Export
◆ =Import/Export

SALES (est): 228.4K **Privately Held**
SIC: 2084 Wines

(G-1487)
TC HEARTLAND LLC (PA)
Also Called: Heartland Food Products Group
14300 Clay Terrace Blvd # 249
(46032-3636)
PHONE.....................317 566-9750
Gene Wolf, *Vice Pres*
Britni Wolfe, *Purch Agent*
Andy Reid, *Accounting Mgr*
Tom Gatherum, *Natl Sales Mgr*
Alexandra Livesey, *Manager*
▼ **EMP:** 475
SALES (est): 216.2MM **Privately Held**
WEB: www.hsweet.com
SIC: 2099 Sorghum syrups: for sweetening

(G-1488)
TELAMON CORPORATION (PA)
1000 E 116th St (46032-3416)
PHONE.....................317 818-6888
Fax: 317 818-6666
Stanley Chen, *CEO*
Keith Gallant, *President*
Robert Kuhlmann, *President*
Randall P Muench, *President*
Albert M Chen, *Chairman*
▲ **EMP:** 200
SQ FT: 130,000
SALES (est): 497.5MM **Privately Held**
WEB: www.ibuybroadband.com
SIC: 4813 8711 3357 ; data telephone
communications; engineering services;
communication wire

(G-1489)
TELAMON ENTP VENTURES LLC
1000 E 116th St (46032-3416)
PHONE.....................317 818-6888
Jessie Wang, *Administration*
EMP: 3 **EST:** 2016
SALES (est): 99.8K **Privately Held**
SIC: 8999 3845 7374 Scientific consult-
ing; electromedical equipment; data pro-
cessing & preparation

(G-1490)
TELAMON INTERNATIONAL CORP (PA)
Also Called: Venture & Alliance Group
1000 E 116th St (46032-3416)
PHONE.....................317 818-6888
Albert Chen, *CEO*
◆ **EMP:** 25
SQ FT: 10,000
SALES (est): 13.6MM **Privately Held**
SIC: 5065 3661 Connectors, electronic;
fiber optics communications equipment

(G-1491)
TELAMON TECHNOLOGIES CORP
Also Called: Telamon International
1000 E 116th St (46032-3416)
PHONE.....................317 818-6888
Albert Chen, *President*
Michael Shen, *President*
John Ludwig, *CFO*
Margaret Chen, *Admin Sec*
▲ **EMP:** 585
SQ FT: 100,000
SALES (est): 492MM
SALES (corp-wide): 497.5MM **Privately Held**
WEB: www.ibuybroadband.com
SIC: 3661 Telephones & telephone appara-
tus
PA: Telamon Corporation
1000 E 116th St
Carmel IN 46032
317 818-6888

(G-1492)
TEMPEST TECHNICAL SALES INC (PA)
13295 Illinois St Ste 329 (46032-3042)
PHONE.....................317 844-9236
Lynn Wuertemberger, *President*
Kevin Chatterton, *Principal*
Susan Edelen, *Accounts Mgr*
Ken Leetch, *Sales Engr*
David Remer, *Sales Engr*
EMP: 12

SQ FT: 1,900
SALES (est): 1.5MM **Privately Held**
WEB: www.tempesttechsales.com
SIC: 3679 5731 5961 3575 Microwave
components; antennas; computer equipment & electronics, mail order; computer
terminals, monitors & components

(G-1493)
TEXAS INSTRUMENTS INCORPORATED
12900 N Meridian St # 175 (46032-5402)
PHONE.....................317 574-2611
Ken Smith, *Branch Mgr*
EMP: 11
SALES (corp-wide): 14.9B **Publicly Held**
WEB: www.ti.com
SIC: 3674 Semiconductors & related de-
vices
PA: Texas Instruments Incorporated
12500 Ti Blvd
Dallas TX 75243
214 479-3773

(G-1494)
TGX MEDICAL SYSTEMS LLC
12220 N Meridian St # 175 (46032-6973)
PHONE.....................317 575-0300
Chris Di Biase, *Opers Staff*
Melissa Achtien, *Controller*
Chris Sogard,
Michael Good,
Jeff Haskett,
EMP: 10
SALES (est): 1MM **Privately Held**
WEB: www.tgxmedical.com
SIC: 7372 Business oriented computer
software

(G-1495)
THM PUBLISHING SACRAMENTO LLC
Also Called: Thm Publishing Indianapolis
301 E Carmel Dr Ste Ce800 (46032-2888)
PHONE.....................317 810-1340
EMP: 2
SALES (est): 60K **Privately Held**
SIC: 2741 Miscellaneous publishing

(G-1496)
THOMAS TOLL
Also Called: Saint Clair Boat Works
1929 W 136th St (46032-9469)
PHONE.....................317 569-2628
Thomas Toll, *Owner*
EMP: 2
SALES (est): 100K **Privately Held**
WEB: www.tollconstruction.com
SIC: 3732 Motorized boat, building & re-
pairing

(G-1497)
TIER 1 MEDICAL LLC
11404 Regency Ln (46033-3971)
PHONE.....................317 316-7871
Kenneth Thurman, *President*
EMP: 2
SALES (est): 130K **Privately Held**
SIC: 3569 5047 8099 Firefighting appara-
tus & related equipment; medical & hospi-
tal equipment; medical rescue squad

(G-1498)
TK SOFTWARE INC (PA)
11495 N Penn St Ste 220 (46032-6935)
PHONE.....................317 569-8887
Arthur Eaton, *Principal*
EMP: 7 **EST:** 2008
SALES (est): 553.5K **Privately Held**
SIC: 7372 Application computer software

(G-1499)
U-NITT LLC
13640 Akers Dr (46074-2316)
PHONE.....................812 251-9980
Julie Feng, *CEO*
▲ **EMP:** 3 **EST:** 2007
SALES (est): 413.3K **Privately Held**
SIC: 5199 5261 5072 3651 Yarns; lawn
ornaments; garden tools, hand; video
camera-audio recorders, household use

(G-1500)
UBER DRAGON STUDIOS INC
1404 Spruce Dr (46033-9373)
PHONE.....................317 520-2837
Adam Fox, *CEO*
Aaron Knirk, *President*
EMP: 2
SALES (est): 117.4K **Privately Held**
SIC: 7372 Home entertainment computer
software

(G-1501)
UBERLUX INC
12579 Pembrooke Cir (46032-8340)
PHONE.....................317 580-0111
Steven Zimmermann, *CEO*
Patrick Haider, *Vice Pres*
EMP: 4
SALES (est): 154.1K **Privately Held**
SIC: 3648 1731 7389 Lighting fixtures,
except electric: residential; lighting con-
tractor

(G-1502)
ULTRA ATHLETE LLC
2800 N Mridian St Ste 125 (46032)
PHONE.....................317 520-9898
Rick Peters,
Thomas Vanneman,
EMP: 2
SALES (est): 210.5K **Privately Held**
SIC: 3842 Braces, orthopedic

(G-1503)
UN COMMUNICATIONS GROUP INC
Also Called: Un Printing & Mailing
1429 Chase Ct (46032-7502)
PHONE.....................317 844-8622
Fax: 317 573-0239
Denise L Purvis, *CEO*
Sayer Ed, *Managing Dir*
Jeff Purvis, *COO*
Mark Shepler, *Exec VP*
James J Purvis, *Vice Pres*
EMP: 35
SQ FT: 30,000
SALES (est): 7.4MM **Privately Held**
WEB: www.uncommunications.com
SIC: 2752 5942 7331 2759 Commercial
printing, offset; book stores; mailing serv-
ice; commercial printing; miscellaneous
publishing; periodicals

(G-1504)
UNITED FEEDS
1513 Brook Mill Ct (46032-9104)
PHONE.....................317 627-5637
James Lease,
EMP: 7
SALES (est): 401.7K **Privately Held**
SIC: 2048 Prepared feeds

(G-1505)
US OILFIELD COMPANY LLC
Also Called: US Solids Control
8925 N Mrdian Ste Ste 120 (46032)
P.O. Box 40704, Indianapolis (46240-0704)
PHONE.....................888 584-7565
John Bales, *President*
Martin Shraeder, *CFO*
EMP: 30
SALES (est): 4.5MM **Privately Held**
SIC: 1389 1381 Oil field services; direc-
tional drilling oil & gas wells

(G-1506)
VITALITY BOWLS
110 W Main St (46032-1796)
PHONE.....................317 581-9496
EMP: 4
SALES (est): 153.1K **Privately Held**
SIC: 2099 Dessert mixes & fillings

(G-1507)
WATERSTONE TECHNOLOGY
12429 Springbrooke Run (46033-9148)
PHONE.....................317 644-0862
Faming Zhang, *Chairman*
Marietta Wu, *COO*
Maximillian Yeh, *Vice Pres*
Susan Cai, *Manager*
▲ **EMP:** 20
SQ FT: 2,000

SALES: 2MM **Privately Held**
SIC: 2819 Industrial inorganic chemicals

(G-1508)
WEAVER AIR PRODUCTS LLC
1033 3rd Ave Sw Ste 212 (46032-7593)
PHONE.....................317 848-4420
Jon Weaver, *Owner*
EMP: 3
SALES (est): 413K **Privately Held**
SIC: 2813 Industrial gases

(G-1509)
WESTWOOD PAPER CO
4489 Camborne Dr (46033-2461)
PHONE.....................317 843-1212
Jill W Sowder, *Owner*
EMP: 6
SALES (est): 288.1K **Privately Held**
SIC: 2754 Stationery & invitation printing,
gravure

(G-1510)
WILEY INDUSTRIES INC
1311 Woodgate Dr (46033-8504)
PHONE.....................317 574-1477
Shannon Wiley, *Principal*
EMP: 2
SALES (est): 133.7K **Privately Held**
SIC: 3999 Manufacturing industries

(G-1511)
YOGURTZ
12561 N Meridian St (46032-9150)
PHONE.....................317 853-6600
Amy P Biggs, *General Mgr*
EMP: 5
SALES (est): 259.4K **Privately Held**
SIC: 2026 Yogurt

Carthage
Rush County

(G-1512)
BC PUBLICATIONS INC
5812 W 850 N (46115-9455)
P.O. Box 309, Dublin (47335-0309)
PHONE.....................765 334-8277
Elizabeth Davis, *Principal*
EMP: 2
SALES (est): 127K **Privately Held**
SIC: 2741 Miscellaneous publishing

(G-1513)
INTEGRATED SYSTEMS MANAGEMENT
7002 W 1000 N B (46115-9584)
P.O. Box 204 (46115-0204)
PHONE.....................765 565-6108
Mark Cosat, *Owner*
EMP: 3
SALES (est): 234.4K **Privately Held**
WEB: www.ismi-gunsprings.com
SIC: 3495 Gun springs, precision

(G-1514)
L L WELDING
501 N East St (46115-0020)
PHONE.....................765 565-6006
EMP: 8 **EST:** 2009
SALES (est): 530K **Privately Held**
SIC: 3444 5051 Mfg Sheet Metalwork
Metals Service Center

(G-1515)
ONU ACRE LLC
9350 W 800 N (46115-9732)
PHONE.....................765 565-1355
James Owen, *Mng Member*
Wendy J Underwood,
EMP: 2
SALES (est): 107.8K **Privately Held**
SIC: 2211 2011 Alpacas, cotton; lamb
products from lamb slaughtered on site

(G-1516)
SIGNS BY SULANE INC
5920 W 850 N (46115-9456)
PHONE.....................765 565-6773
Tom Dennis, *Owner*
Barbara Dennis, *Owner*
EMP: 2 **EST:** 2001

Right margin tab: **GEOGRAPHIC**

SALES (est): 129.9K **Privately Held**
SIC: **3993** Signs & advertising specialties

(G-1517)
TRIPLE J IRONWORKS INC
211 S Main St (46115-9629)
P.O. Box 467 (46115-0467)
PHONE..............................765 544-9152
Joseph Collingwood IV, *President*
Joseph H Collingwood, *Vice Pres*
EMP: 5
SALES (est): 440K **Privately Held**
SIC: **3444** 1791 1796 Sheet metalwork;
structural steel erection; installing building
equipment

Cayuga
Vermillion County

(G-1518)
DANIEL GRIFFIN
Also Called: Griffin Logging
2019 E 50 N (47928-8151)
P.O. Box 236, Newport (47966-0236)
PHONE..............................765 492-3257
Daniel Griffin, *Owner*
EMP: 4
SALES (est): 254.4K **Privately Held**
SIC: **2411** Logging camps & contractors

(G-1519)
FABSTAR INC
200 E Maple St (47928-8243)
PHONE..............................765 230-0261
Fax: 765 492-3660
Steve York, *President*
Mark York, *Vice Pres*
Randal York, *Vice Pres*
EMP: 16
SQ FT: 22,000
SALES (est): 1.6MM **Privately Held**
SIC: **3443** Industrial vessels, tanks & con-
tainers; tanks, standard or custom fabri-
cated: metal plate

(G-1520)
INTERNATIONAL PAPER
COMPANY
2585 E 200 N (47928-8153)
PHONE..............................765 492-3341
Derek Depuydt, *Engineer*
Rusty Akers, *Human Res Mgr*
Michael Reed, *Manager*
EMP: 5
SALES (corp-wide): 21.7B **Publicly Held**
SIC: **2653** Boxes, corrugated: made from
purchased materials
PA: International Paper Company
6400 Poplar Ave
Memphis TN 38197
901 419-9000

(G-1521)
JOHN GEBHART
WOODWORKINGS
Also Called: Gebhart's Woodworking & Lum-
ber
5352 N Fable St (47928-8057)
PHONE..............................765 492-3898
John Gebhart, *Owner*
EMP: 2 EST: 1982
SALES: 50K **Privately Held**
SIC: **2431** 5211 Woodwork, interior & or-
namental; millwork & lumber

Cedar Grove
Franklin County

(G-1522)
SCHINDLER WOODWORK
6006 English Hill Rd (47016-9625)
PHONE..............................513 314-5943
Cody Schindler, *Principal*
EMP: 2
SALES (est): 93.8K **Privately Held**
SIC: **2431** Millwork

(G-1523)
SRK FILTERS LLC
5010 Beesley Rd (47016-9618)
PHONE..............................765 647-9962
Steve Kahles, *Principal*
EMP: 2
SALES (est): 384.8K **Privately Held**
SIC: **3569** Filters

Cedar Lake
Lake County

(G-1524)
A & T CONSTRUCTION AND
EXCVTG
10212 W 128th Ave (46303-8348)
PHONE..............................219 314-2439
Christine Suttinger, *President*
EMP: 3 EST: 2016
SALES (est): 138.9K **Privately Held**
SIC: **3531** 1795 Buckets, excavating:
clamshell, concrete, dragline, etc.; wreck-
ing & demolition work

(G-1525)
AIR TECH COMFORT SYSTEMS
9021 W 141st Ave (46303-8860)
PHONE..............................219 663-9778
James F Todd, *Principal*
EMP: 4
SALES (est): 714.2K **Privately Held**
SIC: **3585** Heating equipment, complete

(G-1526)
CAMILLES STUDIO
11650 Wicker Ave (46303-9793)
PHONE..............................219 365-5902
Edward Mitchell, *Owner*
Catherine Mitchell, *Co-Owner*
EMP: 3
SALES (est): 202.6K **Privately Held**
SIC: **3271** 5032 Concrete block & brick;
brick, stone & related material

(G-1527)
CEDAR SHACK
11300 W 131st Pl (46303-9347)
PHONE..............................219 682-5531
Ralph Ells, *Owner*
EMP: 2
SALES (est): 73.5K **Privately Held**
SIC: **3229** Candlesticks, glass

(G-1528)
GLASS SURGEONS
12604 Havenwood Pass (46303-8692)
PHONE..............................219 374-2500
Jack Olthoff, *Owner*
EMP: 2
SALES (est): 105.1K **Privately Held**
SIC: **3231** Windshields, glass: made from
purchased glass

(G-1529)
GUND COMPANY INC
Also Called: MM&m Electrical Supply
10501 W 133rd Ave (46303-8577)
P.O. Box 376 (46303-0376)
PHONE..............................219 374-9944
Jim Ludwig, *Foreman/Supr*
Becky Heimbuch, *Human Res Mgr*
Jeff Taylor, *Manager*
Judy Webb, *Administration*
EMP: 35
SALES (corp-wide): 70MM **Privately**
Held
WEB: www.thegundcompany.com
SIC: **3644** Insulators & insulation materials,
electrical
PA: The Gund Company Inc
2121 Walton Rd
Saint Louis MO 63114
314 423-5200

(G-1530)
J & J CABINETS
13418 Wicker Ave (46303-9088)
PHONE..............................219 374-6816
Gerald Stenger, *Owner*
EMP: 2 EST: 1964
SALES (est): 153.3K **Privately Held**
SIC: **2434** Wood kitchen cabinets

(G-1531)
JK GRAPHICS INC
Also Called: Ink Spot Printing
12546 Parrish Ave (46303-9260)
PHONE..............................219 374-5930
Kamie Bunge, *President*
James Bunge, *Vice Pres*
EMP: 7
SALES (est): 1.9MM **Privately Held**
SIC: **2752** Commercial printing, litho-
graphic

(G-1532)
OTTOSONS INDUSTRIES INC
12742 Wicker Ave Ste B (46303-9251)
PHONE..............................219 365-8330
Fax: 219 365-5770
Mark Speichert, *President*
Fred Spiechert, *Vice Pres*
EMP: 7
SQ FT: 5,600
SALES (est): 460K **Privately Held**
SIC: **7699** 3599 Hydraulic equipment re-
pair; machine shop, jobbing & repair

(G-1533)
SMITH READY MIX INC
9018 W 133rd Ave (46303-9200)
PHONE..............................219 374-5581
Fax: 219 374-8755
Douglas Smith, *President*
EMP: 8
SALES (corp-wide): 12.7MM **Privately**
Held
SIC: **3273** Ready-mixed concrete
PA: Smith Ready Mix, Inc.
251 Lincolnway
Valparaiso IN 46383
219 462-3191

(G-1534)
STERLING MACHINE CO INC
10501 W 133rd Ave Lot 6 (46303-8578)
P.O. Box 2026 (46303-2026)
PHONE..............................219 374-9360
Anthony Gatto, *President*
Dave Peterson, *Vice Pres*
John Allen, *Treasurer*
EMP: 5
SQ FT: 6,400
SALES (est): 649.7K **Privately Held**
SIC: **3599** Machine shop, jobbing & repair

Celestine
Dubois County

(G-1535)
GESSNER WOODWORKING
106 N 1000 E (47521-9648)
PHONE..............................812 389-2594
Mark Gessner, *Owner*
Joyce Gessner, *Co-Owner*
EMP: 2
SALES: 80K **Privately Held**
SIC: **2499** Decorative wood & woodwork

(G-1536)
MASTERBRAND CABINETS INC
6385 E State Road 164 (47521)
P.O. Box 420, Jasper (47547-0420)
PHONE..............................812 482-2527
Gene Buechlein, *Branch Mgr*
EMP: 100
SALES (corp-wide): 5.2B **Publicly Held**
WEB: www.mbcabinets.com
SIC: **2434** Wood kitchen cabinets
HQ: Masterbrand Cabinets, Inc.
1 Masterbrand Cabinets Dr
Jasper IN 47546
812 482-2527

(G-1537)
SANDER PROCESSING
6614 E State Road 164 (47521-5401)
P.O. Box 68 (47521-0068)
PHONE..............................812 481-0044
James Sander, *Owner*
Chris Sander, *Co-Owner*
Kent Sander, *Co-Owner*
Randy Sander, *Co-Owner*
EMP: 21

SALES: 120K **Privately Held**
SIC: **2013** 2011 Sausages & other prepared meats; meat packing plants

Centerpoint
Clay County

(G-1538)
GREEN MOUNTAIN INDUSTRIES
LLC
603 W State Road 46 (47840-8274)
PHONE..............................812 585-1531
Hansford Mann, *Principal*
EMP: 2
SALES (est): 51.8K **Privately Held**
SIC: **3999** Manufacturing industries

(G-1539)
PARSONS CUSTOM MACHINING
INC
3029 N County Road 100 E (47840-8295)
PHONE..............................812 877-2700
Fax: 812 442-0053
Julie Parsons, *Partner*
Lorren Parsons, *Partner*
EMP: 8 EST: 1931
SQ FT: 14,000
SALES: 700K **Privately Held**
WEB: www.parsonscustom.com
SIC: **3599** Machine shop, jobbing & repair

(G-1540)
R BOOE & SON HARDWOODS
INC
481 N Meridian Rd (47840-8378)
PHONE..............................812 835-2663
Richard Booe, *President*
EMP: 38
SQ FT: 3,000
SALES (est): 5.5MM **Privately Held**
SIC: **2421** Sawmills & planing mills, gen-
eral

Centerville
Wayne County

(G-1541)
CHARLES BANE
Also Called: Pmp Enterprise
2009 Willow Grove Rd (47330-9667)
P.O. Box 116 (47330-0116)
PHONE..............................765 855-5100
Charles Bane, *Owner*
EMP: 3
SQ FT: 1,300
SALES (est): 212.9K **Privately Held**
SIC: **3543** Foundry patternmaking

(G-1542)
GAD-A-BOUT SCREENPRINTING
INC
403 E School St (47330-1528)
PHONE..............................765 855-5681
Raymond Dickerson, *Owner*
EMP: 2
SALES (est): 87K **Privately Held**
SIC: **2261** Screen printing of cotton broad-
woven fabrics

(G-1543)
POLYMER EQUIPMENT CO INC
1219 E Main St (47330-9557)
PHONE..............................765 855-3448
John H Hudson, *President*
Sheila M Hudson, *Vice Pres*
EMP: 5
SQ FT: 7,200
SALES (est): 450K **Privately Held**
SIC: **3089** Injection molding of plastics

(G-1544)
WARM GLOW CANDLE
COMPANY
519 W Water St (47330-1055)
P.O. Box 127 (47330-0127)
PHONE..............................765 855-5483
Jacquelyn Carberry, *President*
EMP: 23

▲ = Import ▼=Export
◆ =Import/Export

SALES (est): 3MM **Privately Held**
SIC: 3999 Candles

Central
Harrison County

(G-1545)
BARKS LUMBER CO INC
1800 Heth Wash Rd Sw (47110-7926)
PHONE.................................812 732-4680
Fax: 812 732-4322
Earl C Barks, *President*
Linda Ferree, *Vice Pres*
Thelma Barks, *Admin Sec*
EMP: 8
SALES (est): 955.6K **Privately Held**
SIC: 2448 5099 Pallets, wood; logs, hewn ties, posts & poles

Chalmers
White County

(G-1546)
BROWN & BROWN FUEL
5774 S State Road 43 (47929-8000)
PHONE.................................219 984-5173
EMP: 3
SALES (est): 143.6K **Privately Held**
SIC: 2869 Fuels

(G-1547)
KEN ANLIKER
Also Called: Anliker Machine
2785 S 75 W (47929-8065)
PHONE.................................219 984-5676
Ken Anliker, *Owner*
EMP: 3 EST: 1998
SQ FT: 30,000
SALES: 450K **Privately Held**
SIC: 3599 3548 Machine & other job shop work; welding apparatus

Chandler
Warrick County

(G-1548)
DWD MILLER INC
10399 Telephone Rd (47610-9669)
PHONE.................................812 853-8497
Wayne Miller, *Partner*
Dennis Miller, *Principal*
EMP: 4
SALES: 300K **Privately Held**
SIC: 3523 Driers (farm): grain, hay & seed

(G-1549)
HOOSIER STAMPING LLC
7988 Gardner Rd (47610-9023)
PHONE.................................812 993-2040
Thomas J Johnson,
▲ EMP: 2 EST: 2010
SALES (est): 290.3K **Privately Held**
SIC: 3469 Metal stampings

(G-1550)
K M SPECIALTY PUMPS INC
8055 Highway 62 W (47610-9341)
P.O. Box 99 (47610-0099)
PHONE.................................812 925-3000
C Russell Welder, *President*
Devin Allen, *Principal*
▲ EMP: 10 EST: 1982
SQ FT: 20,000
SALES (est): 3.6MM **Privately Held**
WEB: www.kmspecialty.com
SIC: 7699 3593 Hydraulic equipment repair; fluid power cylinders, hydraulic or pneumatic

(G-1551)
MID AMERICA POWERED VEHICLES
Also Called: Mid-America Golf Car
1699 S Stevenson Stn Rd (47610-9233)
P.O. Box 5749, Evansville (47716-5749)
PHONE.................................812 925-7745
Toll Free:.................................888 -
Fax: 812 925-7746

Vincent Legeay, *President*
EMP: 7
SQ FT: 9,600
SALES (est): 1.5MM **Privately Held**
WEB: www.electricmotorbike.com
SIC: 5599 5088 7999 7699 Golf cart, powered; golf carts; golf cart, power, rental; golf club & equipment repair; sporting & athletic goods; sheet metalwork

(G-1552)
MIGHTY TRANSPORT LLC
246 Green Valley Dr (47610-9581)
PHONE.................................812 401-7433
EMP: 2
SALES (est): 130K **Privately Held**
SIC: 3799 Mfg Transportation Equipment

(G-1553)
QUALITY COATINGS INC
1700 N State St (47610-9738)
PHONE.................................812 925-3314
Fax: 812 925-7522
Gerald R Lewis, *President*
Troy Ellis Lewis, *Exec VP*
Donald R Lewis, *Vice Pres*
Tricia Lewis, *Controller*
Allen Tompkins, *Sales Staff*
EMP: 15
SQ FT: 50,000
SALES (est): 3.2MM **Privately Held**
SIC: 2851 Paints: oil or alkyd vehicle or water thinned

(G-1554)
STAHL EQUIPMENT INC
718 W Lincoln Ave (47610-9793)
P.O. Box 130 (47610-0130)
PHONE.................................812 925-3341
Fax: 812 925-7503
Norbert Stahl, *President*
Bobbie Stahl, *Treasurer*
EMP: 45
SQ FT: 48,000
SALES (est): 11.8MM **Privately Held**
SIC: 3441 3537 3535 3444 Building components, structural steel; industrial trucks & tractors; conveyors & conveying equipment; sheet metalwork; fabricated plate work (boiler shop)

(G-1555)
WATERWAYS EQUIPMENT EXCHANGE (PA)
1699 S Stevenson Stn Rd (47610-9233)
P.O. Box 5004, Evansville (47716-5004)
PHONE.................................812 925-8104
Paul Legeay III, *President*
EMP: 2
SALES (est): 474.6K **Privately Held**
SIC: 3731 Shipbuilding & repairing

Charlestown
Clark County

(G-1556)
AD PLEX-RHODES INC
100 Quality Ct (47111-1150)
P.O. Box 157 (47111-0157)
PHONE.................................812 256-3396
Fax: 812 256-5246
Joe Kingan, *Principal*
EMP: 4 EST: 2010
SALES (est): 429.3K **Privately Held**
SIC: 2752 Commercial printing, lithographic

(G-1557)
AGGROCK QUARRIES INC
Also Called: Hanson Aggregates
5421 County Road 403 (47111-9646)
P.O. Box 275, Sellersburg (47172-0275)
PHONE.................................812 246-2582
Clay Vibbert, *Manager*
EMP: 20
SALES (est): 2.4MM **Privately Held**
SIC: 5032 1422 Stone, crushed or broken; crushed & broken limestone

(G-1558)
ARTISTIC STONE COMPANY INC
13909 Highway 62 (47111-8623)
P.O. Box 484 (47111-0484)
PHONE.................................812 256-2890
Dan Van Natter, *President*
Linda Van Natter, *Vice Pres*
EMP: 5
SQ FT: 3,900
SALES (est): 306.3K **Privately Held**
SIC: 3281 Building stone products

(G-1559)
C-WAY TOOL AND DIE INC
103 Industrial Way (47111-1246)
PHONE.................................812 256-6341
Fax: 812 256-6343
Bobby W Caudill, *President*
Bob Caudill, *President*
EMP: 9 EST: 1973
SQ FT: 9,600
SALES (est): 690K **Privately Held**
SIC: 3545 7692 3544 Machine tool accessories; welding repair; special dies, tools, jigs & fixtures

(G-1560)
CHEETAH TRIKES INC
7631 High Jackson Rd (47111-9635)
PHONE.................................812 256-9199
Tom Walters, *President*
EMP: 3
SALES (est): 392.9K **Privately Held**
WEB: www.cheetahtrikes.com
SIC: 3751 Motorcycles & related parts

(G-1561)
CHRYSO INC
10600 Highway 62 Unit 7 (47111-1250)
P.O. Box 129 (47111-0129)
PHONE.................................812 256-4220
Eric Berge, *President*
Gary Gilmore, *Principal*
Mark Tlancon, *Corp Secy*
Thomas Green, *Vice Pres*
◆ EMP: 20
SALES (est): 4.2MM
SALES (corp-wide): 13.5MM **Privately Held**
WEB: www.chryso.com
SIC: 3821 Crushing & grinding apparatus, laboratory
HQ: Chryso
19 Place De La Resistance
Issy Les Moulineaux 92130

(G-1562)
DA INC (DH)
1800 Patrol Rd (47111-8509)
PHONE.................................812 503-2302
Fax: 812 256-3352
Yoichiro Kojima, *CEO*
Kenji Kanii, *President*
Eiji Kojima, *Treasurer*
Kunihiko Kawai, *Admin Sec*
▲ EMP: 20
SQ FT: 90,000
SALES (est): 25MM **Privately Held**
SIC: 3089 Plastic processing
HQ: Kojima Press Industry Co.,Ltd.
3-30, Shimoichibacho
Toyota AIC 471-0
565 346-868

(G-1563)
DUAL MACHINE & TOOL CO INC
310 Randolph St (47111-1940)
PHONE.................................812 256-2202
Tom Brown, *President*
Kirk Brown, *Vice Pres*
EMP: 2
SALES: 40K **Privately Held**
SIC: 3549 Metalworking machinery

(G-1564)
E&S WALLCOVERING
9018 Stonemour Way (47111-9697)
PHONE.................................812 256-6668
Jim Elmore, *Owner*
EMP: 4 EST: 1978
SALES (est): 380.8K **Privately Held**
SIC: 2621 Wallpaper (hanging paper)

(G-1565)
EARTH FIRST KENTUCKIANA INC
5511 County Road 403 (47111-9680)
PHONE.................................812 248-0712
Fax: 812 248-0713
John Bisel, *Branch Mgr*
EMP: 6 **Privately Held**
SIC: 2499 5261 5211 Mulch or sawdust products, wood; lawn & garden supplies; lumber & other building materials
PA: Earth First Of Kentuckiana, Inc.
9251 Highway 150
Greenville IN 47124

(G-1566)
EXTREME TRAILER SERVICE LLC
117 Industrial Way (47111-1246)
PHONE.................................812 406-1984
Jeffrey K Wenning, *Principal*
EMP: 7
SALES (est): 780K **Privately Held**
SIC: 3537 Trucks: freight, baggage, etc.: industrial, except mining

(G-1567)
H & H METAL PRODUCTS INC
104 Industrial Way (47111-1247)
PHONE.................................812 256-0444
Kevin Wiggam, *Vice Pres*
Keith Wiggam, *Vice Pres*
EMP: 10
SQ FT: 18,000
SALES (est): 1.8MM **Privately Held**
WEB: www.hhmetalproducts.com
SIC: 3444 Metal roofing & roof drainage equipment; siding, sheet metal

(G-1568)
HARPRING STEEL INC
109 Industrial Way (47111-1246)
P.O. Box 306 (47111-0306)
PHONE.................................812 256-6326
Fax: 812 256-4385
Jerry Cooper, *President*
Julia Cooper, *Corp Secy*
EMP: 5
SQ FT: 18,000
SALES: 528K **Privately Held**
SIC: 3441 1791 Building components, structural steel; structural steel erection

(G-1569)
K&M INDIANA LLC
Also Called: Mitchell Plastics
301 Pike St (47111-8608)
PHONE.................................812 256-3351
Joe D'Angelo, *President*
Rick Cartuyvelles, *General Mgr*
Matthew Merriman, *Opers Staff*
Roger Hand, *Production*
Nathan Borden, *Engineer*
▲ EMP: 160
SQ FT: 200,000
SALES (est): 39.9MM **Privately Held**
SIC: 3089 Automotive parts, plastic

(G-1570)
LOTUS DESIGN GROUP
113 Industrial Way (47111-1246)
PHONE.................................812 206-7281
David Lemay, *Owner*
EMP: 3
SALES (est): 278.8K **Privately Held**
SIC: 3993 Signs & advertising specialties

(G-1571)
LSC COMMUNICATIONS US LLC
100 Quality Ct (47111-1150)
P.O. Box 157 (47111-0157)
PHONE.................................812 256-3396
Marlena Stockdale, *Production*
Ron Terry, *Purch Mgr*
Kyra Stevens, *Manager*
EMP: 250
SALES (corp-wide): 3.6B **Publicly Held**
WEB: www.rrdonnelley.com
SIC: 2752 Commercial printing, offset
HQ: Lsc Communications Us, Llc
191 N Wacker Dr Ste 1400
Chicago IL 60606
844 572-5720

(G-1572)
LUCAS OIL PRO PLLING PRMOTIONS
5511 County Road 403 (47111-9680)
PHONE.................................812 246-3350
Kristi Chastain, *Manager*
EMP: 2
SALES (est): 135K **Privately Held**
SIC: 1389 Construction, repair & dismantling services

(G-1573)
MIKES CREATIVE WOODWORKS LLC
2405 Arrowhead Dr (47111-9312)
PHONE.................................502 649-3665
Michael J Miller,
EMP: 2 EST: 2016
SALES (est): 131.3K **Privately Held**
SIC: 2431 Millwork

(G-1574)
MULZER CRUSHED STONE INC
Also Called: Mulzer Security
15602 Charlstwn Bethlehem (47111-9423)
PHONE.................................812 256-3346
Fax: 812 256-3347
Bob Lingerfelt, *QC Mgr*
Jimmy Bowman, *Manager*
Mark Parr, *Manager*
Caleb Vernon, *Supervisor*
Jerry Ward, *Supervisor*
EMP: 28
SALES (corp-wide): 29.7B **Privately Held**
WEB: www.mulzer.com
SIC: 5032 1422 Brick, stone & related material; crushed & broken limestone
HQ: Mulzer Crushed Stone Inc
　　534 Mozart St
　　Tell City IN 47586
　　812 547-7921

(G-1575)
NEWTON BUSINESS FORMS
104 Bates Dr (47111-8913)
PHONE.................................812 256-5399
Lynn Newton, *Owner*
EMP: 2
SALES (est): 119K **Privately Held**
SIC: 2759 Invitation & stationery printing & engraving

(G-1576)
NIBCO INC
Chemtrol Division
105 Quality Ct (47111-1149)
PHONE.................................812 256-8500
Franco Negron, *Manager*
EMP: 187
SQ FT: 27,000
SALES (corp-wide): 732MM **Privately Held**
WEB: www.nibco.com
SIC: 3089 3084 Fittings for pipe, plastic; plastics pipe
PA: Nibco Inc.
　　1516 Middlebury St
　　Elkhart IN 46516
　　574 295-3000

(G-1577)
NIBCO INC
204 Pike St (47111-9612)
PHONE.................................812 256-8500
Mark Lecker, *Manager*
EMP: 10
SALES (corp-wide): 732MM **Privately Held**
SIC: 3089 Fittings for pipe, plastic
PA: Nibco Inc.
　　1516 Middlebury St
　　Elkhart IN 46516
　　574 295-3000

(G-1578)
OHIO VALLEY FUEL INJECTION
5905 Stacy Rd (47111-9691)
PHONE.................................812 987-5857
Mark Ward, *Owner*
EMP: 4
SALES (est): 292.9K **Privately Held**
SIC: 2869 Fuels

(G-1579)
PATRICIA J NICKELS INC
8324 Cypress Dr (47111-9660)
PHONE.................................502 489-4358
Patricia Mtiberi, *Principal*
EMP: 4
SALES (est): 371.1K **Privately Held**
SIC: 3356 Nickel

(G-1580)
SOUTHERN INDIANA LININGS & COA
113 Industrial Way (47111-1246)
PHONE.................................812 206-7250
Dave Lamy, *Principal*
EMP: 2
SALES (est): 229.2K **Privately Held**
SIC: 3799 Trailer hitches

(G-1581)
SPECIALTY MANUFACTURING OF IND
Also Called: Speciality Manufacturing
15412 Highway 62 Ste 2 (47111-7723)
PHONE.................................812 256-4633
Fax: 812 256-2917
John M Callis, *President*
Rex Callis, *Corp Secy*
Tina Haley, *Purchasing*
Lisa Shaw, *Bookkeeper*
James Clapp, *Shareholder*
▲ **EMP:** 22
SQ FT: 22,000
SALES (est): 5.1MM **Privately Held**
SIC: 3082 3085 3561 Unsupported plastics profile shapes; plastics bottles; pumps & pumping equipment

(G-1582)
SUPERIOR VAULT CO INC (PA)
500 Pike St (47111-8634)
PHONE.................................812 256-5545
Fax: 812 256-5859
Paul Grayson, *President*
Jeffrey Grayson, *Corp Secy*
EMP: 18
SQ FT: 7,000
SALES: 1.4MM **Privately Held**
SIC: 3272 Burial vaults, concrete or precast terrazzo

(G-1583)
TEKNOR APEX CO
6637 Westwood Dr (47111-8771)
PHONE.................................812 246-3357
Gregory Lipps, *Principal*
EMP: 2
SALES (est): 74.4K **Privately Held**
SIC: 2821 Plastics materials & resins

(G-1584)
THOMAS OPTICAL LLC
954 Market St (47111-1951)
PHONE.................................502 548-2163
Phillip Thomas, *Administration*
EMP: 3
SALES (est): 231.5K **Privately Held**
SIC: 3827 Optical instruments & lenses

(G-1585)
WEATHERALL INDIANA INC
Also Called: Weatherall Company
106 Industrial Way (47111-1247)
PHONE.................................812 256-3378
James McCain, *President*
Phyllis Allen, *Safety Mgr*
Bobby McBride, *Engineer*
Michael Carey, *Sales Staff*
Chris Miloe, *Admin Sec*
▼ **EMP:** 17
SQ FT: 14,000
SALES: 2MM **Privately Held**
SIC: 2851 2891 Wood stains; caulking compounds

Chesterfield
Madison County

(G-1586)
A L BREWSTER PLYWOOD INC
Also Called: Brewster Cabinets Paneling Ctr
232 Anderson Rd (46017-1574)
PHONE.................................765 378-1040
Fax: 765 378-1000
Jerry Hoppes, *President*
Cheryl E Hoppes, *Vice Pres*
EMP: 2 EST: 1963
SQ FT: 20,000
SALES (est): 180K **Privately Held**
SIC: 2541 5211 Cabinets, lockers & shelving; lumber & other building materials; lumber products

(G-1587)
ICE LOGGING LLC
515 Linden Ln (46017-1537)
PHONE.................................312 860-0897
Joshua Ice, *Principal*
EMP: 2
SALES (est): 85.7K **Privately Held**
SIC: 2411 Logging

(G-1588)
MORGAN AUTOMOTIVE
4443 State Road 32 E (46017-9525)
PHONE.................................765 378-0593
Mike Morgan, *Owner*
EMP: 5
SALES (est): 403.4K **Privately Held**
SIC: 7538 7539 7694 7699 Engine repair; automotive repair shops; rebuilding motors, except automotive; engine repair & replacement, non-automotive

(G-1589)
SMITHS ENTERPRISES INC
Also Called: Reversible Rollers
1124 Dilts St (46017-1048)
P.O. Box 610, Anderson (46015-0610)
PHONE.................................765 378-6267
Kevin Smith, *President*
Karen Smith, *Vice Pres*
Amy Smith, *Treasurer*
EMP: 8
SQ FT: 6,000
SALES (est): 870K **Privately Held**
SIC: 3089 Molding primary plastic

Chesterton
Porter County

(G-1590)
ACCUCAST INDUSTRIES
1631 Pioneer Trl (46304-9383)
PHONE.................................219 929-1137
Fax: 219 929-1138
Mark Hurson, *Owner*
EMP: 13
SQ FT: 2,184
SALES (est): 1.2MM **Privately Held**
WEB: www.accucastone.com
SIC: 3272 Stone, cast concrete

(G-1591)
AIR PRODUCTS AND CHEMICALS INC
246 Bailey Station Rd (46304-9780)
P.O. Box 949 (46304-0949)
PHONE.................................219 787-9551
Fax: 219 787-8659
Ed Gastonfield, *Branch Mgr*
EMP: 27
SALES (corp-wide): 8.1B **Publicly Held**
WEB: www.airproducts.com
SIC: 2813 Industrial gases
PA: Air Products And Chemicals, Inc.
　　7201 Hamilton Blvd
　　Allentown PA 18195
　　610 481-4911

(G-1592)
ALUMINUM WLDG & MCH WORKS INC
225 W Dunes Hwy (46304-1274)
PHONE.................................219 787-8066

Fax: 219 787-8859
Daryl T Boothe Jr, *CEO*
EMP: 6
SALES (est): 390K **Privately Held**
SIC: 7699 3449 5084 5051 Industrial machinery & equipment repair; miscellaneous metalwork; welding machinery & equipment; tubing, metal; bars, metal; plates, metal; fabricated plate work (boiler shop); fabricated structural metal

(G-1593)
ANCIENT FAITH MINISTRIES
1550 Birdie Way (46304-9158)
P.O. Box 748 (46304-0748)
PHONE.................................219 728-6786
EMP: 2 EST: 2015
SALES (est): 104.9K **Privately Held**
SIC: 2741 Misc Publishing

(G-1594)
APP FACTOR
308 Carmody Dr (46304-1560)
PHONE.................................219 229-1039
Allyson Kazmucha, *Partner*
Thierry Lyles, *Partner*
EMP: 2 EST: 2015
SALES (est): 78.8K **Privately Held**
SIC: 2741

(G-1595)
ARCELORMITTAL USA LLC
250 W Us Highway 12 (46304-9727)
P.O. Box 2928 (46304-5428)
PHONE.................................219 787-2120
Grant Davidson, *General Mgr*
Steven Fortin, *Engineer*
Judy LI, *Engineer*
Kamron Nekoomaram, *Engineer*
Karen Riefe, *Engineer*
EMP: 79 **Privately Held**
SIC: 3312 3325 3356 3316 Blast furnaces & steel mills; rolling mill rolls, cast steel; alloy steel castings, except investment; railroad car wheels, cast steel; tin; tin & tin alloy: rolling, drawing or extruding; cold finishing of steel shapes
HQ: Arcelormittal Usa Llc
　　1 S Dearborn St Ste 1800
　　Chicago IL 60603
　　312 346-0300

(G-1596)
ASHLEYS JEWELRY BY DESIGN LTD
221 Broadway (46304-2421)
PHONE.................................219 926-9039
Fax: 219 926-9960
Craig O'Brien, *President*
EMP: 5
SQ FT: 1,500
SALES (est): 665.4K **Privately Held**
SIC: 5944 3911 Jewelry, precious stones & precious metals; jewelry, precious metal

(G-1597)
BUTLER VINEYARDS
401 Broadway (46304-2347)
PHONE.................................219 929-1400
EMP: 5
SALES (est): 304.5K
SALES (corp-wide): 308.5K **Privately Held**
SIC: 2084 Wines
PA: Butler Vineyards
　　6202 E Robinson Rd
　　Bloomington IN 47408
　　812 332-6660

(G-1598)
CHAD SIMONS
803 Shannon Dr (46304-3162)
PHONE.................................219 405-1620
Chad Simons, *Principal*
EMP: 5
SALES (est): 462.1K **Privately Held**
SIC: 2851 Removers & cleaners

(G-1599)
CHESTERTON TRIBUNE INC
193 S Calumet Rd (46304-2433)
P.O. Box 919 (46304-0919)
PHONE.................................219 926-1131
Fax: 219 926-6389
Warren H Canright, *President*
EMP: 18 EST: 1884

SQ FT: 4,350
SALES (est): 826.8K **Privately Held**
WEB: www.chestertontribune.com
SIC: 2711 Newspapers: publishing only, not printed on site

(G-1600)
CLC EMBROIDERY LLC
332 Wake Robin Dr (46304-2618)
PHONE............................219 395-9600
Joyce M Thomas, *Owner*
EMP: 2
SALES (est): 140K **Privately Held**
SIC: 2395 Embroidery products, except schiffli machine; embroidery & art needlework

(G-1601)
CMS TECHNOLOGIES INC
147 N Jackson Blvd Ste 1x (46304-2079)
PHONE............................219 395-8272
Phil Glaeser, *Principal*
Gary Craig, *Principal*
Mark Schlichting, *Principal*
EMP: 5
SALES (est): 617.5K **Privately Held**
SIC: 3089 Plastic processing

(G-1602)
DESIGN ENGINEERING
Also Called: Design Engineering Company
600 River Dr (46304-1421)
PHONE............................219 926-2170
Al Rioli, *Owner*
EMP: 12
SQ FT: 1,096
SALES (est): 714.9K **Privately Held**
SIC: 3694 8711 3511 Engine electrical equipment; engineering services; turbines & turbine generator sets

(G-1603)
ELECTRO SEAL CORPORATION
Also Called: Northern Indiana Mfg
914 Broadway (46304-2233)
P.O. Box 46 (46304)
PHONE............................219 926-8606
Fax: 219 929-4278
Robert B Dragani, *President*
EMP: 9
SQ FT: 10,000
SALES: 3.5MM **Privately Held**
SIC: 3398 Brazing (hardening) of metal

(G-1604)
ESSENTIAL SEALING PRODUCTS INC
Custom Packing and Seals
307 Melton Rd Ste B (46304-9777)
PHONE............................219 787-8711
Fax: 219 787-8616
Dennis D Errichiello, *Vice Pres*
Susan Pyle, *Purchasing*
EMP: 3
SALES (est): 452.8K
SALES (corp-wide): 1.7MM **Privately Held**
WEB: www.espsealing.com
SIC: 5085 3053 Packing, industrial; seals, industrial; gaskets, packing & sealing devices
PA: Essential Sealing Products, Inc.
10145 Queens Way
Chagrin Falls OH 44023
440 543-8108

(G-1605)
FABRICATED METALS CORP
2180 N State Road 149 (46304-8819)
PHONE............................219 734-6896
William Moore, *President*
EMP: 10
SALES (est): 1.6MM **Privately Held**
SIC: 3441 Fabricated structural metal

(G-1606)
FISH FACTORY
676 Mississinewa Rd (46304-1409)
PHONE............................219 929-9375
EMP: 2
SALES (est): 94.1K **Privately Held**
SIC: 2741 Miscellaneous publishing

(G-1607)
FOUR PART INC
Also Called: Datagraphic Printing
132 S Calumet Rd (46304-2447)
PHONE............................219 926-7777
Fax: 219 926-6662
Catherine Dudak, *President*
Kathrin Dudak, *President*
Ernest Darr, *Shareholder*
Richard Halstead, *Shareholder*
EMP: 5
SALES (est): 296.3K **Privately Held**
SIC: 2752 Commercial printing, offset

(G-1608)
GRAPHIC22 INC
Also Called: Graphic 22
1505 S Calumet Rd Ste 2 (46304-3454)
PHONE............................219 921-5409
Fax: 219 921-0868
Marilyn Busch, *President*
Iain Hursey, *Manager*
EMP: 2
SALES (est): 240.8K **Privately Held**
WEB: www.graphic22.com
SIC: 2261 2262 2759 5099 Printing of cotton broadwoven fabrics; printing: manmade fiber & silk broadwoven fabrics; letterpress & screen printing; signs, except electric; labels, cotton: printed; embroidery products, except schiffli machine

(G-1609)
GRAPHICALLY SPEAKING
349 Sand Creek Dr (46304-1554)
PHONE............................219 921-1572
Lori Clair, *Principal*
EMP: 2 **EST:** 2007
SALES (est): 138.8K **Privately Held**
SIC: 3993 Signs & advertising specialties

(G-1610)
GRINDCO INC
Also Called: Heco
288 W 1050 N (46304-8806)
P.O. Box 819 (46304-0819)
PHONE............................219 763-6130
Adam Bellar, *President*
John Hall, *Engineer*
Joe Bolan, *Manager*
EMP: 44
SQ FT: 20,000
SALES (est): 7.9MM **Privately Held**
WEB: www.hecomach.com
SIC: 3599 Custom machinery; machine shop, jobbing & repair

(G-1611)
HAMPTON IRONWORKS INC
542 Dunewood Dr (46304-3131)
PHONE............................219 929-6448
Bob Hampton, *Principal*
EMP: 2
SALES (est): 262.1K **Privately Held**
SIC: 3446 Architectural metalwork

(G-1612)
HARFORD INDUSTRIES INC
Also Called: Epac
1635 Starwood Dr (46304-1658)
PHONE............................219 929-6455
Susan Harford, *President*
EMP: 2
SQ FT: 2,279
SALES (est): 150K **Privately Held**
WEB: www.harfordindustries.com
SIC: 3545 Precision measuring tools

(G-1613)
INDIANA FLAME SERVICE
250 W Us Highway 12 (46304-9727)
P.O. Box 771, Portage (46368-0771)
PHONE............................219 787-7129
Howard Paterson, *President*
EMP: 29
SALES (est): 4.3MM **Privately Held**
SIC: 3553 Scarfing machines, woodworking

(G-1614)
INDUSTRIAL ORGANIC INKS INC
1608 Fox Point Dr (46304-3147)
PHONE............................219 878-0613
Catherine Swigon, *President*
EMP: 3 **EST:** 1999

SALES (est): 200.7K **Privately Held**
SIC: 2893 Printing ink

(G-1615)
JEFFREYS GOOD SOAP LLC
709 Plaza Dr Ste 151 (46304-1572)
PHONE............................219 926-3447
Rick Fulton,
Cynthia Fulton,
EMP: 2
SALES: 40K **Privately Held**
SIC: 2841 Soap: granulated, liquid, cake, flaked or chip

(G-1616)
JM CHRISTIAN LLC
882 N 350 E (46304-9405)
PHONE............................317 460-0984
James Boyle, *Principal*
EMP: 6
SALES: 500K **Privately Held**
SIC: 3479 Etching & engraving

(G-1617)
LANDMARK SIGNS INC
Also Called: Landmark Signs Group
7424 Industrial Ave (46304-8804)
PHONE............................219 762-9577
Allen C O'Brien, *President*
Mary O'Brien, *Vice Pres*
Sharon Joyce, *Human Res Mgr*
Jason Moorehead, *Mktg Dir*
EMP: 68
SQ FT: 16,000
SALES (est): 9.6MM **Privately Held**
SIC: 3993 Electric signs

(G-1618)
LEGACY SCREEN PRINTING PROMOTI
1086 N State Road 149 (46304-8872)
PHONE............................219 262-4000
EMP: 2
SALES (est): 69.5K **Privately Held**
SIC: 2752 Commercial printing, lithographic

(G-1619)
MARTINSON CABINET SHOP
Also Called: Martinson Custom Kitchens
1245 W Us Highway 20 (46304-9409)
P.O. Box 867 (46304-0867)
PHONE............................219 926-1566
Fax: 219 926-1566
Ronald Martinson, *Owner*
EMP: 4
SQ FT: 6,000
SALES: 300K **Privately Held**
SIC: 2434 Wood kitchen cabinets

(G-1620)
MEADE ELECTRIC CO
246 Bailey Station Rd (46304-9780)
PHONE............................219 787-8317
John Marrion, *Agent*
EMP: 2
SALES (est): 141.2K **Privately Held**
SIC: 3699 Electrical equipment & supplies

(G-1621)
MID-TOWN PETRO ACQUISITION LLC
950 Wabash Ave (46304-2252)
PHONE............................219 728-4110
Dana Leady, *Manager*
EMP: 30
SALES (est): 2.1MM
SALES (corp-wide): 2MM **Privately Held**
SIC: 2911 Petroleum refining
PA: Mid-Town Petroleum Acquisition Llc
2250 Arthur Ave
Elk Grove Village IL 60007
219 728-5149

(G-1622)
MITTAL STEEL USA
71 Detroit Rd (46304-1204)
P.O. Box 2928 (46304-5428)
PHONE............................219 787-2113
Vasudha Seth, *General Mgr*
Richard Burns, *Business Mgr*
Craig Birchette, *Counsel*
Robrecht Himpe, *Exec VP*
Daniel Janczak, *Vice Pres*
EMP: 139 **EST:** 2014

SALES (est): 18.3MM **Privately Held**
SIC: 3312 Blast furnaces & steel mills

(G-1623)
MULLIN SIGN STUDIO
48 E 1050 N (46304-9345)
PHONE............................219 926-8937
John Mullin, *Owner*
EMP: 2
SALES (est): 168.6K **Privately Held**
SIC: 3993 Signs & advertising specialties

(G-1624)
NICHOLSON GROUP LLC
Also Called: Fas-N-Fast
450 E 1400 N (46304-9536)
PHONE............................219 926-3528
William Nicholson, *Mng Member*
Marilyn Nicholson,
Thomas Nicholson,
EMP: 3
SALES (est): 20K **Privately Held**
SIC: 3965 Fasteners

(G-1625)
ONSITE CONSTRUCTION SERVICES
416 Jefferson Ave (46304-3237)
PHONE............................312 723-8060
Kevin Ohare, *CEO*
Brianne Ohare, *Vice Pres*
Zachary Perkitny, *Vice Pres*
Arturo Perkitny, *CFO*
EMP: 25
SALES (est): 835.7K **Privately Held**
SIC: 1795 1799 1389 7349 Demolition, buildings & other structures; construction site cleanup; construction, repair & dismantling services; building maintenance services; cleaning service, industrial or commercial

(G-1626)
OSTERFELD INDUSTRIES
1050 Broadway Stsuite8 (46304-2170)
PHONE............................219 926-4646
Heather Harwood, *Principal*
EMP: 2
SALES (est): 93.9K **Privately Held**
SIC: 3999 Manufacturing industries

(G-1627)
P JS CUSTOM EMBROIDERING LLC
252 Haglund Rd (46304-9757)
PHONE............................219 787-9161
James Constantine, *Principal*
EMP: 2 **EST:** 2010
SALES (est): 91K **Privately Held**
SIC: 2395 Embroidery & art needlework

(G-1628)
PREMIER LUMBER COMPANY
6717 Atcheson Dr (46304)
PHONE............................219 801-6018
Sergio Magana, *President*
Esperanza Magana, *Vice Pres*
EMP: 15 **EST:** 2009
SALES: 500K **Privately Held**
SIC: 2448 Pallets, wood

(G-1629)
PURRFECTPLAY
790 Graham Dr (46304-1660)
PHONE............................219 926-7604
Pamela Wheelock, *Owner*
EMP: 3 **EST:** 2010
SALES: 100K **Privately Held**
SIC: 3944 Games, toys & children's vehicles

(G-1630)
SLEEPY HOLLOW LEATHER INC
Also Called: Sleepy Hollow Lock and Key
108 Lincoln St (46304-1813)
PHONE............................219 926-1071
Fax: 219 926-1071
Kenneth Timm, *Principal*
Lori Timm, *Corp Secy*
EMP: 2
SQ FT: 1,800
SALES (est): 150K **Privately Held**
SIC: 3172 5948 7699 Personal leather goods; luggage & leather goods stores; lock & key services

(G-1631)
SPEEDWAY LLC
Also Called: Speedway Superamerica 5522
502 Gateway Blvd N (46304-9618)
PHONE....................................219 929-1054
EMP: 10 Publicly Held
WEB: www.speedwaynet.com
SIC: 1311 Crude petroleum production
HQ: Speedway Llc
    500 Speedway Dr
    Enon OH 45323
    937 864-3000

(G-1632)
SSP TECHNOLOGIES INC
709 Plaza Dr Ste 2 (46304-1573)
PHONE....................................888 548-4668
Gert F Semler, Administration
EMP: 2 EST: 2016
SALES (est): 226.1K Privately Held
SIC: 3589 Shredders, industrial & commercial

(G-1633)
STORK NEWS NORTHWEST INDIANA
1541 Duffer Dr (46304-8859)
PHONE....................................219 405-0499
Kris Lange, Principal
EMP: 2 EST: 2016
SALES (est): 73.1K Privately Held
SIC: 2721 Periodicals: publishing & printing

(G-1634)
STOUT PLASTIC WELD
Also Called: U-Haul
425 S 15th St (46304-2027)
PHONE....................................219 926-7622
Fax: 219 926-1448
Terry Tharp, Partner
Scott Tharp, Partner
EMP: 10
SQ FT: 1,400
SALES (est): 789.4K Privately Held
SIC: 7513 3829 7692 Truck rental & leasing, no drivers; testing equipment: abrasion, shearing strength, etc.; welding repair

(G-1635)
TWO STICKS INC
147 E Us Highway 20 (46304-9216)
PHONE....................................219 926-7910
EMP: 2
SALES (est): 289.1K Privately Held
SIC: 3537 Trucks: freight, baggage, etc.: industrial, except mining

(G-1636)
UNIQUE SPECIALTY SERVICES LLC
307 S 18th St (46304-2041)
PHONE....................................219 395-8898
Deborah Wilson,
Don Wilson,
EMP: 2
SALES: 70K Privately Held
SIC: 3479 Coating of metals & formed products

(G-1637)
UNIQUE TAPE MANUFACTURING LLC
117 Broadway (46304-2464)
PHONE....................................219 617-4204
Terri Smith, Manager
EMP: 9
SQ FT: 1,600
SALES (est): 349.7K Privately Held
SIC: 3069 Rubber tape

(G-1638)
URSCHEL AIR LEASING LLC
1200 Cutting Edge Dr (46304-3554)
PHONE....................................219 464-4811
Daniel Marchetti, CFO
Robert Urshcel, Mng Member
EMP: 2
SALES (est): 209.6K Privately Held
SIC: 3556 7374 Food products machinery; data processing & preparation

(G-1639)
URSCHEL LABORATORIES INC (PA)
1200 Cutting Edge Dr (46304-3554)
PHONE....................................219 464-4811
Fax: 219 462-3879
Robert R Urschel, Ch of Bd
Patrick C Urschel, President
Maria Degarmo, General Mgr
Steve Johnson, General Mgr
Jack Wright, Managing Dir
◆ EMP: 415 EST: 1910
SQ FT: 250,000
SALES (est): 186.4MM Privately Held
WEB: www.urschel.com
SIC: 3556 Cutting, chopping, grinding, mixing & similar machinery

(G-1640)
VARIED PRODUCTS INDIANA INC
2180 N State Road 149 (46304-8819)
PHONE....................................219 763-2526
Fax: 219 762-5711
Dennis L Willard, President
EMP: 15 EST: 1975
SQ FT: 43,500
SALES (est): 3.2MM Privately Held
WEB: www.variedproducts.com
SIC: 3443 3441 Fabricated plate work (boiler shop); fabricated structural metal

Chrisney
Spencer County

(G-1641)
AMUSEMENT GAMES INC
23b W Market St (47611-8901)
PHONE....................................812 937-7084
Gregory Deller, President
Jeremy Hein, Vice Pres
EMP: 7
SQ FT: 6,000
SALES: 500K Privately Held
SIC: 3999 Barber & beauty shop equipment

Churubusco
Whitley County

(G-1642)
B M C MARKETING CORP
300 E Pleasant St (46723-1809)
PHONE....................................260 693-2193
Steven Barcus, President
EMP: 2
SQ FT: 7,500
SALES: 250K Privately Held
WEB: www.bmcmarketingintl.com
SIC: 3544 Special dies, tools, jigs & fixtures

(G-1643)
BRC RUBBER & PLASTICS INC
Also Called: BRC Rubber Group
589 S Main St (46723-2219)
P.O. Box 227 (46723-0227)
PHONE....................................260 693-2171
Brent Isbell, Plant Mgr
EMP: 250
SALES (corp-wide): 171.4MM Privately Held
SIC: 3061 Mechanical rubber goods
PA: Brc Rubber & Plastics, Inc.
    1029a W State Blvd
    Fort Wayne IN 46808
    260 693-2171

(G-1644)
C & A TOOL ENGINEERING INC (HQ)
4100 N Us 33 (46723)
P.O. Box 94 (46723-0094)
PHONE....................................260 693-2167
Fax: 260 693-3633
Richard Conrow, President
Ralph Bunn, General Mgr
Sara Conrow, Vice Pres
Rob Marr, Vice Pres
Robert Marr, Vice Pres

EMP: 360
SQ FT: 230,000
SALES (est): 132.4MM
SALES (corp-wide): 8.2B Privately Held
SIC: 3544 3545 Diamond dies, metalworking; machine tool accessories
PA: Minebea Mitsumi Inc.
    3-9-6, Mita
    Minato-Ku TKY 108-0
    367 586-711

(G-1645)
C & A TOOL ENGINEERING INC
101 N Main St (46723-1708)
P.O. Box 94 (46723-0094)
PHONE....................................260 693-2167
Richard Conrow, Branch Mgr
Dennis Felger, Maintence Staff
EMP: 250
SALES (corp-wide): 8.2B Privately Held
SIC: 3544 Diamond dies, metalworking
HQ: C & A Tool Engineering Inc.
    4100 N Us 33
    Churubusco IN 46723
    260 693-2167

(G-1646)
C & A TOOL ENGINEERING INC
100 Cole St (46723)
PHONE....................................260 693-2167
Richard Conrow, Branch Mgr
EMP: 2
SALES (corp-wide): 8.2B Privately Held
SIC: 3544 Diamond dies, metalworking
HQ: C & A Tool Engineering Inc.
    4100 N Us 33
    Churubusco IN 46723
    260 693-2167

(G-1647)
C & A TOOL ENGINEERING INC
411 S Mulberry St (46723-2208)
PHONE....................................260 693-2167
Richard Conrow, Principal
Tyler Lash, Project Mgr
Curt Spencer, Project Mgr
EMP: 2
SALES (corp-wide): 8.2B Privately Held
SIC: 3544 Diamond dies, metalworking
HQ: C & A Tool Engineering Inc.
    4100 N Us 33
    Churubusco IN 46723
    260 693-2167

(G-1648)
C & A TOOL ENGINEERING INC
119 S Mulberry St (46723-1714)
PHONE....................................260 693-2167
Richard Conrow, Branch Mgr
EMP: 2
SALES (corp-wide): 8.2B Privately Held
SIC: 3544 Diamond dies, metalworking
HQ: C & A Tool Engineering Inc.
    4100 N Us 33
    Churubusco IN 46723
    260 693-2167

(G-1649)
C & A TOOL ENGINEERING INC
118 N Main St (46723-1709)
P.O. Box 94 (46723-0094)
PHONE....................................260 693-2167
Richard D Conrow, Branch Mgr
EMP: 60
SALES (corp-wide): 8.2B Privately Held
SIC: 3544 Special dies, tools, jigs & fixtures
HQ: C & A Tool Engineering Inc.
    4100 N Us 33
    Churubusco IN 46723
    260 693-2167

(G-1650)
C & A TOOL ENGINEERING INC
105 S Main St (46723-1712)
P.O. Box 194 (46723-0194)
PHONE....................................260 693-2167
Richard D Conrow, Branch Mgr
EMP: 2
SALES (corp-wide): 8.2B Privately Held
SIC: 3544 Special dies, tools, jigs & fixtures
HQ: C & A Tool Engineering Inc.
    4100 N Us 33
    Churubusco IN 46723
    260 693-2167

(G-1651)
CENTERLINE MANUFACTURING
18628 Wappes Rd (46723-9273)
PHONE....................................260 348-7400
Roger Bruck, Principal
EMP: 2
SALES (est): 87.3K Privately Held
SIC: 3599 Industrial machinery

(G-1652)
IDEAL PRO CNC INC
6231 N 650 E (46723-9799)
P.O. Box 217, Laotto (46763-0217)
PHONE....................................260 693-1954
Reynard Herron, President
EMP: 11
SALES (est): 1.9MM Privately Held
SIC: 3423 Hand & edge tools

(G-1653)
KEYSTONE CONCRETE INC (PA)
12628 Us Highway 33 N (46723-9468)
P.O. Box 121 (46723-0121)
PHONE....................................260 693-6437
Fax: 260 693-2789
Mike Hatfield, President
Dan Hatfield, Corp Secy
William Hatfield, Vice Pres
EMP: 26
SQ FT: 8,000
SALES (est): 4.2MM Privately Held
SIC: 3273 Ready-mixed concrete

(G-1654)
KEYSTONE CONSULTING SERVICES
114 Mill St (46723-1817)
PHONE....................................260 693-0250
Mike Galliher, Principal
EMP: 2
SALES (est): 86K Privately Held
SIC: 7372 Prepackaged software

(G-1655)
PERRYS COUNTRY STORE
Also Called: Perry's Specialties
3530 N Us Highway 33 (46723-9343)
PHONE....................................260 693-0084
Scott Perry, Owner
Trissa Perry, Co-Owner
EMP: 2
SALES (est): 143.9K Privately Held
SIC: 2759 Screen printing

(G-1656)
REGAL PUBLICATIONS LLC
120 W Washington St (46723-1717)
PHONE....................................260 693-0698
David Beckman, Owner
Ann Kaplan, CFO
EMP: 3
SALES (est): 241.9K Privately Held
SIC: 2759 Publication printing

(G-1657)
SWAGS WELDING SERVICES LLC
6650 E Mcguire Rd (46723-9333)
PHONE....................................260 417-7510
EMP: 2
SALES (est): 155.3K Privately Held
SIC: 7692 Welding repair

(G-1658)
TACAIR PUBLICATIONS
15922 Wappes Rd (46723-9438)
PHONE....................................260 429-7975
Michael Benolkin, Owner
EMP: 2
SALES: 60K Privately Held
SIC: 2741 Miscellaneous publishing

(G-1659)
TECHNICAL CONTROLS SOLUTIONS
2640 N 825 E (46723-9529)
PHONE....................................260 416-0329
Nancy Guisinger, President
EMP: 7
SALES (est): 95.1K Privately Held
WEB: www.tcsforcomfort.com
SIC: 3829 Measuring & controlling devices

(G-1660)
U S S INC
Also Called: Utility Systems Specialists
9745 E State Road 205-57 (46723-9102)
PHONE....................................260 693-1172
Diane Monroe, *President*
Carl Monroe, *Vice Pres*
EMP: 6
SQ FT: 5,000
SALES: 250K **Privately Held**
WEB: www.usspecialists.com
SIC: 3812 3728 Aircraft control systems, electronic; research & dev by manuf., aircraft parts & auxiliary equip

Cicero
Hamilton County

(G-1661)
GEORGIA SSTNMENT SOLUTIONS INC
1024 Gallium Dr (46034-9113)
PHONE....................................575 621-2372
Daniel Jones, *President*
Steven Ross, *Exec VP*
EMP: 4 EST: 2014
SALES (est): 297.4K **Privately Held**
SIC: 3724 Engine mount parts, aircraft

(G-1662)
IRIS RUBBER COMPANY INC
10 E Jackson St (46034-5040)
P.O. Box 737 (46034-0737)
PHONE....................................317 984-3561
Fax: 317 984-9545
Steve Stewart, *President*
David Evans, *Vice Pres*
EMP: 12 EST: 1956
SQ FT: 7,700
SALES: 1MM **Privately Held**
WEB: www.irisrubber.com
SIC: 3069 3599 3061 3053 Molded rubber products; machine shop, jobbing & repair; mechanical rubber goods; gaskets, packing & sealing devices; synthetic rubber

(G-1663)
MORSE LAKE AUTOMOTIVE
8300 E 216th St (46034-9617)
PHONE....................................317 984-4514
Lou Sams, *Owner*
EMP: 2 EST: 2009
SALES (est): 141K **Privately Held**
SIC: 7694 7549 5531 Armature rewinding shops; lubrication service, automotive; automobile & truck equipment & parts

(G-1664)
PARADIGM SOFTWARE CORP
1020 Seaport Dr (46034-9590)
PHONE....................................317 770-7862
EMP: 2
SALES (est): 81.3K **Privately Held**
SIC: 7372 Prepackaged Software Services

(G-1665)
PING CUSTOM DRAPERY WORKROOM
Also Called: Ping's Custom Drapery
11313 E 234th St (46034-9462)
PHONE....................................317 984-3251
Mary Beth Ping, *Owner*
Thomas Ping, *Co-Owner*
EMP: 2
SQ FT: 2,000
SALES (est): 70K **Privately Held**
SIC: 2211 Draperies & drapery fabrics, cotton

(G-1666)
RANDOLPH CARPET-TILE CLEANING
59 W Armitage Dr (46034-9321)
PHONE....................................317 401-2300
Jeff Randolph, *Manager*
EMP: 2
SALES (est): 79.9K **Privately Held**
SIC: 3582 Commercial laundry equipment

(G-1667)
SIMPLE QUARTERS LLC
2340 Quarter Path Rd (46034-9156)
PHONE....................................812 216-8602
Brett E Snodgrass, *Administration*
EMP: 3
SALES (est): 95.7K **Privately Held**
SIC: 3131 Quarters

(G-1668)
SYSTEM SOLUTIONS INC
4 Forest Bay Ln (46034-9744)
PHONE....................................317 877-7572
Fax: 317 877-7573
Michael O Cull, *President*
EMP: 2
SALES: 300K **Privately Held**
SIC: 3825 Test equipment for electronic & electrical circuits

(G-1669)
TIMBER OX INC
Also Called: Timber Ox Green
2133 E 226th St (46034-9777)
PHONE....................................317 758-5942
Lyn Jackson, *CEO*
EMP: 3
SALES: 950K **Privately Held**
SIC: 2851 Paints & allied products

Clarks Hill
Tippecanoe County

(G-1670)
AMERICAN FIBERTECH CORPORATION
Also Called: Industrial Pallet
11349 Us Highway 52 S (47930-9273)
PHONE....................................219 261-3586
Fax: 765 523-3326
Rob Meister, *CEO*
Rick Hall, *Opers Mgr*
Lloyd Pelfree, *Director*
EMP: 50
SALES (corp-wide): 58.2MM **Privately Held**
WEB: www.ind-pallet-corp.com
SIC: 2448 2449 2441 Pallets, wood & wood with metal; wood containers; nailed wood boxes & shook
PA: American Fibertech Corporation
4 N New York St
Remington IN 47977
219 261-3586

Clarksville
Clark County

(G-1671)
A-1 PALLET CO INC CLARKSVILLE
1507 Progress Way (47129-9231)
PHONE....................................812 288-6339
Fax: 812 288-6847
Billy Waters, *Owner*
EMP: 25 **Privately Held**
SIC: 2448 Wood pallets & skids
PA: A-1 Pallet Company Inc Of Clarksville
940 Cottonwood Dr
Clarksville IN 47129

(G-1672)
A-1 PALLET CO INC CLARKSVILLE (PA)
940 Cottonwood Dr (47129-1042)
P.O. Box 2366 (47131-2366)
PHONE....................................812 288-6339
Billy Waters III, *President*
EMP: 1
SQ FT: 27,000
SALES (est): 2.7MM **Privately Held**
SIC: 2448 2449 Wood pallets & skids; wood containers

(G-1673)
BAIRD ICE CREAM CO
110 N Randolph Ave (47129-2714)
PHONE....................................812 283-3345
Fax: 812 283-8701
Randall C Baird, *Owner*
EMP: 4
SQ FT: 2,500
SALES (est): 273.9K **Privately Held**
SIC: 2023 Ice cream mix, unfrozen: liquid or dry

(G-1674)
BOTTOM LINE MANAGEMENT INC
Also Called: Hearthcraft
1410 Johnson Ln (47129-1402)
PHONE....................................812 944-7388
Fax: 812 945-2500
Shahla Javid, *President*
Kamran Javid, *Vice Pres*
Shahriar Javid, *Vice Pres*
Doug Longest, *Treasurer*
▲ EMP: 15
SQ FT: 30,000
SALES (est): 3.4MM **Privately Held**
WEB: www.hearthcraft.com
SIC: 3429 5199 3589 Fireplace equipment, hardware; andirons, grates, screens; art goods & supplies; commercial cooking & foodwarming equipment

(G-1675)
CD GRAFIX LLC
632 Providence Way Ste 3 (47129-1530)
P.O. Box 3354 (47131-3354)
PHONE....................................812 945-4443
Cindy Farris Loughmiller,
Cynthia Ferris,
EMP: 4 EST: 1999
SALES (est): 395K **Privately Held**
SIC: 2759 Screen printing

(G-1676)
CENTENNIAL BINDERY LLC
1330 Woerner Ave (47129-3105)
PHONE....................................812 472-4655
Rona Durnell, *Project Mgr*
John Durnell,
▲ EMP: 23 EST: 2012
SALES (est): 1.7MM **Privately Held**
SIC: 2789 Binding & repair of books, magazines & pamphlets

(G-1677)
CLASSIC BUILDINGS INC
Also Called: Premier Homes
2709 Blackiston Mill Rd (47129-9020)
PHONE....................................812 944-5821
Jeff Corbett, *President*
Teresa Talley, *Controller*
Joe Bulleit, *Mktg Dir*
Matthew Roth, *Marketing Staff*
EMP: 30
SQ FT: 1,800
SALES (est): 4.9MM **Privately Held**
SIC: 2452 1542 3448 Prefabricated wood buildings; commercial & office buildings, prefabricated erection; prefabricated metal buildings

(G-1678)
CLASSIC TRUSS WD CMPONENTS INC
2709 Blackiston Mill Rd (47129-9020)
PHONE....................................812 944-5821
Jeff Corbett, *President*
Greg Meeks, *Purch Mgr*
Eric Hawkes, *Accounts Mgr*
Cindy Youtsey, *Admin Asst*
EMP: 24
SALES (est): 6.1MM **Privately Held**
SIC: 2439 Trusses, wooden roof

(G-1679)
DNM CONVERTERS & CORES
107 E Lynnwood Dr (47129-1733)
PHONE....................................502 599-5225
Debbie Popplewell, *Partner*
Mike Popplewell, *Partner*
EMP: 2
SALES (est): 158.1K **Privately Held**
SIC: 3356 Precious metals

(G-1680)
F & R DRAPERIES
827 Eastern Blvd Ste R6 (47129-2330)
PHONE....................................812 284-4682
Frances Franklin, *President*
EMP: 2 EST: 1999
SALES (est): 144.5K **Privately Held**
SIC: 2391 Curtains & draperies

(G-1681)
GHK TRUSS LLC
521 N Clark Blvd (47129-2449)
P.O. Box 2696 (47131-2696)
PHONE....................................812 282-6600
Michael G Gilley, *President*
Michael L Harlowe, *Vice Pres*
James M Kulaga, *Vice Pres*
EMP: 33
SALES: 4.4MM **Privately Held**
SIC: 2439 Structural wood members; trusses, wooden roof; trusses, except roof: laminated lumber

(G-1682)
GOH CON INC (PA)
Also Called: Gohmann Asphalt & Construction
1630 Broadway St (47129-7712)
P.O. Box 2428 (47131-2428)
PHONE....................................812 282-1349
Fax: 812 288-2168
Richard L Cripe, *President*
J M Gohmann, *Chairman*
Annette G Dezelan, *Vice Pres*
John R Gohmann, *Vice Pres*
Keith A Kramer, *Treasurer*
EMP: 45
SQ FT: 5,000
SALES (est): 39.9MM **Privately Held**
SIC: 2951 1611 1622 4212 Asphalt & asphaltic paving mixtures (not from refineries); general contractor, highway & street construction; bridge construction; local trucking, without storage; testing laboratories

(G-1683)
GRAPHIC VENTURES INC
648 N Clark Blvd (47129-2404)
P.O. Box 2291 (47131-2291)
PHONE....................................812 288-6093
David S Eve, *President*
EMP: 2
SALES (est): 208.4K **Privately Held**
SIC: 2759 Commercial printing

(G-1684)
H & H HOME IMPROVEMENT INC
1120 N Taggart Ave (47129-1848)
PHONE....................................812 288-8700
Fax: 812 288-8715
Rick Hauber, *President*
Tim Hauber, *Vice Pres*
EMP: 4
SQ FT: 3,500
SALES (est): 432K **Privately Held**
WEB: www.hhhomeimprovement.com
SIC: 1761 1521 1751 3444 Siding contractor; single-family housing construction; window & door (prefabricated) installation; awnings, sheet metal

(G-1685)
HAIR NECESSITIES
1124 Eastern Blvd (47129-1906)
PHONE....................................812 288-5887
Joyce Douglas, *Owner*
EMP: 2
SALES (est): 80K **Privately Held**
SIC: 3999 Hair & hair-based products

(G-1686)
IMI SOUTH LLC
1221 Highway 31 E (47129-9601)
PHONE....................................812 284-9732
Fax: 812 284-0112
Pete Irwing, *Branch Mgr*
EMP: 8
SALES (corp-wide): 800.6MM **Privately Held**
SIC: 3273 Ready-mixed concrete
HQ: Imi South, Llc
1440 Selinda Ave
Louisville KY 40213
502 456-6930

(G-1687)
J & J PALLET CORP
640 Miller Ave (47129-2457)
PHONE....................................812 288-4487
John Jones, *President*
EMP: 35

SALES (corp-wide): 6.5MM **Privately Held**
WEB: www.jjpallet.com
SIC: 2448 Pallets, wood
PA: J & J Pallet Corp
2234 E Market St
New Albany IN 47150
812 944-8670

(G-1688)
JCS ENTERPRISES INC
Also Called: Kentucky Korner
757 E Lewis & Clark Pkwy (47129-2269)
PHONE.................................812 284-4827
Berden Kelly, *Owner*
EMP: 2
SALES (corp-wide): 3MM **Privately Held**
SIC: 2329 Men's & boys' sportswear & athletic clothing
PA: Jcs Enterprises Inc
1034 Trotwood Dr
Lexington KY 40511
859 231-7511

(G-1689)
MUSIC STORE
307 W Lewis & Clark Pkwy (47129-1647)
PHONE.................................812 949-3004
Paul Starks, *Owner*
Nick Starks, *Co-Owner*
EMP: 2
SALES: 110K **Privately Held**
SIC: 3679 5736 Recording heads, speech & musical equipment; musical instrument stores

(G-1690)
PQ CORPORATION
1101 Quartz Rd (47129-3202)
P.O. Box 669, Jeffersonville (47131-0669)
PHONE.................................812 288-7186
Fax: 812 288-4463
Jeff Sayffer, *Manager*
EMP: 41
SALES (corp-wide): 1.4B **Publicly Held**
WEB: www.pqcorp.com
SIC: 2819 Industrial inorganic chemicals
HQ: Pq Corporation
300 Lindenwood Dr
Malvern PA 19355
610 651-4200

(G-1691)
PRECISION AUTOMATION CO INC
Also Called: Altek Mfg. Co.
2120 Addmore Ln (47129-9166)
P.O. Box 2188 (47131-2188)
PHONE.................................812 283-7963
Fax: 812 283-7992
Glen A Morris, *President*
G Frederick Rexon Sr, *Chairman*
Robert J Daily, *Exec VP*
Steven Fischer, *Vice Pres*
J William Huffmon Jr, *Vice Pres*
EMP: 34
SQ FT: 35,000
SALES (est): 7.9MM **Privately Held**
SIC: 3549 3565 Metalworking machinery; packaging machinery

(G-1692)
REEDERS CLEANERS
1205 Eastern Blvd (47129-1701)
PHONE.................................812 945-4833
Douglas Nalley, *President*
EMP: 14
SALES (est): 1.8MM **Privately Held**
SIC: 2842 Drycleaning preparations

(G-1693)
RENEGADE TRIKE CORP
1309 Providence Way (47129-1546)
PHONE.................................812 941-9900
Ron Uesseler, *Manager*
EMP: 3
SALES: 500K **Privately Held**
SIC: 3751 Motorcycles, bicycles & parts

(G-1694)
ROSSWYVERN PRESS LLC
2224 Birch Dr (47129-1214)
PHONE.................................859 421-0864
Neviana Dimova, *Administration*
EMP: 2

SALES (est): 100.5K **Privately Held**
SIC: 2741 Miscellaneous publishing

(G-1695)
SAYBOLT LP
905 Eastern Blvd Ste C (47129-1961)
PHONE.................................812 282-7242
Jim Rasdom, *Manager*
EMP: 3
SALES (corp-wide): 659.8MM **Privately Held**
WEB: www.corelab.com
SIC: 1389 Testing, measuring, surveying & analysis services
HQ: Saybolt Lp
6316 Windfern Rd
Houston TX 77040
713 328-2673

(G-1696)
SEATON SPRINGS INC
Also Called: Signs Now
632 Eastern Blvd B (47129-2454)
PHONE.................................812 282-2440
Fax: 812 282-4077
Greg Hoskinson, *President*
EMP: 3 **Privately Held**
SIC: 3993 Signs & advertising specialties
PA: Seaton Springs, Inc.
1700 Research Dr
Louisville KY 40299

(G-1697)
STEAMIN DEMON INC
1041 S Clark Blvd (47129-3019)
PHONE.................................812 288-6754
Fax: 812 288-7221
Mike Downey, *President*
EMP: 2
SQ FT: 3,000
SALES: 500K **Privately Held**
SIC: 3635 Carpet shampooer

(G-1698)
UNITED SERVICES INC (PA)
Also Called: U.S.I. Custom Blinds
118 W Lewis & Clark Pkwy (47129-1732)
PHONE.................................812 989-3320
Santha Leadingham, *President*
C Daniel Leadingham, *Vice Pres*
EMP: 8
SQ FT: 4,000
SALES: 700K **Privately Held**
SIC: 2591 Window blinds

(G-1699)
VALLEY SCALE COMPANY LLC
Also Called: VSC
751 W Kenwood Ave (47129-2569)
PHONE.................................812 282-5269
Fax: 812 284-6572
Matthew S Guffey, *CEO*
Arlis Guffey, *Ch of Bd*
Marianne Guffey, *Vice Pres*
EMP: 15
SQ FT: 4,500
SALES (est): 4.1MM **Privately Held**
WEB: www.valleyscale.com
SIC: 3596 1389 7699 Railroad track scales; testing, measuring, surveying & analysis services; scale repair service

(G-1700)
WIDOWS WALK
415 E Riverside Dr (47129-3144)
P.O. Box 27073, El Jobean FL (33927-7073)
PHONE.................................812 285-8850
B J McRoy, *Owner*
EMP: 2 **EST:** 1997
SALES (est): 94.9K **Privately Held**
SIC: 5812 2399 Eating places; hammocks & other net products

Clay City
Clay County

(G-1701)
ANGEL FALLS WATER COMPANY
6621 S Old State Road 59 (47841-8074)
PHONE.................................812 939-9107
Fax: 812 939-8417

Russel B Miller Sr, *President*
Donald E Miller, *Admin Sec*
EMP: 5
SQ FT: 4,300
SALES: 188K **Privately Held**
SIC: 2086 Water, pasteurized: packaged in cans, bottles, etc.

(G-1702)
HARRIS BURIAL SERVICES
1440 W County Road 800 S (47841-8229)
PHONE.................................812 939-3605
Eric Harris, *Principal*
EMP: 5
SALES (est): 398.2K **Privately Held**
SIC: 3272 Burial vaults, concrete or pre-cast terrazzo

(G-1703)
IRONHORSE DETAILING INC
8445 S County Road 59 (47841-8206)
P.O. Box 132 (47841-0132)
PHONE.................................812 939-3300
James Zimmerman, *President*
EMP: 2
SALES (est): 234.5K **Privately Held**
SIC: 3449 Bars, concrete reinforcing: fabricated steel

(G-1704)
LOGGERS INCORPORATED
7755 S County Rd 50 (47841)
P.O. Box 122 (47841-0122)
PHONE.................................812 939-2797
Fax: 812 939-3220
Marvin Booe Jr, *President*
James Booe, *Vice Pres*
EMP: 33 **EST:** 1965
SQ FT: 1,800
SALES: 2MM **Privately Held**
SIC: 2421 2431 2411 Sawmills & planing mills, general; millwork; logging

(G-1705)
PIONEER CANE & HANDLE CO
3016 E River Rd (47841-8056)
PHONE.................................812 859-4415
Dale Killion, *Owner*
EMP: 2
SALES (est): 108.5K **Privately Held**
SIC: 2499 Handles, wood

Claypool
Kosciusko County

(G-1706)
LOUIS DREYFUS CO AG INDS LLC
7344 S State Road 15 (46510-9289)
PHONE.................................574 566-2100
Sean Doyle, *President*
EMP: 20
SALES (corp-wide): 44B **Privately Held**
SIC: 6221 2869 Commodity contracts brokers, dealers; glycerin
HQ: Louis Dreyfus Company Agricultural Industries Llc
40 Danbury Rd
Wilton CT 06897

Clayton
Hendricks County

(G-1707)
HUBBARD WELDING
10114 S County Road 100 W (46118-9248)
PHONE.................................317 539-2758
Ray Hubbard, *Owner*
EMP: 2
SALES (est): 111.7K **Privately Held**
SIC: 7692 Welding repair

(G-1708)
TRIVETT CONTRACTING INC
5981 Liberty Pkwy (46118-8838)
PHONE.................................317 539-5150
Fax: 317 539-5170
Daniel V Trivett, *President*
EMP: 28

SALES: 1.6MM **Privately Held**
WEB: www.trivettcontracting.com
SIC: 1541 1799 3449 1796 Renovation, remodeling & repairs: industrial buildings; dock equipment installation, industrial; bars, concrete reinforcing: fabricated steel; machine moving & rigging

(G-1709)
URBAN-ERT SLINGS LLC
1510 E County Road 900 S (46118-9130)
PHONE.................................317 223-6509
Carla Murray, *Persnl Mgr*
Matthew Murray,
EMP: 5
SALES: 80K **Privately Held**
SIC: 3949 Sporting & athletic goods

(G-1710)
WURK METAL PRODUCTS INC
Also Called: Autotwirler
2425 E County Road 800 S (46118-9479)
PHONE.................................317 828-0170
Fax: 812 879-5474
Scott Lands, *President*
Lori Lands, *Shareholder*
◆ **EMP:** 11 **EST:** 2007
SALES: 1.3MM **Privately Held**
SIC: 3559 Automotive related machinery; automotive maintenance equipment

Clermont
Marion County

(G-1711)
DARRINS COFFEE COMPANY
9122 Crawfordsville Rd (46234-1518)
PHONE.................................317 732-5037
Darrin Marion, *Managing Dir*
Deiandra Marion, *COO*
Tiffany Marion, *Exec VP*
Vickie Davidson-Marion, *Director*
▲ **EMP:** 15
SQ FT: 2,250
SALES (est): 2.5MM **Privately Held**
SIC: 5149 2095 Specialty food items; roasted coffee; coffee roasting (except by wholesale grocers); instant coffee

(G-1712)
DR RESTORATIONS INC
Also Called: Exclusive Reality Inc
4252 N Raceway Rd (46234-9248)
PHONE.................................317 646-7150
Ray Hubbard, *Vice Pres*
Bianca Broyles, *CFO*
Joe Robey, *Agent*
EMP: 9
SALES (est): 261K **Privately Held**
SIC: 1799 1742 1721 2431 Construction site cleanup; drywall; painting & paper hanging; window frames, wood

Clinton
Vermillion County

(G-1713)
ARS NEBRASKA LLC
Also Called: DTE
515 E 4th St (47842)
PHONE.................................765 832-5210
Karla Gosnell, *Manager*
EMP: 42
SALES (corp-wide): 111.3MM **Privately Held**
WEB: www.dters.com
SIC: 4789 1389 4911 Railroad car repair; gas field services; electric services
HQ: Ars Nebraska, Llc
1209 S Alda Rd
Grand Island NE 68803
308 382-3880

(G-1714)
B & B PALLET
1301 N 9th St (47842-1514)
EMP: 4 **EST:** 2012
SALES (est): 150K **Privately Held**
SIC: 2448 Mfg Wood Pallets/Skids

▲ = Import ▼=Export
◆ =Import/Export

(G-1715)
BROOKES CANDY CO
247 Maple St (47842)
PHONE...............................765 665-3646
Brooke Schmidt, *President*
EMP: 2
SALES (est): 137.7K **Privately Held**
SIC: 2064 Candy & other confectionery
products

(G-1716)
IEA MANAGEMENT SERVICES INC
3900 White Ave (47842-1160)
P.O. Box 249 (47842-0249)
PHONE...............................765 832-8526
David R Helwig, *President*
David Bostwick, *Admin Sec*
EMP: 2
SALES (est): 327K **Privately Held**
SIC: 3799 Trailers & trailer equipment

(G-1717)
IEA RENEWABLE ENERGY INC
3900 White Ave (47842-1160)
PHONE...............................765 832-8526
EMP: 6 **Privately Held**
SIC: 3799 Carriages, horse drawn
HQ: Iea Renewable Energy, Inc.
2647 Waterfront Parkway E
Indianapolis IN 46214
765 832-8526

(G-1718)
NEW NGC INC
Also Called: National Gypsum Company
75 Ivy Ln (47842-7188)
P.O. Box 367 (47842-0367)
PHONE...............................765 828-0898
Fax: 765 832-1657
George Schmalz, *Plant Mgr*
EMP: 30
SALES (corp-wide): 685.8MM **Privately Held**
SIC: 3275 Gypsum products
HQ: New Ngc, Inc.
2001 Rexford Rd
Charlotte NC 28211

(G-1719)
ROSKOVENSKI SAND & GRAVEL INC
3200 E 1850 S (47842-7207)
PHONE...............................765 832-6748
Fax: 765 832-2771
Thomas Robert Roskovensky, *President*
EMP: 6
SALES (est): 676.2K **Privately Held**
SIC: 1442 Construction sand & gravel

(G-1720)
ROSSKOVENSKI CONCRETE & RDYMX
12927 S State Road 63 (47842-7161)
PHONE...............................765 832-6103
John Rosskovenski, *Owner*
Debbie Rosskovenski, *Co-Owner*
EMP: 5
SQ FT: 5,000
SALES (est): 450K **Privately Held**
SIC: 3272 3273 Burial vaults, concrete or
precast terrazzo; septic tanks, concrete;
ready-mixed concrete

(G-1721)
SIMPLE CREMATIONS BURIALS LLC
459 N 9th St (47842-1227)
PHONE...............................765 592-6226
Michael Papinchock, *Principal*
EMP: 6
SALES (est): 387.6K **Privately Held**
SIC: 3281 Burial vaults, stone

(G-1722)
USELMAN PACKING CO
75 E 4th St (47842-7040)
PHONE...............................765 832-2112
Fax: 765 832-7169
Garry Uselman, *Owner*
EMP: 5 EST: 1975
SALES (est): 43.3K **Privately Held**
SIC: 2011 5147 Meat packing plants;
meats & meat products

Cloverdale
Putnam County

(G-1723)
243 QUARRY
8090 S State Road 243 (46120-9692)
PHONE...............................765 653-4100
Tom Thingst, *Principal*
EMP: 2 EST: 2010
SALES (est): 175.4K **Privately Held**
SIC: 1481 Mine & quarry services, non-
metallic minerals

(G-1724)
BILLY D SNIDER
Also Called: Bills Pallets
294 Bubble Loo Rd (46120-8882)
PHONE...............................765 795-6426
Billy D Snider, *Principal*
EMP: 4
SALES (est): 243.4K **Privately Held**
SIC: 2448 Pallets, wood & wood with metal

(G-1725)
EDTECHZONE LLC
10741 S County Road 850 E (46120-9270)
PHONE...............................317 902-7594
EMP: 3
SALES (est): 150K **Privately Held**
SIC: 7372 Prepackaged Software Services

(G-1726)
HANSON AGGREGATES MIDWEST LLC
State Rd 243 Cty Rd 900 S State Road
(46120)
P.O. Box 328 (46120-0328)
PHONE...............................765 653-7205
Grage Mitchel, *Principal*
EMP: 18
SALES (corp-wide): 20.3B **Privately Held**
SIC: 1422 5032 Limestones, ground;
stone, crushed or broken
HQ: Hanson Aggregates Midwest Llc
207 Old Harrods Creek Rd
Louisville KY 40223
502 244-7550

(G-1727)
HANSON AGRIGOODS MIDWEST INC
8950 S State Road 243 (46120-9698)
P.O. Box 328 (46120-0328)
PHONE...............................317 635-9048
Jack Thompson, *Superintendent*
EMP: 19
SALES (est): 1.8MM **Privately Held**
SIC: 5032 1499 Aggregate; asphalt mining
& bituminous stone quarrying

(G-1728)
LARKIN WOODWORKS
709 S Lafayette St (46120-8716)
PHONE...............................765 795-5332
Linda Larkin, *Owner*
EMP: 2 EST: 2013
SALES (est): 151.5K **Privately Held**
SIC: 2431 Millwork

(G-1729)
MARTIN MRETTA MAGNESIA SPC LLC
2010 E County Road 800 S (46120-8436)
PHONE...............................765 795-3536
Fax: 765 653-0656
Michael Mote, *Branch Mgr*
EMP: 20 **Publicly Held**
SIC: 1411 Limestone, dimension-quarrying
HQ: Martin Marietta Magnesia Specialties,
Llc
755 Lime Rd
Woodville OH 43469
419 849-4223

(G-1730)
MID-STATE AUTOMATION INC
12389 Camp Otto Rd (46120-8098)
PHONE...............................765 795-5500
John Dougherty, *President*
Jacqueline Dougherty, *Controller*
EMP: 5
SQ FT: 4,500

SALES: 300K **Privately Held**
SIC: 3559 3535 1796 ; conveyors & conveying equipment; machinery installation

(G-1731)
MIDWEST CALCIUM CARBONATES LLC
7925 S State Road 243 (46120-5501)
PHONE...............................217 222-1800
Greg Gould,
EMP: 3 EST: 2015
SALES (est): 68.8K **Privately Held**
SIC: 3281 Limestone, cut & shaped

(G-1732)
NALC LLC
8090 S State Road 243 (46120-9692)
PHONE...............................502 548-9590
Greg Gould, *CEO*
Richard Boyd, *Vice Pres*
Thomas Hingst, *Vice Pres*
Cari Hylton, *Accounting Mgr*
EMP: 48 EST: 2014
SQ FT: 10,000
SALES (est): 3.2MM **Privately Held**
SIC: 1422 Crushed & broken limestone

(G-1733)
OHIO RIVER TRADING CO
8090 S State Road 243 (46120-9692)
PHONE...............................765 653-4100
Tom Thingst, *Owner*
EMP: 4
SALES (est): 281.3K **Privately Held**
SIC: 3281 Cut stone & stone products

(G-1734)
POET BRFINING - CLOVERDALE LLC
2265 E County Road 800 S (46120-8431)
PHONE...............................765 795-3235
Luke Logan, *General Mgr*
Jeff Lautt, *CFO*
EMP: 56
SQ FT: 4,000
SALES (est): 14MM **Privately Held**
SIC: 2869 Ethyl alcohol, ethanol
PA: Poet, Llc
4615 N Lewis Ave
Sioux Falls SD 57104

(G-1735)
PUTNAM PLASTICS INC (PA)
30 W Stardust Rd (46120-8699)
P.O. Box 258 (46120-0258)
PHONE...............................765 795-6102
Fax: 765 795-6129
Brad Query, *President*
Chris Query, *Corp Secy*
Marla Corbin, *Vice Pres*
Lawrence Alpert, *Manager*
Debbie Underwood, *Network Mgr*
EMP: 35
SQ FT: 35,000
SALES (est): 6.6MM **Privately Held**
WEB: www.putnamplasticsinc.com
SIC: 2673 Plastic bags: made from pur-
chased materials

(G-1736)
RONNIE ELMORE JR
1193 E State Road 42 (46120-8759)
PHONE...............................765 719-1681
Ronnie Elmore Jr, *Principal*
EMP: 2
SALES (est): 119.7K **Privately Held**
SIC: 2752 Commercial printing, litho-
graphic

(G-1737)
SIGNPLEX LLC
4 W Market St (46120-8424)
P.O. Box 775 (46120-0775)
PHONE...............................765 795-7446
Wayne Meyer, *Owner*
EMP: 3
SALES (est): 183.1K **Privately Held**
SIC: 3993 Signs & advertising specialties

(G-1738)
SPENCER EVENING WORLD
Also Called: Hoostier Topics
1 N Main St (46120-8098)
P.O. Box 226, Spencer (47460-0226)
PHONE...............................765 795-4438

Fax: 765 795-3121
Jenny Snider, *General Mgr*
EMP: 4
SALES (est): 340.5K
SALES (corp-wide): 7.2MM **Privately Held**
WEB: www.spencereveningworld.com
SIC: 2752 2759 5994 2711 Commercial
printing, offset; commercial printing; news
dealers & newsstands; newspapers
PA: Spencer Evening World
114 E Franklin St
Spencer IN 47460
812 829-2255

(G-1739)
STANDARD FOR SUCCESS LLC
10741 S County Road 850 E (46120-9270)
PHONE...............................844 737-3825
Todd Whitlock, *Mng Member*
Kathy Griffey, *Training Spec*
Alan Degener,
Robert Grimes,
EMP: 12
SALES: 1MM **Privately Held**
SIC: 7372 8748 7389 Educational com-
puter software; educational consultant;

(G-1740)
TRIO MILLING INC
Also Called: Smith & Associates
4222 E County Road 1000 S (46120-9016)
PHONE...............................765 795-4088
James R Smith, *President*
Vera I Hughes, *Treasurer*
Anita J Smith, *Admin Sec*
EMP: 2
SALES: 150K **Privately Held**
SIC: 2047 Dog food

Coal City
Owen County

(G-1741)
KECK FINE ART
13855 Bond Rd (47427-7825)
PHONE...............................219 306-9474
James Keck, *Principal*
EMP: 2 EST: 2011
SALES (est): 121.7K **Privately Held**
SIC: 3999 Framed artwork

(G-1742)
LEDGERWOOD & SONS SAWMILL
246 Pleasant View Rd (47427-7948)
PHONE...............................812 939-8212
Fax: 812 939-8303
Larry Ledgerwoodm, *Owner*
EMP: 3
SALES (est): 378.2K **Privately Held**
SIC: 2421 Lumber: rough, sawed or planed

(G-1743)
PATRIOT ARMS
13379 State Highway 246 (47427-8002)
PHONE...............................812 859-4293
Eric Balder, *Manager*
EMP: 2
SALES (est): 137.1K **Privately Held**
SIC: 3484 Guns (firearms) or gun parts, 30
mm. & below

(G-1744)
RODS WELDING SHOP
Also Called: Rod Welding and Auto
2135 Beech Church Rd (47427-7811)
PHONE...............................812 859-4250
Rod Schmaltz, *Owner*
EMP: 2
SQ FT: 3,000
SALES: 40K **Privately Held**
SIC: 7692 Welding repair

GEOGRAPHIC

Coalmont
Clay County

(G-1745)
DUNCAN LOGGING INC
13628 S Watts St (47845-4741)
P.O. Box 114 (47845-0114)
PHONE..............................812 564-2488
Douglas Duncan, *Principal*
EMP: 2
SALES (est): 81.7K **Privately Held**
SIC: 2411 Logging

Coatesville
Putnam County

(G-1746)
ADVANCED PRTCTIVE SLUTIONS LLC
639 Gettysburg (46121-8960)
P.O. Box 131 (46121-0131)
PHONE..............................765 720-9574
Gary Fomich,
EMP: 3 **Privately Held**
SIC: 9711 7381 8299 8742 Military training schools; protective services, guard; self-defense & athletic instruction; management consulting services; machine knives, metalworking

(G-1747)
COMMERCIAL STAR INC
4170 S State Road 75 (46121-9114)
PHONE..............................765 386-2800
Ronald Hayden, *President*
EMP: 10
SQ FT: 38,000
SALES (est): 1.4MM **Privately Held**
WEB: www.commercialstar.com
SIC: 3523 3589 3531 Turf & grounds equipment; shredders, industrial & commercial; hammer mills (rock & ore crushing machines), portable

(G-1748)
CROOKEDSTICK SAWMILL LLC
4546 S State Road 75 (46121-9118)
PHONE..............................317 714-8930
Andrew Gibbs, *Principal*
EMP: 3
SALES (est): 180.1K **Privately Held**
SIC: 2421 Sawmills & planing mills, general

(G-1749)
EXHIBIT A PLASTICS LLC
4170 S State Road 75 (46121-9114)
PHONE..............................765 386-6702
Tom Jackson,
Tom Goode,
EMP: 25
SQ FT: 12,000
SALES (est): 292.8K **Privately Held**
WEB: www.exhibitaplastics.com
SIC: 3089 Injection molding of plastics

(G-1750)
JACOBSEN PROF LAWN CARE INC
6302 E County Road 100 N (46121-9689)
PHONE..............................765 246-7737
Wes Evans, *Branch Mgr*
EMP: 11
SQ FT: 116,000
SALES (corp-wide): 14.2B **Publicly Held**
SIC: 3524 Lawn & garden equipment
HQ: Jacobsen Professional Lawn Care Inc.
11108 Quality Dr
Charlotte NC 28273
704 504-6600

(G-1751)
MAGIC CIRCLE CORPORATION
Also Called: Dixie Chopper
6302 E County Road 100 N (46121-9689)
PHONE..............................765 246-7737
Fax: 765 246-6146
Gary Morgan, *President*
Jeff Haltom, *Vice Pres*
Chris Vernon, *Vice Pres*
Simon Wilson, *CFO*
Arthur Evans, *Shareholder*
EMP: 168
SQ FT: 120,000
SALES (est): 47.9MM **Privately Held**
WEB: www.dixiechopper.com
SIC: 3524 Lawnmowers, residential: hand or power

Colburn
Tippecanoe County

(G-1752)
JC PRINTING & MAILING
3711 Piney Grove Dr (47905-8817)
PHONE..............................765 742-6829
John Whiteman, *Partner*
Charlotte Whiteman, *Partner*
EMP: 2
SALES (est): 180.2K **Privately Held**
SIC: 2759 Commercial printing

(G-1753)
JOHNS FINE CABINETRY
594 N 850 E (47905-9414)
PHONE..............................765 296-2388
EMP: 2
SALES (est): 178.5K **Privately Held**
SIC: 2434 Mfg Wood Kitchen Cabinets

(G-1754)
STEVES CABINETS & MORE
934 S 750 E (47905-9489)
PHONE..............................765 296-9419
Steve Henderson, *Principal*
EMP: 2
SALES (est): 185.4K **Privately Held**
SIC: 2434 Wood kitchen cabinets

(G-1755)
TRI-ESCO INC
101 N 36th St (47905-4784)
P.O. Box 6386, Lafayette (47903-6386)
PHONE..............................765 446-7937
John Wolff, *Vice Pres*
EMP: 8
SALES (est): 887.3K **Privately Held**
SIC: 1542 1771 1794 7692 Commercial & office building contractors; concrete work; excavation work; welding repair

Colfax
Clinton County

(G-1756)
KEVIN COOMER PALLET CO
8930 W County Road 650 S (46035-9420)
PHONE..............................765 324-2294
Kevin Coomer, *Owner*
EMP: 7
SQ FT: 4,800
SALES (est): 706.8K **Privately Held**
SIC: 2448 Pallets, wood

Columbia City
Whitley County

(G-1757)
80/20 INC
1701 S 400 E (46725-8753)
PHONE..............................260 248-8030
Fax: 260 248-8029
Don Wood, *President*
Scott Brown, *Vice Pres*
David Wood, *Vice Pres*
◆ **EMP:** 300
SALES (est): 97.3MM **Privately Held**
WEB: www.8020.net
SIC: 3354 Shapes, extruded aluminum

(G-1758)
ACCU-TOOL INC
831 E Short St (46725-8743)
PHONE..............................260 248-4529
Renee Bauer, *President*
David Bauer, *Vice Pres*
EMP: 7
SQ FT: 9,000
SALES: 650K **Privately Held**
SIC: 3469 Machine parts, stamped or pressed metal

(G-1759)
ACME INDUSTRIAL INC
2380 E Cardinal Dr (46725-8789)
PHONE..............................260 422-6518
Fax: 260 248-9690
Jonathan Joseph, *President*
EMP: 30
SQ FT: 25,000
SALES (est): 3.9MM **Privately Held**
SIC: 3599 Machine & other job shop work

(G-1760)
ADHESIVE SOLUTIONS COMPANY LLC (PA)
4201 N 450 E (46725-9352)
PHONE..............................260 691-0304
Randall Jones,
EMP: 3 **EST:** 1997
SQ FT: 2,000
SALES (est): 280.3K **Privately Held**
WEB: www.hotstik.com
SIC: 2891 5169 5085 Adhesives & sealants; adhesives & sealants; adhesives, tape & plasters

(G-1761)
ADVANCED ASSEMBLY LLC
2101 N 600 E (46725-9029)
PHONE..............................260 244-1700
Jerry Leamere, *Manager*
EMP: 13 **EST:** 2007
SALES (est): 2.2MM **Privately Held**
SIC: 2531 Seats, automobile

(G-1762)
AJ MACHINE INC
507 S Line St (46725-2409)
PHONE..............................260 248-4900
Aaron McClure, *President*
Lon Whitted, *Manager*
Ronda McClure, *Admin Sec*
EMP: 8
SALES (est): 1.3MM **Privately Held**
SIC: 3599 Machine shop, jobbing & repair

(G-1763)
AL-FE SYSTEMS INC
2349 E Cardinal Dr (46725-8789)
PHONE..............................260 483-4411
Kurt H Westman, *President*
EMP: 15
SQ FT: 13,750
SALES (est): 1.2MM **Privately Held**
SIC: 3567 3559 Industrial furnaces & ovens; foundry, smelting, refining & similar machinery

(G-1764)
ASW LLC
Also Called: American Sportworks
2499 S 600 E Ste 102 (46725-9029)
PHONE..............................260 432-1596
Kent Rice,
Tyrone Bello,
Debra Singleton,
EMP: 3
SALES (est): 926.7K **Privately Held**
SIC: 3799 Recreational vehicles

(G-1765)
BAINS PACKING AND RFRGN
Also Called: Bains' Packing & Refrigeration
3922 E Old Trail Rd (46725-9013)
PHONE..............................260 244-5209
Ralph D Bain, *Partner*
George A Bain, *Partner*
Ralph Bain, *Partner*
EMP: 10 **EST:** 1945
SQ FT: 7,000
SALES: 500K **Privately Held**
SIC: 2011 Meat packing plants

(G-1766)
BETTER VISIONS PC
Also Called: City Vision Center
513 N Line St (46725-1229)
PHONE..............................260 244-7542
Andrew B Hogue, *President*
Dennis D Sutton, *Principal*
EMP: 3
SALES (est): 215.1K **Privately Held**
SIC: 5995 3827 Contact lenses, prescription; aiming circles (fire control equipment)

(G-1767)
BREYDEN PRODUCTS INC
4532 E Park 30 Dr (46725-8869)
PHONE..............................260 244-2995
Jay Miller, *President*
Janice Miller, *Corp Secy*
Mike Zuber, *Vice Pres*
◆ **EMP:** 43
SQ FT: 50,000
SALES: 10MM **Privately Held**
WEB: www.breydenproducts.com
SIC: 3496 Miscellaneous fabricated wire products

(G-1768)
BROOKS LANGELOH
465 E Morsches Rd (46725-8917)
PHONE..............................219 691-3577
Brooks Langeloh, *Principal*
EMP: 2
SALES (est): 90.8K **Privately Held**
SIC: 3364 Nonferrous die-castings except aluminum

(G-1769)
BUTLER MILL SERVICE COMPANY
Also Called: Columbia City Mill Service
2734 S 800 E (46725-8892)
PHONE..............................260 625-4930
Fax: 260 625-3783
Tammie Lowrance, *Branch Mgr*
EMP: 32 **Privately Held**
SIC: 3295 Slag, crushed or ground
PA: Butler Mill Service Company
9300 Dix
Dearborn MI 48120

(G-1770)
C & R PLATING CORP
302 Factory St (46725-2761)
P.O. Box 247 (46725-0247)
PHONE..............................586 755-4900
Fax: 260 248-2080
Bob Burger, *CEO*
Dennis Blaugh, *President*
EMP: 36 **EST:** 1965
SQ FT: 13,772
SALES (est): 5MM
SALES (corp-wide): 14.7MM **Privately Held**
WEB: www.kcjplating.com
SIC: 3471 Electroplating of metals or formed products
PA: K.C. Jones Plating Co.
2845 E 10 Mile Rd
Warren MI 48091
586 755-4900

(G-1771)
CAPITOL SOURCE NETWORK
366 E 600 N (46725-8915)
PHONE..............................260 248-9747
Thomas Lehman, *Vice Pres*
▼ **EMP:** 5 **EST:** 2011
SQ FT: 5,000
SALES (est): 239.9K **Privately Held**
SIC: 2086 Carbonated soft drinks, bottled & canned

(G-1772)
CHROMASOURCE INC
2433 S Cr 600 E E (46725)
P.O. Box 8300, Fort Wayne (46898-8300)
PHONE..............................260 420-3000
Fax: 260 420-1833
Jason Brooks, *CEO*
Alexander N Pursley, *President*
Tammy Collier, *Vice Pres*
Gary Ehinger, *Plant Mgr*
Jim Adcox, *Engineer*
▲ **EMP:** 140
SQ FT: 130,000
SALES (est): 34.4MM **Privately Held**
SIC: 2752 7336 Commercial printing, offset; commercial art & graphic design

(G-1773)
CITY OF COLUMBIA CITY
925 E Van Buren St (46725-1916)
PHONE..............................260 248-5118

▲ = Import ▼=Export
◆ =Import/Export

Mike Dear, *Branch Mgr*
EMP: 7 **Privately Held**
SIC: 3589 Water treatment equipment, industrial
PA: City Of Columbia City
112 S Chauncey St Rm C
Columbia City IN 46725
260 248-5100

(G-1774)
CLAYWOOD CREATION
111 S Briarwood Ln (46725-8709)
PHONE..................................260 244-7719
Jerry Krider, *Owner*
EMP: 4
SALES (est): 262.2K **Privately Held**
SIC: 3944 Puzzles

(G-1775)
COUNTRY WOODCRAFTS INC
2283 E State Road 205 (46725-9010)
PHONE..................................260 244-7578
Thomas Mettler, *President*
Cindy Mettler, *Admin Sec*
EMP: 2
SALES (est): 172.3K **Privately Held**
SIC: 3944 Craft & hobby kits & sets

(G-1776)
COUPLED PRODUCTS LLC
2651 S 600 E (46725-9097)
PHONE..................................260 248-3200
John Clark, *Manager*
EMP: 300
SQ FT: 225,000 **Privately Held**
SIC: 3714 3494 3492 3052 Motor vehicle parts & accessories; valves & pipe fittings; fluid power valves & hose fittings; rubber & plastics hose & beltings
PA: Coupled Products Llc
2651 S 600 E
Columbia City IN 46725

(G-1777)
COUPLED PRODUCTS LLC (PA)
2651 S 600 E (46725-9097)
PHONE..................................260 248-3200
Joseph Kochan, *President*
Jonathan Drew, *Exec VP*
Dawn Brazwell, *Vice Pres*
Tina Johnson, *Plant Mgr*
Joe Straub, *QC Mgr*
▼ **EMP:** 311
SQ FT: 50,000
SALES (est): 120.3MM **Privately Held**
SIC: 3714 Motor vehicle parts & accessories

(G-1778)
DEL PALMA ORTHOPEDICS LLC
5865 E State Road 14 (46725-9237)
PHONE..................................260 625-3169
Andrew Palmer, *Mng Member*
Brian More,
EMP: 3
SALES (est): 285.9K **Privately Held**
SIC: 3842 Orthopedic appliances

(G-1779)
DOT AMERICA INC
335 Towerview Dr (46725-8799)
PHONE..................................260 244-5700
Michael Venturini, *President*
EMP: 17
SQ FT: 17,000
SALES (est): 1MM **Privately Held**
SIC: 3471 Finishing, metals or formed products

(G-1780)
DPS PRINTING
950 Liberty Dr (46725-1123)
PHONE..................................260 503-9681
Ryan Carper, *Principal*
EMP: 2
SALES (est): 207.5K **Privately Held**
SIC: 2752 Commercial printing, offset

(G-1781)
DYNAMIC COMPOSITES LLC
2670 S 700 E (46725-9044)
PHONE..................................260 625-8686
Fax: 260 625-8699
Keith E Busse,
Gary E Heasley,
Mark Millett,

Richard P Teets Jr,
EMP: 4
SALES (est): 468.8K **Privately Held**
SIC: 3272 5051 Ties, railroad: concrete; rails & accessories

(G-1782)
EATON HYDRAULICS LLC
1380 S Williams Dr (46725-8750)
PHONE..................................260 248-5800
Tom Schlemmer, *Branch Mgr*
EMP: 4 **Privately Held**
SIC: 3625 Motor controls & accessories
HQ: Eaton Hydraulics Llc
14615 Lone Oak Rd
Eden Prairie MN 55344
952 937-9800

(G-1783)
ERAPSCO
Also Called: Sonobuoytechsystems
4868 E Park 30 Dr (46725-8861)
PHONE..................................260 248-3524
Roland Fritts, *Managing Prtnr*
EMP: 4
SALES (est): 278.3K **Privately Held**
SIC: 3443 Fabricated plate work (boiler shop)

(G-1784)
ESPICH PRINTING INC
107 Hoosier Dr (46725-1013)
PHONE..................................260 244-0132
Fax: 260 248-8001
Mark Espich, *President*
EMP: 3
SQ FT: 1,300
SALES (est): 416.5K **Privately Held**
WEB: www.espichprinting.com
SIC: 2752 Commercial printing, offset

(G-1785)
ESSEX GROUP INC
2580 S 600 E (46725)
PHONE..................................260 248-5500
Fax: 260 461-5494
David Hockerman, *Manager*
EMP: 69
SALES (corp-wide): 105.4MM **Privately Held**
WEB: www.essexwire.com
SIC: 3357 3496 3315 Building wire & cable, nonferrous; miscellaneous fabricated wire products; steel wire & related products
HQ: Essex Group, Inc.
1601 Wall St
Fort Wayne IN 46802
260 461-4000

(G-1786)
ESSEX GROUP INC
Superior Essex
2601 S 600 E (46725-9097)
PHONE..................................260 248-5500
William Nicolson, *Manager*
EMP: 95
SALES (corp-wide): 105.4MM **Privately Held**
WEB: www.essexwire.com
SIC: 3357 Nonferrous wiredrawing & insulating
HQ: Essex Group, Inc.
1601 Wall St
Fort Wayne IN 46802
260 461-4000

(G-1787)
GATOR CASES INC
2499 S 600 E (46725-9029)
PHONE..................................260 627-8070
Crystal Morris, *President*
▲ **EMP:** 10
SALES (est): 1.8MM **Privately Held**
SIC: 3523 Farm machinery & equipment

(G-1788)
GENERAL MACHINE BROKERS INC
1295 E 600 N (46725-8944)
PHONE..................................260 691-3800
Michael D Worthman, *President*
EMP: 5
SALES (est): 232.4K **Privately Held**
SIC: 3599 Machine shop, jobbing & repair

(G-1789)
HINEN PRINTING CO
117 W Market St (46725-2311)
PHONE..................................260 248-8984
Fax: 260 248-8984
Jeff Hinen, *Owner*
EMP: 8
SQ FT: 6,000
SALES (est): 835K **Privately Held**
SIC: 2759 2791 2789 2752 Screen printing; typesetting; bookbinding & related work; commercial printing, lithographic

(G-1790)
HOLMES & COMPANY INC
807 E Ellsworth St (46725-2508)
P.O. Box 370 (46725-0370)
PHONE..................................260 244-6149
Fax: 260 244-5694
Daniel E Almendinger, *President*
Larry Almendinger, *President*
Stephanie J Greer, *President*
Joel Rigueur, *Accountant*
▲ **EMP:** 50 **EST:** 1983
SQ FT: 100,000
SALES (est): 8.1MM **Privately Held**
SIC: 2426 Lumber, hardwood dimension

(G-1791)
HORIZON PUBLICATIONS INC
Also Called: Post and Mail
927 W Connexion Way (46725-1031)
P.O. Box 837 (46725-0837)
PHONE..................................260 244-5153
Doug Brown, *Branch Mgr*
EMP: 38
SALES (corp-wide): 83.1MM **Privately Held**
WEB: www.malvern-online.com
SIC: 2711 Newspapers
PA: Horizon Publications, Inc.
1120 N Carbon St Ste 100
Marion IL 62959
618 993-1711

(G-1792)
HUTHONE LLC
707 Burke St (46725-7751)
PHONE..................................260 248-2384
Charles Grabach, *Principal*
EMP: 3 **EST:** 2015
SALES (est): 154.2K **Privately Held**
SIC: 3471 Plating of metals or formed products

(G-1793)
IAM PETROLEUM INC (PA)
Also Called: Countyline Marathon
5126 W County Line Rd N (46725-8303)
PHONE..................................260 625-9951
Aman Yehdego, *President*
EMP: 8
SALES (est): 7.8MM **Privately Held**
SIC: 1311 Crude petroleum & natural gas

(G-1794)
IMPACT CNC LLC (PA)
1380 S Williams Dr (46725-8750)
P.O. Box 669 (46725-0669)
PHONE..................................260 244-5511
Jerry Busche, *President*
Dwight Busche, *COO*
Shawn Pierce, *Opers Staff*
Dawn Jennings, *Purchasing*
Matthew Hartman, *Engineer*
EMP: 130
SQ FT: 29,400
SALES (est): 41.6MM **Privately Held**
SIC: 3577 Computer peripheral equipment

(G-1795)
INDIANA MATERIALS PROC LLC
5750 E Rail Connect Dr (46725-9498)
PHONE..................................260 244-6026
Abid Bengali, *Owner*
EMP: 15
SALES (est): 1.6MM **Privately Held**
SIC: 3999 Barber & beauty shop equipment

(G-1796)
INK SPOT TATTOO
302 S Main St (46725-2142)
PHONE..................................260 244-0025
Sean Blaine, *Owner*
EMP: 2

SALES (est): 168.9K **Privately Held**
SIC: 2752 Commercial printing, offset

(G-1797)
INTEGRATED MFG & ASSEMBLY LLC
2101 S 600 E (46725-9029)
PHONE..................................260 244-1700
John Forslund, *Branch Mgr*
EMP: 300 **Privately Held**
SIC: 2531 Public building & related furniture
PA: Integrated Manufacturing & Assembly, Llc
6501 E Nevada St
Detroit MI 48234

(G-1798)
IOTRON INDUSTRIES USA INC
4394 E Park 30 Dr (46725-8517)
PHONE..................................260 212-1722
Lloyd Scott, *CEO*
Karin Barber, *President*
EMP: 20
SALES (est): 3.3MM
SALES (corp-wide): 4.9MM **Privately Held**
SIC: 3671 Electron beam (beta ray) generator tubes
PA: Iotron Industries Canada Inc
1425 Kebet Way
Port Coquitlam BC V3C 6
604 945-8838

(G-1799)
J M S MACHINE INC
307 Diamond Ave (46725-2448)
P.O. Box 422 (46725-0422)
PHONE..................................260 244-0077
Jonathan Smith, *President*
Michelle Smith, *Vice Pres*
Jessica Carter, *Admin Sec*
EMP: 2
SALES (est): 306.7K **Privately Held**
WEB: www.jmsmachine.com
SIC: 3599 Custom machinery

(G-1800)
J MILLER CABINETRY INC
Also Called: J Miller Cabinet Company
5874 N 350 E (46725-9341)
PHONE..................................260 691-2032
Fax: 260 691-2599
Steven Marschand, *President*
Bill Lude, *General Mgr*
Cheryl Marschand, *Corp Secy*
EMP: 8 **EST:** 1949
SQ FT: 10,000
SALES (est): 1.8MM **Privately Held**
SIC: 2434 2511 Wood kitchen cabinets; vanities, bathroom: wood; wood household furniture

(G-1801)
JEANNIE AND RACHEL HEIDENREICH
1240 N Airport Rd (46725-8619)
PHONE..................................260 244-4583
Jeannie Heidenreich, *Principal*
EMP: 2
SALES (est): 66.8K **Privately Held**
SIC: 7539 3621 Alternators & generators, rebuilding & repair; starters, for motors

(G-1802)
JIGSAW CREATIONS
5867 N 350 E (46725-9341)
PHONE..................................260 691-2196
Lory Norden, *Owner*
Greg Norden, *Co-Owner*
EMP: 2
SALES (est): 129.5K **Privately Held**
SIC: 3944 Puzzles

(G-1803)
KEEFER GRAPHIC IMAGING INC
2433 S 600 E (46725-8200)
P.O. Box 80513, Fort Wayne (46898-0513)
PHONE..................................260 426-7500
Richard Keefer, *President*
EMP: 2
SALES (est): 175.2K **Privately Held**
SIC: 2759 Commercial printing

GEOGRAPHIC

(G-1804)
KILGORE MANUFACTURING CO INC
Also Called: Kilgore Mfg Plant No 1
445 S Line St (46725-2443)
PHONE....................................260 248-2002
Fax: 260 248-2882
John E Hicks, *President*
Brent Kirkham, *Sales Mgr*
Gary Sims, *Prgrmr*
▲ **EMP:** 63
SQ FT: 25,000
SALES (est): 13.7MM **Privately Held**
WEB: www.kilgoremfg.com
SIC: 3841 3492 5047 3052 Surgical & medical instruments; hose & tube fittings & assemblies, hydraulic/pneumatic; medical & hospital equipment; rubber & plastics hose & beltings

(G-1805)
L B FOSTER COMPANY
2658 S 700 E (46725-9044)
PHONE....................................260 244-2887
Joe Flores, *Principal*
EMP: 5
SALES (corp-wide): 536.3MM **Publicly Held**
SIC: 3312 Railroad crossings, steel or iron
PA: L. B. Foster Company
415 Holiday Dr Ste 1
Pittsburgh PA 15220
412 928-3400

(G-1806)
LAKE STATES VENEER INC
732 S Columbia Pkwy (46725-1515)
PHONE....................................260 244-4767
William Shull, *President*
R D Jones, *Vice Pres*
EMP: 2
SALES (est): 143.9K **Privately Held**
SIC: 2411 Veneer logs

(G-1807)
LAWRENCE INDUSTRIES
2921 E 400 S (46725-8528)
PHONE....................................260 432-9693
EMP: 2
SALES (est): 127.1K **Privately Held**
SIC: 3999 Manufacturing industries

(G-1808)
LEAR CORPORATION
2101 S 600 E (46725-9029)
PHONE....................................260 244-1700
Jackie Daniels, *Plant Mgr*
EMP: 2
SALES (corp-wide): 20.4B **Publicly Held**
SIC: 3714 Motor vehicle parts & accessories
PA: Lear Corporation
21557 Telegraph Rd
Southfield MI 48033
248 447-1500

(G-1809)
MICHFAB MACHINERY
201 Towerview Dr (46725-8799)
PHONE....................................260 244-6117
Scott Richmond, *Principal*
EMP: 2
SALES (est): 81.4K **Privately Held**
SIC: 3599 Industrial machinery

(G-1810)
MICROPULSE iNC (PA)
5865 E State Road 14 (46725-9237)
PHONE....................................260 625-3304
Fax: 260 625-3834
Brian G Emerick, *President*
Tom Line, *Opers Staff*
Brian More, *CFO*
Chris Steffen, *Asst Controller*
Sonya Emerick, *Admin Sec*
EMP: 188
SQ FT: 105,000
SALES (est): 36.3MM **Privately Held**
SIC: 3841 Surgical & medical instruments

(G-1811)
NANOVIS LLC (PA)
5865 E State Road 14 (46725-9237)
PHONE....................................260 625-1502
Matt Hedrick, *Director*

Brian Emerick, *Director*
Steve Gerrish, *Director*
Brian More, *Director*
EMP: 8
SQ FT: 3,000
SALES: 750K **Privately Held**
SIC: 3841 Surgical & medical instruments

(G-1812)
NIBLOCK EXCAVATING INC
1080 Spartan Dr Ste C (46725-1043)
PHONE....................................260 248-2100
Fax: 260 248-4277
Ron Modglin, *Manager*
EMP: 15
SALES (corp-wide): 16.5MM **Privately Held**
SIC: 2951 1794 1771 1611 Asphalt paving mixtures & blocks; excavation work; concrete work; highway & street construction
PA: Niblock Excavating Inc
906 Maple St
Bristol IN 46507
574 848-4437

(G-1813)
NUMERIX INC
406 Diamond Ave Ste B (46725-2451)
PHONE....................................260 248-2942
Jeffrey Johnson, *President*
EMP: 7
SQ FT: 7,000
SALES (est): 1MM **Privately Held**
SIC: 3599 Machine shop, jobbing & repair

(G-1814)
OAK VIEW TOOLING INC
724 E Swihart St (46725-2767)
PHONE....................................260 244-7677
Fax: 260 244-7466
Matthew T Dahms, *President*
Tonnette Dahms, *Vice Pres*
EMP: 14
SQ FT: 5,000
SALES (est): 2.3MM **Privately Held**
WEB: www.oakviewtooling.com
SIC: 3545 Tools & accessories for machine tools

(G-1815)
OLD WORLD FUDGE & CDS DOGS LLC
206 Raleigh Ct (46725-7424)
PHONE....................................260 610-2249
Cris Lamb, *President*
EMP: 2 EST: 2014
SALES (est): 92.3K **Privately Held**
SIC: 2064 Fudge (candy)

(G-1816)
PDQ TOOLING LLC
1100-1 S Williams Dr (46725)
P.O. Box 371 (46725-0371)
PHONE....................................260 244-2984
Jerry Busche, *Mng Member*
EMP: 12 EST: 2013
SQ FT: 1,200
SALES (est): 480.4K **Privately Held**
SIC: 3544 Special dies, tools, jigs & fixtures

(G-1817)
PDQ WORKHOLDING LLC
Also Called: P D Q
1100 S Williams Dr 1 (46725-7527)
P.O. Box 371 (46725-0371)
PHONE....................................260 244-2919
Jerry Busche, *CEO*
Laura Kyler, *Purchasing*
Casey Carpenter, *Engineer*
Chris Hamman, *Engineer*
Jared Sparks, *Engineer*
▲ **EMP:** 25
SALES (est): 6.9MM **Privately Held**
SIC: 3553 Woodworking machinery

(G-1818)
PHILLIPS DIVERSIFIED SERVICES
309 N Washington St (46725-1718)
P.O. Box 161 (46725-0161)
PHONE....................................260 248-2975
John Phillips, *Owner*
B Phillips, *E-Business*
EMP: 6

SALES (est): 235.5K **Privately Held**
SIC: 2759 Invitations: printing

(G-1819)
PRECISION PLASTICS INDIANA INC
900 W Connexion Way (46725-1028)
PHONE....................................260 244-6114
Fax: 260 244-5995
Ronald R Richey, *President*
Terry Farber, *Treasurer*
Keith Boutall, *Manager*
Ryan B Richey, *Admin Sec*
EMP: 150 EST: 1955
SQ FT: 75,000
SALES: 21MM **Privately Held**
WEB: www.pplastic.com
SIC: 3089 3544 Injection molded finished plastic products; industrial molds

(G-1820)
PYROTEK INCORPORATED
4447 E Park 30 Dr (46725-8872)
PHONE....................................260 248-4141
Fax: 260 248-2350
Brigitte Brazda, *Safety Mgr*
Joe Petrecca, *Controller*
Dave Schlicht, *Sales Mgr*
Scott Denning, *Branch Mgr*
Donald Socha, *Analyst*
EMP: 42
SALES (corp-wide): 588.8MM **Privately Held**
WEB: www.pyrotek.info
SIC: 3229 8748 Glass fiber products; business consulting
PA: Pyrotek Incorporated
705 W 1st Ave
Spokane WA 99201
509 926-6212

(G-1821)
QIG LLC
225 Towerview Dr (46725-8799)
PHONE....................................260 244-3591
EMP: 25
SALES (est): 2.5MM **Privately Held**
SIC: 8734 3841 3541 3599 Testing Laboratory Mfg Surgical/Med Instr Mfg Machine Tool-Cutting Mfg Industrial Machinery

(G-1822)
QIG LLC
Also Called: Quality Inspection and Gage
225 Towerview Dr (46725-8799)
PHONE....................................260 244-3591
Fax: 260 244-4365
Kelly Geiger, *President*
Darrin Geiger, *Vice Pres*
EMP: 20
SQ FT: 20,000
SALES: 2.7MM **Privately Held**
SIC: 3599 3541 8734 Custom machinery; machine tools, metal cutting type; calibration & certification

(G-1823)
R & R MANUFACTURING
1150 W 150 N (46725-9586)
PHONE....................................260 244-5621
Randy L Plew, *Owner*
EMP: 3
SQ FT: 5,100
SALES (est): 313K **Privately Held**
SIC: 3444 Mail (post office) collection or storage boxes, sheet metal

(G-1824)
REELCRAFT INDUSTRIES INC
2842 E Business 30 (46725-8451)
PHONE....................................855 634-9109
Fax: 260 248-2605
Robert Law, *President*
Ko Portengen, *Opers Mgr*
James Maggard, *Prdtn Mgr*
Kathleen Keller, *Purch Agent*
Debra Parrett, *Buyer*
▲ **EMP:** 177 EST: 1971
SQ FT: 80,000

SALES (est): 60.8MM
SALES (corp-wide): 294.3MM **Privately Held**
WEB: www.reelcraft.com
SIC: 3496 3499 3429 Miscellaneous fabricated wire products; reels, cable: metal; manufactured hardware (general)
PA: Madison Industries Holdings Llc
500 W Madison St Ste 3890
Chicago IL 60661
312 277-0156

(G-1825)
RESTORATION MED POLYMERS LLC
5865 E State Road 14 (46725-9237)
PHONE....................................260 625-1573
Lou Matrisciano,
EMP: 4 EST: 2015
SALES (est): 499.4K **Privately Held**
SIC: 3841 Diagnostic apparatus, medical

(G-1826)
RICHARD J BAGAN INC
Also Called: Montech USA
1280 S Williams Dr (46725-7528)
P.O. Box 169 (46725-0169)
PHONE....................................260 244-5115
Fax: 260 244-6131
Richard J Bagan, *President*
Lydia McDevitt, *VP Sls/Mktg*
Derek Ellis, *Mktg Coord*
Mike Morgan, *IT/INT Sup*
Sunshine Fry, *Representative*
EMP: 50
SQ FT: 32,000
SALES (est): 13.8MM **Privately Held**
WEB: www.rjbagan.com
SIC: 7629 5084 3613 Electronic equipment repair; electrical measuring instrument repair & calibration; instruments & control equipment; panel & distribution boards & other related apparatus

(G-1827)
RICKIE ALLAN PEASE
Also Called: Rick's Tool Company
406 Diamond Ave (46725-2450)
P.O. Box 151 (46725-0151)
PHONE....................................260 244-7579
Fax: 260 244-6826
Rickie Allan Pease, *Owner*
Rick Pease, *Owner*
EMP: 4
SALES (est): 220K **Privately Held**
SIC: 3542 Thread rolling machines

(G-1828)
RIDGE TRAILERS
3330 E Lincolnway (46725-9099)
PHONE....................................260 244-5443
Matt Thomas, *Principal*
EMP: 2
SALES (est): 158.3K **Privately Held**
SIC: 5599 5013 3799 Utility trailers; trailer parts & accessories; trailers & trailer equipment

(G-1829)
ROBCO ENGINEERED RUBBER PDTS
707 E Short St (46725-7400)
PHONE....................................260 248-2888
Fax: 260 248-4225
Mark Roberts, *President*
Robert Holler, *Vice Pres*
Gwenn Roberts, *Treasurer*
EMP: 10 EST: 1996
SQ FT: 6,500
SALES: 900K **Privately Held**
SIC: 3069 3829 Rubber floor coverings, mats & wallcoverings; measuring & controlling devices

(G-1830)
ROBERT DIETRICK CO INC
777 E Short St (46725-7400)
PHONE....................................260 244-4668
Steve Jones, *Branch Mgr*
EMP: 5
SALES (corp-wide): 14MM **Privately Held**
WEB: www.rd-co.com
SIC: 3537 Loading docks: portable, adjustable & hydraulic

▲ = Import ▼=Export
◆ =Import/Export

PA: Robert Dietrick Co Inc
9051 Technology Dr
Fishers IN 46038
317 842-1991

(G-1831)
RTC
Also Called: RTC Threaders
1901 N Airport Rd (46725-8677)
PHONE.....................260 503-9770
Rick A Pease, *Owner*
EMP: 6
SALES: 1.3MM **Privately Held**
SIC: 3451 7389 Screw machine products;

(G-1832)
RUNNING AROUND SCREEN PRINTING
227 W Van Buren St (46725-2037)
PHONE.....................260 248-1216
Joann Bird, *Owner*
EMP: 6
SALES (est): 490.9K **Privately Held**
SIC: 2752 Commercial printing, offset

(G-1833)
SAILRITE ENTERPRISES INC
2390 E 100 S (46725-9800)
PHONE.....................260 244-4647
Fax: 260 693-2246
Hallie R Grant, *President*
Matthew M Grant, *Vice Pres*
Jeff Frank, *Engineer*
◆ **EMP:** 19
SALES (est): 4.2MM **Privately Held**
WEB: www.sailrite.com
SIC: 5961 3639 Catalog & mail-order houses; sewing machines & attachments, domestic

(G-1834)
SCHWARTZVILLE PALLET
4861 W 300 S (46725-9722)
PHONE.....................260 244-4144
EMP: 4
SALES (est): 275.5K **Privately Held**
SIC: 2448 Pallets, wood & wood with metal

(G-1835)
SOURCE PRODUCTS INC
9875 S Washington Rd (46725-9623)
PHONE.....................260 424-0864
Fax: 260 424-0919
John Wainwright, *President*
EMP: 3
SQ FT: 2,700
SALES: 200K **Privately Held**
SIC: 5063 3646 Lighting fixtures, commercial & industrial; commercial indusl & institutional electric lighting fixtures

(G-1836)
SPEEDWAY REDI MIX INC
Also Called: Columbia City Ready Mix
400 S Whitley St (46725-2629)
P.O. Box 447 (46725-0447)
PHONE.....................260 244-7205
Fax: 260 356-5644
Robert E Hursey, *Opers-Prdtn-Mfg*
EMP: 6 **Privately Held**
SIC: 3273 Ready-mixed concrete
PA: Speedway Redi-Mix Inc
4820 Industrial Rd
Fort Wayne IN 46825

(G-1837)
STEEL DYNAMICS INC
Structural & Rail Division
2601 County Rd 700 E (46725)
PHONE.....................260 248-2600
Fax: 260 625-8950
Johnny Brewer, *Sales Staff*
John Nolan, *Manager*
EMP: 574 **Publicly Held**
SIC: 3312 Plate, sheet & strip, except coated products
PA: Steel Dynamics, Inc.
7575 W Jefferson Blvd
Fort Wayne IN 46804

(G-1838)
STEEL TANK & FABRICATING CORP
Also Called: Stafco
365 S James St (46725-8721)
P.O. Box 210 (46725-0210)
PHONE.....................260 248-8971
Fax: 219 248-8973
Patrick W Kennedy, *President*
Gerald A Hemmelgarn, *Vice Pres*
Carl T Norris, *Vice Pres*
Gene Dietz, *Admin Sec*
Gerald A Scheele, *Asst Sec*
EMP: 20 **EST:** 1952
SQ FT: 15,000
SALES (est): 8MM **Privately Held**
WEB: www.southerntank.net
SIC: 5084 3443 3714 3444 Industrial machinery & equipment; petroleum industry machinery; fabricated plate work (boiler shop); industrial vessels, tanks & containers; motor vehicle parts & accessories; sheet metalwork; fabricated structural metal

(G-1839)
T W MACHINE & GRINDING
7150 N 350 W (46725-9167)
PHONE.....................260 799-4236
Tom Wise, *Principal*
EMP: 2 **EST:** 2008
SALES (est): 163.9K **Privately Held**
SIC: 3599 Grinding castings for the trade

(G-1840)
TESTWORTH LABORATORIES INC
401 S Main St (46725-2143)
PHONE.....................260 244-5137
Lucile M Campbell, *President*
Virginia Campbell, *Vice Pres*
Wil Campbell, *Vice Pres*
Lee R Campbell, *Treasurer*
EMP: 10
SQ FT: 120,000
SALES (est): 677.3K **Privately Held**
SIC: 2891 3087 2851 Adhesives; sealing compounds, synthetic rubber or plastic; custom compound purchased resins; paints & allied products

(G-1841)
THREE RIVERS COMPRSD AR SSTMS
1075 S 50 E (46725-8787)
P.O. Box 476 (46725-0476)
PHONE.....................260 248-8908
Eric Blocher,
EMP: 3
SALES: 400K **Privately Held**
SIC: 3563 Air & gas compressors

(G-1842)
TIMBERLINE SCENERY LLC
700 Hill Dr (46725-1606)
P.O. Box 932 (46725-0932)
PHONE.....................260 244-5588
Jesse Richardson, *Owner*
EMP: 3 **EST:** 2015
SALES (est): 191K **Privately Held**
SIC: 3944 Games, toys & children's vehicles

(G-1843)
ULTRA ELEC PRECSION AIR & LAND
4794 E Park 30 Dr (46725-8871)
PHONE.....................260 327-4112
EMP: 8 **EST:** 1989
SALES (est): 921K **Privately Held**
SIC: 3563 Mfg Air/Gas Compressors

(G-1844)
UNDERSEA SENSOR SYSTEMS INC (HQ)
Also Called: Ultra Electronics
4868 E Park 30 Dr (46725-8861)
PHONE.....................260 244-3500
Joseph Peters, *President*
Jim Majewski, *Senior Buyer*
Nathan Boothby, *Engineer*
Jill Brown, *Engineer*
Thomas Hansel, *Engineer*
◆ **EMP:** 226

SQ FT: 150,000
SALES (est): 86.4MM
SALES (corp-wide): 1B **Privately Held**
WEB: www.ultra-fei.com
SIC: 3812 Nautical instruments; navigational systems & instruments; search & detection systems & instruments
PA: Ultra Electronics Holdings Plc
417 Bridport Road
Greenford MIDDX UB6 8
208 813-4321

(G-1845)
VIKING INC
2740 E Business 30 (46725-8890)
P.O. Box 130 (46725-0130)
PHONE.....................260 244-6141
Fax: 260 244-6124
Mary L Schwenn, *President*
Steven Schwenn, *President*
Donald A Schwenn, *Corp Secy*
EMP: 25
SQ FT: 70,000
SALES (est): 4.1MM **Privately Held**
WEB: www.vikinginc.com
SIC: 3714 3429 3061 Exhaust systems & parts, motor vehicle; manufactured hardware (general); mechanical rubber goods

(G-1846)
WARNER ELECTRIC LLC
4578 E Park 30 Dr (46725-8869)
PHONE.....................260 244-6183
Faith Curry, *Branch Mgr*
EMP: 200
SALES (corp-wide): 876.7MM **Publicly Held**
WEB: www.warnerelectric.com
SIC: 3677 3714 3621 Coil windings, electronic; motor vehicle parts & accessories; motors & generators
HQ: Warner Electric Llc
449 Gardner St
South Beloit IL 61080
815 389-4300

(G-1847)
WEBCO INC
Also Called: Engineering Services
303 Towerview Dr (46725-8799)
PHONE.....................260 244-4233
Fax: 260 244-4633
Bill Blocher, *President*
Delores Blocher, *Corp Secy*
EMP: 5
SQ FT: 9,600
SALES: 1.2MM **Privately Held**
SIC: 3089 8711 Molding primary plastic; engineering services

(G-1848)
YODER & SONS PALLETS
4757 W 300 S (46725-9722)
PHONE.....................260 625-2835
Amos Yoder, *Owner*
EMP: 6
SALES (est): 537.2K **Privately Held**
SIC: 2448 Pallets, wood

Columbus
Bartholomew County

(G-1849)
ACE WELDING AND MACHINE INC
2461 N Indianapolis Rd (47201-3521)
PHONE.....................812 379-9625
Fax: 812 376-9836
Dale L Goddard, *President*
EMP: 6 **EST:** 1969
SQ FT: 10,000
SALES: 250K **Privately Held**
SIC: 7692 3444 3443 Welding repair; sheet metalwork; fabricated plate work (boiler shop)

(G-1850)
ADVANCED MOLD & ENGINEERING
7980 S International Dr (47201-3033)
PHONE.....................812 342-9000
Myron Moorman, *President*
EMP: 12

SQ FT: 7,000
SALES (est): 1.6MM **Privately Held**
WEB: www.advancedmoldandeng.com
SIC: 3544 Industrial molds

(G-1851)
AIM MEDIA INDIANA OPER LLC (PA)
2980 N National Rd A (47201-3234)
P.O. Box 3011 (47202-3011)
PHONE.....................812 372-7811
Jeremy Halbreich, *CEO*
Rick Starks, *COO*
Jeff Rogers, *CFO*
EMP: 80 **EST:** 2015
SQ FT: 23,000
SALES (est): 42.4MM **Privately Held**
SIC: 2741 2711 Miscellaneous publishing; commercial printing & newspaper publishing combined

(G-1852)
AIM MEDIA INDIANA OPER LLC
Republic, The
2980 N National Rd Ste A (47201-3234)
PHONE.....................812 372-7811
Chuck Wells, *Branch Mgr*
EMP: 84
SALES (corp-wide): 42.4MM **Privately Held**
SIC: 2711 Commercial printing & newspaper publishing combined
PA: Aim Media Indiana Operating, Llc
2980 N National Rd A
Columbus IN 47201
812 372-7811

(G-1853)
AK TUBE LLC
150 W 450 S (47201-8872)
PHONE.....................812 341-3200
Randy Davidson, *Senior Engr*
Sheri Redelman, *Branch Mgr*
EMP: 17 **Publicly Held**
SIC: 3317 Steel pipe & tubes
HQ: Ak Tube Llc
30400 E Broadway St
Walbridge OH 43465
419 661-4150

(G-1854)
AMERICAS COML TRNSP RES CO LLC
Also Called: Act Research
4440 Middle Rd (47203-1831)
PHONE.....................812 379-2085
Fax: 812 378-5997
Kenneth Vieth Jr, *President*
Debra Steinbarger, *Sales Mgr*
Frank Maly, *Director*
Jennifer McNealy, *Research Analys*
EMP: 14
SQ FT: 3,000
SALES (est): 1.4MM **Privately Held**
WEB: www.actresearch.net
SIC: 8732 2721 Economic research; statistical reports (periodicals): publishing & printing

(G-1855)
APPLE INC
2448 Woodland Farms Ct (47201-1532)
PHONE.....................812 342-4225
EMP: 2
SALES (corp-wide): 229.2B **Publicly Held**
SIC: 3571 Personal computers (microcomputers)
PA: Apple Inc.
1 Apple Park Way
Cupertino CA 95014
408 996-1010

(G-1856)
APPLIED LABORATORIES INC
3240 N Indianapolis Rd (47201-4859)
P.O. Box 2127 (47202-2127)
PHONE.....................812 372-2607
Fax: 812 372-2631
Anthony Moravec, *CEO*
Susan Harber, *General Mgr*
Brian Crane, *Purch Mgr*
Holli Darlage, *Purch Agent*
Beth Teeters, *Purch Agent*
▲ **EMP:** 100
SQ FT: 80,000

SALES (est): 36.6MM
SALES (corp-wide): 42.1MM **Privately Held**
WEB: www.appliedlabs.com
SIC: **2834** Pharmaceutical preparations
PA: Blairex Laboratories, Inc.
1600 W Brian Dr
Columbus IN 47201
812 378-1864

(G-1857)
AUSTIN POWDER COMPANY
13468 W Old Nashville Rd (47201-8723)
PHONE..................................812 342-1237
Fax: 812 342-0849
David Swango, *Manager*
EMP: 15
SALES (corp-wide): 566.9MM **Privately Held**
SIC: **2892** Black powder (explosive); sporting powder (explosive)
HQ: Austin Powder Company
25800 Science Park Dr # 300
Cleveland OH 44122
216 464-2400

(G-1858)
B B & H TOOL OF COLUMBUS INC
2775 Roadway Dr (47201-7441)
PHONE..................................812 372-3707
Fax: 812 372-3708
Jerrett Deckard, *President*
Dale G Behrman, *Treasurer*
EMP: 18
SQ FT: 7,500
SALES (est): 1.7MM **Privately Held**
SIC: **3544** Special dies & tools

(G-1859)
BETTNER WIRE COATING DYES INC
1230 Jackson St (47201-5774)
P.O. Box 872 (47202-0872)
PHONE..................................812 372-2732
Fax: 812 372-6355
Howard Bettner, *President*
Gerald Bettner, *Vice Pres*
Max Bettner, *Vice Pres*
Nelson Bettner, *Vice Pres*
Edith Bettner, *Treasurer*
EMP: 16
SQ FT: 4,000
SALES (est): 1.1MM **Privately Held**
SIC: **3544** Special dies & tools

(G-1860)
BOOTH SIGNS INC
1307 12th St (47201-5604)
PHONE..................................812 376-7446
Donna Booth, *President*
EMP: 2
SALES (est): 98K **Privately Held**
SIC: **3993** Signs & advertising specialties

(G-1861)
BOYER MACHINE & TOOL CO INC
1080 S Gladstone Ave (47201-9520)
P.O. Box 422 (47202-0422)
PHONE..................................812 379-9581
Fax: 812 378-7278
William Boyer, *CEO*
David Boyer, *President*
Jennifer Wilson, *Treasurer*
▲ EMP: 45 EST: 1964
SQ FT: 33,998
SALES (est): 7.3MM **Privately Held**
WEB: www.boyermachine.com
SIC: **3599 3569 5013** Machine shop, jobbing & repair; assembly machines, nonmetalworking; automotive supplies & parts

(G-1862)
BRIAN T KLEM
Also Called: Laundry Room, The
4270 W Jnathan Moore Pike (47201-9585)
PHONE..................................812 342-4080
Brian Klem, *Owner*
EMP: 5 EST: 2000
SALES (est): 405.7K **Privately Held**
SIC: **3582** Washing machines, laundry: commercial, incl. coin-operated

(G-1863)
BUSINESS & INDUSTRIAL PDTS CO
Also Called: B I P C O
3552 Mockingbird Dr (47203-1333)
PHONE..................................812 376-6149
John Dougherty, *Owner*
EMP: 4
SALES (est): 250K **Privately Held**
WEB: www.bipcousa.com
SIC: **3993** Advertising novelties

(G-1864)
CALTHERM CORPORATION (HQ)
910 S Gladstone Ave (47201-9520)
PHONE..................................812 372-0281
Bruce Abel, *President*
Dennis Sabau, *Vice Pres*
Jason Lucas, *Opers Mgr*
John Oxendine, *Opers Mgr*
Brittany King, *Warehouse Mgr*
▲ EMP: 110
SQ FT: 57,000
SALES (est): 22.8MM **Privately Held**
WEB: www.caltherm.com
SIC: **3714 3822** Thermostats, motor vehicle; auto controls regulating residntl & coml environmt & applncs
PA: Magnumm Corporation
3839 E 10 Mile Rd
Warren MI 48091
586 427-9420

(G-1865)
CALTHERM CORPORATION
Also Called: Permo Wick
835 S Marr Rd (47201-7437)
PHONE..................................812 372-0281
Fax: 812 376-8305
David Rayburn, *QC Mgr*
Randy Cvelbar, *Engineer*
Ryan Prosch, *Engineer*
Jeremiah Hendren, *Design Engr*
Michelle Robison, *Controller*
EMP: 14
SALES (corp-wide): 22.8MM **Privately Held**
WEB: www.caltherm.com
SIC: **3714 3822** Thermostats, motor vehicle; auto controls regulating residntl & coml environmt & applncs
HQ: Caltherm Corporation
910 S Gladstone Ave
Columbus IN 47201
812 372-0281

(G-1866)
CAPCO LLC
1349 Arcadia Dr (47201-8445)
PHONE..................................812 375-1700
Jun Hashizume, *Vice Pres*
Jeff Elkins, *Prdtn Mgr*
Chad Wolf, *QC Mgr*
Shirley Bennett, *Human Resources*
▲ EMP: 84
SQ FT: 24,000
SALES (est): 19.4MM **Privately Held**
SIC: **3469** Stamping metal for the trade

(G-1867)
CARLTON WEST OIL COMPANY LLC
3237 Nugent Blvd (47203-1609)
PHONE..................................812 375-9689
William Haeberle, *Principal*
EMP: 3
SALES (est): 127.8K **Privately Held**
SIC: **1311** Crude petroleum & natural gas

(G-1868)
CE SYSTEMS INC
1045 S Gladstone Ave (47201-9520)
P.O. Box 348 (47202-0348)
PHONE..................................812 372-8234
Joseph Cunningham, *President*
Mike Miller, *Shareholder*
David Smith, *Shareholder*
EMP: 40
SQ FT: 32,000
SALES: 5.4MM **Privately Held**
SIC: **3321 3365 3322** Gray & ductile iron foundries; aluminum foundries; malleable iron foundries

(G-1869)
CHATTIN WALTER R COTTON
2554 Union St (47201-3660)
PHONE..................................812 254-5031
Walter Chattin, *Principal*
EMP: 2 EST: 2001
SALES (est): 96.4K **Privately Held**
SIC: **2261** Finishing plants, cotton

(G-1870)
CIDERLEAF TEA COMPANY INC
4525 Progress Dr (47201-8819)
PHONE..................................812 375-1937
Lalith Paranavitana, *President*
Dr Randall Pflueger, *Vice Pres*
EMP: 2
SALES (est): 64.3K **Privately Held**
SIC: **2099** Food preparations

(G-1871)
CMI PGI HOLDINGS LLC (HQ)
500 Jackson St (47201-6258)
PHONE..................................812 377-5000
Joseph Bernot, *Manager*
Terry Magid, *Manager*
EMP: 2
SALES (est): 236.2K
SALES (corp-wide): 20.4B **Publicly Held**
SIC: **3463** Engine or turbine forgings, nonferrous
PA: Cummins Inc.
500 Jackson St
Columbus IN 47201
812 377-5000

(G-1872)
CNS CUSTOM WOODWORKS INC
1053 Hummingbird Ln (47203-1310)
PHONE..................................812 350-2431
Scott Daugherty, *President*
EMP: 2
SALES (est): 184.6K **Privately Held**
SIC: **2431** Millwork

(G-1873)
COCA-COLA BOTTLING CO INC
1334 Washington St (47201-5724)
PHONE..................................812 376-3381
Fax: 812 372-5238
Albert H Schumaker II, *President*
Kirk Freese, *General Mgr*
William Russell, *Vice Pres*
EMP: 30
SQ FT: 25,000
SALES (est): 9MM **Privately Held**
SIC: **2086** Bottled & canned soft drinks

(G-1874)
COLUMBUS CANVAS LLC
8395 W State Road 46 (47201-8101)
PHONE..................................812 376-9414
Susan K Stier, *Principal*
EMP: 3 EST: 2014
SALES (est): 110.5K **Privately Held**
SIC: **2211** Canvas

(G-1875)
COLUMBUS CSTM CBINETS FURN LLC
4475 Middle Rd (47203-1832)
PHONE..................................812 379-9411
Fax: 812 379-9630
Brian Kiel,
Charles Kiel,
Greg Kiel,
Darren Moore,
EMP: 7
SALES (est): 321.4K **Privately Held**
SIC: **7641 2519 2434** Antique furniture repair & restoration; household furniture, except wood or metal: upholstered; wood kitchen cabinets

(G-1876)
COLUMBUS ENGINEERING INC
Also Called: Cei
6600 S 50 W (47201-3964)
PHONE..................................812 342-1231
Fax: 812 342-2341
Burdett Noblitt, *President*
Ann Noblitt, *Corp Secy*
Mike Noblitt, *Vice Pres*
EMP: 35 EST: 1954
SQ FT: 45,000

SALES (est): 10.9MM **Privately Held**
SIC: **3444** Sheet metalwork

(G-1877)
COLUMBUS INDUSTRIAL ELECTRIC
1625 N Indianapolis Rd (47201-3521)
PHONE..................................812 372-8414
Fax: 812 372-0492
Mary Deppe, *CEO*
Steven M Deppe, *President*
Francis Deppe, *Vice Pres*
Helen A Deppe, *Treasurer*
Susan Chandler, *Admin Sec*
EMP: 13
SQ FT: 31,000
SALES: 5MM **Privately Held**
WEB: www.ciemotors.com
SIC: **7694** Electric motor repair

(G-1878)
COLUMBUS OPTICAL SERVICE INC
Also Called: Columbus Wholesale Optical
2475 Cottage Ave (47201-4476)
PHONE..................................812 372-2678
Fax: 812 378-0245
Charles Oliver, *President*
Robert De Ment, *Vice Pres*
John Oliver, *Vice Pres*
Ron Povaleri, *Sales Mgr*
EMP: 6
SQ FT: 2,200
SALES (est): 963.3K **Privately Held**
WEB: www.columbusoptical.com
SIC: **3851 5995** Eyeglasses, lenses & frames; eyeglasses, prescription

(G-1879)
COLUMBUS PAINT SUPPLY
3800 W C Folger Dr 150 (47201)
PHONE..................................812 375-1118
Fax: 812 372-8636
Ray Butler, *Owner*
EMP: 4
SALES (est): 200K **Privately Held**
SIC: **2851** Paints & allied products

(G-1880)
COLUMBUS PALLET CORPORATION
1520 14th St (47201-5613)
P.O. Box 1189 (47202-1189)
PHONE..................................812 372-7272
Fax: 812 372-3230
Matt A Sebahar, *President*
EMP: 6
SQ FT: 10,000
SALES: 850K **Privately Held**
SIC: **2448** Pallets, wood

(G-1881)
COLUMBUS SIGNS
4540 E State St (47201-2537)
PHONE..................................812 376-7877
Fax: 812 376-7911
Mark Smith, *Owner*
EMP: 2
SQ FT: 8,000
SALES (est): 183.5K **Privately Held**
WEB: www.columbusnet.com
SIC: **3993 7629** Neon signs; electrical repair shops

(G-1882)
COLUMBUS VAULT CO
3100 S Us Highway 31 (47201-9099)
PHONE..................................812 372-3210
Ted Shanks, *Principal*
EMP: 2
SALES (est): 125.1K **Privately Held**
SIC: **3272** Burial vaults, concrete or precast terrazzo

(G-1883)
COSCO INC
2525 State St (47201-7443)
PHONE..................................812 372-0141
Fax: 812 372-0911
Nick Costides, *President*
Richard W Holdeman, *President*
Jon Reynolds, *Exec VP*
Scott Wagner, *Plant Mgr*
Donald Marsh, *VP Finance*
EMP: 1000 EST: 1935

▲ = Import ▼ =Export
◆ =Import/Export

SQ FT: 897,000
SALES: 380MM
SALES (corp-wide): 2.5B Privately Held
WEB: www.djgusa.com
SIC: 3944 2511 2514 Strollers, baby (vehicle); child restraint seats, automotive; walkers, baby (vehicle); high chairs, children's: wood; cribs: wood; cribs: metal; stools, household, padded or plain: metal; serving carts & tea wagons: metal; tables, household: metal
HQ: Dorel U.S.A., Inc.
    2525 State St
    Columbus IN 47201

(G-1884)
CREATIVE TOOL AND MACHINING
4010 Middle Rd (47203-1835)
PHONE..................................812 378-3562
Fax: 812 372-9067
Gregory Exner, President
Angela Bailey, Corp Secy
EMP: 14
SQ FT: 17,500
SALES: 2.5MM Privately Held
WEB: www.creativetool.net
SIC: 3599 3544 Machine shop, jobbing & repair; special dies, tools, jigs & fixtures

(G-1885)
CROSSING CREATIONS
Also Called: Rose Brother Graphics
6562 E 800 N (47203)
PHONE..................................812 587-0212
EMP: 2
SALES (est): 82K Privately Held
SIC: 2759 Commercial Printing

(G-1886)
CUMMINS AMERICAS INC (HQ)
Also Called: Cummins Engine
500 Jackson St (47201-6258)
PHONE..................................812 377-5000
Fax: 812 377-3334
Thomas Linebarger, CEO
Theodore M Solso, President
Marietta Dorathy, General Mgr
Lois Raina, General Mgr
Kobi Wright, Counsel
◆ EMP: 1
SQ FT: 1,000
SALES (est): 14.5MM
SALES (corp-wide): 20.4B Publicly Held
WEB: www.cummins.com
SIC: 5084 3519 Engines & parts, diesel; internal combustion engines
PA: Cummins Inc.
    500 Jackson St
    Columbus IN 47201
    812 377-5000

(G-1887)
CUMMINS DIGITAL VENTURES INC
500 Jackson St (47201-6258)
PHONE..................................812 377-5000
Thad Ewald, Ch of Bd
Rakesh Gangwani, CFO
Preston Ray, Admin Sec
EMP: 28
SALES (est): 552K
SALES (corp-wide): 20.4B Publicly Held
SIC: 7372 Business oriented computer software
PA: Cummins Inc.
    500 Jackson St
    Columbus IN 47201
    812 377-5000

(G-1888)
CUMMINS DIST HOLDCO INC (HQ)
500 Jackson St (47201-6258)
PHONE..................................812 377-5000
David Geraghty, Exec Dir
EMP: 15 EST: 2014
SALES (est): 8.4MM
SALES (corp-wide): 20.4B Publicly Held
SIC: 5091 3519 Sporting & recreation goods; internal combustion engines
PA: Cummins Inc.
    500 Jackson St
    Columbus IN 47201
    812 377-5000

(G-1889)
CUMMINS EMISSION SOLUTIONS INC (HQ)
500 Jackson St (47201-6258)
PHONE..................................608 987-3206
S Padmanabhan, President
R E Harris, Treasurer
Jon Blair, Manager
Barth Weishoff, Manager
M J Sifferlen, Director
EMP: 40
SALES (est): 24.6MM
SALES (corp-wide): 20.4B Publicly Held
SIC: 3714 3519 Exhaust systems & parts, motor vehicle; internal combustion engines
PA: Cummins Inc.
    500 Jackson St
    Columbus IN 47201
    812 377-5000

(G-1890)
CUMMINS ENGINE HOLDING CO INC
500 Jackson St (47201-6258)
PHONE..................................812 377-5000
F Joseph Loughrey, President
Richard Joseph Freeland, President
James A Henderson, Vice Pres
James Lyons, Vice Pres
Mark R Gerstle, Admin Sec
◆ EMP: 11
SALES (est): 2.6MM
SALES (corp-wide): 20.4B Publicly Held
WEB: www.cummins.com
SIC: 3519 Diesel, semi-diesel or duel-fuel engines, including marine
PA: Cummins Inc.
    500 Jackson St
    Columbus IN 47201
    812 377-5000

(G-1891)
CUMMINS INC (PA)
500 Jackson St (47201-6258)
P.O. Box 3005 (47202-3005)
PHONE..................................812 377-5000
N Thomas Linebarger, Ch of Bd
Tracy A Embree, President
Richard J Freeland, President
Norbert Nusterer, President
Srikanth Padmanabhan, President
EMP: 277
SALES: 20.4B Publicly Held
WEB: www.cummins.com
SIC: 3519 3714 3694 3621 Internal combustion engines; engines, diesel & semi-diesel or dual-fuel; diesel engine rebuilding; motor vehicle parts & accessories; motor vehicle engines & parts; crankshaft assemblies, motor vehicle; filters: oil, fuel & air, motor vehicle; engine electrical equipment; generator sets: gasoline, diesel or dual-fuel

(G-1892)
CUMMINS INC
2879 Prairie Stream Way (47203-9046)
PHONE..................................812 377-0150
EMP: 357
SALES (corp-wide): 20.4B Publicly Held
SIC: 3519 Internal combustion engines
PA: Cummins Inc.
    500 Jackson St
    Columbus IN 47201
    812 377-5000

(G-1893)
CUMMINS INC
1460 N National Rd (47201-5577)
PHONE..................................812 377-6072
Per Lange, General Mgr
Thomas Yonushonis, Exec Dir
EMP: 343
SALES (corp-wide): 20.4B Publicly Held
WEB: www.notesbridge.cummins.com
SIC: 3519 Internal combustion engines
PA: Cummins Inc.
    500 Jackson St
    Columbus IN 47201
    812 377-5000

(G-1894)
CUMMINS INC
2851 State St (47201-7449)
PHONE..................................812 377-8601
Bill Bederaux-Cayne, Director
Jim West, Director
EMP: 14
SALES (corp-wide): 20.4B Publicly Held
SIC: 3519 3714 3694 3621 Internal combustion engines; motor vehicle parts & accessories; engine electrical equipment; generator sets: gasoline, diesel or dual-fuel
PA: Cummins Inc.
    500 Jackson St
    Columbus IN 47201
    812 377-5000

(G-1895)
CUMMINS INC
910 S Marr Rd (47201-7440)
PHONE..................................812 377-2932
Chad Rolfe, Branch Mgr
EMP: 20
SALES (corp-wide): 20.4B Publicly Held
SIC: 3519 3714 3694 3621 Internal combustion engines; engines, diesel & semi-diesel or dual-fuel; diesel engine rebuilding; motor vehicle parts & accessories; motor vehicle engines & parts; crankshaft assemblies, motor vehicle; filters: oil, fuel & air, motor vehicle; engine electrical equipment; generator sets: gasoline, diesel or dual-fuel
PA: Cummins Inc.
    500 Jackson St
    Columbus IN 47201
    812 377-5000

(G-1896)
CUMMINS INC
1825 W 450 S (47201-3044)
PHONE..................................812 524-6455
EMP: 21
SALES (corp-wide): 20.4B Publicly Held
SIC: 5013 3519 Motor vehicle supplies & new parts; internal combustion engines
PA: Cummins Inc.
    500 Jackson St
    Columbus IN 47201
    812 377-5000

(G-1897)
CUMMINS INC
3540 W 450 S (47201-8870)
PHONE..................................812 374-4774
Marcie Pierson, Analyst
EMP: 9
SALES (corp-wide): 20.4B Publicly Held
SIC: 3519 Internal combustion engines
PA: Cummins Inc.
    500 Jackson St
    Columbus IN 47201
    812 377-5000

(G-1898)
CUMMINS INC
525 Jackson St (47201)
PHONE..................................765 430-0093
James Kim, Manager
EMP: 4
SALES (corp-wide): 20.4B Publicly Held
SIC: 3714 Motor vehicle parts & accessories
PA: Cummins Inc.
    500 Jackson St
    Columbus IN 47201
    812 377-5000

(G-1899)
CUMMINS INC
Also Called: Cummins Technical Center
1900 Mckinley Ave (47201-6414)
P.O. Box 3005 (47202-3005)
PHONE..................................812 377-7000
Fax: 812 377-7074
Thomas Linebarger, CEO
Ron Chapman, Opers Mgr
Joseph Kelley, Opers Mgr
Coby Pascoe, Opers Mgr
Chris Truman, Opers Mgr
EMP: 350
SALES (corp-wide): 20.4B Publicly Held
WEB: www.cummins.com
SIC: 3519 Internal combustion engines

(G-1900)
CUMMINS POWER GENERATION INC
301 Jackson St (47201-6830)
P.O. Box 3005 (47202-3005)
PHONE..................................812 377-5000
Rich Mills, President
Larry Fetting, General Mgr
Carlos Leon, Business Mgr
Joseph Perkins Jr, Vice Pres
Isaac Coats, Engineer
EMP: 15
SQ FT: 1,000
SALES (est): 4.2MM
SALES (corp-wide): 20.4B Publicly Held
WEB: www.cummins.com
SIC: 5063 5074 5084 3519 Power transmission equipment, electric; heating equipment & panels, solar; instruments & control equipment; internal combustion engines
PA: Cummins Inc.
    500 Jackson St
    Columbus IN 47201
    812 377-5000

(G-1901)
CUMMINS-SCANIA XPI MFG LLC (PA)
1460 N National Rd (47201-5577)
PHONE..................................812 377-5000
Donna Dettmer, Safety Mgr
Steve Ryan, Safety Mgr
Gunrawee Navamark, Purch Mgr
Richard Duncan, Engineer
Eric Hagen, Engineer
EMP: 7
SALES (est): 7.7MM Privately Held
SIC: 3519 Internal combustion engines

(G-1902)
CUNNINGHAM PATTERN & ENGRG INC
4399 N Us Highway 31 (47201-8558)
P.O. Box 854 (47202-0854)
PHONE..................................812 379-9571
Fax: 812 379-9574
Joseph E Cunningham, President
Mike Miller, Vice Pres
Doug Clipp, Project Mgr
Beth Whittington, Office Mgr
Steve Lee, Manager
EMP: 16 EST: 1965
SQ FT: 10,500
SALES: 4.4MM Privately Held
SIC: 3543 3366 3599 Industrial patterns; castings (except die); machine shop, jobbing & repair

(G-1903)
CUSTOM COUNTERS INC
2740 N State Road 9 (47203-8631)
P.O. Box 186, Seymour (47274-0186)
PHONE..................................812 546-0052
Fax: 812 546-0053
Mike Vierling, President
James Vierling, Vice Pres
EMP: 5
SQ FT: 7,000
SALES: 500K Privately Held
SIC: 2541 Counters or counter display cases, wood

(G-1904)
D S E INC
Also Called: Screen Tech Designs
2651 Cessna Dr (47203-1877)
P.O. Box 686 (47202-0686)
PHONE..................................812 376-0310
Fax: 812 372-6617
Paul Saddler, President
Scott Saddler, Vice Pres
Jesse Saddler, Admin Sec
EMP: 30
SQ FT: 18,000
SALES (est): 3.4MM Privately Held
WEB: www.stdesigns.com
SIC: 2759 3479 2396 2851 Screen printing; painting, coating & hot dipping; automotive & apparel trimmings; paints & allied products; surface active agents

G
E
O
G
R
A
P
H
I
C

(G-1905)
DAVIDS INC
905 S Gladstone Ave (47201-9520)
PHONE....................................812 376-6870
Fax: 812 376-0214
Michelle David, *President*
Jeffery David, *Treasurer*
EMP: 11
SQ FT: 4,200
SALES (est): 2.2MM Privately Held
SIC: 3446 7692 3444 Fences, gates, posts & flagpoles; welding repair; sheet metalwork

(G-1906)
DECO CORPORATION
Also Called: Deco Products
6510 S 50 W (47201-9237)
P.O. Box 632 (47202-0632)
PHONE....................................812 342-4767
Fax: 812 342-4452
Robert A Darlage, *President*
John Darlage, *President*
EMP: 20
SQ FT: 40,000
SALES: 900K Privately Held
SIC: 3537 3441 Skids, metal; fabricated structural metal

(G-1907)
DEVENING BLOCK INC (PA)
895 Jonesville Rd (47201-7548)
P.O. Box 566 (47202-0566)
PHONE....................................812 372-4458
Fax: 812 376-3667
Harry E Horn, *President*
Harry Horn, *President*
Steve Horn, *Asst Sec*
EMP: 30
SQ FT: 10,000
SALES (est): 5.2MM Privately Held
SIC: 3271 5032 Concrete block & brick; brick, stone & related material; concrete & cinder building products

(G-1908)
DONUTS N COFFEE INC
2222 State St (47201-7307)
P.O. Box 2305 (47202-2305)
PHONE....................................812 376-2796
Larry Stith, *President*
J David Stith, *Vice Pres*
Carolyn Stith, *Admin Sec*
EMP: 8
SQ FT: 2,800
SALES: 225K Privately Held
SIC: 2045 Flours & flour mixes, from purchased flour

(G-1909)
DOREL HOME FURNISHINGS INC
2525 State St (47201-7443)
PHONE....................................812 372-0141
Troy Franks, *Branch Mgr*
EMP: 410
SALES (corp-wide): 2.5B Privately Held
SIC: 2511 Console tables: wood; tea wagons: wood; coffee tables: wood
HQ: Dorel Home Furnishings, Inc.
410 E 1st St S
Wright City MO 63390
636 745-3351

(G-1910)
DOREL JUVENILE GROUP INC
500 S Gladstone Ave (47201)
PHONE....................................812 314-6629
Dale Fear, *Manager*
EMP: 10
SALES (corp-wide): 2.5B Privately Held
SIC: 3944 Baby carriages & restraint seats
HQ: Dorel Juvenile Group, Inc.
2525 State St
Columbus IN 47201
800 457-5276

(G-1911)
DOREL JUVENILE GROUP INC
505 S Cherry St (47201)
PHONE....................................812 372-0141
Chuck Caldwell, *Manager*
EMP: 3
SALES (corp-wide): 2.5B Privately Held
SIC: 3089 Plastic kitchenware, tableware & houseware

HQ: Dorel Juvenile Group, Inc.
2525 State St
Columbus IN 47201
800 457-5276

(G-1912)
DOREL JUVENILE GROUP INC (DH)
Also Called: Cosco Home & Office Pdts Div
2525 State St (47201-7494)
P.O. Box 2609 (47202-2609)
PHONE....................................800 457-5276
David Taylor, *President*
Jay Caron, *Vice Pres*
Steven E Willeke, *Vice Pres*
◆ EMP: 125
SQ FT: 897,000
SALES (est): 171MM
SALES (corp-wide): 2.5B Privately Held
WEB: www.coscoproducts.com
SIC: 3799 Snowmobiles

(G-1913)
DOREL JUVENILE GROUP INC
Also Called: Safety First
2525 State St (47201-7494)
PHONE....................................812 372-0141
David Taylor, *CEO*
EMP: 111
SALES (corp-wide): 2.5B Privately Held
SIC: 3089 Plastic kitchenware, tableware & houseware
HQ: Dorel Juvenile Group, Inc.
2525 State St
Columbus IN 47201
800 457-5276

(G-1914)
DOREL USA INC (HQ)
Also Called: Dorel Juvenile Group
2525 State St (47201-7443)
PHONE....................................812 372-0141
Nick Costides, *President*
Tim Ferguson, *Exec VP*
Steve Willeke, *Exec VP*
Gary Lauziere, *Credit Mgr*
▲ EMP: 75
SQ FT: 897,000
SALES (est): 552.3MM
SALES (corp-wide): 2.5B Privately Held
SIC: 3944 2511 2514 Strollers, baby (vehicle); child restraint seats, automotive; walkers, baby (vehicle); high chairs, children's: wood; cribs: wood; cribs: metal; stools, household, padded or plain: metal; serving carts & tea wagons: metal; tables, household: metal
PA: Industries Dorel Inc, Les
1255 Av Greene Bureau 300
Westmount QC H3Z 2
514 934-3034

(G-1915)
DWG DESIGN SERVICES CORP
Also Called: .dwg Tooling Technologies
1220 Washington St (47201-5746)
PHONE....................................812 372-0864
Fax: 812 372-0869
William Dirk Rader, *President*
Phil Miles, *Treasurer*
Gary Akin, *Admin Sec*
EMP: 4
SQ FT: 1,800
SALES (est): 490.5K Privately Held
WEB: www.dwgservices.com
SIC: 3544 Special dies, tools, jigs & fixtures

(G-1916)
E F M CORPORATION
Also Called: Product Engineering Company
1480 14th St (47201-5611)
PHONE....................................812 372-4421
James Eversole, *President*
Lloyd D Meyer, *VP Mfg*
EMP: 100
SQ FT: 44,600
SALES (est): 14.1MM Privately Held
WEB: www.efmheating.com
SIC: 3544 Special dies & tools

(G-1917)
ED LLOYD CO
13240 S 100 W (47201-4711)
PHONE....................................812 342-2505
Ed Lloyd, *Owner*

EMP: 2
SALES (est): 100K Privately Held
SIC: 2511 2431 Wood household furniture; interior & ornamental woodwork & trim

(G-1918)
EJL TECH
461 S Mapleton St Ste B (47201-7362)
PHONE....................................812 374-8808
Eric Larsen, *Owner*
EMP: 3
SALES: 250K Privately Held
SIC: 3663 Radio & TV communications equipment

(G-1919)
EM PRINTING & EMBROIDERY LLC
2221 Pear Tree Ct (47201-2740)
PHONE....................................812 373-0082
Michael R Bodart, *Owner*
EMP: 2
SALES (est): 185.7K Privately Held
SIC: 2752 Commercial printing, lithographic

(G-1920)
ENKEI AMERICA INC (PA)
2900 Inwood Dr (47201-9758)
PHONE....................................812 373-7000
Fax: 812 342-6556
Makoto Miura, *CEO*
Todd Howe, *General Mgr*
Rick Merkel, *Exec VP*
Hideo Nakabayashi, *Exec VP*
Mike Boggs, *Vice Pres*
▲ EMP: 645
SQ FT: 246,000
SALES (est): 157.6MM Privately Held
SIC: 3714 3365 Wheels, motor vehicle; aluminum foundries

(G-1921)
ENKEI AMERICA MOLDINGS INC
2680 Norcross Dr (47201-8844)
PHONE....................................812 373-7000
Fax: 812 342-0042
Junichi Suzuki, *President*
▲ EMP: 1
SALES (est): 3.2MM
SALES (corp-wide): 157.6MM Privately Held
SIC: 3363 Aluminum die-castings
PA: Enkei America, Inc.
2900 Inwood Dr
Columbus IN 47201
812 373-7000

(G-1922)
FALCON MANUFACTURING LLC
6200 S International Dr (47201-3034)
PHONE....................................317 884-3600
Gary Sherman,
EMP: 15 EST: 2012
SQ FT: 468,000
SALES (est): 60.9MM Privately Held
SIC: 3511 Turbines & turbine generator sets
PA: The Phoenix Group Inc
164 S Park Blvd
Greenwood IN 46143

(G-1923)
FAURECIA EMISSIONS CONTL TECH
950 W 450 S 4 (47201-1520)
PHONE....................................812 341-2620
EMP: 443
SALES (corp-wide): 342.9MM Privately Held
WEB: www.emcontechnologies.com
SIC: 3714 Exhaust systems & parts, motor vehicle
HQ: Faurecia Emissions Control Technologies Usa, Llc
950 W 450 S
Columbus IN 47201

(G-1924)
FAURECIA EMISSIONS CONTROL
Gladstone Div
601 S Gladstone Ave (47201-9520)
PHONE....................................812 348-4305

Mark Fraser, *Manager*
EMP: 900
SALES (corp-wide): 342.9MM Privately Held
WEB: www.emcontechnologies.com
SIC: 3714 Motor vehicle parts & accessories
HQ: Faurecia Emissions Control Technologies Usa, Llc
950 W 450 S
Columbus IN 47201

(G-1925)
FAURECIA EMISSIONS CONTROL
960 W 450 S (47201)
PHONE....................................937 823-5393
EMP: 2
SALES (corp-wide): 319.5MM Privately Held
SIC: 3714 Mfg Motor Vehicle Parts/Accessories
HQ: Faurecia Emissions Control Technologies Usa, Llc
950 W 450 S
Columbus IN 47201
812 341-2000

(G-1926)
FAURECIA EMISSIONS CONTROL (DH)
Also Called: Emcon Technologies
950 W 450 S (47201-1520)
P.O. Box 3070 (47202-3070)
PHONE....................................812 341-2000
Fax: 812 341-2101
David Degraaf, *President*
Ivo Smutny, *Accounting Mgr*
Christophe Schmidt,
Mark Stidham,
Philippe Vienney,
◆ EMP: 324
SALES (est): 2.5B
SALES (corp-wide): 342.9MM Privately Held
WEB: www.emcontechnologies.com
SIC: 3714 Exhaust systems & parts, motor vehicle; filters: oil, fuel & air, motor vehicle
HQ: Faurecia Usa Holdings, Inc.
2800 High Meadow Cir
Auburn Hills MI 48326
248 724-5100

(G-1927)
FAURECIA EMISSIONS CONTROL
950 W 450 S Bldg 2 (47201-1520)
PHONE....................................812 341-2000
H Wacaser, *Manager*
EMP: 443
SALES (corp-wide): 342.9MM Privately Held
WEB: www.emcontechnologies.com
SIC: 3714 Motor vehicle parts & accessories
HQ: Faurecia Emissions Control Technologies Usa, Llc
950 W 450 S
Columbus IN 47201

(G-1928)
FAURECIA EMISSIONS CONTROL TEC ✪
Also Called: Faurecia Clean Mobility
950 W 450 S (47201-1520)
PHONE....................................812 341-2000
EMP: 4 EST: 2017
SALES (est): 511.4K Privately Held
SIC: 3714 Exhaust systems & parts, motor vehicle

(G-1929)
FAURECIA EXHAUST SYSTEMS LLC
Also Called: Faurecia Emissions Control TEC
950 W 450 S (47201-1520)
PHONE....................................812 341-2079
EMP: 182
SALES (corp-wide): 342.9MM Privately Held
SIC: 3714 Exhaust systems & parts, motor vehicle

▲ = Import ▼=Export
◆ =Import/Export

HQ: Faurecia Emissions Control Systems
Na, Llc
543 Matzinger Rd
Toledo OH 43612
419 727-5000

(G-1930)
FIRST METALS & PLASTICS INC
3805 Jonesville Rd (47201-7703)
P.O. Box 943 (47202-0943)
PHONE...................................812 379-4400
John Counceller, *President*
John D Counceller, *President*
Andrew Counceller, *Manager*
EMP: 32
SQ FT: 50,000
SALES: 3MM **Privately Held**
SIC: 3441 3089 Fabricated structural
metal; plastic processing

(G-1931)
FLAMBEAU INC
4325 Middle Rd (47203-1882)
PHONE...................................812 372-4899
Al Baldwin, *Accounts Mgr*
Valerie Douglas, *Accounts Mgr*
Rick Coffing, *Manager*
EMP: 135
SALES (corp-wide): 320MM **Privately
Held**
SIC: 3089 3949 3944 3469 Pallets, plas-
tic; decoys, duck & other game birds;
games, toys & children's vehicles; metal
stampings; partitions & fixtures, except
wood; metal household furniture
HQ: Flambeau, Inc.
801 Lynn Ave
Baraboo WI 53913
800 352-6266

(G-1932)
**FUTURE TOOL & ENGINEERING
CO**
3400 Scott Dr (47201-4025)
PHONE...................................812 376-8699
Fax: 812 376-8757
Phil Westerfield, *President*
Phyllis Westerfield, *Corp Secy*
Audrey Westerfield, *Financial Exec*
EMP: 12
SQ FT: 6,500
SALES (est): 2.1MM **Privately Held**
SIC: 3544 Special dies & tools

(G-1933)
**GRANITE ENGINEERING & TOOL
CO (PA)**
51 S Us Highway 31 (47201-7807)
PHONE...................................812 375-9077
Fax: 812 375-0169
Joseph Harvey, *President*
Gregg Fields, *General Mgr*
Michael Coons, *Vice Pres*
EMP: 13
SQ FT: 10,000
SALES: 2MM **Privately Held**
WEB: www.graniteengineering.com
SIC: 3544 Special dies & tools; jigs & fix-
tures

(G-1934)
GREGS TOOL & MACHINE
1537 Hutchins Ave Ste D (47201-5602)
PHONE...................................812 373-9329
Greg Westerfield, *Owner*
EMP: 3
SALES: 219K **Privately Held**
SIC: 3312 Tool & die steel

(G-1935)
GRIFFIN INDUSTRIES LLC
345 Water St (47201-6771)
P.O. Box 301 (47202-0301)
PHONE...................................812 379-9528
Fax: 812 379-5539
Tim Shuffet, *Manager*
EMP: 36
SALES (corp-wide): 3.6B **Publicly Held**
WEB: www.griffinind.com
SIC: 2077 2048 2011 Grease rendering,
inedible; tallow rendering, inedible; pre-
pared feeds; meat packing plants
HQ: Griffin Industries Llc
4221 Alexandria Pike
Cold Spring KY 41076
859 781-2010

(G-1936)
H D WILLIAMS CO
1637 Franklin St (47201-5115)
PHONE...................................812 372-6476
Dennis Tibbetts, *Owner*
◆ EMP: 2
SALES (est): 162.3K **Privately Held**
SIC: 3469 Metal stampings

(G-1937)
HARDIGG INDUSTRIES INC
Also Called: Hardigg Battery Products
2405 Norcross Dr (47201-8844)
PHONE...................................812 342-0139
Fax: 812 342-0252
Mike Hacker, *General Mgr*
EMP: 125
SALES (corp-wide): 214.7MM **Privately
Held**
WEB: www.hardigg.com
SIC: 3599 Machine shop, jobbing & repair
HQ: Hardigg Industries, Inc.
147 N Main St
South Deerfield MA 01373
413 665-2163

(G-1938)
HARTLEY J COMPANY INC
101 N National Rd (47201-7848)
P.O. Box 423 (47202-0423)
PHONE...................................812 376-9708
Fax: 812 376-9996
Brent S Hartley, *President*
EMP: 5 EST: 1937
SQ FT: 10,000
SALES (est): 390K **Privately Held**
WEB: www.jhartleyco.com
SIC: 2499 2759 Decorative wood & wood-
work; letterpress printing; trading stamps:
printing

(G-1939)
HITARTH LLC
1609 Cottage Ave Ste G (47201-1200)
PHONE...................................812 372-1744
Vijender Kumar, *Principal*
EMP: 2
SALES (est): 98.6K **Privately Held**
SIC: 3599 Industrial machinery

(G-1940)
**HOME NEWS ENTERPRISES
LLC**
Republic Newspaper
3330 W International Ct (47201-3005)
PHONE...................................812 342-1056
Fax: 812 342-1238
EMP: 50
SALES (corp-wide): 60.8MM **Privately
Held**
SIC: 2711 2752 Newspapers-
Publishing/Printing Lithographic Commer-
cial Printing
PA: Home News Enterprises, L.L.C.
333 2nd St
Columbus IN 47201
800 876-7811

(G-1941)
**HOOSIER METAL PRODUCTS
INC**
1402 Union St (47201-8013)
P.O. Box 28 (47202-0028)
PHONE...................................812 372-5151
Fax: 812 372-5151
EMP: 5
SQ FT: 4,000
SALES (est): 340K **Privately Held**
SIC: 3312 Mfg Steel Forgings

(G-1942)
HOOSIER TOOL & DIE CO INC
Also Called: H T D
2860 N National Rd Ste B (47201-3746)
PHONE...................................812 376-8286
Fax: 812 376-9737
Robert Bosar, *President*
Peter Ariens, *Treasurer*
◆ EMP: 55 EST: 1949
SQ FT: 20,000
SALES: 10MM **Privately Held**
SIC: 3545 3544 Machine tool accessories;
special dies, tools, jigs & fixtures

(G-1943)
HORN PRE-CAST INC
895 Jonesville Rd (47201-7548)
P.O. Box 566 (47202-0566)
PHONE...................................812 372-4458
Fax: 812 372-4458
Harry E Horn, *President*
Harry Horn, *President*
Steve Horn, *Vice Pres*
EMP: 10 EST: 1968
SQ FT: 10,000
SALES (est): 1.6MM
SALES (est): (corp-wide): 5.2MM **Privately
Held**
SIC: 3272 Precast terrazo or concrete
products
PA: Devening Block Inc
895 Jonesville Rd
Columbus IN 47201
812 372-4458

(G-1944)
**IMPACT FORGE GROUP LLC
(DH)**
2805 Norcross Dr (47201-4911)
P.O. Box 1847 (47202-1847)
PHONE...................................812 342-4437
Fax: 812 342-4553
George Thanopolous, *CEO*
Dennis Potter, *Vice Pres*
Michael Keslar, *Admin Sec*
▲ EMP: 1
SALES (est): 180.1MM
SALES (corp-wide): 6.2B **Publicly Held**
SIC: 3462 3463 Iron & steel forgings; non-
ferrous forgings
HQ: Forging Holdings, Llc
1 Dauch Dr
Detroit MI 48211
313 758-2000

(G-1945)
IMPACT FORGE GROUP LLC
2705 Norcross Dr (47201-4910)
PHONE...................................812 342-5527
Andrew Bannoy, *Controller*
EMP: 150
SALES (corp-wide): 6.2B **Publicly Held**
SIC: 3462 Iron & steel forgings
HQ: Impact Forge Group, Llc
2805 Norcross Dr
Columbus IN 47201
812 342-4437

(G-1946)
INDIANA PRECAST INC
895 Jonesville Rd (47201-7548)
PHONE...................................812 372-7771
Keith Bauer, *President*
EMP: 20 EST: 2016
SQ FT: 1,000
SALES (est): 690.8K **Privately Held**
SIC: 3272 Precast terrazo or concrete
products

(G-1947)
**INDIANA RESEARCH INSTITUTE
(PA)**
4571 N Long Rd (47203-9012)
PHONE...................................812 378-4221
Fax: 812 378-5361
Sue Jane Chang, *President*
Benjamin Yen, *Managing Dir*
▲ EMP: 30
SALES (est): 5.1MM **Privately Held**
SIC: 3825 8734 3599 Engine electrical
test equipment; testing laboratories; ma-
chine & other job shop work

(G-1948)
INDIANA RESEARCH INSTITUTE
Also Called: AEC America
1402 Hutchins Ave (47201-5630)
P.O. Box 1815 (47202-1815)
PHONE...................................812 378-5363
Sue Jane Chang, *President*
EMP: 15 **Privately Held**
SIC: 3825 4225 3694 3714 Engine elec-
trical test equipment; general warehous-
ing & storage; engine electrical
equipment; rebuilding engines & trans-
missions, factory basis
PA: Indiana Research Institute
4571 N Long Rd
Columbus IN 47203

(G-1949)
ITSUWA USA LLC
1349 Arcadia Dr (47201-8445)
PHONE...................................812 375-0323
Akira Hayashi, *Principal*
George Chadwell, *Prdtn Mgr*
Shiori Goto, *QC Mgr*
Daniel Gossett, *Manager*
▲ EMP: 14
SALES (est): 1.9MM **Privately Held**
SIC: 3479 Coating of metals & formed
products

(G-1950)
JD METAL CONCEPTS INC
1522 Bridle Way Blvd (47201-8450)
PHONE...................................812 342-9111
Dwayne Back, *Principal*
EMP: 2
SALES (est): 164.7K **Privately Held**
SIC: 3441 Fabricated structural metal

(G-1951)
JEM PRINTING INC
Also Called: PIP Printing
808 3rd St Ste C (47201-2403)
PHONE...................................812 376-9264
Fax: 812 376-9265
Jeanne G Lucas, *President*
Mark A Lucas, *Treasurer*
EMP: 2 EST: 2007
SALES (est): 258.9K **Privately Held**
SIC: 2752 Commercial printing, offset

(G-1952)
**JOHNSON EH CONSTRUCTION
LLC**
8079 Grandview Rd (47201-3336)
PHONE...................................812 344-8450
Even Johnson,
Megan Johnson,
EMP: 2
SALES (est): 156.9K **Privately Held**
SIC: 1771 1522 1389 Flooring contractor;
hotel/motel & multi-family home construc-
tion; construction, repair & dismantling
services

(G-1953)
JOHNSON MATERIALS
450 Franklin St (47201-6753)
PHONE...................................812 373-9044
EMP: 5
SALES (est): 294.1K **Privately Held**
SIC: 1429 Crushed/Broken Stone

(G-1954)
K J PALLETS
10110 S 500 W (47201-4852)
PHONE...................................812 342-6476
EMP: 3 EST: 2010
SALES (est): 130K **Privately Held**
SIC: 2448 Mfg Wood Pallets/Skids

(G-1955)
KOUSEI USA INC
2396 Norcross Dr (47201-8844)
PHONE...................................812 373-7315
Atsuo Suga, *President*
EMP: 6
SALES (est): 368.2K **Privately Held**
SIC: 3465 Body parts, automobile:
stamped metal

(G-1956)
KUSTOM KILMS LLC
2410 Chestnut St (47201-4271)
PHONE...................................317 512-5813
Robert Lebow, *Partner*
Joe Houseberger,
EMP: 5
SALES (est): 301.1K **Privately Held**
SIC: 2491 Wood preserving

(G-1957)
**LEAR MACHINING & WATERJET
INC**
4056 N Long Rd (47203-9057)
P.O. Box 403 (47202-0403)
PHONE...................................812 418-8111
Ron L Long, *President*
James E Long, *Principal*
Andrew A L Long, *Vice Pres*
EMP: 6

GEOGRAPHIC

SALES: 700K **Privately Held**
SIC: 3599 Machine shop, jobbing & repair

(G-1958)
LEES READY-MIX & TRUCKING INC
Also Called: Lee's Ready-Mix
1460 Blessing Rd (47201)
PHONE.................................812 372-1800
Mark Hensley, *Branch Mgr*
EMP: 15
SALES (corp-wide): 9.7MM **Privately Held**
SIC: 3273 4212 1442 Ready-mixed concrete; light haulage & cartage, local; construction sand & gravel
PA: Lees Ready-Mix & Trucking Inc.
1100 W Jfk Dr
North Vernon IN 47265
812 346-9767

(G-1959)
LHP SOFTWARE LLC
Also Called: Lhp Engineering Solutions
1888 Poshard Dr (47203-1897)
PHONE.................................812 373-0870
Landon Stovall, *Manager*
EMP: 137
SALES (corp-wide): 34.9MM **Privately Held**
SIC: 7372 Prepackaged software
PA: Lhp Software Llc
305 Franklin St
Columbus IN 47201
812 373-0870

(G-1960)
LHP SOFTWARE LLC (PA)
Also Called: Lhp Engineering Solutions
305 Franklin St (47201-6731)
PHONE.................................812 373-0870
Fax: 812 373-0875
Richard Crossley, *President*
Aaron Hartman, *Business Mgr*
Joe Skowronek, *Business Mgr*
Jean Hou, *COO*
Joe Shanbaum, *Vice Pres*
EMP: 95
SQ FT: 1,600
SALES (est): 34.9MM **Privately Held**
WEB: www.lhpsoftware.com
SIC: 7371 3999 Computer software development; stage hardware & equipment, except lighting

(G-1961)
LIBERTY ADVANCE MACHINE INC
3210 Scott Dr (47201-4046)
P.O. Box 2247 (47202-2247)
PHONE.................................812 372-1010
Fax: 812 372-6113
Larry Karen Durnil, *President*
Jason Patrick, *Supervisor*
EMP: 3
SQ FT: 5,000
SALES (est): 325K **Privately Held**
SIC: 3728 Aircraft body assemblies & parts

(G-1962)
LINDAL NORTH AMERICA INC
6010 S International Dr (47201-3046)
PHONE.................................812 657-7142
Phil Lever, *President*
Matthias Woelk, *Vice Pres*
◆ EMP: 75
SQ FT: 100,000
SALES: 23MM **Privately Held**
SIC: 3565 Packaging machinery
HQ: Lindal Group Holding Gmbh
Brandstwiete 1
Hamburg
402 000-750

(G-1963)
LLC BLACK JEWELL
Also Called: Black Jewell Popcorn
417 Washington St (47201-6757)
PHONE.................................800 948-2302
Barry Johnson,
EMP: 3
SALES (est): 163.8K **Privately Held**
SIC: 2099 Popcorn, packaged: except already popped

(G-1964)
LLC TIPTON MILLS
835 S Mapleton St (47201-7359)
PHONE.........................716 825-4422
Timothy J Sheehy, *President*
EMP: 2
SALES (est): 400K
SALES (corp-wide): 3.2MM **Privately Held**
SIC: 2066 Chocolate & cocoa products
PA: Buffalo Blends, Inc.
1400 William St
Buffalo NY 14206
716 825-4422

(G-1965)
LUCAS CUSTOM INSTRUMENTS
13360 W Becks Grove Rd (47201-7598)
P.O. Box 1404 (47202-1404)
PHONE.................................812 342-3093
Randy Lucas, *Owner*
EMP: 2
SALES (est): 75K **Privately Held**
SIC: 3931 Guitars & parts, electric & non-electric

(G-1966)
MA METAL CO INC
2860 N National Rd (47201-3746)
PHONE.................................812 526-2666
Peter Ariens, *CEO*
Robert Bosar, *President*
Charlene Mitchell, *Accounting Mgr*
Tim Meier, *Manager*
EMP: 35 EST: 1946
SQ FT: 56,000
SALES: 13MM **Privately Held**
WEB: www.mametal.com
SIC: 3469 Stamping metal for the trade

(G-1967)
MARIAH FOODS CORP
Also Called: Peer Foods
1333 Indiana Ave (47201-6986)
P.O. Box 548 (47202-0548)
PHONE.................................812 378-3366
Larry O Connell, *President*
Paul Wolff, *Purch Mgr*
Donna Recupido, *Treasurer*
Sue Barringer, *Credit Mgr*
Bill Jones, *Human Res Dir*
▲ EMP: 150
SALES (est): 30.2MM
SALES (corp-wide): 33.9MM **Privately Held**
SIC: 2011 Meat packing plants
PA: Peer Foods Group, Inc.
1200 W 35th St Fl 3
Chicago IL 60609
773 927-1440

(G-1968)
MARK & JESSIES FIREWORK SHACK
3515 Hollowell St (47201-7467)
PHONE.................................812 372-3855
EMP: 2
SALES (est): 122.6K **Privately Held**
SIC: 2899 Fireworks

(G-1969)
MARK MURRAY
Also Called: Audio Source
3475 Commerce Dr (47201-2203)
PHONE.................................812 372-8390
Mark Murray, *Owner*
EMP: 4
SALES (est): 1MM **Privately Held**
SIC: 3651 Home entertainment equipment, electronic

(G-1970)
MDL MOLD DIE COMPONENTS INC
4572 N Long Rd (47203-9055)
PHONE.................................812 373-0021
Arthur Beck, *President*
Owen Gall, *Principal*
▲ EMP: 4
SALES (est): 350K **Privately Held**
WEB: www.bencodirect.com
SIC: 3544 Special dies & tools

(G-1971)
MESHBERGER STONE INC
3415 S 650 E (47203-9556)
PHONE.................................812 579-5241
Fax: 317 579-5283
Robert J Simpson, *Ch of Bd*
James C Fehsenfeld, *President*
Mike Hyden, *Superintendent*
John P Vercruysse, *CFO*
Lewis L Davis, *Admin Sec*
EMP: 17 EST: 1937
SQ FT: 4,000
SALES (est): 1.2MM **Privately Held**
SIC: 1422 3274 Limestones, ground; lime

(G-1972)
METAL FABRICATED PRODUCTS CO
925 S Marr Rd (47201-7439)
PHONE.................................812 372-7430
Tom Keith Johnson, *President*
EMP: 2
SQ FT: 2,000
SALES (est): 229.3K **Privately Held**
SIC: 3599 Machine shop, jobbing & repair

(G-1973)
MI TIERRA
1461 Central Ave (47201-5303)
PHONE.................................812 376-0668
Jorge Delgadillo, *Owner*
EMP: 3
SALES (est): 234.8K **Privately Held**
SIC: 2099 5141 5411 5812 Food preparations; groceries, general line; grocery stores; eating places

(G-1974)
MIK MOCHA PRINTS LLC
4637 Clairmont Dr (47203-4763)
PHONE.................................812 376-8891
Mikala Lomax, *Principal*
EMP: 2
SALES (est): 83.9K **Privately Held**
SIC: 2752 Commercial printing, lithographic

(G-1975)
MILESTONE CONTRACTORS LP
3410 S 650 E (47203-9554)
P.O. Box 3004 (47202-3004)
PHONE.................................812 579-5248
Fax: 812 579-6703
Ted Lucas, *President*
Tom Suding, *Plant Mgr*
Mark Thompson, *Human Res Dir*
Cindy Bertram, *Executive Asst*
EMP: 35
SALES (est): 4.5MM
SALES (corp-wide): 186MM **Privately Held**
WEB: www.milestonelp.com
SIC: 1611 1623 1622 2951 Highway & street paving contractor; water, sewer & utility lines; bridge construction; asphalt paving mixtures & blocks; concrete work
PA: Milestone Contractors, Lp
5950 S Belmont Ave
Indianapolis IN 46217
317 788-6885

(G-1976)
MORGAN ADHESIVES COMPANY LLC
Also Called: Mactac
2576 Norcross Dr (47201-3808)
PHONE.................................812 342-2004
Fax: 812 341-2609
Dennis Faltynski, *Manager*
EMP: 100
SALES (corp-wide): 2.3B **Privately Held**
WEB: www.mactac.com
SIC: 2891 3565 2672 Adhesives & sealants; packaging machinery; coated & laminated paper
HQ: Morgan Adhesives Company, Llc
4560 Darrow Rd
Stow OH 44224
330 688-1111

(G-1977)
MOVIE POSTER PRINT
4114 Washington St (47203-1135)
PHONE.................................812 679-7301
Ryan Walton, *Principal*

EMP: 2
SALES (est): 101.4K **Privately Held**
SIC: 2752 Commercial printing, lithographic

(G-1978)
NAGAKURA ENGRG WORKS CO INC
Also Called: N.E.W. Indiana Co.,
630 S Mapleton St (47201-7360)
PHONE.................................812 375-1382
Fax: 812 375-1385
Shuji Nagakura, *President*
Michael Bierlein, *Plant Mgr*
Gary Moore, *Production*
Kristina Day, *Human Res Mgr*
Kozo Nagakura, *Admin Sec*
▲ EMP: 169
SQ FT: 37,500
SALES (est): 27.7MM
SALES (corp-wide): 159.9MM **Privately Held**
WEB: www.nagakurausa.com
SIC: 3714 3462 Motor vehicle transmissions, drive assemblies & parts; iron & steel forgings
PA: Nagakura Mfg.Co.,Ltd.
606, Momozomo
Numazu SZO 410-0
559 671-121

(G-1979)
NAVSPAR INDUSTRIES LLC
1671 Wrenwood Dr (47201-8458)
PHONE.................................812 344-1476
EMP: 2
SALES (est): 96K **Privately Held**
SIC: 3999 Mfg Misc Products

(G-1980)
NEWSOM INDUSTRIES INC
1919 15th St (47201-5301)
PHONE.................................812 372-2844
Fax: 812 375-9255
Jerry L Newsom, *President*
Janet Thompson, *Admin Sec*
EMP: 13 EST: 1950
SQ FT: 8,000
SALES (est): 980K **Privately Held**
WEB: www.newsomindustries.com
SIC: 3451 Screw machine products

(G-1981)
NOBLITT INTERNATIONAL CORP
Also Called: Noblitt Fabricating
4735 N Indianapolis Rd (47203-9440)
P.O. Box 646 (47202-0646)
PHONE.................................812 372-9969
Fax: 812 372-9960
Curt Aton, *President*
EMP: 30 EST: 2008
SALES (est): 7.8MM **Privately Held**
SIC: 3363 Aluminum die-castings

(G-1982)
NTN DRIVESHAFT INC
8251 S International Dr (47201-9329)
PHONE.................................812 342-7000
Fax: 812 342-1155
Tohru Tomiyama, *President*
Nobuo Satoh, *President*
Hidekazu Asaba, *Corp Secy*
Barry Parkhurst, *VP Admin*
Doug Evers, *Vice Pres*
▲ EMP: 1000
SQ FT: 1,200,000
SALES (est): 228.8MM
SALES (corp-wide): 6.9B **Privately Held**
WEB: www.ntndriveshaft.com
SIC: 3714 Motor vehicle parts & accessories
HQ: Ntn Usa Corporation
1600 Bishop Ct
Mount Prospect IL 60056
847 298-4652

(G-1983)
NUGENT SAND COMPANY
5205 W State Road 46 (47201-8725)
P.O. Box 802 (47202-0802)
PHONE.................................812 372-7508
Fax: 812 378-0905
Tim Rose, *Manager*
EMP: 8

▲ = Import ▼=Export
◆ =Import/Export

SALES (corp-wide): 77.5MM **Privately Held**
WEB: www.nugentsand.com
SIC: **1442** Gravel & pebble mining; gravel mining
PA: Nugent Sand Company
1833 River Rd
Louisville KY 40206
502 584-0158

(G-1984)
OESTERLING CHIMNEY SWEEP INC
2360 N National Rd (47201-3732)
PHONE....................................812 372-3512
Daina Ross, *Manager*
EMP: 2
SALES (corp-wide): 803.1K **Privately Held**
SIC: **1741** 3433 Chimney construction & maintenance; stoves, wood & coal burning
PA: Oesterling Chimney Sweep Inc
209 N Walnut St
Batesville IN 47006
812 934-3512

(G-1985)
OLD COPPER STILL DISTLG CO LLC
Also Called: Bear Wallow Distillery
885 Baywood Ct (47201-9747)
PHONE....................................812 342-0765
Susan M Spagnuolo, *Principal*
Susan Spagnuolo, *Principal*
EMP: 5
SALES (est): 518.4K **Privately Held**
SIC: **2869** Grain alcohol, industrial

(G-1986)
ORKA TECHNOLOGIES LLC
2182 W 500 N (47201-9167)
PHONE....................................812 378-9842
Karen Orisich, *President*
EMP: 2
SALES (est): 143.1K **Privately Held**
SIC: **3648** Flashlights

(G-1987)
OSR INC
7715 S International Dr (47201-9329)
PHONE....................................812 342-7642
Fax: 812 342-6660
Shinichi Kimura, *President*
Kenny Canfield, *Project Mgr*
▲ EMP: 10
SALES (est): 2MM
SALES (corp-wide): 158.4MM **Privately Held**
SIC: **3429** Manufactured hardware (general)
PA: Owari Precise Products Co., Ltd.
3-16-85, Yada, Higashi-Ku
Nagoya AIC 461-0
527 217-131

(G-1988)
PACE TOOL AND ENGINEERING INC
2675 Grissom St (47203-1870)
PHONE....................................812 373-9885
Todd Burbrink, *President*
Don Coombs, *Vice Pres*
Mark Thomson, *Treasurer*
EMP: 5
SQ FT: 3,000
SALES: 350K **Privately Held**
WEB: www.pacetool.com
SIC: **3312** Tool & die steel

(G-1989)
PACKAGING CORPORATION AMERICA
Also Called: PCA
3460 Commerce Dr (47201-2204)
PHONE....................................812 376-9301
Fax: 812 376-9891
Bob Haddad, *Mfg Mgr*
Tom Neuman, *Safety Mgr*
Lali Kapanadze, *Human Resources*
Bob Arthur, *Sales Dir*
Denise Little, *Cust Mgr*
EMP: 300

SALES (corp-wide): 6.4B **Publicly Held**
SIC: **2653** Boxes, corrugated: made from purchased materials
PA: Packaging Corporation Of America
1955 W Field Ct
Lake Forest IL 60045
847 482-3000

(G-1990)
PAMELA S TAULMAN
Also Called: Indiana Custom Machining
982 S Marr Rd (47201-7440)
PHONE....................................812 378-5008
Fax: 812 342-3317
Marcus Taulman, *Owner*
Pamela Taulman, *Office Mgr*
EMP: 17
SQ FT: 18,000
SALES: 1.6MM **Privately Held**
SIC: **3599** Machine shop, jobbing & repair

(G-1991)
PCA SUTHERN IND CORRUGATED LLC
3460 Commerce Dr (47201-2204)
PHONE....................................812 376-9301
Thomas A Hassfurther,
EMP: 6
SALES (est): 212.1K
SALES (corp-wide): 6.4B **Publicly Held**
SIC: **2653** Boxes, corrugated: made from purchased materials
PA: Packaging Corporation Of America
1955 W Field Ct
Lake Forest IL 60045
847 482-3000

(G-1992)
PENTZER PRINTING INC
4505 Kelly St (47203-1752)
PHONE....................................812 372-2896
Fax: 812 372-2901
Rosemarie L Settle, *CEO*
Pentzer A Samuel, *President*
John E Settle, *President*
Tom O Vojovich, *Corp Secy*
EMP: 14 EST: 1902
SQ FT: 10,200
SALES (est): 3.9MM **Privately Held**
WEB: www.pentzerprinting.com
SIC: **2752** 2759 Commercial printing, offset; commercial printing

(G-1993)
PERMAWICK COMPANY INC
3110 Permawick Dr (47201-7468)
PHONE....................................812 376-0703
Dennis Sabau, *Enginr/R&D Mgr*
EMP: 10
SALES (est): 1.8MM
SALES (corp-wide): 3.4MM **Privately Held**
WEB: www.permawick.com
SIC: **2992** 2241 Lubricating oils & greases; wicking
PA: Permawick Company, Inc.
255 E Brown St Ste 100
Birmingham MI 48009
248 433-3500

(G-1994)
PHILLIPS COMPANY INC
Also Called: Pdi
6330 E 100 S (47201-9786)
P.O. Box 611 (47202-0611)
PHONE....................................812 378-3797
Fax: 812 378-5941
Valerie A Phillips, *Owner*
Sam Phillips, *Co-Founder*
Jack Sparks, *Business Mgr*
▲ EMP: 52
SQ FT: 9,600
SALES (est): 10.8MM **Privately Held**
SIC: **3714** Motor vehicle parts & accessories

(G-1995)
PHOENIX ASSEMBLY INDIANA LLC
6200 S International Dr (47201-3034)
PHONE....................................317 884-3600
Tom Beck, *Manager*
▲ EMP: 32 EST: 2010

SALES (est): 3.1MM **Privately Held**
SIC: **3569** 4225 4731 8741 Assembly machines, non-metalworking; general warehousing; freight transportation arrangement; industrial management
HQ: Phoenix Assembly, Llc
164 S Park Blvd
Greenwood IN 46143
317 884-3600

(G-1996)
PMG INDIANA LLC (DH)
1751 Arcadia Dr (47201-8712)
PHONE....................................812 379-4606
Dr Michael Krehl, *CEO*
John Von ARX, *President*
Ronald Krause, *Principal*
Robert Pfau, *Principal*
Larry Van Epps, *Exec VP*
▲ EMP: 200
SQ FT: 144,000
SALES (est): 38.9MM **Privately Held**
SIC: **3714** Motor vehicle engines & parts; motor vehicle transmissions, drive assemblies & parts
HQ: Plansee Group Service Gmbh
Metallwerk Plansee-StraBe 71
Reutte 6600
567 260-00

(G-1997)
POWER DRIVES INC
Also Called: Pdi
6077 Acorn Dr (47201-8446)
PHONE....................................812 344-4351
Lou Panvica, *President*
EMP: 2
SALES (est): 123.6K **Privately Held**
SIC: **5084** 3569 Hydraulic systems equipment & supplies; general industrial machinery

(G-1998)
POWER HOUSE BREWING CO
12377 W 50 S (47201-9283)
PHONE....................................812 343-1302
Douglas Memering, *Principal*
EMP: 8
SALES (est): 706.9K **Privately Held**
SIC: **2082** Malt beverages

(G-1999)
PRECISE TOOLING SOLUTIONS INC
Also Called: Precise Mold and Plate
3150 Scott Dr (47201-4045)
PHONE....................................812 378-0247
Fax: 812 378-0431
Donald Dumoulin, *CEO*
Kenny Hall, *Purch Mgr*
▲ EMP: 52
SQ FT: 30,000
SALES (est): 11.9MM **Privately Held**
WEB: www.precisemold.com
SIC: **3544** Industrial molds

(G-2000)
PRESTIGE PRINTING INC
Also Called: You Can Do It Printer
1307 12th St (47201-5604)
PHONE....................................812 372-2500
Fax: 812 372-2793
Frank Miller, *President*
Jenny Miller, *Corp Secy*
Rachel Yancer, *Graphic Designe*
EMP: 11
SQ FT: 7,000
SALES (est): 1.3MM **Privately Held**
WEB: www.prestigeprintingcando.biz
SIC: **2752** Commercial printing, offset

(G-2001)
PROGRESSIVE TOOL & MACHINE
241 Coovert St (47201-7237)
PHONE....................................812 346-1837
Fax: 812 372-1814
Norman Barker, *President*
Scott Barker, *Vice Pres*
EMP: 8
SQ FT: 11,200
SALES: 1MM **Privately Held**
SIC: **3544** 3545 Special dies & tools; machine tool accessories

(G-2002)
PYRAMID PAPER PRODUCTS INC
725 S Mapleton St (47201-7354)
PHONE....................................812 372-0288
Fax: 812 372-0298
Tom Binkowski, *President*
Donald Smith, *Corp Secy*
Bart Fortner, *Project Mgr*
Maritza Meihls, *Project Mgr*
EMP: 40
SQ FT: 40,000
SALES (est): 10.4MM **Privately Held**
SIC: **2653** 3086 Boxes, corrugated: made from purchased materials; packaging & shipping materials, foamed plastic

(G-2003)
QUALITY MACHINE & TOOL WORKS
1201 Michigan Ave (47201-5635)
PHONE....................................812 379-2660
Fax: 812 379-2669
William E Ehrensberger, *President*
Patrick Harrell, *President*
Kippe Detty, *Vice Pres*
Billy Mullins, *Vice Pres*
Gary Carter, *QC Mgr*
▲ EMP: 63 EST: 1951
SQ FT: 90,000
SALES (est): 11.9MM **Privately Held**
WEB: www.qmtw.net
SIC: **3599** Machine shop, jobbing & repair

(G-2004)
QUALTRONICS LLC
4775 Progress Dr (47201-2853)
PHONE....................................812 375-8880
Fax: 812 375-8882
Danielle Short, *Accounts Mgr*
Rob Daly, *Mng Member*
Dennis Albert,
Chris Breeden,
Janice Daly,
EMP: 25
SALES (est): 5.9MM **Privately Held**
WEB: www.qualtronicsllc.com
SIC: **3694** 7389 Harness wiring sets, internal combustion engines;

(G-2005)
QUARTERLY GROUP
5020 Somerset Ln (47201-3129)
PHONE....................................812 526-5600
Torn Thornburg, *Treasurer*
EMP: 2
SALES: 158K **Privately Held**
SIC: **2721** Periodicals

(G-2006)
REPUBLIC INC
333 2nd St (47201-6795)
PHONE....................................812 342-8028
Fax: 812 372-1634
Isaac M Brown, *Owner*
Neil Thompson, *Principal*
Mike Wolanin, *Editor*
EMP: 23
SALES (est): 1.9MM **Privately Held**
WEB: www.republicincorporated.com
SIC: **2711** Commercial printing & newspaper publishing combined; newspapers, publishing & printing

(G-2007)
RICHARD YOUNG
10477 E 600 N (47203-9244)
PHONE....................................812 546-5208
Richard Young, *Owner*
EMP: 2
SALES (est): 158.3K **Privately Held**
SIC: **3523** Driers (farm): grain, hay & seed

(G-2008)
RICHARDSON MOLDING LLC (PA)
2405 Norcross Dr (47201-8844)
PHONE....................................812 342-0139
Steve Dyer, *CEO*
Keith Toll, *Sales Staff*
Mary Hall, *Manager*
Michelle Silence, *Manager*
Daryle Smith, *Executive*
▼ EMP: 107
SQ FT: 150,000

SALES (est): 75.2MM **Privately Held**
SIC: 3089 Pallets, plastic; injection molding of plastics

(G-2009)
RIGHTWAY FASTENERS INC
Also Called: RFI
7945 S International Dr (47201-9329)
PHONE....................................812 342-2700
Fax: 812 342-2720
Yuta Takashima, *President*
Yasutaka Hasegawa, *President*
Ron Miller, *General Mgr*
Satoshi Furuto, *Vice Pres*
Philip Karshner, *Purch Mgr*
▲ **EMP:** 200
SQ FT: 350,000
SALES (est): 38.5MM
SALES (corp-wide): 9.3MM **Privately Held**
WEB: www.rfiusa.com
SIC: 3965 3479 Fasteners; painting, coating & hot dipping
PA: Meido Tekko, K.K.
　　4-5, Sangencho
　　Toyota AIC 471-0
　　565 310-330

(G-2010)
SABIC INNOVATIVE PLAS US LLC
945 S Marr Rd (47201-7439)
PHONE....................................812 372-0197
John Curvey, *Manager*
EMP: 100 **Privately Held**
SIC: 2821 3083 Molding compounds, plastics; laminated plastics plate & sheet
HQ: Sabic Innovative Plastics Us Llc
　　2500 City W Blvd Ste 100
　　Houston TX 77042

(G-2011)
SBS CYBERMETRIX INC
635 S Mapleton St (47201-7361)
PHONE....................................812 378-7960
Garrett Mc Cormick, *Branch Mgr*
EMP: 3
SALES (corp-wide): 6.3B **Privately Held**
SIC: 7371 3825 3625 8711 Computer software development; analog-digital converters, electronic instrumentation type; motor controls, electric; consulting engineer
HQ: Sgs Cybermetrix, Inc.
　　2860 N National Rd A
　　Columbus IN 47201

(G-2012)
SETSER FABRICATING LLC
15601 E 225 N (47203-9609)
PHONE....................................812 546-2169
Jason A Setser, *Mng Member*
EMP: 7
SALES (est): 952K **Privately Held**
SIC: 2381 7389 Fabric dress & work gloves;

(G-2013)
SGS CYBERMETRIX INC (HQ)
2860 N National Rd A (47201-3746)
PHONE....................................800 713-1203
Fax: 812 378-3393
Christine Mullholand, *CEO*
Peter Palladino, *President*
David Bartels, *Vice Pres*
Bruce Thomason, *Chief Engr*
Curt Fiene, *Engineer*
EMP: 3
SALES (est): 11.3MM
SALES (corp-wide): 6.3B **Privately Held**
WEB: www.cybermetrix.com
SIC: 7371 3825 3625 8711 Computer software development; computer software systems analysis & design, custom; analog-digital converters, electronic instrumentation type; motor controls, electric; electric controls & control accessories, industrial; consulting engineer; professional engineer
PA: Fenaco Genossenschaft
　　Erlachstrasse 5
　　Bern BE 3012
　　584 340-000

(G-2014)
SIGN ARAMA
3192 Washington St (47201-2942)
PHONE....................................812 657-7449
Barry Davis, *CEO*
EMP: 2 **EST:** 2012
SALES (est): 159.4K **Privately Held**
SIC: 3993 Signs & advertising specialties

(G-2015)
SIMMONS WINERY & FARM MARKET
8111 E 450 N (47203-8106)
PHONE....................................812 546-0091
David Simmons, *President*
Brenda Simmons, *Treasurer*
EMP: 2
SALES (est): 232.6K **Privately Held**
SIC: 2084 Wines

(G-2016)
STERLING INDUSTRIES INC
4015 N Long Rd (47203-9057)
PHONE....................................812 376-6560
Fax: 812 376-6538
Larry Sterling, *President*
Perry Hayes, *Vice Pres*
Carol Sterling, *Treasurer*
EMP: 25
SQ FT: 20,000
SALES (est): 5.9MM **Privately Held**
WEB: www.sterlingindustriesusa.com
SIC: 3714 Motor vehicle engines & parts

(G-2017)
SUNRIGHT AMERICA INC
6205 S International Dr (47201-3034)
PHONE....................................812 342-3430
Fax: 812 342-3190
Yoshi Ota, *President*
Toshiaki Takeuchi, *Exec VP*
Shannon Rudicel, *Accounting Mgr*
Jon Voelz, *Sales Mgr*
Kenta Takagi, *Sales Staff*
▲ **EMP:** 150
SQ FT: 170,000
SALES (est): 33.6MM
SALES (corp-wide): 211.7MM **Privately Held**
WEB: www.sunrightamerica.com
SIC: 3452 Bolts, nuts, rivets & washers
PA: Sugiura Seisakusho Co.,Ltd.
　　22, Miyakoshi, Terazucho
　　Nishio AIC 444-0
　　563 596-505

(G-2018)
SUPERIOR LAYOUT
1417 Chestnut St (47201-8023)
P.O. Box 4, Hope (47246-0004)
PHONE....................................812 371-1709
Fax: 812 372-0024
Jerry Wilson, *Principal*
EMP: 2 **EST:** 2010
SALES (est): 183.8K **Privately Held**
SIC: 3441 Fabricated structural metal

(G-2019)
SWI
3475 W International Ct (47201-3022)
PHONE....................................812 342-2409
Mitch Arima, *Manager*
EMP: 4
SALES (est): 291K **Privately Held**
SIC: 3312 Stainless steel

(G-2020)
TECHCOM INC
4630 Progress Dr (47201-7825)
PHONE....................................812 372-0960
Fax: 812 373-0960
Bud Mantyla, *Manager*
EMP: 10
SALES (corp-wide): 4.2MM **Privately Held**
WEB: www.techcom.com
SIC: 7336 3999 Graphic arts & related design; models, general, except toy
PA: Techcom, Inc.
　　7515 Company Dr Ste A
　　Indianapolis IN 46237
　　317 865-2530

(G-2021)
TIPTON MILLS FOODS LLC
835 S Mapleton St (47201-7359)
PHONE....................................812 372-0900
David M Harding, *President*
EMP: 8
SALES (est): 846K **Privately Held**
SIC: 2099 Food preparations

(G-2022)
TOOL DYNAMICS LLC
835 S Marr Rd (47201-7437)
PHONE....................................812 379-4243
Fax: 812 379-4243
Todd Schulz, *Owner*
Jeff Spann, *Production*
Shane Hankins, *Sales Engr*
Joe Twerdi, *Sales Engr*
Rebecca Andersen, *Sales Staff*
EMP: 2
SQ FT: 2,500
SALES (est): 357K **Privately Held**
WEB: www.tdynamics1.com
SIC: 3398 Metal heat treating

(G-2023)
TOUCHDOWN MACHINING INC
432 S Mapleton St (47201-7327)
PHONE....................................812 378-0300
Fax: 812 378-0388
Michael T Moore, *President*
Kristine R Moore, *Admin Sec*
EMP: 7
SALES (est): 1.4MM **Privately Held**
SIC: 3599 Machine shop, jobbing & repair; machine & other job shop work

(G-2024)
TOYOTA INDUSTRIAL EQP MFG INC (DH)
Also Called: Tiem
5555 Inwood Dr (47201-9755)
P.O. Box 2487 (47202-2487)
PHONE....................................812 342-0060
Fax: 812 342-1628
Yoshimitsu Ogihara, *President*
Susumu Toyoda, *COO*
Koyu Suzuki, *Exec VP*
Marv Johnson, *Vice Pres*
Bruce Nolting, *Vice Pres*
◆ **EMP:** 277
SQ FT: 600,000
SALES (est): 238.7MM
SALES (corp-wide): 18.8B **Privately Held**
SIC: 3537 Forklift trucks
HQ: Toyota Industries North America, Inc.
　　3030 Barker Dr
　　Columbus IN 47201
　　812 341-3810

(G-2025)
TOYOTA INDUSTRIES N AMER INC (HQ)
3030 Barker Dr (47201-9611)
PHONE....................................812 341-3810
Fax: 812 341-3827
Yoshimitsu Ogihara, *President*
Tom Depalma, *Vice Pres*
Julie Kemp, *Production*
James Brink, *Buyer*
Caleb Alvey, *Engineer*
◆ **EMP:** 259
SALES (est): 1.5B
SALES (corp-wide): 18.8B **Privately Held**
SIC: 3585 5084 Air conditioning, motor vehicle; lift trucks & parts
PA: Toyota Industries Corporation
　　2-1, Toyodacho
　　Kariya AIC 448-0
　　566 222-511

(G-2026)
TWB OF INDIANA
3030 Barker Dr (47201-9611)
PHONE....................................812 342-6000
Gene Jolley, *Principal*
EMP: 2
SALES (est): 87.2K **Privately Held**
SIC: 3714 Motor vehicle parts & accessories

(G-2027)
UNIQUE PRODUCTS
3129 25th St (47203-2436)
PHONE....................................812 376-8887

Jo Ann Swank, *President*
EMP: 2 **EST:** 1992
SQ FT: 2,000
SALES (est): 210.9K **Privately Held**
WEB: www.uniqueinc.com
SIC: 3949 Billiard & pool equipment & supplies, general

(G-2028)
UNITED INDUSTRIAL & WLDG LLC
Also Called: Uiw Supply
8720 N Us Highway 31 (47201-9170)
PHONE....................................812 526-4050
Charles Short, *Mng Member*
Timothy Fox,
EMP: 7
SQ FT: 4,000
SALES: 2.8MM **Privately Held**
SIC: 3548 Welding apparatus

(G-2029)
VICKIE HILDRETH
2331 N Marr Rd (47203-3445)
PHONE....................................812 350-3575
Vickie Hildreth, *Principal*
EMP: 2
SALES (est): 126K **Privately Held**
SIC: 3999 Hair, dressing of, for the trade

(G-2030)
VOGEL BROTHERS CORPORATION
860 Repp Dr (47201-7474)
PHONE....................................812 376-2775
Fax: 812 372-7605
Donald E Vogel, *President*
Virginia B Vogel, *Corp Secy*
David S Vogel, *Vice Pres*
EMP: 70
SQ FT: 10,000
SALES: 1MM **Privately Held**
WEB: www.vogel-brothers.com
SIC: 3421 Scissors, shears, clippers, snips & similar tools

(G-2031)
WEAVER FINE CABINETS FURNITURE
14400 W Georgetown Rd (47201-8716)
PHONE....................................812 342-4833
Rob Weaver, *President*
Diane Weaver, *Vice Pres*
EMP: 3
SALES (est): 481.8K **Privately Held**
SIC: 5712 2519 Cabinet work, custom; household furniture, except wood or metal: upholstered

(G-2032)
WESTROCK CP LLC
3101 State St (47201-7455)
PHONE....................................812 372-8873
Fax: 812 378-4025
Tim Barry, *Branch Mgr*
EMP: 129
SALES (corp-wide): 14.8B **Publicly Held**
WEB: www.sto.com
SIC: 2653 Boxes, corrugated: made from purchased materials
HQ: Westrock Cp, Llc
　　504 Thrasher St
　　Norcross GA 30071

(G-2033)
WESTROCK RKT COMPANY
Also Called: Rock-Tenn Paperboard Products
3101 State St (47201-7455)
PHONE....................................812 372-8873
Fax: 812 378-7322
Rick Hollin, *Manager*
EMP: 128
SALES (corp-wide): 14.8B **Publicly Held**
WEB: www.rocktenn.com
SIC: 2679 2675 2631 Paperboard products, converted; die-cut paper & board; paperboard mills
HQ: Westrock Rkt Company
　　1000 Abernathy Rd Ste 125
　　Atlanta GA 30328
　　770 448-2193

▲ = Import ▼=Export
◆ =Import/Export

(G-2034)
WILBERT SEXTON CORPORATION
3100 S Us Highway 31 (47201-9099)
PHONE................................812 372-3210
Louis Godsey, *Principal*
EMP: 2
SALES (est): 153.2K **Privately Held**
SIC: 3272 Burial vaults, concrete or pre-cast terrazzo

(G-2035)
WINE AND CANVAS DEV LLC
1005 Hawthorne Dr (47203-1621)
PHONE................................317 914-2806
Mary Zwerneman, *Manager*
EMP: 2
SALES (corp-wide): 1.4MM **Privately Held**
SIC: 2084 Wines, brandy & brandy spirits
PA: Wine And Canvas Development Llc
5151 E 82nd St Ste 700
Indianapolis IN 46250
317 345-1567

Commiskey
Jennings County

(G-2036)
QUALITY PALLETS INC
8740 W County Road 700 S (47227-9437)
P.O. Box 725, Seymour (47274-0725)
PHONE................................812 873-6818
Evelyn J Willhite, *President*
Robert D Willhite, *Vice Pres*
EMP: 9
SALES (est): 805.6K **Privately Held**
SIC: 2448 Pallets, wood

(G-2037)
SPARKMAN MFG INC
9197 N Jake Gayle Rd (47227-9322)
PHONE................................812 873-6052
Fax: 812 873-7777
Phillip Sparkman, *President*
Sandra Sparkman, *Corp Secy*
EMP: 9
SQ FT: 14,000
SALES (est): 1.2MM **Privately Held**
SIC: 2448 Wood pallets & skids

Connersville
Fayette County

(G-2038)
ADVANCED PRODUCTS TECH INC
5430 Western Ave (47331-9705)
P.O. Box 247 (47331-0247)
PHONE................................765 827-1166
Fax: 765 827-1167
Tim Hinds, *President*
EMP: 7
SQ FT: 10,000
SALES (est): 771.1K **Privately Held**
WEB: www.advproducts.com
SIC: 3552 3544 Dyeing, drying & finishing machinery & equipment; special dies, tools, jigs & fixtures

(G-2039)
B&B GOODIEZ
911 1/2 Western Ave (47331)
PHONE................................765 338-6833
Chadd Van Winkle, *Owner*
EMP: 4
SALES (est): 83K **Privately Held**
SIC: 2051 Bread, cake & related products

(G-2040)
BELL GRAPHICS AND DESIGN LLC
Also Called: Brunsman Graphic Design
3207 Iowa Ave (47331-2546)
PHONE................................765 827-5441
Craig Bell, *President*
Chris Bell, *Vice Pres*
Reita Brunsman, *Manager*
EMP: 3 EST: 1997
SQ FT: 3,500
SALES (est): 491K **Privately Held**
WEB: www.brunsmangraphicdesign.com
SIC: 2759 Commercial printing

(G-2041)
BEST MACHINE CO INC
1830 Virginia Ave (47331-2832)
P.O. Box 577 (47331-0577)
PHONE................................765 827-0250
Lisa Brown, *President*
EMP: 4
SALES: 150K **Privately Held**
SIC: 3569 Assembly machines, non-metal-working

(G-2042)
C & P ENGINEERING & MFG
1605 Kentucky Ave (47331-1620)
P.O. Box 672 (47331-0672)
PHONE................................765 825-4293
Fax: 765 825-4292
Tim Patterson, *President*
EMP: 20
SQ FT: 15,600
SALES (est): 4MM **Privately Held**
WEB: www.aceofgates.com
SIC: 3441 3535 3444 Fabricated structural metal; conveyors & conveying equipment; sheet metalwork

(G-2043)
COACH LINE MOTORS
Also Called: Cherry Hill Shopping Park
2516 Western Ave (47331-1802)
PHONE................................765 825-7893
Robert Cavins, *Owner*
Sharon Cavins, *Office Mgr*
EMP: 2 EST: 1966
SALES (est): 274.9K **Privately Held**
SIC: 5521 3716 7993 6512 Automobiles, used cars only; recreational van conversion (self-propelled), factory basis; amusement arcade; shopping center, property operation only

(G-2044)
CODYBRO LLC
Also Called: C5 Printing & Graphic Design
3207 Iowa Ave (47331-2546)
P.O. Box 385 (47331-0385)
PHONE................................765 827-5441
Christine Cox,
EMP: 5
SALES (est): 435.5K **Privately Held**
SIC: 2782 2396 2621 2732 Looseleaf forms & fillers, pen ruled or printed only; screen printing on fabric articles; book, bond & printing papers; catalog, magazine & newsprint papers; books: printing & binding

(G-2045)
CP INC
27100 Hall Rd (47331)
P.O. Box 1049 (47331-8049)
PHONE................................765 825-4111
Glen Findley, *President*
Nancy Findley, *Corp Secy*
Scott Findley, *Vice Pres*
Doreen Jarman, *Technology*
Bill Corbett, *Exec Dir*
EMP: 32 EST: 1946
SQ FT: 10,000
SALES (est): 4.8MM **Privately Held**
WEB: www.cpincpaints.com
SIC: 2851 Paints & allied products

(G-2046)
DIECO OF INDIANA INC
5130 Western Ave (47331-9703)
P.O. Box 266 (47331-0266)
PHONE................................765 825-4151
Fax: 765 825-4152
Carson Stevens, *President*
Richard Stevens, *Corp Secy*
EMP: 11
SQ FT: 4,000
SALES: 750K **Privately Held**
SIC: 3544 Special dies & tools

(G-2047)
DUNGAN AERIAL SERVICES INC
4290 N County Road 450 W (47331-9685)
P.O. Box 778 (47331-0778)
PHONE................................765 827-1355
Jeff Dungan, *President*

EMP: 4
SALES (est): 331.5K **Privately Held**
SIC: 2741

(G-2048)
FAYETTE TOOL AND ENGINEERING
5432 Western Ave (47331-9705)
P.O. Box 716 (47331-0716)
PHONE................................765 825-7518
Fax: 765 825-0471
Gary B Adams, *President*
Shelly Goodson, *Corp Secy*
Randy Brock, *Opers Mgr*
Steve Matney, *Engineer*
Mark Stevens, *Engineer*
▲ EMP: 72 EST: 1970
SQ FT: 50,000
SALES (est): 35MM **Privately Held**
WEB: www.fayettetool.com
SIC: 3469 3544 Household cooking & kitchen utensils, metal; special dies & tools

(G-2049)
H&E CUTTER GRINDING INC
6251 Industrial Ave N (47331-7729)
PHONE................................765 825-0541
Fax: 765 825-4964
Jerry D Miller II, *President*
Michael Morgan, *President*
Gene Hood, *Admin Sec*
EMP: 40
SQ FT: 7,200
SALES (est): 6.2MM **Privately Held**
SIC: 3599 Machine shop, jobbing & repair

(G-2050)
HAPPY APPLE EDUCATIONAL SVCS
502 Hill St (47331-1532)
PHONE................................765 338-9293
Terri Wright, *Principal*
EMP: 2
SALES (est): 85.9K **Privately Held**
SIC: 3571 Personal computers (microcomputers)

(G-2051)
HOWARD HOPKINS INC
Also Called: Image Manufacturing
129 Fiant St (47331-3322)
PHONE................................765 827-5666
Fax: 765 825-4037
Howard Hopkins, *President*
EMP: 10
SQ FT: 4,000
SALES: 1MM **Privately Held**
WEB: www.imagemanufacturing.com
SIC: 3599 Machine shop, jobbing & repair

(G-2052)
HOWDEN ROOTS LLC (HQ)
900 W Mount St (47331-1675)
PHONE................................765 827-9200
Constance Pfeiffer, *Buyer*
Gregory Faber, *QC Mgr*
Robert Albers, *Engineer*
David Bitter, *Engineer*
Gary Redelman, *Engineer*
◆ EMP: 147
SALES (est): 82.4MM
SALES (corp-wide): 3.3B **Publicly Held**
SIC: 3564 3563 Blowers & fans; air & gas compressors
PA: Colfax Corporation
420 Natl Bus Pkwy Ste 500
Annapolis Junction MD 20701
301 323-9000

(G-2053)
HYDRO EXTRUDER LLC
5120 Western Ave (47331-9703)
PHONE................................765 825-1141
Charles Straface, *CEO*
Pat Wooley, *Sales Dir*
EMP: 60
SQ FT: 32,000
SALES (corp-wide): 13.8B **Privately Held**
WEB: www.indalex.com
SIC: 3354 Aluminum extruded products
HQ: Hydro Extruder, Llc
Airport Offc Park
Moon Township PA 15108

(G-2054)
I T D INC
Also Called: Industrial Tool & Die
6050 Industrial Ave N (47331-7713)
PHONE................................765 825-0151
Fax: 765 825-0151
Warren Speers, *President*
Darryl Speers, *Vice Pres*
EMP: 7
SQ FT: 7,000
SALES (est): 1MM **Privately Held**
SIC: 3544 Dies & die holders for metal cutting, forming, die casting; die sets for metal stamping (presses)

(G-2055)
INDIANA TOOL INC
6260 Industrial Ave N (47331-7729)
P.O. Box 314 (47331-0314)
PHONE................................765 825-7117
Brian D Fohl, *President*
Bryan Pflum, *Vice Pres*
EMP: 10
SQ FT: 6,000
SALES (est): 1.4MM **Privately Held**
SIC: 3312 Tool & die steel & alloys

(G-2056)
IRVING MATERIALS INC
Also Called: I M I
1998 S State Road 121 (47331-8661)
PHONE................................765 825-2581
Fax: 765 825-0480
Don Steinard, *Opers-Prdtn-Mfg*
EMP: 8
SALES (corp-wide): 800.6MM **Privately Held**
SIC: 3273 Ready-mixed concrete
PA: Irving Materials, Inc.
8032 N State Road 9
Greenfield IN 46140
317 326-3101

(G-2057)
JACOBS & BRICHFORD LLC
2957 S State Road 1 (47331-8942)
PHONE................................765 692-0056
Mathew Brichford,
EMP: 4
SALES (est): 169.3K **Privately Held**
SIC: 2026 Fermented & cultured milk products

(G-2058)
KEENER CORPORATION (PA)
950 Conwell St (47331-2060)
PHONE................................765 825-2100
Fax: 765 825-2885
Gary Keener Sr, *President*
Gary R Keener Jr, *President*
Mark Keener, *Vice Pres*
▲ EMP: 15
SQ FT: 40,000
SALES: 15MM **Privately Held**
SIC: 3535 Conveyors & conveying equipment

(G-2059)
KEENER CORPORATION
950 Conwell St (47331-2060)
PHONE................................765 825-2100
Fax: 765 825-0782
Gary Keener, *President*
EMP: 20
SALES (corp-wide): 15MM **Privately Held**
SIC: 3499 Aerosol valves, metal
PA: Keener Corporation
950 Conwell St
Connersville IN 47331
765 825-2100

(G-2060)
KEENER CORPORATION
Also Called: Keener Corporatio - South
950 Conwell St (47331-2060)
PHONE................................765 825-2711
Fax: 765 827-8550
Mark Keener, *Branch Mgr*
EMP: 63
SALES (corp-wide): 15MM **Privately Held**
SIC: 3535 Conveyors & conveying equipment

PA: Keener Corporation
950 Conwell St
Connersville IN 47331
765 825-2100

(G-2061)
KENLEY CORPORATION
950 Conwell St (47331-2060)
PHONE......................765 825-7150
Gary R Keener Sr, *President*
Mark Keener, *Vice Pres*
EMP: 2
SQ FT: 30,000
SALES (est): 327.9K **Privately Held**
WEB: www.kenleycorporation.com
SIC: 3441 Fabricated structural metal

(G-2062)
**MAC MACHINE & METAL
WORKS INC**
100 N Grand Ave (47331-1937)
P.O. Box 609 (47331-0609)
PHONE......................765 825-5873
Fax: 765 825-0584
John Malone, *President*
David M Krepp, *Vice Pres*
David Krepp, *Vice Pres*
Steven E Krepp, *Vice Pres*
Janet S Malone, *Shareholder*
▼ **EMP:** 34 **EST:** 1951
SQ FT: 25,100
SALES: 3.5MM **Privately Held**
WEB: www.mmmw.com
SIC: 3544 3469 Special dies & tools; jigs
& fixtures; metal stampings

(G-2063)
MCCOMBS AND SON COMPANY
201 W 6th St (47331-1503)
PHONE......................765 825-4581
Fax: 765 825-5404
Marcia S McCombs, *CEO*
Robert McCombs, *President*
Clair McCombs, *President*
Nancy McCombs, *Treasurer*
EMP: 6 **EST:** 1906
SQ FT: 4,784
SALES: 228.3K **Privately Held**
SIC: 3312 Plate, steel

(G-2064)
**MILLER CUSTOM FOREST
PRODUCTS**
4715 W County Road 800 N (47331-9640)
PHONE......................765 478-3057
George Miller, *Partner*
Terry Miller, *Partner*
EMP: 2
SALES (est): 221.9K **Privately Held**
SIC: 2421 Sawmills & planing mills, general

(G-2065)
**MOORE PRECISION MACHINING
LLC (PA)**
1400 Madison St (47331-3342)
PHONE......................765 265-2386
David A Moore, *Mng Member*
Jonathan B Moore, *Mng Member*
EMP: 2
SQ FT: 1,000
SALES (est): 377.5K **Privately Held**
SIC: 3599 Machine shop, jobbing & repair

(G-2066)
**NEWS EXAMINER CIRCULATION
DEPT**
406 N Central Ave (47331-1926)
PHONE......................765 825-2914
Kelly Pierce, *General Mgr*
Tina West, *Principal*
EMP: 3 **EST:** 2007
SALES (est): 106.2K **Privately Held**
SIC: 2711 Newspapers, publishing & printing

(G-2067)
P & E PRODUCTS
637 W 17th St (47331-2214)
PHONE......................765 969-2644
Bruce REA, *Owner*
EMP: 6
SQ FT: 8,000
SALES: 500K **Privately Held**
SIC: 3441 Fabricated structural metal

(G-2068)
POWERRAIL HOLDINGS INC
Also Called: Powerrail Mfg
1321 N Illinois Ave (47331-1606)
PHONE......................765 827-4660
Tom Casper, *Manager*
Shelby Steele, *Maintence Staff*
EMP: 14
SALES (corp-wide): 56.1MM **Privately
Held**
SIC: 3743 Locomotives & parts
PA: Powerrail Holdings, Inc.
205 Clark Rd
Duryea PA 18642
570 883-7005

(G-2069)
QUALITY TOOL DESIGN INC
1645 E County Road 175 N (47331-9135)
PHONE......................765 377-4055
Brian Eddy, *President*
EMP: 2
SALES (est): 110K **Privately Held**
SIC: 3544 Special dies, tools, jigs & fixtures

(G-2070)
**READY MACHINE TOOL & DIE
CORP**
1321 N Illinois Ave (47331-1606)
PHONE......................765 825-3108
Fax: 765 825-1176
Charles Ford, *President*
Jerry L Garriott, *Vice Pres*
EMP: 41 **EST:** 1919
SQ FT: 40,000
SALES (est): 4.1MM **Privately Held**
SIC: 3469 3544 7692 Stamping metal for
the trade; special dies & tools; welding repair

(G-2071)
SPEEDWAY LLC
Also Called: Speedway Superamerica 7556
300 N Central Ave (47331-1925)
PHONE......................765 827-0321
Fax: 765 825-6850
EMP: 10 **Publicly Held**
SIC: 1311 Crude Petroleum & Natural Gas
HQ: Speedway Llc
500 Speedway Dr
Enon OH 45323
937 864-3000

(G-2072)
STANT USA CORP (HQ)
1620 Columbia Ave (47331-1672)
P.O. Box 899 (47331-0899)
PHONE......................765 825-3121
Gary Masse, *CEO*
David Roys, *COO*
Thomas Zambelli, *CFO*
◆ **EMP:** 229
SQ FT: 190,000
SALES (est): 221.7MM **Privately Held**
SIC: 3714 Motor vehicle parts & accessories

(G-2073)
STANT USA CORP
Cv Plant
1620 Columbia Ave (47331-1672)
PHONE......................765 825-3121
Rick Barnett, *Plant Mgr*
EMP: 350 **Privately Held**
SIC: 3714 Motor vehicle parts & accessories
HQ: Stant Usa Corp.
1620 Columbia Ave
Connersville IN 47331

(G-2074)
**TAGGARTS CUSTOM SNDBLST
LLC**
1740 Georgia Ave (47331-1673)
PHONE......................765 825-4584
Jim Taggart, *Owner*
EMP: 3 **EST:** 2007
SALES: 150K **Privately Held**
SIC: 3589 Sandblasting equipment

(G-2075)
TATMAN INC
Also Called: Commercial Printing Service
815 N Central Ave (47331-2049)
P.O. Box 719 (47331-0719)
PHONE......................765 825-2164
Fax: 765 825-4229
Jamison Tatman, *Ch of Bd*
Marilyn Kinzler, *President*
Janet Rose, *Vice Pres*
Melody Crawford, *Treasurer*
EMP: 25
SQ FT: 13,500
SALES (est): 3MM **Privately Held**
WEB: www.cpsprints.com
SIC: 2752 2759 2791 2789 Commercial
printing, offset; letterpress printing; typesetting; bookbinding & related work

(G-2076)
TEC INC
3594 S County Road 350 E (47331-9436)
PHONE......................765 827-3868
Thomas Tressler, *President*
EMP: 2
SALES: 180K **Privately Held**
SIC: 3491 Industrial valves

(G-2077)
VORZEIGEN MACHINING INC
5650 Industrial Ave S (47331-7715)
PHONE......................765 827-1500
Fax: 765 827-1515
Austin B Cummings, *President*
John Godar, *Vice Pres*
Criag Bell, *Engineer*
Mark Myers, *Marketing Staff*
Jen Friend, *Admin Asst*
EMP: 25
SQ FT: 15,000
SALES (est): 4MM **Privately Held**
WEB: www.vorzeigen.com
SIC: 3599 Machine shop, jobbing & repair

(G-2078)
WHITLOCKS PRESSURE WASH
5649 Industrial Ave S (47331-7715)
P.O. Box 391 (47331-0391)
PHONE......................765 825-5868
Fax: 765 827-4446
Bob Whitlock, *Owner*
EMP: 10
SALES (est): 902.9K **Privately Held**
SIC: 7699 7542 5087 3471 Industrial
equipment cleaning; carwash, self-service; carwash equipment & supplies; plating & polishing

---

Converse
Miami County

(G-2079)
JACK HOUSE LLC
106 W Wabash St (46919)
PHONE......................251 990-5960
EMP: 2 **EST:** 2012
SALES (est): 129.4K **Privately Held**
SIC: 2399 Seat belts, automobile & aircraft

(G-2080)
**NORTH CENTRAL IND
SHAVINGS LLC**
307 E Dunn St (46919-2121)
PHONE......................765 395-3875
Toby Middlesworth, *Principal*
EMP: 5 **EST:** 2011
SALES (est): 486.4K **Privately Held**
SIC: 2421 Sawdust & shavings

(G-2081)
OAK HILL WINERY LLC
111 E Marion St (46919-2105)
P.O. Box 549 (46919-0549)
PHONE......................765 395-3632
Betty Moulton, *Vice Pres*
EMP: 2
SALES (est): 181.9K **Privately Held**
SIC: 2084 Wines

(G-2082)
RENCOR INC
12833 S 1000 E (46919-9752)
PHONE......................765 395-7949

Fax: 765 395-7949
Donald Rennaker, *President*
Royce Rennaker, *Corp Secy*
EMP: 5
SALES (est): 474.4K **Privately Held**
SIC: 3599 Machine shop, jobbing & repair

Corunna
Dekalb County

(G-2083)
**CHARLESTON METAL
PRODUCTS INC**
1746 Us Highway 6 (46730-9713)
PHONE......................260 281-9972
Fax: 260 281-9923
Rod Evans, *Branch Mgr*
EMP: 18
SALES (est): 1.4MM
SALES (corp-wide): 20.5MM **Privately
Held**
WEB: www.charlestonmetal.com
SIC: 3599 Machine shop, jobbing & repair
PA: Charleston Metal Products Inc
350 Grant St
Waterloo IN 46793
260 837-8211

(G-2084)
**FRISKNEY GEAR & MACHINE
CORP**
Also Called: Friskney Gear Division
106 N Bridge St (46730-1000)
P.O. Box 122 (46730-0122)
PHONE......................260 281-2200
Fax: 260 281-2200
Randy Thomas, *President*
EMP: 4
SALES: 300K **Privately Held**
SIC: 3599 3568 Machine shop, jobbing &
repair; power transmission equipment

(G-2085)
**PLANT ENGINEERING
SERVICES INC (PA)**
744 County Road 8 (46730-9756)
PHONE......................260 281-2917
Mark A Bohler, *President*
Deborah A Bohler, *Admin Sec*
EMP: 1
SALES (est): 1.6MM **Privately Held**
WEB: www.pltengineering.com
SIC: 3542 7389 Presses: hydraulic &
pneumatic, mechanical & manual;

Corydon
Harrison County

(G-2086)
A F WOLKE CO INC
Also Called: Wolke Paint Manufacturer
723 Quarry Rd Nw (47112-6921)
PHONE......................812 738-4141
Fax: 812 738-0775
Paul Burns, *President*
Chris Williams, *Vice Pres*
EMP: 5 **EST:** 1934
SQ FT: 20,000
SALES (est): 836.8K **Privately Held**
SIC: 2851 Paints & paint additives

(G-2087)
**ACCU-CHEK QULTY SOLUTIONS
LLC**
1015 Old Forest Rd Nw (47112-1909)
PHONE......................812 704-5491
Herschel Smith, *Partner*
EMP: 20 **EST:** 2010
SALES: 400K **Privately Held**
SIC: 3829 Hardness testing equipment

(G-2088)
**AWNINGTEC USA
INCORPORATED**
3265 Highway 62 Nw (47112-6709)
P.O. Box 837 (47112-0837)
PHONE......................812 734-0423
Fax: 812 734-0344
Mansen Way, *President*
Becky Tucker, *General Mgr*

▲ = Import ▼=Export
◆ =Import/Export

Joshua Welch, *Project Mgr*
▲ **EMP:** 20 **EST:** 1997
SQ FT: 15,000
SALES (est): 3.7MM **Privately Held**
WEB: www.awningtecusa.com
SIC: 3444 Awnings & canopies

(G-2089)
BARKS WELDING SUPPLIES
6125 Highway 135 Sw (47112-6068)
PHONE..................812 732-4366
Fax: 812 732-4666
Waunita Barks, *Owner*
Alice Yeager, *Manager*
EMP: 3
SALES (est): 343.7K **Privately Held**
SIC: 7692 5051 Welding repair; steel

(G-2090)
BLUE RIVER SERVICES INC
Also Called: General Mrgans Scrnprint Shppe
101 N Mulberry St (47112-1211)
P.O. Box 547 (47112-0547)
PHONE..................812 738-2437
Daniel Lowe, *Branch Mgr*
EMP: 165
SALES (corp-wide): 17.6MM **Privately Held**
SIC: 2759 Screen printing
PA: Blue River Services, Inc.
1365 N Old Highway 135
Corydon IN 47112
812 738-3836

(G-2091)
BREITBURN OPERATING LP
3761 Corydon Ramsey Rd Nw (47112-6935)
PHONE..................812 738-3338
Duke Green, *Principal*
EMP: 6
SALES (est): 127.1K **Privately Held**
SIC: 1389 1382 Oil & gas field services; oil & gas exploration services

(G-2092)
CHASE N CORYDON
1881 Old Highway 135 Nw (47112-2012)
PHONE..................812 738-3032
Jamie Diamon, *President*
Tony Myers, *Manager*
EMP: 10
SALES (est): 812K **Privately Held**
SIC: 3578 Automatic teller machines (ATM)

(G-2093)
CLINE BROTHERS WELDING
3490 Highway 62 Ne (47112-7714)
PHONE..................812 738-3537
Ron Cline, *Partner*
Don Cline, *Partner*
EMP: 2
SALES (est): 247.4K **Privately Held**
SIC: 3444 7692 Sheet metalwork; welding repair

(G-2094)
COFFMAN LOGGING
2190 Lckford Bridge Rd Sw (47112-6029)
PHONE..................812 732-4857
Allan Coffman, *Owner*
EMP: 4
SALES (est): 387.5K **Privately Held**
SIC: 2411 Logging camps & contractors

(G-2095)
CORYDON MACHINE & TOOL CO INC
615 Quarry Rd Nw (47112-6920)
PHONE..................812 738-3107
Fax: 812 738-3127
Steven Yahraus, *President*
Kevin Rowe, *Vice Pres*
Elsie Yahraus, *Vice Pres*
Scott Shake, *Plant Mgr*
Dale Embrey, *Purch Mgr*
EMP: 38 **EST:** 1979
SQ FT: 27,000
SALES: 5MM **Privately Held**
WEB: www.corydonmachine.com
SIC: 3544 3599 Special dies & tools; machine shop, jobbing & repair

(G-2096)
CORYDON STONE & ASPHALT INC
1100 Quarry Rd Nw (47112-6939)
PHONE..................812 738-2216
Fax: 812 738-8400
Richard Cripe, *President*
EMP: 32 **EST:** 1926
SQ FT: 2,000
SALES (est): 7.5MM
SALES (corp-wide): 39.9MM **Privately Held**
WEB: www.corydonstoneandasphalt.com
SIC: 2951 1422 1442 Asphalt & asphaltic paving mixtures (not from refineries); crushed & broken limestone; construction sand & gravel
PA: Goh Con, Inc.
1630 Broadway St
Clarksville IN 47129
812 282-1349

(G-2097)
DARAMIC LLC
3430 Cline Rd Nw (47112-6908)
PHONE..................812 738-8274
Jean Salvi, *Principal*
EMP: 208
SALES (corp-wide): 19.1B **Privately Held**
WEB: www.daramic.com
SIC: 3069 2499 3269 Roofing, membrane rubber; battery separators, wood; filtering media, pottery
HQ: Daramic, Llc
11430 N Community House R
Charlotte NC 28277

(G-2098)
FERREE LOGGING LLC
2150 Leonard Rd Nw (47112-6867)
PHONE..................812 786-1676
Andrew Ferree, *Principal*
EMP: 2
SALES (est): 81.7K **Privately Held**
SIC: 2411 Logging

(G-2099)
GOH A&C INC
Also Called: Corydon Stone and Asphalt
1100 Quarry Rd Nw (47112-6939)
PHONE..................812 738-2217
John Gohmann, *Owner*
EMP: 27
SALES (corp-wide): 39.9MM **Privately Held**
WEB: www.gohmannasphalt.com
SIC: 1499 Asphalt mining & bituminous stone quarrying
HQ: Goh A&C, Inc.
1630 Broadway St
Clarksville IN 47129
812 282-1349

(G-2100)
HARRISON CNTY DEMOCRATE
229 E Chestnut St (47112-1107)
PHONE..................812 734-0560
EMP: 3
SALES (est): 103.8K **Privately Held**
SIC: 2711 Newspapers, publishing & printing

(G-2101)
HOEHN HARDWOODS
2285 Fogel Rd Se (47112-7959)
PHONE..................812 968-3242
Walter Hoehn, *Owner*
Rowena Hoehn, *Co-Owner*
EMP: 3
SALES (est): 143.4K **Privately Held**
SIC: 2435 Plywood, hardwood or hardwood faced

(G-2102)
ICON METAL FORMING LLC
2190 Landmark Ave Ne (47112-2016)
PHONE..................812 738-5900
Kevin Anderson, *Info Tech Dir*
Robert Wildeboer,
EMP: 380
SALES (est): 70.3MM
SALES (corp-wide): 2.8B **Privately Held**
WEB: www.reedcitytool.com
SIC: 3714 1761 Motor vehicle parts & accessories; sheet metalwork

HQ: Martinrea Industries, Inc.
10501 Mi State Road 52
Manchester MI 48158
734 428-2400

(G-2103)
IMI SOUTH LLC
3060 Cline Rd Nw (47112-6904)
PHONE..................812 738-4173
Fax: 812 738-4923
Rita Ledford, *Branch Mgr*
EMP: 6
SALES (corp-wide): 800.6MM **Privately Held**
SIC: 3273 Ready-mixed concrete
HQ: Imi South, Llc
1440 Selinda Ave
Louisville KY 40213
502 456-6930

(G-2104)
LUCAS OIL RACING INC
3199 Harrison Way Nw (47112-6903)
PHONE..................812 738-1147
Fax: 812 734-0466
Forrest D Lucas, *President*
Robert E Patison, *Vice Pres*
Debbie Wessel, *Safety Dir*
Kim Lucas, *Financial Exec*
Todd Shidler, *Executive*
◆ **EMP:** 15
SALES (est): 4.3MM
SALES (corp-wide): 133.9MM **Privately Held**
SIC: 3533 Well logging equipment
PA: Lucas Oil Products, Inc.
302 N Sheridan St
Corona CA 92880
951 270-0154

(G-2105)
MOSIER PALLET & LUMBER CO
Also Called: Mosier Log Homes
3600 Tee Rd Ne (47112-7459)
PHONE..................812 366-4817
Russell Mosier, *President*
EMP: 5
SALES (est): 499.4K **Privately Held**
SIC: 2452 Prefabricated wood buildings

(G-2106)
NACHURS ALPINE SOLUTIONS CORP
Also Called: Natures Alpine Solutions
3185 Cline Rd Nw (47112-6905)
PHONE..................812 738-1333
Doris Beuser, *Manager*
EMP: 5
SALES (corp-wide): 105.4MM **Privately Held**
WEB: www.nachurs.com
SIC: 2875 5261 Fertilizers, mixing only; fertilizer
HQ: Nachurs Alpine Solutions, Corp.
421 Leader St
Marion OH 43302
740 382-5701

(G-2107)
PEYTON TECHNICAL SERVICES LLC
1548 Highway 62 Nw (47112-5131)
PHONE..................812 738-2016
Trent Peyton, *President*
Troy Wesley, *Project Mgr*
EMP: 10
SALES (est): 1.7MM **Privately Held**
WEB: www.peytontechsvc.com
SIC: 3842 Personal safety equipment

(G-2108)
PFEIFFER WINERY & VINEYARD
Also Called: Trutle Run Winery
940 Saint Peters Ch Rd Ne (47112-8351)
PHONE..................812 952-2650
Laura Pfeiffer, *President*
Jim Pfeiffer, *Vice Pres*
EMP: 2
SALES (est): 179.7K **Privately Held**
SIC: 2084 Wines

(G-2109)
QUICKS MACHINE & TOOL INC
5523 Corydon Ridge Rd Ne (47112-7039)
PHONE..................812 952-2135
Terry Quick, *President*

Virginia Quick, *Treasurer*
EMP: 2
SQ FT: 4,000
SALES (est): 210K **Privately Held**
WEB: www.quickscomputerservices.com
SIC: 3599 Machine shop, jobbing & repair

(G-2110)
ROMAN MARBLENE COMPANY INC
1560 Quarry Rd Nw (47112-6943)
PHONE..................812 738-1367
Frank Triantos, *CEO*
EMP: 15
SQ FT: 20,000
SALES: 1.5MM **Privately Held**
SIC: 3281 Bathroom fixtures, cut stone

(G-2111)
SANDERS SAW MILL INC
2999 N Gethsemane Rd Nw (47112-6802)
PHONE..................812 738-4793
Wayne Sanders, *President*
EMP: 12
SALES (est): 710K **Privately Held**
SIC: 2421 Sawmills & planing mills, general

(G-2112)
SCREWY LEWY LURES INC
1820 Owans Ln Ne (47112-7613)
PHONE..................812 786-7369
James Lewis, *Manager*
EMP: 2
SALES (est): 108.6K **Privately Held**
SIC: 3949 Sporting & athletic goods

(G-2113)
SPORTS SOFTWARE INC
1290 Spencer Ave (47112-2222)
PHONE..................812 738-2735
EMP: 2
SALES (est): 97.7K **Privately Held**
SIC: 7372 Prepackaged Software Services

(G-2114)
TYSON FOODS INC
545 Valley Rd (47112-1747)
P.O. Box 545 (47112-0545)
PHONE..................812 738-3219
Fax: 812 738-5810
Mary Craig, *Purch Agent*
Brandy Wilkerson, *Buyer*
David Wahittington, *Manager*
David Bowman, *Manager*
David Whittington, *Manager*
EMP: 600
SQ FT: 1,000
SALES (corp-wide): 38.2B **Publicly Held**
SIC: 2015 Chicken slaughtering & processing
PA: Tyson Foods, Inc.
2200 W Don Tyson Pkwy
Springdale AR 72762
479 290-4000

(G-2115)
WARREN PRINTING SERVICES LLC
217 E Chestnut St (47112-1107)
PHONE..................812 738-6508
Larry Warren, *Principal*
EMP: 15
SALES (est): 1.8MM **Privately Held**
SIC: 2759 Screen printing

(G-2116)
WHITAKERR DALEMON
Also Called: Whitaker Skid and Crate
1240 Old N Bridge Rd Ne (47112-2259)
PHONE..................812 738-2396
Dale Whitaker, *Owner*
EMP: 4
SALES (est): 322.9K **Privately Held**
SIC: 2448 2441 Wood pallets & skids; cargo containers, wood; pallets, wood & wood with metal; skids, wood; boxes, wood; cases, wood

(G-2117)
ZIMMERMAN ART GLASS COMPANY
300 E Chestnut St (47112-1202)
PHONE..................812 738-2206
Kerry Zimmerman, *Partner*

EMP: 2 EST: 1960
SALES: 110K **Privately Held**
SIC: **3229** Glassware, art or decorative; ashtrays, glass; vases, glass; candlesticks, glass

Covington
Fountain County

(G-2118)
DESIGNS 4 U INC
1350 W 100 N (47932-8107)
PHONE...................................765 793-3026
Brenda Hardy, *President*
Stan Hardy, *Vice Pres*
EMP: 2 EST: 2001
SALES: 40K **Privately Held**
SIC: **3993** 2329 2339 2389 Signs & advertising specialties; men's & boys' athletic uniforms; baseball uniforms: men's, youths' & boys'; basketball uniforms: men's, youths' & boys'; football uniforms: men's, youths' & boys'; uniforms, athletic: women's, misses' & juniors'; uniforms & vestments; band uniforms

(G-2119)
MIDWEST BIO-PRODUCTS INC
618 Liberty St (47932-1531)
PHONE...................................765 793-3426
Masakazu Miyagi, *President*
Mary Patricia Miyagi, *Treasurer*
EMP: 5
SALES (est): 723.6K **Privately Held**
SIC: **2869** Enzymes

(G-2120)
STEEL GRIP INC
1200 Pearl St (47932-1466)
P.O. Box 174 (47932-0174)
PHONE...................................765 793-3652
Fax: 765 793-0335
Vickie Hughes, *Purch Agent*
Dave Mason, *Manager*
EMP: 68
SALES (est): 5.5MM
SALES (corp-wide): 18.6MM **Privately Held**
WEB: www.steelgripinc.com
SIC: **3842** Personal safety equipment
PA: Steel Grip, Inc.
1501 E Voorhees St
Danville IL 61832
217 442-6240

Craigville
Wells County

(G-2121)
COTTONWOOD CORP
Rr 1 (46731)
PHONE...................................260 565-3185
Tim Ringger, *President*
EMP: 2 **Privately Held**
SIC: **2013** Sausages & other prepared meats
PA: Cottonwood Corp
1412 Evergreen Ct
Ossian IN 46777

(G-2122)
HELENA AGRI-ENTERPRISES LLC
2300 N State Road 301 (46731-9758)
P.O. Box 68 (46731-0068)
PHONE...................................260 565-3196
Fax: 260 565-3783
Mike Borne, *Manager*
EMP: 7
SALES (corp-wide): 70.7B **Privately Held**
WEB: www.helenachemical.com
SIC: **2879** Agricultural chemicals
HQ: Helena Agri-Enterprises, Llc
255 Schilling Blvd # 300
Collierville TN 38017
901 761-0050

(G-2123)
MODULAR GREEN SYSTEMS LLC
5889 N 700 W-1 (46731-9505)
PHONE...................................260 547-4121
David Byrd,
EMP: 2
SALES (est): 86.7K **Privately Held**
SIC: **2421** 7389 Outdoor wood structural products;

Crandall
Harrison County

(G-2124)
CORRQUEST AUTOMATION INC
2060 Highway 335 Ne (47114-9407)
PHONE...................................812 596-0049
Brian Wellman, *Branch Mgr*
EMP: 2
SALES (corp-wide): 9MM **Privately Held**
SIC: **1731** 3554 Banking machine installation & service; paper industries machinery; box making machines, paper; corrugating machines, paper; paper mill machinery: plating, slitting, waxing, etc.
PA: Corrquest Automation, Inc.
5253 Old Salem Rd Ne
Albany OR 97321
503 305-3810

Crane
Martin County

(G-2125)
DLA DOCUMENT SERVICES
300 Highway 361 Bldg 18 (47522-4000)
PHONE...................................812 854-1465
Bob Clark, *Manager*
EMP: 2 **Publicly Held**
SIC: **2752** 9711 Commercial printing, lithographic; national security;
HQ: Dla Document Services
5450 Carlisle Pike Bldg 9
Mechanicsburg PA 17050
717 605-2362

(G-2126)
HARRIS CORPORATION
Also Called: Exelis Inc., Electronic
27548 N 1400 E (47522)
PHONE...................................812 202-5171
Dave Melcher, *CEO*
Sara King, *Senior Engr*
Jim Jeffers, *Branch Mgr*
EMP: 3
SALES (corp-wide): 5.9B **Publicly Held**
SIC: **3812** Defense systems & equipment
PA: Harris Corporation
1025 W Nasa Blvd
Melbourne FL 32919
321 727-9100

(G-2127)
HARRIS CORPORATION
27548 N 1400 E (47522)
PHONE...................................812 202-5171
Jim Wantrobski, *Branch Mgr*
EMP: 195
SALES (corp-wide): 5.9B **Publicly Held**
SIC: **3823** 3812 Industrial instrmnts msrmnt display/control process variable; search & navigation equipment
PA: Harris Corporation
1025 W Nasa Blvd
Melbourne FL 32919
321 727-9100

(G-2128)
LEIDOS INC
14064 Westgate Ct (47522-7407)
PHONE...................................812 863-3100
Anthony Moraco, *CEO*
EMP: 189

SALES (corp-wide): 10.1B **Publicly Held**
WEB: www.saic.com
SIC: **8731** 7371 7373 8742 Commercial physical research; energy research; environmental research; medical research, commercial; computer software development; systems engineering, computer related; computer-aided design (CAD) systems service; training & development consultant; recording & playback apparatus, including phonograph; integrated circuits, semiconductor networks, etc.
HQ: Leidos, Inc.
11951 Freedom Dr Ste 500
Reston VA 20190
571 526-6000

(G-2129)
MILITARY FACILITIES
Also Called: Naval Surface Wrfre Cntr Cran
300 Highway 361 (47522-4000)
PHONE...................................812 854-1762
Karl McClure, *Director*
▲ EMP: 6
SALES (est): 2MM **Privately Held**
SIC: **3483** Ammunition, except for small arms

(G-2130)
NSA CRANE ✪
300 Highway 361 (47522-4000)
PHONE...................................812 854-4723
EMP: 2 EST: 2017
SALES (est): 86K **Privately Held**
SIC: **3731** Shipbuilding & repairing

Crawfordsville
Montgomery County

(G-2131)
ACUITY BRANDS INC
1304 E Elmore St (47933-3170)
PHONE...................................765 362-1837
Ray Tamosky, *Vice Pres*
Anthony Melvin, *Buyer*
EMP: 11
SALES (corp-wide): 3.5B **Publicly Held**
SIC: **3646** Commercial indusl & institutional electric lighting fixtures
PA: Acuity Brands, Inc.
1170 Peachtree St Ne
Atlanta GA 30309
404 853-1400

(G-2132)
ACUITY BRANDS LIGHTING INC
Lithonia Lighting
1615 E Elmore St (47933-3122)
PHONE...................................765 362-1837
Bert Kerr, *Branch Mgr*
EMP: 500
SALES (corp-wide): 3.5B **Publicly Held**
SIC: **3646** 3641 Commercial indusl & institutional electric lighting fixtures; electric lamps
HQ: Acuity Brands Lighting, Inc.
1 Acuity Way
Conyers GA 30012

(G-2133)
AMERICAN WATER WORKS CO INC
Also Called: Indiana American Water Company
809 Banjo Dr (47933-9656)
PHONE...................................765 362-3940
Jeffrey Moseley, *Branch Mgr*
EMP: 5
SALES (corp-wide): 3.3B **Publicly Held**
SIC: **5963** 2086 Bottled water delivery; mineral water, carbonated: packaged in cans, bottles, etc.
PA: American Water Works Company, Inc.
1025 Laurel Oak Rd
Voorhees NJ 08043
856 346-8200

(G-2134)
ARCHER-DANIELS-MIDLAND COMPANY
Also Called: ADM
3696 E Elm St (47933-8290)
PHONE...................................765 362-2965

Fax: 765 362-2971
Ken Martin, *Manager*
EMP: 112
SALES (corp-wide): 60.8B **Publicly Held**
WEB: www.admworld.com
SIC: **2041** Flour & other grain mill products
PA: Archer-Daniels-Midland Company
77 W Wacker Dr Ste 4600
Chicago IL 60601
312 634-8100

(G-2135)
BB WIRING LLC
1413 W Us Highway 136 (47933-6109)
PHONE...................................765 376-0190
Brenda Bayless, *Principal*
EMP: 2 EST: 2015
SQ FT: 15,000
SALES (est): 111K **Privately Held**
SIC: **3643** Lamp sockets & receptacles (electric wiring devices)

(G-2136)
C&F FABRICATING LLC
1831 E Elmore St (47933-3126)
PHONE...................................765 362-5922
Jeanette Lowery,
EMP: 2
SALES: 200K **Privately Held**
SIC: **3444** Sheet metalwork

(G-2137)
CALIFORNIA PELLET MILL COMPANY
1114 E Wabash Ave (47933-2698)
PHONE...................................765 362-2600
Fax: 765 362-7551
Larry H Pitsch, *President*
Carl Allis, *Plant Mgr*
Middleton Michael, *Manager*
▲ EMP: 7
SALES (est): 145.8K **Privately Held**
SIC: **3523** Farm machinery & equipment

(G-2138)
CHARLES COONS
Also Called: Hillcrest Mobile Homes Court
2401 Indianapolis Rd (47933-3173)
PHONE...................................765 362-6509
Fax: 765 362-3065
Charles Coons, *Owner*
EMP: 3
SQ FT: 2,400
SALES (est): 177.4K **Privately Held**
SIC: **6515** 1741 6514 2396 Mobile home site operators; masonry & other stonework; dwelling operators, except apartments; automotive & apparel trimmings; pleating & stitching

(G-2139)
CLOSURE SYSTEMS INTL INC
Also Called: Alcoa Csi
1604 E Elmore St (47933-3121)
PHONE...................................765 364-6300
Fax: 765 364-6238
Michael Johnson, *Research*
Julie Harrison, *Engineer*
Jeremiah Migas, *Engineer*
Greg Mishler, *Engineer*
Sarah Worrell, *Controller*
EMP: 2
SALES (est): 250K **Privately Held**
SIC: **3353** Aluminum sheet & strip

(G-2140)
CLOSURE SYSTEMS INTL INC
318 Glenn St (47933)
PHONE...................................317 390-5000
Malcolm Bundey, *Branch Mgr*
EMP: 163 **Privately Held**
SIC: **3334** Primary aluminum
HQ: Closure Systems International, Inc.
7820 Innovation Blvd # 100
Indianapolis IN 46278
317 390-5000

(G-2141)
CLOSURE SYSTEMS INTL INC
Also Called: Csi
1205 E Elmore St (47933-3116)
PHONE...................................765 364-6300
Don Stewart, *Engineer*
Kathy Whitney, *Manager*
EMP: 367 **Privately Held**
WEB: www.alcoacsi.com

SIC: 3334 3089 Primary aluminum; bottle caps, molded plastic
HQ: Closure Systems International, Inc.
7820 Innovation Blvd # 100
Indianapolis IN 46278
317 390-5000

(G-2142)
CPM ACQUISITION CORP
Also Called: California Pellet Mill Company
1114 E Wabash Ave (47933-2635)
P.O. Box 647 (47933-0647)
PHONE.....................765 362-2600
Bill Lippencott, *Safety Mgr*
Carl Allis, *Branch Mgr*
Chris Rowland, *Manager*
Becky Fenters-Silins, *Supervisor*
EMP: 70 **Privately Held**
WEB: www.betaraven.com
SIC: 3523 3559 3312 3544 Feed grinders, crushers & mixers; refinery, chemical processing & similar machinery; blast furnaces & steel mills; special dies, tools, jigs & fixtures
HQ: Cpm Acquisition Corp.
2975 Airline Cir
Waterloo IA 50703
319 232-8444

(G-2143)
CPM CONVEYOR LLC
5119 S Davis Bridge Rd (47933-6825)
PHONE.....................765 918-5190
Donald W Friar, *Principal*
EMP: 5
SALES: 500K **Privately Held**
SIC: 3535 Conveyors & conveying equipment

(G-2144)
CRAWFORD INDUSTRIES LLC (PA)
Also Called: Innovative Consumer Packaging
1414 Crawford Dr (47933-9740)
PHONE.....................800 428-0840
Fax: 765 364-6762
George L Faulstich Jr, *CEO*
Kim McKeown, *Engineer*
Michael Ferguson, *Sales Staff*
Marta Fyffe-Carlile, *Sales Staff*
Lisa Hartman, *Sales Staff*
▲ EMP: 150
SQ FT: 85,000
SALES (est): 66MM **Privately Held**
WEB: www.crawford-industries.com
SIC: 3089 Injection molding of plastics; plastic processing

(G-2145)
CROSSROADS ORTHOTICS & CNSLTN
821 S Washington St (47933-3546)
PHONE.....................765 359-0041
Jenifer L Furness, *Owner*
EMP: 3
SALES (est): 338.5K **Privately Held**
SIC: 3842 Orthopedic appliances

(G-2146)
CROWN CORK & SEAL USA INC
400 N Walnut St (47933-1300)
PHONE.....................765 362-3200
Fax: 765 362-4532
Shelly Leatherman, *Human Res Dir*
Robert Bourque, *Branch Mgr*
Rachel Pena, *Manager*
Bill Perkins, *Maintence Staff*
EMP: 100
SQ FT: 100,000
SALES (corp-wide): 8.7B **Publicly Held**
WEB: www.crowncork.com
SIC: 3411 Metal cans
HQ: Crown Cork & Seal Usa, Inc.
1 Crown Way
Philadelphia PA 19154
215 698-5100

(G-2147)
CURRENT TECHNOLOGIES INC
Frontage Rd (47933)
P.O. Box 21 (47933-0021)
PHONE.....................765 364-0490
Fax: 765 364-1607
Susan Hapak, *President*
EMP: 12
SQ FT: 9,000

SALES (est): 1.9MM **Privately Held**
SIC: 3842 Bandages & dressings; surgical appliances & supplies; laboratory apparatus & furniture

(G-2148)
D AND S PALLET
3174 S 600 W (47933-6914)
PHONE.....................765 866-7263
Dan Searing, *Owner*
EMP: 2
SALES (est): 100K **Privately Held**
SIC: 2448 Pallets, wood & wood with metal

(G-2149)
DISCOUNT DETECTOR SALES INC
7488 S 600 W (47933-6335)
PHONE.....................765 866-0320
Fax: 765 866-0974
EMP: 2 EST: 2000
SALES (est): 150K **Privately Held**
SIC: 3669 Whol Metal Detectors

(G-2150)
DUBOSE STRAPPING INC
4414 E 400 S (47933-7958)
PHONE.....................765 361-0000
Alen Needy, *Branch Mgr*
EMP: 9
SALES (corp-wide): 20.1MM **Privately Held**
SIC: 3499 Strapping, metal
PA: Dubose Strapping, Inc.
906 Industrial Dr
Clinton NC 28328
910 590-1020

(G-2151)
EDW C LEVY CO
Whitesville Mill Service
New Core Rd (47933)
PHONE.....................765 364-9251
Fax: 765 364-0955
Mike Perkins, *Manager*
EMP: 45
SALES (corp-wide): 376.1MM **Privately Held**
WEB: www.edwclevy.com
SIC: 3295 3281 Slag, crushed or ground; cut stone & stone products
PA: Edw. C. Levy Co.
9300 Dix
Dearborn MI 48120
313 429-2200

(G-2152)
FLOW CENTER PRODUCTS INC
2065 S Nucor Rd (47933-7970)
P.O. Box 509 (47933-0509)
PHONE.....................765 364-9460
Roy Kalty, *President*
▲ EMP: 5
SQ FT: 5,600
SALES (est): 322.1K **Privately Held**
WEB: www.flocenter.com
SIC: 3585 Refrigeration & heating equipment

(G-2153)
FRONTIER ADDITIVE MFG LLC
2418 W Co Rd 400 S (47933)
PHONE.....................765 413-5568
Eric Lynch,
EMP: 5
SALES (est): 187.6K **Privately Held**
SIC: 3545 End mills

(G-2154)
GHOST FORGE L T D (PA)
Also Called: Ghost Frge Rubenesque Fashions
1009 S Elm St (47933-3515)
PHONE.....................765 362-8654
Joann Seibert, *CEO*
Joann V Sykes, *President*
James R Shillings, *Vice Pres*
Robert Sykes Jr, *Sales & Mktg St*
▼ EMP: 3 EST: 1998
SALES: 130K **Privately Held**
WEB: www.ghostforge.com
SIC: 2389 Costumes

(G-2155)
GREFCO MINERALS INC
Dicaperl/Mineral Products Div
2510 N Concord Rd (47933-7807)
P.O. Box 48 (47933-0048)
PHONE.....................765 362-6000
Fax: 765 362-3887
Mathew Greenley, *Research*
William Staten, *Manager*
Vern Buman, *Manager*
EMP: 17 **Privately Held**
SIC: 3255 Clay refractories
HQ: Grefco Minerals Inc.
1 Bala Ave Ste 310
Bala Cynwyd PA 19004
610 660-8820

(G-2156)
GUARDIAN TECH GROUP IND LLC
1100 E Elmore St (47933-3573)
PHONE.....................765 364-0863
Brian Hudson, *CEO*
Charles Hudson, *President*
Jason Hudson,
EMP: 7
SQ FT: 24,000
SALES (est): 500K **Privately Held**
SIC: 3451 Screw machine products

(G-2157)
HALLETT ENTERPRISES INC
Also Called: Hallett Gutter Cover
3916 E Traction Rd (47933-8029)
P.O. Box 681484, Indianapolis (46268-7484)
PHONE.....................317 495-7800
Adam Reissner, *Principal*
EMP: 5
SALES (est): 420K **Privately Held**
WEB: www.hallettent.com
SIC: 3444 Gutters, sheet metal

(G-2158)
HERITAGE PRODUCTS INC
2000 Smith Ave (47933-1055)
PHONE.....................765 364-9002
Fax: 765 362-0536
Takaharu Miyake, *President*
Bryan Y Funai, *Principal*
Edmond Simpson, *QC Mgr*
Josh Millikan, *Engineer*
Tatsunori Shigeta, *Treasurer*
▲ EMP: 216
SQ FT: 195,000
SALES (est): 86.7MM
SALES (corp-wide): 192.5MM **Privately Held**
WEB: www.heritageproductsinc.com
SIC: 3465 Body parts, automobile: stamped metal
PA: Hiruta Kogyo Co., Ltd.
1410, Mobira
Kasaoka OKA 714-0
865 663-700

(G-2159)
HOOSIER HRDWOOD RCLAMATION LLC
1471 S 600 W (47933-6912)
PHONE.....................765 299-6507
EMP: 2
SALES (est): 178.6K **Privately Held**
SIC: 2426 Hardwood dimension & flooring mills

(G-2160)
HT ENTERPRISES INC
Also Called: Hi-Temp Refractories
5070 N Old State Road 55 (47933-8138)
P.O. Box 414, Darlington (47940-0414)
PHONE.....................765 794-4174
Tim Foster, *President*
Tom McCormick, *Admin Sec*
EMP: 6
SALES (est): 643.8K **Privately Held**
SIC: 3255 Tile & brick refractories, except plastic

(G-2161)
INTERNATIONAL PAPER COMPANY
801 N Englewood Dr (47933-9741)
PHONE.....................765 364-5342
Gary Huxhold, *Branch Mgr*

Scott Wright, *Manager*
EMP: 88
SALES (corp-wide): 21.7B **Publicly Held**
WEB: www.tin.com
SIC: 2653 Boxes, corrugated: made from purchased materials
PA: International Paper Company
6400 Poplar Ave
Memphis TN 38197
901 419-9000

(G-2162)
INTERNATIONAL PAPER COMPANY
1823 E Elmore St (47933-3126)
PHONE.....................765 359-0107
CJ Wilson, *Branch Mgr*
EMP: 5
SALES (corp-wide): 21.7B **Publicly Held**
SIC: 2631 Paperboard mills
PA: International Paper Company
6400 Poplar Ave
Memphis TN 38197
901 419-9000

(G-2163)
IRVING MATERIALS INC
Also Called: I M I
3350 State Road 32 E (47933-9620)
PHONE.....................765 362-6904
Fax: 765 362-6907
Don Russell, *Manager*
EMP: 8
SALES (corp-wide): 800.6MM **Privately Held**
SIC: 3273 Ready-mixed concrete
PA: Irving Materials, Inc.
8032 N State Road 9
Greenfield IN 46140
317 326-3101

(G-2164)
JARROD ZACHARY WELD
3384 E State Road 32 (47933-9620)
PHONE.....................765 230-6424
Jarrod Zachery, *Principal*
EMP: 2 EST: 2007
SALES (est): 96.8K **Privately Held**
SIC: 7692 Welding repair

(G-2165)
KESSCO WATER LLC (PA)
Also Called: Kinetico Water Systems
2207b Indianapolis Rd (47933-3140)
PHONE.....................765 362-3890
Fax: 765 362-8112
John Kessinger, *Executive*
Margaret Kessinger,
EMP: 4
SQ FT: 6,900
SALES (est): 638.5K **Privately Held**
SIC: 3589 Sewage & water treatment equipment

(G-2166)
KROGER LIMITED PARTNERSHIP II
Pace Dairy Foods
800 N Englewood Dr (47933-9741)
PHONE.....................765 364-5200
Fax: 765 364-5296
Pat Dilts, *Principal*
John Bomba, *Production*
Judy Pennock, *Purch Mgr*
Barry Giggy, *Buyer*
Joyce Gwinnup, *Controller*
EMP: 51
SALES (corp-wide): 122.6B **Publicly Held**
SIC: 2022 Natural cheese
HQ: Kroger Limited Partnership Ii
1014 Vine St
Cincinnati OH 45202
513 762-4000

(G-2167)
LASERWASH
1529 S Washington St (47933-3814)
PHONE.....................765 359-0582
Mark Addler, *Manager*
EMP: 2
SALES (est): 148.4K **Privately Held**
SIC: 3589 Car washing machinery

(G-2168)
LIGHTNING PRINTING
115 N Washington St (47933-1734)
PHONE...................................765 362-5999
EMP: 3
SALES (est): 120K **Privately Held**
SIC: 2759 Commercial printing

(G-2169)
LSC COMMUNICATIONS US LLC
600 W State Road 32 (47933-8967)
PHONE...................................765 362-1300
EMP: 6
SALES (corp-wide): 3.6B **Publicly Held**
SIC: 2732 2721 2621 Book printing; magazines: publishing & printing; catalog, magazine & newsprint papers
HQ: Lsc Communications Us, Llc
　191 N Wacker Dr Ste 1400
　Chicago IL 60606
　844 572-5720

(G-2170)
MAGIC LIGHT NEON SIGN COMPANY
408 California St (47933-1121)
PHONE...................................765 361-5887
Kathy Platipodis, *Owner*
Bill Platipodis, *Manager*
EMP: 5
SALES (est): 275K **Privately Held**
SIC: 3993 Signs & advertising specialties

(G-2171)
MCCLAMROCH AG LLC
Also Called: Perry Equipment
115 W 580 N (47933-7307)
PHONE...................................765 362-4495
Tom McClamroch, *President*
EMP: 7
SALES: 2.3MM **Privately Held**
SIC: 3535 Conveyors & conveying equipment

(G-2172)
MIDWEST BALE TIES INC
1200 E Wabash Ave (47933-2636)
P.O. Box 66 (47933-0066)
PHONE...................................765 364-0113
Randy Francis, *President*
John Kendricks, *Vice Pres*
▲ EMP: 12
SQ FT: 16,000
SALES (est): 2MM **Privately Held**
SIC: 3315 Wire, steel: insulated or armored

(G-2173)
MIDWEST BALE TIES INC
1200 E Wabash Ave (47933-2636)
P.O. Box 66 (47933-0066)
PHONE...................................765 364-0113
Fax: 765 364-0161
John Kendricks, *President*
Jason Ramsey, *Vice Pres*
Susan Sosbe, *Admin Asst*
EMP: 20
SALES: 9MM **Privately Held**
SIC: 3599 Ties, form: metal

(G-2174)
MILAM TOYS INC
Also Called: Pearl of Wisdom
5072 N Us Highway 231 (47933)
PHONE...................................765 362-2826
William T Milam, *President*
Cassandra Mylam, *Vice Pres*
EMP: 2
SALES (est): 133.8K **Privately Held**
WEB: www.pearl-of-wisdom.net
SIC: 3944 Games, toys & children's vehicles

(G-2175)
MILLERS LOCKER PLANT
1979 N Summer Dr (47933-8297)
PHONE...................................765 234-2381
James P Miller, *Partner*
Linda L Miller, *Partner*
EMP: 2
SQ FT: 4,000

SALES (est): 77K **Privately Held**
SIC: 0751 2013 5421 Slaughtering: custom livestock services; sausages & other prepared meats; freezer provisioners, meat

(G-2176)
NOR-COTE INTERNATIONAL INC
506 Lafayette Ave (47933-1336)
PHONE...................................800 488-9180
EMP: 3
SALES (corp-wide): 142.8MM **Privately Held**
SIC: 2893 Printing ink
HQ: Nor-Cote International, Inc.
　605 Lafayette Ave
　Crawfordsville IN 47933
　765 230-7252

(G-2177)
NOR-COTE INTERNATIONAL INC (DH)
605 Lafayette Ave (47933-1339)
P.O. Box 668 (47933-0668)
PHONE...................................765 230-7252
Fax: 765 364-5408
Norman G Wolcott Jr, *Ch of Bd*
Charles McHargue, *COO*
▲ EMP: 42 EST: 1976
SQ FT: 20,000
SALES (est): 12.6MM
SALES (corp-wide): 142.8MM **Privately Held**
WEB: www.norcote.com
SIC: 2893 Duplicating ink; screen process ink

(G-2178)
NOR-COTE INTERNATIONAL INC
605 Lafayette Ave (47933-1339)
P.O. Box 668 (47933-0668)
PHONE...................................765 230-9180
Rick Conrad, *Manager*
EMP: 50
SALES (corp-wide): 142.8MM **Privately Held**
WEB: www.norcote.com
SIC: 2893 Printing ink
HQ: Nor-Cote International, Inc.
　605 Lafayette Ave
　Crawfordsville IN 47933
　765 230-7252

(G-2179)
NORTH ENTERPRISES INC
Also Called: Kwik Kopy Printing
123 E Main St (47933-1710)
PHONE...................................765 362-4410
Fax: 765 362-1439
EMP: 6
SQ FT: 3,000
SALES: 500K **Privately Held**
SIC: 2759 Thermography

(G-2180)
NUCOR CORPORATION
Nucor Steel - Indiana
4537 S Nucor Rd (47933-7969)
P.O. Box 907 (47933-0907)
PHONE...................................765 364-1323
Jeff Powers, *General Mgr*
Calvin Hart, *Opers Staff*
Michael Meade, *Opers Staff*
Drew Kitterman, *Production*
Marta Sweek, *Purch Agent*
EMP: 760
SALES (corp-wide): 20.2B **Publicly Held**
WEB: www.nucor.com
SIC: 3312 3316 Blast furnaces & steel mills; cold finishing of steel shapes
PA: Nucor Corporation
　1915 Rexford Rd Ste 400
　Charlotte NC 28211
　704 366-7000

(G-2181)
NUCOR STEEL CORP
4537 S Nucor Rd (47933-7969)
PHONE...................................765 364-1323
Fax: 765 364-1695
Jeff Moore, *Warehouse Mgr*
Frank Jordan, *Maint Spvr*
Martha Sweek, *Purch Mgr*
Lindsay Chauvin, *Purch Agent*
David Emerson, *Project Engr*

EMP: 39
SALES (est): 16.2MM **Privately Held**
SIC: 3312 Blast furnaces & steel mills

(G-2182)
PALLETS VIVEROS LLC
1815 W 575 N (47933-8165)
PHONE...................................765 307-0112
Edgar Viveros, *Principal*
EMP: 4 EST: 2016
SALES (est): 194.2K **Privately Held**
SIC: 2448 Pallets, wood & wood with metal

(G-2183)
PAPER OF MONTGOMERY COUNTY
201 E Jefferson St # 200 (47933-2881)
PHONE...................................765 361-8888
Tim Timmons, *Partner*
Jeff Bannon, *Partner*
Elizabeth Hedge, *Controller*
EMP: 2
SALES (est): 204.3K **Privately Held**
SIC: 2711 Commercial printing & newspaper publishing combined

(G-2184)
PENGUIN RANDOM HOUSE LLC
1021 N State Road 47 (47933-7131)
PHONE...................................765 362-5125
EMP: 130
SALES (corp-wide): 82.3MM **Privately Held**
WEB: www.anchorbooks.com
SIC: 2731 Books: publishing only
HQ: Penguin Random House Llc
　1745 Broadway
　New York NY 10019
　212 782-9000

(G-2185)
PERFORMANCE MSTR COIL PROC INC
3752 E 350 S (47933-9464)
PHONE...................................765 364-1300
Fax: 765 364-1332
James Harrington, *President*
Antoinette Magnini, *Principal*
James Jensen, *Vice Pres*
Richard Magnini, *Vice Pres*
Anthony Aiardo, *Admin Sec*
EMP: 23
SALES: 2.5MM **Privately Held**
SIC: 3677 Electronic coils, transformers & other inductors

(G-2186)
PHANTOM NEON LLC
Also Called: Phantom Signs
100 E North St (47933-1738)
PHONE...................................765 362-2221
Yvonne Neal, *Owner*
Yvonne Rincon, *Mng Member*
Juan Rincon, *Mng Member*
EMP: 4 EST: 2008
SALES: 400K **Privately Held**
SIC: 3993 2759 Signs & advertising specialties; neon signs; posters, including billboards: printing

(G-2187)
PRAIRIE SCENTS LLC
1817 N State Road 47 (47933-8406)
PHONE...................................765 361-6908
Carla Earl, *Principal*
EMP: 3 EST: 2016
SALES (est): 143.6K **Privately Held**
SIC: 2844 Toilet preparations

(G-2188)
PRECISION MULTI MEDIA
604 Mill St (47933-3439)
PHONE...................................765 359-0466
Matt Gilliland, *Owner*
Denise Gilliland, *Co-Owner*
EMP: 3
SALES: 250K **Privately Held**
SIC: 2396 Printing & embossing on plastics fabric articles

(G-2189)
PURITAN WATER CONDITIONING
216 Lafayette Ave (47933-1609)
P.O. Box 778 (47933-0778)
PHONE...................................765 362-6340

Fax: 765 362-8117
Jeff Hockersmith, *President*
Gary Hockersmith, *Vice Pres*
Jan Cash, *Admin Sec*
EMP: 10
SQ FT: 7,200
SALES (est): 1.3MM **Privately Held**
WEB: www.puritanwater.net
SIC: 3589 5999 7389 Water filters & softeners, household type; water purification equipment, household type; water purification equipment; water softener service

(G-2190)
R B MACHINE COMPANY
2907 S 550 E (47933-7954)
PHONE...................................765 364-6716
Fax: 765 364-7081
Ron Beach, *President*
EMP: 2
SALES (est): 229.1K **Privately Held**
SIC: 3599 Machine shop, jobbing & repair

(G-2191)
RANDOM HOUSE INC
1019 N State Road 47 (47933-7131)
PHONE...................................410 386-7717
Abigail Adams, *Principal*
EMP: 2
SALES (est): 196K **Privately Held**
SIC: 2731 Books: publishing only

(G-2192)
RBM MANUFACTURING INC
566 S 200 E (47933-7932)
PHONE...................................765 364-6933
Fax: 765 364-6944
Ralph R Stevens, *President*
Todd A Stevens, *CFO*
EMP: 5
SQ FT: 4,320
SALES (est): 604.1K **Privately Held**
SIC: 3469 Metal stampings

(G-2193)
RED HAWK CHOPPERS INC
212 N Washington St (47933-1736)
PHONE...................................765 307-2269
Dan Joseph Wemer Jr, *President*
EMP: 2 EST: 2016
SALES (est): 72.7K **Privately Held**
SIC: 3751 Motorcycles & related parts

(G-2194)
RR DONNELLEY & SONS COMPANY
R R Donnelley
1009 Sloan St (47933-2743)
PHONE...................................765 362-1300
Fax: 765 364-3982
Gary Calleo, *Director*
EMP: 1000
SALES (corp-wide): 6.9B **Publicly Held**
WEB: www.rrdonnelley.com
SIC: 2732 2789 Books: printing only; bookbinding & related work
PA: R. R. Donnelley & Sons Company
　35 W Wacker Dr Ste 3650
　Chicago IL 60601
　312 326-8000

(G-2195)
SCAGGS LRGENT SCRNPRINTING LLC
201 E Main St (47933-1831)
PHONE...................................765 362-5477
Kristy Largent,
Jeff Scaggs,
EMP: 2 EST: 2013
SALES: 120K **Privately Held**
SIC: 2211 Print cloths, cotton

(G-2196)
SOLEMA USA INC
315 Glenn St (47933-2363)
P.O. Box 472 (47933-0472)
PHONE...................................765 361-0806
C Scott Ellis, *Principal*
Michelle Ellis, *Vice Pres*
▲ EMP: 4
SALES (est): 339.9K **Privately Held**
WEB: www.solemausa.com
SIC: 2732 Books: printing & binding

▲ = Import ▼=Export
◆ =Import/Export

(G-2197)
STEEL TECHNOLOGIES LLC
3560 S Nucor Rd (47933-7968)
PHONE.....................765 362-3110
John J Ferriola, *Branch Mgr*
EMP: 102 Privately Held
SIC: 3316 3312 Cold-rolled strip or wire; strip steel, cold-rolled: from purchased hot-rolled; sheet, steel, cold-rolled: from purchased hot-rolled; sheet or strip, steel, hot-rolled; coated or plated products; hot-rolled iron & steel products
HQ: Steel Technologies Llc
700 N Hurstbourne Pkwy # 400
Louisville KY 40222
502 245-2110

(G-2198)
SUGAR CREEK FABRICATORS INC
503 W 300 N (47933-9088)
P.O. Box 72 (47933-0072)
PHONE.....................765 361-0891
Greg Funk, *Owner*
EMP: 7
SALES (est): 965K Privately Held
SIC: 3446 Ornamental metalwork

(G-2199)
SUGAR CREEK GRAVEL & STONE
1400 Ladoga Rd (47933-3723)
PHONE.....................765 362-1646
EMP: 2 EST: 2015
SALES (est): 79K Privately Held
SIC: 1442 Construction sand & gravel

(G-2200)
SYSTEMS CONTRACTING CORP
4537 S Nucor Rd (47933-7969)
PHONE.....................765 361-2991
Fax: 765 361-2999
Phil Collins, *Manager*
EMP: 17
SALES (est): 1.2MM Privately Held
SIC: 3547 Pipe & tube mills

(G-2201)
TEMPLE INLAND
801 N Englewood Dr (47933-9741)
PHONE.....................765 362-1074
EMP: 2
SALES (est): 90.5K Privately Held
SIC: 5113 2621 Patterns, paper; paper mills

(G-2202)
U S AGGREGATES INC
3607 N Us Highway 231 (47933-9089)
PHONE.....................765 362-2500
Mark Scott, *Manager*
EMP: 10
SALES (corp-wide): 248.2MM Privately Held
WEB: www.usagg.com
SIC: 1442 Gravel mining
HQ: U S Aggregates Inc
5400 W 86th St
Indianapolis IN 46268
317 872-6010

(G-2203)
W & W FABRICATING INC
2597 S Us Highway 231 (47933-9488)
P.O. Box 602 (47933-0602)
PHONE.....................765 362-2182
Fax: 765 364-9880
Dan D Walden, *President*
Mary Walden, *Treasurer*
EMP: 2
SQ FT: 261,000
SALES (est): 240K Privately Held
SIC: 3444 5051 Sheet metalwork; steel

(G-2204)
WILLS-STOCKTON ACRES LLC
4757 N 360 E (47933-7377)
PHONE.....................765 366-7307
James Wills,
Gary Stockton,
EMP: 2
SALES (est): 118.5K Privately Held
SIC: 2841 Textile soap

(G-2205)
WILSON ENTERPRISES INC (PA)
Also Called: Wilson Autotech
2008 Indianapolis Rd (47933-3136)
PHONE.....................765 362-1089
Fax: 765 362-5447
Diane Wilson, *President*
Mark Wilson, *Treasurer*
EMP: 6
SQ FT: 6,400
SALES (est): 571.9K Privately Held
WEB: www.wilsonbrosracing.com
SIC: 7549 2759 Automotive maintenance services; screen printing

(G-2206)
YES FEED & SUPPLY LLC
Also Called: Associated Mfg & Packg
2065 S Nucor Rd (47933-7970)
PHONE.....................765 361-9821
Randy York,
EMP: 3
SALES (est): 250K Privately Held
SIC: 3999 Manufacturing industries

Cromwell
Noble County

(G-2207)
ALUMINUM CONVERSION INC
204 Parkway (46732)
P.O. Box 137 (46732-0137)
PHONE.....................260 856-2180
Fax: 260 856-2264
Smith Michael A, *President*
Pamela Smith, *Admin Sec*
▲ EMP: 4
SQ FT: 3,500
SALES (est): 900K Privately Held
SIC: 3341 Secondary nonferrous metals

(G-2208)
FREEDOM WIRE INC
458 Olive St (46732-1122)
P.O. Box 278 (46732-0278)
PHONE.....................260 856-3059
Fax: 260 856-3002
Michael E Hatfield, *President*
EMP: 14
SQ FT: 6,000
SALES (est): 2.4MM Privately Held
WEB: www.freedomwire.com
SIC: 3679 Harness assemblies for electronic use: wire or cable

(G-2209)
INDUSTRIAL GRAPHIC DESIGN
203 Industrial Dr (46732-1128)
P.O. Box 277 (46732-0277)
PHONE.....................260 856-2110
Robert H Luellen, *President*
EMP: 2
SQ FT: 2,000
SALES (est): 180K Privately Held
SIC: 2759 Screen printing

(G-2210)
OH HUNT LINES INC
591 N Jefferson St (46732-9547)
PHONE.....................260 856-2126
Dave Martin, *President*
EMP: 7
SALES (est): 665.5K Privately Held
SIC: 3621 Motors, electric

(G-2211)
STEVES PALLETS
3868 N 1025 W (46732-9744)
PHONE.....................260 856-2047
Steve Sturgill, *Owner*
EMP: 8
SALES (est): 861.3K Privately Held
SIC: 2448 Wood pallets & skids

Cross Plains
Ripley County

(G-2212)
FUR REAL TAXIDERMY LLC
4339 E County Road 900 S (47017-8961)
PHONE.....................812 667-6365
Cheryl Mathews, *Principal*
EMP: 2
SALES (est): 99.2K Privately Held
SIC: 3999 Furs

Crothersville
Jackson County

(G-2213)
AISIN CHEMICAL INDIANA LLC
1004 Industrial Way (47229-9415)
PHONE.....................812 793-2888
Yoshiaki Yasui, *President*
Masayuki Isogami, *President*
Masashi Nagino, *Treasurer*
Kevin Buhr, *Finance*
Hiroshi Tanida,
▲ EMP: 50
SALES (est): 14.4MM
SALES (corp-wide): 36.6B Privately Held
SIC: 3499 Friction material, made from powdered metal
HQ: Aisin Chemical Co.,Ltd.
1141-1, Okawagawara, Fujiokainocho
Toyota AIC 470-0
565 766-661

(G-2214)
AISIN DRIVETRAIN INC
1001 Industrial Way (47229-9415)
PHONE.....................812 793-2427
George S Turpin, *President*
Scott Turpin, *President*
Junji Miyagawa, *Exec VP*
Scott Shade, *Vice Pres*
Hiroshi Tanida, *Treasurer*
▲ EMP: 130
SQ FT: 350,000
SALES (est): 36.1MM
SALES (corp-wide): 36.6B Privately Held
WEB: www.aisindrive.com
SIC: 3714 3566 3568 Transmissions, motor vehicle; torque converters, except automotive; power transmission equipment
HQ: Aisin Holdings Of America, Inc.
1665 E 4th Street Rd
Seymour IN 47274
812 524-8144

(G-2215)
ASHLEY ALUMINUM FOUNDRY INC
125 S Armstrong St (47229-1503)
PHONE.....................812 793-2654
Fax: 812 793-2654
Hubert H Ashley Jr, *President*
EMP: 5
SQ FT: 15,000
SALES (est): 539K Privately Held
SIC: 3366 3365 Brass foundry; aluminum foundries

(G-2216)
BISHOP REPAIR
4514 S County Road 700 E (47229-9726)
PHONE.....................812 523-3246
Robert Bishop, *Partner*
EMP: 2 EST: 1993
SALES (est): 227K Privately Held
SIC: 3599 Machine shop, jobbing & repair

(G-2217)
CERRO WIRE LLC
1002 Industrial Way (47229-9415)
PHONE.....................812 793-2929
Rick McDold, *Branch Mgr*
EMP: 70
SALES (corp-wide): 242.1B Publicly Held
WEB: www.cerrowire.com
SIC: 3357 3351 Nonferrous wiredrawing & insulating; wire, copper & copper alloy

HQ: Cerro Wire Llc
1099 Thompson Rd Se
Hartselle AL 35640
256 773-2522

(G-2218)
MASTERSBILT CHASSIS INC
Also Called: Master Built Racing Accessory
6520 S Us Highway 31 (47229-9643)
PHONE.....................812 793-3666
Fax: 812 793-2761
Keith Masters, *President*
Adrian Masters, *Admin Sec*
EMP: 13
SQ FT: 3,200
SALES (est): 1.9MM Privately Held
WEB: www.mastersbilt.com
SIC: 3711 5531 3714 Automobile assembly, including specialty automobiles; automotive parts; motor vehicle parts & accessories

(G-2219)
PRO SERIES PRODUCTS LLC
208 N Armstrong St (47229-1004)
PHONE.....................812 793-3506
Dale Schmelzel,
EMP: 5
SALES: 150K Privately Held
SIC: 3999 Manufacturing industries

(G-2220)
PRO-FORM PLASTICS INC
11624 E State Road 250 (47229-9621)
PHONE.....................812 522-4433
Andrew Nehrt, *President*
Renee Coomer, *General Mgr*
Rob Sherwood, *Sales Dir*
Marlin D Adams, *Admin Sec*
▼ EMP: 30
SQ FT: 32,000
SALES (est): 6.6MM Privately Held
SIC: 2431 3423 3089 Trim, wood; cutting dies, except metal cutting; thermoformed finished plastic products

(G-2221)
S-TECH INC
208 N Armstrong St (47229-1004)
PHONE.....................812 793-3506
Dale Schmelzle, *President*
Mike A Arsoni, *Manager*
EMP: 6
SALES (est): 1.1MM Privately Held
SIC: 7692 Welding repair

Crown Point
Lake County

(G-2222)
ADAMS SMITH (PA)
Also Called: Lakeshore Graphics
10431 Floyd St (46307-2999)
PHONE.....................219 661-2812
Fax: 219 922-9290
Smith Adams, *Owner*
EMP: 6
SALES: 1.5MM Privately Held
WEB: www.lakeshoregraphics.com
SIC: 2759 Commercial printing

(G-2223)
ADVANCED BOILER CTRL SVCS INC (PA)
7515 Cline Ave (46307-9607)
PHONE.....................708 429-7066
Robert Burrink, *President*
EMP: 15
SALES (est): 3.2MM Privately Held
WEB: www.advblr.com
SIC: 3823 Boiler controls: industrial, power & marine type; fluidic devices, circuits & systems for process control; absorption analyzers: infrared, X-ray, etc.: industrial

(G-2224)
ALL N ONE
905 Hub Ct (46307-2733)
PHONE.....................219 226-9263
Jessie Ramos, *President*
EMP: 8
SALES (est): 963.1K Privately Held
SIC: 3444 Gutters, sheet metal

(G-2225)
AMERICAN CHEMICAL SERVICE
12227 S Williams Ct (46307-3673)
PHONE...................................219 613-4114
Erik Johnson, *Principal*
EMP: 2
SALES (est): 62.5K **Privately Held**
SIC: 3999 Manufacturing industries

(G-2226)
ANNABELLA PUBLICATIONS LLC
1385 Tanglewood Ct (46307-5075)
PHONE...................................219 663-4244
Jerry Murdock, *Principal*
EMP: 2
SALES (est): 136.9K **Privately Held**
SIC: 2741 Miscellaneous publishing

(G-2227)
BD MEDICAL DEVELOPMENT INC
1140 Millennium Dr (46307-7533)
PHONE...................................219 310-8551
Bill Depel, *President*
EMP: 5 EST: 2010
SALES (est): 736.5K **Privately Held**
SIC: 3841 2821 Medical instruments & equipment, blood & bone work; molding compounds, plastics

(G-2228)
BLANKET HOG
Also Called: Blanket Buddy
10850 Bell St (46307-8862)
PHONE...................................219 308-9532
Georgi Dukleski,
EMP: 4
SQ FT: 10,000
SALES (est): 115.8K **Privately Held**
SIC: 2392 Blankets, comforters & beddings

(G-2229)
BOBBY LITTLE CREATIONS
610 W Joliet St (46307-3813)
PHONE...................................219 313-5102
Bob Wright, *Owner*
EMP: 5
SALES: 640K **Privately Held**
SIC: 2676 5947 Infant & baby paper products; gift, novelty & souvenir shop

(G-2230)
BOLTTECH MANNINGS INC
1170 Arrowhead Ct (46307-7536)
PHONE...................................219 310-8389
Jeff Fontaine, *President*
EMP: 14
SALES (corp-wide): 460.4MM **Privately Held**
SIC: 3546 Power-driven handtools
HQ: Bolttech Mannings, Inc.
    501 Mosside Blvd
    North Versailles PA 15137
    724 872-4873

(G-2231)
BROGAN PHARMACEUTICALS LLC
9800 Connecticut Dr (46307-7840)
PHONE...................................219 644-3693
Brett Dines,
EMP: 15
SQ FT: 10,500
SALES: 1.2MM **Privately Held**
WEB: www.broganpharma.com
SIC: 2834 Pharmaceutical preparations

(G-2232)
CABINET & COUNTERTOP SOLUTIO
127 Marr Ct (46307-4630)
PHONE...................................219 775-3540
Woody Ramsey, *Principal*
EMP: 4
SALES (est): 292.2K **Privately Held**
SIC: 2434 Wood kitchen cabinets

(G-2233)
CHIEF POWERBOATS INC
280 Wood St (46307-4100)
PHONE...................................219 775-7024
Scott Grady, *President*
Daryl Grady, *Shareholder*

Rosemarie Grady, *Admin Sec*
EMP: 5
SALES: 2.5MM **Privately Held**
SIC: 3732 Boat building & repairing

(G-2234)
CIRCUIT BREAKER SALES CO INC
11181 Virginia St (46307-0083)
PHONE...................................219 575-5420
Finley Ledbetter, *Branch Mgr*
EMP: 2 **Privately Held**
SIC: 3613 Switchgear & switchboard apparatus
HQ: Circuit Breaker Sales Co Inc
    1315 Columbine Dr
    Gainesville TX 76240
    940 665-4444

(G-2235)
CLEAR EDGE FILTRATION INC
202 S Indiana Ave (46307-4114)
PHONE...................................219 306-7339
EMP: 2
SALES (corp-wide): 319.6MM **Privately Held**
SIC: 2295 Coated fabrics, not rubberized
HQ: Clear Edge Filtration, Inc.
    11607 E 43rd St N
    Tulsa OK 74116
    918 728-8111

(G-2236)
CRITSER COMPANIES INC
120 Main St (46307)
P.O. Box 1039 (46308-1039)
PHONE...................................219 663-0052
EMP: 8
SQ FT: 216
SALES (est): 820K **Privately Held**
SIC: 3531 Mfg Construction Machinery

(G-2237)
CROWN BRICK & SUPPLY INC (PA)
820 Thomas St (46307-3497)
PHONE...................................219 663-7880
Fax: 219 662-9096
Danny Martin, *President*
Debbie Dubord, *Vice Pres*
Martin Beenes, *Director*
EMP: 22
SQ FT: 9,000
SALES (est): 7MM **Privately Held**
WEB: www.crownbrick.com
SIC: 5032 3271 Brick, stone & related material; concrete block & brick

(G-2238)
CROWN CAB & COUNTER TOP INC
500 Sheridan St (46307-3398)
PHONE...................................219 663-2725
Fax: 219 663-0818
EMP: 17 EST: 1978
SALES (est): 2MM **Privately Held**
SIC: 2542 2541 2434 Mfg Nonwd Partition/Fixt Mfg Wood Partitions/Fixt Mfg Wood Kitchen Cabinet

(G-2239)
CROWN INDUSTRIES INC
10769 Broadway (46307-7316)
PHONE...................................219 791-9930
Fax: 219 791-9931
Elias Paviadakis, *President*
Michael Paviadakis, *Principal*
Daniel Barajas, *CFO*
Maria Paviadakis, *Treasurer*
▲ EMP: 25
SALES (est): 337.2K **Privately Held**
SIC: 3991 5198 3231 Paint brushes; paint brushes, rollers, sprayers; products of purchased glass

(G-2240)
CROWN MTAL FBRICATORS ERECTORS
1031 E Summit St (46307-2727)
P.O. Box 179 (46308-0179)
PHONE...................................219 661-8277
Fax: 219 663-9997
Gerhard Kurt King, *Owner*
Christine King, *Vice Pres*
EMP: 5

SQ FT: 10,000
SALES (est): 951.7K **Privately Held**
SIC: 3441 Fabricated structural metal

(G-2241)
CROWN POINT SHOPPING NEWS
Also Called: Star
112 W Clark St (46307-3918)
PHONE...................................219 663-4212
Fax: 219 663-2077
Andrew Steel, *Principal*
EMP: 4
SQ FT: 3,000
SALES (est): 236.7K **Privately Held**
SIC: 2741 Shopping news: publishing & printing

(G-2242)
D TIMBER INC
14405 Clark St (46307-9497)
PHONE...................................219 374-8085
Dennis A Ohhof, *Principal*
EMP: 6 EST: 2001
SALES (est): 490.2K **Privately Held**
SIC: 2411 Timber, cut at logging camp

(G-2243)
DANUBIUS MACHINE INC
11205 Delaware Pkwy (46307-7812)
PHONE...................................219 662-7787
Dragan Giurovici, *Principal*
EMP: 7
SALES (est): 1.5MM **Privately Held**
SIC: 3541 Vertical turning & boring machines (metalworking)

(G-2244)
DAWN FOOD PRODUCTS INC
Also Called: Dawn Food Products Frozen Div
9601 Georgia St (46307-9846)
PHONE...................................800 333-3296
W Denson, *Branch Mgr*
EMP: 200
SQ FT: 27,000
SALES (corp-wide): 1.8B **Privately Held**
WEB: www.dawnfoods.com
SIC: 2051 Croissants, except frozen; pastries, e.g. danish: except frozen; yeast goods, sweet: except frozen
HQ: Dawn Food Products, Inc.
    3333 Sargent Rd
    Jackson MI 49201

(G-2245)
DEN-CRAFT DENTAL LABORATORY
1776 E North St (46307-8567)
PHONE...................................219 663-7776
Robert Slepcevich, *President*
EMP: 7
SQ FT: 500
SALES (est): 612.8K **Privately Held**
SIC: 3843 8072 Dental equipment & supplies; dental laboratories

(G-2246)
DONALD L GARD
11629 Burr St (46307-8766)
PHONE...................................219 663-7945
Donald L Gard, *President*
EMP: 3
SALES: 260.6K **Privately Held**
SIC: 3582 Washing machines, laundry: commercial, incl. coin-operated

(G-2247)
DYNA TECHNOLOGY INC
11025 Delaware Pkwy (46307-7895)
PHONE...................................219 663-2920
Veli Ozdemir, *Principal*
EMP: 6
SALES (est): 1.3MM **Privately Held**
SIC: 5031 1531 3354 Doors & windows; ; aluminum extruded products

(G-2248)
EAST CHICAGO MACHINE TOOL SLS
Also Called: Balemaster Division
980 Crown Ct (46307-2732)
PHONE...................................219 663-4525
Fax: 219 663-4591
Cornel E Raab, *President*
Kent Kolodziej, *Division Mgr*

Hilary A Raab Jr, *Vice Pres*
Chris Zale, *Prdtn Mgr*
Mathew Bradley, *Sales Mgr*
▲ EMP: 100
SQ FT: 44,000
SALES (est): 36MM **Privately Held**
WEB: www.balemaster.com
SIC: 3569 3589 Baling machines, for scrap metal, paper or similar material; shredders, industrial & commercial

(G-2249)
ELEMENT HOMES
11061 Broadway (46307-8834)
PHONE...................................219 310-2505
Robert Rossman, *Manager*
EMP: 4
SALES (est): 334.5K **Privately Held**
SIC: 2819 Elements

(G-2250)
ENGINEERED PRODUCTS INC
1203 E Summit St (46307-2730)
PHONE...................................219 662-2080
Robert A Scott Sr, *President*
EMP: 2
SALES (est): 280.1K **Privately Held**
WEB: www.engineeredproducts.net
SIC: 3271 Blocks, concrete: landscape or retaining wall

(G-2251)
EXACT SHEET METAL & SKYLIGHTS
763 Seminole Ct (46307-5200)
PHONE...................................219 670-3520
EMP: 2
SALES (est): 133.7K **Privately Held**
SIC: 3444 Sheet metalwork

(G-2252)
EXPEDITION LOG HOMES
11091 Marion Pl (46307-9428)
PHONE...................................219 663-5555
Stan Fryzel, *Owner*
EMP: 2
SALES (est): 170K **Privately Held**
WEB: www.luvlogs.com
SIC: 2452 1521 Log cabins, prefabricated, wood; single-family housing construction

(G-2253)
FINITE FILTATION COMPANY
120 Las Olas Ct (46307-8432)
PHONE...................................219 789-8084
Rick P Schultz, *CEO*
EMP: 2
SALES (est): 147.1K **Privately Held**
SIC: 3549 Metalworking machinery

(G-2254)
FIVES N AMERCN COMBUSTN INC
730 N Main St (46307-3236)
PHONE...................................219 662-9600
EMP: 4
SALES (corp-wide): 4.3MM **Privately Held**
SIC: 3433 Heating equipment, except electric
HQ: Fives North American Combustion, Inc.
    4455 E 71st St
    Cleveland OH 44105
    216 271-6000

(G-2255)
FUEL FABRICATION LLC
14727 Reeder Ct (46307-8514)
PHONE...................................219 390-7022
Joseph Ponziano, *Principal*
EMP: 2 EST: 2015
SALES (est): 50.6K **Privately Held**
SIC: 3999 Manufacturing industries

(G-2256)
HEARTLAND ADHESIVES INC
7519 Boardwalk (46307-8254)
PHONE...................................219 310-8645
James Pohlman, *President*
Tracy Pohlman, *President*
Matt Scheffer, *Sales Staff*
▲ EMP: 7
SALES (est): 1MM **Privately Held**
SIC: 2891 Adhesives

▲ = Import ▼=Export
◆ =Import/Export

(G-2257)
HOBART LOCKER & MEAT PKG CO
8602 Randolph St (46307-8818)
PHONE....................................219 942-5952
Peter Urenovich, *President*
EMP: 4
SQ FT: 4,000
SALES (est): 348K **Privately Held**
SIC: 2011 5147 Meat packing plants; meats, cured or smoked; meats, fresh

(G-2258)
HOME CITY ICE COMPANY
668 N Madison St (46307-8225)
PHONE....................................219 661-8369
Jason Niewoehner, *Manager*
EMP: 33
SALES (corp-wide): 314.5MM **Privately Held**
SIC: 2097 Ice cubes
PA: The Home City Ice Company
6045 Bridgetown Rd Ste 1
Cincinnati OH 45248
513 574-1800

(G-2259)
HUMPHREY PRINTING COMPANY INC
1001 E Summit St (46307-2727)
PHONE....................................765 452-0093
Fax: 765 452-0099
Ken Humphrey, *President*
Suzanne Meck, *Admin Sec*
EMP: 12 **EST:** 1931
SQ FT: 8,000
SALES (est): 1.3MM **Privately Held**
WEB: www.humphreyprinting.com
SIC: 2752 8742 Offset & photolithographic printing; commercial printing, offset; marketing consulting services

(G-2260)
IMAGE HOUSE INC
1001 E Summit St (46307-2727)
PHONE....................................219 947-0800
Amy Slater, *President*
Steve Slater, *Vice Pres*
EMP: 12
SQ FT: 20,000
SALES (est): 2.1MM **Privately Held**
WEB: www.theimagehouse.net
SIC: 2752 2741 Poster & decal printing, lithographic; promotional printing, lithographic; posters: publishing & printing

(G-2261)
IMCO INDUSTRIAL MACHINE CORP
1201 S Main St (46307-8481)
P.O. Box 943 (46308-0943)
PHONE....................................219 663-6100
Fax: 219 663-5168
Steve Higgins, *President*
Shirley Crapbis, *Corp Secy*
Mark McGurk, *Vice Pres*
EMP: 23
SQ FT: 18,000
SALES (est): 4MM **Privately Held**
SIC: 3599 Machine shop, jobbing & repair

(G-2262)
INDUSTRIAL CONDUCTOR PRODUCTS
10172 Florida Ln (46307-7577)
PHONE....................................219 662-9477
Michael D Haines, *President*
▼ **EMP:** 2 **EST:** 1997
SALES (est): 220K **Privately Held**
SIC: 3625 8711 Industrial controls: push button, selector switches, pilot; engineering services

(G-2263)
INSTANT MEMORABILIA INC
12880 Jefferson Dr (46307-7955)
PHONE....................................219 661-8942
David K De Espinosa, *Principal*
EMP: 2
SALES (est): 130.5K **Privately Held**
SIC: 2752 Commercial printing, lithographic

(G-2264)
JAC JMR INC
Also Called: Quality Imprssons Print Design
1849 E Summit St (46307-2768)
PHONE....................................219 663-6700
Judy Cruse, *President*
EMP: 3
SQ FT: 2,880
SALES (est): 1.1MM **Privately Held**
SIC: 5085 5084 2759 Industrial supplies; printing trades machinery, equipment & supplies; commercial printing

(G-2265)
JADCO LTD
401 N Jackson St (46307-3368)
P.O. Box 267 (46308-0267)
PHONE....................................219 661-2065
John Amodeo, *President*
Charleen Amodeo, *Corp Secy*
Richard Amodeo, *Vice Pres*
▲ **EMP:** 10
SQ FT: 3,000
SALES (est): 2.3MM **Privately Held**
SIC: 5193 3999 Artificial flowers; wreaths, artificial

(G-2266)
JAMES MOBILE OIL CHANGE
291 S Chase Dr (46307-3713)
PHONE....................................219 455-5321
James Kolodziej, *Principal*
EMP: 3
SALES (est): 119.9K **Privately Held**
SIC: 1311 Crude petroleum & natural gas

(G-2267)
JAY COSTAS COMPANIES INC
Also Called: Oil and Go
1492 N Main St (46307-2302)
PHONE....................................219 663-4364
Fax: 219 662-1648
Anne Geary, *Manager*
EMP: 6
SALES (corp-wide): 3.6MM **Privately Held**
SIC: 1389 Oil field services
PA: Jay Costas Companies Inc
121 Lincolnway
Valparaiso IN 46383
219 464-9819

(G-2268)
JD MATERIALS
11563 Baker St (46307-4262)
PHONE....................................219 662-1418
James D Miller, *Principal*
EMP: 2
SALES (est): 241.5K **Privately Held**
SIC: 3537 Industrial trucks & tractors

(G-2269)
JOHNSON CONTROLS INC
2293 N Main St (46307-1854)
PHONE....................................219 736-7105
George Kosides, *Owner*
EMP: 94 **Privately Held**
SIC: 2531 Seats, automobile
HQ: Johnson Controls, Inc.
5757 N Green Bay Ave
Milwaukee WI 53209
414 524-1200

(G-2270)
JP TECHNOLOGY INC
10769 Broadway (46307-7316)
PHONE....................................219 947-2525
Jerry Pagell, *President*
EMP: 3
SALES (est): 351.3K **Privately Held**
SIC: 3651 Home entertainment equipment, electronic

(G-2271)
KIEMLE-HANKINS COMPANY
Also Called: Kh
1011 E Summit St (46307-2727)
PHONE....................................219 213-2643
Mark Martrano, *Manager*
EMP: 11
SALES (corp-wide): 20MM **Privately Held**
SIC: 7694 Electric motor repair

PA: The Kiemle-Hankins Company
94 H St
Perrysburg OH 43551
419 661-2430

(G-2272)
KONECRANES INC
Also Called: Crane Pro Services
1255 Erie Ct Ste B (46307-2770)
PHONE....................................219 661-9602
Fax: 219 763-9838
Heather Hughes, *Manager*
EMP: 16
SALES (corp-wide): 3.7B **Privately Held**
SIC: 3531 Cranes
HQ: Konecranes, Inc.
4401 Gateway Blvd
Springfield OH 45502

(G-2273)
KONRADY GRAPHICS INC
4070 Bush Hill Ct (46307-8953)
P.O. Box 174 (46308-0174)
PHONE....................................219 662-0436
Thomas E Konrady, *President*
Kimberly Konrady, *President*
EMP: 4
SALES: 300K **Privately Held**
SIC: 3993 Signs & advertising specialties

(G-2274)
KUMPLETE AIRWAY SOLUTIONS INC
625 Fairfield Dr (46307-4592)
P.O. Box 1099 (46308-1099)
PHONE....................................219 680-0836
David Kumpbel, *Principal*
David Kumpbell, *Principal*
EMP: 2
SALES (est): 86.6K **Privately Held**
SIC: 3841 Anesthesia apparatus

(G-2275)
LEROY E DOTY CABINET SHOP
Also Called: Doty, Leroy E. Builder
4514 W 105th Ave (46307-2501)
PHONE....................................219 663-1139
Leroy E Doty, *Owner*
Carol Doty, *Co-Owner*
EMP: 3 **EST:** 1955
SALES: 140K **Privately Held**
SIC: 1521 2434 2521 General remodeling, single-family houses; wood kitchen cabinets; cabinets, office: wood

(G-2276)
LGS PLUMBING INC
1112 E Summit St (46307-2729)
PHONE....................................219 663-2177
Fax: 219 662-2788
Sandra K Smith, *President*
Larry G Smith, *Vice Pres*
EMP: 25
SQ FT: 12,000
SALES (est): 6.8MM **Privately Held**
SIC: 3432 1623 Plastic plumbing fixture fittings, assembly; underground utilities contractor

(G-2277)
LITTLE GREEN APPLE HALLMARK
10827 Broadway (46307-7303)
PHONE....................................219 661-0420
EMP: 2
SALES (est): 85.9K **Privately Held**
SIC: 3571 Personal computers (microcomputers)

(G-2278)
MICROWORKS INC
2200 W 97th Pl (46307-2344)
PHONE....................................219 661-8620
Dawn E McIver, *President*
Edward L McIver, *Vice Pres*
Natalie Behm, *QC Mgr*
EMP: 6
SALES (est): 1.1MM **Privately Held**
WEB: www.mwiconsulting.com
SIC: 2835 Microbiology & virology diagnostic products

(G-2279)
NORTH STAR SIGNS INC
9117 Fairbanks St (46307-8854)
PHONE....................................219 365-5935
Ron Sefcik, *President*
Cindy Sefcik, *Vice Pres*
EMP: 3
SALES: 150K **Privately Held**
WEB: www.northstarsign.com
SIC: 3993 Signs & advertising specialties

(G-2280)
NUCOR COLD FINISH
12451 Shelby Pl (46307-9499)
PHONE....................................219 937-1442
EMP: 2 **EST:** 2010
SALES (est): 130K **Privately Held**
SIC: 3312 Blast Furnace-Steel Works

(G-2281)
OH PHARMACEUTICAL CO LTD
9800 Connecticut Dr (46307-7840)
PHONE....................................219 644-3239
GI Bum OH, *CEO*
EMP: 4
SALES (est): 229.4K **Privately Held**
SIC: 2834 Pharmaceutical preparations

(G-2282)
OZINGA BROS INC
1211 E Summit St (46307-2730)
PHONE....................................219 662-0925
Fax: 219 663-7087
Chad Biggs, *Manager*
EMP: 20
SALES (corp-wide): 269.8MM **Privately Held**
SIC: 3273 Ready-mixed concrete
PA: Ozinga Bros., Inc.
19001 Old Lagrange Rd # 30
Mokena IL 60448
708 326-4200

(G-2283)
PHIL & SON INC
871 N Madison St (46307-8212)
PHONE....................................219 663-5757
Fax: 219 663-1066
Alfred Pante, *President*
Vicky Pante, *Admin Sec*
EMP: 12
SQ FT: 7,200
SALES (est): 1.9MM **Privately Held**
WEB: www.philandson.com
SIC: 7699 1731 5063 3699 Locksmith shop; fire detection & burglar alarm systems specialization; burglar alarm systems; security control equipment & systems; security systems services; burglar alarm maintenance & monitoring

(G-2284)
PLOOG ENGINEERING CO INC
814 N Indiana Ave (46307-3447)
PHONE....................................219 663-2854
Fax: 219 663-1373
Max H Ploog, *President*
Ploog Gisela M, *Admin Sec*
EMP: 8 **EST:** 1981
SQ FT: 6,400
SALES (est): 1.2MM **Privately Held**
SIC: 2899 3599 3544 Soil testing kits; machine shop, jobbing & repair; special dies & tools

(G-2285)
POINT MEDICAL CORPORATION (PA)
891 E Summit St (46307-2700)
PHONE....................................219 663-1775
Fax: 219 663-2877
Timothy M Schweikert, *President*
Michelle Cochran, *QC Mgr*
John Cstevens, *Treasurer*
Michael Ibasta, *Director*
▲ **EMP:** 695
SQ FT: 6,000
SALES (est): 70.3MM **Privately Held**
WEB: www.pointmedical.com
SIC: 3841 3842 Surgical & medical instruments; surgical appliances & supplies

GEOGRAPHIC

(G-2286)
POINT MEDICAL CORPORATION
891 E Summit St (46307-2700)
PHONE..............................219 663-1775
Rick Ferraro, *President*
EMP: 140
SALES (est): 6.2MM
SALES (corp-wide): 70.3MM **Privately Held**
WEB: www.pointmedical.com
SIC: 3841 Surgical & medical instruments
PA: Point Medical Corporation
　891 E Summit St
　Crown Point IN 46307
　219 663-1775

(G-2287)
PORTER COUNTY FABRICATORS
13405 Montgomery St (46307-9258)
PHONE..............................219 663-4665
Anthony Brewer, *Owner*
EMP: 8
SALES (est): 766.5K **Privately Held**
SIC: 3498 Fabricated pipe & fittings

(G-2288)
POWDERCOIL TECHNOLOGIES LLC
9800 Connecticut Dr (46307-7840)
PHONE..............................708 634-2343
Robert McShane, *President*
EMP: 2 EST: 2016
SQ FT: 1,000
SALES: 50K **Privately Held**
SIC: 3479 Coating of metals & formed products

(G-2289)
PREFERRED METAL SERVICES INC
1146 Sunnyslope Dr (46307-9312)
PHONE..............................219 988-2386
William M Glass, *President*
D Joyce Glass, *Admin Sec*
EMP: 2 EST: 2001
SQ FT: 1,774
SALES: 75K **Privately Held**
SIC: 5051 3493 Sheets, metal; steel springs, except wire

(G-2290)
PYRO SHIELD INC
1171 Erie Court Crown Pt Crown Point (46307)
PHONE..............................219 661-8600
Donald J Murphy, *President*
Bill Gomez, *Vice Pres*
Andrew Passage, *Admin Sec*
▲ EMP: 15
SQ FT: 23,000
SALES (est): 2.2MM **Privately Held**
SIC: 2211 Canvas & other heavy coarse fabrics: cotton

(G-2291)
RACE ENGINEERING
725 E Goldsborough St # 4 (46307-3393)
PHONE..............................219 661-8904
Fax: 219 661-8904
Dennis Rys, *President*
Kevin Rys, *Vice Pres*
EMP: 2
SALES (est): 259K **Privately Held**
WEB: www.raceengineeringonline.com
SIC: 3711 Automobile assembly, including specialty automobiles

(G-2292)
RED CLOUD ADHESIVES INC
9800 Connecticut Dr (46307-7840)
PHONE..............................219 331-3239
John Sukta, *President*
Taylor Gatz, *Opers Mgr*
EMP: 3
SALES: 300K **Privately Held**
SIC: 2891 Adhesives, paste

(G-2293)
REDAB INDUSTRIES
10425 Maine Dr (46307-7069)
PHONE..............................219 484-8382
Michael Bader, *Principal*
EMP: 2

SALES (est): 177.7K **Privately Held**
SIC: 3999 Manufacturing industries

(G-2294)
REGION COMMUNICATIONS INC
Also Called: Winfield American, The
7590 E 109th Ave (46307-8631)
PHONE..............................219 662-8888
Mike Kucic, *President*
Mike Gooldy, *Vice Pres*
EMP: 2
SALES (est): 151.7K **Privately Held**
SIC: 2711 Newspapers: publishing only, not printed on site

(G-2295)
REGIONAL DATA SERVICES INC
1260 Arrowhead Ct (46307-8222)
PHONE..............................219 661-3200
Fax: 219 661-3210
Rosalind Henderson, *President*
Lori Schuffert, *Manager*
Tish Wilson, *Technology*
Kevin Hanusin, *Software Dev*
Lynda Jones, *Analyst*
EMP: 13
SALES (est): 1.1MM **Privately Held**
WEB: www.regionaldata.com
SIC: 7371 7372 Computer software development; prepackaged software

(G-2296)
RIDDELL TECHNOLOGIES LLC
1351 W 95th Ct (46307-2270)
PHONE..............................219 213-9602
Darrell Riddell,
EMP: 4 EST: 2014
SALES (est): 126.5K **Privately Held**
SIC: 7378 3571 5734 7371 Computer maintenance & repair; computers, digital, analog or hybrid; mainframe computers; computer software & accessories; computer software development

(G-2297)
ROHDER MACHINE & TOOL INC
1023 E Summit St (46307-2794)
PHONE..............................219 663-3697
Fax: 219 662-9718
Daniel J Rohder, *President*
Laurie G Rohder, *Corp Secy*
Matthew Rohder, *Opers Mgr*
EMP: 14
SQ FT: 7,000
SALES (est): 3.3MM **Privately Held**
WEB: www.rohdermachineandbolt.com
SIC: 3452 3599 Bolts, metal; screws, metal; machine shop, jobbing & repair

(G-2298)
ROTA SKIPPER CORPORATION
130 E 168th St (46307)
P.O. Box 219, South Holland IL (60473-0219)
PHONE..............................708 331-0660
Clifford Fitch, *President*
C E Fitch Jr, *Principal*
Clifford Fitch III, *Vice Pres*
Willow J Fitch, *Admin Sec*
EMP: 18 EST: 1940
SQ FT: 10,000
SALES (est): 4.9MM **Privately Held**
WEB: www.pizzamaticusa.com
SIC: 3556 7692 Food products machinery; welding repair

(G-2299)
SCHEFFER INTERNATIONAL INC
1155 Arrowhead Ct (46307-7538)
PHONE..............................219 736-6200
Fax: 219 736-5251
Buddy Scheffer, *President*
Eric Lo, *Admin Sec*
◆ EMP: 15
SQ FT: 9,100
SALES (est): 3.6MM **Privately Held**
SIC: 3555 Printing trades machinery

(G-2300)
SCHMIGBOB LLC
5366 E 111th Ave (46307-5600)
PHONE..............................219 781-7991
Matthew Bigelow, *Principal*
EMP: 3
SALES (est): 188K **Privately Held**
SIC: 3999 Manufacturing industries

(G-2301)
SCOTT STEEL SERVICES INC
1203 E Summit St (46307-2730)
PHONE..............................219 663-4740
Robert A Scott, *President*
Bill Scott, *Vice Pres*
Valerie Scott, *Office Mgr*
EMP: 4
SALES (est): 867.1K **Privately Held**
SIC: 3441 Fabricated structural metal

(G-2302)
SCOTTS COMPANY LLC
825 S Main St (46307-4815)
PHONE..............................219 663-3830
David Louttit, *Branch Mgr*
EMP: 40
SALES (corp-wide): 2.6B **Publicly Held**
WEB: www.scottscompany.com
SIC: 2873 Fertilizers: natural (organic), except compost
HQ: The Scotts Company Llc
　14111 Scottslawn Rd
　Marysville OH 43040
　937 644-3729

(G-2303)
SHAW POLYMERS LLC (PA)
530 N Indiana Ave (46307-3412)
PHONE..............................219 779-9450
Jim Adams, *President*
John O'Keafe, *Business Mgr*
John O'Keafe, *Business Mgr*
Patti Hull, *Opers Mgr*
Kelly Gillig, *CFO*
EMP: 12
SQ FT: 1,500
SALES (est): 10.2MM **Privately Held**
SIC: 2821 5162 Plastics materials & resins; plastics materials & basic shapes

(G-2304)
SIGNS ON TIME INC
10740 Broadway (46307-7310)
PHONE..............................219 661-4488
Fax: 219 661-9930
Roland Brauer, *President*
EMP: 11
SALES (est): 1.2MM **Privately Held**
SIC: 3993 Signs & advertising specialties

(G-2305)
SIMPLIFIED IMAGING LLC
1126 Arrowhead Ct (46307-6801)
PHONE..............................219 663-5122
Gerald G Gross, *Principal*
EMP: 6 EST: 2009
SALES (est): 644.2K **Privately Held**
SIC: 2759 Laser printing

(G-2306)
SITTIN PRETTY LLC
9470 Randolph St (46307-8628)
PHONE..............................219 947-4121
Judith Stevens, *President*
EMP: 3
SALES (est): 195.5K **Privately Held**
SIC: 3999 Pet supplies

(G-2307)
SONAM TECHNOLOGIES LLC
9800 Connecticut Dr (46307-7840)
PHONE..............................844 887-6626
Christopher Hanson, *Principal*
Michael Hanson, *Principal*
Chris Hanson, *Manager*
EMP: 2 EST: 2016
SALES (est): 126.1K **Privately Held**
SIC: 3829 Physical property testing equipment

(G-2308)
SOPHYSA USA INC
503 E Summit St Ste 5 (46307-3477)
PHONE..............................219 663-7711
Philippe Negre, *President*
Steve Egan, *Vice Pres*
EMP: 3
SALES (est): 329.3K **Privately Held**
SIC: 3841 Surgical & medical instruments

(G-2309)
STATION 21 AMERICAN DRILL
201 N Main St (46307-3248)
PHONE..............................219 661-0021
Vernon Segert, *Owner*

EMP: 7
SALES (est): 813K **Privately Held**
SIC: 3541 Drilling & boring machines

(G-2310)
STO-AWAY POWER CRANE INC
9306 Grand Blvd (46307-8829)
PHONE..............................219 942-9797
Cynthia Scegiel, *President*
Cynthia Lynn Scegiel, *President*
Mark Scegiel, *General Mgr*
▲ EMP: 6
SQ FT: 3,400
SALES (est): 1MM **Privately Held**
WEB: www.stoaway.com
SIC: 3537 Cranes, industrial truck

(G-2311)
SUKE INC
2903 Acorn Ct (46307-5191)
PHONE..............................219 689-0321
EMP: 3
SALES (est): 200K **Privately Held**
SIC: 3131 Mfg Footwear Cut Stock

(G-2312)
TDK GRAPHICS INC
1180 N Main St (46307-2715)
PHONE..............................219 663-7799
Tim Koedyker, *President*
Darwin Koedyker, *President*
EMP: 13
SQ FT: 3,200
SALES (est): 2.5MM **Privately Held**
WEB: www.kwikkopyprinting-cp.com
SIC: 2752 7334 7389 Commercial printing, lithographic; photocopying & duplicating services; printers' services: folding, collating

(G-2313)
THERMAL TECH & TEMP INC
772 N Madison St (46307-8210)
PHONE..............................219 808-1258
Tasha Gomez, *Principal*
EMP: 2
SALES: 600K **Privately Held**
SIC: 3567 Induction heating equipment

(G-2314)
TITAN MANUFACTURING CO
13128 Iowa St (46307-9722)
P.O. Box 989 (46308-0989)
PHONE..............................219 662-7238
James Bova, *President*
Ida Novick, *Vice Pres*
EMP: 5 EST: 1966
SQ FT: 14,000
SALES (est): 517.5K **Privately Held**
SIC: 3469 Stamping metal for the trade

(G-2315)
TOP FUEL CROSSFIT
1674 E North St (46307-8568)
PHONE..............................219 281-7001
Michael Young, *Manager*
EMP: 3 EST: 2015
SALES (est): 97.2K **Privately Held**
SIC: 2869 Fuels

(G-2316)
TOWN & COUNTRY INDUSTRIES INC
Also Called: Town & Country Printing
1001 E Summit St (46307-2727)
PHONE..............................219 712-0893
Debera L Hunchy, *President*
EMP: 28 EST: 1970
SQ FT: 21,000
SALES (est): 5.6MM **Privately Held**
WEB: www.townandcountryprinting.com
SIC: 2752 3993 Commercial printing, lithographic; promotional printing, lithographic; signs & advertising specialties

(G-2317)
UTILITIES AVIATION SPECIALISTS
401 W Summit St (46307-2601)
P.O. Box 810 (46308-0810)
PHONE..............................219 662-8175
Robert Feerst, *President*
Patricia Feerst, *Vice Pres*
EMP: 2

▲ = Import ▼=Export
◆ =Import/Export

SALES: 100K Privately Held
WEB: www.helicoptersafety.com
SIC: 3721 8742 Helicopters; planning consultant

(G-2318)
VKF RENZEL USA CORP
1311 Merrillville Rd (46307-2708)
PHONE..................................219 661-6300
Heinz Renzel, *President*
Marc Tacke, *General Mgr*
▲ EMP: 10
SQ FT: 4,000
SALES (est): 1.5MM
SALES (corp-wide): 823.8K **Privately Held**
SIC: 3993 Signs & advertising specialties
HQ: Vkf Renzel Gmbh
Im Geer 15
Isselburg 46419
287 491-00

(G-2319)
VOTER REGISTRATION
2293 N Main St (46307-1854)
PHONE..................................219 755-3795
Sally Lasota, *Exec Dir*
EMP: 3
SALES (est): 200.2K **Privately Held**
SIC: 3579 Office machines

(G-2320)
WILLIE AND ASSOCIATES INC
11188 State St (46307-8608)
PHONE..................................219 662-9046
Terry Willie, *President*
EMP: 5
SALES (est): 291.3K **Privately Held**
SIC: 2599 Cabinets, factory

(G-2321)
WIW INC
424 Wessex Rd (46307)
P.O. Box 704 (46308-0704)
PHONE..................................219 663-7900
Fax: 219 663-7938
Darren Grabek, *President*
Kay Grabek, *Corp Secy*
Brian Sadewasser, *Project Mgr*
EMP: 25
SQ FT: 12,000
SALES (est): 7.7MM **Privately Held**
SIC: 3441 3446 Fabricated structural
metal; architectural metalwork; balconies,
metal; gates, ornamental metal; stairs,
staircases, stair treads: prefabricated
metal

(G-2322)
WOOD SPECIALISTS LLC
12120 Chase St (46307-8740)
PHONE..................................219 779-9026
EMP: 2
SALES (est): 304K **Privately Held**
SIC: 2431 Millwork

(G-2323)
WORTH PUBLICATIONS LLC
13398 Hayes Ct (46307-7807)
P.O. Box 683 (46308-0683)
PHONE..................................219 808-4001
EMP: 2
SALES (est): 87.3K **Privately Held**
SIC: 2741 Miscellaneous publishing

Culver
Marshall County

(G-2324)
ACURA PHARMACEUTICAL TECH
16235 State Road 17 (46511-9010)
PHONE..................................574 842-3305
Peter A Clemens, *Vice Pres*
James Emigh, *Vice Pres*
Robert Seiser, *Treasurer*
EMP: 8
SQ FT: 40,000
SALES (est): 1.4MM
SALES (corp-wide): 2.9MM **Publicly Held**
WEB: www.halseydrug.com
SIC: 2834 Pharmaceutical preparations

PA: Acura Pharmaceuticals, Inc.
616 N North Ct Ste 120
Palatine IL 60067
847 705-7709

(G-2325)
JAY RETAIL SYSTEMS LLC
402 W Cass St (46511-1402)
PHONE..................................574 842-2313
Frederick Jay Bletzinger, *Principal*
▲ EMP: 2
SALES (est): 236.6K **Privately Held**
SIC: 3578 Accounting machines & cash
registers

(G-2326)
SPOTLIGHT LLC
1300 Academy Rd (46511-1234)
PHONE..................................219 616-4421
Hayes Barnes, *Principal*
EMP: 2
SALES (est): 88.3K **Privately Held**
SIC: 3648 Spotlights

(G-2327)
THUNDRBIRD TRADITIONAL ARCHERY
306 N Ohio St (46511-1524)
PHONE..................................812 699-1099
David C Johnson, *Owner*
Dianne Johnson, *Co-Owner*
EMP: 3
SALES: 75K **Privately Held**
SIC: 3949 Bows, archery

Cutler
Carroll County

(G-2328)
CD & WS BORDNER ENTPS INC
Also Called: Bordners Truck Repair & Algnmt
6559 S State Road 75 (46920-9361)
P.O. Box 355 (46920-0355)
PHONE..................................765 268-2120
Dave Bordner, *President*
Wendy Bordner, *Treasurer*
EMP: 2
SQ FT: 4,500
SALES: 240K **Privately Held**
SIC: 1799 7538 3523 7231 Welding on
site; general truck repair; driers (farm):
grain, hay & seed; hairdressers

Cynthiana
Posey County

(G-2329)
B B MINING INC (PA)
11700 Water Tank Rd (47612-9528)
PHONE..................................812 845-2717
Steve Blankenberger, *President*
Donald Blankenberger, *Vice Pres*
David Blankenberger, *Vice Pres*
Rick Blankenberger, *Asst Treas*
Beth Blankenberger, *Admin Sec*
EMP: 3
SALES (est): 3.5MM **Privately Held**
SIC: 1241 Coal mining services

Dale
Spencer County

(G-2330)
ALBERT RANSOM LOGGING INC
7300 Lauderdale Rd (47523-9293)
PHONE..................................812 567-2012
Albert Ransom, *President*
Brenda Ransom, *Admin Sec*
EMP: 3
SALES (est): 374.6K **Privately Held**
SIC: 2411 Logging

(G-2331)
C&S MACHINERY INC
5440 E 2150 N (47523)
P.O. Box 313, Santa Claus (47579-0313)
PHONE..................................812 937-2160
William Sexton, *President*

EMP: 2
SALES (est): 268.5K **Privately Held**
SIC: 3569 General industrial machinery

(G-2332)
MULZER CRUSHED STONE INC
4590 E Aw Mulzer Dr (47523)
P.O. Box 28 (47523-0028)
PHONE..................................812 937-2442
Fax: 812 937-2442
Kenneth Mulzer, *President*
Mathew Bunner, *Safety Dir*
Gloria Allen, *Human Res Mgr*
EMP: 2
SALES (corp-wide): 29.7B **Privately Held**
WEB: www.mulzer.com
SIC: 1422 Crushed & broken limestone
HQ: Mulzer Crushed Stone Inc
534 Mozart St
Tell City IN 47586
812 547-7921

(G-2333)
SPENCER INDUSTRIES INC (PA)
902 Buffaloville Rd (47523-9057)
PHONE..................................812 937-4561
Fax: 812 937-4637
Tom Messmer, *President*
Jarid Hirt, *Vice Pres*
Eric Olinger, *Admin Sec*
▲ EMP: 190
SQ FT: 400,000
SALES (est): 35MM **Privately Held**
WEB: www.spencerindustries.com
SIC: 3089 Thermoformed finished plastic
products; cases, plastic

(G-2334)
THERMWOOD CORPORATION
904 Buffaloville Rd (47523-9057)
P.O. Box 436 (47523-0436)
PHONE..................................812 937-4476
Fax: 812 937-2956
Kenneth Susnjara, *CEO*
David Hildenbrand, *President*
Kishor Dabhade, *General Mgr*
Mike Hardesty, *Exec VP*
Michael Hardesty, *Vice Pres*
◆ EMP: 96
SQ FT: 170,000
SALES (est): 40MM **Privately Held**
WEB: www.thermwood.com
SIC: 3541 Robots for drilling, cutting, grinding, polishing, etc.

(G-2335)
UNIVERSAL PACKAGE LLC
Also Called: Universal Package Systems
4360 E 2150 N (47523)
P.O. Box 88 (47523-0088)
PHONE..................................812 937-3605
JD Kulbeth, *President*
James Davis, *Vice Pres*
Chad Hess, *Controller*
Jim Kulbeth, *Mng Member*
Jim Davis,
EMP: 15
SQ FT: 24,000
SALES (est): 5MM **Privately Held**
SIC: 2671 5085 Plastic film, coated or
laminated for packaging; bins & containers, storage

(G-2336)
YELLOW BANKS CLAY COMPANY INC
Also Called: Yellow Banks Recreation Center
12733 Yellowbanks Trl (47523-8854)
PHONE..................................812 567-4703
James H Marshall, *President*
Patsy Marshall, *Admin Sec*
EMP: 10
SALES (est): 370K **Privately Held**
SIC: 7032 3269 5199 5411 Recreational
camps; cookware: stoneware, coarse
earthenware & pottery; artists' materials;
grocery stores, independent

Daleville
Delaware County

(G-2337)
CASH & CARRY LUMBER CO INC
Also Called: Fuller Architectural Hardwoods
14113 W Main St (47334-9758)
P.O. Box 427 (47334-0427)
PHONE..................................765 378-7575
Fax: 765 378-7545
William Smith, *CEO*
Fred W Fuller II, *President*
Ed Orem, *CFO*
EMP: 12
SQ FT: 40,000
SALES (est): 1.7MM **Privately Held**
WEB: www.fullerarchitectural.com
SIC: 2431 Millwork

(G-2338)
CHESTERFIELD TOOL & ENGRG INC
13710 W Commerce Rd (47334-9347)
P.O. Box 566 (47334-0566)
PHONE..................................765 378-5101
Fax: 765 378-5253
Rick A Ray, *President*
Greg Julian, *General Mgr*
Blake Edwards, *Engineer*
Bruce Hughes, *Project Engr*
Luannen Julian, *CFO*
EMP: 25
SQ FT: 50,000
SALES: 2.9MM **Privately Held**
WEB: www.chesterfieldtool.com
SIC: 3829 3545 7692 3599 Measuring &
controlling devices; gauges (machine tool
accessories); welding repair; machine
shop, jobbing & repair; special dies, tools,
jigs & fixtures

(G-2339)
FILLMANNS INDUSTRIES LLC
3921 S Highbanks Rd (47334-9609)
PHONE..................................765 744-4772
Peter Fillmann, *Principal*
EMP: 2
SALES (est): 110.2K **Privately Held**
SIC: 3999 Manufacturing industries

(G-2340)
JERRY LAMBERT
10010 S County Road 900 W
(47334-9704)
PHONE..................................765 378-7599
Jerry Lambert, *Owner*
EMP: 2 EST: 2000
SALES: 130K **Privately Held**
SIC: 7692 Welding repair

(G-2341)
PRECISION ABRASIVE MACHINERY
14200 W Commerce Rd (47334-9345)
P.O. Box 543 (47334-0543)
PHONE..................................765 378-3315
Fax: 765 378-3316
Edward J Kerr, *President*
Darlene Kerr, *Vice Pres*
EMP: 5
SQ FT: 10,000
SALES: 400K **Privately Held**
WEB: www.precisionabrasive.com
SIC: 3541 Grinding machines, metalworking

Dana
Vermillion County

(G-2342)
DAVERN MACHINE SHOP
Also Called: John Davern
1248 E 500 S (47847-8026)
PHONE..................................765 505-1051
John M Davern, *Owner*
Martha Davern, *Admin Sec*
EMP: 2

SALES: 200K **Privately Held**
SIC: **3523** 1799 Farm machinery & equipment; welding on site

Danville
Hendricks County

(G-2343)
BIO-RESPONSE SOLUTIONS INC
200 Colin Ct (46122-7933)
PHONE.....................317 386-3500
Joseph H Wilson, *CEO*
Lucus J Wilson, *President*
Barbra L Wilson, *Treasurer*
▲ EMP: 10
SQ FT: 9,000
SALES (est): 2.5MM **Privately Held**
SIC: **3589** 5169 Water treatment equipment, industrial; alkalines

(G-2344)
BOOMERANG VENTURES LLC
3367 N County Road 575 E (46122-8690)
PHONE.....................317 852-7786
Joe Gromosky, *Principal*
EMP: 2
SALES (est): 144.1K **Privately Held**
SIC: **3949** Boomerangs

(G-2345)
BUILT BY BILL
360 E Columbia St (46122-1306)
PHONE.....................317 745-2666
William Leisch, *Principal*
EMP: 2
SALES (est): 109.4K **Privately Held**
SIC: **3993** Signs & advertising specialties

(G-2346)
FACET ENGINEERING
1 Hickory Ct (46122-1441)
PHONE.....................317 745-5070
William Bollman, *Owner*
Palmira Bollman, *Co-Owner*
EMP: 2
SALES (est): 121.8K **Privately Held**
SIC: **3544** Special dies, tools, jigs & fixtures

(G-2347)
FLAVOR BURST CO LLP
499 Commerce Dr (46122-7848)
PHONE.....................317 745-2952
Fax: 317 745-2377
Timothy Jay Gerber, *General Ptnr*
Thomas John Gerber, *General Ptnr*
▲ EMP: 18
SQ FT: 35,000
SALES (est): 4.2MM **Privately Held**
WEB: www.flavorburst.com
SIC: **3556** 5149 Ice cream manufacturing machinery; syrups, except for fountain use

(G-2348)
HUNT AND SONS MEMORIAL LLC
2655 E Main St (46122-8468)
PHONE.....................317 745-0940
Matt Hunt, *Principal*
EMP: 3
SALES (est): 306.2K **Privately Held**
SIC: **2759** Engraving

(G-2349)
INCENSE INCENSE ✪
256 Canal West Cir (46122-2517)
PHONE.....................317 544-9444
Amanda Lebrun, *Principal*
EMP: 2 EST: 2017
SALES (est): 74.4K **Privately Held**
SIC: **2899** Incense

(G-2350)
KADEL ENGINEERING CORPORATION
1627 E Main St (46122-9468)
PHONE.....................317 745-2798
Fax: 317 745-2799
Keith Alexander, *Ch of Bd*
David Alexander, *President*
Dolores Alexander, *Corp Secy*
Sheri Lemon, *Vice Pres*

EMP: 35 EST: 1966
SQ FT: 22,000
SALES: 3.5MM **Privately Held**
WEB: www.kadel.com
SIC: **3679** Cryogenic cooling devices for infrared detectors, masers

(G-2351)
LEACH & SONS WATERCARE (PA)
Also Called: Leach and Sons Water Systems
671 E Main St (46122-1939)
PHONE.....................317 248-8954
Fax: 317 745-6971
Paul Leach, *Owner*
EMP: 4
SALES: 400K **Privately Held**
SIC: **7389** 3589 Water softener service; water filters & softeners, household type

(G-2352)
MAGWERKS CORPORATION
501 Commerce Dr (46122-7976)
PHONE.....................317 241-8011
Patrick Jenkins, *President*
▲ EMP: 15
SQ FT: 50,000
SALES (est): 2.6MM **Privately Held**
WEB: www.magwerks.com
SIC: **3829** Physical property testing equipment

(G-2353)
MEARS MACHINE CORP
2983 S County Road 300 E (46122-9447)
PHONE.....................317 745-0656
Jeff Mears, *President*
EMP: 55
SALES (est): 4.9MM
SALES (corp-wide): 15.4MM **Privately Held**
WEB: www.mearsmachine.com
SIC: **3531** Airport construction machinery
PA: Mears Machine Corp
　　9973 E Us Highway 36
　　Avon IN 46123
　　317 271-6041

(G-2354)
OWEN WOODWORKING
3012 S State Road 39 (46122-7961)
PHONE.....................317 331-6936
Jason Owen, *Owner*
EMP: 2
SALES (est): 145.9K **Privately Held**
SIC: **2431** Millwork

(G-2355)
QUALITY HYDRAULIC & MCH SVC
4905 E County Road 450 N (46122-9307)
PHONE.....................317 892-2596
Richard Russell, *President*
Linda Russell, *Vice Pres*
EMP: 3
SALES: 190K **Privately Held**
SIC: **3498** 3699 Tube fabricating (contract bending & shaping); electrical equipment & supplies

(G-2356)
REPUBLICAN
Also Called: Republican Newspaper
6 E Main St (46122-1818)
PHONE.....................317 745-2777
Fax: 317 745-2777
Betty Weesner, *Owner*
EMP: 3
SALES (est): 232.6K **Privately Held**
WEB: www.republicannewspaper.com
SIC: **2711** Newspapers: publishing only, not printed on site

(G-2357)
SCOTTS FASTENERS & SUPPLY LLC
1945 W County Road 300 S (46122-8135)
P.O. Box 671 (46122-0671)
PHONE.....................317 372-8743
Douglas Scott, *Mng Member*
EMP: 2 EST: 2010
SALES (est): 186.1K **Privately Held**
SIC: **3965** Fasteners

(G-2358)
WILSON PRINTING
527 N County Road 50 E (46122-9502)
PHONE.....................317 745-5868
Fax: 317 745-5868
Rex Wilson, *President*
EMP: 2
SALES (est): 121.8K **Privately Held**
SIC: **2759** Letterpress printing

Darlington
Montgomery County

(G-2359)
ANDERSON PRODUCTS
700 E Rd (47940)
P.O. Box 335 (47940-0335)
PHONE.....................765 794-4242
Jack Anderson, *Partner*
Charles Anderson, *Partner*
EMP: 2
SALES (est): 180K **Privately Held**
SIC: **3089** Injection molding of plastics

(G-2360)
B&H INDUSTRIES CORPORATION
6425 E South St (47940-4033)
P.O. Box 460 (47940-0460)
PHONE.....................765 794-4428
Fax: 765 794-4420
Kenneth B Hopper, *President*
Jaye Dee Hopper, *Vice Pres*
Lance R Hopper, *Admin Sec*
EMP: 3
SQ FT: 6,300
SALES (est): 1MM **Privately Held**
SIC: **3965** Fasteners; pins & needles

(G-2361)
SPI BINDING CO INC
610 W South St (47940-7131)
P.O. Box 550 (47940-0550)
PHONE.....................765 794-4992
Fax: 765 794-0035
Linda Crispin, *President*
Dave Crispin, *Vice Pres*
David Crispin, *Vice Pres*
▲ EMP: 50
SALES (est): 4.8MM **Privately Held**
WEB: www.spibinding.com
SIC: **2789** 2782 2396 Bookbinding & related work; blankbooks & looseleaf binders; automotive & apparel trimmings

Dayton
Tippecanoe County

(G-2362)
WEE ENGINEER INC
282 Delaware St (47941-8025)
P.O. Box 39 (47941-0039)
PHONE.....................765 449-4280
Robert Parker, *President*
Charlotte E Parker, *Corp Secy*
Seth Parker, *Vice Pres*
EMP: 12
SQ FT: 8,800
SALES (est): 1.5MM **Privately Held**
SIC: **3563** 3561 5012 Tire inflators, hand or compressor operated; industrial pumps & parts; pumps, domestic: water or sump; trucks, commercial

Decatur
Adams County

(G-2363)
A S M INC
Also Called: Precision Woodcrafters
125 W Grant St (46733-2316)
PHONE.....................260 724-8220
Fax: 260 724-7282
Richard W Steury, *President*
John Kowalczwk, *Principal*
Barbar Kowalczyk, *Principal*
Norm Steury, *Principal*
Patricia Steury, *Principal*

EMP: 5
SQ FT: 5,000
SALES: 350K **Privately Held**
SIC: **2499** 2511 2449 2448 Decorative wood & woodwork; trophy bases, wood; silverware chests: wood; wood containers; wood pallets & skids; nailed wood boxes & shook

(G-2364)
AIP/FW FUNDING INC (PA)
1031 E Us Highway 224 (46733-2737)
PHONE.....................212 627-2360
Dino Cusumano, *President*
Paul Bamatter, *Vice Pres*
EMP: 2
SALES (est): 70.2MM **Privately Held**
SIC: **3716** Motor homes

(G-2365)
ALBERDING WOODWORKING INC
7050 N 200 W (46733-8849)
PHONE.....................260 728-9526
Fax: 260 728-2575
Stephen Alberding, *President*
Jeananne Alberding, *Vice Pres*
EMP: 30
SQ FT: 12,000
SALES (est): 2.8MM **Privately Held**
SIC: **2431** 3272 Doors & door parts & trim, wood; housing components, prefabricated concrete

(G-2366)
ALL AMERICAN HOMES INDIANA LLC
1418 S 13th St (46733-2170)
PHONE.....................260 724-9171
Fax: 260 724-8987
Chad Marchand, *Vice Pres*
EMP: 275
SQ FT: 235,000
SALES (est): 35.9MM **Privately Held**
SIC: **2452** Modular homes, prefabricated, wood
HQ: All American Homes, Llc
　　2831 Dexter Dr
　　Elkhart IN 46514
　　574 266-3044

(G-2367)
ALL AMERICAN HOMES LLC
309 S 13th St (46733-1852)
PHONE.....................260 724-7391
Machelle Bradbury, *Vice Pres*
EMP: 2
SALES (est): 88.9K **Privately Held**
SIC: **3448** Prefabricated metal buildings

(G-2368)
AQUA BLAST CORP
1025 W Commerce Dr (46733-7541)
P.O. Box 547 (46733-0547)
PHONE.....................260 728-4433
Fax: 260 728-4516
David L Tumbleson, *CEO*
Tad Feaster, *Sales Mgr*
Clint Tumbleson, *Info Tech Mgr*
EMP: 11
SQ FT: 12,000
SALES (est): 3.1MM **Privately Held**
WEB: www.aquablast.com
SIC: **3589** 5084 High pressure cleaning equipment; industrial machine parts

(G-2369)
ARCHER-DANIELS-MIDLAND COMPANY
Also Called: ADM
7453 N Piqua Rd (46733-7409)
PHONE.....................260 728-8000
Fax: 260 724-9937
Mike Cecava, *Manager*
EMP: 25
SALES (corp-wide): 60.8B **Publicly Held**
WEB: www.admworld.com
SIC: **2041** Flour & other grain mill products
PA: Archer-Daniels-Midland Company
　　77 W Wacker Dr Ste 4600
　　Chicago IL 60601
　　312 634-8100

▲ = Import ▼=Export
◆ =Import/Export

GEOGRAPHIC

(G-2370)
BEARS DEN EMB & MORE LLC
530 E 900 N (46733-8454)
PHONE............................260 724-4070
Pamela L Berdall, *Mng Member*
EMP: 2
SALES (est): 124.9K **Privately Held**
SIC: 2395 Embroidery & art needlework

(G-2371)
BUCHAN LOGGING INC
3333 E 600 N (46733-9114)
PHONE............................260 728-2136
Fax: 260 749-7557
Dan Buchan, *Principal*
EMP: 3
SALES (est): 314.6K **Privately Held**
SIC: 2411 Logging camps & contractors

(G-2372)
BUNGE NORTH AMERICA INC
1200 N 2nd St (46733-1175)
PHONE............................260 724-2101
Michael Sorg, *Safety Mgr*
Myles Baczynski, *Purch Mgr*
Tammy Knous, *Buyer*
Jocelyn Suman, *Buyer*
Julee Wyatt, *Buyer*
EMP: 60 **Privately Held**
WEB: www.bungemarion.com
SIC: 2075 2079 2077 Soybean oil mills;
edible fats & oils; animal & marine fats &
oils
HQ: Bunge North America, Inc.
1391 Tmberlake Manor Pkwy
Chesterfield MO 63017
314 292-2000

(G-2373)
COMMERCIAL PRINT SHOP INC
Also Called: Complete Printing Service
210 S 2nd St (46733-1667)
P.O. Box 347 (46733-0347)
PHONE............................260 724-3722
Fax: 260 724-3722
Charles A Brune, *President*
EMP: 5
SQ FT: 2,000
SALES (est): 722.3K **Privately Held**
WEB: www.completeprintingservice.com
SIC: 2752 7334 2759 Commercial print-
ing, offset; photocopying & duplicating
services; letterpress printing

(G-2374)
DECATUR PUBLISHING CO INC
Also Called: Decatur Daily Democrat
141 S 2nd St (46733-1664)
PHONE............................260 724-2121
Fax: 260 724-7981
Melanie Radler, *President*
Jesse Lindsey, *Publisher*
Robert Shraluka, *Editor*
Ron Storey, *Manager*
EMP: 20 **EST:** 1857
SQ FT: 3,000
SALES (est): 970K **Privately Held**
SIC: 2711 Newspapers, publishing & print-
ing

(G-2375)
DIETECH CORPORATION
1001 W Commerce Dr (46733-7541)
PHONE............................260 724-8946
Fax: 260 724-8957
Brent Saalfrank, *President*
Bryan Saalfrank, *Treasurer*
Brad Saalfrank, *Admin Sec*
EMP: 8
SALES (est): 1.2MM **Privately Held**
SIC: 3544 3469 Special dies & tools;
metal stampings

(G-2376)
DS WOODS CUSTOM CABINETS
2231 N Us Highway 27 (46733-9353)
PHONE............................260 692-6565
Dale Schwartz, *Owner*
EMP: 3
SALES (est): 272.3K **Privately Held**
SIC: 2434 Wood kitchen cabinets

(G-2377)
DWD INDUSTRIES LLC (DH)
1921 Patterson St (46733-1866)
PHONE............................260 728-9272

Fax: 260 728-9751
Duane Melcher,
▲ **EMP:** 50 **EST:** 1979
SQ FT: 27,000
SALES: 10.5MM
SALES (corp-wide): 41.1K **Privately Held**
WEB: www.estevesgroup.com
SIC: 3544 Wire drawing & straightening
dies
HQ: Diamond Tools Group B.V.
De Vest 1 C
Valkenswaard 5555
402 082-311

(G-2378)
ESTEVES-DWD LLC
Also Called: Esteves Group USA
1921 Patterson St (46733-1866)
PHONE............................260 728-9272
Dan Burtnette,
EMP: 75
SALES (est): 9.8MM
SALES (corp-wide): 41.1K **Privately Held**
SIC: 3544 Wire drawing & straightening
dies
HQ: Diamond Tools Group B.V.
De Vest 1 C
Valkenswaard 5555
402 082-311

(G-2379)
**FUHRMAN PRECISION
SERVICES**
10484 N 200 W (46733-8759)
PHONE............................260 728-9600
John Fuhrman, *President*
Jon Furhman, *President*
Danielle Furhman, *Treasurer*
EMP: 4
SQ FT: 9,000
SALES: 190K **Privately Held**
SIC: 3545 Precision tools, machinists'

(G-2380)
GERKE WELDING INC
Also Called: Gerke Welding & Fabrication
10815 N 000 Rd (46733-8438)
PHONE............................260 724-7701
Fax: 260 724-7701
Mart Gerke, *President*
Julie Gerke, *Vice Pres*
EMP: 2
SALES (est): 75K **Privately Held**
SIC: 7692 Welding repair

(G-2381)
GILPIN INC
1819 Patterson St (46733-1890)
PHONE............................260 724-9155
Fax: 260 724-9849
Todd Gilpin, *President*
Paul Gilpin, *Chairman*
Brad Prather, *VP Opers*
Ron Laurent, *Sales Staff*
▲ **EMP:** 30
SQ FT: 70,000
SALES (est): 6.2MM **Privately Held**
WEB: www.gilpinironworks.com
SIC: 3446 Stairs, fire escapes, balconies,
railings & ladders; fences, gates, posts &
flagpoles

(G-2382)
GOLDSHIELD FIBER GLASS INC
Also Called: Rev Group
2004 Patterson St (46733-1867)
P.O. Box 496 (46733-0496)
PHONE............................260 728-2476
Fax: 260 728-9218
Dino Cusumano, *CEO*
Tim Sullivan, *President*
Matt Buckman, *General Mgr*
Forrest D Theobald, *Senior VP*
Paul Bamatter, *Vice Pres*
EMP: 250
SQ FT: 150,000
SALES: 1.7B
SALES (corp-wide): 2.3B **Privately Held**
SIC: 2221 Fiberglass fabrics
HQ: Fleetwood Enterprises, Inc.
1351 Pomona Rd Ste 230
Corona CA 92882
951 354-3000

(G-2383)
GUERECA WOODWORKING
310 Eastbrook Dr (46733-2912)
PHONE............................260 724-3994
Mario Guereca Jr, *Principal*
EMP: 2
SALES (est): 121.3K **Privately Held**
SIC: 2431 Millwork

(G-2384)
H P SCHMITT PACKING CO INC
976 Waynesboro Rd (46733-2624)
Rural Route 1 Box 7 (46733)
PHONE............................260 724-3146
H P Schmitt Jr, *President*
EMP: 9
SALES (est): 532.7K **Privately Held**
SIC: 2011 Meat packing plants

(G-2385)
HERITAGE WIRE DIE INC
10484 N 200 W (46733-8759)
PHONE............................260 728-9300
Jon M Fuhrman, *President*
EMP: 4
SALES (est): 5MM **Privately Held**
SIC: 3544 Diamond dies, metalworking

(G-2386)
INTELLIRAY INC
10262 N 550 W (46733-7899)
PHONE............................260 547-4399
Timothy Blomenberg, *President*
Kristine Blomenberg, *CFO*
▼ **EMP:** 5
SALES (est): 706.8K **Privately Held**
SIC: 3679 Electronic switches

(G-2387)
JOSEPH M SCHMIDT
Also Called: Triple S Logging
7741 N 200 E (46733-9416)
PHONE............................260 223-3498
Joseph M Schmidt, *Principal*
EMP: 3
SALES (est): 207.7K **Privately Held**
SIC: 2411 Logging camps & contractors

(G-2388)
**JOURNEYMANN PRECISION
PRESS**
10921 N State Road 101 (46733-8169)
PHONE............................260 724-6934
Kristie S Mann, *Principal*
EMP: 2 **EST:** 2015
SALES (est): 59.2K **Privately Held**
SIC: 2741 Miscellaneous publishing

(G-2389)
**KINGSFORD PRODUCTS INC
(PA)**
1819 Patterson St (46733-1846)
PHONE............................740 862-4450
Roland Harrison, *President*
EMP: 6
SALES (est): 2.5MM **Privately Held**
SIC: 3315 3334 3496 Steel wire & related
products; primary aluminum; miscella-
neous fabricated wire products

(G-2390)
**LINGENFELTER PRFMCE
ENGRG INC**
Also Called: Lingenfelter Racing
1557 Winchester Rd (46733-3109)
PHONE............................260 724-2552
Fax: 260 724-8761
Thomas Cress, *President*
▲ **EMP:** 35 **EST:** 1972
SQ FT: 24,000
SALES (est): 1.2MM **Privately Held**
WEB: www.lingenfelter.com
SIC: 7549 5531 3519 3714 High per-
formance auto repair & service; automo-
tive parts; parts & accessories, internal
combustion engines; motor vehicle parts
& accessories; engineering services
PA: Lpe Assets, Llc
1557 Winchester Rd
Decatur IN 46733

(G-2391)
LLAMA CORPORATION
2937 E 900 N (46733-9470)
P.O. Box 702 (46733-0702)
PHONE............................888 701-7432
Robert L Hakes, *President*
EMP: 3
SALES: 200K **Privately Held**
SIC: 8711 3533 3643 3663 Electrical or
electronic engineering; gas field machin-
ery & equipment; oil field machinery &
equipment; lightning protection equip-
ment; radio & TV communications equip-
ment

(G-2392)
MANLEY MEATS INC
302 S 400 E (46733-9095)
PHONE............................260 592-7313
Fax: 260 592-6731
Roger Manley, *President*
Ronald Manley, *Vice Pres*
Steven Manley, *Vice Pres*
Alice Manley, *Treasurer*
Marilyn Guyer, *Admin Sec*
▲ **EMP:** 20 **EST:** 1961
SQ FT: 7,500
SALES (est): 1.4MM **Privately Held**
WEB: www.manleymeats.com
SIC: 5421 2013 2011 Meat markets, in-
cluding freezer provisioners; canned
meats (except baby food) from purchased
meat; meat packing plants

(G-2393)
**MC BRIDE & SON WELDING &
ENGRG**
Also Called: McBride & Son Welding & Engrg
409 Bellmont Rd (46733-2709)
PHONE............................260 724-3534
Brad Mc Bride, *Owner*
EMP: 3
SALES (est): 125K **Privately Held**
SIC: 7692 3444 Welding repair; sheet
metalwork

(G-2394)
**MID-STATES TOOL AND MCH
INC**
2220 Patterson St (46733-1871)
PHONE............................260 728-9797
Fax: 260 728-9795
Jason Scheumann, *Principal*
Sylvia Scheumann, *Corp Secy*
Jeremy Friedt, *QC Mgr*
EMP: 27
SQ FT: 24,200
SALES (est): 4.9MM **Privately Held**
WEB: www.midstatestool.com
SIC: 3599 Machine shop, jobbing & repair

(G-2395)
MIDWEST PRE-FINISHING INC
8826 N 000 Rd (46733-8480)
PHONE............................260 728-9487
Larry A Fullenkamp, *President*
Connie Fullenkamp, *Admin Sec*
EMP: 3
SALES: 350K **Privately Held**
SIC: 3442 Molding, trim & stripping

(G-2396)
MINDS EYE GRAPHICS INC
1019 W Commerce Dr (46733-7541)
P.O. Box 299 (46733-0299)
PHONE............................260 724-2050
Fax: 260 724-4004
Gregory F Kitson, *President*
Teresa Kitson, *Corp Secy*
Laura Farlow, *Purchasing*
EMP: 13
SQ FT: 10,800
SALES (est): 1.4MM **Privately Held**
WEB: www.mindseyeg.com
SIC: 2759 Screen printing

(G-2397)
**PANACEA PAINTS & COATINGS
INC**
1013 W Commerce Dr (46733-7541)
PHONE............................260 728-4222
Fax: 260 728-4984
Mike Vandenburg, *President*
John Hahn, *Vice Pres*
EMP: 8

SQ FT: 11,000
SALES (est): 1MM **Privately Held**
WEB: www.panaceapowder.com
SIC: 3479 Painting of metal products; coating of metals & formed products

(G-2398)
PAUL MARSHALL AND SON LOG
4895 E 600 N (46733-9127)
PHONE..................................260 724-2852
Paul Marshall, *Principal*
EMP: 6 EST: 2010
SALES (est): 392.1K **Privately Held**
SIC: 2411 Logging

(G-2399)
PRESTRESS SERVICES INC
Also Called: Marine Precast
7855 Nw Winchester Rd (46733-8825)
P.O. Box 111 (46733-0111)
PHONE..................................260 724-7117
Fax: 260 724-3349
Bob Sawyer, *President*
Dan Stensrud, *Purch Agent*
Jeff Eyamsom, *Engineer*
Steve Fisher, *Manager*
Norma Jean Yost, *Director*
EMP: 110
SALES (corp-wide): 43.8MM **Privately Held**
SIC: 3272 3441 Prestressed concrete products; concrete stuctural support & building material; fabricated structural metal
PA: Prestress Services, Inc.
5501 Briar Hill Rd
Lexington KY 40516
859 299-0461

(G-2400)
R & K INCINERATOR INC
6125 W 100 S (46733-8355)
PHONE..................................260 565-3214
Fax: 260 565-3149
Mark Kaehr, *President*
EMP: 3 EST: 1974
SALES (est): 2.4MM **Privately Held**
SIC: 3567 Incinerators, metal: domestic or commercial

(G-2401)
REV RECREATION GROUP INC
Also Called: Fleetwood Homes
1031 E Us Highway 224 (46733-2737)
P.O. Box 31 (46733-0031)
PHONE..................................260 728-9564
Chuck Wilkinson, *Branch Mgr*
Jim McDonald, *Maintence Staff*
EMP: 20
SQ FT: 321,600 **Publicly Held**
SIC: 3716 2451 Motor homes; mobile homes
HQ: Rev Recreation Group, Inc.
1031 E Us Highway 224
Decatur IN 46733

(G-2402)
REV RECREATION GROUP INC (HQ)
Also Called: Fleetwood Homes
1031 E Us Highway 224 (46733-2737)
P.O. Box 31 (46733-0031)
PHONE..................................260 728-2121
Fax: 260 728-3009
John Draheim, *CEO*
Jim Jacobs, *President*
John Lowry, *COO*
Steve Heim, *Vice Pres*
Loide Holtzclaw, *Buyer*
▲ EMP: 230
SQ FT: 25,000
SALES (est): 156.8MM **Publicly Held**
SIC: 3716 Motor homes

(G-2403)
REV RECREATION GROUP INC
Also Called: Fleetwood Homes
1803 Winchester St (46733-2187)
PHONE..................................260 724-4217
Larry Rodgers, *Branch Mgr*
EMP: 130 **Publicly Held**
SIC: 3716 2451 Motor homes; mobile homes
HQ: Rev Recreation Group, Inc.
1031 E Us Highway 224
Decatur IN 46733

(G-2404)
SILBERLINE MFG CO INC
Also Called: Silberline of Indiana
2010 Guy Brown Dr (46733-1882)
P.O. Box 815 (46733-0815)
PHONE..................................260 728-2111
Fax: 260 728-2589
Aaron Rhymer, *Engineer*
Thomas E Anderson, *Manager*
EMP: 120
SQ FT: 45,000
SALES (corp-wide): 113.8MM **Privately Held**
WEB: www.silberline.com
SIC: 2816 Metallic & mineral pigments
PA: Silberline Manufacturing Co., Inc.
130 Lincoln Dr
Tamaqua PA 18252
570 668-6050

(G-2405)
SOLAE
1200 N 2nd St (46733-1160)
PHONE..................................260 724-2101
Ted Habegger, *President*
◆ EMP: 5
SALES (est): 384.6K **Privately Held**
SIC: 2075 Soybean oil mills

(G-2406)
SP3
3531 W Us Highway 224 (46733-7504)
PHONE..................................260 547-4150
John Sisco, *Opers Staff*
Shirley Spangler, *Cust Mgr*
Erik Koik, *VP Mktg*
Barbara Frane, *Office Mgr*
Eric Koik, *Branch Mgr*
EMP: 25 **Privately Held**
SIC: 3479 Aluminum coating of metal products
PA: Sp3
1605 Wyatt Dr
Santa Clara CA 95054

(G-2407)
SUIZA DAIRY GROUP LLC
Also Called: Dean Food of Decatur
400 Chamber Dr (46733-1885)
PHONE..................................260 724-2136
Valerie Myers, *Branch Mgr*
EMP: 150 **Publicly Held**
SIC: 2024 Ice cream & ice milk
HQ: Suiza Dairy Group, Llc
2515 Mckinney Ave # 1200
Dallas TX 75201

(G-2408)
TP/ELM ACQUISITION SBUSID INC (HQ)
Also Called: Elm Packaging
2110 Patterson St (46733-1869)
PHONE..................................260 728-2161
Glen Davis, *Controller*
EMP: 100
SQ FT: 100,000
SALES (est): 18.1MM
SALES (corp-wide): 1B **Privately Held**
SIC: 3086 Cups & plates, foamed plastic
PA: Tekni-Plex, Inc.
460 E Swedesford Rd # 3000
Wayne PA 19087
484 690-1520

(G-2409)
TRI TEC SYSTEMS INC
125 W Grant St (46733-2316)
P.O. Box 965 (46733-0965)
PHONE..................................260 724-8874
Fax: 260 724-8530
Gary Sheets, *President*
Robert Mies, *Vice Pres*
Karen Sills, *Manager*
EMP: 25
SQ FT: 12,000
SALES (est): 2MM **Privately Held**
WEB: www.tri-tecsystems.com
SIC: 3679 Harness assemblies for electronic use: wire or cable

(G-2410)
TROYER BROTHERS
6691 W State Road 124 (46733-8330)
PHONE..................................260 589-2244
EMP: 27

SALES (est): 5.1MM **Privately Held**
SIC: 3599 Machine shop, jobbing & repair

(G-2411)
UNIVERSAL METALCRAFT INC
4215 W 750 N (46733-7852)
PHONE..................................260 547-4457
Fax: 260 547-4254
Donald Haines, *President*
Janelle Hartmann, *Admin Sec*
EMP: 35 EST: 1969
SQ FT: 6,400
SALES (est): 6.8MM **Privately Held**
SIC: 3444 3599 Sheet metalwork; machine shop, jobbing & repair

(G-2412)
WHETSTONE INDUSTRIES
1121 Marshall St (46733-1242)
PHONE..................................260 724-2461
Pearl Whetstone, *Owner*
EMP: 3
SALES (est): 100.1K **Privately Held**
SIC: 3999 Manufacturing industries

(G-2413)
XYZ MODEL WORKS
10334 N 500 W (46733-7838)
PHONE..................................260 413-1873
Paul Ruble, *Principal*
EMP: 2 EST: 2010
SALES (est): 109.5K **Privately Held**
SIC: 3999 Novelties, bric-a-brac & hobby kits

Delphi
Carroll County

(G-2414)
ANDERSONS AGRICULTURE GROUP LP
Grain Division
3902 N Anderson Dr (46923-8157)
PHONE..................................765 564-6135
Joe Needham, *Manager*
EMP: 10
SQ FT: 20,000
SALES (corp-wide): 3.6B **Publicly Held**
SIC: 5191 3523 3291 2842 Fertilizer & fertilizer materials; grass seed; fertilizers & agricultural chemicals; farm machinery & equipment; abrasive products; specialty cleaning, polishes & sanitation goods
HQ: The Andersons Agriculture Group L P
1947 Briarfield Blvd
Maumee OH 43537
419 893-5050

(G-2415)
BRIM CONCRETE INC
2485 W Gravel Pit Rd (46923-8422)
PHONE..................................765 564-4975
Bob Williams, *Manager*
EMP: 6
SALES (corp-wide): 3.1MM **Privately Held**
SIC: 3273 3272 Ready-mixed concrete; floor slabs & tiles, precast concrete
PA: Brim Concrete Inc
614 W Fisher St
Monticello IN
574 583-7101

(G-2416)
CARROLL PAPERS INC
Also Called: Carroll County Comet
114 E Franklin St (46923-1210)
PHONE..................................765 564-2222
Joe Moss, *President*
EMP: 8
SALES (corp-wide): 100K **Privately Held**
WEB: www.carrollcountycomet.com
SIC: 2711 Newspapers: publishing only, not printed on site
PA: Carroll Papers Inc
14 E Main St
Flora IN 46929
574 967-4135

(G-2417)
DELPHI BODY WORKS
313 S Washington St (46923-1542)
PHONE..................................765 564-2212

Fax: 765 564-4255
Richard C Bradshaw, *President*
James Huffer, *Admin Sec*
EMP: 17 EST: 1848
SQ FT: 43,000
SALES (est): 3.1MM **Privately Held**
SIC: 3713 5082 3715 3441 Truck bodies (motor vehicles); general construction machinery & equipment; trailer bodies; fabricated structural metal

(G-2418)
DELPHI PRODUCTS CO INC
2065 W Us Highway 421 (46923-8268)
P.O. Box 149 (46923-0149)
PHONE..................................800 382-7903
Blair Underhill, *President*
Alan Girton, *Admin Sec*
EMP: 15
SQ FT: 20,000
SALES (est): 7.8MM **Privately Held**
SIC: 5083 3523 Agricultural machinery & equipment; farm machinery & equipment

(G-2419)
DPC INC
Also Called: Delphi Products Company
2065 W Us Highway 421 (46923-8268)
P.O. Box 149 (46923-0149)
PHONE..................................765 564-3752
Blair Underhill, *President*
Alan Girpon, *Vice Pres*
Alan Girton, *Financial Exec*
EMP: 25
SQ FT: 20,000
SALES (est): 4.6MM **Privately Held**
WEB: www.delphiproducts.com
SIC: 3523 5083 3446 3444 Barn, silo, poultry, dairy & livestock machinery; poultry equipment; livestock equipment; architectural metalwork; sheet metalwork; fabricated plate work (boiler shop); fabricated structural metal

(G-2420)
EFFICIENT PLASTICS SOLUTIONS
9745 N 850 W (46923-9224)
PHONE..................................574 965-4690
Thomas Thompson, *Principal*
EMP: 2 EST: 2016
SALES (est): 90K **Privately Held**
SIC: 2821 Plastics materials & resins

(G-2421)
FRONTIER CARRIAGE
7872 W 1000 N (46923-8623)
PHONE..................................574 965-4444
Shawn Bunnell, *Owner*
Julie Bunnell, *Co-Owner*
EMP: 2
SALES (est): 131.9K **Privately Held**
SIC: 3799 Carriages, horse drawn

(G-2422)
INDIANA PACKERS CORPORATION (HQ)
Hwy 421 S & Cr 100 N (46923)
P.O. Box 318 (46923-0318)
PHONE..................................765 564-3680
Fax: 765 564-3684
Masao Watanabe, *CEO*
Russ Yearwood, *President*
Edward J Nelson, *President*
James Allen, *Vice Pres*
James Hardison, *Vice Pres*
▼ EMP: 1350
SQ FT: 312,000
SALES (est): 360.6MM
SALES (corp-wide): 71B **Privately Held**
SIC: 2011 2013 Pork products from pork slaughtered on site; bacon, slab & sliced from meat slaughtered on site; sausages & other prepared meats
PA: Mitsubishi Corporation
2-3-1, Marunouchi
Chiyoda-Ku TKY 100-0
332 102-121

(G-2423)
MAR-CO PACKAGING INC
Also Called: American Agri Curtains Div
1124 Samuel Milroy Rd (46923-1261)
PHONE..................................765 564-3979
Carolyn Henderson, *Manager*
EMP: 4

SALES (corp-wide): 1.8MM **Privately Held**
SIC: **2391** Curtains, window: made from purchased materials
PA: Mar-Co Packaging, Inc.
1090 S Crystal Ave
Benton Harbor MI 49022
269 925-2222

(G-2424)
MED GRIND INC
7848 N Us Highway 421 (46923-8691)
PHONE................................574 965-4040
Mike Cummings, *President*
EMP: 2
SALES: 94K **Privately Held**
SIC: **3599** Grinding castings for the trade

(G-2425)
P T I MACHINING INC
5395 W 200 N (46923-8265)
P.O. Box 587 (46923-0587)
PHONE................................765 564-9966
Fax: 765 564-6114
Jim W Proffit, *President*
Larry Thompson, *Vice Pres*
Judy Thompson, *Treasurer*
Camille Jones, *Office Mgr*
Janet Proffit, *Admin Sec*
EMP: 6
SQ FT: 15,000
SALES: 3.6MM **Privately Held**
WEB: www.swissparts.com
SIC: **3599** Machine shop, jobbing & repair

(G-2426)
Q GRAPHICS INC (PA)
108 E Main St (46923-1543)
P.O. Box 180 (46923-0180)
PHONE................................765 564-2314
Fax: 765 564-2304
Bret Hanaway, *President*
EMP: 10 EST: 1948
SQ FT: 3,000
SALES (est): 857.6K **Privately Held**
SIC: **2752 5943** Commercial printing, offset; office forms & supplies

(G-2427)
SKYLINE SIGNS INC
Also Called: Skyline Signs & Awnings
1989 W Mill St (46923-8582)
PHONE................................765 564-4422
Fax: 765 564-4433
Rob Johnson, *President*
Sue Johnson, *Vice Pres*
EMP: 2 EST: 2000
SALES (est): 692.1K **Privately Held**
SIC: **3993** Signs & advertising specialties

(G-2428)
TERRYS WELDING INC
9176 W 132 N (46923-9780)
P.O. Box 6384, Lafayette (47903-6384)
PHONE................................765 564-3331
Greg Terry, *Principal*
EMP: 2
SALES (est): 143.6K **Privately Held**
SIC: **7692** Welding repair

(G-2429)
U S AGGREGATES INC
2195 W Us Highway 421 (46923-9325)
P.O. Box 315 (46923-0315)
PHONE................................765 564-2580
Jim Fehsenfeld, *Principal*
EMP: 16
SALES (corp-wide): 248.2MM **Privately Held**
SIC: **1442** Gravel mining
HQ: U S Aggregates Inc
5400 W 86th St
Indianapolis IN 46268
317 872-6010

(G-2430)
U S AGGREGATES INC
Us 421n (46923)
P.O. Box 315 (46923-0315)
PHONE................................765 564-2282
Bill Corbett, *Branch Mgr*
EMP: 20

SALES (corp-wide): 248.2MM **Privately Held**
WEB: www.usagg.com
SIC: **1442 1422 5032** Gravel mining; crushed & broken limestone; limestone
HQ: U S Aggregates Inc
5400 W 86th St
Indianapolis IN 46268
317 872-6010

Demotte
Jasper County

(G-2431)
BABCOCK PAVING INC
6049 Work St (46310-8821)
P.O. Box 729 (46310-0729)
PHONE................................219 987-5450
Toni L Burns, *President*
Rodney Urbano, *Vice Pres*
EMP: 4
SQ FT: 1,100
SALES (est): 320K **Privately Held**
SIC: **2951** Asphalt & asphaltic paving mixtures (not from refineries)

(G-2432)
BOEZEMAN ENTERPRISES INC
Also Called: Boezeman Signs Graphic Design
9941 N 1200 W (46310-9071)
PHONE................................219 345-2732
Fax: 219 345-2733
Lynn Boezeman, *President*
Marcia Boezman, *Vice Pres*
EMP: 2
SALES: 92K **Privately Held**
WEB: www.boezemansigns.com
SIC: **3993** Signs & advertising specialties

(G-2433)
BROKEN MOLD CUSTOMS INC
1207 Daisy St Se (46310-8467)
P.O. Box 648 (46310-0648)
PHONE................................219 863-1008
Becky A Trembly, *Principal*
EMP: 2
SALES (est): 169.5K **Privately Held**
SIC: **3544** Industrial molds

(G-2434)
DEMOTTE DECORATIVE STONE INC
6611 W State Road 10 (46310-7800)
PHONE................................219 987-5461
Scott Walstra, *President*
EMP: 3
SALES (est): 190.4K **Privately Held**
SIC: **1411** Dimension stone

(G-2435)
DEMOTTE MANUFACTURING INC
5844 W State Road 10 (46310-9498)
PHONE................................219 987-6196
Fax: 219 987-6193
John Dyke, *President*
Elaine Dyke, *Vice Pres*
EMP: 9
SALES (est): 1MM **Privately Held**
SIC: **3451 3599 3624 3452** Screw machine products; machine shop, jobbing & repair; carbon & graphite products; bolts, nuts, rivets & washers; copper foundries; nonferrous rolling & drawing

(G-2436)
ELEMENT OF FUN TRAVEL
10327 Forest Hills Dr (46310-5300)
PHONE................................317 435-9185
EMP: 2
SALES (est): 74.4K **Privately Held**
SIC: **2819** Elements

(G-2437)
ELITE MACHINE AND TOOL INC
10192 N 600 E (46310-8528)
PHONE................................219 345-3424
Keith M Smith, *President*
Linda Smith, *Admin Sec*
EMP: 2
SALES (est): 200K **Privately Held**
SIC: **3599** Machine shop, jobbing & repair

(G-2438)
GOLD STANDARD TRUSS LLC
817 15th St Se (46310-9371)
P.O. Box 517 (46310-0517)
PHONE................................219 987-7781
Marv Veldt, *Plant Mgr*
EMP: 3
SALES (est): 275.6K **Privately Held**
SIC: **3999** Manufacturing industries

(G-2439)
GYPSUM EXPRESS LTD
1214 Forsythia St Se (46310-8250)
P.O. Box 501 (46310-0501)
PHONE................................219 987-2181
Fax: 219 987-3136
Tim Shephard, *Branch Mgr*
EMP: 63
SALES (corp-wide): 124.8MM **Privately Held**
SIC: **2741** Miscellaneous publishing
PA: Gypsum Express Ltd.
8280 Sixty Rd
Baldwinsville NY 13027
315 638-2201

(G-2440)
K IRPCHEADSTART PROGRAM
10448 N 450 E (46310-8920)
PHONE................................219 345-2011
Fax: 219 345-2011
Katherine Mendiola, *Branch Mgr*
EMP: 2
SALES (corp-wide): 900K **Privately Held**
SIC: **2752** Commercial printing, lithographic
PA: K Irpcheadstart Program
115 W Pearl St
Winamac IN 46996
574 946-4211

(G-2441)
KANKAKEE VALLEY POST NEWS
Also Called: Action Plus Shopper & Shoppers
827 S Halleck St (46310)
PHONE................................219 987-5111
Fax: 219 987-5119
Dan Hurd, *President*
EMP: 5
SALES (est): 151.9K **Privately Held**
WEB: www.kvpostnews.com
SIC: **2711** Newspapers: publishing only, not printed on site

(G-2442)
KNIP WELDING
8446 W 1000 N (46310-9444)
PHONE................................219 987-5123
Kenny Knip, *Owner*
EMP: 2
SALES: 70K **Privately Held**
SIC: **7692** Welding repair

(G-2443)
LEGACY VULCAN LLC
Also Called: Demotte Yard
832 15th St Se (46310-9371)
P.O. Box 140 (46310-0140)
PHONE................................219 987-3040
Fax: 219 987-5353
John Walstar, *Manager*
EMP: 20 **Publicly Held**
WEB: www.vulcanmaterials.com
SIC: **3272** Concrete products
HQ: Legacy Vulcan, Llc
1200 Urban Center Dr
Vestavia AL 35242
205 298-3000

(G-2444)
MR HEAT INC
11735 N State Road 55 (46310-9612)
PHONE................................219 345-5629
Toll Free:................................866 -
Fax: 219 345-5311
Raymond Thomas, *President*
Joe Thomas, *President*
EMP: 9
SALES (est): 128.5K **Privately Held**
SIC: **3585** Heating & air conditioning combination units

(G-2445)
PRECISE TITLE INC
8917 24th St Sw (46310-9715)
PHONE................................219 987-2286
Peter Georgopoulos, *Principal*
EMP: 2
SALES (est): 156.2K **Privately Held**
SIC: **2389** Apparel & accessories

(G-2446)
RE INDUSTRIES INC
1328 15th St Se Ste 4 (46310-9393)
PHONE................................219 987-1764
David Repko, *President*
EMP: 2
SALES (est): 169K **Privately Held**
SIC: **3999** Manufacturing industries

(G-2447)
SHIELDS MECH & FABRICATION LLC
11474 Chateau Ln (46310-9350)
PHONE................................219 863-3972
David Shields, *Principal*
EMP: 2
SALES (est): 63.9K **Privately Held**
SIC: **3999** Manufacturing industries

(G-2448)
STEVENS IRONWORKS INC
6852 Mercedes Ln (46310-9412)
P.O. Box 730 (46310-0730)
PHONE................................219 987-6332
Melonie Stevens, *President*
Ronald Stevens, *Vice Pres*
EMP: 30
SALES (est): 5MM **Privately Held**
SIC: **3446 3441 1791** Architectural metalwork; fabricated structural metal; structural steel erection

(G-2449)
SUPER HICKSGAS FUEL
5768 E State Road 10 (46310-8888)
PHONE................................219 345-2656
Todd Coady, *Owner*
EMP: 3
SALES (est): 215.2K **Privately Held**
SIC: **2869** Fuels

(G-2450)
VAN KEPPEL REDI-MIX INC
200 5th Ave Ne (46310-9594)
P.O. Box 80 (46310-0080)
PHONE................................219 987-2811
Toll Free:................................866 -
Dave Van Keppel, *President*
EMP: 14 EST: 1950
SQ FT: 5,000
SALES (est): 1.9MM **Privately Held**
SIC: **3273** Ready-mixed concrete

(G-2451)
VARSITY SPORTS INC
603 N Halleck St (46310-9545)
PHONE................................219 987-7200
Fax: 219 987-7200
Scott Ericks, *Principal*
EMP: 5
SALES (est): 343.9K
SALES (corp-wide): 1.3MM **Privately Held**
SIC: **2759 5941 5949 5999** Screen printing; sporting goods & bicycle shops; sewing, needlework & piece goods; trophies & plaques
PA: Varsity Sports Inc
134 N Broad St
Griffith IN 46319
219 924-5110

(G-2452)
WHEELS 4 TOTS INC
10700 W 1300 N (46310-8505)
P.O. Box 221 (46310-0221)
PHONE................................219 987-6812
Fax: 219 987-6824
Jeff Martin, *President*
Donna Martin, *Vice Pres*
▲ EMP: 3 EST: 1999
SQ FT: 8,000
SALES: 100K **Privately Held**
WEB: www.wheels4tots.com
SIC: **3714** Motor vehicle wheels & parts

Denver
Miami County

(G-2453)
BEST FRIENDS INC
252 W Harrison St (46926-9318)
P.O. Box 26 (46926-0026)
PHONE.....................765 985-3872
Kevin Hostetler, *President*
Hayley Hostetler, *Vice Pres*
EMP: 2
SALES (est): 278.2K **Privately Held**
SIC: 2339 7389 Women's & misses' athletic clothing & sportswear;

(G-2454)
IMPERIAL DESIGNS
6599 N State Road 19 (46926-9213)
PHONE.....................765 985-2712
Theresa Armstrong, *Owner*
EMP: 2
SALES (est): 67.6K **Privately Held**
SIC: 2395 Embroidery & art needlework

(G-2455)
WOODCRAFTERS LLC
8472 N 100 E (46926-9120)
PHONE.....................765 469-5103
Chadd A Pattison, *Administration*
EMP: 2 EST: 2012
SALES (est): 122.2K **Privately Held**
SIC: 2511 Wood household furniture

Depauw
Harrison County

(G-2456)
FRED SMITH STORE FIXTURES INC
6405 Highway 337 Nw (47115-8547)
P.O. Box 40 (47115-0040)
PHONE.....................812 347-2363
Fax: 812 347-1304
Dusty Rhodes, *Plant Mgr*
Rodney Shehorn, *Prdtn Mgr*
John Fromme, *Opers Staff*
Janay Hoehn, *Manager*
James Yeager, *Manager*
EMP: 60 EST: 1962
SQ FT: 60,000
SALES (est): 14.2MM **Privately Held**
SIC: 3089 Laminating of plastic

(G-2457)
JOHN S DAVIS INC
Also Called: Davis Crushed Stone & Lime
8605 Big John Rd Nw (47115-8906)
PHONE.....................812 347-2707
Fax: 812 347-1336
Simon Davis, *President*
Selma Lakins, *Admin Sec*
EMP: 10 EST: 1944
SALES: 861.7K **Privately Held**
SIC: 1422 Crushed & broken limestone

Deputy
Jefferson County

(G-2458)
ALDRIDGE CABINETS
10304 W 500 N (47230-9215)
PHONE.....................812 873-6723
EMP: 2
SALES (est): 153.9K **Privately Held**
SIC: 2434 Mfg Wood Kitchen Cabinets

(G-2459)
BAXTER LUMBER LLC
12876 W Deputy Pike Rd (47230-9099)
PHONE.....................812 873-6868
Fax: 812 873-7190
Darla Malcomb, *Project Dir*
Donald Baxter, *Mng Member*
Phil Baxter,
Phillip Baxter,
EMP: 17
SQ FT: 4,000

SALES (est): 2.4MM **Privately Held**
SIC: 2421 Lumber: rough, sawed or planed

(G-2460)
HOMESTEAD PROPERTIES INC
Also Called: Tiny Timbers
10214 W Deputy Pike Rd (47230-9090)
P.O. Box 126 (47230-0126)
PHONE.....................812 866-4415
Fax: 812 866-9221
Sherry Chapo, *President*
Joseph Chapo, *Vice Pres*
EMP: 10
SQ FT: 20,000
SALES: 1MM **Privately Held**
WEB: www.tinytimbers.com
SIC: 2421 2426 Sawmills & planing mills, general; hardwood dimension & flooring mills

(G-2461)
VIRES BACKHOE AND DUMPTRUC
2571 E Doty Mill Rd (47230-9603)
PHONE.....................812 595-1630
Billie Vires, *Principal*
EMP: 2
SALES (est): 216.6K **Privately Held**
SIC: 3531 Backhoes

Derby
Perry County

(G-2462)
RICHARD GREG ETIENNE LOGGING
11133 Trumpet Rd (47525-9506)
PHONE.....................812 843-5132
Richard Greg Etienne, *Owner*
EMP: 2
SALES (est): 96K **Privately Held**
SIC: 2411 Logging camps & contractors

Dillsboro
Dearborn County

(G-2463)
BEVERLY INDUSTRIAL SERVICE
4233 S Farmers Retreat Rd (47018-9297)
PHONE.....................812 667-5047
Cary Snyder, *President*
Howard Snyder, *Owner*
Beverly Snyder, *Corp Secy*
Teresa Meyer, *Vice Pres*
EMP: 11
SQ FT: 20,000
SALES: 1MM **Privately Held**
WEB: www.beverlyind.com
SIC: 7389 3545 Grinding, precision: commercial or industrial; precision tools, machinists'; machine knives, metalworking

(G-2464)
CRAIG HYDRAULIC ENTERPRISES
Also Called: Global Odor Ctrl Tech Mid Amer
9790 Front St (47018-9342)
PHONE.....................812 432-5108
Tom Wafford, *President*
Berneta Wafford, *Treasurer*
EMP: 2
SALES (est): 229.4K **Privately Held**
SIC: 2899 Water treating compounds

(G-2465)
D & D MANUFACTURING INC (PA)
7415 E County Road 50 S (47018-9698)
PHONE.....................812 432-3294
Don Hoffrogge, *President*
Diane Hoffrogge, *Vice Pres*
EMP: 5
SALES (est): 375.1K **Privately Held**
SIC: 3423 Carpet layers' hand tools

(G-2466)
DOBBINS INTERIOR WOODWORKS
5916 E County Road 300 S (47018-7501)
PHONE.....................812 221-0058
Sheila Dobbins, *Principal*
EMP: 2
SALES (est): 10.3K **Privately Held**
SIC: 2431 Millwork

(G-2467)
HELENA AGRI-ENTERPRISES LLC
5262 E Us Highway 50 (47018-8797)
PHONE.....................812 654-3177
Matthew Hirt, *Manager*
EMP: 13
SALES (corp-wide): 70.7B **Privately Held**
WEB: www.helenachemical.com
SIC: 5191 2819 Chemicals, agricultural; industrial inorganic chemicals
HQ: Helena Agri-Enterprises, Llc
255 Schilling Blvd # 300
Collierville TN 38017
901 761-0050

(G-2468)
INDIANA PRECISION TOOLING INC
4233 S Farmers Retreat Rd (47018-9297)
PHONE.....................812 667-5141
Don Gooden, *President*
Judy Gooden, *Vice Pres*
EMP: 10
SQ FT: 20,000
SALES: 750K **Privately Held**
SIC: 3545 3423 Machine tool accessories; machine knives, metalworking; hand & edge tools

(G-2469)
K&D CRAFTS
13020 Southfork Rd (47018-8837)
PHONE.....................812 667-2575
Kimberly Hess, *Owner*
EMP: 2
SALES (est): 87K **Privately Held**
SIC: 3944 Craft & hobby kits & sets

(G-2470)
MULTIPLE MACHINING INC
10150 Lenover St (47018-9421)
P.O. Box 29 (47018-0029)
PHONE.....................812 432-5946
Fax: 812 432-3358
Victor H Farrell Jr, *President*
Chip Farrell, *President*
Sharon E Farrell, *Corp Secy*
EMP: 23
SQ FT: 20,000
SALES (est): 4.5MM **Privately Held**
SIC: 3599 Machine shop, jobbing & repair

(G-2471)
PERFORMANCE MACHINING INC
13350 Us Highway 50 (47018-9603)
PHONE.....................812 432-9180
Fax: 812 432-9181
Steve Ochs, *President*
Lavonne Ochs, *Vice Pres*
EMP: 6
SALES (est): 400K **Privately Held**
WEB: www.performancemachining.com
SIC: 3599 Machine shop, jobbing & repair

(G-2472)
SAVOR FLAVOR LLC
13721 Prosperity Ridge Rd (47018-2500)
PHONE.....................812 667-1030
Linda Hurelbrink, *Manager*
EMP: 2
SALES (est): 62.3K **Privately Held**
SIC: 2087 Flavoring extracts & syrups

(G-2473)
T N Z TECHNOLOGY LLC
5770 Woods Ridge Rd (47018-8880)
PHONE.....................812 438-1205
Tristan Gray, *Managing Prtnr*
Zachary Becker, *Managing Prtnr*
EMP: 2
SQ FT: 2,500

SALES (est): 169K **Privately Held**
SIC: 3577 7378 Computer peripheral equipment; computer maintenance & repair

(G-2474)
VERTICAL VISION INC
2417 S County Road 750 E (47018-9683)
PHONE.....................812 432-3763
Steve Belew, *President*
EMP: 3
SALES (est): 161.4K **Privately Held**
SIC: 2591 Blinds vertical

Dubois
Dubois County

(G-2475)
BIMBO BAKERIES USA INC
Sara Lee Bakery
4878 E 450n (47527-9660)
P.O. Box 218 (47527-0218)
PHONE.....................812 678-3471
Fax: 812 678-5502
Steve Hamilton, *Branch Mgr*
Beth Pfau, *Admin Sec*
EMP: 47
SQ FT: 19,000 **Privately Held**
SIC: 2038 Frozen specialties
HQ: Bimbo Bakeries Usa, Inc
255 Business Center Dr # 200
Horsham PA 19044
215 347-5500

(G-2476)
INDIANA FURNITURE INDS INC
4897 E 45 N (47527)
P.O. Box 12, Jasper (47547-0012)
PHONE.....................812 678-2396
Fax: 812 678-4222
Bret Ackerman, *Principal*
EMP: 110
SALES (corp-wide): 39.9MM **Privately Held**
WEB: www.indianafurniture.com
SIC: 2521 Wood office furniture
PA: Indiana Furniture Industries, Inc.
1224 Mill St
Jasper IN 47546
812 482-5727

(G-2477)
MEYER CUSTOM WOODWORKING INC
2657 E State Road 56 (47527-9541)
PHONE.....................812 695-2021
Fax: 812 695-2021
Melvin Meyer, *President*
Dorothy Meyer, *Treasurer*
EMP: 9
SQ FT: 12,000
SALES (est): 1.1MM **Privately Held**
SIC: 2441 2434 8712 Cases, wood; wood kitchen cabinets; architectural services

(G-2478)
WISEMANS CUSTOM CABINETS INC
4501 E State Road 56 (47527-9505)
PHONE.....................812 678-3601
Hoyt Wiseman, *President*
Doug Wiseman, *Principal*
EMP: 3
SALES (est): 280.8K **Privately Held**
SIC: 2434 Wood kitchen cabinets

Dugger
Sullivan County

(G-2479)
C M ENGINEERING INC
8112 E Main St (47848-8087)
P.O. Box 215 (47848-0215)
PHONE.....................812 648-2038
Fax: 812 648-2385
James M Stringer, *President*
Dean Stringer, *Vice Pres*
Jim Stringer, *Info Tech Mgr*
EMP: 16
SQ FT: 12,000

▲ = Import ▼=Export
◆ =Import/Export

SALES: 2.5MM **Privately Held**
WEB: www.cmengineering.com
SIC: 3599 Machine shop, jobbing & repair

(G-2480)
INDUSTRIAL TRNING UNLMTED CORP (PA)
Also Called: Itu Learnlab
8141 E State St (47848-5041)
P.O. Box 128 (47848-0128)
PHONE...............................812 961-8801
David Carpenter, *President*
Kambi Carpenter, *Vice Pres*
Dawn Sharkus, *Info Tech Mgr*
▼ EMP: 9
SQ FT: 15,800
SALES (est): 1.5MM **Privately Held**
WEB: www.goitu.com
SIC: 3699 Electrical equipment & supplies

(G-2481)
MISNER WELDING & CONSTRUCTION
6922 E County Road 425 S (47848)
P.O. Box 554 (47848-0554)
PHONE...............................812 648-2980
Walter R Misner, *President*
EMP: 8
SALES (est): 376.5K **Privately Held**
SIC: 7692 Welding repair

(G-2482)
NMC INC
Also Called: Northside Machine
8068 E Main St (47848)
PHONE...............................812 648-2636
Fax: 812 648-0128
Richard G Smith, *President*
Debra A Smith, *Corp Secy*
Denny Smith, *Vice Pres*
Mike Smith, *Vice Pres*
Todd Guenther MBA, *Opers Staff*
EMP: 24
SQ FT: 18,900
SALES (est): 4.5MM **Privately Held**
WEB: www.northsidemachine.com
SIC: 3599 Machine shop, jobbing & repair

Dunkirk
Jay County

(G-2483)
ARDAGH GLASS INC
524 E Center St (47336-1365)
P.O. Box 205 (47336-0205)
PHONE...............................765 768-7891
Mike Hart, *Plt & Fclts Mgr*
EMP: 41 **Privately Held**
WEB: www.sgcontainers.com
SIC: 3221 Glass containers
HQ: Ardagh Glass Inc.
10194 Crosspoint Blvd
Indianapolis IN 46256

(G-2484)
GRAPHIC PRINTING CO INC
Also Called: News and Sun
209 S Main St (47336-1243)
P.O. Box 59 (47336-0059)
PHONE...............................765 768-6022
Robert Banser, *Manager*
EMP: 3
SALES (corp-wide): 2.3MM **Privately Held**
SIC: 2711 Commercial printing & newspaper publishing combined
PA: The Graphic Printing Co Inc
309 W Main St
Portland IN 47371
260 726-8141

(G-2485)
HAWTHORNE PRODUCTS INC
16828 N State Road 167n (47336-9126)
P.O. Box 226 (47336-0226)
PHONE...............................765 768-6585
Fax: 765 768-7672
Don Hobson, *President*
Edwin L Kinney, *Vice Pres*
Debbie McCaffery, *Purchasing*
Natalie Smith, *Director*
▲ EMP: 6

SALES (est): 1MM **Privately Held**
WEB: www.hawthorneproducts.com
SIC: 2834 Veterinary pharmaceutical preparations

(G-2486)
MOSEY MANUFACTURING CO INC
11340 W 450 S (47336-8983)
PHONE...............................765 768-7462
Jeff Adams, *Manager*
EMP: 70
SALES (corp-wide): 78.8MM **Privately Held**
WEB: www.moseymfg.com
SIC: 3541 3714 Machine tools, metal cutting type; motor vehicle parts & accessories
PA: Mosey Manufacturing Co Inc
262 Fort Wayne Ave
Richmond IN 47374
765 983-8800

(G-2487)
MOSEY MANUFACTURING CO INC
Also Called: Elwood Operations
11340 W 450 S (47336-8983)
PHONE...............................765 552-3504
Travis Marsh, *Manager*
EMP: 100
SALES (est): 9.5MM
SALES (corp-wide): 78.8MM **Privately Held**
WEB: www.moseymfg.com
SIC: 3541 Machine tools, metal cutting type
PA: Mosey Manufacturing Co Inc
262 Fort Wayne Ave
Richmond IN 47374
765 983-8800

(G-2488)
SDP MANUFACTURING INC
400 Industrial Dr (47336-9607)
P.O. Box 44, Albany (47320-0044)
PHONE...............................765 768-5000
Fax: 765 768-5015
Stanely Douglas Pitman, *President*
Selena D Hall, *Admin Sec*
EMP: 18
SQ FT: 20,000
SALES (est): 6MM **Privately Held**
WEB: www.sdpmfg.com
SIC: 3589 Sewer cleaning equipment, power

(G-2489)
TEAL AUTOMOTIVE INC
450 Industrial Dr (47336-9607)
P.O. Box 100, Albany (47320-0100)
PHONE...............................765 768-7726
Fax: 765 768-1607
Brad Alspaugh, *President*
Beth Fallis, *Marketing Staff*
Sheryl Jackson, *Manager*
EMP: 25 EST: 1978
SALES (est): 4.5MM **Privately Held**
SIC: 3714 Motor vehicle transmissions, drive assemblies & parts

(G-2490)
VERALLIA NORTH AMERICA
524 E Center St (47336-1365)
P.O. Box 205 (47336-0205)
PHONE...............................765 768-7891
EMP: 2
SALES (est): 62.6K **Privately Held**
SIC: 3221 Glass containers

Dupont
Jefferson County

(G-2491)
J W P VINYL DESIGNS
Also Called: JP Signs
5210 E Private Road 415 S (47231-9665)
PHONE...............................812 873-8744
Jeff Petro, *Owner*
EMP: 2 EST: 2000
SQ FT: 2,000
SALES: 92K **Privately Held**
SIC: 3993 Signs & advertising specialties

Dyer
Lake County

(G-2492)
AMERICAN PALLET & RECYCL INC (PA)
1203 Sheffield Ave (46311-1054)
PHONE...............................219 322-4391
Gerald L Piper, *President*
EMP: 2
SALES (est): 1.3MM **Privately Held**
SIC: 2448 7699 Pallets, wood; pallet repair

(G-2493)
DECOR IRONWORKS INC
1483 Joliet St (46311-2026)
P.O. Box 195, Schererville (46375-0195)
PHONE...............................219 865-1222
Robert F Brunner, *Principal*
EMP: 2 EST: 1968
SQ FT: 1,500
SALES (est): 311.2K **Privately Held**
SIC: 3446 Fences or posts, ornamental iron or steel

(G-2494)
DOOR TECH INDUSTRIES INC
2733 Quinn Pl (46311-2349)
PHONE...............................219 322-3465
EMP: 2 EST: 2010
SALES (est): 81K **Privately Held**
SIC: 3999 Mfg Misc Products

(G-2495)
DYER SIGNWERKS INC
1000 Richard Rd (46311-1992)
P.O. Box 312 (46311-0312)
PHONE...............................219 322-7722
Mike Bettenbender, *Principal*
EMP: 2
SALES (est): 110K **Privately Held**
SIC: 2253 T-shirts & tops, knit

(G-2496)
DYER VAULT COMPANY INC
1750 Sheffield Ave (46311-1599)
PHONE...............................219 865-2521
Fax: 219 865-1505
Gerald J Austgen, *President*
Susan Karvasale, *Vice Pres*
EMP: 15 EST: 1938
SQ FT: 4,000
SALES (est): 3MM **Privately Held**
SIC: 3272 Concrete products, precast

(G-2497)
EDDIE S GUITARS
2111 Northwinds Dr (46311-1882)
PHONE...............................219 689-7007
Eddie Jones, *Owner*
EMP: 2
SALES (est): 100K **Privately Held**
SIC: 3931 Guitars & parts, electric & non-electric

(G-2498)
F W A DECKS & FENCING
2401 Hickory Dr (46311-2217)
PHONE...............................219 865-3275
Carolyn Ready, *Owner*
EMP: 6
SALES (est): 494.4K **Privately Held**
SIC: 3446 Fences, gates, posts & flagpoles

(G-2499)
GUARDIAN MOLD PREVENT CORP
906 Jackson Pl (46311-1111)
PHONE...............................708 878-5788
Daniel Redden, *Principal*
EMP: 4
SALES (est): 415.1K **Privately Held**
SIC: 3544 Industrial molds

(G-2500)
HADADY CORPORATION
1832 Lake St (46311-1547)
PHONE...............................219 322-7417
Fax: 219 865-6579

Adam Cook, *Senior Engr*
Bill Froemling, *Design Engr*
Jane Sullivan, *Branch Mgr*
EMP: 150
SALES (corp-wide): 27.6MM **Privately Held**
WEB: www.hadadycorp.com
SIC: 3743 Brakes, air & vacuum: railway
PA: Hadady Corporation
510 W 172nd St
South Holland IL 60473
219 322-7417

(G-2501)
HARRY B HIGLEY & SONS INC
9550 Calumet St (46311-2782)
PHONE...............................219 558-8183
Harry B Higley, *President*
Cora L Higley, *Admin Sec*
EMP: 2
SALES (est): 230K **Privately Held**
SIC: 5072 2741 Screws; miscellaneous publishing

(G-2502)
JOHNS ARCHITECTURAL MEDIA
10544 Mimosa St (46311-7054)
PHONE...............................630 450-7539
EMP: 2
SALES (est): 263.3K **Privately Held**
SIC: 3444 5039 Siding, sheet metal; architectural metalwork

(G-2503)
MODERN MACHINE & GRINDING INC
2001 Clark Rd (46311-1704)
P.O. Box 247 (46311-0247)
PHONE...............................219 322-1201
Fax: 219 322-2058
Bruce Givens, *President*
Tim Holzhauer, *Vice Pres*
Dennis Reed, *Vice Pres*
EMP: 23 EST: 1970
SQ FT: 14,000
SALES (est): 3.9MM **Privately Held**
SIC: 3599 Machine shop, jobbing & repair

(G-2504)
NMM ELECTRIC
1900 Hart St (46311-1731)
PHONE...............................219 864-9688
EMP: 2
SALES (est): 226.2K **Privately Held**
SIC: 3699 Electrical equipment & supplies

(G-2505)
NWI PRINT & MAIL LLC
1050 Flagstone Dr (46311-2184)
PHONE...............................219 916-1358
Doug Pint, *Principal*
EMP: 2 EST: 2014
SALES (est): 180.4K **Privately Held**
SIC: 2752 Commercial printing, lithographic

(G-2506)
OIL TECHNOLOGY INC
1203 Sheffield Ave (46311-1054)
PHONE...............................219 322-2724
Fax: 219 322-1668
Gerald Piper, *Principal*
Jerry Harber, *Corp Secy*
Randall L Holland, *Opers Mgr*
David A Lade, *Controller*
Nick Rovai, *Marketing Mgr*
EMP: 23
SALES (est): 5.3MM **Privately Held**
SIC: 2992 Re-refining lubricating oils & greases

(G-2507)
PDB II INC
2661 Tower Ct (46311-2363)
PHONE...............................219 865-1888
Pat Ballwick, *CEO*
EMP: 2
SALES (est): 106.5K **Privately Held**
SIC: 2389 Apparel & accessories

(G-2508)
PRINTWERK GRAPHICS & DESIGN
1000 Richard Rd (46311-1992)
PHONE...............................219 322-7722

Michael E Bettenbender, *Owner*
EMP: 3
SQ FT: 2,800
SALES (est): 151.1K **Privately Held**
SIC: 2759 7331 Advertising literature: printing; direct mail advertising services

(G-2509)
SIMKO MACHINING INC
51 Chateau Dr (46311-2152)
PHONE..................................219 864-9535
Randy Simko, *President*
Cecilia Derolf, *Manager*
EMP: 8
SALES (est): 609.5K **Privately Held**
SIC: 3599 Machine shop, jobbing & repair

(G-2510)
STAMP N SCRAP INK CORP
1043 Sheffield Ave (46311-1048)
PHONE..................................219 440-7239
Pamela Nachel, *Principal*
EMP: 2
SALES (est): 81.8K **Privately Held**
SIC: 2893 Printing ink

(G-2511)
TRULINESIGNS LLC
13105 81st Ave (46311-2541)
PHONE..................................219 644-7231
Prudence M Montana, *Administration*
EMP: 2
SALES (est): 144.2K **Privately Held**
SIC: 3993 Signs & advertising specialties

(G-2512)
WINDMILL BREWING
2121 Gettler St (46311-1859)
PHONE..................................219 440-2189
EMP: 2
SALES (est): 62.3K **Privately Held**
SIC: 2082 Malt beverages

Earl Park
Benton County

(G-2513)
TRIBUNE SHOWPRINT INC
107 S Oak St (47942)
PHONE..................................574 943-3281
Fax: 219 474-6062
John D Furr, *President*
Mildred Furr, *Treasurer*
Louise Furr, *Admin Sec*
EMP: 9
SQ FT: 4,360
SALES (est): 1MM **Privately Held**
SIC: 2759 Letterpress printing

East Chicago
Lake County

(G-2514)
1632 INC
Also Called: Science Fiction Public
4202 Baring Ave (46312-2509)
PHONE..................................219 398-4155
Eric Flint, *President*
EMP: 2
SALES: 350K **Privately Held**
SIC: 2721 8999 7389 Magazines: publishing & printing; author;

(G-2515)
AMERICAN SCRAP PROCESSING INC
3601 Canal St (46312-1605)
PHONE..................................219 398-1444
Albert Cozzi, *Ch of Bd*
Frank Cozzi, *President*
Gregory Cozzi, *Admin Sec*
EMP: 65
SQ FT: 5,000
SALES (est): 6.2MM **Privately Held**
SIC: 5093 3341 Metal scrap & waste materials; secondary nonferrous metals
HQ: Metal Management, Inc.
200 W Madison St Ste 3600
Chicago IL 60606
312 645-0700

(G-2516)
ARCELORMITTAL HOLDINGS LLC (HQ)
3210 Watling St (46312-1716)
PHONE..................................219 399-1200
Lakshmi Mittal, *Ch of Bd*
Edward Williams, *Division Mgr*
William Ball, *Engng Exec*
Michael G Rippey, *CFO*
Mary Hendrickson, *Manager*
◆ **EMP:** 95
SALES (est): 3.3B **Privately Held**
WEB: www.mittalsteel.com
SIC: 3312 1011 Blast furnaces & steel mills; iron ores
PA: Arcelormittal Sa
Boulevard D'avranches 24-26
Luxembourg
479 21 -

(G-2517)
ARCELORMITTAL INDIANA HBR LLC
Also Called: Arcelormittal Indiana Harbor W
3210 Watling St (46312-1716)
P.O. Box 2928, Chesterton (46304-5428)
PHONE..................................219 399-1200
Rodney B Mott, *CEO*
Louis Schorsch, *Principal*
Lloyd Beattie, *Engineer*
Rick Pintz, *Plant Engr*
▲ **EMP:** 900
SALES (est): 228.8MM **Privately Held**
SIC: 3312 Blast furnaces & steel mills
HQ: Arcelormittal Usa Llc
1 S Dearborn St Ste 1800
Chicago IL 60603
312 346-0300

(G-2518)
ARCELORMITTAL MINORCA MINE INC (DH)
Also Called: Mittal Steel -Ihw- 3 Sp
3210 Watling St (46312-1716)
PHONE..................................219 399-1200
Gary Krall, *CEO*
Peter D Southwich, *Ch of Bd*
Madhu Ranade, *President*
Mark Dutler, *Division Mgr*
Michael Rippey, *Exec VP*
◆ **EMP:** 5
SALES (est): 243.3MM **Privately Held**
SIC: 1011 Open pit iron ore mining; iron ore pelletizing
HQ: Arcelormittal Usa Llc
1 S Dearborn St Ste 1800
Chicago IL 60603
312 346-0300

(G-2519)
ARCELORMITTAL USA LLC
3210 Watling St (46312-1716)
PHONE..................................312 899-3400
Allen Waitkins, *Division Mgr*
Cyril Martinand, *General Mgr*
Owen Decker, *Project Mgr*
Ramesh Sharan, *Project Mgr*
Abel Garcia, *Opers Mgr*
EMP: 4850 **Privately Held**
SIC: 3312 Blast furnaces & steel mills
HQ: Arcelormittal Usa Llc
1 S Dearborn St Ste 1800
Chicago IL 60603
312 346-0300

(G-2520)
ARCELORMITTAL USA LLC
3001 E Columbus Dr (46312-2939)
PHONE..................................219 399-6500
Ken Budge, *Division Mgr*
Joseph Wideman, *Division Mgr*
Arthur Mayo, *Area Mgr*
Leroy Campbell, *Project Mgr*
Edward Levine, *Project Mgr*
EMP: 105 **Privately Held**
SIC: 3312 Blast furnaces & steel mills
HQ: Arcelormittal Usa Llc
1 S Dearborn St Ste 1800
Chicago IL 60603
312 346-0300

(G-2521)
ASPHALT CUTBACKS INC
3000 Gary Rd (46312-3578)
PHONE..................................219 398-4230

Fax: 219 398-7820
Cleopatra Bizoukas, *President*
George Bizoukas, *Vice Pres*
EMP: 11
SALES (est): 4.2MM **Privately Held**
WEB: www.asphaltcutbacks.com
SIC: 2952 2951 Coating compounds, tar; asphalt paving mixtures & blocks

(G-2522)
BEEMSTERBOER SLAG CORP
3210 Watling St (46312-1716)
PHONE..................................219 392-1930
William Mundel, *Owner*
Paul Channell, *Security Dir*
EMP: 71
SALES (corp-wide): 27.6MM **Privately Held**
SIC: 3295 Slag, crushed or ground
PA: Beemsterboer Slag Corp.
3411 Sheffield Ave
Hammond IN 46327
219 931-7462

(G-2523)
BETOS BAR INC
1301 E Chicago Ave (46312-3518)
PHONE..................................219 397-8247
Roberto Abille, *President*
EMP: 5
SALES (est): 536.8K **Privately Held**
SIC: 3631 Barbecues, grills & braziers (outdoor cooking)

(G-2524)
CHICAGO FLAME HARDENING CO
5200 Railroad Ave Ste 1 (46312-3891)
PHONE..................................773 768-3608
Fax: 219 397-4029
Thomas J Farnsworth, *Ch of Bd*
Gwen Farnsworth, *Corp Secy*
John Farnsworth, *Exec VP*
EMP: 28 **EST:** 1956
SQ FT: 25,000
SALES (est): 6.9MM **Privately Held**
WEB: www.cflame.com
SIC: 3398 3312 Metal burning; blast furnaces & steel mills

(G-2525)
DULCERIA GARZA INC
4120 Deal St (46312-2921)
PHONE..................................219 397-1062
Jesus Garza, *Principal*
EMP: 2
SALES (est): 116.2K **Privately Held**
SIC: 2064 Candy & other confectionery products

(G-2526)
EL POPULAR INC
910 E Chicago Ave (46312-3513)
P.O. Box 328 (46312-0328)
PHONE..................................219 397-3728
Edward Garza, *President*
EMP: 12
SALES (est): 1.6MM **Privately Held**
SIC: 2032 Mexican foods: packaged in cans, jars, etc.

(G-2527)
ELECTRIC COATING TECH LLC
Also Called: Material Sciences
4407 Railroad Ave (46312-2654)
PHONE..................................219 378-1930
Steve Tatalovich, *President*
Ed Cochran, *Sales Staff*
Scott Sternhiemer,
Charlie Keene,
James L Todd,
▼ **EMP:** 36
SQ FT: 170,000
SALES (est): 5.1MM
SALES (corp-wide): 148.5MM **Privately Held**
SIC: 3479 Galvanizing of iron, steel or end-formed products
PA: Material Sciences Corporation
6855 Commerce Blvd
Canton MI 48187
734 207-4444

(G-2528)
EUCLID MACHINE & TOOL INC (PA)
4450 Euclid Ave (46312-3045)
PHONE..................................219 397-1374
Fax: 219 392-2466
Jacob D Rakoczy, *President*
Josephine Rakoczy, *Admin Sec*
EMP: 41 **EST:** 1945
SQ FT: 100,000
SALES (est): 3.7MM **Privately Held**
SIC: 3599 3441 Machine shop, jobbing & repair; custom machinery; fabricated structural metal

(G-2529)
GANNON MTAL FBRCATORS ERECTORS
418 E Chicago Ave (46312-3544)
P.O. Box 499 (46312-0499)
PHONE..................................219 398-0299
Fax: 219 397-1949
Nicholas M Paul, *President*
Joseph E Fraley, *Admin Sec*
EMP: 9 **EST:** 1957
SQ FT: 25,000
SALES (est): 1.7MM **Privately Held**
WEB: www.gannongarcialaw.com
SIC: 3441 Fabricated structural metal

(G-2530)
GRC ENTERPRISES INC
Also Called: Taylor Chain
3477 Watling St (46312-1708)
P.O. Box 481 (46312-0481)
PHONE..................................219 932-2220
Gerhard Volkmann, *President*
Henry Walma, *Controller*
EMP: 20
SQ FT: 5,000
SALES (est): 3.4MM **Privately Held**
SIC: 3496 Chain, welded; slings, lifting: made from purchased wire

(G-2531)
GREEN LAKE TUBE LLC (PA)
Also Called: Steel Manufacturing
4500 Euclid Ave (46312-3079)
PHONE..................................219 397-0495
Chris Reid, *President*
Paul Pak,
EMP: 27
SQ FT: 100,000
SALES (est): 2.8MM **Privately Held**
SIC: 3498 Tube fabricating (contract bending & shaping)

(G-2532)
HARSCO CORPORATION
5222 Indianapolis Blvd (46312-3838)
PHONE..................................219 397-0200
Henry W Knueppel, *Branch Mgr*
EMP: 20
SALES (corp-wide): 1.6B **Publicly Held**
SIC: 4953 2899 Refuse systems; chemical preparations
PA: Harsco Corporation
350 Poplar Church Rd
Camp Hill PA 17011
717 763-7064

(G-2533)
HOIST LIFTRUCK MFG LLC (HQ)
4407 Railroad Ave (46312-2654)
PHONE..................................708 552-2722
Vincent Flaska, *President*
EMP: 370 **EST:** 2015
SALES (est): 24.2MM **Privately Held**
SIC: 3537 Forklift trucks

(G-2534)
HUMES & BERG MFG CO INC
4801 Railroad Ave (46312-3359)
PHONE..................................219 391-5880
Fax: 219 397-4534
Irwin Berg, *President*
Michael Berg, *Admin Sec*
▲ **EMP:** 9 **EST:** 1935
SQ FT: 100,000
SALES (est): 1.4MM **Privately Held**
WEB: www.humes-berg.com
SIC: 3931 3161 Stands, music; musical instrument cases

▲ = Import ▼=Export
◆ =Import/Export

(G-2535)
ICO POLYMERS NORTH AMERICA INC
4404 Euclid Ave (46312-3045)
PHONE...................................219 392-3375
John Knapp, *Principal*
EMP: 7
SALES (est): 888K **Privately Held**
SIC: 2821 Plastics materials & resins

(G-2536)
ICO POLYMERS NORTH AMERICA INC
4404 Euclid Ave (46312-3045)
PHONE...................................219 392-3375
EMP: 2
SALES (corp-wide): 2.4B **Publicly Held**
SIC: 2822 Ethylene-propylene rubbers, EPDM polymers
HQ: Ico Polymers North America, Inc.
24624 Interstate 45
Spring TX 77386
832 663-3131

(G-2537)
ILLIANA STEEL INC
Also Called: Illiana Storage & Processing
4407 Railroad Ave (46312-2654)
PHONE...................................219 397-3250
Fax: 219 391-5229
Stanley Frankiewicz, *President*
Steve Strayer, *Corp Secy*
Andrzeji Jach, *Vice Pres*
Gerald Tronjo, *Vice Pres*
EMP: 40
SQ FT: 86,000
SALES (est): 4.8MM **Privately Held**
WEB: www.ihbrr.com
SIC: 5051 3316 Metals service centers & offices; steel; cold-rolled strip or wire

(G-2538)
INDIANA HARBOR COKE COMPANY LP
3210 Watling St (46312-1716)
P.O. Box 240 (46312-0240)
PHONE...................................219 397-5769
Frederick A Henderson, *CEO*
Kenneth J Schuett, *CEO*
▲ EMP: 122 EST: 1996
SALES (est): 69.4MM
SALES (corp-wide): 1.3B **Publicly Held**
SIC: 3312 Blast furnaces & steel mills
PA: Suncoke Energy, Inc.
1011 Warrenville Rd # 600
Lisle IL 60532
630 824-1000

(G-2539)
INDIANA PALLET CO INC
724 E Chicago Ave (46312-6519)
P.O. Box 398 (46312-0398)
PHONE...................................219 398-4223
Fax: 219 398-4302
Sergio Magana, *President*
EMP: 26
SQ FT: 250,000
SALES (est): 4.7MM **Privately Held**
SIC: 2448 Pallets, wood

(G-2540)
INSIGHT EQUITY HOLDINGS LLC
4407 Railroad Ave (46312-2654)
PHONE...................................219 378-1930
Patrick J Murley, *CEO*
EMP: 530
SALES (corp-wide): 1.5B **Privately Held**
SIC: 3312 Sheet or strip, steel, cold-rolled: own hot-rolled
PA: Insight Equity Holdings Llc
1400 Civic Pl Ste 250
Southlake TX 76092
817 488-7775

(G-2541)
KEMIRA WATER SOLUTIONS INC
3761 Canal St (46312-1607)
PHONE...................................219 397-2646
Randy Johnson, *Terminal Mgr*
Jerry Tenny, *CFO*
EMP: 21
SALES (corp-wide): 2.9B **Privately Held**
WEB: www.kemiron.com
SIC: 2899 Chemical preparations

HQ: Kemira Water Solutions, Inc.
1000 Parkwood Cir Se # 500
Atlanta GA 30339
770 436-1542

(G-2542)
KEMIRA WATER SOLUTIONS INC
3761 Canal St (46312-1607)
PHONE...................................219 397-2646
William Wowchuck, *Branch Mgr*
EMP: 2
SALES (corp-wide): 2.9B **Privately Held**
SIC: 2899 Water treating compounds
HQ: Kemira Water Solutions, Inc.
1000 Parkwood Cir Se # 500
Atlanta GA 30339
770 436-1542

(G-2543)
KEMIRON GREAT LAKES LLC
3761 Canal St (46312-1607)
PHONE...................................219 397-2646
Fax: 219 397-2656
Brian Wodetzki, *Vice Pres*
EMP: 20
SALES (est): 3.8MM **Privately Held**
SIC: 2834 Chlorination tablets & kits (water purification)

(G-2544)
KEYSTONE MACHINE SERVICES INC
1520 E Chicago Ave (46312-3575)
P.O. Box 562 (46312-0562)
PHONE...................................219 397-6792
Fax: 219 397-0086
Joseph Spott, *President*
EMP: 5
SQ FT: 5,300
SALES (est): 682.8K **Privately Held**
SIC: 3599 Machine shop, jobbing & repair

(G-2545)
KOCSIS BROTHERS MACHINE CO
4321 Railroad Ave (46312-3455)
PHONE...................................219 397-8400
Fax: 219 398-1234
Jim Belleville, *Manager*
EMP: 30
SALES (corp-wide): 23.3MM **Privately Held**
WEB: www.kocsisbros.com
SIC: 3599 7692 Machine shop, jobbing & repair; welding repair
PA: Kocsis Brothers Machine Company
11755 S Austin Ave
Alsip IL 60803
708 597-8110

(G-2546)
L&N SUPPLY LLC
4016 Deodar St (46312-2809)
P.O. Box 1850, Valparaiso (46384-1850)
PHONE...................................219 397-9500
Lora Kokot, *Mng Member*
EMP: 2
SALES (est): 157.7K **Privately Held**
SIC: 3949 Shooting equipment & supplies, general

(G-2547)
LAFARGE NORTH AMERICA INC
3210 Watling St (46312-1716)
P.O. Box 2974 (46312-7974)
PHONE...................................219 378-1193
Shawn Blacklock, *Project Mgr*
Megan Rittermeyer, *Production*
EMP: 8
SALES (corp-wide): 26.4B **Privately Held**
WEB: www.lafargenorthamerica.com
SIC: 3241 3273 3272 3271 Cement, hydraulic; portland cement; ready-mixed concrete; concrete products; precast terrazo or concrete products; prestressed concrete products; cylinder pipe, prestressed or pretensioned concrete; blocks, concrete or cinder: standard; construction sand & gravel; construction sand mining; gravel mining; asphalt paving mixtures & blocks; paving mixtures; asphalt & asphaltic paving mixtures (not from refineries)

HQ: Lafarge North America Inc.
8700 W Bryn Mawr Ave
Chicago IL 60631
773 372-1000

(G-2548)
LIGHTBEAM TECHNOLOGY
4809 Tod Ave (46312-3405)
PHONE...................................219 397-1684
EMP: 2 EST: 2010
SALES (est): 100K **Privately Held**
SIC: 3599 Mfg Industrial Machinery

(G-2549)
LOCOMOTIVE S PROFESSIONAL
4949 Huish Dr (46312-3768)
PHONE...................................219 398-9123
Adela Ortega, *Owner*
EMP: 6
SALES (est): 686K **Privately Held**
SIC: 3743 Tenders, locomotive

(G-2550)
LTV STEEL CO
3001 Dickey Rd (46312-1610)
PHONE...................................219 391-2076
EMP: 2
SALES (est): 90.8K **Privately Held**
SIC: 3312 Blast furnaces & steel mills

(G-2551)
LUCKY STRAW INC
405 E 151st St (46312-3844)
P.O. Box 9250, Highland (46322-9250)
PHONE...................................219 397-9910
Fax: 219 398-0416
Raymond Scanlon, *Owner*
EMP: 20
SQ FT: 68,000
SALES (est): 2.6MM **Privately Held**
SIC: 2656 Straws, drinking: made from purchased material

(G-2552)
MIDWEST STEEL & TUBE LLC
Also Called: Midwest Steekl Acqusition
4500 Euclid Ave (46312-3079)
PHONE...................................219 398-2200
John Martin,
EMP: 25
SQ FT: 20,000
SALES (est): 3.8MM **Privately Held**
WEB: www.elkhartmetal.com
SIC: 3317 Steel pipe & tubes
PA: Elkhart Metal Distributing, Inc.
3601 County Road 6 E
Elkhart IN 46514

(G-2553)
MINTEQ INTERNATIONAL INC
3001 Dickey Rd (46312-1610)
PHONE...................................219 397-5978
Joe Lozano, *Principal*
EMP: 2 EST: 2016
SALES (est): 62.6K **Privately Held**
SIC: 3297 Nonclay refractories

(G-2554)
NATIONAL MATERIAL LP
National Material Processing
4506 Cline Ave (46312-3181)
PHONE...................................219 397-5088
Nick Savich, *Plant Mgr*
Chris Sekella, *Sales/Mktg Mgr*
Mike Mojzer, *Accounts Mgr*
Allen Landreth, *Sales Staff*
EMP: 119
SQ FT: 60,000
SALES (corp-wide): 1B **Privately Held**
WEB: www.nmlp.com
SIC: 3471 5051 3312 Plating & polishing; metals service centers & offices; blast furnaces & steel mills
PA: National Material L.P.
1965 Pratt Blvd
Elk Grove Village IL 60007
847 806-7200

(G-2555)
NORTHWEST INDUS SPECIALIST
4333 Indianapolis Blvd (46312-2627)
PHONE...................................219 397-7446
Joseph Wargo, *President*
Roger Wargo Jr, *Vice Pres*
Timothy King, *Treasurer*

EMP: 18
SQ FT: 8,000
SALES (est): 3.4MM **Privately Held**
WEB: www.nis4signs.com
SIC: 5099 3993 Signs, except electric; signs & advertising specialties

(G-2556)
PATRIOT RANGE TECHNOLOGIES
4400 Homerlee Ave Ste 1 (46312-2680)
PHONE...................................708 354-3150
EMP: 2
SALES (est): 103.1K **Privately Held**
SIC: 3949 Sporting & athletic goods

(G-2557)
PHOENIX SERVICES LLC
Also Called: Nalco Co
3001 Dickey Rd (46312-1610)
P.O. Box 3070 (46312-8070)
PHONE...................................219 397-0650
Paul Benson, *Prdtn Mgr*
David Price, *Site Mgr*
Walter Murray, *Foreman/Supr*
Ed Front, *Branch Mgr*
Shannon Ortega, *Maintence Staff*
EMP: 38 **Privately Held**
SIC: 3295 Perlite, aggregate or expanded
HQ: Metal Services Llc
148 W State St Ste 301
Kennett Square PA 19348

(G-2558)
PHOENIX SERVICES LLC
3236 Watling St (46312)
P.O. Box 3190 (46312-8190)
PHONE...................................219 399-7808
Tony Cunningham, *Manager*
EMP: 88
SALES (est): 3MM **Privately Held**
SIC: 3312 Blast furnaces & steel mills

(G-2559)
PINDER POLYURETHANE & PLAS INC
481 E 151st St (46312-3844)
P.O. Box 433 (46312-0433)
PHONE...................................219 397-8248
Walter Tokarz, *President*
Janice Gaskill, *Vice Pres*
EMP: 6
SQ FT: 15,000
SALES (est): 1.3MM **Privately Held**
SIC: 2851 5169 Polyurethane coatings; polyurethane products

(G-2560)
PLATEPLUS INC
4303 Kennedy Ave (46312-2723)
PHONE...................................219 392-3400
Fax: 219 398-1194
Mark Hussey, *Branch Mgr*
EMP: 68
SQ FT: 140,000
SALES (corp-wide): 71B **Privately Held**
WEB: www.cargill.com
SIC: 5051 3316 Steel; sheets, galvanized or other coated; strip, metal; sheet, steel, cold-rolled: from purchased hot-rolled; strip steel, cold-rolled: from purchased hot-rolled
HQ: Plateplus Inc.
21 Waterway Ave Ste 525
The Woodlands TX 77380
281 298-0320

(G-2561)
POLLUTION CONTROL INDUSTRIES
4343 Kennedy Ave (46312-2723)
PHONE...................................219 391-7020
John Newell, *President*
EMP: 26
SALES (est): 3.3MM **Privately Held**
SIC: 3999 Manufacturing industries

(G-2562)
PRAXAIR INC
4400 Kennedy Ave (46312-2715)
PHONE...................................219 398-3700
Fax: 219 398-3033
Tim Baird, *Sales Dir*
Dennis Maxwell, *Manager*
EMP: 120

GEOGRAPHIC

SALES (corp-wide): 11.4B **Publicly Held**
SIC: 2813 Industrial gases
PA: Praxair, Inc.
10 Riverview Dr
Danbury CT 06810
203 837-2000

(G-2563)
PRAXAIR INC
2551 Dickie Rd (46312)
PHONE..................................219 397-6940
Dennis Maxwell, *Principal*
EMP: 12
SALES (corp-wide): 11.4B **Publicly Held**
SIC: 2813 Industrial gases
PA: Praxair, Inc.
10 Riverview Dr
Danbury CT 06810
203 837-2000

(G-2564)
PRECISION SURVEILLANCE CORP
Also Called: PSC
3468 Watling St (46312-1709)
PHONE..................................219 397-4295
Fax: 219 397-5867
Paul Smith, *President*
Christopher Cox, *Vice Pres*
Brad Jones, *Opers Mgr*
Tommy Morrison, *Sr Project Mgr*
Pat Furlan, *Admin Sec*
EMP: 50
SQ FT: 40,000
SALES (est): 16.9MM **Privately Held**
WEB: www.psctendon.com
SIC: 1796 1791 3441 8711 Machine moving & rigging; iron work, structural; fabricated structural metal; structural engineering

(G-2565)
PROGRESS RAIL SERVICES CORP
Locomotive & Transit
175 W Chicago Ave (46312-3201)
PHONE..................................219 397-5326
Ricky Todd, *Buyer*
James Shirvinski, *VP Engrg*
Mike Role, *Branch Mgr*
Ed Haynes, *Maintence Staff*
EMP: 200
SALES (corp-wide): 45.4B **Publicly Held**
WEB: www.progressrail.com
SIC: 4789 3312 7389 Railroad maintenance & repair services; railroad car repair; structural & rail mill products; metal cutting services
HQ: Progress Rail Services Corporation
1600 Progress Dr
Albertville AL 35950
256 593-1260

(G-2566)
PRT SOUTH LLC
Also Called: Patriot Range Technologies
4400 Homerlee Ave Ste 1 (46312-2680)
PHONE..................................708 354-3786
James M Corcoran, *Principal*
Thomas Corcoran,
EMP: 4
SALES (est): 360K **Privately Held**
WEB: www.patriotrange.com
SIC: 3949 Target shooting equipment

(G-2567)
REFRACTORY SERVICE CORPORATION (PA)
Also Called: R S C
4900 Cline Ave (46312-3559)
P.O. Box 2276 (46312-7276)
PHONE..................................219 397-7108
Fax: 219 398-4608
Samuel F Bianchi, *President*
Jeffrey Bianchi, *COO*
Laura Eikenmeyer, *Vice Pres*
Cindy Bianchi, *Treasurer*
▲ EMP: 40
SQ FT: 50,000
SALES (est): 15.6MM **Privately Held**
SIC: 3297 7699 Castable refractories, nonclay; industrial equipment services

(G-2568)
SAFETY-KLEEN SYSTEMS INC
601 Riley Rd (46312-1638)
PHONE..................................219 397-1131
Fax: 219 391-6180
Steve Lewis, *Sales Dir*
Scott Miller, *Branch Mgr*
Denny Zawodni, *Manager*
Robin Kaiser, *Admin Asst*
Tom Fleming, *Maintence Staff*
EMP: 15
SALES (corp-wide): 2.9B **Publicly Held**
SIC: 3559 Degreasing machines, automotive & industrial
HQ: Safety-Kleen Systems, Inc.
2600 N Central Expy # 400
Richardson TX 75080
972 265-2000

(G-2569)
SUEZ WTS USA INC
Also Called: General Electric Betz
3210 Watling St (46312-1716)
PHONE..................................219 397-0554
Fax: 219 397-0566
George Grote, *Manager*
EMP: 3
SALES (corp-wide): 86.1MM **Privately Held**
SIC: 3295 Minerals, ground or treated
HQ: Suez Wts Usa, Inc.
4636 Somerton Rd
Trevose PA 19053
215 355-3300

(G-2570)
TMS INTERNATIONAL LLC
3001 Dickey Rd (46312-1610)
PHONE..................................219 881-0155
EMP: 4 **Privately Held**
SIC: 3312 Blast furnaces & steel mills
HQ: Tms International, Llc
12 Monongahela Ave
Glassport PA 15045
412 678-6141

(G-2571)
TMS INTERNATIONAL LLC
Also Called: IMS
3001 Dickey Rd Ste 392 (46312-1610)
PHONE..................................219 397-6550
Fax: 219 398-0565
EMP: 9 **Privately Held**
SIC: 3295 Minerals, Ground Or Treated, Nsk

(G-2572)
TRADEBE GP (DH)
4343 Kennedy Ave (46312-2723)
PHONE..................................800 388-7242
Victor C De Villalonga, *Principal*
Victor Creixell De Villalonga, *Principal*
EMP: 1
SALES (est): 384.2MM
SALES (corp-wide): 137.1K **Privately Held**
SIC: 4953 7699 1389 Hazardous waste collection & disposal; recycling, waste materials; ship boiler & tank cleaning & repair; contractors; industrial equipment cleaning; lease tanks, oil field: erecting, cleaning & repairing
HQ: Tradebe Environmental Services Sl
Avenida Barcelona, 109 - 5
Sant Joan Despi
932 058-100

(G-2573)
TRADEBE INDUSTRIAL SVCS LLC (DH)
1433 E 83rd Ave Ste 200 (46312)
PHONE..................................800 388-7242
Victor Creixell, *CEO*
Sergio Nusimovich Kolodny, *Principal*
Jorge Lopez, *Admin Sec*
EMP: 25 EST: 1981
SQ FT: 35,000
SALES (est): 25.8MM
SALES (corp-wide): 137.1K **Privately Held**
WEB: www.petrosvs.com
SIC: 7699 1389 Ship boiler & tank cleaning & repair; contractors; industrial equipment cleaning; lease tanks, oil field: erecting, cleaning & repairing

(G-2574)
TRI-STATE METALS INC
220 W Chicago Ave (46312-3203)
PHONE..................................219 397-0470
Salvadore Ortiz, *President*
Marrietta Peek, *Treasurer*
EMP: 30
SALES (est): 5.9MM **Privately Held**
WEB: www.tristatemetalinc.com
SIC: 3398 7389 Metal heat treating; metal cutting services

(G-2575)
UNITED STATES GYPSUM COMPANY
301 Riley Rd (46312-1697)
PHONE..................................219 392-4600
Fax: 219 392-4616
John Russell, *Mfg Staff*
Olin Postlethwait, *Buyer*
Bob Salinas, *Electrical Engi*
Kelly Bishop, *Manager*
Marveen Winslow, *Manager*
EMP: 150
SALES (corp-wide): 3.2B **Publicly Held**
WEB: www.usg.com
SIC: 3275 Gypsum products
HQ: United States Gypsum Company Inc
550 W Adams St Ste 1300
Chicago IL 60661
312 606-4000

(G-2576)
UNITED STATES STEEL CORP
101 E 129th St (46312-1650)
PHONE..................................219 391-2045
Dennis Henry, *Branch Mgr*
EMP: 444
SALES (corp-wide): 12.2B **Publicly Held**
SIC: 3325 3312 Steel foundries; blast furnaces & steel mills
PA: United States Steel Corp
600 Grant St Ste 468
Pittsburgh PA 15219
412 433-1121

(G-2577)
UNIVERSAL SERVICES INC
Also Called: Patco Distribution
475 E 151st St (46312-3844)
P.O. Box 500 (46312-0500)
PHONE..................................219 397-4373
Rich Haan, *Manager*
EMP: 4
SQ FT: 43,960
SALES (est): 380K **Privately Held**
SIC: 2911 2899 Greases, lubricating; antifreeze compounds

(G-2578)
US METALS INC
425 W 151st St Ste 2 (46312-3856)
PHONE..................................219 398-1350
Samantha Nadolski, *Sales Mgr*
Bob Qualey, *Branch Mgr*
EMP: 5
SALES (corp-wide): 131.8MM **Privately Held**
SIC: 3449 5051 Bars, concrete reinforcing: fabricated steel; metals service centers & offices
PA: U.S. Metals, Inc.
19102 Gundle Rd
Houston TX 77073
281 443-7473

(G-2579)
VIDIMOS INC
3858 Indiana Harbor Dr (46312-2349)
P.O. Box 480 (46312-0480)
PHONE..................................219 397-2728
Fax: 773 221-2244
Alfred Scott Vidimos, *President*
Jim Companik, *Vice Pres*
Christopher E Lawes, *Vice Pres*
Larry Tetzloff, *Project Mgr*
Adam Vidimos, *Treasurer*
EMP: 80 EST: 1946
SQ FT: 54,000
SALES (est): 24.1MM **Privately Held**
WEB: www.vidimos.com
SIC: 1761 3441 Sheet metalwork; fabricated structural metal

(G-2580)
W R GRACE & CO - CONN
Also Called: W R Grace Davison Chemical Div
5215 Kennedy Ave (46312-3805)
PHONE..................................219 398-2040
Patricia Winkley, *Opers-Prdtn-Mfg*
Paul Taube, *Administration*
EMP: 50
SALES (corp-wide): 1.7B **Publicly Held**
WEB: www.grace.com
SIC: 2819 Industrial inorganic chemicals
HQ: W. R. Grace & Co.-Conn.
7500 Grace Dr
Columbia MD 21044
410 531-4000

Eaton
Delaware County

(G-2581)
ARROWHEAD PLASTIC ENGINEERING
Also Called: Arrowhead Plastic Products
1155 N Hartford St (47338-8774)
P.O. Box 75 (47338-0075)
PHONE..................................765 396-9113
Fax: 765 396-9117
Mildred Jaggers, *Branch Mgr*
EMP: 10
SALES (corp-wide): 14.8MM **Privately Held**
WEB: www.arrowheadinc.com
SIC: 5162 3089 Plastics materials & basic shapes; thermoformed finished plastic products
PA: Arrowhead Plastic Engineering Inc
2909 S Hoyt Ave
Muncie IN 47302
765 286-0533

(G-2582)
EATON SEPTIC TANK COMPANY
14601 N State Road 3n (47338-8936)
PHONE..................................765 396-3275
Jack Ashcraft, *Owner*
EMP: 2
SALES (est): 176.6K **Privately Held**
SIC: 3272 1711 Septic tanks, concrete; septic system construction

(G-2583)
EDEN FOODS INC
Meridian Foods Division
201 E Babb Rd (47338-8807)
P.O. Box 155 (47338-0155)
PHONE..................................765 396-3344
Terry Evans, *General Mgr*
Katie Henry, *QC Mgr*
EMP: 27
SALES (corp-wide): 43.8MM **Privately Held**
WEB: www.edenfoods.com
SIC: 2032 2033 Beans & bean sprouts, canned, jarred, etc.; canned fruits & specialties
PA: Eden Foods, Inc.
701 Tecumseh Rd
Clinton MI 49236
517 456-7424

(G-2584)
GRAPHIC MENUS INC
Also Called: GMI
16555 N State Road 3n (47338-8944)
P.O. Box 400, Muncie (47308-0400)
PHONE..................................765 396-3003
Fax: 765 396-3520
Robert Schwindt, *President*
EMP: 16
SQ FT: 5,000
SALES (est): 1.6MM **Privately Held**
WEB: www.graphicmenus.com
SIC: 2752 2759 Menus, lithographed; commercial printing

(G-2585)
MARTIN ELECTRIC INC
5501 E Eaton Albany Pike (47338-8725)
P.O. Box 2903, Muncie (47307-0903)
PHONE..................................765 288-3254
John Martin, *President*
EMP: 3

SALES (est): 199.4K **Privately Held**
SIC: 3699 1731 7539 Electrical equipment & supplies; electrical work; electrical services

(G-2586)
MERIT TOOL & MANUFACTURING INC
120 N Hartford St (47338)
P.O. Box 365 (47338-0365)
PHONE...............................765 396-9566
Fax: 765 396-9666
Phillip J Reber, *President*
Janet L Reber, *Admin Sec*
EMP: 10
SQ FT: 4,500
SALES (est): 1.5MM **Privately Held**
WEB: www.merittool.com
SIC: 3599 3544 3545 Machine shop, jobbing & repair; custom machinery; jigs & fixtures; gauges (machine tool accessories)

(G-2587)
PALMETTO PLANTERS LLC
1153 N Hartford St (47338)
PHONE...............................765 396-4446
Anita Kishel, *President*
EMP: 3
SALES (est): 276.3K **Privately Held**
SIC: 3229 Glass fiber products

(G-2588)
RODGERS ENTERPRISES LLC
17920 N State Road 3n (47338-8956)
P.O. Box 412 (47338-0412)
PHONE...............................765 396-3143
Richard Rogers, *President*
EMP: 2
SALES (est): 140.6K **Privately Held**
SIC: 1389 Construction, repair & dismantling services

(G-2589)
SHADE TECHNIQUES LLC
4191 E Gregory Rd (47338-8916)
P.O. Box 608 (47338-0608)
PHONE...............................765 396-9903
Fax: 765 396-9904
Dan Vore,
Linda J Vore,
EMP: 7
SQ FT: 5,000
SALES: 500K **Privately Held**
WEB: www.shadetechniques.com
SIC: 3083 Window sheeting, plastic

(G-2590)
WESTROCK RKT COMPANY
800 S Romy St Ste A (47338-8822)
PHONE...............................765 396-3317
Fax: 765 396-9243
Timothy Hagdnduch, *General Mgr*
Dave Hargis, *Purch Agent*
Rick Davis, *Manager*
EMP: 67
SALES (corp-wide): 14.8B **Publicly Held**
WEB: www.rocktenn.com
SIC: 2631 Chip board
HQ: Westrock Rkt Company
1000 Abernathy Rd Ste 125
Atlanta GA 30328
770 448-2193

Economy
Wayne County

(G-2591)
H & H DESIGN & TOOL INC
222 2nd St (47339-9748)
P.O. Box 157 (47339-0157)
PHONE...............................765 886-6199
Fax: 765 886-5259
Jeff Himelick, *President*
Randy Crowe, *General Mgr*
Gene Himelick, *Vice Pres*
Leora Himelick, *Treasurer*
EMP: 8
SQ FT: 3,000

SALES (est): 1.1MM **Privately Held**
SIC: 3599 3535 3544 7692 Machine shop, jobbing & repair; conveyors & conveying equipment; special dies & tools; welding repair

(G-2592)
K-M MACHINE & MFG
12691 Indian Trail Rd (47339-9727)
PHONE...............................765 886-5717
EMP: 2 EST: 2007
SALES (est): 85K **Privately Held**
SIC: 3999 Mfg Misc Products

Edinburgh
Johnson County

(G-2593)
3D ENGINEERING INC
9064 S 600 W (46124-9638)
PHONE...............................317 729-5430
Fax: 317 729-5955
Carlian Niebel, *CEO*
Glen Niebel, *President*
EMP: 3
SALES (est): 371.2K **Privately Held**
SIC: 3714 5013 5531 Motor vehicle engines & parts; automotive engines & engine parts; automobile & truck equipment & parts

(G-2594)
AMERICAN TOURISTER
11891 N Executive Dr (46124-9128)
PHONE...............................812 526-0344
EMP: 2 EST: 2010
SALES (est): 89.5K **Privately Held**
SIC: 3161 Luggage

(G-2595)
AMOS-HILL ASSOCIATES INC
112 Shelby Ave (46124-1042)
P.O. Box 7 (46124-0007)
PHONE...............................812 526-2671
Fax: 812 526-5865
Susanne Renner, *CEO*
William A Costoplos, *President*
Michael Bell, *Controller*
◆ EMP: 150 EST: 1982
SALES (est): 28.5MM **Privately Held**
WEB: www.amoshill.com
SIC: 2435 Veneer stock, hardwood
PA: Koppensteiner Furniere Gmbh & Co. Kg
Unterer Muhlweg 39
Wannweil

(G-2596)
BEACON INDUSTRIES INC (PA)
912 S Walnut St (46124-2001)
P.O. Box 355 (46124-0355)
PHONE...............................812 526-0100
Larry C Sparks, *President*
Michael Senteney, *Treasurer*
Shelley Senteney, *Office Mgr*
Christopher Senteney, *Admin Sec*
EMP: 45
SQ FT: 51,000
SALES (est): 6.6MM **Privately Held**
SIC: 3479 Painting, coating & hot dipping

(G-2597)
BO-WITT PRODUCTS INC
500 N Walnut St (46124-1099)
PHONE...............................812 526-5561
Fax: 812 526-5564
Jon Jacobson, *President*
Jesse Tharp, *President*
Geneva Wilhite, *Manager*
EMP: 35 EST: 1960
SQ FT: 15,000
SALES (est): 7.1MM **Privately Held**
WEB: www.bowitt.com
SIC: 3644 Insulators & insulation materials, electrical

(G-2598)
CENTER LINE MOLD & TOOL INC
703 S Eisenhower Dr (46124-1809)
PHONE...............................812 526-0970
Fax: 812 526-0980
Scott Bringle, *President*

EMP: 15
SQ FT: 13,000
SALES: 1MM **Privately Held**
WEB: www.centerlinemold.com
SIC: 3544 Forms (molds), for foundry & plastics working machinery

(G-2599)
CHALLENGE PLASTIC PRODUCTS INC
110 W Industrial Dr (46124-1457)
PHONE...............................812 526-0582
Fax: 812 526-0590
William Davis, *President*
William R Davis, *Vice Pres*
▲ EMP: 11
SQ FT: 33,000
SALES: 1MM **Privately Held**
SIC: 3089 Injection molded finished plastic products; plastic boats & other marine equipment

(G-2600)
CL TECH INC
216 N Main St (46124-1027)
P.O. Box 277 (46124-0277)
PHONE...............................812 526-0995
Fred C Stadler, *President*
Roberta S Hehman, *Vice Pres*
Vaughan Hehman, *Treasurer*
EMP: 9
SQ FT: 4,000
SALES (est): 1.6MM **Privately Held**
SIC: 3544 3599 Special dies, tools, jigs & fixtures; jigs & fixtures; custom machinery; machine shop, jobbing & repair

(G-2601)
COMPANY PRIDE SHIRTS LLC
8136 W 1200 S (46124-9483)
PHONE...............................812 526-5700
EMP: 2 EST: 2010
SALES (est): 120K **Privately Held**
SIC: 2395 2759 Pleating/Stitching Services Commercial Printing

(G-2602)
COUNTRY COMPONENTS INC
8990 S Edinburgh Rd (46124-9451)
PHONE...............................812 345-9594
Amy Worland,
Heather Franscoviak,
Matthew Franscoviak,
EMP: 3
SALES (est): 208K **Privately Held**
SIC: 3599 Machine & other job shop work

(G-2603)
DANZER SERVICES INC (PA)
206 S Holland St (46124-1431)
P.O. Box 8 (46124-0008)
PHONE...............................812 526-2601
Hans-Joachim Danzer, *CEO*
Dan Sullivan, *President*
Terry Simmonds, *Vice Pres*
Markus Pfister, *CFO*
Mike Bell, *Treasurer*
▲ EMP: 2 EST: 1993
SALES (est): 58MM **Privately Held**
SIC: 2435 Hardwood veneer & plywood

(G-2604)
DANZER VENEER AMERICAS INC
206 S Holland St (46124-1431)
PHONE...............................812 526-6789
Fax: 812 526-6272
Greg Lottes, *President*
Vernon Grider, *Buyer*
EMP: 12
SALES (corp-wide): 297.2MM **Privately Held**
WEB: www.danzerspecialtyveneer.com
SIC: 2435 Hardwood veneer & plywood
HQ: Danzer Veneer Americas, Inc.
119 A I D Dr
Darlington PA 16115

(G-2605)
DAVID R WEBB COMPANY INC (HQ)
206 S Holland St (46124-1431)
P.O. Box 8 (46124-0008)
PHONE...............................812 526-2601
Fax: 812 526-8648

Greg Lottes, *CEO*
Michael Danzer, *Vice Pres*
Mike Maiers, *Vice Pres*
Mike Caffrey, *Treasurer*
Nancy Gardner, *Controller*
◆ EMP: 365
SALES (est): 51.9MM
SALES (corp-wide): 58MM **Privately Held**
WEB: www.davidrwebb.com
SIC: 2435 Hardwood veneer & plywood
PA: Danzer Services, Inc.
206 S Holland St
Edinburgh IN 46124
812 526-2601

(G-2606)
DAVIS MACHINE & TOOL INC
920 S Walnut St (46124-2001)
P.O. Box 157 (46124-0157)
PHONE...............................812 526-2674
Fax: 812 526-0210
Elby McGaha, *President*
EMP: 10 EST: 1982
SQ FT: 15,000
SALES (est): 680K **Privately Held**
SIC: 3544 3542 Industrial molds; machine tools, metal forming type

(G-2607)
DITECH INC
1151 S Walnut St (46124-9037)
P.O. Box 125 (46124-0125)
PHONE...............................812 526-0850
Fax: 812 526-0852
Nathan J Dillingham, *President*
Kimberly Bieker, *Vice Pres*
Christopher A Dillingham, *Vice Pres*
Timothy L Dillingham, *Vice Pres*
Wilma Dillingham, *Vice Pres*
EMP: 75
SQ FT: 50,000
SALES (est): 11.7MM **Privately Held**
SIC: 7389 3444 8742 Packaging & labeling services; sheet metalwork; manufacturing management consultant

(G-2608)
DRUG PLASTICS CLOSURES INC
2875 W 800 N (46124-9572)
PHONE...............................812 526-0555
Dennis Kelley, *Branch Mgr*
Rebecca Simpson, *Executive*
Tim Beeker, *Maintence Staff*
EMP: 55
SALES (corp-wide): 166.9MM **Privately Held**
SIC: 3089 3466 Caps, plastic; crowns & closures
HQ: Drug Plastics Closures, Inc.
850 Montgomery Ave
Boyertown PA 19512
610 367-5000

(G-2609)
DYNO ONE INC
14671 N 250 W (46124-9064)
PHONE...............................812 526-0500
Fax: 812 526-7465
Bill J Willis, *President*
Josh Willis, *Engineer*
Sandra K Willis, *Admin Sec*
EMP: 24
SQ FT: 76,000
SALES (est): 5.8MM **Privately Held**
WEB: www.dyno-one.com
SIC: 3829 Measuring & controlling devices

(G-2610)
ECA ENTERPRISES INC
906 S Walnut St (46124-2001)
P.O. Box 313 (46124-0313)
PHONE...............................812 526-6734
Fax: 812 526-6650
Allan S Miller, *President*
Diane Barringer, *Shareholder*
Gene Nollan, *Shareholder*
Richard A Miller, *Admin Sec*
▲ EMP: 40
SQ FT: 16,000
SALES: 2.8MM **Privately Held**
WEB: www.ecaenterprises.com
SIC: 3432 Plastic plumbing fixture fittings, assembly

GEOGRAPHIC

(G-2611)
EDINBURGH CONNECTOR COMPANY
Also Called: Connectronics
908 S Walnut St (46124-2001)
P.O. Box 246 (46124-0246)
PHONE..........................812 526-8801
Fax: 812 526-9333
Enrique Morales, CEO
Megan Morales, Vice Pres
John Barnes, Engineer
Ronald J Reese, Manager
EMP: 40
SQ FT: 20,000
SALES (est): 7.3MM Privately Held
WEB: www.connectronicsinc.com
SIC: 3678 Electronic connectors

(G-2612)
GEORG UTZ INC
14000 N 250 W (46124-9070)
PHONE..........................812 526-2240
Michael Chiado, General Mgr
Axel Ritzberger, Principal
Matt Huff, Design Engr
Bruno J Bucher, CFO
Chastity Branham, Finance Mgr
EMP: 25
SALES (est): 5.5MM
SALES (corp-wide): 255.8MM Privately Held
WEB: www.us.georgutz.com
SIC: 7389 5131 2542 4225 Authors' agents & brokers; textiles, woven; postal lock boxes, mail racks & related products; warehousing, self-storage; distribution channels consultant
HQ: Georg Utz Ag
   Augraben 4
   Bremgarten AG
   566 487-711

(G-2613)
HISADA AMERICA INC
1191 S Walnut St Ste 102 (46124-9053)
PHONE..........................812 526-0756
Fax: 812 526-0766
Akio Saito, President
Makoto Fukui, President
Toro Mituhara, Vice Pres
Hiro Tsutsui, Director
Marubeni Corp, Shareholder
▲ EMP: 90
SQ FT: 72,000
SALES (est): 22.1MM
SALES (corp-wide): 124.9MM Privately Held
SIC: 3714 Motor vehicle parts & accessories
PA: Hisada Co.,Ltd.
   11, Saburo, Satocho
   Anjo AIC 446-0
   566 979-281

(G-2614)
K & L MACHINING INC
6973 S Us Highway 31 (46124-1068)
PHONE..........................812 526-4840
Pete Knue, President
EMP: 4
SQ FT: 2,500
SALES (est): 448K Privately Held
SIC: 3599 Machine shop, jobbing & repair

(G-2615)
KRAMER FURN & CAB MAKERS INC
12600 N Presidential Way (46124-9069)
PHONE..........................812 526-2711
Fax: 812 526-2035
Thomas H Kramer, President
Michael Wilson, Office Mgr
EMP: 15
SQ FT: 25,000
SALES (est): 2.3MM Privately Held
SIC: 2522 2511 2434 Office bookcases, wallcases & partitions, except wood; cabinets, office: except wood; wood household furniture; wood kitchen cabinets

(G-2616)
LB MOLD INC
1031 S Main St (46124-1378)
PHONE..........................812 526-2030
Fax: 812 526-8286

John Bodine, President
EMP: 20
SQ FT: 15,000
SALES (est): 3.2MM Privately Held
SIC: 3544 Industrial molds

(G-2617)
MANAR INC (PA)
Also Called: Tennplasco
905 S Walnut St (46124-2002)
PHONE..........................812 526-2891
Fax: 812 526-9824
Eugene Nolen, CEO
Dan Barringer, General Mgr
Don Roberts, General Mgr
Larry Johnson, CFO
◆ EMP: 250
SQ FT: 50,000
SALES (est): 49.4MM Privately Held
WEB: www.manarinc.com
SIC: 3089 Molding primary plastic; injection molding of plastics

(G-2618)
MAXIMUM SPNDLE UTILIZATION INC
1141 S Walnut St (46124-9037)
P.O. Box 611, Columbus (47202-0611)
PHONE..........................812 526-8250
Fax: 812 526-8255
Richard E Witkemper, President
Robert Lewellen, VP Opers
Max Boas Director of Engineeri, Mfg Staff
▲ EMP: 42
SQ FT: 17,000
SALES (est): 6.6MM Privately Held
SIC: 3531 Construction machinery attachments

(G-2619)
P M I LLC
12595 N Executive Dr (46124-9067)
PHONE..........................812 374-3856
EMP: 2
SALES (est): 137.7K Privately Held
SIC: 1081 Metal mining services; exploration, metal mining

(G-2620)
PACKAGING CORPORATION AMERICA
Also Called: PCA
12599 N Presidential Way (46124-9039)
PHONE..........................812 526-5919
Robert Groob, Manager
EMP: 20
SALES (corp-wide): 6.4B Publicly Held
WEB: www.columbuscontainer.com
SIC: 2653 Boxes, corrugated: made from purchased materials
PA: Packaging Corporation Of America
   1955 W Field Ct
   Lake Forest IL 60045
   847 482-3000

(G-2621)
PENWAY INC
900 S Walnut St (46124-2001)
P.O. Box 185 (46124-0185)
PHONE..........................812 526-2645
Fax: 812 526-2646
Alan Ryshavy, President
Anu Ryshavy, Admin Sec
EMP: 30
SALES (est): 7.1MM Privately Held
WEB: www.penway.net
SIC: 3443 Tanks, standard or custom fabricated: metal plate

(G-2622)
QUICK TURN ANODIZING LLC
6973 S Us Highway 31 (46124-1068)
PHONE..........................877 716-1150
Jann Powell, President
Trace Powell, Vice Pres
EMP: 5
SQ FT: 11,000
SALES (est): 203.4K Privately Held
SIC: 3471 3479 Anodizing (plating) of metals or formed products; rust proofing (hot dipping) of metals & formed products

(G-2623)
R & R TECHNOLOGIES LLC (PA)
7560 E County Line Rd (46124-1100)
PHONE..........................812 526-2655

Dave Hemmerling, General Mgr
Dennis Cox, Controller
Howard Campbell,
EMP: 30
SQ FT: 55,000
SALES: 6.3MM Privately Held
WEB: www.rrtech.com
SIC: 3089 Injection molding of plastics; plastic processing

(G-2624)
RAPID PROTOTYPING & ENGRG
3340 W Presidential Way (46124-9048)
PHONE..........................812 526-9207
David Flick, President
EMP: 8
SALES: 900K Privately Held
SIC: 3599 Machine shop, jobbing & repair

(G-2625)
RJ FUEL SERVICES INC
6815 W State Road 252 (46124-9461)
P.O. Box 308, Columbus (47202-0308)
PHONE..........................812 350-2897
Rita Gearhart, President
EMP: 2
SALES: 500K Privately Held
SIC: 3586 Oil pumps, measuring or dispensing

(G-2626)
SACOMA INTERNATIONAL LLC
955 S Walnut St (46124-2002)
PHONE..........................812 526-5600
Fax: 812 526-3200
Tom Thornburg, Vice Pres
Clint Coffey, Controller
Tom Hill, Accounts Mgr
Mark Chodan, Program Mgr
Carl Busart, Info Tech Mgr
EMP: 80
SQ FT: 60,000
SALES: 28MM Privately Held
WEB: www.sacoma.com
SIC: 3465 Automotive stampings

(G-2627)
SAPP INC
Also Called: Sapp USA
600 S Kyle St (46124-1606)
PHONE..........................317 512-8353
Diego Mancini, President
Claudio Apollonia, Admin Sec
▲ EMP: 16 EST: 2013
SQ FT: 75,000
SALES: 1MM Privately Held
SIC: 3542 3545 Die casting machines; milling machine attachments (machine tool accessories)

(G-2628)
SHELBY GRAVEL INC
7520 E 650 S (46124-8904)
PHONE..........................812 526-2731
Fax: 812 526-5257
Gregg Hebbe, Branch Mgr
EMP: 10
SALES (corp-wide): 55.5MM Privately Held
SIC: 5032 1442 Concrete mixtures; gravel; gravel mining
PA: Shelby Gravel, Inc
   157 E Rampart St
   Shelbyville IN 46176
   317 398-4485

(G-2629)
SONOCO PRODUCTS COMPANY
6502 S Us Highway 31 (46124-1070)
P.O. Box 188 (46124-0188)
PHONE..........................812 526-5511
Fax: 812 526-0587
Vince Dimino, Branch Mgr
EMP: 200
SALES (corp-wide): 5B Publicly Held
WEB: www.sonoco.com
SIC: 2631 3083 3081 2851 Paperboard mills; laminated plastics plate & sheet; unsupported plastics film & sheet; paints & allied products; commercial printing; packaging paper & plastics film, coated & laminated
PA: Sonoco Products Company
   1 N 2nd St
   Hartsville SC 29550
   843 383-7000

(G-2630)
TSB LLC
12550 N Presidential Way (46124-9039)
PHONE..........................812 314-8331
Mike Ribel, Mng Member
Yoshitaka Psune, Director
EMP: 6
SQ FT: 3,000
SALES: 1MM Privately Held
SIC: 3425 Saw blades & handsaws

(G-2631)
TSUNE AMERICA LLC
12550 N Presidential Way (46124-9039)
PHONE..........................812 378-9875
Mike Riebo, Mng Member
▲ EMP: 17
SQ FT: 3,500
SALES: 11MM Privately Held
WEB: www.rohbiamerica.com
SIC: 3545 5084 Machine tool accessories; industrial machinery & equipment

(G-2632)
YANKEE CANDLE COMPANY INC
11740 Ne Executive Dr (46124-9180)
PHONE..........................812 526-5195
Sharon Canada, Branch Mgr
EMP: 9
SALES (corp-wide): 14.7B Publicly Held
SIC: 5999 5199 3999 Candle shops; candles; barber & beauty shop equipment
HQ: The Yankee Candle Company Inc
   16 Yankee Candle Way
   South Deerfield MA 01373
   413 665-8306

Elberfeld
Warrick County

(G-2633)
DAYLIGHT ENGINEERING INC (PA)
11022 Elberfeld Rd (47613-9449)
PHONE..........................812 983-2518
Thomas E Sawyer, President
Joanne Sawyer, Treasurer
EMP: 3 EST: 1969
SQ FT: 12,200
SALES (est): 1.7MM Privately Held
WEB: www.daylightengineering.com
SIC: 5085 3533 1321 8711 Abrasives; gas field machinery & equipment; natural gas liquids production; engineering services

(G-2634)
EURONIQUE INC
7633 Saint Johns Rd (47613-9167)
P.O. Box 128 (47613-0128)
PHONE..........................812 983-3337
Fax: 812 983-3528
Scott R Hasenour, President
David J Hasenour, Vice Pres
Scott Baehl, Project Mgr
Scott Hasenour, Executive
EMP: 30
SQ FT: 36,000
SALES (est): 6MM Privately Held
WEB: www.euronique.us
SIC: 2541 Cabinets, lockers & shelving; table or counter tops, plastic laminated

(G-2635)
FIBERTECH INC
11744 Blue Bell Rd (47613-9455)
PHONE..........................812 983-2642
William J Scott, President
Angela Felty, Manager
▼ EMP: 60
SALES (est): 1.9MM Privately Held
WEB: www.fibertechinc.net
SIC: 3089 Plastic containers, except foam

(G-2636)
JAMES G HENAGER
8837 S State Road 57 (47613-8445)
PHONE..........................812 795-2230
James G Henager, Owner
EMP: 3

▲ = Import ▼ =Export
◆ =Import/Export

SALES: 75K **Privately Held**
WEB: www.henager.com
SIC: **2431** 2434 2439 Millwork; wood
kitchen cabinets; structural wood members

(G-2637)
NORTH AMERICAN LIGHTING INC
11833 Industrial Park Dr (47613-9038)
PHONE.................................812 983-2663
Makoto Sano, *Manager*
EMP: 625
SALES (corp-wide): 7.9B **Privately Held**
SIC: **3647** Vehicular lighting equipment
HQ: North American Lighting, Inc.
2275 S Main St
Paris IL 61944
217 465-6600

(G-2638)
STOLZ STRUCTURAL INC
7735 Saint Johns Rd (47613-9141)
P.O. Box 420 (47613-0420)
PHONE.................................812 983-4720
Fax: 812 983-3516
Linda Stolz, *President*
John Stolz, *Treasurer*
EMP: 7
SALES (est): 936.2K **Privately Held**
SIC: **3449** Bars, concrete reinforcing: fabricated steel

(G-2639)
SUPERIOR MFG INC
11333 Elberfeld Rd (47613-9452)
PHONE.................................812 983-9900
Fax: 812 983-4220
Lori A Bowman, *President*
Bradley S Lattner, *Admin Sec*
EMP: 12
SALES (est): 2.3MM **Privately Held**
WEB: www.superiortrl.com
SIC: **3715** Truck trailers

(G-2640)
SUPPRESS TEC LLC
7599 Saint Johns Rd (47613-9140)
PHONE.................................812 453-5813
Nicholas Stratman, *Principal*
EMP: 2
SALES (est): 84.2K **Privately Held**
SIC: **3484** Guns (firearms) or gun parts, 30 mm. & below

Elizabeth
Harrison County

(G-2641)
ARTYS LOGGING
7800 E Highway 11 Se (47117-9130)
PHONE.................................812 969-3124
Jeff Lillpop, *Principal*
EMP: 3
SALES (est): 265.8K **Privately Held**
SIC: **2411** Logging

(G-2642)
BEST VINEYARDS
8373 Morgans Ln Se (47117-7408)
PHONE.................................812 969-9463
Wilbert Best, *Owner*
EMP: 3 EST: 2007
SALES (est): 422K **Privately Held**
SIC: **2084** Wines

(G-2643)
BIRKAT ADONAI LLC
4605 N Highway 11 Se (47117-7837)
PHONE.................................219 221-9810
Ruth Ann Watson, *Mng Member*
EMP: 4 EST: 2010
SALES (est): 262.3K **Privately Held**
SIC: **2834** Dermatologicals

(G-2644)
GUY CARDBOARD
2860 N Highway 11 Se (47117-7747)
PHONE.................................812 989-4809
Jason Colligan, *Principal*
EMP: 3
SALES (est): 178.5K **Privately Held**
SIC: **2631** Cardboard

(G-2645)
PRINTING IN TIME INC
8213 Lotticks Cornr Rd Se (47117-7312)
PHONE.................................502 807-3545
Greg Hogle, *President*
EMP: 2
SALES (est): 86.1K **Privately Held**
SIC: **2752** Commercial printing, lithographic

(G-2646)
SIMPSON ALLOY SERVICES INC
7017 Highway 111 Se (47117-8447)
PHONE.................................812 969-2766
Dean Simpson, *President*
Kathy Simpson, *Vice Pres*
EMP: 8
SQ FT: 7,500
SALES (est): 1.6MM **Privately Held**
SIC: **3398** 3724 Metal heat treating; tempering of metal; aircraft engines & engine parts; cooling systems, aircraft engine

(G-2647)
SMALL TOWN PRINTERS LLC
6265 Sand Hill Rd Se (47117-8232)
PHONE.................................812 596-1536
Kristy Hess, *Principal*
EMP: 2
SALES (est): 83.9K **Privately Held**
SIC: **2752** Commercial printing, lithographic

(G-2648)
SMOKESTACK INDUSTRIES LLC
11090 Majestic Blvd Se (47117-8081)
PHONE.................................812 267-8646
EMP: 2 EST: 2010
SALES (est): 113.7K **Privately Held**
SIC: **3999** Manufacturing industries

(G-2649)
SPECIALTY WELDING & MACHINE
9280 Lotticks Cornr Rd Se (47117-7302)
PHONE.................................812 969-2139
Neil Pettit, *President*
Cathi Knear-Petitt, *Vice Pres*
EMP: 3
SQ FT: 2,400
SALES: 100K **Privately Held**
SIC: **7692** 3523 Welding repair; farm machinery & equipment

(G-2650)
WOOD LIGHTER CASES LLC
7705 Pine Hill Dr Se (47117-9139)
PHONE.................................812 969-3908
Jeff Ankrum, *Principal*
EMP: 2 EST: 2014
SALES (est): 138.3K **Privately Held**
SIC: **3523** Farm machinery & equipment

Elizabethtown
Bartholomew County

(G-2651)
SMITHLAND BUTCHERING CO INC
11420 S Us Highway 31 (47232-9578)
PHONE.................................317 729-5398
James Mc Curdy, *President*
Peggy Mc Curdy, *Treasurer*
EMP: 6
SQ FT: 2,400
SALES: 75K **Privately Held**
SIC: **2011** 5147 Meat packing plants; meats, fresh

(G-2652)
WILSON MACHINE SHOP INC
7780 W County Road 800 N (47232-9425)
PHONE.................................812 392-2774
Jeffrey Wilson, *President*
Brenda Reecer, *Corp Secy*
Joseph Wilson, *Vice Pres*
EMP: 4
SQ FT: 7,600
SALES: 250K **Privately Held**
SIC: **3599** 7692 Machine shop, jobbing & repair; welding repair

---

Elkhart
Elkhart County

(G-2653)
(EBS COMPOSITES) ENGINEERED BO
Also Called: Ebsc
3506 Henke St (46514-7653)
PHONE.................................574 266-3471
Ben Pearson, *President*
Jen Snell, *Human Resources*
Dale Dewitt, *Admin Sec*
EMP: 12
SQ FT: 28,000
SALES (est): 2.6MM **Privately Held**
SIC: **3448** 2452 Buildings, portable: prefabricated metal; prefabricated wood buildings

(G-2654)
3W ENTERPRISES LLC
2727 Industrial Pkwy (46516-5402)
PHONE.................................847 366-6555
Dane G Willman,
EMP: 6
SALES (est): 200K **Privately Held**
WEB: www.3wenterprises.com
SIC: **2299** 5084 3561 Burlap, jute; water pumps (industrial); pumps, domestic: water or sump

(G-2655)
A & E SCREEN PRINTING
24266 County Road 45 (46516-6060)
P.O. Box 2644 (46515-2644)
PHONE.................................574 875-4488
EMP: 2 EST: 2008
SALES (est): 100K **Privately Held**
SIC: **2759** Commercial Printing

(G-2656)
A & M SYSTEMS INC
4121 Eastland Dr (46516-9031)
P.O. Box 89 (46515-0089)
PHONE.................................574 522-5000
Fax: 574 522-9099
Jim Miller, *President*
Karey Aenis, *Vice Pres*
▲ EMP: 15
SALES (est): 4MM **Privately Held**
WEB: www.anmsystems.com
SIC: **3542** Headers

(G-2657)
A E TECHRON INC
Also Called: Ae Techron
2507 Warren St (46516-5759)
PHONE.................................574 295-9495
Larry J Shank, *President*
Eric Weaver, *Purchasing*
Jadon Chupp, *Engineer*
Shawn Oltz, *Electrical Engi*
Sonia Shank, *Treasurer*
▲ EMP: 13
SQ FT: 15,000
SALES: 1.8MM **Privately Held**
WEB: www.aetechron.com
SIC: **3651** Household audio equipment

(G-2658)
A NEW COMPANY INC
Also Called: Anewco
4811 Eastland Dr (46516-9634)
P.O. Box 2262 (46515-2262)
PHONE.................................574 293-9088
Fax: 574 522-2855
Rick Hollar, *President*
Nona Hollar, *Admin Sec*
EMP: 17
SQ FT: 70,000
SALES (est): 1.7MM **Privately Held**
WEB: www.anewco.com
SIC: **3231** 2396 Ornamental glass: cut, engraved or otherwise decorated; automotive & apparel trimmings

(G-2659)
A S C INDUSTRIES INC
3604 County Road 6 E (46514-7664)
P.O. Box 1801 (46515-1801)
PHONE.................................574 264-1987
Fax: 574 266-6987
Greg Macri, *President*

Edward Ramsey, *Vice Pres*
▲ EMP: 25
SALES (est): 5.5MM **Privately Held**
WEB: www.ascind.com
SIC: **3498** 3444 Tube fabricating (contract bending & shaping); sheet metalwork

(G-2660)
A-1 WIRE TECH INC
2900 Higgins Blvd (46514-5449)
PHONE.................................815 226-0477
Kenneth D Buck, *President*
Dianna Pigott, *Principal*
▲ EMP: 75
SQ FT: 125,000
SALES (est): 14.7MM
SALES (corp-wide): 242.1B **Publicly Held**
WEB: www.a-1wire.com
SIC: **3315** Wire products, ferrous/iron: made in wiredrawing plants
HQ: Huntington Alloys Corporation
3200 Riverside Dr
Huntington WV 25705
304 526-5100

(G-2661)
AACOA INC (HQ)
2551 County Road 10 W (46514-8786)
PHONE.................................574 262-4685
Daniel Gformsma, *President*
John Jteeple, *Vice Pres*
Tom Elonich, *Production*
Wayne Kampa, *Production*
Scott Markovich, *QC Mgr*
EMP: 145 EST: 1972
SQ FT: 255,000
SALES (est): 90.2MM **Privately Held**
WEB: www.aacoa.com
SIC: **3471** Anodizing (plating) of metals or formed products; electroplating & plating

(G-2662)
ABI PLASTICS LLC
2510 Middlebury St (46516-5512)
PHONE.................................574 294-1700
Fax: 574 294-1313
Glen Unzicker, *Mng Member*
EMP: 2
SALES (est): 345.9K **Privately Held**
SIC: **3089** Injection molding of plastics

(G-2663)
ACADEMY INC
21291 Buckingham Rd (46516-9703)
PHONE.................................574 293-7113
Fax: 574 293-7113
Richard Eysol, *President*
Carolyn Eysol, *Corp Secy*
EMP: 8
SQ FT: 6,000
SALES: 450K **Privately Held**
WEB: www.academy.net
SIC: **2434** 5211 1751 Wood kitchen cabinets; vanities, bathroom: wood; cabinets, kitchen; cabinet & finish carpentry

(G-2664)
ACCENT COMPLEX INC
Also Called: Accent Printing
1201 Richmond St (46516-4150)
PHONE.................................574 522-2368
Fax: 574 295-2221
Joseph J Lidy, *President*
EMP: 2
SQ FT: 43,000
SALES (est): 235.2K **Privately Held**
SIC: **6512** 2752 7389 2451 Commercial & industrial building operation; commercial printing, lithographic; telephone services; mobile homes

(G-2665)
ACCRA-PAC INC
Also Called: Kik-Indiana
1919 Superior St (46516-4707)
PHONE.................................574 295-0000
Jeffrey M Nodland, *CEO*
David Weaver, *CFO*
Aaron Allen, *Finance Mgr*
Patty Yoder, *Supervisor*
Ben Decker, *Network Analyst*
▲ EMP: 70 EST: 1967
SQ FT: 424,000

SALES (est): 12.9MM
SALES (corp-wide): 990.7K **Privately Held**
SIC: **3842** 3633 2834 Personal safety equipment; household laundry equipment; pharmaceutical preparations
PA: Kik Custom Products Inc
101 Macintosh Blvd
Concord ON L4K 4
905 660-0444

(G-2666)
ACCRA-PAC INC (PA)
Also Called: Kik Cusrtom Products
2730 Middlebury St (46516-5582)
P.O. Box 2988 (46515-2988)
PHONE..................................905 660-0444
Fax: 574 522-1468
Jeffrey M Nodland, *CEO*
Stratis Katsiris, *President*
William Smith, *President*
Kingsley Osayande, *Pastor*
Dave Klotter, *Vice Pres*
EMP: 70 EST: 1967
SQ FT: 170,000
SALES (est): 24.5MM **Privately Held**
WEB: www.apgincmd.com
SIC: **3842** 3633 2834 Surgical appliances & supplies; household laundry equipment; pharmaceutical preparations

(G-2667)
ACUTECH LLC
53905 County Road 9 Ste C (46514-5012)
P.O. Box 543, Granger (46530-0543)
PHONE..................................574 262-8228
Joe Bella, *Managing Dir*
Lorrie Branum,
EMP: 15
SQ FT: 7,000
SALES: 2.2MM **Privately Held**
WEB: www.acutech.com
SIC: **3555** Printing trades machinery

(G-2668)
ADAMS & WESTLAKE LTD
Also Called: Adlake
940 N Michigan St (46514-2216)
PHONE..................................574 264-1141
Fax: 574 264-1146
Randy Schneider, *President*
Dg Elmore, *Vice Pres*
Janet Weaver, *Vice Pres*
Jenell Sherman, *Human Res Mgr*
Eric Krall, *Accounts Mgr*
EMP: 35
SQ FT: 65,000
SALES (est): 6.4MM **Privately Held**
WEB: www.adlake.com
SIC: **3743** Train cars & equipment, freight or passenger; interurban cars & car equipment

(G-2669)
ADEC INDUSTRIES
2700 Industrial Pkwy (46516-5401)
PHONE..................................574 522-7729
Fax: 574 294-6018
EMP: 2
SALES (est): 120K **Privately Held**
SIC: **3999** Mfg Misc Products

(G-2670)
AFC INDUSTRIES INC
3604 County Road 6 E (46514-7664)
P.O. Box 1801 (46515-1801)
PHONE..................................574 264-1987
Greg Macri, *President*
EMP: 25
SALES (est): 2.3MM **Privately Held**
SIC: **3441** Fabricated structural metal

(G-2671)
AGDIA INC
52642 County Road 1 (46514-9526)
PHONE..................................574 264-2014
Chester L Sutula, *Ch of Bd*
Baziel Vrient, *President*
Joshua Kuipers, *Research*
Paul Russell, *Research*
Albert Vrient, *Director*
EMP: 55
SQ FT: 55,000

SALES (est): 11.7MM **Privately Held**
WEB: www.agdia.com
SIC: **2835** 8731 Microbiology & virology diagnostic products; agricultural research

(G-2672)
AIRJET INC
2101 Kinro Ct (46514-1697)
P.O. Box 1247 (46515-1247)
PHONE..................................574 264-0123
David Leiter, *President*
EMP: 100
SALES (est): 14.4MM
SALES (corp-wide): 22MM **Privately Held**
WEB: www.airjet.net
SIC: **3564** Ventilating fans: industrial or commercial
PA: Continental Industries Inc
100 W Windsor Ave
Elkhart IN 46514
574 262-4511

(G-2673)
AL-EX INC
3170 Windsor Ct (46514-5556)
PHONE..................................574 206-0100
Rick L Newman, *President*
EMP: 2
SALES (est): 550.5K **Privately Held**
SIC: **3544** Extrusion dies

(G-2674)
ALL AMERICAN GROUP INC (HQ)
Also Called: Viking Formed Products
2831 Dexter Dr (46514-8225)
P.O. Box 1205, Mechanicsburg PA (17055-1205)
PHONE..................................574 262-0123
Fax: 574 266-2559
Richard M Lavers, *President*
Martin L Miranda, *Vice Pres*
Colleen A Zuhl, *CFO*
W Todd Woelfer, *General Counsel*
◆ EMP: 45 EST: 1964
SQ FT: 138,680
SALES (est): 137MM **Privately Held**
WEB: www.coachmen.com
SIC: **3716** 3792 2452 3714 Motor homes; travel trailers & campers; camping trailers & chassis; truck campers (slide-in); modular homes, prefabricated, wood; motor vehicle parts & accessories; single-family housing construction

(G-2675)
ALL AMERICAN GROUP INC
Also Called: Coachmen Recreational Vehicle
1251 N Nappanee St (46514-1733)
PHONE..................................574 262-9889
Mel Williams, *Manager*
EMP: 11 **Privately Held**
SIC: **3716** Motor homes
HQ: All American Group, Inc.
2831 Dexter Dr
Elkhart IN 46514
574 262-0123

(G-2676)
ALL AMERICAN GROUP INC
All American Homes
2831 Dexter Dr (46514-8225)
PHONE..................................574 262-0123
Fax: 574 262-8823
John Trant, *President*
James P Skinner, *Principal*
EMP: 300 **Privately Held**
SIC: **2452** Modular homes, prefabricated, wood
HQ: All American Group, Inc.
2831 Dexter Dr
Elkhart IN 46514
574 262-0123

(G-2677)
ALL AMERICAN HOMES LLC (DH)
2831 Dexter Dr (46514-8225)
P.O. Box 1205, Mechanicsburg PA (17055-1205)
PHONE..................................574 266-3044
Steve Sheinkman, *Principal*
EMP: 20

SALES (est): 39.3MM **Privately Held**
WEB: www.allamericanhomes.com
SIC: **2452** Modular homes, prefabricated, wood
HQ: All American Group, Inc.
2831 Dexter Dr
Elkhart IN 46514
574 262-0123

(G-2678)
ALPHA SYSTEMS LLC
5120 Beck Dr (46516-9512)
PHONE..................................574 295-5206
Brett Griffith, *President*
Greg Donovan, *Business Mgr*
Brad Martin, *Purch Agent*
Troy Huff, *Electrical Engi*
Lj Lawton, *Sales Staff*
EMP: 14
SALES (est): 3.9MM **Privately Held**
SIC: **1761** 2891 2879 Roofing contractor; adhesives; exterminating products, for household or industrial use

(G-2679)
ALTEC ENGINEERING INC (PA)
2401 W Mishawaka Rd (46517-4041)
PHONE..................................574 293-1965
Fax: 574 294-4073
Gary Robinson, *President*
Dennis J Jordan, *Corp Secy*
Joane Robinson, *Exec VP*
EMP: 50
SALES (est): 11.7MM **Privately Held**
WEB: www.altecengineering.com
SIC: **3089** 3088 2221 Molding primary plastic; plastics plumbing fixtures; fiberglass fabrics

(G-2680)
ALUMINUM EXTRUSIONS
3170 Windsor Ct (46514-5556)
PHONE..................................574 206-0100
Rick L Newman, *Principal*
EMP: 3
SALES (est): 224.4K **Privately Held**
SIC: **3354** Aluminum extruded products

(G-2681)
AMC ACQUISITION CORPORATION
Also Called: American Millwork
4840 Beck Dr (46516-9569)
PHONE..................................215 572-0738
Fax: 574 293-5378
Tom Harper, *President*
Tom Stewart, *Business Mgr*
Richard A Horwitz, *Vice Pres*
Larry Piekarz, *Prdtn Mgr*
Scott T Swick, *CFO*
EMP: 100
SQ FT: 170,000
SALES (est): 13.3MM
SALES (corp-wide): 353.3MM **Privately Held**
WEB: www.americanmillwork.com
SIC: **2431** Millwork; moldings & baseboards, ornamental & trim; moldings, wood: unfinished & prefinished; doors & door parts & trim, wood
PA: R.A.F. Industries, Inc.
165 Township Line Rd # 2100
Jenkintown PA 19046
215 572-0738

(G-2682)
AMERICAN ELCTRNIC CMPNENTS INC
Also Called: Durakool
1101 Lafayette St (46516-2615)
PHONE..................................574 295-6330
Fax: 574 293-8013
Tom Henry, *CEO*
Sandy Johnson, *Representative*
▲ EMP: 20
SQ FT: 46,000
SALES (est): 6.7MM **Privately Held**
WEB: www.aecsensors.com
SIC: **3625** Relays, for electronic use; switches, electronic applications

(G-2683)
AMERICAN ELKHART LLC
2304 Charlotte Ave (46517-1196)
PHONE..................................574 293-0333
EMP: 8

SALES (est): 435.4K **Privately Held**
SIC: **2295** Sealing or insulating tape for pipe: coated fiberglass

(G-2684)
AMERICAN LIMB & ORTHOPEDIC CO
58382 State Road 19 # 122 (46517-9291)
PHONE..................................574 522-3643
Norbert Fliess, *President*
EMP: 2
SALES (corp-wide): 1.7MM **Privately Held**
SIC: **3842** 5999 Limbs, artificial; orthopedic & prosthesis applications
PA: American Limb & Orthopedic Co.
2930 Mckinley Ave Ste A
South Bend IN 46615
574 287-3767

(G-2685)
AMERICAN STEEL RULE DIE INC
3401 Reedy Dr (46514-9413)
PHONE..................................574 262-3437
Fax: 574 262-3227
David Catanzarite, *President*
EMP: 8
SQ FT: 5,000
SALES: 650K **Privately Held**
WEB: www.americansteelruledie.com
SIC: **3544** 2675 Dies, steel rule; die-cut paper & board

(G-2686)
AMERICAN STONECAST PDTS INC
4315 Wyland Dr (46516-9501)
P.O. Box 2434 (46515-2434)
PHONE..................................574 206-0097
Fax: 574 206-0098
Kirk Veer, *President*
▼ EMP: 12
SQ FT: 20,000
SALES: 910K **Privately Held**
SIC: **2541** Counter & sink tops

(G-2687)
AMERICAN WAY MARKETING INC
400 Pine Creek Ct (46516-9089)
P.O. Box 1681 (46515-1681)
PHONE..................................574 295-7466
Fax: 574 293-9888
John C Musselman, *President*
▲ EMP: 17
SQ FT: 8,200
SALES (est): 5.2MM **Privately Held**
WEB: www.americanwaymktg.com
SIC: **5099** 3991 Musical instruments parts & accessories; brushes, except paint & varnish

(G-2688)
AMERICANA DEVELOPMENT INC
Also Called: Dexstar Wheel
400 Collins Rd (46516-5437)
PHONE..................................574 295-3535
Angelia Evans, *Purchasing*
Mark Foote, *Purchasing*
Larry Denton, *Mktg Dir*
Joe McGee, *Manager*
Dee Smith, *Manager*
EMP: 60 **Privately Held**
SIC: **3714** Wheel rims, motor vehicle
PA: Americana Development, Inc.
7095 Americana Pkwy
Reynoldsburg OH 43068

(G-2689)
AMS OF INDIANA INC (PA)
3933 E Jackson Blvd (46516-5228)
PHONE..................................574 293-5526
Fax: 574 294-1366
Rex Simpson, *President*
Loraine Simpson, *Admin Sec*
EMP: 40
SQ FT: 40,000
SALES (est): 16MM **Privately Held**
SIC: **5031** 5075 3444 Molding, all materials; warm air heating equipment & supplies; electrical heating equipment; sheet metalwork

▲ = Import ▼=Export
◆ =Import/Export

(G-2690)
AMSAFE PARTNERS INC
Also Called: Am-Safe Commercial Products
3802 Gallatin Way (46514-7650)
PHONE..................................574 266-8330
Jeff Fields, *Manager*
John Hall, *Director*
EMP: 40
SALES (corp-wide): 96.6MM **Privately Held**
WEB: www.amsafe.com
SIC: 3714 Motor vehicle parts & accessories
PA: Amsafe Partners, Inc.
1043 N 47th Ave
Phoenix AZ 85043
602 850-2850

(G-2691)
ANABAPTIST MENNONITE BIBLICAL
Also Called: Institute of Mennonite Studies
3003 Benham Ave (46517-1947)
PHONE..................................574 295-3726
Sara Wenger Shenk, *President*
Ron Ringenberg, *Vice Pres*
Jeffrey Marshall, *Maintenance Dir*
Melissa Troyer, *Mktg Dir*
Barbara Gingerich, *Manager*
EMP: 53
SQ FT: 18,000
SALES (est): 4.8MM **Privately Held**
WEB: www.ambs.edu
SIC: 8221 7372 Theological seminary; application computer software

(G-2692)
ANDERSON PRODUCTS INCORPORATED
Also Called: Anco Products
2500 17th St (46517-1412)
PHONE..................................574 293-5574
Lee R Anderson Sr, *Ch of Bd*
Gregory Keup, *Treasurer*
William Beadie, *Admin Sec*
▲ EMP: 75
SQ FT: 154,000
SALES: 7.9MM
SALES (corp-wide): 3B **Privately Held**
WEB: www.ancoproductsinc.com
SIC: 3296 3089 Fiberglass insulation; ducting, plastic
PA: Api Group Inc.
1100 Old Highway 8 Nw
Saint Paul MN 55112
651 636-4320

(G-2693)
ANDERSON SILVER PLATING CO
541 Industrial Pkwy (46516-5482)
P.O. Box 961 (46515-0961)
PHONE..................................574 294-6447
Fax: 574 295-8884
Michael Anderson, *President*
EMP: 15 EST: 1948
SQ FT: 30,000
SALES: 1.1MM **Privately Held**
WEB: www.andersonsilverplating.com
SIC: 3471 Electroplating of metals or formed products; plating of metals or formed products; gold plating

(G-2694)
APPAREL PROMOTIONS INC
21269 Buckingham Rd (46516-9703)
PHONE..................................574 294-7165
Fax: 574 522-5366
Kent Sager, *President*
Sue Sager, *Corp Secy*
EMP: 5 EST: 1986
SQ FT: 5,000
SALES (est): 430K **Privately Held**
SIC: 2395 2262 2295 5199 Embroidery & art needlework; screen printing: manmade fiber & silk broadwoven fabrics; coated fabrics, not rubberized; advertising specialties

(G-2695)
ARMOR CONTRACT MFG INC
300 Comet Ave (46514-5529)
PHONE..................................574 327-2962
John Cullip, *President*
EMP: 14

SALES (est): 374.8K **Privately Held**
SIC: 3999 Manufacturing industries

(G-2696)
ASHLEY F WARD INC
Also Called: Ashley Ward
56883 Elk Ct (46516-1457)
PHONE..................................574 294-1502
Fax: 574 522-1530
Richard Dudley, *Principal*
EMP: 35
SQ FT: 50,000
SALES (corp-wide): 46.5MM **Privately Held**
WEB: www.ashleyward.com
SIC: 3451 3494 3432 Screw machine products; valves & pipe fittings; plumbing fixture fittings & trim
PA: Ashley F. Ward, Inc.
7490 Easy St
Mason OH 45040
513 398-1414

(G-2697)
ASSA ABLOY DOOR GROUP LLC
Also Called: Dominion Building Products
2300 Johnson St (46514-5577)
PHONE..................................800 826-2617
Fax: 574 264-9682
Rick Weiss, *Manager*
EMP: 15
SALES (corp-wide): 9B **Privately Held**
WEB: www.dominionproducts.com
SIC: 3499 3442 Doors, safe & vault: metal; metal doors, sash & trim
HQ: Assa Abloy Door Group, Llc
9159 Telecom Dr
Milan TN 38358
731 686-8345

(G-2698)
ASSEMBLY MASTERS INC
56624 Elk Park Dr (46516-1400)
PHONE..................................574 293-9026
Debra Hanigosky, *President*
Larry J Gennicks, *Vice Pres*
EMP: 15
SQ FT: 10,000
SALES (est): 2.3MM **Privately Held**
WEB: www.wire-harnesses.net
SIC: 3679 Harness assemblies for electronic use: wire or cable

(G-2699)
ASSISTIVE TECHNOLOGY INC
Also Called: Custom Durable Products
21279 Protecta Dr (46516-9539)
PHONE..................................574 522-7201
Fax: 574 293-0202
EMP: 8
SALES (est): 630K **Privately Held**
SIC: 3842 Mfg Durable Medical Equipment

(G-2700)
ATLAS DIE LLC
Also Called: Atlas Chem-Milling
1627 W Lusher Ave (46517-1421)
PHONE..................................574 295-0277
Fax: 574 293-2359
Shawn Bragg, *Branch Mgr*
EMP: 56
SALES (corp-wide): 50MM **Privately Held**
SIC: 3423 3599 3544 Cutting dies, except metal cutting; machine shop; jobbing & repair; industrial molds
HQ: Atlas Die, Llc
2000 Middlebury St
Elkhart IN 46516
574 295-0050

(G-2701)
ATLAS DIE INC
2000 Middlebury St (46516-5521)
PHONE..................................574 295-0050
Fax: 574 294-2793
Doug Boland, *Manager*
EMP: 24
SALES (est): 1.2MM **Privately Held**
SIC: 3544 Dies, steel rule

(G-2702)
ATWOOD MOBILE PRODUCTS LLC
1120 N Main St (46514-3203)
PHONE..................................574 266-4848
EMP: 91
SALES (corp-wide): 1.6B **Privately Held**
SIC: 3714 Motor vehicle parts & accessories
HQ: Atwood Mobile Products Llc
1120 N Main St
Elkhart IN 46514

(G-2703)
ATWOOD MOBILE PRODUCTS LLC
2040 Toledo Rd (46516-5541)
PHONE..................................574 264-2131
Timothy Stephens, *President*
EMP: 92
SALES (corp-wide): 1.6B **Privately Held**
SIC: 3714 Motor vehicle parts & accessories
HQ: Atwood Mobile Products Llc
1120 N Main St
Elkhart IN 46514

(G-2704)
ATWOOD MOBILE PRODUCTS LLC (DH)
Also Called: Atwood Solutions
1120 N Main St (46514-3203)
P.O. Box 1627 (46515-1627)
PHONE..................................574 264-2131
Fax: 574 264-2136
Mark Nelson, *Mfg Mgr*
George Garrett, *Materials Mgr*
Scott Gregorash, *Maint Spvr*
Tim Brown, *Engineer*
Trey Miller, *Sales Staff*
▲ EMP: 100
SALES (est): 231.3MM
SALES (corp-wide): 1.6B **Privately Held**
SIC: 3714 Motor vehicle parts & accessories

(G-2705)
ATWOOD MOBILE PRODUCTS LLC
3308 Charlotte Ave (46517-1189)
PHONE..................................574 522-7891
Jeff Jones, *Branch Mgr*
EMP: 139
SALES (corp-wide): 1.6B **Privately Held**
SIC: 3714 Motor vehicle parts & accessories
HQ: Atwood Mobile Products Llc
1120 N Main St
Elkhart IN 46514

(G-2706)
ATWOOD MOBILE PRODUCTS LLC
2701 Ada Dr (46514-8646)
PHONE..................................574 264-2131
Rex Poehlman, *Sales Staff*
Robert Alley, *Branch Mgr*
EMP: 99
SALES (corp-wide): 1.6B **Privately Held**
SIC: 3714 Motor vehicle parts & accessories
HQ: Atwood Mobile Products Llc
1120 N Main St
Elkhart IN 46514

(G-2707)
AUSPRO MANUFACTURING CO INC
5320 Beck Dr (46516-9251)
PHONE..................................574 264-3705
Fax: 574 522-3261
Randy Heffner, *President*
EMP: 5 EST: 1953
SQ FT: 12,500
SALES: 337.3K **Privately Held**
WEB: www.auspro.net
SIC: 3451 Screw machine products

(G-2708)
AXIS UNLIMITED LLC
Also Called: Midwest Industrial Tanks
24615 County Road 45 # 2 (46516-5937)
P.O. Box 2897 (46515-2897)
PHONE..................................574 370-8923

Chelsi Bowers, *Principal*
EMP: 9 EST: 2015
SALES (est): 291K **Privately Held**
SIC: 3443 Tanks, lined: metal plate; tanks for tank trucks, metal plate

(G-2709)
AXLE INC
53664 County Road 9 (46514-5028)
P.O. Box 2153 (46515-2153)
PHONE..................................574 264-9434
Thomas R Williams, *President*
Karen E Crelling, *Vice Pres*
EMP: 4
SQ FT: 17,500
SALES (est): 677K **Privately Held**
WEB: www.axle.net
SIC: 3714 Motor vehicle parts & accessories

(G-2710)
B & B INDUSTRIES INC
1121 D I Dr (46514-8232)
PHONE..................................574 262-8551
Fax: 574 262-0624
Bill Bottoms, *President*
Judy Bottoms, *Vice Pres*
Glenn Duncan, *Admin Sec*
▲ EMP: 35
SQ FT: 28,000
SALES (est): 7.4MM **Privately Held**
WEB: www.billbottoms.com
SIC: 3711 Wreckers (tow truck), assembly of; bus & other large specialty vehicle assembly

(G-2711)
B&R MANUFACTURING INC
2503 Marina Dr (46514-8641)
PHONE..................................574 293-5669
Fax: 574 293-5669
Bob Loper, *Owner*
◆ EMP: 3
SALES (est): 203.3K **Privately Held**
SIC: 3999 Manufacturing industries

(G-2712)
B-D INDUSTRIES INC
1715 Fieldhouse Ave (46517-1410)
PHONE..................................574 295-1420
Robert K Denton, *President*
Michael Dills, *Vice Pres*
Carol A Denton, *Admin Sec*
EMP: 12
SQ FT: 13,000
SALES (est): 1MM **Privately Held**
SIC: 3479 3728 3471 Coating of metals & formed products; aircraft parts & equipment; anodizing (plating) of metals or formed products

(G-2713)
BANDIT SIGNS
23970 Byrd Ave (46516-6446)
PHONE..................................574 370-7067
Todd Wise, *Principal*
EMP: 3
SALES (est): 353.2K **Privately Held**
SIC: 3993 Signs, not made in custom sign painting shops

(G-2714)
BARGER PACKAGING INC
2901 Oakland Ave (46517-1508)
PHONE..................................888 525-2845
Mike Nielsen, *Principal*
Scott Felder, *Plant Mgr*
Robert Rehmel, *Design Engr*
Cory Carroll, *Maintence Staff*
EMP: 8 EST: 2015
SALES (est): 168.4K **Privately Held**
SIC: 3053 Packing materials

(G-2715)
BARGER PACKAGING CORPORATION (HQ)
2901 Oakland Ave (46517-1508)
PHONE..................................574 389-1860
Fax: 574 522-6549
Dan Mohs, *CEO*
Patrick J Baert, *CFO*
EMP: 100 EST: 1933
SQ FT: 102,000

SALES (est): 31.4MM
SALES (corp-wide): 48.8MM **Privately Held**
WEB: www.bargerpackaging.com
SIC: 2657 3086 2652 Folding paperboard boxes; packaging & shipping materials, foamed plastic; setup paperboard boxes
PA: Placon Corporation
6096 Mckee Rd
Fitchburg WI 53719
608 271-5634

(G-2716)
BAYER HEALTHCARE LLC
3400 Middlebury St (46516-5586)
PHONE...................................574 262-6136
Mike Kofeldt, *Manager*
EMP: 47
SALES (corp-wide): 41.2B **Privately Held**
SIC: 3841 Diagnostic apparatus, medical
HQ: Bayer Healthcare Llc
100 Bayer Blvd
Whippany NJ 07981
862 404-3000

(G-2717)
BAYER HEALTHCARE LLC
Diabetes Care
1025 N Michigan St (46514-2215)
PHONE...................................574 255-3327
Vince Lisi, *Branch Mgr*
EMP: 54
SALES (corp-wide): 41.2B **Privately Held**
SIC: 2834 Pharmaceutical preparations
HQ: Bayer Healthcare Llc
100 Bayer Blvd
Whippany NJ 07981
862 404-3000

(G-2718)
BBC DISTRIBUTION LLC
53320 Columbia Dr (46514-8153)
PHONE...................................574 266-3601
Bill Dalton, *Manager*
EMP: 7 EST: 2001
SALES (est): 1.6MM **Privately Held**
SIC: 3799 Recreational vehicles

(G-2719)
BEACHFRONT FURNITURE
60874 Ridgepoint Ct (46517-9100)
PHONE...................................574 875-0817
Brian Thompson, *Treasurer*
EMP: 12
SQ FT: 35,000
SALES (est): 1.2MM **Privately Held**
WEB: www.beachfrontfurniture.com
SIC: 2519 Garden furniture, except wood, metal, stone or concrete

(G-2720)
BEEBE CABINET CO INC
22695 State Road 120 (46516-5369)
PHONE...................................574 293-3580
Fax: 574 232-3956
Richard Hunger, *President*
Judith Hunger, *Vice Pres*
EMP: 12 EST: 1935
SQ FT: 10,000
SALES: 900K **Privately Held**
SIC: 2541 2521 2511 2434 Cabinets, except refrigerated: show, display, etc.: wood; wood office furniture; wood household furniture; wood kitchen cabinets

(G-2721)
BENDER WHOLESALE DISTRIBUTORS
2911 Moose Trl (46514-8230)
P.O. Box 1407 (46515-1407)
PHONE...................................574 264-4409
Fax: 574 262-8799
Paul Bender, *President*
Ann Marie Bender, *Vice Pres*
EMP: 10 EST: 1941
SQ FT: 20,000
SALES (est): 1.7MM **Privately Held**
SIC: 2851 5072 5198 Lacquers, varnishes, enamels & other coatings; paints & paint additives; rivets; paints, varnishes & supplies

(G-2722)
BEST FORMED PLASTICS LLC
21209 Protecta Dr (46516-9539)
PHONE...................................574 293-6128

Jane Stewart, *Corp Secy*
James V Stewart, *Mng Member*
EMP: 21
SQ FT: 3,000
SALES (est): 4.7MM **Privately Held**
SIC: 2821 Molding compounds, plastics

(G-2723)
BIG DOG ADHESIVES LLC
615 S 4th St (46516-2717)
PHONE...................................574 299-6768
EMP: 3
SALES (est): 123.2K **Privately Held**
SIC: 2891 Adhesives

(G-2724)
BIOLIFE PLASMA SERVICES LP
2715 Emerson Dr (46514-5645)
PHONE...................................574 264-7204
EMP: 9
SALES (corp-wide): 11.4B **Privately Held**
SIC: 2836 Plasmas
HQ: Biolife Plasma Services L.P.
1435 Lake Cook Rd
Philadelphia PA 19182
847 940-5559

(G-2725)
BKB PETROLEUM INC
22700 Old Us 20 (46516-9149)
PHONE...................................574 389-8159
Lakhwinder Kaur, *Principal*
EMP: 2
SALES (est): 94.3K **Privately Held**
SIC: 1381 Drilling oil & gas wells

(G-2726)
BLACK TIE MANUFACTURING INC
2749 Jami St (46514-8793)
PHONE...................................574 971-6034
William J McEnery, *CEO*
EMP: 7
SALES (est): 670.6K **Privately Held**
SIC: 3088 Tubs (bath, shower & laundry), plastic

(G-2727)
BLESSING TOOL & DIE INC
24366 County Road 45 (46516-6056)
PHONE...................................574 875-1982
James Blessing, *President*
Leah Blessing, *Vice Pres*
EMP: 2
SQ FT: 4,000
SALES (est): 91.5K **Privately Held**
SIC: 3544 Special dies & tools

(G-2728)
BOAT HOLDINGS LLC
Also Called: Bennington Pontoon Boats
2805 Decio Dr (46514-7666)
PHONE...................................574 264-6336
Jacob S Vogel, *CEO*
Steven H Vogel, *Partner*
Diana J Engle, *Vice Pres*
EMP: 3
SALES (est): 117.8K
SALES (corp-wide): 5.4B **Publicly Held**
SIC: 3732 Boat building & repairing
HQ: Polaris Sales Inc.
2100 Highway 55
Hamel MN 55340
763 542-0500

(G-2729)
BOCK INDUSTRIES INC
Also Called: Bull Moose Tube
29851 County Road 20 (46517-8993)
P.O. Box 1037 (46515-1037)
PHONE...................................574 295-8070
Fax: 574 293-6593
John J Meyer, *President*
Stephen H Birk, *Vice Pres*
◆ EMP: 96
SQ FT: 550,000
SALES (est): 23.6MM **Privately Held**
WEB: www.bullmoosetube.com
SIC: 3317 Tubes, wrought: welded or lock joint
HQ: Bull Moose Tube Company
1819 Clarkson Rd Ste 100
Chesterfield MO 63017
636 537-1249

(G-2730)
BODYCOTE THERMAL PROC INC
908 County Road 1 N (46514-8992)
PHONE...................................574 295-2491
Fax: 574 295-1572
Edward Minich, *General Mgr*
Tom Williams, *Branch Mgr*
EMP: 25
SQ FT: 2,700
SALES (corp-wide): 911.9MM **Privately Held**
WEB: www.specialtyheat.com
SIC: 3398 Metal heat treating
HQ: Bodycote Thermal Processing, Inc.
12700 Park Central Dr # 700
Dallas TX 75251
214 904-2420

(G-2731)
BOYD CORPORATION
53208 Columbia Dr (46514-8149)
PHONE...................................574 389-1878
Bill Kuehne, *President*
EMP: 15
SALES (corp-wide): 845.9MM **Privately Held**
SIC: 3069 Bags, rubber or rubberized fabric
HQ: Boyd Corporation
5960 Inglewood Dr Ste 115
Pleasanton CA 94588
209 236-1111

(G-2732)
BRASILIA PRESS INC
2911 Moose Trl (46514-8230)
P.O. Box 2023 (46515-2023)
PHONE...................................574 262-9700
Paul Bender, *President*
Ilaine Bender, *Corp Secy*
EMP: 6
SALES (est): 617.1K **Privately Held**
WEB: www.bendersweb.com
SIC: 5092 2741 Model kits; miscellaneous publishing

(G-2733)
BRIANZA USA CORP
3503 Cooper Dr (46514-8639)
PHONE...................................574 855-9520
Filippo Milani, *Principal*
▲ EMP: 7
SALES (est): 637.6K **Privately Held**
SIC: 3089 Air mattresses, plastic

(G-2734)
BRIDGEVIEW MANUFACTURING LLC
5321 Beck Dr (46516-9251)
PHONE...................................574 970-0116
Jim Brown,
David Hostetler,
EMP: 22
SQ FT: 30,000
SALES: 9MM **Privately Held**
SIC: 3799 Recreational vehicles

(G-2735)
BRIGHT IDEAS LLC
2322 Primrose Ave (46516-4959)
PHONE...................................574 295-5533
Trent Wagner, *Mng Member*
EMP: 3
SALES (est): 360K **Privately Held**
SIC: 2541 Wood partitions & fixtures

(G-2736)
BUDCO TOOL AND DIE
56935 Elk Ct (46516-1460)
PHONE...................................574 522-4004
James Allen, *Owner*
Simon Holly, *Accountant*
EMP: 4 EST: 2016
SALES (est): 184.5K **Privately Held**
SIC: 3544 Special dies & tools

(G-2737)
BULLSEYE TECHNOLOGIES INC
Also Called: Bullseye Leveling
2925 Stephen Pl (46514-7701)
P.O. Box 388, Logansport (46947-0388)
PHONE...................................574 753-0102
R Alan Brink, *President*
EMP: 3

SALES (est): 528.6K **Privately Held**
SIC: 3715 5561 1629 Truck trailers; travel trailers: automobile, new & used; land leveling

(G-2738)
BURKHART ADVERTISING INC
1600 W Beardsley Ave # 110 (46514-1800)
PHONE...................................574 522-4421
Brent Curtis, *Branch Mgr*
EMP: 2
SALES (corp-wide): 16.7MM **Privately Held**
WEB: www.burkhartadv.com
SIC: 3993 7312 Signs & advertising specialties; outdoor advertising services
PA: Burkhart Advertising Inc.
1735 Mishawaka Ave
South Bend IN 46615
574 233-2101

(G-2739)
BURSTON MARKETING INC
2802 Frederic Dr (46514-7638)
P.O. Box 1726 (46515-1726)
PHONE...................................574 262-4005
Fax: 574 262-4487
Thomas Stout, *President*
▲ EMP: 18
SQ FT: 20,000
SALES (est): 3.3MM **Privately Held**
WEB: www.burston.com
SIC: 2396 2395 7336 5199 Screen printing on fabric articles; embroidery & art needlework; graphic arts & related design; advertising specialties

(G-2740)
BY-PASS PAINT SHOP INC (PA)
1132 N Nappanee St (46514-1792)
PHONE...................................574 264-5334
Donato Del Prete, *President*
Florence Del Prete, *Vice Pres*
EMP: 15 EST: 1947
SQ FT: 40,000
SALES (est): 2.1MM **Privately Held**
SIC: 2431 Moldings, wood: unfinished & prefinished

(G-2741)
BYTE BLUE TECHNOLOGY SOLUTIONS
28571 County Road 16 (46516-1531)
PHONE...................................574 903-5637
Edward Collins, *Owner*
EMP: 6
SALES: 400K **Privately Held**
SIC: 5734 7374 7379 3661 Computer & software stores; computer graphics service; ; communication headgear, telephone; computer integrated systems design

(G-2742)
C & G WIRING INC
1824 Leer Dr (46514)
PHONE...................................574 333-3433
Fax: 574 206-8980
Mike Markley, *President*
Cornelis Bergh, *Vice Pres*
EMP: 15
SQ FT: 22,000
SALES (est): 2.7MM **Privately Held**
SIC: 3679 Harness assemblies for electronic use: wire or cable

(G-2743)
C & K MANUFACTURING INC
25943 Forrest Hl (46514-5002)
P.O. Box 3015 (46515-3015)
PHONE...................................574 264-4063
Stephan K Clements, *President*
EMP: 15 EST: 2004
SQ FT: 20,000
SALES (est): 2.2MM **Privately Held**
SIC: 3823 Computer interface equipment for industrial process control

(G-2744)
C M I ENTERPRISES INC
Also Called: C M I Automotive of Indiana
2904 Leer Ct (46514-5448)
PHONE...................................305 685-9651
Fax: 574 262-4782
Jorge Giraldo, *Principal*
EMP: 60

▲ = Import ▼=Export
◆ =Import/Export

SALES (corp-wide): 28.7MM **Privately Held**
WEB: www.cmi-enterprises.com
SIC: 5131 2295 7532 Knit fabrics; textiles, woven; coated fabrics, not rubberized; van conversion
PA: C. M. I. Enterprises, Inc.
13145 Nw 45th Ave
Opa Locka FL 33054
305 622-6410

(G-2745)
C&A WOODWORKING INC
24183 County Road 45 (46516-6024)
PHONE..................574 875-1273
Craig M Stutzman, *President*
Angela S Stutzman, *Admin Sec*
EMP: 3
SALES (est): 289K **Privately Held**
SIC: 2431 Millwork

(G-2746)
C-L BUILDING & LEASING INC
28468 County Road 26 (46517-9786)
PHONE..................574 293-8959
Stella Paff, *Principal*
EMP: 2
SALES (est): 405.1K **Privately Held**
SIC: 6552 3423 5162 Subdividers & developers; hand & edge tools; plastics materials & basic shapes

(G-2747)
CAMCO MANUFACTURING INC
2912 Leer Ct (46514-5448)
PHONE..................574 264-1491
Fax: 574 264-1573
Mike Sommer, *Manager*
EMP: 12
SALES (corp-wide): 162.8MM **Privately Held**
WEB: www.camco.net
SIC: 2899 3594 2842 5561 Antifreeze compounds; fluid power pumps & motors; specialty cleaning, polishes & sanitation goods; recreational vehicle parts & accessories
PA: Camco Manufacturing, Inc.
121 Landmark Dr
Greensboro NC 27409
336 668-7661

(G-2748)
CANA INC (PA)
Also Called: Cana Cabinetry
2712 Old Us 20 W (46514-1350)
PHONE..................574 266-6566
Fax: 574 262-0945
David Geiger, *President*
George Forman, *CFO*
EMP: 80
SQ FT: 94,000
SALES (est): 2MM **Privately Held**
SIC: 2431 Doors & door parts & trim, wood; moldings, wood: unfinished & pre-finished

(G-2749)
CARGO SYSTEMS INC
2603 Glenview Dr (46514-8709)
PHONE..................574 264-1600
Fax: 574 264-9200
John R Coble, *CEO*
Dallis Lindley, *President*
EMP: 5
SQ FT: 9,200
SALES (est): 683.6K **Privately Held**
SIC: 3493 Torsion bar springs

(G-2750)
CARPENTER CO
195 County Road 15 (46516-9785)
PHONE..................574 522-2800
Fax: 574 522-6340
Tommy Stinson, *Manager*
EMP: 400
SQ FT: 50,000
SALES (corp-wide): 2.1B **Privately Held**
WEB: www.carpenter.com
SIC: 3086 Insulation or cushioning material, foamed plastic
PA: Carpenter Co.
5016 Monument Ave
Richmond VA 23230
804 359-0800

(G-2751)
CAST PRODUCTS LP (DH)
Also Called: Colorimetric
3601 Charlotte Ave (46517-1192)
P.O. Box 1368 (46515-1368)
PHONE..................574 294-2684
Fax: 574 295-6921
Dennis Schwartz, *Partner*
Brent Jagla, *Partner*
Thomas Nagy, *Partner*
James Schwartz, *Partner*
Kevin Shrider, *Partner*
▲ **EMP:** 35
SQ FT: 200,000
SALES (est): 15.6MM
SALES (corp-wide): 1.6B **Publicly Held**
WEB: www.castproductscorp.com
SIC: 5074 5014 5084 5031 Plumbing fittings & supplies; tires & tubes; instruments & control equipment; lumber, plywood & millwork; building materials, exterior; adhesives & sealants; caulking compounds; adhesives; sealants; chemicals & allied products
HQ: Dehco, Inc.
3601 Charlotte Ave
Elkhart IN 46517
574 294-2684

(G-2752)
CC MANUFACTURING INC
Also Called: Elk Trailers
54424 Susquehanna Ct (46516-5304)
PHONE..................574 293-1696
Beverly Croxall, *President*
William Croxell, *Vice Pres*
EMP: 12
SQ FT: 40,000
SALES: 2.5MM **Privately Held**
SIC: 3799 Boat trailers

(G-2753)
CENTURY FOAM INC (PA)
2600 S Nappanee St (46517-1082)
P.O. Box 2207 (46515-2207)
PHONE..................574 293-5547
Thomas Teach, *President*
Sandra Teach, *Corp Secy*
Evelyne Leal, *Human Res Mgr*
Kim Bowman, *Sales Mgr*
Robert Leslie, *Director*
▲ **EMP:** 150 **EST:** 1981
SQ FT: 131,000
SALES (est): 27.8MM **Privately Held**
WEB: www.centuryfoam.com
SIC: 3086 Insulation or cushioning material, foamed plastic

(G-2754)
CHAMPION MANUFACTURING INC
2601 Industrial Pkwy (46516-5404)
PHONE..................574 295-6893
Doug Keeslar, *CEO*
Bob Jacobs, *Prdtn Mgr*
Joann Thomas, *Purchasing*
Matt Copeland, *QC Mgr*
Pat Cooper, *Design Engr*
◆ **EMP:** 75
SQ FT: 44,000
SALES (est): 18.6MM
SALES (corp-wide): 966.5MM **Publicly Held**
WEB: www.championchair.com
SIC: 2599 Beds, not household use; hospital beds; hospital furniture, except beds
PA: Invacare Corporation
1 Invacare Way
Elyria OH 44035
440 329-6000

(G-2755)
CHARIOT VANS INC
2998 Paul Dr (46514-8796)
PHONE..................574 264-7577
John Wisolek, *President*
Dennis Peterson, *Vice Pres*
David Durkin, *Treasurer*
EMP: 45 **EST:** 1983
SALES (est): 5.3MM **Privately Held**
SIC: 3716 Recreational van conversion (self-propelled), factory basis

(G-2756)
CHRISTIAN SOUND & SONG INC
56718 Coppergate Dr (46516-5678)
PHONE..................574 294-2893
Charles Cooper, *CEO*
Thomas Lefevre, *COO*
EMP: 3
SALES (est): 163.4K **Privately Held**
WEB: www.soundandsong.com
SIC: 2721 8661 8742 Magazines: publishing & printing; religious organizations; training & development consultant

(G-2757)
CHUBBS STEEL SALES INC
Also Called: Griffin Trailers
57832 County Road 3 (46517-9366)
P.O. Box 64, Osceola (46561-0064)
PHONE..................574 295-3166
Fax: 574 295-6614
Roy Lee Griffin, *President*
Gwen Mae Griffin, *Admin Sec*
EMP: 25
SQ FT: 40,000
SALES (est): 7.9MM **Privately Held**
SIC: 5013 3799 Trailer parts & accessories; trailers & trailer equipment

(G-2758)
CLEER VISION TEMPERED GL LLC
3401 County Road 6 E (46514-7662)
PHONE..................574 262-0449
Rick Collins, *President*
Tim Widner, *General Mgr*
Stephanie Horton, *Office Mgr*
▲ **EMP:** 20
SALES (est): 4.2MM **Privately Held**
SIC: 3211 Tempered glass

(G-2759)
CLEER VISION WINDOWS INC
3401 County Road 6 E (46514-7662)
PHONE..................574 262-0449
John Collins, *Ch of Bd*
Rick Collins, *President*
EMP: 11 **EST:** 1982
SQ FT: 180,000
SALES (est): 842.8K **Privately Held**
SIC: 3231 3442 Strengthened or reinforced glass; metal doors, sash & trim

(G-2760)
CLEER VISION WINDOWS INC
3401 County Road 6 E (46514-7662)
PHONE..................574 262-0449
John Collins, *Ch of Bd*
Rick Collins, *President*
Cynthia Doberenz, *Human Res Mgr*
Tony Chapman, *Sales Mgr*
Diane Sampers, *Sales Executive*
EMP: 15
SQ FT: 18,000
SALES (est): 4.8MM **Privately Held**
SIC: 3231 3442 Strengthened or reinforced glass; metal doors, sash & trim

(G-2761)
CLOVER SHEET METAL COMPANY
28298 Clay St (46517-1072)
PHONE..................574 293-5912
David Collier, *CEO*
Stephen Collier, *President*
EMP: 25
SQ FT: 14,000
SALES (est): 2.9MM **Privately Held**
WEB: www.cloversm.com
SIC: 1761 3444 Sheet metalwork; sheet metalwork

(G-2762)
COLLINS TRAILERS INC
Also Called: J B Enterprises
1053 Middleton Run Rd (46516-9253)
PHONE..................574 294-2561
Fax: 574 293-1828
Joe Collins, *President*
Betty Collins, *Vice Pres*
EMP: 7
SQ FT: 13,000

SALES (est): 1MM **Privately Held**
WEB: www.trailersandwagons.com
SIC: 3799 5599 Trailers & trailer equipment; utility trailers

(G-2763)
COMFORT QUARTERS CONVERSIONS
3507 Cooper Dr (46514-8639)
PHONE..................574 262-3701
EMP: 3 **EST:** 2008
SALES (est): 140K **Privately Held**
SIC: 3131 Mfg Footwear Cut Stock

(G-2764)
COMFYCAPS BY CINDY
1825 Rainbow Bend Blvd (46514-1402)
PHONE..................269 683-6881
EMP: 2
SALES (est): 112.2K **Privately Held**
SIC: 2353 Mfg Hats/Caps/Millinery

(G-2765)
CONN-SELMER INC (DH)
Also Called: Selmer Paris
600 Industrial Pkwy (46516-5414)
P.O. Box 310 (46515-0310)
PHONE..................574 522-1675
John Stonner, *President*
Moeen Hosain, *District Mgr*
Frank Rosso, *District Mgr*
Corkey Trevino, *District Mgr*
Doug White, *Plant Mgr*
▲ **EMP:** 75
SQ FT: 25,000
SALES (est): 204.7MM
SALES (corp-wide): 316.7MM **Privately Held**
WEB: www.conn-selmer.com
SIC: 3931 5736 Musical instruments; pianos, all types: vertical, grand, spinet, player, etc.; brass instruments & parts; woodwind instruments & parts; pianos

(G-2766)
CONN-SELMER INC
Selmer Plant 2
2415 Industrial Pkwy (46516-5406)
P.O. Box 310 (46515-0310)
PHONE..................574 522-1675
Phil Reardon, *District Mgr*
Heinz Mantel, *Manager*
Kathy Sopnicar, *Master*
EMP: 30
SQ FT: 75,888
SALES (corp-wide): 316.7MM **Privately Held**
WEB: www.conn-selmer.com
SIC: 3931 Musical instruments
HQ: Conn-Selmer, Inc.
600 Industrial Pkwy
Elkhart IN 46516
574 522-1675

(G-2767)
CONN-SELMER INC
Vincent Bach Co
500 Industrial Pkwy (46516-5416)
P.O. Box 310 (46515-0310)
PHONE..................574 295-6730
Fax: 574 293-2370
John Stoner, *President*
EMP: 350
SQ FT: 152,320
SALES (corp-wide): 316.7MM **Privately Held**
WEB: www.conn-selmer.com
SIC: 3931 5099 Guitars & parts, electric & nonelectric; musical instruments
HQ: Conn-Selmer, Inc.
600 Industrial Pkwy
Elkhart IN 46516
574 522-1675

(G-2768)
CONN-SELMER INC
1000 Industrial Pkwy (46516-5526)
PHONE..................574 295-0079
Michael R Vickrey, *Exec VP*
Susan Bagnall, *Buyer*
Shelly Matthys, *Manager*
EMP: 640

SALES (corp-wide): 316.7MM **Privately Held**
WEB: www.conn-selmer.com
SIC: 3931 Woodwind instruments & parts; brass instruments & parts; string instruments & parts
HQ: Conn-Selmer, Inc.
600 Industrial Pkwy
Elkhart IN 46516
574 522-1675

(G-2769)
CONSOLIDATED PIPE & VALVE
53903 Juanita Dr (46514-4922)
PHONE...............................574 262-3758
James Morningstar, *Principal*
EMP: 2
SALES (est): 154.5K **Privately Held**
SIC: 3592 Valves

(G-2770)
CONTINENTAL EXPRESS
Also Called: Shade Express
2904 Half Hammond Ave (46516)
PHONE...............................574 294-5684
Charles Youngman, *Owner*
EMP: 2
SQ FT: 5,000
SALES (est): 192.9K **Privately Held**
WEB: www.shadexpress.com
SIC: 2591 Window shades

(G-2771)
CONTINENTAL INDUSTRIES INC (PA)
Also Called: Continental Register Co
100 W Windsor Ave (46514-5503)
P.O. Box 1248 (46515-1248)
PHONE...............................574 262-4511
Fax: 574 262-2075
David Leiter, *President*
Judith Leiter, *Corp Secy*
Paul Leiter, *Vice Pres*
EMP: 93
SQ FT: 170,000
SALES (est): 22MM **Privately Held**
WEB: www.continentalindustries.com
SIC: 3444 3446 Sheet metalwork; registers (air), metal

(G-2772)
CONVERSION COMPONENTS INC
2605 Decio Dr (46514-8627)
PHONE...............................574 264-4181
Fax: 574 264-2823
Jim Shreve, *President*
Beth Shreve, *Corp Secy*
Max Reeder, *Vice Pres*
EMP: 4
SQ FT: 7,500
SALES: 500K **Privately Held**
WEB: www.conversioncomponents.com
SIC: 3714 5013 Motor vehicle parts & accessories; automotive hardware

(G-2773)
COPPER BRASS SALE
3500 Charlotte Ave (46517-1191)
PHONE...............................574 295-3100
Fax: 574 295-5915
Chris Klein, *Principal*
EMP: 3
SALES (est): 211.2K **Privately Held**
SIC: 3353 Aluminum sheet, plate & foil

(G-2774)
CORE WOOD COMPONENTS LLC
612 Kollar St (46514-1358)
PHONE...............................574 370-4457
Wendall Joe Campbell, *President*
Joe Campbell, *Principal*
EMP: 7
SQ FT: 25,000
SALES: 1.2MM **Privately Held**
SIC: 3553 5099 Woodworking machinery; wood & wood by-products

(G-2775)
CRANE COMPOSITES
21067 Protecta Dr (46516-9704)
PHONE...............................574 295-9391
Julie Keith, *Principal*
EMP: 3

SALES (est): 174.8K **Privately Held**
SIC: 3089 Plastics products

(G-2776)
CREATIVE MANUFACTURING RV LLC
330 E Windsor Ave (46514-5565)
P.O. Box 320, North Webster (46555-0320)
PHONE...............................574 333-3302
Rebecca L Belcher, *Partner*
Roger Reiff, *Partner*
EMP: 15
SALES: 400K **Privately Held**
SIC: 3799 6399 Recreational vehicles; warranty insurance, automobile

(G-2777)
CROSBIE FOUNDRY CO INC
1600 Mishawaka St (46514-1898)
PHONE...............................574 262-1502
Fax: 574 262-1503
Daniel J Crosbie, *President*
John F Crosbie, *Corp Secy*
Gregory A Crosbie, *Vice Pres*
Linda Crosbie, *Bookkeeper*
EMP: 35 EST: 1956
SQ FT: 18,500
SALES (est): 5.7MM **Privately Held**
WEB: www.crosbiefoundry.com
SIC: 3369 3366 Nonferrous foundries; copper foundries; castings (except die): copper & copper-base alloy

(G-2778)
CROWN EQUIPMENT CORPORATION
Also Called: Crown Lift Trucks
1125 Herman St (46516-9030)
PHONE...............................574 293-1264
Troy Boyer, *Manager*
EMP: 70
SALES (corp-wide): 3.1B **Privately Held**
SIC: 3537 Lift trucks, industrial: fork, platform, straddle, etc.
PA: Crown Equipment Corporation
44 S Washington St
New Bremen OH 45869
419 629-2311

(G-2779)
CRYSTAL INDUSTRIES INC
28870 Phillips St (46514-1241)
PHONE...............................574 264-6166
Fax: 574 264-3889
Kevin Anthony, *President*
Heather Fite, *Bookkeeper*
James Mark, *Admin Sec*
▲ EMP: 49
SQ FT: 55,000
SALES (est): 8.4MM **Privately Held**
SIC: 3441 Fabricated structural metal

(G-2780)
CTS CORPORATION
1142 W Beardsley Ave (46514-2224)
PHONE...............................574 293-7511
Fax: 574 293-8394
Paul Kelly, *Partner*
Dan Long, *Business Mgr*
Richard Xiong, *Vice Pres*
Allan White, *Plant Mgr*
Omar Corral, *Opers Mgr*
EMP: 43
SALES (corp-wide): 422.9MM **Publicly Held**
SIC: 3678 Electronic connectors
PA: Cts Corporation
4925 Indiana Ave
Lisle IL 60532
630 577-8800

(G-2781)
CTS ELCTRNIC CMPONENTS CAL INC
Also Called: Ierc
905 N West Blvd (46514-1875)
PHONE...............................574 523-3800
Gordon Hunter, *CEO*
Walter S Catlow, *President*
Andrew Herman, *Engineer*
Craig Morris, *Sales Staff*
Frank Lynch, *Manager*
EMP: 6
SQ FT: 6,140

SALES (est): 1.3MM
SALES (corp-wide): 422.9MM **Publicly Held**
WEB: www.ctscorp.com
SIC: 3679 Electronic circuits
PA: Cts Corporation
4925 Indiana Ave
Lisle IL 60532
630 577-8800

(G-2782)
CULLIP INDUSTRIES INC
Also Called: Cullip Tool & Die
300 Comet Ave (46514-5529)
PHONE...............................574 293-8251
Fax: 574 293-8954
John Cullip, *President*
Marie Cullip, *Corp Secy*
EMP: 18 EST: 1959
SQ FT: 10,400
SALES (est): 3MM **Privately Held**
WEB: www.cullipindustries.com
SIC: 3599 Machine shop, jobbing & repair

(G-2783)
CUMMINS POWER GENERATION INC
Also Called: Cummins Onan
5125 Beck Dr Ste A (46516-9094)
PHONE...............................574 262-4611
Mark Fortney, *Manager*
EMP: 42
SALES (corp-wide): 20.4B **Publicly Held**
SIC: 3621 3519 Generators & sets, electric; internal combustion engines
HQ: Cummins Power Generation Inc.
1400 73rd Ave Ne
Minneapolis MN 55432
763 574-5000

(G-2784)
CUSTOM WOOD PRODUCTS INC
1901 W Hively Ave (46517-4028)
PHONE...............................574 522-3300
Kirti P Shah, *President*
Kirit P Shah, *President*
Raju K Shah, *Vice Pres*
▲ EMP: 70
SALES (est): 9MM **Privately Held**
WEB: www.customwoodinc.com
SIC: 2511 2512 3714 2531 Dining room furniture: wood; desks, household: wood; chairs: upholstered on wood frames; motor vehicle parts & accessories; public building & related furniture; wood office furniture

(G-2785)
D & W INC
941 Oak St (46514-2287)
PHONE...............................574 264-9674
Fax: 574 264-9859
Anthony Warning, *President*
Angie Reed, *General Mgr*
Kandee Nutting, *Credit Mgr*
Christy Holdren, *Human Resources*
Paul Warning, *Sales Staff*
▲ EMP: 100
SQ FT: 130,000
SALES (est): 15.8MM **Privately Held**
WEB: www.dwincorp.com
SIC: 3231 5075 Mirrored glass; warm air heating equipment & supplies

(G-2786)
DAILY GRIND CORPORATION
58711 Runway Rd (46516-6265)
PHONE...............................574 875-8389
Fax: 574 293-4864
Tonya Bleiler, *President*
EMP: 10 EST: 1997
SALES (est): 938.7K **Privately Held**
SIC: 3599 Grinding castings for the trade

(G-2787)
DAMON CORPORATION (HQ)
Also Called: Breckenridge Recrtl Pk Trlrs
2958 Gateway Dr (46514-8600)
P.O. Box 1486 (46515-1486)
PHONE...............................574 262-2624
Gary Groom, *President*
Tim Howard, *President*
Craig Weeks, *Corp Secy*
◆ EMP: 15
SQ FT: 8,000

SALES (est): 53.5MM
SALES (corp-wide): 7.2B **Publicly Held**
WEB: www.damonrv.com
SIC: 3716 3792 Motor homes; travel trailers & campers
PA: Thor Industries, Inc.
601 E Beardsley Ave
Elkhart IN 46514
574 970-7460

(G-2788)
DAMON CORPORATION
2824 Jami St (46514-8794)
PHONE...............................574 262-2624
Gary Groom, *President*
EMP: 350
SALES (corp-wide): 7.2B **Publicly Held**
WEB: www.damonrv.com
SIC: 5012 3716 Recreational vehicles, motor homes & trailers; motor homes
HQ: Damon Corporation
2958 Gateway Dr
Elkhart IN 46514
574 262-2624

(G-2789)
DAMON CORPORATION
2958 Paul Dr (46514-8796)
PHONE...............................574 264-2900
Fax: 574 266-6605
Arthur Konecny, *Branch Mgr*
EMP: 12
SALES (corp-wide): 7.2B **Publicly Held**
WEB: www.damonrv.com
SIC: 3711 3716 Buses, all types, assembly of; motor homes
HQ: Damon Corporation
2958 Gateway Dr
Elkhart IN 46514
574 262-2624

(G-2790)
DAMON MOTOR COACH
604 Middleton Run Rd (46516-5447)
P.O. Box 2888 (46515-2888)
PHONE...............................574 536-3781
Bill Fenech, *President*
EMP: 20
SALES (est): 8.3MM
SALES (corp-wide): 7.2B **Publicly Held**
SIC: 3711 Motor vehicles & car bodies
PA: Thor Industries, Inc.
601 E Beardsley Ave
Elkhart IN 46514
574 970-7460

(G-2791)
DEC-O-ART INC
3914 Lexington Park Dr (46514-1194)
PHONE...............................574 294-6451
Fax: 574 295-6534
Anthony J Dosmann, *President*
Ronald Dosmann, *Vice Pres*
Carl Dosmann, *Treasurer*
Fredrick Dosmann, *VP Sales*
EMP: 45
SQ FT: 28,000
SALES (est): 8MM **Privately Held**
WEB: www.deco-art.com
SIC: 2759 Screen printing; letterpress & screen printing

(G-2792)
DEHCO INC (HQ)
Also Called: Recreation Nation
3601 Charlotte Ave (46517-1192)
P.O. Box 1368 (46515-1368)
PHONE...............................574 294-2684
James T Schwartz, *CEO*
Thomas J Nagy, *President*
Ron Wenger, *Exec VP*
Curt Wenger, *Purch Mgr*
Erica Perucci, *Office Mgr*
▲ EMP: 100
SQ FT: 137,000
SALES: 88MM
SALES (corp-wide): 1.6B **Publicly Held**
WEB: www.dehco.net
SIC: 2891 5031 5074 5014 Adhesives & sealants; caulking compounds; adhesives; sealants; lumber, plywood & millwork; building materials, exterior; plumbing fittings & supplies; tires & tubes; instruments & control equipment

PA: Patrick Industries, Inc.
107 W Franklin St
Elkhart IN 46516
574 294-7511

(G-2793)
DELIVERY CONCEPTS INC (PA)
29301 County Road 20 (46517-8990)
PHONE..................................574 522-3981
Fax: 574 522-3423
Anthony M Marchetti, *President*
Daniel Dulmentritt, *Vice Pres*
Rebecca Stanley, *Director*
Aaron A Marchetti, *Admin Sec*
Michael Oliva, *Admin Sec*
EMP: 25
SQ FT: 12,000
SALES (est): 7MM **Privately Held**
WEB: www.deliveryconcepts.com
SIC: 3585 3713 Refrigeration & heating
equipment; specialty motor vehicle bodies

(G-2794)
DEXTER AXLE COMPANY
21611 Protecta Dr (46516-9543)
PHONE..................................574 294-6651
Paul Schwoerer, *Maint Spvr*
Kelly Hunt, *Human Res Mgr*
EMP: 203
SALES (corp-wide): 245.3MM **Privately
Held**
SIC: 3714 5083 Gears, motor vehicle;
lawn & garden machinery & equipment
HQ: Dexter Axle Company
2900 Industrial Pkwy
Elkhart IN 46516

(G-2795)
DEXTER AXLE COMPANY (HQ)
2900 Industrial Pkwy (46516-5491)
P.O. Box 250 (46515-0250)
PHONE..................................574 295-7888
Fax: 574 295-8666
Adam W Dexter, *President*
Tim Meckstroth, *President*
Bill Snider, *General Mgr*
Edward Kopkowski, *COO*
Tom Kelly, *Vice Pres*
◆ EMP: 70
SQ FT: 43,000
SALES (est): 245.3MM **Privately Held**
WEB: www.dexteraxle.com
SIC: 3714 Axles, motor vehicle
PA: Dexko Global Inc.
39555 Orchard Hill Pl
Novi MI 48375
248 533-0029

(G-2796)
DEXTER AXLE COMPANY
Also Called: Al-Ko Kober
21608 Protecta Dr (46516-9532)
PHONE..................................574 294-6651
Robert Murray, *Manager*
EMP: 65
SALES (corp-wide): 245.3MM **Privately
Held**
WEB: www.al-kousa.com
SIC: 3714 Axles, motor vehicle
HQ: Dexter Axle Company
2900 Industrial Pkwy
Elkhart IN 46516

(G-2797)
DIE-RITE MACHINE AND TOOL
CORP
129 Rush Ct (46516-9644)
PHONE..................................574 522-2366
Fax: 574 295-6554
Monty K Craven, *President*
EMP: 8
SQ FT: 12,000
SALES (est): 1.3MM **Privately Held**
SIC: 3544 3599 Special dies & tools; jigs
& fixtures; machine shop, jobbing & repair

(G-2798)
DOMAR MACHINE & TOOL INC
56740 Elk Park Dr (46516-1448)
PHONE..................................574 295-8791
Fax: 574 295-8791
Doug Martin, *President*
Donna Martin, *Vice Pres*
▲ EMP: 6
SQ FT: 10,000

SALES: 1.8MM **Privately Held**
SIC: 3469 Stamping metal for the trade

(G-2799)
DOUBLE T MANUFACTURING
CORP
Also Called: S T Laminating
27139 County Road 6 (46514-5601)
P.O. Box 1371 (46515-1371)
PHONE..................................574 262-1340
Fax: 574 262-2066
Gary Taska, *Chairman*
Marlene Taska, *Corp Secy*
EMP: 10
SQ FT: 15,000
SALES (est): 1.2MM **Privately Held**
WEB: www.double-t-usa.com
SIC: 2541 2434 3714 2521 Counter &
sink tops; vanities, bathroom: wood;
motor vehicle parts & accessories; wood
office furniture

(G-2800)
DREAM LIGHTING INC
2111 Industrial Pkwy (46516-5410)
PHONE..................................574 206-4888
Michael Cole Gilpin, *Principal*
EMP: 8
SALES (est): 800.6K
SALES (corp-wide): 2MM **Privately Held**
SIC: 3646 Commercial indsl & institu-
tional electric lighting fixtures
PA: Power Panda Pty Ltd
U 2 3405 Pacific Hwy
Slacks Creek QLD 4127
731 333-867

(G-2801)
DUBOIS MANUFACTURING INC
30561 Old Us 20 (46514-9471)
PHONE..................................574 674-6988
EMP: 3
SALES (est): 203.8K **Privately Held**
SIC: 3999 Manufacturing industries

(G-2802)
DUMOR WATER SPECIALISTS
INC
4405 Wyland Dr (46516-9501)
PHONE..................................574 522-9500
Brian Stuvzman, *President*
EMP: 20
SALES (est): 3.8MM **Privately Held**
SIC: 2899 Water treating compounds

(G-2803)
DURA AUTOMOTIVE SYSTEMS
OF IND
Also Called: Atwood Mobile Products
2700 Jeanwood Dr (46514-7658)
PHONE..................................574 262-2655
Fax: 574 262-2550
Lawrence A Denton, *President*
Keith Marchiando, *Vice Pres*
J Bryan Williams, *Admin Sec*
EMP: 8
SALES (est): 650K **Privately Held**
SIC: 3714 Motor vehicle parts & acces-
sories

(G-2804)
DURO INC
Also Called: Lee's Wood Products
24478 County Road 45 (46516-6043)
P.O. Box 2341 (46515-2341)
PHONE..................................574 293-6860
Fax: 574 522-2987
Terry Rodino, *President*
EMP: 8
SQ FT: 14,000
SALES (est): 1.3MM **Privately Held**
SIC: 2448 Pallets, wood; cargo containers,
wood & wood with metal

(G-2805)
DURO RECYCLING INC
Also Called: Recycled New
24478 County Road 45 (46516-6043)
P.O. Box 2341 (46515-2341)
PHONE..................................574 522-2572
Terry Rodino, *President*
EMP: 30
SALES (est): 5.1MM **Privately Held**
SIC: 2448 Pallets, wood

(G-2806)
DYNAMIC INDUSTRIAL GROUP
LLC
54347 Highland Blvd (46514-2124)
PHONE..................................574 295-5525
EMP: 2
SALES (est): 86.6K **Privately Held**
SIC: 3441 Fabricated structural metal

(G-2807)
DYNAMIC METALS LLC
Also Called: Dynamic Aerospace and De-
fense
54347 Highland Blvd (46514-2124)
PHONE..................................574 262-2497
Donald Nystrom, *President*
Elaine Stacy, *Transportation*
Nicole Busch, *Asst Controller*
Dennis Nystrom, *Admin Sec*
Andrew Croy, *Technician*
▼ EMP: 85
SQ FT: 80,000
SALES (est): 35.1MM **Privately Held**
WEB: www.dynamicmetalsllc.com
SIC: 3441 Fabricated structural metal

(G-2808)
E INDUSTRIES INC
4526 Chester Dr (46516-9056)
P.O. Box 2983 (46515-2983)
PHONE..................................574 522-7550
Fax: 574 522-7551
Matt Eppers, *President*
Marcia Eppers, *Vice Pres*
EMP: 9
SQ FT: 10,000
SALES (est): 1.4MM **Privately Held**
WEB: www.e-industries.com
SIC: 3069 Molded rubber products

(G-2809)
E T & T POWDER COAT
Also Called: E T and T Enterprises
58391 Ventura Dr (46517-9431)
P.O. Box 1914 (46515-1914)
PHONE..................................574 293-2725
Ted Holland, *President*
Anthony Holland, *Manager*
Blair Hudnall, *Manager*
Brian Jozwiak, *Manager*
Robin Wape, *Manager*
EMP: 3
SQ FT: 27,744
SALES (est): 453.8K **Privately Held**
SIC: 3799 Recreational vehicles

(G-2810)
E Z LOADER BOAT TRAILERS
INC
Also Called: EZ Loader Northcentral
125 W Belvedere Rd (46514-5534)
PHONE..................................574 266-0092
Bill Lang, *Manager*
Rene Boyer, *Info Tech Dir*
EMP: 5
SALES (corp-wide): 65.6MM **Privately
Held**
WEB: www.ezloader.com
SIC: 3799 Boat trailers
PA: E Z Loader Boat Trailers, Inc.
717 N Hamilton St
Spokane WA 99202
574 266-0092

(G-2811)
EASH LLC
Also Called: Eash Design
107 Rush Ct (46516-9644)
PHONE..................................574 295-4450
Damon Marcott, *Mng Member*
EMP: 12
SQ FT: 12,000
SALES: 1MM **Privately Held**
SIC: 2541 5561 Table or counter tops,
plastic laminated; recreational vehicle
parts & accessories

(G-2812)
ECHO MANUFACTURING LLC
21888 Beck Dr (46516-9245)
PHONE..................................574 333-3669
EMP: 8 EST: 2010
SALES (est): 480K **Privately Held**
SIC: 3999 Mfg Misc Products

(G-2806)
(G-2813)
ECM PHOTO TOOLING INC
26082 Heatherfield Dr (46514-6390)
PHONE..................................574 264-4433
Howard Lewis, *President*
EMP: 20
SQ FT: 17,000
SALES (est): 2MM **Privately Held**
SIC: 3599 3544 Machine & other job shop
work; chemical milling job shop; special
dies, tools, jigs & fixtures

(G-2814)
EFP LLC (HQ)
223 Middleton Run Rd (46516-5488)
P.O. Box 2368 (46515-2368)
PHONE..................................574 295-4690
Fax: 574 295-6512
Keith Arenz, *President*
Dennis Orban, *CFO*
Scott Watson, *VP Sales*
Chuck Cook, *Manager*
▲ EMP: 64 EST: 1954
SQ FT: 230,000
SALES (est): 26.6MM
SALES (corp-wide): 1B **Privately Held**
WEB: www.efpcorp.com
SIC: 3086 Plastics foam products; insula-
tion or cushioning material, foamed plas-
tic; packaging & shipping materials,
foamed plastic; ice chests or coolers
(portable), foamed plastic
PA: J. B. Poindexter & Co., Inc
600 Travis St Ste 200
Houston TX 77002
713 655-9800

(G-2815)
ELECTRO-COAT
TECHNOLOGIES
2501 Jeanwood Dr (46514-7615)
PHONE..................................574 266-7356
Fax: 574 266-7361
Dennis Marcott, *CEO*
EMP: 43
SALES (est): 3.5MM **Privately Held**
SIC: 3479 Coating, rust preventive

(G-2816)
ELIXIR INDUSTRIES
Also Called: Diversified Products Div
640 Collins Rd (46516-5421)
PHONE..................................574 294-5685
Fax: 574 293-0946
EMP: 24
SQ FT: 101,478
SALES (corp-wide): 28.3MM **Privately
Held**
SIC: 3469 3631 Mfg Metal Stampings Mfg
Household Cooking Equipment
PA: Elixir Industries
24800 Chrisanta Dr # 210
Mission Viejo CA 92691
949 860-5000

(G-2817)
ELIXIR INDUSTRIES
Also Called: Metals Division
640 Collins Rd (46516-5421)
PHONE..................................574 294-5685
EMP: 44
SALES (corp-wide): 28.3MM **Privately
Held**
SIC: 3469 3441 Mfg Metal Stampings
Structural Metal Fabrication
PA: Elixir Industries
24800 Chrisanta Dr # 210
Mission Viejo CA 92691
949 860-5000

(G-2818)
ELIXIR INDUSTRIES
Also Called: Vent Division
2040 Industrial Pkwy (46516-5411)
PHONE..................................574 294-5685
EMP: 69
SALES (corp-wide): 28.3MM **Privately
Held**
SIC: 3469 3444 3442 3441 Mfg Metal
Stampings Mfg Sheet Metalwork Mfg
Metal Door/Sash/Trim Structural Metal
Fabrctn
PA: Elixir Industries
24800 Chrisanta Dr # 210
Mission Viejo CA 92691
949 860-5000

(G-2819)
ELKCASES INC
Also Called: Sprunger Engineering
23143 Heaton Vis (46514-9340)
PHONE..............................574 295-7700
Dale D Fahlbeck, *CEO*
Vicki Spicer, *Admin Sec*
Kennard R Weaver, *Asst Sec*
EMP: 25
SQ FT: 33,000
SALES (est): 1.3MM **Privately Held**
SIC: 3161 3089 Musical instrument cases;
plastic processing

(G-2820)
ELKHART BEDDING CO INC
2124 Sterling Ave (46516-4999)
PHONE..............................574 293-6200
Fax: 574 522-4667
Chris Darr, *President*
Sandra Darr, *Admin Sec*
EMP: 15
SQ FT: 28,000
SALES (est): 2.3MM **Privately Held**
WEB: www.elkhartbedding.com
SIC: 2515 Mattresses, innerspring or box
spring; box springs, assembled

(G-2821)
ELKHART BINDING INC
51784 State Road 19 (46514-5801)
PHONE..............................574 522-5455
Patrick C Berendt, *President*
EMP: 2
SQ FT: 2,000
SALES (est): 214.9K **Privately Held**
SIC: 2789 Bookbinding & related work

(G-2822)
**ELKHART BRASS
MANUFACTURING CO**
Also Called: Shreve Manufacturing
1302 W Beardsley Ave (46514-1828)
PHONE..............................800 346-0250
Greg Brennecke, *VP Opers*
Jim Peterson, *Engineer*
Fred Wells, *Manager*
Jason Brenneman, *Internal Med*
EMP: 17
SALES (corp-wide): 143.7MM **Privately
Held**
WEB: www.elkhartbrass.com
SIC: 2542 5087 Partitions & fixtures, ex-
cept wood; firefighting equipment
HQ: Elkhart Brass Manufacturing Company
Inc
1302 W Beardsley Ave
Elkhart IN 46514
574 295-8330

(G-2823)
ELKHART CASES INC
Also Called: Sprunger Engineering
23143 Heaton Vis (46514-9340)
PHONE..............................574 295-7700
Fax: 574 295-7761
Dale Fehlbeck, *President*
▲ EMP: 25
SALES: 1.5MM **Privately Held**
SIC: 3089 Injection molding of plastics

(G-2824)
**ELKHART GRINDING SERVICES
INC**
121 Rush Ct (46516-9644)
PHONE..............................574 293-2707
Fax: 574 293-2707
EMP: 2 EST: 2016
SALES (est): 99.2K **Privately Held**
SIC: 3599 Grinding castings for the trade

(G-2825)
ELKHART HINGE CO INC
1839 W Lusher Ave (46517-1394)
PHONE..............................574 293-2841
Fax: 574 293-8288
Steve Holbert, *President*
Jayne Holbert, *Corp Secy*
EMP: 10
SQ FT: 12,000
SALES (est): 1.8MM **Privately Held**
WEB: www.elkharthinge.com
SIC: 3429 Furniture builders' & other
household hardware

(G-2826)
**ELKHART METAL POLISHING
INC**
1926 Leininger Ave (46517-1326)
PHONE..............................574 206-0666
Robert Warren Penney, *Treasurer*
EMP: 2
SALES (est): 74.4K **Privately Held**
SIC: 2842 Metal polish

(G-2827)
ELKHART PLASTICS INC
1400 Leininger Ave (46517-1445)
PHONE..............................574 389-9911
Jan Garber, *Executive Asst*
EMP: 45
SQ FT: 100,000
SALES (corp-wide): 135.7MM **Privately
Held**
SIC: 3089 Plastic containers, except foam
PA: Elkhart Plastics, Inc.
3300 N Kenmore St
South Bend IN 46628
574 232-8066

(G-2828)
ELKHART PLATING CORP
1913 14th St (46516-2278)
P.O. Box 74 (46515-0074)
PHONE..............................574 294-1800
George Malcom, *President*
Don Penzenik, *QC Mgr*
EMP: 18
SQ FT: 15,000
SALES (est): 2.5MM **Privately Held**
WEB: www.elkhartplating.com
SIC: 3471 Electroplating of metals or
formed products

(G-2829)
**ELKHART PRODUCTS
CORPORATION (HQ)**
1255 Oak St (46514-2277)
P.O. Box 701, Matthews NC (28106-0701)
PHONE..............................574 264-3181
Fax: 574 264-0103
Glenn Mosack, *President*
Larry Johnson, *Vice Pres*
Sean P O'Connell, *CFO*
▲ EMP: 300 EST: 1941
SQ FT: 186,000
SALES (est): 120.2MM
SALES (corp-wide): 3.1B **Privately Held**
WEB: www.elkhartproducts.com
SIC: 3498 Tube fabricating (contract bend-
ing & shaping)
PA: Aalberts Industries N.V.
Sandenburgerlaan 4
Langbroek
343 565-080

(G-2830)
**ELKHART STEEL SERVICE INC
(PA)**
Also Called: Lape Steel
23321 C R 106 (46514)
PHONE..............................574 262-2552
Fax: 574 262-8743
Bradford J Miller, *President*
Michelle Miller, *Vice Pres*
James M Hampel, *Admin Sec*
EMP: 35 EST: 1979
SQ FT: 48,400
SALES (est): 17.6MM **Privately Held**
WEB: www.elkhartsteel.com
SIC: 5051 3312 Metals service centers &
offices; steel; hot-rolled iron & steel prod-
ucts; iron & steel: galvanized, pipes,
plates, sheets, etc.

(G-2831)
ELKHART SUPPLY CORP
Also Called: E S C O
1126 Kent St (46514-1799)
PHONE..............................574 264-4156
Lewis Shaum, *President*
Rebecca Mikel, *General Mgr*
Ted Krueger, *Design Engr*
Terry Springer, *Sales Staff*
Connie Kidder, *Department Mgr*
▲ EMP: 23
SQ FT: 15,000

SALES (est): 19.3MM **Privately Held**
WEB: www.escousa.net
SIC: 5063 5074 3643 5065 Light bulbs &
related supplies; wire & cable; electrical
construction materials; electrical fittings &
construction materials; plumbing fittings &
supplies; electric switches; connectors;
electric cord; electronic parts & equipment

(G-2832)
ELKHART TOOL AND DIE INC
2400 15th St (46517-1416)
P.O. Box 1428 (46515-1428)
PHONE..............................574 295-8500
Fax: 574 294-5138
Brent H Brown, *President*
EMP: 28 EST: 1932
SQ FT: 40,000
SALES (est): 4.5MM **Privately Held**
SIC: 3544 Special dies & tools

(G-2833)
ENERSYS
1353 Wade Dr (46514-8229)
PHONE..............................574 266-0658
Stephenie Rahn, *Branch Mgr*
EMP: 88
SALES (corp-wide): 2.5B **Publicly Held**
SIC: 3691 Lead acid batteries (storage bat-
teries)
PA: Enersys
2366 Bernville Rd
Reading PA 19605
610 208-1991

(G-2834)
ENGENAIRE
30068 Westlake Dr (46514-9496)
PHONE..............................574 264-0391
Larry Pendell, *Owner*
EMP: 2
SALES (est): 203.2K **Privately Held**
SIC: 3621 Power generators

(G-2835)
**ENVIRONMENTAL TEST
SYSTEMS**
3504 Henke St (46514-7653)
P.O. Box 389, Loveland CO (80539-0389)
PHONE..............................574 262-2060
John Brew, *Director*
EMP: 13
SALES (est): 1.2MM **Privately Held**
SIC: 3826 8748 Analytical instruments;
business consulting

(G-2836)
EPW LLC
1500 W Hively Ave Ste A (46517-4033)
PHONE..............................574 293-5090
Douglas Lammon,
EMP: 56
SALES (est): 14.3MM **Privately Held**
SIC: 3544 Industrial molds; forms (molds),
for foundry & plastics working machinery

(G-2837)
ESCO INDUSTRIES INC
1701 Conant St (46516-4716)
PHONE..............................574 522-4500
Fax: 574 522-0900
Kelly Rentfrow, *General Mgr*
EMP: 20
SALES (corp-wide): 37.1MM **Privately
Held**
WEB: www.escoindustries.com
SIC: 3275 Gypsum board
PA: Esco Industries, Inc.
185 Sink Hole Rd
Douglas GA 31533
912 384-1417

(G-2838)
**EVANS METAL PRODUCTS CO
INC**
2400 Johnson St (46514-5578)
PHONE..............................574 264-2166
Fax: 574 970-1001
Evans II C David, *President*
Bruce W Reinks, *Vice Pres*
Lorraine S Evans, *Treasurer*
EMP: 14
SQ FT: 12,000

SALES (est): 3.7MM **Privately Held**
WEB: www.evansmetal.com
SIC: 3441 3446 Building components,
structural steel; ladders, for permanent installation: metal; stairs, staircases, stair
treads: prefabricated metal; railings, prefabricated metal

(G-2839)
EXACT-TECH MACHINING INC
1140 County Road 6 W (46514-8218)
PHONE..............................574 970-0197
Fax: 574 522-3506
Edward A Kramer, *President*
Gina R Kramer, *President*
Jennifer Nissley, *Office Mgr*
EMP: 11
SQ FT: 20,000
SALES (est): 2MM **Privately Held**
WEB: www.exact-tech.com
SIC: 3599 Machine shop, jobbing & repair

(G-2840)
EXCEL INDUSTRIES INC
3308 Charlotte Ave (46517-1189)
PHONE..............................574 264-2131
EMP: 2
SALES (est): 128.7K **Privately Held**
SIC: 3999 Manufacturing industries

(G-2841)
EXEMPLARY FOAM INC (PA)
1235 W Hively Ave (46517-1555)
PHONE..............................574 295-8888
John Petrofsky, *President*
Stacey McKee, *General Mgr*
Don Frandsen, *Vice Pres*
Aaron Jenkins, *Marketing Staff*
▲ EMP: 20
SQ FT: 18,000
SALES (est): 3.4MM **Privately Held**
WEB: www.exemplaryfoam.com
SIC: 3069 Foam rubber

(G-2842)
**F & F SCREW MACHINE
PRODUCTS**
4302 Wyland Dr (46516-9519)
PHONE..............................574 293-0362
Blake Slack, *President*
Roger Duffy, *Corp Secy*
Chris Clements, *Opers Mgr*
Jim Tevlin, *Mill Mgr*
Floyd Clements, *Manager*
EMP: 40 EST: 1959
SQ FT: 20,000
SALES (est): 6.7MM **Privately Held**
WEB: www.ffscrewmachine.com
SIC: 3451 Screw machine products

(G-2843)
FAIRVIEW FITTINGS & MFG
23845 County Road 6 (46514-9691)
PHONE..............................574 206-8884
Ryan Yewchuk, *Branch Mgr*
Ryan Yewchuck, *Manager*
John Nowicki, *Representative*
▲ EMP: 3 EST: 1969
SALES (est): 225.8K **Privately Held**
WEB: www.indiana.fairviewfittings.com
SIC: 3089 Fittings for pipe, plastic

(G-2844)
FAN-TASTIC VENT
1120 N Main St (46514-3203)
PHONE..............................800 521-0298
Stephen Milks, *Owner*
EMP: 2
SALES (est): 216.4K **Privately Held**
SIC: 3564 Blowers & fans

(G-2845)
FARIES-MCMEEKAN INC
28858 County Road 20 (46517-9436)
P.O. Box 2388 (46515-2388)
PHONE..............................574 293-3526
George N Mc Meekan, *Ch of Bd*
Scott Mc Meekan, *President*
EMP: 35
SQ FT: 53,000
SALES (est): 3.7MM **Privately Held**
WEB: www.fmmirrors.com
SIC: 3231 Mirrored glass

▲ = Import ▼=Export
◆ =Import/Export

(G-2846)
FARMER TANK INCORPORATED
25575 Woodlawn Ave (46514-3826)
PHONE...................................574 264-4625
Fax: 574 264-6287
Harold Farmer, *President*
Evelyn Farmer, *Vice Pres*
EMP: 7
SQ FT: 12,000
SALES (est): 720K **Privately Held**
SIC: 3272 Septic tanks, concrete

(G-2847)
FENDERS INC
5304 Beck Dr (46516-9251)
P.O. Box 2082 (46515-2082)
PHONE...................................574 293-3717
Herbert L Kirts, *President*
Diane Kirts, *Corp Secy*
EMP: 7
SQ FT: 16,500
SALES (est): 2.9MM **Privately Held**
SIC: 3465 Fenders, automobile: stamped
or pressed metal

(G-2848)
FIBER-TRON CORP
29877 Old Us 33 (46516-1428)
PHONE...................................574 294-8545
Fax: 574 294-2153
William McCaslin, *President*
EMP: 20
SQ FT: 30,000
SALES (est): 4.3MM **Privately Held**
SIC: 3716 3799 Motor homes; recreational
vehicles

(G-2849)
FIBROSAN USA
2926 Paul Dr (46514-8796)
PHONE...................................574 612-4736
EMP: 2
SALES (est): 90.7K **Privately Held**
SIC: 2952 Roof cement: asphalt, fibrous or
plastic

(G-2850)
FIRST PLACE TROPHY INC
Also Called: 1st Place Trophy Shop
24888 County Road 20 (46517-3202)
PHONE...................................574 293-6147
Fax: 574 293-2173
Marvin Boht, *President*
EMP: 4
SALES (est): 300K **Privately Held**
SIC: 5094 3089 5999 Trophies; plastic
hardware & building products; trophies &
plaques

(G-2851)
FLAGER ELECTRIC
224 S Main St (46516-3181)
PHONE...................................574 295-8007
EMP: 2
SALES (est): 128.4K **Privately Held**
SIC: 3699 Electrical equipment & supplies

(G-2852)
FLEXCO PRODUCTS INC
Also Called: Industrial Steel Co Division
2415 Bryant St (46516-5593)
P.O. Box 1582 (46515-1582)
PHONE...................................574 294-2502
Fax: 574 294-1734
Thomas Jellison, *CEO*
Brett Mitchell Jellison, *President*
Susan Jellison, *Corp Secy*
Jeff Greenawalt, *Project Mgr*
Dan Ramirez, *Purchasing*
EMP: 180
SQ FT: 300,000
SALES (est): 56.6MM **Privately Held**
SIC: 5051 3444 Sheets, metal; sheet
metal specialties, not stamped

(G-2853)
FLEXFORM TECHNOLOGIES
LLC
4955 Beck Dr (46516-9092)
PHONE...................................574 295-3777
Gregg Baumbaugh, *CEO*
▲ EMP: 45
SQ FT: 100,000

SALES (est): 9.3MM **Privately Held**
WEB: www.flexformtech.com
SIC: 3711 Automobile assembly, including
specialty automobiles

(G-2854)
FLEXIBLE CONCEPTS INC
1620 Middlebury St (46516-4713)
PHONE...................................574 296-0941
Fax: 574 296-0877
Beth Gerstbauer, *CEO*
Timothy Gerstbauer, *President*
Tom Andrea, *Principal*
Dennis Leyes, *Principal*
Amy Brown, *Treasurer*
EMP: 52
SQ FT: 60,000
SALES (est): 12.9MM **Privately Held**
WEB: www.flexibleconcepts.com
SIC: 3599 3462 Machine shop, jobbing &
repair; iron & steel forgings

(G-2855)
FLEXIBLE MARKETING GROUP
1620 Middlebury St (46516-4713)
PHONE...................................574 296-0941
Elizabeth Gerstbauer, *Principal*
EMP: 2 EST: 2012
SQ FT: 102,957
SALES (est): 156.8K **Privately Held**
SIC: 3482 3499 2899 3483 Cartridge
cases for ammunition, 30 mm. & below;
boxes for packing & shipping, metal; py-
rotechnic ammunition: flares, signals,
rockets, etc.; missile warheads

(G-2856)
FLEXSEALS MANUFACTURING
LLC
2304 Charlotte Ave (46517-1196)
PHONE...................................574 293-0333
Clarence Miller, *Mng Member*
Brad Everett,
EMP: 2 EST: 2014
SALES (est): 281.3K **Privately Held**
SIC: 3089 Extruded finished plastic prod-
ucts

(G-2857)
FLEXTECH CORPORATION
53585 Lakefield Dr (46514-9474)
PHONE...................................574 271-9797
Wesley Jones, *President*
EMP: 3 EST: 1997
SQ FT: 1,700
SALES (est): 331.8K **Privately Held**
SIC: 3365 Aerospace castings, aluminum

(G-2858)
FLORALCRAFT DISTRIBUTORS
(PA)
Also Called: Accessories By Sherwood
1805 Leer Dr (46514-5447)
PHONE...................................574 262-2639
Fax: 574 262-0545
Ronald Ischemenauer, *President*
Steve Schemenauer, *Vice Pres*
David M Schemenauer, *VP Sales*
Elizabeth Sorg, *Shareholder*
Phyllis Schemenauer, *Admin Sec*
▲ EMP: 37
SQ FT: 120,000
SALES (est): 12.2MM **Privately Held**
SIC: 5023 3231 Decorative home furnish-
ings & supplies; framed mirrors

(G-2859)
FLORALCRAFT DISTRIBUTORS
Also Called: Sherwood
52876 Park Six Dr (46514-5431)
PHONE...................................574 262-2639
Steve Schemenauer, *Vice Pres*
EMP: 8 **Privately Held**
SIC: 3999 5023 5193 Plaques, picture,
laminated; decorative home furnishings &
supplies; artificial flowers
PA: Floralcraft Distributors
1805 Leer Dr
Elkhart IN 46514

(G-2860)
FOAMCRAFT INC
900 Industrial Pkwy (46516-5592)
P.O. Box 664076, Indianapolis (46266)
PHONE...................................574 293-8569
Fax: 574 293-4051

Jim Showalter, *Branch Mgr*
EMP: 55
SALES (corp-wide): 69MM **Privately
Held**
SIC: 3086 5199 Padding, foamed plastic;
foams & rubber
PA: Foamcraft Inc
9230 Harrison Park Ct
Indianapolis IN 46216
317 545-3626

(G-2861)
FOREST RIVER INC
2901 County Road 7 N (46514-5199)
PHONE...................................574 264-5179
Tony Cundiff, *Branch Mgr*
EMP: 164
SALES (corp-wide): 242.1B **Publicly
Held**
SIC: 3792 Tent-type camping trailers
HQ: Forest River, Inc.
900 County Road 1 N
Elkhart IN 46514

(G-2862)
FOREST RIVER INC
Dynamax
2745 Northland Dr (46514-7619)
P.O. Box 875 (46515-0875)
PHONE...................................574 262-3474
Peter J Liegl, *President*
EMP: 150
SALES (corp-wide): 242.1B **Publicly
Held**
SIC: 3716 3792 Motor homes; travel trail-
ers & campers
HQ: Forest River, Inc.
900 County Road 1 N
Elkhart IN 46514

(G-2863)
FOREST RIVER INC
Also Called: Battisti Customs
3601 County Road 6 E (46514-7664)
PHONE...................................574 262-5466
EMP: 2
SALES (corp-wide): 242.1B **Publicly
Held**
SIC: 3711 Buses, all types, assembly of
HQ: Forest River, Inc.
900 County Road 1 N
Elkhart IN 46514

(G-2864)
FOREST RIVER INC
Glaval Bus Division
914 County Road 1 N (46514-8992)
PHONE...................................574 262-2212
Phil Hayes, *General Mgr*
EMP: 250
SALES (corp-wide): 242.1B **Publicly
Held**
WEB: www.forestriverinc.com
SIC: 3792 Tent-type camping trailers
HQ: Forest River, Inc.
900 County Road 1 N
Elkhart IN 46514

(G-2865)
FOREST RIVER INC (HQ)
900 County Road 1 N (46514-8992)
P.O. Box 3030 (46515-3030)
PHONE...................................574 389-4600
Fax: 574 296-7558
Peter J Liegl, *President*
Brandon Lott, *General Mgr*
Kevin McArt, *General Mgr*
John Quake, *General Mgr*
Sandy Marschke, *Principal*
▼ EMP: 50
SQ FT: 100,000
SALES (est): 2.9B
SALES (corp-wide): 242.1B **Publicly
Held**
WEB: www.forestriverinc.com
SIC: 5561 3799 Recreational vehicle deal-
ers; recreational vehicles
PA: Berkshire Hathaway Inc.
3555 Farnam St Ste 1140
Omaha NE 68131
402 346-1400

(G-2866)
FOREST RIVER INC
3603 S Nappanee St (46517-1176)
PHONE...................................574 296-7700

Art Colvin, *General Mgr*
Terry Milarczyk, *Cardinal*
Shawn Kaylor, *Regl Sales Mgr*
EMP: 200
SALES (corp-wide): 242.1B **Publicly
Held**
WEB: www.forestriverinc.com
SIC: 3792 3716 5012 Travel trailers &
campers; motor homes; recreational vehi-
cles, motor homes & trailers
HQ: Forest River, Inc.
900 County Road 1 N
Elkhart IN 46514

(G-2867)
FOREST RIVER VIBE
411 County Road 15 (46516-9623)
PHONE...................................574 296-2084
EMP: 2
SALES (est): 202.6K **Privately Held**
SIC: 3792 Travel trailers & campers

(G-2868)
FORMAL AFFAIRS TUXEDO
SHOP
23797 Us Highway 33 (46517-3517)
PHONE...................................574 875-6654
Fax: 574 875-6622
Ingrid Powell, *Co-Owner*
EMP: 3
SALES: 300K **Privately Held**
SIC: 5621 7299 2311 5699 Boutiques;
bridal shops; computer photography or
portrait; tuxedos: made from purchased
materials; formal wear; invitation & sta-
tionery printing & engraving

(G-2869)
FRED SIBLEY SR
Also Called: Fred Sibley Enterprises
25551 Homewood Ave (46514-5025)
PHONE...................................574 264-2237
Fred Sibley Sr, *Owner*
EMP: 2
SQ FT: 5,500
SALES: 100K **Privately Held**
SIC: 3711 Automobile assembly, including
specialty automobiles

(G-2870)
FREDERICK TOOL CORP
24615 County Road 45 # 4 (46516-5957)
PHONE...................................574 295-6700
Jack Wait Sr, *President*
Nancy Wait, *Corp Secy*
Jack Wait Jr,
▲ EMP: 25
SQ FT: 80,000
SALES (est): 2.6MM **Privately Held**
WEB: www.fredericktool.com
SIC: 2491 3546 3545 3429 Wood prod-
ucts, creosoted; power-driven handtools;
machine tool accessories; manufactured
hardware (general); hand & edge tools

(G-2871)
FURRION LLC
52567 Independence Ct (46514-8173)
PHONE...................................574 327-6571
Aaron Fidler, *Mng Member*
Mark Lucas,
EMP: 15 EST: 2007
SQ FT: 16,800
SALES: 200MM
SALES (corp-wide): 19.3MM **Privately
Held**
WEB: www.furrion.com
SIC: 3663 Radio & TV communications
equipment
PA: Furrion Limited
Rm 505-508 5/F Cyberport 3 Core D
Pok Fu Lam HK
285 119-27

(G-2872)
FUSION WOOD PRODUCTS LLC
1600 W Mishawaka Rd (46517-9211)
PHONE...................................574 389-0307
Nathaniel Rhoden, *Mng Member*
EMP: 3
SQ FT: 68,000
SALES (est): 238.5K **Privately Held**
SIC: 2434 Wood kitchen cabinets

(G-2873)
FUTURE WAVE GRAPHICS INC
54257 County Road 7 Apt 4 (46514-3000)
P.O. Box 4568 (46515-4568)
PHONE....................574 389-8803
Laverne Dee Smith, Principal
Teru F Hendrey, Admin Sec
EMP: 9
SALES (est): 510K Privately Held
SIC: 3993 7373 Signs & advertising specialties; computer-aided engineering (CAE) systems service

(G-2874)
G4 TOOL AND TECHNOLOGY INC
1827 Fieldhouse Ave (46517-1316)
P.O. Box 1711 (46515-1711)
PHONE....................574 970-0844
Erin Mullet, President
EMP: 10
SALES (est): 1.3MM Privately Held
SIC: 3452 Bolts, nuts, rivets & washers

(G-2875)
GASKA TAPE INC
1810 W Lusher Ave (46517-1395)
P.O. Box 1968 (46515-1968)
PHONE....................574 294-5431
Fax: 574 293-4504
Jack Boyd Smith Jr, President
Cathy Ruff, General Mgr
Steve Noble, Engineer
Laura Sullivan, Human Res Mgr
Kate Liewald, Sales Mgr
▲ EMP: 100
SQ FT: 150,000
SALES (est): 26.5MM Privately Held
WEB: www.gaska.com
SIC: 3086 2821 3053 Insulation or cushioning material, foamed plastic; thermoplastic materials; gaskets, all materials

(G-2876)
GEMEINHARDT MUSICAL INSTR LLC
Also Called: Gemeinhardt Company, LLC
3302 S Nappanee St (46517-1096)
PHONE....................574 295-5280
Fax: 574 295-8323
Jennifer Baunoch, VP Opers
Kelli Gohn, Prdtn Mgr
Sharon Knepp, Sales Executive
Jennifer Crowell, Mktg Dir
Garland Garth, Info Tech Mgr
▲ EMP: 40
SQ FT: 33,000
SALES (est): 7.8MM Privately Held
WEB: www.gemeinhardt.com
SIC: 3931 5736 Piccolos & parts; flutes & parts; musical instrument stores
PA: Bp Music Holdings Llc
317 Madison Ave
New York NY
212 302-0066

(G-2877)
GENESIS PRODUCTS INC
Also Called: Welformed
2924 County Road 6 E (46514-7678)
PHONE....................574 262-4054
EMP: 20
SALES (corp-wide): 79.2MM Privately Held
SIC: 2522 Panel systems & partitions, office: except wood
PA: Genesis Products, Llc
2608 Almac Ct
Elkhart IN 46514
877 266-8292

(G-2878)
GENESIS PRODUCTS INC
Also Called: Genesis Products, Plant 2
3130 Tuscany Dr (46514-7649)
PHONE....................574 266-8293
Nick Bontrager, Accounts Mgr
Randy Muessig, Accounts Mgr
Caitlin Munch, Marketing Staff
Zack Nickell, Branch Mgr
Morgan Bond, Manager
EMP: 20

SALES (corp-wide): 79.2MM Privately Held
WEB: www.genesisproductsinc.com
SIC: 3479 7389 2431 Aluminum coating of metal products; laminating service; doors, wood
PA: Genesis Products, Llc
2608 Almac Ct
Elkhart IN 46514
877 266-8292

(G-2879)
GENESIS PRODUCTS LLC (PA)
2608 Almac Ct (46514-7628)
PHONE....................877 266-8292
Fax: 574 264-7189
Jonathan Helmuth, President
Dean Powell, Division VP
Matt Hazelbaker, Vice Pres
Jonathan Wenger, Vice Pres
Daniel Acker, Plant Mgr
▲ EMP: 120
SQ FT: 200,000
SALES (est): 79.2MM Privately Held
WEB: www.genesisproductsinc.com
SIC: 7389 2431 Laminating service; doors, wood

(G-2880)
GLACIER BOTTLING COMPANY LLC
23155 Old Us 20 (46516-9000)
PHONE....................574 293-0357
Yuri Cataldo, Principal
EMP: 4
SALES (est): 193.8K Privately Held
SIC: 2086 Water, pasteurized: packaged in cans, bottles, etc.

(G-2881)
GLAZE MFG CO
53612 Tara Ln (46514-9143)
PHONE....................574 612-1401
Philip A Glaze, President
EMP: 10
SALES (est): 50K Privately Held
SIC: 2657 Folding paperboard boxes

(G-2882)
GLOBAL BUILDING PRODUCTS LLC
1121 Herman St (46516-9030)
PHONE....................574 296-6868
Fax: 574 296-6878
Clayton Bjurstrom, Vice Pres
Andrew Carpenter, Mng Member
EMP: 28
SQ FT: 43,000
SALES: 8MM Privately Held
SIC: 3442 Window & door frames

(G-2883)
GLOBAL COMPOSITES INC
Also Called: Global Moulding
58190 County Road 3 (46517-9007)
PHONE....................574 522-9956
Fax: 574 523-0968
Gary L Beck, President
Todd Jones, General Mgr
William Lehman, Vice Pres
Jeff Godfrey, Purch Agent
Marsha Williams, Human Res Dir
EMP: 180
SALES (est): 46.2MM Privately Held
WEB: www.globalcomposites.net
SIC: 3229 Glass fibers, textile

(G-2884)
GLOBAL COMPOSITES INC ○
56807 Elk Park Dr (46516-1451)
PHONE....................574 522-0475
EMP: 2 EST: 2018
SALES (est): 62.6K Privately Held
SIC: 3296 Mineral wool

(G-2885)
GLOBAL GLASS INC
28967 Old Us 33 (46516-1600)
PHONE....................574 294-7681
Gary L Beck, President
Ann M Beck, Treasurer
Stephen M Beck, Admin Sec
EMP: 125
SQ FT: 36,000

SALES (est): 13.8MM Privately Held
WEB: www.globalcompositesinc.com
SIC: 3714 Motor vehicle body components & frame

(G-2886)
GLOBAL OZONE INNOVATIONS LLC
Also Called: Sanitation Equipment
425 Pine Creek Ct (46516-9089)
PHONE....................574 294-5797
Fax: 574 875-9335
Mark Eades,
Rik Kain,
EMP: 2
SALES (est): 250.9K Privately Held
SIC: 3949 5091 5941 7999 Sporting & athletic goods; sporting & recreation goods; sporting goods & bicycle shops; sporting goods rental; sanitation preparations, disinfectants & deodorants

(G-2887)
GLOBAL TRNSP ORGANIZATION LLC
3402 Reedy Dr (46514-7667)
PHONE....................574 226-6372
Dean Crane, Principal
Matthew Strefling, Principal
EMP: 3
SALES (est): 122.5K Privately Held
SIC: 3711 Automobile assembly, including specialty automobiles

(G-2888)
GLUEBOSS ADHESIVE COMPANY LLC
435 Harrison St (46516-2771)
PHONE....................855 458-2677
Phil Curtis, Principal
EMP: 7
SALES (est): 805.1K Privately Held
SIC: 2891 Adhesives

(G-2889)
GOLDEN-HELVEY HOLDINGS INC
1020 County Road 6 W (46514-8299)
PHONE....................574 266-4500
Fax: 574 266-8899
Mark Hillenburg II, President
Linda Boling, Manager
EMP: 10 EST: 1979
SALES (est): 178.3K Privately Held
SIC: 3721 Aircraft

(G-2890)
GOLDEN-HELVEY HOLDINGS INC
1020 County Road 6 W (46514-8299)
PHONE....................574 266-4500
Russell Golden, President
Steve Helvey, Vice Pres
EMP: 80
SQ FT: 55,000
SALES (est): 27.9MM Privately Held
WEB: www.kessington.com
SIC: 3728 3842 Aircraft parts & equipment; implants, surgical

(G-2891)
GOSHEN COACH INC
1826 Leer Dr (46514-5447)
PHONE....................574 970-6300
Troy Snyder, President
Peter Orthwein, Vice Pres
Michael Person, Vice Pres
Amy McCall, Marketing Mgr
Walter Bennett, Admin Sec
▼ EMP: 241
SALES (est): 563.8K Publicly Held
SIC: 3711 Buses, all types, assembly of
PA: Rev Group, Inc.
111 E Kilbourn Ave # 2600
Milwaukee WI 53202

(G-2892)
GR HUBER ENTERPRISES INC
21291 Buckingham Rd (46516-9703)
PHONE....................574 293-7113
Greg Huber, Principal
EMP: 4
SALES (est): 481.2K Privately Held
SIC: 3553 Cabinet makers' machinery

(G-2893)
GRANITECH
3954 Lexington Park Dr (46514-1157)
PHONE....................574 674-6988
Fax: 574 389-1305
Mark Fessenden, President
Rick Farrell Jr, Vice Pres
Steve Jones, Treasurer
▲ EMP: 25
SALES (est): 2.5MM Privately Held
WEB: www.granitech.net
SIC: 3281 2434 Marble, building: cut & shaped; wood kitchen cabinets

(G-2894)
GRAPHIC ARTS & PUBL SVCS
Also Called: Gaps
2121 Roys Ave (46517-2049)
PHONE....................574 294-1770
James Ollan, Owner
EMP: 3
SQ FT: 2,100
SALES (est): 200K Privately Held
SIC: 2752 7336 Commercial printing, offset; commercial art & graphic design

(G-2895)
GRAYSON GRAPHICS
3008 Mobile Dr (46514-5524)
PHONE....................574 264-6466
Lemar Mast, President
EMP: 2
SALES (est): 174.7K Privately Held
WEB: www.graysongraphics.com
SIC: 7336 3993 Commercial art & graphic design; signs & advertising specialties

(G-2896)
GREAT AMERICAN DESK CO INC
1600 W Mishawaka Rd (46517-9211)
P.O. Box 1816, La Porte (46352-1816)
PHONE....................574 293-3591
Kevin Clinton, President
David Gruber, Vice Pres
EMP: 14
SQ FT: 68,000
SALES (est): 2.8MM Privately Held
SIC: 2522 2521 Desks, office: except wood; wood office desks & tables

(G-2897)
GREAT LAKES FOREST PDTS INC
21658 Buckingham Rd (46516-9703)
PHONE....................574 389-9663
EMP: 29
SALES (corp-wide): 66MM Privately Held
SIC: 2421 Resawing lumber into smaller dimensions; lumber: rough, sawed or planed
PA: Great Lakes Forest Products, Inc.
21861 Protecta Dr
Elkhart IN 46516
574 389-9663

(G-2898)
GREAT LAKES FOREST PDTS INC (PA)
21861 Protecta Dr (46516-9544)
PHONE....................574 389-9663
Mark E Smith, President
Jennifer L Smith, Vice Pres
EMP: 93
SALES: 66MM Privately Held
SIC: 2421 5031 Resawing lumber into smaller dimensions; lumber: rough, sawed or planed; lumber, plywood & millwork

(G-2899)
GREEN STREAM COMPANY
29414 Phillips St (46514-1022)
P.O. Box 2341 (46515-2341)
PHONE....................574 293-1949
Amit Shah, President
EMP: 90
SQ FT: 66,000
SALES: 27.5MM Privately Held
SIC: 2448 4953 7699 Pallets, wood; recycling, waste materials; pallet repair

(G-2900)
GRIFFEN PLMBNG-HEATING-COOLING
Also Called: Griffen Plumbing & Heating
2310 Toledo Rd (46516-5537)
PHONE..............................574 295-2440
Fax: 574 295-2520
Todd Mikel, *President*
Todd Mikel, *President*
Dawn Mikel, *Vice Pres*
Debbie Anderson, *Bookkeeper*
Ron Wilson, *Manager*
EMP: 40 EST: 1982
SQ FT: 10,000
SALES (est): 4.3MM Privately Held
SIC: 1711 3585 Plumbing contractors; heating & air conditioning contractors; compressors for refrigeration & air conditioning equipment

(G-2901)
GVS TECHNOLOGIES LLC
5308 Beck Dr (46516-9251)
PHONE..............................574 293-0974
Fax: 574 293-0551
Dan Kirts, *Plant Mgr*
Donald L Breiter, *Treasurer*
Michelle Deleon, *Office Mgr*
Craig Thielen, *Manager*
Vince Scott,
◆ EMP: 18
SQ FT: 12,000
SALES (est): 4.1MM Privately Held
SIC: 3599 3544 Machine shop, jobbing & repair; special dies & tools

(G-2902)
H & A PRODUCTS INC
Also Called: Storm Trailers
28761 Holiday Pl (46517-1109)
P.O. Box 229, Osceola (46561-0229)
PHONE..............................574 226-0079
William D Aust, *President*
William Aust, *President*
EMP: 11
SALES (est): 1.5MM Privately Held
SIC: 2448 Cargo containers, wood & metal combination

(G-2903)
H JOHN ENTERPRISE INC
Also Called: Atlas Specialty Products
21066 Protecta Dr (46516-9537)
PHONE..............................574 293-6008
John Pfanzelt, *President*
Claudia Shumaker, *Corp Secy*
EMP: 25
SQ FT: 18,000
SALES (est): 4.6MM Privately Held
SIC: 3715 2531 Demountable cargo containers; public building & related furniture

(G-2904)
HACH COMPANY
3504 Henke St (46514-7653)
P.O. Box 389, Loveland CO (80539-0389)
PHONE..............................574 262-2060
EMP: 3
SALES (est): 388.9K Privately Held
SIC: 3826 Analytical instruments

(G-2905)
HADLEY PRODUCTS CORPORATION
Hadley Rv, Transit B.u
319 Roske Dr (46516-9084)
PHONE..............................574 266-3700
Michaele Dutton, *Manager*
EMP: 15
SALES (corp-wide): 177.4MM Privately Held
WEB: www.hadley-products.com
SIC: 3799 Trailers & trailer equipment
HQ: Hadley Products Corporation
2851 Prairie St Sw Ste A
Grandville MI 49418
616 530-1717

(G-2906)
HAMPELS WOODLAND PRODUCTS
61292 County Road 7 (46517-8945)
PHONE..............................574 293-2124
EMP: 3
SALES (est): 207.5K Privately Held
SIC: 2491 Wood products, creosoted

(G-2907)
HARMAN MACHINE & ENGINEERING
53905 County Road 9 Ste C (46514-5012)
PHONE..............................574 266-5015
James Harman, *President*
Steven Walls, *Vice Pres*
EMP: 7
SALES: 750K Privately Held
SIC: 3599 Machine & other job shop work

(G-2908)
HARMAN PROFESSIONAL INC
Crown Audio
1718 W Mishawaka Rd (46517-9439)
PHONE..............................574 294-8000
Frank Meredith, *Corp Secy*
Susan Whitfield, *Engineer*
Brian Wachtman, *Electrical Engi*
John Bolstetter, *CFO*
Marc Kellom, *Branch Mgr*
EMP: 450
SQ FT: 200,000
SALES (corp-wide): 148.1B Privately Held
SIC: 3651 3663 3823 Amplifiers: radio, public address or musical instrument; microphones; household audio equipment; transmitting apparatus, radio or television; analyzers, industrial process type
HQ: Harman Professional, Inc.
8500 Balboa Blvd
Northridge CA 91329
818 893-8411

(G-2909)
HART PLASTICS INC
Also Called: Harl Plastics
2907 Park Six Ct (46514-5445)
PHONE..............................574 264-7060
Blake C Miller, *President*
Jennifer White, *Sales Mgr*
EMP: 20
SQ FT: 20,800
SALES (est): 3.4MM Privately Held
SIC: 3089 3714 3429 Thermoformed finished plastic products; motor vehicle parts & accessories; manufactured hardware (general)

(G-2910)
HAVOC MOTOR COMPANY LLC ✪
207 Parkview Ave E (46514-5890)
PHONE..............................973 407-9933
Phil Kozak,
EMP: 4 EST: 2017
SALES (est): 125.1K Privately Held
SIC: 3999 Manufacturing industries

(G-2911)
HAWK ENTERPRISES ELKHART INC (PA)
2902 Park Six Ct (46514-5445)
PHONE..............................574 264-6772
Fax: 574 294-1910
Tom Kershner Jr, *President*
Patrick Rosenlieb, *VP Sales*
▼ EMP: 10
SQ FT: 20,000
SALES (est): 2.5MM Privately Held
WEB: www.hawkenterprises.com
SIC: 3589 Floor washing & polishing machines, commercial

(G-2912)
HELGESON STEEL INC
1130 Verdant St Ste 1 (46516-9330)
PHONE..............................574 293-5576
Fax: 574 293-7099
Fred Helgeson, *President*
Steve Lusher, *Project Mgr*
Joshua Matthews, *Project Mgr*
Nick Bayer, *Sales Mgr*
Bob Gearhart, *Manager*
EMP: 14
SQ FT: 25,000
SALES (est): 3.8MM Privately Held
WEB: www.helgesonsteel.com
SIC: 3441 Building components, structural steel

(G-2913)
HENSLEY COMPOSITES LLC
1705 W Lexington Ave (46514-1941)
PHONE..............................574 202-3840
Dana Cummings, *Co-Founder*
EMP: 3
SALES (est): 238K Privately Held
SIC: 3999 Manufacturing industries

(G-2914)
HERITAGE FINANCIAL GROUP INC (PA)
120 W Lexington Ave # 200 (46516-3117)
PHONE..............................574 522-8000
Fax: 574 522-1801
L Craig Fulmer, *Ch of Bd*
Dan A Morrison, *Co-CEO*
Brian J Smith, *Co-CEO*
Sharon Martin, *Corp Secy*
Debbie Miller, *Loan Officer*
EMP: 55
SQ FT: 75,000
SALES (est): 15.5MM Privately Held
WEB: www.hfgnet.com
SIC: 6531 6141 5521 2451 Real estate managers; consumer finance companies; financing: automobiles, furniture, etc., not a deposit bank; used car dealers; mobile homes; mobile home site operators; financial consultant

(G-2915)
HEYWOOD WILLIAMS INC
601 County Road 17 (46516-9505)
PHONE..............................574 295-8400
Fax: 574 295-1249
Larry Campbell, *President*
EMP: 7 EST: 2011
SALES (est): 782.8K Privately Held
SIC: 3083 Laminated plastics plate & sheet

(G-2916)
HIGHWATER MARINE LLC (PA)
Also Called: Godfrey Marine
4500 Middlebury St (46516-9068)
P.O. Box 1158 (46515-1158)
PHONE..............................574 522-8381
Fax: 574 522-5120
Tim Price, *Manager*
Richard V Gasaway, *Officer*
James Orbik,
▼ EMP: 99
SALES (est): 38.2MM Privately Held
SIC: 3732 Boats, fiberglass: building & repairing

(G-2917)
HINGECRAFT CORPORATION
3601 Lexington Park Dr (46514-1165)
PHONE..............................574 293-6543
Fax: 574 293-3199
Lanny Rogers, *President*
Scott Rogers, *Vice Pres*
Shelley Rogers, *Treasurer*
Carolyn Rogers, *Admin Sec*
EMP: 15 EST: 1976
SQ FT: 50,000
SALES (est): 3.1MM Privately Held
WEB: www.hingecraft.com
SIC: 3429 Builders' hardware; door opening & closing devices, except electrical

(G-2918)
HOLLAND METAL FAB INC
1550 W Lusher Ave (46517-1422)
P.O. Box 1914 (46515-1914)
PHONE..............................574 522-1434
Ted Holland, *President*
Lana Holland, *Admin Sec*
EMP: 15
SQ FT: 19,000
SALES (est): 2.1MM Privately Held
SIC: 3429 Manufactured hardware (general)

(G-2919)
HOMETTE CORPORATION (HQ)
Also Called: Skyline Mainsfield
2520 Bypass Rd (46514-1518)
P.O. Box 743 (46515-0743)
PHONE..............................574 294-6521
Thomas Deranek, *Ch of Bd*
John Pilarski, *CFO*
EMP: 7
SQ FT: 8,000
SALES (est): 61.3MM
SALES (corp-wide): 236.5MM Publicly Held
SIC: 2452 3792 Modular homes, prefabricated, wood; travel trailers & campers
PA: Skyline Champion Corporation
2520 Bypass Rd
Elkhart IN 46514
574 294-6521

(G-2920)
HOOSIER CRANE SERVICE COMPANY
3500 Charlotte Ave (46517-1191)
PHONE..............................574 523-2945
Fax: 574 253-2916
Thomas R Schmidt II, *President*
Jon Harkrider, *Vice Pres*
Laura Yoder, *Sales Staff*
EMP: 30
SQ FT: 29,000
SALES (est): 6.9MM Privately Held
WEB: www.hoosiercrane.com
SIC: 7389 3536 Crane & aerial lift service; cranes, overhead traveling

(G-2921)
HOSE & GO
2623 S Nappanee St (46517-1083)
PHONE..............................574 295-7800
Stephen Lotsbaich, *Owner*
EMP: 2
SALES (est): 134.6K Privately Held
SIC: 3589 Car washing machinery

(G-2922)
HOWARD & SONS CEMENT PRODUCTS
2912 Oakland Ave (46517-1507)
PHONE..............................574 293-1906
James Howard, *President*
Susan Howard, *Treasurer*
EMP: 6
SQ FT: 3,360
SALES (est): 704.3K Privately Held
SIC: 3272 Burial vaults, concrete or precast terrazzo

(G-2923)
HUNTINGTON ALLOYS CORPORATION
2900 Higgins Blvd (46514-5449)
PHONE..............................574 262-3451
Wiliam Belcher, *Branch Mgr*
EMP: 39
SALES (corp-wide): 242.1B Publicly Held
WEB: www.smwpc.com
SIC: 3356 Nickel & nickel alloy pipe, plates, sheets, etc.
HQ: Huntington Alloys Corporation
3200 Riverside Dr
Huntington WV 25705
304 526-5100

(G-2924)
HY-LINE ENTERPRISES INTL INC
25369 Vernon Xing (46514-6260)
PHONE..............................574 294-1112
Fax: 574 293-4672
Mark Horita, *President*
Holly O'Hara, *Chairman*
Scott Dawson, *CFO*
▼ EMP: 75
SQ FT: 36,100
SALES (est): 10.9MM Privately Held
WEB: www.hylinetrailers.com
SIC: 3792 Travel trailers & campers; travel trailer chassis; house trailers, except as permanent dwellings

(G-2925)
HYCO MACHINE & MOLD INC
121 Rush Ct (46516-9644)
PHONE..............................574 522-5847
Fax: 574 522-5847
Barbara High, *President*
Ron High, *Corp Secy*
EMP: 3
SQ FT: 6,000
SALES: 110K Privately Held
SIC: 3599 Machine shop, jobbing & repair

(G-2926)
HYDRO EXTRUDER LLC
3406 Reedy Dr (46516-7667)
PHONE..............................574 262-2667
Charles Straface, *CEO*
Pat Wooley, *Sales Dir*
EMP: 121
SALES (corp-wide): 13.8B **Privately Held**
SIC: 3354 Aluminum extruded products
HQ: Hydro Extruder, Llc
    Airport Offc Park
    Moon Township PA 15108

(G-2927)
IAM AW TL DIE MAKERS LL 229
2618 Lowell Ave (46516-5707)
PHONE..............................574 333-5955
Dennis Williams, *Principal*
EMP: 2
SALES (est): 142.1K **Privately Held**
SIC: 3544 Special dies & tools

(G-2928)
IKON GROUP
330 E Windsor Ave (46514-5565)
PHONE..............................574 326-3661
Brandon Ambris, *Owner*
EMP: 7
SALES (est): 609.5K **Privately Held**
SIC: 3799 Recreational vehicles

(G-2929)
IMPACT TRAILERS
4607 Wyland Dr (46516-9600)
PHONE..............................574 322-4369
EMP: 2
SALES (est): 74.2K **Privately Held**
SIC: 3715 Truck trailers

(G-2930)
IMPERIAL STAMPING CORPORATION
Also Called: Imperial Stamping Company
4801 Middlebury St (46516-9054)
PHONE..............................574 294-3780
John Conner, *President*
Donald Mossey, *Chairman*
Allan J Ludwig, *Corp Secy*
▲ **EMP:** 100
SQ FT: 100,000
SALES (est): 16.1MM **Privately Held**
SIC: 3469 7692 3452 3446 Stamping
metal for the trade; welding repair; bolts,
nuts, rivets & washers; architectural met-
alwork; fabricated structural metal

(G-2931)
INDIANA MICRO MET ETCHING INC
4615 Wyland Dr (46516-9600)
PHONE..............................574 293-3342
Leanne Brekke, *President*
Steve Zimmerman, *Office Mgr*
EMP: 10
SQ FT: 9,000
SALES: 500K **Privately Held**
WEB: www.imei.net
SIC: 3599 Chemical milling job shop

(G-2932)
INDIANA PLASTICS INC
2221 Industrial Pkwy (46516-5497)
PHONE..............................574 294-3253
Jeff Kruis, *President*
Marla Williams, *Corp Secy*
James Kruis, *Vice Pres*
▲ **EMP:** 30
SQ FT: 30,000
SALES (est): 6.8MM **Privately Held**
WEB: www.indianaplastics.com
SIC: 3089 Injection molding of plastics

(G-2933)
INDUSTRIAL AXLE COMPANY LLC
21611 Protecta Dr (46516-9543)
PHONE..............................574 294-6651
EMP: 70
SALES (corp-wide): 245.3MM **Privately Held**
SIC: 3714 Axles, motor vehicle
HQ: Industrial Axle Company, Llc
    21608 Protecta Dr
    Elkhart IN 46516
    574 295-6077

(G-2934)
INDUSTRIAL AXLE COMPANY LLC (DH)
21608 Protecta Dr (46516-9532)
PHONE..............................574 295-6077
Adam Dexter, *President*
Bernie Bolka, *CFO*
EMP: 69
SALES (est): 66MM
SALES (corp-wide): 245.3MM **Privately Held**
SIC: 3714 Axles, motor vehicle

(G-2935)
INNOCOR FOAM TECH - ACP INC
1900 W Lusher Ave (46517-1310)
P.O. Box 2057 (46515-2057)
PHONE..............................574 294-7694
Jerry Eagon, *President*
EMP: 11
SALES (corp-wide): 209.9MM **Privately Held**
SIC: 3069 Bathmats, rubber
HQ: Innocor Foam Technologies - Acp, Inc.
    200 Schulz Dr Ste 2
    Red Bank NJ 07701
    732 945-6222

(G-2936)
INTEGRA CERTIFIED DOCUMENT
605 Mason St (46516-2760)
PHONE..............................574 295-4611
Patrick McCoy,
EMP: 3
SALES (est): 292.9K **Privately Held**
SIC: 3559 Tire shredding machinery

(G-2937)
INTEGRATED BIOMEDICAL TECH
2931 Moose Trl (46514-8230)
PHONE..............................574 264-0025
Wen Wu, *President*
Susan Wu, *Mktg Dir*
EMP: 10
SQ FT: 2,000
SALES: 1MM **Privately Held**
WEB: www.ibtbiomed.com
SIC: 3841 Diagnostic apparatus, medical

(G-2938)
INTERGLOBAL WAY NETWORK LLC
3002 Coast Ct (46514-5504)
PHONE..............................574 971-4490
James L Conway, *Mng Member*
Wayne E Kaylor,
▲ **EMP:** 3
SQ FT: 13,000
SALES (est): 820.4K **Privately Held**
SIC: 3261 Sinks, vitreous china

(G-2939)
IRISH CUPCAKES INC
58727 Baugo Cove Dr (46517-8684)
PHONE..............................574 289-8669
Deborah Rappaport, *Principal*
EMP: 4 **EST:** 2013
SALES (est): 213K **Privately Held**
SIC: 2051 Bread, cake & related products

(G-2940)
IRVINE SHADE & DOOR INC (PA)
Also Called: Irvine Window Coverings
1000 Verdant St (46516-9042)
PHONE..............................574 522-1446
Fax: 574 522-0568
Ben D Mausar Sr, *President*
Ron Green, *President*
Nick Donis, *Vice Pres*
▲ **EMP:** 95
SQ FT: 7,500
SALES (est): 12.5MM **Privately Held**
SIC: 2591 3089 2431 Window blinds;
doors, folding: plastic or plastic coated
fabric; millwork

(G-2941)
J J BABBITT CO
2201 Industrial Pkwy (46516-5486)
P.O. Box 1264 (46515-1264)
PHONE..............................574 315-1639
Fax: 574 293-9465
William Reglein, *President*
Eugene Reglein, *Chairman*
▲ **EMP:** 2 **EST:** 1919
SQ FT: 20,000
SALES (est): 275.2K **Privately Held**
WEB: www.jjbabbitt.com
SIC: 3931 Mouthpieces for musical instru-
ments

(G-2942)
J P INDUSTRIES INC
Also Called: Keline Manufacturing
726 Middleton Run Rd (46516-5424)
PHONE..............................574 293-8763
James E Pettit, *President*
EMP: 10
SALES (est): 1.2MM **Privately Held**
WEB: www.jpengraving.com
SIC: 3743 7389 Railroad equipment; en-
graving service

(G-2943)
J V C RUBBER STAMP COMPANY
816 W Beardsley Ave (46514-2230)
PHONE..............................574 293-0113
Fax: 574 293-0113
Ronald Cataldo, *President*
Nancy Cataldo, *Vice Pres*
EMP: 2
SQ FT: 300
SALES (est): 147.6K **Privately Held**
SIC: 3953 Marking devices

(G-2944)
JAM-KO ENGINEERING COMPANY
21496 Buckingham Rd (46516-9786)
PHONE..............................574 294-7684
Ashok Gupta, *President*
Tyler Whitlow, *General Mgr*
Madhu Gupta, *Vice Pres*
Dave Adam, *Project Engr*
Wayne Kohout, *Supervisor*
EMP: 15 **EST:** 1962
SQ FT: 26,000
SALES (est): 2.6MM **Privately Held**
WEB: www.jamko.com
SIC: 3469 3544 Stamping metal for the
trade; special dies & tools

(G-2945)
JASON INDUSTRIES INC
1500 W Lusher Ave (46517-1422)
PHONE..............................574 294-7595
Fax: 574 522-4874
Lon Franklin, *CEO*
Carol Franklin, *Corp Secy*
Julie Costello, *Executive*
EMP: 86
SALES (est): 27.8MM **Privately Held**
WEB: www.jasoncaps.com
SIC: 3792 5013 Pickup covers, canopies
or caps; automotive supplies & parts;
truck parts & accessories

(G-2946)
JEC STEEL COMPANY (PA)
1137 Verdant St (46516-9045)
PHONE..............................574 326-3829
Jeremy Seniff, *CEO*
EMP: 8
SALES (est): 110K **Privately Held**
SIC: 4212 3325 Steel hauling, local; steel
foundries

(G-2947)
JESSEN MANUFACTURING CO INC
1409 W Beardsley Ave (46514-1827)
P.O. Box 549 (46515-0549)
PHONE..............................574 295-3836
Fax: 574 522-2962
Mark C Jessen, *President*
John Jessen, *COO*
John H Jessen Jr, *Vice Pres*
Douglas Bare, *Safety Mgr*
Jerry Duval, *Purch Mgr*
EMP: 70 **EST:** 1923

SQ FT: 90,000
SALES (est): 19.4MM **Privately Held**
SIC: 3451 Screw machine products

(G-2948)
JET TECHNOLOGIES INC
53893 N Park Ave (46514-5008)
P.O. Box 2848 (46515-2848)
PHONE..............................574 264-3613
Fax: 574 264-3209
Todd G Sullivan, *President*
Jayme Derr, *Vice Pres*
Don Jones, *Manager*
EMP: 50
SQ FT: 35,000
SALES: 10.9MM **Privately Held**
WEB: www.jettechinc.com
SIC: 3089 Injection molding of plastics;
thermoformed finished plastic products

(G-2949)
JMS ELECTRONICS CORPORATION
4400 Wyland Dr (46516-9520)
PHONE..............................574 522-0246
Fax: 574 522-0457
Alex Saharian, *President*
Mike Saharian, *COO*
Matthew Kain, *Vice Pres*
Don Fraser, *Senior Buyer*
John Weber, *Engineer*
▲ **EMP:** 50
SQ FT: 33,000
SALES (est): 10.7MM **Privately Held**
WEB: www.polytron-corp.com
SIC: 3556 3625 3621 Smoking or roast-
ing machinery, including ovens; electric
controls & control accessories; industrial;
motors & generators

(G-2950)
JOLAR ENTERPRISES
58052 Ox Bow Dr (46516-6340)
PHONE..............................574 875-8369
Joyce Parker, *Partner*
Raymond Parker, *Partner*
EMP: 2
SALES (est): 131.7K **Privately Held**
SIC: 2499 5719 Decorative wood & wood-
work; housewares

(G-2951)
JPC LLC
Also Called: Jpc Mat
2926 Paul Dr (46514-8796)
PHONE..............................574 293-8030
Greg Haradine,
▲ **EMP:** 12
SALES: 1.5MM **Privately Held**
SIC: 3069 2273 5561 Mats or matting,
rubber; carpets & rugs; recreational vehi-
cle parts & accessories

(G-2952)
JUS RITE ENGINEERING INC
56977 Elk Ct (46516-1460)
PHONE..............................574 522-9600
Fax: 574 522-0685
David A Bratton, *President*
John Binns, *President*
George P Kelsey, *Vice Pres*
EMP: 28
SQ FT: 26,000
SALES (est): 4.8MM **Privately Held**
WEB: www.jus-rite.com
SIC: 3544 Jigs & fixtures; jigs: inspection,
gauging & checking

(G-2953)
K & K INC
2617 Glenview Dr (46514-8709)
PHONE..............................574 266-8040
Fax: 574 266-9872
Kirk Blank, *President*
Kevin Blank, *General Mgr*
EMP: 16
SQ FT: 18,000
SALES (est): 3MM **Privately Held**
WEB: www.intertoolgroup.com
SIC: 3544 3543 Special dies & tools; in-
dustrial patterns

(G-2954)
K C MACHINE INC
56850 Elk Park Dr (46516-1450)
PHONE..............................574 293-1822

▲ = Import ▼=Export
◆ =Import/Export

Fax: 574 522-2995
Gerald D Cline, *President*
Linda J Cline, *Corp Secy*
EMP: 8 **EST:** 1978
SQ FT: 5,000
SALES (est): 904.7K **Privately Held**
SIC: 3544 3599 Jigs & fixtures; special dies & tools; machine & other job shop work; custom machinery; machine shop, jobbing & repair

(G-2955)
K MIN
2730 Industrial Pkwy (46516-5401)
PHONE..................................574 296-3500
Fax: 574 296-3569
Tina Leonard, *Principal*
EMP: 4
SALES (est): 519.8K **Privately Held**
SIC: 3714 Motor vehicle parts & accessories

(G-2956)
KAMPCO STEEL PRODUCTS INC
57533 County Road 3 (46517-9502)
PHONE..................................574 294-5466
Francis E Freel, *President*
Sue Freel, *Vice Pres*
James Kamp, *Vice Pres*
Tammy Victor, *Sales Associate*
Susan Freel, *Admin Sec*
EMP: 29
SQ FT: 80,000
SALES (est): 6.8MM **Privately Held**
WEB: www.kampco.com
SIC: 3714 Motor vehicle parts & accessories; motor vehicle body components & frame

(G-2957)
KDS INDUSTRIES LLC
21790 Beck Dr (46516-9742)
PHONE..................................574 333-2720
EMP: 2 **EST:** 2012
SALES (est): 98.9K **Privately Held**
SIC: 2231 Upholstery fabrics, wool

(G-2958)
KELLMARK CORPORATION
2501 Ada Dr (46514-8644)
PHONE..................................574 264-9695
George Kelly, *President*
Sue Garber, *President*
Luke A Latimer, *Exec VP*
James J Kelly, *Vice Pres*
Michael W Koestler, *Vice Pres*
EMP: 50
SQ FT: 40,000
SALES (est): 7.5MM **Privately Held**
WEB: www.kellmark.net
SIC: 2752 2771 5199 3993 Calendars, lithographed; greeting cards; calendars; signs & advertising specialties

(G-2959)
KEM KREST CORPORATION
2040 Toledo Rd (46516-5541)
P.O. Box 2977 (46515-2977)
PHONE..................................574 389-2650
Fax: 574 389-2694
Caine Espinoza, *Analyst*
EMP: 11
SALES (est): 2.2MM **Privately Held**
SIC: 2819 Industrial inorganic chemicals

(G-2960)
KEM KREST DEFENSE LLC
3221 Magnum Dr (46516-9021)
PHONE..................................574 389-2650
Amish Shah,
EMP: 10
SALES (est): 631.3K
SALES (corp-wide): 210.8MM **Privately Held**
SIC: 3728 Aircraft parts & equipment
PA: Kem Krest Llc
3221 Magnum Dr
Elkhart IN 46516
574 389-2650

(G-2961)
KENNYLEEHOLMESCOM
25855 Kiser Ct (46514-5226)
PHONE..................................574 612-2526
Kenneth Holmes, *Owner*
Sarah Holmes, *Co-Owner*

EMP: 2
SALES: 10K **Privately Held**
SIC: 7221 2396 5699 7336 Photographic studios, portrait; screen printing on fabric articles; customized clothing & apparel; commercial art & graphic design; screen printing; marketing consulting services

(G-2962)
KESSINGTON LLC
Also Called: Kessington Machine Products
1020 County Road 6 W (46514-8299)
PHONE..................................574 266-4500
Rob Frank, *Prdtn Mgr*
Scott Kolakowski, *Controller*
Graham Vrabel, *Manager*
Linda Boling, *Technology*
Kevin Bailey, *Executive*
EMP: 80
SALES (est): 19.3MM **Privately Held**
SIC: 3365 Aerospace castings, aluminum

(G-2963)
KEYSTONE AUTOMOTIVE INDS INC
2304 Charlotte Ave (46517-1196)
PHONE..................................574 206-1421
Fax: 574 294-2633
Chris Brown, *Manager*
EMP: 6
SALES (corp-wide): 9.7B **Publicly Held**
WEB: www.kool-vue.com
SIC: 3471 7532 Plating of metals or formed products; collision shops, automotive
HQ: Keystone Automotive Industries, Inc.
655 Grassmere Park
Nashville TN 37211
615 781-5200

(G-2964)
KIBBECHEM INC
1139 All Pro Dr (46514-8811)
PHONE..................................574 266-1234
W Glen Kibbe, *President*
Glenn E Killoren, *Principal*
Shane Kibbe, *Exec VP*
Shannon Rice, *Exec VP*
Nci Schemahorn, *Purchasing*
▲ **EMP:** 28
SQ FT: 85,000
SALES (est): 7MM **Privately Held**
SIC: 2899 2865 2816 3086 Foam charge mixtures; color pigments, organic; color pigments; plastics foam products; extruded finished plastic products

(G-2965)
KIEL NA LLC
Also Called: Kiel North America
2009 Middlebury St (46516-5522)
PHONE..................................574 293-3600
Mark Walter, *Finance*
Nicholas R Gwynne, *Mng Member*
Gerhard Hellweg,
▲ **EMP:** 15
SQ FT: 20,000
SALES (est): 3.9MM
SALES (corp-wide): 69.6MM **Privately Held**
SIC: 3713 3743 3499 Truck & bus bodies; train cars & equipment, freight or passenger; automobile seat frames, metal
PA: Franz Kiel Gmbh
Nurnberger Str. 62
Nordlingen 86720
908 121-030

(G-2966)
KIK AEROSOL SOCAL LLC
Also Called: Kik Custom Pdts Los Angeles
1919 Superior St (46516-4707)
PHONE..................................626 363-6200
Jeffrey M Nodland,
▲ **EMP:** 135
SQ FT: 183,000
SALES (est): 9.6MM **Privately Held**
SIC: 2813 Aerosols

(G-2967)
KIK CUSTOM PRODUCTS
1919 Superior St (46516-4707)
PHONE..................................574 294-8695
Dan Williams, *Senior VP*
Tom Kelliher, *Vice Pres*
Dave Klotter, *Vice Pres*

Aaron Brewer, *Prdtn Mgr*
Jason Rump, *Opers Staff*
EMP: 200
SALES (corp-wide): 97.2MM **Privately Held**
SIC: 2842 Specialty cleaning, polishes & sanitation goods
PA: Kik Operating Partnership
101 Macintosh Blvd
Concord ON L4K 4
905 660-0444

(G-2968)
KIK CUSTOM PRODUCTS INC
Also Called: Kik Custom Manufacuring
2730 Middlebury St (46516-5509)
PHONE..................................574 295-0000
Fax: 574 296-1700
Chris Keough, *Project Mgr*
Rema Kunder, *Project Mgr*
Jennifer Moosekian, *Project Mgr*
Alexander Merkel, *Opers Mgr*
Lloyd Moore, *Opers Mgr*
EMP: 29
SALES (corp-wide): 990.7K **Privately Held**
SIC: 7389 2796 2812 Packaging & labeling services; stereotype plates; alkalies
PA: Kik Custom Products Inc
101 Macintosh Blvd
Concord ON L4K 4
905 660-0444

(G-2969)
KINRO MANUFACTURING INC
3501 County Road 6 E (46514-7663)
PHONE..................................574 535-1125
Allan Hammond, *Manager*
EMP: 114
SALES (corp-wide): 2.1B **Publicly Held**
SIC: 3442 Shutters, door or window: metal
HQ: Kinro Manufacturing, Inc.
200 Mmaroneck Ave Ste 301
White Plains NY 10601
817 483-7791

(G-2970)
KINRO MANUFACTURING INC
3501 County Road 6 E (46514-7663)
PHONE..................................574 535-1125
Edward Vonier, *Branch Mgr*
EMP: 175
SALES (corp-wide): 2.1B **Publicly Held**
SIC: 3442 3231 Storm doors or windows, metal; metal doors; products of purchased glass
HQ: Kinro Manufacturing, Inc.
200 Mmaroneck Ave Ste 301
White Plains NY 10601
817 483-7791

(G-2971)
KINRO MANUFACTURING INC (HQ)
Also Called: Starquest Products
3501 County Road 6 E (46514-7663)
PHONE..................................574 535-1125
Jason Lippert, *President*
Scott Mereness, *Principal*
Dominic Gattuso, *Vice Pres*
Refugio Resendiz Estrad, *Plant Mgr*
Michelle Prough, *Materials Mgr*
▲ **EMP:** 35
SQ FT: 9,500
SALES (est): 405.5MM
SALES (corp-wide): 2.1B **Publicly Held**
WEB: www.kinro.com
SIC: 3442 Screen doors, metal; screens, window, metal; storm doors or windows, metal
PA: Lci Industries
3501 County Road 6 E
Elkhart IN 46514
574 535-1125

(G-2972)
KINRO MANUFACTURING INC
3501 County Road 6 E (46514-7663)
PHONE..................................574 535-1125
Jamie Bradley, *Manager*
EMP: 90
SALES (corp-wide): 2.1B **Publicly Held**
WEB: www.kinro.com
SIC: 3442 Screen doors, metal; screens, window, metal; storm doors or windows, metal

HQ: Kinro Manufacturing, Inc.
3501 County Road 6 E
Elkhart IN 46514
574 535-1125

(G-2973)
KOBELCO CMPSR MFG IND INC
3000 Hammond Ave (46516-5919)
PHONE..................................574 295-3145
Fax: 574 293-1641
Kevin O Neill, *President*
Jay Killian, *Vice Pres*
▲ **EMP:** 55 **EST:** 1965
SQ FT: 86,000
SALES: 14MM
SALES (corp-wide): 17.6B **Privately Held**
WEB: www.kocoa.com
SIC: 3563 3599 Air & gas compressors including vacuum pumps; machine shop, jobbing & repair
HQ: Kobe Steel Usa Holdings Inc.
535 Madison Ave Fl 5
New York NY 10022
212 751-9400

(G-2974)
KONAL AUTOMATED SYSTEMS INC
1500 W Hively Ave Ste E (46517-4033)
P.O. Box 100, Centreville MI (49032-0100)
PHONE..................................616 659-4774
Douglas Lammon, *President*
EMP: 75
SQ FT: 10,000
SALES: 5MM **Privately Held**
SIC: 3599 Air intake filters, internal combustion engine, except auto

(G-2975)
KROGER CO
130 W Hively Ave (46517-2113)
PHONE..................................574 294-6092
Joseph Glau, *Branch Mgr*
Brandon Wagner, *Manager*
EMP: 54
SALES (corp-wide): 122.6B **Publicly Held**
WEB: www.kroger.com
SIC: 5411 2051 Supermarkets, chain; bread, cake & related products
PA: The Kroger Co
1014 Vine St Ste 1000
Cincinnati OH 45202
513 762-4000

(G-2976)
KRUIS MOLD & ENGINEERING INC
2221 Industrial Pkwy (46516-5409)
PHONE..................................574 293-4613
Jeff Kruis, *President*
Marla Williams, *Corp Secy*
James Kruis, *Vice Pres*
▲ **EMP:** 16
SQ FT: 13,000
SALES (est): 2.5MM **Privately Held**
SIC: 3544 Industrial molds

(G-2977)
L E JOHNSON PRODUCTS INC (PA)
Also Called: Johnson Hardware
2100 Sterling Ave (46516-4909)
PHONE..................................574 293-5664
Larry A Johnson, *President*
Larry Johnson, *President*
Stephen Johnson, *Vice Pres*
Daniel Schroeder, *Maint Spvr*
John Connon, *Purch Agent*
◆ **EMP:** 93 **EST:** 1959
SQ FT: 200,000
SALES (est): 29.4MM **Privately Held**
WEB: www.johnsonhardware.com
SIC: 3429 Door opening & closing devices, except electrical; furniture hardware

(G-2978)
L E JOHNSON PRODUCTS INC
1133 E Lusher Ave (46516)
PHONE..................................574 293-5664
Larry Johnson, *Branch Mgr*
EMP: 117

SALES (corp-wide): 29.4MM **Privately Held**
SIC: 3429 Door opening & closing devices, except electrical
PA: L E Johnson Products Inc
2100 Sterling Ave
Elkhart IN 46516
574 293-5664

(G-2979)
L S R CONVERSIONS LLC
25771 Miner Rd (46514-5019)
PHONE......................574 206-9610
Fax: 574 206-1870
Sherry Ragland,
Lorri Huspetter,
EMP: 10
SQ FT: 18,000
SALES (est): 990.1K **Privately Held**
SIC: 3792 Travel trailers & campers

(G-2980)
LA MICHOACANA
246 W Lusher Ave (46517-2009)
PHONE......................574 293-9799
Adam Corona, *Principal*
EMP: 5
SALES (est): 417K **Privately Held**
SIC: 2024 Ice cream, bulk

(G-2981)
LABEL LOGIC INC
516 Pine Creek Ct (46516-9093)
P.O. Box 3002 (46515-3002)
PHONE......................574 266-6007
Karen Cripe, *President*
Doug Williams, *General Mgr*
Jeff Cripe, *Vice Pres*
EMP: 38
SQ FT: 48,000
SALES: 10MM **Privately Held**
WEB: www.labellogic1.com
SIC: 2759 Labels & seals: printing

(G-2982)
LACAY FABRICATION AND MFG INC
2801 Glenview Dr (46514-8711)
PHONE......................574 288-4678
Fax: 574 288-2921
Maryann Lacay, *CEO*
Ann M Filley, *President*
EMP: 24
SQ FT: 54,000
SALES (est): 10MM **Privately Held**
WEB: www.lacayfab.com
SIC: 3441 Fabricated structural metal

(G-2983)
LAKE COPPER CONDUCTORS LLC
4430 Eastland Dr (46516-9034)
PHONE......................847 238-3000
Emile Tohme, *President*
Mary Oziemkowski, *CFO*
William Ginter, *Accountant*
William L Runzel,
▲ EMP: 10
SALES (est): 3.5MM **Privately Held**
SIC: 3351 Wire, copper & copper alloy

(G-2984)
LANDJET INTERNATIONAL
21240 Protecta Dr (46516-9535)
PHONE......................574 970-7805
John Dingle, *President*
EMP: 15
SALES (est): 1MM **Privately Held**
SIC: 3799 Recreational vehicles

(G-2985)
LASALLE BRISTOL CORPORATION (HQ)
Also Called: Lasalle Bristol
601 County Road 17 (46516-9505)
P.O. Box 98 (46515-0098)
PHONE......................574 295-4400
Richard W Karcher, *President*
William J Schmuhl Jr, *Principal*
Mike Harris, *Manager*
Don Mowery, *Manager*
Robin L Robb, *Admin Sec*
◆ EMP: 180 EST: 1961

SALES (est): 209.9MM
SALES (corp-wide): 356.3MM **Privately Held**
WEB: www.lasallebristol.com
SIC: 5023 5021 5051 5033 Floor coverings; carpets; resilient floor coverings: tile or sheet; household furniture; aluminum bars, rods, ingots, sheets, pipes, plates, etc.; siding, except wood; residential lighting fixtures; ducting, plastic
PA: Arran Isle Limited
Unit H6, Brindley House
Elland HX5 9
142 232-8850

(G-2986)
LATCH GARD CO INC
1900 Fieldhouse Ave (46517-1315)
PHONE......................574 862-2373
Randall Moyer, *President*
David Geiger, *Vice Pres*
EMP: 7
SALES (est): 1.1MM **Privately Held**
WEB: www.latchgard.com
SIC: 3429 3357 Door locks, bolts & checks; nonferrous wiredrawing & insulating

(G-2987)
LAYTON HOMES CORPORATION (HQ)
2520 Bypass Rd (46514-1518)
P.O. Box 743 (46515-0743)
PHONE......................574 294-6521
Ronald Kloska, *President*
Joseph Fanchi, *Vice Pres*
Richard M Treckelo, *Admin Sec*
EMP: 3 EST: 1962
SALES (est): 13.1MM
SALES (corp-wide): 236.5MM **Publicly Held**
SIC: 3792 Travel trailers & campers
PA: Skyline Champion Corporation
2520 Bypass Rd
Elkhart IN 46514
574 294-6521

(G-2988)
LAYTON HOMES CORPORATION
Also Called: Layton Elkhart
411 County Road 15 (46516-9623)
PHONE......................574 294-6521
Ralph Nichols, *Branch Mgr*
EMP: 60
SALES (corp-wide): 236.5MM **Publicly Held**
SIC: 3792 Travel trailers & campers
HQ: Layton Homes Corporation
2520 Bypass Rd
Elkhart IN 46514
574 294-6521

(G-2989)
LCI INDUSTRIES (PA)
3501 County Road 6 E (46514-7663)
PHONE......................574 535-1125
Jason D Lippert, *CEO*
James F Gero, *Ch of Bd*
Scott T Mereness, *President*
Brian M Hall, *CFO*
Kip A Emenhiser, *Controller*
EMP: 55 EST: 1962
SALES: 2.1B **Publicly Held**
WEB: www.drewindustries.com
SIC: 3711 3714 3715 3442 Chassis, motor vehicle; motor vehicle parts & accessories; trailer bodies; window & door frames; shower stalls, metal

(G-2990)
LCM REALTY LLC
3501 County Road 6 E (46514-7663)
PHONE......................574 535-1125
EMP: 2
SALES (est): 87.2K **Privately Held**
SIC: 3711 Chassis, motor vehicle

(G-2991)
LEARMAN ELECTRONIC TOOL ASSOC
1513 S 6th St (46516-2546)
PHONE......................574 226-0420
Fax: 574 522-7740
Tim Learman, *President*
Pat Learman, *Vice Pres*
EMP: 6 EST: 1955

SQ FT: 15,000
SALES (est): 924.1K **Privately Held**
SIC: 3398 Metal heat treating

(G-2992)
LEER MIDWEST
58391 Ventura Dr (46517-9431)
PHONE......................574 522-5337
Bryan Smith, *Principal*
EMP: 10
SALES (est): 750K **Privately Held**
SIC: 3713 Truck tops

(G-2993)
LEGACY VULCAN LLC
Also Called: Elkhart Yard
2500 W Lusher Ave (46517-1067)
PHONE......................574 293-1536
Chris Weinkauf, *Branch Mgr*
EMP: 16 **Publicly Held**
WEB: www.vulcanmaterials.com
SIC: 3272 Concrete products
HQ: Legacy Vulcan, Llc
1200 Urban Center Dr
Vestavia AL 35242
205 298-3000

(G-2994)
LEONARD EATON TOOLING INC
435 Roske Dr (46516-9086)
PHONE......................574 295-5041
Betty Hartman, *Controller*
EMP: 2
SALES (est): 211.6K **Privately Held**
SIC: 3599 Machine shop, jobbing & repair

(G-2995)
LEPARK MOLD & TOOL
2504 Jeanwood Dr (46514-7656)
PHONE......................574 262-0518
Mike Hoover, *Owner*
Jack Waltermire, *Engineer*
Rick Keen, *Design Engr*
Shaun Phy, *CFO*
Brad Schultheis, *Sales Associate*
EMP: 150
SALES (est): 9.6MM **Privately Held**
SIC: 3089 Injection molding of plastics

(G-2996)
LFD BEARINGS LLC
4505 Wyland Dr Ste 1100 (46516-9682)
PHONE......................574 245-0375
Michael Loeffler, *COO*
▲ EMP: 2
SALES: 1MM **Privately Held**
SIC: 3366 Bushings & bearings

(G-2997)
LIFTCO INC
Also Called: Vb Air Suspension North Amer
3301 Reedy Dr (46514-7665)
PHONE......................574 266-5551
Stanley Disher, *CEO*
John Disher, *President*
Patrick Disher, *Vice Pres*
▲ EMP: 30
SQ FT: 52,000
SALES (est): 5MM **Privately Held**
WEB: www.liftco.net
SIC: 3499 Stabilizing bars (cargo), metal

(G-2998)
LIPPERT CMPONENTS INTL SLS INC
3501 County Road 6 E (46514-7663)
PHONE......................574 312-7480
EMP: 2
SALES (est): 87.2K **Privately Held**
SIC: 3711 Chassis, motor vehicle

(G-2999)
LIPPERT COMPONENTS INC (HQ)
Also Called: Home-Style Industries
3501 County Road 6 E (46514-7663)
P.O. Box 2888 (46515-2888)
PHONE......................800 551-9149
Fax: 574 534-3475
Jason Lippert, *CEO*
L Douglas Lippert, *Ch of Bd*
Shane Duncan, *President*
Marc Grimes, *President*
Scott Mereness, *President*
EMP: 200

SQ FT: 8,000
SALES: 1B
SALES (corp-wide): 2.1B **Publicly Held**
WEB: www.lci1.com
SIC: 3711 3469 3444 3714 Chassis, motor vehicle; stamping metal for the trade; metal roofing & roof drainage equipment; motor vehicle parts & accessories
PA: Lci Industries
3501 County Road 6 E
Elkhart IN 46514
574 535-1125

(G-3000)
LIPPERT COMPONENTS INC
Also Called: Duncan Systems
29391 Old Us 33 (46516-1427)
PHONE......................574 294-6852
Brent Watson, *Manager*
EMP: 72
SALES (corp-wide): 2.1B **Publicly Held**
SIC: 3711 3469 3444 3714 Chassis, motor vehicle; stamping metal for the trade; metal roofing & roof drainage equipment; motor vehicle parts & accessories
HQ: Lippert Components, Inc.
3501 County Road 6 E
Elkhart IN 46514
800 551-9149

(G-3001)
LIPPERT COMPONENTS INC
2503 Banks Ct (46514-7675)
PHONE......................574 295-8166
Jeff Wysong, *Branch Mgr*
EMP: 25
SALES (corp-wide): 2.1B **Publicly Held**
SIC: 2531 Vehicle furniture; seats, automobile
HQ: Lippert Components, Inc.
3501 County Road 6 E
Elkhart IN 46514
800 551-9149

(G-3002)
LIPPERT COMPONENTS MFG INC (HQ)
3501 County Road 6 E (46514-7663)
PHONE......................574 535-1125
Jason Lippert, *CEO*
EMP: 750
SALES (est): 152MM
SALES (corp-wide): 2.1B **Publicly Held**
SIC: 3711 Chassis, motor vehicle
PA: Lci Industries
3501 County Road 6 E
Elkhart IN 46514
574 535-1125

(G-3003)
LIPPERT EXTRUSIONS
1722 W Mishawaka Rd (46517-9404)
PHONE......................574 312-6467
EMP: 2 EST: 2011
SALES (est): 183K **Privately Held**
SIC: 3999 Manufacturing industries

(G-3004)
LITHOTONE INC (PA)
1313 W Hively Ave (46517-1594)
PHONE......................574 294-5521
Fax: 574 294-6851
Robert Priebe, *President*
James Priebe, *Vice Pres*
Jerry Thomas, *Purch Mgr*
Kirk Lehman, *Treasurer*
Timothy Coquillard, *Admin Sec*
EMP: 45 EST: 1962
SQ FT: 41,400
SALES (est): 8.4MM **Privately Held**
WEB: www.lithotone.com
SIC: 2752 Commercial printing, offset

(G-3005)
LITTLE TRAILER CO INC
29877 Old Us 33 (46516-1428)
PHONE......................877 545-4897
David Reynolds, *President*
EMP: 11
SALES (est): 810K **Privately Held**
SIC: 3799 Recreational vehicles

(G-3006)
LIVINGS GRAPHICS INC
Also Called: Printers Plus
2111 Cassopolis St (46514-5115)
PHONE..................................574 264-4114
Fax: 574 262-2112
Kathy Livings, *President*
Joseph Livings, *Vice Pres*
EMP: 6
SALES (est): 530K Privately Held
SIC: 2752 Commercial printing, offset

(G-3007)
LONE STAR INDUSTRIES INC
55284 Corwin Rd (46514-8401)
PHONE..................................574 674-8873
David A Pedzinski, *Manager*
EMP: 3
SQ FT: 2,000
SALES (corp-wide): 287.7MM Privately
Held
SIC: 3241 Portland cement
HQ: Lone Star Industries Inc
10401 N Meridian St # 400
Indianapolis IN 46290
317 706-3314

(G-3008)
LOTEC INC
Also Called: Speedgrip Chuck
2000 Industrial Pkwy (46516-5411)
P.O. Box 596 (46515-0596)
PHONE..................................574 294-1506
Nancy Renaud, *CEO*
David Copp, *Vice Pres*
John Wirt, *Safety Mgr*
Steve Cornelius, *Engineer*
Barry Neilson, *Engineer*
EMP: 48 EST: 1943
SQ FT: 47,200
SALES (est): 7.6MM Privately Held
WEB: www.speedgrip.com
SIC: 3545 Machine tool attachments & ac-
cessories

(G-3009)
M G PRODUCTS INC
4707 Chester Dr (46516-9641)
PHONE..................................574 293-0752
Fax: 574 295-3161
Mark George, *President*
Jeremy George, *Manager*
EMP: 30
SQ FT: 41,000
SALES (est): 5.2MM Privately Held
WEB: www.mgproductscnc.com
SIC: 3599 Machine & other job shop work;
machine shop, jobbing & repair

(G-3010)
M-3 AND ASSOCIATES INC
28244 Clay St (46517-1072)
PHONE..................................574 294-3988
Randy D Wilson, *President*
Linda Wilson, *Corp Secy*
EMP: 20
SQ FT: 20,000
SALES (est): 3.6MM Privately Held
WEB: www.m3assoc.com
SIC: 3493 Torsion bar springs

(G-3011)
M-TEC CORPORATION
701 Collins Rd (46516-5420)
P.O. Box 1064 (46515-1064)
PHONE..................................574 294-1060
Fax: 574 294-1062
William Banks Jr, *CEO*
Dave Devon, *Principal*
John F Hughes, *Admin Sec*
EMP: 105
SALES (est): 10.9MM
SALES (corp-wide): 2.1B Publicly Held
SIC: 3711 Cars, electric, assembly of;
chassis, motor vehicle
HQ: Lippert Components, Inc.
3501 County Road 6 E
Elkhart IN 46514
800 551-9149

(G-3012)
**MACH 1 PAPER AND POLY PDTS
INC**
1801 Minnie St (46516-5736)
PHONE..................................574 522-4500
Thomas Reusser, *President*

EMP: 2
SALES (est): 109.8K Privately Held
SIC: 2679 2655 Paperboard products,
converted; paper products, converted;
tubes, fiber or paper: made from purchased material

(G-3013)
MADDEN MANUFACTURING INC
1317 Princeton St (46516-4106)
P.O. Box 387 (46515-0387)
PHONE..................................574 295-4292
Fax: 574 295-7562
Stuart Barb, *President*
Paula Barb, *Vice Pres*
Aaron Rhoade, *Marketing Staff*
EMP: 10
SQ FT: 11,000
SALES: 800K Privately Held
WEB: www.maddenmfg.com
SIC: 3561 3585 3824 3586 Industrial
pumps & parts; heating equipment, com-
plete; liquid meters; measuring & dispens-
ing pumps; valves & pipe fittings;
fabricated plate work (boiler shop)

(G-3014)
MADILLION PLASTICS INC
836 Summa Dr (46516-9036)
PHONE..................................574 293-4434
Steve Flory, *Manager*
EMP: 2
SALES (est): 88.9K Privately Held
SIC: 3089 Plastics products

(G-3015)
MAG INSTRUMENT INC
25845 Meadow Oak Ln (46514-5217)
PHONE..................................574 262-1521
Adam Mayer, *President*
EMP: 2
SALES (est): 134.8K Privately Held
SIC: 3648 Lighting equipment

(G-3016)
**MANCHESTER TANK &
EQUIPMENT CO**
3630 Manchester Dr (46514-1196)
PHONE..................................574 295-8200
Jim Young, *Opers Mgr*
Pom Doland, *Purch Agent*
Pestrak Jennifer, *Purchasing*
Roger Klein, *Purchasing*
Jim Sommer, *QC Dir*
EMP: 183
SALES (corp-wide): 1.3B Privately Held
WEB: www.mantank.com
SIC: 3443 Cylinders, pressure: metal plate
HQ: Manchester Tank & Equipment Co Inc
1000 Corporate Centre Dr # 300
Franklin TN 37067
615 370-6104

(G-3017)
MAP OF EASTON
3733 Lexington Park Dr (46514-1163)
PHONE..................................574 293-0966
Jim Parson, *Principal*
EMP: 2
SALES (est): 138.4K Privately Held
SIC: 3229 Glass fiber products

(G-3018)
MARKLEY ENTERPRISE INC
800 Lillian Ave (46516-5583)
PHONE..................................574 295-4195
Fax: 574 522-2230
H Timothy Markley, *President*
Nancy Stanner, *Corp Secy*
David Ponsler, *Vice Pres*
Dorothy Anderson, *Project Mgr*
Aaron Peters, *Warehouse Mgr*
EMP: 75 EST: 1962
SQ FT: 16,000
SALES (est): 13.1MM Privately Held
WEB: www.markleyent.com
SIC: 3161 5046 Sample cases; store fix-
tures & display equipment; display equip-
ment, except refrigerated

(G-3019)
MARSHALL & POE LLC (PA)
Also Called: Marshall & Poe Bus Cons & CP
818 Erwin St (46514-3370)
PHONE..................................574 266-5244
Fax: 574 262-5161

Charles Marshall, *Owner*
Richard Kidder, *Principal*
David Weaver, *Principal*
Richard Wooden, *Principal*
Jeff Kaczanowski, *Manager*
EMP: 25
SALES (est): 2.5MM Privately Held
SIC: 7372 Prepackaged software

(G-3020)
MARSON INTERNATIONAL LLC
1001 Sako Ct (46516-9019)
PHONE..................................574 295-4222
Fax: 574 295-5115
Mike Marshall, *President*
Chad Sotebeer, *Purch Agent*
Don Orban, *QC Mgr*
Jason Newburn,
▲ EMP: 40
SALES: 10MM Privately Held
WEB: www.marsonintl.com
SIC: 3441 Fabricated structural metal

(G-3021)
**MARTIN TRUSS
MANUFACTURING**
62332 County Road 1 (46517-9724)
PHONE..................................574 862-4457
Fax: 574 862-1811
Andrew Martin, *Owner*
EMP: 2 EST: 1993
SALES (est): 310.4K Privately Held
SIC: 2439 Trusses, wooden roof

(G-3022)
MAVERICK PACKAGING INC
3505 Reedy Dr (46514-7668)
PHONE..................................574 264-2891
Fax: 574 246-9610
Tom McGlone, *President*
Gena McGlone, *Controller*
▲ EMP: 33
SQ FT: 25,000
SALES (est): 9.3MM Privately Held
SIC: 2844 5122 Hair preparations, includ-
ing shampoos; cosmetics, perfumes &
hair products

(G-3023)
MBSI HOLDINGS LLC
58120 County Road 3 (46517-9007)
PHONE..................................574 295-1214
Rick Bedell, *Mng Member*
Robert E Winks,
EMP: 3
SALES (est): 370K Privately Held
SIC: 2452 Prefabricated wood buildings

(G-3024)
MCDOWELL ENTERPRISES INC
2010 Superior St (46516-4706)
P.O. Box 846 (46515-0846)
PHONE..................................574 293-1042
Fax: 574 293-8484
Carol McDowell, *President*
James Loshbough, *Exec VP*
EMP: 30
SQ FT: 25,000
SALES (est): 4.3MM Privately Held
SIC: 3471 Plating of metals or formed
products

(G-3025)
**MECHANICAL ENGINEERING
CONTROL**
Also Called: Meca
57236 Nagy Dr (46517-1019)
P.O. Box 519 (46515-0519)
PHONE..................................574 294-7580
Jim Bour, *President*
Greg Dean, *Vice Pres*
EMP: 13
SQ FT: 15,000
SALES: 2.6MM Privately Held
SIC: 3613 3599 Panel & distribution
boards & other related apparatus; custom
machinery

(G-3026)
MECK DIE INC
29029 Phillips St (46514-1024)
PHONE..................................574 262-5441
Robert Wilkinson, *President*
Kathy Wilkinson, *Vice Pres*
EMP: 3
SQ FT: 2,400

SALES (est): 350K Privately Held
SIC: 3544 Dies, steel rule

(G-3027)
**MEDICAL STRUCTURES MFG
CORP**
1803 Minnie St (46516-5736)
PHONE..................................574 612-0353
Thomas Cassity, *Principal*
EMP: 9
SALES (est): 893.2K Privately Held
SIC: 3999 Manufacturing industries

(G-3028)
**MEDIX SPECIALTY VEHICLES
LLC**
3008 Mobile Dr (46514-5524)
PHONE..................................574 266-0911
Thomas Moleski, *Director*
▼ EMP: 125
SQ FT: 48,000
SALES: 57.9MM Privately Held
WEB: www.medixambulance.com
SIC: 3711 Ambulances (motor vehicles),
assembly of

(G-3029)
**METALCRAFT PRECISION
MACHINING**
56854 Elk Ct (46516-1456)
PHONE..................................574 293-6700
Don Utz, *President*
Jeff Rhodes, *Vice Pres*
EMP: 15
SQ FT: 20,000
SALES (est): 1.9MM Privately Held
SIC: 3599 Machine shop, jobbing & repair;
machine & other job shop work

(G-3030)
MICHIANA ELKHART INC
51505 State Road 19 (46514-5814)
PHONE..................................574 206-0620
EMP: 3 EST: 2009
SALES (est): 220.9K Privately Held
SIC: 2992 Lubricating oils

(G-3031)
MICHIANA FORKLIFT INC
Also Called: Michiana Compressor
2921 Moose Trl (46514-8230)
PHONE..................................574 326-3702
Jennifer Kowalski, *President*
EMP: 13
SALES (est): 3.2MM Privately Held
SIC: 3537 Forklift trucks

(G-3032)
MICHIANA METAL FABRICATION
1227 W Beardsley Ave (46514-2223)
PHONE..................................574 256-9010
Shawn Winkelmann, *President*
EMP: 5
SQ FT: 18,000
SALES (est): 726.7K Privately Held
SIC: 3544 Special dies & tools; industrial
molds

(G-3033)
**MICHIANA METAL FINISHING
INC**
2805 Frederic Dr (46514-7642)
PHONE..................................574 206-0666
Robert Penney, *Principal*
EMP: 3
SALES (est): 253.4K Privately Held
SIC: 3471 Finishing, metals or formed
products

(G-3034)
MICRO MACHINE WORKS INC
835 Lillian Ave (46516-5525)
P.O. Box 2082 (46515-2082)
PHONE..................................574 293-1354
Herbert L Kirts, *President*
Diane Kirts, *Admin Sec*
EMP: 8 EST: 1992
SQ FT: 1,350
SALES (est): 851.6K Privately Held
WEB: www.micromachineworks.com
SIC: 3599 Machine shop, jobbing & repair

GEOGRAPHIC

(G-3035)
MICROFORM INC
21053 Protecta Dr Ste A (46516-9335)
PHONE....................................574 522-9851
Fax: 574 294-2645
Rose M Darrah, *President*
Neil Darrah, *Treasurer*
EMP: 9
SQ FT: 14,000
SALES: 600K **Privately Held**
WEB: www.microform.com
SIC: 3444 3679 Sheet metalwork; electronic circuits

(G-3036)
MID AMERICA SCREW PRODUCTS
Also Called: M.A.S. Products
21559 Protecta Dr (46516-9542)
PHONE....................................574 294-6905
Fax: 574 522-3090
Steve Nauman, *President*
▲ EMP: 15
SQ FT: 20,000
SALES: 3MM **Privately Held**
SIC: 3451 Screw machine products

(G-3037)
MIDSTATES TOOL & DIE AND ENGRG
3407 Cooper Dr (46514-8638)
PHONE....................................574 264-3521
Fax: 574 266-6938
Michael Masten, *President*
Tonya R Masten, *Admin Sec*
EMP: 22
SQ FT: 16,000
SALES (est): 3.1MM **Privately Held**
WEB: www.mtdsales.com
SIC: 3541 Machine tools, metal cutting type

(G-3038)
MIDWAY SPECIALTY VEHICLES LLC
2940 Dexter Dr (46514-8226)
P.O. Box 1931 (46515-1931)
PHONE....................................574 264-2530
Mike Violi, *President*
Brad Brubaker, *President*
Colleen Pletcher, *Purchasing*
Jack Stouder, *Manager*
Russ Gilpin,
EMP: 48
SQ FT: 78,000
SALES (est): 10.8MM **Privately Held**
SIC: 3711 Automobile assembly, including specialty automobiles

(G-3039)
MIDWEST LEATHER & VINYL
1434 Johnson St (46514-3404)
PHONE....................................574 266-1700
EMP: 2 EST: 2010
SALES (est): 94K **Privately Held**
SIC: 3199 Mfg Leather Goods

(G-3040)
MIDWEST ROTATIONAL MOLDING LLC
22165 Sunset Ln (46516-5398)
PHONE....................................574 294-6891
Gary Wright, *General Ptnr*
EMP: 10
SALES (est): 1.2MM **Privately Held**
SIC: 3089 Molding primary plastic

(G-3041)
MIKE H INC
Also Called: Le Park Mold & Tool
2508 Jeanwood Dr (46514-7656)
PHONE....................................574 262-0518
Mike Hoover, *President*
Bill Faubion, *Vice Pres*
EMP: 5
SALES: 500K **Privately Held**
SIC: 3089 Plastics products

(G-3042)
MILLMARK ENTERPRISES INC
1935 Markle Ave (46517-1321)
P.O. Box 757 (46515-0757)
PHONE....................................574 389-9904
Fax: 574 294-1615
Darin J Miller, *President*

Michelle Miller, *Admin Sec*
EMP: 15
SQ FT: 24,000
SALES (est): 3.6MM **Privately Held**
SIC: 3449 Bars, concrete reinforcing: fabricated steel

(G-3043)
MJB WOOD GROUP INC
1600 Fieldhouse Ave Ste A (46517-1452)
PHONE....................................574 295-5228
Fax: 574 296-7772
Sherry Ohman, *Branch Mgr*
EMP: 6
SALES (corp-wide): 400MM **Privately Held**
WEB: www.mjbwood.com
SIC: 5031 2499 Lumber: rough, dressed & finished; decorative wood & woodwork
PA: Mjb Wood Group, Llc
　　2201 W Royal Ln Ste 250
　　Irving TX 75063
　　972 401-0005

(G-3044)
MODERN MUSCLE CAR FACTORY INC
30446 County Road 12 (46514-8937)
PHONE....................................574 329-6390
Scott Klepinger, *President*
H Klepinger, *Vice Pres*
Heather Klepinger, *Vice Pres*
EMP: 3
SALES (est): 143.1K **Privately Held**
SIC: 2396 Automotive & apparel trimmings

(G-3045)
MOLDED ACSTCAL PDTS EASTON INC
3733 Lexington Park Dr (46514-1163)
PHONE....................................610 253-7135
Sherry McShane, *Manager*
EMP: 50 **Privately Held**
SIC: 3296 Mineral wool
PA: Molded Acoustical Products Of Easton, Inc.
　　3 Danforth Dr
　　Easton PA 18045

(G-3046)
MOR/RYDE INC
Also Called: Mor-Ryde Service Center
1966 Sterling Ave (46516-4221)
P.O. Box 579 (46515-0579)
PHONE....................................574 293-1581
Fax: 574 294-4936
Robert Moore Sr, *Ch of Bd*
Robert G Moore Jr, *President*
Rodney A Moore, *Corp Secy*
Adrian Diaz, *Plant Mgr*
Tim Lies, *Plant Mgr*
EMP: 115
SQ FT: 60,000
SALES (est): 29.8MM **Privately Held**
WEB: www.morryde.com
SIC: 3714 Motor vehicle transmissions, drive assemblies & parts; frames, motor vehicle; motor vehicle body components & frame

(G-3047)
MOR/RYDE INTERNATIONAL INC
1536 Grant St (46514-3756)
PHONE....................................574 293-1581
Robert Moore Sr, *Principal*
Dale Bennett, *Plant Mgr*
EMP: 85 **Privately Held**
SIC: 3448 Buildings, portable: prefabricated metal
PA: Mor/Ryde International Inc
　　1966 Moyer Ave
　　Elkhart IN 46516

(G-3048)
MOR/RYDE INTERNATIONAL INC
23208 Cooper Dr (46514-9741)
PHONE....................................574 293-1581
EMP: 64 **Privately Held**
SIC: 3449 Bars, concrete reinforcing: fabricated steel
PA: Mor/Ryde International Inc
　　1966 Moyer Ave
　　Elkhart IN 46516

(G-3049)
MOR/RYDE INTERNATIONAL INC (PA)
1966 Moyer Ave (46516-4230)
P.O. Box 579 (46515-0579)
PHONE....................................574 293-1581
Robert Moore Sr, *Ch of Bd*
Robert Moore Jr, *President*
Dan Geans, *Accounts Mgr*
Gary Wheeler, *Sales Staff*
Rob Kolean, *Manager*
EMP: 26
SQ FT: 60,000
SALES (est): 47.7MM **Privately Held**
SIC: 3449 3714 Bars, concrete reinforcing: fabricated steel; motor vehicle transmissions, drive assemblies & parts; frames, motor vehicle; motor vehicle body components & frame

(G-3050)
MORAN ENGINEERING LLC
28973 Buttercup Ln (46514-1233)
PHONE....................................574 266-6799
Marty Moran,
EMP: 2
SALES: 200K **Privately Held**
SIC: 3599 Custom machinery

(G-3051)
MOTOR ELECTRIC INC
4700 Eastland Dr (46516-9661)
P.O. Box 1571 (46515-1571)
PHONE....................................574 294-7123
Richard Karenke, *President*
Darren M Karenke, *Vice Pres*
Doris J Karenke, *Admin Sec*
EMP: 7
SQ FT: 10,000
SALES (est): 1.6MM **Privately Held**
WEB: www.motorelectric.com
SIC: 5063 7694 Motors, electric; electric motor repair

(G-3052)
MOYERS INC
3502 Reedy Dr (46514-7668)
P.O. Box 157 (46515-0157)
PHONE....................................574 264-3119
Fax: 574 264-9580
Mark Moyer, *President*
Gunnar Erickson, *Admin Sec*
EMP: 35 EST: 1980
SQ FT: 55,000
SALES: 4MM **Privately Held**
SIC: 3317 3499 3444 Seamless pipes & tubes; tubing, mechanical or hypodermic sizes: cold drawn stainless; chair frames, metal; sheet metalwork

(G-3053)
MR PIN SHI PETER LEE
23329 Century Dr (46514-4941)
PHONE....................................574 264-9754
Peter Lee, *Principal*
EMP: 4
SALES (est): 308.2K **Privately Held**
SIC: 3452 Pins

(G-3054)
MTS PRODUCTS CORP (PA)
28672 Holiday Pl (46517-1111)
P.O. Box 1338 (46515-1338)
PHONE....................................574 295-3142
David E Mount, *President*
Mary E Mount, *Corp Secy*
◆ EMP: 28 EST: 1971
SQ FT: 50,000
SALES: 4.3MM **Privately Held**
WEB: www.mtsproducts.com
SIC: 3161 3651 Cases, carrying; musical instrument cases; briefcases; speaker systems

(G-3055)
MTS PRODUCTS CORP
Also Called: Goshen Case Company
28672 Holiday Pl (46517-1111)
P.O. Box 1338 (46515-1338)
PHONE....................................574 295-3142
Fax: 574 295-1269
David Mount, *President*
EMP: 17

SALES (corp-wide): 4.3MM **Privately Held**
WEB: www.mtsproducts.com
SIC: 3161 3651 Musical instrument cases; speaker systems
PA: Mts Products Corp
　　28672 Holiday Pl
　　Elkhart IN 46517
　　574 295-3142

(G-3056)
NAMACLE LLC
1235 W Hively Ave (46517-1555)
PHONE....................................574 320-1436
Thomas Teach,
EMP: 2
SALES (est): 139.7K **Privately Held**
SIC: 3484 Guns (firearms) or gun parts, 30 mm. & below

(G-3057)
NANOCHEM TECHNOLOGIES LLC
1203 Kent St (46514-1739)
PHONE....................................574 970-2436
Michael Luckett, *Research*
Lila Leonard, *Controller*
Jeff Swartz,
▲ EMP: 50
SALES (est): 18.7MM **Privately Held**
SIC: 2851 Paints & paint additives

(G-3058)
NDA ENERGIZED COATINGS
855 E Mishawaka Rd (46517-2393)
PHONE....................................260 499-0307
EMP: 2
SALES (est): 75.5K **Privately Held**
SIC: 3479 Metal coating & allied service

(G-3059)
NEA LLC
Also Called: Allegra Print & Imaging
131 W Marion St (46516-3206)
PHONE....................................574 295-0024
Chet Nunan,
EMP: 5
SALES (est): 925.3K **Privately Held**
SIC: 3555 2752 Copy holders, printers'; commercial printing, offset

(G-3060)
NESTOR SALES LLC
205 County Road 17 (46516-5449)
PHONE....................................574 295-5535
Dave Rick,
EMP: 6
SALES (corp-wide): 5B **Publicly Held**
SIC: 3423 7699 Hand & edge tools; knife, saw & tool sharpening & repair
HQ: Nestor Sales Llc
　　7337 Bryan Dairy Rd
　　Largo FL 33777
　　727 544-6114

(G-3061)
NEWLETT INC
Also Called: Gemstone
435 Harrison St (46516-2771)
PHONE....................................574 294-8899
Chris Graff, *CEO*
Larry Sensenbaugh, *President*
Ed Jarrett, *Managing Dir*
Jeffrey Smith, *Sales Mgr*
EMP: 52
SALES: 5.5MM **Privately Held**
WEB: www.gemstoness.com
SIC: 2541 Table or counter tops, plastic laminated

(G-3062)
NIBCO INC (PA)
1516 Middlebury St (46516-4740)
P.O. Box 1167 (46515-1167)
PHONE....................................574 295-3000
Rex Martin, *Ch of Bd*
Steven E Malm, *President*
Kenneth J Eme Jr, *Vice Pres*
David Goodling, *Vice Pres*
David L Goodling, *Vice Pres*
◆ EMP: 291
SQ FT: 98,000

SALES (est): 732MM **Privately Held**
WEB: www.nibco.com
SIC: **3494** 3491 3089 Valves & pipe fittings; pipe fittings; plumbing & heating valves; industrial valves; plastic hardware & building products; fittings for pipe, plastic

(G-3063)
NICKELL MOULDING COMPANY INC
3015 Mobile Dr (46514-5525)
P.O. Box 1502 (46515-1502)
PHONE..................................574 295-5223
Fax: 574 264-3853
George Nickell, *President*
Scott McAfoos, *Vice Pres*
Connie Fortson, *Production*
Mark Tavallai, *Purch Mgr*
Sandy Mason, *Human Res Dir*
◆ EMP: 150 EST: 1981
SQ FT: 140,000
SALES (est): 29.1MM **Privately Held**
SIC: **2431** Moldings, wood: unfinished & prefinished

(G-3064)
NORCO INDUSTRIES
2800 Northland Dr (46514-7670)
PHONE..................................800 347-2232
▲ EMP: 3
SALES (est): 90.3K **Privately Held**
SIC: **3999** Manufacturing industries

(G-3065)
NORCO INDUSTRIES INC
Adnik Manufacturing
2600 Jeanwood Dr (46514-7657)
PHONE..................................574 262-3400
Fax: 574 264-2366
Eli Villaba, *Engineer*
Doug Yoder, *Engineer*
Michael Tallman, *CFO*
Jeff Dick, *Manager*
Jan Sutherland, *Manager*
EMP: 210
SALES (corp-wide): 78.8MM **Privately Held**
SIC: **2531** 3714 3452 Public building & related furniture; motor vehicle parts & accessories; bolts, nuts, rivets & washers
PA: Norco Industries, Inc
    365 W Victoria St
    Compton CA 90220
    310 639-4000

(G-3066)
NORTHERN BOX COMPANY INC
1328 Mishawaka St (46514-1809)
P.O. Box 985 (46515-0985)
PHONE..................................574 264-2161
Fax: 574 262-8943
Heidi Linder, *President*
Heidi A Linder, *President*
Christina J Linder, *Admin Sec*
EMP: 27 EST: 1951
SQ FT: 70,000
SALES: 6MM **Privately Held**
SIC: **2653** Boxes, corrugated: made from purchased materials

(G-3067)
NORTHWEST INTERIORS INC
405 Pine Creek Ct (46516-9089)
PHONE..................................574 294-2326
Fax: 574 522-6038
James Mellott, *President*
Jan Mellott, *Corp Secy*
EMP: 25
SQ FT: 24,000
SALES (est): 3.6MM **Privately Held**
SIC: **2391** Draperies, plastic & textile: from purchased materials

(G-3068)
OMEGA NATIONAL PRODUCTS LLC
1010 Rowe St (46516-5507)
PHONE..................................574 295-5353
Michael Van Rooy, *Vice Pres*
Mike Gingrich, *Engineer*
Jane Furfaro, *Marketing Staff*
Kristen Tincher, *Assistant*
EMP: 106

SALES (corp-wide): 22MM **Privately Held**
WEB: www.nationalproducts.com
SIC: **2499** 2452 3231 2431 Decorative wood & woodwork; panels & sections, prefabricated, wood; mirrored glass; millwork
PA: Omega National Products, Llc
    810 Baxter Ave
    Louisville KY 40204
    502 583-3038

(G-3069)
OMNI-TRON TOOLING & ENGRG (PA)
1649 Brookwood Dr (46514-4265)
P.O. Box 1084 (46515-1084)
PHONE..................................574 262-2083
Fax: 574 262-2083
Victor Pixey, *President*
Rita Pixey, *Admin Sec*
EMP: 2
SALES: 100K **Privately Held**
SIC: **3535** 5084 Conveyors & conveying equipment; conveyor systems

(G-3070)
OMNIMAX INTERNATIONAL INC
Amerimax Building Products
160 County Road 15 (46516-9548)
PHONE..................................574 294-8576
EMP: 43
SALES (corp-wide): 854.7MM **Privately Held**
SIC: **3444** 3714 3354 Mfg Sheet Metalwork Mfg Motor Vehicle Parts/Accessories Mfg Aluminum Extruded Products
HQ: Omnimax International, Inc.
    303 Research Dr Ste 400
    Norcross GA 30092
    770 449-7066

(G-3071)
PANEL SOLUTIONS INC (PA)
Also Called: Panel Solutions/Tape Tech
5015 Verdant St (46516-9313)
PHONE..................................574 389-8494
Fax: 574 389-1805
Tom Zurek, *President*
Karen Ponciano, *COO*
Catherine Zurek, *Vice Pres*
Keith Gingerich, *Purchasing*
Mike Person, *Controller*
▲ EMP: 15 EST: 1998
SALES (est): 3.2MM **Privately Held**
WEB: www.panelsolutions.com
SIC: **2621** Wallpaper (hanging paper)

(G-3072)
PANEL SOLUTIONS INC
PS Designs
5015 Berdant Dr (46516)
PHONE..................................574 295-0222
Amanda Zurek, *Branch Mgr*
EMP: 15
SALES (corp-wide): 3.2MM **Privately Held**
SIC: **2211** Draperies & drapery fabrics, cotton
PA: Panel Solutions, Inc.
    5015 Verdant St
    Elkhart IN 46516
    574 389-8494

(G-3073)
PANOLAM INDUSTRIES INC
25603 Borg Rd (46514-5273)
PHONE..................................574 264-0702
Pete Owens, *Branch Mgr*
EMP: 6 **Privately Held**
SIC: **3089** Panels, building: plastic
HQ: Panolam Industries, Inc.
    1 Corporate Dr Ste 725
    Shelton CT 06484
    203 925-1556

(G-3074)
PARAMOUNT PLASTICS INC
2810 Jeanwood Dr (46514-7659)
PHONE..................................574 264-2143
Fax: 574 262-8208
Rex Lim, *President*
Jessie Prugh, *Corp Secy*
Laura Frizzo, *Cust Mgr*
Paramount Stanton, *Maintence Staff*
EMP: 42

SQ FT: 60,000
SALES: 7.8MM **Privately Held**
SIC: **3089** Injection molding of plastics; plastic processing

(G-3075)
PARR CORP
3200 County Road 6 E (46514-9695)
PHONE..................................574 264-9614
David Burger, *President*
Andrew Wiegand, *Admin Sec*
▲ EMP: 4
SALES (est): 447.8K **Privately Held**
SIC: **2891** Adhesives

(G-3076)
PARR TECHNOLOGIES LLC
3200 County Road 6 E (46514-9695)
PHONE..................................574 264-9614
Thomas Joyce, *Principal*
EMP: 15
SALES (est): 3.2MM **Privately Held**
SIC: **2891** Adhesives

(G-3077)
PATHFINDER COMMUNICATIONS CORP (PA)
Also Called: Federated Media
421 S 2nd St Ste 100 (46516-3230)
P.O. Box 487 (46515-0487)
PHONE..................................574 295-2500
Fax: 574 294-4014
John F Dille III, *President*
Robert A Watson, *Corp Secy*
John Lapehn, *CFO*
Janet Robertson, *Finance Mgr*
Claire Svetanoff, *Accountant*
EMP: 25
SQ FT: 1,000
SALES (est): 32.7MM **Privately Held**
WEB: www.federatedmedia.com
SIC: **3993** 2711 Signs & advertising specialties; newspapers: publishing only, not printed on site

(G-3078)
PATHFINDER COMMUNICATIONS CORP
Also Called: Fastsigns
1846 Cassopolis St (46514-3119)
PHONE..................................574 266-5115
Fax: 574 266-6212
Tom Sloma, *Manager*
EMP: 5
SALES (corp-wide): 32.7MM **Privately Held**
WEB: www.federatedmedia.com
SIC: **3993** Signs & advertising specialties
PA: Pathfinder Communications Corporation
    421 S 2nd St Ste 100
    Elkhart IN 46516
    574 295-2500

(G-3079)
PATRICK ALUMINUM INC
Also Called: Yellow Dog Extrusion Company
2708 Frederic Dr (46514-9777)
PHONE..................................574 262-1907
Fax: 574 262-1839
Dominick L Baione, *President*
Mitch Milliner, *Regional Mgr*
Mitchell Milliner, *Manager*
Bryan Spitaels, *Manager*
EMP: 5
SALES (est): 726.4K **Privately Held**
SIC: **3354** Aluminum extruded products

(G-3080)
PATRICK INDUSTRIES INC (PA)
107 W Franklin St (46516-3214)
P.O. Box 638 (46515-0638)
PHONE..................................574 294-7511
Fax: 574 522-5213
Todd M Cleveland, *CEO*
Paul E Hassler, *Ch of Bd*
Andy L Nemeth, *President*
Bill Green, *General Mgr*
Kip B Ellis, *COO*
EMP: 151
SQ FT: 35,000

SALES: 1.6B **Publicly Held**
WEB: www.patrickind.com
SIC: **3275** 2493 2435 5031 Gypsum products; reconstituted wood products; fiberboard, other vegetable pulp; plywood, hardwood or hardwood faced; building materials, exterior; building materials, interior; doors & windows; composite board products, woodboard; roofing & siding materials; insulation materials; adhesives

(G-3081)
PATRICK INDUSTRIES INC
Adorn
1808 W Hively Ave (46517-4026)
PHONE..................................574 522-7710
Fax: 574 522-3931
Todd Cleveland, *Branch Mgr*
EMP: 62
SALES (corp-wide): 1.6B **Publicly Held**
SIC: **2435** Hardwood veneer & plywood
PA: Patrick Industries, Inc.
    107 W Franklin St
    Elkhart IN 46516
    574 294-7511

(G-3082)
PATRICK INDUSTRIES INC
Also Called: Mobilcraft Wood Products
1930 W Lusher Ave (46517-1310)
PHONE..................................574 293-1521
James Johnson, *Manager*
EMP: 120
SQ FT: 20,000
SALES (corp-wide): 1.6B **Publicly Held**
WEB: www.patrickind.com
SIC: **2431** 8741 Doors, wood; management services
PA: Patrick Industries, Inc.
    107 W Franklin St
    Elkhart IN 46516
    574 294-7511

(G-3083)
PATRICK INDUSTRIES INC
Also Called: Nickel Enterprises
3905 Lexington Park Dr (46514-1160)
P.O. Box 638 (46515-0638)
PHONE..................................574 294-5758
Fax: 574 293-4428
Jeff Davis, *General Mgr*
EMP: 30
SQ FT: 20,000
SALES (corp-wide): 1.6B **Publicly Held**
WEB: www.patrickind.com
SIC: **2499** 2541 2493 Decorative wood & woodwork; wood partitions & fixtures; reconstituted wood products
PA: Patrick Industries, Inc.
    107 W Franklin St
    Elkhart IN 46516
    574 294-7511

(G-3084)
PATRICK INDUSTRIES INC
Midwest Laminating Co
1926 W Lusher Ave (46517)
PHONE..................................574 293-1521
Jeff Davis, *General Mgr*
EMP: 35
SALES (corp-wide): 1.6B **Publicly Held**
WEB: www.patrickind.com
SIC: **3089** 2542 2541 2511 Laminating of plastic; partitions & fixtures, except wood; wood partitions & fixtures; wood household furniture; wood kitchen cabinets; laminating service
PA: Patrick Industries, Inc.
    107 W Franklin St
    Elkhart IN 46516
    574 294-7511

(G-3085)
PATRICK INDUSTRIES INC
Also Called: Gustafson
57766 County Road 3 (46517-9363)
PHONE..................................574 522-0871
Todd Cleveland, *CEO*
EMP: 94
SALES (corp-wide): 1.6B **Publicly Held**
SIC: **3647** Automotive lighting fixtures
PA: Patrick Industries, Inc.
    107 W Franklin St
    Elkhart IN 46516
    574 294-7511

GEOGRAPHIC

(G-3086)
PATRICK INDUSTRIES INC
Also Called: Polydyn3
107 Rush Ct (46516-9644)
P.O. Box 638 (46515-0638)
PHONE...................................574 522-6100
EMP: 89
SALES (corp-wide): 1.6B Publicly Held
SIC: 2499 Bungs, wood
PA: Patrick Industries, Inc.
107 W Franklin St
Elkhart IN 46516
574 294-7511

(G-3087)
PATRICK INDUSTRIES INC
Also Called: Mishawaka Sheet Metal
28505 C R 20 W (46517)
PHONE...................................574 294-5959
Fax: 574 294-2202
Jeff Troyer, Manager
EMP: 70
SALES (corp-wide): 1.6B Publicly Held
SIC: 3444 Sheet metalwork
PA: Patrick Industries, Inc.
107 W Franklin St
Elkhart IN 46516
574 294-7511

(G-3088)
PATRICK INDUSTRIES INC
Also Called: L S Manufacturing
56741 Elk Park Dr (46516-1449)
PHONE...................................574 294-8828
EMP: 107
SALES (corp-wide): 1.6B Publicly Held
SIC: 3089 Plastic processing
PA: Patrick Industries, Inc.
107 W Franklin St
Elkhart IN 46516
574 294-7511

(G-3089)
PATRICK INDUSTRIES INC
Also Called: Wire Design
2520 Industrial Pkwy (46516-5405)
P.O. Box 1387 (46515-1387)
PHONE...................................574 293-2990
Micheal Doering, Branch Mgr
EMP: 85
SALES (corp-wide): 1.6B Publicly Held
SIC: 5063 3679 Wire & cable; harness assemblies for electronic use: wire or cable
PA: Patrick Industries, Inc.
107 W Franklin St
Elkhart IN 46516
574 294-7511

(G-3090)
PATRICK INDUSTRIES INC
4906 Hoffman St Ste B (46516-9075)
PHONE...................................574 295-9660
David Daisy, Manager
EMP: 18
SALES (corp-wide): 1.6B Publicly Held
SIC: 3275 Gypsum products
PA: Patrick Industries, Inc.
107 W Franklin St
Elkhart IN 46516
574 294-7511

(G-3091)
PATRICK INDUSTRIES INC
2300 W Mishawaka Rd (46517-4040)
P.O. Box 638 (46515-0638)
PHONE...................................574 294-1975
John Izzard, Branch Mgr
EMP: 89
SALES (corp-wide): 1.6B Publicly Held
SIC: 3275 Gypsum products
PA: Patrick Industries, Inc.
107 W Franklin St
Elkhart IN 46516
574 294-7511

(G-3092)
PAULS CUSTOM MACHINE
30924 County Road 8 (46514-9710)
PHONE...................................574 674-9633
Paul Morehead, Principal
EMP: 2 EST: 2008
SALES (est): 202.8K Privately Held
SIC: 3599 Machine shop, jobbing & repair

(G-3093)
PAULS SEATING INC
56912 Elk Ct (46516-1462)
PHONE...................................574 522-0630
Paul Fizer, President
Brenda Fizer, Vice Pres
EMP: 8
SQ FT: 5,000
SALES: 800K Privately Held
WEB: www.paulsseating.com
SIC: 2531 Seats, automobile

(G-3094)
PHOENIX PALLET INC
2901 Dexter Dr (46514-8227)
P.O. Box 1797 (46515-1797)
PHONE...................................574 262-0458
Michael A Madison, President
EMP: 13
SALES (est): 1.7MM Privately Held
SIC: 2448 Pallets, wood & wood with metal

(G-3095)
PHOENIX USA INC
2601 Marina Dr (46514-8642)
PHONE...................................574 266-2020
Kermit Fisher, President
Carol Sims, Purch Agent
▲ EMP: 25
SQ FT: 40,000
SALES: 10MM Privately Held
WEB: www.phoenixusarv.com
SIC: 3716 Motor homes

(G-3096)
PINNACLE SEATING INC
1011 Herman St (46516-9029)
P.O. Box 1397, Granger (46530-1397)
PHONE...................................574 522-2636
Michael A Spite, President
Andy Spite, Owner
▲ EMP: 5
SQ FT: 20,000
SALES: 600K Privately Held
WEB: www.pinnacleseating.com
SIC: 2514 2522 Chairs, household: metal; office furniture, except wood

(G-3097)
**PIONEER PLASTICS
CORPORATION**
25603 Borg Rd (46514-5273)
PHONE...................................574 264-0702
Fax: 574 264-2398
Rick Posthuma, Manager
EMP: 100 Privately Held
SIC: 3083 Plastic finished products, laminated
HQ: Pioneer Plastics Corporation
1 Corporate Dr Ste 725
Shelton CT 06484
203 925-1556

(G-3098)
PJW INC
56199 Parkway Ave (46516-9300)
PHONE...................................574 295-1203
Pat Welch, Principal
EMP: 2
SALES (est): 225.9K Privately Held
SIC: 3993 Signs & advertising specialties

(G-3099)
PLASTIC COMPONENTS INC
1210 County Road 6 W (46514-8219)
PHONE...................................574 264-7514
Fax: 574 264-6945
Thomas E Graham, President
Kim Ottavi, Corp Secy
Tad Hayden, Vice Pres
Wendi Jay, Human Res Mgr
EMP: 25
SQ FT: 40,000
SALES: 24.9MM Privately Held
WEB: www.plasticcomponentsinc.com
SIC: 3089 Injection molding of plastics; plastic processing

(G-3100)
PLUMROSE USA INC
24402 County Road 45 (46516-6043)
P.O. Box 160 (46515-0160)
PHONE...................................574 295-8190
Fax: 574 294-5335
Mike Wilfert, Branch Mgr

EMP: 250
SQ FT: 60,000 Publicly Held
SIC: 2013 Bacon, side & sliced: from purchased meat
HQ: Plumrose Usa, Inc.
1901 Butterfield Rd # 305
Downers Grove IL 60515

(G-3101)
POLY ELECTRONICS LLC
4400 Wyland Dr (46516-9520)
PHONE...................................574 522-0246
Matthew Kain, Principal
EMP: 65
SALES (est): 3.2MM Privately Held
SIC: 3679 Electronic circuits

(G-3102)
PONTOON BOAT LLC
Also Called: Bennington
2805 Decio Dr (46514-7666)
PHONE...................................574 264-6336
Steven H Vogel, CEO
Diana J Engle, Vice Pres
Scott Kantz, Production
Joel Nafziger, Purch Mgr
Amy S Bateson, Engineer
▼ EMP: 152
SALES (est): 81.1MM Privately Held
SIC: 3732 Boat building & repairing

(G-3103)
POSITRON CORPORATION (PA)
4614 Wyland Dr (46516-9787)
PHONE...................................574 295-8777
Fax: 317 576-0358
Raymond J Sweers, President
Anson Wood, QC Mgr
Mandi Miller, Office Mgr
Sarah Shilling, Executive Asst
EMP: 35
SQ FT: 35,000
SALES (est): 6.9MM Privately Held
WEB: www.positroncorp.com
SIC: 3083 Laminated plastics plate & sheet

(G-3104)
**POSTLE ALUMINUM COMPANY
LLC (HQ)**
511 Pine Creek Ct (46516-9090)
PHONE...................................574 389-0800
Fax: 574 389-0700
Dennis Marcott, CEO
EMP: 31
SALES (est): 9.4MM
SALES (corp-wide): 7.2B Publicly Held
SIC: 1081 Metal mining services
PA: Thor Industries, Inc.
601 E Beardsley Ave
Elkhart IN 46514
574 970-7460

(G-3105)
POSTLE OPERATING LLC (HQ)
Also Called: Postle Aluminum Co
511 Pine Creek Ct (46516-9090)
PHONE...................................574 389-0800
Brad Lemler, Controller
Dennis Marcott, Mng Member
Michael Batts, Technology
▲ EMP: 43 EST: 2006
SQ FT: 112,000
SALES (est): 88.6MM
SALES (corp-wide): 7.2B Publicly Held
WEB: www.postledistributors.com
SIC: 3355 5051 Extrusion ingot, aluminum: made in rolling mills; aluminum bars, rods, ingots, sheets, pipes, plates, etc.
PA: Thor Industries, Inc.
601 E Beardsley Ave
Elkhart IN 46514
574 970-7460

(G-3106)
PRAGMATICS INC
29477 County Road 16 (46516-1313)
PHONE...................................574 295-7908
Claude Gunter, President
Chris Skjold, Vice Pres
EMP: 4
SALES (est): 497.8K Privately Held
SIC: 2833 2835 Medicinals & botanicals; in vitro & in vivo diagnostic substances

(G-3107)
**PRECISION BUFFING AND
POLSG**
Also Called: Precision Building
54194 Adams St (46514-3649)
P.O. Box 1423 (46515-1423)
PHONE...................................574 262-3430
Fax: 574 262-3430
Lori Barry, President
EMP: 3
SQ FT: 9,600
SALES (est): 314.6K Privately Held
SIC: 3471 Polishing, metals or formed products; finishing, metals or formed products

(G-3108)
PRECISION INDUSTRIES CORP
601 Wagner Ave (46516-2357)
P.O. Box 1923 (46515-1923)
PHONE...................................574 522-2626
Fax: 574 522-0009
Sue Ellen Mc Kinnell, President
Jim Hays, Vice Pres
EMP: 12
SQ FT: 30,000
SALES (est): 2.4MM Privately Held
WEB: www.precisionindustriescorp.com
SIC: 3542 Pressing machines; presses; forming, stamping, punching, sizing (machine tools)

(G-3109)
PRECISION STAMPING INC
720 Collins Rd (46516-5419)
P.O. Box 598, Bristol (46507-0598)
PHONE...................................574 522-8987
Jim Checkley, President
Brad Checkley, Vice Pres
Todd Checkley, Treasurer
Brian Checkley, Admin Sec
EMP: 30
SQ FT: 32,000
SALES (est): 5.5MM Privately Held
SIC: 3469 Stamping metal for the trade

(G-3110)
PREMIER FIBERGLASS CO INC
55080 Phillips St (46514-1202)
PHONE...................................574 264-5457
Fax: 574 264-5187
John Kellogg, President
EMP: 40
SQ FT: 40,000
SALES (est): 4.8MM Privately Held
SIC: 3089 Injection molding of plastics

(G-3111)
PREMIER KITCHEN & BATH INC
24615 County Road 45 # 1 (46516-5957)
PHONE...................................574 294-6805
Justin Rockenbaugh, President
EMP: 5
SALES (est): 805.6K Privately Held
SIC: 2541 Counter & sink tops

(G-3112)
PREMIER MOLD
1671 W Franklin St (46516-1912)
PHONE...................................574 293-2846
EMP: 2
SALES (est): 110K Privately Held
SIC: 3544 Mfg Dies/Tools/Jigs/Fixtures

(G-3113)
**PREMIER STRCTRES
ACQSITION INC**
Also Called: Premiere Structures
4200 Middlebury St (46516-5596)
PHONE...................................574 522-4011
Peter Deputy, President
Larry Kantz, Vice Pres
Tom McDaniel, Purchasing
EMP: 60 EST: 2013
SALES: 15MM Privately Held
SIC: 5046 2452 Merchandising machines; modular homes, prefabricated, wood

(G-3114)
PREMIERE BUILDING MTLS INC
Also Called: Orion Lighting
631 Collins Rd (46516-5439)
PHONE...................................574 293-5800
Amy Feil, Branch Mgr
EMP: 8

▲ = Import ▼=Export
◆ =Import/Export

SQ FT: 11,000
SALES (corp-wide): 3MM **Privately Held**
SIC: 3646 Commercial indusl & institutional electric lighting fixtures
PA: Premiere Building Materials, Inc.
8200 Memorial Dr Ste A
Plain City OH 43064
574 293-5800

(G-3115)
PRESERVING PAST
3764 E Jackson Blvd (46516-5205)
PHONE..................................574 835-0833
Julie Cuppy, *Principal*
EMP: 3
SALES (est): 79.1K **Privately Held**
SIC: 2491 Wood preserving

(G-3116)
PRINTED BY ERIK INC
Also Called: AlphaGraphics
660 County Road 15 (46516-9553)
PHONE..................................574 295-1203
Pat Welch, *Principal*
EMP: 7
SALES (est): 798K **Privately Held**
SIC: 2752 Commercial printing, lithographic

(G-3117)
PROAIR LLC (HQ)
2900 County Road 6 W (46514-8297)
PHONE..................................574 264-5494
Fax: 574 264-2194
James Peden, *CEO*
Dennis Mitchell, *President*
David Lavine, *Vice Pres*
▲ EMP: 93
SQ FT: 38,000
SALES (est): 13.8MM **Privately Held**
WEB: www.proairllc.com
SIC: 3585 5075 Air conditioning, motor vehicle; automotive air conditioners
PA: Proair Holdings Corporation
2 University Office Park
Waltham MA 02453
781 891-3066

(G-3118)
PROAIR LLC
2900 County Road 6 W (46514-8297)
PHONE..................................574 264-5494
Dennis Mitchell, *President*
EMP: 10
SALES (corp-wide): 13.8MM **Privately Held**
WEB: www.proairllc.com
SIC: 3585 Air conditioning, motor vehicle
HQ: Proair, Llc
2900 County Road 6 W
Elkhart IN 46514
574 264-5494

(G-3119)
PROLON INC
1040 Sako Ct (46516-9019)
PHONE..................................574 522-8900
Fax: 574 522-3374
Leroy Van Kirk, *Principal*
EMP: 45
SQ FT: 20,000
SALES (est): 9MM **Privately Held**
WEB: www.prolon.com
SIC: 3089 3082 Injection molding of plastics; unsupported plastics profile shapes

(G-3120)
PROTOTYPE BAKER ENGINEERING
53050 Elkhart East Blvd (46514-9479)
PHONE..................................574 266-7223
James Baker, *President*
EMP: 3
SALES (est): 398.5K **Privately Held**
SIC: 3541 Machine tools, metal cutting type

(G-3121)
PT SERVICES INC
2701 Industrial Pkwy # 125 (46516-5441)
PHONE..................................574 970-0512
Patrick Doyle, *President*
Thomas Longcor, *Vice Pres*
EMP: 2

SALES (est): 229.9K **Privately Held**
SIC: 3541 Machine tool replacement & repair parts, metal cutting types

(G-3122)
PUCK SUPPLY & MACHINE LLC
56644 Elk Park Dr (46516-1400)
PHONE..................................574 293-3333
Fax: 574 295-7314
Stevie Nelson, *Sales Associate*
Joe Swald, *Mktg Dir*
EMP: 10
SALES (est): 1.7MM **Privately Held**
SIC: 3089 5085 Injection molding of plastics; industrial supplies; bottler supplies

(G-3123)
PUSSOB APPAREL & PRINTING LLC
1643 Columbian Ave (46514-3439)
PHONE..................................574 229-5795
Ryan Morrison, *Owner*
EMP: 2
SALES (est): 83.9K **Privately Held**
SIC: 2752 Commercial printing, lithographic

(G-3124)
QMP INC
Also Called: Quality Metal Products
2925 Stephen Pl (46514-7701)
PHONE..................................574 262-1575
Fax: 574 262-8765
Shaylor King, *President*
Marjorie King, *Corp Secy*
Tim King, *Vice Pres*
▲ EMP: 40
SALES (est): 6.8MM **Privately Held**
WEB: www.qmp.com
SIC: 3429 3544 3469 Motor vehicle hardware; special dies, tools, jigs & fixtures; metal stampings

(G-3125)
QP INC
530 E Lexington Ave # 155 (46516-3596)
PHONE..................................574 295-6884
Fax: 574 295-6884
Randy Brewers, *President*
Benedict Brewers, *President*
Mike Brewers, *President*
Jack Miller, *Vice Pres*
EMP: 10
SQ FT: 500
SALES (est): 1.1MM **Privately Held**
SIC: 3677 3699 3621 7694 Coil windings, electronic; electrical equipment & supplies; motors & generators; coil winding service

(G-3126)
QUAD 4 PLASTICS INC
1840 Borneman Ave (46517-1334)
PHONE..................................574 293-8660
Fax: 574 293-2869
Fred Pletcher, *President*
Greg Pletcher, *Vice Pres*
Steven Feick, *Treasurer*
Rodney Stamper, *Admin Sec*
EMP: 34
SQ FT: 17,500
SALES (est): 6.5MM **Privately Held**
SIC: 3089 Injection molding of plastics

(G-3127)
QUALITY ENGINEERED PRODUCTS
56802 Elk Ct (46516-1456)
PHONE..................................574 294-6943
Dee Davis, *President*
Laura Bash, *Purchasing*
▲ EMP: 21
SQ FT: 8,000
SALES (est): 3.7MM **Privately Held**
WEB: www.qepdesign.com
SIC: 2672 Adhesive papers, labels or tapes: from purchased material; coated paper, except photographic, carbon or abrasive

(G-3128)
QUALITY PLASTICS AND ENGRG INC
Also Called: D C C
2507 Decio Dr (46514-8647)
PHONE..................................574 262-2621
Fax: 574 264-0089
Rick Donati, *President*
▲ EMP: 30
SQ FT: 33,000
SALES (est): 6.4MM **Privately Held**
SIC: 3089 3679 Injection molding of plastics; harness assemblies for electronic use: wire or cable

(G-3129)
QUALITY PNT PRSTNED FNSHES INC
28827 Us Highway 33 (46516-1625)
PHONE..................................574 294-6944
Fax: 574 293-6891
Jesse Thrash Jr, *President*
Lorraine Thrash, *Admin Sec*
EMP: 6
SQ FT: 8,000
SALES (est): 31.6K **Privately Held**
SIC: 3479 1721 Painting, coating & hot dipping; commercial painting

(G-3130)
QUALITY STEEL & ALUM PDTS INC
Also Called: Dump & Go
28620 County Road 20 (46517-1131)
PHONE..................................574 295-8715
James R Reid, *President*
Carol R Reid, *Admin Sec*
▲ EMP: 22
SALES (est): 13MM **Privately Held**
SIC: 5051 3715 Steel; truck trailers

(G-3131)
QUALITY STEEL & ALUMINIUM
56741 Elk Park Dr (46516-1449)
PHONE..................................574 294-7221
EMP: 2
SALES (est): 164.9K **Privately Held**
SIC: 3544 Special dies & tools

(G-3132)
QUILT DESIGNS INC
Also Called: Quilt Designs At Old Bag Fctry
23669 Wilshire Blvd E (46516-6351)
PHONE..................................574 534-2502
Shirley A Shenk, *President*
J David Shenk, *Corp Secy*
EMP: 6 EST: 1980
SQ FT: 3,000
SALES (est): 523.1K **Privately Held**
WEB: www.quiltdesigns.com
SIC: 2395 5949 2392 Quilting, for the trade; art goods for embroidering, stamped: purchased materials; sewing, needlework & piece goods; household furnishings

(G-3133)
R & R REGULATORS INC
24545 County Road 45 (46516-5959)
PHONE..................................574 522-5846
Thomas Reusser, *President*
EMP: 4
SALES (est): 264.7K **Privately Held**
SIC: 3694 Voltage regulators, automotive

(G-3134)
R & R REGULATORS INC
1801 Minnie St (46516-5736)
PHONE..................................574 522-5846
Tom Reusser, *President*
Terry Malone, *General Mgr*
Ruth Banner, *Corp Secy*
Sabrina Owens, *Manager*
EMP: 14
SQ FT: 9,000
SALES: 700K **Privately Held**
SIC: 3694 5065 5088 3612 Automotive electrical equipment; rectifiers, electronic; electronic parts; pulleys; transformers, except electric; manufactured hardware (general)

(G-3135)
R CONCEPTS INDUSTRIES INC
555 County Road 15 (46516-9784)
PHONE..................................574 295-6641
Fax: 574 295-7537
Chris Curtis, *President*
James Spahn, *Vice Pres*
EMP: 100
SQ FT: 115,000
SALES (est): 17.4MM **Privately Held**
WEB: www.rctoolbox.com
SIC: 3469 3714 3444 3441 Boxes: tool, lunch, mail, etc.: stamped metal; bumpers & bumperettes, motor vehicle; sheet metalwork; fabricated structural metal; partitions & fixtures, except wood

(G-3136)
RAMCO ENGINEERING INC
2805 Frederic Dr (46514-7642)
PHONE..................................574 266-1455
Fax: 574 266-1420
Dee Anna Ryan, *President*
Bill Leeper, *Purch Mgr*
Brian Paul, *Sales Staff*
Deanna K Reed, *Admin Sec*
▲ EMP: 38
SQ FT: 60,000
SALES (est): 7.3MM **Privately Held**
WEB: www.ramco-eng.com
SIC: 3231 3714 3713 Mirrors, truck & automobile: made from purchased glass; motor vehicle parts & accessories; truck & bus bodies

(G-3137)
RANCE ALUMINUM FABRICATION
3012 Mobile Dr (46514-5524)
PHONE..................................574 266-9028
Fax: 574 264-4531
Rod Rance, *President*
Cheryl Rance, *Corp Secy*
EMP: 40
SQ FT: 32,000
SALES (est): 5.9MM **Privately Held**
WEB: www.rancealuminum.com
SIC: 3792 3714 3537 3444 Travel trailers & campers; pickup covers, canopies or caps; motor vehicle body components & frame; industrial trucks & tractors; sheet metalwork

(G-3138)
RANCH FIBERGLASS INC
28564 Holiday Pl (46517-1172)
PHONE..................................574 294-7550
Fax: 574 522-1894
Tim Stankovich, *President*
Sherry Stankovich, *Vice Pres*
Tj Weigand, *Sales Staff*
Howard Roske, *Marketing Mgr*
EMP: 55
SQ FT: 51,000
SALES (est): 10.1MM **Privately Held**
WEB: www.ranchfiberglas.com
SIC: 3792 5561 Pickup covers, canopies or caps; recreational vehicle parts & accessories

(G-3139)
RAYCO MARKETING
29675 Old Us 20 (46514-9351)
PHONE..................................574 293-8416
Ray Petit, *Owner*
EMP: 4
SALES (est): 253.6K **Privately Held**
WEB: www.raycomarketing.com
SIC: 2759 Commercial printing

(G-3140)
RECREATION BY DESIGN LLC
57420 County Road 3 (46517-9798)
PHONE..................................574 294-2117
Randy K Rush,
▼ EMP: 75
SALES (est): 11.8MM **Privately Held**
WEB: www.recreationbydesign.com
SIC: 3792 Travel trailers & campers

(G-3141)
RECYCLING WORKS INC
605 Mason St (46516-2760)
P.O. Box 1492 (46515-1492)
PHONE..................................574 293-3751
Fax: 574 295-8954

G E O G R A P H I C

Charles Himes Jr, *President*
Stephen Himes, *Vice Pres*
EMP: 10
SQ FT: 30,000
SALES (est): 2.4MM **Privately Held**
SIC: 5093 4953 3341 3231 Waste paper; nonferrous metals scrap; refuse systems; secondary nonferrous metals; products of purchased glass; pulp mills

(G-3142)
REDDI-PAC INC
1301 N Nappanee St (46514-1731)
PHONE..................................574 266-6933
Robert Walton, *Principal*
EMP: 25 **Privately Held**
SIC: 2652 Setup paperboard boxes
PA: Reddi-Pac, Inc.
　3700 W Lake Ave
　Glenview IL 60026

(G-3143)
RESCHCOR INC
2711 Industrial Pkwy (46516-5402)
PHONE..................................574 295-2413
Rich Reschly, *Branch Mgr*
EMP: 9
SALES (corp-wide): 23.6MM **Privately Held**
WEB: www.omegaplasticscorp.com
SIC: 3089 Plastic processing
PA: Reschcor, Inc.
　2123 Blakesley Pkwy
　Bristol IN 46507
　574 295-2413

(G-3144)
RESOURCEMFG
3243 Northview Dr (46514-6750)
PHONE..................................574 206-1522
EMP: 2
SALES (est): 101.3K **Privately Held**
SIC: 3999 Manufacturing industries

(G-3145)
RICE FLOORING
58794 Chase Trl (46516-6270)
PHONE..................................574 830-5147
Roger Rice, *Owner*
EMP: 2
SALES (est): 121.6K **Privately Held**
SIC: 2426 Hardwood dimension & flooring mills

(G-3146)
RIM MOLDING AND ENGRG INC
1500 W Hively Ave Ste B (46517-4033)
PHONE..................................574 294-1932
Brian Jagla, *CEO*
Phil Roth, *Vice Pres*
EMP: 15 **EST:** 2010
SALES (est): 3.5MM **Privately Held**
SIC: 2821 Plastics materials & resins; polyurethane resins

(G-3147)
RITE-WAY STEEL INC
25687 Woodlawn Ave (46514-3825)
P.O. Box 28 (46515-0028)
PHONE..................................574 262-3465
Fax: 574 262-8623
Sam Igney, *President*
EMP: 10
SQ FT: 22,000
SALES (est): 850K **Privately Held**
SIC: 3444 Sheet metalwork; studs & joists, sheet metal

(G-3148)
RIVER VALLEY PLASTICS INC
Also Called: Rvp
　1090 D I Dr (46514-8294)
PHONE..................................574 262-5221
Harold J McCracken Jr, *President*
Mitchell Mc Cracken, *Vice Pres*
Paamela K Bidwell, *Admin Sec*
EMP: 28
SQ FT: 22,000
SALES (est): 6.1MM **Privately Held**
WEB: www.rivervalleyplastics.com
SIC: 3089 3544 Injection molding of plastics; special dies & tools

(G-3149)
RIVERSIDE TOOL CORP (DH)
3504 Henke St (46515-7653)
P.O. Box 1425 (46515-1425)
PHONE..................................574 522-6798
Fax: 574 522-6712
Ronald Migedt, *President*
Ron Migedt, *General Mgr*
Brandon Denning, *Production*
Scot Troyer, *Sales Engr*
Dustin Kessler, *Sales Staff*
EMP: 26
SQ FT: 14,000
SALES (est): 9.2MM
SALES (corp-wide): 1.7B **Privately Held**
SIC: 7389 3545 Grinding, precision: commercial or industrial; tools & accessories for machine tools

(G-3150)
ROYALE PHOENIX INC
53972 N Park Ave (46514-5000)
P.O. Box 1664 (46515-1664)
PHONE..................................574 206-1216
Dan R Jourdan, *President*
Glenn J Berden, *Vice Pres*
Glenn Berden, *Vice Pres*
Vicky Jourdan, *Administration*
EMP: 2
SALES: 150K **Privately Held**
SIC: 3711 Motor homes, self-contained, assembly of

(G-3151)
RUCO INC
Also Called: Regal Mold & Die
　1817 Leer Dr (46514-5447)
PHONE..................................574 262-4110
Fax: 574 262-9144
Gary Rheude, *President*
Micheal Leamon, *Vice Pres*
Amy Stutzman, *Manager*
Tom Rogers, *Director*
EMP: 28 **EST:** 1959
SQ FT: 25,000
SALES (est): 5.2MM **Privately Held**
WEB: www.regalmold.com
SIC: 3544 Forms (molds), for foundry & plastics working machinery; industrial molds

(G-3152)
S H LEGGITT COMPANY
Also Called: Marshall Gas Controls
　831 E Windsor Ave Unit 9 (46514-5568)
PHONE..................................574 264-0230
Trey Ywell, *Manager*
EMP: 7
SALES (corp-wide): 53.6MM **Privately Held**
SIC: 3491 3451 3082 Gas valves & parts, industrial; screw machine products; tubes, unsupported plastic
PA: S. H. Leggitt Company
　1000 Civic Center Loop
　San Marcos TX 78666
　956 504-6440

(G-3153)
SAFE FLEET MIRRORS
319 Roske Dr (46516-9084)
PHONE..................................574 266-3700
Laurie Pepple, *President*
EMP: 17
SALES (est): 3.2MM **Privately Held**
SIC: 3714 Motor vehicle parts & accessories

(G-3154)
SAMARON CORP
Also Called: Troyer Products
　3310 Magnum Dr (46516-9020)
PHONE..................................574 970-7070
Fax: 574 848-5825
Daniel Holtz, *CEO*
David Buck, *President*
Jennifer Yoder, *Financial Exec*
EMP: 25
SQ FT: 16,000
SALES (est): 8.5MM **Privately Held**
SIC: 5131 3429 8748 Piece goods & notions; manufactured hardware (general); business consulting

(G-3155)
SAND DESIGNS INC
2609 E Jackson Blvd (46516-5055)
PHONE..................................574 293-5791
Enid Schmitt, *President*
George Schmitt, *Admin Sec*
EMP: 3
SALES: 100K **Privately Held**
SIC: 5199 3199 Fabrics, yarns & knit goods; straps, leather

(G-3156)
SANDMAN PRODUCTS LLC
2604 Glenview Dr (46514-9243)
PHONE..................................574 264-7700
Lloyd Troyer,
EMP: 7
SQ FT: 6,000
SALES: 800K **Privately Held**
SIC: 3553 Sanding machines, except portable floor sanders: woodworking

(G-3157)
SCG ACQUISITION COMPANY LLC
Also Called: Speedgrip Chuck Company
　2000 Industrial Pkwy (46516-5411)
P.O. Box 596 (46515-0596)
PHONE..................................574 294-1506
Nancy Renaud, *CEO*
EMP: 50
SALES (est): 614.3K **Privately Held**
SIC: 3545 Machine tool attachments & accessories

(G-3158)
SCHNEIDER ELECTRIC
4714 Hoffman St (46516-9570)
PHONE..................................574 293-0877
EMP: 3
SALES (est): 106.9K **Privately Held**
SIC: 3613 Switchgear & switchboard apparatus

(G-3159)
SCHUSTER SHEET METAL INC
418 Roske Dr (46516-9085)
PHONE..................................574 293-4802
Fax: 574 522-0426
Doug Livingston, *President*
EMP: 8
SQ FT: 10,500
SALES (est): 1.3MM **Privately Held**
SIC: 3444 Sheet metal specialties, not stamped

(G-3160)
SELECT TOOL & ENG INC
21537 Protecta Dr (46516-9542)
PHONE..................................574 295-6197
Fax: 574 522-5526
Carl Esch, *CEO*
Mark Esch, *President*
EMP: 8
SQ FT: 20,000
SALES (est): 720K **Privately Held**
SIC: 3599 Machine shop, jobbing & repair

(G-3161)
SELKING INTERNATIONAL INC
836 Verdant St (46516-9038)
PHONE..................................574 522-2001
Ken Waite, *Sales Staff*
Alan Jordan, *Manager*
EMP: 9
SALES (corp-wide): 62.9MM **Privately Held**
SIC: 5012 7538 3537 Trucks, commercial; general automotive repair shops; industrial trucks & tractors
HQ: Selking International Inc
　2807 Goshen Rd
　Fort Wayne IN 46808

(G-3162)
SERVICE PRINTERS INC
28574 Phillips St (46514-1236)
PHONE..................................574 266-6710
Fax: 574 266-1689
Barbara J Kujawski, *President*
Tim Kujawski, *Principal*
Barbara Kujawski, *Vice Pres*
Gary Blair, *Prdtn Mgr*
Dan Demeyer, *Sales Staff*
▲ **EMP:** 28

SQ FT: 36,000
SALES (est): 7.2MM **Privately Held**
WEB: www.serviceprinterinc.com
SIC: 2752 2791 2789 Commercial printing, offset; typesetting; bookbinding & related work

(G-3163)
SEW CREATIVE THREADS LLC
189 County Road 6 W (46514-5557)
PHONE..................................574 266-7397
Brenda Miller, *Mng Member*
EMP: 5 **EST:** 2010
SALES: 200K **Privately Held**
SIC: 5131 2517 Thread; sewing machine cabinets & cases, wood

(G-3164)
SHARPS BATON MFG CORP
Also Called: Sharp's Creations
　57330 Orchard Ridge Dr (46516-8904)
PHONE..................................574 214-9389
Fax: 574 522-2172
Jim Sharp, *President*
Mark Sharp, *Treasurer*
Linda Degetter, *Manager*
EMP: 8
SQ FT: 1,600
SALES (est): 873.9K **Privately Held**
WEB: www.sharp-baton.com
SIC: 3949 5949 3446 Batons; notions, including trim; needlework goods & supplies; sewing & needlework; architectural metalwork

(G-3165)
SHERRCOM INDUSTRIES LLC
51005 Twilight Dr (46514-8547)
PHONE..................................574 266-7389
EMP: 2 **EST:** 2010
SALES (est): 75K **Privately Held**
SIC: 3999 Mfg Misc Products

(G-3166)
SHERWOOD INDUSTRIES INC
1805 Leer Dr (46514-5447)
PHONE..................................574 262-2639
Ronald I Schemenauer, *President*
David M Schemenauer, *VP Sales*
Ed Wright, *Director*
Steve Schemenauer, *Executive*
Ronald A Schemenauer, *Shareholder*
▲ **EMP:** 45
SQ FT: 46,000
SALES (est): 6.2MM **Privately Held**
SIC: 3231 Ornamental glass: cut, engraved or otherwise decorated; decorated glassware: chipped, engraved, etched, etc.; mirrored glass; mirrors, truck & automobile: made from purchased glass

(G-3167)
SHIELD RESTRAINT SYSTEMS INC (HQ)
3802 Gallatin Way (46514-7650)
PHONE..................................574 266-8330
Brian Babin, *President*
Gregory Rufus, *Vice Pres*
Jack Curtis, *Engineer*
Myron Hecht, *Engineer*
Anita Hemmingsen, *Human Res Mgr*
▲ **EMP:** 120
SQ FT: 50,000
SALES (est): 73.6MM
SALES (corp-wide): 96.6MM **Privately Held**
WEB: www.amsafecp.com
SIC: 2399 Seat belts, automobile & aircraft
PA: Amsafe Partners, Inc.
　1043 N 47th Ave
　Phoenix AZ 85043
　602 850-2850

(G-3168)
SHROCK MANUFACTURING INC
2746 Jami St (46514-8792)
PHONE..................................574 264-4126
Fax: 574 262-8725
Fred Shrock, *President*
Scott Shrock, *Vice Pres*
Janet Shrock, *Treasurer*
Theresa Burger, *Office Mgr*
EMP: 35
SQ FT: 68,000

SALES: 1.4MM **Privately Held**
WEB: www.shrockmfg.com
SIC: **3499** Furniture parts, metal; automobile seat frames, metal

(G-3169)
SIEMENS AG
2720 E Jackson Blvd (46516-5052)
PHONE....................................574 522-6807
EMP: 2
SALES (est): 88.3K **Privately Held**
SIC: **3661** Telephones & telephone apparatus

(G-3170)
SIGMA SWITCHES PLUS INC
Also Called: Destin Products Division
4703 Wyland Dr (46516-9681)
PHONE....................................574 294-5776
Fax: 574 294-8744
Daniel Rothbauer, *Ch of Bd*
Brian Rothbauer, *President*
Debra May, *Vice Pres*
Adrian Byers, *Sales Staff*
▲ EMP: 21
SQ FT: 12,000
SALES (est): 3.5MM **Privately Held**
SIC: **3625** 3613 Switches, electric power; switchgear & switchboard apparatus

(G-3171)
SIGNODE INDUSTRIAL GROUP LLC
Also Called: Anglebaord
1301 N Nappanee St (46514-1731)
PHONE....................................574 266-6933
Wes Lenig, *Manager*
EMP: 30
SALES (corp-wide): 8.7B **Publicly Held**
SIC: **2679** Paper products, converted
HQ: Signode Industrial Group Llc
3650 W Lake Ave
Glenview IL 60026
847 724-7500

(G-3172)
SIGNS OF TIMES
2201 S Nappanee St (46517-1354)
PHONE....................................574 296-7464
Les Anderson, *Principal*
EMP: 3
SALES (est): 261.8K **Privately Held**
SIC: **3993** Signs, not made in custom sign painting shops

(G-3173)
SISSYS CERAMICS
30803 County Road 20 (46517-9758)
PHONE....................................951 550-7728
EMP: 2
SALES (est): 117.8K **Privately Held**
SIC: **3269** Pottery products

(G-3174)
SJC INDUSTRIES CORP
Also Called: Marque
1110 D I Dr (46514-8231)
PHONE....................................574 264-7511
Fax: 574 262-9236
Chris Graff, *CEO*
Charles Drake, *President*
James Evans, *CFO*
▼ EMP: 215
SQ FT: 120,000
SALES (est): 2.9MM
SALES (corp-wide): 7.2B **Publicly Held**
SIC: **3713** Ambulance bodies
PA: Thor Industries, Inc.
601 E Beardsley Ave
Elkhart IN 46514
574 970-7460

(G-3175)
SKYLINE CHAMPION CORPORATION (PA)
2520 Bypass Rd (46514-1584)
P.O. Box 743 (46515-0743)
PHONE....................................574 294-6521
Fax: 574 295-7061
John C Firth, *Ch of Bd*
Richard W Florea, *President*
Jeffrey A Newport, *COO*
Robert C Davis, *VP Mfg*
Jon S Pilarski, *CFO*
EMP: 277 EST: 1951
SQ FT: 59,000

SALES: 236.5MM **Publicly Held**
WEB: www.skylinecorp.com
SIC: **2451** 2452 3792 Mobile homes; mobile homes, except recreational; prefabricated buildings, wood; travel trailers & campers

(G-3176)
SKYLINE HOMES INC (HQ)
2520 Bypass Rd (46514-1584)
P.O. Box 743 (46515-0743)
PHONE....................................574 294-6521
Jon Pilarski, *CFO*
EMP: 150
SALES: 200.1MM
SALES (corp-wide): 236.5MM **Publicly Held**
WEB: www.skylinerv.com
SIC: **2451** 3792 Mobile homes; travel trailers & campers; travel trailer chassis
PA: Skyline Champion Corporation
2520 Bypass Rd
Elkhart IN 46514
574 294-6521

(G-3177)
SMART CHOICE MOBILE INC
4542 Elkhart Rd (46517-3571)
PHONE....................................574 830-5727
Nabeel Aldeir, *Principal*
EMP: 11
SALES (corp-wide): 6.5MM **Privately Held**
SIC: **3661** Telephone sets, all types except cellular radio
PA: Smart Choice Mobile, Inc.
7667 W 95th St Ste 300
Hickory Hills IL 60457
708 581-4904

(G-3178)
SMCO INC
Also Called: Ferret
2505 Laura Ct (46517-1197)
P.O. Box 35 (46515-0035)
PHONE....................................574 295-1482
Fax: 574 293-9444
Scott McMeekan, *President*
EMP: 30 EST: 1981
SQ FT: 28,000
SALES: 12MM **Privately Held**
SIC: **3441** Fabricated structural metal

(G-3179)
SMOKERS IRON WORKS
Also Called: Plexiclass Awards Disc Tropies
30907 County Road 16 (46516-1037)
PHONE....................................574 674-6683
John Smoker, *Owner*
EMP: 3
SALES (est): 207.1K **Privately Held**
SIC: **3499** 3873 Novelties & giftware, including trophies; clocks, assembly of

(G-3180)
SOLOTAT INDUSTRIES LLC
1233 W Hively Ave (46517-4032)
P.O. Box 2207 (46515-2207)
PHONE....................................574 320-1436
Thomas Teach,
EMP: 3 EST: 2012
SALES (est): 148.6K **Privately Held**
SIC: **3086** 2515 3484 3482 Packaging & shipping materials, foamed plastic; mattresses, containing felt, foam rubber, urethane, etc.; guns (firearms) or gun parts, 30 mm. & below; small arms ammunition; firearms & ammunition, except sporting

(G-3181)
SOUTHSIDE MINI STORAGE
2031 W Mishawaka Rd (46517-4005)
PHONE....................................574 293-3270
Fax: 574 293-3270
Carl Gilley, *President*
Jewelene Gilley, *Corp Secy*
EMP: 5
SQ FT: 6,400
SALES (est): 380K **Privately Held**
SIC: **3716** Recreational van conversion (self-propelled), factory basis

(G-3182)
SOUTHSIDE PLATING WORKS INC
2010 Superior St (46516-4706)
PHONE....................................219 293-5508
EMP: 2 EST: 2012
SALES (est): 76.7K **Privately Held**
SIC: **3471** Plating of metals or formed products

(G-3183)
SPECIAL METALS CORPORATION
2900 Higgins Blvd (46514-5449)
PHONE....................................574 262-3451
William Belcher, *Plant Mgr*
Paul Krewer, *Marketing Staff*
EMP: 40
SALES (corp-wide): 242.1B **Publicly Held**
SIC: **3356** 3341 Nonferrous rolling & drawing; secondary nonferrous metals
HQ: Special Metals Corporation
4832 Richmond Rd Ste 100
Warrensville Heights OH 44128
216 755-3030

(G-3184)
SPECTRUM RV LLC ✪
2801 Dexter Dr (46514-8225)
PHONE....................................574 970-5554
EMP: 2 EST: 2017
SALES (est): 131.3K **Privately Held**
SIC: **3792** Travel trailers & campers

(G-3185)
SPHEROS NORTH AMERICA INC (PA)
22150 Challenger Dr (46514-7005)
PHONE....................................574 264-2190
Casey Cummings, *CEO*
EMP: 11
SALES (est): 19.1MM **Privately Held**
SIC: **3714** Motor vehicle parts & accessories

(G-3186)
STANBIO LABORATORY LP
Efk Life Sciences
1814 Leer Dr (46514-5447)
PHONE....................................830 249-0772
Fax: 574 266-0062
Michael Kuelbs, *QC Mgr*
Cliff Yehle, *Manager*
EMP: 15
SQ FT: 14,250
SALES (corp-wide): 54.9MM **Privately Held**
WEB: www.stanbio.com
SIC: **2835** In vitro & in vivo diagnostic substances; enzyme & isoenzyme diagnostic agents
HQ: Stanbio Laboratory, L.P.
1261 N Main St
Boerne TX 78006
830 824-0772

(G-3187)
STANDARD LABEL CO
4200 Wyland Dr (46516-9509)
PHONE....................................574 522-3548
Fax: 574 522-0070
Tom Wyncott, *President*
Kris Wyncott, *Vice Pres*
EMP: 20 EST: 1980
SQ FT: 20,000
SALES (est): 3.8MM **Privately Held**
WEB: www.standard-label.com
SIC: **2672** Adhesive papers, labels or tapes: from purchased material

(G-3188)
STAR MANUFACTURING LLC
53509 Lakefield Dr (46514-9474)
PHONE....................................574 329-6042
Allen Medford, *Mng Member*
EMP: 5
SALES (est): 331.8K **Privately Held**
SIC: **3999** Manufacturing industries

(G-3189)
STAR TOOL & DIE INC
53088 Faith Ave (46514-9373)
PHONE....................................574 264-3815
Fax: 574 266-6923

Jerry Beck, *President*
Ed Beck, *Vice Pres*
Linda Beck, *Treasurer*
Tom Datena, *Admin Sec*
EMP: 15
SQ FT: 10,000
SALES (est): 1.4MM **Privately Held**
WEB: www.startooldie.com
SIC: **3544** 3599 Special dies & tools; machine shop, jobbing & repair

(G-3190)
STARTRACKS CUSTOM LIFTS
1227 W Beardsley Ave (46514-2223)
PHONE....................................574 596-5331
Bob Helvie, *Principal*
EMP: 3
SALES (est): 165.2K **Privately Held**
SIC: **3999** Manufacturing industries

(G-3191)
STATE WIDE ALUMINUM INC (DH)
Also Called: State Wide Window
3518 County Road 6 E (46514-7663)
P.O. Box 987 (46515-0987)
PHONE....................................574 262-2594
Fax: 574 262-4125
Jim Donohue, *President*
Larry Wolfe, *Vice Pres*
Mike Beckman, *Admin Sec*
◆ EMP: 100 EST: 1971
SQ FT: 75,000
SALES: 25.8MM
SALES (corp-wide): 1B **Privately Held**
WEB: www.statewidealum.com
SIC: **3714** 3231 3444 Motor vehicle body components & frame; strengthened or reinforced glass; doors, glass: made from purchased glass; sheet metalwork
HQ: Truck Accessories Group, Llc
28858 Ventura Dr
Elkhart IN 46517
574 522-5337

(G-3192)
STEINWAY PIANO COMPANY INC (DH)
600 Industrial Pkwy (46516-5414)
PHONE....................................574 522-1675
John Stoner Jr, *President*
EMP: 100
SQ FT: 25,000
SALES (est): 117.8MM
SALES (corp-wide): 316.7MM **Privately Held**
SIC: **3931** Pianos, all types: vertical, grand, spinet, player, etc.
HQ: Conn-Selmer, Inc.
600 Industrial Pkwy
Elkhart IN 46516
574 522-1675

(G-3193)
STEPHENSON BLOCK INC
2211 Grant St (46514-4013)
PHONE....................................574 264-6660
Fax: 574 266-1457
Stephen Hill, *President*
Becky Adams, *Vice Pres*
Jeanne Gove, *Treasurer*
EMP: 6 EST: 1949
SQ FT: 8,600
SALES: 1.3MM **Privately Held**
SIC: **3272** 5032 Concrete products used to facilitate drainage; concrete & cinder building products

(G-3194)
STRAUSS BAKERIES INC (PA)
228 W High St (46516-3130)
PHONE....................................574 293-9027
Fax: 574 522-2137
Daniel Strauss, *CEO*
Stephen F Strauss, *President*
EMP: 100 EST: 1951
SQ FT: 10,000
SALES (est): 5.7MM **Privately Held**
SIC: **2051** 5461 2052 Bread, cake & related products; breads, rolls & buns; cakes, pies & pastries; doughnuts, except frozen; bakeries; pies; doughnuts; cookies; cookies & crackers

(G-3195)
STYRENE SOLUTIONS LLC
115 E Windsor Ave (46514-5546)
PHONE................................574 876-4610
EMP: 2
SALES (est): 74.4K Privately Held
SIC: 2865 Styrene

(G-3196)
SUBURBAN MANUFACTURING COMPANY
1136 Verdant St (46516-9044)
PHONE................................574 294-5681
Fax: 574 293-1685
Michael A Higley, Sales/Mktg Mgr
EMP: 15
SQ FT: 27,000 Privately Held
WEB: www.rvcomfort.com
SIC: 3822 4225 5012 Water heater controls; general warehousing; recreational vehicles, motor homes & trailers
HQ: Suburban Manufacturing Company
676 Broadway St
Dayton TN 37321
423 775-2131

(G-3197)
SUGGS CUSTOM DESIGN SOLUTIONS
336 W Garfield Ave (46516-2501)
PHONE................................574 549-2174
Thadd Suggs, CEO
EMP: 3 EST: 2011
SALES (est): 234K Privately Held
SIC: 3315 Steel wire & related products

(G-3198)
SUMMIT SEATING INC
2601 Northland Dr (46514-7614)
PHONE................................574 264-9636
Ray Fink, Principal
Cindy Philipson, Officer
EMP: 19 EST: 2001
SQ FT: 8,800
SALES: 2.3MM Privately Held
WEB: www.hometheatercollection.com
SIC: 2399 Seat covers, automobile

(G-3199)
SUPERIOR OIL COMPANY INC
Also Called: Superior Fiberglass & Resins
1030 All Pro Dr (46514-8815)
PHONE................................574 264-0161
Wayne Dixon, Manager
EMP: 40
SALES (corp-wide): 199.9MM Privately Held
SIC: 2911 Petroleum refining
PA: Superior Oil Company Inc
1402 N Capitol Ave # 100
Indianapolis IN 46202
317 781-4400

(G-3200)
SUPERIOR SEATING INC
21468 C St (46516-9670)
PHONE................................574 389-9011
Fax: 574 389-8292
Cindy Battisti, President
Angie Campbell, Office Mgr
John S Batisti, Admin Sec
EMP: 20
SQ FT: 8,000
SALES: 2.1MM Privately Held
WEB: www.superior-seats.com
SIC: 2531 Seats, automobile

(G-3201)
SUPERIOR TOOL & DIE COMPANY (PA)
2325 S Nappanee St (46517-1397)
PHONE................................574 293-2591
Fax: 574 295-6348
Roy L Hershberger, President
Thomas Hershberger, Vice Pres
Rick Die, Purchasing
Mary E Hershberger, Treasurer
Lynn Carstens, Accountant
EMP: 26 EST: 1952
SQ FT: 35,000

(G-3202)
T J B INC
2926 Paul Dr (46514-8796)
PHONE................................219 293-8030
Terry Kraus, Principal
EMP: 2
SALES (est): 88.9K Privately Held
SIC: 3443 Fabricated plate work (boiler shop)

(G-3203)
T SHORTER MANUFACTURING INC
2931 Dexter Dr (46514-8227)
PHONE................................574 264-4131
Fax: 574 262-8396
Terry Shorter, President
Jane Shorter, Corp Secy
EMP: 3
SQ FT: 10,000
SALES: 592.8K Privately Held
SIC: 3699 3931 3599 Fire control or bombing equipment, electronic; musical instruments; machine shop, jobbing & repair

(G-3204)
TAIL WIND TRANSPORT
Also Called: Tail Wind Logistics
2991 Paul Dr (46514-8797)
PHONE................................574 343-2157
Vanessa Smithey, Owner
EMP: 15
SALES (est): 993.3K Privately Held
SIC: 3715 Truck trailers

(G-3205)
TAMCO MANUFACTURING CO
2717 Oakland Ave (46517-1558)
P.O. Box 1794 (46515-1794)
PHONE................................574 294-1909
Tony Asoera, Owner
EMP: 4
SQ FT: 25,000
SALES: 150K Privately Held
WEB: www.tamcomfg.com
SIC: 5072 3559 Builders' hardware; plastics working machinery

(G-3206)
TB PLASTIC EXTRUSIONS MICHIANA
54432 Adams St (46514-3647)
PHONE................................574 266-7409
Rodrigo Cortes,
EMP: 50
SALES (est): 3.6MM Privately Held
SIC: 3498 Fabricated pipe & fittings

(G-3207)
TCB ENTERPRISES LLC
4600 Wyland Dr (46516-9787)
PHONE................................574 522-3971
Gretchen Snyder,
Tony Cunnane,
Robert Loper,
▲ EMP: 10
SALES: 2.3MM
SALES (corp-wide): 2.3B Privately Held
SIC: 3743 3647 3498 Trackless trolley buses; vehicular lighting equipment; tube fabricating (contract bending & shaping)
PA: Nfi Group Inc
711 Kernaghan Ave
Winnipeg MB R2C 3
204 224-1251

(G-3208)
TCB INDUSTRIES INC
4519 Wyland Dr (46516-9642)
PHONE................................574 522-3971
Tony Cunnane, Principal
Robert Loper, Principal
Bob Loper, Vice Pres
▲ EMP: 14
SQ FT: 23,000
SALES (est): 119.4K Privately Held
SIC: 3743 Trackless trolley buses

(G-3209)
TEAM SPIRIT TRLRS ELKHART INC
25954 Pierina Dr (46514-5255)
PHONE................................574 266-2966
Fax: 574 266-4076
Dan Stutsman, CEO
EMP: 20
SALES (est): 2.8MM Privately Held
WEB: www.teamspirittrailers.com
SIC: 3715 Truck trailers

(G-3210)
TEKMODO STRUCTURES LLC
1701 Conant St (46516-4716)
PHONE................................574 970-5800
Joan Hahn, Accountant
Marc Lacounte,
EMP: 2
SALES (est): 438.7K Privately Held
SIC: 3089 Composition stone, plastic

(G-3211)
TENNECO AUTOMOTIVE OPER CO INC
4825 Hoffman St (46516-9052)
PHONE................................574 296-9400
Stephen Roseland, Manager
EMP: 70
SALES (corp-wide): 9.2B Publicly Held
WEB: www.tenneco-automotive.com
SIC: 3714 Motor vehicle engines & parts
HQ: Tenneco Automotive Operating Company, Inc.
500 N Field Dr
Lake Forest IL 60045
847 482-5000

(G-3212)
THERMAL CERAMICS INC
Also Called: Morgan Thermal Ceramics
2730 Industrial Pkwy (46516-5401)
PHONE................................574 296-3500
Frank Duchon, Mktg Dir
John Stang, Branch Mgr
EMP: 38
SALES (corp-wide): 1.3B Privately Held
WEB: www.thermalceramics.com
SIC: 3299 3255 3769 3714 Ceramic fiber; brick, clay refractory; guided missile & space vehicle parts & auxiliary equipment; motor vehicle parts & accessories
HQ: Thermal Ceramics Inc.
2102 Old Savannah Rd
Augusta GA 30906
706 796-4200

(G-3213)
THINK NORTH AMERICA INC
3221 Magnum Dr (46516-9021)
PHONE................................313 565-6781
Richard Canny, Branch Mgr
EMP: 30 Privately Held
SIC: 3711 Motor vehicles & car bodies
PA: Think North America, Inc.
22226 Garrison St
Dearborn MI 48124

(G-3214)
THOR INDUSTRIES INC (PA)
601 E Beardsley Ave (46514-3305)
PHONE................................574 970-7460
Peter B Orthwein, Ch of Bd
Robert W Martin, President
Kenneth D Julian, Senior VP
Todd Woelfer, Senior VP
Kenneth Julian, Vice Pres
EMP: 174
SQ FT: 21,000
SALES: 7.2B Publicly Held
WEB: www.thorindustries.com
SIC: 3799 3711 Recreational vehicles; buses, all types, assembly of

(G-3215)
THOR MOTOR COACH
4221 Pine Creek Rd (46516-9557)
PHONE................................574 266-1100
Julie Delapaz, Manager
EMP: 2 EST: 2014
SALES (est): 263.6K Privately Held
SIC: 3716 Motor homes

(G-3216)
THOR MOTOR COACH INC
520 County Road 15 (46514-9552)
P.O. Box 1486 (46515-1486)
PHONE................................574 266-1111
Fax: 574 293-5256
Jeff Kime, President
Fred Palmer, Opers Staff
Mark Smith, Opers Staff
Ryan Burkhart, Sales Staff
Dave Daniels, Sales Staff
▼ EMP: 275
SALES (est): 138MM
SALES (corp-wide): 7.2B Publicly Held
WEB: www.thorindustries.com
SIC: 3716 3792 Motor homes; recreational van conversion (self-propelled), factory basis; travel trailers & campers
PA: Thor Industries, Inc.
601 E Beardsley Ave
Elkhart IN 46514
574 970-7460

(G-3217)
TIME OUT TRAILERS INC
4636 Chester Dr (46516-9056)
PHONE................................574 294-7671
Blake Walters, President
Julie Walters, Vice Pres
EMP: 8
SQ FT: 12,000
SALES: 1.4MM Privately Held
WEB: www.timeout-trailers.com
SIC: 3751 Motorcycle accessories

(G-3218)
TL ENTERPRISES LLC
Also Called: Trailer Life Publishing
2901 E Bristol St Ste D (46514-4385)
PHONE................................574 262-4706
Fax: 574 522-0418
P Gillerlani, Director
EMP: 10
SALES (corp-wide): 488.7MM Privately Held
WEB: www.motorhomemagazine.com
SIC: 7319 2721 7313 Shopping news, advertising & distributing service; periodicals; newspaper advertising representative
HQ: TI Enterprises, Llc
2750 Park View Ct Ste 240
Oxnard CA 93036
805 981-8393

(G-3219)
TL INDUSTRIES INC
21746 Buckingham Rd (46516-9703)
PHONE................................419 666-8144
Randy Rush, President
Bonnie Rush, Corp Secy
EMP: 40 EST: 1966
SQ FT: 25,000
SALES (est): 4.6MM Privately Held
SIC: 3792 Travel trailers & campers

(G-3220)
TOPSTITCH INC
921 Summa Dr (46516-9037)
PHONE................................574 293-6633
Rhonda Pawlowski, President
Alanna Krause, Vice Pres
EMP: 16
SALES (est): 1.6MM Privately Held
SIC: 2395 2759 Embroidery & art needlework; screen printing

(G-3221)
TOUCHTRONICS INC
57315 Nagy Dr Ste A (46517-1081)
PHONE................................574 294-2570
Alice Poseley, President
David Evans, Design Engr
Ron Mathia, Treasurer
Natalie Rose, Shareholder
Joan Young, Admin Sec
EMP: 12
SQ FT: 11,000
SALES (est): 3.1MM Privately Held
WEB: www.touchtronics.com
SIC: 3625 Switches, electronic applications; control equipment, electric

Note on (G-3201) missing closing: SQ FT: 35,000

▲ = Import ▼ =Export
◆ =Import/Export

(G-3222)
TRANSHIELD INC (PA)
2932 Thorne Dr (46514-8228)
PHONE....................................574 742-4333
Fax: 574 266-5220
James Glick, *President*
Matt Peat, *Exec VP*
Brian McKenzie, *Vice Pres*
Mark Schuck, *Vice Pres*
Gregory Todt, *Vice Pres*
◆ EMP: 41
SQ FT: 31,050
SALES (est): 11.3MM **Privately Held**
WEB: www.transhield-usa.com
SIC: 2394 Liners & covers, fabric: made
from purchased materials

(G-3223)
TRIM-LOK INC
1642 Gateway Ct (46514-8216)
PHONE....................................574 227-1143
Darrly Torrey, *Owner*
EMP: 4
SALES (est): 187.1K **Privately Held**
SIC: 3089 Molding primary plastic

(G-3224)
TRP INTERNATIONAL LLC
21840 Protecta Dr (46516-9530)
PHONE....................................574 389-9941
Lyle Townsend, *Manager*
EMP: 15
SALES (est): 2.6MM **Privately Held**
SIC: 3599 Amusement park equipment
PA: Trp International, Llc
5308 Beck Dr
Elkhart IN 46516

(G-3225)
**TRU-FORM METAL PRODUCTS
INC**
1025 D I Dr (46514-8294)
PHONE....................................574 266-8020
Fax: 574 266-8070
Joseph Straughn, *President*
EMP: 12
SQ FT: 15,000
SALES (est): 2MM **Privately Held**
SIC: 3465 Automotive stampings; fenders,
automobile: stamped or pressed metal

(G-3226)
**TRUCK ACCESSORIES GROUP
INC**
Leer Midwest
58288 Ventura Dr (46517-9431)
P.O. Box 1128 (46515-1128)
PHONE....................................574 522-5337
Deborah Molnar, *Human Resources*
Pat Hare, *Manager*
EMP: 165
SALES (corp-wide): 1B **Privately Held**
WEB: www.leer.com
SIC: 3792 Pickup covers, canopies or caps
HQ: Truck Accessories Group, Llc
28858 Ventura Dr
Elkhart IN 46517
574 522-5337

(G-3227)
**TRUTH PUBLISHING COMPANY
INC (PA)**
Also Called: The Truth
421 S 2nd St Ste 100 (46516-3230)
P.O. Box 487 (46515-0487)
PHONE....................................574 294-1661
Fax: 574 294-3895
John F Dille III, *President*
John F Dille III, *President*
David Ogle, *Publisher*
Robert A Watson, *Corp Secy*
▲ EMP: 185 EST: 1889
SQ FT: 30,000
SALES (est): 25MM **Privately Held**
WEB: www.etruth.com
SIC: 2711 Newspapers, publishing & print-
ing

(G-3228)
**TUBE FORM SOLUTIONS LLC
(PA)**
Also Called: Elt Tooling
435 Roske Dr (46516-9086)
PHONE....................................574 295-5041
Jeffrey Jacobs,

Michael Thomas,
▲ EMP: 21
SALES (est): 15.2MM **Privately Held**
SIC: 3549 Metalworking machinery

(G-3229)
TUBE FORM SOLUTIONS LLC
4221 Pine Creek Rd (46516-9557)
PHONE....................................574 266-5230
Jeff Jacobs,
EMP: 20
SALES (corp-wide): 15.2MM **Privately
Held**
SIC: 3549 Metalworking machinery
PA: Tube Form Solutions, Llc
435 Roske Dr
Elkhart IN 46516
574 295-5041

(G-3230)
TWIN AIR PRODUCTS INC
4602 Chester Dr (46516-9056)
PHONE....................................574 295-1129
Fax: 574 295-1087
Roger L Burks, *President*
Charlotte Burks, *Vice Pres*
Chad Burks, *Webmaster*
▲ EMP: 6
SQ FT: 15,000
SALES (est): 730K **Privately Held**
SIC: 3585 7532 Air conditioning, motor ve-
hicle; van conversion

(G-3231)
ULTRA-FAB PRODUCTS INC
57985 State Road 19 (46517-1207)
PHONE....................................574 294-7571
Searer Craig, *President*
Darryl Searer, *Admin Sec*
▲ EMP: 15 EST: 1958
SQ FT: 24,000
SALES (est): 3.3MM **Privately Held**
WEB: www.ultra-fab.com
SIC: 3429 Motor vehicle hardware

(G-3232)
ULTRA-HEAT INC
Also Called: Uhi Worldwide Inc.
1314 Perkins Ave (46516-4913)
P.O. Box 1454 (46515-1454)
PHONE....................................574 522-6594
Fax: 574 522-1967
Donna Temple, *President*
Michael Lewis, *Vice Pres*
EMP: 13
SQ FT: 12,000
SALES (est): 2MM **Privately Held**
WEB: www.ultraheat.com
SIC: 3634 3714 5561 Heaters, space
electric; electric household fans, heaters
& humidifiers; heaters, motor vehicle;
recreational vehicle parts & accessories

(G-3233)
UNITED PET FOODS INC
30809 Corwin Rd (46514-9394)
PHONE....................................574 674-5981
Fax: 574 674-0713
Sally Davis, *President*
Diane Hershberger, *General Mgr*
EMP: 10
SQ FT: 33,000
SALES (est): 1.3MM **Privately Held**
SIC: 2047 Dog & cat food

(G-3234)
UNITED PIES OF ELKHART INC
1016 Middlebury St (46516-4510)
PHONE....................................574 294-3419
Blanche Nichols, *President*
Frank Nichols, *Treasurer*
EMP: 8
SQ FT: 7,200
SALES (est): 650K **Privately Held**
SIC: 2051 2053 Pies, bakery: except
frozen; pies, bakery: frozen

(G-3235)
UNITED ROLL FORMING CORP
58288 County Road 3 (46517-9371)
PHONE....................................574 294-2800
Betty Glaum, *President*
James Glaum, *Vice Pres*
◆ EMP: 35
SQ FT: 65,000

SALES (est): 7.3MM **Privately Held**
WEB: www.unitedrollforming.org
SIC: 3449 Custom roll formed products

(G-3236)
UNITED SHADE LLC
2904 Airport Pkwy (46514-9711)
PHONE....................................574 262-0954
Fax: 574 262-0908
Kyle Dietzen, *Sales Staff*
Braden McCormick,
▲ EMP: 60 EST: 2002
SALES (est): 9.8MM **Privately Held**
SIC: 2591 Window shades

(G-3237)
UNIVERSAL COATINGS LLC
1204 Pierina Dr (46514-5285)
PHONE....................................574 520-3403
Shawn Vertrees, *Administration*
EMP: 2 EST: 2016
SALES (est): 83.4K **Privately Held**
SIC: 3479 Metal coating & allied service

(G-3238)
**UNIVERSAL PRECISION INSTRS
INC**
2921 Lavanture Pl (46514-8233)
PHONE....................................574 264-3997
Ron Drown, *President*
Jamie Prescott, *General Mgr*
Robert Wozny, *Vice Pres*
Chris Kusnierek, *Plant Mgr*
Scott Smith, *Plant Mgr*
EMP: 9
SQ FT: 12,000
SALES (est): 1.4MM **Privately Held**
WEB: www.batesmachine.com
SIC: 3599 3841 Machine shop, jobbing &
repair; surgical & medical instruments

(G-3239)
V THE ELECTRIC BREW
113 E Lexington Ave (46516-3125)
PHONE....................................574 296-7785
Myron Bontrager, *Owner*
EMP: 3
SALES (est): 106.9K **Privately Held**
SIC: 3699 Electrical equipment & supplies

(G-3240)
VAHALA FOAM INC
903 Herman St (46516)
PHONE....................................574 293-1287
Fax: 574 293-1825
Dan Vahala, *Ch of Bd*
Dave Vahala, *President*
EMP: 57
SQ FT: 47,000
SALES (est): 10.7MM **Privately Held**
WEB: www.vahalafoam.com
SIC: 3086 5199 2821 Plastics foam prod-
ucts; insulation or cushioning material;
foamed plastic; foams & rubber; plastics
materials & resins

(G-3241)
VALLEY DISTRIBUTING INC
Also Called: Valley Manufacturing
2820 Lillian Ave (46514-9233)
P.O. Box 1684 (46515-1684)
PHONE....................................574 266-4455
Fax: 574 266-4229
Bill Harris Sr, *President*
EMP: 35
SQ FT: 27,000
SALES (est): 6.8MM **Privately Held**
SIC: 3714 Motor vehicle body components
& frame

(G-3242)
VALMONT INDUSTRIES INC
3403 Charlotte Ave (46517-1190)
PHONE....................................574 295-6942
Fax: 574 295-6998
Aggie Bakken, *Purch Agent*
Scott Brown, *Controller*
Dee Spencer, *Human Res Mgr*
Franco Garcay, *Branch Mgr*
Richard Haskins, *Maintence Staff*
EMP: 75
SQ FT: 400,000
SALES (corp-wide): 2.7B **Publicly Held**
WEB: www.valmont.com
SIC: 3441 Fabricated structural metal

PA: Valmont Industries, Inc.
1 Valmont Plz Ste 500
Omaha NE 68154
402 963-1000

(G-3243)
VERSATILE AUTOMATION TECH
Also Called: Versa Machinery
4850 Green Ct (46516-9596)
PHONE....................................574 266-0780
Lewis Wadsworth, *President*
Lou Edie, *Treasurer*
Harry Washburn, *Admin Sec*
EMP: 6
SQ FT: 1,800
SALES (est): 951.8K **Privately Held**
WEB: www.versamachinery.com
SIC: 3599 Machine shop, jobbing & repair

(G-3244)
VERSATILE FABRICATION LLC
4431 Pine Creek Rd (46516-9561)
PHONE....................................574 293-8504
Will Gury, *President*
EMP: 9
SALES (est): 1.1MM **Privately Held**
SIC: 3469 3599 Ash trays, stamped metal;
machine & other job shop work

(G-3245)
VINCE ROGERS SIGNS INC
400 W Crawford St (46514-2732)
PHONE....................................574 264-0542
Fax: 574 970-0023
Michael Smoot, *President*
EMP: 2
SQ FT: 3,200
SALES: 200K **Privately Held**
SIC: 3993 Signs & advertising specialties

(G-3246)
VINTAGE TRAILERS LTD
4660 Pine Creek Rd (46516-9564)
PHONE....................................574 522-2261
Fax: 574 522-2603
Robert Stone, *CEO*
Roy Stone, *President*
Troy Stone, *President*
Todd Kujawa, *Software Engr*
Susan E Stone, *Admin Sec*
EMP: 34
SQ FT: 48,000
SALES: 9.3MM **Privately Held**
WEB: www.vintagetrailers.com
SIC: 3799 Trailers & trailer equipment; au-
tomobile trailer chassis

(G-3247)
**VISTA MANUFACTURING INC
(PA)**
53345 Columbia Dr (46514-9259)
PHONE....................................574 264-0711
Fax: 574 264-4174
Tod E Tieszen, *President*
Dwayne Tieszen, *Vice Pres*
Nick Bartlett, *QC Mgr*
Alex Tolen, *Electrical Engi*
▲ EMP: 24
SQ FT: 16,000
SALES (est): 6MM **Privately Held**
WEB: www.vistamfg.com
SIC: 3641 5063 Lamps, incandescent fila-
ment, electric; lighting fixtures

(G-3248)
VISTA WORLDWIDE LLC
53345 Columbia Dr (46514-8153)
PHONE....................................574 264-0711
Joe Bonta, *President*
EMP: 4 EST: 2013
SALES (est): 425.9K **Privately Held**
SIC: 3648 3677 3679 Lighting equipment;
transformers power supply, electronic
type; electronic components

(G-3249)
VITRACOAT AMERICA INC (PA)
2807 Marina Dr (46514-7669)
PHONE....................................574 262-2188
Fax: 574 264-2778
Eduardo Mousalli, *President*
Luis Moussali, *Vice Pres*
▼ EMP: 16
SQ FT: 20,000

GEOGRAPHIC

SALES (est): 4.3MM **Privately Held**
WEB: www.vitracoatamerica.com
SIC: 2851 Coating, air curing

(G-3250)
VIXEN COMPOSITES LLC
2965 Lavanture Pl (46514-8233)
PHONE..................................574 970-1224
Gregg Fore, *President*
EMP: 15
SALES (est): 3.2MM **Privately Held**
SIC: 3089 Air mattresses, plastic

(G-3251)
VOMELA
4505 Wyland Dr Ste 800 (46516-9635)
PHONE..................................574 522-6016
EMP: 2 EST: 2011
SALES (est): 134.7K **Privately Held**
SIC: 2752 Commercial printing, lithographic

(G-3252)
WALERKO TOOL AND ENGRG CORP
1935 W Lusher Ave (46517-1348)
PHONE..................................574 295-2233
Fax: 574 522-5510
Edward M Walerko Jr, *President*
▲ EMP: 42
SQ FT: 40,000
SALES: 3.6MM **Privately Held**
WEB: www.walerko.com
SIC: 3599 3724 Machine shop, jobbing & repair; custom machinery; grinding castings for the trade; aircraft engines & engine parts

(G-3253)
WALLAR ADDITIONS INC (PA)
Also Called: American Sunspace
30012 County Road 10 (46514-9776)
PHONE..................................574 262-1989
Fax: 574 264-0904
James Jeffrey Wallar, *President*
William Brad Wallar, *Admin Sec*
EMP: 30
SQ FT: 25,000
SALES (est): 5.1MM **Privately Held**
SIC: 6163 1799 3211 Loan brokers; athletic & recreation facilities construction; flat glass

(G-3254)
WALTER PIANO COMPANY INC
1705 County Road 6 E # 200 (46514-5594)
PHONE..................................574 266-0615
Toll Free:....................................888
Fax: 574 266-0889
Charles R Walter, *President*
Barbara Walter, *Vice Pres*
▲ EMP: 15 EST: 1970
SQ FT: 70,000
SALES: 1.5MM **Privately Held**
WEB: www.walterpiano.com
SIC: 3931 5736 7699 Pianos, all types: vertical, grand, spinet, player, etc.; pianos; piano tuning & repair

(G-3255)
WELCH PACKAGING LLC (HQ)
1020 Herman St (46516-9028)
PHONE..................................574 295-2460
Scott Welch, *President*
Patrick Bennett, *CFO*
Katie Litteral, *Accountant*
Jennifer Hershberger, *Sales Associate*
Christopher Burtner, *Manager*
EMP: 91
SQ FT: 160,000
SALES (est): 34MM
SALES (corp-wide): 224MM **Privately Held**
SIC: 2653 Boxes, corrugated: made from purchased materials
PA: Welch Packaging Group, Inc.
1020 Herman St
Elkhart IN 46516
574 295-2460

(G-3256)
WELCH PACKAGING GROUP INC (PA)
1020 Herman St (46516-9028)
PHONE..................................574 295-2460
M Scott Welch, *President*

Jim Fenner, *Exec VP*
Patrick J Baert, *CFO*
Carl Long, *Officer*
Christopher Welch, *Admin Sec*
▲ EMP: 150
SALES (est): 224MM **Privately Held**
SIC: 2653 Corrugated & solid fiber boxes

(G-3257)
WELLCO HOLDINGS INC (DH)
1503 Mcnaughton Ave (46514-2243)
P.O. Box 728 (46515-0728)
PHONE..................................574 264-9661
Jeffrey M Wells, *President*
Jeff Wells, *Principal*
Gordon Mills, *Plant Mgr*
Mark Olson, *Production*
Bill Peck, *CFO*
▼ EMP: 130 EST: 1958
SQ FT: 55,000
SALES (est): 94.6MM
SALES (corp-wide): 667.9MM **Privately Held**
WEB: www.wellscargo.com
SIC: 3715 Demountable cargo containers

(G-3258)
WESTROCK CP LLC
1535 Fieldhouse Ave (46517-1404)
PHONE..................................574 296-2817
Fax: 574 293-1832
Roger W Stone, *CEO*
EMP: 50
SALES (corp-wide): 14.8B **Publicly Held**
WEB: www.sto.com
SIC: 2631 5113 2653 Paperboard mills; corrugated & solid fiber boxes; corrugated & solid fiber boxes
HQ: Westrock Cp, Llc
504 Thrasher St
Norcross GA 30071

(G-3259)
WHEELCHAIR HELP LLC
515 East St (46516-3611)
PHONE..................................574 295-2220
Joe Lidy, *Owner*
EMP: 3 EST: 2014
SALES (est): 306.2K **Privately Held**
SIC: 3842 Wheelchairs

(G-3260)
WINDSONG K-9 COACH INC
52711 County Road 11 (46514-8306)
PHONE..................................574 971-6358
John Faigh, *President*
EMP: 5
SALES (est): 500K **Privately Held**
SIC: 3999 Manufacturing industries

(G-3261)
WINDSOR STEEL INC
2210 Middlebury St (46516-5518)
P.O. Box 1064 (46515-1064)
PHONE..................................574 294-1060
William Banks Jr, *President*
EMP: 31
SALES (est): 6.9MM **Privately Held**
SIC: 3312 Blast furnaces & steel mills

(G-3262)
WINDSOR WARTCARE
3100 Windsor Ct (46514-5556)
PHONE..................................574 266-6555
Dorwyn Collier, *Owner*
Jenifer Wilkins, *Office Mgr*
EMP: 4
SALES (est): 459.6K **Privately Held**
SIC: 2834 Medicines, capsuled or ampuled

(G-3263)
WINE & CANVAS SOUTH BEND LLC
51213 County Road 11 (46514-8557)
PHONE..................................574 807-1562
EMP: 2
SALES (est): 81K **Privately Held**
SIC: 2211 Canvas

(G-3264)
WISEGUYS SEATING & ACCESSRY CO
2701 Industrial Pkwy (46516-5441)
P.O. Box 211 (46515-0211)
PHONE..................................574 294-6030

Todd Lorang, *CEO*
Jim Wise, *President*
EMP: 3
SALES: 800K **Privately Held**
WEB: www.wiseguys-seats.com
SIC: 2399 Seat covers, automobile

(G-3265)
WOOD CREATIONS INC
800 Industrial Pkwy (46516-5530)
PHONE..................................574 522-7765
Fax: 574 522-6645
Carlos Gonzalez, *Principal*
EMP: 2
SALES (est): 154.5K **Privately Held**
SIC: 2431 Millwork

(G-3266)
WOODPARTS INTERNATIONAL CORP
Also Called: Woodpart International
729 Mason St (46516-2700)
P.O. Box 1011 (46515-1011)
PHONE..................................574 293-0566
Fax: 574 294-4694
Keith Butus, *President*
Peter Butus, *Shareholder*
Carmen Butus, *Admin Sec*
▲ EMP: 12 EST: 1974
SQ FT: 38,000
SALES (est): 1.6MM **Privately Held**
SIC: 2421 Sawmills & planing mills, general; specialty sawmill products; planing mills; kiln drying of lumber

(G-3267)
WOODWRIGHT DOOR & TRIM INC
808 9th St (46516-2653)
P.O. Box 1943 (46515-1943)
PHONE..................................574 522-1667
Fax: 574 522-1667
Bruce Shoup, *President*
EMP: 6
SQ FT: 8,500
SALES (est): 450K **Privately Held**
SIC: 2431 5211 Moldings, wood: unfinished & prefinished; doors & door parts & trim, wood; door & window products

(G-3268)
WORLD RDO MSSNARY FLLWSHIP INC
Also Called: H C J B World Radio
2830 17th St (46517-4008)
PHONE..................................574 970-4252
Fax: 574 293-9910
Scott K McConnell, *Design Engr*
David Pasechnik, *Branch Mgr*
EMP: 23
SALES (corp-wide): 8.8MM **Privately Held**
WEB: www.wb2000.org
SIC: 3663 8711 4832 8661 Transmitter-receivers, radio; engineering services; radio broadcasting stations; Non-denominational church
PA: World Radio Missionary Fellowship, Inc.
1065 Grdn Of The Gods Rd
Colorado Springs CO 80907
719 590-9800

(G-3269)
WORLDWIDE FOAM LTD (PA)
Also Called: Worldcell Extrusions
1806 Conant St (46516-4755)
PHONE..................................574 968-8268
John Petrofsky, *President*
Don Frandsen, *Branch Mgr*
▲ EMP: 5
SALES (est): 2MM **Privately Held**
SIC: 3086 Packaging & shipping materials, foamed plastic

(G-3270)
XANTREX TECHNOLOGY USA INC (DH)
Also Called: Schneder Elc Slar Invrters USA
541 Roske Dr Ste A (46516-9323)
PHONE..................................574 522-9628
Ted Campbell, *President*
▲ EMP: 10
SQ FT: 5,450

SALES (est): 1.2MM
SALES (corp-wide): 200.4K **Privately Held**
SIC: 3629 Inverters, nonrotating: electrical
HQ: Schneider Electric Solar Inverters Usa, Inc
250 S Vasco Rd
Livermore CA 94551
925 245-5400

(G-3271)
YELLOW DOG ANODIZING
2730 Almac Ct (46514-7627)
PHONE..................................574 343-2247
EMP: 3 EST: 2012
SALES (est): 226.1K **Privately Held**
SIC: 3471 Anodizing (plating) of metals or formed products

Ellettsville
Monroe County

(G-3272)
BYBEE STONE COMPANY INC
6293 N Matthews Dr (47429-9424)
P.O. Box 968, Bloomington (47402-0968)
PHONE..................................812 876-2215
Fax: 812 876-6329
William Bybee, *President*
Sharon Myers, *Principal*
George Bybee, *Vice Pres*
Mary Beth Haas, *CFO*
Jeff Chitwood, *Sales Staff*
EMP: 65 EST: 1862
SQ FT: 73,000
SALES (est): 9.3MM **Privately Held**
WEB: www.bybeestone.com
SIC: 3281 Limestone, cut & shaped

(G-3273)
CHADS LLC
Also Called: Chad's Towing and Recovery
6679 W Mcneely St (47429-9444)
PHONE..................................812 323-7377
Chad Stephens, *Principal*
EMP: 4 EST: 2009
SALES (est): 280K **Privately Held**
SIC: 7549 3713 3531 Towing services; automobile wrecker truck bodies; winches

(G-3274)
CHRISTOPHER ENGLE
Also Called: Hamster Press Klingel-Engle Pu
7251 W State Road 46 (47429-1029)
PHONE..................................812 876-3540
Christopher Engle, *Owner*
Terri Klingelhoefer, *Principal*
EMP: 2
SALES: 5K **Privately Held**
SIC: 3944 Games, toys & children's vehicles

(G-3275)
COMPUCOMICS
6079 N Holly Dr (47429-9462)
PHONE..................................812 876-1480
Roy Duncan, *Owner*
EMP: 3
SALES (est): 104.2K **Privately Held**
SIC: 2721 Comic books: publishing only, not printed on site

(G-3276)
COOK GROUP INCORPORATED
Also Called: Cook Medical
6300 N Matthews Dr (47429-9495)
PHONE..................................812 331-1025
Cleve Koehler, *Senior Engr*
EMP: 5
SALES (corp-wide): 980.1MM **Privately Held**
SIC: 3841 Surgical & medical instruments
PA: Cook Group Incorporated
750 N Daniels Way
Bloomington IN 47404
812 339-2235

(G-3277)
COOK INCORPORATED
6600 W Mcneely St (47429-9444)
P.O. Box 489 (47429-0489)
PHONE..................................812 339-2235
Fax: 812 876-3790

▲ = Import ▼=Export
◆ =Import/Export

G
E
O
G
R
A
P
H
I
C

Scott Todd, *Finance Mgr*
Dan Brinson, *Manager*
EMP: 125
SALES (corp-wide): 980.1MM **Privately Held**
WEB: www.cookgroup.com
SIC: 3841 Catheters
HQ: Cook Incorporated
750 N Daniels Way
Bloomington IN 47404
812 339-2235

(G-3278)
DIGITAL CARVINGS LLC
927 E Meadowlands Dr (47429-1086)
PHONE...............................812 269-6123
Bradley Edwards, *Owner*
EMP: 2
SALES (est): 130.9K **Privately Held**
SIC: 2426 8742 Carvings, furniture: wood; general management consultant

(G-3279)
H L SIGNWORKS
616 Robin Dr (47429-1635)
PHONE...............................812 325-5750
Robert Double, *Owner*
EMP: 2
SALES: 75K **Privately Held**
SIC: 3993 Signs & advertising specialties

(G-3280)
HECTOR ENGINEERING CO
123 E Dewey Dr (47429-1705)
PHONE...............................812 876-5274
Fax: 812 876-5223
Dwight Hector, *President*
Rogette Hector, *Corp Secy*
EMP: 2
SALES (est): 120K **Privately Held**
SIC: 3231 Scientific & technical glassware: from purchased glass

(G-3281)
HIGGINS DYAN
Also Called: Costume Delights
5680 W Mcneely St (47429-9411)
PHONE...............................812 876-0754
Dyan Higgins, *Owner*
EMP: 2
SQ FT: 1,800
SALES: 120K **Privately Held**
WEB: www.costumedelights.com
SIC: 2389 5699 7299 Costumes; costumes & wigs; costume rental

(G-3282)
JOURNAL PUBLISHING CO INC
211 N Sale St (47429-1423)
P.O. Box 98 (47429-0098)
PHONE...............................812 876-2254
Fax: 812 876-2853
John T Gillaspy, *President*
EMP: 3 **EST:** 1940
SQ FT: 2,000
SALES (est): 160K **Privately Held**
SIC: 2711 2741 Commercial printing & newspaper publishing combined; shopping news: publishing only, not printed on site

(G-3283)
PARSLEYS SEAL COATING INC
Also Called: Parsley Seal Coating Stripping
305 Ridge Springs Ln (47429-1017)
PHONE...............................812 876-5450
Brent Parsley, *Vice Pres*
EMP: 2
SALES: 45K **Privately Held**
SIC: 2951 Asphalt paving mixtures & blocks

(G-3284)
SNOOKS LAND HOLDING INC
7800 N Mt Tabor Rd (47429-9550)
PHONE...............................812 876-4540
Nonnice Richardson, *Partner*
EMP: 5
SALES (est): 285.8K **Privately Held**
SIC: 3523 Driers (farm): grain, hay & seed

(G-3285)
WOODLAND RIDGE WOODWORKING
5182 W Woodland Rd (47429-9578)
PHONE...............................812 821-8032

Paul C Mizell, *Principal*
EMP: 2
SALES (est): 138.5K **Privately Held**
SIC: 2431 Millwork

Elnora
Daviess County

(G-3286)
BASILOID PRODUCTS CORP
312 N East St (47529-3002)
PHONE...............................812 692-5511
Fax: 812 692-5512
Eric Lane, *President*
EMP: 20 **EST:** 1952
SQ FT: 20,000
SALES (est): 5MM **Privately Held**
WEB: www.basiloid.com
SIC: 3537 5084 3713 2448 Forklift trucks; industrial machinery & equipment; truck & bus bodies; wood pallets & skids

(G-3287)
CAMPBELL PET COMPANY
Also Called: Paws Depot
120 N Odon St (47529-4720)
P.O. Box 128 (47529-0128)
PHONE...............................812 692-5208
Fax: 812 692-5665
Mary Henrichsen, *President*
EMP: 6
SALES (corp-wide): 3.2MM **Privately Held**
WEB: www.campbellpet.com
SIC: 3199 5047 Dog furnishings: collars, leashes, muzzles, etc.: leather; veterinarians' equipment & supplies
PA: Campbell Pet Company
9606 Ne 126th Ave
Vancouver WA 98682
360 892-9786

(G-3288)
CORNELIUS MANUFACTURING INC
5344 E 1250 N (47529-5060)
PHONE...............................812 636-4319
Gerald A Frette, *President*
Brian Frette, *Sales Mgr*
David R Frette, *Admin Sec*
EMP: 60
SQ FT: 90,000
SALES (est): 16.9MM **Privately Held**
SIC: 3523 Trailers & wagons, farm

(G-3289)
GRAHAM CHEESE CORPORATION
Hwy 57 N (47529)
PHONE...............................812 692-5237
Fax: 812 692-5650
Ura Miller, *President*
EMP: 20
SQ FT: 4,800
SALES (est): 2.9MM **Privately Held**
WEB: www.grahamcheese.com
SIC: 2022 5451 Natural cheese; cheese

(G-3290)
JOLLIFF DIESEL SERVICE
Also Called: Jolliff, Phillip
7325 E 1500 N (47529-5031)
PHONE...............................812 692-5725
Phillip Jolliff, *Owner*
EMP: 2
SQ FT: 2,208
SALES: 170K **Privately Held**
SIC: 3519 7538 0115 0116 Diesel engine rebuilding; diesel engine repair: automotive; corn; soybeans

(G-3291)
SALADIN TRAILER SALES INC
637 E Highway 57 (47529-3009)
P.O. Box 6 (47529-0006)
PHONE...............................812 692-5288
Rhonda Saladin, *President*
EMP: 10
SQ FT: 10,800
SALES (est): 1.1MM **Privately Held**
SIC: 3799 5599 Trailers & trailer equipment; utility trailers

(G-3292)
SPECIAL FABRICATION SERVICES
418 E Highway 57 (47529-3019)
PHONE...............................812 384-5384
EMP: 2
SALES (est): 147.5K **Privately Held**
SIC: 3441 Fabricated structural metal

Elwood
Madison County

(G-3293)
AEROMOTIVE MFG INC
8421 N 750 W (46036-8990)
PHONE...............................765 552-0668
Dorcia Stottlemyer, *President*
Charles Stottlemyer, *Admin Sec*
EMP: 2
SALES (est): 196.5K **Privately Held**
SIC: 3441 Fabricated structural metal

(G-3294)
AUNT NETTS COUNTRY CANDLES LLC
Also Called: Dream Mill
7374 W State Rd (46036)
PHONE...............................765 557-2770
Jeanette Middlesworth,
EMP: 3
SALES (est): 161.1K **Privately Held**
SIC: 3999 Manufacturing industries

(G-3295)
DUNN-RITE PRODUCTS INC (PA)
2200 S J St (46036-2506)
PHONE...............................765 552-9433
Edward Dunn Jr, *President*
Douglas Dunn, *Vice Pres*
Nancy Dunn, *Shareholder*
▲ **EMP:** 35
SQ FT: 68,000
SALES (est): 3.8MM **Privately Held**
SIC: 3949 5091 Water sports equipment; swimming pools, equipment & supplies

(G-3296)
ELSA LLC
1240 S State Road 37 (46036-3023)
PHONE...............................765 552-5200
Kiyokazu Sakamoto, *CEO*
Masataka Sakamoto, *Vice Ch Bd*
Yashihito Matsouka, *President*
Hideo Nakamura, *Vice Pres*
Takuya Yoshida, *Vice Pres*
▲ **EMP:** 310
SQ FT: 300,000
SALES (est): 70.9MM
SALES (corp-wide): 21.2MM **Privately Held**
WEB: www.elsallc.com
SIC: 3714 Exhaust systems & parts, motor vehicle; gas tanks, motor vehicle; cleaners, air, motor vehicle; motor vehicle body components & frame
HQ: Elsa Corporation
1240 S State Road 37
Elwood IN 46036
765 552-5200

(G-3297)
ELSA CORPORATION (DH)
1240 S State Road 37 (46036-3023)
PHONE...............................765 552-5200
Fax: 765 552-9282
Kiyokazu Sakamoto, *CEO*
Yashihiko Matsuoka, *President*
Takuya Yoshida, *Principal*
Hideo Nakamura, *Vice Pres*
▲ **EMP:** 350
SQ FT: 400,000
SALES: 130MM
SALES (corp-wide): 21.2MM **Privately Held**
WEB: www.elsallc.com
SIC: 3714 Exhaust systems & parts, motor vehicle; gas tanks, motor vehicle; cleaners, air, motor vehicle; motor vehicle body components & frame

HQ: Sakamoto Industry Co., Ltd.
292, Besshocho
Ota GNM 373-0
276 311-191

(G-3298)
ELWOOD PUBLISHING CO INC (HQ)
Also Called: Call Leader
317 S Anderson St (46036-2018)
P.O. Box 85 (46036-0085)
PHONE...............................765 552-3355
Fax: 765 552-3358
Jack L Barnes, *President*
Robert Naash, *Publisher*
Charles Barnes, *Vice Pres*
Brian Barnes, *Treasurer*
Lori Nash, *Executive*
EMP: 50
SQ FT: 15,000
SALES (est): 4.9MM
SALES (corp-wide): 8.7MM **Privately Held**
WEB: www.dailychiefunion.com
SIC: 2711 Commercial printing & newspaper publishing combined; newspapers: publishing only, not printed on site
PA: Ray Barnes Newspaper Inc
201 E Columbus St 207
Kenton OH 43326
419 674-4066

(G-3299)
GOLDEN THREADS
516 N Anderson St Ste C (46036-1295)
PHONE...............................765 557-7801
Penny Martin, *Owner*
EMP: 2
SALES (est): 85K **Privately Held**
SIC: 2395 Embroidery & art needlework

(G-3300)
IRVING MATERIALS INC
Also Called: I M I
2500 S D St (46036-2621)
PHONE...............................765 552-5041
Beutch Mey, *Branch Mgr*
EMP: 3
SALES (corp-wide): 800.6MM **Privately Held**
SIC: 3273 Ready-mixed concrete
PA: Irving Materials, Inc.
8032 N State Road 9
Greenfield IN 46140
317 326-3101

(G-3301)
J LEWIS SMALL CO INC
9147 W 1000 N (46036-8820)
P.O. Box 426 (46036-0426)
PHONE...............................765 552-5011
John Strack, *President*
Joseph Hertz, *Vice Pres*
EMP: 55
SALES (est): 7.1MM **Privately Held**
SIC: 3911 Rings, finger: precious metal

(G-3302)
JACOBS COUNTRY CANDLES LLC
1420 S K St (46036-2730)
PHONE...............................765 557-0260
Tonya Jacobs, *Principal*
EMP: 2
SALES (est): 122.5K **Privately Held**
SIC: 3999 Candles

(G-3303)
KADET PRODUCTS INC
2403 S J St (46036-2511)
PHONE...............................765 552-7341
Fax: 765 552-7343
Eric Fettig, *President*
Phillip Fettig, *Chairman*
Page Fettig, *Corp Secy*
EMP: 25
SQ FT: 60,000
SALES (est): 3.5MM **Privately Held**
WEB: www.kadetproducts.com
SIC: 3471 Cleaning & descaling metal products; finishing, metals or formed products

---

(G-3304)
LOYS SALES INC
Also Called: Loy's Music Center
715 S 22nd St (46036-2521)
PHONE....................765 552-7250
Leslie J Richardson, *President*
Dan Richardson, *Vice Pres*
EMP: 5
SQ FT: 4,000
SALES: 300K **Privately Held**
SIC: 3651 5731 8299 Household audio & video equipment; radio, television & electronic stores; musical instrument lessons

(G-3305)
MANASEK ACQUISITION CO LLC
Also Called: Warner Bodies
11700 N State Road 37 (46036-9024)
PHONE....................765 551-1600
Fax: 317 773-1715
Rick Manasek, *CEO*
Craig Longstreth, *Exec VP*
EMP: 45
SQ FT: 100,000
SALES: 14.3MM **Privately Held**
SIC: 3713 Truck bodies (motor vehicles)

(G-3306)
MANUFACTURED PRODUCTS
2700 S K St (46036-3109)
PHONE....................765 552-2871
Fax: 765 552-2871
Eric Horn, *Owner*
EMP: 5
SQ FT: 5,500
SALES (est): 398.8K **Privately Held**
SIC: 3599 Machine shop, jobbing & repair

(G-3307)
MODERN DIE SYSTEMS INC
1104 N J St (46036-1164)
PHONE....................765 552-3145
Fax: 765 552-0002
Daniel Neuendorf, *President*
Robert L Davis, *Partner*
Missy Hazelwood, *Corp Secy*
Jeannie Ables, *Manager*
EMP: 20
SQ FT: 10,000
SALES (est): 2.9MM **Privately Held**
WEB: www.moderndiesystems.com
SIC: 3544 3549 3541 Die sets for metal stamping (presses); metalworking machinery; machine tools, metal cutting type

(G-3308)
N & K CABINET INC
2510 S F St (46036-2633)
PHONE....................765 552-6997
Fax: 765 552-7046
Joe Miller, *President*
EMP: 3 EST: 1990
SALES (est): 243.4K **Privately Held**
SIC: 2434 Wood kitchen cabinets

(G-3309)
PROFESSIONAL COMP NASKART INC
1224 S H St (46036-2350)
PHONE....................765 552-9745
Larry Gibson, *Principal*
EMP: 2
SALES (est): 88.8K **Privately Held**
SIC: 3799 Transportation equipment

(G-3310)
PROGRESSIVE PLASTICS INC
2200 S J St (46036-2506)
PHONE....................765 552-2004
Mike Leagre, *President*
Davis Herbert, *Vice Pres*
▲ EMP: 16
SALES (est): 2.7MM **Privately Held**
WEB: www.progressive-plastics.net
SIC: 3089 Injection molding of plastics
PA: Dunn-Rite Products, Inc.
2200 S J St
Elwood IN 46036

(G-3311)
TERRONICS DEVELOPMENT CORP
7565 W 900 N (46036-8907)
PHONE....................765 552-0808
Fax: 765 552-0810

Eduardo C Escallon, *President*
Sam Manghelli, *Corp Secy*
Han Almekinders, *Vice Pres*
Jill Bott, *Financial Exec*
EMP: 3
SQ FT: 4,400
SALES (est): 1.8MM **Privately Held**
WEB: www.terronics.com
SIC: 8731 3564 Commercial research laboratory; blowers & fans

English
Crawford County

(G-3312)
COLLUCI CONSTRUCTION-LOG HOMES
10591 Oriental Rd (47118-7515)
PHONE....................812 843-5607
Bud Colluci, *Owner*
EMP: 2
SALES (est): 105.6K **Privately Held**
WEB: www.collucirivercabins.com
SIC: 2452 7011 Log cabins, prefabricated, wood; hotels & motels

(G-3313)
JIM RHODES LOGGING
2121 W State Road 62 (47118-6003)
PHONE....................812 739-4221
Jim Rhodes, *Owner*
EMP: 2
SALES (est): 140.3K **Privately Held**
SIC: 2411 Logging

(G-3314)
LANDMARK WOOD PRODUCTS INC
118 W Sawmill Rd (47118-6730)
P.O. Box 24 (47118-0024)
PHONE....................812 338-2641
Fax: 812 338-3263
Terry Smith, *President*
Larry Smith, *Vice Pres*
Tim Smith, *Vice Pres*
EMP: 15
SQ FT: 15,000
SALES: 3MM **Privately Held**
SIC: 2499 Kitchen, bathroom & household ware: wood

(G-3315)
MIDWEST CAVIAR LLC
439 E State Road 64 (47118-3609)
PHONE....................812 338-3610
Vicki Cox, *Owner*
EMP: 4
SALES (est): 167K **Privately Held**
SIC: 2091 Caviar, preserved

(G-3316)
MULZER CRUSHED STONE INC
Old Hwy 64e (47118)
PHONE....................812 365-2145
Fax: 812 365-2498
Brad Mulzer, *Vice Pres*
Noel Kessens, *Manager*
EMP: 18
SALES (corp-wide): 29.7B **Privately Held**
WEB: www.mulzer.com
SIC: 1422 3274 Limestones, ground; lime
HQ: Mulzer Crushed Stone Inc
534 Mozart St
Tell City IN 47586
812 547-7921

(G-3317)
OHIO VALLEY CAVIAR
1927 E Shelton Rd (47118-6932)
PHONE....................812 338-4367
Jessica Schigur, *Owner*
EMP: 2
SALES (est): 152.8K **Privately Held**
SIC: 2092 Fresh or frozen packaged fish

(G-3318)
RIDDLE RIDGE WOODWORKS
1731 E Denton Rd (47118-6312)
PHONE....................812 596-4503
EMP: 2
SALES (est): 151.9K **Privately Held**
SIC: 2431 Millwork

(G-3319)
RONALD WRIGHT LOGGING LLC
61 S Pleasant Hill Rd (47118-6709)
PHONE....................812 338-2665
Ronald Wright,
EMP: 5
SALES (est): 448.9K **Privately Held**
SIC: 2411 2421 Logging; sawmills & planing mills, general

Etna Green
Kosciusko County

(G-3320)
EARL CHUPP
Also Called: Woodenware USA
9151 W 750 N (46524-9753)
PHONE....................574 372-8400
Earl Chupp, *Owner*
EMP: 4
SALES (est): 310.4K **Privately Held**
SIC: 2499 Woodenware, kitchen & household

(G-3321)
FASTTIMES FABRICATION CUS
115 S Walnut St (46524-9419)
P.O. Box 210 (46524-0210)
PHONE....................574 858-9222
Heath Roberts, *Owner*
EMP: 3
SALES (est): 333.2K **Privately Held**
SIC: 3441 Fabricated structural metal

(G-3322)
MILLWOOD CUSTOM CABINETS
Also Called: Helmuth Cabinet Shop
7427 N 800 W (46524-9531)
PHONE....................574 646-3009
Earl Mast, *President*
EMP: 3
SQ FT: 4,400
SALES (est): 25.6K **Privately Held**
SIC: 2541 1751 Cabinets, lockers & shelving; cabinet building & installation

(G-3323)
WINONA BUILDING PRODUCTS LLC
9876 W Old Road 30 (46524-9562)
P.O. Box 170 (46524-0170)
PHONE....................574 822-0100
Jamie Veisker, *CEO*
Brian Bailey, *President*
Craig Effenberger, *President*
EMP: 10
SALES (est): 585.7K **Privately Held**
SIC: 3644 Insulators & insulation materials, electrical

(G-3324)
WINONA POWDER COATING INC (PA)
9876 W Old Road 30 (46524-9562)
P.O. Box 170 (46524-0170)
PHONE....................574 267-8311
Fax: 574 353-7882
Jamie Visker, *CEO*
Fred Fribley, *Admin Sec*
▲ EMP: 90 EST: 1963
SQ FT: 25,000
SALES (est): 17.1MM **Privately Held**
WEB: www.winonapowder.com
SIC: 3479 Coating of metals & formed products

Evanston
Spencer County

(G-3325)
SANDY LITTLE COAL CO INC
12568 N State Road 245 (47531)
PHONE....................812 529-8216
Don Foertsch, *President*
Mason Foertsch, *Vice Pres*
Linda Foertsch, *Admin Sec*
EMP: 9
SQ FT: 5,000

SALES (est): 616.3K **Privately Held**
SIC: 1221 Bituminous coal & lignite-surface mining

Evansville
Vanderburgh County

(G-3326)
3-T CORP
Also Called: Clean Air of Evansville
2206 N Grand Ave (47711-3806)
PHONE....................812 424-7878
Fax: 812 424-0568
Barbara Otto, *President*
Andrew Otto, *Vice Pres*
EMP: 7
SQ FT: 12,000
SALES: 525K **Privately Held**
SIC: 3564 5075 7699 Air cleaning systems; air pollution control equipment & supplies; industrial equipment services; filter cleaning

(G-3327)
A & A CUSTOM AUTOMATION INC (PA)
2125 Bergdolt Rd (47711-2845)
PHONE....................812 464-3650
Fax: 812 471-4296
Kristie Chinn, *President*
EMP: 58
SQ FT: 34,000
SALES (est): 14.4MM **Privately Held**
WEB: www.aametal.com
SIC: 3544 Special dies, tools, jigs & fixtures

(G-3328)
A & D CONSTRUCTORS INC (PA)
1449 Kimber Ln Ste 103b (47715-4067)
PHONE....................812 428-3708
Fax: 812 425-8630
Daniel G Felker, *President*
Scott Dilbeck, *Vice Pres*
Kenneth E Wahl, *Admin Sec*
EMP: 175
SQ FT: 1,500
SALES (est): 57MM **Privately Held**
WEB: www.adconstructors.com
SIC: 3441 Fabricated structural metal

(G-3329)
A SCHULMAN INC
2301 St Jseph Indus Pk Dr (47720-1250)
PHONE....................812 253-5238
EMP: 4
SALES (corp-wide): 2.4B **Publicly Held**
SIC: 2821 Molding compounds, plastics
PA: A. Schulman, Inc.
3637 Ridgewood Rd
Fairlawn OH 44333
330 666-3751

(G-3330)
A TIME TO STITCH INC
6916 Hogue Rd (47712-2916)
PHONE....................812 422-5968
Sherry A Titzerr, *Principal*
EMP: 2
SALES (est): 68.4K **Privately Held**
SIC: 2395 Embroidery & art needlework

(G-3331)
A1 PALLETS INC
1801 W Maryland St (47712-5337)
PHONE....................812 425-0381
Larry Dunn, *Owner*
EMP: 5 EST: 1962
SQ FT: 4,000
SALES (est): 471.9K **Privately Held**
SIC: 2448 Pallets, wood

(G-3332)
ABBP LLC
5320 Stringtown Rd (47711-2257)
PHONE....................812 402-5966
Eric J Berensen,
EMP: 7
SQ FT: 2,000
SALES (est): 1MM **Privately Held**
SIC: 3086 Plastics foam products

(G-3333)
ABK TRACKING INC
1201 N Weinbach Ave (47711-4301)
P.O. Box 4715 (47724-0715)
PHONE..........................812 473-9554
Danny P Koester, *President*
Janet L Koester, *Admin Sec*
EMP: 6 EST: 2010
SALES (est): 482.8K **Privately Held**
SIC: 3663

(G-3334)
ACCLAIM GRAPHICS INC
Also Called: Print Tech
908 N Garvin St (47711-5168)
PHONE..........................812 424-5035
Joseph Birkhead, *President*
Kell Y Birkhead, *Vice Pres*
EMP: 8 EST: 1946
SQ FT: 7,600
SALES (est): 1.1MM **Privately Held**
WEB: www.acclaimgraphics.com
SIC: 2754 2791 2789 2759 Job printing,
gravure; typesetting; bookbinding & re-
lated work; commercial printing; commer-
cial printing, lithographic

(G-3335)
ACCURATE TOOL &
ENGINEERING
8501 Neu Rd (47720-7850)
PHONE..........................812 963-6677
Leonard Angermeier, *President*
Susan Angermeier, *Treasurer*
EMP: 2
SQ FT: 2,360
SALES (est): 266.1K **Privately Held**
SIC: 3544 7692 Industrial molds; welding
repair

(G-3336)
ACCURIDE CORPORATION (HQ)
7140 Office Cir (47715-8235)
PHONE..........................812 962-5000
Richard F Dauch, *President*
David G Adams, *President*
Scott D Hazlett, *President*
Gregory A Risch, *President*
Katie Magoteaux, *General Mgr*
EMP: 130
SQ FT: 37,229
SALES: 685.5MM **Privately Held**
SIC: 3714 3713 Wheels, motor vehicle;
wheel rims, motor vehicle; bumpers &
bumperettes, motor vehicle; brake drums,
motor vehicle; truck bodies & parts
PA: Armor Parent Corp.
7140 Office Cir
Evansville IN 47715
812 962-5000

(G-3337)
ACCURIDE EMI LLC
7140 Office Cir (47715-8235)
PHONE..........................940 565-8505
William M Lasky,
EMP: 4
SALES (est): 432K **Privately Held**
SIC: 3714 3713 Motor vehicle parts & ac-
cessories; truck & bus bodies

(G-3338)
ACE EXTRUSION LLC
Extrusion Division
1800 W Maryland St (47712-5338)
P.O. Box 6288 (47719-0288)
PHONE..........................812 463-5230
Randolph Zahn, *President*
EMP: 8
SALES (corp-wide): 17.1MM **Privately**
Held
SIC: 2891 3084 3086 Sealants; adhe-
sives; plastics pipe; packaging & shipping
materials, foamed plastic
PA: Ace Extrusion Llc
14020 Highway 57
Evansville IN 47725
812 868-8640

(G-3339)
ACE EXTRUSION LLC (PA)
14020 Highway 57 (47725-9638)
P.O. Box 6587 (47719-0587)
PHONE..........................812 868-8640
Tim Robards,
EMP: 40

SQ FT: 20,000
SALES (est): 17.1MM **Privately Held**
WEB: www.aceextrusion.com
SIC: 3061 Mechanical rubber goods

(G-3340)
ACE EXTRUSION LLC
Also Called: Extrusion Division
1800 W Maryland St (47712-5338)
P.O. Box 6288 (47719-0288)
PHONE..........................812 463-5230
Fax: 812 463-5229
EMP: 64
SALES (corp-wide): 12.2MM **Privately**
Held
SIC: 2891 3084 3086 Mfg Foam Sealants
& Adhesives
PA: Ace Extrusion Llc
14020 Highway 57
Evansville IN 47725
812 868-8640

(G-3341)
ACE EXTRUSION LLC
Also Called: Pipeconx
701 N 9th Ave (47712-5343)
PHONE..........................812 436-4840
EMP: 29
SALES (corp-wide): 17.1MM **Privately**
Held
SIC: 3272 Pipe, concrete or lined with con-
crete
PA: Ace Extrusion Llc
14020 Highway 57
Evansville IN 47725
812 868-8640

(G-3342)
ACT SYSTEMS INTERNATIONAL
LLC
Also Called: Casters In Motion
1513 N Cullen Ave (47715-2332)
PHONE..........................812 437-4609
John W Smith, *Vice Pres*
John Smith, *Vice Pres*
Aaron M Schapker,
▲ EMP: 10
SALES (est): 740K **Privately Held**
SIC: 3312 Wheels

(G-3343)
AD VISION GRAPHICS INC
Also Called: Zoo Zone
1820 N Hoosier Ave (47715-8542)
PHONE..........................812 476-4932
Greg Gray, *President*
Christina Nobles, *Manager*
EMP: 6
SALES (est): 718.5K **Privately Held**
WEB: www.advisionscreengraphics.com
SIC: 2396 Screen printing on fabric articles

(G-3344)
ADVANCED SIGN & LIGHTING
SVC
13350 N Green River Rd (47725-9768)
PHONE..........................812 430-2817
Benjamin D Boring, *Principal*
EMP: 2
SALES (est): 180K **Privately Held**
SIC: 3993 Signs & advertising specialties

(G-3345)
AIRGAS USA LLC
2300 N Burkhardt Rd (47715-2156)
P.O. Box 5229 (47716-5229)
PHONE..........................812 474-0440
Jeff McCutchan, *Accounts Mgr*
Betty Slaughter, *Manager*
Jeffrey Green, *Director*
EMP: 50
SALES (corp-wide): 164.2MM **Privately**
Held
SIC: 5169 5085 2813 Chemicals & allied
products; industrial supplies; industrial
gases
HQ: Airgas Usa, Llc
259 N Radnor Chester Rd # 100
Radnor PA 19087
610 687-5253

(G-3346)
AJLL LLC
450 Plaza Dr (47715-3548)
PHONE..........................812 477-3611
Jonathan D Keck, *Principal*

EMP: 2
SALES (est): 105K **Privately Held**
SIC: 2084 Wines

(G-3347)
AL PERRY ENTERPRISES INC
(PA)
9203 Petersburg Rd (47725-1479)
PHONE..........................812 867-7727
Al Perry, *President*
EMP: 2
SALES (est): 427.9K **Privately Held**
WEB: www.alperry.com
SIC: 8748 5052 1241 Energy conserva-
tion consultant; coal; coal mining services

(G-3348)
ALL-WEATHER PRODUCTS INC
8346 Baumgart Rd (47725-1514)
PHONE..........................812 867-6403
Fax: 812 867-0257
Roger Feightner, *President*
Juanita Feightner, *Vice Pres*
EMP: 9 EST: 1979
SQ FT: 13,000
SALES (est): 840K **Privately Held**
SIC: 3442 5031 Storm doors or windows,
metal; doors, combination, screen-storm;
windows

(G-3349)
ALTSTADT BUSINESS FORMS
INC (PA)
Also Called: Altstadt Office City
1550 Baker Ave (47710-2510)
P.O. Box 6422 (47719-0422)
PHONE..........................812 425-3393
Fax: 812 425-3410
Mark Altstadt, *President*
Brenda Altstadt, *Vice Pres*
Brenda Atlstadt, *Treasurer*
EMP: 16
SALES (est): 8.4MM **Privately Held**
WEB: www.altstadtofficecity.com
SIC: 5112 2752 5021 2761 Business
forms; business forms, lithographed; of-
fice furniture; manifold business forms;
commercial printing; stationery products

(G-3350)
ALVEYS SIGN CO INC
13100 Highway 57 (47725-7612)
PHONE..........................812 867-2567
Fax: 812 867-1465
Kenneth Alvey, *President*
Helen Alvey, *Vice Pres*
EMP: 45
SQ FT: 51,635
SALES (est): 7.2MM **Privately Held**
WEB: www.alveysigns.com
SIC: 3993 1799 7532 7389 Electric
signs; sign installation & maintenance;
truck painting & lettering; sign painting &
lettering shop

(G-3351)
AMERICAN WHOLESALERS INC
(PA)
3509 American Way (47711-3691)
PHONE..........................812 464-8781
Fax: 812 461-6452
Ric Grant, *Vice Pres*
Douglas N Dockery, *Vice Pres*
Jack Starks, *Treasurer*
Stacy Palstring, *Controller*
Gary Mason, *Office Mgr*
EMP: 27
SALES (est): 11.7MM **Privately Held**
WEB: www.americanwholesalers.biz
SIC: 2952 Siding materials

(G-3352)
AMERICAN WINDOW AND
GLASS INC (PA)
2715 Lynch Rd (47711-2958)
PHONE..........................812 464-9400
Fax: 812 464-3131
Jack Starks, *President*
Michael Smith, *General Mgr*
Douglas Dockery, *Vice Pres*
Ric Grant, *Vice Pres*
Richard Grant, *Treasurer*
EMP: 135
SQ FT: 105,000

SALES (est): 23.7MM **Privately Held**
WEB: www.americanwindowandglass.com
SIC: 3089 3442 3231 Awnings, fiberglass
& plastic combination; doors, folding:
plastic or plastic coated fabric; window
frames & sash, plastic; metal doors, sash
& trim; products of purchased glass

(G-3353)
AMERIQUAL GROUP LLC (HQ)
Also Called: Ameriqual Packaging
18200 Highway 41 N (47725-9300)
PHONE..........................812 867-1300
Timothy Brauer, *Vice Pres*
Shane Shepherd, *Vice Pres*
Mark Oakley, *Purch Mgr*
Doug Diedrich, *Senior Buyer*
Vickie Clemons, *Purch Agent*
◆ EMP: 510
SQ FT: 240,000
SALES (est): 284.5MM
SALES (corp-wide): 38.4MM **Privately**
Held
WEB: www.ameriqual.com
SIC: 2099 Ready-to-eat meals, salads &
sandwiches; box lunches, for sale off
premises
PA: Ameriqual Group Holdings Llc
18200 Highway 41 N
Evansville IN 47725
812 867-1300

(G-3354)
AMERIQUAL GROUP LLC
Also Called: Ameriqual Foods
18200 Highway 41 N (47725-9300)
PHONE..........................812 867-1444
Dennis Straub, *President*
Timothy Brauer, *Vice Pres*
EMP: 30
SQ FT: 111,000
SALES (corp-wide): 38.4MM **Privately**
Held
WEB: www.ameriqual.com
SIC: 2099 Ready-to-eat meals, salads &
sandwiches
HQ: Ameriqual Group, Llc
18200 Highway 41 N
Evansville IN 47725
812 867-1300

(G-3355)
AMERLIGHT LLC (PA)
2800 Lynch Rd Ste B (47711-2928)
PHONE..........................812 602-3452
Sharon Tepool, *Bookkeeper*
Jim Vincent, *Mng Member*
EMP: 8
SQ FT: 110,000
SALES: 3.2MM **Privately Held**
SIC: 3674 3646 5063 Light emitting
diodes; commercial indusl & institutional
electric lighting fixtures; lighting fixtures

(G-3356)
AMROSIA METAL FABRICATION
INC
1701 N Kentucky Ave (47711-3854)
PHONE..........................812 425-5707
James D Burch, *President*
EMP: 2
SALES (est): 65.7K **Privately Held**
SIC: 3499 Fabricated metal products

(G-3357)
ANCHOR INDUSTRIES INC
7701 Highway 41 N (47725-1700)
P.O. Box 7105, Indianapolis (46207-7105)
PHONE..........................812 867-2421
Pete Mogavero, *CEO*
EMP: 73
SALES (corp-wide): 61MM **Privately**
Held
SIC: 3999 Barber & beauty shop equip-
ment
PA: Anchor Industries Inc.
1100 Burch Dr
Evansville IN 47725
812 867-2421

(G-3358)
APEX TOOL AND
MANUFACTURING
2306 N New York Ave (47711-3934)
PHONE..........................812 425-8121
Fax: 812 428-6024

Terry A Babb, *President*
B Jay Babb, *Vice Pres*
Susan B Babb, *Treasurer*
Scott Parker, *Sales Mgr*
Nikki Turner, *Admin Sec*
EMP: 15 **EST:** 1970
SQ FT: 18,000
SALES: 1.3MM **Privately Held**
WEB: www.apextool.org
SIC: 3544 Special dies & tools; jigs & fixtures

(G-3359)
APPLE AMERICAN LANGUAGE INST
9200 Moffett Ln (47725-1430)
PHONE....................812 867-7239
Jacqueline Fenneman, *Principal*
EMP: 2
SALES (est): 117.8K **Privately Held**
SIC: 3571 Personal computers (microcomputers)

(G-3360)
ARBEN CORP
Also Called: Ameristamp Sign-A-Rama
1300 N Royal Ave (47715-7808)
PHONE....................812 477-7763
Fax: 812 477-7989
Walter A Valiant, *President*
Deborah A Valiant, *Vice Pres*
Dawn Sutton, *Prdtn Mgr*
Cindy Lewis, *Accounts Exec*
EMP: 17 **EST:** 1957
SQ FT: 8,400
SALES: 1MM **Privately Held**
SIC: 3953 3993 Marking devices; signs, not made in custom sign painting shops

(G-3361)
ARC INDUSTRIES
615 W Virginia St (47710-1615)
PHONE....................812 471-1633
Margaret Boarman, *President*
◆ **EMP:** 3
SALES (est): 208.1K **Privately Held**
SIC: 3999 Manufacturing industries

(G-3362)
ARCHAEASOLUTIONS INC
911 E Franklin St (47711-5656)
PHONE....................770 487-5303
Michael D Riggs, *CEO*
John Scarbrough, *Vice Pres*
▼ **EMP:** 6
SQ FT: 3,000
SALES (est): 1.8MM **Privately Held**
WEB: www.archaeasolutions.com
SIC: 2835 In vitro & in vivo diagnostic substances

(G-3363)
ARCHER-DANIELS-MIDLAND COMPANY
Also Called: ADM
2350 Broadway Ave (47712-4916)
PHONE....................812 424-3581
Fax: 812 422-5945
Matt Stokerand, *Manager*
EMP: 25
SALES (corp-wide): 60.8B **Publicly Held**
WEB: www.admworld.com
SIC: 2041 Flour & other grain mill products
PA: Archer-Daniels-Midland Company
77 W Wacker Dr Ste 4600
Chicago IL 60601
312 634-8100

(G-3364)
ARCHITECTURAL METAL ROOFG SUP
1400 N Cullen Ave (47715-2331)
PHONE....................812 423-5257
Eric Krupp, *President*
Kenneth Krupp, *Vice Pres*
Caroly Krupp, *Admin Sec*
EMP: 3
SQ FT: 2,500
SALES (est): 1.6MM **Privately Held**
SIC: 2952 Roofing materials

(G-3365)
ARMADA OPTICAL SERVICES INC
701 N Weinbach Ave # 410 (47711-5990)
PHONE....................812 476-6623
Fax: 812 476-6680
Lori L Miller, *President*
Julia Coakley, *Manager*
Fred Miller, *Admin Sec*
EMP: 12
SQ FT: 2,800
SALES (est): 960K **Privately Held**
WEB: www.armadaoptical.com
SIC: 3851 Eyeglasses, lenses & frames

(G-3366)
ARMOR PARENT CORP (PA)
7140 Office Cir (47715-8235)
PHONE....................812 962-5000
Alex Rose, *Principal*
EMP: 10
SALES (est): 685.5MM **Privately Held**
SIC: 3714 3713 Wheel rims, motor vehicle; wheels, motor vehicle; bumpers & bumperettes, motor vehicle; brake drums, motor vehicle; truck bodies & parts

(G-3367)
ATLAS MACHINE AND SUPPLY INC
5001 Hitch Peters Rd (47711-2469)
PHONE....................812 423-7762
Fax: 812 423-7622
Todd Riley, *Manager*
Timothy Smith, *Manager*
Kenny Thompson, *Manager*
EMP: 10
SALES (corp-wide): 43.5MM **Privately Held**
WEB: www.atlasmachine.com
SIC: 5084 3599 Compressors, except air conditioning; machine shop, jobbing & repair
PA: Atlas Machine And Supply, Inc.
7000 Global Dr
Louisville KY 40258
502 584-7262

(G-3368)
AZIMUTH CUSTOM EXTRUSIONS LLC
1618 Lynch Rd (47711-2846)
PHONE....................812 423-6180
Fax: 812 402-6795
Robert K Dickerson, *President*
Charles C Mans, *Vice Pres*
Spencer Parker, *Accounts Mgr*
Robert Dickerson, *Mng Member*
Betty Whitney, *Manager*
EMP: 40
SALES (est): 17MM **Privately Held**
WEB: www.azimuthce.com
SIC: 3081 Unsupported plastics film & sheet

(G-3369)
BAILEY TOOLS & SUPPLY INC
5716 E Morgan Ave Ste 9 (47715-2398)
PHONE....................502 635-6348
Jims Keepes, *Manager*
EMP: 4
SALES (corp-wide): 11.4MM **Privately Held**
SIC: 3541 Electron-discharge metal cutting machine tools
PA: Bailey Tools & Supply, Inc.
1338 S Shelby St
Louisville KY 40217
502 635-6348

(G-3370)
BARGER ENGINEERING INC
2116 Lincoln Ave (47714-1600)
P.O. Box 2507 (47728-0507)
PHONE....................812 476-3077
Gloria Barger, *President*
Hubert S Barger, *President*
EMP: 5
SQ FT: 2,200
SALES (est): 530K **Privately Held**
SIC: 1311 8711 1382 Crude petroleum production; petroleum engineering; oil & gas exploration services

(G-3371)
BCBG MAX AZRIA GROUP LLC
382 W Church St (47715)
PHONE....................515 993-4753
EMP: 2
SALES (corp-wide): 979.1MM **Privately Held**
SIC: 2335 Women's, juniors' & misses' dresses
HQ: Bcbg Max Azria Group, Llc
2761 Fruitland Ave
Vernon CA 90058
323 589-2224

(G-3372)
BENTHALL BROS INC (PA)
15 Read St (47710-1399)
PHONE....................800 488-5995
Fax: 812 424-4750
Dennis M Benthall, *President*
Richard L Zirkle, *President*
Eli Benthall, *Branch Mgr*
EMP: 20 **EST:** 1943
SQ FT: 23,000
SALES (est): 8.7MM **Privately Held**
WEB: www.benthallbros.com
SIC: 5031 3496 3444 Doors, combination, screen-storm; windows; siding, wood; fencing, wood; miscellaneous fabricated wire products; sheet metalwork

(G-3373)
BERENDSEN INC
460 E Sycamore St (47713-2776)
PHONE....................812 423-6468
Fax: 812 424-5940
Caroline Sisbher, *Manager*
Carolyn Fischer, *Info Tech Mgr*
EMP: 4 **Privately Held**
WEB: www.bfpsales.com
SIC: 5084 3535 Hydraulic systems equipment & supplies; pneumatic tube conveyor systems
HQ: Berendsen, Inc.
401 S Boston Ave Ste 1200
Tulsa OK 74103
918 592-3781

(G-3374)
BERRY FILM PRODUCTS CO INC
Also Called: Packerware
101 Oakley St (47710-1237)
PHONE....................812 306-2690
EMP: 3
SALES (est): 97.8K **Privately Held**
SIC: 3089 Plastic containers, except foam; cases, plastic

(G-3375)
BERRY GLOBAL INC
3245 Kansas Rd (47725-9757)
PHONE....................812 867-6671
Fax: 812 867-6289
Mike Morrison, *Plant Mgr*
Heath Tenhumerg, *Purch Agent*
Keith McLemore, *Buyer*
Bob Fella, *Manager*
Brad Fromm, *Maintence Staff*
EMP: 50 **Publicly Held**
SIC: 3089 3081 Bottle caps, molded plastic; unsupported plastics film & sheet
HQ: Berry Global, Inc.
101 Oakley St
Evansville IN 47710
812 424-2904

(G-3376)
BERRY GLOBAL INC (HQ)
Also Called: Berry Plastics
101 Oakley St (47710-1237)
P.O. Box 959 (47706-0959)
PHONE....................812 424-2904
Fax: 812 424-0128
Tom Salmon, *CEO*
Randall J Becker, *President*
Anthony M Civale, *Principal*
Robert V Seminara, *Principal*
Vike Engh, *Vice Pres*
◆ **EMP:** 1200
SALES (est): 4.9B **Publicly Held**
WEB: www.6sens.com
SIC: 3089 3081 Plastic containers, except foam; cups, plastic, except foam; bottle caps, molded plastic; caps, plastic; unsupported plastics film & sheet

(G-3377)
BERRY GLOBAL GROUP INC (PA)
101 Oakley St (47710-1237)
P.O. Box 959 (47706-0959)
PHONE....................812 424-2904
Jonathan D Rich, *Ch of Bd*
Thomas E Salmon, *President*
Curtis L Begle, *President*
Jean-Marc Galvez, *President*
Scott M Tracey, *President*
▼ **EMP:** 10
SALES: 7.1B **Publicly Held**
SIC: 3089 3085 2673 3081 Plastic containers, except foam; cups, plastic, except foam; bottle caps, molded plastic; caps, plastic; plastics bottles; trash bags (plastic film): made from purchased materials; plastic film & sheet; laminated plastics plate & sheet

(G-3378)
BERRY PLASTICS GROUP INC ✪
101 Oakley St (47710-1252)
PHONE....................812 424-2904
Brent Beeler, *President*
Chris Coil, *Engineer*
Joe Nelson, *Maintence Staff*
EMP: 3 **EST:** 2017
SALES (est): 97.8K **Privately Held**
SIC: 3089 Plastics products

(G-3379)
BERRY PLASTICS IK LLC
101 Oakley St (47710-1252)
PHONE....................641 648-5047
Ira Boots, *President*
▲ **EMP:** 70
SQ FT: 96,000
SALES (est): 9.8MM **Publicly Held**
WEB: www.6sens.com
SIC: 3089 2396 Injection molding of plastics; automotive & apparel trimmings
HQ: Berry Global, Inc.
101 Oakley St
Evansville IN 47710
812 424-2904

(G-3380)
BERRY PLASTICS OPCO INC
9845 Hedden Rd (47725-8905)
PHONE....................812 402-2903
EMP: 2 **Publicly Held**
SIC: 3089 Bottle caps, molded plastic
HQ: Berry Plastics Opco, Inc.
101 Oakley St
Evansville IN 47710

(G-3381)
BERRY PLASTICS OPCO INC (DH)
101 Oakley St (47710-1252)
PHONE....................812 424-2904
EMP: 25
SALES (est): 9MM **Publicly Held**
SIC: 3089 Bottle caps, molded plastic
HQ: Berry Global, Inc.
101 Oakley St
Evansville IN 47710
812 424-2904

(G-3382)
BETTER BUILT BARNS INC
4415 E Morgan Ave (47715-2253)
PHONE....................812 477-2001
Terry Turpin, *President*
Frances Turpin, *Vice Pres*
EMP: 2 **EST:** 1997
SALES (est): 210K **Privately Held**
SIC: 2421 Outdoor wood structural products

(G-3383)
BEVERLY G INC
1818 Vann Ave (47714-4054)
PHONE....................812 401-1819
Keith Traphagen, *Principal*
EMP: 3
SALES (est): 104.7K **Privately Held**
SIC: 2711 Newspapers

(G-3384)
BIG B DISTRIBUTORS INC
2727 N Kentucky Ave (47711-6203)
PHONE....................812 425-5235

Robert J Bonenberger, *President*
Richard W Bonenberger, *Vice Pres*
EMP: 10
SQ FT: 2,000
SALES (est): 791.2K **Privately Held**
SIC: 2013 2035 Canned meats (except baby food) from purchased meat; pickles, sauces & salad dressings

(G-3385)
BIMBO BAKERIES USA INC
Also Called: Bimbo Baker US
6717 Toney Ln (47715-1777)
PHONE.................................812 479-6934
EMP: 24
SALES (corp-wide): 13.7B **Privately Held**
SIC: 2051 Mfg Bread/Related Products
HQ: Bimbo Bakeries Usa, Inc
255 Business Center Dr # 200
Horsham PA 19044
215 347-5500

(G-3386)
BLACK EQUIPMENT COMPANY SOUTH
1187 Burch Dr (47725-1701)
PHONE.................................812 477-6481
Jay D Bonnell, *Exec Dir*
EMP: 2 **EST:** 2016
SALES (est): 103.1K **Privately Held**
SIC: 3542 Machine tools, metal forming type

(G-3387)
BLUE RIVER TIMBER LLC
2997 Gethsemane Church Rd (47712)
PHONE.................................812 291-0411
Sandy Meyer, *Principal*
EMP: 6
SALES (est): 490K **Privately Held**
SIC: 2411 Timber, cut at logging camp

(G-3388)
BODY PANELS CO
1101 N Governor St (47711-5069)
PHONE.................................812 962-6262
Fax: 812 962-0680
Mrk Cowan, *Branch Mgr*
EMP: 19
SALES (corp-wide): 12.6MM **Privately Held**
WEB: www.bodypanels.com
SIC: 3465 Fenders, automobile: stamped or pressed metal
PA: Body Panels Co
2282 Whitten Rd
Memphis TN
901 372-6964

(G-3389)
BOEKE ROAD BAPTIST CHURCH INC
Also Called: Faith Music Missions
2601 S Boeke Rd (47714-4933)
P.O. Box 2463 (47728-0463)
PHONE.................................812 479-5342
Fax: 812 474-0483
Ed Russ, *Pastor*
Gayle Russ, *Relg Ldr*
EMP: 7
SALES: 90K **Privately Held**
SIC: 8661 3652 8211 Baptist Church; magnetic tape (audio): prerecorded; private combined elementary & secondary school

(G-3390)
BONDLINE ADHESIVES INC
500 N Woods Ave (47712-6448)
PHONE.................................812 423-4651
Fax: 812 422-2662
Diane D Fisher, *CEO*
Donald Berberich, *Shareholder*
EMP: 10 **EST:** 1966
SQ FT: 8,650
SALES: 3.5MM **Privately Held**
WEB: www.bondlineadhesives.com
SIC: 2891 2851 Adhesives; paints & allied products

(G-3391)
BOOTZ MANUFACTURING CO LLC (PA)
Also Called: Bootz Industries
1400 Park St (47710-2200)
P.O. Box 18010 (47719-1010)
PHONE.................................812 423-5401
Fax: 812 429-2254
Peter J Desocio, *President*
Thomas H Bootz, *Vice Pres*
Bill Weiman, *Treasurer*
▲ **EMP:** 20
SQ FT: 125,000
SALES (est): 38.4MM **Privately Held**
WEB: www.bootz.com
SIC: 3431 Bathtubs: enameled iron, cast iron or pressed metal; sinks: enameled iron, cast iron or pressed metal; lavatories, enameled iron or other metal

(G-3392)
BOOTZ MANUFACTURING CO LLC
Also Called: Bootz Industries
1600 N 1st Ave (47710-2708)
PHONE.................................812 423-5019
Peter J Desocio, *President*
EMP: 7
SALES (corp-wide): 38.4MM **Privately Held**
SIC: 3431 Bathtubs: enameled iron, cast iron or pressed metal; sinks: enameled iron, cast iron or pressed metal; lavatories, enameled iron or other metal
PA: Bootz Manufacturing Company, Llc
1400 Park St
Evansville IN 47710
812 423-5401

(G-3393)
BOOTZ MANUFACTURING COMPANY
Also Called: Bootz Plumbing
2301 W Maryland St (47712-5301)
P.O. Box 18010 (47719-1010)
PHONE.................................812 425-4646
Jim Poor, *Manager*
EMP: 85
SALES (corp-wide): 38.4MM **Privately Held**
WEB: www.bootz.com
SIC: 4225 3432 3431 3261 General warehousing & storage; plumbing fixture fittings & trim; metal sanitary ware; vitreous plumbing fixtures
PA: Bootz Manufacturing Company, Llc
1400 Park St
Evansville IN 47710
812 423-5401

(G-3394)
BOYER ENTERPRISES INC
Also Called: Soltek
12311 Edgewater Dr (47720-7911)
PHONE.................................812 963-9180
Steven D Boyer, *President*
EMP: 2
SALES (est): 331.3K **Privately Held**
WEB: www.solteksystems.com
SIC: 3651 Audio electronic systems

(G-3395)
BP PARALLEL LLC
101 Oakley St (47710-1237)
PHONE.................................812 424-2904
EMP: 3
SALES (est): 20.7K **Publicly Held**
SIC: 3089 Bottle caps, molded plastic
HQ: Berry Global, Inc.
101 Oakley St
Evansville IN 47710
812 424-2904

(G-3396)
BPREX CLOSURE SYSTEMS LLC
101 Oakley St (47710-1237)
P.O. Box 959 (47706-0959)
PHONE.................................812 424-2904
▼ **EMP:** 4
SALES (est): 364.6K **Publicly Held**
SIC: 3089 Bottle caps, molded plastic

HQ: Berry Global, Inc.
101 Oakley St
Evansville IN 47710
812 424-2904

(G-3397)
BPREX CLOSURES LLC (DH)
101 Oakley St (47710-1237)
P.O. Box 959 (47706-0959)
PHONE.................................812 424-2904
EMP: 62
SALES (est): 95.8MM **Publicly Held**
SIC: 3089 Bottle caps, molded plastic
HQ: Berry Global, Inc.
101 Oakley St
Evansville IN 47710
812 424-2904

(G-3398)
BPREX CLOSURES LLC
3245 Kansas Rd (47725-9757)
PHONE.................................812 424-2904
Leslie De Walle, *Branch Mgr*
EMP: 94 **Publicly Held**
SIC: 3089 Plastic containers, except foam
HQ: Bprex Closures, Llc
101 Oakley St
Evansville IN 47710
812 424-2904

(G-3399)
BPREX CLOSURES LLC
Also Called: Manufacturing Facility
3245 Kansas Rd (47725-9757)
PHONE.................................812 867-6671
Leslie De Walle, *Branch Mgr*
EMP: 267 **Publicly Held**
SIC: 3089 Bottle caps, molded plastic
HQ: Bprex Closures, Llc
101 Oakley St
Evansville IN 47710
812 424-2904

(G-3400)
BRACKETT HEATING & AC
5233 Old Boonville Hwy (47715-2124)
PHONE.................................812 476-1138
Fax: 812 471-0638
Wayman E Brackett, *CEO*
David Brackett, *President*
Carla Boulware, *Vice Pres*
Darlene Brackett, *Treasurer*
EMP: 15
SQ FT: 9,000
SALES (est): 2.1MM **Privately Held**
WEB: www.brackettac.com
SIC: 1711 3444 Warm air heating & air conditioning contractor; sheet metalwork

(G-3401)
BRIGGS EXPLORATION PROD CO LLC
4424 Vogel Rd Ste 404 (47715-9003)
PHONE.................................812 249-0564
Brandon Renner, *Administration*
EMP: 2
SALES (est): 178.5K **Privately Held**
SIC: 1311 Crude petroleum & natural gas

(G-3402)
BRINKER MFG JEWELERS INC
111 S Green River Rd Ste C (47715)
PHONE.................................812 476-0651
Fax: 812 479-8493
Roland Brinker, *President*
Dirk Brinker, *Vice Pres*
Kyle Brinker, *CFO*
Dean Brinker, *Treasurer*
Tim Hoehn, *Sales Mgr*
EMP: 18
SQ FT: 7,000
SALES (est): 2.8MM **Privately Held**
WEB: www.brinkersjewelers.com
SIC: 5944 3911 Jewelry, precious stones & precious metals; jewelry apparel

(G-3403)
BRISTOL MYERS
2400 W Lloyd Expy (47712-5095)
PHONE.................................812 428-1927
Fax: 812 429-5526
EMP: 3
SALES (est): 76.6K **Privately Held**
SIC: 2621 Bristols

(G-3404)
BUEHLER FOODS INC
Also Called: Buehler's Buy Low 4182
4635 N 1st Ave (47710-3625)
PHONE.................................812 467-7255
Fax: 812 467-7260
Eric Bedwell, *Manager*
EMP: 120 **Privately Held**
WEB: www.greatpeoplegreatprices.com
SIC: 5411 5912 2052 2051 Supermarkets, independent; drug stores & proprietary stores; cookies & crackers; bread, cake & related products
HQ: Buehler Foods Inc
1100 W 12th Ave
Jasper IN 47546
812 482-1366

(G-3405)
BURKERT-WALTON INC
1561 Allens Ln (47710-3370)
PHONE.................................812 425-7157
Fax: 812 425-7158
William Heierman, *President*
Daniel E Heierman, *Treasurer*
EMP: 5 **EST:** 1906
SQ FT: 6,800
SALES (est): 751.2K **Privately Held**
SIC: 2752 2759 2732 Commercial printing, offset; letterpress printing; pamphlets: printing & binding, not published on site

(G-3406)
BYRD INDUSTRIES
8811 Whispering Tree Ln (47711-1009)
PHONE.................................812 867-5859
Kiah Fuhrer, *Principal*
EMP: 2 **EST:** 2014
SALES (est): 55.1K **Privately Held**
SIC: 3999 Manufacturing industries

(G-3407)
C & K UNITED SHTMTL & MECH
2805 Lincoln Ave Rear (47714-1724)
P.O. Box 16095 (47716-1095)
PHONE.................................812 423-5090
Maurice E Coates Jr, *President*
Catherine Beckley, *Director*
Maurice Coates, *Director*
Pamela Rowe, *Director*
EMP: 30
SQ FT: 4,500
SALES (est): 1.7MM **Privately Held**
SIC: 1711 1761 3444 5033 Mechanical contractor; sheet metalwork; siding contractor; sheet metalwork; siding, except wood

(G-3408)
C & L SHEET METAL LLC
2263 E Tennessee St (47711-4837)
PHONE.................................812 449-9126
Lyman Matherly, *Administration*
EMP: 2
SALES (est): 396.8K **Privately Held**
SIC: 3444 Sheet metalwork

(G-3409)
CAPITAL TECH SOLUTIONS LLC
1112 S Villa Dr (47714-3248)
PHONE.................................812 303-4357
Maverick Taylor, *Owner*
EMP: 6
SALES (est): 891K **Privately Held**
SIC: 3823 Temperature measurement instruments, industrial

(G-3410)
CAPLAS NEPTUNE LLC
101 Oakley St (47710-1237)
PHONE.................................812 424-2904
EMP: 3
SALES (est): 18.3K **Publicly Held**
SIC: 3089 Bottle caps, molded plastic
HQ: Berry Global, Inc.
101 Oakley St
Evansville IN 47710
812 424-2904

(G-3411)
CAPTIVE HOLDINGS LLC
101 Oakley St (47710-1237)
P.O. Box 959 (47706-0959)
PHONE.................................812 424-2904
Iraq Boots, *Principal*
EMP: 6

SALES (est): 621.6K **Publicly Held**
SIC: 3089 Battery cases, plastic or plastic combination
HQ: Berry Global, Inc.
101 Oakley St
Evansville IN 47710
812 424-2904

(G-3412)
CAPTIVE PLASTICS INC (DH)
101 Oakley St (47710-1237)
PHONE.................................812 424-2904
John Dezio, *COO*
Rick Carroll, *Vice Pres*
Rolland Strasser, *Vice Pres*
◆ **EMP:** 170 **EST:** 1969
SQ FT: 228,000
SALES (est): 252.2MM **Publicly Held**
WEB: www.captiveplastics.com
SIC: 3089 Plastic containers, except foam; closures, plastic; injection molding of plastics
HQ: Berry Global, Inc.
101 Oakley St
Evansville IN 47710
812 424-2904

(G-3413)
CASTERS IN MOTION USA LTD LLC
1513 N Cullen Ave (47715-2332)
PHONE.................................812 437-4627
John W Smith, *Mng Member*
EMP: 5 **EST:** 2011
SALES (est): 157.3K **Privately Held**
SIC: 3562 Casters

(G-3414)
CATHOLIC PRESS OF EVANSVILLE
Also Called: Message The
4200 N Kentucky Ave (47711-2752)
P.O. Box 4169 (47724-0169)
PHONE.................................812 424-5536
Fax: 812 424-0907
Tim Lilley, *Director*
Charles Thompson, *Assistant*
EMP: 5
SALES (est): 130K **Privately Held**
SIC: 2711 8661 Newspapers: publishing only, not printed on site; non-church religious organizations

(G-3415)
CHAMP TORQUE CONVERTERS INC
Also Called: Champ Converters
1914 N Denby Ave (47711-3822)
PHONE.................................812 424-2602
Fax: 812 424-2602
Mike McGregor, *President*
Kirk Knight, *President*
Susan Knight, *Vice Pres*
EMP: 5 **EST:** 1960
SQ FT: 2,000
SALES (est): 717.9K **Privately Held**
SIC: 7539 3566 Torque converter repair, automotive; torque converters, except automotive

(G-3416)
CHAMPION OF EVANSVILLE LLC (PA)
6827 Interchange Rd S (47715-8258)
PHONE.................................812 424-2456
Fax: 812 424-2465
Jim Nuning, *District Mgr*
EMP: 17
SALES (est): 1.3MM **Privately Held**
SIC: 3442 3444 Storm doors or windows, metal; awnings, sheet metal

(G-3417)
CHRONOTRACK SYSTEMS CORP (PA)
Also Called: Athlinks
6001 Old Boonville Hwy (47715-2192)
PHONE.................................314 406-7243
Bob Finnegan, *Principal*
EMP: 9
SALES (est): 1MM **Privately Held**
SIC: 2679 Tags & labels, paper

(G-3418)
CLASSIC INDUSTRIES INC
2308 Commercial Ct (47720-1328)
PHONE.................................812 421-4006
Tom Buskavitz, *President*
Diane Buskavitz, *Corp Secy*
EMP: 6 **EST:** 1992
SQ FT: 2,400
SALES (est): 978.2K **Privately Held**
SIC: 3312 Tool & die steel

(G-3419)
CLAYTON HOMES INC
19410 Us 41 N (47725)
PHONE.................................812 423-4052
Ed Marksberry, *Manager*
Lisa Calvert, *Manager*
EMP: 5
SALES (corp-wide): 242.1B **Publicly Held**
WEB: www.clayton.net
SIC: 2451 Mobile homes
HQ: Clayton Homes, Inc.
5000 Clayton Rd
Maryville TN 37804
865 380-3000

(G-3420)
CLONDALKIN PHARMA & HEALTHCARE
1100 E Louisiana St (47711-4748)
PHONE.................................812 464-2461
Fax: 812 426-7578
EMP: 109
SALES (corp-wide): 1.3B **Privately Held**
SIC: 2752 2631 7311 Lithographic Commercial Printing Paperboard Mill Advertising Agency
HQ: Clondalkin Pharma & Healthcare, Inc
1072 Boulder Rd
Greensboro NC 27409
336 292-4555

(G-3421)
COCA-COLA BOTTLING CO CNSLD
3223 Interstate Dr (47715-1780)
PHONE.................................812 228-3200
Johnnie Palmer, *Area Mgr*
EMP: 81
SALES (corp-wide): 4.3B **Publicly Held**
SIC: 2086 Bottled & canned soft drinks
PA: Coca-Cola Bottling Co. Consolidated
4100 Coca Cola Plz # 100
Charlotte NC 28211
704 557-4400

(G-3422)
COLORMAX DIGITAL IMAGING INC (PA)
Also Called: Colormax Imaging
626 Court St (47708-1342)
PHONE.................................812 477-3805
David Odell, *President*
EMP: 20
SQ FT: 2,000
SALES (est): 952.2K **Privately Held**
WEB: www.colormaxdigital.com
SIC: 2711 2752 Commercial printing & newspaper publishing combined; commercial printing, lithographic

(G-3423)
COM-TECH PLASTICS INC (PA)
15000 Highway 41 N (47725-9360)
PHONE.................................812 421-3600
Raymond E Wright, *President*
Michael E Wright, *Treasurer*
EMP: 61
SQ FT: 5,000
SALES (est): 28MM **Privately Held**
WEB: www.matrixxgroup.com
SIC: 3089 Plastic containers, except foam

(G-3424)
COM-TECH PLASTICS INC
9 N Kentucky Ave (47711-5708)
PHONE.................................812 423-8270
Fax: 812 421-3611
Dan Wagner, *Branch Mgr*
Gary Crowe, *Manager*
EMP: 10

SALES (corp-wide): 28MM **Privately Held**
WEB: www.matrixxgroup.com
SIC: 3087 2821 Custom compound purchased resins; plastics materials & resins
PA: Com-Tech Plastics Inc
15000 Highway 41 N
Evansville IN 47725
812 421-3600

(G-3425)
COMMERCIAL COATINGS ASSOC LLC
800 E Oregon St (47711-5112)
PHONE.................................812 483-5130
Kevin Casagrand, *Principal*
EMP: 4
SALES (est): 368.8K **Privately Held**
SIC: 3479 Metal coating & allied service

(G-3426)
COMPLETE LUMBER INC (PA)
5625 Old Boonville Hwy (47715-2132)
P.O. Box 5385 (47716-5385)
PHONE.................................812 473-6400
Fax: 812 473-6409
Peggy Muth, *President*
James N Muth, *Senior VP*
EMP: 13 **EST:** 1961
SQ FT: 12,000
SALES (est): 4MM **Privately Held**
WEB: www.completelumber.com
SIC: 5211 2431 Lumber & other building materials; doors, wood

(G-3427)
CONCRETE SUPPLY LLC (PA)
4300 Vogel Rd (47715-2220)
PHONE.................................812 474-6715
Fax: 812 474-6717
Murl Powell, *Vice Pres*
Jerry Marx,
EMP: 25
SALES (est): 4.5MM **Privately Held**
SIC: 3272 3273 Concrete products; ready-mixed concrete

(G-3428)
CONNECTIONS SIGN LANGUAGE INTE
417 N Weinbach Ave # 107 (47711-6083)
P.O. Box 14492 (47728-6492)
PHONE.................................812 491-6036
Sara Barnett, *Owner*
EMP: 2
SALES (est): 147.1K **Privately Held**
SIC: 3993 Signs & advertising specialties

(G-3429)
CONSTELLATION MOLD INC
4825 Hitch Peters Rd (47711-2481)
PHONE.................................812 424-5338
Fax: 812 424-5338
Donald Kappert, *President*
Joe Baughn, *Vice Pres*
Loretta Kappert, *Vice Pres*
◆ **EMP:** 18
SQ FT: 26,500
SALES (est): 2.7MM **Privately Held**
WEB: www.constmold.com
SIC: 3544 Industrial molds

(G-3430)
CORE MINERALS OPERATING CO INC
25 Nw Riverside Dr # 300 (47708-1211)
PHONE.................................812 759-6950
Fax: 812 759-6960
James P Rode, *President*
Michael McLear, *Exec VP*
John Gasser, *CFO*
EMP: 8
SALES (est): 2.3MM **Privately Held**
SIC: 1311 Crude petroleum production

(G-3431)
CORR-WOOD MANUFACTURING INC
10501 Hedden Rd (47725-8928)
PHONE.................................812 867-0700
Fax: 812 867-1932
Dorothy Moors, *President*
EMP: 25
SQ FT: 17,500

SALES (est): 3.6MM **Privately Held**
SIC: 2499 2448 2449 Reels, plywood; pallets, wood; containers, plywood & veneer wood

(G-3432)
COUNTER DESIGN CO INC
2381 N Cullen Ave (47715-2185)
PHONE.................................812 477-1243
Fax: 812 477-0216
Alvin C Tretter, *President*
EMP: 40 **EST:** 1976
SQ FT: 30,000
SALES: 3.5MM **Privately Held**
WEB: www.counterdesignco.com
SIC: 2541 Table or counter tops, plastic laminated

(G-3433)
COUNTRYMARK COOP HOLDG CORP
7116 Eagle Crest Blvd (47715-8152)
PHONE.................................812 759-6962
Mike Gibdons, *Branch Mgr*
EMP: 50
SALES (corp-wide): 216.4MM **Privately Held**
SIC: 1381 Drilling oil & gas wells
PA: Countrymark Cooperative Holding Corporation
225 S East St Ste 144
Indianapolis IN 46202
800 808-3170

(G-3434)
COVALNCE SPCALTY ADHESIVES LLC (DH)
101 Oakley St (47710-1237)
PHONE.................................812 424-2904
Thomas Salmon, *President*
▼ **EMP:** 500
SALES (est): 283.1MM **Publicly Held**
WEB: www.6sens.com
SIC: 2891 Adhesives & sealants
HQ: Berry Global, Inc.
101 Oakley St
Evansville IN 47710
812 424-2904

(G-3435)
COVALNCE SPCIALTY COATINGS LLC (DH)
Also Called: Covalence Coated Products
101 Oakley St (47710-1237)
PHONE.................................812 424-2904
Jeffrey D Thompson, *President*
◆ **EMP:** 50
SALES (est): 113.6MM **Publicly Held**
SIC: 2672 Coated paper, except photographic, carbon or abrasive
HQ: Berry Global, Inc.
101 Oakley St
Evansville IN 47710
812 424-2904

(G-3436)
CRADDOCK FINISHING CORPORATION
Also Called: Craddock Furniture
1400 W Illinois St (47710-1003)
P.O. Box 269 (47702-0269)
PHONE.................................812 425-2691
Fax: 812 429-1370
Marc C Craddock, *President*
John Craddock, *Treasurer*
Donna Huff, *CTO*
Terry Husk, *Admin Sec*
EMP: 40 **EST:** 1934
SQ FT: 60,000
SALES: 4.2MM **Privately Held**
WEB: www.craddockfinishing.com
SIC: 3479 3089 Painting of metal products; coloring & finishing of plastic products

(G-3437)
CREATIVE CRAFTSMEN INC
5010 N Spring St (47711-2491)
P.O. Box 6144 (47719-0144)
PHONE.................................812 423-2844
Fax: 812 423-1681
Thomas E Pfender, *President*
Pryse Fletcher, *Vice Pres*
Keith Smith, *Treasurer*
Gene Adcock, *Prgrmr*

▲ = Import ▼=Export
◆ =Import/Export

EMP: 45
SQ FT: 42,000
SALES (est): 7.8MM **Privately Held**
WEB: www.creativecraftsmen.net
SIC: **3444** 3443 3599 Sheet metal specialties, not stamped; forming machine
work, sheet metal; trash racks, metal
plate; bins, prefabricated metal plate; machine shop, jobbing & repair

(G-3438)
CREATIVE EMBROIDERY DESIGNS
2545 Mjm Industrial Dr (47715-8526)
PHONE..................................812 479-8280
Donna Smith, *Owner*
Pamela Sanders, *Owner*
EMP: 3
SQ FT: 4,500
SALES: 139K **Privately Held**
WEB: www.cedstitch.com
SIC: **2395** Embroidery & art needlework

(G-3439)
CRESCENT PLASTICS INC (PA)
955 E Diamond Ave (47711-3400)
PHONE..................................812 428-9305
Fax: 812 428-9354
John C Schroeder, *President*
Ken Graves, *Vice Pres*
Penny Pennell, *Sales Staff*
Belle A Fahrer, *Admin Sec*
EMP: 81 **EST:** 1949
SALES (est): 23.3MM **Privately Held**
WEB: www.crescentplastics.com
SIC: **3089** Thermoformed finished plastic
products

(G-3440)
CRESCENT PLASTICS INC
955 E Diamond Ave (47711-3400)
PHONE..................................812 428-9300
John C Schroeder, *Branch Mgr*
EMP: 100
SALES (est): 9.4MM
SALES (corp-wide): 23.3MM **Privately
Held**
WEB: www.crescentplastics.com
SIC: **3089** Thermoformed finished plastic
products
PA: Crescent Plastics, Inc.
955 E Diamond Ave
Evansville IN 47711
812 428-9305

(G-3441)
CRESCENT-CRESLINE-WABASH PLAST
600 N Cross Pointe Blvd (47715-9119)
PHONE..................................812 428-9300
Jerry Brenner, *Principal*
EMP: 2
SALES: 682.9K **Privately Held**
SIC: **3089** Injection molding of plastics

(G-3442)
CRESLINE PLASTIC PIPE CO INC (PA)
600 N Cross Pointe Blvd (47715-9119)
PHONE..................................812 428-9300
Fax: 812 428-9353
John H Schroeder, *Ch of Bd*
Richard A Schroeder, *President*
Gary Richmond, *Vice Pres*
Mike Hatley, *VP Mfg*
Terry Womack, *Purch Agent*
▲ EMP: 35
SQ FT: 8,000
SALES (est): 142.3MM **Privately Held**
WEB: www.creslinepipe.com
SIC: **3084** Plastics pipe

(G-3443)
CRESLINE-NORTHWEST LLC (PA)
600 N Cross Pointe Blvd (47715-9119)
PHONE..................................812 428-9300
Belle Fahrer, *Treasurer*
Richard Schroeder, *Mng Member*
John C Schroeder,
EMP: 48
SQ FT: 15,000
SALES (est): 7.2MM **Privately Held**
WEB: www.cresline-northwest.com
SIC: **3084** Plastics pipe

(G-3444)
CRESLINE-WEST INC (PA)
955 E Diamond Ave (47711-3407)
PHONE..................................812 428-9300
John H Schroeder, *Ch of Bd*
Richard A Schroeder, *President*
Gary B Richmond, *Vice Pres*
Tom Walker, *Vice Pres*
Belle Fahrer, *Admin Sec*
EMP: 5
SQ FT: 15,000
SALES (est): 12.1MM **Privately Held**
WEB: www.cresline-west.com
SIC: **3084** Plastics pipe

(G-3445)
CROSSPOINT POLYMER TECH LLC
2301 St Jseph Indus Pk Dr (47720-1250)
PHONE..................................812 426-1350
Ben Schmidt, *President*
EMP: 55
SALES (est): 11.4MM **Privately Held**
SIC: **3087** Custom compound purchased
resins

(G-3446)
CROWN EQUIPMENT CORPORATION
Also Called: Crown Lift Trucks
2540 Diego Dr (47715-2906)
PHONE..................................812 477-5511
David Smith, *Manager*
EMP: 41
SALES (corp-wide): 3.1B **Privately Held**
WEB: www.okisys.com
SIC: **3537** Lift trucks, industrial: fork, plat-
form, straddle, etc.
PA: Crown Equipment Corporation
44 S Washington St
New Bremen OH 45869
419 629-2311

(G-3447)
CUMMINS CROSSPOINT LLC
7901 Highway 41 N (47725-1525)
PHONE..................................812 867-4400
Fax: 812 867-4411
Ken Hurst, *Branch Mgr*
Mike Kilgore, *Branch Mgr*
EMP: 50
SQ FT: 21,000
SALES (corp-wide): 20.4B **Publicly Held**
SIC: **5084** 5063 3519 Engines & parts,
diesel; generators; internal combustion
engines
HQ: Cummins Crosspoint Llc
2601 Fortune Cir E 300c
Indianapolis IN 46241
317 243-7979

(G-3448)
CURVO LABS INC (PA)
58 Adams Ave (47713-1310)
PHONE..................................619 316-1202
Andrew S Perry, *CEO*
Steve Suhrheinrich, *COO*
EMP: 8 **EST:** 2012
SALES (est): 1.9MM **Privately Held**
SIC: **7372** Business oriented computer
software

(G-3449)
CUSTOM BLIND CO
21 W Sunrise Dr (47710-4659)
PHONE..................................812 867-9280
Jeff Goebel, *President*
EMP: 2
SQ FT: 3,000
SALES: 600K **Privately Held**
SIC: **2591** Drapery hardware & blinds &
shades

(G-3450)
CUSTOM ENGINEERING INC
1900 Lynch Rd (47711-2896)
PHONE..................................812 424-3879
Fax: 812 424-2087
Robert G Klassen, *President*
Jeff Reickers, *Engng Exec*
EMP: 9 **EST:** 1959
SQ FT: 11,000

SALES (est): 950K **Privately Held**
SIC: **3599** 3544 Machine & other job shop
work; custom machinery; special dies &
tools

(G-3451)
CUSTOM SEWING SERVICE
2644 N Heidelbach Ave (47711-3236)
PHONE..................................812 428-7015
Fax: 812 428-7015
Jennifer Ziliak, *Owner*
EMP: 4
SQ FT: 2,100
SALES (est): 390.4K **Privately Held**
SIC: **2221** 5131 5949 5714 Upholstery,
tapestry & wall covering fabrics; com-
forters & quilts, manmade fiber & silk;
piece goods & notions; sewing, needle-
work & piece goods; draperies

(G-3452)
CUSTOM WOODWORKING
Also Called: Custom Wood Floor
3314 Kratzville Rd (47710-3358)
PHONE..................................812 422-6786
Michael Alley, *Owner*
EMP: 4
SALES (est): 505.3K **Privately Held**
SIC: **2431** Millwork

(G-3453)
DANIEL KORB LAUNDRY COMPANY (PA)
Also Called: Pearl Launderers & Cleaners
4905 Bellemeade Ave (47715-4129)
PHONE..................................812 425-6121
Fax: 812 429-1689
Gilbert A Korb Jr, *President*
Bernard Michel, *Corp Secy*
EMP: 75
SQ FT: 40,000
SALES (est): 2.6MM **Privately Held**
SIC: **7211** 7216 7213 2759 Power laun-
dries, family & commercial; drycleaning
plants, except rugs; uniform supply;
screen printing

(G-3454)
DCS CAR AUDIO
Also Called: Dc's Mobile Electronics
1732 W Franklin St A (47712-5107)
PHONE..................................812 437-8488
Fax: 812 437-8488
Dennis Chapman, *Owner*
EMP: 5
SALES (est): 708K **Privately Held**
SIC: **3571** Electronic computers

(G-3455)
DEAN BOSLERS
3820 E Morgan Ave (47715-2242)
PHONE..................................812 476-8787
Steve Waninger, *Principal*
EMP: 3
SALES (est): 101.8K **Privately Held**
SIC: **2211** Furniture denim

(G-3456)
DELILAH CLUB COVERS
4812 Tippecanoe Dr (47715-3234)
PHONE..................................812 401-0012
Delilah Harvey, *Owner*
EMP: 2
SALES (est): 143.7K **Privately Held**
SIC: **3949** Shafts, golf club

(G-3457)
DEXTEROUS MOLD AND TOOL INC
2535 Locust Creek Dr (47720-1558)
PHONE..................................812 422-8046
Fax: 812 422-8047
Eugene Elpers, *President*
Earlene Elpers, *Corp Secy*
Brian Elpers, *Purch Mgr*
EMP: 20 **EST:** 1979
SQ FT: 15,000
SALES (est): 3.5MM **Privately Held**
WEB: www.dexterousmold.com
SIC: **3089** Injection molding of plastics

(G-3458)
DISH EXPRESS
1101 N Fulton Ave (47710-1864)
P.O. Box 1213, Cadiz KY (42211-1213)
PHONE..................................812 962-3982
Nick Cleveland, *Owner*
EMP: 8
SALES (est): 1.5MM **Privately Held**
SIC: **3663** Satellites, communications

(G-3459)
DIST COUNCIL 91
409 Millner Industrial Dr (47710-2545)
PHONE..................................812 962-9191
Steven Stall, *President*
Johnny Alderman, *Treasurer*
Joy Scarlett, *Admin Sec*
EMP: 4
SALES: 1.5MM **Privately Held**
SIC: **2851** 8631 Paints, waterproof; trade
union

(G-3460)
DITTO SALES INC
1817 W Virginia St (47712-5206)
PHONE..................................812 424-4098
John Evans, *Manager*
EMP: 4
SALES (est): 346.2K
SALES (corp-wide): 27.2MM **Privately
Held**
WEB: www.dittosales.com
SIC: **2519** Household furniture, except
wood or metal: upholstered
PA: Ditto Sales, Inc.
2332 Cathy Ln
Jasper IN 47546
812 482-3043

(G-3461)
DON MICHIEL PRINTS LLC ✪
5217 Normandy Pl (47715-2648)
PHONE..................................812 550-7767
Donald Michiel Coffman Jr, *Principal*
EMP: 2 **EST:** 2018
SALES (est): 83.9K **Privately Held**
SIC: **2752** Commercial printing, litho-
graphic

(G-3462)
DONUT BANK INC (PA)
Also Called: Donut Bank Bakery
1031 E Diamond Ave (47711-3901)
PHONE..................................812 426-0011
Fax: 812 422-2839
Harold A Kempf, *President*
Shirley A Kempf, *Corp Secy*
Pat Bretz, *Supervisor*
EMP: 25 **EST:** 1967
SQ FT: 8,000
SALES (est): 19.1MM **Privately Held**
WEB: www.donutbank.com
SIC: **2051** 5461 Doughnuts, except
frozen; pastries, e.g. danish: except
frozen; bakery: wholesale or
wholesale/retail combined; bakeries

(G-3463)
DSM ENGINEERING PLASTICS INC
2267 W Mill Rd (47720-6902)
PHONE..................................812 435-7500
Fax: 248 792-9156
Steve Hartig, *Manager*
EMP: 17
SALES (corp-wide): 10.1B **Privately Held**
SIC: **2821** 3087 3083 Acrylonitrile-butadi-
ene-styrene resins (ABS resins); custom
compound purchased resins; laminated
plastics plate & sheet
HQ: Dsm Engineering Plastics, Inc.
2267 W Mill Rd
Evansville IN 47720

(G-3464)
DSM ENGINEERING PLASTICS INC
Also Called: Unknown
2267 W Mill Rd (47720-6902)
PHONE..................................812 435-7638
Bob Hartmayer, *Branch Mgr*
EMP: 4
SALES (corp-wide): 10.1B **Privately Held**
SIC: **2821** Plastics materials & resins

HQ: Dsm Engineering Plastics, Inc.
2267 W Mill Rd
Evansville IN 47720

(G-3465)
DSM ENGINEERING PLASTICS INC (DH)
Also Called: D S M
2267 W Mill Rd (47720-6902)
PHONE.....................248 530-5500
Fax: 812 435-7702
Richard Pieters, *President*
Debra Dykema, *Vice Pres*
Robert Evans, *Vice Pres*
Jeff Harding, *Design Engr*
Jon Coe, *Admin Sec*
◆ EMP: 230
SQ FT: 150,000
SALES (est): 156.2MM
SALES (corp-wide): 10.1B **Privately Held**
SIC: 2821 3087 3083 Acrylonitrile-butadiene-styrene resins (ABS resins); custom compound purchased resins; laminated plastics plate & sheet

(G-3466)
DUCLAS FITNESS LLC
114 Williamsburg Dr (47715-3456)
PHONE.....................812 217-8544
Edward Duclas,
EMP: 2 EST: 2016
SALES (est): 85.5K **Privately Held**
SIC: 3949 Exercise equipment

(G-3467)
DYNO NOBEL INC
4 Nw 2nd St (47708-1244)
PHONE.....................859 278-4770
Robert A Bingham, *Manager*
EMP: 28 **Privately Held**
SIC: 2892 Explosives
HQ: Dyno Nobel Inc.
2795 E Cottonwood Pkwy # 500
Salt Lake City UT 84121
801 364-4800

(G-3468)
E JAMES DANT (PA)
Also Called: McF Business Products & Svcs
1620 Harmony Way (47720-6107)
PHONE.....................812 476-2271
E James Dant, *Partner*
Andrew Dant, *Partner*
Bryce Dant, *Partner*
David Dant, *Partner*
EMP: 7
SALES: 1.2MM **Privately Held**
SIC: 2759 5045 Commercial printing; computers, peripherals & software

(G-3469)
E JAMES DANT
Also Called: M C F Business Product & Svcs
2520 E Morgan Ave Apt D (47711-4489)
PHONE.....................812 476-2271
Fax: 812 476-7755
Andrew Dants, *Partner*
EMP: 7
SALES (corp-wide): 1.2MM **Privately Held**
SIC: 2759 2761 2752 Commercial printing; manifold business forms; commercial printing, lithographic
PA: E James Dant
1620 Harmony Way
Evansville IN 47720
812 476-2271

(G-3470)
E L S INC
10435 Upper Mt Vernon Rd (47712-9604)
PHONE.....................812 985-2272
Elwanda Shrode, *President*
James W Shrode, *Corp Secy*
EMP: 3 EST: 1971
SQ FT: 10,000
SALES (est): 472.8K **Privately Held**
SIC: 3599 Machine shop, jobbing & repair

(G-3471)
EAGLE RIVER COAL LLC
250 N Cross Pointe Blvd (47715-4073)
PHONE.....................618 252-0490
Thomas Ryan Franks,
Thomas Walker Franks,
Amanda Franks Holland,

Elizabeth Franks Pilcher,
EMP: 2 EST: 2009
SALES (est): 1.5MM **Privately Held**
SIC: 1221 Bituminous coal & lignite-surface mining

(G-3472)
EEMSCO INC
600 W Eichel Ave (47710-2412)
P.O. Box 4717 (47724-0717)
PHONE.....................812 426-2224
Fax: 812 421-4159
John G Mathias Jr, *President*
Walter Kalesia, *Sales Mgr*
Tom Mathias, *Accounts Mgr*
Jenny Utley, *Sales Associate*
Ravonda Murphy, *Manager*
EMP: 27
SQ FT: 42,000
SALES (est): 6.7MM **Privately Held**
WEB: www.eemsco.com
SIC: 3599 7694 Machine shop, jobbing & repair; rewinding services

(G-3473)
ELKO INC
Also Called: Elko Plastic Fabricators Div
940 N Boeke Rd (47711-4902)
PHONE.....................812 473-8400
Fax: 812 473-8402
Randall Kanter, *President*
EMP: 20
SQ FT: 7,000
SALES (est): 3.4MM **Privately Held**
SIC: 3083 5211 5031 2541 Laminated plastics plate & sheet; cabinets, kitchen; counter tops; kitchen cabinets; wood partitions & fixtures; wood kitchen cabinets

(G-3474)
ELPERS TRUCK EQUIPMENT LLC
8136 Baumgart Rd (47725-1510)
PHONE.....................812 423-5787
Fax: 812 423-6039
Greg Wilhite, *CFO*
James Elpers,
EMP: 14
SQ FT: 12,000
SALES (est): 5.2MM **Privately Held**
WEB: www.elperstruck.com
SIC: 3537 Industrial trucks & tractors

(G-3475)
EMI LLC
Also Called: EMI Quality Plating
5701 Old Boonville Hwy (47715-2198)
PHONE.....................812 437-9100
Fran Gilchrist, *President*
Mark Dye, *Vice Pres*
Bill King, *Vice Pres*
EMP: 48
SQ FT: 32,000
SALES (est): 6.3MM **Privately Held**
WEB: www.emiplating.com
SIC: 3471 Electroplating of metals or formed products

(G-3476)
EMP OF EVANSVILLE
Also Called: News 4 U Magazine
4 Chestnut St (47713-1022)
PHONE.....................812 962-1309
Bashar Hamami, *President*
EMP: 15 EST: 2000
SALES (est): 1MM **Privately Held**
WEB: www.news-4u.com
SIC: 2721 Magazines: publishing & printing

(G-3477)
ENCOM INC
Also Called: Encom Polymers
4825 N Spring St (47711-2488)
PHONE.....................812 421-7700
Fax: 812 421-7722
Richard W Kaskel Jr, *President*
Janet M Meeks, *Treasurer*
▲ EMP: 7
SQ FT: 1,200
SALES: 13.7MM **Privately Held**
SIC: 2821 Thermoplastic materials

(G-3478)
ENGLEHARDT CUSTOM WOODWORKING
4125 Kedzie Ave (47712-7894)
PHONE.....................812 425-9282
Barry Englehardt, *Owner*
EMP: 2
SALES (est): 168.9K **Privately Held**
SIC: 2431 Millwork

(G-3479)
ENGLISH RESOURCES INC
816 Nw 2nd St (47708-1018)
P.O. Box 34 (47701-0034)
PHONE.....................812 423-6716
Ken English, *President*
Danny English, *Vice Pres*
Wanda English, *Vice Pres*
Judy Burkhart, *Admin Sec*
▲ EMP: 4
SQ FT: 4,600
SALES (est): 299.7K **Privately Held**
SIC: 1241 Coal mining services

(G-3480)
ENVIROPLAS INC
15220 Foundation Ave (47725-9655)
PHONE.....................812 868-0808
Fax: 812 868-0000
Jim Stratman, *President*
Brian Meredith, *Materials Mgr*
Gayle Arvin, *Accountant*
▲ EMP: 60
SALES (est): 24.5MM **Privately Held**
WEB: www.e-plas.com
SIC: 3087 Custom compound purchased resins

(G-3481)
ESCALADE INCORPORATED (PA)
817 Maxwell Ave (47711-3847)
PHONE.....................812 467-4449
Richard D White, *Ch of Bd*
David L Fetherman, *President*
Dave Fetherman, *Vice Pres*
Patrick J Griffin, *Vice Pres*
Robert Cornell, *Engineer*
EMP: 58
SQ FT: 483,954
SALES: 177.3MM **Publicly Held**
WEB: www.escaladeinc.com
SIC: 3949 3579 Sporting & athletic goods; ping-pong tables; billiard & pool equipment & supplies, general; basketball equipment & supplies, general; paper cutters, trimmers & punches; collating machines for store & office use; perforators (office machines)

(G-3482)
EVANSVILLE ASSN FOR THE BLIND
Also Called: EAB INDUSTRIES
500 N 2nd Ave (47710-1540)
P.O. Box 6445 (47719-0445)
PHONE.....................812 422-1181
Fax: 812 424-3154
Diane Hagler, *Human Res Mgr*
Karla Horrell, *Director*
Michael Lloyd, *Director*
Kathy Coomer, *Admin Asst*
EMP: 120 EST: 1919
SQ FT: 115,000
SALES: 1.7MM **Privately Held**
SIC: 7699 2392 5087 Industrial equipment services; mops, floor & dust; janitors' supplies

(G-3483)
EVANSVILLE BINDERY INC
221 E Columbia St (47711-5047)
PHONE.....................812 423-2222
Gary Beshears, *President*
EMP: 4
SQ FT: 6,000
SALES (est): 424.7K **Privately Held**
SIC: 2759 2752 2789 2791 Business forms: printing; commercial printing, offset; bookbinding & related work; typesetting

(G-3484)
EVANSVILLE BLOCK CO INC
Also Called: Miller Block Co
1700 W Franklin St Ste 14 (47712-5107)
P.O. Box 6325 (47719-0325)
PHONE.....................812 422-2864
Fax: 812 422-9587
Lawrence E Miller, *President*
Keith Milling, *Vice Pres*
EMP: 13
SQ FT: 14,160
SALES: 3.5MM **Privately Held**
SIC: 3271 5032 Architectural concrete: block, split, fluted, screen, etc.; brick, concrete; tile & clay products; brick, except refractory; concrete building products

(G-3485)
EVANSVILLE COURIER CO (DH)
300 E Walnut St (47713-1938)
PHONE.....................812 464-7500
Fax: 812 464-7487
Jack Pate, *President*
Daniel J Castellini, *Vice Pres*
E John Wolfzorn, *Treasurer*
M Denise Kuprionis, *Admin Sec*
EMP: 450 EST: 1845
SQ FT: 140,000
SALES (est): 66.3MM
SALES (corp-wide): 3.1B **Publicly Held**
WEB: www.courierpress.com
SIC: 2711 2791 Newspapers, publishing & printing; typesetting
HQ: Journal Media Group, Inc.
333 W State St
Milwaukee WI 53203
414 224-2000

(G-3486)
EVANSVILLE LITHOGRAPH CO INC
3112 E Walnut St (47714-1468)
PHONE.....................812 477-0506
Fax: 812 477-0506
Joyce Freeman, *President*
J Kirk Freeman, *Vice Pres*
EMP: 4
SQ FT: 3,500
SALES: 200K **Privately Held**
SIC: 2752 Commercial printing, offset

(G-3487)
EVANSVILLE METAL PRODUCTS INC (PA)
Also Called: Refrigeration Sys of Evans
119 Ladonna Blvd (47711-1859)
PHONE.....................812 423-5632
Fax: 812 421-6594
Rahmi Soyugenc, *President*
Marjorie Soyugenc, *Admin Sec*
EMP: 65
SQ FT: 156,000
SALES (est): 13MM **Privately Held**
WEB: www.internationalrevolvingdoors.com
SIC: 3442 3469 3479 3585 Metal doors; store fronts, prefabricated, metal; stamping metal for the trade; coating of metals with plastic or resins; refrigeration & heating equipment

(G-3488)
EVANSVILLE METAL PRODUCTS INC
Refrigeration Systems
2086 N 6th Ave (47710-2812)
PHONE.....................812 421-6589
Leamon Williams, *Manager*
EMP: 25
SALES (corp-wide): 13MM **Privately Held**
WEB: www.internationalrevolvingdoors.com
SIC: 3585 Refrigeration & heating equipment
PA: Evansville Metal Products Inc
119 Ladonna Blvd
Evansville IN 47711
812 423-5632

(G-3489)
EVANSVILLE PALLETS
2203 N Kentucky Ave (47711-3917)
PHONE.....................812 550-0199
EMP: 4
SALES (est): 180K **Privately Held**
SIC: 2448 Pallets, wood & wood with metal

▲ = Import ▼=Export
◆ =Import/Export

(G-3490)
EVANSVILLE PRINT SPECIALIST
2217 W Franklin St (47712-5116)
PHONE......................................812 423-5831
Fax: 812 423-5881
Butch Frank, *President*
Glenda Floyd, *Vice Pres*
Dorothy Wesley, *Vice Pres*
EMP: 2
SQ FT: 2,500
SALES (est): 310.9K **Privately Held**
WEB: www.evprint.com
SIC: 2759 2752 Screen printing; commercial printing, lithographic

(G-3491)
EVANSVILLE SUPER BIKE SHOP
1980 N Burkhardt Rd (47715-2163)
PHONE......................................812 477-1740
Fax: 812 401-0599
Gary Virgin, *Owner*
Travis Durnell, *Manager*
April McDaniel, *Manager*
EMP: 18
SALES (est): 2.8MM **Privately Held**
WEB: www.esuperbike.com
SIC: 3751 Bicycles & related parts

(G-3492)
EVANSVILLE TOOL & DIE INC
4900 N Saint Joseph Ave (47720-1222)
PHONE......................................812 422-7101
Fax: 812 422-7102
Jack Dennis Droste, *President*
Jacob Ward, *Manager*
EMP: 15 EST: 1959
SQ FT: 27,000
SALES (est): 3.2MM **Privately Held**
WEB: www.evansvilletoolanddie.com
SIC: 3544 Special dies & tools

(G-3493)
EVANTEK MANUFACTURING INDS LLC
Also Called: EMI Quality Plating
5701 Old Boonville Hwy (47715-2198)
PHONE......................................812 437-9100
William King, *Mng Member*
EMP: 42
SQ FT: 32,000
SALES (est): 2.9MM **Privately Held**
SIC: 2796 Platemaking services

(G-3494)
EVERGREEN DRILLING LLC
21 Se 3rd St Ste 1 (47708-1412)
P.O. Box 31, Carmi IL (62821-0031)
PHONE......................................812 961-7701
Gary Evans, *President*
EMP: 5
SALES (est): 851.2K **Privately Held**
SIC: 3533 Oil & gas drilling rigs & equipment

(G-3495)
EVILL CYCLES
606 Bell Ave (47712-5612)
PHONE......................................812 401-2045
EMP: 2
SALES (est): 148.2K **Privately Held**
SIC: 3751 5571 7699 Mfg Motorcycles/Bicycles Ret Motorcycles Repair Services

(G-3496)
EXPRESS MOTOR VEHICLE ADM LLC
1111 S Green River Rd # 100 (47715-6811)
PHONE......................................812 909-0116
EMP: 4
SALES (est): 252.8K
SALES (corp-wide): 5.8MM **Privately Held**
SIC: 3469 Automobile license tags, stamped metal
PA: Express Motor Vehicle Administration Llc
3960 Southeastern Ave
Indianapolis IN 46203
317 322-0020

(G-3497)
EXPRESS MOTORS
1059 E Riverside Dr (47714-3454)
PHONE......................................812 437-9495
Fax: 812 437-9495

Aadil Almoudaai, *Owner*
EMP: 4
SALES (est): 346K **Privately Held**
SIC: 2741 Miscellaneous publishing

(G-3498)
FARM BOY MEATS OF EVANSVILLE
2761 N Kentucky Ave (47711-6203)
P.O. Box 996 (47706-0996)
PHONE......................................812 425-5231
Fax: 812 428-8432
Robert J Bononberger, *President*
Greg Merkley, *Prdtn Mgr*
Richard W Bonenberger, *Treasurer*
Stephanie Bonenberger, *Accounts Exec*
Rachael Rheinlander, *Sales Staff*
EMP: 115 EST: 1952
SQ FT: 30,000
SALES (est): 26.2MM **Privately Held**
WEB: www.farmboyfoodservice.com
SIC: 2013 5113 5142 Beef, dried: from purchased meat; pork, cured: from purchased meat; industrial & personal service paper; meat, frozen: packaged; fish, frozen: packaged

(G-3499)
FARMER BROS CO
Also Called: Farmers Brothers Coffee
1905 N Kentucky Ave (47711-3845)
PHONE......................................812 424-3309
Marty Shipper, *Manager*
EMP: 2
SALES (corp-wide): 541.5MM **Publicly Held**
WEB: www.farmerbros.com
SIC: 2095 Coffee roasting (except by wholesale grocers)
PA: Farmer Bros. Co.
1912 Farmer Brothers Dr
Northlake TX 76262
888 998-2468

(G-3500)
FARMERS MACHINE SHOP INC
1511 E Virginia St (47711-5732)
PHONE......................................812 425-1238
Bill Farmer, *Owner*
William Farmer, *General Mgr*
EMP: 2
SQ FT: 2,500
SALES (est): 184.6K **Privately Held**
SIC: 3599 Machine shop, jobbing & repair

(G-3501)
FASTLANE RACEWAY
10040 Brook Meadow Dr (47711-7124)
PHONE......................................812 430-8818
Andrew Kimbrough, *Principal*
EMP: 3
SALES (est): 236.1K **Privately Held**
SIC: 3644 Raceways

(G-3502)
FEHRENBACHER CABINETS INC
8944 Big Cynthiana Rd (47720-7612)
PHONE......................................812 963-3377
Fax: 812 963-3379
Peter Fehrenbacher, *President*
Jim Balbach, *Vice Pres*
Patrick Fehrenbacher, *Vice Pres*
Zach Fehrenbacher, *Vice Pres*
Zachary Fehrenbacher, *Vice Pres*
▲ EMP: 35
SQ FT: 18,000
SALES (est): 5MM **Privately Held**
WEB: www.fci3.com
SIC: 5712 2541 2517 2511 Cabinet work, custom; wood partitions & fixtures; wood television & radio cabinets; wood household furniture; wood kitchen cabinets

(G-3503)
FELLWOCKS AUTOMOTIVE
10004 Darmstadt Rd (47710-5082)
PHONE......................................812 867-3658
Ron Fellwock, *Owner*
EMP: 4
SQ FT: 5,430
SALES (est): 321.2K **Privately Held**
SIC: 3053 3061 Gaskets, packing & sealing devices; automotive rubber goods (mechanical)

(G-3504)
FILTERS PLUS
6227 Calloway Dr (47715-8854)
PHONE......................................812 430-0347
EMP: 2
SALES (est): 168.4K **Privately Held**
SIC: 3569 Mfg General Industrial Machinery

(G-3505)
FISHER & COMPANY INCORPORATED
2301 Saint George Rd (47711-2561)
PHONE......................................586 746-2000
Alfred J Fisher III, *Branch Mgr*
EMP: 135
SALES (corp-wide): 477.2MM **Privately Held**
SIC: 2531 Seats, automobile
PA: Fisher & Company, Incorporated
33300 Fisher Dr
Saint Clair Shores MI 48082
586 746-2000

(G-3506)
FISHER TOOL & DESIGN INC
8231 Burch Park Dr (47725-1707)
PHONE......................................812 867-8350
Fax: 812 867-8351
Timothy L Fisher, *President*
Debra L Fisher, *Vice Pres*
EMP: 10
SQ FT: 24,000
SALES (est): 1.5MM **Privately Held**
WEB: www.fishertool.net
SIC: 3599 Machine shop, jobbing & repair

(G-3507)
FL SMIDTH
1315 N Cullen Ave Ste 102 (47715-8248)
PHONE......................................812 402-9210
T J Rhule, *Branch Mgr*
EMP: 3 EST: 2012
SALES (est): 280.2K **Privately Held**
SIC: 3561 Pumps & pumping equipment

(G-3508)
FLAIR MOLDED PLASTICS INC
2521 Lynch Rd (47711-2954)
PHONE......................................812 425-6155
Fax: 812 452-2932
Albert Brougham, *President*
Benedict A Brougham, *Chairman*
Bert Brougham, *Vice Pres*
Roxanne Bailey, *Engineer*
Jackie Strange, *Treasurer*
EMP: 75 EST: 1965
SQ FT: 91,000
SALES (est): 17.4MM **Privately Held**
WEB: www.flairplastics.com
SIC: 3089 Injection molding of plastics

(G-3509)
FLANDERS ELECTRIC MTR SVC INC
500 E Buena Vista Rd (47711-2722)
PHONE......................................812 867-4014
Allen Patterson, *Branch Mgr*
EMP: 27
SALES (corp-wide): 137.9MM **Privately Held**
SIC: 7694 Electric motor repair
PA: Flanders Electric Motor Service, Inc.
8101 Baumgart Rd
Evansville IN 47725
812 867-7421

(G-3510)
FLANDERS ELECTRIC MTR SVC INC
1050 E Maryland St (47711-4756)
PHONE......................................812 421-4300
Fax: 812 421-4310
Kyle Williams, *Branch Mgr*
Mike Engler, *Technology*
EMP: 26
SALES (corp-wide): 137.9MM **Privately Held**
SIC: 5999 7699 7694 5063 Motors, electric; welding equipment repair; armature rewinding shops; electrical apparatus & equipment

(G-3511)
PA: Flanders Electric Motor Service, Inc.
8101 Baumgart Rd
Evansville IN 47725
812 867-7421

(G-3511)
FOCUS MOLD & MACHINE INC
1145 Indy Ct (47725-6300)
PHONE......................................812 422-9627
Stephen Gardner, *President*
Pam Gardner, *Corp Secy*
Bryan Gardner, *Vice Pres*
EMP: 3
SQ FT: 3,600
SALES (est): 473.5K **Privately Held**
SIC: 3089 3544 Injection molding of plastics; special dies, tools, jigs & fixtures

(G-3512)
FORTERRA CONCRETE INDS INC
1213 Stanley Ave (47711-3569)
PHONE......................................812 426-5353
EMP: 7
SALES (corp-wide): 1.5B **Publicly Held**
SIC: 3999 Pipe cleaners
HQ: Forterra Concrete Industries, Inc.
200 42nd Ave N
Nashville TN 37209
615 889-0700

(G-3513)
FRANK R KOMAR CPA
1431 S Green River Rd (47715-5657)
PHONE......................................812 477-9110
Frank R Komar, *Managing Prtnr*
EMP: 3
SALES (est): 228K **Privately Held**
SIC: 8721 7372 Certified public accountant; prepackaged software

(G-3514)
GALLAGHER DRILLING INC (PA)
115 Se 3rd St Fl 2 (47708-1431)
P.O. Box 8275 (47716-8275)
PHONE......................................812 477-6746
Mary Ellen Gallagher Vieth, *General Ptnr*
Thomas R Bailey, *Corp Secy*
Victor R Gallagher Jr, *Vice Pres*
Michael D Gallagher, *Vice Pres*
Shawn G Gallagher, *Vice Pres*
EMP: 23 EST: 1957
SQ FT: 4,200
SALES (est): 4.1MM **Privately Held**
WEB: www.gallagherdrilling.com
SIC: 1311 1381 1389 Crude petroleum production; natural gas production; drilling oil & gas wells; gas compressing (natural gas) at the fields

(G-3515)
GARRETT PRINTING & GRAPHICS
1405 N 1st Ave (47710-2407)
PHONE......................................812 422-6005
Fax: 812 428-4019
Richard Wooley, *President*
Alicia Cave, *Admin Sec*
Racheal Artis, *Graphic Designe*
EMP: 6
SQ FT: 2,660
SALES (est): 829.9K **Privately Held**
SIC: 2752 Commercial printing, offset

(G-3516)
GAUNT FAMILY LLC
7001 Red Wing Dr (47715-5251)
PHONE......................................812 473-3167
Nancy Gaunt, *Principal*
EMP: 2
SALES (est): 77.6K **Privately Held**
SIC: 2741 Miscellaneous publishing

(G-3517)
GENERAL RBR PLAS OF EVANSVILLE (PA)
1902 N Kentucky Ave (47711-3879)
P.O. Box 4510 (47724-0510)
PHONE......................................812 464-5153
Fax: 812 465-5854
W L Burnett, *President*
Dean Becher, *Vice Pres*
Wanda De Witt, *CFO*
William R Ruez, *Admin Sec*
▲ EMP: 25

SQ FT: 20,000
SALES (est): 20.8MM **Privately Held**
WEB: www.genrub.com
SIC: 5162 5085 3053 3052 Plastics resins; rubber goods, mechanical; hose, belting & packing; gaskets, packing & sealing devices; rubber & plastics hose & beltings

(G-3518)
GENERAL SIGNALS INC
5611 E Morgan Ave (47715-2317)
PHONE..................................812 474-4256
Fax: 812 474-4258
Ronald L Mitchell, *President*
Kirk Mitchell, *Corp Secy*
Michael S Ellenstein Jr, *Vice Pres*
Natalie Feldhaus, *Office Mgr*
Micki Craddock, *Manager*
EMP: 13 **EST:** 1954
SQ FT: 2,000
SALES (est): 3.3MM **Privately Held**
WEB: www.generalsignals.com
SIC: 5088 3229 3743 Railroad equipment & supplies; reflectors for lighting equipment, pressed or blown glass; railroad equipment

(G-3519)
GEORGE KOCH SONS LLC (HQ)
10 S 11th Ave (47712-6800)
PHONE..................................812 465-9600
Fax: 812 465-9676
Robert L Koch II, *President*
Samuel Woehler, *Mfg Dir*
Michael Barnaby, *Engineer*
Bryan Day, *Supervisor*
Scott Wright, *Supervisor*
EMP: 181 **EST:** 1998
SQ FT: 225,000
SALES: 91.6MM
SALES (corp-wide): 1B **Privately Held**
WEB: www.kochllc.com
SIC: 3549 3567 3535 Metalworking machinery; industrial furnaces & ovens; conveyors & conveying equipment
PA: Koch Enterprises, Inc.
14 S 11th Ave
Evansville IN 47712
812 465-9800

(G-3520)
GEORGE KOCH SONS MGT INC
10 S 11th Ave (47712-6800)
PHONE..................................812 422-3257
Sam Wohler, *Principal*
Jenni Bishop, *Accountant*
EMP: 9
SALES: 2.2MM
SALES (corp-wide): 1B **Privately Held**
WEB: www.kochllc.com
SIC: 3363 Aluminum die-castings
HQ: George Koch Sons, Llc
10 S 11th Ave
Evansville IN 47712
812 465-9600

(G-3521)
GOAD CRANKSHAFT SERVICE INC
3514 E Morgan Ave (47715-2236)
PHONE..................................812 477-1127
Larry Goad, *President*
EMP: 2
SALES (est): 121.2K **Privately Held**
SIC: 3599 Crankshafts & camshafts, machining

(G-3522)
GRAFCO INDUSTRIES LTD PARTNR (HQ)
101 Oakley St (47710-1237)
PHONE..................................812 424-2904
Virginia L Campbell, *President*
Timothy Frank, *Partner*
Thomas Frank, *Partner*
EMP: 26
SQ FT: 120,000
SALES (est): 26.7MM **Publicly Held**
SIC: 3089 Plastic containers, except foam; food casings, plastic

(G-3523)
GRAHAM PACKAGING COMPANY LP
5504 Foundation Dr (47725-7652)
PHONE..................................812 868-8012
Fax: 812 868-8015
Jeff Lombard, *Manager*
Kevin Roth, *Maintence Staff*
EMP: 55 **Privately Held**
WEB: www.grahampackaging.com
SIC: 3089 Plastic containers, except foam
HQ: Graham Packaging Company, L.P.
700 Indian Springs Dr # 100
Lancaster PA 17601
717 849-8500

(G-3524)
GREEN TREE PLASTICS LLC
1107 E Virginia St (47711-5724)
PHONE..................................812 402-4127
Bonnie Trafton,
▲ **EMP:** 13
SALES: 900K **Privately Held**
WEB: www.greentreeplastics.com
SIC: 2821 Plastics materials & resins

(G-3525)
GUARDIAN INDUSTRIES LLC
5401 Highway 41 N (47711-1962)
PHONE..................................812 422-6987
EMP: 185
SALES (corp-wide): 44.4B **Privately Held**
SIC: 3211 Flat glass
HQ: Guardian Industries, Llc
2300 Harmon Rd
Auburn Hills MI 48326
248 340-1800

(G-3526)
H & S CUSTOM COUNTERTOPS INC
5705 E Morgan Ave (47715-2319)
PHONE..................................812 422-6314
Roert B Howard, *President*
Robert B Howard, *President*
Bruce W Spaulding, *Admin Sec*
EMP: 2
SALES (est): 253.6K **Privately Held**
SIC: 2541 Table or counter tops, plastic laminated

(G-3527)
H & W MOLDERS INC
1031 W Tennessee St (47710-2349)
PHONE..................................812 423-9340
Lowell Walker, *President*
EMP: 5
SQ FT: 6,000
SALES (est): 435.3K **Privately Held**
SIC: 3089 Injection molding of plastics

(G-3528)
H W MOLDERS
1500 W Missouri St (47710-1844)
PHONE..................................812 423-3552
Robert Koons, *Manager*
EMP: 2
SALES (est): 88.9K **Privately Held**
SIC: 3089 Plastics products

(G-3529)
HAMMER INDUSTRIES INC
1504 N 1st Ave (47710-2410)
P.O. Box 6424 (47719-0424)
PHONE..................................812 422-6953
Fax: 812 422-6957
Ralph E Hammer, *Ch of Bd*
Gregory Hammer, *President*
Kenny Zizzo, *Principal*
Jackie Hammer, *Admin Sec*
EMP: 10
SQ FT: 24,100
SALES (est): 2.4MM **Privately Held**
WEB: www.hammerind.com
SIC: 3011 3499 Tires, cushion or solid rubber; wheels: wheelbarrow, stroller, etc.: disc, stamped metal

(G-3530)
HANDLE WITH CARE PACKAGING
2007 N Green River Rd (47715-1909)
PHONE..................................812 250-1920
Fax: 812 471-1251
Susan Dauldoy, *Principal*

EMP: 2
SALES (est): 130.1K **Privately Held**
SIC: 2499 Handles, wood; packaging & labeling services

(G-3531)
HANGER PROSTHETICS &
Also Called: Hanger Clinic
7145 E Virginia St # 4000 (47715-9144)
PHONE..................................812 479-1121
Sam Liang, *President*
Dale Fries, *Branch Mgr*
EMP: 2
SALES (corp-wide): 1B **Publicly Held**
SIC: 3842 Surgical appliances & supplies
HQ: Hanger Prosthetics & Orthotics East, Inc.
33 North Ave Ste 101
Tallmadge OH 44278

(G-3532)
HANKS NEON & PLASTIC SERVICE
910 Keck Ave (47711-3842)
P.O. Box 4246 (47724-0246)
PHONE..................................812 423-7447
Fax: 812 423-7455
Wade Flake Jr, *President*
Sidney Flake, *Vice Pres*
EMP: 8 **EST:** 1964
SQ FT: 10,500
SALES (est): 530K **Privately Held**
SIC: 3993 Neon signs; electric signs

(G-3533)
HARTFORD BAKERY INC
500 N Fulton Ave (47710-1571)
PHONE..................................812 425-4642
R Jack Lewis Jr, *President*
Kyle Kinder, *General Mgr*
Ken Shelton, *Transptn Dir*
Nathan Ponder, *Plant Mgr*
Rodger L Lesh, *Treasurer*
EMP: 475
SQ FT: 115,000
SALES: 55MM
SALES (corp-wide): 473.3MM **Privately Held**
WEB: www.lewisbakeries.com
SIC: 2051 Bread, all types (white, wheat, rye, etc): fresh or frozen; rolls, bread type: fresh or frozen; cakes, bakery: except frozen
PA: Lewis Brothers Bakeries Inc
500 N Fulton Ave
Evansville IN 47710
812 425-4642

(G-3534)
HARTLAND DISTILLATIONS INC
2410 Lynch Rd (47711-2953)
P.O. Box 3642 (47735-3642)
PHONE..................................812 464-4446
David E Carson, *President*
Paul Carson, *Vice Pres*
Eric Mittlefehldt, *Vice Pres*
David Strahorn, *Treasurer*
EMP: 14
SQ FT: 27,300
SALES (est): 3.3MM **Privately Held**
SIC: 2992 4953 Re-refining lubricating oils & greases; refuse systems

(G-3535)
HARVARD SPORTS INC
817 Maxwell Ave (47711-3847)
PHONE..................................812 467-4449
Robert E Griffin, *Chairman*
EMP: 2
SALES (est): 150K **Privately Held**
SIC: 3949 Sporting & athletic goods

(G-3536)
HAYWARD TYLER INC
12540 Kenai Dr (47725-8040)
PHONE..................................812 867-2848
Paul Cruz, *Manager*
EMP: 2
SALES (est): 230K **Privately Held**
SIC: 3561 Pumps & pumping equipment

(G-3537)
HELFRICH ENGINEERING INC
9401 Hogue Rd (47712-9668)
PHONE..................................812 985-3118
Fax: 812 985-3118

A David Helfrich, *President*
EMP: 7
SQ FT: 5,500
SALES (est): 674.5K **Privately Held**
SIC: 3089 Injection molded finished plastic products

(G-3538)
HERITAGE FINE FURN & CABINETRY
818 E Franklin St (47715-5624)
PHONE..................................812 205-5437
John Faver, *President*
Lisa Faver, *Vice Pres*
EMP: 3
SALES (est): 453K **Privately Held**
WEB: www.heritagefinefurniture.com
SIC: 2434 2511 Wood kitchen cabinets; vanities, bathroom: wood; unassembled or unfinished furniture, household: wood

(G-3539)
HOME - LITTLE CREEK WINERY
4116 Koressel Rd (47720-2236)
PHONE..................................812 319-3951
EMP: 2
SALES (est): 70.4K **Privately Held**
SIC: 2084 Wines

(G-3540)
HOOSIER STAMPING & MFG CORP (PA)
Also Called: Hoosier Wheel
1865 W Franklin St (47712-5108)
P.O. Box 6447 (47719-0447)
PHONE..................................812 426-2778
Fax: 812 426-6908
Thomas J Johnson, *President*
Christina L Webb, *Treasurer*
▲ **EMP:** 25
SQ FT: 38,000
SALES (est): 17.2MM **Privately Held**
WEB: www.hoosierstamping.com
SIC: 3469 Metal stampings

(G-3541)
HOOSIER WHEEL LLC
700 Schrader Dr (47712-4970)
PHONE..................................812 421-6900
Thomas J Johnson, *Manager*
EMP: 2
SALES (est): 217.1K **Privately Held**
SIC: 3312 Wheels

(G-3542)
HOPE MACHINE
3110 Bellemeade Ave (47714-2601)
PHONE..................................502 550-9532
Justin Hope, *Owner*
EMP: 2
SQ FT: 1,000
SALES (est): 94.5K **Privately Held**
SIC: 3599 Machine shop, jobbing & repair

(G-3543)
HOUSE OF BLUEZ
111 S Green Rver Rd Ste F (47715)
PHONE..................................812 401-2583
Jodi Merrick, *Owner*
EMP: 3
SALES (est): 268.1K **Privately Held**
SIC: 5621 2211 Boutiques; denims; jean fabrics

(G-3544)
HRH DOOR CORP
5425 Oak Grove Rd Ste J (47715-2397)
PHONE..................................812 479-5680
Glen Neseau, *Manager*
EMP: 4
SALES (corp-wide): 619.8MM **Privately Held**
WEB: www.waynedalton.com
SIC: 3442 2431 Garage doors, overhead: metal; garage doors, overhead: wood
PA: Hrh Door Corp.
1 Door Dr
Mount Hope OH 44660
850 208-3400

▲ = Import ▼=Export
◆ =Import/Export

(G-3545)
HSM EAGLE LTD
Also Called: Eagle Bearing
6149 Wedeking Ave (47715-8532)
P.O. Box 327, Newburgh (47629-0327)
PHONE.................................812 491-9666
Fax: 812 491-9668
Thomas J Johnson, *President*
▲ EMP: 5
SALES (est): 610K **Privately Held**
WEB: www.eaglebearing.com
SIC: 3823 Differential pressure instruments, industrial process type

(G-3546)
ILPEA INDUSTRIES INC
2500 Lynch Rd (47711-2955)
PHONE.................................812 752-2526
Carlos Medina, *QC Mgr*
Wayne Heverly, *Manager*
Claudio Cataldo, *Manager*
EMP: 10 **Privately Held**
SIC: 3999 Barber & beauty shop equipment
HQ: Ilpea Industries, Inc.
745 S Gardner St
Scottsburg IN 47170
812 752-2526

(G-3547)
IMAGINATION GRAPHICS
2323 W Franklin St (47712-5118)
PHONE.................................812 423-6503
Julie Williams, *Owner*
EMP: 2
SQ FT: 2,500
SALES (est): 110K **Privately Held**
SIC: 2759 Screen printing

(G-3548)
IMI SOUTHWEST INC (HQ)
1816 W Lloyd Expy (47712-5137)
PHONE.................................812 424-3554
Fred Irving, *CEO*
Earl Brinker, *CEO*
Pete Irving, *Ch of Bd*
Mike Harmon, *Vice Pres*
Dennis Lamar, *Plant Mgr*
EMP: 50 EST: 1948
SQ FT: 6,000
SALES (est): 13.2MM
SALES (corp-wide): 800.6MM **Privately Held**
SIC: 3273 Ready-mixed concrete
PA: Irving Materials, Inc.
8032 N State Road 9
Greenfield IN 46140
317 326-3101

(G-3549)
IMPERIAL PETROLEUM INC (PA)
11600 German Pines Dr (47725-9514)
PHONE.................................812 867-1433
Fax: 812 867-1678
Jeffrey T Wilson, *President*
EMP: 9
SALES (est): 4.5MM **Privately Held**
SIC: 1311 2911 1382 1389 Tar sands mining; diesel fuels; oil & gas exploration services; servicing oil & gas wells

(G-3550)
INDIAN INDUSTRIES INC (HQ)
Also Called: Escalade Sports
817 Maxwell Ave (47711-3870)
P.O. Box 889 (47706-0889)
PHONE.................................812 467-1200
Fax: 812 425-1425
David L Fetherman, *CEO*
James Allshouse, *Vice Pres*
Jim Allshouse, *Vice Pres*
Gene Hunter, *Opers Mgr*
Bob Guinn, *Opers Staff*
◆ EMP: 100 EST: 1927
SQ FT: 255,000
SALES (est): 105.5MM
SALES (corp-wide): 177.3MM **Publicly Held**
WEB: www.accudart.com
SIC: 3949 Ping-pong tables; archery equipment, general; billiard & pool equipment & supplies, general; basketball equipment & supplies, general

PA: Escalade, Incorporated
817 Maxwell Ave
Evansville IN 47711
812 467-4449

(G-3551)
INDIANA DRILLING COMPANY INC (PA)
1410 N Cullen Ave (47715-2331)
P.O. Box 5269 (47716-5269)
PHONE.................................812 477-1575
Charles A Robinson, *President*
J Glenn Robinson, *Treasurer*
EMP: 3
SQ FT: 2,500
SALES (est): 437.7K **Privately Held**
SIC: 1381 Drilling oil & gas wells

(G-3552)
INDIANA PETROLEUM CONTRACTORS (PA)
1410 N Cullen Ave (47715-2331)
P.O. Box 5269 (47716-5269)
PHONE.................................812 477-1575
Charles A Robinson, *President*
EMP: 5
SALES (est): 903.6K **Privately Held**
SIC: 1389 Cementing oil & gas well casings

(G-3553)
INDIANA TUBE CORPORATION (DH)
2100 Lexington Rd (47720-1234)
P.O. Box 3005 (47730-3005)
PHONE.................................812 467-7155
Fax: 812 424-0340
John Whitenack, *President*
Ron Hawkins, *VP Opers*
Joel Cunningham, *Finance*
Ron Tenbarge, *VP Sales*
▼ EMP: 251 EST: 1973
SQ FT: 125,000
SALES (est): 53.1MM
SALES (corp-wide): 1.3B **Publicly Held**
WEB: www.indianatube.com
SIC: 3317 Steel pipe & tubes
HQ: Handy & Harman
C/O Steel Partners
New York NY 10022
212 520-2300

(G-3554)
INDUCTION IRON INCORPORATED
403 N 7th Ave (47710-1417)
PHONE.................................813 969-3300
Fax: 812 969-2892
Greg Nun, *Manager*
EMP: 10
SALES (corp-wide): 6.6MM **Privately Held**
SIC: 3449 3341 Miscellaneous metalwork; secondary nonferrous metals
PA: Induction Iron Incorporated
13909 N Dale Mabry Hwy # 203
Tampa FL 33618
813 969-3300

(G-3555)
INDUSTRIAL CONTRS SKANSKA INC
Also Called: Industrial Contrs Shtmtl Div
1001 Mount Auburn Rd (47720-8226)
P.O. Box 208 (47702-0208)
PHONE.................................812 423-7832
Fax: 812 464-7288
Curt Winiger, *Purchasing*
Brent Smith, *Manager*
EMP: 42
SALES (corp-wide): 18.7B **Privately Held**
WEB: www.industrialcontractors.com
SIC: 1541 3471 3446 3444 Industrial buildings, new construction; plating & polishing; architectural metalwork; sheet metalwork; fabricated plate work (boiler shop); fabricated structural metal
HQ: Industrial Contractors Skanska, Inc.
401 Nw 1st St
Evansville IN 47708
812 423-7832

(G-3556)
INDUSTRIAL PLASTICS GROUP LLC
Also Called: Ipg
911 E Virginia St (47711-5657)
PHONE.................................812 831-4053
Barry Cox, *President*
◆ EMP: 23
SALES (est): 5.6MM
SALES (corp-wide): 472.6MM **Privately Held**
SIC: 2821 Plastics materials & resins
PA: Warehouse Services, Inc.
58 S Burty Rd
Piedmont SC 29673
812 831-4053

(G-3557)
INDUSTRIAL RESEARCH INC
Also Called: Hard Chrome Co
510 Dresden St (47710-2402)
PHONE.................................812 401-2333
Fax: 812 422-2855
Bobby G Oglesby, *President*
Darlene Fisher, *Manager*
▲ EMP: 7
SQ FT: 26,000
SALES (est): 902.7K **Privately Held**
SIC: 3471 8748 Electroplating & plating; testing service, educational or personnel

(G-3558)
INDUSTRIAL SEWING MACHINE CO
Also Called: Tom Cooks
2750 N Burkhardt Rd # 107 (47715-1685)
P.O. Box 8243 (47716-8243)
PHONE.................................812 425-2255
Fax: 812 425-2136
Edwina Cook, *Owner*
EMP: 3
SQ FT: 5,000
SALES (est): 110K **Privately Held**
SIC: 7641 2391 5084 5984 Upholstery work; curtains & draperies; sewing machines, industrial; liquefied petroleum gas dealers; household appliance stores

(G-3559)
INDUSTRIAL TOOL & DIE CORP
2201 Lexington Rd (47720-1235)
PHONE.................................812 424-9971
Fax: 812 424-9950
Charles Bryan Coughlin, *President*
Stacey L Coughlin, *Corp Secy*
Angie Meurer, *Office Mgr*
Andy Cox, *Administration*
▲ EMP: 11 EST: 1961
SQ FT: 10,500
SALES (est): 1.3MM **Privately Held**
SIC: 3544 Special dies & tools

(G-3560)
INK WELL BUSINESS CENTER
1326 N Weinbach Ave (47711-4307)
PHONE.................................812 476-9147
James Jarboe, *Owner*
EMP: 2 EST: 2011
SALES (est): 134.5K **Privately Held**
SIC: 2752 Commercial printing, lithographic

(G-3561)
INNER CITY SPORTS TS
3012 Covert Ave (47714-4094)
PHONE.................................812 402-4143
Larry Hooper, *Principal*
EMP: 2
SALES (est): 133.8K **Privately Held**
SIC: 2759 Screen printing

(G-3562)
INTEGRAL TECHNOLOGIES INC
2605 Eastside Park Rd # 1 (47715-2177)
P.O. Box 5676 (47716-5676)
PHONE.................................812 550-1770
James Eagan, *Ch of Bd*
Doug Bathauer, *President*
W Bartlett Snell, *CFO*
EMP: 2
SQ FT: 800
SALES: 96.7K **Privately Held**
WEB: www.itkg.net
SIC: 2821 Plastics materials & resins

(G-3563)
INTEGRATED ENERGY TECHNOLOGIES
225 W Morgan Ave Ste A (47710-2515)
PHONE.................................812 421-7810
Craig Gooding, *President*
Marvin Miller, *Vice Pres*
Wayne Green, *Facilities Mgr*
Randy Arrasmith, *Engineer*
Robert Guiney, *Accountant*
▲ EMP: 40
SQ FT: 55,000
SALES (est): 7.7MM **Privately Held**
SIC: 3724 3714 3511 Exhaust systems, aircraft; exhaust systems & parts, motor vehicle; turbines & turbine generator sets & parts
HQ: Doncasters Inc.
835 Poquonnock Rd
Groton CT 06340

(G-3564)
INTERMETCO PROCESSING INC
1901 W Louisiana St (47710-2268)
P.O. Box 364 (47703-0364)
PHONE.................................812 423-5914
Ron Morgan, *President*
EMP: 3 EST: 2008
SALES (est): 474.8K **Privately Held**
SIC: 3399 Brads: aluminum, brass or other nonferrous metal or wire

(G-3565)
INTERNATIONAL STEEL COMPANY
Also Called: Interntonal Revolving Door Div
2138 N 6th Ave (47710-2814)
PHONE.................................812 425-3311
Rahmi Soyugenc, *President*
Lewis Cheeney, *Vice Pres*
Dean Helvey, *Opers Mgr*
Marjorie Soyugenc, *Admin Sec*
▲ EMP: 70
SQ FT: 156,000
SALES (est): 13MM
SALES (corp-wide): 13MM **Privately Held**
WEB: www.internationalrevolvingdoors.com
SIC: 3442 3231 Metal doors; store fronts, prefabricated, metal; products of purchased glass
PA: Evansville Metal Products Inc
119 Ladonna Blvd
Evansville IN 47711
812 423-5632

(G-3566)
IRD GROUP INC
2138 N 6th Ave (47710-2814)
PHONE.................................812 425-3311
James M Kratochvil, *Principal*
EMP: 20
SQ FT: 135,000
SALES (est): 1MM **Privately Held**
SIC: 3442 Metal doors

(G-3567)
IRVING MATERIALS INC
6000 Oak Grove Rd (47715-2359)
PHONE.................................812 424-3551
EMP: 11
SALES (corp-wide): 800.6MM **Privately Held**
SIC: 3273 Ready-mixed concrete
PA: Irving Materials, Inc.
8032 N State Road 9
Greenfield IN 46140
317 326-3101

(G-3568)
J A SMIT INC
Also Called: Powers Welding Shop
1500 N Fulton Ave (47710-2365)
P.O. Box 6975 (47719-0975)
PHONE.................................812 424-8141
Fax: 812 424-8068
Larry R Smith, *President*
Sharon Smith, *Treasurer*
EMP: 6
SALES (est): 942.9K **Privately Held**
WEB: www.powerswelding.com
SIC: 7692 3446 3443 3441 Welding repair; architectural metalwork; fabricated plate work (boiler shop); fabricated structural metal; gray & ductile iron foundries

GEOGRAPHIC

(G-3569)
J TROCKMAN & SONS INC
1017 Bayse St (47714-4180)
P.O. Box 682 (47704-0682)
PHONE...................................812 425-5271
Fax: 812 425-5277
David Trockman, *President*
Jeffrey Trockman, *Vice Pres*
▼ **EMP:** 36 **EST:** 1985
SQ FT: 28,000
SALES (est): 8.3MM **Privately Held**
SIC: 5093 3341 Ferrous metal scrap &
waste; secondary nonferrous metals

(G-3570)
J&J SPRTS SCREEN PRTG
SPRIT WR
3012 Covert Ave Ste B (47714-4094)
PHONE...................................812 909-2686
Larry Hooper, *Principal*
EMP: 2
SALES (est): 83.9K **Privately Held**
SIC: 2752 Commercial printing, litho-
graphic

(G-3571)
JACK FROST LLC
Also Called: Honeywell Authorized Dealer
1510 Yokel Rd (47711-2867)
PHONE...................................812 477-7244
Fax: 812 479-5217
H Scott Larsen, *President*
Randy Stuckemeyer, *Chairman*
EMP: 40
SQ FT: 11,000
SALES (est): 7.1MM **Privately Held**
WEB: www.jackfrostinc.com
SIC: 1711 3444 Warm air heating & air
conditioning contractor; sheet metalwork

(G-3572)
JBM RACE CARS LLC
7901 Newburgh Rd (47715-4533)
PHONE...................................812 305-3666
Mark McDonald, *Principal*
EMP: 2
SALES (est): 173.6K **Privately Held**
SIC: 3711 Automobile assembly, including
specialty automobiles

(G-3573)
JEF ENTERPRISES INC (PA)
Also Called: Tri-State Trophies
1200 W Columbia St (47710-1400)
P.O. Box 6449 (47719-0449)
PHONE...................................812 425-0628
Fax: 812 425-4983
Lisa Tanner, *President*
Harvey Tanner, *Vice Pres*
Sue A Mullen, *Sales Mgr*
Amy Barnes, *Sales Associate*
Beverley Frederking, *Shareholder*
EMP: 16
SQ FT: 6,000
SALES (est): 1.1MM **Privately Held**
WEB: www.tristatetrophies.com
SIC: 5999 3993 Trophies & plaques; signs
& advertising specialties

(G-3574)
JEFF HURY HARDWOOD
FLOORS PNTG
629 S Norman Ave (47714-2119)
PHONE...................................812 204-8650
Jeff Haury, *Principal*
EMP: 3
SALES (est): 178.5K **Privately Held**
SIC: 1752 1771 2426 Floor laying & floor
work; flooring contractor; flooring, hard-
wood

(G-3575)
JOE W MORGAN INC
Also Called: Henry Fligeltaub Co Div
1901 W Louisiana St (47710-2268)
P.O. Box 928 (47706-0928)
PHONE...................................812 423-5914
Fax: 812 425-5140
Ronald J Morgan, *President*
Alan N Shovers, *Corp Secy*
John Mac Leod, *Vice Pres*
EMP: 65 **EST:** 1971

SALES (est): 16.4MM **Privately Held**
SIC: 3341 5093 Aluminum smelting & refining (secondary); ferrous metal scrap &
waste

(G-3576)
JOHNSON CONTROLS
2225 N Burkhardt Rd (47715-2157)
PHONE...................................812 423-9000
Keenan Carver, *Branch Mgr*
John Baldwin, *Associate*
EMP: 5 **Privately Held**
WEB: www.simplexgrinnell.com
SIC: 3669 Emergency alarms
HQ: Johnson Controls Fire Protection Lp
4700 Exchange Ct Ste 300
Boca Raton FL 33431
561 988-7200

(G-3577)
JOHNSON CONTROLS
800 Canal St (47713-2514)
PHONE...................................812 423-9000
Fax: 812 423-9224
Keenan Carver, *Manager*
EMP: 35 **Privately Held**
WEB: www.simplexgrinnell.com
SIC: 3669 Emergency alarms
HQ: Johnson Controls Fire Protection Lp
4700 Exchange Ct Ste 300
Boca Raton FL 33431
561 988-7200

(G-3578)
JOHNSON CONTROLS INC
8401 N Kentucky Ave Ste H (47725-6301)
PHONE...................................812 868-1374
Fax: 812 868-1379
Billy Payne, *Manager*
EMP: 15 **Privately Held**
SIC: 3822 2531 8744 Building services
monitoring controls, automatic; seats, au-
tomobile; facilities support services
HQ: Johnson Controls, Inc.
5757 N Green Bay Ave
Milwaukee WI 53209
414 524-1200

(G-3579)
JOHNSON PLASTICS & SUP CO
INC
1414 Baker Ave (47710-2508)
PHONE...................................812 424-5554
Fax: 812 421-1265
Richie Johnson, *President*
Mike Anoskey, *Sales Staff*
Gina Johnson, *Admin Sec*
▲ **EMP:** 30
SQ FT: 40,000
SALES (est): 15.3MM **Privately Held**
WEB: www.johnsonplastic.com
SIC: 5162 3086 Plastics materials & basic
shapes; plastics foam products

(G-3580)
JUBILEE HARPS INC
2405 Diefenbach Rd (47720-2650)
PHONE...................................812 426-2547
Rick Woods, *CEO*
Mary Woods, *President*
EMP: 9
SALES: 95K **Privately Held**
WEB: www.jubilee-harps.com
SIC: 3931 Harps & parts

(G-3581)
K S OIL CORP
11625 Ramblewood Ct (47712-9555)
PHONE...................................812 453-3026
Larry Schmitt, *President*
Mildred Kohlmeyer, *Vice Pres*
Melody Schmitt, *Treasurer*
Georgia Nattles, *Admin Sec*
EMP: 9
SALES (est): 795.6K **Privately Held**
WEB: www.ksoils.com
SIC: 1311 1389 Crude petroleum produc-
tion; pumping of oil & gas wells

(G-3582)
KCI CRANE PRO SERVICES
2710 Eastside Park Rd C (47715-8527)
PHONE...................................812 479-0488
Fax: 812 479-0457
Jeff Moss, *Principal*
EMP: 2

SALES (est): 194.3K **Privately Held**
SIC: 2599 Hospital beds

(G-3583)
KENDLE CUSTOM INC
Also Called: Aquathin Air & Water Purifictn
11711 Boberg Rd (47712-8625)
PHONE...................................812 985-5917
Fax: 812 421-9546
George Kendall, *President*
Troy Higgenson, *Vice Pres*
EMP: 2
SALES: 140K **Privately Held**
SIC: 3589 Water purification equipment,
household type

(G-3584)
KENTUCKY-INDIANA LUMBER
CO INC
Also Called: K & I Sash & Door
1700 N Kentucky Ave (47711-3824)
P.O. Box 4099 (47724-0099)
PHONE...................................812 464-2428
Fax: 812 464-2903
Mark C Hansen, *Branch Mgr*
EMP: 33
SALES (corp-wide): 2B **Privately Held**
WEB: www.ki-lumber.com
SIC: 5031 2439 2431 2426 Lumber, ply-
wood & millwork; structural assemblies,
prefabricated: wood; structural wood
members; millwork; hardwood dimension
& flooring mills
HQ: Kentucky-Indiana Lumber Co., Inc.
4010 Collins Ln
Louisville KY 40245
502 637-1401

(G-3585)
KERR GROUP LLC
315 Se 2nd St (47713-1054)
PHONE...................................812 424-2904
Ira Boots, *Branch Mgr*
EMP: 165 **Publicly Held**
SIC: 3089 Closures, plastic
HQ: Kerr Group, Llc
1846 Charter Ln Ste 209
Lancaster PA 17601
812 424-2904

(G-3586)
KERRY INC
DCA Modern Maid
1515 Park St (47710-2295)
PHONE...................................812 464-9151
Fax: 812 464-9196
Joe Sstellern, *Branch Mgr*
EMP: 150
SQ FT: 183,000 **Privately Held**
WEB: www.kerryingredients.com
SIC: 2041 2099 Doughs & batters; food
preparations
HQ: Kerry Inc.
3330 Millington Rd
Beloit WI 53511
608 363-1200

(G-3587)
KERRY INC
1615 N Fulton Ave (47710-2755)
PHONE...................................812 464-9151
EMP: 4 **Privately Held**
SIC: 2041 Doughs & batters
HQ: Kerry Inc.
3330 Millington Rd
Beloit WI 53511
608 363-1200

(G-3588)
KGN SOFTWARE LLC
5100 Vogel Rd (47715-7813)
PHONE...................................812 618-4723
EMP: 2 **EST:** 2011
SALES (est): 100K **Privately Held**
SIC: 7372 Prepackaged Software Services

(G-3589)
KIMALCO INC
Also Called: Kimalco Mattress
213 W Division St Ste J (47710-1368)
PHONE...................................812 463-3105
Kimberly Pike, *President*
EMP: 5

SALES (est): 576.4K **Privately Held**
SIC: 2515 Mattresses & bedsprings; foundations & platforms; mattresses, containing felt, foam rubber, urethane, etc.;
mattresses, innerspring or box spring

(G-3590)
KIMS SCRUB CONNECTION LLC
200 S Green River Rd (47715-7317)
PHONE...................................812 867-1237
Kimberly D Tenhumberg, *Principal*
EMP: 2
SALES (est): 179.2K **Privately Held**
SIC: 2844 Toilet preparations

(G-3591)
KINGS CUSTOM MACHINE
2700 N Cullen Ave (47715-2195)
PHONE...................................812 477-5262
Fax: 812 479-3704
William King, *Owner*
EMP: 8
SQ FT: 4,800
SALES (est): 644.6K **Privately Held**
SIC: 3599 Machine shop, jobbing & repair

(G-3592)
KIRCHOFF CUSTOM SPORTS
311 Eissler Rd (47711-1551)
PHONE...................................812 434-0355
Mike Kirchoff, *Principal*
EMP: 3 **EST:** 2009
SALES (est): 191.1K **Privately Held**
SIC: 2759 Screen printing

(G-3593)
KISSEL PRINTERS INC
901 W Delaware St (47710-1511)
P.O. Box 6342 (47719-0342)
PHONE...................................812 424-5333
Fax: 812 424-5333
Steven A Kissel, *President*
Mary L Kissel, *Admin Sec*
EMP: 3 **EST:** 1946
SALES: 210K **Privately Held**
SIC: 2759 Letterpress printing

(G-3594)
KLEEN-RITE SUPPLY INC
Also Called: Krs
1101 E Diamond Ave (47711-3903)
PHONE...................................812 422-7483
Fax: 812 422-7577
Anthony D Richardt, *President*
Tony Richardt, *Sales Mgr*
Jen Richardt, *Info Tech Mgr*
EMP: 10 **EST:** 1981
SQ FT: 30,000
SALES (est): 2MM **Privately Held**
WEB: www.krssolutions.com
SIC: 5087 2842 Janitors' supplies; clean-
ing or polishing preparations

(G-3595)
KLUEG TOOL & MACHINE INC
14420 Darmstadt Rd (47725-9560)
PHONE...................................812 867-5702
Norman Klueg, *President*
Joanne Klueg, *Treasurer*
EMP: 3
SALES: 225K **Privately Held**
SIC: 3542 3599 3545 Machine tools,
metal forming type; machine shop, job-
bing & repair; machine tool accessories

(G-3596)
KOCH ENTERPRISES INC (PA)
14 S 11th Ave (47712-5020)
PHONE...................................812 465-9800
Kevin R Koch, *President*
Robert Koch, *Chairman*
Susan E Parsons, *CFO*
▲ **EMP:** 7 **EST:** 1873
SALES: 1B **Privately Held**
WEB: www.kochenterprises.com
SIC: 3363 5075 3559 5084 Aluminum
die-castings; air conditioning equipment,
except room units; metal finishing equip-
ment for plating, etc.; industrial machinery
& equipment; sealants; adhesives; alu-
minum smelting & refining (secondary)

144

(G-3597)
KUHN & SONS INC
Also Called: Pro-Tex All Co
210 S Morton Ave (47713-2448)
PHONE..............................812 424-8268
Fax: 812 424-8330
James R Kuhn, *President*
Jim Kuhn, *Managing Prtnr*
J Michael Kuhn, *Admin Sec*
EMP: 20 EST: 1920
SQ FT: 29,500
SALES (est): 4.9MM **Privately Held**
WEB: www.protexall.com
SIC: 2842 5087 5169 Specialty cleaning,
polishes & sanitation goods; janitors' sup-
plies; cleaning & maintenance equipment
& supplies; waxes, except petroleum

(G-3598)
LASERTONE INC
Also Called: Ail
700 N Weinbach Ave # 101 (47711-5966)
PHONE..............................812 473-5945
Fax: 812 473-5980
Mark Daily, *President*
EMP: 15
SQ FT: 5,000
SALES (est): 2.4MM **Privately Held**
SIC: 3861 7629 5112 Toners, prepared
photographic (not made in chemical
plants); business machine repair, electric;
computer & photocopying supplies

(G-3599)
**LEED SELLING TOOLS CORP
(PA)**
9700 Highway 57 (47725-9704)
P.O. Box 3088 (47730-3088)
PHONE..............................812 867-4340
Fax: 812 867-4353
Douglas Edwards, *President*
George K Grace, *Exec VP*
Richard A Edwards, *Vice Pres*
EMP: 42 EST: 1962
SQ FT: 19,000
SALES (est): 32.8MM **Privately Held**
WEB: www.leedsamples.com
SIC: 2789 2782 Swatches & samples;
sample books

(G-3600)
**LEWIS BROTHERS BAKERIES
INC (PA)**
500 N Fulton Ave (47710-1571)
PHONE..............................812 425-4642
Fax: 812 425-7609
R Jack Lewis Jr, *President*
John West, *President*
Harry Lincoln, *General Mgr*
Jack Lewis, *Principal*
Tom Woods Jr, *COO*
▲ EMP: 200 EST: 1925
SQ FT: 100,000
SALES (est): 473.3MM **Privately Held**
WEB: www.lewisbakeries.net
SIC: 2051 5149 Bread, all types (white,
wheat, rye, etc): fresh or frozen; buns,
bread type: fresh or frozen; rolls, sweet:
except frozen; doughnuts, except frozen;
groceries & related products

(G-3601)
**LIBS MIKE & CHOCLAT FCTRY
LLC**
6201 Hogue Rd (47712-2901)
PHONE..............................812 424-8750
R Michael Libs, *Partner*
Patrick Coslett, *Partner*
EMP: 6
SALES (est): 451.9K **Privately Held**
SIC: 2064 Chocolate candy, except solid
chocolate

(G-3602)
LIGHT & INK CORP
Also Called: Link Graphics
1018 E Diamond Ave (47711-3902)
PHONE..............................812 421-1400
Fax: 812 425-5540
Robert Fuchs, *President*
EMP: 8
SQ FT: 9,000
SALES: 1MM **Privately Held**
WEB: www.linkgraphics.com
SIC: 2759 Commercial printing

(G-3603)
LINCS SOFTWARE CORP
1133 W Mill Rd Ste 210 (47710-3806)
PHONE..............................812 204-3619
EMP: 2
SALES (est): 111.4K **Privately Held**
SIC: 7372 Prepackaged software

(G-3604)
LIVELY MACHINE COMPANY INC
4404 Upper Mt Vernon Rd (47712-6418)
PHONE..............................812 425-5060
Fax: 812 425-5477
Jeffrey A Hoefling, *President*
Matt Stennett, *Foreman/Supr*
◆ EMP: 9 EST: 1952
SQ FT: 8,400
SALES (est): 1.3MM **Privately Held**
WEB: www.livelymachine.com
SIC: 3599 Machine shop, jobbing & repair

(G-3605)
LLOYDS MACHINE CO
2214 St Joseph Ind Pk Dr (47720-1207)
PHONE..............................812 422-7064
Fax: 812 422-7064
Mark Lampton, *President*
EMP: 7
SALES: 650K **Privately Held**
WEB: www.lloydsmachine.net
SIC: 3599 7692 Machine shop, jobbing &
repair; welding repair

(G-3606)
LUCENT POLYMERS INC
1800 Lynch Rd (47711-2841)
PHONE..............................812 492-7214
EMP: 5
SALES (corp-wide): 2.4B **Publicly Held**
SIC: 2821 Plastics materials & resins
HQ: Lucent Polymers Inc
1700 Lynch Rd
Evansville IN 47711

(G-3607)
**M & W CONCRETE PIPE &
SUPPLY**
1213 Stanley Ave (47711-3569)
PHONE..............................812 426-2871
Fax: 812 426-2879
Fred Irving, *President*
EMP: 35 EST: 1960
SQ FT: 2,500
SALES (est): 3.4MM
SALES (corp-wide): 800.6MM **Privately
Held**
SIC: 3272 5032 Pipe, concrete or lined
with concrete; sewer pipe, clay
PA: Irving Materials, Inc.
8032 N State Road 9
Greenfield IN 46140
317 326-3101

(G-3608)
MACO REPROGRAHICS LLC
600 Court St (47708-1342)
PHONE..............................812 464-8108
Fax: 812 464-2422
Rick Lents,
Brenda Lents,
EMP: 3
SQ FT: 900
SALES (est): 440K **Privately Held**
WEB: www.macoreprographics.com
SIC: 5049 7334 2752 Engineers' equip-
ment & supplies; drafting supplies; blue-
printing service; commercial printing,
offset

(G-3609)
MADDENCO INC
4847 E Virginia St Ste G (47715-2611)
PHONE..............................812 474-6245
Fax: 812 474-6254
Jay Adams, *President*
Mark Russell, *Vice Pres*
Rhonda Goerges, *Manager*
Patty Mills, *Software Dev*
Beth Herrmann, *Executive*
EMP: 16
SQ FT: 4,500
SALES (est): 3.3MM **Privately Held**
WEB: www.maddenco.com
SIC: 7372 5045 Business oriented com-
puter software; mainframe computers;
word processing equipment

(G-3610)
MAGNOLIA PRODUCTS LLC
314 Ridgeway Ave (47713-1418)
PHONE..............................812 306-8638
Phillip Baker, *Mng Member*
EMP: 2
SALES (est): 124K **Privately Held**
SIC: 2844 5999 5122 Tonics, hair; hair
care products; cosmetics, perfumes &
hair products

(G-3611)
MAGNUM DRILLING SVCS INC
10020 Carmel Ct (47712-9612)
P.O. Box 6481 (47719-0481)
PHONE..............................812 985-3981
Danny L Veeck, *President*
Lisa Veeck, *Office Mgr*
EMP: 10
SALES (est): 1.6MM **Privately Held**
SIC: 1381 Drilling oil & gas wells

(G-3612)
MAJESTIC TOOL INC
9333 W Boonvl New Harmony
(47720-8501)
PHONE..............................812 426-0332
Fax: 812 426-0332
EMP: 6
SQ FT: 4,000
SALES: 400K **Privately Held**
SIC: 3559 Mfg Plastics Working Machinery
Specializing In Hot Stamping & Heat
Sealing Machinery

(G-3613)
MANNON L WALTERS INC
500 N Congress Ave Ste D (47715-2493)
PHONE..............................812 867-5946
Fax: 812 867-5956
Mannon L Walters, *President*
Betty Trabant, *Principal*
Sherry Roberts, *Corp Secy*
Mary Nagle, *Manager*
Mike Newlin, *Admin Sec*
EMP: 10
SQ FT: 2,000
SALES (est): 2.3MM **Privately Held**
WEB: www.mannonoil.com
SIC: 1311 Crude petroleum production

(G-3614)
**MARTIN HOLDING COMPANY
LLC**
Also Called: Indiana Cardinal
605 W Eichel Ave (47710-2411)
PHONE..............................812 401-9988
Kent Haley, *Controller*
Timothy R Martin, *Mng Member*
EMP: 75
SQ FT: 200,000
SALES: 12MM **Privately Held**
SIC: 2821 Plastics materials & resins

(G-3615)
**MASTER MANUFACTURING
COMPANY**
4703 Ohara Dr (47711-2495)
PHONE..............................812 425-1561
Fax: 812 425-4320
John R Gannon Jr, *President*
Tom Miley, *Business Mgr*
Grace Donley, *Corp Secy*
Terri Keller, *Manager*
John Gannon, *CTO*
EMP: 41
SQ FT: 74,000
SALES (est): 8.6MM **Privately Held**
WEB: www.mastermfg.com
SIC: 3469 3423 Stamping metal for the
trade; ironworkers' hand tools

(G-3616)
**MATRIXX GROUP
INCORPORATED**
Citadel Plastics
820 E Columbia St (47711-5146)
PHONE..............................812 421-3600
Mike Huff, *CEO*
EMP: 3
SALES (corp-wide): 2.4B **Publicly Held**
SIC: 2821 Plastics materials & resins

HQ: The Matrixx Group Incorporated
15000 Highway 41 N
Evansville IN 47725
812 421-3600

(G-3617)
**MATRIXX GROUP
INCORPORATED**
Also Called: A. Schulman
15000b Highway 41 N (47725-9360)
PHONE..............................812 421-3600
EMP: 2
SALES (corp-wide): 2.4B **Publicly Held**
SIC: 2821 Thermoplastic materials
HQ: The Matrixx Group Incorporated
15000 Highway 41 N
Evansville IN 47725
812 421-3600

(G-3618)
**MATRIXX GROUP
INCORPORATED**
5001 Ohara Dr (47711-2475)
PHONE..............................812 423-5218
Fax: 812 435-2113
Steven Edge, *Manager*
EMP: 125
SQ FT: 60,000
SALES (corp-wide): 2.4B **Publicly Held**
WEB: www.ferro.com
SIC: 2821 Molding compounds, plastics
HQ: The Matrixx Group Incorporated
15000 Highway 41 N
Evansville IN 47725
812 421-3600

(G-3619)
MATRIXX-QTR INC
15000 Highway 41 N (47725-9360)
PHONE..............................812 429-0901
Mike Huff, *CEO*
▲ EMP: 55
SQ FT: 105,000
SALES (est): 6MM
SALES (corp-wide): 2.4B **Publicly Held**
SIC: 3087 Custom compound purchased
resins
HQ: The Matrixx Group Incorporated
15000 Highway 41 N
Evansville IN 47725
812 421-3600

(G-3620)
**MEAD JOHNSON & COMPANY
LLC (DH)**
Also Called: Mead Johnson Nutrition
2400 W Lloyd Expy (47712-5095)
PHONE..............................812 429-5000
Fax: 812 429-7714
Peter Kasper Jakobsen, *CEO*
Michael Jahn, *General Mgr*
Susan Wentworth, *Business Mgr*
Sandy Mac Pherson, *Senior VP*
Tom De Weerdt, *Vice Pres*
▼ EMP: 277
SQ FT: 875,000
SALES (est): 384MM
SALES (corp-wide): 15.2B **Privately Held**
SIC: 2099 2834 2032 Food preparations;
pharmaceutical preparations; canned
specialties

(G-3621)
MEASURE PRESS INC
526 S Lincoln Park Dr (47714-1542)
PHONE..............................812 473-0361
Robert Griffith, *Owner*
EMP: 2
SALES (est): 9K **Privately Held**
SIC: 2741 Miscellaneous publishing

(G-3622)
MERIDIAN METALFORM INC
1025 W Tennessee St (47710-2349)
PHONE..............................812 422-1524
Fax: 812 423-9346
David Walker, *President*
Mark Stamm, *General Mgr*
EMP: 7
SALES (est): 1.1MM **Privately Held**
SIC: 3442 Casements, aluminum

(G-3623)
METAL MASTERS INC
4600 Broadway Ave (47712-4208)
P.O. Box 3501 (47734-3501)
PHONE..................................812 421-9162
Tony May, *President*
Lynda R Vessel, *Corp Secy*
Steve Vessel, *Vice Pres*
EMP: 3
SALES (est): 390.4K **Privately Held**
SIC: 3441 Fabricated structural metal

(G-3624)
**MEUTH CONSTRUCTION
SUPPLY INC**
2201 Bergdolt Rd (47711-2888)
PHONE..................................812 424-8554
Fax: 812 831-5203
Warren Meuth, *Vice Pres*
Delbert Meuth, *Branch Mgr*
EMP: 11
SALES (corp-wide): 13.5MM **Privately
Held**
SIC: 3273 Ready-mixed concrete
PA: Meuth Construction Supply, Inc.
703 8th St
Henderson KY 42420
270 827-8063

(G-3625)
MICHAEL R HARRIS
Also Called: Harris Oil Co
20 Nw 1st St Rear 208 (47708-1267)
PHONE..................................812 425-9411
R Michael Harris, *Owner*
Karen Baldman, *Admin Sec*
EMP: 2
SALES (est): 110K **Privately Held**
SIC: 1382 1381 Oil & gas exploration
services; drilling oil & gas wells

(G-3626)
**MID-AMERICA ENVIRONMENTAL
LLC**
Also Called: Alpha Laser and Imaging
5815 Metro Center Dr (47715-2651)
PHONE..................................812 475-1644
Fax: 812 476-7419
Miles Hawkins, *Accounts Exec*
Aaron Althaus, *Mng Member*
Jason Althaus,
Scott Althaus,
EMP: 19
SQ FT: 4,500
SALES (est): 1.8MM **Privately Held**
WEB: www.alpha-laser.net
SIC: 3861 7629 Toners, prepared photo-
graphic (not made in chemical plants);
business machine repair, electric

(G-3627)
MIDLAND POWDER LLC
4 Nw 2nd St (47708-1244)
PHONE..................................812 402-4070
David Childs, *Principal*
EMP: 2
SALES (est): 217.4K **Privately Held**
SIC: 2892 Explosives

(G-3628)
**MILLER PLATING & METAL
FINISH**
3200 N 6th Ave (47710-3367)
PHONE..................................812 424-3837
EMP: 2
SALES (est): 140.5K **Privately Held**
SIC: 3471 Plating/Polishing Service

(G-3629)
MILLMADE INC
9 N Kentucky Ave (47711-5708)
PHONE..................................812 424-7778
Fax: 812 424-9839
Billy Grant, *President*
Dennis Grant, *Vice Pres*
EMP: 8
SQ FT: 11,000
SALES (est): 2.8MM **Privately Held**
WEB: www.millmade.com
SIC: 2521 Wood office furniture

(G-3630)
**MINE EQUIPMENT MILL SUPPLY
CO**
4 Nw 2nd St 2 (47708-1244)
PHONE..................................812 402-4070
David Childs, *President*
EMP: 100
SALES (est): 5.2MM **Privately Held**
SIC: 2892 Primary explosives, fuses & det-
onators

(G-3631)
**MOBILE COMMUNICATIONS
TECH**
945 N Peerless Rd (47712-2933)
PHONE..................................812 423-7322
Steven Muensterman, *Vice Pres*
EMP: 2
SALES (est): 175K **Privately Held**
SIC: 3651 4813 4899 FM & AM radio
tuners; telephone communication, except
radio; communication services

(G-3632)
MOBILE DENTAL VAN MFG
800 Cedar Hill Dr (47710-5016)
PHONE..................................812 626-3010
James Kitch, *Principal*
EMP: 2
SALES (est): 99.3K **Privately Held**
SIC: 3999 Manufacturing industries

(G-3633)
MOMINEE STUDIOS INC
5001 Lincoln Ave (47715-4113)
PHONE..................................812 473-1691
Jules Mominee, *Partner*
Terry Mominee, *Corp Secy*
EMP: 4
SALES: 300K **Privately Held**
WEB: www.momineestudios.com
SIC: 3231 5231 Stained glass: made from
purchased glass; glass, leaded or stained

(G-3634)
MONSANTO COTTON
738 Rusher Ln (47725-7842)
PHONE..................................229 759-0035
EMP: 2
SALES (est): 71K **Privately Held**
SIC: 2879 Mfg Agricultural Chemicals

(G-3635)
MOONEY COPY SERVICE INC
40 E Sycamore St (47713-1930)
PHONE..................................812 423-6626
Fax: 812 421-9965
Michael Dejean, *President*
Michael De Jean, *President*
EMP: 4 EST: 1945
SQ FT: 5,000
SALES (est): 390K **Privately Held**
SIC: 2752 2759 Commercial printing, off-
set; letterpress printing

(G-3636)
**MOORE ENGINEERING & PROD
CO (PA)**
Also Called: Mepco
2104 Lincoln Ave (47714-1612)
PHONE..................................812 479-1051
Fax: 812 476-2569
Lester D Moore, *President*
Joyce A Moore, *Admin Sec*
EMP: 12
SQ FT: 3,000
SALES (est): 1.2MM **Privately Held**
SIC: 1311 8711 Crude petroleum produc-
tion; natural gas production; petroleum
engineering

(G-3637)
MOORE MACHINE & GEAR INC
10920 N Saint Joseph Ave (47720-7195)
PHONE..................................812 963-3074
Fax: 812 963-8212
Alan Moore, *President*
Judy Lynch, *Treasurer*
EMP: 6
SQ FT: 2,600
SALES: 600K **Privately Held**
WEB: www.moorecustomgear.com
SIC: 3599 3566 Machine shop, jobbing &
repair; drives, high speed industrial, ex-
cept hydrostatic

(G-3638)
**MOORE METAL WORKS & A/C L
L C**
3712 Upper Mt Vernon Rd (47712-7868)
PHONE..................................812 422-9473
Darlene Moore, *Principal*
EMP: 5
SALES: 500K **Privately Held**
SIC: 3444 Sheet metalwork

(G-3639)
MOTHERSOY INC
424 S Kentucky Ave (47714-1013)
PHONE..................................812 424-5357
Carl Barnaik, *President*
EMP: 2
SALES: 500K **Privately Held**
SIC: 2075 Soybean protein concentrates &
isolates

(G-3640)
MT PUBLISHING COMPANY INC
209 Nw 8th St (47708-1907)
P.O. Box 6802 (47719-0802)
PHONE..................................812 468-8022
Fax: 812 468-7328
Mark A Thompson, *President*
Cathy Thompson, *Vice Pres*
Amanda Becker, *Graphic Designe*
EMP: 8
SALES (est): 786.4K **Privately Held**
WEB: www.mtpublishing.com
SIC: 2741 Miscellaneous publishing

(G-3641)
MULTISEAL INC
4320 Hitch Peters Rd (47711-2831)
PHONE..................................812 428-3422
Fax: 812 428-3432
Gary M Rust, *President*
Robert C Rust, *Vice Pres*
Larry Rust, *Finance*
EMP: 120
SQ FT: 75,000
SALES (est): 35MM **Privately Held**
WEB: www.multiseal-usa.com
SIC: 2891 Sealants; adhesives

(G-3642)
MULZER CRUSHED STONE INC
Also Called: Tell City Concrete Supply
3300 Green River Dr (47715)
PHONE..................................812 547-7921
EMP: 39
SALES (corp-wide): 29.7B **Privately Held**
SIC: 1422 Crushed & broken limestone
HQ: Mulzer Crushed Stone Inc
534 Mozart St
Tell City IN 47586
812 547-7921

(G-3643)
NEW IMAGE TRAVEL LLC
2336 Glenview Dr (47720-1249)
PHONE..................................812 426-1423
Fax: 812 426-7905
Irma Will,
Martin Will,
EMP: 23
SQ FT: 8,000
SALES: 1.2MM **Privately Held**
SIC: 3792 4724 Trailer coaches, automo-
bile; travel agencies

(G-3644)
NICKOLICK DEVELOPMENT
Also Called: Nickolick, Joe J
4209 Highway 41 N Ste 26 (47711-2889)
P.O. Box 5365 (47716-5365)
PHONE..................................812 422-8526
Joe J Nickolick, *Partner*
Mary A Nickolick, *Partner*
EMP: 5
SQ FT: 1,000
SALES (est): 578.8K **Privately Held**
SIC: 6512 1311 Commercial & industrial
building operation; crude petroleum pro-
duction

(G-3645)
NM INDUSTRIES LLC
300 Kirchoff Blvd (47712-5401)
PHONE..................................812 985-3608
Tammy McReynolds, *Owner*
EMP: 2

SALES (est): 74.6K **Privately Held**
SIC: 3999 Manufacturing industries

(G-3646)
NORMAN TOOL INC
15415 Old State Rd (47725-8578)
PHONE..................................812 867-3496
Fax: 812 867-6790
Scott Norman, *President*
EMP: 4
SQ FT: 7,350
SALES: 600K **Privately Held**
WEB: www.normantool.com
SIC: 3823 Industrial instrmnts msrmnt dis-
play/control process variable

(G-3647)
NOV OAK WOODWORKING
913 Washington Ave (47713-2259)
PHONE..................................812 422-1973
Donald Novack, *Principal*
EMP: 2
SALES (est): 130K **Privately Held**
SIC: 2431 Millwork

(G-3648)
**NOVA POLYMERS
INCORPORATED**
2650 Eastside Park Rd (47715-2178)
P.O. Box 8278 (47716-8278)
PHONE..................................812 476-0339
Fax: 812 476-0592
Roger D Chapman, *President*
EMP: 40
SQ FT: 78,000
SALES (est): 9.8MM **Privately Held**
WEB: www.novapolymers.net
SIC: 2821 Plastics materials & resins; ther-
moplastic materials; molding compounds,
plastics

(G-3649)
NUNN MILLING COMPANY INC
4700 New Harmony Rd (47720-1721)
PHONE..................................812 425-3303
Robert J Nunn, *Branch Mgr*
EMP: 33
SALES (corp-wide): 8.1MM **Privately
Held**
WEB: www.nunn-better.com
SIC: 2041 Wheat flour; corn meal
PA: Nunn Milling Company Inc
9634 Hedden Rd
Evansville IN
812 867-4500

(G-3650)
NUSSMEIER ENGRAVING CO
933 Main St (47708-1834)
PHONE..................................812 425-1339
Fax: 812 421-5824
David Nussmeier, *President*
Louis H Nussmeier, *Corp Secy*
Steven D Nussmeier, *Vice Pres*
EMP: 29
SQ FT: 15,000
SALES (est): 2.6MM **Privately Held**
WEB: www.nussmeier.com
SIC: 2754 2791 2759 2752 Stationery &
invitation printing, gravure; cards, except
greeting: gravure printing; invitations:
gravure printing; announcements: gravure
printing; typesetting; commercial printing;
commercial printing, lithographic; blank-
books & looseleaf binders; greeting cards

(G-3651)
**OBRYAN BARREL COMPANY
INC**
5501 Old Boonville Hwy (47715-2130)
PHONE..................................812 479-6741
Fax: 812 474-6187
Arthur J O'Bryan, *President*
Anna O'Bryan, *Corp Secy*
Daniel O'Bryan, *Vice Pres*
Tim O"bryan, *Vice Pres*
Timothy O'Bryan, *Vice Pres*
EMP: 30
SQ FT: 10,000
SALES (est): 13.6MM **Privately Held**
WEB: www.obryanbarrel.com
SIC: 5085 3412 Barrels, new or recondi-
tioned; barrels, shipping: metal

▲ = Import ▼=Export
◆ =Import/Export

(G-3652)
OCE COPIERS
5625 E Virginia St (47715-2652)
PHONE.............................812 479-0000
James Moser, *Principal*
EMP: 2
SALES (est): 112.9K **Privately Held**
SIC: 3579 5044 5065 Duplicating machines; copying equipment; facsimile equipment

(G-3653)
OILFIELD RESEARCH INC
1204 N 1st Ave (47710-2404)
PHONE.............................812 424-2907
Marlin F Krieg, *President*
Carol Sue Roth, *Admin Sec*
EMP: 2 EST: 1960
SALES (est): 190K **Privately Held**
SIC: 8711 1389 Petroleum engineering; oil field services

(G-3654)
OLD JIM CUSTOMS LLC
4001 Vogel Rd (47715-2213)
PHONE.............................812 431-1460
EMP: 4
SALES (est): 320.3K **Privately Held**
SIC: 2816 Chrome pigments: chrome green, chrome yellow, zinc yellow

(G-3655)
OMNI PLASTICS LLC
2300 Lynch Rd (47711-2951)
PHONE.............................812 422-0888
Fax: 812 421-8915
William G Vieth, *President*
▲ EMP: 80
SQ FT: 294,000
SALES (est): 67.3MM
SALES (corp-wide): 6.1B **Publicly Held**
WEB: www.omnithermoplastics.com
SIC: 3083 2821 Laminated plastics plate & sheet; plastics materials & resins
PA: Celanese Corporation
222 Las Colinas Blvd W # 900
Irving TX 75039
972 443-4000

(G-3656)
ORG CHEM GROUP LLC (PA)
2406 Lynch Rd (47711-2953)
PHONE.............................812 464-4446
David Carson, *CEO*
Kevin Harris, *Vice Pres*
Mike Millard, *Vice Pres*
Eric Mittlefehldt, *Vice Pres*
Mike Sturgeon, *CFO*
EMP: 69
SQ FT: 11,000
SALES (est): 40MM **Privately Held**
WEB: www.chem-group.com
SIC: 2869 Industrial organic chemicals

(G-3657)
ORTHOTIC & PROSTHETIC LAB
Also Called: O & P Lab
125 N Weinbach Ave # 330 (47711-6091)
PHONE.............................812 479-6298
Fax: 812 479-6758
Chad Allen, *President*
Elva Allen, *Treasurer*
EMP: 13
SALES (est): 1.7MM **Privately Held**
SIC: 3842 Limbs, artificial; braces, orthopedic

(G-3658)
OTIS ELEVATOR COMPANY
6050 Wedeking Ave Ste 10b (47715-2187)
PHONE.............................812 471-9770
Fax: 812 471-9878
Jason Martin, *Manager*
EMP: 33
SALES (corp-wide): 59.8B **Publicly Held**
WEB: www.otis.com
SIC: 3534 Elevators & equipment
HQ: Otis Elevator Company
1 Carrier Pl
Farmington CT 06032
860 674-3000

(G-3659)
OVATION COMMUNICATIONS INC
Also Called: Kwik Kopy Business Center 130
1326 N Weinbach Ave (47711-4307)
PHONE.............................812 401-9100
Fax: 812 401-9190
Scott Fenneman, *Owner*
EMP: 6
SQ FT: 3,625
SALES (est): 709.9K **Privately Held**
WEB: www.kwikkopyonline.com
SIC: 2752 7334 7311 3993 Commercial printing, offset; photocopying & duplicating services; advertising agencies; signs & advertising specialties; direct mail advertising services

(G-3660)
OVER HILL & DALE SIGN STUDIO
1100 Indy Ct (47725-6300)
PHONE.............................812 867-1664
Fax: 812 867-1664
Dale Wright, *Owner*
Lawrence Wright, *Co-Owner*
EMP: 2
SALES (est): 90K **Privately Held**
SIC: 3993 5099 Signs & advertising specialties; signs, except electric

(G-3661)
PALLET RECYCLERS LLC
4200 Upper Mt Vernon Rd (47712-6429)
PHONE.............................812 402-0095
Fax: 812 402-0096
Art Green, *President*
EMP: 8
SALES (est): 1.1MM **Privately Held**
SIC: 2448 Pallets, wood; pallets, wood & wood with metal

(G-3662)
PARADISE INK INC
619 N Burkhardt Rd Ste G (47715-7296)
PHONE.............................812 402-4465
Julia Hudson, *CEO*
EMP: 2
SALES (est): 278.7K **Privately Held**
SIC: 5084 3577 Printing trades machinery, equipment & supplies; computer peripheral equipment

(G-3663)
PARINGA RESOURCES LIMITED (PA)
6724 E Morgan Ave Ste B (47715-8228)
P.O. Box 449, Calhoun KY (42327-0449)
PHONE.............................314 422-4150
EMP: 3
SALES (est): 1.7MM **Privately Held**
SIC: 8742 1241 Business planning & organizing services; coal mining services

(G-3664)
PARSON ADHESIVES INC
2545 Eastside Park Rd (47715-2175)
PHONE.............................812 401-7277
Pete Shaw, *Owner*
EMP: 20
SALES (corp-wide): 8.3MM **Privately Held**
WEB: www.parsonadhesives.com
SIC: 2891 Adhesives
PA: Parson Adhesives Inc.
3345 W Auburn Rd Ste 107
Rochester Hills MI 48309
248 299-5585

(G-3665)
PAVEMENT COATINGS INC
Also Called: Star-Seal of Tennessee
2120 N Grand Ave (47711-3804)
PHONE.............................812 424-3400
Fax: 812 422-2100
Mark Collins, *President*
Monte Collins, *Vice Pres*
Michael W Collins, *Director*
EMP: 10 EST: 1981
SQ FT: 15,000
SALES (est): 2MM **Privately Held**
WEB: www.pavecoat.com
SIC: 2951 Coal tar paving materials (not from refineries)

(G-3666)
PEABODY BEAR RUN MINING LLC
7100 Eagle Crest Blvd (47715-8152)
PHONE.............................812 659-7126
Keith R Haley, *President*
Walter L Hawkins Jr, *Senior VP*
Bradley E Phillips, *Senior VP*
Darral G Heaton, *Vice Pres*
Kentland D Holcomb, *Vice Pres*
EMP: 574
SALES (est): 25.5MM
SALES (corp-wide): 5.1B **Publicly Held**
SIC: 1221 Bituminous coal & lignite-surface mining
PA: Peabody Energy Corporation
701 Market St
Saint Louis MO 63101
314 342-3400

(G-3667)
PGC MULCH LLC
Also Called: Pgc Landscaping & Mulch
1501 N 7th Ave (47710-2219)
PHONE.............................812 455-0700
Matt Dillon, *Mng Member*
EMP: 9
SALES (est): 500K **Privately Held**
SIC: 2499 7699 Mulch, wood & bark; industrial tool grinding
PA: Pro Grass Cutters, Llc
1119 N Fulton Ave
Evansville IN 47710

(G-3668)
PGP INTERNATIONAL INC
5404 Foundation Blvd (47725-9652)
PHONE.............................812 867-5129
EMP: 9
SALES (corp-wide): 19.7B **Privately Held**
SIC: 2099 Food preparations
HQ: Pgp International, Inc.
351 Hanson Way
Woodland CA 95776
530 662-5056

(G-3669)
PIA AUTOMATION US INC
Also Called: Preh Ima Atomtn Evansville Inc
5825 Old Boonville Hwy (47715-2136)
PHONE.............................812 474-3126
Fax: 812 474-3138
Randy Wire, *President*
Nicole Garrison, *CFO*
Todd Breult, *VP Sales*
EMP: 108 EST: 1963
SQ FT: 50,000
SALES: 24MM **Privately Held**
WEB: www.evana-online.com
SIC: 3535 8711 3549 Robotic conveyors; engineering services; metalworking machinery
HQ: Pia Automation Bad Neustadt Gmbh
Schweinfurter Str. 5-9
Bad Neustadt A.D.Saale 97616
977 192-647

(G-3670)
PILLAR INNOVATIONS LLC
9844 Hedden Rd (47725-8904)
PHONE.............................812 474-9080
Titus Beitzel,
EMP: 6
SALES (corp-wide): 166.3MM **Privately Held**
SIC: 3532 3569 7371 Mining machinery; sprinkler systems, fire: automatic; computer software development & applications
HQ: Pillar Innovations, Llc
92 Corporate Dr
Grantsville MD 21536

(G-3671)
PINCH OF SUGAR
519 N Green River Rd (47715-2472)
PHONE.............................812 476-7650
EMP: 8
SALES (est): 552.6K **Privately Held**
SIC: 2051 Mfg Bread/Related Products

(G-3672)
PIPECONX
701 N 9th Ave (47712-5343)
PHONE.............................800 443-9081
EMP: 8

SALES (est): 966.4K **Privately Held**
SIC: 3084 Mfg Plastic Pipe

(G-3673)
PITTSBURGH GLASS WORKS LLC
424 E Inglefield Rd (47725-9356)
PHONE.............................812 867-6601
Keith Holmes, *Plant Mgr*
James Heacock, *Production*
Donna Offerman, *Purch Mgr*
Barry Jones, *Buyer*
Eric Virgin, *Engineer*
EMP: 500 **Privately Held**
SIC: 3231 Strengthened or reinforced glass
HQ: Pittsburgh Glass Works, Llc
30 Isabella St Ste 500
Pittsburgh PA 15212

(G-3674)
PLASTIC EXTRUSIONS COMPANY
Also Called: Lattice Works
6500 Newburgh Rd (47715-4457)
PHONE.............................812 479-3232
Fax: 812 479-3241
John Michael Cohen, *Owner*
EMP: 3
SQ FT: 3,500
SALES (est): 100K **Privately Held**
SIC: 3089 Extruded finished plastic products

(G-3675)
PLIANT CORP INTERNATIONAL (PA)
101 Oakley St (47710-1237)
PHONE.............................812 424-2904
Jonathan D Rich, *Ch of Bd*
▼ EMP: 3
SALES (est): 1.9MM **Privately Held**
SIC: 3089 Plastic containers, except foam

(G-3676)
PLIANT INTERNATIONAL LLC
Also Called: Pliant Corp International
101 Oakley St (47710-1237)
PHONE.............................812 424-2904
EMP: 3 EST: 2012
SALES (est): 144.2K **Publicly Held**
SIC: 3089 Bottle caps, molded plastic
HQ: Berry Global, Inc.
101 Oakley St
Evansville IN 47710
812 424-2904

(G-3677)
PLIANT PACKAGING CANADA LLC
101 Oakley St (47710-1237)
PHONE.............................812 424-2904
EMP: 3
SALES (est): 230.9K
SALES (corp-wide): 6.4B **Publicly Held**
SIC: 3089 Mfg Plastic Products
HQ: Berry Global, Inc.
101 Oakley St
Evansville IN 47710
812 424-2904

(G-3678)
POLY-SEAL LLC
101 Oakley St (47710-1237)
P.O. Box 959 (47706-0959)
PHONE.............................812 306-2573
◆ EMP: 525 EST: 1969
SQ FT: 240,000
SALES (est): 117.1MM **Publicly Held**
WEB: www.poly-seal.com
SIC: 3089 Closures, plastic; caps, plastic
PA: Berry Global Group, Inc.
101 Oakley St
Evansville IN 47710

(G-3679)
POLYRAM COMPOUNDS LLC
15000 Foundation Ave (47725-7707)
PHONE.............................703 439-7945
Neta Etziony,
EMP: 2
SALES (est): 102K **Privately Held**
SIC: 3087 Custom compound purchased resins

(G-3680)
POWERS ENERGY AMERICA INC
1100 Erie Ave (47715-4858)
PHONE................................812 473-5500
Earl H Powers, *Principal*
EMP: 3 EST: 2008
SALES (est): 300K Privately Held
SIC: 3612 Power & distribution transformers

(G-3681)
PPG INDUSTRIES
424 E Inglefield Rd (47725-9358)
PHONE................................812 867-6601
Fax: 812 867-0474
Harry Nasab, *Principal*
EMP: 3
SALES (est): 275.1K Privately Held
SIC: 2851 Paints & allied products

(G-3682)
PPG INDUSTRIES INC
Also Called: PPG 4380
306 N 7th Ave (47710-1024)
PHONE................................812 424-4774
Chris Shade, *Branch Mgr*
EMP: 24
SALES (corp-wide): 14.2B Publicly Held
WEB: www.ppg.com
SIC: 2851 Paints & allied products
PA: Ppg Industries, Inc.
　　1 Ppg Pl
　　Pittsburgh PA 15272
　　412 434-3131

(G-3683)
PPG INDUSTRIES INC
Also Called: PPG 4382
2211 N Burkhardt Rd Ste D (47715-2194)
PHONE................................812 473-0339
Chris Shade, *Branch Mgr*
EMP: 24
SALES (corp-wide): 14.2B Publicly Held
WEB: www.ppg.com
SIC: 2851 Paints & allied products
PA: Ppg Industries, Inc.
　　1 Ppg Pl
　　Pittsburgh PA 15272
　　412 434-3131

(G-3684)
PREFERRED TANK & TOWER INC (PA)
5444 E Indiana St Pmb 374 (47715-2857)
PHONE................................270 826-7950
Karen Ferguson-Johnston, *President*
Herman Johnston, *Director*
EMP: 7
SQ FT: 7,500
SALES (est): 2MM Privately Held
WEB: www.preferredtower.com
SIC: 3441 Building components, structural steel

(G-3685)
PRIME SOURCE LLC
4609 E Boonv New Harmo Rd (47725)
PHONE................................812 867-8921
Joseph Exum Lewis, *Mng Member*
EMP: 4
SALES (est): 236.5K Privately Held
SIC: 2879 Insecticides & pesticides

(G-3686)
PROKUMA INCORPORATED
110 N Main St (47711-5449)
PHONE................................812 461-1681
Louis Meredith, *President*
Craig Weinzapfel, *Co-President*
EMP: 2
SQ FT: 5,000
SALES: 500K Privately Held
SIC: 3441 Fabricated structural metal

(G-3687)
PROLAM PRODUCTS INC
Also Called: Table Logix
10245 Hedden Rd (47725-8922)
PHONE................................812 867-1662
Fax: 812 867-1665
Thomas D Ancona Jr, *President*
Lori Maihle, *COO*
Mark Plummer, *Vice Pres*
Gary Zimmerman, *Vice Pres*

Darrell Dale, *VP Opers*
EMP: 58
SQ FT: 40,000
SALES: 3.3MM Privately Held
WEB: www.prolamproducts.com
SIC: 2541 7336 2511 2514 Table or counter tops, plastic laminated; graphic arts & related design; dining room furniture: wood; metal kitchen & dining room furniture

(G-3688)
PSC INDUSTRIES INC
Also Called: P S C Fabricating
900 E Virginia St (47711-5645)
PHONE................................812 425-9071
Fax: 812 425-1164
Susanna Durham, *Director*
EMP: 49
SQ FT: 180,000
SALES (corp-wide): 2.2B Privately Held
WEB: www.olsenmedical.com
SIC: 5113 3086 2671 2631 Shipping supplies; plastics foam products; packaging paper & plastics film, coated & laminated; paperboard mills
HQ: Psc Industries, Inc.
　　1100 W Market St
　　Louisville KY 40203
　　502 625-7700

(G-3689)
PSI REPAIR SERVICES INC
5825 Old Boonville Hwy (47715-2136)
PHONE................................812 485-5575
Scott Beasley, *Engineer*
EMP: 2
SALES (est): 106K Privately Held
SIC: 3559 Special industry machinery

(G-3690)
PURINA ANIMAL NUTRITION LLC
2124 Lynch Rd (47711-2947)
PHONE................................812 424-5501
Calvin Scott, *Manager*
EMP: 35
SALES (corp-wide): 12.8B Privately Held
SIC: 2048 Prepared feeds
HQ: Purina Animal Nutrition Llc
　　1080 County Road F W
　　Shoreview MN 55126

(G-3691)
PURINA MILLS LLC
2124 Lynch Rd (47711-2911)
PHONE................................812 424-5501
Fax: 812 424-0746
Calvin Scott, *Manager*
EMP: 12
SQ FT: 20,000
SALES (corp-wide): 12.8B Privately Held
WEB: www.purina-mills.com
SIC: 2048 Stock feeds, dry; poultry feeds; feed supplements
HQ: Purina Mills, Llc
　　555 Maryvle Univ Dr 200
　　Saint Louis MO 63141

(G-3692)
QUICK WELL SERVICE INC
4209 Highway 41 N (47711-2889)
PHONE................................812 426-1924
Gary S Nickolick, *President*
Joe J Nickolick, *Admin Sec*
EMP: 4
SALES (est): 303.6K Privately Held
SIC: 1389 Servicing oil & gas wells

(G-3693)
R & B ASSOCIATES INC
Also Called: Tri-State Trailer and Truck
5920 Oak Grove Rd (47715-2357)
P.O. Box 2541 (47728-0541)
PHONE................................812 471-1550
Fax: 812 471-1868
Daryl Rauscher, *President*
Tanya Rausher, *Vice Pres*
Eric Rauscher, *Admin Sec*
EMP: 5
SQ FT: 400
SALES (est): 1.1MM Privately Held
WEB: www.tstt.com
SIC: 5521 3713 Trucks, tractors & trailers: used; truck bodies & parts

(G-3694)
RAJO GUNS CORP
2106 W Franklin St (47712-5115)
PHONE................................812 422-6945
Stan Diekmann, *President*
EMP: 4 EST: 1953
SQ FT: 5,000
SALES (est): 250K Privately Held
SIC: 3484 5941 Guns (firearms) or gun parts, 30 mm. & below; sporting goods & bicycle shops

(G-3695)
RANDALL CORP
Also Called: Risley's Art Gallery
1105 E Virginia St (47711-5724)
P.O. Box 23264 (47724-1264)
PHONE................................812 425-7122
Fax: 812 421-5656
Randy Chapman, *President*
EMP: 2
SALES (est): 242.4K Privately Held
SIC: 2752 7699 7334 5999 Commercial printing, offset; picture framing, custom; photocopying & duplicating services; art dealers

(G-3696)
RASURE PRINTS
3960 Wood Castle Rd (47711-2776)
PHONE................................812 454-6222
Adena Rasure, *Principal*
EMP: 2
SALES (est): 87.9K Privately Held
SIC: 2752 Commercial printing, lithographic

(G-3697)
RED SPOT PAINT & VARNISH CO (HQ)
1107 E Louisiana St (47711-4747)
P.O. Box 418 (47703-0418)
PHONE................................812 428-9100
Fax: 812 467-2397
Akiro Takedk, *President*
Jeffrey M Scheu, *Vice Pres*
David White, *Vice Pres*
▲ EMP: 350
SQ FT: 200,000
SALES (est): 176.6MM
SALES (corp-wide): 539MM Privately Held
WEB: www.redspot.com
SIC: 2851 Plastics base paints & varnishes
PA: Fujikura Kasei Co., Ltd.
　　2-6-15, Shibakoen
　　Minato-Ku TKY 105-0
　　334 361-101

(G-3698)
RED SPOT PAINT & VARNISH CO
Also Called: A & D Building
1111 E Louisiana St (47711-4747)
PHONE................................812 428-9100
John Phillips, *Manager*
EMP: 50
SALES (corp-wide): 539MM Privately Held
WEB: www.redspot.com
SIC: 2851 Plastics base paints & varnishes
HQ: Red Spot Paint & Varnish Co Inc
　　1107 E Louisiana St
　　Evansville IN 47711
　　812 428-9100

(G-3699)
RED SPOT PAINT & VARNISH CO
1016 E Columbia St (47711-5100)
PHONE................................812 428-9100
Fax: 812 428-0536
Reese Hamilton, *Opers Mgr*
EMP: 400
SALES (corp-wide): 539MM Privately Held
WEB: www.redspot.com
SIC: 2851 3547 Paints & paint additives; painting, coating & hot dipping
HQ: Red Spot Paint & Varnish Co Inc
　　1107 E Louisiana St
　　Evansville IN 47711
　　812 428-9100

(G-3700)
REDSPOT PAINT AND VARNISH CO
1107 E La St (47711)
P.O. Box 418 (47703-0418)
PHONE................................812 428-9100
Fax: 812 428-9167
Akiro Takeda, *CEO*
EMP: 200
SALES (est): 41.5MM Privately Held
SIC: 2851 Paints & allied products

(G-3701)
REFRIGERATION PACKAGE CORP
Also Called: Repaco
11425 N Green River Rd (47725-9728)
PHONE................................812 867-0900
Fax: 812 867-0800
Daniel Myers, *President*
EMP: 6
SQ FT: 5,400
SALES (est): 580K Privately Held
WEB: www.repaco.com
SIC: 3585 Refrigeration equipment, complete; condensers, refrigeration

(G-3702)
REGENCY PAD CORP
2625 Kotter Ave (47715-8508)
PHONE................................731 587-9596
Kenneth Lieblein, *President*
EMP: 56
SQ FT: 50,000
SALES (est): 2.6MM Privately Held
SIC: 2392 Mattress pads

(G-3703)
REISING SON ORIGINALS
5120 Middle Mt Vernon Rd (47712-3710)
PHONE................................812 437-1831
Sean Reising, *Principal*
EMP: 2
SALES (est): 203K Privately Held
SIC: 2499 Decorative wood & woodwork

(G-3704)
REPLAS OF TEXAS INC
15000 Highway 41 N (47725-9360)
PHONE................................812 421-3600
Fax: 812 421-3610
Joe Dalley, *Manager*
EMP: 4
SALES (est): 397.8K Privately Held
SIC: 2821 Molding compounds, plastics

(G-3705)
RESIDUE WEST INC
Also Called: Residue Regency Pad
2625 Kotter Ave (47715-8508)
PHONE................................731 587-9596
Dan Chadwick, *General Mgr*
EMP: 32
SALES (corp-wide): 6.9MM Privately Held
SIC: 3086 Padding, foamed plastic
PA: Residue West Inc.
　　4 Anchor Way
　　Port Washington NY 11050
　　516 883-8294

(G-3706)
RIX PRODUCTS INC
3747 Hogue Rd (47712-6431)
PHONE................................812 426-1749
Rick A Rideout, *President*
EMP: 6
SQ FT: 5,400
SALES: 500K Privately Held
SIC: 3089 3944 Injection molding of plastics; railroad models: toy & hobby

(G-3707)
ROBINSON ENGINEERING & OIL CO (PA)
1410 N Cullen Ave (47715-2331)
P.O. Box 5269 (47716-5269)
PHONE................................812 477-1575
Charles A Robinson, *President*
J Glenn Robinson, *President*
Charles H Robinson, *Vice Pres*
EMP: 10
SQ FT: 2,500

SALES (est): 1.9MM **Privately Held**
WEB: www.earthcadconsulting.com
SIC: 1311 8711 Crude petroleum production; petroleum engineering

(G-3708)
ROLLS-ROYCE CORPORATION
225 W Morgan Ave Ste A (47710-2515)
PHONE.................................812 421-7810
Michael Lampert, *President*
EMP: 66
SALES (corp-wide): 21.5B **Privately Held**
SIC: 3724 3728 Aircraft engines & engine parts; aircraft parts & equipment
HQ: Rolls-Royce Corporation
450 S Meridian St
Indianapolis IN 46225

(G-3709)
ROPPEL INDUSTRIES INC
920 Keck Ave (47711-3842)
PHONE.................................812 425-0267
EMP: 2
SALES (est): 87.2K **Privately Held**
SIC: 3714 Cleaners, air, motor vehicle

(G-3710)
ROYAL CROWN BOTTLING CORP (HQ)
Also Called: RC Cola
1100 Independence Ave (47714-4549)
P.O. Box 2870 (47728-0870)
PHONE.................................812 424-7978
Fax: 812 421-3038
Nancy King Hodge, *President*
Gail L King, *Corp Secy*
Chad Metten, *Vice Pres*
Danny Hill, *Plant Mgr*
David Palmer, *CIO*
EMP: 125 **EST:** 1938
SQ FT: 115,000
SALES (est): 100.3MM **Publicly Held**
SIC: 2086 Soft drinks: packaged in cans, bottles, etc.

(G-3711)
ROYAL INC
Also Called: Royal Feeds
1210 N Fulton Ave (47710-2359)
PHONE.................................812 424-4925
Mike Goodwin, *General Mgr*
EMP: 10 **Privately Held**
SIC: 2085 7841 Distilled & blended liquors; video tape rental
PA: Royal Inc
1212 W Florida St
Evansville IN 47710

(G-3712)
RUTKOWSKI & ASSOCIATES INC
Also Called: Health Employment Law Update
206 Charmwood Ct (47715-3316)
PHONE.................................812 476-4520
Aurthur Rutkowski, *President*
Barbara Rutkowski, *Vice Pres*
EMP: 3
SALES (est): 160K **Privately Held**
SIC: 2741 Miscellaneous publishing

(G-3713)
RYAN OIL CO LLC
123 Nw 4th St Ste 2 (47708-1719)
P.O. Box 507 (47703-0507)
PHONE.................................812 422-4168
Fax: 812 434-6866
Rae Jean Ryan,
William Ryan Hurst,
Kelly Ryan,
EMP: 3 **EST:** 1942
SQ FT: 1,700
SALES (est): 311.9K **Privately Held**
SIC: 1311 Crude petroleum production

(G-3714)
SATER ENTERPRISES
5401 Vogel Rd Ste 430 (47715-7837)
P.O. Box 2509 (47728-0509)
PHONE.................................812 477-1529
Ronald E Sater, *Partner*
Alvrone Sater, *Partner*
EMP: 6
SQ FT: 6,250
SALES (est): 514.9K **Privately Held**
SIC: 1311 6799 Crude petroleum production; investors

(G-3715)
SCHAFFSTEINS TRUCK CLEAN LLC
Also Called: Tc Graphics
601 N 9th Ave (47712-5342)
P.O. Box 6256 (47719-0256)
PHONE.................................812 464-2424
Fax: 812 423-4637
Alan Schaffstein, *President*
Thomas Schaffstein, *President*
Carol Schaffstein, *Admin Sec*
EMP: 15
SQ FT: 20,000
SALES (est): 679.2K **Privately Held**
SIC: 7542 7532 3471 7336 Truck wash; truck painting & lettering; sand blasting of metal parts; commercial art & graphic design

(G-3716)
SCHULMAN
1700 Lynch Rd (47711-2848)
PHONE.................................812 253-5238
EMP: 3
SALES (est): 338.9K **Privately Held**
SIC: 2821 Plastics materials & resins

(G-3717)
SCHUTTE LITHOGRAPHY INC
2716 Kotter Ave (47715-8513)
PHONE.................................812 469-3500
Fax: 812 469-3510
Gary Schutte, *President*
Doris Schutte, *Treasurer*
Christine Schutte, *Sales Staff*
Clarence Nulton, *Manager*
EMP: 30 **EST:** 1977
SQ FT: 22,500
SALES (est): 4.5MM **Privately Held**
SIC: 2752 2789 2759 Color lithography; bookbinding & related work; commercial printing

(G-3718)
SCOTT PRINTING LLC
8823 Old State Rd (47711-6926)
PHONE.................................812 306-7477
Ryan Michael Scott, *President*
EMP: 2
SALES (est): 92.3K **Privately Held**
SIC: 2752 Commercial printing, lithographic

(G-3719)
SEAL CORP USA
1175 E Diamond Ave (47711-3903)
PHONE.................................812 430-8441
Ken Rust, *Principal*
EMP: 6 **EST:** 2013
SALES (est): 572.7K **Privately Held**
SIC: 3953 Embossing seals, corporate & official

(G-3720)
SEALCORPUSA INC
1175 E Diamond Ave (47711-3903)
PHONE.................................866 868-0791
Fax: 812 868-0789
Ken Rust, *Ch of Bd*
Kenneth Rust, *President*
Tim Robards, *Vice Pres*
Barbara Rust, *Vice Pres*
EMP: 32
SQ FT: 35,000
SALES (est): 7MM **Privately Held**
SIC: 2891 8732 Adhesives & sealants; commercial nonphysical research

(G-3721)
SEIB MACHINE & TOOL CO INC
Also Called: Seibs Welding
14314 Bender Rd (47720-7213)
PHONE.................................812 453-6174
George Seib, *President*
EMP: 4
SQ FT: 4,800
SALES: 150K **Privately Held**
SIC: 3699 7692 1761 Teaching machines & aids, electronic; welding repair; sheet metalwork

(G-3722)
SEPARATION BY DESIGN INC
1601 Buchanan Rd (47720-5411)
PHONE.................................812 424-1239

Roy W Jorgensen, *President*
Lee K Jorgensen, *Vice Pres*
Amanda Duggins, *Controller*
John Jarvis, *Manager*
Isaiah Becher, *Technical Staff*
EMP: 6
SQ FT: 17,000
SALES (est): 1.7MM **Privately Held**
SIC: 3586 3569 Measuring & dispensing pumps; gas separators (machinery)

(G-3723)
SERMERSHIEMS FIBERGLASS INC
3817 N Saint Joseph Ave (47720-1201)
PHONE.................................812 424-4701
Fax: 812 428-3584
James Sermersheim, *President*
Carolyn Sermersheim, *Corp Secy*
EMP: 9
SALES (est): 640K **Privately Held**
SIC: 3465 Automotive stampings

(G-3724)
SETCO LLC (DH)
101 Oakley St (47710-1237)
PHONE.................................812 424-2904
Richard Hofmann,
Donald E Parodi,
◆ **EMP:** 450 **EST:** 2003
SQ FT: 288,000
SALES (est): 92.6MM **Publicly Held**
WEB: www.setcobottle.com
SIC: 3085 8711 3544 Plastics bottles; engineering services; special dies, tools, jigs & fixtures
HQ: Berry Global, Inc.
101 Oakley St
Evansville IN 47710
812 424-2904

(G-3725)
SEXTON PLYWOOD & VENEER CO
227 Rosemarie Ct (47715-7425)
PHONE.................................812 454-0488
Caroline Sexton, *Owner*
EMP: 2
SALES (est): 950K **Privately Held**
SIC: 2435 Hardwood veneer & plywood

(G-3726)
SHIRT SHACK
12593 Apache Pass (47720-7502)
PHONE.................................812 550-0158
Michael Knapp, *Principal*
EMP: 2
SALES (est): 111.6K **Privately Held**
SIC: 2759 Screen printing

(G-3727)
SIGN A RAMA
Also Called: Sign-A-Rama
1300 N Royal Ave (47715-7808)
PHONE.................................812 477-7763
Walter Valiant, *Owner*
Matthew Effinger, *Consultant*
EMP: 2
SALES (est): 202.7K **Privately Held**
WEB: www.ameristamp.com
SIC: 3993 3953 Signs & advertising specialties; marking devices

(G-3728)
SIGN CRAFTERS INC (PA)
1508 Stringtown Rd (47711-4593)
P.O. Box 4266 (47724-0266)
PHONE.................................812 424-9011
Fax: 812 428-4973
Bill G Dugan, *President*
Morgan Jones, *Accounts Exec*
EMP: 38
SQ FT: 49,000
SALES (est): 5.7MM **Privately Held**
WEB: www.interior-signs.com
SIC: 3993 Electric signs; neon signs

(G-3729)
SIGN GRAPHICS EVANSVILLE INC
6020 Feitman Dr (47711-1808)
PHONE.................................812 476-9151
Fax: 812 479-5147
Dana Dubuque, *President*
EMP: 6 **EST:** 1973

SQ FT: 4,000
SALES (est): 817.2K **Privately Held**
SIC: 3993 Signs, not made in custom sign painting shops

(G-3730)
SIGNS MAGIC LLC
Also Called: Signs Now
716 N Weinbach Ave (47711-5966)
PHONE.................................812 473-5155
Mark Daily,
EMP: 4
SQ FT: 5,000
SALES: 500K **Privately Held**
SIC: 3993 Signs & advertising specialties

(G-3731)
SILGAN WHITE CAP CORPORATION
2201 W Maryland St (47712-5394)
PHONE.................................812 425-6222
Joan Miller, *Production*
John Bugnitz, *Branch Mgr*
EMP: 250
SALES (corp-wide): 4B **Publicly Held**
WEB: www.silganclosures.com
SIC: 3411 Metal cans
HQ: Silgan White Cap Corporation
4 Landmark Sq Ste 400
Stamford CT 06901

(G-3732)
SINGER OPTICAL COMPANY INC
1401 N Royal Ave (47715-7827)
P.O. Box 3557 (47734-3557)
PHONE.................................812 423-1179
Fax: 812 423-1170
Roger Singer, *President*
Martin E Singer, *Vice Pres*
Scott Brown, *Sales Executive*
Lori Moore, *Manager*
EMP: 16 **EST:** 1948
SQ FT: 15,320
SALES (est): 2.5MM **Privately Held**
WEB: www.singeroptical.com
SIC: 3851 5048 Ophthalmic goods; ophthalmic goods

(G-3733)
SISCO CORPORATION
Also Called: Sisco Box
1231 E Michigan St (47711-5720)
PHONE.................................812 422-2090
Fax: 812 422-2140
Larry Zeitler, *General Mgr*
EMP: 60
SALES (est): 6.1MM
SALES (corp-wide): 11.8MM **Privately Held**
WEB: www.siscobox.com
SIC: 2653 Boxes, corrugated: made from purchased materials
PA: Sisco Corporation
1520 S Mill St
Nashville IL 62263
618 327-3066

(G-3734)
SLEEPMADECOM LLC
2625 Kotter Ave (47715-8508)
PHONE.................................662 350-0999
Matthew Fowler,
EMP: 20
SALES (corp-wide): 2MM **Privately Held**
SIC: 2515 Mattresses & bedsprings
PA: Sleepmade.Com, Llc
179 Tradewinds Dr
Columbus MS 39705
662 386-2222

(G-3735)
SMITH & BUTTERFIELD CO INC (DH)
2800 Lynch Rd Ste D (47711-2928)
P.O. Box 3446 (47733-3446)
PHONE.................................812 422-3261
Fax: 812 429-0532
J Mac Aldridge, *Ch of Bd*
James D Butterfield, *President*
Janie Wessel, *Office Mgr*
Steve Barnes, *Manager*
Teri Grant, *Technology*
EMP: 16 **EST:** 1866
SQ FT: 50,000

SALES (est): 4.5MM **Publicly Held**
WEB: www.smithfield.com
SIC: **5021** 5112 2752 5943 Office furniture; stationery & office supplies; commercial printing, lithographic; office forms & supplies
HQ: Stationers, Inc.
100 Industrial Ln
Huntington WV 25702
304 528-2780

(G-3736)
SMITH & BUTTERFIELD CO INC
Also Called: Ips
2800 Lynch Rd Ste 2 (47711-2913)
P.O. Box 3446 (47733-3446)
PHONE..............................812 422-3261
Jim Butterfield, *President*
EMP: 28
SQ FT: 1,760
SALES (est): 1.9MM **Publicly Held**
WEB: www.smithbutterfield.com
SIC: **5112** 2752 Stationery & office supplies; business forms; commercial printing, lithographic
HQ: Smith & Butterfield Co., Inc.
2800 Lynch Rd Ste D
Evansville IN 47711
812 422-3261

(G-3737)
SMITH RUTH C RN PROF ELECTRLG
715 N 1st Ave Ste 20 (47710-1671)
PHONE..............................812 423-4760
Ruth C Smith, *President*
Nelly Sampson, *Admin Sec*
EMP: 2
SALES (est): 150.2K **Privately Held**
SIC: **3678** Electronic connectors

(G-3738)
SMITHFIELD DIRECT LLC
8426 Baumgart Rd (47725-1516)
PHONE..............................812 867-6644
Fax: 812 867-6673
Andrew Kase, *Branch Mgr*
EMP: 4 **Privately Held**
SIC: **2011** Meat packing plants
HQ: Smithfield Direct, Llc
4225 Naperville Rd # 600
Lisle IL 60532

(G-3739)
SNAPPLE BEVERAGE CORP
1100 Independence Ave (47714-4549)
PHONE..............................812 424-7978
Rick Morse, *Principal*
EMP: 3
SALES (est): 75.4K **Privately Held**
SIC: **2086** Bottled & canned soft drinks

(G-3740)
SOUTHWEST GRAFIX AND AP INC
2229 W Franklin St (47712-5116)
PHONE..............................812 425-5104
Fax: 812 425-5104
Mark Weidner, *President*
Roseann Weidner, *Corp Secy*
EMP: 12
SQ FT: 6,900
SALES (est): 1.6MM **Privately Held**
WEB: www.southwestgrafix.com
SIC: **2759** Screen printing

(G-3741)
SPARKLING CLEAN INC
Also Called: Dallas Towing Service
1018 Bayse St (47714-4129)
PHONE..............................812 422-4871
Fax: 812 428-5461
Jim Ray, *Manager*
EMP: 4
SALES (est): 348.1K **Privately Held**
WEB: www.dallastowingservice.com
SIC: **7549** 5012 3711 Towing service, automotive; commercial vehicles; wreckers (tow truck), assembly of

(G-3742)
SPECIALTY COATINGS LLC
702 Fairway Dr Apt A (47710-5157)
PHONE..............................812 431-3375
Scot William Grossman, *Principal*
EMP: 2

SALES (est): 81.5K **Privately Held**
SIC: **3479** Metal coating & allied service

(G-3743)
SPECIALTY PROCESS EQP CTRL INC
333 Plaza East Blvd Ste G (47715-2860)
P.O. Box 15395 (47716-0395)
PHONE..............................812 473-8528
EMP: 2
SQ FT: 1,000
SALES (est): 130K **Privately Held**
SIC: **7389** 3441 Design And Fabricate Equipment For Control Panels Conveyers And Process Merchandise

(G-3744)
SPECIALTY TOOLING INC
2391 Lexington Rd (47720-1237)
PHONE..............................812 464-8521
Fax: 812 468-4176
Gregory Johann, *President*
Brenda Johann, *Treasurer*
Matthew Lovell, *Sales Mgr*
EMP: 10
SQ FT: 6,400
SALES (est): 1.8MM **Privately Held**
SIC: **3544** 8711 Special dies & tools; dies & die holders for metal cutting, forming, die casting; mechanical engineering

(G-3745)
SRG GLOBAL TRIM INC (DH)
Also Called: Srg Global Evansville
601 N Congress Ave (47715-2448)
PHONE..............................812 473-6200
Kevin Baird, *President*
Doug Girdler, *Treasurer*
Adam Stevens, *Human Res Mgr*
Eva Agee, *Manager*
Gregory J Mulawa, *Director*
▲ EMP: 510 EST: 1964
SQ FT: 400,000
SALES (est): 159.5MM
SALES (corp-wide): 44.4B **Privately Held**
SIC: **3089** Injection molded finished plastic products

(G-3746)
SS&C TECHNOLOGIES INC
110 N Fulton Ave (47710-1036)
PHONE..............................812 266-2000
EMP: 6
SALES (corp-wide): 1.6B **Publicly Held**
SIC: **7372** Prepackaged software
HQ: Ss&C Technologies, Inc.
80 Lamberton Rd
Windsor CT 06095
860 298-4500

(G-3747)
STAR AUTOMATION INC
5625 Vogel Rd Ste B (47715-7828)
PHONE..............................812 475-9947
Tom Kobayashi, *Manager*
EMP: 2
SALES (corp-wide): 98.5MM **Privately Held**
WEB: www.starautomation.com
SIC: **3569** Robots, assembly line: industrial & commercial
HQ: Star Automation, Inc.
N90w14401 Commerce Dr
Menomonee Falls WI 53051

(G-3748)
STEPHEN LIBS CANDY CO INC
Also Called: Stephen Libs Finer Chocolate
6225 Vogel Rd (47715-4033)
PHONE..............................812 473-0048
Fax: 812 473-2086
Stephen R Libs, *President*
Marjorie Libs, *Treasurer*
EMP: 10
SALES (est): 1.1MM **Privately Held**
SIC: **2064** 5441 2068 2066 Candy & other confectionery products; candy; salted & roasted nuts & seeds; chocolate & cocoa products

(G-3749)
STERLING BERRY CORPORATION
101 Oakley St (47710-1237)
PHONE..............................812 424-2904
Martin R Imbler, *President*

Randy Becker, *President*
George Willbrandt, *Vice Pres*
▼ EMP: 8
SALES (est): 637.6K **Publicly Held**
SIC: **3089** Cups, plastic, except foam; molding primary plastic
HQ: Berry Global, Inc.
101 Oakley St
Evansville IN 47710
812 424-2904

(G-3750)
STERLING BOILER AND MECH LLC (PA)
1420 Kimber Ln (47715-4025)
P.O. Box 8004 (47716-8004)
PHONE..............................812 479-5447
Daniel G Felker, *President*
Butch Bradley, *Vice Pres*
Kenneth E Wahl, *Finance Dir*
Brandon Elliott, *Manager*
Kelley Moschner, *Manager*
EMP: 800
SQ FT: 8,000
SALES (est): 158.5MM **Privately Held**
WEB: www.sterlingboiler.com
SIC: **1711** 3443 Mechanical contractor; fabricated plate work (boiler shop)

(G-3751)
STERNBERG INC
Also Called: Sternberg International Isuzu
8950 N Kentucky Ave (47725-1392)
P.O. Box 690, Jasper (47547-0690)
PHONE..............................812 867-0077
Fax: 812 867-7423
Derek Strumberg, *General Mgr*
Tyler Howell, *Foreman/Supr*
Lori Choate, *Parts Mgr*
Nancy Wright, *Human Res Mgr*
EMP: 30
SALES (corp-wide): 71.8MM **Privately Held**
SIC: **5511** 3715 Automobiles, new & used; truck trailers
PA: Sternberg, Inc.
1781 S Us Highway 231
Jasper IN 47546
812 482-5125

(G-3752)
STONE COAL SERVICES LLC
2200 E Boonvle Nw Harmony (47725-8204)
PHONE..............................812 455-8215
Dennis R Wilzbacher, *President*
EMP: 4 EST: 2010
SALES (est): 182K **Privately Held**
SIC: **1241** Coal mining services

(G-3753)
STORM GRAPHICS INC
4707 Bayard Park Dr (47714-0604)
PHONE..............................812 402-5202
Eennis Schwindel, *President*
EMP: 4
SALES (est): 443.2K **Privately Held**
SIC: **7336** 7331 2759 Graphic arts & related design; direct mail advertising services; commercial printing

(G-3754)
SUPERIOR MATTRESS INC
213 W Division St Ste C (47710-1368)
PHONE..............................812 422-5761
Steven Pike, *President*
Alice Ling, *Treasurer*
Kimberly Pike, *Admin Sec*
EMP: 5
SQ FT: 30,000
SALES (est): 347.6K **Privately Held**
SIC: **2515** 5021 Mattresses & bedsprings; beds & bedding

(G-3755)
SWEET LLC
4523 Erinwood Ct (47725-7555)
PHONE..............................812 455-0886
Shani Wiggins, *Executive*
EMP: 4 EST: 2008
SALES (est): 183.6K **Privately Held**
SIC: **2051** Cakes, bakery: except frozen

(G-3756)
SYCAMORE ENTERPRISES INC
Also Called: Asbury Hall
6534 Toney Ln (47715-1772)
P.O. Box 8062 (47716-8062)
PHONE..............................812 491-0901
Fax: 812 476-7683
James R Egen, *President*
Deborah K Egen, *Vice Pres*
Don Bowen, *Treasurer*
EMP: 7
SQ FT: 17,000
SALES (est): 1.1MM **Privately Held**
WEB: www.internest.com
SIC: **5199** 2323 2339 2396 General merchandise, non-durable; men's & boys' neckties & bow ties; neckwear & ties: women's, misses' & juniors'; screen printing on fabric articles

(G-3757)
T S F CO INC
Also Called: Tri State Flasher Co
2930 Saint Philip Rd S (47712-9519)
PHONE..............................812 985-2630
Fax: 812 985-3671
Eugene Barnhart, *President*
Jeanette H Barnhart, *Corp Secy*
Bob Schenk, *Vice Pres*
Mathew Schenk, *Vice Pres*
Patricia Schenk, *Vice Pres*
▼ EMP: 25
SQ FT: 6,000
SALES (est): 4.7MM **Privately Held**
WEB: www.tsfco.com
SIC: **3431** 7359 Portable chemical toilets, metal; equipment rental & leasing; work zone traffic equipment (flags, cones, barrels, etc.); portable toilet rental

(G-3758)
TESTIMONY PUBLICATIONS LLC
901 Jobes Ln (47712-4229)
PHONE..............................812 602-3031
Ralph Michael Kough, *Owner*
EMP: 2
SALES (est): 50K **Privately Held**
SIC: **2741** Miscellaneous publishing

(G-3759)
THERMOSEAL CO ED MUNOZ INC
800 E Oregon St (47711-5112)
P.O. Box 2493 (47728-0493)
PHONE..............................812 428-3343
Fax: 812 428-3343
Ed Munoz, *President*
EMP: 5
SQ FT: 7,180
SALES (est): 770K **Privately Held**
SIC: **2952** Asphalt felts & coatings

(G-3760)
THOMAS E SLADE INC
Also Called: AlphaGraphics
6220 Vogel Rd (47715-4014)
PHONE..............................812 471-7100
Fax: 812 471-1895
Lisa Slade, *President*
Hunter Slade, *General Mgr*
Emily Manzo, *Vice Pres*
Thomas E Slade, *Vice Pres*
Shane Newbanks, *Sales Staff*
EMP: 16
SQ FT: 5,000
SALES (est): 2.8MM **Privately Held**
SIC: **7334** 2759 7336 2791 Photocopying & duplicating services; commercial printing; commercial art & graphic design; typesetting; bookbinding & related work; commercial printing, lithographic

(G-3761)
THRIFY NICKEL WNT ADS EVANSVIL
999 N Congress Ave (47715-2469)
P.O. Box 2431 (47728-0431)
PHONE..............................812 428-8484
Fax: 812 428-4882
James Hall, *President*
Ronald Dukes, *Vice Pres*
EMP: 23
SALES (est): 1.4MM **Privately Held**
SIC: **2741** 2711 Miscellaneous publishing; newspapers

▲ = Import ▼=Export
◆ =Import/Export

(G-3762)
THRUST INDUSTRIES INC
10334 Hedden Rd (47725-8923)
PHONE..................................812 437-3643
Jim Stuteville, *President*
Tracy Stuteville, *Admin Sec*
EMP: 10
SQ FT: 12,000
SALES: 5MM **Privately Held**
WEB: www.thrustin.com
SIC: 3089 3083 Casting of plastic; laminated plastics plate & sheet

(G-3763)
THYME IN KITCHEN LLC
2308 W Franklin St Ste A (47712-5161)
PHONE..................................812 624-0344
Marcia C Jochem, *Principal*
EMP: 3
SALES (est): 170K **Privately Held**
SIC: 2099 Food preparations

(G-3764)
TINT UNLIMITED
204 N 9th Ave Ste C (47712-5173)
PHONE..................................812 402-6102
Melissa Ruffert, *Owner*
EMP: 2
SALES (est): 174.1K **Privately Held**
SIC: 3211 Window glass, clear & colored

(G-3765)
TJS ROASTER
11835 Old Highway 66 (47712-8629)
PHONE..................................812 985-9615
Terry Vanbibber, *Principal*
EMP: 3
SALES (est): 242.6K **Privately Held**
SIC: 2095 Roasted coffee

(G-3766)
TK SALES AND MARKETING LLC
2301 Mount Auburn Rd (47720-5443)
P.O. Box 6805 (47719-0805)
PHONE..................................812 430-5103
Thomas Diehl, *Mng Member*
Kathleen Godeke Diehl,
EMP: 2
SALES (est): 158.1K **Privately Held**
SIC: 3537 Dollies (hand or power trucks), industrial except mining

(G-3767)
TORSION PLASTICS LLC
5400 Foundation Blvd (47725-9652)
P.O. Box 2238, Stow OH (44224-1000)
PHONE..................................330 552-2184
Marc Calcaterra,
EMP: 11
SQ FT: 15,000
SALES (est): 1.7MM **Privately Held**
SIC: 3354 Aluminum extruded products

(G-3768)
TRANE US INC
1024 E Sycamore St (47714-1011)
PHONE..................................812 421-8725
Fax: 812 421-8735
Brett Palmer, *Manager*
EMP: 62 **Privately Held**
SIC: 3585 Refrigeration & heating equipment
HQ: Trane U.S. Inc.
3600 Pammel Creek Rd
La Crosse WI 54601
608 787-2000

(G-3769)
TRANSPORTATION TECH INDS (DH)
7140 Office Cir (47715-8235)
PHONE..................................812 962-5000
Terrence Keating, *President*
Anthony A Donatelli, *Senior VP*
Kenneth M Tallering, *Vice Pres*
▲ EMP: 10
SQ FT: 10,000

SALES (est): 353.7MM
SALES (corp-wide): 685.5MM **Privately Held**
SIC: 2531 3714 3321 4741 Vehicle furniture; motor vehicle wheels & parts; motor vehicle brake systems & parts; brake drums, motor vehicle; ductile iron castings; rental of railroad cars; electroplating of metals or formed products
HQ: Accuride Corporation
7140 Office Cir
Evansville IN 47715
812 962-5000

(G-3770)
TRI STATE CYLINDER HEAD
1712 Read St (47710-2798)
P.O. Box 4008 (47724-0008)
PHONE..................................812 421-0095
Fax: 812 421-0630
Ronald Schmidtt, *President*
▲ EMP: 30
SQ FT: 10,000
SALES (est): 5.5MM **Privately Held**
SIC: 3714 Cylinder heads, motor vehicle; rebuilding engines & transmissions, factory basis; motor vehicle engines & parts

(G-3771)
TRI STATE POWDER COATING LLC
800 Bayse St (47713-2902)
PHONE..................................812 425-7010
Billy G Tibbs, *Administration*
EMP: 4
SALES (est): 450K **Privately Held**
SIC: 3479 Metal coating & allied service

(G-3772)
TRI STATE VALVE INSTRUMENT CO
1200 N Willow Rd Ste 103 (47711-4784)
PHONE..................................812 434-0141
Chrystal Dupont, *Purchasing*
Brian Price, *Manager*
EMP: 2
SALES (est): 161.8K **Privately Held**
SIC: 3592 Valves

(G-3773)
TRI-STATE HOMES AND GARAGES
7703 Baumgart Rd (47725-1501)
PHONE..................................812 867-2411
Billy L Hobgood, *President*
Darrell Hobgood, *Admin Sec*
EMP: 5
SQ FT: 39,400
SALES (est): 600.5K **Privately Held**
SIC: 2452 Prefabricated buildings, wood

(G-3774)
TRI-STATE MACHINE CO INC
2410 N Burkhardt Rd (47715-2154)
PHONE..................................812 479-3159
Fax: 812 479-3150
Chris Scales, *President*
EMP: 10 EST: 1956
SQ FT: 10,000
SALES (est): 1.1MM **Privately Held**
SIC: 3599 7692 Machine shop, jobbing & repair; welding repair

(G-3775)
TRIPLET TOOL AND DIE CO INC
8039 Burch Park Dr (47725-1789)
PHONE..................................812 867-2494
Fax: 812 867-7637
Gary W Turpin, *President*
EMP: 20
SQ FT: 16,800
SALES (est): 2.2MM **Privately Held**
SIC: 3544 3559 Special dies, tools, jigs & fixtures; plastics working machinery

(G-3776)
TRIVALENCE TECHNOLOGIES LLC
3290 Claremont Ave (47712-4930)
PHONE..................................800 209-2517
Eric Stockton, *Vice Pres*
David Richey, *Mng Member*
Mark Larue,
EMP: 5
SQ FT: 44,000

SALES: 2MM **Privately Held**
SIC: 3089 Plastic processing

(G-3777)
TRUARCH INC
3101 N Green River Rd (47715-1369)
PHONE..................................812 402-9511
Ryan Kidwell, *President*
EMP: 5
SALES (est): 431.1K
SALES (corp-wide): 400K **Privately Held**
SIC: 3841 Medical instruments & equipment, blood & bone work
PA: Truarch Inc
2307 S 3rd St
Terre Haute IN 47802
812 232-0910

(G-3778)
TUCKER PUBLISHING GROUP INC
Also Called: Evansville Living
223 Nw 2nd St Ste 200 (47708-1218)
PHONE..................................812 426-2115
Fax: 812 426-2134
Todd Tucker, *President*
Kristin Tucker, *Principal*
Heather Gray, *Treasurer*
Jessica Hoffman, *Accounts Exec*
Jennifer Rhoades, *Accounts Exec*
EMP: 17
SALES (est): 1.7MM **Privately Held**
WEB: www.evansvilleliving.com
SIC: 2721 Magazines: publishing only, not printed on site

(G-3779)
TURONIS FORGET ME NOT INN
4 N Weinbach Ave (47711-6004)
PHONE..................................812 477-7500
Fax: 812 471-3029
Jerry Turner, *President*
EMP: 50
SALES (est): 1.2MM **Privately Held**
SIC: 5812 2082 Eating places; malt beverages

(G-3780)
TWICE DAILY LLC
640 S Bennighof Ave (47714-2020)
P.O. Box 2971 (47728-0971)
PHONE..................................812 484-5417
EMP: 3
SALES (est): 73.3K **Privately Held**
SIC: 2711 Newspapers, publishing & printing

(G-3781)
U S SHEET METAL AND ROOFING CO
1701 N 1st Ave (47710-2700)
P.O. Box 629 (47704-0629)
PHONE..................................812 425-2428
Barry Schnakenburg, *President*
EMP: 2
SALES (est): 142K **Privately Held**
SIC: 3444 Sheet metalwork

(G-3782)
U S VALVES INC
640 S Hebron Ave (47714-4042)
PHONE..................................812 476-6662
Brian Ricci, *President*
EMP: 2
SQ FT: 1,200
SALES (est): 230K **Privately Held**
WEB: www.usvalves.com
SIC: 3491 3599 Valves, automatic control; custom machinery

(G-3783)
UNIQUE-PRESCOTECH INC
Prescotech Division
1900 N New York Ave (47711-3943)
P.O. Box 6117, Fort Smith AR (72906)
PHONE..................................479 646-2973
Fax: 479 646-7968
Charles E Chapman, *Branch Mgr*
EMP: 30
SALES (corp-wide): 175.2MM **Publicly Held**
SIC: 3086 3544 3296 Packaging & shipping materials, foamed plastic; dies, steel rule; mineral wool

HQ: Unique-Prescotech, Inc.
1001 W Oak St
Louisville KY 40210
502 585-5866

(G-3784)
UNISEAL INC (HQ)
1014 Uhlhorn St (47710-2734)
P.O. Box 6288 (47719-0288)
PHONE..................................812 425-1361
Fax: 812 429-1831
Kevin Koch, *Ch of Bd*
Brandon Willis, *President*
Jeff Rock, *General Mgr*
Stephani Catt, *Vice Pres*
Thanikaivelan Veeraraghavan, *Vice Pres*
▲ EMP: 126 EST: 1984
SQ FT: 134,000
SALES: 56.4MM
SALES (corp-wide): 1B **Privately Held**
WEB: www.uniseal.com
SIC: 2891 Sealants; adhesives
PA: Koch Enterprises, Inc.
14 S 11th Ave
Evansville IN 47712
812 465-9800

(G-3785)
UNISEAL INC
1000 Grove St (47710-1824)
PHONE..................................812 425-1361
EMP: 7
SALES (corp-wide): 1B **Privately Held**
SIC: 3084 2891 3568 3498 Plastics pipe; sealants; adhesives; power transmission equipment; fabricated pipe & fittings
HQ: Uniseal, Inc.
1014 Uhlhorn St
Evansville IN 47710
812 425-1361

(G-3786)
UNITED COMPONENTS LLC
14601 Highway 41 N (47725-9357)
PHONE..................................812 867-4156
Scott Felts, *Vice Pres*
Tracy Lettiere, *Manager*
EMP: 13
SALES (corp-wide): 803.2MM **Privately Held**
SIC: 3714 Motor vehicle parts & accessories
HQ: United Components, Llc
2100 International Pkwy
North Canton OH 44720
812 867-4516

(G-3787)
UNITED HERO APPAREL PRINTING
928 Beverly Ave (47710-3130)
PHONE..................................812 306-1998
EMP: 2
SALES (est): 83.9K **Privately Held**
SIC: 2752 Commercial printing, lithographic

(G-3788)
UNITED STATES FILTER
6050 Wedeking Ave (47715-2187)
PHONE..................................812 471-0414
Fax: 812 471-2909
EMP: 2
SALES (est): 161.7K **Privately Held**
SIC: 3569 Filters

(G-3789)
UNIVERSAL OPERATING INC
1521 S Green River Rd (47715-5659)
PHONE..................................812 477-1584
William W Smith, *President*
Nancy L Montgomery, *Treasurer*
EMP: 4 EST: 1953
SQ FT: 1,200
SALES (est): 524.5K **Privately Held**
SIC: 1381 1311 Drilling oil & gas wells; crude petroleum & natural gas production

(G-3790)
UNIVERSITY OF EVANSVILLE
Also Called: University of Evansville Press
1800 Lincoln Ave (47722-1000)
PHONE..................................812 479-2963
William Baer, *Professor*
EMP: 5

G
E
O
G
R
A
P
H
I
C

SALES (corp-wide): 73.2MM **Privately Held**
WEB: www.evansville.edu
SIC: 2731 8221 Book publishing; university
PA: University Of Evansville
　1800 Lincoln Ave
　Evansville IN 47722
　812 488-2000

(G-3791)
UPSIDE PRINTS CORPORATION
727 N Cross Pointe Blvd C (47715-9167)
PHONE.....................................812 319-4883
Anthony Owens, *District Mgr*
EMP: 10 EST: 2014
SALES (est): 236.8K **Privately Held**
SIC: 2752 Commercial printing, lithographic

(G-3792)
VAN ZANDT ENTERPRISES INC
Also Called: Industrial Services Co
1701 N Kentucky Ave (47711-3854)
P.O. Box 6407 (47719-0407)
PHONE.....................................812 423-3511
Fax: 812 423-9567
Edward L Vanzandt, *President*
Debra Van Zandt, *Corp Secy*
EMP: 20
SQ FT: 43,000
SALES: 1MM **Privately Held**
WEB: www.industrialservicesco.com
SIC: 1721 1799 2851 Commercial painting; sandblasting of building exteriors; paints & allied products

(G-3793)
VANDERGRIFF & ASSOCIATES INC
Also Called: Vander Parts Co
1930 Allens Ln (47720-1313)
PHONE.....................................812 422-6033
Fax: 812 422-6577
Gary Van Dergriff, *President*
Gary D Vandergriff, *President*
Steve Vandergriff, *Vice Pres*
Janet Vandergriff, *Admin Sec*
EMP: 5
SQ FT: 30,000
SALES (est): 912.1K **Privately Held**
SIC: 5082 7629 3441 Mining machinery & equipment, except petroleum; electrical repair shops; fabricated structural metal

(G-3794)
VECTREN CORPORATION (PA)
1 Vectren Sq (47708-1209)
PHONE.....................................812 491-4000
Carl L Chapman, *Ch of Bd*
Eric J Schach, *COO*
Wayne Games, *Vice Pres*
Jason Stephenson, *Vice Pres*
Bill Phipps, *Prdtn Mgr*
EMP: 1207
SALES: 2.6B **Publicly Held**
SIC: 4924 4911 1241 1623 Natural gas distribution; electric services; distribution, electric power; generation, electric power; transmission, electric power; coal mining services; water, sewer & utility lines; underground utilities contractor; real estate agents & managers

(G-3795)
VECTREN CORPORATION
20 Nw 4th St (47708-1724)
PHONE.....................................812 424-6411
Daniel Burgher, *President*
Niel C Ellerbrook, *Branch Mgr*
EMP: 35
SALES (corp-wide): 2.6B **Publicly Held**
SIC: 4924 4911 1241 4841 Natural gas distribution; electric services; distribution, electric power; generation, electric power; transmission, electric power; coal mining services; cable & other pay television services; telephone communication, except radio; data telephone communications; local telephone communications; long distance telephone communications
PA: Vectren Corporation
　1 Vectren Sq
　Evansville IN 47708
　812 491-4000

(G-3796)
VERNON A STEVENS
3901 Bergdolt Rd (47711-2591)
PHONE.....................................812 626-0010
Vernon A Stevens, *Owner*
EMP: 5
SALES (est): 278.7K **Privately Held**
SIC: 3579 Postage meters

(G-3797)
VESSELL TRIM CO
955 E Riverside Dr (47713-2898)
PHONE.....................................812 424-2963
Fax: 812 424-2964
Jon Vessell, *President*
Wanda Vessell, *Vice Pres*
EMP: 10 EST: 1949
SQ FT: 10,000
SALES (est): 1.2MM **Privately Held**
WEB: www.vesselltrim.com
SIC: 7532 3714 2394 Body shop, automotive; upholstery & trim shop, automotive; tops (canvas or plastic), installation or repair: automotive; motor vehicle parts & accessories; canvas & related products

(G-3798)
VICKERY DRILLING CO
2526 N Burkhardt Rd (47715-2152)
P.O. Box 9013 (47724-7013)
PHONE.....................................812 473-4671
EMP: 4 EST: 1955
SALES (est): 320K **Privately Held**
SIC: 1311 1382 1381 6519 Operates Oil & Gas Field Properties

(G-3799)
VIDAL PLASTICS LLC
616 N Norman Ave (47711-5872)
PHONE.....................................812 431-8075
Alfonso Vidal, *President*
Kristie Oberhausen, *Opers Mgr*
▲ EMP: 3 EST: 2009
SQ FT: 50,000
SALES: 3MM **Privately Held**
SIC: 2821 Molding compounds, plastics

(G-3800)
VIGO COAF INC
Also Called: Koester Financial Services
250 N Cross Pointe Blvd (47715-4073)
PHONE.....................................812 759-8446
Michael L Schiele, *President*
EMP: 325
SALES (est): 11.9MM **Privately Held**
SIC: 1629 1221 1794 Earthmoving contractor; dredging contractor; surface mining, bituminous; excavation & grading, building construction

(G-3801)
VIGO COAL OPERATING CO INC (PA)
Also Called: Vigo Coal Company
250 N Cross Pointe Blvd (47715-4073)
PHONE.....................................812 759-8446
Fax: 812 759-2625
John C Harman, *President*
Raymond T Purk, *Corp Secy*
EMP: 133
SQ FT: 20,000
SALES (est): 95.9MM **Privately Held**
WEB: www.koesterco.com
SIC: 1221 8748 Surface mining, bituminous; business consulting

(G-3802)
VINDHURST SHEET METAL LLC
2010 N Grand Ave (47711-3802)
PHONE.....................................812 422-0143
Fax: 812 422-4363
Judith A Vindhurst,
Rick J Vindhurst Sr,
Rick J Vindhurst Jr,
EMP: 12
SQ FT: 15,000
SALES (est): 1.5MM **Privately Held**
WEB: www.vindhurstsheetmetal.com
SIC: 3444 1711 Sheet metalwork; heating & air conditioning contractors

(G-3803)
VINTAGE PUBLISHING LLC
7643 Miranda Dr (47711-1501)
PHONE.....................................812 719-7200
Chad Schmidt, *Principal*
EMP: 2
SALES (est): 129.6K **Privately Held**
SIC: 2741 Miscellaneous publishing

(G-3804)
VISION IV INC
14110 Castle Brook Rd (47725-8320)
PHONE.....................................812 423-0119
Jackie Cozgrove, *President*
EMP: 20 EST: 1971
SALES (est): 3.9MM **Privately Held**
WEB: www.visioniv.com
SIC: 2448 Pallets, wood

(G-3805)
W S F FIRE STORE
1279 Maxwell Ave (47711-4141)
PHONE.....................................812 421-3826
Jack Kreny, *Manager*
EMP: 40
SALES (est): 2.5MM **Privately Held**
SIC: 3429 Nozzles, fire fighting

(G-3806)
WABASH PLASTICS INC (PA)
600 N Cross Pointe Blvd (47715-9119)
PHONE.....................................812 428-9300
John C Schroeder, *President*
Roger Kihn, *Maint Spvr*
Chad Cissna, *Engineer*
Logan Robinson, *Project Engr*
Tom Stallings, *Supervisor*
▲ EMP: 275
SALES (est): 61.9MM **Privately Held**
WEB: www.wabashplastics.com
SIC: 3089 Injection molded finished plastic products

(G-3807)
WABASH PLASTICS INC
1300 Burch Dr (47725-1798)
PHONE.....................................812 867-2447
Fax: 812 867-8155
Keith Marvel, *Maint Spvr*
Ed Furniss, *Branch Mgr*
EMP: 21
SALES (est): 4.1MM
SALES (corp-wide): 61.9MM **Privately Held**
SIC: 3089 Injection molding of plastics
PA: Wabash Plastics, Inc.
　600 N Cross Pointe Blvd
　Evansville IN 47715
　812 428-9300

(G-3808)
WAGNER WELDING INCORPORATED
Also Called: Southern Ind Archtectural Pdts
9201 Hogue Rd (47712-9703)
PHONE.....................................812 985-9929
Dennis Wagner, *President*
Beverly Wagner, *Corp Secy*
Bradley Wagner, *Vice Pres*
EMP: 3
SQ FT: 6,480
SALES (est): 150K **Privately Held**
WEB: www.siaproducts.com
SIC: 7692 Welding repair

(G-3809)
WANNEMUEHLER DISTRIBUTION INC
516 N 7th Ave (47710-1420)
PHONE.....................................812 422-3251
Eugene Wannemuehler, *President*
EMP: 15
SALES (est): 1MM **Privately Held**
SIC: 3713 5172 Tank truck bodies; petroleum products

(G-3810)
WCM TOOL & MACHINE INC
810 E Division St (47711-5664)
PHONE.....................................812 422-2315
Fax: 812 422-2369
Joe Winfeild, *President*
Joseph Winfield, *President*
Sam Cutteridge, *Vice Pres*
Samuel Cutteridge, *Vice Pres*
Jan Broshears, *Treasurer*
EMP: 7
SQ FT: 6,000
SALES (est): 390K **Privately Held**
SIC: 3544 Dies, plastics forming

(G-3811)
WHIRLPOOL CORPORATION
5401 Highway 41 N (47711-1962)
PHONE.....................................812 426-4000
Fax: 812 426-4751
Terrie Mathis, *Engineer*
David Winerger, *Controller*
Thomas Webster, *Human Res Dir*
William F Schultz, *Human Resources*
Al Holaday, *Consultant*
EMP: 250
SALES (corp-wide): 21.2B **Publicly Held**
WEB: www.whirlpoolcorp.com
SIC: 3632 3585 Household refrigerators & freezers; freezers, home & farm; refrigeration equipment, complete
PA: Whirlpool Corporation
　2000 N M 63
　Benton Harbor MI 49022
　269 923-5000

(G-3812)
WHITE CAP LLC
2201 W Maryland St (47712-5365)
PHONE.....................................812 425-6221
John Bugnitz, *Principal*
EMP: 2
SALES (est): 138.5K **Privately Held**
SIC: 3999 Manufacturing industries

(G-3813)
WILLIAM F SHIRLEY
Also Called: S & S Machine Co
2721 W Mill Rd (47720-1127)
PHONE.....................................812 426-2599
William F Shirley, *Owner*
June Shirley, *Co-Owner*
EMP: 3
SQ FT: 5,000
SALES (est): 180K **Privately Held**
SIC: 3599 7692 Machine shop, jobbing & repair; welding repair

(G-3814)
WOLFS BAR B Q INC
Also Called: Wolf's Bar-B-Q Restaurant
6600 N 1st Ave (47710-4458)
PHONE.....................................812 424-8891
Fax: 812 424-8905
Terry Wolf, *President*
Kim Wolf, *Vice Pres*
James A Wolf, *Admin Sec*
EMP: 71
SQ FT: 12,500
SALES (est): 2.1MM **Privately Held**
SIC: 5812 5147 2013 Barbecue restaurant; caterers; meats, fresh; sausages & other prepared meats

(G-3815)
WOOD SPC BY FEHRENBACHER INC
8920 Big Cynthiana Rd (47720-7606)
PHONE.....................................812 963-9414
Fax: 812 963-8978
Keith Fehrenbacher, *President*
Gary Fehrenbacher, *Vice Pres*
Chris Fehrenbacher, *Admin Sec*
EMP: 22
SQ FT: 14,000
SALES (est): 3.6MM **Privately Held**
SIC: 2431 Doors & door parts & trim, wood; moldings, wood; unfinished & prefinished; staircases & stairs, wood

(G-3816)
WORLDWIDE BATTERY COMPANY LLC
6050 Wedeking Ave Ste 5 (47715-2187)
PHONE.....................................812 475-1326
EMP: 2
SALES (corp-wide): 26.8MM **Privately Held**
SIC: 5063 3691 Batteries; storage batteries
PA: Worldwide Battery Company, Llc
　9955 Westpoint Dr Ste 120
　Indianapolis IN 46256
　317 845-1330

Fair Oaks
Jasper County

(G-3817)
AMP AMERICAS LLC
Also Called: AMP CNG
5431 E 600 N (47943-8034)
PHONE...................................312 300-6700
EMP: 2
SALES (corp-wide): 3.8MM **Privately Held**
SIC: 2869 5171 Fuels; petroleum bulk stations
PA: Amp Americas, Llc
1130 W Monroe St Ste 1
Chicago IL 60607
312 300-6700

Fairbanks
Sullivan County

(G-3818)
LIFT
6535 W Market St (47849-8081)
PHONE...................................812 394-5438
Jeff Copeland, President
EMP: 4
SALES: 26.1K **Privately Held**
SIC: 3465 Body parts, automobile: stamped metal

Fairland
Shelby County

(G-3819)
ARBUCKLE INDUSTRIES INC
4990 N 550 W (46126-9807)
PHONE...................................317 835-7489
David Arbuckle, President
Cinde Arbuckle, Vice Pres
Ian Harris, Technology
EMP: 2
SALES: 200K **Privately Held**
SIC: 3569 Robots, assembly line: industrial & commercial

(G-3820)
BEGLEY SIGN PAINTING INC
220 N Murnan Ln (46126-2009)
P.O. Box 212 (46126-0212)
PHONE...................................317 835-2027
Fax: 317 835-7546
John Begley, President
EMP: 2
SALES (est): 228.3K **Privately Held**
SIC: 3993 Electric signs

(G-3821)
BROOKFIELD SAND & GRAVEL INC (PA)
8587 N 850 W (46126-9514)
PHONE...................................317 835-2235
Fax: 317 862-3773
Charles Mc Curdy, President
EMP: 25
SQ FT: 15,000
SALES (est): 13.1MM **Privately Held**
SIC: 1442 Sand mining

(G-3822)
JDS PUGH CABINETS INC
Also Called: Pugh's Cabinets
5720 N London Rd (46126-9486)
PHONE...................................317 835-2910
Fax: 317 835-4684
Joseph Pugh, President
Dan Pugh, Vice Pres
Ron Pugh, CFO
EMP: 15
SQ FT: 8,500
SALES (est): 1.5MM **Privately Held**
WEB: www.pughscabinets.com
SIC: 2434 2511 Wood kitchen cabinets; vanities, bathroom: wood; bookcases, household: wood

(G-3823)
JUPITER ALUMINUM CORPORATION
Also Called: Jupiter Coil Coating
205 E Carey St (46126-9694)
PHONE...................................219 932-3322
Alex Gross, Manager
EMP: 45 **Privately Held**
SIC: 3353 3479 Aluminum sheet, plate & foil; painting of metal products
PA: Jupiter Aluminum Corporation
1745 165th St Ste 6
Hammond IN 46320

(G-3824)
MARSTONE PRODUCTS LTD
Also Called: M P L
203 N Edgerton St (46126-2036)
P.O. Box 220 (46126-0220)
PHONE...................................800 466-7465
Fax: 317 835-3050
Thomas Crowley, Principal
Nancy Crawley, Vice Pres
▲ EMP: 32
SQ FT: 20,000
SALES (est): 10.7MM **Privately Held**
SIC: 3281 Table tops, marble; marble, building: cut & shaped

(G-3825)
MGI TRAFFIC CONTROL PDTS INC
102 W Washington St (46126-9661)
P.O. Box 421 (46126-0421)
PHONE...................................317 835-9212
Fax: 317 835-9211
Mike Green, President
EMP: 3
SQ FT: 4,500
SALES (est): 649.8K **Privately Held**
SIC: 3669 5099 Traffic signals, electric; reflective road markers

(G-3826)
PRINTERS GROUP
4485 W 600 N (46126-9774)
PHONE...................................317 835-7720
Gene Taylor, Principal
EMP: 2
SALES (est): 62.9K **Privately Held**
SIC: 2711 Newspapers

(G-3827)
THOMAS L WEHR
Also Called: Wehr Engineering
8192 W 700 N (46126-9507)
PHONE...................................317 835-7824
Fax: 317 835-2992
Thomas Wehr, Owner
Kyle Wehr, Vice Pres
EMP: 4
SQ FT: 2,560
SALES (est): 600K **Privately Held**
WEB: www.glas-master.com
SIC: 3569 3545 Firefighting apparatus & related equipment; machine tool accessories

Fairmount
Grant County

(G-3828)
ALLEN C TERHUNE & ASSOCIATES (PA)
Also Called: News-Sun, The
122 S Main St (46928-1923)
PHONE...................................765 948-4164
Fax: 765 948-4164
Jim Terhune, President
Florence Terhune, Corp Secy
EMP: 4
SQ FT: 5,000
SALES (est): 652.4K **Privately Held**
SIC: 2752 2711 Commercial printing, offset; newspapers

(G-3829)
AMERICAN GORWOOD CORPORATION
Also Called: American Mobile Power
619 E Jefferson St (46928-1817)
P.O. Box 68 (46928-0068)
PHONE...................................765 948-3401
Fax: 765 948-3403
Darrel Brandon, President
Yvonne Brandon, Corp Secy
John Melching, Vice Pres
EMP: 28
SQ FT: 18,000
SALES (est): 4MM **Privately Held**
WEB: www.americanmobilepower.com
SIC: 3714 3594 Motor vehicle transmissions, drive assemblies & parts; fluid power pumps & motors

(G-3830)
BEAST CUSTOM ATHLETIC PRINTING
418 W Fifth St (46928-1320)
PHONE...................................765 610-6802
Philip Parker, Principal
EMP: 2
SALES (est): 83.9K **Privately Held**
SIC: 2752 Commercial printing, lithographic

(G-3831)
FAIRMOUNT NEWS
122 S Main St (46928-1923)
P.O. Box 25 (46928-0025)
PHONE...................................765 948-4164
Jim Terhume, President
EMP: 4 EST: 2001
SALES (est): 188.4K **Privately Held**
SIC: 2711 Newspapers, publishing & printing

(G-3832)
GIBSON BROTHERS WELDING INC
1520 W 900 S (46928-9774)
PHONE...................................765 948-5775
Fax: 765 948-5255
Brian Gibson, President
Dale Gibson, Admin Sec
EMP: 10
SQ FT: 4,200
SALES (est): 1.4MM **Privately Held**
SIC: 7692 3429 Welding repair; fireplace equipment, hardware: andirons, grates, screens

(G-3833)
NORTH AMERICAN MANUFACTURING
619 E Jefferson St (46928-1817)
P.O. Box 65 (46928-0065)
PHONE...................................765 948-3337
Darrell Brandon, President
John Melching, Vice Pres
Yvonne Brandon, Admin Sec
EMP: 40
SALES (est): 11.5MM **Privately Held**
SIC: 3444 Sheet metalwork

(G-3834)
PALLET BUILDER INC
1520 W 900 S (46928-9774)
PHONE...................................765 948-3345
Fax: 765 948-3345
John Remmington, Manager
EMP: 11
SALES (corp-wide): 1MM **Privately Held**
SIC: 2448 Pallets, wood & wood with metal
PA: The Pallet Builder Inc
112 Inks Dr
Winchester IN 47394
765 584-1441

(G-3835)
WIMMER LIME SERVICE INC
7497 S 150 E (46928-9707)
P.O. Box 81 (46928-0081)
PHONE...................................765 948-4001
Fax: 765 948-5463
Tom Wimmer, Owner
Kevin Wimmer, Manager
EMP: 4
SALES (est): 511.5K **Privately Held**
SIC: 3713 Dump truck bodies

Falmouth
Rush County

(G-3836)
BILL BANNER SIGNS
10697 N 600 E (46127-9793)
PHONE...................................765 209-2642
Bill Weaver, Owner
EMP: 2
SALES (est): 72.6K **Privately Held**
SIC: 3993 Signs & advertising specialties

Farmersburg
Sullivan County

(G-3837)
DIRECTIONAL DRILLING CO LLC
112 W Main St (47850-8328)
PHONE...................................812 208-3392
Chad Hardy, Owner
EMP: 4
SALES (est): 411.5K **Privately Held**
SIC: 1381 Directional drilling oil & gas wells

(G-3838)
STONEWARE 3
830a S Charles St (47850-8085)
PHONE...................................812 696-2679
Rita Hawkins, Principal
EMP: 2
SALES (est): 87.4K **Privately Held**
SIC: 3269 Stoneware pottery products

(G-3839)
WRITERS OF VISION
4118 W County Road 975 N (47850-8268)
PHONE...................................812 239-6347
Darrell Case, Principal
EMP: 2
SALES (est): 85.3K **Privately Held**
SIC: 3523 Farm machinery & equipment

Farmland
Randolph County

(G-3840)
BOBS WELDING REPAIR
6447 W 250 S (47340-9562)
PHONE...................................765 744-4192
Robert D Tinsman, Owner
EMP: 2
SALES (est): 107.5K **Privately Held**
SIC: 7692 Welding repair

(G-3841)
CONSOLIDATED PRINTING SVCS INC
201 E Henry St (47340-7006)
PHONE...................................765 468-6033
Fax: 765 468-7652
Daniel Yuska, President
Jeffrey Brooks, Admin Sec
EMP: 11 EST: 1959
SQ FT: 8,000
SALES (est): 976.4K **Privately Held**
SIC: 2752 2791 2789 2759 Commercial printing, offset; typesetting; bookbinding & related work; commercial printing

(G-3842)
MIDWEST RUBBER SALES INC
2135 N 900 W (47340-8942)
PHONE...................................765 468-7105
Rita R Buckner, President
James S Buckner, Treasurer
EMP: 7
SQ FT: 25,000
SALES (est): 1MM **Privately Held**
WEB: www.midwestrubbersales.com
SIC: 3069 Medical & laboratory rubber sundries & related products

GEOGRAPHIC

(G-3843)
MONSANTO
1290 S 1000 W (47340-8909)
PHONE.................................260 341-3227
Telynda Hendrickson, *Principal*
EMP: 2 **EST:** 2016
SALES (est): 74.4K **Privately Held**
SIC: 2879 Agricultural chemicals

(G-3844)
WILLIAMS PRINTING INC
201 E Henry St (47340-7006)
P.O. Box 268 (47340-0268)
PHONE.................................765 468-6033
Tammy Bousman, *President*
EMP: 3
SALES (est): 409.8K **Privately Held**
SIC: 2759 Screen printing

Ferdinand
Dubois County

(G-3845)
AMERICAN WHITETAIL INC
8478 E State Road 62 (47532-7599)
P.O. Box 299 (47532-0299)
PHONE.................................812 937-7185
Fax: 812 937-4157
Ralph Harris, *President*
Kenneth Harris, *Shareholder*
Robert Harris, *Shareholder*
EMP: 10
SQ FT: 18,000
SALES (est): 1.5MM **Privately Held**
WEB: www.archerytargets.com
SIC: 3086 3949 Plastics foam products;
sporting & athletic goods

(G-3846)
BEST CHAIRS INCORPORATED (PA)
1 Best Dr (47532-9233)
P.O. Box 158 (47532-0158)
PHONE.................................812 367-1761
Fax: 812 367-2345
Glenn A Lange, *CEO*
Brian L Lange, *President*
Clement M Lange Jr, *Chairman*
Joseph L Lange, *Exec VP*
Stuart C Curtis, *Vice Pres*
◆ **EMP:** 700
SALES (est): 250MM **Privately Held**
SIC: 2512 Chairs: upholstered on wood
frames

(G-3847)
CARPENTER CO
130 Scenic Industrial Dr (47532-7672)
P.O. Box 175 (47532-0175)
PHONE.................................812 367-2211
Fax: 812 367-1041
Richard Lawrence, *Manager*
EMP: 30
SALES (corp-wide): 2.1B **Privately Held**
WEB: www.carpenter.com
SIC: 3086 Insulation or cushioning mate-
rial, foamed plastic
PA: Carpenter Co.
5016 Monument Ave
Richmond VA 23230
804 359-0800

(G-3848)
DUBOISSPENCER COUNTIES PUBG (PA)
Also Called: Spencer County Leader
113 W 6th St (47532-9517)
P.O. Box 38 (47532-0038)
PHONE.................................812 367-2041
Fax: 812 367-2371
Richard Tretter, *President*
Kathleen Tretter, *Admin Sec*
EMP: 12 **EST:** 1906
SALES (est): 672.3K **Privately Held**
SIC: 2711 Job printing & newspaper pub-
lishing combined; newspapers: publishing
only, not printed on site

(G-3849)
FERDINAND MACHINE SHOP
825 Main St (47532-9792)
PHONE.................................812 367-2590
Leo Giesler Jr, *Partner*

Randy Oser, *Partner*
Jim Weyer, *Partner*
EMP: 4
SQ FT: 5,000
SALES (est): 486K **Privately Held**
SIC: 3599 Machine shop, jobbing & repair

(G-3850)
FERDINAND PROCESSING INC
1182 E 5th St (47532-9780)
PHONE.................................812 367-2073
Paul Gogel, *President*
Paula Gogel, *Vice Pres*
EMP: 4
SALES: 500K **Privately Held**
SIC: 2011 Meat packing plants

(G-3851)
FIVE STARR INC
453 W 9th St (47532-9236)
P.O. Box 10 (47532-0010)
PHONE.................................812 367-1554
Kathy Weyer, *President*
Leisa Weyer, *Manager*
EMP: 2
SALES (est): 145K **Privately Held**
SIC: 3448 Buildings, portable: prefabri-
cated metal

(G-3852)
HERB RAHMAN & SONS INC
9426 E County Road 2100 N (47532-7525)
PHONE.................................812 367-2513
Stan Rahman, *President*
Kenneth Rahman, *Corp Secy*
EMP: 2 **EST:** 1978
SQ FT: 4,000
SALES (est): 225K **Privately Held**
SIC: 2434 Wood kitchen cabinets

(G-3853)
HURST JEFF CUSTOM WOODWORKING
8134 S State Road 162 (47532-9437)
PHONE.................................812 367-1430
Jeff Hurst, *CEO*
EMP: 2
SALES: 110K **Privately Held**
SIC: 2431 Woodwork, interior & ornamen-
tal

(G-3854)
J&L UEBELHOR ENTERPRISES LLC
1440 Virginia St (47532-9192)
P.O. Box 125 (47532-0125)
PHONE.................................812 367-1591
Keith Uebelhor,
Scott Uebelhor,
EMP: 6
SALES (est): 334.1K **Privately Held**
SIC: 3671 Television tubes

(G-3855)
KNU LLC
Also Called: Knu Contract
1 Best Dr (47532-9537)
PHONE.................................812 367-2068
Glenn Lange, *President*
Barbara Donald, *Buyer*
Cindy Boyles, *Purchasing*
Pamela Gibson, *Administration*
EMP: 56
SALES (corp-wide): 27.8MM **Privately Held**
SIC: 2599 Hospital furniture, except beds
PA: Knu, Llc
1300 N Broad St
Leland MS 38756
812 367-1761

(G-3856)
LEIBERING DIMENSION INC
514 W 8th St (47532-9536)
P.O. Box 189 (47532-0189)
PHONE.................................812 367-2971
Shawn N Leibering, *Principal*
EMP: 23
SALES (est): 2.2MM **Privately Held**
SIC: 2511 Wood household furniture

(G-3857)
LELAND MANUFACTURING
1 Best Dr (47532-9537)
PHONE.................................812 367-2068

Faron Lasher, *Principal*
EMP: 2 **EST:** 2014
SALES (est): 96.4K **Privately Held**
SIC: 3999 Manufacturing industries

(G-3858)
MASTERBRAND CABINETS INC
614 W 3rd St (47532-9753)
PHONE.................................812 367-1104
Glen Meservy, *Plant Mgr*
Andrew Hess, *Engineer*
Glen Maservy, *Manager*
Dean Daunhauer, *Manager*
Nicolas Hernandez, *Manager*
EMP: 1000
SALES (corp-wide): 5.2B **Publicly Held**
WEB: www.mbcabinets.com
SIC: 2434 Wood kitchen cabinets; vanities,
bathroom: wood
HQ: Masterbrand Cabinets, Inc.
1 Masterbrand Cabinets Dr
Jasper IN 47546
812 482-2527

(G-3859)
MOBEL INCORPORATED (PA)
2130 Industrial Park Rd (47532-9470)
P.O. Box 130 (47532-0130)
PHONE.................................812 367-1214
Fax: 812 367-1734
Paul Ruhe, *CEO*
Kenneth Lampkin, *President*
EMP: 150
SQ FT: 200,000
SALES (est): 11.9MM **Privately Held**
WEB: www.mobelinc.com
SIC: 2511 Wood bedroom furniture

(G-3860)
OEDING CORPORATION
443 W 16th St (47532-9173)
PHONE.................................812 367-1271
Gary Oeding, *President*
EMP: 3 **EST:** 1945
SALES (est): 574.5K **Privately Held**
WEB: www.oeding.com
SIC: 5984 2511 5712 Propane gas, bot-
tled; wood household furniture; furniture
stores

(G-3861)
PRINTING COMPANY LLC
8765 S Club Rd (47532-9331)
PHONE.................................812 367-2668
Karl Hinson, *Principal*
EMP: 2 **EST:** 2015
SALES (est): 101.5K **Privately Held**
SIC: 2752 Commercial printing, litho-
graphic

(G-3862)
RASCHE BRO LOGGING
12242 E Monte Casino Rd (47532-7638)
PHONE.................................812 357-7782
Alan Rasche, *Principal*
EMP: 6
SALES (est): 285.5K **Privately Held**
SIC: 2411 Logging camps & contractors

(G-3863)
SUPERB TOOLING INC
250 Scenic Industrial Dr (47532-9736)
P.O. Box 227 (47532-0227)
PHONE.................................812 367-2102
Ron Buechler, *President*
EMP: 19
SQ FT: 10,000
SALES (est): 3.4MM **Privately Held**
SIC: 3599 Machine shop, jobbing & repair

(G-3864)
WILMES WINDOW MFG CO INC (PA)
234 W 23rd St (47532-9305)
PHONE.................................812 275-7575
Fax: 812 367-1815
Edward W Wilmes, *President*
EMP: 30 **EST:** 1947
SQ FT: 33,000
SALES: 2MM **Privately Held**
SIC: 3089 5211 3442 3444 Windows,
plastic; windows, storm: wood or metal;
sash, door or window: metal; sheet metal-
work; flat glass; millwork

Fishers
Hamilton County

(G-3865)
ACCENT COATINGS LLC
9915 Glenburr Ct (46038-9025)
PHONE.................................317 712-0017
EMP: 4
SALES (est): 313.5K **Privately Held**
SIC: 3479 Metal coating & allied service

(G-3866)
ACUITY BRANDS LIGHTING INC
12001 Exit 5 Pkwy (46037-7940)
PHONE.................................317 849-1233
David Paulin, *Manager*
EMP: 17
SALES (corp-wide): 3.5B **Publicly Held**
SIC: 3646 Commercial indusl & institu-
tional electric lighting fixtures; fluorescent
lighting fixtures, commercial
HQ: Acuity Brands Lighting, Inc.
1 Acuity Way
Conyers GA 30012

(G-3867)
ALD INDY INC
Also Called: American Leak Detection
12993 Parkside Dr (46038-3864)
PHONE.................................317 826-3833
Mark Dzuba, *President*
EMP: 2 **EST:** 1998
SALES (est): 200K **Privately Held**
SIC: 3599 1711 7389 4939 Water leak
detectors; plumbing, heating, air-condi-
tioning contractors; inspection & testing
services; combination utilities; gas leak-
age detection; water well drilling

(G-3868)
ALEO INC
10396 Lakeland Dr (46037-9323)
P.O. Box 502134, Indianapolis (46250-7134)
PHONE.................................317 324-8583
Mallorie Parrish, *CEO*
EMP: 5
SALES (est): 178.1K **Privately Held**
SIC: 8748 5641 2361 Business consult-
ing; children's wear; infants' wear; t-shirts
& tops: girls', children's & infants'

(G-3869)
ALL-PHASE CONSTRUCTION CO LLC
10182 Orange Blossom Trl (46038-7465)
PHONE.................................317 345-7057
Elisha Madison, *Officer*
Joe Darby Jr, *Officer*
Taj Darby, *Officer*
EMP: 3
SALES (est): 98.5K **Privately Held**
SIC: 1389 1541 0782 1742 Construction,
repair & dismantling services; industrial
buildings & warehouses; renovation, re-
modeling & repairs: industrial buildings;
lawn care services; drywall

(G-3870)
AM PUBLISHING INC
11650 Lantern Rd Ste 103 (46038-3095)
PHONE.................................317 806-0001
Steve Crell, *Administration*
EMP: 2
SALES (est): 80K **Privately Held**
SIC: 2731 Books: publishing & printing

(G-3871)
ANDOVER COILS LLC
13865 Black Canyon Ct (46038-5358)
PHONE.................................765 447-1157
Gregory Steward, *Mng Member*
Kurt Walterhouse, *Mng Member*
Michael Coyle,
Michael Cole,
EMP: 65
SALES (est): 31.1MM **Privately Held**
SIC: 3677 Electronic coils, transformers &
other inductors

▲ = Import ▼=Export
◆ =Import/Export

(G-3872)
ANIPPE
11486 Enclave Blvd (46038-1590)
P.O. Box 41 (46038-0041)
PHONE..................................317 979-1110
EMP: 4 EST: 2011
SALES (est): 305.6K Privately Held
SIC: 2211 Towels & toweling, cotton

(G-3873)
BANGS LABORATORIES INC
9025 Technology Dr (46038-4539)
PHONE..................................317 570-7020
Fax: 317 570-7034
Michael H Ott, Ch of Bd
Chad Owen, President
Ming Peng, Accountant
Amy Royal, Mktg Coord
Toni Dellekamp, Office Mgr
EMP: 16
SQ FT: 9,626
SALES (est): 4.2MM
SALES (corp-wide): 71.2MM Privately
Held
WEB: www.bangslabs.com
SIC: 2899 5169 8731 Chemical prepara-
tions; chemicals & allied products; com-
mercial physical research
PA: Polysciences, Inc.
400 Valley Rd
Warrington PA 18976
215 343-6484

(G-3874)
BARRY COMPANY INC
13317 Britton Park Rd (46038-3500)
PHONE..................................317 578-2486
Fax: 317 578-2551
Nate Wolfe, Manager
EMP: 3
SALES (corp-wide): 21.3MM Privately
Held
WEB: www.barrycompany.net
SIC: 5074 3498 Plumbing fittings & sup-
plies; pipe fittings, fabricated from pur-
chased pipe
PA: Barry Company Inc
1145 E Maryland St
Indianapolis IN 46202
317 637-5327

(G-3875)
BCBG MAX AZRIA GROUP LLC
1132 S Elmhurst (46037)
PHONE..................................515 964-7355
EMP: 2
SALES (corp-wide): 979.1MM Privately
Held
SIC: 2335 Women's, juniors' & misses'
dresses
HQ: Bcbg Max Azria Group, Llc
2761 Fruitland Ave
Vernon CA 90058
323 589-2224

(G-3876)
BEE WINDOW INCORPORATED
Also Called: Faerber's Bee Window
115 Shadowlawn Dr (46038-2432)
PHONE..................................317 283-8522
Fax: 317 921-3052
George Faerber, President
Jeff Todd, CFO
Jeffrey Todd, CFO
Dawn Hawkins, Mktg Dir
Kay Thompson, Director
EMP: 200
SQ FT: 50,000
SALES: 16MM Privately Held
WEB: www.beewindow.com
SIC: 3089 1521 5031 Windows, plastic;
general remodeling, single-family houses;
metal doors, sash & trim

(G-3877)
**BEECHLER WELL DRLG &
PUMP SVC**
10211 E 116th St (46037-9175)
PHONE..................................317 849-2535
Bob Beechler, Owner
EMP: 3
SALES (est): 177.1K Privately Held
SIC: 1381 Service well drilling

(G-3878)
**BENCHMARK CONSUMER
INDUSTRIES**
7538 Timber Springs Dr N (46038-3203)
PHONE..................................317 576-0931
Eric Benner, Owner
EMP: 2
SALES (est): 58K Privately Held
SIC: 3999 Manufacturing industries

(G-3879)
BITTERSWEET PUBLISHING
9936 Boysenberry Dr (46038-3017)
P.O. Box 405 (46038-0405)
PHONE..................................317 640-3943
Carlos Murray, Principal
EMP: 2
SALES (est): 63.5K Privately Held
SIC: 2741 Miscellaneous publishing

(G-3880)
BLEU ROOSTER DESIGNS
7444 River Highlands Dr (46038-1180)
PHONE..................................317 845-0889
Kim Sexson, Partner
EMP: 2
SALES (est): 143.3K Privately Held
SIC: 2392 Cushions & pillows

(G-3881)
BLUSH SALON BOUTIQUE
11631 Maple St (46038-2803)
PHONE..................................317 523-1635
EMP: 2
SALES (est): 80.7K Privately Held
SIC: 2299 Jute & flax textile products

(G-3882)
BROCCOLI PRESS LLC
12624 Largo Dr (46037-8187)
PHONE..................................317 815-4687
Scott Black, Principal
EMP: 2
SALES (est): 89.4K Privately Held
SIC: 2741 Miscellaneous publishing

(G-3883)
CABINETRY GREEN LLC
13818 Promise Rd (46038-3621)
PHONE..................................317 842-1550
Hartman Jean-Christophe, Administration
EMP: 2
SALES (est): 174.4K Privately Held
SIC: 2434 Wood kitchen cabinets

(G-3884)
CAJ FOOD PRODUCTS INC
Also Called: Biotta Juices
11650 Olio Rd Ste 1000 (46037-7621)
PHONE..................................888 524-6882
Matt Herzog, President
John Einsfeld, Vice Pres
▲ EMP: 12
SALES (est): 1MM Privately Held
SIC: 2037 2033 Fruit juices; vegetable
juices: fresh

(G-3885)
CAROUSEL INDUSTRIES
10419 Corning Way (46038-3089)
PHONE..................................317 674-8111
James Sharkey, Principal
EMP: 2
SALES (est): 110.8K Privately Held
SIC: 3999 Manufacturing industries

(G-3886)
CASCADE METRIX LLC
11650 Olio Rd Ste 1000 (46037-7621)
PHONE..................................317 572-7094
Frank Lloyd, President
Kislaya Kunjan, Mng Member
EMP: 3 EST: 2016
SALES (est): 154K Privately Held
SIC: 3845 Patient monitoring apparatus

(G-3887)
**CENTER LINE WOOD WORKS
INC**
14027 Brightwater Dr (46038-7178)
PHONE..................................317 770-9486
EMP: 4 EST: 2008
SALES (est): 210K Privately Held
SIC: 2431 Mfg Millwork

(G-3888)
**CHAPDELLS TREE & PLANT
DESIGN**
11480 E 111th St (46037-3610)
PHONE..................................317 845-9980
Nils Nordell, President
EMP: 2
SQ FT: 1,500
SALES (est): 130K Privately Held
SIC: 3999 Plants, artificial & preserved

(G-3889)
CHILDRESS CORPORATION
Also Called: Budget Blinds
10403 Parmer Cir (46038-5782)
PHONE..................................317 774-8571
Darryl J Childress, Principal
EMP: 2
SALES (est): 142.9K Privately Held
SIC: 2431 Awnings, blinds & shutters,
wood

(G-3890)
CINDYS IN STITCHES
9836 N By Northeast Blvd (46037-9709)
PHONE..................................317 841-1408
Cynthia Hannon, Partner
Cindy Johnson, Partner
EMP: 2
SALES (est): 162.9K Privately Held
WEB: www.cindysinstitches.com
SIC: 2395 Embroidery products, except
schiffli machine

(G-3891)
CLAYTON DANT CORPORATION
Also Called: Tuttle A Dant Clayton Company
120 Shadowlawn Dr (46038-2431)
PHONE..................................317 842-2420
Greg Fischer, CEO
EMP: 5
SALES (est): 619.8K
SALES (corp-wide): 16.4MM Privately
Held
SIC: 2531 Public building & related furni-
ture
PA: Clayton Dant Corporation
1500 Bernheim Ln
Louisville KY 40210
800 626-2177

(G-3892)
COMPOSITION LLC
14048 Woodlark Dr (46038-4524)
PHONE..................................317 979-7214
EMP: 2
SALES (est): 113.9K Privately Held
SIC: 2791 Typesetting

(G-3893)
**CONTECH ENGNERED
SOLUTIONS LLC**
10130 Bahamas Cir (46037-9739)
PHONE..................................317 407-4914
Christa Petzke, Principal
EMP: 4 Privately Held
SIC: 3443 Fabricated plate work (boiler
shop)
HQ: Contech Engineered Solutions Llc
9025 Centre Pointe Dr # 400
West Chester OH 45069
513 645-7000

(G-3894)
CORVANO LLC
11309 Guy St (46038-5452)
PHONE..................................317 403-0471
Gerry Bailey, President
John Millspaugh, Exec VP
EMP: 2 EST: 2016
SALES (est): 62.1K Privately Held
SIC: 7372 8748 Business oriented com-
puter software; systems engineering con-
sultant, ex. computer or professional

(G-3895)
CROWDPIXIE LLC
7594 Timber Springs Dr N (46038-3203)
PHONE..................................317 578-3137
Scott Jones, CEO
Eugene Odonnell, President
EMP: 2
SALES (est): 126K Privately Held
SIC: 7372 7389 Application computer soft-
ware;

(G-3896)
CRYSTAL HEALING ELEMENTS
14018 Parley Ln (46038-5800)
PHONE..................................312 623-1764
Joerg Neumann, Owner
EMP: 2
SALES (est): 74.4K Privately Held
SIC: 2819 Elements

(G-3897)
**DAIRYCHEM LABORATORIES
INC**
9120 Technology Ln (46038-2839)
P.O. Box 6207 (46038-6207)
PHONE..................................317 849-8400
Fax: 317 849-8213
Daniel Church, President
Carol Smallwood, Regl Sales Mgr
Grant Church, Chief Mktg Ofcr
Bill Shazer, Director
Diana Church, Admin Sec
▲ EMP: 16
SQ FT: 16,700
SALES (est): 3.1MM Privately Held
SIC: 2087 Extracts, flavoring

(G-3898)
DAVID INDUS PROCESS PDT CO
Also Called: David Company
10142 Brooks School Rd # 102
(46037-3840)
PHONE..................................317 577-0351
Martha Jane Watrous, President
David Watrous, President
M Jane Watrous, Vice Pres
EMP: 5
SALES (est): 968.9K Privately Held
SIC: 5074 2759 Pipes & fittings, plastic;
visiting cards (including business): print-
ing

(G-3899)
DESIGN WORKS INC
6240 E 116th St (46038-1717)
PHONE..................................317 815-8619
Rachel Cabe, President
EMP: 2
SALES (est): 140.5K Privately Held
SIC: 2512 Upholstered household furniture

(G-3900)
**EATON ELECTRIC HOLDINGS
LLC**
7599 Timber Springs Dr S (46038-2208)
PHONE..................................317 578-7724
EMP: 8 Privately Held
SIC: 3699 Mfg Electrical Equipment/Sup-
plies
HQ: Eaton Electric Holdings Llc
600 Travis St Ste 5600
Houston TX 44122
713 209-8400

(G-3901)
ELAN CORP PLC
11237 Wedgefield Ct (46037-8862)
PHONE..................................317 442-1502
EMP: 2
SALES (est): 74.4K Privately Held
SIC: 2834 Pharmaceutical preparations

(G-3902)
ELENGAS CUSTOMWEAR
12463 Norman Pl (46037-3710)
PHONE..................................317 577-1677
Mike Tittle, Owner
EMP: 2
SALES (est): 107.3K Privately Held
SIC: 2759 Screen printing

(G-3903)
ELI LILLY AND COMPANY
Also Called: Elanco Animal Health
12023 Quarry Ct (46037-3926)
PHONE..................................317 748-1622
Adam M Fivush, Principal
EMP: 144
SALES (corp-wide): 22.8B Publicly Held
SIC: 2834 Pharmaceutical preparations
PA: Eli Lilly And Company
Lilly Corporate Ctr
Indianapolis IN 46285
317 276-2000

GEOGRAPHIC

(G-3904)
EMPLIFY LLC
11787 Lantern Rd Ste 201 (46038-2801)
PHONE...................................800 580-5344
Joseph Loria, *Vice Pres*
Luke McDaniel, *Sales Staff*
Josh Colter, *Marketing Staff*
Joe Horan, *Manager*
Chris Evans, *Executive*
EMP: 49
SQ FT: 9,000
SALES (est): 937.5K Privately Held
SIC: 7372 Application computer software;
business oriented computer software

(G-3905)
ENGINRING CNCPTS UNLIMITED INC
Also Called: Ecu
8950 Technology Dr (46038-2834)
P.O. Box 250 (46038-0250)
PHONE...................................317 826-1558
Fax: 317 849-6475
Adam Suchko, *President*
Diane Ledoux, *VP Opers*
Johnn Marlatt, *Prdtn Mgr*
Alex Suchko, *Electrical Engi*
Susan Suchko, *Admin Sec*
EMP: 4 EST: 1975
SQ FT: 10,000
SALES: 2MM Privately Held
WEB: www.ecu-engine-controls.com
SIC: 3625 Control equipment, electric

(G-3906)
ENTERPRISE MARKING PDTS INC
Also Called: Emp
12840 Ford Dr (46038-2894)
PHONE...................................317 867-7600
Chris Fread, *President*
Carol R Fread, *Vice Pres*
Deb Thompson, *Office Mgr*
EMP: 25
SQ FT: 5,000
SALES (est): 5.3MM Privately Held
SIC: 2754 Intaglio printing

(G-3907)
ESAOTE NORTH AMERICA INC
11907 Exit 5 Pkwy (46037-7939)
P.O. Box 6152 (46038-6152)
PHONE...................................317 813-6000
Glenn Davis, *President*
Tim McNabb, *Vice Pres*
David Struewing, *Opers Mgr*
Jeff Akers, *Traffic Mgr*
Penny Brawner, *Purch Agent*
▲ EMP: 69
SALES: 34MM Privately Held
WEB: www.esaoteusa.com
SIC: 3845 3699 3841 Ultrasonic medical
equipment, except cleaning; electrical
equipment & supplies; surgical & medical
instruments
HQ: Esaote Spa
Via Di Caciolle 15
Firenze FI 50127
055 422-91

(G-3908)
EXCISTA CORPORATION
14213 Calming Waters (46038-6662)
PHONE...................................734 224-3652
Mark Scharboneau, *CEO*
EMP: 2
SALES (est): 207.2K Privately Held
SIC: 2821 Plasticizer/additive based plastic
materials

(G-3909)
F D DESKINS COMPANY INC
12554 Spire View Dr (46037-3701)
PHONE...................................317 284-4014
David Deskins, *President*
EMP: 12
SALES: 3.7MM Privately Held
WEB: www.deskinsinternational.com
SIC: 3569 8748 Filters; environmental
consultant

(G-3910)
FAIRWAY CUSTOM GOLF
12500 Brooks School Rd (46037-9745)
PHONE...................................317 842-0017

Fax: 317 842-1789
Randy Campbell, *Owner*
Diana Campbell, *Administration*
EMP: 2
SALES (est): 148.9K Privately Held
SIC: 3949 7699 5941 Shafts, golf club;
golf club & equipment repair; golf goods &
equipment

(G-3911)
FANSTAND PRINTS
7050 E 116th St Ste 200 (46038-3123)
PHONE...................................317 579-9413
Rory Underwood, *Owner*
EMP: 2
SALES (est): 152.4K Privately Held
SIC: 2752 Commercial printing, litho-
graphic

(G-3912)
FISHERS FIRE STATION 92
11595 Brooks School Rd (46037-9404)
PHONE...................................317 595-3292
Fax: 317 595-3283
Ed Sorg, *Principal*
EMP: 2 EST: 2000
SALES (est): 156.7K Privately Held
SIC: 3711 Fire department vehicles (motor
vehicles), assembly of

(G-3913)
FREIJE TREATMENT SYSTEMS INC
Also Called: Easywater
9715 Kincaid Dr Ste 1100 (46037-8884)
PHONE...................................888 766-7258
William Freije III, *President*
Chad Freije, *General Mgr*
Randy Salatin, *COO*
Dan Hotle, *Sales Mgr*
Brandon Evans, *Sales Staff*
EMP: 25
SALES (est): 6.3MM Privately Held
WEB: www.freije.com
SIC: 3589 Water treatment equipment, in-
dustrial

(G-3914)
FRONT END DIGITAL INC
Also Called: Pyrimont Operating Solutions
11899 Stepping Stone Dr (46037-3918)
PHONE...................................317 652-6134
Matthew David Welch, *CEO*
Kc Cohen, *Corp Secy*
Sean Reiche, *Exec VP*
EMP: 4
SQ FT: 2,500
SALES (est): 1MM Privately Held
WEB: www.pyrimont.com
SIC: 3578 Point-of-sale devices

(G-3915)
GALE FORCE SOFTWARE CORP
11800 Exit 5 Pkwy Ste 102 (46037-7989)
PHONE...................................317 570-4900
Fran Gale, *President*
Russ Mock, *Facilities Dir*
Elliee Gee, *Opers Mgr*
Steven Jenkins, *Engineer*
Marshall Parker, *Engineer*
EMP: 14
SQ FT: 8,000
SALES (est): 1.3MM Privately Held
WEB: www.galeforcecorp.com
SIC: 7372 Business oriented computer
software

(G-3916)
GENERAL MILLS INC
12222 Bedrock Ct (46037-3921)
PHONE...................................317 509-3709
EMP: 54
SALES (corp-wide): 15.7B Publicly Held
SIC: 2043 Cereal breakfast foods
PA: General Mills, Inc.
1 General Mills Blvd
Minneapolis MN 55426
763 764-7600

(G-3917)
GLIDEPATH COM LLC
12175 Visionary Way (46038-3069)
PHONE...................................317 288-4459
Mark Anderson, *Vice Pres*
EMP: 7

SALES (est): 281.6K Privately Held
SIC: 7372 Business oriented computer
software

(G-3918)
GRACIES PAW PRINTS
10053 Parkshore Dr (46038-6858)
PHONE...................................317 910-9969
Karen Hermanson, *Co-Owner*
EMP: 2 EST: 2010
SALES (est): 198.4K Privately Held
SIC: 2752 Commercial printing, litho-
graphic

(G-3919)
GRAPHIC EXPRESSIONS INC
13025 New Britton Dr (46038-1073)
PHONE...................................317 577-9622
Erin Goodwin, *Owner*
EMP: 2
SALES (est): 201.1K Privately Held
SIC: 2752 Commercial printing, litho-
graphic

(G-3920)
H3 SPORTGEAR LLC (HQ)
11988 Fishers Crossing Dr # 161
(46038-2707)
PHONE...................................317 595-7500
Fax: 317 595-7501
Mike Miller, *COO*
Gregg Browne, *VP Sales*
Janet Sarchett, *Director*
Robert Sorensen, *Officer*
Scott H Hines,
▲ EMP: 21
SQ FT: 25,000
SALES (est): 3.2MM Privately Held
WEB: www.h3sportgear.com
SIC: 2339 2329 Women's & misses' ath-
letic clothing & sportswear; men's & boys'
sportswear & athletic clothing

(G-3921)
HAIR HUGGERS LLC
10561 Creektree Ln (46038-6501)
PHONE...................................317 776-9977
Cynthia Kiser, *Mng Member*
EMP: 2
SALES (est): 134.1K Privately Held
SIC: 2339 Scarves, hoods, headbands,
etc.: women's

(G-3922)
HARMONY WINERY
7350 Village Square Ln # 200
(46038-4502)
PHONE...................................317 585-9463
Tatyana Croak, *Owner*
EMP: 2
SALES (est): 279.3K Privately Held
SIC: 2084 Wines

(G-3923)
HAWAIIAN SMOOTHIE LLC
12395 Eddington Pl (46037-5400)
PHONE...................................317 598-1730
Hyon Kim, *Owner*
EMP: 2 EST: 2016
SALES (est): 64.9K Privately Held
SIC: 2037 Frozen fruits & vegetables

(G-3924)
HEARTHMARK LLC (HQ)
Also Called: Jarden Brands Consumables
9999 E 121st St (46037-9727)
P.O. Box 529, Daleville (47334-0529)
PHONE...................................765 557-3000
Chris Scherzinger, *President*
Robert P Totte, *Vice Pres*
Brad NC Cullen, *Transptn Dir*
Ian G H Ashken, *Treasurer*
Jamie Decker, *Manager*
◆ EMP: 120
SALES: 173.7MM
SALES (corp-wide): 14.7B Publicly Held
WEB: www.jardenhomebrands.com
SIC: 3221 Food containers, glass
PA: Newell Brands Inc.
221 River St Ste 13
Hoboken NJ 07030
201 610-6600

(G-3925)
HETZLER OCULAR PROSTHETICS (PA)
10173 Allisonville Rd # 200 (46038-2081)
PHONE...................................317 598-6298
Kathy J Hetzler, *President*
J R Hetzler, *Treasurer*
EMP: 6
SQ FT: 1,950
SALES (est): 773.8K Privately Held
SIC: 3851 Eyes, glass & plastic

(G-3926)
HYMNS2GO LLC
Also Called: Hymns To Go
10315 Stonebridge Ct (46037-9482)
PHONE...................................317 577-0730
Kenneth Booster, *President*
EMP: 1
SALES: 1MM Privately Held
SIC: 3679 Recording & playback appara-
tus, including phonograph

(G-3927)
IMAGE ONE LLC (PA)
Also Called: Awning Innovations
11899 Exit 5 Pkwy (46037-7938)
PHONE...................................317 576-2700
Fax: 317 336-8015
Todd Hayes, *CFO*
Frank I Green, *Mng Member*
Brett Hodges,
EMP: 39
SQ FT: 25,000
SALES (est): 46.7MM Privately Held
SIC: 5039 3993 Awnings; advertising art-
work

(G-3928)
INDIANA BEVEL INC
8605 South St (46038-2907)
PHONE...................................317 596-0001
Steve Gallagher, *President*
EMP: 4
SALES (est): 345.7K Privately Held
SIC: 3211 5231 Flat glass; glass, leaded
or stained

(G-3929)
INDIANAPOLIS WDWKG INTL LLC
9160 Ford Cir (46038-3000)
PHONE...................................317 841-7800
EMP: 22 EST: 2012
SALES (est): 3.6MM Privately Held
SIC: 2431 Millwork

(G-3930)
INFINITY PRINTING PROMOTI
14563 Sowers Dr (46038-5023)
PHONE...................................317 332-4811
EMP: 2 EST: 2014
SALES (est): 83.9K Privately Held
SIC: 2752 Commercial printing, litho-
graphic

(G-3931)
INFO PUBLISHING IMPACT LLC
9869 Worthington Blvd (46038-3068)
PHONE...................................317 912-3642
Kimberly Roach, *Principal*
EMP: 3 EST: 2015
SALES (est): 102.1K Privately Held
SIC: 2711 Newspapers

(G-3932)
INNOVTIVE SRCING SOLUTIONS INC
12752 Broncos Dr (46037-7804)
PHONE...................................317 752-2952
Kyle George, *CEO*
EMP: 2
SALES: 500K Privately Held
SIC: 3724 Aircraft engines & engine parts

(G-3933)
JEDA EQUIPMENT SERVICES INC
13270 Summerwood Ln (46038-7440)
PHONE...................................317 842-9377
Fax: 317 578-2044
Dave Cortner, *President*
Jeannie Cortner, *Treasurer*
EMP: 4

SALES (est): 896.1K **Privately Held**
WEB: www.888jedainc.com
SIC: **5084** 3531 7699 2611 Plastic products machinery; crushers, grinders & similar equipment; industrial machinery & equipment repair; industrial equipment services; pulp mills, mechanical & recycling processing

(G-3934)
JOE TRICKER
13114 Zinfandel Pl (46038-5667)
PHONE.....................................630 759-0251
Joseph Tricker, *Principal*
EMP: 2
SALES (est): 94.5K **Privately Held**
SIC: 3444 Sheet metalwork

(G-3935)
JOHNSON & JOHNSON
10284 Seagrave Dr (46037-9465)
PHONE.....................................732 524-0400
Joyce Kordusky, *Branch Mgr*
EMP: 2
SALES (corp-wide): 76.4B **Publicly Held**
SIC: 2676 Feminine hygiene paper products
PA: Johnson & Johnson
1 Johnson And Johnson Plz
New Brunswick NJ 08933
732 524-0400

(G-3936)
KALDEWEI USA INC
14074 Trade Center Dr # 217
(46038-4575)
PHONE.....................................866 822-2527
Chad Novinger, *Manager*
▲ EMP: 4 EST: 2014
SALES (est): 246.3K **Privately Held**
SIC: 3842 Whirlpool baths, hydrotherapy equipment

(G-3937)
KSM ENTERPRISES
12190 Halite Ln (46038-5491)
PHONE.....................................317 773-7440
Karen Marshall, *Owner*
EMP: 2
SALES (est): 163.9K **Privately Held**
SIC: 3751 Motorcycle accessories

(G-3938)
LEAF HUT SOFTWARE LLC
8430 Weaver Woods Pl (46038-5203)
PHONE.....................................317 770-3632
Charles E Perry III, *Principal*
EMP: 2
SALES (est): 130.3K **Privately Held**
SIC: 7372 Prepackaged software

(G-3939)
LIFOAM INDUSTRIES LLC
9999 E 121st St (46037-9727)
PHONE.....................................410 889-1023
EMP: 4
SALES (corp-wide): 14.7B **Publicly Held**
SIC: 3086 Plastics foam products
HQ: Lifoam Industries, Llc
9999 E 121st
Belcamp MD 21017
866 770-3626

(G-3940)
LOTS OF SOFTWARE LLC
13534 Kelsey Ln (46038-4423)
PHONE.....................................317 578-8120
Bradley Jones, *Owner*
EMP: 2
SALES (est): 84.2K **Privately Held**
SIC: 7372 Prepackaged software

(G-3941)
M & A ORTHOTICS INC
9065 Chadwell Ct Apt 208 (46037-8657)
PHONE.....................................317 281-5253
Paul Burke, *Principal*
EMP: 3 EST: 2000
SALES (est): 179.7K **Privately Held**
SIC: 3842 Orthopedic appliances

(G-3942)
M C L WINDOW COVERINGS INC (PA)
11815 Technology Ln (46038-2890)
PHONE.....................................317 577-2670
Fax: 317 577-2680
Timothy Mc Laughlin, *President*
Geraldyne T Mc Laughlin, *Admin Sec*
EMP: 12
SALES (est): 2.7MM **Privately Held**
SIC: 5714 7359 2221 1799 Drapery & upholstery stores; equipment rental & leasing; upholstery, tapestry & wall covering fabrics; drapery track installation

(G-3943)
MAJESTIC BLOCK & SUPPLY INC
7711 Loma Ct (46038-2524)
PHONE.....................................317 842-6602
Fax: 317 842-4044
Kent Earls, *Owner*
EMP: 8
SALES (est): 731.1K **Privately Held**
SIC: 5032 3271 Lime, except agricultural; concrete block & brick

(G-3944)
MANTRA ENTERPRISE LLC
12694 Balbo Pl (46037-8674)
P.O. Box 7206 (46038-7306)
PHONE.....................................201 428-8709
Kunal Patel,
EMP: 1
SALES (est): 2.2MM **Privately Held**
SIC: 7699 7389 3713 3561 Industrial machinery & equipment repair; ; truck bodies & parts; industrial pumps & parts; industrial machine parts; engines & parts, diesel

(G-3945)
MAXIM AUTOMATION INC
13528 Water Crest Dr (46038-5546)
PHONE.....................................317 418-9561
Jeff Bumgardner, *Vice Pres*
EMP: 7
SALES (est): 660K **Privately Held**
SIC: 3569 Liquid automation machinery & equipment

(G-3946)
METAKITE SOFTWARE LLC
8430 Weaver Woods Pl (46038-5203)
PHONE.....................................317 441-7385
EMP: 2
SALES (est): 117.4K **Privately Held**
SIC: 7372 Prepackaged software

(G-3947)
MM WINDOW FASHIONS
7485 Vineyard Dr (46038-3817)
PHONE.....................................317 585-4933
Mary-Ann Hensley, *Owner*
EMP: 2
SALES (est): 112.1K **Privately Held**
SIC: 2391 Curtains & draperies

(G-3948)
NEXUS VALVE INC
9982 E 121st St (46037-9727)
PHONE.....................................317 257-6050
Kurt Fazekas, *President*
Dustin McGillem, *Engineer*
Richard Wilson, *Engineer*
Kym Allen, *Cust Mgr*
Eva Sitko, *Accounts Exec*
▲ EMP: 40
SQ FT: 10,000
SALES (est): 8.8MM
SALES (corp-wide): 22MM **Privately Held**
SIC: 3491 Industrial valves
PA: Mason-West, Inc.
1601 E Miraloma Ave
Placentia CA 92870
714 630-0701

(G-3949)
PERCH TREE INC
11377 Hawkshead Ln # 200 (46037-4733)
PHONE.....................................630 450-4591
Mary Hoffman, *President*
EMP: 4

SALES (est): 177.3K **Privately Held**
SIC: 3317 Steel pipe & tubes

(G-3950)
PHARMA FORM FINDERS LLC
11164 Muirfield Trce (46037-8830)
PHONE.....................................317 362-1191
Gregory Stephenson, *Principal*
EMP: 3
SALES (est): 150.5K **Privately Held**
SIC: 2834 Pharmaceutical preparations

(G-3951)
PIRO SHOES LLC
8327 Weaver Woods Pl (46038-5202)
PHONE.....................................888 849-0916
Peter Asquini, *Mng Member*
EMP: 16
SALES (est): 1.3MM **Privately Held**
SIC: 3021 Rubber & plastics footwear

(G-3952)
PLAQUEMAKER PLUS INC
Also Called: P M P Design
10080 E 121st St Ste 118 (46037-4211)
PHONE.....................................317 594-5556
Edson Pereira, *President*
Tracy Pereira, *Vice Pres*
Niel Anderson, *Sales Mgr*
EMP: 5
SQ FT: 3,500
SALES (est): 732.6K **Privately Held**
WEB: www.plaquemakerplus.com
SIC: 3999 8743 Plaques, picture, laminated; sales promotion

(G-3953)
PLATINUM INDUSTRIES LLC
11625 Suncatcher Dr (46037-7891)
P.O. Box 333, Selma (47383-0333)
PHONE.....................................765 744-8323
Heather Ane Zeto, *President*
EMP: 3
SALES (est): 132.4K **Privately Held**
SIC: 3999 Manufacturing industries

(G-3954)
PORCHLIGHT GROUP INC
7 Launch Way Ste 610 (46038-1559)
PHONE.....................................317 804-1166
James Brown, *CEO*
EMP: 5 EST: 2014
SQ FT: 18,000
SALES (est): 250K **Privately Held**
SIC: 2741

(G-3955)
POWER WALL SYSTEMS LLC
11253 Tall Trees Dr (46038-4651)
PHONE.....................................317 348-1260
Keith Tully,
EMP: 2
SALES: 900K **Privately Held**
SIC: 3511 Turbines & turbine generator sets

(G-3956)
PPG INDUSTRIES INC
Also Called: PPG 9259
7275 E 116th St (46038-2301)
PHONE.....................................317 577-2344
George Merner, *Branch Mgr*
EMP: 24
SALES (corp-wide): 14.2B **Publicly Held**
WEB: www.ppg.com
SIC: 2851 Paints & allied products
PA: Ppg Industries, Inc.
1 Ppg Pl
Pittsburgh PA 15272
412 434-3131

(G-3957)
PPG INDUSTRIES INC
10564 E 96th St Ste 6 (46037-9643)
PHONE.....................................317 598-9448
Ben Kunkel, *Manager*
EMP: 2
SALES (corp-wide): 14.2B **Publicly Held**
WEB: www.ppg.com
SIC: 2851 Paints & allied products
PA: Ppg Industries, Inc.
1 Ppg Pl
Pittsburgh PA 15272
412 434-3131

(G-3958)
PRECISION CHEMICAL LLC
9723 Kincaid Dr (46037-9791)
PHONE.....................................317 570-1538
Fred Shurtz, *Branch Mgr*
EMP: 6
SALES (est): 615.2K
SALES (corp-wide): 2MM **Privately Held**
WEB: www.precisionchem.com
SIC: 3589 Water treatment equipment, industrial
PA: Precision Chemical Llc
9059 Stonecreek Cir
Newburgh IN 47630
812 858-2431

(G-3959)
QUALITY DATA PRODUCTS INC
10142 Brooks School Rd # 210
(46037-3839)
PHONE.....................................317 595-0700
Dan Falls, *President*
EMP: 2
SALES (est): 176.9K **Privately Held**
WEB: www.qdpi.com
SIC: 7372 Prepackaged software

(G-3960)
QUILT EXPRESSIONS
12514 Reynolds Dr Ste B (46038-9266)
PHONE.....................................317 913-1916
EMP: 4
SALES (est): 170K **Privately Held**
SIC: 2395 Pleating/Stitching Services

(G-3961)
RECREATION INSITES LLC
12237 Westmorland Dr (46037-4406)
PHONE.....................................317 578-0588
Melissa Guffey,
EMP: 2
SALES (est): 229.7K **Privately Held**
SIC: 3949 2531 3069 2273 Playground equipment; picnic tables or benches, park; flooring, rubber: tile or sheet; floor coverings: paper, grass, reed, coir, sisal, jute, etc.

(G-3962)
REDLIN CUSTOM WOODWORKING LLC
8507 Barstow Dr (46038-4448)
PHONE.....................................317 578-1852
David Redlin, *Principal*
EMP: 2
SALES (est): 157.5K **Privately Held**
SIC: 2431 Millwork

(G-3963)
REGISTRATION SYSTEM LLC
7 Launch Way (46038-1559)
PHONE.....................................317 548-4090
Florence May, *President*
EMP: 6
SALES (est): 452.1K **Privately Held**
WEB: www.theregistrationsystem.com
SIC: 7372 Application computer software

(G-3964)
ROOST
7371 E 116th St (46038-2304)
PHONE.....................................317 842-3735
Scott Pipe, *Partner*
Ed Sahm, *Partner*
EMP: 3
SALES (est): 282.7K **Privately Held**
SIC: 7389 3556 Restaurant reservation service; ovens, bakery

(G-3965)
RT SOFTWARE
13534 Kelsey Ln (46038-4423)
PHONE.....................................317 578-8518
Brad Jones, *Principal*
EMP: 2
SALES (est): 107.4K **Privately Held**
SIC: 7372 Prepackaged software

(G-3966)
RUSSELL METAL PRODUCTS
9238 Alton Ct (46037-8909)
PHONE.....................................317 841-9003
Alex Russell, *Owner*
▲ EMP: 15
SQ FT: 5,000

SALES (est): 979.9K **Privately Held**
WEB: www.russellmetalproducts.com
SIC: 3599 Machine shop, jobbing & repair

(G-3967)
SAGAMORE READY-MIX LLC (PA)
9170 E 131st St (46038-3545)
PHONE...................................317 570-6201
Fax: 317 570-6271
Mike Shumaker, *Principal*
Rick Blose, *Vice Pres*
Jay Goad, *CFO*
Rob Shank, *Controller*
Scott Noel, *Sales Mgr*
EMP: 45
SALES (est): 32.5MM **Privately Held**
SIC: 3273 Ready-mixed concrete

(G-3968)
SCOTTS COMPANY LLC
13053 Parkside Dr (46038-8878)
PHONE...................................317 596-7830
Calvin Berg, *Branch Mgr*
EMP: 45
SALES (corp-wide): 2.6B **Publicly Held**
WEB: www.scottscompany.com
SIC: 2873 Fertilizers: natural (organic), except compost
HQ: The Scotts Company Llc
14111 Scottslawn Rd
Marysville OH 43040
937 644-3729

(G-3969)
SHARP PRINTING SERVICES INC
8645 E 116th St (46038-2816)
PHONE...................................317 842-5159
Fax: 317 842-5168
Steven Sharp, *President*
Mike Prater, *Prdtn Mgr*
Walter Sharp, *Treasurer*
Steve Sharp, *Human Res Dir*
Angela Lowe, *Cust Mgr*
EMP: 7
SQ FT: 3,000
SALES (est): 974.6K **Privately Held**
SIC: 2752 7334 Commercial printing, offset; photocopying & duplicating services

(G-3970)
STEAM SPECIALTIES INC
11100 Allisonville Rd (46038-1834)
PHONE...................................317 849-5601
Fax: 317 849-5610
Mark Clapper, *President*
Richard Clapper Jr, *Vice Pres*
Marsha Clapper, *Admin Sec*
EMP: 5 EST: 1965
SQ FT: 8,000
SALES (est): 300K **Privately Held**
SIC: 3582 3546 Pressing machines, commercial laundry & drycleaning; power-driven handtools

(G-3971)
STORAGEWORKS INC
12000 Exit 5 Pkwy (46037-7940)
PHONE...................................317 577-3511
David P Williams, *President*
Jack Fidger, *Principal*
Tom O'Neil, *Vice Pres*
Lee Allison, *Treasurer*
Jon Williams, *Sales Staff*
EMP: 9
SALES (est): 1.4MM **Privately Held**
WEB: www.storageworks.com
SIC: 5046 3537 7699 5084 Commercial equipment; industrial trucks & tractors; industrial equipment services; industrial machinery & equipment

(G-3972)
TC BURTON ENTERPRISES LLC
11764 Marigold Cir (46038-1526)
PHONE...................................317 446-8776
Todd Burton, *President*
EMP: 4
SALES (est): 22.3K **Privately Held**
SIC: 3441 Fabricated structural metal

(G-3973)
TC4LLC
9217 Muir Ln (46037-7959)
PHONE...................................317 709-5429
James Croft, *Principal*

Richard Collins, *Principal*
EMP: 2
SALES (est): 193.9K **Privately Held**
SIC: 5199 3993 7389 Decals; signs & advertising specialties;

(G-3974)
TCT TECHNOLOGIES LLC
10735 Sky Prairie St (46038-7814)
P.O. Box 501527, Indianapolis (46250-6527)
PHONE...................................317 833-6730
Tim O Connell, *President*
EMP: 4 EST: 2007
SALES (est): 500K **Privately Held**
SIC: 3669 Visual communication systems

(G-3975)
TEMPERATURE CONTROL SVCS LLC
13920 Wendessa Dr (46038-6682)
PHONE...................................765 325-2439
Nathan Truitt,
Jennifer Truit,
EMP: 3
SALES: 80K **Privately Held**
SIC: 3822 Temperature controls, automatic

(G-3976)
THOMSON REUTERS CORPORATION
8670 Harrison Pkwy (46038-4456)
PHONE...................................317 570-9387
James Hickerson, *Branch Mgr*
EMP: 2
SALES (corp-wide): 3.2B **Publicly Held**
SIC: 2741 Miscellaneous publishing
HQ: Thomson Reuters Corporation
3 Times Sq
New York NY 10036
646 223-4000

(G-3977)
TODD COUCH REGIONAL OFFICE
10804 Knightsbridge Ln (46037-9287)
PHONE...................................312 863-2520
Todd Church, *President*
EMP: 15
SALES (est): 881.8K **Privately Held**
SIC: 2099 Food preparations

(G-3978)
TOPICS NEWSPAPERS INC
Also Called: Fishers Sun Herald
13095 Publishers Dr (46038-8826)
PHONE...................................888 357-7827
Fax: 317 598-6340
Tom Jeckel, *Manager*
EMP: 60
SQ FT: 40,000
SALES (est): 3.6MM **Privately Held**
WEB: www.topics.com
SIC: 2711 Newspapers, publishing & printing

(G-3979)
TRACKAHEAD LLC
12175 Visionary Way (46038-3069)
P.O. Box 940 (46038)
PHONE...................................800 780-3519
EMP: 2 EST: 2010
SALES (est): 107.9K **Privately Held**
SIC: 7372 Prepackaged Software

(G-3980)
TUTTLE ALUMINUM INTL INC (PA)
Also Called: Western Metal Fabricators
120 Shadowlawn Dr (46038-2433)
P.O. Box 6090 (46038-6090)
PHONE...................................317 842-2420
Peter Q Tuttle I, *President*
Peter Q Tuttle II, *Vice Pres*
Mark Barrett, *Treasurer*
EMP: 20
SQ FT: 30,000
SALES (est): 9.7MM **Privately Held**
SIC: 3441 Fabricated structural metal

(G-3981)
UNIVERSAL TOOL & ENGRG CO
105 Rush Ct (46038-1374)
PHONE...................................317 842-8999
Carl A Grummann, *CEO*

Francis Jenkins, *President*
Robert Rossiter, *Vice Pres*
EMP: 70 EST: 1941
SQ FT: 45,000
SALES (est): 8.2MM **Privately Held**
SIC: 3544 Special dies, tools, jigs & fixtures

(G-3982)
USA TODAY ☉
13095 Publishers Dr (46038-8826)
PHONE...................................212 715-2188
EMP: 2 EST: 2018
SALES (est): 62.9K **Privately Held**
SIC: 2711 Newspapers

(G-3983)
USA VISION SYSTEMS INC
12550 Promise Creek Ln (46038-7717)
PHONE...................................949 583-1519
Joseph Leonard, *Sales Mgr*
EMP: 4
SQ FT: 8,725
SALES (corp-wide): 52.7MM **Privately Held**
SIC: 3699 Security control equipment & systems
HQ: Usa Vision Systems Inc.
9235 Research Dr
Irvine CA 92618
949 583-1519

(G-3984)
WESLEYAN CHURCH CORPORATION (PA)
Also Called: Wesley Publishing House, The
13300 Olio Rd Ste X (46037-7686)
P.O. Box 50434, Indianapolis (46250-0434)
PHONE...................................317 774-7900
Fax: 317 570-5370
Jo Anne Lyon, *President*
Jordan Ellman, *Research*
Kevin Batman, *CFO*
Mario Crifo, *Manager*
Gilbert Skillman, *Professor*
EMP: 69
SQ FT: 15,000
SALES (est): 25.3MM **Privately Held**
WEB: www.greeleywes.com
SIC: 8661 2731 Churches, temples & shrines; books: publishing & printing

(G-3985)
WOLFGANG SOFTWARE
10401 Cotton Blossom Dr (46038-6564)
PHONE...................................317 443-5147
John Dimmett, *Principal*
EMP: 2
SALES (est): 124.6K **Privately Held**
SIC: 7372 Prepackaged software

(G-3986)
WYRCO LLC
13603 E 131st St (46037-6304)
PHONE...................................317 691-2832
Reuben Zielinski,
EMP: 3
SALES (est): 122.5K **Privately Held**
SIC: 3541 Machine tools, metal cutting type

┌─────────────────────┐
Fishers
Hancock County
└─────────────────────┘

(G-3987)
GREEN AIR LLC
13967 Hawkstone Dr (46040-9441)
PHONE...................................317 335-1706
Dhanashree Chakola, *CEO*
EMP: 2
SALES (est): 80K **Privately Held**
SIC: 3822 Switches, thermostatic; thermostats & other environmental sensors

(G-3988)
INFRONT SOFTWARE LLC
10785 Harbor Bay Ct (46040-9017)
PHONE...................................317 501-1871
Daniel Coppersmith, *Principal*
EMP: 2
SALES (est): 113K **Privately Held**
SIC: 7372 Prepackaged software

(G-3989)
IRVING MATERIALS INC
Also Called: I M I
10959 Olio Rd (46040-9628)
PHONE...................................317 335-2121
Fax: 317 335-8796
Scott Gaede, *Branch Mgr*
Brent Neufelder, *Info Tech Dir*
EMP: 23
SALES (corp-wide): 800.6MM **Privately Held**
SIC: 3273 Ready-mixed concrete
PA: Irving Materials, Inc.
8032 N State Road 9
Greenfield IN 46140
317 326-3101

(G-3990)
SOMERSAULTS LLC
Also Called: Somersaults Life Archives
10285 Normandy Ct (46040-1348)
PHONE...................................317 747-7496
Kelli Dalton,
EMP: 3
SALES (est): 235.1K **Privately Held**
SIC: 2834 Pharmaceutical preparations

┌─────────────────────┐
Flat Rock
Shelby County
└─────────────────────┘

(G-3991)
MESHBERGER STONE INC
15 E State Road 252 (47234-7711)
P.O. Box 205 (47234-0205)
PHONE...................................765 525-6442
Fax: 765 525-4260
Mike Henry, *Principal*
EMP: 6
SALES (est): 370K **Privately Held**
SIC: 1422 Crushed & broken limestone

┌─────────────────────┐
Flora
Carroll County
└─────────────────────┘

(G-3992)
CAM CO INC
1776 N 200 E (46929-9299)
PHONE...................................574 967-4496
Maurice E Robeson, *President*
EMP: 4
SALES (est): 202.9K **Privately Held**
SIC: 0213 3599 Hogs; machine shop, jobbing & repair

(G-3993)
CARROLL PAPERS INC (PA)
Also Called: Carroll County Comet
14 E Main St (46929-1351)
P.O. Box 26 (46929-0026)
PHONE...................................574 967-4135
Fax: 574 967-3384
Susan Scholl, *President*
Joe Moss, *Director*
EMP: 8
SQ FT: 2,000
SALES: 100K **Privately Held**
SIC: 2711 Newspapers: publishing only, not printed on site

(G-3994)
EMBROIDERY NATION
209 Manor Dr (46929-1420)
PHONE...................................574 967-3928
EMP: 2
SALES (est): 59K **Privately Held**
SIC: 2395 Pleating/Stitching Services

(G-3995)
EXCEL CO-OP INC
64 W 100 N (46929-9741)
P.O. Box 86 (46929-0086)
PHONE...................................574 967-4166
Fax: 574 967-4167
George Green, *Principal*
EMP: 2
SALES (est): 126.2K **Privately Held**
SIC: 1321 Propane (natural) production

(G-3996)
FLORA WASTEWATER TREATMENT
507 N Division St (46929)
PHONE...........................574 967-3005
Bill McCarty, *Superintendent*
EMP: 3
SALES (est): 307.4K **Privately Held**
SIC: 3589 Water treatment equipment, industrial

(G-3997)
INDIANA LETTERPRESS LLC
315 S Sycamore St (46929-1255)
P.O. Box 5092, Lafayette (47903-5092)
PHONE...........................574 967-0154
EMP: 2
SALES (est): 170.1K **Privately Held**
SIC: 2759 Letterpress printing

(G-3998)
LOUDON PRINTING CO INC
507 W Columbia St (46929-1227)
P.O. Box 177 (46929-0177)
PHONE...........................574 967-3944
Fax: 574 967-3164
Bill Loudon, *President*
Luan Loudon, *Corp Secy*
EMP: 3 EST: 1947
SALES: 300K **Privately Held**
WEB: www.loudounprinting.com
SIC: 2752 Commercial printing, offset

(G-3999)
MIDWEST METER INC
200 Commercial Dr (46929-1528)
PHONE...........................574 967-0175
Joe Ropes, *Manager*
EMP: 5
SALES (est): 600K **Privately Held**
SIC: 3824 Water meters

(G-4000)
MUEHLHAUSEN SPRING COMPANY
488 N 705 E (46929-9360)
PHONE...........................574 859-2481
George Muehlhausen II, *President*
EMP: 8
SQ FT: 2,400
SALES: 150K **Privately Held**
SIC: 3493 Steel springs, except wire

(G-4001)
PARRETTS MEAT PROC & CATRG
Also Called: Parretts Mt Proc Hog Roasting
603 Railroad St (46929-1502)
PHONE...........................574 967-3711
Fax: 574 967-3795
Gary Parrett, *Owner*
Craig Meade, *Co-Owner*
EMP: 12
SALES: 500K **Privately Held**
SIC: 5421 5812 7299 2013 Meat markets, including freezer provisioners; caterers; butcher service, processing only; sausages & other prepared meats; meat packing plants

(G-4002)
Q GRAPHICS INC
103 W Walnut St (46929-1061)
PHONE...........................574 967-3733
Fax: 574 967-3726
Sarah Hanaway, *Manager*
EMP: 5
SALES (corp-wide): 857.6K **Privately Held**
SIC: 2791 Typesetting
PA: Q Graphics Inc
108 E Main St
Delphi IN 46923
765 564-2314

(G-4003)
SISSON & SON MFG JEWELERS
7 W Main St (46929-1354)
P.O. Box 187 (46929-0187)
PHONE...........................574 967-4331
Scott D Sisson, *President*
Eva Sisson, *Admin Sec*
EMP: 3
SQ FT: 2,500

SALES: 120K **Privately Held**
SIC: 5944 3961 7631 Jewelry, precious stones & precious metals; costume jewelry, ex. precious metal & semiprecious stones; jewelry repair services

Florence
Switzerland County

(G-4004)
PROCESS SYSTEMS & SERVICES (PA)
13395 Innovation Dr (47020-9531)
PHONE...........................812 427-2331
Deither Volk, *Owner*
EMP: 4
SALES (est): 463.5K **Privately Held**
SIC: 2821 Plastics materials & resins

(G-4005)
TRENWA INC
13268 Innovation Dr (47020-9530)
PHONE...........................812 427-2217
Lee Wheeler, *Plant Mgr*
James Crockett, *Director*
EMP: 20
SALES (corp-wide): 19.2MM **Privately Held**
WEB: www.trenwa.com
SIC: 3272 Concrete products, precast
PA: Trenwa, Inc.
1419 Alexandria Pike
Fort Thomas KY 41075
859 781-0831

Floyds Knobs
Floyd County

(G-4006)
AQUA NOVA
5914 W Luther Rd (47119-9494)
PHONE...........................812 941-8995
EMP: 5
SQ FT: 5,260
SALES: 825K **Privately Held**
SIC: 3599 Waterjet Cutting Service

(G-4007)
AUTOMATION CONSULTANTS INC
4003 Kendall Ct (47119-9337)
P.O. Box 577 (47119-0577)
PHONE...........................502 552-4995
John Robbins, *President*
EMP: 5
SQ FT: 2,000
SALES: 668.8K **Privately Held**
WEB: www.automacon.com
SIC: 7699 3699 Industrial equipment services; electronic training devices

(G-4008)
B & B SIGNS
5060 Buck Creek Rd (47119-9251)
P.O. Box 7 (47119-0007)
PHONE...........................812 282-5366
Freddie Brennenstuhl, *Owner*
EMP: 3
SQ FT: 2,100
SALES (est): 189.2K **Privately Held**
SIC: 3993 Signs & advertising specialties

(G-4009)
CLOVIS LLC
3333 Buffalo Trl (47119-9725)
PHONE...........................812 944-4791
Philip Sanders, *President*
EMP: 3
SALES (est): 215.4K **Privately Held**
SIC: 3577 Computer peripheral equipment

(G-4010)
FLEXIBLE MATERIALS INC
3595 Lafayette Pkwy (47119-9760)
PHONE...........................812 948-7786
Christopher Brown, *Owner*
EMP: 4
SALES (est): 151K **Privately Held**
SIC: 2435 Hardwood veneer & plywood

(G-4011)
FRENCH TIPS
102 Lafollette Sta S (47119-9772)
PHONE...........................812 923-9055
Don Huynh, *Owner*
EMP: 2
SALES (est): 137.5K **Privately Held**
SIC: 2844 Manicure preparations

(G-4012)
GETTELFINGER HOLDINGS LLC
Also Called: Logo Apparel Plus
5773 Scottsville Rd (47119-9244)
PHONE...........................812 923-9065
Dennis Gettelfinger,
EMP: 4
SALES: 350K **Privately Held**
SIC: 2759 2395 Screen printing; embroidery & art needlework

(G-4013)
HIGHLAND MACHINE TOOL INC
3461 E Luther Rd (47119-9679)
P.O. Box 156 (47119-0156)
PHONE...........................812 923-8884
Fax: 812 923-8886
James E Bezy, *President*
Alan Gahlinger, *Vice Pres*
EMP: 40 EST: 1961
SQ FT: 6,000
SALES (est): 5MM **Privately Held**
WEB: www.highlandmachinetool.com
SIC: 3599 7692 3544 Machine shop, jobbing & repair; welding repair; special dies, tools, jigs & fixtures

(G-4014)
JACK MIX
3400 Lawrence Banet Rd (47119-9605)
PHONE...........................812 923-8679
Jack W Mix, *Principal*
EMP: 3
SALES (est): 132K **Privately Held**
SIC: 3273 Ready-mixed concrete

(G-4015)
JEFF HALLS LOGGING INC
2358 W Riley Rd (47119-9716)
PHONE...........................812 941-8020
Jeffrey Hall, *Owner*
EMP: 6
SALES (est): 453.2K **Privately Held**
WEB: www.jeffhallrealty.com
SIC: 2411 Logging camps & contractors

(G-4016)
MOLD BUSTERS LLC
136 Lee Dr (47119-8918)
PHONE...........................812 989-0008
Chris Moloney, *Principal*
EMP: 2
SALES (est): 89.7K **Privately Held**
SIC: 3544 Industrial molds

(G-4017)
PRINTING SOLUTIONS
6220 Sarles Creek Rd (47119-9407)
PHONE...........................812 923-0756
Richard Chin, *Owner*
EMP: 4 EST: 1996
SALES (est): 1MM **Privately Held**
WEB: www.printing-solutions.org
SIC: 2752 5199 Commercial printing, lithographic; advertising specialties

(G-4018)
PROTON MOLD TOOL INC
6126 Saint Marys Rd (47119-9129)
PHONE...........................812 923-7263
David Gettelfinger, *Owner*
EMP: 2
SALES (est): 169.1K **Privately Held**
SIC: 3544 Special dies & tools

(G-4019)
STROHBECK CABINET INSTALL
4339 Country View Dr (47119-9313)
PHONE...........................812 923-5013
Herman Strohbeck, *Principal*
EMP: 2
SALES (est): 143K **Privately Held**
SIC: 2434 Wood kitchen cabinets

(G-4020)
TECHSHOT LIGHTING LLC
5605 Featheringill Rd # 102 (47119-9583)
PHONE...........................812 923-9591
Rich Bolling, *Business Mgr*
Cole Duffy, *Prdtn Mgr*
John Vellinger,
EMP: 2
SALES: 500K **Privately Held**
SIC: 3647 Vehicular lighting equipment

(G-4021)
TETRAFAB CORPORATION
3429 Knobs Valley Dr (47119-9665)
PHONE...........................812 258-0000
Tony Gutermuth, *Principal*
▲ EMP: 28
SALES (est): 4.7MM **Privately Held**
SIC: 3161 Clothing & apparel carrying cases

(G-4022)
TRISON INDUSTRIES INC
3203 Old Hill Rd (47119-9711)
P.O. Box 10 (47119-0010)
PHONE...........................812 945-7775
EMP: 3
SALES (est): 200K **Privately Held**
SIC: 3599 Mfg Industrial Machinery

(G-4023)
WARD FORGING CO INC
3311 E Luther Rd (47119-9679)
PHONE...........................812 923-7463
Fax: 812 923-7470
Charles Becht Jr, *President*
Carla Becht, *Corp Secy*
EMP: 5 EST: 1920
SQ FT: 14,000
SALES: 500K **Privately Held**
SIC: 3545 3316 Angle rings; bars, steel, cold finished, from purchased hot-rolled

Fontanet
Vigo County

(G-4024)
GREEN LEAF INC
9490 N Baldwin St (47851)
P.O. Box 88 (47851-0088)
PHONE...........................812 877-1546
Pete A Goda, *President*
Curt Owens, *Vice Pres*
Adam Williamson, *Purchasing*
Angela Vikstko, *CFO*
Dawn Blankenbeker, *Human Res Mgr*
▲ EMP: 144
SQ FT: 60,000
SALES (est): 30.5MM **Privately Held**
WEB: www.grnleafinc.com
SIC: 3089 3498 Fittings for pipe, plastic; injection molding of plastics; fabricated pipe & fittings

Fort Branch
Gibson County

(G-4025)
A & T CONCRETE SUPPLY INC
81 E State Road 168 (47648-8041)
P.O. Box 23 (47648-0023)
PHONE...........................812 753-4252
Fax: 812 753-3410
Patricia Pohl, *President*
James Pohl, *Vice Pres*
EMP: 20
SQ FT: 13,000
SALES: 4MM **Privately Held**
SIC: 3273 Ready-mixed concrete

(G-4026)
BARRETT MANUFACTURING INC
Also Called: Tri Star Embroidery
901 E John St (47648-9711)
PHONE...........................812 753-5808
Fax: 812 743-5808
Jeff Barrett, *President*
Joy Barrett, *Admin Sec*
EMP: 3

SQ FT: 10,000
SALES (est): 199.8K **Privately Held**
SIC: 2395 2392 Embroidery products, except schiffli machine; cushions & pillows

(G-4027)
GRANITE TEE SIGNS LLC
7884 S Andee Ln (47648-1549)
PHONE..................................317 670-4967
Brad Lamborne, *Principal*
EMP: 2
SALES (est): 55.7K **Privately Held**
SIC: 3993 Signs & advertising specialties

(G-4028)
NICHOLS OPERATING LLC
8157 S 100 W (47648-8105)
PHONE..................................812 753-3600
Ives Preston, *Principal*
EMP: 4
SALES (est): 580.8K **Privately Held**
SIC: 3569 Gas producers, generators & other gas related equipment

(G-4029)
SOUTH GIBSON STAR-TIMES INC
203 S Mccreary St (47648-1317)
P.O. Box 70 (47648-0070)
PHONE..................................812 753-3553
Fax: 812 753-4251
Frank Heuring, *President*
Phyllis Heuring, *Representative*
EMP: 10
SALES (est): 438.4K **Privately Held**
SIC: 2711 Newspapers, publishing & printing

(G-4030)
WILBERT BURIAL VAULT CO INC
301 S Us Highway 41 (47648-1254)
P.O. Box 67 (47648-0067)
PHONE..................................812 753-3601
Fax: 812 753-4713
Jerry Bickes, *President*
Wayne Bickes, *Admin Sec*
EMP: 25 EST: 1940
SQ FT: 6,000
SALES (est): 3.2MM **Privately Held**
SIC: 3272 Burial vaults, concrete or precast terrazzo

Fort Wayne
Allen County

(G-4031)
101 TOOL & DIE LLC
6716 Metro Park Dr E (46818-9396)
PHONE..................................260 203-2981
Gary Jackson,
David Maberson,
EMP: 8
SQ FT: 6,000
SALES: 800K **Privately Held**
SIC: 3312 Tool & die steel

(G-4032)
1ST CHOICE SAFETY LLC
4642 Pleasant Valley Dr (46825-6812)
P.O. Box 8157 (46898-8157)
PHONE..................................260 797-5338
Ronald V Chidester, *Principal*
Ronald Chidester, *Principal*
EMP: 3
SALES (est): 210.2K **Privately Held**
SIC: 3842 Clothing, fire resistant & protective

(G-4033)
6605 E STATE LLC
2311 Forest Glade (46845-9746)
PHONE..................................260 433-7007
Ronald Kohart, *Mng Member*
EMP: 2
SALES: 100K **Privately Held**
SIC: 3641 Electric light bulbs, complete

(G-4034)
ABSOLUTE MACHINING INC
3834 Vanguard Dr (46809-3300)
PHONE..................................260 747-4568
Fax: 260 747-9505
John Haifley, *President*

Tim Rosswurm, *Vice Pres*
EMP: 4
SQ FT: 2,000
SALES (est): 603.3K **Privately Held**
SIC: 3599 Machine shop, jobbing & repair; machine & other job shop work

(G-4035)
ACCRA PAC HOLDING CO LLC
6435 W Jefferson Blvd # 151 (46804-6203)
PHONE..................................765 326-0005
Samir Shah,
EMP: 2
SALES (est): 62.5K **Privately Held**
SIC: 3999 Manufacturing industries

(G-4036)
ACCU-LABEL INC
2021 Research Dr (46808-3623)
PHONE..................................260 482-5223
Fax: 260 482-5054
David J Manning Jr, *President*
Mj Manning, *Opers Mgr*
Ron Stewart, *Prdtn Mgr*
Catie Manning, *Marketing Staff*
Ben Hendricks, *Manager*
EMP: 30
SQ FT: 22,000
SALES (est): 6.9MM **Privately Held**
WEB: www.acculabel.com
SIC: 2759 2752 2672 2671 Flexographic printing; commercial printing, lithographic; coated & laminated paper; packaging paper & plastics film, coated & laminated

(G-4037)
ACCUGEAR INC
6710 Innovation Blvd (46818-1334)
PHONE..................................260 497-6600
David C Dauch, *CEO*
Richard E Dauch, *Chairman*
Mark S Barrett, *Vice Pres*
▲ EMP: 126
SQ FT: 50,000
SALES (est): 28MM
SALES (corp-wide): 6.2B **Publicly Held**
WEB: www.aam.com
SIC: 3462 Automotive forgings, ferrous: crankshaft, engine, axle, etc.
HQ: American Axle & Manufacturing, Inc.
1 Dauch Dr
Detroit MI 48211

(G-4038)
ACCUTECH MOLD & MACHINE INC
2817 Goshen Rd (46808-1446)
PHONE..................................260 471-6102
Fax: 260 471-8584
Kelly Geiger, *President*
Darrin Geiger, *Vice Pres*
EMP: 130
SQ FT: 8,000
SALES (est): 23MM **Privately Held**
SIC: 3544 3541 Special dies, tools, jigs & fixtures; grinding machines, metalworking; milling machines

(G-4039)
ACCUTEMP PRODUCTS INC (PA)
8415 Clinton Park Dr (46825-3197)
P.O. Box 10090 (46850-0090)
PHONE..................................260 493-0415
Fax: 260 493-0318
Scott Swogger, *President*
Dave Ogram, *President*
John Pennington, *Exec VP*
Doug Myers, *Vice Pres*
Dean Stanley, *Vice Pres*
EMP: 80
SQ FT: 3,000
SALES (est): 16.8MM **Privately Held**
WEB: www.accutemp.net
SIC: 3589 Commercial cooking & food-warming equipment

(G-4040)
ACTIVE TRADING INTERNATIONAL
6015 2 Highway Dr Ste G (46818)
PHONE..................................260 637-1990
Gary Buschman, *President*
EMP: 3
SALES (est): 214.7K **Privately Held**
SIC: 3949 Sporting & athletic goods

(G-4041)
ADAPTEK SYSTEMS INC
14224 Plank St (46818-9092)
PHONE..................................260 637-8660
Fax: 260 637-8597
Joseph G Deprisco, *President*
EMP: 35
SQ FT: 14,000
SALES (est): 10.8MM **Privately Held**
WEB: www.adapteksystems.com
SIC: 3569 3699 3829 Assembly machines, non-metalworking; electrical equipment & supplies; physical property testing equipment

(G-4042)
ADVANCE MACHINE WORKS CORP
2620 Independence Dr (46808-4403)
P.O. Box 8708 (46898-8708)
PHONE..................................260 483-1183
Fax: 260 483-6803
Bryan Neireiter, *President*
Cheryl Wilson, *Office Mgr*
EMP: 30
SQ FT: 10,000
SALES (est): 1.4MM **Privately Held**
WEB: www.advancemachineworks.com
SIC: 3599 Machine shop, jobbing & repair

(G-4043)
ADVANCED CUTTING SYSTEMS INC
4030 Piper Dr (46809-3125)
PHONE..................................260 423-3394
Fax: 260 422-5605
Kevin Koenig, *President*
Tim Lawson, *Treasurer*
David Lawson, *Director*
Jerry Working, *Director*
EMP: 22
SQ FT: 10,200
SALES (est): 4MM **Privately Held**
SIC: 3291 Abrasive products

(G-4044)
ADVANCED MACHINE & TOOL CORP (PA)
Also Called: A M T
3706 Transportation Dr (46818-1388)
PHONE..................................260 489-3572
Fax: 260 489-6720
Frederick Burke, *CEO*
Kyle Koob, *President*
Kyle Kobb, *Senior VP*
Emily Katz, *Purch Mgr*
Walt Kowal, *Engineer*
▲ EMP: 123
SQ FT: 70,000
SALES (est): 25.7MM **Privately Held**
WEB: www.southwestamt.com
SIC: 3599 Custom machinery; machine shop, jobbing & repair

(G-4045)
ADVANCED SYSTEMS INTGRTION LLC
4534 Allen Martin Dr (46806-2801)
PHONE..................................260 447-5555
Heidi Albertson, *Manager*
EMP: 10
SALES (est): 1.5MM **Privately Held**
SIC: 3441 Fabricated structural metal
PA: Advanced Systems & Integration, Llc
8512 Mangum Hollow Dr
Wake Forest NC 27587

(G-4046)
ADVANTAGE CARTRIDGE CO INC
3236 Illinois Rd (46802-4938)
PHONE..................................260 747-9941
Gregory Eshelman, *President*
Rebecca Eshelman, *Admin Sec*
EMP: 11
SALES (est): 1MM **Privately Held**
SIC: 3699 7629 Electrical equipment & supplies; electrical repair shops

(G-4047)
ADVANTAGE DIRECT365 CORP (PA)
Also Called: Advantage Direct
4111 Engleton Dr (46804-3163)
P.O. Box 80067 (46898-0067)
PHONE..................................260 490-1961
Jeffrey A Baker, *CEO*
Jeff Baker, *CEO*
Lisa Thieme, *Vice Pres*
Mary Jane Baker, *Admin Sec*
▲ EMP: 20
SQ FT: 7,500
SALES (est): 2.2MM **Privately Held**
WEB: www.advantagedocument.com
SIC: 2752 Commercial printing, offset

(G-4048)
AEGIS SALES & ENGINEERING INC
5411 Industrial Rd (46825-5121)
PHONE..................................260 483-4160
Fax: 260 484-6480
Joyce Armstrong, *CEO*
Dorsey Roth, *President*
Carey Roth, *Purchasing*
EMP: 18 EST: 1962
SQ FT: 18,000
SALES (est): 3MM **Privately Held**
WEB: www.aegisparts.com
SIC: 3599 3451 Machine shop, jobbing & repair; screw machine products

(G-4049)
AFFORDABLE FOOTWEAR & T-SHRT
4755 Blum Dr (46835-3415)
PHONE..................................260 702-5134
EMP: 2 EST: 2015
SALES (est): 92.3K **Privately Held**
SIC: 2752 Commercial printing, lithographic

(G-4050)
AG APPAREL AND SCREEN PRTG LLC
5515 Planeview Dr (46825-5103)
PHONE..................................260 483-3817
Andy Goodman, *Owner*
EMP: 4
SALES (est): 627.5K **Privately Held**
SIC: 2752 Commercial printing, offset

(G-4051)
AIRGAS USA LLC
4935 New Haven Ave (46803-3020)
PHONE..................................260 749-9576
Scott Latta, *Branch Mgr*
EMP: 10
SALES (corp-wide): 164.2MM **Privately Held**
WEB: www.us.linde-gas.com
SIC: 5085 2813 Welding supplies; industrial gases
HQ: Airgas Usa, Llc
259 N Radnor Chester Rd # 100
Radnor PA 19087
610 687-5253

(G-4052)
AJAX TOOL INC
2828 Commercial Rd (46809-2924)
P.O. Box 9724 (46899-9724)
PHONE..................................260 747-7482
Fax: 260 747-7972
William Osterholt, *President*
EMP: 7 EST: 1963
SQ FT: 12,000
SALES (est): 1.2MM **Privately Held**
WEB: www.ajaxtoolinc.com
SIC: 3544 Special dies & tools

(G-4053)
AL FE HEAT TREATING-OHIO INC (PA)
6920 Pointe Inverness Way # 140 (46804-7938)
PHONE..................................260 747-9422
Kurt H Westman, *President*
Brandon Kocks, *Opers Mgr*
Gary P Peatee, *Purch Mgr*
Renee Ellsworth, *Buyer*
Steve Carr, *Regl Sales Mgr*
EMP: 11

SQ FT: 4,000
SALES (est): 3.2MM **Privately Held**
SIC: 3398 Metal heat treating

(G-4054)
AL-FE HEAT TREATING INC (PA)
Also Called: Al Fe Corporate Group
6920 Pointe Inverness Way # 140
(46804-7938)
PHONE..............................260 747-9422
Kurt Westman, *President*
Kathleen K Westman, *Admin Sec*
EMP: 85
SQ FT: 4,000
SALES (est): 45.5MM **Privately Held**
WEB: www.al-fe.com
SIC: 3398 Metal heat treating

(G-4055)
AL-FE HEAT TREATING INC
Also Called: Piedmont Heat Treating
6920 Pointe Inverness Way (46804-7938)
PHONE..............................888 747-2533
Curt Westman, *President*
EMP: 16
SALES (corp-wide): 45.5MM **Privately Held**
WEB: www.al-fe.com
SIC: 3398 Metal heat treating
PA: Al-Fe Heat Treating Inc
6920 Pointe Inverness Way # 140
Fort Wayne IN 46804
260 747-9422

(G-4056)
ALCONEX SPECIALTY PRODUCTS (PA)
4204 W Ferguson Rd (46809-3143)
PHONE..............................260 744-3446
Fax: 260 745-1938
C David Mc Bane, *President*
Mark A Wilkins, *COO*
▲ EMP: 65
SQ FT: 75,000
SALES (est): 30.9MM **Privately Held**
WEB: www.alconex.com
SIC: 3355 3357 3354 3351 Extrusion ingot, aluminum: made in rolling mills; magnet wire, nonferrous; tube, extruded or drawn, aluminum; copper rolling & drawing

(G-4057)
ALCONEX SPECIALTY PRODUCTS
4201 Piper Dr (46809-3153)
PHONE..............................260 744-3446
C David Mc Bane, *Branch Mgr*
EMP: 26
SALES (corp-wide): 30.9MM **Privately Held**
SIC: 3355 Aluminum rolling & drawing
PA: Alconex Specialty Products Inc
4204 W Ferguson Rd
Fort Wayne IN 46809
260 744-3446

(G-4058)
ALL BORDERS EXPEDITING LLC
1105 River Oak Run (46804-3542)
PHONE..............................260 459-1434
EMP: 4 EST: 2010
SALES (est): 220K **Privately Held**
SIC: 3537 Mfg Industrial Trucks/Tractors

(G-4059)
ALLEN FABRICATORS INC
10106 Smith Rd (46809-9771)
PHONE..............................260 458-0008
Bob Meriwether, *President*
Gregg Owens, *Admin Sec*
EMP: 12
SQ FT: 56,000
SALES (est): 2.6MM **Privately Held**
SIC: 3441 Fabricated structural metal

(G-4060)
ALLIANCE TOOL & EQUIPMENT INC
3919 Engle Rd (46804-4414)
PHONE..............................260 432-2909
Fax: 260 432-9242
James Tomson, *President*
Jane Tomson, *Treasurer*
▲ EMP: 12

SQ FT: 12,000
SALES: 1.3MM **Privately Held**
SIC: 3599 Machine shop, jobbing & repair

(G-4061)
ALLIANCE WINDING EQUIPMENT (PA)
Also Called: Goyal Products
3939 Vanguard Dr (46809-3305)
PHONE..............................260 478-2200
Fax: 260 478-1846
Michael C Khorshid, *CEO*
Mark Carter, *General Mgr*
Dave Wilson, *General Mgr*
Steve Minnich, *Mfg Spvr*
Matt Werling, *Engineer*
▲ EMP: 55
SQ FT: 50,000
SALES (est): 9.5MM **Privately Held**
WEB: www.alliance-winding.com
SIC: 3559 Refinery, chemical processing & similar machinery

(G-4062)
ALLIED MFG PARTNERS INC
Also Called: Tippmann Ordnance
4410 New Haven Ave (46803-1650)
PHONE..............................260 428-2670
Vincent P Tippmann Sr, *President*
Robert Henry, *General Mgr*
William J Federspiel, *Treasurer*
EMP: 3
SQ FT: 15,840
SALES (est): 240K **Privately Held**
SIC: 3699 3489 Electronic training devices; flight simulators (training aids), electronic; teaching machines & aids, electronic; ordnance & accessories

(G-4063)
ALMIGHTY BUSINESS CARDS LLC
9912 White Hill Ct (46804-5984)
PHONE..............................260 615-4663
Paul Heitmann, *Principal*
EMP: 2
SALES (est): 126.1K **Privately Held**
WEB: www.almightybusinesscards.com
SIC: 2752 Business form & card printing, lithographic

(G-4064)
ALRO STEEL CORPORATION
4929 New Haven Ave (46803-3020)
PHONE..............................260 749-1829
Jack Bigham, *Branch Mgr*
EMP: 58
SALES (corp-wide): 1.6B **Privately Held**
WEB: www.alro.com
SIC: 5051 3312 Steel; blast furnaces & steel mills
PA: Alro Steel Corporation
3100 E High St
Jackson MI 49203
517 787-5500

(G-4065)
AMALGAMATED INCORPORATED
6211 Discount Dr (46818-1231)
P.O. Box 8977 (46898-8977)
PHONE..............................260 489-2549
Gary Pipenger, *President*
Paula Pipenger, *Corp Secy*
Randy Walker, *Sales Dir*
▲ EMP: 8
SQ FT: 15,000
SALES: 5MM **Privately Held**
WEB: www.amalgamatedinc.com
SIC: 2819 Industrial inorganic chemicals

(G-4066)
AMANDA ELIZABETH LLC
Also Called: Ae Sport
3711 Vanguard Dr Ste C (46809-3301)
PHONE..............................602 317-9633
Amy Blumenherst, *President*
Joan Abrams, *Treasurer*
EMP: 5 EST: 2011
SQ FT: 2,500
SALES: 2MM **Privately Held**
SIC: 3171 Women's handbags & purses

(G-4067)
AMBANDASH
3826 Walden Run (46815-5260)
PHONE..............................260 415-1709
David Freon, *Principal*
EMP: 3 EST: 2010
SALES (est): 185.6K **Privately Held**
SIC: 2869 Freon

(G-4068)
AMERICAN BOTTLING COMPANY
2711 Independence Dr (46808-1331)
PHONE..............................260 484-4177
Pete Hoffman, *Branch Mgr*
Russ Huglin, *Manager*
EMP: 40 **Publicly Held**
WEB: www.cs-americas.com
SIC: 2086 5149 Bottled & canned soft drinks; groceries & related products
HQ: The American Bottling Company
5301 Legacy Dr
Plano TX 75024

(G-4069)
AMERICAN CHIROPRACTOR MAG INC
Also Called: American Chiropractor, The
5005 Riviera Ct (46825-5805)
PHONE..............................260 471-4090
Richard E Busch, *President*
Jennifer Fortmeyer Busch, *Vice Pres*
Jean I Busch, *Admin Sec*
EMP: 20
SQ FT: 7,000
SALES (est): 1.6MM **Privately Held**
WEB: www.buschchiropractic.com
SIC: 2721 Magazines: publishing only, not printed on site

(G-4070)
AMERICAN FLAME INC
9230 Conservation Way (46809-9642)
PHONE..............................260 459-1703
Corbit Beasey, *CEO*
Christopher Flick, *President*
▲ EMP: 65
SQ FT: 2,000
SALES (est): 381.1K **Privately Held**
SIC: 3429 7699 Fireplace equipment, hardware: andirons, grates, screens; gas appliance repair service

(G-4071)
AMERICAN HYDRO SYSTEMS INC
7201 Engle Rd (46804-2228)
PHONE..............................866 357-5063
Marshall Craig, *President*
EMP: 10
SQ FT: 6,000
SALES (est): 1MM **Privately Held**
WEB: www.americanhydro.com
SIC: 2842 3589 Rust removers; sewage & water treatment equipment

(G-4072)
AMERICAN HYDROFORMERS INC
2320 Meyer Rd (46803-2910)
PHONE..............................260 428-2660
Todd Champany, *Engineer*
Teresa Jones, *Manager*
Mark Blasi, *Officer*
EMP: 19
SALES (est): 3.8MM **Privately Held**
SIC: 3317 Tubing, mechanical or hypodermic sizes: cold drawn stainless

(G-4073)
AMERICAN TOOL SERVICE INC (PA)
7007 Trafalgar Dr (46803-3288)
PHONE..............................260 493-6351
Todd Gibson, *CEO*
Robert Gibson, *Principal*
Jim Doughty, *Natl Sales Mgr*
Dan Coulahan, *Sales Engr*
Lori Lothamer, *Administration*
EMP: 20 EST: 2000
SALES (est): 2.7MM **Privately Held**
WEB: www.a-t-s-i.com
SIC: 3541 Machine tool replacement & repair parts, metal cutting types

(G-4074)
AMERICAN TRUCK COMPANY LLC
7727 Freedom Way (46818-2169)
PHONE..............................260 969-4510
Duncan Sellars,
▲ EMP: 13
SQ FT: 25,000
SALES (est): 1.8MM **Privately Held**
SIC: 3537 Industrial trucks & tractors

(G-4075)
AMT PARTS INTERNATIONAL CORP
Also Called: Amt Precision Parts
3606 Transportation Dr (46818-1374)
PHONE..............................260 490-0223
Rick Burke, *CEO*
EMP: 36
SALES: 5MM **Privately Held**
SIC: 3559 3625 Automotive related machinery; starter, electric motor

(G-4076)
AMT PRECISION PARTS INC
Also Called: Amt Parts International
3606 Transportation Dr (46818-1374)
PHONE..............................260 490-0223
Fax: 260 490-0420
Frederick C Burke Jr, *President*
Cliff Schlatter, *Foreman/Supr*
Teresa Ziegel, *Admin Sec*
◆ EMP: 31
SQ FT: 28,500
SALES: 5.5MM
SALES (corp-wide): 25.7MM **Privately Held**
WEB: www.amtparts.com
SIC: 3599 Machine shop, jobbing & repair
PA: Advanced Machine & Tool Corporation
3706 Transportation Dr
Fort Wayne IN 46818
260 489-3572

(G-4077)
ANOKHI INTERNATIONAL INC
10404 Antelope Ct (46804-4909)
PHONE..............................260 750-0418
Indira D Krishnan, *President*
▲ EMP: 2
SALES (est): 184.5K **Privately Held**
SIC: 2299 5131 7389 Bagging, jute; jute piece goods;

(G-4078)
ANTHONY WAYNE REHABILITATION C (PA)
Also Called: Red Cedar Center
8515 Bluffton Rd (46809-3022)
PHONE..............................260 744-6145
William J Swiss, *President*
Mark Flegge, *CFO*
Eric Weeks, *Human Res Dir*
Jim Palmer, *Manager*
Nancy Bobay, *Director*
EMP: 100
SQ FT: 15,000
SALES: 30.7MM **Privately Held**
WEB: www.awsusa.com
SIC: 8331 7331 3441 3412 Vocational rehabilitation agency; mailing service; fabricated structural metal; metal barrels, drums & pails; wood containers; wood pallets & skids

(G-4079)
ANY REASON SIGNS
9809 Johnson Rd (46818-9458)
PHONE..............................260 450-6756
Dawn Frech, *Principal*
EMP: 2 EST: 2008
SALES (est): 93.7K **Privately Held**
SIC: 3993 Signs & advertising specialties

(G-4080)
APARTMENT ASSN OF FORT WAYNE
3106 Lake Ave Ste A (46805-5441)
PHONE..............................260 482-2916
Beth Wyatt, *Executive*
EMP: 3
SALES: 313.7K **Privately Held**
WEB: www.aafw.org
SIC: 8699 2721 Charitable organization; periodicals

(G-4081)
APOLLO DESIGN TECHNOLOGY INC
4130 Fourier Dr (46818-9384)
PHONE..................................260 497-9191
Fax: 260 497-9192
Joel Nichols, *President*
Caryn Myrice, *CFO*
Keersten Nichols, *Admin Sec*
▲ EMP: 75
SQ FT: 26,000
SALES (est): 12.5MM **Privately Held**
WEB: www.internetapollo.com
SIC: 3229 Pressed & blown glass

(G-4082)
APPLIED COATING CONVERTING LLC
Also Called: A C C
3736 N Wells St (46808-4007)
PHONE..................................260 436-4455
Rick Narramore, *Owner*
▲ EMP: 9
SALES (est): 1.7MM **Privately Held**
SIC: 2679 Paper products, converted

(G-4083)
APPLIED METALS & MCH WORKS INC
1036 Saint Marys Ave (46808-2815)
PHONE..................................260 424-4834
Fax: 260 424-3723
Gary Ecenbarger, *President*
EMP: 25 EST: 1959
SQ FT: 23,000
SALES (est): 4.7MM **Privately Held**
SIC: 3542 3479 3599 7692 Rebuilt machine tools, metal forming types; coating of metals & formed products; machine shop, jobbing & repair; brazing; cracked casting repair; industrial machinery & equipment repair; hydraulic equipment repair; sheet metalwork

(G-4084)
APPLIED TECHNOLOGY GROUP INC
Also Called: A T G
2230 W Coliseum Blvd (46808-3651)
PHONE..................................260 482-2844
Fax: 260 673-0219
Mark Gilpin, *President*
Scott Gillam, *President*
Lakota Morris, *Network Enginr*
Brett Gilpin, *Technician*
EMP: 10
SALES (est): 2.4MM **Privately Held**
SIC: 3699 7382 Security devices; confinement surveillance systems maintenance & monitoring

(G-4085)
APR PLASTIC FABRICATING INC
Lima Rd (46805)
PHONE..................................206 482-8523
Mark Allen, *President*
EMP: 50
SALES (est): 3.3MM **Privately Held**
SIC: 3089 7389 Plastic processing;

(G-4086)
APR PLASTIC FABRICATING INC
2312 Cass St (46808-3110)
PHONE..................................260 482-8523
Fax: 260 483-5616
Mark Allen, *President*
Phil Falls, *General Mgr*
Tammy McDowell, *General Mgr*
Dan Allen, *Vice Pres*
Frank Knaperek, *Safety Mgr*
EMP: 50
SQ FT: 15,000
SALES (est): 8.6MM **Privately Held**
WEB: www.aprtanks.com
SIC: 3089 Injection molding of plastics; plastic processing

(G-4087)
APTERA SOFTWARE INC
201 W Main St (46802-1607)
PHONE..................................260 969-1410
T K Herman, *President*
Conrad Ehiner, *COO*

Nicholas Balcolm, *Web Dvlpr*
David Federspiel, *Sr Software Eng*
EMP: 6
SALES (est): 1.1MM **Privately Held**
WEB: www.apterasoftware.com
SIC: 7372 Business oriented computer software

(G-4088)
APTIMISE COMPOSITES LLC
Also Called: Plastic Composites Co
8301 Clinton Park Dr (46825-3164)
PHONE..................................260 484-3139
Fax: 260 483-2532
EMP: 40 EST: 1957
SALES (est): 8.4MM **Privately Held**
SIC: 3089 Mfg Plastic Products

(G-4089)
ARDEN COMPANIES LLC
Also Called: Arden/Benhar Mills
3510 Piper Dr (46809-3196)
PHONE..................................260 747-1657
Fax: 260 347-2755
Stacey Martin, *Manager*
EMP: 55
SALES (est): 6.1MM
SALES (corp-wide): 219.5MM **Privately Held**
WEB: www.ardencompanies.com
SIC: 2392 3635 2842 Cushions & pillows; household vacuum cleaners; cleaning or polishing preparations
HQ: Arden Companies, Llc
　30400 Telg Rd Ste 200
　Bingham Farms MI 48025
　248 415-8500

(G-4090)
ARISTOLINE CABINET INC
5803 Industrial Rd (46825-5129)
PHONE..................................260 482-9719
Fax: 260 484-9771
Tim Molter, *President*
Rebecca Molter, *Corp Secy*
EMP: 20
SALES (est): 2MM **Privately Held**
SIC: 2434 Wood kitchen cabinets

(G-4091)
ARTEK INC
3311 Enterprise Rd (46808-1398)
P.O. Box 8975 (46898-8975)
PHONE..................................260 484-4222
Fax: 260 484-6914
Dennis Dammeyer, *CEO*
Tony Paulsen, *Project Engr*
Tari Haiflich, *Sales Associate*
Candace Coble, *Admin Asst*
Machelle Suchcicki, *Administration*
▼ EMP: 45
SQ FT: 55,000
SALES (est): 13.4MM **Privately Held**
WEB: www.artek-inc.com
SIC: 3089 Injection molded finished plastic products; plastic processing

(G-4092)
ARTEMIS INTERNATIONAL INC
3711 Vanguard Dr Ste A (46809-3301)
PHONE..................................260 436-6899
Fax: 260 478-6900
Jan Mills, *President*
Leslie Gallo, *General Mgr*
John Sauve, *VP Mktg*
▲ EMP: 6
SQ FT: 4,000
SALES (est): 1.1MM **Privately Held**
WEB: www.anthocyanins.com
SIC: 2861 2834 Dyeing materials, natural; extracts of botanicals: powdered, pilular, solid or fluid

(G-4093)
ASPHALT EQUIPMENT COMPANY INC (PA)
Also Called: Almix
13333 Us Highway 24 W (46814-7457)
PHONE..................................260 672-3004
Fax: 260 672-3020
Michael A Shurtz, *President*
Kathern Shurtz, *Corp Secy*
Grant Shurtz, *Vice Pres*
◆ EMP: 5

SALES (est): 2.5MM **Privately Held**
WEB: www.almix.com
SIC: 3531 5084 3448 3443 Mixers: ore, plaster, slag, sand, mortar, etc.; industrial machinery & equipment; prefabricated metal buildings; fabricated plate work (boiler shop)

(G-4094)
ASSOCIATED MATERIALS LLC
502 Incentive Dr (46825-3376)
PHONE..................................260 451-9072
Albersmeyer Greg, *Branch Mgr*
EMP: 3 **Privately Held**
SIC: 3089 Plastic containers, except foam
HQ: Associated Materials, Llc
　3773 State Rd
　Cuyahoga Falls OH 44223
　330 929-1811

(G-4095)
ATHLETIC EDGE INC
Also Called: Custom Expressions
1133 Old Bridge Pl (46825-3563)
PHONE..................................260 489-6613
Matt P Kostoff, *President*
Cindy Kostoff, *Shareholder*
Michelle Nead, *Shareholder*
Gary Nead, *Admin Sec*
EMP: 10 EST: 1990
SALES (est): 306.5K **Privately Held**
SIC: 7389 2396 3993 Embroidering of advertising on shirts, etc.; screen printing on fabric articles; advertising novelties

(G-4096)
AUTO BUMPER EXCHANGE INC
2321 Bremer Rd (46803-3010)
PHONE..................................260 493-4408
Fax: 260 493-1699
Jerry R Grossman Sr, *President*
Charles Lake, *Corp Secy*
Ralph Grossman, *Shareholder*
Charles W Lehman, *Admin Sec*
▼ EMP: 15 EST: 1954
SQ FT: 8,500
SALES (est): 2.5MM **Privately Held**
WEB: www.abefw.com
SIC: 5013 5015 3714 Bumpers; automotive parts & supplies, used; motor vehicle parts & accessories

(G-4097)
AUTOMATED LASER CORPORATION
14224 Plank St (46818-9092)
PHONE..................................260 637-4140
Joseph Deprisco, *President*
Mike Gigli, *Mfg Staff*
Dustin Geiselman, *Sales Staff*
EMP: 25
SQ FT: 4,800
SALES (est): 2.9MM **Privately Held**
WEB: www.autolase.com
SIC: 3699 8741 Laser systems & equipment; management services

(G-4098)
AVERY DENNISON CORPORATION
Also Called: Fasson Roll North America Div
3011 Independence Dr (46808-1390)
PHONE..................................260 481-4500
Philip Neal, *Chairman*
Todd Riebersal, *Buyer*
Amanda Schneider, *Engineer*
Kris Snepp, *Business Anlyst*
Rita Dailey, *Manager*
EMP: 116
SALES (corp-wide): 6.6B **Publicly Held**
SIC: 2672 Adhesive papers, labels or tapes: from purchased material
PA: Avery Dennison Corporation
　207 N Goode Ave Ste 500
　Glendale CA 91203
　626 304-2000

(G-4099)
AXIS CONTROLS INC
6100 Lower Huntington Rd (46809-9617)
PHONE..................................260 414-4028
Mark Dalman, *President*
John Auer, *Treasurer*
EMP: 2

SALES (est): 226.2K **Privately Held**
WEB: www.axiscontrols.com
SIC: 3625 Industrial controls: push button, selector switches, pilot

(G-4100)
BAE SYSTEMS CONTROLS INC
4250 Airport Expy (46809-9643)
P.O. Box 2232 (46801-2232)
PHONE..................................260 434-5195
Jayson Harris, *Opers Staff*
Scott Swymeler, *Opers Staff*
Stephen Kazmark, *Senior Buyer*
Jon Gallmeyer, *Purch Agent*
Todd Wininger, *QC Mgr*
EMP: 750
SALES (corp-wide): 24.2B **Privately Held**
WEB: www.baesystemscontrols.com
SIC: 3721 3812 Aircraft; search & navigation equipment
HQ: Bae Systems Controls Inc.
　1098 Clark St
　Endicott NY 13760
　607 770-2000

(G-4101)
BAXTER HEATHCARE PLASMA CENTER
7921 Coldwater Rd (46825-3411)
PHONE..................................260 451-8119
EMP: 2
SALES (est): 81.8K **Privately Held**
SIC: 2836 Plasmas

(G-4102)
BCBG MAX AZRIA GROUP LLC
311 S Broadway (46805)
PHONE..................................319 753-0437
EMP: 2
SALES (corp-wide): 979.1MM **Privately Held**
SIC: 2335 Women's, juniors' & misses' dresses
HQ: Bcbg Max Azria Group, Llc
　2761 Fruitland Ave
　Vernon CA 90058
　323 589-2224

(G-4103)
BCBG MAX AZRIA GROUP LLC
1501 M St (46804)
PHONE..................................641 872-1842
EMP: 2
SALES (corp-wide): 979.1MM **Privately Held**
SIC: 2335 Women's, juniors' & misses' dresses
HQ: Bcbg Max Azria Group, Llc
　2761 Fruitland Ave
　Vernon CA 90058
　323 589-2224

(G-4104)
BCBG MAX AZRIA GROUP LLC
41720 Winchester Rd (46825)
PHONE..................................712 243-1965
EMP: 2
SALES (corp-wide): 979.1MM **Privately Held**
SIC: 2335 Women's, juniors' & misses' dresses
HQ: Bcbg Max Azria Group, Llc
　2761 Fruitland Ave
　Vernon CA 90058
　323 589-2224

(G-4105)
BECKYS DIE CUTTING INC
701 Sherman Blvd (46808-2824)
PHONE..................................260 467-1714
Fax: 260 467-1715
Carol R Garrison, *President*
Gregory Garrison, *Vice Pres*
Chris Garrison, *Opers Mgr*
EMP: 4
SALES (est): 651.4K **Privately Held**
SIC: 3544 Special dies & tools

(G-4106)
BHAR INCORPORATED
6509 Moeller Rd (46806-1677)
PHONE..................................260 749-5168
Fax: 260 493-2483
Richard B Kelly, *CEO*
Melissa Smith, *President*
Laurie Kleinhans, *Business Mgr*

▲ = Import ▼=Export
◆ =Import/Export

Jeff Baker, *Vice Pres*
Jim Ross, *Plant Mgr*
EMP: 1
SQ FT: 57,000
SALES (est): 25.5MM
SALES (corp-wide): 536.8MM **Privately Held**
WEB: www.bharinc.com
SIC: 3089 Injection molding of plastics
HQ: Sanko Gosei Technologies Usa, Inc.
6509 Moeller Rd
Fort Wayne IN 46806
260 749-5168

(G-4107)
BIG BRICK HOUSE BAKERY LLP
Also Called: Red Rover Wholesale
4322 Marvin Dr (46806-2596)
P.O. Box 13392 (46868-3392)
PHONE....................260 563-1071
Kevin Rowan, *Partner*
Virginia Leigh Rowan, *Partner*
EMP: 4
SALES (est): 223.4K **Privately Held**
SIC: 2099 2041 7389 Packaged combination products: pasta, rice & potato; wheat flour;

(G-4108)
BIODYNE-MIDWEST LLC
10617 Majic Port Ln (46819-2500)
PHONE....................888 970-0955
Gilman Farley IV, *President*
Tim Weir, *Vice Pres*
Dan Coffin, *CTO*
EMP: 11
SQ FT: 1,000
SALES: 2.3MM **Privately Held**
SIC: 2899 Chemical preparations

(G-4109)
BIOPOLY LLC
7136 Gettysburg Pike (46804-5680)
PHONE....................260 999-6135
Herbert Schwartz, *Mng Member*
EMP: 40 **EST:** 2006
SALES (est): 4.1MM **Privately Held**
SIC: 3842 8731 Orthopedic appliances; medical research, commercial

(G-4110)
BIRCH WOOD
8151 Glencarin Blvd (46804-5799)
PHONE....................260 432-0011
Jeffery Birch, *Principal*
EMP: 4
SALES: 206.1K **Privately Held**
SIC: 2491 Structural lumber & timber, treated wood

(G-4111)
BLACK BOOKS PUBLISHING INC
Also Called: Lyric and Line Tshirt Company
653 Candlelite Ct (46807-3603)
PHONE....................260 225-7479
David L Russell, *CEO*
EMP: 3
SQ FT: 180
SALES: 200K **Privately Held**
SIC: 2731 5699 Book publishing; designers, apparel

(G-4112)
BLACKBOXIT INC
111 E Ludwig Rd Ste 109 (46825-4240)
P.O. Box 518, Avilla (46710-0518)
PHONE....................260 489-8014
Richard S Pulse, *President*
EMP: 7
SQ FT: 2,000
SALES (est): 571.9K **Privately Held**
SIC: 7372 Prepackaged software

(G-4113)
BLOOM PHARMACEUTICAL
Also Called: Erbeco
2831 Union Chapel Rd (46845-9271)
PHONE....................260 615-2633
Cortney Schwartz, *President*
Jerra Myers, *Vice Pres*
EMP: 3

SALES (est): 164K **Privately Held**
SIC: 2834 Ointments; vitamin, nutrient & hematinic preparations for human use; antiseptics, medicinal; medicines, capsuled or ampuled

(G-4114)
BLUERING STENCILS
Also Called: Metal Etching Tech Associates
2248 Research Dr (46808-3628)
PHONE....................260 203-5461
Robert Hall, *Principal*
EMP: 23
SALES (corp-wide): 10MM **Privately Held**
SIC: 3672 Circuit boards, television & radio printed
PA: Blue Ring Stencils Llc
140 Mount Holly By Pass
Lumberton NJ 08048
866 763-3873

(G-4115)
BODYCOTE THERMAL PROC INC
Also Called: Metallurgical Processing
3715 E Washington Blvd (46803-1547)
PHONE....................260 423-1691
Tom Evans, *Branch Mgr*
EMP: 52
SALES (corp-wide): 911.9MM **Privately Held**
WEB: www.mic-houston.com
SIC: 3398 Metal heat treating
HQ: Bodycote Thermal Processing, Inc.
12700 Park Central Dr # 700
Dallas TX 75251
214 904-2420

(G-4116)
BOWMAR LLC
8000 Bluffton Rd (46809-3018)
PHONE....................260 747-3121
Fax: 260 747-9601
Jerry Stephens, *Plant Mgr*
Richard Roberts, *Facilities Mgr*
Kim Sheehan, *Purch Mgr*
Tom Schaffner, *QC Mgr*
Jeff Douglas, *Engineer*
EMP: 40
SQ FT: 75,000
SALES (est): 8.9MM **Privately Held**
SIC: 3575 3674 3643 Computer terminals, monitors & components; semiconductors & related devices; current-carrying wiring devices

(G-4117)
BRANIK INC
3626 Illinois Rd (46804-2062)
PHONE....................260 467-1808
Stanley J Haynes, *President*
Stanley Haynes, *President*
EMP: 2
SALES (est): 338.2K **Privately Held**
WEB: www.branikmotorsports.com
SIC: 2431 Moldings, wood: unfinished & prefinished

(G-4118)
BRC RUBBER & PLASTICS INC (PA)
Also Called: BRC Rubber Group
1029a W State Blvd (46808-3165)
PHONE....................260 693-2171
Fax: 260 693-6511
Charles Chaffee, *CEO*
Joe Dickason, *President*
Dena England, *President*
Todd Haines, *General Mgr*
Karen J Chaffee, *Corp Secy*
▲ **EMP:** 250
SQ FT: 90,000
SALES (est): 171.4MM **Privately Held**
SIC: 3061 3714 3053 Automotive rubber goods (mechanical); motor vehicle parts & accessories; gaskets, packing & sealing devices

(G-4119)
BRC RUBBER & PLASTICS INC
1029 W State Blvd (46808-3165)
PHONE....................260 203-5300
Chuck Chaffee, *Manager*
EMP: 96

SALES (corp-wide): 171.4MM **Privately Held**
SIC: 3061 3714 3053 Automotive rubber goods (mechanical); motor vehicle parts & accessories; gaskets, packing & sealing devices
PA: Brc Rubber & Plastics, Inc.
1029a W State Blvd
Fort Wayne IN 46808
260 693-2171

(G-4120)
BRENMEER LLC
Also Called: Nsignia Screenprinting
5716 Wald Rd (46818-9746)
PHONE....................260 267-0249
Brenda Meerzo, *President*
EMP: 2
SALES (est): 80.6K **Privately Held**
SIC: 2759 Promotional printing; screen printing

(G-4121)
BRISTOL-MYERS SQUIBB COMPANY
7527 Aboite Center Rd (46804-4105)
PHONE....................260 432-2764
Steve Brace, *Manager*
EMP: 89
SALES (corp-wide): 20.7B **Publicly Held**
WEB: www.bms.com
SIC: 2834 Pharmaceutical preparations
PA: Bristol-Myers Squibb Company
430 E 29th St Fl 14
New York NY 10016
212 546-4000

(G-4122)
BROOKS CONSTRUCTION CO INC
6525 Ardmore Ave (46809-9504)
P.O. Box 9560 (46899-9560)
PHONE....................260 478-1990
John Brooks, *Branch Mgr*
EMP: 25
SALES (corp-wide): 100MM **Privately Held**
WEB: www.brooks1st.com
SIC: 3531 Asphalt plant, including gravel-mix type
PA: Brooks Construction Company, Inc.
6525 Ardmore Ave
Fort Wayne IN 46809
260 478-1990

(G-4123)
BROOKWOOD CABINET COMPANY INC
5912 Old Maumee Rd (46803-1705)
PHONE....................260 749-5012
Fax: 260 749-4674
Jerry Kurtz, *President*
Gene L Ruse, *Vice Pres*
EMP: 10
SALES (est): 1.1MM **Privately Held**
SIC: 2434 Wood kitchen cabinets

(G-4124)
BRUCE PAYNE
Also Called: Payne's Die Cutting
5078 Stellhorn Rd (46815-5054)
PHONE....................260 492-2259
Bruce Payne, *Owner*
EMP: 3
SQ FT: 2,400
SALES: 275K **Privately Held**
SIC: 2675 2759 Paper die-cutting; embossing on paper

(G-4125)
BRUNSWICK CORPORATION
Also Called: Harris Kayot
1111 N Hadley Rd (46804-5540)
PHONE....................260 459-8200
Fax: 260 436-6907
James R Poiry, *President*
EMP: 150
SALES (corp-wide): 4.5B **Publicly Held**
WEB: www.brunswick.com
SIC: 3519 3471 3732 Outboard motors; gasoline engines; anodizing (plating) of metals or formed products; pontoons, except aircraft & inflatable

PA: Brunswick Corporation
26125 N Riverwoods Blvd # 500
Mettawa IL 60045
847 735-4700

(G-4126)
BUILDING TEMP SOLUTIONS LLC
3811 Fourier Dr (46818-9381)
P.O. Box 508, Logansport (46947-0508)
PHONE....................260 449-9201
Jeffrey L Secrist, *CFO*
Michael Roads, *Controller*
John Gilbert, *Mng Member*
EMP: 10
SALES (est): 2.5MM **Privately Held**
SIC: 3822 Temperature controls, automatic

(G-4127)
BURKHART ADVERTISING INC
4511 Executive Blvd (46808-1156)
PHONE....................260 482-9566
Fax: 260 483-8971
Tony Wittrock, *Principal*
Steve Depositar, *Prdtn Mgr*
Adam Gerstbauer, *Accounts Exec*
EMP: 20
SALES (corp-wide): 16.7MM **Privately Held**
WEB: www.burkhartadv.com
SIC: 7312 3993 Billboard advertising; neon signs
PA: Burkhart Advertising Inc.
1335 Mishawaka Ave
South Bend IN 46615
574 233-2101

(G-4128)
C & B INDUSTRIES LLC
9009 Coldwater Rd (46825-2072)
PHONE....................260 490-3000
Brian Backstrom, *Principal*
EMP: 2
SALES (est): 136.6K **Privately Held**
SIC: 3999 Manufacturing industries

(G-4129)
C & C INDUSTRIES
10214 Chestnut Plaza Dr (46814-8970)
PHONE....................260 804-6518
Ben Truesdale, *Owner*
EMP: 2
SALES (est): 99.2K **Privately Held**
SIC: 3999 Manufacturing industries

(G-4130)
C & J SERVICES & SUPPLIES INC
Also Called: C & J Security Solutions
5201 Investment Dr (46808-3650)
P.O. Box 80605 (46898-0605)
PHONE....................317 569-7222
Denise Messman, *President*
Chris Sipe, *President*
Dereck Nelsen, *Vice Pres*
Mark Perkins, *Vice Pres*
EMP: 28
SQ FT: 2,200
SALES (est): 4.6MM **Privately Held**
WEB: www.cjssinc.com
SIC: 3715 Truck trailers

(G-4131)
C & P MACHINE SERVICE INC
Also Called: C&P Machine
445 Council Dr (46825-5158)
PHONE....................260 484-7723
Fax: 260 484-7726
Edwin R Baker, *President*
David R Baker, *President*
Charlene Randolph, *Vice Pres*
Hilda Baker, *Treasurer*
Brian Baker, *Sales Mgr*
EMP: 30
SQ FT: 20,000
SALES (est): 4.1MM **Privately Held**
WEB: www.cpmachine.com
SIC: 3599 5013 5531 7538 Machine shop, jobbing & repair; automotive servicing equipment; automotive & home supply stores; engine rebuilding: automotive

(G-4132)
C&B INDUSTRIES LLC
8515 Schwartz Rd (46835-9745)
PHONE....................260 493-3288

Chris Tippmann, *President*
EMP: 2
SALES (est): 26.9K **Privately Held**
SIC: 3999 Manufacturing industries

(G-4133)
CADILLAC COFFEE COMPANY
7221 Innovation Blvd (46818-1333)
PHONE....................260 489-6281
John R Gehlert Jr, *Branch Mgr*
EMP: 40
SALES (corp-wide): 98.8MM **Privately Held**
WEB: www.cadillaccoffee.com
SIC: 2095 Coffee roasting (except by wholesale grocers)
PA: Cadillac Coffee Company
7221 Innovation Blvd
Fort Wayne IN 46818
248 545-2266

(G-4134)
CALHOUN ST SOUP SALAD SPIRITS
112 E Masterson Ave (46803-2327)
PHONE....................260 456-7005
Leo B Vodde, *Principal*
EMP: 3
SALES (est): 163.5K **Privately Held**
SIC: 2099 Salads, fresh or refrigerated

(G-4135)
CALICO PRECISION MOLDING LLC
Also Called: Polytec Packaging Solution
1211 Progress Rd (46808-1261)
PHONE....................260 484-4500
Fax: 260 484-4405
John Soulliere, *President*
Monte Davis, *Opers Staff*
Teresa Gooding, *Purchasing*
Steve Balbaugh, *Engineer*
Steve Offord, *Engineer*
▲ **EMP:** 40
SQ FT: 45,000
SALES (est): 10.7MM **Privately Held**
WEB: www.calicopm.com
SIC: 3089 Synthetic resin finished products; injection molding of plastics

(G-4136)
CALIENTE
1123 E State Blvd (46805-4423)
PHONE....................260 471-0700
Jennifer Voors, *Principal*
EMP: 3
SALES (est): 174.4K **Privately Held**
SIC: 5099 3999 Durable goods; manufacturing industries

(G-4137)
CALIENTE LLC
315 E Wallace St (46803-2342)
PHONE....................260 426-3800
Michael R Kelly,
EMP: 25
SQ FT: 40,000
SALES (est): 7MM **Privately Held**
SIC: 3585 3443 3822 Heating equipment, complete; air coolers, metal plate; pressure controllers, air-conditioning system type

(G-4138)
CANDIES INC
4211 Earth Dr (46809-1513)
PHONE....................260 747-7514
Fax: 260 747-9898
Todd Haines, *President*
EMP: 11
SQ FT: 10,000
SALES (est): 1.3MM **Privately Held**
SIC: 2064 5947 2066 Candy & other confectionery products; gift, novelty & souvenir shop; chocolate & cocoa products

(G-4139)
CANDLES BY DAR INC
Also Called: Darlite Designs
3710 N Clinton St (46805-1202)
PHONE....................260 482-2099
Darwin E Highlen Jr, *President*
▲ **EMP:** 10
SQ FT: 40,000

SALES (est): 2.5MM **Privately Held**
SIC: 5021 5023 5193 3999 Household furniture; home furnishings; florists' supplies; novelties, bric-a-brac & hobby kits; Christmas lights & decorations

(G-4140)
CASTLETON VILLAGE CENTER INC
Also Called: Hightech Signs
6321 Huguenard Rd Ste A (46818-1503)
PHONE....................260 484-2600
Fax: 260 484-2726
Stan Abramowski, *President*
EMP: 12 **Privately Held**
WEB: www.hightech-signs.com
SIC: 3993 Signs & advertising specialties
PA: Castleton Village Center Inc
6321 Huguenard Rd Ste A
Fort Wayne IN 46818

(G-4141)
CASTLETON VILLAGE CENTER INC (PA)
Also Called: Hightech Signs
6321 Huguenard Rd Ste A (46818-1503)
PHONE....................260 471-5959
Fax: 260 471-3707
Marjorie Abramowski, *Ch of Bd*
Doug Abramowski, *President*
Stanley A Abramowski, *President*
Drew Demorest, *Production*
Ellen Bender, *Human Resources*
▲ **EMP:** 11
SALES (est): 2.2MM **Privately Held**
WEB: www.hightech-signs.com
SIC: 3993 Signs, not made in custom sign painting shops

(G-4142)
CENTRAL COCA-COLA BTLG CO INC
5010 Airport Expy (46809-9644)
PHONE....................260 478-2978
Fax: 260 478-1373
Terry Ford, *Manager*
EMP: 150
SQ FT: 200,000
SALES (corp-wide): 35.4B **Publicly Held**
WEB: www.cokecce.com
SIC: 2086 Bottled & canned soft drinks
HQ: Central Coca-Cola Bottling Company, Inc.
555 Taxter Rd Ste 550
Elmsford NY 10523
914 789-1100

(G-4143)
CENTRAL PACKAGING INC
7707 Vicksburg Pike (46804-5549)
PHONE....................260 436-7225
Suteji Takeuchi, *President*
EMP: 150
SQ FT: 160,000
SALES (est): 7.5MM
SALES (corp-wide): 71B **Privately Held**
SIC: 3089 5087 5113 Plastic containers, except foam; janitors' supplies; industrial & personal service paper
HQ: Chuo Kagaku Co., Ltd.
3-5-1, Miyaji
Konosu STM 365-0
485 422-511

(G-4144)
CHAMPION OPCO LLC
Also Called: Champion Window Mfr and Sups
2226 Research Dr (46808-3628)
PHONE....................260 271-4076
Fax: 260 471-5668
Mark George, *Manager*
EMP: 20
SALES (corp-wide): 515.7MM **Privately Held**
SIC: 3442 3444 Storm doors or windows, metal; awnings, sheet metal
PA: Champion Opco, Llc
12121 Champion Way
Cincinnati OH 45241
513 924-4858

(G-4145)
CHEMICALS SOLVENTS & LUBR
8005 N Clinton St (46825-3115)
PHONE....................260 484-2000

Fax: 260 482-6780
Phillip W Bradley, *President*
EMP: 4 **EST:** 1964
SQ FT: 14,000
SALES (est): 594.9K **Privately Held**
SIC: 2851 Paint removers

(G-4146)
CHESSEX MANUFACTURING CO LLC
3415 Centennial Dr (46808-4515)
P.O. Box 80255 (46898-0255)
PHONE....................260 471-9511
Fax: 260 471-8020
Donald Reents,
▲ **EMP:** 13
SALES (est): 1.9MM **Privately Held**
SIC: 3944 Dice & dice cups

(G-4147)
CHICKEN SCRATCH LLC
8003 Young Rd (46835-9542)
PHONE....................260 486-9800
Panayiotis Bourounis, *Principal*
EMP: 2
SALES (est): 69.2K **Privately Held**
SIC: 2711 Newspapers

(G-4148)
CHOPPERS KICKSTAND LLC
3032 Maumee Ave (46803-1514)
PHONE....................260 739-6966
Richard Woodley, *Administration*
EMP: 3 **EST:** 2014
SALES (est): 233.2K **Privately Held**
SIC: 3751 Motorcycles & related parts

(G-4149)
CHUCK BIVENS SERVICES INC
Also Called: States Engineering
10216 Airport Dr (46809-3025)
P.O. Box 9590 (46899-9590)
PHONE....................260 747-6195
Fax: 260 747-4990
Chuck Bivens, *President*
▼ **EMP:** 17 **EST:** 1946
SQ FT: 48,000
SALES: 2.9MM **Privately Held**
WEB: www.statesengineeringinc.com
SIC: 3559 Foundry machinery & equipment

(G-4150)
CINDA B USA LLC
1530 Progress Rd (46808-1181)
PHONE....................260 469-0803
Fax: 260 469-0807
Jon Adams, *President*
▲ **EMP:** 5
SALES (est): 1.8MM **Privately Held**
SIC: 5137 3161 Handbags; women's & children's accessories; traveling bags

(G-4151)
CITY OF FORT WAYNE
Also Called: Biosolid Compost
5510 Lake Ave (46815-7575)
PHONE....................260 749-8040
Stacy Petrovas, *Manager*
EMP: 3 **Privately Held**
SIC: 2875 Compost
PA: City Of Fort Wayne
200 E Berry St
Fort Wayne IN 46802
260 427-1111

(G-4152)
CITY OF FORT WAYNE
Also Called: Street Department
1701 Lafayette St (46803-2320)
PHONE....................260 427-1235
Fax: 260 427-1410
Brad Baumgartner, *Commissioner*
EMP: 100 **Privately Held**
SIC: 3991 Street sweeping brooms, hand or machine
PA: City Of Fort Wayne
200 E Berry St
Fort Wayne IN 46802
260 427-1111

(G-4153)
CJS MENS WEAR
6410 W Jefferson Blvd (46804-6285)
PHONE....................260 436-4788
EMP: 2

SALES (est): 67K **Privately Held**
SIC: 2329 Men's & boys' clothing

(G-4154)
CK PRODUCTS LLC
6230 Innovation Blvd (46818-1399)
PHONE....................260 484-2517
Steve Burdick, *Business Mgr*
Rob Busch, *Opers Mgr*
Randy Thomas, *Maint Spvr*
Scott Osburn, *Accountant*
Tracy Coughlin, *Human Resources*
◆ **EMP:** 83
SQ FT: 55,000
SALES (est): 393K **Privately Held**
SIC: 2064 Candy & other confectionery products
PA: Central Investment Llc
7265 Kenwood Rd Ste 240
Cincinnati OH 45236

(G-4155)
CLASSIC DIE SERVICES INC
6926 Trafalgar Dr Ste D (46803-4206)
PHONE....................260 748-6907
James K Hoffman, *President*
EMP: 22
SALES (est): 2MM **Privately Held**
SIC: 3544 Dies & die holders for metal cutting, forming, die casting; special dies & tools

(G-4156)
CLASSIC GRAPHICS INC
Also Called: Copy Quick
3219 E State Blvd Ste 2 (46805-6801)
PHONE....................260 482-3487
Fax: 260 483-4069
James T Meier, *President*
Victoria Meier, *Vice Pres*
EMP: 13 **EST:** 1971
SQ FT: 2,000
SALES (est): 1.8MM **Privately Held**
WEB: www.classicgraphics.com
SIC: 2752 7336 2791 2789 Commercial printing, offset; commercial art & graphic design; typesetting; bookbinding & related work; commercial printing

(G-4157)
CLASSIC MEDIA LLC
Also Called: Classic Graphics
3219 E State Blvd (46805-6800)
PHONE....................260 482-3487
David M Meier, *Mng Member*
EMP: 5
SQ FT: 4,000
SALES: 300K **Privately Held**
SIC: 2754 7336 Commercial printing, gravure; commercial art & graphic design

(G-4158)
CLASSIC PRODUCTS CORP
6926 Trafalgar Dr Ste D (46803-4206)
PHONE....................260 748-6907
Jim Hoffman, *Branch Mgr*
EMP: 6
SALES (corp-wide): 60.3MM **Privately Held**
WEB: www.classicproducts.com
SIC: 3544 Special dies & tools
PA: Classic Products Corp
4617 Industrial Rd
Fort Wayne IN 46825
260 484-2695

(G-4159)
CLASSIC PRODUCTS CORP (PA)
4617 Industrial Rd (46825-5268)
PHONE....................260 484-2695
Fax: 260 483-7421
Mikel S Eid, *President*
Mike S Eid, *President*
Bob F Jesse, *Chairman*
Bob Gudorf, *Vice Pres*
Steve Potts, *Opers Mgr*
▲ **EMP:** 50
SQ FT: 38,500
SALES (est): 60.3MM **Privately Held**
WEB: www.classicproducts.com
SIC: 5091 2262 2395 5044 Bowling equipment; screen printing: manmade fiber & silk broadwoven fabrics; embroidery & art needlework; photocopy machines

▲ = Import ▼=Export
◆ =Import/Export

(G-4160)
CLASSIC ROCK FACE BLOCK INC
520 Southview Ave (46806-3032)
PHONE..................................260 704-3113
Bart Babis, *Director*
EMP: 5
SALES (est): 265K **Privately Held**
SIC: 1499 Precious stones mining

(G-4161)
CLASSIC TROPHY CO
210 Marciel Dr (46825-5310)
P.O. Box 5487 (46895-5487)
PHONE..................................260 483-1161
Fax: 260 483-4797
Fred Torrence, *President*
Zachary Weidler, *Mktg Dir*
Bill Bader, *Admin Sec*
▲ EMP: 10
SQ FT: 10,000
SALES: 650K **Privately Held**
WEB: www.classictrophy.com
SIC: 3499 5999 3993 Trophies, metal, except silver; trophies & plaques; signs & advertising specialties

(G-4162)
CLOUDBURST LAWN SPRINKLER SYST
1707 Brandywine Trl (46845-1511)
PHONE..................................260 492-8400
Fax: 260 492-8400
Marc Zahn, *President*
Michael Worman, *Vice Pres*
EMP: 10
SALES (est): 1.1MM **Privately Held**
SIC: 3432 1711 Lawn hose nozzles & sprinklers; irrigation sprinkler system installation

(G-4163)
CMA STEEL & FABRICATION INC
3333 Independence Dr (46808-4516)
PHONE..................................260 207-9000
Roger Dammeier, *President*
EMP: 9
SALES (est): 2.2MM **Privately Held**
SIC: 3449 Bars, concrete reinforcing: fabricated steel

(G-4164)
CMA SUPPLY CO FORT WAYNE INC
Also Called: CMA Supply
3333 Independence Dr (46808-4516)
PHONE..................................260 471-9000
Fax: 260 471-4720
Bill Updike, *President*
Roger Dammeier, *Vice Pres*
Jeffery T Degitz, *Vice Pres*
Jeffery Degitz, *Vice Pres*
Jim Weiss, *Manager*
EMP: 18
SQ FT: 15,000
SALES (est): 10.4MM **Privately Held**
WEB: www.cmasupply.com
SIC: 5032 3444 Concrete building products; concrete forms, sheet metal

(G-4165)
CNC INDUSTRIES INC
3810 Fourier Dr (46818-9381)
PHONE..................................260 490-5700
Linda Deam, *President*
Steven Deam Jr, *Principal*
Dustin Kimbrell, *Vice Pres*
EMP: 53
SQ FT: 40,000
SALES (est): 11.3MM **Privately Held**
WEB: www.cncind.com
SIC: 3599 3469 Machine shop, jobbing & repair; custom machinery; machine parts, stamped or pressed metal

(G-4166)
COFFEE LOMONT & MOYER INC
Also Called: Gensic Creative Metals
1205 W Main St (46808-3334)
PHONE..................................260 422-7825
Daniel Lomont, *Exec VP*
Dan Lomont, *Vice Pres*
Jeannine Moyer, *Officer*
Kathleen Lomont, *Admin Sec*
EMP: 15

SQ FT: 9,000
SALES (est): 2.4MM **Privately Held**
WEB: www.gensic.com
SIC: 3449 3446 3444 3443 Miscellaneous metalwork; architectural metalwork; sheet metalwork; fabricated plate work (boiler shop); fabricated structural metal

(G-4167)
COLONY BAY COND OWNERS
2118 Bayside Ct Apt A (46806-7345)
PHONE..................................260 436-4764
Carol Carnall, *Principal*
EMP: 3 EST: 2010
SALES (est): 135.8K **Privately Held**
SIC: 1221 Bituminous coal & lignite-surface mining

(G-4168)
COMMERCIAL SIGNS
Also Called: Commercial School of Lettering
513 E Hawthorne St (46806-3025)
PHONE..................................260 745-2678
Garry Merrills, *President*
Diana Chamber, *Vice Pres*
Diana Chambers, *Vice Pres*
EMP: 7
SQ FT: 5,000
SALES: 120K **Privately Held**
WEB: www.commercialsigns1.com
SIC: 3993 5085 Signs, not made in custom sign painting shops; signmaker equipment & supplies

(G-4169)
COMMERCIAL TECHNICAL SVCS INC
Also Called: Ctsi
2809 Carrington Dr (46804-6062)
PHONE..................................260 436-9898
Vernon C Torres, *President*
EMP: 3
SALES (est): 200K **Privately Held**
SIC: 3999 Manufacturing industries

(G-4170)
COMPLETE CONTROLS INC
3923 Option Pass (46818-1275)
PHONE..................................260 489-0852
Fax: 260 489-0853
Mark A Lewis, *President*
EMP: 5
SALES (est): 1.1MM **Privately Held**
WEB: www.completecontrolsinc.com
SIC: 3823 7699 1731 Temperature measurement instruments, industrial; boiler & heating repair services; electronic controls installation

(G-4171)
COMPLETE DRIVES INC (PA)
Also Called: C D I
6419 Discount Dr (46818-1235)
PHONE..................................260 489-6033
Fax: 260 489-7431
Gregory D Hale, *President*
David Happel, *Vice Pres*
Steve King, *Vice Pres*
John Klopfenstein, *Vice Pres*
Dan Crozier, *Admin Sec*
EMP: 16
SQ FT: 14,000
SALES: 10MM **Privately Held**
SIC: 3366 Bushings & bearings

(G-4172)
COMPOSITES SYNDICATE LLC
Also Called: Plastic Composites Co.
8301 Clinton Park Dr (46825-3164)
PHONE..................................260 484-3139
Fax: 260 483-2532
Ronald Minke,
EMP: 20
SQ FT: 34,000
SALES (est): 1.6MM **Privately Held**
SIC: 3089 Plastic & fiberglass tanks; plastic processing

(G-4173)
CONTINENTAL ENTERPRISES INC
6723 Hanna St (46816-1141)
PHONE..................................260 447-7000
Fax: 260 447-9966
Ronald Clem, *President*

Rick Trump, *Exec VP*
Debbie Clem Felton, *Senior VP*
Lonna Butts, *Vice Pres*
Dave Therkildsen, *Vice Pres*
▲ EMP: 24
SQ FT: 30,000
SALES (est): 5.5MM **Privately Held**
WEB: www.contintl.com
SIC: 3545 Tools & accessories for machine tools

(G-4174)
COPPER KETTLE FUDGE LLC
4714 Union Chapel Rd (46845-9217)
PHONE..................................260 417-1036
Carl Weaver, *Principal*
EMP: 2
SALES (est): 124.4K **Privately Held**
SIC: 2064 Fudge (candy)

(G-4175)
COPY SOLUTIONS INC
5928 W Jefferson Blvd (46804-1677)
PHONE..................................260 436-2679
Fax: 260 436-0196
Kathy L Matthews, *President*
James Matthews, *Vice Pres*
Jim Matthews, *Office Mgr*
EMP: 8
SQ FT: 3,000
SALES (est): 1MM **Privately Held**
WEB: www.yourcopysolution.com
SIC: 7334 2752 Blueprinting service; commercial printing, lithographic

(G-4176)
CORAM USA LLC
6911 Innov Blvd Summi Par Summit Park Ii (46818)
PHONE..................................260 451-8200
Mark Wohlford, *General Mgr*
EMP: 15
SQ FT: 20,000
SALES (est): 2.6MM **Privately Held**
SIC: 3523 Tractors, farm

(G-4177)
CORE BIOLOGIC LLC
3201 Stellhorn Rd (46815-4697)
PHONE..................................888 390-8838
Richard Whipp,
EMP: 2
SALES (est): 74.4K **Privately Held**
SIC: 2835 Microbiology & virology diagnostic products

(G-4178)
CORE LABORATORIES LP
1726 Saint Joe River Dr (46805-1436)
PHONE..................................260 312-0455
Jane Surbeck, *President*
EMP: 13
SALES (corp-wide): 659.8MM **Privately Held**
SIC: 1389 Oil field services
HQ: Core Laboratories Lp
6316 Windfern Rd
Houston TX 77040

(G-4179)
CORE-TECH INC
6000 Maumee Rd (46803-1750)
PHONE..................................260 748-4477
Fax: 260 748-4478
Michael Roselle, *President*
Anthony Roselle, *Vice Pres*
Eric Ames, *Manager*
Jarrod Meeks, *Manager*
▲ EMP: 65
SQ FT: 40,000
SALES (est): 11.7MM **Privately Held**
WEB: www.coretech1.com
SIC: 3543 Industrial patterns

(G-4180)
COREBIOLOGIC LLC
4415 Winding Brook Rd (46814-9449)
PHONE..................................260 437-0353
EMP: 4
SALES (est): 99K **Privately Held**
SIC: 2836 Biological products, except diagnostic

(G-4181)
COTTAGE INDUSTRIES INC
5325 Merchandise Dr (46825-5139)
PHONE..................................260 482-1100
EMP: 2
SALES (est): 121K **Privately Held**
SIC: 3999 Mfg Misc Products

(G-4182)
CPI CARD GROUP - INDIANA INC
613 High St (46808-3440)
P.O. Box 10748 (46853-0748)
PHONE..................................260 424-4920
Anna Rossetti, *President*
Steve Montross, *Principal*
Jerry Dreiling, *Vice Pres*
Diane Jackson, *Vice Pres*
Mary Martinez, *Vice Pres*
▲ EMP: 130 EST: 1947
SQ FT: 28,800
SALES (est): 25.4MM
SALES (corp-wide): 254.8MM **Publicly Held**
WEB: www.didierprinting.com
SIC: 3089 Identification cards, plastic
HQ: Cpi Card Group - Colorado, Inc.
10368 W Centennial Rd A
Littleton CO 80127
303 973-9311

(G-4183)
CRAFT LABORATORIES INC
1901 Lakeview Dr (46808-3919)
PHONE..................................260 432-9467
Fax: 260 436-4161
R William Munsie, *Admin Sec*
EMP: 15
SQ FT: 35,000
SALES (est): 2.1MM **Privately Held**
WEB: www.craftlabs.com
SIC: 2841 2819 5169 2842 Soap & other detergents; industrial inorganic chemicals; chemicals & allied products; specialty cleaning, polishes & sanitation goods; industrial machinery & equipment

(G-4184)
CREATIVE CONTROL SYSTEMS
4115 Clubview Dr (46804-3157)
PHONE..................................260 432-9020
Fax: 260 436-0030
Robert Bailey, *Principal*
EMP: 2 EST: 2011
SALES (est): 192.8K **Privately Held**
SIC: 3822 Appliance regulators

(G-4185)
CREATIVE LIQUID COATINGS INC (PA)
2701 S Coliseum Blvd # 1284 (46803-2976)
P.O. Box 369, Kendallville (46755-0369)
PHONE..................................260 349-1862
Randall R Geist, *President*
Dave Hunt, *Manager*
▲ EMP: 536
SQ FT: 200,000
SALES: 48.8MM **Privately Held**
WEB: www.creativecoatingsinc.com
SIC: 3479 1721 Painting, coating & hot dipping; industrial painting

(G-4186)
CREATIVE POWDER COATINGS LLC
Also Called: Creative Coatings
7505 Freedom Way (46818-2164)
PHONE..................................260 489-3580
Fax: 260 489-3643
Don Harper, *Mng Member*
Richard Lain,
EMP: 60
SQ FT: 106,000
SALES (est): 13.8MM **Privately Held**
SIC: 3399 Powder, metal

(G-4187)
CREATIVE WOODWORKS LLC
9771 Maysville Rd (46815)
PHONE..................................260 450-1742
Tyrone Moore,
EMP: 2
SQ FT: 2,500

SALES (est): 163.5K **Privately Held**
SIC: 2599 Cabinets, factory

(G-4188)
CROWN BATTERY MANUFACTURING CO
3000 E Washington Blvd (46803-1534)
PHONE..................................260 423-3358
Fax: 260 423-3559
Kenneth Talbert, *Principal*
EMP: 5
SALES (corp-wide): 222.1MM **Privately Held**
WEB: www.crownbattery.com
SIC: 3691 Storage batteries
PA: Crown Battery Manufacturing Company
1445 Majestic Dr
Fremont OH 43420
419 332-0563

(G-4189)
CROWN EQUIPMENT CORPORATION
Also Called: Crown Lift Trucks-Ft Wayne
9110 Avionics Dr (46809-9657)
PHONE..................................260 484-0055
Fax: 260 483-8542
Troy Boyer, *Manager*
EMP: 80
SQ FT: 11,000
SALES (corp-wide): 3.1B **Privately Held**
SIC: 3537 Lift trucks, industrial: fork, plat-
form, straddle, etc.
PA: Crown Equipment Corporation
44 S Washington St
New Bremen OH 45869
419 629-2311

(G-4190)
CROWN GROUP CO
Also Called: Indiana Coatings Division
4301 Engle Rd (46804-4422)
PHONE..................................260 432-6900
Fax: 260 432-8982
Marc Lechleitner, *Business Mgr*
Bart Alexander, *Manager*
Nikki Rodriguez, *Clerk*
EMP: 60
SQ FT: 56,000
SALES (corp-wide): 108.1MM **Privately Held**
SIC: 3479 Coating of metals & formed products
PA: The Crown Group Co
2111 Walter Reuther Dr
Warren MI 48091
586 575-9800

(G-4191)
CSL PLASMA INC
108 E Pettit Ave (46806-3003)
PHONE..................................260 454-5083
EMP: 5
SALES (est): 625.4K **Privately Held**
SIC: 2836 Plasmas

(G-4192)
CUMMINS CROSSPOINT LLC
3415 W Coliseum Blvd (46808-1026)
PHONE..................................260 482-3691
Fax: 260 484-8930
Steve Gregg, *Branch Mgr*
EMP: 40
SALES (corp-wide): 20.4B **Publicly Held**
SIC: 5084 3519 Engines & parts, diesel;
internal combustion engines
HQ: Cummins Crosspoint Llc
2601 Fortune Cir E 300c
Indianapolis IN 46241
317 243-7979

(G-4193)
CUSTOM ART SCREEN PRINTING
2800 Wayne Trce (46803-3789)
P.O. Box 15732 (46885-5732)
PHONE..................................260 456-3909
Fax: 260 744-4568
Teresa Sutton, *President*
Keith Hanson, *Principal*
Ray Hanson, *Vice Pres*
EMP: 13
SQ FT: 17,000

SALES (est): 1.7MM **Privately Held**
WEB: www.customartfw.com
SIC: 2759 Screen printing

(G-4194)
CUSTOM CASE PLACE LLC
6435 W Jefferson Blvd (46804-6203)
PHONE..................................260 715-1413
Julie Sellers, *Administration*
EMP: 2
SALES (est): 104K **Privately Held**
SIC: 3523 Farm machinery & equipment

(G-4195)
CUSTOM ENGRG & FABRICATION INC
2211 Freeman St (46802-6926)
PHONE..................................260 745-9299
Fax: 260 745-5461
Bob Hatfield, *Principal*
Jonathon Lawlor, *Engineer*
Brad Herber, *Project Engr*
Rodney Hughes, *Design Engr*
Dale Lutz, *Design Engr*
EMP: 28
SQ FT: 38,000
SALES (est): 6.5MM **Privately Held**
WEB: www.ceandf.com
SIC: 3599 Machine shop, jobbing & repair

(G-4196)
CUSTOM SIGNS UNLIMITED CO
1410 Goshen Ave (46808-2036)
PHONE..................................260 483-4444
Dan Cameron, *Owner*
EMP: 2 EST: 2009
SALES (est): 208.6K **Privately Held**
SIC: 3993 Electric signs

(G-4197)
D AND M ENTERPRISES LLC
Also Called: Custom Poly Packaging
3216 Congressional Pkwy (46808-4417)
PHONE..................................260 483-4008
Fax: 260 484-5166
Kim Schmidt, *Managing Prtnr*
Jim Hansen, *Marketing Mgr*
Michael Carpenter,
EMP: 13
SQ FT: 13,000
SALES (est): 1.9MM **Privately Held**
WEB: www.custompoly.com
SIC: 2673 3081 Plastic bags: made from
purchased materials; unsupported plas-
tics film & sheet

(G-4198)
D&W FINE PACK LLC
Also Called: C&M Fine Pack
7707 Vicksburg Pike (46804-5549)
P.O. Box 12347 (46863-2347)
PHONE..................................260 432-3027
Fax: 260 432-9275
Darrin Claussin, *General Mgr*
EMP: 300
SALES (corp-wide): 614.5MM **Privately Held**
SIC: 3089 Plastic containers, except foam
HQ: D&W Fine Pack Llc
777 Mark St Ste 101
Wood Dale IL 60191

(G-4199)
DANA LIGHT AXLE PRODUCTS LLC (DH)
2100 W State Blvd (46808-1937)
PHONE..................................260 483-7174
Robert Cole, *Manager*
Thomas Stone,
▲ EMP: 81
SALES (est): 130MM **Publicly Held**
SIC: 3714 Motor vehicle parts & acces-
sories

(G-4200)
DATA PRINT INITIATIVES LLC
1710 Dividend Rd (46808-1131)
PHONE..................................260 489-2665
Daniel T Foster, *CEO*
Jim Cawvey, *Vice Pres*
EMP: 9
SALES (est): 1.4MM **Privately Held**
SIC: 2752 Commercial printing, offset

(G-4201)
DAVIS VACHON ARTWORKS
227 W Wallen Rd (46825-2223)
PHONE..................................260 489-9160
Davis Vachon, *Owner*
EMP: 2
SALES (est): 74.4K **Privately Held**
SIC: 3269 Stoneware pottery products

(G-4202)
DCX-CHOL ENTERPRISES INC
1615 E Wallace St (46803-2564)
PHONE..................................260 407-1107
Lola Herron, *Vice Pres*
EMP: 90
SALES (corp-wide): 145.3MM **Privately Held**
SIC: 3812 Aircraft/aerospace flight instru-
ments & guidance systems
PA: Dcx-Chol Enterprises, Inc.
12831 S Figueroa St
Los Angeles CA 90061
310 516-1692

(G-4203)
DEBRAND INC (PA)
Also Called: Debrand Fine Chocolates
10105 Auburn Park Dr (46825-2388)
PHONE..................................260 969-8333
Fax: 260 969-8334
Cathy Brand Beere, *President*
Timothy L Beere, *Corp Secy*
Diane Lampe, *Manager*
Dannielle Goodrich, *Creative Dir*
Timothy Beere, *Executive*
▲ EMP: 90
SQ FT: 3,000
SALES (est): 16.8MM **Privately Held**
WEB: www.debrand.com
SIC: 2064 2066 Chocolate candy, except
solid chocolate; chocolate & cocoa prod-
ucts

(G-4204)
DEISTER CONCENTRATOR LLC
Also Called: 100
9205 Avionics Dr (46809-9637)
PHONE..................................260 747-2700
Larry Adelman, *Mng Member*
Jerry Henry,
Tom O'Neill,
Don Ross,
EMP: 20
SALES (est): 3.7MM **Privately Held**
SIC: 3462 Construction or mining equip-
ment forgings, ferrous

(G-4205)
DEISTER MACHINE COMPANY INC (PA)
1933 E Wayne St (46803-1332)
P.O. Box 1 (46801-0001)
PHONE..................................260 426-7495
Fax: 260 422-1523
Irwin F Deister Jr, *Ch of Bd*
E Mark Deister, *President*
▼ EMP: 200
SQ FT: 65,000
SALES (est): 70.7MM **Privately Held**
WEB: www.deistermachine.com
SIC: 3532 Mining machinery; separating
machinery, mineral; screeners, stationary;
feeders, ore & aggregate

(G-4206)
DEISTER MACHINE COMPANY INC
901 Glasgow Ave (46803-1308)
PHONE..................................260 426-7495
Greg Wood, *Branch Mgr*
EMP: 15
SALES (corp-wide): 70.7MM **Privately Held**
WEB: www.deistermachine.com
SIC: 3532 Mining machinery; separating
machinery, mineral; screeners, stationary;
feeders, ore & aggregate
PA: Deister Machine Company Inc
1933 E Wayne St
Fort Wayne IN 46803
260 426-7495

(G-4207)
DEISTER MACHINE COMPANY INC
1604 E Berry St (46803-1021)
PHONE..................................260 422-0354
Greg Wood, *Manager*
EMP: 250
SALES (est): 19.1MM
SALES (corp-wide): 70.7MM **Privately Held**
WEB: www.deistermachine.com
SIC: 3532 3444 3441 Mining machinery;
separating machinery, mineral; screeners,
stationary; sheet metalwork; fabricated
structural metal
PA: Deister Machine Company Inc
1933 E Wayne St
Fort Wayne IN 46803
260 426-7495

(G-4208)
DENTISSE INC
6415 Mutual Dr (46825-4258)
PHONE..................................260 444-3046
Michael Moore, *President*
Mark Putt, *Vice Pres*
Nate Reusser, *Treasurer*
David Dimberio, *Admin Sec*
EMP: 5 EST: 2007
SALES (est): 700K **Privately Held**
SIC: 2844 Toothpastes or powders, denti-
frices

(G-4209)
DI COLOGNE GROUP ●
14214 Brafferton Pkwy (46814-2301)
PHONE..................................260 616-0158
EMP: 2 EST: 2017
SALES (est): 74.4K **Privately Held**
SIC: 2844 Colognes

(G-4210)
DIGITAL REPROGRAPHICS INC
3311 Congressional Pkwy (46808-4438)
PHONE..................................260 483-8066
James F Scott, *President*
Amy Scott, *Vice Pres*
EMP: 9
SQ FT: 5,000
SALES (est): 940K **Privately Held**
WEB: www.drfw.biz
SIC: 5999 2752 Drafting equipment & sup-
plies; commercial printing, lithographic

(G-4211)
DIRECTV INC
10020 Lima Rd Ste A (46818-9144)
PHONE..................................260 471-3474
Phil McClure, *Manager*
EMP: 2 EST: 2011
SALES (est): 153.7K **Privately Held**
SIC: 3663 Space satellite communications
equipment

(G-4212)
DISKEY ARCHITECTURAL SIGNAGE
450 E Brackenridge St (46802-3521)
P.O. Box 12100 (46862-2100)
PHONE..................................260 424-0233
Mike Butler, *President*
Catherine Butler, *Vice Pres*
Jennifer Gray, *Opers Staff*
EMP: 15
SQ FT: 2,000
SALES: 1MM **Privately Held**
WEB: www.diskeysign.com
SIC: 3993 Signs, not made in custom sign
painting shops

(G-4213)
DISTINCTIVE ELEMENTS
10208 Kilkea Pl (46835-9133)
PHONE..................................260 704-2464
EMP: 3 EST: 2016
SALES (est): 88.5K **Privately Held**
SIC: 2819 Elements

(G-4214)
DIVERSIFIED TOOLS & MACHINE
2701 W Wallen Rd (46818-2240)
PHONE..................................260 489-0272
Fax: 260 497-0882
Richard Eversole, *President*

▲ = Import ▼=Export
◆ =Import/Export

EMP: 7
SQ FT: 5,700
SALES (est): 874.5K **Privately Held**
SIC: 3544 Special dies, tools, jigs & fixtures

(G-4215)
DKM EMBROIDERY INC
Also Called: Sg Trading Post
3203 Caprice Ct (46808-4505)
P.O. Box 8895 (46898-8895)
PHONE..........................260 471-4070
Fax: 260 471-4070
Deborah K Mattox, *President*
▲ **EMP:** 8
SALES (est): 872.5K **Privately Held**
WEB: www.dkmembroidery.com
SIC: 2395 Embroidery products, except schiffli machine; embroidery & art needlework

(G-4216)
DNGCO LLC (PA)
7625 Disalle Blvd (46825-3374)
PHONE..........................800 643-7332
Enoch Stiff, *President*
Laura Hutsell, *General Mgr*
Tom Delong, *Vice Pres*
Rick Miller, *VP Opers*
Kristopher Rice, *Opers Staff*
▲ **EMP:** 50
SALES (est): 18.5MM **Privately Held**
WEB: www.amsportworks.com
SIC: 3751 3799 Motor scooters & parts; go-carts, except children's; off-road automobiles, except recreational vehicles

(G-4217)
DOELL DESIGNS
5211 Stellhorn Rd (46815-5057)
PHONE..........................260 486-4504
Fax: 260 486-4504
Dave Doell, *Owner*
EMP: 2
SQ FT: 3,000
SALES: 80K **Privately Held**
SIC: 7389 3993 Lettering & sign painting services; signs, not made in custom sign painting shops

(G-4218)
DON R FRUCHEY INC
PWC Fabrication
2121 Wayne Haven St (46803-3280)
PHONE..........................260 493-3626
Fax: 260 749-1005
Chuck Brewster, *Branch Mgr*
EMP: 26
SALES (est): 5.8MM
SALES (corp-wide): 18MM **Privately Held**
WEB: www.pwcfabrication.com
SIC: 3443 Fabricated plate work (boiler shop)
PA: Don R Fruchey Inc
5608 Maumee Rd
Fort Wayne IN 46803
260 749-8502

(G-4219)
DOUBLE ENVELOPE CORP
10804 Lake Shasta Ct (46804-6907)
PHONE..........................260 434-0500
Julie Shackley, *Owner*
EMP: 2
SALES (est): 122.7K **Privately Held**
SIC: 5112 2677 Envelopes; envelopes

(G-4220)
DR PEPPER SNAPPLE GROUP I
2711 Independence Dr (46808-1331)
PHONE..........................260 484-4177
EMP: 3
SALES (est): 126.3K **Privately Held**
SIC: 2086 Soft drinks: packaged in cans, bottles, etc.

(G-4221)
DRUMMOND INDUSTRIES
2826 White Oak Ave (46805-2961)
PHONE..........................260 348-5550
Robbie Drummond, *Owner*
EMP: 12
SQ FT: 14,000
SALES (est): 746K **Privately Held**
SIC: 3999 Manufacturing industries

(G-4222)
DRY INC
Also Called: Dry Cleaners Secret
7201 Engle Rd (46804-2228)
PHONE..........................503 977-9204
Scott Heim, *President*
EMP: 11
SALES (est): 1.7MM **Privately Held**
WEB: www.drycleanerssecret.com
SIC: 2842 Drycleaning preparations

(G-4223)
DUESENBURG INC
3330 Congressional Pkwy (46808-4439)
P.O. Box 50311 (46805-0311)
PHONE..........................260 496-9650
Hunar Sakri, *President*
Renee Sakri, *Treasurer*
EMP: 8
SQ FT: 27,000
SALES (est): 442.8K **Privately Held**
WEB: www.duesenburg.com
SIC: 8711 3625 3569 Electrical or electronic engineering; electric controls & control accessories, industrial; liquid automation machinery & equipment

(G-4224)
DUNHAM RUBBER & BELTING CORP
4004 Lower Huntington Rd (46809-9710)
PHONE..........................800 876-5340
Crystal Hues, *Branch Mgr*
EMP: 6
SALES (corp-wide): 27MM **Privately Held**
SIC: 5085 5162 5251 3052 Rubber goods, mechanical; plastics materials & basic shapes; hardware; rubber & plastics hose & beltings
PA: Dunham Rubber & Belting Corporation
682 Commerce Parkway W Dr
Greenwood IN 46143
317 888-3002

(G-4225)
DUPONT 9 BUILDING COMPANY LLC
2518 E Dupont Rd (46825-1675)
PHONE..........................260 432-4913
EMP: 2
SALES (est): 74.4K **Privately Held**
SIC: 2879 Agricultural chemicals

(G-4226)
DUPONT AND TONKEL PARTNERS LLC
10501 Day Lily Dr (46825-2763)
PHONE..........................260 444-2264
EMP: 4 EST: 2013
SALES (est): 186.3K **Privately Held**
SIC: 2879 Agricultural chemicals

(G-4227)
DUPONT COMMONS LLC
10316 Valley Hills Ln (46825-1776)
PHONE..........................260 637-3215
Hugh W Johnston Sr, *Principal*
EMP: 2
SALES (est): 141.1K **Privately Held**
SIC: 2879 Agricultural chemicals

(G-4228)
DUPONT ORTHODONTICS
2121 E Dupont Rd (46825-1546)
PHONE..........................260 490-3554
Allison Bergdoll, *Principal*
EMP: 2
SALES (est): 74.4K **Privately Held**
SIC: 2879 Agricultural chemicals

(G-4229)
DX 4 LLC
Also Called: Proform
3000 Engle Rd (46809-1108)
PHONE..........................260 410-3749
David Tippmann, *Mng Member*
EMP: 10
SALES (est): 1.3MM **Privately Held**
SIC: 3441 Fabricated structural metal

(G-4230)
DYNAMIC HOLDINGS LLC (DH)
7575 W Jefferson Blvd (46804-4131)
PHONE..........................260 969-3500

Theresa E Wagler, *Administration*
EMP: 3
SALES (est): 193K **Publicly Held**
SIC: 3312 Plate, sheet & strip, except coated products
HQ: Stld Holdings, Inc.
6714 Pointe Inverness Way # 100
Fort Wayne IN 46804
260 969-3590

(G-4231)
EAGLE FLOORING BROKERS INC
Also Called: Eagle Tile
220 Fernhill Ave (46805-1017)
PHONE..........................260 422-6100
Brady Wiggins, *President*
▲ **EMP:** 6
SQ FT: 25,000
SALES (est): 1MM **Privately Held**
WEB: www.eagletileonline.com
SIC: 3996 Hard surface floor coverings

(G-4232)
EARTHY INDUSTRIES LLC
2609 East Dr (46805-3614)
PHONE..........................260 483-7588
David A O'Connor, *Principal*
EMP: 2 EST: 2008
SALES (est): 83.9K **Privately Held**
SIC: 3999 Manufacturing industries

(G-4233)
EL MEXICANO INC
Also Called: El Mexicano Newspaper
2301 Fairfield Ave # 102 (46807-1247)
PHONE..........................260 456-6843
Fax: 260 456-2535
Fernando Zapari, *President*
EMP: 4
SALES (est): 271.1K **Privately Held**
SIC: 2741 2711 Miscellaneous publishing; newspapers

(G-4234)
ELECTRIC POWER SERVICE
5423 State Road 930 (46803-1771)
PHONE..........................260 493-4913
Pete Limkemann, *President*
EMP: 5
SQ FT: 6,000
SALES: 80K **Privately Held**
SIC: 7694 5063 Electric motor repair; motors, electric

(G-4235)
ELECTRICAL MOTOR PRODUCTS INC
15009 Dunton Rd (46845-9380)
PHONE..........................877 455-1599
Chuck Koehl, *Owner*
EMP: 2
SALES (est): 305.2K **Privately Held**
SIC: 7694 Electric motor repair

(G-4236)
ELRINGKLINGER MFG IND INC
Also Called: Ekmi
2677 Persistence Dr (46808-1496)
PHONE..........................734 788-1776
Jurgen Weingartner, *President*
EMP: 3
SALES: 10MM
SALES (corp-wide): 1.9B **Privately Held**
SIC: 3711 Automobile assembly, including specialty automobiles
PA: Elringklinger Ag
Max-Eyth-Str. 2
Dettingen An Der Erms 72581
712 372-40

(G-4237)
ENVELOPE SERVICE INC
7101 Lincoln Pkwy (46804-5603)
PHONE..........................260 432-6277
Fax: 260 436-2971
Gary Hilgeman, *President*
EMP: 50 EST: 1978
SQ FT: 36,000
SALES (est): 11.2MM **Privately Held**
SIC: 2677 2752 Envelopes; business form & card printing, lithographic

(G-4238)
ENVIRO INK
6926 Quemetco Ct Ste A (46803-3394)
PHONE..........................260 748-0636
Tony Williams, *Owner*
EMP: 3
SALES (est): 210K **Privately Held**
SIC: 2893 Printing ink

(G-4239)
ENZYME SOLUTIONS INC
10219 River Rapids Run (46845-8950)
PHONE..........................800 523-1323
Jared Hochstedler, *Principal*
EMP: 2
SALES (est): 144.8K **Privately Held**
SIC: 2869 Enzymes

(G-4240)
EPCO PRODUCTS INC
3736 Vanguard Dr (46809-3303)
P.O. Box 9250 (46899-9250)
PHONE..........................260 747-8888
Fredric J Aichele, *President*
J Aichele, *Vice Pres*
Robert Prince, *Vice Pres*
Diana Knight, *Purch Mgr*
Brenda Malicoat, *QC Mgr*
▼ **EMP:** 20 EST: 1980
SQ FT: 25,200
SALES (est): 4.2MM **Privately Held**
WEB: www.epcoproducts.com
SIC: 3451 3429 3541 3494 Screw machine products; marine hardware; motor vehicle hardware; machine tools, metal cutting type; valves & pipe fittings; metal stampings

(G-4241)
ERIE-HAVEN INC (PA)
Also Called: Erie Haven Concrete
3909 Limestone Dr (46809-9709)
P.O. Box 11332 (46857-1332)
PHONE..........................260 478-1674
Fax: 260 747-4889
Larry D Gerig, *President*
Richard Neargarder, *Plant Mgr*
Tim Deal, *Manager*
John Leedy, *Admin Sec*
EMP: 75
SALES (est): 25.2MM **Privately Held**
WEB: www.eriehaven.com
SIC: 3273 3272 Ready-mixed concrete; concrete products

(G-4242)
ES DEICING
3500 Meyer Rd (46806)
PHONE..........................260 422-2020
Eric Hitzfield, *Owner*
Sherry Hitzfield, *Co-Owner*
EMP: 2
SALES (est): 144.3K **Privately Held**
SIC: 2899 Salt

(G-4243)
ESSEX GROUP INC (DH)
Also Called: Superior Essex
1601 Wall St (46802-4352)
P.O. Box 1601 (46801-1601)
PHONE..........................260 461-4000
Fax: 260 461-4199
Justin F Deedy Jr, *President*
Stephen M Carter, *President*
David S Aldridge, *Exec VP*
Debbie Baker-Oliver, *Senior VP*
Matt Odonnell, *Senior VP*
▲ **EMP:** 200 EST: 1973
SQ FT: 500,000
SALES (est): 630.1MM
SALES (corp-wide): 105.4MM **Privately Held**
WEB: www.essexwire.com
SIC: 3357 Communication wire; fiber optic cable (insulated)
HQ: Superior Essex Inc.
6120 Powers Ferry Rd # 150
Atlanta GA 30339
770 657-6000

(G-4244)
ESSEX GROUP INC
Also Called: Telecommunications Pdts Div
1601 Wall St (46802-4352)
PHONE..........................260 461-4000
Chris Mapes, *Branch Mgr*

EMP: 300
SALES (corp-wide): 105.4MM **Privately Held**
WEB: www.essexwire.com
SIC: 3357 3351 Building wire & cable, nonferrous; automotive wire & cable, except ignition sets: nonferrous; communication wire; magnet wire, nonferrous; copper & copper alloy pipe & tube
HQ: Essex Group, Inc.
   1601 Wall St
   Fort Wayne IN 46802
   260 461-4000

(G-4245)
ESSEX GROUP INC
Also Called: Superior Essex
1700 Taylor St (46802)
PHONE...........................260 461-4183
Shafiq Jadallah, *Office Mgr*
EMP: 101
SALES (corp-wide): 105.4MM **Privately Held**
SIC: 3357 Magnet wire, nonferrous
HQ: Essex Group, Inc.
   1601 Wall St
   Fort Wayne IN 46802
   260 461-4000

(G-4246)
ESSEX GROUP INC
3405 Meyer Rd Ste 170 (46803-2982)
PHONE...........................260 461-4994
EMP: 9
SALES (corp-wide): 105.4MM **Privately Held**
SIC: 3357 Nonferrous wiredrawing & insulating
HQ: Essex Group, Inc.
   1601 Wall St
   Fort Wayne IN 46802
   260 461-4000

(G-4247)
ESSEX GROUP INC
601 Wall St (46802)
PHONE...........................704 598-0222
Mike Sears, *Manager*
EMP: 3
SALES (corp-wide): 105.4MM **Privately Held**
SIC: 3357 Magnet wire, nonferrous
HQ: Essex Group, Inc.
   1601 Wall St
   Fort Wayne IN 46802
   260 461-4000

(G-4248)
ESSEX GROUP INC
Also Called: Essex Wire & Cable Division
3405 Meyer Rd Ste 170 (46803-2982)
PHONE...........................260 424-1708
Ron Stiltner, *Branch Mgr*
EMP: 220
SALES (corp-wide): 105.4MM **Privately Held**
WEB: www.essexwire.com
SIC: 4841 3315 Cable television services; steel wire & related products
HQ: Essex Group, Inc.
   1601 Wall St
   Fort Wayne IN 46802
   260 461-4000

(G-4249)
ETERNAL ENERGY LLC
1530 Progress Rd (46808-1181)
PHONE...........................260 410-3056
Kevin Kensinger,
EMP: 2
SALES (est): 185.2K **Privately Held**
SIC: 3675 Electronic capacitors

(G-4250)
EUROPEAN CONCEPTS LLC
Also Called: Anton Alexander
5607 Newland Pl (46835-3880)
PHONE...........................888 797-9005
Anton Babich, *Owner*
EMP: 2
SALES: 45K **Privately Held**
SIC: 2321 7389 Men's & boys' dress shirts;

(G-4251)
EXCELL COLOR GRAPHICS INC
2623 Camino Ct (46808-4427)
P.O. Box 80547 (46898-0547)
PHONE...........................260 482-2720
Fax: 260 482-2257
Thomas Parrot Jr, *President*
Jerry Blaising, *President*
Tracy Green, *Plant Mgr*
James Reutebuch, *Prdtn Mgr*
Jim Isch, *Accounts Exec*
EMP: 35
SQ FT: 40,000
SALES: 6.5MM **Privately Held**
WEB: www.excellcg.com
SIC: 2759 2796 2791 2752 Screen printing; platemaking services; typesetting; commercial printing, lithographic

(G-4252)
FABCORE INDUSTRIES LLC
928 Pencross Dr (46845-1219)
PHONE...........................260 438-3431
Jason Mueller, *Principal*
EMP: 3
SALES (est): 288.7K **Privately Held**
SIC: 3999 Manufacturing industries

(G-4253)
FAIRFIELD GAS WAY
Also Called: Marathon Oil
4230 Fairfield Ave (46807-2740)
PHONE...........................260 744-2186
Brett Bair, *Principal*
EMP: 3
SALES (est): 276.8K **Privately Held**
SIC: 5541 3578 Filling stations, gasoline; automatic teller machines (ATM)

(G-4254)
FALLEN TIMBER BATS LLC
1136 Tina Marie Ct (46825-7256)
PHONE...........................260 387-5841
Daniel Nolan, *Principal*
EMP: 2 EST: 2014
SALES (est): 141.3K **Privately Held**
SIC: 3949 Sporting & athletic goods

(G-4255)
FARM FINDS CANDLE CO LLC
831 Woodland Xing (46825-1529)
PHONE...........................260 437-5403
Lesley Sears, *Principal*
EMP: 2
SALES (est): 62.5K **Privately Held**
SIC: 3999 Candles

(G-4256)
FASHION CITY
1108 E Pontiac St Ste 2 (46803-3400)
PHONE...........................260 744-6753
Hassan Nassor, *President*
EMP: 2
SALES (est): 203.9K **Privately Held**
SIC: 2329 Riding clothes:, men's, youths' & boys'

(G-4257)
FAST PRINT INCORPORATED
3050 E State Blvd (46805-4737)
PHONE...........................260 484-5487
Fax: 260 436-1077
Carolyn Plein, *President*
Caroline Cline, *President*
Stanley Cline, *Corp Secy*
Dan Metzger, *Vice Pres*
Bill Brotherton, *Buyer*
EMP: 8 EST: 1975
SQ FT: 5,400
SALES (est): 840K **Privately Held**
WEB: www.fastprintinc.com
SIC: 2752 Commercial printing, offset

(G-4258)
FASTSIGNS
3014 N Clinton St (46805-1912)
PHONE...........................260 373-0911
Fax: 260 373-1712
Frank Shepler, *Owner*
EMP: 2
SALES (est): 110K **Privately Held**
SIC: 3993 Signs & advertising specialties

(G-4259)
FAURECIA EMISSIONS CONTL TECH
4510 Airport Expy (46809-9658)
PHONE...........................248 758-8160
Michael Manson, *Branch Mgr*
EMP: 100
SALES (corp-wide): 342.9MM **Privately Held**
SIC: 3714 Exhaust systems & parts, motor vehicle; motor vehicle engines & parts
HQ: Faurecia Emissions Control Technologies Usa, Llc
   950 W 450 S
   Columbus IN 47201

(G-4260)
FAZTEK LLC
6935 Lincoln Pkwy (46804-5623)
PHONE...........................260 482-7544
Mark Morton,
Lee Melchi,
Mark E Ruppp,
Wayne Shive,
EMP: 17
SQ FT: 10,000
SALES (est): 4MM **Privately Held**
WEB: www.faztek.net
SIC: 3599 Machine shop, jobbing & repair

(G-4261)
FEDERAL-MOGUL LLC
9602 Coldwater Rd (46825-2095)
PHONE...........................260 497-5563
EMP: 2
SALES (corp-wide): 21.7B **Publicly Held**
SIC: 3559 Degreasing machines, automotive & industrial
HQ: Federal-Mogul Llc
   27300 W 11 Mile Rd # 101
   Southfield MI 48034

(G-4262)
FILMTEC FABRICATIONS LLC
9609 Ardmore Ave (46809-9625)
P.O. Box 9040 (46899-9040)
PHONE...........................419 435-7504
EMP: 2
SALES (est): 62.5K **Privately Held**
SIC: 3999 Manufacturing industries

(G-4263)
FIRST GEAR INC
Also Called: First Gear Engineering & Tech
7606 Freedom Way (46818-2165)
PHONE...........................260 490-3238
Fax: 260 490-4093
Greg Leffler Jr, *President*
Mike Goza, *General Mgr*
Cynthia Leffler, *Vice Pres*
Shane Refeld, *Prdtn Mgr*
Nick Johnson, *Mfg Mgr*
EMP: 17
SQ FT: 16,280
SALES: 1MM **Privately Held**
WEB: www.first-gear.com
SIC: 3559 3728 3812 3841 Automotive related machinery; gears, aircraft power transmission; acceleration indicators & systems components, aerospace; surgical & medical instruments

(G-4264)
FIVE STAR FABULOUS LLC
6931 Lincoln Pkwy (46804-5623)
PHONE...........................260 579-3401
Peter Roesner,
EMP: 2
SALES (est): 67K **Privately Held**
SIC: 2389 Apparel & accessories

(G-4265)
FLARE INC
6210 Discount Dr (46818-1232)
PHONE...........................260 490-1101
Fax: 260 490-1301
Allen Collins, *President*
Kenneth Ehle, *Plant Mgr*
Cherie Collins, *Admin Sec*
▲ EMP: 9 EST: 1976
SALES (est): 1.5MM **Privately Held**
WEB: www.flarebt.com
SIC: 3599 7692 3544 Machine shop, jobbing & repair; welding repair; special dies, tools, jigs & fixtures

(G-4266)
FLAVOREEDS
3535 N Anthony Blvd (46805-1423)
PHONE...........................260 373-2233
Fax: 260 373-2242
Walt Ostermeyer, *Owner*
EMP: 3
SALES (est): 293.5K **Privately Held**
WEB: www.flavoreeds.com
SIC: 3931 Reeds for musical instruments

(G-4267)
FLICKINGER INDUSTRIES INC
1801 Carlton Ave (46802-4576)
PHONE...........................260 432-4527
Fax: 260 436-0684
Ronald Flickinger, *President*
John Flickinger, *Treasurer*
Karen Flickinger, *Admin Sec*
EMP: 45 EST: 1960
SQ FT: 40,000
SALES (est): 13.6MM **Privately Held**
SIC: 3561 Cylinders, pump

(G-4268)
FLP WOODWORKS
1510 Boone St (46808-3708)
PHONE...........................260 424-3904
Philip Koher, *Principal*
EMP: 2
SALES (est): 155.1K **Privately Held**
SIC: 2431 Millwork

(G-4269)
FORT WAYNE AWNING CO INC
7105 Ardmore Ave (46809-9541)
PHONE...........................260 478-1636
Fax: 260 747-0466
Mel K McClain, *President*
Karen S Mc Clain, *Corp Secy*
EMP: 9
SQ FT: 5,000
SALES: 1MM **Privately Held**
SIC: 2394 Canvas & related products; awnings, fabric: made from purchased materials; tents: made from purchased materials; tarpaulins, fabric: made from purchased materials

(G-4270)
FORT WAYNE BOX & PALLET LLC
7739 Hessen Cassel Rd (46816-2627)
PHONE...........................260 409-4067
Nate Oxley,
EMP: 6 EST: 2015
SALES: 500K **Privately Held**
SIC: 2499 Applicators, wood

(G-4271)
FORT WAYNE CLUTCH INC (PA)
Also Called: Fort Wayne Clutch & Driveline
2424 Goshen Rd (46808-1490)
PHONE...........................260 484-8505
Fax: 260 484-8605
Francis De Mayo, *President*
EMP: 14 EST: 1966
SQ FT: 80,000
SALES: 3MM **Privately Held**
WEB: www.fortwayneclutch.com
SIC: 7539 3714 3568 Front end repair, automotive; motor vehicle parts & accessories; power transmission equipment

(G-4272)
FORT WAYNE FABRICATION
3303 Freeman St (46802-4436)
PHONE...........................260 459-8848
Ed Morken, *President*
EMP: 4
SALES (est): 655.9K **Privately Held**
SIC: 3444 Sheet metal specialties, not stamped

(G-4273)
FORT WAYNE METALS RES PDTS
9307 Avionics Dr (46809-9631)
P.O. Box 9040 (46899-9040)
PHONE...........................260 747-4154
Scott Glaze, *CEO*
EMP: 30

SALES (corp-wide): 135.6MM **Privately Held**
WEB: www.fwmetals.com
SIC: 3315 3842 Wire, steel: insulated or armored; surgical appliances & supplies
PA: Fort Wayne Metals Research Products Corp
9609 Ardmore Ave
Fort Wayne IN 46809
260 747-4154

(G-4274)
FORT WAYNE METALS RES PDTS (PA)
9609 Ardmore Ave (46809-9625)
P.O. Box 9040 (46899-9040)
PHONE..............................260 747-4154
Fax: 260 747-0398
Scott Glaze, CEO
Mark Michael, President
Beth Wilges, COO
Kimberly Shoppell, Vice Pres
John Hickey, Project Mgr
▲ EMP: 204 EST: 1970
SQ FT: 50,000
SALES (est): 135.6MM **Privately Held**
WEB: www.fwmetals.com
SIC: 3315 Wire, steel: insulated or armored

(G-4275)
FORT WAYNE METALS RES PDTS
3401 Mcarthur Dr (46809-2884)
PHONE..............................260 747-4154
Mark Michael, Branch Mgr
EMP: 16
SALES (corp-wide): 135.6MM **Privately Held**
SIC: 3315 Steel wire & related products
PA: Fort Wayne Metals Research Products Corp
9609 Ardmore Ave
Fort Wayne IN 46809
260 747-4154

(G-4276)
FORT WAYNE MOLD & ENGRG INC
4501 Earth Dr (46809-1519)
PHONE..............................260 747-9168
Fax: 260 747-3601
Richard A Schmidt, President
Brad Fiedler, President
Richard Schmidt, COO
Darell Beverly, Vice Pres
Roger Marley, Vice Pres
EMP: 44
SQ FT: 25,000
SALES (est): 7.1MM **Privately Held**
WEB: www.fortwaynemold.com
SIC: 3544 Industrial molds

(G-4277)
FORT WAYNE NEWSPAPERS INC
Also Called: News-Sentinel
600 W Main St (46802-1498)
P.O. Box 100 (46801-0100)
PHONE..............................260 461-8444
Fax: 260 461-8777
Micheal Chrisman, President
Russell Sheets, General Mgr
Pete Van Baalen, General Mgr
Dave Benson, Editor
Jamie Duffy, Editor
EMP: 457 EST: 1833
SQ FT: 146,000
SALES (est): 30.8MM
SALES (corp-wide): 903.5MM **Publicly Held**
WEB: www.fortwayne.com
SIC: 2711 2721 2759 Newspapers, publishing & printing; magazines: publishing & printing; commercial printing
HQ: News Publishing Company Inc
600 W Main St
Fort Wayne IN 46802
260 461-8444

(G-4278)
FORT WAYNE PLASTICS INC
Also Called: Fwp
510 Sumpter St (46804-5626)
PHONE..............................260 432-2520

Fax: 260 432-5540
Robb Robertson, President
Phillip Swihart, Vice Pres
Bob Grimes, Purchasing
Ray Linkhart, CFO
Diane Albaugh, Accountant
▲ EMP: 120 EST: 1997
SQ FT: 160,000
SALES (est): 44MM
SALES (corp-wide): 16.1MM **Privately Held**
WEB: www.fortwayneplastics.com
SIC: 3089 Blow molded finished plastic products
HQ: Ftw Holdings Inc.
11840 Westline Indus Dr
Saint Louis MO

(G-4279)
FORT WAYNE POOLS
6930 Gettysburg Pike (46804-5614)
PHONE..............................260 459-4100
Fax: 260 459-4151
Manuel J Perez De La Mesa, CEO
Kurt Heimann, Engineer
Craig Hubbard, CFO
Jeff McDaniel, Regl Sales Mgr
Brian Follis, Sales Executive
EMP: 227
SALES (est): 162.2MM **Publicly Held**
SIC: 5091 3949 Swimming pools, equipment & supplies; swimming pools, plastic
PA: Pool Corporation
109 Northpark Blvd # 400
Covington LA 70433

(G-4280)
FORT WAYNE PRINTING CO INC
909 Production Rd (46808-1270)
PHONE..............................260 471-7744
Fax: 260 471-7746
Gary Bastin, President
Kimberley Bastin, Treasurer
EMP: 17
SQ FT: 14,000
SALES: 3MM **Privately Held**
WEB: www.fortwayneprinting.com
SIC: 2752 2791 Commercial printing, offset; typesetting

(G-4281)
FORT WAYNE WIRE DIE INC (PA)
2424 American Way (46809-3098)
PHONE..............................260 747-1681
Fax: 260 747-4269
Dwight P Bieberich, President
Eric Bieberich, President
Lee Grable, Division Mgr
Don Bieberich, Vice Pres
Donald E Bieberich, Vice Pres
▲ EMP: 177
SQ FT: 50,000
SALES (est): 34.1MM **Privately Held**
WEB: www.fwwd.com
SIC: 3544 Diamond dies, metalworking; special dies & tools

(G-4282)
FORT WAYNE WIRE DIE INC
2424 American Way (46809-3098)
P.O. Box 10794 (46854-0794)
PHONE..............................260 747-1681
EMP: 3
SALES (corp-wide): 34.1MM **Privately Held**
WEB: www.fwwd.com
SIC: 3544 Special dies, tools, jigs & fixtures
PA: Fort Wayne Wire Die, Inc.
2424 American Way
Fort Wayne IN 46809
260 747-1681

(G-4283)
FORT WYNE RDLGY ASSN FUNDATION
Also Called: Breast Diagnostic Center
3707 New Vision Dr (46845-1702)
PHONE..............................260 266-8120
Fax: 260 483-1741
Marita Dwight-Smith, Manager
EMP: 15

SALES (est): 1.5MM
SALES (corp-wide): 6.5MM **Privately Held**
WEB: www.fwradiology.com
SIC: 3841 8011 Diagnostic apparatus, medical; radiologist
PA: Fort Wayne Radiology Association Foundation Inc
3707 New Vision Dr
Fort Wayne IN 46845
260 484-0850

(G-4284)
FRANKE PLATING WORKS INC
2109 E Washington Blvd (46803-1390)
PHONE..............................260 422-8477
Fax: 260 422-8477
Warren T Franke, President
Mitch McAfoose, Business Mgr
Rachel Vergara, Office Mgr
Jeff Buzzard, Manager
EMP: 56
SQ FT: 60,000
SALES (est): 9.1MM **Privately Held**
WEB: www.frankeplatingworks.com
SIC: 3471 Plating of metals or formed products; finishing, metals or formed products

(G-4285)
FRANKLIN ELECTRIC CO INC (PA)
9255 Coverdale Rd (46809-9613)
PHONE..............................260 824-2900
Fax: 260 824-2909
Gregg C Sengstack, Ch of Bd
Delancey W Davis, President
Donald P Kenney, President
Scott Leonard, President
Robert J Stone, President
◆ EMP: 268
SALES: 1.1B **Publicly Held**
WEB: www.franklin-electric.com
SIC: 3621 3561 Motors, electric; electric motor & generator auxillary parts; pumps & pumping equipment; pumps, domestic: water or sump; pumps, oil well & field

(G-4286)
FRANKLIN ELECTRIC INTL (HQ)
9255 Coverdale Rd (46809-9613)
PHONE..............................260 824-2900
Jess B Ford, President
John B Lindsay, Exec VP
Greg Sinstack, Treasurer
EMP: 8
SALES (est): 47.3MM
SALES (corp-wide): 1.1B **Publicly Held**
SIC: 3621 Motors & generators
PA: Franklin Electric Co., Inc.
9255 Coverdale Rd
Fort Wayne IN 46809
260 824-2900

(G-4287)
FRECKER OPTICAL INC
7115 Old Trail Rd (46809-2715)
P.O. Box 9028 (46899-9028)
PHONE..............................260 747-9653
Terry Frecker, President
Allan Frecker, Vice Pres
Bryan Frecker, Treasurer
Brian Frecker, Admin Sec
EMP: 10
SQ FT: 18,000
SALES: 850K **Privately Held**
SIC: 5048 3851 Ophthalmic goods; optometric equipment & supplies; eyeglasses, lenses & frames

(G-4288)
FRIENDS OF THIRD WORLD INC (PA)
Also Called: Co-Op Trading
611 W Wayne St (46802-2167)
PHONE..............................260 422-6821
Fax: 260 422-1650
James Goetsch, President
Howard Traxmor, Chairman
Marian R Waltz, Treasurer
James Curtis Cary, Admin Sec
EMP: 3
SQ FT: 9,000

SALES: 163.1K **Privately Held**
SIC: 8299 2752 5947 Educational services; commercial printing, lithographic; gift shop

(G-4289)
FT WAYNE READER
1301 Lafayette St Ste 202 (46802-3555)
PHONE..............................260 420-8580
Michael Summers, Owner
EMP: 3 EST: 2006
SALES (est): 151.8K **Privately Held**
SIC: 2711 Newspapers, publishing & printing

(G-4290)
FULL PRESS LLC
5714 Evard Rd (46835-1771)
PHONE..............................260 433-7731
EMP: 2
SALES (est): 74K **Privately Held**
SIC: 2741 Miscellaneous publishing

(G-4291)
FXI INC
Also Called: Foamex
3005 Commercial Rd (46809-2927)
PHONE..............................260 747-7485
Fax: 260 747-9166
William Banks, Branch Mgr
EMP: 150
SQ FT: 270,000 **Privately Held**
SIC: 3086 Packaging & shipping materials, foamed plastic
HQ: Fxi, Inc.
1400 N Providence Rd # 2000
Media PA 19063

(G-4292)
G C G INDUSTRIES INC
4636 Newaygo Rd (46808-4103)
PHONE..............................260 482-7454
Fax: 260 482-7552
Terry A Gardner, President
Tamara Gardner, Treasurer
EMP: 25
SQ FT: 12,000
SALES: 500K **Privately Held**
SIC: 3544 Special dies, tools, jigs & fixtures

(G-4293)
GDP INDUSTRIES LLC
7431 Regina Dr (46815-8244)
PHONE..............................260 414-4003
Gary Boyd, Principal
EMP: 2
SALES (est): 149.9K **Privately Held**
SIC: 3999 Manufacturing industries

(G-4294)
GE LEXINGTON LAMP PLANT
433 Council Dr (46825-5101)
PHONE..............................859 277-1161
Mat Barbour, Principal
Greg Maclin, Engineer
Diane Coleman, Manager
EMP: 3
SALES (est): 106.9K **Privately Held**
SIC: 3641 Electric lamps

(G-4295)
GENERAL DYNAMICS CORPORATION
1124 Falcon Creek Pkwy (46845-9043)
PHONE..............................260 637-4773
EMP: 3
SALES (corp-wide): 30.9B **Publicly Held**
SIC: 3731 Shipbuilding & repairing
PA: General Dynamics Corporation
2941 Frview Pk Dr Ste 100
Falls Church VA 22042
703 876-3000

(G-4296)
GENERAL DYNAMICS MISSION
1700 Magnavox Way Ste 200 (46804-1552)
PHONE..............................260 434-9500
Fax: 260 434-9501
William Braun, Engineer
Adam Gerber, Engineer
Adam Greb, Engineer
Timothy Palmer, Engineer
Brian Pattison, Engineer
EMP: 120

GEOGRAPHIC

SALES (corp-wide): 30.9B **Publicly Held**
SIC: 3669 Emergency alarms
HQ: General Dynamics Mission Systems, Inc.
　　12450 Fair Lakes Cir # 200
　　Fairfax VA 22033
　　703 263-2800

(G-4297)
GENERAL ELECTRIC COMPANY
433 Council Dr (46825-5101)
PHONE................................260 439-2000
Fax: 260 439-2071
Michael Bhat, *Buyer*
Jim Rogers, *Branch Mgr*
Sharan Nimesh, *Manager*
Ericka Nolfi, *Manager*
Tom Grimes, *Senior Mgr*
EMP: 300
SALES (corp-wide): 122B **Publicly Held**
SIC: 3621 Motors & generators
PA: General Electric Company
　　41 Farnsworth St
　　Boston MA 02210
　　617 443-3000

(G-4298)
GENTEC INC
3632 Illinois Rd (46804-2062)
PHONE................................260 436-7333
Jessica Weber, *Manager*
EMP: 2
SALES (est): 81.4K **Privately Held**
SIC: 3599 Industrial machinery

(G-4299)
GEORGETOWN DONUTS
6328 E State Blvd (46815-7023)
PHONE................................260 493-6719
Kim Tu, *Owner*
EMP: 4
SALES (est): 140K **Privately Held**
SIC: 2051 Doughnuts, except frozen

(G-4300)
GESCO GROUP LLC (PA) ✿
4422 Earth Dr (46809-1518)
P.O. Box 10474 (46852-0474)
PHONE................................260 747-5088
Timothy Hartigan, *Mng Member*
David Faust,
EMP: 2 EST: 2017
SALES (est): 1.5MM **Privately Held**
SIC: 3533 7353 5999 Gas field machinery & equipment; oil equipment rental services; business machines & equipment

(G-4301)
GOOSE GRAPHICS L L C
4943 Coventry Pkwy (46804-7115)
PHONE................................260 563-4516
Marty Winkleman,
Lisa Winkleman,
▲ EMP: 5
SQ FT: 10,000
SALES: 400K **Privately Held**
WEB: www.goosegraphicsllc.com
SIC: 2759 Screen printing

(G-4302)
GRAPHICS SYSTEMS INC
8421 Mayhew Rd (46835-1003)
PHONE................................260 485-9667
Kurt Leffers, *President*
EMP: 3
SQ FT: 1,300
SALES (est): 210K **Privately Held**
SIC: 3993 Signs & advertising specialties

(G-4303)
GRAPHIK MECHANIX INC
1116 N Wells St (46808-3470)
PHONE................................260 426-7001
William Wright, *CEO*
Sigrid Wright, *Admin Sec*
Gary Gamble, *Administration*
EMP: 6
SQ FT: 2,500
SALES: 350K **Privately Held**
SIC: 2796 7384 Lithographic plates, positives or negatives; film developing services

(G-4304)
GRASSCO INC
Also Called: Peerless of Georgetown
6430 E State Blvd (46815)
PHONE................................260 749-5437
Christine Hoppe, *Manager*
EMP: 3
SALES (corp-wide): 3.7MM **Privately Held**
WEB: www.peerless-cleaners.com
SIC: 3633 Drycleaning machines, household: including coin-operated
PA: Grassco Inc
　　4121 Hillegas Rd
　　Fort Wayne IN 46808
　　260 422-9374

(G-4305)
GRAYCRAFT SIGNS PLUS INC (PA)
2428 Getz Rd (46804-1632)
PHONE................................260 432-3760
Fax: 260 432-8528
Mark A Gray, *President*
Nanette M Gray, *Corp Secy*
EMP: 7
SQ FT: 2,100
SALES (est): 684.3K **Privately Held**
SIC: 3993 Signs, not made in custom sign painting shops; advertising novelties

(G-4306)
GREAT PANES GLASS CO
1307 N Wells St (46808-2793)
PHONE................................260 426-0203
Judy Wire, *President*
EMP: 6
SQ FT: 1,800
SALES (est): 419.4K **Privately Held**
SIC: 5231 3231 Glass; products of purchased glass

(G-4307)
GREATBATCH LTD
Also Called: Greatbatch Medical
4545 Kroemer Rd (46818-9770)
PHONE................................260 755-7300
Thomas Hook, *President*
Leland Junker, *Opers Staff*
Nichole Davis, *Mfg Staff*
John Menth, *Production*
Lori Dingus, *Buyer*
EMP: 5 EST: 2012
SALES (est): 867.2K **Privately Held**
SIC: 3841 Surgical & medical instruments

(G-4308)
GREEN DOG
3421 N Anthony Blvd (46805-2233)
PHCNE................................260 483-1267
Jody Norton, *Principal*
EMP: 2
SALES (est): 139.6K **Privately Held**
SIC: 3999 Pet supplies

(G-4309)
GTA ENTERPRISES INC
4422 Airport Expy Ste 220 (46809-9634)
PHONE................................260 478-7800
Fax: 260 478-7808
Steve Gildea, *President*
Mike Motter, *CFO*
◆ EMP: 34 EST: 2005
SQ FT: 62,000
SALES: 5.5MM **Privately Held**
SIC: 3544 7373 Special dies, tools, jigs & fixtures; computer integrated systems design

(G-4310)
GUIDE ENGINEERING LLC
1515 Dividend Rd (46808-1126)
PHONE................................260 483-1153
Fax: 260 482-6995
Craig S Taylor,
Andrew T Zundel,
Lisa Zundel,
EMP: 32
SQ FT: 18,000
SALES: 8MM **Privately Held**
WEB: www.guideeng.com
SIC: 3599 Custom machinery

(G-4311)
H & E MACHINED SPECIALTIES
1321 E Wallace St (46803-2559)
PHONE................................260 424-2527
Fax: 260 424-2858
Nick Knappenberger, *President*
Carl Ehinger, *President*
Teresa D Bauer, *Admin Sec*
EMP: 15
SQ FT: 33,000
SALES (est): 732K **Privately Held**
SIC: 3599 3451 7539 Machine shop, jobbing & repair; screw machine products; machine shop, automotive

(G-4312)
H & M BAY INC
3410 Meyer Rd (46803-2923)
PHONE................................410 463-5430
Dennis Jones, *Branch Mgr*
EMP: 8
SALES (corp-wide): 150.6MM **Privately Held**
SIC: 2448 Cargo containers, wood & metal combination
PA: H & M Bay, Inc.
　　1800 Industrial Park Rd
　　Federalsburg MD 21632
　　410 754-8001

(G-4313)
H A KING CO INC
3210 Clairmont Ct (46808-4513)
PHONE................................260 482-6376
Owen Roberts, *Manager*
EMP: 15
SALES (corp-wide): 1.8MM **Privately Held**
WEB: www.ha-king.com
SIC: 3069 Molded rubber products
PA: H. A. King Co., Inc.
　　5038 Leafdale Blvd
　　Royal Oak MI 48073
　　248 280-0006

(G-4314)
HAGER INC (PA)
Also Called: Specialized Printed Products
6844 N Clinton St (46825-4920)
PHONE................................260 483-7075
Fax: 260 484-0446
Mark Hager, *President*
EMP: 7
SQ FT: 3,500
SALES (est): 1.1MM **Privately Held**
WEB: www.sppdirect.com
SIC: 2752 7389 2791 2789 Commercial printing, offset; printing broker; typesetting; bookbinding & related work

(G-4315)
HAMILTON NEWS INC
Also Called: Stueben
9115 Sunflower Cv (46819-2555)
PHONE................................260 488-3780
EMP: 3
SALES (est): 140K **Privately Held**
SIC: 2711 Newspapers-Publishing/Printing

(G-4316)
HAMPTON EQUIPMENT LLC
7127 Hessen Cassel Rd (46816-2116)
PHONE................................260 740-8704
Erica Frey, *Owner*
Joe Shaw,
EMP: 2
SALES: 998.9K **Privately Held**
SIC: 7353 3523 1629 Heavy construction equipment rental; farm machinery & equipment; dams, waterways, docks & other marine construction

(G-4317)
HANDLE WITH KARE LLC
1723 Alabama Ave (46805-5013)
PHONE................................260 420-1698
EMP: 2 EST: 2010
SALES (est): 77K **Privately Held**
SIC: 2499 Mfg Wood Products

(G-4318)
HANGER PRSTHETCS & ORTHO INC
Also Called: Hanger Clinic
4666 W Jefferson Blvd (46804-6892)
PHONE................................260 456-5998
Steve Cooper, *Branch Mgr*
EMP: 11
SALES (corp-wide): 1B **Publicly Held**
SIC: 3842 Prosthetic appliances
HQ: Hanger Prosthetics & Orthotics, Inc.
　　10910 Domain Dr Ste 300
　　Austin TX 78758
　　512 777-3800

(G-4319)
HANSON AGGREGATES EAST LLC
1820 W Washington Ctr (46818-1416)
PHONE................................260 490-9006
Tom Meeker, *Branch Mgr*
EMP: 15
SALES (corp-wide): 20.3B **Privately Held**
SIC: 3272 Concrete products
HQ: Hanson Aggregates East Llc
　　3131 Rdu Center Dr
　　Morrisville NC 27560
　　919 380-2500

(G-4320)
HANSON AGGREGATES MIDWEST LLC
6100 Ardmore Ave (46809-9501)
PHONE................................260 747-3105
Sharon Faurote, *Financial Exec*
Peggy Folgel, *Branch Mgr*
EMP: 57
SQ FT: 5,000
SALES (corp-wide): 20.3B **Privately Held**
SIC: 1422 Limestones, ground
HQ: Hanson Aggregates Midwest Llc
　　207 Old Harrods Creek Rd
　　Louisville KY 40223
　　502 244-7550

(G-4321)
HARRIS CORPORATION
Also Called: Electonic Systems Division
1919 W Cook Rd (46818-1165)
P.O. Box 3700 (46801-3700)
PHONE................................260 451-6180
Dave Melcher, *Branch Mgr*
EMP: 99
SALES (corp-wide): 5.9B **Publicly Held**
SIC: 3669 Intercommunication systems, electric
PA: Harris Corporation
　　1025 W Nasa Blvd
　　Melbourne FL 32919
　　321 727-9100

(G-4322)
HARRIS CORPORATION
Night Vsion Cmmnctons Slutions
7310 Innovation Blvd (46818-1370)
P.O. Box 371 (46801)
PHONE................................260 451-6000
Dave Melcher, *CEO*
Nick Bobay, *President*
EMP: 250
SALES (corp-wide): 5.9B **Publicly Held**
WEB: www.ittind.com
SIC: 3625 Control equipment, electric
PA: Harris Corporation
　　1025 W Nasa Blvd
　　Melbourne FL 32919
　　321 727-9100

(G-4323)
HARRIS CORPORATION
ITT Corporation Space Systems
1919 W Cook Rd (46818-1165)
P.O. Box 3700 (46801-3700)
PHONE................................260 451-5597
Fax: 260 487-4017
Ken Peterson, *Branch Mgr*
Brian Plecas, *Art Dir*
EMP: 257
SALES (corp-wide): 5.9B **Publicly Held**
SIC: 3812 3669 3823 Search & navigation equipment; burglar alarm apparatus, electric; industrial instrmnts msrmnt display/control process variable

PA: Harris Corporation
1025 W Nasa Blvd
Melbourne FL 32919
321 727-9100

(G-4324)
HB CONNECT INC
Also Called: Excellon Technologies
1105 Sherman Blvd (46808-3430)
PHONE..................................260 422-1212
Fax: 260 422-8111
Heather Backs, *President*
Denise Hicks, *Human Res Dir*
EMP: 60
SQ FT: 27,000
SALES (est): 14.9MM **Privately Held**
WEB: www.excellontech.com
SIC: 3671 3679 3728 Light sensing &
emitting tubes; harness assemblies for
electronic use: wire or cable; adapter as-
semblies, hydromatic propeller

(G-4325)
**HD SUPPLY CONSTRUCTION
SUPPLY**
Also Called: White Cap 153
4510 Industrial Rd (46825-5204)
PHONE..................................260 471-7619
Fax: 260 483-1243
Eric Solyom, *Branch Mgr*
EMP: 12 **Publicly Held**
SIC: 3272 Concrete products
HQ: Hd Supply Construction Supply, Ltd
3100 Cumberland Blvd Se # 1700
Atlanta GA 30339
770 852-9000

(G-4326)
HEALING ELEMENTS LLC
3102 Mallard Cove Ln (46804-2882)
PHONE..................................260 355-7181
Brandie Nicole Davis, *CEO*
EMP: 3
SALES (est): 99K **Privately Held**
SIC: 2819 Elements

(G-4327)
HEARTCARE LLC
7806 W Jefferson Blvd D (46804-4179)
PHONE..................................260 432-7000
Subhash K Reddy, *Principal*
EMP: 5
SALES (est): 582.5K **Privately Held**
SIC: 3715 Trailers or vans for transporting
horses

(G-4328)
**HEAVY DUTY MANUFACTURING
INC**
4317 Clubview Dr (46804-4404)
PHONE..................................260 432-2480
Michael Miller, *Manager*
Lavon Miller, *Manager*
EMP: 10
SALES (corp-wide): 6.4MM **Privately
Held**
WEB: www.heavydutymfg.com
SIC: 3714 Exhaust systems & parts, motor
vehicle
PA: Heavy Duty Manufacturing, Inc.
1605 Indian Brook Way # 500
Norcross GA 30093
800 241-0551

(G-4329)
**HEBRON VENTURES NORTH
AMERICA**
Also Called: Hebron Ventures Global
344 Field St (46805-1932)
PHONE..................................260 437-7733
Rev William CP, *President*
EMP: 2
SALES (est): 145.9K **Privately Held**
SIC: 3312 Stainless steel

(G-4330)
HECKLEY PRINTING
6134 Constitution Dr (46804-1526)
PHONE..................................260 434-1370
Bill Heckley, *Owner*
EMP: 6
SALES (est): 586.6K **Privately Held**
SIC: 2752 Commercial printing, offset

(G-4331)
HENTZ MFG LLC
1530 Progress Rd (46808-1181)
PHONE..................................260 469-0800
Robert Hinty, *Principal*
EMP: 3
SALES (est): 363.9K **Privately Held**
SIC: 3999 Manufacturing industries

(G-4332)
HIDINGHILDA LLC
1510 Calvert Ct (46845-6138)
PHONE..................................260 760-7093
Dawn Hillyer, *Mng Member*
EMP: 3
SALES (est): 150K **Privately Held**
SIC: 2339 5632 Women's & misses' ac-
cessories; women's accessory & specialty
stores

(G-4333)
**HIGH VELOCITY
MANUFACTURING**
4710 Arden Dr (46804-4400)
PHONE..................................260 413-8429
Terrence W Corbin, *Administration*
EMP: 2 EST: 2015
SALES (est): 162K **Privately Held**
SIC: 3999 Manufacturing industries

(G-4334)
**HIGHMARK TECHNOLOGIES
LLC**
Also Called: Highmark Pack Systems
8343 Clinton Park Dr (46825-3164)
PHONE..................................260 483-0012
Debbie Parrot, *President*
Michael Parrot, *Owner*
Christopher Lake, *Vice Pres*
Kurt Moore, *Vice Pres*
EMP: 20
SQ FT: 22,000
SALES (est): 4.9MM **Privately Held**
SIC: 3355 Aluminum rail & structural
shapes

(G-4335)
HILLSHIRE BRANDS COMPANY
1108 E Pontiac St (46803-3400)
PHONE..................................260 456-4802
EMP: 2
SALES (corp-wide): 38.2B **Publicly Held**
SIC: 2013 Sausages & other prepared
meats
HQ: The Hillshire Brands Company
400 S Jefferson St Fl 1
Chicago IL 60607
312 614-6000

(G-4336)
HILTYS WOODWORK
10615 Schwartz Rd (46835-9249)
PHONE..................................260 627-2905
Jacob Hilty, *Principal*
EMP: 2
SALES (est): 179.7K **Privately Held**
SIC: 2431 Millwork

(G-4337)
**HOLSUM OF FORT WAYNE INC
(HQ)**
136 Murray St (46803-2333)
P.O. Box 11468 (46858-1468)
PHONE..................................260 456-2130
Fax: 260 745-1404
Lewis Jr Jack, *President*
Rodger Lesh, *Vice Pres*
Jeffery J Sankovitch, *Treasurer*
Chris Davidson, *Office Mgr*
Peggy S Lewis, *Admin Sec*
EMP: 160
SQ FT: 34,000
SALES (est): 185.6MM
SALES (corp-wide): 473.3MM **Privately
Held**
SIC: 2051 Bread, all types (white, wheat,
rye, etc): fresh or frozen
PA: Lewis Brothers Bakeries Inc
500 N Fulton Ave
Evansville IN 47710
812 425-4642

(G-4338)
HOME & LAWN SERVICES
7420 Nature Trail Dr (46835-1426)
PHONE..................................260 633-9155
Benjamin Byerline, *Manager*
EMP: 5
SALES (est): 100.5K **Privately Held**
SIC: 0782 2511 0783 Mowing services,
lawn; seeding services, lawn; wood lawn
& garden furniture; removal services,
bush & tree

(G-4339)
HOME RESERVE LLC
Also Called: Home Reserve.com
3015 Cannongate Dr (46808-4508)
PHONE..................................260 969-6939
Scott Anspach, *Asst Treas*
Blaine Wieland, *Mng Member*
Blair Wieland,
Roy Wieland,
▼EMP: 12
SQ FT: 16,500
SALES (est): 1.5MM **Privately Held**
WEB: www.homereserve.com
SIC: 2512 Upholstered household furniture

(G-4340)
HOOK & ARROW
7536 Winchester Rd (46819-2243)
PHONE..................................260 739-6661
Kirk Heem, *Owner*
EMP: 2 EST: 2012
SALES (est): 152.1K **Privately Held**
SIC: 3949 Sporting & athletic goods

(G-4341)
HOOK DEVELOPMENT INC
2731 Brooklyn Ave (46802-3801)
PHONE..................................260 432-7771
Tom Hook, *President*
Kenneth Hook, *Admin Sec*
EMP: 2
SALES (est): 139.3K **Privately Held**
SIC: 3544 Special dies, tools, jigs & fix-
tures

(G-4342)
**HOOK INDUSTRIAL SALES INC
(PA)**
2731 Brooklyn Ave (46802-3801)
P.O. Box 9177 (46899-9177)
PHONE..................................260 432-9441
Fax: 260 436-4152
Thomas G Hook, *President*
Kenneth Hook, *Corp Secy*
Traci Anders, *Purch Mgr*
Herb Pattison, *Engineer*
Donna Cooper, *Office Mgr*
EMP: 65
SQ FT: 79,000
SALES (est): 15.3MM **Privately Held**
WEB: www.hookindustrialsales.com
SIC: 3569 5085 Filter elements, fluid, hy-
draulic line; seals, industrial; gaskets

(G-4343)
**HOOSIER ETHANOL ENERGY
LLC**
110 W Berry St Ste 1200 (46802-2366)
PHONE..................................260 407-6161
Fax: 260 407-6160
Robert O Vegeler,
Robert Vegeler,
EMP: 2
SALES (est): 900K **Privately Held**
WEB: www.vegelerlaw.com
SIC: 2869 Ethyl alcohol, ethanol

(G-4344)
**HOOSIER MANUFACTURING
LLC**
9312 Avionics Dr (46809-9631)
PHONE..................................260 493-9990
Fax: 260 969-1546
Sherman Group, *Owner*
EMP: 2
SALES (est): 160K **Privately Held**
SIC: 3544 Special dies, tools, jigs & fix-
tures

(G-4345)
HOOSIER PRIDE PLASTICS INC
Also Called: Hpp Mold & Tool
6120 Highview Dr (46818-1378)
PHONE..................................260 497-7080
Mike Hoeppner, *President*
Linda Hoeppner, *Vice Pres*
EMP: 20
SQ FT: 30,000
SALES (est): 3.7MM **Privately Held**
WEB: www.hoosierprideplastics.com
SIC: 3089 Injection molding of plastics

(G-4346)
**HOOSIER TOOLMAKING &
ENGRG INC ✪**
6930 Derek Dr (46803-3299)
PHONE..................................260 493-9990
EMP: 2 EST: 2017
SALES (est): 83.2K **Privately Held**
SIC: 3544 Special dies, tools, jigs & fix-
tures

(G-4347)
HORNECO FABRICATION INC
13020 Redding Dr (46814-9773)
PHONE..................................260 672-2064
Bruce Horne, *President*
Gail Fisher, *Admin Sec*
EMP: 2
SALES (est): 180K **Privately Held**
SIC: 3462 Ornamental metal forgings, fer-
rous

(G-4348)
**HORNER INDUSTRIAL
SERVICES INC**
Also Called: Horner Electric
4421 Ardmore Ave (46809-9722)
PHONE..................................260 434-1189
Troy Elder, *Manager*
EMP: 4
SALES (corp-wide): 46.7MM **Privately
Held**
SIC: 3625 7694 7699 5063 Electric con-
trols & control accessories, industrial;
electric motor repair; pumps & pumping
equipment repair; electrical apparatus &
equipment
PA: Horner Industrial Services, Inc.
1521 E Washington St
Indianapolis IN 46201
317 639-4261

(G-4349)
HOSETRACT INDUSTRIES LTD
6433 Discount Dr (46818-1235)
P.O. Box 80008 (46898-0008)
PHONE..................................260 489-8828
Fax: 260 489-6088
James M Schaller, *President*
Mary Delarosa, *Manager*
▲EMP: 15
SQ FT: 12,000
SALES (est): 2.5MM **Privately Held**
WEB: www.hosetract.com
SIC: 3499 Reels, cable: metal

(G-4350)
HUTH TOOL
6930 Derek Dr (46803-3299)
PHONE..................................260 749-9411
David D Richards, *Principal*
EMP: 2 EST: 2011
SALES (est): 118.6K **Privately Held**
SIC: 7389 3599 Grinding, precision: com-
mercial or industrial; machine shop, job-
bing & repair

(G-4351)
HUTH TOOL & MACHINE CORP
6930 Derek Dr (46803-3299)
PHONE..................................260 749-9411
Fax: 260 484-5893
David D Richards, *President*
EMP: 8
SQ FT: 6,000
SALES (est): 1.1MM **Privately Held**
SIC: 3544 7389 Industrial molds; grinding,
precision: commercial or industrial

(G-4352)
HY-TEC FIBERGLASS INC
2201 Suppliers Ct (46818-1172)
PHONE..................................260 489-6601

Fax: 260 489-9084
Gary Onz, *President*
Rick Witzigreuter, *Vice Pres*
EMP: 7
SQ FT: 14,000
SALES: 1MM **Privately Held**
WEB: www.boatshows.com
SIC: 3296 3537 Fiberglass insulation; industrial trucks & tractors

(G-4353)
HYDRO SYSTEMS MFG INC
3632 Illinois Rd Ofc (46804-2062)
PHONE..................260 436-4476
Michael Duff, *President*
Shannon Duff, *Admin Sec*
EMP: 3
SALES (est): 333.3K **Privately Held**
SIC: 3492 Control valves, fluid power: hydraulic & pneumatic

(G-4354)
HYNDMAN INDUSTRIAL PDTS INC
Also Called: Resistance Wire
4031 Merchant Rd Ste A (46818-1266)
PHONE..................260 483-6042
Fax: 260 483-6042
Joseph E Hyndman, *President*
Douglas Maxwell, *Sales Mgr*
Nathan Davidhizar, *Marketing Staff*
▲ **EMP:** 46
SQ FT: 14,000
SALES (est): 8.4MM **Privately Held**
WEB: www.resistancewire.com
SIC: 3634 Electric household cooking appliances

(G-4355)
IASA GROUP LLC (PA)
Also Called: Integrated Custom Components
1905 Production Rd (46808-3647)
P.O. Box 92488, Southlake TX (76092-0488)
PHONE..................260 484-1322
Imtiaz Ahmed, *General Mgr*
Mary Willis, *Info Tech Mgr*
EMP: 2
SALES (est): 307.2K **Privately Held**
SIC: 3728 Aircraft assemblies, subassemblies & parts

(G-4356)
ICON INTERNATIONAL INC (PA)
Also Called: Displaysource
8333 Clinton Park Dr (46825-3164)
PHONE..................260 482-8700
Michael V Parrott, *President*
Bob Morgan, *Sales Staff*
Gary Olinger, *Manager*
Paul Rose, *Director*
Kathryn Parrott, *Admin Sec*
▲ **EMP:** 52
SQ FT: 90,000
SALES (est): 5.1MM **Privately Held**
WEB: www.iconexhibits.com
SIC: 3993 Signs & advertising specialties

(G-4357)
IE PRODUCTS MAD DASHER INC
Also Called: I E Products
4410 Tielker Rd (46809-1543)
PHONE..................260 747-0545
Fax: 260 747-0548
Harry P Laffkas, *President*
Margaret Hyde, *Treasurer*
EMP: 30
SQ FT: 13,500
SALES (est): 4.5MM **Privately Held**
SIC: 3089 2385 3081 Plastic containers, except foam; waterproof outerwear; raincoats, except vulcanized rubber: purchased materials; unsupported plastics film & sheet

(G-4358)
ILLINOIS LUBRICANTS LLC
Also Called: Jiffy Lube
1300 Arprt N Off Park Ste (46825)
PHONE..................260 436-2444
Steve Sanner, *President*
EMP: 6

SALES (est): 132.8K **Privately Held**
SIC: 2911 2992 7549 Oils, lubricating; lubricating oils & greases; high performance auto repair & service

(G-4359)
IM INDIANA HOLDINGS INC
Also Called: Trans-Flo
6300 Ardmore Ave (46809-9502)
PHONE..................260 478-1674
Fax: 260 447-7884
Thomas Irving, *Principal*
Jim Asher, *Safety Mgr*
Rick Neargarder, *Plant Engr*
Larry Schaefer, *Sales/Mktg Mgr*
EMP: 6
SQ FT: 40,000
SALES (corp-wide): 4.8MM **Privately Held**
WEB: www.irving-companies.com
SIC: 3273 Ready-mixed concrete
PA: Indiana Im Holdings Inc
13415 Coldwater Rd
Fort Wayne IN 46845
260 637-3101

(G-4360)
IMAGINE INDUSTRIES LLC
525 Victoria Station Way (46814-8961)
PHONE..................260 494-6530
Vanessa Lauritsen, *Administration*
EMP: 2
SALES (est): 56.3K **Privately Held**
SIC: 3999 Manufacturing industries

(G-4361)
IMPERIAL TROPHY & AWARDS CO
2405 W Jefferson Blvd (46802-4640)
PHONE..................260 432-8161
Fax: 260 432-6081
Rick Loy, *President*
Tom Loy, *Owner*
EMP: 6
SQ FT: 7,000
SALES (est): 300K **Privately Held**
WEB: www.inknewsonline.com
SIC: 5999 5094 3993 3446 Trophies & plaques; trophies; signs & advertising specialties; architectural metalwork; automotive & apparel trimmings; pleating & stitching

(G-4362)
INDIANA BAKING CO
5109 Executive Blvd (46808-1148)
PHONE..................260 483-5997
Ronald W Rice, *President*
Thomas J Casaburo, *President*
Margaret N Rice, *Corp Secy*
EMP: 12
SQ FT: 7,000
SALES (est): 1.5MM **Privately Held**
SIC: 2051 Bread, cake & related products

(G-4363)
INDIANA BARRIER WALL LLC
7107 Smith Rd (46809-9789)
PHONE..................260 747-5777
Fax: 260 747-5775
Scott Fredrick, *Principal*
EMP: 2
SALES (est): 180.5K **Privately Held**
SIC: 3272 Wall & ceiling squares, concrete

(G-4364)
INDIANA HAND PIECE REPAIR
9530 Old Grist Mill Pl (46835-9303)
PHONE..................260 436-0765
John Ball, *President*
EMP: 2
SALES (est): 100K **Privately Held**
SIC: 3541 7699 Machine tool replacement & repair parts, metal cutting types; professional instrument repair services

(G-4365)
INDIANA REFRACTORIES INC
1815 S Anthony Blvd (46803-3605)
P.O. Box 12111 (46862-2111)
PHONE..................260 426-3286
Fax: 260 422-5179
Martin Shepherd, *President*
Al Shepherd, *Vice Pres*
Roger Kilty, *Shareholder*
James Shepherd, *Shareholder*

EMP: 44
SQ FT: 33,000
SALES: 1.1MM **Privately Held**
WEB: www.indianarefractories.com
SIC: 3365 Aluminum foundries

(G-4366)
INDIANA STAMP CO INC (PA)
Also Called: United Ribtype Company
1319 Production Rd (46808-1164)
P.O. Box 8887 (46898-8887)
PHONE..................260 424-8973
Fax: 260 426-5502
Olivia Warner, *President*
Sarah Chesebrough, *Director*
EMP: 40
SQ FT: 32,000
SALES: 3.1MM **Privately Held**
WEB: www.indianastamp.com
SIC: 3953 3993 Embossing seals & hand stamps; signs & advertising specialties

(G-4367)
INDUSTRIAL ENGINEERING INC
Also Called: Industrial Engineering NC
4430 Tielker Rd (46809-1500)
PHONE..................260 478-1514
Fax: 260 747-9574
Harry P Laffkas, *President*
Margaret Hyde, *Corp Secy*
EMP: 80
SQ FT: 13,500
SALES (est): 11.9MM **Privately Held**
SIC: 3599 3544 Machine shop, jobbing & repair; special dies, tools, jigs & fixtures

(G-4368)
INDUSTRIAL METAL PRODUCTS INC
4519 Allen Martin Dr (46806-2851)
PHONE..................260 447-7900
Beverly Rectenwald, *President*
Walter Rectenwald, *Vice Pres*
Jim Rectenwald, *Marketing Staff*
EMP: 12 EST: 1976
SQ FT: 10,000
SALES (est): 2.2MM **Privately Held**
WEB: www.inmetpro.com
SIC: 3599 Machine shop, jobbing & repair

(G-4369)
INFOBIND SYSTEMS INC
1116 N Wells St (46808-3470)
PHONE..................260 248-4989
Stanley Needham, *President*
Carol J Needham, *Corp Secy*
EMP: 2
SALES: 85K **Privately Held**
SIC: 2789 Bookbinding & related work

(G-4370)
INK SPOT
215 W State Blvd (46808-3189)
PHONE..................260 482-4492
Fax: 260 483-3815
Jon Slate, *Owner*
EMP: 2
SQ FT: 1,700
SALES (est): 190.1K **Privately Held**
SIC: 2752 Commercial printing, offset

(G-4371)
INNOVATIONS BY
Also Called: Silva Military Solutions
2611 Lincroft Dr (46845-1918)
PHONE..................260 413-1869
John Taller, *Principal*
Noel Hupp, *Principal*
EMP: 2
SALES (est): 89.9K **Privately Held**
SIC: 3731 7389 Shipbuilding & repairing;

(G-4372)
INNOVATIVE BATTERY POWER INC
10827 Middleford Pl (46818-8896)
PHONE..................260 267-6582
Jeremy Aker, *President*
EMP: 2
SALES (est): 156.7K **Privately Held**
SIC: 3625 Truck controls, industrial battery

(G-4373)
INNOVATIVE TOOLING SOLUTIONS
6225 Commodity Ct (46818-1221)
P.O. Box 15566 (46885-5566)
PHONE..................260 487-9970
Fax: 260 487-9971
Thomas Wheelock, *President*
Joan Wheelock, *Admin Sec*
▲ **EMP:** 8
SQ FT: 10,000
SALES (est): 1.2MM **Privately Held**
WEB: www.innovativetoolingsolutions.com
SIC: 3599 Machine shop, jobbing & repair

(G-4374)
INSTANT AUTO FINANCE INC
2500 Spy Run Ave (46805-3210)
PHONE..................260 483-9000
Tim Allen, *Branch Mgr*
EMP: 6
SALES (est): 601.5K **Privately Held**
SALES (corp-wide): 5.3MM **Privately Held**
SIC: 2752 Commercial printing, lithographic
PA: Instant Auto Finance Inc
1005 N Nappanee St
Elkhart IN 46514
574 262-2617

(G-4375)
INSTATE WELDING SERVICE INC
4911 Industrial Rd (46825-5211)
PHONE..................260 483-0461
EMP: 2
SALES (est): 36.7K **Privately Held**
SIC: 7692 Welding repair

(G-4376)
INSUL-COUSTIC CORPORATION
2701 S Coliseum Blvd (46803-2950)
PHONE..................260 420-1480
Wade Cunningham, *President*
Bob Marsh, *General Mgr*
Steve Alvey, *Vice Pres*
Naomi Cunningham, *Vice Pres*
Tony Mayfield, *Prdtn Mgr*
EMP: 50
SQ FT: 40,000
SALES (est): 13.2MM **Privately Held**
SIC: 3296 Fiberglass insulation

(G-4377)
INTEGER HOLDINGS CORPORATION
Also Called: Greatbatch Medical
4545 Kroemer Rd (46818-9770)
PHONE..................260 373-1664
EMP: 8
SALES (corp-wide): 1.4B **Publicly Held**
SIC: 3675 3692 3691 Electronic capacitors; primary batteries, dry & wet; storage batteries
PA: Integer Holdings Corporation
2595 Dallas Pkwy Ste 310
Frisco TX 75034
214 618-5243

(G-4378)
INTEK MANUFACTURING LLC
11118 Coldwater Rd # 200 (46845-1273)
PHONE..................260 637-4100
Eugene R Tippmann,
EMP: 5
SALES (est): 510K **Privately Held**
WEB: www.intekllc.com
SIC: 3556 Food products machinery

(G-4379)
INTERNATIONAL AUTOMATION INC (PA)
9009 Clubridge Dr (46809-3000)
P.O. Box 9070 (46899-9070)
PHONE..................260 747-6151
Harry M Neff, *President*
Phil Friend, *President*
Pete Cole, *Vice Pres*
Joseph Oberlin, *Treasurer*
William Salin, *Admin Sec*
EMP: 39
SQ FT: 25,000
SALES: 49MM **Privately Held**
SIC: 3593 Fluid power actuators, hydraulic or pneumatic

▲ = Import ▼=Export
◆ =Import/Export

G
E
O
G
R
A
P
H
I
C

(G-4380)
INTERNATIONAL PAPER COMPANY
3904 W Ferguson Rd (46809-3150)
PHONE.....................................260 747-9111
Larry Lamb, *Opers Mgr*
Ross Carolus, *Facilities Mgr*
Mike Kolwalski, *Controller*
Charles Vaughn, *Branch Mgr*
Brenda Berghuis, *Manager*
EMP: 150
SALES (corp-wide): 21.7B **Publicly Held**
WEB: www.internationalpaper.com
SIC: 2621 Paper mills
PA: International Paper Company
6400 Poplar Ave
Memphis TN 38197
901 419-9000

(G-4381)
INTRATEK INC
Also Called: Intratek Engineering
3209 Clearfield Ct (46808-4517)
P.O. Box 80188 (46898-0188)
PHONE.....................................260 484-3377
John Fanning Jr, *President*
EMP: 8
SQ FT: 1,500
SALES (est): 767.8K **Privately Held**
SIC: 3479 Painting, coating & hot dipping

(G-4382)
IPFW STUDENT HOUSING
2101 E Coliseum Blvd # 100 (46805-1499)
PHONE.....................................260 481-4180
Ray Hammond, *Principal*
EMP: 7 EST: 2008
SALES (est): 712.3K **Privately Held**
SIC: 3621 Motor housings

(G-4383)
IRON OUT INC
Also Called: Summit Brands
7201 Engle Rd (46804-2228)
PHONE.....................................800 654-0791
Fax: 260 483-2277
Joel Harter, *CEO*
Charlotte Simonis, *CEO*
Lucas Heckert, *Production*
Mike Brown, *Purch Mgr*
Pannkuk Karen, *Research*
EMP: 50
SQ FT: 18,200
SALES (est): 16.8MM **Privately Held**
WEB: www.ironout.com
SIC: 2899 2891 2842 Water treating compounds; adhesives & sealants; specialty cleaning, polishes & sanitation goods

(G-4384)
IRWIN HODSON GROUP INDIANA LLC
2980 E Coliseum Blvd (46805-1500)
PHONE.....................................260 482-8052
Brad Barondeau, *Owner*
EMP: 6 EST: 2015
SALES (est): 382.1K **Privately Held**
SIC: 3469 Automobile license tags, stamped metal
PA: Irwin Hodson Group Llc
12067 Ne Glenn Widing Dr # 103
Portland OR 97220

(G-4385)
ITT LLC
Also Called: ITT Communications Systems
1919 W Cook Rd (46818-1165)
P.O. Box 3700 (46801-3700)
PHONE.....................................260 451-6000
A Coleman, *Branch Mgr*
EMP: 2
SALES (corp-wide): 2.5B **Publicly Held**
WEB: www.ittind.com
SIC: 3625 Control equipment, electric
HQ: Itt Llc
1133 Westchester Ave N-100
White Plains NY 10604
914 641-2000

(G-4386)
J B TOOL DIE & ENGINEERING CO
1509 Dividend Rd (46808-1159)
PHONE.....................................260 483-9586
Fax: 260 483-9589

David Bear, *President*
David Thompson, *Vice Pres*
Rick Zorger, *Vice Pres*
Gregory Beer, *CFO*
Gregory Christoffel, *Manager*
▲ EMP: 115
SQ FT: 65,000
SALES (est): 22.4MM **Privately Held**
WEB: www.jbtool.com
SIC: 3544 3599 Special dies & tools; machine shop, jobbing & repair

(G-4387)
J T D SPIRAL INC
6212 Highview Dr (46818-1375)
P.O. Box 8007 (46898-8007)
PHONE.....................................260 497-1300
Tim Morris, *President*
Dan Morris, *Corp Secy*
James Morris, *Vice Pres*
EMP: 8
SQ FT: 48,000
SALES (est): 1.1MM **Privately Held**
WEB: www.jtdspiral.com
SIC: 3444 Pipe, sheet metal

(G-4388)
J W SIGNS INC
2511 Alma Ave (46809-2903)
PHONE.....................................260 747-5168
Fax: 260 747-0199
John Walker, *President*
Nancy Woosely, *Treasurer*
EMP: 9
SQ FT: 6,000
SALES (est): 1.1MM **Privately Held**
SIC: 3993 1799 Signs, not made in custom sign painting shops; sign installation & maintenance

(G-4389)
J4 PRINTING LLC
1008 Orlando Dr (46825-4040)
PHONE.....................................260 417-5382
Jeffrey S Junkin, *Administration*
EMP: 2 EST: 2009
SALES (est): 117.4K **Privately Held**
SIC: 2752 Commercial printing, lithographic

(G-4390)
JACYL TECHNOLOGY INC (PA)
Also Called: Jacyl Web Design
6020 Huguenard Rd (46818-1304)
PHONE.....................................260 471-6067
Rhonda Huebner, *CEO*
Joel Huebner, *President*
EMP: 2
SQ FT: 3,400
SALES (est): 500K **Privately Held**
WEB: www.jacyltechnology.com
SIC: 3571 Electronic computers

(G-4391)
JAE ENTERPRISES INC
Also Called: Custom Tube Co
8000 Baer Rd (46809-9781)
PHONE.....................................260 747-0568
Fax: 260 747-4981
Tom Ervin, *Purch Mgr*
Dave Seybert, *Branch Mgr*
EMP: 28
SALES (corp-wide): 2.5MM **Privately Held**
WEB: www.waynesteel.us
SIC: 3498 Tube fabricating (contract bending & shaping)
PA: Jae Enterprises, Inc
7707 Freedom Way
Fort Wayne IN 46818
260 489-6249

(G-4392)
JAE ENTERPRISES INC (PA)
Also Called: Custom Tube Co
7707 Freedom Way (46818-2169)
PHONE.....................................260 489-6249
Dave Seybert, *President*
EMP: 1
SALES (est): 2.5MM **Privately Held**
WEB: www.waynesteel.us
SIC: 3498 Tube fabricating (contract bending & shaping)

(G-4393)
JENNYS BACKERY
4151 Diplomat Plaza Ctr (46806-4531)
PHONE.....................................260 447-9592
Carlo Perez, *Branch Mgr*
EMP: 8 EST: 2011
SALES (est): 420K **Privately Held**
SIC: 2051 Biscuits, baked: baking powder & raised

(G-4394)
JENSEN CABINET INC
205 Murray St (46803-2334)
P.O. Box 10599 (46853-0599)
PHONE.....................................260 456-2131
Fax: 260 456-1912
Thomas L Dedrick, *President*
Jane Franklin, *Treasurer*
Brian K Robertson, *Director*
Daniel D Rohloff, *Director*
David M Wester, *Director*
EMP: 40 EST: 1945
SQ FT: 80,000
SALES (est): 8.1MM **Privately Held**
WEB: www.jensencabinet.com
SIC: 2541 Cabinets, except refrigerated: show, display, etc.: wood; partitions for floor attachment, prefabricated: wood

(G-4395)
JINNINGS EQUIPMENT LLC
4434 Allen Martin Dr (46806-2802)
PHONE.....................................260 447-4343
Fax: 260 447-4363
Justin Arnold, *Sales Staff*
Noel Horvath, *Manager*
Brad Jinnings, *Manager*
Scott H Jinnings, *Manager*
Ryan Eltzroth, *Technician*
▲ EMP: 6
SQ FT: 8,000
SALES (est): 1.5MM **Privately Held**
WEB: www.jinnings.com
SIC: 3531 Pile drivers (construction machinery)

(G-4396)
JM FITTINGS LLC
Also Called: L & L Fittings Mfg
9910 Airport Dr (46809-3041)
P.O. Box 11324 (46857-1324)
PHONE.....................................260 747-9200
Fax: 260 747-9119
Pat Senak, *Controller*
Sharon Sharp, *Personnel*
David Schenkel, *Mng Member*
▲ EMP: 100 EST: 1967
SQ FT: 53,000
SALES (est): 19.6MM **Privately Held**
WEB: www.llfittings.com
SIC: 3494 3463 3498 3492 Pipe fittings; nonferrous forgings; fabricated pipe & fittings; fluid power valves & hose fittings; manufactured hardware (general)

(G-4397)
JOHNSON CONTROLS INC
1300 Airport North Off Pa (46825-6716)
PHONE.....................................260 489-6104
EMP: 80
SALES (corp-wide): 37.1B **Publicly Held**
SIC: 3691 3469 Mfg Storage Batteries Mfg Metal Stampings
PA: Johnson Controls, Inc.
5757 N Green Bay Ave
Milwaukee WI 53209
414 524-1200

(G-4398)
JOHNSON CONTROLS INC
6010 Brandy Chase Cv (46815-7601)
PHONE.....................................260 485-9999
EMP: 2 **Privately Held**
SIC: 2531 Seats, automobile
HQ: Johnson Controls, Inc.
5757 N Green Bay Ave
Milwaukee WI 53209
414 524-1200

(G-4399)
JOHNSON CONTROLS INC
8710 Indianapolis Rd (46809)
PHONE.....................................260 479-4400
Fax: 260 479-2535
Bruce Beach, *Manager*
EMP: 150 **Privately Held**

SIC: 2531 Seats, automobile
HQ: Johnson Controls, Inc.
5757 N Green Bay Ave
Milwaukee WI 53209
414 524-1200

(G-4400)
JOURNAL GAZETTE FOUNDATION
600 W Main St (46802-1498)
PHONE.....................................260 424-5257
Harriett J Inskeep, *President*
Julie Inskeep, *Vice Pres*
Stephen Inskeep, *Vice Pres*
EMP: 6
SALES (est): 343.2K **Privately Held**
WEB: www.jg.net
SIC: 2711 Commercial printing & newspaper publishing combined; newspapers, publishing & printing

(G-4401)
JPT ENTERPRISES INC
6435 W Jefferson Blvd (46804-6203)
PHONE.....................................260 672-1605
Paul Tweet, *CEO*
EMP: 6
SALES (est): 564.6K **Privately Held**
WEB: www.jpr-enterprises.com
SIC: 2911 8999 Oils, fuel; services

(G-4402)
K & S PALLET INC
1025 Osage St (46808-3401)
PHONE.....................................260 422-1264
Fax: 260 422-6968
Steve Lefebvre, *President*
EMP: 17
SQ FT: 7,000
SALES (est): 2.4MM **Privately Held**
SIC: 2448 5031 4953 Pallets, wood; pallets, wood; refuse systems

(G-4403)
KAISER TOOL COMPANY INC
Also Called: Laser Images
3620 Centennial Dr (46808-4514)
P.O. Box 80430 (46898-0430)
PHONE.....................................260 484-3620
Fax: 260 482-1881
Lenore E Perry, *President*
Douglas Perry, *Vice Pres*
EMP: 48 EST: 1955
SQ FT: 20,000
SALES (est): 9.1MM **Privately Held**
SIC: 3545 5085 3541 3423 Machine tool attachments & accessories; industrial supplies; machine tools, metal cutting type; hand & edge tools

(G-4404)
KAUFFMAN ENTERPRISES INC
Also Called: Video Video
7875 Shaker Ct (46804-5708)
PHONE.....................................260 434-1590
Kean Kauffman, *President*
EMP: 6 EST: 1996
SQ FT: 845
SALES (est): 500K **Privately Held**
WEB: www.videovideo.com
SIC: 3651 Compact disk players

(G-4405)
KEEFER PRINTING COMPANY INC
3824 Transportation Dr (46818-1223)
PHONE.....................................260 424-4543
Fax: 260 424-5590
Richard F Keefer, *President*
Tim Tracey, *Plant Mgr*
James M Keefer, *Treasurer*
Pat Keefer, *Marketing Staff*
Chris Schenkel, *Manager*
EMP: 27 EST: 1926
SQ FT: 43,000
SALES: 3.5MM **Privately Held**
SIC: 2759 Letterpress printing

(G-4406)
KELLEY CADILLAC LLC
811 Avenue Of Autos (46804-1182)
PHONE.....................................260 434-4646
Michael McKinney, *Mng Member*
EMP: 2 EST: 2013
SALES (est): 150.7K **Privately Held**
SIC: 3589 Car washing machinery

(G-4407)
KELLY BOX AND PACKAGING CORP (PA)
2801 Covington Rd (46802-6969)
PHONE...................................260 432-4570
Thomas J Kelly, *President*
Adam Kelly, *Controller*
Kristi Roemer, *Human Res Mgr*
Stacy Webb, *Cust Mgr*
Joe Colley, *Sales Staff*
EMP: 95 EST: 1955
SQ FT: 120,000
SALES (est): 21.5MM **Privately Held**
WEB: www.kellybox.com
SIC: 2653 5199 Boxes, corrugated: made from purchased materials; packaging materials

(G-4408)
KEMTUNE INC
2015 S Calhoun St (46802-6411)
P.O. Box 11325 (46857-1325)
PHONE...................................260 745-0722
Fax: 260 456-3598
Gloria Sanderson, *President*
EMP: 4 EST: 1964
SQ FT: 13,000
SALES (est): 444.2K **Privately Held**
SIC: 3589 Water treatment equipment, industrial

(G-4409)
KERHAM INC
Also Called: Mark Fore Sales
205 E Collins Rd (46825-5303)
P.O. Box 80160 (46898-0160)
PHONE...................................260 483-5444
Fax: 260 484-8776
Kevin Gould, *President*
EMP: 25
SQ FT: 23,000
SALES (est): 2.1MM **Privately Held**
WEB: www.markforesales.com
SIC: 5941 5091 2396 2395 Bowling equipment & supplies; bowling equipment; automotive & apparel trimmings; pleating & stitching; signs & advertising specialties

(G-4410)
KEY MILLWORK INC
1830 Wayne Trce (46803-2657)
PHONE...................................260 426-6501
Tom Klaffke, *President*
EMP: 8
SQ FT: 6,500
SALES: 1MM **Privately Held**
SIC: 2431 Millwork

(G-4411)
KISSY FACE LIPSTICK LLC
1542 Reed Rd Apt E (46815-7356)
PHONE...................................260 797-5024
EMP: 2
SALES (est): 74.4K **Privately Held**
SIC: 2844 Mfg Toilet Preparations

(G-4412)
KLOTZ SPECIAL FORMULA PRODUCTS
Also Called: Klotz Synthetic Lubricants
7424 Freedom Way (46818-2100)
PHONE...................................260 490-0489
Fax: 260 490-0490
John C Klotz Jr, *President*
EMP: 11
SQ FT: 30,000
SALES (est): 1.6MM **Privately Held**
WEB: www.klotzlube.com
SIC: 2992 Lubricating oils & greases

(G-4413)
KLX AEROSPACE INC
4250 Airport Expy (46809-9643)
PHONE...................................260 747-0671
EMP: 2
SALES (est): 112K **Privately Held**
SIC: 3721 Aircraft

(G-4414)
KOOMLER & SONS INC
3820 Superior Ridge Dr (46808-4423)
PHONE...................................260 482-7641
Fax: 260 471-7341
Dennis Koomler, *President*

Mark Koomler, *Vice Pres*
Brad Koomler, *Treasurer*
EMP: 10
SALES: 1.2MM **Privately Held**
SIC: 3444 Sheet metalwork

(G-4415)
KPC MEDIA GROUP INC
Also Called: Fort Wayne Business Weekly
3306 Independence Dr (46808-4510)
PHONE...................................260 426-2640
Don Cooper, *Branch Mgr*
Linda Lipp, *Associate*
EMP: 20
SALES (corp-wide): 28.7MM **Privately Held**
SIC: 2711 2791 2752 Newspapers, publishing & printing; typesetting; commercial printing, lithographic
PA: Kpc Media Group Inc.
102 N Main St
Kendallville IN 46755
260 347-0400

(G-4416)
KRONMILLER MACHINE & TOOL
2230 Lakeview Dr (46808-3926)
PHONE...................................260 436-1355
Fax: 260 436-1355
Michael D Kronmiller, *President*
EMP: 7
SQ FT: 4,000
SALES (est): 1.1MM **Privately Held**
SIC: 3544 Special dies, tools, jigs & fixtures

(G-4417)
KT INDUSTRIES LLC
3925 Ardmore Ave (46802-4237)
PHONE...................................260 432-0027
Fax: 260 436-2195
Dan Alt, *Principal*
▼ EMP: 2
SALES (est): 134.7K **Privately Held**
SIC: 3999 Manufacturing industries

(G-4418)
KTI CUTTING TOOLS INC
7007 Trafalgar Dr (46803-3288)
PHONE...................................260 749-1465
Kevin Miguel, *President*
Todd Gibson, *Vice Pres*
EMP: 3
SQ FT: 1,000
SALES: 500K **Privately Held**
SIC: 3545 Cutting tools for machine tools

(G-4419)
L H CARBIDE CORPORATION (HQ)
4420 Clubview Dr (46804-4407)
PHONE...................................260 432-5563
Fax: 260 432-2503
Bruce Emerick, *Ch of Bd*
Leon O Habegger, *Ch of Bd*
Tom Neuenschwander, *Vice Pres*
Shari Nuttle, *Purchasing*
Adam Falk, *Design Engr*
▲ EMP: 195
SQ FT: 92,000
SALES: 19.5MM
SALES (corp-wide): 3.4MM **Privately Held**
WEB: www.lhcarbide.com
SIC: 3544 Special dies & tools
PA: L.H. Industries Corp.
4420 Clubview Dr
Fort Wayne IN 46804
260 432-5563

(G-4420)
L H CONTROLS INC
4208 Clubview Dr (46804-4403)
PHONE...................................260 432-9020
Leon Habegger, *Ch of Bd*
Bruce Emerick, *President*
Bradley N Habegger, *Vice Pres*
Dan Brehm, *CFO*
EMP: 16
SQ FT: 40,000
SALES: 5MM
SALES (corp-wide): 3.4MM **Privately Held**
WEB: www.lhcontrols.com
SIC: 3625 Relays & industrial controls

HQ: L H Carbide Corporation
4420 Clubview Dr
Fort Wayne IN 46804
260 432-5563

(G-4421)
L H STAMPING CORPORATION (HQ)
4420 Clubview Dr (46804-4407)
PHONE...................................260 432-5563
Fax: 260 436-2783
Bruce Emerick, *President*
Leon Habegger, *Chairman*
Bradley Habegger, *Vice Pres*
Jim Turney, *Plant Mgr*
Dan Brehm, *CFO*
EMP: 83
SQ FT: 20,000
SALES: 33MM
SALES (corp-wide): 3.4MM **Privately Held**
WEB: www.lhstamping.com
SIC: 3469 Stamping metal for the trade
PA: L.H. Industries Corp.
4420 Clubview Dr
Fort Wayne IN 46804
260 432-5563

(G-4422)
LAKEVIEW ENGINEERED PDTS INC
2500 W Jefferson Blvd (46802-4641)
PHONE...................................260 432-3479
Fax: 260 432-6239
Donald J Akey, *President*
Alberta Akey, *Vice Pres*
EMP: 7
SALES (est): 1.2MM **Privately Held**
WEB: www.lakeviewengineered.com
SIC: 3443 Fabricated plate work (boiler shop)

(G-4423)
LAMBERT METAL FINISHING INC
Also Called: Smith Metal Finishing
6912 Derek Dr (46803-3299)
PHONE...................................260 493-0529
Chad Lambert, *President*
Robert Muhn, *Vice Pres*
EMP: 8
SALES (est): 842.9K **Privately Held**
SIC: 3471 Finishing, metals or formed products

(G-4424)
LASSUS BROS OIL INC
10225 Illinois Rd (46814-8971)
PHONE...................................260 625-4003
Andy Carmichael, *Branch Mgr*
EMP: 29
SALES (corp-wide): 164.5MM **Privately Held**
SIC: 1311 Crude petroleum & natural gas
PA: Lassus Bros Oil Inc
1800 Magnavox Way
Fort Wayne IN 46804
260 436-1415

(G-4425)
LATHAM MANUFACTURING CORP
Fort Wayne Pools
6932 Gettysburg Pike (46804-5614)
PHONE...................................260 459-4115
Fax: 260 459-4151
EMP: 150 **Publicly Held**
SIC: 3086 Mfg Plastic Foam Products
HQ: Latham Manufacturing Corp.
787 Watervliet Shaker Rd
Latham NY 12110
518 783-7776

(G-4426)
LAUER LOG HOMES
6630 Reed Rd (46835-2271)
PHONE...................................260 486-7010
Connie Lauer, *Owner*
EMP: 2 EST: 1995
SALES: 400K **Privately Held**
WEB: www.lauerloghomes.com
SIC: 2452 Log cabins, prefabricated, wood

(G-4427)
LAWRENCE INDUSTRIES INC
10403 Arbor Trl (46804-4607)
PHONE...................................260 432-9693
Kerry L McAtee, *President*
EMP: 2
SALES (est): 218.4K **Privately Held**
SIC: 3353 Aluminum sheet, plate & foil

(G-4428)
LCF ENTERPRISES LLC
10316 Valley Hills Ln (46825-1776)
PHONE...................................260 483-3248
Fax: 260 471-7407
Hugh W Johnston Sr,
EMP: 5 EST: 1993
SALES (est): 690K **Privately Held**
WEB: www.lcfhomes.com
SIC: 2451 Mobile homes

(G-4429)
LEE MFG LLC
9529 Marquis Ln (46835-9207)
PHONE...................................260 403-2775
Thomas Long, *Principal*
EMP: 2
SALES (est): 87K **Privately Held**
SIC: 3999 Manufacturing industries

(G-4430)
LEEPOXY PLASTICS INC
3706 W Ferguson Rd (46809-3199)
PHONE...................................260 747-7411
Fax: 260 747-7413
Lawrence H Lee, *President*
Tom Weber, *Info Tech Mgr*
EMP: 5 EST: 1965
SQ FT: 14,400
SALES (est): 1.1MM **Privately Held**
WEB: www.leepoxy.com
SIC: 2821 Epoxy resins; polyurethane resins

(G-4431)
LH INDUSTRIES CORP (PA)
4420 Clubview Dr (46804-4407)
PHONE...................................260 432-5563
Leon O Habegger, *President*
Bruce Emerick, *President*
Thomas Neuenschwander, *President*
Joe Siela, *COO*
Jim Tourney, *Plant Mgr*
EMP: 291
SQ FT: 10,000
SALES: 3.4MM **Privately Held**
WEB: www.lhindustries.com/
SIC: 3469 3544 8741 Stamping metal for the trade; special dies, tools, jigs & fixtures; management services

(G-4432)
LH MEDICAL CORPORATION
6932 Gettysburg Pike (46804-5614)
PHONE...................................260 387-5194
Bruce Emerick, *President*
Bradley N Habegger, *Vice Pres*
Leon Habegger, *Director*
Scott Nine, *Director*
Warren Brehm, *Admin Sec*
EMP: 80
SQ FT: 64,000
SALES: 15MM
SALES (corp-wide): 3.4MM **Privately Held**
SIC: 5047 3841 Orthopedic equipment & supplies; surgical instruments & apparatus
HQ: L H Carbide Corporation
4420 Clubview Dr
Fort Wayne IN 46804
260 432-5563

(G-4433)
LICENSED ELIQUID MANUFACTURING
6746 E State Blvd (46815-7762)
PHONE...................................260 687-9213
Shawn Anderson, *Principal*
EMP: 2
SALES (est): 43.6K **Privately Held**
SIC: 3999 Manufacturing industries

(G-4434)
LIDS CORPORATION
Also Called: Lids Kids
4201 Coldwater Rd Ste 506 (46805-1120)
PHONE...................................260 471-4287
Darrell Bureom, *Manager*
EMP: 6
SALES (corp-wide): 2.9B **Publicly Held**
WEB: www.hatworld.com
SIC: 2353 Hats & caps
HQ: Lids Corporation
7555 Woodland Dr
Indianapolis IN 46278

(G-4435)
LIFE MANAGEMENT INC (PA)
Also Called: Airomat
2916 Engle Rd (46809-1106)
PHONE...................................260 747-7408
Fax: 260 747-7409
Joanne K Feasel, *President*
Jody Feasel, *Vice Pres*
Pamela J Peters, *Vice Pres*
EMP: 8 EST: 1958
SQ FT: 6,000
SALES (est): 626.5K **Privately Held**
SIC: 3089 Plastic hardware & building
products

(G-4436)
LIGHTHOUSE PUBL MINISTRIES
9903 Canopy Ln (46835-9330)
P.O. Box 80343 (46898-0343)
PHONE...................................260 209-6948
EMP: 2
SALES (est): 78.1K **Privately Held**
SIC: 2741 Misc Publishing

(G-4437)
**LINCOLN PRINTING
CORPORATION**
3310 Congressional Pkwy (46808-4439)
PHONE...................................260 424-5200
Billy Bradberry, *President*
Liz Hartmann, *General Mgr*
Todd Wiedemann, *Vice Pres*
Max Revere, *Sales Associate*
Mark Linville, *Marketing Staff*
EMP: 40 EST: 1959
SQ FT: 33,000
SALES (est): 6MM
SALES (corp-wide): 585MM **Privately
Held**
WEB: www.consolidatedgraphics.com
SIC: 2752 2791 2789 2761 Commercial
printing, offset; typesetting; bookbinding &
related work; manifold business forms;
commercial printing
PA: R.R. Donnelley Printing Company L.P.
35 W Wacker Dr Ste 3650
Chicago IL 60601
312 326-8000

(G-4438)
LIVE BOLD AEROSPACE LLC
6914 Hiltonia Dr (46819-1326)
PHONE...................................260 438-5710
EMP: 2
SALES (est): 104.8K **Privately Held**
SIC: 3721 Aircraft

(G-4439)
**LOADING DOCK MAINTENANCE
LLC**
5032 Moeller Rd (46806-1504)
PHONE...................................260 424-3635
Rod Sebring,
EMP: 3
SALES (est): 399.2K **Privately Held**
WEB: www.loadingdockmaintenance.com
SIC: 3599 7692 Machine shop, jobbing &
repair; welding repair

(G-4440)
LONE STAR INDUSTRIES INC
4805 Investment Dr (46808-3609)
PHONE...................................260 482-4559
Ken Squires, *Manager*
EMP: 2
SALES (corp-wide): 287.7MM **Privately
Held**
SIC: 3241 Portland cement

HQ: Lone Star Industries Inc
10401 N Meridian St # 400
Indianapolis IN 46290
317 706-3314

(G-4441)
LONG TAIL CORPORATION (PA)
Also Called: Long Tail Technology
5738 Coventry Ln (46804-7141)
PHONE...................................260 918-0489
Brian Hill, *President*
EMP: 6
SALES: 300K **Privately Held**
SIC: 7373 7372 7374 Computer inte-
grated systems design; application com-
puter software; computer graphics service

(G-4442)
LUBE-LINE CORPORATION (PA)
906 Carroll Rd (46845-9778)
PHONE...................................260 637-3779
Thomas Luchies, *President*
EMP: 3
SQ FT: 4,000
SALES (est): 476.2K **Privately Held**
WEB: www.lubetec.com
SIC: 3569 Lubricating systems, centralized

(G-4443)
**LUCAS BUS FORMS & SWIFT
PRTG**
Also Called: Printing Press, The
3020 Cngrnnal Pkwy Ste Ab (46808)
PHONE...................................260 482-7644
Fax: 260 482-6779
James K Lucas, *President*
Margaret E Lucas, *Treasurer*
Bradley Lucas,
Robert Lucas,
EMP: 7
SALES (est): 1MM **Privately Held**
SIC: 2752 5112 Commercial printing, off-
set; business forms

(G-4444)
LUTE SUPPLY
5406 Keystone Dr (46825-5134)
PHONE...................................260 480-2441
Jason Lute, *President*
EMP: 3
SALES (est): 239.3K **Privately Held**
SIC: 5722 5075 3585 Air conditioning
room units, self-contained; warm air heat-
ing equipment & supplies; heating equip-
ment, complete

(G-4445)
LYRA LLC
3711 Astoria Way (46818-8744)
PHONE...................................260 452-4058
Andrew Conner, *Principal*
EMP: 2
SALES (est): 88.3K **Privately Held**
SIC: 3661 3669 7389 Telephone & tele-
graph apparatus; intercommunication sys-
tems, electric;

(G-4446)
**M & J SHELTON ENTERPRISES
INC**
2131 Fairfield Ave (46802-5160)
PHONE...................................260 745-1616
Fax: 260 745-7425
Mike Shelton, *President*
Norma Shelton, *Vice Pres*
EMP: 8
SQ FT: 20,000
SALES (est): 856.7K **Privately Held**
SIC: 3999 1799 Dock equipment & sup-
plies, industrial; dock equipment installa-
tion, industrial; coating, caulking &
weather, water & fireproofing

(G-4447)
**MACALLISTER MACHINERY CO
INC**
Also Called: Caterpillar Authorized Dealer
2500 W Coliseum Blvd (46808-3640)
PHONE...................................260 483-6469
Fax: 260 471-9932
Dennis Sawcett, *Branch Mgr*
Zac Cleary, *Manager*
EMP: 65

SALES (corp-wide): 1B **Privately Held**
WEB: www.mallister.com
SIC: 3492 5082 5084 7699 Hose & tube
fittings & assemblies, hydraulic/pneu-
matic; contractors' materials; engines &
parts, diesel; hydraulic equipment repair;
general automotive repair shops; heavy
construction equipment rental
PA: Macallister Machinery Co Inc
6300 Southeastern Ave
Indianapolis IN 46203
317 545-2151

(G-4448)
**MACHINE REBUILDERS &
SERVICE**
Also Called: Mrs International
4801 Projects Dr (46825-5312)
PHONE...................................260 482-8168
Fax: 260 482-1078
Willi Breuning, *President*
Don Taube, *Vice Pres*
EMP: 12
SQ FT: 15,000
SALES (est): 1.9MM **Privately Held**
WEB: www.mrsinternational.com
SIC: 3599 7694 Machine shop, jobbing &
repair; armature rewinding shops

(G-4449)
MAGIC COMPANY
Also Called: Magic Premium Snacks
405 Lower Huntington Rd (46819-1522)
PHONE...................................260 747-1502
James Godschalk, *President*
▲ EMP: 30
SQ FT: 37,000
SALES: 4.9MM **Privately Held**
SIC: 2096 2099 Potato chips & other po-
tato-based snacks; food preparations

(G-4450)
**MAMON GLOBAL INDUSTRIES
INC**
1009 Manck Dr (46814-8991)
PHONE...................................317 721-1657
Kevin Jemar Mamon, *President*
EMP: 5
SALES (est): 179.9K **Privately Held**
SIC: 3999 Manufacturing industries

(G-4451)
**MANN+HUMMEL FILTRATION
TECHNOL**
9602 Coldwater Rd Ste 104 (46825-2095)
PHONE...................................260 497-5560
Brenda Moore, *Manager*
EMP: 6
SALES (corp-wide): 4.5B **Privately Held**
WEB: www.affiniagroup.com
SIC: 3714 Motor vehicle parts & acces-
sories
HQ: Mann+Hummel Filtration Technology
Group Inc.
1 Wix Way
Gastonia NC 28054
704 869-3300

(G-4452)
MANTECH MANIFOLD
9105 Clubridge Dr (46809-3045)
PHONE...................................260 479-2383
Joe Oberlin, *President*
EMP: 3
SALES (est): 157.1K **Privately Held**
SIC: 3511 Turbines & turbine generator
sets

(G-4453)
MARTIN SPOUTING INC
Also Called: Al-Marco Products
10165 Saint Joe Rd (46835-9549)
PHONE...................................260 485-5703
EMP: 7
SQ FT: 2,000
SALES: 300K **Privately Held**
SIC: 3444 5033 5039 Mfg Aluminum
Spouting & Siding

(G-4454)
MASO INC
Also Called: Masolite
2200 Lafontain St (46802-6967)
PHONE...................................260 432-3568
Fax: 260 436-2788

William Kriesel, *President*
Greg Calhoun, *Plant Mgr*
Jerry Powers, *Plant Mgr*
Steve Ratliff, *Purchasing*
EMP: 16 EST: 1930
SQ FT: 20,000
SALES (est): 3.3MM **Privately Held**
WEB: www.masolite.com
SIC: 3272 Concrete products

(G-4455)
MASTER CORPORATION
Also Called: Master Sports
6206 Discount Dr (46818-1232)
PHONE...................................260 471-0001
Fax: 260 490-7643
EMP: 10
SALES (est): 740K **Privately Held**
SIC: 3949 Sporting And Athletic Goods,
Nec

(G-4456)
MASTER SPAS INC
6927 Lincoln Pkwy (46804-5623)
PHONE...................................260 436-9100
Fax: 260 432-7935
Robert Lauter, *CEO*
Terry Valmassoi, *President*
Deb Moehlenkamp, *Purchasing*
Bruce Kelsey, *QC Mgr*
Nathan Coelho, *Engineer*
▼ EMP: 225
SQ FT: 185,000
SALES (est): 39.7MM **Privately Held**
WEB: www.gazebomaster.com
SIC: 3999 5999 Hot tubs; spas & hot tubs

(G-4457)
**MATSON COUNSULTING
ENGINEERS**
3131 Engle Rd (46809-1109)
PHONE...................................260 478-8813
Fax: 260 478-8815
Lon B Leech, *President*
Jill Leech, *Vice Pres*
Herbert Hildebrand, *Electrical Engi*
EMP: 6
SALES (est): 855.5K **Privately Held**
WEB: www.matsoneng.com
SIC: 3825 Frequency meters: electrical,
mechanical & electronic

(G-4458)
MAXWELL ENGINEERING INC
616 E Wallace St (46803-2368)
PHONE...................................260 745-4991
Matt Maxwell, *President*
EMP: 9
SQ FT: 16,000
SALES (est): 960K **Privately Held**
WEB: www.maxwell-engineering.com
SIC: 3543 3544 3999 Foundry pattern-
making; industrial molds; models, gen-
eral, except toy

(G-4459)
MCCOY BOLT WORKS INC
2811 Congressional Pkwy (46808-1389)
PHONE...................................260 482-4476
Fax: 260 483-6775
Robert M Mc Ardle, *President*
Lisa Houston, *Principal*
Timothy Houston, *Principal*
Marvin Huston, *Principal*
Mark Brown, *Asst Treas*
▲ EMP: 55
SQ FT: 40,000
SALES (est): 11.3MM **Privately Held**
WEB: www.mccoybolt.com
SIC: 3452 Bolts, metal

(G-4460)
MCCRORY PUBLISHING
2530 Deerwood Dr (46825-3918)
PHONE...................................260 485-1812
Greg McCrory, *Owner*
EMP: 2
SALES (est): 137.7K **Privately Held**
SIC: 2741 Miscellaneous publishing

(G-4461)
MCMILLAN EXPRESS
3505 Wayne Trce (46806-4557)
PHONE...................................260 447-7648
J Singh, *Owner*
EMP: 4

SALES (est): 265.4K **Privately Held**
SIC: 2741 Miscellaneous publishing

(G-4462)
MCNEILUS TRUCK AND MFG INC
7520 Freedom Way (46818-2167)
PHONE..................................260 489-3031
Paul Ellingen, *Manager*
EMP: 4
SALES (corp-wide): 6.8B **Publicly Held**
WEB: www.mcneiluscompanies.com
SIC: 3713 Cement mixer bodies
HQ: Mcneilus Truck And Manufacturing, Inc.
　　524 County Rd 34 E
　　Dodge Center MN 55927
　　614 868-0760

(G-4463)
MDL WOODWORKING LLC
1011 W Packard Ave (46807-1753)
PHONE..................................260 242-1824
Michael Liechty, *Administration*
EMP: 2
SALES (est): 79.2K **Privately Held**
SIC: 2431 Millwork

(G-4464)
MEISTER COOK LLC
3217 Stellhorn Rd Ste A (46815-8663)
PHONE..................................260 399-6692
Erik Magner, *Principal*
Myron Yoder, *Sales Staff*
Betsy Magner, *Marketing Mgr*
John Piramalla, *Technician*
EMP: 2
SALES (est): 233K **Privately Held**
SIC: 3589 Food warming equipment, commercial

(G-4465)
MENARD INC
7702 Southtown Xing (46816-2509)
PHONE..................................260 441-0406
Fax: 260 441-8180
John Menard, *Branch Mgr*
EMP: 50
SALES (corp-wide): 13B **Privately Held**
WEB: www.menards.com
SIC: 2431 Millwork
PA: Menard, Inc.
　　5101 Menard Dr
　　Eau Claire WI 54703
　　715 876-5911

(G-4466)
MERIWETHER TOOL & ENGINEERING
10108 Smith Rd (46809-9771)
PHONE..................................260 744-6955
Fax: 260 744-0027
Bob Meriwether, *President*
▲ EMP: 12
SQ FT: 8,000
SALES (est): 211K **Privately Held**
SIC: 3312 3549 Tool & die steel; metalworking machinery

(G-4467)
MET PAK SPECIALTIES INC
2701 S Coliseum Blvd # 1172 (46803-2900)
PHONE..................................260 420-2217
Monty Oakes, *President*
Tim Beery, *Materials Mgr*
EMP: 15
SQ FT: 50,000
SALES (est): 3.3MM **Privately Held**
SIC: 2653 Boxes, corrugated: made from purchased materials

(G-4468)
METROLOGY SERVICES LLC
Also Called: Apex Metrology Solutions
3020 Cngrnonal Pkwy Ste G (46808)
PHONE..................................260 969-8424
Walt Maurer, *President*
EMP: 2
SQ FT: 900
SALES (est): 509.3K
SALES (corp-wide): 155.1MM **Publicly Held**
SIC: 3825 Standards & calibrating equipment, laboratory

PA: Transcat, Inc.
　　35 Vantage Point Dr
　　Rochester NY 14624
　　585 352-7777

(G-4469)
MEXICANO NEWSLETTER
2301 Fairfield Ave # 102 (46807-1253)
PHONE..................................260 704-0682
Fernando Zapari, *Owner*
EMP: 2
SALES (est): 62.9K **Privately Held**
SIC: 2711 Newspapers

(G-4470)
MICHIANA BUSINESS PUBLICATIONS
Also Called: Business People Magazine
7729 Westfield Dr (46825-8313)
PHONE..................................260 497-0433
Fax: 260 497-0822
Daniel Copeland, *President*
Teresa Harmeyer, *Accounts Exec*
Andrea Hatfield, *Accounts Exec*
Megan Mantica, *Accounts Exec*
Lisa Thompson, *Accounts Exec*
EMP: 7
SALES (est): 630K **Privately Held**
SIC: 2721 Magazines: publishing only, not printed on site

(G-4471)
MID AMERICA SIGN CORPORATION (PA)
1319 Production Rd (46808-1164)
PHONE..................................260 744-2200
Fax: 260 456-6114
Richard D Middleton, *President*
EMP: 18
SQ FT: 18,000
SALES (est): 1.9MM **Privately Held**
WEB: www.mid-americasign.net
SIC: 3993 Signs, not made in custom sign painting shops

(G-4472)
MIDWEST ORTHOTIC SERVICES LLC
417 Fernhill Ave (46805-1039)
PHONE..................................574 233-3352
Laura Veldman, *Manager*
EMP: 5
SALES (est): 464.6K
SALES (corp-wide): 14MM **Privately Held**
SIC: 3842 Prosthetic appliances
PA: Midwest Orthotic Services, Llc
　　17530 Dugdale Dr
　　South Bend IN 46635
　　574 233-3352

(G-4473)
MIDWEST PRECISION MACHINING
3626 Illinois Rd (46804-2062)
PHONE..................................260 459-6866
Jeff Bernath, *President*
EMP: 5
SALES (est): 73.8K **Privately Held**
SIC: 3549 Metalworking machinery

(G-4474)
MIDWEST TOOL & DIE CORP
Also Called: Mtd
1126 Sunset Lake Cv (46845-9009)
PHONE..................................260 483-4282
Fax: 260 482-7261
Victor Felger, *President*
David Venderly, *Admin Sec*
EMP: 35 EST: 1974
SQ FT: 40,000
SALES (est): 4.5MM **Privately Held**
WEB: www.midwest-tool.com
SIC: 3544 Special dies & tools

(G-4475)
MIGHTY-QUIP INDUSTRIES
921 E Dupont Rd 894 (46825-1551)
PHONE..................................260 615-1899
Harlan Wheeler, *Owner*
EMP: 2
SALES (est): 166.5K **Privately Held**
SIC: 3621 Motors & generators

(G-4476)
MINNICH MFG INC
2421 W Wallen Rd (46818-2249)
PHONE..................................260 489-5357
Fax: 260 489-4468
Robert J Minnich Jr, *President*
Robert Minnich, *President*
Sharon A Minnich, *Admin Sec*
EMP: 6
SQ FT: 2,400
SALES (est): 650K **Privately Held**
SIC: 3599 Machine shop, jobbing & repair

(G-4477)
MINNICK CONCRETE PRODUCTS INC
Also Called: Minnick Services
222 N Thomas Rd (46808-2910)
P.O. Box 11000 (46855-1100)
PHONE..................................260 432-5031
Mark Minnick, *President*
Alice Minnick, *Corp Secy*
Rick Schaefer, *Vice Pres*
EMP: 28
SQ FT: 45,000
SALES (est): 5.1MM **Privately Held**
WEB: www.curbs.com
SIC: 3272 5032 Burial vaults, concrete or precast terrazzo; concrete products, precast; concrete building products

(G-4478)
MIRTEQ HOLDINGS INC
2201 Suppliers Ct (46818-1172)
PHONE..................................260 490-3706
Thomas Lavin, *CEO*
EMP: 3 EST: 2015
SALES (est): 163.2K **Privately Held**
SIC: 2869 Industrial organic chemicals

(G-4479)
MOBILE MINI INC
5314 Maumee Rd (46803-1727)
PHONE..................................260 749-6611
David Staadt, *Branch Mgr*
EMP: 2
SALES (corp-wide): 533.5MM **Publicly Held**
SIC: 3448 Prefabricated metal buildings
PA: Mobile Mini, Inc.
　　4646 E Van Buren St # 400
　　Phoenix AZ 85008
　　480 894-6311

(G-4480)
MOOSE LAKE PRODUCTS CO
Also Called: First Flash Line
6528 Constitution Dr (46804-1550)
PHONE..................................260 432-2768
Fax: 260 436-6739
Jeff Mettler, *President*
EMP: 15
SQ FT: 5,000
SALES (est): 1.4MM **Privately Held**
WEB: www.firstflash.com
SIC: 7336 2759 Graphic arts & related design; promotional printing

(G-4481)
MORGAN COMMERCIAL LETTERING
434 Merkler St (46825-5228)
PHONE..................................260 482-6430
Gary Morgan, *Owner*
EMP: 2
SALES (est): 146K **Privately Held**
SIC: 3993 Signs & advertising specialties

(G-4482)
MPP INC
Also Called: Metal Plate Polishing
2413 Meyer Rd (46803-2911)
PHONE..................................260 422-5426
James McCall, *President*
Lee Biddle, *General Mgr*
EMP: 40
SQ FT: 30,000
SALES (est): 4.6MM **Privately Held**
WEB: www.mpp.com
SIC: 3471 3599 Finishing, metals or formed products; machine shop, jobbing & repair

(G-4483)
MULLINIX PACKAGES INC (HQ)
3511 Engle Rd (46809-1117)
PHONE..................................260 747-3149
Fax: 260 747-1598
Gene Gentili, *President*
Belinda Glenn, *CFO*
▲ EMP: 161
SQ FT: 409,000
SALES (est): 98.6MM
SALES (corp-wide): 161.6MM **Privately Held**
WEB: www.mullinixpackages.com
SIC: 3089 Plastic containers, except foam
PA: Sabert Corporation
　　2288 Main St
　　Sayreville NJ 08872
　　800 722-3781

(G-4484)
MULTIMATIC NEW HAVEN LLC (PA) ✪
2808 Adams Center Rd (46803-3218)
PHONE..................................260 868-1067
Lance Harris, *Controller*
Peter Czapka, *President*
EMP: 4 EST: 2017
SQ FT: 125,000
SALES (est): 75MM **Privately Held**
SIC: 3465 Body parts, automobile: stamped metal

(G-4485)
MURPAC OF FORT WAYNE LLC
3405 Meyer Rd Ste 135 (46803-2983)
PHONE..................................260 424-2299
EMP: 7
SALES (est): 912.9K **Privately Held**
SIC: 3499 Reels, cable: metal

(G-4486)
MURRAY EQUIPMENT INC
Also Called: Total Control Systems
2515 Charleston Pl (46808-1397)
PHONE..................................260 484-0382
Fax: 260 484-9230
Stephen Murray, *President*
Darren Eavis, *Business Mgr*
Daniel Murray, *Vice Pres*
F David Musselman, *Treasurer*
Shawn Kiefer, *VP Sales*
▲ EMP: 60
SQ FT: 90,000
SALES (est): 58.1MM **Privately Held**
WEB: www.murrayequipment.com
SIC: 5084 3594 Industrial machinery & equipment; materials handling machinery; pumps & pumping equipment; fluid power pumps & motors

(G-4487)
MUZFEED INC
6304 Tanbark Trl (46835-1852)
PHONE..................................815 252-7676
Tyler Berggren, *Principal*
Justin Rix, *Vice Pres*
Dave Sanders, *Vice Pres*
EMP: 3
SALES (est): 124.2K **Privately Held**
SIC: 2721 7389 Periodicals: publishing only;

(G-4488)
N K WELDING PRODUCTS INC
302 W Superior St (46802-1112)
PHONE..................................260 424-1901
Douglas M Kline, *Principal*
EMP: 2
SALES (est): 73.9K **Privately Held**
SIC: 7692 Welding repair

(G-4489)
NANOLAYER TECHNOLOGIES LLC
Also Called: Nanolayer Technology
3523 Knoll Rd (46809-1939)
PHONE..................................260 414-4458
EMP: 10
SALES (est): 690K **Privately Held**
SIC: 2819 Mfg Industrial Inorganic Chemicals

(G-4490)
NATIONAL ATHLETIC SPORTSWEAR
3911 Option Pass (46818-1275)
PHONE..................260 436-2248
Fax: 260 489-0684
Todd Snyder, *President*
EMP: 13
SQ FT: 10,000
SALES (est): 860K Privately Held
SIC: 2395 Embroidery products, except schiffli machine

(G-4491)
NATIONAL RCREATION SYSTEMS INC
Also Called: N R S
1300-D Airport N Off Park (46825-6717)
PHONE..................260 482-6023
Fax: 260 482-7449
Bob Farnsworth, *President*
Karen R Hagan, *Corp Secy*
Rick Vasquez, *Plant Mgr*
Greg Gillig, *Materials Mgr*
Bruce Keuneke, *Purch Mgr*
▼ EMP: 46
SQ FT: 90,000
SALES (est): 9.2MM
SALES (corp-wide): 1.2B Privately Held
WEB: www.bleachers.net
SIC: 2531 Bleacher seating, portable; benches for public buildings
HQ: Playcore Wisconsin, Inc.
544 Chestnut St
Chattanooga TN 37402
423 265-7529

(G-4492)
NATIONWIDE PUBLISHING COMPANY
12110 Glen Lake Dr (46814-4569)
PHONE..................260 312-3924
Michael Kay, *Branch Mgr*
EMP: 4
SALES (corp-wide): 5.7MM Privately Held
SIC: 2741 Telephone & other directory publishing
PA: Nationwide Publishing Company Inc
537 Deltona Blvd
Deltona FL 32725
352 253-0017

(G-4493)
NELSON GLOBAL PRODUCTS INC
Also Called: National Tube Form
3405 Engle Rd (46809-1115)
PHONE..................608 719-1752
Dale Volenberg, *Manager*
EMP: 95 Privately Held
SIC: 3498 Tube fabricating (contract bending & shaping)
PA: Nelson Global Products, Inc.
1560 Williams Dr
Stoughton WI 53589

(G-4494)
NEMCO MEDICAL LTD
8727 Clinton Park Dr (46825-3170)
P.O. Box 263, Hicksville OH (43526-0263)
PHONE..................260 484-1500
Kevin Countryman, *Partner*
EMP: 65
SALES (est): 8.9MM Privately Held
SIC: 3841 Surgical & medical instruments

(G-4495)
NEMCOMED FW LLC
8551 N Clinton St (46825)
PHONE..................260 480-5226
Forrest Whittaker, *CEO*
Rick Link, *Vice Pres*
EMP: 190
SALES (est): 449.9K
SALES (corp-wide): 292.3MM Privately Held
SIC: 3842 Implants, surgical
HQ: Avalign Technologies Inc.
801 Industrial Dr
Hicksville OH 43526

(G-4496)
NEMCOMED INSTRS & IMPLANTS
8727 Clinton Park Dr (46825-3170)
PHONE..................800 255-4576
Forrest R Whittaker, *CEO*
Tony Oneill, *Senior VP*
Scott Gareiss, *Vice Pres*
McNeil Mac Brown, *Vice Pres*
Barbara Sullivan, *CFO*
EMP: 6
SALES (est): 63.9K Privately Held
SIC: 3999 3842 Atomizers, toiletry; surgical appliances & supplies

(G-4497)
NESTLE DREYERS ICE CREAM CO
Also Called: Edys Grd Ice Cream
3426 N Wells St (46808-4001)
PHONE..................260 483-3102
Wayne Clive, *Manager*
EMP: 240
SALES (corp-wide): 90.8B Privately Held
SIC: 2024 Ice cream, bulk
HQ: Nestle Dreyer's Ice Cream Company
5929 College Ave
Oakland CA 94618
510 594-9466

(G-4498)
NEUHAUS INDUSTRIAL MACHINING I
1830 Wayne Trce (46803-2657)
PHONE..................260 710-2845
Kurt Neuhaus, *President*
Kim Neuhaus, *Director*
EMP: 4
SALES (est): 365K Privately Held
SIC: 3541 Machine tool replacement & repair parts, metal cutting types

(G-4499)
NEW DIE CONCEPTS INC
302 E Wallace St (46803-2343)
P.O. Box 12322 (46863-2322)
PHONE..................260 420-9504
Fax: 260 969-6390
EMP: 5
SALES: 200K Privately Held
SIC: 3544 Mfg Dies/Tools/Jigs/Fixtures

(G-4500)
NEW IMAGE PRTG & DESIGN INC
3233 Lafayette St (46806-4049)
PHONE..................260 969-0410
Fax: 260 456-2551
Sharon Miller, *President*
Timothy Spradling, *Engineer*
EMP: 18 EST: 2007
SALES (est): 2.7MM Privately Held
SIC: 2752 Commercial printing, offset

(G-4501)
NEW MLLENNIUM BLDG SYSTEMS LLC (HQ)
7575 W Jefferson Blvd (46804-4131)
PHONE..................260 969-3500
Gary Heasley, *President*
Chris Graham, *Principal*
Bert Hollman, *Principal*
Marvell Williamson, *Maint Spvr*
Christopher Cobbs, *Purch Agent*
▼ EMP: 4
SQ FT: 225,000
SALES (est): 102.1MM Publicly Held
WEB: www.joist-deck.com
SIC: 3441 Joists, open web steel: long-span series

(G-4502)
NEW PROCESS GRAPHICS LLC
310 W Cook Rd (46825-3320)
PHONE..................260 489-1700
Matthew Coffman, *COO*
Christine M Didier-Coffman, *Treasurer*
Corey West, *Accounts Exec*
Jessica Sheets, *Creative Dir*
EMP: 20
SALES (est): 3.2MM Privately Held
SIC: 2759 Screen printing

(G-4503)
NEWS PUBLISHING COMPANY INC (HQ)
600 W Main St (46802-1408)
P.O. Box 100 (46801-0100)
PHONE..................260 461-8444
Scott Mc Gehee, *President*
EMP: 1 EST: 1917
SQ FT: 146,000
SALES (est): 100.5MM
SALES (corp-wide): 903.5MM Publicly Held
SIC: 2711 Newspapers
PA: The Mcclatchy Company
2100 Q St
Sacramento CA 95816
916 321-1846

(G-4504)
NISHIKAWA COOPER LLC
2785 Persistence Dr (46808-1491)
PHONE..................260 593-2156
Steve Folden, *Branch Mgr*
EMP: 250
SALES (corp-wide): 903.4MM Privately Held
SIC: 3069 Weather strip, sponge rubber
HQ: Nishikawa Cooper Llc
324 Morrow St
Topeka IN 46571
260 593-2156

(G-4505)
NORTH COAST ORGANICS LLC
629 E Wash Blvd Fort Wyne (46802)
PHONE..................260 246-0289
Nathan Morin, *Mng Member*
Debbie Morin, *Mng Member*
EMP: 5
SQ FT: 7,000
SALES (est): 157K Privately Held
SIC: 2844 5122 5999 7389 Toilet preparations; toiletries; toiletries, cosmetics & perfumes

(G-4506)
NORTHWEST NEWS & PRINTING
3306 Independence Dr (46808-4510)
PHONE..................260 637-9003
Bob Allman, *Owner*
Ryan Swab, *Manager*
EMP: 2 EST: 1997
SALES (est): 68.9K Privately Held
WEB: www.app-printing.com
SIC: 2711 Newspapers

(G-4507)
OCE CORPORATE PRINTING DIV
6915 Innovation Blvd (46818-1372)
PHONE..................260 436-7395
Ed O'Reilly, *Principal*
EMP: 4
SALES (est): 349.1K Privately Held
SIC: 2752 Commercial printing, lithographic

(G-4508)
ODB INC
Also Called: Our Daily Brew
7203 Wintergreen Dr (46814-8138)
PHONE..................260 673-0062
Lee E Pomerantz, *Principal*
EMP: 3
SALES (est): 112.3K Privately Held
SIC: 2711 Newspapers, publishing & printing

(G-4509)
OFFSET ONE INC
1609 S Calhoun St (46802-5255)
PHONE..................260 456-8828
Fax: 260 744-6839
Kent Whiting, *President*
Bernard Konger, *Principal*
Margaret Konger, *Vice Pres*
EMP: 10 EST: 1981
SQ FT: 18,000
SALES (est): 1.4MM Privately Held
SIC: 2752 2791 2789 2759 Commercial printing, offset; typesetting; bookbinding & related work; commercial printing

(G-4510)
OMNISOURCE LLC (HQ)
Also Called: Omni Auto Parts
7575 W Jefferson Blvd (46804-4131)
PHONE..................260 422-5541
Fax: 260 423-8528
Russell Rinn, *President*
Pat Sitcler, *General Mgr*
Melissa Bain, *Assistant VP*
Mike Hausfeld, *Vice Pres*
Denny Luma, *Vice Pres*
◆ EMP: 220
SQ FT: 30,000
SALES (est): 1.1B Publicly Held
WEB: www.omnisource.com
SIC: 5093 3462 3399 Ferrous metal scrap & waste; nonferrous metals scrap; iron & steel forgings; metal powders, pastes & flakes

(G-4511)
OMNISOURCE HOLDINGS LLC (DH)
7575 W Jefferson Blvd (46804-4131)
PHONE..................260 969-3500
Theresa E Wagler, *Administration*
EMP: 3 EST: 2016
SALES (est): 265.1K Publicly Held
SIC: 3312 Plate, sheet & strip, except coated products
HQ: Stld Holdings, Inc.
6714 Pointe Inverness Way # 100
Fort Wayne IN 46804
260 969-3590

(G-4512)
ORTHO GRIND LLC
7007 Trafalgar Dr (46803-3288)
PHONE..................260 493-1230
Carl Samuel Hoffman, *President*
EMP: 2
SALES (est): 146.9K Privately Held
SIC: 3599 Grinding castings for the trade

(G-4513)
OTTENWELLER CO INC (PA)
3011 Congressional Pkwy (46808-4415)
PHONE..................260 484-3166
Fax: 260 484-9798
Ottenweller Michael, *President*
Michael Ottenweller, *President*
Gary Ottenweller, *Vice Pres*
David Ottenweller, *Opers Mgr*
Kevin Dwire, *QC Mgr*
▼ EMP: 140
SQ FT: 75,000
SALES (est): 50.4MM Privately Held
WEB: www.ottenweller.com
SIC: 3443 3441 3444 Tanks, standard or custom fabricated: metal plate; fabricated structural metal; sheet metalwork

(G-4514)
OUTMAN INDUSTRIES INC
1830 Wayne Trce (46803-2657)
PHONE..................260 467-1576
Tom Outman, *President*
EMP: 9 EST: 1998
SQ FT: 3,000
SALES (est): 1.3MM Privately Held
WEB: www.outmaninc.com
SIC: 3643 Connectors & terminals for electrical devices

(G-4515)
OZA COMPOUND PRODUCTS
1221 Production Rd (46808-1112)
PHONE..................260 483-0406
EMP: 2
SQ FT: 144
SALES: 100K Privately Held
SIC: 2833 5499 Mfg Medicinal/Botanical Products Ret Misc Foods

(G-4516)
P H C INDUSTRIES INC
3115 Pittsburg St (46803-2259)
P.O. Box 11225 (46856-1225)
PHONE..................260 423-9461
Fax: 260 424-0127
Tracey L Lerch, *President*
Chuck Dewey, *Vice Pres*
Ronald Lerch, *Manager*
Kim Araujo, *Admin Sec*
EMP: 6 EST: 1967
SQ FT: 12,500

SALES (est): 3.4MM **Privately Held**
WEB: www.phcindustries.com
SIC: **5085** 3492 7694 Power transmission equipment & apparatus; hose & tube fittings & assemblies, hydraulic/pneumatic; electric motor repair

(G-4517)
PAC CORPORATION
Also Called: Burke Heating Systems Company
211 Soaring Eagle Ct (46845-1166)
PHONE..............................260 637-8792
Joseph Dager, *President*
EMP: 8
SALES (est): 516.9K **Privately Held**
WEB: www.burkeheating.com
SIC: **8741** 3567 Construction management; electrical furnaces, ovens & heating devices, exc. induction

(G-4518)
PAINT THE TOWN GRAPHICS INC
1828 W Main St (46808-3760)
PHONE..............................260 422-9152
Wendy Brown, *President*
Patti Morrison, *Vice Pres*
EMP: 20
SQ FT: 5,000
SALES (est): 2.2MM **Privately Held**
WEB: www.pttgi.com
SIC: **3993** Signs & advertising specialties

(G-4519)
PANORAMIC RENTAL CORP
4321 Goshen Rd (46818-1242)
PHONE..............................800 654-2027
Fax: 260 489-5683
Ryan Loeffler, *President*
Steve Yaggy, *Vice Pres*
Matthew Kline, *Vice Pres*
Carey Sipe, *Vice Pres*
Michelle Kocks, *Purch Agent*
▲ EMP: 35
SQ FT: 18,000
SALES (est): 8.2MM
SALES (corp-wide): 140.1MM **Privately Held**
WEB: www.pancorp.com
SIC: **3843** Dental equipment & supplies
PA: Young Innovations, Inc.
2260 Wendt St
Algonquin IL 60102
847 458-5400

(G-4520)
PARAGON TUBE CORPORATION
1605 Winter St (46803-2513)
PHONE..............................260 424-1266
Fax: 260 422-6631
Jerome F Henry Jr, *President*
Thomas M Carter, *Vice Pres*
Sandra Overman, *Office Mgr*
Brian McClellan, *Executive*
▲ EMP: 22
SQ FT: 91,250
SALES (est): 5.9MM **Privately Held**
WEB: www.paragontube.com
SIC: **3317** Steel pipe & tubes

(G-4521)
PARCO INCORPORATED
9100 Front St (46818-2209)
PHONE..............................260 451-0810
Phillip Roser, *President*
Lisa Roser, *Vice Pres*
Ryan Wilson, *Engineer*
EMP: 18
SQ FT: 60,000
SALES (est): 4.6MM **Privately Held**
WEB: www.parco-inc.com
SIC: **3354** Aluminum extruded products

(G-4522)
PEPSICO INC ✪
3939 N Wells St (46808-4008)
PHONE..............................260 579-3461
EMP: 13 EST: 2017
SALES (est): 2.7MM **Privately Held**
SIC: **2086** Carbonated soft drinks, bottled & canned

(G-4523)
PERDUE PRINTED PRODUCTS INC
1902 S Harrison St (46802-5215)
P.O. Box 10924 (46854-0924)
PHONE..............................260 456-7575
Fax: 260 456-7644
Matthew J Erb, *President*
Judith L Erb, *Corp Secy*
EMP: 7
SQ FT: 3,500
SALES (est): 893.3K **Privately Held**
SIC: **2752** 5112 2759 2395 Commercial printing, offset; business forms; screen printing; embroidery products, except schiffli machine

(G-4524)
PERFECTION BAKERIES INC (PA)
Also Called: Aunt Millie's Bakeries
350 Pearl St (46802-1508)
PHONE..............................260 424-8245
Fax: 260 424-5047
John F Popp, *President*
Jay E Miller, *CFO*
▼ EMP: 230 EST: 1901
SQ FT: 400,000
SALES (est): 515.3MM **Privately Held**
WEB: www.perfectionpastries.com
SIC: **2051** Bread, all types (white, wheat, rye, etc): fresh or frozen; rolls, bread type: fresh or frozen

(G-4525)
PERFECTION BAKERIES INC
Also Called: Aunt Millies Bakeries
4001 Kraft Pkwy (46808-4441)
PHONE..............................260 483-5481
Matt Hinsey, *Manager*
EMP: 57
SALES (corp-wide): 515.3MM **Privately Held**
SIC: **2051** Bakery: wholesale or wholesale/retail combined
PA: Perfection Bakeries, Inc.
350 Pearl St
Fort Wayne IN 46802
260 424-8245

(G-4526)
PETE D LIMKEMANN
724 S Doyle Rd (46803)
PHONE..............................260 403-4297
Pete D Limkemann, *Principal*
EMP: 6
SALES: 1MM **Privately Held**
SIC: **3621** Motors, electric

(G-4527)
PHD INC
9030 Clubridge Dr (46809-3000)
PHONE..............................260 747-6151
EMP: 5
SALES (corp-wide): 49MM **Privately Held**
SIC: **3593** Fluid power cylinders & actuators
HQ: Phd, Inc.
9009 Clubridge Dr
Fort Wayne IN 46809
260 747-6151

(G-4528)
PHENIX TUBE CORP
2701 S Coliseum Blvd # 1148 (46803-2900)
PHONE..............................260 424-3734
Dennis B Weimer, *President*
EMP: 8
SALES (est): 1.1MM **Privately Held**
WEB: www.phenixtube.com
SIC: **2655** Tubes, fiber or paper: made from purchased material

(G-4529)
PHOENIX AMERICA INC
4717 Clubview Dr (46804-4448)
PHONE..............................260 432-9664
Bob Loubier, *President*
John Kaste, *COO*
John Bachle, *Opers Staff*
Julie Lopez, *Manager*
▲ EMP: 29
SQ FT: 24,000

SALES: 4MM **Privately Held**
WEB: www.phoenixamerica.com
SIC: **3824** Tachometer, centrifugal

(G-4530)
PIN-UP CURLS LLC
1835 Marietta Dr (46804-5727)
PHONE..............................260 241-5871
EMP: 3
SALES (est): 153.4K **Privately Held**
SIC: **3452** Pins

(G-4531)
PINUP CURLS SALON
6222 Covington Rd (46804-7312)
PHONE..............................260 267-9659
Carol Triblet, *Manager*
EMP: 5 EST: 2011
SALES (est): 482.2K **Privately Held**
SIC: **3452** Pins

(G-4532)
PLASTIC CARDZ
1925 Wayside Dr (46818-2113)
PHONE..............................260 440-1964
EMP: 2
SALES (est): 83.9K **Privately Held**
SIC: **2752** Commercial printing, lithographic

(G-4533)
PLASTIC CARDZ LLC
12721 Us Highway 24 W (46814-7445)
PHONE..............................260 431-6380
Ryan Messmann, *Principal*
EMP: 2
SALES (est): 194.4K **Privately Held**
SIC: **2752** Commercial printing, lithographic

(G-4534)
PLAYFAIR SHUFFLEBOARD COMPANY
7021 Bluffton Rd (46809-2705)
PHONE..............................260 747-7288
Fax: 260 747-0470
Brian G Crowl, *President*
EMP: 10
SQ FT: 4,500
SALES (est): 752.4K **Privately Held**
SIC: **3949** 5091 5046 Shuffleboards & shuffleboard equipment; billiard equipment & supplies; commercial equipment

(G-4535)
POIRY PARTNERS LLC (PA)
2535 Wayne Trce (46803-3785)
PHONE..............................260 424-1030
Fax: 260 420-4006
Thomas B Poiry, *President*
James Poiry, *Vice Pres*
Jimmy Poiry, *Vice Pres*
John Schoonover, *Plant Mgr*
Amy Jordan, *QC Mgr*
EMP: 50
SALES (est): 6.3MM **Privately Held**
SIC: **3471** Anodizing (plating) of metals or formed products

(G-4536)
POLAR KING INTERNATIONAL INC
4424 New Haven Ave (46803-1650)
PHONE..............................260 428-2530
David C Schenkel, *President*
Todd Ellinger, *General Mgr*
Vincent Tippmann Sr, *Vice Pres*
Bob Erexson, *Prdtn Mgr*
William J Federspiel, *Treasurer*
▼ EMP: 40 EST: 1982
SQ FT: 120,000
SALES (est): 10.2MM **Privately Held**
WEB: www.polarking.com
SIC: **3585** Coolers, milk & water: electric; refrigeration equipment, complete

(G-4537)
POLY HI SOLIDUR INC
2710 American Way (46809-3011)
PHONE..............................260 479-4100
Fax: 260 478-1074
Roland J Finch, *President*
Mark Edede, *Vice Pres*
Harold Epps, *Vice Pres*
Arthur Huge, *Vice Pres*

Daniel Michalak, *Treasurer*
▲ EMP: 280
SQ FT: 60,000
SALES (est): 21.5MM
SALES (corp-wide): 23.5MM **Privately Held**
WEB: www.polyhisolidur.com
SIC: **3089** Injection molding of plastics; plastic processing
PA: Professional Plastics, Inc.
1810 E Valencia Dr
Fullerton CA 92831
714 446-6500

(G-4538)
POLYMOD TECHNOLOGIES INC
4146 Engleton Dr (46804-3162)
P.O. Box 10180 (46850-0180)
PHONE..............................260 436-1322
Fax: 260 432-6051
Ron Zielinski, *President*
Joseph Leto, *Prdtn Mgr*
Ronald Zielinski, *Med Doctor*
Chris Chilson, *Manager*
Caroline Zielinski, *Manager*
EMP: 12
SQ FT: 10,000
SALES (est): 2.2MM **Privately Held**
WEB: www.polymod.com
SIC: **7699** 8731 2821 Plastics products repair; commercial physical research; plastics materials & resins

(G-4539)
POP TIQUE POPCORN
4206 W Jefferson Blvd C3 (46804-6863)
PHONE..............................260 459-3767
Gary Hively, *Owner*
Sarah Kumfer, *Prdtn Mgr*
Abigail Krocker, *Corp Comm Staff*
EMP: 3
SALES (est): 188.1K **Privately Held**
SIC: **2099** Popcorn, packaged: except already popped

(G-4540)
PORTABLE LEFT FOOT ACCELERATOR
429 E Dupont Rd Ste 203 (46825-2051)
PHONE..............................260 637-4447
Becky Marquis, *Principal*
EMP: 2
SALES (est): 118K **Privately Held**
SIC: **3999** Wheelchair lifts

(G-4541)
POSEIDON BARGE LTD
3101 New Haven Ave (46803-2744)
PHONE..............................260 422-8767
Donnie Fain, *CEO*
Mary Habegger-Fox, *President*
Kathleen Buelow, *Regl Sales Mgr*
Austin Fain, *Sales Staff*
David Richhart, *Supervisor*
▲ EMP: 52
SQ FT: 7,200
SALES (est): 29.6MM **Privately Held**
SIC: **5082** 3462 7353 General construction machinery & equipment; construction or mining equipment forgings, ferrous; heavy construction equipment rental

(G-4542)
POWER PLANT SERVICE INC
2500 W Jefferson Blvd (46802-4641)
PHONE..............................260 432-6716
Fax: 260 436-3340
Donald J Akey, *President*
Bart Akey, *Marketing Staff*
Ron Hartman, *Manager*
Matt Maley, *Manager*
Chuck Wyss, *Manager*
EMP: 44 EST: 1911
SQ FT: 70,000
SALES (est): 10.2MM **Privately Held**
WEB: www.powerplantserviceinc.com
SIC: **7699** 3567 5074 3714 Boiler repair shop; oil burner repair service; fuel-fired furnaces & ovens; incinerators, metal: domestic or commercial; plumbing & hydronic heating supplies; motor vehicle parts & accessories; millwork

(G-4543)
POWERCLEAN INC (PA)
Also Called: Powerclean Industrial Services
3404 Metro Dr N Ste B (46898-9399)
P.O. Box 80345 (46898-0345)
PHONE..........................260 483-1375
Fax: 260 483-1375
Steven J Barber, *President*
Sue Pollit, *Treasurer*
EMP: 32 **EST:** 1996
SALES (est): 11.5MM **Privately Held**
SIC: 1521 1799 2842 Patio & deck con-
struction & repair; exterior cleaning, in-
cluding sandblasting; specialty cleaning
preparations

(G-4544)
POWERING ATHLETICS
3711 Vanguard Dr Ste F (46809-3308)
PHONE..........................260 672-1700
Ron Bullch, *Managing Prtnr*
EMP: 9
SALES (est): 832.1K **Privately Held**
SIC: 3949 Exercise equipment

(G-4545)
PPG INDUSTRIES INC
Also Called: PPG 4383
2510 Independence Dr (46808-1324)
PHONE..........................260 373-2373
Mike Nichols, *Branch Mgr*
EMP: 24
SALES (corp-wide): 14.2B **Publicly Held**
WEB: www.ppg.com
SIC: 2851 Paints & allied products
PA: Ppg Industries, Inc.
1 Ppg Pl
Pittsburgh PA 15272
412 434-3131

(G-4546)
PRAXAIR DISTRIBUTION INC
1725 Edsall Ave (46803-2725)
PHONE..........................260 423-4468
EMP: 6
SALES (corp-wide): 11.4B **Publicly Held**
SIC: 2813 5084 5999 Industrial gases;
carbon dioxide; dry ice, carbon dioxide
(solid); oxygen, compressed or liquefied;
welding machinery & equipment; welding
supplies
HQ: Praxair Distribution, Inc.
10 Riverview Dr
Danbury CT 06810
203 837-2000

(G-4547)
PRECISION COLORS LLC
2617 Meyer Rd (46803-2915)
PHONE..........................260 969-6402
Bob Mann, *Mng Member*
Tracy Shellabarger,
Bruce Smith,
Loren Troyer,
EMP: 15
SQ FT: 9,500
SALES: 500K **Privately Held**
SIC: 2821 Plastics materials & resins

(G-4548)
PRECISION DIE TECHNOLOGIES
4716 Speedway Dr (46825-5239)
PHONE..........................260 482-5001
Fax: 260 482-5977
John Frieburger, *President*
Brad Frieburger, *Principal*
Josef Geisler, *Vice Pres*
Brad Freiburger, *Project Mgr*
Sanela Hozanovic, *QC Mgr*
EMP: 40
SQ FT: 5,000
SALES: 4.5MM **Privately Held**
WEB: www.pdtinc.com
SIC: 3544 Wire drawing & straightening
dies; special dies & tools

(G-4549)
PRECISION FABRICATION INC
710 Hanover St (46803-1042)
PHONE..........................260 422-4448
Fax: 260 422-8863
Julia R Isch, *President*
Fred Hagadorn, *Vice Pres*
EMP: 10 **EST:** 1970
SQ FT: 12,000

SALES: 1.5MM **Privately Held**
WEB: www.precisionfabrication.com
SIC: 3441 Fabricated structural metal

(G-4550)
PRECISION HEAT TREATING CORP
2711 Adams Center Rd (46803-3283)
P.O. Box 6162 (46896-0162)
PHONE..........................260 749-5125
Fax: 260 749-0108
Kenneth Vandre Sr, *President*
Kenneth Vandre Jr, *Vice Pres*
Mark Vandre, *Vice Pres*
Mary Vandre, *Admin Sec*
EMP: 21
SQ FT: 29,000
SALES (est): 5.2MM **Privately Held**
WEB: www.phtc.net
SIC: 3398 Metal heat treating

(G-4551)
PRECISION LASER SERVICES INC
14730 Lima Rd (46818-9585)
PHONE..........................260 744-4375
Ed Ferrier, *President*
▼ **EMP:** 32
SQ FT: 30,000
SALES (est): 7.9MM **Privately Held**
WEB: www.plsmfg.com
SIC: 3599 Machine shop, jobbing & repair

(G-4552)
PRECISION PRODUCTS GROUP INC
Also Called: Paramount Tube Division
1430 Progress Rd (46808-1179)
P.O. Box 80400 (46898-0400)
PHONE..........................260 484-4111
Fax: 260 483-0393
Ken Seifert, *Manager*
EMP: 49
SQ FT: 30,000
SALES (est): 15.1MM **Privately Held**
WEB: www.ppgme.com
SIC: 2655 3498 Fiber cans, drums & simi-
lar products; fabricated pipe & fittings
PA: Precision Products Group, Inc.
10201 N Illinois St # 390
Indianapolis IN 46290

(G-4553)
PRECISION UTILITIES GROUP INC
5916 E State Blvd (46815-7637)
PHONE..........................260 485-8300
Dave Schmaucg, *President*
Rich Hamilton, *Senior VP*
Jim Samples, *Vice Pres*
EMP: 200
SALES (est): 35.7MM **Privately Held**
SIC: 3357 Fiber optic cable (insulated)

(G-4554)
PREMIER CONSULTING INC (PA)
Also Called: Premier Wire Die
1712 Dividend Rd (46808-1131)
PHONE..........................260 496-9300
Vincent Griffin, *President*
Tammy L Griffin, *Vice Pres*
▼ **EMP:** 12
SQ FT: 7,000
SALES (est): 1.7MM **Privately Held**
WEB: www.premierconsulting.com
SIC: 3544 Wire drawing & straightening
dies

(G-4555)
PREMIER HYDRAULIC AUGERS INC
2707 Lofty Dr (46808-3927)
PHONE..........................260 456-8518
Fax: 260 456-6868
Greg Seifert, *President*
Bob Meriwether, *President*
Gregg Owens, *Vice Pres*
EMP: 26
SQ FT: 80,000
SALES (est): 1.9MM **Privately Held**
WEB: www.premierauger.com
SIC: 3531 Construction machinery attach-
ments

(G-4556)
PRENTICE PRODUCTS HOLDINGS LLC
4236 W Ferguson Rd (46809-3198)
PHONE..........................260 747-3195
Mark Hagar, *President*
Bryan Stover, *Vice Pres*
Mark Lewis, *VP Sales*
EMP: 21
SQ FT: 16,000
SALES (est): 1.4MM **Privately Held**
SIC: 3993 Signs & advertising specialties

(G-4557)
PRESS-SEAL GASKET CORPORATION
2424 W State Blvd (46808-3934)
P.O. Box 10482 (46852-0482)
PHONE..........................260 436-0521
Fax: 260 436-1908
James W Skinner, *President*
Tonya Steckbeck, *General Mgr*
Erich Smith, *Plant Mgr*
Peter Skinner, *Purch Mgr*
Gary Jones, *Purch Agent*
▼ **EMP:** 145 **EST:** 1954
SQ FT: 150,000
SALES (est): 40MM **Privately Held**
WEB: www.press-seal.com
SIC: 3053 5085 Oil seals, rubber; gaskets,
all materials; gaskets & seals

(G-4558)
PREVAIL PRSTHTICS ORTHTICS INC
7735 W Jefferson Blvd C (46804-4135)
PHONE..........................765 668-0890
John Lee, *Manager*
EMP: 3
SALES (corp-wide): 1.3MM **Privately Held**
SIC: 3842 Prosthetic appliances
PA: Prevail Prosthetics & Orthotics, Inc.
7735 W Jefferson Blvd
Fort Wayne IN 46804
260 483-5219

(G-4559)
PREVAIL PRSTHTICS ORTHTICS INC (PA)
7735 W Jefferson Blvd (46804-4135)
PHONE..........................260 483-5219
Fax: 260 484-2291
Fred W Toenges, *President*
EMP: 25
SQ FT: 10,000
SALES: 1.3MM **Privately Held**
SIC: 3842 Prosthetic appliances

(G-4560)
PREVAIL PRSTHTICS ORTHTICS INC
3906 New Vision Dr (46845-1712)
PHONE..........................260 969-0605
Buck Toenges, *Branch Mgr*
EMP: 3
SALES (corp-wide): 1.3MM **Privately Held**
SIC: 3842 Limbs, artificial
PA: Prevail Prosthetics & Orthotics, Inc.
7735 W Jefferson Blvd
Fort Wayne IN 46804
260 483-5219

(G-4561)
PRINTMASTER LLC
4120 Engleton Dr (46804-3162)
PHONE..........................260 459-1900
Greg Jackson, *Principal*
EMP: 5 **EST:** 2008
SALES (est): 555.5K **Privately Held**
SIC: 3577 Printers & plotters

(G-4562)
PROFESSIONAL METAL REFINISHING
Also Called: Pro-Blast Equip
2415 W State Blvd (46808-3933)
PHONE..........................260 436-2828
Fax: 260 432-1941
Joseph Bruck, *President*
Tonya Vojtkofsky, *Corp Secy*
EMP: 7
SQ FT: 12,000

SALES (est): 829.5K **Privately Held**
WEB: www.prostrip.com
SIC: 3471 Cleaning & descaling metal
products

(G-4563)
PROTECTIVE COATINGS INC
Also Called: Proco
1602 Birchwood Ave (46803-2797)
PHONE..........................260 424-2900
Fax: 260 422-7147
Michael Murrell, *President*
Robert Kaufman, *Vice Pres*
Ken Passmore, *Vice Pres*
Kevin Gerber, *VP Sales*
Angie Pisula, *Office Mgr*
EMP: 40
SQ FT: 100,000
SALES (est): 5.1MM **Privately Held**
WEB: www.proco-fwi.com
SIC: 3069 Molded rubber products

(G-4564)
PRP TECHNOLOGIES LLC
3201 Stellhorn Rd (46815-4697)
PHONE..........................260 433-3769
John Finch, *Administration*
EMP: 4 **EST:** 2013
SALES (est): 327.3K **Privately Held**
SIC: 3841 Surgical & medical instruments

(G-4565)
PWT GROUP LLC
Also Called: Precision Wire Technologies
6320 Highview Dr (46818-1382)
PHONE..........................260 490-6477
Pat Jones, *Plant Mgr*
Ashley Marting, *Marketing Staff*
Lisa Jones, *Office Mgr*
Justin Heins, *Info Tech Mgr*
Wayne Francey,
EMP: 29
SQ FT: 24,900
SALES (est): 5.9MM **Privately Held**
WEB: www.precisionwiretech.com
SIC: 3496 3315 Miscellaneous fabricated
wire products; steel wire & related prod-
ucts

(G-4566)
PYROMATION INC
5211 Industrial Rd (46825-5152)
PHONE..........................260 484-2580
Fax: 260 482-6805
Peter C Wilson, *President*
Melani Wilson, *Corp Secy*
Mark Beckman, *CFO*
EMP: 165
SQ FT: 30,000
SALES (est): 42.7MM **Privately Held**
WEB: www.pyromation.com
SIC: 3823 3829 3822 3812 Temperature
instruments: industrial process type; tem-
perature sensors, except industrial
process & aircraft; auto controls regulat-
ing residntl & coml environmt & applncs;
search & navigation equipment; semicon-
ductors & related devices; relays & indus-
trial controls

(G-4567)
QUAD/GRAPHICS INC
6502 Nelson Rd (46803-1920)
PHONE..........................260 748-5300
EMP: 455
SALES (corp-wide): 4.1B **Publicly Held**
SIC: 2752 Commercial printing, offset
PA: Quad/Graphics Inc.
N61w23044 Harrys Way
Sussex WI 53089
414 566-6000

(G-4568)
QUADRANT EPP USA INC
4115 Polymer Pl (46809-1140)
PHONE..........................260 479-4700
Harold Etts, *Branch Mgr*
EMP: 55
SALES (corp-wide): 34.9B **Privately Held**
WEB: www.quadrantepp.com
SIC: 2824 3082 2821 3052 Nylon fibers;
acrylic fibers; unsupported plastics profile
shapes; rods, unsupported plastic; tubes,
unsupported plastic; nylon resins; plastic
hose

HQ: Quadrant Epp Usa, Inc.
2120 Fairmont Ave
Reading PA 19605
610 320-6600

(G-4569)
QUADRANT EPP USA INC
Also Called: Quadrant Engrg Plastic Pdts
2710 American Way (46809-3011)
PHONE..................................260 479-4100
Nancy Schmidt, *Safety Mgr*
Dan Michalak, *CFO*
Ginger Gadoci, *Human Res Mgr*
Ginger Gaduci, *Human Res Mgr*
Tom West, *Sales Staff*
EMP: 250
SALES (corp-wide): 34.9B **Privately Held**
WEB: www.quadrantepp.com
SIC: 2824 3082 2821 3052 Nylon fibers;
acrylic fibers; unsupported plastics profile
shapes; rods, unsupported plastic; tubes,
unsupported plastic; nylon resins; plastic
hose
HQ: Quadrant Epp Usa, Inc.
2120 Fairmont Ave
Reading PA 19605
610 320-6600

(G-4570)
QUAKE MANUFACTURING INC
3923 Engle Rd (46804-4414)
PHONE..................................260 432-8023
Fax: 260 432-7868
Paul Quake, *CEO*
Hermann Quake, *President*
Sally Quake, *Admin Sec*
EMP: 11
SQ FT: 5,000
SALES (est): 1.9MM **Privately Held**
WEB: www.quakemfg.com
SIC: 3599 Machine shop, jobbing & repair;
machine & other job shop work

(G-4571)
QUALITEX INC
4185 E Park 30 Dr 30th (46814)
PHONE..................................260 244-7839
Richard A Williams, *President*
Logan Williams, *Engineer*
◆ EMP: 10
SQ FT: 10,000
SALES (est): 790K **Privately Held**
WEB: www.qigage.com
SIC: 7549 3674 Inspection & diagnostic
service, automotive; strain gages, solid
state

(G-4572)
QUALITY TOOL CO INC
1431 Production Rd (46808-1166)
PHONE..................................260 484-0187
Fax: 260 484-8727
John L Stump, *President*
Tim Connell, *Design Engr*
Denise Stump, *Office Mgr*
Chris Thomas, *Technology*
Rita M Stump, *Admin Sec*
EMP: 13 EST: 1951
SQ FT: 6,000
SALES (est): 1.9MM **Privately Held**
WEB: www.qualitytoolco.com
SIC: 3544 Special dies & tools

(G-4573)
QUIKCUT INCORPORATED
4630 Allen Martin Dr (46806-2800)
PHONE..................................260 447-8090
EMP: 21 EST: 1997
SALES (est): 3.4MM **Privately Held**
SIC: 3441 Structural Metal Fabrication

(G-4574)
QUIKCUT INCORPORATED (PA)
Also Called: Bruco Industries
4630 Allen Martin Dr (46806-2800)
PHONE..................................260 447-3880
Fax: 260 447-5707
Mark Webb, *President*
Joy Gray, *Vice Pres*
EMP: 27
SQ FT: 48,000
SALES (est): 9.3MM **Privately Held**
SIC: 3443 Fabricated plate work (boiler
shop)

(G-4575)
R&D INVESTMENT HOLDINGS INC
Also Called: Signature Products
6900 Nelson Rd (46803-1928)
PHONE..................................260 749-1301
Robert E Roehm II, *President*
Mark Weber, *CFO*
Deborah Sue Roehm, *Admin Sec*
EMP: 46
SQ FT: 130,000
SALES (est): 3.7MM **Privately Held**
SIC: 2392 3429 2531 Boat cushions;
manufactured hardware (general); public
building & related furniture

(G-4576)
RAYTHEON COMPANY
1010 Production Rd (46808-4106)
PHONE..................................260 429-6000
Fax: 260 459-7170
Albert Perry, *CEO*
Ted Gregory, *Principal*
Steven Sharp, *Principal*
Roy Rodriguez, *Buyer*
Randy Brown, *QC Mgr*
EMP: 700
SALES (corp-wide): 25.3B **Publicly Held**
SIC: 3812 3489 Sonar systems & equip-
ment; ordnance & accessories
PA: Raytheon Company
870 Winter St
Waltham MA 02451
781 522-3000

(G-4577)
RAYTHEON COMPANY
1010 Production Rd (46808-4106)
PHONE..................................310 647-9438
Eric Bemus, *Software Engr*
EMP: 99
SQ FT: 1,000
SALES (corp-wide): 25.3B **Publicly Held**
SIC: 3812 3663 3761 Defense systems &
equipment; space satellite communica-
tions equipment; airborne radio communi-
cations equipment; guided missiles &
space vehicles, research & development;
rockets, space & military, complete
PA: Raytheon Company
870 Winter St
Waltham MA 02451
781 522-3000

(G-4578)
RAYTHEON COMPANY
1010 Production Rd (46808-4106)
PHONE..................................310 647-9438
EMP: 1000
SALES (corp-wide): 25.3B **Publicly Held**
SIC: 3812 Search & navigation equipment
PA: Raytheon Company
870 Winter St
Waltham MA 02451
781 522-3000

(G-4579)
RBC MANUFACTURING CORP
1946 W Cook Rd (46818-1166)
PHONE..................................260 416-5400
Carolyn Springer, *Principal*
▲ EMP: 150
SALES (est): 4.4MM **Privately Held**
SIC: 3999 Manufacturing industries

(G-4580)
REA MAGNET WIRE COMPANY INC
Also Called: REA Magnet Wire NH
4300 New Haven Ave (46803-1648)
PHONE..................................260 421-5400
Fax: 260 424-7073
Ron Foster, *Purch Agent*
Mike Shannon, *Manager*
Susan Boyd, *Manager*
EMP: 400
SALES (corp-wide): 228.8MM **Privately Held**
WEB: www.reawire.com
SIC: 3357 Nonferrous wiredrawing & insu-
lating
PA: Rea Magnet Wire Company, Inc.
3400 E Coliseum Blvd # 200
Fort Wayne IN 46805
260 421-7321

(G-4581)
REBAR CORP OF INDIANA
5601 Industrial Rd (46825-5125)
P.O. Box 15944 (46885-5944)
PHONE..................................260 471-2002
Fax: 260 471-2006
Mark Overhiser, *President*
EMP: 7 EST: 1998
SALES (est): 1.4MM **Privately Held**
SIC: 3449 Fabricated bar joists & concrete
reinforcing bars

(G-4582)
RECKON PLATING INC
5300 Hanna St (46806-3135)
PHONE..................................260 744-4339
Fax: 260 744-6867
Kashem Sarker, *President*
Tanvir Habib, *QC Mgr*
Kristina Miller, *Treasurer*
Cindy Sarker, *Treasurer*
Audrey Rittner, *Supervisor*
EMP: 22
SQ FT: 6,800
SALES (est): 2.3MM **Privately Held**
WEB: www.reckonplating.com
SIC: 3471 Gold plating; chromium plating
of metals or formed products

(G-4583)
RECOVERY TECHNOLOGIES LLC
2001 E Pontiac St Bldg 8 (46803-3653)
PHONE..................................260 745-3902
Fax: 260 747-4700
EMP: 25
SQ FT: 40,000
SALES (est): 1.4MM
SALES (corp-wide): 7.5B **Publicly Held**
SIC: 4953 3341 Refuse System Second-
ary Nonferrous Metal Producer
HQ: Omnisource Corporation
7575 W Jefferson Blvd
Fort Wayne IN 46804
260 422-5541

(G-4584)
RED TORTILLA INC
921 E Dupont Rd Ste 913 (46825-1551)
PHONE..................................260 403-2681
EMP: 3
SALES (est): 88K **Privately Held**
SIC: 2099 Mfg Food Preparations

(G-4585)
REFRACTORY SPECIALISTS LLC
3525 Metro Dr N (46818-9388)
PHONE..................................260 969-1099
Larry Snell, *Mng Member*
EMP: 3
SALES (est): 187.2K **Privately Held**
SIC: 3255 Glasshouse refractories

(G-4586)
REGAL BELOIT AMERICA INC
Also Called: Genteq
1946 W Cook Rd (46818-1166)
PHONE..................................260 416-5400
David Mangrum, *Manager*
EMP: 6
SALES (corp-wide): 3.3B **Publicly Held**
SIC: 3621 Motors & generators
HQ: Regal Beloit America, Inc.
200 State St
Beloit WI 53511
608 364-8800

(G-4587)
REGAL-BELOIT CORPORATION
Also Called: Genteq
1946 W Cook Rd (46818-1166)
PHONE..................................260 416-5400
Mark J Gliebe, *Ch of Bd*
Jonathan J Schlemmer, *COO*
Chuck A Hinrichs, *Vice Pres*
Dennis Mikulecky, *Vice Pres*
Armando Hernandez, *Plant Mgr*
EMP: 56
SALES (est): 9.1MM **Privately Held**
SIC: 7539 5063 3675 Electrical services;
motors, electric; electronic capacitors

(G-4588)
RESIDUAL PAYS DAILY ✪
2313 Florida Dr Apt C15 (46805-3557)
PHONE..................................260 267-1617
Maye Shondiqua, *Principal*
EMP: 2 EST: 2017
SALES (est): 90.7K **Privately Held**
SIC: 2911 Residues

(G-4589)
RESOURCE VENTURES LLC
6714 Pointe Inverness Way # 200
(46804-7936)
PHONE..................................260 432-9177
Theresa E Wagler, *Principal*
EMP: 3
SALES (est): 185.8K **Publicly Held**
SIC: 3312 Plate, sheet & strip, except
coated products
HQ: Stld Holdings, Inc.
6714 Pointe Inverness Way # 100
Fort Wayne IN 46804
260 969-3590

(G-4590)
RESOURCE VENTURES II LLC
7575 W Jefferson Blvd (46804-4131)
PHONE..................................260 969-3500
Theresa E Wagler, *Administration*
EMP: 2
SALES (est): 79.2K **Publicly Held**
SIC: 3312 Plate, sheet & strip, except
coated products
HQ: Stld Holdings, Inc.
6714 Pointe Inverness Way # 100
Fort Wayne IN 46804
260 969-3590

(G-4591)
RHINESTONE SUPPLY LLC
921 E Dupont Rd Ste 233 (46825-1551)
PHONE..................................260 484-2711
Nicole Legere,
EMP: 2
SALES (est): 136.5K **Privately Held**
SIC: 3961 5131 Ornaments, costume, ex-
cept precious metal & gems; trimmings,
apparel

(G-4592)
RICHARDS BAKERY
1130 N Wells St (46808-3470)
PHONE..................................260 424-4012
Michelle Moore, *Partner*
Dick Moore, *Partner*
EMP: 10
SQ FT: 1,500
SALES (est): 816.1K **Privately Held**
SIC: 2051 5461 Bakery: wholesale or
wholesale/retail combined; bakeries

(G-4593)
RIDER PRODUCTIONS
4934 Hillegas Rd (46818-1933)
PHONE..................................260 471-0099
Rob Rider, *President*
EMP: 3
SALES (est): 250K **Privately Held**
SIC: 3651 Audio electronic systems

(G-4594)
RIVERSIDE MFG INC (PA)
14510 Lima Rd (46818-9537)
PHONE..................................260 637-4470
Fred Merritt, *CEO*
Kurt Schneider, *General Mgr*
Angela Snyder, *Project Mgr*
Bryce Carrico, *Engineer*
Scott Maddox, *Engineer*
▲ EMP: 160 EST: 1947
SQ FT: 35,000
SALES (est): 76.3MM **Privately Held**
WEB: www.riversidemfg.com
SIC: 3714 Motor vehicle parts & acces-
sories

(G-4595)
RIVERSIDE MFG LLC (HQ)
14510 Lima Rd (46818-9537)
PHONE..................................260 637-4470
Fred Merritt, *CEO*
EMP: 375
SQ FT: 35,000

G E O G R A P H I C

SALES: 65MM
SALES (corp-wide): 76.3MM **Privately Held**
WEB: www.riversidemfg.com
SIC: 3625 Industrial electrical relays & switches
PA: Riverside Mfg., Inc.
14510 Lima Rd
Fort Wayne IN 46818
260 637-4470

(G-4596)
ROSE INDUSTRIES LLC
6030 Almond Bluff Pass (46804-4258)
PHONE.....................260 348-2610
Joseph F Yovanovitch,
EMP: 2 EST: 2009
SALES (est): 208K **Privately Held**
SIC: 3999 Manufacturing industries

(G-4597)
RUBBER & GASKET CO AMER INC
Also Called: Rga
3328 Congressional Pkwy (46808-4439)
PHONE.....................260 432-9070
Fax: 260 432-9065
Neil Carter, *Managing Dir*
Grant Seltenright, *Marketing Staff*
EMP: 6 **Privately Held**
WEB: www.rgausa.com
SIC: 2399 Belting & belt products
PA: Rubber & Gasket Company Of America, Inc.
3905 E Progress St
North Little Rock AR 72114

(G-4598)
RUGGED STEEL WORKS LLC
Also Called: Ameri-Kan
4325 Meyer Rd (46806-2817)
PHONE.....................260 444-4241
Doug Gunsaullus, *President*
EMP: 16
SQ FT: 93,000
SALES: 1.8MM **Privately Held**
SIC: 7539 3443 Trailer repair; industrial vessels, tanks & containers

(G-4599)
RYAN FUELLING
6928 Nighthawk Dr (46835-9217)
PHONE.....................260 403-6450
Ryan J Fuelling, *Principal*
EMP: 3 EST: 2010
SALES (est): 209.8K **Privately Held**
SIC: 2869 Fuels

(G-4600)
SABERT CORPORATION
3511 Engle Rd (46809-1117)
PHONE.....................260 747-3149
Albert Salama, *CEO*
EMP: 5
SALES (est): 404.5K **Privately Held**
SIC: 2671 Plastic film, coated or laminated for packaging

(G-4601)
SAFELITE GLASS CORP
Also Called: Safelite Autoglass
3927 New Haven Ave (46803-1665)
PHONE.....................260 423-2477
EMP: 5
SALES (corp-wide): 3.7B **Privately Held**
SIC: 3231 Windshields, glass: made from purchased glass
HQ: Safelite Glass Corp.
7400 Safelite Way
Columbus OH 43235
614 210-9000

(G-4602)
SAFETY WEAR FORT WAYNE
Also Called: Soliven Brough
1121 E Wallace St (46803-2555)
P.O. Box B (46899-9900)
PHONE.....................260 456-3535
Daniel Brough, *Owner*
EMP: 20
SALES (est): 1.7MM **Privately Held**
SIC: 3842 Personal safety equipment

(G-4603)
SANCO INDUSTRIES INC
Also Called: Pond Champs
1819 S Calhoun St (46802-5259)
PHONE.....................260 467-1791
Fax: 260 426-3922
Brett Zachary, *Branch Mgr*
EMP: 4
SALES (corp-wide): 3.5MM **Privately Held**
SIC: 2899 1629 Chemical preparations; pond construction
PA: Sanco Industries, Inc.
1819 S Calhoun St
Fort Wayne IN 46802
260 426-6281

(G-4604)
SANCO INDUSTRIES INC (PA)
1819 S Calhoun St (46802-5259)
P.O. Box 11617 (46859-1617)
PHONE.....................260 426-6281
Brett Zachary, *CEO*
Kevin Appenzeller, *President*
EMP: 22
SQ FT: 46,000
SALES (est): 3.5MM **Privately Held**
SIC: 2899 1629 Chemical preparations; pond construction

(G-4605)
SANKO GOSEI TECH USA INC
6509 Moeller Rd (46806-1677)
PHONE.....................260 749-5168
Laurence Tabner, *CEO*
Robert Clark, *Engineer*
EMP: 35
SQ FT: 90,000
SALES (corp-wide): 536.8MM **Privately Held**
SIC: 3089 Injection molding of plastics
HQ: Sanko Gosei Technologies Usa, Inc.
6509 Moeller Rd
Fort Wayne IN 46806
260 749-5168

(G-4606)
SANSHER CORPORATION
8005 N Clinton St (46825-3115)
PHONE.....................260 484-2000
Phillip W Bradley, *President*
Tom Keith, *General Mgr*
EMP: 4
SQ FT: 14,000
SALES (est): 340K **Privately Held**
SIC: 2851 Paint removers; varnish removers

(G-4607)
SCHAEFERS INDIANA TURF CORP
5202 W Washington Ctr Rd (46818-9750)
PHONE.....................260 489-3391
Ryan Schaefer, *President*
EMP: 7
SALES (est): 160.4K **Privately Held**
SIC: 3524 Lawn & garden mowers & accessories

(G-4608)
SCHEUMANN CABINET CO
8809 Winchester Rd (46819-2253)
PHONE.....................260 747-3509
Matthew J Scheumann, *Owner*
EMP: 3
SALES (est): 160K **Privately Held**
SIC: 3553 Woodworking machinery

(G-4609)
SCHMUCKERS WOOD SHOP
9966 Eby Rd (46835-9570)
PHONE.....................260 485-1434
Dan Schmucker, *Owner*
EMP: 6
SALES (est): 368.6K **Privately Held**
SIC: 2499 Decorative wood & woodwork

(G-4610)
SCOTIA CORPORATION
Also Called: Amercan
7707 Freedom Way (46818-2169)
PHONE.....................260 479-8800
David Seybert, *President*
EMP: 25

SALES (est): 2.6MM **Privately Held**
SIC: 3444 Canopies, sheet metal

(G-4611)
SCREEN ART ADVERTISING CO INC
457 Ley Rd Ste B (46825-5269)
PHONE.....................260 483-6514
Paul J Deininger, *President*
Sharon R Deininger, *Corp Secy*
EMP: 4 EST: 1953
SQ FT: 6,000
SALES (est): 362.4K **Privately Held**
SIC: 2759 7336 Screen printing; advertising literature: printing; posters, including billboards: printing; creative services to advertisers, except writers

(G-4612)
SEAL PRODUCTS LLC
10515 Majic Port Ln (46819-2539)
PHONE.....................260 436-5628
Bill Walls, *Opers Mgr*
Seve Sullivan-Doyle, *Cust Mgr*
Jeff S Huntine, *Mng Member*
▲ EMP: 7
SALES (est): 702.6K **Privately Held**
SIC: 3053 Gaskets, packing & sealing devices

(G-4613)
SEASONED SOFTWARE LLC
13030 Callison Ct (46845-2344)
PHONE.....................260 431-5666
Stephen Knilans,
EMP: 2
SALES (est): 77.5K **Privately Held**
SIC: 7372 Prepackaged software

(G-4614)
SEAVAC USA LLC
9304 Yeager Ln (46809-9646)
PHONE.....................260 747-7123
Nathan Froning,
EMP: 6
SALES (est): 704.6K **Privately Held**
SIC: 3479 Coating of metals & formed products

(G-4615)
SELKING INTERNATIONAL INC (HQ)
2807 Goshen Rd (46808-1446)
P.O. Box 80040 (46898-0040)
PHONE.....................260 482-3000
Jerry Selking, *President*
James Selking, *Vice Pres*
Patrick Johnson, *Purch Mgr*
Joseph Selking, *Treasurer*
Jon Rodeffer, *Sales Staff*
EMP: 45
SALES (est): 34.6MM
SALES (corp-wide): 62.9MM **Privately Held**
WEB: www.selkinginternational.com
SIC: 5012 7538 3537 Trucks, commercial; general automotive repair shops; industrial trucks & tractors
PA: Decatur Truck & Tractor Inc
2807 Goshen Rd
Fort Wayne IN 46808
260 482-3000

(G-4616)
SENSORTEC INC
7620 Disalle Blvd (46825-3373)
PHONE.....................260 497-8811
Fax: 260 497-8822
Grant Passwater, *President*
EMP: 20
SQ FT: 15,000
SALES (est): 4.6MM **Privately Held**
WEB: www.sensortecinc.com
SIC: 3829 Thermometers & temperature sensors; temperature sensors, except industrial process & aircraft

(G-4617)
SENSORYCRITTERSCOM
4715 Lima Rd (46808-1203)
PHONE.....................260 373-0900
Lisa Compton, *President*
EMP: 3
SALES: 400K **Privately Held**
SIC: 3842 Technical aids for the handicapped

(G-4618)
SHANK BROTHERS INC (PA)
Also Called: Apsco of Indiana
3710 Piper Dr (46809-3159)
PHONE.....................260 744-4802
Thomas J Shank, *President*
Michael J Shank, *Treasurer*
James Shank, *Admin Sec*
EMP: 12
SQ FT: 2,500
SALES (est): 2.3MM **Privately Held**
SIC: 1711 3431 Warm air heating & air conditioning contractor; metal sanitary ware

(G-4619)
SHAR SYSTEMS INC
3210 Freeman St (46802-4433)
P.O. Box 9196 (46899-9196)
PHONE.....................260 432-5312
Greg Delong, *President*
Perry Parrolsho, *Engineer*
Kerry Roberts, *Engineer*
Scott Smith, *Design Engr*
Linda Rawlins, *Accountant*
▲ EMP: 22
SQ FT: 28,000
SALES (est): 6MM **Privately Held**
WEB: www.sharsystems.com
SIC: 3559 Chemical machinery & equipment

(G-4620)
SHARP SHIRT PRINTING LLC
2831 Union Chapel Rd (46845-9271)
PHONE.....................260 413-9346
EMP: 2
SALES (est): 83.9K **Privately Held**
SIC: 2752 Commercial printing, lithographic

(G-4621)
SHILLING SALES INC
414 E Wayne St (46802-2895)
PHONE.....................260 426-2626
Fax: 260 424-0119
Carol Shilling Nole, *President*
David Foreman, *Warehouse Mgr*
Jama Stemen, *Foreman/Supr*
Marilyn Groves, *Sales Staff*
Christi Wiard, *Sales Staff*
EMP: 23
SQ FT: 6,000
SALES (est): 5.4MM **Privately Held**
WEB: www.shillingsales.com
SIC: 5199 7311 2395 Advertising specialties; advertising agencies; pleating & stitching

(G-4622)
SHOEMAKER INC
12120 Yellow River Rd (46818-9702)
PHONE.....................260 625-4321
Fax: 260 625-4302
John C Shoemaker, *President*
Ruby Shoemaker, *Corp Secy*
John C Shoemaker II, *Vice Pres*
Gena R Hamby, *Asst Treas*
Lora Slates, *Asst Sec*
EMP: 16
SQ FT: 11,500
SALES (est): 2.2MM **Privately Held**
SIC: 3491 Valves, automatic control

(G-4623)
SIGN
2932 E Dupont Rd (46825-1667)
PHONE.....................260 422-7446
EMP: 2
SALES (est): 195.6K **Privately Held**
SIC: 3993 Signs & advertising specialties

(G-4624)
SIGN PRO OF FORT WAYNE INC
7710 Lima Rd (46818-2163)
PHONE.....................260 497-8484
Fax: 260 497-8755
Daron White, *President*
Dave Hayes, *Manager*
Julie Riddle, *Manager*
EMP: 4
SALES (est): 392.1K **Privately Held**
WEB: www.signprofw.com
SIC: 3993 Signs, not made in custom sign painting shops

(G-4625)
SIGN SHOPPE
4619 Lima Rd (46808-1201)
PHONE..............................260 483-1922
Fax: 260 482-4394
Sue Mettler, *Owner*
EMP: 3
SQ FT: 4,600
SALES: 220K **Privately Held**
SIC: 3993 Signs, not made in custom sign painting shops

(G-4626)
SIGNS IN TIME BY GREG INC
4306 Lake Ave (46815-7222)
PHONE..............................260 749-7446
Greg Boley, *President*
Arleen Boley, *Vice Pres*
EMP: 3
SALES: 300K **Privately Held**
SIC: 3993 Signs & advertising specialties

(G-4627)
SIGNS UNLIMITED
1412 Goshen Ave (46808-2036)
PHONE..............................260 484-5769
Marvin Flanery, *Owner*
Christina Flanery, *Co-Owner*
EMP: 6
SALES (est): 556.1K **Privately Held**
WEB: www.signsunlimitedfw.com
SIC: 3993 Electric signs

(G-4628)
SIMPLY SOCKS YARN COMPANY
1408 Clara Ave (46805-3520)
PHONE..............................260 416-2397
EMP: 2
SALES (est): 73.4K **Privately Held**
SIC: 2252 Socks

(G-4629)
SKYTECH II INC
9230 Conservation Way (46809-9642)
PHONE..............................260 459-1703
Christopher Flick, *CEO*
Henry Hall, *President*
Timothy Koesters, *Treasurer*
▲ EMP: 7
SALES (est): 142.3K **Privately Held**
SIC: 3651 3679 Video triggers (remote control TV devices); video triggers, except remote control TV devices

(G-4630)
SKYTECH-SYSTEMS INC
9230 Conservation Way (46809-9642)
PHONE..............................260 459-1703
Christopher Flick, *President*
Steve Tremills, *Vice Pres*
Jenniffer Crawford, *Accounting Mgr*
Corbit W Beasey, *Admin Sec*
▲ EMP: 13
SALES (est): 2.2MM **Privately Held**
SIC: 3651 3679 Video triggers (remote control TV devices); video triggers, except remote control TV devices

(G-4631)
SLIPCOVER XPRESS INC
10607 Leo Rd (46825-2607)
PHONE..............................260 482-7177
Danielle Lopez, *Owner*
EMP: 2
SALES (est): 105.7K **Privately Held**
SIC: 2221 Slip cover fabrics, manmade fiber & silk

(G-4632)
SNUGGY BABY LLC
835 W Berry St (46802-3912)
PHONE..............................260 418-6795
Jo Anderson, *President*
EMP: 2
SALES (est): 170.7K **Privately Held**
SIC: 3944 7389 Baby carriages & restraint seats;

(G-4633)
SOFTWARE PUB LLC
4104 Wyndemere Pass (46835-4638)
PHONE..............................260 486-7839
David Slyby, *Principal*
EMP: 2
SALES (est): 82.6K **Privately Held**
SIC: 7372 Prepackaged software

(G-4634)
SOLFIRE CONTRACT MFG INC
4939 Decatur Rd (46806-3046)
PHONE..............................260 755-2115
Otzo Solis, *President*
EMP: 10
SALES (est): 660K **Privately Held**
SIC: 3639 Major kitchen appliances, except refrigerators & stoves

(G-4635)
SORBASHOCK LLC
204 Barouche Pl (46845-2110)
PHONE..............................574 520-9784
George Woolston, *Business Dir*
Sam Simonson,
Timothy Ovaert,
EMP: 2
SALES (est): 143.6K **Privately Held**
SIC: 3996 Hard surface floor coverings

(G-4636)
SORDELET TOOL & DIE INC
1925 Lakeview Dr (46808-3919)
PHONE..............................260 483-7258
Fax: 260 483-7258
Daniel Sordelet, *President*
Teresa Sordelet, *Admin Sec*
EMP: 5
SQ FT: 12,500
SALES (est): 410K **Privately Held**
SIC: 3599 Machine shop, jobbing & repair

(G-4637)
SORG MILLWORK
10744 Us Highway 27 S (46816-3418)
PHONE..............................260 639-3223
Don L Sorg, *Partner*
Cindy Sorg, *Partner*
Phil Sorg, *Partner*
EMP: 4
SQ FT: 1,248
SALES (est): 280.9K **Privately Held**
SIC: 2431 Millwork

(G-4638)
SPECIALTIES CO LLC
201 S Thomas Rd (46808-2900)
PHONE..............................260 432-3973
Fax: 260 436-4402
Bill Wittenmyer, *Manager*
EMP: 12
SALES (est): 795K **Privately Held**
SIC: 2411 Rails, fence: round or split

(G-4639)
SPEECHLESSTEES LLC
810 Lemonwood Ct (46825-3730)
PHONE..............................260 417-9394
EMP: 2
SALES (est): 94K **Privately Held**
SIC: 2253 Knit Outerwear Mill

(G-4640)
SPEEDWAY CNSTR PDTS CORP
4817 Industrial Rd (46825-5209)
PHONE..............................260 203-9806
Peter Schenkel, *President*
EMP: 2
SALES (est): 328K **Privately Held**
SIC: 3531 Construction machinery

(G-4641)
SPEEDWAY REDI MIX INC
4820 Industrial Rd (46825-5210)
PHONE..............................260 496-8877
Becki Frederick, *President*
EMP: 5 **Privately Held**
SIC: 3273 Ready-mixed concrete
PA: Speedway Redi-Mix Inc
4820 Industrial Rd
Fort Wayne IN 46825

(G-4642)
SPORTSCENTER INC
5511 Coventry Ln (46804-7144)
PHONE..............................260 436-6198
Fax: 260 436-5428
Kevin Rodenbeck, *President*
Tom Rodenbeck, *Vice Pres*
EMP: 6
SQ FT: 3,000
SALES (est): 754K **Privately Held**
SIC: 5941 2396 Team sports equipment; screen printing on fabric articles

(G-4643)
SS CUSTOM CHOPPERS LLC
804 W Wildwood Ave (46807-1643)
PHONE..............................260 415-3793
David Stauffer, *Principal*
EMP: 2
SALES (est): 167.3K **Privately Held**
SIC: 3751 Motorcycles & related parts

(G-4644)
STANDARD PATTERN COMPANY INC
2136 Lafayette St (46803-3373)
PHONE..............................260 456-4870
Fax: 260 456-4725
Keith Peters, *President*
Thad Wagner, *General Mgr*
David Wagner, *Treasurer*
EMP: 5
SALES: 750K **Privately Held**
WEB: www.standardpattern.com
SIC: 3543 Industrial patterns

(G-4645)
STATE BEAUTY SUPPLY
3123 E State Blvd (46805-4738)
PHONE..............................260 755-6361
Yong Yang, *President*
EMP: 2 EST: 2012
SALES (est): 143.6K **Privately Held**
SIC: 5087 3999 Beauty parlor equipment & supplies; barber & beauty shop equipment

(G-4646)
STEEL DYNAMICS INC (PA)
Also Called: SDI
7575 W Jefferson Blvd (46804-4131)
PHONE..............................260 969-3500
Fax: 260 969-3560
Keith E Busse, *Ch of Bd*
Mark D Millett, *President*
Tim Epple, *General Mgr*
Russell B Rinn, *Exec VP*
Christopher A Graham, *Vice Pres*
◆ EMP: 277
SQ FT: 116,000
SALES: 9.5B **Publicly Held**
SIC: 3312 3316 7389 Blast furnaces & steel mills; plate, sheet & strip, except coated products; structural & rail mill products; bar, rod & wire products; cold finishing of steel shapes; scrap steel cutting

(G-4647)
STERITECH-USA INC
314 E Wallace St (46803-2343)
P.O. Box 10816 (46854-0816)
PHONE..............................260 745-7272
Samih Abouhalkah, *President*
EMP: 5
SALES (est): 193.4K **Privately Held**
SIC: 2842 Sanitation preparations, disinfectants & deodorants

(G-4648)
STERLING MANUFACTURING LLC
144 E Collins Rd (46825-5302)
PHONE..............................260 451-9760
Eugene Tippmann Jr, *President*
EMP: 2
SALES (est): 701.4K **Privately Held**
SIC: 3631 Household cooking equipment

(G-4649)
STITCH N FRAME
4220 Bluffton Rd (46809-1752)
PHONE..............................260 478-1301
Fax: 260 478-1301
Paul Schoppman, *Owner*
EMP: 6
SQ FT: 1,800
SALES (est): 456.5K **Privately Held**
SIC: 5999 5945 2499 Artists' supplies & materials; arts & crafts supplies; picture & mirror frames, wood

(G-4650)
STOCK BUILDING SUPPLY LLC
Also Called: Stock 420
2219 Contractors Way (46818-1718)
PHONE..............................260 490-0616
Jeff Clauser, *Branch Mgr*

EMP: 41 **Publicly Held**
WEB: www.stockbuildingsupply.com
SIC: 5211 2431 5031 5713 Millwork & lumber; millwork; lumber: rough, dressed & finished; floor covering stores; builders' hardware
HQ: Bmc East, Llc
8020 Arco Corp Dr Ste 400
Raleigh NC 27617
919 431-1000

(G-4651)
STONE CUSTOM DRUM LLC
2701 S Coliseum Blvd (46803-2950)
PHONE..............................260 403-7519
Bernie Stone, *President*
EMP: 2
SALES (est): 126.4K **Privately Held**
SIC: 3931 Percussion instruments & parts

(G-4652)
STONE INDUSTRIAL INC
1430 Progress Rd (46808-1179)
PHONE..............................301 474-3100
Lawrence E Gloyd, *Ch of Bd*
Tim Kartisek, *General Mgr*
L P Harnois, *Treasurer*
Marshall C Arne, *Admin Sec*
EMP: 150
SQ FT: 112,000
SALES (est): 35.8MM
SALES (corp-wide): 12B **Publicly Held**
SIC: 2655 3082 Tubes, fiber or paper: made from purchased material; tubes, unsupported plastic
HQ: Clarcor Inc.
840 Crescent Centre Dr # 600
Franklin TN 37067
615 771-3100

(G-4653)
STOP & SHRED
5325 Industrial Rd Ste B (46825-5108)
PHONE..............................260 483-6200
Patricia Jaeger, *President*
EMP: 4
SALES (est): 559K **Privately Held**
WEB: www.stopandshred.com
SIC: 3589 Shredders, industrial & commercial

(G-4654)
STOTLAR HILL LLC
4723 E Washington Blvd (46803-1684)
PHONE..............................260 497-0808
Tisha Stotlar, *Principal*
EMP: 4 EST: 2010
SALES (est): 261.2K **Privately Held**
SIC: 3271 Paving blocks, concrete

(G-4655)
STRATAFLO PRODUCTS INC
2010 Lakeview Dr (46808-3922)
P.O. Box 8298 (46898-8298)
PHONE..............................260 482-4366
Thomas Beaver, *President*
EMP: 15 EST: 1939
SQ FT: 10,000
SALES (est): 2MM **Privately Held**
WEB: www.strataflo.com
SIC: 3494 Valves & pipe fittings

(G-4656)
STREAM TEK LLC
4520 Ellenwood Dr (46806-2850)
PHONE..............................260 441-9300
Donna Lenzer, *Partner*
EMP: 3
SALES (est): 390.7K **Privately Held**
WEB: www.streamtekllc.com
SIC: 3599 Machine shop, jobbing & repair

(G-4657)
STRUCTURAL SOURCE
1510 Holliston Trl (46825-7217)
PHONE..............................260 489-0035
Mike Fuller, *Owner*
EMP: 8
SALES (est): 610K **Privately Held**
SIC: 1542 3312 Nonresidential construction; blast furnaces & steel mills

▲ = Import ▼ = Export
◆ = Import/Export

(G-4658)
STUART MANUFACTURING INC
Also Called: Stuart Integrated Systems
1830 Wayne Trce Unit 407 (46803-2657)
PHONE..................................260 403-2003
Fax: 260 456-3486
Lionel Tobin, *President*
EMP: 19
SQ FT: 3,000
SALES (est): 4.1MM **Privately Held**
WEB: www.stuartmfg.com
SIC: 3679 Electronic switches; harness assemblies for electronic use: wire or cable

(G-4659)
SUGAR SPICE CUPCAKE EVENT PLG
443 Pasadena Dr (46807-2750)
PHONE..................................260 610-5103
Donna Masterson, *Owner*
EMP: 2
SALES (est): 68.3K **Privately Held**
SIC: 2051 Bread, cake & related products

(G-4660)
SUGAR TREE INCORPORATED
Also Called: Camo Diva
9185 Lima Rd (46818-1803)
PHONE..................................260 417-3362
Dawn Merriman, *President*
Joanna Uttertack, *Manager*
EMP: 5 EST: 2011
SALES (est): 329.8K **Privately Held**
SIC: 5699 2311 2335 Formal wear; tailored suits & formal jackets; gowns, formal

(G-4661)
SUMMIT BRANDS
3404 Conestoga Dr (46808-4410)
PHONE..................................260 483-2519
Greg Childers, *Exec VP*
Douglas Breeden, *Sales Dir*
EMP: 4
SALES (est): 562.4K **Privately Held**
SIC: 2899 Water treating compounds

(G-4662)
SUMMIT COACHES
6215 Commodity Ct (46818-1221)
PHONE..................................260 489-3556
Fax: 260 489-2582
Robie Ryan, *Admin Sec*
EMP: 2
SALES (est): 133.2K **Privately Held**
SIC: 3714 Motor vehicle parts & accessories

(G-4663)
SUMMIT FOUNDRY SYSTEMS INC
2100 Wayne Haven St (46803-3279)
PHONE..................................260 749-7740
Fax: 260 749-7228
Richard L Meyer, *President*
Sharon Meyer, *Treasurer*
EMP: 14
SQ FT: 18,000
SALES (est): 3.5MM **Privately Held**
WEB: www.summitfoundrysystems.com
SIC: 3559 Foundry machinery & equipment

(G-4664)
SUMMIT INDUSTRIAL TECHNOLOGIES
1400 Arprt N Off Park Ste (46825)
PHONE..................................260 494-3461
Kevin Milliman, *President*
EMP: 3
SQ FT: 5,500
SALES (est): 163.8K **Privately Held**
SIC: 3559 Plastics working machinery

(G-4665)
SUMMIT MANUFACTURING CORP
2320 Meyer Rd (46803-2910)
PHONE..................................260 428-2600
Fax: 260 447-5013
Alan Zemen, *President*
Ellen Blasi, *General Mgr*
Jim De Simone, *Senior VP*
William J Federspiel, *Treasurer*
Greg Rosenfield, *Director*

EMP: 35
SQ FT: 95,000
SALES (est): 6.1MM **Privately Held**
WEB: www.summitmc.com
SIC: 3443 3444 3353 Metal parts; sheet metalwork; aluminum sheet, plate & foil

(G-4666)
SUN CONTROL CENTER LLC
6032 Highview Dr Ste E (46818-1390)
PHONE..................................260 490-9902
Wayne Mshive, *Owner*
Becky Pack, *Admin Sec*
EMP: 10 EST: 1976
SALES: 400K **Privately Held**
SIC: 3442 1799 5719 Storm doors or windows, metal; window treatment installation; window furnishings

(G-4667)
SUPERIOR MACHINE & TOOL CO
6911 Trafalgar Dr (46803-3281)
PHONE..................................260 493-4517
Fax: 260 493-6235
Michael S Perkins, *President*
James C Perkins, *President*
Todd Bauer, *General Mgr*
Michael Perkins, *Vice Pres*
Mike Perkins, *Vice Pres*
EMP: 10 EST: 1946
SQ FT: 15,000
SALES (est): 1.9MM **Privately Held**
SIC: 3599 Machine shop, jobbing & repair

(G-4668)
SUPERIOR MANUFACTURING DIV MAG
2015 S Calhoun St (46802-6411)
P.O. Box 13343 (46868-3343)
PHONE..................................260 456-3596
Terri Parker, *Principal*
EMP: 9
SALES (est): 1.1MM **Privately Held**
SIC: 2899 Water treating compounds

(G-4669)
SUSHIYA-US
14328 Brafferton Pkwy (46814-2304)
PHONE..................................260 444-4263
Yong Lee, *Principal*
EMP: 3 EST: 2011
SALES (est): 328.7K **Privately Held**
SIC: 3421 Table & food cutlery, including butchers'

(G-4670)
SYSTEM SCIENCE INSTITUTE
Also Called: Ssi
4710 Arden Dr Fl 1 (46804-4400)
PHONE..................................260 436-6096
Terry Corbin, *President*
Larry Corbin, *Principal*
EMP: 8
SQ FT: 22,000
SALES (est): 808.5K **Privately Held**
WEB: www.systsci.com
SIC: 3599 Machine shop, jobbing & repair

(G-4671)
SYSTEMS ENGINEERING AND SLS CO
Also Called: SESCO
3805 E Pontiac St (46803-3898)
PHONE..................................260 422-1671
Fax: 260 424-0607
James J Stout, *President*
Keith Coyne, *Purch Agent*
EMP: 8
SQ FT: 21,000
SALES: 4.6MM **Privately Held**
WEB: www.sesco-inc.com
SIC: 3559 3569 5084 3563 Petroleum refinery equipment; lubricating equipment; industrial machinery & equipment; air & gas compressors; oil & gas field machinery

(G-4672)
T F S INC
Also Called: O'Sullivans Italian Pub
1808 W Main St (46808-3759)
PHONE..................................260 422-5896
Tom F Sokolik, *President*
Frank Casagrande, *Vice Pres*

Louis Lecoque, *Manager*
EMP: 9
SQ FT: 2,500
SALES: 39.2K **Privately Held**
SIC: 2599 2531 Bar, restaurant & cafeteria furniture; public building & related furniture

(G-4673)
TAB SOFTWARE
8118 Victoria Woods Pl (46825-6505)
PHONE..................................260 490-7132
Thomas Olinger, *President*
EMP: 2
SALES: 200K **Privately Held**
WEB: www.tabsoftware.com
SIC: 7372 Application computer software

(G-4674)
TARGAMITE LLC
6917 Innovation Blvd (46818-1372)
PHONE..................................260 489-0046
Christopher Alexander, *Design Engr*
Gary Kaufman,
EMP: 2
SALES (est): 229.9K **Privately Held**
SIC: 3699 Electronic training devices

(G-4675)
TARGET PRINTING INC
3233 Lafayette St (46806-4049)
PHONE..................................260 744-6038
Fax: 260 744-8441
Jay Daniel Crance, *President*
Rachel Koussman, *Admin Asst*
EMP: 7
SQ FT: 6,000
SALES (est): 892K **Privately Held**
SIC: 2752 Commercial printing, offset

(G-4676)
TEAM HILLMAN LLC
414 E Wayne St (46802-2815)
PHONE..................................260 426-2626
Carol Shilling Nole, *Mng Member*
EMP: 12
SALES (est): 588.4K **Privately Held**
SIC: 3993 Signs & advertising specialties

(G-4677)
TELECTRO-MEK INC
2700 Nuttman Ave (46802-4210)
P.O. Box 11289 (46857-1289)
PHONE..................................260 747-0586
Fax: 260 747-0588
Ruth Russ, *President*
Scott Aldridge, *Senior VP*
EMP: 7 EST: 1965
SQ FT: 32,000
SALES (est): 1.1MM **Privately Held**
SIC: 3663 Radio broadcasting & communications equipment

(G-4678)
TEREX CORPORATION
Terex Advance Mixer
7727 Freedom Way (46818-2169)
PHONE..................................260 497-0728
Keith Brown, *Purch Dir*
Mark Schulier, *Engineer*
Eric Parent, *Human Res Dir*
Kevin Fix, *Regl Sales Mgr*
Gary Dennis, *Manager*
EMP: 220
SALES (corp-wide): 4.3B **Publicly Held**
WEB: www.terex.com
SIC: 3531 Construction machinery
PA: Terex Corporation
200 Nyala Farms Rd Ste 2
Westport CT 06880
203 222-7170

(G-4679)
TERRAPIN MFG
4109 Evard Rd (46835-1914)
PHONE..................................717 339-6007
Jason Moyer, *Principal*
EMP: 2
SALES (est): 99.5K **Privately Held**
SIC: 3999 Manufacturing industries

(G-4680)
THE BALDUS COMPANY INC
440 E Brackenridge St (46802-3598)
PHONE..................................260 424-2366
George H Baldus, *CEO*

Dave Weadock, *Sales Staff*
EMP: 8 EST: 1950
SQ FT: 25,000
SALES (est): 1.1MM **Privately Held**
WEB: www.balduscompany.com
SIC: 3993 Electric signs

(G-4681)
THE PRO SHEAR CORPORATION CORP
3405 Meyer Rd Ste 100 (46803-2982)
PHONE..................................260 408-1010
Tony Stewart, *CEO*
Scott Krebs, *General Mgr*
Scott Sutherlin, *Facilities Mgr*
Tim Tilbury, *Engineer*
Stacy Smith, *Manager*
EMP: 7
SALES (est): 1.5MM **Privately Held**
SIC: 3465 Automotive stampings

(G-4682)
THERMODYNE FOOD SERVICE PDTS
4418 New Haven Ave (46803-1650)
PHONE..................................260 428-2535
Fax: 260 428-2533
Vincent Tippmann Sr, *President*
William J Federspiel, *Corp Secy*
Gary Price, *Engineer*
Richard Cieslinski, *Natl Sales Mgr*
Brian Markham, *Regl Sales Mgr*
EMP: 22
SQ FT: 50,000
SALES (est): 4.6MM **Privately Held**
WEB: www.tdyne.com
SIC: 3589 5046 3631 Cooking equipment, commercial; commercial equipment; household cooking equipment

(G-4683)
THOROUGHBRED INDUSTRIES INC
6902 Brackenwood Ct (46835-9671)
PHONE..................................260 486-8343
Herb Fuller, *Principal*
EMP: 3
SALES (est): 202.5K **Privately Held**
SIC: 3999 Manufacturing industries

(G-4684)
THREE RIVERS DISTILLING CO LLC
220 E Wallace St (46803-2341)
PHONE..................................260 745-9355
Travis Kraick, *Principal*
EMP: 4 EST: 2013
SALES (est): 178.6K **Privately Held**
SIC: 2085 Distilled & blended liquors

(G-4685)
TIPPMANN PRODUCTS LLC
3905 Goeglein Rd (46815-5731)
PHONE..................................260 438-7946
Gene Tippmann, *President*
EMP: 3 EST: 2013
SALES (est): 343K **Privately Held**
SIC: 2299 Textile goods

(G-4686)
TIPPMANN SPORTS LLC (HQ)
2955 Adams Center Rd (46803-3219)
PHONE..................................800 533-4831
Fax: 260 749-6619
Dennis Tippman Jr, *President*
Huynh Truong, *COO*
David Price, *Site Mgr*
Sean Alford, *Production*
Fer Heiselmann, *Production*
◆ EMP: 92
SQ FT: 23,000
SALES (est): 19MM
SALES (corp-wide): 1.2MM **Privately Held**
SIC: 3546 Guns, pneumatic: chip removal
PA: G.I. Sportz Inc
6000 Rue Kieran
Saint-Laurent QC H4S 2
514 339-1900

(G-4687)
TIPPMANN SPORTS LLC
2955 Adams Center Rd (46803-3219)
PHONE..................................260 749-6022
Lori Sherwood, *CFO*

EMP: 10
SALES (corp-wide): 1.2MM **Privately Held**
WEB: www.tippmann.com
SIC: 3546 3949 Guns, pneumatic: chip removal; sporting & athletic goods
HQ: Tippmann Sports, Llc
2955 Adams Center Rd
Fort Wayne IN 46803
800 533-4831

(G-4688)
TITAN METAL WORX LLC
5225 New Haven Ave (46803-3026)
PHONE.....................................260 422-4433
Justin Reed, *President*
EMP: 28 **EST:** 2015
SALES (est): 1.2MM **Privately Held**
SIC: 3599 Machine shop, jobbing & repair

(G-4689)
TODD K HOCKEMEYER INC
Also Called: K & N Carpet
12108 Us Highway 27 S (46816-9423)
PHONE.....................................260 639-3591
Fax: 260 639-3593
Todd K Hockemeyer, *President*
Kristina Smith, *Manager*
EMP: 5
SQ FT: 18,000
SALES (est): 1.1MM **Privately Held**
WEB: www.kncarpet.com
SIC: 5023 5713 2273 Floor coverings; floor covering stores; carpets & rugs

(G-4690)
TOMLIN ENTERPRISES INC
Also Called: Dennisign
6926 Quemetco Ct (46803-3393)
PHONE.....................................866 994-9200
Mike Berges, *Manager*
EMP: 4
SQ FT: 2,000
SALES (est): 326.5K **Privately Held**
SIC: 3993 Signs & advertising specialties

(G-4691)
TONYA GERHARDT
6134 Constitution Dr (46804-1526)
PHONE.....................................260 434-1370
Tonya Gerhardt, *Executive*
EMP: 2
SALES (est): 83.9K **Privately Held**
SIC: 2752 Commercial printing, lithographic

(G-4692)
TOOLCRAFT LLC
2620 Adams Center Rd (46803-3214)
PHONE.....................................260 749-0454
Fax: 260 493-1666
Mark Parisot, *Project Mgr*
Adam Dall, *Purch Mgr*
John Taylor, *Sales Staff*
Angela Castillo, *Office Mgr*
Bruce Meyer, *Mng Member*
EMP: 22 **EST:** 1960
SQ FT: 28,000
SALES (est): 2.6MM **Privately Held**
WEB: www.toolcraftfw.com
SIC: 3544 3545 7692 Special dies & tools; machine tool accessories; welding repair

(G-4693)
TOOMUCHFUN RUBBERSTAMPS INC
11738 Winchester Rd (46819-9714)
PHONE.....................................260 557-4808
Steve Lindeman, *President*
EMP: 2
SALES: 70K **Privately Held**
SIC: 3953 Cancelling stamps, hand: rubber or metal

(G-4694)
TOTAL CLEANING SOLUTIONS LLC
4620 Lima Rd (46808-1202)
PHONE.....................................260 471-7761
Mark Mendhell,
EMP: 2
SALES (est): 240.4K **Privately Held**
SIC: 2899 Chemical preparations

(G-4695)
TOUCH PLATE TECHNOLOGIES INC
Also Called: Touch Plate Lighting Controls
1830 Wayne Trce Ste 9 (46803-2657)
P.O. Box 10960 (46854-0960)
PHONE.....................................260 426-1565
Douglas Ford, *President*
▲ **EMP:** 17
SQ FT: 8,000
SALES: 1.2MM **Privately Held**
SIC: 3625 3644 3648 Control equipment, electric; face plates (wiring devices); lighting equipment

(G-4696)
TOUCHPLATE TECHNOLOGIES INC
Also Called: Touch Plate
1830 Wayne Trce Ste 9 (46803-2657)
PHONE.....................................260 424-4323
Fax: 260 426-1442
Doug Ford, *President*
▲ **EMP:** 12
SQ FT: 8,500
SALES (est): 2.3MM **Privately Held**
WEB: www.touchplate.com
SIC: 3625 3648 3699 3643 Control equipment, electric; lighting equipment; electrical equipment & supplies; current-carrying wiring devices; switchgear & switchboard apparatus

(G-4697)
TRANE US INC
6602 Innovation Blvd (46818-1389)
PHONE.....................................260 489-0884
Randy Katz, *Manager*
EMP: 25 **Privately Held**
SIC: 3585 Refrigeration & heating equipment
HQ: Trane U.S. Inc.
3600 Pammel Creek Rd
La Crosse WI 54601
608 787-2000

(G-4698)
TRANSFORMATIONS BY WIELAND INC
310 Racquet Dr (46825-4229)
PHONE.....................................800 440-9337
Fax: 260 657-5691
Jaret Wieland, *CEO*
Brace T Wieland, *President*
Stuart Reynolds, *Principal*
Brenda Wieland, *Principal*
Travis Shuman, *Accountant*
EMP: 55 **EST:** 1997
SQ FT: 76,000
SALES (est): 17MM **Privately Held**
WEB: www.trfurniture.com
SIC: 2512 Upholstered household furniture

(G-4699)
TRELLBORG SLING SLTIONS US INC
2531 Bremer Rd (46803-3014)
PHONE.....................................260 748-5895
John McLaughlin, *Research*
Mitchell Schlatter, *Engineer*
Dianna Ryan, *Accountant*
Lori Locke, *Human Resources*
Bob Willis, *Sales Staff*
EMP: 250
SALES (corp-wide): 3.7B **Privately Held**
WEB: www.dowtyauto.com
SIC: 2891 Sealing compounds, synthetic rubber or plastic
HQ: Trelleborg Sealing Solutions Us, Inc.
2531 Bremer Rd
Fort Wayne IN 46803
260 749-9631

(G-4700)
TRELLBORG SLING SLTIONS US INC (DH)
Also Called: Busakshamban
2531 Bremer Rd (46803-3014)
PHONE.....................................260 749-9631
Fax: 260 422-6420
Tim Callison, *President*
Peter Hahn, *President*
Linda Muroski, *President*
Robert White, *VP Admin*
Kevin Alofs, *Vice Pres*

▲ **EMP:** 30
SQ FT: 9,370
SALES (est): 390.6MM
SALES (corp-wide): 3.7B **Privately Held**
WEB: www.dowtyauto.com
SIC: 3089 Plastic processing; bearings, plastic
HQ: Trelleborg Corporation
200 Veterans Blvd Ste 3
South Haven MI 49090
269 639-989 i

(G-4701)
TRI-STATE MACHINING INC
2515 Mcdonald St (46803-1561)
PHONE.....................................260 422-2508
Gary Nuhauf, *President*
Abe Nurser, *Vice Pres*
EMP: 3
SALES (est): 430K **Privately Held**
SIC: 3599 Machine shop, jobbing & repair

(G-4702)
TRI-STATE MECHANICAL INC
4530 Secretary Dr (46808-1199)
PHONE.....................................260 471-0345
Fax: 260 483-3942
Marshall Loveless, *President*
Donna Loveless, *Vice Pres*
EMP: 10
SQ FT: 3,000
SALES: 1.1MM **Privately Held**
SIC: 1711 3441 Heating & air conditioning contractors; fabricated structural metal

(G-4703)
TRI-STATE SHTMTL & MFG LLC ✪
1738 Traders Xing (46845-1536)
PHONE.....................................260 402-8831
EMP: 2 **EST:** 2017
SALES (est): 110.9K **Privately Held**
SIC: 3999 Manufacturing industries

(G-4704)
TRINITY CMMNICATIONS GROUP INC
2524 Merivale St (46805-1532)
P.O. Box 5021 (46895-5021)
PHONE.....................................260 484-1029
Robert Willey, *President*
Leone Willey, *Corp Secy*
Ann Willey, *Vice Pres*
Donald Willey, *Vice Pres*
EMP: 2
SALES: 793.1K **Privately Held**
SIC: 5999 8732 7922 2759 Wheelchair lifts; market analysis or research; concert management service; tickets: printing

(G-4705)
TRITECH MANUFACTURING INC
2728 Commercial Rd (46809-2934)
PHONE.....................................260 747-9154
Fax: 260 747-9181
Edward H Uslar, *President*
Thomas M Uslar, *Corp Secy*
Thomas Uslar, *Treasurer*
EMP: 25
SQ FT: 11,500
SALES (est): 4.1MM **Privately Held**
WEB: www.tritechpcb.com
SIC: 3672 Circuit boards, television & radio printed

(G-4706)
TRIVECTOR MANUFACTURING INC
Also Called: Only Alpha
4404 Engle Ridge Dr (46804-4443)
PHONE.....................................260 637-0141
Thomas Epple, *CEO*
Timothy Saxer, *Exec VP*
Tim Saxer, *VP Sales*
Tom Dwire, *Sales Staff*
Patrick Slusser, *Marketing Staff*
EMP: 45
SALES (est): 29.2MM **Privately Held**
SIC: 5033 3469 Fiberglass building materials; metal stampings

(G-4707)
TT2 LLC
Also Called: Yudu
14516 Lima Rd (46818-9537)
PHONE.....................................260 438-4575
Timothy Burns, *Principal*
Tim Burns, *Mng Member*
Tyler G Eifert, *Mng Member*
EMP: 2
SALES: 30K **Privately Held**
SIC: 5961 2269 7389 Clothing, mail order (except women's); women's apparel, mail order; labels, cotton: printed;

(G-4708)
TUFF TOOL INC
6003 Highgate Pl (46815-7614)
PHONE.....................................262 612-8300
John Schultz, *Principal*
EMP: 5 **EST:** 2012
SALES (est): 459K **Privately Held**
SIC: 3544 Special dies, tools, jigs & fixtures

(G-4709)
TUTHILL CORPORATION
Also Called: Fill-Rite Division
8825 Aviation Dr (46809-9630)
P.O. Box 9100 (46899-9100)
PHONE.....................................260 747-7529
Thomas Headley, *Engineer*
Mike Donley, *Corp Comm Staff*
John Gould, *Branch Mgr*
EMP: 185
SQ FT: 100,000
SALES (corp-wide): 175.8MM **Privately Held**
WEB: www.tuthill.com
SIC: 3561 4813 Pumps & pumping equipment; telephone communication, except radio
PA: Tuthill Corporation
8500 S Madison St
Burr Ridge IL 60527
630 382-4900

(G-4710)
TUTHILL CORPORATION
Also Called: Tuthill Transfer Systems
8825 Aviation Dr (46809-9630)
PHONE.....................................260 747-7529
Tom Carmazzi, *CEO*
David P Groeber, *Treasurer*
Patricia Stuller, *Accountant*
James G Tuthill, *Post Master*
◆ **EMP:** 5
SALES (est): 2MM **Privately Held**
SIC: 3561 Pumps & pumping equipment

(G-4711)
TWO B ENTERPRISES INC
Also Called: Graphics Output
6909 Quemetco Ct (46803-3290)
PHONE.....................................260 245-0119
Richard J Byanski, *President*
Michael D Burgess, *Vice Pres*
Sharon Schiffbauer, *VP Opers*
EMP: 10
SALES (est): 1.5MM **Privately Held**
SIC: 2752 Commercial printing, offset

(G-4712)
U S AIR FILTRATION INC
3450 Stellhorn Rd Ste B (46815-8642)
PHONE.....................................260 486-7399
Ben Perkins, *Sales Mgr*
Joyce Nagy, *Accounts Mgr*
Scott Pitts, *Manager*
EMP: 3
SALES (corp-wide): 2.7MM **Privately Held**
SIC: 3564 Purification & dust collection equipment
PA: U. S. Air Filtration, Inc.
23811 Washington Ave C110176
Murrieta CA 92562
951 491-7282

(G-4713)
UNDER STAIRCASE BREWING CO LLC
4927 S Camden Dr (46825-5511)
PHONE.....................................260 580-2586
Nathan Thornhill, *Principal*
EMP: 2 **EST:** 2016

▲ = Import ▼=Export
◆ =Import/Export

SALES (est): 68.6K **Privately Held**
SIC: 2082 Malt beverages

(G-4714)
UNIQUE OUTDOOR PRODUCTS LLC
4211 Chetham Dr (46835-4635)
PHONE..................................260 486-4955
William Dietsch, *Principal*
EMP: 6
SALES (est): 591.3K **Privately Held**
SIC: 3949 Sporting & athletic goods

(G-4715)
UNITED MEDIA GROUP INC
Also Called: Puff Hut
2801 Freeman St (46802-4426)
PHONE..................................260 436-7417
EMP: 5
SQ FT: 5,000
SALES: 750K **Privately Held**
SIC: 7319 2721 2741 7336 Bus Shelter Advertising

(G-4716)
UNITED OIL CORP
Also Called: Fort Meyers
Hwy 33 And Wash Ctr Rd (46808)
PHONE..................................260 489-3511
Fax: 260 489-3513
Jim Russell, *Manager*
EMP: 5
SALES (corp-wide): 10.8MM **Privately Held**
WEB: www.unitedoilcorp.com
SIC: 1389 Oil field services
PA: United Oil Corp
1609 E Business 30
Columbia City IN 46725
260 244-6000

(G-4717)
UNITED ORTHO
Also Called: United Ortho Enterprises
2235 Pennsylvania St (46803-2138)
PHONE..................................260 422-5827
Russell Moir, *President*
Jeff Mason, *Principal*
Mark Howard, *Principal*
Andrew Opliger, *COO*
Luke Sefton, *Warehouse Mgr*
▲ EMP: 19
SALES (est): 2.9MM **Privately Held**
SIC: 3842 Trusses, orthopedic & surgical

(G-4718)
UNITED SURGICAL INC
Also Called: United Ortho Enterprises
2235 Pennsylvania St (46803-2138)
PHONE..................................260 422-5827
Russell Moir, *President*
Andrew Opliger, *COO*
Kathy McCrady, *Vice Pres*
▲ EMP: 8
SQ FT: 2,400
SALES (est): 1.2MM **Privately Held**
WEB: www.unitedsurgicalassociates.com
SIC: 3842 Surgical appliances & supplies; supports: abdominal, ankle, arch, kneecap, etc.

(G-4719)
UNIVERSAL CONSOLIDATED METHODS
Also Called: Tite-Lok
3522 Astoria Way (46818-8742)
PHONE..................................260 637-2575
Jill Hochstetler, *President*
EMP: 30 EST: 1974
SQ FT: 16,000
SALES (est): 3.3MM **Privately Held**
WEB: www.titelok.com
SIC: 3429 Clamps, metal; marine hardware

(G-4720)
US FOAM CORPORATION
Also Called: US Foam
1829 E Creighton Ave (46803-3631)
PHONE..................................260 456-4998
Fax: 260 744-8599
Paul Becraft, *Manager*
EMP: 9 **Privately Held**
SIC: 3086 Packaging & shipping materials, foamed plastic; padding, foamed plastic

PA: U.S. Foam Corporation
7412 Jager Ct
Cincinnati OH 45230

(G-4721)
USV OPTICAL INC
Also Called: J C Penney Optical
4201 Coldwater Rd Ste 4 (46805-1187)
PHONE..................................260 482-5033
Janet King, *Manager*
EMP: 5
SALES (corp-wide): 492.1MM **Privately Held**
WEB: www.ntouchcomm.net
SIC: 5995 3851 Eyeglasses, prescription; frames & parts, eyeglass & spectacle
HQ: Usv Optical, Inc.
1 Harmon Dr Glen Oaks Par
Glendora NJ 08029

(G-4722)
VALBRUNA SLATER STAINLESS INC
2400 Taylor St (46802-4613)
P.O. Box 630 (46801-0630)
PHONE..................................260 434-2800
Massimo Amenduni Gresele, *President*
Domenico Bellomi, *Vice Pres*
Tom Carlson, *Manager*
Valter Viero, *Admin Sec*
◆ EMP: 110
SALES (est): 31.4MM
SALES (corp-wide): 354.3MM **Privately Held**
SIC: 3312 Ingots, steel; billets, steel; bars & bar shapes, steel, hot-rolled
PA: Acciaierie Valbruna Spa
Viale Della Scienza 25
Vicenza VI 36100
044 496-8211

(G-4723)
VALVE SERVE LLC
2020 E Wa Blvd Ste 550 (46803-1367)
PHONE..................................260 421-1927
Stephen M Mishler, *Principal*
EMP: 2
SALES (est): 155.7K **Privately Held**
SIC: 3592 Valves

(G-4724)
VDK PRINTING LLC ✪
3822 Live Oak Blvd (46804-3938)
PHONE..................................260 602-8212
Brian Vandekeere, *Principal*
EMP: 2 EST: 2017
SALES (est): 94.6K **Privately Held**
SIC: 2752 Commercial printing, lithographic

(G-4725)
VEE ENGINEERING INC
3805 Reynolds St (46803-1682)
PHONE..................................260 424-6635
Fax: 260 424-0260
John Reynolds, *President*
EMP: 80
SQ FT: 30,000
SALES (corp-wide): 11.9MM **Privately Held**
SIC: 3089 3714 Injection molded finished plastic products; motor vehicle parts & accessories
PA: Vee Engineering Inc
3620 W 73rd St
Anderson IN 46011
765 778-7895

(G-4726)
VERTICAL SALE
3838 Sherman Blvd (46808-4017)
PHONE..................................260 438-4299
EMP: 2 EST: 2013
SALES (est): 153.4K **Privately Held**
SIC: 2591 Blinds vertical

(G-4727)
VIKING BUSINESS PRODUCTS INC
Also Called: Proforma Viking
7530 Disalle Blvd (46825-3368)
PHONE..................................260 489-7787
Fax: 260 489-8161
Jack C Sandstrom, *CEO*
Lisa Sandstrom, *President*
Caroline R Sandstrom, *Corp Secy*

EMP: 4
SQ FT: 10,000
SALES (est): 360K **Privately Held**
WEB: www.vikingprod.com
SIC: 2754 Business forms: gravure printing

(G-4728)
VINTAGE CHEMICAL ENTERPRISES
314 E Wallace St (46803-2343)
PHONE..................................260 745-7272
Samih Abouhalkah, *President*
▲ EMP: 6
SALES: 600K **Privately Held**
WEB: www.vintagechemical.com
SIC: 5999 2841 Medical apparatus & supplies; soap & other detergents

(G-4729)
VITA NONWOVENS LLC
9403 Avionics Dr (46809-9632)
PHONE..................................260 747-0990
Fax: 260 399-3731
Jimmie Risner, *Opers Mgr*
Todd Miller, *Prdtn Mgr*
Dwane Church, *Marketing Staff*
EMP: 50
SALES (est): 7.2MM
SALES (corp-wide): 64.8MM **Privately Held**
SIC: 2297 Nonwoven fabrics
PA: Vita Nonwovens Llc
2215 Shore St
High Point NC 27263
336 431-7187

(G-4730)
WAGNER ELECTRIC FORT WAYNE INC
3610 N Clinton St (46805-1898)
PHONE..................................260 484-5532
Fax: 260 484-4485
Peter Bell, *President*
Mary Bell, *Corp Secy*
Andrew Bell, *Vice Pres*
EMP: 9
SQ FT: 11,000
SALES: 5.8MM **Privately Held**
WEB: www.wagnerfw.com
SIC: 5063 7694 Motors, electric; electric motor repair

(G-4731)
WAGNERS PLASTI CRAFT CO
5705 Union Chapel Rd (46845-9614)
PHONE..................................260 627-3147
Mike Wagner, *Owner*
Janelle Wagner, *Co-Owner*
EMP: 2
SALES: 50K **Privately Held**
SIC: 2541 Cabinets, except refrigerated: show, display, etc.: wood

(G-4732)
WAGON TRAIN VENTURES LLC
6712 Felger Rd (46818-9450)
PHONE..................................260 625-5301
Rosemary Imrick, *Owner*
EMP: 2
SALES (est): 131.8K **Privately Held**
SIC: 3944 Games, toys & children's vehicles

(G-4733)
WALL CONTROL SERVICES INC
5742 Industrial Rd (46825-5128)
PHONE..................................260 450-6411
David Wall, *President*
Yan Wall, *Accounts Mgr*
EMP: 3 EST: 2011
SALES (est): 405.1K **Privately Held**
SIC: 3569 3589 7371 7699 Robots, assembly line: industrial & commercial; asbestos removal equipment; software programming applications; industrial machinery & equipment repair;

(G-4734)
WALTERS DEVELOPMENT LLC
6600 Ardmore Ave (46809-9703)
PHONE..................................260 747-7531
Peggy Walters, *Mng Member*
Jeffrey Walters,
Rick Walters,
EMP: 3

SALES (est): 294.3K **Privately Held**
SIC: 2951 Asphalt paving mixtures & blocks

(G-4735)
WARD CORPORATION (PA)
Also Called: Ward Production Machine
642 Growth Ave (46808-3712)
PHONE..................................260 426-8700
Fax: 260 420-1919
Vern Ward, *Ch of Bd*
Marion Ward, *President*
Mary J Atkins, *Vice Pres*
J Hicks, *Plant Mgr*
Treesh Sandy, *Opers Staff*
▲ EMP: 170 EST: 1975
SQ FT: 91,675
SALES (est): 41.2MM **Privately Held**
SIC: 3365 3544 3369 Aluminum foundries; special dies, tools, jigs & fixtures; nonferrous foundries

(G-4736)
WARD CORPORATION
Also Called: Ward Heat Treating
7603 Opportunity Dr (46825-3364)
PHONE..................................260 489-2281
Fax: 260 489-4625
Roy Neilson, *Human Res Mgr*
Bill Jennings, *Manager*
EMP: 20
SALES (corp-wide): 41.2MM **Privately Held**
WEB: www.wardcorp.com
SIC: 3398 3544 Metal heat treating; special dies, tools, jigs & fixtures
PA: Ward Corporation
642 Growth Ave
Fort Wayne IN 46808
260 426-8700

(G-4737)
WATER SCIENCES
327 Ley Rd (46825-5219)
PHONE..................................260 485-4655
Fax: 260 486-6232
Kevin Fuze, *President*
Michael A Fuze, *President*
EMP: 7
SALES (est): 1MM **Privately Held**
WEB: www.watersciences.com
SIC: 2899 Water treating compounds

(G-4738)
WAYNE BLACK OXIDE INC
4505 Executive Blvd (46808-1136)
PHONE..................................260 484-0280
Fax: 260 482-6859
Kent Flaig, *President*
John Flaig, *President*
Michael Carpenter, *Foreman/Supr*
Arlene Flaig, *Treasurer*
EMP: 7
SQ FT: 6,000
SALES (est): 926.4K **Privately Held**
WEB: www.wayneblackoxide.com
SIC: 3471 Finishing, metals or formed products; plating of metals or formed products

(G-4739)
WAYNE CHEMICAL INC
7114 Homestead Rd (46814-4678)
PHONE..................................260 432-1120
Fax: 260 432-1473
William E Spindler, *President*
EMP: 25 EST: 1969
SQ FT: 12,000
SALES (est): 5.9MM **Privately Held**
WEB: www.waynechemical.com
SIC: 3559 2819 2842 Chemical machinery & equipment; industrial inorganic chemicals; specialty cleaning, polishes & sanitation goods

(G-4740)
WAYNE CONCEPTS MFG INC
5005 Speedway Dr (46825-5244)
PHONE..................................260 482-8615
Fax: 260 483-5598
James Gast, *President*
Kenneth Gast, *Vice Pres*
EMP: 8
SQ FT: 10,000

SALES: 1.5MM **Privately Held**
SIC: 2841 Detergents, synthetic organic or inorganic alkaline

(G-4741)
WAYNE MANUFACTURING LLC
5642 Coventry Ln (46804-7140)
PHONE..............................260 432-2233
EMP: 2
SALES (est): 77K **Privately Held**
SIC: 3999 Mfg Misc Products

(G-4742)
WAYNE METAL PROTECTION COMPANY
2413 Meyer Rd (46803-2911)
PHONE..............................260 492-2529
Neal Schaffel, *President*
EMP: 50 **EST:** 1924
SQ FT: 30,000
SALES (est): 4.4MM **Privately Held**
SIC: 3471 2851 Electroplating of metals or formed products; anodizing (plating) of metals or formed products; paints & allied products

(G-4743)
WAYNE PRESS INCORPORATED
Also Called: Garphik Mechanix
1716 S Harrison St (46802-5211)
PHONE..............................260 744-3022
Fax: 260 744-3022
Bill Wright, *President*
Fred S Mertz, *Manager*
EMP: 5
SQ FT: 2,000
SALES (est): 266.2K **Privately Held**
SIC: 2752 2759 Commercial printing, offset; letterpress printing

(G-4744)
WAYNE STEEL SUPPLY INC
7707 Freedom Way (46818-2169)
PHONE..............................260 489-6249
Fax: 260 489-6391
David Seybert, *President*
EMP: 29
SQ FT: 19,200
SALES (est): 3.6MM **Privately Held**
SIC: 3449 Bars, concrete reinforcing: fabricated steel

(G-4745)
WAYNE/SCOTT FETZER COMPANY
Also Called: Wayne Combustion Systems
801 Glasgow Ave (46803-1344)
PHONE..............................260 425-9200
Kenneth J Semelsberger, *President*
Tim Mann, *Plant Mgr*
Ken Kuczmanski, *Mfg Mgr*
Tom Bunn, *Accountant*
Todd Ellinger, *Marketing Staff*
▲ **EMP:** 43
SQ FT: 350,000
SALES (est): 10.8MM **Privately Held**
WEB: www.waynecombustion.com
SIC: 3433 Oil burners, domestic or industrial; gas burners, domestic

(G-4746)
WAYNEDALE MILL INC
6701 Ideal Ave (46809-2429)
PHONE..............................260 436-7100
Fax: 260 747-1615
Richard Freeland, *President*
David Bobilya, *Treasurer*
Deanna Freeland, *Admin Sec*
▲ **EMP:** 10
SALES: 2MM **Privately Held**
WEB: www.waynedalemill.com
SIC: 2431 Millwork

(G-4747)
WAYNEDALE NEWS INC
2505 Lower Huntington Rd A (46809-2692)
PHONE..............................260 747-4535
Robert L Stark, *President*
Cindy Cornwell, *Exec Dir*
EMP: 3
SALES: 160K **Privately Held**
WEB: www.waynedalenews.com
SIC: 2711 Newspapers: publishing only, not printed on site

(G-4748)
WB AUTOMOTIVE HOLDINGS INC
3405 Meyer Rd (46803-2981)
PHONE..............................734 604-8962
Mike Hayes, *Director*
EMP: 11 **Privately Held**
SIC: 5013 3711 Automotive hardware; chassis, motor vehicle
PA: Wb Automotive Holdings, Inc.
3033 Excelsior Blvd # 300
Minneapolis MN 55416

(G-4749)
WEB INDUSTRIES DALLAS INC
Also Called: Web Converting
3925 Ardmore Ave (46802-4237)
PHONE..............................260 432-0027
Don Romine, *CEO*
Robert A Fulton, *Ch of Bd*
Donald Romine, *President*
Blake Batley, *Vice Pres*
Dennis Latimer, *Vice Pres*
▲ **EMP:** 45
SQ FT: 40,000
SALES (est): 8.8MM
SALES (corp-wide): 106.9MM **Privately Held**
SIC: 2679 Paper products, converted
PA: Web Industries Inc.
700 Nickerson Rd Ste 250
Marlborough MA 01752
508 898-2988

(G-4750)
WEB INDUSTRIES FORT WAYNE INC
Also Called: Web Converting of Fort Wayne
3925 Ardmore Ave (46802-4237)
PHONE..............................260 432-0027
Don Romine, *CEO*
Bob Fulton, *Chairman*
Mark Pihl, *COO*
Dennis Latimer, *Exec VP*
Blake Batley, *Vice Pres*
EMP: 47
SQ FT: 110,000
SALES (est): 5.2MM **Privately Held**
WEB: www.ktg.com
SIC: 7389 2241 Tape slitting; electric insulating tapes & braids, except plastic

(G-4751)
WGE EQUIPMENT SOLUTIONS LLC
306 Stable Dr (46825-5249)
PHONE..............................260 636-7218
Steven L Galligher,
EMP: 2 **EST:** 2011
SALES (est): 113.9K **Privately Held**
SIC: 3549 Coil winding machines for springs

(G-4752)
WHIPP IN HOLDINGS LLC (PA)
Also Called: National Tube Form
3405 Engle Rd (46809-1115)
PHONE..............................260 478-2363
Fax: 260 478-1043
Adam Whipp, *President*
Dawn Heiges, *Human Res Mgr*
Rhett Burgess,
Fred Whipp,
Richard Whipp,
▲ **EMP:** 185
SALES (est): 26MM **Privately Held**
WEB: www.nationaltubeform.com
SIC: 3498 Tube fabricating (contract bending & shaping)

(G-4753)
WHITCRAFT ENTERPRISES INC
Also Called: Precise Manufacturing
4323 Merchant Rd (46818-1257)
PHONE..............................260 422-6518
Fax: 260 422-9555
John E Whitcraft, *President*
James E Whitcraft, *Vice Pres*
EMP: 18 **EST:** 1971
SQ FT: 20,000
SALES (est): 5.2MM **Privately Held**
WEB: www.precisemfginc.com
SIC: 3451 Screw machine products

(G-4754)
WHYTE HAUS
1629 Channel Pl (46825-5936)
PHONE..............................260 484-5666
Dana M White, *Owner*
EMP: 2
SALES: 150K **Privately Held**
WEB: www.whytehaus.com
SIC: 3577 Computer peripheral equipment

(G-4755)
WICKS AIR FILTER SERVICE INC
Also Called: Wick's Air Filter
2607 Mcdonald St (46803-1505)
PHONE..............................260 426-1782
Fax: 260 424-2291
Jeanette Carey, *President*
Mike Carey, *Corp Secy*
EMP: 3
SQ FT: 5,000
SALES (est): 390K **Privately Held**
SIC: 5075 3564 Air filters; warm air heating equipment & supplies; blowers & fans

(G-4756)
WILLOWGREEN INC
10351 Dawsons Creek Blvd B (46825-1904)
PHONE..............................260 490-2222
Fax: 260 449-9622
James Miller, *President*
Bernie Miller, *Vice Pres*
EMP: 3
SALES: 250K **Privately Held**
SIC: 2741 Miscellaneous publishing

(G-4757)
WINGS N THINGS FABRICATION
1829 Kroemer Rd (46808-3533)
PHONE..............................260 432-2992
Jeff Moore, *Owner*
Jan Moore, *Vice Pres*
EMP: 3
SALES (est): 158.9K **Privately Held**
SIC: 3441 Fabricated structural metal

(G-4758)
WIRE AMERICA INC
1613 E Wallace St (46803-2564)
PHONE..............................260 969-1700
Lionell Tobin, *President*
Ted Jamison, *Exec VP*
EMP: 43
SQ FT: 45,000
SALES: 91.5MM **Privately Held**
SIC: 4226 Special warehousing & storage; communication wire

(G-4759)
WISE BUSINESS FORMS INC
4301 Merchant Rd (46818-1251)
P.O. Box 8550 (46898-8550)
PHONE..............................260 489-1561
Fax: 260 489-1955
Sally Spur, *Branch Mgr*
David Knappenberger, *Admin Sec*
EMP: 145
SQ FT: 30,000
SALES (corp-wide): 136.8MM **Privately Held**
WEB: www.form-1.com
SIC: 2761 2759 2752 Manifold business forms; commercial printing; commercial printing, lithographic
PA: Wise Business Forms Incorporated
555 Mcfarland 400 Dr
Alpharetta GA 30004
770 442-1060

(G-4760)
WOLF CORPORATION
3434 Adams Center Rd (46803-3230)
P.O. Box 11306 (46857-1306)
PHONE..............................260 749-9393
Fax: 260 749-5829
Anthony E Wolf, *President*
Richard E Wolf, *Chairman*
◆ **EMP:** 40
SQ FT: 95,000
SALES (est): 9.6MM **Privately Held**
WEB: www.wolfcorp.com
SIC: 2515 2299 Mattresses, innerspring or box spring; box springs, assembled; padding & wadding, textile; upholstery filling, textile

(G-4761)
WORKRITE MACHINE & TOOL INC
6319 Discount Dr (46818-1261)
PHONE..............................260 489-4778
Charles Hagan, *President*
Herbert A Beltz Jr, *President*
EMP: 22
SQ FT: 17,400
SALES (est): 3.8MM **Privately Held**
WEB: www.workriteaerostar.com
SIC: 3599 Machine shop, jobbing & repair

(G-4762)
WYNN WIRE DIE SERVICES INC
1919 Lakeview Dr (46808-3919)
PHONE..............................260 471-1395
Rick A Wynn, *President*
Jayne L V Wynn, *Corp Secy*
Brandon Wynn, *Office Mgr*
EMP: 4
SQ FT: 1,200
SALES (est): 574.6K **Privately Held**
WEB: www.wynnwiredie.com
SIC: 3544 Wire drawing & straightening dies

(G-4763)
YELLOW CUP LLC ✪
1025 Northwood Blvd (46805-3440)
PHONE..............................260 403-3489
William Smith,
EMP: 2 **EST:** 2017
SALES (est): 62.5K **Privately Held**
SIC: 3999 Manufacturing industries

(G-4764)
ZEHRHAUS INC
8516 Samantha Dr (46835-1033)
PHONE..............................260 486-3198
David Zehr, *President*
EMP: 4
SQ FT: 5,600
SALES: 65K **Privately Held**
SIC: 2449 2541 Boxes, wood: wirebound; cabinets, except refrigerated: show, display, etc.: wood

(G-4765)
ZEMCO MFG INC
2320 Meyer Rd (46803-2910)
PHONE..............................260 428-2650
Vincent Tippmann Sr, *President*
Cory Zemen, *General Mgr*
Marc Bailey, *Safety Dir*
Todd Champany, *Prdtn Mgr*
Kevin Sholl, *Draft/Design*
EMP: 35
SQ FT: 75,200
SALES: 4.9MM **Privately Held**
WEB: www.zemco.com
SIC: 3714 Motor vehicle parts & accessories

Fortville
Hancock County

(G-4766)
3C COMAN LTD
800 W Ohio St (46040-1241)
PHONE..............................317 650-5156
Thomas Cook, *President*
EMP: 3
SALES (est): 184.1K **Privately Held**
SIC: 1799 1541 3444 Coating of metal structures at construction site; steel building construction; warehouse construction; metal roofing & roof drainage equipment

(G-4767)
ABRASIVE PROCESSING & TECH LLC (PA)
712 E Ohio St (46040-1552)
PHONE..............................317 485-5157
Mikka Gurley, *Office Mgr*
Mike Riggs, *Mng Member*
EMP: 15
SALES (est): 1.3MM **Privately Held**
SIC: 3471 Sand blasting of metal parts

G E O G R A P H I C

(G-4768)
BIG E PUBLICATIONS INC
Also Called: Community Shopper
505 N School St (46040-1054)
PHONE..................................317 485-4097
Fax: 317 485-6800
Sherry Collins, *President*
EMP: 5
SALES (est): 210K **Privately Held**
SIC: 2711 7313 Newspapers; newspaper advertising representative

(G-4769)
CENTRAL TOOL CO INC
461 E Michigan St (46040-1043)
PHONE..................................317 485-5344
Fax: 317 485-5275
James Cooper, *President*
Fred Cooper, *Vice Pres*
William Cooper, *Treasurer*
Mary Louis, *Admin Sec*
EMP: 6 EST: 1946
SQ FT: 8,000
SALES (est): 768.7K **Privately Held**
SIC: 3599 Machine shop, jobbing & repair

(G-4770)
CLM PALLET RECYCLING INC (PA)
3103 W 1000 N (46040-9705)
P.O. Box 19184, Indianapolis (46219-0184)
PHONE..................................317 485-4080
Fax: 317 485-4618
Mark L Loughery, *President*
Charles L Mong III, *Principal*
Derrick Smith, *Vice Pres*
Cody Welch, *Relations*
EMP: 6
SALES (est): 39MM **Privately Held**
SIC: 7699 2499 Pallet repair; mulch, wood & bark

(G-4771)
CROWN COATINGS LLC
770 E Broadway St (46040-1550)
P.O. Box 235 (46040-0235)
PHONE..................................317 482-2766
Al Gibbons, *Principal*
EMP: 5
SALES (est): 459.6K **Privately Held**
SIC: 3471 Finishing, metals or formed products

(G-4772)
D & D BRAKE SALES INC
Also Called: Honeywell Friction Materials
State Rd 234 & Cnty Rd 20 St State Ro (46040)
P.O. Box 160 (46040-0160)
PHONE..................................317 485-5177
Fax: 317 485-5223
Charles E Stewart, *President*
▲ EMP: 60
SQ FT: 130,000
SALES (est): 8.4MM **Privately Held**
SIC: 3714 Motor vehicle brake systems & parts

(G-4773)
DEATONS WATERFRONT SVCS LLC
215 S Madison St (46040-1180)
PHONE..................................317 336-7180
Paul Deaton, *Owner*
Sandy Deaton, *Manager*
EMP: 10 EST: 2011
SALES (est): 1.7MM **Privately Held**
SIC: 3536 Boat lifts

(G-4774)
FORTVILLE AUTOMOTIVE SUP INC
Also Called: NAPA Autoparts Fortville
305 W Broadway St (46040-1408)
PHONE..................................317 485-5114
Aaron Vail, *President*
EMP: 5
SALES (est): 470.1K **Privately Held**
SIC: 3542 Machine tools, metal forming type

(G-4775)
FORTVILLE FEEDERS INC (PA)
750 E Broadway St (46040-1550)
P.O. Box 70 (46040-0070)
PHONE..................................317 485-5095
Fax: 317 485-6182
Michael A Crouse, *President*
Jason Crouse, *Vice Pres*
Joe Hester, *Vice Pres*
John Eckel, *Project Mgr*
Aaron Settles, *Purch Mgr*
EMP: 40
SQ FT: 55,000
SALES (est): 6.4MM **Privately Held**
WEB: www.fortvillefeeders.com
SIC: 3599 Custom machinery

(G-4776)
GENESIS PLASTICS WELDING INC
720 E Broadway St (46040-1550)
PHONE..................................317 485-7887
Fax: 317 485-7888
Tom Ryder, *President*
Dale Wagner, *Opers Mgr*
Nathan Glass, *Engineer*
Robert C Smith, *Admin Sec*
▲ EMP: 30
SQ FT: 15,000
SALES (est): 5.8MM **Privately Held**
WEB: www.genesisrf.com
SIC: 3089 Plastic containers, except foam

(G-4777)
GUARDIAN FIRE SYSTEMS INC
435 W Garden St (46040-1487)
PHONE..................................317 752-2768
Mychal S Nation, *President*
Christian Geiger, *Vice Pres*
EMP: 11 EST: 2006
SALES (est): 920K **Privately Held**
SIC: 3569 Sprinkler systems, fire: automatic

(G-4778)
HALE INDUSTRIES INC
Also Called: Advanced Radiant Systems
315 N Madison St (46040-1160)
P.O. Box 354 (46040-0354)
PHONE..................................317 577-0337
Fax: 317 842-3989
Craig Hale, *President*
Michael Hale, *General Mgr*
Ed Buer, *Train & Dev Mgr*
Nick Reilly, *Sales Engr*
Michael Hawkins, *Marketing Staff*
◆ EMP: 26
SQ FT: 36,000
SALES (est): 10.5MM **Privately Held**
WEB: www.ambirad.com
SIC: 5084 3255 3433 3443 Heat exchange equipment, industrial; heater radiants, clay; room & wall heaters, including radiators; heat exchangers: coolers (after, inter), condensers, etc.; industrial buildings & warehouses

(G-4779)
HOLLOWAY HOUSE INC
309 Business Park Dr (46040-1564)
P.O. Box 158 (46040-0158)
PHONE..................................317 485-4272
Christopher G Eck, *CEO*
Cameron N Eckv, *Vice Pres*
▲ EMP: 27
SQ FT: 27,000
SALES (est): 6.8MM **Privately Held**
WEB: www.hollowayhouse.net
SIC: 2842 2841 Cleaning or polishing preparations; soap & other detergents

(G-4780)
INDIANA AIRCRAFT HARDWARE CO
221 S Main St (46040-1514)
PHONE..................................317 485-6500
Fax: 317 485-6501
Robert Ferrell, *President*
Mike Ferrell, *General Mgr*
Keely Nelson, *General Mgr*
EMP: 9
SQ FT: 3,475

SALES (est): 4MM **Privately Held**
WEB: www.indianaaircraft.com
SIC: 5088 3728 Aircraft & space vehicle supplies & parts; aircraft parts & equipment

(G-4781)
KOMODO PHARMACEUTICALS INC
8064 W 1000 S (46040-9224)
P.O. Box 142 (46040-0142)
PHONE..................................317 485-0023
Jarold McVeigh, *CEO*
Robin McVeigh, *Vice Pres*
EMP: 40
SALES (est): 5.5MM **Privately Held**
WEB: www.komodopharmaceuticals.com
SIC: 2834 5122 Pharmaceutical preparations; pharmaceuticals

(G-4782)
SPECIALIZED SERVICES INC
514 S Main St (46040-1611)
PHONE..................................317 485-8561
EMP: 4 EST: 1996
SALES: 100K **Privately Held**
SIC: 1389 3559 Oil/Gas Field Services

(G-4783)
UNPLUG SOY CANDLES LLC
1360 E Broadway St Ste C (46040-9271)
PHONE..................................317 650-5776
EMP: 2
SALES (est): 62.5K **Privately Held**
SIC: 3999 Candles

Fountain City
Wayne County

(G-4784)
B2 MANUFACTURING LLC
606 Century Dr (47341-9440)
PHONE..................................765 993-4519
Brandon E Blanford, *Administration*
EMP: 2
SALES (est): 138.9K **Privately Held**
SIC: 3999 Manufacturing industries

(G-4785)
ERNEST HEIGHWAY
9347 N State Road 227 (47341-9727)
PHONE..................................765 847-2865
Ernest Heighway, *Owner*
EMP: 3
SALES (est): 201K **Privately Held**
SIC: 3523 Driers (farm): grain, hay & seed

(G-4786)
FOUNTAIN ACRES FOODS
1140 W Whitewater Rd (47341-9540)
PHONE..................................765 847-1897
Stevie Miller, *Owner*
Mary Ann Miller, *Co-Owner*
EMP: 15
SALES (est): 1.9MM **Privately Held**
SIC: 2051 Bakery: wholesale or wholesale/retail combined

(G-4787)
FOUNTAIN FOOD AND FUELING
402 Us Highway 27 N (47341-9409)
PHONE..................................765 847-5257
EMP: 2
SALES (est): 80.3K **Privately Held**
SIC: 2869 Fuels

Fountaintown
Shelby County

(G-4788)
ARK SOFTWARE LLC
8930 N Timberlane Dr (46130-9744)
PHONE..................................317 835-7912
Jay Robinson, *Principal*
EMP: 2
SALES (est): 109.8K **Privately Held**
SIC: 7372 Prepackaged software

(G-4789)
ASH-LIN INC
Also Called: Crates & Pallets
386 E Brookville Rd (46130-9631)
P.O. Box 49 (46130-0049)
PHONE..................................317 861-1540
James Lyddan, *President*
Patricia Lyddan, *Admin Sec*
EMP: 12
SQ FT: 14,500
SALES (est): 1MM **Privately Held**
SIC: 2448 2441 Pallets, wood; boxes, wood

(G-4790)
FOUNTAINTOWN FORGE INC
5513 S 100 E (46130-9441)
P.O. Box 139 (46130-0139)
PHONE..................................317 861-5403
Fax: 317 861-3704
John H Konzen, *CEO*
Jenny Gipson, *Vice Pres*
Jerry Hill, *Vice Pres*
Jeff Kornmann, *CFO*
EMP: 20 EST: 1967
SQ FT: 25,000
SALES (est): 6.9MM **Privately Held**
WEB: www.fountaintownforge.com
SIC: 3462 3463 Iron & steel forgings; machinery forgings, nonferrous

(G-4791)
HARVEST LAND CO-OP INC
1124 W Railroad St (46130-9456)
P.O. Box 73, Finly (46129)
PHONE..................................317 861-5080
Fax: 317 861-5844
Ray Kerkhof, *Manager*
EMP: 5
SALES (corp-wide): 301.4MM **Privately Held**
SIC: 5261 2875 Fertilizer; fertilizers, mixing only
PA: Harvest Land Co-Op, Inc.
1435 Nw 5th St
Richmond IN 47374
765 962-1527

(G-4792)
PATRIOT SAFETY PRODUCTS LLC
11299 N 650 W (46130-9725)
P.O. Box 100, Fairland (46126-0100)
PHONE..................................317 945-7023
Bryan Chastain,
EMP: 4 EST: 2014
SALES (est): 253.3K **Privately Held**
SIC: 3842 Personal safety equipment

(G-4793)
SOLUTIONS FOR PRINT LLC ✪
9530 N 100 W (46130-9780)
PHONE..................................812 584-2701
EMP: 2 EST: 2018
SALES (est): 83.9K **Privately Held**
SIC: 2752 Commercial printing, lithographic

Fowler
Benton County

(G-4794)
AUXILIUS HEAVY INDUSTRIES LLC
301 S Adeway (47944-8411)
P.O. Box 2054, West Lafayette (47996-2054)
PHONE..................................765 885-5099
Katherine Parker, *President*
Carlo Mendoza, *Exec VP*
Michael Parker, *Vice Pres*
EMP: 25 EST: 2015
SQ FT: 3,500
SALES: 4.9MM **Privately Held**
SIC: 3511 Turbines & turbine generator sets

(G-4795)
BENTON REVIEW NEWSPAPER
204 N Adams Ave (47944-1161)
P.O. Box 527 (47944-0527)
PHONE..................................765 884-1902
Fax: 765 884-8110

Karen Moyars, *Owner*
EMP: 4
SQ FT: 2,500
SALES (est): 120K **Privately Held**
SIC: 2711 Newspapers

(G-4796)
BP ALTERNATIVE ENERGY NA INC
91 S 100 E (47944-8201)
PHONE......................765 884-1000
Scott Tomtkins, *Principal*
EMP: 4
SALES (est): 369.7K
SALES (corp-wide): 240.2B **Privately Held**
SIC: 3523 Windmills for pumping water, agricultural
PA: Bp P.L.C.
　1 St. James's Square
　London SW1Y

(G-4797)
BP WIND ENERGY NORTH AMER INC
91 S 100 E (47944-8201)
PHONE......................765 884-1000
Scott Tomtkins, *Branch Mgr*
EMP: 4
SALES (corp-wide): 240.2B **Privately Held**
SIC: 2282 Throwing & winding mills
HQ: Bp Wind Energy North America Inc.
　700 Louisiana St Fl 33
　Houston TX 77002

(G-4798)
BROUILLETTE HEATING & COOLING
403 W 5th St (47944-1413)
PHONE......................765 884-0176
Victor Brouillette, *Owner*
EMP: 3
SALES (est): 261.2K **Privately Held**
SIC: 1711 3567 Warm air heating & air conditioning contractor; industrial furnaces & ovens

(G-4799)
FOWLER RIDGE II WIND FARM LLC
91 S 100 E (47944-8201)
PHONE......................713 354-2100
Matthew Sakurada,
EMP: 27
SALES (est): 3MM
SALES (corp-wide): 240.2B **Privately Held**
SIC: 3621 Windmills, electric generating
HQ: Bp Wind Energy North America Inc.
　700 Louisiana St Fl 33
　Houston TX 77002

(G-4800)
FOWLER RIDGE IV WIND FARM LLC ✪
2870 W State Road 18 (47944-8306)
PHONE......................765 884-1029
Ryan Logan, *Principal*
EMP: 3 **EST:** 2018
SALES (est): 137.5K **Privately Held**
SIC: 2448 Skids, wood

(G-4801)
HOLSCHER PRODUCTS INC
Also Called: Powder Coating/Holscher Pwdr
407 W Main St (47944-1071)
P.O. Box 247 (47944-0247)
PHONE......................765 884-8021
Fax: 765 884-8256
Joseph Holscher, *President*
Marilyn Holscher, *Corp Secy*
▲ **EMP:** 45
SQ FT: 75,000
SALES (est): 6.3MM **Privately Held**
SIC: 3479 Painting of metal products

(G-4802)
MID STATE WATER TREATMENT
1009 E 5th St (47944-1521)
PHONE......................765 884-1220
Lisa Cosby, *Owner*
Alessandra Potenza, *Assoc Editor*
EMP: 4

SALES (est): 198K **Privately Held**
SIC: 3589 Water treatment equipment, industrial

(G-4803)
OXFORD HOUSE INCORPORATED
606 W State Road 18 (47944-8300)
PHONE......................765 884-3265
Polet W Senesac, *President*
Polet Senesac, *President*
Sarah Pickett, *Info Tech Dir*
▲ **EMP:** 65
SQ FT: 34,000
SALES (est): 7.8MM **Privately Held**
SIC: 2591 5521 Blinds vertical; window shades; used car dealers

(G-4804)
POWELL SYSTEMS INC
Fowler Division
604 E 9th St (47944-1652)
P.O. Box 345 (47944-0345)
PHONE......................765 884-0613
Jay Davis, *Branch Mgr*
EMP: 7
SALES (corp-wide): 6MM **Privately Held**
WEB: www.powell-systems.com
SIC: 3444 3537 2448 3412 Sheet metal-work; skids, metal; pallets, metal; skids, wood; pallets, wood; metal barrels, drums & pails; metal cans; corrugated & solid fiber boxes
PA: Powell Systems, Inc.
　162 Churchill Hubbard Rd
　Youngstown OH
　330 759-9220

(G-4805)
POWELL SYSTEMS INC
83 S Meridian Rd (47944-8405)
P.O. Box 345 (47944-0345)
PHONE......................765 884-0980
Fax: 765 884-0308
Larry Fording, *Manager*
EMP: 35
SALES (corp-wide): 6MM **Privately Held**
WEB: www.powell-systems.com
SIC: 3537 3596 3565 3412 Skids, metal; pallets, metal; containers (metal), air cargo; scales & balances, except laboratory; packaging machinery; metal barrels, drums & pails; wood pallets & skids
PA: Powell Systems, Inc.
　162 Churchill Hubbard Rd
　Youngstown OH
　330 759-9220

(G-4806)
SHARYLS HAIR WITH FLARE
104 N Madison Ave (47944-1140)
PHONE......................765 885-5121
EMP: 2
SALES (est): 22.5K **Privately Held**
SIC: 7231 2899 Hairdressers; flares

(G-4807)
SLON INC (PA)
206 N Harrison Ave (47944-1032)
P.O. Box 67 (47944-0067)
PHONE......................765 884-1792
Fax: 765 884-0751
Darrell R Sloniger, *President*
Beverly Sloniger, *Corp Secy*
EMP: 12
SQ FT: 30,000
SALES (est): 1.8MM **Privately Held**
WEB: www.slon.com
SIC: 3281 3272 3271 Stone, quarrying & processing of own stone products; concrete products; concrete block & brick

Francesville
Pulaski County

(G-4808)
ADAPTASOFT INC
106 E Montgomery St (47946-8087)
P.O. Box 68, Monon (47959-0068)
PHONE......................219 567-2547
Fax: 219 567-2548
Timothy C Troxel, *President*
Joel Troxel, *CFO*

EMP: 17
SQ FT: 7,500
SALES (est): 1.2MM **Privately Held**
WEB: www.adaptasoft.com
SIC: 7372 Business oriented computer software

(G-4809)
CLEAR DECISION FILTRATION INC
4571 S 1450 W (47946-8215)
PHONE......................219 567-2008
Anthony Holliday, *President*
Melanie K Holliday, *Corp Secy*
Melanie Holliday, *Office Mgr*
EMP: 17
SQ FT: 4,000
SALES (est): 1.4MM **Privately Held**
SIC: 3569 Filters

(G-4810)
DISINGER MACHINE SHOP
4045 S 1450 W (47946)
P.O. Box 483 (47946-0483)
PHONE......................219 567-2357
Douglas R Disinger, *Owner*
EMP: 4
SALES (est): 342.4K **Privately Held**
SIC: 3599 Machine shop, jobbing & repair

(G-4811)
ELVIN L NUEST SALES AND SERVIC
420 S Bill St (47946-8073)
PHONE......................219 863-5216
Elvin L Nuest, *Owner*
EMP: 3
SALES (est): 192.7K **Privately Held**
SIC: 2875 Compost

(G-4812)
FRANCESVILLE VULCAN MATERIALS
14530 W 700 S (47946-8009)
PHONE......................219 567-9155
Kevin Cox, *President*
EMP: 29
SALES (est): 1.5MM **Privately Held**
SIC: 1422 Crushed & broken limestone

(G-4813)
FTC PRODUCTS CORP
Hwy 421 N One Half Mile (47946)
PHONE......................219 567-2441
Fax: 219 567-2442
Douglas Gutwein, *President*
Mary F Gutwein, *Corp Secy*
EMP: 5
SQ FT: 15,000
SALES: 1MM **Privately Held**
SIC: 3714 Motor vehicle wheels & parts

(G-4814)
LEGACY VULCAN LLC
Also Called: Midwest Division
14530 W 700 S (47946-8009)
PHONE......................219 567-9155
Todd Schultz, *Superintendent*
EMP: 18 **Publicly Held**
WEB: www.vulcanmaterials.com
SIC: 1442 Construction sand & gravel
HQ: Legacy Vulcan, Llc
　1200 Urban Center Dr
　Vestavia AL 35242
　205 298-3000

(G-4815)
SCHLATTERS INC
16179 W 500 S (47946-8636)
P.O. Box 548 (47946-0548)
PHONE......................219 567-9158
Fax: 219 567-9459
Ronald Schlatter, *President*
Jody Schlatter, *Vice Pres*
Nanci Schaltter, *Office Mgr*
EMP: 6
SQ FT: 12,960
SALES: 909.9K **Privately Held**
SIC: 3599 5082 5083 Machine shop, jobbing & repair; general construction machinery & equipment; agricultural machinery & equipment

Francisco
Gibson County

(G-4816)
HOMESTEAD PRIMITIVES INC
704 W School St (47649-9294)
PHONE......................812 782-3521
EMP: 2
SALES (est): 227.2K **Privately Held**
SIC: 2511 Wood household furniture

(G-4817)
PEABODY MIDWEST MINING LLC
Also Called: Francisco Mining
County Rd 850 E (47649)
PHONE......................812 782-3209
Kent Holcomb, *Manager*
EMP: 165
SALES (corp-wide): 5.1B **Publicly Held**
SIC: 1221 Bituminous coal surface mining
HQ: Peabody Midwest Mining Llc
　566 Dickeyville Rd
　Lynnville IN 47619

Frankfort
Clinton County

(G-4818)
ARCHER-DANIELS-MIDLAND COMPANY
Also Called: ADM
2906 S County Road 930 W (46041-7068)
PHONE......................765 523-3286
Fax: 765 523-3210
Jason Buck, *Manager*
EMP: 4
SALES (corp-wide): 60.8B **Publicly Held**
SIC: 2041 Flour & other grain mill products
PA: Archer-Daniels-Midland Company
　77 W Wacker Dr Ste 4600
　Chicago IL 60601
　312 634-8100

(G-4819)
BELL MACHINE COMPANY INC
Also Called: Bastell Perimeter Systems
1400 Magnolia Ave (46041-1028)
PHONE......................765 654-5225
Fax: 765 654-8755
Marshall Bell, *President*
Ron Bell, *Vice Pres*
Ronald Bell, *Benefits Mgr*
Brenda Bell, *Admin Sec*
▲ **EMP:** 10 **EST:** 1946
SQ FT: 5,400
SALES (est): 1.5MM **Privately Held**
WEB: www.basteel.com
SIC: 3544 Wire drawing & straightening dies

(G-4820)
C M WELDING INC
4496 N County Road 0 Ew (46041-7861)
PHONE......................765 258-4024
Don Estes, *Owner*
EMP: 2
SALES (est): 107.9K **Privately Held**
SIC: 7692 Welding repair

(G-4821)
CF GUNWORKS LLC
1157 S County Road 1000 E (46041-8949)
PHONE......................317 538-1122
Brandon Fouch,
Bradly Cline,
EMP: 2 **EST:** 2012
SALES (est): 195.2K **Privately Held**
SIC: 3484 Small arms; guns (firearms) or gun parts, 30 mm. & below; rifles or rifle parts, 30 mm. & below; shotguns or shotgun parts, 30 mm. & below

(G-4822)
CO-ALLIANCE LLP
Also Called: Impact
411b Eb Kellyb Rd (46041)
PHONE......................765 659-2596
Jack Barett, *Manager*
EMP: 6

▲ = Import ▼=Export
◆ =Import/Export

SALES (corp-wide): 483.3MM **Privately Held**
SIC: 2873 5191 Nitrogenous fertilizers; farm supplies
PA: Co-Alliance, Limited Liability Partnership
    5250 E Us Hwy 3
    Avon IN 46123
    317 745-4491

(G-4823)
CO-ALLIANCE LLP
6454 W Rte 28 (46041)
PHONE.................................765 659-3420
EMP: 8
SALES (corp-wide): 483.3MM **Privately Held**
SIC: 5191 5171 5153 2875 Feed; seeds: field, garden & flower; fertilizer & fertilizer materials; petroleum bulk stations & terminals; grains; fertilizers, mixing only
PA: Co-Alliance, Limited Liability Partnership
    5250 E Us Hwy 3
    Avon IN 46123
    317 745-4491

(G-4824)
COOMER & SONS SAWMILL & PALLET
184 Roy Scott Pkwy (46041-8757)
PHONE.................................765 659-2846
Fax: 765 654-7272
Charles Coomer, *Owner*
EMP: 60 EST: 1978
SALES (est): 2.7MM **Privately Held**
WEB: www.coomer.org
SIC: 2448 2421 Pallets, wood; sawmills & planing mills, general

(G-4825)
CTB INC
Brock Grain Systems
1750 W State Road 28 (46041-9146)
PHONE.................................765 654-8517
Doug Niemeyer, *President*
Blain Buttermore, *Manager*
EMP: 30
SALES (corp-wide): 242.1B **Publicly Held**
SIC: 3535 3523 Pneumatic tube conveyor systems; driers (farm): grain, hay & seed
HQ: Ctb, Inc.
    611 N Higbee St
    Milford IN 46542
    574 658-4191

(G-4826)
CTB MN INVESTMENT CO INC
Brock Grain Conditioning Group
1750 W State Road 28 (46041-9146)
PHONE.................................765 654-8517
Bill Crosby, *Manager*
EMP: 40
SALES (corp-wide): 242.1B **Publicly Held**
WEB: www.brockmfg.com
SIC: 3523 3535 Driers (farm): grain, hay & seed; pneumatic tube conveyor systems
HQ: Ctb Mn Investment Co., Inc.
    611 N Higbee St
    Milford IN 46542

(G-4827)
CUSTOM BUILDING PRODUCTS INC
3800 W State Road 28 (46041-8701)
PHONE.................................765 656-0234
Fax: 765 656-0235
Mike Bilek Sr, *Manager*
EMP: 80 **Privately Held**
WEB: www.custombuildingproducts.com
SIC: 5085 2899 2891 Adhesives, tape & plasters; chemical preparations; adhesives & sealants
HQ: Custom Building Products, Inc.
    7711 Center Ave Ste 500
    Huntington Beach CA 92647
    800 272-8786

(G-4828)
DONALDSON COMPANY INC
3260 W State Road 28 (46041-8721)
PHONE.................................765 659-4766
Fax: 765 659-4383
Rich Lewis, *Branch Mgr*

EMP: 300
SQ FT: 120,000
SALES (corp-wide): 2.3B **Publicly Held**
WEB: www.donaldson.com
SIC: 3714 3564 Cleaners, air, motor vehicle; blowers & fans
PA: Donaldson Company, Inc.
    1400 W 94th St
    Minneapolis MN 55431
    952 887-3131

(G-4829)
DSM COATING RESINS INC
3110 W State Road 28 (46041-8718)
PHONE.................................765 659-4721
Steven Dalton, *Branch Mgr*
EMP: 19
SALES (corp-wide): 10.1B **Privately Held**
WEB: www.neoresins.com
SIC: 3069 Floor coverings, rubber
HQ: Dsm Coating Resins, Inc
    1472 Columbia Nitrogen Dr
    Augusta GA 30901
    706 849-6000

(G-4830)
FEDERAL-MOGUL LLC
2845 W State Road 28 (46041-8779)
PHONE.................................765 659-7207
Fax: 765 659-7221
John Geis, *Engineer*
Chuck Hinshaw, *Branch Mgr*
EMP: 820
SQ FT: 175,000
SALES (corp-wide): 21.7B **Publicly Held**
SIC: 3714 Motor vehicle parts & accessories
HQ: Federal-Mogul Llc
    27300 W 11 Mile Rd # 101
    Southfield MI 48034

(G-4831)
FONTANA FASTENERS INC (DH)
Also Called: Lep Special Fasteners
3595 W State Road 28 (46041-6708)
PHONE.................................765 654-0477
Giuseppe Zichella, *CEO*
Jeffrey Goodman, *Purch Agent*
Ross Sharp, *Engineer*
Misty Cochran, *Sales Associate*
▲ EMP: 150
SQ FT: 250,000
SALES (est): 77.8MM **Privately Held**
SIC: 3452 Bolts, metal; screws, metal
HQ: Fontana America Incorporated
    6125 18 Mile Rd
    Sterling Heights MI 48314
    586 997-5600

(G-4832)
FOREST PRODUCTS GROUP INC
Also Called: Forest Products Group Ind Div
901 Blinn Ave (46041-1585)
PHONE.................................765 659-1807
C Marc Robinson, *VP Sales*
Jeff Reinke, *Branch Mgr*
EMP: 20
SQ FT: 1,000
SALES (corp-wide): 30.9MM **Privately Held**
WEB: www.componentstructures.com
SIC: 5031 2431 2426 2421 Lumber: rough, dressed & finished; millwork; hardwood dimension & flooring mills; sawmills & planing mills, general
PA: The Forest Products Group Inc
    1033 Dublin Rd
    Columbus OH 43215
    937 778-0272

(G-4833)
FRANKFORT NEWSPAPER
251 E Clinton St (46041-1906)
PHONE.................................859 254-2385
Jay Frizzo, *Principal*
EMP: 3
SALES (est): 84.3K **Privately Held**
SIC: 2711 Newspapers

(G-4834)
FRITO-LAY NORTH AMERICA INC
323 S County Road 300 W (46041-8780)
PHONE.................................765 659-1831
Fax: 765 654-6610

Liberty Kallner, *Engineer*
Frank Armetta, *Manager*
Daniel Dehn, *Manager*
Brede Evans, *Manager*
EMP: 500
SALES (corp-wide): 63.5B **Publicly Held**
WEB: www.fritolay.com
SIC: 2096 2099 2032 Potato chips & similar snacks; food preparations; canned specialties
HQ: Frito-Lay North America, Inc.
    7701 Legacy Dr
    Plano TX 75024

(G-4835)
FRITO-LAY NORTH AMERICA INC
2611 W County Road 0 Ns (46041-8703)
PHONE.................................765 659-4517
Richard Crick, *Project Mgr*
EMP: 20
SALES (corp-wide): 63.5B **Publicly Held**
WEB: www.fritolay.com
SIC: 2096 2099 Potato chips & similar snacks; food preparations
HQ: Frito-Lay North America, Inc.
    7701 Legacy Dr
    Plano TX 75024

(G-4836)
HI TECH LABEL INC
357 E Washington St (46041-1946)
P.O. Box 765 (46041-0765)
PHONE.................................765 659-1800
Fax: 765 659-1850
Dan W Scott, *President*
Pat Scott, *Vice Pres*
James Elliott, *Mktg Dir*
EMP: 11
SQ FT: 10,000
SALES (est): 1.5MM **Privately Held**
WEB: www.hitechlabel.com
SIC: 2679 2759 2672 Labels, paper: made from purchased material; commercial printing; coated & laminated paper

(G-4837)
INDIANA SKYDIVING CENTER
Also Called: Skydive Indianapolis
3009 W State Road 28 (46041-8712)
P.O. Box 663, Carmel (46082-0663)
PHONE.................................765 659-5557
Bob Dougherty, *President*
EMP: 24
SQ FT: 36,000
SALES (est): 1.2MM **Privately Held**
SIC: 2399 Parachutes

(G-4838)
IRVING MATERIALS INC
28 Lewis Smith Rd (46041)
PHONE.................................765 654-5333
Fax: 765 654-4899
Ron Knowles, *Manager*
EMP: 10
SALES (corp-wide): 800.6MM **Privately Held**
SIC: 3273 Ready-mixed concrete
PA: Irving Materials, Inc.
    8032 N State Road 9
    Greenfield IN 46140
    317 326-3101

(G-4839)
KASPAR BROADCASTING CO INC (PA)
Also Called: Wilo AM & Wshw FM
1401 W Barner St 3 (46041-1506)
P.O. Box 545 (46041-0545)
PHONE.................................765 659-3338
Fax: 765 654-3484
Vernon J Kaspar, *President*
Russell B Kaspar, *Vice Pres*
Russ Kaspar, *Manager*
EMP: 20
SQ FT: 5,500
SALES (est): 4.3MM **Privately Held**
SIC: 4832 2711 Radio broadcasting stations; newspapers

(G-4840)
KAY COMPANY INC
Also Called: Kayco
509 W Barner St (46041-1606)
P.O. Box 429 (46041-0429)
PHONE.................................765 659-3388

Michael S Kay, *President*
EMP: 41
SQ FT: 150,000
SALES (est): 5.3MM **Privately Held**
SIC: 3993 2493 5031 Displays & cutouts, window & lobby; fiberboard, other vegetable pulp; particleboard

(G-4841)
MIDWEST CNSTR COMPONENTS
1729 W State Road 28 (46041-9147)
PHONE.................................765 654-8719
Fax: 765 654-8905
James A Andrew, *President*
George M Palmer III, *Vice Pres*
Ronald Reagan, *Treasurer*
EMP: 6
SQ FT: 10,000
SALES (est): 1.4MM **Privately Held**
WEB: www.midwestcci.com
SIC: 2426 Dimension, hardwood

(G-4842)
NATIONAL CIGAR CORPORATION (PA)
407 N Main St (46041-1729)
PHONE.................................765 659-3326
Fax: 765 654-6932
James K Pogue, *President*
Glenda Baker, *Corp Secy*
Kenneth Wolf, *Vice Pres*
Helen Brandstetter, *Treasurer*
Carl G Berger Jr, *VP Sales*
▼ EMP: 38
SQ FT: 100,000
SALES (est): 614.3K **Privately Held**
WEB: www.broadleafcigars.com
SIC: 0132 2121 Tobacco; cigars

(G-4843)
NEW AGE EQUIPMENT INC
Also Called: Miller Machine Works
3309 Washington Ave (46041-8216)
PHONE.................................765 659-1524
Jeff Kraft, *President*
EMP: 6 EST: 1988
SALES (est): 650.3K **Privately Held**
SIC: 3599 Machine shop, jobbing & repair

(G-4844)
NHK SEATING OF AMERICA INC (DH)
2298 W State Road 28 (46041-9185)
PHONE.................................765 659-4781
Tatsuro Ono, *President*
Dean Hill, *Plant Engr*
Jim Jarrett, *Finance*
Osamu Nakamura, *Manager*
Jim Phillips, *Manager*
▲ EMP: 25
SQ FT: 80,000
SALES (est): 9.4MM
SALES (corp-wide): 6.1B **Privately Held**
WEB: www.nhkseating.com
SIC: 2531 Seats, automobile

(G-4845)
NORTHSIDE MACHINE & TOOL INC
1604 N County Road 0 Ew (46041-7804)
PHONE.................................765 654-4538
Dan Stokes, *President*
EMP: 12
SALES: 500K **Privately Held**
SIC: 3544 3599 5031 Special dies & tools; machine shop, jobbing & repair; lumber: rough, dressed & finished

(G-4846)
NTK PRECISION AXLE CORPORATION
741 S County Road 200 W (46041-8704)
PHONE.................................765 656-1000
Tadao Okamura, *President*
Takashi Tanaka, *Vice Pres*
Jason Smith, *Plant Mgr*
Nick Laughner, *Facilities Mgr*
Patrick Abbott, *Production*
▲ EMP: 252
SQ FT: 200,000

GEOGRAPHIC

SALES (est): 51.6MM
SALES (corp-wide): 6.9B **Privately Held**
WEB: www.ntn.co.jp
SIC: 3312 Axles, rolled or forged; made in steel mills
PA: Ntn Corporation
1-3-17, Kyomachibori, Nishi-Ku
Osaka OSK 550-0
664 435-001

(G-4847)
OSTLER ENTERPRISES INC
Also Called: Landscape Products
1624 W Armstrong Rd (46041-8272)
PHONE....................................765 656-1275
Gary G Ostler, *President*
Gary Ostler, *President*
Melissa Ostler, *Admin Sec*
EMP: 7 EST: 1997
SALES (est): 1.5MM **Privately Held**
SIC: 2499 2875 Mulch, wood & bark; potting soil, mixed

(G-4848)
P & H LLC
309 Harvard Ter (46041-3144)
PHONE....................................765 654-5291
Ed R Pluhar,
Dean Huddleston,
EMP: 2
SALES (est): 184.6K **Privately Held**
SIC: 3471 Sand blasting of metal parts

(G-4849)
PADDACK BROTHERS INC
Also Called: Country Estate Mobile Home Pk
4410 W Old State Road 28 (46041-7245)
PHONE....................................765 659-4777
Fax: 765 659-4779
Jack W Paddack, *President*
Lynn A Paddack, *Admin Sec*
EMP: 15 EST: 1957
SQ FT: 3,400
SALES: 1.5MM **Privately Held**
SIC: 4212 1442 6515 Local trucking, without storage; gravel mining; mobile home site operators

(G-4850)
PEPSI BOTTLING VENTURES LLC
Also Called: Pepsi-Cola
2611 W County Road 0 Ns (46041-8751)
PHONE....................................765 659-7313
Randy Haggard, *Branch Mgr*
EMP: 66
SALES (corp-wide): 76.5MM **Privately Held**
SIC: 2086 Soft drinks: packaged in cans, bottles, etc.; carbonated soft drinks, bottled & canned
HQ: Pepsi Bottling Ventures Llc
4141 Parklake Ave Ste 600
Raleigh NC 27612
919 865-2300

(G-4851)
PRO-TECH TOOL & ENGINEERING
890 E County Road 600 N (46041-7613)
PHONE....................................765 258-3613
Kevin Wilhelm, *Owner*
EMP: 7
SQ FT: 11,000
SALES (est): 1.2MM **Privately Held**
SIC: 5084 5051 3465 Tool & die makers' equipment; stampings, metal; automotive stampings

(G-4852)
PURINA ANIMAL NUTRITION LLC
2472 W State Road 28 (46041-8773)
PHONE....................................765 659-4791
Troy Smith, *Manager*
EMP: 34
SALES (corp-wide): 12.8B **Privately Held**
WEB: www.landolakesidd.com
SIC: 2048 Prepared feeds
HQ: Purina Animal Nutrition Llc
1080 County Road F W
Shoreview MN 55126

(G-4853)
SMITH BUSINESS SUPPLY INC
Also Called: Express Print
358 N Columbia St (46041-1600)
PHONE....................................765 654-4442
Fax: 765 654-4485
Eric Smith, *President*
EMP: 4
SQ FT: 2,700
SALES: 400K **Privately Held**
WEB: www.expressprint.com
SIC: 2752 Commercial printing, offset

(G-4854)
SUN CHEMICAL CORPORATION
General Printing Ink
2642 W State Road 28 (46041-8774)
PHONE....................................765 659-6000
Fax: 765 659-2733
Tom Butera, *Opers-Prdtn-Mfg*
Jeff Shirar, *Maintence Staff*
EMP: 80
SALES (corp-wide): 7B **Privately Held**
WEB: www.sunchemical.com
SIC: 2893 Printing ink
HQ: Sun Chemical Corporation
35 Waterview Blvd Ste 100
Parsippany NJ 07054
973 404-6000

(G-4855)
TECH GROUP NORTH AMERICA INC
2810 W State Road 28 (46041-9197)
PHONE....................................765 650-2300
Fax: 765 650-2301
Robert Hargesheimer, *President*
EMP: 150
SALES (corp-wide): 1.6B **Publicly Held**
SIC: 3089 Injection molding of plastics
HQ: Tech Group North America, Inc.
14677 N 74th St
Scottsdale AZ 85260
480 281-4500

(G-4856)
TIMES
Also Called: Paxton Media Group
211 N Jackson St (46041-1936)
PHONE....................................765 296-3622
Fax: 765 654-7031
David Paxton, *President*
Jay Frizzo, *COO*
Richard Welch, *Vice Pres*
David Mathis, *Treasurer*
Karen Turner, *Admin Sec*
EMP: 45
SQ FT: 17,000
SALES: 1.5MM
SALES (corp-wide): 318.6MM **Privately Held**
WEB: www.ftimes.com
SIC: 2711 4841 2791 2752 Newspapers, publishing & printing; cable television services; typesetting; commercial printing, lithographic
PA: Paxton Media Group, Llc
100 Television Ln
Paducah KY 42003
270 575-8630

(G-4857)
TORDILLERIA DEL VALLE
905 Walnut Ave (46041-1847)
PHONE....................................765 654-9590
Alphonso Ruic, *Owner*
EMP: 3
SALES (est): 204K **Privately Held**
SIC: 2099 Tortillas, fresh or refrigerated

(G-4858)
VICKSMETAL ARMCO ASSOCIATES (PA)
150 S County Road 300 W (46041-8765)
PHONE....................................765 659-5555
Fax: 765 659-5500
Henery Kato, *Partner*
Adriane Lohsl, *Administration*
EMP: 40
SQ FT: 64,000
SALES (est): 9.8MM **Privately Held**
WEB: www.vicksmetal.com
SIC: 7389 3312 Metal slitting & shearing; blast furnaces & steel mills

(G-4859)
WABASH NATIONAL CORPORATION
901 W Morrison St (46041-1603)
PHONE....................................765 659-3856
EMP: 171
SALES (corp-wide): 1.7B **Publicly Held**
SIC: 3715 Truck trailers
PA: Wabash National Corporation
1000 Sagamore Pkwy S
Lafayette IN 47905
765 771-5300

(G-4860)
WINSKI BROTHERS INC
751 W Washington St (46041-1895)
PHONE....................................765 654-5323
Fax: 765 654-0366
Sherman Winski, *President*
Joel Stiller, *Vice Pres*
EMP: 15 EST: 1937
SQ FT: 10,000
SALES: 4.5MM **Privately Held**
SIC: 5093 5051 4953 3341 Metal scrap & waste materials; steel; hazardous waste collection & disposal; secondary nonferrous metals

(G-4861)
ZACHARY CONFECTIONS INC
2130 W State Road 28 (46041-8771)
P.O. Box 219 (46041-0219)
PHONE....................................765 659-4751
Fax: 765 659-1491
John J Zachary Jr, *Ch of Bd*
John J Zachary III, *President*
George Anichini, *Senior VP*
Josh Jakes, *QC Mgr*
Patrick R Kelly, *CFO*
▲ EMP: 220
SQ FT: 300,000
SALES (est): 27.5MM **Privately Held**
WEB: www.zacharyconfections.com
SIC: 2064 Candy & other confectionery products

Franklin
Johnson County

(G-4862)
AGRI-TRONIX CORP
Also Called: Pro Traument Scale
2001 N Morton St (46131-9628)
PHONE....................................317 738-4474
Fax: 317 738-9877
Terry L Clarkson, *President*
Jim Beswick, *Vice Pres*
Brian Nix, *Mfg Mgr*
Stan Hancock, *Cust Mgr*
EMP: 12
SQ FT: 10,000
SALES (est): 2.5MM **Privately Held**
WEB: www.agri-tronix.com
SIC: 3823 7629 Computer interface equipment for industrial process control; electrical equipment repair services

(G-4863)
AIM MEDIA INDIANA OPER LLC
Daily Journal
30 S Water St Ste A (46131-2316)
P.O. Box 699 (46131-0699)
PHONE....................................317 736-7101
Fax: 317 736-2759
J Fred Mattingly, *Adv Dir*
Chris Cosner, *Branch Mgr*
EMP: 26
SALES (corp-wide): 42.4MM **Privately Held**
WEB: www.hjnews.com
SIC: 7313 2752 2711 Newspaper advertising representative; commercial printing, lithographic; newspapers, publishing & printing
PA: Aim Media Indiana Operating, Llc
2980 N National Rd A
Columbus IN 47201
812 372-7811

(G-4864)
AIM MEDIA INDIANA OPER LLC
South Magazine
30 S Water St Ste A (46131-2316)
P.O. Box 699 (46131-0699)
PHONE....................................812 736-7101
Chris Cosner, *Branch Mgr*
EMP: 2
SALES (corp-wide): 42.4MM **Privately Held**
SIC: 2711 Commercial printing & newspaper publishing combined
PA: Aim Media Indiana Operating, Llc
2980 N National Rd A
Columbus IN 47201
812 372-7811

(G-4865)
AIRTOMIC REPAIR STATION
Also Called: Sargent Controls & Aerospace
215 Industrial Dr (46131-9609)
PHONE....................................317 738-0148
Roger Green, *Principal*
Kyle Tourtellot, *Supervisor*
EMP: 2
SALES (est): 200.3K **Privately Held**
SIC: 3724 Aircraft engines & engine parts

(G-4866)
AK TUBE LLC
1001 Hurricane St (46131-1550)
PHONE....................................317 736-8888
EMP: 5
SALES (est): 446.2K **Privately Held**
SIC: 3317 Steel pipe & tubes

(G-4867)
AMCOR RIGID PLASTICS USA LLC
Also Called: Schmalbach-Lubeca
3201 Bearing Dr (46131-7415)
PHONE....................................317 736-4313
Tom Balk, *Branch Mgr*
EMP: 89
SALES (corp-wide): 9.1B **Privately Held**
WEB: www.slpcamericas.com
SIC: 3089 Plastic containers, except foam
HQ: Amcor Rigid Plastics Usa, Llc
935 Technology Dr Ste 100
Ann Arbor MI 48108

(G-4868)
ANNUAL REPORTS INC
Also Called: Annual Reports Services
1250 Park Ave (46131-8868)
P.O. Box 607 (46131-0607)
PHONE....................................317 736-8838
Fax: 317 736-8483
Christopher Doyle, *President*
Jay P Doyle, *Chairman*
Cynthia Doyle, *Vice Pres*
Gloria L Doyle, *Vice Pres*
Chris Doyle, *Manager*
EMP: 50
SQ FT: 1,600
SALES (est): 3.4MM **Privately Held**
WEB: www.annualreportsinc.com
SIC: 7336 8743 2791 Art design services; public relations services; typesetting, computer controlled

(G-4869)
AVBORNE ACCESSORY GROUP INC
Airtomic
215 Industrial Dr (46131-9609)
PHONE....................................317 738-0148
Michael Mislan, *Branch Mgr*
EMP: 30
SALES (corp-wide): 674.9MM **Publicly Held**
WEB: www.doverddi.com
SIC: 3724 Aircraft engines & engine parts
HQ: Avborne Accessory Group, Inc.
7500 Nw 26th St
Miami FL 33122

(G-4870)
B C C PRODUCTS INC
Also Called: Ultimate Bowling Products
2140 Earlywood Dr (46131-8870)
P.O. Box 327 (46131-0327)
PHONE....................................317 494-6420
Fax: 317 736-4872
Roger Brunette Sr, *CEO*

Roger Brunette Jr, *President*
Pauline Brunette, *Treasurer*
Catherine Brunette, *Admin Sec*
▼ **EMP:** 14 **EST:** 1974
SQ FT: 25,000
SALES (est): 4.3MM **Privately Held**
WEB: www.bccproducts.com
SIC: 3087 2851 2821 Custom compound
purchased resins; paints & allied prod-
ucts; plastics materials & resins

(G-4871)
BALL INC
1900 Commerce Pkwy (46131-6965)
PHONE....................................317 736-8236
Frank Brown, *Principal*
EMP: 13 **Privately Held**
SIC: 3411 Metal cans
HQ: Ball Inc.
4201 Congress St Ste 340
Charlotte NC 28209
704 551-1500

(G-4872)
BEST TIRES & WHEELS
320 N Morton St (46131-1648)
PHONE....................................317 306-3379
Colleen McKinnel, *Principal*
EMP: 2 **EST:** 2011
SALES (est): 183.6K **Privately Held**
SIC: 3312 Wheels

(G-4873)
BROADWAVE TECHNOLOGIES
INC
2900 N Graham Rd Ste B (46131-7038)
PHONE....................................317 346-6101
Michael Trulock, *Exec VP*
EMP: 2
SALES (est): 90K **Privately Held**
SIC: 3679 Electronic components

(G-4874)
C L HOLDINGS LLC
Also Called: Pro Industies
1441 Amy Ln (46131-1491)
PHONE....................................317 736-4414
Fax: 317 736-4416
Chris Lynch, *Mng Member*
Shawn Taylor, *Mng Member*
EMP: 8
SALES: 1.3MM **Privately Held**
WEB: www.proindustries.com
SIC: 3949 Exercise equipment; dumbbells
& other weightlifting equipment

(G-4875)
CATERPILLAR REMN POWRTRN
INDNA (HQ)
751 International Dr (46131-9637)
PHONE....................................317 738-2117
James W Owens, *CEO*
John Trueblood, *QC Mgr*
Scott Land, *Director*
▲ **EMP:** 298
SQ FT: 115,000
SALES (est): 63.3MM
SALES (corp-wide): 45.4B **Publicly Held**
SIC: 3714 Rebuilding engines & transmis-
sions, factory basis; motor vehicle en-
gines & parts
PA: Caterpillar Inc.
510 Lake Cook Rd Ste 100
Deerfield IL 60015
224 551-4000

(G-4876)
CLASSIQUE HAIR STYLE
50 S Water St (46131-2316)
PHONE....................................317 738-2104
Sandy Brown, *Partner*
Gloria Crofts, *Partner*
Pam Service, *Partner*
EMP: 8
SALES (est): 134.9K **Privately Held**
SIC: 7231 2844 Unisex hair salons; sham-
poos, rinses, conditioners: hair

(G-4877)
CORPORATE SHIRTS DIRECT
INC
2141 Holiday Ln (46131-2600)
PHONE....................................317 474-6033
Matthew McCall, *Principal*
EMP: 3

SALES (est): 332.2K **Privately Held**
SIC: 2395 Embroidery & art needlework

(G-4878)
COUNTERTOP CONNECTIONS
INC
3042 Hudson St (46131-7203)
PHONE....................................317 822-9858
Rocky Caudill, *Owner*
EMP: 9
SQ FT: 3,600
SALES (est): 620K **Privately Held**
WEB: www.countertopconnection.com
SIC: 2434 2541 Wood kitchen cabinets;
table or counter tops, plastic laminated

(G-4879)
COUNTERTOPS & MORE
500 International Dr (46131-9627)
PHONE....................................317 346-0111
Chuck Hardin, *Owner*
EMP: 2
SALES (est): 206.7K **Privately Held**
SIC: 2434 Wood kitchen cabinets

(G-4880)
CREATIVE COMPUTER
SERVICES
4223 S Shelby 750 W (46131-9205)
PHONE....................................317 729-5779
Sharon Romine-West, *President*
James West, *Manager*
EMP: 6
SALES (est): 400K **Privately Held**
SIC: 7389 2752 Mapmaking services;
maps, lithographed

(G-4881)
DIRECT CONVEYORS LLC
551 Earlywood Dr (46131-9712)
PHONE....................................317 346-7777
Akshay Patwardhan, *Design Engr*
Ron Wood,
▲ **EMP:** 18
SALES: 3MM **Privately Held**
WEB: www.directconveyors.com
SIC: 3535 Conveyors & conveying equip-
ment

(G-4882)
DUALTECH INC
Also Called: Innovative Casting Tech
450 Blue Chip Ct (46131-8825)
P.O. Box 476 (46131-0476)
PHONE....................................317 738-9043
Jack Laugle, *President*
Brian York, *Prdtn Mgr*
Sandy Laugle, *Admin Sec*
Jason Best,
EMP: 25
SQ FT: 10,000
SALES (est): 5.5MM **Privately Held**
WEB: www.dualtech.com
SIC: 3365 Aluminum foundries

(G-4883)
ELECTRO-SPEC INC
1800 Commerce Pkwy (46131-6964)
PHONE....................................317 738-9199
Fax: 317 738-9491
Jeffrey D Smith, *President*
Michele Brasseur, *Purchasing*
Nathan Davis, *Technical Mgr*
David Torok, *Engineer*
Jeffrey Smith, *CFO*
EMP: 85
SQ FT: 20,500
SALES (est): 12.1MM **Privately Held**
WEB: www.electro-spec.com
SIC: 3471 Electroplating of metals or
formed products; gold plating

(G-4884)
ESCO TECHNOLOGIES INC
690 S State St (46131-2553)
PHONE....................................317 346-0393
EMP: 3
SALES (corp-wide): 685.7MM **Publicly**
Held
SIC: 3569 Filters
PA: Esco Technologies Inc.
9900 Clayton Rd Ste A
Saint Louis MO 63124
314 213-7200

(G-4885)
ESSEX GROUP INC
Also Called: Superioir Essex
3200 Essex Dr (46131-9669)
PHONE....................................317 738-4365
Fax: 317 738-7750
Cindy Lara, *Purch Agent*
Dave Mackerel, *Branch Mgr*
EMP: 38
SALES (corp-wide): 105.4MM **Privately**
Held
WEB: www.essexwire.com
SIC: 3357 Magnet wire, nonferrous
HQ: Essex Group, Inc.
1601 Wall St
Fort Wayne IN 46802
260 461-4000

(G-4886)
FAULKENBERG PRINTING CO
INC
1670 Amy Ln (46131-1562)
PHONE....................................317 638-1359
Fax: 317 638-1375
Thomas L Faulkenberg, *President*
James Eugene Faulkenberg, *President*
Brad Rund, *Vice Pres*
Brian Butler, *Info Tech Dir*
EMP: 17 **EST:** 1948
SQ FT: 5,300
SALES: 1.7MM **Privately Held**
WEB: www.faulkenberg.net
SIC: 2752 2789 2759 Commercial print-
ing, offset; bookbinding & related work;
commercial printing

(G-4887)
FRANKS WOOD SHOP
3170 Compass Dr (46131-9807)
PHONE....................................317 738-2039
James Bullock, *Principal*
EMP: 2
SALES (est): 128.6K **Privately Held**
SIC: 2541 Store fixtures, wood

(G-4888)
G & H WIRE COMPANY INC
Also Called: G&H Orthodontics
2165 Earlywood Dr (46131-8879)
PHONE....................................317 346-6655
Kevin McNulty, *President*
Angel Hahn, *Asst Controller*
EMP: 75
SALES (est): 37MM **Privately Held**
SIC: 3843 Dental equipment & supplies

(G-4889)
GLOBAL
600 Ironwood Dr Ste N (46131-8324)
PHONE....................................317 494-6174
Ken Smith, *Principal*
▲ **EMP:** 2
SALES (est): 213.5K **Privately Held**
SIC: 5051 5021 3365 2522 Miscella-
neous nonferrous products; office & pub-
lic building furniture; aluminum foundries;
office furniture, except wood

(G-4890)
GMI CORPORATION
700 International Dr (46131-9733)
PHONE....................................317 736-5116
Fax: 317 736-5125
Fred McWilliams, *President*
Loraine Mc Williams, *Treasurer*
EMP: 65
SQ FT: 68,000
SALES: 12MM **Privately Held**
WEB: www.greenwoodmachine.com
SIC: 3599 Machine shop, jobbing & repair

(G-4891)
GOOD SIGNS
368 S Main St Ste 1 (46131-2414)
PHONE....................................317 738-4663
Fax: 317 738-4663
Jim Crocker, *Owner*
EMP: 5
SQ FT: 1,400
SALES (est): 240K **Privately Held**
SIC: 3993 Signs & advertising specialties

(G-4892)
GRAHAMS WRECKER SERVICE
INC
Also Called: Generations Collision Services
159 W Monroe St (46131-2250)
PHONE....................................317 736-4355
Fax: 317 736-8479
Mark E Graham, *President*
Carole Graham, *Vice Pres*
EMP: 6
SQ FT: 5,200
SALES (est): 860.9K **Privately Held**
WEB: www.grahamwreckerservice.com
SIC: 3713 7549 Automobile wrecker truck
bodies; towing service, automotive

(G-4893)
GRAYSON THERMAL SYSTEMS
CORP
980 Hurricane Rd (46131-9501)
PHONE....................................317 739-3290
Helene Cornils, *CEO*
EMP: 250
SALES (est): 13.2MM
SALES (corp-wide): 35.7MM **Privately**
Held
SIC: 3585 7699 Heating & air conditioning
combination units; thermostat repair
PA: Grayson Automotive Services Limited
Wharfdale House
Birmingham W MIDLANDS B11 2
121 700-5600

(G-4894)
HAGEMIER PRODUCTS
6181 S 550 E (46131-8001)
PHONE....................................812 526-0377
Fax: 812 526-2202
Carolyn Hagemier, *Owner*
EMP: 9
SALES (est): 410K **Privately Held**
SIC: 2448 Pallets, wood

(G-4895)
HOBSON TOOL AND MACHINE
CO
3061 N Morton St (46131-9662)
PHONE....................................317 736-4203
Earl Hobson, *President*
EMP: 10
SALES (est): 1.7MM **Privately Held**
SIC: 3812 Acceleration indicators & sys-
tems components, aerospace

(G-4896)
HOLBROOK MANUFACTURING
INC
291 Province St (46131-1453)
P.O. Box 95 (46131-0095)
PHONE....................................317 736-9387
Fax: 317 736-4395
Avis M Holbrook, *President*
Randy Henson, *General Mgr*
Kenny Thompson, *Managing Dir*
Gabriele Clark, *Business Mgr*
Toni Devore, *Sales Staff*
EMP: 30
SQ FT: 16,400
SALES (est): 5.9MM **Privately Held**
WEB: www.holbrookmfg.com
SIC: 3444 3599 Sheet metalwork; ma-
chine shop, jobbing & repair

(G-4897)
HONEY AND ME
2908 N Graham Rd A (46131-9652)
PHONE....................................317 668-3924
Tonya Pumey, *Principal*
▲ **EMP:** 5
SALES (est): 289.3K **Privately Held**
SIC: 5092 3944 Arts & crafts equipment &
supplies; games, toys & children's vehi-
cles

(G-4898)
IBC US HOLDINGS INC
Also Called: IBC Advanced Alloys
401 Arvin Rd (46131-1549)
PHONE....................................317 738-2558
Mark Wolma, *President*
David Anderson, *Treasurer*
Simon John Anderson, *Director*
Anthony Dutton, *Director*
▲ **EMP:** 7

GEOGRAPHIC

SALES (est): 480.2K Privately Held
SIC: 3325 Steel foundries

(G-4899)
INDIANA SECTION OF PGA OF AMER
2625 Hurricane Rd (46131-7642)
P.O. Box 516 (46131-0516)
PHONE.....................................317 738-9696
Fax: 317 738-9436
Mike David, *Principal*
Keith Clark,
EMP: 2
SALES: 967.4K Privately Held
SIC: 3949 Shafts, golf club

(G-4900)
INDY TUBE FABRICATION LLC
398 Cincinnati St (46131-1415)
P.O. Box 98 (46131-0098)
PHONE.....................................317 883-2000
Brian Russle, *Owner*
EMP: 4
SQ FT: 1,290
SALES (est): 67.7K Privately Held
SIC: 3498 Tube fabricating (contract bending & shaping)

(G-4901)
INNOVATIVE 3D MFG LLC
600 International Dr (46131-9756)
PHONE.....................................317 560-5080
Matthew Egenolf,
EMP: 3
SALES (est): 143.7K Privately Held
SIC: 3599 3499 Machine & other job shop work; friction material, made from powdered metal

(G-4902)
J D PETRO AND ASSOCIATES INC
40 W Court St Ste B (46131-2373)
PHONE.....................................317 736-6566
Fax: 317 736-9120
Jerry D Petro, *President*
Faye E Petro, *Admin Sec*
EMP: 5
SALES: 750K Privately Held
SIC: 2851 Paints & allied products

(G-4903)
KYB AMERICAS CORPORATION (HQ)
2625 N Morton St (46131-8820)
PHONE.....................................317 736-7774
Hiroaki Hirayama, *President*
A Tanaka, *President*
Wade Cunningham, *General Mgr*
Sal Milioto, *General Mgr*
Dan Pierson, *General Mgr*
▲ EMP: 492
SQ FT: 185,000
SALES (est): 187.5MM
SALES (corp-wide): 3.6B Privately Held
WEB: www.kmna-kyb.com
SIC: 3714 8711 Shock absorbers, motor vehicle; engineering services
PA: Kyb Corporation
2-4-1, Hamamatsucho
Minato-Ku TKY 105-0
334 353-511

(G-4904)
KYLE MACHINE & TOOL INC
5228 E 300 S (46131-8131)
PHONE.....................................317 736-4743
Maurice Kyle, *President*
Sue Kyle, *Corp Secy*
EMP: 3
SALES: 160K Privately Held
SIC: 3089 Molding primary plastic

(G-4905)
MCGINN TOOL & ENGINEERING CO
1001 Yandes St (46131-1468)
PHONE.....................................317 736-5512
Fax: 317 736-5608
Joseph L Hudson, *President*
Jacqueline Hudson, *Corp Secy*
Joseph Alt, *Vice Pres*
EMP: 10
SQ FT: 5,200

SALES: 430K Privately Held
SIC: 3544 7692 Special dies & tools; forms (molds), for foundry & plastics working machinery; welding repair

(G-4906)
MEADORS & ASSOC INC
203 Earlywood Dr (46131-9625)
PHONE.....................................317 736-6944
Fax: 317 736-6787
Ed Meadors, *Owner*
EMP: 3
SALES (est): 261.3K Privately Held
SIC: 2439 Trusses, wooden roof

(G-4907)
MICROWAVE DEVICES INC
240 N Forsythe St (46131-1534)
PHONE.....................................317 736-8833
Fax: 317 736-8382
David Mann, *President*
Saralee Mann, *Treasurer*
EMP: 7
SQ FT: 3,000
SALES (est): 1.2MM Privately Held
WEB: www.mwdevices.com
SIC: 3679 3663 Microwave components; radio & TV communications equipment

(G-4908)
MIDSTATE MANUFACTURING CORP
3250 N Graham Rd (46131-8813)
PHONE.....................................317 738-0094
Fax: 317 738-0093
Paul Ambrose, *President*
Jamie Ambrose, *Vice Pres*
EMP: 10
SQ FT: 20,000
SALES (est): 880K Privately Held
SIC: 3599 Custom machinery

(G-4909)
MILLER CHEMICAL TECH & MGT INC
Also Called: Miller Chemical Tech & MGT
980 Hurricane Rd Ste B (46131-9501)
PHONE.....................................317 560-5437
Anthony McCullough, *President*
Michael McCullough, *Vice Pres*
Patricia McCullough, *Admin Sec*
EMP: 7
SALES (est): 1.8MM Privately Held
SIC: 2899 Chemical preparations

(G-4910)
MITSUBISHI HEAVY INDUSTRIES
Also Called: Mhia
1200 N Mitsubishi Pkwy (46131-7560)
PHONE.....................................714 960-3785
Yas Yamata, *Principal*
Mario Santos, *Engineer*
Carl Moore, *Finance Dir*
Joe Dutchinson, *Branch Mgr*
Jeff Trower, *Manager*
EMP: 40
SALES (corp-wide): 38.5B Privately Held
WEB: www.mitsubishicc.net
SIC: 5084 3585 7539 5075 Industrial machinery & equipment; refrigeration & heating equipment; automotive air conditioning repair; warm air heating & air conditioning
HQ: Mitsubishi Heavy Industries Climate Control, Inc.
1200 N Mitsubishi Pkwy
Franklin IN 46131

(G-4911)
MITSUBISHI HEAVY INDUSTRIES (HQ)
Also Called: Mitsubishi Climate Control
1200 N Mitsubishi Pkwy (46131-7560)
PHONE.....................................317 346-5000
Fax: 317 346-6170
Tetsuzo Ukai, *President*
Tenko Ikeea, *Corp Secy*
Yasuaki Kubota, *Corp Secy*
Larry Tichenor, *Prdtn Mgr*
Michelle Zink, *Purch Mgr*
◆ EMP: 214
SQ FT: 200,000

SALES (est): 50.1MM
SALES (corp-wide): 38.5B Privately Held
WEB: www.mitsubishicc.net
SIC: 3585 7519 Air conditioning, motor vehicle;
PA: Mitsubishi Heavy Industries, Ltd.
2-16-5, Konan
Minato-Ku TKY 108-0
367 163-111

(G-4912)
MITSUBSH TRBCHRGR & ENGN AM IN
1200 N Mitsubishi Pkwy A (46131-7560)
PHONE.....................................317 346-5291
Yoshifumi Nuruyu, *Controller*
EMP: 50
SALES (corp-wide): 38.5B Privately Held
SIC: 3566 Speed changers (power transmission equipment), except auto
HQ: Mitsubishi Turbocharger And Engine America Inc
2 Pierce Pl Ste 1100
Itasca IL 60143
630 625-1875

(G-4913)
NITREX INC
350 Blue Chip Ct (46131-8824)
PHONE.....................................317 346-7700
Chris Morawski, *President*
Tiffany Guajardo, *Opers Staff*
Jan Potocki, *Human Res Mgr*
EMP: 21
SQ FT: 16,000
SALES (est): 4.5MM Privately Held
SIC: 3398 Metal heat treating

(G-4914)
NONFERROUS PRODUCTS INC
Also Called: IBC Advanced Alloys Copper
401 Arvin Rd (46131-1549)
P.O. Box 349 (46131-0349)
PHONE.....................................317 738-2558
Mark Wolma, *President*
▲ EMP: 40 EST: 1994
SQ FT: 75,000
SALES (est): 14.1MM
SALES (corp-wide): 15.7MM Privately Held
WEB: www.ibcadvancedalloys.com
SIC: 3312 3369 Blast furnaces & steel mills; nonferrous foundries
PA: Ibc Advanced Alloys Corp
570 Granville St Unit 1200
Vancouver BC V6C 3
604 685-6263

(G-4915)
NSK PRECISION AMERICA INC (DH)
Also Called: NSK Precision America Hq
3450 Bearing Dr (46131-9660)
PHONE.....................................317 738-5000
Christopher Swartwout, *President*
Gus Kontonickas, *President*
Bernard M Lindsay, *Principal*
Matt Smarelli, *QC Mgr*
Dan Williams, *Engineer*
▲ EMP: 7
SQ FT: 42,000
SALES: 30.1MM
SALES (corp-wide): 9.5B Privately Held
SIC: 3562 Ball & roller bearings

(G-4916)
NSK PRECISION AMERICA INC
3450 Bearing Dr (46131-9660)
PHONE.....................................317 738-5000
Christopher Swartwout, *President*
Doug Goeke, *Engineer*
EMP: 157
SALES (corp-wide): 9.5B Privately Held
SIC: 3562 3714 3568 3452 Ball & roller bearings; motor vehicle parts & accessories; power transmission equipment; bolts, nuts, rivets & washers
HQ: Nsk Precision America, Inc.
3450 Bearing Dr
Franklin IN 46131
317 738-5000

(G-4917)
ORTHODONTIC DESIGN AND PROD (PA)
Also Called: O D P
2165 Earlywood Dr (46131-8879)
PHONE.....................................760 734-3995
Richard Bryant, *CEO*
Patrick Roman, *President*
David Brosius, *Vice Pres*
Jack Doyle, *Treasurer*
▲ EMP: 28
SQ FT: 13,000
SALES (est): 3MM Privately Held
WEB: www.odpinc.com
SIC: 3843 3369 5047 Orthodontic appliances; nonferrous foundries; dental equipment & supplies

(G-4918)
OVERTON & SONS TL & DIE CO INC
Also Called: Overton Carbide Tool & Engrg
2155 Mcclain Dr (46131-7573)
PHONE.....................................317 736-7700
Fax: 317 736-7743
Jim Leckron, *COO*
Tony Wells, *Sales Associate*
Dale Bates, *Manager*
EMP: 30
SALES (corp-wide): 18.1MM Privately Held
WEB: www.overtonind.com
SIC: 3353 3547 3545 3544 Tubes, welded, aluminum; rolling mill machinery; machine tool accessories; special dies, tools, jigs & fixtures
PA: Overton & Sons Tool & Die Co., Inc.
1250 S Old State Road 67
Mooresville IN 46158
317 831-4542

(G-4919)
PATRIOT PRODUCTS LLC
3022 Hudson St (46131-7203)
P.O. Box 747 (46131-0747)
PHONE.....................................317 736-8007
Kathleen M Johnson, *CEO*
Mike Saunders, *Vice Pres*
Jeff Wrigley, *Design Engr*
Daniel Johnson, *Controller*
Jerry Johnson,
▲ EMP: 12
SALES (est): 2.7MM Privately Held
SIC: 3462 Armor plate, forged iron or steel

(G-4920)
PILKINGTON NORTH AMERICA INC
1001 Hurricane St (46131-1550)
PHONE.....................................317 346-0621
Susan Gilbert, *Manager*
EMP: 50
SALES (corp-wide): 5.6B Privately Held
SIC: 3211 Flat glass; construction glass
HQ: Pilkington North America, Inc.
811 Madison Ave Fl 1
Toledo OH 43604
614 802-7027

(G-4921)
POWER INVESTMENTS INC (DH)
400 N Forsythe St (46131-1558)
PHONE.....................................317 738-2117
Fax: 317 738-4614
Michael Jarvis, *President*
EMP: 13
SQ FT: 96,000
SALES (est): 63.4MM
SALES (corp-wide): 9.8B Publicly Held
SIC: 3714 3519 5091 5084 Rebuilding engines & transmissions, factory basis; motor vehicle engines & parts; parts & accessories, internal combustion engines; marine engines; diesel engine rebuilding; outboard motors; pumps & pumping equipment; diesel engine repair: automotive
HQ: Reman Holdings, Llc
600 Corporation Dr
Pendleton IN 46064
800 372-5131

(G-4922)
PRECISION FIBER SOLUTIONS LLC
590 Lake Shore Rd (46131-7464)
PHONE..................................317 421-9642
Andrew Aiello, *Principal*
EMP: 2 **EST:** 2016
SALES (est): 91.9K **Privately Held**
SIC: 3599 Industrial machinery

(G-4923)
PRIDGEON & CLAY INC
150 Arvin Rd (46131-1485)
PHONE..................................317 738-4885
Fax: 317 738-0914
David Proctor, *Plant Mgr*
Teresa Denton, *Purch Agent*
Mark Howell, *Engineer*
William Landon, *Human Res Dir*
Doug Hooyer, *Manager*
EMP: 115
SALES (corp-wide): 188.7MM **Privately Held**
WEB: www.pridgeonandclay.com
SIC: 4225 3714 3465 3429 General warehousing & storage; motor vehicle parts & accessories; automotive stampings; manufactured hardware (general)
PA: Pridgeon & Clay, Inc.
    50 Cottage Grove St Sw
    Grand Rapids MI 49507
    616 241-5675

(G-4924)
PRODUCTION HDLG SYSTEMS INC
Also Called: Hovair Automotive
211 Province St (46131-1453)
P.O. Box 474 (46131-0474)
PHONE..................................317 738-0485
Jim Edwards, *CEO*
James M Edwards, *President*
David Benham, *Vice Pres*
▲**EMP:** 15
SQ FT: 60,000
SALES (est): 4.9MM **Privately Held**
SIC: 3535 Conveyors & conveying equipment

(G-4925)
RCO-REED CORPORATION
Also Called: Reed Manufacturing Services
1050 Eastview Dr (46131-9588)
PHONE..................................317 736-8014
Fax: 317 736-6251
Samuel Reed, *President*
▲**EMP:** 25 **EST:** 1965
SQ FT: 30,000
SALES (est): 4.9MM **Privately Held**
SIC: 3451 Screw machine products

(G-4926)
REDI/CONTROLS INC
161 R J Pkwy (46131-7399)
PHONE..................................317 494-6600
Mark Key, *CEO*
Walter Key, *Treasurer*
Lenora Key, *Admin Sec*
EMP: 6
SQ FT: 30,000
SALES: 2MM **Privately Held**
WEB: www.redicontrols.com
SIC: 3585 1711 3822 Refrigeration & heating equipment; plumbing, heating, air-conditioning contractors; auto controls regulating residntl & coml environmt & applncs

(G-4927)
RIVER CITY WINERY
25 N Main St (46131-2335)
PHONE..................................317 868-8223
EMP: 2
SALES (est): 70.4K **Privately Held**
SIC: 2084 Wines

(G-4928)
SARGENT AEROSPACE INC
7500 Nw 26th St (46131)
PHONE..................................305 593-6038
Fax: 317 738-0162
Christopher Bryan, *Principal*
Curtis McCloud, *Inv Control Mgr*
EMP: 2

SALES (est): 190.3K **Privately Held**
SIC: 3721 Aircraft

(G-4929)
SHELBY GRAVEL INC
451 Arvin Rd (46131-1549)
PHONE..................................317 738-3445
Fax: 317 738-4173
Gary Simpson, *Branch Mgr*
EMP: 14
SALES (corp-wide): 55.5MM **Privately Held**
SIC: 3273 3271 1442 Ready-mixed concrete; blocks, concrete or cinder: standard; construction sand & gravel
PA: Shelby Gravel, Inc
    157 E Rampart St
    Shelbyville IN 46176
    317 398-4485

(G-4930)
SHIPSTON ALUM TECH INTL INC (DH)
Also Called: Busche Aluminum Technologies
1450 Commerce Pkwy (46131-6963)
PHONE..................................317 738-0282
Nick Busche, *CEO*
Craig Conaty, *President*
EMP: 5
SALES (est): 40.1MM
SALES (corp-wide): 398.9MM **Privately Held**
SIC: 3365 Aluminum & aluminum-based alloy castings

(G-4931)
SHIPSTON ALUM TECH INTL LLC (HQ)
1450 Commerce Pkwy (46131-6963)
PHONE..................................317 738-0282
Nick Busche, *CEO*
Craig Conaty, *CFO*
EMP: 110
SQ FT: 7,000
SALES (est): 182.9MM
SALES (corp-wide): 398.9MM **Privately Held**
SIC: 3365 Aluminum & aluminum-based alloy castings
PA: Shipston Group U.S., Inc.
    44 Timber Swamp Rd
    Hampton NH 03842
    603 929-6825

(G-4932)
SHIPSTON ALUMINUM TECH IND INC
Also Called: Busche Alum Tchnlgies Franklin
1450 Commerce Pkwy (46131-6963)
PHONE..................................317 738-0282
Fax: 317 738-0262
Nick Busche, *CEO*
EMP: 65
SQ FT: 185,000
SALES (est): 19MM
SALES (corp-wide): 398.9MM **Privately Held**
SIC: 3365 Aluminum foundries
HQ: Shipston Aluminum Technologies International, Inc.
    1450 Commerce Pkwy
    Franklin IN 46131

(G-4933)
SMART TECHNOLOGIES LLC
317 E Creekside Ct W (46131-8993)
PHONE..................................317 738-4338
Lee L Anderson, *President*
Mike Jarvis, *Mng Member*
EMP: 3
SQ FT: 5,000
SALES (est): 253.5K **Privately Held**
SIC: 3714 5013 Fuel systems & parts, motor vehicle; automotive brakes

(G-4934)
STEVES MACHINING & REWORK
1299 Paris Dr (46131-8559)
PHONE..................................317 500-4627
Fax: 317 351-0117
Steve Woodcock, *Principal*
EMP: 2
SALES (est): 119K **Privately Held**
SIC: 3599 Machine shop, jobbing & repair

(G-4935)
SWISS LABS MACHINE & ENGRG INC
2854 N Graham Rd (46131-7676)
PHONE..................................317 346-6190
Joe Bowman, *President*
Amy Bullock, *Office Mgr*
EMP: 6
SQ FT: 4,000
SALES (est): 1.1MM **Privately Held**
SIC: 3545 Precision tools, machinists'

(G-4936)
TERRAFINA INC
2165 Earlywood Dr (46131-8879)
P.O. Box 248, Greenwood (46142-0248)
PHONE..................................317 346-6655
Richard M Jahns, *President*
EMP: 33
SALES (est): 2.9MM **Privately Held**
WEB: www.ghwire.com
SIC: 3843 Dental equipment & supplies; orthodontic appliances

(G-4937)
TEST RITE SYSTEMS & MFG CO LLC
1650 N 800 E (46131-7307)
PHONE..................................317 736-9192
Fax: 317 736-8603
Michael Kaiser, *Owner*
EMP: 2
SQ FT: 7,050
SALES: 250K **Privately Held**
SIC: 3599 Machine shop, jobbing & repair

(G-4938)
VANDIVIER TUDOR MONUMENTS
951 N Main St (46131-1239)
PHONE..................................317 736-5292
EMP: 2
SALES (est): 124.6K **Privately Held**
SIC: 3272 Monuments & grave markers, except terrazo

(G-4939)
W T BOONE ENTERPRISES INC
159 Cincinnati St (46131-1751)
P.O. Box 344 (46131-0344)
PHONE..................................317 738-0275
William T Boone, *President*
Paula S Boone, *Vice Pres*
EMP: 7
SALES (est): 710K **Privately Held**
SIC: 3599 7371 Machine shop, jobbing & repair; computer software systems analysis & design, custom

(G-4940)
WARRIOR OIL SERVICE INC
809 Overstreet St (46131-1545)
PHONE..................................317 738-9777
Fax: 317 738-4105
Joseph Snedegar, *President*
EMP: 17
SQ FT: 1,000
SALES (est): 2.2MM **Privately Held**
SIC: 2992 2869 Re-refining lubricating oils & greases; fuels

(G-4941)
WENDELL DENTON
4257 S 200 E (46131-8978)
PHONE..................................317 736-8397
Wendell Denton, *Owner*
EMP: 4
SALES (est): 269.2K **Privately Held**
SIC: 3399 Primary metal products

(G-4942)
XL GRAPHICS INC
Also Called: Spotlight Strategies
170 Commerce Dr (46131-7312)
P.O. Box 155 (46131-0155)
PHONE..................................317 738-3434
Susan McCarty, *President*
Erin Smith, *President*
Trey Smith, *Opers Staff*
James Bova, *Manager*
EMP: 10
SQ FT: 15,000

SALES (est): 2.1MM **Privately Held**
WEB: www.spotlight-strategies.com
SIC: 2752 2759 3993 2791 Commercial printing, lithographic; commercial printing, offset; promotional printing; screen printing; signs & advertising specialties; typographic composition, for the printing trade

---

Frankton
Madison County

(G-4943)
FOUR STAR PRINTING
1001 E Sigler St (46044-9344)
PHONE..................................765 620-9728
EMP: 2
SALES (est): 83.9K **Privately Held**
SIC: 2752 Commercial printing, lithographic

(G-4944)
VERSATILE METAL WORKS LLC
204 S Washington St (46044)
P.O. Box 2487, Muncie (47307-0487)
PHONE..................................765 754-7470
Jeremi Dobbs, *President*
Shane Stevenson, *COO*
EMP: 12
SQ FT: 18,000
SALES (est): 1.1MM **Privately Held**
WEB: www.versatilemetalworks.com
SIC: 3541 3542 3443 Machine tools, metal cutting type; machine tools, metal forming type; metal parts

---

Fredericksburg
Washington County

(G-4945)
JONES MACHINE & TOOL INC
14710 N Xrd Nw (47120)
PHONE..................................812 364-4588
Fax: 812 364-4546
Danny Jones, *President*
Lincoln Jones, *Prdtn Mgr*
Eugene Dean, *QC Mgr*
Travis Asher, *Marketing Staff*
EMP: 45
SQ FT: 12,000
SALES (est): 9.1MM **Privately Held**
SIC: 3089 3544 3545 3599 Injection molded finished plastic products; industrial molds; dies, plastics forming; machine tool accessories; machine shop, jobbing & repair

---

Freedom
Owen County

(G-4946)
AXTROM INDUSTRIES
Also Called: Axtrom Industries/Pallet Div
170 Mt Calvery Rd (47431-7216)
PHONE..................................812 859-4873
Fax: 812 859-4958
Thomas E Chandler, *CEO*
EMP: 25
SALES (est): 3MM **Privately Held**
SIC: 2448 Pallets, wood

(G-4947)
AYNES UPHOLSTERY LLC
Also Called: Aynes Custom Upholstery
3220 Dunn Rd (47431-7092)
PHONE..................................812 829-1321
Daniel Aynes,
EMP: 2
SALES (est): 140K **Privately Held**
SIC: 1799 2521 Home/office interiors finishing, furnishing & remodeling; wood office furniture

(G-4948)
FREEDOM VALLEY CABINETS
7483 Old Glory Ln (47431-7226)
PHONE..................................812 875-2509
Nathan Lehman, *Partner*
James Lehman, *Partner*

EMP: 8
SALES (est): 1.1MM **Privately Held**
SIC: 2541 1751 Cabinets, except refrigerated; show, display, etc.: wood; cabinet & finish carpentry

(G-4949)
HESSIT WORKS INC
4181 S Us Highway 231 (47431-7329)
PHONE..............................812 829-6246
Friedrich Naether, *President*
Idella Naether, *Vice Pres*
▲ EMP: 6
SALES (est): 749.6K **Privately Held**
WEB: www.hessit.net
SIC: 3271 3272 Paving blocks, concrete; concrete products, precast

---
Freetown
Jackson County

(G-4950)
TWIN WILLOWS LLC
Also Called: Salt Creek Winery
7603 W County Road 925 N (47235-8530)
PHONE..............................812 497-0254
Adrian Lee, *Principal*
Nichole Lee, *Principal*
EMP: 3
SALES (est): 158K **Privately Held**
SIC: 2084 Wines

Fremont
Steuben County

(G-4951)
BARRY A WILCOX
207 S Wayne St (46737-2089)
P.O. Box 121 (46737-0121)
PHONE..............................260 495-3677
Melissa A Wilcox, *Principal*
EMP: 2 EST: 2012
SALES (est): 147.8K **Privately Held**
SIC: 2511 Wood household furniture

(G-4952)
BATTLE CREEK EQUIPMENT CO (PA)
Also Called: Battle Creek Health Eqp Co
702 S Reed Rd (46737-2098)
P.O. Box 629 (46737-0629)
PHONE..............................260 495-3472
David Underhill, *President*
Joyce Underhill, *Vice Pres*
▲ EMP: 40 EST: 1957
SQ FT: 28,000
SALES: 10MM **Privately Held**
SIC: 3949 3842 3634 Sporting & athletic goods; surgical appliances & supplies; electric housewares & fans

(G-4953)
CARDINAL GLASS INDUSTRIES INC
Also Called: Cardina L G
301 E Mcswain Dr (46737-2102)
P.O. Box 99 (46737-0099)
PHONE..............................260 495-4105
Fax: 260 495-4079
Patrick Sills, *Technical Staff*
Dana Stanley, *Director*
Jim Devaney, *Executive*
Odin Clifton, *Maintence Staff*
EMP: 270
SALES (corp-wide): 1B **Privately Held**
WEB: www.cardinalcorp.com
SIC: 3231 5031 Products of purchased glass; lumber, plywood & millwork
PA: Cardinal Glass Industries Inc
　775 Pririe Ctr Dr Ste 200
　Eden Prairie MN 55344
　952 229-2600

(G-4954)
CARVER NON-WOVEN TECH LLC
706 E Depot St (46737-2119)
PHONE..............................260 627-0033
Mark Glidden, *President*
EMP: 149 EST: 2015

SALES (est): 5.3MM
SALES (corp-wide): 48.4MM **Privately Held**
SIC: 2297 Nonwoven fabrics
PA: R3 Composites Corp.
　14123 Roth Rd
　Grabill IN 46741
　260 627-0033

(G-4955)
COLD HEADING CO
900 S Cassell St (46737-2116)
P.O. Box 947 (46737-0947)
PHONE..............................260 495-7003
Fax: 260 495-0178
Ryan Boekhout, *Branch Mgr*
EMP: 90
SALES (corp-wide): 55.6MM **Privately Held**
WEB: www.coldheading.com
SIC: 3452 Bolts, metal
HQ: The Cold Heading Co
　21777 Hoover Rd
　Warren MI 48089
　586 497-7000

(G-4956)
COLD HEADING CO
401 E Sidel St (46737-2138)
P.O. Box 394 (46737-0394)
PHONE..............................260 495-4222
Fax: 260 495-2333
Dominic Blasutti, *Branch Mgr*
EMP: 62
SALES (corp-wide): 55.6MM **Privately Held**
SIC: 3452 Bolts, metal
HQ: The Cold Heading Co
　21777 Hoover Rd
　Warren MI 48089
　586 497-7000

(G-4957)
DALTECH ENTERPRISES INC
Also Called: Daltech Force
810 S Broad St (46737-2113)
P.O. Box 66 (46737-0066)
PHONE..............................260 527-4590
Alex Dallas, *President*
Alexander Dallas, *President*
EMP: 8
SALES (est): 106.7K **Privately Held**
SIC: 3199 Holsters, leather

(G-4958)
DEXTER AXLE COMPANY
301 W Pearl St (46737-2049)
PHONE..............................260 495-5100
Fax: 260 495-1701
Cindy Shuler, *Human Res Dir*
Paula Nevois, *Sales Mgr*
Jerry Nusbaum, *Manager*
Neil Kaiser, *Technology*
EMP: 100
SALES (corp-wide): 245.3MM **Privately Held**
WEB: www.dexteraxle.com
SIC: 3714 Axle housings & shafts, motor vehicle; axles, motor vehicle
HQ: Dexter Axle Company
　2900 Industrial Pkwy
　Elkhart IN 46516

(G-4959)
FREMONT COATINGS DIV
302 E Mcswain Dr (46737-2102)
P.O. Box 659 (46737-0659)
PHONE..............................260 495-4445
Tammy Zarate, *Controller*
EMP: 2
SALES (est): 69.9K **Privately Held**
SIC: 3479 Metal coating & allied service

(G-4960)
GENERAL ALUMINUM MFG COMPANY
Metalloy Fremont Division
303 E Swager St (46737-2148)
P.O. Box 757 (46737-0757)
PHONE..............................260 495-2600
Fax: 260 495-3200
Tom Abernathey, *Plant Mgr*
Thomas Abernathey, *Manager*
Mindy Hantz, *Manager*
EMP: 150

SALES (corp-wide): 1.4B **Publicly Held**
WEB: www.generalaluminum.com
SIC: 3363 3545 3365 Aluminum die-castings; machine tool accessories; aluminum foundries
HQ: General Aluminum Mfg. Company
　6065 Parkland Blvd
　Cleveland OH 44124
　440 947-2000

(G-4961)
HEALTH EQUIPMENT MANUFACTURERS
702 S Reed Rd (46737-2098)
PHONE..............................260 495-3472
Fax: 260 495-1611
Steve Martin, *President*
▲ EMP: 30
SALES (est): 2.6MM **Privately Held**
SIC: 3842 Surgical appliances & supplies

(G-4962)
INDUSTRIAL REP INC
1184 E State Road 120 (46737-9686)
P.O. Box 948 (46737-0948)
PHONE..............................260 316-4973
Bruce W Delucenay, *President*
EMP: 1
SQ FT: 2,400
SALES: 1.5MM **Privately Held**
SIC: 3599 Machine shop, jobbing & repair

(G-4963)
JAMES LAKE VINEYARD INC
Also Called: Satek Winery
6208 N Van Guilder Rd (46737-9340)
PHONE..............................260 495-9463
Larry Satek, *Partner*
Pam Satek, *Partner*
Larry Slater, *Partner*
EMP: 9
SALES (est): 928.3K **Privately Held**
SIC: 2084 5921 Wines; wine

(G-4964)
KOESTER METALS INC (PA)
Also Called: K M I
301 W Water St (46737-2162)
P.O. Box 617 (46737-0617)
PHONE..............................260 495-1818
John M Koester, *Ch of Bd*
Gary Koester, *President*
Ron Mason, *Materials Mgr*
Craig Steinmetz, *Engineer*
Sylvia Koester, *Treasurer*
EMP: 50
SQ FT: 70,000
SALES (est): 8.8MM **Privately Held**
WEB: www.kmienclosures.com
SIC: 3469 3699 3444 Electronic enclosures, stamped or pressed metal; electrical equipment & supplies; sheet metalwork

(G-4965)
LAGRANGE PRODUCTS INC
607 S Wayne St (46737-2170)
P.O. Box 658 (46737-0658)
PHONE..............................260 495-3025
Fax: 260 495-7771
Lynn Blue, *CEO*
Jeff Green, *Maint Spvr*
Ryan Blue, *Purch Mgr*
Chad Brooks, *Purchasing*
Andy Rodenbeck, *QC Mgr*
EMP: 105
SQ FT: 60,000
SALES (est): 14MM **Privately Held**
WEB: www.lagrangeproducts.com
SIC: 3443 Tanks, lined: metal plate

(G-4966)
LETICA CORPORATION
701 E Depot St (46737-2119)
P.O. Box 693 (46737-0693)
PHONE..............................248 652-0557
Fax: 260 495-2603
Paul Limestah, *General Mgr*
John Jenkins, *Plant Mgr*
Mike Fitzgibbon, *Branch Mgr*
Harry Williams, *Maintence Staff*
EMP: 110
SALES (corp-wide): **Privately Held**
WEB: www.letica.com
SIC: 3089 Plastic containers, except foam; pails, plastic

HQ: Letica Corporation
　52585 Dequindre Rd
　Rochester Hills MI 48307
　248 652-0557

(G-4967)
METAL IMPROVEMENT COMPANY LLC
Also Called: M I C Fremont
302 E Mcswain Dr (46737-2102)
P.O. Box 659 (46737-0659)
PHONE..............................260 495-4445
EMP: 47
SALES (corp-wide): 2.1B **Publicly Held**
SIC: 3479 Mfg Corrosion Resistant Coatings
HQ: Metal Improvement Company, Llc
　80 E State Rt 4 Ste 310
　Paramus NJ 07652
　201 843-7800

(G-4968)
METALDYNE BSM LLC
Also Called: Metaldyne Fremont
307 S Tillotson St (46737-2157)
P.O. Box 615 (46737-0615)
PHONE..............................260 495-4315
Thomas A Amato, *CEO*
Thomas Amato, *Principal*
Robert Defauw, *Vice Pres*
Juergen Depp, *Vice Pres*
Cristoph Guhe, *Vice Pres*
▲ EMP: 90 EST: 2009
SALES (est): 26.9MM
SALES (corp-wide): 6.2B **Publicly Held**
WEB: www.metaldyne.com
SIC: 3714 3462 3365 3325 Motor vehicle parts & accessories; iron & steel forgings; aluminum foundries; steel foundries; automotive & home supply stores
HQ: Metaldyne Sinterforged Products, Llc
　197 West Creek Rd
　Saint Marys PA 15857
　814 834-1222

(G-4969)
MOYER PROCESS & CONTROLS CO
105 N Wayne St (46737-2083)
P.O. Box 935 (46737-0935)
PHONE..............................260 495-2405
Fax: 260 495-1290
Jeffrey Duguid, *President*
Jeff Guduid, *Vice Pres*
EMP: 4
SQ FT: 2,400
SALES: 1MM **Privately Held**
WEB: www.moyercompanies.com
SIC: 3829 Physical property testing equipment

(G-4970)
NEW HORIZONS BAKING COMPANY
700 W Water St (46737-2165)
P.O. Box 695 (46737-0695)
PHONE..............................260 495-7055
Fax: 260 495-2307
Mark Duke, *Branch Mgr*
EMP: 100
SALES (est): 12.3MM
SALES (corp-wide): 94MM **Privately Held**
SIC: 2051 Bakery: wholesale or wholesale/retail combined
PA: New Horizons Baking Company Inc
　211 Woodlawn Ave
　Norwalk OH 44857
　419 668-8226

(G-4971)
NORTHERN TOOL AND DIE
501 E Depot St (46737-2117)
P.O. Box 941 (46737-0941)
PHONE..............................260 495-7314
Fax: 260 495-7183
Carl Coburn, *Owner*
EMP: 4
SQ FT: 4,000
SALES (est): 159.7K **Privately Held**
SIC: 3544 Special dies & tools

▲ = Import ▼ =Export
◆ =Import/Export

(G-4972)
REES INC
405 S Reed Rd (46737-2129)
P.O. Box 652 (46737-0652)
PHONE....................................260 495-9811
Debra Kolbow, *President*
Jerome Chebowski, *Rsch/Dvlpt Dir*
Dawn Penner, *Manager*
Sharman Weber, *Manager*
EMP: 15
SQ FT: 32,400
SALES (est): 3.9MM **Privately Held**
WEB: www.reesinc.com
SIC: 5211 3822 3643 Electrical construction materials; auto controls regulating residntl & coml environmnt & applncs; current-carrying wiring devices

(G-4973)
RICHTERS MACHINE & TOOL
4395 E 300 N (46737-9780)
PHONE....................................260 495-5327
Michael P Richter, *Owner*
EMP: 3
SALES: 200K **Privately Held**
SIC: 3599 Machine shop, jobbing & repair

(G-4974)
RICKLES PICKLES
103 W Toledo St (46737-2069)
P.O. Box 490 (46737-0490)
PHONE....................................260 495-9024
Ricky F Corcimiglia, *Principal*
EMP: 4
SALES (est): 325.4K **Privately Held**
SIC: 2035 Pickles, vinegar

(G-4975)
SUR-LOC INC
501 E Swager St (46737-2149)
P.O. Box 750 (46737-0750)
PHONE....................................260 495-4065
Fax: 260 495-4205
Tim Swager, *President*
Lee Swager, *Treasurer*
EMP: 10
SQ FT: 5,000
SALES (est): 1.4MM **Privately Held**
WEB: www.surloc.com
SIC: 3429 3444 Manufactured hardware (general); sheet metalwork

(G-4976)
SWAGER COMMUNICATIONS INC
501 E Swager St (46737-2149)
P.O. Box 656 (46737-0656)
PHONE....................................260 495-2515
Dan J Swager, *President*
Tim Swager, *Corp Secy*
Lee Swager, *Vice Pres*
Jonah Swager, *Project Mgr*
Melissa Wilcox, *Manager*
EMP: 35
SQ FT: 40,000
SALES: 6.3MM **Privately Held**
WEB: www.swager.com
SIC: 3441 1623 Tower sections, radio & television transmission; transmitting tower (telecommunication) construction

(G-4977)
THERMFORM ENGINEERED QULTY LLC
Also Called: Fremont Plastics
500 W Water St (46737-2163)
PHONE....................................260 495-9842
Fax: 260 495-1607
Lyndon Tucker, *President*
EMP: 11
SALES (corp-wide): 685.7MM **Publicly Held**
SIC: 3089 Thermoformed finished plastic products
HQ: Thermoform Engineered Quality Llc
11320 Main St
Huntley IL 60142

(G-4978)
V & P PRINTING
3655 N 300 E (46737-9784)
PHONE....................................260 495-3741
Fax: 260 495-1248
Vernon Strang, *Owner*
EMP: 2

SALES (est): 74.1K **Privately Held**
SIC: 2759 2752 Commercial printing; commercial printing, lithographic

(G-4979)
WENZEL ACQUISITION INC
5610 N West St (46737)
PHONE....................................260 495-9898
Matt Trubergen, *President*
EMP: 2
SALES (est): 115.5K **Privately Held**
SIC: 3469 Spinning metal for the trade

(G-4980)
WENZEL METAL SPINNING INC (PA)
701 W Water St (46737-2165)
P.O. Box 708 (46737-0708)
PHONE....................................260 495-9898
Fax: 260 495-2218
Matthew Tubergen, *President*
Andy Lewis, *Vice Pres*
Mark H Quinlivan, *Vice Pres*
Kerry Hoyer, *Plant Supt*
Mark Peppers, *Plant Mgr*
EMP: 58
SQ FT: 70,000
SALES (est): 14.1MM **Privately Held**
WEB: www.wenzelmetalspinning.com
SIC: 3469 Spinning metal for the trade

(G-4981)
WENZEL METAL SPINNING INC IND
701 W Water St (46737-2165)
P.O. Box 708 (46737-0708)
PHONE....................................260 495-9898
Thomas J Wenzel, *President*
James Hornbacher, *Vice Pres*
EMP: 70
SQ FT: 70,000
SALES (est): 3.6MM **Privately Held**
SIC: 3469 Spinning metal for the trade

(G-4982)
WESTERN CONSOLIDATED TECH INC (DH)
700 W Swager St (46737-2145)
P.O. Box 657 (46737-0657)
PHONE....................................260 495-6866
Fax: 260 495-6109
Kevin Kelly, *President*
Michael J Kelly, *Chairman*
EMP: 75
SQ FT: 185,000
SALES (est): 15.7MM
SALES (corp-wide): 89.4MM **Privately Held**
SIC: 3061 3089 3544 3643 Mechanical rubber goods; automotive rubber goods (mechanical); medical & surgical rubber tubing (extruded & lathe-cut); appliance rubber goods (mechanical); plastic processing; forms (molds), for foundry & plastics working machinery; current-carrying wiring devices; relays & industrial controls; switchgear & switchboard apparatus
HQ: Guardian Electric Manufacturing Co.
1425 Lake Ave
Woodstock IL 60098
815 334-3600

French Lick
Orange County

(G-4983)
ACCENT SIGNS & GRAPHICS
11471 W County Road 75 N (47432-9725)
PHONE....................................866 769-7446
John Liesey, *Owner*
EMP: 6
SALES (est): 568.7K **Privately Held**
WEB: www.accent-graphic.com
SIC: 7336 3993 Graphic arts & related design; signs & advertising specialties

(G-4984)
AHF INDUSTRIES INC
Also Called: Pluto
8647 W State Road 56 (47432-9390)
P.O. Box 391 (47432-0391)
PHONE....................................812 936-9988
Fax: 812 936-2828

Alan J Friedman, *President*
Bernice Friedman, *Vice Pres*
Mark Mills, *Prdtn Mgr*
▲ **EMP:** 210 **EST:** 1913
SQ FT: 120,000
SALES (est): 60.8MM **Privately Held**
WEB: www.plutocorp.com
SIC: 2086 7389 3085 Carbonated beverages, nonalcoholic: bottled & canned; packaging & labeling services; plastics bottles

(G-4985)
FRENCH LICK AUTO SIGNS (PA)
9451 W State Road 56 (47432-8102)
P.O. Box 222, West Baden Springs (47469-0222)
PHONE....................................812 936-7777
Fax: 812 936-4438
Larry Kalb, *Owner*
EMP: 5
SALES (est): 1.6MM **Privately Held**
SIC: 3993 Signs & advertising specialties

(G-4986)
HUGHES PAVING COMPANY INC
11907 Hwy 56 (47432)
PHONE....................................812 678-2126
Fax: 812 678-2306
Curtis W Hughes, *President*
Wayne Hughes, *Vice Pres*
Lena Hughes, *Admin Sec*
EMP: 14
SQ FT: 1,000
SALES: 2.9MM **Privately Held**
SIC: 1771 1611 3531 Blacktop (asphalt) work; highway & street paving contractor; plows: construction, excavating & grading

(G-4987)
JASPER SEATING COMPANY INC
Also Called: Jsi
8084 W County Road 25 S (47432-9022)
PHONE....................................812 936-9977
Michael Eckstein, *Branch Mgr*
EMP: 80
SALES (corp-wide): 228.8MM **Privately Held**
WEB: www.jasperseating.com
SIC: 2521 Chairs, office: padded, upholstered or plain: wood
PA: Jasper Seating Company Inc
225 Clay St
Jasper IN 47546
812 482-3204

(G-4988)
RANDALL LOWE & SONS SAWMILL
6543 W County Road 875 S (47432-9327)
PHONE....................................812 936-2254
Fax: 812 936-4781
Carl Randall Lowe, *Partner*
EMP: 15
SALES (est): 1.7MM **Privately Held**
SIC: 2421 2426 Sawmills & planing mills, general; hardwood dimension & flooring mills

(G-4989)
SPRINGS VALLEY PUBLISHING CO
Also Called: Springs Valley Herald
7303 W County Road 175 S (47432-9347)
PHONE....................................812 936-9630
Fax: 812 936-9559
Robort Denbo, *President*
EMP: 5
SALES (est): 414.3K **Privately Held**
WEB: www.springsvalleyherald.com
SIC: 2711 2752 Newspapers, publishing & printing; commercial printing, lithographic

(G-4990)
TC PRINTING
8381 W State Road 56 (47432-9602)
PHONE....................................812 865-5127
Cecil Rowlett, *Principal*
EMP: 7
SALES (est): 148.6K **Privately Held**
SIC: 2752 Commercial printing, lithographic

Friendship
Ripley County

(G-4991)
CARL DYERS ORIGINAL MOCCASINS
5961 E State Rd 62 (47021)
P.O. Box 31 (47021-0031)
PHONE....................................812 667-5442
Fax: 812 667-4852
Robin Dyer, *President*
EMP: 2
SALES (est): 203.9K **Privately Held**
WEB: www.carldyers.com
SIC: 3149 Moccasins

Fulda
Spencer County

(G-4992)
WANINGER KNNETH SONS LOG TMBER
Also Called: Waninger & Sons Timber Co
Hwy 545 (47536)
PHONE....................................812 357-5200
Kenneth Waninger, *Owner*
Kenneth Waningner, *Owner*
EMP: 18
SALES (est): 1.3MM **Privately Held**
SIC: 5031 2411 Lumber: rough, dressed & finished; logging

Galveston
Cass County

(G-4993)
ANDERSONS AGRICULTURE GROUP LP
8086 E 900 (46932)
PHONE....................................574 626-2522
Tom Weatherwax, *General Mgr*
Joe Johnson, *Manager*
EMP: 40
SALES (corp-wide): 3.6B **Publicly Held**
SIC: 2873 2874 2899 5261 Fertilizers: natural (organic), except compost; ammonium phosphate; deicing or defrosting fluid; fertilizer; fertilizer & fertilizer materials; fertilizers, mixing only
HQ: The Andersons Agriculture Group L P
1947 Briarfield Blvd
Maumee OH 43537
419 893-5050

(G-4994)
ED AND DAVES WOOD CHIPS LLC
419 Sycamore Ct (46932-9783)
PHONE....................................574 699-1263
David Haskin, *Principal*
EMP: 2
SALES (est): 90K **Privately Held**
SIC: 2519 5812 Household furniture; eating places

Garrett
Dekalb County

(G-4995)
ASSMANN CORPORATION AMERICA (PA)
300 N Taylor Rd (46738-1844)
PHONE....................................260 357-3181
Fax: 260 357-3738
David L Crager, *President*
Mary Monce, *Manager*
Vickie S Elliott, *Admin Sec*
EMP: 32
SQ FT: 51,000
SALES (est): 6.5MM **Privately Held**
WEB: www.assmann-usa.com
SIC: 3089 Plastic containers, except foam

(G-4996)
CENTURION INDUSTRIES INC (PA)
Also Called: TFC Canopy
1107 N Taylor Rd (46738-1880)
PHONE..................................260 357-6665
Fax: 260 357-6761
Kenneth L Tharp, *Ch of Bd*
Bradley S Parish, *President*
Thomas Galanis, *General Mgr*
Thomas Patterson, *Vice Pres*
Randy Shinkle, *Vice Pres*
EMP: 60
SQ FT: 80,000
SALES: 162.4MM **Privately Held**
WEB: www.centurionind.com
SIC: 3444 1796 Canopies, sheet metal;
millwright

(G-4997)
CLAYTON HOMES INC
Also Called: Unknown
1850 State Road 8 (46738-1876)
PHONE..................................260 553-5500
Charles Hoefer, *President*
EMP: 2
SALES (corp-wide): 242.1B **Publicly Held**
SIC: 2451 Mobile homes
HQ: Clayton Homes, Inc.
5000 Clayton Rd
Maryville TN 37804
865 380-3000

(G-4998)
CORNERSTONE MILL WORK
106 N Randolph St (46738-1138)
PHONE..................................260 357-0754
Shawn Koble, *Owner*
EMP: 2
SALES (est): 207K **Privately Held**
SIC: 2431 Millwork

(G-4999)
COUNTRYSIDE TOOL
1723 South Rd (46738-1853)
PHONE..................................260 357-3839
Thomas Griffin, *Partner*
EMP: 2
SALES (est): 151.5K **Privately Held**
SIC: 3469 Machine parts, stamped or
pressed metal

(G-5000)
D&A INDUSTRIES INC
5079 County Road 19 (46738-9791)
PHONE..................................260 357-1830
C Thatcher, *Principal*
EMP: 8
SALES (est): 428.7K **Privately Held**
SIC: 3999 Manufacturing industries

(G-5001)
DEKALB TOOL AND ENGRG LLC
700 E Quincy St (46738-1617)
PHONE..................................260 357-1500
Merrill Frame, *President*
EMP: 15
SALES: 1.6MM **Privately Held**
SIC: 3599 Machine shop, jobbing & repair

(G-5002)
E-COLLAR TECHNOLOGIES INC
2120 Forrest Park Dr (46738-1882)
PHONE..................................260 357-0051
Gregory Van Curen, *President*
▲ EMP: 8
SQ FT: 56,000
SALES (est): 1.2MM **Privately Held**
SIC: 3545 Collars (machine tool accessories)

(G-5003)
ELECTRIC MOTORS AND SPC
Also Called: EM&s
701 W King St (46738-1396)
P.O. Box 180 (46738-0180)
PHONE..................................260 357-4141
Fax: 260 357-3888
Judy Morrill, *President*
Keith Bradtmiller, *Admin Sec*
EMP: 155 EST: 1947
SQ FT: 13,000
SALES: 14.2MM **Privately Held**
WEB: www.emsmotors.com
SIC: 3621 Motors, electric

(G-5004)
ENZYME SOLUTIONS INC (PA)
Also Called: E S I
2105 Forrest Park Dr (46738-1882)
PHONE..................................260 553-9100
Fax: 260 497-0512
Timothy Beck, *CEO*
Edwin Fisher Jr, *Admin Sec*
◆ EMP: 15
SQ FT: 39,000
SALES (est): 3.5MM **Privately Held**
WEB: www.enzymesolutions.com
SIC: 2869 Industrial organic chemicals

(G-5005)
GARRETT PRODUCTS
1605 Dekko Dr (46738-1877)
PHONE..................................260 357-5988
Fax: 260 357-3399
Tom Wilcoxson, *Principal*
EMP: 2 EST: 2010
SALES (est): 113.2K **Privately Held**
SIC: 3479 Metal coating & allied service

(G-5006)
GRACE ISLAND SPCALTY FOODS INC
5840 County Road 11 (46738-9743)
PHONE..................................260 357-3336
Kalista A Johnston, *President*
EMP: 3
SALES (est): 200K **Privately Held**
SIC: 2096 2052 Potato chips & similar
snacks; cookies & crackers

(G-5007)
GRIFFITH RBR MILLS OF GARRETT (HQ)
Also Called: Bauman Harnish Rubber Co
400 N Taylor Rd (46738-1846)
PHONE..................................260 357-3125
Fax: 260 357-3130
Howard Laney, *President*
Richard D Hahnert, *Corp Secy*
Donna Laney, *Vice Pres*
Jill D Laney, *Admin Sec*
▲ EMP: 50 EST: 1948
SQ FT: 98,000
SALES: 9.7MM
SALES (corp-wide): 93MM **Privately Held**
SIC: 3061 Mechanical rubber goods; appliance rubber goods (mechanical); automotive rubber goods (mechanical)
PA: Griffith Rubber Mills
2625 Nw Indul St
Portland OR 97210
503 226-6971

(G-5008)
GRIFFITH RBR MILLS OF GARRETT
Also Called: Microwave Plant
507 N Lee St (46738-1045)
PHONE..................................260 357-0876
Fax: 260 357-3868
Max Gregory, *Manager*
EMP: 12
SALES (est): 1.4MM
SALES (corp-wide): 93MM **Privately Held**
SIC: 3069 3053 Molded rubber products;
packing, rubber
HQ: Griffith Rubber Mills Of Garrett Inc
400 N Taylor Rd
Garrett IN 46738
260 357-3125

(G-5009)
GROUP DEKKO INC (HQ)
2505 Dekko Dr (46738-1886)
PHONE..................................260 357-3621
John R May, *CEO*
Jon Jensen, *President*
Joe Haupert, *General Mgr*
Larry Colestock, *Vice Pres*
Tracy Joseph, *Opers Mgr*
▲ EMP: 94
SQ FT: 66,000
SALES (est): 178MM
SALES (corp-wide): 2.5B **Publicly Held**
SIC: 3479 3469 3643 3315 Coating of
metals & formed products; painting of
metal products; metal stampings; current-carrying wiring devices; wire & fabricated
wire products; molding primary plastic
PA: Graham Holdings Company
1300 17th St N Ste 1700
Arlington VA 22209
703 345-6300

(G-5010)
GROUP DEKKO INC
1605 Dekko Dr (46738-1877)
PHONE..................................260 357-5988
Craig Rumsey, *Manager*
EMP: 200
SALES (corp-wide): 2.5B **Publicly Held**
SIC: 3699 Electrical equipment & supplies
HQ: Group Dekko, Inc.
2505 Dekko Dr
Garrett IN 46738

(G-5011)
GROUP DEKKO HOLDINGS INC (HQ)
2505 Dekko Dr (46738-1886)
PHONE..................................260 347-0700
John R May, *CEO*
Timothy White, *President*
Gerald Whiteford, *Vice Pres*
EMP: 2
SALES (est): 132.5MM **Privately Held**
SIC: 3496 Miscellaneous fabricated wire
products

(G-5012)
J & A MACHINE INC
219 E Quincy St (46738-1116)
P.O. Box 89 (46738-0089)
PHONE..................................260 637-6215
Fax: 260 357-5422
Michael Blomberg, *President*
Steve Blomberg, *Vice Pres*
◆ EMP: 6 EST: 1976
SQ FT: 6,624
SALES (est): 802.5K **Privately Held**
SIC: 3599 Machine shop, jobbing & repair

(G-5013)
J & P MACHINE INC
1213 S Franklin St (46738-2025)
PHONE..................................260 357-5157
Fax: 260 357-4418
James C Fike, *President*
Paula J Fike, *Admin Sec*
EMP: 13
SQ FT: 6,000
SALES (est): 980K **Privately Held**
SIC: 3599 Machine shop, jobbing & repair

(G-5014)
J Y DESIGN & PRINT INC
1036 State Road 8 (46738-9703)
PHONE..................................260 357-3759
Fax: 260 357-5995
Julie Yard, *President*
Sherry Shields, *Manager*
EMP: 8
SQ FT: 5,000
SALES (est): 690K **Privately Held**
WEB: www.jydesignandprint.com
SIC: 2759 Commercial printing

(G-5015)
M & S STEEL CORP
217 E Railroad St (46738-1085)
P.O. Box 299 (46738-0299)
PHONE..................................260 357-5184
Fax: 260 357-5900
Walter G Fuller, *President*
Michael Fuller, *Vice Pres*
Joy Goe, *Production*
Adam Parker, *Parts Mgr*
Kent York, *Sales Mgr*
◆ EMP: 27 EST: 1971
SQ FT: 35,000
SALES (est): 8.4MM **Privately Held**
WEB: www.mssteelcorp.com
SIC: 3441 3443 Building components,
structural steel; fabricated plate work
(boiler shop)

(G-5016)
MOLARGIK WOODWORKING INC
1116 S Hamsher St (46738-9628)
PHONE..................................260 357-6625
James Molargik, *President*
EMP: 4
SALES: 850K **Privately Held**
SIC: 2431 2541 Millwork; table or counter
tops, plastic laminated

(G-5017)
MOMENTIVE PERFORMANCE MTLS INC
Also Called: Momentive Performance Mtls
420 N Taylor Rd (46738-1846)
PHONE..................................260 357-2000
Rick Kipley, *Facilities Mgr*
Tom Lapsley, *Branch Mgr*
Chris Jones, *Manager*
EMP: 65
SALES (corp-wide): 2.3B **Publicly Held**
SIC: 2869 3479 Silicones; coating of metals with silicon
HQ: Momentive Performance Materials Inc.
260 Hudson River Rd
Waterford NY 12188

(G-5018)
MOSSBERG INDUSTRIES INC (HQ)
204 N 2nd St (46738-1600)
P.O. Box 37 (46738-0037)
PHONE..................................260 357-5141
Fax: 260 357-5144
Michael Khorshid, *President*
David Fogarty, *Buyer*
Ron Lanoue, *Design Engr*
Debbra Lapp, *Human Res Mgr*
Barry Sordelet, *Marketing Staff*
EMP: 60 EST: 1863
SQ FT: 80,000
SALES (est): 12.6MM
SALES (corp-wide): 52.7MM **Privately Held**
WEB: www.mossbergind.com
SIC: 2499 3499 3089 3086 Spools,
wood; reels, cable: metal; hardware, plastic; plastics foam products
PA: Khorporate Holdings, Inc.
6492 State Road 205
Laotto IN 46763
260 357-3365

(G-5019)
PEERLESS MFG CO
Also Called: Peerless Manufacturing
800 E King St (46738-1613)
PHONE..................................260 357-3271
EMP: 5
SALES (corp-wide): 417MM **Publicly Held**
SIC: 3999 Mfg Misc Products
HQ: Peerless Mfg. Co.
14651 Dallas Pkwy Ste 500
Dallas TX 75254
214 357-6181

(G-5020)
PRINCE MANUFACTURING CORP
320 N Taylor Rd (46738-1844)
P.O. Box En Dr, Avilla (46710)
PHONE..................................260 357-4484
Bernard Talwin, *Office Mgr*
EMP: 30
SALES (corp-wide): 140.7MM **Privately Held**
SIC: 2759 3479 Commercial printing;
coating of metals & formed products
HQ: Prince Manufacturing Corporation
3227 Sunset Blvd Ste E101
West Columbia SC 29169
803 708-4789

(G-5021)
RD RUBBER PRODUCTS INC
1600 South Rd (46738-1726)
P.O. Box 149 (46738-0149)
PHONE..................................260 357-3571
Dan Hoffelder, *President*
Valerie Colburn, *Vice Pres*
EMP: 4

▲ = Import ▼=Export
◆ =Import/Export

SALES (est): 492.7K **Privately Held**
SIC: 3061 8711 Mechanical rubber goods; engineering services

(G-5022)
SCOTT CULBERTSON
Also Called: Garrett Printing
1202 S Hamsher St (46738-9664)
PHONE..................260 357-6430
Fax: 260 357-0822
Scott Culbertson, *Owner*
EMP: 2
SQ FT: 1,800
SALES (est): 163.5K **Privately Held**
SIC: 2754 5943 Stationery & invitation printing, gravure; office forms & supplies

(G-5023)
SUPERIOR WOODCRAFTS LLC
1111 S Franklin St (46738-2023)
PHONE..................260 357-3743
EMP: 2
SALES (est): 111.6K **Privately Held**
SIC: 2511 Wood household furniture

(G-5024)
TR MANUFACTURING LLC
1106 S Cowen St (46738-1910)
PHONE..................260 357-4679
Matt Mason, *Mng Member*
Joe Mattes,
EMP: 6
SALES (est): 1MM **Privately Held**
SIC: 3599 Machine shop, jobbing & repair

Gary
Lake County

(G-5025)
A & T METAL FABRICATORS LLC
7000 W 21st Ave (46406-2404)
PHONE..................219 949-5066
Leonard Nowak,
EMP: 3
SALES (est): 239K **Privately Held**
SIC: 3499 Fabricated metal products

(G-5026)
AARON COMPANY INCORPORATED
Also Called: Family Design
4835 W 45th Ave (46408-3539)
PHONE..................219 838-0852
Fax: 219 972-3704
Gerald A Gearhart, *President*
Henrietta Gearhart, *Admin Sec*
EMP: 13
SQ FT: 3,800
SALES (est): 1.2MM **Privately Held**
SIC: 7359 2512 7641 Home appliance, furniture & entertainment rental services; upholstered household furniture; reupholstery

(G-5027)
AMERICAN PRECISION SVCS INC
7110 W 21st Ave (46406-2406)
PHONE..................219 977-4451
Fax: 219 977-4452
Robert Migliorini, *President*
John Teefel, *Vice Pres*
Jeffery Keith, *CFO*
Alisa Hecim, *Office Mgr*
Allison Booker, *Manager*
EMP: 48
SQ FT: 8,000
SALES (est): 9.2MM **Privately Held**
WEB: www.amprservices.com
SIC: 3599 Machine shop, jobbing & repair

(G-5028)
AMG RESOURCES CORPORATION
459 Cline Ave (46406-1049)
PHONE..................219 949-8150
Fax: 219 949-8129
Nicholas Gord, *Accounts Exec*
Steve Basarab, *Manager*
EMP: 12

SALES (corp-wide): 64.2MM **Privately Held**
SIC: 3341 Detinning of cans & scrap
HQ: Amg Resources Corporation
2 Robinson Plz Ste 350
Pittsburgh PA 15205
412 777-7300

(G-5029)
BADA BOOM FIREWORKS LLC
4601 Cleveland St (46408-3716)
PHONE..................219 472-6700
Matthew Lalich Jr,
EMP: 2
SALES (est): 74.4K **Privately Held**
SIC: 2899 Fireworks

(G-5030)
BMI REFRACTORY SERVICES INC
201 Mississippi St (46402-1546)
PHONE..................219 885-2209
Bill Schleizer, *Manager*
EMP: 8
SALES (corp-wide): 2.2B **Privately Held**
SIC: 3255 Glasshouse refractories
HQ: Bmi Refractory Services, Inc.
250 Parkwest Dr
Pittsburgh PA 15275
412 429-1800

(G-5031)
BRUNOS BREADS LLC
Also Called: Organic Bread of Heaven
2700 W 5th Ave (46404-1248)
PHONE..................219 883-5126
Ron Bruno, *Mng Member*
Pamela Sue Bruno, *Mng Member*
EMP: 15
SQ FT: 2,800
SALES: 509K **Privately Held**
SIC: 2051 5149 5461 Bread, cake & related products; crackers, cookies & bakery products; bakeries

(G-5032)
CALUMET WILBERT VAULT CO INC
1920 W 41st Ave (46408-2399)
PHONE..................219 980-1173
Fax: 219 980-0796
Edward H Carroll Jr, *President*
Nancy Eggbali, *Corp Secy*
EMP: 10
SQ FT: 30,000
SALES (est): 1MM **Privately Held**
SIC: 3272 Burial vaults, concrete or precast terrazzo

(G-5033)
CARMEUSE LIME INC
Also Called: Carmeuse Lime & Stone
1 N Carmeuse Ln (46406-1279)
PHONE..................219 949-1450
Thomas A Buck, *CEO*
EMP: 49 **Privately Held**
SIC: 1422 Crushed & broken limestone
HQ: Carmeuse Lime, Inc.
11 Stanwix St Fl 21
Pittsburgh PA 15222
412 995-5500

(G-5034)
CARMEUSE LIME INC
Also Called: Carmeuse Lime & Stone
1 N Carmeuse Ln (46406-1279)
PHONE..................773 221-9400
EMP: 75 **Privately Held**
SIC: 3274 5032 Mfg Lime Products Whol Brick/Stone Material
HQ: Carmeuse Lime, Inc.
11 Stanwix St Fl 21
Pittsburgh PA 15222
412 995-5500

(G-5035)
CENTRAL ILLINOIS STEEL COMPANY
50 N Bridge St (46404-1074)
PHONE..................219 882-1026
Fax: 219 882-2024
Dan Fleig, *Director*
EMP: 5

SALES (corp-wide): 45MM **Privately Held**
SIC: 3441 5051 Fabricated structural metal; steel; pipe & tubing, steel
PA: Central Illinois Steel Company
21050 Route 4
Carlinville IL 62626
217 854-3251

(G-5036)
CHEMCOATERS LLC
700 Chase St (46404-1246)
PHONE..................219 977-1929
Fax: 219 977-5299
Bill Capizziano,
EMP: 35 **EST:** 1999
SQ FT: 80,000
SALES (est): 7.5MM **Privately Held**
WEB: www.chemcoaters.com
SIC: 3479 Coating or wrapping steel pipe

(G-5037)
CHICAGO STEEL LTD PARTNERSHIP
700 Chase St (46404-1246)
PHONE..................219 949-1111
Bruce Mannakee, *Partner*
William Boak, *Vice Pres*
Ted Katsahnias, *VP Opers*
EMP: 2
SQ FT: 285,000
SALES (est): 206.8K **Privately Held**
SIC: 7389 5051 3312 Metal cutting services; metal slitting & shearing; scrap steel cutting; metals service centers & offices; blast furnaces & steel mills

(G-5038)
CLOVERLEAF FARMS DAIRY
6401 Melton Rd (46403-3010)
PHONE..................219 938-5140
R Curtis, *Owner*
EMP: 3 **EST:** 1999
SALES (est): 143.8K **Privately Held**
SIC: 2024 Ice cream & frozen desserts

(G-5039)
COMMERCIAL GROUP LIFTING PDTS
1601 Cline Ave (46406-2224)
PHONE..................219 944-7200
David Himick, *Principal*
Tony Zonparelli, *Vice Pres*
EMP: 2
SALES (est): 278.7K **Privately Held**
SIC: 3496 Miscellaneous fabricated wire products

(G-5040)
CORSAIR GRAPHICS
1038 E 11th Ct (46403-3545)
PHONE..................219 938-8317
Fax: 219 938-4396
Floyd M Williams, *Owner*
EMP: 3
SALES (est): 180K **Privately Held**
SIC: 3993 Signs & advertising specialties

(G-5041)
DIVINE GRACE HOMECARE
4224 Connecticut St (46409-2106)
PHONE..................219 290-5911
Lloyd Cleveneatha, *Owner*
EMP: 2
SALES (est): 140K **Privately Held**
SIC: 2656 7389 Sanitary food containers;

(G-5042)
DVS REFRACTORIES LLC
1040 N Union St (46403-1460)
PHONE..................219 886-2004
EMP: 3
SALES (est): 256.6K **Privately Held**
SIC: 3255 Clay refractories

(G-5043)
EDSAL INC
700 Chase St Ste 400 (46404-1274)
PHONE..................219 427-1294
▲ EMP: 3 **EST:** 2015
SALES (est): 230K **Privately Held**
SIC: 3999 Manufacturing industries

(G-5044)
ENVIRO FILTRATION INC (PA)
Also Called: Enviro Filters
4719 Roosevelt St (46408-3747)
PHONE..................815 469-2871
Tim Rucinski, *President*
EMP: 3
SQ FT: 4,200
SALES (est): 110K **Privately Held**
WEB: www.envirofiltration.com
SIC: 3569 Filters, general line: industrial

(G-5045)
F R SHEET METAL CO INC
7428 W 15th Ave (46406-2293)
PHONE..................219 949-2290
Fax: 219 949-0972
EMP: 7
SQ FT: 6,000
SALES (est): 550K **Privately Held**
SIC: 1761 3444 Roofing/Siding Contractor Mfg Sheet Metalwork

(G-5046)
FASI COATINGS LLC
3905 W Ridge Rd (46408-1847)
PHONE..................219 985-0788
Timothy Kuiper, *Principal*
James Robshaw, *Principal*
EMP: 4 **EST:** 2016
SALES (est): 133.8K **Privately Held**
SIC: 3479 Metal coating & allied service

(G-5047)
FIRE APARATUS SERVICE INC
Also Called: Fasi Codings
3905 W Ridge Rd (46408-1847)
PHONE..................219 985-0788
Timothy Kuiper, *CEO*
EMP: 4
SALES (est): 460K **Privately Held**
SIC: 5012 7699 3823 Fire trucks; industrial truck repair; thermal conductivity instruments, industrial process type

(G-5048)
FOSBEL INC
1 N Broadway (46402-3101)
PHONE..................219 883-4479
EMP: 2
SALES (est): 160K **Privately Held**
SIC: 2952 Mfg Asphalt Felts/Coatings

(G-5049)
GARY BRIDGE AND IRON CO INC
3700 Roosevelt St (46408-2034)
PHONE..................219 884-3792
Fax: 219 980-0325
Stephan Truchan Jr, *President*
Jean Truchan, *Treasurer*
EMP: 5 **EST:** 1942
SQ FT: 45,000
SALES (est): 730.5K **Privately Held**
WEB: www.gbi1.com
SIC: 3441 3599 7699 4225 Building components, structural steel; machine shop, jobbing & repair; industrial machinery & equipment repair; general warehousing

(G-5050)
GARY METAL MFG LLC
2700 E 5th Ave (46402-1606)
PHONE..................219 885-3232
David J Strilich, *Mng Member*
Jeffrey Strilich,
Frank Zudock,
EMP: 120
SQ FT: 350,000
SALES (est): 17.4MM **Privately Held**
WEB: www.garymetal.com
SIC: 3444 Sheet metal specialties, not stamped; pipe, sheet metal

(G-5051)
GARY MUSLIM CENTER
1473 W 15th Ave (46407-1017)
PHONE..................219 885-3018
Fax: 219 885-0137
Masjid Gary, *Principal*
EMP: 4
SALES (est): 338.2K **Privately Held**
SIC: 2389 Clergymen's vestments

(G-5052)
GARY PRINTING INC
1950 W 11th Ave (46404-2406)
PHONE..................................219 886-1767
Fax: 219 886-1749
Patricia L Eaton, *President*
Helen J Danko, *Treasurer*
EMP: 4 EST: 1946
SQ FT: 925
SALES (est): 533.5K **Privately Held**
SIC: 2752 2791 2796 2759 Commercial printing, offset; typesetting; platemaking services; engraving; labels: gravure printing

(G-5053)
GARY VEHICLE MAINTENANCE-FUEL
1000 Madison St (46402-2834)
PHONE..................................219 881-0219
John Seabrook, *Director*
EMP: 3
SALES (est): 163.1K **Privately Held**
SIC: 2869 Fuels

(G-5054)
GENOA HEALTHCARE LLC
1100 W 6th Ave (46402-1711)
PHONE..................................219 427-1837
EMP: 4 **Privately Held**
SIC: 5912 2834 Drug stores & proprietary stores; pharmaceutical preparations
PA: Genoa Healthcare Llc
707 S Grady Way Ste 700
Renton WA 98057

(G-5055)
GRIFFITH MACHINE & FABRICATING
3750 W 47th Ave (46408-4042)
PHONE..................................219 980-8855
Fax: 219 980-8866
Ernest Dale Voorhies, *President*
Randall Scott Voorhies, *General Mgr*
Randy Voorhies, *Vice Pres*
Norma Voorhies, *Admin Sec*
EMP: 5
SQ FT: 5,000
SALES (est): 763.4K **Privately Held**
SIC: 3441 Fabricated structural metal

(G-5056)
GSP-2700 LLC
2700 E 5th Ave (46402-1606)
PHONE..................................219 885-3232
Fax: 219 885-0528
Frank Zudock, *Partner*
EMP: 2
SALES (est): 247.7K **Privately Held**
SIC: 3444 Sheet metalwork

(G-5057)
HARBISONWALKER INTL INC
Also Called: Anh Refractories Co.
76 N Bridge St (46404-1074)
PHONE..................................219 881-4440
Brian Cavner, *Branch Mgr*
EMP: 4
SALES (corp-wide): 923MM **Privately Held**
SIC: 3255 Clay refractories
HQ: Harbisonwalker International, Inc.
1305 Cherrington Pkwy # 100
Moon Township PA 15108

(G-5058)
HARBISONWALKER INTL INC
76 N Bridge St (46404-1074)
PHONE..................................219 883-3335
Fax: 219 885-3182
Rich Agnew, *Principal*
John Johnson, *Branch Mgr*
EMP: 57
SALES (corp-wide): 923MM **Privately Held**
WEB: www.rhiamerica.com
SIC: 3255 3297 Clay refractories; nonclay refractories
HQ: Harbisonwalker International, Inc.
1305 Cherrington Pkwy # 100
Moon Township PA 15108

(G-5059)
HARRIS BMO BANK NATIONAL ASSN
Also Called: Bmo Harris Bank
6001 Melton Rd (46403-2922)
PHONE..................................219 939-0164
EMP: 5
SALES (corp-wide): 15.2B **Privately Held**
SIC: 3944 Mfg Games/Toys
HQ: Harris Bmo Bank National Association
111 W Monroe St Ste 1200
Chicago IL 60603
312 461-2323

(G-5060)
HARSCO CORPORATION
7100 W 9th Ave (46406-1924)
PHONE..................................219 944-6250
Dave Wollehgan, *Manager*
EMP: 15
SALES (corp-wide): 1.6B **Publicly Held**
SIC: 3295 3291 Roofing granules; abrasive products
PA: Harsco Corporation
350 Poplar Church Rd
Camp Hill PA 17011
717 763-7064

(G-5061)
HEARTS RMNED LIFESTYLE CIR LLC
1052 N County Line Rd (46403-1735)
PHONE..................................800 807-0485
Sheila Rashid, *Mng Member*
Bianca Griffith- Rashid,
EMP: 7
SALES (est): 656.2K **Privately Held**
SIC: 2311 7389 Tailored suits & formal jackets;

(G-5062)
HEAVEN SENT GURMET COOKIES INC
3745 Broadway (46409-1501)
P.O. Box 1796 (46409-0796)
PHONE..................................219 980-1066
Patricia M Johnson, *President*
Glynis Kelly, *Admin Sec*
EMP: 6
SQ FT: 2,000
SALES (est): 656.9K **Privately Held**
SIC: 2052 5812 Cookies & crackers; caterers

(G-5063)
HERALD MACHINE WORKS INC (PA)
7100 Industrial Hwy (46406-1045)
P.O. Box 6331 (46406-0331)
PHONE..................................219 949-0580
Fax: 219 949-0581
Daniel Herald, *President*
Joseph Herald, *Admin Sec*
EMP: 12
SQ FT: 5,200
SALES (est): 1.9MM **Privately Held**
SIC: 3599 Machine shop, jobbing & repair

(G-5064)
HESSVILLE CABLE & SLING CO
1601 Cline Ave (46406-2296)
PHONE..................................773 768-8181
Fax: 219 944-8224
George Randall, *President*
D Kenneth Randall, *Corp Secy*
Tom Randall, *Vice Pres*
▲ EMP: 35
SQ FT: 12,000
SALES (est): 18.7MM **Privately Held**
WEB: www.hessvillecable.com
SIC: 5063 2298 3496 Wire & cable; nets, seines, slings & insulator pads; miscellaneous fabricated wire products

(G-5065)
HOKEY SPOKES
739 N Montgomery St (46403-1240)
PHONE..................................219 938-7360
Richard Barnes, *Principal*
EMP: 3
SALES (est): 270.7K **Privately Held**
SIC: 3647 Bicycle lamps

(G-5066)
HOMEOWNERS EQUITY & RLTY CORP
306 W Ridge Rd (46408)
PHONE..................................219 981-1700
Allan Fefferman, *Principal*
Felipa Ortiz, *Agent*
EMP: 6 EST: 1996
SQ FT: 2,500
SALES (est): 286.4K **Privately Held**
SIC: 3272 Building materials, except block or brick: concrete

(G-5067)
IFC FENCE LLC
3245 W 46th Ave (46408-3653)
PHONE..................................219 977-4000
Luigi Biancardi, *Mng Member*
EMP: 5
SALES: 700K **Privately Held**
SIC: 3315 Chain link fencing

(G-5068)
INDUSTRIAL COMBUSTN ENGINEERS
Also Called: Industrial Combustion Engnrs
7000 W 21st Ave (46406-2404)
PHONE..................................219 949-5066
Fax: 219 944-7683
Leonard G Nowak, *President*
Angela Whitaker, *Office Mgr*
EMP: 20 EST: 1954
SQ FT: 12,000
SALES (est): 4.1MM **Privately Held**
WEB: www.indcomb.com
SIC: 3585 3567 8711 Refrigeration & heating equipment; industrial furnaces & ovens; industrial engineers

(G-5069)
INDUSTRIAL STEEL CNSTR INC
Midwest Freight Services
86 N Bridge St (46404-1074)
PHONE..................................219 885-5610
Fax: 219 881-2744
Jerry Pacific, *Sales Staff*
Daniel Moore, *Manager*
EMP: 200
SALES (corp-wide): 38.1MM **Privately Held**
WEB: www.iscbridge.com
SIC: 3441 3444 3443 3312 Fabricated structural metal; sheet metalwork; fabricated plate work (boiler shop); blast furnaces & steel mills
PA: Industrial Steel Construction, Inc.
413 Old Kirk Rd
Geneva IL 60134
630 232-7473

(G-5070)
INTERSTATE POWER SYSTEMS INC
Also Called: Interstate Powersystems
2601 E 15th Ave (46402-3012)
PHONE..................................952 854-2044
Gordon Galarneau, *CEO*
Mark Goverg, *Branch Mgr*
Mark Govert, *Branch Mgr*
EMP: 27
SALES (corp-wide): 228MM **Privately Held**
SIC: 3714 5084 Motor vehicle parts & accessories; industrial machinery & equipment
HQ: Interstate Power Systems, Inc.
2901 E 78th St
Minneapolis MN 55425
952 854-2044

(G-5071)
JACKSON VISION QUEST
521 Broadway (46402-1910)
PHONE..................................219 882-9397
Alexander Koukiakis, *President*
Dr Dick D Jackson, *President*
EMP: 3 EST: 1929
SALES (est): 291.9K
SALES (corp-wide): 3.8MM **Privately Held**
WEB: www.visionquesteyecare.com
SIC: 3851 5995 Eyeglasses, lenses & frames; optical goods stores

PA: A & K Kouklakis Od Pc
2294 W 81st Ave
Merrillville IN 46410
219 756-1700

(G-5072)
KIDSTUFF PLAYSYSTEMS INC
5400 Miller Ave (46403-2844)
PHONE..................................219 938-3331
Richard Hagelberg, *CEO*
George Mc Guan, *President*
▲ EMP: 25
SQ FT: 28,000
SALES: 3.6MM **Privately Held**
WEB: www.kidstuffplaysystems.com
SIC: 3949 5941 Playground equipment; playground equipment

(G-5073)
MAGNECO/METREL INC
201 Mississippi St (46402-1546)
PHONE..................................219 885-4190
Fax: 219 885-4341
Tom Colander, *Branch Mgr*
EMP: 15
SALES (corp-wide): 65.8MM **Privately Held**
WEB: www.magneco-metrel.com
SIC: 5085 3297 Refractory material; nonclay refractories
PA: Magneco/Metrel, Inc.
223 W Interstate Rd
Addison IL 60101
630 543-6660

(G-5074)
MARGINS PRINTING LLC
4163 Georgia St (46409-2029)
PHONE..................................773 981-4251
Jennifer Gipson-Peterson, *Principal*
EMP: 2
SALES (est): 85.5K **Privately Held**
SIC: 2752 Commercial printing, lithographic

(G-5075)
METAL RESOURCES INC
201 Mississippi St Slip 9 (46402-1548)
PHONE..................................219 886-2710
William R Wilson, *Branch Mgr*
EMP: 3 **Privately Held**
SIC: 3448 Prefabricated metal components
PA: Metal Resources, Inc.
15 Salt Creek Ln Ste 312
Hinsdale IL 60521

(G-5076)
MILLER RACEWAY
4900 Melton Rd (46403-2872)
PHONE..................................219 939-9688
Lakhwinder P Singh, *Principal*
EMP: 3
SALES (est): 275.6K **Privately Held**
SIC: 3644 Raceways

(G-5077)
MINTEQ INTERNATIONAL INC
1 N Broadway (46402-3101)
PHONE..................................219 886-9555
Don Cochran, *Manager*
EMP: 112 **Publicly Held**
SIC: 3297 Nonclay refractories
HQ: Minteq International Inc.
35 Highland Ave
Bethlehem PA 18017

(G-5078)
MODRAK PRODUCTS COMPANY INC
3700 Clark Rd (46408-1308)
PHONE..................................219 838-0308
Fax: 219 838-0660
Larry Modrak, *President*
Judy Modrak, *Vice Pres*
EMP: 10
SQ FT: 15,000
SALES (est): 1.7MM **Privately Held**
SIC: 2842 5087 5999 Specialty cleaning, polishes & sanitation goods; janitors' supplies; cleaning equipment & supplies

(G-5079)
NEW BUSINESS CORPORATION
444 Rutledge St (46404-1011)
PHONE..................................219 886-2700
John Thomas Jr, *President*

▲ = Import ▼=Export
◆ =Import/Export

EMP: 3
SALES: 150K **Privately Held**
WEB: www.gourmetsupreme.com
SIC: **2033** Canned fruits & specialties

(G-5080)
OLD DUTCH SAND CO INC
4600 E 15th Ave (46403-3699)
PHONE....................................219 938-7020
Bernice Gray, *President*
Gary Goldberg, *Vice Pres*
EMP: 5 EST: 1961
SQ FT: 500
SALES: 2.4MM **Privately Held**
SIC: **5032** 1442 Sand, construction; construction sand mining

(G-5081)
ONE EIGHT SEVEN INCORPORATED
1050 Michigan St (46402-3009)
PHONE....................................219 886-2060
Fax: 219 883-6327
Michael R Murton, *VP Opers*
Sue Adkins, *Office Mgr*
Dan Luce, *Manager*
EMP: 6
SALES (est): 643.7K
SALES (corp-wide): 1.4MM **Privately Held**
SIC: **3297** Nonclay refractories
PA: One Eight Seven Incorporated
10485 Frankstown Rd
Pittsburgh PA
412 243-7365

(G-5082)
OZINGA INDIANA RDYMX CON INC
400 Blaine St (46406-1252)
PHONE....................................219 949-9800
Donald Rapley, *President*
Barry N Voorn, *Admin Sec*
EMP: 11
SALES (est): 1.2MM **Privately Held**
SIC: **3273** 5032 Ready-mixed concrete; brick, stone & related material

(G-5083)
PARAMOUNT PRINTING LTD INC
2400 W 47th Ave (46408-4102)
PHONE....................................219 980-0445
Fax: 219 980-0463
Joyce Hazen, *President*
EMP: 2
SQ FT: 2,400
SALES: 200K **Privately Held**
SIC: **2759** Letterpress printing

(G-5084)
PENLINES PUBLISHING LLC
212 W 49th Ave (46408-4519)
PHONE....................................219 884-2632
Onitta Parker, *Principal*
EMP: 2
SALES (est): 97.1K **Privately Held**
SIC: **2741** Miscellaneous publishing

(G-5085)
PRAXAIR INC
Clark & Dean Mitchell Rds (46406)
P.O. Box 6188 (46406-0188)
PHONE....................................219 949-8407
Fax: 219 949-7119
Terri Paton, *Manager*
EMP: 17
SALES (corp-wide): 11.4B **Publicly Held**
SIC: **2813** Industrial gases
PA: Praxair, Inc.
10 Riverview Dr
Danbury CT 06810
203 837-2000

(G-5086)
PRES-DEL ELECTRIC INC
4172 Broadway (46408-2809)
PHONE....................................219 884-3146
Fax: 219 884-3147
Ron Price, *President*
EMP: 6
SQ FT: 18,000
SALES (est): 707K **Privately Held**
SIC: **7694** 5999 Electric motor repair; motors, electric

(G-5087)
PRO PALLET LLC
1584 Blaine St (46406-2220)
PHONE....................................219 292-3389
Matthew Collins, *Principal*
EMP: 7 EST: 2016
SALES (est): 314.8K **Privately Held**
SIC: **2448** Pallets, wood & wood with metal

(G-5088)
RAY KAMMER
Also Called: Midwest Water Controls
6805 Forest Ave (46403-1280)
PHONE....................................219 938-1708
Ray Kammer, *Owner*
EMP: 3
SALES: 500K **Privately Held**
SIC: **3823** Water quality monitoring & control systems

(G-5089)
REED MINERALS
7100 W 9th Ave (46406-1924)
PHONE....................................219 944-6250
Fax: 219 944-6263
Derek Hathaway, *Principal*
EMP: 2
SALES (est): 201.9K **Privately Held**
SIC: **3291** Abrasive products

(G-5090)
REFAX INC
Also Called: Diversified Wear Products
3240 W 5th Ave (46406-1724)
P.O. Box 9018 (46402-9018)
PHONE....................................219 977-0414
Fax: 219 977-2207
Richard A Oliver, *President*
Eva Del Toro, *Purchasing*
Hansel Steuer, *Engineer*
Treavor Mahle, *Sales Mgr*
Harold Josleyn, *Sales Staff*
EMP: 180
SQ FT: 20,000
SALES (est): 44.4MM
SALES (corp-wide): 74.8MM **Privately Held**
SIC: **3441** Fabricated structural metal
PA: Gi Properties, Inc.
6610 Melton Rd
Portage IN 46368
219 763-1177

(G-5091)
REFAX WEAR PRODUCTS INC
3240 W 5th Ave (46406-1724)
PHONE....................................219 977-0414
Richard Oliver, *Principal*
EMP: 2
SALES (est): 257.7K **Privately Held**
WEB: www.refaxinc.com
SIC: **3441** 3446 Fabricated structural metal; architectural metalwork

(G-5092)
RHYNE ENGINES INC
Also Called: Rhyne Competition Engines
5733 W 25th Ave (46406-3127)
PHONE....................................219 845-1218
Fax: 219 845-3012
Joe Rhyne, *President*
EMP: 7
SQ FT: 7,000
SALES (est): 832.3K **Privately Held**
WEB: www.rhynecompetitionengines.com
SIC: **3599** 7549 Machine shop, jobbing & repair; high performance auto repair & service

(G-5093)
RIETH-RILEY CNSTR CO INC
7500 W 5th Ave (46406-1238)
PHONE....................................574 875-5183
Fax: 219 944-2472
Doug Robinson, *Manager*
EMP: 200
SALES (corp-wide): 226.8MM **Privately Held**
WEB: www.reithriley.com
SIC: **1611** 2951 Surfacing & paving; asphalt paving mixtures & blocks
PA: Rieth-Riley Construction Co., Inc.
3626 Elkhart Rd
Goshen IN 46526
574 875-5183

(G-5094)
ROAD EQUIPMENT
3450 Grant St (46408-1010)
PHONE....................................219 887-6400
John Finck, *Accounts Mgr*
Chris Williams, *Manager*
EMP: 2
SALES (est): 87.2K **Privately Held**
SIC: **3714** Motor vehicle parts & accessories

(G-5095)
SAND DUNE PUBLISHING COMPA
8719 Indian Boundary (46403-1410)
P.O. Box 2995 (46403-0995)
PHONE....................................219 938-7118
Winston Simmonds, *Principal*
▲ EMP: 3
SALES (est): 238.6K **Privately Held**
SIC: **2741** Miscellaneous publishing

(G-5096)
SERVSTEEL INC
8880 Mississippi St (46410-7119)
PHONE....................................219 736-6030
Fax: 219 769-0567
Michael McQuillen, *President*
EMP: 39
SALES (corp-wide): 7.6MM **Privately Held**
WEB: www.servsteelinc.com
SIC: **7699** 3297 Power tool repair; nonclay refractories
PA: Servsteel, Inc.
214 W Bridge Dr
Morgan PA 15064
412 221-8600

(G-5097)
SHANXI-INDIANA LLC
Also Called: Dvs Refractories
201 Mississippi St (46402-1546)
PHONE....................................219 885-2209
Jordan Skaltsas,
EMP: 8 EST: 2008
SALES (est): 1MM **Privately Held**
SIC: **3559** Kilns

(G-5098)
SMITHS MEDICAL ASD INC
5700 W 23rd Ave (46406-2617)
PHONE....................................219 554-2196
Jackie Gerner, *Branch Mgr*
EMP: 28
SALES (corp-wide): 4.1B **Privately Held**
WEB: www.smith-medical.com
SIC: **3841** Surgical & medical instruments
HQ: Smiths Medical Asd, Inc.
6000 Nathan Ln N Ste 100
Plymouth MN 55442
763 383-3000

(G-5099)
SMS GROUP INC
Also Called: SMS Technical Services
201 Mssissippi St Ste 12a (46402)
PHONE....................................219 880-0256
Steve Winger, *Principal*
EMP: 50 **Privately Held**
SIC: **3441** 3443 Fabricated structural metal; fabricated plate work (boiler shop)
HQ: Sms Group, Inc.
100 Sandusky St
Pittsburgh PA 15212
412 323-3658

(G-5100)
SOUTHLAKE LIFT TRUCK
3601 Arizona St (46405-3121)
PHONE....................................219 962-4695
Don Glorioso, *Owner*
EMP: 5
SALES (est): 655.9K **Privately Held**
SIC: **3537** 4213 Forklift trucks; trucking, except local

(G-5101)
SSSI INC
1 N Broadway (46402-3101)
P.O. Box 64771 (46401-0771)
PHONE....................................219 880-0818
Rich Soohey, *Branch Mgr*
EMP: 100

SALES (corp-wide): 177MM **Privately Held**
WEB: www.songernet.com
SIC: **1611** 3312 4925 General contractor, highway & street construction; blast furnaces & steel mills; coke oven gas, production & distribution
PA: Sssi, Inc.
2755a Park Ave
Washington PA 15301
724 743-5815

(G-5102)
STYLED RITE COMPANY INC
1500 Polk St (46407-1917)
PHONE....................................219 931-9844
Fax: 219 931-7415
Howard Weiss, *President*
Esther Van Loon, *Vice Pres*
EMP: 6 EST: 1951
SQ FT: 2,000
SALES (est): 480K **Privately Held**
WEB: www.styledrite.com
SIC: **3444** 1521 Awnings, sheet metal; general remodeling, single-family houses

(G-5103)
SUPERIOR TRUSS & PANEL INC
7592 Melton Rd (46403-3147)
PHONE....................................708 339-1200
William Welty, *President*
EMP: 50
SQ FT: 40,000
SALES (est): 8.5MM **Privately Held**
WEB: www.superior-truss.com
SIC: **2439** Trusses, wooden roof

(G-5104)
T K SALES & SERVICE
Also Called: T B K Tarp Sales & Service
669 S Grand Blvd (46403-2901)
P.O. Box 2497 (46403-0497)
PHONE....................................219 962-8982
Anthony J Kettwig, *Owner*
EMP: 4
SQ FT: 3,796
SALES (est): 182.6K **Privately Held**
SIC: **2394** 5199 7692 5251 Tarpaulins, fabric; made from purchased materials; tarpaulins; automotive welding; hardware; inspection services connected with transportation

(G-5105)
THATCHER ENGINEERING CORP
7100 Industrial Hwy (46406-1099)
PHONE....................................219 949-2084
Fax: 773 721-1011
R Stephen Parkison, *President*
Steve Parkison, *General Mgr*
David Cooper, *Safety Dir*
Thomas Wysockey, *Shareholder*
EMP: 90 EST: 1932
SQ FT: 12,000
SALES (est): 7.9MM **Privately Held**
WEB: www.thatchereng.com
SIC: **1741** 1629 3822 1794 Foundation & retaining wall construction; pile driving contractor; auto controls regulating residntl & coml environmt & applncs; excavation work

(G-5106)
TMS INTERNATIONAL LLC
1 N Broadway (46402-3101)
PHONE....................................219 881-0266
EMP: 4 **Privately Held**
SIC: **3312** Blast furnaces & steel mills
HQ: Tms International, Llc
12 Monongahela Ave
Glassport PA 15045
412 678-6141

(G-5107)
TMS INTERNATIONAL LLC
1 N Broadway Stop 380 (46402-3101)
PHONE....................................219 885-7491
EMP: 3 **Privately Held**
SIC: **3312** Blast furnaces & steel mills
HQ: Tms International, Llc
12 Monongahela Ave
Glassport PA 15045
412 678-6141

(G-5108)
TRANS INDUSTRIES INCORPORATED
6325 W 5th Ave (46406-1213)
PHONE..................................219 977-9190
Piagi Phelts, *Principal*
EMP: 3 EST: 2007
SALES (est): 326.3K Privately Held
SIC: 3999 Manufacturing industries

(G-5109)
TRIM-A-SEAL OF INDIANA INC (PA)
Also Called: Styled-Rite
1500 Polk St (46407-1999)
PHONE..................................219 883-2180
Toll Free:...............................888   -
Fax: 219 882-3623
Howard B Weiss, *President*
Lawrence S Weiss, *Vice Pres*
Marlene Weiss, *Treasurer*
Judy Book, *Bookkeeper*
Pamela Weiss, *Admin Sec*
EMP: 15 EST: 1947
SQ FT: 4,000
SALES (est): 2.3MM Privately Held
WEB: www.trimaseal.com
SIC: 3442 3444 Storm doors or windows, metal; louvers, shutters, jalousies & similar items; sheet metalwork

(G-5110)
TRUCK LIFE LLC
7900 Melton Rd (46403-3112)
PHONE..................................219 655-0018
Jana Gaibu, *Owner*
Lee Gaibu, *Mng Member*
EMP: 17
SALES (est): 3.3MM Privately Held
SIC: 3715 Truck trailers

(G-5111)
UNITED STATES STEEL CORP
Also Called: U. S. Steel
1 N Broadway (46402-3199)
PHONE..................................219 888-2000
Fax: 219 888-3390
Darin R Hoffner, *Counsel*
Rick Shank, *Vice Pres*
Michael Williams, *Vice Pres*
Nathaniel E Joseph, *Buyer*
Rich Gilles, *Purchasing*
EMP: 444
SALES (corp-wide): 12.2B Publicly Held
SIC: 3325 3441 3312 Steel foundries; fabricated structural metal; blast furnaces & steel mills
PA: United States Steel Corp
    600 Grant St Ste 468
    Pittsburgh PA 15219
    412 433-1121

(G-5112)
UNIVERSAL EXPORT PARTNR LLC
5528 Melton Rd (46403-2958)
PHONE..................................219 939-9529
Andrea Lyles,
EMP: 2
SALES: 50K Privately Held
SIC: 3253 Ceramic wall & floor tile

(G-5113)
URSERYS LLC
3439 Connecticut St (46409-1012)
PHONE..................................619 206-1761
Ivan D Ursery II,
EMP: 2 EST: 2016
SALES: 7.4K Privately Held
SIC: 2389 Apparel & accessories

(G-5114)
VAN GARD VAULT CO INC
4401 W Ridge Rd (46408-1329)
PHONE..................................219 980-6233
EMP: 3
SALES (est): 251.3K Privately Held
SIC: 3272 Burial vaults, concrete or precast terrazzo

(G-5115)
VAN GARD VAULT CO INC
Also Called: Van Guard Vault
5100 Industrial Hwy (46406-1124)
P.O. Box 629, Griffith (46319-0629)
PHONE..................................219 949-7723
Robert Williams, *President*
EMP: 22
SQ FT: 16,000
SALES (est): 3.2MM Privately Held
WEB: www.vanguardvault.com
SIC: 3272 Burial vaults, concrete or precast terrazzo

(G-5116)
WILLIAM A KADAR
Also Called: Kadar Wood Shop
5015 Broadway (46409-2707)
PHONE..................................219 884-7404
William A Kadar, *Owner*
EMP: 2
SQ FT: 2,500
SALES (est): 134.3K Privately Held
SIC: 1751 2542 2517 2511 Cabinet building & installation; partitions & fixtures, except wood; wood television & radio cabinets; wood household furniture; wood kitchen cabinets

(G-5117)
ZIMCO MATERIALS INC
2555 E 15th Ave (46402-3021)
PHONE..................................219 883-0870
Scott Zimmer, *General Mgr*
EMP: 40
SALES (est): 2.1MM Privately Held
SIC: 3273 5051 5211 Ready-mixed concrete; concrete reinforcing bars; cement; concrete & cinder block

---

Gas City
Grant County

(G-5118)
AMERICAN WOODMARK CORPORATION
5300 Eastside Parkway Dr (46933-1648)
PHONE..................................765 677-1690
Fax: 765 677-1695
Pete Palpant, *Manager*
EMP: 400
SALES (corp-wide): 1.2B Publicly Held
WEB: www.americanwoodmark.com
SIC: 2434 Wood kitchen cabinets
PA: American Woodmark Corporation
    561 Shady Elm Rd
    Winchester VA 22602
    540 665-9100

(G-5119)
ARTISTIC EXPRESSIONS PUBG
111 E South C St (46933-1736)
P.O. Box 308 (46933-0308)
PHONE..................................317 502-6213
EMP: 2
SALES (est): 92.8K Privately Held
SIC: 2741 Miscellaneous publishing

(G-5120)
AVG NORTH AMERICA INC
5133 Eastside Parkway Dr (46933-1601)
PHONE..................................765 748-3162
Karim Suleman, *President*
EMP: 10
SALES (est): 374.7K Privately Held
SIC: 3714 Motor vehicle parts & accessories

(G-5121)
BUTTERWORTH INDUSTRIES INC
5050 Eastside Parkway Dr (46933-1645)
P.O. Box 107 (46933-0107)
PHONE..................................765 677-6725
Fax: 765 677-6735
Frank W Butterworth III, *President*
Frank L Butterworth III, *President*
Alice Butterworth, *Vice Pres*
Donnie Hartley, *Plant Mgr*
Susan Butterworth, *Purch Mgr*
EMP: 50
SQ FT: 32,000

SALES (est): 15.2MM Privately Held
SIC: 3535 Robotic conveyors

(G-5122)
DAVE TURNER
Also Called: Ebenezer Sportswear
109 E South D St (46933-1741)
PHONE..................................765 674-3360
Dave L Turner, *Owner*
EMP: 6
SALES: 280K Privately Held
SIC: 7299 7336 2396 2395 Stitching services; silk screen design; automotive & apparel trimmings; pleating & stitching

(G-5123)
EARTHWISE PLASTICS INC
100 Earthwise Way (46933)
PHONE..................................765 673-0308
Roger Dyson, *President*
Rocci Decamp, *Vice Pres*
Andy Miller, *Vice Pres*
James Harness, *VP Sales*
Scott Bradley, *Manager*
EMP: 45
SQ FT: 10,000
SALES: 13MM Privately Held
SIC: 2899 Plastic wood

(G-5124)
FRANKLIN ELECTRIC CO INC
100 Schaffer Dr (46933-1643)
PHONE..................................765 677-6900
Fax: 765 677-6939
Rd Jones, *Branch Mgr*
EMP: 90
SALES (corp-wide): 1.1B Publicly Held
SIC: 1731 3625 General electrical contractor; relays & industrial controls
PA: Franklin Electric Co., Inc.
    9255 Coverdale Rd
    Fort Wayne IN 46809
    260 824-2900

(G-5125)
GAS CITY B & K INC
928 E Main St (46933-1549)
PHONE..................................765 674-9651
John Thompson, *President*
EMP: 2 EST: 2002
SALES (est): 139.9K Privately Held
SIC: 1389 Cementing oil & gas well casings

(G-5126)
PACKAGING CORPORATION AMERICA
Also Called: PCA/Gas City 323
520 S 1st St (46933-1727)
PHONE..................................765 674-9781
Fax: 765 674-3771
Brad Hazelwood, *Buyer*
Paul Olsen, *Branch Mgr*
Paul Essig, *Manager*
EMP: 100
SALES (corp-wide): 6.4B Publicly Held
WEB: www.packagingcorp.com
SIC: 2653 Boxes, corrugated: made from purchased materials
PA: Packaging Corporation Of America
    1955 W Field Ct
    Lake Forest IL 60045
    847 482-3000

(G-5127)
TWIN CITY JOURNAL REPORTER
407 E Main St (46933-1532)
PHONE..................................765 674-0070
Fax: 765 674-3496
Greg Lenaze, *Owner*
EMP: 2
SALES (est): 75.7K Privately Held
SIC: 2711 Newspapers: publishing only, not printed on site

(G-5128)
WRIGHT REPAIRS INC
5900 Eastside Parkway Dr (46933-1656)
PHONE..................................765 674-3300
Fax: 765 674-1579
Thomas Wright, *President*
Dale Johnson, *Vice Pres*
Bryan Whitehead, *Vice Pres*
Chuck Hood, *Sales Mgr*
EMP: 14

SQ FT: 5,000
SALES: 1.2MM Privately Held
WEB: www.twright.com
SIC: 7694 Electric motor repair

Gaston
Delaware County

(G-5129)
AGBEST COOPERATIVE INC
430 S Sycamore St (47342-9441)
P.O. Box 398 (47342-0398)
PHONE..................................765 358-3388
Fax: 765 358-3808
Marty Clock, *Branch Mgr*
EMP: 8
SALES (corp-wide): 39.4MM Privately Held
WEB: www.agbest.com
SIC: 5261 2875 Fertilizer; fertilizers, mixing only
PA: Agbest Cooperative Inc
    2101 N Granville Ave
    Muncie IN 47303
    765 288-5001

(G-5130)
C & C MAILBOX PRODUCTS
18100 N County Road 925 W (47342-9062)
PHONE..................................765 358-4880
Gerald Clock, *Principal*
EMP: 2
SALES (est): 120.7K Privately Held
SIC: 5021 3444 2441 Outdoor & lawn furniture; mail (post office) collection or storage boxes, sheet metal; nailed wood boxes & shook

(G-5131)
D&D MOTORS
10240 N Langdon Rd (47342-8956)
PHONE..................................765 358-3856
Joe Bourff, *Owner*
EMP: 2
SALES: 150K Privately Held
SIC: 3714 Motor vehicle engines & parts

(G-5132)
G AND G PEPPERS LLC
12245 N County Road 450 W (47342-9423)
P.O. Box 326, Orestes (46063-0326)
PHONE..................................765 358-4519
Gary Reichart, *Partner*
Greg Cox, *Partner*
Michell Reichart, *Partner*
Cara Dennis, *Purchasing*
Michelle Reichart, *Executive*
EMP: 20 EST: 2000
SALES (est): 5MM Privately Held
WEB: www.gandgpeppers.com
SIC: 2099 Chili pepper or powder

Geneva
Adams County

(G-5133)
ADVANCED MANUFACTURING IN
500 W Line St (46740-9202)
PHONE..................................260 273-9669
Robert W Raugh, *President*
EMP: 2
SALES (est): 120.5K Privately Held
SIC: 3999 Manufacturing industries

(G-5134)
CASE AND QUART INC
220 E Shore Dr (46740-9660)
PHONE..................................260 368-7808
Ivan Nevil, *President*
EMP: 3
SALES (est): 184.9K Privately Held
SIC: 3523 Farm machinery & equipment

(G-5135)
ELKHART PRODUCTS CORPORATION
Also Called: Industrial Division
700 Rainbow Rd (46740-9700)
P.O. Box 740 (46740-0740)
PHONE....................260 368-7246
Fax: 260 368-7889
Dave Thompson, *Branch Mgr*
EMP: 125
SALES (corp-wide): 3.1B **Privately Held**
WEB: www.elkhartproducts.com
SIC: 3494 Pipe fittings
HQ: Elkhart Products Corporation
   1255 Oak St
   Elkhart IN 46514
   574 264-3181

(G-5136)
GENEVA MANUFACTURING INC
Also Called: Vgmc
110 5th St (46740-1002)
P.O. Box 219 (46740-0219)
PHONE....................260 368-7555
Fax: 260 368-7210
Terrill Vieth, *President*
Scott Miller, *General Mgr*
Larry J Miller, *Principal*
Julie Amiller, *Corp Secy*
Melissa Garwood, *Office Mgr*
▼ EMP: 39 EST: 1953
SQ FT: 34,000
SALES (est): 8.5MM **Privately Held**
WEB: www.geneva-mfg.com
SIC: 3429 Casket hardware

(G-5137)
O & R PRECISION GRINDING INC
5315 W 900 S (46740-9688)
PHONE....................260 368-9394
Fax: 260 368-9514
Tony Oswalt, *President*
Josh Oswalt, *Vice Pres*
EMP: 41
SQ FT: 26,000
SALES (est): 5.6MM **Privately Held**
SIC: 3544 7692 Special dies & tools;
   welding repair

(G-5138)
RED GOLD INC
Red Gold/Geneva
705 Williams St (46740-1061)
P.O. Box 247 (46740-0247)
PHONE....................260 368-9017
Conrad Heisner, *Plant Mgr*
Jim James, *Maint Spvr*
Kevin Grover, *Purch Agent*
Tom Neuenschwander, *Buyer*
Doug Rains, *Project Engr*
EMP: 101
SALES (corp-wide): 226MM **Privately
Held**
WEB: www.redgold.com
SIC: 2033 2035 Canned fruits & special-
   ties; pickles, sauces & salad dressings
PA: Red Gold, Inc.
   1500 Tomato Country Way
   Elwood IN 46036
   765 557-5500

(G-5139)
SHETLERS FAMOUS STAINELESS
10113 S 450 E (46740-9114)
PHONE....................260 368-9069
William Shetler, *Owner*
▲ EMP: 6 EST: 2010
SALES: 3MM **Privately Held**
SIC: 3312 Stainless steel

Georgetown
Floyd County

(G-5140)
ALL-FLEX INC
6451 S Park Dr (47122-9244)
PHONE....................812 949-8898
Fax: 812 949-8916
David Allen, *President*
Peggy Allen, *Vice Pres*
EMP: 3

SALES (est): 498K **Privately Held**
SIC: 2673 Plastic bags: made from purchased materials

(G-5141)
AREVA PHARMACEUTICALS INC
7112 Areva Dr Ne (47122-7953)
P.O. Box 336 (47122-0336)
PHONE....................855 853-4760
Vivek Swaminathan, *CEO*
Tom Murphy, *President*
Greg Olson, *COO*
EMP: 15
SALES (est): 1.7MM **Privately Held**
SIC: 2834 Pharmaceutical preparations

(G-5142)
DESTINY SOLUTIONS INC
8265 State Road 64 (47122-9056)
PHONE....................502 384-0031
Stan Walk, *President*
Debra Walk, *Shareholder*
EMP: 7
SALES: 2MM **Privately Held**
SIC: 3663 8742 Radio & TV communica-
   tions equipment; management consulting
   services

(G-5143)
DIVERSE WOODWORKING LLC
505 Maplewood Blvd (47122-9261)
PHONE....................812 366-3000
Randy Elliot,
EMP: 3
SALES (est): 455.7K **Privately Held**
SIC: 2431 Millwork

(G-5144)
FABTRATION LLC
526 Maplewood Blvd (47122-9261)
PHONE....................812 989-6730
Rick Keenan, *Mng Member*
Wendy Reisert, *Director*
▼ EMP: 12
SQ FT: 10,000
SALES (est): 2.7MM **Privately Held**
SIC: 3449 3613 Bars, concrete reinforc-
   ing: fabricated steel; control panels, elec-
   tric

(G-5145)
GEORGETOWN TRUSS COMPANY INC
9627 State Road 64 (47122-8842)
P.O. Box 1 (47122-0001)
PHONE....................812 951-2647
Tim Youtsey, *President*
Cindy Youtsey, *Corp Secy*
EMP: 28
SQ FT: 14,000
SALES: 3.2MM **Privately Held**
SIC: 2439 Trusses, except roof: laminated
   lumber; trusses, wooden roof

(G-5146)
KENTUCKIANA MACHINE & TOOL INC
Also Called: Kellco
518 Maplewood Blvd (47122-9261)
PHONE....................502 593-3975
Scott Patterson, *President*
EMP: 5 EST: 1995
SQ FT: 5,500
SALES (est): 619.1K **Privately Held**
SIC: 3599 Machine shop, jobbing & repair

(G-5147)
KS KREATIONS
7700 Greenbrier Rd Ne (47122-9617)
PHONE....................574 514-7366
EMP: 2 EST: 2014
SALES (est): 81.9K **Privately Held**
SIC: 3999 Candles

(G-5148)
LIBERTY GREEN RENEWABLES LLP
5019 Georges Hill Rd Ne (47122-7924)
PHONE....................812 951-3143
Larry W Ott,
EMP: 3
SALES (est): 260.7K **Privately Held**
SIC: 3621 Generating apparatus & parts,
   electrical

(G-5149)
MARTIN GRGORY CNVYOR ENGRG LLC
1549 Pirtle Dr (47122-9109)
P.O. Box 246 (47122-0246)
PHONE....................812 923-9814
Pamela A Villiger,
EMP: 3
SALES (est): 1MM **Privately Held**
WEB: www.martingregoryconveyor.com
SIC: 3535 Unit handling conveying sys-
   tems

(G-5150)
MIKES METAL DECTORS
9350 Indian Bluff Rd Ne (47122-7353)
PHONE....................812 366-3558
Michael Byrn, *Executive Asst*
EMP: 2
SALES (est): 186.5K **Privately Held**
SIC: 3669 Metal detectors

(G-5151)
ODYSSEY MACHINE INC
9627 State Road 64 (47122-8842)
PHONE....................812 951-1160
Robert E Kiper, *Principal*
Jennifer Knigge, *Office Mgr*
EMP: 6 EST: 2014
SALES (est): 62K **Privately Held**
SIC: 7699 3599 3089 Industrial machin-
   ery & equipment repair; crankshafts &
   camshafts, machining; automotive parts,
   plastic

(G-5152)
PIANO SHOP LLC
9161 In 64 (47122)
PHONE....................812 951-2462
Matt Grossman, *Owner*
EMP: 3 EST: 2016
SALES (est): 100.3K **Privately Held**
SIC: 3931 Pianos, all types: vertical, grand,
   spinet, player, etc.

(G-5153)
SPECTRUM
2530 Edwrdsvlle Galena Rd (47122-8745)
PHONE....................812 923-7830
EMP: 2
SALES (est): 76.8K **Privately Held**
SIC: 2759 Commercial printing

(G-5154)
TEAM SUPREME BAIT COMPANY ✪
7565 Pleasant Vly Rd Ne (47122-7547)
PHONE....................812 366-3200
Mark Keehn, *Owner*
EMP: 2 EST: 2017
SALES (est): 69.2K **Privately Held**
SIC: 5091 3949 Swimming pools, equip-
   ment & supplies; baskets (creels), fish &
   bait

(G-5155)
ZTMT INC
1750 Hidden Place Dr (47122-9158)
PHONE....................502 296-4032
Roger Stumler, *President*
Aimee Stumler, *Admin Sec*
EMP: 2
SALES (est): 100.5K **Privately Held**
SIC: 3541 Machine tools, metal cutting
   type

Goodland
Newton County

(G-5156)
3D MACHINE INC
215 S Newton St (47948-8189)
P.O. Box 465 (47948-0465)
PHONE....................219 297-3674
Fax: 219 297-4666
Tim Deno, *President*
Kelly Deno, *Corp Secy*
Tabatha Hall, *Accounts Mgr*
EMP: 40
SQ FT: 72,000

SALES: 7.3MM **Privately Held**
WEB: www.3dmach.com
SIC: 3599 Machine shop, jobbing & repair

(G-5157)
ARCHER-DANIELS-MIDLAND COMPANY
Also Called: ADM
4463 E Us Highway 24 (47948-8195)
P.O. Box 370 (47948-0370)
PHONE....................219 297-4582
Terry Winger, *Branch Mgr*
EMP: 8
SQ FT: 900
SALES (corp-wide): 60.8B **Publicly Held**
WEB: www.admworld.com
SIC: 2041 Flour & other grain mill products
PA: Archer-Daniels-Midland Company
   77 W Wacker Dr Ste 4600
   Chicago IL 60601
   312 634-8100

(G-5158)
BUTLER TOOL & DESIGN INC
641 S Newton St (47948-8128)
PHONE....................219 297-4531
Fax: 219 297-4554
James Butler, *President*
R Kay Butler, *Vice Pres*
EMP: 14
SQ FT: 7,000
SALES (est): 1.1MM **Privately Held**
WEB: www.advatechmfg.com
SIC: 3545 3544 3599 8711 Tools & ac-
   cessories for machine tools; special dies
   & tools; machine shop, jobbing & repair;
   engineering services; machine tools,
   metal cutting type

(G-5159)
GENERATION FOUR MACHINE &
319 N Newton St (47948-8119)
P.O. Box 257 (47948-0257)
PHONE....................219 297-3003
Eric Geravsen, *Principal*
EMP: 2
SALES (est): 266.2K **Privately Held**
SIC: 3599 Machine shop, jobbing & repair

(G-5160)
PARKER-HANNIFIN CORPORATION
Also Called: Cylinder Div
715 S Iroquois St (47948-8178)
PHONE....................219 297-3182
Fax: 219 297-4230
Eric Schultz, *Plant Mgr*
EMP: 46
SALES (corp-wide): 12B **Publicly Held**
WEB: www.parker.com
SIC: 3443 Cylinders, pressure: metal plate
PA: Parker-Hannifin Corporation
   6035 Parkland Blvd
   Cleveland OH 44124
   216 896-3000

(G-5161)
USEFUL PRODUCTS LLC
429 W Jasper St (47948-8005)
PHONE....................877 304-9036
Fax: 219 297-3577
Donald Ringer, *Mng Member*
Allan Adwell,
EMP: 33
SQ FT: 60,000
SALES (est): 5.7MM **Privately Held**
WEB: www.usefulproducts.com
SIC: 2759 3086 Flexographic printing;
   packaging & shipping materials, foamed
   plastic

Goshen
Elkhart County

(G-5162)
A&J WOODWORKING LLC
12263 County Road 36 (46528-6964)
PHONE....................574 642-4551
Arlin Schlabach,
EMP: 9 EST: 2010
SALES: 800K **Privately Held**
SIC: 2431 Millwork

G
E
O
G
R
A
P
H
I
C

(G-5163)
A/C FABRICATING CORP
1821 Century Dr (46528-5044)
P.O. Box 774 (46527-0774)
PHONE................................574 534-1415
Fax: 574 533-5254
Gerie Mast, *President*
Melody Biddle, *Admin Sec*
EMP: 20
SQ FT: 20,000
SALES (est): 3.4MM **Privately Held**
WEB: www.acfabricating.com
SIC: 3498 3542 3355 Tube fabricating (contract bending & shaping); headers; extrusion ingot, aluminum: made in rolling mills

(G-5164)
ABC DENTAL OF GOSHEN
622 W Lincoln Ave (46526-2416)
PHONE................................574 534-8777
Samantha Johnson, *Office Mgr*
Lucinda Good, *Manager*
EMP: 8
SALES (est): 755.1K **Privately Held**
SIC: 3843 Enamels, dentists'

(G-5165)
ADVANCE GREEN MFG CO INC
2482 E Kercher Rd (46526-6466)
PHONE................................574 457-2695
Omer G Kropf, *President*
Kermit Kropf, *General Mgr*
EMP: 6
SQ FT: 1,000
SALES (est): 498K **Privately Held**
SIC: 3999 Coin-operated amusement machines

(G-5166)
ADVANCE MCS ELECTRONICS INC (PA)
67928 Us Highway 33 (46526-8549)
PHONE................................574 642-3501
Fax: 574 642-3503
Michael Snavely, *President*
Charlene Snavely, *Corp Secy*
◆ EMP: 10
SQ FT: 2,200
SALES (est): 2.3MM **Privately Held**
SIC: 5961 3613 Electronic kits & parts, mail order; control panels, electric

(G-5167)
ADVANCED KINEMATICS INC
15593 County Road 28 (46528-9670)
PHONE................................574 533-8178
Bruce Jones, *President*
EMP: 2
SALES (est): 176.8K **Privately Held**
SIC: 3648 Lighting equipment

(G-5168)
AG PROCESSING A COOPERATIVE
Also Called: Supersweet Farm Service
24120 County Road 142 1 (46526-9204)
PHONE................................574 831-2292
Leroy Martin, *Manager*
EMP: 5
SALES (corp-wide): 3.4B **Privately Held**
WEB: www.agp.com
SIC: 2041 Wheat mill feed
PA: Ag Processing Inc A Cooperative
12700 W Dodge Rd
Omaha NE 68154
402 496-7809

(G-5169)
AMERICAN PRINTING COMPANY (PA)
2331 Eisenhower Dr N (46526-8805)
PHONE................................574 533-5399
Jim Magnus, *President*
EMP: 10
SALES (est): 2MM **Privately Held**
SIC: 2752 Commercial printing, offset

(G-5170)
AMISH HILLS WOODWORKING AND MA
64723 County Road 15 (46526-9376)
PHONE................................574 875-3558
Robert Hey, *Principal*
EMP: 2

SALES (est): 126.5K **Privately Held**
SIC: 2431 Millwork

(G-5171)
ARCHER-DANIELS-MIDLAND COMPANY
Also Called: ADM
24120 County Road 142 (46526-9204)
PHONE................................574 831-2292
Robert Gluck, *Manager*
EMP: 3
SALES (corp-wide): 60.8B **Publicly Held**
WEB: www.admworld.com
SIC: 2048 Prepared feeds
PA: Archer-Daniels-Midland Company
77 W Wacker Dr Ste 4600
Chicago IL 60601
312 634-8100

(G-5172)
ARCTIC CLEAR PRODUCTS INC
1808 Barclay Dr (46528-5711)
P.O. Box 452 (46527-0452)
PHONE................................574 533-7671
Fax: 574 533-7671
EMP: 2
SQ FT: 1,800
SALES (est): 212.7K **Privately Held**
SIC: 3677 Manufactures Filtration Devices

(G-5173)
AUSTIN & AUSTIN INC (PA)
Also Called: Ultra Manufacturing
59632 Timberwood Ln (46528-9154)
PHONE................................574 586-2320
Michael Austin, *Principal*
Tammy Austin, *Treasurer*
EMP: 18
SALES (est): 4MM **Privately Held**
SIC: 3599 Machine shop, jobbing & repair

(G-5174)
B & M PRODUCTS
18702 Monticello Dr (46528-8930)
PHONE................................574 238-7468
Fax: 574 294-2476
Roy Edington, *Owner*
EMP: 3
SQ FT: 3,152
SALES (est): 120K **Privately Held**
SIC: 3949 5941 Fishing equipment; bait & tackle

(G-5175)
B & S PRODUCTS CORP
1917 Eisenhower Dr N (46526-5388)
PHONE................................574 537-0770
Fax: 574 537-0880
Colin Black, *President*
Carmen Black, *Treasurer*
Michael Black, *Manager*
EMP: 5
SALES: 500K **Privately Held**
SIC: 2842 Specialty cleaning, polishes & sanitation goods

(G-5176)
B T BTTERY CHARGER SYSTEMS INC
17189 County Road 22 (46528-6612)
PHONE................................574 533-6030
Fax: 574 534-1118
Tom Jewell, *Principal*
EMP: 3
SALES (est): 292.4K **Privately Held**
SIC: 3691 5063 5084 Storage batteries; storage batteries, industrial; materials handling machinery

(G-5177)
BEARCAT CORP
Also Called: Conversions By Bearcat
2431 E Kercher Rd (46526-6465)
P.O. Box 613 (46527-0613)
PHONE................................574 533-0448
Donald Cowan, *President*
Cassandra Cowan, *Admin Sec*
EMP: 35 EST: 1971
SALES (est): 5.7MM **Privately Held**
WEB: www.bearcatcorp.com
SIC: 3444 7532 Sheet metal specialties, not stamped; canopies; sheet metal; customizing services, non-factory basis

(G-5178)
BENTELER AUTOMOTIVE CORP
910 Eisenhower Dr S (46526-5351)
PHONE................................574 534-1499
Fax: 574 533-8975
Missy Berry, *Buyer*
Sandy Chesebro, *Buyer*
Ed Steinebach, *Branch Mgr*
Nick Gromski, *Network Tech*
EMP: 150
SALES (corp-wide): 9.2B **Privately Held**
SIC: 3465 3714 5012 Automotive stampings; motor vehicle parts & accessories; automobiles
HQ: Benteler Automotive Corporation
2650 N Opdyke Rd Ste B
Auburn Hills MI 48326
248 364-7190

(G-5179)
BRISTOL PALLET
64466 State Road 19 (46526-9421)
PHONE................................574 862-1862
EMP: 4
SALES (est): 149.3K **Privately Held**
SIC: 2448 Pallets, wood & wood with metal

(G-5180)
BRUNK CORP (PA)
Also Called: Bartow Warehouse
803 Logan St (46528-3508)
PHONE................................574 533-1109
Steve Bartow, *Ch of Bd*
Tracy Bartow, *President*
David Loeffler, *Project Mgr*
Josh Hunsberger, *QA Dir*
Sandy Hochstetler, *Cust Mgr*
EMP: 50
SQ FT: 125,000
SALES (est): 7.8MM **Privately Held**
WEB: www.brunk-ajp.com
SIC: 3999 5162 Custom pulverizing & grinding of plastic materials; plastics materials & basic shapes

(G-5181)
BUCKLES TOOL AND ENGINEERING
68860 County Road 33 (46526-8538)
PHONE................................574 642-3471
Fax: 574 642-3474
James Buckles II, *President*
Ruby Buckles, *Admin Sec*
EMP: 3
SQ FT: 6,000
SALES: 350K **Privately Held**
SIC: 3599 Machine shop, jobbing & repair

(G-5182)
BURKHOLDER MACHINE
25354 County Road 40 (46526-7433)
PHONE................................574 862-2004
Leon Burkholder, *Owner*
EMP: 2
SQ FT: 3,700
SALES (est): 190K **Privately Held**
SIC: 3599 Machine & other job shop work

(G-5183)
BYLER FAMILY WOOD WORKING
60845 State Road 13 (46528-6581)
PHONE................................574 825-3339
Noah Byler, *Principal*
EMP: 2
SALES (est): 160K **Privately Held**
SIC: 2431 Millwork

(G-5184)
C & L ELECTRIC MOTOR REPR INC
1402 N Chicago Ave (46528-1905)
PHONE................................574 533-2643
Fax: 574 533-1511
Charles Lewallen, *President*
Robert Kauffman, *Vice Pres*
EMP: 4 EST: 1967
SQ FT: 2,400
SALES: 100K **Privately Held**
SIC: 7694 5063 Electric motor repair; motors, electric

(G-5185)
CENTRAL RUBBER & PLASTICS INC
17416 County Road 34 (46528-7513)
P.O. Box 821 (46527-0821)
PHONE................................574 534-6411
Scott Salisbury, *President*
EMP: 24
SQ FT: 20,000
SALES (est): 4.2MM **Privately Held**
WEB: www.centralrubberinc.com
SIC: 3069 Rubber automotive products; molded rubber products

(G-5186)
CENTRUM FORCE FABRICATION
204 W Clinton St (46526-3216)
PHONE................................574 295-5367
Tom Monahan,
EMP: 2
SALES (est): 193.1K **Privately Held**
SIC: 3446 Ornamental metalwork

(G-5187)
CIN-NAN TREASURES
808 Lynwood Dr (46526-1130)
PHONE................................574 533-6593
Larry Unger, *President*
Nancy Unger, *Owner*
EMP: 2
SALES (est): 100.9K **Privately Held**
SIC: 2499 Signboards, wood

(G-5188)
CLINTON CUSTOM WOOD TURNING
62172 County Road 33 (46528-9609)
PHONE................................574 535-0543
Lavern Yoder, *Owner*
EMP: 2
SALES (est): 127.3K **Privately Held**
SIC: 2431 Millwork

(G-5189)
CLINTON HARNESS SHOP
13705 State Road 4 (46528-9650)
PHONE................................574 533-9797
Lloyd Miller, *Owner*
EMP: 2
SALES (est): 173.9K **Privately Held**
SIC: 3111 2386 Leather tanning & finishing; equestrian leather products; shoe leather; leather & sheep-lined garments

(G-5190)
COLBY L STANGER
Also Called: Stanger Excavating
15504 County Road 42 (46528-6945)
PHONE................................574 536-5835
Colby L Stanger, *Owner*
EMP: 3
SALES (est): 344.2K **Privately Held**
SIC: 3531 Construction machinery

(G-5191)
COMMERCIAL STRUCTURES CORP
Speed Space
65213 County Road 31 (46528-9250)
PHONE................................574 773-7931
Fax: 574 642-3071
Steve Miklich, *Vice Pres*
EMP: 3
SALES (corp-wide): 7.1MM **Privately Held**
WEB: www.comstruc.com
SIC: 2451 Mobile buildings: for commercial use
PA: Commercial Structures Corp.
655 N Tomahawk Trl
Nappanee IN 46550
574 773-7931

(G-5192)
COMMODORE CORPORATION
Also Called: Commodore Home Systems
1902 Century Dr (46528-5045)
P.O. Box 729 (46527-0729)
PHONE................................574 534-3067
Brent Olson, *Branch Mgr*
EMP: 120
SQ FT: 152,060

SALES (corp-wide): 122.6MM **Privately Held**
WEB: www.commodorehomes.com
SIC: **2451** Mobile homes, except recreational
PA: The Commodore Corporation
1423 Lincolnway E
Goshen IN 46526
574 533-7100

(G-5193)
COUNTRY VIEW CABINETS LLC
11770 County Road 32 (46528-9646)
PHONE..................................574 825-3150
Mervin L Yoder, *Administration*
EMP: 2
SALES (est): 117.4K **Privately Held**
SIC: **2434** Wood kitchen cabinets

(G-5194)
COUNTRY WOODSHOP LLC
Also Called: Fusion Designs
62870 County Road 43 (46528-6846)
PHONE..................................574 642-3681
Noah Bontrager,
EMP: 20
SALES (est): 2MM **Privately Held**
SIC: **2511** 5031 5021 Kitchen & dining room furniture; kitchen cabinets; dining room furniture

(G-5195)
CRANE COMPOSITES INC
2424 E Kercher Rd (46526-6466)
PHONE..................................815 467-8600
Rob Hancock, *Vice Pres*
Paul Margherio, *Manager*
William Michaels, *Manager*
Michelle Bauer, *Technician*
EMP: 81
SALES (corp-wide): 2.7B **Publicly Held**
SIC: **3089** Panels, building: plastic
HQ: Crane Composites, Inc.
23525 W Eames St
Channahon IL 60410
815 467-8600

(G-5196)
DAIRY FARMERS AMERICA INC
1110 S 9th St (46526-4316)
P.O. Box 557 (46527-0557)
PHONE..................................574 533-3141
Fax: 574 533-2708
Bob Gehlke, *Plant Mgr*
John Brillhart, *Buyer*
Robert Gehlke, *Sales/Mktg Mgr*
EMP: 54
SALES (corp-wide): 14.6B **Privately Held**
WEB: www.dfamilk.com
SIC: **2026** 2023 2021 Milk processing (pasteurizing, homogenizing, bottling); dry, condensed, evaporated dairy products; creamery butter
PA: Dairy Farmers Of America, Inc.
1405 N 98th St
Kansas City KS 66111
816 801-6455

(G-5197)
DAKA MANUFACTURING INC
24578 Copper Ridge Dr (46526-7648)
PHONE..................................574 295-8036
Fax: 574 295-8036
EMP: 6
SQ FT: 5,000
SALES: 500K **Privately Held**
SIC: **3599** Mfg Industrial Machinery

(G-5198)
DANIEL BONTRAGER
Also Called: Bontrager & Sons Projects
14872 County Road 126 (46528-9666)
PHONE..................................574 825-5656
Daniel J Bontrager, *Owner*
EMP: 3
SALES: 250K **Privately Held**
SIC: **2431** Trim, wood

(G-5199)
DIGISTITCH
16123 County Road 40 (46528-6916)
PHONE..................................574 538-3960
EMP: 2
SALES (est): 111.1K **Privately Held**
SIC: **2395** 7389 Embroidery & art needlework;

(G-5200)
DMI HOLDING CORP (HQ)
2164 Caragana Ct (46526-9149)
P.O. Box 2164 (46527-2164)
PHONE..................................574 534-1224
David Hoefer, *President*
Richard W Florea, *President*
Steve Paul, *Vice Pres*
Bill Maki, *CFO*
Larry R Schrock, *Admin Sec*
▲ EMP: 120
SQ FT: 200,000
SALES (est): 85.4MM
SALES (corp-wide): 7.2B **Publicly Held**
WEB: www.dutchmen-rv.com
SIC: **3792** 5012 Travel trailers & campers; travel trailer chassis; recreational vehicles, motor homes & trailers
PA: Thor Industries, Inc.
601 E Beardsley Ave
Elkhart IN 46514
574 970-7460

(G-5201)
DNA ENTERPRISES INC
Also Called: CANTERBURY R V
2470 E Kercher Rd (46526-6466)
P.O. Box 147 (46527-0147)
PHONE..................................574 534-0034
Fax: 574 534-4342
Kevin Wells, *President*
Tyler Steele, *Vice Pres*
EMP: 34
SQ FT: 30,000
SALES: 6.9MM **Privately Held**
WEB: www.canterburyrv.com
SIC: **3792** 5012 Travel trailers & campers; recreational vehicles, motor homes & trailers

(G-5202)
DOMETIC CORPORATION
2482 Century Dr (46528-5021)
PHONE..................................574 389-3759
Tony Short, *Branch Mgr*
EMP: 33
SALES (corp-wide): 1.6B **Privately Held**
SIC: **3634** Personal electrical appliances
HQ: Dometic Corporation
1120 N Main St
Elkhart IN 46514

(G-5203)
DOORS & DRAWERS INC
2302 Dierdorff Rd (46526-6928)
PHONE..................................574 533-3509
Fax: 574 206-0208
Mark Botts, *President*
EMP: 18 EST: 1980
SQ FT: 8,000
SALES (est): 1.4MM **Privately Held**
WEB: www.doorsanddrawersinc.com
SIC: **2431** 2434 Doors & door parts & trim, wood; wood kitchen cabinets

(G-5204)
DOUBLE L WOODWORKING L L C
12478 County Road 34 (46528-6837)
PHONE..................................260 768-3155
Fax: 260 768-4921
Melvin Slabach, *Principal*
EMP: 10
SALES (est): 750K **Privately Held**
SIC: **2431** Millwork

(G-5205)
DS WOOD PRODUCTS INC
14322 County Road 40 (46528-9344)
PHONE..................................574 642-3855
Delmas Davis, *President*
EMP: 2
SALES (est): 135.2K **Privately Held**
SIC: **3161** Musical instrument cases

(G-5206)
DUTCH PARK HOMES INC
2249 Lincolnway E (46526-6429)
PHONE..................................574 642-0150
Fax: 574 642-0155
Omer Kropf, *CEO*
Kermit Kropf, *President*
EMP: 36 EST: 1999
SQ FT: 32,000

SALES (est): 5.9MM **Privately Held**
WEB: www.dutchpark.com
SIC: **3799** All terrain vehicles (ATV)

(G-5207)
E-Z SWEEP & RAKE LLC
2556a Southside Park Dr (46526-6810)
PHONE..................................574 533-2083
EMP: 3
SQ FT: 900
SALES (est): 88K **Privately Held**
SIC: **3261** Mfg Vitreous Plumbing Fixtures

(G-5208)
EAGLE PACKAGING INC
2301 W Wilden Ave (46528-1026)
PHONE..................................260 281-2333
Michael Johnson, *President*
Stephen Holle, *Vice Pres*
EMP: 3
SALES (est): 395.8K **Privately Held**
SIC: **2671** Packaging paper & plastics film, coated & laminated

(G-5209)
EAGLE READY-MIX INC
65723 Us Highway 33 (46526-6924)
PHONE..................................574 642-4455
EMP: 35
SQ FT: 8,000
SALES (est): 8.4MM **Privately Held**
SIC: **3273** Mfg Ready-Mixed Concrete

(G-5210)
ECONOMY OFFSET PRINTERS INC
2516 Industrial Park Dr A (46526-5372)
PHONE..................................574 534-6270
Fax: 574 534-4123
Roy Beaupain, *President*
EMP: 3
SQ FT: 5,000
SALES: 500K **Privately Held**
WEB: www.economyoffset.com
SIC: **2752** Commercial printing, offset

(G-5211)
EL PUENTE LLC
1906 W Clinton St (46526-1618)
P.O. Box 533 (46527-0533)
PHONE..................................574 533-9082
Yizzar Prieto,
EMP: 2
SALES (est): 109.7K **Privately Held**
SIC: **2741** Miscellaneous publishing

(G-5212)
EXTON INC
Also Called: Travel Star Products
2134 Dierdorff Rd 27 (46526-6940)
P.O. Box 513 (46527-0513)
PHONE..................................574 533-0447
Fax: 574 533-0723
Terry Truex, *President*
EMP: 55
SQ FT: 15,000
SALES (est): 8.6MM **Privately Held**
WEB: www.exton.com
SIC: **3089** Injection molded finished plastic products

(G-5213)
FARM FAB
65511 County Road 9 (46526-9236)
PHONE..................................574 862-4775
Isaac Ramer, *Owner*
EMP: 2
SALES: 35K **Privately Held**
SIC: **3441** Fabricated structural metal

(G-5214)
FIEDEKE VINYL COVERINGS INC
811 Eisenhower Dr N (46526-5303)
PHONE..................................574 534-3408
Fax: 574 534-0329
Jackie Fiedeke, *President*
EMP: 15
SQ FT: 10,500
SALES (est): 840K **Privately Held**
SIC: **2396** 3429 7532 Automotive trimmings, fabric; manufactured hardware (general); van conversion

(G-5215)
FLJ TRANSPORT LLC
1025 Lantern Ln (46526-2510)
PHONE..................................574 642-0200
Frisleme Laguerre,
Franck Laguerre,
EMP: 4
SALES (est): 491.2K **Privately Held**
SIC: **3799** Trailers & trailer equipment

(G-5216)
FOAMCRAFT INC
2506 Industrial Park Dr (46526-5370)
PHONE..................................574 534-4343
Fax: 574 534-4049
Curtis Elliot, *Branch Mgr*
EMP: 80
SQ FT: 22,000
SALES (est): 5.3MM
SALES (corp-wide): 69MM **Privately Held**
SIC: **3069** 3086 2821 5199 Foam rubber; plastics foam products; plastics materials & resins; foams & rubber
PA: Foamcraft Inc
9230 Harrison Park Ct
Indianapolis IN 46216
317 545-3626

(G-5217)
FOREST RIVER INC
3010 College Ave (46528-5050)
P.O. Box 124 (46527-0124)
PHONE..................................574 533-5934
Michael Schoeffler, *Manager*
EMP: 146
SALES (corp-wide): 242.1B **Publicly Held**
WEB: www.forestriverinc.com
SIC: **7532** 3792 5012 Van conversion; travel trailers & campers; recreational vehicles, motor homes & trailers
HQ: Forest River, Inc.
900 County Road 1 N
Elkhart IN 46514

(G-5218)
FOREST RIVER INC
2780 County Road 36 (46527)
P.O. Box 124 (46527-0124)
PHONE..................................574 264-2513
Fax: 574 264-7364
Joe Greenlee, *Branch Mgr*
EMP: 164
SALES (corp-wide): 242.1B **Publicly Held**
SIC: **3792** Tent-type camping trailers
HQ: Forest River, Inc.
900 County Road 1 N
Elkhart IN 46514

(G-5219)
FOREST RIVER INC
Also Called: Starcraft Bus
2367 Century Dr (46528-5002)
PHONE..................................574 642-3112
Ray Boyd, *Sales Staff*
Daid Wright, *Branch Mgr*
EMP: 200
SALES (corp-wide): 242.1B **Publicly Held**
WEB: www.forestriverinc.com
SIC: **3792** Tent-type camping trailers
HQ: Forest River, Inc.
900 County Road 1 N
Elkhart IN 46514

(G-5220)
FOREST RIVER CUSTOM EXTRUSIONS
712 Eisenhower Dr S (46526-5347)
PHONE..................................574 975-0206
Don Parsons, *Manager*
EMP: 2 EST: 2010
SALES (est): 174.4K **Privately Held**
SIC: **3792** Travel trailers & campers

(G-5221)
FOURTH FREEDOM FORUM INC
212 S Main St Ste 1 (46526-3742)
PHONE..................................574 534-3402
Fax: 574 534-4937
David B Cortright, *President*
Linda Gerber-Stellingwerf, *COO*
Patrick Pinnick, *CFO*
Alistair Millar, *Exec Dir*

GEOGRAPHIC

EMP: 14
SALES: 3.8MM **Privately Held**
WEB: www.fourthfreedom.org
SIC: 8699 2741 Personal interest organization; newsletter publishing

(G-5222)
GDC INC (PA)
Also Called: G D C
815 Logan St (46528-3508)
P.O. Box 98 (46527-0098)
PHONE..............................574 533-3128
Fax: 574 534-1777
Loretta Miller, *President*
Lonnie Abney, *COO*
Judy Bronge, *Opers Mgr*
Josh Gilbert, *Prdtn Mgr*
Karen Abbs, *Purch Mgr*
▲ **EMP:** 180 **EST:** 1955
SQ FT: 100,000
SALES (est): 45.8MM **Privately Held**
SIC: 3086 3069 2891 2869 Plastics foam products; medical & laboratory rubber sundries & related products; rubber floor coverings, mats & wallcoverings; rubber coated fabrics & clothing; air-supported rubber structures; adhesives & sealants; industrial organic chemicals; synthetic rubber

(G-5223)
GENERAL CRAFTS CORP
602 E Madison St (46526-3436)
PHONE..............................574 533-1936
Fax: 574 534-5675
Thomas Wilhelm, *President*
Michael Wilhelm, *Vice Pres*
Anna Mary Wilhelm, *Shareholder*
EMP: 9 **EST:** 1959
SQ FT: 20,000
SALES (est): 1.5MM **Privately Held**
SIC: 3449 3545 3446 3444 Miscellaneous metalwork; tools & accessories for machine tools; architectural metalwork; sheet metalwork

(G-5224)
GET PRINTING INC
432 Blackport Dr (46528-3664)
PHONE..............................574 533-6827
Fax: 574 533-1926
Marvin Beachy, *President*
Ray Gerber, *Department Mgr*
EMP: 5
SQ FT: 2,600
SALES (est): 830.5K
SALES (corp-wide): 958.3K **Privately Held**
SIC: 2752 Commercial printing, offset
PA: Gospel Echoes Team Association Inc
1809 E Monroe St Ste C
Goshen IN 46528
574 533-0221

(G-5225)
GINDOR INC
66101 Us Highway 33 (46526-9483)
PHONE..............................574 642-4004
Fax: 574 642-4376
Ginny Nichols, *President*
Dorn Nichols, *Vice Pres*
EMP: 6
SQ FT: 8,000
SALES (est): 868K **Privately Held**
WEB: www.gindor.com
SIC: 3053 3993 2672 Gaskets, all materials; signs & advertising specialties; coated & laminated paper

(G-5226)
GLEASON CORPORATION
612 E Reynolds St (46526-4097)
PHONE..............................574 533-1141
Rex Houston, *Manager*
EMP: 150
SALES (corp-wide): 17MM **Privately Held**
WEB: www.gleasoncorporation.com
SIC: 3499 3444 Wheels: wheelbarrow, stroller, etc.: disc, stamped metal; sheet metalwork
PA: Gleason Corporation
10474 Santa Monica Blvd # 400
Los Angeles CA 90025
310 470-6001

(G-5227)
GLEASON INDUSTRIAL PDTS INC
Also Called: Milwaukee Hand Truck
612 E Reynolds St (46526-4097)
PHONE..............................574 533-1141
Fax: 574 534-2131
Morton Kay, *CEO*
Steven Weldy, *Engineer*
William Malone, *CFO*
Shirley Kotler, *Admin Sec*
Howard Simon, *Admin Sec*
▲ **EMP:** 200
SQ FT: 200,000
SALES (est): 45.6MM **Privately Held**
SIC: 3537 Industrial trucks & tractors

(G-5228)
GOSPEL ECHOES TEAM ASSOCIATION (PA)
1809 E Monroe St Ste C (46528-9260)
P.O. Box 555 (46527-0555)
PHONE..............................574 533-0221
Marvin Beachy, *President*
Kathy Yoder, *Manager*
EMP: 9
SQ FT: 5,000
SALES (est): 958.3K **Privately Held**
SIC: 2752 8661 Commercial printing, offset; religious organizations

(G-5229)
GREEN COW POWER LLC
24130 County Road 40 (46526-9210)
P.O. Box 402, Reynolds (47980-0402)
PHONE..............................219 984-5915
Brian Furrer,
EMP: 3
SALES (est): 268.6K **Privately Held**
SIC: 1311 Natural gas production

(G-5230)
GREEN WAY CANDLE COMPANY LLC
63 Greenway Dr (46526-1543)
PHONE..............................574 536-3802
Dianne Martin, *Principal*
EMP: 2
SALES (est): 62.5K **Privately Held**
SIC: 3999 Candles

(G-5231)
GT STAMPING INC
1025 S 10th St (46526-4401)
PHONE..............................574 533-4108
Fax: 574 534-4189
Gerald A Trolz, *Ch of Bd*
Wayne Hart, *Corp Secy*
Randy Kamp, *QC Mgr*
Steve Mueller, *Engineer*
Dave Sparks, *Supervisor*
EMP: 70 **EST:** 1923
SQ FT: 100,000
SALES (est): 16.2MM **Privately Held**
WEB: www.goshenstamping.com
SIC: 3469 Stamping metal for the trade

(G-5232)
GUTIERREZ MEXICAN BAKERY & MKT
122 S Main St (46526-3702)
PHONE..............................574 534-9979
German Gutierrez, *Partner*
Isabel Gutierrez, *Partner*
EMP: 2
SALES (est): 133.1K **Privately Held**
WEB: www.gutzsalina.com
SIC: 2051 Bread, cake & related products

(G-5233)
H-C LIQUIDATING CORP
Also Called: Homecrest Cabinetry
1002 Eisenhower Dr N (46526-5308)
P.O. Box 595 (46527-0595)
PHONE..............................574 535-9300
Fax: 574 534-2550
Warner R S, *President*
John Goebel, *President*
Stephanie Hoover, *Human Resources*
▲ **EMP:** 1025 **EST:** 1969
SALES (est): 85.7MM
SALES (corp-wide): 5.2B **Publicly Held**
WEB: www.homecrestcab.com
SIC: 2434 Wood kitchen cabinets; vanities, bathroom: wood

HQ: Omega Cabinets, Ltd.
1205 Peters Dr
Waterloo IA 50703
319 235-5700

(G-5234)
HAMILTON IRON WORKS INC
208 W Lincoln Ave (46526-3219)
PHONE..............................574 533-3784
Fax: 574 534-3837
Philip M Daub, *President*
EMP: 5 **EST:** 1917
SQ FT: 9,700
SALES (est): 622.8K **Privately Held**
SIC: 3446 3441 Ornamental metalwork; fabricated structural metal

(G-5235)
HARRISON HAULING INC
Also Called: Yellow Creek Gravel Service
64341 County Road 11 (46526-9426)
PHONE..............................574 862-3196
Burnell Weaver, *President*
Lincoln Graybill, *Vice Pres*
Shada Weaver, *Treasurer*
EMP: 3
SALES (est): 596.8K **Privately Held**
SIC: 1442 Construction sand & gravel

(G-5236)
HEARTFELT CREATIONS INC
2147 Eisenhower Dr N (46526-8807)
PHONE..............................574 773-3088
Linda M Bontrager, *President*
Richard A Beechy, *Corp Secy*
EMP: 18
SQ FT: 12,000
SALES (est): 6.4MM **Privately Held**
SIC: 3953 Time stamps, hand: rubber or metal

(G-5237)
HERITAGE UNLIMITED LLC (PA)
11641 County Road 30 (46528-9626)
PHONE..............................574 538-8021
Mervin D Hostetler, *President*
EMP: 14
SALES (est): 300K **Privately Held**
SIC: 2435 Hardwood plywood, prefinished

(G-5238)
HOOGIES SPORTS HOUSE INC
825 Logan St (46528-3508)
PHONE..............................574 533-9875
Fax: 574 533-9875
John Hoogewerf, *President*
Lilli Hoogewerf, *Admin Sec*
EMP: 4
SQ FT: 2,000
SALES (est): 303.7K **Privately Held**
SIC: 5699 5137 2321 2339 Customized clothing & apparel; women's & children's clothing; men's & boys' furnishings; women's & misses' outerwear; bowling equipment & supplies

(G-5239)
HOOSIER INDUSTRIAL SUPPLY
2516 Industrial Park Dr (46526-5372)
P.O. Box 929 (46527-0929)
PHONE..............................574 535-0712
Susan Smith, *President*
EMP: 2 **EST:** 2011
SALES (est): 242.5K **Privately Held**
SIC: 5085 3812 3721 3599 Industrial supplies; aircraft/aerospace flight instruments & guidance systems; aircraft; industrial machinery

(G-5240)
HOOSIER INDUSTRIAL SUPPLY INC
1223 N Chicago Ave (46528-1923)
P.O. Box 929 (46527-0929)
PHONE..............................574 533-8565
Fax: 574 534-1838
Susan B Smith, *President*
Mike Norris, *Regl Sales Mgr*
Mark Davis, *Manager*
Kirk Robison, *Supervisor*
Bruce Barker, *Admin Sec*
EMP: 19
SQ FT: 20,000

SALES (est): 13.7MM **Privately Held**
WEB: www.hoosierind.com
SIC: 5085 5082 5088 3714 Industrial supplies; contractors' materials; marine supplies; aircraft & space vehicle supplies & parts; aeronautical equipment & supplies; aircraft & parts; motor vehicle parts & accessories; measuring & controlling devices

(G-5241)
HOOSIER INTERIOR DOORS INC
523 E Lincoln Ave (46528-3362)
PHONE..............................574 534-3072
Enos Yost Miller, *President*
EMP: 7
SQ FT: 8,400
SALES (est): 1.1MM **Privately Held**
SIC: 2431 5211 Doors & door parts & trim, wood; door & window products

(G-5242)
INDEPENDENT PROTECTION CO INC (PA)
Also Called: Turtle Top
1607 S Main St (46526-4721)
PHONE..............................574 533-4116
Fax: 574 534-3719
Robert E Cripe, *President*
Matthew Sausaman, *General Mgr*
Richard D Cripe, *Vice Pres*
Robert E Cripe Jr, *Vice Pres*
Phillip Tom Jr, *Vice Pres*
▼ **EMP:** 240 **EST:** 1934
SQ FT: 22,000
SALES (est): 58.3MM **Privately Held**
WEB: www.ipclp.com
SIC: 3643 7532 3711 3446 Lightning protection equipment; van conversion; buses, all types, assembly of; architectural metalwork; sheet metalwork

(G-5243)
INDEPENDENT PROTECTION CO INC
Also Called: Terra Transit
1607 S Main St (46526-4721)
P.O. Box 537 (46527-0537)
PHONE..............................574 533-4116
Rob Cripe, *Manager*
EMP: 37
SQ FT: 55,008
SALES (est): 5.4MM
SALES (corp-wide): 58.3MM **Privately Held**
WEB: www.ipclp.com
SIC: 3643 3713 7538 3711 Lightning protection equipment; van bodies; general automotive repair shops; buses, all types, assembly of
PA: Independent Protection Company, Inc.
1607 S Main St
Goshen IN 46526
574 533-4116

(G-5244)
INDUSTRIAL MOTOR & TOOL LLC
60282 County Road 21 (46528-7716)
PHONE..............................574 534-8282
Luke Hoover, *Owner*
Nelba Hoover, *Co-Owner*
Matthew Hoover,
EMP: 3
SALES: 750K **Privately Held**
SIC: 7694 Electric motor repair

(G-5245)
INK ANGEL INC
Also Called: Ink Angel Rubber Stamp
1827 Bashor Rd (46526-1303)
PHONE..............................574 534-4415
Denise Schirr, *President*
Rudi Schirr, *Admin Sec*
EMP: 4
SALES: 253K **Privately Held**
SIC: 3069 Medical & laboratory rubber sundries & related products

(G-5246)
J & J REPAIR
22064 County Road 142 (46526-9201)
PHONE..............................574 831-3075
Elias Martin, *Owner*
EMP: 3

SALES (est): 206.8K **Privately Held**
WEB: www.jjwatchrepair.com
SIC: 7692 1799 3444 7359 Welding repair; welding on site; sheet metalwork; lawn & garden equipment rental

(G-5247)
JBH MANUFACTURING LLC
57210 County Road 23 (46528-7711)
PHONE..................................574 612-1379
Barry R Hines, *Mng Member*
EMP: 3
SQ FT: 4,000
SALES: 100K **Privately Held**
SIC: 3711 Buses, all types, assembly of

(G-5248)
JIM COUCH
Also Called: Software House
1206 Westbrooke Ct (46528-5065)
PHONE..................................574 533-5107
EMP: 2 **EST:** 2000
SALES (est): 110K **Privately Held**
SIC: 7372 Prepackaged Software Services

(G-5249)
JTD ENTERPRISES INC
Also Called: Inventure Electronics
609 N Harrison St (46528-1931)
PHONE..................................574 533-9438
Jennifer Ducheteau, *Principal*
EMP: 13
SQ FT: 15,000
SALES (est): 1.2MM **Privately Held**
SIC: 3672 Printed circuit boards

(G-5250)
K & D CUSTOM COACH INC
2313 Eisenhower Dr N (46526-8805)
PHONE..................................574 537-1716
Ray Lichty, *President*
Pamela Lichty, *Vice Pres*
EMP: 20
SALES (est): 3MM **Privately Held**
SIC: 7549 3711 Automotive customizing services, non-factory basis; automobile assembly, including specialty automobiles

(G-5251)
KELWOOD DESIGNS LLC CABINETRY
25440 County Road 138 (46526-7453)
PHONE..................................574 862-2472
Steve Hunsberger,
EMP: 8
SALES (est): 810K **Privately Held**
SIC: 2434 7389 Wood kitchen cabinets;

(G-5252)
KENNAMETAL INC
1201 Eisenhower Dr N (46526-5311)
PHONE..................................574 534-2585
Mike Omalley, *Branch Mgr*
EMP: 126
SALES (corp-wide): 2.3B **Publicly Held**
SIC: 3545 3548 Cutting tools for machine tools; welding apparatus
PA: Kennametal Inc.
600 Grant St Ste 5100
Pittsburgh PA 15219
412 248-8000

(G-5253)
KENNAMETAL STELLITE LP
1201 Eisenhower Dr N (46526-5311)
PHONE..................................574 534-9532
Fax: 574 534-3417
John Pawlikowski, *Partner*
◆ **EMP:** 80
SQ FT: 56,000
SALES (est): 83.8K
SALES (corp-wide): 2.3B **Publicly Held**
SIC: 3479 Coating of metals & formed products
PA: Kennametal Inc.
600 Grant St Ste 5100
Pittsburgh PA 15219
412 248-8000

(G-5254)
KEYSTONE RV COMPANY
2420 Hackberry Dr (46526-6468)
PHONE..................................574 535-2100
Fax: 574 642-3867
Don Clark, *Sales Staff*
Tonja Lucchese, *Branch Mgr*

Jim Holderman, *IT/INT Sup*
EMP: 120
SALES (corp-wide): 7.2B **Publicly Held**
WEB: www.keystonerv.com
SIC: 3792 Travel trailers & campers
HQ: Keystone Rv Company
2642 Hackberry Dr
Goshen IN 46526

(G-5255)
KEYSTONE RV COMPANY (HQ)
2642 Hackberry Dr (46526-6811)
P.O. Box 2000 (46527-2000)
PHONE..................................574 534-9430
Fax: 574 534-9057
H Coleman Davis III, *President*
David Chupp, *COO*
Tonja Lucchese, *Exec VP*
Tana Clementz, *Plant Mgr*
Jeff Gill, *Purch Dir*
EMP: 70
SQ FT: 66,000
SALES (est): 531.6MM
SALES (corp-wide): 7.2B **Publicly Held**
WEB: www.keystonerv.com
SIC: 3792 Travel trailers & campers; travel trailer chassis; campers, for mounting on trucks
PA: Thor Industries, Inc.
601 E Beardsley Ave
Elkhart IN 46514
574 970-7460

(G-5256)
KEYSTONE RV COMPANY
2425 Davis Dr (46526-6938)
P.O. Box 2000 (46527-2000)
PHONE..................................574 535-2100
Fax: 574 535-1468
David Chupp, *COO*
Randy Mast, *Site Mgr*
Scott Mills, *Purchasing*
Matt Christensen, *Manager*
EMP: 150
SALES (corp-wide): 7.2B **Publicly Held**
SIC: 3792 Travel trailers & campers
HQ: Keystone Rv Company
2642 Hackberry Dr
Goshen IN 46526

(G-5257)
KINRO MANUFACTURING INC
1206 Eisenhower Dr S (46526-5357)
PHONE..................................574 533-8337
Pete Koenecny, *Manager*
EMP: 200
SALES (corp-wide): 2.1B **Publicly Held**
SIC: 3442 3714 3354 5561 Metal doors, sash & trim; motor vehicle parts & accessories; aluminum extruded products; recreational vehicle parts & accessories
HQ: Kinro Manufacturing, Inc.
200 Mmaroneck Ave Ste 301
White Plains NY 10601
817 483-7791

(G-5258)
KROPF INDUSTRIES INC
58647 State Road 15 (46528-8674)
P.O. Box 30 (46527-0030)
PHONE..................................574 533-2171
Fax: 574 533-3723
Don Kropf, *President*
Curt Yoder, *Vice Pres*
Brent Kattau, *Purch Agent*
Trevor Kropf, *Controller*
Sheri Yoder, *Manager*
EMP: 45 **EST:** 1946
SQ FT: 55,600
SALES (est): 8.9MM **Privately Held**
WEB: www.kropfind.com
SIC: 3792 2451 House trailers, except as permanent dwellings; mobile homes

(G-5259)
KUERT CONCRETE INC
18370 Us Highway 20 (46528-9014)
PHONE..................................574 293-0430
Jim Miller, *Manager*
EMP: 13
SALES (corp-wide): 14.4MM **Privately Held**
WEB: www.kuert.com
SIC: 3273 5032 Ready-mixed concrete; concrete building products

PA: Kuert Concrete Inc
3402 Lincoln Way W
South Bend IN 46628
574 232-9911

(G-5260)
L M WOODWORKING
62270 County Road 33 (46528-9609)
PHONE..................................574 534-9177
Larry Miller, *Executive*
EMP: 2
SALES (est): 146.1K **Privately Held**
SIC: 2429 Special product sawmills

(G-5261)
L R NISLEY & SONS
Also Called: Nisley, L R & Sons
62724 County Road 35 (46528-6814)
PHONE..................................574 642-1245
Leroy R Nisley, *Owner*
EMP: 11
SQ FT: 11,000
SALES (est): 878K **Privately Held**
SIC: 2511 Wood household furniture

(G-5262)
LAKEVIEW WOODWORKING
10190 County Road 34 (46528-9639)
PHONE..................................574 642-1335
Felty Lambright, *Principal*
EMP: 2
SALES (est): 114.6K **Privately Held**
SIC: 2431 Millwork

(G-5263)
LARRYS MACHINE
18374 Dennis Ave (46528-9019)
PHONE..................................574 596-4994
EMP: 2 **EST:** 2015
SALES (est): 87K **Privately Held**
SIC: 3599 Mfg Industrial Machinery

(G-5264)
LCM REALTY IV LLC
2469 E Kercher Rd (46526-6465)
PHONE..................................574 312-6182
EMP: 2
SALES (est): 73.4K **Privately Held**
SIC: 3465 Automotive stampings

(G-5265)
LIBERTY HOMES INC (PA)
1101 Eisenhower Dr N (46526-5309)
P.O. Box 35 (46527-0035)
PHONE..................................574 533-0438
Fax: 574 533-0438
Edward J Hussey, *President*
Mitchell Day, *Principal*
Ronald Atkins, *Vice Pres*
Marc A Dosmann, *CFO*
Karl Shively, *CFO*
EMP: 53
SQ FT: 22,000
SALES (est): 19.3MM **Privately Held**
WEB: www.libertyhomesinc.com
SIC: 2451 Mobile homes

(G-5266)
LIPPERT COMPONENTS INC
Also Called: Lippert Interior Solutions
2602 College Ave (46528-5014)
PHONE..................................574 534-8177
Ryan Sailor, *Plant Mgr*
Nathan Hose, *Prdtn Mgr*
Michael Duke, *QC Mgr*
Brock Goodman, *Engineer*
Laura Beach, *Sales Mgr*
EMP: 14
SALES (corp-wide): 2.1B **Publicly Held**
SIC: 2531 Vehicle furniture; seats, automobile
HQ: Lippert Components, Inc.
3501 County Road 6 E
Elkhart IN 46514
800 551-9149

(G-5267)
LIPPERT COMPONENTS INC
2703 College Ave (46528-5040)
PHONE..................................574 537-8900
Jason Lippert, *CEO*
Shannon Angle, *General Mgr*
Braden Weldy, *General Mgr*
Dean Leazenby, *Counsel*
Chuck Bell, *Vice Pres*
EMP: 71

SALES (corp-wide): 2.1B **Publicly Held**
SIC: 3711 Chassis, motor vehicle
HQ: Lippert Components, Inc.
3501 County Road 6 E
Elkhart IN 46514
800 551-9149

(G-5268)
LIPPERT COMPONENTS INC
2703 College Ave (46528-5040)
PHONE..................................574 535-1125
Fax: 574 642-4134
Doug Lippert, *President*
John Ries, *President*
Kevin Gipson, *General Mgr*
Mark Taylor, *General Mgr*
Frank Duong, *Plant Mgr*
EMP: 90
SQ FT: 136,155
SALES (corp-wide): 2.1B **Publicly Held**
WEB: www.lci1.com
SIC: 3711 3469 3444 3714 Chassis, motor vehicle; stamping metal for the trade; metal roofing & roof drainage equipment; motor vehicle parts & accessories; fabricated plate work (boiler shop); mobile homes
HQ: Lippert Components, Inc.
3501 County Road 6 E
Elkhart IN 46514
800 551-9149

(G-5269)
LIPPERT COMPONENTS INC
1701 Century Dr (46528-5048)
PHONE..................................574 537-8900
Dennis Carl, *Engineer*
EMP: 8
SALES (corp-wide): 2.1B **Publicly Held**
SIC: 3441 Fabricated structural metal
HQ: Lippert Components, Inc.
3501 County Road 6 E
Elkhart IN 46514
800 551-9149

(G-5270)
LIPPERT COMPONENTS INC
Also Called: Lippert Interiors
1010 Eisenhower Dr S (46526-5353)
PHONE..................................574 534-2163
Ryan Smith, *Vice Pres*
EMP: 100
SALES (corp-wide): 2.1B **Publicly Held**
SIC: 2531 Vehicle furniture; seats, automobile; chairs, portable folding; chairs, table & arm
HQ: Lippert Components, Inc.
3501 County Road 6 E
Elkhart IN 46514
800 551-9149

(G-5271)
LIPPERT COMPONENTS INC
2703 College Ave (46528-5040)
PHONE..................................574 535-1125
Rick Croton, *Manager*
EMP: 26
SALES (corp-wide): 2.1B **Publicly Held**
WEB: www.lci1.com
SIC: 3711 2451 Chassis, motor vehicle; mobile homes
HQ: Lippert Components, Inc.
3501 County Road 6 E
Elkhart IN 46514
800 551-9149

(G-5272)
LIPPERT COMPONENTS INC
Also Called: Lipper Components
2703 College Ave (46528-5040)
PHONE..................................574 535-1125
Carl Owens, *Manager*
EMP: 32
SALES (corp-wide): 2.1B **Publicly Held**
WEB: www.lci1.com
SIC: 3469 3711 3444 3714 Stamping metal for the trade; chassis, motor vehicle; metal roofing & roof drainage equipment; motor vehicle parts & accessories
HQ: Lippert Components, Inc.
3501 County Road 6 E
Elkhart IN 46514
800 551-9149

GEOGRAPHIC

(G-5273)
LIPPERT COMPONENTS INC
2703 College Ave (46528-5040)
PHONE...................................574 849-0869
Fax: 574 642-4089
Rob Nelson, *Branch Mgr*
EMP: 59
SALES (corp-wide): 2.1B **Publicly Held**
WEB: www.lci1.com
SIC: 3711 3469 3444 3714 Chassis,
motor vehicle; stamping metal for the
trade; metal roofing & roof drainage
equipment; motor vehicle parts & acces-
sories
HQ: Lippert Components, Inc.
3501 County Road 6 E
Elkhart IN 46514
800 551-9149

(G-5274)
LIPPERT COMPONENTS INC
2703 College Ave (46528-5040)
PHONE...................................574 971-4100
Tucker Florea, *Plant Mgr*
Scott Miner, *Branch Mgr*
EMP: 6
SALES (corp-wide): 2.1B **Publicly Held**
WEB: www.lci1.com
SIC: 3714 Motor vehicle parts & acces-
sories
HQ: Lippert Components, Inc.
3501 County Road 6 E
Elkhart IN 46514
800 551-9149

(G-5275)
LIPPERT COMPONENTS INC
2703 College Ave (46528-5040)
PHONE...................................574 971-4320
Fax: 574 642-4373
Todd Driver, *General Mgr*
Ben Shockey, *General Mgr*
Sean N Bentley, *Parts Mgr*
EMP: 170
SALES (corp-wide): 2.1B **Publicly Held**
WEB: www.lci1.com
SIC: 3711 3469 3444 3714 Chassis,
motor vehicle; stamping metal for the
trade; metal roofing & roof drainage
equipment; motor vehicle parts & acces-
sories; travel trailers & campers
HQ: Lippert Components, Inc.
3501 County Road 6 E
Elkhart IN 46514
800 551-9149

(G-5276)
M&M PERFORMANCE INC
16077 Prairie Rose Ave (46528-7304)
PHONE...................................574 536-6103
Bruce McDonald, *President*
EMP: 3
SALES (est): 371.2K **Privately Held**
WEB: www.mandmperformance.com
SIC: 3089 Automotive parts, plastic

(G-5277)
**MAGNUM VENUS PRODUCTS
INC**
Also Called: Magnum Industries
320 N Main St (46528-2826)
PHONE...................................727 573-2955
Stephen E Ciesielski, *Branch Mgr*
EMP: 15
SALES (corp-wide): 34MM **Privately
Held**
WEB: www.gsscs.org
SIC: 5084 3563 Processing & packaging
equipment; spraying outfits: metals,
paints & chemicals (compressor)
PA: Magnum Venus Products, Inc.
2030 Falling Waters Rd # 350
Knoxville TN 37922
865 686-5670

(G-5278)
MAPLE CITY MACHINE INC
1762 E Kercher Rd (46526-6308)
PHONE...................................574 533-6742
Fax: 574 534-8004
Phillip Shank, *President*
Becka Shank, *Admin Sec*
EMP: 14
SQ FT: 18,000
SALES (est): 1.7MM **Privately Held**
SIC: 3599 Machine shop, jobbing & repair

(G-5279)
**MAPLE CITY WOODWORKING
CORP**
2948 Hackberry Dr (46526-6489)
PHONE...................................574 642-3342
Fax: 574 642-3545
Jeff Steine, *President*
EMP: 75
SQ FT: 16,000
SALES (est): 4.3MM **Privately Held**
SIC: 2431 Millwork; interior or ornamental
woodwork & trim; woodwork, interior or or-
namental; exterior & ornamental wood-
work & trim

(G-5280)
MAPLELEAF PRINTING CO INC
301 W Lincoln Ave (46526-3220)
PHONE...................................574 534-7790
Brian Hersherger, *President*
EMP: 6
SALES (est): 896.8K **Privately Held**
SIC: 2752 Commercial printing, offset

(G-5281)
MARTINS WOOD WORKS
66227 County Road 9 (46526-9237)
PHONE...................................574 862-4080
Carlyle Martin, *Owner*
EMP: 4
SALES (est): 319K **Privately Held**
SIC: 2511 5712 5021 Wood household
furniture; custom made furniture, except
cabinets; furniture

(G-5282)
MASTERBRAND CABINETS INC
Also Called: Master Brand Cabinets
1002 Eisenhower Dr N (46526-5308)
PHONE...................................574 535-9300
Christa Guife, *Branch Mgr*
EMP: 5
SALES (corp-wide): 5.2B **Publicly Held**
SIC: 2434 Wood kitchen cabinets
HQ: Masterbrand Cabinets, Inc.
1 Masterbrand Cabinets Dr
Jasper IN 47546
812 482-2527

(G-5283)
MCWANE INC
Also Called: Manchester Tank & Equipment
Co
62626 Stephanie St (46526-9455)
PHONE...................................574 534-9328
Bob Mangas, *Branch Mgr*
EMP: 5
SALES (corp-wide): 1.3B **Privately Held**
WEB: www.mcwane.com
SIC: 3443 Fuel tanks (oil, gas, etc.): metal
plate
PA: Mcwane, Inc.
2900 Highway 280 S # 300
Birmingham AL 35223
205 414-3100

(G-5284)
**MEDTEC AMBULANCE
CORPORATION (DH)**
2429 Lincolnway E (46526-6437)
PHONE...................................574 534-2631
Fax: 574 534-3629
Tim McDonald, *General Mgr*
Ross Munn, *Finance*
David Hill, *Director*
EMP: 120
SALES (est): 11MM
SALES (corp-wide): 6.8B **Publicly Held**
WEB: www.medtecambulance.com
SIC: 3711 Ambulances (motor vehicles),
assembly of; bus & other large specialty
vehicle assembly; fire department vehi-
cles (motor vehicles), assembly of
HQ: Mcneilus Companies, Inc.
524 E Highway St
Dodge Center MN 55927
507 374-6321

(G-5285)
**MEDTEC AMBULANCE
CORPORATION**
2429 Lincolnway E (46526-6437)
PHONE...................................574 533-2924
EMP: 3

(G-5286)
MENNONITE INC INC
1700 S Main St (46526-4724)
PHONE...................................574 535-6050
Fax: 574 535-7438
Everett Thomas, *President*
EMP: 2
SALES: 404.1K **Privately Held**
SIC: 2721 Magazines: publishing & printing

(G-5287)
MICA SHOP INC
2122 Lincolnway E (46526-6426)
PHONE...................................574 533-1102
Verlin Chupp, *President*
Karen Chupp, *Treasurer*
EMP: 20
SQ FT: 40,000
SALES (est): 3.1MM **Privately Held**
WEB: www.micashop.com
SIC: 2541 Counters or counter display
cases, wood; counter & sink tops

(G-5288)
**MICHIANA CARWASH SYSTEMS
LLC**
15228 County Road 22 (46528-9188)
PHONE...................................574 320-2331
Jim Weaver,
EMP: 2
SALES (est): 350K **Privately Held**
SIC: 3589 Car washing machinery

(G-5289)
**MICROLOGY LABORATORIES
LLC**
1303 Eisenhower Dr S (46526-5360)
P.O. Box 340 (46527-0340)
PHONE...................................574 533-3351
Doug Wengerd, *General Mgr*
Rowland G Rose,
Thomas Corson,
Jonathan N Roth,
EMP: 9
SQ FT: 10,000
SALES (est): 1.4MM **Privately Held**
WEB: www.micrologylabs.com
SIC: 2836 Culture media; bacteriological
media

(G-5290)
MIDE PRODUCTS LLC
22420 Forsythia Dr (46528-8332)
PHONE...................................574 333-5906
EMP: 2 EST: 2008
SQ FT: 3,000
SALES (est): 148.3K **Privately Held**
SIC: 3089 Mfg Fence Accessories

(G-5291)
MIKO-HONE MACHINE CO INC
2424 Supreme Ct (46528-7560)
PHONE...................................574 642-4701
EMP: 6
SALES (est): 400K **Privately Held**
SIC: 3541 Mfg Honing Machinery

(G-5292)
**MILLENNIA TECHNOLOGIES
INC**
21948 Shirley Dr (46526-9364)
PHONE...................................574 830-5161
Roger Lange, *CEO*
Roger J Lange, *Administration*
EMP: 5
SALES: 1,000K **Privately Held**
SIC: 3674 Light sensitive devices, solid
state

(G-5293)
**MILLER BROTHERS BUILDERS
INC**
1819 E Monroe St (46528-9260)
PHONE...................................574 533-8602
Daniel B Miller, *President*
Dbradley Plett, *Vice Pres*

Doug Stuckey, *Sales Staff*
Ferman Yutzy, *Sales Staff*
Beth Bontrager, *Office Mgr*
EMP: 25
SQ FT: 5,000
SALES (est): 3.3MM **Privately Held**
WEB: www.millerscorp.com
SIC: 1521 1522 1542 3448 New con-
struction, single-family houses; multi-fam-
ily dwelling construction; commercial &
office building contractors; prefabricated
metal buildings; prefabricated wood build-
ings

(G-5294)
MILLER DOOR & TRIM INC
1702 E Monroe St (46528-4296)
PHONE...................................574 533-8141
Fax: 574 533-8141
Edward Thomas, *President*
EMP: 4
SQ FT: 30,000
SALES (est): 719.5K **Privately Held**
SIC: 2431 Doors, wood; moldings, wood:
unfinished & prefinished; mantels, wood;
stair railings, wood

(G-5295)
MO TRAILER CORPORATION
2211 W Wilden Ave (46528-1147)
P.O. Box 486 (46527-0486)
PHONE...................................574 533-0824
Fax: 574 534-2702
Jeff Mitschelen, *President*
Phil Vail, *Vice Pres*
EMP: 10 EST: 1971
SQ FT: 10,000
SALES (est): 780K **Privately Held**
WEB: www.motrailers.com
SIC: 3799 3621 Trailers & trailer equip-
ment; electric motor & generator parts;
electric motor & generator auxillary parts

(G-5296)
**MOBILE CLIMATE CONTROL
CORP (DH)**
Also Called: McC
17103 State Road 4 (46528-6674)
P.O. Box 803 (46527-0803)
PHONE...................................574 534-1516
Clas Genneberg, *CEO*
▲ EMP: 82 EST: 1987
SQ FT: 80,000
SALES (est): 58.7MM
SALES (corp-wide): 355.7MM **Privately
Held**
WEB: www.acmeair.com
SIC: 5075 3714 Compressors, air condi-
tioning; air conditioner parts, motor vehi-
cle

(G-5297)
MOORES INC
316 W Douglas St (46526-3935)
PHONE...................................574 533-6089
Fax: 574 293-5832
Ronald Moore, *President*
A Ronald Moore, *President*
Kay Mabie, *Purchasing*
EMP: 5
SQ FT: 15,000
SALES: 500K **Privately Held**
SIC: 3582 3552 Rug cleaning, drying or
napping machines: commercial; textile
machinery

(G-5298)
NIBCO INC
Goshen Division
701 Eisenhower Dr N (46526-5301)
PHONE...................................574 296-1240
Fax: 574 296-1241
Steve Seevers, *Manager*
EMP: 200
SQ FT: 89,000
SALES (corp-wide): 732MM **Privately
Held**
WEB: www.nibco.com
SIC: 3089 3432 3088 5162 Fittings for
pipe, plastic; plumbing fixture fittings &
trim; plastics plumbing fixtures; plastics
products
PA: Nibco Inc.
1516 Middlebury St
Elkhart IN 46516
574 295-3000

▲ = Import ▼=Export
◆ =Import/Export

(G-5299)
NOBLE COMPOSITES INC
2424 E Kercher Rd (46526-6466)
PHONE.............................574 533-1462
Fax: 574 533-8970
Larry Farver, *President*
Roger Gowdy, *Vice Pres*
John Gardner, *CFO*
EMP: 118
SALES (est): 15.6MM
SALES (corp-wide): 2.7B **Publicly Held**
WEB: www.noblecomposites.com
SIC: 3492 Control valves, fluid power: hydraulic & pneumatic
HQ: Crane Composites, Inc.
23525 W Eames St
Channahon IL 60410
815 467-8600

(G-5300)
NOLAN BRUBAKER SOFTWARE LLC
434 S Silverwood Ln A (46526-1631)
PHONE.............................574 238-0676
Nolan Brubaker, *Administration*
EMP: 2 **EST:** 2011
SALES (est): 120.9K **Privately Held**
SIC: 7372 Prepackaged software

(G-5301)
OLYMPIA CANDY KITCHEN
136 N Main St (46526-3207)
PHONE.............................574 533-5040
Fax: 574 534-6345
Kathy Andersen, *Owner*
EMP: 13
SQ FT: 1,000
SALES (est): 340K **Privately Held**
SIC: 2064 5812 5441 2066 Candy & other confectionery products; eating places; candy; chocolate & cocoa products

(G-5302)
ORCHARD LANE CABINETS
14425 County Road 126 (46528-9666)
PHONE.............................574 825-7568
Toby Borntrager, *Principal*
EMP: 3 **EST:** 2008
SALES (est): 242.6K **Privately Held**
SIC: 2434 Wood kitchen cabinets

(G-5303)
OZINGA BROS INC
65723 Us Highway 33 (46526-6924)
PHONE.............................574 642-4455
EMP: 35
SALES (corp-wide): 269.8MM **Privately Held**
SIC: 3273 Ready-mixed concrete
PA: Ozinga Bros., Inc.
19001 Old Lagrange Rd # 30
Mokena IL 60448
708 326-4200

(G-5304)
OZINGA BROS INC
1700 Egbert Ave (46528-4214)
PHONE.............................574 971-8239
EMP: 53
SALES (corp-wide): 269.8MM **Privately Held**
SIC: 3273 Ready-mixed concrete
PA: Ozinga Bros., Inc.
19001 Old Lagrange Rd # 30
Mokena IL 60448
708 326-4200

(G-5305)
PAPERS INC
134 S Main St (46526-3794)
PHONE.............................574 534-2591
Ron Baumgartner, *President*
Marilyn Yoder, *Manager*
EMP: 7
SALES (est): 278.3K
SALES (corp-wide): 47.6MM **Privately Held**
WEB: www.the-papers.com
SIC: 2711 Newspapers: publishing only, not printed on site
PA: The Papers Inc
206 S Main St
Milford IN 46542
574 658-4111

(G-5306)
PARAGON PRINTING CENTER INC
117 S Main St (46526-3701)
PHONE.............................574 533-5835
Nyal Weaver, *President*
Rick Vandusen, *Manager*
EMP: 4
SALES (est): 482.7K **Privately Held**
WEB: www.paragonprintingcenter.com
SIC: 2759 Letterpress printing

(G-5307)
PARKER-HANNIFIN CORPORATION
Also Called: Techseal Division
1525 S 10th St (46526-4505)
P.O. Box 517 (46527-0517)
PHONE.............................574 533-1111
Richard Chapman, *Buyer*
Joseph Lotter, *Branch Mgr*
Jon Werbianskyj, *Prgrmr*
EMP: 60
SALES (corp-wide): 12B **Publicly Held**
WEB: www.parker.com
SIC: 3053 3061 3544 2822 Gaskets, all materials; oil seals, rubber; mechanical rubber goods; automotive rubber goods (mechanical); special dies, tools, jigs & fixtures; synthetic rubber
PA: Parker-Hannifin Corporation
6035 Parkland Blvd
Cleveland OH 44124
216 896-3000

(G-5308)
PATRICK INDUSTRIES INC
Also Called: Foremost Fabricators
3352 Maple City Dr (46526-6807)
PHONE.............................574 534-5300
Ryan Berger, *Business Dir*
EMP: 150
SALES (corp-wide): 1.6B **Publicly Held**
SIC: 3275 Gypsum products
PA: Patrick Industries, Inc.
107 W Franklin St
Elkhart IN 46516
574 294-7511

(G-5309)
PLANKS PRINTING SERVICE INC
Also Called: Rapid Ribbons
505 S 9th St (46526-3446)
P.O. Box 222 (46527-0222)
PHONE.............................574 533-1739
Fax: 574 533-0958
David Plank, *President*
David A Plank, *President*
EMP: 9 **EST:** 1946
SQ FT: 2,500
SALES (est): 650K **Privately Held**
WEB: www.rapidribbons.com
SIC: 2759 Commercial printing

(G-5310)
PLETCHERS POULTRY PROCESSING
66786 County Road 17 (46526-9216)
PHONE.............................574 831-2329
Ron Pletcher, *Owner*
Susan Pletcher, *Partner*
EMP: 4
SALES (est): 50K **Privately Held**
SIC: 2015 0751 Poultry slaughtering & processing; poultry services

(G-5311)
PLYMOUTH OIL AND GAS INC
57592 Hearthstone Ct (46528-7852)
PHONE.............................574 875-4808
Onkar Singh, *Principal*
EMP: 2
SALES (est): 158.4K **Privately Held**
SIC: 1382 Oil & gas exploration services

(G-5312)
PREMIERE SIGNS CO INC
Also Called: Premiere Services
400 N Main St (46528-2828)
PHONE.............................574 533-8585
Fax: 574 533-4575
Michael Brown, *President*
Cynthia Brown, *Admin Sec*
EMP: 14
SQ FT: 16,000
SALES (est): 1.5MM **Privately Held**
WEB: www.premiereservices.com
SIC: 3993 1799 5999 Electric signs; sign installation & maintenance; banners, flags, decals & posters

(G-5313)
PROMOTOR ENGINES & COMPONENTS
Also Called: Pro-Motor Engines
1814 Lincolnway E (46526-6411)
PHONE.............................574 533-9898
Fax: 574 533-9756
Doug Tarman, *President*
Justin Tarman, *Manager*
EMP: 3
SQ FT: 8,000
SALES: 480K **Privately Held**
WEB: www.pro-motor.com
SIC: 5531 3599 5013 Automotive parts; automotive accessories; machine shop, jobbing & repair; automotive supplies & parts

(G-5314)
QUALITY MACHINE & TOOL INC
924 E Lincoln Ave (46528-3504)
PHONE.............................574 534-5664
Don Taylor, *President*
Jerry Riley, *Vice Pres*
EMP: 4
SQ FT: 12,000
SALES (est): 800K **Privately Held**
SIC: 3544 3599 Dies, plastics forming; forms (molds), for foundry & plastics working machinery; machine shop, jobbing & repair

(G-5315)
RAECO/PROMO-SPORTS LLC
2249 Lincolnway E (46526-6429)
PHONE.............................574 537-9387
Fax: 574 537-9757
Rae Johnston,
Jean Johnston,
EMP: 40
SALES (est): 3.1MM **Privately Held**
WEB: www.promo-sports.net
SIC: 3993 Signs & advertising specialties; displays & cutouts, window & lobby

(G-5316)
RAMER CHAIR CO
Also Called: Ramer Chair Shop
25445 County Road 38 (46526-7151)
PHONE.............................574 862-4179
Lawrence Ramer, *Owner*
Anna Ramer, *Co-Owner*
EMP: 3
SALES: 125K **Privately Held**
SIC: 2511 Chairs, household, except upholstered: wood; tables, household: wood

(G-5317)
RECREATIONAL CUSTOMS INC
67928 Us Highway 33 (46526-8549)
PHONE.............................574 642-0632
Anita Carpenter, *President*
EMP: 6
SALES (est): 460K **Privately Held**
SIC: 3799 Recreational vehicles

(G-5318)
RIEGSECKERS WOODWORKS INC
15600 County Road 38 (46528-9353)
PHONE.............................574 642-3504
Fax: 574 642-0161
Timothy J Riegsecker, *President*
Larry Riegsecker, *Treasurer*
EMP: 3
SALES (est): 364.3K **Privately Held**
SIC: 2499 Decorative wood & woodwork

(G-5319)
ROANN PUBLISHERS
22425 County Road 42 (46526-9215)
PHONE.............................574 831-2795
Roy Zimmerman, *Owner*
EMP: 2
SALES (est): 27.4K **Privately Held**
SIC: 2721 Magazines: publishing only, not printed on site

(G-5320)
SCHLABACH HARDWOODS
11186 County Road 34 (46528-9628)
PHONE.............................574 642-1157
La Verne Schlabach, *Partner*
John Schlabach Jr, *Partner*
EMP: 5
SQ FT: 3,500
SALES (est): 400K **Privately Held**
SIC: 2431 Planing mill, millwork; moldings, wood: unfinished & prefinished; doors, wood

(G-5321)
SCHUYLER CORP
Also Called: Aquatic Weed Control
2105 Carmen Ct (46526-4500)
P.O. Box 325, Syracuse (46567-0325)
PHONE.............................574 533-2597
James Donahoe, *President*
EMP: 15
SALES (est): 2MM **Privately Held**
SIC: 3317 Tubing, mechanical or hypodermic sizes: cold drawn stainless

(G-5322)
SEATING TECHNOLOGY INC
Also Called: Seat Tech
2703 College Ave (46528-5040)
PHONE.............................574 971-4100
Rick Finnigan, *President*
Marlene Finnigan, *Vice Pres*
Matthew Troyer, *CFO*
▲ **EMP:** 250
SQ FT: 32,000
SALES (est): 19MM
SALES (corp-wide): 2.1B **Publicly Held**
WEB: www.seatingtechnologyinc.com
SIC: 2512 2514 2515 Recliners: upholstered on wood frames; couches, sofas & davenports: upholstered on wood frames; household furniture: upholstered on metal frames; sofa beds (convertible sofas)
HQ: Lippert Components, Inc.
3501 County Road 6 E
Elkhart IN 46514
800 551-9149

(G-5323)
SIGNTECH SIGN SERVICES INC
1508 Bashor Rd (46528-1903)
P.O. Box 835 (46527-0835)
PHONE.............................574 537-8080
Fax: 574 537-8088
Todd Lehman, *President*
Jan Plummer, *Principal*
EMP: 4
SALES (est): 469.3K **Privately Held**
SIC: 3993 Signs & advertising specialties

(G-5324)
SOUTH BEND TRIBUNE
114 S Main St (46526-3702)
PHONE.............................574 971-5651
EMP: 2
SALES (est): 62.9K **Privately Held**
SIC: 2711 Newspapers

(G-5325)
SOUTHWEST WELDING
25389 State Road 119 (46526-7460)
PHONE.............................574 862-4453
John D Martin, *Owner*
EMP: 3
SALES (est): 300K **Privately Held**
SIC: 7692 1799 Welding repair; welding on site

(G-5326)
STABILITY AMERICA INC
Also Called: Parent Co. Glassteel
2928 Elder Dr (46526-8926)
PHONE.............................574 642-3029
EMP: 2
SALES (est): 148.1K **Privately Held**
SIC: 3229 Glass fiber products

(G-5327)
STAMINA METAL PRODUCTS INC
901 E Madison St (46528-3510)
PHONE.............................574 534-7410
Randy Huber, *President*
Mary Huber, *Vice Pres*
EMP: 2

GEOGRAPHIC

SQ FT: 2,500
SALES (est): 283.1K **Privately Held**
SIC: 3469 3544 3599 Stamping metal for
the trade; special dies & tools; machine &
other job shop work; machine shop, jobbing & repair

(G-5328)
STARCRAFT CORPORATION
Also Called: Starcraft Accessories
2006 Century Dr (46528-5000)
P.O. Box 12, Middlebury (46540-0012)
PHONE..............................574 534-7705
Sherry Roberts, *Principal*
EMP: 6
SQ FT: 30,000
SALES (est): 713.2K **Privately Held**
SIC: 3714 Motor vehicle parts & acces-
sories
HQ: Starcraft Corporation
1123 S Indiana Ave
Goshen IN 46526
574 534-7827

(G-5329)
STARCRAFT CORPORATION (HQ)
1123 S Indiana Ave (46526-6207)
P.O. Box 12, Middlebury (46540-0012)
PHONE..............................574 534-7827
Fax: 574 534-1238
Michael H Schoeffler, *CEO*
Kelly L Rose, *Ch of Bd*
Douglass C Goad, *Exec VP*
Joseph E Katona III, *CFO*
▼ EMP: 26
SQ FT: 5,000
SALES (est): 2.3MM **Privately Held**
SIC: 3714 3792 3716 3713 Motor vehicle
parts & accessories; travel trailers &
campers; motor homes; truck & bus bod-
ies

(G-5330)
STARQUEST PRODUCTS LLC
2006 Century Dr (46528-5000)
PHONE..............................574 537-0486
EMP: 4 EST: 2005
SALES (est): 530K
SALES (corp-wide): 901.1MM **Publicly
Held**
SIC: 3089 Manufactures Plastic Products
HQ: Kinro Manufacturing, Inc.
3501 County Road 6 E
Elkhart IN 46514
574 971-4100

(G-5331)
SUPERIOR LAMINATING INC
60894 County Road 19 (46528-7409)
PHONE..............................574 361-7266
Fax: 574 533-8170
Elroy Bontrager, *President*
Andrea Rosevelle, *Admin Sec*
EMP: 17
SQ FT: 19,820
SALES (est): 2.5MM **Privately Held**
WEB: www.superiorlaminating.com
SIC: 5031 2434 Kitchen cabinets; wood
kitchen cabinets; vanities, bathroom:
wood

(G-5332)
SUPREME CORPORATION (DH)
2581 Kercher Rd (46528-7556)
P.O. Box 463 (46527-0463)
PHONE..............................574 642-4888
Fax: 574 642-4540
Herbert M Gardner, *Ch of Bd*
Robert W Wilson, *President*
Christopher Allison, *General Mgr*
Steve Odell, *General Mgr*
Al Schroeder, *General Mgr*
◆ EMP: 1100
SQ FT: 280,000
SALES (est): 310.3MM
SALES (corp-wide): 1.7B **Publicly Held**
WEB: www.supremecorp.com
SIC: 3713 3792 3585 Truck bodies (motor
vehicles); bus bodies (motor vehicles);
van bodies; travel trailers & campers; re-
frigeration & heating equipment
HQ: Supreme Industries, Inc.
2581 Kercher Rd
Goshen IN 46528
574 642-3070

(G-5333)
SUPREME CORPORATION
2581 Kercher Rd (46528-7556)
PHONE..............................574 642-4888
Mark Weber, *CEO*
EMP: 308
SALES (corp-wide): 1.7B **Publicly Held**
SIC: 3713 Truck cabs for motor vehicles
HQ: Supreme Corporation
2581 Kercher Rd
Goshen IN 46528
574 642-4888

(G-5334)
SUPREME CORPORATION
2581 Kercher Rd (46528-7556)
PHONE..............................574 642-4888
Robert Wilson, *Manager*
EMP: 1300
SALES (corp-wide): 1.7B **Publicly Held**
SIC: 3713 Truck & bus bodies
HQ: Supreme Corporation
2581 Kercher Rd
Goshen IN 46528
574 642-4888

(G-5335)
SUPREME CORPORATION GEORGIA
2581 Kercher Rd (46528-7556)
PHONE..............................574 228-4130
Mark D Weber, *President*
EMP: 1
SALES (est): 6.2MM
SALES (corp-wide): 1.7B **Publicly Held**
SIC: 3537 Industrial trucks & tractors
HQ: Supreme Corporation
2581 Kercher Rd
Goshen IN 46528
574 642-4888

(G-5336)
SUPREME INDUSTRIES INC (HQ)
2581 Kercher Rd (46528-7556)
P.O. Box 463 (46527-0463)
PHONE..............................574 642-3070
Fax: 574 642-3208
Brent L Yeagy, *President*
Mike Garner, *Partner*
Fred Ballowe, *General Mgr*
Rod Cook, *General Mgr*
Mike Oium, *General Mgr*
◆ EMP: 75 EST: 1974
SQ FT: 26,000
SALES: 300MM
SALES (corp-wide): 1.7B **Publicly Held**
SIC: 3537 3713 3799 Industrial trucks &
tractors; truck & bus bodies; stake, plat-
form truck bodies; trailers & trailer equip-
ment
PA: Wabash National Corporation
1000 Sagamore Pkwy S
Lafayette IN 47905
765 771-5300

(G-5337)
SWARTZNDRBER HRDWOOD CREAT LLC
17229 County Road 18 (46528-8681)
PHONE..............................574 534-2502
Fax: 574 534-2504
Larion Swartzendruber,
Nancy Swartzendruber,
EMP: 40
SQ FT: 30,000
SALES (est): 5.4MM **Privately Held**
SIC: 2426 2511 2521 Furniture stock &
parts, hardwood; wood household furni-
ture; chairs, household, except uphol-
stered: wood; desks, household: wood;
dining room furniture: wood; wood office
furniture; bookcases, office: wood; desks,
office: wood; tables, office: wood

(G-5338)
T & M RUBBER INC
1102 S 10th St (46526-4487)
P.O. Box 516 (46527-0516)
PHONE..............................574 533-3173
Fax: 574 533-7599
Jerry Bernard, *President*
Martina Dawson, *Vice Pres*
Karl Shively, *CFO*
◆ EMP: 30 EST: 1948

SQ FT: 62,000
SALES: 3MM **Privately Held**
WEB: www.tmrubber.com
SIC: 3061 2822 3053 Mechanical rubber
goods; synthetic rubber; oil seals, rubber;
gaskets, all materials

(G-5339)
TECHKNOWLEDGEY INC (PA)
1840 W Lincoln Ave (46526-5918)
PHONE..............................574 971-4267
Boyd Smith, *President*
Krista L Smith, *Vice Pres*
EMP: 4 EST: 2006
SALES (est): 587K **Privately Held**
SIC: 3572 7371 Computer storage de-
vices; custom computer programming
services

(G-5340)
TRIANGLE RUBBER CO LLC (PA)
Also Called: Tri-Seals Division
1924 Elkhart Rd (46526-1174)
P.O. Box 95 (46527-0095)
PHONE..............................574 533-3118
Fax: 574 534-0416
Charles H Gerwels,
Edward V Gerwels,
Paul Gerwels,
▲ EMP: 105 EST: 1950
SQ FT: 68,000
SALES (est): 19.8MM **Privately Held**
WEB: www.trianglerubberco.com
SIC: 2821 3053 3061 3083 Elastomers,
nonvulcanizable (plastics); gaskets &
sealing devices; mechanical rubber
goods; laminated plastics plate & sheet;
industrial organic chemicals; synthetic
rubber

(G-5341)
TRIANGLE RUBBER CO LLC
1801 Eisenhower Dr N (46526-5386)
PHONE..............................574 533-3118
Kevin Gerwells, *Manager*
EMP: 20
SQ FT: 36,500
SALES (corp-wide): 19.8MM **Privately
Held**
WEB: www.trianglerubberco.com
SIC: 2821 Plastics materials & resins
PA: Triangle Rubber Co., Llc
1924 Elkhart Rd
Goshen IN 46526
574 533-3118

(G-5342)
TRIPLE CROWN MEDIA LLC
Also Called: The Goshen News
114 S Main St (46526-3702)
P.O. Box 569 (46527-0569)
PHONE..............................574 533-2151
Fax: 574 533-0839
John Reynolds, *Principal*
EMP: 90
SALES (corp-wide): 19.6MM **Privately
Held**
WEB: www.graycommunication.com
SIC: 2711 2791 2759 2752 Commercial
printing & newspaper publishing com-
bined; typesetting; commercial printing;
commercial printing, lithographic
HQ: Triple Crown Media, Llc
725 Old Norcross Rd
Lawrenceville GA 30046
770 483-5910

(G-5343)
TURTLE TOP MINI MOTOR HOMES
1607 S Main St (46526-4721)
PHONE..............................574 831-4340
Rob Cripe, *Owner*
Thomas Craig, *CFO*
EMP: 6
SALES (est): 758.9K **Privately Held**
WEB: www.turtletop.com
SIC: 3711 Buses, all types, assembly of

(G-5344)
TWO EL EXITO
117 Brookside Mnr (46526-8833)
PHONE..............................574 830-5104
Adrian Villalobos, *Principal*
EMP: 2

SALES (est): 94.4K **Privately Held**
SIC: 7372 Publishers' computer software

(G-5345)
WAVE EXPRESS
67952 Us Highway 33 (46526-8549)
P.O. Box 67, Syracuse (46567-0067)
PHONE..............................574 642-0630
Anita Carpenter, *Principal*
EMP: 3
SALES (est): 435.4K **Privately Held**
SIC: 3711 Motor vehicles & car bodies

(G-5346)
WILDWOOD MILLWORK LLC
2408 Lincolnway E (46526-6424)
PHONE..............................574 535-9104
Derrick Otto, *Purch Agent*
Ed Stahley, *Sales Mgr*
Janell Helmuth, *Office Mgr*
Galen Helmuth, *Department Mgr*
Dennis Helmuth,
EMP: 8
SALES (est): 1.3MM **Privately Held**
SIC: 2431 Millwork

(G-5347)
ZIEMAN MANUFACTURING COMPANY
Also Called: Design Time
2475 E Kercher Rd (46526-6465)
PHONE..............................574 522-5202
Fax: 574 533-5181
Denise Rodewald, *Branch Mgr*
EMP: 3
SALES (corp-wide): 2.1B **Publicly Held**
WEB: www.zieman.com
SIC: 3715 3441 2451 3799 Truck trailer
chassis; fabricated structural metal; mo-
bile homes; trailers & trailer equipment
HQ: Zieman Manufacturing Company Inc
2703 College Ave
Goshen IN 46528
574 535-1125

(G-5348)
ZIMMER METAL SALES LLC
64470 State Road 19 (46526-9421)
PHONE..............................574 862-1800
David Zimmerman, *Mng Member*
Marv Zimmerman, *Mng Member*
EMP: 5
SQ FT: 9,600
SALES (est): 819.9K **Privately Held**
SIC: 3444 5211 Siding, sheet metal; siding

Gosport
Owen County

(G-5349)
ALEXANDER MACHINE
7847 Jones Rd (47433-7712)
PHONE..............................812 879-4982
Mark Alexander, *Owner*
EMP: 4
SQ FT: 10,000
SALES: 500K **Privately Held**
SIC: 3678 Electronic connectors

(G-5350)
GOSPORT MANUFACTURING CO INC
Also Called: King of Tarpaulins The
11 Lousisa St (47433)
P.O. Box 26 (47433-0026)
PHONE..............................812 879-4224
Fax: 812 879-4227
Joseph B King, *President*
Brad King, *Sales Mgr*
Marsha Pemberton, *Manager*
▲ EMP: 35
SQ FT: 22,000
SALES (est): 4.5MM **Privately Held**
WEB: www.gosportmfg.com
SIC: 2394 Tarpaulins, fabric: made from
purchased materials

(G-5351)
INDIANA QUARRIERS & CARVERS
8383 N Stinesville Rd (47433-9505)
PHONE..............................812 935-8383
John Steckling, *President*

EMP: 12
SALES (est): 1.7MM Privately Held
SIC: 1411 Dimension stone

(G-5352)
KINSER TIMBER PRODUCTS INC
Also Called: Kinser Trucking
8283 W Hedrick Rd (47433-9515)
PHONE..................812 876-4775
Fax: 812 876-9649
Jerry Kinser, *President*
Julia Kinser, *Admin Sec*
EMP: 7
SALES (est): 815.6K Privately Held
SIC: 2411 2421 5211 5031 Logging camps & contractors; sawmills & planing mills, general; lumber products; lumber: rough, dressed & finished

(G-5353)
LIBERTY CUT STONE INC
9921 N Liberty Hollow Rd (47433-9521)
PHONE..................812 935-5515
Phil Wampler, *President*
Mike Wampler, *Vice Pres*
Marybeth Wampler, *Treasurer*
EMP: 3
SQ FT: 5,000
SALES (est): 230K Privately Held
SIC: 3281 Cut stone & stone products

(G-5354)
OHM ENTERPRISE LLC
Also Called: Custom Manufacturing Solutions
2534 State Highway 67 (47433-7722)
PHONE..................812 879-5455
AMI Shah, *President*
Sonny Shah, *Vice Pres*
EMP: 4
SALES (est): 326.8K Privately Held
SIC: 3599 Tubing, flexible metallic

(G-5355)
STAG TOOL
3755 W Burma Rd (47433-9587)
PHONE..................812 876-3281
Roy Spivey, *Owner*
EMP: 4
SALES: 180K Privately Held
SIC: 3544 3599 Special dies, tools, jigs & fixtures; machine shop, jobbing & repair

(G-5356)
TSF TOOL LLC
5044 S Salem Church Rd (47433-8930)
PHONE..................765 537-9008
Sandra Fish,
Tim Fish,
EMP: 2
SALES: 40K Privately Held
SIC: 3599 Machine shop, jobbing & repair

(G-5357)
WHIFFEN MACHINE AND PRESS REPR
9967 N Brown Ln (47433-9411)
PHONE..................812 876-1257
Fax: 812 876-1257
Don Whiffen, *President*
Cheryl Whiffen, *Vice Pres*
EMP: 2
SQ FT: 1,200
SALES: 200K Privately Held
SIC: 7699 3599 Printing trades machinery & equipment repair; machine shop, jobbing & repair

Grabill
Allen County

(G-5358)
BRINDLE PRODUCTS INC (PA)
13633 David Dr (46741)
P.O. Box 227 (46741-0227)
PHONE..................260 627-2156
Fax: 260 627-5145
Fred Gage, *Ch of Bd*
Joseph F Gage, *President*
Mike Demoss, *Plant Mgr*
Andrea Gage, *Office Mgr*
EMP: 20
SQ FT: 38,000

SALES (est): 4.3MM Privately Held
WEB: www.brindleproducts.com
SIC: 3714 3715 3713 Motor vehicle parts & accessories; truck trailers; truck bodies (motor vehicles)

(G-5359)
CEDAR CREEK SAWMILL LLC
15010 Page Rd (46741-9680)
P.O. Box 605 (46741-0605)
PHONE..................260 627-3985
Benjamin S Graber, *Owner*
EMP: 25
SALES (est): 4.2MM Privately Held
SIC: 2421 Sawmills & planing mills, general

(G-5360)
CHRIS SCHWARTZ
Also Called: Schwartz's Custom Woodworking
13631 Spencerville Rd (46741-9675)
PHONE..................260 615-9574
Chris Schwartz, *Principal*
EMP: 2
SALES: 80K Privately Held
SIC: 2431 5712 Woodwork, interior & ornamental; furniture stores

(G-5361)
CONTINENTAL STRL PLAS INC
13811 Roth Rd (46741-9678)
PHONE..................260 627-0890
Rod Swann, *Manager*
EMP: 21
SALES (corp-wide): 7.8B Privately Held
SIC: 3714 Motor vehicle parts & accessories
HQ: Continental Structural Plastics, Inc.
255 Rex Blvd
Auburn Hills MI 48326
248 237-7800

(G-5362)
COURIER PRINTING CO ALLEN CNTY
13720 Main St (46741-2011)
P.O. Box 77 (46741-0077)
PHONE..................260 627-2728
Fax: 260 627-2519
Charles A Dick, *President*
Judy Dick, *Vice Pres*
Waldo P Dick, *Treasurer*
EMP: 9 EST: 1949
SQ FT: 6,400
SALES (est): 230K Privately Held
SIC: 2711 2791 2789 2759 Job printing & newspaper publishing combined; newspapers: publishing only, not printed on site; typesetting; bookbinding & related work; commercial printing; commercial printing, lithographic

(G-5363)
DUTCH MADE INC (PA)
10415 Roth Rd (46741-9637)
P.O. Box 310 (46741-0310)
PHONE..................260 657-3311
Fax: 260 657-5778
Lester R Zehr, *President*
Corey Graber, *Opers Mgr*
Del Pask, *Project Engr*
Dave Korus, *CFO*
Steve Krug, *Controller*
EMP: 105 EST: 1968
SQ FT: 11,000
SALES (est): 12.6MM Privately Held
SIC: 2434 Wood kitchen cabinets

(G-5364)
FIBERGLASS PDTS & BOAT REPR
12401 Bay Heights Blvd (46741-9605)
PHONE..................260 627-3209
Thomas J Miller, *Principal*
EMP: 2
SALES (est): 152K Privately Held
SIC: 3732 Boat building & repairing

(G-5365)
GRABER BOX & PALLET FMLY LMT P
16301 Trammel Rd (46741-9769)
PHONE..................260 657-5657
Toby Graber,

Joshua Graber,
Norman Graber,
EMP: 34
SALES (est): 5.5MM Privately Held
SIC: 2448 7389 Pallets, wood & wood with metal;

(G-5366)
GRABER CABINETRY LLC
Also Called: Cabinets & Furniture
15210 Grabill Rd (46741-9719)
PHONE..................260 627-2243
Fax: 260 627-3162
Chris Graber, *President*
Vincent Tipman Sr, *Principal*
Solomon Graber, *Vice Pres*
Kristi Abel, *Manager*
EMP: 50
SQ FT: 10,500
SALES (est): 6.9MM Privately Held
WEB: www.cabinetsbygraber.com
SIC: 2541 2517 2521 2434 Cabinets, except refrigerated: show, display, etc.: wood; home entertainment unit cabinets, wood; wood office furniture; wood kitchen cabinets; plastics materials & resins

(G-5367)
GRABER MANUFACTURING LLC
12836 Cuba Rd (46741-9721)
PHONE..................260 657-3400
James G Graber,
Joseph R Graber Jr,
EMP: 3 EST: 2000
SALES: 200K Privately Held
SIC: 3089 2511 Window frames & sash, plastic; storage chests, household; wood

(G-5368)
GRABILL CABINET COMPANY INC
13844 Sawmill Dr (46741-9481)
P.O. Box 40 (46741-0040)
PHONE..................877 472-2782
Fax: 260 627-3539
Martin Heiny, *President*
David Carnahan, *Admin Sec*
EMP: 210 EST: 1946
SQ FT: 105,000
SALES (est): 35MM Privately Held
WEB: www.grabillcabinets.com
SIC: 2431 2434 2511 Panel work, wood; wood kitchen cabinets; wood household furniture

(G-5369)
GRABILL COUNTRY MEAT 1 INC
Also Called: Grabill Home Food Service
13211 West St (46741-2031)
P.O. Box 190 (46741-0190)
PHONE..................260 627-3691
Patrick Fonner, *President*
Dennis Fonner, *Corp Secy*
EMP: 11
SQ FT: 10,000
SALES: 5MM Privately Held
SIC: 5149 2038 2013 Canned goods: fruit, vegetables, seafood, meats, etc.; frozen specialties; sausages & other prepared meats

(G-5370)
GRABILL TRUSS INCORPORATED
Also Called: Grabill Truss Manufacturing
14005 David Ln (46741)
P.O. Box 250 (46741-0250)
PHONE..................260 627-0933
Fax: 260 627-0934
William Kaufman, *President*
EMP: 6
SQ FT: 12,800
SALES (est): 975.7K Privately Held
SIC: 3443 Truss plates, metal

(G-5371)
GRABILL WOODWORKING SPECIALTY
13830 Grabill Rd (46741-2000)
PHONE..................260 627-5982
Fax: 260 627-2401
Steve Jones, *President*
EMP: 5
SQ FT: 9,000

SALES: 400K Privately Held
SIC: 2434 2499 Wood kitchen cabinets; woodenware, kitchen & household

(G-5372)
HOME GUARD INDUSTRIES INC
13101 Main St (46741-2021)
P.O. Box 39 (46741-0039)
PHONE..................260 627-6060
Fax: 260 627-0969
Brian G Barbieri, *President*
Joseph Barbieri Jr, *Vice Pres*
Bill Parrish, *Plant Mgr*
▲ EMP: 100
SQ FT: 170,000
SALES (est): 21.5MM Privately Held
WEB: www.home-guard.net
SIC: 3442 3089 Metal doors; windows, plastic

(G-5373)
J & N STONE INC
13729 David Dr (46741)
P.O. Box 294 (46741-0294)
PHONE..................260 627-2404
Fax: 260 627-2404
Jack Langcher Jr, *President*
Tong N Nokaya, *General Mgr*
EMP: 16
SALES (est): 1.5MM Privately Held
WEB: www.jnstone.com
SIC: 3281 Cut stone & stone products

(G-5374)
J M WOODWORKING CO INC
10832 Witmer Rd (46741-9752)
PHONE..................260 627-8362
John E Langacher, *President*
Maryanne Langacher, *Vice Pres*
EMP: 2
SALES (est): 236.1K Privately Held
SIC: 2499 Decorative wood & woodwork

(G-5375)
J R GRABER & SONS INC
12916 Cuba Rd (46741-9721)
PHONE..................260 657-5620
Joseph R Graber Jr, *Partner*
Michael Graber, *Partner*
Ruben Graber, *Partner*
David Nolt, *Partner*
James Witmer, *Partner*
EMP: 15 EST: 1965
SQ FT: 14,000
SALES (est): 1.9MM Privately Held
SIC: 2449 Boxes, wood: wirebound

(G-5376)
JOHNNY GRABER WOODWORKING
11522 Notestine Rd (46741-9735)
PHONE..................260 466-4957
Johnny Graber, *Owner*
EMP: 5
SALES: 250K Privately Held
SIC: 2434 1799 7389 Wood kitchen cabinets; kitchen cabinet installation;

(G-5377)
JR GRBER SONS FMLY LTD PRTNR
15822 Trammel Rd (46741-9767)
PHONE..................260 657-1071
Joseph Graber Jr, *Managing Prtnr*
Ruben Graber, *Partner*
EMP: 9
SALES (est): 1.2MM Privately Held
SIC: 2441 2448 Boxes, wood; pallets, wood

(G-5378)
LENGACHER MACHINE INC
17305 Grabill Rd (46741-9538)
PHONE..................260 657-3114
Eli Lengacher, *President*
Anna Lengacher, *Corp Secy*
EMP: 10
SQ FT: 13,000
SALES: 1.5MM Privately Held
SIC: 3599 Machine shop, jobbing & repair

(G-5379)
LSM MANUFACTURING LLC
15303 Roth Rd (46741-9618)
PHONE..................260 409-4030

Sheryl Lyons, *Principal*
EMP: 3
SALES (est): 282K **Privately Held**
SIC: 3999 Bleaching & dyeing of sponges

(G-5380)
MILLER CABINETRY & FURN LLC
16016 Trammel Rd (46741-9723)
PHONE.....................................260 657-5052
Steven Miller, *Owner*
EMP: 2
SALES (est): 231.6K **Privately Held**
SIC: 2434 Wood kitchen cabinets

(G-5381)
OLD FORT DISTILLERY INC
12311 Saint Joe Rd (46741-9411)
PHONE.....................................260 705-5128
Paul Grush, *President*
Kristal Grush, *Treasurer*
EMP: 2
SALES (est): 62.3K **Privately Held**
SIC: 2085 Distilled & blended liquors

(G-5382)
OLD LUMBER YARD CLAY FACTORY
Also Called: Clay Factory, The
13716 3rd St (46741-2004)
P.O. Box 371 (46741-0371)
PHONE.....................................260 627-3567
Karen Roseberry, *President*
EMP: 15
SQ FT: 4,000
SALES (est): 923.9K **Privately Held**
SIC: 3944 5945 Craft & hobby kits & sets; arts & crafts supplies

(G-5383)
R3 COMPOSITES CORP (PA)
14123 Roth Rd (46741-9678)
PHONE.....................................260 627-0033
Mark Glidden, *President*
Michael Parrish, *Opers Mgr*
Kirk Klein, *CFO*
Geoffrey Newman, *Program Mgr*
Ron Gerken, *Maintence Staff*
EMP: 81 **EST:** 2000
SQ FT: 235,000
SALES (est): 48.4MM **Privately Held**
WEB: www.r3composites.com
SIC: 3089 Fiberglass doors

(G-5384)
SAUDER WOODWORKING CO
13737 Main St (46741-2037)
PHONE.....................................800 537-1530
EMP: 3
SALES (corp-wide): 500MM **Privately Held**
SIC: 2531 Chairs, portable folding
PA: Sauder Woodworking Co.
502 Middle St
Archbold OH 43502
419 446-3828

(G-5385)
WOOD TECHNOLOGIES LLC
13804 Antwerp Rd (46741-9716)
PHONE.....................................260 627-8858
Ben Lengacher, *Vice Pres*
Benjamin E Lengacher, *Mng Member*
▼ **EMP:** 25
SQ FT: 40,000
SALES: 9MM **Privately Held**
SIC: 5046 2541 Store fixtures & display equipment; store & office display cases & fixtures

Grandview
Spencer County

(G-5386)
CORN ISLAND SHIPYARD INC
9447 Indiana 66 (47615)
P.O. Box 125, Lamar (47550-0125)
PHONE.....................................812 362-8808
Fax: 812 362-8809
Don Foertsch, *President*
Linda Foertsch, *Corp Secy*
David Foertsch, *Vice Pres*
▲ **EMP:** 4

SALES (est): 1.2MM **Privately Held**
WEB: www.cornislandshipyard.com
SIC: 3731 Barges, building & repairing

(G-5387)
GRANDVIEW ALUMINUM PRODUCTS
110 W 4th St (47615-9483)
P.O. Box 687 (47615-0687)
PHONE.....................................812 649-2569
Fax: 812 649-2526
Harold L Banks, *President*
Georgia Lee Banks, *Corp Secy*
Brett Banks, *Vice Pres*
Leslie Banks, *Vice Pres*
▲ **EMP:** 35 **EST:** 1965
SQ FT: 13,000
SALES (est): 7MM **Privately Held**
WEB: www.gapalum.com
SIC: 3363 3993 3366 3365 Aluminum die-castings; signs & advertising specialties; copper foundries; aluminum foundries; platemaking services

Granger
St. Joseph County

(G-5388)
AAM-EQUIPCO INC (PA)
12838 Loop Ct (46530-9289)
PHONE.....................................574 272-8886
John Finks, *President*
Nancy Finks, *Corp Secy*
EMP: 3
SALES (est): 1.5MM **Privately Held**
SIC: 5084 3549 Industrial machinery & equipment; metalworking machinery

(G-5389)
ALLEGIANCE TOOL & DIE INC
12888 Industrial Park Dr (46530-8868)
PHONE.....................................574 277-1819
Donald Litznerski, *President*
EMP: 7
SQ FT: 5,600
SALES (est): 660K **Privately Held**
SIC: 3544 Special dies & tools

(G-5390)
ASHLEY WORLDWIDE INC (PA)
Also Called: Gerber Manufacturing
13388 State Road 23 (46530-8621)
PHONE.....................................574 259-2481
Fax: 574 255-6849
Terry L Gerber, *Ch of Bd*
Deron Gerber, *President*
Maria Patterson, *Plant Mgr*
Nancy D Gerber, *Admin Sec*
▲ **EMP:** 5
SQ FT: 1,500
SALES (est): 9.6MM **Privately Held**
SIC: 2311 Men's & boys' uniforms; policemen's uniforms: made from purchased materials

(G-5391)
B & B SPECIALTIES INC
14234 Cleveland Rd (46530-9653)
PHONE.....................................574 277-0499
Fax: 574 277-0499
Richard Bennett, *President*
Virginia Bennett, *Vice Pres*
EMP: 2
SALES (est): 223.7K **Privately Held**
WEB: www.bennettbuilt.com
SIC: 3944 5945 Airplane models, toy & hobby; models, toy & hobby

(G-5392)
B C WELDING INC
12801 Industrial Park Dr (46530-8868)
P.O. Box 257 (46530-0257)
PHONE.....................................574 272-9008
Fax: 574 272-9067
William Carnes, *Principal*
EMP: 6
SQ FT: 15,000
SALES: 1.5MM **Privately Held**
WEB: www.bcwelding.net
SIC: 3441 Fabricated structural metal

(G-5393)
B Y M ELECTRONICS INC
10288 Anderson Rd (46530-7263)
PHONE.....................................574 674-5096
Brian Y McCay, *CEO*
Brian Y Mc Cay, *President*
Suzanne M Mc Cay, *Vice Pres*
EMP: 2
SALES: 500K **Privately Held**
SIC: 3699 Welding machines & equipment, ultrasonic

(G-5394)
BIRDS NEST INC
Also Called: Wild Birds Unlimited
421 E University Dr (46530-4499)
PHONE.....................................574 247-0201
David Gunter, *President*
Kathy Gunter, *Owner*
EMP: 2
SALES (est): 150K **Privately Held**
WEB: www.birdsnways.com
SIC: 5999 2048 Pets & pet supplies; bird food, prepared

(G-5395)
BT&F LLC
Also Called: Grip-Tite
12441 Beckley St Ste 8 (46530-9660)
PHONE.....................................574 272-6128
Brian Harker, *Managing Dir*
Hamendar Agarwal,
James Larkin,
▲ **EMP:** 7
SQ FT: 23,000
SALES (est): 2.4MM **Privately Held**
SIC: 3423 Hand & edge tools

(G-5396)
BUCK & COMPANY INC
12000 Buttercup Cir (46530-7153)
PHONE.....................................574 292-0874
T Lee Buck, *Manager*
EMP: 4
SALES (est): 331.7K **Privately Held**
SIC: 3564 Blowers & fans

(G-5397)
CORNERSTONE CABINETRY LLC
15510 Cleveland Rd (46530-8559)
PHONE.....................................574 250-2690
EMP: 2
SALES (est): 156.9K **Privately Held**
SIC: 2434 Wood kitchen cabinets

(G-5398)
CT INDUSTRIES LLC
51622 Steeple Chase Dr (46530-9373)
PHONE.....................................574 675-9422
Robin Tooley, *Principal*
EMP: 2
SALES (est): 74.6K **Privately Held**
SIC: 3999 Manufacturing industries

(G-5399)
CUSTOM CANDY WRAPPERS COMPANY
52092 Larkspur Cir (46530-8956)
PHONE.....................................574 247-0756
Beth Anne Jackson, *Owner*
EMP: 2
SALES (est): 126.7K **Privately Held**
SIC: 2759 5947 Wrappers: printing; gift, novelty & souvenir shop

(G-5400)
DAUGHERTY CABINETS
51719 Gumwood Rd (46530-3304)
PHONE.....................................574 272-9205
Douglas Daugherty, *Principal*
EMP: 2
SALES (est): 152K **Privately Held**
SIC: 2434 Wood kitchen cabinets

(G-5401)
DIMENSIONS IN TOOLING INC
12635 Sandy Dr (46530-4306)
PHONE.....................................574 273-1505
Fax: 574 968-0036
Ross A Dickey, *President*
Randy Weirich, *Technology*
EMP: 10
SQ FT: 1,100

SALES (est): 1.6MM **Privately Held**
SIC: 3545 Machine tool attachments & accessories; bits for use on lathes, planers, shapers, etc.; tools & accessories for machine tools

(G-5402)
DON R KILL PUBLISHING INC
50742 Old Lantern Trl (46530-9175)
PHONE.....................................574 271-9381
Donald R Kill, *President*
Nancy Kill, *Corp Secy*
EMP: 2
SALES (est): 80K **Privately Held**
SIC: 7311 2721 Advertising agencies; trade journals: publishing only, not printed on site

(G-5403)
EDNA B LLC
51265 Golfview Ct (46530-6501)
PHONE.....................................574 271-4300
EMP: 2
SALES (est): 145.4K **Privately Held**
SIC: 2399 Mfg Fabricated Textile Products

(G-5404)
ELEMENT PRO SERVICES LLC
50961 Partridge Woods Dr (46530-7540)
PHONE.....................................574 271-5259
William Steele, *Principal*
EMP: 2
SALES (est): 81.8K **Privately Held**
SIC: 2819 Elements

(G-5405)
EMNET LLC
12441 Beckley St Ste 6 (46530-9660)
PHONE.....................................574 360-1093
Luis Montestruque, *Owner*
EMP: 2 **EST:** 2015
SALES (est): 114.4K **Privately Held**
SIC: 3825 Instruments to measure electricity

(G-5406)
EMT INDUSTRIES INC
Also Called: Excel Rubber
12065 Covered Wagon Ct (46530-7100)
PHONE.....................................574 533-1273
Thomas J Taylor, *President*
Philip T Everett, *Exec VP*
J Patrick McManus, *Admin Sec*
EMP: 50
SQ FT: 14,500
SALES (est): 7.4MM **Privately Held**
WEB: www.excelrubber.com
SIC: 3061 3053 Mechanical rubber goods; gaskets & sealing devices

(G-5407)
FIRST CHOICE FORESTRY & LOG
51101 Old Cottage Dr (46530-4713)
PHONE.....................................574 271-9425
Joseph B Hines, *Owner*
EMP: 2
SALES (est): 81.7K **Privately Held**
SIC: 2411 Logging

(G-5408)
GBI AIR SYSTEMS INC
50867 Post Rd (46530-6853)
PHONE.....................................574 272-0600
Ray Ritchey, *President*
Diane Ritchey, *Vice Pres*
EMP: 2
SALES (est): 371K **Privately Held**
WEB: www.gbiairsystems.com
SIC: 3564 4961 Blowers & fans; purification & dust collection equipment; exhaust fans: industrial or commercial; ventilating fans: industrial or commercial; air conditioning supply services

(G-5409)
GILLIS COMPANY
51093 Bittersweet Rd (46530)
PHONE.....................................574 273-9086
Fax: 574 273-9625
Greg Gillis, *President*
Brian Gillis, *Vice Pres*
▲ **EMP:** 7
SQ FT: 2,600

▲ = Import ▼ =Export
◆ =Import/Export

SALES (est): 1.1MM **Privately Held**
SIC: **2842** 5094 Cleaning or polishing preparations; specialty cleaning preparations; polishing preparations & related products; jewelers' findings

(G-5410)
GRANGER GAZETTE
50841 Stonebridge Dr (46530-8268)
P.O. Box 16 (46530-0016)
PHONE..................................574 277-2679
Kerry Byler, *President*
EMP: 5
SALES (est): 311.6K **Privately Held**
SIC: **2711** 2791 2789 2752 Newspapers; typesetting; bookbinding & related work; commercial printing, lithographic

(G-5411)
GREAT LAKES WATERJET INC
53100 Corydon Ct (46530-5838)
PHONE..................................574 651-2158
Stacey E Curtiss, *President*
EMP: 2
SALES: 175K **Privately Held**
SIC: **3999** 7389 Manufacturing industries; metal cutting services

(G-5412)
HESTAD INDUSTRIES INC
52265 Wood Haven Dr (46530-5605)
PHONE..................................574 271-7609
Ron Hestad, *President*
EMP: 2
SALES (est): 92K **Privately Held**
SIC: **3999** Manufacturing industries

(G-5413)
HOMESTEAD INDUSTRIES INC
53193 Chelle Ln (46530-8997)
PHONE..................................574 273-5274
Elizabeth Huge, *Owner*
EMP: 4
SQ FT: 17,000
SALES: 250K **Privately Held**
SIC: **3999** 5947 Candles; gift, novelty & souvenir shop

(G-5414)
INDIANA INTGRATED CIRCUITS LLC
Also Called: Iic
14659 Horseshoe Bend Ct (46530-8231)
PHONE..................................724 244-4560
Jason M Kulick,
EMP: 2
SALES (est): 121.2K **Privately Held**
SIC: **3674** Semiconductors & related devices

(G-5415)
INTERACTIVE ENGINEERING INC
15925 Fair Banks Ct (46530-7067)
PHONE..................................574 272-5851
Thomas E Henry, *President*
Sarah Henry, *Corp Secy*
EMP: 3 EST: 1992
SQ FT: 2,000
SALES (est): 310.4K **Privately Held**
SIC: **3089** Injection molded finished plastic products

(G-5416)
ITALMAC USA INC
12743 Heather Park Dr # 104 (46530-4317)
PHONE..................................574 243-0217
Mattia Marchiotto, *President*
Thomas J Hall, *Principal*
Roberto Ghizzoni, *Vice Pres*
▲ EMP: 4
SALES (est): 516.2K **Privately Held**
SIC: **3444** Sheet metalwork

(G-5417)
K MOLD AND ENGINEERING INC
51383 Bittersweet Rd (46530-6204)
P.O. Box 96 (46530-0096)
PHONE..................................574 271-9122
Fax: 574 272-5858
Kenneth Kasner, *President*
Phyllis Kasner, *Vice Pres*
EMP: 12 EST: 1982
SQ FT: 18,000

SALES (est): 2MM **Privately Held**
SIC: **3544** Industrial molds

(G-5418)
LAZAR SCIENTIFIC INCORPORATED
Also Called: LSI
12692 Sandy Dr Ste 116 (46530-4340)
P.O. Box 1128 (46530-1128)
PHONE..................................574 271-7020
Gregory G Lazarczyk, *President*
Michael J Finn, *Sales/Mktg Mgr*
Susan Y Lazarczyk, *Admin Sec*
EMP: 4 EST: 1998
SQ FT: 1,400
SALES (est): 1.3MM **Privately Held**
SIC: **5049** 3826 Analytical instruments; petroleum product analyzing apparatus

(G-5419)
MARCOTTE CABINETS
51286 Ironwood Rd (46530-7622)
PHONE..................................574 520-1342
Faye Marcotte, *CFO*
EMP: 2
SALES (est): 255.4K **Privately Held**
SIC: **2434** Wood kitchen cabinets

(G-5420)
MICHIANA CABINET & REFACING LL
50520 Park Ln E (46530-7526)
PHONE..................................574 277-0801
Don Wierenga, *Principal*
EMP: 2
SALES (est): 120K **Privately Held**
SIC: **2434** Wood kitchen cabinets

(G-5421)
MICRO TOOL & MACHINE CO INC
51836 Purdue Ct (46530-9566)
PHONE..................................574 272-9141
Fax: 574 256-0829
Michael Casini, *President*
Joseph Kertes, *Vice Pres*
Thomas Pauwels, *Treasurer*
EMP: 8
SQ FT: 6,000
SALES: 1.2MM **Privately Held**
SIC: **3544** 3541 Industrial molds; machine tools, metal cutting type

(G-5422)
MIDWEST FABRICATION LLC
16100 Branchwood Ln (46530-8986)
PHONE..................................574 276-5041
Matthew Hunsberger,
EMP: 2 EST: 2010
SALES: 12K **Privately Held**
SIC: **3569** General industrial machinery

(G-5423)
MISHAWAKA BREWING COMPANY
408 W Cleveland Rd (46530-9577)
PHONE..................................574 256-9993
Tom R Schmidt Sr, *President*
Sally J Foster, *Admin Sec*
EMP: 40
SQ FT: 1,800
SALES (est): 3MM **Privately Held**
SIC: **2082** 5181 5813 5812 Beer (alcoholic beverage); ale (alcoholic beverage); porter (alcoholic beverage); stout (alcoholic beverage); beer & ale; drinking places; eating places

(G-5424)
MOLDED ACSTCAL PDTS EASTON INC
13065 Anderson Rd (46530-9283)
PHONE..................................574 968-3124
Frank Peters, *CFO*
Robert Snyder, *Branch Mgr*
EMP: 200 **Privately Held**
WEB: www.mapeaston.com
SIC: **3269** Cookware: stoneware, coarse earthenware & pottery
PA: Molded Acoustical Products Of Easton, Inc.
3 Danforth Dr
Easton PA 18045

(G-5425)
MORSE METAL FAB INC
51111 Bittersweet Rd (46530-7880)
PHONE..................................574 674-6237
Kevin Montague, *President*
Chip Tompkins, *Marketing Staff*
Troy Turnock, *Admin Sec*
EMP: 21
SQ FT: 28,000
SALES (est): 3.3MM **Privately Held**
WEB: www.morsemetalfab.com
SIC: **3444** 3441 Sheet metalwork; fabricated structural metal

(G-5426)
NEETA SWEET CUPCAKES N MINIS
52101 Goldenrod Ln (46530-7150)
PHONE..................................574 286-7032
EMP: 3 EST: 2013
SALES (est): 90.2K **Privately Held**
SIC: **2051** Bread, cake & related products

(G-5427)
NIELSEN ENTERPRISES INC
Also Called: Proforma Corporate Solutions
51950 Chicory Ln (46530-7587)
P.O. Box 719 (46530-0719)
PHONE..................................574 277-3748
Jon R Nielsen, *President*
EMP: 2
SALES (est): 162.2K **Privately Held**
SIC: **2759** Promotional printing

(G-5428)
PAIGE MARSCHALL
Also Called: Paige's Custom Lettering
12622 Alexander Dr (46530-9619)
P.O. Box 412 (46530-0412)
PHONE..................................574 277-1631
Fax: 574 277-1601
Paige Marschall, *Owner*
EMP: 9
SQ FT: 6,000
SALES (est): 800K **Privately Held**
SIC: **7389** 2395 Textile & apparel services; embroidery products, except schiffli machine

(G-5429)
PREMIER PRINT & SVCS GROUP INC
6910 N Main St Unit 11 (46530-9681)
PHONE..................................574 273-2525
Carl Digirolomo, *Manager*
James Buell, *Software Dev*
EMP: 10
SALES (corp-wide): 16.7MM **Privately Held**
SIC: **2759** 5943 Business forms: printing; office forms & supplies
PA: Premier Print & Services Group, Inc.
10 S Riverside Plz # 1810
Chicago IL 60606
312 648-2266

(G-5430)
RC FUN PARKS LLC
12990 Adams Rd (46530-7895)
PHONE..................................574 217-7715
Donna Shearer, *Owner*
EMP: 2 EST: 2012
SALES (est): 213.4K **Privately Held**
SIC: **3944** Electronic toys

(G-5431)
RIDG-U-RAK INC
51738 Foxdale Ln (46530-8437)
PHONE..................................574 273-8036
John Pellegrino, *Branch Mgr*
EMP: 5
SALES (corp-wide): 73.6MM **Privately Held**
SIC: **2448** Pallets, wood
PA: Ridg-U-Rak Inc.
120 S Lake St
North East PA 16428
814 725-8751

(G-5432)
SENTINEL SERVICES INC
Also Called: Chikol Equities
51618 Autumn Ridge Dr (46530-7009)
P.O. Box 774 (46530-0774)
PHONE..................................574 360-5279

David Kebrdle, *President*
Trixie Hawley, *Administration*
EMP: 15
SALES (est): 1MM **Privately Held**
SIC: **8721** 7389 7322 8742 Accounting, auditing & bookkeeping; auditing services; accounting services, except auditing; financial services; adjustment & collection services; financial consultant; business consulting; fur stripping

(G-5433)
SHELTON POWDER COATING LLC
51345 Bittersweet Rd (46530-6204)
PHONE..................................574 323-8369
Kent Shelton, *Owner*
EMP: 4
SALES (est): 439.8K **Privately Held**
SIC: **3399** Powder, metal

(G-5434)
SHIVOM JAY STEELS INTL LLC
14260 Meridian Xing (46530-4284)
PHONE..................................574 271-7222
▲ EMP: 2
SALES (est): 160K **Privately Held**
SIC: **3315** Mfg Steel Wire/Related Products

(G-5435)
SINCERELY DIFFERENT LLC
51860 Sharon Ct (46530-6823)
PHONE..................................574 292-1727
Sarah Dwigans, *Administration*
EMP: 2
SALES (est): 157.3K **Privately Held**
SIC: **2844** Toilet preparations

(G-5436)
SIR GRAPHICS INC
Also Called: Screen Printing
12599 Industrial Park Dr (46530-6872)
P.O. Box 1452 (46530-1452)
PHONE..................................574 272-9330
Fax: 574 272-9349
Leonard Shidaker, *President*
Donna Smink, *Corp Secy*
EMP: 6
SQ FT: 10,000
SALES (est): 593K **Privately Held**
SIC: **2759** 2396 Screen printing; automotive & apparel trimmings

(G-5437)
SPECTRUM SERVICES INC
12911 Industrial Park Dr # 7 (46530-4603)
P.O. Box 363 (46530-0363)
PHONE..................................574 272-7605
Dan Courtney, *President*
EMP: 4
SALES (est): 590.2K **Privately Held**
SIC: **3545** 7699 Machine tool accessories; sewing machine repair shop

(G-5438)
SPORTCRAFTERS INC (PA)
Also Called: Spin Zone
51345 Bittersweet Rd (46530-6204)
P.O. Box 452 (46530-0452)
PHONE..................................574 243-4994
Peter Colan, *President*
Cole Shearer, *Marketing Staff*
EMP: 2
SQ FT: 2,500
SALES (est): 315K **Privately Held**
WEB: www.sportcrafters.com
SIC: **5941** 3429 5091 Bicycle & bicycle parts; bicycle racks, automotive; bicycle equipment & supplies

(G-5439)
SR PETROLEUM INC
15482 Bryanton Ct (46530-8212)
PHONE..................................574 383-5879
Sarwan Singh, *Principal*
EMP: 2
SALES (est): 112.1K **Privately Held**
SIC: **1381** Drilling oil & gas wells

(G-5440)
STAINLESS STEEL KITCHENS
12911 Industrial Park Dr # 3 (46530-4604)
P.O. Box 877, Mishawaka (46546-0877)
PHONE..................................574 272-2530
Fax: 574 259-6310

Linda Bergling, *Owner*
Craig Bergling, *Co-Owner*
EMP: 2
SALES: 500K **Privately Held**
SIC: 2514 Kitchen cabinets: metal

(G-5441)
STANTON & ASSOCIATES INC
6910 N Main St Unit 15 (46530-9681)
PHONE....................574 247-5522
Brian J Milnamow, *President*
Jeffrey B Rothermel, *Vice Pres*
EMP: 3
SALES: 320K **Privately Held**
SIC: 3585 5078 Refrigeration equipment, complete; refrigeration equipment & supplies

(G-5442)
SYSGENOMICS LLC
51210 Lexingham Dr (46530-8256)
PHONE....................574 302-5396
Steven Buechler, *Mng Member*
Sunil Dadve, *Mng Member*
Yesim Gokmen-Polar, *Mng Member*
EMP: 3 **EST:** 2014
SALES (est): 49.8K **Privately Held**
SIC: 2835 2834 In vitro diagnostics; pharmaceutical preparations

(G-5443)
TEAM ONEWAY
12911 Industrial Park Dr (46530-4603)
PHONE....................574 387-5417
Josh Holt, *President*
EMP: 2
SALES (est): 87.2K **Privately Held**
SIC: 3714 Motor vehicle parts & accessories

(G-5444)
TECHNICAL WATER TREATMENT INC
51431 Autumn Ridge Dr (46530-7006)
PHONE....................574 277-1949
Rex McHenry, *Principal*
EMP: 2
SALES (est): 344K **Privately Held**
SIC: 5084 3589 Industrial machinery & equipment; sewage & water treatment equipment

(G-5445)
UFP GRANGER LLC
Also Called: Universal Forest Products
50415 Herbert St (46530-9161)
PHONE....................574 277-7670
David A Tutas, *Mng Member*
EMP: 32 **EST:** 2010
SALES (est): 3.2MM
SALES (corp-wide): 3.9B **Publicly Held**
SIC: 5031 2448 2421 2439 Lumber: rough, dressed & finished; wood pallets & skids; building & structural materials, wood; structural wood members
PA: Universal Forest Products, Inc.
2801 E Beltline Ave Ne
Grand Rapids MI 49525
616 364-6161

(G-5446)
UNIVERSAL FOREST PRODUCTS INC
50415 Herbert St (46530-9161)
PHONE....................574 277-7670
Fax: 574 277-0547
Dewayne Creighton, *Branch Mgr*
EMP: 20
SALES (corp-wide): 3.9B **Publicly Held**
SIC: 2421 Building & structural materials, wood
PA: Universal Forest Products, Inc.
2801 E Beltline Ave Ne
Grand Rapids MI 49525
616 364-6161

(G-5447)
UNIVERSAL FOREST PRODUCTS INDI
51070 Bittersweet Rd (46530-7879)
P.O. Box 129 (46530-0129)
PHONE....................574 273-6326
Dick McBride, *General Ptnr*
EMP: 200

SALES (est): 13.7MM **Privately Held**
SIC: 2491 2435 2431 2426 Wood preserving; hardwood veneer & plywood; millwork; hardwood dimension & flooring mills; sawmills & planing mills, general; logging

(G-5448)
URBAN SWIRL (PA)
7130 Heritage Square Dr # 440 (46530-5644)
PHONE....................574 387-4035
Christopher Hildebrandt, *Principal*
EMP: 6 **EST:** 2012
SALES (est): 665.3K **Privately Held**
SIC: 2026 Yogurt

(G-5449)
VTI PACKAGING SPECIALTIES
12912 Industrial Park Dr (46530-8837)
P.O. Box 320 (46530-0320)
PHONE....................574 277-4119
Margaret Anne Lavanture, *President*
EMP: 20
SALES (est): 314.7K **Privately Held**
SIC: 2671 Packaging paper & plastics film, coated & laminated

(G-5450)
VYTEC INC
12912 Industrial Park Dr (46530-8837)
P.O. Box 1148 (46530-1148)
PHONE....................574 277-4295
Fax: 574 277-2973
Margaret A Lavanture, *President*
Robert W Lavanture, *Vice Pres*
EMP: 30
SQ FT: 30,000
SALES: 5MM **Privately Held**
WEB: www.vytec.com
SIC: 3089 Extruded finished plastic products

(G-5451)
WAIT INDUSTRIES LLC
Also Called: M-3 & Associates
11930 Pacific Dr (46530-6071)
PHONE....................574 347-4320
Doug Wait,
EMP: 2
SALES (est): 214.5K **Privately Held**
SIC: 3444 Sheet metalwork

(G-5452)
WIGGINS PRESS LLC
15945 Preswick Ln (46530-6518)
PHONE....................574 273-1769
John F Zwerneman, *Owner*
EMP: 2
SALES (est): 50K **Privately Held**
SIC: 2741 Miscellaneous publishing

Greencastle
Putnam County

(G-5453)
A&M COMMERCIAL CLEANING LLC
1138 Avenue D St (46135-1840)
PHONE....................765 720-3737
Manuwell Ross,
EMP: 5
SALES: 900K **Privately Held**
SIC: 3589 Commercial cleaning equipment

(G-5454)
CASH CONCRETE PRODUCTS INC (PA)
1541 S County Road 450 E (46135-7951)
PHONE....................765 653-4007
Fax: 765 653-4007
Thomas C Cash, *President*
Tim Cash, *Treasurer*
Neal Cash, *Marketing Staff*
Brian Brinkman, *Technology*
EMP: 14
SQ FT: 13,000
SALES (est): 2.4MM **Privately Held**
SIC: 3273 3271 3272 Ready-mixed concrete; blocks, concrete or cinder: standard; concrete products

(G-5455)
CASH CONCRETE PRODUCTS INC
State Road 240 (46135)
PHONE....................765 653-4887
Tom Cash, *President*
EMP: 2
SALES (corp-wide): 2.4MM **Privately Held**
SIC: 3273 Ready-mixed concrete
PA: Cash Concrete Products Inc
1541 S County Road 450 E
Greencastle IN 46135
765 653-4007

(G-5456)
CROWN EQUIPMENT CORPORATION
Also Called: Crown Lift Trucks
2600 State Rd 240 E (46135)
P.O. Box 840 (46135-0840)
PHONE....................765 653-4240
Fax: 765 653-3538
Vince Wallace, *Plant Mgr*
EMP: 469
SALES (corp-wide): 3.1B **Privately Held**
SIC: 3537 Lift trucks, industrial: fork, platform, straddle, etc.
PA: Crown Equipment Corporation
44 S Washington St
New Bremen OH 45869
419 629-2311

(G-5457)
D & E MACHINE INC
944 W County Road 350 N (46135-8597)
PHONE....................765 653-8919
Fax: 765 653-2053
Dennis Flora, *President*
EMP: 7
SQ FT: 5,000
SALES: 800K **Privately Held**
SIC: 3599 3544 Machine shop, jobbing & repair; special dies & tools

(G-5458)
GREENCASTLE OFFSET INC
Also Called: Greencastle Offset Printing
20 S Jackson St (46135-1514)
PHONE....................765 653-4026
Fax: 765 653-7471
Terry Mc Carter, *President*
Pat Carter, *Vice Pres*
Pat Mc Carter, *Vice Pres*
EMP: 2 **EST:** 1961
SQ FT: 7,200
SALES (est): 304.7K **Privately Held**
WEB: www.greencastleoffsetprinting.com
SIC: 2752 2789 2721 Commercial printing, offset; bookbinding & related work; periodicals

(G-5459)
GYREWIDE PUBLICATIONS & BAD
1925 Windemere Dr (46135-9213)
PHONE....................765 721-7676
Donovan Wheeler, *Principal*
EMP: 2
SALES (est): 59.2K **Privately Held**
SIC: 2741 Miscellaneous publishing

(G-5460)
HARRIS SUGAR BUSH LLC (PA)
999 E County Road 325 N (46135-8025)
PHONE....................765 653-5108
Arthur Harris, *Principal*
EMP: 6
SALES (est): 576K **Privately Held**
SIC: 2099 Sugar, industrial maple

(G-5461)
HARTMAN LOGGING
1158 W Us Highway 40 (46135-8794)
PHONE....................765 653-3889
Darrell Minor, *Partner*
Daryle Minor, *Partner*
EMP: 3
SALES (est): 310.7K **Privately Held**
SIC: 2411 Logging camps & contractors

(G-5462)
HEARTLAND AUTOMOTIVE INC
300 S Warren Dr (46135-7573)
P.O. Box 648 (46135-0648)
PHONE....................765 653-4263
Fax: 765 653-6455
Toshio Kawashima, *Principal*
Todd Anderson, *District Mgr*
Ronan Miot, *Admin Sec*
▲ **EMP:** 600
SQ FT: 132,000
SALES (est): 228.8MM **Privately Held**
WEB: www.hauto.net
SIC: 3714 Motor vehicle parts & accessories

(G-5463)
HEARTLAND AUTOMOTIVE LLC
300 S Warren Dr (46135-7573)
P.O. Box 648 (46135-0648)
PHONE....................765 653-4263
Gary Hazlett, *QC Mgr*
Yusuke Sakuma, *Treasurer*
Atsuo Shoda, *Director*
Kaji Sawabe, *Director*
Ronan Miot, *Admin Sec*
EMP: 8
SALES (est): 251.6K **Privately Held**
SIC: 3714 Motor vehicle parts & accessories

(G-5464)
HENDERSHOT SERVICE CENTER INC
711 N Jackson St (46135-1036)
P.O. Box 56 (46135-0056)
PHONE....................765 653-2600
Gregory Hendershot,
Darcy Hendershot,
EMP: 10
SQ FT: 40,000
SALES (est): 905.5K **Privately Held**
SIC: 7538 7549 3621 General automotive repair shops; towing services; generating apparatus & parts, electrical

(G-5465)
JTN SERVICES INC
4421 S Us Highway 231 (46135-8711)
PHONE....................765 653-7158
Bill Newgent, *President*
Tammy Newgetn, *Corp Secy*
EMP: 4
SALES (est): 547.1K **Privately Held**
SIC: 5261 3647 Lawn & garden equipment; flasher lights, automotive

(G-5466)
LEAR CORPORATION
750 S Fillmore Rd (46135-7322)
PHONE....................765 653-2511
Fax: 765 653-7381
Carl Beckwith, *Manager*
EMP: 9
SALES (corp-wide): 20.4B **Publicly Held**
WEB: www.lear.com
SIC: 3714 Motor vehicle parts & accessories
PA: Lear Corporation
21557 Telegraph Rd
Southfield MI 48033
248 447-1500

(G-5467)
LEWIS JERRY CNSTR & EXCVTG
Also Called: Jerry Lewis Cnstr & Excvtg
1249 N Jackson St (46135-8929)
PHONE....................765 653-2800
Fax: 765 653-5733
Jerry Lewis, *President*
Barbara Lewis, *Admin Sec*
EMP: 8
SQ FT: 11,000
SALES (est): 790K **Privately Held**
SIC: 1794 1771 3273 Excavation work; concrete work; ready-mixed concrete

(G-5468)
MILLSTONE SPECIALTIES INC
1001 Sherwood Dr (46135-1156)
PHONE....................765 653-7382
Richard Taylor, *President*
Ellen Taylor, *Admin Sec*
EMP: 2
SALES (est): 140K **Privately Held**
SIC: 7372 Prepackaged software

(G-5469)
MY COUNTY PUBLISHING LLC
15 1/2 S Indiana St (46135-1509)
PHONE..................765 630-8221
EMP: 4
SALES (est): 180K Privately Held
SIC: 2741 Misc Publishing

(G-5470)
OBRIEN JACK & PAT ENTERPRISES
Also Called: Jack O'Brien Welding Service
1208 W County Road 125 S (46135-8479)
PHONE..................765 653-5070
Jack O'Brien, President
Joyce Obrian, Corp Secy
Pat O'Brien, Vice Pres
EMP: 2
SALES: 60K Privately Held
SIC: 7692 Welding repair

(G-5471)
PDK INDUSTRIES INC
6145 S County Road 375 W (46135-8629)
PHONE..................765 721-3085
EMP: 2
SALES (est): 102.8K Privately Held
SIC: 3999 Manufacturing industries

(G-5472)
PHOENIX CLOSURES INC
2000 S Jackson St (46135-2050)
PHONE..................765 658-1800
Chris Henderson, Production
Ken Skrypek, Regl Sales Mgr
Morgan Mullenix, Office Mgr
Bill Benton, Manager
EMP: 98
SALES (corp-wide): 94.5MM Privately Held
SIC: 3069 3089 5031 Molded rubber products; injection molding of plastics; molding, all materials
PA: Phoenix Closures, Inc.
1899 High Grove Ln
Naperville IL 60540
630 420-4750

(G-5473)
PINGLETON SAWMILL INC
525 S County Road 550 W (46135-8362)
PHONE..................765 653-2878
Fax: 765 653-7057
Lee Pingleton, President
Robert Pingleton, Vice Pres
Linda Pingleton, Treasurer
Ardell Pingleton, Admin Sec
EMP: 20
SALES (est): 3.4MM Privately Held
WEB: www.pingletonsawmillinc.com
SIC: 2421 2426 2411 Sawmills & planing mills, general; hardwood dimension & flooring mills; logging

(G-5474)
PRINTING PHANTOM
3101 W County Road 100 S (46135-8492)
PHONE..................765 719-2097
Payne Chestnut, Principal
EMP: 2
SALES (est): 125.7K Privately Held
SIC: 2752 Commercial printing, lithographic

(G-5475)
PROGRESSIVE PRINTING CO INC
115 N Jackson St Ste 1 (46135-1233)
P.O. Box 4 (46135-0004)
PHONE..................765 653-3814
Fax: 765 653-7318
Gary Gram, President
Cathy Lowery, Vice Pres
S James Gram, Shareholder
EMP: 3 EST: 1949
SQ FT: 6,000
SALES: 400K Privately Held
SIC: 2752 2791 2789 2759 Commercial printing, offset; typesetting; bookbinding & related work; commercial printing

(G-5476)
R B ANNIS INSTRUMENTS INC
117 W Franklin St (46135-1223)
PHONE..................765 848-1621

Michael E Scott, President
Sylvia M Scott, Treasurer
EMP: 8
SQ FT: 6,000
SALES: 800K Privately Held
WEB: www.rbannis.com
SIC: 3629 3695 3677 3651 Electronic generation equipment; magnetic & optical recording media; electronic coils, transformers & other inductors; household audio & video equipment; transformers, except electric; computer storage devices

(G-5477)
RUST PUBLISHING IN LLC
100 N Jackson St (46135-1240)
PHONE..................765 653-5151
Diana Dick, Receptionist
EMP: 2
SALES (est): 132.2K Privately Held
SIC: 2741 Miscellaneous publishing

(G-5478)
SPECKIN SIGN SERVICE INC
845 Indianapolis Rd (46135-1451)
PHONE..................317 539-5133
William Speckin III, President
EMP: 3
SALES (est): 224.6K Privately Held
SIC: 3993 Signs & advertising specialties

(G-5479)
TAYLOR MADE ENTERPRISES
Also Called: Taylor Made Awards
1292 N Jackson St (46135-8929)
P.O. Box 492 (46135-0492)
PHONE..................765 653-8481
Lawrence Taylor Jr, President
EMP: 6
SALES (est): 64.6K Privately Held
WEB: www.tm-awards.com
SIC: 3353 Plates, aluminum

(G-5480)
TRUTH PUBLISHING COMPANY INC
Also Called: Banner Graphic
100 N Jackson St (46135-1240)
P.O. Box 509 (46135-0509)
PHONE..................765 653-5151
Fax: 765 653-2063
Joey Bennett, Editor
Steve Hendershot, Branch Mgr
EMP: 30
SALES (est): 1.7MM
SALES (corp-wide): 25MM Privately Held
WEB: www.etruth.com
SIC: 2711 2791 2752 Newspapers: publishing only, not printed on site; typesetting; commercial printing, lithographic
PA: Truth Publishing Company, Inc
421 S 2nd St Ste 100
Elkhart IN 46516
574 294-1661

(G-5481)
WASSER BREWING COMPANY LLC
102 E Franklin St (46135-1220)
PHONE..................765 653-3240
Chris Weeks,
EMP: 6 EST: 2014
SALES (est): 205.4K Privately Held
SIC: 2082 5812 Beer (alcoholic beverage); eating places

Greendale
Dearborn County

(G-5482)
ANCHOR GLASS CONTAINER CORP
200 Belleview Dr (47025-1485)
PHONE..................812 537-1655
Fax: 812 537-4903
Katie Petty, Human Res Mgr
Mike Whiting, Personnel
Randy Becker, Manager
Jerry Bowles, Manager
EMP: 300

SALES (corp-wide): 264.1K Privately Held
WEB: www.anchorglass.com
SIC: 3221 Glass containers
HQ: Anchor Glass Container Corporation
401 E Jackson St Ste 1100
Tampa FL 33602

(G-5483)
B/C PRECISION TOOL INC
1000b Schenley Pl (47025-1571)
PHONE..................812 577-0642
Glenn Bryant, President
EMP: 2
SALES: 200K Privately Held
SIC: 3544 Special dies & tools

(G-5484)
CAUBLE PRECISION MACHINE INC
1224 Foxwood Ct (47025-8523)
PHONE..................812 537-4884
Michelle Rothzeid, Principal
EMP: 2
SALES (est): 130K Privately Held
SIC: 3599 Machine shop, jobbing & repair

(G-5485)
CM REED LLC (PA)
Also Called: Pur-SE
18463 Running Deer Ln (47025-8246)
PHONE..................517 546-4100
Carolyn Reed, Owner
EMP: 4
SQ FT: 1,800
SALES (est): 452.1K Privately Held
SIC: 5621 3171 2339 Women's clothing stores; women's specialty clothing stores; women's handbags & purses; women's & misses' accessories

(G-5486)
GILES CHEMICAL CORPORATION
Also Called: Giles Manufacturing
200 Brown St (47025-1583)
PHONE..................812 537-4852
Rick Skipton, Principal
EMP: 4
SALES (corp-wide): 60.2MM Privately Held
WEB: www.gilescorp.com
SIC: 2899 2819 Salt; magnesium compounds or salts, inorganic
HQ: Giles Chemical Corporation
102 Commerce St
Waynesville NC 28786
828 452-4784

(G-5487)
GILES MANUFACTURING COMPANY
200 Brown St (47025-1583)
PHONE..................812 537-4852
Fax: 812 537-2382
Richard Wrenn, President
EMP: 3 EST: 1988
SALES (est): 230K Privately Held
SIC: 2834 2819 Pharmaceutical preparations; industrial inorganic chemicals

(G-5488)
HARPER DIRECT LLC
5100 Schenley Pl (47025-2181)
PHONE..................214 245-5026
Eric Hanent, CEO
EMP: 300
SALES (est): 27.7MM Privately Held
SIC: 2621 Catalog paper

(G-5489)
HREZO INDUSTRIAL EQP & ENGRG
Also Called: Hrezo Engineering
1025 Ridge Ave (47025-1324)
PHONE..................812 537-4700
Fax: 812 537-5054
Bob Hrezo, Owner
Robert J Hrezo, Owner
EMP: 12
SQ FT: 6,000

SALES: 950K Privately Held
WEB: www.hrezoengineering.com
SIC: 5084 5074 3585 8711 Pumps & pumping equipment; convectors; heating equipment, complete; heat pumps, electric; consulting engineer

(G-5490)
LYNCH FIREWORKS DISPLAY INC
56 Oakey Ave (47025-1539)
PHONE..................812 537-1750
Kevin J Lynch, President
▲ EMP: 2
SALES (est): 118.1K Privately Held
SIC: 2899 Fireworks

(G-5491)
MGPI PROCESSING INC
7 Ridge Ave (47025-1637)
PHONE..................812 532-4100
EMP: 16
SALES (corp-wide): 318.2MM Publicly Held
SIC: 2085 Distilled & blended liquors
HQ: Mgpi Processing, Inc.
100 Commercial St
Atchison KS 66002
913 367-1480

(G-5492)
OMNI TECHNOLOGIES INC (PA)
779 Rudolph Way (47025-8378)
PHONE..................812 537-4102
Donald Culberson, President
Zane White, Safety Mgr
Dan Culbertson, Production
Craig Linter, Purch Mgr
Ed Risinger, Controller
EMP: 65
SQ FT: 50,000
SALES: 8MM Privately Held
SIC: 3089 Plastic processing; molding primary plastic

(G-5493)
PRI-PAK INC
2000 Schenley Pl (47025-1593)
PHONE..................812 260-2291
John Kaiser, CEO
John W Fisher, Ch of Bd
John A Hillenbrand, Vice Ch Bd
Joe Marunowski, Plant Mgr
Tammy Phillips, Treasurer
◆ EMP: 200
SQ FT: 200,000
SALES (est): 45.3MM Privately Held
WEB: www.pripak.com
SIC: 2085 2086 2084 Cordials, alcoholic; cocktails, alcoholic; soft drinks: packaged in cans, bottles, etc.; wine coolers (beverages)

(G-5494)
QUEEN CITY CANDY LLC
601 Rudolph Way (47025-8377)
PHONE..................812 537-5203
Vince Klee, President
Vincent Klee, Opers Staff
Jennifer Klee Riffle, Administration
EMP: 2
SALES (est): 62.3K Privately Held
SIC: 2064 7336 Chewing candy, not chewing gum; package design

(G-5495)
TRI-STATE HYDRAULICS INDUS SUP
Also Called: Tri State Hydraulic Indus Sup
752 Oberting Rd (47025-9441)
PHONE..................812 537-3485
Steven Harris, President
EMP: 2
SALES: 350K Privately Held
SIC: 3492 3429 3052 Fluid power valves & hose fittings; hose & tube fittings & assemblies, hydraulic/pneumatic; manufactured hardware (general); rubber & plastics hose & beltings

(G-5496)
TY BOWELLS FARRIER SERVICE
Also Called: Bowell Ty & Michelle
170 Us Highway 50 E (47025-8401)
PHONE..................812 537-3990
Ty Bowell, *Owner*
Michelle Bowell, *Managing Prtnr*
EMP: 2 EST: 1988
SALES (est): 107.8K **Privately Held**
SIC: 3462 Horseshoes

Greenfield
Hancock County

(G-5497)
AIM MEDIA INDIANA OPER LLC
Daily Reporter
22 W New Rd (46140-1090)
PHONE..................317 462-5528
Fax: 317 467-6017
Rich Torres, *Editor*
Jeff Rogers, *CFO*
Kathy Braun, *Human Res Mgr*
John Senger, *Branch Mgr*
Carrie Lacy, *CIO*
EMP: 21
SALES (corp-wide): 42.4MM **Privately Held**
WEB: www.hjnews.com
SIC: 2711 2791 2752 Newspapers, publishing & printing; typesetting; commercial printing, lithographic
PA: Aim Media Indiana Operating, Llc
2980 N National Rd A
Columbus IN 47201
812 372-7811

(G-5498)
AIM MEDIA INDIANA OPER LLC
New Palestine Press
22 W New Rd (46140-1090)
PHONE..................317 462-5528
John Senger, *Branch Mgr*
EMP: 2
SALES (corp-wide): 42.4MM **Privately Held**
SIC: 2711 Commercial printing & newspaper publishing combined
PA: Aim Media Indiana Operating, Llc
2980 N National Rd A
Columbus IN 47201
812 372-7811

(G-5499)
AIM MEDIA INDIANA OPER LLC
Aim Media Printing
22 W New Rd (46140-1090)
PHONE..................317 462-5528
Larry Ham, *Branch Mgr*
EMP: 43
SALES (corp-wide): 42.4MM **Privately Held**
SIC: 2711 Commercial printing & newspaper publishing combined
PA: Aim Media Indiana Operating, Llc
2980 N National Rd A
Columbus IN 47201
812 372-7811

(G-5500)
AMERICAS CABINET CO OF IND
7367 E Us Highway 40 (46140-9411)
PHONE..................317 788-9533
Wilford Listenfelt, *Vice Pres*
EMP: 6
SALES (est): 303.7K **Privately Held**
SIC: 2434 Wood kitchen cabinets

(G-5501)
APEX ELECTRIC & SIGN INC
4328 E State Road 234 (46140-9043)
PHONE..................317 326-1325
Gregory L Heuer, *Branch Mgr*
EMP: 2
SALES (corp-wide): 348.5K **Privately Held**
SIC: 3993 Signs & advertising specialties
PA: Apex Electric & Sign Inc
500 N Range Line Rd
Morristown IN 46161
317 326-1325

(G-5502)
API INTERNATIONAL INC
6219 W Stoner Dr (46140-7307)
PHONE..................317 894-1100
Shawn Merrill, *Manager*
EMP: 12
SALES (corp-wide): 24.1MM **Privately Held**
SIC: 3541 Flange facing machines
PA: Api International, Inc.
12505 Sw Herman Rd
Tualatin OR 97062
503 692-3800

(G-5503)
APPLICATION SOFTWARE
117 Wood St (46140-2164)
PHONE..................317 814-8010
William Hodson, *Principal*
EMP: 2
SALES (est): 114.9K **Privately Held**
WEB: www.erebar.com
SIC: 7372 Prepackaged software

(G-5504)
ATKINS NUTRITIONALS INC
3023 N Dist Way Unit 200 (46140)
PHONE..................317 622-4154
Joseph E Scalzo, *CEO*
EMP: 2
SALES (corp-wide): 41.7MM **Publicly Held**
SIC: 2099 Food preparations
HQ: Atkins Nutritionals, Inc.
1225 17th St Ste 1000
Denver CO 80202

(G-5505)
AVERY DENNISON CORPORATION
Also Called: Avery Dennison Fasson
870 Anderson Blvd (46140-7997)
PHONE..................317 462-1988
Steve Borse, *Plant Mgr*
Steve Riley, *Engineer*
George Boyd, *Project Engr*
Jeff Hagg, *Project Engr*
Jeff Russell, *Human Res Mgr*
EMP: 58
SALES (corp-wide): 6.6B **Publicly Held**
WEB: www.avery.com
SIC: 2672 Adhesive backed films, foams & foils
PA: Avery Dennison Corporation
207 N Goode Ave Ste 500
Glendale CA 91203
626 304-2000

(G-5506)
B AND R ENGRAVING INC
5825 W 300 N (46140-8305)
PHONE..................317 894-3599
Fax: 317 894-3599
Rosie Burk, *President*
Rosalind Burk, *Admin Secy*
EMP: 4
SALES: 100K **Privately Held**
SIC: 2759 Engraving

(G-5507)
BASTIAN AUTOMATION ENGRG LLC
Also Called: Bastian Solutions
2155 Fields Blvd (46140-3012)
PHONE..................317 467-2583
Fax: 317 866-0014
William A Bastian II, *CEO*
EMP: 60
SALES (est): 72.6MM
SALES (corp-wide): 256.2MM **Privately Held**
WEB: www.bluearc.biz
SIC: 3579 7699 Forms handling equipment; industrial equipment services
HQ: Bastian Solutions, Llc
10585 N Meridian St Fl 3
Indianapolis IN 46290
317 575-9992

(G-5508)
BATH & BODY WORKS LLC
1519 N State St (46140-1066)
PHONE..................317 468-0834
Phyllis Ficorilli, *Manager*
EMP: 18

SALES (corp-wide): 12.6B **Publicly Held**
WEB: www.bath-and-body.com
SIC: 5999 2844 Perfumes & colognes; toilet preparations
HQ: Bath & Body Works, Llc
7 Limited Pkwy E
Reynoldsburg OH 43068

(G-5509)
BRENDA SUE WARE EATON LLC
840 E Ridge Dr (46140-8713)
PHONE..................317 462-2058
Brenda Sue Ware Eaton, *Owner*
EMP: 2 EST: 2013
SALES (est): 122.7K **Privately Held**
SIC: 3625 Motor controls & accessories

(G-5510)
BWI INDIANA INC
Also Called: Bwi Group
989 Opportunity Pkwy (46140-0010)
PHONE..................937 260-2460
Thomas P Gold, *President*
Karis Troncoso, *Finance*
Zijian Zhao, *Admin Secy*
EMP: 20
SALES (est): 498.7K **Privately Held**
SIC: 3714 Motor vehicle brake systems & parts; motor vehicle steering systems & parts

(G-5511)
CATERPILLAR INC
6719 W 350 N (46140-9617)
PHONE..................630 743-4094
Jim Owens, *CEO*
▲ EMP: 100
SALES: 9.7MM **Privately Held**
SIC: 3531 5082 Construction machinery; construction & mining machinery

(G-5512)
CEMEX MATERIALS LLC
Also Called: Rinker Materials
6662 W 350 N (46140-9617)
PHONE..................317 891-7500
Tom Hartley, *Manager*
EMP: 30 **Privately Held**
SIC: 3273 Ready-mixed concrete
HQ: Cemex Materials, Llc
1501 Belvedere Rd
West Palm Beach FL 33406
561 833-5555

(G-5513)
CEMEX MATERIALS LLC
6662 W 350 N (46140-9617)
PHONE..................317 891-3015
Tom Hartley, *Regional Mgr*
EMP: 45 **Privately Held**
WEB: www.rinkermaterials.com
SIC: 3273 Ready-mixed concrete
HQ: Cemex Materials, Llc
1501 Belvedere Rd
West Palm Beach FL 33406
561 833-5555

(G-5514)
CHAMELEON LIFESTYLES LLC
1678 E Grey Feather Trl (46140-7155)
PHONE..................317 468-3246
Matt Mueller, *Manager*
EMP: 2 EST: 2012
SALES (est): 222.4K **Privately Held**
SIC: 2752 Commercial printing, lithographic

(G-5515)
COMMON SENSE PRODUCING LLC
1041 N Village Greene Dr (46140-8288)
PHONE..................317 622-1682
John Sifferlen, *Principal*
EMP: 3 EST: 2015
SALES (est): 155.9K **Privately Held**
SIC: 1311 Crude petroleum & natural gas

(G-5516)
CORROSION TECHNOLOGIES INC
6268 W Stoner Dr Ste C (46140-7306)
PHONE..................317 894-0627
Kay Squires, *CEO*
Kevin Squires, *President*

Lynn Bryant, *Cust Mgr*
EMP: 3 EST: 1999
SQ FT: 2,500
SALES (est): 606.1K **Privately Held**
WEB: www.corrosiontech.com
SIC: 3084 Plastics pipe

(G-5517)
D & V PRECISION SHEETMETAL
205 S 400 W (46140-8500)
PHONE..................317 462-2601
Fax: 317 462-2680
Dan Mattingly Sr, *CEO*
Dan Mattingly Jr, *President*
Vicki Mattingly, *Corp Secy*
EMP: 20
SQ FT: 14,000
SALES (est): 4.2MM **Privately Held**
WEB: www.dvsheetmetal.com
SIC: 3444 Sheet metal specialties, not stamped

(G-5518)
DAED TOOLWORKS
3255 W Birdsong Ct (46140-9298)
PHONE..................317 861-7419
Raney Nelson, *Principal*
EMP: 2 EST: 2012
SALES (est): 109.2K **Privately Held**
SIC: 2499 Decorative wood & woodwork

(G-5519)
DANIELS VINEYARD LLC
6311 W Stoner Dr (46140-7413)
PHONE..................317 894-6860
Randy Degan, *Administration*
EMP: 4
SALES (est): 295K **Privately Held**
SIC: 2084 Wines, brandy & brandy spirits

(G-5520)
DEAN CO INC
Also Called: Spitzer Enterprises
6153 W 400 N (46140-9641)
PHONE..................317 891-2518
Mike Spitzer, *Owner*
EMP: 4
SALES (est): 335.6K **Privately Held**
SIC: 2895 Carbon black

(G-5521)
DORMA ✛
215 W New Rd (46140-1095)
PHONE..................317 468-6742
EMP: 2 EST: 2017
SALES (est): 73.4K **Privately Held**
SIC: 3429 Manufactured hardware (general)

(G-5522)
EDWARDS STEEL INC
Also Called: Custom Metal Industries
2042 E Main St (46140-8130)
PHONE..................317 462-9451
Skylar T Edwards, *President*
EMP: 6
SQ FT: 22,600
SALES: 1.5MM **Privately Held**
SIC: 3444 Sheet metalwork

(G-5523)
ELANCO US INC (HQ)
2500 Innovation Way N (46140-9163)
PHONE..................877 352-6261
Joseph Burkett, *CEO*
Robert Jones, *President*
Brian Reeve, *Vice Pres*
Chad Montgomery, *Manager*
Dan Mars, *Info Tech Mgr*
▲ EMP: 202
SALES (est): 134.1MM
SALES (corp-wide): 22.8B **Publicly Held**
WEB: www.petwellness.com
SIC: 2834 Pharmaceutical preparations
PA: Eli Lilly And Company
Lilly Corporate Ctr
Indianapolis IN 46285
317 276-2000

(G-5524)
ELI LILLY AND COMPANY
Also Called: Elanco Animal Health
2500 Innovation Way N (46140-9163)
P.O. Box 708 (46140-0708)
PHONE..................317 276-2000
Fax: 317 277-5002

William Blackwelder, *Project Mgr*
Chuck Rutledge, *Project Mgr*
Dan Sweat, *Opers Staff*
Patrick W Thomas, *Opers Staff*
Matt Deacon, *Mfg Staff*
EMP: 14
SALES (corp-wide): 22.8B **Publicly Held**
WEB: www.lilly.com
SIC: 2834 Pharmaceutical preparations
PA: Eli Lilly And Company
Lilly Corporate Ctr
Indianapolis IN 46285
317 276-2000

(G-5525)
EMERSON CLIMATE TECH INC
6579 W 350 N Ste A (46140-7233)
PHONE..................................937 498-3671
Bob Labbett, *VP Corp Comm*
Ibidayo Awosola, *Technology*
Glenn Russell, *Director*
EMP: 9
SALES (corp-wide): 15.2B **Publicly Held**
SIC: 3585 Condensers, refrigeration
HQ: Emerson Climate Technologies, Inc.
1675 Campbell Rd
Sidney OH 45365
937 498-3011

(G-5526)
EMERSON CLIMATE TECH INC
6579 W 350 N Ste A (46140-7233)
PHONE..................................317 968-4250
Fax: 317 894-1830
Glenn Russell, *Manager*
EMP: 112
SALES (corp-wide): 15.2B **Publicly Held**
WEB: www.copeland-corp.com
SIC: 3585 Condensers, refrigeration
HQ: Emerson Climate Technologies, Inc.
1675 Campbell Rd
Sidney OH 45365
937 498-3011

(G-5527)
ENGINEERED MACHINED PDTS INC
Also Called: E M P
125 N Blue Rd (46140-8900)
PHONE..................................317 462-8894
Fax: 317 462-2687
Ted Ochs, *Branch Mgr*
EMP: 100
SQ FT: 60,000
SALES (est): 17.9MM **Privately Held**
WEB: www.emp-corp.com
SIC: 3714 Oil pump, motor vehicle
PA: Engineered Machined Products, Inc.
3111 N 28th St
Escanaba MI 49829

(G-5528)
ENGINEERED MACHINED PDTS INC
Also Called: Emp
317462 8894 (46140)
PHONE..................................317 462-8894
Ted Ochs, *Plant Mgr*
EMP: 150
SQ FT: 60,000 **Privately Held**
WEB: www.emp-corp.com
SIC: 3714 Motor vehicle parts & accessories; internal combustion engines
PA: Engineered Machined Products, Inc.
3111 N 28th St
Escanaba MI 49829

(G-5529)
ENTERKIN MANUFACTURING CO INC
165 W New Rd (46140-1093)
PHONE..................................317 462-4477
Dennis Enterkin, *President*
EMP: 20
SALES (est): 1.7MM **Privately Held**
WEB: www.hangerbolt.com
SIC: 3965 3452 Fasteners; bolts, nuts, rivets & washers

(G-5530)
ENVIGO RMS INC
6825 W 400 N Ste 170 (46140-6606)
PHONE..................................317 806-6080
EMP: 4

SALES (corp-wide): 2MM **Privately Held**
SIC: 0279 2048 2836 3821 Laboratory animal farm; prepared feeds; veterinary biological products; laboratory apparatus & furniture
HQ: Envigo Rms, Inc.
8520 Allison Pointe Blvd # 400
Indianapolis IN 46250
317 806-6080

(G-5531)
EXCEL MACHINE
3103 W Us Highway 40 (46140-8320)
PHONE..................................317 467-0299
Gene Gray Jr, *Owner*
EMP: 4
SQ FT: 3,000
SALES: 450K **Privately Held**
SIC: 3599 Chemical milling job shop

(G-5532)
FRUGAL TIMES
2309 W 100 N (46140-8487)
P.O. Box 925 (46140-0925)
PHONE..................................317 326-4165
M Babcock, *Supervisor*
EMP: 2
SALES (est): 83.2K **Privately Held**
SIC: 2731 Book publishing

(G-5533)
GREENFIELD COFFEE COMPANY
303 E Lincoln St (46140-1624)
PHONE..................................317 498-9568
Nora Apple, *Principal*
EMP: 2 **Privately Held**
SIC: 3571 Personal computers (microcomputers)

(G-5534)
GREENFIELD FEEDERS INC
3599 W Us Highway 40 (46140-9590)
PHONE..................................317 462-6363
Fax: 317 462-5408
Charlie Wilkerson, *President*
EMP: 11
SQ FT: 8,400
SALES (est): 1.8MM **Privately Held**
WEB: www.greenfieldfeeders.com
SIC: 3444 3443 Sheet metalwork; fabricated plate work (boiler shop)

(G-5535)
GREENFIELD SIGNS INC
716 W Main St (46140-2061)
PHONE..................................317 469-3095
EMP: 3
SALES (est): 178.5K **Privately Held**
SIC: 3993 Electric signs

(G-5536)
HARMON COATINGS LLC
4528 N 25 W (46140-8634)
PHONE..................................317 326-4298
David Harmon, *Principal*
EMP: 2 EST: 2010
SALES (est): 161.2K **Privately Held**
SIC: 3479 Metal coating & allied service

(G-5537)
IDENITEE
3626 W Us Highway 40 (46140-8590)
PHONE..................................317 462-4606
EMP: 2 EST: 2007
SALES (est): 81K **Privately Held**
SIC: 2759 Commercial Printing

(G-5538)
INDIANA AUTOMOTIVE FAS INC
1300 Anderson Blvd (46140-7934)
PHONE..................................317 467-0100
Fax: 317 467-0400
Heisaburo Hidaka, *President*
Chris Crafton, *General Mgr*
Mark Vance, *General Mgr*
Pete Murray, *Vice Pres*
Randall Shepherd, *Plant Mgr*
▲ **EMP:** 401
SQ FT: 849,780
SALES: 89.5MM
SALES (corp-wide): 711.6MM **Privately Held**
WEB: www.iafi.com
SIC: 3452 3714 Screws, metal; motor vehicle parts & accessories

PA: Aoyama Seisakusho Co.,Ltd.
1-8, Takahashi, Oguchicho
Niwa-Gun AIC 480-0
587 951-151

(G-5539)
INDIANA BOX COMPANY
2200 Royal Dr (46140-7441)
PHONE..................................317 462-7743
Johnnie Jones, *Manager*
EMP: 33
SALES (corp-wide): 702.7MM **Privately Held**
SIC: 2653 Boxes, corrugated: made from purchased materials
HQ: Indiana Box Company
1200 Riverfork Dr
Huntington IN 46750
260 356-9660

(G-5540)
INDIANA KNITWEAR CORPORATION (PA)
230 E Osage St (46140-2423)
P.O. Box 309 (46140-0309)
PHONE..................................317 462-4413
Fax: 317 462-0994
Gene Bate, *CEO*
Roger Denisar, *Mfg Staff*
Patrick Jeffers, *CFO*
Christi Vanness, *Controller*
Diana Gross, *Human Res Mgr*
◆ **EMP:** 32
SQ FT: 85,000
SALES (est): 12.1MM **Privately Held**
WEB: www.indyknit.com
SIC: 2329 2369 Shirt & slack suits: men's, youths' & boys'; girls' & children's outerwear

(G-5541)
INFRARED TECHNOLOGIES LLC
6531 E 200 N (46140-9450)
PHONE..................................317 326-2019
Art Tompkins,
EMP: 9
SALES (est): 1.1MM **Privately Held**
SIC: 3567 Infrared ovens, industrial

(G-5542)
IRVING MATERIALS INC (PA)
Also Called: I M I
8032 N State Road 9 (46140-9097)
PHONE..................................317 326-3101
Fax: 317 326-7799
Earl G Brinker, *President*
Pete Irving, *Chairman*
Brian Newlin, *Sheriff*
Bill Avey, *Plant Mgr*
Randy Cornelius, *Plant Mgr*
EMP: 60
SQ FT: 36,000
SALES (est): 800.6MM **Privately Held**
WEB: www.irvmat.com
SIC: 3273 3271 5032 2951 Ready-mixed concrete; concrete block & brick; sand, construction; gravel; stone, crushed or broken; asphalt paving blocks (not from refineries)

(G-5543)
J & J ENGINEERING INC
610 W Osage St (46140-2396)
PHONE..................................317 462-2309
Fax: 317 462-7944
Jerry M Bow, *President*
Marisue Bow, *Business Mgr*
Mary Sue Bow, *Treasurer*
EMP: 15
SALES (est): 337K **Privately Held**
SIC: 3559

(G-5544)
JOB SHOP COATING INC
18 E Pierson St (46140-2442)
P.O. Box 923 (46140-0923)
PHONE..................................317 462-9714
Fax: 317 466-9714
Joseph Strodtman, *President*
EMP: 35
SQ FT: 15,500
SALES (est): 3MM **Privately Held**
SIC: 3479 Coating of metals with plastic or resins; hot dip coating of metals or formed products

(G-5545)
JOSTENS INC
5220 N Sugar Hills Dr (46140-8653)
PHONE..................................317 326-2782
Gordy Pope, *Manager*
EMP: 3
SALES (corp-wide): 14.7B **Publicly Held**
WEB: www.jostens.com
SIC: 3911 Rings, finger: precious metal
HQ: Jostens, Inc.
7760 France Ave S Ste 400
Minneapolis MN 55435
952 830-3300

(G-5546)
KBC MACHINE
408 Woodland East Dr (46140-8887)
PHONE..................................317 446-6163
Keith Coleman, *Owner*
EMP: 2
SALES (est): 232.8K **Privately Held**
SIC: 3555 Printing presses

(G-5547)
KEIHIN IPT MFG LLC
400 W New Rd (46140-3001)
PHONE..................................317 462-3015
Koki Onuma, *President*
Gregory S Young, *Vice Pres*
Tony Harvey, *Purch Mgr*
Mamoru Tanaka, *Treasurer*
▲ **EMP:** 2000
SALES (est): 228.8MM
SALES (corp-wide): 3.3B **Privately Held**
WEB: www.kipt-inc.com
SIC: 3714 Fuel systems & parts, motor vehicle
HQ: Keihin North America, Inc.
2701 Enterprise Dr # 100
Anderson IN 46013
765 298-6030

(G-5548)
KH WOODWORKING
739 W North St (46140-2034)
PHONE..................................317 702-5094
Ken Harris, *Principal*
EMP: 2 EST: 2016
SALES (est): 71.9K **Privately Held**
SIC: 2431 Millwork

(G-5549)
LITTLE I PUBLICATIONS LLC
120 Lake View Ct N (46140-1355)
PHONE..................................317 467-9297
Walter Brown, *Owner*
EMP: 2
SALES (est): 62.4K **Privately Held**
SIC: 2741 Miscellaneous publishing

(G-5550)
MEYER MILL OAK WOODCRAFTERS
Also Called: Meyer Mill Weddings
1539 E 300 N (46140-8333)
PHONE..................................317 462-1413
Al Meyer, *Owner*
Judy Meyer, *Partner*
EMP: 5 EST: 1974
SQ FT: 1,800
SALES: 100K **Privately Held**
SIC: 2499 5719 Woodenware, kitchen & household; housewares

(G-5551)
MF PRINTING LLC
133 Mcclellan Rd (46140-1226)
PHONE..................................317 462-6895
Rodney G Fleming, *Principal*
EMP: 2 EST: 2010
SALES (est): 18.6K **Privately Held**
SIC: 2752 Commercial printing, lithographic

(G-5552)
MID-AMERICA SOUND CORPORATION
Also Called: Mid American Sound
6643 W 400 N (46140-9116)
PHONE..................................317 947-9880
Robert Williams, *CEO*
Jason Wells, *Principal*
EMP: 17 EST: 2016
SQ FT: 25,000

SALES (est): 253.3K **Privately Held**
SIC: 7922 3648 Concert management
service; lighting equipment

(G-5553)
MIKES BOAT WORKS LLC
610 Pratt St (46140-1661)
PHONE..............................317 410-4981
Michael P Coffey, *Administration*
EMP: 2
SALES (est): 116.8K **Privately Held**
SIC: 3732 Boat building & repairing

(G-5554)
MITCHELL-FLEMING PRINTING INC
420 W Osage St (46140-2231)
P.O. Box 477 (46140-0477)
PHONE..............................317 462-5467
Fax: 317 462-5088
EMP: 10 EST: 1954
SQ FT: 37,500
SALES: 1.1MM **Privately Held**
SIC: 2732 2789 2752 Book Printing Book-
binding/Related Work Lithographic Com-
mercial Printing

(G-5555)
MITER CRAFT INC
708 Lake Dr (46140-1121)
PHONE..............................317 462-3621
Darrell Carter, *President*
Curtis Crawford, *Exec VP*
EMP: 7 EST: 1998
SALES (est): 600K **Privately Held**
SIC: 2431 Interior & ornamental woodwork
& trim

(G-5556)
MOAN RACING PRODUCTS LLC
Also Called: Www.psychmxgrafix.com
4812 S 50 W (46140-9243)
PHONE..............................317 644-3100
Jay Moan, *Principal*
EMP: 4
SQ FT: 8,500
SALES (est): 438K **Privately Held**
SIC: 2752 Poster & decal printing, litho-
graphic

(G-5557)
MODERNFOLD INC (DH)
215 W New Rd (46140-1095)
PHONE..............................800 869-9685
Fax: 765 521-6234
Lewis N Stryke, *President*
Brian Hurley, *President*
Cathy Dugan, *Buyer*
Michael Lohaus, *Purchasing*
Adam Burke, *Engineer*
▲ EMP: 204
SQ FT: 200,000
SALES (est): 90.5MM
SALES (corp-wide): 2.5B **Privately Held**
SIC: 2542 2522 Partitions for floor attach-
ment, prefabricated: except wood; panel
systems & partitions, office: except wood
HQ: Dormakaba Usa Inc.
100 Dorma Dr
Reamstown PA 17567
717 336-3881

(G-5558)
MONROE CUSTOM UTILITY BODIES
Also Called: MCB Accessories
3312 N 600 W (46140-8006)
PHONE..............................317 894-8684
Fax: 317 894-1896
Dennis R Cowan, *President*
Chad Cowan, *Prdtn Mgr*
Lloyd Terry, *Engineer*
Justin Groover, *Sales Staff*
Larry Patterson, *Chief Mktg Ofcr*
EMP: 60 EST: 1969
SQ FT: 30,000
SALES: 5.3MM **Privately Held**
WEB: www.monroebodies.com
SIC: 3713 3469 Specialty motor vehicle
bodies; utility truck bodies; van bodies;
boxes: tool, lunch, mail, etc.: stamped
metal

(G-5559)
MOORFEED CORPORATION
4162 N Ems Blvd (46140-5502)
PHONE..............................317 545-7171
Fax: 317 542-7317
Domenic Angelicchio, *President*
Brian Bego, *General Mgr*
Dennis O'Donnell, *Vice Pres*
EMP: 40
SQ FT: 56,000
SALES (est): 10MM **Privately Held**
SIC: 3559 Electronic component making
machinery

(G-5560)
MOSELEY LABORATORIES INC
6108 W Stoner Dr (46140-7383)
PHONE..............................317 866-8460
Wesley D Sing, *President*
Ethel P Sing, *Corp Secy*
Wesley Sing, *Vice Pres*
Francine Sing-Borsa, *Vice Pres*
EMP: 23
SQ FT: 10,000
SALES: 200K **Privately Held**
SIC: 8734 2087 Product testing laborato-
ries; flavoring extracts & syrups

(G-5561)
NORTH STREET COMPANIES LLC
216 W North St (46140-2022)
PHONE..............................317 457-4520
Felicia Harcourt, *Principal*
EMP: 3
SALES (est): 202.9K **Privately Held**
SIC: 2087 Beverage bases

(G-5562)
NOVARTIS ANIMAL HEALTH US INC
2500 Innovation Way N (46140-9163)
PHONE..............................317 276-2348
Robert Jones, *President*
EMP: 2
SALES (est): 68.6K **Privately Held**
SIC: 2048 Prepared feeds

(G-5563)
PGG ENTERPRISES LLC
6331 E Us Highway 40 (46140-9724)
PHONE..............................317 462-2871
Paul Glenzer, *Mng Member*
EMP: 3
SALES: 100K **Privately Held**
SIC: 7692 Automotive welding

(G-5564)
PRECOAT METALS CORP (DH)
1950 E Main St (46140-8128)
PHONE..............................317 462-7761
Fax: 317 467-6475
Gerard Dombek, *President*
Gerard M Dombek, *President*
Gerald Clouse, *Plant Mgr*
Victoria Stanley, *Human Resources*
Warren Craft, *Sales Staff*
▲ EMP: 50
SALES (est): 270.5MM
SALES (corp-wide): 3.6B **Publicly Held**
SIC: 3479 Painting of metal products;
painting, coating & hot dipping
HQ: Precoat Metals, Inc.
1310 Papin St Ste 300
Saint Louis MO 63103
314 436-7010

(G-5565)
PRECOAT METALS CORP
1950 E Main St (46140-8128)
PHONE..............................317 462-7761
Gary Hollo, *COO*
Joe Morgan, *Admin Mgr*
EMP: 152
SALES (corp-wide): 3.6B **Publicly Held**
SIC: 3479 3471 Painting of metal prod-
ucts; plating & polishing
HQ: Precoat Metals Corp.
1950 E Main St
Greenfield IN 46140
317 462-7761

(G-5566)
RECON GROUP LLP
6719 W 350 N (46140-9617)
PHONE..............................855 874-8741
Sender Shamiss, *President*
EMP: 2
SALES (corp-wide): 250MM **Privately Held**
SIC: 8742 7372 5731 3651 Marketing
consulting services; prepackaged soft-
ware; radio, television & electronic stores;
household audio & video equipment
PA: The Recon Group Llp
20200 W Dixie Hwy # 1005
Miami FL 33180
855 874-8741

(G-5567)
ROSE-WALL MFG INC
5827 W Us Highway 40 (46140-8881)
PHONE..............................317 894-4497
Fax: 317 894-4493
Theodore Rossell, *President*
Brad Rosell, *Vice Pres*
Chris Rossell, *Admin Sec*
EMP: 6
SQ FT: 7,200
SALES: 1MM **Privately Held**
SIC: 1781 3533 Water well drilling; water
well drilling equipment

(G-5568)
ROYAL BOX GROUP LLC
2200 Royal Dr (46140-7441)
PHONE..............................317 462-7743
Johnny Jones, *COO*
EMP: 4
SALES (corp-wide): 702.7MM **Privately Held**
SIC: 2653 Corrugated & solid fiber boxes
HQ: Royal Box Group, Llc
1301 S 47th Ave
Cicero IL 60804
708 656-2020

(G-5569)
RPH ON CALL LLC
1115 N 300 W (46140-8488)
PHONE..............................317 622-4800
Brian Durham, *Mng Member*
EMP: 25
SALES (est): 1.6MM **Privately Held**
SIC: 2834 Pharmaceutical preparations

(G-5570)
RWH WOODWORKING
240 W Osage St (46140-2227)
PHONE..............................317 714-5179
Ronny W Holliday, *Owner*
EMP: 2
SALES: 80K **Privately Held**
SIC: 2426 Carvings, furniture: wood

(G-5571)
SCHNEDER ELC BLDNGS AMRCAS INC
Also Called: Control Solutions
6191 W 400 N Ste 100 (46140-7449)
PHONE..............................317 894-6374
Dan Cook, *Branch Mgr*
EMP: 7
SALES (corp-wide): 200.4K **Privately Held**
SIC: 1711 3613 Warm air heating & air
conditioning contractor; switchgear &
switchboard apparatus
HQ: Schneider Electric Buildings Americas,
Inc.
1650 W Crosby Rd
Carrollton TX 75006
972 323-1111

(G-5572)
SEALWRAP SYSTEMS LLC
325 E Main St (46140-2307)
PHONE..............................317 462-3310
Curtis D Wilson, *CEO*
Melvin C Brewer, *Mng Member*
EMP: 4 EST: 1997
SQ FT: 5,000
SALES (est): 57.6K **Privately Held**
WEB: www.sealwrap.com
SIC: 2822 Synthetic rubber; silicone rub-
bers

(G-5573)
SIGN-A-RAMA
842 S State St (46140-2536)
PHONE..............................317 477-2400
Cheryl Edon, *Owner*
EMP: 3
SALES (est): 296.6K **Privately Held**
SIC: 3993 Signs & advertising specialties

(G-5574)
SIMS-LOHMAN INC
725 E Main St (46140-2618)
PHONE..............................317 467-0710
EMP: 4
SALES (corp-wide): 115.8MM **Privately Held**
SIC: 5031 2435 Kitchen cabinets; hard-
wood veneer & plywood
PA: Sims-Lohman, Inc.
6325 Este Ave
Cincinnati OH 45232
513 651-3510

(G-5575)
SOFTWARE INFORMATICS GROUP LLC
869 N 300 W (46140-7996)
PHONE..............................317 326-2598
Larry Myers, *Principal*
EMP: 2
SALES (est): 157K **Privately Held**
SIC: 7372 Business oriented computer
software

(G-5576)
SONICU LLC
19 W Main St (46140-2340)
PHONE..............................317 468-2345
Christopher Smith, *Mng Member*
EMP: 3 EST: 2007
SALES (est): 568.7K **Privately Held**
SIC: 3677 Filtration devices, electronic

(G-5577)
SPITZERS RACING ENTERPRISES
6135 W 400 N (46140-9641)
PHONE..............................317 894-9533
Fax: 317 894-9619
Michael D Spitzer, *President*
Karen Spitzer, *Treasurer*
EMP: 12
SQ FT: 30,000
SALES (est): 1.9MM **Privately Held**
WEB: www.gospitzer.com
SIC: 3711 3714 Automobile assembly, in-
cluding specialty automobiles; motor vehi-
cle parts & accessories

(G-5578)
STANLEY FASTENING SYSTEMS LP
Also Called: Stanley-Bostitch
501 W New Rd (46140-3004)
PHONE..............................317 398-0761
Fax: 317 392-5609
John Sendler, *Business Mgr*
Ron Mahan, *Mfg Staff*
Blair Brimmir, *Sales Staff*
EMP: 87
SQ FT: 70,000
SALES (corp-wide): 12.7B **Publicly Held**
SIC: 3496 3546 3452 3325 Staples,
made from purchased wire; power-driven
handtools; bolts, nuts, rivets & washers;
steel foundries
HQ: Stanley Fastening Systems Lp
2 Briggs Dr
East Greenwich RI 02818

(G-5579)
TEAM IMAGE LLC (PA)
121 S Pennsylvania St (46140-2478)
PHONE..............................317 468-0802
Leisa D Morris,
EMP: 50
SALES (est): 6.2MM **Privately Held**
SIC: 2759 Screen printing

(G-5580)
TEAM IMAGE LLC
212 E Main St (46140-2305)
PHONE..............................317 477-7468
EMP: 32

▲ = Import ▼=Export
◆ =Import/Export

SALES (corp-wide): 6.2MM **Privately Held**
SIC: 2759 Screen printing
PA: Team Image, Llc
121 S Pennsylvania St
Greenfield IN 46140
317 468-0802

(G-5581)
TIFFANY MARBLE OF INDIANAPOLIS
6301 W 400 N (46140-9641)
PHONE.....................................317 894-9141
Fax: 317 894-0606
Robert Spragg, *President*
EMP: 7
SQ FT: 10,500
SALES: 700K **Privately Held**
SIC: 3431 Bathroom fixtures, including sinks

(G-5582)
TSUDA USA CORPORATION
2934 Jannetides Blvd (46140-9334)
PHONE.....................................317 468-9177
Tatsuya Kinoshita, *President*
▲ EMP: 12 EST: 2012
SALES (est): 3.5MM **Privately Held**
SIC: 3714 Transmissions, motor vehicle

(G-5583)
VIVOLAC CULTURES CORPORATION
6108 W Stoner Dr (46140-7383)
PHONE.....................................317 866-9528
Wesley D Sing, *President*
David Jaramillo, *CFO*
EMP: 40
SALES (est): 8.2MM **Privately Held**
SIC: 2099 Baking powder & soda, yeast & other leavening agents

(G-5584)
WILDMAN ENTERPRISE
516 Grove St (46140-2220)
PHONE.....................................317 985-0924
Kendall Wildman, *Principal*
EMP: 2
SALES (est): 103.3K **Privately Held**
SIC: 3949 Sporting & athletic goods

(G-5585)
WONDER NAIL LLC
1909 Melody Ln (46140-1199)
PHONE.....................................317 462-8404
Scott Tian, *Principal*
EMP: 2
SALES (est): 149.3K **Privately Held**
SIC: 2844 Manicure preparations

(G-5586)
ZIG-ZAG CRNR QILTS BASKETS LLC
7872 N Troy Rd (46140-9028)
PHONE.....................................317 326-3115
Jennifer L Titus,
EMP: 2
SQ FT: 1,200
SALES (est): 130K **Privately Held**
WEB: www.zigzagcorner.com
SIC: 2395 2211 7299 Quilting, for the trade; basket weave fabrics, cotton; quilting for individuals

---

Greens Fork
Wayne County

(G-5587)
L & S LUMBER ✪
7501 State Road 38 (47345-9708)
PHONE.....................................765 886-1452
Stephen Stoltzfus, *Owner*
Levi Stoltzfus, *Co-Owner*
EMP: 2 EST: 2017
SALES (est): 77.6K **Privately Held**
SIC: 3429 Builders' hardware

Greensburg
Decatur County

(G-5588)
ACRO ENGINEERING INC
1120 W Washington St (47240-9504)
PHONE.....................................812 663-6236
Fax: 812 663-3600
Rollin N Harpring, *President*
Sonny Neisius, *Vice Pres*
Christopher L Harpring, *Admin Sec*
▲ EMP: 20 EST: 2000
SQ FT: 13,000
SALES (est): 3.5MM **Privately Held**
WEB: www.acroeng.com
SIC: 3599 7692 3544 Machine shop, jobbing & repair; welding repair; special dies, tools, jigs & fixtures

(G-5589)
ADVANCED BEARING MATERIALS LLC
1515 W Main St (47240-9585)
PHONE.....................................812 663-3401
Robert Ewing,
EMP: 36
SALES (est): 7MM **Privately Held**
WEB: www.miba-us.com
SIC: 3568 Bearings, bushings & blocks

(G-5590)
BLASDEL ENTERPRISES INC
495 W Mckee St (47240-2067)
PHONE.....................................812 663-3213
Fax: 812 663-4968
William Blasdel, *President*
Elizabeth Blasdel, *Vice Pres*
Beth Blasdel, *Plant Mgr*
Allan McKellar, *Sales Mgr*
EMP: 10 EST: 1982
SQ FT: 30,000
SALES: 1.9MM **Privately Held**
WEB: www.blasdel.net
SIC: 3567 3565 Infrared ovens, industrial; bag opening, filling & closing machines

(G-5591)
BODYCOTE THERMAL PROC INC
1930 N Montgomery Rd (47240-1276)
PHONE.....................................812 662-0500
Martin Swan, *Principal*
EMP: 35
SALES (corp-wide): 911.9MM **Privately Held**
SIC: 3398 Metal heat treating
HQ: Bodycote Thermal Processing, Inc.
12700 Park Central Dr # 700
Dallas TX 75251
214 904-2420

(G-5592)
BROTHERS INDUSTRIES
803 E Washington St (47240-2214)
PHONE.....................................812 560-6224
EMP: 2
SALES (est): 106.4K **Privately Held**
SIC: 3999 Manufacturing industries

(G-5593)
CIRCLE PRINTING LLC
130 W Main St (47240-1601)
PHONE.....................................812 663-7367
Fax: 812 663-7368
Jan Gunter, *Mng Member*
Monica Gunter,
EMP: 2
SQ FT: 2,000
SALES (est): 100K **Privately Held**
WEB: www.circleprinting.net
SIC: 5331 2752 Variety stores; commercial printing, offset

(G-5594)
COMMUNITY HOLDINGS INDIANA INC
Also Called: Greensburg Daily News
135 S Franklin St (47240-2023)
P.O. Box 106 (47240-0106)
PHONE.....................................812 663-3111
Fax: 812 663-2985
Jerry Stader, *Manager*

EMP: 25 **Privately Held**
WEB: www.clintonnc.com
SIC: 2711 2791 2752 Newspapers, publishing & printing; typesetting; commercial printing, lithographic
HQ: Community Holdings Of Indiana, Inc.
3500 Colonnade Pkwy # 600
Birmingham AL 35243

(G-5595)
CREATIVE FINISHING
6417 S County Road 220 Sw (47240-7425)
PHONE.....................................812 591-8111
David Cherry, *Principal*
EMP: 2
SALES (est): 199K **Privately Held**
SIC: 3479 Painting, coating & hot dipping

(G-5596)
CUSTOM CONTROLS & ENGINEERING
346 E North St (47240-1718)
PHONE.....................................812 663-0755
Dan Schutte, *President*
Rick Colee, *Vice Pres*
EMP: 2
SQ FT: 4,000
SALES: 375K **Privately Held**
SIC: 3824 1731 Controls, revolution & timing instruments; computerized controls installation

(G-5597)
CUSTOM SECURE HANDLES LLC
6283 W County Road 600 S (47240-7546)
PHONE.....................................812 764-4948
Terry Garland,
EMP: 8
SALES (est): 740.2K **Privately Held**
SIC: 3449 7389 Bars, concrete reinforcing: fabricated steel;

(G-5598)
DANCE WORLD BAZAAR CORPORATION
Also Called: McLean's Screen Printing
1553 N Commerce East Dr (47240-1291)
PHONE.....................................812 663-7679
Fax: 812 663-4150
Sandy McLean, *President*
EMP: 9
SQ FT: 9,000
SALES: 1MM **Privately Held**
WEB: www.dawobaz.com
SIC: 2396 2759 Screen printing on fabric articles; commercial printing

(G-5599)
DELTA FAUCET COMPANY
1425 W Main St (47240-9730)
PHONE.....................................812 663-4433
EMP: 3 EST: 1984
SALES (est): 160.3K
SALES (corp-wide): 7.6B **Publicly Held**
SIC: 3432 Plumbing fixture fittings & trim
HQ: Masco Corporation Of Indiana
55 E 111th St
Indianapolis IN 46280
317 848-1812

(G-5600)
FOREMOST FLEXIBLE FABRICATING
Also Called: Foremost Flexible Products
824 N Michigan Ave (47240-1484)
PHONE.....................................812 663-4756
Fax: 812 663-4806
Daniel Wenning, *President*
Dam Huffmeyer, *Vice Pres*
Deanna Wenning, *Vice Pres*
EMP: 7
SQ FT: 8,000
SALES: 863K **Privately Held**
WEB: www.foremostflex.com
SIC: 2391 Curtains, window: made from purchased materials

(G-5601)
G E C O M CORP (HQ)
1025 E Barachel Ln (47240-1269)
PHONE.....................................812 663-2270
Fax: 812 663-2230
Makoto Sakamoto, *President*
Toru Shibata, *Principal*

Brian Burke, *Vice Pres*
Hiromasa Iwaya, *Vice Pres*
Gary Hash, *Facilities Mgr*
▲ EMP: 900
SQ FT: 210,000
SALES (est): 284.4MM
SALES (corp-wide): 4.8B **Privately Held**
WEB: www.gecomcorp.com
SIC: 3714 Motor vehicle body components & frame
PA: Mitsui Mining And Smelting Company, Limited
1-11-1, Osaki
Shinagawa-Ku TKY 141-0
354 378-000

(G-5602)
GAME PLAN GRAPHICS LLC
123 N Broadway St (47240-2002)
PHONE.....................................812 663-3238
Fax: 812 222-4263
Angie Willson, *President*
Keith Greiwe, *Vice Pres*
EMP: 3
SQ FT: 3,000
SALES (est): 250K **Privately Held**
SIC: 5661 5941 2396 5999 Footwear, athletic; sporting goods & bicycle shops; screen printing on fabric articles; trophies & plaques

(G-5603)
GREEN SIGN CO INC
Also Called: Greensignco.com
1045 E Freeland Rd (47240-9435)
PHONE.....................................812 663-2550
Fax: 812 663-6563
Shawn C Green, *President*
Rose Perdue, *Vice Pres*
Bud Perdue, *Admin Sec*
EMP: 11
SQ FT: 10,000
SALES (est): 1.6MM **Privately Held**
WEB: www.greensignco.com
SIC: 3993 Electric signs

(G-5604)
GREENSBURG PRINTING CO INC
116 N Franklin St (47240-2046)
PHONE.....................................812 663-8265
Fax: 812 663-0714
Wayne Peetz, *President*
John Wenning, *Treasurer*
EMP: 3 EST: 1971
SQ FT: 3,000
SALES: 150K **Privately Held**
WEB: www.greensburgprinting.com
SIC: 2752 2791 2789 2759 Commercial printing, offset; typesetting; bookbinding & related work; commercial printing; automotive & apparel trimmings

(G-5605)
H & M TOOL & DIE INC
242 W Mckee St (47240-1999)
PHONE.....................................812 663-8252
Norbert Hoeing, *President*
La Donna Hoeing, *Corp Secy*
EMP: 10 EST: 1971
SQ FT: 11,200
SALES: 1MM **Privately Held**
WEB: www.hm-tool.com
SIC: 3544 Special dies & tools

(G-5606)
HARRISON SAND AND GRAVEL CO (PA)
992 S County Road 800 E (47240-8854)
PHONE.....................................812 663-2021
Kenneth T Wanstrath, *President*
John R Wanstrath, *Corp Secy*
EMP: 15 EST: 1954
SQ FT: 2,800
SALES: 1.4MM **Privately Held**
SIC: 1442 Common sand mining; gravel mining

(G-5607)
HERBERT S SAWMILL
Also Called: Herbert Vernon Sawmill
3438 E County Road 700 S (47240-9645)
PHONE.....................................812 663-9347
Fax: 812 663-9347
Vernon Herbert, *Owner*
Dina Herbert, *Co-Owner*

EMP: 10
SQ FT: 12,160
SALES: 1MM **Privately Held**
SIC: 2421 2426 Sawmills & planing mills, general; hardwood dimension & flooring mills

(G-5608)
HERBERTS TRUCK & VAN
1625 N Carver St (47240-9353)
PHONE...............................812 663-6970
Fax: 812 663-6970
Sharon M Herbert, *Owner*
EMP: 4
SALES (est): 128.7K **Privately Held**
SIC: 3713 Van bodies

(G-5609)
HH RELLIM INC
Also Called: Streetscape Products Limited
3494 E Base Rd (47240-7967)
PHONE...............................812 662-9944
Jeff Miller, *President*
EMP: 2
SALES: 750K **Privately Held**
SIC: 3229 Glass furnishings & accessories

(G-5610)
HITACHI POWDERED MTLS USA INC (PA)
1024 E Barachel Ln (47240-1277)
P.O. Box 588 (47240-0588)
PHONE...............................812 663-5058
Fax: 812 663-8118
Jun Sakai, *Ch of Bd*
Greg Owens, *Vice Pres*
Thomas Robertson, *Safety Dir*
John Zola, *Materials Mgr*
Brumback Jim, *Opers Staff*
▲ EMP: 121
SQ FT: 148,000
SALES (est): 26.9MM **Privately Held**
SIC: 3714 Motor vehicle parts & accessories

(G-5611)
HOMETOWN ENERGY
1430 W Main St (47240-9730)
PHONE...............................812 663-3391
Lori Pilz, *Principal*
EMP: 3 EST: 2007
SALES (est): 310.6K **Privately Held**
SIC: 2911 Gases & liquefied petroleum gases

(G-5612)
HONDA MANUFACTURING IND LLC
2755 N Michigan Ave (47240-9341)
PHONE...............................812 222-6000
Bob Nelson, *President*
Kiyoshi Ikeyama, *Vice Pres*
Chuck Alexander, *Production*
Zachary Crisp, *Production*
Renea Oltman, *Production*
◆ EMP: 2300
SALES (est): 228.8MM
SALES (corp-wide): 144.1B **Privately Held**
SIC: 3711 Automobile assembly, including specialty automobiles
HQ: American Honda Motor Co., Inc.
    1919 Torrance Blvd
    Torrance CA 90501
    310 783-2000

(G-5613)
HOTMIX INC
992 S County Road 800 E (47240-8854)
PHONE...............................812 663-2020
Randy Wanstrath, *Manager*
EMP: 2
SALES (corp-wide): 1.5MM **Privately Held**
SIC: 2951 Asphalt & asphaltic paving mixtures (not from refineries)
PA: Hotmix Inc
    110 Forest Ave
    Aurora IN 47001
    812 926-1471

(G-5614)
HOUCK INDUSTRIES INC
814 E Randall St (47240-2311)
P.O. Box 8 (47240-0008)
PHONE...............................812 663-5675

Fax: 812 663-5803
Richard C Fayette, *President*
Vicky Ostendorf, *Vice Pres*
EMP: 42
SALES (est): 6.9MM **Privately Held**
WEB: www.houckind.com
SIC: 3429 2434 Cabinet hardware; wood kitchen cabinets

(G-5615)
INDIANA WIRE PRODUCTS INC
915 N Ireland St (47240-1136)
PHONE...............................812 663-7441
Fax: 812 663-5997
Jerry C Westhafer, *Ch of Bd*
Steven Westhafer, *President*
Julie Kuehl, *Corp Secy*
William Burr, *Vice Pres*
Carlle Burr, *Shareholder*
EMP: 13 EST: 1960
SQ FT: 24,000
SALES (est): 1.3MM **Privately Held**
WEB: www.indianawireproducts.com
SIC: 3496 Fencing, made from purchased wire; mesh, made from purchased wire

(G-5616)
JOHN REMMLER WELL DRILLING
Also Called: Remmler Drilling & Pump Svc
3970 N County Rd 500 N (47240)
PHONE...............................812 663-8178
John Remmler, *Owner*
EMP: 2
SALES (est): 309.8K **Privately Held**
SIC: 1381 1781 Drilling oil & gas wells; water well drilling

(G-5617)
K AND S FARM AND MACHINE SHOP
4620 S County Road 550 E (47240-8638)
PHONE...............................812 663-8567
Fax: 812 663-8698
Kenny Peters, *President*
Rita Peters, *Admin Sec*
EMP: 10
SQ FT: 15,000
SALES (est): 700K **Privately Held**
SIC: 7699 3449 Agricultural equipment repair services; miscellaneous metalwork

(G-5618)
K FAB INC
1940 N Montgomery Rd (47240-1276)
PHONE...............................812 663-6299
Sam Koester, *President*
EMP: 3
SQ FT: 11,000
SALES (est): 240K **Privately Held**
SIC: 7692 Welding repair

(G-5619)
KLENE PIPE STRUCTURES INC
515 N Anderson St (47240-1410)
PHONE...............................812 663-6445
Fax: 812 663-4151
Robin Klene, *President*
EMP: 6
SQ FT: 10,500
SALES (est): 817.9K **Privately Held**
WEB: www.klenepipe.com
SIC: 3498 Fabricated pipe & fittings

(G-5620)
KOVA FERTILIZER INC (PA)
1330 N Anderson St (47240-1011)
PHONE...............................812 663-5081
Fax: 812 663-5370
Bradley Reed, *President*
Paul Barnard, *General Mgr*
Brain Reed, *Vice Pres*
Todd Reed, *Vice Pres*
Roger Dumond, *Safety Mgr*
EMP: 20 EST: 1947
SQ FT: 50,000
SALES (est): 91.6MM **Privately Held**
WEB: www.ekova.com
SIC: 5191 2875 Fertilizers & agricultural chemicals; fertilizers, mixing only

(G-5621)
LOWES PELLETS AND GRAIN INC (PA)
2372 W State Road 46 (47240-9056)
PHONE...............................812 663-7863
Fax: 812 663-7943
Floyd Alan Lowe, *President*
Don Lowe, *Principal*
Regina Lowe, *Vice Pres*
David A Leas, *Controller*
Kristi Lowe, *Admin Sec*
EMP: 26
SQ FT: 10,000
SALES (est): 19.6MM **Privately Held**
WEB: www.lowespellets.com
SIC: 5153 2048 1542 Grains; cereal-, grain-, & seed-based feeds; farm building construction

(G-5622)
MESCO MANUFACTURING LLC
900 E Randall St (47240-2328)
PHONE...............................812 663-3870
Bryan Messer, *Mng Member*
Greg Mason,
Larry Rogers,
EMP: 65 EST: 2011
SQ FT: 77,000
SALES (est): 9.5MM **Privately Held**
SIC: 3599 Custom machinery

(G-5623)
MEYER ENGINEERING INC
1420 W Main St (47240-9730)
PHONE...............................812 663-6535
Fax: 812 663-3619
John S Meyer, *President*
Andy Meyer, *COO*
Pam Meyer, *Treasurer*
EMP: 12
SQ FT: 6,000
SALES (est): 990K **Privately Held**
SIC: 3544 Jigs & fixtures

(G-5624)
MSSH INC
Also Called: Ashley Machine
901 N Carver St (47240-1014)
P.O. Box 2 (47240-0002)
PHONE...............................812 663-2180
Fax: 812 663-5405
E Thomas Barnes, *President*
EMP: 7
SQ FT: 9,000
SALES (est): 133.1K **Privately Held**
WEB: www.mssh.com
SIC: 3523 3556 3444 Poultry brooders, feeders & waterers; food products machinery; sheet metalwork

(G-5625)
MY PNEUMATIC TOOLS AND SERVICE
7032 E Shelby 1100 S (47240)
PHONE...............................317 364-3324
Michael Young, *Owner*
EMP: 2
SALES: 60K **Privately Held**
SIC: 3544 Special dies, tools, jigs & fixtures

(G-5626)
NAPOLEON HARDWOOD LBR CO INC
1522 S Mill Creek Rd (47240-6321)
P.O. Box 40, Napoleon (47034-0040)
PHONE...............................812 852-4090
Fax: 812 852-4091
Lawrence W Dean, *President*
EMP: 48
SQ FT: 10,000
SALES (est): 7.2MM **Privately Held**
SIC: 2448 2421 2431 2426 Pallets, wood; skids, wood; sawmills & planing mills, general; millwork; hardwood dimension & flooring mills; logging

(G-5627)
NEW POINT STONE CO INC (PA)
Also Called: Harris City Stone Company
992 S County Road 800 E (47240-8854)
PHONE...............................812 663-2021
Fax: 812 662-6088
Kenneth T Wanstrath, *President*
James Wanstrath, *Principal*

Russell Wanstrath, *Principal*
William Wanstrath, *Principal*
John R Wanstrath, *Corp Secy*
▲ EMP: 17 EST: 1924
SQ FT: 2,800
SALES: 12.3MM **Privately Held**
SIC: 1422 Crushed & broken limestone

(G-5628)
NEW POINT STONE CO INC
Harris City Stone Co Div
3671 S County Road 220 Sw (47240-8985)
PHONE...............................812 663-2422
Fax: 812 663-9631
Eldred Borgman, *General Mgr*
Randy Wanstrath, *Personnel*
EMP: 12
SALES (corp-wide): 12.3MM **Privately Held**
SIC: 1429 3274 1422 Igneous rock, crushed & broken-quarrying; lime; crushed & broken limestone
PA: New Point Stone Co Inc
    992 S County Road 800 E
    Greensburg IN 47240
    812 663-2021

(G-5629)
PRINTPACK INC
Flexible Packaging Group
930 E Barachel Ln Ste 200 (47240-3254)
PHONE...............................812 663-5091
Fax: 812 663-3820
Sheila Pake, *Financial Exec*
Julie Holloway, *Human Res Mgr*
Christine Shirreffs, *Sales Staff*
Bob Wangsley, *Manager*
EMP: 300
SQ FT: 80,000
SALES (corp-wide): 1.3B **Privately Held**
WEB: www.printpack.com
SIC: 2673 3081 2759 Bags: plastic, laminated & coated; plastic film & sheet; commercial printing
HQ: Printpack, Inc.
    2800 Overlook Pkwy Ne
    Atlanta GA 30339
    404 460-7000

(G-5630)
PROWLER INDUSTRIES LLC
1220 N Liberty Cir E (47240-6682)
PHONE...............................877 477-6953
Amy Ward, *Mng Member*
◆ EMP: 13
SALES (est): 154.9K **Privately Held**
SIC: 3999 Manufacturing industries

(G-5631)
RAVER READY MIX CONCRETE LLC
7935 E State Road 46 (47240-7215)
PHONE...............................812 662-7900
Julie Raver,
Joseph Raver,
EMP: 8
SALES: 2MM **Privately Held**
SIC: 3273 Ready-mixed concrete

(G-5632)
S & J MANUFACTURING LLC
712 S Christy Rd (47240-2386)
PHONE...............................812 662-6640
Steve Fasnacht, *Owner*
EMP: 4
SALES (est): 282.4K **Privately Held**
SIC: 3315 Wire & fabricated wire products

(G-5633)
SCHEIDLER MACHINE INCORPORATED
3551 N Old Us Highway 421 (47240-9371)
PHONE...............................812 662-6555
Jerome Scheidler, *CEO*
EMP: 2
SALES (est): 178.7K **Privately Held**
SIC: 3545 Precision tools, machinists'

(G-5634)
STANDARD FERTILIZER COMPANY
2006 S County Road 60 Sw (47240-8299)
PHONE...............................812 663-8391
Fax: 812 663-8485
Sheldon J Roberts Sr, *President*

Danny Bausback, *Vice Pres*
Kendra Trenkamtp, *Office Mgr*
EMP: 17 **EST:** 1925
SQ FT: 4,000
SALES (est): 3.2MM **Privately Held**
SIC: 2077 Meat meal & tankage, except as animal feed; bone meal, except as animal feed; animal fats, oils & meals

(G-5635)
STEEL TECHNOLOGIES LLC
1811 N Montgomery Rd (47240-2519)
PHONE...............................812 663-9704
Fax: 812 663-9468
Ronda Lee, *Branch Mgr*
EMP: 100 **Privately Held**
SIC: 3316 Bars, steel, cold finished, from purchased hot-rolled
HQ: Steel Technologies Llc
700 N Hurstbourne Pkwy # 400
Louisville KY 40222
502 245-2110

(G-5636)
TAYLOR MADE CANDLES
7864 W County Road 80 N (47240-7910)
PHONE...............................812 663-6634
James Taylor, *Partner*
Eileen Taylor, *Partner*
EMP: 2
SALES: 220K **Privately Held**
SIC: 5999 3999 Candle shops; candles

(G-5637)
TOP NOTCH TOOL & ENGINEERING
930 E Main St (47240-2305)
PHONE...............................812 663-2184
Chris Bruns, *President*
Roger Meyer, *Corp Secy*
Donald Lecher, *Vice Pres*
EMP: 6
SQ FT: 4,500
SALES: 1.5MM **Privately Held**
SIC: 3599 Machine shop, jobbing & repair

(G-5638)
TREE CITY SAW MILL
Also Called: Tree City Sawmill
2663 E County Road 500 S (47240-7877)
PHONE...............................812 663-6363
Fax: 812 662-6132
Paul Stuehrenberg, *Owner*
EMP: 8
SQ FT: 3,200
SALES (est): 815.6K **Privately Held**
SIC: 2421 Sawmills & planing mills, general

(G-5639)
TREE CITY TOOL & ENGRG CO INC
1954 N Montgomery Rd (47240-1276)
P.O. Box 409 (47240-0409)
PHONE...............................812 663-4196
Fax: 812 663-4220
Steve Simmonds, *President*
Robert Simmonds, *Vice Pres*
Thor Henrikson, *Buyer*
Butch Simmonds, *Sls & Mktg Exec*
Gerald Lawrence, *Sales Mgr*
▼ **EMP:** 69
SALES (est): 17.1MM **Privately Held**
WEB: www.treecitytool.com
SIC: 3599 3544 Custom machinery; special dies, tools, jigs & fixtures

(G-5640)
VALEO NORTH AMERICA INC
Also Called: Valeo Engine Cooling
1100 E Barachel Ln (47240-1200)
PHONE...............................812 663-8541
EMP: 600 **Privately Held**
SIC: 3714 Motor vehicle parts & accessories
HQ: Valeo North America, Inc.
150 Stephenson Hwy
Troy MI 48083

(G-5641)
VALEO NORTH AMERICA INC
Also Called: Valeo Engine Cooling
1100 E Barachel Ln (47240-1200)
PHONE...............................812 663-8541
Peter Henry, *General Mgr*
Pierrick Veirier, *Project Mgr*

Dave Garvey, *Mfg Spvr*
Deborah Broughton, *Opers Staff*
Barbara Sembach, *Production*
EMP: 493 **Privately Held**
WEB: www.valeoinc.com
SIC: 3714 Motor vehicle parts & accessories; radiators & radiator shells & cores, motor vehicle; clutches, motor vehicle; transmissions, motor vehicle
HQ: Valeo North America, Inc.
150 Stephenson Hwy
Troy MI 48083

(G-5642)
WITTROCK ENTERPRISES LLC
Also Called: Wittrock Healthcare
8829 E State Road 46 (47240-7449)
PHONE...............................812 222-0373
Patrick Matthews,
EMP: 26 **EST:** 2016
SALES (est): 5MM **Privately Held**
SIC: 2599 Hospital furniture, except beds

Greentown
Howard County

(G-5643)
ACCENT WIRE PRODUCTS
324 Shamrock Ave (46936-9302)
PHONE...............................765 628-3587
EMP: 2
SALES (est): 138.4K **Privately Held**
SIC: 3496 Miscellaneous fabricated wire products

(G-5644)
BLONDIES COOKIES INC (PA)
303 N Meridian St (46936-1225)
PHONE...............................765 628-3978
Brenda Coffman, *President*
Mark A Coffman, *Corp Secy*
Beverly Austin, *Vice Pres*
EMP: 12
SALES (est): 10.6MM **Privately Held**
SIC: 2052 5461 Cookies; cookies

(G-5645)
FLODDERS SAWMILL
10861 E 100 N (46936)
PHONE...............................765 628-0280
Ross Flodder, *President*
EMP: 9
SALES (est): 892.5K **Privately Held**
SIC: 2421 Sawmills & planing mills, general

Greenville
Floyd County

(G-5646)
502 MOLD POLISHING LLC
1007 Wagon Trl (47124-8614)
PHONE...............................502 436-0239
Richard Cochran, *Principal*
EMP: 3
SALES (est): 168.1K **Privately Held**
SIC: 3471 Polishing, metals or formed products

(G-5647)
CAPRIOLE INC
10329 New Cut Rd (47124-9202)
PHONE...............................812 923-9408
Fax: 812 923-9408
Judith Schad, *President*
Paula Lambert, *Treasurer*
EMP: 5
SALES (est): 482.5K **Privately Held**
WEB: www.capriolegoatcheese.com
SIC: 2022 Natural cheese

(G-5648)
EARTH FIRST KENTUCKIANA INC (PA)
9251 Highway 150 (47124-9636)
P.O. Box 123, Sellersburg (47172-0123)
PHONE...............................812 923-1227
Fax: 812 923-0113
Damian Cristiani, *President*
Danny Cristiani, *Admin Sec*

EMP: 5
SQ FT: 6,400
SALES: 190K **Privately Held**
SIC: 5251 5261 2499 Tools; lawn & garden supplies; mulch or sawdust products, wood

(G-5649)
EMBROIDERY SOLUTIONS U S
8301 Pekin Rd Ste 1 (47124-9403)
PHONE...............................812 923-9152
John Schillingberger, *Owner*
Anita Schillingberber, *Manager*
EMP: 2
SALES (est): 91K **Privately Held**
SIC: 2395 Embroidery & art needlework

(G-5650)
LYNX MOTION TECHNOLOGY CORP
9540 Highway 150 (47124-9683)
P.O. Box 250 (47124-0250)
PHONE...............................812 923-7474
Jerald Chalfin, *CEO*
Roy L Kessinger Jr, *Ch of Bd*
Robert J Westerkamp, *President*
EMP: 2
SQ FT: 4,000
SALES (est): 243.5K **Privately Held**
WEB: www.lynxmotiontechnology.com
SIC: 6794 3621 Patent buying, licensing, leasing; motors, electric

(G-5651)
NALLEYS WOODWORKING
4747 Saint Johns Rd (47124-9334)
PHONE...............................812 923-1299
William Nalley, *Principal*
EMP: 2
SALES (est): 198.2K **Privately Held**
SIC: 2431 Millwork

(G-5652)
RICHARDS PRINTERY
9357 Arthur Coffman Rd (47124-9436)
PHONE...............................812 406-0295
Rich Mullins, *Owner*
EMP: 2
SALES (est): 123K **Privately Held**
SIC: 2752 Commercial printing, offset

(G-5653)
ROL PUBLICATIONS
3600 Amy Ln Ne (47124-7802)
PHONE...............................812 366-4154
Larry Rol, *Principal*
EMP: 2
SALES (est): 151.7K **Privately Held**
SIC: 2741 Miscellaneous publishing

(G-5654)
SLIP HARRIS COMPANY LLC
5971 Buttontown Rd (47124-9542)
PHONE...............................812 923-5674
Chris Tisheuar, *Owner*
Theresa Tisheuar,
EMP: 2
SALES (est): 164.4K **Privately Held**
SIC: 2097 Manufactured ice

(G-5655)
TECHSHOT INC
7200 Highway 150 (47124-9515)
PHONE...............................812 923-9591
Mark S Deuser, *President*
Mark Deuser, *General Mgr*
Ken Barton, *Manager*
Bobby Holland, *Manager*
EMP: 28
SQ FT: 20,000
SALES (est): 6.5MM **Privately Held**
WEB: www.shot.com
SIC: 3679 Electronic circuits

(G-5656)
YELLOW DOG WOODWORKING LLC
4747 Saint Johns Rd (47124-9334)
PHONE...............................502 817-9395
William Nalley, *Principal*
EMP: 4
SALES (est): 371.1K **Privately Held**
SIC: 2431 Millwork

Greenwood
Johnson County

(G-5657)
3D PRINTING & PROTOTYPING LLC ✪
823 Cypress S (46143-3030)
PHONE...............................317 319-8515
Jeff Reynolds, *Principal*
EMP: 2 **EST:** 2017
SALES (est): 97.7K **Privately Held**
SIC: 2752 Commercial printing, lithographic

(G-5658)
ABELL TOOL CO INC
446 Park 800 Dr (46143-9525)
P.O. Box 1014 (46142-0968)
PHONE...............................317 887-0021
Fax: 317 882-6422
Jeffery Abell, *President*
A Donna Abell, *Vice Pres*
EMP: 8
SQ FT: 7,500
SALES: 800K **Privately Held**
SIC: 3549 Metalworking machinery

(G-5659)
ADVANTAGE ELECTRONICS INC
525 E Stop 18 Rd (46143-9808)
P.O. Box 407 (46142-0407)
PHONE...............................317 888-1946
Fax: 317 889-9703
Steven E Wash, *President*
Jon Andrews, *Electrical Engi*
Terry Fellers, *Sales Executive*
Jeff Manifold, *Mktg Dir*
Karl Williams, *Programmer Anys*
EMP: 15
SQ FT: 5,000
SALES (est): 3.2MM **Privately Held**
SIC: 3625 3825 Control equipment, electric; test equipment for electronic & electric measurement

(G-5660)
ADVANTAGE ENGINEERING INC (PA)
525 E Stop 18 Rd (46143-9808)
P.O. Box 407 (46142-0407)
PHONE...............................317 887-0729
Fax: 317 881-1277
Jon Gunderson, *President*
Susan Schaub, *Exec VP*
Randy Goode, *Vice Pres*
Ron Wolfe, *Vice Pres*
Doug Short, *Purch Mgr*
EMP: 100
SQ FT: 60,000
SALES (est): 24.7MM **Privately Held**
WEB: www.advantagerep.com
SIC: 3822 3585 3443 Temperature controls, automatic; refrigeration equipment, complete; cooling towers, metal plate

(G-5661)
ADVANTIS MEDICAL INC
2121 Southtech Dr Ste 600 (46143-6395)
PHONE...............................317 859-2300
Forrest Whittaker, *President*
Michael Bettini, *Vice Pres*
Sue Fawbush, *Vice Pres*
Brian McRoberts, *Vice Pres*
Kevin Wagner, *Opers Spvr*
▼ **EMP:** 129
SQ FT: 400,000
SALES (est): 32.8MM **Privately Held**
WEB: www.advantismedical.com
SIC: 3841 Surgical & medical instruments
PA: Avalign Technologies, Inc.
2275 Half Day Rd Ste 126
Bannockburn IL 60015

(G-5662)
AFFORDABLE FURNITURE
816 Us Highway 31 N (46142-4401)
PHONE...............................317 881-7726
Angela Ritter, *Manager*
EMP: 2 **EST:** 2011
SALES (est): 120.7K **Privately Held**
SIC: 5712 5021 2599 Mattresses; furniture; furniture & fixtures

(G-5663)
AIR FEET LLC
191 Us Highway 31 S Ste C (46143-3575)
PHONE..............................317 441-1817
Wayne Purcell,
EMP: 7 EST: 2011
SQ FT: 5,000
SALES (est): 633.7K **Privately Held**
SIC: 3131 Inner parts for shoes

(G-5664)
AIRGAS INC
415 Park 800 Dr Ste A (46143-7894)
PHONE..............................812 376-9155
Wayne Lovelace, *Manager*
EMP: 5
SALES (corp-wide): 164.2MM **Privately
Held**
WEB: www.airproducts.com
SIC: 2813 Industrial gases
HQ: Airgas, Inc.
    259 N Radnor Chester Rd # 100
    Radnor PA 19087
    610 687-5253

(G-5665)
AMERICAN INDUSTRIAL CORP
1400 American Way (46143-8466)
P.O. Box 859 (46142-0859)
PHONE..............................317 859-9900
Fax: 765 859-9901
David M Jacks, *President*
Mark Kerner, *President*
Paul D Jacks, *Vice Pres*
Melanie J Gorrell, *Admin Sec*
EMP: 50 EST: 1969
SQ FT: 64,000
SALES (est): 20.6MM **Privately Held**
WEB: www.teamaic.com
SIC: 3531 Finishers & spreaders (construction equipment)

(G-5666)
**AMERICAN REUSABLE ENERGY
LLC**
801 N Madison Ave (46142-4128)
PHONE..............................317 965-2604
Joseph Aker,
EMP: 3
SQ FT: 8,000
SALES (est): 147.2K **Privately Held**
SIC: 2077 Animal fats, oils & meals

(G-5667)
APPLE AMERICAN GROUP
1251 Us Highway 31 N (46142-4503)
PHONE..............................317 889-1167
EMP: 2
SALES (est): 118.2K **Privately Held**
SIC: 3571 Personal computers (microcomputers)

(G-5668)
AVON SPORTS APPAREL CORP
3115 Meridian Parke Dr D (46142-9414)
PHONE..............................317 887-2673
Phil Orlando, *Branch Mgr*
EMP: 2
SALES (corp-wide): 3.6MM **Privately
Held**
WEB: www.avonsportsapparel.com
SIC: 2395 5941 Embroidery products, except schiffli machine; soccer supplies
PA: Avon Sports Apparel Corp.
    7710 E Us Highway 36
    Avon IN 46123
    317 272-3831

(G-5669)
BEAUTI PLEAT DRAPERIES INC
201 Moccosin Ct (46142-7305)
PHONE..............................317 887-1728
Fax: 317 887-1728
Janet Swigert, *President*
Shirley Roller, *Vice Pres*
EMP: 2 EST: 1960
SALES: 120K **Privately Held**
SIC: 5714 2591 Draperies; drapery hardware & blinds & shades; curtain & drapery rods, poles & fixtures

(G-5670)
**BILL BALDWINS
SCREENPRINTING**
129 Totten Dr (46143-1122)
PHONE..............................317 881-2712
Bill Baldwin, *Principal*
EMP: 2
SALES (est): 120.6K **Privately Held**
SIC: 2759 Screen printing

(G-5671)
**BROADWAVE TECHNOLOGIES
INC**
500 Polk St Ste 25 (46143-1638)
PHONE..............................317 888-8316
Joetta J Truelock, *President*
Joetta Trulock, *President*
Mike Arbesem, *Vice Pres*
EMP: 15
SALES (est): 2.4MM **Privately Held**
WEB: www.broadwavetech.com
SIC: 3699 Electrical equipment & supplies

(G-5672)
BSB TRANS INC
711 Legacy Blvd (46143-6437)
PHONE..............................317 919-8778
Baljit Singh Boparai, *President*
EMP: 2
SALES (est): 259.1K **Privately Held**
SIC: 3715 Truck trailers

(G-5673)
C R GRAPHICS
485 E Pearl St (46143-1348)
PHONE..............................317 881-6192
Fax: 317 889-9608
Russel Poamey, *Owner*
EMP: 2
SALES (est): 108.8K **Privately Held**
SIC: 2759 Screen printing

(G-5674)
**CELLOFOAM NORTH AMERICA
INC**
2615 Endress Pl (46143-8684)
P.O. Box 406, Conyers GA (30012-0406)
PHONE..............................317 535-0826
Fax: 317 535-9837
Mel Owens, *General Mgr*
EMP: 15
SALES (corp-wide): 119.7MM **Privately
Held**
WEB: www.cellofoam.com
SIC: 2821 Plastics materials & resins
PA: Cellofoam North America Inc.
    1917 Rockdale Indstrl Blv
    Conyers GA 30012
    770 929-3688

(G-5675)
CHRISTYS DESIGN & SIGN CO
500 Polk St Ste 17 (46143-1629)
P.O. Box 703 (46142-0703)
PHONE..............................317 882-5444
Fax: 317 882-9442
Christine Holt, *President*
William Hanley, *President*
EMP: 2
SQ FT: 5,000
SALES: 250K **Privately Held**
SIC: 3993 7389 Signs, not made in custom sign painting shops; sign painting & lettering shop

(G-5676)
CORNER CABINET
405 E Main St (46143-1363)
PHONE..............................317 859-6336
Ross Agresta, *Owner*
EMP: 4
SALES (est): 473.9K **Privately Held**
SIC: 2434 Wood kitchen cabinets

(G-5677)
CRASH BEDS LLC
545 Christy Dr Ste 2101 (46143-1086)
PHONE..............................317 601-4436
Brandon Landes, *Principal*
EMP: 2
SQ FT: 2,700
SALES: 60K **Privately Held**
SIC: 5021 5712 2392 Mattresses; mattresses; mattress pads

(G-5678)
CRYSTAL CLEAR INC
2257 Willow Lake Dr (46143-9325)
P.O. Box 661 (46142-0661)
PHONE..............................317 753-5393
Brad Colwell, *President*
Jamie Hays, *Vice Pres*
EMP: 9
SALES: 250K **Privately Held**
SIC: 7349 3452 Window cleaning; washers

(G-5679)
CRYSTAL MACHINING INC
1144 Tampico Rd (46143-1931)
PHONE..............................317 727-8984
Tom Smith, *Principal*
EMP: 2 EST: 2007
SALES (est): 197.1K **Privately Held**
SIC: 3599 Machine shop, jobbing & repair

(G-5680)
CTP CORPORATION
2615 Endress Pl (46143-8684)
PHONE..............................317 787-5747
Clyde Griffith, *Branch Mgr*
EMP: 60
SALES (est): 5.5MM **Privately Held**
SIC: 2836 Tuberculins

(G-5681)
**DISTANCE LEARNING SYSTEMS
IND**
107 N State Road 135 # 302 (46142-1351)
PHONE..............................888 955-3276
Fax: 317 884-0202
David Christy, *President*
Derrick Christy, *CFO*
Sarah Benson, *Exec Dir*
EMP: 40
SQ FT: 10,000
SALES (est): 4.6MM **Privately Held**
WEB: www.dlsii.com
SIC: 2731 7389 Book publishing; personal service agents, brokers & bureaus

(G-5682)
DOOR SERVICE SUPPLY
4075 Primrose Path (46142-8391)
PHONE..............................317 496-0391
Pat Fischer, *Owner*
EMP: 2
SALES (est): 199.4K **Privately Held**
SIC: 3442 Window & door frames

(G-5683)
**DUNHAM RUBBER & BELTING
CORP (PA)**
682 Commerce Parkway W Dr
(46143-7532)
P.O. Box 47249, Indianapolis (46247-0249)
PHONE..............................317 888-3002
Fax: 317 888-2335
Gary Buchanan, *President*
James Wainwright, *Vice Pres*
▲ **EMP:** 42
SQ FT: 36,000
SALES (est): 27MM **Privately Held**
SIC: 5085 5162 5251 3052 Rubber goods, mechanical; plastics materials & basic shapes; hardware; rubber & plastics hose & beltings

(G-5684)
EARTHWISE WOODWORKS LLC
1119 Falkirk Ct (46143-3154)
PHONE..............................317 887-0142
William J Gromer, *Principal*
EMP: 2 EST: 2016
SALES (est): 65.4K **Privately Held**
SIC: 2431 Millwork

(G-5685)
ELITE PROTECTIVE COATINGS
3632 Woodland Streams Dr (46143-9462)
PHONE..............................317 476-1712
Mark Whitaker, *Principal*
EMP: 2
SALES (est): 81.5K **Privately Held**
SIC: 3479 Metal coating & allied service

(G-5686)
ENDRESS + HAUSER INC (DH)
2350 Endress Pl (46143-9672)
PHONE..............................317 535-7138

(G-5687) (continued from above)
Fax: 317 535-9357
Klaus Endress, *President*
Jurgen Schrempp, *Division Mgr*
Peter Blaser-Hans, *General Mgr*
Peter Hans, *General Mgr*
Codd Lucey, *General Mgr*
▲ **EMP:** 200
SQ FT: 250,000
SALES: 62MM
SALES (corp-wide): 2.6B **Privately Held**
WEB: www.us.endress.com
SIC: 3823 Industrial instrmnts msrmnt display/control process variable
HQ: Endress+Hauser (International) Holding Ag
    Kagenstrasse 2
    Reinach BL 4153
    617 157-575

(G-5687)
ENDRESS + HAUSER INC
2413 Endress Pl (46143-8683)
PHONE..............................317 535-7138
EMP: 108
SALES (corp-wide): 2.6B **Privately Held**
SIC: 3823 Industrial instrmnts msrmnt display/control process variable
HQ: Endress + Hauser Inc
    2350 Endress Pl
    Greenwood IN 46143
    317 535-7138

(G-5688)
**ENDRESS + HUSER FLOWTEC
AG INC**
Also Called: Endresshauser
2330 Endress Pl (46143-9772)
PHONE..............................317 535-7138
Gerhard Jost, *CEO*
Hans-Peter Blaser, *General Mgr*
Luc Reibel, *Project Mgr*
Massimo Allegritti, *Buyer*
Mathieu Weibel, *Research*
▲ **EMP:** 120
SALES (est): 205.9MM
SALES (corp-wide): 2.6B **Privately Held**
SIC: 3823 Flow instruments, industrial process type
HQ: Endress+Hauser (International) Holding Ag
    Kagenstrasse 2
    Reinach BL 4153
    617 157-575

(G-5689)
**ENDRESS+HAUSER (USA)
AUTOMATIO**
2340 Endress Pl (46143-9772)
PHONE..............................317 535-2121
John Schnake, *General Mgr*
Jon McCullum, *Controller*
EMP: 95
SALES (est): 8.6MM
SALES (corp-wide): 2.6B **Privately Held**
SIC: 3823 Industrial instrmnts msrmnt display/control process variable
HQ: Endress + Hauser Inc
    2350 Endress Pl
    Greenwood IN 46143
    317 535-7138

(G-5690)
**ENDRESS+HAUSER WETZER
USA INC**
2413 Endress Pl (46143-8683)
PHONE..............................317 535-1362
Patrick Ncglothen, *General Mgr*
Jayson Norris, *Controller*
◆ **EMP:** 24
SQ FT: 2,000
SALES (est): 5MM
SALES (corp-wide): 2.6B **Privately Held**
SIC: 3823 Industrial instrmnts msrmnt display/control process variable
HQ: Endress + Hauser Inc
    2350 Endress Pl
    Greenwood IN 46143
    317 535-7138

(G-5691)
ENTREE VOUS GREENWOOD
1642 Olive Br Parke Ln (46143-9821)
PHONE..............................317 881-0800
EMP: 2
SALES (est): 57K **Privately Held**
SIC: 2099 Food preparations

▲ = Import ▼=Export
◆ =Import/Export

(G-5692)
EQUIPPE ADVANCED MOBILITY
Also Called: Equippe Mobility Resources
3209 W Smi Val Rd Ste 146 (46142)
PHONE....................................317 807-6789
David Dokmanovich, *Principal*
EMP: 2
SQ FT: 220
SALES: 250K **Privately Held**
SIC: 3842 Wheelchairs

(G-5693)
EXCLUSIVELY ORTHODONTICS LAB
Also Called: Pam Franz
4475 Country Ln (46142-9050)
PHONE....................................317 887-1076
Pam Franz, *President*
Larry Franz, *Admin Sec*
EMP: 2
SALES (est): 140K **Privately Held**
SIC: 3843 Orthodontic appliances

(G-5694)
EXECUTIVE IMAGE BLDG SVCS INC
500 Polk St Ste 11 (46143-1629)
PHONE....................................317 865-1366
Blake Clements, *CEO*
Ray Jackson, *Director*
EMP: 12
SQ FT: 3,000
SALES: 3.5MM **Privately Held**
SIC: 3822 Building services monitoring controls, automatic

(G-5695)
FIRE STAR INDUSTRIES LLC
4644 Brentridge Pkwy (46143-9360)
PHONE....................................317 432-3212
Jason Stits, *CEO*
EMP: 3
SALES (est): 241.7K **Privately Held**
SIC: 3999 Manufacturing industries

(G-5696)
FRANKLIN PUBLISHING INC
Also Called: Road Runner Expediting
5373 Ashby Ct (46143-6268)
PHONE....................................800 634-1993
Michael Jones, *President*
▲ EMP: 5
SALES: 900K **Privately Held**
WEB: www.fastfoodfacts.com
SIC: 2732 Pamphlets: printing & binding, not published on site

(G-5697)
GLANDER
1678 Ashwood Dr (46143-8823)
PHONE....................................317 889-1039
Karl Glander, *Principal*
EMP: 3
SALES (est): 240K **Privately Held**
SIC: 3579 Shorthand machines

(G-5698)
GRAFTON PEEK INCORPORATED
Also Called: Hartwell's Premium Products
280 W Main St (46142-3128)
PHONE....................................317 557-8377
Jason West, *CEO*
Charles Bryant, *Executive*
EMP: 24
SALES (est): 799.4K **Privately Held**
SIC: 5812 7299 2035 Caterers; banquet hall facilities; dressings; salad: raw & cooked (except dry mixes)

(G-5699)
GREENWOOD DRAPERIE CORP
Also Called: Greenwood Draperies
965 Apple Valley Rd (46142-5018)
PHONE....................................317 882-0130
Fax: 317 881-5635
Nancy Buxton, *President*
Don Buxton, *Treasurer*
John T Kutney, *Admin Sec*
EMP: 3
SQ FT: 3,200
SALES: 200K **Privately Held**
SIC: 2391 2591 5714 Curtains & draperies; drapery hardware & blinds & shades; draperies

(G-5700)
GREENWOOD MODELS INC
350 Commerce Parkway W Dr (46142-7046)
PHONE....................................317 859-2988
Fax: 317 535-7758
Val J Weakley, *President*
John Weakley, *Corp Secy*
EMP: 7
SQ FT: 14,000
SALES (est): 700K **Privately Held**
SIC: 3444 3599 7692 2396 Sheet metal-work; machine shop, jobbing & repair; welding repair; automotive & apparel trimmings

(G-5701)
HARTS HANDMADE NATURALS LLC
1354 Westridge Ct (46142-2119)
PHONE....................................317 407-9988
Katherine Hart,
EMP: 2
SALES (est): 191.2K **Privately Held**
SIC: 2841 Textile soap

(G-5702)
HAWAIIAN SMOOTHIE LLC
1251 Us Highway 31 N (46142-4503)
PHONE....................................317 881-7290
Hyon Kim, *Administration*
EMP: 4
SALES (est): 159.8K **Privately Held**
SIC: 2037 Frozen fruits & vegetables

(G-5703)
HORIZON BIOTECHNOLOGIES LLC
1740 S Morgantown Rd (46143-8348)
PHONE....................................317 534-2540
Jonathan P Northrup,
EMP: 2
SALES (est): 119.5K **Privately Held**
SIC: 2834 Pharmaceutical preparations

(G-5704)
HUBBARD SERVICES INC
Also Called: Fastsigns
1280 Us Highway 31 N T (46142-4525)
PHONE....................................317 881-2828
Fax: 317 881-1122
John Hubbard, *President*
Marilyn Hubbard, *Corp Secy*
EMP: 7
SQ FT: 850
SALES (est): 815.8K **Privately Held**
SIC: 3993 Signs & advertising specialties

(G-5705)
IKE NEWTON LLC
949 Fry Rd (46142-1822)
PHONE....................................317 902-1772
Isaac Daniel,
EMP: 2
SALES: 60K **Privately Held**
SIC: 8742 7372 7389 Marketing consulting services; application computer software;

(G-5706)
INDUSTRIAL WATER MGT INC
140 S Park Blvd (46143-8837)
P.O. Box 511 (46142-0511)
PHONE....................................317 889-0836
William Yost, *President*
EMP: 3
SQ FT: 4,000
SALES (est): 490K **Privately Held**
SIC: 5084 2819 Chemical process equipment; industrial inorganic chemicals

(G-5707)
INDY MOBILE APPS LLC
264 Legacy Blvd (46143-6774)
PHONE....................................508 685-5240
Chandramouli Kesavan,
EMP: 2
SALES (est): 65.5K **Privately Held**
SIC: 7372 Application computer software

(G-5708)
IRVING MATERIALS INC
Also Called: IMI Irving Material
6695 W Fifth Valley Rd (46142)
PHONE....................................317 888-0157
Fax: 317 888-8066
Brian Duncan, *Manager*
EMP: 7
SALES (corp-wide): 800.6MM **Privately Held**
SIC: 3273 Ready-mixed concrete
PA: Irving Materials, Inc.
8032 N State Road 9
Greenfield IN 46140
317 326-3101

(G-5709)
JIFFY LUBE
320 S Emerson Ave (46143-1900)
PHONE....................................317 882-5823
Steve Stanner, *Owner*
EMP: 11
SALES (est): 308.8K **Privately Held**
SIC: 7549 3443 Lubrication service, automotive; fuel tanks (oil, gas, etc.): metal plate

(G-5710)
JOSEPH LEE
Also Called: J & L Cabinet Design Group
438 S Emerson Ave 211 (46143-1948)
PHONE....................................317 931-9446
Joseph Less, *Owner*
EMP: 2 EST: 2016
SALES (est): 90.4K **Privately Held**
SIC: 2599 Cabinets, factory

(G-5711)
K&P INDUSTRIES LLC
1200 Tanglewood Dr (46142-5225)
PHONE....................................317 881-9245
Kenneth Fair, *Principal*
EMP: 2
SALES (est): 117.8K **Privately Held**
SIC: 3999 Manufacturing industries

(G-5712)
KAWNEER COMPANY INC
1040 Sierra Dr Ste 1500 (46143-7022)
PHONE....................................317 882-2314
Jeff Hance, *Manager*
EMP: 20
SALES (corp-wide): 12.9B **Publicly Held**
SIC: 3446 Architectural metalwork
HQ: Kawneer Company, Inc.
555 Guthridge Ct
Norcross GA 30092
770 449-5555

(G-5713)
KENNEY ORTHPDICS INDNPOLIS LLC (HQ)
33 E County Line Rd Ste E (46143-1078)
PHONE....................................317 300-0814
John M Kenney, *Mng Member*
Patrick Conley,
William Lester,
Thomas McIntosh,
Timothy C Ruth,
EMP: 6
SALES: 1.2MM
SALES (corp-wide): 15MM **Privately Held**
SIC: 3842 Surgical appliances & supplies
PA: Kenney Ortho Group, Inc.
208 Normandy Ct
Nicholasville KY 40356
859 241-1015

(G-5714)
KYB AMERICAS CORPORATION
850 N Graham Rd (46143-4600)
PHONE....................................317 881-7772
Kazumi Fujikawa, *CEO*
Matt Ault, *Mfg Spvr*
Jack Moore, *Maint Spvr*
Ana Rangel, *Purchasing*
Jeremy Keusch, *Engineer*
EMP: 13
SALES (corp-wide): 3.6B **Privately Held**
SIC: 3714 Motor vehicle parts & accessories
HQ: Kyb Americas Corporation
2625 N Morton St
Franklin IN 46131
317 736-7774

(G-5715)
KYB AMERICAS CORPORATION
850 N Graham Rd Ste C (46143-4601)
PHONE....................................630 620-5555

Kazumi Fujikawa, *CEO*
Rob Africano, *Regl Sales Mgr*
Dave Livingston, *Manager*
EMP: 50
SALES (corp-wide): 3.6B **Privately Held**
SIC: 3714 Shock absorbers, motor vehicle
HQ: Kyb Americas Corporation
2625 N Morton St
Franklin IN 46131
317 736-7774

(G-5716)
L&E ENGINEERING LLC
Also Called: L&E Engineering Company
254 N Graham Rd (46142)
P.O. Box 607, Franklin OH (45005-0607)
PHONE....................................317 884-0017
Bryan Perkins, *President*
Earl Larkin, *Co-CEO*
EMP: 70 EST: 1952
SQ FT: 27,000
SALES (est): 7.5MM
SALES (corp-wide): 163.1MM **Privately Held**
SIC: 3728 Aircraft parts & equipment
PA: Novaria Group, L.L.C.
6300 Ridglea Pl Ste 800
Fort Worth TX 76116
817 381-3810

(G-5717)
LANGUELL PRINTING INC
547 N Greenbriar Dr (46142-1212)
PHONE....................................317 889-3545
Roger Dean Languell, *President*
Roger Languell, *President*
EMP: 5
SALES (est): 300K **Privately Held**
SIC: 2759 Commercial printing

(G-5718)
LENSTECH OPTICAL LAB INC
Also Called: Lens Tech
1064 Greenwood Sprng Blvd (46143-6402)
PHONE....................................317 882-1249
William Harding, *President*
Greg Kyle, *Vice Pres*
Greg Dallas, *Admin Sec*
EMP: 33
SALES (est): 4.1MM **Privately Held**
SIC: 3851 Frames, lenses & parts, eyeglass & spectacle

(G-5719)
LESTER RECREATION DESIGNS LLC
751 Nonchalant Ct (46142-8335)
PHONE....................................317 888-2071
John M Lester, *Owner*
EMP: 2
SALES: 120K **Privately Held**
SIC: 3949 Playground equipment

(G-5720)
LIFT WORKS INC
5253 Mount Pleasant S St (46142-8941)
PHONE....................................812 797-0479
Zacheriah Cole, *President*
EMP: 4 EST: 2016
SALES (est): 159.4K **Privately Held**
SIC: 3728 Aircraft parts & equipment

(G-5721)
LOGICAL CONCEPTS
494 S Emerson Ave Ste E1 (46143-1913)
PHONE....................................317 885-6330
Tom Ward, *President*
EMP: 73
SALES (est): 9.9MM **Privately Held**
WEB: www.omni-site.net
SIC: 3669 5063 Burglar alarm apparatus, electric; electrical apparatus & equipment

(G-5722)
M R S PRINTING ERECTORS INC
4258 Redman Dr (46142-7346)
PHONE....................................317 888-1314
Fax: 317 634-4820
John Michel, *President*
James Spencer, *Vice Pres*
▲ EMP: 7
SQ FT: 23,000

SALES (est): 416.2K **Privately Held**
WEB: www.mrsprintingerectors.com
SIC: 7699 1796 3542 Printing trades machinery & equipment repair; machinery installation; machine tools, metal forming type

(G-5723)
MAPLEHURST BAKERIES LLC
1760 Industrial Dr (46143-9526)
PHONE...............................317 858-9000
Pete Kresge, *Site Mgr*
Art Mulholland, *VP Finance*
Mike Swanson, *Branch Mgr*
EMP: 135
SALES (corp-wide): 37.8B **Privately Held**
WEB: www.maplehurstbakeries.com
SIC: 2051 Bakery: wholesale or wholesale/retail combined
HQ: Maplehurst Bakeries, Llc
    50 Maplehurst Dr
    Brownsburg IN 46112
    317 858-9000

(G-5724)
MAY AND CO INC
Also Called: Scandinavian Sleep Products
3210 Greensview Dr (46143-9579)
PHONE...............................317 236-6500
Fax: 317 236-6503
Lawrence T May, *CEO*
Robert G May, *President*
Maria May, *CFO*
EMP: 23 EST: 1952
SQ FT: 74,000
SALES (est): 2.7MM **Privately Held**
WEB: www.mayandcompany.com
SIC: 2515 Mattresses & foundations; bedsprings, assembled

(G-5725)
MCNEIL COATINGS CONSULTANTS
1132 Kay Dr (46142-2204)
PHONE...............................317 885-1557
Malcom McNeil, *President*
Lenora McNeil, *General Mgr*
EMP: 2
SALES: 100K **Privately Held**
SIC: 8742 3479 Industrial consultant; painting, coating & hot dipping

(G-5726)
NACHI AMERICA INC (HQ)
715 Pushville Rd (46143-9782)
PHONE...............................317 535-5527
Fax: 317 530-1012
Tony Inoue, *President*
Kazuhide Maruyama, *General Mgr*
David Petrimoulx, *General Mgr*
Masanobu Tsuruga, *General Mgr*
Keith Hasuike, *Regional Mgr*
▲ EMP: 150
SQ FT: 53,000
SALES: 65.7MM **Privately Held**
SALES (corp-wide): 2B **Privately Held**
WEB: www.nachiamerica.com
SIC: 3545 3568 3542 3569 Machine tool accessories; bearings, bushings & blocks; machine tools, metal forming type; robots, assembly line: industrial & commercial; jacks, hydraulic; stainless steel
PA: Nachi-Fujikoshi Corp.
    1-9-2, Higashishimbashi
    Minato-Ku TKY 105-0
    355 685-111

(G-5727)
NACHI TECHNOLOGY INC
713 Pushville Rd (46143-9782)
PHONE...............................317 535-5000
Fax: 317 535-8484
Robert Komasara, *President*
Hidehito Miyata, *VP Opers*
Joe Schmidt, *Safety Mgr*
Harold Llewellyn, *Controller*
Kevin Dhonau, *Branch Mgr*
◆ EMP: 150
SQ FT: 137,000
SALES (est): 31.8MM **Privately Held**
SALES (corp-wide): 2B **Privately Held**
WEB: www.nachitech.com
SIC: 3562 Ball & roller bearings

HQ: Nachi America Inc.
    715 Pushville Rd
    Greenwood IN 46143
    317 535-5527

(G-5728)
NACHI TOOL AMERICA INC
717 Pushville Rd (46143-9782)
PHONE...............................317 535-0320
Kirk Blumenstock, *Manager*
EMP: 19
SALES (est): 3.5MM **Privately Held**
SIC: 3545 Machine tool accessories; drills (machine tool accessories)

(G-5729)
NU LED LIGHTING
1147 Old Vines Ct (46143-3411)
PHONE...............................317 989-7352
Shane Jardine, *Administration*
EMP: 2
SALES (est): 170.1K **Privately Held**
SIC: 3648 Lighting equipment

(G-5730)
OAKEN BARREL BREWING CO INC
Also Called: Oakenbarrel.com
50 Airport Pkwy Ste L (46143-1438)
PHONE...............................317 887-2287
Fax: 317 887-2446
William J Fulton, *President*
Brook P Belli, *Vice Pres*
Kwang Y Casey, *Admin Sec*
EMP: 48
SQ FT: 7,700
SALES: 2.1MM **Privately Held**
WEB: www.oakenbarrel.com
SIC: 5813 2082 Bars & lounges; malt beverages

(G-5731)
PERFECT PLASTIC PRINTING CORP
3967 Woodmore Dr (46142-9761)
PHONE...............................317 888-9447
Joe Renforth, *Manager*
EMP: 2
SALES (est): 129.5K **Privately Held**
SIC: 2759 Commercial printing

(G-5732)
PHOENIX ASSEMBLY LLC (HQ)
164 S Park Blvd (46143-8837)
PHONE...............................317 884-3600
Harry Sherman, *CEO*
Gary Sherman, *President*
Patrick Sherman, *Corp Secy*
▲ EMP: 91
SQ FT: 9,106
SALES (est): 52MM **Privately Held**
SIC: 5013 3569 4731 8741 Motor vehicle supplies & new parts; assembly machines, non-metalworking; freight transportation arrangement; industrial management

(G-5733)
PLASTER SHAK
1797 Old State Road 37 (46143-9186)
PHONE...............................317 881-6518
Don Weaver, *Owner*
EMP: 3
SQ FT: 6,200
SALES (est): 50K **Privately Held**
SIC: 3843 3299 5032 3272 Plaster, dental; plaques: clay, plaster or papier mache; drywall materials; concrete products

(G-5734)
POLY-TAINER INC
999 Gerdt Ct Ste C (46143-6114)
PHONE...............................317 883-2072
Fax: 317 883-2077
Kevin George, *Principal*
EMP: 170
SALES (corp-wide): 80MM **Privately Held**
WEB: www.polytainer.com
SIC: 3085 Plastics bottles
PA: Poly-Tainer, Inc.
    450 W Los Angeles Ave
    Simi Valley CA 93065
    805 526-3424

(G-5735)
POYNTER SHEET METAL INC
775 Commerce Parkway W Dr (46143-7535)
PHONE...............................317 893-1193
Fax: 812 935-6472
Joseph Lanstell, *CEO*
Jeff Milligan, *Superintendent*
Scott Lollar, *Safety Dir*
Randy Neal, *Project Mgr*
Floyd Vandagriff, *Project Mgr*
EMP: 275
SQ FT: 72,000
SALES: 52MM
SALES (corp-wide): 665MM **Privately Held**
SIC: 5075 3444 7349 Fans, heating & ventilation equipment; sheet metalwork; air duct cleaning
PA: Wilhelm Construction, Inc.
    3914 Prospect St
    Indianapolis IN 46203
    317 359-5411

(G-5736)
PREMIER CSTM COATINGS LLC IND
4676 Rainmaker Row (46143-7433)
PHONE...............................317 557-7841
Chris Foutz, *Principal*
EMP: 2 EST: 2016
SALES (est): 75.5K **Privately Held**
SIC: 3479 Metal coating & allied service

(G-5737)
PRESS CONTROL SYSTEMS
1864 S Crooked Ln (46143-8755)
PHONE...............................317 887-1369
Doug Wright, *Principal*
EMP: 4
SALES (est): 153.5K **Privately Held**
SIC: 2741 Miscellaneous publishing

(G-5738)
QUALITY REPAIR SERVICES INC
411 Knight Dr (46142-9372)
PHONE...............................317 881-0205
Fax: 317 881-0294
Larry Jordan, *President*
EMP: 15 EST: 1979
SQ FT: 6,768
SALES: 1.5MM **Privately Held**
SIC: 7694 Electric motor repair

(G-5739)
RITTERS FROZEN CUSTARD INC
3219 W County Line Rd (46142-9402)
PHONE...............................317 859-1038
Fax: 317 859-1038
Philip Barnheart, *General Mgr*
EMP: 6 **Privately Held**
SIC: 2024 Ice cream, bulk
HQ: Ritter's Frozen Custard, Inc.
    351 N Morton St
    Franklin IN 46131

(G-5740)
ROBERT J ROBINSON AIRCRAFT
904 N Matthews Rd (46143-9778)
PHONE...............................317 787-7809
Robert J Robinson MD, *Principal*
EMP: 2
SALES (est): 110.9K **Privately Held**
SIC: 3721 Aircraft

(G-5741)
ROBERTSON MACHINE CO INC
Also Called: Clark Dairy Equipment
430 E Main St (46143-1364)
P.O. Box 157 (46142-0157)
PHONE...............................317 881-9405
Fax: 317 881-9489
Michael T Robertson, *President*
Nancy Robertson, *Corp Secy*
EMP: 6 EST: 1999
SQ FT: 10,000
SALES (est): 796.4K **Privately Held**
SIC: 3599 3523 Machine shop, jobbing & repair; sprayers & spraying machines, agricultural

(G-5742)
ROGERS ENTERPRISES INC
Also Called: Rogers & Hollands Jewelers
1251 Us Highway 31 N (46142-4503)
PHONE...............................317 851-5500
Gina Anapachelli, *Manager*
EMP: 5
SALES (corp-wide): 113.9MM **Privately Held**
SIC: 5944 7631 3911 Jewelry stores; jewelry repair services; jewelry mountings & trimmings
PA: Rogers Enterprises, Inc.
    20821 S Cicero Ave
    Matteson IL 60443
    708 679-7588

(G-5743)
ROWE CONVEYOR LLC (PA)
1729 Us Highway 31 S Fj (46143-4100)
PHONE...............................317 602-1024
William A Rowe,
EMP: 2
SALES (est): 302.2K **Privately Held**
SIC: 3535 3537 3499 Conveyors & conveying equipment; stacking machines, automatic; strapping, metal

(G-5744)
ROYAL PIN LEISURE CENTERS INC
Also Called: Southern Bowl
1010 Us Highway 31 S (46143-2407)
PHONE...............................317 881-8686
Kenneth Howard, *Branch Mgr*
Howard Majors, *Executive*
EMP: 30
SALES (corp-wide): 1.7MM **Privately Held**
SIC: 3452 Pins
PA: Royal Pin Leisure Centers Inc
    8463 Castlewood Dr # 103
    Indianapolis IN 46250
    317 841-1002

(G-5745)
RUNNING COMPANY LLC
1251 Us Highway 31 N # 112 (46142-4558)
PHONE...............................317 887-0606
EMP: 3
SALES (est): 119K
SALES (corp-wide): 743.3K **Privately Held**
SIC: 3949 Sporting & athletic goods
PA: Running Company, Llc
    1079 Broad Ripple Ave
    Indianapolis IN 46220
    317 202-0202

(G-5746)
SABCO SIGN CO INC
1620 W Smith Valley Rd C (46142-1550)
PHONE...............................317 882-3380
Fax: 317 881-4635
Richard Simpson, *President*
EMP: 3
SQ FT: 4,000
SALES: 200K **Privately Held**
WEB: www.sabcosign.com
SIC: 3993 Signs, not made in custom sign painting shops

(G-5747)
SAN JO STEEL INC
610 W Main St Ste A (46142-2098)
PHONE...............................317 888-6227
Fax: 317 882-1760
Jeffrey T Cave, *President*
Dean Martin, *Vice Pres*
Sherry Kelley, *Project Mgr*
Brad Pugh, *Treasurer*
David Martin, *Shareholder*
EMP: 18
SQ FT: 10,000
SALES (est): 5.8MM **Privately Held**
WEB: www.sanjosteel.com
SIC: 3446 3441 Architectural metalwork; fabricated structural metal

(G-5748)
SCHWANS HOME SERVICE INC
1763 Industrial Dr (46143-9526)
PHONE...............................317 882-6624
Fax: 317 887-3303
Bruce Cochrin, *President*
EMP: 23

▲ = Import ▼=Export
◆ =Import/Export

SALES (corp-wide): 4.6B **Privately Held**
SIC: 2038 4215 Pizza, frozen; parcel delivery, vehicular
HQ: Schwan's Home Service, Inc.
115 W College Dr
Marshall MN 56258
507 532-3274

(G-5749)
SIGN SOLUTIONS INC
505 Commerce Parkway W Dr
(46143-6483)
PHONE.............................317 881-1818
Monty Hopkins, *President*
Thomas Hopkins, *Sales Staff*
Lisa Rains, *Office Mgr*
EMP: 14
SALES (est): 2.2MM **Privately Held**
SIC: 3993 Electric signs

(G-5750)
SPRING VENTURES INFOVATION LLC
1846 Saratoga Dr (46143-6879)
PHONE.............................317 847-1117
V RAO Bhamidipati,
EMP: 4
SALES (est): 206.6K **Privately Held**
SIC: 8742 7379 8748 7371 Management consulting services; computer related consulting services; systems analysis & engineering consulting services; custom computer programming services; prepackaged software

(G-5751)
SUMITOMO ELECTRIC CARBIDE INC
595 S Emerson Ave (46143-1951)
PHONE.............................317 859-1601
EMP: 3
SALES (corp-wide): 28.9B **Privately Held**
SIC: 3699 Electrical equipment & supplies
HQ: Sumitomo Electric Carbide Inc
1001 E Business Center Dr
Mount Prospect IL 60056
847 635-0044

(G-5752)
TEMPTEK INC
525 E Stop 18 Rd (46143-9808)
P.O. Box 1152 (46142-0276)
PHONE.............................317 887-6352
Jon Gunderson, *President*
Mike Oswalt, *General Mgr*
Susan Schaub, *Exec VP*
Randy Goode, *Vice Pres*
Ron Wolfe, *Vice Pres*
EMP: 5
SQ FT: 20,000
SALES (est): 1.3MM **Privately Held**
WEB: www.temptek.com
SIC: 3822 1711 3443 3433 Temperature controls, automatic; plumbing, heating, air-conditioning contractors; fabricated plate work (boiler shop); heating equipment, except electric

(G-5753)
TNEMEC COMPANY INC
458 Park 800 Dr (46143-9525)
PHONE.............................317 884-1806
Jeff Payton, *Branch Mgr*
EMP: 3
SALES (corp-wide): 118.3MM **Privately Held**
WEB: www.tnemec.com
SIC: 2851 Coating, air curing; lacquers, varnishes, enamels & other coatings
PA: Tnemec Company, Inc.
6800 Corporate Dr
Kansas City MO 64120
816 483-3400

(G-5754)
TOCO INC
4307 Blackwood Ct (46143-7909)
PHONE.............................317 627-8854
Laura McIntosh, *President*
EMP: 3
SALES: 50K **Privately Held**
SIC: 3559 Special industry machinery

(G-5755)
TRADEMARK SCREEN PRINTING
173 E Broadway St (46143-1306)
PHONE.............................317 885-3258
EMP: 2 EST: 2001
SALES (est): 90K **Privately Held**
SIC: 2759 Commercial Printing

(G-5756)
TRUE CHEM INC
283 Innisbrooke Ave (46142-9215)
P.O. Box 1424 (46142-6324)
PHONE.............................317 769-2701
Leslie Sherry, *President*
EMP: 4
SALES: 300K **Privately Held**
SIC: 3589 7389 Water purification equipment, household type;

(G-5757)
TUPY AMERICAN FOUNDRY CORP
200 N Emerson Ave Ste C (46143-7015)
PHONE.............................317 859-0066
Javier Ruiz, *Branch Mgr*
EMP: 3 **Privately Held**
SIC: 3325 Steel foundries
HQ: Tupy American Foundry Corp
39205 Country Club Dr C22
Farmington Hills MI 48331
248 324-0167

(G-5758)
VISION AID SYSTEMS INC
Also Called: Low Vision Store
916 E Main St Ste 114 (46143-1500)
P.O. Box 1369 (46142-6269)
PHONE.............................317 888-0323
James Fortman, *President*
Lisa Preston, *Admin Sec*
EMP: 2
SQ FT: 750
SALES (est): 180K **Privately Held**
WEB: www.visionaidsystems.com
SIC: 3827 4841 Optical instruments & apparatus; cable & other pay television services

(G-5759)
WESSELS COMPANY
Also Called: Rnk Intl C/O
101 Tank St (46143-1203)
PHONE.............................317 888-9800
Fax: 317 865-7411
James Fuller, *President*
Guy Kirk Jr, *Vice Pres*
Mike Anderson, *Mfg Staff*
Megan McDaniel, *Purch Agent*
Todd May, *Purchasing*
▲ EMP: 80
SQ FT: 103,000
SALES (est): 24.4MM
SALES (corp-wide): 116.4MM **Privately Held**
WEB: www.wesselscompany.com
SIC: 3443 Tanks, standard or custom fabricated: metal plate
PA: Nm Group Global, Llc
161 Greenfield St
Tiffin OH 44883
419 447-5211

Griffith
Lake County

(G-5760)
ACME CABINETS CORP
1331 E Main St (46319-2932)
PHONE.............................219 924-1800
Fax: 219 924-1801
Donald Elman, *President*
Richard Elman, *Admin Sec*
EMP: 8 EST: 1959
SQ FT: 5,400
SALES: 886.6K **Privately Held**
WEB: www.acmecabinets.com
SIC: 2434 Wood kitchen cabinets

(G-5761)
AEROMET INDUSTRIES INC
739 S Arbogast St (46319-3149)
PHONE.............................219 924-7442

Fax: 219 924-6732
Fred Wahlberg, *President*
Drew Wahlberg, *Corp Secy*
Gus Sitaras, *Vice Pres*
Greg Caputo, *Production*
Terry Chopps, *Buyer*
▲ EMP: 55
SQ FT: 25,500
SALES (est): 11.4MM **Privately Held**
WEB: www.aerometindustries.com
SIC: 3599 3545 Machine shop, jobbing & repair; machine tool attachments & accessories

(G-5762)
AMERICAN NATURAL RESOURCES LLC
Also Called: American Natural Resources Str
120 N Broad St (46319-2219)
PHONE.............................219 922-6444
Fax: 219 922-6642
Edward Leep, *Mng Member*
EMP: 15
SALES: 1.5MM **Privately Held**
WEB: www.leepstaxidermy.com
SIC: 7699 2599 5021 5712 Taxidermists; boards: planning, display, notice; furniture; furniture stores

(G-5763)
ATCO-GARY METAL TECH LLC
1931 E Main St (46319-2921)
PHONE.............................219 885-3232
David A Strilich, *Mng Member*
EMP: 110
SALES (est): 15.5MM **Privately Held**
SIC: 3444 Sheet metalwork

(G-5764)
B K & M INC
210 S Lindberg St (46319-2694)
PHONE.............................219 924-0184
Toni Gwiazda, *President*
Vince Gwiazda, *Vice Pres*
EMP: 3
SALES (est): 328.7K **Privately Held**
SIC: 3452 Bolts, metal

(G-5765)
BEARING SERVICE COMPANY PA
1951 N Griffith Blvd (46319-1043)
PHONE.............................773 734-5132
Janet July, *Manager*
EMP: 4
SALES (corp-wide): 51.8MM **Privately Held**
WEB: www.bearing-service.com
SIC: 3562 3568 Roller bearings & parts; power transmission equipment
PA: Bearing Service Company Of Pennsylvania
630 Alpha Dr
Pittsburgh PA 15238
412 963-7710

(G-5766)
BLYTHES SPORT SHOP INC (PA)
138 N Broad St (46319-2287)
P.O. Box 539 (46319-0539)
PHONE.............................219 924-4403
Fax: 219 922-3240
Rodger Blythe, *President*
Lester Blythe, *Corp Secy*
Michael Blythe, *Vice Pres*
EMP: 15
SQ FT: 6,000
SALES (est): 5.6MM **Privately Held**
SIC: 3484 5099 3482 Guns (firearms) or gun parts, 30 mm. & below; firearms & ammunition, except sporting; cores, bullet: 30 mm. & below

(G-5767)
BM CREATIONS INC
1313 E Main St (46319-2932)
PHONE.............................219 922-8935
Shyam Hathi, *Principal*
EMP: 2
SALES (est): 184.4K **Privately Held**
SIC: 2759 Commercial printing

(G-5768)
CATALYST SERVICES INC
1940 N Lafayette Ct (46319-1000)
PHONE.............................219 972-7803

Fax: 219 972-7826
Greg Kraus, *President*
EMP: 20
SALES (est): 3.8MM
SALES (corp-wide): 1.4B **Privately Held**
SIC: 2819 Catalysts, chemical
HQ: Ceda International, Inc.
2600 S Shore Blvd Ste 300
League City TX 77573
281 478-2600

(G-5769)
CCMP INC
Also Called: Beryl Martin
1313 E Main St (46319-2932)
PHONE.............................219 922-8935
J Kim Sorenson, *President*
Brian Tucker, *General Mgr*
EMP: 47
SQ FT: 50,000
SALES: 2.3MM **Privately Held**
WEB: www.ccmp.com
SIC: 2759 Commercial printing

(G-5770)
CHEMICAL CONTROL SYSTEMS INC (PA)
403 Industrial Dr (46319-3811)
PHONE.............................219 465-5103
Fax: 219 922-9633
Mike Walker, *President*
Susy Walker, *Corp Secy*
Jim Flannery, *Vice Pres*
EMP: 3
SQ FT: 8,000
SALES: 1.5MM **Privately Held**
SIC: 3589 3586 Water treatment equipment, industrial; measuring & dispensing pumps

(G-5771)
CHICAGO SPECIALTY STEEL CORP
505 Industrial Dr (46319-2696)
PHONE.............................219 922-8888
Andrew S Kern, *President*
Jason Kern, *Vice Pres*
EMP: 28
SALES (est): 7.2MM **Privately Held**
SIC: 3441 Fabricated structural metal

(G-5772)
EASON MANUFACTURING INC
601 Industrial Dr Ste B (46319-2695)
PHONE.............................312 310-9430
Fax: 219 922-6207
Earl Hokens Jr, *President*
EMP: 3
SQ FT: 4,200
SALES (est): 210K **Privately Held**
SIC: 3599 Machine shop, jobbing & repair

(G-5773)
GARY MACHINERY LLC
1931 E Main St (46319-2921)
PHONE.............................219 980-5700
Fax: 219 980-0405
Mike Golec, *General Mgr*
Lee Donahoe, *Sales Staff*
▲ EMP: 20
SQ FT: 30,000
SALES: 5MM **Privately Held**
WEB: www.garymachinery.com
SIC: 3549 Cutting & slitting machinery

(G-5774)
GORDON LUMBER COMPANY
806 W Avenue H (46319-3012)
PHONE.............................219 924-0500
Fax: 219 924-1069
Vincent Gwiazda, *President*
Conrad Swalwell, *Vice Pres*
Louis Piattoni, *Admin Sec*
EMP: 4 EST: 1940
SQ FT: 7,500
SALES (est): 405.4K
SALES (corp-wide): 559K **Privately Held**
SIC: 2449 5031 Wood containers; lumber: rough, dressed & finished
PA: Continental Custom Crate Inc
806 W Avenue H
Griffith IN

(G-5775)
GREENWOOD TOOL & DIE CO INC
231 S Lindberg St (46319-2694)
PHONE....................................219 924-9663
Fax: 219 924-9667
Myron Kurth, *President*
David Kurth, *Treasurer*
Gail Kurth, *Admin Sec*
EMP: 2
SQ FT: 6,000
SALES (est): 327.2K **Privately Held**
SIC: 3599 3544 Machine shop, jobbing & repair; special dies, tools, jigs & fixtures

(G-5776)
HD MECHANICAL INC
507 Industrial Dr (46319-2696)
PHONE....................................219 924-6050
Erik Hansen, *President*
Keith Best, *Admin Sec*
EMP: 4
SQ FT: 10,000
SALES: 2.2MM **Privately Held**
SIC: 1623 3498 3317 Pipe laying construction; fabricated pipe & fittings; piping systems for pulp paper & chemical industries; steel pipe & tubes

(G-5777)
HUDEC CONSTRUCTION COMPANY
Also Called: Hudec Woodworking Company
148 N Ivanhoe Ct (46319-3457)
PHONE....................................219 922-9811
John Hudec, *President*
Julie Hudec, *Corp Secy*
EMP: 20
SALES (est): 3.9MM **Privately Held**
WEB: www.hudecjaffna.org
SIC: 2431 1521 Millwork; general remodeling, single-family houses

(G-5778)
HYDRO-EXC INC
321 E Main St (46319-2214)
PHONE....................................219 922-9886
Fax: 219 922-9819
Colleen Ravesloot, *President*
Michael Ravesloot, *Vice Pres*
Gregg Nadess, *CFO*
EMP: 27
SQ FT: 20,000
SALES (est): 4.7MM **Privately Held**
SIC: 1794 1629 1381 Excavation & grading, building construction; trenching contractor; directional drilling oil & gas wells

(G-5779)
ICE CREAM ON WHEELS INC ✪
2011 N Griffith Blvd (46319-1009)
PHONE....................................800 884-9793
Thomas Benedict Renwald, *Chairman*
EMP: 3 EST: 2017
SALES (est): 120.1K **Privately Held**
SIC: 2024 5451 Ice cream, packaged: molded, on sticks, etc.; ice cream (packaged)

(G-5780)
INSTELLUS INC (PA)
Also Called: Instellus Technology Solutions
425 N Broad St Ste 4 (46319-2223)
PHONE....................................734 415-3013
Ethan Adams, *CEO*
Paul Aguiano,
Preston Teters,
EMP: 2
SQ FT: 5,200
SALES (est): 236.2K **Privately Held**
SIC: 3724 3699 Aircraft engines & engine parts; security control equipment & systems

(G-5781)
KEYWEST METAL
2034 N Griffith Blvd (46319-1009)
PHONE....................................219 513-8429
EMP: 3 EST: 2012
SALES (est): 184.1K **Privately Held**
SIC: 3399 Primary metal products

(G-5782)
MAINLINE MANUFACTURING COMPANY
329 N Colfax St (46319-2849)
PHONE....................................219 237-0770
Joseph Novosel, *Principal*
EMP: 2
SALES (est): 151.6K **Privately Held**
SIC: 3999 Manufacturing industries

(G-5783)
MARGARET MACHINE AND TOOL CO
206 S Lindberg St (46319-2694)
PHONE....................................219 924-0859
Fax: 219 924-6458
Vincent G Wiazda, *President*
EMP: 9
SQ FT: 10,000
SALES (est): 1MM **Privately Held**
SIC: 3599 Machine shop, jobbing & repair

(G-5784)
MARQUETTE COUNCIL 3631 KN
1400 S Broad St (46319-3212)
PHONE....................................219 864-3255
EMP: 2
SALES (est): 158.7K **Privately Held**
SIC: 3944 Mfg Games/Toys

(G-5785)
MIDWEST MACHINING & FABG
711 W Main St (46319-2634)
P.O. Box D (46319-0498)
PHONE....................................219 924-0206
Fax: 219 924-2406
Ronald W Stassin, *President*
Stanley Majkowski, *Corp Secy*
EMP: 10 EST: 1973
SQ FT: 5,000
SALES (est): 900K **Privately Held**
SIC: 3599 7692 Machine shop, jobbing & repair; welding repair

(G-5786)
MITEK USA INC
905 W Glen Park Ave (46319-2028)
PHONE....................................219 924-3835
EMP: 75
SALES (corp-wide): 210.8B **Publicly Held**
SIC: 3443 3999 Mfg Fabricated Plate Work Mfg Misc Products
HQ: Mitek Usa, Inc.
16023 Swingley Ridge Rd
Chesterfield MO 63017
314 434-1200

(G-5787)
PRO-WELD LLC
4710 Oaklane Dr (46319-2560)
PHONE....................................219 922-8861
Walter Cassoday,
EMP: 8
SALES (est): 1.2MM **Privately Held**
WEB: www.pro-weld.com
SIC: 7692 Welding repair

(G-5788)
RCR METAL FAB LLC
713 N Oakwood St (46319-2427)
PHONE....................................219 923-9104
Richard Rentschler, *Owner*
EMP: 4
SALES (est): 336.5K **Privately Held**
SIC: 3441 Fabricated structural metal

(G-5789)
REACTOR SERVICES INTL INC
Also Called: RSI
238 S Linburg (46319)
P.O. Box 614 (46319-0614)
PHONE....................................219 924-0507
Fax: 219 924-0705
Mark Sleeman, *General Mgr*
EMP: 30
SALES (corp-wide): 83.3MM **Privately Held**
WEB: www.reactorservices.com
SIC: 2819 Catalysts, chemical
PA: Reactor Services International, Inc.
200 Avenue I Bldg G
Alvin TX
281 824-0841

(G-5790)
SPRY-CLEAR EAR INC
Also Called: Clear Ear Hearing Aid Center
827 W Glen Park Ave (46319-2027)
PHONE....................................219 934-9747
Bob Spry, *President*
Tammy Spry, *Vice Pres*
EMP: 4
SQ FT: 1,700
SALES: 529.4K **Privately Held**
SIC: 3842 Hearing aids

(G-5791)
TEC HOIST LLC
1349 E Main St (46319-2932)
PHONE....................................708 598-2300
William C Kratochvil,
▲ EMP: 12
SQ FT: 10,000
SALES (est): 1.4MM
SALES (corp-wide): 47.6MM **Privately Held**
WEB: www.imperialcrane.com
SIC: 3534 3536 Elevators & moving stairways; hoisting slings
PA: Imperial Crane Services, Inc.
7500 Imperial Dr
Bridgeview IL 60455
708 598-2300

(G-5792)
TECHNICAL WEIGHING SVCS INC
1000 Reder Rd (46319-3116)
PHONE....................................219 924-3433
Fax: 219 924-0254
Randy Purty, *Owner*
EMP: 2
SALES (corp-wide): 3.3MM **Privately Held**
SIC: 7692 Welding repair
PA: Technical Weighing Services, Inc.
1004 Reder Rd
Griffith IN 46319
219 924-3366

(G-5793)
TECHNICAL WEIGHING SVCS INC (PA)
Also Called: TECH WEIGH MANUFACTURING
1004 Reder Rd (46319-3116)
PHONE....................................219 924-3366
Fax: 219 924-4566
Jack L Clark, *President*
Jane Wright, *Accounts Mgr*
Sandra L Clark, *Admin Sec*
▲ EMP: 32
SQ FT: 30,000
SALES: 3.3MM **Privately Held**
SIC: 5046 7699 3596 3825 Scales, except laboratory; scale repair service; weighing machines & apparatus; electrical energy measuring equipment

(G-5794)
UPRIGHT IRON WORKS INC
1036 Reder Rd (46319-3116)
PHONE....................................219 922-1994
Elizabeth Matelundin, *President*
Elizabeth Mate-Lundin, *President*
EMP: 9
SALES (est): 1.5MM **Privately Held**
SIC: 3446 Ornamental metalwork

Grovertown
Starke County

(G-5795)
F & F CONTRACTING
7315 E 300 N (46531-9206)
PHONE....................................574 867-4471
John Frank Atkins, *Owner*
Freda Atkins, *Co-Owner*
EMP: 5
SALES (est): 250K **Privately Held**
SIC: 2441 2653 2449 2448 Boxes, wood; pallets, corrugated: made from purchased materials; wood containers; wood pallets & skids

---

Guilford
Dearborn County

(G-5796)
ALPACA HOLLER LLC ✪
25327 Jacobs Rd (47022-9272)
PHONE....................................513 544-6866
Stephanie Rack, *Principal*
EMP: 2 EST: 2017
SALES (est): 73.4K **Privately Held**
SIC: 2231 Alpacas, mohair: woven

(G-5797)
BES RACING ENGINES INC
27545 State Route 1 (47022-9334)
PHONE....................................812 576-2371
Anthony Bischoff, *President*
EMP: 10
SALES: 1.4MM **Privately Held**
SIC: 3519 Gasoline engines

(G-5798)
DOLE
6575 Stonegate Dr (47022-9754)
PHONE....................................812 576-2186
EMP: 2 EST: 2010
SALES (est): 24.7K **Privately Held**
SIC: 2099 Food preparations

(G-5799)
STEPHENS WOODWORKING
5928 Bonnell Rd (47022-9600)
PHONE....................................812 487-2818
Terry Stephens, *Owner*
EMP: 3 EST: 2008
SALES (est): 266K **Privately Held**
SIC: 2431 Millwork

Gwynneville
Shelby County

(G-5800)
PEARL CUSTOM PLASTIC MOLDING
7072 E Mulberry St (46144-5502)
PHONE....................................765 763-6961
Fax: 765 763-7361
Nancy J Grimes, *Owner*
EMP: 9
SQ FT: 5,000
SALES (est): 937.8K **Privately Held**
SIC: 3843 Dental equipment & supplies

Hagerstown
Wayne County

(G-5801)
ABBOTTS CANDY AND GIFTS INC (PA)
Also Called: Abbott's Candy Shop
48 E Walnut St (47346-1542)
PHONE....................................765 489-4442
Fax: 765 489-5501
Suanna Goodnight, *President*
Gordon Goodnight, *Vice Pres*
Richard Federico, *Admin Sec*
EMP: 20
SQ FT: 12,000
SALES: 780K **Privately Held**
WEB: www.abbottscandy.com
SIC: 2064 5947 5441 2066 Candy & other confectionery products; gift shop; candy; chocolate & cocoa products

(G-5802)
ALL AMERICAN SCREEN PRTG LLC
16914 Massey Rd (47346-9400)
PHONE....................................765 914-7600
Ricky J Estes, *Principal*
EMP: 2
SALES (est): 83.9K **Privately Held**
SIC: 2752 Commercial printing, lithographic

▲ = Import ▼=Export
◆ =Import/Export

(G-5803)
AUTOCAR LLC
551 S Washington St (47346-1557)
PHONE..................................765 489-5499
Fax: 765 489-5230
Jim Johnston, *President*
Ed Steyn, *President*
Andrew Taitz, *Chairman*
James M Johnston, *Mng Member*
Ryan Billet,
▲ EMP: 200
SQ FT: 200,000
SALES (est): 103.3MM
SALES (corp-wide): 156.7MM **Privately Held**
WEB: www.autocartruck.com
SIC: 3713 Garbage, refuse truck bodies
PA: Gvw Group, Llc
625 Roger Williams Ave
Highland Park IL 60035
847 681-8417

(G-5804)
BRIAN BEX REPORT INC
Also Called: American Communications Netwrk
100 N Woodpecker Rd (47346-1431)
PHONE..................................765 489-5566
Brian Bex, *President*
Kristopher Bex, *Vice Pres*
EMP: 3 EST: 1966
SQ FT: 15,000
SALES (est): 368.8K **Privately Held**
SIC: 2721 Periodicals: publishing only

(G-5805)
CUSTOM MTAL FNSHNG-INDIANA LLC
9705 State Road 38 (47346-9520)
PHONE..................................765 489-4089
James M Canfield, *Owner*
EMP: 3
SALES (est): 373.8K **Privately Held**
SIC: 3571 Computers, digital, analog or hybrid

(G-5806)
HAGERSTOWN GRAVEL & CNSTR
14064 Olive Branch Rd (47346-9719)
PHONE..................................765 489-4812
Fred A House, *President*
Sabrina Joanes, *Principal*
Herbert Dunford, *Vice Pres*
Roselyn House, *Treasurer*
EMP: 5 EST: 1953
SQ FT: 500
SALES: 400K **Privately Held**
SIC: 1794 1442 1799 Excavation work; gravel mining; swimming pool construction

(G-5807)
HARVEST LAND CO-OP INC
4379 Jacksonburg Rd (47346-9624)
PHONE..................................765 489-4141
Marlin Larson, *President*
EMP: 15
SALES (corp-wide): 301.4MM **Privately Held**
WEB: www.harvestland.com
SIC: 5191 2879 2875 2048 Fertilizers & agricultural chemicals; agricultural chemicals; fertilizers, mixing only; prepared feeds; crop preparation services for market
PA: Harvest Land Co-Op, Inc.
1435 Nw 5th St
Richmond IN 47374
765 962-1527

(G-5808)
MANCHESTER INDUSTRIES INC VA
63 Paul R Foulke Pkwy (47346-1632)
P.O. Box 229 (47346-0229)
PHONE..................................765 489-4521
Ranse McKinney, *Manager*
EMP: 30 **Publicly Held**
SIC: 2679 Paperboard products, converted
HQ: Manchester Industries Inc. Of Virginia
200 Orleans St
Richmond VA 23231
804 226-4250

(G-5809)
MAXWELL MILLING INDIANA INC
4359 N State Road 1 (47346-9620)
P.O. Box 230 (47346-0230)
PHONE..................................765 489-3506
James L Maxwell III, *President*
Joe Baldwin, *Opers Mgr*
J Walter Pelletier III, *Treasurer*
EMP: 7
SALES (est): 1.3MM **Privately Held**
SIC: 3541 Milling machines

(G-5810)
PB METAL WORKS
50 Paul R Foulke Pkwy (47346-1626)
PHONE..................................765 489-1311
Melvin Teachey, *Owner*
EMP: 2
SALES: 150K **Privately Held**
SIC: 1761 5719 5031 3443 Sheet metalwork; metalware; trim, sheet metal; cupolas, metal plate

(G-5811)
PHEONIX INC
Also Called: Logo Shop, The
98 W Main St (47346-1215)
PHONE..................................765 489-3030
EMP: 6
SALES (est): 340K **Privately Held**
SIC: 2759 7336 Commercial Printing Commercial Art/Graphic Design

(G-5812)
PRECISION WIRE ASSEMBLIES INC
551 E Main St (47346-1421)
PHONE..................................765 489-6302
Fax: 765 489-4240
Penny Wickes, *President*
Richard Ramey, *General Mgr*
William M Wickes, *Vice Pres*
Jeff Combs, *Buyer*
Tom Kelly, *Engineer*
EMP: 75
SQ FT: 265,000
SALES (est): 13.1MM **Privately Held**
SIC: 3679 Harness assemblies for electronic use: wire or cable

(G-5813)
SYLTECH EXPERIMENTAL
13931 Clyde Oler Rd (47346-9764)
PHONE..................................765 489-1777
Ray Rigaud, *Owner*
EMP: 2
SALES (est): 166K **Privately Held**
SIC: 3599 Machine shop, jobbing & repair

(G-5814)
TEDCO INC (PA)
Also Called: Tedco Toys
498 S Washington St (47346-1596)
PHONE..................................765 489-4527
Fax: 765 489-5752
Ralph R Meyer, *President*
Marjorie T Meyer, *Corp Secy*
Sue Ellen Childs, *Controller*
◆ EMP: 15 EST: 1982
SQ FT: 9,000
SALES (est): 2.1MM **Privately Held**
WEB: www.tedcotoys.com
SIC: 3944 Games, toys & children's vehicles

(G-5815)
TEDCO INC
303 W Main St (47346-1143)
PHONE..................................765 489-5807
Mark Marlat, *Manager*
EMP: 2
SALES (corp-wide): 2.1MM **Privately Held**
WEB: www.tedcotoys.com
SIC: 3089 Injection molding of plastics
PA: Tedco Inc
498 S Washington St
Hagerstown IN 47346
765 489-4527

(G-5816)
WHITE WATER TRUSS LLC
79 Paul R Foulke Pkwy (47346-1632)
PHONE..................................765 489-6261

Mark Wilkins, *Manager*
Dan Lapp,
EMP: 8
SALES (est): 1.3MM **Privately Held**
SIC: 2439 Trusses, except roof: laminated lumber

(G-5817)
WILLOW WAY LLC
Also Called: Soapequipment.com
12873 We Oler Rd (47346-9716)
PHONE..................................765 886-4640
Ron Jonas, *CEO*
▼ EMP: 9
SALES (est): 1.5MM **Privately Held**
SIC: 3556 Cutting, chopping, grinding, mixing & similar machinery

Hamilton
Steuben County

(G-5818)
AAA GALVANIZING - JOLIET INC
Also Called: Azz Galvanizing Hamilton
7825 S Homestead Dr (46742-9622)
PHONE..................................260 488-4477
Jeff Reynolds, *Branch Mgr*
EMP: 53
SALES (corp-wide): 810.4MM **Publicly Held**
SIC: 3479 Hot dip coating of metals or formed products; coating of metals & formed products
HQ: Aaa Galvanizing - Joliet, Inc.
625 Mills Rd
Joliet IL 60433

(G-5819)
AIR WAY MFG
7540 S Homestead Dr (46742-9622)
PHONE..................................269 749-2161
Jeff Hanson, *Plant Mgr*
EMP: 4
SALES (est): 587.8K **Privately Held**
SIC: 3999 Manufacturing industries

(G-5820)
CHUCKS CLEANERS
3820 E Bellefontaine Rd (46742-9363)
P.O. Box 433 (46742-0433)
PHONE..................................260 488-3362
Charles J Ott, *Owner*
EMP: 2 EST: 1988
SALES (est): 108.9K **Privately Held**
SIC: 7216 3582 Cleaning & dyeing, except rugs; ironers, commercial laundry & drycleaning

(G-5821)
E M F CORP
Also Called: Indiana Wire Assembly
7335 S Enterprise Dr (46742-9662)
P.O. Box 484 (46742-0484)
PHONE..................................260 488-2479
Fax: 260 488-2031
Richard Poe, *President*
EMP: 25
SALES (corp-wide): 40.4MM **Privately Held**
WEB: www.emfusa.com
SIC: 3643 3351 3694 Current-carrying wiring devices; wire, copper & copper alloy; engine electrical equipment
PA: E M F Corp
505 Pokagon Trl
Angola IN 46703
260 665-9541

(G-5822)
G&L MACHINE
5920 County Road 4 (46742-9743)
P.O. Box 314 (46742-0314)
PHONE..................................260 488-2100
Gary Laupzenhiser,
EMP: 5
SALES (est): 630.2K **Privately Held**
SIC: 3334 Primary aluminum

(G-5823)
HAMILTON INDUSTRIAL INC
6610 S State Road 1 (46742-9519)
PHONE..................................260 488-3662
Lloyd J Bartels, *CEO*

EMP: 2
SALES (est): 97.2K **Privately Held**
SIC: 3599 Machine shop, jobbing & repair

(G-5824)
INDUSTRIAL STEERING PDTS INC (PA)
7790 S Homestead Dr (46742-9622)
P.O. Box 868, Bryan OH (43506-0868)
PHONE..................................260 488-1880
Fax: 419 636-3366
Terri Freudenberger, *President*
John Freudenberger, *Vice Pres*
Tricia Baughman, *Engineer*
EMP: 50
SQ FT: 100,000
SALES (est): 8MM **Privately Held**
WEB: www.industrialsteering.com
SIC: 3714 Steering mechanisms, motor vehicle

(G-5825)
MAGITEK LLC
5618 County Road 6 (46742-9730)
PHONE..................................260 488-2226
Fax: 260 488-4676
Stephan Lautzenhiser,
EMP: 8
SALES (est): 869.1K **Privately Held**
SIC: 3841 Diagnostic apparatus, medical

(G-5826)
PITTSFIELD PRODUCTS INC
Also Called: Pittsfield of Indiana
7365 S Enterprise Dr (46742-9662)
P.O. Box 126 (46742-0126)
PHONE..................................260 488-2124
Fax: 260 488-2223
Charles Ackman, *Branch Mgr*
EMP: 80
SALES (corp-wide): 35.1MM **Privately Held**
WEB: www.pittsfieldproducts.com
SIC: 3569 Filters, general line: industrial
PA: Pittsfield Products, Inc.
5741 Jackson Rd
Ann Arbor MI 48103
734 665-3771

(G-5827)
PLASTIC PROCESSORS INC
7450 S Homestead Dr (46742-9361)
P.O. Box 508 (46742-0508)
PHONE..................................260 488-3999
Fax: 260 488-2170
Jackson Wetzel, *President*
Jay Wetzel, *Vice Pres*
EMP: 13
SQ FT: 30,000
SALES (est): 2.4MM **Privately Held**
WEB: www.plasticprocessorsinc.com
SIC: 3089 Extruded finished plastic products; plastic processing

(G-5828)
SCOTT FETZER COMPANY
7715 S Homestead Dr (46742-9622)
PHONE..................................260 488-3531
John Obrien, *Manager*
EMP: 65
SALES (corp-wide): 242.1B **Publicly Held**
SIC: 3634 Personal electrical appliances
HQ: The Scott Fetzer Company
28800 Clemens Rd
Westlake OH 44145
440 892-3000

(G-5829)
SUPERIOR CANOPY CORPORATION
2435 E Bellefontaine Rd (46742-9619)
PHONE..................................260 488-4065
Fax: 260 488-4063
George Stamper, *President*
Ralph Lingo, *Principal*
Kristina Vilders, *Admin Asst*
EMP: 21
SALES (est): 5.7MM **Privately Held**
WEB: www.superiorcanopy.com
SIC: 3444 3281 Canopies, sheet metal; building stone products

G
E
O
G
R
A
P
H
I
C

(G-5830)
TRITON METAL PRODUCTS INC
7790 S Homestead Dr (46742-9622)
PHONE..........................260 488-1800
Terri Freudenberger, *President*
Shawn Sabins, *General Mgr*
John Freudenberger Jr, *Vice Pres*
Rick Snyder, *Maint Spvr*
Patty Ferreira, *Human Resources*
EMP: 35
SALES (est): 8.8MM
SALES (corp-wide): 8MM **Privately Held**
SIC: 3441 Fabricated structural metal
PA: Industrial Steering Products, Inc.
　7790 S Homestead Dr
　Hamilton IN 46742
　260 488-1880

Hamlet
Starke County

(G-5831)
NORTON PACKAGING INC
5190 N Industrial Pkwy (46532-9596)
PHONE..........................574 867-6002
Fax: 574 867-6207
Tom Kenny, *Opers Staff*
Jim Koch, *Manager*
EMP: 25
SALES (corp-wide): 69.3MM **Privately Held**
WEB: www.nortonpackaging.com
SIC: 3089 3411 Plastic containers, except foam; metal cans
PA: Norton Packaging, Inc.
　20670 Corsair Blvd
　Hayward CA 94545
　510 786-1922

(G-5832)
PRO CLEAN LLC
607 E Plymouth St (46532-9514)
P.O. Box 443, Valparaiso (46384-0443)
PHONE..........................574 867-1000
Wayne Watson,
EMP: 5
SALES: 241K **Privately Held**
SIC: 3564 Blowers & fans

Hammond
Lake County

(G-5833)
A IS FOR APPLE LEARNING CENTER
1510 173rd St (46324-2879)
PHONE..........................219 629-3514
EMP: 2
SALES (est): 85.9K **Privately Held**
SIC: 3571 Personal computers (microcomputers)

(G-5834)
ACCUCRAFT IMAGING INC
5920 Hohman Ave (46320-2423)
PHONE..........................219 933-3007
Fax: 219 933-3052
Leon Dombrowski, *President*
Mary Hall, *Production*
Don Wiltfong, *Representative*
EMP: 6
SALES (est): 610K **Privately Held**
SIC: 2796 Color separations for printing

(G-5835)
ADVANTAGE SIGNS & GRAPHICS INC
6223 Hohman Ave Ste 3 (46324-1071)
PHONE..........................219 853-1427
Margaret R Smith, *Principal*
EMP: 6
SALES (est): 623.2K **Privately Held**
SIC: 3993 Signs & advertising specialties

(G-5836)
AFFORDABLE SIGN & NEON INC
534 Conkey St Ste 1 (46324-1146)
PHONE..........................219 853-1855
Fax: 219 853-1857
Lisa Thomas, *President*

EMP: 3
SALES (est): 342.8K **Privately Held**
WEB: www.a-1affordablesigns.com
SIC: 3993 Signs & advertising specialties

(G-5837)
AH PRINTING SERVICE
7421 Van Buren Ave (46324-2549)
PHONE..........................219 933-7686
Herbert Waldron, *Owner*
EMP: 2
SALES (est): 88.9K **Privately Held**
SIC: 2752 Commercial printing, lithographic

(G-5838)
ALLIN PLASTICS ENGRAVING
2845 Garfield Ave (46322-1639)
PHONE..........................219 972-2223
Jacqueline A Jarecki, *Owner*
EMP: 2
SALES (est): 144K **Privately Held**
SIC: 3089 Engraving of plastic

(G-5839)
ALMIRAS BAKERY
2635 169th St (46323-1507)
PHONE..........................219 844-4334
Frank Vantil, *President*
Ronald Karner, *Treasurer*
EMP: 30
SQ FT: 4,000
SALES (est): 1MM **Privately Held**
WEB: www.almirasbakery.net
SIC: 5461 2052 2051 Cakes; cookies & crackers; bread, cake & related products

(G-5840)
AMERICAN FABRICATORS INC
5832 Cline Ave (46323-1201)
P.O. Box 531, East Chicago (46312-0531)
PHONE..........................219 844-4744
Fax: 219 844-4787
Joseph Fraley, *President*
Michael Fraley, *Treasurer*
EMP: 20
SQ FT: 18,000
SALES (est): 4.8MM **Privately Held**
WEB: www.americanfabricators.com
SIC: 3441 Fabricated structural metal

(G-5841)
AMERICAN STAIR CORPORATION INC
3510 Calumet Ave (46320-1123)
PHONE..........................815 886-9600
Fax: 815 372-3683
Gordon Fitzsimmons, *President*
Ross Johnson, *Vice Pres*
Rocco Maggio, *Accounts Mgr*
EMP: 90 **EST:** 1956
SQ FT: 66,000
SALES (est): 29.3MM **Privately Held**
WEB: www.americanstair.com
SIC: 3446 Architectural metalwork; railings, bannisters, guards, etc.: made from metal pipe; stairs, staircases, stair treads: prefabricated metal

(G-5842)
AMORE FORTE LLC
Also Called: Amore Forte By Moni
7556 Monroe Ave (46324)
P.O. Box 4501 (46324-0501)
PHONE..........................702 763-2550
Stephanie M Baldwin, *Mng Member*
Danielle Kreachbaum,
EMP: 2
SALES: 150K **Privately Held**
SIC: 3911 5094 7389 Jewelry, precious metal; bracelets, precious metal; medals, precious or semiprecious metal; jewelry & precious stones;

(G-5843)
AMSTED RAIL COMPANY INC
Also Called: Asf Keystones
4831 Hohman Ave (46327-1579)
PHONE..........................219 931-1900
Bob Cantwell, *Vice Pres*
EMP: 100
SALES (corp-wide): 2.3B **Privately Held**
WEB: www.asf-keystone.com
SIC: 3743 Railroad equipment

HQ: Amsted Rail Company, Inc.
　311 S Wacker Dr Ste 5300
　Chicago IL 60606

(G-5844)
ASHE INDUSTRIES
17 Highland St (46320-2418)
PHONE..........................219 852-6040
Nico Ross, *Principal*
EMP: 2
SALES (est): 117.1K **Privately Held**
SIC: 3999 Manufacturing industries

(G-5845)
BAXTER HEALTHCARE CORP
7048 Hohman Ave (46324-1841)
PHONE..........................847 948-2000
EMP: 2
SALES (est): 86.6K **Privately Held**
SIC: 3841 Surgical & medical instruments

(G-5846)
BEATTY INTERNATIONAL INC (PA)
940 150th St (46327-1805)
PHONE..........................219 931-3000
William C Beatty, *President*
Phyllis Henkelmann, *Corp Secy*
Phillip Beatty, *Vice Pres*
Deborah Wilson, *Asst Treas*
Brian Beatty, *Asst Sec*
EMP: 25
SQ FT: 180,000
SALES (est): 12.3MM **Privately Held**
SIC: 3599 3542 3569 5084 Machine shop, jobbing & repair; punching & shearing machines; bridge or gate machinery, hydraulic; metalworking machinery

(G-5847)
BEATTY MACHINE & MFG CO
940 150th St (46327-1805)
PHONE..........................219 931-3000
Fax: 219 937-1662
William C Beatty, *President*
Brian Beatty, *Vice Pres*
Deborah Wilson, *Asst Treas*
EMP: 65 **EST:** 1917
SQ FT: 125,000
SALES (est): 7.8MM **Privately Held**
WEB: www.beattymachine.com
SIC: 3599 3542 Machine shop, jobbing & repair; punching & shearing machines
PA: Beatty International, Inc
　940 150th St
　Hammond IN 46327

(G-5848)
BEEMSTERBOER SLAG CORP (PA)
3411 Sheffield Ave (46327-1004)
PHONE..........................219 931-7462
Fax: 219 931-7463
Steven Beemsterboer, *President*
Dave Oram, *General Mgr*
Alan Beemsterboer, *Principal*
Michael Beemsterboer, *Vice Pres*
Mike Beemsterboer, *Vice Pres*
EMP: 25 **EST:** 1933
SQ FT: 1,200
SALES (est): 27.6MM **Privately Held**
SIC: 3295 Minerals, ground or treated

(G-5849)
BEEMSTERBOER SLAG CORP
3411 Sheffield Ave (46327-1004)
PHONE..........................219 931-7462
Peter Beemsterboer, *Manager*
EMP: 50
SALES (corp-wide): 27.6MM **Privately Held**
SIC: 3471 3295 Finishing, metals or formed products; minerals, ground or treated
PA: Beemsterboer Slag Corp.
　3411 Sheffield Ave
　Hammond IN 46327
　219 931-7462

(G-5850)
BEMCOR INC
940 150th St (46327-1805)
PHONE..........................219 937-1600
Fax: 219 937-1661
Willian C Beatty, *CEO*
Daniel J Lazar, *President*

Phyllis Henkelmann, *Corp Secy*
Brian Beatty, *Vice Pres*
Troy Reader, *Purch Agent*
EMP: 15
SQ FT: 18,000
SALES (est): 4.5MM **Privately Held**
SIC: 3569 3599 5084 3542 Bridge or gate machinery, hydraulic; machine shop, jobbing & repair; metalworking machinery; machine tools, metal forming type; industrial trucks & tractors; cutlery
PA: Beatty International, Inc
　940 150th St
　Hammond IN 46327

(G-5851)
BETTER METAL SYSTEMS LLC
7604 Oakdale Ave (46324-3017)
PHONE..........................219 290-2539
EMP: 2
SALES (est): 182.1K **Privately Held**
SIC: 1081 Metal mining services

(G-5852)
BEVERLY TENT & AWNING CO
7126 Calumet Ave (46324-2406)
PHONE..........................219 931-3723
Fax: 219 931-6894
William Kaminski, *Owner*
EMP: 5
SALES (est): 376.7K **Privately Held**
SIC: 2394 7359 Awnings, fabric: made from purchased materials; party supplies rental services

(G-5853)
BIMBO BAKERIES USA INC
3420 179th St (46323-3050)
PHONE..........................219 844-0465
EMP: 24 **Privately Held**
SIC: 2051 Bakery: wholesale or wholesale/retail combined
HQ: Bimbo Bakeries Usa, Inc
　255 Business Center Dr # 200
　Horsham PA 19044
　215 347-5500

(G-5854)
BRENCO LLC (PA)
Also Called: Brenco Exotic Woods
2300 Michigan St (46320-1464)
PHONE..........................219 844-9570
Jeff Brennan,
▲ **EMP:** 2 **EST:** 2002
SQ FT: 80,000
SALES (est): 514.5K **Privately Held**
SIC: 2439 5023 Timbers, structural: laminated lumber; wood flooring

(G-5855)
CALUMET ABRASIVES CO INC
Also Called: Cabco
3039 169th Pl (46323-2346)
PHONE..........................219 844-2695
Fax: 219 989-4272
John G Anderson, *President*
▼ **EMP:** 30
SQ FT: 14,000
SALES (est): 10.4MM **Privately Held**
WEB: www.calumetabrasives.com
SIC: 3291 Abrasive wheels & grindstones, not artificial

(G-5856)
CALUMET BREWERIES INC
6535 Osborne Ave (46320-2998)
PHONE..........................219 845-2242
Fax: 219 845-2338
John J Kiernan, *President*
Mark J Kiernan, *Vice Pres*
Damain Walker, *Sales Mgr*
Daniel Guzek, *Manager*
EMP: 45
SQ FT: 80,000
SALES (est): 7.1MM **Privately Held**
WEB: www.calbrew.com
SIC: 2082 5149 5181 Beer (alcoholic beverage); groceries & related products; beer & ale

(G-5857)
CARESTONE INC
1646 Summer St (46320-2218)
PHONE..........................219 853-0600
EMP: 50
SQ FT: 40,000

SALES (est): 490.6K **Privately Held**
SIC: 2842 Mfg Mill Type Cylinders

(G-5858)
CARGILL INCORPORATED
1100 Indianapolis Blvd (46320-1019)
PHONE..............................402 533-4227
Jim Fritz, *Principal*
EMP: 260
SALES (corp-wide): 88.8B **Privately Held**
WEB: www.cargill.com
SIC: 0723 2075 2046 2048 Corn drying
services; hay baling services; cotton seed
delinting services; flour milling custom
services; soybean oil, cake or meal; corn
oil, refined; corn oil, meal; gluten meal;
high fructose corn syrup (HFCS); prepared feeds; meat packing plants; beef
products from beef slaughtered on site;
pork products from pork slaughtered on
site; poultry slaughtering & processing
PA: Cargill, Incorporated
15407 Mcginty Rd W
Wayzata MN 55391
952 742-7575

(G-5859)
CENTRIFUGE CHICAGO CORPORATION
1721 Summer St (46320-2235)
PHONE..............................219 852-5200
Douglas E Rivich, *President*
John Bargoz, *Vice Pres*
EMP: 7
SQ FT: 3,500
SALES (est): 1.1MM **Privately Held**
SIC: 3569 Centrifuges, industrial

(G-5860)
CHICAGO COLOR GRAPHICS
7258 Forest Ave (46324-1842)
PHONE..............................312 856-1433
Paul Dombrowski, *President*
EMP: 5
SALES (est): 500K **Privately Held**
SIC: 7389 2752 2396 Printing broker;
commercial printing, lithographic; automo-
tive & apparel trimmings

(G-5861)
CHINET COMPANY
6629 Indianapolis Blvd (46320-2833)
PHONE..............................219 989-7040
EMP: 2 **EST:** 2010
SALES (est): 120K **Privately Held**
SIC: 2491 Wood Preserving

(G-5862)
CJ PRINTING
9445 Indianapolis Blvd A (46322-2649)
PHONE..............................219 924-1685
Chuck Pease, *Owner*
Margaret Ellis, *Treasurer*
Dave Luken, *Manager*
EMP: 4
SALES (est): 344.3K **Privately Held**
SIC: 2752 Commercial printing, offset

(G-5863)
CKMT ASSOCIATES INC
Also Called: Calumet Press, The
6405 Olcott St (46320-2835)
PHONE..............................219 924-2820
Philip E Cartwright PHD, *President*
Dennis Van Kooten, *Purch Dir*
Konnie Kuiper, *Shareholder*
Nancy Minas, *Shareholder*
Randy Minas, *Shareholder*
EMP: 28 **EST:** 1938
SQ FT: 6,200
SALES: 1.3MM **Privately Held**
SIC: 2711 2791 2789 2752 Commercial
printing & newspaper publishing com-
bined; typesetting; bookbinding & related
work; commercial printing, lithographic

(G-5864)
CONOPCO INC
1200 Calumet Ave (46320-1015)
PHONE..............................219 659-3200
Louie Gibuffone, *Manager*
EMP: 150
SQ FT: 25,000
SALES (corp-wide): 63B **Privately Held**
SIC: 2844 Toilet preparations

HQ: Conopco, Inc.
700 Sylvan Ave
Englewood Cliffs NJ 07632
201 894-2727

(G-5865)
CONTROL CONSULTANTS OF AMERICA (PA)
Also Called: Ccoa of Indiana
3800 179th St (46323-3035)
PHONE..............................219 989-3311
Robert J Lewis, *CEO*
John R Coyne, *President*
Donald H Henrich, *Treasurer*
Patrick S Dolan, *Admin Sec*
Michael Khoury,
▼ **EMP:** 3
SALES (est): 403.4K **Privately Held**
SIC: 3613 3625 Control panels, electric;
control equipment, electric; industrial con-
trols: push button, selector switches, pilot

(G-5866)
CR PUBLICATIONS
640 Conkey St (46324-1142)
P.O. Box 2097 (46323-0097)
PHONE..............................219 931-6700
Jake Jacobs, *Manager*
EMP: 5
SALES (est): 420.6K **Privately Held**
SIC: 2721 2731 8748 Magazines: pub-
lishing only, not printed on site; book pub-
lishing; business consulting

(G-5867)
CUSTOM DRAPERIES OF INDIANA
Also Called: Hammond Drapery
7205 Calumet Ave (46324-2407)
PHONE..............................219 924-2500
Fax: 219 931-3409
Samuel R Gershman, *President*
EMP: 9
SALES (est): 530K **Privately Held**
WEB: www.custom-draperies.com
SIC: 2391 2591 2431 Draperies, plastic &
textile: from purchased materials; drapery
hardware & blinds & shades; millwork

(G-5868)
D & D INDUSTRIES INC
Also Called: Calumet Surface Hardening
6805 Mccook Ave (46323-1554)
PHONE..............................219 844-5600
Fax: 219 845-1046
Don Doffin, *President*
EMP: 9 **EST:** 1962
SQ FT: 12,500
SALES: 1.8MM **Privately Held**
SIC: 3398 Brazing (hardening) of metal

(G-5869)
DAVIES-IMPERIAL COATINGS INC
1275 State St (46320-1633)
P.O. Box 790 (46325-0790)
PHONE..............................219 933-0877
Fax: 219 932-4201
Davies Donn T, *President*
Adele Davies, *Vice Pres*
Joann Davies, *Admin Sec*
▲ **EMP:** 40
SQ FT: 55,000
SALES (est): 12.7MM **Privately Held**
WEB: www.daviesimperial.com
SIC: 2851 2819 2891 Paints & paint addi-
tives; lacquers, varnishes, enamels &
other coatings; industrial inorganic chemi-
cals; adhesives & sealants

(G-5870)
DIETRICH INDUSTRIES INC
1435 165th St (46320-2816)
PHONE..............................219 931-3741
Fax: 219 931-2269
Tim Short, *Manager*
EMP: 180
SALES (corp-wide): 3.5B **Publicly Held**
WEB: www.dietrichmetalframing.com
SIC: 3316 3312 3444 3443 Cold finishing
of steel shapes; blast furnaces & steel
mills; sheet metalwork; fabricated plate
work (boiler shop)

HQ: Dietrich Industries, Inc.
200 W Old Wilson Brdge Rd
Worthington OH 43085
800 873-2604

(G-5871)
DOVER CHEMICAL CORPORATION
Also Called: Hammond Works
3000 Sheffield Ave (46327-1013)
PHONE..............................219 852-0042
Robert Glaze, *Principal*
Joyce Gorczynski, *Human Resources*
Mike Bonomo, *Manager*
Mike Prising, *Info Tech Mgr*
Dave Fulton, *Technology*
EMP: 31
SALES (corp-wide): 1.1B **Privately Held**
SIC: 2819 2869 Industrial inorganic chem-
icals; industrial organic chemicals
HQ: Dover Chemical Corporation
3676 Davis Rd Nw
Dover OH 44622
330 343-7711

(G-5872)
DOW THEORY FORECASTS INC
7412 Calumet Ave Ste 1 (46324-2692)
PHONE..............................219 931-6480
Fax: 219 931-6487
Charles Carlson, *CEO*
Cheryl Evans, *Admin Sec*
EMP: 35 **EST:** 1946
SQ FT: 17,000
SALES (est): 3MM **Privately Held**
WEB: www.dowtheory.com
SIC: 2741 7311 Business service newslet-
ters: publishing & printing; advertising
agencies
PA: Horizon Management Services Inc
7412 Calumet Ave
Hammond IN 46324

(G-5873)
E Z CHOICE
5529 Calumet Ave (46320-2019)
PHONE..............................219 852-4281
Issa Batarseh, *Principal*
EMP: 2
SALES (est): 145.1K **Privately Held**
SIC: 1389 Excavating slush pits & cellars

(G-5874)
ECO SERVICES OPERATIONS CORP
2000 Michigan St (46320-1462)
PHONE..............................219 932-7651
Greg Yates, *Branch Mgr*
EMP: 42
SALES (corp-wide): 1.4B **Publicly Held**
WEB: www.food.us.rhodia.com
SIC: 2819 2812 2865 2869 Boric acid;
phosphates, except fertilizers: defluori-
nated & ammoniated; soda ash, sodium
carbonate (anhydrous); phenol, alkylated
& cumene; diphenylamines; isocyanates;
fluorinated hydrocarbon gases; silicones;
chemical preparations
HQ: Eco Services Operations Corp.
2002 Timberloch Pl
The Woodlands TX 77380
844 812-1812

(G-5875)
ECONOMY SIGNS INC
546 Conkey St (46324-1153)
PHONE..............................219 932-1233
Fax: 219 932-2741
Walt Swets, *President*
▲ **EMP:** 7
SALES (est): 708.1K **Privately Held**
SIC: 5099 3993 Signs, except electric;
signs & advertising specialties

(G-5876)
ELECTRIC MOTOR SERVICES INC (PA)
6350 Indianapolis Blvd (46320-2231)
PHONE..............................219 931-2850
Joseph Kotso, *President*
Hector Graciano, *President*
Albert Burgos, *Vice Pres*
Michael Kotso, *Admin Sec*
EMP: 36
SQ FT: 40,000

SALES (est): 10.8MM **Privately Held**
SIC: 7694 Electric motor repair

(G-5877)
ELECTRO-TECH INC
5334 Sohl Ave (46320-1615)
PHONE..............................219 937-0826
Fax: 219 937-3744
Pete Bambic, *President*
Rudy Bambic, *Vice Pres*
EMP: 8 **EST:** 1998
SALES (est): 770K **Privately Held**
SIC: 3599 Custom machinery

(G-5878)
ELEPHANT ENTERPRISES
7618 Tapper Ave (46324-3021)
PHONE..............................248 366-5383
EMP: 2
SALES (est): 62.9K **Privately Held**
SIC: 2711 Newspapers

(G-5879)
FEHRING F N & SON PRINTERS
Also Called: Fehring Printers
7336 Calumet Ave (46324-2620)
PHONE..............................219 933-0439
Fax: 219 931-8814
Frank N Fehring, *Owner*
EMP: 3 **EST:** 1937
SQ FT: 5,000
SALES (est): 300K **Privately Held**
SIC: 2752 2759 Commercial printing, off-
set; letterpress printing

(G-5880)
FLAT ROCK
6732 Calumet Ave (46324-1646)
PHONE..............................219 852-5262
Kevin Hardesty, *Principal*
EMP: 4
SALES (est): 399.3K **Privately Held**
SIC: 2599 Bar, restaurant & cafeteria furni-
ture

(G-5881)
FLYING TURTLE PUBLISHING LLC
7216 Birch Ave (46324-2449)
PHONE..............................219 221-8488
Mari L Barnes, *Administration*
EMP: 2 **EST:** 2010
SALES (est): 103.8K **Privately Held**
SIC: 2741 Miscellaneous publishing

(G-5882)
FUENTES DISTRIBUTING
6811 New Hampshire Ave (46323-1959)
PHONE..............................219 808-2147
Dave Fuentes, *Owner*
EMP: 2
SALES (est): 171.3K **Privately Held**
SIC: 3537 Trucks: freight, baggage, etc.:
industrial, except mining

(G-5883)
H A INDUSTRIES
4527 Columbia Ave (46327-1666)
PHONE..............................219 931-6304
Fax: 219 931-6050
Dick Mork, *President*
◆ **EMP:** 8
SALES (est): 1.2MM **Privately Held**
SIC: 3999 Barber & beauty shop equip-
ment

(G-5884)
HAMMOND GROUP INC (PA)
Also Called: Halstab
1414 Field St Bldg B (46320-2678)
P.O. Box 6408 (46325-6408)
PHONE..............................219 931-9360
Fax: 219 937-2372
Terry Murphy, *President*
Kenneth Reed, *Counsel*
Gordon C Beckley, *Vice Pres*
Charles T Miller, *CFO*
Peter F Murphy III, *Treasurer*
◆ **EMP:** 33 **EST:** 1930
SQ FT: 22,000
SALES (est): 33.3MM **Privately Held**
WEB: www.hmndgroup.com
SIC: 2819 Lead compounds or salts, inor-
ganic, not used in pigments

(G-5885)
HAMMOND GROUP INC
Also Called: Halox Division
6530 Schneider St (46320-2900)
PHONE..................................219 933-1560
Ray Rex, *Branch Mgr*
EMP: 38
SALES (corp-wide): 33.3MM **Privately Held**
WEB: www.hmndgroup.com
SIC: 2816 2865 2851 Inorganic pigments; cyclic crudes & intermediates; paints & allied products
PA: Hammond Group, Inc.
 1414 Field St Bldg B
 Hammond IN 46320
 219 931-9360

(G-5886)
HAMMOND GROUP INC
Also Called: Hammond Lead Products
2323 165th St (46320-2906)
P.O. Box 6408 (46325-6408)
PHONE..................................219 845-0031
Sudhir Patel, *Branch Mgr*
EMP: 24
SALES (corp-wide): 33.3MM **Privately Held**
WEB: www.hmndgroup.com
SIC: 3441 3356 Expansion joints (structural shapes), iron or steel; nonferrous rolling & drawing
PA: Hammond Group, Inc.
 1414 Field St Bldg B
 Hammond IN 46320
 219 931-9360

(G-5887)
HAMMOND LEAD PRODUCTS LLC
1414 Field St Bldg B (46320-2678)
PHONE..................................219 931-9360
Sudhir Patel, *President*
▲ EMP: 7
SALES (est): 300.5K
SALES (corp-wide): 33.3MM **Privately Held**
SIC: 3356 Lead & lead alloy: rolling, drawing or extruding
PA: Hammond Group, Inc.
 1414 Field St Bldg B
 Hammond IN 46320
 219 931-9360

(G-5888)
HAMMOND STEEL COMPONENTS LLC
3200 Sheffield Ave (46327-1001)
PHONE..................................630 816-1343
EMP: 2
SALES (est): 217.1K **Privately Held**
SIC: 3315 Steel wire & related products

(G-5889)
HANGER PRSTHETCS & ORTHO INC
7324 Indianapolis Blvd (46324-2908)
PHONE..................................219 844-2021
Fax: 219 989-9690
Brian Steinbeger, *Manager*
EMP: 10
SALES (corp-wide): 1B **Publicly Held**
SIC: 3842 5999 Limbs, artificial; orthopedic & prosthesis applications
HQ: Hanger Prosthetics & Orthotics, Inc.
 10910 Domain Dr Ste 300
 Austin TX 78758
 512 777-3800

(G-5890)
HARVEST PETROLEUM INC
9518 Primrose Ln (46321-3614)
PHONE..................................219 924-8236
Paul Runick Jr, *President*
EMP: 2
SALES (est): 145.8K **Privately Held**
SIC: 3731 Drilling & production platforms, floating (oil & gas)

(G-5891)
HENRY PRATT COMPANY LLC
403 Conkey St (46324-1116)
PHONE..................................219 931-0405
Scott Burda, *Buyer*
Kim Shelton, *Manager*

EMP: 12
SALES (corp-wide): 826MM **Publicly Held**
SIC: 3491 Industrial valves
HQ: Henry Pratt Company, Llc
 401 S Highland Ave
 Aurora IL 60506
 630 844-4000

(G-5892)
HETTY INCORPORATED
Also Called: Miss Print
6937 Calumet Ave (46324-2045)
PHONE..................................219 933-0833
Fax: 219 937-4883
Rick Baltensberger, *Principal*
EMP: 5
SALES (est): 420.8K
SALES (corp-wide): 739.7K **Privately Held**
SIC: 2752 7336 2791 2789 Commercial printing, offset; graphic arts & related design; typesetting; bookbinding & related work
PA: Hetty Incorporated
 8244 Calumet Ave
 Munster IN 46321
 219 836-2517

(G-5893)
HOOSIER ROLL SHOP SERVICES LLC
7020 Cline Ave (46323-2502)
PHONE..................................219 844-8077
Fax: 219 844-8095
Anthony Tauber,
Brian Majcher,
Roger Toczek,
EMP: 14
SALES (est): 1.5MM **Privately Held**
SIC: 3547 Rolling mill machinery

(G-5894)
HORIZON MANAGEMENT SERVICES (PA)
7412 Calumet Ave (46324-2622)
PHONE..................................219 852-3200
Robert T Evans, *CEO*
Richard Moroney, *Vice Pres*
Shelby Cavanaugh, *Marketing Staff*
Thomas Hathoot, *Officer*
Cheryl Evans, *Admin Sec*
EMP: 30
SQ FT: 18,000
SALES (est): 2.4MM **Privately Held**
WEB: www.lowpricedstocks.com
SIC: 2741 Business service newsletters: publishing & printing

(G-5895)
HORIZON PUBLISHING COMPANY LLC
7412 Calumet Ave Ste 100 (46324-2622)
PHONE..................................219 852-3200
Robert T Evans, *President*
EMP: 25
SALES (est): 3.3MM **Privately Held**
WEB: www.horizonpublishing.com
SIC: 7389 6282 2731 2721 Hotel & motel reservation service; investment advice; book publishing; periodicals

(G-5896)
HUHTAMAKI INC
Also Called: Huhtamaki Foodservice
6629 Indianapolis Blvd (46320-2833)
PHONE..................................219 972-4264
Rich Blastic, *Branch Mgr*
Chris Quist, *Maintence Staff*
EMP: 110
SQ FT: 26,000
SALES (corp-wide): 35.2B **Privately Held**
WEB: www.huhtamaki.com
SIC: 2621 2823 2671 Molded pulp products; cellulosic manmade fibers; packaging paper & plastics film, coated & laminated
HQ: Huhtamaki, Inc.
 9201 Packaging Dr
 De Soto KS 66018
 913 583-3025

(G-5897)
IES SUBSIDIARY HOLDINGS INC
1825 Summer St (46320-2237)
PHONE..................................219 937-0100
Fran Finn, *Manager*
EMP: 54 **Publicly Held**
WEB: www.magnetech.com
SIC: 3264 7694 Magnets, permanent: ceramic or ferrite; motor repair services
HQ: Ies Subsidiary Holdings, Inc
 5433 Westheimer Rd # 500
 Houston TX 77056
 713 860-1500

(G-5898)
ILLIANA REMEDIAL ACTION INC
6550 Osborne Ave (46320-2913)
PHONE..................................219 844-4862
James Hough, *President*
EMP: 9
SQ FT: 4,500
SALES (est): 282K **Privately Held**
SIC: 1442 Sand mining

(G-5899)
INDUSTRIAL TOOL & MFG CO
4901 Calumet Ave (46327-1898)
PHONE..................................219 932-8670
Fax: 219 932-0519
Stanley Sobilo Jr, *President*
EMP: 7 EST: 1947
SQ FT: 14,000
SALES (est): 880K **Privately Held**
SIC: 3599 Machine shop, jobbing & repair

(G-5900)
INSULATION FABRICATORS INC (HQ)
2501 165th St Ste 3 (46320-2933)
PHONE..................................219 845-2008
Ted McNabb, *President*
Nick Oakley, *Foreman/Supr*
Mark Horvat, *VP Sales*
EMP: 70 EST: 1979
SQ FT: 15,000
SALES (est): 71.8MM
SALES (corp-wide): 433.8MM **Privately Held**
WEB: www.insulationfabricators.com
SIC: 5033 3296 Mineral wool insulation materials; fiberglass insulation
PA: Distribution International, Inc.
 9000 Railwood Dr
 Houston TX 77078
 713 428-3740

(G-5901)
INTERNATIONAL PAPER COMPANY
2501 165th St Ste 3 (46320-2933)
PHONE..................................219 844-6509
Fax: 219 844-1277
Phil Glenn, *Manager*
EMP: 133
SALES (corp-wide): 21.7B **Publicly Held**
WEB: www.internationalpaper.com
SIC: 2621 Paper mills
PA: International Paper Company
 6400 Poplar Ave
 Memphis TN 38197
 901 419-9000

(G-5902)
JANETTE WALKER
1050 Eaton St (46320-2613)
PHONE..................................219 937-9160
Jeanette Walker, *Principal*
EMP: 2
SALES (est): 77.1K **Privately Held**
SIC: 3911 Jewelry, precious metal

(G-5903)
JUPITER ALUMINUM CORPORATION (PA)
1745 165th St Ste 6 (46320-2800)
PHONE..................................219 932-3322
Fax: 219 933-2720
Dietrich M Gross, *CEO*
Loren Jahn, *CFO*
▲ EMP: 200
SQ FT: 7,000
SALES (est): 156.4MM **Privately Held**
SIC: 3353 3354 Aluminum sheet, plate & foil; coils, rod, extruded, aluminum

(G-5904)
KAPLAN ENTERPRISES INC
4334 Calumet Ave (46320-1135)
PHONE..................................219 933-7993
EMP: 3
SALES (est): 183.1K **Privately Held**
SIC: 2899 Fireworks
PA: Kaplan Enterprises, Inc
 3740 179th St
 Hammond IN 46323

(G-5905)
KEIL CHEMICAL CORPORATION
3000 Sheffield Ave (46327-1013)
PHONE..................................219 931-2630
Fax: 219 931-0895
Dwain Colvin, *President*
Scott Warner, *Engineer*
Dan Atteberry, *Info Tech Mgr*
EMP: 100
SALES (est): 9.6MM
SALES (corp-wide): 1.1B **Privately Held**
WEB: www.doverchem.com
SIC: 2911 2992 Fuel additives; lubricating oils & greases
HQ: Dover Chemical Corporation
 3676 Davis Rd Nw
 Dover OH 44622
 330 343-7711

(G-5906)
LANSING METALLIZING & GRINDING
Also Called: Lansing Metaliizing & Grinding
4742 Calumet Ave (46327-1610)
PHONE..................................219 931-1785
Fax: 219 931-6423
Thomas Alb, *President*
Cheryl Alb, *Vice Pres*
Rayn Alb, *Treasurer*
EMP: 2 EST: 1968
SQ FT: 6,200
SALES (est): 211.4K **Privately Held**
WEB: www.lansingmetalizing.com
SIC: 3479 3599 Coating of metals & formed products; machine shop, jobbing & repair

(G-5907)
LEAR CORPORATION
1401 165th St (46320-2816)
PHONE..................................219 852-0014
Fax: 219 852-0018
Dave Brown, *Plant Mgr*
EMP: 500
SALES (corp-wide): 20.4B **Publicly Held**
WEB: www.lear.com
SIC: 3714 2531 Motor vehicle parts & accessories; public building & related furniture
PA: Lear Corporation
 21557 Telegraph Rd
 Southfield MI 48033
 248 447-1500

(G-5908)
LINDE GAS NORTH AMERICA LLC
3930 Michigan St (46323-1203)
PHONE..................................219 989-9304
Jack Taylor, *Plant Mgr*
Jim Flack, *Manager*
EMP: 19
SALES (corp-wide): 20.1B **Privately Held**
SIC: 2813 Oxygen, compressed or liquefied
HQ: Linde Gas North America Llc
 200 Somerset Corp Blvd # 7000
 Bridgewater NJ 08807

(G-5909)
M M PALTECH INC
518 Hoffman St (46327-1516)
PHONE..................................219 932-5308
Clif Moore, *Principal*
EMP: 3
SALES (est): 238K **Privately Held**
SIC: 2448 Pallets, wood & wood with metal

(G-5910)
MAD HATTERS UNLIMITED
4846 Pine Ave (46327-1843)
PHONE..................................219 852-6011
Fred Denton, *Partner*
Brett Denton, *Partner*

Diane Denton, *Partner*
Beth Volpe, *Partner*
EMP: 3
SALES (est): 210K **Privately Held**
SIC: 3199 2353 Leather goods; hats, caps
& millinery

(G-5911)
MAGNETECH INDUSTRIAL SVC
1825 Summer St (46320-2237)
PHONE.................................219 937-0100
Fax: 219 933-1209
Mauder Bill, *Traffic Mgr*
Fran Finn, *Manager*
EMP: 6 EST: 2010
SALES (est): 624.9K **Privately Held**
SIC: 7694 Electric motor repair

(G-5912)
MARIE S EMBROIDERY
7132 Madison Ave (46324-1908)
PHONE.................................219 931-2561
Marie Gruszka, *Owner*
EMP: 2
SALES (est): 96.4K **Privately Held**
WEB: www.mariesembroidery.com
SIC: 2395 2759 Embroidery & art needle-
work; commercial printing

(G-5913)
MARIOS ATHLETIC ZONE
6942 Indianapolis Blvd (46324-2206)
PHONE.................................219 845-1800
Mario Porras, *Owner*
EMP: 4
SALES (est): 348.9K **Privately Held**
SIC: 3149 Athletic shoes, except rubber or
plastic

(G-5914)
MATRIX NAC
Also Called: Matrix North American Cnstr
4508 Columbia Ave (46327-1665)
PHONE.................................219 931-6600
Jason W Turner, *President*
D Troy Blair, *Vice Pres*
James C Faroh, *Vice Pres*
Douglas J Montalbano, *Vice Pres*
Terry D Stewart, *Vice Pres*
EMP: 14
SALES (est): 2.8MM **Privately Held**
SIC: 1541 5051 1389 3621 Industrial
buildings, new construction; metal wires,
ties, cables & screening; construction, re-
pair & dismantling services; electric motor
& generator parts; general warehousing

(G-5915)
MELISSA KING ✪
3542 170th Pl (46323-2548)
PHONE.................................219 989-1497
EMP: 2 EST: 2017
SALES (est): 62.3K **Privately Held**
SIC: 2084 Wines, Brandy, And Brandy
Spirits, Nsk

(G-5916)
MILLS ELECTRIC CO INC
4828 Calumet Ave (46327-1899)
PHONE.................................219 931-3114
Fax: 219 931-9431
Richard Mills Jr, *President*
Richard Mills III, *Vice Pres*
EMP: 9
SQ FT: 10,000
SALES (est): 1.3MM **Privately Held**
SIC: 7694 5084 Rewinding services; elec-
tric motor repair; pumps & pumping
equipment

(G-5917)
**MOLD REMOVAL TEAM OF
HAMMOND**
6938 Grand Ave (46323-2570)
PHONE.................................219 554-9719
EMP: 2 EST: 2011
SALES (est): 110K **Privately Held**
SIC: 3544 Mfg Dies/Tools/Jigs/Fixtures

(G-5918)
**MOTION & CONTROL ENTPS
LLC**
Also Called: Primet Fluid Power
7917 New Jersey Ave (46323-3040)
PHONE.................................219 844-4224

Fax: 219 844-4284
Timothy Hall, *President*
Daniel Lafontaine, *Opers Mgr*
Dan Lafontaine, *Purch Agent*
George Traicoff, *Sales Staff*
Bill Bestow, *Sales Associate*
EMP: 10
SALES (corp-wide): 57.5MM **Privately
Held**
SIC: 5084 7699 3629 Hydraulic systems
equipment & supplies; pneumatic tools &
equipment; hydraulic equipment repair;
electronic generation equipment
HQ: Motion & Control Enterprises Llc
100 Williams Dr
Zelienople PA 16063
724 452-6000

(G-5919)
MR TINTZ
6806 Indianapolis Blvd D (46324-1739)
PHONE.................................219 844-5500
John Mancilla, *Principal*
EMP: 2 EST: 2009
SALES (est): 160.7K **Privately Held**
SIC: 3211 Window glass, clear & colored

(G-5920)
MUNSTER STEEL CO INC
1501 Huehn St (46327-0001)
PHONE.................................219 924-5198
Fax: 219 924-1794
Jeanne Robbins, *President*
Patricia Martin, *Vice Pres*
Debbie Dorsey, *Marketing Staff*
EMP: 43
SQ FT: 200,000
SALES (est): 12.2MM **Privately Held**
SIC: 3441 Building components, structural
steel

(G-5921)
**NIAGARA LASALLE
CORPORATION**
Also Called: Fluid Power Division
1412 150th St (46327-1743)
PHONE.................................800 262-2558
Dean Duncan, *Opers Mgr*
Edwina Mierwa, *Human Res Mgr*
Amy Seiluns, *Sales Staff*
Ken Pritchard, *Manager*
Mike Vercimak, *Manager*
EMP: 35
SQ FT: 50,000
SALES (corp-wide): 491.1MM **Privately
Held**
WEB: www.niag.com
SIC: 3316 3714 3398 3312 Bars, steel,
cold finished, from purchased hot-rolled;
motor vehicle parts & accessories; metal
heat treating; blast furnaces & steel mills
HQ: Niagara Lasalle Corporation
1412 150th St
Hammond IN 46327
219 853-6000

(G-5922)
**NIAGARA LASALLE
CORPORATION (HQ)**
1412 150th St (46327-1743)
PHONE.................................219 853-6000
Joel Hawthorne, *CEO*
Michael Salamon, *President*
Michael Burchwell, *General Mgr*
Kevin Kirkland, *General Mgr*
David Ascher, *Vice Pres*
▲ **EMP:** 180
SALES (est): 226.8MM
SALES (corp-wide): 491.1MM **Privately
Held**
WEB: www.niagaralasalle.com
SIC: 3316 Bars, steel, cold finished, from
purchased hot-rolled
PA: Specialty Steel Works Incorporated
1412 150th St
Hammond IN 46327
877 289-2277

(G-5923)
**NORTHWEST ALUM
FABRICATORS INC**
6103 Kennedy Ave (46323-1045)
PHONE.................................219 844-4354
George Heldt Jr, *President*
EMP: 8 EST: 2003

SALES (est): 1.1MM **Privately Held**
SIC: 3441 Fabricated structural metal

(G-5924)
O-M DISTRIBUTORS INC
Also Called: Tortillas Nuevo Leon
724 Hoffman St (46327-1827)
PHONE.................................219 853-1900
Fax: 219 853-1903
Oscar Martinez, *President*
Maria S Martinez, *Corp Secy*
◆ **EMP:** 35 EST: 1979
SQ FT: 50,000
SALES: 7MM **Privately Held**
SIC: 2099 Tortillas, fresh or refrigerated

(G-5925)
P & H IRON & SUPPLY INC
1435 Summer St (46320-2213)
PHONE.................................219 853-0240
Fax: 219 853-0240
Richard Hughes, *Manager*
Lori Kovacich, *Admin Sec*
EMP: 10
SALES (est): 1.6MM **Privately Held**
SIC: 5093 3341 Metal scrap & waste ma-
terials; secondary nonferrous metals

(G-5926)
PERIMETER SOLUTIONS LP
Halox
1326 Summer St (46320-2240)
PHONE.................................219 933-1560
Fax: 219 933-1570
Micheal Wagner, *Branch Mgr*
EMP: 120 **Privately Held**
WEB: www.hmndgroup.com
SIC: 2819 Lead compounds or salts, inor-
ganic, not used in pigments
HQ: Perimeter Solutions Lp
373 Marshall Ave
Saint Louis MO 63119
314 983-7500

(G-5927)
PICKLE BITES
7451 Olcott Ave (46323-2610)
PHONE.................................219 902-6315
EMP: 2 EST: 2015
SALES (est): 124.3K **Privately Held**
SIC: 2035 Pickled fruits & vegetables

(G-5928)
QUAD PLUS LLC
3535 165th St (46323-1226)
PHONE.................................219 844-9214
Raul Torres, *Branch Mgr*
EMP: 22
SALES (corp-wide): 19MM **Privately
Held**
SIC: 3566 Speed changers, drives & gears
PA: Quad Plus Llc
1921 Cherry Hill Rd
Joliet IL 60433
815 740-0860

(G-5929)
QUALITY GRAPHICS CORP
7801 Northcote Ave (46324-3337)
PHONE.................................219 845-7084
John Harrigan, *President*
Wiliam Harrigan, *Vice Pres*
EMP: 5
SALES: 600K **Privately Held**
SIC: 2752 Commercial printing, litho-
graphic

(G-5930)
**QUANEX CORP LASALLE STEEL
DIV**
1412 150th St (46327-1743)
PHONE.................................219 853-6202
Fax: 219 853-6208
Frank Archer, *President*
EMP: 5 EST: 2012
SALES (est): 533.5K **Privately Held**
SIC: 3316 Cold finishing of steel shapes

(G-5931)
**R P S HYDRAULICS SALES &
SVC**
Also Called: RPS Hydraulic Sales & Service
3550 179th St Ste 7 (46323-3066)
PHONE.................................219 845-5526
Fax: 219 845-5699

▼ **EMP:** 24
SQ FT: 11,000
SALES (est): 4.6MM **Privately Held**
SIC: 3561 3494 3594 3593 Mfg
Pumps/Pumping Equip Mfg Valves/Pipe
Fittings Mfg Fluid Power Pump/Mtr Mfg
Fluid Power Cylinder

(G-5932)
**REFRACTORY SERVICE
CORPORATION**
4902 Calumet Ave (46327-1817)
P.O. Box 2276, East Chicago (46312-7276)
PHONE.................................219 853-0885
Fax: 219 937-9529
Jeff Tianchi, *Branch Mgr*
EMP: 25
SALES (est): 1.8MM
SALES (corp-wide): 15.6MM **Privately
Held**
SIC: 5085 3297 Refractory material; non-
clay refractories
PA: Refractory Service Corporation Inc
4900 Cline Ave
East Chicago IN 46312
219 397-7108

(G-5933)
RESCO PRODUCTS INC
5501 Kennedy Ave (46323-1168)
P.O. Box 2128 (46323-0128)
PHONE.................................219 844-7830
Frank Stumpo, *Principal*
EMP: 75
SALES (corp-wide): 216.3MM **Privately
Held**
SIC: 3297 Nonclay refractories
PA: Resco Products, Inc.
6600 Steubenville Pike # 1
Pittsburgh PA 15205
888 283-5505

(G-5934)
RHI US LTD
2929 Carlson Dr Ste 201 (46323-0018)
PHONE.................................219 237-2420
Phil Poulin, *President*
Joseph Plunkett, *Vice Pres*
◆ **EMP:** 2
SALES (est): 524K **Privately Held**
SIC: 3652 Pre-recorded records & tapes

(G-5935)
RMG CABINET
6809 Columbia Ave (46324-1600)
PHONE.................................219 712-6129
Robert M Gates, *President*
EMP: 2
SALES (est): 198.1K **Privately Held**
SIC: 2434 Wood kitchen cabinets

(G-5936)
**SCREW CONVEYOR
CORPORATION (PA)**
700 Hoffman St (46327-1827)
PHONE.................................219 931-1450
Fax: 219 931-0209
Garry M Abraham, *CEO*
Curtis F Abraham, *President*
Randy Block, *Vice Pres*
Walter W Geisler, *Vice Pres*
Richard G Young, *Admin Sec*
▼ **EMP:** 34 EST: 1933
SQ FT: 90,000
SALES (est): 31.2MM **Privately Held**
SIC: 3535 Conveyors & conveying equip-
ment

(G-5937)
**SCREW CONVEYOR PACIFIC
CORP (PA)**
700 Hoffman St (46327-1827)
PHONE.................................219 931-1450
Garry M Abraham, *CEO*
Curtis F Abraham, *President*
Randolph Block, *Vice Pres*
Richard G Young, *Admin Sec*
EMP: 36
SALES (est): 20.5MM **Privately Held**
WEB: www.screwconveyor.com
SIC: 3535 Conveyors & conveying equip-
ment

(G-5938)
SERVICE PUBLICATION INC
Also Called: Bargain Finder, The
7147 Kennedy Ave (46323-2226)
P.O. Box 1445, Portage (46368-9245)
PHONE..................................219 845-4445
Fax: 219 989-7173
Richard Paulsin, *President*
EMP: 2
SQ FT: 5,000
SALES (est): 951.4K Privately Held
SIC: 2711 2741 Newspapers: publishing only, not printed on site; miscellaneous publishing

(G-5939)
SILGAN CONTAINERS MFG CORP
2501 165th St Ste 2 (46320-2933)
PHONE..................................219 845-1500
Roger Mentz, *Branch Mgr*
EMP: 80
SALES (corp-wide): 4B Publicly Held
WEB: www.silgancontainers.com
SIC: 3411 Metal cans
HQ: Silgan Containers Manufacturing Corporation
21600 Oxnard St Ste 1600
Woodland Hills CA 91367

(G-5940)
SIMKO INDUSTRIAL FABRICATORS
4545 Ash Ave (46327-1622)
P.O. Box 2919, East Chicago (46312-7919)
PHONE..................................219 933-9100
Fax: 219 933-0980
Daniel Simko, *President*
EMP: 30
SQ FT: 25,000
SALES: 5MM Privately Held
WEB: www.simkofab.com
SIC: 3441 Fabricated structural metal

(G-5941)
SIMKO SONS INDUS REFRACTORIES
4545 Ash Ave (46327-1622)
P.O. Box 2919, East Chicago (46312-7919)
PHONE..................................219 933-9100
Daniel Simko, *President*
Elaine Simko, *Shareholder*
Jon Simko, *Shareholder*
EMP: 15
SQ FT: 50,000
SALES (est): 2MM Privately Held
SIC: 3297 Nonclay refractories

(G-5942)
SMART MACHINE INC
9941 Express Dr (46322-2610)
PHONE..................................219 922-0706
Michael Rohder, *President*
EMP: 6
SALES (est): 466K Privately Held
SIC: 3965 Fasteners

(G-5943)
SOUTH SHORE SLAG LLC (PA)
3411 Sheffield Ave (46327-1004)
PHONE..................................219 881-6544
Alan C Beemsterboer,
EMP: 18
SALES (est): 8.1MM Privately Held
SIC: 3295 Slag, crushed or ground

(G-5944)
SOUTHERN ELECTRIC COIL LLC
5025 Columbia Ave (46327-1759)
PHONE..................................219 931-5500
Ron Rossetto, *President*
Rich Skurka, *President*
Dennis Nardoni, *General Ptnr*
Greg Dubrick, *CFO*
▲ EMP: 50
SQ FT: 64,000
SALES (est): 12.6MM Privately Held
SIC: 3621 3677 Coils, for electric motors or generators; electronic coils, transformers & other inductors

(G-5945)
SPARKS BELTING COMPANY INC
3420 179th St 3b (46323-3050)
PHONE..................................800 451-4537
Jim Staley, *Regional Mgr*
EMP: 6
SALES (corp-wide): 596.1MM Privately Held
SIC: 3535 3568 3429 Conveyors & conveying equipment; power transmission equipment; manufactured hardware (general)
HQ: Sparks Belting Company, Inc.
3800 Stahl Dr Se
Grand Rapids MI 49546

(G-5946)
SPECIALTY STEEL WORKS INC (PA)
1412 150th St (46327-1743)
PHONE..................................877 289-2277
Joel Hawthorne, *CEO*
Michael Salamon, *COO*
Mike Eberth, *Vice Pres*
Anthony Verkruyse, *CFO*
Steven Doner, *Director*
EMP: 5
SALES (est): 491.1MM Privately Held
SIC: 3317 Tubes, seamless steel

(G-5947)
SWANEL INC
Also Called: Swanel Beverage
6044 Erie Ave (46320-2532)
P.O. Box 1186 (46325-1186)
PHONE..................................219 932-7676
Fax: 219 853-7441
Edward Roviaro, *President*
EMP: 65 EST: 1942
SQ FT: 10,000
SALES (est): 31.6MM Privately Held
WEB: www.swanel.com
SIC: 5078 5169 5145 2086 Beverage coolers; ice making machines; carbon dioxide; syrups, fountain; soft drinks: packaged in cans, bottles, etc.

(G-5948)
TAP-A-LITE INC
820 165th St (46324-1394)
PHONE..................................219 932-8067
Fax: 219 933-7036
William Hayden, *President*
Margaret Schmidt, *Corp Secy*
EMP: 25 EST: 1966
SQ FT: 10,000
SALES (est): 3.6MM
SALES (corp-wide): 3.6B Publicly Held
WEB: www.uhaul.com
SIC: 3679 3643 3699 3641 Harness assemblies for electronic use: wire or cable; plugs, electric; electrical equipment & supplies; electric lamps
HQ: U-Haul International, Inc.
2727 N Central Ave
Phoenix AZ 85004
602 263-6011

(G-5949)
THOMAS CUBIT INC
110 Brunswick St (46327-1553)
PHONE..................................219 933-0566
Fax: 219 931-5542
Thomas E Cubit II, *President*
Rosemarie Roesel, *Vice Pres*
EMP: 5 EST: 1946
SQ FT: 3,600
SALES (est): 543.4K Privately Held
SIC: 3599 3441 7692 3444 Machine shop, jobbing & repair; fabricated structural metal; welding repair; sheet metalwork

(G-5950)
THOMASVILLE FURNITURE INDS INC
442 165th St (46324-1328)
PHONE..................................336 476-2175
Salvador Balderas, *Principal*
EMP: 2 EST: 2016
SALES (est): 72.9K Privately Held
SIC: 2511 Wood household furniture

(G-5951)
TRI-STATE INDUSTRIES INC
4923 Columbia Ave (46327-1853)
PHONE..................................219 933-1710
Donald Keller, *President*
Frances Keller, *Admin Sec*
▲ EMP: 62
SQ FT: 35,000
SALES (est): 12.4MM Privately Held
SIC: 3548 3545 Welding apparatus; gas welding equipment; machine tool attachments & accessories

(G-5952)
TRIFAB & CONSTRUCTION INC (PA)
2433 167th St (46323-1422)
PHONE..................................219 845-1300
Fax: 219 845-4047
William O Stott, *President*
Robert Wajda, *Corp Secy*
Leonard Pysh, *Vice Pres*
▼ EMP: 6
SQ FT: 6,800
SALES: 2.5MM Privately Held
SIC: 1541 3053 7699 Renovation, remodeling & repairs: industrial buildings; gaskets & sealing devices; tank repair

(G-5953)
UNILEVER UNITED STATES INC
Also Called: Unilever Hpc USA
1200 Calumet Ave (46320-1097)
PHONE..................................219 659-3200
Brad Tieke, *Manager*
EMP: 32
SALES (corp-wide): 63B Privately Held
WEB: www.unilever.com
SIC: 2841 Soap & other detergents
HQ: Unilever United States, Inc.
700 Sylvan Ave
Englewood Cliffs NJ 07632
201 894-4000

(G-5954)
VANS INDUSTRIAL INC
231 Condit St (46320-1923)
PHONE..................................219 931-4881
Donald Van Camp, *President*
Frances V Camp, *Treasurer*
Renee Vancamp, *Admin Sec*
EMP: 25
SQ FT: 33,000
SALES (est): 6.3MM Privately Held
WEB: www.vansindustrial.com
SIC: 1711 3441 1611 Mechanical contractor; fabricated structural metal; general contractor, highway & street construction

(G-5955)
VERMETTE MACHINE COMPANY INC
7 143rd St (46327-1395)
PHONE..................................219 931-5406
Fax: 219 931-8652
Joseph Geisen, *President*
Edward Hayes, *Vice Pres*
EMP: 11 EST: 1946
SQ FT: 42,000
SALES (est): 2.9MM Privately Held
WEB: www.vermettlifts.com
SIC: 3537 Lift trucks, industrial: fork, platform, straddle, etc.

(G-5956)
VIDICOM CORPORATION
124 Sibley St (46320-1726)
PHONE..................................219 923-7475
Fax: 219 923-7475
John Jage, *CEO*
EMP: 17
SALES (est): 1MM Privately Held
SIC: 3651 1731 Television receiving sets; closed circuit television installation

(G-5957)
WATER TEC LLC
7020 Cline Ave (46323-2502)
P.O. Box 708, Chesterton (46304-0708)
PHONE..................................219 554-1790
William Tutlewski, *Principal*
EMP: 6
SALES (est): 600K Privately Held
SIC: 3589 Water treatment equipment, industrial

(G-5958)
AUTO WOOD RESTORATION
Also Called: Rodman's Auto Wood Restoration
24 S Pennsylvania St (46340-9600)
P.O. Box 86 (46340-0086)
PHONE..................................219 797-3775
James Rodman, *Owner*
EMP: 2 EST: 1974
SQ FT: 1,000
SALES (est): 190.6K Privately Held
WEB: www.autowood.net
SIC: 2426 Vehicle stock, hardwood

(G-5959)
BULK TRUCK & TRANSPORT SERVICE
659 W Lagrange Rd (47243-9433)
P.O. Box 28 (47243-0028)
PHONE..................................812 866-2155
Fax: 812 866-5765
Maurice Auxier, *President*
Dave Auxier, *Vice Pres*
Patrick Auxier, *Treasurer*
Darrell Auxier, *Shareholder*
Warren Auxier, *Admin Sec*
EMP: 28
SQ FT: 13,400
SALES (est): 7.2MM Privately Held
WEB: www.btandt.com
SIC: 3443 5012 7699 Tanks, standard or custom fabricated: metal plate; trucks, commercial; tank repair

(G-5960)
FAS PLASTIC ENTERPRISES INC
3408 W State Road 56 (47243-9063)
PHONE..................................812 265-2928
Fax: 812 265-2517
Frank G Mingione, *President*
L Steve Ball, *Vice Pres*
Steve Ball, *Vice Pres*
Frank J Mingione, *Vice Pres*
Carol L Lee, *Treasurer*
▲ EMP: 60
SQ FT: 25,000
SALES (est): 11.4MM Privately Held
WEB: www.fasplastics.com
SIC: 3089 Injection molding of plastics

(G-5961)
HANOVER MACHINE & TOOL INC
3408 W State Road 56 (47243-9063)
PHONE..................................812 265-6265
Frank G Mingione, *President*
Frank J Mingione, *Corp Secy*
EMP: 5
SQ FT: 4,000
SALES (est): 608.3K Privately Held
SIC: 3544 Special dies & tools

(G-5962)
LINDAS
4630 W Lea Ln (47243-9247)
PHONE..................................812 265-0099
Linda Ondera, *Manager*
EMP: 3
SALES (est): 293.4K Privately Held
SIC: 3559 Plastics working machinery

(G-5963)
PATES SLAUGHTERING & PROC
Off Hwy 62 (47243)
PHONE..................................812 866-4710
Tim Morrison, *Owner*
EMP: 6
SALES (est): 217.5K Privately Held
SIC: 0751 2011 2013 Slaughtering: custom livestock services; meat packing plants; sausages & other prepared meats

▲ = Import ▼=Export
◆ =Import/Export

Hardinsburg
Washington County

(G-5964)
DMRAY SAWMILL INC
6001 E Us Highway 150 (47125-6401)
PHONE.....................................812 723-1109
Donald W Ray, *President*
Marcella Ray, *Vice Pres*
EMP: 8
SALES: 1MM **Privately Held**
SIC: 2421 Lumber: rough, sawed or planed

(G-5965)
TURKEY ROOST PUBLISHING LLC
4500 S Calloway Dr (47125-6496)
PHONE.....................................402 972-6388
Daniel Fennessey, *Principal*
EMP: 2
SALES (est): 72.5K **Privately Held**
SIC: 2711 Newspapers

Harlan
Allen County

(G-5966)
BA ROMINES SHEET METAL INC
11827 Hood St (46743-5403)
P.O. Box 242 (46743-0242)
PHONE.....................................260 657-5500
Fax: 260 657-5551
Brent Romines, *President*
EMP: 35
SQ FT: 3,000
SALES (est): 9.5MM **Privately Held**
SIC: 3444 Ducts, sheet metal

(G-5967)
CAC WALL PANELS LP
14329 Rupert Rd (46743-7412)
PHONE.....................................260 437-4003
Leroy Eicher, *Managing Prtnr*
EMP: 5
SALES (est): 707.9K **Privately Held**
SIC: 2431 Panel work, wood

(G-5968)
CLOVER PRINTING LLC
16840 State Road 37 (46743-9789)
P.O. Box 224 (46743-0224)
PHONE.....................................260 657-3003
EMP: 2 **EST:** 2015
SALES (est): 88.6K **Privately Held**
SIC: 2759 Commercial printing

(G-5969)
CUMMINS REPAIR INC
11110 Scipio Rd (46743-9708)
PHONE.....................................260 632-4800
James Cummins, *President*
EMP: 3
SALES (est): 476.5K **Privately Held**
SIC: 7699 3519 Industrial machinery & equipment repair; internal combustion engines

(G-5970)
DUTCH MADE INC
Also Called: Kitchen/Bath Design Center
16836 State Road 37 (46743-9789)
PHONE.....................................260 657-3331
Fax: 260 657-3421
Don Prichard, *General Mgr*
Martin Graber, *Branch Mgr*
EMP: 4
SALES (est): 181.5K
SALES (corp-wide): 12.6MM **Privately Held**
SIC: 5399 2434 2431 2426 Catalog showrooms; wood kitchen cabinets; millwork; hardwood dimension & flooring mills
PA: Dutch Made Inc
10415 Roth Rd
Grabill IN 46741
260 657-3311

(G-5971)
FISHER SPECIALTIES INC
11515 Roberts Rd (46743)
PHONE.....................................260 385-8251
Fax: 260 657-5705
Joseph A Fisher, *President*
Terri L Fisher, *Admin Sec*
EMP: 8
SALES (est): 375.4K **Privately Held**
SIC: 2541 Counter & sink tops

(G-5972)
HARLAN CABINETS INC
12707 Spencerville Rd (46743-7497)
P.O. Box 307 (46743-0307)
PHONE.....................................260 657-5154
Fax: 260 657-5151
Simon Wagler, *President*
Omer Wagler, *President*
Michelle Hershberger, *Safety Mgr*
Lee Hershberger, *Marketing Staff*
Ray Wagler, *Admin Sec*
EMP: 60 **EST:** 1955
SQ FT: 100,000
SALES (est): 8.2MM **Privately Held**
WEB: www.harlancabinets.com
SIC: 2434 Wood kitchen cabinets

(G-5973)
KENT BRENNEKE
Also Called: Maumee Machine & Tool
14038 Scipio Rd (46743-9711)
PHONE.....................................260 446-5383
Kent Brenneke, *Owner*
EMP: 2 **EST:** 2000
SALES (est): 127.6K **Privately Held**
SIC: 3545 3451 3452 Machine tool accessories; screw machine products; bolts, nuts, rivets & washers; washers; bolts, metal

(G-5974)
OUR COUNTRY HOME ENTPS INC (PA)
Also Called: Sunequinox
12120 Water St (46743-5415)
P.O. Box 429, Grabill (46741-0429)
PHONE.....................................260 657-5605
Fax: 260 627-6311
Thomas Blake Sr, *President*
Tom Blake Jr, *Vice Pres*
Elmer Lengacher, *Plant Mgr*
Chris Rohrbaugh, *CFO*
▲ **EMP:** 96
SQ FT: 24,000
SALES: 29MM **Privately Held**
WEB: www.ochinc.com
SIC: 2541 3433 5074 Wood partitions & fixtures; solar heaters & collectors; heating equipment & panels, solar

Harmony
Clay County

(G-5975)
LAWSON WELDING SHOP
10516 N County 200e (47853)
P.O. Box 26 (47853-0026)
PHONE.....................................812 448-8984
Ronald Lawson, *Owner*
EMP: 2 **EST:** 1969
SQ FT: 7,000
SALES (est): 491.8K **Privately Held**
SIC: 7692 Welding repair

Hartford City
Blackford County

(G-5976)
3M COMPANY
304 S 075 E (47348-9796)
PHONE.....................................765 348-3200
Fax: 765 348-2793
Bob Cooper, *Engineer*
Ray Lorenv, *Branch Mgr*
Dan Carlson, *Manager*
Corey Martin, *Manager*
Doug Osborn, *Manager*
EMP: 270

SALES (corp-wide): 31.6B **Publicly Held**
WEB: www.mmm.com
SIC: 3291 2672 2671 Abrasive products; coated & laminated paper; packaging paper & plastics film, coated & laminated
PA: 3m Company
3m Center
Saint Paul MN 55144
651 733-1110

(G-5977)
ADM CUSTOM CREATIONS LLC
6 Belfast Ct (47348-9755)
PHONE.....................................765 499-0584
Allen D Johnson, *President*
EMP: 2 **EST:** 2014
SALES (est): 131.8K **Privately Held**
SIC: 3993 Signs & advertising specialties

(G-5978)
BRC RUBBER & PLASTICS INC
Also Called: Hartford City Division
1133 Gilkey Ave (47348-9549)
P.O. Box 611 (47348-0611)
PHONE.....................................260 693-2171
Fax: 765 348-4811
Dave Huffman, *Branch Mgr*
EMP: 160
SALES (corp-wide): 171.4MM **Privately Held**
SIC: 3061 3053 Automotive rubber goods (mechanical); gaskets, packing & sealing devices
PA: Brc Rubber & Plastics, Inc.
1029a W State Blvd
Fort Wayne IN 46808
260 693-2171

(G-5979)
D J INVESTMENTS INC
Also Called: Hearing Aid Outlet
1608 N Cherry St (47348-1356)
PHONE.....................................765 348-3558
Dan Ahrens, *Branch Mgr*
EMP: 3
SALES (corp-wide): 540K **Privately Held**
SIC: 5999 3842 Hearing aids; hearing aids
PA: D J Investments Inc
0660 E 200 S
Hartford City IN 47348
765 348-4381

(G-5980)
G & S RURAL WOODWORKING
1102 S 200 E (47348-8884)
PHONE.....................................765 348-7781
Legalzoom, *Principal*
EMP: 2
SALES (est): 75.1K **Privately Held**
SIC: 2431 Millwork

(G-5981)
HAROLD PRECISION PRODUCTS INC
Also Called: H P Products
1600 Gilkey Ave (47348-9549)
P.O. Box 350 (47348-0350)
PHONE.....................................765 348-2710
Fax: 765 348-2825
Michael Baughey, *CEO*
Dan Baughey, *President*
Mark Baughey, *Vice Pres*
Jim Toll, *QC Mgr*
Mike Baughey, *Executive*
EMP: 22
SQ FT: 70,000
SALES (est): 4.5MM **Privately Held**
WEB: www.p-h-p.net
SIC: 3469 Stamping metal for the trade

(G-5982)
HARTFORD CITY NEWS TIMES
Also Called: News-Times
100 N Jefferson St (47348-2201)
PHONE.....................................765 348-0110
Fax: 765 348-0112
Larry Perrotto, *President*
EMP: 161 **EST:** 1914
SQ FT: 4,800
SALES (est): 5.6MM **Privately Held**
WEB: www.hartfordcitynewstimes.com
SIC: 2711 2752 Newspapers, publishing & printing; commercial printing, offset

(G-5983)
HARTFORD TEC GLASS CO INC (PA)
735 E Water St (47348-2264)
P.O. Box 613 (47348-0613)
PHONE.....................................765 348-1282
Fax: 765 348-5435
George M Reidy, *President*
Michael Patrick Reidy, *Admin Sec*
EMP: 20 **EST:** 1939
SQ FT: 40,000
SALES (est): 2.6MM **Privately Held**
SIC: 3231 5039 1793 Stained glass: made from purchased glass; glass construction materials; glass & glazing work

(G-5984)
MAYCO INTERNATIONAL LLC
Also Called: Mayco Intl Hartford Cy
1701 W Mcdonald St (47348-9599)
PHONE.....................................765 348-5780
Patricia Stephens, *Principal*
EMP: 15 **Privately Held**
SIC: 3089 Plastic processing
PA: Mayco International Llc
42400 Merrill Rd
Sterling Heights MI 48314

(G-5985)
MIDDLETOWN ENTERPRISES INC
Also Called: Sinclair Glass
105 N Wabash Ave (47348-2366)
P.O. Box 527 (47348-0527)
PHONE.....................................765 348-3100
Fax: 765 348-3823
Gavin Mair, *President*
Rita Hudson, *Purch Mgr*
▲ **EMP:** 40
SQ FT: 65,000
SALES (est): 5MM **Privately Held**
WEB: www.sinclairglass.com
SIC: 3231 Ornamental glass: cut, engraved or otherwise decorated

(G-5986)
NEW-INDY HARTFORD CITY LLC (DH)
Also Called: New-Indy Containerboard
501 S Spring St (47348-2500)
P.O. Box 30 (47348-0030)
PHONE.....................................765 348-5440
Philip Freel, *General Mgr*
Jon Pierce, *General Mgr*
Aaron Richards, *Accountant*
EMP: 86
SALES (est): 20.7MM
SALES (corp-wide): 36.5MM **Privately Held**
WEB: www.hcpaper.com
SIC: 2621 Wrapping & packaging papers; bag paper
HQ: New-Indy Containerboard Llc
3500 Porsche Way Ste 150
Ontario CA 91764
909 296-3400

(G-5987)
PETOSKEY PLASTICS INC
1100 W Grant St (47348-1970)
PHONE.....................................765 348-9808
Shane Duncan, *Department Mgr*
EMP: 102
SQ FT: 208,000
SALES (corp-wide): 81.3MM **Privately Held**
SIC: 3081 Polyethylene film
PA: Petoskey Plastics, Inc.
1 Petoskey St
Petoskey MI 49770
231 347-2602

(G-5988)
PRINTERS EXPRESS INC
Also Called: Event Print
112 N Jefferson St (47348-2201)
P.O. Box 361 (47348-0361)
PHONE.....................................765 348-0069
Fax: 765 348-4514
Cecelia Richardson, *President*
Mike Richardson, *Exec VP*
Shannon Richardson,
EMP: 8
SQ FT: 3,600

SALES (est): 975.2K **Privately Held**
WEB: www.printersexpress.biz
SIC: 2759 Screen printing

(G-5989)
QUALITY PALLET
1506 W Park Ave (47348-8739)
PHONE..............................765 348-4840
Ding Goodnight, *Owner*
Matt Goodnight, *Plant Mgr*
EMP: 20
SALES: 170K **Privately Held**
SIC: 2448 Pallets, wood & wood with metal

(G-5990)
SHALEE OILS LLC
400 Bob Barry Dr (47348)
P.O. Box 425 (47348-0425)
PHONE..............................765 329-4057
Bill Knapp, *Mng Member*
EMP: 6 **EST**: 2016
SALES (est): 391.8K **Privately Held**
SIC: 2992 Rust arresting compounds, animal or vegetable oil base

(G-5991)
STAN CLAMME (PA)
725 E Water St (47348-2264)
PHONE..............................765 348-0008
Stan Clamme, *Principal*
EMP: 5
SALES (est): 1.1MM **Privately Held**
SIC: 3523 Sprayers & spraying machines, agricultural

(G-5992)
STUTZ PRODUCTS CORP
606 S Walnut St (47348-2627)
P.O. Box 468 (47348-0468)
PHONE..............................765 348-2510
Fax: 765 348-1001
Bill Musselman, *President*
Helen Muffelman, *Corp Secy*
EMP: 6 **EST**: 1930
SQ FT: 6,500
SALES (est): 702.3K **Privately Held**
WEB: www.stutzproducts.com
SIC: 3556 Cutting, chopping, grinding, mixing & similar machinery

(G-5993)
TRU-FORM STEEL & WIRE INC (PA)
1204 Gilkey Ave (47348-9549)
P.O. Box 266 (47348-0266)
PHONE..............................765 348-5001
Jeffrey Tuttle, *President*
Monty Tuttle, *Vice Pres*
▲ **EMP**: 30
SALES (est): 17.1MM **Privately Held**
SIC: 3089 3315 3441 3412 Plastic processing; wire & fabricated wire products; fabricated structural metal; metal barrels, drums & pails; partitions & fixtures, except wood

(G-5994)
TRU-FORM STEEL & WIRE INC
1822 Joe Bonham Dr (47348-9265)
P.O. Box 266 (47348-0266)
PHONE..............................765 348-5001
Keith Rodarnel, *Manager*
EMP: 50
SALES (corp-wide): 17.1MM **Privately Held**
SIC: 3441 3089 Fabricated structural metal; plastic processing
PA: Tru-Form Steel & Wire, Inc.
　1204 Gilkey Ave
　Hartford City IN 47348
　765 348-5001

(G-5995)
VENTURE INDUS
1701 W Mcdonald St (47348-9599)
PHONE..............................765 348-5780
Paul Hague, *Partner*
EMP: 3
SALES (est): 234.3K **Privately Held**
SIC: 2821 Molding compounds, plastics

(G-5996)
VICTORIAS VINEYARD
426 S Willman Rd (47348-9703)
PHONE..............................765 348-3070
Gordon Jackson, *Principal*

EMP: 4 **EST**: 2011
SALES (est): 232.1K **Privately Held**
SIC: 2084 Wines, brandy & brandy spirits

Haubstadt
Gibson County

(G-5997)
BAILEY CHASSIS COMPANY LLC
78 W 1100 S (47639-8837)
PHONE..............................615 822-7041
Floyd Bailey, *President*
EMP: 7
SQ FT: 5,000
SALES: 1MM **Privately Held**
SIC: 5531 3799 Automotive parts; automobile trailer chassis

(G-5998)
DEWIG BROS MEATS
100 W Maple St (47639-8100)
PHONE..............................812 768-6208
Thomas E Dewig, *Owner*
EMP: 4 **EST**: 2014
SALES (est): 261.8K **Privately Held**
SIC: 2011 Meat packing plants; meat by-products from meat slaughtered on site; lamb products from lamb slaughtered on site

(G-5999)
DEWIG BROS PACKING CO INC
100 E Maple St (47639)
PHONE..............................812 768-6208
Fax: 812 768-6220
Thomas Dewig, *President*
Janet Dewig, *Vice Pres*
EMP: 35 **EST**: 1915
SQ FT: 8,000
SALES (est): 2.8MM **Privately Held**
SIC: 5421 2011 Meat markets, including freezer provisioners; pork products from pork slaughtered on site

(G-6000)
EDS WOOD CRAFT
300 E Gibson St (47639-8203)
P.O. Box 362 (47639-0362)
PHONE..............................812 768-6617
Fax: 812 768-6617
Edward C May, *Owner*
EMP: 3
SALES: 70K **Privately Held**
SIC: 2521 1752 2541 2517 Cabinets, office: wood; carpet laying; wood partitions & fixtures; wood television & radio cabinets; wood kitchen cabinets

(G-6001)
GIBSON COUNTY SAND & GRAV INC
2997 W State Road 68 (47639-8631)
PHONE..............................812 851-5800
EMP: 2
SALES (est): 144.4K **Privately Held**
SIC: 1442 Construction sand & gravel

(G-6002)
HILLTOP MCH SP HAUBSTADT LLC
4958 E 1200 S (47639-7907)
PHONE..............................812 768-5717
Kenneth I Langford, *Principal*
EMP: 3 **EST**: 2008
SALES (est): 244K **Privately Held**
SIC: 3599 Machine shop, jobbing & repair

(G-6003)
HOOSIER HOT RODS CLASSICS INC
189 E State Road 68 (47639-8840)
PHONE..............................812 768-5221
Kent Mann, *President*
EMP: 6 **EST**: 2007
SALES (est): 679.3K **Privately Held**
SIC: 3711 7532 Automobile assembly, including specialty automobiles; antique & classic automobile restoration

(G-6004)
PRODIGY MOLD & TOOL INC
88 E 1100 S (47639-8836)
PHONE..............................812 753-3029
Fax: 812 753-5001
Shawn McGrew, *President*
Darrin Schmitt, *Vice Pres*
Brett Duncan, *Officer*
EMP: 22
SQ FT: 14,500
SALES (est): 3.5MM **Privately Held**
WEB: www.prodigymold.com
SIC: 3599 3451 3089 Custom machinery; screw machine products; injection molding of plastics

(G-6005)
S&C MACHINE LLC
1197 W 1000 S (47639-8603)
PHONE..............................812 768-6731
Cynthia M Shoemaker, *Principal*
EMP: 5 **EST**: 2007
SALES (est): 615.5K **Privately Held**
SIC: 3599 Machine & other job shop work

(G-6006)
TNT TRUCK ACCESSORIES LLC
152 W 1275 S (47639-8712)
PHONE..............................812 305-0714
Michele Elpers,
EMP: 2
SALES: 118K **Privately Held**
SIC: 3714 Motor vehicle parts & accessories

(G-6007)
VOGLER COPPERWORKS LLC
308 S Vine St (47639-8151)
PHONE..............................812 630-9010
Aaron Vogler, *Owner*
EMP: 3
SALES (est): 209.5K **Privately Held**
SIC: 3444 Sheet metalwork

(G-6008)
WEST SIDE AUTOMATION
78 W 1100 S (47639-8837)
PHONE..............................812 768-6878
Fax: 812 753-4664
Lanny Schmidt, *Owner*
Kathy Schmidt, *Corp Secy*
EMP: 12
SQ FT: 4,000
SALES (est): 3.1MM **Privately Held**
SIC: 3625 Relays & industrial controls

Hazleton
Gibson County

(G-6009)
ELLIS MACHINE SHOP LLC
1318 E 870 N (47640-9248)
PHONE..............................812 779-7477
Chad Ellis, *Principal*
EMP: 2
SALES (est): 81.4K **Privately Held**
SIC: 3599 Machine shop, jobbing & repair

(G-6010)
PAUL E POTTS
8689 W Private Road 375 N (47640-9631)
PHONE..............................812 354-3241
Paul E Potts, *Owner*
EMP: 3
SALES (est): 417.9K **Privately Held**
SIC: 1311 Crude petroleum production

Hebron
Porter County

(G-6011)
DAVID M PSZONKA
93 S 695 W (46341-9722)
PHONE..............................219 988-2235
David M Pszonka, *Owner*
Joan Pszonka, *Co-Owner*
EMP: 2 **EST**: 2013
SALES (est): 105.8K **Privately Held**
SIC: 2064 7389 Lollipops & other hard candy;

(G-6012)
FABRICATED SPECIALTIES INC
511 N Main St (46341-8701)
PHONE..............................219 996-4787
Amanda Rhoades, *President*
EMP: 2
SALES (est): 185.8K **Privately Held**
SIC: 3613 Control panels, electric

(G-6013)
GRANITE INNOVATIONS INC
18178 Clay St (46341-9304)
PHONE..............................219 690-1081
Steve Han, *President*
EMP: 6
SALES (est): 736.2K **Privately Held**
SIC: 3281 Granite, cut & shaped

(G-6014)
HOCHBAUM MACHINE SERVICES INC
11 Wood Ct (46341-9064)
PHONE..............................219 996-6830
Fax: 219 996-6840
Jamie Hochbaum, *President*
Mike Sweitzer, *Vice Pres*
Greg Gallagher, *Opers Mgr*
EMP: 20
SQ FT: 5,000
SALES (est): 4.6MM **Privately Held**
SIC: 3599 Machine shop, jobbing & repair

(G-6015)
LAKE AIR BALANCE
639 W 250 S (46341-9226)
PHONE..............................219 988-2449
Wanda Vajner, *Principal*
EMP: 2
SALES (est): 188.8K **Privately Held**
SIC: 3444 Sheet metalwork

(G-6016)
LDN WELDING CORP
17907 Union St (46341-9072)
PHONE..............................219 996-5643
Darrick Nykaza, *Principal*
EMP: 2
SALES (est): 127.5K **Privately Held**
SIC: 7692 Welding repair

(G-6017)
LENNON INDUSTRIES
1102 Norbeh Dr (46341-8511)
PHONE..............................219 996-6024
Jim Williams, *Principal*
EMP: 8
SALES (est): 725.9K **Privately Held**
SIC: 3999 Manufacturing industries

(G-6018)
LENNON INDUSTRIES INC
3629 E 157th Ave (46341-9221)
PHONE..............................219 996-6838
Jim Williams, *President*
Jamie Hochbaum, *Vice Pres*
EMP: 7
SQ FT: 2,000
SALES (est): 629K **Privately Held**
SIC: 3599 Machine shop, jobbing & repair

(G-6019)
NATHAN MILLIS TOOLS LLC
115 Poplar Ct (46341-8890)
PHONE..............................219 996-3305
Nathan A Millis, *Principal*
EMP: 2
SALES (est): 81.4K **Privately Held**
SIC: 3599 Industrial machinery

(G-6020)
PORTER COUNTY IR & MET RECYCLE
552 S 600 W Ste 1 (46341-8822)
PHONE..............................219 996-7630
Fax: 219 996-6217
John Perzee, *President*
Janet Perzee, *Treasurer*
EMP: 15
SQ FT: 2,640
SALES (est): 3MM **Privately Held**
SIC: 5093 3341 Ferrous metal scrap & waste; nonferrous metals scrap; secondary nonferrous metals

(G-6021)
PREMIER COMPONENTS LLC
346 S 725 W (46341-9709)
PHONE...................................219 776-9372
Michael Williams, *Mng Member*
EMP: 5
SALES: 500K **Privately Held**
SIC: 3547 Steel rolling machinery

(G-6022)
RUSS PRINT SHOP
Also Called: Advertiser
131 N Main St (46341-8972)
P.O. Box 2 (46341-0002)
PHONE...................................219 996-3142
Fax: 219 996-3144
Russ Franzman Sr, *President*
EMP: 10
SQ FT: 1,856
SALES (est): 1.3MM **Privately Held**
WEB: www.russprintshop.com
SIC: 2752 2741 2791 2711 Commercial printing, offset; newsletter publishing; typesetting; newspapers

(G-6023)
VAN SCHOUWEN FARMS
19306 Clay St (46341-9347)
PHONE...................................219 696-0877
Jacob Van Schouwen, *Partner*
Marvin Van Schouwen, *Partner*
EMP: 5
SALES (est): 2.4MM **Privately Held**
SIC: 2035 Onions, pickled

(G-6024)
VAUTERBUILT INC
16448 Clay St (46341-9006)
PHONE...................................219 712-2384
Andrew Vauter, *President*
Sue Vauter, *Bookkeeper*
EMP: 2
SALES: 150K **Privately Held**
SIC: 3559 Automotive related machinery

(G-6025)
WOODLAND RESTORATION LLC
96 Hickory Ave (46341-9117)
PHONE...................................219 509-3078
Michaelina Houghtaling, *Principal*
EMP: 2
SALES (est): 207.1K **Privately Held**
SIC: 2499 Wood products

Heltonville
Lawrence County

(G-6026)
DWIGHT SMITH LOGGING
815 Roberts Ln (47436-8674)
PHONE...................................812 834-5546
Dwight Smith, *President*
EMP: 6
SALES (est): 509.1K **Privately Held**
SIC: 2411 Logging camps & contractors

(G-6027)
KINSERS HARDWOOD
7805 Bartlettsville Rd (47436-8550)
PHONE...................................812 834-5568
Mickey L Kinser, *Owner*
EMP: 5
SQ FT: 4,000
SALES (est): 450.4K **Privately Held**
SIC: 2421 2426 Sawmills & planing mills, general; lumber, hardwood dimension

(G-6028)
SPECIAL IDEAS INCORPORATED
Also Called: Interfaith Resources
511 Diamond Rd (47436-8503)
PHONE...................................812 834-5691
Jusitce Strain, *Owner*
Karen St Rain, *Owner*
EMP: 2
SALES (est): 166K **Privately Held**
WEB: www.special-ideas.com
SIC: 2711 Newspapers

(G-6029)
TURNER DOLLS INC
3522 Pleasant Run Rd (47436-9630)
P.O. Box 36 (47436-0036)
PHONE...................................812 834-5065
Fax: 812 834-1501
Virginia Turner, *President*
Boyde Turner, *Principal*
EMP: 8
SQ FT: 4,800
SALES (est): 978.5K **Privately Held**
WEB: www.turnerdolls.com
SIC: 3942 5945 Dolls, except stuffed toy animals; dolls & accessories

(G-6030)
VIRGINIAS VERY OWN LLC
3522 Pleasant Run Rd (47436-9630)
P.O. Box 36 (47436-0036)
PHONE...................................812 834-5065
Virginia Turner, *Mng Member*
EMP: 2
SALES (est): 126.5K **Privately Held**
SIC: 3942 Dolls, except stuffed toy animals

Henryville
Clark County

(G-6031)
A & A LOGGING ✪
7006 Henryville Otisco Rd (47126-8932)
PHONE...................................502 553-4132
EMP: 2 EST: 2017
SALES (est): 81.7K **Privately Held**
SIC: 2411 Logging

(G-6032)
S & M PRECAST INC
16700 Sima Gray Rd (47126-8626)
PHONE...................................812 294-3703
Fax: 812 294-4862
Raymond Grass, *President*
Becky A Graf, *Vice Pres*
EMP: 5 EST: 1995
SALES (est): 1MM **Privately Held**
SIC: 3272 Concrete products, precast

(G-6033)
SULLIVAN ENGINEERED SERVICES
Also Called: S.E.S.
316 Mount Zion Rd (47126-8657)
P.O. Box 410 (47126-0410)
PHONE...................................812 294-1724
Larry Sullivan, *President*
EMP: 6
SQ FT: 2,000
SALES: 500K **Privately Held**
WEB: www.ses.net
SIC: 3613 3542 7371 Control panels, electric; machine tools, metal forming type; custom computer programming services

Highland
Lake County

(G-6034)
AC PRINTING INC
2647 Highway Ave (46322-1614)
PHONE...................................708 418-9100
Lee F Simmons, *President*
William Simmons, *Vice Pres*
EMP: 5
SQ FT: 1,500
SALES: 1MM **Privately Held**
SIC: 2752 Commercial printing, offset

(G-6035)
APPLE LY EVER AFTER INC
3542 Highway Ave (46322-1712)
PHONE...................................219 838-9397
Lori A Sitter, *President*
EMP: 2
SALES (est): 128.6K **Privately Held**
SIC: 3571 Personal computers (microcomputers)

(G-6036)
B & W SPECIALIZED DRILLING
9002 Indianapolis Blvd B (46322-2501)
PHONE...................................219 746-9463
Thomas K Witherow, *President*
Carl Bowling, *Vice Pres*
Neal E Witherow, *Treasurer*
EMP: 5
SQ FT: 2,500
SALES: 400K **Privately Held**
SIC: 3545 Boring machine attachments (machine tool accessories)

(G-6037)
BAXTER PRINTING INC
3837 Ridge Rd (46322-2294)
PHONE...................................219 923-1999
Fax: 219 923-1936
Betty Turoci, *President*
David Turoci, *Sales Staff*
EMP: 7
SQ FT: 2,300
SALES (est): 1.1MM **Privately Held**
SIC: 2759 2752 2789 Screen printing; commercial printing, offset; bookbinding & related work

(G-6038)
BETTER METAL SYSTEMS LLC
9445 Indianapolis Blvd J (46322-2649)
PHONE...................................888 958-5945
Gregory Ullstam, *Director*
EMP: 3
SALES (est): 217.3K **Privately Held**
SIC: 3471 Cleaning & descaling metal products

(G-6039)
C E R METAL MARKING CORP
2224 Industrial Dr Ste C (46322-2652)
PHONE...................................219 924-9710
Fax: 219 924-9718
Edward J Siska, *President*
Robert Bernal, *Vice Pres*
Ernesto Santos, *Treasurer*
EMP: 5
SQ FT: 1,500
SALES: 150K **Privately Held**
WEB: www.cermetalmark.com
SIC: 3469 Stamping metal for the trade

(G-6040)
C J P CORPORATION
9445 Indianapolis Blvd A (46322-2648)
PHONE...................................219 924-1685
Charles J Pease, *President*
David Dahms, *Corp Secy*
EMP: 8
SQ FT: 4,500
SALES (est): 760K **Privately Held**
WEB: www.cjpcorp.com
SIC: 2752 2791 2789 Commercial printing, offset; typesetting; bookbinding & related work

(G-6041)
CUSTOM URETHANES INC
10010 Express Dr (46322-2612)
PHONE...................................219 924-1644
Fax: 219 924-2770
Jerry Lawhorn, *President*
Marie Lawhorn, *Corp Secy*
EMP: 7
SQ FT: 10,000
SALES (est): 918.4K **Privately Held**
SIC: 3089 Injection molded finished plastic products; injection molding of plastics

(G-6042)
DEFRUKUSCN LLC
2158 45th St 520 (46322-3742)
PHONE...................................219 718-2128
Guangchang Zhou, *President*
EMP: 3
SALES (est): 244.3K **Privately Held**
SIC: 5122 2869 5169 Drugs & drug proprietaries; laboratory chemicals, organic; organic chemicals, synthetic

(G-6043)
DXD SIGNS
9231 Spring St (46322-2538)
PHONE...................................219 588-4403
Tracy Day, *Principal*
EMP: 2

SALES (est): 135.5K **Privately Held**
SIC: 3993 Signs & advertising specialties

(G-6044)
ECONOMY ELECTRIC HTG & COOLG
9031 Grace St (46322-2166)
PHONE...................................219 923-4441
David Rivera, *Owner*
EMP: 2
SALES (est): 170.3K **Privately Held**
SIC: 1711 3699 Heating systems repair & maintenance; electrical equipment & supplies

(G-6045)
ENGINEERED STEEL CONCEPTS INC
9241 Spring St (46322-2538)
P.O. Box 3306, Munster (46321-0306)
PHONE...................................219 924-9056
▲ EMP: 10
SALES (est): 660K **Privately Held**
SIC: 3559 Mfg Misc Industry Machinery

(G-6046)
GERARD
9311 Southmoor Ave (46322-2518)
PHONE...................................219 924-6388
Sarah McMahon, *Principal*
EMP: 3
SALES (est): 252.4K **Privately Held**
SIC: 3355 Structural shapes, rolled, aluminum

(G-6047)
GRINDING EXPERTS
2736 Condit St Ste C (46322-1689)
PHONE...................................219 838-7773
Wanda Siko, *President*
Kevin Siko, *Vice Pres*
EMP: 2
SALES (est): 240K **Privately Held**
SIC: 3599 Amusement park equipment

(G-6048)
GROWLERS
2816 Highway Ave (46322-1629)
PHONE...................................219 924-0245
Myron Chapman, *Owner*
EMP: 2 EST: 2007
SALES (est): 180K **Privately Held**
SIC: 2599 Bar, restaurant & cafeteria furniture

(G-6049)
HEADCO INDUSTRIES INC
Also Called: Bearing Headquarters Co
9922 Express Dr (46322-2609)
PHONE...................................219 924-7758
Carl Kator, *Manager*
EMP: 4
SALES (corp-wide): 162.5MM **Privately Held**
SIC: 5085 5084 3599 Bearings; hydraulic systems equipment & supplies; machine shop, jobbing & repair
PA: Headco Industries, Inc.
2601 Parkes Dr
Broadview IL 60155
708 681-4400

(G-6050)
IT FACTOR PUBLICATIONS INC
Also Called: Noir Magazine
2158 45th St Ste 224 (46322-3742)
PHONE...................................219 228-8424
Gina Vaughn, *CEO*
Dee Johnson, *CFO*
EMP: 21
SALES: 780K **Privately Held**
SIC: 2721 Periodicals

(G-6051)
KIN NATURALS LLC
2158 45th St (46322-3742)
PHONE...................................219 213-9516
Katrina Pickett, *Administration*
EMP: 2
SALES (est): 64.6K **Privately Held**
SIC: 2844 Lotions, shaving

(G-6052)
NATURAL ANSWERS
2300 Ramblewood Dr Ste C (46322-3627)
PHONE...............................(219) 922-3663
Sarah Leep, *Principal*
EMP: 3
SALES (est): 263.9K **Privately Held**
SIC: 2099 5149 8049 Food preparations; health foods; nutritionist

(G-6053)
P C COMMUNICATION INC
2301 Ridgewood St (46322-1537)
PHONE...............................219 838-2546
Peter Calderon, *CEO*
Jeannine Calderon, *Vice Pres*
EMP: 5
SALES (est): 262K **Privately Held**
SIC: 7291 3829 Tax return preparation services; measuring & controlling devices

(G-6054)
REWRIGHT PRINTING
9222 Indianapolis Blvd D (46322-2559)
PHONE...............................219 513-8133
EMP: 2
SALES (est): 83.9K **Privately Held**
SIC: 2752 Commercial printing, lithographic

(G-6055)
SHEET METAL SERVICES INC
9944 Express Dr (46322-2688)
PHONE...............................219 924-1206
Fax: 219 922-8640
Robin Longfellow, *President*
Terry Longfellow, *Vice Pres*
EMP: 17
SQ FT: 7,210
SALES (est): 2.6MM **Privately Held**
SIC: 3444 Sheet metalwork

(G-6056)
TASCO INDUSTRIES INC
10018 Express Dr (46322-2612)
PHONE...............................219 922-6100
Fax: 219 922-3900
Yucel Turan, *President*
Nalan Turan, *Vice Pres*
EMP: 5
SQ FT: 6,000
SALES: 699K **Privately Held**
SIC: 3599 Machine & other job shop work

(G-6057)
TORTI PRODUCTS INC
2735 Glenwood St (46322-1046)
PHONE...............................219 730-2071
Fernando Gutierrez, *President*
EMP: 4
SALES (est): 304.1K **Privately Held**
SIC: 2051 2099 Bakery: wholesale or wholesale/retail combined; tortillas, fresh or refrigerated

(G-6058)
VIANNOS VILLAGE CRETAN OIL
2011 Idlewild Ct (46322-2319)
PHONE...............................219 513-6720
Jordan Tsolakides, *Principal*
EMP: 2
SALES (est): 116.5K **Privately Held**
SIC: 1311 Crude petroleum & natural gas

(G-6059)
VITAMORPH LABS LLC
9445 Indianapolis Blvd # 1049 (46322-2648)
PHONE...............................219 237-0174
Jeff Carlson,
EMP: 2
SALES (est): 62.3K **Privately Held**
SIC: 2023 5999 Dietary supplements, dairy & non-dairy based; miscellaneous retail stores

(G-6060)
WOODHOLLOW LLC
9603 Spring St Rear (46322-2636)
PHONE...............................219 384-2802
Daniel Elzinga, *Principal*
EMP: 2 EST: 2016
SALES (est): 55.2K **Privately Held**
SIC: 2499 Wood products

Hillsdale
Vermillion County

(G-6061)
NEWPORT PALLET INC
1110 W Industrial Dr (47854-8117)
PHONE...............................765 505-9463
Adam Winland, *President*
EMP: 20
SALES (est): 822K **Privately Held**
SIC: 2448 Pallets, wood & wood with metal

Hoagland
Allen County

(G-6062)
ALL AMRCAN SHTTER CMPNENTS LLC
14525 Bruick Ln (46745-9623)
PHONE...............................260 639-0112
James B Knapke,
EMP: 2
SALES (est): 88.9K **Privately Held**
SIC: 3089 Shutters, plastic

(G-6063)
BK INTERNATIONAL LLC
Also Called: All American Components
14525 Bruick Ln (46745-9623)
PHONE...............................260 639-0112
Bill Faderston, *CEO*
Jim Knapke, *Manager*
EMP: 1
SALES: 7MM **Privately Held**
SIC: 3089 Shutters, plastic

(G-6064)
DWD INDUSTRIES LLC
Also Called: Decatur Wire Die
11117 English St (46745-7402)
P.O. Box 65 (46745-0065)
PHONE...............................260 639-3254
Fred Sauer, *Manager*
EMP: 2
SALES (corp-wide): 41.1K **Privately Held**
SIC: 3544 Wire drawing & straightening dies
HQ: Dwd Industries, Llc
　　1921 Patterson St
　　Decatur IN 46733
　　260 728-9272

(G-6065)
KNAPKE & SONS INC
Also Called: Woodworking By Design
14525 Bruick Ln (46745-9623)
PHONE...............................260 639-0112
Fax: 260 639-3475
James Knapke Jr, *President*
Tony Knapke, *Admin Sec*
▲ EMP: 20
SQ FT: 40,000
SALES (est): 3.3MM **Privately Held**
SIC: 2431 Moldings, wood: unfinished & prefinished

(G-6066)
MADISON CABINETS INC
14727 Bruick Dr (46745-1500)
P.O. Box 188 (46745-0188)
PHONE...............................260 639-3915
Fax: 260 639-6692
Herman Guenin, *President*
Craig Guenin, *Corp Secy*
Heath Guenin, *Vice Pres*
EMP: 8
SQ FT: 4,000
SALES (est): 1MM **Privately Held**
WEB: www.madisoncabinets.com
SIC: 2434 2517 2511 Wood kitchen cabinets; wood television & radio cabinets; wood household furniture

(G-6067)
STONE STREET QUARRIES INC
5536 Hoagland Rd (46745-9619)
P.O. Box 9246, Fort Wayne (46899-9246)
PHONE...............................260 639-6511
Fax: 260 639-7109
William Sovers, *President*
Larry Gerig, *Vice Pres*
EMP: 21 EST: 1917
SQ FT: 1,000
SALES: 1.6MM **Privately Held**
SIC: 1422 3281 Limestones, ground; cut stone & stone products

---

Hobart
Lake County

(G-6068)
ADVANCE ENERGY LLC
3580 N Hobart Rd C (46342-1442)
PHONE...............................312 665-0022
Tom Collins II, *Principal*
Vance Kenney, *Mng Member*
EMP: 2
SQ FT: 4,000
SALES (est): 389.3K **Privately Held**
SIC: 5172 2911 Engine fuels & oils; oils, fuel

(G-6069)
ARISTO LLC
Also Called: Aristo Catalyst Technology
4410 W 37th Ave Frnt (46342-1654)
PHONE...............................219 962-1032
Andreas Proimos, *President*
Robert Kolar, *Plant Mgr*
Andrius Malinauskas, *Engineer*
Matt Bapple, *CFO*
Nancy Rochester, *Manager*
▲ EMP: 50 EST: 1991
SALES (est): 10.9MM **Privately Held**
WEB: www.aristo.com
SIC: 3694 3714 Armatures, automotive; motor vehicle parts & accessories

(G-6070)
CAL PIPE MANUFACTURING INC
6451 Northwind Pkwy (46342-2496)
PHONE...............................219 844-6800
Fax: 219 844-6884
Bob Westerfield, *Manager*
EMP: 13
SALES (est): 2.4MM
SALES (corp-wide): 9.5MM **Privately Held**
WEB: www.calpipe.com
SIC: 3498 Fabricated pipe & fittings
PA: Cal Pipe Manufacturing Inc
　　19440 S Dminguez Hills Dr
　　Compton CA 90220
　　562 803-4388

(G-6071)
CALPIPE INDUSTRIES LLC
Calbrite
6451 Northwind Pkwy (46342-2496)
PHONE...............................219 844-6800
Daniel J Markus, *CEO*
EMP: 2 **Publicly Held**
SIC: 5051 3498 Metals service centers & offices; fabricated pipe & fittings
HQ: Calpipe Industries, Llc
　　19440 S Dminguez Hills Dr
　　Rancho Dominguez CA 90220

(G-6072)
CALUMET ORTHPD PROSTHETICS CO
7554 Grand Blvd (46342-6672)
PHONE...............................219 942-2148
Fax: 219 947-2143
Ronald Pawlowski, *President*
Micalea Pawlowski, *Vice Pres*
EMP: 9
SALES (est): 1.1MM **Privately Held**
SIC: 3842 Braces, orthopedic; limbs, artificial; orthopedic appliances; elastic hosiery, orthopedic (support)

(G-6073)
CARCAPSULE USA INC
4590 W 61st Ave (46342-6474)
PHONE...............................219 945-9493
Phillip Potocki,
▲ EMP: 3
SALES (est): 175.5K **Privately Held**
SIC: 2399 Automotive covers, except seat & tire covers

(G-6074)
CHAPPOS INC
101 N Wabash St (46342-4031)
PHONE...............................219 942-8101
Martin T Chappo, *President*
Judith Chappo, *Corp Secy*
EMP: 4
SALES (est): 222.9K **Privately Held**
SIC: 7692 7538 Automotive welding; engine rebuilding: automotive

(G-6075)
CJ DEVELOPERS INC
Also Called: Quick Sign & Shirt
150 N Illinois St (46342-3224)
PHONE...............................219 942-5051
Cynthia Lahaie, *President*
EMP: 4
SALES (est): 279.4K **Privately Held**
SIC: 3993 Signs & advertising specialties

(G-6076)
COIL TRAN CORP (PA)
Also Called: Hobart Electronics Division
160 S Illinois St (46342-4512)
PHONE...............................219 942-8511
Fax: 219 942-0017
Nicholas N Kriadis, *CEO*
Gary N Kriadis, *President*
Demetra Kriadis, *Corp Secy*
Steve Stavrinoudis, *Engineer*
Stephen Stavrinovdis, *Engineer*
▲ EMP: 90
SQ FT: 30,000
SALES (est): 24.8MM **Privately Held**
WEB: www.hobart-electronics.com
SIC: 3677 5065 3621 3612 Electronic coils, transformers & other inductors; electronic parts & equipment; motors & generators; transformers, except electric

(G-6077)
CONNIES SATIN STITCH
829 E 3rd St (46342-4501)
PHONE...............................219 942-1887
Fax: 219 947-2537
Harry Decausemaker, *President*
Connie Decausemaker, *Partner*
EMP: 5
SQ FT: 2,500
SALES (est): 310K **Privately Held**
SIC: 7389 2395 Sewing contractor; pleating & stitching

(G-6078)
EASTONS LETTERING SERVICE
514 E 3rd St (46342-4418)
PHONE...............................219 942-5101
Fax: 219 942-5101
Mark Easton, *Owner*
EMP: 2 EST: 1960
SQ FT: 1,600
SALES (est): 152.6K **Privately Held**
SIC: 3999 Novelties, bric-a-brac & hobby kits

(G-6079)
HARDINS SPEED SERVICE CO
3649 Illinois St (46342-1056)
PHONE...............................219 962-8080
Eddie Hardin, *Owner*
EMP: 6
SQ FT: 3,500
SALES: 250K **Privately Held**
SIC: 5531 3711 3799 Automotive parts; motor vehicles & car bodies; trailer hitches

(G-6080)
HIELO SERVICES LLC
3011 Crabapple Ln (46342-3815)
PHONE...............................219 973-1952
Maria Guillen,
EMP: 3
SALES: 10K **Privately Held**
SIC: 2711 Newspapers

(G-6081)
INDIANA BOTANIC GARDENS INC
Also Called: Botanic Choice
3401 W 37th Ave (46342-1751)
P.O. Box 5, Hammond (46325-0005)
PHONE...............................219 947-4040
Fax: 219 947-4148

Harvey Cleland, *Ch of Bd*
Timothy D Cleland, *President*
John Kaplan, *Vice Pres*
David Meyer, *Vice Pres*
Greg Villaroman, *Purchasing*
◆ **EMP:** 157 **EST:** 1910
SQ FT: 50,000
SALES: 18.8MM **Privately Held**
WEB: www.botanicchoice.com
SIC: 5961 2833 Mail order house; botanical products, medicinal: ground, graded or milled

(G-6082)
J V CRANE & ENGINEERING INC
425 S Shelby St (46342-4721)
P.O. Box 543 (46342-0543)
PHONE..................................219 942-8566
Philip Victor, *President*
Wayne Sabin, *Treasurer*
EMP: 23 **EST:** 1978
SQ FT: 21,500
SALES: 5MM **Privately Held**
WEB: www.jvcrane.com
SIC: 3536 1731 Cranes, overhead traveling; general electrical contractor

(G-6083)
KARBACH HOLDINGS CORPORATION
1701 Northwind Pkwy (46342-6549)
PHONE..................................219 924-2454
Kevin Huseman, *President*
Connie Huseman, *Corp Secy*
EMP: 17
SQ FT: 10,000
SALES (est): 1.8MM **Privately Held**
SIC: 3993 Signs & advertising specialties

(G-6084)
KEYWEST METAL
6338 E 35th Ave (46342-1463)
PHONE..................................219 654-4063
Michael Clark, *Administration*
EMP: 2
SALES (est): 197.1K **Privately Held**
SIC: 5051 3399 Metals service centers & offices; primary metal products

(G-6085)
KNITTING MILL SPECIALTIES
Also Called: Kms
291 N County Line Rd (46342-7103)
PHONE..................................219 942-8031
Fax: 219 947-7909
Fred Karrle, *President*
EMP: 5
SQ FT: 2,000
SALES (est): 790.7K **Privately Held**
SIC: 3843 Dental materials

(G-6086)
LAFF OR DIE PRODUCTIONS
221 N Colorado St (46342-2921)
PHONE..................................219 942-3790
EMP: 2 **EST:** 2009
SALES (est): 120K **Privately Held**
SIC: 3544 Mfg Dies/Tools/Jigs/Fixtures

(G-6087)
LAKE GEORGE MATERIAL & SUP CO
450 S Ohio St (46342-4661)
PHONE..................................219 942-1912
Vincent R Boyd, *President*
James Hamilton, *Branch Mgr*
EMP: 5
SALES (corp-wide): 1MM **Privately Held**
SIC: 5211 3273 Masonry materials & supplies; ready-mixed concrete
PA: Lake George Material & Supply Co Inc
450 S Ohio St
Hobart IN 46342
219 942-3215

(G-6088)
LCAS INC
233 Center St (46342-4427)
PHONE..................................541 219-0229
Randall Brant,
EMP: 7
SALES (est): 261K **Privately Held**
SIC: 2741 Miscellaneous publishing

(G-6089)
LINDAS GONE BUGGIE
28 E 36th Pl (46342-1031)
PHONE..................................219 299-0174
EMP: 2 **EST:** 2012
SALES (est): 208.3K **Privately Held**
SIC: 3531 Concrete buggies, powered

(G-6090)
MAKE IT BLACK SEAL COATING
824 Lake St (46342-5228)
PHONE..................................219 629-6230
Thomas Ross Jr, *Owner*
EMP: 2
SALES (est): 72K **Privately Held**
SIC: 3479 Metal coating & allied service

(G-6091)
MELLON TAX SERVICE
101 Center St (46342-4425)
PHONE..................................219 947-1660
James Mellon, *Partner*
Pamela Mellon, *Partner*
EMP: 3
SALES (est): 231.4K **Privately Held**
SIC: 7389 7372 Legal & tax services; prepackaged software

(G-6092)
MIDWEST PRODUCTS CO INC (PA)
400 S Indiana St (46342-4541)
P.O. Box 564 (46342-0564)
PHONE..................................219 942-1134
Fax: 219 947-2347
Jon Zaloum, *President*
Diane Bilderback, *Mfg Spvr*
Donna Giricz, *Controller*
Angie Flesher, *Bookkeeper*
Hannah Snyder, *Accounts Mgr*
▲ **EMP:** 85 **EST:** 1952
SQ FT: 61,000
SALES (est): 12.4MM **Privately Held**
WEB: www.midwestproducts.com
SIC: 3944 2493 Airplane models, toy & hobby; boat & ship models, toy & hobby; hardboard & fiberboard products

(G-6093)
RUWALDT PACKING CO INC
6510 E Ridge Rd (46342-2302)
P.O. Box 563 (46342-0563)
PHONE..................................219 942-2911
Edward Oedzes, *President*
EMP: 30
SQ FT: 1,000
SALES (est): 3.9MM **Privately Held**
SIC: 2011 2013 Lamb products from lamb slaughtered on site; mutton from meat slaughtered on site; veal from meat slaughtered on site; sausages & other prepared meats

(G-6094)
SAPPERS MARKET AND GREENHOUSES
Also Called: Sapper's Farm Market
1155 S Lake Park Ave (46342-5959)
PHONE..................................219 942-4995
Fax: 219 942-9780
Janet Kraynik, *Owner*
EMP: 9
SALES (est): 325.6K **Privately Held**
SIC: 0181 0161 2048 5261 Ornamental nursery products; vegetables & melons; bird food, prepared; Christmas trees (natural)

(G-6095)
SIGN SOURCE ONE I GROUP INC
3429 Michigan St (46342-1170)
PHONE..................................219 736-5865
Scott Billeck, *President*
EMP: 3
SQ FT: 2,500
SALES: 200K **Privately Held**
SIC: 3993 Electric signs

(G-6096)
SMOKE SMOKE SMOKE
1165 W 37th Ave (46342-2012)
PHONE..................................219 942-3331
Omar Alburei, *Owner*
EMP: 3

SALES (est): 174.6K **Privately Held**
SIC: 3999 Cigarette & cigar products & accessories

(G-6097)
STORK NEWS NORTHWEST INDIANA
2880 Tulip Ln (46342-7521)
PHONE..................................219 808-5221
David Parsanko, *Principal*
EMP: 3
SALES (est): 140K **Privately Held**
SIC: 2721 Periodicals: publishing & printing

(G-6098)
THOMPSON
421 Driftwood Dr (46342-3909)
PHONE..................................219 942-8133
Harold Thompson, *Manager*
EMP: 3
SALES (est): 220.7K **Privately Held**
SIC: 3841 Veterinarians' instruments & apparatus

(G-6099)
TITANIUM RAILS NUTRITION LLC
1709 E 37th Ave (46342-2576)
PHONE..................................219 940-3704
Martin Amaya, *Manager*
EMP: 4
SALES (est): 143.5K **Privately Held**
SIC: 3356 Titanium

(G-6100)
WICKER GALLERY
619 E 3rd St (46342-4419)
PHONE..................................219 942-0783
Jan Rains, *Principal*
EMP: 2 **EST:** 2007
SALES (est): 188.1K **Privately Held**
SIC: 3272 Furniture, garden: concrete

(G-6101)
WISE INDUSTRIES INC (DEL)
1596 Lilac Ct (46342-5978)
P.O. Box 2040, Weirton WV (26062-1240)
PHONE..................................219 947-5333
Rae Weisburd, *President*
EMP: 4 **EST:** 1993
SALES (est): 451.7K **Privately Held**
SIC: 3021 7389 Protective footwear, rubber or plastic; safety inspection service

(G-6102)
X PRESS STORAGE LLC
401 S Shelby St (46342-4721)
PHONE..................................219 942-1227
Robert Czarney, *Principal*
EMP: 2
SALES (est): 12K **Privately Held**
SIC: 2741 Miscellaneous publishing

(G-6103)
YOUNIQUELY YOURS
955 Duck Creek Ct (46342-5335)
PHONE..................................219 942-1489
Fax: 219 763-4384
Sue Johnson, *Partner*
EMP: 2
SALES (est): 186.9K **Privately Held**
SIC: 3499 5961 5999 Novelties & giftware, including trophies; gift items, mail order; artificial flowers

---

Holland
Dubois County

(G-6104)
BRATCO INC
502 N 2nd St (47541-9675)
PHONE..................................812 536-4071
James Wire, *President*
Karen Wire, *Co-Owner*
EMP: 9
SALES (est): 872.3K **Privately Held**
WEB: www.bratco-operating.com
SIC: 2431 Millwork

(G-6105)
EAST SIDE JERSEY DAIRY INC
300 W Main St (47541-9653)
P.O. Box 70 (47541-0070)
PHONE..................................812 536-2207
EMP: 3
SALES (corp-wide): 1.8B **Privately Held**
SIC: 2026 Milk processing (pasteurizing, homogenizing, bottling)
HQ: East Side Jersey Dairy Inc
1100 Broadway
Carlinville IL 62626
217 854-2547

(G-6106)
WOODS PRINTING COMPANY INC
601 W Main St (47541-9687)
P.O. Box 99 (47541-0099)
PHONE..................................812 536-2261
Fax: 812 536-2151
Maurice C Woods, *CEO*
David Springston, *President*
Emma Lou Woods, *Corp Secy*
Sharon Springston, *Vice Pres*
Steve Curtice, *Accounts Mgr*
EMP: 16 **EST:** 1971
SQ FT: 8,800
SALES (est): 3MM **Privately Held**
SIC: 2752 Commercial printing, offset

Holton
Ripley County

(G-6107)
GUYS WOOD N THINGS
340 N County Road 300 W (47023-8508)
PHONE..................................812 689-0433
Sara Lee, *Owner*
EMP: 2
SALES: 50K **Privately Held**
SIC: 2431 Woodwork, interior & ornamental

(G-6108)
HOLMAN SEPTIC TANK SLS REDYMIX
Also Called: Holman's Septic Tank Sales
4896 S Old Michigan Rd (47023-9115)
PHONE..................................812 689-1913
Harry Holman, *President*
Bernette Holman, *Vice Pres*
EMP: 14
SQ FT: 7,500
SALES: 3MM **Privately Held**
SIC: 3272 Septic tanks, concrete

Homer
Rush County

(G-6109)
SAMPLER INC (PA)
7138 W 235 S (46146-9812)
PHONE..................................765 663-2233
Avis Brown, *President*
Bruce Levi, *Manager*
EMP: 14 **EST:** 1946
SQ FT: 10,000
SALES: 392.4K **Privately Held**
SIC: 2511 5719 Wood household furniture; wood bedroom furniture; dining room furniture: wood; housewares

---

Hope
Bartholomew County

(G-6110)
ACTION FILTRATION INC (PA)
221 Raymond St (47246-9356)
PHONE..................................812 546-6262
Fax: 812 546-0055
Les Benesh, *President*
Paul M Trotta Jr, *Vice Pres*
▼ **EMP:** 5
SQ FT: 12,000

SALES (est): 7MM **Privately Held**
WEB: www.actionfiltration.com
SIC: 3569 Filters, general line: industrial; filters

(G-6111)
CUSTOM STEEL TECHNOLOGIES LLC
701 South St (47246-9345)
P.O. Box 2 (47246-0002)
PHONE..................................812 546-2299
David Hobbs, *Sls & Mktg Exec*
Timothy Jordan,
EMP: 8 EST: 2009
SALES (est): 1.5MM **Privately Held**
SIC: 3441 Building components, structural steel

(G-6112)
FLW PLASTICS INC
Also Called: Air Support Medical
199 Raymond St (47246-9382)
P.O. Box 99 (47246-0099)
PHONE..................................812 546-0050
Fax: 812 546-0049
Kathy Walters, *President*
Lori Wiltsey, *General Mgr*
EMP: 25
SQ FT: 12,000
SALES (est): 931.7K **Privately Held**
SIC: 3089 3841 Injection molding of plastics; anesthesia apparatus

(G-6113)
FOURMAN ENTERPRISES INC
701 South St (47246-9345)
PHONE..................................812 546-5734
Fax: 812 546-1734
Gary Bailey, *President*
Boyd Emerson, *Sales Executive*
EMP: 14
SQ FT: 7,200
SALES (est): 2.4MM **Privately Held**
SIC: 3599 7699 Custom machinery; hydraulic equipment repair

(G-6114)
HOPE HARDWOODS INC
1006 Seminary St (47246-1427)
P.O. Box 37 (47246-0037)
PHONE..................................812 546-4427
Fax: 812 546-5607
D Thomas Miller, *President*
Lowell Miller, *Corp Secy*
Ben Miller, *Vice Pres*
Gary M Miller, *Vice Pres*
EMP: 10 EST: 1972
SQ FT: 13,000
SALES (est): 2MM **Privately Held**
SIC: 5084 2421 Sewing machines, industrial; sawmills & planing mills, general

(G-6115)
HOPE POWDER COAT INC
220 Raymond St (47246-9356)
PHONE..................................812 546-5555
Brian McKinley, *President*
Christi Law, *Vice Pres*
David Law, *Vice Pres*
▼ EMP: 3
SQ FT: 1,000
SALES (est): 180K **Privately Held**
SIC: 3399 Powder, metal

(G-6116)
INDIANA NEWS MEDIA LLC
Also Called: Hope Star Journal
645 Harrison St (47246-1203)
PHONE..................................812 546-4940
Larry D Simpson, *Principal*
EMP: 5
SALES (est): 227.3K **Privately Held**
SIC: 2711 Job printing & newspaper publishing combined

(G-6117)
PADEN ENGINEERING CO INC
100 Raymond St (47246-9382)
P.O. Box 100 (47246-0100)
PHONE..................................812 546-4447
Fax: 812 546-5312
Dennis Schulz, *President*
Patricia Schulz, *Vice Pres*
EMP: 7
SQ FT: 16,000

SALES (est): 1.1MM **Privately Held**
SIC: 3441 8711 Fabricated structural metal; engineering services

(G-6118)
PRICE MOTOR SPORT ENGINEERING
205 Main St (47246-1524)
PHONE..................................812 546-4220
Fax: 812 546-5111
Mary K Price, *President*
William F Price, *Corp Secy*
EMP: 5
SALES (est): 380K **Privately Held**
WEB: www.pricemotorsport.com
SIC: 3714 5531 3519 Motor vehicle parts & accessories; speed shops, including race car supplies; internal combustion engines

(G-6119)
RUSACH INTERNATIONAL INC
100 Raymond St (47246-9382)
PHONE..................................317 638-0298
Fax: 317 632-8594
Rudi Sachs, *Exec VP*
Kevin McIntosh, *Vice Pres*
▲ EMP: 15
SQ FT: 24,000
SALES (est): 3.1MM **Privately Held**
WEB: www.eimeldingen-us.com
SIC: 3545 5085 Machine tool attachments & accessories; rotary tables; industrial tools

---

Howe
Lagrange County

(G-6120)
CRUISER RV LLC
Also Called: Shadow Cruiser
160 W 750 N (46746-9236)
P.O. Box 130 (46746-0130)
PHONE..................................260 562-3500
Fax: 260 562-2210
David E Fought, *President*
Dan E Vanliew, *Treasurer*
EMP: 60
SQ FT: 30,000
SALES (est): 16.3MM
SALES (corp-wide): 7.2B **Publicly Held**
WEB: www.shadowcruiser.com
SIC: 3792 Truck campers (slide-in)
HQ: Heartland Recreational Vehicles Llc
2831 Dexter Dr
Elkhart IN 46514
574 266-8726

(G-6121)
D RV LUXURY SUITES LLC
1000 Interchange Dr (46746)
P.O. Box 235 (46746-0235)
PHONE..................................260 562-1075
David Fought, *President*
EMP: 75
SALES (est): 8.3MM **Privately Held**
SIC: 3799 Recreational vehicles

(G-6122)
DRV LLC
160 W 750 N (46746-9236)
P.O. Box 235 (46746-0235)
PHONE..................................260 562-1075
David E Fought, *President*
▲ EMP: 35
SALES (est): 8.5MM
SALES (corp-wide): 7.2B **Publicly Held**
WEB: www.doubletreervsuites.com
SIC: 3799 Recreational vehicles
HQ: Heartland Recreational Vehicles Llc
2831 Dexter Dr
Elkhart IN 46514
574 266-8726

(G-6123)
EXO-S US LLC
6505 N State Road 9 (46746-9702)
PHONE..................................260 562-4131
Bernard Lynk, *Manager*
EMP: 264
SALES (corp-wide): 115.9MM **Privately Held**
SIC: 3089 Injection molding of plastics

HQ: Exo-S Us Llc
6505 N State Road 9
Howe IN 46746
260 562-4100

(G-6124)
EXO-S US LLC
6505 N State Road 9 (46746-9702)
PHONE..................................260 562-4100
Bernie Lynk, *Branch Mgr*
EMP: 150
SALES (corp-wide): 115.9MM **Privately Held**
SIC: 3089 Injection molding of plastics
HQ: Exo-S Us Llc
6505 N State Road 9
Howe IN 46746
260 562-4100

(G-6125)
EXO-S US LLC (DH)
Also Called: Camoplast Crocker
6505 N State Road 9 (46746-9702)
P.O. Box 69 (46746-0069)
PHONE..................................260 562-4100
Emmanuel Duchesne, *CEO*
Sylvain Dupuis, *President*
Daniel Denault, *CFO*
◆ EMP: 112
SQ FT: 725
SALES: 86MM
SALES (corp-wide): 115.9MM **Privately Held**
SIC: 3089 Injection molding of plastics
HQ: Exo-S Inc
2100 Rue King O Bureau 240
Sherbrooke QC J1J 2
819 346-3967

(G-6126)
HENSCHEN SAND AND GRAVEL
4635 N 800 E (46746-9767)
PHONE..................................260 367-2636
EMP: 3 EST: 2012
SALES (est): 229.6K **Privately Held**
SIC: 1442 Construction sand & gravel

(G-6127)
LGIN LLC
6825 N 375 E (46746-9684)
PHONE..................................260 562-2233
John Larimer, *Principal*
EMP: 3
SALES (est): 131.9K **Privately Held**
SIC: 2068 Salted & roasted nuts & seeds

(G-6128)
MAKE IT MOBILE LLC
770 E State Road 120 (46746-9218)
P.O. Box 10 (46746-0010)
PHONE..................................260 562-1045
William Gibson,
EMP: 35
SALES (est): 200K **Privately Held**
SIC: 3714 Motor vehicle parts & accessories

(G-6129)
MICHIANA LAMINATED PRODUCTS
7130 N 050 E (46746-9706)
PHONE..................................260 562-2871
Fax: 260 562-3759
Michael R Sutter, *CEO*
Matthew R Sutter, *President*
Matthew Sutter, *President*
EMP: 12
SQ FT: 20,000
SALES (est): 2MM **Privately Held**
WEB: www.michianalaminated.com
SIC: 2541 Table or counter tops, plastic laminated

(G-6130)
NELSON J HOCHSTETLER
Also Called: Ban Transit
1935 W 450 N (46746-9609)
PHONE..................................260 499-0315
Nelson Hochstetler, *Owner*
Elizabeth Hochstetler, *Admin Sec*
EMP: 2 EST: 2004
SALES (est): 283.2K **Privately Held**
SIC: 3537 7389 Industrial trucks & tractors;

(G-6131)
RAPID SENSORS INC
6060 N 160 W (46746-9436)
P.O. Box 188 (46746-0188)
PHONE..................................260 562-3614
Larry Hedeen, *President*
EMP: 6
SALES (est): 490K **Privately Held**
WEB: www.rapidsensors.com
SIC: 3674 Ultra-violet sensors, solid state

Hudson
Steuben County

(G-6132)
COLD HEADING CO
103 W State Road 4 (46747-9336)
PHONE..................................260 587-3231
Fax: 260 587-3231
EMP: 50
SALES (corp-wide): 55.6MM **Privately Held**
WEB: www.coldheading.com
SIC: 3452 Bolts, metal
HQ: The Cold Heading Co
21777 Hoover Rd
Warren MI 48089
586 497-7000

(G-6133)
LA ZEE TEK
5610 S State Road 327 (46747-9704)
PHONE..................................260 351-3274
Barbara Kjendalen, *CEO*
James E Kjendalen, *President*
EMP: 3
SALES (est): 304.3K **Privately Held**
WEB: www.lazeetek.com
SIC: 3577 8731 Computer peripheral equipment; computer (hardware) development

---

Huntertown
Allen County

(G-6134)
ASPHALT DRUM MIXERS INC
Also Called: ADM
1 Adm Pkwy (46748-9790)
PHONE..................................260 637-5729
Fax: 260 637-3164
Wayne Boyd, *CEO*
Michael Devine, *President*
Linda Boyd, *Admin Sec*
▼ EMP: 50
SQ FT: 45,000
SALES (est): 16.8MM **Privately Held**
WEB: www.admasphaltplants.com
SIC: 3531 Mixers: ore, plaster, slag, sand, mortar, etc.

(G-6135)
CLUTE ENTERPRISES INC
Also Called: O3 Solutions
18706 Coldwater Rd (46748-9732)
PHONE..................................260 413-0810
Kevin Clute, *President*
John Langston, *Principal*
EMP: 2
SALES (est): 257K **Privately Held**
SIC: 3589 Sewage & water treatment equipment

(G-6136)
CREATIVE TOOL INC
2403 W Shoaff Rd (46748-9484)
PHONE..................................260 338-1222
Thomas Lowe, *President*
EMP: 4
SQ FT: 3,000
SALES (est): 680.9K **Privately Held**
SIC: 3541 Machine tool replacement & repair parts, metal cutting types

(G-6137)
EAGLE PRECISION MACHINING INC
2420 Shoaff R (46748)
PHONE..................................260 637-4649
Fax: 260 327-3999

▲ = Import ▼=Export
◆ =Import/Export

John Stieren, *President*
Joanne Stieren, *Admin Sec*
EMP: 8
SQ FT: 4,700
SALES (est): 605K **Privately Held**
SIC: 3541 Machine tool replacement & repair parts, metal cutting types

(G-6138)
FITCH INC
3708 Mccomb Rd (46748-9448)
PHONE..............................260 637-0835
Richard Fitch, *Branch Mgr*
EMP: 3
SALES (corp-wide): 17.7B **Privately Held**
SIC: 3491 Industrial valves
HQ: Fitch Inc
   585 Suth Front St Ste 300
   Columbus OH 43215
   614 885-3453

(G-6139)
H & H SALES COMPANY INC
16339 Lima Rd (46748-9756)
P.O. Box 686 (46748-0686)
PHONE..............................260 637-3177
Fax: 260 637-6880
John Hawkins, *CEO*
Phil Randall, *President*
Tom Hiser, *Vice Pres*
Rex Yant, *Vice Pres*
◆ **EMP:** 16
SQ FT: 23,000
SALES: 3MM **Privately Held**
WEB: www.hhsalescompany.com
SIC: 3713 3715 3499 Truck bodies (motor vehicles); trailer bodies; aerosol valves, metal

(G-6140)
INDIGO PRINTING & GRAPHICS
15732 Golden Eagle Cv (46748-9223)
PHONE..............................260 432-1320
Fax: 260 436-0748
Thoburn Hatch, *President*
Michael Oetting, *Vice Pres*
EMP: 8
SQ FT: 6,000
SALES (est): 750K **Privately Held**
SIC: 2752 Commercial printing, offset

(G-6141)
INNOVATIVE RFID INC
105 Twin Eagles Blvd W (46748-9296)
PHONE..............................260 433-5835
Stephen L Fink, *President*
Michael Westrick, *President*
EMP: 4
SALES (est): 290K **Privately Held**
SIC: 3825 Oscillators, audio & radio frequency (instrument types); radio frequency measuring equipment

(G-6142)
MANAGED CMMUNICATIONS SVCS LLC
18511 Lima Rd (46748-9703)
P.O. Box 387 (46748-0387)
PHONE..............................260 480-7885
Paul Prestia,
EMP: 15
SQ FT: 1,550
SALES (est): 1.3MM **Privately Held**
SIC: 3663 Airborne radio communications equipment

(G-6143)
PARAMETRIC MACHINING INC
16335 Lima Rd Ste 3 (46748-9302)
PHONE..............................260 338-1564
Michael Sutton, *President*
Sandra Sutton, *Admin Sec*
EMP: 13
SQ FT: 16,000
SALES: 1.1MM **Privately Held**
SIC: 3599 Machine shop, jobbing & repair; machine & other job shop work

(G-6144)
PRECISION WELDING CORPORATION
16403 Lima Rd (46748-9756)
P.O. Box 511 (46748-0511)
PHONE..............................260 637-5514
Fax: 260 637-5517
Orville E Hantz, *President*

Janice Hantz, *Corp Secy*
Kelly Kovets, *Vice Pres*
EMP: 4
SQ FT: 10,000
SALES (est): 584.1K **Privately Held**
SIC: 7692 3544 Welding repair; special dies, tools, jigs & fixtures

(G-6145)
PREVAIL DESIGN SYSTEMS LLC
5130 Willow Bluff Trl (46748-9798)
PHONE..............................260 245-1245
Aaron Engle, *President*
EMP: 5 **EST:** 2011
SALES (est): 255.2K **Privately Held**
SIC: 3571 Electronic computers; computers, digital, analog or hybrid; minicomputers

(G-6146)
RMT INC
2420 W Shoaff Rd (46748-9484)
P.O. Box 431 (46748-0431)
PHONE..............................260 637-4649
Fax: 260 637-6839
Paul Russell, *President*
Timothy Pease, *Vice Pres*
EMP: 15
SQ FT: 1,800
SALES (est): 2MM **Privately Held**
WEB: www.rmt-tooling.com
SIC: 3599 Machine shop, jobbing & repair

(G-6147)
SOMMER LETTER COMPANY LLC
3916 N County Line Rd E (46748-9486)
PHONE..............................260 414-6686
Kyle Sommer, *Principal*
EMP: 2
SALES (est): 62.9K **Privately Held**
SIC: 2711 Newspapers

(G-6148)
US AUTOMATION LLC
7143 State Road 3 (46748-9605)
PHONE..............................260 338-1100
Dale Duncan, *Mng Member*
Dee Duncan,
EMP: 8
SQ FT: 10,000
SALES (est): 1.4MM **Privately Held**
WEB: www.usautomationllc.com
SIC: 3599 Machine shop, jobbing & repair

(G-6149)
YB NORMAL CUSTOM WOOD WORKING
16335 Lima Rd (46748-9302)
PHONE..............................260 338-2003
Ted Geers, *Owner*
EMP: 3 **EST:** 2010
SALES (est): 250.5K **Privately Held**
SIC: 7389 5712 5021 2499 Design services; furniture stores; office & public building furniture; decorative wood & woodwork

---

Huntingburg
Dubois County

(G-6150)
B & A CNSTR & DESIGN INC
772 W 3rd St (47542-1206)
P.O. Box 135 (47542-0135)
PHONE..............................812 683-4600
Roger Thacker, *President*
EMP: 15
SQ FT: 12,500
SALES (est): 3.2MM **Privately Held**
SIC: 3448 Trusses & framing: prefabricated metal

(G-6151)
BY THE SWORD INC
304 E Sunset Dr (47542-9317)
PHONE..............................877 433-9368
David Rothgeb, *President*
EMP: 10
SALES: 950K **Privately Held**
SIC: 3312 Armor plate

(G-6152)
C & L LUMBER INC
8836 W State Road 64 (47542-9759)
PHONE..............................812 536-2171
Chuck Jones, *President*
Larry Jones, *Vice Pres*
EMP: 6
SALES (est): 380K **Privately Held**
WEB: www.cllumber.com
SIC: 2421 Sawmills & planing mills, general

(G-6153)
CECILS PRINTING & OFFICE SUPS
319 E 4th St (47542-1337)
PHONE..............................812 683-4416
Fax: 812 683-4416
Sue Fraze, *President*
Jeff Fraze, *Vice Pres*
EMP: 3
SQ FT: 1,000
SALES (est): 313.4K **Privately Held**
SIC: 2759 2752 5943 2796 Letterpress printing; commercial printing, offset; office forms & supplies; platemaking services; typesetting; bookbinding & related work

(G-6154)
CYCLONE SHOP INC
2403 S 600w (47542-9592)
PHONE..............................812 683-2887
Eugene Hopf, *President*
Jerry Hopf, *Corp Secy*
EMP: 2
SQ FT: 10,000
SALES: 175K **Privately Held**
SIC: 3441 1542 Fabricated structural metal; commercial & office building, new construction

(G-6155)
DMI FURNITURE INC
703 N Chestnut St (47542)
PHONE..............................812 683-2123
Fax: 812 683-5150
Rick Rosbottom, *VP Mfg*
Rick Rofbottom, *Manager*
EMP: 4
SQ FT: 28,798
SALES (corp-wide): 468.7MM **Publicly Held**
WEB: www.dmifurniture.com
SIC: 2521 2511 Desks, office: wood; desks, household: wood
HQ: Dmi Furniture, Inc.
   9780 Ormsby Station Rd # 2000
   Louisville KY 40223
   502 426-4351

(G-6156)
DMI FURNITURE INC
213 W 1st St (47542-9483)
P.O. Box 450 (47542-0450)
PHONE..............................812 683-4035
Mark Gogel, *Manager*
EMP: 15
SALES (corp-wide): 468.7MM **Publicly Held**
WEB: www.dmifurniture.com
SIC: 2511 2426 Wood household furniture; hardwood dimension & flooring mills
HQ: Dmi Furniture, Inc.
   9780 Ormsby Station Rd # 2000
   Louisville KY 40223
   502 426-4351

(G-6157)
DUBOIS COUNTY FREE PRESS LLC
4288 W 630s (47542-9660)
P.O. Box 46 (47542-0046)
PHONE..............................812 639-9651
Matthew Crane-Mcroberts,
EMP: 2 **EST:** 2011
SALES: 100K **Privately Held**
SIC: 2711 Newspapers: publishing only, not printed on site

(G-6158)
DUBOIS WOOD PRODUCTS INC (PA)
707 E 6th St (47542-1131)
P.O. Box 386 (47542-0386)
PHONE..............................812 683-3613

Fax: 812 683-3847
Jack B Parker, *CEO*
Bryan Meyerholtz, *President*
Paul Lueken, *Vice Pres*
Jerry Egloff, *Project Mgr*
Callie Meunier, *Project Mgr*
EMP: 160 **EST:** 1979
SQ FT: 200,000
SALES (est): 32.2MM **Privately Held**
SIC: 2511 Novelty furniture: wood

(G-6159)
DUBOIS WOOD PRODUCTS INC
610 E 5th St (47542-1403)
P.O. Box 386 (47542-0386)
PHONE..............................812 683-5105
Tud Allen, *Principal*
EMP: 20
SALES (corp-wide): 32.2MM **Privately Held**
SIC: 2511 2431 Tables, household: wood; millwork
PA: Dubois Wood Products, Inc.
   707 E 6th St
   Huntingburg IN 47542
   812 683-3613

(G-6160)
DUBOIS WOOD REALTY INC
Also Called: Dubois Wood Products
707 E 6th St (47542-1131)
P.O. Box 386 (47542-0386)
PHONE..............................812 683-3613
Bryan Myerholtz, *President*
Phil Leuken, *Corp Secy*
Paul Leuken, *Vice Pres*
EMP: 163
SQ FT: 73,000
SALES (est): 8.8MM **Privately Held**
WEB: www.duboiswood.com
SIC: 2521 Wood office furniture

(G-6161)
DURCHOLZ EXCAVATING & CNSTR CO
Also Called: Durcholz Excvtg & Cnstr Co In
4308 S State Road 162 (47542-9467)
PHONE..............................812 634-1764
Robert Anthony Durcholz, *President*
Mary Jane Durcholz, *Corp Secy*
EMP: 6
SQ FT: 1,200
SALES: 852.5K **Privately Held**
SIC: 1794 3715 Excavation work; trailer bodies

(G-6162)
ELEMENTAL INC
512 S Park Dr (47542-9244)
PHONE..............................812 684-8036
Robert Lamberson, *Owner*
EMP: 2
SALES (est): 74.4K **Privately Held**
SIC: 2819 Elements

(G-6163)
ENGLERT & MEYER CORPORATION
Also Called: Blessinger Brothers
6720 S 585w (47542-9232)
PHONE..............................812 683-3540
Randy Englert, *President*
Genin Robert, *Principal*
Annette Englert, *Vice Pres*
Carol Meyer, *Vice Pres*
Allen Meyer, *Treasurer*
EMP: 3
SQ FT: 4,000
SALES (est): 243.8K **Privately Held**
SIC: 1794 7692 5251 Excavation work; welding repair; hardware

(G-6164)
FARBEST FARMS INC
4689 S 400w (47542-9199)
P.O. Box 480 (47542-0480)
PHONE..............................812 481-1034
Theodore Seger, *President*
Gerald Jones, *Corp Secy*
EMP: 10
SALES (est): 2.3MM **Privately Held**
SIC: 2015 Poultry slaughtering & processing

GEOGRAPHIC

(G-6165)
FARBEST FOODS INC
4689 S 400w (47542-9199)
P.O. Box 480 (47542-0480)
PHONE....................................812 683-4200
Fax: 812 683-4226
Ted J Segar, *President*
Brian Hawkins, *Vice Pres*
Gerald K Jones, *Vice Pres*
Joseph Michael, *Vice Pres*
Dave Burkholder, *Plant Mgr*
EMP: 900
SQ FT: 100,000
SALES (est): 204.5MM **Privately Held**
WEB: www.farbestfoods.com
SIC: 2015 Turkey, processed

(G-6166)
FARBEST FOODS INTL INC
4689 S 400w (47542-9199)
PHONE....................................812 683-4200
Ted J Segar, *President*
EMP: 2 EST: 2014
SALES (est): 88.9K **Privately Held**
SIC: 2015 Turkey, processed

(G-6167)
GLOBAL CUTTING SOLUTIONS
613 E 7th St (47542-1103)
PHONE....................................812 683-5808
Randy Bolin, *Owner*
EMP: 13
SALES (est): 1MM **Privately Held**
SIC: 3545 Cutting tools for machine tools

(G-6168)
HUCKS FOOD FUEL
Also Called: Citgo
601 N Main St (47542-1043)
PHONE....................................812 683-5566
Mike Tubbs, *Manager*
EMP: 3
SALES (est): 192.1K **Privately Held**
SIC: 2869 Fuels

(G-6169)
HUNTINGBURG MACHINE WORKS INC
309 N Main St (47542-1344)
PHONE....................................812 683-3531
Fax: 812 683-4750
Mark Gasser, *President*
Mary Ann Lauderdale, *Office Mgr*
EMP: 16 EST: 1918
SQ FT: 7,100
SALES (est): 2.2MM **Privately Held**
WEB: www.huntingburg.org
SIC: 1711 5074 3599 Plumbing contractors; warm air heating & air conditioning contractor; plumbing & hydronic heating supplies; machine shop, jobbing & repair

(G-6170)
HURST CUSTOM CABINETS INC
1003 S Cherry St (47542-9493)
PHONE....................................812 683-3378
John Hurst, *President*
Janice Hurst, *Admin Sec*
EMP: 5
SALES: 450K **Privately Held**
SIC: 2434 Wood kitchen cabinets

(G-6171)
INDIANA SOUTHERN HARDWOODS
2739 S Saint Anthony Rd W (47542-8802)
PHONE....................................812 326-2053
Gene Merkley, *President*
Jolene Rogge, *General Mgr*
Frank Merkley, *Shareholder*
Joe Merkley, *Shareholder*
Richard Merkley, *Shareholder*
EMP: 30
SQ FT: 9,500
SALES (est): 4.1MM **Privately Held**
SIC: 2421 2449 Lumber: rough, sawed or planed; wood containers

(G-6172)
IRVING MATERIALS INC
Also Called: I M I
615 W 12th St (47542-9335)
PHONE....................................812 683-4444
Fax: 812 683-5776
Calvin Cash, *Branch Mgr*
EMP: 15
SALES (corp-wide): 800.6MM **Privately Held**
SIC: 3273 Ready-mixed concrete
PA: Irving Materials, Inc.
8032 N State Road 9
Greenfield IN 46140
317 326-3101

(G-6173)
KNIES SAWMILL INC
Also Called: Charles W Knies Sawmill
2238 E 550s (47542-9417)
PHONE....................................812 683-3402
Fax: 812 683-3402
Charles Knies, *President*
Chad Knies, *Principal*
Rachel Knies, *Principal*
Carla Kniles, *Principal*
David Kniles, *Principal*
EMP: 8
SQ FT: 20,000
SALES (est): 650K **Privately Held**
SIC: 2426 Flooring, hardwood

(G-6174)
LOEWENSTEIN FURNITURE INC
1204 E 6th St (47542-9375)
PHONE....................................800 521-5381
Bruce Albertson, *President*
EMP: 2
SALES (est): 207.5K **Privately Held**
SIC: 2519 2515 Furniture, household: glass, fiberglass & plastic; chair & couch springs, assembled; foundations & platforms

(G-6175)
MASTERBRAND CABINETS INC
Also Called: Production Systems Assoc
1009 N Geiger St (47542-8914)
P.O. Box 420, Jasper (47547-0420)
PHONE....................................812 482-2527
Fax: 812 683-2252
Steven Clifton, *General Mgr*
Shona Brown, *Purch Mgr*
Brian Mehringer, *Buyer*
John Roos, *Buyer*
Diane Webb, *Buyer*
EMP: 200
SALES (corp-wide): 5.2B **Publicly Held**
WEB: www.mbcabinets.com
SIC: 2434 Wood kitchen cabinets
HQ: Masterbrand Cabinets, Inc.
1 Masterbrand Cabinets Dr
Jasper IN 47546
812 482-2527

(G-6176)
NORTHSIDE MACHINING INC
407 W 12th St (47542-9226)
PHONE....................................812 683-3500
Fax: 812 683-3500
Paul Betz, *President*
Joseph A Betz, *Corp Secy*
EMP: 7
SQ FT: 4,500
SALES (est): 946.2K **Privately Held**
SIC: 3599 7692 3544 Machine shop, jobbing & repair; welding repair; special dies, tools, jigs & fixtures

(G-6177)
OFS BRANDS HOLDINGS INC
1204 E 6th St (47542-9375)
P.O. Box 100 (47542-0100)
PHONE....................................800 521-5381
Joseph Bellino, *Ch of Bd*
Robert H Menke Jr, *President*
Loretta Shamsey, *District Mgr*
Scott Hall, *Area Mgr*
Jane Colclasure, *Business Mgr*
▲ EMP: 2000 EST: 1937
SQ FT: 1,600,000
SALES (est): 228.8MM **Privately Held**
SIC: 2521 2522 2511 2599 Wood office furniture; office furniture, except wood; wood household furniture; hospital furniture, except beds

(G-6178)
PRECISION STONE WORKS
1984 W 950s (47542-9097)
PHONE....................................812 683-1102
Todd Brittain, *Owner*
▲ EMP: 15 EST: 2008

SALES (est): 1MM **Privately Held**
SIC: 2541 Counter & sink tops

(G-6179)
STEINKAMP WAREHOUSES INC
Also Called: Southern Indiana Treating
1000 N Main St (47542-1050)
P.O. Box 535 (47542-0535)
PHONE....................................812 683-3860
Fax: 812 683-2232
Scott A Steinkamp, *President*
Tony Bailey, *Admin Sec*
EMP: 45 EST: 1885
SQ FT: 18,000
SALES (est): 7.7MM **Privately Held**
SIC: 2491 5211 Preserving (creosoting) of wood; lumber & other building materials

(G-6180)
SUN ENERGY GROUP LLC
2740 W 1100s (47542-9403)
PHONE....................................812 683-1178
Thomas Chandler, *President*
EMP: 15
SALES (est): 2.7MM **Privately Held**
SIC: 1241 Coal mining services

(G-6181)
TAILGATERS INC
802 S Main St (47542-9167)
PHONE....................................812 827-3600
Sue E Potter, *President*
EMP: 2
SALES (est): 119.4K **Privately Held**
SIC: 2099 Sauces: gravy, dressing & dip mixes

(G-6182)
TRETTER BOEGLIN INC
Also Called: Huntingburg Vault Co
475 W 19th St (47542-8908)
PHONE....................................812 683-4598
Fax: 812 683-5336
Dennis Boeglin, *President*
Mike Tretter, *Vice Pres*
EMP: 8 EST: 1953
SQ FT: 8,000
SALES (est): 944.6K **Privately Held**
SIC: 3272 Burial vaults, concrete or precast terrazzo

(G-6183)
UNIMIN CORPORATION
1405 Industrial Park Dr (47542-9818)
P.O. Box 194 (47542-0194)
PHONE....................................812 683-2179
Kevin Heckel, *Manager*
EMP: 8
SALES (corp-wide): 136.2MM **Publicly Held**
WEB: www.unimin.com
SIC: 1455 3295 3281 Ball clay mining; minerals, ground or treated; cut stone & stone products
HQ: Covia Holdings Corporation
8834 Mayfield Rd
Chesterland OH 44026
800 255-7263

Huntington
Huntington County

(G-6184)
ADVANCED ENGINEERING INC
5299 N Mishler Rd (46750-8322)
PHONE....................................260 356-8077
Fax: 260 356-4197
Phillip Layman, *President*
Frances Stouffer, *QC Mgr*
John Layman, *Treasurer*
Dan Thompson, *Admin Sec*
EMP: 11
SQ FT: 10,000
SALES: 800K **Privately Held**
SIC: 3312 Tool & die steel

(G-6185)
ALTERNATIVE FUEL SOLUTIONS LLC
8380 N 200 W (46750-9724)
PHONE....................................260 224-1965
Hal Hoffman,
EMP: 6

SALES (est): 790.3K **Privately Held**
SIC: 2869 Fuels

(G-6186)
APPALACHIAN LOG HMS FULTN ELC
1268 Waterworks Rd (46750-3846)
PHONE....................................260 356-5431
EMP: 2
SALES (est): 200K **Privately Held**
SIC: 2452 Mfg Prefabricated Wood Buildings

(G-6187)
ATI PRODUCTS INC
Also Called: A & I Products
855 N Broadway St (46750-2584)
P.O. Box 8, Rock Valley IA (51247-0008)
PHONE....................................260 358-9254
Fax: 260 358-9256
Dawn Linzey, *Branch Mgr*
EMP: 8
SALES (corp-wide): 91.3MM **Privately Held**
SIC: 3469 Stamping metal for the trade
PA: Ati Products, Inc.
5100 W W T Harris Blvd H
Charlotte NC 28269
704 596-4493

(G-6188)
AUTO TRUCK GROUP LLC
1640 Riverfork Dr (46750-8444)
PHONE....................................260 356-1610
Brandon Fruechte, *Plant Mgr*
EMP: 15
SALES (corp-wide): 1.7B **Privately Held**
SIC: 3599 7692 3444 Machine shop, jobbing & repair; welding repair; sheet metalwork
HQ: Auto Truck Group, Llc
1420 Brewster Creek Blvd
Bartlett IL 60103
630 860-5600

(G-6189)
AVNET
3650 W 200 N (46750-9002)
PHONE....................................260 359-9513
EMP: 2
SALES (est): 116.6K **Privately Held**
SIC: 5065 3679 Electronic parts; electronic components

(G-6190)
BECKLER POWER EQUIPMENT
1255 S Jefferson St (46750-3824)
PHONE....................................260 356-1188
Timothy J Beckler, *Owner*
EMP: 2
SALES: 125K **Privately Held**
SIC: 5261 3546 Lawnmowers & tractors; saws & sawing equipment

(G-6191)
BENDIX COML VHCL SYSTEMS LLC
Bendix Wpdc
1850 Riverfork Dr (46750-9004)
PHONE....................................260 356-9720
Mike Pogorelc, *Plant Mgr*
Randy Seaman, *Opers Mgr*
Robert Laux, *Mfg Mgr*
Anelle James, *Engineer*
Melissa Thompson, *Controller*
EMP: 371
SQ FT: 102,000 **Privately Held**
SIC: 3714 4225 Motor vehicle parts & accessories; general warehousing & storage
HQ: Bendix Commercial Vehicle Systems Llc
901 Cleveland St
Elyria OH 44035
440 329-9000

(G-6192)
BENDIX MC II
1230 Sabine St (46750-2427)
PHONE....................................260 356-9720
Chris Camp, *Principal*
Tom Geren, *Human Res Mgr*
Cheryl Smart, *Cust Mgr*
Ken Harrell, *Sales Executive*
▲ EMP: 2 EST: 2009
SALES (est): 195.7K **Privately Held**
SIC: 2499 Shoe & boot products, wood

(G-6193)
BENSON SOLAR ENTERPRISES LLC
Also Called: Solar Goes Green
1140 E Franklin St (46750-2575)
P.O. Box 5156 (46750-5156)
PHONE...................................855 533-7467
Jodi Benson, *Mng Member*
Brady L Benson
EMP: 2 **EST:** 2011
SALES: 100K **Privately Held**
SIC: 3674 Solar cells

(G-6194)
BLUE COLLAR
23 E Washington St (46750-2726)
PHONE...................................260 359-8030
Art Easterday, *Owner*
EMP: 4
SALES (est): 327.4K **Privately Held**
SIC: 2599 Bar, restaurant & cafeteria furniture

(G-6195)
BRYAN MACHINE SERVICE INC
345 Commerce Dr (46750-9098)
PHONE...................................260 356-5530
Fax: 260 356-5234
Steven Bryan, *President*
EMP: 8
SQ FT: 12,000
SALES (est): 620K **Privately Held**
WEB: www.bryanmachine.com
SIC: 3599 3544 Machine shop, jobbing & repair; special dies, tools, jigs & fixtures

(G-6196)
CARRIER CORPORATION
3650 W 200 N (46750-9002)
PHONE...................................260 358-0888
Joel Jerabek, *Manager*
EMP: 750
SALES (corp-wide): 59.8B **Publicly Held**
WEB: www.carrier.com
SIC: 3672 Printed circuit boards
HQ: Carrier Corporation
    13995 Pasteur Blvd
    Palm Beach Gardens FL 33418
    800 379-6484

(G-6197)
CAUSE PRINTING COMPANY
5448 W 400 S (46750-8139)
PHONE...................................260 224-3515
EMP: 2
SALES (est): 83.9K **Privately Held**
SIC: 2752 Commercial printing, lithographic

(G-6198)
COACHES CONNECTION INC
200 E Park Dr (46750-2718)
P.O. Box 1123 (46750-1123)
PHONE...................................260 356-0400
James L Schroeder, *President*
Linda Schroeder, *Admin Sec*
EMP: 7
SALES (est): 740K **Privately Held**
WEB: www.coaches-connection.com
SIC: 5091 5941 2759 2752 Sporting & recreation goods; sporting goods & bicycle shops; commercial printing; commercial printing, lithographic; automotive & apparel trimmings; pleating & stitching

(G-6199)
CONTINENTAL STRL PLAS INC
1890 Riverfork Dr (46750-9004)
PHONE...................................260 355-4011
EMP: 234
SALES (corp-wide): 7.8B **Privately Held**
SIC: 3089 Plastic processing
HQ: Continental Structural Plastics, Inc.
    255 Rex Blvd
    Auburn Hills MI 48326
    248 237-7800

(G-6200)
D K ENTERPRISES LLC
1675 Riverfork Dr (46750-8427)
P.O. Box 151 (46750-0151)
PHONE...................................260 356-9011
Daniel M Drummond, *Administration*
EMP: 3

SALES (est): 168.8K **Privately Held**
SIC: 2295 Metallizing of fabrics

(G-6201)
E & B PAVING INC
875 N Broadway St (46750-2586)
PHONE...................................260 356-0828
Fax: 260 358-0454
Mike Jackson, *Superintendent*
Jared Hill, *Project Mgr*
Larry Booth, *Branch Mgr*
EMP: 16
SALES (corp-wide): 800.6MM **Privately Held**
SIC: 3273 Ready-mixed concrete
HQ: E & B Paving, Inc.
    286 W 300 N
    Anderson IN 46012
    765 643-5358

(G-6202)
ECOLAB INC
970 E Tipton St (46750-1611)
PHONE...................................260 359-3280
Fredric Ratliff, *Buyer*
Scott Pierce, *Plant Engr*
Tracey Hartman, *HR Admin*
Chris Petersen, *Branch Mgr*
Hattie Meekin, *Manager*
EMP: 80
SALES (corp-wide): 13.8B **Publicly Held**
WEB: www.ecolab.com
SIC: 2842 2841 Specialty cleaning, polishes & sanitation goods; disinfectants, household or industrial plant; deodorants, nonpersonal; floor waxes; soap & other detergents
PA: Ecolab Inc.
    1 Ecolab Pl
    Saint Paul MN 55102
    800 232-6522

(G-6203)
EL SHADDAI INC
517 N Jefferson St (46750-2748)
PHONE...................................260 359-9080
Randy Fields, *President*
Jason Fields, *Vice Pres*
Linda Fields, *Treasurer*
EMP: 5
SALES (est): 463.6K **Privately Held**
SIC: 2759 Screen printing

(G-6204)
FOIL DIE INTERNATIONAL INC
1054 W 900 N (46750-9772)
PHONE...................................260 359-9011
Fax: 260 359-1940
Lanie Creech, *President*
Cory Reust, *Manager*
Rhonda Creech, *Admin Sec*
EMP: 14
SQ FT: 3,600
SALES (est): 1.6MM **Privately Held**
WEB: www.foildie.com
SIC: 3544 Special dies, tools, jigs & fixtures

(G-6205)
FOIL FORM INC
1054 W 900 N (46750-9772)
PHONE...................................260 359-9011
Lanie Creech, *President*
Christopher Eckert, *Admin Sec*
EMP: 5
SALES (est): 498.6K **Privately Held**
SIC: 3544 Special dies, tools, jigs & fixtures

(G-6206)
GENERAL ALUMINUM MFG COMPANY
Also Called: Park Ohio
1345 Henry St (46750-3837)
P.O. Box 709 (46750-0709)
PHONE...................................260 356-3900
Gary Barlow, *Principal*
Tina Romano-Allen, *Human Res Dir*
EMP: 100
SALES (corp-wide): 1.4B **Publicly Held**
WEB: www.generalaluminum.com
SIC: 3365 Aluminum & aluminum-based alloy castings

HQ: General Aluminum Mfg. Company
    6065 Parkland Blvd
    Cleveland OH 44124
    440 947-2000

(G-6207)
GERDAU MACSTEEL INC
Heat Treating Division
25 Commercial Rd (46750-8805)
PHONE...................................260 356-9520
Ron Kensky, *Branch Mgr*
EMP: 48 **Privately Held**
WEB: www.quanex.com
SIC: 3398 Metal heat treating
HQ: Gerdau Macsteel, Inc.
    5591 Morrill Rd
    Jackson MI 49201

(G-6208)
HART PUBLISHERS INC
2955 E 630 N (46750-9673)
PHONE...................................260 672-8978
Susan C Hart, *Principal*
EMP: 2
SALES (est): 106.1K **Privately Held**
WEB: www.hartpublishers.com
SIC: 2741 Miscellaneous publishing

(G-6209)
HELENA AGRI-ENTERPRISES LLC
321 Thurman Poe Way (46750-4317)
PHONE...................................574 268-4762
Doug Goff, *Branch Mgr*
EMP: 30
SALES (corp-wide): 70.7B **Privately Held**
SIC: 5191 2879 Chemicals, agricultural; agricultural chemicals
HQ: Helena Agri-Enterprises, Llc
    255 Schilling Blvd # 300
    Collierville TN 38017
    901 761-0050

(G-6210)
HERITAGE TOOL AND DIE INC
Also Called: Heritage Arms
679 W Markle Rd (46750-9369)
PHONE...................................260 359-8121
Fax: 260 359-8403
John Wegmann, *President*
Jerry Smith, *Vice Pres*
Kevin Scheiber, *Admin Sec*
EMP: 5
SQ FT: 7,200
SALES (est): 700K **Privately Held**
SIC: 3544 Special dies, tools, jigs & fixtures

(G-6211)
HUNTINGTON COUNTY TAB INC
1670 Etna Ave (46750-4132)
P.O. Box 391 (46750-0391)
PHONE...................................260 356-1107
Fax: 260 356-1177
Scott Trauner, *President*
EMP: 13
SALES (est): 652.4K **Privately Held**
WEB: www.huntingtoncountytab.com
SIC: 2711 Newspapers: publishing only, not printed on site

(G-6212)
HUNTINGTON SHEET METAL INC
2060 Old Us Highway 24 (46750-1679)
PHONE...................................260 356-9011
Dan Drummond, *Branch Mgr*
EMP: 15
SALES (corp-wide): 27.4MM **Privately Held**
WEB: www.hsmetal.com
SIC: 3441 Fabricated structural metal
PA: Huntington Sheet Metal Inc
    1675 Riverfork Dr
    Huntington IN 46750
    260 356-9011

(G-6213)
HUNTINGTON SHEET METAL INC (PA)
1675 Riverfork Dr (46750-8427)
P.O. Box 151 (46750-0151)
PHONE...................................260 356-9011
Fax: 260 358-0762
Dan Drummond, *President*

Mike Easley, *Design Engr*
David Drummond, *Treasurer*
Brice Kaylor, *Sales Staff*
Roger Hubartt, *Manager*
EMP: 85
SQ FT: 90,000
SALES (est): 27.4MM **Privately Held**
WEB: www.hsmetal.com
SIC: 3444 7692 Sheet metal specialties, not stamped; welding repair

(G-6214)
HUNTINGTON TOOL & DIE INC
9 Commercial Rd (46750-8805)
PHONE...................................260 356-5940
Fax: 260 356-2931
Mark L Thompson, *President*
Jane Spears, *Manager*
EMP: 10 **EST:** 1965
SQ FT: 6,000
SALES: 720K **Privately Held**
SIC: 3544 Special dies & tools; jigs & fixtures

(G-6215)
INDIANA BOX COMPANY (DH)
1200 Riverfork Dr (46750-9054)
PHONE...................................260 356-9660
Fax: 765 728-5056
Robert L McIlvane, *CEO*
J Jordan Nerenberg, *Ch of Bd*
Jay King, *President*
Scott M Clary, *Treasurer*
Mike Davis, *VP Sales*
EMP: 40
SQ FT: 2,500
SALES (est): 10.7MM
SALES (corp-wide): 702.7MM **Privately Held**
SIC: 2653 Corrugated & solid fiber boxes
HQ: Royal Box Group, Llc
    1301 S 47th Ave
    Cicero IL 60804
    708 656-2020

(G-6216)
INDUSTRIAL CONTROL SERVICE
Also Called: I C S
1321 W Park Dr (46750-8028)
P.O. Box 1141 (46750-1141)
PHONE...................................260 356-4698
Mark Reust, *President*
EMP: 11
SQ FT: 3,000
SALES (est): 1.9MM **Privately Held**
WEB: www.icscontrolnet.com
SIC: 3599 Machine & other job shop work; machine shop, jobbing & repair

(G-6217)
INNOVATIVE PACKAGING ASSOC INC (PA)
1312 Flaxmill Rd (46750-1370)
PHONE...................................260 356-6577
Eugene Fleck, *CEO*
Chris Fleck, *Principal*
Brien Blackburn, *Vice Pres*
EMP: 12
SQ FT: 130,000
SALES: 10.1MM **Privately Held**
WEB: www.innpac.com
SIC: 2653 3086 Corrugated & solid fiber boxes; packaging & shipping materials, foamed plastic

(G-6218)
IRVING MATERIALS INC
500 Erie Stone Rd (46750-9682)
PHONE...................................574 653-2749
Fax: 574 653-2727
Fred Irving, *President*
Earl Brinker, *CFO*
EMP: 15
SALES (est): 1.4MM **Privately Held**
SIC: 1442 Sand mining; gravel mining

(G-6219)
IRVING MATERIALS INC
Also Called: I M I
500 Erie Stone Rd (46750-9682)
PHONE...................................260 356-7214
Larry Rich, *Branch Mgr*
EMP: 19

GEOGRAPHIC

SALES (corp-wide): 800.6MM Privately Held
SIC: 3273 Ready-mixed concrete
PA: Irving Materials, Inc.
　8032 N State Road 9
　Greenfield IN 46140
　317 326-3101

(G-6220)
J O WOLF TOOL & DIE INC
550 Condit St (46750-2506)
PHONE....................................260 672-2605
Keith Miller, President
Dawn L Miller, Vice Pres
EMP: 6
SQ FT: 4,800
SALES (est): 993.9K Privately Held
WEB: www.wolftool.com
SIC: 3544 Special dies & tools

(G-6221)
JOB SCHOLAR LLC
4399 E 300 N (46750-9519)
PHONE....................................419 564-9574
Trey Calver,
Jacob Bagley,
Aaron Wolf,
EMP: 3
SALES (est): 110.9K Privately Held
SIC: 2741 7375 7389 ; information re-
　trieval services;

(G-6222)
KOCH INDUSTRIES INC
502 E Hosler Rd (46750-9501)
PHONE....................................260 356-7191
Shawn Kimberly, Manager
EMP: 4
SALES (corp-wide): 44.4B Privately Held
WEB: www.kochind.com
SIC: 2879 Agricultural disinfectants
PA: Koch Industries, Inc.
　4111 E 37th St N
　Wichita KS 67220
　316 828-5500

(G-6223)
**LILLSUN MANUFACTURING CO
INC**
1350 Harris St (46750-4302)
P.O. Box 767 (46750-0767)
PHONE....................................260 356-6514
Lillian Sunderman, President
William Sunderman, Vice Pres
Sharon Sunderman Ulrich, Admin Sec
EMP: 9 EST: 1951
SALES (est): 680K Privately Held
WEB: www.lillsun.com
SIC: 2499 Woodenware, kitchen & house-
　hold

(G-6224)
LIME CITY MANUFACTURING CO
1470 Etna Ave (46750-3640)
P.O. Box 509 (46750-0509)
PHONE....................................260 356-6826
Fax: 260 356-3427
Randall C Rider, CEO
Karen J Keller Rider, President
Cory Reber, Corp Secy
Mandy Reber, COO
Mark Shultz, Vice Pres
EMP: 22 EST: 1941
SQ FT: 30,000
SALES: 3.5MM Privately Held
WEB: www.limecitymfg.com
SIC: 3469 3465 3643 7699 Stamping
　metal for the trade; automotive stamp-
　ings; current-carrying wiring devices;
　metal reshaping & replating services

(G-6225)
LIME CITY PRESS LLC
9712 N 300 W (46750-9726)
PHONE....................................260 344-3435
Thomas N Mills, Principal
EMP: 2
SALES (est): 76.3K Privately Held
SIC: 2741 Miscellaneous publishing

(G-6226)
**M & S INDUS MET FBRICATORS
INC**
Also Called: M & S Indus Met Fabricators
5 Commercial Rd (46750-8805)
PHONE....................................260 356-0300

Fax: 260 356-0398
Gary Mickley, Ch of Bd
Jason Mickley, President
Nancy Mickley, Vice Pres
Christian Brown, Purch Mgr
Zack Swain, Supervisor
EMP: 100
SQ FT: 72,000
SALES: 9MM Privately Held
SIC: 3444 Sheet metalwork

(G-6227)
M S POWDER COATING
5 Commercial Rd (46750-8805)
PHONE....................................260 356-0300
EMP: 2
SALES (est): 175.4K Privately Held
SIC: 3479 Metal coating & allied service

(G-6228)
MEMCOR INC
Also Called: Memcor-Truohm
1320 Flaxmill Rd (46750-4405)
PHONE....................................260 356-4300
Fax: 260 356-7376
Jeffrey R Crawford, President
Jeffrey Crawford, General Mgr
EMP: 15
SQ FT: 7,000
SALES: 1MM Privately Held
WEB: www.memcorinc.com
SIC: 3824 Mechanical & electromechanical
　counters & devices

(G-6229)
METALLOID CORPORATION
500 Jackson St (46750-2583)
P.O. Box 5139 (46750-5139)
PHONE....................................260 356-3200
Fax: 260 356-3201
Sheila Russ, Vice Pres
Kristi Schlotter, Purchasing
Robert McKay, Exec Dir
EMP: 20
SALES (corp-wide): 15MM Privately
Held
SIC: 2992 Lubricating oils & greases
PA: Metalloid Corporation
　1160 White St
　Sturgis MI 49091
　800 686-3201

(G-6230)
**MIDWEST INDUS MET
FBRCTION INC**
281 Thurman Poe Way (46750-4319)
P.O. Box 903 (46750-0903)
PHONE....................................260 356-5262
Fax: 260 356-5336
Blaine Kaylor, President
Stephanie Cutting, Technology
EMP: 45
SQ FT: 75,000
SALES (est): 9.5MM Privately Held
SIC: 3499 Fire- or burglary-resistive prod-
　ucts

(G-6231)
MIDWEST INDUSTRIAL METAL
2080 Old Us Highway 24 (46750-1679)
PHONE....................................260 358-0373
Blaine Kaylor, President
EMP: 7
SALES (est): 1MM Privately Held
SIC: 3499 Fabricated metal products

(G-6232)
**NORTHERN INDIANA PACKG CO
INC (DH)**
1200 Riverfork Dr (46750-9054)
PHONE....................................260 356-9660
Fax: 260 356-2754
Tim Tootle, President
EMP: 19
SALES (est): 3.9MM
SALES (corp-wide): 702.7MM Privately
Held
SIC: 2653 Boxes, corrugated: made from
　purchased materials
HQ: Schwarz Partners Packaging, Llc
　3600 Woodview Trce # 300
　Indianapolis IN 46268
　317 290-1140

(G-6233)
**ONWARD MANUFACTURING
COMPANY (DH)**
1000 E Market St (46750-2576)
PHONE....................................260 358-4111
Ted Witzel, CEO
◆ EMP: 73
SALES (est): 40.3MM
SALES (corp-wide): 11.5MM Privately
Held
SIC: 3631 5023 Barbecues, grills & bra-
　ziers (outdoor cooking); home furnishings
HQ: Onward Manufacturing Company Lim-
　ited
　585 Kumpf Dr
　Waterloo ON N2V 1
　519 885-4540

(G-6234)
OWENS FUEL CENTER
2718 Guilford St (46750-9701)
PHONE....................................260 358-1211
Dave Weaver, Manager
EMP: 3
SALES (est): 186.1K Privately Held
SIC: 2869 Fuels

(G-6235)
PATHFINDER AMRAMP LLC
2824 Theater Ave (46750-7978)
P.O. Box 1001 (46750-1001)
PHONE....................................260 356-0500
John Niederman,
Diana Laux,
EMP: 2
SALES (est): 219.7K Privately Held
SIC: 3448 Ramps: prefabricated metal

(G-6236)
**PATHFINDER SERVICES INC
(PA)**
Also Called: Pathfinder Cmnty Connection
2824 Theater Ave (46750-7978)
P.O. Box 1001 (46750-1001)
PHONE....................................260 356-0500
Fax: 260 356-3141
John J Niederman, President
Diana Laux, CFO
Tammy Fearnow, Human Res Dir
Jessica Miller, Marketing Staff
Matthew Miller, Administration
EMP: 50 EST: 1966
SQ FT: 10,000
SALES: 22.4MM Privately Held
WEB: www.pathfinderservices.org
SIC: 8331 7389 2652 Vocational rehabili-
　tation agency; sheltered workshop; pack-
　aging & labeling services; document &
　office record destruction; setup paper-
　board boxes

(G-6237)
PERFECTION WHEEL LLC
255 N Briant St (46750-2957)
PHONE....................................260 358-9239
Roger McClellan, Principal
Tony Hunnicutt, Prdtn Mgr
Karl Sorg, Prdtn Mgr
Larry Goken, Sales Staff
Teresa McClellan, Officer
EMP: 13 EST: 2010
SALES (est): 2.1MM Privately Held
SIC: 3714 Motor vehicle parts & acces-
　sories

(G-6238)
PHD INC
4763 N Us Highway 24 E (46750-9617)
PHONE....................................260 356-0120
Fax: 260 356-9369
Nelson Broman, COO
Frank Nunley, Maint Spvr
Ron Bradford, Engineer
Jodi Radziewicz, Human Res Mgr
Ron Cardin, Branch Mgr
EMP: 108
SALES (corp-wide): 49MM Privately
Held
WEB: www.phdinc.com
SIC: 3561 3494 Cylinders, pump; valves &
　pipe fittings
HQ: Phd, Inc.
　9009 Clubridge Dr
　Fort Wayne IN 46809
　260 747-6151

(G-6239)
POLAR SEAL INC
4461 W 500 N (46750-8941)
PHONE....................................260 356-2369
Joyce Rethlake, President
David Rethlake, Vice Pres
EMP: 3
SALES (est): 300K Privately Held
WEB: www.polarsealinc.com
SIC: 2952 Roofing materials

(G-6240)
PULLEY-KELLAM CO INC (PA)
Also Called: Premier Powder Coating
245 Erie St (46750-2999)
PHONE....................................260 356-6326
Fax: 260 356-1928
Marla A Foster, CEO
James L Foster, President
Dena M Kellam, Vice Pres
EMP: 22 EST: 1959
SQ FT: 100,000
SALES (est): 8.1MM Privately Held
SIC: 2522 3444 Office furniture, except
　wood; sheet metalwork

(G-6241)
QUANEX HEAT TREAT
25 Commercial Rd (46750-8999)
PHONE....................................260 356-9520
Fax: 260 356-9522
Ron Kensky, Manager
EMP: 40 EST: 2008
SALES (est): 2.5MM Privately Held
SIC: 3433 Heating equipment, except elec-
　tric

(G-6242)
QUICKBLADES
1640 Riverfork Dr Ste A (46750-8445)
PHONE....................................260 359-2072
Tim Delong, Regl Sales Mgr
EMP: 2
SALES (est): 117.5K Privately Held
SIC: 3479 Painting, coating & hot dipping

(G-6243)
RED LARK PRESS INC
230 George St (46750-2045)
PHONE....................................260 224-7974
Zachary C Weimann, President
EMP: 2
SALES (est): 85.4K Privately Held
SIC: 2741 Miscellaneous publishing

(G-6244)
ROYAL BOX GROUP LLC
Indiana Box Company
1200 Riverfork Dr (46750-9054)
PHONE....................................765 728-2416
Robert L McIlvane, CEO
Greg Wildman, Opers Mgr
Cynthia Seebold, Sales Staff
EMP: 54
SALES (corp-wide): 702.7MM Privately
Held
SIC: 2653 Boxes, corrugated: made from
　purchased materials
HQ: Royal Box Group, Llc
　1301 S 47th Ave
　Cicero IL 60804
　708 656-2020

(G-6245)
ROYER ENTERPRISES INC
Also Called: Indiana Wire Die Co
6780 N 362 W (46750-8882)
PHONE....................................260 359-0689
Brian Royer, President
Nancy Carpenter, Manager
EMP: 16
SQ FT: 12,000
SALES (est): 1.9MM Privately Held
WEB: www.indianawiredie.com
SIC: 3544 3291 Wire drawing & straight-
　ening dies; abrasive products

(G-6246)
SCHACHTPFISTER INC
232 E Washington St Ste 3 (46750-2749)
PHONE....................................260 356-9775
Fax: 260 356-0736
Steve Pfister, President
Jane Young, Admin Sec
▲ EMP: 5
SQ FT: 5,000

SALES (est): 370K **Privately Held**
SIC: 3069 Molded rubber products

(G-6247)
SCHNEIDER ELECTRIC USA INC
6 Commercial Rd (46750-8805)
PHONE..................................260 356-2060
Fax: 260 356-7451
Jim Harden, *Plant Mgr*
Sandra Merritt, *Safety Mgr*
Christine Troxell, *Human Res Mgr*
Claudia Estrada, *Manager*
Erick Walberth, *Director*
EMP: 16
SQ FT: 45,000
SALES (corp-wide): 200.4K **Privately Held**
WEB: www.squared.com
SIC: 5063 3612 Electrical apparatus &
   equipment; transformers, except electric
HQ: Schneider Electric Usa, Inc.
   800 Federal St
   Andover MA 01810
   978 975-9600

(G-6248)
SHUTTLEWORTH LLC (HQ)
Also Called: Shuttleworth North America
10 Commercial Rd (46750-8805)
PHONE..................................260 356-8500
Fax: 260 356-1315
Mark W Anderson, *President*
William M Schult, *President*
Ken Tinnell, *General Mgr*
Bret Ranc, *COO*
Richard Harrison, *Sr Corp Ofcr*
▲ EMP: 75 EST: 1962
SQ FT: 50,700
SALES (est): 23.3MM
SALES (corp-wide): 641.6MM **Privately Held**
WEB: www.shuttleworth.com
SIC: 3535 Conveyors & conveying equipment
PA: Pro Mach, Inc.
   50 E Rivercntr Blvd 180
   Covington KY 41011
   513 831-8778

(G-6249)
SPECIALTY ENGRG TL & DIE LLC
875 E State St (46750-2927)
P.O. Box 5171 (46750-5171)
PHONE..................................260 356-2678
Fax: 260 359-9027
David Goodpasture, *Mng Member*
EMP: 5
SQ FT: 8,000
SALES (est): 645.5K **Privately Held**
WEB: www.specialtyengineering.net
SIC: 3544 Special dies & tools

(G-6250)
SPEEDWAY REDI MIX INC
1217 W Park Dr (46750-8027)
PHONE..................................260 356-5600
Steve Turner, *Manager*
EMP: 12 **Privately Held**
SIC: 3273 Ready-mixed concrete
PA: Speedway Redi-Mix Inc
   4820 Industrial Rd
   Fort Wayne IN 46825

(G-6251)
SPORTSMOBILE INC
250 Court St (46750-2820)
PHONE..................................260 356-5435
Fax: 260 358-0328
Charles Borskey, *President*
Jane Borskey, *Corp Secy*
James Friermood, *Vice Pres*
EMP: 10
SQ FT: 12,000
SALES: 2.1MM **Privately Held**
WEB: www.sportsmobile.com
SIC: 3716 Recreational van conversion
   (self-propelled), factory basis

(G-6252)
STE INC
855 N Broadway St (46750-2584)
P.O. Box 566 (46750-0566)
PHONE..................................260 358-9254
Fax: 260 358-9256
Don Lindsey, *President*

EMP: 10
SQ FT: 12,800
SALES (est): 580K **Privately Held**
SIC: 3544 Special dies, tools, jigs & fix-
   tures

(G-6253)
STINES PRINTING
549 Warren St (46750-2723)
PHONE..................................260 356-5994
Fax: 260 356-6964
Rodney Stine, *President*
Kay Stine, *Vice Pres*
EMP: 3
SALES (est): 338.4K **Privately Held**
SIC: 2759 2752 2791 2789 Envelopes:
   printing; stationery: printing; visiting cards
   (including business): printing; commercial
   printing, lithographic; typesetting; book-
   binding & related work; automotive & ap-
   parel trimmings

(G-6254)
SUIZA DAIRY GROUP LLC
Also Called: Schenkel's All-Star Dairy
1019 Flaxmill Rd (46750-1362)
P.O. Box 642 (46750-0642)
PHONE..................................260 355-2273
Jim Lanciotti, *Branch Mgr*
EMP: 100 **Publicly Held**
SIC: 2026 Fluid milk
HQ: Suiza Dairy Group, Llc
   2515 Mckinney Ave # 1200
   Dallas TX 75201

(G-6255)
TRANSMETCO CORPORATION
Also Called: Keystone Automotive Industries
1750 Riverfork Dr (46750-8443)
PHONE..................................260 355-0089
Rob Wagman, *President*
Victor Casini, *Vice Pres*
John Quinn, *Vice Pres*
Vaughn Hooks, *Warden*
▲ EMP: 15
SQ FT: 42,500
SALES (est): 3MM
SALES (corp-wide): 9.7B **Publicly Held**
WEB: www.transmetcocorp.com
SIC: 3341 Aluminum smelting & refining
   (secondary)
PA: Lkq Corporation
   500 W Madison St Ste 2800
   Chicago IL 60661
   312 621-1950

(G-6256)
TRANSWHEEL CORPORATION (HQ)
Also Called: Coast To Coast
3000 Yeoman Way (46750-9003)
PHONE..................................260 358-8660
Fax: 260 358-2537
Jim Devlin, *Vice Pres*
Roger McClellan, *Vice Pres*
▲ EMP: 195
SQ FT: 53,000
SALES (est): 20.8MM
SALES (corp-wide): 9.7B **Publicly Held**
SIC: 3714 5521 Wheels, motor vehicle;
   used car dealers
PA: Lkq Corporation
   500 W Madison St Ste 2800
   Chicago IL 60661
   312 621-1950

(G-6257)
TWO EES WINERY
6808 N Us Highway 24 E (46750-9690)
PHONE..................................260 672-2000
Eric Harris, *Principal*
EMP: 7 EST: 2012
SALES (est): 610.8K **Privately Held**
SIC: 2084 Wines

(G-6258)
UNITED BRETHREN IN CHRIST
Also Called: Church Untd Brethern In Chrst
302 Lake St (46750-1264)
PHONE..................................260 356-2312
Phil Whipple, *Principal*
Ron Ramsey, *Pastor*
EMP: 11
SQ FT: 2,500

SALES (est): 960K **Privately Held**
WEB: www.ub.org
SIC: 2721 5942 Periodicals; book stores

(G-6259)
UNITED STATES MINERAL PDTS CO
Also Called: Isolatek International
701 N Broadway St (46750-2577)
P.O. Box 5006 (46750-5006)
PHONE..................................260 356-2040
Fax: 260 356-2337
Noah Price, *Plant Mgr*
Thomas Lund, *Opers Mgr*
Vergil Joe Underwood, *Production*
Todd England, *Engineer*
Dan Redner, *Finance Mgr*
EMP: 70
SQ FT: 1,000 **Privately Held**
WEB: www.cafco.com
SIC: 3296 2899 Mineral wool; chemical
   preparations
HQ: United States Mineral Products Com-
   pany Inc
   41 Furnace St
   Stanhope NJ 07874
   973 347-1200

(G-6260)
UNITED TECHNOLOGIES ELECTR
Also Called: UT Electronic Controls
3650 W 200 N (46750-9002)
PHONE..................................260 359-3514
Donald Cawley, *President*
Mike Roher, *General Mgr*
Kelly A Romano, *Principal*
Ronald Bruehlman, *Vice Pres*
Keith Heigl, *Engineer*
▲ EMP: 550
SALES (est): 163MM
SALES (corp-wide): 59.8B **Publicly Held**
SIC: 3822 Auto controls regulating residntl
   & coml environmt & applncs
HQ: Carrier Corporation
   13995 Pasteur Blvd
   Palm Beach Gardens FL 33418
   800 379-6484

(G-6261)
WILSON BURIAL VAULT INC
446 W Markle Rd (46750-9363)
P.O. Box 429 (46750-0429)
PHONE..................................260 356-5722
Garland Wilson, *President*
Greg L Wilson, *Corp Secy*
Everett Wilson, *Vice Pres*
EMP: 5 EST: 1970
SQ FT: 25,000
SALES (est): 598.2K **Privately Held**
WEB: www.wilsonburialvault.com
SIC: 3272 1799 Burial vaults, concrete or
   precast terrazzo; grave excavation

Indianapolis
Hamilton County

(G-6262)
BELDEN INC
401 Pennsylvania Pkwy (46280-1385)
PHONE..................................317 818-6300
Denis Suggs, *President*
Peter Cox, *Project Mgr*
Kathie Leffel, *Sales Associate*
Karis Davis, *Manager*
Geoff Webb, *Manager*
EMP: 239
SALES (corp-wide): 2.3B **Publicly Held**
WEB: www.cdtc.com
SIC: 3357 Nonferrous wiredrawing & insu-
   lating
PA: Belden Inc.
   1 N Brentwood Blvd Fl 15
   Saint Louis MO 63105
   314 854-8000

(G-6263)
EMPIRE LACROSSE & SPORTS INC
9700 Lake Shore Dr E B (46280-1997)
PHONE..................................317 574-4529
Chris Berju, *Owner*
Byron Stankus, *Principal*

EMP: 4
SALES (est): 200K **Privately Held**
WEB: www.empirelax.com
SIC: 3949 Lacrosse equipment & supplies,
   general

(G-6264)
FAST HOLSTER LLC
10376 Harrow Pl (46280-1449)
PHONE..................................317 727-5243
Jerry Clark, *President*
EMP: 3
SALES (est): 223.4K **Privately Held**
SIC: 3199 Holsters, leather

(G-6265)
GALBE MAGAZINE LLC
10540 Combs Ave (46280-1440)
PHONE..................................248 742-5231
Shellyn Ponder,
EMP: 2
SALES (est): 140K **Privately Held**
SIC: 2721 7389 Magazines: publishing &
   printing;

(G-6266)
HALO LLC (PA)
Also Called: Bastian Solutions
10585 N Meridian St Fl 3 (46290-1069)
PHONE..................................317 575-9992
William A Bastian II, *CEO*
▼ EMP: 90
SQ FT: 69,000
SALES (est): 256.2MM **Privately Held**
SIC: 8711 3535 Engineering services;
   conveyors & conveying equipment

(G-6267)
HANGER PRSTHETCS & ORTHO INC
Also Called: Hanger Orthopedics
10435 N Pennsylvna St (46280-1097)
PHONE..................................317 818-1459
Fax: 317 684-7797
Doug Hodgef, *Manager*
EMP: 5
SALES (corp-wide): 1B **Publicly Held**
SIC: 3842 Prosthetic appliances
HQ: Hanger Prosthetics & Orthotics, Inc.
   10910 Domain Dr Ste 300
   Austin TX 78758
   512 777-3800

(G-6268)
HP INC
10201 N Illinois St # 240 (46290-1114)
PHONE..................................317 566-6200
Fax: 317 582-4500
Charla Ireland, *Manager*
EMP: 90
SQ FT: 40,000
SALES (corp-wide): 52B **Publicly Held**
SIC: 3571 Personal computers (microcom-
   puters)
PA: Hp Inc.
   1501 Page Mill Rd
   Palo Alto CA 94304
   650 857-1501

(G-6269)
IP SOFTWARE INC
10333 N Meridian St (46290-1150)
PHONE..................................317 569-1313
Thomas Millay, *CEO*
EMP: 2
SALES (est): 150.4K **Privately Held**
SIC: 7372 Prepackaged software

(G-6270)
JOSTENS INC
9700 Lake Shore Dr E D (46280-2941)
PHONE..................................317 843-1958
Bill Palmer, *Manager*
EMP: 4
SALES (corp-wide): 14.7B **Publicly Held**
WEB: www.jostens.com
SIC: 3911 Rings, finger: precious metal
HQ: Jostens, Inc.
   7760 France Ave S Ste 400
   Minneapolis MN 55435
   952 830-3300

(G-6271)
LONE STAR INDUSTRIES INC (DH)
Also Called: Buzzi Unicem
10401 N Meridian St # 400 (46290-1154)
PHONE.................................317 706-3314
Fax: 317 805-3250
Massimo Toso, *President*
Patrick Lydon, *Vice Pres*
Nancy Krial, *CFO*
▲ EMP: 100 EST: 1919
SALES (est): 256.5MM
SALES (corp-wide): 287.7MM **Privately Held**
SIC: 3241 3273 Portland cement; ready-mixed concrete

(G-6272)
MARTIN MARIETTA MATERIALS INC
Also Called: Carmel Sand & Gravel
11010 Hazel Dell Pkwy (46280-2923)
PHONE.................................317 846-8540
EMP: 20 **Publicly Held**
WEB: www.martinmarietta.com
SIC: 1422 Crushed & broken limestone
PA: Martin Marietta Materials Inc
2710 Wycliff Rd
Raleigh NC 27607

(G-6273)
MASCO CORPORATION OF INDIANA (HQ)
55 E 111th St (46280-1071)
P.O. Box 40980 (46240-0980)
PHONE.................................317 848-1812
Fax: 317 848-0713
Keith J Allman, *CEO*
John G Sznewajs, *President*
Amit Bhargava, *Vice Pres*
Kenneth G Cole, *Vice Pres*
Richard G Hosteller, *Vice Pres*
◆ EMP: 300
SQ FT: 125,000
SALES (est): 452.6MM
SALES (corp-wide): 7.6B **Publicly Held**
SIC: 3432 Plumbing fixture fittings & trim; faucets & spigots, metal & plastic; plastic plumbing fixture fittings, assembly
PA: Masco Corporation
17450 College Pkwy
Livonia MI 48152
313 274-7400

(G-6274)
NEPTUNE FLOTATION LLC
101 W 103rd St (46290-1102)
PHONE.................................317 588-3600
Andrew W Elder, *President*
EMP: 10
SALES (est): 1.4MM **Privately Held**
SIC: 3089 Molding primary plastic

(G-6275)
PDMA INC
10201 N Illinois St # 420 (46290-1155)
PHONE.................................317 844-7750
Timothy L Wagner, *President*
EMP: 2
SALES (est): 326.3K **Privately Held**
SIC: 3825 Instruments to measure electricity

(G-6276)
PRECISION PRODUCTS GROUP INC (PA)
Also Called: Paramount Tube Division
10201 N Illinois St # 390 (46290-1148)
PHONE.................................330 698-4711
Dave Hooe, *President*
George Ondiek, *CFO*
▲ EMP: 384
SQ FT: 118,891
SALES (est): 85.1MM **Privately Held**
WEB: www.ppgme.com
SIC: 3495 3493 3496 2655 Wire springs; steel springs, except wire; miscellaneous fabricated wire products; tubes, mailing: made from purchased paper fiber; tubes, unsupported plastic

(G-6277)
PRECISION PRODUCTS GROUP INC
Also Called: Stone Industrial Division
10201 N Illinois St # 390 (46290-1148)
PHONE.................................301 474-3100
Timothy Kartisek, *Principal*
EMP: 132 **Privately Held**
WEB: www.ppgme.com
SIC: 2655 3089 3082 Tubes, fiber or paper: made from purchased material; plastic processing; unsupported plastics profile shapes
PA: Precision Products Group, Inc.
10201 N Illinois St # 390
Indianapolis IN 46290

(G-6278)
PRIORITY PRESS INC
Also Called: Press 96
9609 N College Ave (46280-1627)
PHONE.................................317 848-9695
Norm Melzer, *Owner*
EMP: 2
SALES (est): 130.2K
SALES (corp-wide): 17.4MM **Privately Held**
WEB: www.prioritygroupinc.com
SIC: 2759 5112 5049 Commercial printing; computer paper; engineers' equipment & supplies
PA: Priority Press, Inc.
4026 W 10th St
Indianapolis IN 46222
317 241-4234

(G-6279)
QUANTUMGRAPHIX LLC
10302 N College Ave (46280-1435)
PHONE.................................317 819-0009
Kevin Dowd, *Branch Mgr*
EMP: 3
SALES (est): 185.6K
SALES (corp-wide): 4.6MM **Privately Held**
SIC: 2752 Commercial printing, lithographic
PA: Quantumgraphix, Llc
2130 Watterson Trl
Louisville KY 40299
502 493-5933

(G-6280)
SAGAMORE READY MIX
5001 E 106th St (46280-2943)
PHCNE.................................317 573-5410
EMP: 2
SALES (est): 83.1K **Privately Held**
SIC: 5211 3273 1771 Cement; ready-mixed concrete; concrete work

(G-6281)
STRAHMAN HOLDINGS INC (HQ)
10201 N Illinois St # 200 (46290-1114)
PHONE.................................317 818-5030
John Aplin, *Managing Dir*
Brent Showalter, *Principal*
Eric Derheimer, *Asst Director*
EMP: 1 EST: 2013
SALES (est): 6.4MM
SALES (corp-wide): 19.8MM **Privately Held**
SIC: 3494 Valves & pipe fittings
PA: Cid Capital, Inc.
10201 N Illinois St # 200
Indianapolis IN 46290
317 818-5030

(G-6282)
TELECOM LLC
Also Called: Priority Communications
10401 N Meridian St # 401 (46290-1151)
PHONE.................................317 805-1090
Robert Brack, *President*
Steve Maddox, *Vice Pres*
Nathan McCord, *Opers Mgr*
EMP: 8
SALES (est): 156.5K **Privately Held**
SIC: 3661 Telephone answering machines

(G-6283)
WOODFIELD PRINTING INC
9700 Lake Shore Dr E (46280-1997)
PHONE.................................317 848-2000
Fax: 317 848-9900
Greg Pinkman, *President*
Bonnie Pinkman, *Treasurer*
EMP: 4
SQ FT: 2,100
SALES (est): 650K **Privately Held**
WEB: www.woodfieldprinting.com
SIC: 2752 2759 Commercial printing, off-set; commercial printing

---

Indianapolis
Marion County

(G-6284)
2 BEARS LLC
4725 Brookville Rd (46201-4707)
PHONE.................................317 375-1634
Michael Farley, *Mng Member*
Lawrence Bell, *Mng Member*
EMP: 2
SALES (est): 108.7K **Privately Held**
SIC: 2395 Embroidery & art needlework

(G-6285)
250OK LLC
9247 N Meridian St # 301 (46260-1879)
PHONE.................................855 250-6529
Greg Kraios, *CEO*
Jeff Hansen, *Vice Pres*
Joe Montgomery, *VP Mktg*
Paul Fearnow, *Director*
EMP: 3
SALES (est): 196K **Privately Held**
SIC: 7372 Business oriented computer software

(G-6286)
2FRESH PRINTS LLC
10329 Galena Ct (46239-8602)
PHONE.................................317 947-7164
Collin Wickware, *Principal*
EMP: 2
SALES (est): 83.9K **Privately Held**
SIC: 2752 Commercial printing, lithographic

(G-6287)
2SWEET PRINTING SERVICE LLC
3320 Falcon Dr (46222-4638)
PHONE.................................317 476-4402
Latonia Humphrey, *Owner*
EMP: 2
SALES (est): 86.6K **Privately Held**
SIC: 2752 Commercial printing, lithographic

(G-6288)
3M COMPANY
5457 W 79th St (46268-1675)
PHONE.................................317 692-6666
Denise Rutherford, *President*
Robert Klun, *Vice Pres*
Gene Brown, *Project Mgr*
Feng Cai, *Materials Mgr*
Dave Albean, *Engineer*
EMP: 332
SALES (corp-wide): 31.6B **Publicly Held**
SIC: 3841 3842 3291 2842 Surgical instruments & apparatus; bandages & dressings; abrasive products; specialty cleaning, polishes & sanitation goods; tape, pressure sensitive: made from purchased materials; adhesives & sealants
PA: 3m Company
3m Center
Saint Paul MN 55144
651 733-1110

(G-6289)
3M INDIANAPOLIS
7911 Zionsville Rd (46268-1650)
PHONE.................................317 692-3000
Inge G Thulin, *Ch of Bd*
Randy Mallitz, *Vice Pres*
EMP: 7
SALES (est): 472.2K **Privately Held**
SIC: 5731 8082 1446 Consumer electronic equipment; home health care services; industrial sand

(G-6290)
3RD DIMENSION LLC
Also Called: 3rd Dimension Indus 3d Prtg
7168 Zionsville Rd (46268-2163)
PHONE.................................317 941-7958
Robert Markley,
EMP: 7
SALES (est): 381.2K **Privately Held**
SIC: 3599 Machine shop, jobbing & repair

(G-6291)
4BOARD LLC
802 N Meridian St (46204-1118)
PHONE.................................317 997-3354
Timothy Bowen,
EMP: 3
SALES (est): 187.8K **Privately Held**
SIC: 3499 Novelties & specialties, metal

(G-6292)
55 MONUMENT CIR LEVEL OFF LLC
55 E Market St (46204-3016)
PHONE.................................317 423-9472
EMP: 3
SALES (est): 147.1K **Privately Held**
SIC: 3272 Monuments & grave markers, except terrazo

(G-6293)
A C MALLORY CAPACITORS LLC (PA)
4411 S High School Rd (46241-6404)
PHONE.................................317 612-1000
Ronald Voegele, *CFO*
Wayne Hodges,
EMP: 78
SQ FT: 45,000
SALES (est): 9.6MM **Privately Held**
WEB: www.mallory-ac.com
SIC: 3675 Electronic capacitors

(G-6294)
A CREATE SPACE INC
2750 E 55th St Ste D (46220-3667)
PHONE.................................317 254-2600
Tom Hayes, *Principal*
EMP: 3
SALES (est): 379.1K **Privately Held**
SIC: 3261 Bathroom accessories/fittings, vitreous china or earthenware

(G-6295)
A G A GAS INC
5825 Elmwood Ave (46203-6032)
PHONE.................................317 783-2331
Fax: 317 786-6015
Bob Hilliard, *President*
EMP: 20
SALES (est): 1.8MM **Privately Held**
SIC: 2813 Industrial gases

(G-6296)
A HARRIS VERL INC
Also Called: Sign-A-Rama
1331 N Capitol Ave (46202-2313)
PHONE.................................317 736-4680
Fax: 317 290-0493
Verl Allen Harris, *President*
Judith Caroline Harris, *Vice Pres*
EMP: 4
SQ FT: 3,200
SALES: 500K **Privately Held**
WEB: www.signarama.com
SIC: 3993 Signs & advertising specialties

(G-6297)
A L E ENTERPRISES
4623 S High School Rd (46241-7652)
PHONE.................................317 856-2981
Anthony L Elrod, *Owner*
EMP: 5
SALES (est): 302.7K **Privately Held**
SIC: 1521 1542 2511 2521 General remodeling, single-family houses; commercial & office building, new construction; wood household furniture; cabinets, office: wood

(G-6298)
A MAYES ING INC
3335 N Keystone Ave (46218-2075)
PHONE.................................317 925-5777
David Mayes, *President*
Ann Mayes, *Vice Pres*

Georgia Watson, *Treasurer*
EMP: 6
SQ FT: 1,700
SALES (est): 229.7K
SALES (corp-wide): 1.4MM **Privately Held**
WEB: www.3dtrophyamayesinginc.com
SIC: 7389 3089 2759 Engraving service; engraving of plastic; screen printing
PA: 3-D Trophy & Engraving Co Inc
3335 N Keystone Ave
Indianapolis IN 46218
317 925-5777

(G-6299)
A PALLET COMPANY
1305 Bedford St (46221-1409)
PHONE...................................317 687-9020
SA Mencer, *President*
Scott Mencer, *Manager*
EMP: 8
SALES (est): 1.3MM **Privately Held**
SIC: 2448 Pallets, wood

(G-6300)
A PLUS IMAGES I N C
5700 W Minn St Ste A5 (46241-3855)
PHONE...................................317 405-8955
Robert Straka, *President*
Doug Straka, *Vice Pres*
EMP: 2
SALES (est): 300K **Privately Held**
SIC: 2759 Screen printing

(G-6301)
A-1 AWARDS INC
2500 N Ritter Ave (46218-3294)
PHONE...................................317 546-9000
Fax: 317 542-1900
Stephen L Capper, *President*
Nora Capper, *Treasurer*
Chris Alstott, *Technology*
▲ EMP: 15
SQ FT: 15,000
SALES (est): 2MM **Privately Held**
WEB: www.a-1awards.com
SIC: 3914 2789 2396 2395 Trophies, silver; trophies, pewter; trophies, plated (all metals); trophies, stainless steel; bookbinding & related work; automotive & apparel trimmings; pleating & stitching

(G-6302)
A-1 LETTER SHOP INC
Also Called: A-1 Letter & Print Shop
417 E Ohio St (46204-2121)
PHONE...................................317 632-7212
Fax: 317 638-0547
Gary R Hollingsworth, *President*
Larry Palmer, *Treasurer*
Jenny L Hollingsworth, *Admin Sec*
EMP: 4
SQ FT: 3,000
SALES (est): 479.7K **Privately Held**
SIC: 2752 Commercial printing, offset

(G-6303)
A-1 SHADE CO
5550 Marnette St (46241-1244)
PHONE...................................317 247-6447
EMP: 2
SQ FT: 3,000
SALES (est): 135.2K **Privately Held**
SIC: 2591 5719 Mfg Drapery Hardware/Blinds Ret Misc Homefurnishings

(G-6304)
A-1VET LLC
4411 Dunn St (46226-3935)
PHONE...................................317 498-1804
Nicholas Biddy, *President*
EMP: 3
SALES (est): 134.8K **Privately Held**
SIC: 3679 7389 Harness assemblies for electronic use: wire or cable;

(G-6305)
AARVEE ASSOCIATES LLC
Also Called: Signs By Tmrrow Indanapolis NW
9541 Valparaiso Ct (46268-1130)
PHONE...................................312 222-5665
Rajesh Patnaik,
Vidhya Patnaik,
EMP: 2 EST: 2012

SALES (est): 128.5K **Privately Held**
SIC: 3993 Signs, not made in custom sign painting shops

(G-6306)
ABARI PROPERTIES DEVELOPMENT
5137 Red Yarrow Way (46254-5303)
PHONE...................................317 721-9230
Shirlaun Hubbard, *Principal*
EMP: 6
SQ FT: 2,250
SALES (est): 170.4K **Privately Held**
SIC: 8741 1521 1389 Management services; single-family housing construction; construction, repair & dismantling services

(G-6307)
ABB FLEXIBLE AUTOMATION INC
Also Called: ABB Robotics
8401 Northwest Blvd (46278-1382)
PHONE...................................317 876-9090
Fax: 317 872-4129
Edward Gross, *Branch Mgr*
EMP: 40
SALES (corp-wide): 34.3B **Privately Held**
SIC: 3569 3625 3563 Robots, assembly line: industrial & commercial; relays & industrial controls; air & gas compressors
HQ: Abb Flexible Automation Inc.
1250 Brown Rd
Auburn Hills MI 48326
248 391-9000

(G-6308)
ABBOTT CONTROLS INC
Also Called: Honeywell Authorized Dealer
3535 Kessler Blvd N Dr (46222-1831)
PHONE...................................317 697-7102
Dave Abbott, *President*
Kristi Abbott, *Vice Pres*
EMP: 4
SALES (est): 603.5K **Privately Held**
SIC: 3822 Temperature controls, automatic

(G-6309)
ABBOTT LABORATORIES
7155 Wadsworth Way (46219-1751)
PHONE...................................317 356-5478
Michael Writt, *Manager*
EMP: 34
SALES (corp-wide): 27.3B **Publicly Held**
WEB: www.abbott.com
SIC: 2834 Vitamin, nutrient & hematinic preparations for human use
PA: Abbott Laboratories
100 Abbott Park Rd
Abbott Park IL 60064
224 667-6100

(G-6310)
ABELL ENGINEERING & MFG
2229 E New York St (46201-3148)
PHONE...................................317 687-1174
Fax: 317 687-1175
George Abell, *President*
Nicole Abell, *Vice Pres*
EMP: 10
SQ FT: 5,000
SALES (est): 1.5MM **Privately Held**
SIC: 3444 Sheet metalwork

(G-6311)
ABLE WOODCRAFTERS LLC
8180 River Bay Dr E (46240-2997)
PHONE...................................317 915-1225
Cheryl Bole, *Principal*
EMP: 3
SALES (est): 179.5K **Privately Held**
SIC: 2511 Wood household furniture

(G-6312)
ABRASIVE PRODUCTS LLC
701 W Henry St (46225-1182)
PHONE...................................317 423-3957
EMP: 2
SALES (est): 66.9K **Privately Held**
SIC: 3291 Abrasive products

(G-6313)
ACCU-TECH AUTOMATION INC
1752 Lutherwood Dr (46219-1957)
PHONE...................................317 352-1490

Fax: 317 352-1500
Brian Rhinehart, *President*
EMP: 10
SQ FT: 6,000
SALES (est): 1.5MM **Privately Held**
WEB: www.accu-techautomation.com
SIC: 3535 Conveyors & conveying equipment

(G-6314)
ACCUCAST INC
9705 Decatur Dr (46256-9655)
PHONE...................................317 849-5521
Fax: 317 849-5521
Steven A Robinson, *President*
James A Robinson Sr, *Corp Secy*
EMP: 2 EST: 1990
SQ FT: 1,000
SALES: 200K **Privately Held**
SIC: 3321 8711 Gray iron castings; ductile iron castings; consulting engineer

(G-6315)
ACD SUPPLIERS LLC
5426 Wood Hollow Dr (46239-6899)
PHONE...................................317 527-9715
Anh Dinh, *Principal*
EMP: 2 EST: 2015
SALES (est): 76.1K **Privately Held**
SIC: 5015 3661 5113 7999 Automotive supplies, used; telephone central office equipment, dial or manual; sanitary food containers; night club, not serving alcoholic beverages; office & public building furniture

(G-6316)
ACE MOBILITY INC
9850 E 30th St (46229-3608)
PHONE...................................317 241-2444
Tim Roberts, *President*
◆ EMP: 16
SQ FT: 16,000
SALES (est): 1.4MM **Privately Held**
WEB: www.ahnafield.com
SIC: 3089 Automotive parts, plastic

(G-6317)
ACI CONSTRUCTION COMPANY INC
5108 Topp Dr (46218-3259)
PHONE...................................317 549-1833
Fax: 317 549-1880
Lindsey Lewis, *President*
EMP: 15
SALES (est): 2.5MM **Privately Held**
SIC: 2851 Paints, asphalt or bituminous; putty, wood fillers & sealers; putty

(G-6318)
ACS SIGN SOLUTION (PA)
1110 E 22nd St (46202-1848)
PHONE...................................317 925-2835
Joseph Lehner, *Principal*
EMP: 10
SALES (est): 982.6K **Privately Held**
SIC: 3993 Electric signs

(G-6319)
ACS SIGN SOLUTION
Also Called: ACS Sign Systems
115 E 21st St (46202-1423)
PHONE...................................317 201-4838
Richard Lutin, *Branch Mgr*
EMP: 3
SALES (corp-wide): 982.6K **Privately Held**
SIC: 3993 Signs & advertising specialties
PA: Acs Sign Solution
1110 E 22nd St
Indianapolis IN 46202
317 925-2835

(G-6320)
ACTERNA LLC
5808 Churchman Byp (46203-6109)
PHONE...................................317 788-9351
Joe Banich, *Plant Mgr*
Gerald Rudolf, *Engineer*
Troy Thorpe, *Engineer*
Dale Boyle, *Branch Mgr*
Robert Flask, *Manager*
EMP: 25

SALES (corp-wide): 811.4MM **Publicly Held**
SIC: 3669 7379 3825 5065 Intercommunication systems, electric; computer related consulting services; ; instruments to measure electricity; test equipment for electronic & electric measurement; electronic parts & equipment; electronic circuits; testing laboratories
HQ: Acterna Llc
20250 Century Blvd # 100
Germantown MD 20874
301 353-1550

(G-6321)
ACTION BRACE AND PROSTHETICS
5942 W 71st St (46278-1728)
PHONE...................................317 347-4222
Fax: 317 347-4227
EMP: 10 EST: 1998
SQ FT: 3,600
SALES: 710K **Privately Held**
SIC: 3842 Retails Prosthetics

(G-6322)
ACTIVE SENSORS INCORPORATED
8520 Allison Pointe Blvd # 220 (46250-5700)
PHONE...................................317 713-2973
Christopher Smith, *President*
EMP: 2
SALES: 950K **Privately Held**
SIC: 3672 Printed circuit boards

(G-6323)
ADAPTIVE MOBILITY INC
7040 Guion Rd (46268-4812)
PHONE...................................317 347-6400
Fax: 317 347-6409
F Keith Conaway, *CEO*
Janice Conaway, *President*
EMP: 14
SQ FT: 24,000
SALES (est): 1MM **Privately Held**
SIC: 3999 5047 Wheelchair lifts; medical equipment & supplies

(G-6324)
ADDENDA CORPORATION (HQ)
5929 Lakeside Blvd (46278-1996)
PHONE...................................317 290-5007
Gary R Mitchener, *President*
Mark S McCaughey, *Vice Pres*
EMP: 3
SALES (est): 695.7K
SALES (corp-wide): 17MM **Privately Held**
WEB: www.addendacorporation.com
SIC: 2899 Chemical preparations
PA: Metals And Additives, Llc
5929 Lakeside Blvd
Indianapolis IN 46278
317 290-5007

(G-6325)
ADHESIVE PRODUCTS INC
9635 Park Davis Dr (46235-5202)
P.O. Box 6434, Fishers (46038-6434)
PHONE...................................317 899-0565
Dave Rebholc, *President*
EMP: 5
SALES (est): 726K **Privately Held**
WEB: www.apcglue.com
SIC: 2672 5169 Adhesive backed films, foams & foils; chemicals & allied products

(G-6326)
ADIDAS GROUP
8677 Logo Athletic Ct (46219-1430)
PHONE...................................317 895-7000
Blake Lunberg, *President*
Bruce Neff, *Traffic Mgr*
Remedios Arguello, *Manager*
Kristen Lasorsa, *Manager*
Jeremy Ronnebaum, *Analyst*
EMP: 2
SALES (est): 470K **Privately Held**
SIC: 3021 Canvas shoes, rubber soled

(G-6327)
ADM MOBILITY SOLUTIONS INC
8360 W Washington St (46231-1349)
PHONE...................................317 481-8707
Ronald Beaman, *President*

Shannon L Beaman, *Vice Pres*
EMP: 2
SALES (est): 417.9K **Privately Held**
SIC: 7532 3711 Van conversion; automobile bodies, passenger car, not including engine, etc.

(G-6328)
ADMIRAL MEDICAL CENTER INC
Also Called: Professional Diabetes Center
5435 Emerson Way Ste 210 (46226-1469)
PHONE....................................317 924-3757
Richard Graves, *President*
EMP: 6 EST: 2008
SQ FT: 2,500
SALES (est): 532.9K **Privately Held**
SIC: 3841 Surgical & medical instruments

(G-6329)
ADRIAN ORCHARDS INC
500 W Epler Ave (46217-3620)
PHONE....................................317 784-0550
Fax: 317 784-6605
George J Adrian, *President*
Janet Adrian-Nixon, *Treasurer*
Monika Adrian, *Sales Executive*
EMP: 6
SQ FT: 2,000
SALES (est): 420K **Privately Held**
SIC: 0175 0171 2099 Apple orchard; berry crops; cider, nonalcoholic

(G-6330)
ADVANCE PRTECTIVE COATINGS INC
Also Called: Line-X of Indy
8448 Moller Rd (46268-1507)
PHONE....................................317 228-0123
Dave Unger, *President*
Michael Smith, *Vice Pres*
Lucia Smith, *Treasurer*
EMP: 8
SQ FT: 10,000
SALES: 450K **Privately Held**
SIC: 2821 3714 Plastics materials & resins; pickup truck bed liners

(G-6331)
ADVANCE STORES COMPANY INC
Also Called: Advance Auto Parts
5125 N Keystone Ave (46205-1559)
PHONE....................................317 253-5034
Carl T Hansen Jr, *CPA*
Jessica Christensen, *Branch Mgr*
EMP: 9
SALES (corp-wide): 9.3B **Publicly Held**
SIC: 5531 3825 Automobile & truck equipment & parts; battery testers, electrical
HQ: Advance Stores Company Incorporated
5008 Airport Rd Nw
Roanoke VA 24012
540 362-4911

(G-6332)
ADVANCED CONTROL TECH INC
Also Called: Act
6805 Hillsdale Ct (46250-2039)
P.O. Box 40965 (46240-0965)
PHONE....................................317 806-2750
Gary Colip, *President*
Judith Colip, *Vice Pres*
▲ **EMP:** 5
SQ FT: 16,000
SALES (est): 933.5K **Privately Held**
WEB: www.act-solutions.com
SIC: 3822 3674 3643 3625 Thermostats & other environmental sensors; semiconductors & related devices; light emitting diodes; current-carrying wiring devices; relays & industrial controls

(G-6333)
ADVANCED DRAINAGE SYSTEMS
420 S Belmont Ave (46222-4269)
PHONE....................................317 917-7960
EMP: 3 EST: 2016
SALES (est): 112.8K **Privately Held**
SIC: 3317 Steel pipe & tubes

(G-6334)
ADVANCED ORTHOPRO INC (PA)
1820 N Illinois St (46202-1318)
PHONE....................................317 924-4444
Fax: 317 924-6319
Mohamad Mansoori, *President*
Pamela Julian, *General Mgr*
Aboul Mansoori, *Corp Secy*
Karen Mansoori, *Vice Pres*
EMP: 25
SQ FT: 7,600
SALES (est): 2.7MM **Privately Held**
WEB: www.advancedorthopro.com
SIC: 3842 8011 Braces, orthopedic; prosthetic appliances; offices & clinics of medical doctors

(G-6335)
ADVANCED RACG SUSPENSIONS INC
1698 Midwest Blvd (46214-2281)
PHONE....................................317 896-3306
Fax: 317 271-1225
Corey Fillip, *President*
EMP: 11
SQ FT: 2,500
SALES: 1.5MM **Privately Held**
WEB: www.advancedracingsusp.com
SIC: 3714 Shock absorbers, motor vehicle

(G-6336)
ADVANCED SERVICES LLC
5426 Elmwood Ave (46203-6025)
PHONE....................................317 780-6909
Fax: 317 786-8265
Paul Clark, *Mng Member*
EMP: 15
SALES (est): 2MM **Privately Held**
WEB: www.paulclark.com
SIC: 2273 Carpets & rugs

(G-6337)
ADVANTAGE COMPONENTS CORP
2233 S West St (46225-2063)
PHONE....................................317 784-0299
George Hilgemeier, *CEO*
Steve Vogel, *President*
Roger Beal, *Vice Pres*
EMP: 5 EST: 1999
SALES (est): 497.2K **Privately Held**
SIC: 3599 Machine shop, jobbing & repair

(G-6338)
ADVANTAGE FLUID SYSTEMS LLC
Also Called: Afs Fluid Controls
8170 Zionsville Rd (46268-1625)
PHONE....................................800 317-1570
Doug Wilber, *Mng Member*
EMP: 2
SALES (est): 444.6K **Privately Held**
SIC: 3593 Fluid power actuators, hydraulic or pneumatic

(G-6339)
ADVANTAGE MANUFACTURING
1802 W 10th St (46222-3804)
PHONE....................................317 237-4289
Fax: 317 237-4548
Richard Bryant, *Owner*
EMP: 4
SQ FT: 8,000
SALES: 500K **Privately Held**
SIC: 3444 Sheet metalwork

(G-6340)
ADVENT PRECISION INC
1740 Industry Dr Ste F (46219-2738)
PHONE....................................317 908-6937
Timothy Brenamen, *President*
Mark Earls, *Vice Pres*
EMP: 4
SQ FT: 2,400
SALES: 150K **Privately Held**
SIC: 3545 Precision tools, machinists'

(G-6341)
AEARO TECHNOLOGIES LLC (HQ)
Also Called: Aearo Company
5457 W 79th St (46268-1675)
P.O. Box 33331, Saint Paul MN (55133-3331)
PHONE....................................317 692-6666
Fax: 317 692-6772
Julie Bushman, *President*
Robert D Anderson, *Principal*
Brian S McGinley, *Principal*
Ron Reed, *Finance*
Robert T Cimperman, *Mng Member*
▲ **EMP:** 600
SQ FT: 200,000
SALES: 318.3MM
SALES (corp-wide): 31.6B **Publicly Held**
WEB: www.aearo.com
SIC: 3842 3851 3643 Ear plugs; noise protectors, personal; protective eyewear; plugs, electric
PA: 3m Company
3m Center
Saint Paul MN 55144
651 733-1110

(G-6342)
AEARO TECHNOLOGIES LLC
E-A-R Specialty Composites
7911 Zionsville Rd (46268-1650)
PHONE....................................317 692-6666
Fax: 317 692-3111
Randy Mallitz, *Branch Mgr*
EMP: 200
SALES (corp-wide): 31.6B **Publicly Held**
WEB: www.aearo.com
SIC: 3086 3444 3443 3296 Plastics foam products; sheet metalwork; fabricated plate work (boiler shop); mineral wool; gaskets, packing & sealing devices; plastics materials & resins
HQ: Aearo Technologies Llc
5457 W 79th St
Indianapolis IN 46268
317 692-6666

(G-6343)
AERIAL DRONE EXPOSURES INC
2869 N Moreland Ave (46222-2122)
PHONE....................................404 641-5563
Reginald Krow, *Principal*
EMP: 2
SALES (est): 86K **Privately Held**
SIC: 3721 Motorized aircraft

(G-6344)
AERIAL IMAGING RESOURCES LLC
712 N New Jersey St (46202-3359)
PHONE....................................317 550-5970
Matthew Austin,
EMP: 3
SALES: 100K **Privately Held**
SIC: 3861 Photographic equipment & supplies

(G-6345)
AERIAL SIGN CO
1205 Cannonero Ct (46217-4303)
PHONE....................................317 258-9696
EMP: 2
SALES (est): 120K **Privately Held**
SIC: 3993 Mfg Signs/Advertising Specialties

(G-6346)
AERO INDUSTRIES INC (PA)
4243 W Bradbury Ave (46241-5253)
PHONE....................................317 808-1923
Fax: 317 244-1311
James R Tuerk, *CEO*
Robert P Tuerk, *Ch of Bd*
David L Boyd, *President*
Ron Eggers, *Business Mgr*
Steve White, *Plant Mgr*
▲ **EMP:** 100 EST: 1946
SQ FT: 46,000
SALES (est): 44.2MM **Privately Held**
WEB: www.aeroindustries.com
SIC: 3714 Motor vehicle parts & accessories

(G-6347)
AERODINE COMPOSITES LLC
8201 Indy Ln (46214-2327)
PHONE....................................317 271-1207
Fax: 317 271-4455
Craig McCarthy, *Engineer*
Amber Simpson, *Office Mgr*
EMP: 10
SQ FT: 12,000
SALES (est): 1.5MM **Privately Held**
WEB: www.aerodinecomposites.com
SIC: 3624 Carbon & graphite products

(G-6348)
AERODINE ENGINEERING GROUP LLC
8201 Indy Ln (46214-2327)
PHONE....................................317 271-1207
Randall Rodine,
EMP: 3
SALES: 200K **Privately Held**
SIC: 3624 Carbon & graphite products

(G-6349)
AEROPRO HOLDINGS LLC
7035 E 86th St (46250-1547)
PHONE....................................317 849-9555
Paul Thompson,
EMP: 2
SALES (est): 77.4K **Privately Held**
SALES (corp-wide): 600.2MM **Privately Held**
SIC: 3069 Rubber automotive products
HQ: Deflecto, Llc
7035 E 86th St
Indianapolis IN 46250
317 849-9555

(G-6350)
AF OHAB COMPANY INC
Also Called: Afequip.com
2346 S Lynhurst Dr # 302 (46241-5171)
PHONE....................................317 225-4740
Abdul Feroze Ohab, *CEO*
Glenn Perdue, *Business Mgr*
EMP: 45
SALES: 23MM **Privately Held**
SIC: 3531 5082 Construction machinery; graders, road (construction machinery); construction machinery attachments; general construction machinery & equipment

(G-6351)
AFTER ACTION MED DNTL SUP LLC
4444 Decatur Blvd Ste 100 (46241-9601)
PHONE....................................317 831-2699
Jerry Aytes,
EMP: 2
SALES: 250K **Privately Held**
SIC: 5047 3841 Medical equipment & supplies; surgical & medical instruments; biopsy instruments & equipment

(G-6352)
AGI INTERNATIONAL INC
2525 N Shadeland Ave D5 (46219-1770)
P.O. Box 30544, Charlotte NC (28230-0544)
PHONE....................................317 536-2415
E Jerome Agnew, *President*
EMP: 17
SQ FT: 1,200
SALES: 2MM **Privately Held**
WEB: www.agiinternational.com
SIC: 8742 4225 8741 8748 Management consulting services; management engineering; manufacturing management consultant; quality assurance consultant; general warehousing & storage; management services; business consulting; assembly machines, non-metalworking; shims, metal

(G-6353)
AIR ENERGY SYSTEMS INC (PA)
4790 W 73rd St (46268-2115)
PHONE....................................317 290-8500
Fax: 317 290-1900
William C Maher, *President*
Dorothy G Maher, *Treasurer*
Collin Maher, *Sales Associate*
EMP: 6
SQ FT: 24,000

SALES (est): 550K **Privately Held**
WEB: www.aesrack.com
SIC: 5075 3634 Warm air heating equipment & supplies; ventilating equipment & supplies; electric household fans, heaters & humidifiers

(G-6354)
AIRGAS INC
1441 Bates St (46201-3943)
PHONE..................................317 632-7106
Fax: 317 632-8201
Scott Neeton, *Manager*
EMP: 22
SALES (corp-wide): 164.2MM **Privately Held**
WEB: www.painenterprise.com
SIC: 2813 2097 2911 Dry ice, carbon dioxide (solid); manufactured ice; petroleum refining
HQ: Airgas, Inc.
259 N Radnor Chester Rd # 100
Radnor PA 19087
610 687-5253

(G-6355)
AIRGAS USA LLC
Also Called: Airgas Puritan Medical
5701 Fortune Cir S Ste M (46241-5534)
PHONE..................................317 248-8072
Patty Powell, *Business Mgr*
Keany Earl, *Manager*
EMP: 12
SALES (corp-wide): 164.2MM **Privately Held**
SIC: 3842 3841 2813 Respirators; surgical & medical instruments; industrial gases
HQ: Airgas Usa, Llc
259 N Radnor Chester Rd # 100
Radnor PA 19087
610 687-5253

(G-6356)
AIRGAS USA LLC
5825 Elmwood Ave (46203-6032)
PHONE..................................317 783-2331
Stephen Gee, *Plant Mgr*
Steve Gee, *Manager*
EMP: 17
SALES (corp-wide): 164.2MM **Privately Held**
SIC: 2813 Industrial gases
HQ: Airgas Usa, Llc
259 N Radnor Chester Rd # 100
Radnor PA 19087
610 687-5253

(G-6357)
AJAX TOCCO MAGNETHERMIC CORP
2525 N Shadeland Ave A6 (46219-1787)
PHONE..................................317 352-9880
Gary Teise, *Branch Mgr*
EMP: 2
SALES (corp-wide): 1.4B **Publicly Held**
WEB: www.ajaxtocco.com
SIC: 3567 3612 7699 Metal melting furnaces, industrial: electric; electric furnace transformers; industrial machinery & equipment repair
HQ: Ajax Tocco Magnethermic Corporation
1745 Overland Ave Ne
Warren OH 44483
330 372-8511

(G-6358)
AK SUPPLY INC
10501 E Washington St (46229-2609)
PHONE..................................317 895-0410
Kevin Drake, *President*
Areli Drake, *Vice Pres*
EMP: 11
SALES (est): 1MM **Privately Held**
SIC: 2394 Shades, canvas: made from purchased materials

(G-6359)
ALACHERI PUBLISHING LLC
8335 Catamaran Dr (46236-9587)
PHONE..................................317 755-6670
Kathryn Gillette, *Mng Member*
EMP: 2
SALES: 260K **Privately Held**
SIC: 2741 Miscellaneous publishing

(G-6360)
ALEBRO LLC
7690 Zionsville Rd (46268-2173)
PHONE..................................317 876-9212
Gino Lucchese, *Principal*
EMP: 7
SALES (est): 836.8K **Privately Held**
SIC: 2899 Salt

(G-6361)
ALEX AND ANI LLC
8702 Keystone Xing (46240-7621)
PHONE..................................317 575-8449
EMP: 4 **Privately Held**
SIC: 3915 Jewelers' materials & lapidary work
PA: Alex And Ani, Llc
2000 Chapel View Blvd # 360
Cranston RI 02920

(G-6362)
ALEXANDER SCREW PRODUCTS INC
Also Called: Stiffler Handy Product
8750 Pendleton Pike (46226-4110)
P.O. Box 26084 (46226-0084)
PHONE..................................317 898-5313
Fax: 317 897-8317
Larry Alexander, *CEO*
Jesse Alexander, *Vice Pres*
Oren D Alexander, *Vice Pres*
Kevin Summers, *Sales Associate*
Jeremiah Alexander, *Manager*
EMP: 49 EST: 1961
SQ FT: 50,000
SALES (est): 12.1MM **Privately Held**
WEB: www.alexanderscrew.com
SIC: 3451 3449 Screw machine products; miscellaneous metalwork

(G-6363)
ALEXANDRIA EXTRUSION COMPANY
Also Called: Alexandria Extrsion Midamerica
4925 Aluminum Dr (46218-3156)
PHONE..................................317 545-1221
Thomas Schabel, *Principal*
EMP: 43
SALES (corp-wide): 228.8MM **Privately Held**
SIC: 3354 Shapes, extruded aluminum
PA: Alexandria Extrusion Company
401 County Road 22 Nw
Alexandria MN 56308
320 762-7657

(G-6364)
ALGAEWHEEL INC
Also Called: Fish Boys, The
201 N Illinois St # 1200 (46204-4209)
PHONE..................................317 582-1400
Christopher Limcaco, *President*
Leon Shelton, *Vice Pres*
Huon Matthews, *Director*
Joel Johnston, *Admin Sec*
EMP: 3
SALES (est): 413.9K **Privately Held**
SIC: 3589 Water treatment equipment, industrial

(G-6365)
ALGALCO LLC
6532 Castle Knoll Ct (46250-1439)
PHONE..................................317 361-2787
Kc Cohen, *Administration*
EMP: 2 EST: 2007
SALES (est): 261.7K **Privately Held**
SIC: 3399 Aluminum atomized powder

(G-6366)
ALL CITY METAL CRAFT INC
121 W Sumner Ave (46217-3256)
PHONE..................................317 782-9340
Terry Donald Choates, *President*
Pamela Choate, *Admin Sec*
EMP: 4
SQ FT: 6,000
SALES (est): 290K **Privately Held**
SIC: 3446 3441 Ornamental metalwork; fabricated structural metal

(G-6367)
ALL PRO SHEARING INC
1905 Lawton Ave (46203-2994)
P.O. Box 1744, Mishawaka (46546-1744)
PHONE..................................317 691-1005
Danny Fey, *President*
EMP: 11 EST: 2003
SQ FT: 87,120
SALES: 2MM **Privately Held**
SIC: 3341 Secondary nonferrous metals

(G-6368)
ALLEN INDUSTRIES INC (PA)
6874 Hawthorn Park Dr (46220-3909)
PHONE..................................317 595-0730
Eugene Allen Jr, *President*
EMP: 5
SQ FT: 15,000
SALES (est): 704K **Privately Held**
SIC: 7349 2819 2844 Building & office cleaning services; industrial inorganic chemicals; cosmetic preparations

(G-6369)
ALLIED STEEL RULE DIES INC
5811 W Minnesota St (46241-3845)
PHONE..................................317 634-9835
Fax: 317 634-8835
Kelly Russell, *President*
Bill Hankins, *Sales Staff*
EMP: 15
SQ FT: 17,000
SALES (est): 2.2MM **Privately Held**
WEB: www.allieddies.com
SIC: 3544 Dies, steel rule; special dies & tools

(G-6370)
ALLISON PAYMENT SYSTEMS LLC (PA)
2200 Production Dr (46241-4912)
P.O. Box 102 (46206-0102)
PHONE..................................317 808-2400
Fax: 317 808-2477
Joseph H Thomas, *Chairman*
Renee Durre, *Vice Pres*
Dale J Eland, *Vice Pres*
Kevin Thomas, *Vice Pres*
William M Thomas, *Vice Pres*
EMP: 180
SQ FT: 60,000
SALES (est): 55.1MM **Privately Held**
WEB: www.apsllc.com
SIC: 2752 5112 Commercial printing, offset; business forms

(G-6371)
ALLISON TRANSM HOLDINGS INC (PA)
1 Allison Way (46222-3271)
PHONE..................................317 242-5000
David S Graziosi, *President*
David Coulter, *General Mgr*
Kevin Koonce, *General Mgr*
John M Coll, *Senior VP*
Michael A Dick, *Senior VP*
EMP: 66
SALES: 2.2B **Publicly Held**
SIC: 3714 Motor vehicle parts & accessories; motor vehicle transmissions, drive assemblies & parts

(G-6372)
ALLISON TRANSMISSION INC
6040 W 62nd St (46278-2909)
PHONE..................................317 280-6206
Greg Rotvold, *Finance*
Terence Molloy, *Branch Mgr*
Scott Kluemper, *Exec Dir*
EMP: 1730 **Publicly Held**
WEB: www.allisontransmission.com
SIC: 3714 3728 Motor vehicle parts & accessories; aircraft power transmission equipment
HQ: Allison Transmission, Inc.
1 Allison Way
Indianapolis IN 46222

(G-6373)
ALLISON TRANSMISSION INC (HQ)
1 Allison Way (46222-3271)
P.O. Box 894 (46206-0894)
PHONE..................................317 242-5000
Fax: 317 242-0450

David S Graziosi, *President*
Randall Kirk, *President*
Teresa J Van Niekerk, *President*
Ram S Amarnath, *Managing Dir*
James Coleman, *Managing Dir*
◆ EMP: 2500
SALES (est): 923.4MM **Publicly Held**
WEB: www.allisontransmission.com
SIC: 3714 Transmissions, motor vehicle

(G-6374)
ALLISON TRANSMISSION INC
Also Called: Allison Transmission Division
901 Grande Ave (46222-3276)
P.O. Box 894 (46206-0894)
PHONE..................................317 242-5000
Fax: 317 242-0389
Paul Nicholas, *Executive*
EMP: 15 **Publicly Held**
WEB: www.allisontransmission.com
SIC: 3714 Motor vehicle parts & accessories
HQ: Allison Transmission, Inc.
1 Allison Way
Indianapolis IN 46222

(G-6375)
ALLISON TRANSMISSION INC
2840 Fortune Cir Dr W A (46241)
PHONE..................................317 242-2080
William Klenk, *Branch Mgr*
EMP: 60 **Publicly Held**
WEB: www.allisontransmission.com
SIC: 3714 Transmissions, motor vehicle
HQ: Allison Transmission, Inc.
1 Allison Way
Indianapolis IN 46222

(G-6376)
ALLISON TRANSMISSION INC
Also Called: Allison Parts Distribution
5902 Decatur Blvd (46241-9579)
PHONE..................................317 821-5104
Scott Smale, *Auditor*
Ron Sauer, *Branch Mgr*
Teri Miller, *Manager*
EMP: 200 **Publicly Held**
WEB: www.allisontransmission.com
SIC: 3714 3511 Motor vehicle parts & accessories; turbines & turbine generator sets
HQ: Allison Transmission, Inc.
1 Allison Way
Indianapolis IN 46222

(G-6377)
ALOCIT USA
1128 S West St (46225-1463)
PHONE..................................317 631-9111
Kenny Boehm, *President*
▲ EMP: 3 EST: 2013
SALES (est): 150.9K **Privately Held**
SIC: 3479 Coating of metals & formed products

(G-6378)
ALRO STEEL CORPORATION
Also Called: Alro Group
5620 Churchman Ave (46203-6007)
PHONE..................................317 781-3800
Fax: 317 781-3810
Mark Timberlake, *Branch Mgr*
EMP: 50
SALES (corp-wide): 1.6B **Privately Held**
WEB: www.alro.com
SIC: 5051 3444 Steel; sheet metalwork
PA: Alro Steel Corporation
3100 E High St
Jackson MI 49203
517 787-5500

(G-6379)
ALTEC INDUSTRIES INC
Also Called: Northern Division
5201 W 84th St (46268-1532)
P.O. Box 681308 (46268-7308)
PHONE..................................317 872-3460
Fax: 317 876-3620
Richard Hershman, *Materials Mgr*
Bryan Shotts, *Engineer*
Trista Bailey, *Senior Engr*
Hugh Cate, *Branch Mgr*
EMP: 160

SALES (corp-wide): 765.5MM **Privately Held**
WEB: www.altec.com
SIC: 3531 Aerial work platforms: hydraulic/elec. truck/carrier mounted
HQ: Altec Industries, Inc.
210 Inverness Center Dr
Birmingham AL 35242
205 991-7733

(G-6380)
AMA USA INC
7998 Georgetown Rd # 400 (46268-1697)
PHONE................................317 329-6590
Giuliano Cacucci, *President*
Craig Hartwick, *Sales Dir*
▲ EMP: 4
SQ FT: 10,000
SALES: 5MM **Privately Held**
SIC: 3531 Construction machinery

(G-6381)
AMBRE BLENDS
7825 E 89th St (46256-1239)
PHONE................................317 257-0202
Amber Crocket, *Owner*
Stephanie Harris, *Sales Staff*
EMP: 3
SALES (est): 373.3K **Privately Held**
SIC: 2844 Toilet preparations

(G-6382)
AMD GROUP LLC
Also Called: AMD Lasers
8925 N Meridian St # 250 (46260-5372)
PHONE................................317 202-9530
Alan Miller, *CEO*
Bart Waclawik, *COO*
EMP: 12 EST: 2016
SALES (est): 531.2K **Privately Held**
SIC: 3841 Surgical lasers

(G-6383)
AMERAWHIP INC
1735 W 18th St (46202-1056)
PHONE................................317 639-5248
John Clifford, *President*
▲ EMP: 4
SALES (est): 265.9K **Privately Held**
SIC: 3629 Electronic generation equipment

(G-6384)
AMERIBRIDGE LLC
5425 Poindexter Dr (46235-9040)
PHONE................................317 826-2000
Fax: 317 826-2005
Kevin Steingart, *President*
Dustin Sloan, *Vice Pres*
Gary Sloan, *Vice Pres*
Tim Keyes,
EMP: 53
SALES (est): 17MM **Privately Held**
SIC: 3531 Airport construction machinery

(G-6385)
AMERICAN ART CLAY CO INC (PA)
Also Called: A M A C O
6060 Guion Rd (46254-1222)
PHONE................................317 243-0066
Lester B Sandoe Jr, *CEO*
William E Berry, *President*
Valri P Sandoe, *Vice Chairman*
Karen Gephart, *CFO*
Larena Moore, *Accounting Mgr*
◆ EMP: 128 EST: 1919
SQ FT: 163,000
SALES (est): 15.9MM **Privately Held**
WEB: www.amaco.com
SIC: 3295 3559 5092 3083 Clay, ground or otherwise treated; pottery making machinery; kilns; toys & hobby goods & supplies; plastic finished products, laminated

(G-6386)
AMERICAN CLASSIFIEDS
Also Called: Thrifty Nickel Want ADS
359 E Thompson Rd (46227-1624)
PHONE................................317 782-8111
Fax: 317 782-0882
Minni Dhanjal, *President*
Daljit Dhanjal, *Vice Pres*
EMP: 25
SQ FT: 2,500

SALES (est): 2MM **Privately Held**
SIC: 2741 2711 Miscellaneous publishing; newspapers

(G-6387)
AMERICAN CONTACT LENS SERVICE
5617 W 74th St (46278-1753)
PHONE................................317 347-2900
Fax: 317 347-2910
Myrna Brady, *President*
Crystal H Bell, *Corp Secy*
EMP: 5
SQ FT: 2,800
SALES: 600K **Privately Held**
WEB: www.aclsindy.com
SIC: 3851 Contact lenses

(G-6388)
AMERICAN HERITAGE SHUTTERS
Also Called: Mk Interiors
9450 Timberline Dr (46256-4722)
PHONE................................317 598-6908
Fax: 317 823-8895
Mark Keenan,
EMP: 2
SALES: 600K **Privately Held**
SIC: 2431 Windows & window parts & trim, wood; awnings, blinds & shutters, wood

(G-6389)
AMERICAN LAWN MOWER
7444 Shadeland Stn Way (46256-3925)
PHONE................................800 633-1501
Kate Hemming, *Manager*
EMP: 2
SALES (est): 69.4K **Privately Held**
SIC: 5083 3524 Lawn & garden machinery & equipment; lawn & garden mowers & accessories

(G-6390)
AMERICAN SENIOR HOMECARE
4519 E 82nd St Ofc (46250-5641)
PHONE................................317 849-4968
Fax: 317 849-0145
Diane Anderson, *Director*
EMP: 12
SALES (est): 368.4K **Privately Held**
SIC: 2711 Newspapers, publishing & printing

(G-6391)
AMERICAN TOOL SERVICE INC
3955 Industrial Blvd Frnt (46254-2539)
PHONE................................317 782-3551
Chris Walden, *Branch Mgr*
Erik Jackson, *Supervisor*
EMP: 10
SALES (est): 1.1MM
SALES (corp-wide): 2.7MM **Privately Held**
WEB: www.a-t-s-i.com
SIC: 3541 Machine tool replacement & repair parts, metal cutting types
PA: American Tool Service, Inc
7007 Trafalgar Dr
Fort Wayne IN 46803
260 493-6351

(G-6392)
AMERICAN WIRE ROPE & SLING OF
5760 Dividend Rd (46241-4304)
PHONE................................877 634-2545
EMP: 7
SALES (est): 85K **Privately Held**
SIC: 3496 Miscellaneous fabricated wire products

(G-6393)
AMERIFAB INC
3501 E 9th St (46201-2509)
PHONE................................317 231-0100
Fax: 317 231-0144
Gabe Carinci, *President*
Rick Manasek, *COO*
Andy Akers, *Exec VP*
Joseph P Hochgesang, *Vice Pres*
Brian Wilson, *Safety Mgr*
▲ EMP: 70
SQ FT: 85,000

SALES (est): 15.9MM **Privately Held**
WEB: www.amerifabinc.com
SIC: 3547 Ferrous & nonferrous mill equipment, auxiliary

(G-6394)
AMERIFLO INC
1936 S Lynhurst Dr Ste P (46241-4636)
PHONE................................317 844-2019
Rebecca Voege, *President*
Jim Voege, *President*
EMP: 30
SQ FT: 2,500
SALES (est): 9MM **Privately Held**
WEB: www.ameriflo.com
SIC: 3823 Flow instruments, industrial process type

(G-6395)
AMERIFLO2 INC
1936 S Lynhurst Dr Ste P (46241-4636)
PHONE................................317 844-2019
Rebecca Voege, *President*
Jim Voege, *Vice Pres*
EMP: 13
SQ FT: 2,000
SALES: 2.4MM **Privately Held**
SIC: 3841 Surgical & medical instruments

(G-6396)
AMG ENGINEERING MACHINING INC
4030 Guion Ln (46268-2564)
P.O. Box 681245 (46268-7245)
PHONE................................317 329-4000
Fax: 317 329-4010
Theaodis Gary, *President*
Chris Chadd, *General Mgr*
Helen Randolph, *Corp Secy*
Santosh Binwade, *Mfg Staff*
Larry Summers, *Supervisor*
▲ EMP: 20
SQ FT: 30,000
SALES: 5.5MM **Privately Held**
WEB: www.amgindy.com
SIC: 3599 Machine shop, jobbing & repair

(G-6397)
AMG LLC
Also Called: Regin Manufacturing
4030 Guion Ln (46268-2564)
P.O. Box 781108 (46278-8108)
PHONE................................317 329-4004
Theaodis Gary Jr, *Mng Member*
EMP: 40
SALES (est): 8.3MM **Privately Held**
SIC: 3823 3491 Flow instruments, industrial process type; industrial valves

(G-6398)
ANATOLIA GROUP LTD PARTNERSHIP
640 E Michigan St (46202-0008)
PHONE................................203 343-7808
Arif Ugur, *Principal*
EMP: 4
SQ FT: 1,650
SALES (est): 244.6K **Privately Held**
SIC: 3559 Semiconductor manufacturing machinery

(G-6399)
ANCIENT CELLARS
360 W 63rd St (46260-4718)
PHONE................................503 437-4827
EMP: 4
SALES (est): 122.9K **Privately Held**
SIC: 2084 Wines

(G-6400)
ANDON SPECIALTIES INC ○
5736 W 79th St (46278-1708)
PHONE................................317 983-1700
EMP: 2 EST: 2017
SALES (est): 99K **Privately Held**
SIC: 3677 Filtration devices, electronic

(G-6401)
ANDYS GLOBAL INC
8445 Castlewood Dr Ste C (46250-4582)
PHONE................................317 595-8825
Arvind Mistry, *President*
Jyoti A Mistry, *Vice Pres*
Shital A Mistry, *Treasurer*
▲ EMP: 4

SQ FT: 2,400
SALES: 135K **Privately Held**
SIC: 3421 Scissors, shears, clippers, snips & similar tools

(G-6402)
ANODIZING TECHNOLOGIES INC
5868 N New Jersey St (46220-2535)
P.O. Box 502770 (46250-7770)
PHONE................................317 253-5725
John L Chesterfield, *President*
EMP: 3
SALES (est): 534.9K **Privately Held**
WEB: www.anodizingtechnologies.com
SIC: 3559 Metal finishing equipment for plating, etc.

(G-6403)
ANTHONY WAYNE REHABILITATION C
Also Called: Postmasters
2762 Rand Rd (46241-5506)
PHONE................................317 972-1000
Gary Johloz, *Manager*
EMP: 20
SALES (corp-wide): 30.7MM **Privately Held**
WEB: www.awsusa.com
SIC: 2759 7331 Commercial printing; laser printing; mailing service
PA: Anthony Wayne Rehabilitation Center For Handicapped And Blind, Inc
8515 Bluffton Rd
Fort Wayne IN 46809
260 744-6145

(G-6404)
ANTREASIAN DESIGN INC
3124 Ridgeview Dr (46226-6152)
PHONE................................317 546-3234
Fax: 317 546-0253
Mark B Antreasian, *President*
Cris Antreasian, *Vice Pres*
EMP: 15
SQ FT: 17,000
SALES (est): 2.3MM **Privately Held**
WEB: www.adiarchwood.com
SIC: 2511 2521 2431 Wood household furniture; wood office furniture; millwork

(G-6405)
AOM BOOKSHOP
5239 Rockville Rd Ste B (46224-9109)
P.O. Box 532532 (46253-2532)
PHONE................................317 493-8095
Quinton Blackwell, *President*
Andre Blackwell, *Publisher*
John Mitchell, *Business Mgr*
Madison Blackwell, *Development*
Erika Watkins, *Accountant*
EMP: 6
SALES (est): 254K **Privately Held**
SIC: 2731 2782 5015 Textbooks: publishing only, not printed on site; textbooks: publishing & printing; scrapbooks, albums & diaries; automotive supplies, used

(G-6406)
AP SIGN GROUP LLC
Also Called: Sommer Awning Group
1160 W 16th St (46202-2162)
PHONE................................317 257-1869
Fax: 317 257-1973
Chris Sommer, *Vice Pres*
Sheila Shaw, *Accounting Mgr*
Mike Blodgett, *Sales Staff*
Steve Summer, *Mng Member*
Garrett Thomas, *Project Leader*
EMP: 27
SALES (est): 4.8MM **Privately Held**
SIC: 3993 Electric signs; advertising artwork

(G-6407)
APP ENGINEERING INCORPORATED
5234 Elmwood Ave (46203-5915)
PHONE................................317 755-3422
Greg Bradley, *President*
Francis Wai, *Vice Pres*
Wing-Kin Wai, *Vice Pres*
EMP: 10
SQ FT: 6,000

▲ = Import ▼=Export
◆ =Import/Export

SALES (est): 2MM **Privately Held**
WEB: www.appengineering.com
SIC: 3825 Instruments to measure electricity

(G-6408)
APP PRESS LLC
435 Virginia Ave Unit 607 (46203-1967)
PHONE....................................317 661-4759
Lauren Schommer, *Manager*
Joe Doyle, *Prgrmr*
Corey Phillips, *Software Dev*
Grant Glas,
Kevin Smith,
EMP: 2
SALES (est): 218.3K **Privately Held**
SIC: 7372 7371 Business oriented computer software; computer software development; software programming applications

(G-6409)
APPLE PRESS INC
6327 Ferguson St (46220-1707)
PHONE....................................317 253-7752
Fax: 317 254-0330
Mark Finch, *President*
EMP: 4
SQ FT: 10,000
SALES (est): 270K **Privately Held**
SIC: 2752 Commercial printing, lithographic

(G-6410)
APPLICATION SOFTWARE INC
9801 Fall Creek Rd 101 (46256-4802)
PHONE....................................317 823-3525
Roger Welter, *President*
EMP: 2
SALES (est): 139.8K **Privately Held**
SIC: 7372 Business oriented computer software

(G-6411)
APPLIED COMPOSITES ENGRG INC
705 S Girls School Rd (46231-1131)
PHONE....................................317 243-4225
Fax: 317 243-4227
Leigh R Sargent, *President*
Jeff Rybolt, *Vice Pres*
Matthew Torzewski, *VP Opers*
John Pettit, *Production*
Adam Sullivan, *Buyer*
EMP: 44
SQ FT: 45,000
SALES (est): 11.1MM
SALES (corp-wide): 30.3MM **Privately Held**
WEB: www.appliedcomposites.com
SIC: 3544 3624 3083 2823 Industrial molds; fibers, carbon & graphite; laminated plastics plate & sheet; cellulosic manmade fibers
HQ: Ac&A Enterprises, Llc
25692 Atlantic Ocean Dr
Lake Forest CA 92630
949 716-3511

(G-6412)
AQUATIC RENOVATION SYSTEMS INC
Also Called: Renosys
2825 55th Pl Ste G (46220-3531)
PHONE....................................317 251-0207
Fax: 317 251-0360
Stewart J Mart, *President*
Steve Comstock, *Vice Pres*
Gary Novitski, *Vice Pres*
EMP: 45
SQ FT: 24,800
SALES (est): 8.4MM **Privately Held**
WEB: www.renosys.com
SIC: 3949 Swimming pools, plastic

(G-6413)
ARCAMED LLC
5101 Decatur Blvd Ste A (46241-9529)
PHONE....................................317 375-7733
Jon Desalvo, *Mng Member*
▼ EMP: 42
SQ FT: 20,000
SALES (est): 6.8MM **Privately Held**
SIC: 3841 Medical instruments & equipment, blood & bone work

(G-6414)
ARCHER PRODUCTS INC
8756 E 33rd St (46226-6516)
PHONE....................................317 899-0700
Fax: 317 899-0702
Perry A Benson, *President*
EMP: 4
SQ FT: 2,021
SALES (est): 530.4K **Privately Held**
WEB: www.archerblades.com
SIC: 3425 Saw blades & handsaws

(G-6415)
ARCHER-DANIELS-MIDLAND COMPANY
Also Called: ADM
1901 S Sherman Dr (46203-3308)
PHONE....................................317 784-2200
Fax: 317 786-8795
George Greenwoood, *Branch Mgr*
EMP: 12
SALES (corp-wide): 60.8B **Publicly Held**
SIC: 2041 Flour & other grain mill products
PA: Archer-Daniels-Midland Company
77 W Wacker Dr Ste 4600
Chicago IL 60601
312 634-8100

(G-6416)
ARCONIC INC
Also Called: Alcoa
2334 Production Dr (46241-4914)
PHONE....................................317 241-9393
Gene Bleke, *Manager*
EMP: 135
SALES (corp-wide): 12.9B **Publicly Held**
SIC: 3353 Aluminum sheet & strip
PA: Arconic Inc.
390 Park Ave Fl 12
New York NY 10022
212 836-2758

(G-6417)
ARCTRANS LLC
1414 S West St Ste B (46225-1530)
PHONE....................................317 231-1620
Carl Allen,
EMP: 14
SQ FT: 1,500
SALES: 850K **Privately Held**
SIC: 3537 Trucks: freight, baggage, etc.: industrial, except mining

(G-6418)
ARDAGH GLASS INC (HQ)
Also Called: Verallia North America
10194 Crosspoint Blvd (46256-3328)
P.O. Box 50487 (46250-0487)
PHONE....................................317 558-1002
Niall Wall, *CEO*
Eric Dirlam, *President*
Joseph R Grewe, *President*
John M Haack, *Senior VP*
Jim Keener, *Vice Pres*
◆ EMP: 299
SQ FT: 60,000
SALES (est): 850.9MM **Privately Held**
WEB: www.sgcontainers.com
SIC: 3221 Glass containers; bottles for packing, bottling & canning: glass
PA: Ard Holdings Sa
Rue Charles Martel 56
Luxembourg
262 585-55

(G-6419)
ARIZONA SPORT SHIRTS INC
100 Gasoline Aly Ste Az (46222-5916)
PHONE....................................317 481-2160
Fax: 317 247-4392
Karl Korbacher, *President*
Cheryl Korbacher, *Vice Pres*
Rosemary Chadd, *Office Mgr*
EMP: 30
SQ FT: 10,000
SALES (est): 7.7MM **Privately Held**
WEB: www.arizonasportshirts.com
SIC: 5136 5137 3993 2396 Sportswear, men's & boys'; sportswear, women's & children's; signs & advertising specialties; automotive & apparel trimmings; pleating & stitching

(G-6420)
ARK MODEL AND STAMPINGS INC
2401 N Ritter Ave (46218-4019)
PHONE....................................317 549-3394
Fax: 317 549-3449
Charles Kevin Walsh, *President*
Kelley Fidler, *Admin Sec*
EMP: 16
SQ FT: 20,000
SALES (est): 2.5MM **Privately Held**
SIC: 3469 3544 Stamping metal for the trade; special dies & tools

(G-6421)
ARROW CONTAINER LLC
5343 Commerce Square Dr (46237-9743)
PHONE....................................317 882-6444
Fax: 317 889-4885
Walter Gill, *Exec VP*
Nick Brummett, *Purch Agent*
Danielle Emery, *Sales Staff*
Debbie Gill, *Office Mgr*
James R La Sarre Jr,
EMP: 100
SQ FT: 60,000
SALES (est): 32.7MM **Privately Held**
WEB: www.arrowcontainer.com
SIC: 2631 Boxboard

(G-6422)
ARROW POWDER COATING LLC
1030 E New York St (46202-3730)
P.O. Box 2005 (46206-2005)
PHONE....................................317 822-8002
Troy Simmerman, *QC Mgr*
Donald Hodina,
Brian Staggs,
EMP: 20
SQ FT: 17,000
SALES (est): 2.5MM **Privately Held**
SIC: 3479 Coating of metals & formed products

(G-6423)
ARTSY CANVAS
9900 Westpoint Dr Ste 138 (46256-3338)
PHONE....................................855 206-9045
EMP: 2
SALES (est): 73.4K **Privately Held**
SIC: 2211 Canvas

(G-6424)
ASAP IDENTIFICATION SEC INC
212 W 10th St Ste F100 (46202-5697)
PHONE....................................317 488-1030
Sheila Brown, *President*
Thomas E Brown, *Vice Pres*
EMP: 3
SQ FT: 650
SALES (est): 310.4K **Privately Held**
SIC: 3999 5044 Identification badges & insignia; photocopy machines

(G-6425)
ASBESTOS ABATEMENT & MOLD
816 E Elbert St (46227-1631)
PHONE....................................317 783-0350
Rick Smallwood, *Owner*
EMP: 2
SALES (est): 249.7K **Privately Held**
SIC: 3544 Industrial molds

(G-6426)
ASPHALT MATERIALS INC (PA)
5400 W 86th St (46268-1537)
P.O. Box 68123 (46268-0123)
PHONE....................................317 872-6010
Fax: 317 872-6327
David N Blackburn, *President*
Bob Khanna, *Business Mgr*
Eric Werner, *Vice Pres*
Cory Larue, *Plant Mgr*
John P Vercruysse, *Treasurer*
EMP: 370 EST: 1957
SQ FT: 2,500
SALES (est): 248.2MM **Privately Held**
SIC: 2951 1442 Asphalt & asphaltic paving mixtures (not from refineries); sand mining; gravel mining

(G-6427)
ASPHALT MATERIALS INC
Heritage Research Group
7901 W Morris St (46231-1366)
P.O. Box 68123 (46268-0123)
PHONE....................................317 243-8304
Dave Bowering, *Engineer*
Tony Kriech, *Enginr/R&D Mgr*
EMP: 35
SALES (corp-wide): 248.2MM **Privately Held**
SIC: 2951 Asphalt paving mixtures & blocks
PA: Asphalt Materials, Inc.
5400 W 86th St
Indianapolis IN 46268
317 872-6010

(G-6428)
ASPHALT MATERIALS INC
Also Called: Heritage Group Safety
5400 W 86th St (46268-1537)
PHONE....................................317 875-4670
Mike Kelly, *President*
John Kossos, *Director*
EMP: 9
SALES (corp-wide): 248.2MM **Privately Held**
SIC: 2951 1442 8748 5099 Asphalt & asphaltic paving mixtures (not from refineries); sand mining; gravel mining; safety training service; safety equipment & supplies
PA: Asphalt Materials, Inc.
5400 W 86th St
Indianapolis IN 46268
317 872-6010

(G-6429)
ASPHALT MATERIALS INC
Also Called: Asphalt Refining Co
4902 W 86th St (46268-1652)
P.O. Box 68123 (46268-0123)
PHONE....................................317 872-5580
Randy Foley, *Manager*
EMP: 20
SALES (corp-wide): 248.2MM **Privately Held**
SIC: 2951 Asphalt & asphaltic paving mixtures (not from refineries)
PA: Asphalt Materials, Inc.
5400 W 86th St
Indianapolis IN 46268
317 872-6010

(G-6430)
ASSURANCE LOCKING SYSTEMS LLC
5673 Misty Ridge Cir (46237-2735)
PHONE....................................317 786-8724
Doanld L Walls,
EMP: 3
SALES: 950K **Privately Held**
SIC: 3429 Manufactured hardware (general)

(G-6431)
ASTBURY WATER TECHNOLOGY INC (PA)
Also Called: A W T
5940 W Raymond St (46241-4349)
PHONE....................................317 328-7153
Fax: 317 328-7159
Daniel T Astbury, *CEO*
Michael J Gillespie, *Vice Pres*
Kathryn B Astbury, *CFO*
Mark Bruce, *Sr Project Mgr*
Robert Clark, *Info Tech Dir*
EMP: 62
SQ FT: 16,000
SALES (est): 12.5MM **Privately Held**
WEB: www.astburygroup.com
SIC: 3589 1629 Water filters & softeners, household type; water purification equipment, household type; water treatment equipment, industrial; waste water & sewage treatment plant construction

(G-6432)
ASTEC CORP
7750 Zionsville Rd # 650 (46268-5126)
PHONE....................................317 872-7550
Fax: 317 872-7562
James J Arlington, *President*
Robert A Salem, *Vice Pres*

EMP: 6
SQ FT: 8,600
SALES (est): 1MM **Privately Held**
WEB: www.walbernize.com
SIC: 2842 2819 Cleaning or polishing preparations; industrial inorganic chemicals

(G-6433)
ASTERION LLC
5425 W 84th St (46268-1520)
P.O. Box 68809 (46268-0809)
PHONE.............................317 875-0051
Blair R Vandivier, *President*
Roger Sowinski, *President*
Charles Bowens, *Plant Mgr*
Brad Martin, *Controller*
Kenneth Harasyn, *Sales Staff*
◆ EMP: 23
SQ FT: 32,000
SALES: 10MM **Privately Held**
SIC: 2899 Chemical preparations; plating compounds

(G-6434)
AT&T CORP
Also Called: AT&T Publishing
7144 Lakeview Pkwy W Dr (46268-4104)
PHONE.............................317 347-2163
Fax: 317 685-7609
Steven Herrera, *Manager*
Paul Anderson, *Manager*
David Kennedy, *Associate*
EMP: 222
SALES (corp-wide): 160.5B **Publicly Held**
WEB: www.att.com
SIC: 2741 Miscellaneous publishing
HQ: At&T Corp.
　　1 At&T Way
　　Bedminster NJ 07921
　　800 403-3302

(G-6435)
ATC PLASTICS LLC (PA)
8425 Woodfield Crossing B (46240-0050)
PHONE.............................317 469-7552
Tom Stevning, *Mng Member*
Richard Mejia,
EMP: 1
SQ FT: 1,000
SALES (est): 7.9MM **Privately Held**
SIC: 2821 Plastics materials & resins

(G-6436)
ATHENA ARTS & GRAPHICS INC
Also Called: Resumes Today
3500 Depauw Blvd Ste 1000 (46268-1136)
PHONE.............................317 876-8916
Fax: 317 879-9654
J Sue Wagner, *President*
Joan Green, *President*
Jsue Wagner, *President*
Sue Wagner, *Vice Pres*
EMP: 4
SQ FT: 5,000
SALES (est): 343.6K **Privately Held**
SIC: 2752 2791 2741 2789 Commercial printing, offset; typesetting; miscellaneous publishing; bookbinding & related work

(G-6437)
ATHLETES MANAGEMENT & SERVICE
3750 Guion Rd Ste 315 (46222-1669)
P.O. Box 22547 (46222-0547)
PHONE.............................317 925-8200
Fax: 317 925-8200
Garry H Donna, *President*
EMP: 2
SALES (est): 238.9K **Privately Held**
SIC: 7941 2721 Sports clubs, managers & promoters; magazines: publishing & printing

(G-6438)
ATI
6635 E 30th St (46219-1138)
PHONE.............................317 238-3073
Ken Hammond, *Principal*
▲ EMP: 4
SALES (est): 561.9K **Privately Held**
SIC: 3312 Stainless steel

(G-6439)
AUBRY LANE LLC
5333 W 86th St (46268-1501)
PHONE.............................317 644-6372
Jordan Hetlund,
EMP: 4 EST: 2016
SALES: 15K **Privately Held**
SIC: 3171 Handbags, women's

(G-6440)
AUS EMBROIDERY INC
8745 Rawles Ave Ste C (46219-7831)
PHONE.............................317 899-1225
Jay Conway, *President*
Richard Conway, *Treasurer*
Carla Conway, *Admin Sec*
EMP: 4
SQ FT: 1,200
SALES (est): 417.3K **Privately Held**
SIC: 3999 Embroidery kits

(G-6441)
AUSTIN-WESTRAN LLC (PA)
2876 Wooded Glen Ct (46268-4246)
PHONE.............................815 234-2811
Bill Diemel, *President*
Gordon Murphy, *Materials Mgr*
Chris Osterholz, *Director*
▲ EMP: 125 EST: 2001
SQ FT: 200,000
SALES (est): 37.9MM **Privately Held**
WEB: www.austinwestran.com
SIC: 3567 3444 2514 Industrial furnaces & ovens; sheet metalwork; tables, household: metal

(G-6442)
AUTO CENTER INC
Also Called: Pre-Owned Auto Center
5461 Massachusetts Ave (46218-2463)
PHONE.............................317 545-3360
Gus Rajabi, *President*
David Brumley, *Vice Pres*
EMP: 2
SQ FT: 20,000
SALES (est): 197.6K **Privately Held**
SIC: 7538 3599 General automotive repair shops; machine shop, jobbing & repair

(G-6443)
AUTOMATED WEAPON SECURITY INC
9324 E 10th St (46229-2505)
PHONE.............................860 559-7176
Charles Phersele, *President*
EMP: 2
SALES: 80K **Privately Held**
SIC: 3842 Linemen's safety belts

(G-6444)
AUTOMATIC FASTNER TOOLS
3250 Payne Dr (46227-7680)
PHONE.............................317 784-4111
Fax: 317 781-9468
Kay Ralston, *Owner*
Dan Ralston, *Co-Owner*
EMP: 6
SALES: 500K **Privately Held**
SIC: 3559 Automotive related machinery

(G-6445)
AUTOMATIC TOOL CONTROL
Also Called: A T C
4037 Guion Ln (46268-2564)
PHONE.............................317 328-8492
Hemi Sagi, *President*
Sarah Sagi, *President*
Billy Recker, *Design Engr*
EMP: 30
SQ FT: 32,000
SALES (est): 9.2MM **Privately Held**
WEB: www.atcinc.net
SIC: 3829 Liquid leak detection equipment

(G-6446)
AUTOMOBILE DEALERS ASSN OF IND (PA)
150 W Market St Ste 812 (46204-2886)
PHONE.............................317 635-1441
Fax: 317 232-0137
Timothy Dowling, *Exec VP*
EMP: 8
SQ FT: 2,068

SALES: 398K **Privately Held**
SIC: 8611 2741 5943 8748 Trade associations; business service newsletters: publishing & printing; office forms & supplies; business consulting

(G-6447)
AUTUMN INTERIORS
11717 E Washington St (46229-2947)
PHONE.............................317 894-1494
Nancy Schantz, *Owner*
EMP: 2
SQ FT: 1,800
SALES (est): 175.3K **Privately Held**
SIC: 2211 7641 Draperies & drapery fabrics, cotton; upholstery work

(G-6448)
AVALON ENTERPRISES INC
Also Called: Avalon Drinkware
12010 E Washington St (46229-2954)
PHONE.............................317 894-8666
J Gregory Kroetz, *President*
Patti Kroetz, *Treasurer*
EMP: 5
SQ FT: 4,000
SALES (est): 569.5K **Privately Held**
WEB: www.avalondrinkware.com
SIC: 2752 Commercial printing, lithographic

(G-6449)
B AND D LIGHTING
5635 Hickory Rd (46239-1842)
P.O. Box 39089 (46239-0089)
PHONE.............................317 414-8056
Brian Distel, *Principal*
EMP: 5
SALES (est): 691.5K **Privately Held**
SIC: 3648 Lighting equipment

(G-6450)
B Q PRODUCTS INC
6233 Brookville Rd (46219-8213)
P.O. Box 430, Beech Grove (46107-0430)
PHONE.............................317 786-5500
Fax: 317 786-0599
Dennis Laswell, *President*
Rick Mc Garvey, *Opers Mgr*
EMP: 23
SQ FT: 8,000
SALES (est): 2.4MM **Privately Held**
WEB: www.bqproducts.com
SIC: 3679 Electronic circuits

(G-6451)
B6 MANUFACTURING LLC
4701 Massachusetts Ave (46218-3144)
PHONE.............................317 549-4290
Allan Bir Jr, *CEO*
Steven Hedges, *CFO*
EMP: 8
SQ FT: 10,000
SALES (est): 384.7K **Privately Held**
SIC: 3499 Friction material, made from powdered metal

(G-6452)
BACKDOOR BAKING COMPANY LLC
301 Buckingham Dr (46208-3627)
PHONE.............................317 927-7275
Laura Harris, *Principal*
EMP: 3
SALES (est): 112.3K **Privately Held**
SIC: 2051 Bread, cake & related products

(G-6453)
BACKYARD COMPANY
5621 Woodland Trace Blvd (46237-3186)
PHONE.............................317 727-0298
John Hingle, *Principal*
EMP: 2
SALES (est): 169.5K **Privately Held**
SIC: 3446 Fences, gates, posts & flagpoles

(G-6454)
BAD BOYS BLLARD PRDUCTIONS LLC
9037 Matterhorn Rd (46234-2079)
PHONE.............................702 738-4950
Richard Jones,
EMP: 2

SALES (est): 181.4K **Privately Held**
SIC: 3949 Billiard & pool equipment & supplies, general

(G-6455)
BANE-CLENE CORP (PA)
Also Called: William F Bane Co
3940 N Keystone Ave (46205-2911)
PHONE.............................317 546-5448
Fax: 317 543-2222
William F Bane Jr, *President*
Wm Bane, *General Mgr*
William F Bane Sr, *Chairman*
Donald A Bane, *CFO*
Dan Willis, *Cust Mgr*
EMP: 20
SQ FT: 27,000
SALES: 2.7MM **Privately Held**
WEB: www.baneclene.com
SIC: 7217 5169 5087 2842 Carpet & upholstery cleaning on customer premises; chemicals & allied products; carpet & rug cleaning equipment & supplies, commercial; specialty cleaning, polishes & sanitation goods

(G-6456)
BANTAM INDUSTRIES INC
2346 S Lynhurst Dr # 601 (46241-8607)
PHONE.............................714 561-6122
EMP: 2
SALES (est): 77K **Privately Held**
SIC: 3999 Manufacturing industries

(G-6457)
BATCH SMALL PRESS LLC ⊙
240 Newhart St (46217-3546)
PHONE.............................317 410-8923
Joel Goodwin, *Owner*
EMP: 2 EST: 2017
SALES (est): 59.2K **Privately Held**
SIC: 2741 Miscellaneous publishing

(G-6458)
BATTERY XPRESS
12549 Marina View Dr (46256-9607)
PHONE.............................765 759-2288
Ryan Stout,
EMP: 7 EST: 2008
SALES (est): 425.3K **Privately Held**
SIC: 2086 Carbonated soft drinks, bottled & canned

(G-6459)
BAXTER HEALTHCARE CORPORATION
6812 Corporate Dr (46278-1935)
PHONE.............................317 291-0620
Fax: 317 297-2983
David Hoffman, *Manager*
EMP: 40
SALES (corp-wide): 10.5B **Publicly Held**
SIC: 3841 Surgical & medical instruments
HQ: Baxter Healthcare Corporation
　　1 Baxter Pkwy
　　Deerfield IL 60015
　　224 948-2000

(G-6460)
BECKMAN COULTER INC
5355 W 76th St (46268-4166)
PHONE.............................317 471-8029
Coulter Beckman, *Branch Mgr*
Ryan Britt, *Manager*
Kyle Buren, *Manager*
Emily Edeburn, *Manager*
Andres Garcia, *Manager*
EMP: 82
SALES (corp-wide): 18.3B **Publicly Held**
WEB: www.beckman.com
SIC: 3826 3821 2869 Analytical instruments; chemical laboratory apparatus; centrifuges, laboratory; laboratory chemicals, organic
HQ: Beckman Coulter, Inc.
　　250 S Kraemer Blvd
　　Brea CA 92821
　　714 993-5321

(G-6461)
BECKMAN COULTER INC
5350 Lakeview Pkwy (46268)
PHONE.............................317 808-4200
Scott Atkin, *Branch Mgr*
EMP: 82

▲ = Import ▼=Export
◆ =Import/Export

SALES (corp-wide): 18.3B **Publicly Held**
WEB: www.beckman.com
SIC: 3826 Analytical instruments; liquid chromatographic instruments
HQ: Beckman Coulter, Inc.
250 S Kraemer Blvd
Brea CA 92821
714 993-5321

(G-6462)
BECKMAN COULTER INC
7451 Winton Dr (46268-5103)
PHONE.............................317 808-4200
Fax: 317 808-4395
Scott Atkin, *Manager*
Rusty Hitch, *Manager*
Ron Shipman, *Manager*
EMP: 2 EST: 2014
SALES (est): 220.5K **Privately Held**
SIC: 3826 Analytical instruments

(G-6463)
BEDDER WAY COMPANY INC
Also Called: Meridian Closet
3450 Developers Rd (46227-3585)
PHONE.............................317 783-5105
Fax: 317 783-5021
Chris Kosten, *President*
Nathan Harman, *CFO*
Jason Parsley, *Sales Staff*
Megan Tackett, *Marketing Staff*
▼ EMP: 25 EST: 2001
SALES (est): 3.9MM **Privately Held**
WEB: www.bedderway.com
SIC: 2511 Wood bedroom furniture

(G-6464)
BEEMAK PLASTICS INC
7035 E 86th St (46250-1547)
PHONE.............................317 841-4398
Chris Braun, *Principal*
EMP: 4
SALES (est): 318.1K **Privately Held**
SIC: 3089 Plastics products

(G-6465)
BEEMAN JORGENSEN INC
Also Called: Tpr
7510 Allisonville Rd (46250-2354)
PHONE.............................317 841-7677
Dr Brett Johnson, *President*
Julie Johnson, *Admin Sec*
EMP: 5
SALES: 100K **Privately Held**
WEB: www.tpr-inc.com
SIC: 2731 Textbooks: publishing only, not printed on site; books: publishing only

(G-6466)
BEER BARON LLC
Also Called: Triton Brewing
5764 Wheeler Rd (46216-1038)
PHONE.............................317 735-2706
David Waldman, *Mng Member*
Michael Deweese, *Mng Member*
Jon Lang, *Mng Member*
EMP: 3
SALES (est): 407.9K **Privately Held**
SIC: 2082 Beer (alcoholic beverage)

(G-6467)
BERNARD HASTEN
Also Called: Speedread Technologies
4525 Saguaro Trl (46268-2557)
PHONE.............................317 824-4544
Fax: 317 824-4547
Bernard Hasten, *Owner*
Laurie Hasten, *CFO*
Lois Pardue, *Manager*
EMP: 6
SALES (est): 962K **Privately Held**
WEB: www.speedreadtech.com
SIC: 3824 Water meters

(G-6468)
BEST EQUIPMENT & WELDING CO
1960 Midwest Blvd (46214-2337)
PHONE.............................317 271-8652
Glenn N Foy, *President*
Richard Gilbert, *Vice Pres*
Dick Gilbert, *Sales Executive*
Richard B Gilbert Jr, *Admin Sec*
EMP: 25
SQ FT: 17,000

SALES (est): 5.1MM **Privately Held**
SIC: 3548 7692 Welding apparatus; welding repair

(G-6469)
BEST EQUIPMENT CO INC (PA)
5550 Poindexter Dr (46235-9041)
PHONE.............................317 823-3050
Mike Dahlmann, *President*
Michael Dahlmann, *President*
Maria Dahlmann, *CFO*
Ben Wanner, *Sales Staff*
Robert Halstead, *Manager*
EMP: 28
SALES (est): 24MM **Privately Held**
SIC: 5084 7629 3699 Waste compactors; trucks, industrial; electrical equipment repair services; welding machines & equipment, ultrasonic

(G-6470)
BEX SCREEN PRINTING INC
5602 Elmwood Ave Ste 214 (46203-6072)
PHONE.............................317 791-0375
Fax: 317 791-0383
Rebecca Miller, *President*
Beth Lucas, *CFO*
EMP: 3
SQ FT: 1,400
SALES (est): 260K **Privately Held**
SIC: 2759 Commercial printing

(G-6471)
BEYOND MONUMENTAL
202 E Market St (46204-3306)
PHONE.............................317 454-8519
EMP: 3
SALES (est): 298.8K **Privately Held**
SIC: 3272 Monuments & grave markers, except terrazo

(G-6472)
BHAR PRINTING INC
8745 Rawles Ave (46219-7800)
PHONE.............................317 899-1020
Fax: 317 898-8196
Ram Bhargava, *President*
Madhu Bhargava, *Vice Pres*
Jenina Enley, *Manager*
EMP: 7
SQ FT: 10,000
SALES: 900K **Privately Held**
WEB: www.bharprinting.com
SIC: 2752 Commercial printing, offset

(G-6473)
BIG GUY SIGNS LLC
5575 Elmwood Ave Ste C (46203-6046)
PHONE.............................317 780-6000
Angel Crawford, *Mng Member*
EMP: 5
SALES (est): 547.8K **Privately Held**
SIC: 3993 Signs, not made in custom sign painting shops

(G-6474)
BIGGERSTAFF & SON EXCAVATING
5002 E Thompson Rd (46237-1945)
PHONE.............................317 784-6034
Howard Biggerstaff, *President*
EMP: 7
SALES (est): 1.3MM **Privately Held**
SIC: 3531 1521 Excavators: cable, clamshell, crane, derrick, dragline, etc.; general remodeling, single-family houses

(G-6475)
BIMBO BAKERIES USA INC
8121 W 10th St (46214-2431)
PHONE.............................317 273-0444
EMP: 24
SALES (corp-wide): 13.7B **Privately Held**
SIC: 2051 Mfg Bread/Related Products
HQ: Bimbo Bakeries Usa, Inc
255 Business Center Dr # 200
Horsham PA 19044
215 347-5500

(G-6476)
BIONODE LLC
7987 Clearwater Pkwy (46240-4902)
PHONE.............................317 292-7686
Murray Firestone, *CEO*
EMP: 2

SALES (est): 86.6K **Privately Held**
SIC: 3845 Electrotherapeutic apparatus

(G-6477)
BIOSAFE ENGINEERING LLC
5750 W 80th St (46278-1340)
PHONE.............................317 858-8099
Phillip Mervis, *CEO*
Shanon Jones, *Business Mgr*
Brandon Ross, *Engineer*
Scott Bacon, *Project Engr*
Brian Bading, *Project Engr*
EMP: 20
SQ FT: 16,000
SALES (est): 5.5MM **Privately Held**
WEB: www.biosafeengineering.com
SIC: 8711 2836 Mechanical engineering; biological products, except diagnostic

(G-6478)
BITTERSWEET CANDLE COMPANY LLC
5230 Park Emerson Dr (46203-6932)
PHONE.............................317 782-3170
Gene Kramer,
EMP: 17
SALES (est): 1.2MM **Privately Held**
SIC: 3999 Candles

(G-6479)
BITUMINOUS MATERIALS & SUP LP
5400 W 86th St (46268-1502)
PHONE.............................317 228-8203
Dave Blackburn, *Managing Prtnr*
Gary Lindgren, *Vice Pres*
EMP: 2
SALES (est): 246.3K **Privately Held**
SIC: 2952 Asphalt felts & coatings

(G-6480)
BIZCARD
9745 Fall Creek Rd (46256-4728)
PHONE.............................317 436-8649
EMP: 2
SALES (est): 164.9K **Privately Held**
SIC: 2752 Commercial printing, lithographic

(G-6481)
BLACK & DECKER (US) INC
Also Called: Dewalt Service Center 017
5999 Crawfordsville Rd (46224-3789)
PHONE.............................317 241-1200
David Fahrenholz, *General Mgr*
EMP: 7
SQ FT: 500
SALES (corp-wide): 12.7B **Publicly Held**
WEB: www.dewalt.com
SIC: 3546 Power-driven handtools
HQ: Black & Decker (U.S.) Inc.
1000 Stanley Dr
New Britain CT 06053
860 225-5111

(G-6482)
BLACK EMBER LLC
1332 Cliff Ridge Ct (46217-2753)
PHONE.............................317 840-5523
EMP: 2
SALES (est): 130K **Privately Held**
SIC: 7372 Prepackaged Software Services

(G-6483)
BLACK PLATE CATERING
2025 E 46th St (46205-1412)
PHONE.............................317 634-8030
Keith Little, *Owner*
EMP: 2 EST: 2013
SALES (est): 229K **Privately Held**
SIC: 3312 Black plate

(G-6484)
BLINKLESS POWER EQUIPMENT LLC
8802 Bash St Ste F (46256-1288)
PHONE.............................317 844-7328
Rand Gengenbach,
EMP: 8 EST: 2011
SALES (est): 673K **Privately Held**
SIC: 3621 3613 Motors & generators; phase or rotary converters (electrical equipment); inverters, rotating: electrical; control panels, electric; power switching equipment

(G-6485)
BLUE GUARDIAN PUBLISHING CO
5252 Brianna Ln (46235-6811)
PHONE.............................317 506-0763
Jon A Daggy, *Principal*
EMP: 2
SALES (est): 97.5K **Privately Held**
SIC: 2741 Miscellaneous publishing

(G-6486)
BLUE MARBLE COCKTAILS INC
6008 Corporate Way (46278-2923)
PHONE.............................888 400-3090
Alan Miller, *President*
EMP: 30
SQ FT: 18,000
SALES: 13MM **Privately Held**
SIC: 2085 Cocktails, alcoholic

(G-6487)
BLUE OCTOPUS PRINTING COMPANY
2431 Directors Row (46241-4972)
PHONE.............................317 247-1997
Gary Johnloz, *Vice Pres*
Kj Williams, *Manager*
EMP: 2
SALES (est): 148.6K **Privately Held**
SIC: 2759 Screen printing

(G-6488)
BLUE PILLAR INC
9025 River Rd Ste 150 (46240-6447)
PHONE.............................317 723-6601
Tana Linback, *Business Anlyst*
Paul Schuler, *Info Tech Mgr*
EMP: 22 **Privately Held**
SIC: 7372 Application computer software
PA: Blue Pillar, Inc.
2 N Market St Fl 4
Frederick MD 21701

(G-6489)
BLUE RIBBON PRODUCTS INC
8188 Allison Ave (46268-1615)
P.O. Box 781043 (46278-8043)
PHONE.............................317 972-7970
Fax: 317 972-7981
Mark J Studley, *President*
Ethan Blocher-Smith, *Info Tech Mgr*
EMP: 5
SQ FT: 10,000
SALES (est): 1.2MM **Privately Held**
WEB: www.blueribboninc.com
SIC: 2842 Cleaning or polishing preparations

(G-6490)
BLUE SUN VENTURES LTD
Also Called: Bakesmart
525 S Meridian St (46225-1108)
PHONE.............................317 426-0001
Michael Clements, *President*
EMP: 3
SALES (est): 253.8K **Privately Held**
SIC: 7372 Application computer software

(G-6491)
BO-MAR INDUSTRIES INC
3838 S Arlington Ave (46203-6107)
PHONE.............................317 899-1240
Fax: 317 899-1241
Robert Buchanan, *President*
Jill Buchanan, *Corp Secy*
Mark Buchanan, *Vice Pres*
EMP: 45
SQ FT: 42,000
SALES: 6.1MM **Privately Held**
WEB: www.bo-marind.com
SIC: 3444 3993 2514 Sheet metal specialties, not stamped; signs & advertising specialties; metal household furniture

(G-6492)
BOARDER MAGIC BY J & A
902 W Banta Rd (46217-3828)
PHONE.............................317 545-4401
Jim Ault, *Manager*
EMP: 2
SALES (est): 165K **Privately Held**
SIC: 3531 Construction machinery

(G-6493)
BODYCOTE THERMAL PROC INC
500 W 21st St (46202-1195)
P.O. Box 1226 (46206-1226)
PHONE.................................317 924-4321
John Hillenbrand, *Sales Executive*
Seth Walradth, *Office Mgr*
Ray Thompson, *Branch Mgr*
EMP: 40
SALES (corp-wide): 911.9MM **Privately Held**
SIC: 3398 Metal heat treating
HQ: Bodycote Thermal Processing, Inc.
12700 Park Central Dr # 700
Dallas TX 75251
214 904-2420

(G-6494)
BOLINGER MACHINE CO
23 N Alton Ave (46222-3908)
PHONE.................................317 241-2989
Fax: 317 241-7736
Alan Bolinger, *Owner*
Jerry Bolinger, *Owner*
EMP: 12
SQ FT: 13,000
SALES: 500K **Privately Held**
SIC: 3599 Machine shop, jobbing & repair

(G-6495)
BONNIER CORPORATION
Also Called: Corporation Bonnier
838 N Delaware St (46204-1127)
PHONE.................................317 231-5862
EMP: 2
SALES (corp-wide): 3.1B **Privately Held**
SIC: 2721 Periodicals
HQ: Bonnier Corporation
460 N Orlando Ave Ste 200
Winter Park FL 32789

(G-6496)
BOOMSTICK INTERACTIVE LLC
6346 Stockwell Dr (46237-3138)
PHONE.................................812 528-4875
Jeremy Wagner, *CEO*
Monette Viduya, *Vice Pres*
EMP: 2
SALES (est): 100.2K **Privately Held**
SIC: 7372 7389 Application computer software;

(G-6497)
BOSPHORUS BREAKFAST HOOKAH BAR
937 S East St (46225-1377)
PHONE.................................317 624-1700
EMP: 2
SALES (est): 116.2K **Privately Held**
SIC: 2064 Breakfast bars

(G-6498)
BOWMAN BROTHERS INC
1831 E 64th St (46220-2101)
PHONE.................................317 253-6043
Ward Bowman, *President*
Joseph Gromek, *Director*
EMP: 19
SALES (est): 2.6MM **Privately Held**
SIC: 2951 Asphalt paving mixtures & blocks

(G-6499)
BRADEN SUTPHIN INK CO
1340 Sadlier Circle E Dr (46239-1052)
PHONE.................................317 352-8781
Fax: 317 352-8785
Brian Chronister, *Principal*
EMP: 2
SALES (est): 193.8K **Privately Held**
SIC: 2893 Printing ink

(G-6500)
BRAINSTORM PRINT LLC
2603 55th Pl (46220-3527)
PHONE.................................317 466-1600
Richard Gold, *Managing Prtnr*
EMP: 5
SALES (est): 298.1K **Privately Held**
SIC: 2752 Commercial printing, offset

(G-6501)
BRALLAN PRESS LLC
5835 N Tacoma Ave (46220-2844)
PHONE.................................765 337-7909
EMP: 2
SALES (est): 82K **Privately Held**
SIC: 2741 Misc Publishing

(G-6502)
BRAMA INC
Also Called: Big Red
5855 Kopetsky Dr Ste I (46217-9636)
PHONE.................................317 786-7770
Dennis Blong, *President*
▲ EMP: 20
SALES (est): 4.8MM **Privately Held**
WEB: www.bigred.org
SIC: 3563 Air & gas compressors

(G-6503)
BRAND PRTG & PHOTO-LITHO CO (PA)
Also Called: Brand Quick Printing
8745 Rawles Ave Ste D (46219-7831)
P.O. Box 324, Carmel (46082-0324)
PHONE.................................317 921-4095
Fax: 317 921-4098
Kyle Brand, *President*
EMP: 5 EST: 1950
SQ FT: 3,600
SALES (est): 1MM **Privately Held**
WEB: www.quikprinting.com
SIC: 2893 2752 5112 2791 Letterpress or offset ink; lithographing on metal; business forms; typesetting; bookbinding & related work; commercial printing

(G-6504)
BRASS RING
1245 Shelby St (46203-1950)
PHONE.................................317 635-7464
Patricia E Perrin, *Administration*
EMP: 6
SALES (est): 548.1K **Privately Held**
SIC: 2599 Bar, restaurant & cafeteria furniture

(G-6505)
BREDENSTEINER & ASSOC INC
1920 Dr Martin Luther Kin (46202-1108)
PHONE.................................317 921-2226
Jim Bredenstein, *President*
EMP: 2
SALES (est): 200.3K **Privately Held**
SIC: 2759 Commercial printing

(G-6506)
BRICKYARD CROSSING
2572 Moller Rd (46224-3381)
PHONE.................................317 492-6573
EMP: 2 EST: 2010
SALES (est): 156K **Privately Held**
SIC: 3949 Shafts, golf club

(G-6507)
BRICS
901 E 64th St (46220-1101)
PHONE.................................317 257-5757
David Gabovitch, *Owner*
EMP: 7
SALES (est): 439.2K **Privately Held**
SIC: 2024 Ice cream, bulk

(G-6508)
BRIGHT SHEET METAL COMPANY INC (PA)
Also Called: A To Z Sheet Metal
4212 W 71st St Ste A (46268-2274)
PHONE.................................317 291-7600
Fax: 317 328-4613
Phil Meyers, *President*
Gary Aletto, *COO*
Jim Meyers, *Vice Pres*
EMP: 110
SQ FT: 35,500
SALES (est): 41.9MM **Privately Held**
WEB: www.brightsheetmetal.com
SIC: 1761 3444 Sheet metalwork; sheet metalwork

(G-6509)
BRIGHTER DAYZ PUBLISHING LLC
7210 Mars Dr (46241-3693)
PHONE.................................317 793-1364
Elenora Stretshberry, *Principal*
EMP: 2
SALES (est): 51.4K **Privately Held**
SIC: 2741 Miscellaneous publishing

(G-6510)
BRIGHTON COLLECTIBLES LLC
8702 Keystone Xing 142a (46240-7815)
PHONE.................................317 580-0912
Fax: 317 580-0681
Jerry Kohl, *Owner*
EMP: 32
SALES (corp-wide): 375.3MM **Privately Held**
SIC: 2339 Women's & misses' accessories
PA: Brighton Collectibles, Llc
14022 Nelson Ave
City Of Industry CA 91746
626 961-9381

(G-6511)
BRINKMAN PRESS INC
6945 Hawthorn Park Dr (46220-3910)
PHONE.................................317 722-0305
Fax: 317 722-0312
Thomas Brinkman, *President*
Darla Leffert, *General Mgr*
Sandra L Brinkman, *Admin Sec*
Julia Molloy, *Graphic Designe*
EMP: 9
SQ FT: 2,800
SALES (est): 1.5MM **Privately Held**
WEB: www.brinkmanpress.com
SIC: 2752 Commercial printing, offset

(G-6512)
BROWNSBURG CUSTOM CABINETS
1747 Country Club Rd (46234-1828)
P.O. Box 198, Brownsburg (46112-0198)
PHONE.................................317 271-1887
Fax: 317 273-1877
Robert Overman, *President*
David Roberts, *Treasurer*
EMP: 6
SQ FT: 10,000
SALES: 500K **Privately Held**
SIC: 3083 Plastic finished products, laminated

(G-6513)
BRULIN HOLDING COMPANY INC (PA)
2920 Aj Brown Ave (46205-4066)
P.O. Box 270 (46206-0270)
PHONE.................................317 923-3211
Charles Pollnow, *President*
Jolee R Chartrand, *Vice Pres*
Kim Essenburg, *CFO*
EMP: 22
SALES (est): 13.3MM **Privately Held**
SIC: 2842 2841 Cleaning or polishing preparations; floor waxes; sanitation preparations; disinfectants, household or industrial plant; soap: granulated, liquid, cake, flaked or chip

(G-6514)
BRULIN HOLDING COMPANY INC
2920 Dr Andrew J Brown (46205-4066)
PHONE.................................317 923-3211
EMP: 100
SALES (corp-wide): 13.3MM **Privately Held**
SIC: 2842 2841 Cleaning or polishing preparations; floor waxes; sanitation preparations; disinfectants, household or industrial plant; soap: granulated, liquid, cake, flaked or chip
PA: Brulin Holding Company, Inc.
2920 Aj Brown Ave
Indianapolis IN 46205
317 923-3211

(G-6515)
BRUMATE LLC
640 E Michigan St C135 (46202-0008)
PHONE.................................317 474-7352
Dylan Jacob, *Mng Member*
EMP: 1
SQ FT: 13,000
SALES: 2MM **Privately Held**
SIC: 2084 Wine coolers (beverages)

(G-6516)
BRYTON CORPORATION
4011 Championship Dr (46268-2588)
P.O. Box 68177 (46268-0177)
PHONE.................................317 334-8700
Bob Samuels, *President*
R T Samuels, *Principal*
Martha Samuels, *Vice Pres*
▲ EMP: 15
SQ FT: 10,000
SALES (est): 3.5MM **Privately Held**
SIC: 3842 5047 Surgical appliances & supplies; medical equipment & supplies

(G-6517)
BUCHANAN PUBLISHING
7835 E 56th St Apt B (46226-1380)
PHONE.................................317 546-4524
N A Buchanan, *Principal*
EMP: 2
SALES (est): 102.7K **Privately Held**
SIC: 2741 Miscellaneous publishing

(G-6518)
BUCKAROOS INC (PA)
9855 Crosspoint Blvd # 142 (46256-3353)
PHONE.................................317 899-9100
Jeffrey Rebholz, *President*
Arnold Rebholz, *Treasurer*
Pat Stephens, *Sales Mgr*
EMP: 14
SQ FT: 10,000
SALES (est): 2.8MM **Privately Held**
WEB: www.buckaroos.com
SIC: 3444 2499 3432 5072 Metal housings, enclosures, casings & other containers; dowels, wood; plastic plumbing fixture fittings, assembly; hand tools; power tools & accessories

(G-6519)
BUCKEYE CORRUGATED INC
4001 S High School Rd B (46241-6448)
PHONE.................................330 576-0590
Robert Butterfield, *Branch Mgr*
Randy Wright, *Info Tech Mgr*
EMP: 56
SALES (corp-wide): 194.1MM **Privately Held**
SIC: 2653 Corrugated & solid fiber boxes
PA: Buckeye Corrugated, Inc
822 Kumho Dr Ste 400
Fairlawn OH 44333
330 576-0590

(G-6520)
BUCKNER INC (PA)
Also Called: Sundae's
9922 E 79th St (46256-4824)
PHONE.................................317 570-0533
Fax: 317 846-4477
David Bucker, *President*
Steve Buckner, *Vice Pres*
EMP: 18
SQ FT: 1,600
SALES (est): 1.1MM **Privately Held**
SIC: 5812 2024 5149 Restaurant, family: independent; ice cream stands or dairy bars; ice cream, bulk; coffee & tea

(G-6521)
BULL HN INFO SYSTEMS INC
1099 N Meridian St # 200 (46204-1075)
PHONE.................................317 686-5500
Danny Allee, *Branch Mgr*
EMP: 20
SALES (corp-wide): 170.3MM **Privately Held**
SIC: 3571 3577 7378 7373 Mainframe computers; computer peripheral equipment; computer & data processing equipment repair/maintenance; computer peripheral equipment repair & maintenance; systems integration services; electrical work
HQ: Bull Hn Information Systems Inc.
285 Billerica Rd Ste 200
Chelmsford MA 01824
978 294-6000

(G-6522)
BURRIS ENGINEERING INC
5430 S Franklin Rd (46239-9646)
PHONE.................................317 862-1046
Fax: 317 862-1048
Mark Burris, *President*

David Smith, *Corp Secy*
EMP: 16
SQ FT: 15,000
SALES (est): 3.1MM **Privately Held**
SIC: 3728 Aircraft parts & equipment

(G-6523)
BUTLER-MACDONALD INC
5955 W 80th St (46278-1322)
PHONE..............................317 872-5115
Fax: 317 872-5660
J Scott Johnson, *President*
Tim Cash, *Vice Pres*
Rana Sayre, *Human Resources*
Susan B Johnson, *Admin Sec*
▲ **EMP:** 70
SQ FT: 120,000
SALES (est): 15MM **Privately Held**
WEB: www.butlermacdonald.com
SIC: 3089 Plastic processing

(G-6524)
BUZZI UNICEM USA INC
1112 W Thompson Rd (46217-9264)
PHONE..............................317 780-9860
Mike Glaze, *Manager*
EMP: 23
SALES (corp-wide): 287.7MM **Privately Held**
SIC: 3241 Portland cement
HQ: Buzzi Unicem Usa Inc.
100 Brodhead Rd Ste 230
Bethlehem PA 18017
610 882-5000

(G-6525)
BWAY CORPORATION
6061 Guion Rd (46254-1221)
PHONE..............................317 297-4638
Ron Bowman, *Vice Pres*
Ken Muncy, *Plant Mgr*
Byron Johnson, *Opers Mgr*
Dave Carter, *Purch Mgr*
Doug Bedee, *QC Mgr*
EMP: 16
SALES (corp-wide): 787.1MM **Privately Held**
SIC: 3089 Plastic containers, except foam
HQ: Bway Corporation
8607 Roberts Dr Ste 250
Atlanta GA 30350

(G-6526)
C & G LABELING
4057 Vincennes Rd (46268-3008)
PHONE..............................317 396-2953
Robert Copeland, *Owner*
EMP: 2 **EST:** 2016
SALES (est): 85.9K **Privately Held**
SIC: 3577 Computer peripheral equipment

(G-6527)
C & W INKD
6300 Brookville Rd Bldg B (46219-8251)
PHONE..............................317 352-1000
Fax: 317 352-1001
Tommy L Cooper, *President*
EMP: 16 **EST:** 2007
SQ FT: 10,000
SALES (est): 3MM **Privately Held**
WEB: www.cwdie.com
SIC: 3554 2789 2675 7319 Die cutting & stamping machinery, paper converting; binding only: books, pamphlets, magazines, etc.; die-cut paper & board; distribution of advertising material or sample services

(G-6528)
C H ELLIS LLC
Also Called: C. H. Ellis
2432 Se Ave (46201)
PHONE..............................317 636-3351
Fax: 317 635-5140
Clay Barnes, *CEO*
Jeffrey Hale, *President*
Robert Able, *Vice Pres*
EMP: 40
SALES (est): 1.2MM **Privately Held**
SIC: 3161 Luggage

(G-6529)
C&C POLO ENTERPRISES INC
Also Called: UPS
9801 Fall Creek Rd (46256-4802)
PHONE..............................317 577-8266

Roshelle Polo, *Principal*
EMP: 2
SALES (est): 134.6K **Privately Held**
SIC: 7389 4783 3053 Mailbox rental & related service; packing goods for shipping; packing materials

(G-6530)
C&R RACING INCORPORATED (DH)
Also Called: C & R
6950 Guion Rd (46268-2576)
PHONE..............................317 293-4100
Fax: 317 293-4110
Chris B Paulsen, *President*
Debra Paulsen, *Corp Secy*
▲ **EMP:** 60
SQ FT: 35,000
SALES: 11MM
SALES (corp-wide): 35.9MM **Privately Held**
WEB: www.crracing.com
SIC: 3599 Machine shop, jobbing & repair
HQ: P.W.R Performance Products Pty Ltd
103 Lahrs Rd
Ormeau QLD 4208
755 471-600

(G-6531)
C-CAT INC
1726 W 15th St (46202-2025)
PHONE..............................317 568-2899
Kristi Johnson, *President*
Justin Treadway, *Vice Pres*
Brook Crist, *Project Mgr*
Jake Nierman, *Project Mgr*
Kaley Gregg, *Opers Mgr*
EMP: 14
SQ FT: 4,472
SALES (est): 2.5MM **Privately Held**
SIC: 2298 Cable, fiber

(G-6532)
CABINETRY IDEAS INC
6113 Allisonville Rd (46220-4607)
PHONE..............................317 722-1300
Nancy L Barbee, *Principal*
Raymond Giehll, *Opers Mgr*
Sarah Massari, *Production*
EMP: 4
SALES (est): 487.9K **Privately Held**
SIC: 2434 Wood kitchen cabinets

(G-6533)
CAKE BAKE SHOP INC
6515 Carrollton Ave (46220-1616)
PHONE..............................317 257-2253
Gwendolyn Rogers, *President*
EMP: 3
SALES (est): 68.6K **Privately Held**
SIC: 2051 Cakes, pies & pastries

(G-6534)
CALUMET FINANCE CORP
2780 Waterfront Pkwy (46214)
PHONE..............................317 328-5660
EMP: 3
SALES (est): 256.8K
SALES (corp-wide): 3.7B **Publicly Held**
SIC: 2911 Petroleum refining
PA: Calumet Specialty Products Partners
Lp
2780 Waterfront Pkwy
Indianapolis IN 46214
317 328-5660

(G-6535)
CALUMET GP LLC
2780 Wtrfrnt Pkwy Dr St (46214)
PHONE..............................317 328-5660
Fred Fehsenfeld,
EMP: 11
SALES (est): 2.2MM **Privately Held**
SIC: 2911 Petroleum refining

(G-6536)
CALUMET INTERNATIONAL INC
2780 Waterfront (46214)
PHONE..............................317 328-5660
Bill Grube, *President*
Allan Moyes, *Vice Pres*
EMP: 2
SALES (est): 211.9K **Privately Held**
WEB: www.calumetlub.com
SIC: 2911 Petroleum refining

(G-6537)
CALUMET KARNS CITY REF LLC (HQ)
Also Called: Calumet Penreco, LLC
2780 Waterfront (46214)
PHONE..............................317 328-5660
F W Grube, *CEO*
Tom Readal, *President*
▼ **EMP:** 60
SALES (est): 20.5MM
SALES (corp-wide): 3.7B **Publicly Held**
SIC: 2911 Petroleum refining
PA: Calumet Specialty Products Partners
Lp
2780 Waterfront Pkwy
Indianapolis IN 46214
317 328-5660

(G-6538)
CALUMET MISSOURI LLC (HQ)
2780 Waterfront Pkwy E Dr (46214-2044)
PHONE..............................318 795-3800
Donna Meyers, *Finance*
David Volpe, *Manager*
▲ **EMP:** 30 **EST:** 1990
SQ FT: 958,320
SALES (est): 9.6MM
SALES (corp-wide): 3.7B **Publicly Held**
SIC: 2911 Solvents
PA: Calumet Specialty Products Partners
Lp
2780 Waterfront Pkwy
Indianapolis IN 46214
317 328-5660

(G-6539)
CALUMET OPERATING LLC (HQ)
2780 Waterfront Pkwy (46214)
PHONE..............................317 328-5660
R Patrick Murray II, *Vice Pres*
EMP: 11
SALES (est): 292.5MM
SALES (corp-wide): 3.7B **Publicly Held**
SIC: 2992 Lubricating oils
PA: Calumet Specialty Products Partners
Lp
2780 Waterfront Pkwy
Indianapolis IN 46214
317 328-5660

(G-6540)
CALUMET REFINING LLC (DH)
Also Called: Calumet Spcialty Pdts Partners
2780 Waterfront Pkwy (46214)
PHONE..............................317 328-5660
Fax: 317 328-5668
F W Grube, *Managing Prtnr*
Harji Gill, *Vice Pres*
Grady Lee, *Safety Dir*
Jeff Lang, *Plant Mgr*
James Stoker, *Project Mgr*
◆ **EMP:** 47
SQ FT: 10,000
SALES (est): 287.3MM
SALES (corp-wide): 3.7B **Publicly Held**
WEB: www.calumetspecialty.com
SIC: 2911 Petroleum refining
HQ: Calumet Operating, L.L.C.
2780 Waterfront Pkwy
Indianapolis IN 46214
317 328-5660

(G-6541)
CALUMET SHREVEPORT LLC
2780 Waterfront Pkwy E Dr (46214-2044)
PHONE..............................317 328-5660
Roy Jacobsen, *Principal*
EMP: 77 **EST:** 2004
SALES (est): 10.7MM
SALES (corp-wide): 3.7B **Publicly Held**
SIC: 2911 Petroleum refining
HQ: Calumet Refining, Llc
2780 Waterfront Pkwy
Indianapolis IN 46214
317 328-5660

(G-6542)
CALUMET SPCLTY PDTS PRTNERS LP (PA)
2780 Waterfront Pkwy (46214)
PHONE..............................317 328-5660
Timothy Go, *CEO*
Calumet GP, *General Ptnr*
Ralph Lockman, *District Mgr*

Greg Morical, *Vice Pres*
Michael Rhoades, *Vice Pres*
▼ **EMP:** 277
SQ FT: 58,501
SALES: 3.7B **Publicly Held**
WEB: www.calumetlubricants.com
SIC: 2911 Solvents; mineral waxes, natural; fuel additives

(G-6543)
CALUMET SUPERIOR LLC
2780 Waterfront Pkwy 20 (46214)
PHONE..............................317 328-5660
Jeff Barnaby, *Accountant*
F W Grube,
EMP: 200
SALES (est): 36.6MM
SALES (corp-wide): 3.7B **Publicly Held**
SIC: 5983 2999 Fuel oil dealers; fuel briquettes & waxes
PA: Calumet Specialty Products Partners
Lp
2780 Waterfront Pkwy
Indianapolis IN 46214
317 328-5660

(G-6544)
CAMERABEE LLC
7507 Crews Dr (46226-3988)
PHONE..............................317 546-2999
Derek Hammer, *Principal*
EMP: 2 **EST:** 2014
SALES (est): 91.9K **Privately Held**
SIC: 3861 Cameras & related equipment

(G-6545)
CAMPBELL VENTILATION INC
Also Called: CVI Sheet Metal Contractors
1544 Kennington St (46225-1816)
PHONE..............................317 636-7211
Fax: 317 636-7224
Michael Campbell, *Ch of Bd*
David Campbell, *President*
Lori Fresher, *Corp Secy*
Leland Campbell, *Executive*
Diane Campbell, *Shareholder*
EMP: 15
SQ FT: 6,500
SALES: 1.8MM **Privately Held**
WEB: www.campbellventilation.com
SIC: 3444 Sheet metalwork

(G-6546)
CANDY CENTS VENDING INC
7515 Somerset Bay Apt B (46240-3445)
PHONE..............................317 378-9197
Juan Meka Anderson, *President*
EMP: 5 **EST:** 2014
SALES (est): 218.1K **Privately Held**
SIC: 2096 Potato chips & similar snacks

(G-6547)
CAPITAL CITY TRANSIT LLC
3421 W Washington St (46222-3933)
PHONE..............................317 813-5800
Fax: 317 813-5810
Buck Retmier, *CEO*
Cathy Retmier, *President*
Sherry Byram, *Manager*
EMP: 2
SALES (est): 230K **Privately Held**
SIC: 3711 Buses, all types, assembly of

(G-6548)
CAPITAL MACHINE COMPANY INC (PA)
Also Called: Capital Machines International
2801 Roosevelt Ave (46218-3667)
P.O. Box 18340 (46218-0340)
PHONE..............................317 638-6661
Fax: 317 636-5122
William L Koss, *President*
Andy Klotz, *President*
Mary Joan Koss Rothenberger, *Director*
EMP: 17 **EST:** 1887
SQ FT: 35,000
SALES (est): 2.4MM **Privately Held**
SIC: 3553 3545 3541 Veneer mill machines; machine tool accessories; machine tools, metal cutting type

(G-6549)
CAPITOL CITY CONTAINER CORP
8240 Zionsville Rd (46268-1627)
PHONE..............................317 875-0290

Fax: 317 876-6694
Richard Purcell, *President*
John Mike Purcell, *Vice Pres*
Mike Purcell, *Vice Pres*
Kaye McTighe, *Accounting Mgr*
Adriana Jackson, *Sales Staff*
EMP: 43 EST: 1974
SQ FT: 75,000
SALES (est): 10.5MM **Privately Held**
WEB: www.capcitycont.com
SIC: 2653 Boxes, corrugated: made from purchased materials

(G-6550)
CAPITOL CITY GLASS INC
1424 S East St (46225-1806)
PHONE..................................317 635-2556
Fax: 317 217-1326
Mark J Eads, *President*
EMP: 3
SALES: 400K **Privately Held**
SIC: 3211 Flat glass

(G-6551)
CARDINAL CONTAINER CORP
750 S Post Rd (46239-9745)
PHONE..................................317 898-2715
Fax: 317 899-6747
D E Ferguson, *CEO*
H Dale Farmer, *President*
Duane Stoots, *Vice Pres*
Mark A Prosser, *CFO*
EMP: 40
SQ FT: 60,000
SALES (est): 10.1MM **Privately Held**
WEB: www.cardinalcontainercorp.com
SIC: 2653 Boxes, corrugated: made from purchased materials

(G-6552)
CARDINAL HEALTH 414 LLC
4343 W 62nd St (46268-2514)
PHONE..................................317 981-4100
Alyssa Carter, *Branch Mgr*
EMP: 65
SALES (corp-wide): 129.9B **Publicly Held**
SIC: 2834 2835 Pharmaceutical preparations; in vitro & in vivo diagnostic substances
HQ: Cardinal Health 414, Llc
   7000 Cardinal Pl
   Dublin OH 43017
   614 757-5000

(G-6553)
CARDINAL MANUFACTURING CO INC
1095 E 52nd St (46205-1204)
PHONE..................................317 283-4175
Fax: 317 283-1336
Jim Mulligan, *President*
Steve Baumgardner, *Manager*
EMP: 10
SALES (est): 1.6MM **Privately Held**
SIC: 3993 3444 Signs, not made in custom sign painting shops; sheet metalwork

(G-6554)
CARECYCLE LLC
8302 E 33rd St (46226-6503)
PHONE..................................317 372-7444
Brian Evans,
Lance Denardin,
EMP: 3
SQ FT: 10,000
SALES (est): 117.4K **Privately Held**
SIC: 3841 Surgical & medical instruments; surgical instruments & apparatus

(G-6555)
CARGILL DRY CORN INGRDENTS INC
1730 W Michigan St (46222-3855)
PHONE..................................317 632-1481
Mike Smith, *Branch Mgr*
EMP: 80
SALES (corp-wide): 88.8B **Privately Held**
SIC: 2041 2048 Corn meal; corn grits & flakes, for brewers' use; livestock feeds
HQ: Cargill Dry Corn Ingredients, Inc.
   616 S Jefferson St
   Paris IL 61944
   217 465-5331

(G-6556)
CARLTON VENTURES INC
Also Called: Ink Well
1815 N Meridian St # 100 (46202-1489)
PHONE..................................317 637-2590
Fax: 317 637-2593
Karen Carlton, *President*
EMP: 8
SQ FT: 3,500
SALES (est): 1.1MM **Privately Held**
SIC: 2752 Commercial printing, offset

(G-6557)
CARPENTER CO INC
Also Called: Carpenter Realtors
5751 W 56th St (46254-1604)
PHONE..................................317 297-2900
Fax: 317 290-2414
Regina Jones, *Principal*
Jennifer Blandford, *Sales Staff*
EMP: 32
SALES (corp-wide): 20MM **Privately Held**
WEB: www.gmaccarpenter.com
SIC: 3423 Carpenters' hand tools, except saws: levels, chisels, etc.
PA: Carpenter Co Inc
   8901 S Meridian St
   Indianapolis IN 46217
   317 888-3303

(G-6558)
CARR METAL PRODUCTS INC
3735 N Arlington Ave (46218-1867)
PHONE..................................317 542-0691
Fax: 317 542-0694
Bernie B Berry III, *President*
EMP: 140 EST: 1963
SQ FT: 65,000
SALES (est): 15.6MM **Privately Held**
WEB: www.carrmetalproducts.com
SIC: 2542 3089 3469 3444 Cabinets: show, display or storage: except wood; thermoformed finished plastic products; metal stampings; sheet metalwork; fabricated plate work (boiler shop); luggage

(G-6559)
CARRIER CORPORATION
7310 W Morris St (46231-1355)
P.O. Box 70 (46206-0070)
PHONE..................................317 243-0851
Fax: 317 240-5253
Halsey Cook, *President*
David Meyers, *Vice Pres*
Greg Maupai, *Project Mgr*
Scott White, *Project Mgr*
Richard Conway, *Engineer*
EMP: 80
SALES (corp-wide): 59.8B **Publicly Held**
WEB: www.carrier.com
SIC: 3585 3433 Refrigeration & heating equipment; heating equipment, except electric
HQ: Carrier Corporation
   13995 Pasteur Blvd
   Palm Beach Gardens FL 33418
   800 379-6484

(G-6560)
CARSON MANUFACTURING CO INC
5451 N Rural St (46220-3691)
P.O. Box 20464 (46220-0464)
PHONE..................................317 257-3191
Fax: 317 254-2667
Barbara S Ferguson, *President*
William H Carson, *Corp Secy*
Lisa Yates, *Purch Mgr*
◆ EMP: 19
SQ FT: 47,000
SALES: 3MM **Privately Held**
WEB: www.carson-mfg.com
SIC: 3625 3679 3577 3669 Relays & industrial controls; electronic circuits; computer peripheral equipment; sirens, electric: vehicle, marine, industrial & air raid

(G-6561)
CARTER-LEE BUILDING COMPONENTS
1717 W Washington St (46222-4542)
PHONE..................................317 639-5431
Dave N Carter, *Ch of Bd*

John Carter, *Vice Pres*
EMP: 40
SALES (est): 5MM **Privately Held**
SIC: 2439 3448 Trusses, wooden roof; trusses & framing: prefabricated metal

(G-6562)
CARTRIDGE SPECIALIST INC
Also Called: Csi Print Supply
2440 E 57th St (46220-5821)
PHONE..................................317 257-4465
James R Beck, *President*
EMP: 5
SALES (est): 410K **Privately Held**
SIC: 3955 Print cartridges for laser & other computer printers

(G-6563)
CASE INDY PRODUCTS INC
1810 S Lynhurst Dr Ste L (46241-4451)
PHONE..................................317 677-0200
Jake Klemann, *President*
EMP: 5
SALES: 500K **Privately Held**
WEB: www.indycase.com
SIC: 2449 Shipping cases, wood: wire-bound

(G-6564)
CASPER INC
4310 Stout Field North Dr (46241-4002)
PHONE..................................660 221-5906
Leslie Exendine, *COO*
EMP: 2
SALES (est): 130K **Privately Held**
SIC: 7372 Publishers' computer software

(G-6565)
CASTLETON VILLAGE CENTER INC
Also Called: Hightech Signs
450 E 96th St (46240-5703)
PHONE..................................317 577-1995
Fax: 317 577-2295
Doug Abramowski, *Principal*
EMP: 3 **Privately Held**
WEB: www.hightech-signs.com
SIC: 3993 Signs & advertising specialties
PA: Castleton Village Center Inc
   6321 Huguenard Rd Ste A
   Fort Wayne IN 46818

(G-6566)
CATALYST INC (PA)
Also Called: Catalyst USA
5420 W Sthern Ave Ste 104 (46241)
PHONE..................................317 227-3499
Fax: 317 227-3489
Steven T Sudler Sr, *President*
EMP: 6
SALES (est): 3.6MM **Privately Held**
WEB: www.catalystusa.com
SIC: 7372 Prepackaged software

(G-6567)
CATCHRS LLC
365 E 75th St (46240-2845)
PHONE..................................310 902-9723
Jonathan Henrichsen, *Principal*
Matthew Geddie,
EMP: 4
SALES (est): 219K **Privately Held**
SIC: 2076 Coconut oil

(G-6568)
CATHETER RESEARCH INC (PA)
Also Called: Thomas Medical
6102 Victory Way (46278-2934)
PHONE..................................317 872-0074
Fax: 317 872-0169
Phil H Sheingold, *President*
John A Steen, *Chairman*
John Delaney, *Vice Pres*
Glenn Uhrich, *Vice Pres*
Daniel Rich, *Mfg Mgr*
▲ EMP: 148
SQ FT: 37,000
SALES (est): 29.4MM **Privately Held**
WEB: www.catheterresearch.com
SIC: 3841 Surgical & medical instruments

(G-6569)
CBFC LLC
7698 Zionsville Rd (46268-2173)
P.O. Box 68618 (46268-0618)
PHONE..................................317 352-0444

Geff Hays, *Vice Pres*
Albert Leatherberry, *Director*
EMP: 12 EST: 2007
SALES: 3MM **Privately Held**
SIC: 2099 Ready-to-eat meals, salads & sandwiches

(G-6570)
CCTS TECHNOLOGY GROUP INC
Also Called: CLEAN EXHAUST
8403 N Illinois St (46260-2319)
PHONE..................................305 209-5743
Theodore Sputh, *President*
EMP: 2
SALES: 107.2K **Privately Held**
SIC: 3519 5084 7538 Diesel, semi-diesel or duel-fuel engines, including marine; engines & parts, diesel; engine repair, except diesel: automotive

(G-6571)
CDE INDUSTRIES LLC
4470 N Delaware St (46205-1718)
PHONE..................................317 573-6790
Kenneth Kleinknecht, *President*
EMP: 2 EST: 2013
SALES (est): 149.8K **Privately Held**
SIC: 3999 Manufacturing industries

(G-6572)
CECO METAL DOORS AND FRAMES
4010 S Meridian St (46217-3310)
PHONE..................................317 787-3455
EMP: 3
SALES (est): 160.3K **Privately Held**
SIC: 3442 Mfg Metal Doors/Sash/Trim

(G-6573)
CELEBRATION CREATIONS INC
Also Called: Celebration Halloween
5860 Michigan Rd (46228-1731)
PHONE..................................800 762-8286
Fax: 317 257-9446
Elizabeth Stanley, *President*
◆ EMP: 20
SQ FT: 10,000
SALES: 4MM **Privately Held**
WEB: www.celebrationhalloween.com
SIC: 2389 Costumes

(G-6574)
CELLAR MASTERS LLC
Also Called: Kahn's Fine Wines Marketplace
8310 Allison Pointe Blvd (46250-1981)
PHONE..................................317 817-9473
Jim Arnold,
Joe Husar,
EMP: 40
SALES (est): 3.9MM **Privately Held**
SIC: 2084 Wines

(G-6575)
CEMEX
1051 S Emerson Ave (46203-1606)
PHONE..................................317 351-9912
EMP: 2
SALES (est): 100.5K **Privately Held**
SIC: 3273 Ready-mixed concrete

(G-6576)
CEMEX MATERIALS LLC
Also Called: Indianapolis - Pipe
1501 S Holt Rd (46241-4107)
PHONE..................................317 891-3015
Fax: 317 241-1857
John Susong, *Branch Mgr*
EMP: 23 **Privately Held**
WEB: www.prestressservices.com
SIC: 3273 Ready-mixed concrete
HQ: Cemex Materials, Llc
   1501 Belvedere Rd
   West Palm Beach FL 33406
   561 833-5555

(G-6577)
CENTERLINE STUDIO
1011 E Beecher St (46203-3989)
PHONE..................................317 423-3220
Dane Sauer, *Partner*
EMP: 2
SALES (est): 237.3K **Privately Held**
SIC: 3441 Fabricated structural metal

▲ = Import ▼=Export
◆ =Import/Export

(G-6578)
**CENTRAL BRACE & LIMB CO
INC (PA)**
1901 N Capitol Ave (46202-1265)
PHONE............................317 925-4296
Miles A Hobbs, *President*
Michael Hobbs, *President*
Justin Hobbs, *Vice Pres*
Patricia Hobbs, *Treasurer*
EMP: 13 EST: 1961
SQ FT: 3,100
SALES (est): 4MM **Privately Held**
SIC: 3842 5999 Orthopedic appliances;
prosthetic appliances; orthopedic & pros-
thesis applications

(G-6579)
**CENTRAL BRACE & LIMB CO
INC**
1901 N Capitol Ave (46202-1265)
PHONE............................317 872-1596
Pat Hobbs, *Manager*
EMP: 2
SALES (est): 145.7K
SALES (corp-wide): 4MM **Privately Held**
SIC: 3842 5999 Braces, orthopedic; ortho-
pedic & prosthesis applications
PA: Central Brace & Limb Co Inc
1901 N Capitol Ave
Indianapolis IN 46202
317 925-4296

(G-6580)
**CENTRAL COCA-COLA BTLG
CO INC**
5000 W 25th St (46224-3378)
PHONE............................317 398-0129
Fax: 317 398-0129
Larry Rife, *Manager*
Darrell Jutte, *Director*
EMP: 25
SALES (corp-wide): 35.4B **Publicly Held**
WEB: www.cokecce.com
SIC: 2086 Soft drinks: packaged in cans,
bottles, etc.
HQ: Central Coca-Cola Bottling Company,
Inc.
555 Taxter Rd Ste 550
Elmsford NY 10523
914 789-1100

(G-6581)
**CENTRAL COCA-COLA BTLG
CO INC**
3830 Hanna Cir (46241-7202)
PHONE............................317 243-3771
Fax: 317 240-6715
Marvin Herb, *Ch of Bd*
EMP: 20
SALES (corp-wide): 35.4B **Publicly Held**
WEB: www.cckokomo.com
SIC: 2086 5149 2087 Carbonated soft
drinks, bottled & canned; groceries & re-
lated products; flavoring extracts & syrups
HQ: Central Coca-Cola Bottling Company,
Inc.
555 Taxter Rd Ste 550
Elmsford NY 10523
914 789-1100

(G-6582)
**CENTRAL IND MULDINGS
MLLWK INC**
2721 N Emerson Ave (46218-3267)
PHONE............................317 568-1639
William Doss, *President*
Rodney J Zigler, *Vice Pres*
EMP: 17
SQ FT: 13,000
SALES (est): 2.1MM **Privately Held**
SIC: 2431 Millwork

(G-6583)
CENTRAL IND OIL CO
5656 N Pennsylvania St (46220-3026)
PHONE............................317 253-1131
W Appel, *Owner*
EMP: 2
SALES (est): 117K **Privately Held**
SIC: 1389 Oil field services

(G-6584)
**CENTRAL INDIANA
WOODWORKERS**
1702 Misty Lake Dr (46260-6124)
PHONE............................317 407-9228
EMP: 2
SALES (est): 110K **Privately Held**
SIC: 2431 Millwork

(G-6585)
CENTRAL WELDING INC
6040 Gray Rd (46237-2827)
PHONE............................317 784-7730
Terry Boyer, *Owner*
EMP: 3 EST: 2001
SALES (est): 75K **Privately Held**
SIC: 7692 Welding repair

(G-6586)
**CENTURY PHARMACEUTICALS
INC**
10377 Hague Rd (46256-3399)
PHONE............................317 849-4210
Fax: 317 849-4263
Ross A Deardorff, *President*
Carol Deardorff, *Opers Mgr*
EMP: 17
SQ FT: 28,000
SALES (est): 3.8MM **Privately Held**
WEB: www.centurypharmaceuticals.com
SIC: 2834 7389 3841 2844 Pharmaceuti-
cal preparations; vitamin, nutrient &
hematinic preparations for human use;
packaging & labeling services; surgical &
medical instruments; toilet preparations

(G-6587)
**CENTURY TOOL &
ENGINEERING**
1330 Deloss St (46203-1159)
PHONE............................317 685-0942
Fax: 317 685-1332
David J Yanasak, *President*
EMP: 6
SQ FT: 4,500
SALES (est): 700K **Privately Held**
SIC: 3544 7692 3545 Special dies &
tools; welding repair; machine tool acces-
sories

(G-6588)
CENVEO INC
6302 Churchman Byp (46203-6119)
PHONE............................317 791-5250
Jim Buzzard, *Principal*
Rick Stevens, *Opers Staff*
EMP: 68 Publicly Held
SIC: 2677 Envelopes
PA: Cenveo, Inc.
200 1st Stamford Pl # 200
Stamford CT 06902

(G-6589)
CERAMICA INC
6695 E 34th St (46226-6121)
PHONE............................317 546-0087
Fax: 317 546-4080
Dick Light, *Ch of Bd*
Doug Light, *President*
Marianne Townley, *Corp Secy*
Keith Light, *Vice Pres*
▲ **EMP:** 12
SQ FT: 6,000
SALES (est): 1.3MM **Privately Held**
WEB: www.ceramicainc.com
SIC: 3251 3281 3471 Structural brick &
blocks; structural clay tile; cut stone &
stone products; plating & polishing

(G-6590)
CES COMPANY LLC
Also Called: Sign-A-Rama
1331 N Capitol Ave (46202-2313)
PHONE............................317 290-0491
Chad Smith, *CEO*
EMP: 3 EST: 2016
SALES (est): 110.6K **Privately Held**
SIC: 3993 Signs & advertising specialties

(G-6591)
CGENETECH INC
7202 E 87th St Ste 100 (46256-1200)
PHONE............................317 295-1925
Qiang Yu, *President*
Fengping WEI, *Admin Sec*

EMP: 2
SALES (est): 140K **Privately Held**
WEB: www.cgenetech.com
SIC: 2833 Medicinal chemicals

(G-6592)
CH ELLIS CO INC (PA)
Also Called: Howe Industries
2432 Southeastern Ave (46201-4161)
P.O. Box 1005 (46206-1005)
PHONE............................317 636-3351
Robert N Able, *CEO*
Bob Able, *General Mgr*
Brad Harper, *Business Mgr*
Wanda K Cooney, *CFO*
Wanda Cooney, *CFO*
▲ **EMP: 40 EST:** 1902
SQ FT: 53,000
SALES (est): 7.3MM **Privately Held**
WEB: www.chellis.com
SIC: 3161 2449 Cases, carrying; shipping
cases & drums, wood: wirebound & ply-
wood

(G-6593)
**CHANCE INDIANA STANDARDS
LAB**
Also Called: Indiana Standards Laboratory
2919 Shelby St (46203-5236)
PHONE............................317 787-6578
Fax: 317 787-6580
Richard Chance, *President*
Mark Cook, *Vice Pres*
EMP: 14
SQ FT: 4,000
SALES: 1MM **Privately Held**
WEB: www.indianastandards.com
SIC: 7629 3825 Electrical measuring in-
strument repair & calibration; test equip-
ment for electronic & electric
measurement

(G-6594)
CHASE SOUTHPORT EMERSON
7120 Emblem Dr (46237-8502)
PHONE............................317 266-7470
Deanna Eagan, *Principal*
EMP: 2
SALES (est): 122.2K **Privately Held**
SIC: 3578 Automatic teller machines (ATM)

(G-6595)
CHEDDAR STACKS INC
5875 Castle Crk (46250-4331)
PHONE............................317 566-0425
Aaron M Wilson, *CEO*
EMP: 2
SALES (est): 56.5K **Privately Held**
SIC: 7372 Prepackaged software

(G-6596)
CHELI FUEL
2551 N Emerson Ave (46218-3233)
PHONE............................317 377-1480
Ahmed Bessaiah, *Principal*
EMP: 5 EST: 2013
SALES (est): 383.7K **Privately Held**
SIC: 2869 Fuels

(G-6597)
CHEM-AQUA
8401 E 33rd St (46226-6504)
PHONE............................317 899-3660
Joe Fisher, *Principal*
EMP: 2
SALES (est): 218.4K **Privately Held**
SIC: 3589 Water treatment equipment, in-
dustrial

(G-6598)
CHEP (USA) INC
606 W Troy Ave (46225-2238)
PHONE............................317 780-0700
Bernard Redmond, *Human Res Mgr*
Brian Cutcher, *Manager*
EMP: 50 Privately Held
WEB: www.ifcosystems.com
SIC: 3952 2448 Palettes, artists'; cargo
containers, wood & wood with metal
HQ: Chep (U.S.A.) Inc.
5897 Windward Pkwy
Alpharetta GA 30005
770 379-6900

(G-6599)
CHEYENNE ENTERPRISES LLC
6949 Antelope Dr (46278-2822)
PHONE............................317 253-7795
Sheila Thomas, *Principal*
EMP: 2
SALES (est): 110K **Privately Held**
SIC: 2741 Miscellaneous publishing

(G-6600)
CHICAGO CASE COMPANY (PA)
2432 Southeastern Ave (46201-4161)
PHONE............................317 636-3351
Stanley Barrish, *President*
Mark Gewirtz, *Vice Pres*
▲ **EMP:** 9
SQ FT: 18,750
SALES (est): 909K **Privately Held**
WEB: www.chicagocase.com
SIC: 3949 Sporting & athletic goods

(G-6601)
**CHISHOLM LUMBER & SUP CO
INC**
3419 Roosevelt Ave (46218-3795)
P.O. Box 18280 (46218-0280)
PHONE............................317 547-3535
Fax: 317 547-3536
Douglas Chisholm Jr, *President*
Michael B Chisholm, *Vice Pres*
Paul Krfebs, *Project Mgr*
Brian Rooksberry, *Project Mgr*
Francine Francis, *Financial Exec*
EMP: 35
SQ FT: 4,000
SALES (est): 17.4MM **Privately Held**
WEB: www.chisholmlumber.com
SIC: 5031 2431 3444 2435 Lumber:
rough, dressed & finished; millwork; sheet
metalwork; hardwood veneer & plywood;
hardwood dimension & flooring mills;
sawmills & planing mills, general

(G-6602)
CHRISTIAN CANDLE COMPANY
1509 Mary Dr (46241-2809)
PHONE............................317 427-8070
EMP: 2 EST: 2015
SALES (est): 62.5K **Privately Held**
SIC: 3999 Candles

(G-6603)
**CHRISTIE MACHINE WORKS CO
INC**
Also Called: Indianapolis Welding Co
425 W Mccarty St (46225-1237)
PHONE............................317 638-8840
Fax: 317 638-8841
John R Humphrey Sr, *President*
Joseph H Humphrey, *Corp Secy*
EMP: 5 EST: 1909
SQ FT: 7,300
SALES (est): 572.6K **Privately Held**
SIC: 3599 1799 Machine shop, jobbing &
repair; welding on site

(G-6604)
CHUCKS STACE-ALLEN INC
2246 W Minnesota St # 50 (46221-1842)
P.O. Box 21216 (46221-0216)
PHONE............................317 632-2401
Fax: 317 637-7563
Marcia Grimes, *President*
Tim Grimes, *Corp Secy*
Larry E Grimes, *Vice Pres*
James Timmons, *Vice Pres*
Bob Smith, *Project Mgr*
EMP: 20 EST: 1946
SQ FT: 12,000
SALES (est): 3.5MM **Privately Held**
SIC: 3545 Chucks: drill, lathe or magnetic
(machine tool accessories)

(G-6605)
**CINDYS CROSSSTITCH &
PATTERNS**
2265 Reformers Ave (46203-2982)
PHONE............................317 410-0764
EMP: 2
SALES (est): 155.2K **Privately Held**
SIC: 3543 Industrial patterns

(G-6606)
CINEMATIC CAPTIONING SYSTEMS
8111 Bel Moore Blvd (46259-9789)
PHONE..................................317 862-3418
Roland L Hodges, *President*
EMP: 2
SALES (est): 182.5K **Privately Held**
WEB: www.moviecaptions.com
SIC: 2531 Theater furniture

(G-6607)
CIRCLE CITY HEAT TREATING INC
2243 Massachusetts Ave (46218-4395)
PHONE..................................317 638-2252
Fax: 317 638-2181
Richard W Krug, *President*
Marla Reel, *Office Mgr*
Kathy S Krug, *Admin Sec*
EMP: 10
SQ FT: 14,000
SALES (est): 1.7MM **Privately Held**
WEB: www.circlecityheattreating.com
SIC: 3398 3471 Metal heat treating; plating & polishing

(G-6608)
CIRCLE CITY REBAR LLC
4002 Industrial Blvd (46254-2512)
PHONE..................................317 917-8566
Fax: 317 917-8729
Frank Davis,
EMP: 12
SALES (est): 4.4MM **Privately Held**
SIC: 3449 Bars, concrete reinforcing: fabricated steel

(G-6609)
CIRCLE CITY SONORANS LLC
Also Called: Circle City Kombucha
1121 N Arlington Ave (46219-3226)
PHONE..................................317 401-9787
Matthew Whiteside, *CEO*
EMP: 3
SQ FT: 2,000
SALES (est): 100.5K **Privately Held**
SIC: 2086 Carbonated beverages, nonalcoholic: bottled & canned

(G-6610)
CIRCLE CITY WOODWORKING
5574 Alcott Ln (46221-4869)
PHONE..................................765 637-6687
Kyle Mooneyhan, *Principal*
EMP: 2
SALES (est): 85.2K **Privately Held**
SIC: 2431 Millwork

(G-6611)
CIRCLE MEDICAL PRODUCTS INC
8202 Indy Ln (46214-2326)
PHONE..................................317 271-2626
Fax: 317 357-8349
Jon S Watson, *President*
EMP: 6
SQ FT: 7,000
SALES: 500K **Privately Held**
SIC: 3841 4953 Surgical & medical instruments; medical waste disposal

(G-6612)
CITADEL ARCHITECTURAL PDTS INC
3131 N Franklin Rd Ste A (46226-6390)
PHONE..................................317 894-9400
Fax: 317 894-6333
Scott Swisher, *CEO*
Greg Beresford, *Purch Agent*
Debbie Maynard, *Controller*
Mike Nelson, *Sales Mgr*
Sean Walker, *Marketing Mgr*
EMP: 45
SQ FT: 80,000
SALES (est): 17MM **Privately Held**
WEB: www.citadelap.com
SIC: 3444 Sheet metalwork

(G-6613)
CITIZENS BY-PRODUCTS COAL CO (HQ)
2020 N Meridian St (46202-1306)
PHONE..................................317 927-4738

Dave Griffiths, *President*
Kerry Lykins, *President*
EMP: 12
SALES (est): 3.1MM
SALES (corp-wide): 711.4MM **Privately Held**
SIC: 1321 8742 Natural gas liquids; marketing consulting services
PA: Citizens Energy Group
    2020 N Meridian St
    Indianapolis IN 46202
    317 924-3341

(G-6614)
CITIZENS ENERGY GROUP
366 Kentucky Ave (46225-1165)
PHONE..................................317 261-8794
David Tombs, *General Mgr*
Leon Pappas, *Plant Engr*
EMP: 89
SALES (corp-wide): 711.4MM **Privately Held**
WEB: www.citizensgas.com
SIC: 4925 3312 Gas: mixed, natural & manufactured; chemicals & other products derived from coking
PA: Citizens Energy Group
    2020 N Meridian St
    Indianapolis IN 46202
    317 924-3341

(G-6615)
CITY OPTICAL CO INC (PA)
Also Called: Dr Tavel's One Hour Optical
2839 Lafayette Rd (46222-2147)
PHONE..................................317 924-1300
Fax: 317 924-3741
Lawrence S Tavel MD, *President*
Alan G Tavel Od, *Vice Pres*
Brian C Coyle, *Mktg Dir*
Steven Crook, *Info Tech Dir*
EMP: 60
SQ FT: 21,000
SALES (est): 46.1MM **Privately Held**
WEB: www.taveloptical.com
SIC: 5048 5049 5995 8042 Ophthalmic goods; optical goods; optical goods stores; offices & clinics of optometrists; ophthalmic goods

(G-6616)
CITY OPTICAL CO INC
Also Called: Dr Tavel Premium Optical
3636 S East St (46227-1239)
PHONE..................................317 788-4243
Sue Miller, *Manager*
EMP: 5
SALES (corp-wide): 46.1MM **Privately Held**
WEB: www.taveloptical.com
SIC: 5049 3851 Optical goods; lens grinding, except prescription: ophthalmic
PA: City Optical Co., Inc.
    2839 Lafayette Rd
    Indianapolis IN 46222
    317 924-1300

(G-6617)
CLASSIC CABINETRY
10665 E 59th St (46236-8334)
PHONE..................................317 823-1853
Darrel Thomas, *Partner*
Ron Buckley, *Partner*
EMP: 5
SQ FT: 3,000
SALES (est): 620K **Privately Held**
SIC: 5031 2541 Kitchen cabinets; counters or counter display cases, wood

(G-6618)
CLASSIC CHEMICAL CORP
7750 Zionsville Rd # 700 (46268-5126)
P.O. Box 781493 (46278-8493)
PHONE..................................812 934-3289
Frank Desmond, *President*
▼ EMP: 4 EST: 2000
SQ FT: 9,000
SALES: 1MM **Privately Held**
WEB: www.degreaser.net
SIC: 2869 2843 Industrial organic chemicals; surface active agents

(G-6619)
CLEAR CHANNEL OUTDOOR INC
511 Madison Ave (46225-1185)
PHONE..................................317 686-2350
Brett Beshore, *President*
EMP: 33 **Publicly Held**
WEB: www.clearchanneloutdoor.com
SIC: 7312 3993 Billboard advertising; signs & advertising specialties
HQ: Clear Channel Outdoor, Inc.
    2325 E Camelback Rd # 400
    Phoenix AZ 85016

(G-6620)
CLIF BAR & COMPANY
7575 Georgetown Rd (46268-4132)
PHONE..................................510 596-6451
Kevin Cleary, *CEO*
EMP: 8 **Privately Held**
SIC: 2052 Cookies & crackers
PA: Clif Bar & Company
    1451 66th St
    Emeryville CA 94608

(G-6621)
CLIFF A OSTERMEYER
Also Called: Music Town Distributors
9375 College Dr Apt A (46240-4199)
PHONE..................................615 361-7902
Cliff A Ostermeyer, *Owner*
EMP: 8
SQ FT: 3,000
SALES (est): 436.7K **Privately Held**
SIC: 2711 6794 3652 7389 Newspapers: publishing only, not printed on site; copyright buying & licensing; pre-recorded records & tapes; music & broadcasting services

(G-6622)
CLINICAL DRUG INFORMATION LLC (DH)
8425 Woodfield (46240)
PHONE..................................317 735-5300
Roy Mulder, *Manager*
EMP: 6
SALES (est): 539.8K
SALES (corp-wide): 5.2B **Privately Held**
SIC: 2731 Book publishing
HQ: Wolters Kluwer Health, Inc.
    2001 Market St Ste 5
    Philadelphia PA 19103
    215 521-8300

(G-6623)
CLONDALKIN PHARMA & HEALTHCARE
Also Called: Essentra
6454 Saguaro Ct (46268-2545)
P.O. Box 78005 (46278-0005)
PHONE..................................317 328-7355
Fax: 317 328-7365
EMP: 145
SALES (corp-wide): 1.3B **Privately Held**
SIC: 2752 2791 2759 Lithographic Commercial Printing Typesetting Services Commercial Printing
HQ: Clondalkin Pharma & Healthcare, Inc
    1072 Boulder Rd
    Greensboro NC 27409
    336 292-4555

(G-6624)
CLOSURE SYSTEMS INTL INC (DH)
Also Called: C S I
7820 Innovation Blvd # 100 (46278-0016)
PHONE..................................317 390-5000
Fax: 317 390-5079
Malcolm P Bundey, *President*
Thomas Degnan, *President*
Ken Averitte, *Business Mgr*
Lawrence R Purtell, *Exec VP*
Ronald D Dickel, *Vice Pres*
◆ EMP: 163 EST: 1932
SQ FT: 64,000
SALES (est): 278.6MM **Privately Held**
WEB: www.alcoacsi.com
SIC: 3334 3565 Primary aluminum; bottling machinery: filling, capping, labeling

(G-6625)
CLOVER INDUSTRIAL SERVICES LLC
1555 S Franklin Rd Ste D (46239-8575)
PHONE..................................317 879-5001
Troy Gamble, *President*
Troy M Gamble, *President*
EMP: 28 EST: 2010
SQ FT: 21,000
SALES (est): 3MM **Privately Held**
SIC: 3589 Vacuum cleaners & sweepers, electric: industrial

(G-6626)
CMG INC
455 Rawles Ct (46229-3147)
PHONE..................................317 890-1999
Chris Julka, *General Mgr*
EMP: 5
SALES (corp-wide): 12.6MM **Privately Held**
SIC: 3444 Sheet metalwork; metal roofing & roof drainage equipment
PA: Cmg, Inc.
    301 Yard Dr
    Verona WI 53593
    608 826-0356

(G-6627)
COBAR INDUSTRIES INC
8302 Christiana Ln (46256-3414)
PHONE..................................317 691-7124
EMP: 3
SQ FT: 2,000
SALES (est): 128.3K **Privately Held**
SIC: 3999 Mfg Misc Products

(G-6628)
COBO INDUSTRIES
6831 Ridge Vale Pl Apt 2b (46237-7826)
PHONE..................................812 341-4318
Colin Bouillon, *Principal*
EMP: 2
SALES (est): 67K **Privately Held**
SIC: 3999 Manufacturing industries

(G-6629)
CODEWELD INC
905 E Edgewood Ave (46227-2037)
P.O. Box 17913 (46217-0913)
PHONE..................................317 784-4140
Larry Groce, *President*
EMP: 4
SALES (est): 360K **Privately Held**
SIC: 3443 Heat exchangers, condensers & components

(G-6630)
COLA VOCE MUSIC INC
4600 Sunset Ave (46208-3443)
PHONE..................................317 466-0624
Fred Hatfield, *Owner*
EMP: 2 EST: 2008
SALES (est): 144.9K **Privately Held**
SIC: 2741 Music book & sheet music publishing

(G-6631)
COLLEGE NETWORK INC (PA)
Also Called: Itestout.com
3815 River Crossing Pkwy # 260 (46240-7758)
P.O. Box 80016 (46280-0016)
PHONE..................................800 395-3276
Fax: 317 876-3276
Gary L Eyler, *President*
David Knight, *COO*
William Fitton, *CFO*
Ryan Sallee, *CIO*
EMP: 5
SQ FT: 25,000
SALES (est): 25.9MM **Privately Held**
WEB: www.college-net.com
SIC: 2741 Guides: publishing only, not printed on site

(G-6632)
COLLIER PUBG & CONSULTING
5351 E Thompson Rd # 227 (46237-4094)
PHONE..................................317 513-8176
Latonya Collier, *President*
EMP: 25
SALES: 49.5MM **Privately Held**
SIC: 2732 Book printing

(G-6633)
COLORCON INC
3702 E 21st St (46218-4487)
PHONE..................................317 545-6211
Fax: 317 545-6218
Martin Megregian, *Plant Engr*
Steven Bennett, *Branch Mgr*
Tara Blahnik, *Director*
Ben Pitt, *Director*
Joe Reynolds, *Maintence Staff*
EMP: 36
SALES (corp-wide): 3B **Privately Held**
SIC: 2834 2046 Pharmaceutical preparations; wet corn milling
HQ: Colorcon, Inc.
420 Moyer Blvd
West Point PA 19486
215 699-7733

(G-6634)
COLORCON INC ✪
6585 E 30th St (46219-1101)
PHONE..................................317 545-6211
EMP: 4 EST: 2017
SALES (est): 186.3K **Privately Held**
SIC: 2834 Pharmaceutical preparations

(G-6635)
COLORCON INC
6585 E 30th St (46219-1101)
PHONE..................................317 545-6211
EMP: 3
SALES (corp-wide): 3B **Privately Held**
SIC: 2834 Pharmaceutical preparations
HQ: Colorcon, Inc.
420 Moyer Blvd
West Point PA 19486
215 699-7733

(G-6636)
COMCAST SPOTLIGHT
8415 Allison Pointe Blvd # 500
(46250-4204)
PHONE..................................317 502-5098
Kevin Van Housen, *Sales Mgr*
Lisa A Byrne, *Accounts Mgr*
Reanna Bechdolt, *Accounts Exec*
Amber Guthrie, *Marketing Staff*
Lynette Irwin, *Manager*
EMP: 6 EST: 2014
SALES (est): 312.3K **Privately Held**
SIC: 3648 Spotlights

(G-6637)
COMMERCIAL FINISHING CORP
7199 English Ave (46219-7406)
PHONE..................................317 267-0377
Fax: 317 546-1453
Timothy B Hughes, *President*
EMP: 25 EST: 1971
SQ FT: 13,000
SALES (est): 3.3MM **Privately Held**
SIC: 3479 3471 Coating of metals & formed products; enameling, including porcelain, of metal products; plating & polishing

(G-6638)
COMMERCIAL LAUNDRY EQUIPMENT
5560 W Ralston Rd (46221-9675)
P.O. Box 37, Camby (46113-0037)
PHONE..................................317 856-1234
Fax: 317 856-0432
Bill Thompson, *President*
EMP: 4 EST: 1987
SQ FT: 2,500
SALES: 350K **Privately Held**
WEB: www.commercial-laundry.com
SIC: 3582 Dryers, laundry: commercial, including coin-operated

(G-6639)
COMMUNITY PAPERS INC
Also Called: West Side Community News
608 S Vine St (46241-0815)
PHONE..................................317 241-7363
Fax: 317 240-6397
Jackie Deppe, *President*
EMP: 4
SALES (est): 305.5K **Privately Held**
SIC: 2711 2791 Newspapers: publishing only, not printed on site; typesetting

(G-6640)
COMPANION DIAGNOSTICS INC
8206 Rockville Rd # 282 (46214-3113)
PHONE..................................860 227-9028
Richard Selinfreund, *President*
EMP: 6 EST: 2010
SALES (est): 632K **Privately Held**
SIC: 2835 In vitro & in vivo diagnostic substances

(G-6641)
COMPASSIONATE PROCEDURES LLC
8140 Morningside Dr (46240-2531)
PHONE..................................317 259-4656
Eric Yancy,
EMP: 7 EST: 2010
SALES (est): 466.4K **Privately Held**
SIC: 3841 Surgical & medical instruments

(G-6642)
COMPONENT MACHINE INC
1631 Gent Ave (46202-2185)
PHONE..................................317 635-8929
Fax: 317 756-7807
Thomas Crowe Jr, *President*
Donna Crowe, *Corp Secy*
EMP: 7
SQ FT: 14,400
SALES: 410K **Privately Held**
WEB: www.componentmachine.com
SIC: 3599 5531 3714 Machine shop, jobbing & repair; automotive parts; motor vehicle parts & accessories

(G-6643)
COMPOSITECH INC
Also Called: Zipp Speed Weaponry
5315 Walt Pl (46254-5797)
PHONE..................................800 231-6755
Fax: 317 243-3879
Andrew Ording, *President*
Todd Winget, *Prdtn Mgr*
Chris Dunlap, *Engineer*
Ben Waite, *Design Engr*
Nathan Schickel, *Manager*
▲ EMP: 45
SQ FT: 17,400
SALES (est): 6.3MM
SALES (corp-wide): 554.2MM **Privately Held**
SIC: 3949 3751 3714 Sporting & athletic goods; motorcycles, bicycles & parts; motor vehicle parts & accessories
PA: Sram, Llc
1000 W Fulton Market Fl 4
Chicago IL 60607
312 664-8800

(G-6644)
CONAGRA BRANDS INC
4300 W 62nd St (46268-2520)
PHONE..................................317 329-3700
EMP: 154
SALES (corp-wide): 7.9B **Publicly Held**
SIC: 2099 Food preparations
PA: Conagra Brands, Inc.
222 Merchandise Mart Plz
Chicago IL 60654
312 549-5000

(G-6645)
CONAGRA BRANDS INC
7579 Georgetown Rd (46268-4132)
PHONE..................................402 240-5000
EMP: 400
SALES (corp-wide): 7.9B **Publicly Held**
SIC: 2099 2038 2013 Food preparations; dessert mixes & fillings; seasonings & spices; ready-to-eat meals, salads & sandwiches; frozen specialties; dinners, frozen & packaged; lunches, frozen & packaged; sausages & other prepared meats
PA: Conagra Brands, Inc.
222 Merchandise Mart Plz
Chicago IL 60654
312 549-5000

(G-6646)
CONAGRA BRANDS INC
4300 W 62nd St (46268-2520)
PHONE..................................317 329-3700
Michael Pfeiffer, *Branch Mgr*
EMP: 420

SALES (corp-wide): 7.9B **Publicly Held**
WEB: www.conagra.com
SIC: 2021 Creamery butter
PA: Conagra Brands, Inc.
222 Merchandise Mart Plz
Chicago IL 60654
312 549-5000

(G-6647)
CONAGRA DAIRY FOODS COMPANY
4300 W 62nd St (46268-2520)
PHONE..................................317 329-3700
Michael Pfeiffer, *Branch Mgr*
EMP: 420
SQ FT: 30,000
SALES (corp-wide): 7.9B **Publicly Held**
SIC: 2026 Whipped topping, except frozen or dry mix
HQ: Conagra Dairy Foods Company Inc
222 Merchandise Mart Plz # 1300
Chicago IL 60654
630 848-0975

(G-6648)
CONCEPT PRINTS INC
6707 Guion Rd (46268-4810)
PHONE..................................317 290-1222
Fax: 317 290-1954
Thomas Hackett, *President*
▲ EMP: 16
SQ FT: 15,000
SALES (est): 1.6MM **Privately Held**
WEB: www.conceptprints.com
SIC: 2395 7389 2261 Embroidery & art needlework; design services; screen printing of cotton broadwoven fabrics

(G-6649)
CONFECTIONERY PRODUCTS MFG INC
Also Called: Choco-Pan
1725 S Franklin Rd Ste A (46239-2170)
PHONE..................................317 269-7363
Joe Shonk, *President*
EMP: 4 EST: 2010
SQ FT: 4,000
SALES: 600K **Privately Held**
SIC: 2051 Bread, cake & related products

(G-6650)
CONMOTO ENTERPRISES INC
Also Called: Advanced Inspection Solutions
6226 Graham Rd (46220-4940)
PHONE..................................219 787-1622
John D Sullivan, *President*
EMP: 2
SALES: 500K **Privately Held**
SIC: 3827 Optical instruments & lenses

(G-6651)
CONNECTA CORPORATION
3363 Boulevard Pl (46208-4611)
P.O. Box 88241 (46208-0241)
PHONE..................................317 923-9282
Fax: 317 923-1560
Alan R Pyle, *President*
▲ EMP: 12
SQ FT: 7,300
SALES (est): 2.3MM **Privately Held**
WEB: www.connecta.com
SIC: 3643 Electric connectors

(G-6652)
CONOVER CUSTOM FABRICATION INC
2625 S Pennsylvania St (46225-2320)
PHONE..................................317 784-1904
Fax: 317 788-7685
John Conover, *President*
Claire Conover, *Corp Secy*
EMP: 15
SALES (est): 3.1MM **Privately Held**
WEB: www.conofab.com
SIC: 1799 3444 Food service equipment installation; sheet metalwork

(G-6653)
CONTAINER LIFE CYCLE MGT LLC
Also Called: Indianapolis Drum Service
3619 Terrace Ave (46203-2250)
PHONE..................................317 357-9853
Fax: 317 357-8796
Dennis Long, *General Mgr*

EMP: 75
SALES (est): 10.4MM **Privately Held**
SIC: 3412 Metal barrels, drums & pails

(G-6654)
CONTAINMENT TECH GROUP INC (PA)
5460 Victory Dr Ste 300 (46203-5970)
PHONE..................................317 862-5945
Michelle Moore, *President*
Janet Rahe, *Vice Pres*
Greg Herron, *Sales Dir*
Angie Harris, *Manager*
Doug Weaver, *Manager*
EMP: 5 EST: 1994
SQ FT: 10,000
SALES (est): 1.3MM **Privately Held**
WEB: www.mic4.com
SIC: 3829 Ion chambers

(G-6655)
CONTECH ENGNERED SOLUTIONS LLC
7164 Graham Rd Ste 120 (46250-2675)
PHONE..................................317 842-7766
Fax: 317 845-0753
Robert Trees, *Manager*
EMP: 10 **Privately Held**
SIC: 3443 Fabricated plate work (boiler shop)
HQ: Contech Engineered Solutions Llc
9025 Centre Pointe Dr # 400
West Chester OH 45069
513 645-7000

(G-6656)
CONTINENTAL CARBONIC PDTS INC
4140 Cashard Ave (46203-6019)
P.O. Box 421219 (46242-1219)
PHONE..................................317 784-3311
Fax: 317 784-3668
Bill Risley, *Branch Mgr*
EMP: 8
SALES (corp-wide): 34.9B **Privately Held**
WEB: www.ccpidryice.com
SIC: 3585 Refrigeration & heating equipment; refrigeration equipment, complete; condensers, refrigeration
HQ: Continental Carbonic Products, Inc.
3985 E Harrison Ave
Decatur IL 62526
217 428-2068

(G-6657)
CONTINNTAL BROADCAST GROUP LLC
Also Called: Wedj-FM
1800 N Meridian St # 605 (46202-1433)
PHONE..................................317 924-1071
Fax: 317 924-7766
Marvin Kosossky, *Owner*
Amiee McGrath, *Business Mgr*
Jeffrey Warshaw, *Treasurer*
Ana Saldana, *Accounts Exec*
Rafael Ayala, *Marketing Staff*
EMP: 21
SALES: 1.8MM **Privately Held**
SIC: 4832 3651 Radio broadcasting stations; FM & AM radio tuners

(G-6658)
CONTINUUM GAMES INCORPORATED
221 S Franklin Rd (46219-7734)
PHONE..................................877 405-2662
Greg Hughes, *President*
▲ EMP: 4
SALES (est): 1MM **Privately Held**
SIC: 5092 3944 Board games; bingo boards (games); board games, children's & adults'

(G-6659)
CONTOUR HARDENING INC
Also Called: Real Power
8227 Northwest Blvd # 130 (46278-1387)
PHONE..................................317 876-1530
Vincent L Laplante, *Sales Staff*
Donald Smith, *Manager*
EMP: 4
SALES (corp-wide): 13MM **Privately Held**
SIC: 3621 Motors & generators

PA: Contour Hardening, Inc.
8401 Northwest Blvd
Indianapolis IN 46278
888 867-2184

(G-6660)
CONTOUR HARDENING INC (PA)
8401 Northwest Blvd (46278-1382)
PHONE...................................888 867-2184
Fax: 317 879-2484
John Storm, *President*
John M Storm, *President*
Brian Steinkamp, *Vice Pres*
Jim Cochrane, *Purchasing*
Chrissy Sottong, *Purchasing*
▲ EMP: 50
SQ FT: 59,000
SALES (est): 13MM **Privately Held**
WEB: www.contourhardening.com
SIC: 3567 8731 5084 3621 Heating units
& devices, industrial: electric; commercial
physical research; metalworking machin-
ery; motors & generators

(G-6661)
COOKS FABRICATION INC
6011 E Hanna Ave Ste H (46203-6120)
PHONE...................................317 782-1722
Danae Cook, *President*
EMP: 2
SALES (est): 328.2K **Privately Held**
SIC: 3842 3843 Orthopedic appliances;
dental equipment & supplies

(G-6662)
COOL PLANET LLC
Also Called: Cool Planet Awning Co
340 S Mitthoeffer Rd (46229-3065)
PHONE...................................317 927-9000
Fax: 317 927-9003
Matthew Garvey, *President*
EMP: 7 EST: 1998
SALES (est): 907.5K **Privately Held**
WEB: www.coolplanetawnings.com
SIC: 2394 Awnings, fabric: made from pur-
chased materials

(G-6663)
COOL-SHIRTS INC
7654 Geist Estates Cir (46236-8661)
PHONE...................................317 826-1674
John Lewis, *Principal*
EMP: 2
SALES (est): 90K **Privately Held**
SIC: 3679 Electronic components

(G-6664)
COPIA VINEYARDS AND WINERY LLC
435 Virginia Ave Unit 707 (46203-1968)
PHONE...................................805 835-6094
Varinder Sahi, *President*
EMP: 2
SALES (est): 69.4K **Privately Held**
SIC: 2084 Wines

(G-6665)
COPYFIRE TYPESETTING INC
1513 Touchstone Dr (46239-8864)
PHONE...................................317 894-0408
EMP: 2
SALES (est): 115.6K **Privately Held**
SIC: 2791 Typesetting

(G-6666)
CORBETT PHRMCEUTICALS DVCS LLC
7101 Red Lake Ct (46217-7011)
PHONE...................................765 513-0674
Aaron Rivers,
EMP: 30
SQ FT: 10,000
SALES: 1.6MM **Privately Held**
SIC: 3841 8734 Surgical & medical instru-
ments; product testing laboratories

(G-6667)
CORK MEDICAL LLC
8000 Castleway Dr (46250-1943)
PHONE...................................317 361-4651
Patrick McGinley, *President*
EMP: 5
SQ FT: 20,000

SALES (est): 368.7K
SALES (corp-wide): 903.7K **Privately Held**
SIC: 3841 2394 Inhalation therapy equip-
ment; air cushions & mattresses, canvas
PA: Cork Medical, Llc
8000 Castleway Dr
Indianapolis IN 46250
317 849-2675

(G-6668)
CORNELIUS PRINTED PRODUCTS INC
Also Called: Hoosier Data Forms
1002 E 25th St (46205-4400)
PHONE...................................317 923-1340
Fax: 317 923-1341
David J Cornelius, *President*
Debbie Madison, *CIO*
Kevin Terek, *Administration*
EMP: 24 EST: 1989
SQ FT: 36,000
SALES (est): 4MM
SALES (corp-wide): 370.1MM **Publicly Held**
SIC: 2761 Manifold business forms
PA: Ennis, Inc.
2441 Presidential Pkwy
Midlothian TX 76065
972 775-9801

(G-6669)
CORNERSTONE COMMUNICATIONS LLC
8910 Purdue Rd Ste 750 (46268-6102)
PHONE...................................317 802-0107
Kevin Calhoun, *Mng Member*
Christa Key, *Director*
Allen Handt,
EMP: 15
SQ FT: 1,900
SALES (est): 2MM **Privately Held**
WEB: www.cstoneindy.com
SIC: 7372 Prepackaged software

(G-6670)
CORNERSTONE EXPEDITING LLC
7730 Gordon Way (46237-9663)
PHONE...................................317 893-2891
Ruben Rojas, *Principal*
EMP: 4
SALES (est): 435.9K **Privately Held**
SIC: 2655 Fiber shipping & mailing con-
tainers

(G-6671)
CORPORATE SYSTEMS ENGRG LLC
1215 Brookville Way (46239-1049)
PHONE...................................317 322-7984
Fax: 317 375-3610
Steve Taylor, *President*
John D Lutz, *CFO*
Angelo Kostarides, *Director*
EMP: 65
SQ FT: 10,000
SALES (est): 8.8MM **Privately Held**
WEB: www.corporatesystems.com
SIC: 7379 3663 Computer related consult-
ing services; radio & TV communications
equipment; transmitter-receivers, radio

(G-6672)
COSMOPROF
9455 E Washington St (46229-3085)
PHONE...................................317 897-0124
EMP: 2
SALES (est): 60K **Privately Held**
SIC: 5087 3999 Electrolysis equipment &
supplies; cigar & cigarette holders

(G-6673)
COSWORTH LLC (HQ)
5355 W 86th St (46268-1501)
PHONE...................................844 278-6941
Hal Reisiger, *CEO*
Pierre Wildman, *Mng Member*
▲ EMP: 88 EST: 1977
SQ FT: 60,000

SALES (est): 8.6MM
SALES (corp-wide): 71.1MM **Privately Held**
WEB: www.cosworth.com
SIC: 3519 Parts & accessories, internal
combustion engines
PA: Cosworth Group Holdings Limited
The Octagon
Northampton NORTHANTS NN5 5
160 459-8300

(G-6674)
COSWORTH ELECTRONICS LLC
5355 W 86th St (46268-1501)
PHONE...................................317 808-3800
Ryan Tindall, *Mng Member*
EMP: 2
SQ FT: 3,000
SALES (est): 907.5K
SALES (corp-wide): 71.1MM **Privately Held**
WEB: www.piresearch.com
SIC: 3823 Data loggers, industrial process
type
PA: Cosworth Group Holdings Limited
The Octagon
Northampton NORTHANTS NN5 5
160 459-8300

(G-6675)
COUNTRY CLUB COMPUTER
8247 Indy Ct (46214-2300)
PHONE...................................317 271-4000
Mark Genung, *Owner*
EMP: 5
SALES (est): 120.6K **Privately Held**
SIC: 7997 5734 5045 3571 Country club,
membership; computer & software stores;
computers, peripherals & software; elec-
tronic computers

(G-6676)
COUNTRYMARK COOP HOLDG CORP (PA)
225 S East St Ste 144 (46202-4059)
PHONE...................................800 808-3170
Charles Smith, *President*
John Deaton, *Vice Pres*
Bryant Garibay, *Safety Dir*
Mike Willman, *Opers Mgr*
Jamie McKee, *Site Mgr*
EMP: 20
SQ FT: 3,000
SALES (est): 216.4MM **Privately Held**
WEB: www.countrymark.com
SIC: 5172 2911 1382 1311 Petroleum
brokers; petroleum refining; aerial geo-
physical exploration oil & gas; crude pe-
troleum & natural gas production;
investment holding companies, except
banks

(G-6677)
COUNTRYMARK REF LOGISTICS LLC
225 S East St Ste 144 (46202-4059)
PHONE...................................800 808-3170
Charles E Smith,
Nina Zike, *Admin Sec*
EMP: 2
SALES (est): 74.4K **Privately Held**
SIC: 2869 Fuels

(G-6678)
COUNTY MATERIALS CORP
2050 S Harding St (46221-1948)
P.O. Box 8, Maxwell (46154-0008)
PHONE...................................317 262-4920
EMP: 5
SALES (est): 565.8K **Privately Held**
SIC: 3272 Concrete products

(G-6679)
COURTNEY SIGNS & GRAPHICS INC
Also Called: Courtney Signs & Lighting
7535 E 71st St (46256-1909)
PHONE...................................317 841-3297
Fax: 317 532-4899
Ron Courtney, *Owner*
Ethel Courtney, *Vice Pres*
EMP: 2 EST: 1999
SALES (est): 230.2K **Privately Held**
WEB: www.courtneysigns.com
SIC: 3993 Signs & advertising specialties

(G-6680)
COVERS OF INDIANA INC
2906 Kentucky Ave (46221-2102)
PHONE...................................317 244-0291
Boyd Warren Jr, *President*
Edith Warren, *Treasurer*
EMP: 6
SQ FT: 10,000
SALES: 55K **Privately Held**
SIC: 2211 7641 Broadwoven fabric mills,
cotton; canvas; sail cloth; reupholstery

(G-6681)
COWAN SYSTEMS LLC
6238 W Minnesota St (46241-4215)
PHONE...................................317 241-4158
Marvin Herb, *Principal*
EMP: 2
SALES (est): 170K **Privately Held**
SIC: 3713 Beverage truck bodies

(G-6682)
COY & ASSOCIATES
2305 E Banta Rd (46227-4908)
PHONE...................................317 787-5089
Chester Coy, *Owner*
EMP: 2
SALES (est): 140K **Privately Held**
SIC: 5943 2791 5734 Office forms & sup-
plies; typesetting; computer & software
stores

(G-6683)
CRA-WAL INC
Also Called: Crawal Division
4001 S High School Rd (46241-6448)
PHONE...................................317 856-3701
Doug Bosnik, *President*
Mark Husted, *Vice Pres*
EMP: 80
SQ FT: 100,000
SALES (est): 16.9MM
SALES (corp-wide): 194.1MM **Privately Held**
WEB: www.cra-wal.com
SIC: 2653 Boxes, corrugated: made from
purchased materials
PA: Buckeye Corrugated, Inc
822 Kumho Dr Ste 400
Fairlawn OH 44333
330 576-0590

(G-6684)
CRAFT METAL PRODUCTS INC
2751 N Emerson Ave (46218-3267)
PHONE...................................317 545-3252
Fax: 317 545-3288
Kenneth Knauss, *President*
Janet Knauss, *Admin Sec*
▼ EMP: 9
SQ FT: 17,000
SALES (est): 1.6MM **Privately Held**
WEB: www.craftmetal.com
SIC: 3646 5023 5033 5021 Commercial
indusl & institutional electric lighting fix-
tures; carpets; fiberglass building materi-
als; office & public building furniture

(G-6685)
CRAFTMARK BAKERY LLC
5202 Exploration Dr (46241-9003)
PHONE...................................317 548-3929
Ahmad Hamade, *CEO*
Bennie M Bray,
EMP: 10 EST: 2013
SALES (est): 4.8MM **Privately Held**
SIC: 2051 5461 Breads, rolls & buns; bak-
eries
PA: Cic Partners I Lp
3879 Maple Ave Ste 400
Dallas TX 75219

(G-6686)
CREATEC CORPORATION
6835 Guion Rd Ste A (46268-6811)
PHONE...................................317 566-0022
Fax: 317 259-7733
▲ EMP: 25
SALES (est): 41.6MM **Privately Held**
WEB: www.createccorp.com
SIC: 3086 2821 Packaging & shipping ma-
terials, foamed plastic; plastics materials
& resins

(G-6687)
CREATIVE IMPRESSIONS INC
6908 Carlsen Ave (46214-3243)
PHONE....................................317 244-9842
John E Richards, *President*
Steve Richards, *President*
Norda Richards, *Admin Sec*
EMP: 14 **EST:** 1976
SQ FT: 2,000
SALES: 1MM **Privately Held**
SIC: 7812 2752 7819 Audio-visual program production; commercial printing, lithographic; commercial printing, offset; services allied to motion pictures

(G-6688)
CREATIVE INDUSTRIES INC
1024 Western Dr (46241-1437)
PHONE....................................317 248-1102
Fax: 317 247-4953
Larry Clark, *Ch of Bd*
Mark Clark, *President*
Brett Cooper, *Prdtn Mgr*
Ed Bopp, *Traffic Mgr*
Mike Clark, *Treasurer*
EMP: 12 **EST:** 1969
SQ FT: 19,400
SALES: 2MM **Privately Held**
WEB: www.creativeind.com
SIC: 2542 3231 Partitions & fixtures, except wood; strengthened or reinforced glass

(G-6689)
CREATIVE LOGIC EQUIPMENT CORP
5482 Ashurst St (46220-4829)
PHONE....................................317 271-1100
Carl Elvers, *Administration*
EMP: 2
SALES (est): 85.9K **Privately Held**
SIC: 3571 Electronic computers

(G-6690)
CREEK CHASSIS INC
Also Called: Creek Motor Sports
312 Gasoline Aly (46222-3984)
PHONE....................................317 247-4480
Greg Creek, *Owner*
Tim Jennings, *General Mgr*
EMP: 2
SALES (est): 150K **Privately Held**
SIC: 3429 Motor vehicle hardware

(G-6691)
CRESCENT OIL COMPANY INC
1751 W Raymond St (46221-2025)
P.O. Box 1266 (46206-1266)
PHONE....................................317 634-1415
Fax: 317 232-4146
EMP: 3 **EST:** 1893
SQ FT: 7,200
SALES (est): 570.7K **Privately Held**
SIC: 2992 Mfg Lubricating Oils/Greases

(G-6692)
CRICHLOW INDUSTRIES INC
Also Called: Indianapolis Badge Name Plate
6848 Hawthorn Park Dr (46220-3909)
PHONE....................................317 925-5178
Fax: 317 921-1156
David C Crichlow, *President*
EMP: 4
SQ FT: 18,000
SALES (est): 493K **Privately Held**
WEB: www.indybadge.com
SIC: 3999 2796 3993 3479 Badges, metal: policemen, firemen, etc.; embossing plates for printing; plates & cylinders for rotogravure printing; lithographic plates, positives or negatives; signs, not made in custom sign painting shops; name plates: engraved, etched, etc.; metal stampings; packaging paper & plastics film, coated & laminated

(G-6693)
CRITERION PRESS INC
Also Called: The Criterion Newspaper
1400 N Meridian St (46202-2305)
P.O. Box 1410 (46206-1410)
PHONE....................................317 236-1570
Fax: 317 236-1593
Daniel M Buechlein, *President*
EMP: 16
SQ FT: 5,300

SALES: 1.2MM **Privately Held**
SIC: 2711 2759 2741 Newspapers: publishing only, not printed on site; commercial printing; directories: publishing only, not printed on site

(G-6694)
CROSS PRINTWEAR INC
3466 N Raceway Rd (46234-9201)
PHONE....................................317 293-1776
Fax: 317 387-1776
Kenneth Mierke, *President*
Paul Summers, *Admin Sec*
EMP: 14
SQ FT: 3,500
SALES (est): 1.1MM **Privately Held**
SIC: 2396 Screen printing on fabric articles

(G-6695)
CROSSPOINT POWER AND RFRGN LLC (PA)
4301 W Morris St (46241-2503)
PHONE....................................317 240-1967
Lee Cox, *Parts Mgr*
Chris Harper, *Manager*
EMP: 34 **EST:** 2015
SALES (est): 5.8MM **Privately Held**
SIC: 3585 Refrigeration & heating equipment

(G-6696)
CROSSRADS CNTRTOPS CBNETRY LLC
604 S Audubon Rd (46219-8112)
PHONE....................................317 908-9254
John Dicken, *Principal*
EMP: 2
SALES (est): 89.6K **Privately Held**
SIC: 2434 Wood kitchen cabinets

(G-6697)
CROSSRADS RHBILITATION CTR INC
Crossroads Industrial Services
8302 E 33rd St (46226-6503)
PHONE....................................317 897-7320
Fax: 317 897-9763
Curtiss Quirin, *COO*
Jack Costello, *Marketing Staff*
Bill Love, *Marketing Staff*
Jeff Gore, *Executive*
EMP: 110
SQ FT: 18,000
SALES (est): 7.8MM
SALES (corp-wide): 12.7MM **Privately Held**
WEB: www.x-roads.org
SIC: 7389 3599 7331 3469 Finishing services; packaging & labeling services; mailing & messenger services; machine shop, jobbing & repair; direct mail advertising services; metal stampings; fabricated structural metal; bookbinding & related work
PA: Crossroads Rehabilitation Center, Inc.
4740 Kingsway Dr
Indianapolis IN 46205
317 466-1000

(G-6698)
CROSSWIND PHARMACEUTICALS LLC
9402 Uptown Dr Ste 1200 (46256-1042)
PHONE....................................317 436-8522
Phillip Berry,
EMP: 3
SALES (est): 225.5K **Privately Held**
SIC: 2834 Pharmaceutical preparations

(G-6699)
CROWN BIOSCIENCE INDIANA INC
7918 Zionsville Rd (46268-1649)
PHONE....................................317 872-6001
Fax: 317 872-6002
Jean-Pierre Wery, *CEO*
Yixin Wang, *Director*
EMP: 7
SALES (est): 1.2MM **Privately Held**
WEB: www.preclinomics.com
SIC: 8733 2834 8731 Medical research; solutions, pharmaceutical; commercial physical research

PA: Crown Bioscience, Inc.
11011 Torreyana Rd # 200
San Diego CA 92121

(G-6700)
CROWN TECHNOLOGY INC
7513 E 96th St (46256-1009)
P.O. Box 50426 (46250-0426)
PHONE....................................317 845-0045
Fax: 317 845-9086
Joseph C Peterson, *President*
Shaun Slinkard, *General Mgr*
Eric Hodapp, *QC Mgr*
Dave Jaap, *Sales Mgr*
Jeff Buckner, *Manager*
▲ **EMP:** 35
SQ FT: 65,000
SALES (est): 10.5MM **Privately Held**
WEB: www.crowntech.com
SIC: 2899 2819 6794 Foam charge mixtures; iron (ferric/ferrous) compounds or salts; patent buying, licensing, leasing

(G-6701)
CRUST N MORE INC
6815 E 34th St (46226-6125)
PHONE....................................317 890-7878
Mick R Holt, *President*
EMP: 14
SQ FT: 19,000
SALES (est): 2MM **Privately Held**
SIC: 2041 Pizza mixes

(G-6702)
CRYOVAC INC
Also Called: Cryovac Division
7950 Allison Ave (46268-1612)
PHONE....................................317 876-4100
Dennis Nuhfer, *Principal*
EMP: 134
SALES (corp-wide): 4.4B **Publicly Held**
WEB: www.cryovac.com
SIC: 3086 Packaging & shipping materials, foamed plastic
HQ: Cryovac, Inc.
2415 Cascade Pointe Blvd
Charlotte NC 28208
980 430-7000

(G-6703)
CSL PLASMA INC
2750 E 46th St (46205-2311)
PHONE....................................317 688-5852
EMP: 2
SALES (est): 74.4K
SALES (corp-wide): 6.9B **Privately Held**
SIC: 2836 Plasmas
HQ: Csl Plasma Inc.
900 Broken Sound Pkwy Nw # 4
Boca Raton FL 33487
561 981-3700

(G-6704)
CSL PLASMA INC
5550 E Washington St (46219-6426)
PHONE....................................317 352-9157
Michael Deen, *Manager*
EMP: 70
SALES (corp-wide): 6.9B **Privately Held**
WEB: www.zlbplasma.com
SIC: 2836 Blood derivatives; plasmas
HQ: Csl Plasma Inc.
900 Broken Sound Pkwy Nw # 4
Boca Raton FL 33487
561 981-3700

(G-6705)
CUMMINS - ALLISON CORP
Also Called: Cummins-Allison
5696 W 74th St (46278-1752)
PHONE....................................317 872-6244
Fax: 317 872-6245
Mark Winter, *Sales/Mktg Mgr*
EMP: 6
SALES (corp-wide): 377.9MM **Privately Held**
WEB: www.gsb.com
SIC: 5044 7629 3519 Office equipment; business machine repair, electric; internal combustion engines
PA: Cummins - Allison Corp.
852 Feehanville Dr
Mount Prospect IL 60056
847 759-6403

(G-6706)
CUMMINS CROSSPOINT LLC (HQ)
2601 Fortune Cir E 300c (46241-5567)
PHONE....................................317 243-7979
R David Smitson, *President*
Chris Harlow, *Vice Pres*
Mike Patterson, *Vice Pres*
John R Smitson, *Vice Pres*
April Beaman, *Controller*
EMP: 28 **EST:** 1981
SQ FT: 8,000
SALES (est): 148.8MM
SALES (corp-wide): 20.4B **Publicly Held**
SIC: 5084 7538 5063 3519 Engines & parts, diesel; diesel engine repair: automotive; generators; internal combustion engines
PA: Cummins Inc.
500 Jackson St
Columbus IN 47201
812 377-5000

(G-6707)
CUMMINS CROSSPOINT LLC
Also Called: Crosspoint Solutions
3621 W Morris St (46241-2703)
PHONE....................................317 244-7251
EMP: 30
SALES (corp-wide): 20.4B **Publicly Held**
SIC: 5084 3519 Engines & parts, diesel; internal combustion engines
HQ: Cummins Crosspoint Llc
2601 Fortune Cir E 300c
Indianapolis IN 46241
317 243-7979

(G-6708)
CUMMINS CROSSPOINT LLC
Also Called: OEM Solution Center
4557 W Bradbury Ave Ste 3 (46241-5236)
PHONE....................................317 484-2146
John Canellas, *Branch Mgr*
EMP: 3
SALES (corp-wide): 20.4B **Publicly Held**
SIC: 7538 3519 Engine repair; internal combustion engines
HQ: Cummins Crosspoint Llc
2601 Fortune Cir E 300c
Indianapolis IN 46241
317 243-7979

(G-6709)
CUMMINS INC
3621 W Morris St (46241-2703)
PHONE....................................317 244-7251
Jay Goad, *Vice Pres*
Mike Westbrooks, *Human Res Mgr*
Betty Gilbert, *Branch Mgr*
Jim Abraham, *Manager*
Colleen Koeberlin, *Manager*
EMP: 2
SALES (corp-wide): 20.4B **Publicly Held**
SIC: 3519 3714 3694 3621 Internal combustion engines; motor vehicle parts & accessories; engine electrical equipment; generator sets: gasoline, diesel or dual-fuel
PA: Cummins Inc.
500 Jackson St
Columbus IN 47201
812 377-5000

(G-6710)
CUMMINS INC
Also Called: Cummins Sales and Service
301 E Market St (46204-2847)
PHONE....................................317 610-2493
Angela Harker, *Branch Mgr*
EMP: 3
SALES (corp-wide): 20.4B **Publicly Held**
SIC: 3519 3714 3694 3621 Internal combustion engines; engines, diesel & semi-diesel or dual-fuel; diesel engine rebuilding; motor vehicle parts & accessories; motor vehicle engines & parts; crankshaft assemblies, motor vehicle; filters: oil, fuel & air, motor vehicle; engine electrical equipment; generator sets: gasoline, diesel or dual-fuel
PA: Cummins Inc.
500 Jackson St
Columbus IN 47201
812 377-5000

(G-6711)
CUNNINGHAM QUALITY PAINTING
2060 Yandes St　(46202-1939)
PHONE..................................317 925-8852
Donna Cunningham, *President*
John Cunningham, *Vice Pres*
EMP: 6
SQ FT: 20,000
SALES (est): 475.9K　**Privately Held**
SIC: 3479　Painting of metal products

(G-6712)
CUSTOM DRAPERY SERVICE INC
1540 E 86th St　(46240-1986)
PHONE..................................317 587-1518
Fax: 317 894-8637
Janice Walter, *President*
Judith W Benner, *Corp Secy*
EMP: 7
SQ FT: 1,500
SALES (est): 380K　**Privately Held**
SIC: 2391 5714　Draperies, plastic & textile: from purchased materials; draperies

(G-6713)
CUSTOM GAGE & TOOL CO INC
7305 E 30th St　(46219-1191)
PHONE..................................317 547-8257
Devon Allison, *President*
EMP: 4
SQ FT: 4,000
SALES: 380K　**Privately Held**
WEB: www.daveallison.com
SIC: 3545 3544 7692　Machine tool attachments & accessories; special dies & tools; jigs & fixtures; welding repair

(G-6714)
CUSTOM INTERIOR DYNAMICS LLC
3314 Prospect St　(46203-2234)
PHONE..................................317 632-0477
Fax: 317 632-0478
Richard Delacruz,
EMP: 10
SQ FT: 40,000
SALES (est): 1.2MM　**Privately Held**
WEB: www.custominteriordynamics.com
SIC: 2431 3446 7389　Interior & ornamental woodwork & trim; woodwork, interior & ornamental; architectural metalwork; interior decorating

(G-6715)
CUSTOM KEEPSAKES MACHINE EMB
915 Tanninger Dr　(46239-9474)
PHONE..................................317 894-5506
Kathleen Harrison, *Principal*
EMP: 2 EST: 2015
SALES (est): 96.9K　**Privately Held**
SIC: 3599　Industrial machinery

(G-6716)
CUSTOM OUTFITTED PROTECTION
9309 Memorial Park Dr 1b　(46216-2262)
PHONE..................................317 373-2092
Jeffrey Weaver, *Principal*
EMP: 2
SALES (est): 108.1K　**Privately Held**
SIC: 3842　Ear plugs

(G-6717)
CUSTOM PACKAGING INC
7248 Haverhill Ct　(46250-2442)
PHONE..................................317 876-9559
Fax: 317 876-9785
Bert Wilhoite, *President*
EMP: 14
SQ FT: 44,800
SALES: 2.8MM　**Privately Held**
SIC: 2653 2759 2671　Boxes, corrugated: made from purchased materials; display items, corrugated: made from purchased materials; commercial printing; packaging paper & plastics film, coated & laminated

(G-6718)
CUTTING EDGE CRAFTSMEN LLC
1125 Brookside Ave C20　(46202-0041)
PHONE..................................317 757-6975
Michael A Fisher, *Mng Member*
Jeffrey Mack,
EMP: 4
SQ FT: 2,400
SALES: 100K　**Privately Held**
SIC: 3441　Fabricated structural metal

(G-6719)
CYBERIA LTD
Also Called: Club Cyberia
6800 E 30th St　(46219-1104)
PHONE..................................317 721-2582
Jason Voyles, *Ch of Bd*
David Norris, *President*
Franklin Robison, *Treasurer*
Mic Owens, *Mktg Dir*
Austin Owens, *Admin Sec*
EMP: 5
SALES (est): 66K　**Privately Held**
SIC: 8331 8322 3541 7371　Sheltered workshop; community center; home workshop machine tools, metalworking; custom computer programming services; noncommercial research organizations

(G-6720)
D & S MACHINE INC
10640 Deme Dr Ste R　(46236-4713)
PHONE..................................317 826-2900
Martin Patterson, *President*
Monet Patterson, *Vice Pres*
EMP: 7
SQ FT: 4,000
SALES (est): 670K　**Privately Held**
SIC: 3544　Special dies, tools, jigs & fixtures

(G-6721)
D D MCKAY AND ASSOCIATES
Also Called: Next Day Signs
4068 Pendleton Way　(46226-5224)
PHONE..................................317 546-7446
Fax: 317 546-7008
David McKay, *President*
EMP: 3
SQ FT: 1,600
SALES (est): 500K　**Privately Held**
WEB: www.nextdaysigns.com
SIC: 3993　Signs, not made in custom sign painting shops

(G-6722)
D M SALES & ENGINEERING INC
1325 Sunday Dr　(46217-9334)
PHONE..................................317 783-5493
Fax: 317 787-5642
David D Mickel, *President*
Richard Mickel, *President*
Rich Mickel, *Vice Pres*
Patricia A Mickel, *Admin Sec*
EMP: 24
SQ FT: 20,000
SALES: 1.2MM　**Privately Held**
WEB: www.dmsales-eng.com
SIC: 3089　Thermoformed finished plastic products

(G-6723)
DAECHANG SEAT CO LTD USA
8150 Woodland Dr　(46278-1347)
PHONE..................................317 755-3663
Wi-In Cho, *CEO*
EMP: 17 EST: 2016
SALES (est): 4.3MM　**Privately Held**
SIC: 3312　Sheet or strip, steel, hot-rolled

(G-6724)
DAN GOODE CABINET
3839 Englewood Dr　(46226-5105)
PHONE..................................317 541-9878
Dan Cabinet, *Principal*
EMP: 2
SALES (est): 151.8K　**Privately Held**
SIC: 2434　Wood kitchen cabinets

(G-6725)
DANCE SOPHISTICATES
1605 Prospect St　(46203-2024)
PHONE..................................317 634-7728
Denise L Dennis, *Owner*

Cindy De Moulin, *Vice Pres*
Kelly McGaha, *Office Mgr*
EMP: 20
SQ FT: 3,000
SALES (est): 1.6MM　**Privately Held**
WEB: www.dancesoph.com
SIC: 2389 2339 2326　Uniforms & vestments; band uniforms; women's & misses' outerwear; men's & boys' work clothing

(G-6726)
DAREDEVIL BREWING CO
1151 Main St　(46224-6976)
PHONE..................................317 512-2202
Jonathan Shane Pearson, *President*
EMP: 7
SALES (est): 100.4K　**Privately Held**
SIC: 2082　Malt beverages

(G-6727)
DARLING INGREDIENTS INC
700 W Southern Ave　(46225-2062)
P.O. Box 33639　(46203-0639)
PHONE..................................317 784-4486
Tony Croteau, *Manager*
Kristy Porento, *Manager*
EMP: 45
SALES (corp-wide): 3.6B　**Publicly Held**
WEB: www.darlingii.com
SIC: 2077　Animal & marine fats & oils
PA: Darling Ingredients Inc.
　251 Oconnor Ridge Blvd
　Irving TX 75038
　972 717-0300

(G-6728)
DAVIS INDUSTRIES INC
4090 Westover Dr　(46268-1843)
PHONE..................................317 871-0103
Thomas W Davis, *President*
EMP: 8
SALES (est): 855.7K　**Privately Held**
WEB: www.davisindustries.net
SIC: 3999　Manufacturing industries

(G-6729)
DBISP LLC
Also Called: Dbfederal
5847 W 74th St　(46278-1757)
PHONE..................................317 222-1671
Johnnie Winstead, *Accounts Mgr*
John M Miller,
EMP: 10
SQ FT: 2,585
SALES (est): 3.9MM　**Privately Held**
WEB: www.dbisp.net
SIC: 4813 5734 2521 5112　; modems, monitors, terminals & disk drives: computers; wood office furniture; office supplies; hardware; office equipment

(G-6730)
DC CONSTRUCTION SERVICES INC
9465 Counselors Row # 200　(46240-6423)
PHONE..................................317 577-0276
Dustin Calhoun, *President*
Christopher M Wirth, *CFO*
Aaron Grinstead, *Human Res Mgr*
Mike Todd, *Accounts Exec*
EMP: 50 EST: 2013
SALES (est): 8.1MM　**Privately Held**
SIC: 1542 2951　Commercial & office buildings, renovation & repair; asphalt paving mixtures & blocks

(G-6731)
DEEM & LOUREIRO INC
8111 Bayberry Ct　(46250-1629)
PHONE..................................770 652-9871
Edwina Loureiro, *Principal*
Karen Deem, *COO*
EMP: 2 EST: 1999
SALES (est): 138.9K　**Privately Held**
WEB: www.deemloureiro.com
SIC: 7336 7389 2541 8712　Commercial art & graphic design; art design services; graphic arts & related design; interior design services; cabinets, except refrigerated: show, display, etc.; wood; architectural engineering

(G-6732)
DEFLECTO LLC (DH)
7035 E 86th St　(46250-1547)
P.O. Box 50057　(46250-0057)
PHONE..................................317 849-9555
Fax: 317 841-4395
Paul Thompson, *CEO*
Thomas H Quinn, *President*
Jay Bray, *Vice Pres*
Keith Huffman, *Vice Pres*
Craig Scachitti, *Vice Pres*
▲ **EMP:** 300 EST: 1960
SALES: 177.8MM
SALES (corp-wide): 600.2MM　**Privately Held**
WEB: www.deflecto.com
SIC: 3089 2542　Plastic hardware & building products; ducting, plastic; office & store showcases & display fixtures
HQ: Jordan Specialty Plastics, Inc.
　1751 Lake Cook Rd Ste 550
　Deerfield IL 60015
　847 945-5591

(G-6733)
DELP PRINTING & MAILING INC
7750 Zionsville Rd # 200　(46268-2195)
PHONE..................................317 872-9744
Fax: 317 872-0415
Lorie Darland, *President*
EMP: 21
SQ FT: 7,200
SALES (est): 2.1MM　**Privately Held**
WEB: www.delpprintingandmailing.com
SIC: 7331 2752　Mailing service; commercial printing, lithographic

(G-6734)
DENVER STONE
Also Called: Denver Stone Machine Co
3148 S Holt Rd　(46221-2225)
PHONE..................................317 244-5889
Fax: 317 244-5889
Mark Stone, *Owner*
EMP: 40
SALES (est): 3.4MM　**Privately Held**
SIC: 3479 3599 7692　Coating of metals with plastic or resins; machine shop, jobbing & repair; welding repair

(G-6735)
DESIGN MEDIA CONNECTIONS LLC
9365 Counselors Row # 104　(46240-6418)
PHONE..................................317 819-2022
Keith Smith, *Architect*
Rick Fetz, *Mng Member*
Robert Boyd,
Kerrie Dunn,
Jim Jefferson,
EMP: 4
SQ FT: 2,000
SALES: 1.8MM　**Privately Held**
WEB: www.dm-online.com
SIC: 2759　Commercial printing

(G-6736)
DEUXFRERES LLC
1351 S Girls School Rd　(46231-1352)
PHONE..................................317 241-7600
Thomas R Brouillard, *Principal*
EMP: 80
SQ FT: 10,000
SALES (est): 3.7MM　**Privately Held**
SIC: 3471　Electroplating of metals or formed products

(G-6737)
DEVELOPMENTAL NATURAL RES
8750 Sugar Pine Pt　(46256-4350)
PHONE..................................317 543-4886
Fax: 317 543-4880
Arthur Widgery, *President*
Kenneth Widgery, *Vice Pres*
EMP: 9
SQ FT: 15,000
SALES (est): 1.5MM　**Privately Held**
WEB: www.dnrsite.com
SIC: 2833　Botanical products, medicinal: ground, graded or milled

(G-6738)
DGP INTELSIUS LLC
7696 Zionsville Rd (46268-2173)
PHONE...................................317 452-4006
Andrew Mills, *CEO*
Carl Rubenstein,
▲ EMP: 70 EST: 2008
SQ FT: 14,000
SALES (est): 15.1MM
SALES (corp-wide): 215.5K **Privately
Held**
SIC: 2652 Setup paperboard boxes
HQ: Dgp Intelsius Limited
1 Harrier Court
York YO41
190 460-7390

(G-6739)
**DIAMOND CHAIN COMPANY INC
(HQ)**
402 Kentucky Ave (46225-1174)
PHONE...................................800 872-4246
Fax: 317 633-2243
John Roach, *President*
Scott Web, *Opers Mgr*
Jalaine Kane, *Engineer*
Adam Bee, *CFO*
Jo Koenig, *Finance*
▲ EMP: 174
SALES (est): 53MM
SALES (corp-wide): 2.3B **Privately Held**
WEB: www.diamondchain.com
SIC: 3462 Chains, forged steel
PA: Amsted Industries Incorporated
180 N Stetson Ave # 1800
Chicago IL 60601
312 645-1700

(G-6740)
DIAMOND MINING LEAD
929 Evening Dr Ste A (46201)
PHONE...................................317 340-7760
Brian D Williams, *Owner*
EMP: 2
SALES (est): 170K **Privately Held**
SIC: 1081 Metal mining services

(G-6741)
**DIAMOND TOOLS TECHNOLOGY
INC**
9339 Castlegate Dr (46256-1002)
PHONE...................................847 537-8686
Jiang Xia, *President*
Yan LI, *Vice Pres*
▲ EMP: 13 EST: 2010
SQ FT: 3,000
SALES (est): 2MM **Privately Held**
WEB: www.diamondtoolstechnology.com
SIC: 3915 Diamond cutting & polishing

(G-6742)
DIGIOP INC
9340 Priority Way West Dr (46240-1468)
PHONE...................................800 968-3606
Rich Mellott, *President*
EMP: 35
SALES (est): 5.1MM **Privately Held**
SIC: 3699 Electrical equipment & supplies

(G-6743)
**DIMPLEX NORTH AMERICA
LIMITED**
221 S Franklin Rd Ste 300 (46219-7735)
PHONE...................................317 890-0809
Martyn Camp, *Branch Mgr*
EMP: 9
SALES (corp-wide): 328.1K **Privately
Held**
SIC: 3822 Electric heat controls; appliance
regulators
HQ: Glen Dimplex Americas Limited
1367 Industrial Rd Suite 768
Cambridge ON N3H 4
519 650-3630

(G-6744)
DISTINCT IMAGES INC
6830 Hawthorn Park Dr (46220-3909)
PHONE...................................317 613-4413
Fax: 317 536-4699
James Pike, *President*
EMP: 16
SQ FT: 5,000

SALES: 2MM **Privately Held**
SIC: 2759 Promotional printing; screen
printing

(G-6745)
DIVERS SUPPLY COMPANY INC
Also Called: Ikelite Underwater Systems
50 W 33rd St (46208-4638)
P.O. Box 88100 (46208-0100)
PHONE...................................317 923-4523
Fax: 317 924-7988
Jean M Brigham, *President*
Duane Brigham, *Vice Pres*
David Combs, *Plant Mgr*
James Livers, *Marketing Staff*
Gale Livers, *Manager*
▼ EMP: 80
SQ FT: 20,000
SALES (est): 9.5MM **Privately Held**
WEB: www.ikelite.com
SIC: 3949 Skin diving equipment, scuba
type

(G-6746)
**DIVERSE FABRICATION
SERVICES**
5508 Elmwood Ave Ste 317 (46203-6073)
PHONE...................................317 781-8800
Kristofer C Deckard, *Principal*
EMP: 6
SALES (est): 349.5K **Privately Held**
SIC: 7692 Welding repair

(G-6747)
**DIVERSE SALES SOLUTIONS
LLC**
4947 Oakbrook Ct (46254-1116)
PHONE...................................317 514-2403
Sterling Davis, *Principal*
Peter Le, *Principal*
EMP: 4 EST: 2013
SALES (est): 177.8K **Privately Held**
SIC: 2396 2752 2796 7389 Fabric print-
ing & stamping; commercial printing, off-
set; calendar & card printing, lithographic;
engraving on copper, steel, wood or rub-
ber: printing plates;

(G-6748)
DIVERSE TECH SERVICES INC
Also Called: Diverse Managed Services
7176 Waldemar Dr (46268-2183)
PHONE...................................317 432-6444
Clyde Harris, *President*
Rj McConnell, *Principal*
Amber Amores-Villalobos, *Manager*
George Apgar, *Admin Sec*
EMP: 14
SALES (est): 1.8MM **Privately Held**
SIC: 7371 7372 7373 7378 Computer
software systems analysis & design, cus-
tom; computer software development &
applications; business oriented computer
software; computer systems analysis &
design; computer peripheral equipment
repair & maintenance

(G-6749)
**DIVERSFIED CMMUNICATIONS
GROUP**
Also Called: Digital Color Graphics
2629 Rand Rd (46241-5501)
PHONE...................................317 755-3191
Fax: 317 635-1909
Robert Christopher Hutson, *President*
EMP: 13
SQ FT: 16,000
SALES (est): 3.1MM **Privately Held**
WEB: www.dcgindy.biz
SIC: 2752 Commercial printing, offset

(G-6750)
**DIVERSIFIED OPHTHALMICS
INC**
4555 Independence Sq (46203-5591)
PHONE...................................317 780-1677
Danny Lawrence, *Div Sub Head*
Patricia Koss, *Prdtn Mgr*
EMP: 13
SALES (corp-wide): 285.4MM **Privately
Held**
WEB: www.divopt.com
SIC: 5048 3851 3229 Ophthalmic goods;
ophthalmic goods; pressed & blown glass

HQ: Diversified Ophthalmics, Inc.
250 Mccullough St
Cincinnati OH
800 852-8089

(G-6751)
DIVERSITY PRESS LLC
4026 W 10th St (46222-3203)
PHONE...................................317 241-4234
Darrell Johnson, *President*
Donna Merchant, *Vice Pres*
EMP: 2
SALES (est): 119K **Privately Held**
SIC: 2752 Commercial printing, offset

(G-6752)
DIVSYS INTERNATIONAL LLC
8110 Zionsville Rd (46268-1625)
PHONE...................................317 405-9427
Nita Conaway, *Finance Mgr*
Tammie Fish, *Mng Member*
Belinda Carol Bentle,
Nicolita Bentle,
EMP: 24
SQ FT: 20,000
SALES (est): 4MM **Privately Held**
WEB: www.divsys.com
SIC: 8734 3672 Testing laboratories;
printed circuit boards

(G-6753)
DIXIE METAL SPINNING CORP
4730 Industrial Pkwy (46226-2900)
PHONE...................................317 541-1330
Fax: 317 541-1764
David Terhune, *President*
Jack Proctor, *Admin Sec*
EMP: 6
SQ FT: 14,400
SALES (est): 628K **Privately Held**
SIC: 3469 Spinning metal for the trade

(G-6754)
DJ WREATH CREATIONS LLC
6829 Meadowgreen Dr (46236-8014)
PHONE...................................317 723-3268
Diane J Fischer, *Administration*
EMP: 2
SALES (est): 107.2K **Privately Held**
SIC: 3999 Wreaths, artificial

(G-6755)
DMG MORI USA INC
6848 Hillsdale Ct (46250-2001)
PHONE...................................317 913-0978
Brian McGirk, *President*
EMP: 3
SALES (corp-wide): 3.9B **Privately Held**
SIC: 3541 Machine tools, metal cutting
type
HQ: Dmg Mori Usa, Inc.
2400 Huntington Blvd
Hoffman Estates IL 60192
847 593-5400

(G-6756)
DOERR PRINTING CO
4222 E 18th St (46218-4576)
PHONE...................................317 568-0135
Fax: 317 543-9218
Jan Doerr, *Principal*
EMP: 3
SALES: 450K **Privately Held**
WEB: www.doerrprinting.com
SIC: 2752 2791 2789 2759 Commercial
printing, offset; typesetting; bookbinding &
related work; commercial printing

(G-6757)
DOG EAR PUBLISHING
4011 Vincennes Rd (46268-3008)
PHONE...................................317 228-3656
Nelson Miles, *Publisher*
EMP: 2
SALES (est): 73.2K **Privately Held**
SIC: 2759 Commercial printing

(G-6758)
DORMAKABA USA INC
Also Called: Best Access Solutions
6161 E 75th St (46250-2701)
PHONE...................................317 806-4605
Richard Monahan, *Branch Mgr*
EMP: 750

SALES (corp-wide): 2.5B **Privately Held**
SIC: 3429 3446 Door locks, bolts &
checks; door opening & closing devices,
except electrical; railings, bannisters,
guards, etc.: made from metal pipe; railings, prefabricated metal
HQ: Dormakaba Usa Inc.
100 Dorma Dr
Reamstown PA 17567
717 336-3881

(G-6759)
DORON DISTRIBUTION INC
Also Called: Traffic Signal Company
10625 Deme Dr Ste C (46236-4709)
PHONE...................................317 594-9259
Fax: 317 594-9406
Christine Doron, *President*
William Doron, *Vice Pres*
Katharine Doron, *VP Mktg*
EMP: 6 EST: 1982
SQ FT: 6,000
SALES (est): 880K **Privately Held**
WEB: www.trafficsignalcompany.com
SIC: 3625 5063 Control equipment, elec-
tric; signaling equipment, electrical

(G-6760)
DOTSTAFF LLC
5875 Castle Creek Pkwy N (46250-4331)
PHONE...................................317 806-6100
Sarah Webb, *Program Mgr*
Joseph Bielawski,
Dave Stenger,
EMP: 40
SALES (est): 5.4MM **Privately Held**
WEB: www.dotstaff.com
SIC: 7372 Prepackaged software

(G-6761)
DOVE PRINTING SERVICES
8425 Wdfld Xing Blvd (46240-7315)
PHONE...................................317 843-8222
EMP: 2
SALES (est): 207.8K **Privately Held**
SIC: 2752 Lithographic Commercial Print-
ing

(G-6762)
DOW AGROSCIENCES LLC
5110 E 69th St (46220-3830)
PHONE...................................317 252-5602
EMP: 4
SALES (corp-wide): 62.4B **Publicly Held**
SIC: 2879 Agricultural chemicals
HQ: Dow Agrosciences Llc
9330 Zionsville Rd
Indianapolis IN 46268
317 337-3000

(G-6763)
DOW AGROSCIENCES LLC (DH)
9330 Zionsville Rd (46268-1053)
PHONE...................................317 337-3000
Tim Hassinger, *Mng Member*
Patrick Bell, *Manager*
Mark Jackson, *Executive*
John Wallace, *Representative*
◆ EMP: 1200
SQ FT: 1,205,000
SALES (est): 370MM
SALES (corp-wide): 62.4B **Publicly Held**
SIC: 2879 5191 0721 8731 Agricultural
chemicals; insecticides & pesticides;
fungicides, herbicides; seeds & bulbs;
crop protecting services; agricultural re-
search
HQ: The Dow Chemical Company
2030 Dow Ctr
Midland MI 48674
989 636-1000

(G-6764)
DOWNEY CREATIONS LLC
1811 Executive Dr Ste R (46241-4361)
PHONE...................................317 248-9888
Fax: 317 244-6823
David G Downey,
Alan Heritier,
EMP: 65
SALES (est): 6.5MM **Privately Held**
SIC: 5094 3911 Diamonds (gems); pre-
cious stones (gems); jewel settings &
mountings, precious metal

(G-6765)
DRAKE CORPORATION
9930 E 56th St (46236-2810)
PHONE...................................636 464-5070
Greg Harris, *Manager*
EMP: 10
SQ FT: 6,000
SALES (corp-wide): 8.8MM **Privately Held**
SIC: 3545 3546 Drill bits, metalworking; saws & sawing equipment
PA: Drake Corporation
1180 Wernsing Rd
Jasper IN 47546
636 464-5070

(G-6766)
DREAM KRAFT LLC
4037 N Drexel Ave (46226-4534)
PHONE...................................317 545-2988
Robert H Lee, *Owner*
EMP: 3
SALES (est): 132K **Privately Held**
SIC: 2022 Processed cheese

(G-6767)
DRINKGP LLC
5707 Brockton Dr Apt 115 (46220-5476)
PHONE...................................317 410-4748
Erin Jones, *CEO*
James Edds, *COO*
EMP: 2
SALES (est): 68.6K **Privately Held**
SIC: 2082 7389 Malt beverages;

(G-6768)
DRS GRAPHIX GROUP INC
Also Called: PIP Printing
3855 E 96th St Ste L (46240-2070)
PHONE...................................317 569-1855
Carol Sandberg, *President*
EMP: 4
SALES: 500K **Privately Held**
SIC: 2752 7334 7373 Business form & card printing, lithographic; graphic arts & related design; systems integration services

(G-6769)
DUAL MACHINE CORPORATION
Also Called: Klincher Locknut
1951 Bloyd Ave (46218-3590)
PHONE...................................317 921-9850
Fax: 317 925-3205
John A Bratt, *President*
John Bratt, *General Mgr*
Carol Schnyder, *Corp Secy*
Nancy Wiarek, *Mfg Staff*
EMP: 10
SQ FT: 18,000
SALES (est): 1MM **Privately Held**
SIC: 3451 Screw machine products

(G-6770)
DUEL & TOOL & GAGE INC
1553 S Concord St (46241-4542)
PHONE...................................317 244-0129
Mike D Shively, *President*
Brad Collins, *Senior VP*
EMP: 4
SALES: 250K **Privately Held**
SIC: 3599 Machine shop, jobbing & repair

(G-6771)
DURM VINEYARD INC
Also Called: Buck Creek Winery
11747 Indian Creek Rd S (46259-1056)
PHONE...................................317 862-9463
Jeffrey A Durm, *President*
Kelly Drum, *Vice Pres*
Josett Randolph, *Admin Sec*
EMP: 8
SQ FT: 2,400
SALES (est): 460K **Privately Held**
SIC: 5182 2084 Wine; wines, brandy & brandy spirits

(G-6772)
DYER CHARLES B AND RATLIFF CO
238 S Meridian St Fl 3 (46225-1024)
P.O. Box 3061 (46206-3061)
PHONE...................................317 634-3381
EMP: 9 **EST:** 1890

SALES (est): 85.8K **Privately Held**
SIC: 3911 5944 Mfg Jewelry & Rings & Ret Jewelry

(G-6773)
DYNALOY LLC
6445 Olivia Ln (46226-6157)
PHONE...................................317 788-5694
Fax: 317 788-5690
Guillermo Novo, *President*
James Brady, *Asst Mgr*
Steven Dwyer,
◆ **EMP:** 19
SALES (est): 9.2MM
SALES (corp-wide): 1.1B **Publicly Held**
WEB: www.dynaloy.com
SIC: 5169 2842 Specialty cleaning & sanitation preparations; specialty cleaning, polishes & sanitation goods
PA: Versum Materials, Inc.
8555 S River Pkwy
Tempe AZ 85284
602 282-1000

(G-6774)
DYNAMARK GRAPHICS GROUP INC
Also Called: PIP Printing
3855 E 96th St Ste L (46240-2070)
PHONE...................................317 569-1855
EMP: 6
SALES (est): 689.3K
SALES (corp-wide): 8.5MM **Privately Held**
SIC: 2752 Commercial printing, offset
PA: Dynamark Graphics Group, Inc.
7210 Zionsville Rd
Indianapolis IN 46268
317 328-2555

(G-6775)
DYNAMARK GRAPHICS GROUP INC (PA)
Also Called: PIP Printing
7210 Zionsville Rd (46268-2165)
PHONE...................................317 328-2555
Fax: 317 328-2567
Thomas D Fulner, *President*
Cindy Parris, *Accounts Mgr*
Wanda Degalliford, *Sales Staff*
Dianne Robinson, *Admin Sec*
EMP: 23
SQ FT: 25,000
SALES (est): 8.5MM **Privately Held**
WEB: www.dggink.com
SIC: 7389 7334 2752 2791 Printing broker; presorted mail service; photocopying & duplicating services; commercial printing, offset; typesetting; bookbinding & related work

(G-6776)
DYNAMARK GRAPHICS GROUP INC
Also Called: PIP Printing
7210 Zionsville Rd (46268-2165)
PHONE...................................317 328-2565
Fax: 317 241-2825
Larrie Dillard, *General Mgr*
EMP: 15
SALES (corp-wide): 8.5MM **Privately Held**
WEB: www.dggink.com
SIC: 2752 Commercial printing, offset
PA: Dynamark Graphics Group, Inc.
7210 Zionsville Rd
Indianapolis IN 46268
317 328-2555

(G-6777)
DYNAMARK GRAPHICS GROUP INC
Also Called: PIP Printing
7210 Zionsville Rd (46268-2165)
PHONE...................................317 634-2963
Fax: 317 634-2969
Laurie Grandys, *Manager*
EMP: 3
SALES (corp-wide): 8.5MM **Privately Held**
WEB: www.dggink.com
SIC: 2752 2791 2789 Commercial printing, offset; typesetting; bookbinding & related work

PA: Dynamark Graphics Group, Inc.
7210 Zionsville Rd
Indianapolis IN 46268
317 328-2555

(G-6778)
DYNAMIC DIES INC
2321 Executive Dr (46241-5008)
PHONE...................................317 247-4706
Fax: 317 248-9759
Doug Ringle, *General Mgr*
Douglas Ringle, *General Mgr*
Brian Shaw, *Manager*
EMP: 30
SQ FT: 4,500
SALES (corp-wide): 24.4MM **Privately Held**
WEB: www.dynamicdies.com
SIC: 3544 2796 Paper cutting dies; platemaking services
PA: Dynamic Dies, Inc.
1705 Commerce Rd
Holland OH 43528
419 865-0249

(G-6779)
DYNAMIC LANDSCAPES LLC
Also Called: Dynamic Landscape & Design Co
1022 Halifax Ln (46231-1876)
PHONE...................................317 409-3487
Brandon Preston, *Mng Member*
EMP: 34
SALES (est): 3.9MM **Privately Held**
SIC: 2951 0781 7389 Concrete, asphaltic (not from refineries); landscape services;

(G-6780)
DYNO NOBEL INC
905 Burbank Rd (46219-5022)
PHONE...................................219 253-2525
EMP: 2
SALES (est): 99.5K **Privately Held**
SIC: 2892 Explosives

(G-6781)
E & R MACHINE COMPANY INC
8910 Crawfordsville Rd (46234-3313)
P.O. Box 34566 (46234-0566)
PHONE...................................317 293-1550
Fax: 317 293-8045
Earl J Rouille, *President*
Delores Rouille, *Treasurer*
EMP: 2 **EST:** 1971
SQ FT: 630
SALES: 95K **Privately Held**
SIC: 3599 Machine shop, jobbing & repair

(G-6782)
E FAB INCORPORATED
513 National Ave Ste A (46227-1282)
PHONE...................................317 786-9593
Gony Eldridde, *President*
EMP: 3
SALES (est): 476.4K **Privately Held**
WEB: www.metalarcinc.net
SIC: 3444 Sheet metalwork

(G-6783)
E-TANK LTD
999 W Troy Ave (46225-2243)
PHONE...................................317 296-0510
Williams Hallene, *Branch Mgr*
EMP: 17
SALES (corp-wide): 14.2MM **Privately Held**
SIC: 3443 Industrial vessels, tanks & containers
PA: E-Tank, Ltd.
4113 Millennium Blvd Se
Massillon OH 44646
330 837-5100

(G-6784)
E3 DIAGNOSTICS INC
Also Called: E3 Gordon Stowe
8770 Commerce Park Pl D (46268-3172)
PHONE...................................317 334-2000
Fax: 317 334-0033
Julie Renshaw, *Manager*
EMP: 4 **Privately Held**
SIC: 3845 Audiological equipment, electromedical

HQ: E3 Diagnostics, Inc.
3333 N Kennicott Ave
Arlington Heights IL 60004
847 459-1770

(G-6785)
EAGLE CONSULTING INC
7968 Zionsville Rd (46268-1649)
PHONE...................................317 590-0485
Raymond T Miller, *President*
Alyce M Miller, *Principal*
EMP: 6 **EST:** 2001
SALES (est): 1.1MM **Privately Held**
SIC: 3559 Automotive related machinery

(G-6786)
EAGLE MAGNETIC COMPANY INC
7417 Crawfordsville Rd (46214-1571)
P.O. Box 24283 (46224-0283)
PHONE...................................317 297-1030
Fax: 317 299-1323
Alice Coddington, *President*
Ron Jaggers, *Vice Pres*
Steve Gillespie, *Prdtn Mgr*
Kristen Patterson, *Purch Agent*
Dennis Graham, *QC Mgr*
EMP: 43 **EST:** 1970
SQ FT: 35,000
SALES (est): 10.1MM **Privately Held**
WEB: www.eaglemagnetic.com
SIC: 3444 Sheet metalwork

(G-6787)
EARTH MAMA COMPOST
10830 Lafayette Rd (46278-5029)
PHONE...................................317 759-4589
Heather Maybury, *Principal*
EMP: 2
SALES (est): 74.4K **Privately Held**
SIC: 2875 Compost

(G-6788)
EARTHCHAIN MAGNETIC PRO
9930 E 56th St (46236-2810)
PHONE...................................317 803-8034
Michael Harris, *Principal*
Brian Haskett, *Sales Mgr*
EMP: 2
SALES (est): 100.4K **Privately Held**
SIC: 3544 Special dies, tools, jigs & fixtures

(G-6789)
EASLEY ENTERPRISES INC
Also Called: Easley Winery
205 N College Ave (46202-3701)
PHONE...................................317 636-4516
Fax: 317 974-0128
Mark Easley, *President*
Meredith Easley, *Manager*
Kimberly Utterback, *Manager*
EMP: 38
SQ FT: 20,000
SALES (est): 6.5MM **Privately Held**
WEB: www.easleywine.com
SIC: 2084 2085 Wine cellars, bonded: engaged in blending wines; distilled & blended liquors

(G-6790)
EAST HEAT WOOD PELLETS LLC
217 S Belmont Ave Ste E (46222-4286)
PHONE...................................317 638-4840
Melinda Saxton,
EMP: 2 **EST:** 2012
SALES (est): 211.6K **Privately Held**
SIC: 2299 Wool waste processing

(G-6791)
EAST PENN MANUFACTURING CO
Also Called: Deka Battery
918 S Senate Ave (46225-1456)
PHONE...................................317 236-6288
EMP: 2
SALES (corp-wide): 2.4B **Privately Held**
SIC: 3694 Battery cable wiring sets for internal combustion engines
PA: East Penn Manufacturing Co.
102 Deka Rd
Lyon Station PA 19536
610 682-6361

▲ = Import ▼=Export
◆ =Import/Export

(G-6792)
EAST SIDE WELDING INC
10148 Pendleton Pike (46236-2827)
PHONE...................................317 823-4065
Joanne Sensney, *President*
EMP: 2
SALES (est): 100K **Privately Held**
SIC: 7692 Welding repair

(G-6793)
EASTSIDE MACHINE SHOP
4500 Dunn St (46226-3938)
PHONE...................................317 549-2216
Fax: 317 549-2880
Jeannie Smith, *Partner*
Denver Smith, *Partner*
EMP: 8
SQ FT: 2,000
SALES (est): 1MM **Privately Held**
SIC: 3599 Machine shop, jobbing & repair

(G-6794)
EAT HERE INDY LLC (PA)
5255 Winthrop Ave Ste 110 (46220-3574)
PHONE...................................317 502-4419
Bradley Houser, *Mng Member*
Austin Burris,
EMP: 2
SALES (est): 181.4K **Privately Held**
SIC: 7372 Application computer software

(G-6795)
EATON & HANCOCK ASSOCIATES
2066 Oldfields Cir (46228)
PHONE...................................317 291-6513
EMP: 2
SALES (est): 240K **Privately Held**
SIC: 3625 Mfg Relays/Industrial Controls

(G-6796)
EATON CORPORATION
Eaton Logistics Center
7365 Winton Dr (46268-5101)
PHONE...................................317 704-2520
Fax: 317 704-2528
Rob Haynes, *Branch Mgr*
EMP: 12 **Privately Held**
WEB: www.eaton.com
SIC: 8741 8111 3714 3713 Management
  services; legal services; motor vehicle
  parts & accessories; truck & bus bodies;
  power transmission equipment
HQ: Eaton Corporation
  1000 Eaton Blvd
  Cleveland OH 44122
  440 523-5000

(G-6797)
EBWA INDUSTRIES INC
Also Called: Electron Beam Welding
1556 Deloss St (46201-3904)
PHONE...................................317 637-5860
Daniel Diehl, *President*
EMP: 10
SALES (est): 100.8K **Privately Held**
SIC: 7692 Welding repair

(G-6798)
ECHO ENGRG & PROD SUPS INC (PA)
Also Called: Echo Supply
5406 W 78th St (46268-4149)
PHONE...................................317 876-8848
Kingdon Offenbacker, *CEO*
John Offenbacker, *President*
John Seitz, *COO*
Albert Chew, *Vice Pres*
Matt Becker, *Engineer*
▲ EMP: 43
SQ FT: 21,600
SALES (est): 17.2MM **Privately Held**
WEB: www.echosupply.com
SIC: 2821 Plastics materials & resins

(G-6799)
ECKHART & COMPANY INC
4011 W 54th St (46254-4789)
PHONE...................................317 347-2665
Fax: 317 347-2666
Chris Eckhart, *President*
Gary Neidlinger, *Plant Mgr*
Mike Carlberg, *Manager*
Brad Gargus, *Manager*
Cari Medaris, *Manager*
EMP: 45 EST: 1918
SQ FT: 60,000
SALES (est): 7.1MM **Privately Held**
WEB: www.eckhartandco.com
SIC: 2789 2782 Binding only: books, pam-
  phlets, magazines, etc.; blankbooks &
  looseleaf binders

(G-6800)
ECO LIGHTING SOLUTIONS LLC
8730 Corporation Dr (46256-1289)
PHONE...................................866 897-1234
Jeff Pinyot, *President*
David Packard, *COO*
EMP: 13
SALES (est): 2MM **Privately Held**
SIC: 3646 Commercial indusl & institu-
  tional electric lighting fixtures

(G-6801)
ECO-BAT AMERICA LLC
Also Called: Quemetco
7870 W Morris St (46231-1365)
PHONE...................................317 247-1303
Fax: 317 244-4653
Glen Harold, *Branch Mgr*
EMP: 244
SALES (corp-wide): 6.3MM **Privately Held**
SIC: 3356 3341 3339 Nonferrous rolling &
  drawing; secondary nonferrous metals;
  lead smelting & refining (primary)
HQ: Eco-Bat America Llc
  2777 N Stemmons Fwy # 1800
  Dallas TX 75207
  214 688-4000

(G-6802)
ED BOILINI
24 E 40th St (46205-2625)
PHONE...................................317 921-0155
EMP: 2
SALES (est): 86.6K **Privately Held**
SIC: 3841 Surgical And Medical Instru-
  ments

(G-6803)
ED SONS INC (PA)
Also Called: PIP Printing
8335 Pendleton Pike (46226-4017)
PHONE...................................317 897-8821
Fax: 317 897-8822
Paul Edson, *President*
Lurette Edson, *Vice Pres*
Dale R Edson, *Treasurer*
EMP: 12 EST: 1969
SQ FT: 4,200
SALES (est): 1.2MM **Privately Held**
SIC: 2752 7334 2791 2789 Commercial
  printing, offset; photocopying & duplicat-
  ing services; typesetting; bookbinding &
  related work; commercial printing

(G-6804)
EDCO WELDING AND HYDRAULIC INC
861 W Troy Ave (46225-2241)
PHONE...................................317 783-2323
Melvin E Vanmeter, *President*
Donna Vanmeter, *Principal*
EMP: 12
SALES (est): 836.8K **Privately Held**
SIC: 7692 Welding repair

(G-6805)
EDGE TECHNOLOGIES INC
4455 W 62nd St (46268-2521)
PHONE...................................317 408-0116
Fax: 317 293-2185
George Kim, *President*
Vada Kim, *COO*
EMP: 9
SQ FT: 5,500
SALES (est): 922.9K **Privately Held**
SIC: 3599 Custom machinery

(G-6806)
EDITIONS LTD GALLERY FINE ARTS
838 E 65th St (46220-1896)
PHONE...................................317 466-9940
Fax: 317 466-0113
Chris Mallen, *Manager*
EMP: 4
SALES (est): 230K **Privately Held**
SIC: 2499 5023 5999 8412 Picture frame
  molding, finished; frames & framing, pic-
  ture & mirror; art, picture frames & deco-
  rations; art gallery

(G-6807)
EDM SPECIALTIES INC
7746 Milhouse Rd (46241-9550)
PHONE...................................317 856-4700
Richard Sharp, *President*
EMP: 4
SALES (est): 486.2K **Privately Held**
SIC: 3541 Machine tools, metal cutting
  type

(G-6808)
EDUCATION CONNECTION PUBG LLC
4923 W 78th St (46268-4170)
PHONE...................................317 876-3355
EMP: 2
SALES (est): 86K **Privately Held**
SIC: 2741 Misc Publishing

(G-6809)
EDWARD E PETRI COMPANY
20 N Meridian St Ste 206 (46204-3023)
PHONE...................................317 636-5007
Fax: 317 636-9640
Charles Walker, *President*
EMP: 4
SQ FT: 1,498
SALES (est): 400K **Privately Held**
WEB: www.petrijewelers.com
SIC: 3911 5944 Jewelry, precious metal;
  jewelry, precious stones & precious met-
  als

(G-6810)
EDWARD ONEIL ASSOCIATES
Also Called: Balfour Company
1810 S Raceway Rd (46231-1852)
PHONE...................................317 244-5400
Edward O'Neil, *Owner*
EMP: 3
SALES (est): 1MM **Privately Held**
SIC: 5094 5112 7389 2754 Jewelry &
  precious stones; watches & parts; tro-
  phies; stationery & office supplies; en-
  graving service; commercial printing,
  gravure

(G-6811)
EFURNITUREMAX LLC
8070 Castleton Rd 117 (46250-2005)
PHONE...................................317 697-9504
Cameron Paterson, *Mng Member*
EMP: 2
SALES (est): 630K **Privately Held**
SIC: 2511 7389 Wood household furniture;

(G-6812)
EGENOLF CONTG & RIGGING II INC
350 Wisconsin St (46225-1536)
PHONE...................................317 787-5301
Peter Egenolf, *President*
Michael Egenolf, *Exec VP*
R Joseph Jansen, *Vice Pres*
EMP: 55
SALES (est): 4MM **Privately Held**
SIC: 1796 1541 3599 Machine moving &
  rigging; industrial buildings & ware-
  houses; catapults

(G-6813)
EGENOLF ENTERPRISE INC
Also Called: Capstone Commerce Company
2855 N Evanklin Rd Ste (46226)
PHONE...................................317 501-5069
Pat Egenolf, *President*
EMP: 2
SALES (est): 292.4K **Privately Held**
SIC: 3524 Lawn & garden tractors & equip-
  ment

(G-6814)
EGENOLF MACHINE INC
2916 Bluff Rd Ste A (46225-2296)
PHONE...................................317 787-5301
Fax: 317 787-5018
James Egenolf, *President*
Joseph Egenolf, *Exec VP*
R Joseph Jansen III, *Vice Pres*
Mary T Egenolf, *Treasurer*
Eileen Egenolf, *Admin Sec*
EMP: 90
SQ FT: 55,000
SALES (est): 8.8MM **Privately Held**
WEB: www.egenolfmachine.com
SIC: 1796 3599 7692 7629 Machine
  moving & rigging; machinery installation;
  machine shop, jobbing & repair; welding
  repair; electrical repair shops; printing
  trades machinery; machine tools, metal
  forming type

(G-6815)
EHOB INC
250 N Belmont Ave (46222-4265)
PHONE...................................317 972-4600
Fax: 317 972-4601
Scott D Rogers, *President*
Matt Hawthorne, *COO*
Brian Conway, *Exec VP*
Dave Denton, *Vice Pres*
Kimberly Greene, *Vice Pres*
▲ EMP: 120
SQ FT: 53,000
SALES (est): 27MM **Privately Held**
WEB: www.ehob.com
SIC: 3842 Surgical appliances & supplies

(G-6816)
EHRGOTTS SIGNS & STAMPS INC
7173 W Us Highway 40 (46229-4214)
PHONE...................................317 353-2222
Sarah Barker Clevenger, *President*
EMP: 2 EST: 2013
SALES (est): 120K **Privately Held**
SIC: 3953 Marking devices

(G-6817)
EISELES HONEY LLC
8146 Zionsville Rd (46268-1625)
PHONE...................................317 896-5830
Jeffrey Peterson,
EMP: 3
SQ FT: 3,600
SALES: 535K **Privately Held**
SIC: 2099 Honey, strained & bottled

(G-6818)
EJ USA INC
201 N Illinois St # 1900 (46204-1904)
PHONE...................................765 744-1184
EMP: 12 **Privately Held**
SIC: 3321 Manhole covers, metal
HQ: Ej Usa, Inc.
  301 Spring St
  East Jordan MI 49727
  800 874-4100

(G-6819)
ELEKTRISOLA INCORPORATED
2400 N Shadeland Ave B (46219-1737)
PHONE...................................317 375-8192
Eddie Forte, *Manager*
EMP: 3
SALES (corp-wide): 30MM **Privately Held**
WEB: www.elektrisola.com
SIC: 3357 Magnet wire, nonferrous
PA: Elektrisola Incorporated
  126 High St
  Boscawen NH 03303
  603 796-2114

(G-6820)
ELEMENTS ELEARNING LLC
4543 Melbourne Rd (46228-2771)
PHONE...................................317 986-2113
Constance Carlisle, *Principal*
EMP: 3 EST: 2014
SALES (est): 186.9K **Privately Held**
SIC: 2819 Industrial inorganic chemicals

(G-6821)
ELEVATOR ONE LLC
120 E Market St (46204-3250)
PHONE...................................317 634-8001
Chance Felling, *Mng Member*
EMP: 8
SALES (est): 680.3K **Privately Held**
SIC: 3534 Elevators & equipment

GEOGRAPHIC

(G-6822)
ELI LILLY AND COMPANY (PA)
Lilly Corporate Ctr (46285-0001)
PHONE...................................317 276-2000
Fax: 317 276-2000
David A Ricks, *Ch of Bd*
Derica W Rice, *Exec VP*
Melissa S Barnes, *Senior VP*
Michael J Harrington, *Senior VP*
Martin Bott, *Vice Pres*
EMP: 4000 EST: 1876
SALES: 22.8B **Publicly Held**
WEB: www.lilly.com
SIC: 2834 Pharmaceutical preparations;
　drugs affecting parasitic & infective dis-
　eases; analgesics; veterinary pharmaceu-
　tical preparations

(G-6823)
ELI LILLY AND COMPANY
1400 W Raymond St (46221-2004)
PHONE...................................317 276-2000
John Benitez, *Counsel*
John Beyrau, *Project Mgr*
Cindy Hammill, *Research*
Cecilia Mur, *Research*
Anne Renton, *Research*
EMP: 15
SALES (corp-wide): 22.8B **Publicly Held**
WEB: www.lilly.com
SIC: 2834 Pharmaceutical preparations
PA: Eli Lilly And Company
　Lilly Corporate Ctr
　Indianapolis IN 46285
　317 276-2000

(G-6824)
ELI LILLY AND COMPANY
Also Called: Elanco Animal Health
2401 Directors Row (46241-4907)
PHONE...................................317 276-2000
Robert Behrend, *Engineer*
Angela Bryant, *Branch Mgr*
David Kutoloski, *Business Dir*
Yugong Cheng, *Associate*
EMP: 14
SALES (corp-wide): 22.8B **Publicly Held**
WEB: www.lilly.com
SIC: 2834 Pharmaceutical preparations
PA: Eli Lilly And Company
　Lilly Corporate Ctr
　Indianapolis IN 46285
　317 276-2000

(G-6825)
ELI LILLY AND COMPANY
1223 W Morris St Dock 312 (46221)
PHONE...................................317 277-1079
Holly Cannon, *Project Mgr*
Kevin Cisa, *Manager*
Kimberly Shields, *Manager*
John Stanciu, *Manager*
Chris Froggatt, *Consultant*
EMP: 19
SALES (corp-wide): 22.8B **Publicly Held**
SIC: 2834 Pharmaceutical preparations
PA: Eli Lilly And Company
　Lilly Corporate Ctr
　Indianapolis IN 46285
　317 276-2000

(G-6826)
ELI LILLY AND COMPANY
355 E Merrill St (46225-1340)
PHONE...................................317 276-7907
EMP: 18
SALES (corp-wide): 22.8B **Publicly Held**
SIC: 2834 Pharmaceutical preparations
PA: Eli Lilly And Company
　Lilly Corporate Ctr
　Indianapolis IN 46285
　317 276-2000

(G-6827)
ELI LILLY AND COMPANY
450 S Meridian St (46225-1103)
PHONE...................................317 276-2000
Boris Lin, *Oncology*
EMP: 8
SALES (corp-wide): 22.8B **Publicly Held**
SIC: 2834 Pharmaceutical preparations
PA: Eli Lilly And Company
　Lilly Corporate Ctr
　Indianapolis IN 46285
　317 276-2000

(G-6828)
ELI LILLY AND COMPANY
1223 S Harding St (46221)
PHONE...................................317 651-7790
John Lechleiter, *President*
Brad Reaman, *Info Tech Mgr*
Mary Benmachiche, *Representative*
Cindy Payne, *Associate*
EMP: 6
SQ FT: 60,000
SALES (corp-wide): 22.8B **Publicly Held**
SIC: 2834 Pharmaceutical preparations
PA: Eli Lilly And Company
　Lilly Corporate Ctr
　Indianapolis IN 46285
　317 276-2000

(G-6829)
ELI LILLY AND COMPANY
Lilly Corporate Center (46285-0001)
PHONE...................................317 276-2000
Steven Ring, *Opers Staff*
Paul Thompson, *Accounts Mgr*
Daniel Boehm, *Branch Mgr*
Manuel Lopez, *Project Leader*
Ralph Forey, *Consultant*
EMP: 14
SALES (corp-wide): 22.8B **Publicly Held**
SIC: 2834 Pharmaceutical preparations
PA: Eli Lilly And Company
　Lilly Corporate Ctr
　Indianapolis IN 46285
　317 276-2000

(G-6830)
ELI LILLY AND COMPANY
Also Called: Elanco Animal Health
30 S Meridian St Fl 5 (46204-3564)
PHONE...................................317 277-0147
Tinggui Yin, *Research*
Monica Dickenson, *Branch Mgr*
Carlisa Richards, *Manager*
Valerie Brown, *Consultant*
Jennie Deem, *Consultant*
EMP: 25
SALES (corp-wide): 22.8B **Publicly Held**
WEB: www.lilly.com
SIC: 2834 Pharmaceutical preparations
PA: Eli Lilly And Company
　Lilly Corporate Ctr
　Indianapolis IN 46285
　317 276-2000

(G-6831)
ELI LILLY AND COMPANY
1280 S Dakota St (46225-1581)
PHONE...................................317 276-7907
D Kyle Thompson, *Branch Mgr*
EMP: 14
SALES (corp-wide): 22.8B **Publicly Held**
WEB: www.lilly.com
SIC: 2834 Pharmaceutical preparations
PA: Eli Lilly And Company
　Lilly Corporate Ctr
　Indianapolis IN 46285
　317 276-2000

(G-6832)
ELI LILLY AND COMPANY
Also Called: Elanco Animal Health
1402 S Dakota St (46225)
PHONE...................................317 276-5925
EMP: 11
SALES (corp-wide): 22.8B **Publicly Held**
WEB: www.lilly.com
SIC: 2834 Pharmaceutical preparations
PA: Eli Lilly And Company
　Lilly Corporate Ctr
　Indianapolis IN 46285
　317 276-2000

(G-6833)
ELI LILLY AND COMPANY
Also Called: Elanco Animal Health
1555 S Harding St (46221-1873)
PHONE...................................317 276-2000
Marie Abbott, *Principal*
Bob Mark, *Engineer*
Erin Lewis, *Manager*
Dan Neumann, *Consultant*
Stephanie Drenning, *Senior Mgr*
EMP: 11
SALES (corp-wide): 22.8B **Publicly Held**
WEB: www.lilly.com
SIC: 2834 Pharmaceutical preparations

PA: Eli Lilly And Company
　Lilly Corporate Ctr
　Indianapolis IN 46285
　317 276-2000

(G-6834)
ELI LILLY AND COMPANY
Also Called: Elanco Animal Health
639 S Delaware St (46225-1392)
PHONE...................................317 276-2118
Fax: 317 276-0427
Kerry Dunlavey, *Principal*
Pierre V Abraham, *Sales Mgr*
Patty Hines, *Manager*
Richard Chipelewski, *Technology*
Charlene Brundage, *Software Engr*
EMP: 4
SALES (corp-wide): 22.8B **Publicly Held**
WEB: www.lilly.com
SIC: 2834 Pharmaceutical preparations
PA: Eli Lilly And Company
　Lilly Corporate Ctr
　Indianapolis IN 46285
　317 276-2000

(G-6835)
ELI LILLY AND COMPANY
Also Called: Elanco Animal Health
2301 Executive Dr (46241-5008)
PHONE...................................317 276-2000
Richard Justice, *Branch Mgr*
Mike Griffith, *Manager*
EMP: 14
SALES (corp-wide): 22.8B **Publicly Held**
WEB: www.lilly.com
SIC: 2834 Pharmaceutical preparations
PA: Eli Lilly And Company
　Lilly Corporate Ctr
　Indianapolis IN 46285
　317 276-2000

(G-6836)
ELI LILLY INTERNATIONAL CORP (HQ)
893 S Delaware St (46225-1782)
PHONE...................................317 276-2000
David Ricks, *President*
James B Lootens, *Principal*
J A Harper, *Vice Pres*
Mark Ryan, *Vice Pres*
Richard Smith, *Vice Pres*
EMP: 15
SALES (est): 353.4MM
SALES (corp-wide): 22.8B **Publicly Held**
SIC: 8742 2834 8731 3841 Business
　consultant; pharmaceutical preparations;
　commercial physical research; surgical &
　medical instruments; agricultural chemi-
　cals
PA: Eli Lilly And Company
　Lilly Corporate Ctr
　Indianapolis IN 46285
　317 276-2000

(G-6837)
ELIE CLEANING SERVICES LLC
10475 Crosspoint Blvd # 250 (46256-3386)
PHONE...................................317 983-3388
Richardo Elie,
EMP: 14
SALES (est): 28.6K **Privately Held**
SIC: 7542 7349 2842 Washing & polish-
　ing, automotive; carwash, automatic; car-
　wash, self-service; cleaning service,
　industrial or commercial; polishing prepa-
　rations & related products

(G-6838)
ELITE INDUSTRIES LLC
6331 Muirfield Way (46237-9584)
PHONE...................................317 407-6869
Steven Ell, *Administration*
EMP: 2
SALES (est): 78.9K **Privately Held**
SIC: 3999 Manufacturing industries

(G-6839)
ELITE PRINTING INC
4239 Madison Ave (46227-1530)
PHONE...................................317 781-9701
Tim Derloshon, *Branch Mgr*
EMP: 2
SALES (corp-wide): 450K **Privately Held**
SIC: 2752 Commercial printing, offset

PA: Elite Printing Inc
　2138 E 52nd St
　Indianapolis IN 46205
　317 257-2744

(G-6840)
ELITE PRINTING INC (PA)
2138 E 52nd St (46205-1408)
PHONE...................................317 257-2744
Jim V Renterghem, *President*
Suzy Van Renterghem, *President*
Suzette Van Renterghem, *Principal*
Jim Van Renterghem, *Vice Pres*
EMP: 4
SQ FT: 2,200
SALES (est): 450K **Privately Held**
WEB: www.eliteprinting.net
SIC: 2752 Commercial printing, offset

(G-6841)
ELL ENTERPRISES INC
2950 E Hanna Ave (46227-3557)
PHONE...................................317 783-7838
Fax: 317 783-7839
Phillip M Ell, *President*
Sherri Ell, *Corp Secy*
John V Greengoss, *Accountant*
▼ EMP: 8
SQ FT: 10,000
SALES (est): 1.3MM **Privately Held**
SIC: 2541 5046 Display fixtures, wood;
　store fixtures

(G-6842)
ELLIOTT CO OF INDIANAPOLIS
Also Called: Elliott Company
9200 Zionsville Rd (46268-1081)
PHONE...................................317 291-1213
Fax: 317 291-1219
Bryan C Elliott, *President*
Charles Elliott, *Vice Pres*
Linda M Elliott, *Admin Sec*
EMP: 14
SQ FT: 30,000
SALES (est): 5.2MM **Privately Held**
WEB: www.elliottfoam.com
SIC: 3086 Insulation or cushioning mate-
　rial, foamed plastic

(G-6843)
ELLIOTT-WILLIAMS COMPANY INC
3500 E 20th St (46218-4485)
PHONE...................................317 453-2295
Fax: 317 453-1977
Michael M Elliott Sr, *President*
Michael M Elliott Jr, *Vice Pres*
Richard A Fiorelli, *VP Mfg*
EMP: 70
SQ FT: 110,000
SALES (est): 8.5MM **Privately Held**
SIC: 3585 3822 5078 1799 Refrigeration
　equipment, complete; air conditioning &
　refrigeration controls; refrigeration equip-
　ment & supplies; appliance installation

(G-6844)
ELMCO ENGINEERING INC (PA)
6107 Churchman Road Byp Bypass
(46203)
PHONE...................................317 788-4114
Fax: 317 788-0220
Robert E Behrens, *CEO*
Larry E Emery, *President*
EMP: 50
SQ FT: 35,000
SALES (est): 8.3MM **Privately Held**
SIC: 3599 Machine shop, jobbing & repair

(G-6845)
ELWOOD FUEL AND CIGS LLC
1050 S High School Rd (46241-3120)
PHONE...................................317 244-5744
Kevin Cleveland, *Principal*
EMP: 3
SALES (est): 250.1K **Privately Held**
SIC: 2869 Fuels

(G-6846)
EMARSYS NORTH AMERICA INC
10 W Market St Ste 1350 (46204-2930)
PHONE...................................844 693-6277
Hagai Hartman, *CEO*
Sean Brady, *President*
Josef Ahorner, *Chairman*

▲ = Import ▼ = Export
◆ = Import/Export

Daniel Eisenhut, *Vice Pres*
Guy Hanin, *Opers Staff*
EMP: 50 **EST:** 2015
SQ FT: 20,000
SALES (est): 1.5MM **Privately Held**
SIC: 7372 8742 Prepackaged software; marketing consulting services

(G-6847)
EMB FISHING LLC
Also Called: Accent Fishing Product
8133 Winterset Cir (46214-2287)
PHONE......................317 244-8741
Luther E Rounsaville, *Mng Member*
EMP: 2
SALES (est): 146.5K **Privately Held**
SIC: 3949 7389 Lures, fishing: artificial;

(G-6848)
EMBROIDERY PLUS INC
5514 W Washington St (46241-2103)
PHONE......................317 243-3445
Fax: 317 243-2444
Stan Wisehart, *President*
EMP: 6
SALES: 180K **Privately Held**
SIC: 2395 Embroidery & art needlework

(G-6849)
EMC CORPORATION
8888 Keystone Xing # 700 (46240-4609)
PHONE......................317 706-8600
Fax: 317 566-1312
Michael Pratt, *Manager*
EMP: 30
SALES (corp-wide): 78.6B **Publicly Held**
WEB: www.emc.com
SIC: 3572 Computer storage devices
HQ: Emc Corporation
　　176 South St
　　Hopkinton MA 01748
　　508 435-1000

(G-6850)
EMC PROJECTS
1409 N New Jersey St (46202-2623)
PHONE......................317 420-8005
EMP: 2
SALES (est): 85.9K **Privately Held**
SIC: 3572 Computer storage devices

(G-6851)
EMC2
3539 N Colorado Ave (46218-1509)
P.O. Box 18713 (46218-0713)
PHONE......................317 435-8021
EMP: 3
SALES (est): 171.5K **Privately Held**
SIC: 3572 Computer storage devices

(G-6852)
EMCO GEARS INC
703 S Girls School Rd (46231-3129)
PHONE......................317 243-3836
Fax: 317 243-3873
Dan Cota, *Manager*
EMP: 6
SALES (est): 753.8K
SALES (corp-wide): 5.5MM **Privately Held**
WEB: www.emco-gears.com
SIC: 3462 Gear & chain forgings
PA: Emco Gears, Inc.
　　160 King St
　　Elk Grove Village IL 60007
　　847 220-4327

(G-6853)
EMERSON ELECTRIC CO
8320 Brookville Rd Ste E (46239-8914)
PHONE......................317 322-2055
EMP: 5
SALES (corp-wide): 15.2B **Publicly Held**
SIC: 3823 Industrial instrmnts msrmnt display/control process variable
PA: Emerson Electric Co.
　　8000 West Florissant Ave
　　Saint Louis MO 63136
　　314 553-2000

(G-6854)
EMMIS COMMUNICATIONS CORP (PA)
40 Monument Cir Ste 700 (46204-3017)
PHONE......................317 266-0100
Jeffrey H Smulyan, *Ch of Bd*

Patrick M Walsh, *President*
J Scott Enright, *Exec VP*
Bob Richards, *Vice Pres*
Traci Thomson, *Vice Pres*
EMP: 60
SQ FT: 91,500
SALES: 148.4MM **Publicly Held**
WEB: www.emmis.com
SIC: 4832 2721 Radio broadcasting stations; periodicals: publishing & printing

(G-6855)
EMMIS OPERATING COMPANY (HQ)
40 Monument Cir Ste 700 (46204-3017)
PHONE......................317 266-0100
Jefferey Smulyan, *CEO*
Jeff Snulyan, *CEO*
Richard F Cummings, *President*
Gary Thoe, *President*
Michael Levitan, *Exec VP*
EMP: 31
SQ FT: 142,000
SALES (est): 23.7MM
SALES (corp-wide): 148.4MM **Publicly Held**
SIC: 4832 4833 2721 Radio broadcasting stations; television broadcasting stations; magazines: publishing only, not printed on site
PA: Emmis Communications Corp
　　40 Monument Cir Ste 700
　　Indianapolis IN 46204
　　317 266-0100

(G-6856)
EMMIS PUBLISHING LP (HQ)
Also Called: Texas Monthly
40 Monument Cir Ste 100 (46204-3045)
PHONE......................317 266-0100
Fax: 317 684-2080
Evan Smith, *CEO*
Jeff Ditmire, *President*
Elynn Russell, *President*
Greg Loewen, *Partner*
Barbara Brill, *Partner*
EMP: 46
SALES (est): 95.8MM
SALES (corp-wide): 148.4MM **Publicly Held**
WEB: www.indianapolismagazine.com
SIC: 2721 Magazines: publishing only, not printed on site
PA: Emmis Communications Corp
　　40 Monument Cir Ste 700
　　Indianapolis IN 46204
　　317 266-0100

(G-6857)
EMMIS PUBLISHING CORPORATION (HQ)
40 Monument Cir Ste 700 (46204-3017)
PHONE......................317 266-0100
Patrick M Walsh, *President*
Scott Enright, *Admin Sec*
EMP: 2
SALES (est): 3MM
SALES (corp-wide): 148.4MM **Publicly Held**
SIC: 2721 Periodicals: publishing & printing
PA: Emmis Communications Corp
　　40 Monument Cir Ste 700
　　Indianapolis IN 46204
　　317 266-0100

(G-6858)
EMPHYMAB BIOTECH LLC
351 W 10th St (46202-4118)
PHONE......................317 274-5935
Joseph Trebley, *Manager*
EMP: 3
SALES (est): 272.8K **Privately Held**
SIC: 2834 Pharmaceutical preparations

(G-6859)
EMPRO MANUFACTURING CO INC
10920 E 59th St (46236-8337)
P.O. Box 26060 (46226-0060)
PHONE......................317 823-3000
Fax: 317 823-4835
Gary J Graf, *President*
Shelly Schultz, *General Mgr*
Mike Harriman, *Engineer*
Jennifer Evans, *Office Mgr*

Gretchen E Graf, *Admin Sec*
▲ **EMP:** 20 **EST:** 1950
SQ FT: 5,000
SALES (est): 5.7MM **Privately Held**
WEB: www.emproshunts.com
SIC: 3629 Test equipment for electronic & electrical circuits; electronic generation equipment

(G-6860)
EMQUIP CORPORATION
6909 E 32nd St (46226-6158)
PHONE......................317 849-3977
Fax: 317 547-0739
Donald Wilson, *President*
Shirley Wilson, *Corp Secy*
EMP: 5 **EST:** 1965
SQ FT: 8,500
SALES (est): 929.3K **Privately Held**
SIC: 3533 Oil & gas field machinery

(G-6861)
ENDOWMENT DEVELOPMENT SERVICES
Also Called: EDS
921 E 86th St Ste 100 (46240-1841)
PHONE......................317 542-9829
Fax: 317 549-9470
James R Marshell, *President*
Judith Epperson, *Vice Pres*
EMP: 10
SALES (est): 250K **Privately Held**
SIC: 2741 2721 Miscellaneous publishing; periodicals

(G-6862)
ENER1 INC (HQ)
8740 Hague Rd Bldg 7 (46256-1246)
PHONE......................317 703-1800
Michael Canada, *CEO*
Tim Hans, *Plant Mgr*
James Bowman, *Opers Staff*
Gabriel Holmes, *Electrical Engi*
John T Warner, *Chief Mktg Ofcr*
EMP: 23
SQ FT: 3,500
SALES (est): 147.9MM
SALES (corp-wide): 165.2MM **Privately Held**
SIC: 3691 Storage batteries
PA: Enerdel, Inc.
　　8740 Hague Rd Bldg 7
　　Indianapolis IN 46256
　　317 703-1800

(G-6863)
ENERDEL INC (PA)
8740 Hague Rd Bldg 7 (46256-1246)
PHONE......................317 703-1800
Fax: 317 585-3444
Michael Canada, *CEO*
Andrew Balog, *Exec VP*
James Bowman, *Senior VP*
Mike Frossard, *Mfg Mgr*
Dr Tomasz Poznar, *VP Bus Dvlpt*
▲ **EMP:** 136
SALES (est): 165.2MM **Privately Held**
WEB: www.enerdel.com
SIC: 3691 8731 Storage batteries; commercial physical research

(G-6864)
ENERGY ACCESS INC
5344 W 79th St (46268-1631)
PHONE......................317 329-1676
Tom Peine, *President*
Malcolm McClure, *Vice Pres*
▲ **EMP:** 12 **EST:** 1998
SQ FT: 2,000
SALES (est): 2.6MM **Privately Held**
WEB: www.energyaccess.com
SIC: 3629 3699 Battery chargers, rectifying or nonrotating; electrical equipment & supplies

(G-6865)
ENERGY QUEST INC
8553 Bash St Ste 107 (46250-5534)
PHONE......................317 827-9212
Ronald Foster, *President*
Albert Hyde, *Manager*
EMP: 4 **Publicly Held**
SIC: 2869 Industrial organic chemicals
PA: Energy Quest, Inc.
　　103 Firetower Rd
　　Leesburg GA 31763

(G-6866)
ENERGY SAVER LIGHTS INC
2530 Brandywine Ct (46241-5199)
PHONE......................202 544-7868
Carlet Auguste, *President*
EMP: 10
SALES (est): 540K **Privately Held**
SIC: 3999 3641 Stage hardware & equipment, except lighting; electric light bulbs, complete

(G-6867)
ENGHOUSE NETWORKS (US) INC (HQ)
333 N Alabama St Ste 240 (46204-2151)
PHONE......................317 262-4666
Michael J Reinarts, *Ch of Bd*
Manfred Hanuschek, *President*
Martin Sparks, *Project Mgr*
Nathan Habegger, *CFO*
EMP: 65
SQ FT: 15,931
SALES (est): 18.3MM
SALES (corp-wide): 262.6MM **Privately Held**
WEB: www.ctigroup.com
SIC: 7372 Business oriented computer software
PA: Enghouse Systems Limited
　　80 Tiverton Crt Suite 800
　　Markham ON L3R 0
　　905 946-3200

(G-6868)
ENGINEERED INDUSTRIAL PRODUCTS
5652 W 74th St (46278-1752)
P.O. Box 114 (46206-0114)
PHONE......................317 684-4280
Fax: 317 684-4284
Donald W Fink, *Ch of Bd*
Steve Fink, *President*
Thomas Kuhn, *Vice Pres*
EMP: 5
SALES (est): 602.2K **Privately Held**
SIC: 3599 Hose, flexible metallic

(G-6869)
ENGINEERED MEDICAL SYSTEMS
Also Called: E M S
2055 Executive Dr (46241-4311)
PHONE......................317 246-5500
Jeffrey J Quinn, *President*
Brad H Quinn, *Vice Pres*
Andrew Shurig, *Vice Pres*
▲ **EMP:** 70
SQ FT: 20,000
SALES (est): 15.7MM **Privately Held**
WEB: www.engmedsys.com
SIC: 3841 Surgical & medical instruments

(G-6870)
ENHANCEMENT POWER PRODUCTS
398 N Mitchner Ave (46219-5114)
PHONE......................317 359-3461
Gregory Head, *President*
Mark Chapple, *Vice Pres*
Robert R Atherton, *Treasurer*
EMP: 4
SALES: 700K **Privately Held**
SIC: 3519 Governors, pump, for diesel engines

(G-6871)
ENVIGO RMS INC (DH)
Also Called: Teklad Diets
8520 Allison Pointe Blvd # 400 (46250-5700)
PHONE......................317 806-6080
Fax: 317 806-6090
David Broecker, *President*
Yarnin Gal, *President*
Denise Cox, *General Mgr*
Mark Bibi, *Vice Pres*
Joseph Bondi, *Vice Pres*
▲ **EMP:** 150
SQ FT: 48,000

SALES (est): 9MM
SALES (corp-wide): 2MM **Privately Held**
WEB: www.harlan.com
SIC: 0279 2048 2836 3821 Laboratory animal farm; prepared feeds; veterinary biological products; laboratory apparatus & furniture
HQ: Envigo Crs Limited
  Woolley Road
  Huntingdon CAMBS PE28
  148 089-2000

(G-6872)
ENVIRNMNTAL CTRL SOLUTIONS LLC
5115 N Richardt Ave (46226-2740)
PHONE....................317 358-5985
Claude Jones, *CEO*
EMP: 2
SALES (est): 104.2K **Privately Held**
SIC: 3823 Industrial instrmnts msrmnt display/control process variable

(G-6873)
ENVIROPEEL USA
1128 S West St (46225-1463)
PHONE....................317 631-9100
Ivan Hess, *Vice Pres*
Mark Hanselman, *Sales Staff*
Corey Pierce, *Manager*
EMP: 6
SALES (est): 491.9K **Privately Held**
SIC: 1382 Oil & gas exploration services

(G-6874)
EON PERFORMANCE LLC
1526 Woodson Dr Apt 209 (46227-1599)
PHONE....................847 997-8619
Nicholas Beyer, *CEO*
Colin Hawk, *President*
EMP: 2
SALES (est): 56.5K **Privately Held**
SIC: 7372 7389 Application computer software;

(G-6875)
EPI PRINTERS INC
Also Called: E P I
7502 E 86th St (46256-1210)
PHONE....................317 579-4870
Fax: 317 579-4880
Dean Wolf, *Vice Pres*
Andrew Counceller, *Manager*
EMP: 88
SALES (corp-wide): 216MM **Privately Held**
WEB: www.epiinc.com
SIC: 2752 2789 Commercial printing, offset; bookbinding & related work
PA: Epi Printers, Inc.
  5404 Wayne Rd
  Battle Creek MI 49037
  800 562-9733

(G-6876)
ESCO ENTERPRISES INDIANA INC
Also Called: Earl's Indy
302 Gasoline Aly (46222-4076)
PHONE....................317 241-0318
Fax: 317 247-1128
Thomas Meko, *President*
Mark J Meko, *Vice Pres*
Sara A Meko, *Admin Sec*
EMP: 13
SQ FT: 15,000
SALES (est): 1.4MM **Privately Held**
WEB: www.earlsindy.com
SIC: 3599 7549 Hose, flexible metallic; automotive maintenance services

(G-6877)
ESSENTRA PACKAGING US INC
6454 Saguaro Ct (46268-2545)
PHONE....................317 328-7355
EMP: 10
SALES (corp-wide): 1.3B **Privately Held**
SIC: 2673 Bags: plastic, laminated & coated
HQ: Essentra Packaging U.S. Inc.
  2 Westbrook Corp Ctr
  Westchester IL 60154
  704 418-8692

(G-6878)
ESSILOR LABORATORIES AMER INC
Also Called: Bell Duffens Optical
1718 Lafayette Rd (46222-2809)
PHONE....................317 637-2391
Travis Miller, *General Mgr*
Jennifer Rzeszewski, *General Mgr*
Erick Peterson, *Opers Mgr*
David Goff, *Technician*
EMP: 90 **Privately Held**
WEB: www.crizal.com
SIC: 3851 Eyeglasses, lenses & frames
HQ: Essilor Laboratories Of America, Inc.
  13515 N Stemmons Fwy
  Dallas TX 75234
  972 241-4141

(G-6879)
ESSROC CORP
1051 S Emerson Ave (46203-1606)
PHONE....................317 351-9910
EMP: 9
SALES (corp-wide): 20.3B **Privately Held**
SIC: 3241 Cement, hydraulic
HQ: Essroc Corp.
  3251 Bath Pike
  Nazareth PA 18064
  610 837-6725

(G-6880)
ESTES DESIGN AND MANUFACTURING
470 S Mitthoeffer Rd (46229-3058)
PHONE....................317 899-2203
Fax: 317 898-2034
Larry Estes, *President*
Ron Estes, *Vice Pres*
Mark Visser, *Production*
Greg Gillon, *Purch Mgr*
Tim H Hughes, *Purch Mgr*
EMP: 90
SQ FT: 52,000
SALES (est): 32MM **Privately Held**
WEB: www.estesdm.com
SIC: 3444 Sheet metal specialties, not stamped

(G-6881)
ESTES DESIGNS
7510 E 39th St (46226-5164)
PHONE....................317 899-5556
Roland Smith, *CFO*
Larry Ruble, *Manager*
Christopher Estes, *Manager*
EMP: 4
SALES (est): 499.9K **Privately Held**
SIC: 3398 Metal burning

(G-6882)
ETCHING INDUSTRIES CORPORATION
Also Called: St Reigs Crystal
3233 N Post Rd (46226-6533)
PHONE....................317 591-3500
Fax: 800 969-3824
Richard Firkser, *President*
EMP: 40
SALES (est): 6.9MM **Privately Held**
WEB: www.keepsakebottles.com
SIC: 3499 3231 Novelties & giftware, including trophies; products of purchased glass

(G-6883)
EVERYTHING UNDERGROUND INC
6945 Westlake Rd (46214-3825)
PHONE....................317 491-8148
Lashell Daniels, *CEO*
EMP: 2
SALES (est): 92.7K **Privately Held**
SIC: 7372 Business oriented computer software

(G-6884)
EVOQUA WATER TECHNOLOGIES LLC
6111 Guion Rd (46254-1223)
PHONE....................317 280-4255
EMP: 5
SALES (corp-wide): 1.1B **Publicly Held**
SIC: 3589 Sewage & water treatment equipment

HQ: Evoqua Water Technologies Llc
  210 6th Ave Ste 3300
  Pittsburgh PA 15222
  724 772-0044

(G-6885)
EVOQUA WATER TECHNOLOGIES LLC
6125 Guion Rd (46254-1223)
PHONE....................317 280-4251
Fax: 317 280-4268
Dave Fowler, *Manager*
EMP: 20
SALES (corp-wide): 1.1B **Publicly Held**
SIC: 5074 2821 Water heaters & purification equipment; plastics materials & resins
HQ: Evoqua Water Technologies Llc
  210 6th Ave Ste 3300
  Pittsburgh PA 15222
  724 772-0044

(G-6886)
EWING LIGHT METALS CO INC
Also Called: E L M
3451 Terrace Ave (46203-2247)
PHONE....................317 926-4591
Fax: 317 926-4670
Cayne Inocencio, *President*
Carlos Inocencio, *Vice Pres*
Michelle Inocencio, *Vice Pres*
EMP: 12
SQ FT: 18,000
SALES (est): 1.9MM **Privately Held**
WEB: www.ewinglightmetals.com
SIC: 3365 3366 3369 3322 Aluminum & aluminum-based alloy castings; castings (except die); brass; nonferrous foundries; malleable iron foundries

(G-6887)
EWIRELESS LLC
4625 N Capitol Ave (46208-3553)
PHONE....................317 536-0400
Kirby Goble,
EMP: 3
SALES: 300K **Privately Held**
SIC: 3571 Electronic computers

(G-6888)
EXACTO MACHINE & TOOL INC
3402 W 79th St (46268-1912)
PHONE....................317 872-3136
George Lemcke, *President*
EMP: 5
SQ FT: 1,800
SALES (est): 332.7K **Privately Held**
SIC: 3599 Machine shop, jobbing & repair

(G-6889)
EXACTSEAL INC
7601 E 88th Pl Ste 3b (46256-1396)
PHONE....................317 559-2220
Hiren Jetani, *CEO*
EMP: 2
SALES: 1MM **Privately Held**
SIC: 3053 3052 3069 5085 Gaskets, packing & sealing devices; rubber & plastics hose & beltings; rubber hose; rubber automotive products; rubber goods, mechanical; silicone rubbers

(G-6890)
EXACTTARGET INC (HQ)
20 N Meridian St Ste 200 (46204-3023)
PHONE....................317 423-3928
Marc Benioff, *Ch of Bd*
Andrew J Kofoid, *COO*
Steven A Collins, *CFO*
Timothy B Kopp, *Chief Mktg Ofcr*
Traci M Dolan,
EMP: 145 **EST:** 2000
SQ FT: 66,536
SALES (est): 7.5MM
SALES (corp-wide): 10.4B **Publicly Held**
WEB: www.exacttarget.com
SIC: 7372 Prepackaged software
PA: Salesforce.Com, Inc.
  1 Market Ste 300
  San Francisco CA 94105
  415 901-7000

(G-6891)
EXCEL BUSINESS PRINTING INC
6302 Rucker Rd Ste A (46220-4853)
PHONE....................317 259-1075

Michael R Miller, *President*
EMP: 6
SQ FT: 1,200
SALES: 600K **Privately Held**
SIC: 2752 5112 Commercial printing, lithographic; business forms

(G-6892)
EXECUTIVE MGT SVCS IND INC
1605 Prospect St (46203-2024)
P.O. Box 501818 (46250-6818)
PHONE....................317 594-6000
Brian Wyatt, *Branch Mgr*
EMP: 3
SALES (corp-wide): 205.3MM **Privately Held**
SIC: 3599 Machine & other job shop work
PA: Executive Management Services Of Indiana, Inc.
  4177 N Ems Blvd
  Indianapolis IN 46250
  317 813-1490

(G-6893)
EXELEAD INC
6925 Guion Rd (46268-2582)
PHONE....................317 347-2800
John Rigg, *Vice Pres*
John Jones, *Buyer*
Valarie Gossage, *Human Res Mgr*
Raymond Destefano, *HR Admin*
Tom Busby, *Manager*
EMP: 113
SALES (est): 29.3MM
SALES (corp-wide): 86.5K **Privately Held**
SIC: 2834 Pharmaceutical preparations
HQ: Leadiant Biosciences, Inc.
  9841 Wash Blvd Ste 500
  Gaithersburg MD 20878
  301 948-1041

(G-6894)
EXIDE TECHNOLOGIES
5945 W 84th St Ste B (46278-1397)
PHONE....................317 876-7475
Robbin Neal, *Human Resources*
Rick King, *Manager*
EMP: 93
SALES (corp-wide): 2.6B **Privately Held**
SIC: 3691 Lead acid batteries (storage batteries)
PA: Exide Technologies (Inc.)
  13000 Deerfield Pkwy # 200
  Milton GA 30004
  678 566-9000

(G-6895)
EXOTIC METAL TREATING INC
6234 E Hanna Ave (46203-6129)
PHONE....................317 784-8565
Fax: 317 784-8569
Kathy Susko, *President*
Keith Susko, *Vice Pres*
Keith A Susko, *Manager*
Kelli Hall, *Admin Sec*
▲ **EMP:** 10
SQ FT: 14,000
SALES: 1.5MM **Privately Held**
WEB: www.exoticmetaltreating.com
SIC: 3398 Metal heat treating; brazing (hardening) of metal

(G-6896)
EXPO DESIGNERS CO INC
Also Called: Expodesign
720 S Belmont Ave (46221-1100)
PHONE....................317 784-5610
Mark Thornton, *President*
Manash Sahoo, *Vice Pres*
Samantha Sullivan, *Office Admin*
Galen Conley, *Admin Asst*
EMP: 23
SQ FT: 59,000
SALES (est): 2.4MM **Privately Held**
WEB: www.expodesign.net
SIC: 7389 2399 Design, commercial & industrial; banners, made from fabric; flags, fabric

(G-6897)
EXPRESS BINDINGS
212 W 10th St Ste F130 (46202-5692)
PHONE....................317 269-8114
John Dicklin, *President*
EMP: 5

SALES (est): 551.8K **Privately Held**
SIC: 2789 Bookbinding & related work

(G-6898)
EXTRANET TALENT
3502 Woodview Trce (46268-3181)
PHONE.................................317 362-0140
EMP: 2
SALES (est): 74.4K **Privately Held**
SIC: 2836 Extracts

(G-6899)
F E HARDING PAVING CO INC
5145 E 96th St (46240-1440)
PHONE.................................317 846-7401
Fred Harding, *President*
EMP: 4
SALES (corp-wide): 33.6MM Privately
Held
SIC: 2951 Asphalt paving mixtures &
blocks
PA: F E Harding Paving Co Inc
10151 Hague Rd
Indianapolis IN
317 849-9666

(G-6900)
F ROBERT GARDNER CO INC
1621 E New York St (46201-3095)
PHONE.................................317 634-2333
Fax: 317 634-2334
Brian F Gardner, *President*
Bonnie Gardner, *Corp Secy*
Brian D Gardner, *Vice Pres*
EMP: 9
SQ FT: 12,000
SALES: 600K **Privately Held**
WEB: www.rfginc.com
SIC: 2752 3083 2759 2672 Commercial
printing, offset; laminated plastics plate &
sheet; commercial printing; coated & lami-
nated paper; automotive & apparel trim-
mings

(G-6901)
**FABRICATED STEEL
CORPORATION**
9809 Park Davis Dr (46235-2393)
PHONE.................................317 899-0012
Fax: 317 899-0015
Derek Romeril, *President*
EMP: 7
SQ FT: 20,000
SALES (est): 800K **Privately Held**
SIC: 3535 3441 Conveyors & conveying
equipment; fabricated structural metal

(G-6902)
**FALCON METAL FABRICATION
INC**
2210 W 60th St (46228-1148)
PHONE.................................317 255-9365
Fax: 317 255-9379
Bruce Crum, *President*
Jerry Robertson, *Principal*
EMP: 10
SQ FT: 20,000
SALES (est): 1.7MM **Privately Held**
SIC: 3448 Prefabricated metal buildings

(G-6903)
FAMILY LEISURECOM INC
11811 Pendleton Pike (46236-3910)
PHONE.................................317 823-4448
Kevin Presontanie, *President*
EMP: 5 **EST:** 2011
SALES (est): 1.5MM **Privately Held**
SIC: 5021 3944 Furniture; board games,
puzzles & models, except electronic

(G-6904)
FAMILY VINEYARD
3944 N Delaware St (46205-2650)
PHONE.................................812 322-1720
Eric B Weddle, *Principal*
EMP: 4
SALES (est): 307.1K **Privately Held**
SIC: 2084 Wines

(G-6905)
FARIS MAILING INC
701 N Holt Rd Ste 3 (46222-3455)
PHONE.................................317 246-3315
Fax: 317 246-3330
Robert L Faris Jr, *President*

Jane Faris Parsons, *Treasurer*
Pat Adam, *Human Resources*
EMP: 15
SQ FT: 25,000
SALES: 3.9MM **Privately Held**
WEB: www.farismailing.com
SIC: 7331 2752 Mailing service; commer-
cial printing, lithographic

(G-6906)
FATHEADZ INC
Also Called: Fatheadz Eyewear
1125 W 16th St (46202-2107)
PHONE.................................800 561-6640
Eric Elmore, *CEO*
Michael Hayden, *CFO*
Andrew Poe, *Controller*
Justin Myers, *Mktg Dir*
Sam David, *Marketing Mgr*
▲ **EMP:** 10
SQ FT: 15,000
SALES (est): 2.6MM **Privately Held**
SIC: 3851 Glasses, sun or glare

(G-6907)
FEDERAL-MOGUL LLC
8325 N Norfolk St (46268-1695)
PHONE.................................317 875-7259
Fax: 317 876-7207
Trish Drews, *Principal*
Chuck Kerschen, *Branch Mgr*
EMP: 270
SALES (corp-wide): 21.7B **Publicly Held**
SIC: 3714 Motor vehicle parts & acces-
sories
HQ: Federal-Mogul Llc
27300 W 11 Mile Rd # 101
Southfield MI 48034

(G-6908)
**FEDEX OFFICE & PRINT SVCS
INC**
120 Monument Cir Ste 107 (46204-4902)
PHONE.................................317 631-6862
Joe Rutter, *Manager*
EMP: 20
SALES (corp-wide): 65.4B **Publicly Held**
SIC: 7334 2791 2789 2752 Photocopying
& duplicating services; typesetting; book-
binding & related work; commercial print-
ing, lithographic
HQ: Fedex Office And Print Services, Inc.
7900 Legacy Dr
Plano TX 75024
214 550-7000

(G-6909)
**FEDEX OFFICE & PRINT SVCS
INC**
10 S West St (46204-2709)
PHONE.................................317 974-0378
Fax: 317 974-0521
Maverick Zander, *Manager*
EMP: 11
SALES (corp-wide): 65.4B **Publicly Held**
SIC: 7389 7334 5099 2752 Packaging &
labeling services; photocopying & dupli-
cating services; signs, except electric;
commercial printing, lithographic
HQ: Fedex Office And Print Services, Inc.
7900 Legacy Dr
Plano TX 75024
214 550-7000

(G-6910)
**FEDEX OFFICE & PRINT SVCS
INC**
241 W Washington St (46204-3435)
PHONE.................................317 917-1529
Fax: 317 917-1570
EMP: 11
SALES (corp-wide): 65.4B **Publicly Held**
SIC: 7389 7334 5099 2752 Packaging &
labeling services; photocopying & dupli-
cating services; signs, except electric;
commercial printing, lithographic
HQ: Fedex Office And Print Services, Inc.
7900 Legacy Dr
Plano TX 75024
214 550-7000

(G-6911)
**FEDEX OFFICE & PRINT SVCS
INC**
6091 E 82nd St (46250-1524)
PHONE.................................317 849-9683
Tony Pennington, *Manager*
EMP: 20
SALES (corp-wide): 65.4B **Publicly Held**
WEB: www.kinkos.com
SIC: 7334 2791 2789 Photocopying & du-
plicating services; typesetting; bookbind-
ing & related work
HQ: Fedex Office And Print Services, Inc.
7900 Legacy Dr
Plano TX 75024
214 550-7000

(G-6912)
**FEDEX OFFICE & PRINT SVCS
INC**
3269 W 86th St Ste A (46268-3822)
PHONE.................................317 337-2679
Fred Lechance, *Manager*
EMP: 20
SALES (corp-wide): 65.4B **Publicly Held**
WEB: www.kinkos.com
SIC: 7334 2791 2789 2672 Photocopying
& duplicating services; typesetting; book-
binding & related work; coated & lami-
nated paper
HQ: Fedex Office And Print Services, Inc.
7900 Legacy Dr
Plano TX 75024
214 550-7000

(G-6913)
**FEDEX OFFICE & PRINT SVCS
INC**
5030 W Pike Plaza Rd (46254-3001)
PHONE.................................317 295-1063
Micah Cain, *Manager*
EMP: 3
SALES (corp-wide): 65.4B **Publicly Held**
WEB: www.kinkos.com
SIC: 7334 2791 2789 Photocopying & du-
plicating services; typesetting; bookbind-
ing & related work
HQ: Fedex Office And Print Services, Inc.
7900 Legacy Dr
Plano TX 75024
214 550-7000

(G-6914)
**FEDEX OFFICE & PRINT SVCS
INC**
1050 Broad Ripple Ave (46220-2035)
PHONE.................................317 251-2406
Laura Andersen-Bailes, *Manager*
EMP: 13
SALES (corp-wide): 65.4B **Publicly Held**
WEB: www.kinkos.com
SIC: 7334 2791 2789 2759 Photocopying
& duplicating services; typesetting; book-
binding & related work; commercial print-
ing
HQ: Fedex Office And Print Services, Inc.
7900 Legacy Dr
Plano TX 75024
214 550-7000

(G-6915)
**FEDEX OFFICE & PRINT SVCS
INC**
8231 Us 31 S (46227-6228)
PHONE.................................317 885-6480
Mike Ficher, *Branch Mgr*
EMP: 24
SALES (corp-wide): 65.4B **Publicly Held**
WEB: www.kinkos.com
SIC: 7334 2791 2789 Photocopying & du-
plicating services; typesetting; bookbind-
ing & related work
HQ: Fedex Office And Print Services, Inc.
7900 Legacy Dr
Plano TX 75024
214 550-7000

(G-6916)
FERGUSON
1057 E 54th St Ste A (46220-3590)
PHONE.................................317 254-5965
EMP: 2

SALES (est): 160.3K **Privately Held**
SIC: 5085 5074 3432 Industrial supplies;
plumbing fittings & supplies; plumbing fixture fittings & trim

(G-6917)
FIBERGLAS & PLASTIC FABG
2832 N Webster Ave (46219-1013)
PHONE.................................317 549-1779
Fax: 317 546-3682
Karl A Spandau, *President*
George L Craig, *Vice Pres*
EMP: 20
SQ FT: 21,000
SALES: 1MM **Privately Held**
SIC: 3089 Plastic processing

(G-6918)
**FIBERGLASS ENGRG & DESIGN
INC**
Also Called: F.E.D.
7421 Crawfordsville Rd (46214-1571)
P.O. Box 34154 (46234-0154)
PHONE.................................317 293-0002
Michael Moody, *President*
EMP: 9
SQ FT: 12,000
SALES (est): 1.2MM **Privately Held**
SIC: 2531 Vehicle furniture

(G-6919)
**FIDELITY DENTAL HANDPIECE
SVC**
4330 Black Oak Dr (46228-3110)
PHONE.................................317 254-0277
Francis Feeney, *Owner*
EMP: 2
SALES (est): 135.2K **Privately Held**
SIC: 7699 3843 Dental instrument repair;
hand pieces & parts, dental

(G-6920)
FINELINE DIGITAL GROUP INC
8081 Zionsville Rd (46268-1624)
PHONE.................................317 872-4490
Richard Miller, *President*
Dan Clark, *VP Opers*
Rick Kappel, *Production*
Rich Mathiesen, *VP Sales*
EMP: 20
SALES (est): 1.7MM **Privately Held**
SIC: 2791 Typesetting

(G-6921)
**FINELINE GRAPHICS
INCORPORATED**
Also Called: Fineline Printing Group
8081 Zionsville Rd (46268-1624)
PHONE.................................317 872-4490
Fax: 317 870-4410
Richard Miller, *President*
Paul Doerfler, *Vice Pres*
Lisa Young, *Vice Pres*
Rich Mathiesen, *Accounts Mgr*
Guy Vreeman, *Director*
EMP: 56
SQ FT: 48,000
SALES (est): 19.2MM **Privately Held**
WEB: www.finelink.com
SIC: 2752 7331 2791 Commercial print-
ing, offset; mailing service; typesetting

(G-6922)
FINISH ALTERNATIVES
705 Northfield Ct (46227-1617)
PHONE.................................317 440-2899
Robert Lyle, *Owner*
EMP: 2
SALES: 250K **Privately Held**
SIC: 2434 Wood kitchen cabinets

(G-6923)
FIRESMOKE ORG
323 N Delaware St (46204-1801)
PHONE.................................317 690-2542
Jason Krusen, *Vice Pres*
EMP: 2
SALES (est): 133.7K **Privately Held**
SIC: 2515 Foundations & platforms

(G-6924)
**FIRESTONE INDUSTRIAL PDTS
INC (DH)**
250 W 96th St Fl 2 (46260-1316)
PHONE.................................317 575-7000

G
E
O
G
R
A
P
H
I
C

Scott Damon, *President*
Michael Sigillito, *Vice Pres*
Jose Anes, *Treasurer*
Brian Fritts, *Admin Sec*
EMP: 2
SALES (est): 590.9K
SALES (corp-wide): 32.5B **Privately Held**
SIC: 3714 Motor vehicle parts & accessories

(G-6925)
FIRST CLASS PRINTING
6800 E 30th St (46219-1104)
PHONE................................317 808-2222
Mark Zainey, *Principal*
EMP: 2
SALES (est): 121.3K **Privately Held**
SIC: 2759 Commercial printing

(G-6926)
FIRST DATABANK INC
500 E 96th St Ste 500 # 500 (46240-3767)
P.O. Box 40930 (46240-0930)
PHONE................................317 571-7200
Fax: 317 571-7255
Pete Curnutt, *General Mgr*
Susie Rhodes, *Research*
Mary Dial, *Branch Mgr*
Kathy Chadwick, *Manager*
Pankaj Rastogi, *Analyst*
EMP: 7
SALES (corp-wide): 6.7B **Privately Held**
SIC: 2741 7375 Technical manuals: publishing only, not printed on site; micropublishing; information retrieval services; data base information retrieval
HQ: First Databank, Inc.
701 Gateway Blvd Ste 600
South San Francisco CA 94080
800 633-3453

(G-6927)
FIRST QUALITY PRINTING INC
8745 Rawles Ave Ste D (46219-7831)
PHONE................................317 506-8633
Keith Rand, *President*
Joyce Rand, *Vice Pres*
EMP: 3
SQ FT: 2,000
SALES (est): 368.8K **Privately Held**
SIC: 2752 2791 Commercial printing, offset; typesetting

(G-6928)
FIRST QUALITY PRINTING CENTER
5498 Emerson Way (46226-1408)
PHONE................................317 546-5531
Fax: 317 255-9787
Joyce Rand, *Principal*
EMP: 2
SALES (est): 118.3K **Privately Held**
SIC: 2752 Commercial printing, offset

(G-6929)
FISERV INC
2307 Directors Row (46241-4905)
PHONE................................317 576-6700
Fax: 317 576-6730
Kevin Wachtel, *Senior VP*
EMP: 400
SQ FT: 100,000
SALES (corp-wide): 5.7B **Publicly Held**
WEB: www.fiserv.com
SIC: 2759 2752 Commercial printing; commercial printing, lithographic
PA: Fiserv, Inc.
255 Fiserv Dr
Brookfield WI 53045
262 879-5000

(G-6930)
FISHER CLINICAL SERVICES INC
1220 W Morris St (46221-1710)
PHONE................................317 277-0337
Jen Griffith, *General Mgr*
EMP: 100
SALES (corp-wide): 20.9B **Publicly Held**
SIC: 2834 Pharmaceutical preparations
HQ: Fisher Clinical Services Inc.
7554 Schantz Rd
Allentown PA 18106
610 391-0800

(G-6931)
FLAG & BANNER COMPANY INC
Also Called: Fabco Publishing
5450 Lafayette Rd Ste 5 (46254-1655)
PHONE................................317 299-4880
Fax: 317 299-4896
Karen E Bush, *President*
Clifton H Bush IV, *Vice Pres*
Nancy Wood, *Admin Sec*
EMP: 10
SQ FT: 3,500
SALES (est): 1.8MM **Privately Held**
WEB: www.fabco-usa.com
SIC: 5131 5999 5199 2396 Flags & banners; flags; banners; advertising specialties; screen printing on fabric articles; signs & advertising specialties; architectural metalwork

(G-6932)
FLAWLESS BEAUTY LLC
4951 Tuscany Ln (46254-5459)
PHONE................................317 914-7952
Elaine M Andrews, *Owner*
EMP: 2
SALES (est): 81.5K **Privately Held**
SIC: 3911 5999 Jewelry apparel; cosmetics

(G-6933)
FLEMING ASSOC CALIBRATION INC
Also Called: Fleming Air Flow
1060 N Capitol Ave E100 (46204-1044)
PHONE................................317 631-4605
Fax: 317 631-4611
Ronald J Fleming, *President*
EMP: 8
SQ FT: 2,600
SALES: 800K **Privately Held**
SIC: 3829 Vibration meters, analyzers & calibrators

(G-6934)
FLETCHS APPLE LANE
5441 Senour Rd (46239-1933)
PHONE................................317 489-2697
EMP: 2
SALES (est): 85.9K **Privately Held**
SIC: 3571 Personal computers (microcomputers)

(G-6935)
FLEX-TECH INC
5108 Massachusetts Ave (46218-2418)
PHONE................................317 546-0183
Fax: 317 549-2211
Steven R Brandhoff, *President*
EMP: 15
SQ FT: 8,000
SALES (est): 2.4MM **Privately Held**
SIC: 3585 Refrigeration & heating equipment

(G-6936)
FLINT GROUP US LLC
Also Called: Flint Group Print Media N Amer
4910 W 78th St (46268-4169)
PHONE................................317 471-8435
David Van Blarcum, *Plant Mgr*
John Louzon, *Opers Mgr*
William A Tasseff, *Sales & Mktg St*
Todd Miller, *Accounts Exec*
John Weber, *Accounts Exec*
EMP: 34
SQ FT: 20,000
SALES (corp-wide): 3.5B **Privately Held**
WEB: www.flintink.com
SIC: 2893 Printing ink; lithographic ink
PA: Flint Group Us Llc
14909 N Beck Rd
Plymouth MI 48170
734 781-4600

(G-6937)
FLINT GROUP US LLC
Also Called: Flint Ink North America Div
4910 W 78th St (46268-4169)
PHONE................................317 870-4422
Fax: 317 870-4426
Dave Foster, *Sales/Mktg Mgr*
Marcia Hodges, *Office Mgr*
EMP: 30
SALES (corp-wide): 3.5B **Privately Held**
WEB: www.flintink.com
SIC: 2893 Printing ink

PA: Flint Group Us Llc
14909 N Beck Rd
Plymouth MI 48170
734 781-4600

(G-6938)
FLO REALTY LLC
1 Indiana Sq (46204-2004)
PHONE................................317 636-6481
Ann Page, *Principal*
EMP: 2
SALES (est): 87.6K **Privately Held**
SIC: 3949 Batons

(G-6939)
FLOORTECH
1280 W Southport Rd (46217-4175)
PHONE................................317 887-6825
Fax: 317 887-6886
Jeff Montfort, *Owner*
EMP: 5
SALES: 950K **Privately Held**
SIC: 2426 Flooring, hardwood

(G-6940)
FLUID HANDLING TECHNOLOGY INC
7692 Zionsville Rd (46268-2173)
PHONE................................317 216-9629
Tim Burlingame, *General Mgr*
Stephen Burlingame, *Opers Mgr*
Jim Betz,
EMP: 4
SALES (est): 2MM **Privately Held**
SIC: 5051 3069 Tubing, metal; tubing, rubber

(G-6941)
FLUTES INC (PA)
8252 Zionsville Rd (46268-1627)
PHONE................................317 870-6010
Tony Reiley, *President*
Jack Schwarz, *Principal*
Terry Walles, *Principal*
Jeffrey Schwarz, *Vice Pres*
Kevin Collins, *Opers Mgr*
EMP: 71 **EST:** 2006
SQ FT: 160,000
SALES: 80MM **Privately Held**
WEB: www.flutesllc.com
SIC: 2679 Corrugated paper: made from purchased material

(G-6942)
FLYNN MEDIA LLC
Also Called: Flynn Interactive
9334 Champton Dr (46256-1061)
P.O. Box 503068 (46250-8068)
PHONE................................317 536-2972
Patrick Flynn, *CEO*
EMP: 3
SALES: 30K **Privately Held**
SIC: 7371 7372 7373 Computer software systems analysis & design, custom; computer software writing services; computer software development; business oriented computer software; computer integrated systems design

(G-6943)
FOAMCRAFT INC (PA)
Also Called: Bestway Foam
9230 Harrison Park Ct (46216-1090)
PHONE................................317 545-3626
Fax: 317 543-3416
Robert W Elliott, *President*
Robert B Green, *Vice Pres*
Michael D Rich, *VP Mfg*
Jennifer E Chapman, *Treasurer*
▲ **EMP:** 180
SQ FT: 48,000
SALES (est): 69MM **Privately Held**
SIC: 3086 Plastics foam products

(G-6944)
FOCUS SURGERY INC
4000 Pendleton Way (46226-5224)
PHONE................................317 541-1580
Fax: 317 541-1581
Narendra T Sanghvi, *President*
EMP: 16
SQ FT: 7,400
SALES (est): 2.8MM **Privately Held**
WEB: www.focus-surgery.com
SIC: 3845 Ultrasonic medical equipment, except cleaning

PA: Sonacare Medical, Llc
10130 Perimeter Pkwy # 250
Charlotte NC 28216

(G-6945)
FOOD SPECIALTIES INC
Also Called: Tasty Rich
1727 Expo Ln (46214-2334)
PHONE................................317 271-0862
John Bradshaw, *President*
Wayne Johnson, *Sales Staff*
Ned Hornback, *Admin Sec*
EMP: 3 **EST:** 1941
SQ FT: 18,000
SALES: 500K **Privately Held**
SIC: 2035 Dressings, salad: raw & cooked (except dry mixes); mustard, prepared (wet)

(G-6946)
FOODS PEER
1825 Stout Field Ter (46241-4028)
PHONE................................317 735-4283
EMP: 3 **EST:** 2011
SALES (est): 262.5K **Privately Held**
SIC: 2011 Meat packing plants

(G-6947)
FOOT LOCKER RETAIL INC
6020 E 82nd St Ste 632 (46250-0029)
PHONE................................317 578-1892
Miranda Stockdall, *Branch Mgr*
EMP: 6
SALES (corp-wide): 7.7B **Publicly Held**
SIC: 3949 Sporting & athletic goods
HQ: Foot Locker Retail, Inc.
330 W 34th St
New York NY 10001

(G-6948)
FORECAST SALES INC
2719 Tobey Dr (46219-1417)
PHONE................................317 829-0147
Brian L McCoy, *President*
Steven L McCoy, *Vice Pres*
Ben Jones, *Design Engr*
Sally Andis, *Office Mgr*
Curtis Sanchez, *Creative Dir*
EMP: 5
SALES (est): 117.1K **Privately Held**
SIC: 3589 Sandblasting equipment

(G-6949)
FOREMOST FARMS USA COOPERATIVE
7202 E 87th St Ste 112 (46256-1200)
PHONE................................317 842-7755
Fax: 317 841-4192
Gregg Elliott, *Manager*
EMP: 7 **Privately Held**
WEB: www.foremostfarms.com
SIC: 2022 Cheese, natural & processed
PA: Foremost Farms Usa Cooperative
E10889 Penny Ln
Baraboo WI 53913

(G-6950)
FORGET ME NOT PRINTING LTD
7858 Bosinney Cir (46256-4027)
PHONE................................317 508-7401
Kathleen L McKinney, *Principal*
Kathleen McKinney, *Principal*
EMP: 2
SALES (est): 163.5K **Privately Held**
SIC: 2752 Commercial printing, lithographic

(G-6951)
FOUR POINTS DEVELOPMENT CORP
Also Called: Signs Now
6368 Harrison Ridge Blvd (46236-7816)
PHONE................................317 357-3275
Fax: 317 357-7484
Dave Humes, *President*
Lil Jett, *Corp Secy*
Ellen Humes, *Vice Pres*
Dale Jett, *Vice Pres*
EMP: 16
SQ FT: 2,700
SALES (est): 100K **Privately Held**
SIC: 5921 3993 Liquor stores; signs, not made in custom sign painting shops

(G-6952)
FOURTH SHIFT INC
2145 Ransdell St (46225-1865)
PHONE..................................317 567-3072
David Hunt, *Principal*
EMP: 15
SALES (est): 2.2MM **Privately Held**
SIC: 2431 Staircases, stairs & railings

(G-6953)
FOX STUDIOS INC
6027 Gladden Dr (46220-2567)
PHONE..................................317 253-0135
Fax: 317 253-5647
Clare Fox Acheson, *President*
Mary Fox, *Corp Secy*
Ann Fox Clark, *Vice Pres*
EMP: 12
SQ FT: 5,500
SALES (est): 600K **Privately Held**
WEB: www.foxstudios.com
SIC: 3211 Flat glass; plate & sheet
glass; window glass, clear & colored; an-
tique glass; products of purchased glass

(G-6954)
FOY INDUSTRIES
6953 Dean Rd (46220-3809)
PHONE..................................317 727-3905
Dave Strobel, *Principal*
EMP: 2
SALES (est): 71.4K **Privately Held**
SIC: 3999 Manufacturing industries

(G-6955)
FR CHINOOK LLC
7441 Chinook Cir (46219-7534)
PHONE..................................317 356-1666
Adam McNeal, *Partner*
EMP: 4
SALES (est): 303.7K **Privately Held**
SIC: 2451 Mobile homes

(G-6956)
FRAKES ENGINEERING INC
7950 Castleway Dr Ste 160 (46250-1994)
PHONE..................................317 577-3000
Fax: 317 577-3005
James L Frakes, *President*
Scott Newsom, *Business Mgr*
Anthony Sebastian, *Business Mgr*
Joe Worland, *Business Mgr*
Lisa Frakes-Bratcher, *Corp Secy*
EMP: 30
SQ FT: 22,000
SALES (est): 8.3MM **Privately Held**
WEB: www.frakesengineering.com
SIC: 7373 3625 Systems integration serv-
ices; relays & industrial controls

(G-6957)
**FRANK WISS RACG
COMPONENTS INC**
140 Gasoline Aly (46222-3965)
PHONE..................................317 248-4764
Fax: 317 484-1736
Frank W Weiss, *President*
Wade Weiss, *Vice Pres*
Shawna Greves, *Admin Sec*
Christina Weiss, *Admin Sec*
EMP: 23
SQ FT: 8,800
SALES: 2.1MM **Privately Held**
WEB: www.fwrc.com
SIC: 7539 3714 5013 Machine shop, au-
tomotive; motor vehicle parts & acces-
sories; motor vehicle supplies & new
parts

(G-6958)
FRANKINSTEIN INDUSTRIES INC
6800 E 30th St (46219-1104)
PHONE..................................217 918-4548
Franklin Robison, *Principal*
EMP: 2
SALES (est): 104.2K **Privately Held**
SIC: 3999 Manufacturing industries

(G-6959)
FRANKLIN BARRY GALLERY
Also Called: Frame Shop, The
617 Massachusetts Ave (46204-1606)
PHONE..................................317 822-8455
Don Elliot, *President*
EMP: 2

SALES: 170K **Privately Held**
SIC: 5999 8999 2752 Art, picture frames
& decorations; actuarial consultant; advertising posters, lithographed

(G-6960)
**FRANKLIN TOWNSHIP CIVIC
LEAGUE**
Also Called: FRANKLIN TOWNSHIP IN-
FORMER
8822 Southeastern Ave (46239-1341)
PHONE..................................317 862-1774
Kathy Burton, *President*
EMP: 4
SALES: 105.5K **Privately Held**
SIC: 2711 Newspapers

(G-6961)
FRAZIER PRODUCTS
3445 S Harding St (46217-3141)
PHONE..................................317 781-9781
Edward Frazier, *Owner*
EMP: 10
SALES (est): 450.1K **Privately Held**
WEB: www.frazierproducts.com
SIC: 2399 3523 Horse harnesses & riding
crops, etc.: non-leather; farm machinery &
equipment

(G-6962)
FRED WEBER INC
2050 S Harding St (46221-1948)
PHONE..................................317 262-4920
Douglas K Weible, *CEO*
EMP: 15
SALES (corp-wide): 368.8MM **Privately
Held**
SIC: 3272 5074 Pipe, concrete or lined
with concrete; pipes & fittings, plastic
PA: Fred Weber, Inc.
2320 Creve Coeur Mill Rd
Maryland Heights MO 63043
314 344-0070

(G-6963)
FREEDOM CORRUGATED LLC
5505 W 74th St (46268-4184)
PHONE..................................317 290-1140
Thomas E Bennett, *Principal*
EMP: 5
SALES (est): 416.9K **Privately Held**
SIC: 2653 Corrugated & solid fiber boxes

(G-6964)
**FREIJE TREATMENT SYSTEMS
INC**
7435 E 86th St (46256-1207)
PHONE..................................317 508-3848
Gregory Lloyd, *Principal*
EMP: 2
SALES (est): 79.9K **Privately Held**
SIC: 3589 Service industry machinery

(G-6965)
FRONTIER ENGINEERING
12469 E 65th St (46236-9720)
PHONE..................................317 823-6885
Fax: 317 823-6005
Steve Jourdan, *Owner*
Lila Jourdan, *Owner*
EMP: 2
SALES: 50K **Privately Held**
SIC: 3559 3535 ; unit handling conveying
systems

(G-6966)
**FUEL PRFMCE ENHANCEMENT
LLC**
10640 Deme Dr Ste H (46236-4713)
PHONE..................................317 979-2316
Kreshaune Martinez, *General Mgr*
EMP: 5
SALES (est): 336.8K **Privately Held**
SIC: 2869 Fuels

(G-6967)
FUEL RECOVERY SERVICE INC
125 W South St Unit 2690 (46206-4696)
P.O. Box 2690 (46206-2690)
PHONE..................................317 372-3029
Richard Raymond, *CEO*
EMP: 2
SALES (est): 200.4K **Privately Held**
SIC: 2911 Oils, fuel

(G-6968)
FULL COLOR DIRECT LLC
3808 Churchman Woods Blvd
(46203-6094)
PHONE..................................317 538-4500
Tracy McClain,
Marcia McClain,
EMP: 7
SQ FT: 3,000
SALES: 410.1K **Privately Held**
WEB: www.fullcolordirect.com
SIC: 2759 Commercial printing

(G-6969)
FUNDEX GAMES LTD
Also Called: Great American Puzzle Factory
1901 W 16th St (46202-2034)
PHONE..................................317 248-1080
Fax: 317 248-1086
Carl E Voigt IV, *President*
Chip Voigt, *President*
Pete Voigt, *Vice Pres*
▲ EMP: 60
SQ FT: 10,000
SALES (est): 19.9MM **Privately Held**
WEB: www.fundexgames.com
SIC: 3944 Board games, children's &
adults'

(G-6970)
**FURNITURE SALES &
MARKETING**
7219 Knollvalley Ln (46256-2190)
PHONE..................................317 849-1508
Don Morris, *Owner*
EMP: 2
SALES (est): 113.5K **Privately Held**
SIC: 2512 Upholstered household furniture

(G-6971)
FUTON FACTORY INC (PA)
Also Called: Eclipse Imports
5920 E 34th St (46218-1809)
PHONE..................................317 549-8639
Margaret Brady, *President*
Darwin Bostrom, *Vice Pres*
EMP: 12
SQ FT: 49,000
SALES (est): 5.5MM **Privately Held**
WEB: www.futonfactory.com
SIC: 5712 2515 Bedding & bedsprings;
mattresses & bedsprings

(G-6972)
FUTURETEK
535 N Livingston Ave (46222-3401)
PHONE..................................317 631-0098
Mitchell Lewis, *Owner*
EMP: 2
SALES (est): 146.9K **Privately Held**
SIC: 3571 Electronic computers

(G-6973)
FUZION PRODUCTS LLC
6312 Southeastern Ave (46203-5828)
PHONE..................................317 536-0745
Scott Brown, *CEO*
Chris Felger, *CFO*
EMP: 3
SALES (est): 228.4K **Privately Held**
SIC: 3315 Nails, steel: wire or cut

(G-6974)
G & G METAL SPINNERS INC
1717 Cornell Ave (46202-1898)
PHONE..................................317 923-3225
Fax: 317 923-9507
Kenneth T Young, *President*
Scott Kauffman, *Marketing Staff*
Linda J Young, *Admin Sec*
EMP: 20 EST: 1949
SQ FT: 50,000
SALES (est): 4.3MM **Privately Held**
WEB: www.ggmetalspinners.com
SIC: 3542 3444 Spinning machines,
metal; sheet metalwork

(G-6975)
**G K OPTICAL COMPANY INC
(DH)**
2902 N Mitthoeffer Pl (46229-1398)
PHONE..................................317 881-2585
Fax: 317 881-6950
Mark Haubry, *Manager*
Betty Peery, *Admin Sec*

EMP: 42
SQ FT: 15,000
SALES (est): 2.3MM **Privately Held**
WEB: www.gkoptical.com
SIC: 3827 3851 3229 Optical instruments
& lenses; ophthalmic goods; pressed &
blown glass
HQ: Essilor Of America, Inc.
13555 N Stemmons Fwy
Dallas TX 75234
214 496-4000

(G-6976)
G L D INC (PA)
6427 N Ewing St (46220-4425)
PHONE..................................317 924-7981
David Combs, *President*
Larry Ostendorf, *Vice Pres*
EMP: 3
SQ FT: 1,800
SALES: 240K **Privately Held**
SIC: 3949 Skin diving equipment, scuba
type

(G-6977)
G THRAPP JEWELERS INC
5609 N Illinois St (46208-1554)
PHONE..................................317 255-5555
Fax: 317 253-0760
Gary Thrapp, *President*
Barbara Thrapp, *Corp Secy*
Ryan Thrapp, *Buyer*
EMP: 21
SQ FT: 2,800
SALES (est): 3.3MM **Privately Held**
WEB: www.gthrapp.com
SIC: 5944 3911 Jewelry, precious stones
& precious metals; jewelry, precious metal

(G-6978)
GAC CHEMICAL CORPORATION
Also Called: General Alum & Chemical
1598 S Senate Ave (46225-1516)
PHONE..................................317 917-0319
Fax: 317 917-0322
Chalie Osbourne, *Manager*
EMP: 6 **Privately Held**
SIC: 2819 Aluminum compounds
PA: Gac Chemical Corporation
34 Kidder Point Rd
Searsport ME 04974

(G-6979)
GALE ENAMELING CO INC
10095 Old National Rd (46231-1990)
PHONE..................................317 839-7474
Fax: 317 839-8493
Curtis Ping, *President*
Doreen Ping, *Vice Pres*
Samuel Ping, *Treasurer*
EMP: 8 EST: 1971
SQ FT: 6,000
SALES: 240K **Privately Held**
SIC: 3479 Coating of metals & formed
products

(G-6980)
GAME VAULT
3734 Pursley Ln (46235-9102)
PHONE..................................317 209-7795
EMP: 3
SALES (est): 237.1K **Privately Held**
SIC: 3272 Burial vaults, concrete or pre-
cast terrazzo

(G-6981)
GAMEOTO LLC
3400 Bloomsbury Ln (46228)
PHONE..................................317 883-9322
John Justice,
EMP: 2
SALES (est): 74K **Privately Held**
SIC: 3944 Games, toys & children's vehi-
cles

(G-6982)
**GAMMONS METAL & MFG CO
INC**
Also Called: Colorworks
2900 N Richardt Ave (46219-1119)
PHONE..................................317 546-7091
Jeffery F Slipher, *President*
Kipp Keller, *Facilities Mgr*
Jeff Slipher, *Human Res Dir*
Wade Yensel, *Sales Mgr*
▲ EMP: 54

SQ FT: 33,600
SALES (est): 14.8MM **Privately Held**
WEB: www.gammonsmetal.com
SIC: 3444 3469 3479 7389 Sheet metalwork; stamping metal for the trade; coating of metals & formed products; metal cutting services; special dies, tools, jigs & fixtures; architectural metalwork

(G-6983)
GAPCO INC
1817 Inisheer Ct (46217-5430)
PHONE.............................317 787-6440
Fax: 317 787-6476
Gary C Gray, *President*
EMP: 7 EST: 1952
SQ FT: 7,023
SALES (est): 730.8K **Privately Held**
SIC: 3451 Screw machine products

(G-6984)
GARDNER GLASS PRODUCTS INC
Also Called: Division 60
1705 Lafayette Rd (46222-2808)
PHONE.............................317 464-0881
Pamela Harris, *Manager*
EMP: 14
SALES (corp-wide): 104.7MM **Privately Held**
SIC: 3231 Products of purchased glass
PA: Gardner Glass Products, Inc.
    301 Elkin Hwy
    North Wilkesboro NC 28659
    336 651-9300

(G-6985)
GARRITY STONE INC
3137 N Ritter Ave (46218-2502)
PHONE.............................317 546-0893
Brandon Garrity, *President*
Kenneth Kalal, *Vice Pres*
EMP: 3
SALES (est): 569K **Privately Held**
SIC: 1411 5032 Dimension stone; aggregate

(G-6986)
GARRITY TOOL COMPANY LLC
3555 Developers Rd Ste A (46227-3577)
PHONE.............................317 541-1400
Fax: 317 541-8930
Betty Garrity, *CEO*
Donald Garrity, *President*
Michael Ottenweller, *President*
Dwight Griggs, *COO*
Tony Parsley, *Purch Mgr*
EMP: 65
SQ FT: 45,000
SALES (est): 14.1MM
SALES (corp-wide): 50.4MM **Privately Held**
WEB: www.garritytoolcompany.com
SIC: 3599 Machine shop, jobbing & repair
PA: Ottenweller Co., Inc.
    3011 Congressional Pkwy
    Fort Wayne IN 46808
    260 484-3166

(G-6987)
GC SOLUTIONS INC
Also Called: Fastsigns
3702 W 86th St Ste B (46268-1903)
PHONE.............................317 334-1149
August Ciresi, *President*
EMP: 4
SQ FT: 6,600
SALES (est): 324.1K **Privately Held**
SIC: 3993 Signs & advertising specialties

(G-6988)
GE POWER ELECTRONICS INC
3148 E 48th St (46205-1623)
PHONE.............................317 259-9264
EMP: 4
SALES (corp-wide): 122B **Publicly Held**
SIC: 3661 Telephone & telegraph apparatus
HQ: Ge Power Electronics, Inc.
    601 Shiloh Rd
    Plano TX 75074
    972 244-9288

(G-6989)
GEIGER & PETERS INC
761 S Sherman Dr (46203-1584)
P.O. Box 33807 (46203-0807)
PHONE.............................317 322-7740
Fax: 317 359-9525
Stephen H Kitter, *President*
James Colzani, *President*
Robert Elsner, *President*
Carl Peters, *Chairman*
Barry Hochstedler, *Vice Pres*
EMP: 62 EST: 1905
SQ FT: 130,000
SALES (est): 23.9MM **Privately Held**
SIC: 3441 Building components, structural steel

(G-6990)
GEIST BIKE AND HOBBY COMPANY
8150 Oaklandon Rd Ste 103 (46236-7522)
PHONE.............................317 855-1346
Margaret Corey, *President*
EMP: 5
SQ FT: 3,000
SALES (est): 195.4K **Privately Held**
SIC: 3944 5941 5945 7699 Games, toys & children's vehicles; sporting goods & bicycle shops; hobby, toy & game shops; recreational sporting equipment repair services; fitness & sporting goods, mail order

(G-6991)
GENER8 LLC
1901 W 16th St (46202-2034)
PHONE.............................317 253-8737
Carl E Voigt IV, *Mng Member*
EMP: 7
SALES (est): 1.2MM **Privately Held**
SIC: 3944 5092 Games, toys & children's vehicles; toys & games

(G-6992)
GENERAL AUTOMATION COMPANY
9325 Uptown Dr Ste 700 (46256-1079)
PHONE.............................317 849-7483
Gabriel Effing, *President*
Nancy Smith, *General Mgr*
Jason Hart, *Engineer*
Bill Gurney, *Marketing Staff*
EMP: 10
SQ FT: 3,300
SALES (est): 1.2MM **Privately Held**
WEB: www.aicweb.net
SIC: 3625 8742 Relays & industrial controls; automation & robotics consultant

(G-6993)
GENERAL CABLE INDUSTRIES INC
Also Called: Indianapolis, In Plant
7950 Rockville Rd (46214-3107)
PHONE.............................317 271-8447
Buck Wright, *Plant Mgr*
William Wright, *Manager*
EMP: 45
SQ FT: 45,000
SALES (corp-wide): 1.3B **Privately Held**
WEB: www.generalcable.com
SIC: 3357 Nonferrous wiredrawing & insulating
HQ: General Cable Industries, Inc.
    4 Tesseneer Dr
    Highland Heights KY 41076

(G-6994)
GENERAL CABLE INDUSTRIES INC
Also Called: In, Technology Center
7920 Rockville Rd (46214-3107)
PHONE.............................317 271-8447
Mark Easter, *Engineer*
Daniel Jessop, *Branch Mgr*
Sherrie Vincent, *Manager*
EMP: 45
SQ FT: 50,000
SALES (corp-wide): 1.3B **Privately Held**
WEB: www.generalcable.com
SIC: 3357 7379 Communication wire;
HQ: General Cable Industries, Inc.
    4 Tesseneer Dr
    Highland Heights KY 41076

(G-6995)
GENERAL DEVICES CO INC
1410 S Post Rd Ste 100 (46239-9788)
P.O. Box 39100 (46239-0100)
PHONE.............................317 897-7000
Fax: 317 898-2917
Maxwell S Fall, *President*
Martin K Fall, *Vice Pres*
Ken Lamaster, *Engineer*
Jera Hughes, *Manager*
Dave Willis, *Manager*
EMP: 32 EST: 1953
SQ FT: 143,500
SALES (est): 9MM **Privately Held**
SIC: 3469 Metal stampings

(G-6996)
GENERAL FABRICATORS INC
5230 S Harding St (46217-9572)
PHONE.............................317 787-9354
Fax: 317 783-6287
Mark Blackard, *President*
Jeff Aucoin, *Project Mgr*
EMP: 8
SQ FT: 21,500
SALES: 1.3MM **Privately Held**
SIC: 3089 3083 Plastic hardware & building products; laminated plastics plate & sheet

(G-6997)
GENERAL FURNITURE & BEDG PDTS
7249 Fulham Dr (46250-2775)
PHONE.............................317 849-2670
B D Basil, *CEO*
Hugh Ann Conley, *Ch of Bd*
Debbie Mc Analley, *Treasurer*
EMP: 6 EST: 1954
SQ FT: 40,000
SALES: 2MM **Privately Held**
SIC: 3069 5087 Foam rubber; upholsterers' equipment & supplies

(G-6998)
GENERAL MATERIAL HANDLING CO
1302 Kings Cove Ct (46260-1671)
P.O. Box 47662 (46247-0662)
PHONE.............................317 888-5735
John M Drey, *President*
Ann Drey, *Vice Pres*
EMP: 2
SALES: 680K **Privately Held**
SIC: 5084 3535 Materials handling machinery; unit handling conveying systems

(G-6999)
GENERAL STEEL
5335 N Tacoma Ave Ste 16 (46220-3648)
PHONE.............................317 251-9583
Eric Smith, *Principal*
EMP: 2
SALES (est): 66K **Privately Held**
SIC: 1099 Metal ores

(G-7000)
GENESYS TELECOM LABS INC
Also Called: Interactive Intelligence
5501 W 79th St (46268-1607)
PHONE.............................317 715-8545
EMP: 3
SALES (corp-wide): 69.9MM **Privately Held**
SIC: 7372 Business oriented computer software
HQ: Genesys Telecommunications Laboratories, Inc.
    2001 Junipero Serra Blvd
    Daly City CA 94014
    650 466-1100

(G-7001)
GENESYS TELECOM LABS INC
Interactive Intelligence
7601 Interactive Way (46278-2727)
PHONE.............................317 872-3000
Dustin Goad, *Regional Mgr*
Paul McGuire, *Business Mgr*
David Girard, *Project Mgr*
Evan Byl, *Engineer*
Chris Covert, *Engineer*
EMP: 849

SALES (corp-wide): 69.9MM **Privately Held**
SIC: 7372 Business oriented computer software
HQ: Genesys Telecommunications Laboratories, Inc.
    2001 Junipero Serra Blvd
    Daly City CA 94014
    650 466-1100

(G-7002)
GEORGE P STEWART PRINTING CO
Also Called: Indianapolis Recorder
2901 N Tacoma Ave (46218-2737)
P.O. Box 18499 (46218-0499)
PHONE.............................317 924-5143
Fax: 317 924-5148
Caroleen Mays, *President*
Angie Kuhn, *Business Mgr*
EMP: 21 EST: 1896
SQ FT: 12,000
SALES: 26.9K **Privately Held**
WEB: www.indianapolisrecorder.com
SIC: 2711 Commercial printing & newspaper publishing combined; newspapers, publishing & printing

(G-7003)
GETSAYDO LLC
5255 Winthrop Ave (46220-3573)
PHONE.............................317 800-8319
Lawrence McGlown, *CEO*
Michael Manross, *Mng Member*
EMP: 2
SQ FT: 20,000
SALES (est): 91.9K **Privately Held**
SIC: 7372 Business oriented computer software

(G-7004)
GHOST TRAIL WINERY LLC
5528 W 62nd St (46268-2404)
PHONE.............................317 387-0052
John Taylor, *Principal*
EMP: 2
SALES (est): 86.7K **Privately Held**
SIC: 2084 Wines

(G-7005)
GILES AGENCY INCORPORATED
7002 Graham Rd Ste 219 (46220-4282)
PHONE.............................317 842-5546
Debra Giles, *President*
EMP: 7
SALES (est): 955.1K **Privately Held**
SIC: 2752 7389 Commercial printing, lithographic; promotional printing, lithographic;

(G-7006)
GIMME CHARGE LLC
2245 Kessler Blvd E Dr (46220-2404)
PHONE.............................317 759-4067
Trevor Back,
Tyler Back,
EMP: 5 EST: 2013
SALES (est): 455.2K **Privately Held**
SIC: 3679 7389 Static power supply converters for electronic applications;

(G-7007)
GIRAFFE X GRAPHICS INC
5746 Wheeler Rd (46216-1038)
PHONE.............................317 546-4944
Sharon Maurer, *President*
Pat Hirschfeld, *Vice Pres*
EMP: 9
SQ FT: 3,000
SALES (est): 750K **Privately Held**
WEB: www.itye-dye.com
SIC: 2759 2395 Screen printing; embroidery products, except schiffli machine

(G-7008)
GLOBAL AIR INC (PA)
913 Bates St (46202-4018)
PHONE.............................317 634-5300
Fax: 317 638-7486
Spitznogle, *President*
Arnold H Breeden, *Shareholder*
EMP: 17
SQ FT: 35,000
SALES (est): 35K **Privately Held**
SIC: 3599 Chemical milling job shop

(G-7009)
GLOBAL AIR INC
6450 Rucker Rd (46220-4841)
PHONE.................................317 251-1251
Natasha Schriver, *Coordinator*
EMP: 9
SALES (corp-wide): 35K **Privately Held**
SIC: 3599 Chemical milling job shop
PA: Global Air Inc.
913 Bates St
Indianapolis IN 46202
317 634-5300

(G-7010)
GLOBAL AIR INC
6450 Rucker Rd (46220-4841)
PHONE.................................317 251-1251
Josh Hill, *Plant Mgr*
EMP: 7
SALES (est): 294.5K **Privately Held**
SIC: 3724 Aircraft engines & engine parts

(G-7011)
GLOBAL FORMING LLC
913 Bates St (46202-4018)
PHONE.................................317 290-1000
Victor Dance,
▲ EMP: 25
SALES (est): 7.2MM **Privately Held**
SIC: 3714 Motor vehicle parts & accessories

(G-7012)
GLOBAL PLASTICS INC
6739 Guion Rd (46268-4810)
PHONE.................................317 299-2345
Fax: 317 298-1328
J R Spitznogle, *President*
James G Spitznogle, *Admin Sec*
EMP: 100
SQ FT: 35,500
SALES (est): 33.3MM **Privately Held**
SIC: 3089 3544 Injection molding of plastics; special dies, tools, jigs & fixtures

(G-7013)
GLOBAL WATER
TECHNOLOGIES INC
351 W 10th St Ste 537 (46202-4103)
P.O. Box 702 (46206-0702)
PHONE.................................317 452-4488
Fax: 317 452-4489
Erik Hromadka, *President*
Rana S Gill, *Vice Pres*
Tony Sandlin, *Treasurer*
EMP: 5
SQ FT: 3,000
SALES (est): 734K **Privately Held**
WEB: www.gwtr.com
SIC: 3589 Water treatment equipment, industrial

(G-7014)
GLOBALVUE INTERNATIONAL
LLC
6402 Corporate Dr (46278-2913)
PHONE.................................866 974-1968
EMP: 2 EST: 2012
SALES (est): 140K **Privately Held**
SIC: 3629 Mfg Electrical Industrial Apparatus

(G-7015)
GLOBE ASPHALT PAVING CO
INC
6445 E 30th St (46219-1006)
P.O. Box 19168 (46219-0168)
PHONE.................................317 568-4344
Fax: 317 635-1569
William Shumaker, *President*
Jane P Shumaker, *Vice Pres*
John Shumaker, *Admin Sec*
EMP: 50
SQ FT: 10,000
SALES (est): 9.6MM **Privately Held**
WEB: www.globeasphalt.com
SIC: 1794 2951 1611 Excavation work; asphalt paving blocks (not from refineries); grading

(G-7016)
GMP HOLDINGS LLC
Also Called: Crossroads Lighting
2525 N Shadeland Ave (46219-1787)
PHONE.................................317 353-6580

Gerald Peterson, *President*
Nilza Gonzalez, *Chief Mktg Ofcr*
EMP: 9
SQ FT: 12,000
SALES: 2MM **Privately Held**
SIC: 3433 3648 8711 Solar heaters & collectors; lighting equipment; engineering services

(G-7017)
GOAT INDUSTRIES LLC ✪
17 S Pennsylvania St (46204)
PHONE.................................770 940-0433
Jeffrey Batson,
EMP: 3 EST: 2017
SALES (est): 122.2K **Privately Held**
SIC: 3999 Manufacturing industries

(G-7018)
GOLD N GEMS
10202 E Washington St # 1325
(46229-2599)
PHONE.................................317 895-6002
Salim Ali, *Owner*
EMP: 2
SALES (est): 120K **Privately Held**
SIC: 3911 Jewelry, precious metal

(G-7019)
GOLDEN BEAM METALS LLC
6805 Hillsdale Ct (46250-2039)
P.O. Box 40965 (46240-0965)
PHONE.................................317 806-2750
Gary Colip, *President*
Brad Smith, *Treasurer*
▲ EMP: 3 EST: 2015
SALES (est): 239K **Privately Held**
SIC: 3399 Iron ore recovery from open hearth slag

(G-7020)
GOLDEN PRIDE HAIR COMPANY
LLC
1226 N Illinois St S205 (46202-2325)
PHONE.................................812 777-9604
Toya Marie Gordon,
EMP: 3
SALES (est): 100K **Privately Held**
SIC: 2389 Apparel & accessories

(G-7021)
GOLDEN TRNGLE LBRCANT
SVCS LLC
5009 W 81st St (46268-1639)
PHONE.................................317 875-9465
EMP: 5 EST: 2005
SALES (est): 710K **Privately Held**
SIC: 2992 Mfg Lubricating Oils/Greases

(G-7022)
GOLDLEAF PROMOTIONAL
PRODUCTS
6630 Ferguson St (46220-1151)
PHONE.................................317 202-2754
Shelby Goldblatt, *President*
EMP: 5
SQ FT: 2,000
SALES: 550K **Privately Held**
WEB: www.goldleafpromotions.com
SIC: 7311 2759 Advertising agencies; commercial printing

(G-7023)
GONZALEZ PALLETS
105 S Denny St (46201-4409)
PHONE.................................317 644-1242
Arnulfa Tigre, *Principal*
EMP: 4
SALES (est): 335.5K **Privately Held**
SIC: 2448 Wood pallets & skids

(G-7024)
GOODLIFE INDUSTRIES INC
3925 E 26th St (46218-3074)
PHONE.................................317 339-6341
Nathan E Oatts, *Principal*
EMP: 2
SALES (est): 125K **Privately Held**
SIC: 3999 Manufacturing industries

(G-7025)
GOODPRINT LLC
611 N Park Ave Apt 106 (46204-1681)
PHONE.................................201 926-0133
EMP: 2

SALES (est): 83.9K **Privately Held**
SIC: 2752 Commercial printing, lithographic

(G-7026)
GOODTIME MANUFACTURING
LLC
Also Called: Goodtime Technology Dev
5136 W 81st St (46268-1640)
PHONE.................................317 876-3661
EMP: 5 EST: 2012
SQ FT: 50,000
SALES (est): 310K **Privately Held**
SIC: 3069 Fabricated Rubber Products, Nec, Nsk

(G-7027)
GOODWILL INDUSTRIES
9704 Beaumont Rd (46216-1026)
PHONE.................................317 546-7251
EMP: 3 EST: 2010
SALES (est): 132.5K **Privately Held**
SIC: 3999 Manufacturing industries

(G-7028)
GOODWILL INDUSTRIES
1635 W Michigan St (46222-3899)
PHONE.................................317 524-4293
Fax: 317 524-4336
Toni Thompson, *Owner*
Jim Humphrey, *COO*
Cindy Graham, *Vice Pres*
Justin Warner, *Human Res Dir*
Joy Bosley, *Manager*
▲ EMP: 46
SALES (est): 6.6MM **Privately Held**
SIC: 3999 Manufacturing industries

(G-7029)
GORILLA PLASTIC RBR GROUP
LLC
3401 Newton Ave (46201-4340)
PHONE.................................317 635-9616
Fax: 317 635-9617
Don Katz, *Mng Member*
EMP: 18
SALES (est): 2.7MM **Privately Held**
SIC: 3069 Molded rubber products

(G-7030)
GOULD SOLENOID VALVE CO
4707 Massachusetts Ave (46218-3144)
PHONE.................................317 547-5289
John Gould, *President*
Phil Hubbs, *Opers Staff*
Chad Morin, *Sales Staff*
Andrea Mead, *Office Mgr*
EMP: 13
SALES (est): 157.8K **Privately Held**
SIC: 3491 Solenoid valves

(G-7031)
GOULDING & WOOD INC
823 Massachusetts Ave (46204-1610)
PHONE.................................317 637-5222
Fax: 317 637-5236
Jason Overall, *President*
Mark Goulding, *Corp Secy*
Brandon Woods, *Vice Pres*
Kurt Ryll, *Design Engr*
Phil Lehman, *Master*
EMP: 14
SQ FT: 10,500
SALES (est): 1.4MM **Privately Held**
WEB: www.gouldingandwood.com
SIC: 3931 7699 Pipes, organ; organ tuning & repair

(G-7032)
GRACE DIGITAL PRINTING
7304 Atmore Dr (46217-3082)
PHONE.................................317 903-6172
EMP: 2
SALES (est): 135K **Privately Held**
SIC: 2752 Lithographic Commercial Printing

(G-7033)
GRACE W R & CO-CO
7950 Allison Ave (46268-1612)
PHONE.................................317 876-4100
EMP: 2
SALES (est): 74.4K **Privately Held**
SIC: 2821 Plastics materials & resins

(G-7034)
GRAND PRODUCTS INC
1650 S Girls School Rd (46231-1308)
PHONE.................................317 870-3122
EMP: 201
SALES (corp-wide): 34.1MM **Privately Held**
SIC: 3999 Coin-operated amusement machines
PA: Grand Products, Inc.
1718 Hampshire Dr
Elk Grove Village IL 60007
800 621-6101

(G-7035)
GRANDMA HAMS FARM LLC
5436 N Delaware St (46220-3014)
PHONE.................................317 253-0635
K M Carr, *Principal*
EMP: 3
SALES (est): 118.9K **Privately Held**
SIC: 2013 Prepared pork products from purchased pork

(G-7036)
GRAPHICORP
Also Called: Park 100 Business Printing
8587 Zionsville Rd 206 (46268-1511)
PHONE.................................317 867-3099
Janet Sexson, *President*
Randy Zentz, *Corp Secy*
EMP: 5
SQ FT: 1,850
SALES (est): 375K **Privately Held**
SIC: 2752 7336 Commercial printing, offset; graphic arts & related design

(G-7037)
GRAVEL DOCTOR
INDIANAPOLIS LLC
7611 Dornock Dr (46237-9675)
PHONE.................................317 399-4585
EMP: 2
SALES (est): 66K **Privately Held**
SIC: 1442 Construction sand & gravel

(G-7038)
GRAVIS EBIKES INC
7220 N Audubon Rd (46250-2618)
PHONE.................................317 690-0616
Todd Embree, *President*
EMP: 9
SALES (est): 428.4K **Privately Held**
SIC: 3751 Motorcycles, bicycles & parts

(G-7039)
GRAYBULL ORGANIC WINES
INC
7365 Lakeside Dr (46278-1618)
PHONE.................................317 797-2186
EMP: 2
SALES (est): 75.4K **Privately Held**
SIC: 2084 Wines

(G-7040)
GREAT STATES CORPORATION
Also Called: American Lawn Mower Co.
7444 Shadeland Stn Way (46256-3925)
PHONE.................................317 392-3615
Fax: 317 392-4118
Robert E Kersey, *CEO*
Micheal Kersey, *President*
James W Hewitt, *VP Sales*
Gary Smith, *Marketing Staff*
Patrick D Hellman, *Admin Sec*
▲ EMP: 20
SQ FT: 100,000
SALES: 35MM **Privately Held**
WEB: www.reelin.com
SIC: 3524 Lawnmowers, residential: hand or power

(G-7041)
GREEN PLUS PLASTICS LLC
3131 N Franklin Rd Ste L (46226-6390)
PHONE.................................317 672-2410
Kumar Aeneni, *Mng Member*
EMP: 9
SALES (est): 1MM **Privately Held**
SIC: 3089 Plastic processing

(G-7042)
GREEN PLUS PLASTICS LLC
3131 N Franklin Rd Ste L (46226-6390)
PHONE.................................931 510-0525

EMP: 2
SALES (est): 129.1K **Privately Held**
SIC: 2821 Plastics materials & resins

(G-7043)
GREENCYCLE OF INDIANA INC
1103 W Troy Ave (46225-2247)
PHONE...............................317 780-8175
John Repenning, *Branch Mgr*
EMP: 9 **Privately Held**
SIC: 2499 Mulch or sawdust products, wood
HQ: Greencycle Of Indiana, Inc
　　400 Central Ave Ste 115
　　Northfield IL 60093

(G-7044)
GREENLIGHT LLC
Also Called: GREENLIGHT COLLECTIBLES
5855 W 74th St (46278-1757)
PHONE...............................317 287-0600
Russell Hughes,
Tara Petty, *Administration*
▲ EMP: 13
SALES: 11.7MM **Privately Held**
SIC: 3944 Automobile & truck models, toy & hobby

(G-7045)
GREENLINE SCREEN PRINTING
6830 Hawthorn Park Dr (46220-3909)
PHONE...............................317 572-1155
Jim Pike, *President*
EMP: 2
SALES (est): 119.9K **Privately Held**
SIC: 2752 Commercial printing, offset

(G-7046)
GREENSGROOMER WORLDWIDE INC (PA)
10992 E Us Highway 136 A (46234-9095)
P.O. Box 34151 (46234-0151)
PHONE...............................317 388-0695
Fax: 317 298-8852
Michael Davis, *President*
Jill Davis, *Vice Pres*
EMP: 5
SQ FT: 23,000
SALES (est): 3MM **Privately Held**
WEB: www.greensgroomerww.com
SIC: 3441 Fabricated structural metal

(G-7047)
GREGORY & APPEL
11738 Capistrano Dr (46236-8841)
PHONE...............................317 823-0131
Ken Tomozawa, *Vice Pres*
EMP: 2
SALES (est): 85.9K **Privately Held**
SIC: 3571 Personal computers (microcomputers)

(G-7048)
GREYS AUTOMOTIVE INC
1604 W Minnesota St (46221-1833)
PHONE...............................317 632-3562
Charles Grey, *President*
Patricia Grey, *Treasurer*
EMP: 2
SQ FT: 3,600
SALES: 300K **Privately Held**
SIC: 5531 3599 Automotive parts; machine shop, jobbing & repair

(G-7049)
GRIND CITY CUSTOMS
7145 E 46th St (46226-3803)
PHONE...............................317 981-5462
EMP: 2
SALES (est): 87.9K **Privately Held**
SIC: 3599 Mfg Industrial Machinery

(G-7050)
GRINDING AND POLSG MCHY CORP
Also Called: G & P Machinery
2801 Tobey Dr (46219-1481)
PHONE...............................317 898-0750
Fax: 317 899-1627
James Reiman, *President*
Sarah Chaille, *Treasurer*
▲ EMP: 15 EST: 1952
SQ FT: 30,000

SALES: 1.9MM **Privately Held**
WEB: www.gandpmachinery.com
SIC: 3549 3541 3553 Metalworking machinery; machine tools, metal cutting type; woodworking machinery

(G-7051)
GRINON INDUSTRIES LLC
7649 Winton Dr (46268-4142)
PHONE...............................317 388-5100
Josh Springer, *CEO*
Dustin Worrell, *Business Mgr*
Mike Price, *Vice Pres*
Kyle Johnson, *Sales Dir*
Mathew Muncy, *Cust Mgr*
▲ EMP: 26
SQ FT: 25,000
SALES (est): 5.2MM **Privately Held**
SIC: 3585 Beer dispensing equipment

(G-7052)
GROWING SMILES INC
7210 Madison Ave Ste O (46227-5227)
P.O. Box 56022 (46256-0022)
PHONE...............................317 787-6404
Fax: 317 787-5618
Ellen M Ahlers, *Manager*
EMP: 4
SALES (est): 366.7K **Privately Held**
SIC: 3843 Orthodontic appliances

(G-7053)
GRRK HOLDINGS INC
Also Called: Ds Smith Rapak
7430 New Augusta Rd (46268-2291)
PHONE...............................317 872-0172
Fax: 317 872-1242
Gary W Smith, *CEO*
Daniel A Cunningham, *President*
Richard W Smith, *Vice Pres*
Brent W Todd, *Vice Pres*
Richard Smith, *VP Mfg*
▲ EMP: 50 EST: 1960
SQ FT: 28,000
SALES: 12.1MM
SALES (corp-wide): 5.9B **Privately Held**
SIC: 3089 3565 2673 Injection molding of plastics; packaging machinery; plastic & pliofilm bags
PA: Ds Smith Plc
　　7th Floor 350 Euston Road
　　London NW1 3
　　207 756-1800

(G-7054)
GRUNAU COMPANY INC
4341 W 96th St (46268-1178)
PHONE...............................317 872-7360
Robert Harlow, *Manager*
EMP: 30
SALES (corp-wide): 3B **Privately Held**
SIC: 3669 1711 Fire detection systems, electric; mechanical contractor
HQ: Grunau Company, Inc.
　　1100 W Anderson Ct
　　Oak Creek WI 53154
　　414 216-6900

(G-7055)
GRUNDFOS PUMPS MFG CORP
2005 Dr Martin L King Jr (46202-1165)
PHONE...............................317 925-9661
Andrew Warrington, *Principal*
EMP: 15
SALES (corp-wide): 4B **Privately Held**
SIC: 3561 Pumps & pumping equipment
HQ: Grundfos Pumps Manufacturing Corporation
　　5900 E Shields Ave
　　Fresno CA 93727

(G-7056)
GSI GROUP INC
Farm Fans
5900 Elmwood Ave (46203-6033)
PHONE...............................317 787-3047
EMP: 20
SALES (corp-wide): 10.7B **Publicly Held**
SIC: 3564 Farm Fan Sales & Marketing Division
HQ: The Gsi Group Llc
　　1004 E Illinois St
　　Assumption IL 62510
　　217 226-4421

(G-7057)
GUIDE BOOK PUBLISHING
5929 Haverford Ave (46220-2752)
P.O. Box 20643 (46220-0643)
PHONE...............................317 259-0599
Bob Vogt, *Principal*
EMP: 2
SALES (est): 62.9K **Privately Held**
SIC: 2711 Newspapers

(G-7058)
GUIDE TECHNOLOGIES LLC (PA)
250 E 96th St Ste 525 (46240-3736)
PHONE...............................317 844-3162
Fred Cramer, *VP Sls/Mktg*
Dave Meadows,
Sheri George, *Sr Consultant*
Nick Stoltzfus, *Sr Consultant*
EMP: 3 EST: 1997
SQ FT: 1,750
SALES (est): 3.9MM **Privately Held**
WEB: www.guidetechnologies.com
SIC: 7372 Prepackaged software

(G-7059)
GULSAD INC
Also Called: Ship It Now Store, The
4084 Pendleton Way (46226-5224)
PHONE...............................317 541-1940
Arif Sadruddin, *CEO*
EMP: 2
SALES (est): 224.3K **Privately Held**
SIC: 2754 Commercial printing, gravure

(G-7060)
GUTTER ONE SUPPLY
8026 Woodland Dr (46278-1349)
PHONE...............................317 872-1257
EMP: 2
SALES (est): 96.3K **Privately Held**
SIC: 5211 5031 2431 Lumber & other building materials; composite board products, woodboard; millwork

(G-7061)
GWIN ENTERPRISES
7294 S Delaware St (46227-2434)
PHONE...............................317 881-6401
Barry L Gwin, *Principal*
EMP: 4
SALES (est): 346.7K **Privately Held**
SIC: 3663 Airborne radio communications equipment

(G-7062)
H C SCHUMACHER MACHINE CO INC
3619 S Arlington Ave (46203-6104)
PHONE...............................317 787-9361
Fax: 317 784-6991
Clair W Golay, *President*
Jackie Golay, *Vice Pres*
Michael Hope, *Vice Pres*
EMP: 20 EST: 1929
SQ FT: 20,000
SALES (est): 2.7MM **Privately Held**
SIC: 3559 Glass making machinery: blowing, molding, forming, etc.

(G-7063)
HACKETT PUBLISHING COMPANY (PA)
3333 Massachusetts Ave (46218-3754)
P.O. Box 44937 (46244-0937)
PHONE...............................317 635-9250
Fax: 800 783-9213
James N Hullett, *CEO*
Frances Hackett, *President*
Deborah D Wilkes, *President*
Elizabeth Wilson, *Editor*
Eddie Ellis, *Warehouse Mgr*
EMP: 30
SQ FT: 51,000
SALES: 6.9MM **Privately Held**
WEB: www.hackettpublishing.com
SIC: 2731 Textbooks: publishing only, not printed on site

(G-7064)
HACKETT PUBLISHING COMPANY
832 Pierson St (46204-1109)
P.O. Box 44937 (46244-0937)
PHONE...............................317 635-9250

Sherry Brown, *Manager*
EMP: 15
SALES (est): 1.3MM
SALES (corp-wide): 6.9MM **Privately Held**
WEB: www.hackettpublishing.com
SIC: 2731 Book publishing
PA: Hackett Publishing Company Inc
　　3333 Massachusetts Ave
　　Indianapolis IN 46218
　　317 635-9250

(G-7065)
HACKNEY HOME FURNISHINGS INC
Also Called: Holland House
9420 E 33rd St (46235-4204)
PHONE...............................317 895-4300
EMP: 28
SALES (corp-wide): 22.3MM **Privately Held**
SIC: 2511 Mfg Wood Household Furniture
HQ: Hackney Home Furnishings, Inc.
　　1050 Topside Rd
　　Louisville TN 46235

(G-7066)
HALO METALWORKS INC
4000 W 10th St (46222-3203)
PHONE...............................317 481-0100
James Spencer, *President*
EMP: 15
SALES (est): 1.6MM **Privately Held**
SIC: 3441 Fabricated structural metal

(G-7067)
HAMILTON BROS INC
1840 Midwest Blvd (46214-2376)
PHONE...............................317 241-2571
Larry Hamilton, *President*
EMP: 12 EST: 1949
SALES: 1.2MM **Privately Held**
WEB: www.hamiltonbros.com
SIC: 7699 1381 Pumps & pumping equipment repair; drilling water intake wells

(G-7068)
HAMILTON EXHIBITS LLC (PA)
9150 E 33rd St (46235-3605)
PHONE...............................317 898-9300
Fax: 317 898-9353
Dan Cantor, *CEO*
Mindy Baxter, *Vice Pres*
Lynne Damer, *Vice Pres*
Jason Weddle, *VP Opers*
Joe Fox, *Project Mgr*
▲ EMP: 100 EST: 1997
SQ FT: 195,200
SALES (est): 15.4MM **Privately Held**
WEB: www.hamilton-exhibits.com
SIC: 2653 Display items, corrugated: made from purchased materials

(G-7069)
HANGER PRSTHETCS & ORTHO INC
Also Called: Hanger Orthotics
1330 N Illinois St (46202-2321)
PHONE...............................317 923-2351
Doug Hodge, *Manager*
EMP: 7
SALES (corp-wide): 1B **Publicly Held**
SIC: 3842 Prosthetic appliances
HQ: Hanger Prosthetics & Orthotics, Inc.
　　10910 Domain Dr Ste 300
　　Austin TX 78758
　　512 777-3800

(G-7070)
HANSFORD CO
7420 N Park Ave (46240-3029)
PHONE...............................317 255-4756
David Hansford, *Principal*
EMP: 2
SALES (est): 112.7K **Privately Held**
SIC: 1382 Oil & gas exploration services

(G-7071)
HANSFORD PREVENT LLC
5658 Buck Pond Ct (46237-8423)
P.O. Box 39223 (46239-0223)
PHONE...............................317 985-2346
Michael Hansford, *Principal*
EMP: 2
SALES (est): 144.9K **Privately Held**
SIC: 3582 Commercial laundry equipment

(G-7072)
HANSON AGGRGATES SOUTHEAST INC
4200 S Harding St (46217-9537)
PHONE.................................317 788-4086
Fax: 317 787-5067
Randy Jones, *General Mgr*
Don Roadruck, *Sales Staff*
EMP: 60
SALES (corp-wide): 20.3B Privately Held
SIC: 1442 1422 1429 Sand mining; gravel mining; limestones, ground; boulder, crushed & broken-quarrying
HQ: Hanson Aggregates Southeast, Inc.
3237 Satellite Blvd # 210
Duluth GA 30096
770 491-2777

(G-7073)
HARDING MATERIALS INC
5145 E 96th St (46240-1440)
PHONE.................................317 846-7401
Shawn Angle, *Manager*
EMP: 4
SALES (corp-wide): 1.2MM Privately Held
SIC: 3531 Asphalt plant, including gravel-mix type
PA: Harding Materials, Inc.
10151 Hague Rd
Indianapolis IN 46256
317 849-9666

(G-7074)
HARDINGPOORMAN INC
Also Called: Full Court Press
4923 W 78th St (46268-4170)
PHONE.................................317 876-3355
Fax: 317 876-3398
David A Harding, *President*
Steve Anzalone, *COO*
Lynn Churchill, *Vice Pres*
Bob Poorman, *Vice Pres*
Robert Poorman, *Vice Pres*
EMP: 134
SQ FT: 52,800
SALES (est): 48.1MM Privately Held
WEB: www.spggraphics.com
SIC: 2752 Commercial printing, offset

(G-7075)
HARDINGPOORMAN GROUP INC
Also Called: Full Court Press Printing
4923 W 78th St (46268-4170)
PHONE.................................317 876-3355
David A Harding, *CEO*
Steve Anzalone, *President*
Keith Craig, *Vice Pres*
Max Phillips, *Vice Pres*
Jim Wachob, *Mfg Staff*
EMP: 6
SALES (est): 2MM Privately Held
SIC: 2752 Commercial printing, offset

(G-7076)
HARLAN DEVELOPMENT COMPANY
404 S Kitley Ave (46219-7401)
PHONE.................................317 352-1583
Hal Harlan, *Principal*
EMP: 3
SALES (est): 240K Privately Held
SIC: 2836 Biological products, except diagnostic

(G-7077)
HARMAN EMBEDDED AUDIO LLC
6602 E 75th St Ste 520 (46250-2870)
PHONE.................................317 849-8175
Fax: 317 849-8178
Chris Welsh, *Mng Member*
Jeffrey P McAteer,
Alan Michel,
▲ EMP: 45
SQ FT: 5,000
SALES (est): 7.9MM
SALES (corp-wide): 148.1B Privately Held
WEB: www.mwmacoustics.com
SIC: 5065 3651 Electronic parts & equipment; audio electronic systems

HQ: Harman International Industries Incorporated
400 Atlantic St Ste 15
Stamford CT 06901
203 328-3500

(G-7078)
HARRY & IZZYS NORTHSIDE LLC
4050 E 82nd St (46250-1620)
PHONE.................................317 915-8045
Jeff Smith, *Principal*
EMP: 4 EST: 2011
SALES (est): 535.4K Privately Held
SIC: 3421 Table & food cutlery, including butchers'

(G-7079)
HARVEST CAFE COFFEE & TEA LLC
2225 E 54th St Ste A (46220-3435)
P.O. Box 20603 (46220-0603)
PHONE.................................317 585-9162
Larry French, *Sales Staff*
Andy Wolf, *Mng Member*
Reggie Faxton,
EMP: 5
SALES (est): 305K Privately Held
SIC: 5812 5149 2095 Cafe; coffee & tea; roasted coffee

(G-7080)
HAYABUSA LLC
5025 E 82nd St (46250-5600)
PHONE.................................317 594-1188
Shang Song, *Principal*
EMP: 6 EST: 2008
SALES (est): 778.8K Privately Held
SIC: 3421 Table & food cutlery, including butchers'

(G-7081)
HCO HOLDING I CORPORATION
Monsey Bakor
4351 W Morris St (46241-2503)
PHONE.................................317 248-1344
Fax: 317 243-6613
Clarence Cook, *Safety Dir*
Rob Franklin, *Plant Mgr*
EMP: 35
SALES (corp-wide): 263.6MM Privately Held
WEB: www.henry.com
SIC: 2952 2951 2891 Roofing felts, cements or coatings; asphalt paving mixtures & blocks; adhesives & sealants
HQ: Hco Holding I Corporation
999 N Sepulveda Blvd
El Segundo CA 90245
323 583-5000

(G-7082)
HDH MANUFACTURING INC
4008 W 10th St (46222-3203)
PHONE.................................317 918-4088
Austin Hall, *President*
EMP: 3
SALES (est): 141.6K
SALES (corp-wide): 300K Privately Held
SIC: 3599 Machine shop, jobbing & repair
PA: Hdh Manufacturing Inc.
3534 Nolen Dr
Indianapolis IN 46234
317 918-4088

(G-7083)
HDH MANUFACTURING INC (PA)
3534 Nolen Dr (46234-1410)
PHONE.................................317 918-4088
Austin Hall, *President*
Roger Detmering, *Vice Pres*
Gabe Hall, *Vice Pres*
EMP: 3
SALES: 300K Privately Held
SIC: 3599 7389 Machine shop, jobbing & repair;

(G-7084)
HEARTLAND DISTILLERS LLC
9402 Uptown Dr Ste 1000 (46256-1042)
PHONE.................................317 598-9775
Stuart Hobson, *Mng Member*
EMP: 8 EST: 2008
SALES (est): 864.6K Privately Held
SIC: 2085 Distilled & blended liquors

(G-7085)
HEARTLAND FILM INC
1043 Virginia Ave Ste 2 (46203-1761)
PHONE.................................317 464-9405
Stuart Lowry, *President*
Derek Hulsey, *Marketing Staff*
Allison Ackmann, *Manager*
Susan Frenzel, *Manager*
Louise Henderson, *Director*
EMP: 9
SQ FT: 4,970
SALES: 1.4MM Privately Held
WEB: www.heartlandfilmfestival.com
SIC: 3861 Motion picture film

(G-7086)
HEAT EXCHANGER DESIGN INC
Also Called: H E D
901 E Beecher St (46203-3974)
P.O. Box 524 (46206-0524)
PHONE.................................317 917-1566
Fax: 317 686-9100
Hesham Derazi, *President*
Cliff Shipley, *Vice Pres*
Kaleb Ratcliff, *Manager*
Heather McDaniel, *Admin Asst*
▲ EMP: 50
SQ FT: 114,000
SALES (est): 13.5MM Privately Held
WEB: www.hed-inc.com
SIC: 3443 Heat exchangers: coolers (after, inter); condensers, etc.

(G-7087)
HELIOS LLC
8001 Woodland Dr (46278-1332)
PHONE.................................317 554-9911
Scott Bogden, *Mng Member*
EMP: 35
SALES (est): 3.7MM Privately Held
WEB: www.gohelios.com
SIC: 7372 Application computer software

(G-7088)
HELLBENT INC
833 N Denny St (46201-2636)
P.O. Box 2987 (46206-2987)
PHONE.................................765 631-4934
EMP: 2 EST: 2011
SALES (est): 97K Privately Held
SIC: 3949 Mfg Sporting/Athletic Goods

(G-7089)
HERFF JONES LLC
4625 W 62nd St (46268-2546)
P.O. Box 36, Marceline MO (64658-0036)
PHONE.................................317 612-3400
Tom James, *Manager*
EMP: 33
SALES (corp-wide): 1.1B Privately Held
WEB: www.herffjones.com
SIC: 2741 2752 2732 2731 Yearbooks: publishing & printing; commercial printing, lithographic; book printing; book publishing
HQ: Herff Jones, Llc
4501 W 62nd St
Indianapolis IN 46268
800 419-5462

(G-7090)
HERFF JONES LLC
4601 W 62nd St (46268-2570)
PHONE.................................620 365-5181
Tony Leavitt, *Mfg Mgr*
EMP: 80
SALES (corp-wide): 1.1B Privately Held
WEB: www.herffjones.com
SIC: 3911 Rings, finger: precious metal
HQ: Herff Jones, Llc
4501 W 62nd St
Indianapolis IN 46268
800 419-5462

(G-7091)
HERFF JONES LLC
4601 W 62nd St (46268-2570)
PHONE.................................800 837-4235
EMP: 3
SALES (corp-wide): 798.6MM Privately Held
SIC: 3911 Mfg Precious Metal Jewelry
PA: Herff Jones, Llc
4501 W 62nd St
Indianapolis IN 46268
800 837-4235

(G-7092)
HERFF JONES LLC (DH)
Also Called: Camera Art
4501 W 62nd St (46268-2569)
PHONE.................................800 419-5462
Fax: 317 329-3309
Jeffrey Webb, *CEO*
Adam Blumenfeld, *President*
David A Burkert, *President*
Kenneth G Langlois, *President*
Donald J Agin, *Vice Pres*
◆ EMP: 200
SQ FT: 42,700
SALES (est): 658.5MM
SALES (corp-wide): 1.1B Privately Held
WEB: www.herffjones.com
SIC: 3911 2721 2741 Rings, finger: precious metal; periodicals; yearbooks: publishing & printing
HQ: Varsity Brands, Llc
6745 Lenox Center Ct # 300
Memphis TN 38115
901 387-4306

(G-7093)
HERFF JONES CO INDIANA - INC
4625 W 62nd St (46268-2546)
PHONE.................................317 297-3740
Fax: 317 329-3308
Scott Cool, *Principal*
EMP: 9
SALES (est): 807.4K Privately Held
SIC: 3911 Jewelry, precious metal

(G-7094)
HERFF JONES YEARBOOKS
4625 W 62nd St (46268-2546)
PHONE.................................717 334-9123
Marshall Scott, *Owner*
EMP: 2
SALES (est): 118.8K Privately Held
SIC: 2759 2731 Publication printing; book publishing

(G-7095)
HERITAGE ASPHALT LLC
5400 W 86th St (46268-1502)
P.O. Box 68123 (46268-0123)
PHONE.................................317 872-6010
Bradley Mullen, *President*
EMP: 5
SALES (est): 565.4K Privately Held
SIC: 2951 Asphalt paving mixtures & blocks

(G-7096)
HERNANDEZ SIGNS LLC ✪
2937 S Rybolt Ave (46241-5919)
PHONE.................................317 500-1303
Patricio Hernandez, *Principal*
EMP: 2 EST: 2017
SALES (est): 72.6K Privately Held
SIC: 3993 Signs & advertising specialties

(G-7097)
HERON PRINTING CO INC
159 Walnut St (46227-5166)
PHONE.................................317 865-0007
Fax: 317 889-8797
Nicholas Schmoll, *President*
Susan Schmoll, *Treasurer*
EMP: 3
SQ FT: 2,500
SALES (est): 248K Privately Held
WEB: www.heronprinting.net
SIC: 2752 Commercial printing, offset

(G-7098)
HF CHLOR-ALKALI LLC (PA)
9307 E 56th St (46216-2068)
P.O. Box 489, Eddyville IA (52553-0489)
PHONE.................................317 591-0000
Timothy Harris, *President*
▲ EMP: 27
SALES (est): 8.1MM Privately Held
SIC: 2812 Caustic soda, sodium hydroxide

(G-7099)
HG METAL FABRICATION
1426 N Graham Ave (46219-3134)
PHONE.................................317 491-3381
Oscar Hilario, *Principal*
EMP: 2
SALES (est): 161.6K Privately Held
SIC: 3499 Fabricated metal products

(G-7100)
HGL DYNAMICS INC
2461 Directors Row Ste J (46241-4937)
PHONE.....................317 782-3500
James Hones, *President*
Robert Sparkman, *Vice Pres*
Aliza Sparkman, *Info Tech Mgr*
EMP: 5
SALES: 750K **Privately Held**
SIC: 8711 3825 Engineering services; instruments to measure electricity

(G-7101)
HGMC SUPPLY INC
Also Called: Hg Metals
5402 Massachusetts Ave (46218-2451)
PHONE.....................317 351-9500
Cynthia B Gardner, *President*
Sean E Gardner, *Vice Pres*
Lawrence Casey, *Project Mgr*
Gene Gardner, *Prdtn Mgr*
EMP: 18
SQ FT: 26,000
SALES (est): 5.3MM **Privately Held**
WEB: www.gardnercon.com
SIC: 1541 8741 1791 3446 Industrial buildings & warehouses; construction management; structural steel erection; stairs, fire escapes, balconies, railings & ladders

(G-7102)
HI TECH FOAM PRODUCTS INC
9900 Westpoint Dr Ste 116 (46256-3338)
PHONE.....................317 614-1515
Fax: 317 614-1520
Randall Knox, *CEO*
EMP: 2
SALES (est): 77.4K **Privately Held**
SIC: 3053 Gaskets, packing & sealing devices

(G-7103)
HI TECH SYSTEMS INC (PA)
8575 Zionsville Rd (46268-1511)
PHONE.....................317 704-1077
Kenjiro Tanoue, *President*
Richard Wheeler, *Business Anlyst*
EMP: 5
SQ FT: 1,800
SALES (est): 3.7MM **Privately Held**
SIC: 3599 Custom machinery

(G-7104)
HI-PERFRMNCE SPERABRASIVES INC
9133 Pendleton Pike Ste G (46236-3244)
PHONE.....................317 899-1050
Travis L Rhoden Sr, *President*
Kevin Brown, *Vice Pres*
Bill West, *Vice Pres*
EMP: 9
SQ FT: 3,000
SALES (est): 2.1MM **Privately Held**
WEB: www.hps-usa.com
SIC: 3291 Abrasive metal & steel products

(G-7105)
HI-TECH FOAM PRODUCTS LLC (HQ)
550 Bell St (46202-3593)
P.O. Box 21280, Owensboro KY (42304-1280)
PHONE.....................270 684-8331
John Metaxas, *President*
▲ **EMP:** 22
SQ FT: 50,000
SALES (est): 2.8MM
SALES (corp-wide): 1B **Privately Held**
SIC: 3053 3086 3069 Gaskets & sealing devices; packaging & shipping materials; foamed plastic; foam rubber
PA: Hickory Springs Manufacturing Company
235 2nd Ave Nw
Hickory NC 28601
828 328-2201

(G-7106)
HIGH END CONCEPTS INC
Also Called: National Screen Printing Co
225 E 10th St (46202-3303)
PHONE.....................317 630-9901
William M Kessler, *President*
EMP: 10

SQ FT: 7,000
SALES: 1.1MM **Privately Held**
WEB: www.highendconcepts.com
SIC: 8743 2759 7389 Promotion service; screen printing; embroidering of advertising on shirts, etc.

(G-7107)
HIGHLAND PARK SERVICES INC
5345 Winthrop Ave (46220-3278)
PHONE.....................317 954-0456
Christian J Franke, *President*
Nicholas Guemes, *Principal*
Robert J Mocek, *Admin Sec*
EMP: 3
SALES (est): 190K **Privately Held**
SIC: 3531 Construction machinery

(G-7108)
HILL & GRIFFITH COMPANY
3637 Farnsworth St (46241-5310)
PHONE.....................317 241-9233
Mark Anderson, *Production*
Jeff Anderson, *Engineer*
Timothy Bolton, *Engineer*
Michael Lawry, *Manager*
Ryan Canfield, *Manager*
EMP: 22
SALES (corp-wide): 12.1MM **Privately Held**
SIC: 5051 3364 3363 3297 Foundry products; nonferrous die-castings except aluminum; aluminum die-castings; non-clay refractories; lubricating oils & greases
PA: Hill & Griffith Company
1085 Summer St
Cincinnati OH 45204
513 921-1075

(G-7109)
HIRATA CORPORATION OF AMERICA (HQ)
5625 Decatur Blvd (46241-9509)
PHONE.....................317 856-8600
Biagio Longo, *President*
David Schneck, *Division Mgr*
Kenichiro Otomaru, *Exec VP*
Keith Coe, *Project Mgr*
Joe Ratajczak, *Project Mgr*
◆ **EMP:** 30 **EST:** 1980
SQ FT: 30,000
SALES: 101.9MM
SALES (corp-wide): 883.8MM **Privately Held**
WEB: www.hirata.com
SIC: 3535 3537 8711 Conveyors & conveying equipment; industrial trucks & tractors; engineering services
PA: Hirata Corporation
111, Hitotsugi, Uekimachi, Kita-Ku
Kumamoto KUM 861-0
962 720-555

(G-7110)
HKN INTERNATIONAL LLC
Also Called: Aerosmith Fastening Systems
5621 Dividend Rd (46241-4301)
PHONE.....................317 243-5959
Christy Reed, *Sales Staff*
Robert Shluzas, *Mng Member*
Timia Washington, *Admin Sec*
▲ **EMP:** 6
SALES (est): 1.3MM **Privately Held**
SIC: 3542 Nail heading machines

(G-7111)
HOGEN INDUSTRIES INC INDIANA
4655 Massachusetts Ave (46218-3143)
PHONE.....................317 591-5070
Allan Bir, *CEO*
EMP: 25
SQ FT: 2,500
SALES: 125K **Privately Held**
WEB: www.hogenindustries.com
SIC: 3444 5085 3423 Sheet metalwork; industrial supplies; hand & edge tools

(G-7112)
HOME CITY ICE COMPANY
55 S State Ave (46201-3802)
PHONE.....................317 638-0437
EMP: 22

SALES (corp-wide): 314.5MM **Privately Held**
SIC: 2097 Manufactured ice
PA: The Home City Ice Company
6045 Bridgetown Rd Ste 1
Cincinnati OH 45248
513 574-1800

(G-7113)
HOME CITY ICE COMPANY
2000 Dr M Lther Kng Dr Martin (46202)
PHONE.....................317 926-2451
Jim Serger, *Branch Mgr*
Todd Ellingwood, *Maintence Staff*
EMP: 25
SALES (corp-wide): 314.5MM **Privately Held**
WEB: www.homecityice.com
SIC: 2097 5999 Manufactured ice; ice
PA: The Home City Ice Company
6045 Bridgetown Rd Ste 1
Cincinnati OH 45248
513 574-1800

(G-7114)
HOME CITY ICE COMPANY
Also Called: Polar Ice
3602 W Washington St (46241-1625)
PHONE.....................317 926-2451
Scott Beil, *General Mgr*
EMP: 25
SALES (corp-wide): 314.5MM **Privately Held**
WEB: www.homecityice.com
SIC: 2097 Block ice; ice cubes
PA: The Home City Ice Company
6045 Bridgetown Rd Ste 1
Cincinnati OH 45248
513 574-1800

(G-7115)
HONEYCOMB PRODUCTS INC
Also Called: Indianapolis Thermal Proc
405 W Raymond St (46225-1944)
PHONE.....................317 787-9351
Fax: 317 787-0951
Phillip Olley, *President*
EMP: 23
SQ FT: 10,000
SALES (est): 4.7MM **Privately Held**
SIC: 3398 Metal heat treating

(G-7116)
HONEYWELL INTERNATIONAL INC
9355 Delegates Row (46240-3803)
PHONE.....................317 580-6165
Fax: 317 580-6010
Scott Maynard, *Manager*
EMP: 60
SALES (corp-wide): 40.5B **Publicly Held**
WEB: www.honeywell.com
SIC: 3724 Aircraft engines & engine parts
PA: Honeywell International Inc.
115 Tabor Rd
Morris Plains NJ 07950
973 455-2000

(G-7117)
HONEYWELL INTERNATIONAL INC
1775 N Sherman Dr Ste A (46218-4493)
PHONE.....................317 359-9505
Richard Groves, *Manager*
EMP: 5
SALES (corp-wide): 40.5B **Publicly Held**
WEB: www.adilink.com
SIC: 3724 Aircraft engines & engine parts
PA: Honeywell International Inc.
115 Tabor Rd
Morris Plains NJ 07950
973 455-2000

(G-7118)
HONING STL HSPTLITY CNCPTS INC
5807 Tempest Dr (46237-4433)
PHONE.....................317 332-5170
Matthew M Kennedy, *President*
EMP: 2
SALES (est): 89.6K **Privately Held**
SIC: 3599 Grinding castings for the trade

(G-7119)
HOOK INDUSTRIAL SALES INC
2138 N Olney St (46218-3714)
PHONE.....................317 545-8100
Fax: 317 549-2767
Ken Hook, *General Mgr*
Kenneth Hook, *Manager*
EMP: 10
SALES (corp-wide): 15.3MM **Privately Held**
WEB: www.hookindustrialsales.com
SIC: 7699 3593 Industrial machinery & equipment repair; fluid power cylinders & actuators
PA: Hook Industrial Sales Inc
2731 Brooklyn Ave
Fort Wayne IN 46802
260 432-9441

(G-7120)
HOOSIER BADGE & TROPHIES INC
6161 Hillside Ave Fl 1 (46220-2597)
PHONE.....................317 257-4441
Fax: 317 257-4447
Stuart B Countryman, *President*
Alice M Countryman, *Vice Pres*
EMP: 7 **EST:** 1964
SQ FT: 7,000
SALES (est): 1.3MM **Privately Held**
SIC: 3089 3479 5999 Engraving of plastic; etching & engraving; trophies & plaques; rubber stamps

(G-7121)
HOOSIER GASKET CORPORATION (PA)
2400 Enterprise Park Pl (46218-4291)
PHONE.....................317 545-2000
Fax: 317 545-5500
Jeffery Jackson, *President*
Ben Jackson, *Vice Pres*
Dan Jackson, *Vice Pres*
Daniel Jackson, *Vice Pres*
Mark Smith, *Vice Pres*
▲ **EMP:** 95 **EST:** 1960
SQ FT: 130,000
SALES (est): 27.5MM **Privately Held**
WEB: www.hoosiergasket.com
SIC: 3452 3053 Washers; gaskets, all materials

(G-7122)
HOOSIER MACHINE & WELDING INC
451 Arbor Ave (46221-1257)
P.O. Box 21204 (46221-0204)
PHONE.....................317 638-6286
Fax: 317 638-9712
Randy Routier, *President*
Cecelia Routier, *Admin Sec*
EMP: 12 **EST:** 1966
SQ FT: 8,000
SALES: 1MM **Privately Held**
SIC: 7692 Welding repair

(G-7123)
HOOSIER SHRED
9325 Uptown Dr Ste 1400 (46256-1080)
PHONE.....................317 915-7473
Chuck Dickinson, *Owner*
George Artz, *Opers Mgr*
EMP: 2 **EST:** 2010
SALES (est): 222.3K **Privately Held**
SIC: 3554 Cutting machines, paper

(G-7124)
HOOSIER SHRED LLC
9525 Brigantine Ct (46256-9546)
PHONE.....................317 989-9333
Aaron Metelko,
EMP: 3
SALES (est): 270K **Privately Held**
SIC: 3559 Tire shredding machinery

(G-7125)
HOOSIER TRIM PRODUCTS LLC
1850 Expo Ln (46214-2335)
PHONE.....................317 271-4007
Fax: 317 271-7440
Howard Thomas,
Wallace Bryant,
Richard Hauser,
Joshua Mellentine,
EMP: 25

SQ FT: 50,000
SALES: 3MM **Privately Held**
WEB: www.hoosiertrim.com
SIC: **3469** 3354 3449 Metal stampings;
shapes, extruded aluminum; custom roll
formed products

(G-7126)
HOOSIER TRUCK & TRAILER SRV
4301 W Southport Rd (46217-9328)
PHONE..................................317 887-4887
Fax: 317 881-4887
Jason Jenkins, *President*
Skip Jenkins, *Vice Pres*
EMP: 3 EST: 1997
SALES (est): 370K **Privately Held**
SIC: **3589** Sandblasting equipment

(G-7127)
HORNER APG LLC (PA)
Also Called: Horner Advanced Products
Group
59 S State Ave (46201-3876)
PHONE..................................317 916-4274
Phil Horner, *CEO*
Philip Horner, *CEO*
Tom Berkopes, *CFO*
Allen Horner,
Mary Horner,
▲ EMP: 57
SALES (est): 11.2MM **Privately Held**
WEB: www.heapg.com
SIC: **3625** 5063 7694 Electric controls &
control accessories, industrial; electrical
apparatus & equipment; electric motor re-
pair

(G-7128)
HORNER INDUSTRIAL SERVICES INC
59 S State Ave (46201-3876)
PHONE..................................317 916-4274
Richard Copper, *Principal*
EMP: 4
SALES (corp-wide): 46.7MM **Privately Held**
SIC: **3625** 7694 7699 7629 Electric controls & control accessories, industrial;
electric motor repair; pumps & pumping
equipment repair; electrical equipment repair, high voltage; electrical apparatus &
equipment
PA: Horner Industrial Services, Inc.
1521 E Washington St
Indianapolis IN 46201
317 639-4261

(G-7129)
HORNER INDUSTRIAL SERVICES INC
Also Called: Indiana Fan & Fabrication
2045 E Washington St (46201-4184)
PHONE..................................317 634-7165
Fax: 317 685-0810
Marc Dardeen, *Manager*
EMP: 13
SALES (corp-wide): 46.7MM **Privately Held**
SIC: **3564** 3444 5084 5075 Blowing fans:
industrial or commercial; sheet metal-
work; industrial machinery & equipment;
warm air heating & air conditioning; motor
vehicle parts & accessories; fabricated
structural metal
PA: Horner Industrial Services, Inc.
1521 E Washington St
Indianapolis IN 46201
317 639-4261

(G-7130)
HORNER INDUSTRIAL SERVICES INC
Also Called: Scherer Industrial Group
1521 E Washington St (46201-3848)
PHONE..................................317 639-4261
Fax: 317 639-4342
Mark Wolma, *Director*
EMP: 75
SALES (corp-wide): 46.7MM **Privately Held**
SIC: **7694** 5063 Motor repair services;
electric motor repair; electrical apparatus
& equipment

PA: Horner Industrial Services, Inc.
1521 E Washington St
Indianapolis IN 46201
317 639-4261

(G-7131)
HORSEPOWER INDY LLC
4 Gasoline Aly Ste D (46222-5920)
PHONE..................................317 757-8668
James Light, *Mng Member*
EMP: 2 EST: 2012
SALES: 650K **Privately Held**
SIC: **3751** Motorcycles, bicycles & parts

(G-7132)
HOT CAKE
6845 Bluff Rd (46217-3926)
PHONE..................................317 889-2253
EMP: 4
SALES (corp-wide): 908.5K **Privately Held**
SIC: **7299** 5949 2759 Tanning salon;
sewing & needlework; screen printing
PA: Hot Cake
8555 Ditch Rd
Indianapolis IN 46260
317 254-5993

(G-7133)
HOT OFF PRESS
5838 Bonnie Brae St (46228-1842)
PHONE..................................317 253-5987
Dave Overman, *President*
Rita Overman, *Partner*
EMP: 2
SALES (est): 170.7K **Privately Held**
SIC: **2759** Commercial printing

(G-7134)
HOT ROD CAR CARE LLC
Also Called: Indy Auto Graphics
7242 E 86th St (46250-3597)
PHONE..................................317 660-2077
Kyle Davenport, *President*
EMP: 9
SQ FT: 4,000
SALES (est): 796.8K **Privately Held**
WEB: www.indyautographics.com
SIC: **3993** 7532 7336 Signs & advertising
specialties; lettering, automotive; creative
services to advertisers, except writers

(G-7135)
HOTEL TANGO WHISKEY INC
Also Called: Hotel Tango Distillery
702 Virginia Ave (46203-0017)
PHONE..................................317 653-1806
Travis Barnes, *President*
Nick Ladig, *Vice Pres*
Brian Willsey, *Vice Pres*
EMP: 28
SQ FT: 3,500
SALES (est): 1MM **Privately Held**
SIC: **2084** Brandy & brandy spirits

(G-7136)
HOTEL VANITIES INTL LLC (PA)
5514 Stockwell Ct (46237-3153)
PHONE..................................317 787-2330
Tiffany Beam, *Project Mgr*
Jessica Hess, *Project Mgr*
Kevin Smith, *Project Mgr*
John Schroeder, *VP Sales*
Elizabeth Hatfield, *Manager*
▲ EMP: 12
SALES (est): 1.9MM **Privately Held**
WEB: www.hotelvanities.com
SIC: **3088** Bathroom fixtures, plastic

(G-7137)
HOUGHTON MIFFLIN HARCOURT CO
Also Called: Hmh
2700 N Richardt Ave (46219-1117)
PHONE..................................317 359-5585
Fax: 317 351-3636
Dennis Carey, *Owner*
EMP: 6
SALES (corp-wide): 1.4B **Publicly Held**
SIC: **3999** 2731 Education aids, devices &
supplies; book publishing
PA: Houghton Mifflin Harcourt Company
125 High St Ste 900
Boston MA 02110
617 351-5000

(G-7138)
HOUGHTON MIFFLIN HARCOURT PUBG
2700 N Richardt Ave (46219-1117)
PHONE..................................317 359-5585
Dennis Carey, *Branch Mgr*
EMP: 150
SALES (corp-wide): 1.4B **Publicly Held**
WEB: www.hmco.com
SIC: **2731** Book publishing
HQ: Houghton Mifflin Harcourt Publishing
Company
125 High St Ste 900
Boston MA 02110
617 351-5000

(G-7139)
HOVERSTREAM LLC
4801 Van Cleave St (46226-2942)
PHONE..................................317 489-0075
Jason Kuehn, *Owner*
▲ EMP: 3
SALES: 248.5K **Privately Held**
SIC: **3599** Propellers, ship & boat: ma-
chined

(G-7140)
HOWERTON RACECAR WORKS INC
Also Called: Howerton Racing Products
360 Gasoline Aly (46222-3967)
PHONE..................................317 241-0868
Fax: 317 241-0898
Jack Howerton, *President*
EMP: 10
SQ FT: 3,000
SALES (est): 1.1MM **Privately Held**
SIC: **3711** Motor vehicles & car bodies

(G-7141)
HP INC
7520 Georgetown Rd (46268-4131)
PHONE..................................317 334-3400
Kevin Bales, *Manager*
Keith Hangarage, *Director*
Migdalia Ruiz, *Training Spec*
EMP: 2500
SALES (corp-wide): 52B **Publicly Held**
SIC: **3571** Personal computers (microcom-
puters)
PA: Hp Inc.
1501 Page Mill Rd
Palo Alto CA 94304
650 857-1501

(G-7142)
HSM
9525 Delegates Row (46240-3807)
PHONE..................................317 573-8700
Darren Gray, *Sales Executive*
EMP: 2
SALES (est): 86K **Privately Held**
SIC: **3724** Aircraft engines & engine parts

(G-7143)
HUEHLS SEAL COATING & LAWN CAR
312 E Epler Ave (46227-1927)
PHONE..................................317 782-4069
Christopher Huehls, *Mng Member*
EMP: 2
SALES: 132.1K **Privately Held**
SIC: **0782** 1611 7692 Lawn care services;
surfacing & paving; welding repair

(G-7144)
HUMPHREY PRINTING CO
2346 S Lynhurst Dr 407c (46241-8621)
PHONE..................................317 241-6049
EMP: 2
SALES (est): 113.3K **Privately Held**
SIC: **2752** Lithographic Commercial Print-
ing

(G-7145)
HUMPHREYS WELDING SERVICE
810 Front Royal Dr (46227-2774)
PHONE..................................317 881-9024
George Humphrey, *Owner*
EMP: 3
SQ FT: 2,000
SALES: 250K **Privately Held**
SIC: **7692** 3599 Welding repair; machine
shop, jobbing & repair

(G-7146)
HURCO COMPANIES INC (PA)
1 Technology Way (46268-5106)
P.O. Box 68180 (46268-0180)
PHONE..................................317 293-5309
Fax: 317 328-2812
Michael Doar, *Ch of Bd*
Gregory S Volovic, *President*
John P Donlon, *Exec VP*
Sonja K McClelland, *CFO*
Robert W Cruickshank, *Director*
▲ EMP: 200
SQ FT: 165,000
SALES: 243.6MM **Publicly Held**
WEB: www.hurco.com
SIC: **3823** 7372 Computer interface equip-
ment for industrial process control;
prepackaged software

(G-7147)
HURCO COMPANIES INC
7220 Winton Dr (46268-5142)
PHONE..................................317 347-6208
Jason Strachman, *Manager*
EMP: 7
SALES (corp-wide): 243.6MM **Publicly Held**
SIC: **3823** Computer interface equipment
for industrial process control
PA: Hurco Companies, Inc.
1 Technology Way
Indianapolis IN 46268
317 293-5309

(G-7148)
HUTCHISON SIGN CO INC
215 S Munsie St (46229-2823)
PHONE..................................317 894-8787
William P Hutchison II, *President*
James Devine, *Executive Asst*
EMP: 20
SQ FT: 40,000
SALES (est): 2.7MM **Privately Held**
SIC: **3993** 1799 Electric signs; sign instal-
lation & maintenance

(G-7149)
HWH EMBROIDERY INC
5255 N Tacoma Ave Ste 2 (46220-3646)
PHONE..................................317 895-0201
Mark Hagerty, *President*
EMP: 18
SALES (est): 1.3MM **Privately Held**
SIC: **2395** Embroidery & art needlework

(G-7150)
HYDRAULIC PRESS BRICK COMPANY (HQ)
3600 Woodview Trce # 300 (46268-3123)
PHONE..................................317 290-1140
Jack W Schwarz, *Ch of Bd*
Thomas E Bennett, *President*
EMP: 25 EST: 1868
SQ FT: 3,000
SALES (est): 4MM
SALES (corp-wide): 702.7MM **Privately Held**
WEB: www.hpbhaydite.com
SIC: **3295** Shale, expanded
PA: Schwarz Partners, L.P.
3600 Woodview Trce # 300
Indianapolis IN 46268
317 290-1140

(G-7151)
HYDRO FIRE PROTECTION INC
5851 S Harding St (46217-9592)
PHONE..................................317 780-6980
Fax: 317 882-9707
Robert Birk, *President*
Tracy Branneman, *Treasurer*
Mary Birk, *Admin Sec*
EMP: 25
SQ FT: 7,500
SALES: 4.6MM **Privately Held**
SIC: **1711** 3569 Fire sprinkler system in-
stallation; sprinkler systems, fire: auto-
matic

(G-7152)
HYDRO-GEAR INC
5101 Decatur Blvd (46241-9528)
PHONE..................................317 821-0477
EMP: 9

SALES (corp-wide): 6.8B Privately Held
SIC: 3594 Hydrostatic drives (transmissions)
HQ: Hydro-Gear Inc
1411 S Hamilton St
Sullivan IL 61951
217 728-2581

(G-7153)
I F S CORP
Also Called: Fastsigns
9433 E Washington St (46229-3085)
PHONE...................................317 898-6118
Fax: 317 898-6149
August Cirdsi, President
Jerry C Walker, President
Jeffrey Parsons, Finance
EMP: 3
SALES (est): 1MM Privately Held
SIC: 3993 Signs & advertising specialties

(G-7154)
I LOVE SALAD LLC
4825 E 96th St (46240-3800)
PHONE...................................317 688-7512
Hee Lee, Principal
EMP: 6
SALES (est): 366.8K Privately Held
SIC: 2099 Salads, fresh or refrigerated

(G-7155)
IAIRE LLC (PA)
6805 Hillsdale Ct (46250-2039)
P.O. Box 40965 (46240-0965)
PHONE...................................317 806-2750
Joe Finkan, Mng Member
Gary Colip,
EMP: 8
SALES (est): 5.7MM Privately Held
SIC: 3564 Air purification equipment

(G-7156)
IBJ CORPORATION
Also Called: Indianapolis Business Journal
41 E Washington St # 200 (46204-3517)
PHONE...................................317 634-6200
Fax: 317 263-5060
Michael Maurer, President
Lou Harry, Editor
Greg Morris, Vice Pres
Jeff Basch, CFO
Robert Schloss, Treasurer
EMP: 75
SQ FT: 13,500
SALES (est): 6.4MM Privately Held
WEB: www.indnext.com
SIC: 2711 Newspapers: publishing only,
not printed on site; newspapers, publishing & printing

(G-7157)
IKIO LED LIGHTING LLC
8470 Allison Pointe Blvd # 128
(46250-4368)
PHONE...................................765 414-0835
Hardeep Singh, Mng Member
Ekam Singh, Mng Member
▲ EMP: 15
SALES: 2.4MM Privately Held
SIC: 3648 7349 Lighting equipment; lighting maintenance service

(G-7158)
ILAB LLC
111 Monument Cir Ste 882 (46204-5173)
PHONE...................................317 218-3258
Vaughn Young, Business Mgr
Gerry Bailey, Mng Member
Gordon Leibbrandt, Mng Member
Jethro Lloyd, Mng Member
Sherry Wooldridge, Program Mgr
EMP: 54
SALES (est): 6.3MM Privately Held
SIC: 7371 7372 5045 Custom computer
programming services; prepackaged software; computer software

(G-7159)
ILLINOIS TOOL WORKS INC
ITW Specialty Products
7130 W Mccarty St (46241-1464)
P.O. Box 1869, Akron OH (44309-1869)
PHONE...................................317 390-5940
Fax: 317 390-5999
George Duvall, Manager
EMP: 45

SALES (corp-wide): 14.3B Publicly Held
SIC: 3559 3714 Sewing machines & hat &
zipper making machinery; motor vehicle
parts & accessories
PA: Illinois Tool Works Inc.
155 Harlem Ave
Glenview IL 60025
847 724-7500

(G-7160)
ILLINOIS TOOL WORKS INC
Also Called: ITW Gema
4141 W 54th St (46254-3728)
PHONE...................................317 298-5000
Chris Merritt, General Mgr
EMP: 50
SQ FT: 63,000
SALES (corp-wide): 14.3B Publicly Held
WEB: www.itwgema.us
SIC: 3549 3621 Assembly machines, including robotic; control equipment for
electric buses & locomotives
PA: Illinois Tool Works Inc.
155 Harlem Ave
Glenview IL 60025
847 724-7500

(G-7161)
IMAGE INKS COMPANY
7363 Red Rock Rd (46236-9358)
PHONE...................................317 432-5041
Zachary L Grider, President
EMP: 2
SALES (est): 124K Privately Held
SIC: 3861 Printing equipment, photographic

(G-7162)
IMAGINEERING ENTERPRISES INC
2719 N Emerson Ave Ste A (46218-3283)
PHONE...................................317 635-8565
F James Hammer, President
EMP: 15
SQ FT: 50,000
SALES (est): 1.5MM
SALES (corp-wide): 20.7MM Privately Held
SIC: 3479 8711 Painting, coating & hot
dipping; engineering services
PA: Imagineering Enterprises Inc
1302 W Sample St
South Bend IN 46619
574 287-2941

(G-7163)
IMH FABRICATION INC (PA)
Also Called: Imh Products
1121 E 46th St (46205-2016)
P.O. Box 20814 (46220-0814)
PHONE...................................317 252-5566
Fax: 317 252-5565
Eric Odmark, President
Mark Seger, COO
Darrell Hansel, Prdtn Mgr
Cindy Noble, Manager
EMP: 10 EST: 1955
SQ FT: 25,000
SALES (est): 12.9MM Privately Held
WEB: www.imh.com
SIC: 3444 3469 Sheet metal specialties,
not stamped; stamping metal for the trade

(G-7164)
IMH FABRICATION INC
2073 Dr Andrew J Brown (46202-1932)
P.O. Box 20814 (46220-0814)
PHONE...................................317 252-5566
Mike Kennedy, President
EMP: 12
SALES (corp-wide): 12.9MM Privately Held
WEB: www.imh.com
SIC: 3444 3469 Sheet metal specialties,
not stamped; metal stampings
PA: Imh Fabrication Inc.
1121 E 46th St
Indianapolis IN 46205
317 252-5566

(G-7165)
IMINE CORPORATION
8520 Allison Pointe Blvd (46250-5700)
PHONE...................................877 464-6388
EMP: 2

SALES (est): 66K Privately Held
SIC: 1481 Nonmetallic mineral services

(G-7166)
IMMUNORES-THERAPEUTICS LLC
Noyes Pavillion 5th Fl E (46202)
PHONE...................................860 514-0526
Linda Sharkus, Principal
EMP: 2 EST: 2014
SALES (est): 140K Privately Held
SIC: 3841 Surgical & medical instruments

(G-7167)
IMPACT SAFETY INC
7991 W 21st St Ste D1 (46214-4304)
PHONE...................................317 852-3067
Robby Pierce, CEO
▲ EMP: 2
SALES (est): 168.7K Privately Held
SIC: 3949 Sporting & athletic goods

(G-7168)
IMPRESSIONS THAT COUNT INC
917 Greer St (46203-1717)
PHONE...................................317 423-0581
Gregory Townsend, President
EMP: 3
SALES (est): 250K Privately Held
SIC: 3953 Marking devices; printing dies,
rubber or plastic, for marking machines;
numbering stamps, hand: rubber or metal

(G-7169)
INCHROMATICS LLC
1545 Trace Ln (46260-2740)
PHONE...................................317 872-7401
David Nurok,
EMP: 3
SALES (est): 221.5K Privately Held
SIC: 3826 Chromatographic equipment,
laboratory type

(G-7170)
INDEPENDENT CONCRETE PIPE CO (PA)
2050 S Harding St (46221-1948)
PHONE...................................419 841-3361
Fax: 317 262-4926
Barry Bundrant, Ch of Bd
Edward Higgins, Exec VP
George J Langenderfer Jr, Vice Pres
John Bearss, Treasurer
EMP: 25
SQ FT: 10,000
SALES (est): 13.9MM Privately Held
SIC: 3272 Pipe, concrete or lined with concrete; sewer pipe, concrete; culvert pipe,
concrete; manhole covers or frames, concrete

(G-7171)
INDEPENDENT CONCRETE PIPE CO
2050 S Harding St (46221-1948)
PHONE...................................800 875-4920
Fax: 574 256-2704
Jeff Swann, Principal
EMP: 20
SALES (corp-wide): 13.9MM Privately Held
SIC: 3272 5032 Pipe, concrete or lined
with concrete; sewer pipe, clay
PA: Independent Concrete Pipe Co
2050 S Harding St
Indianapolis IN 46221
419 841-3361

(G-7172)
INDEPENDENT CONCRETE PIPE CO
2050 S Harding St (46221-1948)
PHONE...................................317 262-4920
Mike Pepper, Branch Mgr
EMP: 35
SALES (corp-wide): 13.9MM Privately Held
SIC: 3272 5032 5211 5051 Pipe, concrete or lined with concrete; brick, stone &
related material; masonry materials &
supplies; pipe & tubing, steel
PA: Independent Concrete Pipe Co
2050 S Harding St
Indianapolis IN 46221
419 841-3361

(G-7173)
INDEPENDENT CONCRETE PIPE CO
2050 S Harding St (46221-1948)
PHONE...................................317 262-4920
Tony Blair, Plant Mgr
Roger Parker, Sales Staff
EMP: 16
SALES (corp-wide): 13.9MM Privately Held
SIC: 3272 Culvert pipe, concrete; sewer
pipe, concrete
PA: Independent Concrete Pipe Co
2050 S Harding St
Indianapolis IN 46221
419 841-3361

(G-7174)
INDEPENDENT CONCRETE PIPE CO
Also Called: Indiana Division
2050 S Harding St (46221-1948)
PHONE...................................317 262-4920
Scott Bundrant, Manager
EMP: 30
SALES (corp-wide): 13.9MM Privately Held
SIC: 3272 Pipe, concrete or lined with concrete
PA: Independent Concrete Pipe Co
2050 S Harding St
Indianapolis IN 46221
419 841-3361

(G-7175)
INDEPENDENT RAIL CORPORATION
Also Called: Indierail
6233 Brookville Rd (46219-8213)
P.O. Box 430, Beech Grove (46107-0430)
PHONE...................................317 780-8480
Fax: 317 784-8481
Robert Driggers, President
Dennis L Laswell, Admin Sec
EMP: 23
SQ FT: 5,000
SALES (est): 5.3MM Privately Held
SIC: 3542 Mechanical (pneumatic or hydraulic) metal forming machines

(G-7176)
INDIANA BUSINESS MAGAZINE
1100 Waterway Blvd (46202-2156)
PHONE...................................317 692-1200
Elissa Cronk, Principal
EMP: 2
SALES (est): 73.1K Privately Held
SIC: 2721 Periodicals

(G-7177)
INDIANA CITY BREWING LLC
24 Shelby St (46202-3941)
PHONE...................................317 643-1103
Ray Kamstra,
EMP: 15
SQ FT: 6,000
SALES (est): 501.7K Privately Held
SIC: 5813 2082 5181 Tavern (drinking
places); bars & lounges; beer (alcoholic
beverage); beer & ale

(G-7178)
INDIANA CONCESSION SUPPLY LLC
2402 N Shadeland Ave R (46219-1774)
PHONE...................................317 353-1667
Fax: 317 353-1702
Dave Battas, Owner
Dave Battas Jr, Mng Member
Dave Battas Sr,
EMP: 10
SQ FT: 15,000
SALES (est): 4.3MM Privately Held
SIC: 3589 Popcorn machines, commercial

(G-7179)
INDIANA FIBER WORKS
625 E 11th St (46202-2727)
PHONE...................................317 524-5711
Rob McNabb, Principal
EMP: 3 EST: 2008
SALES (est): 304.9K Privately Held
SIC: 3554 Paper industries machinery

▲ = Import ▼=Export
♦ =Import/Export

(G-7180)
INDIANA INSTRUMENTS INC
8032 Gordon Dr (46278-1316)
P.O. Box 53731 (46253-0731)
PHONE...................................317 875-8032
Barry J Stern, *President*
Judy Stern, *Corp Secy*
EMP: 3
SALES (est): 230K **Privately Held**
SIC: 3699 Teaching machines & aids, electronic

(G-7181)
INDIANA LASER SPINE CENTER
8202 Clearvista Pkwy 9e (46256-1457)
PHONE...................................317 577-1800
Phillip Kingma, *President*
Wenda Kingma, *Manager*
EMP: 2
SALES (est): 257K **Privately Held**
SIC: 3845 Surgical support systems: heartlung machine, exc. iron lung

(G-7182)
INDIANA LOGO SIGN GROUP
600 E 96th St Ste 460 (46240-3823)
PHONE...................................800 950-1093
EMP: 2 EST: 2015
SALES (est): 99.1K **Privately Held**
SIC: 3993 Signs & advertising specialties

(G-7183)
INDIANA METAL TREATING INC
512 S Harding St (46221-1137)
PHONE...................................317 636-2421
Fax: 317 636-4902
Rusella Keifer, *President*
Rod Wininger, *Vice Pres*
EMP: 10
SQ FT: 4,000
SALES: 540K **Privately Held**
SIC: 3398 Metal heat treating

(G-7184)
INDIANA MODEL COMPANY INC
Also Called: IMC
6136 E Hanna Ave (46203-6127)
PHONE...................................317 787-6358
Fax: 317 787-1274
Ernest E Huber, *President*
Paula M Huber, *Corp Secy*
Mark Carson, *Purchasing*
Ernie Huber, *Executive*
Paula Huber, *Executive*
EMP: 63 EST: 1963
SQ FT: 50,000
SALES (est): 14MM **Privately Held**
WEB: www.imc4cnc.com
SIC: 3444 3599 3544 Sheet metalwork; machine shop, jobbing & repair; special dies, tools, jigs & fixtures

(G-7185)
INDIANA NANOTECH LLC
Also Called: Research
7750 Centerstone Dr (46259-1485)
PHONE...................................317 385-1578
Robert Karlinsey, *Mng Member*
EMP: 6
SQ FT: 2,500
SALES (est): 918K **Privately Held**
SIC: 2844 Toilet preparations

(G-7186)
INDIANA NEWSPAPERS LLC (HQ)
Also Called: Indianapolis Star, The
130 S Meridian St (46225-1046)
PHONE...................................317 444-4000
Fax: 317 444-7222
Karen Crotchfelt, *President*
Gracia C Martore, *Vice Pres*
Michael A Hart, *Treasurer*
Craig A Dubow, *Director*
Todd A Mayman, *Admin Sec*
EMP: 900 EST: 1998
SQ FT: 324,000
SALES (est): 209.9MM
SALES (corp-wide): 3.1B **Publicly Held**
SIC: 2711 2752 Commercial printing & newspaper publishing combined; commercial printing, lithographic
PA: Gannett Co., Inc.
7950 Jones Branch Dr
Mc Lean VA 22102
703 854-6000

(G-7187)
INDIANA NEWSPAPERS LLC
Also Called: Indianapolis Star
8278 Georgetown Rd (46268-1622)
PHONE...................................317 444-3800
EMP: 11
SALES (corp-wide): 3.1B **Publicly Held**
SIC: 2711 Commercial printing & newspaper publishing combined; newspapers, publishing & printing
HQ: Indiana Newspapers Llc
130 S Meridian St
Indianapolis IN 46225
317 444-4000

(G-7188)
INDIANA OXYGEN COMPANY INC (PA)
Also Called: Hoosier Oxygen Company
6099 Corporate Way (46278-2923)
P.O. Box 78588 (46278-0588)
PHONE...................................317 290-0003
Fax: 317 328-5009
Walter L Brant, *Ch of Bd*
Anne Hayes, *President*
Michael Gunnels, *Exec VP*
Mike Gunnels, *Exec VP*
Gary Halter, *Exec VP*
EMP: 55 EST: 1915
SQ FT: 31,000
SALES (est): 60.1MM **Privately Held**
WEB: www.indianaoxygen.com
SIC: 5169 5084 2813 Industrial gases; welding machinery & equipment; industrial gases

(G-7189)
INDIANA PICKLE COMPANY LLC
8434 Silverado Dr (46237-8246)
PHONE...................................317 698-7292
Robert Carmack, *Administration*
EMP: 2 EST: 2015
SALES (est): 162.2K **Privately Held**
SIC: 2035 Pickled fruits & vegetables

(G-7190)
INDIANA SEAL
9329 Castlegate Dr (46256-1002)
PHONE...................................317 841-3547
Brian McConnell, *Manager*
EMP: 3
SALES (est): 186.7K **Privately Held**
SIC: 3494 Pipe fittings

(G-7191)
INDIANA SIGN & BARRICADE INC
5240 E 25th St (46218-3934)
PHONE...................................317 377-8000
Janet L Schutt, *President*
Steve A Apple, *Director*
Sheila M McNelis, *Director*
EMP: 26
SQ FT: 37,000
SALES (est): 4.2MM **Privately Held**
SIC: 3993 Signs & advertising specialties

(G-7192)
INDIANA STATE MEDICAL ASSN
Also Called: I S M A Report
322 Canal Walk Ste Cl (46202-3265)
PHONE...................................317 261-2060
Fax: 317 261-2076
Mark Ingold, *Finance*
Kathleen Hopper, *Manager*
Richard R King, *Director*
Stacy Cook, *General Counsel*
Jill Bruce, *Administration*
EMP: 34
SQ FT: 11,585
SALES: 3.6MM **Privately Held**
WEB: www.ismanet.org
SIC: 8621 2721 Medical field-related associations; periodicals

(G-7193)
INDIANA STEEL FABRICATING INC (PA)
4545 W Bradbury Ave (46241-5210)
P.O. Box 421547 (46242-1547)
PHONE...................................317 247-4545
Fax: 317 241-6223
Stephen Porter, *President*
Steve Dowden, *Treasurer*
Barbara E Osborne, *Admin Sec*

EMP: 31 EST: 1954
SQ FT: 36,000
SALES: 18.4MM **Privately Held**
WEB: www.indianasteelfab.com
SIC: 3441 Fabricated structural metal

(G-7194)
INDIANA STEEL RULE DIE INC
Also Called: Indiana Steel Rule & Die
6331 English Ave (46219-8267)
P.O. Box 33843 (46203-0843)
PHONE...................................317 352-9859
Fax: 317 352-9859
Rick Lee, *President*
EMP: 2
SALES (est): 262K **Privately Held**
SIC: 3544 Dies & die holders for metal cutting, forming, die casting

(G-7195)
INDIANA THERMAL SOLUTIONS LLC
6872 Hillsdale Ct # 375 (46250-2001)
PHONE...................................317 570-5400
Chris Adkins,
Dan Adams,
Paul Mattingly,
EMP: 10
SQ FT: 2,700
SALES (est): 4.3MM **Privately Held**
SIC: 3823 Thermal conductivity instruments, industrial process type

(G-7196)
INDIANA VENEERS CORP (PA)
1121 E 24th St (46205-4425)
PHONE...................................317 926-2458
Fax: 317 926-8569
Werner L Lorenz, *President*
Peter Lorenz, *President*
▼ EMP: 53 EST: 1892
SQ FT: 200,000
SALES (est): 10.9MM **Privately Held**
WEB: www.indianaveneers.com
SIC: 2435 Veneer stock, hardwood

(G-7197)
INDIANA WHOLESALE WINE LQ CO
1240 Brookville Way Ste J (46239-1099)
PHONE...................................317 667-0231
Kevin Paschke, *Owner*
▲ EMP: 5
SALES (est): 802.3K **Privately Held**
SIC: 5182 2084 Wine; wines

(G-7198)
INDIANAPOLIS FABRICATIONS LLC
Also Called: Lfab
1125 Brookside Ave G50 (46202-2778)
PHONE...................................317 600-3522
Owen Jones, *Project Mgr*
Randy Domeck,
▲ EMP: 12
SALES (est): 2MM **Privately Held**
SIC: 3441 Fabricated structural metal

(G-7199)
INDIANAPOLIS GATORADE
5858 Decatur Blvd (46241-9575)
PHONE...................................317 821-6400
Lance Oxley, *Director*
EMP: 4
SALES (est): 264.8K **Privately Held**
SIC: 2086 Bottled & canned soft drinks

(G-7200)
INDIANAPOLIS GRANITE & MBL INC
5360 Winthrop Ave (46220-3258)
PHONE...................................317 259-4478
Carol E King, *President*
Fred King, *Vice Pres*
EMP: 3
SQ FT: 10,000
SALES (est): 249.1K **Privately Held**
SIC: 3281 Granite, cut & shaped

(G-7201)
INDIANAPOLIS INDUSTRIAL PDTS
Also Called: Matjack Division Indianapolis
2320 Duke St (46205-2240)
PHONE...................................317 359-3078

Fax: 317 359-3079
John Sweezy Jr, *CEO*
Bradley Sweezy, *Vice Pres*
Cherie Owens, *Admin Sec*
Susan Sweezy, *Admin Sec*
EMP: 7
SQ FT: 6,000
SALES (est): 1.2MM **Privately Held**
WEB: www.matjack.com
SIC: 3069 Air-supported rubber structures

(G-7202)
INDIANAPOLIS MARINE CO
Also Called: Smitty's Indianapolis Marine
4979 Massachusetts Ave (46218-3146)
PHONE...................................317 545-4646
Fax: 317 547-6535
Charles R Smith, *Partner*
David T Smith, *Partner*
Steven Smith, *General Mgr*
EMP: 11
SQ FT: 6,200
SALES (est): 780K **Privately Held**
SIC: 2394 3732 Tarpaulins, fabric: made from purchased materials; convertible tops, canvas or boat: from purchased materials; boat building & repairing

(G-7203)
INDIANAPOLIS METAL SPINNING CO
1924 Midwest Blvd (46214-2337)
PHONE...................................317 273-7440
Fax: 317 273-7450
James C Kaufman, *President*
▲ EMP: 12 EST: 1924
SQ FT: 50,000
SALES (est): 1.8MM **Privately Held**
WEB: www.imspinning.com
SIC: 3469 Spinning metal for the trade; stamping metal for the trade

(G-7204)
INDIANAPOLIS RUBBER STAMP CO
Also Called: Irsco Marking Products
955 N Pennsylvania St (46204-1031)
P.O. Box 44787 (46244-0787)
PHONE...................................317 263-9540
Fax: 317 263-9543
David Schilling, *CEO*
Mark Schilling, *President*
Barbara Handy, *Treasurer*
Vivian Surface, *Admin Sec*
EMP: 14 EST: 1919
SQ FT: 14,000
SALES (est): 930K **Privately Held**
WEB: www.indremcs.org
SIC: 3953 Marking devices

(G-7205)
INDIANAPOLIS SIGNWORKS INC
5349 W 86th St (46268-1501)
PHONE...................................317 872-8722
Fax: 317 872-8724
Andy Chapman, *President*
EMP: 22
SQ FT: 15,000
SALES (est): 3.6MM **Privately Held**
WEB: www.indianapolissignworks.com
SIC: 3993 7336 Signs & advertising specialties; commercial art & illustration

(G-7206)
INDUSTRIAL ADHESIVES INDIANA
8202 Indy Ln (46214-2326)
PHONE...................................317 271-2100
Jon Scott Watson, *President*
Mary Jane Watson, *Vice Pres*
EMP: 5
SALES: 2MM **Privately Held**
WEB: www.thebestglue.com
SIC: 2891 Adhesives

(G-7207)
INDUSTRIAL ANODIZING CO INC
1610 W Washington St (46222-4594)
P.O. Box 1363 (46206-1363)
PHONE...................................317 637-4641
Fax: 317 634-7316
William Wimmenauer Jr, *President*
EMP: 50 EST: 1963
SQ FT: 30,000

SALES (est): 5.6MM **Privately Held**
WEB: www.industrialanodizing.com
SIC: **3471** Anodizing (plating) of metals or formed products

(G-7208)
INDUSTRIAL HYDRAULICS INC
1005 Western Dr (46241-1436)
PHONE...............................317 247-4421
Fax: 317 240-4384
Ronald P Dilley, *President*
Duane Harris, *Vice Pres*
William Duane Harris Jr, *Vice Pres*
Matthew Pogue, *Parts Mgr*
Victor Hutton, *Buyer*
EMP: 24
SQ FT: 18,000
SALES (est): 5.8MM **Privately Held**
WEB: www.ihi-indy.com
SIC: **7699 3599** Hydraulic equipment repair; custom machinery

(G-7209)
INDUSTRIAL SALES & SUPPLY INC
Also Called: Zoofari Gardens
5640 Professional Cir (46241-5015)
PHONE...............................317 240-0560
Patti Luc, *President*
Max Rettig, *Sales Executive*
EMP: 18
SALES (est): 3.7MM **Privately Held**
SIC: **3334 3545** Primary aluminum; machine tool accessories

(G-7210)
INDUSTRIAL SERVICES GROUP INC
6450 Guion Rd (46268-2531)
PHONE...............................317 334-0921
David Nirschl, *President*
EMP: 10
SALES (est): 17.4K **Privately Held**
SIC: **3589** Commercial cleaning equipment

(G-7211)
INDUSTRIAL SOFTWARE LLC
7657 Stones River Ct (46259-6727)
PHONE...............................317 862-0650
Dana Stephenson, *President*
EMP: 2
SALES (est): 127.8K **Privately Held**
SIC: **7372** Prepackaged software

(G-7212)
INDY AEROSPACE INC
2801 Fortune Cir E Ste J (46241-5551)
PHONE...............................817 521-6508
Jose Rodriguez, *CEO*
Austin Mielczarek, *Principal*
EMP: 5
SALES: 2MM **Privately Held**
SIC: **1799 4581 3499** Renovation of aircraft interiors; aircraft upholstery repair; aerosol valves, metal

(G-7213)
INDY COLOR PRINTING LLC
6220 Hardegan St (46227-4907)
PHONE...............................317 371-8829
Jeanne McCullough, *Owner*
EMP: 2 EST: 2011
SALES (est): 179.9K **Privately Held**
SIC: **2752** Commercial printing, lithographic

(G-7214)
INDY COMPOSITE WORKS INC
3945 Guion Ln Ste A (46268-2677)
PHONE...............................317 280-9766
Greg Strydesky, *President*
Russ Polak, *Engineer*
EMP: 35
SALES (est): 6.4MM **Privately Held**
SIC: **2824** Organic fibers, noncellulosic

(G-7215)
INDY CUSTOM MACHINE INC
8267 Indy Ct (46214-2300)
PHONE...............................317 271-1544
Jeff Rapp, *President*
Jene McVay, *Vice Pres*
Tammy Powell, *Vice Pres*
EMP: 7
SQ FT: 5,600

SALES (est): 1MM **Privately Held**
SIC: **3599** Machine shop, jobbing & repair; machine & other job shop work

(G-7216)
INDY CYLINDER HEAD
8621 Stheastern Ave Ste B (46239)
PHONE...............................317 862-3724
Fax: 317 862-6300
Russell E Flagle, *President*
▼ EMP: 22
SQ FT: 3,000
SALES (est): 3.8MM **Privately Held**
WEB: www.indyheads.com
SIC: **3714** Cylinder heads, motor vehicle

(G-7217)
INDY GLASS CENTER INC
6366 E 32nd Ct (46226-6168)
PHONE...............................317 591-5000
Fax: 317 591-5010
Paul Davis, *President*
Jack Ferrell, *Vice Pres*
EMP: 18
SQ FT: 25,000
SALES (est): 3.4MM **Privately Held**
WEB: www.indyglasscenter.com
SIC: **3211 5039 3231** Insulating glass, sealed units; glass construction materials; architectural metalwork; products of purchased glass

(G-7218)
INDY METRO WOMAN MAGAZINE
8961 Crystal Lake Dr (46240-6413)
PHONE...............................317 843-1344
Mark Burg, *Publisher*
EMP: 2 EST: 2008
SALES (est): 138.8K **Privately Held**
SIC: **7313 2721** Printed media advertising representatives; magazines: publishing & printing

(G-7219)
INDY PARTS INC
2 Gasoline Aly A (46222-3963)
PHONE...............................317 243-7171
Scott Jasek, *President*
EMP: 5
SALES (est): 457.7K **Privately Held**
SIC: **3089** Automotive parts, plastic

(G-7220)
INDY POWDER COATING INC
4300 W 10th St (46222-3208)
PHONE...............................317 244-2231
Fax: 317 244-2232
Gary K Farber, *President*
EMP: 5
SALES (est): 694.8K **Privately Held**
SIC: **3479** Painting, coating & hot dipping

(G-7221)
INDY RAPID 3D LLC
10117 Falcon Cove Cir (46236-8495)
PHONE...............................812 243-4175
Danielle Homsangpradit,
EMP: 2
SALES (est): 107.6K **Privately Held**
SIC: **2821 7389 8711 8713** Plastics materials & resins; ; engineering services; photogrammetric engineering; business consulting

(G-7222)
INDY SPORTS PREVIEW PROGRAM
Also Called: Indy Sports Magazine
1089 3rd Ave Sw Ste 207 (46205)
PHONE...............................317 259-0570
Fax: 317 271-7917
Paul Shockley, *President*
EMP: 20
SALES: 500K **Privately Held**
SIC: **2721** Magazines: publishing only, not printed on site

(G-7223)
INDY STUD WELDING
2654 Allen Ave (46203-5144)
PHONE...............................317 416-3617
Kenneth M Pologruto, *Owner*
EMP: 2

SALES: 230K **Privately Held**
SIC: **3423** Ironworkers' hand tools

(G-7224)
INDY WEB INC
3151 Madison Ave A (46227-1160)
PHONE...............................317 356-3622
David Nelson, *President*
Rich Jensen, *Exec VP*
John Goldberg, *Manager*
EMP: 4
SQ FT: 2,400
SALES (est): 560.9K **Privately Held**
WEB: www.indyweb.net
SIC: **4813 3571 8748** ; ; personal computers (microcomputers); systems engineering consultant, ex. computer or professional

(G-7225)
INDYS SIGN SOURCE INC
5501 W 86th St Ste C (46268-1583)
PHONE...............................317 372-2260
Scott Mize, *President*
Jack Stroud, *Vice Pres*
Gregory Mize, *Admin Sec*
EMP: 3
SALES (est): 220.4K **Privately Held**
SIC: **3993** Signs & advertising specialties

(G-7226)
INFINIAS LLC
9340 Priority Way West Dr (46240-1468)
PHONE...............................317 348-1249
Wayne Jared,
▼ EMP: 9
SQ FT: 1,600
SALES: 2MM **Privately Held**
SIC: **3679** Electronic switches

(G-7227)
INFINITY PERFORMANCE INC
7002 N Park Ave (46220-1040)
PHONE...............................317 479-1017
George Atkinson, *President*
EMP: 43
SQ FT: 30,000
SALES: 4.6MM **Privately Held**
WEB: www.infinityperformance.com
SIC: **3069** Rubber floor coverings, mats & wallcoverings

(G-7228)
INFRASTRUCTURE AND ENERGY (PA)
2647 Waterfront Pkwy (46214)
PHONE...............................765 828-2580
Mohsin Y Meghji, *Ch of Bd*
John Paul Roehm, *President*
Andrew Layman, *CFO*
EMP: 10
SALES (est): 49MM **Publicly Held**
SIC: **3621 8711** Windmills, electric generating; energy conservation engineering

(G-7229)
INGREDION INCORPORATED
5521 W 74th St (46268-4184)
PHONE...............................317 295-4122
EMP: 14
SALES (corp-wide): 5.8B **Publicly Held**
SIC: **2046** Wet corn milling; corn starch; corn oil products; corn sugars & syrups
PA: Ingredion Incorporated
5 Westbrook Corporate Ctr # 500
Westchester IL 60154
708 551-2600

(G-7230)
INGREDION INCORPORATED
1050 W Raymond St (46221-2010)
P.O. Box 1084 (46206-1084)
PHONE...............................317 635-4400
Steve Mundell, *Warehouse Mgr*
Judy Wooden, *Manager*
◆ EMP: 23
SALES (corp-wide): 5.8B **Publicly Held**
SIC: **3999** Lawn ornaments
PA: Ingredion Incorporated
5 Westbrook Corporate Ctr # 500
Westchester IL 60154
708 551-2600

(G-7231)
INGREDION INCORPORATED
1515 Drover St (46221-1735)
PHONE...............................317 635-4455
Bob Stefansic, *Manager*
EMP: 71
SALES (corp-wide): 5.8B **Publicly Held**
SIC: **2046** Corn starch
PA: Ingredion Incorporated
5 Westbrook Corporate Ctr # 500
Westchester IL 60154
708 551-2600

(G-7232)
INGROUP
200 W Washington St M12 (46204-2728)
P.O. Box 383, Noblesville (46061-0383)
PHONE...............................317 817-9997
Edward Feigenbaum, *Owner*
EMP: 2
SQ FT: 120
SALES (est): 106.5K **Privately Held**
WEB: www.ingrouponline.com
SIC: **2741 8748** Newsletter publishing; publishing consultant

(G-7233)
INHABIT INC
211 S Ritter Ave Ste B (46219-7151)
PHONE...............................317 636-1699
Jennifer Tuttle, *President*
Michael Tuttle, *Vice Pres*
▲ EMP: 9
SQ FT: 6,500
SALES (est): 925.8K **Privately Held**
WEB: www.inhabitliving.com
SIC: **2392** Household furnishings

(G-7234)
INLAND PAPER BOARD & PACKAGING
5461 W 79th St (46268-1675)
PHONE...............................317 879-9710
Steve Raine, *Principal*
EMP: 3
SALES (est): 332K **Privately Held**
SIC: **2621** Wrapping & packaging papers

(G-7235)
INNOVATIVE CHEMICAL RESOURCES
Also Called: I C R
6464 Rucker Rd (46220-4841)
PHONE...............................317 695-6001
John Hulen, *President*
Clay F Cox, *Vice Pres*
EMP: 5
SQ FT: 1,000
SALES (est): 515.6K **Privately Held**
SIC: **2899 8999** Chemical preparations; chemical consultant

(G-7236)
INNOVATIVE CONCEPTS GROUP
8624 Quarterhorse Dr (46256-4322)
PHONE...............................317 408-0292
Robert Puma, *President*
EMP: 5
SALES (est): 367.9K **Privately Held**
SIC: **2048 5199** Prepared feeds; pet supplies

(G-7237)
INNOVATIVE FABRICATION LLC
Also Called: Indy Hanger
801 S Emerson Ave (46203-1602)
PHONE...............................317 215-5988
Roger A Crowder, *Mng Member*
Walt Smith,
EMP: 70
SQ FT: 80,000
SALES: 17MM **Privately Held**
SIC: **3315** Hangers (garment), wire

(G-7238)
INNOVATIVE MOLD & MACHINE INC
2702 Brill Rd (46225-2303)
PHONE...............................317 634-1177
Michael D Thomas, *President*
Jodi Lawrence, *Office Mgr*
EMP: 3 EST: 1995
SQ FT: 2,000

▲ = Import ▼=Export
◆ =Import/Export

SALES (est): 597.1K **Privately Held**
SIC: 3089 3549 Injection molding of plastics; metalworking machinery

(G-7239)
INNOVTIVE HYDRLIC SLUTIONS LLC
Also Called: Protect Perry
3015 S Harding St (46217-3133)
PHONE...................................317 252-0120
Ian Harley,
EMP: 8
SALES (est): 742.4K **Privately Held**
SIC: 3492 Hose & tube fittings & assemblies, hydraulic/pneumatic

(G-7240)
INSERTEC INC (PA)
4011 W 54th St (46254-4789)
PHONE...................................800 556-1911
Fax: 317 824-5758
David M Harrison, *President*
Robert Roy, *Vice Pres*
EMP: 64
SQ FT: 75,000
SALES (est): 5.6MM **Privately Held**
WEB: www.insertec.com
SIC: 7372 7389 Prepackaged software; packaging & labeling services

(G-7241)
INSIGN INC
Also Called: Real Estate Sign Services
5812 Linton Ln (46220-5355)
PHONE...................................317 251-0131
Laura J Tomlin, *President*
EMP: 2
SALES (est): 234.9K **Privately Held**
WEB: www.realestatesignservices.com
SIC: 3993 Signs & advertising specialties

(G-7242)
INSIGNIA SIGN SHOP LLC
7225 E Raymond St (46239-9583)
PHONE...................................317 356-4639
Amy Waterman, *Owner*
EMP: 3
SALES (est): 210.1K **Privately Held**
SIC: 3993 Signs & advertising specialties

(G-7243)
INSTANT REFUND TAX SERVICE
10059 E Washington St (46229-2623)
PHONE...................................317 536-1689
David Franklin, *Principal*
EMP: 2
SALES (est): 18K **Privately Held**
SIC: 2752 Commercial printing, lithographic

(G-7244)
INSTANTWHIP-INDIANAPOLIS INC
9125 Burk Rd (46229-3083)
PHONE...................................317 899-1533
Fax: 317 899-1544
Ted Wadsworth, *General Mgr*
EMP: 10
SALES (corp-wide): 5MM **Privately Held**
SIC: 2026 5143 Whipped topping, except frozen or dry mix; dairy products, except dried or canned
PA: Instantwhip-Indianapolis Inc
2200 Cardigan Ave
Columbus OH 43215
614 488-2536

(G-7245)
INSTY-PRINTS
930 E Hanna Ave (46227-1306)
PHONE...................................317 788-1504
Fax: 317 788-1543
Robin Heldman, *Principal*
EMP: 2
SALES (est): 140.5K **Privately Held**
SIC: 2752 Commercial printing, lithographic

(G-7246)
INTEGER HOLDINGS CORPORATION
Also Called: Greatbatch Medical
3737 N Arlington Ave (46218-1867)
PHONE...................................317 454-8800
Charlie Wemhoff, *Opers Staff*

Chris Albers, *Engineer*
Bill Schulenberg, *Manager*
EMP: 130
SALES (corp-wide): 1.4B **Publicly Held**
SIC: 3089 Cases, plastic
PA: Integer Holdings Corporation
2595 Dallas Pkwy Ste 310
Frisco TX 75034
214 618-5243

(G-7247)
INTEGRATED DE ICING SERVI
7899 S Service Rd Ste H (46241-4214)
PHONE...................................317 517-1643
EMP: 3
SALES (est): 231.1K **Privately Held**
SIC: 3728 Aircraft parts & equipment

(G-7248)
INTEGRATED INSTRUMENT SERVICES
5601 Fortune Cir S Ste A (46241-5533)
P.O. Box 51013 (46251-0013)
PHONE...................................317 248-1958
Fax: 317 247-8502
Al Chamen, *President*
Hasan Al Mahrovq, *Vice Pres*
Kassab Sayel, *Vice Pres*
EMP: 10
SQ FT: 10,000
SALES (est): 500K **Privately Held**
WEB: www.i2sinc.com
SIC: 8734 3821 Testing laboratories; vacuum pumps, laboratory

(G-7249)
INTEGRATED TECH RESOURCES
2445 Directors Row Ste J (46241-4936)
PHONE...................................317 757-5432
Diane Fleete, *President*
EMP: 4
SALES: 1MM **Privately Held**
SIC: 3613 Control panels, electric

(G-7250)
INTEGRATORCOM INC
6161 E 75th St (46250-2701)
PHONE...................................317 849-2250
Mark Shumaker, *Principal*
EMP: 2
SALES (est): 154.2K **Privately Held**
SIC: 3669 Communications equipment

(G-7251)
INTEMPO SOFTWARE INC
8777 Purdue Rd Ste 340 (46268-3121)
PHONE...................................800 950-2221
Matt Hopp, *General Mgr*
EMP: 5
SALES (corp-wide): 3MM **Privately Held**
SIC: 7372 Prepackaged software
PA: Intempo Software Inc.
191 Chestnut St Fl 5
Springfield MA 01103
800 950-2221

(G-7252)
INTERNATIONAL CODE COUNCIL INC
Also Called: Icbo
1223 S Richland St (46221-1604)
PHONE...................................317 879-1677
Brent Snyder, *Office Mgr*
EMP: 4
SALES (corp-wide): 42.2MM **Privately Held**
SIC: 2741 Directories: publishing only, not printed on site
PA: International Code Council, Inc.
500 New Jersey Ave Nw # 6
Washington DC 20001
202 370-1800

(G-7253)
INTERNATIONAL CRYOGENICS INC
4040 Championship Dr (46268-2588)
PHONE...................................317 297-4777
Fax: 317 297-7988
Donna Jung, *President*
Raymond Moncrief, *Vice Pres*
EMP: 16
SQ FT: 28,000

SALES (est): 3.9MM **Privately Held**
SIC: 3559 Cryogenic machinery, industrial

(G-7254)
INTERNATIONAL METALS PROC INC
3131 N Franklin Rd Ste E (46226-6390)
PHONE...................................317 895-4141
Fax: 317 895-4142
Robert O'Neal, *President*
EMP: 34 **EST:** 1998
SALES (est): 8.3MM **Privately Held**
SIC: 3441 Fabricated structural metal

(G-7255)
INTERNATIONAL PAPER COMPANY
4901 W 79th St (46268-1662)
PHONE...................................317 871-6999
John Falk, *Manager*
EMP: 35
SALES (corp-wide): 21.7B **Publicly Held**
WEB: www.internationalpaper.com
SIC: 2621 Paper mills
PA: International Paper Company
6400 Poplar Ave
Memphis TN 38197
901 419-9000

(G-7256)
INTERNATIONAL PAPER COMPANY
7536 Miles Dr (46231-3344)
PHONE...................................317 481-4000
Mark Crevonis, *Branch Mgr*
EMP: 10
SALES (corp-wide): 21.7B **Publicly Held**
SIC: 2621 Paper mills
PA: International Paper Company
6400 Poplar Ave
Memphis TN 38197
901 419-9000

(G-7257)
INTERNATIONAL PAPER COMPANY
4350 Sam Jones Expy (46241-5259)
PHONE...................................317 510-6410
EMP: 133
SALES (corp-wide): 22.3B **Publicly Held**
SIC: 2621 2653 2656 2631 Paper Mill Mfg Corrugated/Fiber Box
PA: International Paper Company
6400 Poplar Ave
Memphis TN 38197
901 419-9000

(G-7258)
INTERNATIONAL PAPER COMPANY
8501 Moller Rd (46268-1510)
PHONE...................................317 715-9080
EMP: 11
SALES (corp-wide): 21.7B **Publicly Held**
SIC: 2621 Paper mills
PA: International Paper Company
6400 Poplar Ave
Memphis TN 38197
901 419-9000

(G-7259)
INTERNATIONAL PAPER COMPANY
8501 Moller Rd (46268-1510)
PHONE...................................317 875-4101
EMP: 20
SALES (corp-wide): 21.7B **Publicly Held**
WEB: www.tin.com
SIC: 2653 Boxes, corrugated: made from purchased materials
PA: International Paper Company
6400 Poplar Ave
Memphis TN 38197
901 419-9000

(G-7260)
INTERNATIONAL PAPER COMPANY
2135 Stout Field East Dr (46241-4014)
PHONE...................................317 390-3300
Ann Grecu, *Controller*
Ray Shannon, *Accounts Mgr*
Kyle Drew, *Branch Mgr*
EMP: 92

SALES (corp-wide): 21.7B **Publicly Held**
WEB: www.tin.com
SIC: 2653 Boxes, corrugated: made from purchased materials
PA: International Paper Company
6400 Poplar Ave
Memphis TN 38197
901 419-9000

(G-7261)
INTERNATIONAL RESOURCES INC
9325 Uptown Dr Ste 900 (46256-1039)
PHONE...................................317 813-5300
Darrell White, *President*
Jeffrey Beuoy, *Vice Pres*
EMP: 2
SALES (est): 377.1K **Privately Held**
WEB: www.intlresources.com
SIC: 3661 Telephones & telephone apparatus

(G-7262)
INTERNTNAL DAMND GOLD EXCH LTD
Also Called: Patora Fine Jewelers
6010 W 86th St Ste 114 (46278-1407)
PHONE...................................317 872-6666
Pamela Hickman, *President*
Tony Freije, *Manager*
EMP: 15
SQ FT: 3,200
SALES (est): 1.5MM **Privately Held**
SIC: 5944 3911 7631 7389 Jewelry stores; jewelry, precious metal; jewelry repair services; auction, appraisal & exchange services

(G-7263)
INTERVENTION DIAGNOSTICS INC
6925 Hawthorn Park Dr (46220-3910)
PHONE...................................317 432-6091
James Connolly, *Owner*
EMP: 7
SALES (est): 546.9K **Privately Held**
SIC: 2835 In vitro & in vivo diagnostic substances

(G-7264)
INVENSYS PROCESSS SYSTEMS INC
101 W Ohio St (46204-1906)
PHONE...................................317 372-2839
EMP: 2000
SALES (corp-wide): 200.4K **Privately Held**
SIC: 3822 Temperature controls, automatic
HQ: Invensys Processs Systems, Inc.
10900 Equity Dr
Houston TX 77041
713 329-1600

(G-7265)
IPHEION DEVELOPMENT CORP
Also Called: ipheion Custom Technologies
3421 Breckenridge Dr (46228-2751)
PHONE...................................240 281-1619
Elsa Rose Hoffmann, *President*
Dominik Hoffmann, *Chief Engr*
EMP: 2
SALES (est): 98.4K **Privately Held**
SIC: 8999 8748 8711 3826 Scientific consulting; systems analysis & engineering consulting services; engineering services; analytical instruments

(G-7266)
IPS-INTEGRATED PRJ SVCS LLC
Also Called: Ips Indiana
320 N Meridian St Ste 212 (46204-1721)
PHONE...................................317 247-1200
Fax: 317 247-0776
Michael Vitello, *Branch Mgr*
EMP: 5
SALES (corp-wide): 119.8MM **Privately Held**
WEB: www.ipsdb.com
SIC: 2834 Solutions, pharmaceutical
PA: Ips-Integrated Project Services, Llc
721 Arbor Way Ste 100
Blue Bell PA 19422
610 828-4090

(G-7267)
IRA PRESERVATION PARTNERS
3271 E 79th St Apt C (46240-3364)
PHONE....................................317 722-0710
EMP: 2
SALES (est): 88.9K **Privately Held**
SIC: 3443 Fabricated Plate Work (Boiler Shop)

(G-7268)
IRVING MATERIALS INC
Also Called: I M I
5560 S Belmont Ave (46217-9749)
PHONE....................................317 784-5433
Kerry Webb, *QC Mgr*
Audrey Adamson, *Cust Mgr*
Ron Averidge, *Branch Mgr*
EMP: 20
SALES (corp-wide): 800.6MM **Privately Held**
SIC: 3273 Ready-mixed concrete
PA: Irving Materials, Inc.
　　8032 N State Road 9
　　Greenfield IN 46140
　　317 326-3101

(G-7269)
IRVING MATERIALS INC
Also Called: I M I
4700 W 96th St (46268-2917)
PHONE....................................317 872-0152
Fax: 317 872-2852
Roger Ronk, *Branch Mgr*
EMP: 15
SALES (corp-wide): 800.6MM **Privately Held**
SIC: 3273 Ready-mixed concrete
PA: Irving Materials, Inc.
　　8032 N State Road 9
　　Greenfield IN 46140
　　317 326-3101

(G-7270)
IRVING MATERIALS INC
Also Called: I M I
5244 E 96th St (46240-3747)
PHONE....................................317 843-2944
Fax: 317 843-2944
Jeromy Kendall, *Manager*
EMP: 7
SALES (corp-wide): 800.6MM **Privately Held**
SIC: 3273 Ready-mixed concrete
PA: Irving Materials, Inc.
　　8032 N State Road 9
　　Greenfield IN 46140
　　317 326-3101

(G-7271)
IRVING MATERIALS INC
Also Called: I M I
4200 S Harding St Ste X (46217-9593)
PHONE....................................317 783-3381
Phillip Blaylock, *Branch Mgr*
EMP: 18
SALES (corp-wide): 800.6MM **Privately Held**
SIC: 3273 Ready-mixed concrete
PA: Irving Materials, Inc.
　　8032 N State Road 9
　　Greenfield IN 46140
　　317 326-3101

(G-7272)
IRVING MATERIALS INC
4330 W Morris St (46241-2504)
PHONE....................................317 243-7391
Fax: 317 243-7391
Phil Blaylock, *Manager*
EMP: 17
SALES (corp-wide): 800.6MM **Privately Held**
SIC: 3273 Ready-mixed concrete
PA: Irving Materials, Inc.
　　8032 N State Road 9
　　Greenfield IN 46140
　　317 326-3101

(G-7273)
IRVING MATERIALS INC
3130 N Post Rd (46226)
PHONE....................................317 899-2187
Fax: 317 899-2187
Mike Jackson, *Manager*
EMP: 15

SALES (corp-wide): 800.6MM **Privately Held**
SIC: 3273 Ready-mixed concrete
PA: Irving Materials, Inc.
　　8032 N State Road 9
　　Greenfield IN 46140
　　317 326-3101

(G-7274)
ISF INC
Also Called: Sign Fab
6468 Rucker Rd (46220-4841)
PHONE....................................317 251-1219
Fax: 317 251-1224
Adam Walsh, *President*
Holly Walsh, *Admin Sec*
EMP: 24
SQ FT: 12,000
SALES (est): 5.3MM **Privately Held**
WEB: www.isfsigns.com
SIC: 3993 Electric signs

(G-7275)
ISI INC
1212 E Michigan St (46202-3554)
PHONE....................................317 631-7980
Fax: 317 631-7981
William Witchger, *Ch of Bd*
Guy Driggers, *President*
EMP: 15
SQ FT: 20,000
SALES (est): 3.1MM
SALES (corp-wide): 53.8MM **Privately Held**
WEB: www.isi-inc.com
SIC: 5199 2295 Packaging materials; tape, varnished: plastic & other coated (except magnetic)
PA: Marian Worldwide, Inc.
　　1011 E Saint Clair St
　　Indianapolis IN 46202
　　317 638-6525

(G-7276)
ITECH HOLDINGS LLC
Also Called: Itech Digital
6330 E 75th St Ste 132 (46250-2717)
PHONE....................................317 567-5160
Fax: 317 704-0450
Mark Nazarenus, *President*
Bryan McCorkle, *Prdtn Mgr*
Steve Spiech, *CFO*
Benjamyn Bell, *Technical Staff*
Patrick Goffinet, *Executive*
◆ EMP: 35
SQ FT: 10,000
SALES (est): 8.7MM **Privately Held**
WEB: www.itechdigital.com
SIC: 3651 Video camera-audio recorders, household use

(G-7277)
ITW GEMA
4141 W 54th St (46254-3728)
PHONE....................................317 298-5000
Fax: 317 298-5117
Mark Fooksman, *Director*
▲ EMP: 24
SALES (est): 4.2MM **Privately Held**
SIC: 3399 Powder, metal

(G-7278)
IVY WOODWORKS LLC
8634 Burrell Ln (46256-6306)
PHONE....................................317 842-4085
EMP: 2
SALES (est): 150K **Privately Held**
SIC: 2431 Mfg Millwork

(G-7279)
J & K ASSOCIATES
6302 Rucker Rd Ste C (46220-4853)
P.O. Box 734, Greencastle (46135-0734)
PHONE....................................317 255-3588
John R Means, *Partner*
Howard Thomas, *Partner*
EMP: 3
SQ FT: 2,600
SALES (est): 302K **Privately Held**
SIC: 3469 Machine parts, stamped or pressed metal

(G-7280)
J & T MARINE SPECIALISTS INC
810 S Mitthoeffer Rd (46239-9640)
PHONE....................................317 890-9444

SALES (corp-wide): 800.6MM **Privately Held**
SIC: 3273 Ready-mixed concrete
PA: Irving Materials, Inc.
　　8032 N State Road 9
　　Greenfield IN 46140
　　317 326-3101

James Booe, *President*
Tinka Booe, *Admin Sec*
▲ EMP: 2
SALES (est): 302.4K **Privately Held**
WEB: www.turboprop.com
SIC: 3324 3599 Commercial investment castings, ferrous; machine & other job shop work

(G-7281)
J 2 SYSTEMS AND SUPPLY LLC
Also Called: J2 S&S
803 E 38th St (46205-2823)
PHONE....................................317 602-3940
James Ibaugh, *Office Mgr*
Rickey Steenberger, *Office Mgr*
James Leonard, *Mng Member*
John Thompson,
EMP: 6
SQ FT: 2,500
SALES (est): 3.9MM **Privately Held**
WEB: www.thomdist.com
SIC: 5169 2992 2842 2841 Industrial chemicals; lubricating oils & greases; specialty cleaning, polishes & sanitation goods; soap & other detergents; industrial inorganic chemicals; petroleum products

(G-7282)
J A LARR & CO
4040 E 82nd St Ste C9 (46250-4209)
PHONE....................................317 627-3192
Joseph A Larr, *Owner*
EMP: 2
SALES (est): 750K **Privately Held**
SIC: 3669 Pedestrian traffic control equipment

(G-7283)
J C SIPE INC
Also Called: J C Sipe Jewelers
3000 E 96th St (46240-3717)
PHONE....................................317 848-0215
Fax: 317 848-1979
Sam H Sipe, *Ch of Bd*
Laura C Sipe, *President*
EMP: 5
SQ FT: 4,338
SALES (est): 726.8K **Privately Held**
WEB: www.jcsipe.com
SIC: 5944 3911 Jewelry, precious stones & precious metals; jewel settings & mountings, precious metal; pearl jewelry, natural or cultured; watchbands, precious metal

(G-7284)
J COFFEY METAL MASTERS INC
2514 Bethel Ave (46203-3034)
P.O. Box 33001 (46203-0001)
PHONE....................................317 780-1864
Fax: 317 780-7968
James L Coffey, *President*
William Rinnert, *Vice Pres*
Janet S Coffey, *Treasurer*
EMP: 75
SQ FT: 35,000
SALES: 151.8K **Privately Held**
WEB: www.mmindy.com
SIC: 1761 3441 Sheet metalwork; fabricated structural metal

(G-7285)
J D GOULD COMPANY INC
4707 Massachusetts Ave (46218-3144)
PHONE....................................317 542-1876
Fax: 317 547-5234
John E Gould, *President*
Phillip Hubbs, *Business Mgr*
Brian Kent, *QC Mgr*
Charles Phil Hubbs, *Manager*
EMP: 14 EST: 1951
SQ FT: 12,000
SALES (est): 3.2MM **Privately Held**
WEB: www.gouldvalve.com
SIC: 3491 Solenoid valves

(G-7286)
J HENRYS MACHINE SHOP LLC
1111 S East St (46225-1325)
PHONE....................................317 917-1052
Michele Young, *President*
EMP: 2
SALES (est): 175.2K **Privately Held**
SIC: 3599 Machine shop, jobbing & repair

(G-7287)
J L SQUARED INC
1347 Sadlier Circle S Dr (46239-1059)
P.O. Box 807, Beech Grove (46107-0807)
PHONE....................................317 354-1513
Fax: 317 354-1586
Leann Jenkins, *President*
EMP: 2
SQ FT: 8,100
SALES: 1MM **Privately Held**
SIC: 3441 Fabricated structural metal

(G-7288)
J M MCCORMICK
8214 Allison Ave (46268-1616)
PHONE....................................317 874-4444
Ed Espey, *Owner*
EMP: 2
SALES (est): 219.3K **Privately Held**
SIC: 5031 2421 Lumber: rough, dressed & finished; sawmills & planing mills, general

(G-7289)
J N P CUSTOM DESIGNS INC
Also Called: Jnp Custom Designs
550 W 65th St (46260-4604)
P.O. Box 68854 (46268-0854)
PHONE....................................317 253-2198
Portia O Neal, *President*
John Oneal, *Vice Pres*
EMP: 2 EST: 1985
SALES: 30K **Privately Held**
WEB: www.jpcustomdesigns.com
SIC: 2759 2395 Screen printing; embroidery & art needlework

(G-7290)
J W MODEL & ENGINEERING INC
5508 Elmwood Ave Ste 406 (46203-6039)
PHONE....................................317 788-7471
Fax: 317 788-0552
Larry Woempner, *President*
EMP: 8 EST: 1981
SQ FT: 14,300
SALES (est): 929.1K **Privately Held**
SIC: 3544 Special dies, tools, jigs & fixtures

(G-7291)
J&L LIGHTING SOLUTIONS LLC
21 N Pennsylvania St (46204-3140)
PHONE....................................317 413-8768
Elizabeth L Coram,
EMP: 2
SALES (est): 108.2K **Privately Held**
SIC: 3648 Lighting equipment

(G-7292)
JACK HOWARD
1915 S State Ave (46203-4184)
PHONE....................................317 788-7643
Fax: 317 788-8046
Jack Howard, *Owner*
EMP: 3
SALES (est): 160K **Privately Held**
SIC: 3444 Sheet metalwork

(G-7293)
JACK LAURIE COML FLOORS INC
7998 Georgetown Rd # 1000 (46268-5631)
PHONE....................................317 569-2095
Tierra Maesch, *Project Mgr*
Logan Moore, *Project Mgr*
John Laurie, *Branch Mgr*
EMP: 3
SALES (corp-wide): 1.4MM **Privately Held**
SIC: 5713 3081 5198 Floor covering stores; floor or wall covering, unsupported plastic; paints, varnishes & supplies
PA: Jack Laurie Commercial Floors, Inc.
　　430 W Coliseum Blvd
　　Fort Wayne IN 46805
　　317 704-1100

(G-7294)
JACKSON GROUP INC
5804 Churchman Byp (46203-6109)
PHONE....................................317 791-9000
Katherine S Jackson, *President*
Michael McQueary, *Prdtn Mgr*
Lee A Miller, *VP Sales*
Jackie Korellis, *Accounts Mgr*

Becky Allen, *Accounts Exec*
EMP: 180
SALES (est): 21.6MM
SALES (corp-wide): 6.9B **Publicly Held**
SIC: 2752 Commercial printing, litho-
graphic
HQ: Consolidated Graphics, Inc.
5858 Westheimer Rd # 200
Houston TX 77057
713 787-0977

(G-7295)
JACKSON SYSTEMS LLC
5418 Elmwood Ave (46203-6025)
PHONE...................................317 788-6800
Joe Jackson, *Vice Pres*
Dustin S Peddycord, *Opers Mgr*
Jennifer Dremonas, *Buyer*
Elijah Montgomery, *Senior Engr*
Jim Dufault, *Sales Dir*
EMP: 27
SQ FT: 10,000
SALES (est): 7.9MM **Privately Held**
WEB: www.jacksonsystems.com
SIC: 3822 7389 Electric heat controls; de-
sign services

(G-7296)
JAH COATINGS LLC
6415 E 11th St (46219-3419)
PHONE...................................317 550-7169
Joseph Hubbard, *Principal*
EMP: 2
SALES (est): 83.5K **Privately Held**
SIC: 3479 Metal coating & allied service

(G-7297)
JAMES R MCNUTT
3130 N Mitthoefer Rd (46235-2400)
P.O. Box 36550 (46236-0550)
PHONE...................................317 899-6955
Jim McNutt Jr, *Owner*
EMP: 2
SALES (est): 119.4K **Privately Held**
SIC: 3578 Change making machines

(G-7298)
JAT INC LLC
1638 Lancashire Ct Apt E (46260-2164)
PHONE...................................317 201-3684
EMP: 2
SALES: 5K **Privately Held**
SIC: 2396 Screen Printing

(G-7299)
**JAY ORNER SONS BILLIARD CO
INC (PA)**
6333 Rockville Rd (46214-3920)
PHONE...................................317 243-0046
Fax: 317 247-7743
Steve Orner, *President*
Daniele Orner, *Corp Secy*
Tom Orner, *Vice Pres*
▲ **EMP:** 8 **EST:** 1968
SQ FT: 5,000
SALES (est): 1.6MM **Privately Held**
WEB: www.ornerbilliards.com
SIC: 3949 5091 7699 Billiard & pool
equipment & supplies, general; billiard
equipment & supplies; billiard table repair

(G-7300)
JDSU ACTERNA HOLDINGS LLC
5808 Churchman Byp (46203-6109)
PHONE...................................317 788-9351
Stephen Liao, *Engineer*
Mark Ortel, *Sales Staff*
Joe Budano, *Manager*
Steven Windle, *Manager*
Bruce Chrisp, *Technology*
EMP: 5
SALES (corp-wide): 811.4MM **Publicly
Held**
SIC: 3674 Optical isolators
HQ: Jdsu Acterna Holdings Llc
1 Milestone Center Ct
Germantown MD 20876
240 404-1550

(G-7301)
JENSON INDUSTRIES INC
Also Called: Alternative Container
8219 Zionsville Rd (46268-1628)
PHONE...................................317 871-0122
EMP: 8

SALES (est): 1.5MM **Privately Held**
SIC: 2631 Paperboard Mill

(G-7302)
JETER WINERY INC
7302 Kita Dr (46259-7608)
PHONE...................................317 862-9193
EMP: 2 **EST:** 2004
SALES (est): 100K **Privately Held**
SIC: 2084 Mfg Wines/Brandy/Spirits

(G-7303)
JEWELERS BOUTIQUE INC
3320 Madison Ave (46227-1130)
PHONE...................................317 788-7679
Fax: 317 788-3188
Charles Gardner, *President*
Elaine Gardner, *Vice Pres*
EMP: 4
SQ FT: 1,800
SALES (est): 380K **Privately Held**
WEB: www.jewelersboutique.com
SIC: 3911 5944 Jewelry, precious metal;
jewelry stores

(G-7304)
**JFW INDUSTRIES
INCORPORATED**
5134 Commerce Square Dr (46237-9705)
PHONE...................................317 887-1340
Fax: 317 881-6790
Fred D Walker, *President*
James W Leach, *Vice Pres*
Vicki Lemen, *Purch Dir*
Brett Chermansky, *Engineer*
Kerry Lynch, *Controller*
EMP: 105
SQ FT: 14,000
SALES: 11.1MM **Privately Held**
SIC: 3825 Radio apparatus analyzers

(G-7305)
JIMCO ENGINEERING CO
3315 Sutherland Ave (46218-1904)
PHONE...................................317 923-2290
Daniel Noland, *Owner*
EMP: 2
SQ FT: 6,500
SALES (est): 600K **Privately Held**
SIC: 3599 Machine shop, jobbing & repair

(G-7306)
JL WALTER & ASSOCIATES INC
1211 Roosevelt Ave (46202-2790)
PHONE...................................317 524-3600
Lloyd Webber, *Principal*
EMP: 40
SALES (est): 15.3MM **Privately Held**
SIC: 3441 7699 Fabricated structural
metal; metal reshaping & replating serv-
ices

(G-7307)
JOHN KING
6515 Olivia Ln (46226-6167)
PHONE...................................317 801-3080
John King, *Administration*
EMP: 2
SALES (est): 62.3K **Privately Held**
SIC: 2084 Wines, brandy & brandy spirits

(G-7308)
JOHNCO CORP
8770 Commerce Park Pl F (46268-3128)
PHONE...................................317 576-4417
Nadia Miller, *President*
EMP: 5
SALES (est): 915.5K **Privately Held**
SIC: 5112 5087 2521 5251 Stationery &
office supplies; janitors' supplies; wood of-
fice furniture; hardware; modems, moni-
tors, terminals & disk drives; computers

(G-7309)
JOHNSON CONTROLS
11820 Pendleton Pike (46236-3929)
PHONE...................................317 826-2130
Fax: 317 826-2140
Terry Dollar, *Branch Mgr*
Kurt Kleine, *Manager*
EMP: 140 **Privately Held**
WEB: www.simplexgrinnell.com
SIC: 1711 5999 1731 3498 Fire sprinkler
system installation; fire extinguishers; fire
detection & burglar alarm systems spe-
cialization; fabricated pipe & fittings

HQ: Johnson Controls Fire Protection Lp
4700 Exchange Ct Ste 300
Boca Raton FL 33431
561 988-7200

(G-7310)
JOINT & CLUTCH SERVICE INC
2075 Kentucky Ave (46221-1968)
PHONE...................................317 264-5038
Christy Andy, *Manager*
EMP: 2
SALES (est): 81.4K **Privately Held**
SIC: 3599 Industrial machinery

(G-7311)
**JONES & WEBB ASSOCIATES
INC**
151 N Delaware St Ste 120 (46204-2508)
PHONE...................................317 236-9755
Dave Webb, *President*
David Jones, *Vice Pres*
EMP: 4
SQ FT: 800
SALES (est): 451K **Privately Held**
SIC: 2759 Commercial printing

(G-7312)
JOSEPH & JONES LLC
Also Called: Mobile Distillery
6170 Guilford Ave (46220-1919)
PHONE...................................317 691-0328
Anthony Joseph, *CEO*
James Jones,
EMP: 2
SALES: 30K **Privately Held**
SIC: 2085 Vodka (alcoholic beverage)

(G-7313)
JOSSEY-BASS PUBLISHERS
10475 Crosspoint Blvd (46256-3386)
PHONE...................................877 762-2974
William Pesce, *Principal*
EMP: 2
SALES (est): 84K **Privately Held**
SIC: 2741 Miscellaneous publishing

(G-7314)
JOY MI INDUSTRIES INC
8707 Arbor Lake Dr # 1523 (46268-4284)
PHONE...................................317 876-3917
Milton Manuel, *Principal*
EMP: 2
SALES (est): 95.9K **Privately Held**
SIC: 3999 Manufacturing industries

(G-7315)
JOYCE CONSULTING LLC
9132 Sargent Manor Ct (46256-1392)
PHONE...................................317 577-8504
Christine Joyce, *Managing Prtnr*
James R Joyce, *Principal*
▲ **EMP:** 2 **EST:** 2007
SQ FT: 6,000
SALES: 2MM **Privately Held**
SIC: 3531 Bulldozers (construction ma-
chinery)

(G-7316)
**JOYFUL NOISE RECORDINGS
LLC**
1030 Orange St (46203-1870)
PHONE...................................317 632-3220
Karl Hofstetter, *President*
EMP: 2
SALES (est): 189.2K **Privately Held**
SIC: 2741 Miscellaneous publishing

(G-7317)
JP OWNERSHIP GROUP INC
5804 Churchman Byp (46203-6109)
PHONE...................................317 791-1122
Patsy Koepke, *President*
EMP: 53
SQ FT: 125,000
SALES (est): 7.6MM **Privately Held**
WEB: www.jacksonpress.com
SIC: 2752 Commercial printing, offset

(G-7318)
JRP MACHINE CO
1607 Deloss St Ste B (46201-3968)
PHONE...................................317 955-1905
Randy Humphrey Jr, *President*
Tatiana L Hiese, *Corp Secy*
EMP: 2

SQ FT: 4,800
SALES (est): 276.5K **Privately Held**
WEB: www.jrpmachine.net
SIC: 3451 Screw machine products

(G-7319)
JSN ADVERTISING INC
Also Called: Just Signs Now Advertising
8522 Madison Ave (46227-6192)
PHONE...................................317 888-7591
Jerry Nesses, *President*
EMP: 4
SQ FT: 3,000
SALES: 800K **Privately Held**
SIC: 3993 Signs & advertising specialties

(G-7320)
JT COMPOSITES LLC
312 Gasoline Aly Ste C (46222-3990)
PHONE...................................317 297-9520
Julian Bailey, *General Ptnr*
Tony Holl, *Manager*
EMP: 3 **EST:** 2009
SALES (est): 250K **Privately Held**
SIC: 2813 2655 Carbon dioxide; cans,
composite: foil-fiber & other: from pur-
chased fiber

(G-7321)
JUNCOS RACING ✪
4401 Gilman St (46224-6982)
PHONE...................................317 640-2348
Jason Marksberry, *CFO*
EMP: 3 **EST:** 2017
SALES (est): 97.2K **Privately Held**
SIC: 3644 Raceways

(G-7322)
JURGEN ASSOCIATES INC
5180 Commerce Cir (46237-9744)
PHONE...................................317 786-3513
Fax: 317 887-6671
Robert A Jurgen, *President*
James Jurgen, *Vice Pres*
EMP: 8
SQ FT: 6,000
SALES (est): 1.1MM **Privately Held**
WEB: www.zyfer.com
SIC: 2541 Wood partitions & fixtures

(G-7323)
JUST DESSERTS INC
7768 Zionsville Rd # 300 (46268-2100)
PHONE...................................317 872-2253
Fax: 317 870-5620
Kevin J Goudie, *President*
EMP: 11
SALES (est): 1.6MM **Privately Held**
SIC: 2051 Bakery: wholesale or whole-
sale/retail combined

(G-7324)
JUST FOR GRANITE
5277 Emco Dr (46220-4850)
PHONE...................................317 842-8255
Fax: 317 257-8564
Pete Rusomaroff, *Owner*
EMP: 8
SALES (est): 454.4K **Privately Held**
SIC: 1799 3441 Counter top installation;
fabricated structural metal

(G-7325)
JUST STANDOUT LLC
951 E 86th St Ste 200e (46240-2092)
PHONE...................................317 531-6956
Matthew Jones, *Mng Member*
Raymond Mack, *Mng Member*
EMP: 2
SALES (est): 171.8K **Privately Held**
SIC: 2252 Socks

(G-7326)
K & K FENCE INC
6520 Brookville Rd (46219-8219)
PHONE...................................317 359-5425
Fax: 317 352-7723
Frederick C Poe, *President*
EMP: 25
SQ FT: 2,500
SALES (est): 7.3MM **Privately Held**
WEB: www.kandkfence.com
SIC: 1799 5211 3446 Fence construction;
fencing; fences or posts, ornamental iron
or steel

(G-7327)
K C CREATIONS
11612 Breckenridge Ct (46236-3829)
PHONE....................................937 748-8181
Ken Cleveland, *President*
Sandra Love, *Vice Pres*
EMP: 3
SQ FT: 10,000
SALES (est): 282.5K **Privately Held**
WEB: www.cultureworks.org
SIC: 7389 3499 Design, commercial & industrial; novelties & giftware, including trophies

(G-7328)
K J S ASSOCIATES
8431 Castlewood Dr (46250-1534)
PHONE....................................317 842-7500
Roger Lavalley, *Engineer*
EMP: 2
SALES (est): 104.2K **Privately Held**
SIC: 3825 3679 Instruments to measure electricity; electronic components

(G-7329)
KAISER PRESS LLC
2525 E 91st St (46240-2064)
PHONE....................................317 619-7092
Nathan Hopman, *Principal*
EMP: 4
SALES (est): 83.8K **Privately Held**
SIC: 2711 Newspapers

(G-7330)
KALEMS ENTERPRISES INC
Also Called: Metro Area Printing
8455 Castlewood Dr Ste H (46250-1565)
PHONE....................................317 399-1645
Lee Daniels, *President*
Karen Daniels, *Principal*
EMP: 3
SALES (est): 163.5K **Privately Held**
SIC: 2752 Commercial printing, offset

(G-7331)
KAMPLAIN MACHINE CO INC
6360 La Pas Trl (46268-2511)
PHONE....................................317 388-9111
Fax: 317 388-9124
Greg Kamplain, *President*
Judy Kamplain, *Admin Sec*
EMP: 5
SQ FT: 14,500
SALES (est): 836.1K **Privately Held**
WEB: www.kamplainmachine.com
SIC: 3599 Machine shop. jobbing & repair

(G-7332)
KAMPS INC
1905 S Belmont Ave (46221-1924)
PHONE....................................317 634-8360
Matt Scott, *Branch Mgr*
EMP: 33
SALES (corp-wide): 157.4MM **Privately Held**
SIC: 2448 Pallets, wood
PA: Kamps, Inc.
2900 Peach Ridge Ave Nw
Grand Rapids MI 49534
616 453-9676

(G-7333)
KAPLAN INC
7835 Woodland Dr Ste 100 (46278-2742)
P.O. Box 68520 (46268-0520)
PHONE....................................317 872-7220
Don Fischer, *Principal*
EMP: 85
SALES (corp-wide): 2.5B **Publicly Held**
WEB: www.kaplan.com
SIC: 7375 2731 7372 7374 Information retrieval services; book publishing; prepackaged software; data processing service; business training services
HQ: Kaplan, Inc.
6301 Kaplan Univ Ave
Fort Lauderdale FL 33309
212 492-5800

(G-7334)
KASTING PRINTING SERVICE
7146 S Meridian St (46217-4042)
PHONE....................................317 881-9411
Betty Kasting, *Owner*
EMP: 2

SALES (est): 120K **Privately Held**
SIC: 2752 Commercial printing, lithographic

(G-7335)
KAYS GRAPHICS INC
Also Called: Quick Copy & Design
151 N Delaware St Ste 120 (46204-2508)
PHONE....................................317 236-9755
Fax: 317 236-9756
David Webb, *President*
John Jones, *Vice Pres*
EMP: 3
SQ FT: 1,000
SALES (est): 240K **Privately Held**
SIC: 7334 2759 2789 Photocopying & duplicating services; commercial printing; bookbinding & related work

(G-7336)
KBC MACHINE INC
1740 Wales Ave (46218-4592)
PHONE....................................317 638-7865
Keith Coleman, *President*
Barbara A Coleman, *Vice Pres*
Phillip Coleman, *Opers Mgr*
EMP: 4
SQ FT: 8,000
SALES (est): 290.3K **Privately Held**
SIC: 3599 Machine shop, jobbing & repair

(G-7337)
KC ENGINEERING INC
5602 Elmwood Ave Ste 118 (46203-6071)
PHONE....................................317 352-9742
Fax: 317 352-9742
Thomas L Covington, *President*
Sue A Covington, *Vice Pres*
EMP: 8
SQ FT: 11,000
SALES (est): 1MM **Privately Held**
SIC: 3544 Forms (molds), for foundry & plastics working machinery

(G-7338)
KECO ENGINEERED COATINGS INC (PA)
1030 S Kealing Ave (46203-1516)
PHONE....................................317 356-7279
Fax: 317 356-6725
Michael Klinge, *President*
▲ EMP: 15
SQ FT: 25,000
SALES (est): 2.3MM **Privately Held**
WEB: www.kecocoatings.com
SIC: 3479 Coating of metals & formed products

(G-7339)
KEESLING CUSTOM POOLS & PATIOS
10424 Rainbow Ln (46236-9558)
PHONE....................................317 823-3526
Jeffrey A Keesling, *President*
EMP: 5
SALES (est): 579.1K **Privately Held**
SIC: 3949 Swimming pools, except plastic

(G-7340)
KEIHIN IPT MFG
9900 Westpoint Dr (46256-3358)
PHONE....................................317 578-5260
Yasumichi Ohama, *Principal*
EMP: 8
SALES (est): 808.9K **Privately Held**
SIC: 3999 Manufacturing industries

(G-7341)
KENNAMETAL INC
9217 Backwater Dr (46250-4134)
PHONE....................................317 696-8798
EMP: 120
SALES (corp-wide): 2.3B **Publicly Held**
SIC: 3545 Machine tool accessories
PA: Kennametal Inc.
600 Grant St Ste 5100
Pittsburgh PA 15219
412 248-8000

(G-7342)
KENNEDY TANK & MFG CO
833 E Sumner Ave (46227-1345)
P.O. Box 47070 (46247-0070)
PHONE....................................317 787-1311
Fax: 317 783-7772

Patrick W Kennedy, *President*
Paul K Bolin, *Vice Pres*
Paul Bolin, *Vice Pres*
John Cochran, *Vice Pres*
Scot W Evans, *Vice Pres*
EMP: 130
SQ FT: 51,000
SALES: 30MM **Privately Held**
WEB: www.kennedytank.com
SIC: 3443 Tanks, standard or custom fabricated: metal plate

(G-7343)
KENRA PROFESSIONAL LLC (HQ)
Also Called: Elucence Products
7445 Company Dr (46237-9296)
PHONE....................................317 356-6491
Patrick Ludwig, *President*
Robert Schaeffler, *General Mgr*
Jessica Costello, *Regional Mgr*
Patrina Hall, *Regional Mgr*
Ron Kelsen, *Regional Mgr*
EMP: 10
SQ FT: 48,500
SALES (est): 9.7MM
SALES (corp-wide): 1.9MM **Privately Held**
WEB: www.kenra.com
SIC: 2844 7231 2899 Hair preparations, including shampoos; cosmetic preparations; beauty shops; chemical preparations
PA: Imperial Capital Corporation
200 King St W Suite 1701
Toronto ON M5H 3
416 362-3658

(G-7344)
KEY MADE NOW
317 N Kenyon St (46219-6109)
PHONE....................................317 664-8582
EMP: 2
SALES (est): 113.1K **Privately Held**
SIC: 3429 Keys, locks & related hardware

(G-7345)
KEY SHEET METAL INC
1128 E Maryland St (46202-3975)
PHONE....................................317 546-7151
Dave Key, *President*
EMP: 5
SQ FT: 3,800
SALES (est): 1MM **Privately Held**
SIC: 3444 3546 Awnings, sheet metal; drills & drilling tools

(G-7346)
KEYS R US
3210 E Thompson Rd (46227-6623)
PHONE....................................317 616-0267
EMP: 2
SALES (est): 85.5K **Privately Held**
SIC: 3429 Keys, locks & related hardware

(G-7347)
KEYWEST LLC
4811 S High School Rd (46221-3601)
P.O. Box 310, Camby (46113-0310)
PHONE....................................317 821-8419
EMP: 6
SALES (est): 589.5K **Privately Held**
SIC: 2099 Food preparations

(G-7348)
KHAMIS FINE JEWELERS INC
9763 Fall Creek Rd (46256-4713)
PHONE....................................317 841-8440
Mary J Khamis, *President*
EMP: 2
SQ FT: 1,600
SALES (est): 265.1K **Privately Held**
WEB: www.khamisfinejewelers.com
SIC: 5944 7631 7389 3479 Jewelry, precious stones & precious metals; jewelry repair services; auction, appraisal & exchange services; engraving jewelry silverware, or metal

(G-7349)
KIMBALL ELEC INDIANAPOLIS
2950 N Catherwood Ave (46219-1011)
PHONE....................................812 634-4000
Don Charron, *CEO*
Michael Sergesketter, *CFO*
EMP: 67

SALES (est): 4.5MM
SALES (corp-wide): 930.9MM **Publicly Held**
SIC: 3672 Printed circuit boards
HQ: Kimball Electronics Group, Llc
1205 Kimball Blvd
Jasper IN 47546

(G-7350)
KIMBALL ELECTRONICS INC
2402 N Shadeland Ave (46219-1137)
PHONE....................................317 357-3175
Curtis Bilbrey, *Branch Mgr*
EMP: 73
SALES (corp-wide): 930.9MM **Publicly Held**
SIC: 3089 Injection molded finished plastic products
PA: Kimball Electronics, Inc.
1205 Kimball Blvd
Jasper IN 47546
812 634-4000

(G-7351)
KIMBALL ELECTRONICS INC
6205 E 30th St (46219-1003)
PHONE....................................317 545-5383
Bob Pratt, *Opers Mgr*
Bill Groves, *Safety Mgr*
Jerry Clark, *Manager*
Fred Otto, *Manager*
Carol Hutchinson, *Info Tech Mgr*
EMP: 100
SALES (corp-wide): 930.9MM **Publicly Held**
SIC: 3089 3544 3499 3469 Injection molded finished plastic products; special dies, tools, jigs & fixtures; metal household articles; metal stampings
PA: Kimball Electronics, Inc.
1205 Kimball Blvd
Jasper IN 47546
812 634-4000

(G-7352)
KING MACHINING INC
1213 Indy Way (46214-4302)
PHONE....................................317 271-3132
Barry King, *President*
Jeanna King, *CFO*
EMP: 6
SQ FT: 1,850
SALES: 201K **Privately Held**
WEB: www.customnozzlesinc.com
SIC: 3599 Machine shop, jobbing & repair

(G-7353)
KING-TUESLEY ENTERPRISES INC (PA)
Also Called: Road Solutions
5616 Progress Rd (46241-4333)
P.O. Box 42387 (46242-0387)
PHONE....................................800 428-3266
Fax: 317 244-8461
Charles Linsky, *CEO*
Gary King, *President*
Joseph Stafford, *CFO*
Malcolm J Tuesley, *Admin Sec*
EMP: 26
SQ FT: 25,000
SALES: 4MM **Privately Held**
SIC: 2879 Agricultural chemicals

(G-7354)
KINGERY GROUP INC
Also Called: National Printfast
6574 Breckenridge Dr (46236-3827)
PHONE....................................317 823-9585
Pat Kingery, *President*
EMP: 21
SQ FT: 24,000
SALES (est): 1.4MM **Privately Held**
WEB: www.printfast.com
SIC: 2759 Commercial printing

(G-7355)
KITE & KEY LLC
5825 Alpine Ave (46224-2135)
PHONE....................................317 654-7703
Chameleon Porter, *Principal*
EMP: 2
SALES (est): 114.2K **Privately Held**
SIC: 3944 Kites

▲ = Import ▼=Export
◆ =Import/Export

(G-7356)
KITTY MAC INC
Also Called: Fresh Air Screens
4010 W 86th St Ste D (46268-1779)
PHONE..................................888 549-0783
Marvin F Miller, *President*
Carolyn R Miller, *Treasurer*
EMP: 5
SALES: 700K **Privately Held**
SIC: 3442 Screen doors, metal

(G-7357)
KLEMMS MEAT MARKET
Also Called: Klemm's Sausage Company
1845 Shelby St (46203-4043)
PHONE..................................317 632-1963
Gerhard Klemm, *Owner*
EMP: 6 **EST:** 1913
SQ FT: 3,200
SALES (est): 219.8K **Privately Held**
SIC: 2013 5421 Sausages from pur-
chased meat; meat markets, including
freezer provisioners

(G-7358)
**KLH HOLDING CORPORATION
(HQ)**
2002 Lafayette Rd (46222-2325)
PHONE..................................317 634-3976
Fax: 317 634-3968
Kevin Neighbours, *President*
Bryan J Hite, *Admin Sec*
EMP: 21 **EST:** 1976
SQ FT: 25,000
SALES (est): 2.6MM **Privately Held**
SIC: 3069 Rubber automotive products

(G-7359)
**KLINGE ENAMELING COMPANY
INC**
Also Called: Klinge Coatings
5001 Prospect St (46203-2499)
PHONE..................................317 359-8291
Fax: 317 359-8294
Philip Klinge, *President*
Sheila Shaw, *Vice Pres*
David Druetzler, *Purchasing*
Jerry Butner, *QC Mgr*
Michael Overway, *Engineer*
EMP: 45 **EST:** 1956
SQ FT: 30,000
SALES (est): 5.9MM **Privately Held**
WEB: www.klingecoatings.com
SIC: 3479 2899 3471 8711 Enameling,
including porcelain, of metal products;
chemical preparations; sand blasting of
metal parts; mechanical engineering

(G-7360)
KLIPSCH GROUP INC (HQ)
3502 Woodview Trce # 200 (46268-3182)
PHONE..................................317 860-8100
Fax: 317 860-9100
Fred S Klipsch, *Ch of Bd*
Paul Jacobs, *President*
Mark Casavant, *President*
Paul Thielman, *General Mgr*
Oscar Bernardo, *Vice Pres*
◆ **EMP:** 150
SQ FT: 12,200
SALES (est): 50.5MM
SALES (corp-wide): 507MM **Publicly
Held**
WEB: www.paulklipsch.com
SIC: 3651 Household audio & video equip-
ment; loudspeakers, electrodynamic or
magnetic
PA: Voxx International Corporation
2351 J Lawson Blvd
Orlando FL 32824
800 645-7750

(G-7361)
KLOSTERMAN BAKING CO
5867 Churchman Ave (46203-6012)
PHONE..................................317 359-5545
Fax: 317 359-3759
Steve Faulstich, *Principal*
EMP: 35
SALES (corp-wide): 207.2MM **Privately
Held**
SIC: 2051 Bread, cake & related products

PA: Klosterman Baking Co.
4760 Paddock Rd
Cincinnati OH 45229
513 242-5667

(G-7362)
KNOTTS AND FRYE INC
Also Called: Costumes By Margie By Cher
3818 N Illinois St (46208-4017)
PHONE..................................317 925-6406
Fax: 317 925-6407
Cheryl Harmon, *President*
EMP: 4
SQ FT: 5,000
SALES: 250K **Privately Held**
SIC: 7299 2389 Costume rental; masquer-
ade costumes

(G-7363)
KNOX ENTERPRISES INC
1 Technology Way (46268-5106)
PHONE..................................317 714-3073
Randall Knox, *President*
EMP: 8
SALES: 650K **Privately Held**
SIC: 3053 3069 3086 Gaskets, packing &
sealing devices; fabricated rubber prod-
ucts; plastics foam products

(G-7364)
KOCHS ELECTRIC INC
202 E Palmer St (46225-1640)
PHONE..................................317 639-5624
Fax: 317 684-9253
Kevin Koch, *President*
Kristi Williams, *Vice Pres*
Betty Koch, *Shareholder*
EMP: 12
SQ FT: 1,500
SALES (est): 2.3MM **Privately Held**
SIC: 7699 7694 Pumps & pumping equip-
ment repair; electric motor repair

(G-7365)
KOMUN SCENTS
4635 Falcon Run Way (46254-2073)
PHONE..................................317 308-0714
Anthony Dix, *Principal*
EMP: 2
SALES (est): 107.4K **Privately Held**
SIC: 2844 Toilet preparations

(G-7366)
KONECRANES INC
Also Called: Crane Pro Services
1345 Brookville Way Ste E (46239-1036)
PHONE..................................317 546-8122
Fax: 317 352-8128
Sallie Disser, *President*
Eric Bloodworth, *Manager*
EMP: 12
SALES (corp-wide): 3.7B **Privately Held**
WEB: www.kciusa.com
SIC: 3536 Hoists, cranes & monorails
HQ: Konecranes, Inc.
4401 Gateway Blvd
Springfield OH 45502

(G-7367)
**KORTZENDORF MACHINE &
TOOL**
1450 Sunday Dr (46217-9339)
PHONE..................................317 783-5449
Fax: 317 784-6484
Tom Kortzendorf, *President*
Robert Kortzendorf, *Corp Secy*
EMP: 19 **EST:** 1956
SQ FT: 15,000
SALES (est): 2.9MM **Privately Held**
WEB: www.kortzendorf.com
SIC: 3599 7692 3544 Machine shop, job-
bing & repair; welding repair; special dies,
tools, jigs & fixtures

(G-7368)
KRAZY KLOTHES LTD (PA)
1101 S Illinois St (46225-1411)
PHONE..................................317 687-8310
Fax: 317 687-8317
Dan Murphy, *President*
EMP: 4
SQ FT: 13,000

SALES (est): 593.4K **Privately Held**
WEB: www.krazyklothes.com
SIC: 2341 2322 Pajamas & bedjackets:
women's & children's; nightwear, men's &
boys': from purchased materials

(G-7369)
KREIG DE VAULT
1 Indiana Sq Ste 2050 (46204-2020)
PHONE..................................317 238-6234
Fax: 317 238-6350
Steven Sherman, *Senior Partner*
EMP: 3
SALES (est): 154.5K **Privately Held**
SIC: 3272 Burial vaults, concrete or pre-
cast terrazzo

(G-7370)
L R GREEN CO INC
Also Called: Poster Display Co
5650 Elmwood Ave (46203-6029)
PHONE..................................317 781-4200
Fax: 317 781-4210
Lawrence R Green, *President*
Patricia S Green, *Corp Secy*
Karen Beckham, *Finance*
▲ **EMP:** 75 **EST:** 1974
SQ FT: 65,000
SALES (est): 12.1MM **Privately Held**
WEB: www.poster-display.com
SIC: 3993 Displays & cutouts, window &
lobby; signs, not made in custom sign
painting shops

(G-7371)
L5 SOLUTIONS LLC
7950 Castleway Dr Ste 160 (46250-1994)
PHONE..................................317 436-1044
Anthony Sebastian, *Business Mgr*
David Boesch, *Engineer*
Howard Snyder, *Engineer*
Tom N Walker, *Engineer*
Frank Howard, *Mng Member*
EMP: 5 **EST:** 2006
SALES (est): 665.4K **Privately Held**
SIC: 3571 5045 Electronic computers;
computers, peripherals & software; com-
puter peripheral equipment

(G-7372)
LA OLA LATINO AMERICANA
2401 W Washington St (46222-4178)
P.O. Box 22056 (46222-0056)
PHONE..................................317 822-0345
Ildefonso Carbajal, *Owner*
EMP: 10 **EST:** 1997
SALES (est): 489.8K **Privately Held**
SIC: 2711 Newspapers

(G-7373)
LA VOZ DE INDIANA INC
Also Called: La Voz De Ind Blingual Newsppr
2911 W Washington St (46222-4053)
PHONE..................................317 423-0957
Liliana Hamnik Parod, *CEO*
Jose Gonzalez, *Vice Pres*
EMP: 8
SQ FT: 5,000
SALES (est): 511.9K **Privately Held**
SIC: 2711 Newspapers, publishing & print-
ing

(G-7374)
LAIBE CORPORATION
1414 Bates St (46201-3944)
PHONE..................................317 231-2250
Mark Laibe, *Ch of Bd*
James R Hopkins, *President*
Stephen Gessner, *Engineer*
Calvin Moore, *Engineer*
William Fields, *Design Engr*
▲ **EMP:** 55
SALES (est): 14.8MM **Privately Held**
SIC: 3533 Oil & gas drilling rigs & equip-
ment

(G-7375)
LAIRD PLASTICS INC
3439 N Shadeland Ave # 5 (46226-5787)
PHONE..................................317 890-1808
Fax: 317 890-1804
Jason Jenkins, *Branch Mgr*
EMP: 6

SALES (corp-wide): 437.7MM **Privately
Held**
SIC: 3089 5162 Windows, plastic; plastics
film; plastics materials; plastics sheets &
rods
PA: Laird Plastics, Inc.
5800 Campus Circle Dr E # 1508
Irving TX 75063
469 299-7000

(G-7376)
LAMB MACHINE & TOOL CO
3510 E Raymond St (46203-4745)
PHONE..................................317 780-9106
Kenneth Boehm, *President*
EMP: 2
SALES (est): 81.4K **Privately Held**
SIC: 3599 Industrial machinery

(G-7377)
LAMBEL CORPORATION
7902 E 88th St (46256-1236)
PHONE..................................317 849-6828
Fax: 317 577-1510
Richard M Cook, *President*
Susan Cook, *Treasurer*
EMP: 12 **EST:** 1965
SQ FT: 10,000
SALES (est): 990K **Privately Held**
WEB: www.lambel.com
SIC: 2759 2672 Labels & seals: printing;
coated & laminated paper

(G-7378)
**LAMBERT ASPHLTING
SLCATING INC**
12649 White Rabbit Dr (46235-6116)
PHONE..................................317 985-8061
Brian Lambert, *President*
EMP: 5
SALES (est): 420K **Privately Held**
SIC: 2851 Removers & cleaners

(G-7379)
LAMCO FINISHERS INC
8260 Zionsville Rd (46268-1627)
P.O. Box 78258 (46278-0258)
PHONE..................................317 471-1010
James R Vivian, *President*
Kay Vivian, *Chairman*
Kelly Vernon, *Vice Pres*
Jenny Church, *Project Mgr*
EMP: 35
SQ FT: 33,000
SALES (est): 4MM **Privately Held**
WEB: www.lamcofinishers.com
SIC: 3999 2759 7389 2789 Plaques, pic-
ture, laminated; laser printing; engraving;
laminating services; finishing services;
bookbinding & related work; blankbooks &
looseleaf binders; coated & laminated
paper

(G-7380)
LANTZS COACHWORKS INC
505 S Tibbs Ave Lot 3251 (46241-1630)
PHONE..................................317 487-1111
Fax: 317 487-1255
Don Claycomb, *Manager*
Rebecca Lantzpatton, *Manager*
EMP: 5
SALES (corp-wide): 2.3MM **Privately
Held**
WEB: www.lantzscoachworks.com
SIC: 3715 Truck trailer chassis; demount-
able cargo containers
PA: Lantz's Coachworks, Inc.
100 S Kentucky Ave
Evansville IN 47714
812 425-4439

(G-7381)
**LARRY ROBERTSON
ASSOCIATES**
Also Called: Beveled Glass & Ltg Designs
1056 Millwood Ct (46260-2230)
PHONE..................................812 537-4090
Fax: 317 547-1926
Larry Robertson, *President*
Ronald Slagle, *Corp Secy*
▲ **EMP:** 20
SALES (est): 2.2MM **Privately Held**
WEB: www.beveledglassdesigns.com
SIC: 3231 2431 Leaded glass; doors &
door parts & trim, wood

(G-7382)
LARRYS TLS HYDRAULIC JACK SVCS
702 S Lynhurst Dr (46241-2135)
PHONE..................................317 243-8666
Larry Dorris, *Owner*
EMP: 2
SALES: 150K **Privately Held**
SIC: 3549 Cutting & slitting machinery

(G-7383)
LATICRETE INTERNATIONAL INC
4620 W 84th St Ste 200 (46268-3820)
PHONE..................................317 298-8510
David A Rothberg, *President*
Henry B Rothberg, *Admin Sec*
▲ EMP: 8
SALES (est): 973.4K **Privately Held**
SIC: 3253 5032 Ceramic wall & floor tile; ceramic wall & floor tile

(G-7384)
LATICRETE INTERNATIONAL INC
4620 W 84th St Ste 200 (46268-3820)
PHONE..................................317 298-8510
Fax: 317 298-4237
Ron Roach, *Manager*
EMP: 8
SALES (corp-wide): 149.3MM **Privately Held**
WEB: www.laticrete.com
SIC: 2891 Adhesives & sealants
PA: Laticrete International, Inc.
91 Amity Rd
Bethany CT 06524
203 393-0010

(G-7385)
LAUCK MANUFACTURING CO INC
735 Bacon St (46227-1113)
PHONE..................................317 787-6269
Fax: 317 787-3855
Dan Slightom, *President*
Laurie A Slightom, *Corp Secy*
Andrew Slightom, *Prdtn Mgr*
EMP: 13
SQ FT: 12,000
SALES (est): 2.6MM **Privately Held**
WEB: www.lauckmfg.com
SIC: 3444 7692 3496 3469 Sheet metal specialties, not stamped; welding repair; miscellaneous fabricated wire products; metal stampings

(G-7386)
LAVA LIPS
6821 Grosvenor Pl (46220-4136)
PHONE..................................317 965-6629
Michael T Siemer, *Vice Pres*
EMP: 2
SALES (est): 104.7K **Privately Held**
SIC: 2035 Pickles, sauces & salad dressings

(G-7387)
LCA-VISION INC
Also Called: Lasikplus Vision Center
8930 Keystone Xing (46240-2179)
PHONE..................................317 818-3980
Randy Poynter, *Director*
EMP: 6
SALES (corp-wide): 33.8MM **Privately Held**
SIC: 3841 8042 Ophthalmic lasers; offices & clinics of optometrists
HQ: Lca-Vision Inc.
7840 Montgomery Rd
Cincinnati OH 45236
513 792-9292

(G-7388)
LDI LTD LLC (PA)
54 Monument Cir Ste 800 (46204-2949)
PHONE..................................317 237-5400
J A Lacy, *CEO*
Andre B Lacy, *Ch of Bd*
Margot Eccles, *Vice Pres*
Margot L Eccles, *Vice Pres*
Ryan Polk, *Vice Pres*
EMP: 10

SALES (est): 1.4B **Privately Held**
SIC: 2671 Packaging paper & plastics film, coated & laminated

(G-7389)
LEADTRACK SOFTWARE
11415 Sturgen Bay Ln (46236-9026)
PHONE..................................317 823-0748
Jim Labelle, *CEO*
Amy Wilson, *Info Tech Dir*
EMP: 5
SALES (est): 336.4K **Privately Held**
WEB: www.leadtrack.com
SIC: 7372 Prepackaged software

(G-7390)
LEAP FROGZ SCREANPRINTING EMB
3307 Madison Ave (46227-1129)
PHONE..................................317 786-2441
Todd Kenzig, *Owner*
EMP: 3 EST: 2007
SALES (est): 282.2K **Privately Held**
SIC: 2759 3552 2241 Screen printing; embroidery machines; fabric tapes

(G-7391)
LEAR CORPORATION
4409 W Morris St (46241-2401)
PHONE..................................317 481-0530
EMP: 4
SALES (corp-wide): 20.4B **Publicly Held**
SIC: 3714 Motor vehicle electrical equipment
PA: Lear Corporation
21557 Telegraph Rd
Southfield MI 48033
248 447-1500

(G-7392)
LEASENET INCORPORATED
8888 Keystone Xing # 1300 (46240-4609)
PHONE..................................317 575-4098
Michael Osborne, *Principal*
EMP: 2
SALES (est): 232.7K **Privately Held**
SIC: 3569 Lubrication equipment, industrial

(G-7393)
LEED THERMAL PROCESSING INC
1718 N Luett Ave (46222-2529)
PHONE..................................317 637-5102
Fax: 317 637-0259
Pamela Bowman, *President*
James Friedt, *Corp Secy*
EMP: 7
SALES (est): 750K **Privately Held**
SIC: 3312 3398 Blast furnaces & steel mills; metal heat treating

(G-7394)
LEGACY RESOURCES CO LP (PA)
2780 Wtrfrnt Pw E Dr # 200 (46214-2030)
PHONE..................................317 328-5660
F W Grube, *General Ptnr*
Barbara Meranda, *Controller*
EMP: 3
SQ FT: 2,500
SALES (est): 4.6MM **Privately Held**
WEB: www.legacyresourcesco.com
SIC: 1382 Oil & gas exploration services

(G-7395)
LENNOX IND PRODUCTION LXUD 240
6542 E Westfield Blvd (46220-1110)
PHONE..................................317 253-0353
EMP: 2
SALES (est): 105.2K **Privately Held**
SIC: 3585 Refrigeration & heating equipment

(G-7396)
LENNOX LIR LENNOX INDS INTL
8148 Woodland Dr (46278-1347)
PHONE..................................317 334-1339
EMP: 2
SALES (est): 79.9K **Privately Held**
SIC: 3585 Refrigeration & heating equipment

(G-7397)
LEON R DIXON
Also Called: Beak It Bronze
5206 Fawn Hill Ct (46226-1412)
PHONE..................................317 545-1956
EMP: 2 EST: 2000
SALES (est): 120K **Privately Held**
SIC: 3366 Copper Foundry

(G-7398)
LESCO INC
8569 Zionsville Rd (46268-1511)
PHONE..................................317 876-7968
Roger Smith, *Branch Mgr*
EMP: 3
SALES (corp-wide): 29.7B **Publicly Held**
WEB: www.lesco.com
SIC: 2875 Fertilizers, mixing only
HQ: Lesco, Inc.
1385 E 36th St
Cleveland OH 44114
216 706-9250

(G-7399)
LESSONLY INC
407 Fulton St 302 (46202-3758)
PHONE..................................317 469-9194
John M Yoder, *President*
Conner Burt, *COO*
Clifford Justin, *Accounting Mgr*
Katie Townsend, *Sales Staff*
EMP: 52
SALES (est): 1.7MM **Privately Held**
SIC: 7372 Educational computer software

(G-7400)
LEXINGTON PHARMACEUTICALS
8496 Georgetown Rd (46268-1672)
PHONE..................................317 870-0370
Michael D Becker, *Principal*
EMP: 4 EST: 2010
SALES (est): 326.4K **Privately Held**
SIC: 2834 Pharmaceutical preparations

(G-7401)
LH SOFTWARE CONCEPTS LLC
3601 W 69th St (46268-2523)
PHONE..................................317 222-1779
Patrick Hess,
EMP: 2
SALES (est): 118.6K **Privately Held**
SIC: 7372 7389 Application computer software;

(G-7402)
LIBERTY BOOK & BB MANUFACTURES (PA)
901 E Maryland St (46202-3931)
PHONE..................................317 633-1450
Fax: 317 633-1453
Robert Van Horn, *President*
Henry Jones, *Vice Pres*
Ted Pitrelli, *Vice Pres*
Tom Ross, *Treasurer*
Marshall Gage, *Admin Sec*
▲ EMP: 38
SQ FT: 40,000
SALES (est): 3.2MM **Privately Held**
SIC: 3111 2789 2759 Bookbinders' leather; edging books, cards or paper; gilding books, cards or paper; labels & seals: printing

(G-7403)
LIFE LESS ORDINARY LLC
9032 Sargent Creek Dr (46256-1366)
PHONE..................................317 727-4277
Scott Drake, *Mng Member*
EMP: 2
SALES: 8K **Privately Held**
SIC: 7371 3949 Computer software development & applications; sporting & athletic goods

(G-7404)
LIFE PATH NUMEROLOGY CENTER
Also Called: Life Path Business Sevices
108 S Elder Ave (46222-4522)
PHONE..................................317 638-9752
Daniel Hardt, *President*
Timothy Phipps, *Vice Pres*
Timothy Thipps, *Vice Pres*
Cynthia A Coplen, *Treasurer*

Donna Winsted, *Admin Sec*
EMP: 3
SALES: 50K **Privately Held**
WEB: www.lifepathnum.com
SIC: 8742 2711 General management consultant; commercial printing & newspaper publishing combined

(G-7405)
LIGHT MINE CANDLE COMPANY LLC
1701 Redbay Dr (46234-0167)
PHONE..................................317 353-7786
Johnathon Brown, *Principal*
EMP: 2
SALES (est): 66.2K **Privately Held**
SIC: 3999 Candles

(G-7406)
LIL GIRLS GLAM LLC
Also Called: Lil Girl's Glam Spa Bus
2333 Rostock Ct (46229-2397)
PHONE..................................317 507-3443
Jenise Dunn, *CEO*
EMP: 2
SALES (est): 98.4K **Privately Held**
SIC: 3999 Fingernails, artificial

(G-7407)
LINEAR PUBLISHING CORP
Also Called: Midwest Parenting Publications
921 E 86th St Ste 108 (46240-1841)
PHONE..................................317 722-8500
Fax: 317 722-8510
Gregory Wynne, *President*
Susan Bryant, *Editor*
Wendy Cox, *Editor*
Roxanne Burns, *Business Mgr*
Jennica Zalewski, *Sales Staff*
EMP: 3
SQ FT: 2,499
SALES (est): 543.7K **Privately Held**
WEB: www.lps1.com
SIC: 2721 Magazines: publishing only, not printed on site

(G-7408)
LINK PRINTING SERVICES LLC
12237 Old Stone Dr (46236-9222)
PHONE..................................317 826-9852
William L Cole II, *Principal*
EMP: 2
SALES (est): 187.5K **Privately Held**
SIC: 2752 Commercial printing, lithographic

(G-7409)
LITHO PRESS INC
1747 Massachusetts Ave (46201-1040)
PHONE..................................317 634-6468
Joseph B Lacy, *President*
Bernard Lacy, *Vice Pres*
John Lacy, *Vice Pres*
▲ EMP: 25 EST: 1953
SQ FT: 36,000
SALES (est): 5.9MM **Privately Held**
WEB: www.lithopress.com
SIC: 2752 Commercial printing, offset

(G-7410)
LLOYD JR FRANK P AND ASSOC
4461 Sylvan Rd (46228-2844)
PHONE..................................317 388-9225
Frank P Lloyd Jr, *Principal*
EMP: 2
SALES (est): 177.7K **Privately Held**
SIC: 3826 Analytical instruments

(G-7411)
LLOYDS OF INDIANA INC
2507 Roosevelt Ave (46218-3642)
PHONE..................................317 251-5430
Fax: 317 251-6371
Gary Jones, *President*
Scott Maxfield, *Sales Dir*
Rosanne Bohman, *Manager*
EMP: 6
SQ FT: 2,400
SALES (est): 600K **Privately Held**
WEB: www.lloydsofindiana.com
SIC: 3999 Plaques, picture, laminated

▲ = Import ▼=Export
◆ =Import/Export

(G-7412)
LOADED PHARMACEUTICALS INC
3417 Pinetop Dr (46227-7822)
PHONE....................317 300-1996
David Fulkerson, *Principal*
EMP: 3
SALES (est): 143.6K **Privately Held**
SIC: 2834 Pharmaceutical preparations

(G-7413)
LOCKERBIE SQUARE CAB CO INC
4350 W 10th St (46222-3208)
PHONE....................317 635-1134
Fax: 317 635-1319
Tracy Godfrey, *President*
Cathy Burch, *Admin Sec*
EMP: 5
SQ FT: 7,000
SALES: 1MM **Privately Held**
SIC: 2431 3083 2511 2434 Millwork; laminated plastics plate & sheet; wood household furniture; wood kitchen cabinets

(G-7414)
LOCKHEED MARTIN CORPORATION
5101 Decatur Blvd Ste A (46241-9529)
PHONE....................317 821-4000
David Jacobs, *Branch Mgr*
EMP: 435 **Publicly Held**
WEB: www.lockheedmartin.com
SIC: 3721 Aircraft; research & development on aircraft by the manufacturer
PA: Lockheed Martin Corporation
6801 Rockledge Dr
Bethesda MD 20817

(G-7415)
LOGICAL LIGHTING AND CONTROLS
5054 Crawfordsville Rd (46224-5665)
PHONE....................317 244-8234
Keith Sheffer, *Owner*
EMP: 2
SALES (est): 115.4K **Privately Held**
SIC: 3648 Lighting equipment

(G-7416)
LONE STAR INDUSTRIES INC
1112 W Thompson Rd (46217-9264)
PHONE....................317 780-9860
Michael Glave, *Branch Mgr*
EMP: 2
SALES (corp-wide): 287.7MM **Privately Held**
SIC: 3241 Portland cement
HQ: Lone Star Industries Inc
10401 N Meridian St # 400
Indianapolis IN 46290
317 706-3314

(G-7417)
LONN MANUFACTURING INC
5450 W 84th St (46268-1523)
PHONE....................317 897-1440
Fax: 317 898-4561
Scott Guenther, *President*
Jim Russell, *Vice Pres*
▼ EMP: 4
SQ FT: 30,000
SALES (est): 700.6K **Privately Held**
SIC: 3589 Water purification equipment, household type

(G-7418)
LORD CORPORATION
Also Called: Thermoset Plastics Division
5101 E 65th St (46220-4816)
PHONE....................317 259-4161
Fax: 317 252-8419
Joe Luchik, *Manager*
EMP: 100
SALES (corp-wide): 929.8MM **Privately Held**
SIC: 2891 Adhesives
PA: Lord Corporation
111 Lord Dr
Cary NC 27511
919 468-5979

(G-7419)
LORD FMS GAMES
7244 Rooses Way (46217-7484)
PHONE....................317 710-2253
Joseph McCurdy,
EMP: 3
SALES (est): 116.4K **Privately Held**
SIC: 7371 7372 7389 Computer software development; home entertainment computer software;

(G-7420)
LOUTSA INC
7435 W 10th St (46214-2517)
PHONE....................317 273-0123
Toris Naples, *President*
EMP: 15
SALES (est): 1.1MM **Privately Held**
SIC: 2043 Cereal breakfast foods

(G-7421)
LOVETT PALLET RECYCLING LLC
217 S Belmont Ave Ste E (46222-4286)
PHONE....................317 638-4840
Fax: 317 638-4848
Paul Lovett,
Brad Lovett,
EMP: 55
SQ FT: 20,000
SALES (est): 11.1MM **Privately Held**
SIC: 2448 Pallets, wood

(G-7422)
LOYAL MFG CORP
1121 S Shortridge Rd (46239-1081)
PHONE....................317 359-3185
Fax: 317 353-9284
Ronald Lambert, *President*
Todd Fox, *General Mgr*
Mike Taylor, *Engineer*
Christine Gray, *Manager*
EMP: 12
SQ FT: 13,000
SALES: 1.3MM **Privately Held**
SIC: 3444 Sheet metal specialties, not stamped

(G-7423)
LUCAS OIL RACEWAY
10267 E Us Highway 136 (46234-9089)
P.O. Box 34300 (46234-0300)
PHONE....................317 291-4090
Mike Lewis, *Senior VP*
EMP: 12 EST: 2011
SALES (est): 1.3MM **Privately Held**
SIC: 3644 Raceways

(G-7424)
LUCKMANN INDUSTRIES
3135 Jackson St (46222-4039)
PHONE....................317 464-0323
EMP: 2
SALES (est): 129.1K **Privately Held**
SIC: 3999 Manufacturing industries

(G-7425)
LUI PLUS
7933 Valley Stream Dr (46237-8540)
PHONE....................812 309-9350
EMP: 2
SALES (est): 84.8K **Privately Held**
SIC: 5021 2522 Office & public building furniture; office furniture, except wood

(G-7426)
LUMEN CACHE INC
11216 Fall Creek Rd (46256-9406)
PHONE....................317 222-1314
Derek Cowburn, *President*
Lynn Cowburn, *Officer*
EMP: 2 EST: 2011
SALES (est): 132.4K **Privately Held**
SIC: 3648 Lighting equipment

(G-7427)
LUSH
4507 E 82nd St (46250-1670)
PHONE....................317 842-5874
David White, *Owner*
EMP: 3
SALES (est): 374.3K **Privately Held**
SIC: 2841 Soap & other detergents

(G-7428)
LUXOTTICA RETAIL N AMER INC
Also Called: Lenscrafters
4020 Lafayette Rd (46254-2506)
PHONE....................317 293-9999
Elizabeth Young, *Manager*
EMP: 23 **Privately Held**
WEB: www.lenscrafters.com
SIC: 5995 8042 3851 Eyeglasses, prescription; offices & clinics of optometrists; ophthalmic goods
HQ: Luxottica Retail North America Inc.
4000 Luxottica Pl
Mason OH 45040

(G-7429)
M & M SVC STN EQP SPCALIST INC
Also Called: Mid Valley Supply Co
2228 Yandes St (46205-4534)
PHONE....................317 347-8001
John Childes, *Manager*
EMP: 7
SALES (corp-wide): 7.7MM **Privately Held**
SIC: 3492 Hose & tube couplings, hydraulic/pneumatic
PA: M & M Service Station Equipment Specialist, Inc.
4489 Mary Ingle Hwy
Silver Grove KY 41085
859 781-0402

(G-7430)
M & M TRIM INC
6525 Capitol Reef Ln (46237-4484)
P.O. Box 33488 (46203-0488)
PHONE....................317 791-7009
Patrick Fritz, *President*
EMP: 2
SALES (est): 273.1K **Privately Held**
SIC: 2431 Interior & ornamental woodwork & trim

(G-7431)
M & S CURTIS LLC
10015 Chester Dr (46240)
PHONE....................317 946-8440
Michael D Curtis, *Mng Member*
EMP: 8
SALES: 100K **Privately Held**
SIC: 3999 Manufacturing industries

(G-7432)
M A C CORPORATION
4717 Massachusetts Ave (46218-3144)
PHONE....................317 545-3341
Fax: 317 545-8570
Roger Hobbs, *President*
Bill Featherstone, *Regional Mgr*
Ray Hobbs, *Exec VP*
A Kay Hobbs, *Treasurer*
Ida Young, *Admin Sec*
EMP: 60 EST: 1975
SQ FT: 60,000
SALES (est): 14MM **Privately Held**
SIC: 3443 Dumpsters, garbage

(G-7433)
M RI SOLUTIONS
8805 N Meridian St (46260-2760)
PHONE....................317 218-3006
Edward Kolowitz, *General Mgr*
EMP: 50
SALES (est): 3.6MM **Privately Held**
SIC: 3829 Medical diagnostic systems, nuclear

(G-7434)
M2M HOLDINGS INC
450 E 96th St Ste 300 (46240-3797)
PHONE....................317 249-1700
Vincent Burkett, *President*
Jeff Tognoni, *President*
Kathy Kinder, *Vice Pres*
Brenda Padgett, *Vice Pres*
Don Melton, *Asst Sec*
EMP: 650
SALES (est): 23.4MM **Privately Held**
SIC: 7372 Prepackaged software

(G-7435)
MACHINING CENTER INC
5935 Kopetsky Dr Ste E (46217-9008)
PHONE....................317 787-1965

Fax: 317 787-1973
Daniel D Medcalf, *President*
EMP: 10
SQ FT: 12,000
SALES (est): 1.2MM **Privately Held**
SIC: 3544 Special dies, tools, jigs & fixtures

(G-7436)
MAE OF AMERICA INC
7960 Castleway Dr Ste 131 (46250-1979)
PHONE....................765 561-4539
Joseph Kemple, *CEO*
EMP: 3
SALES (est): 236.2K **Privately Held**
SIC: 3547 Straightening machinery (rolling mill equipment)

(G-7437)
MAGIC CANDLE INC
203 S Audubon Rd (46219-7214)
PHONE....................317 357-1101
Janet Deferbrache, *President*
EMP: 2
SALES: 60K **Privately Held**
SIC: 3999 Candles

(G-7438)
MAGNETIC INSTRUMENTATION INC (PA)
Also Called: Utility Systems
8431 Castlewood Dr (46250-1534)
PHONE....................317 842-9000
Fax: 317 849-7600
Todd McMullen, *CEO*
Jon Goodson, *Manager*
Jim Kinsley, *Software Engr*
EMP: 44 EST: 1978
SQ FT: 30,000
SALES (est): 6.9MM **Privately Held**
WEB: www.maginst.com
SIC: 3699 3825 Electrical equipment & supplies; test equipment for electronic & electric measurement

(G-7439)
MAGNETIC INSTRUMENTATION LLC
Also Called: Utility Systems
8431 Castlewood Dr (46250-1534)
PHONE....................317 842-7500
David Miller, *President*
EMP: 28
SQ FT: 15,000
SALES: 4MM **Privately Held**
SIC: 3699 Electrical equipment & supplies

(G-7440)
MAGNIFISCENTS
5207 E 38th St (46218-1718)
PHONE....................317 549-3880
Dwayne Tyler, *Owner*
EMP: 2
SALES: 180K **Privately Held**
SIC: 2899 Incense

(G-7441)
MAHOMED SALES & WHSNG LLC
Also Called: M S W
8258 Zionsville Rd (46268-1627)
PHONE....................317 472-5800
Fax: 317 472-5801
Yousuf Mohamed, *CEO*
James Brown, *President*
Keith Kanipe, *Vice Pres*
Misty Kuntz, *Engineer*
EMP: 80 EST: 1997
SQ FT: 150,000
SALES (est): 59MM **Privately Held**
WEB: www.whse.com
SIC: 4225 3714 General warehousing; motor vehicle parts & accessories

(G-7442)
MAIN EVENT MDSG GROUP LLC
6880 Hillsdale Ct (46250-2001)
PHONE....................317 570-8900
Fax: 317 570-8989
Brian Fahle, *President*
Penny East, *Opers Staff*
Peggy Burris, *Accounts Mgr*
Jennifer Dezelan, *Accounts Mgr*
Whitey Kapsalis, *Accounts Exec*
▲ EMP: 18

GEOGRAPHIC

SQ FT: 4,000
SALES (est): 5.1MM **Privately Held**
WEB: www.mainevt.com
SIC: 2262 7336 Screen printing: man-made fiber & silk broadwoven fabrics; silk screen design

(G-7443)
MAIN1MEDIA LLC
Also Called: Main One Media
8459 Castlewood Dr Ste D (46250-4581)
PHONE.................................317 841-7000
Rick Terry,
EMP: 7
SQ FT: 3,000
SALES: 300K **Privately Held**
WEB: www.main1media.com
SIC: 2731 Pamphlets: publishing & printing

(G-7444)
MAINGATE INC
7900 Rockville Rd (46214-3107)
PHONE.................................317 243-2000
David I Moroknek, President
Mark Lynn, General Mgr
Ned Walliser, Senior VP
Mark Bragg, Vice Pres
Tim Labelle, Vice Pres
▲ EMP: 100
SQ FT: 30,000
SALES (est): 24.2MM **Privately Held**
WEB: www.maingateinc.com
SIC: 2339 2396 2395 6794 Women's & misses' athletic clothing & sportswear; screen printing on fabric articles; embroidery & art needlework; copyright buying & licensing

(G-7445)
MAJESTIC MARBLE IMPORTS INC
1100 E Maryland St (46202-3975)
PHONE.................................317 237-4400
Fax: 317 237-4462
Jose Alejos, President
Barcia Alejos, Admin Sec
▲ EMP: 18
SQ FT: 6,200
SALES (est): 1.7MM **Privately Held**
SIC: 3281 Cut stone & stone products

(G-7446)
MAJOR TOOL AND MACHINE INC
1458 E 19th St (46218-4289)
PHONE.................................317 636-6433
Fax: 317 634-9420
J Stephen Weyreter, Ch of Bd
Mike Trosen, General Mgr
Rick Ogden, Superintendent
John Huter, Vice Pres
Bjorn Lissman, Vice Pres
▲ EMP: 320 EST: 1949
SQ FT: 450,000
SALES (est): 54.7MM **Privately Held**
WEB: www.majortool.com
SIC: 7692 3599 3769 3544 Welding repair; machine & other job shop work; guided missile & space vehicle parts & auxiliary equipment; special dies, tools, jigs & fixtures; industrial trucks & tractors; sheet metalwork

(G-7447)
MALIBU WELLNESS INC
Also Called: Malibu C
6050 E Hanna Ave Ste 1 (46203-6288)
PHONE.................................317 624-7560
Thomas G Porter, CEO
Debra Porter, Corp Secy
Randy Jones, Opers Mgr
Doug Peelle, Finance
Trisha Kemp, Manager
▲ EMP: 45
SQ FT: 97,000
SALES: 7MM **Privately Held**
SIC: 2844 Hair preparations, including shampoos; cosmetic preparations

(G-7448)
MALLORY SONALERT PRODUCTS INC
4411 S High School Rd (46241-6404)
P.O. Box 2064 (46206-2064)
PHONE.................................317 612-1000

Wayne Hodges, President
Dan Obrien, Vice Pres
Joe Heath, Safety Mgr
Christopher Baldwin, QC Dir
Ronald Voegele, CFO
▲ EMP: 35
SQ FT: 22,500
SALES (est): 7.3MM **Privately Held**
WEB: www.mallory-sonalert.com
SIC: 3679 Electronic circuits

(G-7449)
MANN DISTRIBUTION INC
7 Barbara Ct (46222-1414)
PHONE.................................317 293-6785
John Mann, Owner
EMP: 2
SALES (est): 193.4K **Privately Held**
SIC: 2621 Tissue paper

(G-7450)
MANSFIELD - KING LLC
6501 Julian Ave (46219-6603)
PHONE.................................317 788-0750
Charles Haywood, President
▲ EMP: 75
SQ FT: 200,000
SALES (est): 31.8MM **Privately Held**
SIC: 2844 Toilet preparations

(G-7451)
MARC WOODWORKING INC
1719 English Ave (46201-4006)
PHONE.................................317 635-9663
Fax: 317 635-9673
Joseph A Hirsch, President
Mary Ann Lutz, Controller
EMP: 65 EST: 1972
SQ FT: 60,000
SALES (est): 9.7MM **Privately Held**
WEB: www.marcwoodworking.com
SIC: 2499 Decorative wood & woodwork

(G-7452)
MARGCO INTERNATIONAL LLC
6445 E 30th St (46219-1006)
PHONE.................................317 568-4274
Louis Schiesz,
William Shumaker,
▲ EMP: 6
SQ FT: 3,500
SALES (est): 564.4K **Privately Held**
SIC: 2851 Paints & allied products

(G-7453)
MARIAN INC
1011 E Saint Clair St (46202-3569)
PHONE.................................317 638-6525
Eugene J Witchger, President
▲ EMP: 3000
SALES (est): 179.7MM **Privately Held**
SIC: 3699 Electrical welding equipment; electron beam metal cutting, forming or welding machines; electron linear accelerators; electronic training devices

(G-7454)
MARIAN WORLDWIDE INC (PA)
1011 E Saint Clair St (46202-3569)
PHONE.................................317 638-6525
Witchger William J, President
Bill Witchger, President
Eugene J Witchger, Vice Pres
Kerry Crabbe, Opers Mgr
Gene Witchger, Opers Mgr
▲ EMP: 80 EST: 1954
SQ FT: 200,000
SALES (est): 53.8MM **Privately Held**
WEB: www.marianinc.com
SIC: 3679 3053 2672 2891 Electronic circuits; gaskets, all materials; tape, pressure sensitive: made from purchased materials; adhesives & sealants; laminated plastics plate & sheet

(G-7455)
MARIETTA MARTIN MATERIALS INC
Also Called: Belmont Sand
5620 S Belmont Ave (46217-9712)
P.O. Box 47217 (46247-0217)
PHONE.................................317 789-4020
Roy Smith, Branch Mgr
EMP: 13 **Publicly Held**
WEB: www.martinmarietta.com
SIC: 1422 Crushed & broken limestone

PA: Martin Marietta Materials Inc
2710 Wycliff Rd
Raleigh NC 27607

(G-7456)
MARKETING SERVICES GROUP INC
2601 S Holt Rd (46241-5736)
P.O. Box 421268 (46242-1268)
PHONE.................................317 381-2268
Jennifer Rode, Surgery Dir
EMP: 324
SALES (est): 7.8MM
SALES (corp-wide): 16.3B **Publicly Held**
SIC: 7336 2759 Commercial art & graphic design; commercial printing
HQ: Balkamp Inc
2601 Stout Heritage Pkwy # 100
Plainfield IN 46168
317 754-3900

(G-7457)
MARMON HIGHWAY TECH LLC
Also Called: Fontaine Truck Equipment Co
2770 Bluff Rd (46225-2205)
PHONE.................................317 787-0718
Fax: 317 787-0794
Joseph A Stoutner, Manager
EMP: 27
SQ FT: 2,400
SALES (corp-wide): 242.1B **Publicly Held**
WEB: www.fontaineindustries.com
SIC: 5013 7538 7532 3713 Wheels, motor vehicle; general automotive repair shops; top & body repair & paint shops; truck & bus bodies
HQ: Marmon Highway Technologies Llc
5915 Chalkville Rd 300
Birmingham AL 35235
205 508-2000

(G-7458)
MARQUISE ENTERPRISES LTD
7330 E 86th St Ste 100 (46256-1252)
PHONE.................................317 578-3400
Fax: 317 578-3401
Mark Wolf, Branch Mgr
EMP: 8
SALES (corp-wide): 5.1MM **Privately Held**
SIC: 1751 2431 5084 Carpentry work; millwork; woodworking machinery
PA: Marquise Enterprises Ltd.
5248 Port Royal Rd
Springfield VA 22151
703 912-6727

(G-7459)
MARTECK INC
7998 Georgetown Rd # 600 (46268-5631)
PHONE.................................317 824-0240
Robert Copeland, CEO
Andy Hazelgrove, Representative
EMP: 20
SQ FT: 3,000
SALES (est): 4.2MM **Privately Held**
SIC: 3577 Bar code (magnetic ink) printers

(G-7460)
MARTIN SIGNS & CRANE SERVICES
7204 E 46th St (46226-3800)
PHONE.................................317 908-9708
Fax: 317 545-6100
Fred Martin, President
EMP: 3
SQ FT: 2,500
SALES (est): 100K **Privately Held**
SIC: 7532 3993 Truck painting & lettering; electric signs; neon signs

(G-7461)
MARTINSVILLE MILLING CO INC
8391 N Illinois St (46260-2944)
PHONE.................................317 253-2581
Elizabeth Carpenter, President
Sarah Lugar, Corp Secy
▲ EMP: 2
SALES (est): 111.1K **Privately Held**
SIC: 2041 Flour & other grain mill products

(G-7462)
MARY JONAS
Also Called: Df Global Mfg
2104 Dr Andrw J Brwn Ave (46202-1935)
PHONE.................................317 500-0600
Mary Jonas, Owner
Gregory Trusty, Consultant
EMP: 12
SALES (est): 537.1K **Privately Held**
SIC: 3089 3492 3444 Injection molded finished plastic products; injection molding of plastics; windshields, plastic; hose & tube fittings & assemblies, hydraulic/pneumatic; radiator shields or enclosures, sheet metal

(G-7463)
MASCO CORPORATION OF INDIANA
300 S Carroll Rd (46229-3959)
PHONE.................................317 848-1812
Jim Flood, Safety Mgr
Steve McCall, Opers Staff
Jeff Slinker, Mfg Staff
Michelle Huff, Purch Dir
Charles W Hettrick, Technical Mgr
EMP: 100
SALES (corp-wide): 7.6B **Publicly Held**
SIC: 2759 3993 2789 2752 Promotional printing; signs & advertising specialties; bookbinding & related work; commercial printing, lithographic; automotive & apparel trimmings
HQ: Masco Corporation Of Indiana
55 E 111th St
Indianapolis IN 46280
317 848-1812

(G-7464)
MASSON M ROSS CO INC
Also Called: M Ross Masson
567 N Highland Ave (46202-3545)
PHONE.................................317 632-8021
William Witchger, President
C Joseph Koehler, Vice Pres
Cindy Edwards, Plant Mgr
Tina Marsh, Controller
EMP: 12 EST: 1907
SQ FT: 22,000
SALES (est): 990K **Privately Held**
WEB: www.mrossmasson.com
SIC: 2241 Strapping webs

(G-7465)
MATAM CORP
1434 N New Jersey St (46202-2624)
P.O. Box 44238 (46244-0238)
PHONE.................................317 264-9908
Joseph McIntosh, President
▼ EMP: 3
SQ FT: 1,700
SALES (est): 317.3K **Privately Held**
SIC: 2048 Kelp meal & pellets: prepared as animal feed

(G-7466)
MATERIALS PROCESSING INC
3500 Depauw Blvd (46268-1170)
PHONE.................................317 803-3010
Donald K Densborn, Principal
EMP: 3 EST: 2011
SALES (est): 233K **Privately Held**
SIC: 3443 Fabricated plate work (boiler shop)

(G-7467)
MATRIX PHOTO LABORATORIES INC
Also Called: Matrix Imaging
118 W North St (46204-1229)
PHONE.................................317 635-4756
Fax: 317 632-9592
Teresa D Freije, CEO
Brian M Freije, President
Joe Freije, Vice Pres
EMP: 18
SQ FT: 17,000
SALES (est): 1.5MM **Privately Held**
WEB: www.matrixdigitalphoto.com
SIC: 2759 Commercial printing

(G-7468)
MATTOX & MOORE INC
1503 E Riverside Dr (46202-2097)
PHONE.................................317 632-7534

▲ = Import ▼=Export
◆ =Import/Export

Richard Feigh, *President*
Brett Breht, *Vice Pres*
Greg Feigh, *Admin Sec*
EMP: 6 EST: 1950
SQ FT: 4,000
SALES: 1MM **Privately Held**
SIC: 2834 3841 3829 Veterinary pharmaceutical preparations; surgical & medical instruments; measuring & controlling devices

(G-7469)
MAURY BOYD & ASSOCIATES INC
9241 Castlegate Dr (46256-1004)
PHONE...................317 849-6110
Richard A Boyd, *President*
Thomas Hicks, *Treasurer*
Michael Moxley, *Consultant*
EMP: 19 **EST:** 1949
SQ FT: 10,000
SALES (est): 2MM **Privately Held**
SIC: 7389 2796 2791 2789 Printing broker; platemaking services; typesetting; bookbinding & related work; commercial printing, lithographic

(G-7470)
MAYS+RED SPOT COATINGS LLC
5611 E 71st St (46220-3920)
PHONE...................317 558-2024
Damon J Wilson,
William Mays,
Matthew B Murphy,
John B Phillips,
Charles D Storm,
EMP: 5
SALES: 2.3MM **Privately Held**
SIC: 3479 Coating, rust preventive

(G-7471)
MCBROOM ELECTRIC CO INC
Also Called: McBroom Industrial Services
800 W 16th St (46202-2202)
PHONE...................317 926-3451
Fax: 317 927-0759
Richard McBroom, *President*
Collin Massie, *Accounting Mgr*
Michelle Weissert, *Human Res Dir*
Bob Campbell, *VP Sales*
Robert Hoquim, *CTO*
EMP: 65
SQ FT: 46,800
SALES (est): 15.7MM **Privately Held**
WEB: www.mcbroomelectric.com
SIC: 7694 5063 3549 Rebuilding motors, except automotive; motors, electric; metalworking machinery

(G-7472)
MCGINTY CONVEYORS INC
5002 W Washington St (46241-2299)
PHONE...................317 240-4315
Fax: 317 240-4323
John W McGinty III, *President*
John W Mc Ginty III, *President*
▲ **EMP:** 6
SQ FT: 12,000
SALES (est): 2.9MM **Privately Held**
WEB: www.mcgintyconveyors.com
SIC: 5084 3535 Materials handling machinery; conveyor systems; conveyors & conveying equipment

(G-7473)
MD LAIRD INC
Also Called: PIP Printing
8255 Craig St Ste 110 (46250-4583)
PHONE...................317 842-6338
Fax: 317 842-6348
Mike Laird, *President*
EMP: 2
SALES (est): 301.1K **Privately Held**
WEB: www.ilectris.com
SIC: 2752 Commercial printing, offset

(G-7474)
MED DEVICES LLC
6335 Old Orchard Rd (46226-1040)
PHONE...................317 508-1699
Gabe Browne, *President*
EMP: 2
SALES (est): 152.7K **Privately Held**
SIC: 3841 Surgical & medical instruments

(G-7475)
MED2950 LLC
2950 N Catherwood Ave (46219-1011)
P.O. Box 18189 (46218-0189)
PHONE...................317 545-5383
Ron Lyon, *President*
David Berry,
Bryan Bowman,
Timothy Franklin,
▲ **EMP:** 15
SQ FT: 8,000
SALES (est): 4MM **Privately Held**
WEB: www.medivative.com
SIC: 3841 Surgical & medical instruments

(G-7476)
MEDICAL DEVICE BUS SVCS INC
8904 Bash St Ste A (46256-1286)
PHONE...................317 596-3320
Fax: 317 596-3324
Gay Davis, *Manager*
EMP: 5
SALES (corp-wide): 76.4B **Publicly Held**
SIC: 3842 Surgical appliances & supplies
HQ: Medical Device Business Services, Inc.
700 Orthopaedic Dr
Warsaw IN 46582

(G-7477)
MELROSE GROUP LLC
6833 Fair Ridge Dr (46221-4059)
PHONE...................317 437-6784
EMP: 3
SALES (est): 269.6K **Privately Held**
SIC: 3569 Liquid automation machinery & equipment

(G-7478)
MEMORIES BY DESIGN INC
5615 Central Ave (46220-3011)
PHONE...................317 254-1708
Stuart Winternheimer, *President*
Charles Winternheimer, *Principal*
EMP: 2
SALES (est): 108K **Privately Held**
SIC: 3999 Flowers, artificial & preserved

(G-7479)
MERCER MACHINE COMPANY INC
1421 S Holt Rd (46241-4105)
PHONE...................317 241-9903
Fax: 317 241-5726
Tracy Robinson, *President*
Brian Robinson, *Vice Pres*
EMP: 15 **EST:** 1954
SQ FT: 13,000
SALES: 1.4MM **Privately Held**
WEB: www.mercermachine.net
SIC: 3599 Machine shop, jobbing & repair; chemical milling job shop

(G-7480)
MERCHANTS METALS INC
6701 Bluff Rd (46217-3986)
PHONE...................317 783-7678
Ryan Riggins, *Branch Mgr*
EMP: 10
SALES (corp-wide): 2.2B **Privately Held**
SIC: 3315 Steel wire & related products
HQ: Merchants Metals Llc
211 Perimeter Center Pkwy
Atlanta GA 30346
770 741-0300

(G-7481)
MERCK SHARP & DOHME CORP
8440 Woodfld Xing 490 (46240-4347)
PHONE...................317 286-3038
Laura Pawelek, *Manager*
EMP: 12
SALES (corp-wide): 40.1B **Publicly Held**
SIC: 2834 Pharmaceutical preparations
HQ: Merck Sharp & Dohme Corp.
2000 Galloping Hill Rd
Kenilworth NJ 07033
908 740-4000

(G-7482)
MERIN INTERIORS INDIANAPOLIS
1145 Woodmere Dr (46260-4003)
PHONE...................317 251-6603

Harry A Merin, *Owner*
EMP: 2
SALES: 200K **Privately Held**
SIC: 2591 2391 Window blinds; window shades; curtains & draperies

(G-7483)
MERRITT MANUFACTURING INC
1350 W Southport Rd Ste C (46217-5394)
P.O. Box 17152 (46217-0152)
PHONE...................317 409-0148
Jammie Shayne Merritt, *President*
Barbara G Merritt, *Corp Secy*
EMP: 2
SQ FT: 1,000
SALES: 75K **Privately Held**
SIC: 3944 Child restraint seats, automotive

(G-7484)
MERSS CORPORATION
1017 W 23rd St (46208-5442)
PHONE...................317 632-7299
Fax: 317 632-5822
Robert Polk, *President*
Christopher Polk, *Vice Pres*
Sharron Polk, *Shareholder*
Beverly Polk, *Admin Sec*
EMP: 6
SQ FT: 20,000
SALES (est): 540K **Privately Held**
WEB: www.mersscorporation.com
SIC: 3821 7699 5047 Sterilizers; medical equipment repair, non-electric; medical equipment & supplies

(G-7485)
MET-PRO TECHNOLOGIES LLC
Dean Pump Division
6040 Guion Rd (46254-1222)
PHONE...................317 293-2930
Fax: 317 297-7028
Jerry D'Alterio, *General Mgr*
Ron Reece, *Purch Agent*
John Ryan, *Engineer*
Robert Plummer, *Marketing Staff*
EMP: 35
SALES (corp-wide): 345MM **Publicly Held**
WEB: www.met-pro.com
SIC: 3561 3594 Pumps & pumping equipment; fluid power pumps & motors
HQ: Met-Pro Technologies Llc
4625 Red Bank Rd
Cincinnati OH 45227
513 458-2600

(G-7486)
METAL FINISHING CO INC
3901 E 26th St (46218-3003)
PHONE...................317 546-9004
Fax: 317 546-9009
Damian Mc Dowell, *President*
Ruth McClellan, *Admin Sec*
EMP: 6 **EST:** 1941
SQ FT: 4,000
SALES: 300K **Privately Held**
SIC: 3471 Electroplating of metals or formed products; polishing, metals or formed products

(G-7487)
METAL IMPROVEMENT COMPANY LLC
5945 W 84th St Ste D (46278-1397)
PHONE...................317 875-6030
Dan Richardson, *Manager*
Randall Benjamin, *Manager*
EMP: 6
SALES (corp-wide): 2.2B **Publicly Held**
WEB: www.mic-houston.com
SIC: 3398 Metal heat treating; shot peening (treating steel to reduce fatigue)
HQ: Metal Improvement Company, Llc
80 E Rte 4 Ste 310
Paramus NJ 07652
201 843-7800

(G-7488)
METAL SOLUTIONS INC
5756 Churchman Ave (46203-6009)
PHONE...................317 781-6734
Fax: 317 786-6747
Michael Burdine, *President*
EMP: 16

SALES: 1.5MM **Privately Held**
WEB: www.metalsolutionsusa.com
SIC: 3441 Fabricated structural metal

(G-7489)
METALLIC SEALS INC
2735 Brill Rd (46225-2302)
PHONE...................317 780-0773
Virginia Allen, *President*
EMP: 3
SQ FT: 3,500
SALES (est): 259.1K **Privately Held**
SIC: 3053 Gaskets, all materials

(G-7490)
METALS AND ADDITIVES LLC (PA)
Also Called: Omni Oxide
5929 Lakeside Blvd (46278-1996)
PHONE...................317 290-5007
Fax: 317 290-5011
Greg Stevens, *President*
Mark Mc Caughey, *Vice Pres*
Gregg R Bennett, *CFO*
▼ **EMP:** 18
SQ FT: 6,000
SALES (est): 17MM **Privately Held**
SIC: 2819 Lead compounds or salts, inorganic, not used in pigments

(G-7491)
METALWORKING LUBRICANTS CO
1509 S Senate Ave (46225-1573)
PHONE...................317 269-2444
Fax: 317 269-2443
Michael Zielinski, *Plant Engr*
Garry Baize, *Manager*
EMP: 50
SALES (corp-wide): 221.8MM **Privately Held**
WEB: www.mwlco.com
SIC: 2992 2899 2842 2841 Cutting oils, blending; made from purchased materials; chemical preparations; specialty cleaning, polishes & sanitation goods; soap & other detergents; industrial inorganic chemicals
PA: Metalworking Lubricants Company
25 W Silverdome Indus Par
Pontiac MI 48342
248 332-3500

(G-7492)
METFAB INC
1329 Sadlier Circle W Dr (46239-1055)
PHONE...................317 322-0385
William Wycoff, *President*
EMP: 2
SALES (est): 132.3K **Privately Held**
SIC: 3441 Fabricated structural metal

(G-7493)
MEYER PLASTICS INC (PA)
Also Called: Sila Seal
5167 E 65th St (46220-4816)
PHONE...................317 259-4131
Fax: 317 252-4687
Ralph R Meyer, *President*
Chad Cecil, *Vice Pres*
Rick Sproull, *Vice Pres*
Jeff Scott, *Warehouse Mgr*
Tim Richards, *Purch Mgr*
▲ **EMP:** 60 **EST:** 1950
SQ FT: 84,000
SALES (est): 24.8MM **Privately Held**
WEB: www.meyerplastics.com
SIC: 3089 5162 Thermoformed finished plastic products; plastics materials & basic shapes

(G-7494)
MGTC INC
5757 Kopetsky Dr Ste D (46217-9282)
PHONE...................317 786-1693
Tom Wilson, *Branch Mgr*
EMP: 4
SALES (corp-wide): 313.3MM **Publicly Held**
SIC: 2339 Sportswear, women's
HQ: Mgtc, Inc.
11541 Trail Ridge Pl
Zionsville IN 46077
317 780-0609

(G-7495)
MI-TECH TUNGSTEN METALS LLC
4701 Massachusetts Ave (46218-3144)
PHONE....................................317 549-4290
Allan C Bir Jr, *Mng Member*
EMP: 100
SQ FT: 90,000
SALES: 25MM **Privately Held**
SIC: 3356 Tungsten, basic shapes

(G-7496)
MICHELE L GRAVEL
8607 Depot Dr (46217-5202)
PHONE....................................317 889-0521
Michele Gravel, *Principal*
EMP: 5
SALES (est): 240.7K **Privately Held**
SIC: 1442 Construction sand & gravel

(G-7497)
MICRO METL CORPORATION (PA)
3035 N Shadeland Ave # 300
(46226-6281)
PHONE....................................800 662-4822
Fax: 317 543-5499
Gerald E Schultz, *President*
Barbara E Schultz, *Principal*
Barry Smith, *Project Mgr*
Eugene Sikorovsky, *Admin Sec*
EMP: 144
SQ FT: 180,000
SALES (est): 83.7MM **Privately Held**
WEB: www.micrometl.net
SIC: 3444 Sheet metalwork

(G-7498)
MICRO MOTION INC
8525 Northwest Blvd (46278-1384)
PHONE....................................317 334-1893
Fax: 317 870-2977
Joe Almond, *Manager*
EMP: 2
SALES (corp-wide): 15.2B **Publicly Held**
SIC: 3824 Liquid meters
HQ: Micro Motion, Inc.
        7070 Winchester Cir
        Boulder CO 80301
        303 530-8400

(G-7499)
MICROMETL INDIANAPOLIS
3035 N Shadeland Ave (46226-6200)
PHONE....................................317 524-5400
Gerald Schultz, *Owner*
EMP: 4
SALES (est): 447.2K **Privately Held**
SIC: 3441 Fabricated structural metal

(G-7500)
MICRONUTRIENTS USA LLC
Also Called: Micronutrients Division
1550 Research Way (46231-3350)
PHONE....................................317 486-5880
Fax: 317 486-5888
Bruce Crutcher, *CEO*
Fred Steward, *President*
▲ **EMP:** 60
SQ FT: 30,000
SALES (est): 24.2MM **Privately Held**
WEB: www.micronutrients.net
SIC: 2048 Feed supplements
HQ: Trouw Nutrition Usa, Llc
        115 Executive Dr
        Highland IL 62249
        618 654-2070

(G-7501)
MICROSOFT CORPORATION
8702 Keystone Xing Ste 66 (46240-7621)
PHONE....................................317 705-6900
Neha Mishra, *Partner*
Steve Piper, *Principal*
Dustin Gates, *Accounts Mgr*
Pamela Sellers, *Accounts Mgr*
Rusty Fishel, *Manager*
EMP: 15
SALES (corp-wide): 110.3B **Publicly Held**
WEB: www.microsoft.com
SIC: 7372 Application computer software

PA: Microsoft Corporation
        1 Microsoft Way
        Redmond WA 98052
        425 882-8080

(G-7502)
MID AMERICA COOP EDUCATION
6302 Rucker Rd (46220-4886)
PHONE....................................317 726-6910
Rod Kelsay, *Principal*
EMP: 2
SALES: 114.5K **Privately Held**
SIC: 2754 Business form & card printing, gravure

(G-7503)
MIDLAND PLASTICS CO DIVISION
3001 E 30th St (46218-2850)
PHONE....................................317 352-7785
Daniel D Pratt Jr, *Principal*
EMP: 13
SALES (est): 2MM **Privately Held**
SIC: 2653 Corrugated & solid fiber boxes

(G-7504)
MIDWEST EMPIRE LLC
Also Called: ASG Unlimited
3747 S Meridian St (46217-3265)
PHONE....................................317 786-7446
Scott Femler, *Mng Member*
EMP: 2 EST: 2004
SALES (est): 230K **Privately Held**
SIC: 2752 Commercial printing, offset

(G-7505)
MIDWEST ENERGY PARTNERS LLC
201 S Capitol Ave Ste 510 (46225-1025)
PHONE....................................317 600-3235
William Herrick, *President*
EMP: 2
SALES (est): 150K **Privately Held**
SIC: 1381 Drilling oil & gas wells

(G-7506)
MIDWEST GRAPHICS INC
5550 Elmwood Ct (46203-6043)
PHONE....................................317 780-4600
Fax: 317 780-4611
Michael L La Londe, *President*
John Hannon, *Vice Pres*
James Timmerman, *Vice Pres*
Janice Martinez, *Sales Staff*
Molly Schneider, *Sales Staff*
EMP: 50
SQ FT: 30,000
SALES (est): 8.2MM **Privately Held**
SIC: 2759 Commercial printing

(G-7507)
MIDWEST MFG RESOURCES INC
3902 Hanna Cir Ste J (46241-7207)
PHONE....................................317 821-9872
Fax: 317 821-9874
Gene Haas, *Branch Mgr*
EMP: 6 **Privately Held**
WEB: www.hfomidwest.com
SIC: 3541 Machine tools, metal cutting type
HQ: Midwest Manufacturing Resources, Inc.
        1993 Case Pkwy
        Twinsburg OH 44087
        330 405-4227

(G-7508)
MIDWEST NONWOVENS INDIANA LLC
4555 W Bradbury Ave Ste 4 (46241-5209)
PHONE....................................317 241-8956
Bryan Speight, *CEO*
Christopher Look, *COO*
EMP: 23
SALES (est): 5.6MM **Privately Held**
SIC: 2297 Nonwoven fabrics

(G-7509)
MIDWEST ORTHOTIC SERVICES LLC
Also Called: Midwest Orthotic and Tech Ctr
3445 W 96th St (46268-1102)
PHONE....................................317 334-1114
Josh Ahlstrom, *Manager*

EMP: 2
SALES (est): 247.1K
SALES (corp-wide): 14MM **Privately Held**
SIC: 3842 Orthopedic appliances
PA: Midwest Orthotic Services, Llc
        17530 Dugdale Dr
        South Bend IN 46635
        574 233-3352

(G-7510)
MIDWEST REMEDIATION
5858 Thunderbird Rd (46236-2869)
PHONE....................................317 826-0940
David Sweet, *Owner*
Ruben Sanchez, *Project Mgr*
Brad Arnold, *Accountant*
Ryan Elfreich, *Marketing Staff*
Chris Dunn, *Manager*
EMP: 21
SALES (est): 3.6MM **Privately Held**
SIC: 3544 Industrial molds

(G-7511)
MIDWEST RUBBER PRODUCTS INC
2457 E Washington St (46201-4155)
PHONE....................................317 237-4037
Anthony Schlichte, *President*
EMP: 7
SALES (est): 1.7MM **Privately Held**
SIC: 3069 Floor coverings, rubber

(G-7512)
MIDWEST STL RULE CUTNG DIE INC
5570 Elmwood Ct (46203-6043)
PHONE....................................317 780-4600
Michael Lalonde, *President*
John Hannon, *Vice Pres*
Renee Farley, *Purchasing*
Robert A Morr, *Treasurer*
Dave Jeffries, *Sales Executive*
EMP: 28 EST: 1997
SQ FT: 19,000
SALES (est): 3.7MM **Privately Held**
SIC: 3544 Dies, steel rule

(G-7513)
MIDWEST SURFACE PREP LLC
5835 White Oak Ct (46220-5229)
PHONE....................................317 726-1336
Christopher J Theriac, *Mng Member*
EMP: 5 EST: 2008
SALES (est): 456.4K **Privately Held**
SIC: 3471 Sand blasting of metal parts

(G-7514)
MIKE BURROUGHS SFTWR DEV LLC
4001 N Meridian St (46208-4012)
PHONE....................................317 927-7195
EMP: 2 EST: 2009
SALES (est): 120K **Privately Held**
SIC: 7372 Prepackaged Software Services

(G-7515)
MIKE JONES SOFTWARE
8903 Powderhorn Ln (46256-1350)
PHONE....................................317 845-7479
Mike Jones, *Owner*
EMP: 2
SALES (est): 96.2K **Privately Held**
SIC: 7372 Prepackaged software

(G-7516)
MIKE-SELLS WEST VIRGINIA INC
5767 Dividend Rd (46241-4303)
PHONE....................................317 241-7422
Larry Ore, *Manager*
EMP: 15
SALES (corp-wide): 65.7MM **Privately Held**
SIC: 2052 2096 2099 Pretzels; corn chips & other corn-based snacks; potato chips & other potato-based snacks; food preparations
PA: Mike-Sell's West Virginia, Inc.
        333 Leo St
        Dayton OH 45404
        937 228-9400

(G-7517)
MILES PRINTING CORPORATION
4923 W 78th St (46268-4170)
PHONE....................................317 870-6115
Fax: 317 243-8575
Lynne A Churchill, *President*
EMP: 10
SQ FT: 2,500
SALES (est): 1.8MM **Privately Held**
WEB: www.milespress.com
SIC: 2752 Commercial printing, offset

(G-7518)
MILL END DRAPERY INC
4720 N Keystone Ave (46205-1513)
PHONE....................................317 257-4800
Fax: 317 257-4807
Greg Stone, *President*
EMP: 7
SALES: 90K **Privately Held**
SIC: 5714 2591 2391 Drapery & upholstery stores; drapery hardware & blinds & shades; curtains & draperies

(G-7519)
MILLCRAFT PAPER COMPANY
2735 Fortune Cir W Ste A (46241-5520)
PHONE....................................317 240-3500
Fax: 317 240-0400
Donald Chamness, *Branch Mgr*
EMP: 40 **Privately Held**
SIC: 5111 5112 2789 2675 Printing paper; envelopes; bookbinding & related work; die-cut paper & board; industrial & personal service paper
HQ: The Millcraft Paper Company
        6800 Grant Ave
        Cleveland OH 44105
        216 441-5505

(G-7520)
MILLER MAID CABINETS INC
6815 S Emerson Ave Ste D (46237-3362)
PHONE....................................317 786-0418
Charles Kincaid, *Principal*
Tom Davis, *Vice Pres*
EMP: 15
SALES (est): 1.1MM **Privately Held**
SIC: 2434 Wood kitchen cabinets

(G-7521)
MILLER VENEERS INC
3724 E 13th St (46201-1502)
P.O. Box 11085 (46201-0085)
PHONE....................................317 638-2326
Fax: 317 634-0555
Thomas A Miller, *President*
Sally M Sando, *Vice Pres*
Benjamin R Miller, *Treasurer*
▼ **EMP:** 140 EST: 1930
SQ FT: 12,000
SALES (est): 23.2MM **Privately Held**
WEB: www.millerveneers.com
SIC: 2435 Hardwood veneer & plywood

(G-7522)
MILLER WASTE MILLS INC
Also Called: R T P Company
8111 Zionsville Rd (46268-1626)
PHONE....................................507 454-6900
Fax: 317 802-9107
Greg Whitten, *General Mgr*
Chuck Hess, *Associate*
EMP: 45
SALES (corp-wide): 330.1MM **Privately Held**
WEB: www.millerwastemills.com
SIC: 3087 3083 Custom compound purchased resins; laminated plastics plate & sheet
PA: Miller Waste Mills, Incorporated
        580 E Front St
        Winona MN 55987
        507 454-6906

(G-7523)
MILLTRONICS USA INC (HQ)
Also Called: Hurco Usa, Inc.
1 Technology Way (46268-5106)
PHONE....................................317 293-5309
Fax: 317 347-6201
Michael Doar, *CEO*
▲ **EMP:** 35

▲ = Import ▼=Export
◆ =Import/Export

SALES (est): 32.9MM
SALES (corp-wide): 243.6MM **Publicly Held**
SIC: 3823 7372 Computer interface equipment for industrial process control; prepackaged software
PA: Hurco Companies, Inc.
1 Technology Way
Indianapolis IN 46268
317 293-5309

(G-7524)
MINING MEDIA INC
6043 Primrose Ave (46220-2349)
PHONE....................317 802-7116
Peter Johnson, *Branch Mgr*
EMP: 2
SALES (corp-wide): 1MM **Privately Held**
SIC: 2741 Miscellaneous publishing
PA: Mining Media Inc.
8751 E Hampden Ave Ste B1
Denver CO 80231
303 283-0640

(G-7525)
MINUTEMAN PRESS
6377 Rockville Rd (46214-3920)
PHONE....................317 209-1677
Evan Walters, *Owner*
EMP: 4
SALES (est): 478.4K **Privately Held**
SIC: 2752 2759 Commercial printing, offset; commercial printing

(G-7526)
MITCHEL & SCOTT MACHINE CO
Also Called: Bar Steel Service Center
1841 Ludlow Ave (46201-1035)
PHONE....................317 639-5331
Thomas L Mitchel, *Ch of Bd*
Richard G Siler, *President*
Stephen Mitchel, *Vice Pres*
David Mitchel, *VP Mfg*
Gary Williams, *Treasurer*
EMP: 300
SQ FT: 94,000
SALES (est): 20.2MM **Privately Held**
SIC: 3451 Screw machine products

(G-7527)
MITCHEL GROUP INCORPORATED (PA)
Also Called: Mitchel & Scott Machine Co
1841 Ludlow Ave (46201-1035)
PHONE....................317 639-5331
Fax: 317 684-8245
Bradley Smith, *President*
David Mitchel, *Vice Pres*
Pat Mitchel, *Plant Mgr*
Kent Edwards, *Production*
Eric Jones, *Purch Agent*
▲ **EMP:** 200 **EST:** 1933
SQ FT: 120,000
SALES (est): 38MM **Privately Held**
WEB: www.mitsco.com
SIC: 3451 Screw machine products

(G-7528)
MITCHUM-SCHAEFER INC
Also Called: Schaefer Technologies
4901 W Raymond St (46241-4733)
PHONE....................317 546-4081
Fax: 317 546-4095
Michael G Schaefer, *Ch of Bd*
Steven J Schaefer, *President*
Mike Rizzi, *Vice Pres*
EMP: 55 **EST:** 1932
SQ FT: 60,000
SALES (est): 6.9MM **Privately Held**
SIC: 3599 7692 Custom machinery; machine shop, jobbing & repair; welding repair

(G-7529)
MJP & COMPANY LLC
Also Called: Sandpaper America
1728 E New York St (46201-3025)
PHONE....................317 631-7263
Janet Pflum, *CEO*
EMP: 7 **EST:** 2012
SQ FT: 9,000
SALES (est): 314.1K **Privately Held**
SIC: 3291 Abrasive products; cloth, abrasive: garnet, emery, aluminum oxide coated

(G-7530)
MJS BUSINESSES LLC
Also Called: Sign Factory
5381 E 82nd St (46250-4510)
PHONE....................317 845-1932
Fax: 317 845-1963
Montell Staples,
Telisa Staples,
EMP: 2
SQ FT: 1,200
SALES: 105K **Privately Held**
SIC: 3993 Signs & advertising specialties

(G-7531)
MOBILE DRILL OPERATING CO LLC
Also Called: Mobile Drill Intl
3807 Madison Ave (46227-1372)
PHONE....................317 260-8108
Fax: 317 784-5661
Tim Sabo, *Mng Member*
Mike Johnson,
Brad Todd,
▲ **EMP:** 42
SALES (est): 15MM **Privately Held**
WEB: www.mobiledrill.net
SIC: 3533 Oil & gas drilling rigs & equipment

(G-7532)
MOBILE MINI INC
2104 W Epler Ave (46217-9612)
PHONE....................317 782-1513
Ibrahim Iilyas, *Manager*
EMP: 10
SALES (corp-wide): 533.5MM **Publicly Held**
WEB: www.mobilemini.com
SIC: 3448 Buildings, portable: prefabricated metal
PA: Mobile Mini, Inc.
4646 E Van Buren St # 400
Phoenix AZ 85008
480 894-6311

(G-7533)
MOELLER PRINTING CO INC
4401 E New York St (46201-3646)
P.O. Box 11288 (46201-0288)
PHONE....................317 353-2224
Fax: 317 353-2037
David Moeller Sr, *President*
David Moeller Jr, *Vice Pres*
Charles T Moeller, *Admin Sec*
EMP: 20 **EST:** 1931
SQ FT: 9,000
SALES: 3.5MM **Privately Held**
SIC: 2759 2752 Embossing on paper; commercial printing, offset

(G-7534)
MOHAWK LABORATORIES
8401 E 33rd St (46226-6504)
PHONE....................317 899-3660
Lester Levy, *President*
▲ **EMP:** 4
SALES (est): 788.4K **Privately Held**
SIC: 3589 Sewage & water treatment equipment

(G-7535)
MONITORING SOLUTIONS INC
4440 S High School Rd C (46241-6402)
PHONE....................317 856-9400
Fax: 317 856-9410
Tom Barr, *Manager*
EMP: 20 **Privately Held**
WEB: www.monsol.com
SIC: 3823 Water quality monitoring & control systems
PA: Monitoring Solutions, Incorporated
78 State Route 173 Ste 7
Hampton NJ 08827

(G-7536)
MONROE MANUFACTURING TECH INC
5508 Elmwood Ave Ste 422 (46203-6074)
P.O. Box 91, Beech Grove (46107-0091)
PHONE....................317 782-1005
Anita Monroe, *President*
Joseph Monroe Jr, *Corp Secy*
EMP: 5
SQ FT: 3,600

SALES: 500K **Privately Held**
SIC: 3599 Machine shop, jobbing & repair

(G-7537)
MONROE WOOD WORKS
10203 Heather Hills Rd (46229-2120)
PHONE....................317 979-0964
Susan Laurel Thompson, *Owner*
EMP: 2
SALES (est): 85.2K **Privately Held**
SIC: 2431 Millwork

(G-7538)
MONTGOMERY TENT & AWNING CO
5054 E 10th St (46201-2864)
P.O. Box 11516 (46201-0516)
PHONE....................317 357-9759
Fax: 317 357-9761
James W Montgomery, *President*
Kenneth Montgomery, *Vice Pres*
EMP: 10 **EST:** 1955
SALES (est): 1.3MM **Privately Held**
SIC: 5999 2394 5941 Tents; tents: made from purchased materials; awnings, fabric: made from purchased materials; camping & backpacking equipment

(G-7539)
MONUMENT CHEMICAL LLC (PA)
6510 Telecom Dr Ste 425 (46278-6330)
PHONE....................317 223-2630
Amy Schumacher, *President*
William Gibson, *Engineer*
Chris Svoboda, *VP Human Res*
Dan Malone, *VP Sales*
Albert Bernhardt, *Sales Dir*
EMP: 17
SALES (est): 92.3MM **Privately Held**
SIC: 2821 5033 2951 Thermoplastic materials; asphalt felts & coating; asphalt paving mixtures & blocks

(G-7540)
MONUMENT CONSTRUCTION INC
430 Msschstts Ave Ste 104 (46204)
PHONE....................317 472-0271
Brad Richey, *President*
EMP: 7
SALES (est): 1MM **Privately Held**
SIC: 3272 Monuments, concrete

(G-7541)
MONUMENT LIGHTHOUSE CHART
8503 Summertree Ln (46256-3487)
PHONE....................317 657-0160
EMP: 3
SALES (est): 114.6K **Privately Held**
SIC: 3272 Monuments & grave markers, except terrazo

(G-7542)
MOORFEED ACQUISITION LLC
Also Called: Moorfeed Parts Automation
1445 Brookville Way Ste R (46239-1197)
PHONE....................317 545-7171
Jason Troxel,
EMP: 14
SALES (est): 2.8MM **Privately Held**
SIC: 3559

(G-7543)
MORRIS MACHINE CO INC
6480 S Belmont Ave (46217-9767)
PHONE....................317 788-0371
Fax: 317 788-9248
Robert J Chylaszek, *CEO*
Tom Gregory, *Plant Mgr*
Cecil Williams, *CFO*
Lily Jenkins, *Office Mgr*
Christopher D Morris, *Admin Sec*
EMP: 70
SQ FT: 24,000
SALES (est): 26.5MM **Privately Held**
WEB: www.morrismachine.net
SIC: 3599 Machine shop, jobbing & repair

(G-7544)
MORRIS MOLD AND MACHINE CO
912 E 21st St (46202-1838)
PHONE....................317 923-6653

Fax: 317 923-8453
Morris Fishburn Jr, *President*
Ray Fishburn, *Treasurer*
EMP: 6
SQ FT: 8,500
SALES (est): 746.5K **Privately Held**
SIC: 3544 7699 3545 Industrial molds; plastics products repair; industrial machinery & equipment repair; machine tool accessories

(G-7545)
MORRIS PRINTING COMPANY INC
1502 N College Ave (46202-2799)
PHONE....................317 639-5553
Fax: 317 639-5554
Daniel M Evard, *President*
EMP: 7 **EST:** 1877
SQ FT: 5,000
SALES (est): 1MM **Privately Held**
WEB: www.morrisprinting.com
SIC: 2752 Commercial printing, offset

(G-7546)
MOSS L GLASS CO INC
Also Called: Moss Glass
5265 E 82nd St (46250-1627)
PHONE....................765 642-4946
Fax: 765 643-0439
Rickie B Moss, *President*
Wes Shoup, *General Mgr*
Ted Moss, *Vice Pres*
Sue Evans, *Office Mgr*
EMP: 19
SQ FT: 30,000
SALES (est): 2MM **Privately Held**
WEB: www.mossglass.com
SIC: 1793 5231 3231 Glass & glazing work; glass; products of purchased glass

(G-7547)
MOTIONWEAR LLC
1315 Sunday Dr (46217-9334)
PHONE....................317 780-4182
Robert Wilson, *CEO*
Jeff Billig, *Controller*
Summer Rogers, *Creative Dir*
EMP: 175
SALES (est): 13.2MM **Privately Held**
SIC: 5699 2339 Customized clothing & apparel; belts, apparel: custom; sports apparel; riding apparel; athletic clothing: women's, misses' & juniors'; sportswear, women's; uniforms, athletic: women's, misses' & juniors'; leotards: women's, misses' & juniors'

(G-7548)
MOTOROLA SOLUTIONS INC
2461 Directors Row Ste C (46241-4937)
PHONE....................317 716-8064
EMP: 4 **EST:** 2013
SALES (est): 331.3K **Privately Held**
SIC: 3663 Radio & TV communications equipment

(G-7549)
MOTSINGER AUTO SUPPLY INC
345 W Hanna Ave (46217-5107)
PHONE....................317 782-8484
Jack Whitaker, *President*
Cynthia S Whitaker, *Vice Pres*
EMP: 6 **EST:** 1952
SQ FT: 2,500
SALES (est): 475.7K **Privately Held**
SIC: 3599 5013 7692 Machine & other job shop work; automotive supplies & parts; welding repair

(G-7550)
MOUNTJOY WOODING
1221 Schleicher Ave (46229-2330)
PHONE....................317 897-6792
Peter Mountjoy, *Owner*
EMP: 2
SALES (est): 137.3K **Privately Held**
SIC: 2431 Millwork

(G-7551)
MOURON & COMPANY INC
1025 Western Dr (46241-1436)
PHONE....................317 243-7955
Fax: 317 243-2514
Thomas Mouron, *President*
Gwenda R Mouron, *Vice Pres*

Mark Bryan, *Controller*
EMP: 15
SQ FT: 15,000
SALES (est): 3.1MM **Privately Held**
WEB: www.mouronandco.com
SIC: 2521 2541 2514 2434 Tables, office: wood; counters or counter display cases, wood; metal household furniture; wood kitchen cabinets

(G-7552)
MPS INDIANAPOLIS INC
Also Called: Multi Packaging Solutions Ind
2020 Production Dr (46241-4325)
PHONE..................................317 241-2020
John D Howard, *President*
William Hogan, *Corp Secy*
Julie Eaton, *Sales Executive*
▲ **EMP:** 110
SQ FT: 20,000
SALES (est): 15.5MM
SALES (corp-wide): 14.8B **Publicly Held**
SIC: 2759 Advertising literature: printing
HQ: Mps Holdco, Inc.
5800 W Grand River Ave
Lansing MI 48906

(G-7553)
MR MHAMMADS SWEET-BEAN SNACKS
4212 Village Bend Ln (46254-6244)
PHONE..................................317 519-0728
George Muhammad, *CEO*
EMP: 2
SALES (est): 131.8K **Privately Held**
SIC: 2051 7389 Cakes, pies & pastries;

(G-7554)
MS WHEELCHAIR INDIANA INC
9106 Tansel Ct (46234-1371)
PHONE..................................317 408-0947
Geraldine Padgett, *Owner*
EMP: 2
SALES (est): 86.6K **Privately Held**
SIC: 3842 Wheelchairs

(G-7555)
MTD PRODUCTS INC
5353 W 79th St (46268-1699)
PHONE..................................317 986-2042
EMP: 399
SALES (corp-wide): 2.5B **Privately Held**
SIC: 3524 Lawn & garden equipment
HQ: Mtd Products Inc
5965 Grafton Rd
Valley City OH 44280
330 225-2600

(G-7556)
MUD CREEK PUBLISHING INC
8335 Allison Pointe Trl # 200 (46250-1790)
PHONE..................................317 577-9659
EMP: 2
SALES (est): 210K **Privately Held**
SIC: 2741 Misc Publishing

(G-7557)
MULRY MANUFACTURING LLC
Also Called: Sharbade
4261 Kessler Lane East Dr (46220-5203)
PHONE..................................317 253-2756
Thomas Mulry, *Mng Member*
Joan Mulry,
EMP: 2
SALES: 85K **Privately Held**
SIC: 3949 Sporting & athletic goods

(G-7558)
MULTI PACKAGING SOLUTIONS INC
Also Called: Ivy Hill Packaging Division
2020 Production Dr (46241-4325)
PHONE..................................317 241-2020
Dennis Stephenson, *Sales Executive*
Bill Radaker, *Info Tech Mgr*
EMP: 280
SQ FT: 10,000
SALES (corp-wide): 14.8B **Publicly Held**
WEB: www.ivyhill-wms.com
SIC: 2752 2759 Commercial printing, litho-graphic; commercial printing
HQ: Multi Packaging Solutions, Inc.
150 E 52nd St Ste 2800
New York NY 10022

(G-7559)
MULTIPLE RESOURCE SOLUTION
6925 S Carroll Rd (46259-1067)
PHONE..................................317 862-2584
David B Fagel, *Senior VP*
EMP: 2
SALES (est): 155.6K **Privately Held**
SIC: 3442 Molding, trim & stripping

(G-7560)
MUROPLEX THERAPEUTICS INC
5701 Carrollton Ave (46220-2640)
P.O. Box 44219 (46244-0219)
PHONE..................................317 502-0545
Larry Blaszczak, *President*
EMP: 2
SALES (est): 102.7K **Privately Held**
SIC: 2834 Pharmaceutical preparations

(G-7561)
MURRELL OPTICAL LLC
4150 Lafayette Rd Ste C (46254-2491)
PHONE..................................317 280-0114
Steve Murrell, *CEO*
EMP: 2 EST: 2016
SALES (est): 107.6K **Privately Held**
SIC: 3827 Optical instruments & apparatus

(G-7562)
MVO USA INC
8802 Bash St Ste A (46256-1288)
P.O. Box 501910 (46250-6910)
PHONE..................................317 585-5785
Tammy Borden-Dennis, *President*
John Naidus, *President*
Kelvin J Tiedman, *Vice Pres*
Jessica Roberts, *Accountant*
◆ **EMP:** 15
SQ FT: 40,000
SALES (est): 4MM
SALES (corp-wide): 2.2B **Privately Held**
WEB: www.bishopsteering.com
SIC: 3559 3714 3728 Automotive related machinery; motor vehicle parts & acces-sories; military aircraft equipment & arma-ment
HQ: Gmh Stahlverarbeitung Gmbh
Nikolaus-Otto-Str. 1
Schwabisch Gmund 73529
540 139-0

(G-7563)
MY DAILY WEDDING DEALS LLC
4822 Crystal River Ct (46240-6435)
PHONE..................................812 603-6149
EMP: 2
SALES (est): 97.7K **Privately Held**
SIC: 2711 Newspapers, publishing & print-ing

(G-7564)
MY-TE PRODUCTS INC
9880 E 30th St (46229-3608)
PHONE..................................317 897-9880
Fax: 317 897-9811
Brian S King, *President*
Brent Burris, *Vice Pres*
David L Moody, *Vice Pres*
Ross King, *Manager*
EMP: 18 EST: 1941
SQ FT: 21,600
SALES: 2.7MM **Privately Held**
WEB: www.myte.com
SIC: 3531 Winches

(G-7565)
MYCOGEN CORPORATION (DH)
9330 Zionsville Rd (46268-1053)
PHONE..................................317 337-3000
Jerome Periberie, *President*
W Pete Siggelko, *Vice Pres*
William W Wales, *Vice Pres*
Geoffrey E Merszer, *Treasurer*
▼ **EMP:** 10
SQ FT: 22,917
SALES: 384.9MM
SALES (corp-wide): 62.4B **Publicly Held**
SIC: 5191 2879 0721 8731 Seeds & bulbs; seeds: field, garden & flower; agri-cultural chemicals; crop protecting serv-ices; crop disease control services; crop related entomological services (insect control); agricultural research

(G-7566)
MYCOGEN CROP PROTECTION INC
9330 Zionsville Rd (46268-1053)
PHONE..................................317 337-3000
Joseph Velovitch, *Principal*
EMP: 48
SALES (est): 3.6MM
SALES (corp-wide): 62.4B **Publicly Held**
SIC: 2879 Agricultural chemicals
HQ: Mycogen Corporation
9330 Zionsville Rd
Indianapolis IN 46268
317 337-3000

(G-7567)
N ROLLS-ROYCE AMERCN TECH INC
Also Called: Libertyworks
2059 S Tibbs Ave (46241-4812)
P.O. Box 420 (46206-0420)
PHONE..................................317 230-4347
Mark Wilson, *COO*
Sandra Jackson, *Supervisor*
EMP: 245
SALES (est): 43.2MM
SALES (corp-wide): 21.5B **Privately Held**
SIC: 3764 Guided missile & space vehicle engines, research & devel.
HQ: Rolls-Royce Corporation
450 S Meridian St
Indianapolis IN 46225

(G-7568)
N3 LLC
Also Called: N3 Boatworks
7001 Hawthorn Park Dr A (46220-3912)
PHONE..................................317 845-9253
Mark Dougherty, *Mng Member*
Andrew Cornelius, *Manager*
Michael Vincz, *Manager*
EMP: 3
SQ FT: 18,000
SALES (est): 606.8K **Privately Held**
SIC: 3732 Boat building & repairing

(G-7569)
NANOSONICS INC
7205 E 87th St (46256-1204)
PHONE..................................844 876-7466
Ron Bacskai, *President*
EMP: 40
SQ FT: 5,000
SALES: 25MM **Privately Held**
SIC: 3845 Ultrasonic scanning devices, medical

(G-7570)
NATIONAL DENTEX LLC
Ito & Koby Dental Studio
6402 Castleplace Dr (46250-1904)
PHONE..................................317 849-5143
Fax: 317 849-5530
John Sebring, *President*
Tom Daulton, *President*
EMP: 55
SALES (corp-wide): 147.8MM **Privately Held**
WEB: www.nationaldentex.com
SIC: 8072 8021 3843 3842 Crown & bridge production; offices & clinics of den-tists; dental equipment & supplies; surgi-cal appliances & supplies
HQ: National Dentex, Llc
11601 Kew Gardens Ave # 200
Palm Beach Gardens FL 33410
561 537-8300

(G-7571)
NATIONAL FEDERATION OF (PA)
690 W Washington St (46204-2725)
P.O. Box 690 (46206-0690)
PHONE..................................317 972-6900
Fax: 317 822-5700
Davis Whitfield, *COO*
Joanne Bennett, *CFO*
Kathleen Rodewald, *CFO*
Mautrice Meriweather, *Human Res Mgr*
Robert F Kanaby, *Exec Dir*
EMP: 40
SQ FT: 41,700

SALES: 15MM **Privately Held**
WEB: www.nfhs.com
SIC: 2731 7812 5136 5137 Books: pub-lishing only; pamphlets: publishing only, not printed on site; video tape production; uniforms, men's & boys'; uniforms, women's & children's

(G-7572)
NATIONAL ICE CORP
5333 Commerce Square Dr F (46237-8627)
PHONE..................................317 887-9446
James Heady, *Principal*
EMP: 3
SALES (est): 122.7K **Privately Held**
SIC: 2024 5099 Ice cream & frozen desserts; durable goods

(G-7573)
NATIONAL LIB BINDERY CO OF IND
55 S State Ave Ste 100 (46201-3800)
PHONE..................................317 636-5606
Joseph Cox, *President*
Eric Lindseth, *Vice Pres*
Janet Cox, *Admin Sec*
EMP: 8 EST: 1938
SALES (est): 916.3K **Privately Held**
WEB: www.nlbco.com
SIC: 2789 Binding only: books, pamphlets, magazines, etc.; rebinding books, maga-zines or pamphlets

(G-7574)
NATIONAL NOTIFICATION CTR LLC
20 N Meridian St Ste 300 (46204-3028)
PHONE..................................317 613-6060
Debra Myers, *CFO*
EMP: 2
SALES (est): 74.4K **Privately Held**
SIC: 2844 Toilet preparations

(G-7575)
NATIONAL OILWELL VARCO INC
9870 E 30th St (46229-3608)
PHONE..................................317 897-3099
Ryan Corn, *Manager*
Richard Cole, *Representative*
EMP: 9
SALES (corp-wide): 7.3B **Publicly Held**
SIC: 3533 Oil field machinery & equipment
PA: National Oilwell Varco, Inc.
7909 Parkwood Circle Dr
Houston TX 77036
713 346-7500

(G-7576)
NATIONAL RETAIL HARDWARE ASSN
Also Called: Hardware Retailing
136 N Delaware St Ste 200 (46204-2529)
PHONE..................................317 290-0338
Fax: 317 275-9403
Tom Smith, *CFO*
Bill Mancuso, *Sales Staff*
Katie McHone-Jones, *Manager*
William Lee, *Director*
EMP: 31
SQ FT: 20,700
SALES (est): 4.8MM **Privately Held**
SIC: 2721 8611 Magazines: publishing & printing; business associations

(G-7577)
NATURES WOODSHOP LLC
7438 Cotherstone Ct (46256-2077)
PHONE..................................317 691-1462
Jan J Syphers, *Mng Member*
EMP: 2
SALES (est): 112K **Privately Held**
SIC: 2499 Applicators, wood

(G-7578)
NAVISTAR CMPONENT HOLDINGS LLC (DH)
5565 Brookville Rd (46219-7109)
PHONE..................................317 352-4500
Jerry Sweetland, *President*
Gary Mitchell,
William D Graf,
▲ **EMP:** 372
SQ FT: 500,000

SALES (est): 101.5MM
SALES (corp-wide): 8.5B **Publicly Held**
WEB: www.internationaldelivers.com
SIC: 3321 6719 Gray iron castings; investment holding companies, except banks
HQ: Navistar, Inc.
2701 Navistar Dr
Lisle IL 60532
331 332-5000

(G-7579)
NCH CORPORATION
Chemsearch Division
8401 E 33rd St (46226-6504)
PHONE...................................317 899-3660
Joe Fisher, *Principal*
Eric Stidd, *Maintence Staff*
EMP: 37
SQ FT: 1,000
SALES (corp-wide): 996.6MM **Privately Held**
WEB: www.nch.com
SIC: 2842 Specialty cleaning, polishes & sanitation goods
PA: Nch Corporation
2727 Chemsearch Blvd
Irving TX 75062
972 438-0211

(G-7580)
NCS PEARSON INC
2629 Waterfront Pkwy E Dr (46214-2076)
PHONE...................................317 297-0259
EMP: 99
SALES (corp-wide): 5.9B **Privately Held**
SIC: 3577 Optical scanning devices
HQ: Ncs Pearson Inc
5601 Green Valley Dr # 220
Bloomington MN 55437
952 681-3000

(G-7581)
ND PRINTS
3924 W Washington St (46241-0941)
EMP: 2
SALES (est): 140.9K **Privately Held**
SIC: 2752 Lithographic Commercial Printing

(G-7582)
NECHANNA ONE PRODUCTIONS CORP
11252 Redskin Ln Apt G (46235-9241)
PHONE...................................317 400-8908
Denise Harris, *CEO*
EMP: 2
SALES (est): 85.2K **Privately Held**
SIC: 7372 8249 Business oriented computer software; educational computer software; business training services

(G-7583)
NERX BIOSCIENCES INC
351 W 10th St Ste 510 (46202-4100)
PHONE...................................317 251-7408
EMP: 10
SALES (est): 760K **Privately Held**
SIC: 2836 Mfg Biological Products

(G-7584)
NEW CASTLE MODULAR INC
6990 W Washington St (46241-2939)
PHONE...................................765 521-0788
Richard Salewicz, *President*
EMP: 11
SQ FT: 100,000
SALES (est): 866.6K **Privately Held**
SIC: 2452 Modular homes, prefabricated, wood

(G-7585)
NEW ENGLAND SHEETS LLC
3600 Wdview Trce Ste 300 (46268)
PHONE...................................978 487-2500
Fred Hamilton, *Mng Member*
EMP: 43
SALES (corp-wide): 8.5MM **Privately Held**
SIC: 3444 Sheet metalwork
PA: New England Sheets, Llc
36 Saratoga Blvd
Devens MA 01434
978 487-2500

(G-7586)
NEWSLETTER EXPRESS LTD
3500 Depauw Blvd Ste 1000 (46268-1136)
PHONE...................................317 876-8916
Sue Wagner, *Principal*
EMP: 2
SALES (est): 191.1K **Privately Held**
SIC: 2752 Commercial printing, lithographic

(G-7587)
NIDEC MOTOR CORPORATION
Indianplis Admn/Ngineering Ctr
2831 Waterfront Pkwy E Dr (46214-2016)
PHONE...................................317 328-4079
Lowell Kligus, *President*
J P Russell, *Branch Mgr*
EMP: 650
SALES (corp-wide): 13.9B **Privately Held**
WEB: www.gotoemerson.com
SIC: 3625 3822 3643 Relays & industrial controls; auto controls regulating residntl & coml environmt & applncs; current-carrying wiring devices
HQ: Nidec Motor Corporation
8050 West Florissant Ave
Saint Louis MO 63136

(G-7588)
NOAH WORCESTER DERM SOCIETY
8365 Keystone Xing (46240-2684)
PHONE...................................317 257-5907
James Ertle, *Principal*
EMP: 5
SALES (est): 391.6K **Privately Held**
SIC: 2834 Dermatologicals

(G-7589)
NOCHAR INC
8650 Commerce Park Pl K (46268-3126)
PHONE...................................317 613-3046
Fax: 317 613-3052
Carl Gehlhausen, *President*
Carolyn Gehlhausen, *Corp Secy*
EMP: 3
SALES (est): 901.1K **Privately Held**
WEB: www.nochar.com
SIC: 5169 2899 2819 Industrial chemicals; chemical preparations; industrial inorganic chemicals

(G-7590)
NOEL-SMYSER ENGINEERING CORP
4005 Industrial Blvd (46254-2511)
PHONE...................................317 293-2215
Fax: 317 293-0397
Jeff Noel, *President*
John Noel, *Vice Pres*
Anthony Noel, *Engineer*
Noel Alexander, *Finance Mgr*
EMP: 15
SQ FT: 20,000
SALES: 5.7MM **Privately Held**
WEB: www.noel-smyser.com
SIC: 3694 3825 Automotive electrical equipment; test equipment for electronic & electric measurement

(G-7591)
NORTH AMERICA PACKAGING CORP
Also Called: Nampac
6061 Guion Rd (46254-1221)
PHONE...................................317 291-2396
Fax: 317 298-6153
Bruce Smith, *Branch Mgr*
EMP: 200
SALES (corp-wide): 787.1MM **Privately Held**
WEB: www.nampac.com
SIC: 3412 3085 Barrels, shipping: metal; drums, shipping: metal; milk (fluid) shipping containers, metal; pails, shipping: metal; plastics bottles
HQ: North America Packaging Corp
1515 W 22nd St Ste 550
Oak Brook IL 60523
630 203-4100

(G-7592)
NORTHEAST MACHINE & TOOL CO
10655 E 59th St (46236-8334)
PHONE...................................317 823-6594
Earl McHenry, *Owner*
EMP: 3
SQ FT: 4,000
SALES: 200K **Privately Held**
SIC: 3599 7692 7629 Machine shop, jobbing & repair; welding repair; electrical repair shops

(G-7593)
NORTHERN INDIANA OIL LLC
Also Called: Pure Edible Oils
212 W 10th St Ste D365 (46202-5684)
PHONE...................................765 749-3791
Dulce Martinez Belcher, *Principal*
EMP: 3
SALES (est): 122K **Privately Held**
SIC: 2079 Edible oil products, except corn oil

(G-7594)
NORTHFIELD BLOCK COMPANY
901 E Troy Ave (46203-5135)
PHONE...................................800 424-0190
EMP: 3
SALES (corp-wide): 29.7B **Privately Held**
SIC: 3271 Blocks, concrete or cinder: standard
HQ: Northfield Block Company
1 Hunt Ct
Mundelein IL 60060
847 816-9000

(G-7595)
NORTHSIDE PATTERN WORKS INC
4370 Saguaro Trl (46268-2552)
PHONE...................................317 290-0501
Fax: 317 290-0639
Don Holbrook, *President*
Diane Holbrook, *Admin Sec*
EMP: 4
SQ FT: 5,000
SALES: 800K **Privately Held**
SIC: 3543 Industrial patterns

(G-7596)
NORTHWIND ELECTRONICS LLC
8875 Bash St (46256-1276)
PHONE...................................317 288-0787
Phillip Berry, *CEO*
Rhoda Capps, *General Mgr*
Steve Fox, *General Mgr*
EMP: 15
SALES (est): 3MM **Privately Held**
SIC: 5999 3714 3679 Electronic parts & equipment; automotive wiring harness sets; harness assemblies for electronic use: wire or cable

(G-7597)
NORTHWIND PHARMACEUTICALS LLC
212 W 10th St Ste A310 (46202-5686)
PHONE...................................800 722-0772
Phillip Berry, *CEO*
EMP: 6
SQ FT: 918
SALES (corp-wide): 3MM **Privately Held**
SIC: 2834 Pharmaceutical preparations
PA: Northwind Pharmaceuticals, Llc
9402 Uptown Dr Ste 1100
Indianapolis IN 46256
317 522-1637

(G-7598)
NOVA FLEX GROUP
7812 Moller Rd (46268-2117)
PHONE...................................317 334-1444
Ian Donnelly, *President*
EMP: 13
SALES (corp-wide): 22.8MM **Privately Held**
WEB: www.novaflexhose.com
SIC: 3052 Rubber hose
HQ: Nova Flex Group
1024 Industrial Dr
West Berlin NJ 08091

(G-7599)
NOVA GRAPHICS INC
Also Called: Novaprints
7805 E 89th St (46256-1239)
PHONE...................................317 577-6682
Julie Snyder, *Principal*
Julie Baldwin, *Sales Staff*
EMP: 11
SQ FT: 20,000
SALES (est): 2.6MM **Privately Held**
WEB: www.novaprints.com
SIC: 2752 7334 Commercial printing, offset; photocopying & duplicating services

(G-7600)
NOVACOVE LLC
4162 Viva Ln (46239-1913)
PHONE...................................219 775-2966
Brendon Steele,
EMP: 3
SALES (est): 74.9K **Privately Held**
SIC: 7372 Application computer software

(G-7601)
NOVIPAX LLC
7950 Allison Ave (46268-1612)
PHONE...................................201 791-7600
Mike Vanatsky, *Branch Mgr*
Jerry Kelly, *Manager*
EMP: 64
SALES (corp-wide): 2.2B **Privately Held**
SIC: 2673 Plastic & pliofilm bags
HQ: Novipax Llc
2215 York Rd Ste 504
Oak Brook IL 60523
630 686-2735

(G-7602)
NPS XOFIGO MFG PLANT 5889
4343 W 62nd St (46268-2514)
PHONE...................................317 981-4129
EMP: 2
SALES (est): 108.2K **Privately Held**
SIC: 3999 Manufacturing industries

(G-7603)
NTR METALS LLC
4014 W 10th St (46222-3203)
PHONE...................................317 522-2891
Aaron Stewart, *Branch Mgr*
EMP: 3
SALES (corp-wide): 98.2MM **Privately Held**
SIC: 3961 Costume jewelry, ex. precious metal & semiprecious stones
HQ: Ntr Metals Llc
10720 Composite Dr
Dallas TX 75220
469 522-1111

(G-7604)
NUCLEAR MEASUREMENTS CORP
2460 N Arlington Ave (46218-4160)
P.O. Box 18248 (46218-0248)
PHONE...................................317 546-2415
Fax: 317 543-4420
Lg Vaughn, *Ch of Bd*
Donald Demoss, *President*
EMP: 4 **EST:** 1948
SQ FT: 10,000
SALES (est): 677.9K **Privately Held**
SIC: 3829 Nuclear radiation & testing apparatus

(G-7605)
NUVO INC (PA)
Also Called: Nuvo Newsweekly
3951 N Meridian St # 200 (46208-4078)
PHONE...................................317 254-2400
Fax: 317 254-2405
Kevin McKinney, *President*
Emily Taylor, *Editor*
Katelyn Calhoun, *Accounts Mgr*
Jessie Davis, *Accounts Exec*
Vicki Knorr, *Accounts Exec*
EMP: 30
SQ FT: 6,090
SALES (est): 2.2MM **Privately Held**
WEB: www.nuvo.net
SIC: 2711 Newspapers: publishing only, not printed on site

(G-7606)
NUWAVE MANUFACTURING
68 N Gale St Ste G (46201-3508)
PHONE..................................317 987-8229
Brian Fabel, *Principal*
▲ EMP: 8
SALES (est): 1MM **Privately Held**
SIC: 3999 Barber & beauty shop equipment

(G-7607)
NVB PLAYGROUNDS INC
Also Called: AAA State of Play.com
10725 Hidden Oak Way (46236-8436)
PHONE..................................317 826-2777
Nicolas Breedlove, *Principal*
Victor Breedlove, *Principal*
Kevin Van Wye, *Sales Staff*
▲ EMP: 6
SALES (est): 835.5K **Privately Held**
SIC: 5941 2531 Playground equipment; picnic tables or benches, park

(G-7608)
OAK SECURITY GROUP LLC
8904 Bash St Ste K (46256-1286)
PHONE..................................317 585-9830
Fax: 317 585-9834
Lawrence E Rogers, *CEO*
Lawrence Rogers, *CEO*
Steve Atkinson, *General Mgr*
Jim McCrory, *Opers Mgr*
Travis Wilson, *CFO*
▲ EMP: 11
SQ FT: 8,000
SALES (est): 2.3MM **Privately Held**
WEB: www.oaksecurity.com
SIC: 3429 Door opening & closing devices, except electrical

(G-7609)
OCTIV INC
54 Monument Cir Ste 200 (46204-2943)
PHONE..................................317 550-0148
David Kerr, *CEO*
Dustin Sapp, *CEO*
Antony Rine, *Business Mgr*
John Ludwig, *CFO*
Domenic Fish, *Treasurer*
EMP: 51
SALES (est): 4.5MM **Privately Held**
SIC: 7372 8742 Prepackaged software; marketing consulting services

(G-7610)
ODIN CORPORATION OF DELAWARE
6736 E 82nd St (46250-1506)
P.O. Box 50187 (46250-0187)
PHONE..................................317 849-3770
Fax: 317 842-9021
Josef Y Dahlstrand Jr, *Ch of Bd*
Kim Dahlstrand, *President*
EMP: 5
SQ FT: 8,775
SALES: 500K **Privately Held**
WEB: www.odincorporation.com
SIC: 3568 Couplings, shaft: rigid, flexible, universal joint, etc.

(G-7611)
OFFICE FURNITURE WAREHOUSE INC
7121 Royal Oakland Ct (46236-9153)
PHONE..................................317 872-6477
David Nash, *Principal*
Mary Nash, *Principal*
EMP: 4
SALES: 800K **Privately Held**
WEB: www.ofwinc.net
SIC: 2522 Office furniture, except wood

(G-7612)
OFFSET HOUSE INC
Also Called: OFFSET HOUSE PRINTING
9374 Castlegate Dr (46256-1001)
PHONE..................................317 849-5155
Robert E Bon Jour Jr, *President*
Rob Bonjour, *General Mgr*
Renee E Bon Jour Weiberg, *Corp Secy*
Jay Williamson, *Accounts Mgr*
Lois J Bonjour, *Admin Sec*
EMP: 13 EST: 1965
SQ FT: 11,000

SALES: 1.7MM **Privately Held**
WEB: www.offsethouseinc.com
SIC: 2752 2759 2791 2789 Commercial printing, offset; publication printing; typesetting; bookbinding & related work

(G-7613)
OIL PALACE LIMITED
4525 Lafayette Rd Ste L (46254-2011)
PHONE..................................317 679-9187
Julia Pettigrew, *Principal*
Ismaila Ndiaye, *Principal*
EMP: 2 EST: 2010
SALES (est): 163.5K **Privately Held**
SIC: 2844 Perfumes & colognes

(G-7614)
OKAYA USA
8227 Northwest Blvd (46278-1387)
PHONE..................................317 362-0696
Ippei Okuyama, *Principal*
EMP: 2
SALES (est): 98.6K **Privately Held**
SIC: 3599 Industrial machinery

(G-7615)
OLDCASTLE APG MIDWEST INC (HQ)
Also Called: Schuster's Building Products
901 E Troy Ave (46203-5135)
PHONE..................................317 786-0971
Fax: 317 788-5906
Marcia Gibson, *President*
John Nimmo, *Vice Pres*
Keith Brady, *Vice Pres*
Greg Jacot, *Vice Pres*
Matt Austin, *CFO*
▲ EMP: 650
SALES (est): 62.2MM
SALES (corp-wide): 29.7B **Privately Held**
SIC: 3272 Concrete products
PA: Crh Public Limited Company
Stonemasons Way
Dublin 14
140 410-00

(G-7616)
OLDCASTLE BUILDINGENVELOPE INC
8441 Bearing Dr (46268-1686)
PHONE..................................317 876-1155
Barb Peirson, *General Mgr*
EMP: 9
SALES (corp-wide): 29.7B **Privately Held**
SIC: 3231 Products of purchased glass
HQ: Oldcastle Buildingenvelope, Inc.
5005 Lndn R Jnsn Fwy 10
Dallas TX 75244
214 273-3400

(G-7617)
OLDCASTLE BUILDINGENVELOPE INC
Also Called: Glasmont
8441 Bearing Dr (46268-1686)
P.O. Box 68596 (46268-0596)
PHONE..................................317 876-1155
Fax: 317 876-1221
Dwayne Pierson, *Plant Mgr*
Amy Poteet, *Financial Exec*
EMP: 100
SALES (corp-wide): 29.7B **Privately Held**
WEB: www.oldcastleglass.com
SIC: 3231 5231 Tempered glass: made from purchased glass; insulating glass: made from purchased glass; glass
HQ: Oldcastle Buildingenvelope, Inc.
5005 Lndn B Jnsn Fwy 10
Dallas TX 75244
214 273-3400

(G-7618)
OMEGA ONE CONNECT INC
3825 E 78th St (46240-3401)
P.O. Box 40953 (46240-0953)
PHONE..................................317 626-3445
Michael Falkner, *President*
Daniel Pierson, *Vice Pres*
EMP: 2 EST: 2012
SALES: 12K **Privately Held**
SIC: 2721 7389 Magazines: publishing & printing;

(G-7619)
OMG CUPCAKES & SWEETS LLC
9797 Hidden Hills Ln (46234-3199)
PHONE..................................317 281-7926
Julie Allen, *Principal*
EMP: 4 EST: 2010
SALES (est): 131.7K **Privately Held**
SIC: 2051 Bread, cake & related products

(G-7620)
OMNISOURCE MARKETING GROUP INC
Also Called: Housefield Marketing
8925 N Meridian St # 150 (46260-5363)
PHONE..................................317 575-3300
Janet Goldberg, *President*
Linda Maurer, *Vice Pres*
Michael Rudy, *CFO*
◆ EMP: 43
SALES (est): 15.8MM **Privately Held**
WEB: www.omnisourcemarketing.com
SIC: 5199 2759 Advertising specialties; commercial printing

(G-7621)
ON GUARD
10329 Vandergriff Rd (46239-9593)
PHONE..................................317 753-5312
Michelle Moore, *President*
EMP: 3
SALES (est): 166.7K
SALES (corp-wide): 1.3MM **Privately Held**
WEB: www.mic4.com
SIC: 3841 Surgical & medical instruments
PA: Containment Technologies Group, Inc.
5460 Victory Dr Ste 300
Indianapolis IN 46203
317 862-5945

(G-7622)
ONFIELD APPAREL GROUP LLC
8677 Logo Athletic Ct (46219-1430)
PHONE..................................317 895-7249
Janie Lewis, *CFO*
Scott Cobb, *Sales Staff*
Scott Landreth, *Marketing Staff*
EMP: 2
SALES (est): 107.9K **Privately Held**
SIC: 3149 Athletic shoes, except rubber or plastic

(G-7623)
ONION ENTERPRISES INC
Also Called: Zvibleman, Barry
5705 W 73rd St (46278-1741)
PHONE..................................317 762-6007
Barry Zvibleman, *Branch Mgr*
EMP: 2
SALES (corp-wide): 2.7MM **Privately Held**
WEB: www.onionenterprises.com
SIC: 3589 Water treatment equipment, industrial
PA: Onion Enterprises, Inc.
14713 Reserve Ln
Naples FL 34109
239 272-6655

(G-7624)
OOSHIRTS INC
7800 Records St Ste C (46226-3986)
PHONE..................................317 246-9083
Raymond Lei, *President*
EMP: 2
SALES (est): 174.6K **Privately Held**
SIC: 2759 Screen printing

(G-7625)
OOTEN PATTERN WORKS
1101 N Eleanor St (46214-3440)
PHONE..................................317 244-7348
William Baker, *Owner*
EMP: 2
SALES (est): 97K **Privately Held**
SIC: 3543 Industrial patterns

(G-7626)
OPEN CONTROL SYSTEMS LLC
905 N Capitol Ave Ste 200 (46204-1004)
PHONE..................................317 429-0627
Jennifer Baker, *Human Resources*
Anthony Wilkerson, *Mng Member*
Michael Martin,

Steve Haley, *Representative*
EMP: 5
SALES (est): 1.3MM **Privately Held**
SIC: 3822 Temperature controls, automatic

(G-7627)
OPFLEX SOLUTIONS INC
733 S West St (46225-1253)
PHONE..................................800 568-7036
Scott Charles Smith, *President*
EMP: 75
SALES (est): 10.1MM **Privately Held**
SIC: 3086 Plastics foam products

(G-7628)
OPFLEX TECHNOLOGIES LLC
2525 N Shadeland Ave (46219-1787)
PHONE..................................317 731-6123
EMP: 6
SALES (corp-wide): 4.9MM **Privately Held**
SIC: 3086 Cups & plates, foamed plastic
HQ: Opflex Technologies, Llc
733 S West St
Indianapolis IN 46225
518 568-7036

(G-7629)
OPFLEX TECHNOLOGIES LLC (HQ)
Also Called: Opflex Environmental Tech
733 S West St (46225-1253)
PHONE..................................518 568-7036
Mitchell T Stoltz, *President*
Patrick A Trefun, *Treasurer*
James E Lacrosse, *Manager*
John J Baker, *Admin Sec*
EMP: 20 EST: 2012
SALES: 3MM
SALES (corp-wide): 4.9MM **Privately Held**
SIC: 3086 Plastics foam products
PA: Nws Holdings, Llc
733 S West St
Indianapolis IN 46225
317 602-6644

(G-7630)
OPTICAL MEDIA MFG INC
310 N Alabama St Ste 320 (46204-2154)
PHONE..................................317 822-1850
Charles Viering, *President*
Holly Viering, *Exec VP*
EMP: 50
SALES: 250K **Privately Held**
WEB: www.opticaldisc-systems.com
SIC: 3695 Magnetic & optical recording media

(G-7631)
ORORA NORTH AMERICA
Also Called: Landsberg Indianapolis Div 1015
4635 W 84th St Ste 500 (46268-1792)
PHONE..................................317 879-4628
Jim Birch, *Marketing Staff*
Heather Grisel, *Marketing Staff*
Katie Polly, *Marketing Staff*
Steve Pittler, *Branch Mgr*
EMP: 28
SALES (corp-wide): 3B **Privately Held**
SIC: 5113 2653 Paper & products, wrapping or coarse; boxes, corrugated: made from purchased materials
HQ: Orora Packaging Solutions
6600 Valley View St
Buena Park CA 90620
714 562-6000

(G-7632)
ORTHOCONCEPTS INC
10947 Echo Grove Cir (46236-9069)
PHONE..................................317 727-0100
John Alley, *President*
EMP: 3
SALES (est): 279.9K **Privately Held**
SIC: 3845 Ultrasonic scanning devices, medical

(G-7633)
ORTHOTIC & PROSTHETIC DESIGNS
5120 Commerce Cir Ste 104 (46237-9717)
PHONE..................................317 882-9002
Julia Kean, *Principal*
EMP: 7

▲ = Import ▼=Export
◆ =Import/Export

SALES (est): 600.8K **Privately Held**
SIC: 3842 Surgical appliances & supplies

(G-7634)
OSCAR TELECOM INC
802 N Grant Ave (46201-2657)
PHONE...................................317 359-7000
Donald Campbell, *President*
EMP: 2
SALES (est): 198.7K **Privately Held**
SIC: 3651 Household video equipment

(G-7635)
OSI SPECIALTIES INC
6299 Guion Rd (46268-2530)
PHONE...................................317 293-4858
Debbie Williams, *President*
EMP: 50
SALES (est): 2.3MM **Privately Held**
SIC: 3842 Surgical appliances & supplies

(G-7636)
OSWALT MENU COMPANY INC
1433 Alimingo Dr (46260-4058)
PHONE...................................317 257-8039
Fax: 765 348-3137
EMP: 2 EST: 1949
SALES (est): 242.1K **Privately Held**
SIC: 7311 2752 Specialty Advertising/Design Service And Printing Company

(G-7637)
OTTINGER MACHINE CO
Also Called: Ottinger Machine Shop
2900 N Richardt Ave (46219-1119)
PHONE...................................317 654-1700
Fax: 317 769-6460
Jeffrey Ottinger, *Partner*
Candy Buckmaster, *Partner*
EMP: 2 EST: 1950
SQ FT: 7,000
SALES: 100K **Privately Held**
SIC: 3599 Machine shop, jobbing & repair

(G-7638)
OUT OF SIGHT SCREEN CO INC
3910 Cranbrook Dr (46240-3624)
PHONE...................................317 430-1705
Christopher Shepherd, *President*
EMP: 2
SALES (est): 150K **Privately Held**
SIC: 2511 Screens, privacy: wood

(G-7639)
OVR THERE INDUSTRIES INC
5825 Bonnie Brae St (46228-1841)
PHONE...................................317 946-8365
Jeffrey R Piper, *Principal*
EMP: 2
SALES (est): 143.9K **Privately Held**
SIC: 3999 Manufacturing industries

(G-7640)
OXFORD INDUSTRIES INC
8701 Keystone Xing 14b (46240-4641)
PHONE...................................317 569-0160
Terry Pillow, *Branch Mgr*
EMP: 3
SALES (corp-wide): 1B **Publicly Held**
SIC: 3161 Clothing & apparel carrying
  cases
PA: Oxford Industries, Inc.
  999 Peachtree St Ne # 688
  Atlanta GA 30309
  404 659-2424

(G-7641)
P & A MACHINE INC
3025 English Ave (46201-4345)
P.O. Box 3305 (46206-3305)
PHONE...................................317 634-3673
Fax: 317 464-9725
Paul A Coffey, *President*
Lisa Coffey, *Treasurer*
EMP: 7
SQ FT: 3,000
SALES: 450K **Privately Held**
SIC: 3599 3469 Machine shop, jobbing &
  repair; machine parts, stamped or
  pressed metal

(G-7642)
P & J TOOL CO INC
3525 Massachusetts Ave (46218-3899)
PHONE...................................317 546-4858
Fax: 317 549-9429

Frank S Johnson, *President*
Gerald Johnson, *Principal*
Charles W Johnson Jr, *Vice Pres*
Joanne Johnson, *Manager*
EMP: 7
SQ FT: 15,000
SALES (est): 825.6K **Privately Held**
WEB: www.pandjtoolco.com
SIC: 3599 Machine shop, jobbing & repair

(G-7643)
P H DREW INCORPORATED
2450 N Raceway Rd (46234-9152)
P.O. Box 34295 (46234-0295)
PHONE...................................317 297-5152
Fax: 317 297-5313
Philip H Drew, *President*
Christopher Drew, *Vice Pres*
Rhea Cain, *Human Resources*
Roy McDaniel, *Manager*
EMP: 31
SQ FT: 18,000
SALES (est): 9.8MM **Privately Held**
WEB: www.phdrew.com
SIC: 3441 Building components, structural
  steel

(G-7644)
P-AMERICAS LLC
Also Called: Pepsico
5411 W 78th St (46268-4150)
PHONE...................................317 876-6800
Fax: 317 876-6914
Rachel Kelly, *Traffic Mgr*
Kelly A Haywood, *Buyer*
Dean Senesac, *QC Mgr*
Steve Coston, *Branch Mgr*
Tim Donnelly, *Manager*
EMP: 123
SALES (corp-wide): 63.5B **Publicly Held**
SIC: 2086 5149 Bottled & canned soft
  drinks; groceries & related products
HQ: P-Americas Llc
  1 Pepsi Way
  Somers NY 10589
  336 896-5740

(G-7645)
PACK PRINTING
1916 Haynes Ave (46240-3236)
PHONE...................................317 437-9779
Brian V Powers, *Principal*
EMP: 2
SALES (est): 159K **Privately Held**
SIC: 2752 Commercial printing, litho-
  graphic

(G-7646)
**PACKAGING CORPORATION
AMERICA**
7752 W Morris St (46231-1363)
PHONE...................................317 247-0193
Rob Rop, *Manager*
EMP: 6
SALES (corp-wide): 6.4B **Publicly Held**
WEB: www.columbuscontainer.com
SIC: 2653 Boxes, corrugated: made from
  purchased materials
PA: Packaging Corporation Of America
  1955 W Field Ct
  Lake Forest IL 60045
  847 482-3000

(G-7647)
PACKETVAC LLC
7018 W 71st St (46278-1610)
PHONE...................................317 414-6137
John Hall, *President*
EMP: 3
SALES (est): 150.5K **Privately Held**
SIC: 3571 7389 Electronic computers;

(G-7648)
PAG HOLDINGS INC (HQ)
Also Called: Polymer Additives Group
5929 Lakeside Blvd (46278-1996)
PHONE...................................317 290-5006
Stephen J Groves, *CEO*
Greg Stevens, *President*
Greg Bennett, *CFO*
◆ EMP: 5
SALES (est): 1.8MM
SALES (corp-wide): 17MM **Privately
Held**
SIC: 2861 Gum & wood chemicals

PA: Metals And Additives, Llc
  5929 Lakeside Blvd
  Indianapolis IN 46278
  317 290-5007

(G-7649)
**PANHANDLE EASTRN PIPE LINE
LP**
9371 Zionsville Rd (46268-1035)
P.O. Box 38, Zionsville (46077-0038)
PHONE...................................317 873-2410
Fax: 317 733-3204
Carl Kaiser, *Enginr/R&D Mgr*
EMP: 40
SALES (corp-wide): 40.5B **Publicly Held**
SIC: 1389 Processing service, gas
HQ: Panhandle Eastern Pipe Line Com-
  pany, Lp
  8111 Westchester Dr # 600
  Dallas TX 75225
  214 981-0700

(G-7650)
PANTHER GRAPHICS LLC
5740 Decatur Blvd (46241-9561)
P.O. Box 4330, Carmel (46082-4330)
PHONE...................................317 223-3845
John Barnes, *Mng Member*
Nicolas Baumann,
EMP: 3
SALES (est): 269.1K **Privately Held**
SIC: 2759 Decals: printing

(G-7651)
PAPER TIGERS INC
Also Called: Papyrus
8702 Keystone Xing (46240-7621)
PHONE...................................317 573-9040
Fax: 317 573-9539
Theresa Mertes, *Manager*
EMP: 6
SALES (est): 498.8K **Privately Held**
WEB: www.papertigers.net
SIC: 5943 2759 Stationery stores; invita-
  tion & stationery printing & engraving

(G-7652)
PAR DIGITAL IMAGING
3330 Madison Ave (46227-1130)
PHONE...................................317 787-3330
Fax: 317 787-3305
Ray Wilkisin, *President*
Vaughn Rathburn, *Principal*
EMP: 4
SQ FT: 3,000
SALES (est): 250K **Privately Held**
WEB: www.parprinting.com
SIC: 2752 Commercial printing, offset

(G-7653)
**PARADISE MACHINE & TOOL
CORP**
6820 W Minnesota St (46241-2943)
PHONE...................................317 247-4606
Fax: 317 247-0442
Francis N Paradise, *President*
Rita Paradise, *Vice Pres*
Dennis Paradise, *Shareholder*
Mark Paradise, *Shareholder*
EMP: 5
SQ FT: 30,000
SALES: 400K **Privately Held**
SIC: 3544 Special dies, tools, jigs & fix-
  tures

(G-7654)
PARAGON MEDICAL INC
Also Called: Indianapolis I&I
7350 E 86th St (46256-1206)
PHONE...................................317 570-5830
Sairajkiran Nagboth, *Branch Mgr*
Scott Boltz, *Prgrmr*
Celeste Griffin, *Clerk*
EMP: 9
SALES (corp-wide): 191.6MM **Privately
Held**
SIC: 3842 Surgical appliances & supplies
PA: Paragon Medical, Inc.
  8 Matchett Dr
  Pierceton IN 46562
  574 594-2140

(G-7655)
PARIAH
5702 Crittenden Ave (46220-2805)
PHONE...................................317 250-0612

(G-7656)
EMP: 2
SALES (est): 120.2K **Privately Held**
SIC: 2339 Women's & misses' outerwear

(G-7656)
PARK 100 FOODS INC
Also Called: A & L Spcialty Foods H C Trnsp
6908 E 30th St (46219-1105)
PHONE...................................317 549-4545
Jim Washburn, *Branch Mgr*
EMP: 50
SALES (corp-wide): 95MM **Privately
Held**
WEB: www.park100foods.com
SIC: 2013 2032 2035 Frozen meats from
  purchased meat; cooked meats from pur-
  chased meat; soups, except seafood:
  packaged in cans, jars, etc.; pickles,
  sauces & salad dressings
PA: Park 100 Foods Inc
  326 E Adams St
  Tipton IN 46072
  765 675-3480

(G-7657)
PARRISH OF INDIANA INC
1020 Beal Ct (46217-5338)
PHONE...................................317 859-0934
Debra Parrish, *President*
EMP: 6
SALES (est): 805.6K **Privately Held**
WEB: www.parrishwaste.com
SIC: 2611 Pulp manufactured from waste
  or recycled paper

(G-7658)
PARTS CLEANING TECH LLC
2263 Distributors Dr (46241-5004)
PHONE...................................317 241-9379
Roy Richards, *Manager*
EMP: 3
SALES (corp-wide): 20.8MM **Privately
Held**
WEB: www.partscleaning.net
SIC: 2842 Cleaning or polishing prepara-
  tions; degreasing solvent
PA: Parts Cleaning Technologies, Llc
  26400 Capitol
  Redford MI 48239
  313 952-2646

(G-7659)
PASTELERIA GRESIL LLC
5348 W 38th St (46254-2916)
PHONE...................................317 299-8801
Silvia Y Gordon, *Principal*
EMP: 8
SALES (est): 619.4K **Privately Held**
SIC: 2051 Cakes, bakery: except frozen

(G-7660)
PATHFINDER SCHOOL LLC
Also Called: Self Reliance Outfitters
6050 Churchman Byp (46203-6064)
PHONE...................................317 791-8777
David M Canterbury,
David Canterbury,
James Canterbury,
Kim Canterbury,
EMP: 12
SALES (est): 755.1K **Privately Held**
SIC: 8211 3949 Public adult education
  school; camping equipment & supplies

(G-7661)
**PATRIOT SOFTWARE
SOLUTIONS INC**
1311 W 96th St Ste 220 (46260-1173)
PHONE...................................317 573-5431
Scott Martin, *President*
Pamela Marra, *Admin Sec*
EMP: 5 EST: 2001
SQ FT: 1,500
SALES (est): 306.1K **Privately Held**
SIC: 7372 Business oriented computer
  software

(G-7662)
PATRIOTIC FIREWORKS INC
Also Called: Rons Halloween
1314 S High School Rd (46241-3129)
PHONE...................................317 381-0529
Ron Surenkamp, *President*
Sally Surenkamp, *Admin Sec*
▲ EMP: 3

SALES (est): 535.4K **Privately Held**
SIC: 2899 Fireworks

(G-7663)
PATTERSON DRIVESHAFT INC
8360 W Washington St (46231-1349)
PHONE................................317 481-0495
Ron Beaman, *President*
EMP: 5 EST: 1972
SALES (est): 598.9K **Privately Held**
SIC: 3714 Drive shafts, motor vehicle

(G-7664)
PAVER RESCUE INC
7802 E 88th St (46256-1234)
PHONE................................317 259-4880
Parker Weber, *Principal*
EMP: 2
SALES (est): 233.2K **Privately Held**
SIC: 3531 Pavers

(G-7665)
PBS MFG LLC
5693 Federalist Ct (46254-1043)
PHONE................................317 515-2875
Bruce E Meyer, *President*
EMP: 2
SALES (est): 99.1K **Privately Held**
SIC: 3999 Manufacturing industries

(G-7666)
PCA PUBLISHING INC
8845 Jackson St (46231-1147)
PHONE................................317 658-2055
John Lee Couch, *Owner*
EMP: 2 EST: 2011
SALES (est): 110.5K **Privately Held**
SIC: 2741 Miscellaneous publishing

(G-7667)
PEANUT BUTTER AND JELLY
5501 E 71st St Ste 4 (46220-3900)
PHONE................................317 205-9211
Anita Beck, *Director*
EMP: 9
SALES: 427.3K **Privately Held**
SIC: 2099 Peanut butter

(G-7668)
PEARSON EDUCATION INC
Also Called: Financial Times-Prentice Hall
800 E 96th St Ste 300 (46240-3759)
PHONE................................317 428-3049
Greg Wiegand, *Editor*
Laurie Casey, *Opers Staff*
Julie Nahil, *Production*
Sandra Schroeder, *Art Dir*
EMP: 30
SALES (corp-wide): 5.9B **Privately Held**
WEB: www.phgenit.com
SIC: 2731 Books: publishing & printing
HQ: Pearson Education, Inc.
　　221 River St
　　Hoboken NJ 07030
　　201 236-7000

(G-7669)
PEARSON EDUCATION INC
5550 W 74th St (46268-4183)
PHONE................................317 715-2150
John Mawer, *Sales Mgr*
AMI Sponseller, *Accounts Exec*
Tim Martin, *Branch Mgr*
EMP: 25
SALES (corp-wide): 5.9B **Privately Held**
WEB: www.phgenit.com
SIC: 2731 Books: publishing only
HQ: Pearson Education, Inc.
　　221 River St
　　Hoboken NJ 07030
　　201 236-7000

(G-7670)
PENTERA GROUP INC
921 E 86th St Ste 100 (46240-1841)
PHONE................................317 543-2055
Judith Cohn, *President*
Kim Trittin, *Treasurer*
Amy Rector, *Senior Editor*
EMP: 14
SQ FT: 2,500
SALES (est): 1.6MM **Privately Held**
WEB: www.pgiresources.com
SIC: 2741 Miscellaneous publishing

(G-7671)
PEPSICO
5010 W 81st St (46268-1638)
PHONE................................317 334-0153
David Williams, *Principal*
Brandon Reed, *Sales Staff*
Kevin C Knight, *Manager*
EMP: 10
SALES (est): 2.4MM **Privately Held**
SIC: 2086 Carbonated soft drinks, bottled
& canned

(G-7672)
PEPSICO
5858 Decatur Blvd (46241-9575)
PHONE................................317 821-6400
Bob Harper, *Principal*
Tom Richter, *Engineer*
Eugene Crawford, *Manager*
Eric Jones, *Manager*
James Stevens, *Manager*
▲ EMP: 41
SALES (est): 9.2MM
SALES (corp-wide): 63.5B **Publicly Held**
SIC: 2086 Carbonated soft drinks, bottled
& canned
PA: Pepsico, Inc.
　　700 Anderson Hill Rd
　　Purchase NY 10577
　　914 253-2000

(G-7673)
PERANIS HOCKEY WORLD
7325 E 96th St Ste F (46250-3307)
PHONE................................317 288-5183
Matthew Walker, *Owner*
EMP: 2 EST: 2015
SALES (est): 151.3K **Privately Held**
SIC: 3949 Sporting & athletic goods

(G-7674)
**PERFECT IMPRESSIONS
PRINTING**
Also Called: Interchurch Print Shop
3901 N Meridian St Ste 15 (46208-4026)
P.O. Box 90311 (46290-0311)
PHONE................................317 923-1756
Fax: 317 925-4820
Debbie S Smith, *Owner*
EMP: 6
SQ FT: 1,500
SALES (est): 484.7K **Privately Held**
SIC: 2752 7334 Commercial printing, off-
set; photocopying & duplicating services

(G-7675)
**PERFECT MANUFACTURING
LLC**
450 W 16th Pl (46202-1167)
PHONE................................317 924-5284
Mark Haag,
EMP: 6
SALES (est): 1.1MM **Privately Held**
SIC: 3089 Pallets, plastic
PA: Perfect Pallets, Inc.
　　450 W 16th Pl
　　Indianapolis IN 46202

(G-7676)
PERFECT PALLETS INC (PA)
450 W 16th Pl (46202-1167)
PHONE................................888 553-5559
Fax: 317 924-5309
Mark E Haag, *President*
Marylyn Haag, *Manager*
Marilyn S Haag, *Admin Sec*
EMP: 53
SQ FT: 50,000
SALES (est): 9.6MM **Privately Held**
WEB: www.perfectpallets.com
SIC: 3089 Pallets, plastic

(G-7677)
PERFECTA USA
Also Called: Absolute Printing Equipment
5505 S Franklin Rd (46239-9646)
PHONE................................317 862-7371
Paul Myer, *President*
Brett Stow, *Assistant VP*
▲ EMP: 30
SALES (est): 3.4MM **Privately Held**
WEB: www.perfectausa.com
SIC: 3555 Printing trades machinery

(G-7678)
**PERI FORMWORK SYSTEMS
INC**
5550 S East St Stc E (46227-1991)
PHONE................................317 390-0062
Fax: 317 390-0067
Tom Ameel, *Manager*
EMP: 10
SALES (corp-wide): 59.7MM **Privately
Held**
SIC: 3444 Concrete forms, sheet metal
HQ: Peri Formwork Systems, Inc.
　　7135 Dorsey Run Rd
　　Elkridge MD 21075
　　410 712-7225

(G-7679)
PERMA LUBRICATION
2346 S Lynhurst Dr Ste J (46241-8621)
PHONE................................317 241-0797
Exel Woodcock, *Manager*
EMP: 3
SALES (est): 132.7K **Privately Held**
SIC: 7514 3569 Passenger car rental; lu-
bricating equipment

(G-7680)
PETROCHOICE HOLDINGS INC
Also Called: Miller Industrial Fluids
1751 W Raymond St (46221-2025)
PHONE................................317 634-7300
Fax: 317 636-6761
Ross Smith, *General Mgr*
EMP: 25
SALES (corp-wide): 816.5MM **Privately
Held**
SIC: 2992 5172 Oils & greases, blending
& compounding; lubricating oils & greases
HQ: Petrochoice Holdings, Inc.
　　1300 Virginia Dr Ste 405
　　Fort Washington PA 19034
　　267 705-2015

(G-7681)
PFORTUNE ART & DESIGN INC
Also Called: Pfortune Art & Design
9549 Valparaiso Ct (46268-1130)
PHONE................................317 872-4123
Ned Sutton, *President*
Sheri Sutton, *Corp Secy*
Pete Weaver, *Vice Pres*
EMP: 2
SQ FT: 1,800
SALES (est): 200.4K **Privately Held**
SIC: 2499 5999 Picture frame molding,
finished; art dealers

(G-7682)
PGW INDUSTRIES INC
1445 Brookville Way Ste S (46239-1197)
PHONE................................317 322-3599
Fax: 317 322-3596
Eric Walker, *Manager*
EMP: 2
SALES (est): 110.2K **Privately Held**
SIC: 3999 Manufacturing industries

(G-7683)
PHIL IRWIN ADVERTISING INC
Also Called: Ad-Sign & Display Division
5995 E 30th St (46218-3317)
PHONE................................317 547-5117
Fax: 317 568-0519
Phil Irwin Jr, *President*
Pamela Polovich, *Office Mgr*
Sarah Arney, *Manager*
EMP: 10
SQ FT: 12,000
SALES (est): 700K **Privately Held**
SIC: 2759 7359 Screen printing; tent &
tarpaulin rental

(G-7684)
PHILIPS ULTRASOUND INC
Also Called: A T L
7518 E 39th St (46226-5164)
PHONE................................317 591-5242
Dan Tallent, *Principal*
EMP: 10
SALES (corp-wide): 20.9B **Privately Held**
SIC: 3845 Electromedical apparatus
HQ: Philips Ultrasound, Inc.
　　22100 Bothell Everett Hwy
　　Bothell WA 98021
　　800 982-2011

(G-7685)
PHOENIX BRANDS LLC (PA)
2601 Fortune Cir E 102b (46241-5523)
PHONE................................203 975-0319
Sanjiv Mehra, *Mng Member*
Mark Landry,
◆ EMP: 10
SQ FT: 7,000
SALES (est): 23.3MM **Privately Held**
SIC: 2841 Soap & other detergents

(G-7686)
PHOENIX BRANDS LLC
2601 Fortune Cir E 102b (46241-5523)
PHONE................................317 231-8044
Diane K Zimmerman, *Principal*
EMP: 60
SALES (corp-wide): 23.3MM **Privately
Held**
SIC: 2841 Soap & other detergents
PA: Phoenix Brands Llc
　　2601 Fortune Cir E 102b
　　Indianapolis IN 46241
　　203 975-0319

(G-7687)
PHOENIX SIGN WORKS INC
5345 Lexington Ave (46219-7025)
PHONE................................317 432-4027
Hal Paul, *President*
Mark Schutte, *Director*
EMP: 9 EST: 2010
SALES: 750K **Privately Held**
SIC: 3993 Electric signs

(G-7688)
PHOTO SCREEN SERVICE INC
1505 Southeastern Ave (46201-3980)
PHONE................................317 636-7712
Fax: 317 636-7717
Brian M Chambers, *President*
Sebrina Chambers, *Admin Sec*
EMP: 5 EST: 1948
SQ FT: 8,000
SALES (est): 685.9K **Privately Held**
WEB: www.photoscreenservice.com
SIC: 2759 Screen printing

(G-7689)
PIEDMONT PLASTICS INC
7768 Zionsville Rd (46268-5125)
PHONE................................317 947-4500
EMP: 2
SALES (corp-wide): 190.6MM **Privately
Held**
SIC: 3081 Plastic film & sheet
PA: Piedmont Plastics, Inc.
　　5010 W Wt Harris Blvd
　　Charlotte NC 28269
　　704 597-8200

(G-7690)
PIEZOTECH LLC (HQ)
Also Called: Meggitt Sensing Systems
8431 Georgetown Rd # 300 (46268-5628)
PHONE................................317 876-4670
Fax: 317 876-4681
John Jaqua Jr, *CEO*
Richard D Barton, *CEO*
Randall S Coakes, *COO*
James M Dallas, *Vice Pres*
Dane Delozier, *Vice Pres*
EMP: 30
SQ FT: 30,000
SALES (est): 11.5MM
SALES (corp-wide): 2.6B **Privately Held**
WEB: www.piezotechnologies.com
SIC: 3829 Measuring & controlling devices
PA: Meggitt Plc
　　Atlantic House, Aviation Park West
　　Christchurch BH23
　　120 259-7597

(G-7691)
PIN POINT AV LLC
8226 Kentallen Ct (46236-8380)
PHONE................................317 750-3120
Dave Anderson, *Principal*
EMP: 5
SALES (est): 436.8K **Privately Held**
SIC: 3452 Pins

(G-7692)
PINK LIPSTICK AND COMPANY
5744 Brendon Way West Dr (46226-7209)
PHONE................................317 992-6818

Ashia Lynn Hambrick, *President*
EMP: 2
SALES (est): 74.4K **Privately Held**
SIC: 2844 Lipsticks

(G-7693)
**PINNACLE EQUIPMENT
COMPANY INC**
1616 Milburn St (46202-2126)
P.O. Box 88637 (46208-0637)
PHONE....................................317 259-1180
Andre Jones, *President*
Shelley Jones, *Human Resources*
George Piche, *Sales Engr*
Chris Carson, *Sales Staff*
EMP: 8
SQ FT: 11,000
SALES (est): 3.1MM **Privately Held**
WEB: www.pinnaclequipment.com
SIC: 3444 Sheet metalwork

(G-7694)
**PINNACLE MANUFACTURING
GROUP**
Also Called: PMG
5622 Liberty Creek Dr E (46254-1005)
PHONE....................................317 691-2460
Ollie J Whitmore, *President*
EMP: 3
SALES: 500K **Privately Held**
SIC: 3999 Manufacturing industries

(G-7695)
PINNACLE OIL HOLDINGS LLC
8175 Allison Ave (46268-1648)
PHONE....................................317 875-9465
John Fought, *Manager*
EMP: 15 **Privately Held**
SIC: 2992 5172 8742 Lubricating oils &
greases; lubricating oils & greases; mar-
keting consulting services
PA: Pinnacle Oil Holdings, Llc
5009 W 81st St
Indianapolis IN 46268

(G-7696)
**PINNACLE OIL HOLDINGS LLC
(PA)**
5009 W 81st St (46268-1639)
PHONE....................................317 875-9465
Fax: 317 875-0889
Gregory Morris, *Exec VP*
John J Massel, *Vice Pres*
Tom Gunter, *Prdtn Mgr*
Denice Hansen, *Accountant*
Kenton L Morris, *Mng Member*
EMP: 26
SQ FT: 275,000
SALES (est): 127MM **Privately Held**
SIC: 2992 5172 8742 Lubricating oils &
greases; lubricating oils & greases; mar-
keting consulting services

(G-7697)
PINNACLE OIL TRADING LLC
8175 Allison Ave (46268-1648)
PHONE....................................317 875-9465
Kenton L Morris,
EMP: 3
SALES: 12MM **Privately Held**
SIC: 1389 Gas field services
PA: Pinnacle Oil Holdings, Llc
5009 W 81st St
Indianapolis IN 46268

(G-7698)
PITNEY BOWES INC
5071 W 74th St (46268-5112)
PHONE....................................260 436-7395
Philip A Koehl, *Controller*
Ed Oreily, *Manager*
EMP: 35
SALES (corp-wide): 3.5B **Publicly Held**
SIC: 3579 7359 Postage meters; business
machine & electronic equipment rental
services
PA: Pitney Bowes Inc.
3001 Summer St Ste 3
Stamford CT 06905
203 356-5000

(G-7699)
**PIZO OPERATING COMPANY
LLC**
7901 W Morris St (46231-1366)
PHONE....................................317 243-0811
Nigel Morrison,
EMP: 40
SALES (est): 4MM
SALES (corp-wide): 207.5MM **Privately
Held**
SIC: 3312 Hoops, iron & steel
HQ: Heritage Environmental Services, Llc
7901 W Morris St
Indianapolis IN 46231
317 243-0811

(G-7700)
PLASTIC ASSEMBLY TECH INC
8445 Castlewood Dr Ste B (46250-4570)
PHONE....................................317 841-1202
Fax: 317 841-2717
Gary Clodfelter, *President*
Mary Clodfelter, *Vice Pres*
EMP: 6
SQ FT: 5,500
SALES (est): 1.2MM **Privately Held**
WEB:
www.plasticassemblytechnologies.com
SIC: 5047 3845 Medical equipment & sup-
plies; electromedical equipment

(G-7701)
PLATINUM DISPLAY GROUP
5855 Kopetsky Dr (46217-9635)
PHONE....................................317 731-5026
Adam Lickliter, *President*
EMP: 5 EST: 2011
SALES (est): 489.4K **Privately Held**
SIC: 2541 Store fixtures, wood

(G-7702)
PLAYN2WIN LLC
7948 Preservation Dr (46278-9545)
PHONE....................................317 345-4653
Gary Johnson, *CEO*
Susan Clarke-Johnson, *CFO*
Aydin Garth, *Director*
EMP: 3
SALES (est): 78.2K **Privately Held**
SIC: 8999 3952 Artists & artists' studios;
mixtures, gold or bronze: artists'; water
colors, artists'; canvas, prepared on
frames: artists'; pencils & leads, including
artists'

(G-7703)
PMW HOLDINGS LLC ✪
2255 Colfax Ln (46260-6601)
PHONE....................................317 339-4685
Erik C Morris, *Chief Mktg Ofcr*
Steve Watkins, *CTO*
Russel Polak,
EMP: 3 EST: 2017
SALES (est): 109.5K **Privately Held**
SIC: 8742 3087 2295 2821 Management
consulting services; custom compound
purchased resins; chemically coated &
treated fabrics; vinyl resins; resins

(G-7704)
POINT CARE ULTRASOUND LP
5904 E Southport Rd (46237-9341)
PHONE....................................317 459-8113
Michael Welsh, *Partner*
▲ EMP: 6
SALES (est): 461.6K **Privately Held**
SIC: 3845 Ultrasonic medical equipment,
except cleaning

(G-7705)
POLYGON
2346 S Lynhurst Dr F201e (46241-8628)
PHONE....................................317 240-1130
Adrian Topete, *Principal*
EMP: 2
SALES (est): 159.1K **Privately Held**
SIC: 5085 5033 3089 Industrial supplies;
fiberglass building materials; plastic pro-
cessing

(G-7706)
**POLYMER TECHNOLOGY
SYSTEMS INC (HQ)**
Also Called: Pts Diagnostics
7736 Zionsville Rd (46268-2175)
PHONE....................................317 870-5610
Fax: 317 870-5608
Robert Huffstodt, *President*
Keith Moskowitz, *Vice Pres*
Jennifer Grandidier, *Human Res Mgr*
Cathleen Alaimo, *Director*
Lance Bury, *General Counsel*
▲ EMP: 90
SQ FT: 32,000
SALES (est): 37MM
SALES (corp-wide): 155.9MM **Privately
Held**
WEB: www.cardiochek.com
SIC: 3841 Diagnostic apparatus, medical
PA: Sinocare Inc.
No.265, Guyuan Rd., High-Tech Indus-
trial Development Zone
Changsha 41020
731 899-3552

(G-7707)
PORT SERVICES LLC
6127 Gunyon Way (46237-9575)
PHONE....................................317 840-7606
Bryan Black,
EMP: 6
SALES (est): 270K **Privately Held**
WEB: www.portservicesllc.com
SIC: 3669 Communications equipment

(G-7708)
POSITRAX INC
Also Called: Allied OSI Labs
6299 Guion Rd (46268-2530)
PHONE....................................317 293-4858
Fax: 317 299-1367
Anthony Miller DPM, *President*
Debbie Williams, *General Mgr*
Scott Ludlow, *QC Dir*
Brian Williams, *Technology*
EMP: 65
SQ FT: 14,000
SALES (est): 9.3MM **Privately Held**
WEB: www.aolabs.com
SIC: 3842 Foot appliances, orthopedic

(G-7709)
POSTERS 2 PRINTS LLC
9900 Westpoint Dr Ste 138 (46256-3338)
PHONE....................................800 598-5837
David Hosei, *Principal*
EMP: 10
SALES (est): 1.4MM **Privately Held**
SIC: 2752 Commercial printing, litho-
graphic

(G-7710)
POSTERS2PRINTS LLC
10428 Starboard Way (46256-9514)
PHONE....................................317 414-8972
Michael Slate, *Principal*
Leslie Kiffmeyer, *Consultant*
EMP: 4
SALES (est): 281K **Privately Held**
SIC: 2752 Commercial printing, litho-
graphic

(G-7711)
**POWDER METAL TECHNICIANS
INC**
8462 Brookville Rd (46239-9491)
P.O. Box 358, Greenwood (46142-0358)
PHONE....................................317 353-2812
Riley Bennett, *Principal*
EMP: 3
SALES (est): 615.7K **Privately Held**
SIC: 3599 Machine shop, jobbing & repair

(G-7712)
**POWER TRAIN CORP FORT
WAYNE (PA)**
2334 Production Dr (46241-4990)
PHONE....................................317 241-9393
Lyle Bass, *President*
Bob Biggs, *Vice Pres*
Joe Leffel, *Admin Sec*
EMP: 14

SALES (est): 5.3MM **Privately Held**
SIC: 5015 3714 3446 Motor vehicle parts,
used; motor vehicle parts & accessories;
architectural metalwork

(G-7713)
**PPG ARCHITECTURAL FINISHES
INC**
Also Called: Glidden Professional Paint Ctr
7025 Madison Ave (46227-5203)
PHONE....................................317 787-9393
Fax: 317 889-1102
Ricky Mitchel, *Manager*
EMP: 7
SALES (corp-wide): 14.2B **Publicly Held**
WEB: www.gliddenpaint.com
SIC: 2891 Adhesives
HQ: Ppg Architectural Finishes, Inc.
1 Ppg Pl
Pittsburgh PA 15272
412 434-3131

(G-7714)
PPG INDUSTRIES INC
Also Called: PPG 4367
5977 E 82nd St (46250-1523)
PHONE....................................317 849-2340
EMP: 24
SALES (corp-wide): 15.3B **Publicly Held**
SIC: 2851 Mfg Paints/Allied Products
PA: Ppg Industries, Inc.
1 Ppg Pl
Pittsburgh PA 15272
412 434-3131

(G-7715)
PPG INDUSTRIES INC
Also Called: PPG 4361
952 N Delaware St (46202-3375)
PHONE....................................317 267-0511
Douglas Ve, *Branch Mgr*
EMP: 24
SALES (corp-wide): 14.2B **Publicly Held**
WEB: www.ppg.com
SIC: 2851 Paints & allied products
PA: Ppg Industries, Inc.
1 Ppg Pl
Pittsburgh PA 15272
412 434-3131

(G-7716)
PPG INDUSTRIES INC
Also Called: PPG 4365
10009 E Washington St (46229-2623)
PHONE....................................317 897-3836
Jim Skweres, *Manager*
EMP: 24
SALES (corp-wide): 14.2B **Publicly Held**
WEB: www.ppg.com
SIC: 2851 Paints & allied products
PA: Ppg Industries, Inc.
1 Ppg Pl
Pittsburgh PA 15272
412 434-3131

(G-7717)
PPG INDUSTRIES INC
Also Called: PPG 4364
7025 Madison Ave (46227-5203)
PHONE....................................317 787-9393
Kevin Lannan, *Branch Mgr*
EMP: 24
SALES (corp-wide): 14.2B **Publicly Held**
WEB: www.ppg.com
SIC: 2851 Paints & allied products
PA: Ppg Industries, Inc.
1 Ppg Pl
Pittsburgh PA 15272
412 434-3131

(G-7718)
PPG INDUSTRIES INC
Also Called: PPG 4363
2311 E 53rd St (46220-3429)
PHONE....................................317 251-9494
Fax: 317 251-9495
Roy Moore, *Branch Mgr*
EMP: 2
SALES (corp-wide): 14.2B **Publicly Held**
WEB: www.ppg.com
SIC: 2851 Paints & allied products
PA: Ppg Industries, Inc.
1 Ppg Pl
Pittsburgh PA 15272
412 434-3131

GEOGRAPHIC

(G-7719)
PPG INDUSTRIES INC
Also Called: PPG 5547
6951 E 30th St Ste E (46219-1190)
PHONE...........................317 546-5714
Nathan Pittman, *Manager*
EMP: 24
SALES (corp-wide): 14.2B **Publicly Held**
WEB: www.ppg.com
SIC: 2851 Paints & allied products
PA: Ppg Industries, Inc.
　　1 Ppg Pl
　　Pittsburgh PA 15272
　　412 434-3131

(G-7720)
PRATT VISUAL SOLUTIONS COMPANY
3035 N Shadeland Ave (46226-6200)
PHONE...........................800 428-7728
EMP: 50 **EST:** 2012
SQ FT: 50,000
SALES: 27MM
SALES (corp-wide): 155MM **Privately Held**
SIC: 2759 Commercial printing
PA: Vomela Specialty Company
　　274 Fillmore Ave E
　　Saint Paul MN 55107
　　651 228-2200

(G-7721)
PRAXAIR INC
1500 Polco St (46222-3285)
PHONE...........................317 240-2500
EMP: 3
SALES (est): 143.6K **Privately Held**
SIC: 2813 Industrial gases

(G-7722)
PRAXAIR DISTRIBUTION INC
1400 Polco St (46222-5210)
PHONE...........................317 481-4550
Ron Flood, *Sales Staff*
Neil Faucett, *Branch Mgr*
EMP: 2
SQ FT: 1,900
SALES (corp-wide): 11.4B **Publicly Held**
SIC: 2813 5084 5999 Industrial gases; carbon dioxide; dry ice, carbon dioxide (solid); oxygen, compressed or liquefied; welding machinery & equipment; welding supplies
HQ: Praxair Distribution, Inc.
　　10 Riverview Dr
　　Danbury CT 06810
　　203 837-2000

(G-7723)
PRAXAIR DISTRIBUTION INC
1400 Polco St (46222-5210)
PHONE...........................317 481-4550
Joe Feeser, *Manager*
EMP: 40
SQ FT: 15,000
SALES (corp-wide): 11.4B **Publicly Held**
WEB: www.mittler.com
SIC: 2813 Industrial gases
HQ: Praxair Distribution, Inc.
　　10 Riverview Dr
　　Danbury CT 06810
　　203 837-2000

(G-7724)
PRAXAIR SURFACE TECH INC
1555 Main St (46224-6539)
PHONE...........................317 240-2500
EMP: 180
SALES (corp-wide): 11.4B **Publicly Held**
SIC: 3479 Coating of metals & formed products
HQ: Praxair Surface Technologies, Inc.
　　1500 Polco St
　　Indianapolis IN 46222
　　317 240-2500

(G-7725)
PRAXAIR SURFACE TECH INC (HQ)
1500 Polco St (46222-3285)
PHONE...........................317 240-2500
Fax: 317 240-2380
Pierre Luthi, *President*
Dean Hackett, *Vice Pres*
Thomas Lewis, *Vice Pres*

Alan Draper, *Finance*
E Hartford, *Sales Staff*
◆ **EMP:** 132
SQ FT: 58,000
SALES (est): 841.3MM
SALES (corp-wide): 11.4B **Publicly Held**
SIC: 3479 3548 3563 Painting, coating & hot dipping; coating, rust preventive; hot dip coating of metals or formed products; electric welding equipment; spraying outfits: metals, paints & chemicals (compressor)
PA: Praxair, Inc.
　　10 Riverview Dr
　　Danbury CT 06810
　　203 837-2000

(G-7726)
PRAXAIR SURFACE TECH INC
1245 Main St (46224-6533)
PHONE...........................317 240-2544
Dan Fillenworth, *Manager*
EMP: 200
SALES (corp-wide): 11.4B **Publicly Held**
SIC: 3471 Plating & polishing
HQ: Praxair Surface Technologies, Inc.
　　1500 Polco St
　　Indianapolis IN 46222
　　317 240-2500

(G-7727)
PRAXAIR SURFACE TECH INC
1555 Main St (46224-6539)
PHONE...........................317 240-2192
EMP: 5
SALES (corp-wide): 11.4B **Publicly Held**
SIC: 3479 Painting, coating & hot dipping; coating, rust preventive; hot dip coating of metals or formed products
HQ: Praxair Surface Technologies, Inc.
　　1500 Polco St
　　Indianapolis IN 46222
　　317 240-2500

(G-7728)
PRC - DESOTO INTERNATIONAL INC
Also Called: PPG Aerospace
6022 Corporate Way (46278-2923)
PHONE...........................317 290-1600
Roald Johanssan, *Branch Mgr*
EMP: 37
SALES (corp-wide): 14.2B **Publicly Held**
SIC: 2891 3089 Sealing compounds, synthetic rubber or plastic; adhesives; plastic containers, except foam
HQ: Prc - Desoto International, Inc.
　　24811 Ave Rockefeller
　　Valencia CA 91355
　　661 678-4209

(G-7729)
PRECISE PRINTING PLUS SIGNS
4501 N Edmondson Ave (46226-3636)
PHONE...........................317 545-5117
Bobbie J Howard, *President*
EMP: 2
SALES (est): 201.6K **Privately Held**
SIC: 7389 5999 3993 Printers' services: folding, collating; rubber stamps; signs & advertising specialties

(G-7730)
PRECISELY WRITE INC
9801 Fall Creek Rd 202 (46256-4802)
PHONE...........................317 585-7701
Ruth Nickolich, *President*
EMP: 3
SQ FT: 1,240
SALES (est): 235.6K **Privately Held**
WEB: www.precisely.com
SIC: 2741 7338 8999 Technical manual & paper publishing; editing service; technical writing; technical manual preparation

(G-7731)
PRECISION CAMS INC (PA)
Also Called: Enviropeel USA
3510 E Raymond St (46203-4745)
PHONE...........................317 631-9100
Kenneth L Boehm, *President*
EMP: 22
SQ FT: 31,000
SALES (est): 4.6MM **Privately Held**
SIC: 3545 Cams (machine tool accessories)

(G-7732)
PRECISION CAMS INC
Also Called: US Exploration Eqp Co Div
3510 E Raymond St (46203-4745)
PHONE...........................317 780-0117
William Knorr, *Branch Mgr*
EMP: 2
SALES (corp-wide): 4.6MM **Privately Held**
SIC: 3545 Cams (machine tool accessories)
PA: Precision Cams Inc
　　3510 E Raymond St
　　Indianapolis IN 46203
　　317 631-9100

(G-7733)
PRECISION CRYOGENIC SYSTEMS
7804 Rockville Rd (46214-3105)
PHONE...........................317 273-2800
Fax: 317 273-2802
Roy Larrison, *President*
Paul Coverdale, *Vice Pres*
Richard Gummer, *Vice Pres*
EMP: 15
SQ FT: 7,000
SALES (est): 3MM **Privately Held**
WEB: www.precisioncryo.com
SIC: 3443 Cryogenic tanks, for liquids & gases

(G-7734)
PRECISION POLISHING & BUFFING
1038 S Kealing Ave (46203-1516)
PHONE...........................317 352-0165
Fax: 317 356-2813
Fred Mullen, *President*
EMP: 8
SQ FT: 17,850
SALES (est): 780K **Privately Held**
SIC: 3471 Buffing for the trade; polishing, metals or formed products

(G-7735)
PRECISION RACG COMPONENTS LLC
Also Called: PRC
140 Gasoline Aly (46222-3965)
PHONE...........................317 248-4764
Christopher Sumner, *President*
EMP: 11
SQ FT: 11,000
SALES (est): 2.2MM **Privately Held**
SIC: 3599 3714 3444 Machine shop, jobbing & repair; custom machinery; oil pump, motor vehicle; sheet metalwork; sheet metal specialties, not stamped

(G-7736)
PRECISION RINGS INCORPORATED
5611 Progress Rd (46241-4332)
P.O. Box 421189 (46242-1189)
PHONE...........................317 247-4786
Fax: 317 248-9781
Jay S Crannell, *Ch of Bd*
Joseph L Crannell, *President*
Richard Cuculick, *General Mgr*
Rob Wilson, *Chief Engr*
Jordan Thralls, *Design Engr*
EMP: 50 **EST:** 1950
SQ FT: 49,000
SALES (est): 13.7MM **Privately Held**
WEB: www.precisionrings.com
SIC: 3592 Pistons & piston rings

(G-7737)
PRECISION RUBBER PLATE CO INC
5620 Elmwood Ave (46203-6029)
PHONE...........................317 783-3226
Fax: 317 788-5680
Lawrence R Green, *President*
Susan Green, *Corp Secy*
Manuel S Green, *COO*
James A Green, *Vice Pres*
▲ **EMP:** 55 **EST:** 1938
SQ FT: 36,000
SALES (est): 12.9MM **Privately Held**
WEB: www.prpflexo.com
SIC: 3555 Printing plates

(G-7738)
PRECISION TUBES INC
Also Called: Penn Tool
5730 Kopetsky Dr Ste C (46217-9006)
PHONE...........................317 783-2339
Fax: 317 783-5600
Richard E Warren, *President*
Patricia Warren, *Admin Sec*
EMP: 5
SALES: 400K **Privately Held**
WEB: www.precisiontubes.com
SIC: 3544 7692 3545 Special dies & tools; welding repair; machine tool accessories

(G-7739)
PREFERRED PRINT
6220 Hardegan St (46227-4907)
PHONE...........................317 371-8829
EMP: 2
SALES (est): 161.4K **Privately Held**
SIC: 2752 Commercial printing, lithographic

(G-7740)
PREFERRED SEATING COMPANY LLC
633 Yosemite Dr (46217-3961)
P.O. Box 17622 (46217-0622)
PHONE...........................317 782-3323
Frank Sumner, *President*
Billie Sumner, *Vice Pres*
EMP: 2
SALES: 1MM **Privately Held**
SIC: 5021 2531 Theater seats; stadium seating

(G-7741)
PREMIER SIGN GROUP INC
740 E 52nd St Ste 7 (46205-1175)
PHONE...........................317 613-4411
Fax: 317 613-4412
Jim Leahy, *President*
Greg Cunningham, *Vice Pres*
EMP: 7
SQ FT: 3,500
SALES: 1.4MM **Privately Held**
SIC: 3993 Electric signs

(G-7742)
PREMIERE ADVERTISING
2704 E 62nd St Ste B (46220-2985)
PHONE...........................317 722-2400
Andrew H Auch, *President*
Jon Wainscott, *Accounts Exec*
Travis Wilken, *Accounts Exec*
EMP: 3
SQ FT: 2,500
SALES: 620K **Privately Held**
WEB: www.premiereadv.com
SIC: 5199 2759 Advertising specialties; commercial printing

(G-7743)
PRESSURE SYSTEMS INC
16 Gazebo Dr (46227-3005)
PHONE...........................317 755-3050
Louie Bowser, *President*
EMP: 12
SALES: 950K **Privately Held**
SIC: 3589 High pressure cleaning equipment

(G-7744)
PRETTY IN PRINTS LLC
4022 Carrollton Ave (46205-2702)
PHONE...........................317 252-3672
Ryan Blalock, *Principal*
EMP: 2
SALES (est): 112.2K **Privately Held**
SIC: 2752 Commercial printing, lithographic

(G-7745)
PREVAIL PRSTHTICS ORTHTICS INC
6330 E 75th St Ste 126 (46250-2717)
PHONE...........................317 577-2273
Stephanie Jones Cutler, *Branch Mgr*
EMP: 3
SQ FT: 600
SALES (corp-wide): 1.3MM **Privately Held**
SIC: 3842 Prosthetic appliances

PA: Prevail Prosthetics & Orthotics, Inc.
7735 W Jefferson Blvd
Fort Wayne IN 46804
260 483-5219

(G-7746)
PRIME TECH INC
3131 N Franklin Rd Ste B (46226-6390)
PHONE.................................317 715-1162
A Desida, *Director*
EMP: 3
SALES (est): 118.7K **Privately Held**
SIC: 3511 Turbines & turbine generator
sets

(G-7747)
PRIMED & READY LLC
5036 E 65th St (46220-4585)
PHONE.................................317 694-2028
Paul Jesch, *Owner*
EMP: 2
SALES (est): 288K **Privately Held**
SIC: 3273 Ready-mixed concrete

(G-7748)
PRINT AND SAVE LLP
4420 W Washington St (46241-0824)
PHONE.................................317 567-1459
EMP: 4
SALES (est): 101.5K **Privately Held**
SIC: 2752 Commercial printing, litho-
graphic

(G-7749)
PRINT IDEAS
2233 Country Club Rd (46234-1838)
PHONE.................................317 299-8766
William Yount, *Owner*
EMP: 3
SALES: 400K **Privately Held**
SIC: 2752 Commercial printing, offset

(G-7750)
PRINT SHARP ENTERPRISES
INC
Also Called: Minuteman Press
4371 Sellers St (46226-7109)
PHONE.................................317 899-2754
Fax: 317 899-2763
Timothy Newberry, *President*
David L Ruse, *Admin Sec*
EMP: 4
SQ FT: 5,000
SALES: 500K **Privately Held**
SIC: 2752 Commercial printing, litho-
graphic

(G-7751)
PRINTEC SOLUTIONS INC
8130 Wysong Dr (46219-1835)
PHONE.................................317 289-6510
Steve Zachary, *President*
Jay Ehlers, *Vice Pres*
Beth Willner, *Shareholder*
EMP: 4 EST: 2006
SALES (est): 468.7K **Privately Held**
SIC: 2752 3993 Commercial printing, litho-
graphic; signs & advertising specialties

(G-7752)
PRINTEGRA CORP
Also Called: Pintegra/Whosser Data Forms
1002 E 25th St (46205-4400)
PHONE.................................317 328-0022
Kevin Santon, *General Mgr*
Mark Keller, *Facilities Mgr*
EMP: 55
SALES (corp-wide): 370.1MM **Publicly
Held**
WEB: www.printegra.com
SIC: 2761 2782 Continuous forms, office
& business; blankbooks & looseleaf
binders
HQ: Printegra Corp
5040 Highlands Pkwy Se
Smyrna GA 30082
770 487-5151

(G-7753)
PRINTING CENTER INC
Also Called: Printing Complex, The
3503 N Shadeland Ave (46226-5708)
PHONE.................................317 545-8518
Fax: 317 545-8519
Gregory Ernest, *President*
Doris Ernest, *Corp Secy*

EMP: 7
SQ FT: 2,400
SALES (est): 892.8K **Privately Held**
SIC: 2752 Commercial printing, offset

(G-7754)
PRINTING CONCEPTS INC
Also Called: Minuteman Press
4371 Sellers St (46226-7109)
PHONE.................................317 899-2754
Frank Endicott, *President*
Robert Ylinen, *President*
Jack Panzer, *Area Mgr*
Shane Anderson, *Production*
EMP: 5
SQ FT: 6,000
SALES (est): 493.6K **Privately Held**
SIC: 2752 Commercial printing, offset

(G-7755)
PRINTING PARTNERS INC (PA)
Also Called: Partners Marketing
929 W 16th St (46202-2214)
PHONE.................................317 635-2282
Michael O Brien, *President*
Joel O Brien, *Vice Pres*
Joe Brower, *CFO*
EMP: 92
SQ FT: 53,000
SALES (est): 14.6MM **Privately Held**
WEB: www.printingpartners.net
SIC: 2752 7331 2759 Commercial print-
ing, offset; mailing service; letterpress
printing

(G-7756)
PRINTING PARTNERS EAST INC
Also Called: Insty-Prints
929 W 16th St (46202-2214)
PHONE.................................317 356-2522
Michael O'Brien, *President*
Joel O'Brien, *Admin Sec*
EMP: 6
SQ FT: 2,140
SALES (est): 558.5K **Privately Held**
SIC: 2752 7334 Commercial printing, litho-
graphic; photocopying & duplicating serv-
ices

(G-7757)
PRINTING SERVICES INC
5333 Commerce Square Dr (46237-8627)
PHONE.................................317 300-0363
EMP: 2
SALES (est): 117.5K **Privately Held**
SIC: 2759 Commercial printing

(G-7758)
PRINTING TECHNOLOGIES INC
6266 Morenci Trl (46268-4827)
PHONE.................................800 428-3786
Fax: 317 299-2325
Walter Alfred, *President*
Joseph Walkes, *Vice Pres*
Scott Begbie, *VP Sales*
EMP: 45
SQ FT: 30,000
SALES (est): 14MM **Privately Held**
WEB: www.ptionaroll.com
SIC: 3861 Sensitized film, cloth & paper

(G-7759)
PRIORITY PRESS INC (PA)
Also Called: Priority Business Forms
4026 W 10th St (46222-3282)
PHONE.................................317 241-4234
Fax: 317 240-3858
Joseph Straka, *President*
Robert Straka, *Vice Pres*
Patty Birch, *Accounts Exec*
Mark O'Sickey, *Accounts Exec*
Rob Straka, *Sales Staff*
EMP: 35
SQ FT: 52,000
SALES (est): 17.4MM **Privately Held**
WEB: www.prioritygroupinc.com
SIC: 2759 5112 5049 Commercial print-
ing; computer paper; engineers' equip-
ment & supplies

(G-7760)
PRIORITY PRESS INC
Press 96
4026 W 10th St (46222-3282)
PHONE.................................317 240-0103
Fax: 317 848-9762

Gary Weatherholt, *Branch Mgr*
EMP: 3
SALES (corp-wide): 17.4MM **Privately
Held**
WEB: www.prioritygroupinc.com
SIC: 2759 2752 Commercial print-
ing; photocopying & duplicating services;
commercial printing, offset
PA: Priority Press, Inc.
4026 W 10th St
Indianapolis IN 46222
317 241-4234

(G-7761)
PRIORITY PRINTING LLC
4026 W 10th St (46222-3203)
PHONE.................................317 241-4234
Jay Straka,
EMP: 3
SQ FT: 1,000
SALES (est): 126.1K **Privately Held**
SIC: 2732 2752 2791 Book printing; pam-
phlets: printing & binding, not published
on site; commercial printing, offset; busi-
ness form & card printing, lithographic;
linotype composition, for the printing trade

(G-7762)
PRIZED POSSESSION
Also Called: Websters Tom Custom WD Turn-
ing
6606 Avalon Forest Dr (46250-2804)
PHONE.................................317 842-1498
Tom Webster, *Owner*
EMP: 3
SALES (est): 175.2K **Privately Held**
SIC: 2426 Turnings, furniture: wood

(G-7763)
PRN GRAPHICS LLC
3822 N Illinois St (46208-4017)
PHONE.................................317 426-3545
Kelly Jones, *General Mgr*
Greg Brenner, *Mng Member*
EMP: 3
SQ FT: 1,000
SALES: 130K **Privately Held**
WEB: www.prngraphics.com
SIC: 2759 Screen printing

(G-7764)
PRN INCORPORATED
9449 Priority Way West Dr (46240-6425)
PHONE.................................317 624-4401
Lawrence Sage, *Exec VP*
EMP: 2
SALES: 36.3K **Privately Held**
SIC: 2759 Screen printing

(G-7765)
PRO EPUIPMENT SERVICE
451 S Kenmore Rd (46219-7422)
PHONE.................................317 322-7858
EMP: 2
SALES (est): 140K **Privately Held**
SIC: 3535 Mfg Conveyors/Equipment

(G-7766)
PRO FOODS AMERICA INC
11971 Promontory Ct (46236-8985)
PHONE.................................317 826-8526
Edward Wooton, *Principal*
EMP: 3
SALES (est): 213.7K **Privately Held**
SIC: 2099 Food preparations

(G-7767)
PRO-KOTE INDY
8813 Robbins Rd (46268-1024)
PHONE.................................317 872-0001
John Griffin, *Owner*
Ben Griffin, *Opers Mgr*
EMP: 4
SALES (est): 464K **Privately Held**
SIC: 3399 Silver powder

(G-7768)
PROCOAT INC
920 E New York St (46202-3729)
PHONE.................................317 263-5071
Fax: 317 263-5098
Kenneth P Gootee, *President*
Penny L Gootee, *Vice Pres*
EMP: 3

SALES (est): 258.7K **Privately Held**
SIC: 3479 5091 Painting, coating & hot
dipping; sporting & recreation goods

(G-7769)
PRODUCTION PLASTIC
MOLDING
3402 W 79th St (46268-1912)
PHONE.................................317 872-4669
Fax: 317 872-1227
George A Lemcke, *President*
Suzanne Lemcke, *Vice Pres*
▲ EMP: 4
SQ FT: 1,500
SALES: 500K **Privately Held**
SIC: 3089 Injection molding of plastics

(G-7770)
PROFESSIONAL BOWLING
BALL SVC
Also Called: Flying W Trophy Div
2630 Madison Ave (46225-2180)
PHONE.................................317 786-4329
Fax: 317 786-6150
Charles Guedel, *President*
Christa Dunham, *Vice Pres*
Christopher Guedel, *Vice Pres*
Linda Guedel, *Vice Pres*
EMP: 9
SQ FT: 5,000
SALES (est): 640K **Privately Held**
SIC: 3499 3479 Trophies, metal, except
silver; engraving jewelry silverware, or
metal

(G-7771)
PROFESSIONAL GIFTING INC
6366 Guilford Ave 300 (46220-1750)
PHONE.................................317 257-3466
Ken Reinstrom, *Principal*
Danielle Esmits, *Manager*
EMP: 17
SALES (est): 2.1MM **Privately Held**
SIC: 2253 T-shirts & tops, knit

(G-7772)
PROFESSIONAL GRADE SVCS
LLC
10428 Windward Dr (46234-3667)
P.O. Box 531451 (46253-1451)
PHONE.................................317 688-8898
Damien Blain, *Principal*
EMP: 9
SALES (est): 689.9K **Privately Held**
SIC: 3646 7349 0782 Commercial indusl
& institutional electric lighting fixtures; flu-
orescent lighting fixtures, commercial;
building maintenance services; lawn &
garden services

(G-7773)
PROFIT FINDERS
INCORPORATED
Also Called: Indiana Custom Embroidery
6438 Rucker Rd (46220-4839)
PHONE.................................317 251-7792
Fax: 317 252-5741
Kris Maynard, *President*
Karla J Maynard, *Admin Sec*
EMP: 12
SQ FT: 7,500
SALES: 841.6K **Privately Held**
SIC: 2395 Embroidery products, except
schiffli machine; embroidery & art needle-
work

(G-7774)
PROFORMA PREMIER PRINTING
10252 Eastwind Ct (46256-9782)
PHONE.................................317 842-9181
Al Elskus, *President*
Lynn Elskus, *Vice Pres*
EMP: 2 EST: 2001
SALES (est): 299K **Privately Held**
SIC: 2752 Commercial printing, litho-
graphic

(G-7775)
PROGRESSIVE DESIGN
APPAREL INC
Also Called: Sugar Abd Bruno
7260 Georgetown Rd (46268-4125)
PHONE.................................317 293-5888
Fax: 317 293-5886
Challen L Powers, *President*

Stefani Merchant, *Accounts Exec*
Jasmine Moses, *Sales Staff*
Steven L Powers, *Admin Sec*
Stewart Forrest, *Graphic Designe*
EMP: 25
SQ FT: 14,000
SALES (est): 2.2MM **Privately Held**
WEB: www.pdacoolstuff.com
SIC: 3993 2395 2396 Signs & advertising specialties; embroidery & art needlework; screen printing on fabric articles

(G-7776)
PROGRESSIVE PLATING COMPANY
Also Called: Production Plating
2064 Columbia Ave (46202-1994)
PHONE..................................317 923-2413
Fax: 317 924-4969
Allen L Williamson, *President*
Betty Williamson, *Corp Secy*
David Williamson, *Vice Pres*
Allen Williamson, *Sales Executive*
EMP: 49
SQ FT: 27,000
SALES (est): 5MM **Privately Held**
WEB: www.progressiveplating.com
SIC: 3471 Electroplating of metals or formed products

(G-7777)
PROMETHIUS CONSULTING LLC
9519 Valparaiso Ct (46268-1130)
PHONE..................................317 733-2388
Denver Abernathy, *President*
Tony Valle, *Partner*
Anthony W Valle, *Principal*
Aaron Toops, *Vice Pres*
Cindy Moore, *Office Mgr*
EMP: 11
SALES: 1.4MM **Privately Held**
SIC: 3825 Network analyzers

(G-7778)
PROMEX TECHNOLOGIES LLC
Also Called: US Biopsy
7510 E 82nd St (46256-1410)
PHONE..................................317 736-0128
Sean Miller,
Deborah Beck,
John Gilligan,
Greg Haney,
Joseph Mark,
EMP: 25
SQ FT: 20,000
SALES (est): 2.8MM
SALES (corp-wide): 292.3MM **Privately Held**
WEB: www.usbiopsy.com
SIC: 3841 Surgical & medical instruments
HQ: Argon Medical Devices, Inc.
　　2600 Dallas Pkwy Ste 440
　　Frisco TX 75034
　　903 675-9321

(G-7779)
PROSCO INC
3818 Prospect St (46203-2203)
PHONE..................................317 353-2920
EMP: 7
SQ FT: 18,000
SALES (est): 1MM **Privately Held**
SIC: 5169 2899 2842 2819 Whol Chemicals/Products Mfg Chemical Preparation Mfg Polish/Sanitation Gd Mfg Indstl Inorgan Chem

(G-7780)
PROSHRED INDIANAPOLIS INC
Also Called: Kendall Enterprise
3140 N Shadeland Ave (46226-6292)
PHONE..................................317 578-3650
Ken Carite, *CEO*
EMP: 10
SALES: 300K **Privately Held**
SIC: 3589 Shredders, industrial & commercial

(G-7781)
PROSOLIA INC
6500 Tech Ctr Dr Ste 200 (46278)
PHONE..................................317 275-5794
Justin Wiseman, *Ch of Bd*
John Graves, *Business Mgr*
Brian Laughlin, *Vice Pres*

EMP: 8
SALES (est): 2MM **Privately Held**
WEB: www.prosolia.com
SIC: 3826 Analytical instruments

(G-7782)
PROSPERUS LLC
Also Called: Test Gauge & Backflow Supply
5644 S Meridian St Ste E (46217-2759)
PHONE..................................317 786-8990
James Probst,
EMP: 4
SALES (est): 400K **Privately Held**
SIC: 3824 Gauges for computing pressure temperature corrections

(G-7783)
PROTEUS SOLUTIONS LLC
2367 Black Gold Dr (46234-1279)
PHONE..................................317 222-1138
John C Hanes, *Mng Member*
Jason Christensen, *Mng Member*
Julie Christensen, *Mng Member*
Christine Hanes, *Mng Member*
EMP: 4
SALES (est): 290K **Privately Held**
SIC: 3613 Control panels, electric

(G-7784)
PRP WINE INTERNATIONAL
8310 Allison Pointe Blvd # 205
(46250-1998)
PHONE..................................317 288-0005
EMP: 2
SALES (est): 138.9K **Privately Held**
SIC: 5921 5182 2084 Wine; wine; wines

(G-7785)
PSC INDUSTRIES INC
Also Called: Glasrite Div
6790 E 32nd St (46226-6163)
PHONE..................................317 547-5439
Fax: 317 546-7315
Rick Harvey, *Plant Mgr*
EMP: 30
SALES (corp-wide): 2.2B **Privately Held**
WEB: www.olsenmedical.com
SIC: 1742 3296 2891 Plastering, drywall & insulation; mineral wool; adhesives & sealants
HQ: Psc Industries, Inc.
　　1100 W Market St
　　Louisville KY 40203
　　502 625-7700

(G-7786)
PSI GROUP INC
5071 W 74th St (46268-5112)
PHONE..................................317 297-3211
Fax: 317 297-1894
Troy Evans, *Vice Pres*
EMP: 2
SALES (est): 239.5K **Privately Held**
SIC: 3444 Mail (post office) collection or storage boxes, sheet metal

(G-7787)
PTF CABINETS & TOPS LLC
1310 W Troy Ave Ste A (46225-2252)
PHONE..................................317 786-4367
Jason Buis, *President*
Dustin Donovan, *Vice Pres*
EMP: 7
SQ FT: 40,000
SALES (est): 255.4K **Privately Held**
SIC: 2541 Table or counter tops, plastic laminated

(G-7788)
PTS SIGNS & WRAPS
1720 Orchid Ct (46219-2829)
PHONE..................................317 653-1807
Marcia Luterman, *Administration*
EMP: 2
SALES (est): 74.2K **Privately Held**
SIC: 3993 Signs & advertising specialties

(G-7789)
PUMPALARMCOM LLC
203 W Morris St (46225-1440)
PHONE..................................888 454-5051
Thomas Ward, *President*
EMP: 5
SALES (est): 644.2K **Privately Held**
SIC: 3669 Signaling apparatus, electric

(G-7790)
PURE IMAGE LASER AND SPA LLC
5222 S East St Ste B1 (46227-1983)
PHONE..................................317 306-6603
Christina Thomas, *Co-Owner*
Mechelle Castor, *Co-Owner*
EMP: 2 **EST:** 2015
SALES (est): 106K **Privately Held**
SIC: 3999 Massage machines, electric: barber & beauty shops

(G-7791)
PURSUIT DEFENSE TECHNOLOGY LLC ✪
1405 Barth Ave (46203-2702)
PHONE..................................630 687-3826
Agueda F Mayan, *Manager*
Alyn Brown, *Manager*
EMP: 4 **EST:** 2017
SALES (est): 191.6K **Privately Held**
SIC: 3674 Solid state electronic devices

(G-7792)
QFS HOLDINGS LLC
Also Called: Quality Fabricated Solutions
2457 E Washington St B (46201-4155)
PHONE..................................317 634-2543
Charley Powers, *President*
Ernest F Rathz, *Mfg Staff*
EMP: 5 **EST:** 1883
SQ FT: 30,000
SALES (est): 550K **Privately Held**
WEB: www.melaun.com
SIC: 3449 Miscellaneous metalwork

(G-7793)
QSENS EQUIPMENT SOLUTIONS LLC
7602 Dartmouth Rd (46260-3325)
PHONE..................................317 443-6167
James Terry,
EMP: 4 **EST:** 2009
SALES: 300K **Privately Held**
SIC: 3585 Refrigeration & heating equipment

(G-7794)
QTG PEPSI CO LARRY DAVI
9101 Orly Rd (46241-9605)
PHONE..................................317 830-4020
EMP: 8 **EST:** 2010
SALES (est): 725.3K **Privately Held**
SIC: 2086 Soft drinks: packaged in cans, bottles, etc.

(G-7795)
QUAKER OATS COMPANY
5858 Decatur Blvd (46241-9575)
PHONE..................................317 821-6442
John Kossos, *Safety Mgr*
David Copeland, *Human Res Dir*
Edwin Wiley, *Manager*
EMP: 20
SALES (corp-wide): 63.5B **Publicly Held**
WEB: www.quakeroats.com
SIC: 2086 Bottled & canned soft drinks
HQ: The Quaker Oats Company
　　555 W Monroe St Fl 1
　　Chicago IL 60661
　　312 821-1000

(G-7796)
QUALIDIE CORP
515 N Luett Ave (46222-3311)
PHONE..................................317 632-6845
Fax: 317 632-4297
Michael K Beasley, *President*
Tom Sterrett, *Foreman/Supr*
Cynthia A Beasley, *Admin Sec*
EMP: 11
SQ FT: 6,000
SALES (est): 1MM **Privately Held**
WEB: www.qualidie.com
SIC: 3544 Special dies & tools

(G-7797)
QUALITY IMAGINATION CORP
4405 Massachusetts Ave (46218-3142)
PHONE..................................317 753-0042
Jorge Senisse, *President*
EMP: 2
SALES (est): 185.2K **Privately Held**
SIC: 2759 Commercial printing

(G-7798)
QUALITY MCH REPR & ENGRG INC
4032 S East St (46227-1413)
P.O. Box 39231 (46239-0231)
PHONE..................................317 375-1366
Robert Laugell, *President*
Susan Laugle, *Vice Pres*
EMP: 5
SALES (est): 450.5K **Privately Held**
SIC: 3599 Machine shop, jobbing & repair

(G-7799)
QUALITY STEEL TREATING CO INC
3860 Prospect St (46203-2292)
PHONE..................................317 357-8691
Fax: 317 357-8695
Lloyd R Mattson Jr, *President*
Kevin Mattson, *Vice Pres*
Chris Palmer, *QC Mgr*
Sonja Mattson, *Treasurer*
Carol Gordy, *Controller*
EMP: 32 **EST:** 1949
SQ FT: 40,000
SALES (est): 6.8MM **Privately Held**
SIC: 3398 Metal heat treating; brazing (hardening) of metal

(G-7800)
QUALITY SYSTEMS LLC
5603 W Raymond St Ste N (46241-4356)
PHONE..................................317 326-4660
Barry Dematas, *Mng Member*
EMP: 13
SQ FT: 8,000
SALES (est): 2.4MM **Privately Held**
SIC: 3532 Feeders, ore & aggregate

(G-7801)
QUALITY TANK TRUCKS & EQP INC
3301 Moore Ave (46201-4305)
PHONE..................................317 635-0000
Robert Bray, *President*
EMP: 7
SQ FT: 1,000
SALES (est): 640K **Privately Held**
SIC: 3713 3272 Truck & bus bodies; septic tanks, concrete

(G-7802)
QUALITY TYPESETTING
5501 S East St (46227-1901)
PHONE..................................317 787-4466
Fax: 317 787-4422
Dan Turner, *Owner*
EMP: 5
SALES (est): 190K **Privately Held**
WEB: www.floridawest.com
SIC: 2791 Typesetting

(G-7803)
QUANTUMTECH LLC
5042 Brandywine Dr # 322 (46241-8612)
PHONE..................................786 512-0827
Jose Disotuar, *Owner*
EMP: 2
SALES (est): 94.6K **Privately Held**
SIC: 3572 Computer storage devices

(G-7804)
QUICK WALK SYSTEMS INC
5315 N Pennsylvania St (46220-3058)
PHONE..................................317 255-2247
Sam Rogers, *President*
EMP: 2
SALES (est): 210K **Privately Held**
SIC: 3996 Tile, floor: supported plastic

(G-7805)
QUIKRETE COMPANIES INC
3100 E 56th St (46220-3624)
PHONE..................................317 251-2281
Danny Hubbard, *Sales Executive*
John B Shank, *Office Mgr*
John Shank, *Manager*
EMP: 35 **Privately Held**
WEB: www.quikrete.com
SIC: 3272 3273 3255 1442 Building materials, except block or brick: concrete; ready-mixed concrete; clay refractories; construction sand & gravel

HQ: The Quikrete Companies Llc
5 Concourse Pkwy Ste 1900
Atlanta GA 30328
404 634-9100

(G-7806)
R & M ENTERPRISES
2908 N Routiers Ave (46219-1551)
Rural Route 2 Box 193a, Cloverdale
(46120)
PHONE...............................765 795-6395
Ron Collier, *Owner*
EMP: 3
SQ FT: 25,000
SALES (est): 147.7K **Privately Held**
SIC: 2421 Custom sawmill; kiln drying of
lumber

(G-7807)
R & S PLATING INC
2302 Bloyd Ave (46218-3527)
PHONE...............................317 925-2396
Fax: 317 925-4939
James Raymond, *President*
Joe Raymond, *President*
EMP: 9 EST: 1946
SQ FT: 5,000
SALES (est): 585.6K **Privately Held**
SIC: 3471 Plating of metals or formed
products; electroplating of metals or
formed products

(G-7808)
R C ELECTRIC
3659 W 10th St (46222-3376)
PHONE...............................317 600-3001
Earl B Walker, *Principal*
EMP: 21 EST: 2011
SALES (est): 4.3MM **Privately Held**
SIC: 3699 Electrical equipment & supplies

(G-7809)
**R FALCONE POWERSPORTS
INC**
2416 W 16th St (46222-2836)
PHONE...............................317 803-2432
Chuck Hatten, *Sales Staff*
EMP: 2
SALES (est): 71.7K **Privately Held**
SIC: 3751 Motorcycles & related parts

(G-7810)
R R DONNELLEY INC
Also Called: More Wallace
201 S Capitol Ave Ste 201 # 201
(46225-1095)
PHONE...............................317 631-2203
Mark Angelson, *President*
EMP: 10
SALES (est): 535.2K **Privately Held**
SIC: 2711 Commercial printing & newspa-
per publishing combined

(G-7811)
**RABB & HOWE CABINET TOP
CO**
2571 Winthrop Ave (46205-4464)
PHONE...............................317 926-6442
Fax: 317 926-9285
Philip C Rabb, *Partner*
Philip B Rabb, *Partner*
EMP: 12
SQ FT: 18,000
SALES: 1.5MM **Privately Held**
SIC: 2521 2599 2541 2434 Cabinets, of-
fice; wood; cabinets, factory; wood parti-
tions & fixtures; wood kitchen cabinets

(G-7812)
RACEWAY COMMONS
55 S Raceway Rd (46231-1060)
PHONE...............................303 503-4333
EMP: 2
SALES (est): 88.3K **Privately Held**
SIC: 3644 Mfg Nonconductive Wiring De-
vices

(G-7813)
RAD CUBE LLC
9449 Priority Way West Dr (46240-6425)
PHONE...............................317 456-7560
Sandeep Allam,
EMP: 15

SALES (est): 335.7K **Privately Held**
SIC: 7372 8748 Application computer software; business consulting

(G-7814)
**RADIATION PHYSICS
CONSULTING**
7022 Warwick Rd (46220-1051)
PHONE...............................317 251-0193
Thomas Schumacher, *President*
Laurie Schumacher, *Vice Pres*
EMP: 3
SALES (est): 235.5K **Privately Held**
SIC: 3845 Ultrasonic scanning devices,
medical

(G-7815)
RAM SERVICES RFRGN & MECH
5170 Atherton North Dr (46219-6904)
PHONE...............................317 679-8541
David Leach, *President*
Debra Leach, *Corp Secy*
EMP: 5
SALES (est): 240K **Privately Held**
SIC: 3585 Refrigeration & heating equip-
ment

(G-7816)
RAPPID MFG INC
8219 Indy Ct (46214-2300)
PHONE...............................317 440-8084
Tammy Powell, *Principal*
EMP: 2
SALES (est): 158.4K **Privately Held**
SIC: 3999 Manufacturing industries

(G-7817)
RAPT PEN LLC
3614 N Grant Ave (46218-1428)
PHONE...............................317 547-8113
Ja'net Edwards, *Principal*
EMP: 2
SALES (est): 67.5K **Privately Held**
SIC: 2711 Newspapers

(G-7818)
RAVEN COMMUNICATIONS INC
Also Called: Carlson Report
6939 Lantern Rd (46256-2109)
PHONE...............................317 576-9889
Fax: 317 576-0441
William R Wilburn, *President*
EMP: 2
SQ FT: 2,000
SALES (est): 156.8K **Privately Held**
WEB: www.jonesreportplus.com
SIC: 2721 Trade journals: publishing only,
not printed on site

(G-7819)
**RAYCO MCH & ENGRG GROUP
INC**
970 Western Dr (46241-1435)
PHONE...............................317 291-7848
Gregory A Cox, *President*
Angela Cox, *Vice Pres*
EMP: 21
SQ FT: 7,500
SALES: 3MM **Privately Held**
SIC: 3599 3714 3728 Air intake filters, in-
ternal combustion engine, except auto;
motor vehicle parts & accessories; aircraft
parts & equipment

(G-7820)
RAYMOND LITTLE PRINT SHOP
7800 Records St Ste C (46226-3986)
PHONE...............................317 246-9083
EMP: 2
SALES (est): 117.9K **Privately Held**
SIC: 2759 Commercial printing

(G-7821)
RAYTHEON COMPANY
6125 E 21st St (46219-2058)
PHONE...............................317 306-4872
Kevin Wood, *QA Dir*
Patrick Avery, *Engineer*
Roy Brammer, *Engineer*
Jay Friedlander, *Engineer*
Chad Godina, *Engineer*
EMP: 35

SALES (corp-wide): 25.3B **Publicly Held**
SIC: 3812 3663 3674 3721 Defense systems & equipment; radio & TV communications equipment; semiconductors &
related devices; aircraft
PA: Raytheon Company
870 Winter St
Waltham MA 02451
781 522-3000

(G-7822)
RAYTHEON COMPANY
6125 E 21st St (46219-2058)
PHONE...............................317 306-8471
Steve Casper, *CEO*
Danielle Figlio, *Business Mgr*
Steve Kaspar, *Vice Pres*
EMP: 200
SALES (corp-wide): 25.3B **Publicly Held**
WEB: www.raytheon.com
SIC: 7629 3812 Electrical equipment re-
pair services; search & navigation equip-
ment
PA: Raytheon Company
870 Winter St
Waltham MA 02451
781 522-3000

(G-7823)
RC ENTERPRISE LLC
1389 W 86th St Ste 143 (46260-2101)
PHONE...............................317 225-6747
Mark Cabbell,
Dawnrell Reece,
EMP: 2
SALES (est): 95.3K **Privately Held**
SIC: 1389 7389 Construction, repair & dis-
mantling services;

(G-7824)
READING BAKERY SYSTEMS TA
7517 Winton Dr (46268-5105)
PHONE...............................317 337-0000
◆ EMP: 11 EST: 2010
SALES (est): 1.7MM **Privately Held**
SIC: 3556 Bakery machinery

(G-7825)
**RED LINE GRAPHICS
INCORPORATED (PA)**
6430 S Belmont Ave (46217-9767)
PHONE...............................317 591-9400
EMP: 30
SQ FT: 19,000
SALES (est): 2.3MM **Privately Held**
SIC: 2752 Lithographic Commercial Print-
ing

(G-7826)
**REED IMMUNODIAGNOSTICS
LLC**
351 W 10th St (46202-4118)
PHONE...............................317 446-3582
R Aleks Davis, *Ch of Bd*
Sam Florance Jr III, *President*
Ronald Bowsher,
EMP: 3
SALES (est): 182K **Privately Held**
SIC: 3841 Diagnostic apparatus, medical

(G-7827)
REGENCY TECHNOLOGIES INC
3880 Pendleton Way # 900 (46226-7627)
P.O. Box 269010 (46226-9010)
PHONE...............................317 543-9740
▲ EMP: 8
SQ FT: 5,000
SALES: 800K **Privately Held**
SIC: 3679 Mfg Electronic Components

(G-7828)
REIBERG CERAMICS
5723 N Meridian St (46208-1563)
PHONE...............................317 283-8441
Robert Reiberg, *Principal*
EMP: 3
SALES (est): 166.7K **Privately Held**
SIC: 3269 Pottery products

(G-7829)
REILLY INDUSTRIES INC
1500 S Tibbs Ave (46241-4537)
PHONE...............................317 247-8141
Fax: 317 248-6558
Timothy Zappala, *Principal*

EMP: 3
SALES (est): 288.1K **Privately Held**
SIC: 3999 Manufacturing industries

(G-7830)
**REISS ORNA & STRUCTURALL
PDTS**
3739 N Illinois St (46208-4229)
PHONE...............................317 925-2371
Paul R Reiss, *President*
Waneta L Reiss, *Admin Sec*
EMP: 20 EST: 1886
SQ FT: 14,000
SALES (est): 4.3MM **Privately Held**
SIC: 3446 Architectural metalwork

(G-7831)
RELATIONAL GRAVITY INC
12623 Tealwood Dr (46236-8174)
PHONE...............................317 855-7685
Jeffrey D Hutson, *Principal*
EMP: 2
SALES (est): 104.4K **Privately Held**
SIC: 7372 Prepackaged software

(G-7832)
RELIANT ENGINEERING INC
1329 Sadlier Circle W Dr (46239-1055)
PHONE...............................317 322-9084
Fax: 317 322-9110
Bill Wycoff, *President*
Sharon K Wycoff, *Admin Sec*
EMP: 11
SQ FT: 4,800
SALES (est): 1.4MM **Privately Held**
SIC: 3599 Machine shop, jobbing & repair

(G-7833)
**RENAISSNCE ELECTRONIC
SVCS LLC**
Also Called: Premier Claim Services
1502 W Edgewood Ave Ste A
(46217-9293)
PHONE...............................317 786-2235
Erick J Paul, *President*
EMP: 31
SALES (est): 5.3MM **Privately Held**
SIC: 7372 Business oriented computer
software

(G-7834)
REO-USA INC
8450 E 47th St (46226-2925)
PHONE...............................317 899-1395
Frediel Twellsieca, *President*
Barbara Miller, *Vice Pres*
Rhonda Hoffman, *Purchasing*
▲ EMP: 11
SALES (est): 2.1MM **Privately Held**
WEB: www.reo-usa.com
SIC: 3677 Inductors, electronic

(G-7835)
REVERE INDUSTRIES
111 Monument Cir Ste 3200 (46204-0066)
PHONE...............................317 638-1521
Julie Campbell, *Principal*
Ryan Southwell, *Engineer*
EMP: 3
SALES (est): 209.5K **Privately Held**
SIC: 3355 Aluminum rolling & drawing

(G-7836)
RHEEM SALES COMPANY INC
1240 Brookville Way (46239-1041)
PHONE...............................479 648-4900
EMP: 5
SALES (est): 449.7K
SALES (corp-wide): 394.3MM **Privately
Held**
SIC: 3585 Refrigeration & heating equip-
ment
HQ: Rheem Manufacturing Company Inc
1100 Abernathy Rd # 1700
Atlanta GA 30328
770 351-3000

(G-7837)
RHR CORPORATION
Also Called: Direct Cnnect Prtg Dgital Svcs
930 E Hanna Ave (46227-1306)
PHONE...............................317 788-1504
Robin K Heldman, *President*
EMP: 4 EST: 1973
SQ FT: 3,600

SALES: 470K **Privately Held**
SIC: 2752 7334 2791 2789 Commercial printing, offset; photocopying & duplicating services; typesetting; bookbinding & related work

(G-7838)
RHYNE & ASSOCIATES INC
Also Called: Rhyne, R E & Company
3560 Madison Ave (46227-1352)
PHONE..................317 786-4459
Fax: 317 781-8352
Robert E Rhyne, *President*
Mary A Rhyne, *Corp Secy*
Deborah Moore, *Vice Pres*
EMP: 14 EST: 1957
SQ FT: 12,500
SALES (est): 1.1MM **Privately Held**
SIC: 7641 2392 Reupholstery; slipcovers: made of fabric, plastic etc.

(G-7839)
RICHARDSON MOLDING LLC
Engineering Division
5601 S Meridian St Ste B (46217-2738)
PHONE..................317 787-9463
George Noel, *Engineer*
EMP: 3
SALES (corp-wide): 75.2MM **Privately Held**
SIC: 3089 5211 Molding primary plastic; lumber & other building materials
PA: Richardson Molding Incorporated
2405 Norcross Dr
Columbus IN 47201
812 342-0139

(G-7840)
RICHESON CONTRACTING INC
Also Called: Richeson Cabinet
5325 Commerce Square Dr (46237-9743)
PHONE..................317 889-5995
Fax: 317 889-4191
Kimberly Richeson, *President*
Dale Richeson, *Vice Pres*
Ryan Richeson, *Project Mgr*
EMP: 30
SALES (est): 5.1MM **Privately Held**
WEB: www.richesoncabinets.com
SIC: 2599 Cabinets, factory

(G-7841)
RICKER OIL COMPANY INC
4002 S East St (46227-1413)
PHONE..................317 780-1777
Quinn Ricker, *Branch Mgr*
EMP: 34
SALES (corp-wide): 240MM **Privately Held**
SIC: 1389 Construction, repair & dismantling services
PA: Ricker Oil Company, Inc.
30 W 11th St
Anderson IN 46016
765 643-3016

(G-7842)
RICKER OIL COMPANY INC
3750 E Fall Creek Parkway (46205-3631)
PHONE..................317 920-0850
EMP: 51
SALES (corp-wide): 240MM **Privately Held**
SIC: 2051 Cakes, bakery: except frozen
PA: Ricker Oil Company, Inc.
30 W 11th St
Anderson IN 46016
765 643-3016

(G-7843)
RICS SOFTWARE INC
129 E Market St Ste 1100 (46204-3295)
PHONE..................317 455-5338
Jason Becker, *CEO*
Mark Brown, *CFO*
EMP: 35
SALES: 8MM **Privately Held**
SIC: 7372 Business oriented computer software

(G-7844)
RIEBEL ROQUE INC
Also Called: Riebel Roque Publishing Co
6027 Castlebar Cir (46220-4107)
PHONE..................317 849-3680
Richard Osborne, *President*

Josie Osborne, *Vice Pres*
EMP: 2
SALES (est): 130K **Privately Held**
SIC: 2741 Directories: publishing only, not printed on site

(G-7845)
RINKER MATERIALS
1501 S Holt Rd (46241-4107)
PHONE..................317 241-8237
R Woodrum, *Executive*
EMP: 5
SALES (est): 133.7K **Privately Held**
SIC: 3272 Concrete products

(G-7846)
RINKER MATERIALS CORP
1030 S Kitley Ave (46203-2623)
PHONE..................317 353-2118
John Kirby, *Purch Agent*
EMP: 2
SALES (est): 66K **Privately Held**
SIC: 1442 Construction sand & gravel

(G-7847)
RIVARS INC (PA)
9900 Westpoint Dr Ste 132 (46256-3338)
PHONE..................765 789-6119
Beth Slusher, *CEO*
Tara Holcomb, *Sales Dir*
Brady Bader, *Accounts Mgr*
Matt Quinn, *Manager*
Timothy Slusher,
▲ EMP: 24
SQ FT: 21,000
SALES (est): 2.3MM **Privately Held**
WEB: www.rivars.com
SIC: 2389 5699 Costumes; costumes, masquerade or theatrical

(G-7848)
RLR ASSOCIATES INC
1302 N Illinois St (46202-2321)
PHONE..................317 632-1300
Rodney Reid, *President*
EMP: 8
SQ FT: 4,000
SALES (est): 750K **Privately Held**
SIC: 7336 7389 3993 Graphic arts & related design; interior design services; signs & advertising specialties

(G-7849)
ROBERT PEREZ
Also Called: Neodyne Technologies
3945 Guion Ln Ste A (46268-2677)
PHONE..................317 291-7311
Robert Perez, *Owner*
EMP: 5 EST: 2010
SALES (est): 396.8K **Privately Held**
SIC: 3724 8711 Aircraft engines & engine parts; mechanical engineering; aviation &/or aeronautical engineering

(G-7850)
ROCHE DIABETES CARE INC
9115 Hague Rd (46256-1025)
PHONE..................317 521-2000
Debbie Waltz, *Counsel*
Tom Abkins, *Senior VP*
Ilona Torontali, *Vice Pres*
Bob Werner, *Vice Pres*
Josh Hatheway, *Research*
▲ EMP: 99
SALES (est): 71.6MM
SALES (corp-wide): 53.9B **Publicly Held**
SIC: 3841 Surgical & medical instruments
HQ: Roche Holdings, Inc.
1 Dna Way
South San Francisco CA 94080

(G-7851)
ROCHE DIAGNOSTICS CORPORATION (DH)
9115 Hague Rd (46256-1045)
P.O. Box 50457 (46250-0457)
PHONE..................800 428-5076
Fax: 317 521-2090
Jack Phillips, *CEO*
Marco Tiberi, *General Mgr*
Christine Blinco, *Business Mgr*
Henry Bennett, *Vice Pres*
Steve A Oldham, *Vice Pres*
◆ EMP: 1000 EST: 1998
SQ FT: 700,000

SALES (est): 1.5B
SALES (corp-wide): 53.9B **Publicly Held**
WEB: www.roche.com
SIC: 2835 In vitro & in vivo diagnostic substances

(G-7852)
ROCHE DIAGNOSTICS CORPORATION
Also Called: Roche Applied Sciences
7988 Centerpoint Dr (46256-3377)
PHONE..................317 521-2000
Ronni Bertelsen, *Accounts Mgr*
Ben Molter, *Branch Mgr*
Tim Juergens, *Manager*
Carol Darling, *Consultant*
Diana Ivanova, *Director*
EMP: 9
SALES (corp-wide): 53.9B **Publicly Held**
SIC: 3826 Analytical instruments
HQ: Roche Diagnostics Corporation
9115 Hague Rd
Indianapolis IN 46256
800 428-5076

(G-7853)
ROCHE HEALTH SOLUTIONS INC
9115 Hague Rd (46256-1025)
PHONE..................317 570-5100
David Barnes, *Vice Pres*
EMP: 180
SQ FT: 30,000
SALES (est): 29.7MM
SALES (corp-wide): 53.9B **Publicly Held**
WEB: www.disetronicusa.com
SIC: 5047 5999 3841 Medical equipment & supplies; medical apparatus & supplies; surgical & medical instruments
HQ: Roche Holdings, Inc.
1 Dna Way
South San Francisco CA 94080

(G-7854)
ROCORE THERMAL SYSTEMS LLC (PA)
2401 Directors Row Ste R (46241-4907)
PHONE..................317 227-2929
Fax: 317 227-2939
Travis Nichols, *Vice Pres*
Lonnie Fultz, *Technology*
Dave Rollings, *Technology*
Stuart Eden,
EMP: 20
SQ FT: 4,100
SALES (est): 12.9MM **Privately Held**
SIC: 3714 Motor vehicle parts & accessories

(G-7855)
ROI MARKETING COMPANY
5868 W 71st St 101 (46278-1730)
P.O. Box 78092 (46278-0092)
PHONE..................317 644-0797
Adell Means, *President*
EMP: 3
SALES (est): 410.4K **Privately Held**
SIC: 7389 8742 5946 3089 Advertising, promotional & trade show services; marketing consulting services; camera & photographic supply stores; identification cards, plastic; business form paper; security systems services

(G-7856)
ROLL COATER INC
9908 Blue Ridge Way (46234-5045)
PHONE..................317 652-1102
Jennifer Radwin, *Principal*
EMP: 3
SALES (est): 147.4K **Privately Held**
SIC: 3471 Plating & polishing

(G-7857)
ROLLS-ROYCE CORPORATION
2840 Fortune Cir W (46241-5505)
PHONE..................317 437-9326
Jim Tilton, *Manager*
EMP: 4000
SALES (corp-wide): 21.5B **Privately Held**
SIC: 3724 Aircraft engines & engine parts
HQ: Rolls-Royce Corporation
450 S Meridian St
Indianapolis IN 46225

(G-7858)
ROLLS-ROYCE CORPORATION (DH)
450 S Meridian St (46225-1103)
P.O. Box 420 (46206-0420)
PHONE..................317 230-2000
Fax: 317 230-4020
Warren East Cbe, *CEO*
Tom Bell, *President*
Chris Cholerton, *President*
Daniel Longbottom, *President*
Andy Draine, *General Mgr*
▲ EMP: 4000
SQ FT: 2,700,000
SALES (est): 1.9B
SALES (corp-wide): 21.5B **Privately Held**
SIC: 3724 3443 3462 3731 Aircraft engines & engine parts; industrial vessels, tanks & containers; nuclear power plant forgings, ferrous; submarines, building & repairing; railroad locomotives & parts, electric or nonelectric; yachts, building & repairing
HQ: Rolls-Royce North America Holdings Inc.
1875 Explorer St Ste 200
Reston VA 20190
703 834-1700

(G-7859)
ROMCULINARY LLC
1933 N Talbott St (46202-1533)
PHONE..................630 235-3338
Steven Romweber, *Mng Member*
EMP: 3
SALES (est): 174.7K **Privately Held**
SIC: 3556 Food products machinery

(G-7860)
RONLEWHORN INDUSTRIES LLC
4226 Sunset Ave (46208-3766)
PHONE..................765 661-9343
Aaron Scamihorn, *Principal*
EMP: 2
SALES (est): 84.2K **Privately Held**
SIC: 3999 Manufacturing industries

(G-7861)
ROOFING & INSULATION SUP INC
6555 E 30th St Ste D2 (46219-1187)
PHONE..................317 547-4373
Sprague Mullikin, *President*
EMP: 2
SALES: 1MM **Privately Held**
SIC: 3272 Concrete stuctural support & building material

(G-7862)
ROSE ENGINEERING CO INC
1105 Martin St (46227-3198)
PHONE..................317 788-4446
Fax: 317 781-9219
David Howard, *President*
Charles N Howard, *Vice Pres*
EMP: 9
SQ FT: 10,000
SALES (est): 638K **Privately Held**
SIC: 3599 3452 Machine shop, jobbing & repair; lock washers

(G-7863)
ROSS-GAGE INC (PA)
8502 Brookville Rd (46239-9427)
P.O. Box 8 (46206-0008)
PHONE..................317 283-2323
Fax: 317 931-2108
Thomas W Ross, *President*
Bill Main, *Vice Pres*
Paco Fernandez, *Shareholder*
▼ EMP: 70
SALES (est): 13.2MM **Privately Held**
WEB: www.rossgage.com
SIC: 2675 Die-cut paper & board

(G-7864)
ROUND TOWN BREWERY LLC
950 S White River Pkwy W (46204)
PHONE..................317 657-6397
Mackenzie Schenk, *CEO*
Jerry Sutherlin, *Vice Pres*
David Castor, *Bd of Directors*
Keith Reilly, *Bd of Directors*
Mitchell Schenk, *Bd of Directors*

▲ = Import ▼=Export
◆ =Import/Export

EMP: 2
SQ FT: 12,000
SALES (est): 109.9K **Privately Held**
SIC: 2082 Beer (alcoholic beverage)

(G-7865)
ROYAL FOOD PRODUCTS INC
7001 Hawthorn Park Dr A (46220-3912)
PHONE..............................317 782-2660
James Heidt, *President*
John J Heidt, *Chairman*
Joe Mc Carthy, *Corp Secy*
Doug Carns, *VP Sales*
EMP: 55
SQ FT: 84,000
SALES (est): 11.5MM **Privately Held**
WEB: www.royalfp.com
SIC: 2035 2026 Seasonings & sauces, ex-
cept tomato & dry; mayonnaise; cream,
sour

(G-7866)
ROYAL PIN LEISURE CTR
6441 W Washington St (46241-3024)
PHONE..............................317 247-4426
Fax: 317 248-8008
J B West, *Principal*
Howard Majors, *Human Res Dir*
Taylor Comeau, *Mktg Dir*
EMP: 2
SALES (est): 110K **Privately Held**
SIC: 3949 5812 5945 Bowling pins; pizza
restaurants; toys & games

(G-7867)
ROYAL SPA CORPORATION (PA)
Also Called: Royal Spa Manufacturing
2041 W Epler Ave (46217-9695)
PHONE..............................317 781-0828
Fax: 317 781-1115
Richard Bartlett, *President*
Robert Dapper, *Vice Pres*
▲ EMP: 70
SQ FT: 78,000
SALES (est): 13.1MM **Privately Held**
SIC: 3088 3949 3634 Plastics plumbing
fixtures; bathroom fixtures, plastic; hot
tubs, plastic or fiberglass; tubs (bath,
shower & laundry), plastic; sporting & ath-
letic goods; electric housewares & fans

(G-7868)
RPI CONSULTANTS LLC
Also Called: Imaj Data Company
5666 Winthrop Ave (46220-3265)
PHONE..............................317 803-7431
Greg Pollard,
EMP: 19
SALES (corp-wide): 5.8MM **Privately
Held**
SIC: 3695 Computer software tape &
disks; blank, rigid & floppy
PA: Rpi Consultants, Llc
101 N Haven St Ste 201
Baltimore MD 21224
410 276-6090

(G-7869)
RRC CORPORATION
Also Called: King's Copies
1002 E Garfield Dr (46203-4216)
PHONE..............................317 687-8325
Robert Cosby, *President*
EMP: 12
SALES: 168K **Privately Held**
SIC: 7334 2752 2791 Photocopying & du-
plicating services; commercial printing,
offset; typesetting

(G-7870)
**RST CUSTOM WOODWORKING
LL**
1015 E 42nd St (46205-2001)
PHONE..............................317 602-2490
EMP: 2
SALES (est): 85.2K **Privately Held**
SIC: 2431 Millwork

(G-7871)
RUBENSTEIN LLC
Also Called: Edibleindy
7982 Fishback Rd (46278-9717)
PHONE..............................317 946-2752
Jeff Rubenstein,
EMP: 5

SALES: 62K **Privately Held**
SIC: 2759 7389 Magazines: printing;

(G-7872)
RUBICON FOODS LLC
7320 E 86th St Ste 400 (46256-1250)
PHONE..............................317 826-8793
Steve Hockemeyer,
EMP: 10 EST: 2006
SALES (est): 898K **Privately Held**
SIC: 2013 Sausages & other prepared
meats

(G-7873)
RUSSEL WARFIELD INC
1132 Rosner Dr (46224-6946)
PHONE..............................317 243-7650
EMP: 2
SALES (est): 110K **Privately Held**
SIC: 2731 Books-Publishing/Printing

(G-7874)
RUSSELLS TUBE FORMING INC
220 Gasoline Aly (46222-3909)
PHONE..............................317 241-4072
Fax: 317 241-5382
John Russell, *President*
Nancy Russell, *Corp Secy*
Tim Russell, *Vice Pres*
EMP: 20 EST: 1971
SQ FT: 17,500
SALES (est): 4.7MM **Privately Held**
WEB: www.russellstubeforming.com
SIC: 3498 Tube fabricating (contract bend-
ing & shaping)

(G-7875)
RUSTIC GLOW CANDLE CO LLC
7605 Indian Lake Rd (46236-9520)
PHONE..............................317 696-4264
Brandyn Allen Hall, *President*
EMP: 2
SALES (est): 67K **Privately Held**
SIC: 3999 Candles

(G-7876)
RX HELP CENTERS LLC
3905 Vincennes Rd Ste 200 (46268-3039)
P.O. Box 34555 (46234-0555)
PHONE..............................866 478-9593
Jeffery Paul Christensen, *CEO*
William Lee Stafford, *President*
EMP: 2
SALES (est): 86.6K **Privately Held**
SIC: 3841 Surgical & medical instruments

(G-7877)
S & R WELDING INC
113 Pennsylvania Ct (46225-2327)
PHONE..............................317 710-0360
Fax: 317 786-9325
Steve Rusomaroff, *President*
Terry Rusomaroff, *Admin Sec*
EMP: 3
SQ FT: 1,500
SALES: 100K **Privately Held**
SIC: 3052 7699 Rubber hose; rubber
product repair

(G-7878)
S C PRYOR INC
Also Called: Pryor Safe & Lock
5424 Brookville Rd (46219-7103)
PHONE..............................317 352-1281
Fax: 317 352-1213
Stanley C Pryor, *President*
Mary Pryor, *Vice Pres*
▲ EMP: 26
SQ FT: 1,500
SALES (est): 4.8MM **Privately Held**
WEB: www.pryorco.com
SIC: 5044 5099 1799 7699 Vaults &
safes; locks & lock sets; safe or vault in-
stallation; lock & key services; fire- or bur-
glary-resistive products; manufactured
hardware (general)

(G-7879)
S CJ INCORPORATED
2021 W Raymond St (46221-2013)
PHONE..............................317 822-3477
Fax: 317 822-3479
Cathy Houston, *Owner*
EMP: 11 EST: 2008
SALES (est): 1.6MM **Privately Held**
SIC: 3713 Dump truck bodies

(G-7880)
S S M INC
Also Called: Unit Step
4000 Southeastern Ave (46203-1563)
PHONE..............................317 357-4552
Fax: 317 352-0561
James W Marten, *President*
◆ EMP: 5
SQ FT: 12,000
SALES (est): 475K **Privately Held**
WEB: www.mss.com
SIC: 3446 3272 Architectural metalwork;
concrete products, precast

(G-7881)
S T PRAXAIR TECHNOLOGY INC
1500 Polco St (46222-3274)
PHONE..............................317 240-2500
EMP: 5
SALES (est): 357.4K
SALES (corp-wide): 11.4B **Publicly Held**
SIC: 3479 3548 Painting, coating & hot
dipping; electric welding equipment
PA: Praxair, Inc.
10 Riverview Dr
Danbury CT 06810
203 837-2000

(G-7882)
S W INDUSTRIES INC
2024 Bluff Rd (46225-1996)
P.O. Box 1944 (46206-1944)
PHONE..............................317 788-4221
Fax: 317 788-4224
EMP: 15
SQ FT: 14,000
SALES (est): 3.5MM **Privately Held**
SIC: 5093 3341 3312 Whol Scrap/Waste
Mat Secndry Nonfrs Mtl Prdcr Blast Fur-
nace-Steel Work

(G-7883)
SAC ACQUISITION LLC
8702 Keystone Xing # 165 (46240-7621)
PHONE..............................317 575-1795
Emily Valencia, *Branch Mgr*
EMP: 2
SALES (corp-wide): 131.5MM **Privately
Held**
SIC: 5021 2499 5023 Furniture; decora-
tive wood & woodwork; decorative home
furnishings & supplies
PA: Sac Acquisition Llc
2 Landmark Sq Ste 300
Stamford CT 06901
888 636-1223

(G-7884)
SAFETY VEHICLE EMBLEM INC
5235 Commerce Cir (46237-9747)
PHONE..............................317 885-7565
Fax: 317 885-7574
Shelley Warrick, *President*
Lynnette Deogracias, *Principal*
Rhonda Chatfield, *Corp Secy*
EMP: 15
SQ FT: 6,000
SALES (est): 1.1MM **Privately Held**
WEB: www.safetyvehicle.com
SIC: 3993 2396 2395 Signs, not made in
custom sign painting shops; automotive &
apparel trimmings; pleating & stitching

(G-7885)
**SAFRAN NCLLES SVCS
AMRICAS LLC**
725 S Girls School Rd (46231-1131)
PHONE..............................317 789-8188
Michael Robinson, *Mng Member*
EMP: 12 EST: 2014
SQ FT: 18,234
SALES: 1.6MM
SALES (corp-wide): 650.9MM **Privately
Held**
SIC: 3728 Nacelles, aircraft
PA: Safran
2 Bd Du General Martial Valin
Paris 75015
140 608-080

(G-7886)
SAGAMORE READY-MIX LLC
4550 S Harding St (46217-9552)
PHONE..............................317 783-3768
EMP: 88

SALES (corp-wide): 32.5MM **Privately
Held**
SIC: 3273 Ready-mixed concrete
PA: Sagamore Ready-Mix, Llc
9170 E 131st St
Fishers IN 46038
317 570-6201

(G-7887)
**SAHASRA TECHNOLOGIES
CORP (PA)**
Also Called: Stlogics
9449 Priority Way West Dr (46240-6425)
PHONE..............................317 845-5326
Priya Prasad, *CEO*
Brad Robbins, *Director*
EMP: 50
SQ FT: 2,300
SALES (est): 800K **Privately Held**
WEB: www.esahasra.com
SIC: 7371 7372 Computer software devel-
opment; custom computer programming
services; publishers' computer software

(G-7888)
SALDANA RACING TANKS INC
Also Called: Saldana Racing Products
3754 N Raceway Rd (46234-9225)
PHONE..............................317 852-4193
Fax: 317 852-0158
Keith Wagoner, *President*
▼ EMP: 14
SQ FT: 11,000
SALES (est): 2.5MM **Privately Held**
WEB: www.saldanaracingproducts.com
SIC: 3714 Radiators & radiator shells &
cores, motor vehicle; fuel systems &
parts, motor vehicle

(G-7889)
**SAMS TECHNICAL PUBLISHING
LLC**
9850 E 30th St (46229-3608)
PHONE..............................317 396-9850
Scott Weaver,
Richard White,
EMP: 15
SALES (est): 1MM **Privately Held**
SIC: 2741 Technical manual & paper pub-
lishing

(G-7890)
SANBAR OF INDIANA INC
Also Called: Hoover Sheet Metal
1721 S Franklin Rd # 100 (46239-2170)
PHONE..............................317 375-6220
John W Kraus, *President*
Allen Heyd, *Vice Pres*
Michael M Kraus, *Treasurer*
Sandra K Kraus, *Admin Sec*
EMP: 4 EST: 1958
SQ FT: 4,750
SALES (est): 57.7K **Privately Held**
WEB: www.hoversheetmetal.com
SIC: 3444 3441 Sheet metalwork; fabri-
cated structural metal

(G-7891)
**SANBORN SOFTWARE
SYSTEMS LLC**
402 E 43rd St (46205-1706)
PHONE..............................317 283-7735
Robert C Sanborn, *Partner*
EMP: 2
SALES (est): 68.4K **Privately Held**
SIC: 7372 Prepackaged software

(G-7892)
SANDPAPER AMERICA INC
1728 E New York St (46201-3025)
PHONE..............................317 631-7263
Fax: 317 631-7266
Earl Powers, *President*
Lawrence Powers, *Corp Secy*
▲ EMP: 9
SQ FT: 9,000
SALES (est): 1.3MM **Privately Held**
WEB: www.sandpaperamerica.com
SIC: 3291 Sandpaper

(G-7893)
SANDRA RICE NOODLE
10625 Pendleton Pike A11 (46236-3098)
PHONE..............................317 823-8323
Sandra Noodle, *Principal*

EMP: 8 **EST:** 2007
SALES (est): 534.5K **Privately Held**
SIC: 2098 Noodles (e.g. egg, plain & water), dry

(G-7894)
SANOFI US SERVICES INC
5225 W 81st St (46268-1643)
PHONE..................................317 228-5750
David Groth, *Manager*
EMP: 25
SALES (corp-wide): 609.6MM **Privately Held**
WEB: www.aventispharma-us.com
SIC: 2834 Pharmaceutical preparations
HQ: Sanofi Us Services Inc.
  55 Corporate Dr
  Bridgewater NJ 08807
  336 407-4994

(G-7895)
SANTAROSSA MOSAIC TILE CO INC (PA)
2707 Roosevelt Ave (46218-3646)
P.O. Box 18181 (46218-0181)
PHONE..................................317 632-9494
Ketchum Todd, *President*
David M Santarossa, *President*
Santarossa John, *Corp Secy*
▲ **EMP:** 200 **EST:** 1924
SQ FT: 24,000
SALES (est): 28.7MM **Privately Held**
WEB: www.santarossa.com
SIC: 1743 5023 1752 3251 Terrazzo work; mosaic work; tile installation, ceramic; marble installation, interior; carpets; floor laying & floor work; wood floor installation & refinishing; carpet laying; linoleum installation; flooring brick, clay; flooring contractor; flooring, hardwood

(G-7896)
SATCO INC
4221 S High School Rd (46241-6452)
PHONE..................................317 856-0301
Fax: 317 856-2803
Robert Duvall, *Manager*
EMP: 23
SALES (corp-wide): 62.7MM **Privately Held**
WEB: www.satco-inc.com
SIC: 2448 Cargo containers, wood & metal combination
PA: Satco, Inc.
  1601 E El Segundo Blvd
  El Segundo CA 90245
  310 322-4719

(G-7897)
SATELLITE OASIS
8464 Brookville Rd (46239-9491)
PHONE..................................317 375-1097
▲ **EMP:** 2
SALES (est): 146.4K **Privately Held**
SIC: 3663 Space satellite communications equipment

(G-7898)
SATURDAY EVENING POST SOC INC
Also Called: Childrens Better Health Inst
1100 Waterway Blvd (46202-2174)
PHONE..................................317 634-1100
Fax: 317 637-4630
Joan Servaas, *President*
Robert Silvers, *Treasurer*
Dwight Lamb, *Manager*
EMP: 53
SQ FT: 32,000
SALES: 6.9MM **Privately Held**
WEB: www.cbhi.org
SIC: 2721 Magazines: publishing only, not printed on site

(G-7899)
SB FINISHING
6844 Hawthorn Park Dr (46220-3909)
PHONE..................................317 598-0965
Anita Hays, *Principal*
EMP: 2 **EST:** 2008
SALES (est): 151.5K **Privately Held**
SIC: 3949 Playground equipment

(G-7900)
SCALABLE PRESS ✪
7800 Records St (46226-3984)
PHONE..................................510 396-5226
EMP: 2 **EST:** 2017
SALES (est): 107.2K **Privately Held**
SIC: 2741 Miscellaneous publishing

(G-7901)
SCALE COMPUTING INC (PA)
525 S Meridian St (46225-1108)
PHONE..................................317 856-9959
Fax: 317 534-3040
Jeff Ready, *President*
Ehren Maedge, *COO*
Clint McVey, *Senior VP*
Dave Demlow, *Vice Pres*
Peter Fuller, *Vice Pres*
EMP: 25
SALES: 10MM **Privately Held**
SIC: 3572 Computer storage devices

(G-7902)
SCHAEFER TECHNOLOGIES INC
4901 W Raymond St (46241-4733)
PHONE..................................317 241-9444
Fax: 317 546-4096
Steven J Schaefer, *CEO*
Kevin Schaefer, *President*
Ronald Silvers, *General Mgr*
Bob Huser, *Engineer*
Scott Rizzi, *Engineer*
EMP: 85
SQ FT: 60,000
SALES (est): 18.3MM **Privately Held**
WEB: www.schaefer-technologies.com
SIC: 3599 Machine shop, jobbing & repair

(G-7903)
SCHOUTEN METAL CRAFT INC
2211 E 44th St (46205-2204)
PHONE..................................317 546-2639
Ron Schouten, *President*
EMP: 6
SQ FT: 4,300
SALES: 475K **Privately Held**
WEB: www.schoutenmetalcraft.com
SIC: 3446 Ornamental metalwork

(G-7904)
SCHWARZ PARTNERS LP (PA)
3600 Woodview Trce # 300 (46268-3123)
PHONE..................................317 290-1140
Jack Schwarz, *Partner*
Gaye H Schwarz, *Partner*
Jeff Schwarz, *Partner*
John Schwarz, *Partner*
Stephanie Blackman, *Vice Pres*
EMP: 35
SQ FT: 6,000
SALES (est): 702.7MM **Privately Held**
SIC: 2679 Paper products, converted

(G-7905)
SCOTT BILLMAN
5411 Maplewood Dr (46224-3329)
PHONE..................................317 293-9921
Scott Billman, *Owner*
EMP: 2
SALES (est): 131.8K **Privately Held**
SIC: 3577 Computer peripheral equipment

(G-7906)
SCREENPRINT SPECIAL TEES LLC
4353 W 96th St Ste 200 (46268-1439)
PHONE..................................317 396-0349
Jaime Bennette,
EMP: 4
SALES (est): 398K **Privately Held**
SIC: 2759 Screen printing

(G-7907)
SEARLE EXHIBIT TECH INC
3500 E 20th St Ste 3 (46218-4477)
PHONE..................................317 787-3012
EMP: 10
SQ FT: 7,500
SALES (est): 720K **Privately Held**
SIC: 3999 Mfg Misc Products

(G-7908)
SELECO INC
8427 Zionsville Rd (46268-1525)
P.O. Box 68809 (46268-0809)
PHONE..................................317 872-4148
Blair Vandivier, *President*
Paul Kaupisch, *Opers Mgr*
EMP: 25
SQ FT: 15,000
SALES (est): 2.7MM **Privately Held**
WEB: www.seleco.com
SIC: 3471 Plating of metals or formed products

(G-7909)
SELF CARE LLC
4816 Bridgefield Dr (46254-5802)
PHONE..................................317 295-8279
Carol Lamb,
Thomas Lamb,
EMP: 2
SALES (est): 120.3K **Privately Held**
SIC: 3931 Musical instruments

(G-7910)
SEND A SCENT ARROW CO INC
4257 Wedgewood Ct (46254-3411)
PHONE..................................317 297-5232
Robert K Lyon, *President*
Deanna Lyon, *Corp Secy*
EMP: 8
SALES (est): 620K **Privately Held**
SIC: 3949 Arrows, archery

(G-7911)
SENTECH CORPORATION
8358 Masters Rd (46250-1538)
PHONE..................................317 596-1988
Jerry W Spore, *CEO*
Jerry R Coonrod, *President*
Joel R Eder, *General Mgr*
EMP: 8
SQ FT: 10,000
SALES (est): 1.7MM **Privately Held**
WEB: www.sentechcorp.com
SIC: 3826 Gas testing apparatus

(G-7912)
SENTINEL ALARM SYSTEMS INC
7520 E 88th Pl (46256-1253)
PHONE..................................317 842-6482
Bruce W Chandler, *President*
EMP: 10
SQ FT: 7,800
SALES (est): 960K **Privately Held**
WEB: www.sentinelalarm.net
SIC: 3699 Security devices

(G-7913)
SERMATECH INTL CANADA CORP
1500 Polco St (46222-3274)
PHONE..................................317 240-2500
George Bradley, *President*
EMP: 4 **EST:** 2014
SALES (est): 357.4K
SALES (corp-wide): 11.4B **Publicly Held**
SIC: 3479 Coating of metals & formed products
HQ: Praxair Surface Technologies, Inc.
  1500 Polco St
  Indianapolis IN 46222
  317 240-2500

(G-7914)
SERVAAS INC (PA)
1100 Waterway Blvd (46202-2156)
PHONE..................................317 633-2020
Amy Servaas, *President*
Joan S Durham, *Admin Sec*
EMP: 6
SQ FT: 3,500
SALES (est): 823.7K **Privately Held**
WEB: www.curtislicensing.com
SIC: 3462 3069 2842 2721 Iron & steel forgings; rubber automotive products; specialty cleaning, polishes & sanitation goods; magazines: publishing only, not printed on site

(G-7915)
SERVAAS LABORATORIES INC
Also Called: Bar Keepers Friend
5240 Walt Pl (46254-5795)
PHONE..................................317 636-7760

Fax: 317 264-2192
Paul Servaas, *President*
Tony Patterson, *Vice Pres*
Matthew Selig, *CFO*
Christina Dietz, *Controller*
Amy Reismeyer, *Admin Sec*
▲ **EMP:** 50 **EST:** 1957
SALES (est): 19.1MM **Privately Held**
WEB: www.barkeepersfriend.com
SIC: 2842 Cleaning or polishing preparations

(G-7916)
SERVER PARTNERS LLC
101 E Michigan St (46204-1505)
P.O. Box 29234 (46229-0234)
PHONE..................................317 917-2000
Kim J Brand, *Manager*
EMP: 8
SALES (est): 58.6K **Privately Held**
SIC: 3575 Computer terminals

(G-7917)
SERVICE GRAPHICS INC
Also Called: S G I
8350 Allison Ave (46268-1660)
PHONE..................................317 471-8246
Michael P Burks, *President*
Jack Burns, *President*
Bernie Weitekamp, *Corp Secy*
Forrest Adam, *COO*
Wendy Prescott, *Vice Pres*
EMP: 65
SQ FT: 200,000
SALES (est): 8.6MM **Privately Held**
WEB: www.sgi-net.com
SIC: 7389 7334 7331 2752 Packaging & labeling services; multilithing; mailing service; lithographing on metal; bookbinding & related work; commercial printing

(G-7918)
SEW UNIQUE INC
9054 Sweet Bay Ct (46260-1554)
PHONE..................................317 257-0503
Judy Himelstein, *President*
EMP: 3
SQ FT: 800
SALES: 24.4K **Privately Held**
SIC: 2395 Emblems, embroidered; decorative & novelty stitching, for the trade

(G-7919)
SHACKELFORD GRAPHICS
5640 S Meridian St Ste C (46217-2761)
PHONE..................................317 783-3582
Paul J Shackelford, *Owner*
EMP: 2
SALES (est): 300K **Privately Held**
SIC: 2752 Commercial printing, offset

(G-7920)
SHADE BY DESIGN INC
10501 E Washington St (46229-2609)
PHONE..................................317 602-3513
Kevin Drake, *President*
Larry Marietta, *Principal*
EMP: 7
SQ FT: 6,600
SALES: 600K **Privately Held**
SIC: 2394 1799 Canvas awnings & canopies; awning installation

(G-7921)
SHADOW CUSTOM GRAPHICS
4703 W Vermont St (46222-3258)
PHONE..................................317 481-9710
Fax: 317 481-9711
Daren Merkle, *Owner*
Jason Burgess, *Manager*
EMP: 4
SALES (est): 302.9K **Privately Held**
WEB: www.shadowgraphix.com
SIC: 2759 Commercial printing

(G-7922)
SHADOW GRAPHIX INC
4703 W Vermont St (46222-3258)
PHONE..................................317 481-9710
Daren Merkle, *President*
Keith Wethington, *Prdtn Mgr*
EMP: 7
SQ FT: 6,400

SALES (est): 742.1K **Privately Held**
SIC: **7373** 2759 7336 Computer-aided manufacturing (CAM) systems service; wrappers: printing; decals: printing; commercial art & illustration

(G-7923)
SHARPEN TECHNOLOGIES INC
211 N Penn St Ste 400 (46204-1969)
P.O. Box 55526 (46205-0526)
PHONE..............................855 249-3357
Cameron Weeks, *CEO*
Seth Daniels, *Opers Staff*
Bracken Fields, *CFO*
Ryan Wharton, *Manager*
Jon Sparks, *Technology*
EMP: 62 EST: 2011
SALES (est): 8MM **Privately Held**
SIC: **7372** Prepackaged software

(G-7924)
SHE LETTERED
555 Pine Dr (46260-1452)
PHONE..............................317 844-4555
EMP: 2
SALES (est): 92K **Privately Held**
SIC: **2253** Knit Outerwear Mill

(G-7925)
SHEET METAL MODELS INC
Also Called: Sheet Metal Models/Machine TI
2702 National Ave (46227-3531)
PHONE..............................317 783-1303
Fax: 317 783-1388
Joseph A Gilliland, *President*
EMP: 15 EST: 1959
SQ FT: 12,500
SALES (est): 2.5MM **Privately Held**
WEB: www.shtmod.com
SIC: **3444** Sheet metal specialties, not stamped

(G-7926)
SHEET MTL WKRS LOCAL NO 20
2828 E 45th St Ste A (46205-2403)
PHONE..............................317 541-0050
Michael D Patrick, *Principal*
Joseph Potesta, *Programmer Anys*
EMP: 12
SALES: 3MM **Privately Held**
SIC: **3444** Sheet metalwork

(G-7927)
SHEETS LLC
3600 Woodview Trce # 300 (46268-3123)
PHONE..............................317 290-1140
Jack Schwarx,
EMP: 5
SQ FT: 12,000
SALES (est): 3.7MM **Privately Held**
SIC: **2679** Corrugated paper: made from purchased material

(G-7928)
SHELBY ENGINEERING CO INC
2233 S West St (46225-2063)
P.O. Box 1544 (46206-1544)
PHONE..............................317 784-1135
Fax: 317 780-1846
George F Hilgemeier Jr, *President*
EMP: 42
SQ FT: 20,000
SALES: 1.8MM **Privately Held**
SIC: **3523** Harvesters, fruit, vegetable, tobacco, etc.

(G-7929)
SHELBY GRAVEL INC
2701 S Emerson Ave (46203-4822)
PHONE..............................317 784-6678
Fax: 317 782-4292
Parker Haehl, *Project Mgr*
John D Haehl Sr, *Branch Mgr*
EMP: 21
SALES (corp-wide): 55.5MM **Privately Held**
SIC: **3273** Ready-mixed concrete
PA: Shelby Gravel, Inc
157 E Rampart St
Shelbyville IN 46176
317 398-4485

(G-7930)
SHELBY GRAVEL INC
Also Called: Shelby Materials
10770 E County Road 300 N (46234-9415)
PHONE..............................317 216-7556
Randy Sperry, *Branch Mgr*
EMP: 12
SALES (corp-wide): 55.5MM **Privately Held**
SIC: **5084** 5211 3273 Materials handling machinery; cement; ready-mixed concrete
PA: Shelby Gravel, Inc
157 E Rampart St
Shelbyville IN 46176
317 398-4485

(G-7931)
SHELBY WESTSIDE UPHOLSTERING
Also Called: Shelby Upholstering Interiors
3136 W 16th St (46222-2781)
PHONE..............................317 631-8911
Fax: 317 631-7626
Donald R Quass, *President*
Betty Quass, *Corp Secy*
Donald P Quass, *Controller*
EMP: 7
SQ FT: 4,800
SALES (est): 666.8K **Privately Held**
WEB: www.shelbyupholstering.com
SIC: **7641** 5713 5714 2512 Reupholstery; carpets; draperies; living room furniture: upholstered on wood frames

(G-7932)
SHEPHERD DISTRIBUTING
2154 S Lynhurst Dr (46241-4716)
PHONE..............................317 991-3877
Reva J Shepherd Capalla, *President*
EMP: 6
SALES (est): 88.8K **Privately Held**
SIC: **5149** 5099 2086 Beverages, except coffee & tea; durable goods; bottled & canned soft drinks

(G-7933)
SHIMP OPTICAL CORP
Also Called: V J Shimp Optical
932 S Meridian St Ste 101 (46225-1307)
PHONE..............................317 636-4448
Fax: 317 638-6032
Michael Shimp, *President*
Diane Shimp, *Vice Pres*
EMP: 2
SALES: 500K **Privately Held**
SIC: **3995** 3851 Eyeglasses, prescription; lens grinding, except prescription: ophthalmic

(G-7934)
SHIRLEY ENGRAVING CO INC
4026 W 10th St (46222-3203)
PHONE..............................317 634-4084
Fax: 317 685-2524
Donald J Margason Jr, *President*
Teri Margason, *Treasurer*
EMP: 10 EST: 1965
SQ FT: 20,000
SALES: 1MM **Privately Held**
WEB: www.shirleyengraving.com
SIC: **2759** 2796 2791 2752 Engraving; thermography; platemaking services; typesetting; commercial printing, lithographic; die-cut paper & board

(G-7935)
SHIRTS N THINGS S N T GRAPHICS
Also Called: Snt Graphics
1115 Country Club Rd (46234-1816)
PHONE..............................317 271-3515
Fax: 317 271-7895
Jane Butler, *Owner*
EMP: 5
SQ FT: 4,300
SALES: 400K **Privately Held**
WEB: www.sntgraphics.com
SIC: **5699** 2396 2395 Sports apparel; screen printing on fabric articles; embroidery & art needlework

(G-7936)
SIEMENS ENERGY INC
201 S Capitol Ave A (46225-1000)
PHONE..............................317 677-1340

EMP: 37
SALES (corp-wide): 97.7B **Privately Held**
SIC: **3511** Gas turbine generator set units, complete
HQ: Siemens Energy, Inc.
4400 N Alafaya Trl
Orlando FL 32826
407 736-2000

(G-7937)
SIEMENS INDUSTRY INC
7800 Col H Weir Cook Mem (46241-8003)
PHONE..............................317 381-0734
EMP: 87
SALES (corp-wide): 97.7B **Privately Held**
SIC: **3822** Air conditioning & refrigeration controls
HQ: Siemens Industry, Inc.
100 Technology Dr
Alpharetta GA 30005
770 740-3000

(G-7938)
SIG MEDIA LLC (PA)
5423 Landrum Dr (46234-3734)
PHONE..............................317 858-7624
James Byers, *Principal*
T Adams, *Opers Mgr*
EMP: 8
SALES (est): 926.4K **Privately Held**
SIC: **3993** 7312 7319 7336 Signs & advertising specialties; advertising novelties; outdoor advertising services; transit advertising services; bus card advertising; display advertising service; graphic arts & related design

(G-7939)
SIGMA MICRO CORP
714 N Senate Ave (46202-3763)
PHONE..............................317 631-6580
EMP: 2 EST: 2010
SALES (est): 110K **Privately Held**
SIC: **7372** Prepackaged Software Services

(G-7940)
SIGN CRAFT INDUSTRIES INC
Also Called: Quicksign
8816 Corporation Dr (46256-1291)
PHONE..............................317 842-8664
Fax: 317 842-3015
Greg Beyerl, *President*
Phil Sheingold, *COO*
Emily Dixon, *Purch Mgr*
Steve McVicker, *VP Sales*
Michael Dierdorf, *Manager*
EMP: 49
SQ FT: 43,000
SALES (est): 7.7MM **Privately Held**
WEB: www.signcraftind.com
SIC: **3993** 5999 5046 Electric signs; alarm signal systems; signs, electrical

(G-7941)
SIGN GROUP INC (PA)
Also Called: S G I
5370 W 84th St (46268-1517)
PHONE..............................317 875-6969
Fax: 317 875-6644
Robert Scherer, *President*
Danielle Wills, *Vice Pres*
EMP: 17
SALES (est): 2.5MM **Privately Held**
WEB: www.frontrowscoring.com
SIC: **1799** 7629 3993 Sign installation & maintenance; electrical equipment repair services; electric signs

(G-7942)
SIGN GROUP INC
Front Row Sports Technology
5370 W 84th St (46268-1517)
PHONE..............................317 228-8049
Robert Scherer, *President*
EMP: 7
SALES (est): 597.8K
SALES (corp-wide): 2.5MM **Privately Held**
WEB: www.frontrowscoring.com
SIC: **3993** Scoreboards, electric
PA: The Sign Group Inc
5370 W 84th St
Indianapolis IN 46268
317 875-6969

(G-7943)
SIGN GUYS INC
Also Called: Next Day Signs
5442 W 86th St (46268-1502)
PHONE..............................317 875-7446
Mike Ford, *President*
Chris Nash, *President*
EMP: 5
SALES (est): 433K **Privately Held**
SIC: **3993** 5999 Signs & advertising specialties; banners, flags, decals & posters

(G-7944)
SIGN HERE LTD
4444 Decatur Blvd # 1200 (46241-9537)
PHONE..............................317 487-8001
Diana Scalph, *Owner*
Steven Scalph, *Co-Owner*
EMP: 4
SALES (est): 271.7K **Privately Held**
SIC: **3993** Signs & advertising specialties

(G-7945)
SIGN SERVICES
1305 W 29th St (46208-4942)
PHONE..............................317 546-1111
Fax: 317 546-5881
Mickey Levy, *Principal*
EMP: 6
SALES (est): 895.8K **Privately Held**
SIC: **3993** Signs & advertising specialties

(G-7946)
SIGNDOC IDENTITY LLC
3150 Rand Rd (46241-5408)
P.O. Box 42264 (46242-0264)
PHONE..............................317 247-9670
Daniel Gayde, *Principal*
EMP: 8
SQ FT: 25,000
SALES (est): 1.1MM **Privately Held**
SIC: **3444** 5046 3993 1799 Awnings & canopies; signs, electrical; electric signs; neon signs; sign installation & maintenance; lighting contractor

(G-7947)
SIM 2 K INC
6330 E 75th St Ste 336 (46250-2708)
PHONE..............................317 251-7920
Christy Finegan, *CEO*
Mark Finegan, *President*
EMP: 15
SALES (est): 2.3MM **Privately Held**
WEB: www.sim2k.com
SIC: **7372** 7379 Prepackaged software; computer related maintenance services

(G-7948)
SIMS CABINET CO INC (PA)
431 N Holmes Ave (46222-3747)
P.O. Box 22385 (46222-0385)
PHONE..............................317 634-1747
Fax: 317 634-0889
James Sims, *President*
Richard Sims, *Principal*
Becky Sparks, *Corp Secy*
EMP: 35
SQ FT: 16,000
SALES (est): 6.6MM **Privately Held**
WEB: www.simscabinetco.com
SIC: **3083** 2541 2434 Plastic finished products, laminated; wood partitions & fixtures; wood kitchen cabinets

(G-7949)
SINDEN RACING SERVICE INC
1201 Main St (46224-6533)
PHONE..............................317 243-7171
Fax: 317 243-7185
Jeff Sinden, *President*
Joseph Kennedy, *Corp Secy*
Patty Crull, *Manager*
EMP: 15
SQ FT: 21,000
SALES (est): 2.3MM **Privately Held**
WEB: www.sindenracing.com
SIC: **3559** 3949 3596 3441 Automotive related machinery; sporting & athletic goods; scales & balances, except laboratory; fabricated structural metal; metal heat treating

(G-7950)
SKINNY AND COMPANY LLC
5762 W 74th St Ste 117 (46278-1754)
PHONE....................................888 865-4278
Matt Geddie, *Principal*
Monique Wallace, *Sales Mgr*
Mary Pempek, *Accounts Mgr*
EMP: 10
SALES (est): 1MM **Privately Held**
SIC: 2076 Coconut oil

(G-7951)
SKYWARD PUBLISHING LLC
2709 Westbrook Ave (46241-5647)
PHONE....................................317 791-2212
Jeffery C Reuter,
EMP: 2
SALES (est): 140K **Privately Held**
SIC: 2741 Miscellaneous publishing

(G-7952)
SLM INDUSTRIES LLC
8606 Allsnvlle Rd Ste 134 (46250)
PHONE....................................317 537-1090
Mark Rottler, *Principal*
EMP: 2
SALES (est): 84.2K **Privately Held**
SIC: 3999 Manufacturing industries

(G-7953)
SMITSON CMMNICATIONS GROUP LLC
Also Called: American Speedy Printing
3500 Depauw Blvd Ste 1000 (46268-1136)
PHONE....................................317 876-8916
Harrison A Smitson III,
Noelani Langille, *Graphic Designe*
EMP: 6
SALES (est): 958.1K **Privately Held**
SIC: 2752 Commercial printing, offset

(G-7954)
SMOCK MATERIAL HANDLING CO
3420 Park Davis Cir (46235-2397)
PHONE....................................317 890-3200
Fax: 317 890-3210
William B Smock, *President*
Robert Smock, *General Mgr*
John T Smock, *Vice Pres*
Steve Styer, *Purch Mgr*
Robert M Smock, *Admin Sec*
EMP: 18 EST: 1970
SQ FT: 20,000
SALES: 3.3MM **Privately Held**
WEB: www.smockmh.com
SIC: 3535 5084 Conveyors & conveying
equipment; materials handling machinery

(G-7955)
SNODGRASS SHEET METAL
1930 S State Ave (46203-4185)
PHONE....................................317 783-3181
Philip Meyers, *President*
EMP: 14
SALES (est): 5.4MM **Privately Held**
SIC: 3444 Sheet metalwork
PA: Bright Sheet Metal Company, Inc.
4212 W 71st St Ste A
Indianapolis IN 46268

(G-7956)
SNYKIN INC
Also Called: Fastsigns
3915 E 96th St (46240-1419)
PHONE....................................317 818-0618
Fax: 317 845-4428
Wes Snyder, *President*
EMP: 7
SALES (est): 967.3K **Privately Held**
SIC: 3993 Signs & advertising specialties

(G-7957)
SOCKS FOR THE HOMELESS INC
3518 N Gladstone Ave (46218-1570)
PHONE....................................317 568-3942
Shay Spivey-Mays, *Owner*
EMP: 3
SALES (est): 118.7K **Privately Held**
SIC: 2252 Socks

(G-7958)
SOJANE TECHNOLOGIES INC
Also Called: Info-Lite
7526 E 82nd St Ste 110 (46256-1462)
PHONE....................................317 915-1059
Rajesh J Shah, *President*
EMP: 7
SALES: 1MM **Privately Held**
WEB: www.doctorshah.com
SIC: 3993 Electric signs

(G-7959)
SOLAR AMERICA SOLUTIONS LLC
9263 Castlegate Dr (46256-1004)
PHONE....................................317 688-8581
Dave Crawmer, *Mng Member*
EMP: 5
SALES (est): 426.4K **Privately Held**
SIC: 3433 Solar heaters & collectors

(G-7960)
SOLAR SOURCES INC (PA)
6755 Gray Rd (46237-3254)
P.O. Box 47068 (46247-0068)
PHONE....................................317 788-0084
Fax: 317 787-0592
Felson Bowman, *President*
Fred Bowman, *Vice Pres*
David Bricker, *Vice Pres*
Donald A Keller, *Vice Pres*
Jerry Hargus, *Foreman/Supr*
▲ EMP: 16
SQ FT: 10,000
SALES (est): 186.3MM **Privately Held**
WEB: www.solarsources.com
SIC: 1221 Strip mining, bituminous

(G-7961)
SOLAR SOURCES UNDERGROUND LLC (PA)
6755 Gray Rd (46237-3254)
P.O. Box 567, Petersburg (47567-0567)
PHONE....................................317 788-0084
Felson Bowman, *Mng Member*
Tracy Ellis,
EMP: 5
SALES (est): 20.9MM **Privately Held**
SIC: 1222 Bituminous coal-underground
mining

(G-7962)
SOLEY ORTHOTICS LLC
5787 W 74th St (46278-1755)
PHONE....................................317 373-7395
Brian Raynor, *Principal*
EMP: 3 EST: 2014
SALES (est): 293.2K **Privately Held**
SIC: 3842 Orthopedic appliances

(G-7963)
SONACARE MEDICAL LLC
4000 Pendleton Way (46226-5224)
PHONE....................................888 874-4384
Narendra T Sanghvi, *CEO*
EMP: 25
SALES (est): 3.6MM **Privately Held**
SIC: 3845 Ultrasonic medical equipment,
except cleaning
PA: Sonacare Medical, Llc
10130 Perimeter Pkwy # 250
Charlotte NC 28216

(G-7964)
SOUTHSIDER
Also Called: Southside Publishing
6025 Madison Ave Ste B (46227-4722)
PHONE....................................317 781-0023
Denise Summers, *Owner*
Kelly Sawyers, *Principal*
EMP: 2 EST: 2009
SALES (est): 142.8K **Privately Held**
SIC: 2711 Commercial printing & newspa-
per publishing combined; newspapers,
publishing & printing

(G-7965)
SOUTHWARK METAL MFG CO
Also Called: Indianapolis Division
10401 E 59th St (46236-8332)
PHONE....................................317 823-5300
Christine Powers, *Mktg Coord*
Terry Mulder, *Manager*
John Moran, *Director*
Lanora Huskisson, *Executive*

EMP: 150
SALES (corp-wide): 119.5MM **Privately Held**
SIC: 3444 3498 3433 Ducts, sheet metal;
fabricated pipe & fittings; heating equipment, except electric
PA: Southwark Metal Manufacturing Company
2800 Red Lion Rd
Philadelphia PA 19154
215 735-3401

(G-7966)
SPACE KRAFT
4901 W 79th St (46268-1662)
PHONE....................................317 871-6999
Mark Jones, *Manager*
◆ EMP: 18
SALES (est): 3.7MM **Privately Held**
SIC: 2621 Paper mills

(G-7967)
SPECIALTY COATING SYSTEMS INC (HQ)
7645 Woodland Dr (46278-2707)
PHONE....................................317 451-8549
Terry Bush, *CEO*
Eugene J Boros, *Principal*
James Heise, *Plant Mgr*
Alex Dix, *Prdtn Mgr*
Adam Larrison, *Buyer*
▲ EMP: 11
SQ FT: 60,224
SALES (est): 76.1MM **Privately Held**
WEB: www.scscoatings.com
SIC: 3479 Coating of metals & formed
products
PA: Royal Electronic Co., Ltd.
46, Ta Lien 4th St.,
Taoyuan City TAY
335 526-51

(G-7968)
SPECIALTY STAINLESS (PA)
4337 W 96th St Ste 500 (46268-6122)
PHONE....................................317 337-9800
Matt Dittemore, *President*
EMP: 5
SALES (est): 60.5K **Privately Held**
SIC: 3312 Stainless steel

(G-7969)
SPECIALTY TOOL LLC
6011 E Hanna Ave Ste D (46203-6120)
PHONE....................................260 493-6351
Tom Martin, *Manager*
EMP: 16
SALES (corp-wide): 280.8MM **Privately Held**
SIC: 3541 5084 3545 Machine tools,
metal cutting type; industrial machinery &
equipment; machine tool accessories
HQ: Specialty Tool Llc
6925 Trafalgar Dr
Fort Wayne IN 46803
260 493-6351

(G-7970)
SPECIFIED LIGHTING FIXS OF IND (PA)
8904 Bash St Ste B (46256-1286)
PHONE....................................317 577-8100
Paul Brock, *President*
EMP: 12
SALES (est): 1.4MM **Privately Held**
SIC: 3646 Commercial indusl & institu-
tional electric lighting fixtures

(G-7971)
SPECIFIED LTG SYSTEMS IND INC
8904 Bash St Ste B (46256-1286)
PHONE....................................317 577-8100
Paul Brock, *Manager*
EMP: 17
SALES (est): 3.1MM **Privately Held**
SIC: 3646 Commercial indusl & institu-
tional electric lighting fixtures

(G-7972)
SPECTACLES OF CARMEL INC
7945 Lieber Rd (46260-2834)
PHONE....................................317 475-9011
Bradley M Subrin, *President*
EMP: 2

SALES (est): 150.8K **Privately Held**
SIC: 3851 Spectacles

(G-7973)
SPECTRA METAL SALES INC
1711 W New York St (46222-4370)
PHONE....................................317 822-8291
Jim Dotson, *Manager*
EMP: 6
SALES (corp-wide): 301.3MM **Privately Held**
WEB: www.spectrametals.net
SIC: 3355 5051 Aluminum rolling & draw-
ing; aluminum bars, rods, ingots, sheets,
pipes, plates, etc.
PA: Spectra Metal Sales, Inc.
6104 Boat Rock Blvd Sw
Atlanta GA 30336
404 344-4305

(G-7974)
SPEEDWAY LLC
Also Called: Speedway Superamerica 7102
5960 S East St (46227-2020)
PHONE....................................317 783-6361
Cindy Bewley, *Branch Mgr*
EMP: 10 **Publicly Held**
WEB: www.speedwaynet.com
SIC: 1311 Crude petroleum production
HQ: Speedway Llc
500 Speedway Dr
Enon OH 45323
937 864-3000

(G-7975)
SPORTS CHRONICLE LLC
1934 Alvee Cir (46239-8779)
PHONE....................................317 353-9365
Robert M Kelly, *Principal*
EMP: 4
SALES (est): 172.5K **Privately Held**
SIC: 2711 Newspapers, publishing & print-
ing

(G-7976)
SPORTS LICENSED DIVISION
8677 Logo Athletic Ct (46219-1430)
PHONE....................................508 758-6101
Paul Fireman, *Manager*
EMP: 10
SALES (corp-wide): 25B **Privately Held**
WEB: www.groupathletica.com
SIC: 3949 Sporting & athletic goods
HQ: Sports Licensed Division Of The Adi-
das Group
25 Drydock Ave Ste 110e
Boston MA 02210

(G-7977)
SPORTS LICENSED DIVISION
Also Called: Sld of The Adidas Group
8677 Logo Athletic Ct (46219-1430)
PHONE....................................317 895-7000
Alecia Monett, *Engineer*
Sherry Hedge, *Human Res Dir*
Debbie Wisenan, *Manager*
EMP: 1100
SALES (corp-wide): 25B **Privately Held**
SIC: 2329 2339 Men's & boys' sportswear
& athletic clothing; women's & misses'
athletic clothing & sportswear
HQ: Sports Licensed Division Of The Adi-
das Group, Llc
25 Drydock Ave Ste 110e
Boston MA 02210

(G-7978)
SPORTS SELECT USA INC
1920 N Shadeland Ave (46219-1732)
PHONE....................................317 631-4011
Anthony Kroot, *President*
Jon Sinder, *CFO*
Jonathan Sinder, *Director*
▲ EMP: 4
SALES (est): 433.8K **Privately Held**
SIC: 3651 Household audio & video equip-
ment

(G-7979)
SRAM LLC
5315 Walt Pl (46254-5797)
PHONE....................................317 481-1120
Jason Fowler, *Manager*
Pamela Baker, *Master*
EMP: 4

▲ = Import ▼=Export
◆ =Import/Export

SALES (corp-wide): 554.2MM **Privately Held**
SIC: **3751** Gears, motorcycle & bicycle
PA: Sram, Llc
1000 W Fulton Market Fl 4
Chicago IL 60607
312 664-8800

(G-7980)
ST CLAIR PRESS
1203 E Saint Clair St (46202-3590)
PHONE.................................317 612-9100
Judy Huntley, *Principal*
EMP: 2
SALES (est): 83.9K **Privately Held**
SIC: **2752** Commercial printing, lithographic

(G-7981)
ST LOUIS GROUP LLC
8888 Keystone Xing # 650 (46240-4640)
PHONE.................................317 975-3121
Megan Borns, *Materials Mgr*
Jennifer Mattice, *Sales Mgr*
Alyssa Nash, *Sales Staff*
Rhonda Burgess, *Manager*
Dago Hornedo,
▲ EMP: 24
SALES (est): 5.6MM **Privately Held**
SIC: **3669** Smoke detectors

(G-7982)
ST REGIS CULVERT INC
1101 S Kitley Ave (46203-2639)
PHONE.................................317 353-8065
Fax: 317 356-0925
Robert Mooney, *Manager*
EMP: 15
SALES (corp-wide): 4.4MM **Privately Held**
WEB: www.stregisculvert.com
SIC: **3498 3432 3272** Fabricated pipe & fittings; plumbing fixture fittings & trim; concrete products
PA: St. Regis Culvert, Inc.
202 Morrell St
Charlotte MI 48813
517 543-3430

(G-7983)
STAAB SHEET METAL INC
2720 S Tibbs Ave Ste 1x (46241-5301)
PHONE.................................317 241-2553
Fax: 317 241-5109
John Staab, *President*
Judy Staab, *Vice Pres*
EMP: 7
SQ FT: 2,600
SALES (est): 730K **Privately Held**
SIC: **3441** Fabricated structural metal

(G-7984)
STACKMAN SIGNS/GRAPHICS INC
Also Called: United Sign Advertising
5520 S Harding St (46217-9578)
PHONE.................................317 784-6120
Fax: 317 784-6142
John Walker, *President*
Dana Walker, *Admin Sec*
EMP: 23
SQ FT: 6,800
SALES (est): 2.4MM **Privately Held**
WEB: www.usadv.net
SIC: **3993** Electric signs

(G-7985)
STAGE NINJA LLC
1060 N Capitol Ave E350 (46204-1097)
PHONE.................................317 829-1507
Brent Eskew, *Co-CEO*
Clayton Willis, *Co-CEO*
EMP: 6
SQ FT: 1,000
SALES: 600K **Privately Held**
WEB: www.stewartdevelopment.net
SIC: **3699** Electrical equipment & supplies

(G-7986)
STANBINGER FLUTES INC
5920 S East St (46227-2020)
PHONE.................................317 784-3012
Fax: 317 784-1735
David Straubinger, *Principal*
EMP: 3

SALES (est): 366.2K **Privately Held**
SIC: **3931** Musical instruments

(G-7987)
STANDARD CHANGE-MAKERS INC (PA)
Also Called: Distrbteurs De Monnaie Std Inc
3130 N Mitthoefer Rd (46235-2400)
P.O. Box 36550 (46236-0550)
PHONE.................................317 899-6955
Fax: 317 899-6977
James Robert McNutt, *CEO*
Michael Hassfurder, *Vice Pres*
Kevin Smith, *Mfg Dir*
Bruce Jones, *Purch Agent*
John Gibbs, *Electrical Engi*
▲ EMP: 110 EST: 1955
SQ FT: 36,000
SALES (est): 17.4MM **Privately Held**
WEB: www.standardchange.com
SIC: **3578 3581 7359** Change making machines; locks, coin-operated; equipment rental & leasing

(G-7988)
STANDARD CHANGE-MAKERS INC
Also Called: Nik-O-Lok Company
3130 N Mitthoefer Rd (46235-2400)
PHONE.................................317 899-6955
Jeff Kagan, *Branch Mgr*
EMP: 10
SALES (corp-wide): 17.4MM **Privately Held**
WEB: www.standardchange.com
SIC: **7699 5072 3578** Vending machine repair; security devices, locks; change making machines
PA: Standard Change-Makers, Inc.
3130 N Mitthoefer Rd
Indianapolis IN 46235
317 899-6955

(G-7989)
STANDARD DIE SUPPLY OF INDIANA (PA)
927 S Pennsylvania St (46225-1395)
PHONE.................................317 236-6200
Fax: 317 236-6205
Charles F Wolfred, *President*
Lorraine Allen, *President*
Rebecca Menso, *President*
Angela Still, *President*
EMP: 45 EST: 1946
SQ FT: 60,000
SALES (est): 13.4MM **Privately Held**
WEB: www.getstandard.com
SIC: **5085 3544 3452** Industrial supplies; die sets for metal stamping (presses); industrial molds; bolts, nuts, rivets & washers

(G-7990)
STANDOUT SOCKS
3704 Ontario Cir (46268-1981)
PHONE.................................317 531-6950
EMP: 2
SALES (est): 77.6K **Privately Held**
SIC: **2252** Socks

(G-7991)
STANLEY SECURITY SOLUTIONS INC
Also Called: Best Access Systems
6161 E 75th St (46250-2701)
PHONE.................................317 598-0421
Marta Vosberg, *Manager*
Michael McCoy, *Manager*
EMP: 30
SALES (corp-wide): 12.7B **Publicly Held**
WEB: www.bestlock.com
SIC: **3429 5099 5072** Locks or lock sets; locks & lock sets; hardware
HQ: Stanley Security Solutions, Inc.
9998 Crosspoint Blvd # 3
Indianapolis IN 46256
317 849-2255

(G-7992)
STANLEY SECURITY SOLUTIONS INC
Also Called: Best Access Systems
6161 E 75th St (46250-2701)
PHONE.................................678 533-3846
Tom Ryan, *Manager*

EMP: 20
SALES (corp-wide): 12.7B **Publicly Held**
SIC: **3429** 5072 Locks or lock sets; security devices, locks
HQ: Stanley Security Solutions, Inc.
9998 Crosspoint Blvd # 3
Indianapolis IN 46256
317 849-2255

(G-7993)
STANLEY SECURITY SOLUTIONS INC
Also Called: Best Access Systems
6161 E 75th St (46250-2701)
PHONE.................................317 849-2250
Toll Free:.................................877 -
Fax: 317 806-3127
Joe Peoples, *Manager*
Valarie Harris, *Representative*
EMP: 100
SALES (corp-wide): 12.7B **Publicly Held**
WEB: www.bestlock.com
SIC: **3429 5099** Locks or lock sets; locks & lock sets
HQ: Stanley Security Solutions, Inc.
9998 Crosspoint Blvd # 3
Indianapolis IN 46256
317 849-2255

(G-7994)
STANS SIGN DESIGN
6373 Rucker Rd (46220-4836)
PHONE.................................317 251-3838
Fax: 317 251-3377
Stanley Charles, *President*
Caroline Charles, *Vice Pres*
Carolyn Charles, *Vice Pres*
EMP: 4
SALES (est): 362.4K **Privately Held**
SIC: **3993** Signs, not made in custom sign painting shops

(G-7995)
STAPERT TOOL & MACHINE CO INC
2958 Carson Ave (46203-5220)
PHONE.................................317 787-2387
Steve Stapert, *President*
EMP: 8
SQ FT: 6,600
SALES: 700K **Privately Held**
SIC: **3545** Machine tool accessories

(G-7996)
STAR METAL PRODUCTS
2075 S Belmont Ave (46221-1909)
PHONE.................................317 631-5902
Rick Manasick, *Owner*
EMP: 28
SALES (est): 2.2MM **Privately Held**
SIC: **3548** Welding & cutting apparatus & accessories

(G-7997)
STAR PACKAGING COMPANY INC
4001 Prospect St (46203-2347)
PHONE.................................317 357-3707
Fax: 317 357-3717
Jane H Morrison, *President*
William W Morrison, *Vice Pres*
EMP: 8
SQ FT: 17,000
SALES: 700K **Privately Held**
WEB: www.starpackaging.net
SIC: **2655** Fiber spools, tubes & cones

(G-7998)
STATE GEAR COMPANY INC
3510 E Raymond St (46203-4745)
PHONE.................................317 634-3521
Fax: 317 687-9385
Jay D Robinson, *President*
Charles Farmer, *Vice Pres*
EMP: 14 EST: 1969
SQ FT: 18,000
SALES (est): 2MM **Privately Held**
WEB: www.statetoolgear.com
SIC: **3566** Speed changers, drives & gears

(G-7999)
STEEL SERVICES INC
1110 W Thompson Rd (46217-9264)
PHONE.................................317 783-5255
Timothy J Watkins, *President*

Valerie Ardrey, *Receptionist*
EMP: 8
SALES (est): 4.4MM **Privately Held**
WEB: www.steelservices.biz
SIC: **3441** Fabricated structural metal

(G-8000)
STENNO CARBON CO
1410 S Post Rd Ste 100 (46239-9788)
PHONE.................................317 890-8710
Fax: 317 890-8813
Joe Kinney, *Manager*
EMP: 11
SALES (corp-wide): 4.3MM **Privately Held**
WEB: www.stennocarbon.com
SIC: **3955** Carbon paper for typewriters, sales books, etc.
PA: Stenno Carbon Co.
6600 N Saint Louis Ave
Portland OR 97203
503 533-4561

(G-8001)
STERLING ELECTRIC INC (PA)
7997 Allison Ave (46268-1613)
PHONE.................................317 872-0471
Raymond E Helton, *CEO*
Bryan Moeller, *President*
Mark Varys, *Vice Pres*
Walter Mashburn, *Sls & Mktg Exec*
Barb Feldbauer, *Sales Mgr*
▲ EMP: 43
SQ FT: 80,000
SALES (est): 11MM **Privately Held**
SIC: **3566 3621** Speed changers, drives & gears; motors, electric

(G-8002)
STERLING ELECTRIC INC
7973 Allison Ave (46268-1613)
PHONE.................................317 872-0471
Walter Mashburn, *Manager*
EMP: 6
SALES (corp-wide): 11MM **Privately Held**
SIC: **3621** Motors, electric
PA: Sterling Electric, Inc.
7997 Allison Ave
Indianapolis IN 46268
317 872-0471

(G-8003)
STERLING FLUID SYSTEMS USA LLC (DH)
Also Called: Peerless Pump Company
2005 Dr Mrtn Lthr Kng Jr (46202-1165)
PHONE.................................317 925-9661
Fax: 317 924-7388
Dean Douglas, *President*
◆ EMP: 250
SQ FT: 300,000
SALES (est): 208MM
SALES (corp-wide): 4B **Privately Held**
WEB: www.peerlesspump.com
SIC: **3561** Industrial pumps & parts
HQ: Grundfos Holding Ag
C/O Bratschi Ag, Zweigniederlassung
Zug
Zug ZG
417 692-222

(G-8004)
STEVE SCHMIDT RACING ENGINES
8560 E 30th St (46219-1423)
PHONE.................................317 898-1831
Fax: 317 898-1829
Steve Schmidt, *President*
▲ EMP: 12
SQ FT: 28,000
SALES (est): 1.6MM **Privately Held**
WEB: www.steveschmidtracing.com
SIC: **3599** Machine shop, jobbing & repair

(G-8005)
STEWART WARNER SOUTH WIND
2445 Directors Row Ste G (46241-4936)
PHONE.................................812 547-7071
Fax: 317 486-2607
Robert Graham, *Principal*
Ron Fisher, *Vice Pres*
Lisa Dauby, *Manager*
EMP: 5

G
E
O
G
R
A
P
H
I
C

SALES (est): 507.9K **Privately Held**
SIC: 3443 3585 Finned tubes, for heat transfer; evaporative condensers, heat transfer equipment

(G-8006)
STFRANCIS MDWEST HART VLVE CTR
5330 E Stop 11 Rd (46237-6345)
PHONE.................................877 788-2583
Joe Sagorsky, *Principal*
EMP: 2
SALES (est): 169.9K **Privately Held**
SIC: 3592 Valves

(G-8007)
STICKLE STEAM SPECIALTIES CO
2215 Valley Ave (46218-4388)
PHONE.................................317 636-6563
Fax: 317 637-3249
Stickle Roger Harris, *President*
David Schulze, *COO*
Chad Stickle, *Vice Pres*
Lynn Stickle, *Treasurer*
John Ward, *Sales Mgr*
EMP: 19 EST: 1907
SQ FT: 10,000
SALES (est): 4.7MM **Privately Held**
WEB: www.sticklesteam.com
SIC: 3554 Paper industries machinery

(G-8008)
STONE ARTISANS LTD
7952 Zionsville Rd (46268-1649)
PHONE.................................317 362-0107
Cory Kroger, *President*
EMP: 4
SALES (est): 460.3K **Privately Held**
SIC: 3423 3259 3281 Stonecutters' hand tools; architectural clay products; curbing, granite or stone

(G-8009)
STONE CENTER OF INDIANA LLC (PA)
5272 E 65th St (46220-4877)
PHONE.................................317 849-9100
Fax: 317 849-9794
John Reissner Smitson, *President*
Mark Sawyer, *Vice Pres*
Alan Drane, *Director*
EMP: 24
SQ FT: 30,000
SALES: 8MM **Privately Held**
SIC: 5032 5211 3281 1411 Brick, stone & related material; building stone; masonry materials & supplies; cut stone & stone products; dimension stone

(G-8010)
STRAND DIAGNOSTICS LLC
5770 Decatur Blvd Ste A (46241-9561)
PHONE.................................317 455-2100
Ted Schenberg, *CEO*
Laura Beggrow, *President*
Travis Morgan, *CFO*
EMP: 20
SALES (est): 3.6MM **Privately Held**
SIC: 2835 In vitro & in vivo diagnostic substances

(G-8011)
STRATEGIC TALENT LLC
Also Called: Extract Talent
3502 Woodview Trce (46268-3181)
PHONE.................................317 489-4000
Nancy Newman,
EMP: 3
SALES (est): 114.8K **Privately Held**
SIC: 1311 Crude petroleum & natural gas

(G-8012)
STRITTO SIGN ART COMPANY
1401 N Sherman Dr (46201-1515)
PHONE.................................317 356-2126
Fax: 317 356-2126
Joseph Allio, *President*
EMP: 4
SQ FT: 1,680
SALES: 50K **Privately Held**
SIC: 3993 Signs, not made in custom sign painting shops

(G-8013)
STRUCTURAL LLC
54 Monument Cir (46204-2942)
PHONE.................................317 713-7500
Eric Tobias, *Partner*
Kristian Andersen, *Partner*
EMP: 5
SQ FT: 1,500
SALES (est): 287.7K **Privately Held**
SIC: 7372 Business oriented computer software

(G-8014)
STURM HEAT TREATING INC
1110 S Drexel Ave (46203-2301)
PHONE.................................317 357-2368
Fax: 317 356-2417
Eric Ambler, *President*
EMP: 10 EST: 1983
SQ FT: 15,000
SALES: 900K **Privately Held**
SIC: 3398 Metal heat treating

(G-8015)
SUMCO LLC
1351 S Girls School Rd (46231-1352)
PHONE.................................317 241-7600
Fax: 317 248-2352
Michele Gross, *Purch Mgr*
Michael Brouillard, *Engineer*
Michael Smith, *Engineer*
Fred Wittman, *Engineer*
David Smith, *Sales Staff*
▲ **EMP:** 94
SQ FT: 120,000
SALES (est): 21.6MM **Privately Held**
SIC: 3471 Electroplating of metals or formed products

(G-8016)
SUMMIT MANUFACTURING CORP
10586 E 59th St (46236-8333)
PHONE.................................317 823-2848
Fax: 317 823-2850
Weldon Wright, *President*
Linda Wright, *Corp Secy*
Burch Johnson, *Vice Pres*
Cliff Johnson, *Office Mgr*
EMP: 7
SQ FT: 2,200
SALES (est): 1.1MM **Privately Held**
WEB: www.summithosereels.com
SIC: 3569 Lubricating equipment

(G-8017)
SUN KING BREWING COMPANY LLC
Also Called: Sk Beer
135 N College Ave (46202-3801)
PHONE.................................317 602-3702
Steve Koers, *President*
Ryan Baker, *Maintenance Dir*
Brad Cornelius, *CFO*
Aryn Coomes, *Merchandise Mgr*
Elizabeth Belange, *Marketing Staff*
▲ **EMP:** 5
SALES (est): 2.9MM **Privately Held**
SIC: 5181 2082 Beer & other fermented malt liquors; beer (alcoholic beverage)

(G-8018)
SUNCOAST COFFEE INC (PA)
Also Called: Hubbard & Cravens Coffee
1114 E 52nd St (46205-1213)
PHONE.................................317 251-3198
Fax: 317 251-3297
Rick Hubbard, *President*
Jerry Cravens, *Vice Pres*
Erni Mann, *CFO*
Sam Edrington, *Sales Executive*
Nicholas Hubbard, *Director*
EMP: 25
SQ FT: 2,500
SALES (est): 27.3MM **Privately Held**
SIC: 5149 7389 2095 Coffee, green or roasted; coffee service; coffee roasting (except by wholesale grocers)

(G-8019)
SUNDANCE ENTERPRISES INC
Also Called: Sundance Solutions
3902 Hanna Cir Ste E (46241-7207)
PHONE.................................317 856-9780
Fax: 914 946-2955

William J Purdy, *CEO*
Robert Purdy, *President*
Mary Hamilton, *Regional Mgr*
Ellen Henson, *Accounts Mgr*
Barbara Purdy, *Manager*
▲ **EMP:** 30
SALES (est): 723.2K **Privately Held**
SALES (corp-wide): 9.3B **Privately Held**
SIC: 3841 5999 Diagnostic apparatus, medical; medical apparatus & supplies
HQ: Molnlycke Health Care Ab
Gamlestadsvagen 3c
Goteborg 415 0
317 223-000

(G-8020)
SUNYATA SOFTWARE LLC
8415 Autumn Leaf Ct Apt E (46268-3675)
PHONE.................................310 923-1821
Bharath Sheelam, *Principal*
EMP: 2 EST: 2015
SALES (est): 56.5K **Privately Held**
SIC: 7372 Prepackaged software

(G-8021)
SUPERIOR DISTRIBUTION
2570 N Shadeland Ave (46219-1739)
PHONE.................................618 242-5560
Fax: 317 308-5524
Joe Vaal, *Principal*
EMP: 5
SALES (est): 1MM **Privately Held**
SIC: 5075 3585 1711 Warm air heating equipment & supplies; heating equipment, complete; ventilation & duct work contractor

(G-8022)
SUPERIOR METAL TECH LLC
Also Called: Morgan Francis Flagpoles & ACC
9850 E 30th St (46229-3608)
PHONE.................................317 897-9850
Alan Symons, *CEO*
Steve Blackburn, *President*
Tom Galloway, *Principal*
Tim Gross, *Vice Pres*
Curt Lamb, *Manager*
▲ **EMP:** 85
SALES (est): 16.2MM **Privately Held**
WEB: www.superiormetaltechnologies.net
SIC: 3471 3479 Anodizing (plating) of metals or formed products; painting of metal products

(G-8023)
SUPREMEX MIDWEST INC (PA)
5331 N Tacoma Ave (46220-3613)
PHONE.................................317 253-4321
Stewart Emerson, *CEO*
Ken Orlando, *Plant Mgr*
David J Bailey, *Sales Executive*
EMP: 51 EST: 2016
SQ FT: 76,000
SALES (est): 6.9MM **Privately Held**
SIC: 2621 Stationery, envelope & tablet papers

(G-8024)
SUPREMEX MIDWEST INC
Bowers Envelope Company
5331 N Tacoma Ave (46220-3613)
PHONE.................................317 253-4321
EMP: 38
SALES (corp-wide): 6.9MM **Privately Held**
SIC: 2621 Paper mills
PA: Supremex Midwest Inc.
5331 N Tacoma Ave
Indianapolis IN 46220
317 253-4321

(G-8025)
SWAROVSKI NORTH AMERICA LTD
6020 E 82nd St Ste 430 (46250-5530)
PHONE.................................317 841-0037
EMP: 7
SALES (corp-wide): 3.7B **Privately Held**
SIC: 3961 Costume jewelry
HQ: Swarovski North America Limited
1 Kenney Dr
Cranston RI 02920
401 463-6400

(G-8026)
SWEET ART INC
Also Called: Sweet Art Gallery
8320 Brookville Rd Ste P (46239-8914)
PHONE.................................317 787-3647
Linda Shonk, *President*
EMP: 3
SQ FT: 3,500
SALES (est): 338.8K **Privately Held**
SIC: 2051 5992 Pastries, e.g. danish: except frozen; florists

(G-8027)
SWEET N SASSY CUPCAKES
8440 Coppel Ln (46259-1400)
PHONE.................................317 652-6132
Erin Garvey, *Principal*
EMP: 4
SALES (est): 167.2K **Privately Held**
SIC: 2051 Bread, cake & related products

(G-8028)
SWEET THINGS INC (PA)
Also Called: Sweet Things Candy & Gifts
2288 W 86th St (46260-1944)
PHONE.................................317 872-8720
Fax: 317 872-4959
Penni Brodey, *President*
Ronald Brodey, *Admin Sec*
EMP: 10
SQ FT: 2,695
SALES (est): 647.3K **Privately Held**
WEB: www.sweetthingsinc.com
SIC: 5441 5145 2066 Candy; confectionery produced for direct sale on the premises; confectionery; chocolate & cocoa products

(G-8029)
SYMANTEC CORPORATION
8888 Keystone Xing # 1300 (46240-4609)
PHONE.................................317 575-4010
Scott Berkel, *Branch Mgr*
EMP: 6
SALES (corp-wide): 4B **Publicly Held**
WEB: www.symantec.com
SIC: 7372 Prepackaged software
PA: Symantec Corporation
350 Ellis St
Mountain View CA 94043
650 527-8000

(G-8030)
SYNTAG RFLD
602 N Park Ave (46204-1615)
PHONE.................................317 685-5292
Peter Hanson, *Principal*
EMP: 2
SALES (est): 163.9K **Privately Held**
SIC: 3577 Bar code (magnetic ink) printers

(G-8031)
SYSTEC CORPORATION
Also Called: Systec Conveyors
3245 N Mitthoefer Rd (46235-3489)
PHONE.................................317 890-9230
Fax: 317 890-9232
Richard D Harris, *CEO*
Michael F Harris, *President*
Teresa L Harris, *Corp Secy*
Christopher W Harris, *Vice Pres*
John Gould, *Controller*
EMP: 85
SQ FT: 60,000
SALES (est): 25.1MM **Privately Held**
SIC: 3535 Unit handling conveying systems; robotic conveyors

(G-8032)
T & M EQUIPMENT COMPANY INC
6501 Guion Rd (46268-4808)
PHONE.................................317 293-9255
Vicky Thompson, *Office Mgr*
Michael Malatestinic, *Manager*
EMP: 15
SALES (corp-wide): 34.8MM **Privately Held**
SIC: 7699 5013 5084 3536 Industrial equipment services; motor vehicle supplies & new parts; industrial machinery & equipment; hoists, cranes & monorails; crane & aerial lift service

PA: T & M Equipment Company Inc
2880 E 83rd Pl
Merrillville IN 46410
219 942-2299

(G-8033)
T H S INTERNATIONAL INC
Also Called: Accordion Medical
3510 E 96th St Ste 27 (46240-3735)
PHONE.................................317 759-2869
Kazuo Takai, *Ch of Bd*
David Quigley, *President*
Heather Conner, *Opers Staff*
EMP: 5
SQ FT: 1,000
SALES (est): 768.5K
SALES (corp-wide): 15.1MM **Privately Held**
WEB: www.thsinternational.com
SIC: 5047 3841 Medical equipment & supplies; catheters
PA: Takai Hospital Supply Co., Ltd.
2-31-25, Yushima
Bunkyo-Ku TKY 113-0
338 147-761

(G-8034)
TAMWALL INC
Also Called: Tamwall Demountable Partitions
4362 Sellers St (46226-7107)
PHONE.................................317 546-5055
Fax: 317 545-7160
Thomas Mills, *President*
Susan Mills, *Admin Sec*
EMP: 11
SQ FT: 18,000
SALES (est): 1.1MM **Privately Held**
SIC: 2542 Partitions for floor attachment, prefabricated: except wood

(G-8035)
TANGLEWOOD PUBLISHING INC
Also Called: Tanglewood Press
1060 N Capitol Ave E395 (46204-1068)
PHONE.................................812 877-9488
Peggy Tierney, *President*
▲ **EMP:** 3
SALES (est): 239.2K **Privately Held**
SIC: 2741 Miscellaneous publishing

(G-8036)
TARPENNING-LAFOLLETTE CO INC
404 W Gimber St (46225-2269)
PHONE.................................317 780-1500
Fax: 317 780-1600
Kim Martin, *Ch of Bd*
Rex A Martin, *President*
Chad G Martin, *Vice Pres*
Rodney H Pittman, *Admin Sec*
EMP: 28 **EST:** 1920
SQ FT: 48,000
SALES (est): 5.7MM **Privately Held**
WEB: www.tarp-laff.com
SIC: 3444 7699 Sheet metalwork; industrial equipment services

(G-8037)
TARTAN PROPERTIES LLC
3419 Roosevelt Ave (46218-3761)
P.O. Box 18280 (46218-0280)
PHONE.................................317 714-7337
John D Chisholm, *Principal*
EMP: 4
SALES (est): 412.1K **Privately Held**
SIC: 5211 2431 6512 5251 Lumber & other building materials; trim, wood; non-residential building operators; builders' hardware; hand tools

(G-8038)
TASCON CORP
2213 Duke St (46205-2237)
PHONE.................................317 547-6127
Fax: 317 542-0779
Stephen E Schmidt, *President*
Eve Schmidt, *Treasurer*
EMP: 20
SQ FT: 4,800
SALES (est): 2.5MM **Privately Held**
WEB: www.tasconcorp.com
SIC: 3545 3541 Diamond cutting tools for turning, boring, burnishing, etc.; machine tools, metal cutting type

(G-8039)
TAUGHT IT LLC
8440 Wdfld Xing Blvd (46240-2488)
PHONE.................................317 469-4120
Jason Orbaugh,
Yuval Kordov,
EMP: 2
SALES (est): 68.9K **Privately Held**
SIC: 2741

(G-8040)
TAVISTOCK RESTAURANTS LLC
Also Called: Alcatraz Brewing Co.
49 W Maryland St Ste 104 (46204-3523)
PHONE.................................317 488-1230
Fax: 317 488-1231
Erik Stukenberg, *Manager*
EMP: 85
SALES (corp-wide): 58.4MM **Privately Held**
WEB: www.tavistockrestaurants.com
SIC: 2082 5181 5812 Beer (alcoholic beverage); beer & ale; eating places
HQ: Tavistock Restaurants Llc
2024 N Woodlawn St # 417
Wichita KS 67208
510 594-4262

(G-8041)
TC HEARTLAND LLC
Also Called: Heartland Food Products Group
4635 W 84th St Ste 300 (46268-3721)
PHONE.................................317 876-7121
EMP: 150
SALES (corp-wide): 216.2MM **Privately Held**
SIC: 2099 Sorghum syrups: for sweetening
PA: Tc Heartland Llc
14300 Clay Terrace Blvd # 249
Carmel IN 46032
317 566-9750

(G-8042)
TCLOGIC LLC
429 N Penn St Ste 300 (46204-1888)
PHONE.................................317 464-5152
Fax: 317 464-5153
Thomas Uhrig, *Vice Pres*
Cindy Uhrig, *VP Opers*
EMP: 8 **EST:** 1997
SQ FT: 2,000
SALES (est): 1.2MM **Privately Held**
WEB: www.tclogic.com
SIC: 3695 5045 Computer software tape & disks: blank, rigid & floppy; computer software

(G-8043)
TEAM GREEN INC
7615 Zionsville Rd (46268-2174)
PHONE.................................317 872-2700
Fax: 317 872-2600
Kim Green, *President*
Kevin Savoree, *CFO*
EMP: 90
SALES: 8.7MM **Privately Held**
SIC: 7948 3711 Motor vehicle racing & drivers; automobile assembly, including specialty automobiles

(G-8044)
TEC-TOOL INC
220 N Main St (46214)
PHONE.................................812 526-3158
Victor Burgos, *President*
EMP: 2
SALES (est): 153.4K **Privately Held**
SIC: 3399 Metal fasteners

(G-8045)
TECH ENTERPRISES INCORPORATED
5868 Haverford Ave (46220-2760)
PHONE.................................317 251-3816
Jean Gierke, *President*
Carl Gierke, *Admin Sec*
EMP: 2
SALES (est): 241.6K **Privately Held**
SIC: 3695 Computer software tape & disks: blank, rigid & floppy

(G-8046)
TECH INNOVATION LLC
8517 Oakmont Ln (46260-5340)
PHONE.................................317 506-8343

John Leitgeb, *Manager*
John R Gayman,
EMP: 3
SALES (est): 319.8K **Privately Held**
SIC: 7372 Application computer software

(G-8047)
TECH SOLUTIONS AND SALES INC
6898 Hawthorn Park Dr (46220-3909)
P.O. Box 3689, Carmel (46082-3689)
PHONE.................................317 536-5846
Dave Fellabaum, *Principal*
EMP: 2
SALES (est): 237.4K **Privately Held**
SIC: 3651 Audio electronic systems

(G-8048)
TECHCOM INC (PA)
7515 Company Dr Ste A (46237-9635)
P.O. Box 39206 (46239-0206)
PHONE.................................317 865-2530
Ilene N Adams, *President*
Greg Moore, *General Mgr*
Pat Adams, *Treasurer*
Gary Creamer, *Marketing Mgr*
John Louden, *Producer*
▲ **EMP:** 32 **EST:** 1976
SQ FT: 16,400
SALES: 4.2MM **Privately Held**
WEB: www.techcom.com
SIC: 3999 7336 Models, general, except toy; graphic arts & related design

(G-8049)
TECHNALYSIS INC
7172 Waldemar Dr (46268-2183)
P.O. Box 44316 (46244-0316)
PHONE.................................317 291-1985
Fax: 317 291-7281
Jason R Lemon, *Ch of Bd*
Akin Ecer, *President*
Hasan Akay, *Vice Pres*
EMP: 35
SQ FT: 13,500
SALES (est): 2.4MM **Privately Held**
WEB: www.technalysis.com
SIC: 8711 7371 7372 Consulting engineer; computer software development; prepackaged software

(G-8050)
TECHNOLOGY DYNAMICS
9105 E 56th St Ste 2150 (46216-2233)
PHONE.................................317 524-6338
Brian Scott, *Principal*
EMP: 2
SALES (est): 90K **Privately Held**
SIC: 3679 Electronic components

(G-8051)
TECHNUITY INC
6040 W 79th St (46278-1727)
PHONE.................................800 887-2557
◆ **EMP:** 2 **EST:** 2010
SALES (est): 130K **Privately Held**
SIC: 3694 Mfg Engine Electrical Equipment

(G-8052)
TEEKI HUT CUSTOM TEES INC
807 Broad Ripple Ave (46220-1960)
PHONE.................................317 205-3589
Matthew Stuart, *Owner*
EMP: 2
SALES (est): 194.5K **Privately Held**
SIC: 2759 Screen printing

(G-8053)
TEMPLETON MYERS INC
Also Called: BCT
351 S Post Rd (46219-7900)
PHONE.................................317 898-6688
Doug Keller, *President*
Tom Keller, *Opers Mgr*
EMP: 48
SALES (est): 8.9MM **Privately Held**
SIC: 2752 Commercial printing, lithographic

(G-8054)
TERRECORP INC
2121 Hillside Ave (46218-3569)
PHONE.................................317 951-8325
Fax: 317 951-8329
Michael Lanza, *President*

Kurt Cargnino, *Vice Pres*
EMP: 16
SQ FT: 25,000
SALES (est): 2.5MM **Privately Held**
WEB: www.terrecorp.com
SIC: 3463 Bearing & bearing race forgings, nonferrous

(G-8055)
TFI INC
Also Called: Tf Fulfillment
6355 Morenci Trl (46268-2592)
PHONE.................................317 290-1333
James Purcell, *President*
Jodi Jiles, *Exec VP*
Leigh Purcell, *CFO*
Shawn Dickensheets, *Sales Mgr*
Matthew Hale, *Sales Mgr*
▲ **EMP:** 15
SQ FT: 22,000
SALES: 15MM **Privately Held**
WEB: www.thetimefactory.com
SIC: 5199 4225 2752 Calendars; general warehousing; calendar & card printing, lithographic

(G-8056)
TGF ENTERPRISES LLC
Also Called: Bigasspizzacutter.com
11075 Woods Bay Ln (46236-9021)
PHONE.................................440 840-9704
Thomas Faludy, *Mng Member*
EMP: 2
SALES: 350K **Privately Held**
SIC: 8742 8732 3556 7389 Business consultant; merger, acquisition & reorganization research; slicers, commercial, food;

(G-8057)
THE EMINENCE HAIR COLLECTN LLC ✪
5401 S East St Ste 107 (46227-2076)
PHONE.................................317 222-5085
Barbara Spencer, *President*
EMP: 2 **EST:** 2017
SALES (est): 62.8K **Privately Held**
SIC: 3999 Hair & hair-based products

(G-8058)
THERMODYNAMIC PROCESS CTRL LLC
5730 Kopetsky Dr Ste B (46217-9006)
P.O. Box 17912 (46217-0912)
PHONE.................................317 780-5743
Fax: 317 780-0988
Norman Muerer, *Principal*
EMP: 8 **EST:** 2009
SALES (est): 843.8K **Privately Held**
SIC: 3443 Boiler shop products: boilers, smokestacks, steel tanks

(G-8059)
THERMOGRAPHY INDIANAPOLIS LLC
4000 N Meridian St Apt 10 (46208-4034)
PHONE.................................317 370-5111
EMP: 2
SALES (est): 119.1K **Privately Held**
SIC: 2759 Thermography

(G-8060)
THERMOVISION THERMOGRAPHY
3815 River Crosng Pkwy Ste 100 (46240)
PHONE.................................317 306-6622
EMP: 2
SALES (est): 80.6K **Privately Held**
SIC: 2759 Thermography

(G-8061)
THICKSTAT INC
5251 S East St Ste 331 (46227-2038)
PHONE.................................201 294-1896
Dharini Ganesan,
Gayathri Arunachalam,
EMP: 2
SALES (est): 148K **Privately Held**
SIC: 7372 7371 Prepackaged software; business oriented computer software; computer software systems analysis & design, custom; computer software development & applications

(G-8062)
THIS THAT EMB SCREEN PRTG LLC
3724 N Dequincy St (46218-1641)
PHONE...................................317 541-8548
Lorraine Johnson, *Principal*
EMP: 2
SALES (est): 147.8K **Privately Held**
SIC: 2752 Commercial printing, lithographic

(G-8063)
THOMAS & SKINNER INC (PA)
1120 E 23rd St (46205-4590)
P.O. Box 150 (46206-0150)
PHONE...................................317 923-2501
Fax: 317 923-5919
Norris E Krall, *Ch of Bd*
Vernon Detlef, *President*
Neil Moehring, *Corp Secy*
EMP: 467
SQ FT: 28,000
SALES (est): 81.5MM **Privately Held**
WEB: www.thomas-skinner.com
SIC: 3499 Magnets, permanent: metallic

(G-8064)
THOMAS GREEN LLC
7517 Winton Dr (46268-5105)
PHONE...................................317 337-0000
Fax: 317 337-0007
Terry Groff, *President*
Michael Johnson, *VP Mfg*
Kim Bloom,
▲ EMP: 2
SALES (est): 470K **Privately Held**
WEB: www.readingbakery.com
SIC: 3589 Commercial cooking & food-warming equipment

(G-8065)
THOMAS MONUMENTS INC
7009 W Washington St (46241-2840)
PHONE...................................317 244-6525
Fax: 317 243-6850
June Bolton, *President*
Glen Bolton, *Vice Pres*
EMP: 6
SQ FT: 1,500
SALES: 1MM **Privately Held**
SIC: 5999 3281 Monuments, finished to custom order; monument or burial stone, cut & shaped

(G-8066)
THOMAS/EUCLID INDUSTRIES INC
Also Called: EUCLID MACHINE CO
2575 Bethel Ave (46203-3000)
P.O. Box 33459 (46203-0459)
PHONE...................................317 783-7171
Fax: 317 787-7126
Billy R Thomas, *President*
Jeanette Thomas, *Corp Secy*
Ron Merrill, *Vice Pres*
Roynal Merrill, *Vice Pres*
Ryan Merrill, *Project Mgr*
▲ EMP: 78 EST: 1946
SQ FT: 32,000
SALES: 6.4MM **Privately Held**
WEB: www.thomaseuclid.com
SIC: 3599 Machine shop, jobbing & repair

(G-8067)
THOMCO INC
1414 Sadlier Circle W Dr (46239-1058)
PHONE...................................317 359-3539
Fax: 317 359-3151
Tom Spicklemire, *President*
Tom Yocum, *Vice Pres*
Tracey Gruell, *Admin Sec*
EMP: 4
SQ FT: 5,500
SALES (est): 480K **Privately Held**
WEB: www.thomcometals.com
SIC: 3444 Sheet metalwork

(G-8068)
THOMPSON PRINTING SERVICE INC
447 E Elbert St (46227-1656)
PHONE...................................317 783-7448
Michael A Thompson, *President*
Mary R Thompson, *Corp Secy*
Mike Thompson, *Corp Secy*

Wesley H Thompson, *Vice Pres*
EMP: 3
SALES: 150K **Privately Held**
SIC: 2752 Commercial printing, offset

(G-8069)
THOUGHTS ARE THINGS
Also Called: T A T Apparel and Promotions
8035 Clearwater Dr (46256-4613)
PHONE...................................317 585-8053
Nancy Paul, *Owner*
EMP: 2 EST: 1995
SALES: 71K **Privately Held**
SIC: 2759 Promotional printing; letterpress & screen printing

(G-8070)
THREE CUPS LLC
310 W Michigan St Ste A (46202-3227)
PHONE...................................317 633-8082
Tony Townsley, *Mng Member*
Scott Willy,
EMP: 2
SALES (est): 80.9K **Privately Held**
SIC: 2731 Books: publishing only

(G-8071)
THREE DOG SOFTWARE INC
5258 Hickory Lake Dr (46235-6801)
PHONE...................................317 823-7080
David Baker, *Principal*
EMP: 2
SALES (est): 137.7K **Privately Held**
SIC: 7372 Prepackaged software

(G-8072)
THUGS INC CHOPPERS
735 N Lynhurst Dr (46224-6871)
PHONE...................................317 454-3762
Vince Ballard, *Owner*
EMP: 2 EST: 2009
SALES (est): 199.4K **Privately Held**
SIC: 3751 Motorcycles & related parts

(G-8073)
THUNDERBIRD AVIATION LLC
8623 E Washington St (46219-6823)
PHONE...................................847 303-3100
Robert P Thomas, *Administration*
EMP: 2
SALES (est): 134.8K **Privately Held**
SIC: 3721 Aircraft

(G-8074)
THYSSENKRUPP ELEVATOR CORP
8665 Bash St (46256-1202)
PHONE...................................317 595-1125
Rick Wilheite, *Branch Mgr*
Mike Corey, *Branch Mgr*
EMP: 33
SQ FT: 1,500
SALES (corp-wide): 48.7B **Privately Held**
WEB: www.tyssenkrupp.com
SIC: 7699 1796 5084 3999 Elevators: inspection, service & repair; elevator installation & conversion; elevators; wheelchair lifts
HQ: Thyssenkrupp Elevator Corporation
11605 Haynes Bridge Rd # 650
Alpharetta GA 30009
678 319-3240

(G-8075)
TIMBER CREEK DESIGN CO INC
7230 Guion Rd (46268-4888)
PHONE...................................317 297-5336
Doug Schister, *President*
EMP: 14
SALES (est): 1.2MM **Privately Held**
WEB: www.timbercreekdesignconstruction.com
SIC: 2511 Wood household furniture

(G-8076)
TIMES LEADER PUBLICATIONS LLC
Also Called: Southside Times The
7670 Us 31 S (46227-8547)
PHONE...................................317 300-8782
Brian Kelly, *CEO*
Brian Ruckle, *Sales Mgr*
Roger Huntzinger,
Rick Miers,
EMP: 10

SALES (est): 693.5K **Privately Held**
SIC: 2711 Newspapers, publishing & printing

(G-8077)
TLS BY DESIGN
10737 Sand Key Cir (46256-9533)
PHONE...................................765 683-1971
Elizabeth U Day, *President*
Jeffrey A Day, *Principal*
EMP: 10
SALES (est): 740K **Privately Held**
SIC: 2531 Public building & related furniture

(G-8078)
TO A TEE INC
7125 Girls School Ave (46241-2805)
PHONE...................................317 757-8842
Barbara A Young, *President*
William Gilbreath, *Vice Pres*
Richard Meyer, *Vice Pres*
Richard Young, *Vice Pres*
EMP: 14
SQ FT: 13,000
SALES (est): 2.1MM **Privately Held**
SIC: 2759 Screen printing

(G-8079)
TOM DOHERTY COMPANY INC
Also Called: Cardinal Publishers Group
2402 N Shadeland Ave A (46219-1137)
PHONE...................................317 352-8200
Thomas Doherty, *President*
Kelsey Schnieders, *Editor*
Adrianne Doherty, *Vice Pres*
Adriane Doherty, *Opers Staff*
Thomas McLean, *Sales Staff*
▲ EMP: 8
SQ FT: 13,500
SALES (est): 2MM **Privately Held**
WEB: www.cardinalpub.com
SIC: 2741 2731 5192 Music books: publishing & printing; book publishing; books

(G-8080)
TOMLINSON MANUFACTURING
1125 Brookside Ave Ste C1 (46202-3164)
PHONE...................................800 881-9769
EMP: 3
SALES (est): 271.6K **Privately Held**
SIC: 3999 Manufacturing industries

(G-8081)
TOP SHELF ACOUSTICS LLC
8175 Ehlerbrook Rd (46237-9789)
PHONE...................................317 512-4569
Miranda Gahimer, *Principal*
EMP: 2
SALES (est): 159K **Privately Held**
SIC: 3679 Electronic components

(G-8082)
TOPGARD LLC
1125 Brookside Ave (46202-3587)
PHONE...................................317 525-0700
Bob Cameron, *Principal*
EMP: 2
SALES (est): 156.5K **Privately Held**
SIC: 3999 Manufacturing industries

(G-8083)
TOUCHWOOD TRANS INC
7142 Chesterton Ln (46237-8308)
PHONE...................................317 941-0009
Manjinder Singh, *Principal*
EMP: 2
SALES (est): 73.5K **Privately Held**
SIC: 2499 Wood products

(G-8084)
TOWNE POST NETWORK INC
11216 Fall Creek Rd 125 (46256-9406)
PHONE...................................317 288-7101
Tom Britt, *CEO*
EMP: 6
SALES (est): 779K **Privately Held**
SIC: 2721 Magazines: publishing only, not printed on site

(G-8085)
TOWNEPOST LLC
12135 Southcreek Ct (46236-6200)
PHONE...................................317 288-7101
Keenan Hauke, *Principal*
EMP: 6 EST: 2011

SALES (est): 259K **Privately Held**
SIC: 2711 Newspapers, publishing & printing

(G-8086)
TOYOSHIMA INDIANA INC
Also Called: Toyoshima Special Steel USA
735 Saint Paul St (46203-1466)
PHONE...................................317 638-3511
Fax: 317 631-7729
Yoshikazu Tanabe, *President*
Anthony York, *Vice Pres*
Mary McAllister, *Purch Mgr*
Kyle Cooper, *Sales Mgr*
▲ EMP: 19
SQ FT: 57,000
SALES (est): 3.3MM
SALES (corp-wide): 43.9MM **Privately Held**
WEB: www.gssu.com
SIC: 3537 Lift trucks, industrial: fork, platform, straddle, etc.
PA: Ts Shoji, K.K.
1-1-6, Sumiyoshi
Ikeda OSK 563-0
727 619-610

(G-8087)
TPG MT VERNON MARINE LLC
Also Called: Mt. Vernon Barge Service
1341 N Capitol Ave (46202-2313)
PHONE...................................317 631-0234
Daniel B Altman, *CEO*
Don W Miller, *President*
Steve Siemers, *Vice Pres*
Daniel O'Leary, *CFO*
EMP: 175
SALES (est): 14.9MM **Privately Held**
WEB: www.mvbarge.com
SIC: 4731 3731 Freight transportation arrangement; shipbuilding & repairing

(G-8088)
TRADERS POINT WINERY
5520 W 84th St (46268-1521)
PHONE...................................317 879-9463
William Durr, *Manager*
EMP: 5
SALES (est): 465.5K **Privately Held**
SIC: 2084 Wines

(G-8089)
TRAFFIC SIGN COMPANY INC
9402 Uptown Dr Ste 1500 (46256-1076)
PHONE...................................317 845-9305
Doug Fehribach, *President*
EMP: 3 EST: 1970
SALES: 260K **Privately Held**
WEB: www.trafficsigninc.com
SIC: 5099 3993 Signs, except electric; signs & advertising specialties

(G-8090)
TRANE US INC
5355 N Post Rd (46216-1114)
PHONE...................................317 255-8777
James Fischer, *Branch Mgr*
Tim Tomasic, *Executive*
EMP: 90 **Privately Held**
SIC: 3585 Refrigeration & heating equipment
HQ: Trane U.S. Inc.
3600 Pammel Creek Rd
La Crosse WI 54601
608 787-2000

(G-8091)
TRAVELING SATCHEL LLC
1501 Oakwood Trl (46260-4074)
PHONE...................................317 502-3241
Savannah Whitson, *Principal*
EMP: 2
SALES (est): 77.4K **Privately Held**
SIC: 3161 Satchels

(G-8092)
TRAVIS BRITTON
Also Called: T1design
315 N Franklin Rd (46219-5213)
PHONE...................................317 762-6018
Travis Britton, *Owner*
EMP: 2

SALES (est): 54.1K **Privately Held**
SIC: 7389 2396 3993 5999 Design services; screen printing on fabric articles; signs, not made in custom sign painting shops; banners, flags, decals & posters; screen printing

(G-8093)
TREMAIN CERAMIC TILE & FLR CVG
8105 E 47th St (46226-2970)
PHONE................................317 542-1491
Fax: 317 542-1508
Jesse R Tremain Jr, *President*
Stephen M Winter, *President*
Grover Kahler, *Vice Pres*
EMP: 25
SQ FT: 2,000
SALES (est): 2.6MM **Privately Held**
SIC: 1743 5211 3281 2541 Tile installation, ceramic; marble installation, interior; lumber & other building materials; cut stone & stone products; wood partitions & fixtures; masonry & other stonework; dimension stone

(G-8094)
TRENDWAY CORPORATION
5273 Lakeview Pkwy S Dr (46268-4111)
PHONE................................317 870-3269
Don Heeringa, *Branch Mgr*
EMP: 11
SALES (corp-wide): 76.4MM **Privately Held**
SIC: 2522 Panel systems & partitions, office: except wood
PA: Trendway Corporation
13467 Quincy St
Holland MI 49424
616 399-3900

(G-8095)
TRI STAR FILTRATION INC
5319 W 86th St (46268-1501)
PHONE................................317 337-0940
Jeff Hangan, *President*
EMP: 4
SALES (est): 679.2K **Privately Held**
SIC: 3677 Filtration devices, electronic

(G-8096)
TRI-STATE FOREST PRODUCTS INC
6740 Guion Rd (46268-2547)
PHONE................................317 328-1850
Fax: 317 328-1836
Tom Lathan, *President*
Alan Johnson, *Mktg Dir*
Kirk Westerbeck, *Manager*
EMP: 16 **Privately Held**
WEB: www.tsfpi.com
SIC: 2411 Logging
PA: Tri-State Forest Products Inc
2105 Sheridan Ave
Springfield OH 45505

(G-8097)
TRIANGLE ENGINEERING CORP
2206 Production Dr (46241-4998)
PHONE................................317 243-8549
Fax: 317 243-8780
Jon Reeves, *President*
Doug Staten, *General Mgr*
Douglas Staten, *Vice Pres*
David Golay, *Admin Sec*
EMP: 51
SQ FT: 31,300
SALES (est): 9.7MM **Privately Held**
SIC: 3599 Machine shop, jobbing & repair

(G-8098)
TRIANGLE PRINTING INC
6107 Homestead Dr (46227-4839)
PHONE................................317 786-3488
Fax: 317 787-6539
James E Eads, *Vice Pres*
EMP: 5 EST: 1946
SQ FT: 5,500
SALES: 400K **Privately Held**
WEB: www.triangleprinting.us
SIC: 2752 2675 Commercial printing, offset; die-cut paper & board

(G-8099)
TRILITHIC INC (HQ)
5808 Churchman Byp (46203-6109)
PHONE................................317 895-3600
Fax: 317 895-3613
Terry W Bush, *CEO*
Jeffrey Hale, *President*
Gregg Rodgers, *Vice Pres*
Gary Sinde, *Vice Pres*
Daniel Dillon, *Purch Dir*
▲ EMP: 110
SQ FT: 120,000
SALES (est): 15.1MM
SALES (corp-wide): 811.4MM **Publicly Held**
WEB: www.trilithic.com
SIC: 3826 8999 1731 Analytical instruments; communication services; communications specialization
PA: Viavi Solutions Inc.
6001 America Center Dr # 6
San Jose CA 95002
408 404-3600

(G-8100)
TRILLIUM CABINET COMPANY INC
4357 W 96th St (46268-1178)
PHONE................................317 471-8870
Steve Campbell, *President*
Scott Campbell, *Vice Pres*
EMP: 3
SALES: 302K **Privately Held**
WEB: www.trilliumcabinet.com
SIC: 2434 Wood kitchen cabinets

(G-8101)
TRINITY METALS LLC
2440 N Shadeland Ave (46219-1737)
PHONE................................317 358-8265
EMP: 2 **Privately Held**
SIC: 3399 Tacks, nonferrous metal or wire
HQ: Trinity Metals Llc
6400 English Ave
Indianapolis IN 46219

(G-8102)
TRINITY METALS LLC (HQ)
Also Called: Shupan & Sons
6400 English Ave (46219-8227)
PHONE................................317 358-8265
Wade Conner, *CEO*
Hari Agrawal,
◆ EMP: 2
SALES (est): 2.6MM **Privately Held**
SIC: 3399 Tacks, nonferrous metal or wire

(G-8103)
TRUE STORIES PUBLISHING CO LLC
48 N Whitcomb Ave (46224-8727)
PHONE................................765 425-8224
Rebecca Harbert, *Principal*
EMP: 2
SALES (est): 104.3K **Privately Held**
SIC: 2741 Miscellaneous publishing

(G-8104)
TRULITE GL ALUM SOLUTIONS LLC
Also Called: Arch Amarlite
7701 W New York St (46214-2989)
PHONE................................317 273-0646
Fax: 317 273-1990
Terry Britt, *Manager*
Dan Wagner, *Director*
EMP: 100 **Privately Held**
SIC: 3449 Miscellaneous metalwork
PA: Trulite Glass & Aluminum Solutions, Llc
403 Westpark Ct Ste 201
Peachtree City GA 30269

(G-8105)
TSA AMERICA LLC
6898 Hawthorn Park Dr (46220-3909)
PHONE................................317 915-1950
Mariano Cunill,
Brian D Beck,
EMP: 3
SQ FT: 1,100
SALES (est): 272.1K **Privately Held**
SIC: 3541 Gear cutting & finishing machines

(G-8106)
TUBE PROCESSING CORP
604 E Legrande Ave (46203-3907)
PHONE................................317 787-5747
Fax: 317 782-9489
Mike Gill, *Vice Pres*
EMP: 208
SALES (corp-wide): 152.9MM **Privately Held**
SIC: 3498 Fabricated pipe & fittings; tube fabricating (contract bending & shaping)
PA: Tube Processing Corp
604 E Legrande Ave
Indianapolis IN 46203
317 787-1321

(G-8107)
TUBE PROCESSING CORP (PA)
Also Called: Aerofab
604 E Legrande Ave (46203-3907)
PHONE................................317 787-1321
Fax: 317 786-3074
George J Seybert, *President*
Dean Mantha, *General Mgr*
Steven R Dreyer, *Vice Pres*
Eddie Deal, *Mfg Mgr*
Richard Ashcraft, *Engineer*
▲ EMP: 475
SQ FT: 164,000
SALES (est): 152.9MM **Privately Held**
SIC: 3498 3356 3469 7692 Fabricated pipe & fittings; tube fabricating (contract bending & shaping); nickel & nickel alloy pipe, plates, sheets, etc.; machine parts, stamped or pressed metal; brazing; sheet metalwork; aircraft parts & equipment

(G-8108)
TUBE PROCESSING CORP
Ctp Division
3750 Shelby St (46227-3361)
PHONE................................317 782-9486
Matt McIntyre, *Foreman/Supr*
Mike Gill, *Branch Mgr*
Steve Trego, *Supervisor*
Peter Devarakonda, *Executive*
EMP: 200
SALES (corp-wide): 152.9MM **Privately Held**
SIC: 3498 3444 3441 3317 Tube fabricating (contract bending & shaping); sheet metalwork; fabricated structural metal; steel pipe & tubes
PA: Tube Processing Corp
604 E Legrande Ave
Indianapolis IN 46203
317 787-1321

(G-8109)
TUBE PROCESSING CORP
Ctp Sheetmetal Division
3555 Madison Ave (46227-1351)
PHONE................................317 264-7760
Russ Chisham, *Branch Mgr*
EMP: 208
SALES (corp-wide): 152.9MM **Privately Held**
SIC: 3498 3356 3469 7692 Fabricated pipe & fittings; tube fabricating (contract bending & shaping); nickel & nickel alloy pipe, plates, sheets, etc.; machine parts, stamped or pressed metal; brazing; sheet metalwork; aircraft parts & equipment
PA: Tube Processing Corp
604 E Legrande Ave
Indianapolis IN 46203
317 787-1321

(G-8110)
TUBE PROCESSING CORP
Aerofab Division
604 E Legrande Ave (46203-3907)
PHONE................................317 787-1321
Tony Gentry, *Manager*
EMP: 150
SALES (corp-wide): 152.9MM **Privately Held**
SIC: 3498 Fabricated pipe & fittings
PA: Tube Processing Corp
604 E Legrande Ave
Indianapolis IN 46203
317 787-1321

(G-8111)
TUFF SHED
4250 W Morris St (46241-2502)
PHONE................................317 481-8388
Tom Saurey, *President*
EMP: 2
SALES (est): 150.3K **Privately Held**
SIC: 2452 Prefabricated wood buildings

(G-8112)
TULIP TREE CREAMERY LLC
6330 Corporate Dr Ste D (46278-2937)
PHONE................................317 331-5469
Laura Davenport, *Sales Staff*
Fons Smits,
EMP: 6 EST: 2013
SALES (est): 369.3K **Privately Held**
SIC: 2022 2021 Processed cheese; creamery butter

(G-8113)
TUNGSTEN COMPANY LLC
6124 Lazy Ln (46259-6809)
PHONE................................317 788-6732
Andrew Tromp,
EMP: 2
SALES: 1MM **Privately Held**
WEB: www.tungstenco.com
SIC: 3499 Fabricated metal products

(G-8114)
TURNKEY INSTRUMENT SOLUTIONS
1132 Southeastern Ave (46202-3947)
PHONE................................317 946-6354
Pat Roche, *President*
John Ferguson, *Vice Pres*
EMP: 3
SALES (est): 343.8K **Privately Held**
WEB: www.turnkeyinstrumentsolutions.com
SIC: 3999 Dock equipment & supplies, industrial

(G-8115)
TW PERFORMANCE COATINGS LLC
8110 Christian Ln (46217-4409)
PHONE................................317 331-8664
Pamela M Shafer, *Principal*
EMP: 2
SALES (est): 134.4K **Privately Held**
SIC: 3479 Metal coating & allied service

(G-8116)
TWAY COMPANY INCORPORATED
Also Called: Tway Lifting Products
1609 Oliver Ave (46221-1145)
P.O. Box 1525 (46206-1525)
PHONE................................317 636-2591
Fax: 317 634-1213
Robert S Hansen, *CEO*
Peter G Hansen, *President*
Stan R Deal, *Treasurer*
K Arlene Hansen, *Admin Sec*
EMP: 20
SQ FT: 9,400
SALES: 6MM **Privately Held**
WEB: www.twaycompany.com
SIC: 5051 3315 5084 5085 Cable, wire; cable, steel: insulated or armored; hoists; rope, except wire rope

(G-8117)
TWIN COATINGS & FINISHES
10216 E 25th St (46229-1326)
PHONE................................317 557-0633
Michael Eggers, *Owner*
EMP: 2
SALES (est): 51.5K **Privately Held**
SIC: 3479 Metal coating & allied service

(G-8118)
TWISTED LIME BARTENDING
6459 N Lynnfield Ct (46254-4930)
PHONE................................317 607-6836
Anthony Barnett, *Principal*
EMP: 2
SALES (est): 114.4K **Privately Held**
SIC: 3274 Lime

(G-8119)
TYSON CORPORATION (PA)
2301 S Holt Rd (46241-2998)
PHONE................................317 241-8396

Fax: 317 241-6892
Brent Claymon, *Principal*
Matthew Claymon, *Principal*
Michael Clark, *COO*
Ken Willis, *Pastor*
Bryan Patrick Ferry, *Vice Pres*
◆ **EMP:** 25 **EST:** 1966
SQ FT: 180,000
SALES (est): 3.3MM **Privately Held**
WEB: www.ncreditc.com
SIC: 2451 Mobile homes

(G-8120)
U S AGGREGATES INC (HQ)
5400 W 86th St (46268-1502)
P.O. Box 68123 (46268-0123)
PHONE..............................317 872-6010
Robert Simpson, *Ch of Bd*
James C Fehsenfeld, *President*
Lewis Davis, *Vice Pres*
John P Vercruysee, *Vice Pres*
▲ **EMP:** 3
SQ FT: 2,500
SALES (est): 35.8MM
SALES (corp-wide): 248.2MM **Privately Held**
WEB: www.usagg.com
SIC: 1442 Gravel mining
PA: Asphalt Materials, Inc.
     5400 W 86th St
     Indianapolis IN 46268
     317 872-6010

(G-8121)
U S FILTER
6125 Guion Rd (46254-1223)
PHONE..............................317 280-4251
David Fowler, *Principal*
EMP: 2
SALES (est): 249.4K **Privately Held**
SIC: 3569 Filters

(G-8122)
U S FILTER DISTRIBUTION
1680 Expo Ln (46214-2332)
PHONE..............................317 271-1463
Larry Hanley, *Manager*
EMP: 2
SALES (est): 416.9K **Privately Held**
SIC: 3569 Filters

(G-8123)
U S O OF INDIANA INC
3905 Vincennes Rd Ste 204 (46268-3025)
PHONE..............................317 704-2400
John Gilliland, *Principal*
EMP: 2
SALES (est): 312.7K **Privately Held**
SIC: 3711 Military motor vehicle assembly

(G-8124)
UEBELHORS GOLF
Also Called: Custom Golf By Uebelhor
7611 S Meridian St (46217-4257)
PHONE..............................317 881-4109
Fax: 317 887-5979
Robert N Uebelhor, *President*
EMP: 4
SALES (est): 373.9K **Privately Held**
SIC: 3949 5091 5941 Golf equipment;
     golf equipment; golf goods & equipment

(G-8125)
ULRICH CHEMICAL INC
3111 N Post Rd (46226-6566)
PHONE..............................317 898-8632
Fax: 317 895-0614
Edward M Pitkin, *President*
Stephen J Hiatt, *Exec VP*
James W Collins, *Vice Pres*
Suzanne P Shaw, *Vice Pres*
James P Fohl, *Treasurer*
▲ **EMP:** 75 **EST:** 1919
SQ FT: 103,000
SALES (est): 14.2MM **Privately Held**
SIC: 5169 2812 Chemicals, industrial &
     heavy; chlorine, compressed or liquefied

(G-8126)
UNCLE ALBERTS AMPLIFIER INC
7709 Hague Rd (46256-1751)
PHONE..............................317 845-3037
Kevin Silva, *President*
Jan Silva, *Treasurer*
EMP: 3

SQ FT: 1,600
SALES: 120K **Privately Held**
SIC: 3651 7699 Amplifiers: radio, public
     address or musical instrument; profes-
     sional instrument repair services

(G-8127)
UNITED AIR WORKS INC
9715 Decatur Dr (46256-9656)
PHONE..............................317 576-0040
Lora L Gandy, *President*
EMP: 3
SALES (est): 352.6K **Privately Held**
SIC: 3495 Sash balances, spring

(G-8128)
UNITED PRECISION GEAR CO INC
4937 Camden St (46227-1683)
PHONE..............................317 784-4665
Fax: 317 784-4665
Don Le Masters, *President*
Marilyn Le Masters, *Corp Secy*
EMP: 3 **EST:** 1946
SQ FT: 2,000
SALES: 250K **Privately Held**
SIC: 3566 Gears, power transmission, ex-
     cept automotive; reduction gears & gear
     units for turbines, except automotive

(G-8129)
UNIVERSAL DOOR CARRIER INC
1609 S Sigsbee St (46241-2903)
P.O. Box 42165 (46242-0165)
PHONE..............................317 241-3447
Fax: 317 241-3528
Daniel Y Shattuck Sr, *President*
Daniel Shattuck, *Vice Pres*
Daniel Y Shattuck Jr, *Vice Pres*
Ruth Ann Shattuck, *Admin Sec*
Ruth Shattuck, *Admin Sec*
EMP: 7 **EST:** 1904
SQ FT: 10,000
SALES (est): 790K **Privately Held**
WEB: www.universaldoor.com
SIC: 2431 3441 3567 3442 Millwork; fab-
     ricated structural metal; industrial fur-
     naces & ovens; metal doors, sash & trim

(G-8130)
UNIVERSAL TRANSPARENT BAG CO
230 W Mccarty St (46225-1234)
P.O. Box 985 (46206-0985)
PHONE..............................317 634-6425
Needham S Hurst, *President*
Rick Hurst, *General Mgr*
William C Hurst, *Corp Secy*
EMP: 4 **EST:** 1951
SQ FT: 45,000
SALES (est): 462.9K **Privately Held**
WEB: www.nkhurst.com
SIC: 2673 Plastic bags: made from pur-
     chased materials

(G-8131)
UPLAND BREWING COMPANY
4842 N College Ave (46205-1964)
PHONE..............................317 602-3931
Doug Dayhoff, *Owner*
EMP: 7 **EST:** 2009
SALES (est): 359.9K **Privately Held**
SIC: 2082 Beer (alcoholic beverage)

(G-8132)
UPPER LEVEL SPORTS LLC
2303 E Riverside Dr (46208-5247)
PHONE..............................317 681-3754
Gregory Ash-Buck, *Principal*
EMP: 3 **EST:** 2013
SALES (est): 213.8K **Privately Held**
SIC: 3131 Uppers

(G-8133)
URBAN LOGGING COMPANY LLC
404 W 44th St (46208-3736)
PHONE..............................317 710-4070
Christopher Cottingham, *Mng Member*
Gerry Cottingham,
EMP: 11
SQ FT: 2,000
SALES: 800K **Privately Held**
SIC: 2499 Decorative wood & woodwork

(G-8134)
UREAS MUSIC GROUP LLC
4340 N Illinois St (46208-3781)
PHONE..............................317 426-3103
EMP: 2
SALES (est): 74.4K **Privately Held**
SIC: 2873 Mfg Nitrogenous Fertilizers

(G-8135)
URIDYNAMICS INC
Also Called: Hydratrend
6786 Hawthorn Park Dr (46220-3947)
PHONE..............................317 915-7896
Myron Rapkin, *President*
Jack Mulgrew, *Vice Pres*
Bruce Shull PHD, *Vice Pres*
EMP: 14
SQ FT: 4,000
SALES (est): 1.9MM **Privately Held**
WEB: www.uridynamics.com
SIC: 2835 In vitro & in vivo diagnostic sub-
     stances

(G-8136)
US CENTRIFUGE SYSTEMS LLC
1428 W Henry St Ste C (46221-1273)
P.O. Box 47, Logansport (46947-0047)
PHONE..............................317 299-2020
Steven Wallace, *General Mgr*
Jessica Domby, *Sales Staff*
William Spencer,
▲ **EMP:** 19
SALES (est): 3.5MM
SALES (corp-wide): 4.7MM **Privately Held**
SIC: 3569 Centrifugal purifiers
PA: Dilling Group, Inc.
     111 E Mildred St
     Logansport IN 46947
     574 753-3182

(G-8137)
US INNOVATION GROUP INC
Also Called: U.S. Centrifuge
1428 W Henry St Ste C (46221-1273)
P.O. Box 47, Logansport (46947-0047)
PHONE..............................800 899-2040
Scott Behrens, *President*
Patricia M Deeds, *Treasurer*
▲ **EMP:** 14
SQ FT: 15,000
SALES (est): 2.2MM **Privately Held**
WEB: www.uscentrifuge.com
SIC: 3569 Centrifuges, industrial

(G-8138)
US WATER SYSTEMS INC
1209 Country Club Rd (46234-1818)
PHONE..............................317 209-0889
Mark Timmons, *President*
Patricia Anies, *President*
Travis O'Meara, *Cust Mgr*
Shawn McGinnis, *Info Tech Dir*
EMP: 10
SALES (est): 1.3MM **Privately Held**
WEB: www.uswatersystems.com
SIC: 8748 3589 5046 5999 Environmen-
     tal consultant; water purification equip-
     ment, household type; restaurant
     equipment & supplies; water purification
     equipment; water purification equipment

(G-8139)
USA MEDICAL SUPPLIERS LTD
9658 Oakhaven Ct (46256-2199)
PHONE..............................608 782-1855
Polly Ann Mihalovic, *President*
EMP: 2
SQ FT: 2,500
SALES: 0 **Privately Held**
SIC: 3842 Surgical appliances & supplies

(G-8140)
USE WHAT YOUVE GOT MINISTRY
3549 Boulevard Pl (46208-4403)
P.O. Box 1521 (46206-1521)
PHONE..............................317 924-4124
Cecelia Whitfield, *President*
EMP: 2
SALES: 46.4K **Privately Held**
SIC: 3799 Recreational vehicles

(G-8141)
USER WISE SOFTWARE LTD
11720 E Washington St (46229-3978)
PHONE..............................317 894-1385
Craig A Burns, *President*
EMP: 2
SALES (est): 108.7K **Privately Held**
SIC: 7372 Prepackaged software

(G-8142)
V GLOBAL HOLDINGS LLC
Also Called: Vertellus
6330 E 75th St Ste 144 (46250-2717)
PHONE..............................317 247-8141
Rich Preziotti, *President*
Anne Frye, *CFO*
Philip Gillespie, *CFO*
EMP: 1000
SALES (est): 7.1MM
SALES (corp-wide): 58.1MM **Privately Held**
SIC: 0711 2819 2821 2879 Soil chemical
     treatment services; ammonium salts &
     compounds; epoxy resins; polyurethane
     resins; insecticides & pesticides; invest-
     ment holding companies, except banks
PA: Vertellus Holdings Llc
     201 N Illinois St # 1800
     Indianapolis IN 46204
     317 247-8141

(G-8143)
V M INTEGRATED
8501 Bash St Ste 1000 (46250-5505)
PHONE..............................877 296-0621
Adam Rolfsen, *President*
Linda Rolfsen, *CFO*
EMP: 3
SALES (est): 109.6K **Privately Held**
SIC: 1761 3952 Roof repair; chalk: car-
     penters', blackboard, marking, tailors',
     etc.

(G-8144)
VAL ROLLERS INC
2345 N Butler Ave (46218-3910)
PHONE..............................317 542-1968
Fax: 317 542-1920
William J Williams, *President*
Andrew Williams, *Treasurer*
EMP: 7
SALES (est): 1.1MM **Privately Held**
WEB: www.valrollers.com
SIC: 3728 Aircraft parts & equipment

(G-8145)
VALIDATED CUSTOM SOLUTIONS LLC (PA)
905 N Capitol Ave 200 (46204-1004)
PHONE..............................317 259-7604
John Thompson, *Managing Prtnr*
Anthony Wilkerson, *Partner*
Beth Slaninka, *Controller*
Matt Kruse, *Sales Engr*
Jim Van, *Sales Engr*
EMP: 3
SALES (est): 1.7MM **Privately Held**
WEB: www.vc-solutions.com
SIC: 3585 Heating & air conditioning com-
     bination units

(G-8146)
VAN WESTRUM CORPORATION
1750 E 37th St (46218-1015)
PHONE..............................317 926-3200
Fax: 317 926-1750
Mark S Van Westrum, *President*
Mark S Westrum, *President*
Edith Westrum, *Corp Secy*
EMP: 5 **EST:** 1946
SQ FT: 33,000
SALES (est): 460K **Privately Held**
WEB: www.vanwestrum.com
SIC: 3479 Painting, coating & hot dipping

(G-8147)
VANDELAY INDUSTRIES
348 Palmyra Dr (46239-9169)
PHONE..............................317 657-6205
Gregory Truex, *Owner*
EMP: 2
SALES (est): 80.4K **Privately Held**
SIC: 3999 Manufacturing industries

▲ = Import ▼=Export
◆ =Import/Export

(G-8148)
VART GRAFIX
5102 Sandhurst Dr (46217-9461)
P.O. Box 17008 (46217-1080)
PHONE.....................................317 513-5522
V Grafix, *Principal*
EMP: 2
SALES (est): 164.7K **Privately Held**
SIC: 3993 Signs & advertising specialties

(G-8149)
VASMO INC
Also Called: Polymicrospheres Division
4101 E 30th St Ste 2 (46218-3068)
PHONE.....................................317 549-3722
Fax: 317 549-3722
Dr S Mohan, *Director*
EMP: 10
SQ FT: 45,000
SALES (est): 1.3MM **Privately Held**
SIC: 2836 3841 Biological products, except diagnostic; surgical & medical instruments

(G-8150)
VENEER SERVICES LLC
1457 Sunday Dr (46217-9338)
PHONE.....................................317 346-0711
Tim Brown, *Sales Staff*
Dane Floyd, *Mng Member*
◆ **EMP:** 16
SALES (est): 4.1MM **Privately Held**
WEB: www.veneerservices.com
SIC: 3553 Bandsaws, woodworking

(G-8151)
VERONA LLC
2346 S Lynhurst Dr C101 (46241-5169)
PHONE.....................................317 248-9888
Meir Alon,
EMP: 5 **EST:** 2010
SALES (est): 194.1K **Privately Held**
SIC: 3911 Shirt studs, precious & semi-precious metal or stone

(G-8152)
VERSATILE PROCESSING GROUP INC (PA)
9820 Westpoint Dr Ste 300 (46256-3363)
PHONE.....................................317 577-8930
Rob Van Vliet, *CEO*
Ron Rickter, *Vice Pres*
Scott Severson, *CFO*
Terrance Shipp, *Director*
EMP: 7
SQ FT: 6,000
SALES (est): 127.1MM **Privately Held**
WEB: www.versatileprocessing.com
SIC: 3341 Secondary nonferrous metals

(G-8153)
VERTELLUS HOLDINGS LLC (PA)
201 N Illinois St # 1800 (46204-1904)
PHONE.....................................317 247-8141
Rich Preziotti, *President*
EMP: 1
SALES (est): 58.1MM **Privately Held**
SIC: 2869 Industrial organic chemicals

(G-8154)
VERTELLUS INTGRTED PYRDNES LLC
201 N Illinois St # 1800 (46204-1904)
PHONE.....................................317 247-8141
Richard V Preziotti, *President*
Anne Frye, *Vice Pres*
David Schwind, *Treasurer*
EMP: 128
SALES (est): 128.1MM **Privately Held**
SIC: 5191 5169 2833 Chemicals, agricultural; industrial chemicals; medicinal chemicals

(G-8155)
VERTELLUS LLC (PA)
201 N Illinois St # 1800 (46204-1904)
PHONE.....................................317 247-8141
Anne Frye, *Vice Pres*
EMP: 45 **EST:** 2016
SALES (est): 480MM **Privately Held**
SIC: 2869 Industrial organic chemicals

(G-8156)
VERTELLUS SBH HOLDINGS LLC
201 N Illinois St # 1800 (46204-1904)
PHONE.....................................317 247-8141
Anne Frye, *President*
Craig Wian, *CFO*
David Schwind, *Treasurer*
EMP: 45
SALES: 50MM **Privately Held**
SIC: 2869 Amines, acids, salts, esters
PA: Vsi Holdings Llc
201 N Illinois St # 1800
Indianapolis IN 46204

(G-8157)
VESTA INGREDIENTS INC
5767 Thunderbird Rd (46236-2866)
PHONE.....................................317 895-9000
Sam Kwoen, *President*
EMP: 8
SALES (est): 1MM **Privately Held**
SIC: 2834 Druggists' preparations (pharmaceuticals)

(G-8158)
VESTA PHARMACEUTICALS INC
5767 Thunderbird Rd (46236-2866)
PHONE.....................................317 895-9000
Fax: 317 895-9340
Sam Kwon, *President*
Lacey O Connell, *Project Dir*
▲ **EMP:** 20
SQ FT: 6,000
SALES (est): 4.8MM **Privately Held**
WEB: www.vestapharm.com
SIC: 2023 Dietary supplements, dairy & non-dairy based

(G-8159)
VF OUTDOOR LLC
8702 Keystone Xing (46240-7621)
PHONE.....................................317 843-9419
Sarah Musgrove, *Branch Mgr*
EMP: 16
SALES (corp-wide): 11.8B **Publicly Held**
SIC: 2329 Men's & boys' leather, wool & down-filled outerwear
HQ: Vf Outdoor, Llc
2701 Harbor Bay Pkwy
Alameda CA 94502
510 618-3500

(G-8160)
VIARILOC DISTRIBUTORS INC
1717 Expo Ln (46214-2334)
PHONE.....................................317 273-0089
Richard Pare, *President*
EMP: 2 **EST:** 1992
SALES (est): 224.4K **Privately Held**
WEB: www.icpcitation.com
SIC: 3714 Motor vehicle parts & accessories

(G-8161)
VIAVI SOLUTIONS INC
5808 Churchman Byp (46203-6109)
PHONE.....................................317 788-9351
Angie Pons, *Buyer*
Terry Rochioli, *Buyer*
Nick Johnson, *Engineer*
Christian Orphall, *Engineer*
Joseph Banich, *Branch Mgr*
EMP: 275
SALES (corp-wide): 811.4MM **Publicly Held**
WEB: www.jdsuniphase.com
SIC: 3674 Optical isolators
PA: Viavi Solutions Inc.
6001 America Center Dr # 6
San Jose CA 95002
408 404-3600

(G-8162)
VICTORY MFG
Also Called: Vtty
933 N Lynhurst Dr (46224-6875)
PHONE.....................................317 731-5063
Heath Wright, *Owner*
EMP: 6
SALES (est): 286.8K **Privately Held**
SIC: 3999 Manufacturing industries

(G-8163)
VIN ELITE IMPORTS INC
55 S State Ave Ste 358 (46201-3896)
PHONE.....................................317 264-9250
David M Hunter, *President*
Debra Hunter, *Admin Sec*
▲ **EMP:** 2
SQ FT: 1,800
SALES: 2.5MM **Privately Held**
SIC: 5182 2086 Wine; bottling wines & liquors; carbonated beverages, nonalcoholic: bottled & canned

(G-8164)
VINEYARD FISHERY PRODUCTS LLC
3032 Ruckle St (46205-3968)
PHONE.....................................317 902-0753
EMP: 2
SALES (est): 138.5K **Privately Held**
SIC: 2084 Wines

(G-8165)
VISIONS PRINTING LLC
6015 E 34th St Ste A (46226-6109)
PHONE.....................................317 960-2322
EMP: 2
SALES (est): 78.4K **Privately Held**
SIC: 2752 Commercial printing, lithographic

(G-8166)
VISTA GRPHIC CMMUNICATIONS LLC
7915 E 30th St (46219-1235)
PHONE.....................................317 898-2000
Timothy Rolfsen, *Owner*
Carol Ratliff, *Human Res Dir*
Benjamin Rolfsen, *Marketing Staff*
David Marr, *Manager*
Pam Wickham, *Administration*
EMP: 18
SQ FT: 58,500
SALES: 5MM **Privately Held**
WEB: www.vistapkg.com
SIC: 2671 Paper coated or laminated for packaging

(G-8167)
VIZAI LLC
7151 Jessman Road East Dr E (46256-4222)
PHONE.....................................630 677-6583
Ethan Owen Petersen, *Mng Member*
Shannon Michele Anderson,
EMP: 2
SALES (est): 56.5K **Privately Held**
SIC: 7372 7389 Prepackaged software;

(G-8168)
VON DUPRIN LLC (DH)
Also Called: Glynn Johnson
2720 Tobey Dr (46219-1428)
PHONE.....................................317 429-2866
Fax: 800 525-0337
Randy Smith, *President*
Tim Eckersley, *President*
Mike Cain, *Vice Pres*
Barbara Santoro, *Admin Sec*
▲ **EMP:** 500 **EST:** 1908
SQ FT: 225,000
SALES (est): 101.6MM **Privately Held**
WEB: www.vonduprin.com
SIC: 3429 Builders' hardware
HQ: Schlage Lock Company Llc
11819 N Pennsylvania St
Carmel IN 46032
317 810-3700

(G-8169)
VON DUPRIN LLC
2720 Tobey Dr (46219-1428)
PHONE.....................................317 899-2760
EMP: 3 **Privately Held**
SIC: 3429 Mfg Hardware
HQ: Von Duprin Llc
2720 Tobey Dr
Indianapolis IN 46219
317 429-2866

(G-8170)
VSI ACQUISITION CORP
201 N Illinois St (46204-1904)
PHONE.....................................317 247-8141
Richard V Preziott, *President*

Craig Wian, *CFO*
Anne M Frye, *Admin Sec*
◆ **EMP:** 200 **EST:** 2014
SALES: 25MM **Privately Held**
SIC: 2833 Organic medicinal chemicals: bulk, uncompounded

(G-8171)
VSI LIQUIDATING INC (DH)
Also Called: Vertellus Agriculture & Ntrtn
201 N Illinois St # 1800 (46204-1904)
PHONE.....................................317 247-8141
Richard Preziotti, *President*
Susan Elrod, *Purch Mgr*
Philip Gillespie, *CFO*
Christina Walling, *Executive Asst*
Tim Cox, *Admin Asst*
▼ **EMP:** 28
SQ FT: 30,000
SALES (est): 269.5MM
SALES (corp-wide): 1.5B **Privately Held**
WEB: www.reillyind.com
SIC: 2865 Cyclic crudes, coal tar; tar
HQ: Vertellus Specialties Holdings Corp.
201 N Illinois St # 1800
Indianapolis IN 46204
317 247-8141

(G-8172)
W W G INC
5602 Elmwood Ave Ste 222 (46203-6072)
PHONE.....................................317 783-6413
Fax: 317 783-0983
William Watson, *President*
Virgil Warren, *Treasurer*
EMP: 6
SQ FT: 2,200
SALES (est): 750K **Privately Held**
SIC: 3544 Special dies & tools; jigs & fixtures

(G-8173)
W/S PACKAGING GROUP INC
8444 Castlewood Dr # 400 (46250-5535)
PHONE.....................................317 578-4454
Fax: 317 578-4464
Chris Doerr, *Manager*
EMP: 7
SALES (corp-wide): 760.8MM **Privately Held**
SIC: 2752 Commercial printing, lithographic
PA: W/S Packaging Group, Inc.
2571 S Hemlock Rd
Green Bay WI 54229
920 866-6300

(G-8174)
WABCOINDUSTRIES LLC
5540 W Henry St (46241-0620)
PHONE.....................................317 361-3653
Gregory W Rettig, *President*
EMP: 2
SALES (est): 70.1K **Privately Held**
SIC: 3999 Manufacturing industries

(G-8175)
WAGNER SIGNS INC
2802 E Troy Ave (46203-5585)
PHONE.....................................317 788-0202
Fax: 317 788-1579
Gene Wagner, *President*
EMP: 21
SQ FT: 4,200
SALES: 10MM **Privately Held**
WEB: www.wagnersigns.com
SIC: 7336 7389 3993 Silk screen design; sign painting & lettering shop; signs & advertising specialties

(G-8176)
WALKER INFORMATION INC
8940 River Crossing Blvd (46240-2290)
PHONE.....................................317 843-3939
Steve Walker, *Branch Mgr*
EMP: 10
SALES (corp-wide): 21MM **Privately Held**
SIC: 3842 Walkers
PA: Walker Information, Inc.
301 Pennsylvania Pkwy # 400
Indianapolis IN 46280
317 843-3939

(G-8177)
WAMINGO PUBLISHING LLP
5441 Hibben Ave (46219-6413)
PHONE.................................317 443-1326
Darren Parsons, *Principal*
EMP: 2
SALES (est): 67.8K **Privately Held**
SIC: 2741 Miscellaneous publishing

(G-8178)
WANAFEED CORPORATION
Also Called: Wanamaker Feed & Seed Company
4410 Northeastern Ave (46239-1659)
PHONE.................................317 862-4032
Fax: 317 862-9677
James R Trimble, *President*
EMP: 5
SQ FT: 12,000
SALES: 1MM **Privately Held**
SIC: 2048 5261 5191 Livestock feeds; bird food, prepared; fertilizer; nursery stock, seeds & bulbs; seeds: field, garden & flower; fertilizer & fertilizer materials

(G-8179)
WAYNE BURIAL VAULT COMPANY
602 S Emerson Ave (46203-1664)
PHONE.................................317 357-4656
Fax: 317 357-5441
Donald C Davis, *President*
David L Preist, *Corp Secy*
Philip Davis, *Manager*
EMP: 8 EST: 1928
SQ FT: 10,000
SALES (est): 1.3MM **Privately Held**
SIC: 3272 Burial vaults, concrete or pre-cast terrazzo

(G-8180)
WBH INC (PA)
Also Called: Aerospace Products Company
123 N Pine St (46202-3844)
PHONE.................................317 269-1510
Fax: 317 269-1522
John Fazli, *President*
Dawn Fazli, *CFO*
Linda Young, *Info Tech Mgr*
Jeremy A Fazli, *Admin Sec*
EMP: 15
SQ FT: 50,000
SALES (est): 5MM **Privately Held**
WEB: www.aerospaceproducts.com
SIC: 3724 3829 3545 5088 Aircraft engines & engine parts; gauges, motor vehicle: oil pressure, water temperature; machine tool accessories; combat vehicles

(G-8181)
WEBBER MANUFACTURING COMPANY
8498 Brookville Rd (46239-9491)
P.O. Box 19449 (46219-0449)
PHONE.................................317 357-8681
Fax: 317 357-8685
David E Lovett, *President*
Doug Nering, *Treasurer*
Sandra L Nering, *Admin Sec*
EMP: 21 EST: 1946
SQ FT: 29,800
SALES (est): 5MM **Privately Held**
SIC: 3569 3826 3535 3565 Testing chambers for altitude, temperature, ordnance, power; environmental testing equipment; conveyors & conveying equipment; packaging machinery; refrigeration & heating equipment; metal stampings

(G-8182)
WEBSTERS SPORTING GOODS INC
Also Called: Pro-Prep
5060 E 62nd St Ste 114 (46220-5398)
PHONE.................................317 255-4855
Fax: 317 255-4585
Richard C Webster, *President*
Jane E Webster, *Corp Secy*
EMP: 10
SALES (est): 841.7K **Privately Held**
WEB: www.pro-prep.com
SIC: 5941 5699 3949 Fishing equipment; hunting equipment; sports apparel; baseball equipment & supplies, general

(G-8183)
WELLS ROBE SALES & RENTAL
Also Called: Wells Unlimited Robes Service
5702 E 40th St (46226-4865)
PHONE.................................317 542-9062
Salathiel E Wells, *Owner*
EMP: 2
SALES: 50K **Privately Held**
SIC: 2384 Robes & dressing gowns

(G-8184)
WERT FIXTURE & DISPLAY INC
6951 E 30th St Ste C (46219-1190)
PHONE.................................317 577-0905
Fax: 317 844-6739
Richard A Wert, *President*
Joan Wert, *Vice Pres*
EMP: 3
SQ FT: 2,000
SALES: 650K **Privately Held**
WEB: www.wertfixture.com
SIC: 5046 2541 Store fixtures & display equipment; cabinets, except refrigerated: show, display, etc.: wood

(G-8185)
WEST FORK WHISKEY CO
1660 Bellefontaine St (46202-1811)
PHONE.................................812 583-9797
Julian Ross Jones, *President*
Blake Jones, *Co-Owner*
Robert McIntyre, *Co-Owner*
EMP: 3
SALES (est): 162.9K **Privately Held**
SIC: 2085 Bourbon whiskey

(G-8186)
WESTFIELD OUTDOOR INC
8675 Purdue Rd (46268-1116)
PHONE.................................317 334-0364
Charlie Cai, *CEO*
Liping Yuan, *President*
Daoqing Yang, *Director*
▲ EMP: 150 EST: 2004
SQ FT: 18,000
SALES: 150K **Privately Held**
SIC: 3949 Camping equipment & supplies

(G-8187)
WESTROCK MWV LLC
Envelope Division
6302 Churchman Byp (46203-6119)
PHONE.................................317 787-3361
Fax: 317 791-5282
Bill Stinger, *General Mgr*
EMP: 250
SQ FT: 65,000
SALES (corp-wide): 14.8B **Publicly Held**
WEB: www.meadwestvaco.com
SIC: 2677 Envelopes
HQ: Westrock Mwv, Llc
　　501 S 5th St
　　Richmond VA 23219
　　804 444-1000

(G-8188)
WHB INTERNATIONAL INC
101 W Ohio St Ste 810 (46204-4207)
PHONE.................................317 820-3001
Adriano Hubner, *President*
Magaly Hunter Busato, *Vice Pres*
▲ EMP: 4
SQ FT: 1,600
SALES: 20.6MM **Privately Held**
WEB: www.whbbrasil.com.br
SIC: 5531 3363 Automotive parts; aluminum die-castings

(G-8189)
WHEEL GROUP HOLDINGS LLC
Also Called: Wheel One
5720 Kopetsky Dr Ste I (46217-9281)
PHONE.................................317 780-1661
Pam Goss, *Branch Mgr*
EMP: 6
SALES (corp-wide): 44MM **Privately Held**
SIC: 3714 Wheel rims, motor vehicle
PA: Wheel Group Holdings, Llc
　　1050 N Vineyard Ave
　　Ontario CA 91764
　　888 399-8885

(G-8190)
WHEELCHAIR OF INDIANA
4717 Boulevard Pl (46208-3501)
PHONE.................................317 627-6560
Julie Fritz, *Principal*
EMP: 2
SALES (est): 86.6K **Privately Held**
SIC: 3842 Wheelchairs

(G-8191)
WHISKEY BUSINESS
11915 Pendleton Pike D (46236-9711)
PHONE.................................317 823-5078
Taja Rumble, *Manager*
EMP: 5 EST: 2007
SALES (est): 126.9K **Privately Held**
SIC: 2064 Candy bars, including chocolate covered bars

(G-8192)
WHITE RIVER GRAVEL COMPANY INC
10151 Hague Rd (46256-3312)
PHONE.................................317 834-6818
Richard Wallace, *CEO*
Roger Davee, *Vice Pres*
Mike Davee, *Treasurer*
Rita Specker, *Admin Sec*
Josh Wallace, *Admin Sec*
EMP: 8
SALES (est): 1.3MM **Privately Held**
SIC: 1442 Construction sand & gravel

(G-8193)
WHITEHEAD SIGNS INC
1801 Deloss St (46201-4004)
PHONE.................................317 632-1800
Fax: 317 632-4397
Charles S Whitehead, *President*
Charles Toby, *Vice Pres*
Steven T Whitehead, *Admin Sec*
EMP: 10
SQ FT: 8,000
SALES (est): 1.2MM **Privately Held**
WEB: www.whiteheadsigns.com
SIC: 3993 1799 7389 Neon signs; sign installation & maintenance; sign painting & lettering shop

(G-8194)
WIESE HOLDING COMPANY
4549 W Bradbury Ave (46241-5210)
P.O. Box 421009 (46242-1009)
PHONE.................................317 241-8600
Fax: 317 241-8864
Bruce Schwierman, *Senior VP*
Don Turk, *Branch Mgr*
EMP: 50
SALES (corp-wide): 209.4MM **Privately Held**
WEB: www.wieseusa.com
SIC: 5084 3537 Industrial machinery & equipment; industrial trucks & tractors
PA: Wiese Holding Company
　　1445 Woodson Rd
　　Saint Louis MO 63132
　　314 997-4444

(G-8195)
WILBERT BURIAL VAULT CO INC
2165 N Sherman Dr (46218-3817)
P.O. Box 18126 (46218-0126)
PHONE.................................317 547-1387
Fax: 317 547-2460
Robert Rose, *President*
Judith Rose, *Treasurer*
▲ EMP: 13
SQ FT: 28,000
SALES (est): 1.9MM **Privately Held**
SIC: 3272 Burial vaults, concrete or precast terrazzo

(G-8196)
WILCO CORPORATION
5352 W 79th St (46268-1631)
PHONE.................................317 228-9320
Jerry Carroll, *President*
Roger D Carroll, *Admin Sec*
EMP: 17 EST: 1953
SQ FT: 12,500
SALES (est): 2.6MM **Privately Held**
WEB: www.wilcocorp.com
SIC: 3679 Electronic circuits

(G-8197)
WILDWOOD FLORAL CO LLC
6347 Forest View Dr (46260-4709)
PHONE.................................916 220-4900
Ashley Sassoon, *Principal*
EMP: 2 EST: 2015
SALES (est): 66.8K **Privately Held**
SIC: 2499 Wood products

(G-8198)
WILEY PUBLISHING INC
Also Called: John Wiley and Sons Publishing
10475 Croinpoint Blvd 100 (46256)
PHONE.................................317 842-2032
Fax: 317 572-4000
Amy Fandrei, *Editor*
Steve Hayes, *Editor*
Paul Reese, *Editor*
Beth McDougall, *Facilities Mgr*
Michelle Dombrosky, *Opers Staff*
EMP: 300
SALES (corp-wide): 1.8B **Publicly Held**
WEB: www.mcp.com
SIC: 2731 8299 Books: publishing & printing; educational service, nondegree granting: continuing educ.
HQ: Wiley Publishing Llc
　　111 River St
　　Hoboken NJ 07030
　　201 748-6000

(G-8199)
WILLIAM ROAM LLC
6501 Julian Ave (46219-6603)
PHONE.................................317 356-2715
A Murphy, *Owner*
EMP: 4
SALES (est): 529.2K **Privately Held**
SIC: 2844 Toilet preparations

(G-8200)
WILLIAM WESLEY PROFESSIONAL
5605 W 73rd St (46278-1739)
PHONE.................................317 635-1000
William C Perkins, *President*
Wesley Spiller, *Vice Pres*
EMP: 11
SALES (est): 1.2MM **Privately Held**
SIC: 3843 8072 Teeth, artificial (not made in dental laboratories); dental laboratories

(G-8201)
WILLIAMS WOODS PUBG SVCS LLC
3921 English Ave (46201-4571)
PHONE.................................317 270-0976
Deborah J Williams, *Administration*
EMP: 2 EST: 2008
SALES (est): 125.2K **Privately Held**
SIC: 2741 Miscellaneous publishing

(G-8202)
WILLIS CURTIS GENIE JR
4606 N Ritter Ave (46226-2214)
PHONE.................................317 377-4711
Curtis Willis, *Principal*
EMP: 2
SALES (est): 86.6K **Privately Held**
SIC: 2752 Commercial printing, lithographic

(G-8203)
WINDOW MAN INC
Also Called: All American Vending
5575 Elmwood Ave Ste B (46203-6046)
PHONE.................................317 755-3207
Rance Kleiber, *President*
EMP: 2 EST: 2001
SALES (est): 368.2K **Privately Held**
SIC: 3581 5046 Mechanisms & parts for automatic vending machines; vending machines, coin-operated

(G-8204)
WINE AND CANVAS DEV LLC (PA)
5151 E 82nd St Ste 700 (46250-5643)
PHONE.................................317 345-1567
Steve Gentry, *Manager*
EMP: 10
SALES (est): 1.4MM **Privately Held**
SIC: 2211 Canvas

(G-8205)
WIRECUT TECHNOLOGIES INC
5328 Commerce Square Dr (46237-9742)
PHONE..................................317 885-9915
Fax: 317 885-9916
James Ditman, *President*
Kimberly Young, *Office Mgr*
Valerie Ditman, *Admin Sec*
EMP: 8
SQ FT: 5,400
SALES (est): 850K **Privately Held**
WEB: www.wirecuttechnologies.com
SIC: 3599 Electrical discharge machining (EDM)

(G-8206)
WISE PRINTING INC
Also Called: Allegra Print & Imaging
1429 Sadlier Circle W Dr (46239-1057)
PHONE..................................317 351-9477
David Wise, *President*
Karen Wise, *Exec VP*
EMP: 2
SQ FT: 3,600
SALES (est): 250K **Privately Held**
SIC: 2752 Commercial printing, offset

(G-8207)
WNC OF DAYTON LLC
3969 E 82nd St (46240-2468)
PHONE..................................937 999-8868
Philip Davis, *Principal*
EMP: 2 EST: 2013
SALES (est): 140K **Privately Held**
SIC: 2211 Canvas

(G-8208)
WOLF PRINTING LLC
7120 Graham Rd (46250-2649)
PHONE..................................317 577-1771
Fax: 317 577-4213
Cindy Wolf, *Mng Member*
Scott Wolf,
EMP: 5
SQ FT: 3,000
SALES: 500K **Privately Held**
SIC: 2752 Commercial printing, offset

(G-8209)
WOLF TECHNICAL ENGINEERING LLC
9855 Crnpint Blvd Ste 126 (46256)
PHONE..................................800 783-9653
Amy Wortman,
James Casassa,
Stuart Nightenhelser,
EMP: 3 EST: 2012
SALES (est): 158.7K **Privately Held**
SIC: 8711 2399 2531 3728 Mechanical engineering; seat belts, automobile & aircraft; seats, aircraft; research & dev by manuf., aircraft parts & auxiliary equip

(G-8210)
WOLFE AND SWICKARD MCH CO INC
1344 S Tibbs Ave (46241-4130)
P.O. Box 42817 (46242-0817)
PHONE..................................317 241-2589
Fax: 317 240-4228
Samuel W Swickard, *President*
Carolyn Swickard, *Shareholder*
EMP: 80 EST: 1945
SQ FT: 50,000
SALES (est): 13.4MM **Privately Held**
SIC: 3599 3625 Machine shop, jobbing & repair; relays & industrial controls

(G-8211)
WOOD-MIZER LLC
8180 W 10th St (46214-2430)
PHONE..................................317 271-1542
Mark Thompson, *CFO*
EMP: 4
SALES (est): 221K
SALES (corp-wide): 116MM **Privately Held**
SIC: 3541 Milling machines
PA: Wood-Mizer Holdings, Inc.
   8180 W 10th St
   Indianapolis IN 46214
   317 271-1542

(G-8212)
WOOD-MIZER HOLDINGS INC (PA)
Also Called: Lastec
8180 W 10th St (46214-2430)
PHONE..................................317 271-1542
Fax: 317 273-1011
Richard Vivers, *President*
John Donk, *Maint Spvr*
Jay Burdine, *Production*
Chad Stevens, *Production*
Antonio Castro, *Senior Buyer*
◆ EMP: 150 EST: 1972
SQ FT: 148,000
SALES (est): 116MM **Privately Held**
WEB: www.lastec.com
SIC: 3553 3524 3425 2431 Sawmill machines; lawn & garden mowers & accessories; saw blades & handsaws; doors & door parts & trim, wood

(G-8213)
WOODEN CONCEPT INC
7410 Dobson St (46268-2132)
PHONE..................................317 293-3137
Steven Munn, *President*
Mike Kelly, *Plant Mgr*
EMP: 4
SQ FT: 8,000
SALES (est): 276.2K **Privately Held**
WEB: www.woodenconcept.be
SIC: 2511 5712 Wood household furniture; custom made furniture, except cabinets

(G-8214)
WOODWIND & BRASSWIND INC
Musician's Friend
6625 Network Way Ste 200 (46278-1683)
PHONE..................................574 251-3547
Fax: 574 251-3501
Dennis Bamber, *President*
Kurt Witt, *Marketing Staff*
EMP: 16 **Privately Held**
WEB: www.wwbw.com
SIC: 3931 Musical instruments
HQ: Woodwind & Brasswind, Inc.
   5795 Lindero Canyon Rd
   Westlake Village CA 91362
   818 735-8800

(G-8215)
WORKERS IN VINEYARD INC
8650 Coralberry Ln (46239-1709)
PHONE..................................317 245-7256
James Collier, *Principal*
EMP: 2 EST: 2015
SALES (est): 75.4K **Privately Held**
SIC: 2084 Wines, brandy & brandy spirits

(G-8216)
WORLD MEDIA GROUP INC
Also Called: W M G
2301 Whispering Dr (46239-9678)
PHONE..................................317 549-8484
Fax: 317 549-8484
Michael Cantor, *President*
Julia Whistler, *Vice Pres*
Dick Helm, *Info Tech Mgr*
Jeff Mellentine, *Officer*
▲ EMP: 130
SQ FT: 70,000
SALES (est): 26.4MM **Privately Held**
WEB: www.wmg-inc.com
SIC: 3652 7336 Pre-recorded records & tapes; art design services

(G-8217)
WOUNDVISION
212 W 10th St Ste F180 (46202-5433)
PHONE..................................317 775-6054
Brett Whigham, *COO*
Nick McMurray, *Director*
James Spahn,
EMP: 5
SALES (est): 602.6K **Privately Held**
SIC: 3578 Billing machines

(G-8218)
WRIGHT COATINGS CORPORATION
8620 W 82nd St (46278-1009)
PHONE..................................317 937-6768
Charles S Wright, *Principal*
EMP: 2

SALES (est): 189.8K **Privately Held**
SIC: 3479 Metal coating & allied service

(G-8219)
WRITEGUARD BUSINESS SYSTEMS
5102 E 65th St (46220-4817)
P.O. Box 20113 (46220-0113)
PHONE..................................317 849-7292
Fax: 317 849-7385
Larry La Hue, *President*
Kathleen Smith, *General Mgr*
Linda Boyle, *Controller*
EMP: 4
SQ FT: 6,000
SALES (est): 450K **Privately Held**
SIC: 2761 2782 2791 2759 Computer forms, manifold or continuous; checkbooks; ledgers & ledger sheets; typesetting; commercial printing; commercial printing, lithographic

(G-8220)
WRITT SALES & SUPPLY CO INC
Also Called: Major Medical Sales
7155 Wadsworth Way (46219-1751)
PHONE..................................317 356-5478
Fax: 317 353-2268
Michael Writt, *President*
Lisa Hess, *Manager*
Mike Writt, *Manager*
EMP: 7
SQ FT: 8,000
SALES: 3MM **Privately Held**
WEB: www.nutra-balance-products.com
SIC: 2834 Vitamin, nutrient & hematinic preparations for human use

(G-8221)
WRR INC
Also Called: State Plating
8908 Gary Pl (46256-1388)
PHONE..................................317 577-1149
W R Railing, *President*
Randy Railing, *President*
EMP: 110 EST: 1962
SQ FT: 300,000
SALES (est): 5.5MM **Privately Held**
WEB: www.stateplating.com
SIC: 3471 Chromium plating of metals or formed products

(G-8222)
XTRAC INC
6183 W 80th St (46278-1344)
PHONE..................................317 472-2451
Fax: 317 472-2455
Andrew Hood, *Vice Pres*
Andrew Heard, *Vice Pres*
Lisa Lamott, *Administration*
Rebecca Bacon, *Personnel Assit*
EMP: 10
SALES (corp-wide): 440.2K **Privately Held**
SIC: 3714 Motor vehicle parts & accessories
HQ: Xtrac Limited
   Gables Way Kennet Park
   Thatcham BERKS RG19
   163 529-3800

(G-8223)
YAMAHA MARINE PRECISION PROPEL
2427 N Ritter Ave (46218-4019)
PHONE..................................317 545-9080
Fax: 317 542-1176
Ben M Speciale, *President*
Phil Dyskow, *Vice Pres*
James Booe, *Plant Mgr*
Steve McLelland, *Sales Executive*
Tinka Booe, *Admin Sec*
▲ EMP: 32
SQ FT: 62,000
SALES (est): 8.7MM
SALES (corp-wide): 14.9B **Privately Held**
SIC: 3366 Propellers
HQ: Yamaha Motor Corporation Usa
   6555 Katella Ave
   Cypress CA 90630
   714 761-7300

(G-8224)
YANNIS FURS INC
8805 Crestview Dr (46240-5915)
PHONE..................................317 580-0914

Ioannis Apostolidis, *Principal*
EMP: 2
SALES (est): 127.7K **Privately Held**
SIC: 2371 5632 Fur coats & other fur apparel; fur apparel

(G-8225)
YURTS OF AMERICA INC
4375 Sellers St (46226-7109)
PHONE..................................317 377-9878
Kenneth Lawrence, *Vice Pres*
EMP: 5
SALES (est): 788.3K **Privately Held**
WEB: www.yurtsofamerica.com
SIC: 3792 Tent-type camping trailers

(G-8226)
ZIMMER WELDING CO
16 N Harding St (46222-4400)
PHONE..................................317 632-5212
Bob J Marshall, *Owner*
EMP: 4
SQ FT: 1,600
SALES (est): 497.7K **Privately Held**
SIC: 7692 1799 3444 Welding repair; welding on site; sheet metalwork

(G-8227)
ZOLLMAN PLASTIC SURGERY PC
8227 Northwest Blvd # 290 (46278-1377)
PHONE..................................317 328-1100
Charles W Zollman, *President*
Wally Zollman, *Plastic Surgeon*
EMP: 3
SALES (est): 283K **Privately Held**
SIC: 8011 3842 Plastic surgeon; implants, surgical

(G-8228)
ZPS AMERICA LLC
4950 W 79th St (46268-1665)
PHONE..................................317 452-4030
Peter Julina, *Opers Mgr*
Craig Coffey, *Engineer*
Andrew Suja, *Engineer*
John Ross, *Natl Sales Mgr*
Olaf Tessarzyk, *Mng Member*
▲ EMP: 26
SALES (est): 5.6MM **Privately Held**
SIC: 3541 3545 Machine tools, metal cutting type; vertical turning & boring machines (metalworking); gear cutting & finishing machines; numerically controlled metal cutting machine tools; milling machine attachments (machine tool accessories)

Ireland
Dubois County

(G-8229)
LEED SELLING TOOLS CORP
5312 W Ireland Center St (47545)
P.O. Box 68 (47545-0068)
PHONE..................................812 482-7888
Fax: 812 482-9738
Pat Kersteins, *Personnel*
Richard Edwards, *Manager*
EMP: 165
SQ FT: 40,000
SALES (corp-wide): 32.8MM **Privately Held**
WEB: www.leedsamples.com
SIC: 2782 3161 Blankbooks & looseleaf binders; luggage
PA: Leed Selling Tools Corp
   9700 Highway 57
   Evansville IN 47725
   812 867-4340

Jamestown
Boone County

(G-8230)
FUKAI TOYOTETSU INDIANA CORP
Also Called: Ftic
1100 N Lebanon St (46147)
PHONE..................................765 676-4800

Kenzo Enishi, *President*
Mari Yamamoto Regnier, *Principal*
EMP: 11
SQ FT: 151,000
SALES (est): 371.8K **Privately Held**
SIC: 3465 Body parts, automobile:
stamped metal

(G-8231)
JRS CUSTOM FABRICATION
5998 S 500 W (46147-9470)
PHONE.................................765 676-4170
John Stanbrough, *Owner*
EMP: 2
SALES (est): 129.5K **Privately Held**
SIC: 3499 Novelties & giftware, including
trophies

(G-8232)
P & H ENGINEERING INC
6745 Middle Jamestown Rd (46147-9212)
PHONE.................................765 676-6323
Howard Ferland, *President*
Pricilla Ferland, *Treasurer*
EMP: 3
SALES: 175K **Privately Held**
SIC: 3599 7692 3544 Machine shop, job-
bing & repair; welding repair; special dies,
tools, jigs & fixtures

(G-8233)
WILLIAMS TOOL & MACHINE CORP
54 W Main St (46147-9131)
P.O. Box 183 (46147-0183)
PHONE.................................765 676-5859
Fax: 765 676-6454
Gary Williams, *President*
Louis Williams, *Vice Pres*
EMP: 10
SQ FT: 50,000
SALES (est): 627K **Privately Held**
SIC: 3444 3599 Sheet metalwork; ma-
chine shop, jobbing & repair

Jasonville
Greene County

(G-8234)
ERC MINING INDIANA CORP
15127 W 700 N (47438-6160)
PHONE.................................812 665-9780
Mark Jensen, *President*
EMP: 8 EST: 2015
SALES (est): 228.6K **Privately Held**
SIC: 1241 Mining services: anthracite

Jasper
Dubois County

(G-8235)
AIR RIDE TECHNOLOGIES INC
350 S Saint Charles St (47546-7807)
PHONE.................................812 482-2932
Fax: 812 634-6632
Bret Voelkel, *Owner*
Sharon Voelkel, *Admin Sec*
▲ **EMP:** 40
SQ FT: 12,000
SALES (est): 7.1MM **Privately Held**
WEB: www.ridetech.com
SIC: 3714 Motor vehicle parts & acces-
sories

(G-8236)
ARISTOCRAT INC
1 Masterbrand Cabinets Dr (47546-2248)
PHONE.................................812 634-0460
S Pfister, *Principal*
▲ **EMP:** 2
SALES (est): 288.5K **Privately Held**
SIC: 2519 Household furniture, except
wood or metal: upholstered

(G-8237)
B JS ELECTRONICS
Also Called: Joe Lorey Music
265 S Clay St (47546-3344)
PHONE.................................812 482-3484
Joseph Lorey, *Owner*

EMP: 4
SQ FT: 2,400
SALES (est): 263K **Privately Held**
SIC: 3663 Radio broadcasting & communi-
cations equipment

(G-8238)
BAWEL INDUSTRIES LP
2667 S Meridian Rd (47546-3957)
PHONE.................................812 634-8004
Douglas A Bawel, *Partner*
EMP: 2
SALES (est): 20.1K **Privately Held**
SIC: 3999 Manufacturing industries

(G-8239)
BWT CUSTOM WOODWORKING LLC
1325 Franklin St (47546-2210)
PHONE.................................812 634-1800
Angie Traylor, *Principal*
EMP: 2
SALES (est): 264.1K **Privately Held**
SIC: 2431 Millwork

(G-8240)
CELEBRATION ICE LLC
4525 W Church Ave (47546-8173)
P.O. Box 43, Ireland (47545-0043)
PHONE.................................812 634-9801
Mark Seibert,
EMP: 4
SQ FT: 5,500
SALES (est): 564K **Privately Held**
SIC: 2097 Manufactured ice

(G-8241)
CENTRAL COCA-COLA BTLG CO INC
641 Wernsing Rd (47546-8137)
PHONE.................................812 482-7475
EMP: 2
SALES (corp-wide): 35.4B **Publicly Held**
SIC: 5149 2086 8741 Soft drinks; soft
drinks: packaged in cans, bottles, etc.;
management services
HQ: Central Coca-Cola Bottling Company,
Inc.
555 Taxter Rd Ste 550
Elmsford NY 10523
914 789-1100

(G-8242)
CENTRAL CONCRETE SUPPLY LLC
801 E 230s (47546-7300)
P.O. Box 147 (47547-0147)
PHONE.................................812 481-2331
Brad Persohn, *Owner*
Jerry Max,
Merle Powell,
Steve Rudolph,
EMP: 13
SALES (est): 2.2MM **Privately Held**
SIC: 3273 Ready-mixed concrete

(G-8243)
DADS ROOT BEER COMPANY LLC
950 S Saint Charles St (47546-2688)
PHONE.................................812 482-5352
Steve Williams, *Sales Staff*
Keith G Hedinger,
Andrea Hedinger,
EMP: 2
SALES (est): 261.9K **Privately Held**
SIC: 2086 Carbonated soft drinks, bottled
& canned

(G-8244)
DE MASQU PRODUCTIONS LTD
601 Main St (47546-3040)
PHONE.................................812 556-0061
EMP: 4 EST: 2011
SALES (est): 160K **Privately Held**
SIC: 3199 Mfg Leather Goods

(G-8245)
DITTO SALES INC (PA)
Also Called: Versteel
2332 Cathy Ln (47546-7705)
PHONE.................................812 482-3043
G Scott Schwinghammer, *President*
Audra Hamlin, *Managing Dir*
Cassie Schaeffer, *Buyer*

Brian Anderson, *Engineer*
Chris Dewig, *Engineer*
▲ **EMP:** 25
SQ FT: 90,000
SALES (est): 27.2MM **Privately Held**
WEB: www.dittosales.com
SIC: 3499 5072 Furniture parts, metal;
hardware

(G-8246)
DRAKE CORPORATION
Also Called: Carbide Cutting Tools-Drake
1180 Wernsing Rd (47546-8171)
PHONE.................................812 683-2101
Fax: 812 683-2108
Dennis Kunkler, *Branch Mgr*
EMP: 30
SALES (corp-wide): 8.8MM **Privately Held**
SIC: 3545 3568 3541 3425 Cutting tools
for machine tools; power transmission
equipment; machine tools, metal cutting
type; saw blades & handsaws; abrasive
products
PA: Drake Corporation
1180 Wernsing Rd
Jasper IN 47546
636 464-5070

(G-8247)
DUBOIS CNTY BLOCK & BRICK INC
Also Called: Dubois Co Block & Brick
2208 Newton St (47546-1501)
P.O. Box 1030 (47547-1030)
PHONE.................................812 482-6293
Dennis Persohn, *President*
Roger Cox, *Vice Pres*
Steve Jahn, *Treasurer*
EMP: 17
SALES (est): 4MM **Privately Held**
WEB: www.dcblockbrick.com
SIC: 5032 3271 Brick, stone & related ma-
terial; concrete block & brick

(G-8248)
DUBOIS EQUIPMENT COMPANY LLC
620 3rd Ave (47546-3601)
PHONE.................................812 482-3644
James F Arvin, *CEO*
EMP: 30 EST: 2015
SALES (est): 778.4K
SALES (corp-wide): 25.7MM **Privately Held**
SIC: 3999 Barber & beauty shop equip-
ment
HQ: Timesavers, Llc
11123 89th Ave N
Maple Grove MN 55369
763 488-6600

(G-8249)
DUBOIS MACHINE CO INC
Also Called: Du Bois Equipment Company
620 3rd Ave (47546-3601)
P.O. Box 749 (47547-0749)
PHONE.................................812 482-3644
Fax: 812 482-3544
Robert Williams, *President*
Kurt Tretter, *Principal*
Brian Ackrierman, *Vice Pres*
Benjamin W Hasenourf, *Treasurer*
Scott Spayd, *Manager*
EMP: 30
SQ FT: 20,000
SALES (est): 131.6K **Privately Held**
WEB: www.duboisequipment.com
SIC: 3553 3559 3549 Woodworking ma-
chinery; plastics working machinery; met-
alworking machinery

(G-8250)
ERNY SHEET METAL INC
1020 2nd Ave (47546-3409)
PHONE.................................812 482-1044
David Erny, *President*
Barbara Erny, *Corp Secy*
EMP: 14 EST: 1940
SQ FT: 1,500
SALES (est): 2.1MM **Privately Held**
SIC: 3444 Sheet metalwork

(G-8251)
FOREST PRODUCTS MFG CO (PA)
51 E 30th St (47546-1300)
P.O. Box 606 (47547-0606)
PHONE.................................812 482-5625
Fax: 812 482-9148
John Seng, *President*
Phil Gramelspacher, *Vice Pres*
David Seng, *Treasurer*
Joseph Seng, *Admin Sec*
EMP: 40
SQ FT: 40,000
SALES: 3MM **Privately Held**
SIC: 2421 2426 Sawmills & planing mills,
general; furniture dimension stock, hard-
wood

(G-8252)
G & T INDUSTRIES INC
290 E 30th St (47546-1308)
PHONE.................................812 634-2252
Jason Whitsitt, *General Mgr*
Paul Wise, *Manager*
Theresa Sourerdike, *Info Tech Mgr*
EMP: 40
SALES (corp-wide): 50.1MM **Privately Held**
WEB: www.gtindustries.com
SIC: 3086 Insulation or cushioning mate-
rial, foamed plastic
PA: G & T Industries, Inc.
1001 76th St Sw
Byron Center MI 49315
616 452-8611

(G-8253)
G & T INDUSTRIES OF INDIANA
2741 Cathy Ln (47546-9463)
PHONE.................................812 634-2252
Fax: 812 634-2875
Frank Daugul, *Sales Mgr*
Paul Wise, *Manager*
EMP: 30
SALES (corp-wide): 50.1MM **Privately Held**
WEB: www.foamproductsgroup.com
SIC: 5087 2821 2671 Upholsterers'
equipment & supplies; plastics materials
& resins; packaging paper & plastics film,
coated & laminated
HQ: G & T Industries Of Indiana Inc
1001 76th St Sw
Byron Center MI

(G-8254)
HELMING BROS INC (PA)
Also Called: Copper Box, The
1030 Fairview Ave (47546-2407)
PHONE.................................812 634-9797
Fax: 812 634-9797
Joseph Helming, *President*
Jennifer Rasche, *Corp Secy*
Kathleen Helming, *Vice Pres*
EMP: 5
SQ FT: 7,500
SALES (est): 912.5K **Privately Held**
SIC: 1761 1721 1799 1793 Sheet metal-
work; commercial painting; industrial
painting; steeple jacks; glass & glazing
work; sheet metalwork

(G-8255)
JASPER CHAIR COMPANY INC
534 E 8th St (47546-2953)
P.O. Box 331 (47547-0331)
PHONE.................................812 482-5239
Fax: 812 482-1066
Jeff S Barth, *President*
Fred A Barth, *President*
Chad Barth, *Admin Sec*
▲ **EMP:** 100
SQ FT: 75,000
SALES (est): 20.3MM **Privately Held**
WEB: www.jasperchair.com
SIC: 2522 2521 2531 2512 Office furni-
ture, except wood; chairs, office: padded,
upholstered or plain: wood; school furni-
ture; upholstered household furniture;
wood household furniture

▲ = Import ▼=Export
◆ =Import/Export

(G-8256)
JASPER DESK COMPANY INC (PA)
415 E 6th St (47546-2918)
P.O. Box 111 (47547-0111)
PHONE..............................812 482-4132
Fax: 812 482-9552
James Arvin, *President*
Phillip Gramelspacher, *General Mgr*
John Wright, *Vice Pres*
Steven Kieser, *Engineer*
James Seifert, *Treasurer*
EMP: 13 **EST:** 1876
SQ FT: 2,000
SALES (est): 9.6MM **Privately Held**
WEB: www.jasperdesk.com
SIC: 2521 Desks, office: wood; tables, office: wood

(G-8257)
JASPER DESK COMPANY INC
415 E 6th St (47546-2918)
P.O. Box 111 (47547-0111)
PHONE..............................812 482-6827
Phil Gramelstacher, *General Mgr*
EMP: 69
SALES (corp-wide): 9.6MM **Privately Held**
WEB: www.jasperdesk.com
SIC: 2521 Desks, office: wood; tables, office: wood
PA: Jasper Desk Company, Inc.
415 E 6th St
Jasper IN 47546
812 482-4132

(G-8258)
JASPER ELECTRIC MOTOR INC (HQ)
815 Wernsing Rd (47546-8141)
P.O. Box 650 (47547-0650)
PHONE..............................812 482-1660
Gervase Schwenk, *Ch of Bd*
Doug Bawel, *President*
Mike Schwenk, *Vice Pres*
Raymond Schwenk, *Treasurer*
E Ray Bawel, *Admin Sec*
EMP: 9
SQ FT: 2,500
SALES: 2.3MM
SALES (corp-wide): 501.9MM **Privately Held**
WEB: www.jasperelectricmotors.com
SIC: 7694 5063 5999 Electric motor repair; motors, electric; motors, electric
PA: Jasper Engine Exchange, Inc.
815 Wernsing Rd
Jasper IN 47546
812 482-1041

(G-8259)
JASPER ELECTRIC MOTOR INC
733 W Division Rd (47546-9711)
PHONE..............................812 482-1660
Fax: 812 634-1561
Jeff Bawel, *Manager*
EMP: 15
SALES (corp-wide): 501.9MM **Privately Held**
WEB: www.jasperelectricmotors.com
SIC: 7694 5063 Electric motor repair; motors, electric
HQ: Jasper Electric Motor Inc
815 Wernsing Rd
Jasper IN 47546
812 482-1660

(G-8260)
JASPER EMB & SCREEN PRTG
Also Called: Jasper EMB & Screenprinting
310 Main St (47546-3315)
PHONE..............................812 482-4787
Fax: 812 482-4787
Paul Voegerl, *President*
EMP: 6
SQ FT: 3,000
SALES (est): 620.8K **Privately Held**
WEB: www.jasperemb.com
SIC: 2395 2396 Embroidery products, except schiffli machine; screen printing on fabric articles

(G-8261)
JASPER ENGINE EXCHANGE INC (PA)
Also Called: Jasper Engines & Transmissions
815 Wernsing Rd (47546-8141)
P.O. Box 650 (47547-0650)
PHONE..............................812 482-1041
Fax: 812 634-1820
Douglas Bawel, *CEO*
Zachery Bawel, *President*
Jason Hulsman, *Division Mgr*
Craig Leuck, *General Mgr*
John Schroeder, *Vice Pres*
◆ **EMP:** 900 **EST:** 1952
SQ FT: 220,000
SALES (est): 501.9MM **Privately Held**
WEB: www.jasperengines.com
SIC: 3714 7538 6512 Rebuilding engines & transmissions, factory basis; fuel systems & parts, motor vehicle; gears, motor vehicle; general automotive repair shops; nonresidential building operators

(G-8262)
JASPER OPTICAL LAB
231 S Us Highway 231 (47546-3244)
PHONE..............................812 634-9020
Fax: 812 634-9888
Gregory Gordon, *Owner*
EMP: 8
SALES (est): 456.5K **Privately Held**
SIC: 5995 3851 Eyeglasses, prescription; ophthalmic goods

(G-8263)
JASPER RUBBER PRODUCTS INC (PA)
1010 1st Ave W (47546-3201)
PHONE..............................812 482-3242
Fax: 812 482-0816
Jeffrey Geisler, *Ch of Bd*
Douglas Mathias, *President*
Laura Mohr, *President*
Rebecca Beckman, *General Mgr*
Scott Gehlhausen, *Exec VP*
▲ **EMP:** 749 **EST:** 1949
SQ FT: 330,000
SALES (est): 178MM **Privately Held**
WEB: www.jasperrubber.com
SIC: 3061 Mechanical rubber goods

(G-8264)
JASPER SEATING COMPANY INC (PA)
Also Called: Jasper Group
225 Clay St (47546-3306)
PHONE..............................812 482-3204
Elliott Michael, *President*
Ronald Beck, *Vice Pres*
Dean Schmitt, *Prdtn Mgr*
Tonya Hief, *Opers Staff*
Christine Sander, *CFO*
▲ **EMP:** 1185
SQ FT: 207,000
SALES (est): 228.8MM **Privately Held**
WEB: www.jasperseating.com
SIC: 2521 2531 2522 Wood office furniture; chairs, office: padded, upholstered or plain: wood; school furniture; office furniture, except wood

(G-8265)
JASPER VENEER INC
810 W 14th St (47546-1838)
P.O. Box 226 (47547-0226)
PHONE..............................812 482-4245
George Gramelspacher, *Principal*
EMP: 43
SALES (est): 3.6MM **Privately Held**
SIC: 2435 Veneer stock, hardwood

(G-8266)
JASPER WILLOW SPRINGS MO LLC
815 Wernsing Rd (47546-8141)
PHONE..............................800 827-7455
Raymond Schwenk, *Administration*
EMP: 2
SALES (est): 122.1K **Privately Held**
SIC: 3714 Motor vehicle parts & accessories

(G-8267)
JOFCO INC (PA)
Also Called: Jofco, International
225 Clay St (47546-3306)
P.O. Box 71 (47547-0071)
PHONE..............................812 482-5154
Fax: 812 634-2392
William A Rubino, *CEO*
Bill Rubino, *President*
Joseph F Steurer, *Chairman*
Gregory Sturm, *Vice Pres*
Steve Pleck, *Purch Dir*
◆ **EMP:** 221 **EST:** 1922
SQ FT: 265,000
SALES (est): 51.6MM **Privately Held**
WEB: www.jofco.com
SIC: 5021 2521 Office furniture; chairs, office: padded, upholstered or plain: wood

(G-8268)
JOFCO INC
305 E 12th Ave (47546-7908)
P.O. Box 71 (47547-0071)
PHONE..............................812 482-5154
Joseph Steurar, *Director*
EMP: 219
SALES (corp-wide): 51.6MM **Privately Held**
WEB: www.jofco.com
SIC: 2521 Chairs, office: padded, upholstered or plain: wood; desks, office: wood; cabinets, office: wood; panel systems & partitions (free-standing), office: wood
PA: Jofco Inc
225 Clay St
Jasper IN 47546
812 482-5154

(G-8269)
JUST MONOGRAMS LLC
535 University Dr (47546-8084)
PHONE..............................812 827-3693
Sherri Schwenk, *Principal*
EMP: 7
SALES (est): 314.1K **Privately Held**
SIC: 2395 Embroidery & art needlework

(G-8270)
KENNETH FUHRMAN
6711 N 550w (47546-8701)
PHONE..............................812 482-4612
Kenneth Fuhrman, *Partner*
EMP: 2
SALES (est): 167.1K **Privately Held**
WEB: www.kfuhrman.com
SIC: 3523 Driers (farm): grain, hay & seed

(G-8271)
KEUSCH GLASS INC
403 E 23rd St (47546-8172)
P.O. Box 487 (47547-0487)
PHONE..............................812 482-2566
Fax: 812 482-9365
Timothy Keusch, *President*
Elisabeth Anderson, *Train & Dev Mgr*
Melissa Goldman, *Technology*
Ronald C Keusch, *Shareholder*
Elisabeth R Anderson, *Admin Sec*
EMP: 15
SQ FT: 15,600
SALES: 4.7MM **Privately Held**
WEB: www.keuschglass.com
SIC: 5039 3089 Glass construction materials; windows, plastic

(G-8272)
KIMBALL ELECTRONICS INC
1038 E 15th St (47546-2225)
PHONE..............................812 634-4200
Fax: 812 634-4330
Bob McKenzie, *General Mgr*
Marvin Fajardo, *Business Mgr*
Jim Huelster, *Business Mgr*
Kevin Kurtz, *Business Mgr*
Chris Thyen, *Vice Pres*
EMP: 464
SALES (corp-wide): 930.9MM **Publicly Held**
SIC: 3571 3672 Electronic computers; printed circuit boards
PA: Kimball Electronics, Inc.
1205 Kimball Blvd
Jasper IN 47546
812 634-4000

(G-8273)
KIMBALL ELECTRONICS GROUP LLC (HQ)
1205 Kimball Blvd (47546-0017)
PHONE..............................812 634-4000
Donald D Charron, *President*
John H Kahle, *Vice Pres*
Michael K Sergesketter, *CFO*
Adam Smith, *Treasurer*
Judith Brosseau, *Human Res Dir*
◆ **EMP:** 750
SQ FT: 1,000,000
SALES (est): 844.9MM
SALES (corp-wide): 930.9MM **Publicly Held**
SIC: 3571 Electronic computers
PA: Kimball Electronics, Inc.
1205 Kimball Blvd
Jasper IN 47546
812 634-4000

(G-8274)
KIMBALL ELECTRONICS MFG INC
1600 Royal St (47549-1022)
PHONE..............................812 482-1600
Douglas Habig, *Ch of Bd*
Don Charron, *President*
EMP: 825
SALES (est): 631.8MM
SALES (corp-wide): 930.9MM **Publicly Held**
SIC: 3679 Electronic circuits
HQ: Kimball Electronics Group, Llc
1205 Kimball Blvd
Jasper IN 47546

(G-8275)
KIMBALL ELECTRONICS TAMPA INC (DH)
1205 Kimball Blvd (47546-0017)
PHONE..............................812 634-4000
Donald D Charron, *President*
Michelle R Schroeder, *Vice Pres*
Felipe Martinez, *Engineer*
Michael K Sergesketter, *CFO*
Gregory R Kincer, *Treasurer*
▲ **EMP:** 952
SQ FT: 150,000
SALES (est): 202.5MM
SALES (corp-wide): 930.9MM **Publicly Held**
WEB: www.reptron.com
SIC: 3679 3672 Electronic circuits; printed circuit boards

(G-8276)
KIMBALL FURNITURE GROUP LLC
Also Called: Kimball Office
1037 E 15th St (47549-0001)
PHONE..............................812 482-8517
Denise Friedman, *Purch Mgr*
Paul McCord, *Engineer*
Kathy Sigler, *Branch Mgr*
Patrick Prondzinski, *Director*
EMP: 120
SALES (corp-wide): 669.9MM **Publicly Held**
SIC: 2522 Office furniture, except wood
HQ: Kimball Furniture Group, Llc
1600 Royal St
Jasper IN 47549

(G-8277)
KIMBALL FURNITURE GROUP LLC
National Office Furniture
340 E 11th Ave (47549-0001)
PHONE..............................812 634-3526
Barry Richardson, *Mfg Mgr*
Richard Farr, *Branch Mgr*
Vince Cooke, *Director*
EMP: 300
SALES (corp-wide): 669.9MM **Publicly Held**
SIC: 2522 Office furniture, except wood
HQ: Kimball Furniture Group, Llc
1600 Royal St
Jasper IN 47549

GEOGRAPHIC

(G-8278)
KIMBALL FURNITURE GROUP LLC
Also Called: Kimball Office
1620 Cherry St (47549-0001)
PHONE..................................812 482-8401
Brian N Esch, *Engineer*
Richard Farr, *Branch Mgr*
EMP: 90
SQ FT: 72,000
SALES (corp-wide): 669.9MM **Publicly Held**
SIC: 2436 2435 Softwood veneer & plywood; hardwood veneer & plywood
HQ: Kimball Furniture Group, Llc
1600 Royal St
Jasper IN 47549

(G-8279)
KIMBALL FURNITURE GROUP LLC (HQ)
1600 Royal St (47549-1022)
PHONE..................................812 482-1600
Donald W Van Winkle, *President*
James C Thyen, *Vice Pres*
Michelle R Schroeder, *CFO*
R Gregory Kincer, *Treasurer*
John H Kahle, *Admin Sec*
◆ EMP: 185
SQ FT: 133,000
SALES (est): 1.1B
SALES (corp-wide): 669.9MM **Publicly Held**
SIC: 2521 2522 Wood office furniture; office furniture, except wood
PA: Kimball International, Inc.
1600 Royal St
Jasper IN 47549
812 482-1600

(G-8280)
KIMBALL HOSPITALITY INC
1180 E 16th St (47549-0001)
PHONE..................................812 482-8090
Fax: 812 482-8188
Kimberly Walker, *District Mgr*
Kevin Meadows, *Design Engr*
EMP: 19
SALES (corp-wide): 669.9MM **Publicly Held**
SIC: 2599 Hotel furniture
HQ: Kimball Hospitality Inc
1600 Royal St
Jasper IN 47549

(G-8281)
KIMBALL HOSPITALITY INC (DH)
1600 Royal St (47549-1022)
PHONE..................................812 482-8090
Fax: 812 634-4325
Kourtney Smith, *President*
Douglas A Habig, *Chairman*
Robert W Bomholt, *Vice Pres*
Robert F Schneider, *Vice Pres*
Chris Thyen, *Vice Pres*
▲ EMP: 61
SALES (est): 72.1MM
SALES (corp-wide): 669.9MM **Publicly Held**
SIC: 2599 Hospital furniture, except beds

(G-8282)
KIMBALL INTERNATIONAL INC (PA)
1600 Royal St (47549-1022)
PHONE..................................812 482-1600
Fax: 812 482-8300
Robert F Schneider, *Ch of Bd*
Kathy Sigler, *President*
Kourtney Smith, *President*
Kourtney L Smith, *President*
Kourtney Smith, *President*
◆ EMP: 277 EST: 1939
SALES: 669.9MM **Publicly Held**
WEB: www.kimball.com
SIC: 2511 2512 2521 2522 Wood household furniture; upholstered household furniture; wood office furniture; office furniture, except wood; stereo cabinets, wood; television cabinets, wood

(G-8283)
KIMBALL NATIONAL OFFICE F
340 E 11th Ave (47549-0001)
PHONE..................................812 634-3356

▲ EMP: 4
SALES (est): 370.2K **Privately Held**
SIC: 2522 Office furniture, except wood

(G-8284)
KIMBALL OFFICE INC
1155 W 12th Ave (47546-8195)
PHONE..................................812 634-3220
Deena Toy, *Coordinator*
Alex Mlsna, *Associate*
EMP: 19
SALES (corp-wide): 669.9MM **Publicly Held**
SIC: 2522 Office desks & tables: except wood
HQ: Kimball Office Inc.
1600 Royal St
Jasper IN 47549

(G-8285)
KIMBALL OFFICE INC (DH)
1600 Royal St (47549-1022)
PHONE..................................812 482-1600
Douglas A Habig, *Ch of Bd*
Thomas L Habig, *Vice Ch Bd*
Michael Wagner, *President*
James C Thyen, *President*
C Allen Parker, *Vice Pres*
▲ EMP: 500
SQ FT: 195,000
SALES (est): 329MM
SALES (corp-wide): 669.9MM **Publicly Held**
SIC: 2522 Office desks & tables: except wood

(G-8286)
KITCHEN JEWELS INC (PA)
1330 Franklin St (47546-2209)
PHONE..................................812 482-9663
Fax: 812 482-1226
Dale Gress, *President*
Virgil Gress, *President*
Joseph H Fehribach, *Vice Pres*
Micki Gress, *Vice Pres*
EMP: 31
SQ FT: 54,000
SALES (est): 4.4MM **Privately Held**
WEB: www.kitchenjewels.com
SIC: 2434 Wood kitchen cabinets

(G-8287)
LECLERE MANUFACTURING INC
2905 Newton St (47546-1335)
P.O. Box 846 (47547-0846)
PHONE..................................812 683-5627
James M Le Clere, *President*
Rhonda K Le Clere, *Treasurer*
EMP: 9
SALES (est): 1.1MM **Privately Held**
SIC: 2448 2441 Pallets, wood; nailed wood boxes & shook

(G-8288)
M & C LLC
Also Called: Mailboxes and Parcel Depot
3626 N Newton St (47546)
PHONE..................................812 482-7447
Fax: 812 482-7297
Cathy Siebert,
EMP: 3
SQ FT: 1,500
SALES: 175K **Privately Held**
SIC: 3086 Packaging & shipping materials, foamed plastic

(G-8289)
MAGNOLIA
311 W 36th St (47546-9521)
PHONE..................................317 831-3221
Cherryl A Jedele, *Principal*
EMP: 3 EST: 2007
SALES (est): 258.9K **Privately Held**
SIC: 3842 Prosthetic appliances

(G-8290)
MASTERBRAND CABINETS INC
Also Called: Kitchen Craft Cabinetry
1 Masterbrand Cabinets Dr (47546-2248)
PHONE..................................812 482-2527
Randy Knott, *Manager*
EMP: 5
SALES (corp-wide): 5.2B **Publicly Held**
WEB: www.mbcabinets.com
SIC: 2434 Wood kitchen cabinets

HQ: Masterbrand Cabinets, Inc.
1 Masterbrand Cabinets Dr
Jasper IN 47546
812 482-2527

(G-8291)
MASTERBRAND CABINETS INC (HQ)
Also Called: Homecrest
1 Masterbrand Cabinets Dr (47546-2248)
P.O. Box 420 (47547-0420)
PHONE..................................812 482-2527
Fax: 812 482-5977
David M Randich, *President*
Brian Eckman, *Exec VP*
Sean Fisher, *Exec VP*
Gary Lautzehiser, *Exec VP*
Rob Mullally, *Exec VP*
▲ EMP: 300
SALES (est): 2.7B
SALES (corp-wide): 5.2B **Publicly Held**
WEB: www.mbcabinets.com
SIC: 2434 Wood kitchen cabinets
PA: Fortune Brands Home & Security, Inc.
520 Lake Cook Rd
Deerfield IL 60015
847 484-4400

(G-8292)
MASTERBRAND CABINETS INC
Also Called: Decora Cabinets
1491 S Meridian Rd (47546-3831)
P.O. Box 420 (47547-0420)
PHONE..................................812 482-2513
Fax: 812 482-7410
Laura Kessens, *Human Resources*
Joe Schaffer, *Manager*
Eric Harpenau, *Manager*
Ted O'Bryan, *Manager*
John Kunkel, *Director*
EMP: 229
SALES (corp-wide): 5.2B **Publicly Held**
WEB: www.mbcabinets.com
SIC: 2434 Wood kitchen cabinets
HQ: Masterbrand Cabinets, Inc.
1 Masterbrand Cabinets Dr
Jasper IN 47546
812 482-2527

(G-8293)
MASTERBRAND CABINETS INC
1 Masterbrand Cabinets Dr (47546-2248)
PHONE..................................256 362-5530
Dave Randich, *President*
Rich Forbes, *Branch Mgr*
EMP: 280
SALES (corp-wide): 5.2B **Publicly Held**
WEB: www.mbcabinets.com
SIC: 2434 Wood kitchen cabinets
HQ: Masterbrand Cabinets, Inc.
1 Masterbrand Cabinets Dr
Jasper IN 47546
812 482-2527

(G-8294)
MEHRINGER METAL DESIGN LLC
919 E 14th St Ste 102 (47546-2274)
PHONE..................................812 634-6100
Jeffrey W Mehringer,
EMP: 8
SALES: 350K **Privately Held**
SIC: 2514 Metal household furniture

(G-8295)
MERKLEY & SONS INC
Also Called: Merkley Packing Co
3994 W 180n (47546-8498)
PHONE..................................812 482-7020
Fax: 812 482-7033
James Merkley, *President*
David Merkley, *Vice Pres*
Selma Merkley, *Treasurer*
Karen Altmann, *Admin Sec*
EMP: 30 EST: 1950
SQ FT: 21,000
SALES: 6MM **Privately Held**
SIC: 5421 5147 2011 2013 Meat markets, including freezer provisioners; meats, fresh; meat packing plants; sausages & other prepared meats

(G-8296)
MO-WOOD PRODUCTS INC (HQ)
51 E 30th St (47546-1300)
P.O. Box 606 (47547-0606)
PHONE..................................812 482-5625
John W Seng, *President*
EMP: 3 EST: 1977
SQ FT: 3,200
SALES: 2.5MM
SALES (corp-wide): 3MM **Privately Held**
SIC: 2426 Furniture dimension stock, hardwood
PA: Forest Products Manufacturing Company
51 E 30th St
Jasper IN 47546
812 482-5625

(G-8297)
NAP ASSET HOLDINGS LTD (PA)
Also Called: Nap Gladu
1180 Wernsing Rd (47546-8171)
PHONE..................................812 482-2000
Fax: 812 457-7458
Bradley Stack, *President*
Brad Munch, *Engineer*
Brad Bottoms, *Controller*
Doug Buggle, *Sales Staff*
Michael Bowers, *Manager*
◆ EMP: 75
SQ FT: 55,000
SALES (est): 45.7MM **Privately Held**
WEB: www.naptools.com
SIC: 7699 3541 3545 Knife, saw & tool sharpening & repair; saws, power (metalworking machinery); tools & accessories for machine tools

(G-8298)
NATIONAL OFFICE FURNITURE INC (DH)
1610 Royal St (47549-0001)
PHONE..................................812 482-1600
Fax: 812 482-8980
Keefe Collins, *Division Mgr*
Lyndee Cook, *Division Mgr*
Spencer Henderson, *Division Mgr*
Danny Stingley, *Division Mgr*
Kirt Bachman, *District Mgr*
◆ EMP: 115
SQ FT: 200,000
SALES (est): 208.1MM
SALES (corp-wide): 669.9MM **Publicly Held**
SIC: 2521 Wood office furniture

(G-8299)
PACKAGING CORPORATION AMERICA
Also Called: PCA
240 S Truman Rd (47546-9768)
PHONE..................................812 482-4598
Fax: 812 482-3455
Jay Stilmeyer, *Branch Mgr*
EMP: 7
SALES (corp-wide): 6.4B **Publicly Held**
WEB: www.columbuscontainer.com
SIC: 2653 Boxes, corrugated: made from purchased materials
PA: Packaging Corporation Of America
1955 W Field Ct
Lake Forest IL 60045
847 482-3000

(G-8300)
PEPSI-COLA
Also Called: Pepsico
2811 Market St (47546-1409)
PHONE..................................812 634-1844
EMP: 2
SALES (est): 62.3K **Privately Held**
SIC: 2086 Carbonated soft drinks, bottled & canned

(G-8301)
PHAZE ONE LLC
4533 Baden Strasse (47546-9175)
PHONE..................................812 634-9545
Robert Hamm, *Mng Member*
EMP: 2
SALES (est): 109.7K **Privately Held**
SIC: 2851 7389 Removers & cleaners;

(G-8302)
ROBERT L WEHR
Also Called: Wehr Welding & Repair Shop
1527 W 100s (47546-8204)
PHONE...................................812 482-2673
Robert L Wehr, *Owner*
EMP: 2
SALES (est): 133.4K **Privately Held**
SIC: 7692 Welding repair

(G-8303)
SCHMIDT CONTRACTING INC
1111 Maurice St (47546-3748)
PHONE...................................812 482-3923
Fax: 812 482-3900
Phillip A Schmidt, *President*
Thomas R Schmidt, *Corp Secy*
Carol L Schmidt, *Vice Pres*
EMP: 18
SQ FT: 10,200
SALES (est): 1.8MM **Privately Held**
WEB: www.schmidtcontracting.com
SIC: 1711 1761 3441 3433 Warm air
heating & air conditioning contractor; roof-
ing contractor; fabricated structural metal;
heating equipment, except electric;
plumbing fixture fittings & trim; asphalt
felts & coatings

(G-8304)
SCHROCK CABINET
5231 Oak Grove Rd (47547)
P.O. Box 420 (47547-0420)
PHONE...................................812 482-2527
Paul Bertanard, *Principal*
EMP: 4
SALES (est): 353.5K **Privately Held**
SIC: 2434 Wood kitchen cabinets

(G-8305)
SEMINOLE STONE INC
1503 S Meridian Rd (47546-3832)
P.O. Box 13 (47547-0013)
PHONE...................................812 634-7115
Joseph R Knies, *President*
Jeff Knies, *Corp Secy*
EMP: 10
SQ FT: 800
SALES (est): 427.8K **Privately Held**
SIC: 1422 Limestones, ground

(G-8306)
SERVANTS INC (PA)
3145 Lottes Dr (47546-3264)
P.O. Box 848 (47547-0848)
PHONE...................................812 634-2201
Sharon Montgomery, *President*
John Besaw, *Principal*
Werner Ariel, *Engineer*
Mary Schnaus, *Cust Mgr*
EMP: 60
SQ FT: 106,000
SALES: 12.6MM **Privately Held**
WEB: www.servants.com
SIC: 2653 5113 5031 2448 Boxes, corru-
gated: made from purchased materials;
industrial & personal service paper; lum-
ber, plywood & millwork; wood pallets &
skids

(G-8307)
SERVANTS INC
3145 Lottes Dr (47546-3264)
PHONE...................................812 634-2201
Mike Hurt, *Manager*
EMP: 4
SALES (corp-wide): 12.6MM **Privately
Held**
WEB: www.servants.com
SIC: 2653 5113 2448 Boxes, corrugated:
made from purchased materials; corru-
gated & solid fiber boxes; wood pallets &
skids
PA: Servants Inc
3145 Lottes Dr
Jasper IN 47546
812 634-2201

(G-8308)
SHAMROCK CABINETS INC
5785 W 150n (47546-9733)
P.O. Box 724, Ireland (47545-0724)
PHONE...................................812 482-7969
Fax: 812 482-7969
Clara M Brauneker, *President*
Dennis Wickman, *Corp Secy*

Jeff Brauneker, *Vice Pres*
Julie Brauneker, *Office Mgr*
Debbie Wickman, *Shareholder*
EMP: 33 EST: 1962
SALES: 3.2MM **Privately Held**
SIC: 2434 2431 2511 2542 Wood kitchen
cabinets; vanities, bathroom: wood; mantels, wood; bookcases, household: wood;
partitions & fixtures, except wood; wood
office furniture; wood television & radio
cabinets

(G-8309)
SMOKER FRIENDLY
2913 Newton St (47546-1335)
PHONE...................................812 556-0244
Susan Garloch, *General Mgr*
EMP: 2 EST: 2013
SALES (est): 115.1K **Privately Held**
SIC: 5993 5194 2111 Cigarette store;
smoking tobacco; cigarettes

(G-8310)
SNAPPY MINDS LLC
1330 Cobblestone Rd (47546-8050)
PHONE...................................812 661-8506
Michael Park, *CEO*
Bill Heyman, *Partner*
EMP: 2
SALES (est): 99.6K **Privately Held**
SIC: 7372 7389 Business oriented com-
puter software; educational computer
software;

(G-8311)
**SOUTHERN INDIANA SUPPLY
INC**
1059 Wernsing Rd (47546-7911)
PHONE...................................812 482-2267
Jim Ruhe, *President*
Stephanie Stark, *Office Mgr*
Paul Giesler, *Manager*
EMP: 5 EST: 1996
SALES: 400K **Privately Held**
SIC: 3272 Building materials, except block
or brick: concrete

(G-8312)
**UNITED CABINET
CORPORATION NIT**
1 Masterbrand Cabinets Dr (47546-2248)
PHONE...................................812 482-2561
Martin V Doren, *Principal*
EMP: 2 EST: 2007
SALES (est): 155.1K **Privately Held**
SIC: 2599 Cabinets, factory

(G-8313)
WERNER SAWMILL INC
3545 N 550w (47546-9797)
PHONE...................................812 482-7565
Fax: 812 482-4883
Kevin Werner, *President*
Mary J Werner, *Admin Sec*
EMP: 35
SQ FT: 21,000
SALES (est): 3.4MM **Privately Held**
SIC: 2421 2426 Sawmills & planing mills,
general; hardwood dimension & flooring
mills

(G-8314)
**WHITE OAK LAND & TIMBER
LLC**
560 E 25th St (47546-8117)
PHONE...................................812 482-5102
Michael K Braun, *Principal*
EMP: 3
SALES (est): 172.2K **Privately Held**
SIC: 2411 Timber, cut at logging camp

Jeffersonville
Clark County

(G-8315)
1ST SOURCE PRODUCTS INC
2822 Sable Mill Ln (47130-9247)
PHONE...................................812 288-7466
Fax: 812 288-7971
Donald L Sandusky, *President*
B Scott Sparks, *Vice Pres*
Suzanne Mowry, *Human Resources*
John Webb, *Sales Mgr*

Sarah Gould, *Accounts Mgr*
▲ EMP: 12
SALES: 7.5MM **Privately Held**
WEB: www.1stsourceproducts.com
SIC: 3535 3315 Conveyors & conveying
equipment; fence gates posts & fittings:
steel

(G-8316)
323INK LLC
2818 Sable Mill Ln (47130-9247)
PHONE...................................812 282-3620
Fax: 812 282-3620
Carrie Comingore, *Owner*
EMP: 5 EST: 1968
SQ FT: 1,500
SALES (est): 330K **Privately Held**
WEB: www.tandlprinting.com
SIC: 2752 Commercial printing, offset

(G-8317)
**ACL PROFESSIONAL SERVICES
INC**
1701 Utica Pike (47130-4747)
PHONE...................................812 288-0100
Mike Ryan, *CEO*
EMP: 464
SALES (est): 14MM **Privately Held**
SIC: 4449 3731 Water transportation of
freight; shipbuilding & repairing
HQ: Commercial Barge Line Company
1701 E Market St
Jeffersonville IN 47130
812 288-0100

(G-8318)
**ACOUSTICAL AUDIO DESIGNS
LLC**
2008 Coopers Ln (47130-9225)
PHONE...................................812 282-7522
Fax: 812 282-3435
Mike Dewees,
EMP: 11
SALES (est): 2.1MM **Privately Held**
SIC: 3663 Radio & TV communications
equipment

(G-8319)
ACTION EMBROIDERY INC
4400 Charlestown Pike (47130-8744)
PHONE...................................850 626-1796
Denise Harper-Higgs, *President*
Melony Worall, *Vice Pres*
EMP: 2
SALES (est): 95K **Privately Held**
SIC: 7299 2261 Stitching services; screen
printing of cotton broadwoven fabrics

(G-8320)
ACTIVE ANKLE SYSTEMS INC
233 Quartermaster Ct (47130-3669)
P.O. Box 1001, Gardner KS (66030-1001)
PHONE...................................812 258-0663
Fax: 812 258-0664
Glen R Snow, *President*
Henry H Porter Jr, *Chairman*
Scott Morton, *COO*
Diane Lilly, *CFO*
Doug Stetner, *Shareholder*
EMP: 15
SQ FT: 4,480
SALES (est): 1.6MM **Privately Held**
WEB: www.activeankle.com
SIC: 3842 5047 Supports: abdominal,
ankle, arch, kneecap, etc.; medical equip-
ment & supplies

(G-8321)
AEDS & SAFETY SERVICES LLC
12 Abby Chase (47130-9762)
P.O. Box 20595, Louisville KY (40250-
0595)
PHONE...................................502 641-3118
Melvin Canter, *Mng Member*
EMP: 3 EST: 2003
SALES: 150K **Privately Held**
SIC: 3845 7389 Defibrillator;

(G-8322)
AMATROL INC (PA)
Also Called: Oxygen Education
2400 Centennial Blvd (47130-8538)
PHONE...................................812 288-8285
Paul S Perkins, *President*
Kimberly Perkins, *Vice Pres*
Jim Steele, *Vice Pres*

Tim Tyler, *Mfg Staff*
Shannon Norton, *Buyer*
EMP: 150 EST: 1981
SQ FT: 26,000
SALES (est): 25MM **Privately Held**
WEB: www.amatrol.com
SIC: 3569 3823 Robots, assembly line: in-
dustrial & commercial; industrial instrmnts
msrmnt display/control process variable

(G-8323)
**AMERICAN BARGE LINE
COMPANY (DH)**
1701 E Market St (47130-4755)
PHONE...................................812 288-0100
Mark Holden, *President*
EMP: 1
SALES (est): 860.3MM **Privately Held**
SIC: 4449 3731 4491 Canal barge opera-
tions; barges, building & repairing; marine
terminals
HQ: American Commercial Lines, Inc.
1701 E Market St
Jeffersonville IN 47130
812 288-0100

(G-8324)
**AMERICAN COML BARGE LINE
LLC (HQ)**
1701 E Market St (47130-4717)
PHONE...................................812 288-0100
Fax: 812 288-0256
Mark K Knoy, *CEO*
Paul A Tobin, *COO*
Robert M Blocker, *Senior VP*
Marty Hettel, *Vice Pres*
David J Huls, *CFO*
EMP: 200
SQ FT: 165,000
SALES (est): 750MM **Privately Held**
WEB: www.aclines.com
SIC: 4449 3731 4491 Canal barge opera-
tions; barges, building & repairing; marine
terminals

(G-8325)
**AMERICAN COMMERCIAL LINES
INC (HQ)**
Also Called: Acl
1701 E Market St (47130-4755)
P.O. Box 610 (47131-0610)
PHONE...................................812 288-0100
Fax: 812 288-1664
Mark K Knoy, *CEO*
Paul A Tobin, *COO*
Robert M Blocker, *Senior VP*
David J Huls, *Senior VP*
Dawn R Landry, *Senior VP*
EMP: 170
SQ FT: 165,000
SALES (est): 1B **Privately Held**
SIC: 4449 3731 4491 Canal barge opera-
tions; barges, building & repairing; marine
terminals

(G-8326)
ANCHOR ENTERPRISES
10 Arctic Spgs (47130-4701)
PHONE...................................812 282-7220
Judy Lloyd, *Owner*
EMP: 2
SALES: 100K **Privately Held**
SIC: 2752 2759 2761 Commercial print-
ing, lithographic; commercial printing, off-
set; letterpress printing; screen printing;
manifold business forms

(G-8327)
**AUTONEUM NORTH AMERICA
INC**
100 River Ridge Pkwy (47130-7762)
PHONE...................................248 848-0100
John Lenga, *Branch Mgr*
EMP: 2
SALES (corp-wide): 2.2B **Privately Held**
SIC: 3714 Motor vehicle parts & acces-
sories
HQ: Autoneum North America, Inc.
29293 Haggerty Rd
Novi MI 48377
248 848-0100

(G-8328)
BEACH MOLD & TOOL INC
4600 New Middle Rd (47130-8540)
PHONE..................................502 649-9915
Susan Katzman, *Branch Mgr*
EMP: 2
SALES (corp-wide): 228.8MM **Privately Held**
SIC: 3089 Injection molding of plastics
PA: Beach Mold & Tool, Inc.
999 Progress Blvd
New Albany IN 47150
812 945-2688

(G-8329)
BENITOS PRINTING
214 E Maple St (47130-3420)
PHONE..................................812 282-4855
EMP: 2 **EST:** 2008
SALES (est): 110K **Privately Held**
SIC: 2752 Lithographic Commercial Printing

(G-8330)
BLITZ MANUFACTURING CO IND
263 America Pl (47130-4285)
P.O. Box 846 (47131-0846)
PHONE..................................812 284-2548
Fax: 812 288-7766
Howard Sturm, *President*
Richard Spiers, *Opers Mgr*
Robert Solensky, *CFO*
Lanna Berkun, *Sales Mgr*
Bess Rick, *Manager*
▼ **EMP:** 60
SQ FT: 4,000
SALES (est): 10.1MM **Privately Held**
WEB: www.blitzinc.com
SIC: 3471 2842 Cleaning, polishing & finishing; metal polish

(G-8331)
BRIDGEWELL RESOURCES LLC
1274 Dutch Ln (47130-6371)
PHONE..................................812 285-1811
EMP: 7
SALES (corp-wide): 1.5B **Privately Held**
SIC: 5031 2491 5039 5153 Whol Lumber/Plywd/Millwk Wood Preserving Whol Cnstn Materials Whol Grain/Field Beans
HQ: Bridgewell Resources Llc
10200 Sw Greenburg Rd # 500
Tigard OR 97223

(G-8332)
BRINLY-HARDY COMPANY (PA)
3230 Industrial Pkwy (47130-9632)
PHONE..................................812 218-7200
Jane W Hardy, *CEO*
Michael Schmitt, *President*
◆ **EMP:** 100 **EST:** 1839
SALES (est): 59.4MM **Privately Held**
WEB: www.brinly.com
SIC: 3524 3423 Lawn & garden equipment; carts or wagons for lawn & garden; cultivators (garden tractor equipment); hand & edge tools

(G-8333)
BRIOVARX
1050 Patrol Rd (47130-7750)
PHONE..................................812 256-8600
Brian Laird, *Vice Pres*
Matt Powers, *Vice Pres*
Melissa Anderson, *Opers Staff*
Michael Jobe, *Opers Staff*
Kerry Mello, *Opers Staff*
EMP: 15
SALES (est): 2.3MM **Privately Held**
SIC: 2834 Pharmaceutical preparations

(G-8334)
BUDGET PRINTING CENTERS INC (PA)
Also Called: Budget Instant Print
902 E 10th St (47130-4141)
PHONE..................................812 282-8832
Fax: 812 282-4057
Roger W Fisher, *President*
Lisa Green, *Manager*
EMP: 5 **EST:** 1981
SQ FT: 2,000
SALES: 325K **Privately Held**
WEB: www.budgetinstantprint.com
SIC: 2752 7384 Commercial printing, offset; photo-offset printing; film processing & finishing laboratory

(G-8335)
CARMAN INDUSTRIES INC (PA)
1005 W Riverside Dr (47130-3143)
P.O. Box 579 (47131-0579)
PHONE..................................812 288-4710
Fax: 812 288-4708
C James Hyslop, *President*
Bill Wetherton, *Vice Pres*
William Wetherton, *Vice Pres*
Richard Geiger, *Design Engr*
J L Ising, *CFO*
EMP: 50 **EST:** 1961
SQ FT: 60,000
SALES (est): 12.7MM **Privately Held**
WEB: www.carmanindustries.com
SIC: 3535 Conveyors & conveying equipment

(G-8336)
CHEMTRUSION INC
Also Called: Chemtrusion-Indiana
1403 Port Rd (47130-8411)
PHONE..................................812 280-2910
Fax: 812 280-2915
Leo Visser, *Plant Mgr*
Joe Bina, *Technical Mgr*
Jeremy Foushee, *Financial Analy*
Carol Allen, *Human Res Dir*
Deborah Weatherholt, *Manager*
EMP: 60
SALES (corp-wide): 40.6MM **Privately Held**
WEB: www.chemtrusion.com
SIC: 2821 3714 Thermoplastic materials; motor vehicle parts & accessories
PA: Chemtrusion, Inc.
7115 Clinton Dr
Houston TX 77020
713 675-1616

(G-8337)
CLARCOR AIR FILTRATION PDTS (DH)
100 River Ridge Cir (47130-8974)
PHONE..................................502 969-2304
Chris Conway, *CEO*
Douglas Griffin, *President*
Kevin Bush, *Principal*
Jon Gallisdorfer, *Vice Pres*
Joseph Hovekamp, *Vice Pres*
◆ **EMP:** 70 **EST:** 1964
SQ FT: 7,500
SALES (est): 262.6MM
SALES (corp-wide): 12B **Publicly Held**
WEB: www.airguard.com
SIC: 3564 Air cleaning systems
HQ: Clarcor Inc.
840 Crescent Centre Dr # 600
Franklin TN 37067
615 771-3100

(G-8338)
CLARKE AMERICAN CHECKS INC
Also Called: Harland Clarke
240 America Pl (47130-4272)
PHONE..................................812 283-9598
Ronald Ryder, *Branch Mgr*
EMP: 163 **Privately Held**
SIC: 2782 Checkbooks
HQ: Clarke American Checks Inc.
15955 La Cantera Pkwy
San Antonio TX 78256
210 697-8888

(G-8339)
CLARKE AMERICAN CHECKS INC
239 America Pl (47130-4272)
PHONE..................................812 283-9598
Fax: 812 283-7204
Bob Armor, *Plant Mgr*
EMP: 160
SQ FT: 40,000
SALES (est): 170K **Privately Held**
WEB: www.clarkeamerican.com
SIC: 2782 2791 2789 2759 Blankbooks & looseleaf binders; typesetting; bookbinding & related work; commercial printing; commercial printing, lithographic

HQ: Clarke American Checks Inc.
15955 La Cantera Pkwy
San Antonio TX 78256
210 697-8888

(G-8340)
CLARKE AMERICAN CHECKS INC
239 America Pl (47130-4272)
PHONE..................................812 283-9598
Fax: 812 283-7204
EMP: 2
SALES (est): 170K **Privately Held**
SIC: 2759 Commercial Printing

(G-8341)
COMMERCIAL BARGE LINE COMPANY (DH)
1701 E Market St (47130-4755)
PHONE..................................812 288-0100
Mark K Knoy, *President*
Paul Tobin, *COO*
Robert M Blocker, *Senior VP*
Dawn R Landry, *Senior VP*
David J Huls, *CFO*
EMP: 11
SALES (est): 864.8MM **Privately Held**
SIC: 4449 4491 3731 Canal barge operations; marine terminals; barges, building & repairing
HQ: American Barge Line Company
1701 E Market St
Jeffersonville IN 47130
812 288-0100

(G-8342)
COMPLETE METAL FABRICATION INC
200 Salem Rd (47130-7752)
PHONE..................................812 284-4470
Fax: 812 284-4480
Hugh Willeford, *President*
Kate Merchant, *Safety Mgr*
Roger A Harshey Jr, *Admin Sec*
EMP: 20
SQ FT: 22,400
SALES (est): 3.7MM **Privately Held**
SIC: 3599 Machine shop, jobbing & repair

(G-8343)
COMPLETE PRTG SOLUTIONS INC
2199 Hamburg Pike (47130-6317)
PHONE..................................812 285-9200
David H Leuhart, *CEO*
Shan Leuhart, *President*
EMP: 3
SQ FT: 15,000
SALES (est): 7.3K **Privately Held**
SIC: 2752 Commercial printing, offset

(G-8344)
COMPUTER TECHNOLOGY
1101 Watt St (47130-3843)
P.O. Box 2774, Clarksville (47131-2774)
PHONE..................................812 283-5094
Neal Altman, *President*
EMP: 4
SALES (est): 190K **Privately Held**
SIC: 3469 Machine parts, stamped or pressed metal

(G-8345)
COOK COMPRESSION INC
2540 Centennial Blvd (47130-8535)
PHONE..................................502 515-6900
Frank Wierengo, *President*
Jim Prendergast, *Vice Pres*
Bill Martin, *Controller*
▲ **EMP:** 655
SALES (est): 44.1MM
SALES (corp-wide): 7.8B **Publicly Held**
WEB: www.cookmanley.com
SIC: 7699 3563 Compressor repair; air & gas compressors
PA: Dover Corporation
3005 Highland Pkwy # 200
Downers Grove IL 60515
630 541-1540

(G-8346)
CORBETTS CUSTOM CABINETRY LLC
6104 Carr Cir (47130-9244)
PHONE..................................812 670-6211
EMP: 2
SALES (est): 169.9K **Privately Held**
SIC: 2434 Wood kitchen cabinets

(G-8347)
CORONADO STONE INC
4306 Charlestown Pike (47130-8702)
PHONE..................................812 284-2845
Fax: 812 282-1520
Carolyn Ward, *President*
Carolyn T Ward, *President*
Jim Blanton, *COO*
Jeremy Ward, *Vice Pres*
EMP: 45
SALES: 6MM **Privately Held**
WEB: www.coronadostone.com
SIC: 3281 1752 Furniture, cut stone; vinyl floor tile & sheet installation

(G-8348)
CREATIVE CONCEPT VENTURES INC
Also Called: Insty-Prints
590 Missouri Ave (47130-3083)
P.O. Box 812 (47131-0812)
PHONE..................................812 282-9442
Fax: 812 282-9498
Mike Rich, *President*
Denise Freville, *Vice Pres*
Carlotta Simpson, *Vice Pres*
EMP: 5
SQ FT: 3,000
SALES (est): 550K **Privately Held**
SIC: 7336 2752 7334 2791 Graphic arts & related design; offset & photolithographic printing; photocopying & duplicating services; typesetting; bookbinding & related work

(G-8349)
CYLICRON LLC
5171 Maritime (47130-8452)
P.O. Box 4185 (47131-4185)
PHONE..................................812 283-4600
K Michael Roberts, *President*
Karen Cane, *CFO*
Adam Gabbard, *CFO*
Larry Jordan, *Sales Associate*
Randy Brewer, *Manager*
▲ **EMP:** 63
SQ FT: 140,000
SALES (est): 10.8MM **Privately Held**
WEB: www.cylicron.com
SIC: 2796 Plates & cylinders for rotogravure printing

(G-8350)
DALLAS GROUP OF AMERICA INC
Magnesol Div
1402 Fabricon Blvd (47130-9607)
PHONE..................................812 283-6675
Fax: 812 282-5409
Walter Mulflur, *Vice Pres*
David Cousins, *Plant Mgr*
Doug Rudy, *Research*
Dan Hicks, *Engineer*
Oscar Martinez, *Engineer*
EMP: 60
SQ FT: 6,000
SALES (corp-wide): 122.3MM **Privately Held**
SIC: 2819 3339 Magnesium compounds or salts, inorganic; primary nonferrous metals
PA: The Dallas Group Of America Inc
374 Rte 22
Whitehouse NJ 08888
908 534-7800

(G-8351)
DIAMOND BILLIARD PRODUCTS INC
4700 New Middle Rd (47130-8539)
PHONE..................................812 288-7665
Robert G Sullivan, *President*
Chad Scharlow, *Vice Pres*
Brian Miller, *Sales Dir*
Aaron Berger, *Sales Staff*
Paul Smith, *Sales Associate*
◆ **EMP:** 50
SQ FT: 71,000

SALES: 6MM **Privately Held**
WEB: www.diamondbilliardproducts.com
SIC: 5091 3949 Billiard equipment & supplies; billiard & pool equipment & supplies, general

(G-8352)
DOVER CORPORATION (PA)
Also Called: C Lee Cook
2540 Centennial Blvd (47130-8535)
PHONE....................................502 587-6783
Don York, *President*
EMP: 200
SALES (est): 35.1MM **Privately Held**
SIC: 3592 Carburetors, pistons, rings, valves

(G-8353)
EAGLE INDUSTRIES INC
Also Called: Nolan Co
131 E Court Ave Ste 200 (47130-3603)
P.O. Box 1059 (47131-1059)
PHONE....................................812 282-1393
Fax: 812 282-0171
Chris Nolan, *President*
EMP: 10
SQ FT: 3,500
SALES (est): 1.5MM **Privately Held**
WEB: www.eagleindustries.net
SIC: 2673 Plastic bags: made from purchased materials

(G-8354)
ENERGY DELIVERY SOLUTIONS LLC
Also Called: EDS
3315 Industrial Pkwy (47130-9633)
PHONE....................................502 271-8753
William Ehringer, *Mng Member*
EMP: 5
SQ FT: 7,500
SALES (est): 742.7K **Privately Held**
SIC: 2834 2844 Pharmaceutical preparations; cosmetic preparations

(G-8355)
ENGLISH INDUSTRIES LLC
2781 Jefferson Centre Way (47130-8265)
PHONE....................................812 218-9882
Jon Stricker, *Owner*
EMP: 2 EST: 2010
SALES (est): 100K **Privately Held**
SIC: 3999 Manufacturing industries

(G-8356)
ENJOY LIFE NATURAL BRANDS LLC
301 Salem Rd (47130-7764)
PHONE....................................773 632-2163
EMP: 10 **Publicly Held**
SIC: 2046 2051 Wheat gluten; bread, cake & related products
HQ: Enjoy Life Natural Brands, Llc
8770 W Bryn Mawr Ave
Chicago IL 60631
773 632-2163

(G-8357)
ERNEST A COOPER
Also Called: Competitive Pallet Service
1502 Production Rd (47130-9604)
PHONE....................................812 284-0436
Fax: 812 284-9560
Ernest Cooper, *Owner*
Caryn Cooper, *Co-Owner*
EMP: 25
SQ FT: 9,600
SALES (est): 2MM **Privately Held**
SIC: 2448 Pallets, wood; pallets, wood & wood with metal

(G-8358)
ERNSTBERGER ENTERPRISES INC
211 Eastern Blvd (47130-2801)
PHONE....................................812 282-0488
Fax: 812 282-3297
Dean Collins, *Vice Pres*
▲ EMP: 70
SQ FT: 85,000
SALES (est): 20.5MM **Privately Held**
WEB: www.munichwelding.com
SIC: 3441 7692 Fabricated structural metal; welding repair

(G-8359)
ESTES WASTE SOLUTIONS LLC
5005 Hamburg Pike (47130-9203)
P.O. Box 578, Floyds Knobs (47119-0578)
PHONE....................................812 283-6400
Kathy Estes,
Bill White,
EMP: 7
SALES (est): 143.3K **Privately Held**
SIC: 3443 Dumpsters, garbage

(G-8360)
FINISH DESIGN WOODWORKING INC
2819 Sable Mill Ln (47130-9248)
PHONE....................................812 284-9240
Fax: 812 284-9234
Harold Snook, *President*
Brian Rauck, *Sales Mgr*
Bonnie Stewart, *Executive*
EMP: 20
SQ FT: 21,000
SALES (est): 2.7MM **Privately Held**
WEB: www.fdwinc.com
SIC: 2431 2531 Millwork; public building & related furniture

(G-8361)
FLEXIBLE MATERIALS INC (PA)
3101 Hamburg Pike Ste B (47130-9645)
PHONE....................................812 280-7000
Ronald W Humin, *CEO*
Rodney Beyl, *President*
Chris Brown, *President*
Edward J Krawiec, *Principal*
Greg Hublar, *Vice Pres*
▲ EMP: 87
SQ FT: 25,000
SALES (est): 17.4MM **Privately Held**
SIC: 2435 Hardwood veneer & plywood

(G-8362)
FLEXIBLE MATERIALS INC
3101 Hamburg Pike Ste A (47130-9645)
PHONE....................................812 280-9578
Rod Beyl, *Principal*
EMP: 60
SALES (corp-wide): 17.4MM **Privately Held**
SIC: 2435 3083 2891 2671 Hardwood veneer & plywood; laminated plastics plate & sheet; adhesives & sealants; packaging paper & plastics film, coated & laminated
PA: Flexible Materials, Inc.
3101 Hamburg Pike Ste B
Jeffersonville IN 47130
812 280-7000

(G-8363)
FORM WOOD INDUSTRIES INC
1601 Production Rd (47130-9624)
PHONE....................................812 284-3676
Fax: 812 285-5074
Todd Smith, *President*
▲ EMP: 40
SQ FT: 80,000
SALES (est): 10MM **Privately Held**
WEB: www.formwood.com
SIC: 2435 3469 Veneer stock, hardwood; architectural panels or parts, porcelain enameled

(G-8364)
FREUDENBERG MEDICAL MIS INC (DH)
Also Called: Medventure Technology
2301 Centennial Blvd (47130-8975)
PHONE....................................812 280-2400
Mitch Moeller, *President*
Mark Sterett, *VP Opers*
Kimberly W Wray, *Opers Mgr*
Bryan Ogle, *Prdtn Mgr*
Anthony Appling, *Engineer*
EMP: 169
SQ FT: 100,000
SALES: 51.4MM
SALES (corp-wide): 8.3B **Privately Held**
SIC: 3841 Medical instruments & equipment, blood & bone work
HQ: Freudenberg Medical, Llc
1110 Mark Ave
Carpinteria CA 93013
805 684-3304

(G-8365)
FULL METAL SOLUTIONS LLC
295a America Pl (47130)
PHONE....................................812 725-9660
Chad Webb, *Mng Member*
EMP: 9 EST: 2011
SALES (est): 1.2MM **Privately Held**
SIC: 3448 Ramps: prefabricated metal

(G-8366)
GABRIEL PRODUCTS INC
2303 Cypress Pt (47130-6775)
PHONE....................................502 291-5388
Gabriel Appiah, *President*
EMP: 2 EST: 2010
SALES (est): 260.7K **Privately Held**
SIC: 2899 Corrosion preventive lubricant

(G-8367)
GATEWAY GALVINIZING INC
1117 Brown Forman Rd (47130-8418)
PHONE....................................812 284-5241
Fax: 812 284-5257
Julian Dozier, *President*
Steve Reitz, *Plant Mgr*
EMP: 45
SQ FT: 35,000
SALES (est): 6.7MM **Privately Held**
SIC: 3479 Galvanizing of iron, steel or end-formed products

(G-8368)
GENESIS PLASTICS SOLUTIONS LLC
2200 Centennial Blvd (47130-8533)
PHONE....................................812 283-4435
Jim Gladden, *CEO*
Kenny Ulrich, *Plant Mgr*
EMP: 2
SALES (est): 490K **Privately Held**
SIC: 3089 Injection molded finished plastic products

(G-8369)
GEO PFAUS SONS COMPANY INC
800 Wall St (47130-3619)
P.O. Box 7 (47131-0007)
PHONE....................................800 732-8645
Fax: 812 283-0765
Norman E Pfau Jr, *President*
Kari Pfau Hall, *Corp Secy*
Sue D Pfau, *Admin Sec*
EMP: 50 EST: 1869
SALES (est): 9.4MM **Privately Held**
WEB: www.pfauoil.com
SIC: 2077 Animal & marine fats & oils

(G-8370)
GOODRICH CORPORATION
Goodrich Cabin Systems
510 Patrol Rd (47130-7755)
PHONE....................................812 704-5200
Roger Wolfe, *President*
EMP: 70
SALES (corp-wide): 59.8B **Publicly Held**
SIC: 3728 Aircraft parts & equipment
HQ: Goodrich Corporation
2730 W Tyvola Rd
Charlotte NC 28217
704 423-7000

(G-8371)
GORDON B CRAWFORD DMD
1804 E Park Pl (47130-4811)
PHONE....................................812 288-8560
Gordon B Crawford, *Owner*
Gordon B Crawford DMD, *Owner*
EMP: 3
SALES (est): 200K **Privately Held**
SIC: 3843 Enamels, dentists'

(G-8372)
HERITAGE HARDWOODS KY INC (PA)
1507 Production Rd (47130-9624)
PHONE....................................812 288-5855
Maurice Smith, *Ch of Bd*
Todd Smith, *Director*
EMP: 70 EST: 1977
SALES (est): 6.9MM **Privately Held**
WEB: www.formwood.win.net
SIC: 2435 2426 Veneer stock, hardwood; hardwood dimension & flooring mills

(G-8373)
HI TECH VENEER LLC
276 America Pl (47130-4286)
PHONE....................................812 284-9775
Fax: 812 284-9042
Jason Crapo, *CEO*
Tim Griffin, *General Mgr*
Shane Sharp, *General Mgr*
Chris Totten, *CFO*
Tony Crawford, *Supervisor*
▲ EMP: 50
SALES (est): 4.4MM **Privately Held**
SIC: 2436 Softwood veneer & plywood

(G-8374)
HIGHWAY PRESS INC
2199 Hamburg Pike (47130-6397)
PHONE....................................812 283-6462
Fax: 812 283-6962
Jack Leuthart, *President*
Jo Ann Leuthart, *Corp Secy*
Robert Leuthart, *Vice Pres*
EMP: 6 EST: 1947
SQ FT: 5,500
SALES (est): 739.9K **Privately Held**
SIC: 2752 2759 Commercial printing, offset; letterpress printing

(G-8375)
HOME PHONE INC
414 Spring St (47130-3452)
PHONE....................................812 280-3657
Kenneth Calkins, *President*
EMP: 2
SALES (est): 124.1K **Privately Held**
SIC: 2451 Mobile homes

(G-8376)
HOOSIER PENN OIL CO INC
Also Called: H P Oil
2990 Industrial Pkwy (47130-9629)
PHONE....................................812 284-9433
Jack Hedges, *Manager*
EMP: 7
SALES (est): 1.1MM
SALES (corp-wide): 14.4MM **Privately Held**
WEB: www.hpoil.com
SIC: 5171 2869 Petroleum bulk stations; solvents, organic
PA: Hoosier Penn Oil Co Inc.
4060 W 10th St
Indianapolis IN 46222
317 390-5406

(G-8377)
HORIZON TERRA INCORPORATED (HQ)
Also Called: Idx - Louisville
101 River Ridge Cir (47130-8974)
PHONE....................................812 280-0000
Fax: 812 280-0377
Terrence Schultz, *President*
Fritz Baumgartner, *Admin Sec*
▲ EMP: 80
SQ FT: 150,000
SALES (est): 15MM
SALES (corp-wide): 394.6MM **Privately Held**
WEB: www.idxcorp.com
SIC: 1793 2541 Glass & glazing work; cabinets, lockers & shelving
PA: Idx Corporation
1 Rider Trail Plaza Dr
Earth City MO 63045
314 739-4120

(G-8378)
IDEMITSU LUBRICANTS AMER CORP (DH)
701 Port Rd (47130-8425)
PHONE....................................812 284-3300
Shoichi Tominaga, *President*
Masashi Yokomura, *President*
Erick Esparza, *Division Mgr*
Heather Couch, *General Mgr*
Tammi Walts, *General Mgr*
◆ EMP: 55
SQ FT: 150,000
SALES: 248.2MM
SALES (corp-wide): 35B **Privately Held**
WEB: www.apolloamerica.com
SIC: 2992 Lubricating oils & greases

HQ: Apollo Idemitsu Corporation
1831 16th St
Sacramento CA 95811
916 443-0890

(G-8379)
IDX CORPORATION
101 River Ridge Cir (47130-8974)
PHONE......................812 280-0000
Dennis Dugan, *Manager*
EMP: 195
SALES (corp-wide): 394.6MM **Privately Held**
WEB: www.idxcorporation.com
SIC: 2542 Office & store showcases & display fixtures
PA: Idx Corporation
1 Rider Trail Plaza Dr
Earth City MO 63045
314 739-4120

(G-8380)
INDIANA IMPRINT LLC
3006 Bishop Rd (47130-8835)
PHONE......................812 704-2773
Kari McGilvra, *Administration*
EMP: 3
SALES (est): 293.8K **Privately Held**
SIC: 3555 Printing presses

(G-8381)
INSCOPE MEDICAL SOLUTIONS INC
2533 Centennial Blvd (47130-8535)
P.O. Box 726 (47131-0726)
PHONE......................502 882-0183
Margaret Galloway, *CEO*
EMP: 2 EST: 2016
SQ FT: 1,200
SALES (est): 115.3K **Privately Held**
SIC: 3841 Surgical & medical instruments

(G-8382)
JC DISTRIBUTERS INC
505 Amelie Dr Ste 2 (47130-5275)
PHONE......................502 276-6311
Christopher Stiles, *President*
EMP: 9 EST: 2008
SALES (est): 524K **Privately Held**
SIC: 2086 Bottled & canned soft drinks

(G-8383)
JC MOAG CORPORATION
249 America Pl (47130-4272)
P.O. Box 1415 (47131-1415)
PHONE......................812 284-8400
Fax: 812 284-8420
John T Moag, *CEO*
James C Moag, *President*
J C Moag, *Vice Pres*
▲ EMP: 75 EST: 1946
SQ FT: 80,000
SALES (est): 13.8MM **Privately Held**
WEB: www.jcmoag.com
SIC: 2541 3231 Store fixtures, wood; products of purchased glass

(G-8384)
JDC VENEERS INC
Also Called: HI Tech Veneer
276 America Pl (47130-4286)
PHONE......................812 284-9775
Jason Crato, *President*
Jason Crapo, *Principal*
Chris Totten, *CFO*
Steve Webster, *Controller*
James Grubbs, *Sales Staff*
▲ EMP: 53
SQ FT: 30,000
SALES (est): 11.6MM **Privately Held**
WEB: www.hitechveneer.com
SIC: 2436 Plywood, softwood

(G-8385)
JEFFBOAT LLC
1701 E Market St (47130-4755)
P.O. Box 610 (47131-0610)
PHONE......................812 288-0200
Fax: 812 288-0343
Mark K Knoy, *President*
Paul A Tobin, *COO*
Robert M Blocker, *Senior VP*
David J Huls, *CFO*
Barker Price, *Mng Member*
▲ EMP: 117

SALES (est): 62.5MM **Privately Held**
SIC: 3531 Marine related equipment
HQ: Commercial Barge Line Company
1701 E Market St
Jeffersonville IN 47130
812 288-0100

(G-8386)
KENTUCKIANA WIRE ROPE & SUPPLY
3335 Industrial Pkwy (47130-9619)
PHONE......................812 282-3667
Fax: 812 282-4059
John P Fireovid, *President*
Todd Stites, *Plant Mgr*
Tim Coombs, *Sales Associate*
Carol Lowry, *Office Mgr*
Fireovid L Patricia, *Admin Sec*
EMP: 13
SQ FT: 15,500
SALES (est): 7.3MM **Privately Held**
WEB: www.kwrinc.com
SIC: 5072 5051 2298 3496 Hardware; chains; rope, wire (not insulated); rope, except asbestos & wire; wire chain; slings, lifting: made from purchased wire

(G-8387)
KENTUCKIANA YACHT SERVICES LLC
Also Called: Kys
700 E Market St (47130-3924)
PHONE......................812 282-2660
Bill Molnar, *Sales Mgr*
David Shaw,
EMP: 2
SALES: 1.1MM **Privately Held**
SIC: 3732 5561 Yachts, building & repairing; recreational vehicle parts & accessories

(G-8388)
KENTUCKY CONCRETE INDIANA LLC
Also Called: Ohio Valley Ready Mix
2220 Hamburg Pike (47130-6320)
P.O. Box 9, Elizabethtown KY (42702-0009)
PHONE......................812 282-6671
Sharon H Schlatter, *President*
Fred Schlatter, *Vice Pres*
EMP: 20
SALES: 4MM **Privately Held**
SIC: 3273 Ready-mixed concrete

(G-8389)
KEY ELECTRONICS INC
2533 Centennial Blvd (47130-8535)
PHONE......................812 206-2500
A Thomas Hardy, *President*
Larry Porter, *COO*
Brian Doherty, *Engineer*
David Meece, *CFO*
▲ EMP: 185
SQ FT: 104,000
SALES (est): 79.7MM **Privately Held**
WEB: www.keyelectronics.com
SIC: 3679 Electronic circuits

(G-8390)
KITCHEN KOMPACT INC
911 E 11th St (47130-4172)
P.O. Box 868 (47131-0868)
PHONE......................812 282-6681
Fax: 812 282-7880
Walter Dwight Gahm, *Ch of Bd*
Walter Dwight Gahm Jr, *President*
Robert G Wilson, *Vice Pres*
Gordon Gahm, *Treasurer*
Brett Gahm, *Sales Staff*
EMP: 200 EST: 1937
SQ FT: 390,000
SALES (est): 39.2MM **Privately Held**
WEB: www.kitchenkompact.com
SIC: 2434 Wood kitchen cabinets; vanities, bathroom: wood

(G-8391)
LINK ELECTRICAL SERVICE
1018 E 7th St (47130-4451)
PHONE......................812 288-8184
Susan Link, *Principal*
EMP: 2

SALES (est): 144.4K **Privately Held**
SIC: 5099 3993 1731 Signs, except electric; signs & advertising specialties; general electrical contractor

(G-8392)
M2 INDUSTRIES LLC
2200 Utica Pike (47130-5019)
PHONE......................812 246-0651
Dale Mills, *Principal*
EMP: 2
SALES (est): 172.9K **Privately Held**
SIC: 3999 Manufacturing industries

(G-8393)
MACPACTOR INC
414 Spring St (47130-3452)
P.O. Box 145 (47131-0145)
PHONE......................502 643-7845
Dale Mills, *Vice Pres*
EMP: 4 EST: 2013
SALES (est): 393K **Privately Held**
SIC: 3496 Miscellaneous fabricated wire products

(G-8394)
MAJOR LEAGUE ELECTRONICS LLC
2533 Cenennial Blvd (47130)
PHONE......................812 670-4174
Fax: 812 944-7268
Douglas R Coffman, *President*
Sue Lynn Ross, *Manager*
EMP: 22
SQ FT: 18,500
SALES (est): 6MM **Privately Held**
WEB: www.mlelectronics.com
SIC: 3678 Electronic connectors

(G-8395)
MALONEY GROUP INC
6300 E Highway 62 (47130-8770)
PHONE......................812 285-7400
Michael Maloney, *President*
Gary Maloney, *Vice Pres*
EMP: 10
SALES (est): 849.6K **Privately Held**
WEB: www.maloneyoutdoor.com
SIC: 2211 3171 3172 Denims; women's handbags & purses; handbags, regardless of material: men's

(G-8396)
MARINE BUILDERS INC
208 Church St (47130-9411)
P.O. Box 2215, Clarksville (47131-2215)
PHONE......................812 283-7932
Fax: 812 282-1485
David W Evanczyk, *President*
Sarah Evanczyk, *Corp Secy*
Byron Evanczyk, *Vice Pres*
Matthew Evanczyk, *Project Mgr*
Yusef Norris, *Purch Mgr*
EMP: 92
SQ FT: 18,000
SALES (est): 19MM **Privately Held**
WEB: www.marinebuilders.com
SIC: 3731 3441 Towboats, building & repairing; commercial passenger ships, building & repairing; fabricated structural metal

(G-8397)
MARK HEDGE
1501 Cameron Dr (47130-6609)
PHONE......................812 288-8037
EMP: 2
SALES (est): 134.7K **Privately Held**
SIC: 3743 Mfg Railroad Equipment

(G-8398)
MARWOOD INC
2901 Hamburg Pike (47130-6722)
PHONE......................812 288-8344
Fax: 812 282-0734
James C Martin, *President*
Lyman C Martin III, *Vice Pres*
▲ EMP: 11
SQ FT: 17,000
SALES (est): 3.1MM **Privately Held**
WEB: www.marwoodveneer.com
SIC: 5031 2435 Veneer; veneer stock, hardwood

(G-8399)
MAXIMUM SCREEN PRINTING
3310 E 10th St (47130-7285)
PHONE......................502 802-4652
EMP: 2
SALES (est): 101.2K **Privately Held**
SIC: 2752 Commercial printing, lithographic

(G-8400)
MICRO BUSINESSWARE INC
1008 E 10th St (47130-4225)
PHONE......................502 424-6613
Richard Bergstrom, *Principal*
EMP: 2
SALES (est): 106.5K **Privately Held**
SIC: 7372 Prepackaged software

(G-8401)
MIDWEST MOLD REMEDIATION
912 Webster Blvd (47130-6530)
PHONE......................502 386-6559
Terry Tuggle, *President*
EMP: 6
SALES (est): 64K **Privately Held**
SIC: 3544 Industrial molds

(G-8402)
MYTEX POLYMERS US CORP
1403 Port Rd (47130-8411)
PHONE......................812 280-2900
Masayuki Arai, *President*
Mamoru Hirasawa, *Vice Pres*
Joseph Bina, *Opers Mgr*
Kohei Ichiya, *Treasurer*
Shinichiro Iguchi, *Treasurer*
▲ EMP: 30
SQ FT: 235,000
SALES (est): 11.4MM
SALES (corp-wide): 34.9B **Privately Held**
SIC: 3089 Plastic containers, except foam; plastic processing
HQ: Mitsubishi Chemical Corporation
1-1-1, Marunouchi
Chiyoda-Ku TKY 100-0
367 487-300

(G-8403)
NEW HOPE SERVICES INC (PA)
Also Called: Aberdeen Woods Apartments
725 Wall St (47130-3616)
PHONE......................812 288-8248
Fax: 812 288-1206
James A Bosley, *CEO*
Bonnie Long, *Vice Pres*
Kimberly Tungate, *Manager*
Elizabeth Boyd, *Director*
Johnathan Watkins, *Executive*
EMP: 50
SQ FT: 30,000
SALES: 8.9MM **Privately Held**
WEB: www.newhopeservices.org
SIC: 8322 2396 8331 3993 Child related social services; automotive & apparel trimmings; sheltered workshop; signs & advertising specialties

(G-8404)
NEWS AND TRIBUNE ◆
221 Spring St (47130-3353)
PHONE......................812 206-2168
E Newland, *Business Mgr*
EMP: 2 EST: 2017
SALES (est): 62.9K **Privately Held**
SIC: 2711 Newspapers

(G-8405)
NICHOLSON & SONS PRINTING INC
Also Called: Nicholson Printing
209 Eastern Blvd (47130-2801)
PHONE......................812 283-1200
Fax: 812 284-3705
Martha Nicholson, *President*
Marvin Nicholson, *Corp Secy*
Chris Nicholson, *Vice Pres*
Mike Nicholson, *Vice Pres*
EMP: 15
SQ FT: 10,500
SALES (est): 2.2MM **Privately Held**
WEB: www.nicholsonprinting.com
SIC: 2752 Commercial printing, offset; letters, circular or form: lithographed

(G-8406)
OHIO RIVER METAL SERVICES INC
5150 Loop Rd (47130-8412)
PHONE...................................812 282-4770
Fax: 812 282-5873
Shirley Ohta, *CEO*
Charles R Moore, *President*
Rita Moore, *Corp Secy*
Henry Taylor, *Exec VP*
EMP: 115
SQ FT: 200,000
SALES (est): 36.1MM
SALES (corp-wide): 9.7B **Publicly Held**
WEB: www.eaglesteel.com
SIC: 3316 Cold-rolled strip or wire
HQ: Metals Usa, Inc.
4901 Nw 17th Way Ste 405
Fort Lauderdale FL 33309
954 202-4000

(G-8407)
OHIO VALLEY READY MIX INC
2220 Hamburg Pike (47130-6398)
P.O. Box 9, Elizabethtown KY (42702-0009)
PHONE...................................812 282-6671
Fax: 812 282-6687
Gerald Ayres, *President*
Marsha Gardner, *Corp Secy*
Todd Ayres, *Vice Pres*
EMP: 38
SQ FT: 2,000
SALES (est): 5MM **Privately Held**
SIC: 3273 Ready-mixed concrete

(G-8408)
OLON INDUSTRIES INC (US)
600 Patrol Rd (47130-7700)
PHONE...................................812 256-6400
Louis Cajka, *Director*
EMP: 16
SALES (corp-wide): 23.3MM **Privately Held**
SIC: 2426 Furniture dimension stock, hardwood
HQ: Olon Industries Inc. (Us)
411 Union St
Geneva IL 60134
630 232-4705

(G-8409)
ORICA USA INC
2000 Coopers Ln Ste A1 (47130-9201)
PHONE...................................812 256-7800
Fax: 812 256-7804
Rick Beck, *Manager*
EMP: 13
SALES (corp-wide): 3.9B **Privately Held**
SIC: 5169 2892 Explosives; explosives
HQ: Orica Usa Inc.
33101 E Quincy Ave
Watkins CO 80137

(G-8410)
OUR LITTLE BOOKS LLC
306 Brighton Ave (47130-4704)
PHONE...................................812 987-2475
EMP: 2
SALES (est): 110K **Privately Held**
SIC: 2731 Book Publishing

(G-8411)
OXINAS PARTNERS LLC ✪
702 N Shore Dr Ste 101 (47130-3109)
PHONE...................................812 725-8649
Brian Coxon,
EMP: 5 **EST:** 2018
SALES (est): 104.7K **Privately Held**
SIC: 7389 7372 Financial services; application computer software

(G-8412)
PARKER-HANNIFIN CORPORATION
100 River Ridge Cir (47130-8974)
PHONE...................................502 810-5823
EMP: 2
SALES (est): 85.9K
SALES (corp-wide): 12B **Publicly Held**
SIC: 3594 Fluid power pumps & motors
PA: Parker-Hannifin Corporation
6035 Parkland Blvd
Cleveland OH 44124
216 896-3000

(G-8413)
PGP CORP
Also Called: Voss Industries
701 Loop Rd (47130-8428)
PHONE...................................812 285-7700
Fax: 812 285-7704
Joseph Rhodea, *Branch Mgr*
Timothy Bilkey, *CIO*
EMP: 90
SQ FT: 180,000
SALES (corp-wide): 91MM **Privately Held**
WEB: www.pgpcorp.com
SIC: 5051 3559 7389 Steel; metal pickling equipment; metal slitting & shearing
PA: Pgp Corp.
7925 Beech Daly Rd
Taylor MI 48180

(G-8414)
PHANTOM INDUSTRIES LLC
734 Spring St (47130-3556)
PHONE...................................812 276-5956
Sean Fitzgerald, *President*
EMP: 3 **EST:** 2015
SALES (est): 315.8K **Privately Held**
SIC: 3999 Manufacturing industries

(G-8415)
PPG INDUSTRIES INC
Also Called: PPG 4315
3310 E Highway 62 Ste 6 (47130)
PHONE...................................812 285-0546
Douglas Gill, *Branch Mgr*
EMP: 2
SALES (corp-wide): 14.2B **Publicly Held**
WEB: www.ppg.com
SIC: 2851 Paints & allied products
PA: Ppg Industries, Inc.
1 Ppg Pl
Pittsburgh PA 15272
412 434-3131

(G-8416)
PREMIER PRINTS
3018 Seminole Dr (47130-5866)
PHONE...................................812 987-1129
Reganel Burgess, *Principal*
EMP: 2 **EST:** 2013
SALES (est): 225.7K **Privately Held**
SIC: 2752 Commercial printing, lithographic

(G-8417)
PRINTING INC LOUISVILLE KY
Also Called: Pretty Incrdbl Communications
1600 Dutch Ln Ste A (47130-6302)
PHONE...................................502 368-6555
Kelly Abney, *President*
Ken Minogue, *Vice Pres*
◆ **EMP:** 25
SQ FT: 75,000
SALES (est): 4.8MM **Privately Held**
WEB: www.pilouisville.com
SIC: 2752 Commercial printing, offset

(G-8418)
PUROLATOR PDTS A FILTRATION CO (DH)
Also Called: Air Filters Sales & Service
100 River Ridge Cir (47130-8974)
PHONE...................................866 925-2247
Bill Pappas, *President*
Alan H Spicer, *President*
▲ **EMP:** 250
SQ FT: 250,000
SALES (est): 191MM
SALES (corp-wide): 12B **Publicly Held**
WEB: www.afss.net
SIC: 3564 3433 Filters, air: furnaces, air conditioning equipment, etc.; heating equipment, except electric
HQ: Clarcor Inc.
840 Crescent Centre Dr # 600
Franklin TN 37067
615 771-3100

(G-8419)
REVERE PLASTICS SYSTEMS LLC
5171 Maritime (47130-8452)
PHONE...................................812 670-2240
Nathan Coleman, *Engineer*
Joe Nelson, *Engineer*
Kyle Dalton, *Manager*
Crystal Ries, *Manager*
EMP: 8 **Privately Held**
SIC: 3089 Injection molding of plastics
HQ: Revere Plastics Systems, Llc
401 Elm St
Clyde OH 43410

(G-8420)
RO VIC WOOD PRODUCTS INC
254 America Pl C (47130-4297)
P.O. Box 1014 (47131-1014)
PHONE...................................812 283-9199
Fax: 812 283-1145
Robert Mondun, *President*
Vickie Mondun, *Corp Secy*
EMP: 35
SQ FT: 53,200
SALES (est): 3.9MM **Privately Held**
SIC: 2511 2431 Bookcases, household: wood; millwork

(G-8421)
ROLL FORMING CORPORATION
1205 N Access Dr (47130-8477)
PHONE...................................812 284-0650
Nick Garber, *Project Engr*
Chad Shaffer, *Branch Mgr*
Rick Foxx, *Manager*
Sharon Alonso, *Director*
EMP: 55
SALES (corp-wide): 16B **Privately Held**
SIC: 3449 Miscellaneous metalwork; custom roll formed products
HQ: Roll Forming Corporation
1070 Brooks Industrial Rd
Shelbyville KY 40065
502 633-4435

(G-8422)
SAMPAN SCREEN PRINT NEW IMAGE
202 Ash St (47130-9408)
PHONE...................................812 282-8499
Fax: 812 285-0451
Lynn Murchy, *Owner*
EMP: 5
SQ FT: 4,800
SALES (est): 572.3K **Privately Held**
SIC: 2759 Screen printing

(G-8423)
SCHIMPFF CONFECTIONERY
347 Spring St (47130-3449)
PHONE...................................812 283-8367
Fax: 812 288-2229
Warren Schimpff, *Owner*
Jill Schimpff, *Co-Owner*
EMP: 11
SQ FT: 5,000
SALES (est): 602.3K **Privately Held**
WEB: www.schimpffs.com
SIC: 5441 2064 5812 Candy; confectionery; candy & other confectionery products; restaurant, lunch counter

(G-8424)
SMITH ESTILL MARINE SERVICE
4210 E Hwy 62 (47130)
PHONE...................................812 282-7944
Estill Smith, *President*
Helen Smith, *Admin Sec*
EMP: 2
SALES: 200K **Privately Held**
SIC: 3731 Barges, building & repairing

(G-8425)
SOUTHERN INDIANA PLASTICS INC (PA)
Also Called: Si Plastics
1606 Dutch Ln (47130-6302)
P.O. Box 7066, Indianapolis (46207-7066)
PHONE...................................812 280-7474
Fax: 812 218-8480
Roger Smallwood, *President*
John Sampson, *Plant Mgr*
Ryan Riggs, *Opers Mgr*
Tammy Schoenfeld, *Administration*
EMP: 50
SQ FT: 60,000
SALES: 7.8MM **Privately Held**
WEB: www.siplastics.com
SIC: 3089 Injection molding of plastics

(G-8426)
SPENCER MACHINE AND TL CO INC
6205 Gheens Mill Rd (47130-9214)
PHONE...................................812 282-6300
Fax: 812 282-7272
Glenn Spencer, *President*
Glenn Spainhour, *General Mgr*
Betty J Spencer, *Corp Secy*
Bradley Spencer, *Vice Pres*
EMP: 20
SQ FT: 24,000
SALES (est): 5.1MM **Privately Held**
SIC: 3569 3599 Filters; machine shop, jobbing & repair

(G-8427)
STADRY ENCLOSURE CO
213 Riverwood Dr (47130-5641)
P.O. Box 472 (47131-0472)
PHONE...................................812 284-2244
Kevin Baggerly, *Owner*
EMP: 3
SALES (est): 307.6K **Privately Held**
SIC: 3444 Metal housings, enclosures, casings & other containers

(G-8428)
STEEL DYNAMICS INC
Also Called: Flat Roll Div - Jeffersonville
5134 Loop Rd (47130-8412)
PHONE...................................812 218-1490
Fax: 812 284-9278
Mark McCartin, *Warehouse Mgr*
Chase Ault, *Engineer*
Diana Maynard, *Accountant*
Chris Winger, *Branch Mgr*
Jordan Breiner, *Branch Mgr*
EMP: 100 **Publicly Held**
SIC: 3312 3479 Plate, sheet & strip, except coated products; galvanizing of iron, steel or end-formed products
PA: Steel Dynamics, Inc.
7575 W Jefferson Blvd
Fort Wayne IN 46804

(G-8429)
STEEL STRUCTURAL PRODUCTS LLC (HQ)
Also Called: Tri-S
1195 Port Rd (47130-8478)
PHONE...................................812 670-4195
Scott Stuzkert, *President*
Eric Lambert,
EMP: 10
SQ FT: 11,000
SALES (est): 1.4MM
SALES (corp-wide): 319.1MM **Privately Held**
SIC: 3312 Structural shapes & pilings, steel
PA: The Mill Steel Co
5116 36th St Se
Grand Rapids MI 49512
616 949-6700

(G-8430)
STEWART GRAPHICS INC (PA)
Also Called: Voluforms
1419 Fabricon Blvd (47130-9603)
P.O. Box 402, Sellersburg (47172-0402)
PHONE...................................812 283-0455
Fax: 812 283-1346
Charles H Stewart, *CEO*
Wendy Eckert, *COO*
Gay Collings, *Vice Pres*
Jim Hutchinson, *Vice Pres*
Jeff Waiz, *Vice Pres*
EMP: 34
SALES (est): 19.1MM **Privately Held**
WEB: www.voluforms.com
SIC: 5112 2761 7384 Business forms; manifold business forms; photographic services

(G-8431)
SWEET PROPERTIES LLC
347 Spring St (47130-3449)
PHONE...................................812 283-8367
Warren Schimpff, *Principal*
EMP: 2
SALES (est): 84.4K **Privately Held**
SIC: 2064 Candy & other confectionery products

(G-8432)
SWIFTTRIP LLC
702 N Shore Dr (47130-3104)
PHONE................................812 206-5200
Fax: 812 206-5309
Lee Thomas, *Principal*
EMP: 2 EST: 2008
SALES (est): 210.2K Privately Held
SIC: 7372 Prepackaged software

(G-8433)
TC PALLETS & PEDDLER SWEET LLC
1414 E 10th St (47130-4205)
PHONE................................812 283-1090
Dave Wooten,
EMP: 5
SALES (est): 318.9K Privately Held
SIC: 2448 Pallets, wood

(G-8434)
THE OFFICE SUP OF SOUTHERN IND (PA)
Also Called: Kopy Kat
417 Spring St (47130-3451)
PHONE................................812 283-5523
Fax: 812 288-7063
Jeffery E Frey, *President*
EMP: 6 EST: 1970
SQ FT: 5,000
SALES (est): 3.1MM Privately Held
SIC: 5112 2752 5044 Office supplies;
commercial printing, offset; office equipment

(G-8435)
TRIDENT ENGRAVING INC
3114 New Chapel Rd (47130-8916)
PHONE................................812 282-2098
Ronald Woodward, *Principal*
EMP: 2
SALES (est): 97.5K Privately Held
SIC: 2759 Commercial printing

(G-8436)
TWIN SPIRES CABINETRY LLC
316 E Court Ave (47130-3412)
PHONE................................502 644-4183
EMP: 2
SALES (est): 158.3K Privately Held
SIC: 2434 Wood kitchen cabinets

(G-8437)
UTC AEROSPACE SYSTEMS
510 Patrol Rd (47130-7755)
PHONE................................812 704-5200
Emily Smith, *Principal*
EMP: 2
SALES (est): 140K Privately Held
SIC: 3721 Aircraft

(G-8438)
VAPOURFLOW LLC
590 Missouri Ave Ste 105 (47130-3085)
PHONE................................812 284-5204
Henry Webster, *CEO*
Michael Abner, *President*
Blake Woodbury, *Vice Pres*
Don Ledwidge, *Manager*
EMP: 6
SALES (est): 1MM Privately Held
SIC: 3671 Gas or vapor tubes

(G-8439)
VOICE OF GOD RECORDINGS INC
5911 Charlestown Pike (47130-3879)
P.O. Box 950 (47131-0950)
PHONE................................812 246-2137
Fax: 812 256-6187
Joseph M Branham, *President*
William P Branham Sr, *Vice Pres*
William Paul Brewer Jr, *Controller*
◆ EMP: 84
SQ FT: 60,000
SALES: 26.2MM Privately Held
WEB: www.branham.org
SIC: 5961 3652 2791 2789 Record &/or
tape (music or video) club, mail order;
pre-recorded records & tapes; typesetting; bookbinding & related work; commercial printing, lithographic; book
publishing

(G-8440)
WATER ENERGIZERS INC
3008 Middle Rd Ste A (47130-5500)
PHONE................................812 288-6900
Fax: 812 288-2142
C L Harris, *Ch of Bd*
Rhonda R Harris, *President*
Dr Robert E Harris, *Exec VP*
Ronald D Harris, *Shareholder*
Lahna H Barnes, *Admin Sec*
EMP: 10
SQ FT: 12,000
SALES (est): 1.6MM Privately Held
WEB: www.waterenergizers.com
SIC: 3589 Water treatment equipment, industrial

(G-8441)
WENDELL CONGER
Also Called: Conger Signs
3730 Utica Sellersburg Rd (47130-8636)
PHONE................................812 282-2564
Wendell Conger, *Owner*
EMP: 2 EST: 1956
SALES (est): 183.8K Privately Held
SIC: 3993 Electric signs

(G-8442)
WHITESELL PRCSION CMPNENTS INC
100 Technology Way (47130-9644)
PHONE................................812 282-4014
Neil L Whitesell, *CEO*
Bob Wiese, *Corp Secy*
Hart Vogt, *COO*
EMP: 150 EST: 2011
SQ FT: 286,000
SALES (est): 32.1MM Privately Held
SIC: 3541 Machine tools, metal cutting
type

(G-8443)
XTREME GRAPHICS
3301 Justinian (47130-8631)
P.O. Box 1452 (47131-1452)
PHONE................................812 989-6948
Tonya Nolan, *Principal*
EMP: 2 EST: 2007
SALES (est): 152.2K Privately Held
SIC: 2759 5699 5941 5949 Screen printing; sports apparel; sporting goods & bicycle shops; sewing, needlework & piece
goods

Jonesboro
Grant County

(G-8444)
EXEON PROCESSORS LLC (PA)
232 W Pearl St (46938-1054)
PHONE................................765 674-2266
Steve Lundergan, *Vice Pres*
Jason Kozin, *Mng Member*
Ron Stiltner,
EMP: 20
SQ FT: 30,000
SALES (est): 5MM Privately Held
SIC: 2611 Pulp mills, mechanical & recycling processing

(G-8445)
H A P INDUSTRIES INC
Also Called: Rich Glas Products
7220 S 200 W (46938-9769)
PHONE................................765 948-3385
Fax: 765 948-3386
Allen J Fox, *President*
Paul Fox, *Corp Secy*
▲ EMP: 6
SALES (est): 720.6K Privately Held
SIC: 3089 3431 Plastic kitchenware, tableware & houseware; metal sanitary ware

(G-8446)
JROTTEN CHOPPER
6563 Wheeling Pike (46938-9702)
PHONE................................765 517-1779
John Armes, *Principal*
EMP: 2 EST: 2010
SALES (est): 189K Privately Held
SIC: 3751 Motorcycles & related parts

Jonesville
Bartholomew County

(G-8447)
BRICK
309 Walnut St (47247-4718)
PHONE................................812 522-8636
Bill Jefferies, *Owner*
EMP: 2
SALES (est): 228.2K Privately Held
SIC: 2599 Bar, restaurant & cafeteria furniture

(G-8448)
C & G TOOL INC
706 W Chestnut St (47247-4724)
PHONE................................812 524-7061
Curt Price, *President*
Greg Price, *Vice Pres*
EMP: 6
SALES (est): 300K Privately Held
SIC: 3312 Tool & die steel

(G-8449)
L & P MANUFACTURING COMPANY
207 Rodgers Ln (47247-4731)
PHONE................................812 405-2093
Roselyn Long, *CEO*
James Long, *President*
Jason Patrick, *Manager*
EMP: 5 EST: 2015
SALES: 300K Privately Held
SIC: 3599 Machine shop, jobbing & repair

Kendallville
Noble County

(G-8450)
A-1 PRODUCTION INC
5809 E Leighty Rd (46755-9700)
PHONE................................260 347-0960
Fax: 260 347-4727
Chris Behnke, *President*
David Snyder, *Admin Sec*
▼ EMP: 32 EST: 1949
SQ FT: 50,000
SALES (est): 4.4MM Privately Held
WEB: www.a1production.com
SIC: 3599 Machine shop, jobbing & repair

(G-8451)
AFFORDABLE SIGNS
700 S Orchard St (46755-2022)
PHONE................................260 349-1710
Fax: 260 349-1710
Brian Anderson, *Owner*
EMP: 2
SALES (est): 150K Privately Held
SIC: 3993 Signs & advertising specialties

(G-8452)
ALPHA PRIME COMPUTERS
113 S Main St (46755-1715)
PHONE................................260 347-4800
Adam Knisely, *Owner*
EMP: 3
SALES (est): 160.4K Privately Held
SIC: 5734 3571 Computer peripheral
equipment; electronic computers

(G-8453)
ALUM-ELEC STRUCTURES INC
250 W Grove St (46755-1409)
PHONE................................260 347-9362
Fax: 260 347-9326
Joseph Taylor, *President*
Nancy Taylor, *Corp Secy*
EMP: 6
SQ FT: 7,600
SALES (est): 1MM Privately Held
WEB: www.alumelec.com
SIC: 3441 Building components, structural
steel

(G-8454)
APPLE TERRACE LLC
515 Professional Way (46755-2928)
P.O. Box 633 (46755-0633)
PHONE................................260 347-9400

Fax: 260 347-0692
Michael M Yoder, *Principal*
EMP: 8
SALES (est): 98.1K Privately Held
SIC: 3571 Personal computers (microcomputers)

(G-8455)
ARCHIMEDES INC
2705 Marion Dr (46755-3280)
PHONE................................260 347-3903
Steve Paddock, *President*
EMP: 5
SALES (est): 130.1K
SALES (corp-wide): 726.5MM Privately
Held
SIC: 3965 Fasteners
HQ: Bollhoff Beteiligungsges. Mbh
Archimedesstr. 1-4
Bielefeld
521 448-201

(G-8456)
ASHLEY INDUSTRIAL MOLDING INC
100 S Progress Dr W (46755-3261)
PHONE................................260 349-1982
Rod Schoon, *Branch Mgr*
EMP: 5
SALES (est): 589.1K
SALES (corp-wide): 41.3MM Privately
Held
SIC: 3089 Molding primary plastic
PA: Ashley Industrial Molding Inc
310 S Wabash St
Ashley IN 46705
260 587-9155

(G-8457)
AWOL METAL CONTORSION LLC
439 Prospect Ave (46755-2250)
PHONE................................260 909-0411
Jacob Farver,
EMP: 2
SALES (est): 113.4K Privately Held
SIC: 3441 7538 Fabricated structural
metal; general automotive repair shops

(G-8458)
B & J SPECIALTY INC
B & J Medical
4268 E Us Highway 6 (46755-9343)
PHONE................................260 636-2067
John Wicker, *Branch Mgr*
EMP: 14 Privately Held
SIC: 3845 Electromedical equipment
PA: B & J Specialty, Inc.
7919 N 100 E
Wawaka IN 46794

(G-8459)
B&J INTERNATIONAL LLC
4268 E Us Highway 6 (46755-9343)
PHONE................................260 854-2215
John Wicker,
▲ EMP: 6
SQ FT: 1,000
SALES (est): 2.4MM Privately Held
SIC: 3089 3469 Injection molding of plastics; spinning metal for the trade

(G-8460)
BANCO INDUSTRIES INC
11542 N State Road 3 (46755-9732)
P.O. Box 5191 (46755-5191)
PHONE................................260 347-9524
Fax: 260 347-1134
Marvin Nagel, *President*
Dianne Nagel, *Co-Owner*
Glen Nagel, *Vice Pres*
Marlene Nagle, *Admin Sec*
EMP: 12
SQ FT: 6,000
SALES: 937K Privately Held
WEB: www.bancoindustries.com
SIC: 3599 Machine shop, jobbing & repair

(G-8461)
BOLLHOFF INC (DH)
2705 Marion Dr (46755-3280)
PHONE................................260 347-3903
Steve Paddock, *President*
Chris Lautzenhiser, *Plant Mgr*
Shane La Rocca, *Project Mgr*
Sharon Maley, *Purch Agent*

▲ = Import ▼=Export
◆ =Import/Export

Tyler Grimm, *QC Mgr*
▲ **EMP:** 23
SQ FT: 100,000
SALES (est): 5.8MM
SALES (corp-wide): 726.5MM **Privately Held**
WEB: www.bollhoff-rivnut.com
SIC: 3452 3965 Bolts, nuts, rivets & washers; fasteners
HQ: Bollhoff Gmbh
Archimedesstr. 1-4
Bielefeld 33649
521 448-203

(G-8462)
BUSCHE PERFORMANCE GROUP INC
811 Commerce Dr (46755-9381)
PHONE..................................260 349-0070
Anthony Jagger, *Vice Pres*
EMP: 70
SALES (corp-wide): 398.9MM **Privately Held**
WEB: www.busche-cnc.com
SIC: 3599 Machine shop, jobbing & repair
HQ: Busche Performance Group, Inc.
1563 E State Road 8
Albion IN 46701
260 636-7030

(G-8463)
CHARMARAN CORPORATION
1451 Stonebraker Dr (46755-1027)
PHONE..................................260 347-3347
David Brenay, *President*
EMP: 12
SQ FT: 30,000
SALES: 1.2MM **Privately Held**
SIC: 3466 3469 3444 2655 Closures, stamped metal; machine parts, stamped or pressed metal; culverts, flumes & pipes; fiber spools, tubes & cones

(G-8464)
COLWELL INC (HQ)
2605 Marion Dr (46755-3273)
P.O. Box 308 (46755-0308)
PHONE..................................260 347-1981
Fax: 260 347-2079
William V Byars, *CEO*
Donovan Freeland, *President*
Patrick Van Arnam, *President*
Kevin C Gurney, *Senior VP*
Eric Daniels, *Warehouse Mgr*
▲ **EMP:** 108
SQ FT: 200,000
SALES (est): 104.2MM
SALES (corp-wide): 122.1MM **Privately Held**
WEB: www.colwellcolour.com
SIC: 2752 Cards, lithographed; color lithography
PA: Colwell Industries, Inc.
1611 County Road B W # 315
Saint Paul MN 55113
612 340-0365

(G-8465)
COLWELL INC
231 S Progress Dr E (46755-3269)
P.O. Box 308 (46755-0308)
PHONE..................................260 347-1981
David Brayton, *Manager*
EMP: 200
SALES (corp-wide): 122.1MM **Privately Held**
SIC: 2752 Cards, lithographed; color lithography
HQ: Colwell, Inc.
2605 Marion Dr
Kendallville IN 46755
260 347-1981

(G-8466)
CONLEY WELDING SPECIALTIES INC
605 S Orchard St (46755-2011)
PHONE..................................260 343-9051
Latesa Conley, *President*
Jeffrey Conley, *Admin Sec*
EMP: 3
SALES (est): 214.6K **Privately Held**
SIC: 7692 Welding repair

(G-8467)
COUNTRY SEWING
8929 E 1125 N (46755-9745)
PHONE..................................260 347-9733
Homer Morgan, *Owner*
Pam Morgan, *Owner*
EMP: 2
SALES (est): 61.3K **Privately Held**
SIC: 7219 2399 Garment alteration & repair shop; fabricated textile products

(G-8468)
COURIER COMMUNICATIONS LLC
Also Called: Courier Printing
2500 Marion Dr (46755-3270)
PHONE..................................260 347-3044
Sybella Wilder, *Manager*
EMP: 300
SALES (corp-wide): 3.6B **Publicly Held**
SIC: 2752 Commercial printing, lithographic
HQ: Courier Communications Llc
15 Wellman Ave
North Chelmsford MA 01863
978 251-6000

(G-8469)
COURIER KENDALLVILLE INC (DH)
2500 Marion Dr (46755-3270)
PHONE..................................260 347-3044
Fax: 260 347-3507
James F Conway III, *President*
Rajeev Balakrishna, *Senior VP*
Sharon Dobias, *Mfg Dir*
Kathy Baker, *Purch Agent*
Peter M Folger, *CFO*
▲ **EMP:** 50
SQ FT: 200,000
SALES (est): 96.4MM
SALES (corp-wide): 3.6B **Publicly Held**
SIC: 2732 Book printing
HQ: Courier Communications Llc
15 Wellman Ave
North Chelmsford MA 01863
978 251-6000

(G-8470)
CREATIVE LIQUID COATINGS INC
2620 Marion Dr (46755-3272)
P.O. Box 369 (46755-0369)
PHONE..................................260 349-1862
Dan St Germain, *Branch Mgr*
EMP: 144 **Privately Held**
WEB: www.creativecoatingsinc.com
SIC: 3479 Painting, coating & hot dipping
PA: Creative Liquid Coatings, Inc.
2701 S Coliseum Blvd # 1284
Fort Wayne IN 46803

(G-8471)
DA-MAR INDUSTRIES INC (PA)
Also Called: Lewger Machine & Tool
201 W Ohio St (46755-2015)
PHONE..................................260 347-1662
David Vangessel, *President*
EMP: 10 **EST:** 1951
SQ FT: 25,000
SALES (est): 2.3MM **Privately Held**
WEB: www.lewger.com
SIC: 3599 3549 3469 7692 Machine shop, jobbing & repair; assembly machines, including robotic; stamping metal for the trade; welding repair

(G-8472)
DEKKO ACQUISITION PARENT INC (PA)
6928 N 400 E (46755-9346)
PHONE..................................260 347-0700
Robert Bergmann, *President*
Gerald Whiteford, *Vice Pres*
Michael Schnabel, *Admin Sec*
▲ **EMP:** 6
SALES (est): 145.1MM **Privately Held**
SIC: 3496 Wire fasteners

(G-8473)
DEPENDABLE METAL TREATING INC
902 Dowling St (46755-9401)
P.O. Box 276 (46755-0276)
PHONE..................................260 347-5744
Fax: 260 347-5944
Ross L Noble, *President*
EMP: 18
SQ FT: 23,600
SALES (est): 4MM **Privately Held**
WEB: www.dependablemetaltreating.com
SIC: 3398 Metal heat treating

(G-8474)
DOW SILICONES CORPORATION
111 S Progress Dr E (46755-3268)
PHONE..................................260 347-5813
Fax: 260 347-5819
Greg Collins, *Manager*
EMP: 15
SQ FT: 23,427
SALES (corp-wide): 62.4B **Publicly Held**
WEB: www.dowcorning.com
SIC: 2869 Silicones
HQ: Dow Silicones Corporation
2200 W Salzburg Rd
Auburn MI 48611
989 496-4000

(G-8475)
FLINT & WALLING INC
Also Called: Star Water Systems
95 N Oak St (46755-1736)
PHONE..................................260 347-1781
Fax: 260 347-6662
Scott M Lechner, *President*
Ben Painter, *Regional Mgr*
Scott Wallen, *Vice Pres*
Greg Emerick, *Plant Mgr*
Terry Mendenhall, *Plant Mgr*
◆ **EMP:** 150
SQ FT: 232,080
SALES (est): 101.2MM
SALES (corp-wide): 164.8MM **Privately Held**
WEB: www.flintandwalling.com
SIC: 3561 Industrial pumps & parts; pumps, domestic: water or sump
PA: Zoeller Company
3649 Cane Run Rd
Louisville KY 40211
502 778-2731

(G-8476)
GRAPHIC PACKAGING INTL LLC
301 S Progress Dr E (46755-3266)
PHONE..................................260 347-7612
Mike Taube, *Safety Dir*
Sandi Schlup, *Buyer*
Morgan Gillery, *Manager*
Connie Gottfried, *Manager*
Larry Deardorf, *Supervisor*
EMP: 409 **Publicly Held**
SIC: 2631 Paperboard mills
HQ: Graphic Packaging International, Llc
1500 Riveredge Pkwy # 100
Atlanta GA 30328

(G-8477)
GROUP DEKKO INC
6928 N 400 E Dock101 (46755-9346)
PHONE..................................260 599-3405
Jamie Prescott, *Branch Mgr*
EMP: 30
SALES (corp-wide): 2.5B **Publicly Held**
SIC: 3841 Surgical & medical instruments
HQ: Group Dekko, Inc.
2505 Dekko Dr
Garrett IN 46738

(G-8478)
HENDRICKSON INTERNATIONAL CORP
Hendrickson Truck Suspension
101 S Progress Dr W (46755-3262)
PHONE..................................260 349-6400
Fax: 260 347-2711
Gary Hake, *Manager*
EMP: 202
SALES (corp-wide): 1.1B **Privately Held**
SIC: 3714 3713 Motor vehicle parts & accessories; truck & bus bodies

HQ: Hendrickson International Corporation
500 Park Blvd Ste 450
Itasca IL 60143
630 874-9700

(G-8479)
HY-MATIC MFG INC
205 W Ohio St (46755-2015)
P.O. Box 98 (46755-0098)
PHONE..................................260 347-3651
Fax: 260 347-4467
Richard Borger, *President*
Mary Alice Norris, *Vice Pres*
EMP: 22
SQ FT: 39,000
SALES: 1.2MM **Privately Held**
SIC: 3451 3594 3494 Screw machine products; fluid power pumps & motors; valves & pipe fittings

(G-8480)
ILLINOIS TOOL WORKS INC
Also Called: ITW Tomco
2720 Marion Dr (46755-3279)
P.O. Box 5140 (46755-5140)
PHONE..................................260 347-8040
Fax: 260 347-3930
Chris Carns, *Branch Mgr*
EMP: 125
SALES (corp-wide): 14.3B **Publicly Held**
SIC: 3089 3499 3672 3714 Injection molded finished plastic products; strapping, metal; printed circuit boards; motor vehicle parts & accessories
PA: Illinois Tool Works Inc.
155 Harlem Ave
Glenview IL 60025
847 724-7500

(G-8481)
JOHNSON CONTROLS INC
300 S Progress Dr E (46755-3266)
PHONE..................................260 347-0500
Bill Johns, *Branch Mgr*
EMP: 94 **Privately Held**
SIC: 2531 Seats, automobile
HQ: Johnson Controls, Inc.
5757 N Green Bay Ave
Milwaukee WI 53209
414 524-1200

(G-8482)
K LASH & SON INC
910 Harlash St (46755-1026)
PHONE..................................260 347-3660
Larry Lash, *President*
Ellen Lash, *Corp Secy*
Steven W Lash, *Corp Secy*
EMP: 4
SQ FT: 5,000
SALES: 250K **Privately Held**
SIC: 1521 5211 2431 New construction, single-family houses; lumber & other building materials; millwork

(G-8483)
KAMMERER DYNAMICS INC
5780 E Concrete Dr (46755-9395)
PHONE..................................260 349-9098
Klint Kammerer, *President*
Kelly Kammerer, *Principal*
EMP: 18 **EST:** 2014
SQ FT: 5,000
SALES (est): 969.5K **Privately Held**
SIC: 3441 Fabricated structural metal

(G-8484)
KAMMERER INC
303 W Wayne St (46755-1484)
PHONE..................................260 349-9098
Kelly Kammerer, *Branch Mgr*
EMP: 4
SALES (est): 209.5K
SALES (corp-wide): 678.2K **Privately Held**
SIC: 7692 5051 3312 1542 Welding repair; steel; blast furnaces & steel mills; nonresidential construction
PA: Kammerer Inc.
2348 E Kammerer Rd
Kendallville IN 46755
260 347-0389

(G-8485)
KAMMERER INC (PA)
2348 E Kammerer Rd (46755-3067)
PHONE.................................260 347-0389
Fax: 260 347-0389
Sherril Kammerer, *Owner*
Kevin Bortner, *Sales Mgr*
Kelly Kammerer, *Manager*
EMP: 2
SALES (est): 678.2K **Privately Held**
SIC: 7692 3444 3443 3441 Welding repair; sheet metalwork; fabricated plate work (boiler shop); fabricated structural metal

(G-8486)
KENDALLVILLE IRON & METAL INC
243 E Lisbon Rd (46755-3618)
P.O. Box 69 (46755-0069)
PHONE.................................260 347-1958
Fax: 260 347-1966
Gary Spidel, *President*
Susan Norris, *Vice Pres*
Lynn R Spidel, *Vice Pres*
EMP: 26
SALES (est): 6.1MM **Privately Held**
SIC: 5093 4212 3341 Metal scrap & waste materials; local trucking, without storage; secondary nonferrous metals

(G-8487)
KITCHEN-QUIP INC
Also Called: Americhef USA
338 S Oak St (46755-1759)
P.O. Box 548 (46755-0548)
PHONE.................................260 837-8311
Fax: 260 837-7919
Winston B Sparling, *Ch of Bd*
Stephen B Sparling, *President*
Treva E Sparling, *Exec VP*
Jeffery Musick, *Vice Pres*
EMP: 45 **EST:** 1946
SQ FT: 70,000
SALES (est): 9.3MM **Privately Held**
WEB: www.kqcasting.com
SIC: 3363 3369 3556 Aluminum die-castings; nonferrous foundries; food products machinery

(G-8488)
KPC MEDIA GROUP INC (PA)
Also Called: Advance Leader
102 N Main St (46755-1714)
PHONE.................................260 347-0400
Terry R Ward, *CEO*
Terry Housholder, *President*
George B Witwer, *President*
Lucretia Cardenas, *Editor*
Susan Carpenter, *Editor*
EMP: 110
SQ FT: 40,000
SALES (est): 28.7MM **Privately Held**
WEB: www.kpcnews.net
SIC: 2711 2791 2752 Commercial printing & newspaper publishing combined; typesetting; commercial printing, lithographic

(G-8489)
KRAFT HEINZ FOODS COMPANY
151 W Ohio St (46755-2033)
PHONE.................................260 347-1300
Fax: 260 347-5590
Bob Bortner, *Manager*
EMP: 25
SALES (corp-wide): 26.2B **Publicly Held**
WEB: www.kraftfoods.com
SIC: 2141 Tobacco stemming & redrying
HQ: Kraft Heinz Foods Company
1 Ppg Pl Ste 3200
Pittsburgh PA 15222
412 456-5700

(G-8490)
LEGGETT & PLATT INCORPORATED
Kendallville 5801
2225 Production Rd (46755-3255)
PHONE.................................260 347-2600
Ruff Dunton, *General Mgr*
Russell Dunton, *Branch Mgr*
Jeremy Binkley, *Technology*
EMP: 125

SALES (corp-wide): 3.9B **Publicly Held**
WEB: www.leggett.com
SIC: 3495 2515 Mechanical springs, precision; furniture springs, unassembled; mattresses & bedsprings
PA: Leggett & Platt, Incorporated
1 Leggett Rd
Carthage MO 64836
417 358-8131

(G-8491)
LUXEMBURG MACHINE LLC
5638 E Us Highway 6 (46755-9364)
PHONE.................................260 347-4192
Ray Luxemburg, *Principal*
EMP: 2 **EST:** 2007
SALES (est): 126.4K **Privately Held**
SIC: 3599 Machine shop, jobbing & repair

(G-8492)
M&M MACHINES
111 W Lisle St (46755-2034)
P.O. Box 376, Wolcottville (46795-0376)
PHONE.................................260 349-1922
EMP: 2
SALES (est): 218.9K **Privately Held**
SIC: 3544 Mfg Dies/Tools/Jigs/Fixtures

(G-8493)
MAHONEY FOUNDRIES INC (PA)
Also Called: Vermont Foundry Company
209 W Ohio St (46755-2015)
PHONE.................................260 347-1768
Fax: 260 347-1768
Stephen Patrick Mahoney, *President*
Brad Heath, *Superintendent*
Don Wells, *Superintendent*
Joan Mahoney, *CFO*
Christine M Krehl, *Treasurer*
EMP: 100
SQ FT: 29,000
SALES (est): 20.1MM **Privately Held**
SIC: 3366 3365 Castings (except die): brass; aluminum & aluminum-based alloy castings

(G-8494)
MD MOXIE LLC
Also Called: Advantage Thermal Service
5966 E Concrete Dr (46755-9361)
PHONE.................................260 347-1203
Michael Moxie, *Mng Member*
EMP: 25
SALES (est): 2.2MM **Privately Held**
SIC: 3585 Heating & air conditioning combination units

(G-8495)
MODERN PRINTING CO
Also Called: Ossian Printing
117 E Williams St (46755-1743)
P.O. Box 181 (46755-0181)
PHONE.................................260 347-1679
Fax: 260 347-9511
Verlin Lung, *Owner*
EMP: 4
SALES: 850K **Privately Held**
SIC: 2752 Commercial printing, offset; lithographing on metal

(G-8496)
MP STEEL INDIANA LLC (PA)
5966 E Concrete Dr (46755-9361)
P.O. Box 876 (46755-0876)
PHONE.................................260 347-1203
Michael Pitterich,
EMP: 50
SALES (est): 7.2MM **Privately Held**
SIC: 3398 Metal heat treating

(G-8497)
MR BS SPORTS & DESIGN
Also Called: Mr B'S Sporting Goods
117 S Main St (46755-1715)
PHONE.................................260 347-4830
Fax: 260 347-4830
Ronald N Bruce, *Owner*
EMP: 2
SALES: 81K **Privately Held**
SIC: 2759 Screen printing

(G-8498)
MURRAYS TIN CUP
2004 W North St (46755-2856)
PHONE.................................260 349-1002
Wendy Potter, *Manager*

EMP: 3 **EST:** 2009
SALES (est): 205.8K **Privately Held**
SIC: 3356 Tin

(G-8499)
NEW-INDY HARTFORD CITY LLC
Also Called: Kendallville Recycle Center
606 Uhl Dr (46755-1057)
P.O. Box 5118 (46755-5118)
PHONE.................................260 347-4739
Jim Sizemore, *Branch Mgr*
EMP: 11
SALES (corp-wide): 36.5MM **Privately Held**
WEB: www.hcpaper.com
SIC: 2621 Wrapping & packaging papers; bag paper
HQ: New-Indy Hartford City Llc
501 S Spring St
Hartford City IN 47348
765 348-5440

(G-8500)
NO SAG
2225 Production Rd (46755-3255)
PHONE.................................260 347-2600
Fax: 260 347-4764
Russ Dunton, *COO*
Bill Schmitt, *Manager*
EMP: 12
SALES (est): 2MM **Privately Held**
WEB: www.nosag.net
SIC: 2599 Furniture & fixtures

(G-8501)
PENT ASSEMBLIES
6928 N 400 E (46755-9346)
PHONE.................................260 347-5828
Charles Schrimper, *CEO*
Steve Hankins, *President*
Robert Kozlowski, *COO*
Dianne Gerencser, *Admin Sec*
EMP: 100
SQ FT: 10,000
SALES (est): 35.8MM **Privately Held**
SIC: 3679 3643 3089 Harness assemblies for electronic use: wire or cable; current-carrying wiring devices; injection molding of plastics

(G-8502)
PENT PLASTICS INC (PA)
6928 N 400 E (46755-9346)
PHONE.................................260 897-3775
Charles Schrimper, *CEO*
Rick Nowels, *President*
Robert Kozlowski, *COO*
Dianne Gerencser, *Admin Sec*
▲ **EMP:** 118
SQ FT: 50,000
SALES (est): 6.7MM **Privately Held**
SIC: 3089 3641 3469 Molding primary plastic; injection molded finished plastic products; plastic processing; electric lamps; metal stampings

(G-8503)
QUICK TANKS INC (PA)
522 Krueger St (46755-1421)
P.O. Box 338 (46755-0338)
PHONE.................................260 347-3850
Thomas R Quick, *President*
James Sulier, *General Mgr*
Jon Luttman, *Purchasing*
Rex Fischer, *Research*
Scott Powell, *Chief Engr*
EMP: 25 **EST:** 1950
SQ FT: 3,000
SALES (est): 10.3MM **Privately Held**
WEB: www.quicktanks.com
SIC: 3443 3479 Tanks, standard or custom fabricated: metal plate; galvanizing of iron, steel or end-formed products

(G-8504)
QUICK TANKS INC
522 Krueger St (46755-1421)
PHONE.................................260 347-3850
Thomas R Quick, *President*
EMP: 6
SALES (corp-wide): 10.3MM **Privately Held**
WEB: www.quicktanks.com
SIC: 3443 4225 Tanks, standard or custom fabricated: metal plate; general warehousing & storage

PA: Quick Tanks Inc
522 Krueger St
Kendallville IN 46755
260 347-3850

(G-8505)
RACEWAY HAND CAR WASH LLC
606 Fairview Blvd (46755-2924)
PHONE.................................260 242-9866
Sateesh Rachamadugu, *President*
EMP: 4 **EST:** 2011
SALES (est): 219.2K **Privately Held**
SIC: 3644 Raceways

(G-8506)
RELIABLE TOOL & MACHINE CO (PA)
Also Called: Reliable Prod Machining & Wldg
301 W Ohio St (46755-2017)
P.O. Box 757 (46755-0757)
PHONE.................................260 343-7150
Fax: 260 347-5552
Tom Walterhouse, *CEO*
Owen Drerup, *Ch of Bd*
Charles Drerup, *President*
Chuck Drerup, *President*
EMP: 70 **EST:** 1946
SALES (est): 16.3MM **Privately Held**
SIC: 3714 3599 Wheels, motor vehicle; brake drums, motor vehicle; axles, motor vehicle; machine shop, jobbing & repair

(G-8507)
RELIABLE TOOL & MACHINE CO
902 S Main St (46755-2025)
PHONE.................................260 347-4000
Herman Lehman, *Branch Mgr*
EMP: 30
SALES (corp-wide): 16.3MM **Privately Held**
SIC: 3599 Machine shop, jobbing & repair
PA: Reliable Tool & Machine Company Inc
301 W Ohio St
Kendallville IN 46755
260 343-7150

(G-8508)
RELIABLE TOOL & MACHINE CO
800 Weston Ave (46755-2041)
PHONE.................................260 347-4000
Andy Hampshire, *Branch Mgr*
EMP: 30
SALES (corp-wide): 16.3MM **Privately Held**
SIC: 3599 Machine shop, jobbing & repair
PA: Reliable Tool & Machine Company Inc
301 W Ohio St
Kendallville IN 46755
260 343-7150

(G-8509)
SACRED SELECTIONS
Also Called: RE Winset Music
112 N Shore Dr (46755-2632)
PHONE.................................260 347-3758
Fax: 260 347-9299
Janella Turansky,
EMP: 3
SALES (est): 244.4K **Privately Held**
SIC: 2731 5961 Book music: publishing only, not printed on site; catalog & mail-order houses

(G-8510)
SLATERS CONCRETE PRODUCTS
322 E Wayne St (46755-1458)
PHONE.................................260 347-0164
Fax: 260 347-6893
Jeff Slater, *President*
Marylin Slater, *Corp Secy*
Joe Schroeder, *Vice Pres*
EMP: 7 **EST:** 1923
SQ FT: 10,000
SALES (est): 1.1MM **Privately Held**
SIC: 3271 5211 5032 Blocks, concrete or cinder: standard; concrete & cinder block; concrete & cinder block

(G-8511)
STIEN DESIGNS & GRAPHICS INC
106 S Main St (46755-1716)
PHONE.................................260 347-9136

▲ = Import ▼=Export
◆ =Import/Export

Fax: 260 347-9136
Diann Stienbarger, *President*
Doug Younce, *Vice Pres*
Gerry Stienbarger, *Treasurer*
Pam Younce, *Admin Sec*
EMP: 3
SALES: 500K **Privately Held**
SIC: 2754 7336 7389 3089 Commercial printing, gravure; silk screen design; embroidering of advertising on shirts, etc.; engraving of plastic

(G-8512)
TAYLOR MADE GROUP HOLDINGS INC
Also Called: Taylor Made Systems Indiana
1101 Stonebraker Dr (46755-1028)
PHONE..................................260 347-1368
Fax: 260 347-4618
John Schoonover, *Plant Mgr*
Randy Beery, *Opers Mgr*
Marc Rhinehart, *Purchasing*
Jerry Akey, *QC Mgr*
Ryan Carper, *Engineer*
EMP: 150
SALES (corp-wide): 228.8MM **Privately Held**
WEB: www.taylormadegroup.com
SIC: 3714 3732 3231 Wipers, windshield, motor vehicle; boat building & repairing; products of purchased glass
PA: Taylor Made Group Holdings, Inc.
66 Kingsboro Ave
Gloversville NY 12078
518 725-0681

(G-8513)
WAUSEON MCHNE&MFG-KNDLVLLE DIV
708 S Orchard St (46755-2022)
PHONE..................................260 347-5095
Fax: 260 347-1345
Douglas A Weddelman, *President*
Matt Bombic, *Finance*
EMP: 20
SALES (est): 2.5MM **Privately Held**
SIC: 3599 Machine shop, jobbing & repair

(G-8514)
WOLFPACK CHASSIS LLC
800 Weston Ave (46755-2041)
PHONE..................................260 349-1887
Steve Hawk, *President*
EMP: 30
SALES: 5MM **Privately Held**
SIC: 3315 3792 Steel wire & related products; camping trailers & chassis

(G-8515)
YANFENG US AUTOMOTIVE
300 S Progress Dr E (46755-3266)
PHONE..................................260 347-0500
Bart Alexander, *Manager*
EMP: 250
SQ FT: 60,000 **Privately Held**
SIC: 3089 Plastic containers, except foam
HQ: Yanfeng Us Automotive Interior Systems I Llc
41935 W 12 Mile Rd
Novi MI 48377
248 319-7333

Kennard
Henry County

(G-8516)
GOODS CANDIES
State Rd 234 (47351)
P.O. Box 41 (47351-0041)
PHONE..................................765 785-6776
Terry Vickery, *Owner*
EMP: 7
SQ FT: 2,000
SALES (est): 567K **Privately Held**
SIC: 2064 Candy & other confectionery products

Kentland
Newton County

(G-8517)
BON L MANUFACTURING COMPANY
508 Wilson St (47951-9700)
PHONE..................................815 351-6802
David Asher, *Branch Mgr*
EMP: 150
SQ FT: 120,000
SALES (corp-wide): 1B **Publicly Held**
WEB: www.bonlalum.com
SIC: 3354 3471 3444 Aluminum extruded products; plating & polishing; sheet metalwork
HQ: Bon L Manufacturing Company
25 Bonnell St
Newnan GA 30263
770 253-2020

(G-8518)
CONTINENTAL MACHINING PRODUCTS
306 S 3rd St (47951-1311)
PHONE..................................219 474-5061
Fax: 219 279-2984
Garry Hixson, *President*
Brad Hixson, *Vice Pres*
Alan Adwell, *Treasurer*
EMP: 4
SQ FT: 3,000
SALES: 250K **Privately Held**
WEB: www.continentalmachining.com
SIC: 3599 Machine shop, jobbing & repair

(G-8519)
CPX INC (PA)
410 E Kent St (47951-8625)
PHONE..................................219 474-5280
Fax: 219 474-5478
Michael Sanders, *President*
Candace Sanders, *Purch Dir*
Douglas K Miller, *Treasurer*
Tamar Luecke, *Manager*
Mike Miller, *Admin Sec*
▲ **EMP:** 100
SQ FT: 40,000
SALES (est): 93.1MM **Privately Held**
WEB: www.cpxinc.com
SIC: 3089 3694 Molding primary plastic; harness wiring sets, internal combustion engines

(G-8520)
HOOSIER METAL POLISH INC
Also Called: Lehman Manufacturing
304 N Fairground Rd (47951)
P.O. Box 85 (47951-0085)
PHONE..................................219 474-6011
Luanne Watt, *President*
Keith E Watt, *Vice Pres*
Eric G Watt, *CFO*
Ronald G Watt, *Shareholder*
EMP: 15
SALES: 750K **Privately Held**
SIC: 5084 3567 Industrial machinery & equipment; ceramic kilns & furnaces

(G-8521)
ICE RIVER SPRINGS KENTLAND LLC
306 E Bailie St (47951-1399)
PHONE..................................219 474-6300
James F Gott, *President*
Alexandra Gott, *Vice Pres*
EMP: 25
SALES (est): 3.8MM
SALES (corp-wide): 29.9MM **Privately Held**
SIC: 2086 Mineral water, carbonated: packaged in cans, bottles, etc.
PA: Ice River Springs Water Co. Inc
485387 County Rd 11
Shelburne ON L9V 3
519 925-2929

(G-8522)
NEWTON COUNTY ENTERPRISES INC
Also Called: Community Media Group
305 E Graham St (47951-1235)
PHONE..................................219 474-5532
Fax: 219 474-5354
David Paxton, *President*
Don Hurd, *Principal*
EMP: 3
SALES (est): 224.4K **Privately Held**
WEB: www.newtoncountyenterprise.com
SIC: 2711 Newspapers, publishing & printing
HQ: The Times Republic
1492 E Walnut St
Watseka IL 60970
815 432-5227

(G-8523)
ROGERS GROUP INC
Also Called: Newton County Stone Co
235 E Us Highway 24 (47951-8623)
PHONE..................................219 474-5125
Fax: 219 474-3275
Tom Goyett, *Superintendent*
Kelly Krause, *Safety Mgr*
EMP: 20
SALES (corp-wide): 1B **Privately Held**
WEB: www.rogersgroupinc.com
SIC: 1422 5032 3274 Limestones, ground; stone, crushed or broken; lime
PA: Rogers Group, Inc.
421 Great Circle Rd
Nashville TN 37228
615 242-0585

(G-8524)
TRILL MACHINE LLC
104 W Washington St (47951-1154)
PHONE..................................219 730-0744
Joanne Mendes, *Partner*
Sean Patwell, *Partner*
EMP: 2
SALES (est): 105.3K **Privately Held**
SIC: 7372 7389 Application computer software;

Kewanna
Fulton County

(G-8525)
KEWANNA METAL SPECIALTIES INC (PA)
419 W Main St (46939-9527)
P.O. Box 367 (46939-0367)
PHONE..................................574 653-2554
Fax: 574 653-2556
Allen Finke, *President*
James B Finke, *Vice Pres*
Paul Schaeffner, *QC Mgr*
Amy Kwiatkowski, *Manager*
Jeffrey A Finke, *Admin Sec*
EMP: 65 **EST:** 1959
SQ FT: 160,000
SALES (est): 9.8MM **Privately Held**
WEB: www.fultonsquare.com
SIC: 3496 Grilles & grillework, woven wire; kitchen wire goods; mats & matting; mesh, made from purchased wire

(G-8526)
KEWANNA SCREEN PRINTING INC
109 Toner St (46939)
P.O. Box 397 (46939-0397)
PHONE..................................574 653-2683
Fax: 574 653-2737
Benjamin Fehrer, *President*
▼ **EMP:** 9
SALES (est): 1.3MM **Privately Held**
SIC: 2759 2396 Screen printing; decals: printing; automotive & apparel trimmings

(G-8527)
PLYMOUTH TUBE COMPANY
718 E Main St (46939)
P.O. Box 246 (46939-0246)
PHONE..................................574 653-2575
Fax: 574 653-2896
Lloyd Jennings, *Branch Mgr*
EMP: 4

SALES (corp-wide): 277.4MM **Privately Held**
WEB: www.plymouth.com
SIC: 3317 Steel pipe & tubes
PA: Plymouth Tube Company
29w 150 Warrenville Rd
Warrenville IL 60555
630 393-3550

(G-8528)
WINAMAC COIL SPRING INC
512 N Smith St (46939-2039)
P.O. Box 278 (46939-0278)
PHONE..................................574 653-2186
Fax: 574 653-2645
Daniel Pesaresi Sr, *Ch of Bd*
Joseph Pesaresi, *President*
Andrew Pesaresi, *Vice Pres*
Samantha Johnson, *Purchasing*
Kyle Mollencupp, *Engineer*
EMP: 194 **EST:** 1948
SQ FT: 120,000
SALES (est): 40MM **Privately Held**
WEB: www.winamaccoilspring.com
SIC: 3495 3496 3493 Mechanical springs, precision; miscellaneous fabricated wire products; steel springs, except wire

Kimmell
Noble County

(G-8529)
BOYD MACHINE & REPAIR CO INC
Also Called: Bmr Group
3794 W 50 S (46760-9766)
P.O. Box 93, Wolflake (46796-0093)
PHONE..................................260 635-2195
Fax: 260 635-2329
Larry L Boyd, *President*
Mark Boyd, *Treasurer*
Bill Shultz, *Manager*
Carolyn Boyd, *Admin Sec*
EMP: 30 **EST:** 1974
SQ FT: 50,000
SALES (est): 4.9MM **Privately Held**
SIC: 7699 3398 Industrial machinery & equipment repair; metal heat treating

(G-8530)
LIGHT BEAM TECHNOLOGIES INC
3794 W 50 S (46760-9766)
P.O. Box 308, Wolflake (46796-0308)
PHONE..................................260 635-2195
Larry L Boyd, *President*
EMP: 5
SALES (est): 535.4K **Privately Held**
SIC: 3567 Industrial furnaces & ovens

(G-8531)
METZGER DAIRY INC
4837 W 100 S (46760-9679)
PHONE..................................260 564-5445
Jack D Metzger, *President*
Jack J Metzger, *President*
John Metzger, *Vice Pres*
Susan Metzger, *Treasurer*
Kimery Metzger, *Admin Sec*
EMP: 10
SALES (est): 1.3MM **Privately Held**
SIC: 3556 Dairy & milk machinery

Kingman
Fountain County

(G-8532)
JRS WOOD SHOP
6950 W 1025 N (47952-7240)
PHONE..................................765 498-2663
Kenneth Asbury Jr, *Owner*
EMP: 5
SALES (est): 257.2K **Privately Held**
SIC: 2431 Trim, wood

GEOGRAPHIC

(G-8533)
STEEL GRIP INC
Also Called: Steel Grip Safety Apparel
42233 S Kingman Rd (47952)
P.O. Box 247 (47952-0247)
PHONE....................................765 397-3344
Fax: 765 397-3220
Dick Minnette, *Manager*
EMP: 90
SALES (corp-wide): 18.6MM **Privately Held**
WEB: www.steelgripinc.com
SIC: 3842 2381 2326 Personal safety
  equipment; fabric dress & work gloves;
  men's & boys' work clothing
PA: Steel Grip, Inc.
  1501 E Voorhees St
  Danville IL 61832
  217 442-6240

(G-8534)
YORK TANK AND MFG LLC
4438 S Roberts St (47952-8402)
PHONE....................................765 401-0667
Randal York,
EMP: 11
SALES (est): 739.4K **Privately Held**
SIC: 3999 Manufacturing industries

Kingsbury
Laporte County

(G-8535)
D & M PRECISION MACHINING INC
1 Kingsbury Indstrl Park (46345)
PHONE....................................219 393-5132
Ron Gross, *President*
Tonya Gross, *Vice Pres*
EMP: 4
SALES: 400K **Privately Held**
SIC: 3599 Machine shop, jobbing & repair

(G-8536)
ELECTRO CORPORATION
1st Rd Kingsbury Indus Pa (46345)
PHONE....................................219 393-5571
Fax: 219 393-5283
Mitch Juszkiewicz, *President*
Linda Juszkiewicz, *Corp Secy*
EMP: 13
SQ FT: 15,000
SALES (est): 1.7MM **Privately Held**
WEB: www.electrocorp.com
SIC: 7694 5063 3625 3621 Electric
  motor repair; motors, electric; relays & in-
  dustrial controls; motors & generators; in-
  stalling building equipment

(G-8537)
ENVIRONMENTAL PRODUCTS INC
Also Called: E P I
Fourth Road Kingsbury (46345)
P.O. Box 6, La Porte (46352-0006)
PHONE....................................219 393-3446
Tom Robinson, *President*
◆ EMP: 10
SALES (est): 720K **Privately Held**
WEB: www.environmentalproducts.com
SIC: 2522 2521 Chairs, office: padded or
  plain, except wood; desks, office: except
  wood; wood office furniture

(G-8538)
ESM GROUP INC
5th Rd Bldg 4 (46345)
P.O. Box 78 (46345-0078)
PHONE....................................219 393-5502
Pat Dragmister, *Manager*
EMP: 15
SALES (corp-wide): 241.5MM **Privately Held**
WEB: www.esmgroup.com
SIC: 2819 2899 Nonmetallic compounds;
  chemical preparations
HQ: Esm Group Inc.
  300 Corporate Pkwy 118n
  Amherst NY 14226
  716 446-8914

(G-8539)
INDUSTRIAL MINT WLDG MACHINING (PA)
Also Called: Imw
2nd & Hupp Rd (46345)
P.O. Box 385 (46345-0385)
PHONE....................................219 393-5531
Matthew Sularski, *President*
Gene Berchem, *President*
Robert Sularski, *Vice Pres*
Stephen Sularski, *Treasurer*
▲ EMP: 50
SQ FT: 85,000
SALES (est): 23.5MM **Privately Held**
SIC: 3569 3599 4212 Assembly ma-
  chines, non-metalworking; machine shop,
  jobbing & repair; heavy machinery trans-
  port, local

(G-8540)
M C WELDING & MACHINING CO
I Kingsbury Industrial Pa (46345)
PHONE....................................219 393-5718
Fax: 219 393-5750
Marian Cetera, *President*
Martha Cetera, *Vice Pres*
Brad Mrozinski, *Plant Mgr*
EMP: 4
SQ FT: 13,000
SALES (est): 599.9K **Privately Held**
SIC: 3599 Machine shop, jobbing & repair

(G-8541)
MAYFIELD-GLENN GROUP INC
Also Called: Master Roll Mfg's
3999 Hupp Rd Bldg R23 (46345)
PHONE....................................219 393-7117
Fax: 219 393-7217
Rodney E Mayfield, *President*
Jim D Glenn, *Treasurer*
EMP: 17
SQ FT: 11,000
SALES (est): 1.5MM **Privately Held**
WEB: www.masterrollmfgs.com
SIC: 3315 Steel wire & related products

(G-8542)
MELROSE PYROTECHNICS INC (PA)
Kingsbury Industrial Park (46345)
P.O. Box 302 (46345-0302)
PHONE....................................219 393-5522
Fax: 574 393-5710
Michael Cartolano, *President*
Rosaria Cartolano, *Admin Sec*
◆ EMP: 2
SALES (est): 1.6MM **Privately Held**
SIC: 2899 Fireworks

(G-8543)
NATIONAL PRODUCTS LLC
1st Rd Kingsbury Indus Pa (46345)
PHONE....................................219 393-5536
Fax: 574 393-5060
Bill Allen,
Randy Allen,
Ray Allen,
Rick Allen,
Rodney Amor,
EMP: 130
SALES (est): 18.4MM **Privately Held**
SIC: 2842 7389 Specialty cleaning, pol-
  ishes & sanitation goods; rug, upholstery,
  or dry cleaning detergents or spotters;
  packaging & labeling services

(G-8544)
ON POINT MACHINING INC
7111 Union Center Rd (46345)
PHONE....................................219 393-5132
Matthew R Kalucki, *President*
EMP: 5
SQ FT: 5,000
SALES (est): 289.4K **Privately Held**
SIC: 3599 Machine & other job shop work

(G-8545)
R & R PLASTICS INC
4th Rd Kingsbury Indus Pa (46345)
PHONE....................................219 393-5505
Fax: 574 393-3944
Robert Jackson, *President*
Maynard Searing, *Vice Pres*
EMP: 52 EST: 1979
SQ FT: 72,000
SALES: 2.9MM **Privately Held**
SIC: 3089 Injection molding of plastics

Kingsford Heights
Laporte County

(G-8546)
PROTERO CORPORATION
Also Called: Dental Enterprises
605 Grayton Rd (46346-3330)
P.O. Box 600 (46346-0600)
PHONE....................................219 393-5591
Fax: 219 393-5593
Jeffrey A Maki, *President*
EMP: 23
SQ FT: 14,000
SALES (est): 5.4MM **Privately Held**
WEB: www.dentalmodelsplus.com
SIC: 3843 Orthodontic appliances

Kirklin
Clinton County

(G-8547)
CARMEL ENGINEERING INC
413 E Madison St (46050-9028)
P.O. Box 67 (46050-0067)
PHONE....................................765 279-8955
Fax: 765 279-8966
Paul Weaver, *CEO*
Sonny Brunes, *President*
Randy Weaver, *Vice Pres*
Allan Roden, *Engineer*
Arlene Weaver, *Admin Sec*
EMP: 12
SQ FT: 1,200
SALES (est): 2.5MM **Privately Held**
WEB: www.carmelengineering.com
SIC: 1799 3999 3556 3443 Food service
  equipment installation; custom machinery;
  machine shop, jobbing & repair; food
  products machinery; fabricated plate work
  (boiler shop)

(G-8548)
E & R MANUFACTURING COMPANY
504 N Illinois St (46050)
P.O. Box 68 (46050-0068)
PHONE....................................765 279-8826
Fax: 765 279-8828
Paul Mangis, *President*
Martha Mangis, *Chairman*
Ronald E Neese, *Corp Secy*
EMP: 8 EST: 1954
SQ FT: 13,000
SALES (est): 1.2MM **Privately Held**
WEB: www.ermanufacturing.com
SIC: 3559 Stone working machinery

(G-8549)
KIRKLIN WASTE WATER TREATMENT
800 N Main St (46050)
P.O. Box 147 (46050-0147)
PHONE....................................765 279-5251
EMP: 2
SALES (est): 120.5K **Privately Held**
SIC: 3589 Water treatment equipment, in-
  dustrial

Knightstown
Henry County

(G-8550)
HOOSIER FEEDER COMPANY INC
100 W Morgan St (46148-9363)
PHONE....................................765 445-3333
Fax: 765 445-3335
Greg Schombert, *President*
Chris Schombert, *Vice Pres*
Ron Stoeffler, *Vice Pres*
Tonnie Addison, *Purch Mgr*
EMP: 22 EST: 2007
SQ FT: 15,000
SALES (est): 5MM **Privately Held**
SIC: 3559 Pharmaceutical machinery

(G-8551)
HY-FLEX CORPORATION
8774 S State Road 109 (46148-5503)
PHONE....................................765 571-5125
Ben Mills, *President*
Esther Mills, *Corp Secy*
Allen Mills, *Vice Pres*
EMP: 35
SQ FT: 18,000
SALES (est): 11.7MM **Privately Held**
WEB: www.hyflexcorp.com
SIC: 3561 3444 Industrial pumps & parts;
  sheet metalwork

(G-8552)
JAG METAL SOLUTIONS INC
234 W Warrick St (46148-1150)
P.O. Box 382, Monrovia (46157-0382)
PHONE....................................765 445-4459
Fax: 765 445-4456
Connie Peacock, *President*
EMP: 9
SALES (est): 1.8MM **Privately Held**
SIC: 3399 Primary metal products

(G-8553)
JATECH SCIENTIFIC INC (PA)
117 S Franklin St (46148-1307)
PHONE....................................765 345-2085
Edward Jackson, *President*
George Kannapel, *Vice Pres*
EMP: 9
SALES (est): 700K **Privately Held**
WEB: www.jatechscientific.com
SIC: 3589 Sewage & water treatment
  equipment

(G-8554)
KNIGHTSTOWN BANNER LLC
24 N Washington St (46148-1275)
P.O. Box 116 (46148-0116)
PHONE....................................765 345-2292
Eric Cox,
EMP: 41
SALES (est): 2MM **Privately Held**
SIC: 2711 Newspapers: publishing only,
  not printed on site

(G-8555)
MAURICE LUKENS JR
Also Called: Quality Hardwood Sales
38 W Grant St (46148-1313)
PHONE....................................765 345-2971
Jim Lukens Jr, *Owner*
Maurice Lukens Jr, *Owner*
EMP: 5 EST: 1960
SALES: 1.4MM **Privately Held**
SIC: 5099 5031 2426 2421 Logs, hewn
  ties, posts & poles; lumber, plywood &
  millwork; hardwood dimension & flooring
  mills; sawmills & planing mills, general;
  logging

(G-8556)
MAYHILL PUBLICATIONS INC (PA)
Also Called: Farmweek
27 N Jefferson St (46148-1242)
PHONE....................................765 345-5133
Fax: 800 695-8153
R Thomas Mayhill, *CEO*
Gary A Thoe, *President*
Margaret A Mayhill, *Vice Pres*
Rachel Shallenberg, *Production*
Diane Mc Roberts, *Sales Staff*
EMP: 35
SQ FT: 39,924
SALES (est): 4.1MM **Privately Held**
WEB: www.farmweek.net
SIC: 2711 Newspapers, publishing & print-
  ing

(G-8557)
MIDCOUNTRY MEDIA INC
27 N Jefferson St (46148-1242)
P.O. Box 90 (46148-0090)
PHONE....................................765 345-5133
Gary Thoe, *President*
Carol Johnson, *President*
Ann Hinch, *Editor*
Rachel Shallenberg, *Editor*
Merry Thoe, *Vice Pres*
EMP: 75
SQ FT: 10,500

SALES (est): 6.4MM **Privately Held**
WEB: www.midcountrymedia.com
SIC: 2711 2721 Job printing & newspaper
publishing combined; periodicals: publishing & printing

(G-8558)
**MOBILITY VEHICLES INDIANA
LLC**
11389 N Goose Rd (46148-9226)
PHONE..................................317 471-7169
Bryce Ahnafield, *Managing Prtnr*
EMP: 2
SALES (est): 139.5K **Privately Held**
SIC: 3842 5999 Technical aids for the
handicapped; technical aids for the handi-
capped

(G-8559)
PINNACLE WOODWORKING LLC
9708 S County Road 650 W (46148-9243)
PHONE..................................765 345-2301
Dennis Muncy, *President*
EMP: 2
SALES (est): 258.2K **Privately Held**
SIC: 2431 Millwork

(G-8560)
SMITHS TAC SHACK
117 E Main St (46148-1250)
PHONE..................................765 345-5590
Ronald Smith Jr, *Managing Prtnr*
Ronald A Smith, *Partner*
James Smith, *Mng Member*
EMP: 3
SALES (est): 171K **Privately Held**
SIC: 2399 Horse & pet accessories, textile;
horse harnesses & riding crops, etc.: non-
leather

Knightsville
Clay County

(G-8561)
**INTERIOR FIXS & MLLWK CO
INC**
995 E Barnett St (47857-8012)
P.O. Box 157 (47857-0157)
PHONE..................................812 446-0933
Fax: 812 446-9403
Ray Jones, *CEO*
EMP: 9
SQ FT: 12,000
SALES (est): 907.5K **Privately Held**
SIC: 2434 2431 Wood kitchen cabinets;
millwork

Knox
Starke County

(G-8562)
ALLIANCE COATING LLC
204 E Danker St (46534-2017)
P.O. Box 212 (46534-0212)
PHONE..................................574 772-3372
Dana Baker, *President*
EMP: 2
SALES (est): 91.3K **Privately Held**
SIC: 3479 Metal coating & allied service

(G-8563)
**CARTERS MANUFACTURING &
WELD**
3270 S County Road 210 (46534-7965)
PHONE..................................630 464-1520
Carter Comella, *Principal*
EMP: 2 EST: 2012
SALES (est): 131.1K **Privately Held**
SIC: 3999 Manufacturing industries

(G-8564)
DAUBERT VCI INC
1805 Pacific Ave (46534-9489)
PHONE..................................574 772-9310
M Lawrence Garman, *President*
EMP: 40
SALES (corp-wide): 73.1MM **Privately
Held**
WEB: www.daubertvci.com
SIC: 2672 Coated & laminated paper

HQ: Daubert Vci, Inc.
1333 Burr Ridge Pkwy # 200
Burr Ridge IL 60527
630 203-6800

(G-8565)
**DRAGON INDUSTRIES
INCORPORATED**
2120 E State Road 10 (46534-8512)
PHONE..................................574 772-3508
Fax: 574 772-3580
Mike Bailey, *Owner*
EMP: 3
SALES (est): 189.7K **Privately Held**
SIC: 3999 Manufacturing industries

(G-8566)
FONTAINE TRAILER COMPANY
1201 W Culver Rd (46534-8558)
PHONE..................................574 772-6673
Michael Eberwein, *Manager*
EMP: 3
SALES (corp-wide): 242.1B **Publicly
Held**
WEB: www.road-gear.com
SIC: 3715 Trailer bodies
HQ: Fontaine Commercial Trailer, Inc.
430 Sam Letson Indus Rd
Haleyville AL 35565
205 486-5251

(G-8567)
**HOOSIER CUSTOM PLASTICS
LLC**
Also Called: Eco Golf
201 Hamilton Dr (46534-8118)
PHONE..................................574 772-2120
Craig Dulworth, *Partner*
Gordon Schenk, *Mng Member*
Mike Tetzlofs,
▲ EMP: 35
SQ FT: 16,000
SALES (est): 7.1MM **Privately Held**
WEB: www.hcplastic.com
SIC: 3089 Injection molded finished plastic
products

(G-8568)
INDIANA FINE BLANKING
1200 Kloeckner Dr (46534-7500)
PHONE..................................574 772-3850
Alex Weisheit, *Plant Mgr*
Ron Bede, *Controller*
EMP: 2
SALES (est): 178.6K **Privately Held**
SIC: 3469 Stamping metal for the trade

(G-8569)
J AIME MUSIC PUBLISHING LLC
10040 E 50 S (46534-8230)
PHONE..................................574 772-2934
Jaime Bradley, *Principal*
EMP: 2
SALES (est): 62.9K **Privately Held**
SIC: 2711 Newspapers

(G-8570)
**KNOX FERTILIZER COMPANY
INC**
2660 E 100 S (46534-8768)
P.O. Box 248 (46534-0248)
PHONE..................................574 772-6275
Fax: 574 772-5878
Robert Shaw Jr, *President*
Craig Filley, *Sales Mgr*
Mark C Shaw, *Admin Sec*
◆ EMP: 3 EST: 1950
SALES (est): 2.9MM **Privately Held**
WEB: www.knoxfert.com
SIC: 0782 2873 Lawn & garden services;
nitrogenous fertilizers

(G-8571)
KRUZ INC (PA)
1201 W Culver Rd (46534-8558)
P.O. Box 129 (46534-0129)
PHONE..................................574 772-6673
Kent P Kruzick, *President*
Kyle Kruzick, *Sales Staff*
Adam Collins, *Manager*
▲ EMP: 40
SQ FT: 63,000

SALES (est): 10.9MM **Privately Held**
WEB: www.kruz.com
SIC: 3713 3715 Dump truck bodies; truck
trailers

(G-8572)
MAIN STREET COMPUTERS
4 S Main St Apt A (46534-0015)
PHONE..................................574 772-7890
Fax: 574 772-7889
Obet Pabon, *CEO*
EMP: 2
SALES (est): 200.5K **Privately Held**
SIC: 3575 Computer terminals, monitors &
components

(G-8573)
MANITEX INTERNATIONAL INC
Also Called: Manitex Sabre
5420 E State Road 8 (46534-9696)
PHONE..................................574 772-5380
David J Langevin, *Ch of Bd*
EMP: 124 **Publicly Held**
SIC: 3443 Containers, shipping (bombs,
etc.): metal plate
PA: Manitex International, Inc.
9725 Industrial Dr
Bridgeview IL 60455

(G-8574)
MANITEX SABRE INC
5420 E State Road 8 (46534-9696)
PHONE..................................574 772-5380
Andrew Rooke, *President*
Jeff James, *Plant Mgr*
EMP: 70
SALES (est): 11.2MM **Privately Held**
SIC: 3443 Tanks, standard or custom fabri-
cated: metal plate

(G-8575)
MPI PRODUCTS LLC
Also Called: Indiana Fine Blanking
1200 Kloeckner Dr (46534-7500)
PHONE..................................574 772-3850
Bob Johnston, *Engineer*
Tom Burnham, *Branch Mgr*
Stephen Beckett, *Manager*
Chris Martin, *Manager*
Jeanie Mixis, *Manager*
EMP: 301
SQ FT: 50,000
SALES (corp-wide): 317.6MM **Privately
Held**
WEB: www.mpi-int.com
SIC: 3469 3465 Stamping metal for the
trade; automotive stampings
HQ: Mpi Products Llc
2129 Austin Ave
Rochester Hills MI 48309

(G-8576)
PHILIP KONRAD & SONS INC
1315 E State Road 10 (46534-8506)
PHONE..................................574 772-3966
Fax: 574 772-4176
Phillip W Konrad, *President*
Dennis P Konrad, *Corp Secy*
Carole Konrad, *Vice Pres*
Donald P Konrad, *Vice Pres*
Dennis Konrad, *Treasurer*
EMP: 11 **EST: 1957**
SQ FT: 16,000
SALES (est): 1.1MM **Privately Held**
SIC: 2431 2434 Millwork; wood kitchen
cabinets

(G-8577)
REAGENT CHEMICAL & RES INC
Also Called: White Flyer Targets
317 Kloeckner Dr (46534-7720)
PHONE..................................574 772-3271
EMP: 100
SALES (corp-wide): 375MM **Privately
Held**
SIC: 2819 Industrial inorganic chemicals
PA: Reagent Chemical & Research, Inc.
115 Rte 202
Ringoes NJ 08551
908 284-2800

(G-8578)
REAGENT CHEMICAL & RES INC
1705 Pacific Ave (46534-1001)
PHONE..................................574 772-7424
EMP: 12

SALES (corp-wide): 375MM **Privately
Held**
SIC: 3949 2819 Targets, archery & rifle
shooting; sulfur, recovered or refined, incl.
from sour natural gas
PA: Reagent Chemical & Research, Inc.
115 Rte 202
Ringoes NJ 08551
908 284-2800

(G-8579)
**ROAD APPLE
PSYCHOTHERAPY ✪**
740 S 1100 E (46534-9664)
PHONE..................................574 230-3449
Char Riale, *Principal*
EMP: 2 EST: 2017
SALES (est): 85.9K **Privately Held**
SIC: 3571 Personal computers (microcom-
puters)

(G-8580)
SAMSWOODWORKING
4725 S 750 E (46534-9553)
PHONE..................................574 772-6482
Samuel Sopt, *Principal*
EMP: 2
SALES (est): 85.2K **Privately Held**
SIC: 2431 Millwork

(G-8581)
SCP BUILDING PRODUCTS LLC
Also Called: Barber & Ross of Indiana
1001 W Culver Rd (46534-8553)
PHONE..................................574 772-2955
Sam Khoury,
Dave Heimstra,
EMP: 5
SALES (est): 71.6K **Privately Held**
SIC: 2431 Millwork

(G-8582)
SPECIALTY SHOPPE
1307 S Heaton St (46534-2352)
PHONE..................................574 772-7873
Fax: 574 772-7816
Robin Marshall, *Owner*
Susan A Marshall, *Manager*
EMP: 2
SALES (est): 120K **Privately Held**
SIC: 5999 2396 7389 Trophies & plaques;
fabric printing & stamping; engraving
service

(G-8583)
**SPORTS UNLIMITED PRINTED
AP**
6 S Cleveland St (46534-2402)
PHONE..................................574 772-4239
Albert Einstein, *Owner*
EMP: 2
SALES (est): 159.6K **Privately Held**
SIC: 2759 Screen printing

(G-8584)
**STARKE COUNTY RECYCLING
INC**
3055 S Us Highway 35 (46534-9706)
PHONE..................................574 772-2594
James Campbell, *President*
EMP: 10
SALES (est): 1.1MM **Privately Held**
SIC: 2611 Pulp manufactured from waste
or recycled paper

(G-8585)
STUDIO PRINTERS
1202 S Heaton St (46534-2394)
PHONE..................................574 772-0900
Fax: 574 772-3907
Michael C Reimbold, *President*
Mike Reimbold, *Principal*
EMP: 7 EST: 1945
SQ FT: 2,500
SALES (est): 861.7K **Privately Held**
WEB: www.studioprinters.com
SIC: 2759 Commercial printing

(G-8586)
V & H FIBERGLASS REPAIR
680 N Us Highway 35 (46534-8932)
PHONE..................................574 772-4920
Fax: 574 772-4280
Victor Hughes, *Owner*
EMP: 2

G
E
O
G
R
A
P
H
I
C

SALES: 60K **Privately Held**
SIC: 3229 Glass fiber products

(G-8587)
WESTROCK CP LLC
Also Called: Rocktenn-Knox
6595 E State Road 10 (46534-8462)
PHONE..............................574 772-5545
Wes Lenig, *General Mgr*
EMP: 34
SQ FT: 50,000
SALES (corp-wide): 14.8B **Publicly Held**
SIC: 2653 Boxes, corrugated: made from purchased materials
HQ: Westrock Cp, Llc
504 Thrasher St
Norcross GA 30071

(G-8588)
WHITE FLYER TARGETS
317 Kloeckner Dr (46534-7720)
P.O. Box 130 (46534-0130)
PHONE..............................574 772-3271
EMP: 8
SALES (est): 40.3K **Privately Held**
SIC: 3949 Mfg Sporting/Athletic Goods

Kokomo
Howard County

(G-8589)
A D I SCREEN PRINTING
4758 E 00 Ns (46901-6676)
PHONE..............................765 457-8580
Fax: 765 457-8582
Larry Amthauer, *Owner*
EMP: 7
SQ FT: 4,400
SALES: 900K **Privately Held**
SIC: 2261 2395 Screen printing of cotton broadwoven fabrics; embroidery & art needlework

(G-8590)
ALLIED TUBE & CONDUIT CORP
101 E Broadway St (46901-2919)
PHONE..............................765 459-8811
Fax: 765 459-0246
Richard Paul, *Manager*
EMP: 46 **Publicly Held**
WEB: www.alliedtube.com
SIC: 3312 3498 Tubes, steel & iron; fabricated pipe & fittings
HQ: Allied Tube & Conduit Corporation
16100 Lathrop Ave
Harvey IL 60426
708 339-1610

(G-8591)
APTIV SERVICES US LLC
Delphi Electronics and Safety
1 Corporate Dr (46902-4000)
P.O. Box 9005 (46904-9005)
PHONE..............................765 451-5011
Jeffrey J Owens, *Manager*
EMP: 19
SALES (corp-wide): 16.6B **Privately Held**
SIC: 3714 3625 3812 5013 Instrument board assemblies, motor vehicle; electric controls & control accessories, industrial; aircraft/aerospace flight instruments & guidance systems; motor vehicle supplies & new parts; chassis, motor vehicle
HQ: Aptiv Services Us, Llc
5725 Innovation Dr
Troy MI 48098

(G-8592)
APTIV SERVICES US LLC
Also Called: Delphi
1 Corporate Dr (46902-4000)
PHONE..............................765 451-5011
Steve Felix, *Branch Mgr*
Kathy Lutgen, *Director*
EMP: 2
SALES (corp-wide): 16.6B **Privately Held**
WEB: www.delphiauto.com
SIC: 3714 Motor vehicle parts & accessories
HQ: Aptiv Services Us, Llc
5725 Innovation Dr
Troy MI 48098

(G-8593)
APTIV SERVICES US LLC
Also Called: Delphi
2151 E Lincoln Rd (46902-3773)
PHONE..............................765 451-0732
Daniel Frazier, *Manager*
EMP: 209
SALES (corp-wide): 16.6B **Privately Held**
WEB: www.delphiauto.com
SIC: 3714 Motor vehicle parts & accessories
HQ: Aptiv Services Us, Llc
5725 Innovation Dr
Troy MI 48098

(G-8594)
APTIV SERVICES US LLC
Also Called: Delphi
2705 S Goyer Rd (46902-7403)
P.O. Box 9005 (46904-9005)
PHONE..............................765 451-5011
Robert Hayes, *Purchasing*
Ronald Webster, *Engineer*
Delphi Kokomo, *Branch Mgr*
David Wohleen, *Branch Mgr*
EMP: 209
SALES (corp-wide): 16.6B **Privately Held**
WEB: www.delphiauto.com
SIC: 3714 Motor vehicle parts & accessories
HQ: Aptiv Services Us, Llc
5725 Innovation Dr
Troy MI 48098

(G-8595)
B & D MANUFACTURING INC
2100 E Carter St (46901-5660)
PHONE..............................765 452-2761
Fax: 765 452-9671
Mike Green, *President*
EMP: 6
SQ FT: 10,000
SALES (est): 872.3K **Privately Held**
SIC: 3544 Special dies & tools; jigs & fixtures; forms (molds), for foundry & plastics working machinery

(G-8596)
B&D LIGHTS LLC
2100 E Carter St (46901-5660)
PHONE..............................765 452-2761
Charles Daine, *Owner*
EMP: 2
SALES (est): 170K **Privately Held**
SIC: 3646 Fluorescent lighting fixtures, commercial

(G-8597)
BEACHY MACHINE SHOP LLC
3884 E 400 N (46901-9359)
PHONE..............................765 452-9051
Ezra Beachy, *President*
EMP: 6
SALES (est): 550.9K **Privately Held**
SIC: 3462 Automotive forgings, ferrous: crankshaft, engine, axle, etc.

(G-8598)
BLACKHAWK MILLWRIGHT & RIGGING
1316 Ann St (46901-2200)
P.O. Box 35, Greentown (46936-0035)
PHONE..............................765 662-7922
Patrick Lee, *President*
Jody Lee, *Treasurer*
EMP: 5
SALES (est): 834.3K **Privately Held**
SIC: 3441 Fabricated structural metal

(G-8599)
BLUE CREEK TRAIL MAP CO
3506 Hawthorne Ln (46902-4521)
PHONE..............................765 455-9867
Archie Wills, *Principal*
Scott Pendleton, *Supervisor*
EMP: 2 **EST:** 2008
SALES (est): 162.7K **Privately Held**
SIC: 2752 Maps, lithographed

(G-8600)
BOB LOW DISCOUNT TOBACCO
221 W Morgan St (46901-2252)
PHONE..............................765 868-9713
Brinda William, *Manager*
EMP: 4

SALES (est): 267.2K **Privately Held**
SIC: 2121 Cigars

(G-8601)
BOBS QUICK COPY SHOP
1128 Emery St (46902-2635)
PHONE..............................765 457-9160
EMP: 2
SALES (est): 125.5K **Privately Held**
SIC: 2752 Commercial printing, offset

(G-8602)
BRYANT ICE CO INC
824 S Armstrong St (46901-5328)
PHONE..............................765 459-4543
Daniel J Bryant, *President*
EMP: 3
SALES (est): 340K **Privately Held**
SIC: 2097 Ice cubes

(G-8603)
C LASER INC
613 W Lincoln Rd Ste A (46902-3460)
PHONE..............................317 641-5185
Pattanam Srinivasan, *CEO*
EMP: 2
SALES (est): 86.6K **Privately Held**
SIC: 3845 Laser systems & equipment, medical

(G-8604)
CARDINAL METAL FINISHING LLC (PA)
1500 E Murden St (46901-5667)
PHONE..............................866 585-8024
Lisa Guarnieri, *Principal*
Scott Zemnick, *Principal*
EMP: 110
SALES (est): 6MM **Privately Held**
SIC: 3559 Metal finishing equipment for plating, etc.

(G-8605)
CENTRAL BRACE & LIMB CO INC
802 S Berkley Rd Ste B (46901-5110)
PHONE..............................765 457-4868
Ann Vent, *Branch Mgr*
EMP: 3
SALES (corp-wide): 4MM **Privately Held**
SIC: 3842 Limbs, artificial
PA: Central Brace & Limb Co Inc
1901 N Capitol Ave
Indianapolis IN 46202
317 925-4296

(G-8606)
CHALK PRECISION MACHINING LLC
3095 N Washington St (46901-5857)
PHONE..............................765 452-9202
EMP: 2 **EST:** 2011
SALES (est): 110K **Privately Held**
SIC: 3599 Mfg Industrial Machinery

(G-8607)
COCA COLA BTLG CO KOKOMO IND (PA)
Also Called: Coca-Cola
2305 Davis Rd (46901-2176)
P.O. Box 1049 (46903-1049)
PHONE..............................765 457-4421
Fax: 765 452-2138
Edmond P Severns Jr, *President*
Virginia Severns, *Vice Pres*
▲ **EMP:** 72 **EST:** 1915
SQ FT: 70,000
SALES: 2.2MM **Privately Held**
WEB: www.cckokomo.com
SIC: 2086 Bottled & canned soft drinks

(G-8608)
COMMUNITY HOLDINGS INDIANA INC
Also Called: Kokomo Tribune
300 N Union St (46901-4612)
P.O. Box 9014 (46904-9014)
PHONE..............................765 459-3121
Fax: 765 456-7207
Connie Alexander, *Principal*
EMP: 16 **Privately Held**
WEB: www.clintonnc.com
SIC: 2711 2791 2752 Newspapers: publishing only, not printed on site; typesetting; commercial printing, lithographic

HQ: Community Holdings Of Indiana, Inc.
3500 Colonnade Pkwy # 600
Birmingham AL 35243

(G-8609)
CUMULUS INTRMDATE HOLDINGS INC
Also Called: Sign Pro
4834 N Parkway (46901-3970)
PHONE..............................765 452-5704
Fax: 765 456-1195
Bob Wall, *Branch Mgr*
EMP: 3
SALES (corp-wide): 1.1B **Publicly Held**
WEB: www.citadelradio.com
SIC: 3993 Signs & advertising specialties
HQ: Cumulus Intermediate Holdings Inc.
3280 Peachtree Rd Ne # 2300
Atlanta GA 30305

(G-8610)
CUSTOM BUILT BARNS INC (PA)
Also Called: Custom Built Storage Sheds
2312 N Plate St (46901-1692)
PHONE..............................765 457-9037
Fax: 765 459-9414
John D Bass, *President*
EMP: 2
SQ FT: 2,300
SALES (est): 579.2K **Privately Held**
SIC: 2452 2511 Prefabricated buildings, wood; wood lawn & garden furniture; novelty furniture: wood

(G-8611)
DD STOOPS LASER ENGRAVING
315 W Markland Ave (46901-6106)
PHONE..............................765 868-4999
Dan Stoops, *Owner*
EMP: 2
SALES (est): 137.7K **Privately Held**
SIC: 7389 3479 Engraving service; etching & engraving

(G-8612)
DELCO ELECTRONICS ❂
3700 Orleans Dr (46902-4344)
PHONE..............................765 455-9713
Pete Moody, *Engineer*
EMP: 2 **EST:** 2017
SALES (est): 87.2K **Privately Held**
SIC: 3714 Motor vehicle parts & accessories

(G-8613)
DELCO ELECTRONICS
4221 Coventry Dr (46902-9409)
PHONE..............................765 451-9325
EMP: 2
SALES (est): 88.3K **Privately Held**
SIC: 3694 Engine electrical equipment

(G-8614)
DELPHI E & S MORGAN STREET OPS
1501 E 200 N (46901-8909)
PHONE..............................765 451-2571
EMP: 2
SALES (est): 245.6K **Privately Held**
SIC: 3714 Motor vehicle parts & accessories

(G-8615)
DELPHI POWERTRAIN SYSTEMS LLC
Also Called: Kokomo Power Electronics
1501 E 200 N (46901-8909)
PHONE..............................765 236-0025
Lisa Hardwick, *Branch Mgr*
EMP: 12
SALES (corp-wide): 1.5MM **Privately Held**
SIC: 3714 Motor vehicle parts & accessories
HQ: Delphi Powertrain Systems, Llc
5820 Innovation Dr
Troy MI 48098
248 813-2000

(G-8616)
DELPHI POWERTRAIN SYSTEMS LLC
2151 E Lincoln Rd (46902-3773)
PHONE..............................765 451-0732
EMP: 3

▲ = Import ▼=Export
◆ =Import/Export

SALES (corp-wide): 1.5MM **Privately Held**
SIC: **3714** Motor vehicle parts & accessories
HQ: Delphi Powertrain Systems, Llc
5820 Innovation Dr
Troy MI 48098
248 813-2000

(G-8617)
DONNIE MICHAELS KICKS
3780 S Reed Rd (46902-3829)
PHONE................................765 457-4083
Donald Michaels, *Owner*
EMP: 2
SALES (est): 103.2K **Privately Held**
SIC: **7999** 2721 Karate instruction; periodicals

(G-8618)
DUNCAN SERVICE COMPANY
701 S Main St (46901-5459)
PHONE................................765 452-6799
Jeffrey Duncan, *Owner*
EMP: 6
SALES (est): 426.9K **Privately Held**
WEB: www.duncanservicecompany.com
SIC: **3585** Parts for heating, cooling & refrigerating equipment

(G-8619)
ECHELBARGER MACHINING CO LLC
Also Called: Echelbrger Precision Machining
2614 Precision Dr (46902-8500)
PHONE................................765 252-1965
Brad Carney, *President*
Brian Eckelbarger, *Mng Member*
Dan Carney, *Mng Member*
EMP: 11
SQ FT: 8,000
SALES (est): 1.5MM **Privately Held**
SIC: **3599** Custom machinery; machine shop, jobbing & repair

(G-8620)
ELECTRONIC SERVICES LLC
Also Called: CSI ELECTRONICS
1942 S Elizabeth St (46902-2432)
PHONE................................765 457-3894
Fax: 765 457-4395
Shep Beyland, *Managing Prtnr*
Patricia A Beyland, *Vice Pres*
Kaye Becker, *Purch Mgr*
Amanda Olsan, *Marketing Mgr*
Chris Sullivan, *Marketing Staff*
EMP: 32
SQ FT: 11,600
SALES: 4.9MM **Privately Held**
WEB: www.csielectronics.com
SIC: **1731** 3679 General electrical contractor; electronic circuits

(G-8621)
ENGINEERED CONVEYORS INC (PA)
1055 Home Ave (46902-1624)
P.O. Box 1112 (46903-1112)
PHONE................................765 459-4545
Fax: 765 459-4565
John Puckebaum, *Ch of Bd*
EMP: 18
SQ FT: 12,500
SALES (est): 3.2MM **Privately Held**
WEB: www.engineeredconveyors.com
SIC: **1796** 3441 Machinery installation; fabricated structural metal

(G-8622)
FCA US LLC
Also Called: Chrysler Transmission
2401 S Reed Rd (46902-7902)
P.O. Box 9007 (46904-9007)
PHONE................................765 454-1705
Dan Grizzle, *Principal*
Larry Swain, *Safety Mgr*
Ryan Houck, *Engineer*
Greg Rhees, *Engineer*
Craig Shoemaker, *Engineer*
EMP: 1126
SALES (corp-wide): 130.8B **Privately Held**
SIC: **3714** Motor vehicle transmissions, drive assemblies & parts

HQ: Fca Us Llc
1000 Chrysler Dr
Auburn Hills MI 48326

(G-8623)
FCA US LLC
3660 State Rd 931 (46901)
PHONE................................765 854-4234
Jeremy Keaping, *Branch Mgr*
EMP: 1500
SALES (corp-wide): 130.8B **Privately Held**
SIC: **3714** Transmissions, motor vehicle
HQ: Fca Us Llc
1000 Chrysler Dr
Auburn Hills MI 48326

(G-8624)
FCA US LLC
Also Called: Chrysler Foundry
1947 S Elizabeth St (46902-2431)
PHONE................................765 454-0018
Daniel Gadberry, *Production*
Humberto De Luca, *Engineer*
Bob Bowers, *Branch Mgr*
EMP: 1150
SALES (corp-wide): 130.8B **Privately Held**
SIC: **3365** 3714 3519 3325 Aluminum foundries; motor vehicle parts & accessories; internal combustion engines; steel foundries
HQ: Fca Us Llc
1000 Chrysler Dr
Auburn Hills MI 48326

(G-8625)
FCA US LLC
Also Called: Kokomo Castings
1001 E Boulevard (46902-5740)
P.O. Box 9007 (46904-9007)
PHONE................................765 454-1005
Fax: 765 454-1513
Keith Hughes, *Research*
Scott Wiggers, *Plant Engr*
Michael Tuberty, *Branch Mgr*
EMP: 1075
SALES (corp-wide): 130.8B **Privately Held**
SIC: **3714** 3365 3363 Motor vehicle parts & accessories; aluminum foundries; aluminum die-castings
HQ: Fca Us Llc
1000 Chrysler Dr
Auburn Hills MI 48326

(G-8626)
G & J
Also Called: Handle Bar, The
1252 N Main St (46901-2849)
PHONE................................765 457-9889
Sherri Dewitt, *Manager*
EMP: 3
SALES (est): 269K **Privately Held**
SIC: **2499** Handles, wood

(G-8627)
G E KERR COMPANIES INC
Also Called: Co Experts
2600 W Jefferson St (46901-1750)
PHONE................................417 426-5504
George E Kerr, *President*
Della R Kerr, *Corp Secy*
EMP: 2 EST: 1958
SALES (est): 182.9K **Privately Held**
WEB: www.coexperts.com
SIC: **1389** Detection & analysis service, gas

(G-8628)
GM COMPONENTS HOLDINGS LLC
Also Called: Kokomo Electronic Assembly
2100 E Lincoln Rd (46902-3774)
PHONE................................765 451-8440
Steve Hartwig, *Plant Mgr*
EMP: 300 **Publicly Held**
SIC: **3714** Motor vehicle parts & accessories
HQ: Gm Components Holdings, Llc
300 Renaissance Ctr
Detroit MI 48243

(G-8629)
GM COMPONENTS HOLDINGS LLC
Gmch Kokomo Plt 9
2033 E Blvd Plant 9 9 Plant (46904)
P.O. Box 9005 (46904-9005)
PHONE................................765 451-9049
Steve Hartwig, *Branch Mgr*
EMP: 4 **Publicly Held**
SIC: **3651** 3625 3714 3812 Audio electronic systems; electric controls & control accessories, industrial; instrument board assemblies, motor vehicle; aircraft/aerospace flight instruments & guidance systems
HQ: Gm Components Holdings, Llc
300 Renaissance Ctr
Detroit MI 48243

(G-8630)
GM COMPONENTS HOLDINGS LLC
Gmch Kokomo Fab 3
2150 E Lincoln Rd (46902-3774)
P.O. Box 9005 (46904-9005)
PHONE................................765 451-5011
Steve Hartwig, *Branch Mgr*
EMP: 5 **Publicly Held**
SIC: **3694** Automotive electrical equipment
HQ: Gm Components Holdings, Llc
300 Renaissance Ctr
Detroit MI 48243

(G-8631)
GOUDY BROTHERS BOILER CO INC
100 W Spraker St (46901-2240)
P.O. Box 537 (46903-0537)
PHONE................................765 459-4416
Fax: 765 459-4615
Vicki Spall, *President*
Donald Spall, *Corp Secy*
Jeffrey Spall II, *Shareholder*
EMP: 25 EST: 1919
SQ FT: 10,000
SALES (est): 1.7MM **Privately Held**
SIC: **7699** 3446 3444 3443 Gas appliance repair service; architectural metalwork; sheet metalwork; fabricated plate work (boiler shop)

(G-8632)
GRAPHICS LAB UV PRINTING INC
Also Called: Throttle Jockey
1041 S Union St (46902-1630)
PHONE................................765 457-5784
Fax: 765 457-4028
Robert Davis, *President*
Matthew Davis, *Vice Pres*
Jamie Lubben, *Admin Sec*
EMP: 2
SALES (est): 1.4MM **Privately Held**
WEB: www.graphicslab.com
SIC: **2759** 5571 Screen printing; decals; printing; motorcycle dealers

(G-8633)
GREEN CUBES TECHNOLOGY CORP (PA)
4124 Cartwright Dr (46902-4388)
PHONE................................502 416-1060
Chris Tecca, *CEO*
Mohammed Alobaidi, *President*
Anthony Cooper, *President*
Jennifer Payton, *VP Opers*
▲ EMP: 46
SQ FT: 7,000
SALES: 7K **Privately Held**
SIC: **3679** Electronic loads & power supplies

(G-8634)
H & H PARTNERSHIP INC
Also Called: Fast Land Food
174 E North St (46901-2959)
PHONE................................765 513-4739
Charnpreet Kaur, *President*
Inderjit Singh, *Vice Pres*
EMP: 5
SQ FT: 3,000

SALES (est): 209.8K **Privately Held**
SIC: **7215** 2032 2092 Laundry, coin-operated; chicken broth: packaged in cans, jars, etc.; prepared fish or other seafood cakes & sticks

(G-8635)
H & R INDUSTRIAL LLC
816 Millbrook Ln (46901-5129)
PHONE................................765 868-8408
Fax: 765 868-8308
Jim Rezo, *President*
Scott Ronk, *Vice Pres*
Chris Fairchild, *Project Mgr*
Sam Layman, *Project Mgr*
Greg Crisp, *Engineer*
EMP: 72
SQ FT: 28,000
SALES: 15MM **Privately Held**
SIC: **3449** Bars, concrete reinforcing: fabricated steel

(G-8636)
HARVEY HINKLEMEYERS
1554 S Dixon Rd (46902-5997)
PHONE................................765 452-1942
Harvey Hinklemeyers, *Principal*
EMP: 2
SALES (est): 77.4K **Privately Held**
SIC: **5812** 2099 Eating places; food preparations

(G-8637)
HAYNES INTERNATIONAL INC
2000 W Defenbaugh St (46902-6015)
P.O. Box 9013 (46904-9013)
PHONE................................765 457-3790
August Cigan, *Vice Pres*
Larry Yarosz, *Engineer*
Sarah Oldfather, *Accountant*
Susan Bickel, *Manager*
Lee Mumaw, *Manager*
EMP: 700
SALES (corp-wide): 395.2MM **Publicly Held**
WEB: www.hastelloy.com
SIC: **3356** Gold & gold alloy: rolling, drawing or extruding
PA: Haynes International, Inc.
1020 W Park Ave
Kokomo IN 46901
765 456-6000

(G-8638)
HAYNES INTERNATIONAL INC (PA)
1020 W Park Ave (46901-6330)
P.O. Box 9013 (46904-9013)
PHONE................................765 456-6000
Fax: 765 456-6905
Michael Shor, *CEO*
John C Corey, *Ch of Bd*
Eric Jansen, *Superintendent*
Janice W Gunst, *Vice Pres*
Mellen Karen, *Vice Pres*
EMP: 748
SALES: 395.2MM **Publicly Held**
WEB: www.hastelloy.com
SIC: **3356** Nickel; titanium

(G-8639)
HOOSIER SPLINE BROACH CORP
1401 Touby Pike (46901-2503)
P.O. Box 538 (46903-0538)
PHONE................................765 452-8273
Fax: 765 457-7629
Gilbert Larison, *President*
Mary Larison, *Corp Secy*
Jeff Larison, *Vice Pres*
Amy Shiflet, *Office Mgr*
Linda Lovell, *Admin Asst*
EMP: 22
SQ FT: 15,000
SALES: 3.5MM **Privately Held**
WEB: www.hoosierbroach.com
SIC: **3545** 7692 3541 Machine tool attachments & accessories; broaches (machine tool accessories); welding repair; machine tools, metal cutting type

G E O G R A P H I C

(G-8640)
HOROHO PRINTING COMPANY INC
500 N Philips St (46901-4259)
PHONE................765 452-8862
Fax: 765 452-8862
Merrill L Horoho, *President*
Gregory E Horoho, *Vice Pres*
Gregory Horoho, *Vice Pres*
Linda Beachy, *Treasurer*
Marjorie Horoho, *Admin Sec*
EMP: 4
SQ FT: 2,016
SALES: 185K **Privately Held**
WEB: www.horohoprinting.com
SIC: 2752 Commercial printing, offset

(G-8641)
HOWARD PRINT SHOP
2111 W Alto Rd (46902-4810)
PHONE................765 453-6161
Fax: 765 453-0054
David Howard, *Owner*
EMP: 6
SQ FT: 2,000
SALES: 550K **Privately Held**
WEB: www.howardps.com
SIC: 2752 2791 2789 Commercial printing, offset; typesetting; bookbinding & related work

(G-8642)
HYNES KOKOMO LLC
1817 W Defenbaugh St (46902-6014)
PHONE................330 799-3221
Tom Sheridan, *Mng Member*
EMP: 4
SALES (est): 692.7K **Privately Held**
SIC: 3312 Stainless steel

(G-8643)
IDEAL INC
Also Called: Ideal Janitor Supply
1037 S Union St (46902-1630)
P.O. Box 203 (46903-0203)
PHONE................765 457-6222
Fax: 765 457-1200
Brad Bourff, *President*
EMP: 7
SQ FT: 6,000
SALES (est): 626.9K **Privately Held**
WEB: www.idealjanitorsupply.com
SIC: 7218 5087 2842 Treated equipment supply: mats, rugs, mops, cloths, etc.; janitors' supplies; dusting cloths, chemically treated

(G-8644)
IDRA NORTH AMERICA INC
1510 Ann St (46901-2242)
PHONE................765 459-0085
Ricardo Ferario, *President*
EMP: 4
SALES (est): 1.3MM **Privately Held**
SIC: 3542 Die casting machines

(G-8645)
INDALEX INC
1500 E Murden St (46901-5667)
PHONE................765 457-1117
Tim Stubbs, *CEO*
EMP: 2
SALES (est): 99.9K **Privately Held**
SIC: 3354 Aluminum extruded products

(G-8646)
INFINEON TECH AMERICAS CORP
2529 Commerce Dr Ste H (46902-7815)
PHONE................765 454-2144
John Bartow, *Manager*
EMP: 3
SALES (corp-wide): 8.3B **Privately Held**
WEB: www.irf.com
SIC: 3674 Semiconductors & related devices
HQ: Infineon Technologies Americas Corp.
101 N Pacific Coast Hwy
El Segundo CA 90245
310 726-8000

(G-8647)
INTENSE INCENSE
1211 N Morrison St (46901-2761)
PHONE................765 457-3602

EMP: 2 EST: 2012
SALES (est): 110K **Privately Held**
SIC: 2899 Mfg Chemical Preparations

(G-8648)
INVESTWELL ELECTRONICS INC
329 E Firmin St (46902-2240)
PHONE................765 457-1911
Bradley A Johnson, *President*
EMP: 4
SQ FT: 6,000
SALES: 140K **Privately Held**
WEB: www.investwellelectronics.com
SIC: 3679 Electronic circuits

(G-8649)
IRVING MATERIALS INC
Also Called: I M I
1315 S Dixon Rd (46902-6056)
PHONE................765 452-4044
Wayne Sears, *Opers Mgr*
Gary Jones, *Branch Mgr*
EMP: 15
SALES (corp-wide): 800.6MM **Privately Held**
SIC: 3273 Ready-mixed concrete
PA: Irving Materials, Inc.
8032 N State Road 9
Greenfield IN 46140
317 326-3101

(G-8650)
JASON RANDALL DESIGNS
361 W 300 S (46902-5124)
PHONE................317 319-6747
Randall Jason, *Owner*
EMP: 2
SALES (est): 72.9K **Privately Held**
SIC: 2511 Wood household furniture

(G-8651)
KINDER GROUP INC
1915 E North St (46901-3169)
PHONE................765 457-5966
Fax: 765 452-6603
Jeff Cardwell, *President*
Matthew Kinder, *Corp Secy*
EMP: 150
SQ FT: 7,500
SALES (est): 8MM **Privately Held**
SIC: 3993 1799 Electric signs; sign installation & maintenance

(G-8652)
KOKOMO CABINETRY
1516 N Locke St (46901-2428)
PHONE................765 457-2385
Steve Hite, *Owner*
EMP: 2
SALES (est): 129.4K **Privately Held**
SIC: 2434 Wood kitchen cabinets

(G-8653)
KOKOMO METAL FABRICATORS INC
1931 E North St (46901-3169)
PHONE................765 459-8173
Fax: 765 459-8127
Jeff Jones, *President*
Terry Etchison, *Vice Pres*
EMP: 4 EST: 1960
SQ FT: 5,000
SALES: 400K **Privately Held**
SIC: 3599 3444 3443 3441 Custom machinery; sheet metalwork; fabricated plate work (boiler shop); fabricated structural metal

(G-8654)
KOKOMO OPALESCENT GLASS CO
1310 S Market St (46902-1633)
P.O. Box 2265 (46904-2265)
PHONE................765 457-8136
Fax: 765 459-5177
John O'Donald, *CEO*
Richard H Elliott, *President*
Lynn Smith, *Corp Secy*
Tom Giles, *Vice Pres*
Cindy Locke, *Sales Staff*
◆ EMP: 32 EST: 1888
SQ FT: 63,000

SALES: 3MM **Privately Held**
SIC: 3231 Decorated glassware: chipped, engraved, etched, etc.

(G-8655)
KOKOMO OPTICAL COMPANY INC
501 E Lincoln Rd (46902-3742)
P.O. Box 2132 (46904-2132)
PHONE................765 459-5137
Fax: 765 455-1810
Jack Ellis, *President*
Jill Reeb, *Owner*
EMP: 5 EST: 1951
SQ FT: 4,000
SALES (est): 339.9K **Privately Held**
SIC: 5995 3851 5048 Eyeglasses, prescription; eyeglasses, lenses & frames; ophthalmic goods

(G-8656)
KOKOMO SPRING COMPANY INC
320 Rainbow Dr (46902-3796)
PHONE................765 459-5156
Fax: 765 459-4567
Sheila Rossman, *President*
Christopher Fry, *Vice Pres*
Douglas G Bailey, *Shareholder*
Ralph E Bailey, *Shareholder*
William J Drake, *Shareholder*
EMP: 15
SQ FT: 110,000
SALES (est): 2.2MM **Privately Held**
WEB: www.kokomospring.com
SIC: 3493 Coiled flat springs

(G-8657)
KOKOMO TRUCK STORE
901 E Markland Ave (46901-6218)
PHONE................765 459-5118
Kenny Pollard, *Owner*
EMP: 4
SALES (est): 240K **Privately Held**
SIC: 3537 Trucks, tractors, loaders, carriers & similar equipment

(G-8658)
LESLIE-FISHER ENGINEERING INC
2832 E Boulevard (46902-2770)
PHONE................765 457-7796
Hugh L Nixon, *President*
Ruth Nixon, *Admin Sec*
EMP: 7
SQ FT: 10,000
SALES (est): 1MM **Privately Held**
SIC: 3589 Commercial cooking & food-warming equipment

(G-8659)
LINK ENGINEERING LLC (PA)
Also Called: Shotmizer Unit Dose Packaging
1719 N Main St (46901-2268)
PHONE................765 457-1166
Christopher Eikenberry,
EMP: 5
SQ FT: 24,000
SALES (est): 680.6K **Privately Held**
SIC: 3089 Injection molding of plastics

(G-8660)
LORENTSON MANUFACTURING CO (PA)
1111 Rank Pkwy (46901-3124)
P.O. Box 932 (46903-0932)
PHONE................765 452-4425
Fax: 765 452-7940
Christian Sawyer, *CEO*
Creda J Lorentson, *President*
Michelle Brooks, *Warehouse Mgr*
David Mashino, *Engineer*
Ron Mickelson, *Engineer*
▲ EMP: 45 EST: 1949
SQ FT: 15,000
SALES (est): 14MM **Privately Held**
SIC: 3089 3544 Injection molding of plastics; industrial molds

(G-8661)
M PRO LLC
4812 N Parkway (46901-3941)
PHONE................765 459-4750
Michael Polk, *Principal*
EMP: 3

SALES (est): 281.9K **Privately Held**
SIC: 3535 Conveyors & conveying equipment

(G-8662)
MACS EXPRESS INC
428 E Center Rd (46902-5321)
PHONE................765 865-9700
Maria Farrington, *Principal*
EMP: 4
SALES (est): 326.4K **Privately Held**
SIC: 2741 Miscellaneous publishing

(G-8663)
MARIETTA MARTIN MATERIALS INC
Also Called: Martin Marietta Aggregates
2400 W 50 S (46902-5964)
PHONE................765 459-3194
Fax: 765 452-1837
Dan Yentis, *Manager*
EMP: 16 **Publicly Held**
WEB: www.martinmarietta.com
SIC: 1422 Crushed & broken limestone
PA: Martin Marietta Materials Inc
2710 Wycliff Rd
Raleigh NC 27607

(G-8664)
MARTIN BROWN PUBLISHERS LLC
1138 S Webster St (46902-6357)
PHONE................765 459-8258
Martin Brown, *Principal*
EMP: 2
SALES (est): 106.2K **Privately Held**
SIC: 2741 Miscellaneous publishing

(G-8665)
MERVIS INDUSTRIES INC
Also Called: Mervis & Sons
990 E Carter St (46901-4919)
P.O. Box 827, Danville IL (61834-0827)
PHONE................765 454-5800
Fax: 765 459-8890
Michael Mervis, *Manager*
EMP: 56
SALES (corp-wide): 161.2MM **Privately Held**
SIC: 5093 3341 Metal scrap & waste materials; secondary nonferrous metals
PA: Mervis Industries, Inc.
3295 E Main St Ste C
Danville IL 61834
217 442-5300

(G-8666)
MIER PRODUCTS INC
Also Called: Bw Manufacturing
1500 Ann St (46901-2242)
PHONE................765 457-0223
Fax: 765 457-0607
Robert Hullinger, *President*
C Scott Hullinger, *Vice Pres*
EMP: 25
SQ FT: 30,000
SALES (est): 5.8MM **Privately Held**
WEB: www.mierproducts.com
SIC: 3469 3679 Electronic enclosures, stamped or pressed metal; electronic circuits

(G-8667)
MILLWOOD BOX & PALLET
4665 E 600 N (46901-9241)
PHONE................765 628-7330
Homer Miller, *Owner*
EMP: 4 EST: 2014
SALES (est): 221.2K **Privately Held**
SIC: 2448 Pallets, wood & wood with metal

(G-8668)
MOBILE DYNAMOMETER LLC
1309 E Markland Ave (46901-6226)
PHONE................765 271-5080
Mark Harrell, *Principal*
EMP: 2 EST: 2015
SALES (est): 152.8K **Privately Held**
SIC: 3714 Motor vehicle parts & accessories

(G-8669)
MOMS HOMEMADE PIES CO LLC
3700 S Lafountain St (46902-3805)
PHONE................................765 453-4417
Dave Puckett, *President*
Olena Puckett, *Vice Pres*
EMP: 5
SALES (est): 364.5K **Privately Held**
SIC: 2051 Cakes, bakery: except frozen

(G-8670)
MOON FABRICATING CORP
700 W Morgan St (46901-2159)
P.O. Box 567 (46903-0567)
PHONE................................765 459-4194
Fax: 765 452-6090
Greg Veach, *President*
EMP: 43
SQ FT: 60,000
SALES (est): 5.2MM **Privately Held**
WEB: www.moontanks.com
SIC: 3443 Fabricated plate work (boiler shop); tanks, lined: metal plate

(G-8671)
MOONLIGHT MOLD & MACHINE INC
924 Millbrook Ln (46901-5127)
PHONE................................765 868-9860
Timothy Skaggs, *President*
Rusty Ritchie, *Vice Pres*
EMP: 5 EST: 1998
SQ FT: 1,080
SALES (est): 840.8K **Privately Held**
WEB: www.moonlightmold.com
SIC: 3544 Industrial molds

(G-8672)
MOORES PIE SHOP INC
115 W Elm St (46901-2839)
PHONE................................765 457-2428
Fax: 765 459-0238
Greg Lukas, *President*
Patty A Parrett, *President*
Patty Parrett, *President*
EMP: 6
SQ FT: 3,000
SALES (est): 500K **Privately Held**
SIC: 2051 2053 Pies, bakery: except frozen; pies, bakery: frozen

(G-8673)
MOTOROLA INC
2723 Albright Rd (46902-3996)
PHONE................................765 455-5100
James Cronin, *Principal*
EMP: 2
SALES (est): 49K **Privately Held**
SIC: 5399 3577 Miscellaneous general merchandise; computer peripheral equipment

(G-8674)
MULLIGANS SPORTS PUB
1134 Home Ave (46902-1623)
PHONE................................765 868-8230
William Isenhower, *President*
EMP: 6
SALES (est): 644.2K **Privately Held**
SIC: 2599 Bar, restaurant & cafeteria furniture

(G-8675)
NANO UNIVERSE LLC
514 Rudgate Ln (46901-3816)
PHONE................................765 457-5860
EMP: 5
SALES (est): 350K **Privately Held**
SIC: 3825 Mfg Electrical Measuring Instruments

(G-8676)
NO PASS LLC
2512 Lauren Ln (46901-7088)
PHONE................................516 713-6885
Ladonna Powell, *CEO*
EMP: 3
SALES (est): 71.1K **Privately Held**
SIC: 7372 Application computer software

(G-8677)
NXP USA INC
2733 Albright Rd (46902-3996)
PHONE................................765 455-5100

James Cronin, *Director*
EMP: 20
SALES (corp-wide): 9.2B **Privately Held**
WEB: www.freescale.com
SIC: 3674 Semiconductors & related devices
HQ: Nxp Usa, Inc.
6501 W William Cannon Dr
Austin TX 78735
512 933-8214

(G-8678)
PATS CUSTOM PRINTING AND EMB
1003 N Buckeye St (46901-2853)
PHONE................................765 456-1532
EMP: 2 EST: 2011
SALES (est): 100K **Privately Held**
SIC: 2752 Lithographic Commercial Printing

(G-8679)
PEPKA SPRING COMPANY INC
810 S Waugh St (46901-5502)
P.O. Box 2825 (46904-2825)
PHONE................................765 459-3114
Fax: 765 459-3112
John V Pepka, *President*
Paul C Pepka, *Vice Pres*
Rita S Pepka, *Treasurer*
EMP: 10 EST: 1946
SQ FT: 9,000
SALES (est): 1.5MM **Privately Held**
WEB: www.pepkaspr.com
SIC: 3495 3493 Precision springs; steel springs, except wire

(G-8680)
PERFORMANCE POWDER COATING
1124 S Union St (46902-1662)
PHONE................................765 438-5224
Danny Miller, *Owner*
EMP: 5
SALES (est): 120K **Privately Held**
SIC: 3471 Sand blasting of metal parts

(G-8681)
PLANET MIND LLC
Also Called: Planet Mind Learning Store
108 N Main St (46901-4625)
PHONE................................765 452-2341
Fax: 765 452-6893
EMP: 2
SALES (est): 100K **Privately Held**
SIC: 3944 Mfg Games/Toys

(G-8682)
PLATING PRODUCTS INC
1020 S Main St (46902-1609)
P.O. Box 699, Dayton NV (89403-0699)
PHONE................................775 241-0416
Fax: 765 457-1196
David Young, *President*
Richard Hamilton, *Corp Secy*
Jane Young, *Shareholder*
EMP: 4 EST: 1949
SQ FT: 20,000
SALES (est): 400K **Privately Held**
SIC: 3559 Metal finishing equipment for plating, etc.

(G-8683)
PRAXAIR INC
2100 E Lincoln Rd (46902-3774)
PHONE................................765 456-1128
EMP: 20
SALES (corp-wide): 11.4B **Publicly Held**
SIC: 2813 Industrial gases
PA: Praxair, Inc.
10 Riverview Dr
Danbury CT 06810
203 837-2000

(G-8684)
PREFERRED ENTERPRISES INC
2215 Carr Dr (46902-9543)
PHONE................................765 457-0637
Fax: 765 457-1116
Mark Dupouy, *President*
Ruth Dupouy, *Admin Sec*
EMP: 2
SQ FT: 1,100

SALES: 300K **Privately Held**
WEB: www.preferredenterprises.com
SIC: 5199 2759 Advertising specialties; commercial printing

(G-8685)
PREMIER PRINTING
1708 W Taylor St (46901-4218)
PHONE................................765 459-8339
Keith Krzeminski, *Owner*
EMP: 4
SALES: 120K **Privately Held**
SIC: 2759 Commercial printing

(G-8686)
PRINTCRAFT PRESS INC
524 S Union St (46901-5498)
PHONE................................765 457-2141
Fax: 765 457-5243
David Pelgen, *President*
Peggy Debard, *Corp Secy*
Kevin Debard, *Vice Pres*
EMP: 5 EST: 1956
SQ FT: 2,000
SALES (est): 768K **Privately Held**
WEB: www.printcraftpress.com
SIC: 2752 Commercial printing, offset

(G-8687)
REED CONTRACTING COMPANY
113 W Jefferson St (46901-4538)
P.O. Box 329 (46903-0329)
PHONE................................765 452-2638
Charlie Reed, *Owner*
EMP: 15
SQ FT: 30,000
SALES: 1.2MM **Privately Held**
SIC: 1542 1541 3479 1799 Commercial & office buildings, renovation & repair; renovation, remodeling & repairs: industrial buildings; coating of metals & formed products; sandblasting of building exteriors

(G-8688)
REED SIGN SERVICE INC
113 W Jefferson St (46901-4538)
PHONE................................765 459-4033
Fax: 765 452-4848
Jay Reed, *President*
Charlie Reed, *Vice Pres*
EMP: 5
SQ FT: 28,000
SALES (est): 464.2K **Privately Held**
SIC: 3993 7389 Signs & advertising specialties; sign painting & lettering shop

(G-8689)
REX BYERS HTG & COOLG SYSTEMS
4108 Cartwright Dr (46902-4388)
PHONE................................765 459-8858
Fax: 765 963-2271
Rex A Byers, *President*
EMP: 14
SALES (est): 2.3MM **Privately Held**
WEB: www.rexbyers.com
SIC: 1711 3432 1731 Warm air heating & air conditioning contractor; plumbing fixture fittings & trim; electronic controls installation

(G-8690)
SARAN INDUSTRIES LLC (PA)
1500 E Murden St (46901-5667)
PHONE................................317 897-2170
Fax: 317 895-8185
Anthony Pesavento, *CEO*
Nick Saran, *Vice Pres*
Greg Smith, *QC Mgr*
Jeff Frazee, *Engineer*
Randall Bruns, *Info Tech Mgr*
EMP: 54 EST: 2014
SALES (est): 44.8MM **Privately Held**
SIC: 3398 7699 4225 Metal heat treating; industrial equipment services; general warehousing & storage

(G-8691)
SCHLABACH WINDOW & GLASS LLC
5337 E 250 N (46901-8470)
PHONE................................765 628-2024
Melvin A Schlabach,
EMP: 3

SALES (est): 320K **Privately Held**
SIC: 3089 1542 5083 Window frames & sash, plastic; farm building construction; agricultural machinery & equipment

(G-8692)
SEARCHLIGHT SOCIAL LLC
1694 S 200 E (46902-4142)
PHONE................................317 983-3802
Seth Crowder, *Principal*
EMP: 2
SALES (est): 88.3K **Privately Held**
SIC: 3648 Searchlights

(G-8693)
SELBY PUBLISHING & PRINTING
3405 Zartman Rd (46902-2979)
PHONE................................765 453-5417
Phyllis Selby, *Partner*
Robert Selby, *Partner*
EMP: 2
SALES (est): 120.6K **Privately Held**
SIC: 2759 7299 Commercial printing; genealogical investigation service

(G-8694)
SEMICNDCTOR CMPONENTS INDS LLC
Also Called: On Semiconductor
2529 Commerce Dr Ste B (46902-7815)
PHONE................................765 868-5015
Brad Yount, *Manager*
Sandy Butler, *Admin Asst*
EMP: 8
SALES (corp-wide): 5.5B **Publicly Held**
WEB: www.onsemi.com
SIC: 3674 Semiconductors & related devices
HQ: Semiconductor Components Industries, Llc
5005 E Mcdowell Rd
Phoenix AZ 85008
800 282-9855

(G-8695)
SHEARER PRINTING SERVICE INC
Also Called: Shearer Business Products
107 W Markland Ave (46901-6102)
P.O. Box 668 (46903-0668)
PHONE................................765 457-3274
Fax: 765 457-1639
Brian G Shearer, *President*
Stephen K Shupperd, *Corp Secy*
Jo Hall, *Vice Pres*
Jenny Hunt, *Accounts Exec*
David Lovegrove, *Accounts Exec*
EMP: 25 EST: 1937
SQ FT: 7,800
SALES (est): 4.8MM **Privately Held**
WEB: www.shearerbusiness.com
SIC: 2752 5712 5943 7629 Commercial printing, offset; office furniture; office forms & supplies; business machine repair, electric

(G-8696)
SIGNS XP INC
1609 Cherry Hill Ln (46902-3129)
PHONE................................765 453-4812
EMP: 2 EST: 2009
SALES (est): 120K **Privately Held**
SIC: 3993 Mfg Signs/Advertising Specialties

(G-8697)
SLATE MECHANICAL INC
4602 W 100 N (46901-3889)
PHONE................................765 452-9611
Fax: 765 452-2251
Ted Slate, *President*
Rick Slate, *Vice Pres*
Miriam Slate, *Admin Sec*
EMP: 14
SQ FT: 7,000
SALES (est): 1.2MM **Privately Held**
WEB: www.slatemechanical.com
SIC: 1711 3444 Mechanical contractor; plumbing contractors; warm air heating & air conditioning contractor; sheet metalwork

(G-8698)
SPECIALTY TOOL & DIE COMPANY
1614 Rank Parkway Ct (46901-3123)
PHONE....................................765 452-9209
Fax: 765 452-8411
Gordon L Riley, *President*
Brian Riley, *Vice Pres*
Gordon B Riley, *Admin Sec*
EMP: 14
SQ FT: 10,000
SALES (est): 3.1MM **Privately Held**
SIC: 3544 Special dies & tools

(G-8699)
STAHL WELDING INC
2610 S Goyer Rd (46902-4198)
PHONE....................................765 457-3386
Frederick E Stahl, *President*
Georgia Stahl, *Corp Secy*
Jeff Stahl, *Vice Pres*
EMP: 4
SQ FT: 30,000
SALES (est): 287.2K **Privately Held**
SIC: 7692 7353 1796 5051 Welding repair; cranes & aerial lift equipment, rental or leasing; machine moving & rigging; steel

(G-8700)
STAR NAIL
1500 E Markland Ave (46901-6229)
PHONE....................................765 453-0743
Chris Phan, *Owner*
EMP: 2
SALES (est): 158.7K **Privately Held**
SIC: 2844 Manicure preparations

(G-8701)
STEPHENS FABRICATION INC
1817 W Defenbaugh St (46902-6014)
PHONE....................................765 459-9770
Fax: 765 459-4968
Gregory A Stephens, *President*
EMP: 34
SQ FT: 32,500
SALES (est): 4.8MM **Privately Held**
SIC: 3441 Fabricated structural metal

(G-8702)
STEPHENS MACHINE INC (PA)
Also Called: SD
1600 Dodge St (46902-2407)
PHONE....................................765 459-4017
Fax: 765 457-1410
Gregory A Stephens, *President*
Adrian Tharp, *Sales Staff*
Stephens Greg, *Admin Sec*
Dawn Wisler, *Clerk*
EMP: 55
SQ FT: 14,400
SALES: 10.4MM **Privately Held**
WEB: www.stephensmachine.com
SIC: 3599 Machine shop, jobbing & repair

(G-8703)
STEPHENS MACHINE INC
1801 S Berkley Rd (46902-6085)
PHONE....................................765 459-9770
Richard Stephens, *Manager*
EMP: 38
SALES (corp-wide): 10.4MM **Privately Held**
WEB: www.stephensmachine.com
SIC: 3599 Machine shop, jobbing & repair
PA: Stephens Machine Inc
   1600 Dodge St
   Kokomo IN 46902
   765 459-4017

(G-8704)
SYNDICATE SALES INC (PA)
2025 N Wabash Ave (46901-2063)
P.O. Box 756 (46903-0756)
PHONE....................................765 457-7277
Fax: 765 454-6748
Delmar Demaree, *Ch of Bd*
Brian Hite, *Accounting Mgr*
Alice Bowers, *Accountant*
Holly Moore, *Human Res Dir*
Jen Masiello, *Natl Sales Mgr*
▼ EMP: 410
SQ FT: 85,000
SALES (est): 193.3MM **Privately Held**
SIC: 3089 Injection molding of plastics

(G-8705)
T G R INC
Also Called: T G R Signs
1257 E Morgan St (46901-2557)
PHONE....................................765 452-8225
Fax: 765 457-0173
Timothy Ryberg, *President*
Gayle Ryberg, *Corp Secy*
Jim Williams, *Site Mgr*
EMP: 15
SQ FT: 25,000
SALES: 1.2MM **Privately Held**
WEB: www.tgrfinishing.com
SIC: 3479 3993 Coating of metals & formed products; hot dip coating of metals or formed products; rust proofing (hot dipping) of metals & formed products; signs & advertising specialties

(G-8706)
T L TATE MANUFACTURING INC
1500 N Webster St (46901-2123)
PHONE....................................765 452-8283
Timothy L Tate, *President*
EMP: 7 EST: 2000
SQ FT: 18,500
SALES (est): 803.9K **Privately Held**
SIC: 3599 Machine shop, jobbing & repair

(G-8707)
TATE SOAPS & SURFACTANTS INC
1500 N Webster St (46901-2123)
PHONE....................................765 868-4488
Troy L Tate, *President*
Michael F Hartz, *Vice Pres*
Thomas J Kronk, *Vice Pres*
EMP: 7
SQ FT: 64,000
SALES (est): 1.2MM **Privately Held**
WEB: www.tatesoaps.com
SIC: 2842 Cleaning or polishing preparations

(G-8708)
TITANIUM LLC
847 N 300 E (46901-5768)
PHONE....................................765 236-6906
Eric Newman, *Principal*
EMP: 2
SALES (est): 90.8K **Privately Held**
SIC: 3356 Titanium

(G-8709)
TOWN COUNTRY PRINTING ◆
315 N Main St (46901-4621)
PHONE....................................765 452-0093
EMP: 2 EST: 2018
SALES (est): 83.9K **Privately Held**
SIC: 2752 Commercial printing, lithographic

(G-8710)
TRUE PRECISION TECH INC
1602 Ehavens St (46901)
PHONE....................................765 252-9766
Andrew I Jay, *Principal*
Derek H Krause, *Principal*
EMP: 3
SALES (est): 189.4K **Privately Held**
SIC: 3999 Atomizers, toiletry

(G-8711)
USEFUL HOME PRODUCTS LLC
186 Champagne Ct (46901-9565)
PHONE....................................765 459-0095
Garold B Bitner II, *CEO*
R Kay Bitner,
EMP: 9
SQ FT: 720
SALES (est): 738.5K **Privately Held**
SIC: 2519 Furniture, household: glass, fiberglass & plastic

(G-8712)
VICKERS GRAPHICS INC
329 S 00 Ew (46902-5102)
P.O. Box 2525 (46904-2525)
PHONE....................................765 868-4646
Matthew Brake, *CEO*
EMP: 6
SQ FT: 12,000
SALES: 354.6K **Privately Held**
SIC: 2759 2395 Screen printing; embroidery & art needlework

(G-8713)
VITAL SIGNS MARKETING LLC
2850 Bridgestone Cir (46902-7008)
PHONE....................................765 453-5088
James Johnson, *Principal*
EMP: 2
SALES (est): 80.2K **Privately Held**
SIC: 3993 Signs & advertising specialties

(G-8714)
WALTERS CABINET SHOP
471 E 1300 S (46901-7629)
PHONE....................................765 452-9634
Fax: 765 452-9634
Jim Walters, *Owner*
▲ EMP: 3
SALES: 300K **Privately Held**
SIC: 2434 2541 2517 2511 Wood kitchen cabinets; wood partitions & fixtures; wood television & radio cabinets; wood household furniture

(G-8715)
WDMI INC
1397 E Havens St (46901-3199)
PHONE....................................765 868-9646
Fax: 765 868-9675
Will Lorance, *Owner*
EMP: 13
SALES (corp-wide): 10.4MM **Privately Held**
WEB: www.transit-mix.com
SIC: 3273 Ready-mixed concrete
PA: Wdmi, Inc.
   2341 W Jefferson St
   Plymouth IN 46563

(G-8716)
WEB SOFTWARE LLC
Also Called: 1 Up
2115 W Alto Rd Ste A (46902-5398)
PHONE....................................765 452-3936
David McChesney, *Partner*
Maureen Mall, *Business Dir*
EMP: 11
SALES (est): 1.1MM **Privately Held**
WEB: www.hubclassifieds.com
SIC: 7372 7371 Prepackaged software; computer software systems analysis & design, custom

---

Kouts
Porter County

(G-8717)
LEGGETT & PLATT INCORPORATED
Also Called: Leggett & Platt 0714
State Road 8 (46347)
P.O. Box 609 (46347-0609)
PHONE....................................219 766-2261
Greg Hoagland, *Safety Mgr*
EMP: 100
SALES (corp-wide): 3.9B **Publicly Held**
WEB: www.leggett.com
SIC: 2515 Mattresses & bedsprings
PA: Leggett & Platt, Incorporated
   1 Leggett Rd
   Carthage MO 64836
   417 358-8131

(G-8718)
TIMBERLINE WOODWORKING INC
304 E Mentor St (46347-7011)
P.O. Box 322 (46347-0322)
PHONE....................................219 766-2733
Fax: 219 766-2818
Shannon Kingsbury, *President*
EMP: 4
SQ FT: 2,000
SALES (est): 512.6K **Privately Held**
SIC: 2541 2517 Cabinets, except refrigerated: show, display, etc.: wood; home entertainment unit cabinets, wood

---

La Crosse
Laporte County

(G-8719)
CANNON TIMBER LLC
418 E Oneida St (46348-9551)
PHONE....................................219 754-1088
Jesse Cannon, *Principal*
EMP: 3 EST: 2008
SALES (est): 226.1K **Privately Held**
SIC: 2411 Timber, cut at logging camp

(G-8720)
KIEL MEDIA LLC
16 E Main St (46348-9515)
P.O. Box 53 (46348-0053)
PHONE....................................219 544-2060
Justin Kiel, *Mng Member*
Kelly Kiel, *Mng Member*
EMP: 2
SALES: 80K **Privately Held**
SIC: 2741 Miscellaneous publishing

(G-8721)
LABRAID INC
Also Called: Country Maid
9404 W 2100 S (46348-9745)
PHONE....................................219 754-2501
Lyla Frank, *President*
Curtis Frank, *Corp Secy*
EMP: 5
SQ FT: 1,800
SALES (est): 446.6K **Privately Held**
SIC: 2053 Pastries (danish): frozen

La Fontaine
Wabash County

(G-8722)
G & G MILLWRIGHT SERVICE LLC
11052 S 600 E (46940-9217)
PHONE....................................260 571-4908
Danny Gifford,
Brenda J Gifford,
EMP: 5
SALES (est): 367.5K **Privately Held**
SIC: 3541 Machine tool replacement & repair parts, metal cutting types

(G-8723)
LA FONTAINE GENERATOR EXCHANGE
202 Logan St (46940-2825)
P.O. Box 308 (46940-0308)
PHONE....................................765 981-4561
Fax: 765 981-2333
Michael Loschiavo, *President*
Linda E Loschiavo, *Treasurer*
Jeremy Steel, *Manager*
EMP: 7 EST: 1973
SQ FT: 10,000
SALES: 300K **Privately Held**
SIC: 3694 Breaker point sets, internal combustion engine; generators, automotive & aircraft; alternators, automotive

(G-8724)
LA FONTAINE GRAVEL INC
1244 E 1050 S (46940-9196)
PHONE....................................765 981-4849
James Derck, *President*
Andrew King, *Vice Pres*
EMP: 3
SALES (est): 432.7K **Privately Held**
SIC: 1442 Gravel mining

La Porte
Laporte County

(G-8725)
A & A SHEET METAL PRODUCTS (PA)
Also Called: Se-Cur-All Cabinets
5122 N State Road 39 (46350-8354)
P.O. Box 1848 (46352-1848)
PHONE....................................219 326-1288

▲ = Import ▼=Export
◆ =Import/Export

Fax: 219 324-3780
David E Williams, *President*
Michael H Williams, *Vice Pres*
Larry Wilke, *Plant Mgr*
Jack Williams, *Treasurer*
Rebecca Stanton, *Controller*
▼ EMP: 72
SQ FT: 155,000
SALES (est): 13.5MM **Privately Held**
WEB: www.securalldoors.com
SIC: 3442 2542 Fire doors, metal; lockers (not refrigerated): except wood

(G-8726)
ACCURATE CASTINGS INC
Also Called: Kingsbury Castings Div
3232 3rd Rd (46350)
P.O. Box 639 (46352-0639)
PHONE...................................219 393-3122
Fax: 574 393-5030
William Lange, *Branch Mgr*
EMP: 70
SALES (corp-wide): 24.8MM **Privately Held**
WEB: www.hilerindustries.com
SIC: 3321 3369 3322 Ductile iron castings; nonferrous foundries; malleable iron foundries
PA: Accurate Castings Inc
118 Koomler Dr
La Porte IN 46350
219 362-8531

(G-8727)
AERO METALS INC (PA)
1201 E Lincolnway (46350-3955)
PHONE...................................219 326-1976
Fax: 574 326-1972
Robert Stowell, *CEO*
James Fleming, *President*
Linda Stowell, *Vice Pres*
Jerry Hart, *Plant Mgr*
Rex Wiesemann, *Purchasing*
▲ EMP: 324
SQ FT: 76,000
SALES (est): 55.5MM **Privately Held**
WEB: www.aerometals.com
SIC: 3324 3364 Commercial investment castings, ferrous; aerospace investment castings, ferrous; brass & bronze die-castings

(G-8728)
AERO-FLO INDUSTRIES INC
3999 E Hupp Rd Bldg R34 (46350-7694)
PHONE...................................219 393-3555
Fax: 219 393-5857
Jack Rich Jr, *President*
Margaret E Rich, *Admin Sec*
▲ EMP: 9
SQ FT: 25,000
SALES (est): 1.7MM **Privately Held**
WEB: www.aero-flo.com
SIC: 3564 5075 Blowers & fans; air conditioning & ventilation equipment & supplies

(G-8729)
ALEXANDRIA MW LLC
Also Called: Alex Mid West
4747 W State Road 2 Ste B (46350-6561)
PHONE...................................219 324-9541
Fax: 219 326-5952
Marty Hurlbut, *Mng Member*
Linda Rixe,
Jacques Sholepte,
▲ EMP: 5
SALES (est): 2.2MM **Privately Held**
SIC: 2431 Moldings & baseboards, ornamental & trim

(G-8730)
ALPHA BAKING CO INC
360 N Fail Rd (46350-7051)
PHONE...................................219 324-7440
Fax: 574 324-4271
Larry Mitchell, *President*
David Curry, *Transptn Dir*
Rich McIndoo, *Chief Engr*
EMP: 170
SALES (corp-wide): 228.8MM **Privately Held**
WEB: www.alphabaking.com
SIC: 2051 2053 Breads, rolls & buns; frozen bakery products, except bread

PA: Alpha Baking Co., Inc.
5001 W Polk St
Chicago IL 60644
773 261-6000

(G-8731)
AMERICAN LICORICE COMPANY (PA)
1900 Whirlpool Dr S (46350-2594)
PHONE...................................510 487-5500
John R Kretchmer, *CEO*
Tim Walsh, *Ch of Bd*
Clint Christensen, *Manager*
Timothy R Walsh, *Admin Sec*
Amy Drake, *Administration*
▲ EMP: 35 EST: 1914
SQ FT: 3,500
SALES (est): 114.3MM **Privately Held**
WEB: www.redvines.com
SIC: 2064 Licorice candy

(G-8732)
AMERICAN LICORICE COMPANY
1900 Whirlpool Dr S (46350-2594)
PHONE...................................219 362-5790
Vince Galleos, *Ltd Ptnr*
EMP: 250
SALES (corp-wide): 114.3MM **Privately Held**
WEB: www.redvines.com
SIC: 2064 Licorice candy
PA: American Licorice Company
1900 Whirlpool Dr S
La Porte IN 46350
510 487-5500

(G-8733)
AMERICAN RENOLIT CORPORATION (DH)
1207 E Lincolnway (46350-3987)
PHONE...................................219 324-6886
Fax: 219 324-5332
Renaat Demeulemeester, *President*
Michael Krause, *Plant Mgr*
Qi Zhang, *Research*
Nils Dietz, *CFO*
James Shellito, *Accounts Mgr*
▲ EMP: 180
SQ FT: 125,000
SALES: 80MM
SALES (corp-wide): 1.9B **Privately Held**
WEB: www.americanrenolit.com
SIC: 3081 5162 Plastic film & sheet; plastics film
HQ: Renolit Se
Horchheimer Str. 50
Worms 67547
624 130-30

(G-8734)
APPLETON GRP LLC
2362 N Us Highway 35 (46350-8380)
PHONE...................................219 326-5936
Claudette Harrison, *Branch Mgr*
EMP: 90
SALES (corp-wide): 15.2B **Publicly Held**
SIC: 3644 Electric conduits & fittings
HQ: Appleton Grp Llc
9377 W Higgins Rd
Rosemont IL 60018
847 268-6000

(G-8735)
ATHENTIC INC
702 Ohio St (46350-4166)
P.O. Box 1663 (46352-1663)
PHONE...................................219 362-8508
Fax: 574 324-8090
EMP: 10
SALES (est): 600K **Privately Held**
SIC: 2731 2741 Books-Publishing/Printing Misc Publishing

(G-8736)
ATI CASTING SERVICE LLC (DH)
300 Philadelphia St (46350-3927)
PHONE...................................219 362-1000
Joe Walker, *President*
Jordan Larson, *Business Mgr*
R J Harshman,
David Hogan,
▼ EMP: 26
SALES (est): 11.1MM **Publicly Held**
SIC: 3369 White metal castings (lead, tin, antimony), except die

(G-8737)
B & B MANUFACTURING INC
Also Called: B&B Manufacturing
712 N Fail Rd (46350-9020)
PHONE...................................219 324-0247
Fax: 219 324-2694
Bob Hamilton, *President*
Dave Lee, *Corp Secy*
Brian Mulligan, *Vice Pres*
Rick Talbert, *Vice Pres*
Cheryl Flemington, *Materials Mgr*
▲ EMP: 80
SQ FT: 105,000
SALES (est): 23.6MM **Privately Held**
WEB: www.bbman.com
SIC: 3714 Motor vehicle parts & accessories

(G-8738)
BEV CAN PRINTERS LLC
1705 State St Bldg B (46350-3118)
PHONE...................................219 617-6181
Dave Strupeck, *President*
EMP: 2
SQ FT: 12,500
SALES: 2.7MM **Privately Held**
SIC: 2759 Commercial printing

(G-8739)
BIDWHIST INDUSTRIES
5276 N Verma Dr (46350-8437)
PHONE...................................219 879-2508
Bill Lott, *Owner*
EMP: 4
SALES (est): 220K **Privately Held**
SIC: 3543 Industrial patterns

(G-8740)
BOSS INDUSTRIES LLC
1761 Genesis Dr (46350-2492)
PHONE...................................219 324-7776
Fax: 219 324-7470
Patrick A Wilkins, *President*
Ed Ketcham, *Vice Pres*
Andy Foster, *Inv Control Mgr*
Nikki Strong, *Buyer*
Teresa Tulacz, *Buyer*
◆ EMP: 32
SQ FT: 50,000
SALES (est): 11.4MM **Privately Held**
WEB: www.bossair.com
SIC: 3563 Air & gas compressors

(G-8741)
BRASHEAR
8804 N 200 E (46350-8934)
PHONE...................................219 778-2422
Mercedes Brashaer, *Owner*
EMP: 3
SALES (est): 145.3K **Privately Held**
WEB: www.brashear.com
SIC: 3581 Automatic vending machines

(G-8742)
BRICK ROAD BREWERY CORP
308 Perry St (46350-3216)
PHONE...................................219 362-7623
Charles Krcilek, *President*
Gerald Krcilek, *Corp Secy*
EMP: 2
SALES: 150K **Privately Held**
WEB: www.backroadbrewery.com
SIC: 2082 Beer (alcoholic beverage)

(G-8743)
C FABCO/L INC
9811 W State Road 2 Ste 1 (46350-7061)
PHONE...................................219 785-4181
Fax: 574 785-4880
John E Roach, *President*
EMP: 22
SQ FT: 30,000
SALES: 1.5MM **Privately Held**
SIC: 3441 Fabricated structural metal

(G-8744)
CADDO CONNECTIONS INC
2833 N Goldring Rd (46350-7134)
PHONE...................................219 874-8119
Fax: 219 873-0003
Joseph Demorrow, *President*

HQ: Tdy Industries, Llc
1000 Six Ppg Pl
Pittsburgh PA 15222
412 394-2896

Ronald Caddo, *President*
EMP: 23
SQ FT: 13,500
SALES: 6.4MM **Privately Held**
SIC: 3679 3613 3694 Harness assemblies for electronic use: wire or cable; control panels, electric; engine electrical equipment

(G-8745)
CORIANT OPERATIONS INC
Also Called: Tellabs
3393 S Coulter Creek Dr (46350-7675)
PHONE...................................219 785-1737
James Menifee, *Branch Mgr*
EMP: 70 **Privately Held**
WEB: www.tellabsoperations.com
SIC: 3661 Telephones & telephone apparatus
PA: Coriant Operations, Inc.
1415 W Diehl Rd
Naperville IL 60563

(G-8746)
COUNTRY STITCHES EMBROIDERY
606 E 400 N (46350-4470)
PHONE...................................219 324-7625
Norm Eggert, *President*
Maxine Eggert, *Vice Pres*
Michelle Eggert, *Treasurer*
Kathy Johnson, *Admin Sec*
EMP: 8
SALES: 187.4K **Privately Held**
SIC: 5699 5611 2395 T-shirts, custom printed; hats, men's & boys'; embroidery & art needlework

(G-8747)
CREATIONS IN GLASS
725 Pine Lake Ave (46350-2320)
PHONE...................................219 326-7941
Al Gardner, *Owner*
Carolyn Gardner, *Manager*
EMP: 2
SALES: 70K **Privately Held**
WEB: www.creationsinglass.net
SIC: 3229 5947 Pressed & blown glass; gift, novelty & souvenir shop

(G-8748)
DANNYS FIREWORKS
2415 Monroe St (46350-5262)
PHONE...................................219 324-5757
Daniel Strieter, *Owner*
Christi Strieter, *Co-Owner*
EMP: 10
SALES (est): 762.8K **Privately Held**
SIC: 2899 Fireworks

(G-8749)
DANWOOD INDUSTRIES
7606 S Young Rd (46350-9252)
PHONE...................................219 369-1484
William Dankert, *Owner*
EMP: 4
SQ FT: 11,000
SALES (est): 339.9K **Privately Held**
SIC: 2448 Wood pallets & skids

(G-8750)
DEATH STUDIOS
431 Pine Lake Ave (46350-2303)
PHONE...................................219 362-4321
Jeff Keim, *Owner*
EMP: 4
SQ FT: 1,200
SALES (est): 247.3K **Privately Held**
WEB: www.deathstudios.com
SIC: 2389 Masquerade costumes

(G-8751)
DIEDRICH DRILL INC
5 Fisher St (46350-4768)
PHONE...................................219 326-7788
Fax: 574 324-5962
Thomas S Ledonne, *Principal*
Jean F Lange, *Admin Sec*
▲ EMP: 42
SQ FT: 25,000
SALES (est): 13.1MM **Privately Held**
WEB: www.diedrichdrill.com
SIC: 3533 3546 Drill rigs; drills & drilling tools

(G-8752)
DWYER INSTRUMENTS INC
Also Called: EMC Stamping
3999 E Hupp Rd Bldg R64 (46350-0007)
PHONE.................................219 393-5250
Fax: 219 393-3546
Jeff Belkiewitz, *Manager*
EMP: 20
SALES (corp-wide): 100MM **Privately Held**
WEB: www.dwyer-inst.com
SIC: 3679 3469 Electronic switches; metal stampings
PA: Dwyer Instruments Inc
    102 Indiana Highway 212
    Michigan City IN 46360
    219 879-8868

(G-8753)
E-PAK MACHINERY INC
1535 S State Road 39 (46350-6301)
PHONE.................................219 393-5541
Fax: 219 324-2884
Ronald Sarto, *CEO*
Tony Swedersky, *Vice Pres*
Bobby Bradford, *Prdtn Mgr*
Jesse Koontz, *Safety Mgr*
Tony Swederski, *Opers Staff*
▼ **EMP:** 50
SQ FT: 52,000
SALES (est): 16.3MM **Privately Held**
WEB: www.epakmachinery.com
SIC: 3565 Bottling machinery: filling, capping, labeling

(G-8754)
ELECTRIK CONNECTION INC
Also Called: S & W Electric
106 Washington St (46350-2426)
PHONE.................................219 362-4581
John T Barnhart, *President*
Lola N Barnhart, *Corp Secy*
EMP: 5
SQ FT: 9,700
SALES (est): 1.4MM **Privately Held**
SIC: 5063 7694 Motors, electric; electrical supplies; electric motor repair

(G-8755)
ELF MACHINERY LLC
1535 S State Road 39 (46350-6301)
PHONE.................................219 393-5541
Fax: 574 324-0063
Rick Allegretti, *President*
Tracy Connors, *Controller*
EMP: 130
SQ FT: 80,000
SALES (est): 16.5MM **Privately Held**
SIC: 3565 Packaging machinery; bottling machinery: filling, capping, labeling

(G-8756)
EMPROTECH STEEL SERVICES LLC
3234 N State Road 39 (46350-8605)
PHONE.................................219 326-6900
Ron Johnson, *Controller*
Karen Swanson, *Office Mgr*
EMP: 100
SALES (est): 12MM **Privately Held**
SIC: 3599 Machine shop, jobbing & repair

(G-8757)
F D RAMSEY & CO INC
Also Called: Ramsey's Sheet Metal
708 Ridgeway St (46350-3853)
P.O. Box 636 (46352-0636)
PHONE.................................219 362-2452
Fax: 574 324-0691
Logan Walker, *President*
Robert Allen, *Admin Sec*
EMP: 14
SALES (est): 1.9MM **Privately Held**
SIC: 1761 3564 3496 3444 Sheet metalwork; blowers & fans; miscellaneous fabricated wire products; sheet metalwork; fabricated plate work (boiler shop); office furniture, except wood

(G-8758)
GREGORY THOMAS INC (PA)
Also Called: Gti Static Solutions
1823 N Circle View Ln (46350-2132)
PHONE.................................219 324-3801
Thomas G Smith, *President*
EMP: 3

SALES (est): 556.4K **Privately Held**
WEB: www.swisscontrols.com
SIC: 5063 3629 Electrical apparatus & equipment; static elimination equipment, industrial

(G-8759)
GTW ENTERPRISES INC
183 W 800 N (46350-8743)
PHONE.................................219 362-2278
Fax: 219 362-2278
George Wroblewski, *President*
Vera Wroblewski, *Vice Pres*
EMP: 20
SQ FT: 12,000
SALES (est): 1.4MM **Privately Held**
WEB: www.gtwenterprises.com
SIC: 3554 Paper industries machinery

(G-8760)
HARPERCOLLINS PUBLISHERS LLC
Also Called: Harpercollins Return Center
2205 E Lincolnway (46350-8732)
PHONE.................................219 324-4880
Fax: 219 324-4970
Harper Collins, *Owner*
EMP: 68
SALES (corp-wide): 9B **Publicly Held**
WEB: www.harpercollins.com
SIC: 2731 Books: publishing only
HQ: Harpercollins Publishers L.L.C.
    195 Broadway Fl 2
    New York NY 10007
    212 207-7000

(G-8761)
HARRIS PRE CAST INC (PA)
Also Called: Kovenz Memorial Shop
1877 W Severs Rd (46350-6915)
PHONE.................................219 362-2457
Fax: 219 326-7747
Jeffery Scott Harris, *President*
EMP: 3
SQ FT: 6,820
SALES (est): 418.5K **Privately Held**
SIC: 5999 3272 Monuments, finished to custom order; burial vaults, concrete or precast terrazzo

(G-8762)
HAYNES INTERNATIONAL INC
3238 N Hwy 39 (46352)
PHONE.................................219 326-8530
Fax: 765 456-6305
Dave Mahan, *Manager*
EMP: 201
SALES (corp-wide): 395.2MM **Publicly Held**
WEB: www.hastelloy.com
SIC: 3356 3341 Nickel; secondary nonferrous metals
PA: Haynes International, Inc.
    1020 W Park Ave
    Kokomo IN 46901
    765 456-6000

(G-8763)
HESTON LOG HOMES INC
10409 N 200 E (46350-8862)
PHONE.................................219 778-4074
EMP: 2
SALES (est): 160K **Privately Held**
SIC: 2452 Mfg Prefabricated Wood Buildings

(G-8764)
HICKMAN WILLIAMS & COMPANY
Also Called: Hickman Williams & Co
2321 W Progress Dr (46350-7782)
PHONE.................................708 656-8818
Fax: 708 442-3793
V Valaenziano, *Division Mgr*
Scott McClain, *Vice Pres*
Dan Baran, *Engineer*
John Kalinowski, *Manager*
Lawrence Gebhardt, *Manager*
EMP: 17
SQ FT: 132,000
SALES (corp-wide): 190.1MM **Privately Held**
WEB: www.hicwilco.com
SIC: 1221 4225 3624 Coal preparation plant, bituminous or lignite; general warehousing; carbon & graphite products

PA: Hickman, Williams & Company
    250 E 5th St Ste 300
    Cincinnati OH 45202
    513 621-1946

(G-8765)
HJJ INC
Also Called: Art Gallery, The
1533 Weller Ave (46350-4657)
PHONE.................................219 362-4421
Harry Jorgenson, *President*
Judy Jorgenson, *Corp Secy*
EMP: 2
SQ FT: 800
SALES (est): 167.2K **Privately Held**
SIC: 5999 2499 Art dealers; picture & mirror frames, wood

(G-8766)
HOLSUM OF FORT WAYNE INC
Also Called: Lewis Bakeries
800 Boyd Blvd (46350-4419)
P.O. Box 426 (46352-0426)
PHONE.................................219 362-4561
Fax: 574 325-0030
Dean Allen, *President*
Jim Hudock, *Controller*
John West, *Sales Executive*
Jim McMann, *Manager*
Ronald Stallings, *Supervisor*
EMP: 175
SQ FT: 69,000
SALES (corp-wide): 473.3MM **Privately Held**
SIC: 2051 Bread, cake & related products
HQ: Holsum Of Fort Wayne Inc
    136 Murray St
    Fort Wayne IN 46803
    260 456-2130

(G-8767)
HOWMET CASTINGS & SERVICES INC
Alcoa Howmet, Laporte
1110 E Lincolnway (46350-3954)
PHONE.................................219 326-7400
Fax: 574 324-3193
Chris Kraynak, *Branch Mgr*
EMP: 645
SQ FT: 160,000
SALES (corp-wide): 12.9B **Publicly Held**
SIC: 3324 3369 3341 Steel investment foundries; nonferrous foundries; secondary nonferrous metals
HQ: Howmet Castings & Services, Inc.
    1616 Harvard Ave
    Newburgh Heights OH 44105
    216 641-4400

(G-8768)
HRR ENTERPRISES INC
1755 Genesis Dr (46350-2492)
PHONE.................................219 362-9050
Fax: 219 362-9051
W D Tarpley, *President*
EMP: 30
SQ FT: 13,000
SALES: 5.6MM
SALES (corp-wide): 39.5MM **Privately Held**
WEB: www.hrrenterprises.com
SIC: 2077 2011 Animal & marine fats & oils; meat packing plants
PA: Kane-Miller Corp.
    1 S School Ave Ste 401
    Sarasota FL 34237
    941 346-2003

(G-8769)
HULL AIRCRAFT SUPPORT LLC
602 Lakeside St (46350-2210)
P.O. Box 1637 (46352-1637)
PHONE.................................219 324-6247
Eric Hull, *Principal*
Jamie Hull,
EMP: 2
SALES (est): 197.9K **Privately Held**
SIC: 3721 Airplanes, fixed or rotary wing

(G-8770)
INDUSTRIAL LUMBER PRODUCTS INC
251 N State Road 39 (46350-2052)
PHONE.................................219 324-7697
Fax: 574 324-3707
Everett Atwood, *President*

Debora Atwood, *Corp Secy*
EMP: 9
SQ FT: 10,000
SALES (est): 1.5MM **Privately Held**
SIC: 2448 5031 Cargo containers, wood; pallets, wood; lumber, plywood & millwork

(G-8771)
INDUSTRIAL PATTERN WORKS INC
119 Koomler Dr (46350-2545)
PHONE.................................219 362-4547
Fax: 219 324-7081
Frank Pinkepank, *President*
Vicki Easton, *Manager*
EMP: 10
SQ FT: 17,500
SALES (est): 1.9MM **Privately Held**
SIC: 3599 Machine shop, jobbing & repair

(G-8772)
J & J INDUSTRIAL SERVICES INC
2204 E Lincolnway Bldg D (46350-6556)
P.O. Box 1737 (46352-1737)
PHONE.................................219 362-4973
Fax: 219 324-7346
James Jablonski, *President*
Scott Kessler, *Principal*
EMP: 2
SQ FT: 800
SALES (est): 365.8K **Privately Held**
SIC: 3823 3613 Panelboard indicators, recorders & controllers: receiver; panel & distribution boards & other related apparatus

(G-8773)
J & L DIMENSIONAL SERVICES INC
16 Industrial Pkwy (46350-7055)
P.O. Box 1629 (46352-1629)
PHONE.................................219 325-3588
Fax: 219 362-7350
Lisa Corey, *President*
Larry Corey, *Vice Pres*
EMP: 45
SQ FT: 20,000
SALES (est): 5.6MM **Privately Held**
WEB: www.j-ldimensional.com
SIC: 3471 7334 Cleaning, polishing & finishing; blueprinting service

(G-8774)
JAEGER-NTEK SLING SLUTIONS INC
115 Koomler Dr (46350-2545)
PHONE.................................219 324-1111
Mark S Dilley, *President*
Hans Ulrich Von Tippelskirch, *Chairman*
Raymond A Young, *Vice Pres*
Roger Schuster, *Purch Mgr*
Ray Young, *Engineer*
▲ **EMP:** 60
SQ FT: 132,000
SALES (est): 16.8MM
SALES (corp-wide): 166MM **Privately Held**
WEB: www.jaeger-unitek.com
SIC: 3083 Laminated plastics plate & sheet
PA: Arnold Jager Holding Gmbh
    Bissendorfer Str. 6
    Hannover 30625
    511 535-80

(G-8775)
KANE-MILLER CORP
Also Called: American Meat Packing Div
1755 Genesis Dr (46350-2492)
PHONE.................................219 362-9050
Dan Tarpley, *Branch Mgr*
EMP: 30
SQ FT: 200,000
SALES (corp-wide): 39.5MM **Privately Held**
WEB: www.kanemiller.com
SIC: 2077 2011 Tallow rendering, inedible; pork products from pork slaughtered on site
PA: Kane-Miller Corp.
    1 S School Ave Ste 401
    Sarasota FL 34237
    941 346-2003

▲ = Import ▼=Export
◆ =Import/Export

(G-8776)
KELLERS LIMESTONE SERVICE
2074 N 50 W (46350-8009)
PHONE..................................219 326-1688
Fax: 219 324-5390
Larry Keller, *President*
Jane L Keller, *Admin Sec*
EMP: 10 EST: 1947
SQ FT: 6,000
SALES: 1.1MM **Privately Held**
SIC: 4212 1794 1422 Dump truck haulage; excavation work; excavation & grading, building construction; crushed & broken limestone

(G-8777)
KENCO PLASTICS INC
Also Called: Train Co
809 Pine Lake Ave (46350-2322)
PHONE..................................219 324-6621
Connie Coates, *Manager*
EMP: 11
SALES (corp-wide): 7.4MM **Privately Held**
WEB: www.kenco.net
SIC: 3089 3559 Injection molded finished plastic products; plastics working machinery
PA: Kenco Plastics Inc
2022 W 450 N
La Porte IN 46350
219 362-7565

(G-8778)
KENCO PLASTICS INC (PA)
2022 W 450 N (46350-8324)
P.O. Box 364 (46352-0364)
PHONE..................................219 362-7565
Fax: 574 362-7568
Kenneth W Coates III, *President*
Barbara Coates, *Corp Secy*
EMP: 18
SQ FT: 5,500
SALES (est): 7.4MM **Privately Held**
WEB: www.kenco.net
SIC: 3089 Injection molded finished plastic products

(G-8779)
KENCO PLASTICS INC
Also Called: In Line Industries
809 Pine Lake Ave (46350-2322)
PHONE..................................219 326-5501
Fax: 219 324-6110
Kerry Hickok, *Branch Mgr*
EMP: 11
SALES (est): 1.5MM
SALES (corp-wide): 7.4MM **Privately Held**
SIC: 3089 Injection molded finished plastic products
PA: Kenco Plastics Inc
2022 W 450 N
La Porte IN 46350
219 362-7565

(G-8780)
KENNAMETAL INC
Also Called: Casting Service
300 Philadelphia St (46350-3927)
PHONE..................................219 362-1000
Fax: 219 362-4413
Henry Wojciechowski, *General Mgr*
Joe Walker, *Vice Pres*
Brian Hayes, *Opers Mgr*
Jose Diaz, *Maint Spvr*
Ryan Estand, *Opers Staff*
EMP: 6
SALES (corp-wide): 2.3B **Publicly Held**
SIC: 2819 Tungsten carbide powder, except abrasive or metallurgical
PA: Kennametal Inc.
600 Grant St Ste 5100
Pittsburgh PA 15219
412 248-8000

(G-8781)
KFC COMPOSITE ENGINEERING INC
3451 S State Road 104 (46350-6808)
PHONE..................................219 369-9093
Fax: 219 369-1923
Todd Hornig, *President*
Mary Hornig, *Admin Sec*
EMP: 3
SQ FT: 6,800

SALES (est): 250K **Privately Held**
SIC: 3711 Automobile bodies, passenger car, not including engine, etc.

(G-8782)
LA PORTE PRCSION MCH WORKS LLC
1756 Genesis Dr (46350-2492)
PHONE..................................219 326-7000
Gary Ledenbach,
EMP: 6
SQ FT: 6,000
SALES (est): 639.5K **Privately Held**
SIC: 3599 Machine shop, jobbing & repair

(G-8783)
LA PORTE SMOKES AND BEVERAGES
609 E Lincolnway (46350-3835)
PHONE..................................219 575-7754
Ashokkumar S Patel, *Principal*
EMP: 2
SALES (est): 192.9K **Privately Held**
SIC: 2131 Smoking tobacco

(G-8784)
LA PORTE TECHNOLOGIES LLC (PA)
300 Philadelphia St (46350-3927)
PHONE..................................219 362-1000
Joe Walker, *Plant Mgr*
Kenji Scott,
Srinath Narayanan,
Billy J Parrott,
EMP: 12
SALES (est): 909K **Privately Held**
SIC: 3321 Gray & ductile iron foundries

(G-8785)
LAKESHORE FOODS CORP
Also Called: Al's
702 E Lincolnway Ste 1 (46350-3890)
PHONE..................................219 362-8513
Fax: 574 362-8515
Donald Gonser, *Manager*
EMP: 140
SALES (corp-wide): 46.3MM **Privately Held**
WEB: www.alssupermarket.com
SIC: 5411 5912 2051 Grocery stores, chain; drug stores & proprietary stores; bread, cake & related products
PA: Lakeshore Foods Corp.
100 Commerce Sq
Michigan City IN 46360
219 326-7500

(G-8786)
LINDE LLC
7996 N State Road 39 (46350-8607)
PHONE..................................219 324-0498
Tom Zolvinski, *Branch Mgr*
EMP: 77
SALES (corp-wide): 20.1B **Privately Held**
SIC: 2813 Nitrogen; oxygen, compressed or liquefied
HQ: Linde Llc
200 Somerset Corporate Bl
Bridgewater NJ 08807
908 464-8100

(G-8787)
LIQUID PACKAGING SOLUTIONS INC
3999 E Hupp Rd Bldg R43 (46350-7696)
PHONE..................................219 393-3600
Fax: 219 393-5260
James Kyle, *CEO*
Theresa Mago, *President*
▼ **EMP:** 26
SQ FT: 11,000
SALES (est): 6.8MM **Privately Held**
WEB: www.liquidpackagingsolution.com
SIC: 3565 Packaging machinery

(G-8788)
M & R PATTERN INC
6205 Fail Rd (46350-8830)
PHONE..................................219 778-4675
Fax: 574 324-7911
Gary McMahon, *President*
Mike Barber, *Vice Pres*
EMP: 3
SQ FT: 5,000

SALES (est): 210K **Privately Held**
SIC: 3544 Industrial molds; forms (molds), for foundry & plastics working machinery

(G-8789)
MARK HEISTER DESIGN INC
1600 Indiana Ave (46350-5202)
PHONE..................................312 527-0422
Mark Heister, *President*
Gloria Clark, *Manager*
EMP: 6
SQ FT: 2,500
SALES: 3MM **Privately Held**
WEB: www.markheister.com
SIC: 2335 Women's, juniors' & misses' dresses

(G-8790)
MECHANOVENT CORPORATION
171 Factory St (46350-2622)
PHONE..................................219 326-1767
Fax: 574 325-6805
Dana Wade, *Sales Mgr*
Dan Curry, *Manager*
EMP: 5 EST: 1981
SQ FT: 32,000
SALES (est): 1MM
SALES (corp-wide): 146.6MM **Privately Held**
WEB: www.mechanovent.com
SIC: 3564 Blowers & fans
PA: The New York Blower Company
7660 S Quincy St
Willowbrook IL 60527
630 794-5700

(G-8791)
METALIZED COATINGS LLC
1540 Genesis Dr (46350-2593)
PHONE..................................219 851-0683
Jeff Maki, *Mng Member*
EMP: 3 EST: 2014
SALES (est): 129.8K **Privately Held**
SIC: 3479 Coating of metals & formed products

(G-8792)
METALTEC INC
11 Pine Lake Ave Ste C (46350-3076)
PHONE..................................219 362-9811
Fax: 574 362-9833
Dorena Corley, *President*
Jack Corley, *Admin Sec*
▲ **EMP:** 6
SQ FT: 35,000
SALES (est): 1MM **Privately Held**
SIC: 3599 3441 Custom machinery; fabricated structural metal

(G-8793)
MIDWEST BC
755 S 500 W (46350-9757)
PHONE..................................219 369-4839
Justin Wright, *Principal*
EMP: 6 EST: 2010
SALES (est): 422.6K **Privately Held**
SIC: 2493 Strandboard, oriented

(G-8794)
MILLBURN PEAT COMPANY INC
1733 E Division Rd (46350-8041)
P.O. Box 1160, Milan IL (61264-1160)
PHONE..................................219 362-7025
Fax: 219 324-2308
Ronald D Bjustrom, *President*
Robert Render, *President*
Kenneth McBright, *CFO*
Jon Yung, *Manager*
EMP: 48
SQ FT: 50,000
SALES (est): 4.8MM **Privately Held**
SIC: 1499 2875 5191 5032 Peat mining & processing; potting soil, mixed; garden supplies; soil, potting & planting; brick, stone & related material; brick, except refractory; stone, crushed or broken; industrial sand

(G-8795)
MILLWORK SPECIALTIES CO INC
Also Called: MSC Property Management Div
1405 Lake St (46350-3168)
PHONE..................................219 362-2960
Willard Dorman, *President*
June Dorman, *Corp Secy*

EMP: 3 EST: 1957
SQ FT: 5,000
SALES (est): 296.3K **Privately Held**
SIC: 6531 2421 Real estate managers; planing mills

(G-8796)
MOBILE STADIUM LIGHTING LLC
707 N Fail Rd (46350-9021)
PHONE..................................219 325-0000
Jason Brissette, *Administration*
EMP: 2
SALES (est): 157.3K **Privately Held**
SIC: 3648 Lighting equipment

(G-8797)
MONOSOL LLC
1609 Genesis Dr (46350-2493)
PHONE..................................219 324-9459
Joseph Olesh, *Project Mgr*
Tim Boyle, *Branch Mgr*
EMP: 25
SALES (corp-wide): 4.6B **Privately Held**
SIC: 2671 Plastic film, coated or laminated for packaging
HQ: Monosol, Llc
707 E 80th Pl Ste 301
Merrillville IN 46410
219 762-3165

(G-8798)
MOOSE LODGE
Also Called: Moose Lodge No 492
925 Boyd Blvd (46350-4420)
PHONE..................................219 362-2446
Larry Reuille, *Principal*
Edward Pace, *Administration*
Ed Pays, *Administration*
EMP: 3
SALES: 65.9K **Privately Held**
SIC: 2389 Lodge costumes

(G-8799)
NEW YORK BLOWER COMPANY
171 Factory St (46350-2699)
PHONE..................................217 347-3233
Fax: 574 325-6801
Paul Novotny, *President*
Kal Oneal, *General Mgr*
Matthew Denzine, *Mfg Mgr*
Laken Adams, *Purch Mgr*
Rhonda McGee, *Purch Mgr*
EMP: 200
SALES (corp-wide): 146.6MM **Privately Held**
WEB: www.nyb.com
SIC: 3564 Ventilating fans: industrial or commercial
PA: The New York Blower Company
7660 S Quincy St
Willowbrook IL 60527
630 794-5700

(G-8800)
NRP JONES LLC (PA)
Also Called: Screw Machine Products
302 Philadelphia St (46350-3927)
P.O. Box 310 (46352-0310)
PHONE..................................219 362-4508
Mark Prast, *Vice Pres*
▲ **EMP:** 63
SQ FT: 15,000
SALES (est): 15.3MM **Privately Held**
SIC: 3492 3533 3829 Control valves, aircraft: hydraulic & pneumatic; oil field machinery & equipment; testing equipment: abrasion, shearing strength, etc.

(G-8801)
OLD BARN CREATIONS LLC
2634 N Vermeer Ln (46350-8439)
PHONE..................................219 324-2553
Emiley Blakes, *Owner*
EMP: 2
SALES (est): 113.2K **Privately Held**
SIC: 2511 Wood household furniture

(G-8802)
P M FABRICATING INCORPORATED
2008 Ohio St (46350-8053)
PHONE..................................219 362-9926
Fax: 574 324-6674
Van Risley, *President*
Patrick Meaney, *Chairman*

(PA)=Parent Co (HQ)=Headquarters (DH)=Div Headquarters
✪ = New Business established in last 2 years

Kathleen Meaney, *Admin Sec*
EMP: 9
SQ FT: 13,125
SALES (est): 1.2MM **Privately Held**
SIC: 3599 Machine & other job shop work; machine shop, jobbing & repair

(G-8803)
PACKAGING LOGIC INC
239 Factory St (46350-2624)
P.O. Box 338 (46352-0338)
PHONE.................................219 326-1350
Fax: 219 326-1272
Richard T Parrette Jr, *President*
Dennis Bardon, *Senior VP*
Cindy Hoehne, *Vice Pres*
Chad Parrette, *Vice Pres*
EMP: 39
SQ FT: 178,000
SALES (est): 10.1MM **Privately Held**
WEB: www.packaginglogic.com
SIC: 2653 Boxes, corrugated: made from purchased materials

(G-8804)
PLASTIC PACKAGE LLC
1900 Whirlpool Dr Ste 300 (46350-2708)
PHONE.................................916 921-3399
John Walter, *Branch Mgr*
EMP: 12
SALES (corp-wide): 21MM **Privately Held**
SIC: 3089 Plastic containers, except foam
PA: Plastic Package, Llc
　　4600 Beloit Dr
　　Sacramento CA 95838
　　916 921-3399

(G-8805)
PRAXAIR INC
3076 N State Road 39 (46350-8604)
PHONE.................................219 326-7808
Roy Downs, *President*
EMP: 20
SALES (corp-wide): 11.4B **Publicly Held**
SIC: 2813 Oxygen, compressed or liquefied; nitrogen; argon
PA: Praxair, Inc.
　　10 Riverview Dr
　　Danbury CT 06810
　　203 837-2000

(G-8806)
PRECISIONAIR LLC
1828 N Summit Dr (46350-2107)
PHONE.................................219 380-9267
Scott Schreeg, *Manager*
EMP: 2
SALES (est): 202.7K **Privately Held**
SIC: 3563 Air & gas compressors

(G-8807)
PRECOAT METALS CORP
858 E Hupp Rd (46350-7691)
PHONE.................................219 393-3561
Fax: 219 393-2104
Todd Ryan, *Branch Mgr*
EMP: 67
SQ FT: 155,000
SALES (corp-wide): 3.6B **Publicly Held**
SIC: 3479 Painting of metal products
HQ: Precoat Metals Corp.
　　1950 E Main St
　　Greenfield IN 46140
　　317 462-7761

(G-8808)
QUALITY INDUSTRIAL SUPPLIES
Also Called: Quality Industrial Services
517 Brighton St (46350-2612)
P.O. Box 1702 (46352-1702)
PHONE.................................219 324-2654
Fax: 574 325-3599
John Blind, *Ch of Bd*
Richard Weller, *President*
EMP: 11
SQ FT: 7,000
SALES (est): 1MM **Privately Held**
SIC: 3613 3823 3549 Control panels, electric; industrial instrmnts msrmnt display/control process variable; metalworking machinery

(G-8809)
R & B MOLD AND DIE INC
1560 Lake St (46350-3173)
PHONE.................................219 324-4176
Fax: 219 324-4176
David Brantley, *President*
EMP: 5
SQ FT: 4,560
SALES: 600K **Privately Held**
WEB: www.rbmoldanddie.com
SIC: 3599 Machine shop, jobbing & repair

(G-8810)
R & R TOOL MANUFACTURING INC
1540 Lake St (46350-3173)
PHONE.................................219 362-1681
Fax: 219 325-9222
Mike Rollins, *President*
EMP: 34
SQ FT: 33,000
SALES: 2MM **Privately Held**
SIC: 3599 7692 3469 3444 Machine shop, jobbing & repair; welding repair; metal stampings; sheet metalwork

(G-8811)
REUER MACHINE & TOOL INC
1733 E State Road 2 (46350-4490)
PHONE.................................219 362-2894
Fax: 574 324-6253
Robert Reuer, *President*
Dean Tuholski, *Vice Pres*
Mary Rucker, *Office Mgr*
EMP: 8 **EST:** 1980
SQ FT: 6,000
SALES (est): 866.3K **Privately Held**
SIC: 3599 Machine shop, jobbing & repair

(G-8812)
RIDEN INC
Also Called: Hawkins Print Shop
315 Lincolnway (46350-2412)
PHONE.................................219 362-5511
Fax: 574 362-5511
Christopher Hawkins, *President*
Greg Hawkins, *Vice Pres*
EMP: 5
SQ FT: 20,000
SALES (est): 660.6K **Privately Held**
SIC: 2752 2791 2789 Commercial printing, offset; typesetting; bookbinding & related work

(G-8813)
ROTATION DYNAMICS CORPORATION
1164 E 150 N (46350-9119)
PHONE.................................219 325-8808
Fax: 219 325-0921
Dave Koepke, *Opers Mgr*
Barb Nykiel, *Human Res Mgr*
Steve Aker, *Manager*
Mike Yearick, *Manager*
EMP: 21
SALES (corp-wide): 164.4MM **Privately Held**
SIC: 3555 2796 Printing trades machinery; platemaking services
PA: Rotation Dynamics Corporation
　　1101 Windham Pkwy
　　Romeoville IL 60446
　　630 769-9255

(G-8814)
RS PRECISION MACHINING
7909 N Wilhelm Rd (46350-8631)
PHONE.................................219 362-4560
Rudy Schlager, *Owner*
EMP: 2
SALES (est): 209.4K **Privately Held**
SIC: 3599 Machine shop, jobbing & repair

(G-8815)
SALIWANCHIK & SONS WELDING & F
3707 N Us Highway 35 (46350-8383)
P.O. Box 68 (46352-0068)
PHONE.................................219 362-9009
Ted Saliwanchik, *Owner*
EMP: 2
SALES: 250K **Privately Held**
SIC: 7692 Welding repair

(G-8816)
SCHMIDT MARKEN DESIGNS
3403 S Wozniak Rd (46350-7820)
PHONE.................................219 785-4238
Karen Marken, *Partner*
Douglas Schmidt, *Partner*
EMP: 3
SALES (est): 227.5K **Privately Held**
SIC: 5719 3269 Pottery; pottery household articles, except kitchen articles

(G-8817)
SEMCOR INC
Also Called: Semcor Manufacturing
1500 Genesis Dr (46350-2593)
PHONE.................................219 362-0222
Scott Siefker, *President*
Mark Siefker, *Vice Pres*
EMP: 15
SQ FT: 50,000
SALES (est): 736.4K **Privately Held**
SIC: 3613 3621 3646 Panel & distribution boards & other related apparatus; generator sets: gasoline, diesel or dual-fuel; commercial indusl & institutional electric lighting fixtures

(G-8818)
SEVENOKS INC
Also Called: Sterno Delivery
3539 Monroe St (46350-6178)
P.O. Box 870 (46352-0870)
PHONE.................................800 523-8715
Fax: 574 324-7124
Don Hinshaw, *President*
EMP: 8 **EST:** 2011
SALES (est): 5MM **Publicly Held**
SIC: 3086 Cups & plates, foamed plastic
HQ: Sterno Products, Llc
　　1880 Compton Ave Ste 101
　　Corona CA 92881
　　951 682-9600

(G-8819)
SHADOWHOUSE JIU-JITSU INC
Also Called: Contact Concealment
3707 N Promenade Cir (46350-8287)
PHONE.................................219 873-4556
Bruce Weiler, *President*
EMP: 2
SALES (est): 132.5K **Privately Held**
SIC: 3089 Cases, plastic

(G-8820)
SHF MICROWAVE PARTS CO
7102 W 500 S (46350-9575)
PHONE.................................219 785-2602
Pierette Rutz, *Owner*
EMP: 2
SALES: 18K **Privately Held**
WEB: www.shfmicro.com
SIC: 5065 3663 Communication equipment; radio & TV communications equipment

(G-8821)
SILCOTEC INC
707 Boyd Blvd (46350-4416)
PHONE.................................219 324-4411
Fax: 574 324-7252
Brian Sauers, *CEO*
Clifford E Myers, *President*
Charles B Sauers, *Admin Sec*
▲ **EMP:** 10
SQ FT: 22,000
SALES (est): 3.7MM **Privately Held**
WEB: www.silcotec.com
SIC: 2851 Paints & paint additives

(G-8822)
SILGAN CONTAINERS MFG CORP
300 N Fail Rd (46350-7051)
PHONE.................................219 362-7002
EMP: 14
SALES (est): 2.2MM **Privately Held**
SIC: 3411 Mfg Metal Cans

(G-8823)
SILGAN CONTAINERS MFG CORP
300 N Fail Rd (46350-7051)
PHONE.................................219 362-7002
Fax: 574 325-3817
Randy Rhodes, *Manager*

EMP: 82
SALES (corp-wide): 4B **Publicly Held**
WEB: www.silgancontainers.com
SIC: 3411 Metal cans
HQ: Silgan Containers Manufacturing Corporation
　　21600 Oxnard St Ste 1600
　　Woodland Hills CA 91367

(G-8824)
STRATIKORE
1714 E Lincolnway (46350-4479)
P.O. Box 689 (46352-0689)
PHONE.................................574 807-0028
Ray Wolff, *President*
▲ **EMP:** 4
SALES (est): 440.8K **Privately Held**
SIC: 3082 8711 Rods, unsupported plastic; consulting engineer

(G-8825)
TALL COTTON MARKETING LLC
Also Called: Soap Guy, The
3522 S State Road 104 (46350-6806)
PHONE.................................312 320-5862
Jeffrey Dorrian, *CEO*
EMP: 2
SALES (est): 363.2K **Privately Held**
SIC: 5122 2841 Toilet soap; soap: granulated, liquid, cake, flaked or chip

(G-8826)
TALON TERRA LLC
399 E Hupp Rd (46350)
PHONE.................................219 393-1400
Jon Yung, *Manager*
EMP: 5
SALES (est): 1MM **Privately Held**
SIC: 3524 Lawn & garden equipment

(G-8827)
TDY INDUSTRIES LLC
Also Called: ATI Casting Service
300 Philadelphia St (46350-3927)
PHONE.................................219 362-1000
Patrick Hassey, *CEO*
David Neil, *President*
Jon D Walton, *Senior VP*
Dennis Basham, *Plant Mgr*
Paul Frushour, *Manager*
EMP: 158
SALES (est): 64.7MM **Publicly Held**
SIC: 3369 Zinc & zinc-base alloy castings, except die-castings
PA: Allegheny Technologies Incorporated
　　1000 Six Ppg Pl
　　Pittsburgh PA 15222

(G-8828)
TERRY LIQUIDATION III INC (PA)
Also Called: Hytek Hose & Coupling Div
210 Philadelphia St (46350-3925)
P.O. Box 310 (46352-0310)
PHONE.................................219 362-9908
Fax: 574 324-0815
Terry Jones, *Vice Pres*
Terry H Jones, *Vice Pres*
Brian K Jones, *Treasurer*
Lois Weeden, *Admin Sec*
▲ **EMP:** 60
SQ FT: 60,000
SALES (est): 13MM **Privately Held**
SIC: 3492 5085 Hose & tube fittings & assemblies, hydraulic/pneumatic; industrial supplies

(G-8829)
TERRY LIQUIDATION III INC
Hy-Tek Hose & Coupling
28 Industrial Pkwy (46350-7055)
PHONE.................................219 362-3557
Fax: 219 362-1317
Kelly Donahoe, *Financial Exec*
EMP: 20
SALES (corp-wide): 13MM **Privately Held**
SIC: 5084 3594 3451 3429 Hydraulic systems equipment & supplies; fluid power pumps & motors; screw machine products; manufactured hardware (general)
PA: Terry Liquidation Iii, Inc.
　　210 Philadelphia St
　　La Porte IN 46350
　　219 362-9908

▲ = Import ▼=Export
◆ =Import/Export

(G-8830)
TFCO INCORPORATED (PA)
2606 N State Road 39 (46350-2034)
P.O. Box 339 (46352-0339)
PHONE...................................219 324-4166
Fax: 219 324-4866
Brad M Childress, *President*
Mike Gormley, *General Mgr*
▲ EMP: 8
SALES (est): 1.2MM **Privately Held**
WEB: www.tfcoinc.com
SIC: 3053 Gasket materials

(G-8831)
THERMCO INSTRUMENT CORPORATION
1201 W Us Highway 20 (46350-8613)
P.O. Box 309 (46352-0309)
PHONE...................................219 362-6258
Fax: 219 324-3568
Dennis Richardson, *President*
Kent Richardson, *Principal*
Glen Richardson, *Corp Secy*
Dan Flodder, *Purch Agent*
EMP: 14
SQ FT: 24,670
SALES (est): 3.6MM **Privately Held**
WEB: www.thermco.com
SIC: 3823 On-stream gas/liquid analysis instruments, industrial

(G-8832)
TRUSSLINK
512 Washington St (46350-3334)
PHONE...................................219 362-3968
Fax: 219 324-2091
Pat South, *Owner*
EMP: 3 EST: 1976
SALES (est): 116.7K **Privately Held**
SIC: 2439 Structural wood members

(G-8833)
WINN MACHINE INC
720 Boyd Blvd (46350-4417)
PHONE...................................219 324-2978
Fax: 219 874-9104
Damon Gasaway, *President*
Dina Gasaway, *Treasurer*
Virginia Winn, *Admin Sec*
Stephanie Zeno, *Assistant*
EMP: 8
SQ FT: 11,000
SALES (est): 1.5MM **Privately Held**
SIC: 3599 3451 Machine shop, jobbing & repair; screw machine products

(G-8834)
YANDT BOAT WORKS
308 Grayson Rd (46350-2249)
PHONE...................................219 851-8311
Andrew F Yandt, *Owner*
EMP: 2 EST: 2015
SALES (est): 171.4K **Privately Held**
SIC: 3732 Boat building & repairing

Laconia
Harrison County

(G-8835)
A NEW COVENANT WOODWORK LLC
4305 Hooptown Rd Se (47135-9132)
PHONE...................................812 737-2929
Ken Buzek, *Mng Member*
Debbie Buzek, *Mng Member*
EMP: 5
SALES: 560K **Privately Held**
SIC: 2426 Hardwood dimension & flooring mills

(G-8836)
GRACE AMAZING GRAPHICS ✪
250 W Highway 11 Se (47135-8829)
PHONE...................................812 737-2841
Edward Farrow, *Principal*
EMP: 2 EST: 2017
SALES (est): 83.9K **Privately Held**
SIC: 2752 Commercial printing, lithographic

(G-8837)
LACONIA LASER ENGRAVING
2825 Mosquito Creek Rd Se (47135-9070)
PHONE...................................812 786-3641
Jeffrey W Lehman, *Owner*
EMP: 2
SALES (est): 69.3K **Privately Held**
SIC: 2759 Commercial printing

Ladoga
Montgomery County

(G-8838)
BRADLEY INNOVATION GROUP LLC
Also Called: Bradley Environmental
7442 S 750 E (47954-7214)
PHONE...................................765 942-7127
James Bradley, *Principal*
William Blythe,
EMP: 4
SALES (est): 289.5K **Privately Held**
SIC: 3561 Pumps & pumping equipment

(G-8839)
CHELSEAS MODEL HORSES
7889 S Ladoga Rd (47954-7289)
PHONE...................................765 366-1082
Chelsea Benge, *Owner*
EMP: 2
SALES (est): 127.6K **Privately Held**
SIC: 3944 Games, toys & children's vehicles

(G-8840)
EMERALD CAST RNEWABLE FUEL LLC
Also Called: ECR Fuel
329 W College St (47954-7307)
PHONE...................................765 942-5019
Steve Weir,
EMP: 7
SALES: 1.4MM **Privately Held**
SIC: 2911 Diesel fuels

(G-8841)
NEW MARKET PLASTICS INC (PA)
Also Called: Gator Buckets
10099 S Us Highway 231 (47954-8036)
P.O. Box 57, New Market (47965-0057)
PHONE...................................317 758-5494
Fax: 765 866-1345
Kerry Hopkins, *President*
EMP: 12
SQ FT: 22,000
SALES (est): 1.9MM **Privately Held**
SIC: 3089 Injection molded finished plastic products; injection molding of plastics

(G-8842)
STULLS MACHINING CENTER INC
209 E College St (47954-7041)
P.O. Box 353 (47954-0353)
PHONE...................................765 942-2717
Ryan Stull, *President*
Warren Boling, *Shareholder*
EMP: 2 EST: 1993
SALES (est): 293.9K **Privately Held**
SIC: 3549 Wiredrawing & fabricating machinery & equipment, ex. die

(G-8843)
STULLS MCH & FABRICATION INC
213 E Locust St (47954-7045)
P.O. Box 353 (47954-0353)
PHONE...................................765 942-2717
Ryan Stull, *President*
Scott Stull, *Vice Pres*
EMP: 2
SALES: 100K **Privately Held**
SIC: 3599 3499 Machine shop, jobbing & repair; machine bases, metal

Lafayette
Tippecanoe County

(G-8844)
20 MINUTE SIGNS PLUS
3032 E 800 S (47909-9124)
PHONE...................................765 413-1046
Mike Moll, *President*
Terri A Moll, *Admin Sec*
EMP: 2 EST: 2010
SALES (est): 167.8K **Privately Held**
SIC: 3993 Signs & advertising specialties

(G-8845)
ACELL INC
3589 Sgmre Pkwy N 220 (47904)
PHONE...................................765 464-8198
Fax: 765 464-8947
Sherry Dibro, *President*
EMP: 12
SALES (est): 2MM
SALES (corp-wide): 59.3MM **Privately Held**
SIC: 2833 Medicinals & botanicals
PA: Acell, Inc.
6640 Eli Whitney Dr # 200
Columbia MD 21046
800 826-2926

(G-8846)
ADVANCE REPAIR & MACHINING
3311 Imperial Pkwy Ste B (47909-5114)
PHONE...................................765 474-8000
Kyle D Garrett, *President*
EMP: 7
SALES (est): 570K **Privately Held**
SIC: 3599 Machine shop, jobbing & repair

(G-8847)
ADVANCED VSCULAR THERAPIES INC
1125 N 13th St (47904-2012)
PHONE...................................765 423-1720
Kerry Logan, *President*
Kathryn Logan, *President*
EMP: 2 EST: 2010
SALES (est): 157K **Privately Held**
SIC: 3841 Surgical & medical instruments

(G-8848)
AG PRINTING SPECIALISTS LLC
2880 Us Highway 231 S # 200 (47909-2874)
PHONE...................................866 445-6824
Tim Powers,
Steve Roswaski,
EMP: 4
SALES (est): 429.6K **Privately Held**
SIC: 2752 Commercial printing, offset

(G-8849)
ALCOA INC
160 N 36th St (47905-4701)
PHONE...................................765 447-1707
Greg Clayton, *Manager*
EMP: 135
SALES (corp-wide): 12.9B **Publicly Held**
SIC: 3353 Aluminum sheet & strip
PA: Arconic Inc.
390 Park Ave Fl 12
New York NY 10022
212 836-2758

(G-8850)
ALLOY CUSTOM PRODUCTS LLC
9701 Old State Road 25 N (47905-9734)
P.O. Box 198, Delphi (46923-0198)
PHONE...................................765 564-4684
Ted Boatman, *President*
▼ EMP: 94
SQ FT: 101,000
SALES (est): 21.7MM
SALES (corp-wide): 3.6B **Publicly Held**
SIC: 3443 Cryogenic tanks, for liquids & gases; vessels, process or storage (from boiler shops): metal plate

PA: Trinity Industries, Inc.
2525 N Stemmons Fwy
Dallas TX 75207
214 631-4420

(G-8851)
AMERICAN ORTHPDICS PROSTHETICS
720 Farabee Ct (47905-5917)
PHONE...................................765 447-0111
Brian Creighton, *President*
EMP: 6
SQ FT: 3,600
SALES (est): 1MM **Privately Held**
WEB: www.amerortho.com
SIC: 5999 2399 Artificial limbs; orthopedic & prosthesis applications; hammocks & other net products

(G-8852)
ARCONIC INC
Also Called: Arconic Forgings & Extrusions
3131 Main St (47905-2272)
PHONE...................................765 771-3600
Fax: 765 771-3576
Diane Schrader, *Buyer*
Jodi Yim, *Engineer*
Ron McClure, *Finance Mgr*
Jody Koontz, *Human Res Mgr*
Marisa Kosney, *Human Res Mgr*
EMP: 850
SALES (corp-wide): 12.9B **Publicly Held**
SIC: 3354 Tube, extruded or drawn, aluminum
PA: Arconic Inc.
390 Park Ave Fl 12
New York NY 10022
212 836-2758

(G-8853)
ARROW VAULT CO INC
1312 Underwood St (47904-1122)
PHONE...................................765 742-1704
Robert Burris, *President*
Kathleen Burris, *Corp Secy*
EMP: 6 EST: 1946
SQ FT: 6,000
SALES (est): 701.8K **Privately Held**
SIC: 3272 Burial vaults, concrete or precast terrazzo

(G-8854)
ASH ACCESS TECHNOLOGY INC
3601 Sagamore Pkwy N B (47904-5033)
PHONE...................................765 742-4813
Stephen R Ash MD, *Ch of Bd*
Robert B Truitt, *President*
Carmine J Durham, *Vice Pres*
Roland Winger, *Vice Pres*
Nels Bergmark, *Treasurer*
EMP: 9
SQ FT: 8,500
SALES (est): 620K **Privately Held**
WEB: www.ashaccess.com
SIC: 8733 3841 Medical research; surgical & medical instruments

(G-8855)
AUDIO DIAGNOSTICS INC
Also Called: Audiodiagnostics
2320 Concord Rd Ste A (47909-2710)
PHONE...................................765 477-7016
Susan Berner, *President*
Shari Haillsamer, *Corp Secy*
EMP: 2
SALES (est): 194.4K **Privately Held**
SIC: 3842 8099 8049 Hearing aids; hearing testing service; audiologist

(G-8856)
AUTO ART & SIGNS
420 Sagamore Pkwy N (47904-2826)
PHONE...................................765 448-6800
Ken Klim, *Principal*
EMP: 2
SALES (est): 146.9K **Privately Held**
SIC: 3993 Signs & advertising specialties

(G-8857)
AUTO SPECIALTY OF LAFAYETTE
313 Teal Rd (47905-2310)
PHONE...................................765 446-2311
Connie Budreau, *President*

G
E
O
G
R
A
P
H
I
C

Greg Budreau, *Vice Pres*
EMP: 9
SALES (est): 1MM **Privately Held**
WEB: www.autospecialtyperformance.com
SIC: 7538 7549 7539 7533 General automotive repair shops; inspection & diagnostic service, automotive; brake repair, automotive; muffler shop, sale or repair & installation; machine shop, jobbing & repair

(G-8858)
AWARDS UNLIMITED INC
3031 Union St (47904-2756)
PHONE.................................765 447-9413
Fax: 765 447-2005
Stacey Shirar, *President*
Darrel Shirar, *Treasurer*
Ashley Smith, *Asst Mgr*
EMP: 7
SQ FT: 5,180
SALES (est): 560K **Privately Held**
WEB: www.awardsunlimitedinc.com
SIC: 5999 5199 3993 Trophies & plaques; advertising specialties; signs & advertising specialties

(G-8859)
B & M ELECTRICAL CO INC
710 Navco Dr (47905-4719)
P.O. Box 4795 (47903-4795)
PHONE.................................765 448-4532
Fax: 765 447-9136
Mark J Buche, *President*
Kathleen S Buche, *Admin Sec*
▼ **EMP:** 13 **EST:** 1979
SQ FT: 8,400
SALES: 1.3MM **Privately Held**
WEB: www.bmelectrical.com
SIC: 3625 3694 7539 Starter, electric motor; alternators, automotive; automotive repair shops; electrical services

(G-8860)
BEUTLER MEAT PROCESSING CO
802 Wabash Ave (47905)
PHONE.................................765 742-7285
Stephen Beutler, *President*
EMP: 15
SALES (est): 808.5K **Privately Held**
SIC: 2011 7299 Meat packing plants; butcher service, processing only

(G-8861)
BIONIC PROSTH & ORTHOS GRP LLC ◘
5 Executive Dr Ste D-2 (47905-3832)
PHONE.................................765 838-8222
EMP: 2 **EST:** 2017
SALES (est): 86.6K **Privately Held**
SIC: 3842 Surgical appliances & supplies

(G-8862)
BLUE PRINT SPECIALTIES INC
1500 Union St (47904-2156)
PHONE.................................765 742-6976
Fax: 765 742-2060
Neil Klinker, *President*
Carolyn Schnelle, *Admin Sec*
EMP: 3
SALES: 583.7K **Privately Held**
WEB: www.blueprintspecialties.net
SIC: 7334 5049 2752 Blueprinting service; engineers' equipment & supplies; commercial printing, lithographic

(G-8863)
BLUMLING DESIGN AND GRAPHICS
3228 Olympia Dr Ste C (47909-5116)
PHONE.................................765 477-7446
Thomas K Blumling, *President*
EMP: 5
SQ FT: 2,500
SALES (est): 379.6K **Privately Held**
WEB: www.blumlingdesigngroup.com
SIC: 3993 5198 Signs, not made in custom sign painting shops; wallcoverings

(G-8864)
BOLLOCK INTERPRISES INC
900 Farabee Ct (47905-5922)
PHONE.................................765 448-6000
Fax: 765 446-1126

Alfred A Bollock Jr, *President*
Carol Bollock, *Vice Pres*
Sharon Bollock, *Treasurer*
Stewart Bollock, *Marketing Mgr*
Steve Young, *Shareholder*
EMP: 17
SQ FT: 21,000
SALES (est): 1.3MM **Privately Held**
SIC: 2599 5712 Factory furniture & fixtures; furniture stores

(G-8865)
BROWELL ENTERPRISES INC
Also Called: Custom Machine Shop
711 N 31st St (47904-2709)
PHONE.................................765 447-2292
Fax: 765 447-7280
Debbie Browell, *President*
Brian Browell, *President*
Rick Chester, *Admin Sec*
EMP: 15
SQ FT: 7,500
SALES (est): 2.8MM **Privately Held**
WEB: www.browellent.com
SIC: 3599 Machine shop, jobbing & repair

(G-8866)
CARGILL INCORPORATED
1502 Wabash Ave (47905-1038)
PHONE.................................765 423-4302
Fax: 765 420-6770
John Zoss, *Superintendent*
EMP: 38
SALES (corp-wide): 88.8B **Privately Held**
WEB: www.cargill.com
SIC: 2075 2079 Soybean oil mills; edible fats & oils
PA: Cargill, Incorporated
     15407 Mcginty Rd W
     Wayzata MN 55391
     952 742-7575

(G-8867)
CARLEX INDIANA ASSEMBLY (DH)
Also Called: Carlex Glass Company
3701 David Howarth Dr (47909-9360)
PHONE.................................765 471-9399
Sam Aoki, *President*
Jim Melton, *Engineer*
Ted Hathaway, *Controller*
EMP: 30
SQ FT: 24,000
SALES (est): 8MM
SALES (corp-wide): 2.1B **Privately Held**
SIC: 3211 Flat glass
HQ: Central Glass America, Inc.
     7200 Centennial Blvd
     Nashville TN 37209
     423 884-1105

(G-8868)
CARTESIAN CORP
230 Walnut St (47905-1001)
PHONE.................................765 742-0293
Stephen M Rush, *President*
Jim Peters, *Vice Pres*
EMP: 20
SQ FT: 60,000
SALES (est): 4MM **Privately Held**
WEB: www.cartcorp.com
SIC: 3444 Sheet metalwork

(G-8869)
CASINO PRINTING FOR LESS
1400 Canal Rd (47904-4053)
PHONE.................................765 742-0000
EMP: 2 **EST:** 2011
SALES (est): 110K **Privately Held**
SIC: 2752 Lithographic Commercial Printing

(G-8870)
CASSINI - D & D MFG INC
800 S Earl Ave (47904-3350)
P.O. Box 4428 (47903-4428)
PHONE.................................765 449-7992
David Caffini, *President*
EMP: 9
SALES (est): 710.4K **Privately Held**
SIC: 1761 2434 3281 Sheet metalwork; vanities, bathroom: wood; curbing, granite or stone

(G-8871)
CATERPILLAR INC
3701 South St (47905-4856)
PHONE.................................765 448-5000
Fax: 765 448-5282
Jim Albert, *Engineer*
Steve Bloch, *Engineer*
Welch Chad, *Engineer*
Nick Clinkenbeard, *Engineer*
Kristie Denovich, *Engineer*
EMP: 120
SQ FT: 30,000
SALES (corp-wide): 45.4B **Publicly Held**
WEB: www.cat.com
SIC: 3531 Construction machinery
PA: Caterpillar Inc.
     510 Lake Cook Rd Ste 100
     Deerfield IL 60015
     224 551-4000

(G-8872)
CATHOLIC MOMENT
610 Lingle Ave (47901-1740)
P.O. Box 260 (47902-0260)
PHONE.................................765 742-2050
Thomas Russel, *Manager*
EMP: 5
SALES (est): 209.3K **Privately Held**
SIC: 2711 Newspapers

(G-8873)
CENTRAL COCA-COLA BTLG CO INC
830 N 6th St (47904-1803)
PHONE.................................765 423-5668
Dan Artis, *General Mgr*
EMP: 50
SALES (corp-wide): 35.4B **Publicly Held**
WEB: www.cokecce.com
SIC: 2086 Soft drinks: packaged in cans, bottles, etc.
HQ: Central Coca-Cola Bottling Company, Inc.
     555 Taxter Rd Ste 550
     Elmsford NY 10523
     914 789-1100

(G-8874)
CERES SOLUTIONS LLP
3354 Us Highway 52 S (47905-7701)
PHONE.................................765 477-6542
Cathy Deanman, *Branch Mgr*
EMP: 7
SALES (corp-wide): 309.8MM **Privately Held**
SIC: 1311 Crude petroleum & natural gas
PA: Ceres Solutions, Llp
     2112 Indianapolis Rd
     Crawfordsville IN 47933
     765 362-6108

(G-8875)
COLEMAN CABLE LLC
3400 Union St (47905-4448)
PHONE.................................765 449-7227
John Semyen, *Manager*
EMP: 115
SALES (corp-wide): 2.5B **Privately Held**
WEB: www.copperfielddllc.com
SIC: 3061 3548 2891 2822 Mechanical rubber goods; welding apparatus; adhesives & sealants; synthetic rubber
HQ: Coleman Cable, Llc
     1530 S Shields Dr
     Waukegan IL 60085
     847 672-2300

(G-8876)
CONCORD REALSTATE CORP
Also Called: Concord Window Manufacturing
308 Erie St (47904-2553)
PHONE.................................765 423-5555
Fax: 765 423-8118
E G Kenworthy, *President*
Merle Kenworthy, *Vice Pres*
EMP: 10
SALES (est): 800K **Privately Held**
WEB: www.bestwindowanddoor.com
SIC: 2431 5211 1751 1521 Windows & window parts & trim, wood; door & window products; window & door (prefabricated) installation; single-family home remodeling, additions & repairs

(G-8877)
COPY-PRINT SHOP INC
Also Called: National Group, The
627 S Earl Ave Ste A (47904-3600)
PHONE.................................765 447-6868
Fax: 765 448-9603
Leo S Farrell, *President*
Eric Wright, *Production*
Tom McCain, *Info Tech Mgr*
EMP: 21
SQ FT: 12,000
SALES (est): 5.3MM **Privately Held**
SIC: 2752 7334 Commercial printing, offset; photocopying & duplicating services

(G-8878)
COPYMAT SERVICE INC
135 S Chauncey Ave (47906-3722)
PHONE.................................765 743-5995
Fax: 765 743-7015
Donald Steele, *President*
EMP: 4
SQ FT: 2,400
SALES (est): 445.5K **Privately Held**
SIC: 7334 2752 2791 Photocopying & duplicating services; commercial printing, offset; typesetting

(G-8879)
COZY CAT INC
2101 Indian Trail Dr (47906-2030)
P.O. Box 2823 (47996-2823)
PHONE.................................765 463-1254
Linda Stafford, *President*
EMP: 4
SALES (est): 310.3K **Privately Held**
SIC: 7331 7338 2759 1542 Mailing service; resume writing service; invitations: printing; agricultural building contractors; barber shops; boarding services, kennels

(G-8880)
CP GROUP INC
867 Shawnee Ave (47905-1455)
PHONE.................................765 551-7768
J Scott Huggins, *President*
John A Huggins, *Admin Sec*
EMP: 2 **EST:** 1992
SALES (est): 188.8K **Privately Held**
SIC: 2893 Printing ink

(G-8881)
CPP FILTER CORPORATION
730 Farabee Ct (47905-5917)
P.O. Box 5602 (47903-5602)
PHONE.................................765 446-8416
Fax: 765 448-2870
John Gleason, *President*
Milo Reinhardt, *Vice Pres*
EMP: 5
SQ FT: 3,700
SALES (est): 853.4K **Privately Held**
WEB: www.cppfilter.com
SIC: 3569 Filters

(G-8882)
CREATIVE INC
Also Called: Sign Experts
150 N 36th St (47905-4701)
PHONE.................................765 447-3500
Fax: 765 447-7079
Lucy Borga, *President*
Shawn Borga, *Vice Pres*
EMP: 8
SALES (est): 1MM **Privately Held**
WEB: www.signxperts.com
SIC: 3993 Signs & advertising specialties

(G-8883)
CROSSROADS GALVANIZING LLC
4877 E Old 350 S (47905-7723)
PHONE.................................765 421-6741
Brent Williams, *Manager*
EMP: 12
SALES (corp-wide): 15MM **Privately Held**
SIC: 3479 Galvanizing of iron, steel or end-formed products
PA: Crossroads Galvanizing, Llc
     400 Industrial Dr
     Glasgow MO 65254
     660 338-2242

▲ = Import ▼=Export
◆ =Import/Export

(G-8884)
CUSTOM FORMS INC (PA)
1400 Canal Rd Ste B (47904-4031)
P.O. Box 2277, West Lafayette (47996-2277)
PHONE..................................765 463-6162
Fax: 765 463-1655
Maria E Goble, *President*
Gary R Goble, *Vice Pres*
Linda Lamb, *Treasurer*
▲ EMP: 5
SQ FT: 4,000
SALES (est): 5.2MM **Privately Held**
WEB: www.casinoforms.com
SIC: 5112 2752 Business forms; commercial printing, offset

(G-8885)
CUSTOM TEES
Also Called: Rock N' Roll Alley
1516 Sherwood Dr (47909-3746)
PHONE..................................765 449-4893
Fax: 765 447-7859
Paul Miller, *Owner*
EMP: 5
SALES (est): 246.5K **Privately Held**
SIC: 5699 3552 T-shirts, custom printed; silk screens for textile industry

(G-8886)
CUSTOMIZED MACHINING INC
5596 Keeneland Way (47905-0637)
PHONE..................................765 490-7894
Troy Boggs, *Principal*
EMP: 2
SALES (est): 185.1K **Privately Held**
SIC: 3599 Machine shop, jobbing & repair

(G-8887)
DEPENDABLE RUBBER INDUSTRIAL
201 Farabee Dr S Ste C (47905-4703)
P.O. Box 6081 (47903-6081)
PHONE..................................765 447-5654
Fax: 765 447-9273
Paul Swinford, *President*
EMP: 3
SQ FT: 2,400
SALES (est): 939.9K **Privately Held**
SIC: 5085 7699 3599 3492 Valves, pistons & fittings; hydraulic equipment repair; flexible metal hose, tubing & bellows; hose & tube fittings & assemblies, hydraulic/pneumatic

(G-8888)
DESIRABLE SCENTS
3843 Daisy Dr (47905-4904)
PHONE..................................317 504-4976
EMP: 2
SALES (est): 90K **Privately Held**
SIC: 2844 Toilet preparations

(G-8889)
DESTRO MACHINES LLC
1905 Mulligan Way Apt D (47909-3935)
PHONE..................................412 999-1619
Charles Destro, *Mng Member*
EMP: 2
SALES (est): 70.9K **Privately Held**
SIC: 3949 Water sports equipment

(G-8890)
DEWILDE GLASS INC
Also Called: Magic Glass Lafayette
712 Ste 1 Wide Water Dr (47904)
PHONE..................................765 742-0229
Michael Dewilde, *President*
EMP: 7
SALES (est): 673.4K **Privately Held**
SIC: 7536 5231 3231 Automotive glass replacement shops; glass; windshields, glass: made from purchased glass

(G-8891)
DILDEN BROS INC
Also Called: Dilden Bros Well & Drilling
1426 Canal Rd (47904-1832)
P.O. Box 1538 (47902-1538)
PHONE..................................765 742-1717
Wayne Findlay, *President*
Dottie Findlay, *Manager*
Don Findlay, *Admin Sec*
EMP: 12
SQ FT: 9,000
SALES (est): 3.2MM **Privately Held**
SIC: 3533 1781 Water well drilling equipment; water well servicing

(G-8892)
DUNCAN SUPPLY CO INC
Also Called: Johnson Contrls Authorized Dlr
510 Morland Dr (47905-4716)
PHONE..................................765 446-0105
Todd Brumley, *Manager*
EMP: 5
SALES (corp-wide): 50.1MM **Privately Held**
SIC: 5722 5078 3585 Household appliance stores; commercial refrigeration equipment; refrigeration equipment, complete
PA: Duncan Supply Co Inc
910 N Illinois St
Indianapolis IN 46204
317 634-1335

(G-8893)
E-BEAM SERVICES INC
3400 Union St (47905-4448)
PHONE..................................765 447-6755
Fax: 765 449-1085
Robb Huff, *Branch Mgr*
EMP: 2
SALES (corp-wide): 5MM **Privately Held**
WEB: www.e-beamservices.com
SIC: 3999 Sterilizers, barber & beauty shop
PA: E-Beam Services, Inc.
270 Duffy Ave Ste H
Hicksville NY 11801
516 622-1422

(G-8894)
EVONIK CORPORATION
Also Called: Tippecanoe Laboratories
1650 Lilly Rd (47909-9201)
PHONE..................................765 477-4300
Fax: 765 477-4818
Kevin Walters, *Maint Spvr*
Tom Mecklenburg, *Production*
Dawn Lehman, *Purch Mgr*
Bonnie Lutz, *Purch Mgr*
Sarah Parks, *Buyer*
EMP: 650
SALES (corp-wide): 2.4B **Privately Held**
WEB: www.lilly.com
SIC: 2869 Industrial organic chemicals
HQ: Evonik Corporation
299 Jefferson Rd
Parsippany NJ 07054
973 929-8000

(G-8895)
FAIRFIELD MANUFACTURING CO INC
Also Called: Oerlikon Fairfield
2309 Concord Rd (47909-2707)
PHONE..................................765 772-4547
Jeff Miller, *Engineer*
Jeff Potrzebowski, *CFO*
Vickie Clark, *Human Res Mgr*
Susanne Qualkenbush, *Human Res Mgr*
John Easton, *Regl Sales Mgr*
EMP: 26
SALES (corp-wide): 2.8B **Privately Held**
WEB: www.fairfieldmfg.com
SIC: 3714 3568 3545 Differentials & parts, motor vehicle; gears, motor vehicle; power transmission equipment; machine tool accessories
HQ: Fairfield Manufacturing Company, Inc.
2400 Sagamore Pkwy S
Lafayette IN 47905

(G-8896)
FAIRFIELD MANUFACTURING CO INC (HQ)
Also Called: Oerlikon Fairfield
2400 Sagamore Pkwy S (47905-5116)
P.O. Box 7940 (47903-7940)
PHONE..................................765 772-4000
Fax: 765 772-4001
David Evans, *President*
Gary McGrady, *Area Mgr*
Jose Orozco, *Area Mgr*
Garry Francis, *Vice Pres*
Dave Martin, *Vice Pres*
▲ EMP: 800
SQ FT: 600,000

SALES (est): 234.1MM
SALES (corp-wide): 2.8B **Privately Held**
WEB: www.fairfieldmfg.com
SIC: 3462 3714 5085 Gear & chain forgings; gears, motor vehicle; gears
PA: Oc Oerlikon Corporation Ag, Pfaffikon
Churerstrasse 120
PfAffikon SZ
583 609-696

(G-8897)
FEDEX OFFICE & PRINT SVCS INC
3520 South St (47905-4724)
PHONE..................................765 449-4950
Eric Ingram, *Manager*
EMP: 10
SALES (corp-wide): 65.4B **Publicly Held**
WEB: www.kinkos.com
SIC: 7334 2796 2791 2789 Photocopying & duplicating services; platemaking services; typesetting; bookbinding & related work; commercial printing, lithographic
HQ: Fedex Office And Print Services, Inc.
7900 Legacy Dr
Plano TX 75024
214 550-7000

(G-8898)
FENWICK PHARMA LLC
8812 Fenwick Ct (47905-7929)
PHONE..................................765 296-7443
Daniel T Smith, *Principal*
EMP: 2
SALES (est): 140.3K **Privately Held**
SIC: 2834 Pharmaceutical preparations

(G-8899)
FLAT ELECTRONICS LLC
4315 Commerce Dr 440-101 (47905-3822)
PHONE..................................765 414-6635
Shameer Hassan,
EMP: 2
SALES (est): 48.6K **Privately Held**
SIC: 7371 3629 5065 Computer software development & applications; battery chargers, rectifying or nonrotating; mobile telephone equipment

(G-8900)
FRECKLES GRAPHICS INC
3835 Fortune Dr (47905-4879)
PHONE..................................765 448-4692
Fax: 765 448-4692
Gerry Rogers, *President*
EMP: 15
SQ FT: 20,000
SALES (est): 1.3MM **Privately Held**
WEB: www.frecklesgraphics.com
SIC: 7389 7336 2759 2395 Sewing contractor; commercial art & graphic design; screen printing; embroidery products, except schiffli machine

(G-8901)
FRITO-LAY NORTH AMERICA INC
3435 S 460 E (47905-7727)
PHONE..................................765 471-1833
Kris Kilkipkil, *Manager*
EMP: 166
SALES (corp-wide): 63.5B **Publicly Held**
SIC: 2096 Potato chips & similar snacks
HQ: Frito-Lay North America, Inc.
7701 Legacy Dr
Plano TX 75024

(G-8902)
GANNETT CO INC
Also Called: Journal and Courier
823 Park East Blvd Ste C (47905-0811)
PHONE..................................765 423-5512
Fax: 765 420-5246
Gary M Suisman, *Publisher*
Travis Komidar, *Opers Staff*
Rod Lowe, *Production*
Nancy J Trafton, *Director*
EMP: 217
SALES (corp-wide): 3.1B **Publicly Held**
WEB: www.gannett.com
SIC: 2711 2752 Newspapers: publishing only, not printed on site; commercial printing, lithographic

PA: Gannett Co., Inc.
7950 Jones Branch Dr
Mc Lean VA 22102
703 854-6000

(G-8903)
GANNETT CO INC
Journal and Courier
1501 Veterans Mem Pkwy E (47905-8917)
PHONE..................................765 423-5511
Tim Braybrooks, *Manager*
EMP: 8
SALES (est): 561.1K
SALES (corp-wide): 3.1B **Publicly Held**
SIC: 2711 7375 Newspapers, publishing & printing; information retrieval services
PA: Gannett Co., Inc.
7950 Jones Branch Dr
Mc Lean VA 22102
703 854-6000

(G-8904)
GARDINER RENTALS BILL
510 Veterans Mem Pkwy E (47905-8790)
PHONE..................................765 447-5111
Bill Gardiner, *Principal*
EMP: 4
SALES (est): 270.1K **Privately Held**
SIC: 3799 Recreational vehicles

(G-8905)
GARY RATCLIFF
Also Called: Ratcliff Enterprises
9950 Us Highway 231 S (47909-9050)
PHONE..................................765 538-3170
Gary Ratcliff, *Owner*
EMP: 2 EST: 1986
SALES (est): 163K **Privately Held**
SIC: 3441 Fabricated structural metal

(G-8906)
GEO SPECIALTY CHEMICALS INC (PA)
401 S Earl Ave Ste 3 (47904-3606)
P.O. Box 4747 (47903-4747)
PHONE..................................765 448-9412
Kenneth A Ghazey, *CEO*
Shawn Cannon, *Plant Mgr*
Shelly McConnaughey, *Finance*
Jorge Tena, *Mktg Dir*
Caren Shedd, *Compensation Mg*
▲ EMP: 9
SALES (est): 151.1MM **Privately Held**
WEB: www.geosc.com
SIC: 2819 Industrial inorganic chemicals

(G-8907)
GIBBS SUSIE FRAMING & ART
514 Main St (47901-1445)
PHONE..................................765 428-2434
Susie Gibbs, *Owner*
EMP: 2
SALES: 95K **Privately Held**
SIC: 2499 8999 5999 Picture frame molding, finished; artist; art dealers

(G-8908)
GOLDDEN CORPORATION (PA)
Also Called: Crowd Factor
3601 Sagamore Pkwy N E (47904-5041)
PHONE..................................765 423-4366
Fax: 765 423-2936
Gary E Edmondson, *President*
EMP: 11 EST: 1980
SQ FT: 12,000
SALES (est): 10.1MM **Privately Held**
WEB: www.purduegear.com
SIC: 5947 5699 2759 Souvenirs; sports apparel; screen printing

(G-8909)
GOLDEN LION INC
Also Called: Golden Lion Jewelers
3416 State Road 38 E (47905-5120)
PHONE..................................765 446-9557
Fax: 765 446-8797
Millie Nelson, *Principal*
Paul Nelson, *Principal*
EMP: 2
SALES (est): 156.8K **Privately Held**
SIC: 3911 5944 7631 5932 Jewelry, precious metal; jewelry stores; jewelry repair services; pawnshop

(G-8910)
GRATEFUL HEART ENTERPRISES LLC
Also Called: Grateful Heart Gallery & Gifts
5082 Glacier Way (47909-9189)
PHONE......................................765 838-2266
Diane L Gee, *Principal*
EMP: 9
SQ FT: 2,400
SALES (est): 725.4K **Privately Held**
SIC: 3269 Art & ornamental ware, pottery

(G-8911)
HARRISON MACDONALD & SONS
Also Called: Macdonald Classified Service
302 Ferry St Ste 300 (47901-1186)
PHONE......................................765 742-9012
Fax: 765 742-2843
Patrick Macdonald, *President*
Justin Rice, *Partner*
Nichole Kocher, *Graphic Designe*
EMP: 11 EST: 1927
SALES (est): 1.8MM **Privately Held**
WEB: www.macdonaldadvertisingservices.com
SIC: 7311 2741 Advertising agencies; advertising consultant; miscellaneous publishing

(G-8912)
HAYWOOD PRINTING CO INC
300 N 5th St (47901-1117)
PHONE......................................765 742-4085
Fax: 765 742-6647
Donald Benham, *President*
Dona Benham, *Vice Pres*
Jeff Benham, *Vice Pres*
Scott Benham, *Vice Pres*
Warren Benham, *Vice Pres*
EMP: 25
SQ FT: 48,700
SALES (est): 3.5MM **Privately Held**
SIC: 2759 2752 Letterpress printing; commercial printing, offset

(G-8913)
HEMOCLEANSE INC (PA)
3601 Sagamore Pkwy N B (47904-5033)
PHONE......................................765 742-4813
Robert B Truitt, *President*
Stephen R Ash MD, *Chairman*
EMP: 13
SQ FT: 10,000
SALES (est): 1.7MM **Privately Held**
WEB: www.hemocleanse.com
SIC: 3841 Surgical & medical instruments

(G-8914)
HI-TECH CONCRETE INC
3691 S 500 E (47905-0510)
PHONE......................................765 477-5550
Tom Berhammer, *President*
Ned Derhammer, *Vice Pres*
EMP: 8
SALES (est): 637.1K **Privately Held**
SIC: 3272 Concrete products

(G-8915)
HIGHWAY SAFETY SERVICES INC
3215 Imperial Pkwy (47909-5103)
PHONE......................................765 474-1000
Michael Madrid, *President*
Douglas Nagel, *Opers Staff*
EMP: 2
SALES (est): 423.1K **Privately Held**
SIC: 3669 7389 Pedestrian traffic control equipment; flagging service (traffic control)

(G-8916)
HOLDER BEDDING INC (PA)
Also Called: HB
230 Farabee Dr N (47905-5912)
PHONE......................................765 447-7907
Fax: 765 447-7907
Daphine Holder, *President*
Allen Holder, *Vice Pres*
Gary Holder, *Vice Pres*
Scott Holder, *Vice Pres*
Carol Holder, *Treasurer*
EMP: 4
SQ FT: 6,200

SALES (est): 889.7K **Privately Held**
SIC: 5712 2515 Mattresses; mattresses & foundations; furniture springs

(G-8917)
HOMER BANES
Also Called: Banes Machine Shop
520 S Earl Ave (47904-3262)
PHONE......................................765 449-8551
Homer Banes, *Owner*
EMP: 2
SALES (est): 229.2K **Privately Held**
SIC: 3569 General industrial machinery

(G-8918)
HOWE HOUSE LTD EDITIONS INC (PA)
624 South St (47901-1469)
PHONE......................................765 742-6831
William H Baugh, *President*
Rick Spies, *Vice Pres*
EMP: 4
SALES: 90K **Privately Held**
WEB: www.howehouse.com
SIC: 5199 2656 Gifts & novelties; Christmas novelties; paper cups, plates, dishes & utensils

(G-8919)
ICE CREAM SPECIALTIES INC
Also Called: North Star Distributing
2600 Concord Rd (47905-2773)
P.O. Box 679 (47902-0679)
PHONE......................................765 474-2989
Fax: 765 474-6150
Robert Burkey, *Ltd Ptnr*
EMP: 100
SALES (corp-wide): 1.8B **Privately Held**
SIC: 2024 Ice cream & frozen desserts
HQ: Ice Cream Specialties, Inc.
　　8419 Hanley Industrial Ct
　　Saint Louis MO 63144
　　314 962-2550

(G-8920)
IMPRESSIONS LLC
3007 1/2 Kossuth St (47904-3252)
PHONE......................................765 490-2575
Lorna D Smith,
EMP: 2
SALES (est): 177.1K **Privately Held**
SIC: 2752 Commercial printing, lithographic

(G-8921)
INDIANA LOGGING COMPANY CORP
8228 S 350 E (47909-9125)
PHONE......................................765 523-2616
Joshua Stinson, *Owner*
EMP: 3
SALES (est): 196.4K **Privately Held**
SIC: 2411 Logging

(G-8922)
INDIANA STEEL FABRICATING INC
925 S 1st St (47905-1034)
P.O. Box 748 (47902-0748)
PHONE......................................765 742-1031
Fax: 765 742-2632
Stephen Porter, *President*
EMP: 11
SALES (corp-wide): 18.4MM **Privately Held**
WEB: www.indianasteelfab.com
SIC: 3312 3441 Structural shapes & pilings, steel; fabricated structural metal
PA: Indiana Steel Fabricating Inc
　　4545 W Bradbury Ave
　　Indianapolis IN 46241
　　317 247-4545

(G-8923)
INDIANAPOLIS SCALE COMPANY
3619 N 500 E (47905-7866)
PHONE......................................317 856-6606
Richard T Robley, *President*
EMP: 3
SALES (corp-wide): 3.2MM **Privately Held**
SIC: 3596 Industrial scales

PA: Indianapolis Scale Company Inc
　　10262 Leases Corner Ct
　　Camby IN 46113
　　317 856-6606

(G-8924)
INDUSTRIAL PLATING INC
120 N 36th St (47905-4786)
PHONE......................................765 447-5036
Fax: 765 447-7023
William Uerkwitz, *Ch of Bd*
Darrell Uerkwitz, *President*
Charles Williams, *Vice Pres*
EMP: 57 EST: 1955
SQ FT: 50,000
SALES (est): 6.3MM **Privately Held**
SIC: 3471 Plating of metals or formed products

(G-8925)
INSPIRED FIRE GLASS STUDIO & G
2124 State Road 25 W (47909-9229)
PHONE......................................765 474-1981
Sharon Owens, *Owner*
EMP: 2
SALES (est): 123.2K **Privately Held**
SIC: 3229 Glassware, art or decorative

(G-8926)
IRVING MATERIALS INC
Also Called: I M I
2903 Old State Road 25 N (47905-7891)
P.O. Box 2220, West Lafayette (47996-2220)
PHONE......................................765 423-2533
Fax: 765 423-1775
Ron Knowles, *Branch Mgr*
EMP: 40
SALES (corp-wide): 800.6MM **Privately Held**
SIC: 3273 Ready-mixed concrete
PA: Irving Materials, Inc.
　　8032 N State Road 9
　　Greenfield IN 46140
　　317 326-3101

(G-8927)
J ROBERT SWITZER
1020 Beck Ln (47909-3067)
PHONE......................................765 474-1307
Robert Switzer, *Owner*
Sandra K Awitzer, *Principal*
EMP: 2
SALES (est): 110K **Privately Held**
SIC: 2411 Logging

(G-8928)
JACOBS MFG LLC
218 Trowbridge Dr (47909-6925)
PHONE......................................765 490-6111
EMP: 2
SALES (est): 108.6K **Privately Held**
SIC: 3999 Manufacturing industries

(G-8929)
JAMES A ANDREW INC
Also Called: Home Works
665 Maple Point Dr (47904)
PHONE......................................765 269-9807
Fax: 765 448-6414
James Andrew, *Branch Mgr*
EMP: 9
SALES (corp-wide): 17.5MM **Privately Held**
WEB: www.henrypoor.com
SIC: 2426 Flooring, hardwood
PA: James A Andrew Inc
　　3315 Brady Ln
　　Lafayette IN 47909
　　765 474-1388

(G-8930)
JAVA ROASTER
130 N 3rd St (47901-1225)
PHONE......................................765 742-2037
Pete Walker, *Owner*
EMP: 9
SALES (est): 260K **Privately Held**
SIC: 5812 2095 Coffee shop; coffee roasting (except by wholesale grocers)

(G-8931)
JESSUP PAPER BOX LLC
4775 Dale Dr (47905-7709)
PHONE......................................765 588-9137

John D Huber Jr, *President*
EMP: 25
SALES (est): 764.1K **Privately Held**
SIC: 2652 Setup paperboard boxes

(G-8932)
JG AND JG INDUSTRIES LLC
1609 Hart St (47904-1410)
PHONE......................................765 742-0260
EMP: 2 EST: 2010
SALES (est): 73K **Privately Held**
SIC: 3999 Mfg Misc Products

(G-8933)
JOHN WALLACE BUILDER INC
301 S 675 E (47905-8729)
PHONE......................................765 447-3614
John Wallace, *Owner*
Carolyn Wallace, *Co-Owner*
EMP: 3
SALES: 500K **Privately Held**
SIC: 2679 Building, insulating & packaging paper

(G-8934)
JT-FENCING LLC
4027 Amethyst Dr (47909-8084)
PHONE......................................765 323-8591
Johnny Trombley,
EMP: 2
SALES: 100K **Privately Held**
SIC: 2499 Fencing, docks & other outdoor wood structural products

(G-8935)
K-MOTION RACING ENGINES
2381 N 24th St (47904-1244)
PHONE......................................765 742-8494
Fax: 765 742-1363
Robert H Kamp, *Owner*
EMP: 8 EST: 1970
SQ FT: 12,000
SALES (est): 710K **Privately Held**
SIC: 5531 5013 3599 Speed shops, including race car supplies; motor vehicle supplies & new parts; machine shop, jobbing & repair

(G-8936)
KALEIDOSCOPE INC
1214 North St (47904-2561)
PHONE......................................765 423-1951
Fax: 765 423-1951
Susan Delong, *President*
Susan De Long, *President*
EMP: 4
SQ FT: 1,600
SALES (est): 200K **Privately Held**
SIC: 3231 1793 Stained glass: made from purchased glass; glass & glazing work

(G-8937)
KARMA INDUSTRIES INC
525 Wabash Ave (47905-1048)
PHONE......................................765 742-9200
Adriana Corbin, *Principal*
EMP: 2
SALES (est): 94K **Privately Held**
SIC: 3999 Manufacturing industries

(G-8938)
KEN TEX CRUDE PRODUCERS INC
2401 Mondavi Blvd (47909-8444)
P.O. Box 230, Paoli (47454-0230)
PHONE......................................812 723-2108
William Reynolds, *President*
EMP: 2
SALES (est): 91.6K **Privately Held**
SIC: 1389 Oil & gas field services

(G-8939)
KINKOS INC
3520 South St (47905-4724)
PHONE......................................765 449-4950
Fax: 765 447-5443
Sylvia Zerbes, *Manager*
Eric Ingram, *Manager*
EMP: 2 EST: 2010
SALES (est): 197.7K **Privately Held**
SIC: 2752 Commercial printing, lithographic

(G-8940)
KIRBY RISK CORPORATION (PA)
Also Called: Kirby Risk Electrical Supply
1815 Sagamore Pkwy N (47904-1765)
P.O. Box 5089 (47903-5089)
PHONE.................................765 448-4567
Fax: 765 448-1342
James K Risk III, *President*
Jason Bricker, *Vice Pres*
Doug Gutridge, *Vice Pres*
Stephanie Laorange, *Vice Pres*
John Mack, *Plant Mgr*
▲ **EMP:** 100
SQ FT: 55,000
SALES (est): 401.3MM **Privately Held**
WEB: www.kirbyrisk.com
SIC: 5063 7694 3599 3679 Electrical supplies; electric motor repair; machine shop, jobbing & repair; harness assemblies for electronic use: wire or cable; capacitors, fixed or variable

(G-8941)
KIRBY RISK CORPORATION
Also Called: Kirby Risk Electric Motor Repr
714 S 1st St (47905-1009)
PHONE.................................765 423-4205
Marty Guy, *Manager*
EMP: 31
SALES (corp-wide): 401.3MM **Privately Held**
WEB: www.kirbyrisk.com
SIC: 5063 7694 Electrical supplies; electric motor repair
PA: Kirby Risk Corporation
1815 Sagamore Pkwy N
Lafayette IN 47904
765 448-4567

(G-8942)
KIRBY RISK CORPORATION
Also Called: Kirby Risk Servicenter
3574 Mccarty Ln (47905-4895)
P.O. Box 5089 (47903-5089)
PHONE.................................765 447-1402
Fax: 765 449-7557
Robert White, *Engineer*
Kurt Jenkins, *Manager*
Todd Jackson, *Info Tech Mgr*
EMP: 300
SALES (corp-wide): 401.3MM **Privately Held**
WEB: www.kirbyrisk.com
SIC: 5063 3825 3714 3694 Electrical supplies; instruments to measure electricity; motor vehicle parts & accessories; engine electrical equipment; electronic connectors; current-carrying wiring devices
PA: Kirby Risk Corporation
1815 Sagamore Pkwy N
Lafayette IN 47904
765 448-4567

(G-8943)
KIRBY RISK CORPORATION
Also Called: Kirby Risk Precision Machining
1700 Schuyler Ave (47904-1120)
P.O. Box 5387 (47903-5387)
PHONE.................................765 742-2254
Jim Smith, *Manager*
Loren Randall, *Director*
EMP: 92
SALES (corp-wide): 401.3MM **Privately Held**
WEB: www.kirbyrisk.com
SIC: 3599 Machine shop, jobbing & repair
PA: Kirby Risk Corporation
1815 Sagamore Pkwy N
Lafayette IN 47904
765 448-4567

(G-8944)
KLS SANTAS
4406 Chisholm Trl (47909-3612)
PHONE.................................765 474-6951
Kevin D Sweeney, *Owner*
EMP: 2
SALES (est): 92.6K **Privately Held**
SIC: 3942 Dolls & doll clothing

(G-8945)
KNOY APPAREL
1164 S Creasy Ln (47905-4959)
PHONE.................................765 448-1031
Brad Knoy, *President*

EMP: 3
SALES (est): 235.6K **Privately Held**
SIC: 2759 5941 Screen printing; sporting goods & bicycle shops

(G-8946)
KROMET AMERICA INC
2700 Concord Rd (47909-2775)
PHONE.................................812 346-5117
Tom Mantini, *President*
EMP: 40
SQ FT: 47,800
SALES (est): 3MM
SALES (corp-wide): 33.4MM **Privately Held**
WEB: www.kromet.com
SIC: 3471 Electroplating of metals or formed products
PA: Kromet International Inc
200 Sheldon Dr
Cambridge ON N1R 7
519 623-2511

(G-8947)
LAFAYETTE DENTAL LABORATORY
5628 Roseberry Rdg (47905-8508)
PHONE.................................765 447-9341
Fax: 765 447-9341
Randall Jackson, *President*
Randy W Jackson, *Corp Secy*
Rick Jackson, *Exec VP*
Joe Rock, *Vice Pres*
EMP: 22
SQ FT: 9,000
SALES (est): 2MM **Privately Held**
SIC: 8072 3843 3842 Crown & bridge production; dental equipment & supplies; surgical appliances & supplies

(G-8948)
LAFAYETTE INSTRUMENT CO INC (PA)
Also Called: LI
3700 Sagamore Pkwy N (47904-1066)
P.O. Box 5729 (47903-5729)
PHONE.................................765 423-1505
Fax: 765 423-4111
Jennifer D Rider, *President*
Terry Echard, *Vice Pres*
Steve Rider, *Vice Pres*
Brent Smitley, *Engineer*
Troy Walters, *Engineer*
▲ **EMP:** 47
SQ FT: 43,000
SALES (est): 8.9MM **Privately Held**
WEB: www.licmef.com
SIC: 3829 Measuring & controlling devices; polygraph devices

(G-8949)
LAFAYETTE PUZZLE FACTORY LLC
4315 Commerce Dr (47905-3822)
PHONE.................................800 883-6408
John Paul Clauson, *President*
EMP: 6
SALES (est): 308.6K **Privately Held**
SIC: 3944 Puzzles
PA: Larose Industries Llc
1578 Sussex Tpke
Randolph NJ 07869

(G-8950)
LAFAYETTE QUALITY PRODUCTS INC
111 Farabee Dr S (47905-4704)
P.O. Box 5827 (47903-5827)
PHONE.................................765 446-0890
Fax: 765 448-6788
Gordon D Wimberly, *Ch of Bd*
Roland Kuntz, *President*
Bunch Dienna, *Manager*
EMP: 17
SQ FT: 41,600
SALES: 3MM **Privately Held**
SIC: 3599 Machine shop, jobbing & repair

(G-8951)
LAFAYETTE TENT & AWNING CO
125 S 5th St (47901-1618)
PHONE.................................765 742-4277
Fax: 765 742-4462
Scott Ebershoff, *President*
Henry Ebershoff, *President*

Craig Ebershoff, *Vice Pres*
Daniel Meyer, *Manager*
Richard Ebershoff, *Admin Sec*
EMP: 25 **EST:** 1913
SQ FT: 65,000
SALES: 4.5MM **Privately Held**
WEB: www.lafayettetent.com
SIC: 2394 5999 Awnings, fabric: made from purchased materials; tents: made from purchased materials; tents

(G-8952)
LAFAYETTE WIRE PRODUCTS INC
2700 Concord Rd (47909-2775)
P.O. Box 4552 (47903-4552)
PHONE.................................765 474-7896
Fax: 765 474-7114
John S Castell, *Ch of Bd*
Sam Newton, *President*
Patricia C Castell, *Admin Sec*
▲ **EMP:** 65
SQ FT: 100,000
SALES (est): 12.5MM **Privately Held**
WEB: www.lafayettewire.com
SIC: 3496 3537 Shelving, made from purchased wire; industrial trucks & tractors

(G-8953)
LANDIS GYR UTILITIES SVCS INC
2800 Duncan Rd (47904-5012)
PHONE.................................765 742-1001
John Grad, *President*
Saieb Alrawi, *Engineer*
Kristy Murray, *Human Resources*
EMP: 22
SALES (est): 3.7MM **Privately Held**
SIC: 3613 Metering panels, electric

(G-8954)
LANDIS+GYR INC
2800 Duncan Rd (47904-5012)
PHONE.................................765 742-1001
Fax: 765 742-0936
Rebecca Lorentz, *Opers Staff*
Justin Hall, *Design Engr*
Gretchen Evans, *Accounting Mgr*
Jeana Stone, *Accounting Mgr*
Paul Berger, *Finance*
EMP: 21
SALES (corp-wide): 48.4B **Privately Held**
SIC: 3825 Meters: electric, pocket, portable, panelboard, etc.; measuring instruments & meters, electric; demand meters, electric
HQ: Landis+Gyr Inc.
30000 Mill Creek Ave # 100
Alpharetta GA 30022
678 258-1500

(G-8955)
LANSING BUILDING PRODUCTS INC
1425 Industrial Dr (47905-4871)
PHONE.................................765 448-4363
Tom Richardson, *Principal*
EMP: 8
SALES (corp-wide): 396.9MM **Privately Held**
SIC: 3442 5031 5211 5251 Screens, window, metal; windows; siding; hardware
PA: Lansing Building Products, Inc.
2221 Edward Holland Dr
Richmond VA 23230
804 266-8893

(G-8956)
LAS PERLAS TAPATIAS INC
Also Called: Las Perlas Tapatias Mexican RE
11 N Earl Ave (47904-2812)
PHONE.................................765 447-0601
Pablo Alvarez, *President*
Joel Herrera, *Vice Pres*
EMP: 5
SALES (est): 150.8K **Privately Held**
SIC: 5812 2052 Mexican restaurant; bakery products, dry

(G-8957)
LIGHT HOUSE HOMES CENTER (PA)
3918 Harry Ave (47905-5285)
PHONE.................................765 448-4502
Fax: 765 448-4245

James Tarvin, *President*
Harry Van Der Noord, *Shareholder*
Tom Santefort, *Shareholder*
EMP: 15 **EST:** 1983
SQ FT: 2,400
SALES (est): 2.3MM **Privately Held**
SIC: 5271 5211 3241 2452 Mobile homes; modular homes; cement, hydraulic; prefabricated wood buildings

(G-8958)
LIMELIGHT PUBLISHING
1600 Main St (47904-2919)
PHONE.................................765 448-4461
John Hiem, *Owner*
EMP: 2
SALES (est): 73.1K **Privately Held**
SIC: 2721 Periodicals

(G-8959)
LIQUIDSPRING LLC
4899 E 400 S (47905-9371)
PHONE.................................765 474-7816
Gary Ford, *Vice Pres*
Peter Schmid, *Engineer*
Wayne Wells, *Sales Staff*
Carl Harr, *Marketing Staff*
Dean Bartolone,
EMP: 6
SQ FT: 2,000
SALES (est): 1.7MM **Privately Held**
SIC: 3446 Acoustical suspension systems, metal

(G-8960)
LOU MARY DONUTS INC
Also Called: Mary Lou Donuts
1830 S 4th St (47905-2134)
PHONE.................................765 474-9131
Jeff Walden, *Principal*
EMP: 10
SQ FT: 3,000
SALES (est): 812.8K **Privately Held**
SIC: 2051 Bakery: wholesale or wholesale/retail combined

(G-8961)
LPF LIMITED
4315 Commerce Dr (47905-3822)
PHONE.................................765 447-0939
JP Clauson, *Principal*
Cora Fung, *Creative Dir*
EMP: 7
SALES (est): 585.3K **Privately Held**
SIC: 3944 Puzzles

(G-8962)
LUDO FACT USA LLC
4775 Dale Dr (47905-7709)
PHONE.................................765 588-9137
Horst Walz,
Fabian Walz,
EMP: 53
SALES: 1MM **Privately Held**
SIC: 3944 Board games, children's & adults'
HQ: Ludo Fact Usa Inc.
1000 Essington Rd
Joliet IL

(G-8963)
LUND INTERNATIONAL HOLDING CO
Also Called: Roadworks Manufacturing
3565 E 300 N (47905-8819)
PHONE.................................765 742-7200
Fax: 765 742-7270
EMP: 20 **Privately Held**
SIC: 3647 3713 Headlights (fixtures), vehicular; truck & bus bodies
PA: Lund International Holding Company
4325 Hamilton Mill Rd
Buford GA 30518

(G-8964)
MCKINNEY CORPORATION
4710 Fastline Dr (47905-7914)
PHONE.................................765 448-4800
Fax: 765 448-4885
Lawrence McKinney, *President*
EMP: 27
SALES (est): 5.9MM **Privately Held**
SIC: 3354 Aluminum extruded products; aluminum rod & bar; aluminum pipe & tube

GEOGRAPHIC

(G-8965)
MEDTRIC LLC
3000 Kent Ave Ste D1-104 (47906-1075)
PHONE...765 586-8228
Sean Connell, *President*
Robert Einterz, *Mktg Dir*
Jianming LI, *Info Tech Mgr*
EMP: 3
SQ FT: 600
SALES (est): 267K **Privately Held**
SIC: 2833 Medicinals & botanicals

(G-8966)
MENTAL REHABILITATION
1322 Fairfax Dr (47909-7312)
P.O. Box 4456 (47903-4456)
PHONE...765 414-5590
Russell W Burry, *President*
EMP: 6
SALES (est): 245.1K **Privately Held**
SIC: 7372 Prepackaged software

(G-8967)
MEYER PLASTICS INC
Sagamore Div
100 Creasy Ct (47905-6529)
PHONE...765 447-2195
Fax: 765 449-4109
Bryan Young, *Manager*
EMP: 7
SALES (corp-wide): 24.8MM **Privately
Held**
WEB: www.meyerplastics.com
SIC: 5162 3089 Plastics materials & basic
shapes; plastic processing
PA: Meyer Plastics Inc
5167 E 65th St
Indianapolis IN 46220
317 259-4131

(G-8968)
MID AMERICA PRINT COUNCIL
2217 Miami Trl (47906-1923)
PHONE...765 463-3971
Michal Hathaway, *Principal*
EMP: 2
SALES (est): 115.2K **Privately Held**
SIC: 2752 Commercial printing, litho-
graphic

(G-8969)
MIDWEST COIL LLC
2304 Brothers Dr Ste A (47909-2292)
PHONE...765 807-5429
Michael E Corcoran, *Mng Member*
Marvin K White,
▲ EMP: 13
SALES (est): 2.5MM **Privately Held**
SIC: 3677 Electronic coils, transformers &
other inductors

(G-8970)
MILESTONE CONTRACTORS LP
3301 S 460 E (47905-7727)
PHONE...765 772-7500
Fax: 765 772-7541
Justin Patterson, *Project Mgr*
Ryan Whitaker, *Project Mgr*
Jim Gross, *Manager*
EMP: 200
SALES (corp-wide): 186MM **Privately
Held**
WEB: www.milestonelp.com
SIC: 1611 2951 Highway & street paving
contractor; asphalt paving mixtures &
blocks
PA: Milestone Contractors, Lp
5950 S Belmont Ave
Indianapolis IN 46217
317 788-6885

(G-8971)
MITCHELL FABRICS INC
3532 Coleman Ct Ste B (47905-4455)
PHONE...309 674-8631
Mitchell Favus, *President*
EMP: 30 EST: 1945
SALES (est): 16.4MM **Privately Held**
WEB: www.mitchellfabrics.com
SIC: 5131 2591 Drapery material, woven;
blinds vertical

(G-8972)
MODERN BIOLOGY INCORPORATED
2211 South St (47904-2968)
PHONE...765 523-3338
Fax: 765 743-7612
Martha J Anderson, *President*
EMP: 4
SALES (est): 443K **Privately Held**
WEB: www.modernbio.com
SIC: 3999 Education aids, devices & sup-
plies

(G-8973)
MTA TECHNOLOGY LLC
2624 Salem St (47904-2726)
PHONE...765 447-2221
Maung Than, *Mng Member*
EMP: 10 EST: 2016 **Privately Held**
SIC: 3089 7389 Corrugated panels, plas-
tic;

(G-8974)
NANSHN AMRC ADV ALUM TECH LLC
3600 Us Highway 52 S (47905-7706)
PHONE...765 838-8645
John Linson, *President*
Jeff Stringer, *General Mgr*
Brandy Balser, *Purchasing*
Mike Bond, *Manager*
Scott Evans, *Manager*
▲ EMP: 230
SQ FT: 600,000
SALES: 110MM
SALES (corp-wide): 2.5B **Privately Held**
SIC: 3334 3341 Primary aluminum; alu-
minum smelting & refining (secondary)
PA: Shandong Nanshan Aluminium Co.,Ltd.
Nanshan Village, Dongjiang Town
Longkou 26570
535 866-6352

(G-8975)
NEON CACTUS
360 Brown St (47901)
PHONE...765 743-6081
Fax: 765 743-6639
Jim Cochran, *Owner*
EMP: 2
SALES (est): 156.3K **Privately Held**
SIC: 3993 Neon signs

(G-8976)
NEW CONCEPT METAL DETECTOR
511 N Earl Ave (47904-2818)
PHONE...765 447-2681
Iris Perez, *Owner*
EMP: 7
SALES (est): 1.2MM **Privately Held**
SIC: 3669 Metal detectors

(G-8977)
OLIVE BRANCH ETC INC
Also Called: Sign Art Etc
181 Sagamore Pkwy S (47905-4744)
PHONE...765 449-1884
Doug Ellenberger, *Owner*
Randy Tessier, *Production*
Jeff Ward, *CIO*
Derick Marshall, *Graphic Designe*
Max Robertson, *Graphic Designe*
▲ EMP: 9
SQ FT: 8,000
SALES (est): 475K **Privately Held**
WEB: www.signartetc.com
SIC: 3993 Signs, not made in custom sign
painting shops

(G-8978)
PAYNES FINE CABRINETRY
7705 E 300 N (47905-9624)
PHONE...765 589-9176
Charles Payne, *Owner*
EMP: 3
SALES (est): 183.5K **Privately Held**
SIC: 2434 Wood kitchen cabinets

(G-8979)
PEERLESS PATTERN & MACHINE CO
3521 Coleman Ct (47905-4484)
PHONE...765 477-7719
Fax: 765 474-9395
Nathan D Scaggs, *President*
Joyce Scaggs, *Treasurer*
EMP: 9
SQ FT: 10,000
SALES (est): 2MM **Privately Held**
SIC: 7692 3599 3543 Welding repair; ma-
chine & other job shop work; industrial
patterns

(G-8980)
PERRY FOAM PRODUCTS INC (PA)
Also Called: Diskit Sales Division
2335 S 30th St (47909-2702)
P.O. Box 6419 (47903-6419)
PHONE...765 474-3404
Richard Landrum, *President*
Scott Kempin, *President*
David P Holder, *Treasurer*
▲ EMP: 35 EST: 1960
SQ FT: 40,000
SALES (est): 7.2MM **Privately Held**
WEB: www.perrychemical.com
SIC: 3086 Plastics foam products

(G-8981)
PPG ARCHITECTURAL FINISHES INC
Also Called: Glidden Professional Paint Ctr
15 N Earl Ave (47904-2812)
PHONE...765 447-9334
Fax: 765 447-7465
Tim Johnston, *Sales/Mktg Mgr*
EMP: 5
SALES (corp-wide): 14.2B **Publicly Held**
WEB: www.gliddenpaint.com
SIC: 2891 Adhesives
HQ: Ppg Architectural Finishes, Inc.
1 Ppg Pl
Pittsburgh PA 15272
412 434-3131

(G-8982)
PRAXAIR INC
2655 Teal Rd Ste E (47905-2254)
PHONE...765 447-8171
Missy Willhite, *Manager*
EMP: 2
SALES (corp-wide): 11.4B **Publicly Held**
SIC: 2813 Industrial gases
PA: Praxair, Inc.
10 Riverview Dr
Danbury CT 06810
203 837-2000

(G-8983)
PRINT WORKS OF LAFAYETTE INC
3217 Olympia Dr (47909-5167)
P.O. Box 94, Stockwell (47983-0094)
PHONE...765 446-9735
Fax: 765 446-2346
Stan Mitchell, *President*
EMP: 7
SALES: 300K **Privately Held**
WEB: www.printworks.lafayette.in.us
SIC: 2752 Commercial printing, litho-
graphic

(G-8984)
PURDY CONCRETE INC (PA)
3633 Old Us Highway 231 S (47909-2422)
PHONE...765 477-7687
Fax: 765 474-8993
Carol A Purdy, *President*
Edward Purdy, *Corp Secy*
EMP: 45
SALES (est): 6.6MM **Privately Held**
WEB: www.purdyconcrete.com
SIC: 3273 Ready-mixed concrete

(G-8985)
PURDY MATERIALS INC
3633 Old Us Highway 231 S (47909-2422)
PHONE...765 474-8993
Edward Purdy, *President*
Carol Purdy, *Principal*
EMP: 13
SALES (est): 2.5MM **Privately Held**
WEB: www.purdymaterials.com
SIC: 3273 Ready-mixed concrete

(G-8986)
PYRAMID SIGN & DESIGN INC
515 Farabee Dr S (47905-4712)
PHONE...765 447-4174
Fax: 765 447-4174
Rex Deaton, *President*
Brian Roark, *Corp Secy*
Robert Vandergraff II, *Vice Pres*
EMP: 4
SQ FT: 3,600
SALES: 350K **Privately Held**
SIC: 3993 7532 5999 Signs & advertising
specialties; lettering, automotive; decals

(G-8987)
R & A GOODMAN ENTERPRISES
1109 S 1025 E (47905-9425)
PHONE...765 296-3446
Randy Goodman, *President*
Daniel Goodman, *Corp Secy*
EMP: 3
SALES (est): 101.7K **Privately Held**
SIC: 7692 1751 7363 Welding repair; win-
dow & door installation & erection; truck
driver services

(G-8988)
RADIAN RESEARCH INC
3852 Fortune Dr (47905-4879)
PHONE...765 449-5500
Timothy C Everidge, *President*
Martin Rogers, *Vice Pres*
◆ EMP: 60
SQ FT: 22,000
SALES (est): 14.1MM **Privately Held**
WEB: www.radianresearch.com
SIC: 3825 8748 Power measuring equip-
ment, electrical; energy measuring equip-
ment, electrical; systems analysis or
design

(G-8989)
REA MAGNET WIRE COMPANY INC
2800 Concord Rd (47909-3399)
PHONE...765 477-8000
Fax: 765 477-8100
Eric Foster, *Opers Mgr*
Peter Von Stein, *Engineer*
Kyle Long, *Electrical Engi*
John Hake, *Branch Mgr*
Diane West, *Manager*
EMP: 290
SALES (corp-wide): 228.8MM **Privately
Held**
WEB: www.reawire.com
SIC: 3351 3643 3357 3355 Wire, copper
& copper alloy; current-carrying wiring de-
vices; nonferrous wiredrawing & insulat-
ing; aluminum rolling & drawing; steel
wire & related products
PA: Rea Magnet Wire Company, Inc.
3400 E Coliseum Blvd # 200
Fort Wayne IN 46805
260 421-7321

(G-8990)
REPROCOMM INC
Lafayette Printing
511 Ferry St (47901-1141)
PHONE...765 423-2578
Fax: 765 742-1242
David R Sattler, *Branch Mgr*
EMP: 15
SALES (est): 2MM
SALES (corp-wide): 15MM **Privately
Held**
SIC: 2752 2789 Commercial printing, off-
set; bookbinding & related work
PA: Reprocomm Inc
179 N Miami St
Peru IN 46970
765 472-5700

(G-8991)
RICK BLACK ASSOCIATES LLC
Also Called: Wildcat Creek Winery
3233 E 200 N (47905-8801)
PHONE...765 838-3498
Richard Black, *Mng Member*
EMP: 7
SALES (est): 690.7K **Privately Held**
SIC: 2084 Wines

▲ = Import ▼=Export
◆ =Import/Export

(G-8992)
RICO AROMA LLC
Also Called: Papa Murphy's
2324 Teal Rd (47905-2219)
P.O. Box 6324, Fishers (46038-6324)
PHONE..................................765 471-1700
Robert Arnold,
EMP: 9
SALES (est): 300K Privately Held
SIC: 5812 2041 Pizzeria, chain; pizza
mixes

(G-8993)
RIETH-RILEY CNSTR CO INC
Also Called: Area 340
3425 Ofarrell Rd Ste 1 (47905-3947)
PHONE..................................765 447-2324
Tom Buck, Branch Mgr
EMP: 75
SALES (corp-wide): 226.8MM Privately
Held
WEB: www.reithriley.com
SIC: 1771 2951 Blacktop (asphalt) work;
asphalt paving mixtures & blocks
PA: Rieth-Riley Construction Co., Inc.
3626 Elkhart Rd
Goshen IN 46526
574 875-5183

(G-8994)
S & S PROGRAMMING INC
3601 Sagamore Pkwy N F (47904-5033)
PHONE..................................765 423-4472
Keith Schuman, President
EMP: 6
SQ FT: 2,000
SALES (est): 624.9K Privately Held
WEB: www.sspro.com
SIC: 7372 5045 Business oriented com-
puter software; computers, peripherals &
software

(G-8995)
SCALAR DESIGN ENGRG & DIST
LLC
836 Shawnee Ave (47905-1456)
PHONE..................................765 429-5545
Joseph P Joyce,
Stephanie L Joyce,
EMP: 2
SALES: 100K Privately Held
SIC: 3824 8711 Mechanical & electro-
mechanical counters & devices; design-
ing: ship, boat, machine & product

(G-8996)
SCHUG AWARDS LLC
229 S 30th St (47909)
PHONE..................................765 447-0002
Sharon A Schug, Mng Member
EMP: 4
SALES (est): 217.6K Privately Held
SIC: 5999 2499 Trophies & plaques; tro-
phy bases, wood

(G-8997)
SCHUMAKER TECHNICAL
ASSEMBLY
681 N 36th St (47905-4475)
P.O. Box 439 (47902-0439)
PHONE..................................765 742-7176
Fax: 765 742-7176
Daniel A Schumaker, Owner
EMP: 8
SQ FT: 3,500
SALES: 1MM Privately Held
WEB: www.schumakertech.com
SIC: 3679 Electronic circuits; harness as-
semblies for electronic use: wire or cable

(G-8998)
SCOTTORSVILLE SALES AND
SVC
602 S Earl Ave (47904-3264)
PHONE..................................765 250-5245
EMP: 5 EST: 2012
SALES (est): 26.5K Privately Held
SIC: 3621 Motors, electric

(G-8999)
SMR MANAGEMENT INC
2139 Klondike Rd (47906-5124)
PHONE..................................765 252-0257
Tom Houck, Branch Mgr
EMP: 2

SALES (corp-wide): 675K Privately Held
SIC: 3714 Motor vehicle parts & accessories
PA: Smr Management Inc.
1728 Coral Way
Coral Gables FL 33145
305 529-2488

(G-9000)
SNYDER & CO INC
406 S Earl Ave (47904-3261)
PHONE..................................765 447-3452
Fax: 765 447-3452
EMP: 6
SQ FT: 5,000
SALES (est): 530K Privately Held
SIC: 1761 1711 3444 3443 Roofing/Sid-
ing Contr Plumbing/Heat/Ac Contr Mfg
Sheet Metalwork Mfg Fabricated Plate
Wrk Structural Metal Fabrctn

(G-9001)
SPOTLIGHT CYBERSECURITY
LLC
250 Main St Ste 590 (47901-1249)
PHONE..................................805 886-4456
Jacob Crisp, CEO
Robert Morton,
EMP: 2 Privately Held
SIC: 9711 7372 7371 National security;
business oriented computer software; ap-
plication computer software; custom com-
puter programming services

(G-9002)
STALL & KESSLER INC
Also Called: Stall Kessler's Diamond Center
333 Columbia St (47901-1315)
P.O. Box 938 (47902-0938)
PHONE..................................765 742-1259
Fax: 765 742-1393
Jeffery Kessler, President
EMP: 7
SQ FT: 2,000
SALES (est): 1MM Privately Held
WEB: www.stallandkessler.com
SIC: 5944 3911 7631 Watches; jewelry,
precious stones & precious metals; jew-
elry, precious metal; watch, clock & jew-
elry repair

(G-9003)
STEADY DEMAND LLC
3200 South St Ste 6 (47904-3184)
PHONE..................................765 404-1763
David Lindahl, General Mgr
EMP: 2
SALES (est): 120K Privately Held
SIC: 7372 Utility computer software

(G-9004)
STEINER ENTERPRISES INC
3532 Coleman Ct Ste B (47905-4455)
PHONE..................................765 429-6409
Fax: 765 807-3033
Ed Steiner, President
Thomas P Hicks, President
David Barrett, Opers Mgr
Matt Jewell, Sls & Mktg Exec
▲ EMP: 18
SQ FT: 4,500
SALES (est): 4.9MM Privately Held
WEB: www.steineronline.com
SIC: 3824 Mechanical & electromechanical
counters & devices

(G-9005)
SUGARCUBE SYSTEMS INC
2746 Margesson Xing (47909-8092)
PHONE..................................765 543-6709
Jason Clark, President
EMP: 2
SALES (est): 160.9K Privately Held
SIC: 3559 7389 Semiconductor manufac-
turing machinery;

(G-9006)
SURPLUS STORE AND
EXCHANGE
Also Called: Vierks Fine Jewelry
1650 Main St (47904-2919)
PHONE..................................765 447-0200
Dan Vierk, President
EMP: 12
SQ FT: 10,000

SALES (est): 3.2MM Privately Held
WEB: www.vierks.com
SIC: 5094 5944 3911 Jewelry; jewelry,
precious stones & precious metals; jewel
settings & mountings, precious metal

(G-9007)
TATE LYLE INGRDNTS AMRICAS
LLC
3300 Us Highway 52 S (47905-7701)
P.O. Box 7977 (47903-7977)
PHONE..................................765 474-5474
Daniel Kirk, Plant Mgr
Amy Hale, Engineer
Joe Sauer, Engineer
Chuck Jones, Controller
Keith Oliger, Branch Mgr
EMP: 262
SALES (corp-wide): 3.8B Privately Held
WEB: www.aestaley.com
SIC: 2046 2087 Wet corn milling; flavoring
extracts & syrups
HQ: Tate & Lyle Ingredients Americas Llc
2200 E Eldorado St
Decatur IL 62521
217 423-4411

(G-9008)
TATE LYLE INGRDNTS AMRICAS
LLC
Also Called: Pate & Lyle
2245 Sagamore Pkwy N (47904-1620)
P.O. Box 1398 (47902-1398)
PHONE..................................765 448-7123
Brandon Johnson, Opers Mgr
Kevin Niaburgge, Opers-Prdtn-Mfg
Cory Hanson, Engineer
Ronald Rechkemmer, Human Res Mgr
Gerrit Ladage, Director
EMP: 86
SALES (corp-wide): 3.8B Privately Held
WEB: www.aestaley.com
SIC: 2046 Wet corn milling
HQ: Tate & Lyle Ingredients Americas Llc
2200 E Eldorado St
Decatur IL 62521
217 423-4411

(G-9009)
TERRYS WELDING INC
707 Widewater Dr (47904-1060)
P.O. Box 6384 (47903-6384)
PHONE..................................765 742-4191
Fax: 765 742-4191
Greg Terry, Manager
EMP: 4
SALES (est): 216.2K Privately Held
SIC: 7692 Welding repair

(G-9010)
THIEME AND WAGNER
BREWING CO
1619 Stonevalley Ct (47909-7211)
PHONE..................................765 477-0667
Brian Thieme, Principal
EMP: 3
SALES (est): 75.4K Privately Held
SIC: 2082 Malt beverages

(G-9011)
TRV INDUSTRIES
1213 Hartford St Apt 5 (47904-2066)
PHONE..................................765 413-2301
EMP: 2 EST: 2010
SALES (est): 72K Privately Held
SIC: 3999 Mfg Misc Products

(G-9012)
TRW AUTOMOTIVE US LLC
Also Called: TRW Automotive Commercial
Stee
800 Heath St (47904-1863)
P.O. Box 60 (47902-0060)
PHONE..................................765 423-5377
Fax: 765 429-1868
Keith Davis, Materials Dir
Sandra Herring, Safety Mgr
Frank Maggio, Buyer
Kevin Tilton, Chief Engr
David Welker, Chief Engr
EMP: 655 Privately Held
WEB: www.trw.mediaroom.com
SIC: 3714 Motor vehicle parts & acces-
sories

HQ: Trw Automotive U.S. Llc
12001 Tech Center Dr
Livonia MI 48150
734 855-2600

(G-9013)
TRW COMMERCIAL STEERING
800 Heath St (47904-1863)
P.O. Box 60 (47902-0060)
PHONE..................................765 423-5377
Fax: 765 429-1697
Lynn Honsey, Vice Pres
▲ EMP: 650
SALES: 19.3K Privately Held
SIC: 3714 Motor vehicle parts & acces-
sories

(G-9014)
TWIN PRINTS INC
Also Called: Instant Copy
701 Main St (47901-1459)
PHONE..................................765 742-8656
James Speed, President
William Freeman, Vice Pres
EMP: 6
SQ FT: 6,000
SALES (est): 871.2K Privately Held
SIC: 2752 Commercial printing, offset

(G-9015)
VICTORIAN HOUSE SCONES
LLC
1305 Richards St (47904-2658)
P.O. Box 8094 (47903-8094)
PHONE..................................765 742-2709
Deborah Anderson,
EMP: 2
SALES: 10K Privately Held
SIC: 2052 Bakery products, dry

(G-9016)
VOIDTEAM STUDIOS
Also Called: Voidteam Network
2930 Greenbush St (47904-2434)
PHONE..................................765 414-9777
Christian Terry, Partner
Travis Adamczyk, Partner
Alan Sauer, Partner
EMP: 7
SALES (est): 273.5K Privately Held
SIC: 7372 7389 Home entertainment com-
puter software;

(G-9017)
WABASH NATIONAL LP (HQ)
1000 Sagamore Pkwy S (47905-4727)
P.O. Box 6129 (47903-6129)
PHONE..................................765 771-5300
Richard Zivny, President
EMP: 70
SALES (est): 22.8MM
SALES (corp-wide): 1.7B Publicly Held
SIC: 3715 3792 Truck trailers; travel trail-
ers & campers
PA: Wabash National Corporation
1000 Sagamore Pkwy S
Lafayette IN 47905
765 771-5300

(G-9018)
WABASH NATIONAL
CORPORATION (PA)
1000 Sagamore Pkwy S (47905-4727)
P.O. Box 6129 (47903-6129)
PHONE..................................765 771-5300
Fax: 765 447-9405
Brent L Yeagy, President
Kevin Page, President
Dustin Smith, President
Mark J Weber, President
Donnie Holland, General Mgr
EMP: 277
SQ FT: 1,200,000
SALES: 1.7B Publicly Held
WEB: www.wabashnational.com
SIC: 3715 3714 5012 Truck trailers; trailer
bodies; motor vehicle parts & acces-
sories; automobiles & other motor vehi-
cles; trailers for trucks, new & used

(G-9019)
WABASH NATIONAL MFG LP
1000 Sagamore Pkwy S (47905-4727)
P.O. Box 6129 (47903-6129)
PHONE..................................765 771-5310
EMP: 81

SALES (est): 95.9K
SALES (corp-wide): 1.7B **Publicly Held**
SIC: 3715 Truck trailers
PA: Wabash National Corporation
1000 Sagamore Pkwy S
Lafayette IN 47905
765 771-5300

(G-9020)
WARREN INDUSTRIES INC (HQ)
Also Called: Mega Brands America
3200 South St (47904-3183)
PHONE.................................765 447-2151
Fax: 765 448-1313
Marc Bertrand, *President*
Peter Ferrante, *Vice Pres*
▲ EMP: 75
SQ FT: 100,000
SALES (est): 6.9MM
SALES (corp-wide): 248MM **Privately Held**
WEB: www.megabrandsamerica.com
SIC: 3944 Puzzles; board games, children's & adults'
PA: Mega Brands Inc
4505 Rue Hickmore
Saint-Laurent QC H4T 1
514 333-5555

(G-9021)
WASTE 1
3304 Concord Rd (47909-5128)
PHONE.................................765 477-9138
Fax: 765 477-6560
Tom McDonald, *Principal*
EMP: 4
SALES (est): 328.1K **Privately Held**
SIC: 3089 Garbage containers, plastic

(G-9022)
WASU INC
Also Called: Aardvark Furniture
24 N Earl Ave (47904-2813)
PHONE.................................765 448-4450
Fax: 765 448-9198
Carl R Mullen, *President*
Michelle Mullen, *Vice Pres*
Willard Casey, *Admin Sec*
EMP: 3
SQ FT: 19,000
SALES (est): 496.5K **Privately Held**
WEB: www.wasu.com
SIC: 5999 2395 Infant furnishings & equipment; cribs; children's furniture; embroidery & art needlework

(G-9023)
WHITE ASPEN WOODWORKING LLC ✪
4241 Fletcher Dr (47909-8274)
PHONE.................................765 471-4962
Stuart White, *Principal*
EMP: 2 EST: 2017
SALES (est): 105.1K **Privately Held**
SIC: 2431 Millwork

(G-9024)
WHITETOWER COLLECTION LLC
976 Wexford Dr (47905-8549)
PHONE.................................847 826-0927
Paola Torreblanca-Fischer, *CEO*
Paola Fischer, *Principal*
Ricardo Torreblanca, *Vice Pres*
EMP: 3
SALES (est): 181.1K **Privately Held**
SIC: 2211 Drills, cotton; piques, cotton; airplane cloth, cotton

(G-9025)
WILLIAMS SIGNS INC
6407 Whippoorwill Ln (47905-8724)
PHONE.................................765 448-6725
Norman Williams, *Owner*
Ruth Williams, *Co-Owner*
EMP: 2 EST: 1991
SALES (est): 174.1K **Privately Held**
SIC: 3993 Signs & advertising specialties

(G-9026)
WORWAG COATINGS LLC (DH)
3420 Kossuth St (47905-4714)
PHONE.................................765 447-2137
Elizabeth Brown, *Purchasing*
Mike Grandy,
▲ EMP: 25

SQ FT: 42,000
SALES (est): 4.6MM
SALES (corp-wide): 242.1MM **Privately Held**
WEB: www.worwagcoatings.com
SIC: 2851 Paints & allied products
HQ: Karl Worwag Gmbh & Co. Industrielacke
Strohgaustr. 28
Stuttgart 70435
711 829-60

(G-9027)
ZF NORTH AMERICA INC
9th & Greenbush (47904)
PHONE.................................765 429-1678
Brian Kipp, *Branch Mgr*
EMP: 3 **Privately Held**
SIC: 3469 Metal stampings
HQ: Trw Automotive U.S. Llc
12001 Tech Center Dr
Livonia MI 48150
734 855-2600

(G-9028)
ZF NORTH AMERICA INC
4820 Dale Dr (47905-7709)
PHONE.................................765 429-1984
EMP: 273 **Privately Held**
SIC: 3469 3679 3089 Metal stampings; electronic switches; plastic processing
HQ: Trw Automotive U.S. Llc
12001 Tech Center Dr
Livonia MI 48150
734 855-2600

(G-9029)
ZOJILA LLC
2004 N 9th St (47904)
PHONE.................................765 404-3767
Rony Joseph,
EMP: 2
SALES (est): 300K **Privately Held**
WEB: www.zojila.com
SIC: 7389 3469 Design services; kitchen fixtures & equipment: metal, except cast aluminum

---

Lagrange
Lagrange County

(G-9030)
ALUMINUM CARGO TRAILERS INC
Also Called: Act
2840 N State Road 9 (46761-9346)
P.O. Box 210 (46761-0210)
PHONE.................................260 463-0185
Michael Baxley, *President*
EMP: 15
SALES (est): 1.3MM **Privately Held**
SIC: 3715 Truck trailers

(G-9031)
ANR PIPELINE COMPANY
2255 W Us Highway 20 (46761-8626)
PHONE.................................260 463-3342
Fax: 260 463-2066
Myron Pschyoda, *Manager*
EMP: 5
SALES (corp-wide): 10.5B **Privately Held**
SIC: 4922 1311 1221 Pipelines, natural gas; crude petroleum & natural gas; bituminous coal & lignite-surface mining
HQ: Anr Pipeline Company
700 Louisiana St Ste 700 # 700
Houston TX 77002
832 320-2000

(G-9032)
AUTOMATED PRODUCTS INTL LLC
Also Called: API
2840 N State Road 9 (46761-9346)
PHONE.................................260 463-2515
Ronald Yoder,
Elvie J Frey Sr,
Freeman Helmuth,
EMP: 15
SQ FT: 18,000
SALES (est): 2.8MM **Privately Held**
WEB: www.apiclamps.com
SIC: 3714 Pickup truck bed liners

(G-9033)
BEAVER MOULDINGS LLC
3565 S 300 W (46761-8819)
PHONE.................................260 463-4822
Jongs Weaver, *Mng Member*
EMP: 4
SQ FT: 130
SALES (est): 199.6K **Privately Held**
SIC: 2431 7699 Moldings, wood: unfinished & prefinished; horseshoeing

(G-9034)
CENTERLINE WOODWORKING ✪
695 S 600 W (46761-8633)
PHONE.................................260 768-4116
EMP: 2 EST: 2017
SALES (est): 85.2K **Privately Held**
SIC: 2431 Millwork

(G-9035)
COUNTY OF LAGRANGE
Also Called: La Grange County
300 E Factory St (46761-1507)
PHONE.................................260 499-6353
Fax: 260 463-7838
Jeff Brill, *Manager*
EMP: 25 **Privately Held**
WEB: www.lagrangesd.com
SIC: 4959 3531 Road, airport & parking lot maintenance services; road construction & maintenance machinery
PA: County Of Lagrange
114 W Michigan St Ste 1
Lagrange IN 46761
260 499-6380

(G-9036)
D W STEWART
104 E Wayne St (46761-1847)
PHONE.................................260 463-2607
Fax: 260 463-4068
D W Stewart, *Owner*
EMP: 2
SALES (est): 110K **Privately Held**
SIC: 3559 Automotive related machinery

(G-9037)
DOMETIC CORPORATION
509 S Poplar St (46761-2317)
PHONE.................................260 463-7657
Fax: 260 463-7602
John Waters, *President*
EMP: 375
SQ FT: 240,000
SALES (corp-wide): 1.6B **Privately Held**
WEB: www.edometic.com
SIC: 3585 3714 2394 Air conditioning units, complete: domestic or industrial; heating equipment, complete; refrigeration equipment, complete; motor vehicle parts & accessories; canvas & related products
HQ: Dometic Corporation
1120 N Main St
Elkhart IN 46514

(G-9038)
DUTCH COUNTRY WOODWORKING INC
Also Called: Shur Ply
200 Industrial Pkwy (46761-1144)
PHONE.................................260 499-4847
Delbert Schrock, *President*
EMP: 2
SALES (est): 198.3K **Privately Held**
SIC: 2499 1751 Decorative wood & woodwork; carpentry work

(G-9039)
DUTCHCRAFT CORPORATION
50 S 375 W (46761-9470)
PHONE.................................260 463-8366
Fax: 260 463-8366
Wayne Yoder, *President*
Naomi Yoder, *Vice Pres*
EMP: 5
SQ FT: 17,000
SALES (est): 564.5K **Privately Held**
SIC: 2431 Millwork

(G-9040)
E & S WOOD CREATIONS LLC
Also Called: Excell
2030 N 450 W (46761-8611)
PHONE.................................260 768-3033
Ervin J Miller,
EMP: 15
SALES (est): 1.9MM **Privately Held**
SIC: 2434 2511 Wood kitchen cabinets; wood bedroom furniture

(G-9041)
F & N WOODWORKING LLC
2105 W 450 S (46761-9726)
PHONE.................................260 463-8938
Freeman P Miller, *Mng Member*
EMP: 12
SALES (est): 1.3MM **Privately Held**
SIC: 2511 Chairs, household, except upholstered: wood

(G-9042)
FISHERMAN S LURECRAFT SHOP INC
513 W Central Ave (46761-2112)
PHONE.................................260 829-1274
Kim Straley, *President*
EMP: 3
SALES (est): 238.7K **Privately Held**
SIC: 3949 5199 Fishing tackle, general; bait, fishing

(G-9043)
GROH INC
406 W North St (46761-1106)
PHONE.................................260 463-2410
Cynthia A Troyer, *President*
Ronald S Troyer, *Admin Sec*
EMP: 2
SALES (est): 300K **Privately Held**
SIC: 3732 Non-motorized boat, building & repairing

(G-9044)
HOCHSTETLER WELDING
2520 W 350 N (46761-9449)
PHONE.................................260 463-2793
Samuel Hochstetler, *Principal*
EMP: 5
SALES (est): 227.5K **Privately Held**
SIC: 7692 Welding repair

(G-9045)
HOSTETLER CARRIAGE
3200 W 300 S (46761-9481)
PHONE.................................260 463-9920
Marvin Hostetler, *Owner*
EMP: 5
SALES (est): 628K **Privately Held**
SIC: 3799 Carriages, horse drawn

(G-9046)
INDIANA CUSTOM TRUCKS LLC (PA)
Also Called: Ict
2840 N State Road 9 2 (46761-9346)
PHONE.................................260 463-3244
Fax: 260 463-2603
Michael Baxley, *Mng Member*
Elwin Eash,
Elvie Frey,
Fritz Helmuth,
EMP: 35
SQ FT: 60,000
SALES (est): 3.8MM **Privately Held**
WEB: www.indianacustomtrucks.com
SIC: 3713 3714 7532 3429 Truck cabs for motor vehicles; motor vehicle parts & accessories; top & body repair & paint shops; clamps, metal

(G-9047)
INDIANA INTERSTATE ENTPS LLC
Also Called: Cross Rv Sales
1695 E Us Highway 20 (46761-8783)
PHONE.................................260 463-8100
Paul Cross, *Mng Member*
EMP: 6
SALES (est): 712.6K **Privately Held**
SIC: 3792 Campers, for mounting on trucks

G
E
O
G
R
A
P
H
I
C

(G-9048)
JAG WIRE LLC
130 E 200 N (46761-9345)
P.O. Box 218 (46761-0218)
PHONE..................................260 463-8537
Fax: 219 463-8990
Kevin M Myers, President
Ranay Uhl,
EMP: 12 EST: 2000
SQ FT: 20,000
SALES (est): 2.1MM **Privately Held**
WEB: www.jagwirellc.com
SIC: 3679 Harness assemblies for electronic use: wire or cable

(G-9049)
JEMDD LLC
5680 W 100 N (46761-8605)
PHONE..................................260 768-4156
Fax: 260 768-4354
Paul R Mishler, President
Mike Monson, Corp Secy
EMP: 24
SQ FT: 7,000
SALES (est): 1.8MM **Privately Held**
SIC: 5147 5421 2011 2013 Meats, fresh; meat markets, including freezer provisioners; beef products from beef slaughtered on site; pork products from pork slaughtered on site; sausages & other prepared meats

(G-9050)
JOHNNY BONTRAGER
Also Called: Jr & Sons Woodworking
1735 N 400 W (46761-8608)
PHONE..................................260 463-8912
EMP: 2
SALES (est): 130K **Privately Held**
SIC: 2434 2511 5211 5712 Mfg Retail & Wholesale Wooden Cabinets And Household Furniture

(G-9051)
KUNTRY LUMBER AND FARM SUP LTD
2875 S 00ew (46761-8844)
P.O. Box 126 (46761-0126)
PHONE..................................260 463-3242
Fax: 260 463-8204
William Connelly, President
Bryant Gilliland, Vice Pres
EMP: 24
SALES (est): 4.3MM **Privately Held**
WEB: www.kuntrylumber.com
SIC: 5211 2431 5191 Lumber & other building materials; millwork; farm supplies

(G-9052)
LA GRANGE PUBLISHING CO INC
Also Called: Waddell Printing Co
Hc 9 Box S (46761)
PHONE..................................260 463-3243
Fax: 260 463-2734
William Connelly, President
Charlette Connelly, Corp Secy
Eugene N Marten, Vice Pres
Joyce Marten, Asst Treas
EMP: 18 EST: 1856
SALES (est): 1.2MM **Privately Held**
SIC: 2711 2791 2789 2759 Commercial printing & newspaper publishing combined; job printing & newspaper publishing combined; typesetting; bookbinding & related work; commercial printing; commercial printing, lithographic

(G-9053)
LAGRANGE PUBLISHING CO INC
Also Called: Standard & News
50 W 100 S (46761-9401)
PHONE..................................260 463-2166
William Connelly, President
EMP: 10 EST: 1994
SALES (est): 567.6K **Privately Held**
SIC: 2711 Newspapers: publishing only, not printed on site

(G-9054)
LAGWANA PRINTING INC
Also Called: People's Exchange, The
4425 W Us Highway 20 # 3 (46761-8407)
P.O. Box 70, Shipshewana (46565-0070)
PHONE..................................260 463-4901
Daniel Byler, President
Roger Wenger, Vice Pres
Jerry Hostetler, Treasurer
Justin R Geigley, Admin Sec
EMP: 30
SALES (est): 4.4MM **Privately Held**
SIC: 2752 Commercial printing, lithographic

(G-9055)
LAKESTREET ENTERPRISES LLC
75 N 700 W (46761-8687)
PHONE..................................260 768-7991
Menno Petersheim,
Inez Petersheim,
EMP: 2
SALES (est): 175.7K **Privately Held**
SIC: 2399 Horse & pet accessories, textile

(G-9056)
LAMBRIGHTS INC
2450 W Us Highway 20 (46761-8772)
P.O. Box 295 (46761-0295)
PHONE..................................260 463-2178
Fax: 260 463-7444
Richard Lambright, President
Joe Walter, Treasurer
EMP: 52 EST: 1949
SQ FT: 90,000
SALES (est): 4.7MM **Privately Held**
WEB: www.lambrights.com
SIC: 5144 5191 2048 2015 Eggs; animal feeds; prepared feeds; poultry slaughtering & processing

(G-9057)
LARRYS CANVAS CLEANING
403 E Central Ave (46761-2329)
PHONE..................................260 463-2220
Larry Bontrager, Owner
EMP: 2
SALES (est): 211.5K **Privately Held**
SIC: 2394 Awnings, fabric: made from purchased materials

(G-9058)
LILLICH SIGN CO INC
1333 Industrial Dr N (46761-1159)
P.O. Box 240 (46761-0240)
PHONE..................................260 463-3930
Fax: 260 463-4947
Joe Lillich, President
EMP: 10
SALES (est): 670K **Privately Held**
WEB: www.lillichsign.net
SIC: 3993 Displays & cutouts, window & lobby; signs, not made in custom sign painting shops

(G-9059)
MAPLE LEAF WOODWORKING
3950 W 200 N (46761-8769)
PHONE..................................260 768-8166
EMP: 2
SALES (est): 112.5K **Privately Held**
SIC: 2431 Millwork

(G-9060)
MASTERCRAFT INC (PA)
711 S Poplar St (46761-2407)
P.O. Box 97 (46761-0097)
PHONE..................................260 463-8702
Clifton D Reynolds, Principal
Doug Cline, Vice Pres
Dave Toney, Vice Pres
Richard Garman, Director
EMP: 150 EST: 1971
SALES (est): 71.8MM **Privately Held**
WEB: www.apticallc.com
SIC: 2512 2514 2515 Upholstered household furniture; metal household furniture; mattresses, innerspring or box spring; box springs, assembled

(G-9061)
MIDWEST CUSTOM WOODWORKING
409 E Lafayette St (46761-1910)
PHONE..................................574 349-1645
Wyatt Martin, Principal
EMP: 2
SALES (est): 85.2K **Privately Held**
SIC: 2431 Millwork

(G-9062)
OHIO TABLE PAD OF INDIANA
1400 N Detroit St (46761-1142)
PHONE..................................260 463-2139
Fax: 260 463-3593
EMP: 32
SQ FT: 10,000
SALES (corp-wide): 10.7MM **Privately Held**
SIC: 2392 Mfg Household Furnishings
HQ: Ohio Table Pad Of Indiana (Inc)
350 3 Meadows Dr
Perrysburg OH 43551
419 872-6400

(G-9063)
RAINBOW DESIGN INC
1100 W Us Highway 20 (46761-9477)
PHONE..................................260 593-2856
Keith Hershberger, President
EMP: 20
SALES (est): 1.5MM **Privately Held**
SIC: 2434 Wood kitchen cabinets

(G-9064)
SIGNATURE INDUSTRIES INC
1775 E Us Highway 20 # 4 (46761-9072)
PHONE..................................260 350-3688
Lorne Hershberger, President
EMP: 3 EST: 2012
SALES (est): 257.6K **Privately Held**
SIC: 2431 Windows & window parts & trim, wood

(G-9065)
SIX MILE WELDING
40 S 600 W (46761-9428)
PHONE..................................260 768-3126
Norman J Mishler, Owner
EMP: 5
SALES (est): 298.5K **Privately Held**
SIC: 7692 Welding repair

(G-9066)
SPECTRUM FINISHING LLC
1340 Industrial Dr N (46761-1143)
PHONE..................................260 463-7300
Freeman Miller,
EMP: 32
SQ FT: 37,000
SALES (est): 2.7MM **Privately Held**
SIC: 2431 5021 Millwork; furniture

(G-9067)
SPREUER & SON INC
115 E Spring St (46761-1897)
PHONE..................................260 463-3513
Fax: 260 463-4297
Ron Troyer, Owner
Ronald Troyer, President
Roberta Craig, Corp Secy
EMP: 18 EST: 1944
SQ FT: 1,000
SALES (est): 5.7MM **Privately Held**
WEB: www.hoosiertrailer.com
SIC: 3799 3441 3444 3443 Boat trailers; fabricated structural metal; sheet metalwork; fabricated plate work (boiler shop); machine shop, jobbing & repair

(G-9068)
STANLEY OLIVER PRODUCTS LLC
3545 E 100 N (46761-9696)
P.O. Box 243 (46761-0243)
PHONE..................................260 499-3506
David Merrifield, President
EMP: 5
SALES (est): 320K **Privately Held**
SIC: 3431 3432 Bathroom fixtures, including sinks; plumbing fixture fittings & trim

(G-9069)
SUPER BLEND INC
105 S 500 E (46761-9511)
PHONE..................................260 463-7486
Fax: 260 463-7486
Rose Miller, President
Phil Miller, Vice Pres
Helen Mischler, Treasurer
EMP: 6
SALES: 1.5MM **Privately Held**
SIC: 2048 8611 Feed supplements; business associations

(G-9070)
SWINGS N THINGS
4755 W Us Highway 20 (46761-9425)
PHONE..................................260 336-8811
Levi Miller, Owner
EMP: 2
SALES (est): 85.7K **Privately Held**
SIC: 2511 Wood household furniture

(G-9071)
W & M WOODWORKING
3180 E 450 S (46761-9782)
PHONE..................................260 854-3126
William Bontrager, Principal
EMP: 2
SALES (est): 128K **Privately Held**
SIC: 2431 Millwork

Lagro
Wabash County

(G-9072)
COMMERCIAL PRINTING OF LAGRO
400 Clinton St (46941-9683)
P.O. Box 127 (46941-0127)
PHONE..................................260 782-2421
Thomas Tucker, President
Dan Tucker, Corp Secy
EMP: 2
SQ FT: 3,200
SALES: 110K **Privately Held**
SIC: 2752 Commercial printing, offset

(G-9073)
VICE BROS PATTERN SHOP & FNDRY
1010 W State Road 524 (46941-5416)
P.O. Box 327 (46941-0327)
PHONE..................................260 782-2585
Fax: 260 782-2585
Phyllis Bowman, CEO
Stanley K Bowman, President
▲ EMP: 2
SQ FT: 8,700
SALES: 175K **Privately Held**
WEB: www.vicebrothers.com
SIC: 3365 Aluminum & aluminum-based alloy castings

Lake Station
Lake County

(G-9074)
A SIGN ODYSSEY LLC
727 Central Ave (46405-1511)
PHONE..................................219 962-1247
Dee Tucker, Vice Pres
Cheryl Hullinger, Manager
Rick Besmehn,
EMP: 3
SALES (est): 273.6K **Privately Held**
SIC: 3993 Signs & advertising specialties

(G-9075)
GREENWALD SURGICAL CO INC
2688 Dekalb St (46405-1519)
PHONE..................................219 962-1604
Fax: 219 962-4009
Christopher Reynolds, President
Thomas S Reynolds, Vice Pres
Kathy Couture, Purchasing
Pete Morganelli, Purchasing
Kathy Bryant, Bookkeeper
EMP: 22 EST: 1930
SQ FT: 13,500

SALES (est): 3.6MM **Privately Held**
WEB: www.greenwaldsurgical.com
SIC: **3841** 3845 Surgical instruments &
apparatus; electromedical equipment

(G-9076)
S & S INDUSTRY &
MANUFACTURING
3311 Liverpool Rd (46405-3041)
PHONE.................................219 963-0213
Eduardo Loza, *President*
EMP: 15
SALES (est): 1.5MM **Privately Held**
SIC: **1799** 1611 3496 Fence construction;
surfacing & paving; miscellaneous fabri-
cated wire products

(G-9077)
SOUND & GRAPHICS
2580 Central Ave A (46405-2124)
P.O. Box 5064, Gary (46405-0064)
PHONE.................................219 963-7293
Henry Delbre, *Owner*
EMP: 3 EST: 1999
SALES (est): 160K **Privately Held**
SIC: **2752** Commercial printing, litho-
graphic

(G-9078)
SUN ENGINEERING INC
950 Marquette Rd (46405-1548)
PHONE.................................219 962-1191
Fax: 219 962-5880
Walter E Williams, *President*
Melinda Rhodes, *Admin Sec*
EMP: 50 EST: 1959
SQ FT: 85,000
SALES (est): 9.7MM **Privately Held**
SIC: **3599** 7692 3443 Machine shop, job-
bing & repair; welding repair; fabricated
plate work (boiler shop)

(G-9079)
TITANIUM EAGLES NUTRITION
4700 Central Ave (46405-2517)
PHONE.................................219 781-6018
Suyapa Figueroa, *Principal*
EMP: 2
SALES (est): 90.8K **Privately Held**
SIC: **3356** Titanium

(G-9080)
US CRANE & HOIST INC
721 E 25th Pl (46405-1503)
PHONE.................................219 963-1400
Zeb Foster, *President*
EMP: 3
SQ FT: 18,000
SALES: 1MM **Privately Held**
SIC: **3536** 5084 Hoists, cranes & mono-
rails; industrial machinery & equipment

(G-9081)
WUNDER CO INC
3200 E 37th Ave (46405-3001)
P.O. Box 5272 (46405-0272)
PHONE.................................219 962-8573
Fax: 219 962-8574
Rick Tubbs, *President*
Ilyas Frenkel, *Director*
EMP: 15
SQ FT: 2,000
SALES (est): 2.2MM **Privately Held**
SIC: **5211** 3089 Fencing; fences, gates &
accessories: plastic

Lake Village
Newton County

(G-9082)
EXPERT WOODWORKS
9126 N 200 E (46349-9389)
PHONE.................................219 345-2705
Linda Phelps, *Principal*
EMP: 2 EST: 2008
SALES (est): 159.5K **Privately Held**
SIC: **2431** Millwork

(G-9083)
MIDCOUNTY MACHINING INC
Also Called: Mid-County Machining
9313 N 300 W (46349-9531)
PHONE.................................219 992-9380

Herb Dresbaugh, *President*
Judy Dresbaugh, *Vice Pres*
EMP: 4
SQ FT: 2,750
SALES (est): 310K **Privately Held**
SIC: **3599** Machine shop, jobbing & repair

(G-9084)
PHOENIX SPECIALTIES LTD
2798 W 800 N (46349)
PHONE.................................219 345-5812
Nancey Heughes, *President*
EMP: 3
SALES (est): 299K **Privately Held**
SIC: **3317** Welded pipe & tubes

(G-9085)
PHOENIX SPECIALTIES LTD
2279 E State Road 10 (46349-9254)
PHONE.................................219 345-5812
John Piechocki, *Owner*
EMP: 2
SALES (est): 130K **Privately Held**
SIC: **3441** Fabricated structural metal

(G-9086)
REESE FORGE ORNA
IRONWORK
6873 W 700 N (46349-9520)
PHONE.................................219 775-1039
David Reese, *Principal*
EMP: 5 EST: 2008
SALES (est): 321K **Privately Held**
SIC: **1791** 3446 3699 Iron work, struc-
tural; gates, ornamental metal; security
devices

(G-9087)
RING INDUSTRIES INC
3572 W State Road 10 # 13 (46349-9484)
PHONE.................................219 204-1577
EMP: 2
SALES (est): 109.6K **Privately Held**
SIC: **3999** Manufacturing industries

(G-9088)
TJ MAINTENANCE LLC
8591 N 300 W (46349)
PHONE.................................219 776-8427
John Maciejko,
EMP: 9 EST: 2013
SALES (est): 1MM **Privately Held**
SIC: **3089** 3443 1791 Plastic & fiberglass
tanks; industrial vessels, tanks & contain-
ers; tanks, lined: metal plate; storage
tanks, metal: erection

(G-9089)
WORLDWIDE DOOR CMPNNTS
IND INC
8218 N 279 W (46349-9498)
PHONE.................................219 992-9225
Jerry Monts De Oca, *President*
Jerry M Deoca, *President*
▲ EMP: 2
SQ FT: 15,000
SALES (est): 165.6K **Privately Held**
SIC: **3442** Metal doors, sash & trim

Laketon
Wabash County

(G-9090)
LAKETON REFINING
CORPORATION
2784 W Lukens Lake Rd (46943-0198)
P.O. Box 231 (46943)
PHONE.................................260 982-0703
Fax: 260 982-2091
Lewis L Davis, *Exec VP*
EMP: 20
SALES (corp-wide): 248.2MM **Privately Held**
SIC: **5171** 2951 Petroleum terminals; as-
phalt paving mixtures & blocks
HQ: Laketon Refining Corporation
5400 W 86th St
Indianapolis IN 46268
260 982-2171

(G-9091)
SEBASTY MANUFACTURING INC
10321 N Troyer Rd (46943-0180)
PHONE.................................574 505-1511
EMP: 2
SALES (est): 100.7K **Privately Held**
SIC: **3999** Manufacturing industries

Lakeville
St. Joseph County

(G-9092)
124 PUBLISHING LLC
124 S Michigan St (46536-7704)
PHONE.................................574 784-0046
EMP: 2 EST: 2014
SALES (est): 95.3K **Privately Held**
SIC: **2741** Miscellaneous publishing

(G-9093)
BRANIFF GAME BIRDS
67510 Mulberry Rd (46536-9450)
PHONE.................................574 784-3919
Fax: 574 784-3919
Beverly Braniff, *Owner*
EMP: 5
SALES (est): 80K **Privately Held**
SIC: **3949** Decoys, duck & other game
birds

(G-9094)
CORBY PUBLISHING LP
11961 Tyler Rd (46536-9603)
PHONE.................................574 229-1107
James Langford, *Partner*
EMP: 2
SALES (est): 110K **Privately Held**
SIC: **2731** 7389 Book publishing;

(G-9095)
CREED & DYER PRECAST INC
68186 Us Highway 31 (46536-9738)
PHONE.................................574 784-3361
Keith Dyer, *President*
EMP: 3
SALES (est): 336.8K **Privately Held**
SIC: **3272** 5039 Septic tanks, concrete;
septic tanks

(G-9096)
HOOSIER RACING TIRE CORP
Also Called: Hoosier Tire
65465 Sr 931 (46536)
PHONE.................................574 784-3409
Fax: 860 646-2054
Joyce L Newton, *President*
Dave Morrow, *COO*
Dennis Sherman, *Vice Pres*
Brad Hicks, *Plant Mgr*
Melanie Strain, *Purchasing*
▼ EMP: 75
SALES: 44.4MM
SALES (corp-wide): 51.9B **Privately Held**
WEB: www.hoosiertire.com
SIC: **5014** 5531 3011 5699 Automobile
tires & tubes; automotive tires; tires &
inner tubes; sports apparel
HQ: Continental Tire The Americas, Llc
1830 Macmillan Park Dr
Fort Mill SC 29707
800 450-3187

(G-9097)
SPECIALTY INDUS COATINGS
CORP
555 N Michigan Rd (46536-7004)
PHONE.................................574 784-3711
Jeff Cornett, *President*
EMP: 6
SALES: 400K **Privately Held**
SIC: **3479** Painting, coating & hot dipping

(G-9098)
ULTRA/GLAS OF LAKEVILLE
INC
520 Industrial Dr (46536-9557)
P.O. Box 407 (46536-0407)
PHONE.................................574 784-8958
Fax: 574 784-3048
Herbert Davidson, *President*
Ronald Davidson, *Vice Pres*
EMP: 15

SQ FT: 8,000
SALES (est): 2.4MM **Privately Held**
SIC: **3088** Shower stalls, fiberglass & plas-
tic; tubs (bath, shower & laundry), plastic

Lamar
Spencer County

(G-9099)
FOERTSCH CONSTRUCTION CO
INC (PA)
12724 N State Road 245 (47550-7200)
PHONE.................................812 529-8211
Fax: 812 529-8381
Mason Foertsch, *President*
Don Foertsch, *Vice Pres*
EMP: 60
SQ FT: 5,000
SALES (est): 17.4MM **Privately Held**
SIC: **1221** 1794 1622 Strip mining, bitumi-
nous; excavation work; bridge, tunnel &
elevated highway

(G-9100)
HILLTOP PROCESSING INC
Also Called: Big Chops Famous Bbq
13371 N State Road 245 (47550-7202)
PHONE.................................812 544-2174
EMP: 2
SALES (est): 88K **Privately Held**
SIC: **7299** 2013 2011 Misc Personal Serv-
ices Mfg Prepared Meats Meat Packing
Plant

Lanesville
Harrison County

(G-9101)
JBS POWDER COATING LLC
7320 Thomas Ave Ne (47136-8638)
PHONE.................................812 952-1204
John Butler, *Mng Member*
EMP: 2
SALES (est): 139.6K **Privately Held**
SIC: **3399** Powder, metal

(G-9102)
KENTUCKIANA MACHINE &
TOOL
4550 Lazy Creek Rd Ne (47136-8812)
PHONE.................................502 301-9005
H Cobb, *President*
EMP: 2
SALES (est): 327.3K **Privately Held**
SIC: **3531** Construction machinery

(G-9103)
S & S SERVICE
7608 Main St Ne (47136-8612)
PHONE.................................812 952-2306
Don Schickel, *Owner*
EMP: 2
SALES: 70K **Privately Held**
SIC: **7699** 0782 7692 Agricultural equip-
ment repair services; bermuda sprigging
services; welding repair

Laotto
Noble County

(G-9104)
BEAL SYSTEMS INC
Also Called: Glowire
10772 E State Road 205 (46763-9709)
PHONE.................................260 693-0772
Janet S Beal, *President*
James D Beal, *Admin Sec*
EMP: 2
SALES (est): 180.1K **Privately Held**
WEB: www.glowire.com
SIC: **3496** Woven wire products

▲ = Import ▼=Export
◆ =Import/Export

(G-9105)
COUNTRY HRITG WNERY VINYRD INC
185 County Road 68 (46763-9614)
P.O. Box 371 (46763-0371)
PHONE..................................260 637-2980
Jeremy R Lutter, *President*
Jennifer L Lutter, *Admin Sec*
EMP: 15
SALES (est): 1.7MM **Privately Held**
SIC: 2084 Wines

(G-9106)
COUNTRY MILL CABINET CO INC
7590 E 400 S (46763-9786)
PHONE..................................260 693-9289
Fax: 260 693-9289
Robert B Green, *President*
Dianne Green, *Corp Secy*
Richard Green, *Vice Pres*
EMP: 10
SQ FT: 6,560
SALES: 1MM **Privately Held**
SIC: 2599 1751 Cabinets, factory; cabinet building & installation

(G-9107)
FULK INC
Also Called: A1 Machine
40 County Road 70 (46763-9602)
P.O. Box 7, Huntertown (46748-0007)
PHONE..................................260 338-1012
Kenneth Fulk, *President*
EMP: 3
SALES (est): 23.1K **Privately Held**
SIC: 3542 Machine tools, metal forming type

(G-9108)
GLENWOOD M BROWN CO LLC
209 County Road 56 (46763-9605)
PHONE..................................260 710-4428
Glenwood M Brown,
EMP: 3 EST: 2008
SALES (est): 198.5K **Privately Held**
SIC: 3511 Turbines & turbine generator sets

(G-9109)
GROUP DEKKO INC
Also Called: Dekko Techinal Center
11913 E 450 S (46763-9750)
PHONE..................................260 637-3964
Fax: 260 637-5641
Robert Einhaus, *Manager*
EMP: 12
SALES (corp-wide): 2.5B **Publicly Held**
SIC: 3643 Current-carrying wiring devices
HQ: Group Dekko, Inc.
2505 Dekko Dr
Garrett IN 46738

(G-9110)
KHORPORATE HOLDINGS INC (PA)
Also Called: Mossberg Industries
6492 State Road 205 (46763-9609)
PHONE..................................260 357-3365
Fax: 260 356-7891
Michael Khorshid, *President*
Tim Gerst, *Plant Mgr*
Greg Baker, *Opers Mgr*
Scott Lancaster, *Foreman/Supr*
Todd Muehlmeyer, *Purchasing*
▲ EMP: 102 EST: 1950
SQ FT: 20,000
SALES: 52.7MM **Privately Held**
WEB: www.huntingtonelectric.com
SIC: 3496 3676 3089 5084 Cable, uninsulated wire: made from purchased wire; wire winding; electronic resistors; injection molding of plastics; tool & die makers' equipment

(G-9111)
KML INC (PA)
108 S Main St (46763-4818)
P.O. Box 380 (46763-0380)
PHONE..................................260 897-3723
Fax: 260 897-3433
Andrew W Peterson, *President*
EMP: 27
SQ FT: 16,000
SALES (est): 6.3MM **Privately Held**
WEB: www.kml.net
SIC: 2819 Chemicals, high purity: refined from technical grade; industrial chemicals

(G-9112)
LAKE LITE INC
105 W Simon St (46763-4813)
P.O. Box 414 (46763-0414)
PHONE..................................260 918-2758
Jeffrey Martzall, *President*
Keith L Henley Jr, *Vice Pres*
EMP: 3
SALES (est): 15.8K **Privately Held**
WEB: www.lakelite.com
SIC: 3731 5551 Lighters, marine: building & repairing; marine supplies & equipment

(G-9113)
LANCON ELECTRIC INC
101 S Main St (46763-4818)
PHONE..................................260 897-3285
Andrew J Langohr Sr, *President*
EMP: 4
SALES (est): 300.6K **Privately Held**
SIC: 5063 3699 1731 Generators; electrical equipment & supplies; electrical work

(G-9114)
PEERLESS MANUFACTURING
103 W Simon St (46763-4813)
PHONE..................................260 897-3070
EMP: 2
SALES (est): 75K **Privately Held**
SIC: 3999 Mfg Misc Products

(G-9115)
WAYNE MANUFACTURING CORP
6505 State Road 205 (46763-9618)
P.O. Box 188 (46763-0188)
PHONE..................................260 637-5586
Fax: 260 357-4193
Monty Dickerhoof, *President*
Ken Gnau, *Vice Pres*
Kenneth Gnau, *Vice Pres*
Loren Snow, *Plant Mgr*
Joel Reed, *Engineer*
EMP: 50
SQ FT: 95,000
SALES (est): 14.4MM **Privately Held**
SIC: 3469 Metal stampings
PA: Wayne Manufacturing, Llc
6505 State Road 205
Laotto IN 46763
260 637-8888

Lapaz
Marshall County

(G-9116)
A HOMESTEAD SHOPPE INC (PA)
330 E Vandalia St (46537)
P.O. Box 254 (46537-0254)
PHONE..................................574 784-2307
Fax: 574 784-3271
Bruce Albert, *President*
▲ EMP: 40
SQ FT: 85,000
SALES (est): 5.8MM **Privately Held**
SIC: 3645 5063 Lamp & light shades; lamp shades, metal; lighting fixtures; lighting fixtures, residential; lighting fittings & accessories

(G-9117)
INJECTION PLASTIC & MFG CO
12140 Us Hwy 6 E (46537)
PHONE..................................574 784-2070
Fax: 574 784-2220
Robert Strang Jr, *President*
John Strang, *Vice Pres*
Bunni Strang, *Treasurer*
Gail Strang, *Admin Sec*
EMP: 14 EST: 1968
SQ FT: 12,000
SALES (est): 2MM **Privately Held**
SIC: 3544 3089 3599 Special dies & tools; industrial molds; forms (molds), for foundry & plastics working machinery; injection molding of plastics; custom machinery

(G-9118)
INJECTION PLASTICS
12798 2a Rd St 2 (46537)
PHONE..................................574 784-2070
EMP: 3 EST: 2013
SALES (est): 210K **Privately Held**
SIC: 2821 Plasticizer/additive based plastic materials

Lapel
Madison County

(G-9119)
HEWLETT-PACKARD CO
9471 Tiger Ct (46051-9547)
PHONE..................................765 534-4468
Ken Knepp, *Owner*
EMP: 2
SALES (est): 85.9K **Privately Held**
SIC: 3571 Electronic computers

(G-9120)
WESTLUND CONCEPTS
806 N Woodward St (46051-5564)
P.O. Box 1051 (46051-1051)
PHONE..................................317 819-0611
Doug Westlund, *Partner*
Dan Westlund, *Partner*
EMP: 17
SQ FT: 10,000
SALES (est): 500K **Privately Held**
SIC: 7389 3993 3441 Design services; signs & advertising specialties; fabricated structural metal

Larwill
Whitley County

(G-9121)
DOUGLAS INDUSTRIES LLC
2277 N Binkley Rd (46764-9561)
PHONE..................................260 327-3692
Douglas Reiff, *Mng Member*
EMP: 2
SALES (est): 156.2K **Privately Held**
SIC: 2441 5085 Ammunition boxes, wood; boxes, crates, etc., other than paper

(G-9122)
INDIANA FACTORY OUTLET MARINE
3450 S 1100 W-57 (46764-9601)
PHONE..................................260 799-4764
Dan Lees, *President*
EMP: 5
SALES: 2MM **Privately Held**
SIC: 3069 Pontoons, rubber

(G-9123)
J G CABINET & COUNTER INC
2571 S State Road 5 (46764-9766)
PHONE..................................260 723-4275
Fax: 260 723-4157
Jerry Grube, *President*
Brian Adams, *Sales Staff*
Sandra Grube, *Admin Sec*
EMP: 5
SQ FT: 12,000
SALES (est): 676.7K **Privately Held**
SIC: 2434 Wood kitchen cabinets

(G-9124)
PYRAMID PLASTIC GROUP INC
1560 N State Road 5 (46764-9791)
PHONE..................................260 327-3145
Karen Buesching, *Principal*
EMP: 2
SALES (est): 206.5K **Privately Held**
SIC: 3089 Injection molding of plastics

(G-9125)
RED STAR CONTRACT MFG INC
1560 N State Road 5 (46764-9791)
PHONE..................................260 327-3145
Fax: 260 327-3297
Scott Werstler, *President*
EMP: 4
SALES: 2.5MM **Privately Held**
SIC: 3089 Molding primary plastic

(G-9126)
REDSTAR CONTRACT MANUFACTURING
1560 N State Road 5 (46764-9791)
PHONE..................................260 327-3145
Scott Werstler, *Principal*
EMP: 3
SALES (est): 211.9K **Privately Held**
SIC: 3999 Manufacturing industries

Laurel
Franklin County

(G-9127)
A SIGN ABOVE
25033 Us Highway 52 (47024-9644)
PHONE..................................317 392-2144
Millton Cain, *Owner*
EMP: 2
SALES (est): 170.8K **Privately Held**
SIC: 3993 Signs & advertising specialties

(G-9128)
NEW POINT STONE CO INC
Also Called: Harris City Stone Co
24031 Derbyshire Rd (47024-9757)
PHONE..................................765 698-2227
Fax: 765 698-2104
Nathan Wanstrath, *Branch Mgr*
EMP: 12
SALES (corp-wide): 12.3MM **Privately Held**
SIC: 3281 1422 Stone, quarrying & processing of own stone products; crushed & broken limestone
PA: New Point Stone Co Inc
992 S County Road 800 E
Greensburg IN 47240
812 663-2021

(G-9129)
TREEHUGGER MAPLE SYRUP LLC
15203 Ott Rd (47024-9744)
PHONE..................................765 698-3728
Deirdre Schirmer, *Owner*
EMP: 2
SALES (est): 62.3K **Privately Held**
SIC: 2099 Maple syrup

Lawrenceburg
Dearborn County

(G-9130)
ALL ABOUT ORGANIZING
253 Charles A Liddle Dr # 1 (47025-2987)
PHONE..................................513 238-8157
Mark Grismore, *Owner*
EMP: 3 EST: 2006
SQ FT: 5,000
SALES (est): 364.5K **Privately Held**
SIC: 1799 5047 2434 Closet organizers, installation & design; medical & hospital equipment; wood kitchen cabinets

(G-9131)
AT THE BARN WINERY
1726 Einsel Rd (47025-8773)
PHONE..................................513 310-8810
Debby Stutz, *Principal*
EMP: 2
SALES (est): 83.1K **Privately Held**
SIC: 2084 Wines

(G-9132)
B N OIL LLC
622 Arch St (47025-1710)
PHONE..................................859 816-2244
Devanshi Patel, *Principal*
EMP: 2
SALES (est): 90.1K **Privately Held**
SIC: 1311 Crude petroleum & natural gas

(G-9133)
BATESVILLE PRODUCTS INC (PA)
434 Margaret St (47025-1747)
PHONE..................................513 381-2057
Fax: 812 537-5693
Richard E Weber, *President*

Thomas Kersting, *Vice Pres*
Terry Mc Carthy, *Vice Pres*
Tim Weber, *Vice Pres*
Tim Williams, *Purch Mgr*
▲ **EMP:** 63 **EST:** 1945
SQ FT: 24,000
SALES (est): 10.5MM **Privately Held**
WEB: www.batesvilleproducts.com
SIC: 3429 3544 3471 3443 Manufactured hardware (general); special dies, tools, jigs & fixtures; plating & polishing; fabricated plate work (boiler shop); nonferrous foundries; aluminum die-castings

(G-9134)
BEACON PUBLISHING CO INC
Also Called: Bright Beacon
24486 Stateline Rd Ste F (47025-9802)
P.O. Box 4022 (47025-4022)
PHONE.................................812 637-0660
Elizabeth Morris, *President*
EMP: 2
SALES: 70K **Privately Held**
SIC: 2711 Newspapers, publishing & printing

(G-9135)
CREATIVE CABINET DESIGNS
414 White Ridge Rd (47025-9163)
PHONE.................................812 637-3300
EMP: 4 **EST:** 1997
SALES: 175K **Privately Held**
SIC: 2599 Manufacture Custom Cabinets

(G-9136)
DEARBORN COATINGS LLC
25768 Mount Pleasant Rd (47025-9729)
PHONE.................................513 600-9580
Michael Robert Schallick, *Administration*
EMP: 2
SALES (est): 101.8K **Privately Held**
SIC: 3479 Metal coating & allied service

(G-9137)
DELPHOS HERALD OF INDIANA (PA)
Also Called: Register Publications
126 W High St (47025-1908)
PHONE.................................812 537-0063
EMP: 50
SALES: 1.8MM **Privately Held**
SIC: 2711 Newspapers-Publishing/Printing

(G-9138)
DELPHOS HERALD OF INDIANA INC (HQ)
Also Called: EAGLE PRINT
126 W High St (47025-1908)
PHONE.................................812 537-0063
Fax: 812 537-5576
Murray Cohen, *President*
April Fritch, *General Mgr*
Jim Buchberger, *Editor*
Janet Essert, *Adv Mgr*
John Reiniger, *Director*
EMP: 50 **EST:** 1825
SQ FT: 9,000
SALES: 1.3MM
SALES (corp-wide): 1.1MM **Privately Held**
WEB: www.registerpublications.com
SIC: 2711 2752 Commercial printing & newspaper publishing combined; commercial printing, lithographic; commercial printing, offset
PA: Herald Delphos Inc
　　405 N Main St
　　Delphos OH 45833
　　419 695-0015

(G-9139)
DONALDSON COMPANY INC
1802 Boardwalk Dr (47025-6722)
PHONE.................................812 637-9200
Fax: 812 637-9201
William Cook, *CEO*
EMP: 4
SALES (corp-wide): 2.3B **Publicly Held**
SIC: 3564 Blowers & fans
PA: Donaldson Company, Inc.
　　1400 W 94th St
　　Minneapolis MN 55431
　　952 887-3131

(G-9140)
ENGRAVE INC
140 Industrial Dr (47025-1116)
PHONE.................................812 537-8693
Fax: 812 537-8696
Robert E Polewski, *Ch of Bd*
Robert G Polewski, *President*
EMP: 12
SQ FT: 13,000
SALES (est): 1.9MM **Privately Held**
SIC: 3089 3544 Molding primary plastic; industrial molds

(G-9141)
FILCA LLC
22806 Stateline Rd (47025-9128)
PHONE.................................812 637-3559
Jonathon Wood, *Principal*
EMP: 2 **EST:** 2015
SALES (est): 112.9K **Privately Held**
SIC: 3599 Industrial machinery

(G-9142)
GABBARD AND SON ELECTRIC
252 Charles A Liddle Dr # 7 (47025-2978)
PHONE.................................812 747-7621
EMP: 2
SALES (est): 124.7K **Privately Held**
SIC: 3699 Electrical equipment & supplies

(G-9143)
GABRIEL INTL GROUP LLC (PA)
136 Industrial Dr (47025-1116)
P.O. Box 15396, Cincinnati OH (45215-0396)
PHONE.................................812 537-5400
Fax: 812 537-5501
Rick Kaup, *President*
Ronald Gibbons, *Manager*
EMP: 6
SQ FT: 5,100
SALES (est): 468.5K **Privately Held**
SIC: 3559 Tire shredding machinery

(G-9144)
GC FULLER MFG CO INC
1 Shurlite Dr (47025-2945)
PHONE.................................812 539-2831
Fax: 812 539-4029
Richard C Haneberg, *President*
Robert Haneberg, *Treasurer*
Sandy Laclair, *Office Mgr*
Sandra Le Clair, *Manager*
Roman Welter, *Admin Sec*
▲ **EMP:** 11 **EST:** 1917
SQ FT: 30,000
SALES (est): 2.3MM **Privately Held**
WEB: www.shurlite.com
SIC: 3548 Welding apparatus

(G-9145)
HOOSIER WALLBEDS INCORPORATED
23036 Stateline Rd (47025-7799)
PHONE.................................812 747-7154
Daniel J Badinghaus, *President*
EMP: 4
SALES (est): 259.8K **Privately Held**
SIC: 2679 Wallboard, decorated: made from purchased material

(G-9146)
KOI ENTERPRISES INC
Also Called: Federated Auto Parts
601 Saint Clair St (47025-1760)
PHONE.................................812 537-2335
Fax: 812 537-1231
Dave Eldridge, *Branch Mgr*
EMP: 7
SALES (corp-wide): 644.2MM **Privately Held**
SIC: 5531 5015 5013 3599 Automotive parts; motor vehicle parts, used; automotive supplies & parts; machine shop, jobbing & repair
HQ: K.O.I. Enterprises, Inc.
　　2701 Spring Grove Ave
　　Cincinnati OH 45225
　　513 357-2400

(G-9147)
LEISURE POOL & SPA
159 Florence Dr (47025-1198)
PHONE.................................812 537-0071
Fax: 812 537-0071

Thomas Cheek, *Mng Member*
EMP: 4
SALES (est): 368.6K **Privately Held**
SIC: 3949 5091 5999 Water sports equipment; swimming pools, equipment & supplies; swimming pool chemicals, equipment & supplies

(G-9148)
NEON ACCENTS
Also Called: Custom Signs
101 W Eads Pkwy (47025-1174)
PHONE.................................812 537-0102
Fax: 812 537-2320
Donald Gigerich, *Owner*
EMP: 2
SQ FT: 2,700
SALES: 250K **Privately Held**
WEB: www.trucknvans.com
SIC: 3993 Signs, not made in custom sign painting shops

(G-9149)
OHIO VALLEY ELECTRIC
800 Aep Dr (47025-2510)
PHONE.................................812 532-5288
EMP: 2
SALES (est): 104.8K **Privately Held**
SIC: 3699 1731 Electrical equipment & supplies; electrical work

(G-9150)
OSSENBECK MACH CO
4755 Eileens Way (47025-8573)
PHONE.................................937 564-6092
Robert Ossenbeck, *Owner*
EMP: 2 **EST:** 2015
SALES (est): 108.4K **Privately Held**
SIC: 3599 Industrial machinery

(G-9151)
OVIDEON LLC
135 Short St Side (47025-2007)
PHONE.................................812 577-3274
Tony Wiggins, *Partner*
EMP: 5
SALES: 1MM **Privately Held**
SIC: 3823 Digital displays of process variables

(G-9152)
PLANET PETS
1099 W Eads Pkwy (47025-1162)
PHONE.................................812 539-7316
Mac Renburen, *Owner*
EMP: 5
SALES (est): 401.6K **Privately Held**
SIC: 3999 Pet supplies

(G-9153)
PRAXAIR INC
601 Front St (47025-2607)
PHONE.................................812 537-2898
Barry Nanz, *Branch Mgr*
EMP: 21
SALES (corp-wide): 11.4B **Publicly Held**
SIC: 2813 Industrial gases
PA: Praxair, Inc.
　　10 Riverview Dr
　　Danbury CT 06810
　　203 837-2000

(G-9154)
QUILTERS GARDEN
9 E Center St (47025-1849)
PHONE.................................812 539-4939
Betty Warwick, *Principal*
EMP: 2
SALES (est): 146.1K **Privately Held**
SIC: 2395 Quilting & quilting supplies

(G-9155)
RIX LASER PROCESSING
252 Charles A Liddle Dr (47025-2978)
PHONE.................................812 537-9230
Richard Rees, *Principal*
EMP: 2
SALES (est): 206.9K **Privately Held**
SIC: 3599 Machine shop, jobbing & repair

(G-9156)
RON OSBORNE MACHINING INC
25660 Mount Pleasant Rd (47025-9721)
PHONE.................................812 637-1045
Ron Osborne, *President*
EMP: 5

SALES (est): 431.7K **Privately Held**
SIC: 3599 Machine shop, jobbing & repair

(G-9157)
SIGN A RAMA
Also Called: Sign-A-Rama
1210 W Eads Pkwy (47025-1165)
PHONE.................................812 537-5516
Fax: 812 537-5518
Kevin McCord, *Owner*
EMP: 5
SALES (est): 292.3K **Privately Held**
SIC: 3993 Signs & advertising specialties

(G-9158)
THINKING MACHINE LLC
798 Greentree Rd (47025-7674)
PHONE.................................812 539-2968
Jeff King, *Owner*
EMP: 2
SALES (est): 114.4K **Privately Held**
SIC: 3599 Industrial machinery

(G-9159)
TRADE LINE FABRICATING INC
22422 Stateline Rd (47025-7306)
PHONE.................................812 637-1444
James Klem, *President*
Eric Klem, *Corp Secy*
Kurt Klem, *Vice Pres*
Mark Klem, *Vice Pres*
EMP: 35
SQ FT: 27,000
SALES (est): 5.4MM **Privately Held**
SIC: 3599 7692 3444 3441 Machine shop, jobbing & repair; welding repair; sheet metalwork; fabricated structural metal

(G-9160)
TRI-STATE POWER SUPPLY LLC
48 Doughty Rd (47025-2939)
PHONE.................................812 537-2500
Terry Miller, *Mng Member*
EMP: 5 **EST:** 2010
SALES (est): 562.4K **Privately Held**
SIC: 5531 3691 5085 Batteries, automotive & truck; storage batteries; alkaline cell storage batteries; batteries, rechargeable; nickel cadmium storage batteries; industrial supplies

(G-9161)
W & M ENTERPRISES INC
370 Industrial Dr (47025-2900)
PHONE.................................812 537-4656
Fax: 812 537-5463
William Lawrence, *President*
Wendell Lawrence, *Vice Pres*
Carlos Lawrence, *Treasurer*
Shannon Clark, *Admin Sec*
EMP: 25
SQ FT: 30,000
SALES: 3MM **Privately Held**
WEB: www.wmtrailers.com
SIC: 3537 2449 Containers (metal), air cargo; wood containers

(G-9162)
WOODYS HOT RODZ LLC
23950 Salt Fork Rd (47025-9177)
PHONE.................................812 637-1933
Fax: 812 637-2370
Christopher Sondles, *President*
Gabrielle Sauerland, *Director*
EMP: 8
SALES (est): 1MM **Privately Held**
SIC: 3714 Propane conversion equipment, motor vehicle

Leavenworth
Crawford County

(G-9163)
CRAWFORD COUNTY CONCRETE
7172 S Tower Rd (47137-8304)
PHONE.................................812 739-2707
EMP: 2
SALES (est): 131.3K **Privately Held**
SIC: 5032 3273 Stone, crushed or broken; ready-mixed concrete

(G-9164)
JASPER ENGINE EXCHANGE INC
6400 E Industrial Ln (47137-8316)
PHONE....................................812 482-1041
Matt Williams, *Engineer*
Michele Harris, *Branch Mgr*
EMP: 100
SALES (corp-wide): 501.9MM **Privately Held**
WEB: www.jasperengines.com
SIC: 3714 Rebuilding engines & transmissions, factory basis; fuel systems & parts, motor vehicle; gears, motor vehicle
PA: Jasper Engine Exchange, Inc.
815 Wernsing Rd
Jasper IN 47546
812 482-1041

(G-9165)
MULZER CRUSHED STONE INC
Also Called: Cape Sandy Quarry
19925 S Alton Fredonia Rd (47137-7209)
PHONE....................................812 739-4777
Fax: 812 739-4105
Mike Rickenbaugh, *Maint Spvr*
Greg Cox, *QC Mgr*
Mart A Tarr, *Branch Mgr*
EMP: 150
SALES (corp-wide): 29.7B **Privately Held**
WEB: www.mulzer.com
SIC: 1429 Grits mining (crushed stone)
HQ: Mulzer Crushed Stone Inc
534 Mozart St
Tell City IN 47586
812 547-7921

Lebanon
Boone County

(G-9166)
AIR SYSTEMS COMPENTS LP
Also Called: ASC
843 Indianapolis Ave (46052-2829)
P.O. Box 646 (46052-0646)
PHONE....................................765 483-5841
Thomas Kristin, *COO*
EMP: 4
SALES (est): 997.4K **Privately Held**
SIC: 3585 Refrigeration & heating equipment

(G-9167)
AMERICAN AIR FILTER CO INC
Also Called: AAF International
210 N Enterprise Blvd (46052-8192)
PHONE....................................888 223-2003
Fax: 765 483-3673
Scott Swanson, *Manager*
EMP: 100
SQ FT: 200,000
SALES (corp-wide): 21.5B **Privately Held**
SIC: 3564 Filters, air: furnaces, air conditioning equipment, etc.
HQ: American Air Filter Company, Inc.
9920 Corporate Campus Dr # 2200
Louisville KY 40223
502 637-0011

(G-9168)
AMERICAN ULTRAVIOLET COMPANY (PA)
Also Called: American Ultraviolet Co., Inc.
212 S Mount Zion Rd (46052-9479)
PHONE....................................765 483-9514
Fax: 765 483-9525
Meredith C Stines, *President*
Diana Plunkett, *Purch Mgr*
◆ EMP: 60 EST: 1960
SQ FT: 70,000
SALES: 14MM **Privately Held**
SIC: 3674 3641 Ultra-violet sensors, solid state; ultraviolet lamps

(G-9169)
ARC OF GREATER BOONE CNTY INC
Also Called: ARC Rehab Services
912 W Main St (46052-2318)
PHONE....................................765 482-0051
Fax: 765 482-0051
Shannon Riley, *Consultant*
Brit Cartin, *Exec Dir*
EMP: 11 **Privately Held**
SIC: 8322 8331 3999 Rehabilitation services; job training & vocational rehabilitation services; atomizers, toiletry
PA: Arc Of Greater Boone County, The Inc.
900 W Main St
Lebanon IN 46052

(G-9170)
ATP WELDING INC
Also Called: Atp Steel & Welding Supplies
930 Hendricks Dr (46052-2973)
P.O. Box 212 (46052-0212)
PHONE....................................765 483-9273
Fax: 765 483-9316
Rick Scott, *President*
Joyce Scott, *Admin Sec*
EMP: 9
SALES: 1MM **Privately Held**
WEB: www.atpwelding.com
SIC: 7692 Welding repair

(G-9171)
C D VENTURES INC
820 Hendricks Dr (46052-2971)
PHONE....................................765 482-9179
Nathan M Fouch, *President*
Rose Mary Fouch, *Vice Pres*
Pat Willis, *Manager*
Brenda L Fouch, *Admin Sec*
EMP: 4
SQ FT: 13,000
SALES: 350K **Privately Held**
SIC: 2621 Paper mills; packaging paper

(G-9172)
CASE NEW HOLLAND LLC
420 S Enterprise Blvd (46052-8888)
PHONE....................................765 482-5446
Jeffrey Case, *Principal*
▲ EMP: 14
SALES (est): 2.7MM **Privately Held**
SIC: 3523 Farm machinery & equipment

(G-9173)
CENTRE TOWNSHIP
525 Ransdell Rd (46052-2372)
PHONE....................................765 482-1729
Pat McGinley, *Chief*
EMP: 30 **Privately Held**
SIC: 9224 1389 Fire department, not including volunteer; fire fighting, oil & gas field
PA: Centre Township
1122 N Lebanon St E
Lebanon IN 46052

(G-9174)
CNH INDUSTRIAL AMERICA LLC
400 S Enterprise Blvd (46052-8888)
PHONE....................................765 482-5409
Keith Hansen, *Manager*
Holly Derose, *Manager*
EMP: 208
SALES (corp-wide): 27.9B **Privately Held**
SIC: 3523 Farm machinery & equipment
HQ: Cnh Industrial America Llc
700 State St
Racine WI 53404
262 636-6011

(G-9175)
COMMUNITY HOLDINGS INDIANA INC
Also Called: Lebanon Reporter, The
117 E Washington St (46052-2209)
PHONE....................................765 482-4650
Greta Sanderson, *Manager*
EMP: 25 **Privately Held**
WEB: www.clintonnc.com
SIC: 2711 2791 2752 Newspapers: publishing only, not printed on site; typesetting; commercial printing, lithographic
HQ: Community Holdings Of Indiana, Inc.
3500 Colonnade Pkwy # 600
Birmingham AL 35243

(G-9176)
COMMUNITY HOLDINGS INDIANA INC
Also Called: Zionsville Times Sentinel
117 E Washington St (46052-2209)
PHONE....................................317 873-6397
Fax: 317 873-6259
Greta Sanderson, *Manager*
EMP: 7 **Privately Held**
SIC: 2711 Newspapers, publishing & printing
HQ: Community Holdings Of Indiana, Inc.
3500 Colonnade Pkwy # 600
Birmingham AL 35243

(G-9177)
CROSSROADS IMPRINTS INC
107 W Main St (46052-2522)
PHONE....................................765 482-2931
Steve Horton, *President*
EMP: 2
SALES (est): 158.3K **Privately Held**
SIC: 2752 Commercial printing, lithographic

(G-9178)
CUSTOM COVERS INC
4548 W 50 S (46052-9465)
PHONE....................................765 481-7800
Todd Stewart, *CEO*
Jodi Kinsler, *President*
EMP: 5
SQ FT: 2,400
SALES (est): 675.6K **Privately Held**
WEB: www.customcovers.com
SIC: 3081 Floor or wall covering, unsupported plastic

(G-9179)
DAVID W MILLER MILLER LONGBOW
1304 S East St Apt C (46052-2892)
PHONE....................................765 482-3234
David Miller, *Principal*
EMP: 2
SALES (est): 110.5K **Privately Held**
SIC: 3949 Bows, archery

(G-9180)
DE VOLS ORNAMENTAL IRON
4540 E State Road 32 (46052-9605)
PHONE....................................765 482-1171
Fax: 765 482-1141
Don Devol, *Partner*
Alice Devol, *Partner*
EMP: 3 EST: 1967
SQ FT: 3,500
SALES (est): 285.3K **Privately Held**
WEB: www.apexweb.com
SIC: 3446 5712 Architectural metalwork; gates, ornamental metal; outdoor & garden furniture

(G-9181)
DONALDSONS CHOCOLATES INC
Also Called: Donaldson Country Home
600 S State Road 39 (46052-9401)
PHONE....................................765 482-3334
Fax: 765 482-7994
George Donaldson, *President*
EMP: 12
SALES (est): 1.5MM **Privately Held**
WEB: www.donaldsonschocolates.com
SIC: 2064 2066 Candy bars, including chocolate covered bars; chocolate & cocoa products

(G-9182)
FALL CREEK CORPORATION
Also Called: Fall Creek Enterprises
917 E Walnut St (46052-2870)
P.O. Box 92, Whitestown (46075-0092)
PHONE....................................765 482-1861
Fax: 765 482-1861
A J Fulks, *President*
EMP: 6
SQ FT: 3,000
SALES (est): 500K **Privately Held**
WEB: www.fcsutler.com
SIC: 2389 5932 Uniforms & vestments; used merchandise stores

(G-9183)
GIGGLING WENCHES HANDCRAFTS
2123 Hannah Ct (46052-4016)
PHONE....................................765 482-9776
EMP: 2 EST: 2003
SALES: 6.4K **Privately Held**
SIC: 2389 Mfg Apparel/Accessories

(G-9184)
H W HASTY WELDING INC
125 W 300 N (46052-9538)
PHONE....................................765 482-8925
Fax: 765 482-8983
H Wayne Hasty, *President*
Kathryn Hasty, *Vice Pres*
EMP: 8
SALES (est): 682.2K **Privately Held**
SIC: 7692 Welding repair

(G-9185)
HACHETTE BOOK GROUP INC
121 N Enterprise Blvd (46052-8193)
PHONE....................................765 483-9900
John Baker, *Buyer*
Alisha Fisher, *Manager*
Jim Dicarlo, *Manager*
Ron Olsen, *Manager*
EMP: 250
SALES (corp-wide): 70.7MM **Privately Held**
SIC: 2731 5192 Books: publishing only; books, periodicals & newspapers
HQ: Hachette Book Group, Inc.
1290 Ave Of The Americas
New York NY 10104
800 759-0190

(G-9186)
HANGOUT AT FLAMES LLC
Also Called: Promotion Extras
3776 N State Road 39 (46052-9598)
PHONE....................................765 483-2009
Lucia Smith,
EMP: 2
SALES: 10K **Privately Held**
SIC: 3999 Manufacturing industries

(G-9187)
HENDRICKSON INTERNATIONAL CORP
Also Called: Hendrickson Trlr Suspntn
180 N Mount Zion Rd (46052-8329)
PHONE....................................765 483-5350
Fax: 765 482-2928
Perry Bahr, *Manager*
EMP: 250
SALES (corp-wide): 1.1B **Privately Held**
SIC: 3715 3714 3713 Truck trailers; motor vehicle parts & accessories; truck & bus bodies
HQ: Hendrickson International Corporation
500 Park Blvd Ste 450
Itasca IL 60143
630 874-9700

(G-9188)
IBC COATINGS TECHNOLOGIES LTD
902 Hendricks Dr (46052-2973)
PHONE....................................317 418-3725
Solomon Berman, *President*
David Stanton, *Opers Mgr*
Eugene Popov, *Project Engr*
Ilya Y Soyfer, *Controller*
Caity King, *Human Resources*
▲ EMP: 20
SQ FT: 15,000
SALES (est): 3.8MM **Privately Held**
WEB: www.ibccoatings.com
SIC: 3479 Coating of metals & formed products

(G-9189)
IBC MATERIALS & TECH LLC
902 Hendricks Dr (46052-2973)
PHONE....................................765 482-9802
Solomon Berman, *President*
Ashok Ramaswamy, *President*
Kyla Dunn, *Info Tech Mgr*
EMP: 15
SALES (est): 2.4MM **Privately Held**
SIC: 3479 Coating of metals & formed products

(G-9190)
IGH STEEL FABRICATION INC
1001 Ransdell Rd (46052-2352)
PHONE....................................765 482-7534
Scott Nirider, *President*
EMP: 5
SALES (est): 1.1MM **Privately Held**
SIC: 3441 Fabricated structural metal

(G-9191)
INDIANA BATON TWIRLING ASSOC
6920 S 280 E (46052-9780)
PHONE....................................317 769-6826
Larry Leap, *Principal*
EMP: 2
SALES (est): 122K **Privately Held**
SIC: 3949 Batons

(G-9192)
INTERPAK INC
820 Hendricks Dr (46052-2971)
PHONE....................................765 482-9179
Fax: 765 482-9175
Nathan Fouch, *President*
Rose Mary Fouch, *Vice Pres*
EMP: 5 EST: 1972
SALES (est): 540K **Privately Held**
SIC: 2679 Paperboard products, converted

(G-9193)
IRVING MATERIALS INC
417 S West St (46052)
PHONE....................................765 482-5620
Fax: 765 482-5661
Mike Swank, *Manager*
EMP: 7
SALES (corp-wide): 800.6MM **Privately Held**
SIC: 3273 Ready-mixed concrete
PA: Irving Materials, Inc.
8032 N State Road 9
Greenfield IN 46140
317 326-3101

(G-9194)
K & M TOOL & DIE INC
406 S Patterson St (46052-2334)
P.O. Box 645 (46052-0645)
PHONE....................................765 482-9464
Fax: 765 482-0348
John Kouns, *CEO*
Norma Kouns, *President*
Steven Kouns, *Vice Pres*
EMP: 6
SQ FT: 72,000
SALES (est): 904.1K **Privately Held**
SIC: 3544 Special dies, tools, jigs & fixtures

(G-9195)
KAUFFMAN ENGINEERING INC (PA)
701 Ransdell Rd (46052-2385)
PHONE....................................765 483-4919
Fax: 765 483-4930
Michael W Buis, *President*
Otto N Frenzel IV, *Treasurer*
Kent Howard, *Admin Sec*
▲ EMP: 90
SQ FT: 70,000
SALES (est): 87.5MM **Privately Held**
WEB: www.tmmorrismfg.com
SIC: 3679 Harness assemblies for electronic use: wire or cable

(G-9196)
KAUFFMAN ENGINEERING INC LLC
202 S Mount Zion Rd (46052-9479)
PHONE....................................765 482-5640
Gary Hake, *Manager*
EMP: 75
SALES (corp-wide): 87.5MM **Privately Held**
SIC: 3679 Harness assemblies for electronic use: wire or cable
PA: Kauffman Engineering Inc
701 Ransdell Rd
Lebanon IN 46052
765 483-4919

(G-9197)
LAMINIQUE INC
540 Ransdell Rd (46052-2373)
PHONE....................................765 482-4222
Fax: 765 482-4266
Keith Hammer, *President*
Robert Brown, *Vice Pres*
EMP: 27
SQ FT: 13,800

SALES (est): 4MM **Privately Held**
WEB: www.laminique.com
SIC: 2519 2541 2434 Fiberglass & plastic furniture; wood partitions & fixtures; wood kitchen cabinets

(G-9198)
LEBANON BERG VAULT CO INC
730 E Elm St (46052-2620)
PHONE....................................765 482-0302
Marion Galvin, *President*
EMP: 5
SQ FT: 8,000
SALES (est): 494.7K **Privately Held**
SIC: 3272 5087 Burial vaults, concrete or precast terrazzo; concrete burial vaults & boxes

(G-9199)
LEBANON CORP (PA)
Also Called: David Alan Chocolatier
1700 N Lebanon St (46052-1501)
P.O. Box 588 (46052-0588)
PHONE....................................765 482-7273
Fax: 765 482-5660
David Honan, *President*
Paul R Honan Jr, *President*
Jon Silverderg, *Vice Pres*
Kathleen Honan, *Admin Sec*
EMP: 5
SQ FT: 5,750
SALES (est): 813.7K **Privately Held**
SIC: 3841 Eye examining instruments & apparatus

(G-9200)
LEBANON REPORTER
117 E Washington St (46052-2200)
PHONE....................................765 482-4650
EMP: 15
SALES (est): 105.8K **Privately Held**
SIC: 2711 Newspapers-Publishing/Printing

(G-9201)
LOGOS EXPRESS INC
1225 Ransdell Ct (46052-2377)
PHONE....................................317 272-1200
Mark A Scott, *President*
Matthew Beem, *Vice Pres*
EMP: 3
SALES (est): 270K **Privately Held**
SIC: 2396 Screen printing on fabric articles

(G-9202)
MARSHALL COMPANIES INDIANA
Also Called: Marshall Crane
6850 S 280 E (46052-9780)
PHONE....................................317 769-2666
Toll Free:..........................866   -
Fax: 317 769-3169
Jim Marshall, *President*
Rod Marshall, *Vice Pres*
EMP: 8 EST: 1997
SQ FT: 7,800
SALES (est): 1.2MM **Privately Held**
SIC: 3531 1542 Cranes; commercial & office building contractors

(G-9203)
MARVELOUS WOODWORKING LLC
5475 S 175 W (46052-9740)
PHONE....................................317 679-5890
Douglas S Marvel, *Administration*
EMP: 2 EST: 2009
SALES (est): 211.4K **Privately Held**
SIC: 2431 Millwork

(G-9204)
MC GINLEY FIRE APPARATUS
901 W Washington St (46052-2082)
PHONE....................................765 482-3152
Fax: 765 482-0558
James McGinley, *Owner*
James Mc Ginley, *Owner*
EMP: 4 EST: 1975
SALES (est): 454K **Privately Held**
SIC: 3711 7539 Fire department vehicles (motor vehicles), assembly of; automotive repair shops

(G-9205)
METAL TECHNOLOGY OF INDIANA
Also Called: M T I
810 Hendricks Dr (46052-2971)
PHONE....................................765 482-1100
Fax: 765 482-1133
Donna E Hoyt, *President*
Bryan L Hoyt, *Exec VP*
Darrell E Morlan, *Admin Sec*
EMP: 20
SQ FT: 12,000
SALES: 2.6MM **Privately Held**
WEB: www.metaltechcoatings.com
SIC: 3449 7699 Miscellaneous metalwork; professional instrument repair services

(G-9206)
MINUTE PRINT IT INC
312 W South St (46052-2458)
PHONE....................................765 482-9019
Fax: 765 482-9050
Yancy Stults, *President*
Anne Brown, *Manager*
EMP: 8
SQ FT: 7,200
SALES: 850K **Privately Held**
SIC: 2752 2791 Commercial printing, offset; typesetting

(G-9207)
MODELS LLC (PA)
2275 S 500 W (46052-8948)
P.O. Box 624 (46052-0624)
PHONE....................................765 676-6700
Chip Mc Mann,
▲ EMP: 20 EST: 1961
SQ FT: 4,000
SALES (est): 2MM **Privately Held**
WEB: www.modelsllc.net
SIC: 3089 3444 3599 Injection molding of plastics; sheet metalwork; machine shop, jobbing & repair

(G-9208)
MOSSMAN METAL WORKS
3595 W 200 S (46052-8936)
PHONE....................................765 676-6055
Matthew Mossman, *Owner*
EMP: 3
SALES: 400K **Privately Held**
SIC: 3444 Sheet metalwork

(G-9209)
NEWJAC INC
415 S Grant St (46052-3605)
PHONE....................................765 483-2190
Loren Gard, *President*
Anthony D Haag, *President*
Barry Newton, *Vice Pres*
Mike Nolan, *Facilities Dir*
Mike Carter, *Project Mgr*
EMP: 100
SQ FT: 86,000
SALES (est): 32.1MM **Privately Held**
WEB: www.newjac.com
SIC: 3399 Iron ore recovery from open hearth slag

(G-9210)
PALMOR PRODUCTS INC (PA)
1990 John Bart Rd (46052-1212)
PHONE....................................800 872-2822
Fax: 765 436-2490
Deborah M Crum, *President*
Stanley Morton, *President*
Karen L Morton, *Treasurer*
Morton Stanley G, *Admin Sec*
EMP: 40 EST: 1975
SQ FT: 56,000
SALES (est): 5.8MM **Privately Held**
WEB: www.trac-vac.com
SIC: 3524 3444 Blowers & vacuums, lawn; sheet metalwork

(G-9211)
PEARSON EDUCATION INC
199 Pearson Pkwy (46052-2798)
PHONE....................................765 483-6500
John Lytle, *Branch Mgr*
EMP: 230
SALES (corp-wide): 5.9B **Privately Held**
SIC: 2721 Periodicals

HQ: Pearson Education, Inc.
221 River St
Hoboken NJ 07030
201 236-7000

(G-9212)
PEARSON EDUCATION INC
150 Pearson Pkwy (46052-2798)
PHONE....................................765 483-6738
EMP: 237
SALES (corp-wide): 5.9B **Privately Held**
SIC: 2721 Periodicals
HQ: Pearson Education, Inc.
221 River St
Hoboken NJ 07030
201 236-7000

(G-9213)
PENGUIN RANDOM HOUSE LLC
199 Pearson Pkwy (46052-2798)
PHONE....................................800 672-7836
David Shanks, *CEO*
EMP: 3
SALES (corp-wide): 82.3MM **Privately Held**
SIC: 2731 Books: publishing only
HQ: Penguin Random House Llc
1745 Broadway
New York NY 10019
212 782-9000

(G-9214)
PERDUE FARMS INC
5490 N 500 E (46052-8214)
PHONE....................................765 325-2997
Camillo Ramaro, *Manager*
EMP: 9
SALES (corp-wide): 5.5B **Privately Held**
WEB: www.perdue.com
SIC: 2015 Chicken, processed: fresh
PA: Perdue Farms Inc.
31149 Old Ocean City Rd
Salisbury MD 21804
410 543-3000

(G-9215)
PERFECTION PRODUCTS INC
1320 Indianapolis Ave (46052-2949)
PHONE....................................765 482-7786
Fax: 765 482-7792
John Vickery, *President*
EMP: 30
SQ FT: 32,000
SALES (est): 4.6MM **Privately Held**
WEB: www.perfection-products.com
SIC: 3674 Semiconductors & related devices

(G-9216)
PHOENIX SAFE INTERNATIONAL LLC
382 N Mount Zion Rd (46052-8330)
P.O. Box 608 (46052-0608)
PHONE....................................765 483-0954
Paul Carsaro, *President*
Alfred J McQueen, *President*
Janet L Pape, *President*
Penny S Cooper, *Vice Pres*
Janet Pape, *Vice Pres*
▲ EMP: 4
SQ FT: 2,150
SALES (est): 878.4K **Privately Held**
WEB: www.phoenixsafeusa.com
SIC: 3499 Safe deposit boxes or chests, metal

(G-9217)
PICTURE PERFECT PRINTING
1301 Ashley Dr (46052-1081)
PHONE....................................765 482-4241
Robert Patterson, *Principal*
EMP: 2
SALES (est): 114.1K **Privately Held**
SIC: 2752 Commercial printing, lithographic

(G-9218)
QUALITY DRAPERY CORPORATION
1334 W Main St (46052-2326)
PHONE....................................765 481-2370
Fax: 765 481-2380
Michael Lewellyn, *President*
EMP: 20
SQ FT: 24,000

▲ = Import ▼=Export
◆ =Import/Export

SALES (est): 1MM **Privately Held**
SIC: 2391 5023 Curtains & draperies; draperies

(G-9219)
QUICKSILVER METALS INC
2805 N State Road 39 (46052-9192)
PHONE.....................................765 482-1782
Anthony Holmes, *President*
Catherine Holmes, *Admin Sec*
EMP: 2
SALES: 50K **Privately Held**
SIC: 3599 Machine shop, jobbing & repair

(G-9220)
RICH MANUFACTURING INC
1990 John Bart Rd (46052-1212)
PHONE.....................................765 436-2744
Fax: 765 436-2521
Stan Morton, *President*
EMP: 6
SALES (est): 1MM **Privately Held**
SIC: 3524 3423 Lawn & garden equipment; hand & edge tools

(G-9221)
SAINT ADRIAN MEATS SAUSAGE LLC
6115 E State Road 47 (46052-9227)
PHONE.....................................317 403-3305
Ryan West,
Amelia West,
EMP: 2 **EST:** 2014
SALES (est): 208.5K **Privately Held**
SIC: 2013 Sausages & related products, from purchased meat; frozen meats from purchased meat; smoked meats from purchased meat

(G-9222)
SEMSTREAM LP
550 W 125 S (46052-9403)
P.O. Box 568 (46052-0568)
PHONE.....................................765 482-8105
Fax: 765 482-8119
John Fansher, *Manager*
EMP: 4
SALES (est): 249.4K **Privately Held**
SIC: 1321 Propane (natural) production

(G-9223)
SHARK-CO MFG LLC
1231 Indianapolis Ave (46052-2932)
PHONE.....................................317 670-6397
Monica Sharkey, *Principal*
Jason Sharkey, *Principal*
Ryan Walden, *Principal*
EMP: 5
SALES (est): 307.9K **Privately Held**
SIC: 3999 Manufacturing industries

(G-9224)
SKJODT-BRRETT CNTRACT PCKG LLC
401 S Enterprise Blvd (46052-8888)
PHONE.....................................765 482-6856
Dan Skjodt, *President*
Ben Chen, *Credit Mgr*
▲ **EMP:** 300
SQ FT: 220,000
SALES (est): 109.8MM **Privately Held**
SIC: 2099 Food preparations

(G-9225)
SMART MANUFACTURING INC
515 N State Road 75 (46052-8261)
PHONE.....................................765 482-7481
Dale W Thompson, *President*
Gary Cummins, *Vice Pres*
EMP: 4
SALES (est): 500.6K **Privately Held**
WEB: www.smartmfg.net
SIC: 3728 1799 Deicing equipment, aircraft; welding on site

(G-9226)
SPAN INC
724 Esplanade St (46052-1654)
PHONE.....................................317 347-2646
Fax: 317 347-2640
William Baker, *President*
Andy Kaffenberger, *Vice Pres*
EMP: 12
SQ FT: 10,000

SALES (est): 2MM **Privately Held**
WEB: www.spaninc.com
SIC: 3691 8711 Batteries, rechargeable; electrical or electronic engineering; marine engineering

(G-9227)
TAB TECHNOLOGIES
437 W 150 S (46052-8184)
PHONE.....................................765 482-7561
Steve O'Hara, *Owner*
EMP: 3
SALES (est): 296.1K **Privately Held**
SIC: 8731 3511 Computer (hardware) development; turbo-generators

(G-9228)
THREE K RACING ENTERPRISES
Also Called: 3-K Racing
2685 S 25 W (46052-9748)
PHONE.....................................765 482-4273
Melvin Kenyon, *President*
Donald Kenyon, *Corp Secy*
EMP: 2 **EST:** 1969
SALES: 500K **Privately Held**
SIC: 7538 3799 Engine rebuilding: automotive; midget autos, power driven

(G-9229)
TRIANGLE ASPHALT PAVING CORP
501 Sam Ralston Rd (46052-1339)
PHONE.....................................765 482-5701
Fax: 765 482-1405
Steven L Day, *President*
John Day, *Vice Pres*
Elizabeth Lewis, *Treasurer*
EMP: 25
SQ FT: 4,200
SALES (est): 4.3MM **Privately Held**
WEB: www.triangleasphalt.com
SIC: 1611 2951 2952 Surfacing & paving; asphalt & asphaltic paving mixtures (not from refineries); asphalt felts & coatings

(G-9230)
TRUCKPRO LLC
Also Called: Power Train
450 N Enterprise Blvd (46052-8185)
PHONE.....................................765 482-6525
Bob Baumgardp, *Manager*
EMP: 10
SALES (corp-wide): 1.8B **Privately Held**
SIC: 7537 3714 3315 Automotive transmission repair shops; motor vehicle parts & accessories; steel wire & related products
HQ: Truckpro, Llc
1900 Charles Bryan Rd
Cordova TN 38016
901 252-4200

(G-9231)
UNITED STATES COLD STORAGE INC
415 S Mount Zion Rd (46052-8897)
PHONE.....................................765 482-2653
Fax: 765 482-2652
Jacob McChristian, *Engineer*
Adam Ashley, *Branch Mgr*
EMP: 44
SALES (corp-wide): 9.8B **Privately Held**
SIC: 4222 2097 Warehousing, cold storage or refrigerated; block ice; ice cubes
HQ: United States Cold Storage, Inc.
2 Aquarium Dr Ste 400
Camden NJ 08103
856 354-8181

(G-9232)
WHITAKER GLASS & MIRROR LLC
104 E Superior St (46052-2535)
PHONE.....................................765 482-1500
Troy Whitaker,
EMP: 8
SALES (est): 888K **Privately Held**
SIC: 3231 5231 Products of purchased glass; glass, leaded or stained

Leesburg
Kosciusko County

(G-9233)
BRICK STREET EMBROIDERY
205 E Prairie St (46538-7719)
P.O. Box 193 (46538-0193)
PHONE.....................................574 453-3729
Helen Smoker, *Owner*
EMP: 2
SALES (est): 60K **Privately Held**
SIC: 3993 Signs & advertising specialties

(G-9234)
CLUNETTE ELEVATOR CO INC
4316 W 600 N (46538-9210)
PHONE.....................................574 858-2281
Fax: 574 858-2558
John Anglin, *President*
John Anglin Jr, *President*
Dan Anglin, *Vice Pres*
Tom Anglin, *Treasurer*
Jessica Ayers, *Sales Executive*
EMP: 15 **EST:** 1951
SQ FT: 25,000
SALES: 10MM **Privately Held**
SIC: 5191 5153 2041 2875 Fertilizer & fertilizer materials; feed; grain elevators; flour & other grain mill products; fertilizers, mixing only

(G-9235)
COMPOSITE DESIGNS INC
Also Called: C D I
306 School St (46538-7726)
P.O. Box 176 (46538-0176)
PHONE.....................................574 453-2902
Raymond Doss, *President*
Sean Alderfer, *Principal*
Karl Schmucker, *Admin Sec*
EMP: 6 **EST:** 2008
SALES (est): 434.4K **Privately Held**
SIC: 2439 Arches, laminated lumber

(G-9236)
GALLOWAY FABRICATING
3776 E 750 N (46538-9161)
PHONE.....................................574 453-3802
Fax: 574 453-3802
Larry A Galloway, *Owner*
EMP: 4
SQ FT: 8,000
SALES (est): 404K **Privately Held**
SIC: 3469 Spinning metal for the trade

(G-9237)
J L HARRIS MACHINE CO INC
4953 N 700 E (46538-8940)
PHONE.....................................574 834-2866
Fax: 574 834-2866
James L Harris, *President*
Sandra Harris, *Admin Sec*
EMP: 3
SALES (est): 419.8K **Privately Held**
SIC: 3599 Machine shop, jobbing & repair

(G-9238)
MAPLE LEAF INC (PA)
Also Called: Maple Leaf Farms
101 E Church St (46538-7701)
P.O. Box 167 (46538-0167)
PHONE.....................................574 453-4455
Terry L Tucker B S, *President*
John Tucker, *Principal*
Scott Tucker, *Co-President*
Mike Turk, *Vice Pres*
Mike Vint, *Maint Spvr*
◆ **EMP:** 455
SALES (est): 25.5MM **Privately Held**
SIC: 0259 2015 5159 Duck farm; ducks, processed; chicken, processed; feathers

Leo
Allen County

(G-9239)
BETTER VISIONS PC
Also Called: City Vision Center
10529 Hosler Rd A (46765-9736)
PHONE.....................................260 627-2669
Andrew B Hogue, *President*

Dennis D Sutton, *Principal*
EMP: 3 **EST:** 1999
SALES (est): 234.7K **Privately Held**
SIC: 5995 3827 Contact lenses, prescription; aiming circles (fire control equipment)

(G-9240)
C&M WOODWORKING LLC
10225 Donald Ave (46765-9507)
PHONE.....................................260 403-4555
Charles A Biller, *Administration*
EMP: 2 **EST:** 2014
SALES (est): 110.5K **Privately Held**
SIC: 2431 Millwork

(G-9241)
CEDAR CREEK STUDIOS INC
7030 Hosler Rd (46765-9547)
P.O. Box 480 (46765-0480)
PHONE.....................................260 627-7320
Nancy Walters, *President*
Jim Walters, *Vice Pres*
EMP: 2
SQ FT: 1,200
SALES (est): 246.1K **Privately Held**
WEB: www.caiminc.com
SIC: 3089 3714 3053 Injection molding of plastics; motor vehicle parts & accessories; gaskets, packing & sealing devices

(G-9242)
DAVID KECHEL
Also Called: Miltec Circuits
12921 Leo Rd (46765-9656)
PHONE.....................................260 627-2749
David Kechel, *Owner*
EMP: 9 **EST:** 1988
SQ FT: 6,000
SALES: 1.5MM **Privately Held**
WEB: www.2miltec.com
SIC: 3672 Printed circuit boards

(G-9243)
K GRIMMER INDUSTRIES INC (PA)
Also Called: Hurricane Compressor Company
17301 Juniper Ln (46765-9340)
PHONE.....................................317 736-3800
Fax: 317 736-3801
John E Grimmer, *Ch of Bd*
Kenneth Grimmer, *President*
◆ **EMP:** 50
SQ FT: 50,000
SALES (est): 24.3MM **Privately Held**
SIC: 3563 4924 Air & gas compressors including vacuum pumps; natural gas distribution

(G-9244)
MOORES WELDING SERVICE INC
13131 Leo Rd (46765-9628)
PHONE.....................................260 627-2177
Fax: 260 627-8477
Michael B Moore, *President*
Anne Moore, *Vice Pres*
▲ **EMP:** 5
SQ FT: 3,500
SALES (est): 400K **Privately Held**
SIC: 7692 1799 Welding repair; welding on site

(G-9245)
POCO A POCO LLC
7611 Hursh Rd (46765-9538)
PHONE.....................................317 443-5753
Samuel Steury, *Principal*
EMP: 2
SALES (est): 68.4K **Privately Held**
SIC: 2084 Wines, brandy & brandy spirits

(G-9246)
TRUDEL FAMILY LTD PARTNERSHIP
14101 Leo Rd (46765-9666)
PHONE.....................................260 627-5626
Theodore G Trudel, *General Ptnr*
EMP: 2
SALES: 50K **Privately Held**
SIC: 3524 Lawn & garden mowers & accessories

Leroy
Lake County

(G-9247)
COPE BROTHERS MACHINE SHOP
5301 E State Rd 231 (46355)
PHONE..........................219 663-5561
Fax: 219 226-1575
Larry Cope, *President*
Sheryl Cope, *Vice Pres*
EMP: 4 EST: 1946
SQ FT: 4,000
SALES (est): 484K Privately Held
SIC: 3599 Machine shop, jobbing & repair

Lewisville
Henry County

(G-9248)
APM&CO INC
616 W Us Highway 40 (47352-9711)
PHONE..........................317 409-5639
Arlen McBride, *President*
Joseph A McBride, *Vice Pres*
EMP: 7
SQ FT: 12,134
SALES (est): 350K Privately Held
SIC: 2046 Corn oil, crude

Lexington
Scott County

(G-9249)
BURTON LUMBER CO INC
13980 W Polk Rd (47138-6924)
PHONE..........................812 866-4438
Fax: 812 866-4438
Bobby Burton, *President*
Christine Burton, *Corp Secy*
Henry L Burton, *Vice Pres*
EMP: 18
SALES (est): 3.2MM Privately Held
SIC: 2448 2426 2421 2411 Pallets, wood; furniture dimension stock, hardwood; sawmills & planing mills, general; logging

(G-9250)
GLDN RULE TRUSS & METAL SALES
4886 S 850 W (47138-7620)
PHONE..........................812 866-1800
Milt Kinsinder, *Owner*
EMP: 2
SALES: 400K Privately Held
SIC: 5051 3443 Plates, metal; truss plates, metal

(G-9251)
HANSON AGGREGATES MIDWEST LLC
313 S State Road 203 (47138-9002)
P.O. Box 130, Scottsburg (47170-0130)
PHONE..........................812 889-2120
Darrell Owsley, *Opers Mgr*
Roger Hawkins, *Facilities Mgr*
EMP: 12
SALES (corp-wide): 20.3B Privately Held
SIC: 1422 3281 3274 Limestones, ground; cut stone & stone products; lime
HQ: Hanson Aggregates Midwest Llc
207 Old Harrods Creek Rd
Louisville KY 40223
502 244-7550

(G-9252)
KEITH BIXLER
Also Called: Bixlers Logging
352 S Getty Rd (47138-8403)
PHONE..........................812 866-1637
Keith Bixler, *Owner*
EMP: 4
SALES (est): 175.4K Privately Held
SIC: 2411 Logging

(G-9253)
LONGBOW MACHINING LLC
1666 S Rogers Rd (47138-7772)
PHONE..........................812 599-6728
Tonie A Wycoff, *Partner*
EMP: 4
SALES: 100K Privately Held
SIC: 3545 Machine tool accessories

(G-9254)
NIELSEN COMPANY
1602 S 1066 W (47138-7064)
PHONE..........................812 889-3493
EMP: 2
SALES (est): 108.3K Privately Held
SIC: 2752 Commercial printing, lithographic

(G-9255)
RBG INC
Also Called: Clown Room, The
9186 W Henry Rd (47138-7933)
PHONE..........................812 866-3983
Ron Gregory, *Owner*
EMP: 3 EST: 2010
SALES (est): 121.4K Privately Held
SIC: 3949 Bowling balls

(G-9256)
WAGLER MACHINING LLC
11778 W State Road 256 (47138-6817)
PHONE..........................812 866-2904
Joshua Wagler, *Manager*
Jill Wagler,
EMP: 4
SQ FT: 1,200
SALES: 150K Privately Held
SIC: 3599 Machine shop, jobbing & repair

Liberty
Union County

(G-9257)
C & F INDUSTRIES
5282 W Booth Rd (47353-8477)
PHONE..........................765 580-0378
EMP: 3
SALES (est): 183.9K Privately Held
SIC: 3999 Manufacturing industries

(G-9258)
CHARLES KOLB LOGGING
7096 S Snowden Rd (47353-8972)
PHONE..........................765 458-7766
Charles F Kolb, *Partner*
James Kolb, *Partner*
Thomas Kolb, *Partner*
EMP: 3 EST: 1957
SALES (est): 338.9K Privately Held
WEB: www.charleskolblogging.com
SIC: 2411 Logging camps & contractors

(G-9259)
COFFMAN & FAIRBANKS INDUSTRIES
5282 W Booth Rd (47353-8477)
PHONE..........................765 458-7896
Christyanne Coffman, *Principal*
EMP: 2
SALES (est): 86K Privately Held
SIC: 3999 Manufacturing industries

(G-9260)
EATON PARTNERS LLC
5282 W Booth Rd (47353-8477)
PHONE..........................765 458-7896
Shane Coffman, *Owner*
EMP: 2
SALES (est): 149K Privately Held
SIC: 3625 Motor controls & accessories

(G-9261)
JAMES E BARNHIZER
Also Called: Barnhizer Machining and Wldg
2302 Omar Fields Dr (47353-9620)
PHONE..........................765 458-9344
James E Barnhizer, *Owner*
EMP: 5
SALES (est): 484K Privately Held
SIC: 3544 Special dies, tools, jigs & fixtures

(G-9262)
KITCHEN KRAFTS
302 E Union St (47353-1211)
PHONE..........................765 458-6858
Kenneth C Hoog, *Owner*
EMP: 2
SALES (est): 62.3K Privately Held
SIC: 2022 Processed cheese

(G-9263)
LARRY G BYRD
Also Called: B & B Washer Assemblies
2312 W County Road 250 S (47353-9056)
PHONE..........................765 458-7285
Fax: 765 458-7285
Larry G Byrd, *Owner*
Carol S Byrd, *Partner*
EMP: 10 EST: 1982
SALES: 450K Privately Held
SIC: 3069 Washers, rubber

(G-9264)
LIBERTY HERALD
10 N Market St (47353-1122)
PHONE..........................765 458-5114
Fax: 765 458-5115
Gary Wolf, *President*
EMP: 6
SALES (est): 315K Privately Held
SIC: 2711 Newspapers, publishing & printing

(G-9265)
MEDRECO INC
757 S State Road 101 (47353-8974)
P.O. Box 100 (47353-0100)
PHONE..........................765 458-7444
Fax: 765 458-7446
Gerald S Paul, *President*
EMP: 9
SQ FT: 30,000
SALES: 1.3MM Privately Held
WEB: www.medreco.com
SIC: 2599 Hospital beds

(G-9266)
NAPIER & NAPIER
2369 S Us Highway 27 (47353-9796)
PHONE..........................765 580-9116
Fax: 765 458-6879
Theresa Schwegman, *Partner*
Tara Mc Creary, *Partner*
Robert D Napier, *Partner*
EMP: 5
SQ FT: 10,000
SALES: 450K Privately Held
SIC: 3644 3471 3444 3354 Insulators & insulation materials, electrical; plating & polishing; sheet metalwork; aluminum extruded products; steel pipe & tubes

(G-9267)
NSK CORPORATION
Also Called: NSK Corporation, Liberty Plant
1112 E Kitchel Rd (47353-8985)
PHONE..........................765 458-5000
Fax: 765 458-7832
Brian Grissom, *Plant Mgr*
Andrew McCashland, *Buyer*
Joyce Lake, *Purchasing*
Andy Boger, *Engineer*
Michael Charlton, *Engineer*
EMP: 209
SALES (corp-wide): 9.5B Privately Held
WEB: www.nsk-corp.com
SIC: 3562 5085 3714 3568 Ball bearings & parts; bearings; motor vehicle parts & accessories; power transmission equipment; bolts, nuts, rivets & washers
HQ: Nsk Corporation
4200 Goss Rd
Ann Arbor MI 48105
734 913-7500

(G-9268)
OUTDOOR PERFORMANCE
2920 S Us Highway 27 (47353-8516)
PHONE..........................765 732-3335
Travis Walters, *Owner*
EMP: 8 EST: 2009
SALES (est): 1MM Privately Held
SIC: 3751 Motorcycles & related parts

(G-9269)
OXFORD CABINET COMPANY LLC
141 S Us Highway 27 (47353-9076)
PHONE..........................765 223-2101
Terry Hupp, *Principal*
EMP: 3
SALES (est): 227.3K Privately Held
SIC: 2434 Wood kitchen cabinets

(G-9270)
PROLINE BOWSTRINGS
1957 S Hubble Rd (47353-9622)
PHONE..........................513 259-3738
Joe Hamilton, *Owner*
EMP: 3
SALES (est): 162.4K Privately Held
SIC: 3949 Archery equipment, general

(G-9271)
RPC MACHINERY INC
424 N Industrial Park Rd (47353-8575)
PHONE..........................765 458-5655
Edmond Reaser, *President*
EMP: 4 EST: 1994
SQ FT: 3,000
SALES (est): 590.1K Privately Held
WEB: www.rpmachineryserviceinc.com
SIC: 3554 1796 Paper industries machinery; installing building equipment

(G-9272)
WHITEWATER VALLEY RVS INC
853 S State Road 101 (47353-9045)
PHONE..........................765 458-5171
Fax: 765 458-7416
Mary Evans Munsing, *President*
Darren Redpath, *Owner*
EMP: 6
SQ FT: 1,400
SALES (est): 859.8K Privately Held
SIC: 3715 Truck trailers; demountable cargo containers

(G-9273)
WINSLOW-BROWNING INC
Also Called: W B I
215 Brownsville Ave (47353-1002)
PHONE..........................765 458-5157
W John Browning, *President*
Karen Capps, *VP Admin*
Ronald Herring, *Vice Pres*
Carl Peraino, *Sales Staff*
Kay Bishop, *Director*
EMP: 20
SQ FT: 28,000
SALES (est): 4.8MM Privately Held
SIC: 2851 Coating, air curing

Ligonier
Noble County

(G-9274)
ACADIA
1201 Gerber St (46767-2420)
PHONE..........................260 894-7125
Fax: 260 894-4896
Ken Wiese, *Manager*
EMP: 2
SALES (est): 331.6K Privately Held
SIC: 3714 Motor vehicle parts & accessories

(G-9275)
ADVANCED METAL ETCHING INC
801 Gerber St (46767-2412)
PHONE..........................260 894-4189
Fax: 260 894-4190
Blake Geer, *President*
Scott Seniff, *President*
EMP: 26
SQ FT: 22,000
SALES: 2.6MM Privately Held
WEB: www.metaletching.com
SIC: 3678 3599 Electronic connectors; chemical milling job shop

(G-9276)
ANNIE OAKLEY ENTERPRISES INC
300 Johnson St (46767-2309)
P.O. Box 203 (46767-0203)
PHONE..................................260 894-7100
Fax: 260 894-7218
Renee Gabet, *President*
Charles Gabet, *Vice Pres*
▲ **EMP:** 12 **EST:** 1971
SQ FT: 2,400
SALES (est): 720K **Privately Held**
SIC: 3961 2844 Costume jewelry, ex. precious metal & semiprecious stones; perfumes, natural or synthetic

(G-9277)
BLACKPOINT ENGINEERING LLC
Also Called: Jet City Specialties
601 Sroufe St Ste 200 (46767-0010)
PHONE..................................574 642-3152
Steve Wygant, *Mng Member*
EMP: 7 **EST:** 1996
SQ FT: 6,000
SALES (est): 1MM **Privately Held**
WEB: www.partdaddy.com
SIC: 3599 Machine shop, jobbing & repair

(G-9278)
BRC RUBBER & PLASTICS INC
Ligonier Rubber
1497 Gerber St (46767-2422)
P.O. Box 71 (46767-0071)
PHONE..................................260 894-4121
Fax: 260 894-7263
Richard Nieno, *Opers-Prdtn-Mfg*
EMP: 165
SQ FT: 32,000
SALES (corp-wide): 171.4MM **Privately Held**
SIC: 3061 3714 3053 Mechanical rubber goods; motor vehicle parts & accessories; gaskets, packing & sealing devices
PA: Brc Rubber & Plastics, Inc.
1029a W State Blvd
Fort Wayne IN 46808
260 693-2171

(G-9279)
CARLEX GLASS AMERICA LLC
Carlex Glass Ind Inc-Ligonier
860 W Us Highway 6 (46767-2543)
PHONE..................................260 894-7750
Fax: 260 894-4999
Bill Barnhart, *Engineer*
Russell Ebeid, *Manager*
EMP: 470
SALES (corp-wide): 2.1B **Privately Held**
SIC: 3231 Products of purchased glass
HQ: Carlex Glass America, Llc
7200 Centennial Blvd
Nashville TN 37209

(G-9280)
CUSTOM CUT CANVAS LLC
401 W Union St (46767-1234)
PHONE..................................260 221-3000
Linfred Unternahrer, *Principal*
EMP: 2
SALES (est): 56.3K **Privately Held**
SIC: 2211 Canvas

(G-9281)
EDNA TROYER
Also Called: Apple Designs
6316 W 825 N (46767-9541)
PHONE..................................260 894-4405
Edna Troyer, *Owner*
EMP: 2
SQ FT: 6,000
SALES (est): 133.6K **Privately Held**
SIC: 2452 2511 Panels & sections, prefabricated, wood; chairs, household, except upholstered: wood

(G-9282)
EMERGENCY RADIO SERVICE LLC (PA)
9144 N 900 W (46767-9236)
P.O. Box 110 (46767-0110)
PHONE..................................317 821-0422
Fax: 260 894-7581
Brian T Hull, *President*
Rick Helstrom, *Area Mgr*

John Hull, *Vice Pres*
Mark T Hull, *Vice Pres*
Karen Kieper, *CFO*
EMP: 35
SQ FT: 6,000
SALES: 17MM **Privately Held**
WEB: www.erssite.com
SIC: 5065 3441 Communication equipment; tower sections, radio & television transmission

(G-9283)
ERS HOLDING COMPANY INC (PA)
9144 N 900 W (46767-9236)
PHONE..................................260 894-4145
Brian T Hull, *President*
EMP: 21 **EST:** 2014
SALES (est): 8.6MM **Privately Held**
SIC: 3441 Tower sections, radio & television transmission

(G-9284)
ERS TOWER LLC
Also Called: MISSION 1 COMMUNICATIONS
9144 N 900 W (46767-9236)
P.O. Box 110 (46767-0110)
PHONE..................................260 894-4145
John Hull, *President*
Jon Shultz, *General Mgr*
EMP: 25
SALES: 8.6MM **Privately Held**
SIC: 3441 Tower sections, radio & television transmission
PA: Ers Holding Company, Inc.
9144 N 900 W
Ligonier IN 46767
260 894-4145

(G-9285)
FREUDENBERG-NOK GENERAL PARTNR
Also Called: Automotive Vibration Division
1497 Gerber St (46767-2422)
PHONE..................................260 894-7183
Fax: 260 894-4960
Steve Sperlazza, *Manager*
EMP: 450
SALES (corp-wide): 8.3B **Privately Held**
WEB: www.freudenberg-nok.com
SIC: 3714 3594 3444 Motor vehicle engines & parts; fluid power pumps & motors; sheet metalwork
HQ: Freudenberg-Nok General Partnership
47774 W Anchor Ct
Plymouth MI 48170
734 451-0020

(G-9286)
GROTRIAN TOOL & DIE
300 Sroufe St (46767-1246)
P.O. Box 171 (46767-0171)
PHONE..................................260 894-3558
Fax: 260 894-3552
Mark Grotrian, *Owner*
EMP: 3
SQ FT: 1,000
SALES (est): 200K **Privately Held**
SIC: 3544 Special dies & tools

(G-9287)
HITACHI AUTOMOTIVE SYSTEMS
925 N Main St (46767-2060)
PHONE..................................859 734-9451
Steve Meadows, *Branch Mgr*
EMP: 300
SALES (corp-wide): 87.9B **Privately Held**
SIC: 3694 3714 3699 3625 Alternators, automotive; ignition systems, high frequency; motor vehicle parts & accessories; electrical equipment & supplies; relays & industrial controls
HQ: Hitachi Automotive Systems Americas, Inc.
955 Warwick Rd
Harrodsburg KY 40330
859 734-9451

(G-9288)
JELD-WEN INC
Jeld-Wen Doors
200 Gerber St (46767-1518)
P.O. Box 259 (46767-0259)
PHONE..................................260 894-7111

Steve Crawford, *Branch Mgr*
EMP: 115
SQ FT: 22,000 **Publicly Held**
WEB: www.jeld-wen.com
SIC: 3442 Metal doors
HQ: Jeld-Wen, Inc.
2645 Silver Crescent Dr
Charlotte NC 28273
800 535-3936

(G-9289)
LIGONIER WOODWORKING
1068 E Perry Rd (46767-9568)
PHONE..................................260 894-9969
Richard Hochstetler, *Co-Owner*
Irene Hochstetler, *Co-Owner*
EMP: 7
SALES (est): 450K **Privately Held**
SIC: 2431 7389 Millwork;

(G-9290)
MULTITECH SWISS MACHINING LLC
711 Gerber St (46767-2410)
PHONE..................................260 894-4180
Rahul Parikh, *President*
Joel Brown, *Director*
Thomas Falcone, *Admin Sec*
EMP: 9
SQ FT: 20,000
SALES (est): 333.4K **Privately Held**
SIC: 3451 Screw machine products
PA: Multitech Industries, Inc.
350 Village Dr
Carol Stream IL 60188

(G-9291)
P & J INDUSTRIES INC
1494 Gerber St (46767-2421)
PHONE..................................260 894-7143
Fax: 260 894-4893
Chris Judt, *Manager*
EMP: 30
SALES (corp-wide): 11.4MM **Privately Held**
SIC: 3471 Chromium plating of metals or formed products; electroplating of metals or formed products
PA: P & J Industries, Inc.
4934 Lewis Ave
Toledo OH 43612
419 726-2675

(G-9292)
PARKER-HANNIFIN CORPORATION
Also Called: Integrated Sealing Systems Div
1201 Gerber St (46767-2420)
P.O. Box 29 (46767-0029)
PHONE..................................260 894-7125
Christopher Overmyer, *Engineer*
Jason Brown, *Branch Mgr*
Del Owen, *Manager*
Stephanie Reese, *Manager*
EMP: 150
SALES (corp-wide): 12B **Publicly Held**
WEB: www.parker.com
SIC: 3714 3568 3053 Transmission housings or parts, motor vehicle; power transmission equipment; gaskets, packing & sealing devices
PA: Parker-Hannifin Corporation
6035 Parkland Blvd
Cleveland OH 44124
216 896-3000

(G-9293)
PRO TECH METAL FINISHING
214 Heckner Dr (46767-2062)
PHONE..................................260 894-4011
Randall Pollem, *Owner*
EMP: 20
SALES (est): 1.7MM **Privately Held**
SIC: 3471 Finishing, metals or formed products

(G-9294)
ROYAL IMPRINTS INC
711 Gerber St (46767-2410)
P.O. Box 599, Sunman (47041-0599)
PHONE..................................800 894-3151
Fax: 260 894-3822
EMP: 45
SALES (est): 6.1MM
SALES (corp-wide): 2.8B **Privately Held**
SIC: 2621 Paper Mills

HQ: The Occasions Group Inc
1750 Tower Blvd
North Mankato MN 56003
507 625-0800

(G-9295)
SILGAN PLASTICS LLC
910 Gerber St (46767-2425)
PHONE..................................260 894-3118
Fax: 260 894-7805
EMP: 100
SALES (corp-wide): 3.6B **Publicly Held**
SIC: 3085 Mfg Plastic Bottles
HQ: Silgan Plastics Llc
14515 North Outer 40 Rd # 210
Chesterfield MO 63017
800 274-5426

(G-9296)
STRUCTURAL COMPOSITES IND INC
Also Called: SCI
1118 Gerber St (46767-2417)
PHONE..................................260 894-4083
Fax: 260 894-4289
Jim Fearnow, *President*
Lynette Gerard, *COO*
Ken Baranowski, *Admin Sec*
EMP: 100
SQ FT: 40,000
SALES (est): 18MM
SALES (corp-wide): 1.6B **Publicly Held**
SIC: 2221 3799 Fiberglass fabrics; automotive fabrics, manmade fiber; recreational vehicles
PA: Patrick Industries, Inc.
107 W Franklin St
Elkhart IN 46516
574 294-7511

(G-9297)
SUPERIOR SAMPLE CO INC
520 Gerber St (46767-2405)
P.O. Box 550 (46767-0550)
PHONE..................................260 894-3136
Fax: 260 894-7636
Nancy Hagen, *CEO*
Peggy Daniels, *President*
Rex Hagen, *Chairman*
▲ **EMP:** 40
SQ FT: 120,000
SALES (est): 6.3MM **Privately Held**
WEB: www.superiorsample.com
SIC: 2789 Swatches & samples

(G-9298)
SUPREME CORPORATION
Also Called: Tower Structural Laminating
1491 Gerber St (46767-2422)
PHONE..................................260 894-9191
Fax: 260 894-9199
Al Schroeder, *Branch Mgr*
EMP: 275
SALES (corp-wide): 1.7B **Publicly Held**
SIC: 3713 3792 3585 Truck bodies (motor vehicles); travel trailers & campers; refrigeration & heating equipment
HQ: Supreme Corporation
2581 Kercher Rd
Goshen IN 46528
574 642-4888

(G-9299)
TENNECO AUTOMOTIVE OPER CO INC
1490 Gerber St (46767-2421)
PHONE..................................260 894-9214
Fax: 574 894-9495
Tim Holland, *Branch Mgr*
EMP: 204
SALES (corp-wide): 9.2B **Publicly Held**
WEB: www.tenneco-automotive.com
SIC: 3714 Mufflers (exhaust), motor vehicle
HQ: Tenneco Automotive Operating Company, Inc.
500 N Field Dr
Lake Forest IL 60045
847 482-5000

(G-9300)
TI AUTOMOTIVE LIGONIER CORP
925 N Main St (46767-2060)
PHONE..................................260 894-3163

G E O G R A P H I C

William Kozyra, *President*
Mike Zdroik, *President*
Dale Freel, *Engineer*
Don Lamkin, *Engineer*
Kevin Shell, *Engineer*
◆ **EMP:** 400 **EST:** 1990
SQ FT: 160,000
SALES: 131.4K
SALES (corp-wide): 4B **Privately Held**
SIC: 3714 Motor vehicle parts & accessories
HQ: Ti Group Automotive Systems, Llc
2020 Taylor Rd
Auburn Hills MI 48326
248 296-8000

(G-9301)
VIBRACOUSTIC NORTH AMERICA L P
1496 Gerber St (46767-2421)
PHONE...................260 894-7199
William Tobin, *Manager*
EMP: 150
SALES (corp-wide): 2.1B **Privately Held**
SIC: 3559 Automotive related machinery
HQ: Vibracoustic North America, L. P.
400 Aylworth Ave
South Haven MI 49090

(G-9302)
VIBRATION CONTROL TECH LLC
1492 Gerber St (46767-2421)
PHONE...................260 894-7199
Bob Schultz, *CFO*
▲ **EMP:** 2 **EST:** 2011
SALES (est): 250.2K **Privately Held**
SIC: 3559 Special industry machinery

Linden
Montgomery County

(G-9303)
CARLSON MOTORSPORTS
Also Called: Carlson Racing
215 N High St (47955-8108)
P.O. Box 153 (47955-0153)
PHONE...................765 339-4407
Brian Carlson, *Partner*
Sarah Carlson, *Partner*
EMP: 2
SALES (est): 205.3K **Privately Held**
WEB: www.carlsonmotorsports.com
SIC: 3519 5599 Internal combustion engines; go-carts

(G-9304)
LINDEN MACHINE SHOP LLC
220 N Main St (47955-8091)
P.O. Box 382 (47955-0382)
PHONE...................765 339-7244
Fax: 765 339-4732
Darryl Smith,
Tammy Smith,
EMP: 4
SQ FT: 9,200
SALES (est): 545.9K **Privately Held**
SIC: 3599 7692 3471 Machine shop, jobbing & repair; welding repair; plating & polishing

(G-9305)
SPURLINO MTLS INDIANAPOLIS LLC
11528 N Us Highway 231 (47955-8004)
PHONE...................765 339-4055
Jim Spurlino,
EMP: 40
SALES (est): 1.9MM **Privately Held**
SIC: 3273 Ready-mixed concrete

Linton
Greene County

(G-9306)
D & M PRINTING INC
Also Called: Smith Printing
13 N Main St (47441-1762)
PHONE...................812 847-4837
Fax: 812 847-4837
Mike Smith, *President*

EMP: 2
SQ FT: 840
SALES (est): 245.5K **Privately Held**
SIC: 2752 2791 Commercial printing, offset; typesetting

(G-9307)
H AND H 3D PLASTICS INC
12759 W 300 N (47441-6112)
PHONE...................812 699-0379
Jason Habich, *Principal*
EMP: 2
SALES (est): 107.6K **Privately Held**
SIC: 3089 Monofilaments, nontextile

(G-9308)
JACKSON BROTHERS LUMBER CO
59 State Rd S (47441)
PHONE...................812 847-7812
Rick Destrom, *President*
Bobbie Ferguson, *Admin Sec*
EMP: 14
SALES: 740K **Privately Held**
SIC: 2421 2431 2426 Lumber: rough, sawed or planed; millwork; hardwood dimension & flooring mills

(G-9309)
LANDIS EQUIPMENT & TOOL RENTAL
Also Called: A Rental Center
390 S Main St (47441-2116)
PHONE...................812 847-2582
Scott Landis, *Owner*
EMP: 3
SALES (est): 220.1K **Privately Held**
SIC: 3599 5084 7513 Machine shop, jobbing & repair; industrial machinery & equipment; truck rental & leasing, no drivers

(G-9310)
MARKLE MUSIC
Also Called: Markle Classic Signs
44 S Main St (47441-1819)
PHONE...................812 847-2103
Fax: 812 847-2103
Fred Markle, *Owner*
Kathy Markle, *Co-Owner*
Merritt Houldson,
EMP: 3 **EST:** 1978
SQ FT: 4,000
SALES (est): 274.7K **Privately Held**
WEB: www.marklemusic.com
SIC: 5736 7699 3993 String instruments; musical instrument repair services; signs & advertising specialties

(G-9311)
PITTMAN MINE SERVICE LLC
2878 N State Road 59 (47441-6199)
PHONE...................812 847-2340
Raymond Pittman, *Owner*
Victor Daiber, *Vice Pres*
EMP: 30
SALES (est): 4.3MM **Privately Held**
SIC: 1241 7353 8741 Bituminous coal mining services, contract basis; heavy construction equipment rental; construction management

(G-9312)
PRO-MARK BLDG SOLUTIONS LLC
575 N 1000 W (47441-5297)
P.O. Box 633 (47441-0633)
PHONE...................812 798-1178
EMP: 11
SALES (est): 487.9K **Privately Held**
SIC: 2952 Roofing materials

(G-9313)
RUSS PUBLISHING
Also Called: Linton Daily Citizen
79 S Main St (47441-1818)
P.O. Box 129 (47441-0129)
PHONE...................812 847-4487
Randy Lift, *CEO*
Chris Pruett, *Publisher*
EMP: 19
SQ FT: 10,000

SALES (est): 982.6K **Privately Held**
SIC: 2711 Commercial printing & newspaper publishing combined; newspapers, publishing & printing

(G-9314)
SUPERIOR ICE CO INC
492 A St Nw (47441-6704)
P.O. Box 4 (47441-0004)
PHONE...................812 847-4312
Fax: 812 847-3494
Blaine Lannan, *President*
EMP: 15
SQ FT: 7,500
SALES (est): 2.5MM **Privately Held**
SIC: 5999 2097 Ice; manufactured ice

(G-9315)
WILKES PRINTING INC
1089 1st St Se (47441-5635)
PHONE...................812 847-0005
EMP: 2 **EST:** 2016
SALES (est): 83.9K **Privately Held**
SIC: 2752 Lithographic Commercial Printing

Lizton
Hendricks County

(G-9316)
INDUSTRIAL TUBE COMPONENTS INC
6114 N County Road 50 W (46149-9485)
PHONE...................317 431-2188
Kimberly Russell, *Principal*
Matt Russell, *Principal*
EMP: 6
SALES (est): 625.4K **Privately Held**
SIC: 3498 Tube fabricating (contract bending & shaping)

(G-9317)
LASTEC LLC
7865 N County Road 100 E (46149-9402)
PHONE...................317 892-4444
Mark Thompson, *Principal*
Dave Baylif, *Principal*
David Bayless, *Sales Mgr*
Brian Ashley, *Regl Sales Mgr*
Darryl Floyd, *Manager*
EMP: 13
SALES (est): 2.4MM **Privately Held**
SIC: 3524 Lawn & garden mowers & accessories

(G-9318)
WOOD-MIZER HOLDINGS INC
Also Called: Lastec
7865 N County Rd Ste 100 (46149)
PHONE...................317 892-4188
Fax: 317 892-4188
Bill Etienne, *COO*
Scott Dufek, *Branch Mgr*
EMP: 55
SALES (corp-wide): 116MM **Privately Held**
WEB: www.lastec.com
SIC: 3524 Lawn & garden mowers & accessories
PA: Wood-Mizer Holdings, Inc.
8180 W 10th St
Indianapolis IN 46214
317 271-1542

Logansport
Cass County

(G-9319)
A RAYMOND TINNERMAN AUTO INC
Also Called: A Raymond Tinnerman
800 W County Road 250 S (46947-8269)
PHONE...................574 722-5168
Wes Carden, *Engineer*
Keith Holmes, *Branch Mgr*
Dee Butz, *Manager*
Lloyd Knight, *Manager*
Tony Hillman, *Planning*
EMP: 240 **Privately Held**
WEB: www.tinnermanpalnut.com

SIC: 3471 3495 3469 3429 Plating & polishing; wire springs; metal stampings; manufactured hardware (general); metal heat treating; copper foundries
HQ: A. Raymond Tinnerman Automotive, Inc.
3091 Research Dr
Rochester Hills MI 48309
248 260-2121

(G-9320)
AMERI-TEK MANUFACTURING INC
3332 Billiard Dr (46947-8272)
P.O. Box 359 (46947-0359)
PHONE...................574 753-8058
Fax: 574 722-3117
Joe B Bowyer, *President*
Steven E Bowyer, *Vice Pres*
Debbie Bowyer, *Admin Sec*
EMP: 14
SQ FT: 17,600
SALES (est): 2.6MM **Privately Held**
WEB: www.ameri-tekmfg.com
SIC: 3469 3544 Stamping metal for the trade; special dies & tools

(G-9321)
ANDERSONS AGRICULTURE GROUP LP
2345 S 400 E (46947)
PHONE...................574 753-4974
Rod Erny, *Manager*
EMP: 12
SALES (corp-wide): 3.6B **Publicly Held**
SIC: 2874 2873 2875 Phosphatic fertilizers; nitrogenous fertilizers; fertilizers, mixing only
HQ: The Andersons Agriculture Group L P
1947 Briarfield Blvd
Maumee OH 43537
419 893-5050

(G-9322)
ANDERSONS CLYMERS ETHANOL LLC
3389 W County Road 300 S (46947-8924)
PHONE...................574 722-2627
EMP: 2
SALES (corp-wide): 3.6B **Publicly Held**
SIC: 2869 Ethyl alcohol, ethanol
HQ: The Andersons Clymers Ethanol Llc
1947 Briarfield Blvd
Maumee OH 43537

(G-9323)
BACCHUS WINERY GOLF VINYRD LLC
14 Golfview Dr (46947-4104)
PHONE...................574 732-4663
Amanda Crain, *Administration*
EMP: 2
SALES (est): 115.6K **Privately Held**
SIC: 2084 Wines

(G-9324)
BHJ USA INC
Also Called: Cass County Byproducts
81 E Industrial Blvd (46947-6712)
PHONE...................574 722-3933
Fax: 574 737-8606
TI Montgomery, *Plant Mgr*
Chris Hallam, *Branch Mgr*
EMP: 40 **Privately Held**
SIC: 5149 2047 Pet foods; dog & cat food
HQ: Bhj Usa, Inc.
2510 Edward Babe Gmez Ave
Omaha NE 68107
402 734-8030

(G-9325)
BILLMAN MONUMENT & SIGN CO
1137 Pleasant HI (46947-1924)
PHONE...................574 753-2394
Fax: 574 732-0149
Charlie Gaumer, *Owner*
EMP: 2 **EST:** 1889
SQ FT: 3,600
SALES (est): 138.7K **Privately Held**
SIC: 5999 3993 Monuments, finished to custom order; signs, not made in custom sign painting shops

(G-9326)
CAL-COMP USA (INDIANA) INC
Also Called: Total Electronics
1 Technology Way (46947-1710)
PHONE.............................956 342-5061
Jack Chang, *CEO*
Tom Conrad, *COO*
John Yerger, *COO*
Ronald L Rehberger, *Vice Pres*
Mark Martin, *Facilities Mgr*
▲ EMP: 400
SQ FT: 72,000
SALES (est): 137.8MM
SALES (corp-wide): 3.2B **Privately Held**
WEB: www.totalems.com
SIC: 3672 Circuit boards, television & radio
printed
PA: Cal-Comp Electronics (Thailand) Public
Company Limited
191/54, 191/57 Ratchadaphisek Road
Klong Toei 10110
226 150-33

(G-9327)
CARMICHAEL ELECTRIC LLC
4334 Logansport Rd (46947-8862)
PHONE.............................574 722-4028
Anthony Carmichael,
EMP: 7 EST: 2009
SALES (est): 896.7K **Privately Held**
SIC: 3699 Electrical equipment & supplies

(G-9328)
CARTER FUEL SYSTEMS LLC (HQ)
101 E Industrial Blvd (46947-6994)
PHONE.............................574 722-6141
Michael Muller, *Purch Mgr*
Robert Henderson, *Mng Member*
▲ EMP: 270
SALES (est): 129.5MM
SALES (corp-wide): 816.9MM **Privately Held**
SIC: 3714 5989 Fuel pumps, motor vehicle; coal
PA: Crowne Group, Llc
127 Public Sq Ste 5110
Cleveland OH 44114
216 589-0198

(G-9329)
CARTER FUEL SYSTEMS LLC
91 E Industrial Blvd (46947-6712)
PHONE.............................574 735-0235
Brad Angel, *Plant Mgr*
EMP: 400
SALES (corp-wide): 816.9MM **Privately Held**
SIC: 3714 Motor vehicle parts & accessories
HQ: Carter Fuel Systems, Llc
101 E Industrial Blvd
Logansport IN 46947
574 722-6141

(G-9330)
CARTERS CONCRETE BLOCK INC (PA)
Also Called: Kokomo Masonry & Supply
5110 W Us Highway 24 (46947-7079)
PHONE.............................574 722-2644
Fax: 574 722-5614
Steve Carter, *President*
Linda Carter, *Corp Secy*
David Carter, *Vice Pres*
EMP: 20 EST: 1943
SQ FT: 2,000
SALES (est): 3.2MM **Privately Held**
WEB: www.cartersconcreteblock.com
SIC: 3272 5211 Concrete stuctural support
& building material; lintels, concrete;
brick; masonry materials & supplies

(G-9331)
CASS COUNTY MACHINE INC
2915 Green Hills Dr (46947-1311)
PHONE.............................574 722-5714
Fax: 574 722-2920
Larry D Bruck, *President*
Steve Bodony, *Finance Mgr*
Karen Cox, *Office Mgr*
EMP: 13 EST: 1947
SQ FT: 7,500
SALES: 500K **Privately Held**
SIC: 3599 Machine shop, jobbing & repair

(G-9332)
COMMUNITY HOLDINGS INDIANA INC
Also Called: Pharos Tribune
517 E Broadway (46947-3154)
P.O. Box 210 (46947-0210)
PHONE.............................574 722-5000
Robyn McClosky, *Branch Mgr*
EMP: 16 **Privately Held**
WEB: www.clintonnc.com
SIC: 2711 2752 Newspapers, publishing &
printing; commercial printing, lithographic
HQ: Community Holdings Of Indiana, Inc.
3500 Colonnade Pkwy # 600
Birmingham AL 35243

(G-9333)
CRAFTSNMOREGALORE LLC
710 W Melbourne Ave (46947-3055)
PHONE.............................574 303-2231
Carma Veil, *Principal*
EMP: 2
SALES (est): 116.1K **Privately Held**
SIC: 5999 2893 Banners, flags, decals &
posters; letterpress or offset ink

(G-9334)
EIS FIBERCOATING INC
616 E Main St (46947-5003)
PHONE.............................574 722-5192
Fax: 574 722-6452
Paul Rossomme, *President*
Linda Rossomme, *Vice Pres*
EMP: 50
SQ FT: 8,000
SALES (est): 7.4MM **Privately Held**
WEB: www.fibercoating.com
SIC: 3069 3089 Hard rubber & molded
rubber products; plastic processing

(G-9335)
GRABLE BURIAL VAULT SERVICES
322 Highland St (46947-4936)
P.O. Box 1079 (46947-0979)
PHONE.............................574 753-4514
Mike Grable, *President*
EMP: 3
SALES: 400K **Privately Held**
SIC: 3272 Burial vaults, concrete or precast terrazzo

(G-9336)
HOPPER DEVELOPMENT INC
Also Called: H D I
1332 18th St (46947-4464)
P.O. Box 296 (46947-0296)
PHONE.............................574 753-6621
Fax: 574 753-6670
Robert J Hopper, *President*
John Hopper, *President*
Joan Hopper, *Corp Secy*
Doug Lucy, *Foreman/Supr*
Jason Hopper, *Officer*
EMP: 17 EST: 1970
SQ FT: 14,000
SALES (est): 1.7MM **Privately Held**
WEB: www.teamhdi.com
SIC: 3089 3544 3543 3469 Injection
molding of plastics; forms (molds), for
foundry & plastics working machinery; industrial patterns; metal stampings

(G-9337)
HTI
500 W Clinton St Ste 2 (46947-4684)
P.O. Box 741 (46947-0741)
PHONE.............................574 722-2814
Fax: 574 722-8460
Chico Rodriguez, *General Mgr*
Matthew Gluth, *Plant Engr*
EMP: 18 EST: 1976
SQ FT: 27,000
SALES (est): 4.1MM **Privately Held**
WEB: www.callhti.com
SIC: 3398 Metal heat treating

(G-9338)
HUMPHREY TOOL CO INC
120 Water St (46947-1874)
P.O. Box 48 (46947-0048)
PHONE.............................574 753-3853
Fax: 574 722-7219
Ron Bunger, *President*
EMP: 4

SQ FT: 3,600
SALES: 467.7K **Privately Held**
SIC: 3469 3544 Stamping metal for the
trade; special dies & tools

(G-9339)
I N C O M WHOLESALE SUPPLY
2865 E Market St (46947-2070)
PHONE.............................574 722-2442
Mike McCord, *Owner*
Stephanie Tatacsil, *Manager*
EMP: 3
SALES (est): 150K **Privately Held**
SIC: 2899 Chemical supplies for foundries

(G-9340)
INDIANA DIMENSION INC
Also Called: I D I
1621 W Market St (46947-9728)
P.O. Box 568 (46947-0568)
PHONE.............................574 739-2319
Fax: 574 739-2818
Byron Roy Rentschler, *President*
William M Cole, *Chairman*
Jeremy Rentschler, *Corp Secy*
Ken Gibbs, *Opers Staff*
John A Land, *CFO*
▲ EMP: 55
SQ FT: 180,000
SALES (est): 7.5MM **Privately Held**
WEB: www.indianadimension.com
SIC: 2431 Millwork; panel work, wood;
moldings, wood: unfinished & prefinished

(G-9341)
INTERACTIONS INC
Also Called: Pepsi-Cola
1031 N 3rd St (46947-2619)
P.O. Box 449 (46947-0449)
PHONE.............................574 722-6207
Fax: 574 722-5185
Gary Enders, *Principal*
Bobbi Pearcy, *Production*
Gary L Enders, *Controller*
Pete Nelson, *Sales Staff*
Lamont Pryor, *Sales Staff*
EMP: 75
SQ FT: 66,000
SALES (est): 10.2MM **Privately Held**
WEB: www.interactions.com
SIC: 2086 Soft drinks: packaged in cans,
bottles, etc.

(G-9342)
IRVING MATERIALS INC
Also Called: I M I
2245 S County Road 150 E (46947-8007)
P.O. Box 842 (46947-0842)
PHONE.............................574 722-3420
Adam Reeser, *Branch Mgr*
EMP: 4
SALES (corp-wide): 800.6MM **Privately Held**
SIC: 3273 Ready-mixed concrete
PA: Irving Materials, Inc.
8032 N State Road 9
Greenfield IN 46140
317 326-3101

(G-9343)
JC PRINTING
301 Burlington Ave (46947-4834)
PHONE.............................574 721-9000
Jorge Ceron, *Principal*
EMP: 2
SALES (est): 168.8K **Privately Held**
SIC: 2752 Commercial printing, lithographic

(G-9344)
KAUFFMAN ENGINEERING INC
830 State Road 25 S (46947-4682)
P.O. Box 658 (46947-0658)
PHONE.............................574 722-3800
Mike Coplen, *Manager*
EMP: 90
SALES (corp-wide): 87.5MM **Privately Held**
WEB: www.tmmorrismfg.com
SIC: 3679 Harness assemblies for electronic use: wire or cable
PA: Kauffman Engineering Inc
701 Ransdell Rd
Lebanon IN 46052
765 483-4919

(G-9345)
KENT NUTRITION GROUP INC
2407 S County Road 400 E (46947-8576)
PHONE.............................574 722-5368
Dave Mayhill, *Purchasing*
Duke Tanguy, *Manager*
EMP: 20
SQ FT: 60,000
SALES (corp-wide): 637MM **Privately Held**
WEB: www.kentfeeds.com
SIC: 2048 Livestock feeds; poultry feeds
HQ: Kent Nutrition Group, Inc.
1600 Oregon St
Muscatine IA 52761
866 647-1212

(G-9346)
KEP CHEM INC
616 Center Ave (46947-2936)
P.O. Box 1141 (46947-7141)
PHONE.............................574 739-0501
James E Keplinger, *President*
EMP: 5
SALES (est): 380K **Privately Held**
SIC: 2879 Agricultural chemicals

(G-9347)
LEHIGH CEMENT COMPANY LLC
3084 W County Road 225 S (46947-8476)
PHONE.............................877 534-4442
John Morris, *Branch Mgr*
EMP: 2
SALES (corp-wide): 20.3B **Privately Held**
SIC: 3241 3273 5032 Portland cement;
ready-mixed concrete; aggregate
HQ: Lehigh Cement Company Llc
300 E John Carpenter Fwy
Irving TX 75062
877 534-4442

(G-9348)
LEHIGH HANSON ECC INC
3084 W County Road 225 S (46947-8476)
PHONE.............................574 753-5121
Fax: 574 722-2168
Ken Gillespie, *Branch Mgr*
EMP: 110
SALES (corp-wide): 20.3B **Privately Held**
WEB: www.essroc.com
SIC: 3241 2899 Portland cement; chemical preparations
HQ: Lehigh Hanson Ecc, Inc.
3251 Bath Pike
Nazareth PA 18064
610 837-6725

(G-9349)
LOGAN STAMPINGS INC
1100 E Main St (46947-5013)
P.O. Box 298 (46947-0298)
PHONE.............................574 722-3101
Fax: 574 722-5543
Robert Baker, *President*
Harold McKee, *Director*
EMP: 50
SQ FT: 76,000
SALES (est): 10.6MM **Privately Held**
WEB: www.loganstampings.com
SIC: 3469 Stamping metal for the trade

(G-9350)
LOGANSPORT MACHINE CO INC
Also Called: LMC Workholding
1200 W Linden Ave (46947-2950)
P.O. Box 7006 (46947-7006)
PHONE.............................574 735-0225
Fax: 574 753-5596
Gordon J Duerr III, *President*
Pat Klein, *Vice Pres*
Royal Parker Lancaster Jr, *Vice Pres*
James Ringer, *Production*
Willie Turner, *Purch Mgr*
▲ EMP: 40 EST: 1937
SQ FT: 60,000
SALES: 8MM **Privately Held**
WEB: www.logan-mmk.com
SIC: 3545 3593 5084 Machine tool attachments & accessories; chucks: drill,
lathe or magnetic (machine tool accessories); fluid power cylinders & actuators;
industrial machinery & equipment

(G-9351)
LOGANSPORT PHAROS PRESS
3175 Billiard Dr (46947-8273)
PHONE............................574 753-4169
Robyn McCloskey, *Principal*
EMP: 2 EST: 2013
SALES (est): 160.2K **Privately Held**
SIC: 2741 Miscellaneous publishing

(G-9352)
LOGO ZONE INC
731 Lakeview Dr (46947-2204)
PHONE............................574 753-7569
Tim Senesac, *President*
EMP: 2
SALES (est): 265.6K **Privately Held**
SIC: 3552 Textile machinery

(G-9353)
M H EBY INC
2909 W County Road 300 S (46947-5206)
PHONE............................574 753-4000
Troy Miller, *Branch Mgr*
EMP: 10
SALES (corp-wide): 100MM **Privately Held**
SIC: 3713 Truck bodies (motor vehicles)
PA: M. H. Eby Inc.
1194 Main St
Blue Ball PA 17506
800 292-4752

(G-9354)
MATTHEW WARREN INC
Also Called: Matthew Warren Spring
500 E Ottawa St (46947-2610)
PHONE............................574 722-8200
Fax: 574 722-8241
Mike Kime, *Engineer*
Don Paul, *Engineer*
William Marcum, *Branch Mgr*
Carol Mund, *Asst Mgr*
EMP: 14
SALES (corp-wide): 169MM **Privately Held**
SIC: 3493 Steel springs, except wire
HQ: Matthew Warren, Inc.
9501 Tech Blvd Ste 401
Rosemont IL 60018
847 349-5760

(G-9355)
MOUNTVILLE MATS
5270 E Country Club Rd (46947-8451)
PHONE............................574 753-8858
David Hart, *Owner*
EMP: 2
SALES (est): 85.2K **Privately Held**
SIC: 2273 Mats & matting

(G-9356)
MYERS DESIGNS INC
6061 Logansport Rd # 140 (46947-8866)
PHONE............................317 955-2450
Jason Myers, *President*
EMP: 2
SALES (est): 207.5K **Privately Held**
SIC: 2519 Furniture, household: glass, fiberglass & plastic

(G-9357)
MYERS SPRING CO INC
720 Water St (46947-1735)
PHONE............................574 753-5105
Fax: 574 722-5902
Todd A Miller, *President*
Craig L Miller, *Admin Secy*
Gretchen G Miller, *Admin Secy*
EMP: 40 EST: 1946
SQ FT: 28,800
SALES (est): 11.6MM **Privately Held**
WEB: www.myers-spring.com
SIC: 3495 3496 3493 Mechanical springs, precision; miscellaneous fabricated wire products; steel springs, except wire

(G-9358)
NELSON ACQUISITION LLC
Also Called: Nelson Tube Company
130 E Industrial Blvd (46947-6994)
PHONE............................574 753-6377
Fax: 574 739-2265
David Holt,
Michael Rans,
EMP: 80
SQ FT: 40,000

SALES (est): 10.7MM **Privately Held**
SIC: 3312 Tubes, steel & iron

(G-9359)
NF FRICTION COMPOSITES INC
1441 Holland St (46947-1720)
PHONE............................414 365-1550
Joyce Butzen, *President*
Noel Nixon, *General Mgr*
R Christopher Butzen, *Vice Pres*
EMP: 5
SQ FT: 100,000
SALES (est): 550K **Privately Held**
SIC: 3299 Mica products, built-up or sheet

(G-9360)
NICK-EM BUILDERS LLC
Also Called: Foppers Gourmet Pet Treat Bky
1005 W Broadway (46947-2903)
PHONE............................574 516-1060
Michelle Leffert, *Mng Member*
Clark Leffert, *Mng Member*
EMP: 8
SQ FT: 45,000
SALES (est): 1.2MM **Privately Held**
WEB: www.foppers.com
SIC: 3999 Pet supplies

(G-9361)
QUALITY DIE SET CORP
600 Water St (46947-1804)
PHONE............................574 967-4411
Fax: 574 967-4160
Jerry Shank, *President*
Christi Shank, *Corp Secy*
Raymond Shank, *Vice Pres*
EMP: 32
SQ FT: 60,000
SALES (est): 7.4MM **Privately Held**
SIC: 3469 3542 7692 3544 Stamping metal for the trade; rebuilt machine tools, metal forming types; welding repair; special dies, tools, jigs & fixtures

(G-9362)
ROGERS CABINETRY
2527 N County Road 925 E (46947-7794)
PHONE............................574 664-9931
William Cassidy, *Principal*
EMP: 2
SALES (est): 172.3K **Privately Held**
SIC: 2434 Wood kitchen cabinets

(G-9363)
RUBEN MARTINEZ
1936 E Private Road 340 N (46947-6843)
PHONE............................574 735-0803
Ruben Martinez, *Owner*
EMP: 6
SALES (est): 290.4K **Privately Held**
SIC: 4214 7389 3537 Local trucking with storage; ; trucks: freight, baggage, etc.: industrial, except mining

(G-9364)
SMALL PARTS INC (HQ)
600 Humphrey St (46947-4999)
P.O. Box 7002 (46947-7002)
PHONE............................574 753-6323
Fax: 574 753-6660
John E Barnes, *CEO*
Clay T Barnes, *President*
Clay Jackson, *President*
Jim Bauer, *Vice Pres*
John Farmani, *Treasurer*
◆ EMP: 335
SQ FT: 135,000
SALES (est): 139.9MM
SALES (corp-wide): 144.6MM **Privately Held**
WEB: www.smallpartsinc.com
SIC: 3443 Metal parts
PA: Materials Processing, Inc.
3500 Depauw Blvd
Indianapolis IN 46268
317 803-3010

(G-9365)
SMALL PARTS INC
112 E Mildred St (46947-4979)
P.O. Box 7002 (46947-7002)
PHONE............................574 739-6236
Carl Methner, *Principal*
Tony Firmami, *CFO*
EMP: 385

SALES (corp-wide): 144.6MM **Privately Held**
SIC: 3469 Metal stampings
HQ: Small Parts, Inc.
600 Humphrey St
Logansport IN 46947
574 753-6323

(G-9366)
SUMMIT/EMS CORPORATION
1509 Woodlawn Ave (46947-4459)
PHONE............................574 722-1317
Larry Graf, *Principal*
Jennifer Kelley, *Purch Agent*
Gina Moore, *Admin Mgr*
▲ EMP: 30
SQ FT: 10,000
SALES (est): 6.1MM **Privately Held**
SIC: 3621 Generating apparatus & parts, electrical

(G-9367)
SUS CAST PRODUCTS INC
Also Called: S U S
1825 W Market St (46947-1746)
P.O. Box 268 (46947-0268)
PHONE............................574 753-4111
Fax: 574 753-4112
Kenneth Merlau, *CEO*
Jeff Todd, *Vice Pres*
Randall G Martin, *CFO*
◆ EMP: 65
SQ FT: 80,000
SALES (est): 14.8MM **Privately Held**
WEB: www.suscastproducts.com
SIC: 3363 3365 Aluminum die-castings; aluminum foundries

(G-9368)
T & L TOOL & DIE II CO INC
911 Calla St (46947-1705)
PHONE............................574 722-6246
Fax: 574 722-6247
Kirby Dillon, *President*
Margaret L Dillon, *Admin Sec*
EMP: 5 EST: 1955
SQ FT: 9,075
SALES (est): 800K **Privately Held**
SIC: 3544 Special dies & tools

(G-9369)
THERAPTIC ELMNTS BY LORI MYERS ✪
3901 High St (46947-2562)
PHONE............................765 480-2525
EMP: 2 EST: 2017
SALES (est): 74.4K **Privately Held**
SIC: 2819 Elements

(G-9370)
TRANSCO RAILWAY PRODUCTS INC
1331 18th St (46947)
P.O. Box 706 (46947-0706)
PHONE............................574 753-6227
Fax: 574 753-6228
Tom Cavanaugh, *QC Mgr*
Eric Nichols, *Manager*
EMP: 80
SQ FT: 10,000
SALES (corp-wide): 96.7MM **Privately Held**
SIC: 3743 Railroad equipment
HQ: Transco Railway Products Inc.
200 N La Salle St # 1550
Chicago IL 60601
312 427-2818

(G-9371)
TRIBINE INDUSTRIES LLC
6991 E 750 N (46947-9301)
PHONE............................316 282-8011
Ben Dillon, *President*
EMP: 2
SALES (est): 75.4K **Privately Held**
SIC: 2041 Grain mills (except rice)

(G-9372)
TUBE FABRICATION INDS INC
130 E Industrial Blvd (46947-6994)
PHONE............................574 753-6377
Peter A Ferentinos, *CEO*
Julie Ellis, *President*
Troy Zimmerman, *Vice Pres*
Chris Worthington, *Administration*
▲ EMP: 42

SALES (est): 15.7MM **Privately Held**
SIC: 2655 Ammunition cans or tubes, board laminated with metal foil

(G-9373)
TYSON FOODS INC
2125 S County Road 125 W (46947-8477)
PHONE............................574 753-6121
Fax: 574 722-8601
Kathy Rozzi, *Purch Dir*
Dave Backman, *Plant Engr*
Daryell Schmidt, *Manager*
Howard Duncan, *Manager*
Randy Wescott, *Comp Tech*
EMP: 1000
SQ FT: 800,000
SALES (corp-wide): 38.2B **Publicly Held**
SIC: 2011 2013 Meat packing plants; sausages & other prepared meats
PA: Tyson Foods, Inc.
2200 W Don Tyson Pkwy
Springdale AR 72762
479 290-4000

(G-9374)
TYSON FRESH MEATS INC
Hwy 35 S (46947)
PHONE............................574 753-6134
Darrell Schmidt, *Manager*
Michael Cunningham, *Technology*
EMP: 394
SALES (corp-wide): 38.2B **Publicly Held**
SIC: 2011 Pork products from pork slaughtered on site
HQ: Tyson Fresh Meats, Inc.
800 Stevens Port Dr
Dakota Dunes SD 57049
605 235-2061

(G-9375)
VALLEY TOOL & DIE STAMPINGS
6408 W Us Highway 24 (46947-6901)
P.O. Box 6, Lake Cicott (46942-0006)
PHONE............................574 722-4566
Fax: 574 753-0225
Norman E Miller, *President*
Michael A Holcomb, *Vice Pres*
Lynn Burton, *Treasurer*
EMP: 26
SQ FT: 32,600
SALES (est): 4.3MM **Privately Held**
SIC: 3469 3544 3496 3495 Stamping metal for the trade; special dies, tools, jigs & fixtures; miscellaneous fabricated wire products; wire springs; steel springs, except wire

---

Long Beach
Laporte County

(G-9376)
CAINE PUBLISHING LLC
2721 Floral Trl (46360-1671)
PHONE............................312 215-5253
Francesca Caine, *Principal*
EMP: 4
SALES (est): 167.3K **Privately Held**
SIC: 2741 Miscellaneous publishing

(G-9377)
KOLOSSOS INC
2715 Duffy Ln (46360-1552)
P.O. Box 309, Michigan City (46361-0309)
PHONE............................312 952-6991
Edward Billys, *President*
Giorgios Karayannis, *Vice Pres*
Michael Karayannis, *Admin Sec*
▲ EMP: 3
SALES: 200K **Privately Held**
SIC: 2035 5169 Seasonings, seafood sauces (except tomato & dry); food additives & preservatives

(G-9378)
LANGLEY FINE ART PRINTS
2019 Somerset Rd (46360-1432)
PHONE............................219 872-0087
Joan Langley, *Principal*
EMP: 2 EST: 2009
SALES (est): 151.2K **Privately Held**
SIC: 2752 Commercial printing, lithographic

▲ = Import ▼=Export
◆ =Import/Export

(G-9379)
PRINT CENTER INC
2902 Ridge Rd (46360-1724)
PHONE..................................219 874-9683
Jennifer Rucinski, *Owner*
EMP: 2 EST: 2013
SALES (est): 200.6K Privately Held
SIC: 2752 Commercial printing, lithographic

Loogootee
Martin County

(G-9380)
CUSTOM DOOR MANUFACTURING
8076 N 1100 E (47553-5630)
PHONE..................................812 636-3667
Dave Graber, *Owner*
EMP: 4
SALES (est): 411.9K Privately Held
SIC: 2431 Doors & door parts & trim, wood

(G-9381)
DELMAR KNEPP LOGGING
10293 E 600 N (47553-5581)
PHONE..................................812 486-2565
Delmar Knepp, *Principal*
EMP: 2
SALES (est): 156.8K Privately Held
SIC: 2411 Logging camps & contractors

(G-9382)
EDS MACHINE & TOOL ✪
1250 Mount Pleasant Rd (47553-4964)
PHONE..................................812 295-7264
Ed Searl, *Owner*
EMP: 2 EST: 2017
SALES (est): 85.9K Privately Held
SIC: 3599 Industrial machinery

(G-9383)
GRABER FURNITURE
6377 N 1200 E (47553-5607)
PHONE..................................812 295-4939
Enos Graber, *Owner*
EMP: 9
SALES (est): 877.2K Privately Held
SIC: 2426 5712 2434 Furniture stock & parts, hardwood; furniture stores; wood kitchen cabinets

(G-9384)
GREENWELL SOFTWARE LLC
9750 N 1300 E (47553-5176)
PHONE..................................812 295-4665
Tyler Wagler, *Owner*
EMP: 2
SALES (est): 145.3K Privately Held
SIC: 7372 Prepackaged software

(G-9385)
HICKORY VALLEY WOODWORKING LLC
10432 E 625 N (47553-5583)
PHONE..................................812 486-2857
Phil Stoll,
EMP: 6
SALES (est): 659K Privately Held
SIC: 2431 Millwork

(G-9386)
J & R TOOL INC
11919 E 250 N (47553-5489)
P.O. Box 143 (47553-0143)
PHONE..................................812 295-2557
Rick Bell, *President*
Adam Crouse, *Partner*
Jean Bell, *Vice Pres*
EMP: 5
SQ FT: 3,200
SALES (est): 570K Privately Held
SIC: 3599 Machine shop, jobbing & repair

(G-9387)
KNEPP LOGGING
2946 N 900 E (47553-5423)
PHONE..................................812 486-3741
David Knepp, *Owner*
EMP: 6
SALES (est): 323.4K Privately Held
SIC: 2411 Timber, cut at logging camp

(G-9388)
KQ SERVICING LLC
22383 Third Rd (47553-4683)
PHONE..................................812 486-9244
Kyla Quick, *Mng Member*
Jammie Quick,
EMP: 5 EST: 2013
SALES (est): 206.2K Privately Held
SIC: 1241 1542 Coal mining services; commercial & office building contractors

(G-9389)
LOOGOOTEE TRIBUNE INC
514 N John F Kennedy Ave (47553-1102)
P.O. Box 277 (47553-0277)
PHONE..................................812 295-2500
Fax: 812 295-5221
Larry D Hatmbree, *President*
EMP: 7
SQ FT: 1,200
SALES: 200K Privately Held
SIC: 2711 Newspapers: publishing only, not printed on site

(G-9390)
LOUGHMILLER MCH TL DESIGN INC
Also Called: Loughmiller Mch Tl & Design
12851 E 150 N (47553-5385)
PHONE..................................812 295-3903
Fax: 812 295-3646
Jason Loughmiller, *President*
Pamela Loughmiller, *Corp Secy*
Richard Hoke, *Vice Pres*
EMP: 30
SQ FT: 3,600
SALES (est): 7MM Privately Held
SIC: 3545 7692 3544 3541 Machine tool accessories; welding repair; special dies, tools, jigs & fixtures; machine tools, metal cutting type; machine shop, jobbing & repair

(G-9391)
MAIN MUSIC
12958 E Us Highway 50 (47553-5211)
PHONE..................................812 295-2020
Chris Main, *Manager*
EMP: 2
SALES (est): 150.7K Privately Held
SIC: 3931 Musical instruments

(G-9392)
R & M WELDING & FABRICATING SP (PA)
1192 State Road 550 (47553-4755)
PHONE..................................812 295-9130
Fax: 812 295-4123
Robert Wathen, *Owner*
EMP: 3
SALES (est): 500K Privately Held
SIC: 1799 3411 7692 3444 Welding on site; metal cans; welding repair; sheet metalwork

(G-9393)
REGAL MILLS ODON
2805 N 1200 E (47553-5493)
PHONE..................................812 295-2299
Jerome Ginerich, *Principal*
EMP: 2
SALES (est): 83.7K Privately Held
SIC: 2048 Prepared feeds

(G-9394)
RONALD LEE ALLEN
8271 S 1125 E (47553-5335)
PHONE..................................812 644-7649
Ronald Lee Allen, *Principal*
EMP: 3
SALES (est): 175.9K Privately Held
SIC: 2411 7389 Logging;

(G-9395)
VALESCO MANUFACTURING INC
7857 N 1100 E (47553-5628)
PHONE..................................812 636-6001
Ammon Weaver, *Branch Mgr*
EMP: 2
SALES (est): 297K
SALES (corp-wide): 732K Privately Held
SIC: 3523 Weeding machines, agricultural; hulling machinery, agricultural

PA: Valesco Manufacturing Inc.
9875 N County Road 600 E
Roachdale IN 46172
765 522-2740

(G-9396)
W & S WOODWORKING
6460 N 1100 E (47553-5591)
PHONE..................................812 486-3673
Willard F Toll, *Owner*
EMP: 6
SALES (est): 350K Privately Held
SIC: 2499 Decorative wood & woodwork

(G-9397)
WAGLER WOODWORKING
19866 Us Highway 231 (47553-4652)
PHONE..................................812 486-6357
Jason Wagler, *Principal*
EMP: 2 EST: 2010
SALES (est): 243.1K Privately Held
SIC: 2431 Millwork

(G-9398)
WILLIAM R ARVIN
Also Called: Arvin's Creative Woodworking
200 Brooks Ave (47553-1411)
PHONE..................................812 486-5255
William R Arvin, *Owner*
EMP: 2
SALES (est): 222.6K Privately Held
SIC: 2434 Wood kitchen cabinets

Lowell
Lake County

(G-9399)
AVERY DENNISON CORPORATION
270 Westmeadow Pl (46356-1678)
PHONE..................................219 696-7777
Fax: 219 690-4071
Keith Barstow, *Manager*
EMP: 100
SALES (corp-wide): 6.6B Publicly Held
WEB: www.avery.com
SIC: 2672 3081 3497 2678 Adhesive papers, labels or tapes: from purchased material; unsupported plastics film & sheet; metal foil & leaf; stationery products; pressed fiber & molded pulp products except food products
PA: Avery Dennison Corporation
207 N Goode Ave Ste 500
Glendale CA 91203
626 304-2000

(G-9400)
BLUMENAU ALPACAS
19950 Austin St (46356-9691)
PHONE..................................219 713-6171
EMP: 2
SALES (est): 138.5K Privately Held
SIC: 2231 Alpacas, mohair: woven

(G-9401)
BUTCHER BLOCK
17918 Grant Pl (46356-9511)
PHONE..................................219 696-9111
Fax: 219 696-9150
Robert Reed, *President*
Diana Reed, *Vice Pres*
EMP: 12
SQ FT: 3,168
SALES (est): 547.5K Privately Held
SIC: 0751 2013 2011 Slaughtering: custom livestock services; sausages & other prepared meats; meat packing plants

(G-9402)
CENTRAL OVERHEAD DOOR
2080 W 172nd Ln (46356-9307)
PHONE..................................219 696-1566
EMP: 2
SALES (est): 157.1K Privately Held
SIC: 2431 Mfg Millwork

(G-9403)
CUSTOM CABINET & MILLWORK
17804 Holtz Rd (46356-2144)
PHONE..................................219 696-9827
Dan Weaver, *Owner*
EMP: 2

SALES (est): 171.9K Privately Held
SIC: 2434 Wood kitchen cabinets

(G-9404)
DOCUTECH DOCUMENT SERVICE
1601 Northview Dr (46356-2598)
PHONE..................................219 690-3038
EMP: 2 Privately Held
SIC: 2759 Publication printing

(G-9405)
ECHO PUBLICATIONS
15863 Stevenson Pl (46356-1005)
PHONE..................................219 696-3756
Mike Alcantar, *Owner*
EMP: 2
SALES (est): 92K Privately Held
SIC: 2741 Miscellaneous publishing

(G-9406)
GRAPHEX INTERNATIONAL
792 W 181st Ave (46356-9529)
PHONE..................................219 696-4849
Ellen Bowers, *President*
EMP: 3
SALES (est): 229.5K Privately Held
SIC: 3993 Signs & advertising specialties

(G-9407)
GREIF INC
17405 Holtz Rd (46356-2135)
PHONE..................................219 746-3753
Richard Salverson, *Technical Mgr*
EMP: 2
SALES (est): 65.4K Privately Held
SIC: 2493 Reconstituted wood products

(G-9408)
INDIANA SPRAY FOAM
17958 Grant Pl Unit A (46356-7204)
PHONE..................................219 696-6100
Mike Young, *Mng Member*
EMP: 8
SALES (est): 790.5K Privately Held
SIC: 3069 Foam rubber

(G-9409)
INNOVATIVE ENERGY INC
Also Called: Ratech Industries
10653 W 181st Ave (46356-9451)
PHONE..................................219 696-3639
Fax: 219 696-5220
Robert Wadsworth, *President*
Mary Wadsworth, *Treasurer*
Kerry Smith, *Manager*
▲ EMP: 35 EST: 1980
SQ FT: 248,000
SALES: 8MM Privately Held
WEB: www.insul.net
SIC: 2671 5033 Packaging paper & plastics film, coated & laminated; insulation materials

(G-9410)
JRS CUSTOM CABINETS CO
16855 Mississippi St (46356-9521)
PHONE..................................219 696-7205
Fax: 219 696-5526
James A Mitsch Jr, *President*
Joe Long, *Vice Pres*
Joseph E Long, *Admin Sec*
EMP: 20
SQ FT: 8,000
SALES (est): 2.7MM Privately Held
SIC: 2434 Wood kitchen cabinets

(G-9411)
JTM HOME & BUILDING
16005 Chestnut St (46356-9326)
PHONE..................................219 690-1445
Tom McFarlane, *President*
EMP: 3
SALES (est): 240K Privately Held
SIC: 1389 Construction, repair & dismantling services

(G-9412)
KOZS QUALITY PRINTING INC
17934 Grant Pl A (46356-9511)
PHONE..................................219 696-6711
John Kozlowski, *President*
Debbie Kozlowski, *Vice Pres*
EMP: 5
SQ FT: 1,000

G E O G R A P H I C

SALES (est): 440K **Privately Held**
SIC: 2759 2752 Letterpress printing; commercial printing, offset

(G-9413)
LEEPS SUPPLY CO
7332 Mcconnell Ave (46356-1775)
PHONE..................................219 696-9511
John Hamster, *President*
EMP: 3
SALES (est): 228.6K **Privately Held**
SIC: 2591 5099 Venetian blinds; firearms & ammunition, except sporting

(G-9414)
LEGACY VULCAN LLC
Also Called: Lowell Quarry
9331 W 205th Ave (46356-9606)
PHONE..................................219 696-5467
Kevin Cox, *Manager*
EMP: 15 **Publicly Held**
WEB: www.vulcanmaterials.com
SIC: 1411 Dimension stone
HQ: Legacy Vulcan, Llc
1200 Urban Center Dr
Vestavia AL 35242
205 298-3000

(G-9415)
LOWELL CONCRETE PRODUCTS INC
9312 W 181st Ave (46356-9452)
P.O. Box 247 (46356-0247)
PHONE..................................219 696-3339
Fax: 219 696-3937
William Austgen, *President*
Linda Savage, *Vice Pres*
EMP: 31
SQ FT: 2,000
SALES (est): 5.2MM **Privately Held**
SIC: 3272 Concrete products, precast; pipe, concrete or lined with concrete

(G-9416)
MATTS REPAIR INC
9412 W 181st Ave (46356-9651)
P.O. Box 373 (46356-0373)
PHONE..................................219 696-6765
Fax: 219 696-1939
Roberta Bryant, *President*
Sue Starr, *Office Mgr*
Kevin Starr, *Manager*
Mark Starr, *Manager*
Darlene Roy, *Asst Mgr*
EMP: 10
SQ FT: 5,000
SALES (est): 1.1MM **Privately Held**
SIC: 3599 7692 Machine shop, jobbing & repair; welding repair

(G-9417)
MIDWEST ACCURATE GRINDING SVC
17211 Morse St (46356-1432)
PHONE..................................219 696-4060
Fax: 219 696-4062
John Conley Sr, *President*
Cathy Womack, *Corp Secy*
Carolyn Conley, *Vice Pres*
EMP: 10
SQ FT: 8,500
SALES (est): 1MM **Privately Held**
WEB: www.midwestaccurate.com
SIC: 7389 3599 Grinding, precision: commercial or industrial; machine shop, jobbing & repair

(G-9418)
NICHOLS MFG CO INC
1006 W 203rd Ave (46356-9747)
PHONE..................................219 696-8577
Fax: 219 696-7665
James Nichols, *President*
William J Nichols, *President*
EMP: 10 **EST:** 1937
SQ FT: 13,300
SALES (est): 1MM **Privately Held**
SIC: 7692 3523 Welding repair; sprayers & spraying machines, agricultural

(G-9419)
PILCHER PUBLISHING CO INC
Also Called: Lowell Tribune
318 E Commercial Ave (46356-1708)
P.O. Box 191 (46356-0191)
PHONE..................................219 696-7711

Fax: 219 696-7713
Mary Jeanette, *President*
EMP: 20 **EST:** 1943
SQ FT: 15,000
SALES (est): 1.3MM **Privately Held**
SIC: 2711 Commercial printing & newspaper publishing combined

(G-9420)
PRECISION AGRONOMY
23305 Whitcomb St (46356-7504)
PHONE..................................219 552-0032
Garrett Corning, *Principal*
EMP: 2
SALES (est): 81.4K **Privately Held**
SIC: 3599 Industrial machinery

(G-9421)
PURPLE DOOR PRESS
8833 W 156th Ct (46356-9438)
PHONE..................................219 690-1046
Jean Lahm, *Principal*
EMP: 2
SALES (est): 75.2K **Privately Held**
SIC: 2741 Miscellaneous publishing

(G-9422)
SACO INDUSTRIES INC
17151 Morse St (46356-1433)
P.O. Box 342 (46356-0342)
PHONE..................................219 690-9900
Fax: 219 696-2232
Ronald Bergstrom, *President*
Paulette Bergstrom, *Corp Secy*
Jodie Wasserott, *Project Mgr*
Jennifer Kidd, *Financial Exec*
Douglas Newlin, *VP Sales*
EMP: 370 **EST:** 1952
SQ FT: 200,000
SALES (est): 79.6MM **Privately Held**
WEB: www.sacoindustries.com
SIC: 2434 Wood kitchen cabinets; vanities, bathroom: wood

(G-9423)
SUPERIOR ELECTRIC NWI LLC
8900 W 156th Ave (46356-7719)
PHONE..................................219 696-0717
Steve Galecki, *Administration*
EMP: 2 **EST:** 2014
SALES (est): 215.2K **Privately Held**
SIC: 3699 Electrical equipment & supplies

(G-9424)
UNITED STARTER ALTERNATOR LLC
404 Mocking Bird Ln (46356-2435)
PHONE..................................219 696-9095
Fax: 219 696-9037
Henry Henke, *Mng Member*
EMP: 3
SALES (est): 100K **Privately Held**
WEB: www.unitedstarter.com
SIC: 3694 Engine electrical equipment

(G-9425)
V N C INC
Also Called: Better Built Products
585 N Nichols St (46356-1649)
PHONE..................................219 696-5031
Vincent Anderson, *President*
Cindy Anderson, *Admin Sec*
EMP: 12
SQ FT: 22,000
SALES (est): 1MM **Privately Held**
SIC: 3353 3089 3444 Aluminum sheet, plate & foil; shutters, plastic; sheet metalwork

Lynn
Randolph County

(G-9426)
ENVIRONMENTAL MANAGEMENT & DEV
105 W Sherman St (47355)
P.O. Box 126 (47355-0126)
PHONE..................................765 874-1539
Dennis Thurston, *President*
EMP: 3
SALES: 300K **Privately Held**
SIC: 3589 Water treatment equipment, industrial

(G-9427)
GOLIATH CASKET INC
8261 S 350 E (47355-9362)
PHONE..................................765 874-2380
Fax: 765 874-2380
Keith Davis, *President*
B Julane Davis, *Vice Pres*
EMP: 8
SQ FT: 6,000
SALES (est): 421.6K **Privately Held**
WEB: www.oversizecasket.com
SIC: 3995 Burial caskets

(G-9428)
KABERT INDUSTRIES INC
514 W Church St (47355-9624)
PHONE..................................765 874-2335
Fax: 765 874-1254
Lucille Gibson, *Persnl Dir*
Rick Gibson, *Asst Mgr*
EMP: 91
SALES (corp-wide): 13.5MM **Privately Held**
WEB: www.kabert.com
SIC: 2221 3564 Glass & fiberglass broad-woven fabrics; blowers & fans
PA: Kabert Industries Inc
321 W Saint Charles Rd
Villa Park IL 60181
630 833-2115

(G-9429)
KABERT INDUSTRIES INC
Also Called: Kabert Fiberglass
2681 E 800 S (47355-9140)
P.O. Box 327 (47355-0327)
PHONE..................................765 874-1300
Fax: 765 874-1255
Lucille Gibson, *Manager*
EMP: 30
SALES (corp-wide): 13.5MM **Privately Held**
WEB: www.kabert.com
SIC: 2221 Fiberglass fabrics
PA: Kabert Industries Inc
321 W Saint Charles Rd
Villa Park IL 60181
630 833-2115

(G-9430)
LYNN TOOL COMPANY INC
107 Elm St (47355)
P.O. Box 366 (47355-0366)
PHONE..................................765 874-2471
Fax: 765 874-1634
Stephen Baker, *President*
EMP: 8 **EST:** 1966
SQ FT: 3,000
SALES (est): 1MM **Privately Held**
SIC: 3599 3469 3443 Custom machinery; metal stampings; weldments

(G-9431)
POWERHOUSE ENGINES LLC
10771 S 100 E (47355-9432)
PHONE..................................765 576-1418
George Bradley Rhoades,
EMP: 2
SQ FT: 2,400
SALES: 120K **Privately Held**
SIC: 3519 Internal combustion engines

(G-9432)
T F & T INC
Also Called: Hinshaw Tool & Die
603 Linden St (47355)
P.O. Box 615 (47355-0615)
PHONE..................................765 874-1628
Fax: 765 874-1628
Fred Green, *President*
Todd Green, *Vice Pres*
EMP: 7
SQ FT: 9,000
SALES (est): 829.3K **Privately Held**
SIC: 3599 Machine shop, jobbing & repair

(G-9433)
YAHWEH DESIGN AND PRINTING
6567 E 700 S (47355-9394)
PHONE..................................765 874-1003
Traci Craig, *Owner*
EMP: 2
SALES (est): 91.5K **Privately Held**
SIC: 2752 Commercial printing, lithographic

Lynnville
Warrick County

(G-9434)
DOUG WILCOX
Also Called: Custom Polishing
1188 W State Route 68 (47619-8273)
PHONE..................................812 476-1957
Doug Wilcox, *Owner*
EMP: 2
SALES (est): 75.8K **Privately Held**
SIC: 3471 Polishing, metals or formed products

(G-9435)
MYSTIQUE WINERY AND VINYRD LLC
13000 Gore Rd (47619-8026)
PHONE..................................812 922-5612
Steven Clutter, *Principal*
EMP: 5
SALES (est): 374.4K **Privately Held**
SIC: 2084 Wines

(G-9436)
PEABODY MIDWEST MINING LLC (HQ)
Also Called: Black Beauty Mining Div
566 Dickeyville Rd (47619-8257)
P.O. Box 400, Huntingburg (47542-0400)
PHONE..................................812 434-8500
C A Burggraf, *President*
J F Quinn, *Vice Pres*
W L Hawkins Jr, *Treasurer*
Mary Ann Ball, *Human Res Mgr*
Steven Chancellor, *Mng Member*
EMP: 50
SALES (est): 826MM
SALES (corp-wide): 5.1B **Publicly Held**
SIC: 1221 1222 1241 Bituminous coal surface mining; bituminous coal-underground mining; coal mining services
PA: Peabody Energy Corporation
701 Market St
Saint Louis MO 63101
314 342-3400

(G-9437)
PEABODY WILD BOAR MINING LLC
566 Dickeyville Rd (47619-8257)
PHONE..................................812 434-8500
EMP: 5
SALES (est): 228.1K **Privately Held**
SIC: 1221 Bituminous Coal/Lignite Surface Mining

(G-9438)
WILD BOAR MINE
2277 Tecumseh Rd (47619)
PHONE..................................812 922-1015
Tom Peck, *Manager*
EMP: 2
SALES (est): 124.8K **Privately Held**
SIC: 1479 Mineral pigment mining

Lyons
Greene County

(G-9439)
KAHO BROTHERS INC
460 E Broad St (47443)
PHONE..................................812 659-2901
H Scot Kaho, *President*
Jay D Kaho, *Treasurer*
EMP: 3
SALES (est): 309.3K **Privately Held**
SIC: 2411 Logging camps & contractors

Macy
Miami County

(G-9440)
BURNS CONSTRUCTION INC
Also Called: Burns Buldings
6676 S Old Us Highway 31 (46951-8639)
PHONE..................................574 382-2315
Dan Burns, *President*
Michael Burns, *Sales Mgr*
EMP: 28
SQ FT: 1,500
SALES: 1.7MM **Privately Held**
SIC: 1542 3448 2452 Commercial & of-
fice building, new construction; farm build-
ing construction; garage construction;
prefabricated metal buildings; prefabri-
cated wood buildings

Madison
Jefferson County

(G-9441)
AJ EXPRESS BROKER SERVICE
73 N Rogers Rd (47250-7781)
PHONE..................................812 866-1380
Andrew Le Grand, *Principal*
EMP: 2
SALES (est): 143.3K **Privately Held**
SIC: 2741 Miscellaneous publishing

(G-9442)
ALAN W LONG
Also Called: Gifts That Last
120 E Main St (47250-3411)
PHONE..................................812 265-6717
Alan Long, *Owner*
EMP: 2
SQ FT: 2,600
SALES: 125K **Privately Held**
SIC: 5944 3911 5947 Jewelry stores; jew-
elry apparel; gift shop

(G-9443)
ALLIED TUBE & CONDUIT CORP
Also Called: Century Tube
4004 N Us 421 (47250-9800)
PHONE..................................812 265-9255
Fax: 812 265-9355
Mark A Acosta, *Branch Mgr*
EMP: 138 **Publicly Held**
WEB: www.alliedtube.com
SIC: 3317 3714 3498 Welded pipe &
tubes; motor vehicle parts & accessories;
fabricated pipe & fittings
HQ: Allied Tube & Conduit Corporation
16100 Lathrop Ave
Harvey IL 60426
708 339-1610

(G-9444)
ARVIN SANGO INC (DH)
Also Called: A S I
2905 Wilson Ave (47250-3834)
PHONE..................................812 265-2888
Fax: 812 273-8339
Dan N Baughman, *President*
Greg Edwards, *Vice Pres*
Scott Hubbard, *Vice Pres*
Kevin Orrill, *Vice Pres*
▲ EMP: 600
SQ FT: 323,000
SALES: 800MM
SALES (corp-wide): 25.6MM **Privately
Held**
WEB: www.arvinsango.com
SIC: 3714 Exhaust systems & parts, motor
vehicle; instrument board assemblies,
motor vehicle; motor vehicle body compo-
nents & frame
HQ: Sango Co.,Ltd.
1-1, Miyashita, Fukutacho
Miyoshi HIR 470-0
561 340-035

(G-9445)
BAD APPLE MACS LLC
605 W Main St (47250-3738)
PHONE..................................812 274-0469
Janet McIntosh, *Principal*
EMP: 2

SALES (est): 85.9K **Privately Held**
SIC: 3571 Personal computers (microcomputers)

(G-9446)
BELTONE HEARING CARE
219 Clifty Dr Ste D (47250-1603)
PHONE..................................812 274-4116
EMP: 2
SALES (est): 86.6K **Privately Held**
SIC: 3842 Absorbent cotton, sterilized

(G-9447)
CARL HUGNESS PUBLISHING
318 Mulberry St (47250-3498)
P.O. Box 225 (47250-0225)
PHONE..................................812 273-2472
Carl Hungness, *Principal*
EMP: 2 EST: 2013
SALES (est): 125.4K **Privately Held**
SIC: 2741 Miscellaneous publishing

(G-9448)
CENTURY TUBE LLC
4004 N Us 421 (47250-9800)
PHONE..................................812 265-9255
Patrick James, *CEO*
Stephen Graham, *CFO*
EMP: 125
SQ FT: 240
SALES (est): 100MM
SALES (corp-wide): 816.9MM **Privately
Held**
WEB: www.crownegroupinc.com
SIC: 3317 Steel pipe & tubes
PA: Crowne Group, Llc
127 Public Sq Ste 5110
Cleveland OH 44114
216 589-0198

(G-9449)
CHRISTMAN LOGGING
7641 N Bacon Ridge Rd (47250-9367)
PHONE..................................502 525-2649
Tara Richmond, *Principal*
EMP: 3
SALES (est): 98.8K **Privately Held**
SIC: 2411 Logging

(G-9450)
CHRISTYS CANDLES INC
Also Called: Christy's Candles & Gifts
2631 Michigan Rd (47250-1875)
PHONE..................................812 273-3072
Christy Brogan, *Mng Member*
Jon Brogan,
EMP: 5
SQ FT: 6,000
SALES: 400K **Privately Held**
WEB: www.christyscountrycandles.com
SIC: 3999 Candles

(G-9451)
CHURCHILL CIGARS
605 W 2nd St (47250-3747)
PHONE..................................812 273-2249
Edward Roszczynski, *Principal*
EMP: 2
SALES (est): 112.7K **Privately Held**
SIC: 3999 Cigarette & cigar products & ac-
cessories

(G-9452)
**CLIFTY ENGINEERING AND
TOOL CO**
2949 Clifty Dr (47250-1680)
PHONE..................................812 273-3272
Fax: 812 273-4841
Robert D Hughes, *CEO*
Raymond H Combs, *President*
Betty L Helton, *Corp Secy*
Arnold W Curry, *Senior VP*
Cecil Dunn, *Vice Pres*
EMP: 105 EST: 1961
SQ FT: 57,000
SALES (est): 15.9MM **Privately Held**
WEB: www.cliftyengineering.com
SIC: 3544 3599 Special dies & tools; elec-
trical discharge machining (EDM)

(G-9453)
COLLINS TOOL & DIE INC
2902 Wilson Ave (47250-1831)
PHONE..................................812 273-4765
Fax: 812 265-4183
Ronnie Collins, *President*

Diann Collins, *Corp Secy*
EMP: 9
SQ FT: 6,000
SALES (est): 1.2MM **Privately Held**
SIC: 3544 7692 Special dies & tools;
welding repair

(G-9454)
COLUMBUS EMBROIDERY
617 Green Rd (47250-2141)
PHONE..................................812 273-0860
Fax: 812 273-8811
Kevin Fry, *President*
EMP: 4
SALES: 400K **Privately Held**
WEB: www.columbusembroidery.com
SIC: 2395 Embroidery products, except
schiffli machine

(G-9455)
**CRESTWOOD EQUITY
PARTNERS LP**
Also Called: Blue Flame
3625 Clifty Dr (47250-1649)
PHONE..................................812 265-3313
Fax: 812 265-2819
Ted Klopfenstein, *Manager*
EMP: 5
SALES (corp-wide): 3.8B **Publicly Held**
WEB: www.inergypropane.com
SIC: 5984 3589 Propane gas, bottled;
water treatment equipment, industrial
PA: Crestwood Equity Partners Lp
811 Main St Ste 3400
Houston TX 77002
832 519-2200

(G-9456)
**DIE-MENSIONAL METAL
STAMPING**
2950 Wilson Ave (47250-1831)
P.O. Box 756 (47250-0756)
PHONE..................................812 265-3946
Fax: 812 265-4311
Fred Swinney, *President*
Dianna Swinney, *Admin Sec*
EMP: 10
SQ FT: 12,000
SALES (est): 1MM **Privately Held**
SIC: 3469 3441 3542 3444 Metal stamp-
ings; fabricated structural metal; machine
tools, metal forming type; sheet metal-
work

(G-9457)
**DIGITAL PRINTING
INCORPORATED**
Also Called: Dpi
2906 Clifty Dr (47250-1641)
PHONE..................................812 265-2205
Fax: 812 273-6402
George Jackson, *President*
Orme Wilson, *Principal*
Julie Hoskins, *Admin Sec*
EMP: 12
SQ FT: 12,000
SALES (est): 1.1MM **Privately Held**
WEB: www.dpimad.com
SIC: 2752 2791 2789 Commercial print-
ing, offset; typesetting; bookbinding & re-
lated work

(G-9458)
DOE RUN TOOLING INC
8550 E Doe Run Rd (47250-8541)
PHONE..................................812 265-3057
Jerry Hunter, *President*
Laura Hunter, *Vice Pres*
EMP: 2
SALES (est): 120K **Privately Held**
SIC: 3544 Special dies, tools, jigs & fix-
tures

(G-9459)
EAST INDUSTRIES LLC
831 W Main St (47250-3131)
PHONE..................................812 273-4358
Joshua Nichter, *Principal*
EMP: 5
SALES (est): 601.7K **Privately Held**
SIC: 3999 Barber & beauty shop equip-
ment

(G-9460)
**ELECTRIC MOTOR SALES &
SERVICE**
1540 W Jpg Niblo Rd (47250-9734)
PHONE..................................812 574-3233
EMP: 2
SALES (est): 100K **Privately Held**
SIC: 3699 Mfg Electrical Equipment/Sup-
plies

(G-9461)
**EXTREME PRECISION
PRODUCTS LLC**
Also Called: 1st Choice Machining & Tooling
11388 N West Fork Rd (47250-7326)
PHONE..................................812 839-0101
Calvin Daugherty, *Owner*
EMP: 2
SALES (est): 283.4K **Privately Held**
SIC: 3599 Machine shop, jobbing & repair

(G-9462)
FORCE CNC LLC
940 Lanier Dr (47250-2014)
PHONE..................................812 273-0218
Greg Goldsmith, *President*
Allen Wingham, *General Ptnr*
Jerry Ousley, *Buyer*
EMP: 6
SQ FT: 8,000
SALES (est): 1.1MM **Privately Held**
WEB: www.forcecnc.com
SIC: 3599 Machine shop, jobbing & repair

(G-9463)
GROTE INDUSTRIES INC (PA)
2600 Lanier Dr (47250-1797)
PHONE..................................812 273-2121
Fax: 812 265-8440
William D Grote III, *Ch of Bd*
William Dominic Grote IV, *President*
Mike Grote, *General Mgr*
James L Braun, *Vice Pres*
Ken Hoskins, *Plant Mgr*
◆ EMP: 822
SQ FT: 435,000
SALES (est): 291MM **Privately Held**
WEB: www.grote.com
SIC: 3231 3647 Mirrors, truck & automo-
bile: made from purchased glass; vehicu-
lar lighting equipment

(G-9464)
GROTE INDUSTRIES LLC
2600 Lanier Dr (47250-1797)
PHONE..................................812 265-8273
William Grote IV, *President*
James Braun, *CFO*
John Grote, *Admin Sec*
EMP: 1200
SQ FT: 435,000
SALES (est): 40.1MM **Privately Held**
SIC: 3647 3231 Vehicular lighting equip-
ment; mirrors, truck & automobile: made
from purchased glass

(G-9465)
HI DEF MACHINING LLC
3508 N State Road 7 (47250-7961)
PHONE..................................812 493-9943
Sean Alderman, *General Mgr*
EMP: 4 EST: 2016
SALES (est): 113.4K **Privately Held**
SIC: 3549 Wiredrawing & fabricating ma-
chinery & equipment, ex. die

(G-9466)
HIGHPOINT MFG LLC
3501 N Jefferson Lake Rd (47250-9277)
PHONE..................................812 273-8987
EMP: 2 EST: 2004
SALES (est): 71K **Privately Held**
SIC: 3999 Mfg Misc Products

(G-9467)
HILLTOP WOOD WORKING
4406 W County Road 1050 S
(47250-9616)
PHONE..................................270 604-1962
Caesar Stoltzfus, *Owner*
EMP: 12
SALES: 1MM **Privately Held**
SIC: 2499 Applicators, wood

G E O G R A P H I C

(G-9468)
HILLTOP WOODWORKING
4406 W County Road 1050 S
(47250-9616)
PHONE................................812 689-3462
Caesar Stoltzfus, *Principal*
EMP: 3
SALES (est): 370.3K Privately Held
SIC: 2431 Millwork

(G-9469)
HK PETROLEUM LTD
606 E Main St (47250-4708)
P.O. Box 224 (47250-0224)
PHONE................................229 366-1313
Rick Kay, *Partner*
EMP: 5
SQ FT: 1,800
SALES (est): 415.9K Privately Held
SIC: 2911 Fractionation products of crude
petroleum, hydrocarbons

(G-9470)
**HOOSIER DRILLING CONTRS
INC**
8364 S Us 421 (47250-9632)
PHONE................................812 689-1260
Robert Sumler, *President*
Robert S Sumler Jr, *Vice Pres*
Tonya B Sumler, *Vice Pres*
Tim Johnson, *Manager*
EMP: 10
SALES (est): 2.4MM Privately Held
WEB: www.hoosierdrilling.com
SIC: 1381 Directional drilling oil & gas
wells

(G-9471)
HYPERBOLE SOFTWARE UNLTD
Also Called: Hyperbole Creations
9383 E Tate Ridge Rd (47250-8754)
P.O. Box 104 (47250-0104)
PHONE................................812 839-6635
Carl W Reynolds, *Owner*
EMP: 8
SALES: 100K Privately Held
SIC: 7372 Business oriented computer
software

(G-9472)
IMI SOUTH LLC
3650 N Hwy 7 (47250)
PHONE................................812 273-1428
Edward Campbol, *Branch Mgr*
EMP: 4
SALES (corp-wide): 800.6MM Privately
Held
SIC: 3273 Ready-mixed concrete
HQ: Imi South, Llc
1440 Selinda Ave
Louisville KY 40213
502 456-6930

(G-9473)
**INTERSTATE BLOCK
CORPORATION**
3148 Clifty Dr (47250-1645)
P.O. Box 566, Columbus (47202-0566)
PHONE................................812 273-1742
Fax: 812 265-5267
Harry E Horn, *President*
EMP: 4
SALES (est): 258.5K Privately Held
SIC: 3273 Ready-mixed concrete

(G-9474)
JPG MACHINE & TOOL LLC
1263 W Jpg Woodfill Rd # 212
(47250-9731)
PHONE................................812 265-4512
Fax: 812 265-4412
Debbie Ford, *Mng Member*
Charlene Jenkins, *Mng Member*
EMP: 6
SALES: 900K Privately Held
SIC: 3549 Metalworking machinery

(G-9475)
KENTUCKIANA PUBLISHING
Also Called: Roundabout Entertainment
Guide
307 Jefferson St (47250-3408)
PHONE................................812 273-2259
Don Ward, *President*
EMP: 6

SALES (est): 393.5K Privately Held
WEB: www.roundaboutmadison.com
SIC: 2711 Newspapers: publishing only,
not printed on site

(G-9476)
**KOEHLER WELDING SUPPLY
INC**
2352 Michigan Rd (47250-2443)
PHONE................................812 574-4103
David J Ungru, *President*
Suzanna Ungru, *CFO*
Ted Herbert, *Accounts Mgr*
Todd Ungru, *Sales Staff*
Kai Kempker, *Office Mgr*
◆ EMP: 14
SQ FT: 8,300
SALES: 16MM Privately Held
SIC: 5085 3535 5999 5172 Welding sup-
plies; robotic conveyors; welding supplies;
lubricating oils & greases; specialty clean-
ing & sanitation preparations

(G-9477)
**LANTHIER WINERY &
RESTAURANT**
123 Mill St (47250-3132)
PHONE................................812 273-2409
Chris Lanthier, *Owner*
EMP: 12
SALES (est): 520K Privately Held
WEB: www.lanthierwinery.com
SIC: 2084 5812 5947 Wines; eating
places; gift, novelty & souvenir shop

(G-9478)
MACKS WELDING
Also Called: Madison Boat & Barge
2890 Wilson Ave (47250-1830)
PHONE................................812 265-6255
Mack Breeck, *Principal*
EMP: 12
SALES (est): 885.7K Privately Held
WEB: www.madisonboatandbarge.com
SIC: 3732 3731 Boats, fiberglass: building
& repairing; barges, building & repairing

(G-9479)
MADISON COURIER
Also Called: Weekly Herald, The
310 Courier Sq (47250-9919)
PHONE................................812 265-3641
Fax: 812 273-6903
Jane Wallis Jacobs, *President*
Don Wallis Jr, *Vice Pres*
Curtis Jacobs Jr, *Admin Sec*
EMP: 33 EST: 1837
SQ FT: 4,480
SALES (est): 1.6MM Privately Held
WEB: www.madisoncourier.com
SIC: 2711 2752 Newspapers: publishing
only, not printed on site; commercial print-
ing, lithographic

(G-9480)
MADISON PLATING INC
2520 Lanier Dr Ste A (47250-4011)
P.O. Box 758 (47250-0758)
PHONE................................812 273-2211
Fax: 812 265-9923
Claude O Routon, *President*
Rebecca Routon, *Treasurer*
EMP: 10
SQ FT: 8,000
SALES (est): 840K Privately Held
WEB: www.thermalchemical.com
SIC: 3471 Electroplating of metals or
formed products

(G-9481)
**MADISON PRECISION
PRODUCTS INC**
94 E 400 N (47250-9599)
PHONE................................812 273-4702
Fax: 812 273-2451
Michihiko Kato, *President*
Kazuyoshi Matsushita, *Principal*
Ken Degler, *Exec VP*
Don Bentley, *Assistant VP*
Randy Boyd, *Vice Pres*
▲ EMP: 500
SQ FT: 176,500

SALES (est): 160.5MM
SALES (corp-wide): 144.1B Privately
Held
WEB: www.madisonprecision.com
SIC: 3363 3365 Aluminum die-castings;
aluminum foundries
HQ: Metts Corporation
1620, Matoba
Kawagoe STM 350-1
492 375-900

(G-9482)
MADISON TOOL AND DIE INC
3000 Michigan Rd (47250-1801)
PHONE................................812 273-2250
Fax: 812 273-3018
Terry Sparks, *President*
Gary Sparks, *Vice Pres*
▲ EMP: 75
SQ FT: 75,000
SALES (est): 13.9MM Privately Held
SIC: 3544 3451 Special dies & tools;
screw machine products

(G-9483)
MADISON TRUSS COMPANY
5426 N Olive Branch Rd (47250-9376)
PHONE................................812 273-5482
David A Gosman, *President*
EMP: 4
SQ FT: 9,000
SALES (est): 470K Privately Held
SIC: 2439 Counter tops; cabinet & finish
carpentry

(G-9484)
MADISON VINEYARDS INC
1456 E 400 N (47250-9387)
PHONE................................812 273-6500
Steven Palmer, *President*
Sandra Palmer, *Vice Pres*
EMP: 4
SALES: 56K Privately Held
SIC: 2084 Wines

(G-9485)
MEESE INC
Also Called: Meese Orbitron Dunne Co
1745 Cragmont St (47250-2807)
PHONE................................812 273-1008
Fax: 812 273-1878
Michael Bruce, *Manager*
EMP: 67
SQ FT: 120,000
SALES (corp-wide): 107.8MM Privately
Held
WEB: www.modroto.com
SIC: 2393 3089 3496 3444 Canvas
bags; tubs, plastic (containers); miscella-
neous fabricated wire products; sheet
metalwork; canvas & related products
HQ: Meese, Inc.
535 N Midland Ave
Saddle Brook NJ 07663
201 796-4490

(G-9486)
MIDWEST GYM SUPPLY INC (PA)
775 Scott Ct (47250-1829)
PHONE................................812 265-4099
Paul Kemp, *President*
▼ EMP: 15
SQ FT: 32,000
SALES (est): 1.2MM Privately Held
WEB: www.midwestgymsupply.com
SIC: 3949 5091 Gymnasium equipment;
athletic goods

(G-9487)
MIDWEST TUBE MILLS INC (PA)
2855 Michigan Rd (47250-1814)
P.O. Box 830 (47250-0830)
PHONE................................812 265-1553
Fax: 812 265-1623
Rick Russell, *CEO*
Larry Brown, *Sales Staff*
EMP: 85
SQ FT: 10,000
SALES (est): 36.7MM Privately Held
WEB: www.midwesttubemills.com
SIC: 3312 Tubes, steel & iron

(G-9488)
MILLENNIUM TOOL INC
619 Thomas Hill Rd (47250-2537)
PHONE................................812 273-1566

Fax: 812 273-0546
Kyle Lyon, *President*
Jeremy Dykes, *General Mgr*
Cheryl Lyon, *CFO*
EMP: 40
SQ FT: 17,000
SALES (est): 6.4MM Privately Held
WEB: www.millenniumtoolinc.com
SIC: 3544 Special dies & tools

(G-9489)
MPS PRINTING INC
339 Clifty Dr (47250-1605)
PHONE................................812 273-4446
Jeff Daghir, *President*
Sharon Daghir, *Treasurer*
Roy Graham, *Cust Mgr*
EMP: 4
SQ FT: 3,000
SALES (est): 360K Privately Held
WEB: www.mpsprinting.com
SIC: 2752 7334 2759 Commercial print-
ing, offset; photocopying & duplicating
services; commercial printing

(G-9490)
**PATHOLOGY COMPUTER
SYSTEMS**
Also Called: Division of Clones Plus
131 E Main St (47250-3459)
PHONE................................812 265-3264
Dan Helman, *President*
EMP: 2
SALES (est): 218.9K Privately Held
SIC: 7372 Prepackaged software

(G-9491)
RAINBOWS STAINED GLASS
1782 E Telegraph Hill Rd (47250-8790)
PHONE................................812 265-0030
Rick Collier, *Owner*
Karen Collier, *Owner*
EMP: 3
SALES (est): 159.1K Privately Held
SIC: 3231 Products of purchased glass

(G-9492)
RKO ENTERPRISES LLC
2850 Clifty Dr (47250-1699)
PHONE................................812 273-8813
Fax: 812 273-5145
Michelle Pratt, *General Mgr*
Keith Olson,
◆ EMP: 8
SQ FT: 16,000
SALES (est): 1.4MM Privately Held
WEB: www.rkoenterprises.com
SIC: 3499 Fire- or burglary-resistive prod-
ucts

(G-9493)
ROYER CORPORATION
805 East St (47250-3210)
PHONE................................800 457-8997
Fax: 812 265-3207
Roger Williams, *President*
Pat Berry, *Exec VP*
Tena Perry, *Vice Pres*
Justin Murray, *Engineer*
Lauren Marsh, *Accounting Mgr*
▲ EMP: 65
SQ FT: 62,000
SALES (est): 13.4MM Privately Held
WEB: www.royercorp.com
SIC: 3089 Novelties, plastic

(G-9494)
**S L THOMAS FAMILY WINERY
INC**
208 E 2nd St (47250-3420)
PHONE................................812 273-3755
Steven Thomas, *President*
Elizabeth Thomas, *Corp Secy*
EMP: 2
SALES (est): 170K Privately Held
SIC: 2084 Wines

(G-9495)
SISWD PROCESSING (PA)
Also Called: Southeast Ind Solid Waste Proc
6556 N Shun Pike Rd 534 (47250-9723)
PHONE................................812 574-4080
Fax: 812 574-4082
Aaron Bell, *Director*
EMP: 6

SALES (est): 767.6K **Privately Held**
SIC: 1389 Processing service, gas

(G-9496)
STAR QUALITY AWARDS INC
322 Crestwood Dr (47250-2353)
PHONE.................................812 273-1740
Toll Free:..................................888 -
Fax: 812 265-2522
Pamela Moon, *President*
Linda Cummins, *Data Proc Dir*
EMP: 2
SALES (est): 164.1K **Privately Held**
SIC: 7389 2396 5199 3479 Engraving service; screen printing on fabric articles; advertising specialties; etching & engraving

(G-9497)
TAUNYAS CREATIVE CUTS
220 Clifty Dr (47250-1696)
PHONE.................................812 574-7722
EMP: 2 **EST:** 2008
SALES (est): 82.8K **Privately Held**
SIC: 3999 Barber & beauty shop equipment

(G-9498)
THORNTONS MTRCYCLE SLS - MDSON
217 Clifty Dr (47250-1603)
PHONE.................................812 574-6347
Tammy Schwagmeier, *Co-Owner*
EMP: 4
SALES (est): 1.7MM **Privately Held**
SIC: 5012 3799 Motorcycles; all terrain vehicles (ATV)

(G-9499)
VEHICLE SERVICE GROUP LLC
Rotary Lift
2700 Lanier Dr (47250-1753)
P.O. Box 1560 (47250-0560)
PHONE.................................812 273-1622
Matt Webster, *Vice Pres*
Lawrence Chase, *Branch Mgr*
Doug Spiller, *Manager*
EMP: 22
SALES (corp-wide): 7.8B **Publicly Held**
WEB: www.doverindustries.com
SIC: 3711 Chassis, motor vehicle
HQ: Vehicle Service Group, Llc
2700 Lanier Dr
Madison IN 47250

(G-9500)
VEHICLE SERVICE GROUP LLC
Also Called: Chief Automotive Technologies
996 Industrial Dr (47250-3901)
PHONE.................................800 445-9262
EMP: 6
SALES (corp-wide): 7.8B **Publicly Held**
SIC: 3711 Chassis, motor vehicle
HQ: Vehicle Service Group, Llc
2700 Lanier Dr
Madison IN 47250

(G-9501)
VEHICLE SERVICE GROUP LLC (HQ)
Also Called: Chief Automotive Technologies
2700 Lanier Dr (47250-1753)
PHONE.................................800 640-5438
Fax: 812 265-9596
Niclas Ytterdahl, *President*
Jim Dirksen, *Vice Pres*
James Wysinski, *Vice Pres*
Jeff Hay, *Controller*
Michelle Hoene, *Accountant*
◆ **EMP:** 277
SALES: 279.6MM
SALES (corp-wide): 7.8B **Publicly Held**
SIC: 3711 Chassis, motor vehicle
PA: Dover Corporation
3005 Highland Pkwy # 200
Downers Grove IL 60515
630 541-1540

Magnet
Perry County

(G-9502)
ANTHONY D ETIENNE LOGGING
Also Called: Doyle Logging Etienne
15502 N State Road 66 (47520-5069)
PHONE.................................812 843-5872
Anthony D Etienne, *Owner*
Lana Etienne, *Owner*
EMP: 7
SALES (est): 390K **Privately Held**
SIC: 2411 Logging

Manilla
Rush County

(G-9503)
E & L CONSTRUCTION INC
Also Called: Log Home Construction Indiana
1375 N 800 E (46150-9609)
PHONE.................................765 525-7081
Paul Weaver Jr, *President*
Pansy Weaver, *Vice Pres*
EMP: 3
SALES (est): 391.1K **Privately Held**
SIC: 1521 2452 New construction, single-family houses; log cabins, prefabricated, wood

Marengo
Crawford County

(G-9504)
EASTERN RED CEDAR PRODUCTS LLC (PA)
9611 S County Road 425 E (47140-7305)
PHONE.................................812 365-2495
Richard Newton,
EMP: 8
SALES (est): 1.3MM **Privately Held**
WEB: www.cedarusa.com
SIC: 2421 Sawmills & planing mills, general

(G-9505)
WALTON LOGGING
991 S State Road 66 (47140-8419)
PHONE.................................812 365-9635
Pamela Walton, *Principal*
EMP: 3
SALES (est): 173K **Privately Held**
SIC: 2411 Logging

Marion
Grant County

(G-9506)
ADVANCED CABINET SYSTEMS INC
1629 S Joaquin Dr (46953-9635)
P.O. Box 167 (46952-0167)
PHONE.................................765 677-8000
Greg Bowers, *President*
Philip Bowers, *Vice Pres*
Thomas Reto, *CFO*
EMP: 65
SQ FT: 70,000
SALES (est): 9.5MM **Privately Held**
SIC: 2434 Wood kitchen cabinets

(G-9507)
AGRICOR INC
Also Called: Grain Millers
1626 S Joaquin Dr (46953-9633)
P.O. Box 807 (46952-0807)
PHONE.................................765 662-0606
Fax: 765 662-7189
Steve Wickes, *President*
Bill Cramer, *Opers Staff*
Dave Hermanson, *Controller*
Tadashi Sugimoto, *Sales Mgr*
Chanda Hiatt, *Sales Staff*
▼ **EMP:** 52
SQ FT: 3,200

SALES (est): 11.9MM
SALES (corp-wide): 232.6MM **Privately Held**
WEB: www.agricor.org
SIC: 2041 Flour & other grain mill products; oat flour
PA: Grain Millers, Inc.
10400 Viking Dr Ste 301
Eden Prairie MN 55344
952 829-8821

(G-9508)
ARDAGH GLASS INC
123 E Mckinley St (46952-2271)
P.O. Box 249 (46952-0249)
PHONE.................................765 651-1260
Roger Erb, *Senior VP*
EMP: 14 **Privately Held**
SIC: 3221 Glass containers
HQ: Ardagh Glass Inc.
10194 Crosspoint Blvd
Indianapolis IN 46256

(G-9509)
ARDAGH GLASS INC
Also Called: Ardagh Is Services
123 E Mckinley St (46952-2271)
PHONE.................................765 662-1172
Gordon Love, *Vice Pres*
EMP: 7 **Privately Held**
SIC: 3221 Glass containers; bottles for packing, bottling & canning: glass
HQ: Ardagh Glass Inc.
10194 Crosspoint Blvd
Indianapolis IN 46256

(G-9510)
ATLAS FOUNDRY COMPANY INC
601 N Henderson Ave (46952-3348)
PHONE.................................765 662-2525
James M Gartland Jr, *Ch of Bd*
William F Gartland, *President*
Joseph C Gartland, *Vice Pres*
EMP: 125 **EST:** 1893
SALES: 25.7MM **Privately Held**
SIC: 3321 Gray & ductile iron foundries; gray iron castings

(G-9511)
AVIONIC STRUCTURES OF INDIANA
4589 N Wabash Rd (46952-9738)
P.O. Box 1246 (46952-7646)
PHONE.................................765 671-7865
Charles E Herriman, *Principal*
EMP: 2
SALES (est): 243.7K **Privately Held**
SIC: 3714 Motor vehicle parts & accessories

(G-9512)
BAHR BROS MFG INC
Also Called: Bahr Brothers Manufacturing
2545 S Lincoln Blvd (46953-3802)
P.O. Box 411 (46952-0411)
PHONE.................................765 664-6235
Fax: 765 662-1340
Jefferey P Jackson, *Ch of Bd*
Jeffrey P Jackson, *Ch of Bd*
Timothy Street, *President*
Scott Bratcher, *Vice Pres*
Steve Carl, *Safety Dir*
EMP: 48 **EST:** 1909
SQ FT: 45,000
SALES (est): 12.9MM **Privately Held**
WEB: www.bahrbros.com
SIC: 3325 3554 3321 3312 Steel foundries; paper industries machinery; gray iron castings; ductile iron castings; stainless steel

(G-9513)
BURNSIDE ENTERPRISES
4796 N 300 E (46952-6819)
PHONE.................................765 664-4032
Larry Burnside, *Principal*
EMP: 2
SALES (est): 167.2K **Privately Held**
SIC: 2452 Log cabins, prefabricated, wood

(G-9514)
CANINES CHOICE INC
1019 E 26th St (46953-3709)
PHONE.................................765 662-2633
Robert Kramer, *President*
Barb Kinzie, *Vice Pres*

Joan Williams, *Supervisor*
▲ **EMP:** 7
SQ FT: 23,000
SALES (est): 1.1MM **Privately Held**
WEB: www.canineschoice.com
SIC: 2047 Dog food

(G-9515)
CARICO ENTERPRISES LLC
Also Called: Carico Systems
3426 W Delphi Pike (46952-9266)
P.O. Box 1313 (46952-7713)
PHONE.................................765 384-4451
Jeanna Riddle, *CEO*
Justin Riddle, *President*
EMP: 7
SQ FT: 100,000
SALES (est): 795.8K **Privately Held**
SIC: 3315 Wire carts: grocery, household & industrial

(G-9516)
CAUSE PRINTING COMPANY
1102 W Ontario St (46953-3900)
PHONE.................................765 573-3330
Valerie Jullierat, *President*
EMP: 3
SALES (est): 107.2K **Privately Held**
SIC: 2759 Screen printing

(G-9517)
CENTRAL INDIANA ETHANOL LLC
Also Called: Cie
2955 W Delphi Pike (46952-9265)
PHONE.................................765 384-4001
Fax: 765 384-4001
Ryan Drook, *CEO*
Gary Drook, *General Mgr*
Jeff Rusine, *Buyer*
Shelly Obenchain, *VP Finance*
Jeff Harts, *Chief Mktg Ofcr*
EMP: 58
SALES (est): 32.7MM **Privately Held**
WEB: www.cie.us
SIC: 2819 Nuclear fuel & cores, inorganic

(G-9518)
COMPUTER AGE ENGINEERING INC
Also Called: C A E
867 E 38th St (46953-4402)
P.O. Box 3268 (46953-0268)
PHONE.................................765 674-8551
Fax: 765 674-3964
Michael Bartrom, *President*
Sherri Bartrom, *Vice Pres*
Ted Fiock, *Project Mgr*
Patricia Payne, *Purch Agent*
Michael Pollen, *Engineer*
EMP: 30
SQ FT: 12,500
SALES (est): 7MM **Privately Held**
WEB: www.caeweb.com
SIC: 8711 3559 Electrical or electronic engineering; automotive related machinery

(G-9519)
D E KEY MACHINE SHOP
1442 E 450 N (46952-9020)
PHONE.................................765 664-1720
David Key, *Principal*
EMP: 2
SALES (est): 148.6K **Privately Held**
SIC: 3599 Machine shop, jobbing & repair

(G-9520)
DANA DRIVESHAFT PRODUCTS LLC
400 S Miller Ave (46953-1137)
PHONE.................................260 432-2903
Kirk Alderman, *Mfg Staff*
Sam Simons, *QC Dir*
Robert Bragg, *Manager*
Paul Larochelle, *Manager*
Peggy Lyons, *Programmer Anys*
EMP: 400 **Publicly Held**
SIC: 3714 3713 Universal joints, motor vehicle; drive shafts, motor vehicle; truck & bus bodies
HQ: Dana Driveshaft Products, Llc
3939 Technology Dr
Maumee OH 43537

GEOGRAPHIC

(G-9521)
DOUBLE H MANUFACTURING CORP
Also Called: Double H Plastics
2548 W 26th St (46953-9414)
PHONE......................................765 664-9090
Fax: 765 664-1002
Joseph Harp, *President*
David Harp, *Vice Pres*
Harry Harp, *Vice Pres*
▲ EMP: 70
SQ FT: 20,000
SALES (est): 12.1MM **Privately Held**
WEB: www.doublehplastics.com
SIC: 2821 Plastics materials & resins

(G-9522)
E & B PAVING INC
3888 S Garthwaite Rd (46953-5621)
PHONE......................................765 674-5848
Dave Coverdale, *Manager*
EMP: 20
SALES (corp-wide): 800.6MM **Privately Held**
SIC: 1611 2951 1771 Surfacing & paving; asphalt paving mixtures & blocks; concrete work
HQ: E & B Paving, Inc.
286 W 300 N
Anderson IN 46012
765 643-5358

(G-9523)
EXPERT ELECTRIC
2916 E Bocock Rd (46952-8665)
PHONE......................................765 664-6642
Chad Dixon, *Principal*
EMP: 2
SALES (est): 178.2K **Privately Held**
SIC: 7623 3699 1731 1711 Refrigeration service & repair; electrical equipment & supplies; electrical work; warm air heating & air conditioning contractor

(G-9524)
GENERAL CABLE INDUSTRIES INC
Also Called: Marion, In Plant
440 E 8th St (46953-2088)
PHONE......................................765 664-2321
Fax: 765 668-0700
Jay Buehler, *Plant Mgr*
Erik Gangstad, *Safety Mgr*
Robert McMillan, *Purch Agent*
Carrie Silvers, *Purch Agent*
Dennis Summerlot, *Engineer*
EMP: 279
SQ FT: 1,000,000
SALES (corp-wide): 1.3B **Privately Held**
WEB: www.generalcable.com
SIC: 3357 Communication wire
HQ: General Cable Industries, Inc.
4 Tesseneer Dr
Highland Heights KY 41076

(G-9525)
GENERAL MOTORS LLC
2400 W 2nd St (46952-3249)
PHONE......................................765 668-2000
Fax: 765 668-2058
Paul Buetow, *Plant Mgr*
Anthony Maynard, *Safety Mgr*
Mark Sanders, *Purch Agent*
Michael Baldwin, *Engineer*
Joel Piatt, *Manager*
EMP: 277 **Publicly Held**
SIC: 3465 3711 3544 3469 Automotive stampings; motor vehicles & car bodies; special dies, tools, jigs & fixtures; metal stampings; sheet metalwork
HQ: General Motors Llc
300 Renaissance Ctr L1
Detroit MI 48243

(G-9526)
GILLESPIE MRRELL GEN CONTG LLC
1240 S Adams St (46953-2327)
PHONE......................................765 618-4084
Andrew Morrell, *President*
Charles E Gillespie, *Vice Pres*
EMP: 1

SALES (est): 201.4K **Privately Held**
SIC: 5211 3567 3822 Roofing material; metal melting furnaces, industrial: electric; air conditioning & refrigeration controls

(G-9527)
GRANT COUNTY STEEL INC
2201 S Branson St (46953-3258)
P.O. Box 1285 (46952-7685)
PHONE......................................765 668-7547
Fax: 765 668-4803
Dinh Ngo, *President*
Hai Nguyen, *Vice Pres*
EMP: 15
SQ FT: 15,000
SALES (est): 6.2MM **Privately Held**
WEB: www.ngos.com
SIC: 5051 3441 3444 3443 Steel; fabricated structural metal; sheet metalwork; fabricated plate work (boiler shop)

(G-9528)
HAMBY
2104 S Valley Ave (46953-2913)
PHONE......................................765 664-4045
George E Hamby, *Principal*
EMP: 2
SALES (est): 144.6K **Privately Held**
SIC: 3672 Printed circuit boards

(G-9529)
HARTSON-KENNEDY CABINET TOP CO (PA)
522 W 22nd St (46953-2926)
P.O. Box 3095 (46953-0095)
PHONE......................................765 668-8144
Fax: 765 662-3452
William Kennedy, *President*
Christopher L Kennedy, *Vice Pres*
Michael R Kennedy, *Vice Pres*
Michael Kennedy, *Vice Pres*
Glen Devitt, *Opers Mgr*
EMP: 279 EST: 1948
SQ FT: 121,435
SALES (est): 99.2MM **Privately Held**
WEB: www.hartson-kennedy.com
SIC: 3083 Plastic finished products, laminated

(G-9530)
HELVIE & SONS INC
5418 S Lincoln Blvd (46953-6203)
PHONE......................................765 674-1372
Jim Helvie, *President*
Kenneth Helvie, *Vice Pres*
EMP: 5 EST: 1953
SALES (est): 646.5K **Privately Held**
SIC: 1781 1389 Water well drilling; water well servicing; oil & gas wells: building, repairing & dismantling

(G-9531)
HOOSIER REPRODUCTION SERVICES
1417 W Kem Rd (46952-1856)
PHONE......................................765 664-3162
Fax: 765 664-3171
Wally Rec, *Owner*
Larry Campbell, *Co-Owner*
EMP: 5
SALES (est): 230K **Privately Held**
SIC: 2752 Commercial printing, offset

(G-9532)
HUHTAMAKI INC
1001 E 38th St Ste B (46953-4477)
PHONE......................................765 664-2330
EMP: 320
SALES (corp-wide): 35.2B **Privately Held**
SIC: 2656 3565 Sanitary food containers; labeling machines, industrial
HQ: Huhtamaki, Inc.
9201 Packaging Dr
De Soto KS 66018
913 583-3025

(G-9533)
INDIANA OXYGEN COMPANY INC
2215 S Western Ave (46953-2826)
PHONE......................................765 662-8700
Fax: 765 664-9775
Gary Morrison, *Branch Mgr*
EMP: 4

SALES (corp-wide): 60.1MM **Privately Held**
WEB: www.indianaoxygen.com
SIC: 3541 5084 5169 Machine tools, metal cutting type; welding machinery & equipment; industrial gases; chemicals, industrial & heavy
PA: Indiana Oxygen Company Inc
6099 Corporate Way
Indianapolis IN 46278
317 290-0003

(G-9534)
IRVING MATERIALS INC
I M I
3888 S Garthwaite Rd (46953-5621)
PHONE......................................765 922-7285
Fax: 765 677-5243
Kevin Holcum, *Branch Mgr*
EMP: 10
SALES (corp-wide): 800.6MM **Privately Held**
SIC: 3273 1442 1611 3295 Ready-mixed concrete; construction sand & gravel; resurfacing contractor; minerals, ground or treated; cement, hydraulic
PA: Irving Materials, Inc.
8032 N State Road 9
Greenfield IN 46140
317 326-3101

(G-9535)
IRVING MATERIALS INC
Also Called: I M I
3892 S Garthwaite Rd (46953-5621)
PHONE......................................765 674-2271
Mike Borum, *Branch Mgr*
EMP: 14
SALES (corp-wide): 800.6MM **Privately Held**
SIC: 3273 Ready-mixed concrete
PA: Irving Materials, Inc.
8032 N State Road 9
Greenfield IN 46140
317 326-3101

(G-9536)
J G BOWERS INC
Also Called: Advanced Cabinet Systems
1629 S Joaquin Dr (46953-9635)
P.O. Box 167 (46952-0167)
PHONE......................................765 668-7000
Fax: 765 677-9000
Greg Bowers, *President*
Phil Herring, *Manager*
Jane Bowers, *Admin Sec*
EMP: 30
SQ FT: 15,000
SALES (est): 13.8MM **Privately Held**
SIC: 1542 2541 Commercial & office building, new construction; commercial & office buildings, renovation & repair; showcases, except refrigerated: wood; display fixtures, wood

(G-9537)
J R NEWBY
405 N Henderson Ave (46952-3303)
P.O. Box 374, Van Buren (46991-0374)
PHONE......................................765 664-3501
J R Newby, *Principal*
EMP: 2
SALES (est): 147.2K **Privately Held**
SIC: 2499 Wood products

(G-9538)
JBD MACHINING
1702 W Jeffras Ave (46952-3345)
PHONE......................................765 671-9050
Jerzy Radomski, *Owner*
EMP: 3
SALES (est): 278.9K **Privately Held**
SIC: 3599 Machine shop, jobbing & repair

(G-9539)
JUJUBERRY LLC
2020 S Western Ave (46953-2800)
PHONE......................................765 673-0058
EMP: 4
SALES (est): 293.3K **Privately Held**
SIC: 2026 Mfg Fluid Milk

(G-9540)
KIRBY RISK CORPORATION
1221 S Adams St (46953-2328)
PHONE......................................765 664-5185

Fax: 765 664-4818
Gary Spall, *Sales Staff*
Tim Schmidt, *Branch Mgr*
Tim Smith, *Manager*
EMP: 10
SQ FT: 10,000
SALES (corp-wide): 401.3MM **Privately Held**
WEB: www.kirbyrisk.com
SIC: 5063 5085 7694 Electrical supplies; industrial sewing thread; electric motor repair; rewinding services
PA: Kirby Risk Corporation
1815 Sagamore Pkwy N
Lafayette IN 47904
765 448-4567

(G-9541)
L & L PRESS INC
Also Called: Hoosier Jiffy Print
1417 W Kem Rd (46952-1856)
P.O. Box 802 (46952-0802)
PHONE......................................765 664-3162
Rob Wilson, *President*
Lori McGillem, *Vice Pres*
EMP: 12
SQ FT: 2,000
SALES: 1.2MM **Privately Held**
SIC: 2752 2791 2789 2759 Commercial printing, offset; typesetting; bookbinding & related work; commercial printing; coated & laminated paper

(G-9542)
LEIN CORPORATION
3301 S Hamaker St (46953-4229)
P.O. Box 3064 (46953-0064)
PHONE......................................765 674-6950
Fax: 765 674-6970
David Compton, *President*
Lisa E Compton, *Corp Secy*
JD Lutton, *CFO*
EMP: 47
SQ FT: 14,000
SALES (est): 4.6MM **Privately Held**
WEB: www.leincorporation.com
SIC: 3479 Coating of metals & formed products; painting of metal products

(G-9543)
MARION METAL PRODUCTS INC
401 N Henderson Ave (46952-3303)
PHONE......................................765 662-8333
Fax: 765 662-8409
Tom Brubaker, *President*
Jerri Henderson, *Corp Secy*
Mark Brubaker, *Vice Pres*
EMP: 30
SQ FT: 20,000
SALES (est): 5.2MM **Privately Held**
SIC: 3441 Boat & barge sections, prefabricated metal

(G-9544)
MARION PAPER BOX COMPANY
600 E 18th St (46953-3304)
P.O. Box 276 (46952-0276)
PHONE......................................765 664-6435
Fax: 765 664-6440
David Wilson, *President*
Joseph McCoy, *Principal*
Margaret Wilson, *Vice Pres*
EMP: 10
SQ FT: 15,000
SALES (est): 1.5MM **Privately Held**
WEB: www.marionpaperboxco.com
SIC: 2653 Boxes, corrugated: made from purchased materials

(G-9545)
MARION STEEL FABRICATION INC
1819 S Branson St (46953-3237)
P.O. Box 1478 (46952-7878)
PHONE......................................765 664-1478
James Swan, *President*
EMP: 30
SALES (est): 3.3MM
SALES (corp-wide): 7.8MM **Privately Held**
WEB: www.marionsteelfab.com
SIC: 3441 3444 3443 Building components, structural steel; sheet metalwork; fabricated plate work (boiler shop)

▲ = Import ▼=Export
◆ =Import/Export

PA: Marion Steel Fabrication, Inc.
333 W 4th St
Marion IN 46952
765 664-1478

(G-9546)
MARION TENT & AWNING CO
225 W Swayzee St (46952-2709)
PHONE...................................765 664-7722
Fax: 765 664-7722
Roger Krumel, Owner
Caroline Krumel, Co-Owner
EMP: 3 EST: 1936
SALES: 350K Privately Held
SIC: 2394 3444 Awnings, fabric: made
from purchased materials; awnings, sheet
metal

(G-9547)
MIDWEST CABINET SOLUTIONS INC
1001 E 24th St (46953-3324)
PHONE...................................765 664-3938
Fax: 765 664-3942
Jeremey E McCord, Mng Member
Ken Nichols, Manager
Derrick A Brown,
EMP: 14
SQ FT: 14,000
SALES (est): 2.4MM Privately Held
SIC: 2519 3083 Radio cabinets, plastic;
laminated plastic sheets

(G-9548)
NOVA PACKAGING GROUP INC
Also Called: Nova Pak
2409 W 2nd St (46952-3248)
P.O. Box 338 (46952-0338)
PHONE...................................765 651-2600
William Craig Dobbs, CEO
John R Irving, President
Gilbert McDaniel, General Mgr
Beth Dilley, Purch Agent
EMP: 43 EST: 1999
SQ FT: 214,000
SALES (est): 10.6MM Privately Held
SIC: 2653 3412 Boxes, corrugated: made
from purchased materials; metal barrels,
drums & pails

(G-9549)
PAGES EDITORIAL SERVICES INC
113 E Old Kokomo Rd (46953-6005)
PHONE...................................765 674-4212
Fax: 765 674-2475
Shirley Planck, President
Jae Brown, Editor
Jae Berry, Vice Pres
EMP: 10
SQ FT: 1,400
SALES (est): 1MM Privately Held
WEB: www.pagesmag.com
SIC: 2721 8231 Magazines: publishing &
printing; libraries

(G-9550)
PAXTON MEDIA GROUP LLC
Also Called: Chronicle-Tribune
610 S Adams St (46953-2041)
PHONE 765 664-5111
Fax: 765 668-4256
Amy Eads, Branch Mgr
EMP: 49
SALES (corp-wide): 318.6MM Privately
Held
WEB: www.jonesborosun.com
SIC: 2711 Commercial printing & newspa-
per publishing combined; newspapers,
publishing & printing
PA: Paxton Media Group, Llc
100 Television Ln
Paducah KY 42003
270 575-8630

(G-9551)
PEARSON PRINTING COMPANY
3239 S Washington St (46953-4025)
PHONE...................................765 664-8769
Kevin Pearson, Owner
EMP: 5
SALES (est): 353.2K Privately Held
SIC: 2759 Letterpress printing

(G-9552)
PEERLESS MACHINE & TOOL CORP
1804 W 2nd St (46952-3362)
P.O. Box 385 (46952-0385)
PHONE...................................765 662-2586
Fax: 765 662-6067
Jeffrey D Carson, President
Robert D Carson, Chairman
Barry Conrad, Vice Pres
◆ EMP: 60
SQ FT: 75,000
SALES (est): 11.4MM Privately Held
WEB: www.peerlessmachine.com
SIC: 3554 3559 Paper industries machin-
ery; plastics working machinery

(G-9553)
PEERLESS PRINTING CORP
Also Called: Peerless Printing & Off Sups
513 S Washington St (46953-1962)
P.O. Box 962 (46952-0962)
PHONE...................................765 664-8341
Fax: 765 664-9769
Kurt Kohlmorgen, President
Jane Kohlmorgen, Corp Secy
Ann Kohlmorgen, Vice Pres
Christy Whitton, Pub Rel Mgr
EMP: 16 EST: 1910
SQ FT: 5,800
SALES (est): 2.1MM Privately Held
WEB: www.ppcprint.com
SIC: 5112 2752 Office supplies; commer-
cial printing, offset

(G-9554)
PORTALS OF LIGHT INC
1186 E 700 N (46952-9401)
PHONE...................................765 981-2651
Nancy A Malley, President
EMP: 2
SALES (est): 124.8K Privately Held
SIC: 2741 Miscellaneous publishing

(G-9555)
PPI ACQUISITION LLC
Also Called: Pro Prints Gear
1424 W 35th St (46953-3454)
PHONE...................................765 674-8627
Steve Turner, President
Sue Farthing, Bookkeeper
Nicole Stancil, Sales Staff
EMP: 18 EST: 2013
SALES (est): 2.3MM Privately Held
SIC: 2759 5091 Screen printing; athletic
goods

(G-9556)
PRECISION TOOL & DIE INC
1735 W Factory Ave (46952-2424)
P.O. Box 808 (46952-0808)
PHONE...................................765 664-4786
Dennis Florek, President
C Greg Hearn, Corp Secy
EMP: 6
SQ FT: 5,900
SALES (est): 767.7K Privately Held
SIC: 3599 Machine shop, jobbing & repair

(G-9557)
QUAKER CHEMICAL CORP
2400 W 2nd St (46952-3249)
PHONE...................................765 668-2441
Jim Greemy, Manager
EMP: 3
SALES (est): 308.9K Privately Held
SIC: 4226 2899 Petroleum & chemical
bulk stations & terminals for hire; chemi-
cal preparations

(G-9558)
RACING FUEL IGNITE
2950 W Delphi Pike (46952-9265)
PHONE...................................765 733-0833
EMP: 3
SALES (est): 88.3K Privately Held
SIC: 2869 Fuels

(G-9559)
REALITY MOTOR SPORTS INC
1322 N Baldwin Ave (46952-1932)
PHONE...................................765 662-3000
Warren Thomas, President
Lori Thomas, Corp Secy
EMP: 5 EST: 1999

SALES (est): 1.5MM Privately Held
WEB: www.realitymotorsports.net
SIC: 3751 Motorcycles & related parts

(G-9560)
RONALD L MILLER
1102 N Wabash Ave (46952-2510)
PHONE...................................765 662-3881
Ronald Miller, Principal
EMP: 2
SALES (est): 121.7K Privately Held
SIC: 3843 Enamels, dentists'

(G-9561)
SCOTTS GRANT COUNTY ASP INC
2686 S 300 W (46953-9706)
PHONE...................................765 664-2754
Don Scott, President
EMP: 8
SALES (est): 836.3K Privately Held
SIC: 2951 5032 1611 Asphalt paving mix-
tures & blocks; paving materials; surfac-
ing & paving

(G-9562)
SIGN PROS OF MARION
4260 S 400 W (46953-9733)
PHONE...................................765 677-1234
Fax: 765 677-0765
Lee Cabe, Owner
EMP: 2
SALES (est): 198.7K Privately Held
SIC: 3993 Signs & advertising specialties

(G-9563)
SPEEDWAY REDI MIX INC
Also Called: Grant County Ready Mix
1620 W Factory Ave (46952-2427)
PHONE...................................765 671-1020
Bill Miller, Manager
EMP: 5 Privately Held
SIC: 3273 8611 Ready-mixed concrete;
business associations
PA: Speedway Redi-Mix Inc
4820 Industrial Rd
Fort Wayne IN 46825

(G-9564)
SPORTS HOTLINE
1950 W Westholme Dr (46952-9332)
P.O. Box 1183 (46952-7583)
PHONE...................................765 664-8732
Fax: 765 664-3378
Kenneth Hill, Owner
EMP: 3
SALES (est): 124.4K Privately Held
SIC: 2711 Newspapers: publishing only,
not printed on site

(G-9565)
SWAN REAL ESTATE MGMT INC
815 N Western Ave (46952-2507)
P.O. Box 1478 (46952-7878)
PHONE...................................765 664-1478
James Swan, Real Est Agnt
EMP: 2
SALES (est): 86.6K Privately Held
SIC: 3441 Fabricated structural metal

(G-9566)
T & J PLATING INC
2439 W 11th St (46953-1020)
P.O. Box 1390 (46952-7790)
PHONE...................................765 664-9669
Fax: 765 662-6141
Terry Hill, President
Virginia Hill, Treasurer
EMP: 7
SQ FT: 16,200
SALES (est): 859K Privately Held
SIC: 3471 Electroplating of metals or
formed products

(G-9567)
TRIANGLE PUBLISHING
4201 S Washington St (46953-4974)
PHONE...................................765 677-2544
Nathan Birky, Manager
EMP: 2
SALES (est): 136.7K Privately Held
SIC: 2741 Miscellaneous publishing

(G-9568)
TULOX PLASTICS CORPORATION
1007 W Overlook Rd (46952-1330)
PHONE...................................765 664-5155
Fax: 765 664-0257
John C Sciaudone, President
Thomas P Glynn, Vice Pres
William E Patuzzi, Vice Pres
▲ EMP: 125
SQ FT: 36,000
SALES (est): 18.6MM Privately Held
WEB: www.tulox.com
SIC: 3089 Plastic containers, except foam

(G-9569)
ULTIMATE MFG
4794 S Lincoln Blvd (46953-5508)
PHONE...................................765 517-1160
EMP: 2
SALES (est): 84.7K Privately Held
SIC: 3999 Manufacturing industries

(G-9570)
VIA DEVELOPMENT CORP (PA)
867 E 38th St (46953-4402)
PHONE...................................888 225-5842
Michael Bartrom, President
Sherri Bartrom, Vice Pres
EMP: 20
SQ FT: 14,000
SALES (est): 3.6MM Privately Held
SIC: 3569 7371 Robots, assembly line: in-
dustrial & commercial; custom computer
programming services

(G-9571)
VITA VET LABORATORIES INC
1920 W Westholme Dr (46952-9332)
P.O. Box 567, Converse (46919-0567)
PHONE...................................765 662-9398
William Clevenger, President
Christine N Clevenger, Admin Sec
EMP: 5
SQ FT: 20,000
SALES (est): 360K Privately Held
SIC: 2834 Veterinary pharmaceutical
preparations

(G-9572)
WELCH PACKAGING MARION LLC
2409 W 2nd St (46952-3248)
PHONE...................................765 651-2600
Fax: 260 375-3731
M Scott Welch,
EMP: 100
SALES (est): 9.9MM
SALES (corp-wide): 224MM Privately
Held
SIC: 2653 Boxes, corrugated: made from
purchased materials
HQ: Welch Packaging, Llc
1020 Herman St
Elkhart IN 46516
574 295-2460

(G-9573)
WILEY METAL FABRICATING INC (PA)
4589 N Wabash Rd (46952-9738)
P.O. Box 1246 (46952-7646)
PHONE...................................765 671-7865
Fax: 765 671-7875
Edward M Wiley, President
Tom Reto, COO
Rob Wiley, Vice Pres
Robert Wiley, Vice Pres
Mike Adkins, Director
EMP: 160 EST: 1982
SQ FT: 110,000
SALES (est): 49MM Privately Held
WEB: www.wileymetal.com
SIC: 3444 Sheet metalwork

(G-9574)
WILEY METAL FABRICATING INC
816 W 34th St (46953-4256)
P.O. Box 1246 (46952-7646)
PHONE...................................765 674-9707
Fax: 765 664-2025
Robert Wiley, Branch Mgr
EMP: 55

SALES (corp-wide): 49MM **Privately Held**
SIC: 3444 Sheet metalwork
PA: Wiley Metal Fabricating Inc
4589 N Wabash Rd
Marion IN 46952
765 671-7865

Markle
Wells County

(G-9575)
AFFORDABLE LUXURY HOMES INC
Also Called: Alh Building Systems
49 S 500 E (46770-5448)
PHONE.................................260 758-2141
Fax: 260 758-2177
Kevin Cossairt, President
David Cossairt, Vice Pres
EMP: 100
SQ FT: 12,000
SALES (est): 27.9MM **Privately Held**
WEB: www.alh-building.com
SIC: 2452 5031 Prefabricated wood buildings; lumber, plywood & millwork; plywood

(G-9576)
CONVERTASTEP LLC
4654 E Markle Rd (46770-9632)
PHONE.................................260 969-8645
Steve Kitchin, President
Susan Honegger, Director
EMP: 9
SQ FT: 1,000
SALES (est): 1MM **Privately Held**
SIC: 3534 Stair elevators, motor powered

(G-9577)
HARE CANVAS PRODUCTS
300 N Tracy St (46770-9557)
PHONE.................................260 758-8800
Fax: 260 758-2053
Mark Hauenstein, Owner
EMP: 4
SQ FT: 3,000
SALES: 190K **Privately Held**
WEB: www.harekrishnaexports.com
SIC: 5999 2394 Canvas products; canvas & related products

(G-9578)
K-K TOOL AND DESIGN INC
50 Countryside Dr (46770-9563)
P.O. Box 456 (46770-0456)
PHONE.................................260 758-2940
Fax: 260 758-3181
Jim Blake, Owner
Kim Kinline, Treasurer
EMP: 20
SALES (est): 3.9MM **Privately Held**
SIC: 3544 7692 3545 3444 Special dies, tools, jigs & fixtures; welding repair; machine tool accessories; sheet metalwork; fabricated structural metal

(G-9579)
LATHER UP LLC
2040 W 900 N-90 (46770-9742)
PHONE.................................260 638-4978
Jean Bayless, Owner
EMP: 2
SALES (est): 137.6K **Privately Held**
SIC: 2841 Soap & other detergents

(G-9580)
MARKLE WATER TREATMENT PLANT
460 Parkview Dr (46770)
PHONE.................................260 758-3482
Stephen Jeffers, Manager
EMP: 2
SALES (est): 129.5K **Privately Held**
SIC: 3589 5999 7389 Water treatment equipment, industrial; water purification equipment; water softener service

(G-9581)
NOVAE CORP (PA)
Also Called: I-69 Trailer Center
1 Novae Pkwy (46770-9087)
PHONE.................................260 758-9800

Fax: 260 758-9839
Steve Bermes, CEO
Kevin Bermes, General Mgr
Christopher Storie, COO
Mike Bermes, Vice Pres
Paul Riseborough, Broker
▲ EMP: 73
SQ FT: 30,000
SALES (est): 100.2MM **Privately Held**
WEB: www.novaecorp.com
SIC: 5084 3524 Trailers, industrial; lawn & garden mowers & accessories

(G-9582)
STRUCTURAL IRON & FAB INC
480 W Scott St (46770-5401)
P.O. Box 166 (46770-0166)
PHONE.................................260 758-2273
Garland K Smith, President
EMP: 4
SALES (est): 692.5K **Privately Held**
SIC: 3441 Fabricated structural metal

(G-9583)
W C GRANT COMPANY INCORPORATED
9665 N 100 W-90 (46770-9756)
PHONE.................................260 484-6688
Fax: 260 489-4428
Dale Dolby, President
Max Jones, Vice Pres
EMP: 12
SQ FT: 21,600
SALES: 2MM **Privately Held**
WEB: www.wcgrant.com
SIC: 3582 3567 Washing machines, laundry: commercial, incl. coin-operated; fuel-fired furnaces & ovens

(G-9584)
WAYNE METALS LLC (PA)
400 E Logan St (46770-9514)
PHONE.................................260 758-3121
Fax: 260 758-2521
Greg Myers, CEO
Greg Stucky, General Mgr
Rollyn Coverdale, Senior VP
Kris Morrison, Vice Pres
John Berish, Mfg Dir
EMP: 127
SQ FT: 170,000
SALES (est): 39.6MM **Privately Held**
WEB: www.waynemetal.com
SIC: 3443 Metal parts

Markleville
Madison County

(G-9585)
BAGS BY BRENDA
3674 E 575 S (46056-9793)
PHONE.................................765 779-4287
Brenda L Lewis, Owner
EMP: 2 EST: 2000
SALES: 25K **Privately Held**
SIC: 2392 Bags, garment storage: except paper or plastic film

(G-9586)
BECKS BIRD FEEDERS
8909 S State Road 109 (46056-9784)
PHONE.................................765 874-1496
David Reed, Owner
EMP: 3
SALES: 500K **Privately Held**
SIC: 3999 0211 Pet supplies; beef cattle feedlots

(G-9587)
DOSE SHIELD CORPORATION
530 Oakmont Ln (46056)
PHONE.................................317 576-0183
John Zehner, Principal
EMP: 2
SALES (est): 177.3K
SALES (corp-wide): 1.4MM **Publicly Held**
SIC: 3829 Medical diagnostic systems, nuclear
PA: Positron Corporation
550 Oakmont Ln
Westmont IL 60559
317 576-0183

(G-9588)
MARK TOOL & DIE INC
50 W Main St (46056)
PHONE.................................765 533-4932
Fax: 765 533-2134
Jeffrey Davis, President
EMP: 10
SQ FT: 5,500
SALES: 1MM **Privately Held**
SIC: 3544 Special dies, tools, jigs & fixtures

(G-9589)
REFLECTIX INC
1 School St (46056)
P.O. Box 108 (46056-0108)
PHONE.................................765 533-4332
Fax: 765 533-2327
Dale Tokarski, President
Lamont Millspaugh, Vice Pres
Connie Mc Laughlin, MIS Dir
◆ EMP: 100
SQ FT: 10,000
SALES (est): 39.6MM
SALES (corp-wide): 4.4B **Publicly Held**
WEB: www.reflectixinc.com
SIC: 2679 1711 Insulating paper: batts, fills & blankets; plumbing, heating, air-conditioning contractors
PA: Sealed Air Corporation
2415 Cascade Pointe Blvd
Charlotte NC 28208
980 221-3235

Marshall
Parke County

(G-9590)
COUNTRYSIDE CABINETRY LLC
2881 E Lucas Rd (47859-8875)
PHONE.................................765 597-2391
Alfred Stoltzfus, Principal
EMP: 2
SALES (est): 170.6K **Privately Held**
SIC: 2434 Wood kitchen cabinets

(G-9591)
FUTUREX INDUSTRIES INC
Futurex Automotive
101 Guionrd Rd (47859)
P.O. Box 56 (47859-0056)
PHONE.................................765 597-2221
Fax: 765 597-2227
Richard Kremer, Owner
EMP: 35
SALES (corp-wide): 89.5MM **Privately Held**
WEB: www.futurexind.com
SIC: 3081 5521 Plastic film & sheet; used car dealers
PA: Futurex Industries, Inc.
80 E Smith St
Bloomingdale IN 47832
765 498-3900

(G-9592)
IRON BULL MFG LLC
5947 N 350 E (47859-8827)
PHONE.................................765 597-2480
Emmanuel King, Mng Member
EMP: 5
SALES (est): 813.5K **Privately Held**
SIC: 3535 Unit handling conveying systems

(G-9593)
UWAY EXTRUSION LLC
48 N Parke Ave (47859)
P.O. Box 92 (47859-0092)
PHONE.................................765 592-6089
Dustin Kremer, President
EMP: 15
SQ FT: 6,000
SALES: 3MM **Privately Held**
SIC: 3599 Custom machinery

Martinsville
Morgan County

(G-9594)
AIR EQUIPMENT & ENGRG INC
60 Industrial Dr (46151-8074)
PHONE.................................765 349-9259
Fax: 765 349-3378
Donald G Cox, President
Rob Donnelly, Sales Mgr
Glenn Iacobucci, Technician
EMP: 20
SQ FT: 7,200
SALES (est): 6MM **Privately Held**
WEB: www.ae-e.com
SIC: 3535 Pneumatic tube conveyor systems

(G-9595)
ALLERGYFREE INC
3755 Adams Dr (46151-9201)
PHONE.................................765 349-0006
W Bryant Green III, Principal
EMP: 2
SALES (est): 77K **Privately Held**
SIC: 3999 Manufacturing industries

(G-9596)
C & R WOODWORKS
8880 Huggin Hollow Rd (46151-7675)
PHONE.................................317 422-9603
Roger Anders, Owner
EMP: 2
SALES (est): 139.8K **Privately Held**
SIC: 2434 Wood kitchen cabinets

(G-9597)
CEDAR CREEK WINERY
3820 Leonard Rd (46151-5600)
PHONE.................................765 342-9000
Bryce Elsner, Administration
EMP: 7
SALES (est): 640.3K **Privately Held**
SIC: 2084 Wines

(G-9598)
CEG & SUPPLY LLC
1858 Haven Trl (46151-6206)
P.O. Box 343, Monrovia (46157-0343)
PHONE.................................317 435-6398
Brian Clark,
EMP: 2 EST: 2016
SALES (est): 73.4K **Privately Held**
SIC: 3421 Cutlery

(G-9599)
CRONE LUMBER CO INC
501 N Park Ave (46151-1093)
P.O. Box 1171 (46151-0171)
PHONE.................................765 342-1160
Fax: 765 342-2259
Harmon Crone, President
Steve Crone, Vice Pres
Rick Zimmerman, CFO
Nancy Crone, Admin Sec
EMP: 32 EST: 1972
SQ FT: 27,000
SALES: 5MM **Privately Held**
SIC: 2421 Lumber: rough, sawed or planed

(G-9600)
DANIEL SKAGGS & COMPANY
610 W Dickson St (46151-2746)
PHONE.................................765 342-0071
Daniel Skaggs, Owner
EMP: 2
SALES: 500K **Privately Held**
WEB: www.danielskaggs.com
SIC: 2411 0191 0115 0111 Logging camps & contractors; general farms, primarily crop; corn; wheat

(G-9601)
DG GRAPHICS LLC
1809 E Morgan St (46151-1388)
PHONE.................................765 349-9500
Deric Gayde, President
EMP: 3
SALES (est): 255.7K **Privately Held**
SIC: 3993 Signs & advertising specialties

(G-9602)
DRP MOLD INC
70 James Baldwin Dr (46151-8080)
PHONE..................................765 349-3355
Fax: 765 349-3366
Donald L Parker, *President*
Linda Parker, *Corp Secy*
EMP: 5
SALES (est): 653.3K **Privately Held**
WEB: www.drpmold.com
SIC: 3544 Industrial molds

(G-9603)
FBF ORIGINALS INC
1201 S Ohio St (46151-2914)
PHONE..................................765 349-7474
Kelly Baugh, *President*
Valeka Turner, *Cust Mgr*
Gregory Mills, *Manager*
Andru Bruning, *Graphic Designe*
▲ EMP: 4 EST: 2015
SALES (est): 160.8K **Privately Held**
SIC: 3111 2252 5139 Accessory products,
leather; socks; footwear

(G-9604)
FIDELI PUBLISHING
119 W Morgan St (46151-1449)
PHONE..................................888 343-3542
Robin Surface, *Owner*
EMP: 3 EST: 2008
SALES (est): 219.8K **Privately Held**
SIC: 2731 Books: publishing & printing

(G-9605)
FLOSOURCE INC
489 Gardner Ave (46151-9420)
PHONE..................................765 342-1360
Amy Macowan, *President*
Kean Macowan, *Vice Pres*
Jim Nelson, *Sales Engr*
Matt Macowan, *Admin Sec*
EMP: 22
SALES (est): 10.4MM **Privately Held**
SIC: 3491 3625 5074 Industrial valves;
actuators, industrial; steam fittings

(G-9606)
FOR BARE FEET INC
1201 S Ohio St (46151-2914)
PHONE..................................765 349-7474
Fax: 765 349-7470
Sharon Rivenbark, *President*
Tina Bode, *VP Admin*
Kelly Rivenbark Baugh, *Vice Pres*
Randy Bode, *Vice Pres*
Alan Zellmer, *Vice Pres*
▲ EMP: 140
SQ FT: 90,000
SALES (est): 27.1MM **Privately Held**
SIC: 2252 Anklets & socks

(G-9607)
FOREST COMMODITIES INC (PA)
1789 S Old State Road 67 (46151-6252)
PHONE..................................765 349-3291
Fax: 765 349-3297
Daniel T Wooley, *President*
EMP: 2
SALES (est): 360.2K **Privately Held**
WEB: www.forestcommodities.com
SIC: 3524 Lawn & garden equipment

(G-9608)
FORM/TEC PLASTICS INCORPORATED
Also Called: Shields Designs
1000 Industrial Dr (46151-8095)
P.O. Box 1672 (46151-0672)
PHONE..................................765 342-2300
Fax: 765 342-0567
William D Shields, *President*
Brad Shields, *General Mgr*
Jacqueline K Shields, *Corp Secy*
Sarah Hansen, *Opers Mgr*
Karen Shields, *Finance Mgr*
EMP: 40
SQ FT: 18,000
SALES (est): 7.3MM **Privately Held**
WEB: www.racingshields.com
SIC: 3089 Plastic processing

(G-9609)
GILL CARBIDE SAW & TL SVC LLC
8471 Waverly Rd (46151-7616)
PHONE..................................317 698-6787
Karyn Cleveland, *Principal*
EMP: 2
SALES (est): 74.4K **Privately Held**
SIC: 2819 Carbides

(G-9610)
HAM ENTERPRISE LLC
160 E Morgan St (46151-1543)
PHONE..................................317 831-2902
Fax: 765 342-6788
Richard M Bryant,
EMP: 9
SQ FT: 1,500
SALES (est): 1.1MM **Privately Held**
SIC: 3599 Amusement park equipment

(G-9611)
HAM ENTERPRISES MACHINE CO
4590 Jordan Rd (46151-6544)
PHONE..................................765 342-7966
Opal Ham, *President*
Jerry Ham, *Manager*
EMP: 7
SQ FT: 2,500
SALES (est): 470K **Privately Held**
WEB: www.hamenterprisemachine.com
SIC: 3451 Screw machine products

(G-9612)
HILLTOP LEATHER
1820 Observatory Rd (46151-7128)
PHONE..................................317 508-3404
Thomas Thompson, *Owner*
EMP: 2
SALES: 200K **Privately Held**
SIC: 2386 5699 Garments, leather; leather
garments

(G-9613)
HOOSIER TIMES INC
60 S Jefferson St (46151-1968)
P.O. Box 1636 (46151-0636)
PHONE..................................765 342-3311
Mayer Maloney, *Manager*
EMP: 20
SALES (corp-wide): 882.7MM **Publicly Held**
WEB: www.htinteractive.com
SIC: 2711 Newspapers, publishing & printing
HQ: Hoosier Times, Inc.
1900 S Walnut St
Bloomington IN 47401
812 331-4270

(G-9614)
IMPRESSION PRINTING
389 E Walnut St (46151-2060)
PHONE..................................765 342-6977
Fax: 765 342-6977
Randy Foley, *Owner*
Phyllis J Foley, *Partner*
Randy D Foley, *Partner*
EMP: 6
SALES (est): 340K **Privately Held**
SIC: 2752 Commercial printing, offset

(G-9615)
INDIANA GRATINGS INC
210 W Douglas St (46151-1001)
P.O. Box 1762 (46151-0762)
PHONE..................................765 342-7191
Fax: 765 342-0382
Debra S Lenahan, *CEO*
Debra Lenahan, *President*
Charles Maginn, *President*
Douglas Maginn, *Vice Pres*
Tony Payne, *Production*
▼ EMP: 19 EST: 1976
SQ FT: 32,000
SALES (est): 4.8MM **Privately Held**
WEB: www.indianagratingsinc.com
SIC: 3446 3444 3441 3364 Architectural
metalwork; open flooring & grating for
construction; sheet metalwork; fabricated
structural metal; nonferrous die-castings
except aluminum; aluminum extruded
products

(G-9616)
INSTANT WAREHOUSE
1290 Morton Ave (46151-3029)
PHONE..................................765 342-3430
Robert Bennet, *President*
EMP: 2
SALES (est): 125.4K **Privately Held**
SIC: 2752 Commercial printing, litho-
graphic

(G-9617)
INTEGRITY QNTUM INNVATIONS LLC
6830 Hancock Ridge Rd (46151-9679)
PHONE..................................765 537-9037
Timothy J Spear, *Owner*
EMP: 3
SALES (est): 170.4K **Privately Held**
SIC: 3572 Computer storage devices

(G-9618)
IRVING MATERIALS INC
1502 Rogers Rd (46151-3250)
PHONE..................................765 342-3369
Fax: 765 342-9479
Luke Owings, *Branch Mgr*
EMP: 5
SALES (corp-wide): 800.6MM **Privately Held**
SIC: 3273 Ready-mixed concrete
PA: Irving Materials, Inc.
8032 N State Road 9
Greenfield IN 46140
317 326-3101

(G-9619)
KARYN K CLEVELAND
8471 Waverly Rd (46151-7616)
PHONE..................................317 698-6787
Karyn Cleveland, *Principal*
EMP: 2
SALES (est): 74.4K **Privately Held**
SIC: 2819 Carbides

(G-9620)
LIGHTHOUSE CREAT CANDLES GIFTS
1190 E Morgan St (46151-1745)
PHONE..................................765 342-2920
EMP: 2
SALES (est): 62.5K **Privately Held**
SIC: 3999 Candles

(G-9621)
MANN ROAD SAWMILL INC
7060 New Harmony Rd (46151-9263)
PHONE..................................765 342-2700
Robert Leland Baker, *President*
EMP: 2
SALES (est): 171.6K **Privately Held**
SIC: 2421 Sawmills & planing mills, gen-
eral

(G-9622)
MARIETTA MARTIN MATERIALS INC
Also Called: Martin Marietta Aggregates
8520 Old State Road 37 N (46151-8339)
PHONE..................................317 831-7391
Fax: 317 834-0586
Keith Hurlbert, *Manager*
EMP: 7 **Publicly Held**
WEB: www.martinmarietta.com
SIC: 5032 1442 Aggregate; construction
sand & gravel
PA: Martin Marietta Materials Inc
2710 Wycliff Rd
Raleigh NC 27607

(G-9623)
MARTINSVILLE VAULT COMPANY
5910 Hacker Creek Rd (46151-8761)
PHONE..................................765 342-4576
James Asher, *President*
Pamela Asher, *Vice Pres*
EMP: 2
SALES: 100K **Privately Held**
SIC: 3272 5032 Solid containing units,
concrete; concrete & cinder building prod-
ucts

(G-9624)
MATCHLESS MACHINE & TOOL CO
55 James Baldwin Dr (46151-8081)
P.O. Box 1733 (46151-0733)
PHONE..................................765 342-4550
Fax: 765 342-5647
Gerald L Etter, *President*
Ellen Pruitt, *Office Mgr*
Ellen Eilson Pruitt, *Manager*
▲ EMP: 35
SQ FT: 21,500
SALES: 3.7MM **Privately Held**
SIC: 3544 Industrial molds

(G-9625)
METCALF ENGINEERING INC
Also Called: Hopkins & Woods
290 E Morgan St (46151-1545)
PHONE..................................765 342-6792
Fax: 765 342-6790
Steve Metcalf, *President*
Julie Metcalf, *Treasurer*
EMP: 9 EST: 1942
SQ FT: 8,762
SALES: 1MM **Privately Held**
SIC: 3599 7692 Machine shop, jobbing &
repair; welding repair

(G-9626)
MIDWEST LOGGING & VENEER
50 Rose St (46151-8055)
P.O. Box 1146 (46151-0146)
PHONE..................................765 342-2774
Mike Dow, *Owner*
EMP: 3
SALES (est): 500K **Privately Held**
SIC: 2411 Logging camps & contractors

(G-9627)
MODERN POWDER COATING LLC
801 S Ohio St (46151-2556)
PHONE..................................765 342-7039
Justin Hickman, *Owner*
EMP: 2
SALES (est): 100K **Privately Held**
SIC: 3479 Metal coating & allied service

(G-9628)
MYERS CABINET COMPANY
409 E Pike St (46151-1624)
PHONE..................................765 342-7781
Terry Myers, *Principal*
EMP: 2
SALES (est): 217.5K **Privately Held**
SIC: 2434 Wood kitchen cabinets

(G-9629)
NAPTOWN VAPORS LLC (PA)
339 Morton Ave Ste B (46151-2439)
PHONE..................................765 315-0554
Douglas Todd Scott,
EMP: 3
SALES (est): 583.8K **Privately Held**
SIC: 3634 Cigarette lighters, electric

(G-9630)
OLIVER MACHINE & TL CORP
110 Industrial Dr (46151-8083)
PHONE..................................765 349-2271
Eric Strahmayer, *President*
EMP: 14
SALES (est): 1.3MM **Privately Held**
SIC: 3599 Machine shop, jobbing & repair

(G-9631)
ONEAL WOOD PRODUCTS INC
1120 Lenvoil Rd (46151-8639)
PHONE..................................765 342-2709
Marvin O'Neal, *President*
Judy O'Neall, *Vice Pres*
EMP: 6
SALES (est): 727.6K **Privately Held**
SIC: 2421 Sawmills & planing mills, gen-
eral

(G-9632)
PAUL NELSON
4009 E Rembrandt Dr (46151-6033)
PHONE..................................765 352-0698
Paul Nelson, *Owner*
EMP: 7 EST: 2008
SALES (est): 604.9K **Privately Held**
SIC: 3674 Solid state electronic devices

G E O G R A P H I C

(G-9633)
POPLAR LOG HOMES INC
Also Called: Lnl Logging
2635 Little Hurricane Rd (46151-8580)
PHONE.................................765 342-9910
Leonard Kernel, *President*
EMP: 6
SALES (est): 370.4K **Privately Held**
SIC: 2411 Logging

(G-9634)
ROGERS GROUP INC
Also Called: Martinsville Asphalt & Cnstr
1500 Rogers Rd (46151-3250)
PHONE.................................765 342-9655
Donnie Campbell, *Branch Mgr*
EMP: 7
SALES (corp-wide): 1B **Privately Held**
WEB: www.rogersgroupinc.com
SIC: 1442 Construction sand & gravel
PA: Rogers Group, Inc.
     421 Great Circle Rd
     Nashville TN 37228
     615 242-0585

(G-9635)
ROGERS GROUP INC
Also Called: Morgan County Sand & Gravel
Co
1500 Rogers Rd (46151-3250)
PHONE.................................765 342-6898
Fax: 765 349-0350
Donnie Camuple, *Superintendent*
EMP: 8
SQ FT: 2,400
SALES (corp-wide): 1B **Privately Held**
WEB: www.rogersgroupinc.com
SIC: 1442 3274 3272 2951 Construction
sand & gravel; lime; concrete products;
asphalt paving mixtures & blocks
PA: Rogers Group, Inc.
     421 Great Circle Rd
     Nashville TN 37228
     615 242-0585

(G-9636)
ROLLS-ROYCE PLC
4151 Arnold Ave (46151-6941)
PHONE.................................317 306-2441
Robert Killian, *Engineer*
EMP: 3
SALES (est): 118.7K **Privately Held**
SIC: 3511 Turbines & turbine generator
sets

(G-9637)
**SCURVY PALACE PUBLISHING
LLC**
6149 New Harmony Rd (46151-7519)
PHONE.................................317 809-4591
EMP: 2 EST: 2013
SALES (est): 86.6K **Privately Held**
SIC: 2741 Miscellaneous publishing

(G-9638)
**SHIRLEY MACHINE & ENGRG
INC (PA)**
200 Robert Curry Dr (46151-8078)
PHONE.................................765 349-9040
Fax: 765 349-8997
Stacey Siemantel, *President*
Matthew Siemantel, *Vice Pres*
EMP: 31
SALES (est): 4.8MM **Privately Held**
SIC: 3599 Machine shop, jobbing & repair

(G-9639)
T&S SIGNS
6205 Beech Grove Rd (46151-9505)
PHONE.................................317 996-3027
Tina Sample, *Principal*
EMP: 2
SALES (est): 119.3K **Privately Held**
SIC: 3993 Signs & advertising specialties

(G-9640)
TARTER WOODWORKING LLC
440 Rolling Woods Dr (46151-7068)
PHONE.................................765 349-4193
Larry Tarter,
EMP: 2
SALES (est): 207K **Privately Held**
SIC: 2431 Millwork

(G-9641)
TERRY L RAY
Also Called: Ray's Wood Products
340 S Sycamore St (46151-2246)
PHONE.................................765 342-3180
Terry L Ray, *Owner*
EMP: 3
SALES (est): 261.8K **Privately Held**
SIC: 2421 Sawmills & planing mills, gen-
eral

(G-9642)
TIMBERLIGHT MFG CO
1155 S Shore Dr (46151-8873)
PHONE.................................317 694-1317
Robin R Livesay, *President*
EMP: 2
SALES (est): 123.9K **Privately Held**
SIC: 3999 Candles

(G-9643)
**TOWNSEND TRANSMISSIONS
LLC**
1051 S Old State Road 67 (46151-6256)
PHONE.................................765 342-0042
Thomas Scott Townsend,
EMP: 4
SALES (est): 405K **Privately Held**
SIC: 3714 Rebuilding engines & transmis-
sions, factory basis

(G-9644)
TWIGG CORPORATION (HQ)
659 E York St (46151-2500)
PHONE.................................765 342-7126
Fax: 765 342-1553
Roy W Rapp II, *Ch of Bd*
Rana Mathers, *President*
Roy W Rapp IV, *President*
Ryan Robertson, *General Mgr*
Cheryl L Rapp, *Corp Secy*
EMP: 80 EST: 1971
SQ FT: 110,000
SALES: 19.4MM
SALES (corp-wide): 36.2MM **Privately
Held**
WEB: www.twiggcorp.com
SIC: 3724 7699 Aircraft engines & engine
parts; engine repair & replacement, non-
automotive
PA: Rapp & Sons Inc
     3767 11th St
     Wyandotte MI 48192
     734 283-1000

(G-9645)
**TWISOD WICK CANDLE
COMPANY**
1115 Twin Br (46151-8542)
PHONE.................................317 490-4789
Richard Scheve, *Partner*
EMP: 2
SALES (est): 98.1K **Privately Held**
SIC: 3999 Candles

(G-9646)
USA TRAVEL MAGAZINE
7213 Bethany Park (46151-7820)
PHONE.................................317 834-3683
Melody Schubert, *Owner*
EMP: 2
SALES: 7.8K **Privately Held**
SIC: 2721 Magazines: publishing only, not
printed on site

(G-9647)
WALLACE CONSTRUCTION INC
Also Called: W A P Company
9790 Old State Road 37 N (46151-8342)
P.O. Box 1432 (46151-0432)
PHONE.................................317 422-5356
Fax: 317 422-5296
Richard E Wallace Jr, *President*
Roger Huff, *Admin Sec*
EMP: 15
SALES (est): 3.2MM **Privately Held**
SIC: 1611 2951 1442 Highway & street
paving contractor; paving mixtures; con-
struction sand & gravel

(G-9648)
WHITES WOODWORKS
1835 Pumpkinvine Hill Rd (46151-7402)
PHONE.................................765 341-6678
James White, *Principal*

EMP: 2
SALES (est): 85.2K **Privately Held**
SIC: 2431 Millwork

Marysville
Clark County

(G-9649)
**AEROSPACE WATERJET SVCS
LLC**
21608 New Market Rd (47141-9752)
PHONE.................................502 836-1112
Denise Edington, *Principal*
EMP: 2
SALES (est): 162.5K **Privately Held**
SIC: 3721 Aircraft

(G-9650)
**OPTIMUM SYSTEM PRODUCTS
INC**
20304 New Market Rd (47141-9621)
PHONE.................................812 289-1905
EMP: 12
SALES (corp-wide): 11.7MM **Privately
Held**
SIC: 2752 Lithographic Commercial Print-
ing
PA: Optimum System Products, Inc.
     921 Eastwind Dr Ste 133
     Westerville OH 43081
     614 885-4464

(G-9651)
SOLOMON M EICHER
Also Called: Ace Metal Sales
7809 Henderson Rd (47141-9765)
PHONE.................................812 289-1252
Solomon M Eicher, *Owner*
EMP: 2
SALES (est): 206.3K **Privately Held**
SIC: 3541 Home workshop machine tools,
metalworking

Matthews
Grant County

(G-9652)
JENNERJAHN MACHINE INC
901 S Massachusetts Ave (46957-1508)
P.O. Box 379 (46957-0379)
PHONE.................................765 998-2733
Fax: 765 998-2468
Chris Jennerjahn, *President*
Joe Gall, *Plant Supt*
Diana Wells, *Purch Agent*
Roger Vogel, *Engineer*
Kris Kimmerling, *Treasurer*
▲ EMP: 40 EST: 1979
SQ FT: 30,000
SALES: 14.2MM **Privately Held**
WEB: www.jennerjahn.com
SIC: 3554 3599 Paper industries machin-
ery; custom machinery

Mauckport
Harrison County

(G-9653)
CARVERS LOGGING LLP
1801 Overlook Dr Sw (47142-9249)
PHONE.................................812 732-4932
Robert Carver, *Principal*
EMP: 3
SALES (est): 197.6K **Privately Held**
SIC: 2411 Logging

(G-9654)
DEER RUN SAWMILL LLC
8242 Vly Cy Mckport Rd Sw (47142)
PHONE.................................812 732-4608
Chris Schneider, *Principal*
EMP: 3 EST: 2012
SALES (est): 179.1K **Privately Held**
SIC: 2421 Sawmills & planing mills, gen-
eral

(G-9655)
MAUCKPORT SAND & GRAVEL
3200 W Highway 11 Sw (47142-9530)
PHONE.................................812 732-8800
Kevin Lucas, *Partner*
CL Lucas Jr, *Partner*
EMP: 4 EST: 2009
SALES: 500K **Privately Held**
SIC: 1442 Construction sand & gravel

(G-9656)
MICHAEL SKAGGS
Also Called: Timber & Logging
Rr 1 (47142)
PHONE.................................812 732-8809
Micheal Skaggs, *Owner*
EMP: 2
SALES (est): 105.6K **Privately Held**
SIC: 2411 Logging

(G-9657)
MILLENNIAL FIREWORKS
10645 Highway 135 Sw (47142)
PHONE.................................812 732-5126
Michael Lagrange, *Principal*
EMP: 3 EST: 2001
SALES (est): 340.7K **Privately Held**
SIC: 2899 Fireworks

(G-9658)
NORSTAM VENEERS INC
2990 Overlook Dr Sw (47142-9234)
P.O. Box 32 (47142-0032)
PHONE.................................812 732-4391
Mark Fitzgerald, *President*
Dana Mc Carty, *Vice Pres*
Dana McCarty, *Vice Pres*
V P Veneer, *Sales Mgr*
EMP: 88 EST: 1970
SQ FT: 89,700
SALES (est): 13.1MM **Privately Held**
SIC: 2421 2435 2426 Lumber: rough,
sawed or planed; veneer stock, hard-
wood; hardwood dimension & flooring
mills

(G-9659)
WILLIAMS BROS LOGGING LLC
2880 Overlook Dr Sw (47142-9232)
PHONE.................................270 547-0266
Rick Williams, *Principal*
EMP: 5
SALES (est): 342.5K **Privately Held**
SIC: 2411 Logging camps & contractors

Maxwell
Hancock County

(G-9660)
COUNTY MATERIALS CORP
119 N Main St (46154-9718)
PHONE.................................317 323-6000
Tim Sonnentag, *President*
EMP: 28
SALES (corp-wide): 426.8MM **Privately
Held**
SIC: 3272 Pipe, concrete or lined with con-
crete
PA: County Materials Corp.
     205 North St
     Marathon WI 54448
     715 443-2434

(G-9661)
**INDEPENDENT CONCRETE PIPE
CO**
8 E Junction St (46154-9702)
P.O. Box 8 (46154-0008)
PHONE.................................317 326-2600
Fax: 317 326-4185
Mark Wilson, *Manager*
EMP: 20
SALES (corp-wide): 13.9MM **Privately
Held**
SIC: 3272 Pipe, concrete or lined with con-
crete
PA: Independent Concrete Pipe Co
     2050 S Harding St
     Indianapolis IN 46221
     419 841-3361

(G-9662)
KLINE CABINET MAKERS LLC
16 S Main St (46154-9720)
P.O. Box 12 (46154-0012)
PHONE...............................317 326-3049
Doug Dayhoff, *Mng Member*
Dan Hayes,
EMP: 14
SQ FT: 12,000
SALES: 1.1MM **Privately Held**
WEB: www.klinecabinetmakers.com
SIC: 2434 2541 5211 Wood kitchen cabinets; wood partitions & fixtures; counter tops

Mays
Rush County

(G-9663)
P O C INDUSTRIES INC
8944 N Crossway (46155-9800)
PHONE...............................765 645-5015
Fax: 765 645-5256
Paris O Cross Jr, *President*
John Wooldridge, *Treasurer*
Donna Trout, *Admin Sec*
EMP: 8 EST: 1969
SQ FT: 15,000
SALES (est): 972.6K **Privately Held**
SIC: 3599 Machine shop, jobbing & repair

McCordsville
Hancock County

(G-9664)
ADVANCED FINISHING CORPORATION
7724 Depot St Bldg A (46055-6173)
P.O. Box 51 (46055-0051)
PHONE...............................317 335-2210
Fax: 317 335-3378
George Wanamaker, *CEO*
Marjorie Wanamaker, *President*
EMP: 6
SQ FT: 30,000
SALES (est): 635.1K **Privately Held**
SIC: 3479 Enameling, including porcelain, of metal products

(G-9665)
CHAMPION RACING ENGINES
5002 W State Road 234 (46055-9595)
PHONE...............................317 335-2491
Richard Fox, *Owner*
EMP: 3
SQ FT: 5,400
SALES: 200K **Privately Held**
WEB: www.gochampion.com
SIC: 7539 3714 3519 Machine shop, automotive; motor vehicle engines & parts; internal combustion engines

(G-9666)
FABRI-TECH INC
8236 N 600 W (46055-9802)
PHONE...............................317 849-7755
Fax: 317 331-9413
Donald L Menchhofer, *CEO*
Jeffrey C Menchhofer, *President*
◆ **EMP:** 45 EST: 1971
SQ FT: 30,000
SALES: 3.5MM **Privately Held**
SIC: 2399 3429 Horse & pet accessories, textile; saddlery hardware

(G-9667)
FFESAR INC
6564 W Black Tail Way (46055-4456)
P.O. Box 1497, Columbus (47202-1497)
PHONE...............................812 378-4220
Roger Eng, *CEO*
▲ **EMP:** 3
SALES: 2MM **Privately Held**
SIC: 3469 5021 Furniture components, porcelain enameled; furniture

(G-9668)
HARVEST MOON WINERY LLC
9407 N Captain Cir (46055-9338)
PHONE...............................317 258-4615

EMP: 2
SALES (est): 62.3K **Privately Held**
SIC: 2084 Wines

(G-9669)
HELLWEG HOLDINGS LLC
12940 Rocky Pointe Rd (46055-9580)
PHONE...............................317 909-6764
David Hellweg, *CEO*
Mary Amos, *COO*
EMP: 2
SALES (est): 98K **Privately Held**
SIC: 1389 7389 Hydraulic fracturing wells;

(G-9670)
INNERPRINT INC
12940 Rocky Pointe Rd (46055-9580)
P.O. Box 30442, Charlotte NC (28230-0442)
PHONE...............................317 509-6511
Mary King, *CEO*
EMP: 3
SALES: 950K **Privately Held**
SIC: 2752 Commercial printing, lithographic

Mccordsville
Hancock County

(G-9671)
INTEL CORPORATION
6088 Crossfield Trl (46055-9570)
PHONE...............................317 336-5464
EMP: 2
SALES (est): 90K **Privately Held**
SIC: 3674 Microprocessors

McCordsville
Hancock County

(G-9672)
IRISH INDUSTRIES
13006 Rocky Pointe Rd (46055-9581)
PHONE...............................773 213-2422
Nicole Wawok, *Principal*
EMP: 2
SALES (est): 62.5K **Privately Held**
SIC: 3999 Manufacturing industries

(G-9673)
LUMEN CACHE INCORPORATED
13402 Chrisfield Ln (46055-9646)
PHONE...............................317 739-4218
Derek Cowburn, *CEO*
Derek Cownburn, *CEO*
Lynn Shinkel, *Principal*
▲ **EMP:** 2
SALES: 200K **Privately Held**
SIC: 3699 7373 Electrical equipment & supplies; office computer automation systems integration

(G-9674)
PROPORTION-AIR INC (PA)
8250 N 600 W (46055-9367)
P.O. Box 218 (46055-0218)
PHONE...............................317 335-2602
Fax: 317 335-3853
Daniel E Cook, *President*
Tom Becknell, *Regional Mgr*
Brent L Archer, *Vice Pres*
Kevin Baldwin, *Project Mgr*
Mark Fox, *Foreman/Supr*
EMP: 58
SQ FT: 115,000
SALES (est): 11.6MM **Privately Held**
WEB: www.proportionair.com
SIC: 3492 3491 Fluid power valves & hose fittings; industrial valves

(G-9675)
SCHATZI PRESS
10004 Springstone Rd (46055-9630)
PHONE...............................317 335-2335
Joseph Krauter Jr, *Principal*
EMP: 2
SALES (est): 87K **Privately Held**
SIC: 2741 Miscellaneous publishing

(G-9676)
SIGNATURE METALS INC
6315 Pin Oak Dr (46055-9418)
PHONE...............................317 335-2207
Steven Duhamell, *President*
EMP: 2
SALES (est): 194.4K **Privately Held**
WEB: www.signaturemetals.com
SIC: 3446 Ornamental metalwork

(G-9677)
SYZYGY MEDIA INC
12940 Rocky Pointe Rd (46055-9580)
PHONE...............................317 509-8987
EMP: 2
SALES (est): 281.9K **Privately Held**
SIC: 2759 Commercial Printing

Mecca
Parke County

(G-9678)
GRIFFIN LOGGING LLC
4967 W Craig St (47860-8028)
PHONE...............................765 592-5701
Michael Griffin, *Owner*
EMP: 2
SALES (est): 81.7K **Privately Held**
SIC: 2411 Logging

Medaryville
Pulaski County

(G-9679)
HIVELY WELDING CO INC
14695 W State Road 14 (47957-8150)
PHONE...............................219 843-5111
Rex Hively, *President*
Debra Hively, *Admin Sec*
EMP: 2
SQ FT: 6,250
SALES: 116.4K **Privately Held**
SIC: 7692 Welding repair

Medora
Jackson County

(G-9680)
BENNETT PRINTING
1245 S County Road 925 W (47260-9550)
PHONE...............................812 966-2917
Larry Bennett, *Owner*
EMP: 2
SALES: 10K **Privately Held**
SIC: 2759 Commercial printing

(G-9681)
BUNDY BROS & SONS INC
3 David St (47260)
PHONE...............................812 966-2551
Fax: 812 966-2221
Leland R Bundy Jr, *President*
Leora Gossman, *Vice Pres*
Virginia Robertson, *Treasurer*
EMP: 12
SQ FT: 1,350
SALES (est): 5.1MM **Privately Held**
SIC: 5153 5191 2875 2048 Grain elevators; feed; fertilizer & fertilizer materials; seeds & bulbs; fertilizers, mixing only; prepared feeds; flour & other grain mill products

(G-9682)
PUMPHREYS PERFORMANCE ENGINES
1820 S State Road 235 (47260-9569)
PHONE...............................812 358-4704
Mitchell Pumphrey, *Principal*
EMP: 2
SALES (est): 81.4K **Privately Held**
SIC: 3599 Machine shop, jobbing & repair

Memphis
Clark County

(G-9683)
INDEPENDENT CABINETS
12910 Highway 60 (47143-9608)
PHONE...............................502 594-6026
Jerry Longest, *Principal*
EMP: 2
SALES (est): 164.5K **Privately Held**
SIC: 2434 Wood kitchen cabinets

Mentone
Kosciusko County

(G-9684)
A & B FABRICATING & MAINT INC
516 N Morgan St (46539-9293)
P.O. Box 623 (46539-0623)
PHONE...............................574 353-1012
Fax: 574 353-8172
Jeff Beasley, *President*
EMP: 15
SQ FT: 12,000
SALES (est): 2.6MM **Privately Held**
WEB: www.abfabricating.com
SIC: 3441 3444 3443 Fabricated structural metal; sheet metalwork; fabricated plate work (boiler shop)

(G-9685)
CARGILL INCORPORATED
104 N Etna St (46539-9115)
P.O. Box 336 (46539-0336)
PHONE...............................574 353-7621
Fax: 574 353-8162
Larry Whipple, *Manager*
EMP: 2
SALES (corp-wide): 88.8B **Privately Held**
WEB: www.cargill.com
SIC: 2048 2041 Prepared feeds; flour & other grain mill products
PA: Cargill, Incorporated
15407 Mcginty Rd W
Wayzata MN 55391
952 742-7575

(G-9686)
CARGILL INCORPORATED
104 N Etna St (46539-9115)
PHONE...............................574 353-7623
Larry Whipple, *General Mgr*
EMP: 30
SQ FT: 20,000
SALES (corp-wide): 88.8B **Privately Held**
WEB: www.cargill.com
SIC: 2048 Prepared feeds
PA: Cargill, Incorporated
15407 Mcginty Rd W
Wayzata MN 55391
952 742-7575

(G-9687)
CRAIG WELDING AND MFG INC
5158 N 825 E (46539-9605)
PHONE...............................574 353-7912
Fax: 574 353-8132
Donald K Craig, *President*
John Craig, *Vice Pres*
Thomas Evans, *Vice Pres*
Chris Peterson, *Vice Pres*
Mark Metzger, *Mfg Staff*
EMP: 47 EST: 1971
SQ FT: 75,000
SALES (est): 6.4MM **Privately Held**
WEB: www.craigwelding.com
SIC: 7692 3441 Welding repair; fabricated structural metal

(G-9688)
MID-WEST SPRING MFG CO
Also Called: Midwest Spring & Stamping
105 N Etna St (46539-9116)
P.O. Box 337 (46539-0337)
PHONE...............................574 353-1409
Fax: 574 353-7388
Jeff Fuller, *Buyer*
Tammy Newsome, *Human Resources*
Brain Duke, *Marketing Staff*

GEOGRAPHIC

Joe Vernon, *Marketing Staff*
C J Overmyer, *Branch Mgr*
EMP: 98
SALES (corp-wide): 17.6MM **Privately Held**
SIC: 3495 3469 3496 3423 Wire springs; stamping metal for the trade; miscellaneous fabricated wire products; hand & edge tools
PA: Spring Mid-West Manufacturing Company
1404 N Joliet Rd Ste C
Romeoville IL 60446
630 739-3800

(G-9689)
MIDWEST POULTRY SERVICES LP (PA)
Also Called: Midwest Pullet Farm
9951 W State Road 25 (46539-9131)
P.O. Box 307 (46539-0307)
PHONE..................................574 353-7232
Fax: 574 353-7223
Robert Krouse, *CEO*
Daniel Krouse, *General Mgr*
Brent Westendorf, *Opers Mgr*
Stacey Harsh, *Safety Mgr*
Jennifer Taylor, *Sales Mgr*
▲ **EMP:** 16
SQ FT: 20,000
SALES: 174.9MM **Privately Held**
SIC: 0751 2015 Poultry services; egg processing

Merrillville
Lake County

(G-9690)
2020 LAB INC
Also Called: Vision Quest
2294 W 81st Ave (46410-5339)
PHONE..................................219 756-8703
Kathy Kouklakis, *President*
Maria Hronopoulos, *President*
EMP: 4
SALES (est): 448.8K **Privately Held**
SIC: 3851 Eyeglasses, lenses & frames

(G-9691)
AALAND GEM COMPANY INC
8102 Georgia St (46410-6225)
PHONE..................................219 769-4492
Fax: 219 793-9766
Thomas Moriarty, *President*
Virginia Moriarty, *Treasurer*
EMP: 4
SQ FT: 900
SALES: 800K **Privately Held**
SIC: 3911 3915 Jewelry apparel; rings, finger: precious metal; gems, real & imitation: preparation for settings; diamond cutting & polishing

(G-9692)
AD CRAFT PRINTERS INCORPORATED
3201 E 83rd Pl (46410-6542)
PHONE..................................219 942-9799
EMP: 2 EST: 2007
SALES (est): 153.4K **Privately Held**
SIC: 2752 Lithographic Commercial Printing

(G-9693)
ALBANESE CONF GROUP INC (PA)
5441 E Lincoln Hwy (46410-5947)
PHONE..................................219 942-1877
Fax: 219 942-1899
Scott Albanese, *President*
Richard Albanese, *Vice Pres*
Dorothy Albanese, *Treasurer*
Leslie Simonovski, *Marketing Mgr*
Ashley V Tuuk, *Marketing Staff*
◆ **EMP:** 125
SQ FT: 12,000
SALES (est): 39.3MM **Privately Held**
WEB: www.albaneseconfectionery.com
SIC: 2064 5141 Candy & other confectionery products; groceries, general line

(G-9694)
ALBANESE CONF GROUP INC
Also Called: Albanese Candy Retail
1910 W Us 30 (46410)
PHONE..................................219 738-2333
Scott Albanese, *Director*
EMP: 2
SALES (corp-wide): 39.3MM **Privately Held**
SIC: 2064 Candy & other confectionery products
PA: Albanese Confectionery Group, Inc.
5441 E Lincoln Hwy
Merrillville IN 46410
219 942-1877

(G-9695)
ALL METAL POLISHING
2777 E 83rd Pl (46410-6409)
PHONE..................................219 980-3011
EMP: 6
SALES (est): 470K **Privately Held**
SIC: 2842 Mfg Polish/Sanitation Goods

(G-9696)
AMERICAN EAGLE SECURITY INC
6111 Harrison St Ste 126 (46410-2971)
PHONE..................................219 980-1177
Rose Ann Colon, *President*
Daniel R Colon, *Vice Pres*
EMP: 6
SQ FT: 1,259
SALES (est): 58.9K **Privately Held**
SIC: 7382 4841 4899 7389 Security systems services; fire alarm maintenance & monitoring; protective devices, security; closed circuit television services; data communication services; fire extinguisher servicing; emergency alarms

(G-9697)
AMERICAN INDUSTRIAL MCHY INC
4015 W 83rd Pl (46410-6054)
PHONE..................................219 755-4090
Fax: 219 755-4091
Michael F Dolder, *President*
Marilyn Dolder, *Admin Sec*
EMP: 17
SQ FT: 7,500
SALES (est): 4.5MM **Privately Held**
WEB: www.aimmachinery.com
SIC: 3599 3537 Custom machinery; trucks, tractors, loaders, carriers & similar equipment

(G-9698)
ARMCO
6071 Broadway (46410-2619)
PHONE..................................219 981-8864
Larry Rizer, *Owner*
EMP: 2
SALES (est): 115.2K **Privately Held**
SIC: 3312 Blast furnaces & steel mills

(G-9699)
BARSTEEL CORPORATION
1000 E 80th Pl Ste 425n (46410-5603)
PHONE..................................219 650-7100
Pete Schroeder, *Branch Mgr*
EMP: 6 **Privately Held**
SIC: 3312 Blast furnaces & steel mills
PA: Barsteel Corporation
484 Central Ave Ste 201
Highland Park IL 60035

(G-9700)
BCBG MAX AZRIA GROUP LLC
380 Huku Lii Pl (46410)
PHONE..................................712 277-3937
EMP: 2
SALES (corp-wide): 979.1MM **Privately Held**
SIC: 2335 Women's, juniors' & misses' dresses
HQ: Bcbg Max Azria Group, Llc
2761 Fruitland Ave
Vernon CA 90058
323 589-2224

(G-9701)
BIONIC PROSTHETICS AND ORTHO (PA)
8695 Connecticut St Ste E (46410-6240)
PHONE..................................219 791-9200
Sumesh Saxena,
EMP: 2
SALES (est): 633.8K **Privately Held**
SIC: 3842 Prosthetic appliances

(G-9702)
BLESSING ENTERPRISES INC
Also Called: Merrillville Awning & Tent
1420 E 91st Dr (46410-7174)
PHONE..................................219 736-9800
Fax: 219 736-9100
Mike Blessing, *President*
Nita Blessing, *Corp Secy*
EMP: 14
SQ FT: 10,000
SALES (est): 1.5MM **Privately Held**
WEB: www.awningguy.com
SIC: 2394 Awnings, fabric: made from purchased materials

(G-9703)
BOB PRESCOTT
Also Called: Sign's By Tomorrow
101 W 78th Pl (46410-5468)
PHONE..................................219 736-7804
Fax: 219 736-7853
Bob Prescott, *Owner*
EMP: 4
SALES (est): 320.1K **Privately Held**
SIC: 3993 Signs & advertising specialties

(G-9704)
BROADWAY AUTO GLASS LLC
6491 Broadway (46410-3007)
PHONE..................................219 884-5277
Todd Oday, *General Mgr*
Joseph Davis,
EMP: 17
SALES (est): 1.4MM **Privately Held**
SIC: 7536 7699 3993 5531 Automotive glass replacement shops; china & glass repair; signs & advertising specialties; automotive accessories; glass tinting, architectural or automotive

(G-9705)
BT MANAGEMENT INC
Also Called: Custom Imprint
8605 Indiana Pl (46410-6369)
PHONE..................................219 794-9546
John Immordino, *President*
Tammy Immordino, *Treasurer*
EMP: 7
SQ FT: 2,520
SALES (est): 890.2K **Privately Held**
SIC: 2759 Screen printing

(G-9706)
C & C IRON INC
6409 Hendricks St (46410-2805)
PHONE..................................219 769-2511
Fax: 219 769-2999
Michael R Crist, *President*
Sharon Crist, *Corp Secy*
Lorenzo J Crist, *Vice Pres*
EMP: 25
SQ FT: 12,400
SALES (est): 6.5MM **Privately Held**
WEB: www.cnciron.com
SIC: 3441 Building components, structural steel

(G-9707)
CAPRICORN FOODS LLC (PA)
8880 Louisiana St (46410-7153)
PHONE..................................219 670-1872
Gregory Lawson Stephan, *President*
EMP: 4
SALES: 2MM **Privately Held**
SIC: 2023 Condensed, concentrated & evaporated milk products

(G-9708)
CROWN TRAINING & DEVELOPMENT
2642 E 84th Pl (46410-6424)
PHONE..................................219 947-0845
Fax: 219 945-1868
Dave Maksimovich, *President*

David Maksimovich, *General Mgr*
Dawn Maksimovich, *Treasurer*
EMP: 30
SQ FT: 6,600
SALES: 800K **Privately Held**
WEB: www.crowntraining.com
SIC: 8748 2741 7373 8249 Business consulting; miscellaneous publishing; computer integrated systems design; vocational schools; engineering services; management services

(G-9709)
CUSTOM IMPRINT CORPORATION
8605 Indiana Pl (46410-6369)
PHONE..................................800 378-3397
Fax: 219 794-9548
Tamara Immordino, *President*
John Immordino, *Vice Pres*
EMP: 20 EST: 2015
SALES (est): 501.6K **Privately Held**
SIC: 2395 2396 Embroidery products, except schiffli machine; screen printing on fabric articles

(G-9710)
DENTAL PROFESSIONAL LABS
8040 Cleveland Pl (46410-5302)
PHONE..................................219 769-6225
Fax: 219 769-3949
Michael Suris, *President*
Dorothy Suris, *Vice Pres*
EMP: 25
SALES (est): 1.9MM **Privately Held**
SIC: 8072 3843 Crown & bridge production; dental equipment & supplies

(G-9711)
DRONE1260WRX LLC
6841 E 85th Ct (46410-7443)
PHONE..................................773 957-3625
Benjamin L Toles, *Principal*
EMP: 2
SALES (est): 100.2K **Privately Held**
SIC: 3721 Motorized aircraft

(G-9712)
ED NICKELS
5793 Taney Pl (46410-2167)
PHONE..................................219 887-6128
Ed Nickels, *Principal*
EMP: 3 EST: 2010
SALES (est): 228.4K **Privately Held**
SIC: 3356 Nickel

(G-9713)
ENTERPRISE MGT SOLUTIONS LLC (PA)
1900 W 62nd Ave (46410-2372)
PHONE..................................219 545-8544
Tasha Figueroa, *CEO*
Tina Mahone, *COO*
EMP: 2
SALES (est): 142K **Privately Held**
SIC: 8711 8748 8111 8742 Engineering services; business consulting; legal services; management consulting services; small arms

(G-9714)
EXHAUST PRODUCTIONS INC (PA)
Also Called: E P I
2777 E 83rd Pl (46410-6409)
PHONE..................................219 942-0069
Fax: 219 942-0700
Terry L Daniel, *Ch of Bd*
Louis Pringle, *President*
EMP: 55
SQ FT: 40,000
SALES (est): 10.1MM **Privately Held**
WEB: www.epiflex.com
SIC: 3714 Exhaust systems & parts, motor vehicle

(G-9715)
FIRST IMAGE
1447 E 86th Pl (46410-6341)
PHONE..................................219 791-9900
Joanne Nary, *Principal*
EMP: 2
SALES (est): 254.6K **Privately Held**
SIC: 2842 Laundry cleaning preparations

(G-9716)
FORTES BROS ELECTRIC
3931 W 77th Pl (46410-5060)
PHONE.................................219 472-0111
EMP: 2
SALES (est): 88.3K **Privately Held**
SIC: 3699 Electrical equipment & supplies

(G-9717)
GRAPHIC EXPRESSIONS
6707 Broadway (46410-3531)
PHONE.................................219 663-2085
Rich Lambie, *Owner*
EMP: 3
SALES (est): 144.9K **Privately Held**
SIC: 2752 Commercial printing, litho-
graphic

(G-9718)
HAIRE MACHINE CORPORATION
3019 E 84th Pl (46410-6431)
P.O. Box 11030 (46411-1030)
PHONE.................................219 947-4545
Fax: 219 947-1199
Douglas J Muller, *President*
◆ EMP: 26
SQ FT: 25,000
SALES (est): 4.8MM **Privately Held**
SIC: 3554 Corrugating machines, paper

(G-9719)
HMMCOPL LLC
1000 E 80th Pl Ste 777s (46410-5652)
PHONE.................................219 757-3575
Fax: 219 757-3541
Paul Sharkey,
John Howard,
Patricia Natili,
EMP: 35
SQ FT: 6,000
SALES (est): 7.4MM **Privately Held**
WEB: www.profile-systems.com
SIC: 3822 Auto controls regulating residntl
& coml environmt & applncs

(G-9720)
HMT LLC
4100 W 82nd Ave (46410-6065)
PHONE.................................219 736-9901
Fax: 219 736-9908
E Lusk, *Branch Mgr*
Chad Reinwald, *Manager*
EMP: 13
SALES (corp-wide): 133.2MM **Privately
Held**
SIC: 7699 3443 7389 1791 Tank repair;
fuel tanks (oil, gas, etc.): metal plate; in-
dustrial & commercial equipment inspec-
tion service; storage tanks, metal:
erection
PA: Hmt Llc
19241 David Memorial Dr # 150
Shenandoah TX 77385
281 681-7000

(G-9721)
IJS CUSTOM PRINTING LLC
2023 W 75th Pl Unit 33 (46410-4792)
PHONE.................................219 769-2050
Maurice Tisby, *Principal*
EMP: 4
SALES (est): 315K **Privately Held**
SIC: 2752 Commercial printing, litho-
graphic

(G-9722)
**ILLIANA GRINDING MACHINING
INC**
5341 Broadway (46410-1554)
PHONE.................................219 884-5828
Fax: 219 884-2583
Ray Hunt, *President*
EMP: 7
SQ FT: 7,000
SALES (est): 697K **Privately Held**
SIC: 7389 3599 3423 Grinding, precision:
commercial or industrial; machine & other
job shop work; knives, agricultural or in-
dustrial

(G-9723)
J W HICKS INC (PA)
8955 Louisiana St (46410-7114)
PHONE.................................219 736-2212
Fax: 219 736-2526

James W Hicks, *President*
Bill Nirschel, *Regional Mgr*
James R Hicks, *Vice Pres*
Joshua Diehl, *Engineer*
Linda Herod, *Controller*
▲ EMP: 25
SQ FT: 30,000
SALES (est): 7.2MM **Privately Held**
WEB: www.jwhicks.com
SIC: 3297 Castable refractories, nonclay

(G-9724)
KYLES INCENSE LLC
5330 Delaware St (46410-1633)
P.O. Box 10124 (46411-0124)
PHONE.................................219 682-4278
Sylvia Franklin-Kyle, *Principal*
EMP: 2
SALES (est): 81.8K **Privately Held**
SIC: 2899 Incense

(G-9725)
**LAKE COUNTY SAND & GRAVEL
LLC**
2115 W Lincoln Hwy (46410-5334)
PHONE.................................219 988-4540
Gerald M Bishop, *Principal*
EMP: 2
SALES (est): 90.7K **Privately Held**
SIC: 1442 Construction sand & gravel

(G-9726)
LEEPS SUPPLY CO INC (PA)
Also Called: Do It Best
8001 Tyler St (46410-5345)
PHONE.................................219 756-5337
Fax: 219 756-4922
John Hamstra, *President*
Josh Hamstra, *Vice Pres*
Brad Gossman, *Store Mgr*
Bob Jubera, *Store Mgr*
Sharon Gluth, *Financial Exec*
EMP: 72 EST: 1954
SQ FT: 24,500
SALES (est): 53.9MM **Privately Held**
WEB: www.leeps.com
SIC: 5074 3261 5251 Plumbing fittings &
supplies; vitreous plumbing fixtures; hard-
ware

(G-9727)
LIFE DME LLC
8896 Louisiana St (46410-7153)
PHONE.................................219 795-1296
Fax: 219 795-1349
Mubarak Amine, *President*
EMP: 9
SALES (est): 1.4MM **Privately Held**
SIC: 3841 Surgical instruments & appara-
tus

(G-9728)
**LOVING CARE
PTNT/WHEELCHAIR TR**
6115 Johnson St (46410-2957)
PHONE.................................219 427-1137
Gwenell F White, *Owner*
EMP: 2
SALES (est): 86.6K **Privately Held**
SIC: 3842 Wheelchairs

(G-9729)
LUXOTTICA RETAIL N AMER INC
Also Called: Lenscrafters
2212 Southlake Mall (46410-6441)
PHONE.................................219 736-0141
Fax: 219 736-2958
Sherry Merriman, *Branch Mgr*
EMP: 25 **Privately Held**
WEB: www.lenscrafters.com
SIC: 5995 3851 Eyeglasses, prescription;
ophthalmic goods
HQ: Luxottica Retail North America Inc.
4000 Luxottica Pl
Mason OH 45040

(G-9730)
MARKET PLACE PUBLICATIONS
7091 Broadway Ste D (46410-3537)
PHONE.................................219 769-7733
Steven Gallovick, *Owner*
EMP: 3
SALES: 200K **Privately Held**
SIC: 5411 2721 Grocery stores; maga-
zines: publishing & printing

(G-9731)
MENDOZA MEXICAN MIX
7425 Madison St (46410-4607)
PHONE.................................219 791-9034
Scott Embury, *Principal*
EMP: 2
SALES (est): 115.8K **Privately Held**
SIC: 3273 Ready-mixed concrete

(G-9732)
MENDOZAS INC
7425 Madison St (46410-4607)
PHONE.................................219 791-9034
Mellonie A Mendoza, *President*
EMP: 4
SALES (est): 255.2K **Privately Held**
SIC: 3273 Ready-mixed concrete

(G-9733)
**MIDWEST ORTHOTIC SERVICES
LLC**
114 E 90th Dr (46410-7160)
PHONE.................................219 736-9960
Bernie Veldman, *Branch Mgr*
EMP: 26
SALES (est): 1MM
SALES (corp-wide): 14MM **Privately
Held**
SIC: 3842 Braces, orthopedic
PA: Midwest Orthotic Services, Llc
17530 Dugdale Dr
South Bend IN 46635
574 233-3352

(G-9734)
MILANI CUSTOM HOMES LLC
5222 Connecticut St (46410-1545)
PHONE.................................219 455-5804
Brandi Shotwell, *President*
EMP: 3
SALES (est): 201.5K **Privately Held**
SIC: 6514 1542 1742 1541 Residential
building, four or fewer units: operation;
nonresidential construction; commercial &
office building, new construction; plaster
& drywall work; renovation, remodeling &
repairs: industrial buildings; wood floor installation & refinishing; electronic computers

(G-9735)
MILESTONE CABINETRY
2916 E 83rd Pl (46410-6414)
PHONE.................................219 947-0600
EMP: 7
SALES (est): 562.6K **Privately Held**
SIC: 2434 Wood kitchen cabinets

(G-9736)
**MODERN DROP FORGE
COMPANY**
8757 Colorado St (46410-7204)
P.O. Box 429, Blue Island IL (60406-0429)
PHONE.................................708 388-1806
Gregory Heim, *President*
Thomas Holmes, *General Mgr*
Virginia Heim, *Vice Pres*
Melissa Rodriguez, *Opers Mgr*
Brian Yazumbek, *QC Mgr*
EMP: 13
SQ FT: 5,000
SALES (est): 188.8K
SALES (corp-wide): 8.8MM **Privately
Held**
WEB: www.modernforge.com
SIC: 3544 Special dies, tools, jigs & fix-
tures
PA: Modern Drop Forge Company, Llc
8757 Colorado St
Merrillville IN 46410
708 489-4208

(G-9737)
**MODERN DROP FORGE
COMPANY LLC (PA)**
8757 Colorado St (46410-7204)
PHONE.................................708 489-4208
Gregory Heim, *CEO*
Patrick Thompson, *CFO*
Richard Heim, *Director*
▲ EMP: 430
SQ FT: 250,000

SALES: 8.8MM **Privately Held**
WEB: www.modernforge.com
SIC: 3544 3462 Special dies & tools; iron
& steel forgings

(G-9738)
**MODERN FORGE COMPANIES
LLC**
8757 Colorado St (46410-7204)
PHONE.................................708 388-1806
Sadie Farmer,
EMP: 700
SALES (est): 7.5MM **Privately Held**
SIC: 8711 3429 Engineering services;
manufactured hardware (general); door
opening & closing devices, except electri-
cal

(G-9739)
MODERN FORGE INDIANA LLC
8757 Colorado St (46410-7204)
PHONE.................................219 945-5945
EMP: 15 EST: 2011
SALES (est): 5.8MM **Privately Held**
SIC: 3462 Iron & steel forgings

(G-9740)
MOMAKI PUBLISHING LLC
1701 W 55th Ave (46410-1878)
PHONE.................................847 454-4641
EMP: 2
SALES (est): 59.2K **Privately Held**
SIC: 2741 Miscellaneous publishing

(G-9741)
MONOSOL LLC (DH)
707 E 80th Pl Ste 301 (46410-5683)
PHONE.................................219 762-3165
Fax: 219 755-4062
P Scott Bening, *CEO*
Laura Grunzinger, *Owner*
Mike Arana, *Maint Spvr*
Chuck Jones, *Opers Spvr*
Aaron Schmick, *QC Mgr*
▲ EMP: 19
SALES (est): 74MM
SALES (corp-wide): 4.6B **Privately Held**
WEB: www.monosol.com
SIC: 2671 Plastic film, coated or laminated
for packaging

(G-9742)
OLD GARY INC
1433 E 83rd Ave (46410-6307)
PHONE.................................941 755-0976
Michelle Marshall-Smith, *Executive*
EMP: 2
SALES (est): 38.1K **Privately Held**
SIC: 8742 7372 7361 6552 Management
consulting services; prepackaged soft-
ware; employment agencies; subdividers
& developers

(G-9743)
ORNAMENTAL IRON WORKS
5300 Massachusetts St (46410-1696)
PHONE.................................219 988-4929
EMP: 4
SQ FT: 4,000
SALES: 500K **Privately Held**
SIC: 3446 Stairs, fire escapes, balconies,
railings & ladders

(G-9744)
**PARKER-HANNIFIN
CORPORATION**
Also Called: Medical Systems Division
1201 E 86th Pl Ste H (46410-6377)
PHONE.................................219 736-0400
William Depel, *Principal*
Ferguson Poliquin, *Plant Mgr*
Kathleen Joslyn, *Human Res Mgr*
Mary Depel, *Manager*
EMP: 14
SALES (corp-wide): 12B **Publicly Held**
SIC: 3594 Fluid power pumps & motors
PA: Parker-Hannifin Corporation
6035 Parkland Blvd
Cleveland OH 44124
216 896-3000

(G-9745)
PHILIP PINS
3701 W 79th Pl (46410-5011)
PHONE.................................219 769-1059

G
E
O
G
R
A
P
H
I
C

Philip Pins, *Principal*
EMP: 5
SALES (est): 453K **Privately Held**
SIC: 3452 Pins

(G-9746)
PIONEER SIGNS INC
Also Called: Gary Sign Co
3289 E 83rd Pl (46410-6542)
PHONE..............................219 884-7587
Fax: 219 942-3077
Paul Grochowski, *President*
Gerald Mick, *Vice Pres*
Muriel Grochowski, *Treasurer*
EMP: 11 EST: 1960
SQ FT: 5,000
SALES (est): 1.2MM **Privately Held**
WEB: www.pioneersigns.com
SIC: 3993 1799 7389 3999 Electric
signs; neon signs; sign installation &
maintenance; sign painting & lettering
shop; chairs, hydraulic, barber & beauty
shop

(G-9747)
**PLASTIC LINE
MANUFACTURING**
9070 Louisiana St (46410-7155)
PHONE..............................219 769-8022
Fax: 219 769-8105
Marjorie Wallace, *President*
Karen Ragan, *Controller*
EMP: 37 EST: 1960
SQ FT: 30,000
SALES: 2.5MM **Privately Held**
WEB: www.plasticlinecountertops.com
SIC: 2542 2541 2434 Counters or counter
display cases: except wood; wood parti-
tions & fixtures; wood kitchen cabinets

(G-9748)
POLYCON INDUSTRIES INC
8919 Colorado St (46410-7208)
PHONE..............................219 738-1000
Fax: 219 738-1024
Berle Blitstein, *President*
Patrick Ignas, *Prdtn Mgr*
Matthew Muta, *Plant Engr*
William Hansen, *CFO*
Joe Nelson, *Accounting Mgr*
EMP: 250
SQ FT: 200,000
SALES (est): 78.6MM
SALES (corp-wide): 79.1MM **Privately
Held**
WEB: www.crown-polycon-inc.com
SIC: 3089 3085 Plastic containers, except
foam; plastics bottles
PA: Crown Packaging International, Inc.
8919 Colorado St
Merrillville IN 46410
219 738-1000

(G-9749)
PRIME CONVEYOR INC
8903 Louisiana St (46410-7114)
PHONE..............................219 736-1994
Fax: 219 736-5880
James Robinson, *President*
Marilynn Robinson, *Regional Mgr*
Dennis Armstrong, *Vice Pres*
EMP: 35
SQ FT: 28,000
SALES (est): 12.2MM **Privately Held**
WEB: www.primeconveyor.com
SIC: 3535 Conveyors & conveying equip-
ment

(G-9750)
ROCK HARD STONES CUSTOM
2023 W 75th Pl (46410-4791)
PHONE..............................219 613-0112
EMP: 2
SALES (est): 83.9K **Privately Held**
SIC: 2752 Commercial printing, litho-
graphic

(G-9751)
ROMANART INC
7302 Taft St (46410-4549)
P.O. Box 879, Crown Point (46308-0879)
PHONE..............................219 736-9150
Roman Perez, *President*
Kurt Pack, *Vice Pres*
EMP: 6

SALES: 750K **Privately Held**
WEB: www.romanartinc.com
SIC: 2759 Screen printing

(G-9752)
SCRIBE PUBLICATIONS INC
2050 W 86th Ave (46410-8822)
PHONE..............................219 791-9254
Charity A Nelson, *Principal*
EMP: 2 EST: 2009
SALES (est): 105.8K **Privately Held**
SIC: 2741 Miscellaneous publishing

(G-9753)
SHARON SPERRY
Also Called: Sharon's Tollebooth
1106 W 73rd Ave (46410-3818)
PHONE..............................219 736-0121
Sharon Sperry, *Owner*
EMP: 2 EST: 1991
SALES (est): 78K **Privately Held**
SIC: 2499 Decorative wood & woodwork

(G-9754)
**SITEONE LANDSCAPE SUPPLY
LLC**
Also Called: John Deere Landscapes
4068 W 82nd Ct (46410-6473)
PHONE..............................219 769-2351
EMP: 4
SALES (corp-wide): 1.8B **Publicly Held**
SIC: 5261 5083 3432 Lawn & garden
equipment; lawn & garden machinery &
equipment; lawn hose nozzles & sprin-
klers
HQ: Siteone Landscape Supply, Llc
300 Colonial Center Pkwy # 600
Roswell GA 30076
770 255-2100

(G-9755)
**T & M EQUIPMENT COMPANY
INC (PA)**
2880 E 83rd Pl (46410-6412)
PHONE..............................219 942-2299
Fax: 219 942-1180
William Malatestinic, *President*
Peter Turek, *Vice Pres*
Phil Young, *Plant Mgr*
EMP: 37
SQ FT: 35,000
SALES (est): 34.8MM **Privately Held**
SIC: 5084 3536 7699 Materials handling
machinery; hoists, cranes & monorails; in-
dustrial machinery & equipment repair

(G-9756)
T M E INC
9100 Lane St Bldg C-2 (46410)
PHONE..............................219 769-6627
Edwin A Tylenda Jr, *President*
Mary Lou Tylenda, *Admin Sec*
EMP: 2
SQ FT: 9,600
SALES: 220K **Privately Held**
SIC: 3599 7699 Machine shop, jobbing &
repair; pumps & pumping equipment re-
pair

(G-9757)
**TECHNOLOGY CONS GROUP
LLC**
1421 E 91st Dr (46410-7175)
PHONE..............................219 525-4064
Richard Cannon,
EMP: 4
SQ FT: 2,000
SALES (est): 645.9K **Privately Held**
SIC: 3651 5999 7812 Household audio &
video equipment; audio-visual equipment
& supplies; audio-visual program produc-
tion

(G-9758)
TERRYS SEWER SERVICE
8235 Lincoln St (46410-6132)
PHONE..............................219 756-5238
Tammie Kilburn, *Partner*
Terry Kilburn, *Partner*
EMP: 2
SALES: 200K **Privately Held**
SIC: 3272 Sewer pipe, concrete

(G-9759)
**TRADEBE ENVIRONMENTAL
SVCS LLC (DH)**
1433 E 83rd Ave Ste 200 (46410-6307)
PHONE..............................800 388-7242
Jeff Beswick, *CEO*
Bob O'Brien, *Exec VP*
EMP: 1
SALES: 200MM
SALES (corp-wide): 137.1K **Privately
Held**
SIC: 4953 7699 1389 Hazardous waste
collection & disposal; recycling, waste
materials; ship boiler & tank cleaning &
repair, contractors; industrial equipment
cleaning; lease tanks, oil field: erecting,
cleaning & repairing
HQ: Tradebe Gp
4343 Kennedy Ave
East Chicago IN 46312
800 388-7242

(G-9760)
UPS STORE 5219
417 W 81st Ave (46410-5317)
PHONE..............................219 750-9597
Fax: 219 736-7550
Adele Molinaro, *President*
EMP: 3
SQ FT: 2,000
SALES (est): 150K **Privately Held**
SIC: 4215 2752 Package delivery, vehicu-
lar; calendar & card printing, lithographic

(G-9761)
WHITECO INDUSTRIES INC (PA)
Also Called: Celebration Station
1000 E 80th Pl Ste 700n (46410-5676)
PHONE..............................219 769-6601
Dean White, *President*
John Lannon, *General Mgr*
Bill Wellman, *Vice Pres*
John Peterman, *Treasurer*
Ted Marek, *Training Dir*
EMP: 1000 EST: 1935
SQ FT: 16,000
SALES (est): 154.5MM **Privately Held**
WEB: www.morningsidecp.com
SIC: 7312 7011 7922 6552 Billboard ad-
vertising; motel, franchised; inns; theatri-
cal production services; land subdividers
& developers, commercial; data process-
ing service; signs & advertising special-
ties

Metamora
Franklin County

(G-9762)
**ALL OCCASIONS GIFT SHOP
LLC**
Also Called: Smelly Gourmet, The
19062 S Main St (47030-9756)
P.O. Box 58 (47030-0058)
PHONE..............................513 314-5693
Steven Collier,
EMP: 2
SQ FT: 2,400
SALES (est): 102.1K **Privately Held**
SIC: 5947 5963 5812 2844 Gift shop;
food service, coffee-cart; fast food restau-
rants & stands; face creams or lotions;
hotels & motels

Michigan City
La Porte County

(G-9763)
**NEWCOMB PRINTING SERVICES
INC**
605 E 9th St (46360-3651)
PHONE..............................219 874-3201
EMP: 2 EST: 2013
SALES (est): 97K **Privately Held**
SIC: 2752 Lithographic Commercial Print-
ing

Michigan City
Laporte County

(G-9764)
ADIDAS NORTH AMERICA INC
Also Called: Adidas Outlet Store Mich Cy
601 Wabash St Ste 1205 (46360-3415)
PHONE..............................219 878-5822
Jaimi Dudzik-Bolz, *Manager*
Rachit Rawal, *Assistant*
EMP: 17
SALES (est): 25B **Privately Held**
SIC: 2329 Athletic (warmup, sweat & jog-
ging) suits: men's & boys'; men's & boys'
athletic uniforms; knickers, dress (sepa-
rate): men's & boys'
HQ: Adidas North America, Inc.
5055 N Greeley Ave
Portland OR 97217
971 234-2300

(G-9765)
**AMERICAN ENCODER REPAIR
SERVIC**
7115 W Lynwood Dr (46360-9162)
PHONE..............................219 872-2822
Fax: 219 872-2823
Karen Lagrou, *Owner*
EMP: 99
SALES (est): 1.2MM **Privately Held**
SIC: 7694 Electric motor repair

(G-9766)
APERION CARE
1101 E Coolspring Ave (46360-6310)
PHONE..............................219 874-5211
EMP: 2
SALES (est): 81.8K **Privately Held**
SIC: 2841 Soap & other detergents

(G-9767)
ASHLEY F WARD INC
Also Called: Fitech Divison
2031 Tryon Rd (46360-2813)
PHONE..............................219 879-4177
Todd Tirotta, *Manager*
EMP: 25
SQ FT: 27,000
SALES (corp-wide): 46.5MM **Privately
Held**
WEB: www.ashleyward.com
SIC: 3451 3494 3462 3452 Screw ma-
chine products; valves & pipe fittings; iron
& steel forgings; bolts, nuts, rivets &
washers; plumbing fixture fittings & trim
PA: Ashley F. Ward, Inc.
7490 Easy St
Mason OH 45040
513 398-1414

(G-9768)
BIELA PRINTING
1004 Kentucky St (46360-4034)
PHONE..............................219 874-8094
David Biela, *Owner*
EMP: 3
SALES (est): 209.3K **Privately Held**
SIC: 2752 Commercial printing, litho-
graphic

(G-9769)
**BIONIC PROSTHETICS AND
ORTHO**
1200 S Woodland Ave Ste A (46360-7389)
PHONE..............................219 221-6119
Dheeraj Bhambhani, *Branch Mgr*
EMP: 2 **Privately Held**
SIC: 3842 Prosthetic appliances
PA: Bionic Prosthetics And Orthotics Group
Llc
8695 Connecticut St Ste E
Merrillville IN 46410

(G-9770)
BLOCKSOM & CO (PA)
450 Saint John Rd Ste 710 (46360-7385)
P.O. Box 2007 (46361-8007)
PHONE..............................219 878-4455
Fax: 219 874-9785
Andrew Swan, *President*
Douglas Smith, *Chairman*
Lindsay Grant, *Traffic Mgr*
Charlene Grant, *Accounting Dir*

▲ = Import ▼=Export
◆ =Import/Export

Dennice Adrian, *Accountant*
◆ **EMP:** 7 **EST:** 1919
SALES: 10MM **Privately Held**
WEB: www.blocksom.com
SIC: 3564 Filters, air: furnaces, air conditioning equipment, etc.

(G-9771)
BLOCKSOM & CO
Also Called: Paratex Products
420 E 5th St (46360-3344)
P.O. Box 2007 (46361-8007)
PHONE.................................219 878-4458
Fax: 219 874-3752
Andrew Swan, *President*
EMP: 40
SALES (est): 5.7MM
SALES (corp-wide): 10MM **Privately Held**
WEB: www.blocksom.com
SIC: 2299 3564 Batting, wadding, padding & fillings; blowers & fans
PA: Blocksom & Co.
450 Saint John Rd Ste 710
Michigan City IN 46360
219 878-4455

(G-9772)
CALUMET PALLET COMPANY INC
4333 Ohio St (46360-7743)
P.O. Box 736 (46361-0736)
PHONE.................................219 932-4550
Fax: 219 937-4550
Jeffery Bridegroom, *President*
Bridegroom Allison L, *President*
Carol Bridegroom, *Corp Secy*
EMP: 72
SQ FT: 35,000
SALES (est): 17.4MM **Privately Held**
WEB: www.calumetpallet.com
SIC: 2448 Pallets, wood

(G-9773)
CENTRAL STATES MFG INC
2051 Tryon Rd (46360-2813)
PHONE.................................219 879-4770
Fax: 219 879-9670
Debbie Jordan, *Branch Mgr*
EMP: 90
SALES (corp-wide): 219.5MM **Privately Held**
WEB: www.centralstatesmfg.com
SIC: 3448 3444 3441 2952 Panels for prefabricated metal buildings; sheet metalwork; fabricated structural metal; asphalt felts & coatings
PA: Central States Manufacturing, Inc.
302 Jane Pl
Lowell AR 72745
479 770-0188

(G-9774)
CHANCE ABRASIVES
217 Twilight Dr (46360-1250)
PHONE.................................219 871-0977
Diane Kendrick, *Owner*
EMP: 2
SALES (est): 158.8K **Privately Held**
SIC: 3291 Abrasive products

(G-9775)
COLLINS CAVIAR COMPANY
113 York St (46360-3653)
PHONE.................................269 231-5100
Rachel Collins, *Owner*
EMP: 4
SALES (est): 280.3K **Privately Held**
WEB: www.collinscaviar.com
SIC: 2092 Seafoods, frozen: prepared

(G-9776)
CRITERION CATALYSTS & TECH LP
Also Called: Criterion Catalyst Technologys
1800 E Us Highway 12 (46360-2098)
PHONE.................................219 874-6211
Fax: 219 861-4254
Mik Burke, *Manager*
EMP: 125
SALES (corp-wide): 305.1B **Privately Held**
WEB: www.criterioncatalysts.com
SIC: 2819 Catalysts, chemical

HQ: Criterion Catalysts & Technologies L.P.
910 Louisiana St Ste 2900
Houston TX 77002
713 241-3000

(G-9777)
CUSTOM COMPRESSOR SVCS CORP
104 Woodland Ct Ste A (46360-7391)
P.O. Box 326 (46361-0326)
PHONE.................................219 879-4966
Scott Schermer, *President*
EMP: 6 **EST:** 1999
SALES (est): 352.6K **Privately Held**
SIC: 3563 Air & gas compressors

(G-9778)
CVG SPRAGUE DEVICES LLC
527 W Us Highway 20 (46360-6835)
PHONE.................................614 289-5360
EMP: 2
SALES (corp-wide): 755.2MM **Publicly Held**
SIC: 3714 Motor vehicle parts & accessories
HQ: Sprague Cvg Devices Llc
7800 Walton Pkwy
New Albany OH 43054
219 872-7295

(G-9779)
D & J CUSTOM EMBROIDERY
Also Called: D&J Custom Embroidery
707 E 11th St (46360-3619)
PHONE.................................219 874-9061
Deb Jordan, *Partner*
J Dobkins, *Partner*
EMP: 2
SALES (est): 83K **Privately Held**
SIC: 2395 Embroidery & art needlework

(G-9780)
DAGE-MTI MICHIGAN CITY INC
701 N Roeske Ave (46360-2671)
PHONE.................................219 872-5514
Fax: 219 872-5559
John B Moore, *President*
Peggy Moore, *Vice Pres*
Lori Osos, *Purch Agent*
Brian Henderlong, *QC Mgr*
John Bogan, *Manager*
EMP: 8
SQ FT: 22,000
SALES (est): 1.5MM **Privately Held**
WEB: www.dage-mti.com
SIC: 3651 Household video equipment

(G-9781)
DEKKER VACUUM TECHNOLOGIES INC
935 S Woodland Ave (46360-5672)
PHONE.................................219 861-0661
Fax: 219 861-0662
Rick Jan Dekker, *CEO*
Charles Mitchell, *President*
▲ **EMP:** 43 **EST:** 1998
SQ FT: 45,000
SALES: 18MM **Privately Held**
WEB: www.dekkervacuum.com
SIC: 5084 3563 Pumps & pumping equipment; vacuum (air extraction) systems, industrial

(G-9782)
DIAMOND MANUFACTURING COMPANY
Also Called: Diamond Mfg Co Midwest
600 Royal Rd (46360-2744)
PHONE.................................219 874-2374
Fax: 219 874-8028
Phil Guba, *Branch Mgr*
EMP: 42
SALES (corp-wide): 9.7B **Publicly Held**
WEB: www.diamondman.com
SIC: 3469 3471 3479 3089 Perforated metal, stamped; cleaning, polishing & finishing; coating of metals & formed products; plastic processing
HQ: Diamond Manufacturing Company
243 W Eigth St
Wyoming PA 18644
570 693-0300

(G-9783)
DPA INVESTMENTS INC
1750 E Us Highway 12 (46360-2076)
PHONE.................................219 873-0914
Fax: 219 873-0946
Peter Askew, *Manager*
EMP: 7
SALES (corp-wide): 43.2MM **Privately Held**
WEB: www.usalco.com
SIC: 2819 Industrial inorganic chemicais
PA: Dpa Investments, Inc.
2601 Cannery Ave
Baltimore MD 21226
410 918-2230

(G-9784)
DUNELAND ALPACAS LTD
1394 N County Line Rd (46360-9522)
PHONE.................................219 877-4417
Michael W Small, *Principal*
EMP: 2 **EST:** 2008
SALES (est): 118.5K **Privately Held**
SIC: 2231 Alpacas, mohair: woven

(G-9785)
DWYER INSTRUMENTS INC
Mercoid Divsion Dwyer Instrs
102 Hwy 212 (46360-1956)
P.O. Box 373 (46361-0373)
PHONE.................................219 879-8000
Fax: 219 872-9057
Steven Clark, *President*
Crystal Kaczmarek, *Buyer*
Kelly Wenzel, *Buyer*
Andrew Orlowski, *Engineer*
Michael Popp, *Design Engr*
EMP: 200
SALES (corp-wide): 100MM **Privately Held**
WEB: www.dwyer-inst.com
SIC: 3823 Industrial instrmnts msrmnt display/control process variable
PA: Dwyer Instruments Inc
102 Indiana Highway 212
Michigan City IN 46360
219 879-8868

(G-9786)
DWYER INSTRUMENTS INC
Also Called: Love Controls
102 Indiana Highway 212 (46360-1956)
P.O. Box 338 (46361-0338)
PHONE.................................219 879-8000
EMP: 11
SALES (corp-wide): 100MM **Privately Held**
WEB: www.dwyer-inst.com
SIC: 3823 Industrial instrmnts msrmnt display/control process variable
PA: Dwyer Instruments Inc
102 Indiana Highway 212
Michigan City IN 46360
219 879-8868

(G-9787)
DYNAMIC DESIGNS SCOTTYS
3409 Franklin St (46360-7008)
PHONE.................................219 809-7268
Scott Roberts, *Principal*
EMP: 3
SALES (est): 284K **Privately Held**
SIC: 2499 Trophy bases, wood

(G-9788)
ELKHART PLASTICS INC
316 Lake Shore Dr (46360-2356)
PHONE.................................574 370-1079
Bonnie Turner, *Principal*
EMP: 2
SALES (est): 88.9K **Privately Held**
SIC: 3089 Plastics products

(G-9789)
EXPLODING BRAIN PRESS
607 Franklin St (46360-3411)
PHONE.................................219 393-0796
Nichole Sheaffer, *Principal*
EMP: 2
SALES (est): 101.5K **Privately Held**
SIC: 2741 Miscellaneous publishing

(G-9790)
FABRICATED METALS CORP
4991a W Us Highway 20 (46360-6638)
PHONE.................................219 871-0230

William Moore, *President*
EMP: 10
SQ FT: 12,000
SALES (est): 1.3MM **Privately Held**
SIC: 3441 Fabricated structural metal

(G-9791)
FAITH WALKERS
Also Called: Faith Walkers Screen Printing
7358 W Johnson Rd (46360-2926)
PHONE.................................219 873-1900
Donald Brooks, *Partner*
Mary Brooks, *Partner*
EMP: 5
SALES (est): 339.2K **Privately Held**
SIC: 2759 Screen printing

(G-9792)
FAST LANE FOODS INC
Also Called: Cigarette Discount Outlet
4211 Franklin St (46360-7805)
PHONE.................................219 879-3300
Fax: 219 879-3300
Tara Leslie, *Manager*
EMP: 10
SALES (corp-wide): 4.4MM **Privately Held**
SIC: 2111 Cigarettes
PA: Fast Lane Foods Inc
8008 Kennedy Ave
Highland IN 46322
219 838-6600

(G-9793)
FILTRATION PLUS INC
4208 N 900 W (46360-9346)
PHONE.................................219 879-0663
Fax: 219 879-0670
William Ruckel, *President*
Jeff Hunter, *General Mgr*
Donna Stich, *Vice Pres*
EMP: 40
SQ FT: 8,500
SALES (est): 7.4MM **Privately Held**
SIC: 5085 3569 Filters, industrial; filters, general line: industrial

(G-9794)
FITECH INC
2031 Tryon Rd (46360-2813)
PHONE.................................513 398-1414
Fax: 219 874-8284
Thomas Fitzgerald, *President*
Brian Scalf, *Vice Pres*
Dan Wilson, *Vice Pres*
Anthony Baron, *Sales Mgr*
EMP: 20
SQ FT: 25,000
SALES (est): 3.1MM **Privately Held**
WEB: www.fitech.net
SIC: 3599 3451 Machine shop, jobbing & repair; screw machine products

(G-9795)
FRECH U S A INC
6000 Ohio St (46360-7757)
PHONE.................................219 874-2812
Fax: 219 874-2434
Ioannis Ioannidis, *Ch of Bd*
Bob Tracy, *General Mgr*
Robert Tracy, *General Mgr*
Norbert Erhard, *Treasurer*
Connie Sager, *Controller*
▲ **EMP:** 14
SQ FT: 30,000
SALES (est): 5.1MM
SALES (corp-wide): 107.1MM **Privately Held**
SIC: 3542 Machine tools, metal forming type
PA: Oskar Frech Gmbh + Co. Kg
Schorndorfer Str. 32
Schorndorf 73614
718 170-20

(G-9796)
FREEZING SYSTEMS AND SVC INC
107 Freyer Rd (46360-2224)
PHONE.................................219 879-6236
Christopher Redlarczyk, *President*
Stefanie Willett, *Human Resources*
David Detullio, *Marketing Staff*
EMP: 16
SQ FT: 60,000

SALES: 850K **Privately Held**
SIC: 3632 Household refrigerators & freezers

(G-9797)
GEBERIT MANUFACTURING INC
Also Called: Chicago Faucet Company
1100 Boone Dr (46360-7730)
PHONE..................................219 879-4466
Fax: 219 872-8003
Keith D Kramer, *President*
Bruce Reidel, *Vice Pres*
Valentin F Lopez, *CFO*
◆ EMP: 42
SALES (est): 7.9MM
SALES (corp-wide): 2.9B **Privately Held**
SIC: 3432 3088 Plumbing fixture fittings & trim; plastics plumbing fixtures
HQ: Geberit International Ag
　　Schachenstrasse 77
　　Jona SG
　　552 216-300

(G-9798)
GUARDIAN COUPLINGS LLC
300 Indiana 212 (46360-2859)
PHONE..................................219 874-5248
EMP: 3
SALES (est): 355.2K **Privately Held**
SIC: 3568 Power transmission equipment

(G-9799)
GUARDIAN IND INC
Also Called: Guardian Industries
300 Indiana Highway 212 (46360-2859)
PHONE..................................219 874-5248
R Keith Sandin, *President*
Valorie Ingram, *Admin Sec*
▲ EMP: 40
SQ FT: 45,000
SALES (est): 8.2MM
SALES (corp-wide): 876.7MM **Publicly Held**
WEB: www.guardiancouplings.com
SIC: 3429 3568 Clamps & couplings, hose; couplings, shaft: rigid, flexible, universal joint, etc.
PA: Altra Industrial Motion Corp.
　　300 Granite St Ste 201
　　Braintree MA 02184
　　781 917-0600

(G-9800)
HANSON PIPE PRECAST
302 Elmwood Dr (46360-1943)
PHONE..................................219 873-9509
Lorie Anderson, *Principal*
EMP: 3
SALES (est): 272.3K **Privately Held**
SIC: 3272 Precast terrazo or concrete products

(G-9801)
HARRISON ELECTRIC INC
10855 W 400 N (46360-9474)
PHONE..................................219 879-0444
Fax: 219 879-0402
Thomas E Walma, *President*
Patricia A Walma, *Corp Secy*
Jonathan T Walma, *Vice Pres*
EMP: 19
SQ FT: 17,500
SALES (est): 4.4MM **Privately Held**
WEB: www.harrison-elec.com
SIC: 7694 5063 Electric motor repair; motors, electric

(G-9802)
HEARTHSIDE FOOD SOLUTIONS LLC
Also Called: Michigan City Baking
502 W Us Highway 20 (46360-6836)
PHONE..................................219 878-1522
Fax: 219 873-1882
Dave Dolan, *Plant Mgr*
EMP: 300 **Privately Held**
SIC: 2052 2051 Cookies; bread, cake & related products
PA: Hearthside Food Solutions, Llc
　　3500 Lacey Rd Ste 300
　　Downers Grove IL 60515

(G-9803)
ILLINOIS TOOL WORKS INC
1919 E Us Highway 12 (46360-2151)
PHONE..................................219 874-4217

Mary Lou McFadden, *Personnel*
Brent Thompson, *Manager*
EMP: 62
SQ FT: 100,000
SALES (corp-wide): 14.3B **Publicly Held**
SIC: 5085 3546 3429 3272 Fasteners & fastening equipment; drill attachments, portable; manufactured hardware (general); concrete products
PA: Illinois Tool Works Inc.
　　155 Harlem Ave
　　Glenview IL 60025
　　847 724-7500

(G-9804)
J & J WELDING
Also Called: J&J Welding
4100 W 700 N (46360-9761)
PHONE..................................219 872-7282
James E Ames Sr, *Owner*
EMP: 2
SALES: 200K **Privately Held**
SIC: 7692 Welding repair

(G-9805)
JOSAM COMPANY (PA)
525 W Us Highway 20 (46360-6835)
P.O. Box T (46361-0360)
PHONE..................................219 872-5531
Fax: 219 874-9539
B Scott Holloway Sr, *CEO*
Scott Holloway Jr, *CEO*
Steven J Holloway, *Vice Ch Bd*
Barry J Hodgekins, *COO*
Barry Hodgekins, *Exec VP*
▲ EMP: 51
SQ FT: 120,000
SALES (est): 12.8MM **Privately Held**
WEB: www.josam.com
SIC: 3431 3432 3444 3423 Plumbing fixtures: enameled iron cast iron or pressed metal; plumbing fixture fittings & trim; sheet metalwork; hand & edge tools; vitreous plumbing fixtures

(G-9806)
KELLEY PAGELS ENTERPRISES LLC
Also Called: Mc Kay Printing Services
500 Huron (46360-3368)
PHONE..................................219 872-8552
Fax: 219 872-8531
Tom Kuczymski,
Laurel Kuczymski,
EMP: 16
SQ FT: 33,000
SALES (est): 5MM **Privately Held**
WEB: www.mckayprinting.com
SIC: 2752 2759 Commercial printing, offset; publication printing

(G-9807)
KTR CORPORATION
122 Anchor Rd (46360-2802)
P.O. Box 9065 (46361-9065)
PHONE..................................219 872-9100
Fax: 219 872-9150
Dr Joseph Gerstner, *Ch of Bd*
Megan James, *Regional Mgr*
Benjamin Stark, *Regional Mgr*
Tim Young, *Materials Mgr*
Michael Ford, *Production*
▲ EMP: 35
SQ FT: 35,000
SALES (est): 9.8MM
SALES (corp-wide): 225.7MM **Privately Held**
SIC: 3568 Power transmission equipment
HQ: Ktr Systems Gmbh
　　Carl-Zeiss-Str. 25
　　Rheine 48432
　　597 179-80

(G-9808)
LANDMARK HOME & LAND CO INC (PA)
1902 Washington St (46360-4476)
PHONE..................................219 874-4065
Frank Tuma, *President*
Michael Curran, *Director*
EMP: 3
SALES (est): 380.2K **Privately Held**
WEB: www.lhlc.com
SIC: 1799 2452 1521 Building site preparation; prefabricated wood buildings; single-family housing construction

(G-9809)
LEGACY SCREEN PRTG PRMTONS LLC ✪
503 Gardena St (46360-6218)
PHONE..................................219 262-4000
EMP: 2 EST: 2017
SALES (est): 83.9K **Privately Held**
SIC: 2752 Commercial printing, lithographic

(G-9810)
LESAC CORPORATION (PA)
700 W Michigan Blvd (46360-3285)
PHONE..................................219 879-3215
Fax: 219 874-8930
Richard D Kirsgalvis, *President*
▼ EMP: 38
SALES (est): 5.9MM **Privately Held**
WEB: www.alchemyradio.com
SIC: 3569 2674 Filters, general line: industrial; bags: uncoated paper & multiwall

(G-9811)
LIGHTHOUSE INDUSTRIES INC (PA)
107 Eastwood Rd Ste D (46360-2403)
P.O. Box 8905 (46361-8905)
PHONE..................................219 879-1550
Fax: 219 879-1509
Todd J Holloway Sr, *President*
John Wojcik, *President*
▲ EMP: 21
SQ FT: 25,000
SALES (est): 7.6MM **Privately Held**
WEB: www.lighthouseindustries.com
SIC: 3089 Injection molding of plastics

(G-9812)
LITERATURE SALES
613 Franklin St (46360-3411)
PHONE..................................219 873-3093
Debra Strelesky, *Principal*
EMP: 2 EST: 2009
SALES (est): 111.6K **Privately Held**
SIC: 2721 Magazines: publishing & printing

(G-9813)
M T M MACHINING INC
Also Called: Peters & Marske
311 Indiana Highway 212 (46360-2858)
P.O. Box 9348 (46361-9348)
PHONE..................................219 872-8677
Fax: 219 872-8679
Todd Weist, *President*
Donna Weist, *Corp Secy*
EMP: 10
SQ FT: 15,000
SALES (est): 930K **Privately Held**
SIC: 3599 7692 3444 Machine shop, jobbing & repair; welding repair; sheet metalwork

(G-9814)
MAGAZINE FULFILLMENT CORP
613 Franklin St (46360-3411)
PHONE..................................219 874-4245
Robert W Lake, *President*
Ruth Mokrycki, *Vice Pres*
EMP: 25
SALES (est): 4.2MM **Privately Held**
WEB: www.pubco-printing.com
SIC: 5192 2721 Magazines; periodicals

(G-9815)
MARLEY-WYLAIN COMPANY (HQ)
Also Called: Weil-Mclain
500 Blaine St (46360-2387)
PHONE..................................630 560-3703
Fax: 219 877-0556
Tom Blashill, *President*
Mark Richardson, *President*
Tony Curran, *Senior VP*
Greg Brennxcke, *Vice Pres*
Keith McLeod, *Vice Pres*
▲ EMP: 159 EST: 2009
SALES (est): 49MM
SALES (corp-wide): 1.4B **Publicly Held**
SIC: 3433 Boilers, low-pressure heating: steam or hot water
PA: Spx Corporation
　　13320a Balntyn Corp Pl
　　Charlotte NC 28277
　　980 474-3700

(G-9816)
MARLEY-WYLAIN COMPANY
Also Called: Weil-Mclain
500 Blaine St (46360-2387)
PHONE..................................219 879-6561
Fax: 219 879-4025
John Swann, *President*
EMP: 2
SALES (corp-wide): 1.4B **Publicly Held**
SIC: 3433 Boilers, low-pressure heating: steam or hot water
HQ: The Marley-Wylain Company
　　500 Blaine St
　　Michigan City IN 46360
　　630 560-3703

(G-9817)
MICHIGAN CITY PAPER BOX CO
1206 Pine St (46360-3732)
P.O. Box 275 (46361-0275)
PHONE..................................219 872-8383
Fax: 219 872-6035
Albert A Hoodwin, *CEO*
Linda Hardesty, *Admin Sec*
◆ EMP: 70 EST: 1904
SQ FT: 25,000
SALES (est): 20.4MM **Privately Held**
WEB: www.buyabox.com
SIC: 2631 Paperboard mills

(G-9818)
MIDWEST CUSTOM FINISHING INC
800 Royal Rd (46360-2746)
PHONE..................................219 874-0099
Fax: 219 874-0068
Rich Hamm, *Vice Pres*
EMP: 18
SALES (est): 1.7MM **Privately Held**
SIC: 3479 Painting, coating & hot dipping; coating of metals & formed products
PA: Midwest Custom Finishing, Inc.
　　1906 Clover Rd
　　Mishawaka IN 46545

(G-9819)
MIDWEST METAL PRODUCTS INC
111 Mariner Dr (46360-2824)
PHONE..................................219 879-8595
Fax: 219 879-8566
Geoff Wendt, *President*
Kevin Smith, *Vice Pres*
Doug Campbell, *QC Mgr*
EMP: 50
SQ FT: 28,000
SALES (est): 15.3MM **Privately Held**
WEB: www.midwestmetalproducts.net
SIC: 3312 Structural & rail mill products

(G-9820)
MIDWEST WHEELCOATERS LLC
800 Royal Rd (46360-2746)
PHONE..................................219 874-0099
Fax: 219 264-6721
Janet Wegiel, *Accounting Mgr*
Richard Hamm, *Mng Member*
Rich Hamm, *Exec Dir*
EMP: 30
SALES (est): 3.3MM **Privately Held**
SIC: 3479 Painting, coating & hot dipping

(G-9821)
MONTGOMERY & ASSOCIATES INC
Also Called: Beacher Business Printers
911 Franklin St (46360-3595)
PHONE..................................219 879-0088
Fax: 219 879-8070
G A Montgomery, *Ch of Bd*
Donald Montgomery, *President*
Andrew Tallackson, *Editor*
Thomas Montgomery, *Vice Pres*
Sally Montgomery, *Admin Sec*
EMP: 12 EST: 1976
SQ FT: 3,000
SALES (est): 1MM **Privately Held**
WEB: www.bbpnet.com
SIC: 2752 2711 2789 Commercial printing, offset; newspapers, publishing & printing; bookbinding & related work

(G-9822)
MULHERN BELTING INC
910 Indiana Highway 212 (46360-3025)
PHONE......................................219 879-2385
Dan Jonker, *Manager*
EMP: 6
SALES (corp-wide): 20MM **Privately Held**
SIC: 3052 Rubber & plastics hose & belt-
ings
PA: Mulhern Belting, Inc.
148 Bauer Dr
Oakland NJ 07436
201 337-5700

(G-9823)
NEWS DISPATCH (HQ)
Also Called: Michigan City News Dispatch
422 Franklin St Ste B (46360-3267)
PHONE......................................219 874-7211
Fax: 219 872-8511
J Fred Paxton, *President*
Patrick Keller, *Publisher*
Isis Cains, *Marketing Staff*
▲ EMP: 110
SQ FT: 25,000
SALES (est): 6.8MM
SALES (corp-wide): 318.6MM **Privately
Held**
WEB: www.thenewsdispatch.com
SIC: 2711 Newspapers: publishing only,
not printed on site
PA: Paxton Media Group, Llc
100 Television Ln
Paducah KY 42003
270 575-8630

(G-9824)
NIKE INC
917 Lighthouse Pl (46360-3462)
PHONE......................................219 879-1320
Katie McGarry, *Manager*
EMP: 38
SALES (corp-wide): 36.4B **Publicly Held**
SIC: 3021 Rubber & plastics footwear
PA: Nike, Inc.
1 Sw Bowerman Dr
Beaverton OR 97005
503 671-6453

(G-9825)
**ONLINE PACKAGING
INCORPORATED**
124 Tri Quad Dr (46360-3182)
PHONE......................................219 872-0925
Fax: 219 872-0928
Tim Wyman, *Branch Mgr*
EMP: 20
SALES (est): 1.5MM **Privately Held**
SIC: 5169 2842 Specialty cleaning & sani-
tation preparations; specialty cleaning,
polishes & sanitation goods
PA: Online Packaging, Incorporated
4311 Liberty Ln
Plover WI 54467

(G-9826)
PACKAGING GROUP CORP (PA)
2125 E Us Highway 12 C (46360-2198)
PHONE......................................219 879-2500
Fax: 219 874-9007
Elliott Weller, *President*
Daniel Goolsby, *Vice Pres*
EMP: 20
SQ FT: 35,000
SALES (est): 4.3MM **Privately Held**
SIC: 2992 4783 Oils & greases, blending
& compounding; packing & crating

(G-9827)
PANICCIA HEATING & COOLING
Also Called: Honeywell Authorized Dealer
5076 N Bleck Rd (46360-9142)
PHONE......................................219 872-2198
Mark Paniccia, *President*
Sheri Paniccia, *Vice Pres*
EMP: 3
SALES (est): 456.1K **Privately Held**
SIC: 3444 1711 Sheet metalwork; heating
& air conditioning contractors

(G-9828)
**PENDLETON WOOLEN MILLS
INC**
401 Lighthouse Pl (46360-3471)
P.O. Box 3030, Portland OR (97208-3030)
PHONE......................................219 879-0326
EMP: 51
SALES (corp-wide): 352.3MM **Privately
Held**
SIC: 2231 Wool Broadwoven Fabric Mill
PA: Pendleton Woolen Mills, Inc.
220 Nw Broadway
Portland OR 97209
503 226-4801

(G-9829)
PRINOVA SOLUTIONS
1700 E Us Highway 12 (46360-2076)
PHONE......................................219 879-7356
Darren Salyer, *General Mgr*
EMP: 15
SALES (est): 1.5MM **Privately Held**
SIC: 2041 Wheat flour

(G-9830)
PUBCO INC
613 Franklin St (46360-3411)
PHONE......................................219 874-4245
Fax: 219 873-3014
Robert Lake, *President*
EMP: 10
SALES (est): 553.9K **Privately Held**
SIC: 2741 2791 2752 Miscellaneous pub-
lishing; typesetting; commercial printing,
lithographic

(G-9831)
**PUBLISHERS CONSULTING
CORP**
613 Franklin St (46360-3411)
PHONE......................................219 874-4245
Robert W Lake Jr, *President*
EMP: 20
SQ FT: 25,000
SALES (est): 1.2MM **Privately Held**
WEB: www.mag-full.com
SIC: 2741 2791 2752 Miscellaneous pub-
lishing; typesetting; commercial printing,
lithographic

(G-9832)
PYRAMID METALLIZING INC
3155 W Dunes Hwy (46360-6764)
PHONE......................................219 879-9967
Bill Cristea, *President*
Kevin Downing, *Treasurer*
Roger Growden, *Admin Sec*
EMP: 7
SQ FT: 12,000
SALES: 900K **Privately Held**
SIC: 3479 Painting, coating & hot dipping

(G-9833)
R & E PALLET INC
1843 E Us Highway 12 (46360-2075)
PHONE......................................219 873-9671
Salvador Gomez, *President*
Isaias Gomez, *Vice Pres*
EMP: 4
SALES (est): 821.8K **Privately Held**
SIC: 2448 Pallets, wood & wood with metal

(G-9834)
REXFORD RAND CORP (PA)
2123 E Us Highway 12 (46360-2153)
P.O. Box 9005 (46361-9005)
PHONE......................................219 872-5561
Fax: 219 872-4571
Selwyn J Ancel, *Ch of Bd*
Albert I Ancel, *President*
Megan Rice, *Marketing Staff*
Doris A Ancel, *Admin Sec*
EMP: 25
SQ FT: 16,000
SALES (est): 2.1MM **Privately Held**
WEB: www.rexfordrand.com
SIC: 2842 Specialty cleaning preparations;
sanitation preparations, disinfectants &
deodorants

(G-9835)
ROSEDALE FILTERS LLC
700 W Michigan Blvd (46360-3285)
P.O. Box 9004 (46361-9004)
PHONE......................................219 879-4700

Dan Racek, *Principal*
EMP: 2
SALES (est): 285.1K **Privately Held**
SIC: 3569 Filters

(G-9836)
**ROYAL ACRES EQUESTRIAN
CENTER**
9375 W 300 N (46360-9315)
PHONE......................................219 874-7519
Fax: 219 874-7519
Todd Much, *President*
EMP: 6 EST: 1996
SALES (est): 430K **Privately Held**
WEB: www.royalacres.com
SIC: 3111 7948 0752 Equestrian leather
products; racing, including track opera-
tion; animal specialty services

(G-9837)
**SAGER METAL STRIP COMPANY
LLC**
100 Boone Dr (46360-7703)
PHONE......................................219 874-3609
Fax: 219 874-3649
Kay Frank, *Controller*
Jerry Eapmon, *Manager*
Peter Pairitz,
Jon Ahoborn, *Administration*
Michael Brennan,
▼ EMP: 35 EST: 1976
SQ FT: 88,000
SALES (est): 11.9MM **Privately Held**
WEB: www.sagermetal.com
SIC: 3535 Conveyors & conveying equip-
ment

(G-9838)
SAMCO GROUP INC (PA)
Also Called: Peepers Reading Glasses
9935 E Us Highway 12 (46360-1315)
P.O. Box 739 (46361-0739)
PHONE......................................219 872-4413
Fax: 219 872-4695
Paul Sammann, *President*
Diane Reed, *Office Mgr*
Teress Sammann, *Admin Sec*
◆ EMP: 7
SQ FT: 8,500
SALES (est): 1MM **Privately Held**
WEB: www.peeperspecs.com
SIC: 3851 3421 Eyeglasses, lenses &
frames; scissors, shears, clippers, snips &
similar tools

(G-9839)
SANDIN MFG INC
250 Indiana Highway 212 (46360-2857)
PHONE......................................219 872-2253
Keith Sandin, *President*
Todd Miller, *CFO*
Heather Swistek, *Executive Asst*
Helen C Sandlin, *Admin Sec*
▲ EMP: 59
SQ FT: 40,000
SALES: 9.7MM **Privately Held**
SIC: 2298 Wire rope centers

(G-9840)
**SANDUSKY ABRASIVE WHEEL
CO**
Also Called: Sandusky-Chicago Abrasive Whl
532 W 4th St (46360-3868)
P.O. Box 9233 (46361-9233)
PHONE......................................219 879-6601
Fax: 219 872-8139
Anthony Llorens, *President*
EMP: 40
SQ FT: 35,000
SALES (est): 4.2MM **Privately Held**
WEB: www.sanduskychicago.com
SIC: 3291 Wheels, abrasive

(G-9841)
SANLO INC
400 Hwy 212 (46360-2821)
PHONE......................................219 879-0241
Paul From, *CEO*
Rhonda Shank, *Purchasing*
Patty Hawkins, *Controller*
Luke Vandercar, *Sales Engr*
▲ EMP: 100
SQ FT: 100,000

SALES (est): 29.5MM
SALES (corp-wide): 19.6MM **Privately
Held**
WEB: www.sanlo.com
SIC: 3315 3568 3496 3357 Cable, steel:
insulated or armored; couplings, shaft:
rigid, flexible, universal joint, etc.; joints &
couplings; miscellaneous fabricated wire
products; nonferrous wiredrawing & insulating
HQ: Central Wire, Inc.
6509 Olson Rd
Union IL 60180
815 923-2131

(G-9842)
SECORP INC
Also Called: Michiana Impreglon Center
205 Woodcreek Dr 1 (46360-3180)
PHONE......................................219 874-5010
Thomas J Kramer, *President*
Sue Ann Kramer, *Admin Sec*
EMP: 5
SQ FT: 7,000
SALES (est): 615.3K **Privately Held**
WEB: www.michianaimpreglon.com
SIC: 3479 Coating of metals & formed
products

(G-9843)
SHADY CREEK VINEYARD
2030 Tryon Rd (46360-2814)
PHONE......................................219 874-9463
Tim Anderson, *Principal*
EMP: 8
SALES (est): 754.8K **Privately Held**
SIC: 2084 Wines

(G-9844)
SMITH READY MIX INC
3608 E Michigan Blvd (46360-6526)
P.O. Box 489, Valparaiso (46384-0489)
PHONE......................................219 874-6219
Doug Smith, *President*
EMP: 15
SALES (corp-wide): 12.7MM **Privately
Held**
SIC: 3273 Ready-mixed concrete
PA: Smith Ready Mix, Inc.
251 Lincolnway
Valparaiso IN 46383
219 462-3191

(G-9845)
SOUTHWATER SOURCING LLC
200 Tomahawk Dr (46360-2752)
PHONE......................................219 809-7106
Tom Stayanoff, *Mng Member*
▲ EMP: 2
SALES (est): 134.6K **Privately Held**
SIC: 3629 Electronic generation equipment

(G-9846)
SPX CORPORATION
Marley
500 Blaine St (46360-2387)
PHONE......................................219 879-6561
Gordon Stretch, *President*
Rick Millar, *Branch Mgr*
EMP: 250
SQ FT: 460,000
SALES (corp-wide): 1.4B **Publicly Held**
WEB: www.spx.com
SIC: 3443 Cooling towers, metal plate
PA: Spx Corporation
13320a Balntyn Corp Pl
Charlotte NC 28277
980 474-3700

(G-9847)
STANDARD INDUSTRIES INC
Also Called: GAF Materials
505 N Roeske Ave (46360-2668)
PHONE......................................219 872-1111
Fax: 219 878-5888
Daniel Jackson, *Purch Mgr*
Don Bulyar, *Project Engr*
Dwain Dodson, *Manager*
Lynn Russell, *Manager*
Fred Barbari, *Maintence Staff*
EMP: 150
SALES (corp-wide): 1.5B **Privately Held**
SIC: 2493 2952 Insulation & roofing mate-
rial, reconstituted wood; asphalt felts &
coatings

G E O G R A P H I C

HQ: Standard Industries Inc.
1 Campus Dr
Parsippany NJ 07054

(G-9848)
STRANCO INC
1306 W Us Highway 20 (46360-6899)
PHONE..................................219 874-5221
Fax: 219 872-2835
Steve Depalma, *President*
John Mickey, *Transptn Dir*
Reed Ellis, *Plant Mgr*
Jen Nowak, *Opers Mgr*
Donna Cooper, *Admin Sec*
EMP: 14
SQ FT: 25,000
SALES: 2MM Privately Held
WEB: www.strancoinc.com
SIC: 2759 Labels & seals: printing

(G-9849)
SULLAIR LLC (HQ)
3700 E Michigan Blvd (46360-6527)
PHONE..................................219 879-5451
Fax: 219 874-1221
Scott Nelson, *CEO*
Mark Benzel, *Regional Mgr*
Kent Vansickle, *Area Mgr*
David Booth, *Vice Pres*
Jon Hilberg, *Vice Pres*
◆ EMP: 277 EST: 2006
SQ FT: 138,600
SALES (est): 172.4MM
SALES (corp-wide): 87.9B Privately Held
WEB: www.sullair.com
SIC: 3569 3563 Filters, general line: industrial; air & gas compressors including vacuum pumps
PA: Hitachi, Ltd.
1-6-6, Marunouchi
Chiyoda-Ku TKY 100-0
332 581-111

(G-9850)
SULLIVAN-PALATEK INC
1201 W Us Highway 20 (46360-6851)
PHONE..................................219 874-2497
Fax: 219 872-5043
Robert McFee, *Ch of Bd*
Bruce McFee, *President*
Lori La Tour, *Office Mgr*
▲ EMP: 75
SQ FT: 180,000
SALES (est): 54.1MM
SALES (corp-wide): 5.8MM Privately Held
WEB: www.sullivanind.com
SIC: 3563 Air & gas compressors including vacuum pumps
PA: G.H.S. Corporation
2813 Wilbur St
Springfield MI 49037
800 388-4447

(G-9851)
TAMARA EATON
1213 E Coolspring Ave (46360-6319)
PHONE..................................219 872-9151
Tamara Eaton, *Principal*
EMP: 2
SALES (est): 209.3K Privately Held
SIC: 3625 Motor controls & accessories

(G-9852)
TEACO INC
2117 Ohio St (46360-5830)
P.O. Box E (46361-0290)
PHONE..................................219 874-6234
Fax: 219 874-6080
Ross Terry, *President*
Steve Terry, *General Mgr*
Diane Navarro, *Manager*
Margaret Terry, *Executive*
EMP: 10
SQ FT: 5,600
SALES: 554K Privately Held
SIC: 7629 7389 3825 3672 Electronic equipment repair; inspection & testing services; test equipment for electronic & electrical circuits; printed circuit boards; relays & industrial controls; switchgear & switchboard apparatus

(G-9853)
TMAK INC
Also Called: Quality Industrial Service
200 Winski Dr (46360-4174)
P.O. Box 738 (46361-0738)
PHONE..................................219 874-7661
Fax: 219 874-7684
Timothy Johnson, *President*
Michelle Bazin-Johnson, *Vice Pres*
Joe Schindler, *Research*
Tina Havlin, *Office Mgr*
▲ EMP: 27
SQ FT: 10,700
SALES: 2.4MM Privately Held
WEB: www.mctd.com
SIC: 3544 3599 Special dies & tools; custom machinery

(G-9854)
TRINITY DISPLAYS INC
50 Marine Dr Apt E8 (46360-1309)
PHONE..................................219 201-8733
Robert Swiatek, *CEO*
Martin McGinnis, *CEO*
EMP: 5
SALES (est): 447K Privately Held
SIC: 3999 7389 Advertising display products;

(G-9855)
TRIPLEX PLATING INC
1555 E Us Highway 12 (46360-2002)
PHONE..................................219 879-9607
Fax: 219 879-9607
James A Baldwin, *CEO*
Debra Sydrow, *Admin Sec*
EMP: 40
SQ FT: 28,200
SALES (est): 4.8MM Privately Held
SIC: 3471 Electroplating of metals or formed products

(G-9856)
TT MACHINING & FABRICATING LLC
228 Indiana Highway 212 (46360-2857)
PHONE..................................219 878-0399
Thomas Lynch, *Manager*
EMP: 6
SALES (est): 510K Privately Held
SIC: 3599 Machine & other job shop work

(G-9857)
VANAIR MANUFACTURING INC (PA)
10896 W 300 N (46360-9466)
PHONE..................................219 879-5100
Ralph Kokot, *CEO*
Greg Kokot, *President*
John Graun Sr, *Vice Pres*
Ralph Kokot III, *Vice Pres*
Ted Pulaski, *Vice Pres*
▲ EMP: 112 EST: 1972
SQ FT: 18,000
SALES (est): 20.8MM Privately Held
SIC: 3713 3563 3621 3566 Truck & bus bodies; air & gas compressors including vacuum pumps; motors & generators; speed changers, drives & gears

(G-9858)
VERA BRADLEY INC
505 Lighthouse Pl (46360-3472)
PHONE..................................219 878-1093
Vera Jania, *Branch Mgr*
EMP: 49
SALES (corp-wide): 454.6MM Publicly Held
SIC: 3171 Women's handbags & purses
PA: Vera Bradley, Inc.
12420 Stonebridge Rd
Roanoke IN 46783
877 708-8372

(G-9859)
VITAMINS INC
1700 E Us Highway 12 (46360-2076)
PHONE..................................219 879-7356
Fax: 219 879-4858
Chuck Bilderback, *Production*
Darin Salyer, *Branch Mgr*
Jeff Filipiak, *Manager*
EMP: 24

SALES (corp-wide): 7.4MM Privately Held
WEB: www.vitamins.com
SIC: 2041 2833 5122 2087 Wheat germ; vitamins, natural or synthetic: bulk, uncompounded; drugs, proprietaries & sundries; flavoring extracts & syrups; canned specialties; pharmaceutical preparations
PA: Vitamins, Inc.
315 Fullerton Ave
Carol Stream IL 60188

(G-9860)
WILLIAMS WEST & WITTS PDTS CO
Also Called: Integrative Flavors
3501 W Dunes Hwy (46360-6717)
P.O. Box 209 (46361-0209)
PHONE..................................219 879-8236
Fax: 219 879-8237
Georgeann Quealy, *President*
Brian Quealy, *Exec VP*
Fermin Medina, *Plant Mgr*
Joe Batayeh, *Sales Mgr*
John True, *Director*
EMP: 9
SALES (est): 1.1MM Privately Held
WEB: www.williamswestandwitts.com
SIC: 2034 2099 Dried & dehydrated soup mixes; sauces: gravy, dressing & dip mixes

(G-9861)
WOODLAND LBOR RLTONS CNSULTING
15 Bristol Dr (46360-1977)
PHONE..................................219 879-6095
Douglas Bobillo, *Principal*
EMP: 2
SALES (est): 50.2K Privately Held
SIC: 2499 Wood products

(G-9862)
YACHT BRITE PROFFESIONAL CARE
101 Kenwood Pl (46360-7046)
PHONE..................................219 874-1181
Laura Jahnz, *Owner*
EMP: 8
SALES (est): 543.9K Privately Held
SIC: 3732 Yachts, building & repairing

(G-9863)
ZIP-A-TEE SHIRT INC
120 Glencove Dr (46360-7711)
PHONE..................................219 879-5556
James E Cross, *President*
Linda Cross, *Admin Sec*
EMP: 6
SQ FT: 650
SALES (est): 33.2K Privately Held
SIC: 2253 T-shirts & tops, knit

Michigantown
Clinton County

(G-9864)
CO-ALLIANCE LLP
805 East St (46057-9558)
P.O. Box 26 (46057-0026)
PHONE..................................765 249-2233
Joe Rule, *Branch Mgr*
EMP: 8
SALES (corp-wide): 483.3MM Privately Held
SIC: 5153 5171 5191 2875 Grains; petroleum bulk stations & terminals; feed; fertilizers, mixing only
PA: Co-Alliance, Limited Liability Partnership
5250 E Us Hwy 3
Avon IN 46123
317 745-4491

(G-9865)
CRENSHAW PAVING INC
7304 E County Road 100 N (46057-9774)
PHONE..................................765 249-2342
Robert Crenshaw, *President*
Janet Crenshaw, *Corp Secy*
Bryan Crenshaw, *Vice Pres*
EMP: 8

SALES (est): 1.2MM Privately Held
SIC: 3272 Paving materials, prefabricated concrete; burial vaults, concrete or precast terrazzo; concrete products, precast

Middlebury
Elkhart County

(G-9866)
A & R MACHINE SHOP LLP
14719 County Road 20 (46540-9649)
PHONE..................................574 825-5686
Rudy J Miller, *Partner*
Earnest Lehman, *Partner*
Calvin Miller, *Partner*
Delbert R Miller, *Partner*
Wayne Miller, *Partner*
EMP: 42
SQ FT: 34,000
SALES (est): 6MM Privately Held
SIC: 3599 Machine shop, jobbing & repair

(G-9867)
ABERCROMBIE TEXTILES I LLC
300 Wayne St (46540-9263)
P.O. Box 1140 (46540-1140)
PHONE..................................574 825-9800
Laura Long, *Manager*
EMP: 2
SALES (corp-wide): 5.6MM Privately Held
SIC: 2299 Batting, wadding, padding & fillings
PA: Abercrombie Textiles I, Llc
1322 Mount Sinai Ch Rd
Shelby NC 28152
704 487-1245

(G-9868)
ALL AMERICAN GROUP INC
Shasta Industries
14489 Us Highway 20 (46540-9733)
P.O. Box 30 (46540-0030)
PHONE..................................574 825-8555
Fax: 574 825-9573
Robert Adasiak, *Branch Mgr*
EMP: 268
SQ FT: 80,000
SALES (corp-wide): Privately Held
WEB: www.coachmen.com
SIC: 3792 5012 Travel trailers & campers; recreational vehicles, motor homes & trailers
HQ: All American Group, Inc.
2831 Dexter Dr
Elkhart IN 46514
574 262-0123

(G-9869)
ALL AMERICAN GROUP INC
All American Specialty Vehicle
51165 Greenfield Pkwy (46540-8220)
PHONE..................................574 825-1720
Don Roberts, *Office Mgr*
EMP: 100 Privately Held
SIC: 3716 Motor homes
HQ: All American Group, Inc.
2831 Dexter Dr
Elkhart IN 46514
574 262-0123

(G-9870)
AMERICAN PETROLEUM
11044 County Road 2 (46540-9632)
PHONE..................................269 223-4135
EMP: 2
SALES (est): 90.7K Privately Held
SIC: 2911 Petroleum refining

(G-9871)
ARBOC SPECIALTY VEHICLES LLC
51165 Greenfield Pkwy (46540-8220)
PHONE..................................574 825-1720
Donald Roberts, *CEO*
EMP: 99
SALES: 20.4MM
SALES (corp-wide): 2.3B Privately Held
SIC: 3713 Truck & bus bodies
PA: Nfi Group Inc
711 Kernaghan Ave
Winnipeg MB R2C 3
204 224-1251

(G-9872)
ARBOR INDUSTRIES INC
117 14th Ave (46540-9222)
P.O. Box 313 (46540-0313)
PHONE............................574 825-2375
David Sheeley, *President*
David Baylis, *Vice Pres*
EMP: 20
SQ FT: 24,000
SALES (est): 3.4MM **Privately Held**
SIC: 2421 Custom sawmill; specialty sawmill products; resawing lumber into smaller dimensions; furniture dimension stock, softwood

(G-9873)
ARTISAN INTERIORS INC (PA)
526 S Main St (46540-9701)
P.O. Box 165, Nappanee (46550-0165)
PHONE............................574 825-9494
Fax: 574 825-2878
Jane E Yoder, *President*
Eli Yoder, *Admin Sec*
EMP: 23
SQ FT: 30,000
SALES (est): 6.9MM **Privately Held**
WEB: www.artisan-interiors.com
SIC: 2391 2392 Draperies, plastic & textile: from purchased materials; bedspreads & bed sets: made from purchased materials

(G-9874)
B&J ROCKET AMERICA INC
325 N Main St (46540-9003)
PHONE............................574 825-5802
Andreas Muller, *CEO*
Marcos Guzman, *Plant Mgr*
Caitlin Smith, *Sales Staff*
▲ **EMP:** 20
SQ FT: 38,000
SALES (est): 5.9MM **Privately Held**
SIC: 3469 3599 3544 3398 Stamping metal for the trade; machine shop, jobbing & repair; special dies & tools; metal heat treating; brazing (hardening) of metal; sheet metalwork; tube fabricating (contract bending & shaping)

(G-9875)
CLASSEE VINYL WINDOWS LLC
59323 County Road 35 (46540-8850)
PHONE............................574 825-7863
David Lehman,
Karen Lehman,
EMP: 6
SALES (est): 941.1K **Privately Held**
SIC: 3442 5211 Louver windows, metal; windows, storm: wood or metal

(G-9876)
COACHMEN RECRTL VEHICLES CO
423 N Main St (46540-9218)
Mike Terlep, *Vice Pres*
Colleen Zuhl, *Treasurer*
James A Bartel, *Manager*
Robert Ledbetter, *Admin Sec*
EMP: 7
SALES (est): 825.7K **Privately Held**
SIC: 3711 Bus & other large specialty vehicle assembly

(G-9877)
CORNERSTONE BUSINESS PRTG LLC
510 Skyview Dr (46540-9427)
PHONE............................574 642-4060
EMP: 2
SALES (est): 83.9K **Privately Held**
SIC: 2752 Commercial printing, lithographic

(G-9878)
COUNTRY CORNER WOODWORKS LLC
52133 State Road 13 (46540-9622)
PHONE............................574 825-6782
Lavern Lambright, *Mng Member*
Jerry Bontrager,
EMP: 3
SALES (est): 193.1K **Privately Held**
SIC: 2599 1751 Cabinets, factory; cabinet building & installation

(G-9879)
COUNTY LINE CABINETRY LLC
705 N 1200 W (46540-9301)
PHONE............................574 642-1202
Verlin Lehman, *Principal*
EMP: 4
SALES (est): 387.2K **Privately Held**
SIC: 2434 Wood kitchen cabinets

(G-9880)
CULVER DUCK FARMS INC
12215 County Road 10 (46540-9694)
P.O. Box 910 (46540-0910)
PHONE............................574 825-9537
Fax: 574 825-2613
Herbert R Culver, *President*
Stephanie Isola Torres, *Purch Mgr*
Norma Barrera-Miles, *Human Resources*
Dayton Frey, *Admin Sec*
◆ **EMP:** 200 **EST:** 1977
SQ FT: 35,000
SALES (est): 42.1MM **Privately Held**
WEB: www.culverduck.com
SIC: 2015 Duck slaughtering & processing; poultry slaughtering & processing

(G-9881)
DIAMONDS COMPONETS INC
420 N Main St Ste 6 (46540-8986)
PHONE............................574 358-0452
Eric J Stutzman, *CEO*
EMP: 21
SQ FT: 14,000
SALES: 2.5MM **Privately Held**
SIC: 3715 Truck trailers

(G-9882)
DIRTY SQUEEGEE SCREEN PRTG LLC
57319 County Road 35 (46540-9720)
PHONE............................574 358-0003
Amy Miller, *Principal*
EMP: 2
SALES (est): 288.1K **Privately Held**
SIC: 2752 Commercial printing, lithographic

(G-9883)
ELKHART COUNTY GRAVEL INC
56570 County Road 35 (46540-8755)
PHONE............................574 825-7913
Barney Beer, *Manager*
EMP: 3
SALES (corp-wide): 5.4MM **Privately Held**
SIC: 1442 Sand mining
PA: Elkhart County Gravel Inc
19242 Us Highway 6
New Paris IN 46553
574 831-2815

(G-9884)
ELKHART PLASTICS INC
51703 Packard Dr (46540-9664)
PHONE............................574 825-9797
Fax: 574 825-1129
Jack Welter, *President*
Chuck Huston, *President*
Jeff Giacchino, *Vice Pres*
Jake Hixson, *Natl Sales Mgr*
Jeff Harms, *Maintence Staff*
EMP: 190
SALES (corp-wide): 135.7MM **Privately Held**
SIC: 3089 Plastic processing
PA: Elkhart Plastics, Inc.
3300 N Kenmore St
South Bend IN 46628
574 232-8066

(G-9885)
ESSENHAUS INC
Also Called: Essenhaus Foods
240 W Us Highway 20 (46540-9713)
PHONE............................574 825-6790
Fax: 574 825-0455
Robert Miller, *Ch of Bd*
Lance Miller, *President*
Joel Miller, *Admin Sec*
EMP: 300 **EST:** 1971
SQ FT: 65,000
SALES: 19.3MM **Privately Held**
WEB: www.essenhaus.com
SIC: 5812 2098 Restaurant, family: independent; noodles (e.g. egg, plain & water), dry

(G-9886)
EVERGREEN RECRTL VEHICLES LLC (PA)
Also Called: Evergreen Rv
10758 County Road 2 (46540-9630)
P.O. Box 12 (46540-0012)
PHONE............................574 825-4298
Michael Schoeffler, *CEO*
Doug Lantz,
Kelly Rose,
▼ **EMP:** 18
SQ FT: 1,000
SALES (est): 4.2MM **Privately Held**
SIC: 3792 Travel trailers & campers

(G-9887)
FOREST RIVER INC
Forest River Marine
51773 County Road 39 (46540-9661)
PHONE............................574 389-4636
Fax: 574 825-6170
Eric Rose, *Sales Executive*
Tom McCudby, *Manager*
EMP: 16
SALES (corp-wide): 242.1B **Publicly Held**
SIC: 3792 Travel trailers & campers
HQ: Forest River, Inc.
900 County Road 1 N
Elkhart IN 46514

(G-9888)
FOUR STAR WELDING
11400 W 300n (46540)
PHONE............................574 825-3856
EMP: 2
SALES (est): 111.1K **Privately Held**
SIC: 7692 Welding repair

(G-9889)
GOHN BROS MANUFACTURING CO
105 S Main St (46540-4001)
P.O. Box 1110 (46540-1110)
PHONE............................574 825-2400
John Swartzentruber, *Owner*
EMP: 8
SQ FT: 6,000
SALES (est): 440K **Privately Held**
SIC: 2326 5611 5331 5949 Work apparel, except uniforms; clothing accessories: men's & boys'; variety stores; fabric stores piece goods

(G-9890)
GRAND DESIGN RV LLC
Also Called: Black Bear Recrtl Vehicles
11333 County Road 2 (46540-9632)
PHONE............................574 825-8000
Donald Clark, *President*
EMP: 625
SALES (est): 53.6MM
SALES (corp-wide): 1.5B **Publicly Held**
SIC: 7519 3799 Recreational vehicle rental; recreational vehicles
PA: Winnebago Industries, Inc.
605 W Crystal Lake Rd
Forest City IA 50436
641 585-3535

(G-9891)
IDEAL COATINGS LLC
11431 County Road 10 (46540-8927)
PHONE............................574 358-0182
EMP: 2
SALES (est): 123.8K **Privately Held**
SIC: 3479 Metal coating & allied service

(G-9892)
INDIANA GALVANIZING LLC
51702 Lovejoy (46540-9591)
PHONE............................574 822-9102
John Monnig, *President*
EMP: 35
SQ FT: 95
SALES: 5MM **Privately Held**
SIC: 3479 Hot dip coating of metals or formed products

(G-9893)
INDIANA WOOD PRODUCTS INC
58228 County Road 43 (46540-9555)
P.O. Box 1168 (46540-1168)
PHONE............................574 825-2129
Daniel Sherman, *Ch of Bd*

Mary Lou Hetler, *President*
Richard A Hetler Jr, *President*
Rick Hetler, *Vice Pres*
Jennifer Davis, *Treasurer*
EMP: 85
SQ FT: 55,000
SALES (est): 15.5MM **Privately Held**
SIC: 2426 2448 2421 2441 Lumber, hardwood dimension; pallets, wood; skids, wood; cargo containers, wood; sawmills & planing mills, general; lumber: rough, sawed or planed; specialty sawmill products; sawdust, shavings & wood chips; nailed wood boxes & shook

(G-9894)
IP MOULDING INC
219 W Us Highway 20 (46540-9713)
PHONE............................574 825-5845
John Young, *CEO*
EMP: 83 **EST:** 2013
SALES (est): 15.4MM **Privately Held**
SIC: 2821 Plastics materials & resins
PA: Inteplast Group Corporation
9 Peach Tree Hill Rd
Livingston NJ 07039

(G-9895)
IZZY PLUS
Also Called: Izzy Better Together
11451 Harter Dr (46540-9663)
PHONE............................574 821-1200
Chuck Saylor, *CEO*
▲ **EMP:** 9 **EST:** 2009
SALES (est): 1.2MM **Privately Held**
SIC: 2521 5712 Wood office furniture; furniture stores

(G-9896)
JAYCO INC (HQ)
Also Called: Bottom Line Rv
903 S Main St (46540-8529)
P.O. Box 460 (46540-0460)
PHONE............................574 825-5861
Fax: 574 825-7354
Derald Bontrager, *President*
Richardson James, *General Mgr*
Keith Altiere, *Maint Spvr*
Laren Stayton, *Purch Mgr*
Angela Baker, *Purch Agent*
▼ **EMP:** 1550
SQ FT: 700,000
SALES (est): 904.5MM
SALES (corp-wide): 7.2B **Publicly Held**
WEB: www.jayco.com
SIC: 5013 3716 3792 Trailer parts & accessories; motor homes; recreational van conversion (self-propelled), factory basis; house trailers, except as permanent dwellings; campers, for mounting on trucks; camping trailers & chassis
PA: Thor Industries, Inc.
601 E Beardsley Ave
Elkhart IN 46514
574 970-7460

(G-9897)
JOMAR MACHINING & FABG INC
13393 County Road 22 (46540-9039)
PHONE............................574 825-9837
Lavon Detweiler, *President*
Geff Fisher, *Corp Secy*
Matt Troyer, *CFO*
Rachel Lee, *Manager*
EMP: 30
SQ FT: 15,700
SALES (est): 6.4MM **Privately Held**
SIC: 3599 7692 3594 1799 Machine shop, jobbing & repair; welding repair; fluid power pumps & motors; welding on site

(G-9898)
JSJ FURNITURE CORPORATION
Also Called: Zoom Seating
11451 Harter Dr (46540-9663)
PHONE............................256 768-2871
Chuck Saylor, *CEO*
EMP: 109
SALES (corp-wide): 596.1MM **Privately Held**
WEB: www.harter.com
SIC: 2531 Stadium seating; bleacher seating, portable; seats, miscellaneous public conveyances

HQ: Jsj Furniture Corporation
    17237 Van Wagoner Rd
    Spring Lake MI 49456
    616 847-6534

(G-9899)
JSJ FURNITURE CORPORATION
Harter
11451 Harter Dr (46540-9663)
PHONE....................................574 825-5871
Chuck Saylor, *CEO*
EMP: 140
SALES (corp-wide): 596.1MM **Privately Held**
WEB: www.harter.com
SIC: 2522 2521 5021 Office furniture, except wood; wood office furniture; office furniture
HQ: Jsj Furniture Corporation
    17237 Van Wagoner Rd
    Spring Lake MI 49456
    616 847-6534

(G-9900)
L & W ENGINEERING INC
107 Industrial Pkwy E (46540-8511)
PHONE....................................574 825-5351
Fax: 574 825-1006
Wilbur Bontrager, *Ch of Bd*
Roger Huffman, *President*
Kennard Weaver, *Corp Secy*
Robert M Sutter, *Vice Pres*
EMP: 80
SQ FT: 100,000
SALES (est): 22.5MM **Privately Held**
WEB: www.lw-eng.com
SIC: 3714 3429 3499 3498 Motor vehicle body components & frame; manufactured hardware (general); motor vehicle hardware; bicycle racks, automotive; metal ladders; fabricated pipe & fittings; sheet metalwork; fabricated structural metal

(G-9901)
LANE SHADY WELDING
56322 County Road 35 (46540-8753)
PHONE....................................574 825-5553
James E Miller, *Administration*
EMP: 5
SALES (est): 209.8K **Privately Held**
SIC: 7692 Welding repair

(G-9902)
LEGGETT & PLATT INCORPORATED
Leggett & Platt 0168
402 N Main St (46540-9216)
P.O. Box 70 (46540-0070)
PHONE....................................574 825-9561
EMP: 142
SQ FT: 2,000
SALES (corp-wide): 3.7B **Publicly Held**
SIC: 2542 Mfg Partitions/Fixtures-Non-wood
PA: Leggett & Platt, Incorporated
    1 Leggett Rd
    Carthage MO 64836
    417 358-8131

(G-9903)
LGS PACE INTERNATIONAL INC
Also Called: Look Trailers
11550 Harter Dr (46540-9663)
PHONE....................................574 848-5665
EMP: 2
SALES (est): 159.4K **Privately Held**
SIC: 3792 Mfg Travel Trailers/Campers

(G-9904)
LIPPERT COMPONENTS INC
51040 Greenfield Pkwy (46540-8981)
PHONE....................................574 312-7445
Fax: 574 825-3797
Steve Slowki, *Manager*
EMP: 100
SALES (corp-wide): 2.1B **Publicly Held**
WEB: www.lci1.com
SIC: 3711 3469 3444 3714 Chassis, motor vehicle; stamping metal for the trade; metal roofing & roof drainage equipment; motor vehicle parts & accessories
HQ: Lippert Components, Inc.
    3501 County Road 6 E
    Elkhart IN 46514
    800 551-9149

(G-9905)
LOUISIANA-PACIFIC CORPORATION
Also Called: LP Middlebury
219 W Us Highway 20 (46540-9713)
PHONE....................................574 825-5845
Fax: 574 825-6595
Mercer Dave, *CEO*
EMP: 100
SALES (corp-wide): 2.7B **Publicly Held**
WEB: www.lpcorp.com
SIC: 2431 Moldings & baseboards, ornamental & trim
PA: Louisiana-Pacific Corporation
    414 Union St Ste 2000
    Nashville TN 37219
    615 986-5600

(G-9906)
MIDDLEBURY CHEESE COMPANY LLC (HQ)
Also Called: Deutsch Kase Haus Inc
11275 W 250 N (46540-7708)
PHONE....................................574 825-9511
Fax: 574 825-1102
Richard Guggisber, *President*
EMP: 35
SQ FT: 40,000
SALES (est): 6.4MM
SALES (corp-wide): 11.2MM **Privately Held**
WEB: www.guggisberg.com
SIC: 2022 Cheese spreads, dips, pastes & other cheese products
PA: Guggisberg Cheese, Inc.
    5060 State Route 557
    Millersburg OH 44654
    330 893-2550

(G-9907)
MIDDLEBURY HARDWOOD PDTS INC (HQ)
101 Joan Dr (46540)
PHONE....................................574 825-9524
Chuck Lamb, *CEO*
Charles E Lamb, *President*
Mike Wagner, *President*
Al Herzog, *Production*
Sean Nolan, *Purch Mgr*
▲ EMP: 135
SQ FT: 2,000
SALES (est): 22.5MM
SALES (corp-wide): 1.6B **Publicly Held**
WEB: www.middleburyhardwoodproducts.com
SIC: 2431 2541 2511 1751 Doors & door parts & trim, wood; door frames, wood; cabinets, except refrigerated: show, display, etc.: wood; chairs, household, except upholstered: wood; tables, household: wood; cabinet & finish carpentry
PA: Patrick Industries, Inc.
    107 W Franklin St
    Elkhart IN 46516
    574 294-7511

(G-9908)
MILLERS MILL
55514 County Road 8 (46540-9539)
PHONE....................................574 825-2010
Alta Miller, *Owner*
EMP: 6
SALES: 60K **Privately Held**
WEB: www.millersmill.com
SIC: 2099 2033 Cider, nonalcoholic; canned fruits & specialties

(G-9909)
MILLERS SUPERIOR ENTPS INC (PA)
Also Called: Cargo Express
11550 Harter Dr (46540-9663)
PHONE....................................877 475-5665
Lyle Miller, *President*
John Miller Jr, *Vice Pres*
EMP: 15
SQ FT: 93,500
SALES (est): 8.6MM **Privately Held**
WEB: www.cargoexpress.com
SIC: 3715 Demountable cargo containers

(G-9910)
MILLERS WINDMILL SERVICE
Also Called: Sam's Windmill Service
14386 County Road 14 (46540-9527)
PHONE....................................574 825-2877
Duane Miller, *Owner*
EMP: 4
SALES: 240K **Privately Held**
SIC: 3523 Windmills for pumping water, agricultural

(G-9911)
MILLERS WOODNTHINGS INC
11894 County Road 14 (46540-9642)
P.O. Box 725 (46540-0725)
PHONE....................................574 825-2996
Fax: 574 825-7967
Jerry Miller, *President*
EMP: 13
SALES (est): 800K **Privately Held**
SIC: 2511 2499 End tables: wood; coffee tables: wood; tables, household: wood; chairs, household, except upholstered: wood; decorative wood & woodwork

(G-9912)
NRC MODIFICATIONS INC
51045 Greenfield Pkwy (46540-8982)
PHONE....................................574 825-3646
Fax: 574 825-3586
Nick Cook, *President*
J Michael Lapp, *Vice Pres*
Gerald Flack, *Plant Mgr*
Jerry Flack, *Prdtn Mgr*
EMP: 14
SQ FT: 20,000
SALES (est): 2.4MM **Privately Held**
WEB: www.nrcmod.com
SIC: 3713 3711 Truck bodies (motor vehicles); motor vehicles & car bodies

(G-9913)
OLD HOOSIER MEATS
101 Wayne St (46540-9221)
PHONE....................................574 825-2940
Len Miller, *Owner*
EMP: 5
SALES (est): 220.4K **Privately Held**
SIC: 2011 Meat by-products from meat slaughtered on site

(G-9914)
PACE AMERICAN ENTERPRISES INC (HQ)
11550 Harter Dr (46540-9663)
PHONE....................................800 247-5767
Fax: 574 825-5409
James R Tennant, *CEO*
Jack Cordan, *President*
Richard J Mullin, *VP Finance*
Kendall Miller, *Info Tech Dir*
Peter Y Lee, *Admin Sec*
EMP: 45
SQ FT: 400,000
SALES (est): 34.6MM
SALES (corp-wide): 13.3B **Privately Held**
WEB: www.paceamerican.com
SIC: 3715 Demountable cargo containers
PA: Sun Capital Partners, Inc.
    5200 Town Center Cir # 400
    Boca Raton FL 33486
    561 962-3400

(G-9915)
PUMPKIN PATCH MARKET INC
10532 Us Highway 20 (46540-9557)
PHONE....................................574 825-3312
Glen Miller, *President*
Lyle Chupp, *Vice Pres*
Janice Miller, *Treasurer*
EMP: 5
SALES (est): 500K **Privately Held**
WEB: www.pumpkinpatchmarket.com
SIC: 2491 2434 2499 Wood products, creosoted; wood kitchen cabinets; decorative wood & woodwork

(G-9916)
PUMPKINVINE QUILTING INC
500 Spring Valley Dr # 3 (46540-9281)
PHONE....................................574 825-1151
Dawn Briskie, *Principal*
EMP: 2
SALES (est): 92.9K **Privately Held**
SIC: 5949 2395 Fabric stores piece goods; quilted fabrics or cloth

(G-9917)
ROUND TWO BEGINS CORPORATION
300 Wayne St (46540-9263)
PHONE....................................574 825-9800
John Regan, *President*
EMP: 3
SALES (est): 212.8K **Privately Held**
SIC: 2241 Bindings, textile

(G-9918)
SHOWHAULERS TRUCKS INC
114 Industrial Pkwy E (46540-8510)
P.O. Box 9 (46540-0009)
PHONE....................................574 825-6764
Kermit L Troyer, *President*
Chad Troyer, *Admin Sec*
EMP: 35
SQ FT: 23,500
SALES: 12MM **Privately Held**
WEB: www.showhauler.com
SIC: 3799 Recreational vehicles

(G-9919)
SONNER INDUSTRIES LLC
58639 County Road 35 (46540-8817)
PHONE....................................574 370-9387
Jacob Sonner, *Principal*
EMP: 2
SALES (est): 97.3K **Privately Held**
SIC: 3999 Manufacturing industries

(G-9920)
STALTER GLASS INC
400 N Main St (46540-9216)
P.O. Box 248 (46540-0248)
PHONE....................................574 825-2225
Fax: 574 825-2225
Dennis Stalter, *President*
Richard Stalter, *Vice Pres*
EMP: 4 EST: 1947
SQ FT: 3,600
SALES (est): 509.2K **Privately Held**
SIC: 1793 3423 Glass & glazing work; cutters, glass

(G-9921)
STARCRAFT RV INC
903 S Main St (46540-8529)
P.O. Box 460 (46540-0460)
PHONE....................................800 945-4787
Fax: 260 593-2579
Donald Walter, *President*
Fred A Davis, *Principal*
Bob Miller, *Regl Sales Mgr*
Aaron Mortrud, *Regl Sales Mgr*
Steve Schumacher, *Regl Sales Mgr*
◆ EMP: 386
SQ FT: 282,000
SALES (est): 46.6MM
SALES (corp-wide): 7.2B **Publicly Held**
WEB: www.starcraftrv.com
SIC: 3792 Travel trailers & campers; tent-type camping trailers; camping trailers & chassis; campers, for mounting on trucks
HQ: Jayco, Inc.
    903 S Main St
    Middlebury IN 46540
    574 825-5861

(G-9922)
STEELMASTER MACHINE & TL CORP
106 Industrial Pkwy E (46540-8510)
PHONE....................................574 825-7670
Fax: 574 825-2419
Paul Culp, *President*
Kathy Culp, *Corp Secy*
EMP: 15
SALES (est): 2.5MM **Privately Held**
SIC: 3469 Stamping metal for the trade

(G-9923)
WARD INDUSTRIES INC
58582 State Road 13 (46540-8805)
PHONE....................................574 825-2548
Fax: 574 825-5645
Derek G Ward, *President*
EMP: 11
SQ FT: 20,000

SALES (est): 1.2MM **Privately Held**
WEB: www.wardindustries.com
SIC: **3648** 3645 3446 3993 Lanterns:
electric, gas, carbide, kerosene or gasoline; decorative area lighting fixtures; outdoor lighting equipment; residential
lighting fixtures; lamp posts, metal; signs
& advertising specialties; commercial indusl & institutional electric lighting fixtures; manufactured hardware (general)

(G-9924)
WASHBURN HEATING & AC
Also Called: Honeywell Authorized Dealer
54761 County Road 8 (46540-9516)
P.O. Box 1428 (46540-1428)
PHONE......................................574 825-7697
Fax: 574 825-0135
Eugene Washburn, *President*
Darcy Washburn, *Admin Sec*
EMP: 4
SALES (est): 500K **Privately Held**
WEB: www.washburnair.com
SIC: **3585** 1711 Heating & air conditioning
combination units; heating & air condition-
ing contractors

(G-9925)
WHITETAIL HEARTBEAT
61755 State Road 13 (46540-9758)
PHONE......................................260 336-1052
Faron Yoder, *Principal*
EMP: 3
SALES (est): 171K **Privately Held**
SIC: **2721** Periodicals: publishing only

(G-9926)
WINNEBAGO OF INDIANA LLC
Also Called: Sunnybrook Rv
201 14th Ave (46540-9647)
PHONE......................................574 825-5250
Fax: 574 825-5433
John Hernandez, *President*
Elvie Frey, *President*
Chad Boardrow, *Purchasing*
Sheldon Troyer, *Info Tech Mgr*
▼ EMP: 200
SALES (est): 65.3MM
SALES (corp-wide): 1.5B **Publicly Held**
SIC: **3792** Travel trailers & campers; trailer
coaches, automobile; travel trailer chas-
sis; campers, for mounting on trucks
PA: Winnebago Industries, Inc.
605 W Crystal Lake Rd
Forest City IA 50436
641 585-3535

(G-9927)
WOODLAND PARK INC
111 Crystal Heights Blvd (46540-8553)
P.O. Box 1309 (46540-1309)
PHONE......................................574 825-2104
Fax: 574 825-2487
Ernie Yoder, *President*
Derald Bontrager, *Vice Pres*
Edna Yoder, *Treasurer*
Nancy Kauffman, *Admin Sec*
EMP: 54
SQ FT: 25,000
SALES (est): 9.1MM **Privately Held**
WEB: www.woodland-park.com
SIC: **2451** Mobile homes, personal or pri-
vate use

(G-9928)
YODER & SONS
13781 County Road 20 # 1 (46540-9644)
PHONE......................................574 642-1196
Abraham J Yoder, *Partner*
Allen Yoder, *Partner*
Marlin Yoder, *Partner*
EMP: 3 EST: 1978
SQ FT: 1,000
SALES (est): 438K **Privately Held**
SIC: **3599** Machine shop, jobbing & repair

(G-9929)
YODER WOODWORKING
60157 County Road 35 (46540-9750)
PHONE......................................574 825-0402
Lavon Yoder, *Principal*
EMP: 2
SALES (est): 175.6K **Privately Held**
SIC: **2431** Millwork

(G-9930)
YODERS MONUMENTS INC ✪
409 Bristol Ave (46540-9049)
PHONE......................................260 768-7934
Lydia Myoder, *Admin Sec*
EMP: 2 EST: 2017
SALES (est): 109K **Privately Held**
SIC: **3272** Monuments & grave markers,
except terrazo

(G-9931)
ZIGGITY SYSTEMS INC
101 Industrial Pkwy E (46540-8549)
PHONE......................................574 825-5849
Fax: 574 825-7674
Dale Hostetler, *President*
Kelvin Wittmer, *General Mgr*
Robert Hostetler, *Vice Pres*
EMP: 40
SALES (est): 9.1MM **Privately Held**
WEB: www.ziggity.com
SIC: **3523** Poultry brooders, feeders & wa-
terers

(G-9932)
ZOOM SEATING
11451 Harter Dr (46540-9663)
PHONE......................................574 825-3368
EMP: 2
SALES (est): 90.4K **Privately Held**
SIC: **2599** Furniture & fixtures

Middletown
Henry County

(G-9933)
BELGIAN HORSE WINERY LLC
7122 W County Road 625 N (47356-9750)
PHONE......................................765 779-3002
Harry Harter, *Principal*
EMP: 2
SALES (est): 124.9K **Privately Held**
SIC: **2084** Wines

(G-9934)
**DOWN-LITE INTERNATIONAL
INC**
8984 W State Road 236 (47356-9326)
PHONE......................................513 229-3696
James Lockhart, *Principal*
David Lueder, *Vice Pres*
▲ EMP: 4
SALES (est): 93.1K **Privately Held**
SIC: **2211** Bedspreads, cotton

(G-9935)
EVART ENGINEERING CO INC
1340 State St (47356-9357)
P.O. Box 10 (47356-0010)
PHONE......................................765 354-2232
Fax: 765 354-6027
Maurice Kemerly, *President*
Carol Kemerly, *Corp Secy*
Brett J Kemerly, *Vice Pres*
Jim Coomer, *Sales Mgr*
EMP: 11 EST: 1953
SQ FT: 18,400
SALES (est): 4MM **Privately Held**
SIC: **3599** 3544 Custom machinery; spe-
cial dies & tools; jigs & fixtures

(G-9936)
HOLIC LLC
710 Norfleet Dr W (47356-9551)
PHONE......................................765 444-8115
Frances Torres, *Mng Member*
Antony Torres,
EMP: 14 EST: 2013
SQ FT: 36,000
SALES: 5MM **Privately Held**
SIC: **2033** 8742 Chili sauce, tomato: pack-
aged in cans, jars, etc.; marketing con-
sulting services

(G-9937)
**LIBERTY TOOL AND
ENGINEERING**
277 N 11th St (47356-1707)
P.O. Box 67 (47356-0067)
PHONE......................................765 354-9550
Fax: 765 354-6035
Richard Schwalm, *President*

Patricia Schwalm, *Vice Pres*
EMP: 5
SQ FT: 3,000
SALES: 250K **Privately Held**
SIC: **3599** 3545 3544 Machine shop, job-
bing & repair; machine tool accessories;
special dies, tools, jigs & fixtures

(G-9938)
METAL ART INC
7730 N Raider Rd (47356-9401)
P.O. Box 191 (47356-0191)
PHONE......................................765 354-4571
Lisa Anderson, *President*
Danny Barrett, *Foreman/Supr*
EMP: 5
SALES (est): 967.6K **Privately Held**
SIC: **3444** Sheet metalwork

(G-9939)
MUDHOLE MACHINE SHOP LLC
5121 N County Road 200 W (47356-9417)
PHONE......................................765 533-4228
Steven Province, *Principal*
EMP: 2 EST: 2015
SALES (est): 106K **Privately Held**
SIC: **3599** Machine shop, jobbing & repair

(G-9940)
**R & Y PROFESSIONAL TOOLS
LLC**
102 S 15th St (47356-9335)
PHONE......................................765 354-9076
Ronald Helsley, *Principal*
EMP: 2
SALES (est): 98.1K **Privately Held**
SIC: **3599** Industrial machinery

(G-9941)
**SLICK ENGINEERING
INDUSTRIES**
8768 W State Road 236 (47356-9326)
P.O. Box 39 (47356-0039)
PHONE......................................765 354-2822
Fax: 765 354-4759
Richard Russell, *President*
Ruthanne Russell, *Corp Secy*
Ruth Anne Fattic, *Admin Sec*
EMP: 8 EST: 1947
SQ FT: 7,700
SALES (est): 600K **Privately Held**
WEB: www.slickeng.com
SIC: **3599** 3545 3544 Machine shop, job-
bing & repair; machine tool accessories;
special dies, tools, jigs & fixtures

(G-9942)
TRACE ENGINEERING INC
400 Locust St (47356-1433)
P.O. Box 159 (47356-0159)
PHONE......................................765 354-4351
Fax: 765 354-2033
Kaye Stephenson, *President*
Edgar Dunkin, *Vice Pres*
Beth Dunkin, *Admin Sec*
EMP: 8
SQ FT: 7,500
SALES: 900K **Privately Held**
SIC: **3599** Machine shop, jobbing & repair

(G-9943)
**TUFF STUFF SALES AND SVC
INC**
8520 W State Road 236 (47356-9326)
PHONE......................................765 354-4151
Robert Butterfield, *Principal*
EMP: 3 EST: 2016
SALES (est): 172.8K **Privately Held**
SIC: **3499** Safes & vaults, metal

Milan
Ripley County

(G-9944)
GERALD S ZINS
12988 E State Road 48 (47031-9679)
PHONE......................................812 623-4980
Gerald S Zins, *Principal*
EMP: 2
SALES (est): 137.1K **Privately Held**
SIC: **3713** 7389 Dump truck bodies;

(G-9945)
MILAN FOOD BANK
Also Called: Wayne Meats
201 Josephine St (47031-1107)
P.O. Box 648 (47031-0648)
PHONE......................................812 654-3682
Wayne Worhrig, *Owner*
EMP: 6
SALES (est): 320K **Privately Held**
SIC: **2011** 5812 Meat packing plants;
caterers

(G-9946)
ROEDER INDUSTRIES
406 W Carr St (47031-1114)
P.O. Box 728 (47031-0728)
PHONE......................................812 654-3322
Russ Roeder, *Owner*
EMP: 6
SQ FT: 14,000
SALES: 1MM **Privately Held**
SIC: **3541** 3542 5084 Machine tools,
metal cutting type; presses: forming,
stamping, punching, sizing (machine
tools); machine tools & accessories

(G-9947)
UNITED METHODIST PUBG HSE
6358 E County Road 50 N (47031-9001)
PHONE......................................812 654-1325
EMP: 231
SALES (corp-wide): 45.9MM **Privately
Held**
SIC: **2731** Books: publishing & printing
PA: The United Methodist Publishing House
2222 Rosa L Parks Blvd
Nashville TN 37228
615 749-6000

Milford
Kosciusko County

(G-9948)
AGILE MFG INC
720 Industrial Park Rd (46542)
P.O. Box 2000 (46542-2000)
PHONE......................................417 845-6065
▲ EMP: 6
SALES (est): 768.8K **Privately Held**
SIC: **3999** Manufacturing industries

(G-9949)
BISON COACH LLC
1002 N Old State Road 15 (46542-9140)
PHONE......................................574 658-4161
Fax: 574 658-4476
Scott Tuttle, *President*
EMP: 25
SALES (est): 6.4MM
SALES (corp-wide): 7.2B **Publicly Held**
SIC: **3792** Travel trailers & campers
PA: Thor Industries, Inc.
601 E Beardsley Ave
Elkhart IN 46514
574 970-7460

(G-9950)
BISON HORSE TRAILERS LLC
804 S Higbee St (46542-9608)
PHONE......................................574 658-4161
Joshua Chipps, *Principal*
EMP: 2
SALES (est): 116.1K **Privately Held**
SIC: **3716** Motor homes

(G-9951)
CTB INC
Also Called: Chore-Time Plty Prod Systems
410 N Higbee St (46542-9147)
P.O. Box 2000 (46542-2000)
PHONE......................................574 658-4191
Fax: 574 658-3220
Chris Stoler, *Sales Mgr*
EMP: 22
SALES (corp-wide): 242.1B **Publicly
Held**
SIC: **3523** Farm machinery & equipment
HQ: Ctb, Inc.
611 N Higbee St
Milford IN 46542
574 658-4191

(G-9952)
CTB INC (HQ)
Also Called: Chore-Time Plty Prod Systems
611 N Higbee St (46542-9752)
P.O. Box 2000 (46542-2000)
PHONE..............................574 658-4191
Fax: 574 658-4133
Victor A Mancinelli, *CEO*
Tom Brackett, *President*
Douglas J Niemeyer, *President*
Randy S Eveler, *Vice Pres*
William Mabee, *Vice Pres*
◆ **EMP:** 700
SQ FT: 600,000
SALES (est): 333.4MM
SALES (corp-wide): 242.1B **Publicly Held**
WEB: www.ctbinc.com
SIC: 3443 3523 Bins, prefabricated metal plate; farm storage tanks, metal plate; hog feeding, handling & watering equipment; poultry brooders, feeders & waterers
PA: Berkshire Hathaway Inc.
3555 Farnam St Ste 1140
Omaha NE 68131
402 346-1400

(G-9953)
CTB INC
Chore Time/Brock International
611 N Kigby St (46542)
P.O. Box 2000 (46542-2000)
PHONE..............................574 658-9323
EMP: 6
SALES (corp-wide): 242.1B **Publicly Held**
SIC: 3443 Bins, prefabricated metal plate; farm storage tanks, metal plate
HQ: Ctb, Inc.
611 N Higbee St
Milford IN 46542
574 658-4191

(G-9954)
CTB INC
Chore Time
410 N Higbee St (46542-9147)
P.O. Box 2000 (46542-2000)
PHONE..............................574 658-4191
Jeff Miller, *Vice Pres*
EMP: 5
SALES (corp-wide): 242.1B **Publicly Held**
SIC: 3443 Bins, prefabricated metal plate
HQ: Ctb, Inc.
611 N Higbee St
Milford IN 46542
574 658-4191

(G-9955)
CTB MN INVESTMENT CO INC (HQ)
611 N Higbee St (46542-9752)
P.O. Box 2000 (46542-2000)
PHONE..............................574 658-4191
Victor A Mancinelli, *President*
Don Steinhilber, *CFO*
Michael J Kissane, *Admin Sec*
◆ **EMP:** 50
SQ FT: 611,000
SALES (est): 110.3MM
SALES (corp-wide): 242.1B **Publicly Held**
WEB: www.brockmfg.com
SIC: 3443 3523 3564 3556 Farm storage tanks, metal plate; farm machinery & equipment; blowers & fans; food products machinery; prefabricated metal buildings
PA: Berkshire Hathaway Inc.
3555 Farnam St Ste 1140
Omaha NE 68131
402 346-1400

(G-9956)
M M PRINTING PLUS
634 E Beer Rd (46542-9057)
PHONE..............................574 658-9345
Michelle Hurst, *Owner*
EMP: 2
SALES (est): 137.1K **Privately Held**
SIC: 2752 Commercial printing, lithographic

(G-9957)
MAPLE LEAF FARMS INC (HQ)
Also Called: Serenade Foods
9166 N 200 E (46542-9722)
P.O. Box 167, Leesburg (46538-0167)
PHONE..............................574 453-4500
Fax: 574 658-2208
Terry L Tucker, *Ch of Bd*
John Tucker, *President*
Robert Ditto, *Vice Pres*
Don Ratliff, *VP Opers*
Don Slater, *Opers Staff*
◆ **EMP:** 650
SALES (est): 25.5MM **Privately Held**
WEB: www.mapleleaffarms.com
SIC: 0259 2015 Duck farm; duck slaughtering & processing
PA: Maple Leaf, Inc.
101 E Church St
Leesburg IN 46538
574 453-4455

(G-9958)
MAPLE LEAF FARMS INC
Also Called: Serenade Foods
9179 N 200 E (46542-9722)
PHONE..............................574 658-4121
Fax: 574 658-2246
EMP: 7
SALES (corp-wide): 25.5MM **Privately Held**
SIC: 2015 Duck slaughtering & processing
HQ: Maple Leaf Farms, Inc.
9166 N 200 E
Milford IN 46542
574 453-4500

(G-9959)
MILLER CANVAS SHOP
13279 N 400 W (46542-9609)
PHONE..............................574 658-3563
Ernest Miller, *Owner*
EMP: 4
SALES (est): 368.6K **Privately Held**
SIC: 2394 Canvas & related products

(G-9960)
MILLERS CUSTOM CARE CANDES
12711 N 400 W (46542-9644)
PHONE..............................574 658-4976
Willis Miller, *Owner*
EMP: 2 EST: 2008
SALES (est): 208K **Privately Held**
SIC: 2211 Canvas

(G-9961)
PHEND AND BROWN INC (PA)
367 E 1250 N (46542-9052)
P.O. Box 150 (46542-0150)
PHONE..............................574 658-4166
Daniel F Brown, *President*
Andrew J Brown, *Vice Pres*
Douglas V Brown, *Vice Pres*
Douglas Brown, *Vice Pres*
Don Miller, *QA Dir*
EMP: 48 EST: 1922
SQ FT: 17,084
SALES: 31.5MM **Privately Held**
WEB: www.phend-brown.com
SIC: 1611 1442 1623 1794 Highway & street paving contractor; resurfacing contractor; gravel & pebble mining; water, sewer & utility lines; excavation work

(G-9962)
PURINA ANIMAL NUTRITION LLC
346 W 1350 N (46542-9187)
PHONE..............................574 658-4137
Larry Moorman, *Manager*
EMP: 35
SALES (corp-wide): 12.8B **Privately Held**
SIC: 2048 Prepared feeds
HQ: Purina Animal Nutrition Llc
1080 County Road F W
Shoreview MN 55126

(G-9963)
PURINA MILLS LLC
346 W 1350 N (46542-9187)
PHONE..............................574 658-4137
Fax: 574 658-4159
Judy Burkins, *Principal*
Larry G Moorman, *Manager*
EMP: 21

SALES (corp-wide): 12.8B **Privately Held**
WEB: www.purina-mills.com
SIC: 2048 Prepared feeds
HQ: Purina Mills, Llc
555 Maryvle Univ Dr 200
Saint Louis MO 63141

(G-9964)
ROYAL OUTDOOR PRODUCTS INC
401 E Syracuse St (46542-3010)
P.O. Box 610, Marion VA (24354-0610)
PHONE..............................574 658-9442
Paul Carrico, *CEO*
Dennis Yoder, *President*
EMP: 101
SQ FT: 135,000
SALES (est): 15.1MM **Privately Held**
WEB: www.royalcrownltd.com
SIC: 3089 Plastic hardware & building products; hardware, plastic

(G-9965)
SLABAUGH WELDING LLC
3942 W 1350 N (46542)
PHONE..............................574 773-5410
Nelson D Slabaugh, *Principal*
EMP: 5
SALES (est): 231.4K **Privately Held**
SIC: 7692 Welding repair

(G-9966)
VANS CABINET SHOP
1704 E Mock Rd (46542-9732)
PHONE..............................574 658-9625
Fax: 574 658-4025
Steve Van Laningham, *President*
Steve Vanlaningham, *President*
Susan Vanlaningham, *Admin Sec*
EMP: 4
SQ FT: 3,200
SALES (est): 395.9K **Privately Held**
SIC: 2434 5712 Wood kitchen cabinets; cabinet work, custom

(G-9967)
ZIMMERMAN-NEWCOMER GRAVEL
1775 E 1150 N (46542-9011)
PHONE..............................574 658-4063
Gary Newcomer, *Owner*
EMP: 3
SALES (est): 266.9K **Privately Held**
SIC: 1442 Construction sand & gravel

Millersburg
Elkhart County

(G-9968)
A & M WOODWORKING
5545 S 1125 W (46543-9546)
PHONE..............................574 642-4555
Anthony Yoder,
EMP: 4
SALES (est): 296.3K **Privately Held**
SIC: 2431 Millwork

(G-9969)
CUSTOM WOOD FINISHING
10561 County Road 44 (46543-9708)
PHONE..............................574 642-1213
Glen Graber, *Principal*
EMP: 2 EST: 2008
SALES (est): 182K **Privately Held**
SIC: 2431 Millwork

(G-9970)
HOOSIER CUSTOM WOODWORKING
67348 County Road 33 (46543-9407)
PHONE..............................574 642-3764
Myron Slabach, *Owner*
EMP: 2 EST: 2010
SALES (est): 158.3K **Privately Held**
SIC: 2431 Millwork

(G-9971)
LAWNCREATIONS LLC
10592 County Rd (46543)
PHONE..............................574 536-1546
Adrian Fry,
Arlin Fry,

EMP: 2
SALES: 12K **Privately Held**
SIC: 3648 Decorative area lighting fixtures

(G-9972)
ROCK RUN INDUSTRIES LLC
11665 W 600 S (46543-9611)
PHONE..............................574 361-0848
Freeman D Schlabach, *Principal*
Gary Yoder, *VP Sales*
EMP: 45 EST: 2009
SALES: 13.7MM **Privately Held**
SIC: 3446 Architectural metalwork

(G-9973)
SCHWARTZ WOODWORKING
4810 S 950 W (46543-9607)
PHONE..............................260 593-3193
Marvin Schwartz, *Owner*
EMP: 4
SALES (est): 271.2K **Privately Held**
SIC: 2431 Millwork

(G-9974)
STONEY CREEK WASH MACHINE SHOP
66365 E County Line Rd (46543-9742)
PHONE..............................574 642-1155
EMP: 2
SALES (est): 154.7K **Privately Held**
SIC: 3599 Machine shop, jobbing & repair

(G-9975)
STONEY CREEK WINERY
10315 County Road 146 (46543-9711)
PHONE..............................574 642-4454
Gary Plank, *Executive*
EMP: 2
SALES (est): 126.1K **Privately Held**
SIC: 2084 Wines

Milltown
Crawford County

(G-9976)
ROBERTSON CRUSHED STONE INC
6300 Hwy 64 Nw (47145)
P.O. Box 97 (47145-0097)
PHONE..............................812 633-4881
Fax: 812 633-4881
Charlie Robertson, *President*
William Robertson, *Vice Pres*
Kathy Robertson Shank, *Vice Pres*
EMP: 14 EST: 1970
SQ FT: 300
SALES: 1.4MM **Privately Held**
SIC: 1422 Crushed & broken limestone

Milroy
Rush County

(G-9977)
BILLS INDUSTRIES LLC
7794 S 175 W (46156)
P.O. Box 274 (46156-0274)
PHONE..............................765 629-0227
Rick A Bills,
Angela M Bills,
EMP: 6
SALES (est): 515.7K **Privately Held**
SIC: 2759 Engraving

(G-9978)
CANNON FABRICATION COMPANY
7957 S State Road 3 (46156-9770)
P.O. Box 218 (46156-0218)
PHONE..............................765 629-2277
Fax: 765 629-8282
John McDaniel, *President*
Tom Simasko, *Vice Pres*
▲ **EMP:** 10
SQ FT: 12,000
SALES (est): 2MM **Privately Held**
SIC: 3053 Gaskets, all materials

(G-9979)
DETWEILERS CABINET SHOP
6053 W State Road 244 (46156-9704)
PHONE...................................765 629-2698
Levi Detweiler, *Owner*
EMP: 2
SALES: 60K **Privately Held**
SIC: 2499 Woodenware, kitchen & household

(G-9980)
HARCOURT INDUSTRIES INC
Also Called: Harcourt Outlines
7765 S 175 W (46156-9668)
P.O. Box 128 (46156-0128)
PHONE...................................765 629-2625
Fax: 765 629-2849
Jean Ann Harcourt, *President*
Rick Bills, *Vice Pres*
Joseph Harcourt, *Vice Pres*
Brad Sizemore, *CFO*
Joseph C Harcourt, *Admin Sec*
▲ **EMP:** 45
SQ FT: 70,000
SALES (est): 13.3MM **Privately Held**
WEB: www.harcourtoutlines.com
SIC: 3952 5112 2782 2759 Pencils & leads, including artists'; pens &/or pencils; blankbooks & looseleaf binders; commercial printing; die-cut paper & board

(G-9981)
HOOSIER PALLET
4126 W 900 S (46156-9505)
PHONE...................................765 629-2899
Abe Keim, *Owner*
EMP: 3 **EST:** 1996
SALES (est): 526.7K **Privately Held**
SIC: 2448 Pallets, wood & wood with metal

(G-9982)
MIDWEST GASKET CORPORATION
100 S Railroad St (46156)
PHONE...................................765 629-2221
Fax: 765 629-2645
Robert Tobian, *President*
▲ **EMP:** 20
SQ FT: 15,000
SALES (est): 2.9MM **Privately Held**
SIC: 3053 Gaskets, all materials

(G-9983)
MILROY CANNING COMPANY
100 S Railroad St (46156)
P.O. Box 125 (46156-0125)
PHONE...................................765 629-2221
Bob Tovian, *President*
Bob Tobian, *Manager*
EMP: 5
SQ FT: 25,000
SALES (est): 527.8K **Privately Held**
SIC: 2033 0191 Tomato products: packaged in cans, jars, etc.; general farms, primarily crop

(G-9984)
MILROY PALLET INC
Also Called: H & M Pallet
3018 W 1050 S (46156-9511)
PHONE...................................765 629-2919
Fax: 765 629-2053
Steve Keim, *President*
Abe Keim, *Vice Pres*
Olivia Atherton, *Admin Sec*
EMP: 3
SQ FT: 12,000
SALES (est): 680.4K **Privately Held**
SIC: 2448 Pallets, wood; pallets, wood & wood with metal

(G-9985)
RUSH COUNTY STONE CO INC
5814 W State Road 244 (46156-9568)
PHONE...................................765 629-2211
Fax: 765 629-2400
Joe S Columbe, *President*
EMP: 6 **EST:** 1941
SALES (est): 619.3K **Privately Held**
SIC: 1411 3281 3274 Limestone, dimension-quarrying; cut stone & stone products; lime

(G-9986)
RUSH COUNTY WOOD PRODUCTS
2437 W 900 S (46156-9699)
PHONE...................................765 629-0603
Richard Schrock, *Owner*
EMP: 3
SALES (est): 253.7K **Privately Held**
SIC: 2434 Wood kitchen cabinets

Milton
Wayne County

(G-9987)
DIMENSIONAL IMPRINTING INC
13579 Whitaker Dr (47357-9703)
PHONE...................................260 417-0202
Mahlon Whitaker, *President*
EMP: 2
SALES: 500K **Privately Held**
SIC: 2759 Promotional printing

Mishawaka
St. Joseph County

(G-9988)
ABI ATTACHMENTS INC
520 S Byrkit St (46544-3019)
PHONE...................................877 788-7253
Sam Methuselah, *President*
Malcolm J Tuesley, *Principal*
Scott Homes, *Vice Pres*
Pat Dowling, *Sales Mgr*
Jack Owens, *Sales Associate*
▼ **EMP:** 20
SALES (est): 7.3MM **Privately Held**
WEB: www.absoluteinnovations.net
SIC: 3446 Gratings, open steel flooring

(G-9989)
ACCU-MOLD LLC (HQ)
1702 E 7th St (46544-3213)
PHONE...................................269 323-0388
David Felicijan, *President*
Troland Clay,
EMP: 23
SALES (est): 3.8MM
SALES (corp-wide): 7.5MM **Privately Held**
SIC: 3544 3089 3678 3841 Forms (molds), for foundry & plastics working machinery; injection molding of plastics; electronic connectors; surgical & medical instruments
PA: Mno-Bmadsen
415 E Prairie Ronde St
Dowagiac MI 49047
269 783-4111

(G-9990)
ACTUANT CORPORATION
Also Called: Power Gear
1217 E 7th St (46544-2851)
P.O. Box 2888, Elkhart (46515-2888)
PHONE...................................574 254-1428
Fax: 574 256-6743
Tari Blazei, *Finance*
EMP: 47
SALES (corp-wide): 1.1B **Publicly Held**
WEB: www.actuant.com
SIC: 3593 Fluid power cylinders, hydraulic or pneumatic
PA: Actuant Corporation
N86w12500 Westbrook Xing
Menomonee Falls WI 53051
262 293-1500

(G-9991)
ADVANCED METAL FABRICATORS INC
1204 E 6th St (46544-2822)
PHONE...................................574 259-1263
John Ford, *Director*
EMP: 10
SALES (est): 1.1MM **Privately Held**
WEB: www.am-fab.com
SIC: 3469 Metal stampings

(G-9992)
AK TOOL AND DIE
13990 Early Rd (46545-4527)
PHONE...................................574 286-9010
Kenny Beckham, *President*
EMP: 6
SALES (est): 525K **Privately Held**
SIC: 3423 2675 Hand & edge tools; diecut paper & board

(G-9993)
ALLEN-DAVIS ENTERPRISES INC
920 Brook Run Dr Apt 3b (46544-9009)
P.O. Box 1484 (46546-1484)
PHONE...................................574 303-2173
William W Allen, *President*
William C Davis, *Vice Pres*
▲ **EMP:** 2
SALES: 112.7K **Privately Held**
WEB: www.lobster-louie.com
SIC: 3421 Scissors, hand

(G-9994)
ALLIED SPECIALTY PRECISION INC
815 E Lowell Ave (46545-6480)
P.O. Box 543 (46546-0543)
PHONE...................................574 255-4718
Pam Rubenstein, *CEO*
Eric Kurzhal, *President*
Larry De Later, *Vice Pres*
Michael EBY, *Buyer*
Seth Jordan, *Engineer*
EMP: 65 **EST:** 1954
SQ FT: 26,000
SALES (est): 15.9MM **Privately Held**
WEB: www.aspi-nc.com
SIC: 3599 Machine shop, jobbing & repair

(G-9995)
AM GENERAL LLC
13200 Mckinley Hwy (46545-7530)
P.O. Box 650 (46546-0650)
PHONE...................................574 258-7523
Fax: 574 258-7509
Jerry Moore, *Mfg Staff*
Larry Mueller, *QC Mgr*
Todd Leahy, *Engineer*
Tyler See, *Engineer*
Thomas Mc Gillicuddy, *Human Resources*
EMP: 800
SQ FT: 16,200 **Privately Held**
WEB: www.amgmil.com
SIC: 3711 3795 3537 7381 Military motor vehicle assembly; tanks & tank components; industrial trucks & tractors; security guard service
HQ: Am General Llc
105 N Niles Ave
South Bend IN 46617
574 237-6222

(G-9996)
AN-MAR WIRING SYSTEMS INC
711 E Grove St (46545-6863)
PHONE...................................574 255-5523
Fax: 574 255-5355
Dean W Johnson, *President*
Ann Mary Johnson, *Treasurer*
EMP: 10
SQ FT: 6,000
SALES: 1MM **Privately Held**
WEB: www.anmarwiring.com
SIC: 3643 3621 3566 Current-carrying wiring devices; motors & generators; speed changers, drives & gears

(G-9997)
ART WORKS SIGN CO INC
55581 Currant Rd (46545-4741)
PHONE...................................574 360-9290
Fax: 574 255-9112
Steve Depositar, *President*
Shelly Depositar, *Admin Sec*
EMP: 7
SQ FT: 5,200
SALES (est): 1MM **Privately Held**
WEB: www.artworkssigns.com
SIC: 3993 Signs, not made in custom sign painting shops

(G-9998)
ASCENSIA DIABETES CARE US INC
430 S Beiger St (46544-3207)
PHONE...................................201 875-8066
Ed Ramsey, *Branch Mgr*
EMP: 26 **Publicly Held**
SIC: 3841 2835 5047 Inhalation therapy equipment; barium diagnostic agents; industrial safety devices: first aid kits & masks
HQ: Ascensia Diabetes Care Us inc.
5 Woodhollow Rd Ste 3
Parsippany NJ 07054
973 560-6500

(G-9999)
ASSEMBLY MASTERS INC
55807 Currant Rd (46545-4805)
PHONE...................................574 293-9026
Fax: 574 257-9885
Al Spencer, *Owner*
EMP: 2 **EST:** 2010
SALES (est): 133.1K **Privately Held**
SIC: 3678 Electronic connectors

(G-10000)
AUNT BETHS PRODUCTS INC
Also Called: Aunt Beth's Cookies
1828 Clover Rd (46545-7247)
PHONE...................................574 259-6244
Fax: 574 259-2940
Beth Modlin, *President*
Ted E Modlin, *Corp Secy*
EMP: 8 **EST:** 1987
SQ FT: 8,000
SALES (est): 838.6K **Privately Held**
WEB: www.auntbethscookies.com
SIC: 2052 Cookies; bakery products, dry

(G-10001)
AUNTIE ANNES
6501 Grape Rd Ste 670a (46545-1039)
PHONE...................................574 271-8740
Fax: 574 273-2956
Tracy Vervynckt, *General Mgr*
EMP: 8
SALES (est): 141.7K **Privately Held**
SIC: 5461 2052 Pretzels; pretzels

(G-10002)
B & F MACHINE PRODUCTS
606 S Byrkit St (46544-3008)
PHONE...................................574 255-7447
Robert Frederick, *President*
Glenda Frederick, *Vice Pres*
EMP: 5
SQ FT: 8,700
SALES (est): 679.3K **Privately Held**
SIC: 3599 Machine shop, jobbing & repair

(G-10003)
B&B MOLDERS LLC
58471 Fir Rd (46544-5834)
PHONE...................................574 259-7838
Fax: 574 259-7939
Britt Murphey, *Principal*
Paul Bergin, *Principal*
Richard Layher, *Supervisor*
▲ **EMP:** 65
SQ FT: 60,000
SALES (est): 14.6MM **Privately Held**
WEB: www.bandbmolders.com
SIC: 3089 Injection molding of plastics

(G-10004)
BAYER HEALTHCARE LLC
3930 Edison Lakes Pkwy (46545-3418)
PHONE...................................574 252-4734
Katherine Page, *Finance Mgr*
Robert Hurley, *Finance*
Bayer Care, *Branch Mgr*
Charles Sharkey, *Manager*
EMP: 13
SALES (corp-wide): 41.2B **Privately Held**
SIC: 2834 Pharmaceutical preparations
HQ: Bayer Healthcare Llc
100 Bayer Blvd
Whippany NJ 07981
862 404-3000

(G-10005)
BAYER HEALTHCARE LLC
4100 Edison Lakes Pkwy (46545-3465)
PHONE...................................574 252-4735

G
E
O
G
R
A
P
H
I
C

Dianne Nagy, *Business Mgr*
EMP: 134
SALES (corp-wide): 41.2B **Privately Held**
SIC: 2834 Pharmaceutical preparations
HQ: Bayer Healthcare Llc
100 Bayer Blvd
Whippany NJ 07981
862 404-3000

(G-10006)
BBS ENTERPRISES INC
Also Called: F & F Machine Specialties
55980 Russell Indus Pkwy (46545-7545)
PHONE.................................574 255-3173
Fax: 574 255-4837
David A Behrens, *President*
Karen M Behrens, *Admin Sec*
EMP: 29 **EST:** 1967
SQ FT: 16,000
SALES (est): 5.6MM **Privately Held**
WEB: www.ffmachine.com
SIC: 3841 3599 Diagnostic apparatus, medical; surgical instruments & apparatus; machine shop, jobbing & repair; custom machinery

(G-10007)
BENCH & FIELD PET FOODS LLC
1025 W 11th St (46544-4818)
P.O. Box 6 (46546-0006)
PHONE.................................800 525-4802
Mark Bennett,
EMP: 2
SALES (est): 172.9K **Privately Held**
WEB: www.benchandfield.com
SIC: 2047 5999 Dog food; pet supplies

(G-10008)
BENDER MOLD & MACHINE INC
55951 Russell Indus Pkwy (46545-5198)
PHONE.................................574 255-5176
Fax: 574 258-9652
Richard Bender, *President*
EMP: 10
SALES (est): 977.2K **Privately Held**
SIC: 3089 Injection molding of plastics

(G-10009)
BENDER PRODUCTS INC
Also Called: Bender Plastics
55951 Russell Indus Pkwy (46545-7544)
PHONE.................................574 255-5350
Fax: 574 258-2554
Nevin Siqueira, *President*
EMP: 50
SQ FT: 40,000
SALES (est): 11.9MM **Privately Held**
WEB: www.benderplastics.com
SIC: 3089 3714 3643 3496 Injection molding of plastics; motor vehicle parts & accessories; current-carrying wiring devices; miscellaneous fabricated wire products

(G-10010)
BILL WALTERS CONCRETE INC
1134 E 12th St (46544-5704)
PHONE.................................574 259-0056
Bill D Walters, *President*
EMP: 10
SQ FT: 4,500
SALES (est): 980K **Privately Held**
SIC: 3272 Battery wells or boxes, concrete

(G-10011)
BONNIE DOON ICE CREAM CORP
2704 Lincolnway W (46544-1520)
PHONE.................................574 255-9841
EMP: 10
SALES (corp-wide): 1.3MM **Privately Held**
SIC: 5812 2024 Eating Place Mfg Ice Cream/Frozen Desert
PA: Bonnie Doon Ice Cream Corp
505 S 3rd St Ste 110
Elkhart IN
574 264-3390

(G-10012)
BORECO INDUSTRIES INC
54530 Clover Rd (46545-1704)
PHONE.................................574 255-4149
William F Bodish Sr, *President*
EMP: 3

SALES (est): 214.6K **Privately Held**
SIC: 3599 Machine shop, jobbing & repair

(G-10013)
BRADFORD PRESS
302 W 3rd St (46544-1922)
PHONE.................................574 876-3601
Ruth J Smith, *Principal*
EMP: 2
SALES (est): 106K **Privately Held**
SIC: 2741 Miscellaneous publishing

(G-10014)
BUILDERS IRON WORKS INC
1016 E 12th St (46544-5706)
PHONE.................................574 254-1553
Fax: 574 287-1598
Elvis Balentine, *President*
Mary Wunder, *Corp Secy*
EMP: 20
SQ FT: 15,500
SALES (est): 4.7MM **Privately Held**
WEB: www.buildersironworks.com
SIC: 3441 3446 Fabricated structural metal; architectural metalwork; stairs, staircases, stair treads: prefabricated metal

(G-10015)
C & J CORPORATION
Also Called: Pro Fab
1530 Ken Mcintee Ct (46544-3021)
PHCNE.................................574 255-6793
Bruce E Coleman, *President*
Charles Coleman, *Principal*
Kathy James, *Vice Pres*
EMP: 8 **EST:** 1998
SQ FT: 19,000
SALES (est): 918.7K **Privately Held**
SIC: 2796 Steel line engraving for the printing trade

(G-10016)
C & P DISTRIBUTING LLC
2500 Miracle Ln Ste D (46545-3017)
PHONE.................................574 256-1138
Fax: 574 256-1144
John Pierce, *President*
Jay Mead, *Sales Mgr*
EMP: 20
SQ FT: 24,000
SALES (est): 4.3MM **Privately Held**
WEB: www.cpdist.com
SIC: 3575 3999 5045 5099 Computer terminals, monitors & components; coin-operated amusement machines; computers; coin-operated machines & mechanisms; computer & data processing equipment repair/maintenance; computer peripheral equipment repair & maintenance; vending machine repair

(G-10017)
CAST PRODUCTS LP
Colorimeteric Division
1711 Clover Rd (46545-7248)
PHONE.................................574 255-9619
Roy Strong, *General Mgr*
EMP: 55
SALES (corp-wide): 1.6B **Publicly Held**
WEB: www.castproductscorp.com
SIC: 2891 Caulking compounds
HQ: Cast Products, L.P.
3601 Charlotte Ave
Elkhart IN 46517
574 294-2684

(G-10018)
CLAYMORE TOOLS INC
1619 N Home St (46545-7238)
PHONE.................................574 255-6483
Fax: 574 255-6412
David Adamson, *President*
Isobel Adamson, *Treasurer*
Ray Lada, *Admin Sec*
EMP: 9
SQ FT: 10,000
SALES (est): 740K **Privately Held**
SIC: 3544 3541 3546 3545 Special dies & tools; machine tools, metal cutting: exotic (explosive, etc.); power-driven hand-tools; machine tool accessories; mining machinery

(G-10019)
COLORIMETRIC INC
1711 Clover Rd (46545-7292)
PHONE.................................574 255-9619
Fax: 574 259-0211
John Hendricks, *President*
Gregory Querry, *Vice Pres*
EMP: 45 **EST:** 1977
SQ FT: 47,000
SALES (est): 5.7MM
SALES (corp-wide): 1.6B **Publicly Held**
WEB: www.castproductscorp.com
SIC: 2891 Caulking compounds
HQ: Cast Products, L.P.
3601 Charlotte Ave
Elkhart IN 46517
574 294-2684

(G-10020)
COMMUNITY VAULT INC
1120 N Merrifield Ave (46545-6711)
PHONE.................................574 255-3033
Mike Laudenbacke, *President*
Tina Laudenbacke, *Admin Sec*
EMP: 3 **EST:** 1997
SALES (est): 416.1K **Privately Held**
SIC: 3272 Burial vaults, concrete or pre-cast terrazzo

(G-10021)
CONCRETE & ASPHALT RECYCL INC (DH)
2010 Went Ave (46545-6447)
PHONE.................................574 237-1928
David L Schrock, *President*
EMP: 13
SALES (est): 3.4MM
SALES (corp-wide): 2.2MM **Privately Held**
SIC: 2951 4953 Concrete, asphaltic (not from refineries); asphalt & asphaltic paving mixtures (not from refineries); recycling, waste materials

(G-10022)
CONRAD MACHINE CO INC
926 E Mckinley Ave (46545-4126)
PHONE.................................574 259-1190
Fax: 574 259-1190
David Conrad, *President*
EMP: 2
SQ FT: 4,000
SALES (est): 257.1K **Privately Held**
SIC: 3599 Machine shop, jobbing & repair

(G-10023)
COR-A-VENT INC (PA)
2529 Lincolnway W (46544-1523)
P.O. Box 428 (46546-0428)
PHONE.................................574 255-1910
Fax: 574 258-6162
Gary L Sells, *Ch of Bd*
Mark Keller, *COO*
Tom Osborn, *Manager*
Shirley Sells, *Admin Sec*
◆ **EMP:** 12
SQ FT: 6,000
SALES (est): 3.9MM **Privately Held**
WEB: www.cor-a-vent.com/
SIC: 3089 1711 Extruded finished plastic products; ventilation & duct work contractor

(G-10024)
COR-A-VENT INC
945 E 6th St (46544-2825)
PHONE.................................574 258-6161
Gary Sells, *Manager*
EMP: 20
SALES (corp-wide): 3.9MM **Privately Held**
SIC: 3089 3564 Plastic hardware & building products; blowers & fans
PA: Cor-A-Vent Inc
2529 Lincolnway W
Mishawaka IN 46544
574 255-1910

(G-10025)
CRESSY MEMORIAL GROUP INC
3925 Glaser Ct (46545-4539)
PHONE.................................574 258-1800
Mary Cressy, *President*
Steve Lyons, *Principal*

Sarah Tepe, *Sales Staff*
EMP: 2 **EST:** 2006
SALES (est): 160.5K **Privately Held**
SIC: 3995 Burial vaults, fiberglass

(G-10026)
CUMMINS CROSSPOINT LLC
3025 N Home St (46545-4439)
PHONE.................................574 252-2154
Carrie Buisman, *Branch Mgr*
EMP: 36
SALES (corp-wide): 20.4B **Publicly Held**
SIC: 5084 3519 Engines & parts, diesel; internal combustion engines
HQ: Cummins Crosspoint Llc
2601 Fortune Cir E 300c
Indianapolis IN 46241
317 243-7979

(G-10027)
CUSTOM METAL FABRICATION LLC
603 W 9th St (46544-4916)
PHONE.................................574 257-8851
Kris Kruger, *Principal*
EMP: 2
SALES (est): 180.8K **Privately Held**
SIC: 3499 Fabricated metal products

(G-10028)
CUSTOM PLASTICS LLC
1950 E Mckinley Ave (46545-7206)
PHONE.................................574 259-2340
Fax: 574 259-2342
William Morlock, *Manager*
EMP: 17
SALES (corp-wide): 3MM **Privately Held**
WEB: www.spinwelding.com
SIC: 3089 Injection molding of plastics
PA: Custom Plastics, Llc
1305 Brooks St
Ontario CA 91762
909 984-0200

(G-10029)
DAMAGE INDUSTRIES II LLC
55685 Currant Rd (46545-4811)
PHONE.................................574 256-7006
Amy Robison,
EMP: 2
SQ FT: 3,700
SALES (est): 70.5K **Privately Held**
SIC: 3999 Manufacturing industries

(G-10030)
DAMAN PRODUCTS COMPANY INC
1811 N Home St (46545-7267)
PHONE.................................574 259-7841
Fax: 574 259-7665
Larry Davis, *President*
Mike Linsky, *Purchasing*
Krysten Shoulders, *Human Res Dir*
Terri Linsky, *HR Admin*
David Jaeckel, *Manager*
EMP: 93
SQ FT: 50,000
SALES (est): 19.5MM **Privately Held**
WEB: www.damanifolds.com
SIC: 3492 Control valves, fluid power: hydraulic & pneumatic

(G-10031)
DAMPING TECHNOLOGIES INC
12970 Mckinley Hwy Ste 1 (46545-7500)
PHONE.................................574 258-7916
James Schmucker, *QC Mgr*
Joe Herman, *Branch Mgr*
EMP: 25
SALES (est): 2.4MM **Privately Held**
WEB: www.dampingtechnologies.com
SIC: 3625 8711 3829 3823 Relays & industrial controls; noise control equipment; engineering services; acoustical engineering; measuring & controlling devices; industrial instrmnts msrmnt display/control process variable; household audio & video equipment
PA: Damping Technologies, Inc.
55656 Currant Rd
Mishawaka IN 46545

(G-10032)
DAMPING TECHNOLOGIES INC (PA)
55656 Currant Rd (46545-4802)
PHONE.................................574 258-7916
Fax: 574 258-7911
Michael L Parin, *President*
Adam Parin, *Mfg Staff*
Warren Barham, *Purchasing*
Tom Joughin, *Engineer*
Tom Lewis, *Senior Engr*
EMP: 25
SQ FT: 40,000
SALES (est): 4.4MM Privately Held
WEB: www.dampingtechnologies.com
SIC: 3625 8711 Relays & industrial controls; noise control equipment; engineering services; acoustical engineering

(G-10033)
DATA-VISION INC
4215 Edison Lakes Pkwy # 140 (46545-1425)
PHONE.................................574 243-8625
Fax: 574 243-8630
Randy Schmidt, *President*
John Dempsey, *Vice Pres*
Dendy McNeer, *Admin Sec*
EMP: 18
SALES (est): 2.7MM Privately Held
WEB: www.d-vision.com
SIC: 7372 4813 Prepackaged software;

(G-10034)
DAVE JONES MACHINISTS LLC
1212 N Merrifield Ave (46545-6709)
PHONE.................................574 256-5500
Fax: 574 256-1543
Davis P Jones,
Kathy Butterbaugh,
◆ EMP: 4
SQ FT: 4,500
SALES: 325K Privately Held
WEB: www.davejonesmachinists.com
SIC: 3827 Optical instruments & apparatus

(G-10035)
DEARBORN CRANE AND ENGRG CO (PA)
Also Called: Dearborn Overhead Crane
1133 E 5th St (46544-2831)
PHONE.................................574 259-2444
Fax: 574 256-6612
Yatish Joshi, *President*
Joan Joshi, *Vice Pres*
Debra Wilson, *Controller*
Ray Lyvers, *Manager*
EMP: 31
SQ FT: 43,000
SALES: 14MM Privately Held
SIC: 3536 7389 Hoists, cranes & monorails; industrial & commercial equipment inspection service

(G-10036)
DIGI INTERNATIONAL INC
Also Called: Smart Temps
435 Park Place Cir # 100 (46545-3576)
PHONE.................................877 272-3111
EMP: 5
SALES (corp-wide): 181.6MM Publicly Held
SIC: 3822 Refrigeration thermostats
PA: Digi International Inc.
11001 Bren Rd E
Minnetonka MN 55343
952 912-3444

(G-10037)
DULEY PRESS INC
2906 N Home St (46545-4491)
P.O. Box 484 (46546-0484)
PHONE.................................574 259-5203
Fax: 574 256-5935
Judd Lowenhar, *Ch of Bd*
Michael Lowenhar, *President*
EMP: 30 EST: 1936
SQ FT: 14,000
SALES (est): 5.5MM Privately Held
WEB: www.duleypress.com
SIC: 2752 Commercial printing, offset

(G-10038)
EAGLE PET PRODUCTS INC
1025 W 11th St (46544-4818)
PHONE.................................574 259-7834
EMP: 80
SALES (corp-wide): 2.9B Privately Held
SIC: 2047 Mfg Dog & Cat Foods
HQ: Eagle Pet Products, Inc.
1025 W 11th St
Mishawaka IN 46544
574 259-7834

(G-10039)
ECKCO INC
12962 Jefferson Blvd (46545-7534)
PHONE.................................574 257-0299
Gary Eck, *Principal*
EMP: 3
SALES (est): 246K Privately Held
SIC: 3089 Injection molding of plastics

(G-10040)
ELECTRO TRANSFER SYSTEMS INC (PA)
Also Called: E T S
1810 Clover Rd (46545-7247)
PHONE.................................574 234-0600
Fax: 574 289-0107
Thomas Richardson, *President*
Scott A Lee, *Vice Pres*
Norman F Sagon, *Vice Pres*
EMP: 85
SQ FT: 50,000
SALES (est): 7.7MM Privately Held
SIC: 3679 3089 Harness assemblies for electronic use: wire or cable; molding primary plastic

(G-10041)
ENGINEERED RUBBER & PLASTICS
646 Rivers Edge Ct (46544-4173)
PHONE.................................574 254-1405
Edwin E Hatton, *President*
Lori Stubbs, *Treasurer*
Sue Schleis, *Office Mgr*
Dorothy J Hatton, *Admin Sec*
EMP: 14
SQ FT: 7,000
SALES: 600K Privately Held
SIC: 3089 3449 3061 Molding primary plastic; injection molded finished plastic products; extruded finished plastic products; miscellaneous metalwork; mechanical rubber goods

(G-10042)
ENVISIO DESIGN LLC
Also Called: Envisioit
2406 Schumacher Dr (46545-3344)
PHONE.................................574 274-4394
Lynn M Fitzpatrick, *President*
Joe Power, *COO*
Dennis Fitzpatrick, *Treasurer*
Joseph Power, *Info Tech Mgr*
Phil Power, *Director*
EMP: 3
SALES (est): 216K Privately Held
SIC: 7371 7372 Custom computer programming services; computer software systems analysis & design, custom; computer software development & applications; computer software development; application computer software

(G-10043)
ETS INTERNATIONAL LLC
1810 Clover Rd (46545-7247)
PHONE.................................574 234-0700
Hamender Agarwal, *President*
◆ EMP: 70
SQ FT: 50,000
SALES (est): 9.8MM Privately Held
SIC: 3679 Harness assemblies for electronic use: wire or cable

(G-10044)
FOSTEK
201 S Main St (46544-2006)
PHONE.................................540 587-5870
EMP: 11 EST: 2012
SALES (est): 1.8MM Privately Held
SIC: 3086 Plastics foam products

(G-10045)
GARYRAE INC
Also Called: Precision Wood Products
800 Cleveland St (46544-4861)
PHONE.................................574 255-7141
Fax: 574 255-7705
Gary Matt, *President*
Rae Matt, *Vice Pres*
EMP: 15
SQ FT: 10,000
SALES: 700K Privately Held
WEB: www.garyrae.com
SIC: 2431 2541 Millwork; doors & door parts & trim, wood; interior & ornamental woodwork & trim; wood partitions & fixtures

(G-10046)
GENESIS MOLDING INC
55901 Currant Rd (46545-4803)
PHONE.................................574 256-9271
James Deren, *President*
Tim Morris, *Partner*
Brandon Geisel, *Vice Pres*
Jeff Gilbert, *Manager*
▲ EMP: 75
SQ FT: 20,000
SALES: 9.4MM Privately Held
SIC: 3089 Injection molded finished plastic products; injection molding of plastics

(G-10047)
GLOBAL MOLD SOLUTIONS INC
1702 E 7th St (46544-3213)
PHONE.................................574 259-6262
Michael A Vaughn, *President*
EMP: 30
SQ FT: 35,000
SALES (est): 2.1MM Privately Held
WEB: www.globalmoldsolutions.com
SIC: 3544 Special dies, tools, jigs & fixtures

(G-10048)
HARD SURFACE FABRICATIONS INC
810 S Beiger St (46544-3215)
PHONE.................................574 259-4843
Fax: 574 259-4844
Everett H Behnke, *President*
Constance Behnke, *Corp Secy*
EMP: 7
SQ FT: 9,000
SALES: 850K Privately Held
WEB: www.hardsurfacekormax.com
SIC: 2221 Acrylic broadwoven fabrics

(G-10049)
HEATHER SOUND AMPLIFICATION
1717 E 6th St (46544-3208)
PHONE.................................574 255-6100
Richard Johnson, *President*
EMP: 3
SQ FT: 3,200
SALES (est): 200K Privately Held
WEB: www.hsarolltops.com
SIC: 3679 2517 Electronic circuits; wood television & radio cabinets

(G-10050)
HOOSIER BOX AND SKID INC
2401 Schumacher Dr (46545-3343)
P.O. Box 8123, South Bend (46660-8123)
PHONE.................................574 256-2111
Fax: 574 256-1221
Neal Stanfield, *President*
James Hansen, *Vice Pres*
Suzanne Stanfield, *Admin Sec*
EMP: 8
SQ FT: 45,000
SALES (est): 1MM Privately Held
SIC: 2448 2441 Pallets, wood; cargo containers, wood & wood with metal; cargo containers, wood; skids, wood; nailed wood boxes & shook

(G-10051)
HOOSIER ROASTER LLC
2212 Lincolnway W (46544-1617)
PHONE.................................574 257-1415
Chris Skodinski, *Owner*
EMP: 2

SALES (est): 164.4K Privately Held
SIC: 3634 2095 Roasters, electric; roasted coffee

(G-10052)
IMAGINATION PUBLICATIONS LLC
203 N Main St (46544-1410)
PHONE.................................574 256-6666
Rick Singleton, *Principal*
EMP: 2
SALES (est): 114.5K Privately Held
WEB: www.imaginationpublications.com
SIC: 2741 Miscellaneous publishing

(G-10053)
INDIANA RUG COMPANY
900 Cleveland St (46544-4859)
PHONE.................................574 252-4653
Pam Richards, *Owner*
EMP: 3
SALES (est): 446.5K Privately Held
WEB: www.indianarugco.com
SIC: 2273 5713 Carpets & rugs; floor covering stores

(G-10054)
INTERPLASTIC CORPORATION
Also Called: North American Composites
1460 E 12th St (46544-5824)
PHONE.................................574 259-1505
Floyd Linch, *Branch Mgr*
EMP: 15
SALES (corp-wide): 302.9MM Privately Held
SIC: 2821 Plastics materials & resins
PA: Interplastic Corporation
1225 Willow Lake Blvd
Saint Paul MN 55110
651 481-6860

(G-10055)
J H J INC
Also Called: Madison, The
15314 Harrison Rd (46544-5721)
PHONE.................................574 256-6966
Fax: 574 256-6966
Craig Nowicki, *President*
John J Hoffman, *President*
Paul Schuchman, *Vice Pres*
Scott Baker, *Opers Mgr*
Jody Primmer, *Purchasing*
EMP: 50 EST: 1972
SQ FT: 45,000
SALES (est): 17MM Privately Held
WEB: www.jackelinc.com
SIC: 3089 Injection molding of plastics; plastic hardware & building products; hardware, plastic

(G-10056)
J Q TEX INC
Also Called: Trailmaster
1033 E 5th St (46544-2833)
PHONE.................................574 259-0329
Fax: 574 258-1132
V Q Kreiger, *President*
Tex Galloway, *Treasurer*
Michelle Doan, *Administration*
EMP: 40
SQ FT: 30,000
SALES (est): 6.6MM Privately Held
SIC: 3799 Boat trailers

(G-10057)
JACKSON HEWITT TAX SERVICE
922 S Beiger St (46544-3216)
PHONE.................................574 255-2200
Tony Magaldi, *President*
EMP: 190
SALES (est): 4.2MM Privately Held
WEB: www.jacksonhewitt.com
SIC: 7291 2899 Tax return preparation services; fireworks

(G-10058)
JAMES F REILLY 3 ENT
1969 E Mckinley Ave (46545-7205)
PHONE.................................574 277-8267
James Reilly, *President*
EMP: 2
SALES (est): 80.5K Privately Held
SIC: 1081 Mine development, metal

G
E
O
G
R
A
P
H
I
C

(G-10059)
JAMIL PACKAGING
CORPORATION (PA)
1420 Industrial Dr (46544-5720)
P.O. Box 684 (46546-0684)
PHONE.....................................574 256-2600
David A Diroll, *President*
Mary E Diroll, *Corp Secy*
▲ EMP: 106
SQ FT: 160,000
SALES: 30.1MM **Privately Held**
WEB: www.jamilpackaging.com
SIC: 2653 5199 Boxes, corrugated: made
  from purchased materials; pallets, corru-
  gated: made from purchased materials;
  packaging materials

(G-10060)
JANCO ENGINEERED
PRODUCTS LLC
1217 E 7th St (46544-2851)
PHONE.....................................574 255-3169
Peter Giczewski, *President*
Daniel Crowell, *Plant Mgr*
Jamie Joyce, *Mfg Staff*
Craig Humphries, *Engineer*
Eugene Pucuk, *Treasurer*
▲ EMP: 140
SQ FT: 80,000
SALES (est): 39.5MM **Privately Held**
WEB: www.jancoengineeredproducts.com
SIC: 3613 Switchgear & switchboard appa-
  ratus

(G-10061)
JC METAL FABRICATION
15393 Kelly Rd (46544-9204)
PHONE.....................................574 340-1109
Joseph R Campoli, *Administration*
EMP: 2
SALES (est): 244.1K **Privately Held**
SIC: 3499 Fabricated metal products

(G-10062)
KANOFF ENTERPRISES
928 W Berry Ave (46545-8842)
PHONE.....................................574 575-6787
Benjamin Kanoff, *Owner*
EMP: 3
SALES (est): 182.7K **Privately Held**
SIC: 3312 3462 Pipes & tubes; gears,
  forged steel

(G-10063)
KENDRION (MISHAWAKA) LLC
56733 Magnetic Dr (46545-7481)
PHONE.....................................574 257-2422
Fax: 574 257-2421
Corey Hurcomb, *Managing Dir*
Brad Price, *Managing Dir*
Poehls Joerg, *Executive*
EMP: 30
SQ FT: 22,000
SALES: 6MM
SALES (corp-wide): 544.7MM **Privately Held**
WEB: www.tri-techllc.com
SIC: 3679 3677 3089 3824 Electronic cir-
  cuits; solenoids for electronic applica-
  tions; electronic coils, transformers &
  other inductors; plastic processing; injec-
  tion molded finished plastic products; me-
  chanical & electromechanical counters &
  devices; current-carrying wiring devices;
  motors & generators
PA: Kendrion N.V.
  Utrechtseweg 33
  Zeist 3704
  306 997-250

(G-10064)
KNOX TOOL & DIE INC
2027 N Merrifield Ave (46545-6406)
P.O. Box 413 (46546-0413)
PHONE.....................................574 255-1256
Fax: 574 255-1501
Phillip Knox II, *President*
Phillip A Knox, *Treasurer*
▲ EMP: 4 EST: 1975
SQ FT: 6,000
SALES: 784.9K **Privately Held**
SIC: 3544 Special dies & tools

(G-10065)
KRA INTERNATIONAL LLC (PA)
1810 Clover Rd (46545-7247)
PHONE.....................................574 259-3550
Hari Agarwal, *President*
Greg Pollock, *Plant Engr*
Pankaj Yadav, *Info Tech Mgr*
▲ EMP: 59
SQ FT: 28,000
SALES: 11.8MM **Privately Held**
WEB: www.krainternational.com
SIC: 3679 Harness assemblies for elec-
  tronic use: wire or cable; electronic cir-
  cuits

(G-10066)
KRAIGS CUSTOM
WOODWORKING
1810 E 12th St (46544-5928)
PHONE.....................................574 904-7501
Kraig Pehling, *Principal*
EMP: 2
SALES (est): 184K **Privately Held**
SIC: 2431 Millwork

(G-10067)
LAIDIG INC
14535 Dragoon Trl (46544-6814)
PHONE.....................................574 256-0204
Fax: 574 255-5575
Daniel Laidig, *President*
Wyn Laidig, *President*
Tom Lindenman, *President*
Jeff Walker, *Transptn Dir*
Tony Steele, *Purch Agent*
EMP: 50
SQ FT: 45,000
SALES (est): 16.7MM **Privately Held**
WEB: www.laidig.com
SIC: 3523 3537 3448 3423 Silo fillers &
  unloaders; industrial trucks & tractors;
  prefabricated metal buildings; hand &
  edge tools

(G-10068)
LANDRUMS MCH TL REPR &
SVCS
1002 Saint Jerome St (46544-5735)
PHONE.....................................574 256-0312
James Landrum, *President*
Beverly Landrum, *Vice Pres*
EMP: 4
SQ FT: 570
SALES (est): 579.6K **Privately Held**
WEB: www.gettysservocontrols.com
SIC: 3541 Machine tool replacement & re-
  pair parts, metal cutting types

(G-10069)
LE HUE MACHINE & TOOL CO
INC
1915 N Cedar St (46545-6466)
PHONE.....................................574 255-8404
Fax: 574 255-8207
Dale Le Hue, *President*
Susan Le Hue, *Treasurer*
EMP: 7
SQ FT: 12,200
SALES (est): 600K **Privately Held**
SIC: 3544 3599 Special dies & tools; ma-
  chine shop, jobbing & repair

(G-10070)
LOGO BOYS INC
3102 N Home St (46545-4438)
PHONE.....................................574 256-6844
Fax: 574 256-6855
Dean A Himelick, *President*
Cathy Young, *Opers Staff*
Brad Bennett, *Regl Sales Mgr*
Bob Nicol, *Admin Sec*
EMP: 8
SQ FT: 2,400
SALES (est): 1MM **Privately Held**
WEB: www.logoboys.net
SIC: 7336 2395 Silk screen design; em-
  broidery products, except schiffli machine

(G-10071)
LONGHORN SAND AND GRAVEL
LLC
1434 Fallcreek Dr (46544-5850)
PHONE.....................................574 532-2788
EMP: 3 EST: 2011

SALES (est): 220K **Privately Held**
SIC: 1442 Construction sand & gravel

(G-10072)
MACOR
1025 W 11th St (46544-4818)
PHONE.....................................574 255-2658
Fax: 574 259-0730
Jim Cocquyt, *Owner*
EMP: 2
SALES (est): 19.2K **Privately Held**
SIC: 2047 Dog & cat food

(G-10073)
MAJESTIC DRAPERIES
400 S West St (46544-1926)
PHONE.....................................574 259-3080
Verna Huston, *Principal*
EMP: 2
SALES (est): 189.3K **Privately Held**
SIC: 2211 Draperies & drapery fabrics, cot-
  ton

(G-10074)
MARON PRODUCTS
INCORPORATED
1301 Industrial Dr (46544-5799)
PHONE.....................................574 259-1971
Fax: 574 259-1978
Paul Mc Mahon, *President*
Ed Quiett, *Purchasing*
Heidi Przygoda, *Human Res Mgr*
EMP: 85
SQ FT: 200,000
SALES (est): 25.6MM **Privately Held**
WEB: www.maronproducts.com
SIC: 3444 3469 Sheet metalwork; stamp-
  ing metal for the trade

(G-10075)
MATRIX TOOL INC
1210 S Merrifield Ave (46544-5711)
PHONE.....................................574 259-3093
Fax: 574 259-3552
Andrew Bryant, *President*
EMP: 12
SALES (est): 1.6MM **Privately Held**
WEB: www.matrixtool.com
SIC: 2821 3544 Molding compounds,
  plastics; special dies, tools, jigs & fixtures

(G-10076)
MC METALCRAFT INC
Also Called: Reliable Metalcraft Corp
1210 Willow St (46545-6762)
PHONE.....................................574 259-8101
Scott Chakan, *President*
Blair Melvin, *COO*
EMP: 7 EST: 2015
SQ FT: 20,000
SALES: 1.5MM **Privately Held**
SIC: 3469 3312 Stamping metal for the
  trade; tool & die steel

(G-10077)
MC METALCRAFT INC
Also Called: Reliable Metalcraft
1210 Willow St (46545-6762)
PHONE.....................................574 259-8101
Scott Chakan, *President*
Blair Melvin, *COO*
EMP: 8 EST: 2015
SQ FT: 20,000
SALES (est): 535.4K **Privately Held**
SIC: 3469 Stamping metal for the trade

(G-10078)
MERRILL CORPORATION
Also Called: Merrill Pharmacy
606 N Main St (46545-6620)
PHONE.....................................574 255-2988
Fax: 574 258-5945
Marc O Merrill, *President*
Christopher Merrill, *Corp Secy*
EMP: 17
SQ FT: 7,560
SALES: 6MM **Privately Held**
SIC: 5912 5047 2834 Drug stores; med-
  ical & hospital equipment; medical equip-
  ment & supplies; dental equipment &
  supplies; ointments

(G-10079)
MICHANA USED MUSIC AND
MEDIA
4609 Grape Rd Ofc (46545-8257)
PHONE.....................................574 247-1188
EMP: 2 EST: 2005
SALES (est): 130K **Privately Held**
SIC: 3651 Mfg Home Audio/Video Equip-
  ment

(G-10080)
MICHIANA EXECUTIVE
JOURNAL
Also Called: Business To Business
203 N Main St (46544-1410)
PHONE.....................................574 256-6666
Fax: 574 258-6107
Rick Singleton, *Owner*
EMP: 30
SALES (est): 1.5MM **Privately Held**
SIC: 2721 Trade journals: publishing &
  printing

(G-10081)
MICHIANA GLOBAL MOLD INC
1702 E 7th St (46544-3213)
PHONE.....................................574 259-6262
Eric Seigel, *President*
Angi Tuveson, *Admin Asst*
▲ EMP: 11
SALES (est): 915.8K **Privately Held**
SIC: 3544 Forms (molds), for foundry &
  plastics working machinery

(G-10082)
MICHIANA LIFT EQUIPMENT INC
709 S Byrkit St (46544-3018)
P.O. Box 1092 (46546-1092)
PHONE.....................................574 257-1665
Fax: 574 257-0484
Dennis D Gadacz, *President*
John Clemens, *Shareholder*
Rosemary Gadacz, *Shareholder*
EMP: 7
SQ FT: 1,736
SALES (est): 450K **Privately Held**
SIC: 3999 1796 Wheelchair lifts; elevator
  installation & conversion

(G-10083)
MICHIANA METAL FABRICATIO
1310 E 6th St (46544-2820)
PHONE.....................................574 256-9010
Fax: 574 256-0103
EMP: 2
SALES (est): 100K **Privately Held**
SIC: 3499 Mfg Misc Fabricated Metal
  Products

(G-10084)
MICHIANA PLASTICS INC
1702 E 7th St (46544-3219)
PHONE.....................................574 259-6262
Fax: 574 256-2780
James Orszulak, *President*
Michael A Vaughn, *Vice Pres*
Bill Stickley, *Manager*
▲ EMP: 35 EST: 1964
SQ FT: 34,450
SALES (est): 4.3MM **Privately Held**
SIC: 3544 Forms (molds), for foundry &
  plastics working machinery; industrial
  molds

(G-10085)
MIDWEST BLIND & SHADE CO
4115 Grape Rd (46545-2609)
PHONE.....................................574 271-0770
Fax: 574 271-0880
Charles Prichard, *Owner*
June S Prichard, *Corp Secy*
EMP: 5
SQ FT: 2,500
SALES (est): 310K **Privately Held**
WEB: www.midwestblindandshade.com
SIC: 2591 5719 5023 Window blinds; win-
  dow furnishings; vertical blinds

(G-10086)
MIDWEST CUSTOM FINISHING
INC (PA)
1906 Clover Rd (46545-7245)
PHONE.....................................574 258-0099
Jerry Cunningham, *President*
Rich Hamm, *Vice Pres*

Bill Thompson, *Vice Pres*
EMP: 2
SQ FT: 23,000
SALES (est): 2.6MM **Privately Held**
SIC: 3479 Painting, coating & hot dipping; coating of metals & formed products

(G-10087)
MIDWEST FINISHING SYSTEMS INC
1906 Clover Rd (46545-7245)
PHONE.....................................574 257-0099
Jerry Cunningham, *President*
William Thompson, *President*
Allen Campbell, *General Mgr*
Pete Finchum, *Plant Mgr*
Chris Jacobsen, *Project Mgr*
EMP: 40
SQ FT: 23,000
SALES (est): 9.5MM **Privately Held**
SIC: 3991 8711 3567 3563 Brooms & brushes; industrial engineers; industrial furnaces & ovens; air & gas compressors

(G-10088)
MILITARY NEON SIGNS
3304 Wild Cherry Rdg W (46544-6901)
PHONE.....................................574 258-9804
Ted Spear, *Owner*
EMP: 2
SALES (est): 91K **Privately Held**
SIC: 3993 Neon signs

(G-10089)
MISHAWAKA LLC
609 E Jefferson Blvd (46545-6524)
PHONE.....................................574 259-1981
James G Johnson,
EMP: 3
SALES (est): 89.1K **Privately Held**
SIC: 3542 Magnetic forming machines

(G-10090)
MISHAWAKA DOOR LLC
58743 Executive Dr (46544-6845)
PHONE.....................................574 259-2822
Martin Madden, *General Mgr*
EMP: 4 EST: 2008
SALES (est): 619.5K **Privately Held**
SIC: 2431 Door frames, wood

(G-10091)
MISHAWAKA FOOD PANTRY INC
315 Lincolnway W (46544-1903)
PHONE.....................................574 220-6213
Michael Hayes, *Director*
EMP: 3
SALES (est): 553.9K **Privately Held**
SIC: 2099 Food preparations

(G-10092)
MISHAWAKA FROZEN CUSTARD
Also Called: Ritter's Frozen Custard
3921 N Main St (46545-3107)
PHONE.....................................574 255-8000
Bob Jaques, *Owner*
EMP: 30
SALES (est): 1.8MM **Privately Held**
SIC: 2024 8322 5451 5812 Ice cream & frozen desserts; hotline; ice cream (packaged); eating places

(G-10093)
MISHAWAKA WHSE & DISTRG LLC
2017 Elder Rd (46545-7323)
PHONE.....................................574 259-6011
George Derbin,
Dolores J Derbin,
EMP: 2
SQ FT: 28,300
SALES: 250K **Privately Held**
SIC: 2541 Sink tops, plastic laminated

(G-10094)
NCP COATINGS INC
Also Called: Mishawaka Devision
1413 Clover Rd (46545-7271)
PHONE.....................................574 255-9678
Fax: 574 255-9679
Sherman Drew, *Manager*
EMP: 6

SALES (corp-wide): 17.9MM **Privately Held**
WEB: www.ncpcoatings.com
SIC: 2851 2899 Paints & allied products; core oil or binders
PA: Ncp Coatings, Inc.
225 Fort St
Niles MI 49120
269 683-3377

(G-10095)
NEXT DAY SIGNS
Also Called: Next Day Signs & Images
13565 Us 20 (46545)
PHONE.....................................574 259-7446
Fax: 574 259-7170
Marlene Iza, *Owner*
EMP: 2
SQ FT: 2,000
SALES (est): 148.1K **Privately Held**
SIC: 3993 Signs & advertising specialties

(G-10096)
NOODLE ALLEY
2370 Miracle Ln (46545-3012)
PHONE.....................................574 258-1889
Naya Sursag, *Owner*
EMP: 8 EST: 2009
SALES (est): 672.4K **Privately Held**
SIC: 2098 Noodles (e.g. egg, plain & water), dry

(G-10097)
NORTH WOODS VILLAGE
1409 E Day Rd (46545-3671)
PHONE.....................................574 247-1866
North Woods, *Principal*
EMP: 8
SALES (est): 1.3MM **Privately Held**
SIC: 2499 Wood products

(G-10098)
NYLONCRAFT INC (HQ)
Also Called: Techniplas
616 W Mckinley Ave (46545-5597)
PHONE.....................................574 256-1521
Mark Hagan, *President*
Bob Krzozowski, *COO*
Roland Erb, *Vice Pres*
Dennis Wasikowski, *Vice Pres*
Tim Schrock, *Plant Mgr*
▲ EMP: 357
SQ FT: 165,000
SALES (est): 174.1MM
SALES (corp-wide): 303.3MM **Privately Held**
WEB: www.nyloncraft.com
SIC: 3089 Injection molding of plastics
PA: Techniplas, Llc
N44w33341 Wtrtwn Plnk Rd
Nashotah WI 53058
262 369-5555

(G-10099)
PANGLOSS INDUSTRIES INC
2215 Waters Edge Ct (46545-7281)
PHONE.....................................574 217-8505
Jill Judge, *Principal*
EMP: 2
SALES (est): 149K **Privately Held**
SIC: 3999 Manufacturing industries

(G-10100)
PATRICK INDUSTRIES INC
Also Called: West Executive Offices
5020 Lincolnway E (46544-4206)
PHONE.....................................574 255-9692
Dale Smith, *Branch Mgr*
EMP: 225
SALES (corp-wide): 1.6B **Publicly Held**
WEB: www.patrickind.com
SIC: 2295 Coated fabrics, not rubberized
PA: Patrick Industries, Inc.
107 W Franklin St
Elkhart IN 46516
574 294-7511

(G-10101)
PATRICK INDUSTRIES INC
Metals Division
5020 Lincolnway E (46544-4206)
PHONE.....................................574 255-9692
Red Wiedner, *Manager*
EMP: 150

SALES (corp-wide): 1.6B **Publicly Held**
WEB: www.patrickind.com
SIC: 3354 5031 Aluminum extruded products; lumber, plywood & millwork
PA: Patrick Industries, Inc.
107 W Franklin St
Elkhart IN 46516
574 294-7511

(G-10102)
PAUL TIROTTA
Also Called: Maverick Molding
1701 E 6th St (46544-3208)
PHONE.....................................574 255-4101
Fax: 574 255-4114
Paul Tirotta, *Owner*
EMP: 10
SQ FT: 14,000
SALES: 750K **Privately Held**
SIC: 3089 Injection molding of plastics

(G-10103)
PENZ PRODUCTS INC
1320 S Merrifield Ave (46544-5709)
PHONE.....................................574 255-4736
Fax: 574 256-0624
David A Penzenik, *President*
Richard Penzenik, *President*
Gregory Penzenik, *Vice Pres*
Bryan Rozmarynowski, *Prdtn Mgr*
Jim Severns, *Maint Spvr*
▲ EMP: 40
SQ FT: 70,000
SALES (est): 11.2MM **Privately Held**
WEB: www.penzproductsinc.com
SIC: 3441 3089 Fabricated structural metal; plastic processing

(G-10104)
PLASTIMATIC ARTS CORP
Also Called: Pac Banner Works
3622 N Home St (46545-4316)
PHONE.....................................574 254-9000
Timothy Rink, *President*
Lisa Rink, *Corp Secy*
Melanie Horvath, *Finance Mgr*
Mary Anne Riffel, *Finance Other*
Dan Clark, *Marketing Staff*
EMP: 25
SQ FT: 30,000
SALES (est): 4.2MM **Privately Held**
WEB: www.pacbannerworks.com
SIC: 3993 3999 3953 2759 Signs & advertising specialties; plaques, picture, laminated; embossing seals & hand stamps; screen printing; screen printing on fabric articles; bookbinding & related work

(G-10105)
POWER COMPONENTS OF MIDWEST
56641 Twin Branch Dr (46545-7479)
P.O. Box 1348 (46546-1348)
PHONE.....................................574 256-6990
Fax: 574 256-6643
Todd Webster, *President*
Larry Jante, *Vice Pres*
Gary Holvoet, *Treasurer*
James D Waters, *Admin Sec*
EMP: 180
SQ FT: 84,000
SALES (est): 20.9MM **Privately Held**
SIC: 3625 3674 5063 Switches, electric power; semiconductors & related devices; switchgear

(G-10106)
PRECISION ELECTRIC INC
Also Called: Precision Electronics
1508 W 6th St (46544-1640)
P.O. Box 451 (46546-0451)
PHONE.....................................574 256-1000
Joe Chamberlin, *President*
Kerry R Dodd, *Vice Pres*
Jason Billmaier, *Project Mgr*
Patrick Joyce, *Sales Staff*
Ryan Chamberlin, *Marketing Staff*
▲ EMP: 22 EST: 1987
SQ FT: 28,000
SALES (est): 5.9MM **Privately Held**
WEB: www.precision-elec.com
SIC: 7694 3599 Electric motor repair; machine shop, jobbing & repair

(G-10107)
PRECISION PIECE PARTS INC
712 S Logan St (46544-4892)
PHONE.....................................574 255-3185
Fax: 574 255-2086
Gregory C Rogers, *President*
Joe Norris, *Mfg Mgr*
Joe Przygoda, *QC Mgr*
Jim Lawrence, *Engineer*
Karen Steele, *Controller*
EMP: 60 EST: 1943
SQ FT: 25,000
SALES (est): 9.4MM **Privately Held**
WEB: www.ppp-inc.com
SIC: 3728 3842 3451 Aircraft parts & equipment; surgical appliances & supplies; implants, surgical; screw machine products

(G-10108)
PRINT MY MERCH LLC ✪
14208 Dragoon Trl (46544-6831)
PHONE.....................................765 269-6772
Jacob Dobransky, *CEO*
EMP: 2 EST: 2017
SALES (est): 83.9K **Privately Held**
SIC: 2752 Commercial printing, lithographic

(G-10109)
PRINTING EMPORIUM INC
Also Called: Zipp Print
235 E Mckinley Ave Ste 2 (46545-6260)
PHONE.....................................574 256-0059
Fax: 574 256-0093
Mark Sirok, *Manager*
EMP: 2
SALES (est): 220K **Privately Held**
WEB: www.zip-printing.com
SIC: 2752 2791 Lithographing on metal; typesetting

(G-10110)
PRO TOOL & ENGINEERING INC
3723 N Home St (46545-4313)
PHONE.....................................574 256-5911
Fax: 574 256-5911
Paul Kitkowski, *President*
Kathy Kitkowski, *Corp Secy*
EMP: 13
SQ FT: 10,000
SALES: 600K **Privately Held**
SIC: 3544 Industrial molds

(G-10111)
PROFESSIONAL PERMITS
2319 Lincolnway E (46544-3314)
PHONE.....................................574 257-2954
Doug Merritt, *Owner*
EMP: 3
SALES (est): 327.8K **Privately Held**
SIC: 3993 Signs & advertising specialties

(G-10112)
PULLIAM ENTERPRISES INC
Also Called: Pull Rite
13790 Jefferson Blvd (46545-7345)
PHONE.....................................574 259-1520
Fax: 574 258-0289
Andrew Pulliam, *Ch of Bd*
Randall A Pulliam, *President*
Linda Hampton, *Vice Pres*
Leota Pulliam, *Admin Sec*
EMP: 50 EST: 1978
SQ FT: 25,000
SALES (est): 9.3MM **Privately Held**
SIC: 3714 Trailer hitches, motor vehicle

(G-10113)
R & D MOLD & ENGINEERING INC
1710 Clover Rd (46545-7272)
PHONE.....................................574 257-1070
Robert Roose, *President*
Karen Egendoerfer-Roose, *Corp Secy*
EMP: 8
SQ FT: 6,400
SALES: 900K **Privately Held**
WEB: www.rdmold.com
SIC: 3544 Industrial molds

(G-10114)
R & R BOWLING INC
Also Called: Randy Harvey Pro Shop
1504 Chestnut St (46545-6464)
PHONE............................574 252-4123
Randy Harvey, *President*
EMP: 2
SQ FT: 2,500
SALES (est): 125K **Privately Held**
WEB: www.randyharveysproshop.com
SIC: 3949 Bowling equipment & supplies

(G-10115)
RACEWAY DISTRIBUTING INC
2803 N Main St (46545-3305)
PHONE............................574 850-8191
EMP: 3
SALES (est): 238.2K **Privately Held**
SIC: 3644 Raceways

(G-10116)
RENSEW INC
706 E Broadway St (46545-6741)
PHONE............................574 257-0665
Richard R Howell, *Principal*
EMP: 2
SALES (est): 102.9K **Privately Held**
SIC: 2395 Embroidery & art needlework

(G-10117)
RICK SINGLETON
Also Called: Studio A Advertising
203 N Main St (46544-1410)
PHONE............................574 259-5555
Rick Singleton, *Owner*
Ron Martin, *Graphic Designe*
EMP: 25
SQ FT: 20,000
SALES (est): 2.8MM **Privately Held**
WEB: www.studioaadvertising.com
SIC: 7311 2721 Advertising agencies;
magazines: publishing only, not printed on
site

(G-10118)
RIVER VALLEY SHEET METAL INC
Also Called: Air & Energy
58785 Executive Dr (46544-6845)
P.O. Box 591 (46546-0591)
PHONE............................574 259-2538
Fax: 574 256-2293
Mark Siebert, *President*
Kurt Siebert, *Exec VP*
Marlene Siebert, *Vice Pres*
Kurt Jeff Siebert, *Admin Sec*
EMP: 26
SQ FT: 27,000
SALES (est): 3.5MM **Privately Held**
SIC: 1761 3444 5039 Roofing, siding &
sheet metal work; sheet metalwork; air
ducts, sheet metal

(G-10119)
RX HONING MACHINE CORP
1301 E 5th St (46544-2899)
PHONE............................574 259-1606
Fax: 574 259-9163
R J Watson, *President*
Vickie Watson, *Treasurer*
EMP: 4
SQ FT: 6,000
SALES (est): 320K **Privately Held**
SIC: 3541 7699 Honing & lapping ma-
chines; knife, saw & tool sharpening & re-
pair

(G-10120)
SAMPSON FIBERGLASS INC
2424 N Home St (46545-4426)
PHONE............................574 255-4356
Fax: 574 255-4623
Edwin Sampson, *President*
Konnie Sampson, *Vice Pres*
EMP: 31
SALES (est): 4.1MM **Privately Held**
SIC: 2221 Fiberglass fabrics

(G-10121)
SCHURZ COMMUNICATIONS INC (HQ)
1301 E Douglas Rd Ste 200 (46545-1732)
PHONE............................574 247-7237
Todd Schurz, *President*
Gary N Hoipkemier, *CFO*

EMP: 15 EST: 1872
SQ FT: 1,500
SALES (est): 667.1MM
SALES (corp-wide): 882.7MM **Publicly Held**
WEB: www.schurz.com
SIC: 4833 2711 Television broadcasting
stations; newspapers, publishing & print-
ing
PA: Gray Television, Inc.
4370 Peachtree Rd Ne # 500
Brookhaven GA 30319
404 504-9828

(G-10122)
SCITT INC
Also Called: Science For Today and Tomor-
row
1840 E 12th St (46545-5904)
P.O. Box 7037, Fishers (46038-7037)
PHONE............................574 208-6649
Fax: 574 258-5594
Timothy Ludwig, *President*
Arnold F Ludwig, *Admin Sec*
EMP: 4
SALES (est): 473.9K **Privately Held**
WEB: www.scittkits.com
SIC: 3944 8732 Science kits: micro-
scopes, chemistry sets, etc.; commercial
nonphysical research

(G-10123)
SIGN FACTORY
55811 Elder Rd (46545-4605)
PHONE............................574 255-7446
EMP: 2 EST: 2009
SALES (est): 118.8K **Privately Held**
SIC: 3993 Signs & advertising specialties

(G-10124)
SIGNS UNLIMITED
4121 Lincolnway E (46544-4022)
PHONE............................574 255-0500
Mike Stowe, *Owner*
EMP: 3
SALES (est): 258.7K **Privately Held**
SIC: 3993 Signs & advertising specialties

(G-10125)
SLB CORPORATION
Also Called: Hose Assemblies
1906 E Mckinley Ave (46545-7206)
PHONE............................574 255-9774
Fax: 574 255-0932
Matthew B Veldman, *President*
Sue Matthys, *Athletic Dir*
▲ EMP: 18
SALES (est): 4.3MM **Privately Held**
WEB: www.hoseassem.com
SIC: 3052 3492 3429 Rubber hose; fluid
power valves & hose fittings; manufac-
tured hardware (general)

(G-10126)
SMART SYSTEMS
303 S Byrkit St (46544-2904)
PHONE............................800 348-0823
Michael Miller, *Partner*
Melissa Miller, *Office Mgr*
EMP: 4
SALES (est): 140K **Privately Held**
SIC: 2842 Sanitation preparations

(G-10127)
SMART TEMPS LLC
435 Park Place Cir # 100 (46545-3578)
PHONE............................574 217-8847
John Miller, *President*
Michael McKay, *COO*
Jason Driscoll, *Opers Staff*
Kristin Agostino, *CFO*
Evan Barnum-Steggerd, *Regl Sales Mgr*
EMP: 5
SALES (est): 1MM **Privately Held**
SIC: 3822 Refrigeration thermostats

(G-10128)
SMITH SIGNS INC
Also Called: Smith Graphics & Design
317 Capital Ave (46545-3343)
PHONE............................574 255-6446
Fax: 574 255-8055
Douglas Smith, *President*
EMP: 9

SALES (est): 1.3MM **Privately Held**
SIC: 3993 Signs, not made in custom sign
painting shops

(G-10129)
SNARK PUBLISHING LLC
340 Park Ave (46545-6905)
PHONE............................574 256-1027
Lori Scaskey-Sigety, *Principal*
EMP: 2
SALES (est): 88.3K **Privately Held**
SIC: 2711 Newspapers

(G-10130)
SNOW MANAGEMENT GROUP
14009 Jefferson Blvd (46545-7338)
PHONE............................574 252-5253
Thomas Lovisa, *Principal*
EMP: 3
SALES (est): 221K **Privately Held**
SIC: 2851 Removers & cleaners

(G-10131)
SOUTH BEND CLUTCH INC
709 W Jefferson Blvd (46545-5843)
PHONE............................574 256-5064
Fax: 574 256-2568
Walter Pyfer, *President*
Andrew Pyfer, *Vice Pres*
Dave Winter, *Mfg Staff*
Peter Pyfer, *Director*
Mary A Bauer, *Admin Sec*
▲ EMP: 24
SQ FT: 6,000
SALES (est): 6.1MM **Privately Held**
WEB: www.southbendclutch.com
SIC: 3714 Clutches, motor vehicle

(G-10132)
SOUTH BEND MODERN MOLDING INC
605 Laurel St (46544-2328)
P.O. Box 850 (46546-0850)
PHONE............................574 255-0711
Charles Zimmerman, *President*
Donald Zimmerman, *Vice Pres*
Russ Johnson, *Engineer*
Brian Kanouse, *Engineer*
Penny Holderman, *Sales Staff*
▲ EMP: 60 EST: 1942
SQ FT: 100,000
SALES (est): 17.3MM **Privately Held**
WEB: www.sbmm.com
SIC: 3061 3069 Mechanical rubber goods;
rubber automotive products

(G-10133)
SOUTH BEND SCREEN PROCESS INC (PA)
Also Called: Shape Man
3622 N Home St (46545-4316)
PHONE............................574 254-9000
Robert Kistler, *President*
Sue Kistler, *Admin Sec*
EMP: 7 EST: 1954
SQ FT: 11,000
SALES (est): 820.1K **Privately Held**
WEB: www.southbendscreen.com
SIC: 2759 Screen printing; decals: printing;
posters, including billboards: printing

(G-10134)
SOUTHLAND METALS INC
4042 Southampton Dr (46544-9139)
PHONE............................574 252-4441
Keith Crawford, *President*
EMP: 5
SALES (corp-wide): 5.8MM **Privately Held**
SIC: 3325 Steel foundries
PA: Southland Metals, Inc.
115 Carnahan Dr Ste 2
Maumelle AR 72113
501 851-1166

(G-10135)
STANDARD MOTOR PRODUCTS INC
Also Called: Ristance
1718 N Home St (46545-7237)
PHONE............................574 259-6253
Fax: 574 259-6945
Mike Schreiber, *Prdtn Mgr*
Dean Petros, *Materials Mgr*
Jim Goodnough, *Purch Agent*

Beth Carpenter, *Human Res Mgr*
Gerald Anton, *Persnl Mgr*
EMP: 136
SALES (corp-wide): 1.1B **Publicly Held**
WEB: www.smpcorp.com
SIC: 3694 Ignition apparatus, internal com-
bustion engines
PA: Standard Motor Products, Inc.
3718 Northern Blvd # 600
Long Island City NY 11101
718 392-0200

(G-10136)
STEEL AVENUE INC
3848 Cottage Ave (46544-3857)
PHONE............................517 238-2220
Andrew Bonham, *President*
Kim Bonham, *Corp Secy*
EMP: 2
SALES (est): 331.3K **Privately Held**
SIC: 3312 Slabs, steel

(G-10137)
SUBSTRATE TREATMENTS LUBR INC
Also Called: ST&I
1309 S Byrkit Ave (46544-5837)
P.O. Box 1966 (46546-1966)
PHONE............................574 258-0904
Fax: 574 258-0944
Robert Kvietkus, *President*
EMP: 9
SALES (est): 160.1K **Privately Held**
SIC: 2819 Industrial inorganic chemicals

(G-10138)
SUPERIOR PIECE PARTS INC
54015 Fir Rd (46545-1701)
PHONE............................574 277-4236
Fax: 574 259-6607
Harvey Ludwig, *President*
Gale Meisner, *Vice Pres*
EMP: 15 EST: 1965
SQ FT: 14,900
SALES (est): 800K **Privately Held**
SIC: 3599 Machine shop, jobbing & repair

(G-10139)
T PRODUCTIONS INC
504 S Byrkit St (46544-3010)
PHONE............................574 257-8610
Tony Kozlowski, *President*
Deanna Kozlowski, *Vice Pres*
EMP: 11 EST: 1999
SALES (est): 1MM **Privately Held**
WEB: www.t-productions.com
SIC: 2759 Screen printing

(G-10140)
TOOLMASTERS INC
1203 E 6th St (46544-2896)
PHONE............................574 256-1881
Fax: 574 259-7123
Ron Newcomer, *President*
Donald Barbour, *Vice Pres*
EMP: 8
SQ FT: 10,000
SALES: 750K **Privately Held**
SIC: 3544 3542 Special dies & tools;
welding positioners (jigs); machine tools,
metal forming type

(G-10141)
TRIPLEX INDUSTRIES INC
55901 Currant Rd (46545-4803)
PHONE............................574 256-9253
Fax: 574 258-4284
Kevin Geisel, *President*
Larry Geisel, *Vice Pres*
Kathleen Geisel, *Shareholder*
▲ EMP: 14
SQ FT: 8,000
SALES (est): 1.7MM **Privately Held**
WEB: www.genesismolding.com
SIC: 3544 Industrial molds

(G-10142)
UNITED CONVEYOR CORPORATION
13077 Mckinley Hwy (46545-7598)
PHONE............................574 256-0991
Fax: 574 256-3765
Mark Pajakowski, *Branch Mgr*
EMP: 40

SALES (corp-wide): 183.7MM **Privately Held**
WEB: www.unitedconveyorsupply.com
SIC: 3535 3532 5084 Conveyors & conveying equipment; mining machinery; conveyor systems
HQ: United Conveyor Corporation
2100 Norman Dr
Waukegan IL 60085
847 473-5900

(G-10143)
UNITED TOOL & ENGINEERING INC
337 Campbell St (46544-2898)
PHONE..................................574 259-1953
Fax: 574 258-6721
Richard Penn, *President*
John R Penn, *Treasurer*
EMP: 42
SQ FT: 40,000
SALES (est): 6.9MM **Privately Held**
WEB: www.unitedtleng.com
SIC: 3544 Special dies, tools, jigs & fixtures; special dies & tools; jigs & fixtures

(G-10144)
VALLEY SCREEN PROCESS CO INC
58740 Executive Dr (46544-6898)
PHONE..................................574 256-0901
Fax: 574 255-7966
Jerome E Bauer, *CEO*
Karen M Barnett, *President*
Martin Hess, *Vice Pres*
Carol Bauer, *Admin Sec*
▲ EMP: 77 EST: 1967
SQ FT: 60,000
SALES (est): 19.1MM **Privately Held**
SIC: 2759 Screen printing

(G-10145)
VAN COM INC
Also Called: Welded Products Div
1030 N Merrifield Ave (46545-6713)
PHONE..................................574 255-9689
Fax: 574 256-1885
Kamiel Vandevoorde, *President*
Jay Rantz, *Purchasing*
EMP: 35
SQ FT: 26,000
SALES (est): 5.8MM **Privately Held**
SIC: 3599 Machine shop, jobbing & repair

(G-10146)
VERTICAL PLUS MRI AMERICA LLC
3838 N Main St Ste 1a (46545-3100)
PHONE..................................574 257-4674
Roalsen Merritt, *Branch Mgr*
EMP: 6
SALES (est): 582.9K
SALES (corp-wide): 129.4K **Privately Held**
SIC: 2591 Blinds vertical
PA: Vertical Plus Mri Of America, Llc
3330 W 177th St Ste 1d
Hazel Crest IL 60429
708 799-4940

(G-10147)
VIRTUOSO DISTILLERS LLC
4211 Grape Rd (46545-2657)
PHONE..................................574 876-4450
Steven Ross, *President*
EMP: 5
SALES (est): 276.5K **Privately Held**
SIC: 2085 Distilled & blended liquors

(G-10148)
VISION MACHINE WORKS INC
Also Called: K & P Products
56540 Twin Branch Dr (46545-7477)
PHONE..................................574 259-6500
James Niemier, *President*
Michael Szymczak, *Vice Pres*
Rj Hohl, *Plant Mgr*
Mike Rowe, *Manager*
EMP: 14
SQ FT: 14,000
SALES (est): 2.5MM **Privately Held**
WEB: www.vmwinc.net
SIC: 3599 7692 3544 Machine shop, jobbing & repair; welding repair; special dies, tools, jigs & fixtures

(G-10149)
WAKA MFG INC
945 E 5th St (46544-2835)
PHONE..................................574 258-0019
Fax: 574 258-1807
Joseph J Gyarmati Sr, *President*
Joseph J Gyarmati Jr, *Vice Pres*
EMP: 5
SQ FT: 8,000
SALES (est): 430K **Privately Held**
SIC: 3599 Machine shop, jobbing & repair

(G-10150)
WELLPET LLC
1025 W 11th St (46544-4818)
PHONE..................................574 259-7834
Doug Mitchell, *Plant Mgr*
EMP: 100
SALES (corp-wide): 98.5MM **Privately Held**
SIC: 2047 Dog & cat food
PA: Wellpet Llc
200 Ames Pond Dr Ste 200 # 200
Tewksbury MA 01876
877 869-2971

(G-10151)
WESTROCK CP LLC
1925 Stone Ct (46545-4441)
PHONE..................................574 256-0318
Fax: 574 259-7898
Bob Feeney, *Branch Mgr*
EMP: 135
SALES (corp-wide): 14.8B **Publicly Held**
WEB: www.smurfit-stone.com
SIC: 2653 5113 Boxes, corrugated: made from purchased materials; corrugated & solid fiber boxes
HQ: Westrock Cp, Llc
504 Thrasher St
Norcross GA 30071

(G-10152)
YELLOW DOOR PUBLISHING LLC
637 Misty Harbour Ct (46544-4153)
PHONE..................................574 256-5797
Richard Kuehl, *Owner*
EMP: 2
SALES (est): 106.2K **Privately Held**
SIC: 2741 Miscellaneous publishing

(G-10153)
ZH BROTHERS INTERNATIONAL INC
5625 Irish Way Apt 2 (46545-1457)
PHONE..................................313 718-6732
Guoqzang Zhu, *President*
Eric Seigel, *Principal*
▲ EMP: 5
SALES (est): 420K **Privately Held**
SIC: 3678 3751 Electronic connectors; bicycles & related parts

---

Mitchell
Lawrence County

(G-10154)
ADKINS SAWMILL INC
2929 Fleenor Rd (47446)
PHONE..................................812 849-4036
Paul Adkin, *Owner*
EMP: 2
SALES (est): 238.5K **Privately Held**
SIC: 2421 Sawmills & planing mills, general

(G-10155)
AKKA PLASTICS INC
1100 Teke Burton Dr (47446-5398)
P.O. Box 525 (47446-0525)
PHONE..................................812 849-9256
Fax: 812 849-9257
Marvin Stahl, *President*
EMP: 25
SQ FT: 25,000
SALES (est): 5.5MM **Privately Held**
WEB: www.akkainc.net
SIC: 3089 Injection molded finished plastic products; injection molding of plastics

(G-10156)
C T C CORPORATION
3030 Poplar St (47446-8025)
PHONE..................................812 849-2500
Bryan Curl, *President*
EMP: 5
SALES (est): 753.4K **Privately Held**
SIC: 3535 Conveyors & conveying equipment

(G-10157)
C&M CONVEYOR INC
Also Called: Automated Systems Technology
4598 State Road 37 (47446-5388)
PHONE..................................812 849-5647
Fax: 812 849-6166
Don Laipple, *CEO*
Randy Grube, *President*
EMP: 160
SQ FT: 84,000
SALES (est): 57.9MM
SALES (corp-wide): 61.8MM **Privately Held**
WEB: www.cmconveyor.com
SIC: 3535 5084 Conveyors & conveying equipment; conveyor systems
PA: Hammond, Kennedy, Whitney & Company, Inc.
420 Lexington Ave Rm 402
New York NY 10170
212 867-1010

(G-10158)
CAROUSEL WINERY
6058 Lawrenceport Rd (47446-6038)
PHONE..................................812 849-1005
EMP: 2
SALES (est): 135K **Privately Held**
SIC: 2084 Wines

(G-10159)
CONTECH ENGNERED SOLUTIONS LLC
Metric Industrial Park (47446)
PHONE..................................812 849-3933
Fax: 812 849-5974
Joe Behne, *Superintendent*
EMP: 35 **Privately Held**
SIC: 3443 Fabricated plate work (boiler shop)
HQ: Contech Engineered Solutions Llc
9025 Centre Pointe Dr # 400
West Chester OH 45069
513 645-7000

(G-10160)
CONTECH ENGNERED SOLUTIONS LLC
200 John R Williams Ave (47446-8021)
PHONE..................................812 849-3933
Scott Foy, *Accounts Mgr*
Joseph Behne, *Branch Mgr*
EMP: 40 **Privately Held**
SIC: 3443 3444 Fabricated plate work (boiler shop); sheet metalwork
HQ: Contech Engineered Solutions Llc
9025 Centre Pointe Dr # 400
West Chester OH 45069
513 645-7000

(G-10161)
COUPLED PRODUCTS LLC
Preferred Technical Group
1201 Orchard St (47446-1621)
PHONE..................................812 849-5304
Fax: 812 849-3966
Arthur Carter, *General Mgr*
EMP: 400
SQ FT: 90,000 **Privately Held**
SIC: 3714 Motor vehicle parts & accessories
PA: Coupled Products Llc
2651 S 600 E
Columbia City IN 46725

(G-10162)
DREWS DEER PROCESSING
8122 Us Highway 50 W (47446-5439)
PHONE..................................812 279-6246
Denny Perkins, *Principal*
EMP: 3
SALES (est): 167K **Privately Held**
SIC: 2011 Meat packing plants

(G-10163)
FOAMCRAFT INC
100 N Industrial Pkwy (47446-8037)
PHONE..................................812 849-3350
Fax: 812 359-9514
Dick Yerington, *Branch Mgr*
EMP: 46
SQ FT: 32,000
SALES (est): 3.9MM
SALES (corp-wide): 69MM **Privately Held**
SIC: 3086 Plastics foam products
PA: Foamcraft Inc
9230 Harrison Park Ct
Indianapolis IN 46216
317 545-3626

(G-10164)
LAWRENCE CNTY FABRICATION CORP
240 S Meridian Rd (47446-8015)
PHONE..................................812 849-0124
Fax: 812 849-6415
Melissa Barnes, *President*
Dean Barnes, *COO*
▲ EMP: 30
SQ FT: 15,000
SALES (est): 16MM **Privately Held**
SIC: 3441 Fabricated structural metal

(G-10165)
LEHIGH CEMENT COMPANY LLC
180 N Meridian Rd (47446-1144)
P.O. Box 97 (47446-0097)
PHONE..................................812 849-2191
Fax: 812 849-6045
Mike Atchison, *Financial Exec*
Ed Epping, *Branch Mgr*
EMP: 152
SALES (corp-wide): 20.3B **Privately Held**
WEB: www.lehighcement.com
SIC: 3273 3241 Ready-mixed concrete; cement, hydraulic
HQ: Lehigh Cement Company Llc
300 E John Carpenter Fwy
Irving TX 75062
877 534-4442

(G-10166)
MAMMOTH HATS INC
1773 Huron Williams Rd (47446-7470)
PHONE..................................812 849-2772
Charles Clifford, *President*
EMP: 11
SALES: 854.4K **Privately Held**
SIC: 5611 7389 2353 2253 Hats, men's & boys'; ; hats, caps & millinery; hats & headwear, knit; hats: women's, children's & infants'

(G-10167)
MITCHELL INDUSTRIES INC
1407 W Main St (47446-9250)
P.O. Box 559 (47446-0559)
PHONE..................................812 849-4931
Randy Nahvi, *President*
Brenda Bebout, *Vice Pres*
Daniel Talbott, *Plant Mgr*
EMP: 10
SALES (est): 910K **Privately Held**
SIC: 3312 Blast furnaces & steel mills

(G-10168)
NOVELS BY NELLOTIE
393 Sonny Dorsett Rd (47446-7355)
PHONE..................................812 583-1196
Nellotie Chastain, *Principal*
EMP: 2 EST: 2015
SALES (est): 90.1K **Privately Held**
SIC: 2741 Miscellaneous publishing

(G-10169)
RED BULL ARMORY LLC
440 Peaceful Valley Rd (47446-6822)
PHONE..................................757 287-7738
Christopher Higgins, *CEO*
EMP: 2
SALES (est): 149.4K **Privately Held**
SIC: 3484 7389 Guns (firearms) or gun parts, 30 mm. & below; inspection & testing services

---

(G-10170)
ROGERS GROUP INC
Also Called: Mitchell Crushed Stone
3020 State Road 60 W (47446-7556)
PHONE..........................812 849-3530
Fax: 812 849-6483
David Knight, *Foreman/Supr*
Craig Huffine, *Sales Executive*
Danny Powell, *Manager*
EMP: 23
SALES (corp-wide): 1B Privately Held
WEB: www.rogersgroupinc.com
SIC: 1442 5032 3295 3274 Construction
sand & gravel; stone, crushed or broken;
minerals, ground or treated; lime
PA: Rogers Group, Inc.
421 Great Circle Rd
Nashville TN 37228
615 242-0585

(G-10171)
SPX CORPORATION
4598 State Road 37 (47446-5388)
P.O. Box 379 (47446-0379)
PHONE..........................812 849-5647
Jeff Smithers, *President*
EMP: 120
SALES (corp-wide): 1.4B Publicly Held
WEB: www.spx.com
SIC: 3443 Cooling towers, metal plate
PA: Spx Corporation
13320a Balntyn Corp Pl
Charlotte NC 28277
980 474-3700

(G-10172)
STEELTECH PARTNERS LLC
240 S Meridian Rd (47446-8015)
PHONE..........................812 849-0124
Mark Suvak, *CEO*
Dean Barnes, *COO*
Dan Brown, *CFO*
EMP: 6
SALES (est): 477.4K Privately Held
SIC: 3441 Fabricated structural metal

Modoc
Randolph County

(G-10173)
GRO-TEC INC
10324 W Us Highway 36 (47358-9371)
PHONE..........................765 853-1246
Fax: 765 853-5886
Richard Martin, *President*
Tyler Martin, *Vice Pres*
Penny Martin, *Admin Sec*
EMP: 14
SQ FT: 9,000
SALES: 2.2MM Privately Held
SIC: 2048 Feed premixes; mineral feed
supplements

(G-10174)
**M & S SCREW MACHINE
PRODUCTS**
S Main St (47358)
P.O. Box 223, Lynn (47355-0223)
PHONE..........................765 853-5022
Fax: 765 853-5068
Richard Million, *President*
EMP: 7
SQ FT: 15,000
SALES: 500K Privately Held
SIC: 3599 Machine shop, jobbing & repair

Monon
White County

(G-10175)
DEERWOOD GROUP
792 E State Road 16 (47959-8503)
PHONE..........................219 866-5521
Harold A Smith, *Owner*
EMP: 4
SQ FT: 1,500
SALES (est): 199.6K Privately Held
WEB: www.enigami.com
SIC: 2522 2599 Cabinets, office: except
wood; cabinets, factory

(G-10176)
LEGACY VULCAN LLC
Midwest Division
6857 N Us Highway 421 (47959-8000)
PHONE..........................219 253-6686
Fax: 219 253-8498
Bob Agley, *Opers-Prdtn-Mfg*
EMP: 11 Publicly Held
WEB: www.vulcanmaterials.com
SIC: 1442 Construction sand & gravel
HQ: Legacy Vulcan, Llc
1200 Urban Center Dr
Vestavia AL 35242
205 298-3000

(G-10177)
**MONON MEAT PACKING
COMPANY**
402 N Railroad St (47959-8177)
P.O. Box 776 (47959-0776)
PHONE..........................219 253-6363
Fax: 219 253-6363
Scott Wiggins, *President*
Sandy Wiggins, *Treasurer*
EMP: 6
SQ FT: 10,000
SALES (est): 998.6K Privately Held
SIC: 2011 Meat packing plants

(G-10178)
ROSE ACRE FARMS INC
Also Called: White County Egg Farms
5408 W State Road 16 (47959-8067)
PHONE..........................219 253-6681
Fax: 219 253-7296
David Gibson, *Manager*
EMP: 60
SALES (corp-wide): 665.1MM Privately
Held
WEB: www.roseacre.com
SIC: 0191 2015 0252 General farms, pri-
marily crop; poultry slaughtering & pro-
cessing; chicken eggs
PA: Rose Acre Farms Inc
1657 W Tipton St
Seymour IN 47274
812 497-2557

(G-10179)
**VANGUARD NATIONAL TRAILER
CORP (HQ)**
289 Water Tower Dr (47959-8160)
P.O. Box 748, Monticello (47960-0748)
PHONE..........................219 253-2000
Fax: 219 253-7386
Charles Mudd, *CEO*
Mary Blanchette, *Regional Mgr*
Jeff Hyatt, *Vice Pres*
Kevin Black, *Plant Mgr*
William Caudill, *Materials Mgr*
▲ EMP: 277
SQ FT: 400,000
SALES: 333.7MM
SALES (corp-wide): 11.5B Privately Held
WEB: www.vanguardtrailer.com
SIC: 3715 3713 Truck trailers; truck bod-
ies & parts
PA: China International Marine Containers
(Group) Co., Ltd.
Cimc R&D Center, No.2 Gangwan Av-
enue,Shekou Industrial Zone,Nans
Shenzhen 51806
755 268-0263

(G-10180)
WHISTLE STOP
10012 N Us Highway 421 (47959-8253)
PHONE..........................219 253-4100
Dale Ward, *Owner*
EMP: 2
SALES (est): 121.7K Privately Held
SIC: 3999 Whistles

Monroe
Adams County

(G-10181)
ECKHART WOODWORKING INC
424 S Van Buren St (46772-9308)
PHONE..........................260 692-6218
Fax: 260 592-7008
Joe Eckhart, *President*
Tim Eckhart, *Vice Pres*

EMP: 29
SQ FT: 11,000
SALES (est): 3.9MM Privately Held
SIC: 2431 Moldings & baseboards, orna-
mental & trim

(G-10182)
GOTOKIOSK LLC
109 E Andrews St (46772-7010)
P.O. Box 157 (46772-0157)
PHONE..........................800 206-0177
EMP: 2
SALES (est): 273.1K Privately Held
SIC: 2541 Counters or counter display
cases, wood

(G-10183)
JOHNSON CONTROLS
424 S Vanburen St (46772)
PHONE..........................260 692-6666
Fax: 260 692-6189
Joe Johnson, *Manager*
EMP: 24 Privately Held
WEB: www.simplexgrinnell.com
SIC: 3669 Emergency alarms
HQ: Johnson Controls Fire Protection Lp
4700 Exchange Ct Ste 300
Boca Raton FL 33431
561 988-7200

(G-10184)
PHAZPAK INC
Also Called: Pems
259 N Van Buren St (46772-9700)
PHONE..........................260 692-6416
Fax: 260 692-6417
Kenneth D Parrish, *President*
John Parrish, *Vice Pres*
Ruth Parrish, *Admin Sec*
▲ EMP: 6
SQ FT: 10,000
SALES (est): 765.3K Privately Held
WEB: www.phazpak.com
SIC: 5063 7694 Motors, electric; electric
motor repair

(G-10185)
STRICK CORPORATION
301 N Polk St (46772-9703)
PHONE..........................260 692-6121
Fax: 260 692-6622
Les Quay, *General Mgr*
Jason Chaney, *Senior Mgr*
Ken Gleason, *Technology*
EMP: 350
SALES (corp-wide): 84.1MM Privately
Held
WEB: www.stricktlr.com
SIC: 3715 Truck trailers
PA: Strick Corporation
225 Lincoln Hwy
Fairless Hills PA 19030
215 949-3600

(G-10186)
STRICK TRAILERS LLC
301 N Polk St (46772-9703)
PHONE..........................260 692-6121
Frank Katz,
EMP: 9
SALES (est): 2.4MM Privately Held
SIC: 3715 Trailer bodies

(G-10187)
SWISS METAL SPINNING CO
2301 W 200 S (46772-9765)
PHONE..........................260 692-1401
Amos Schwartz, *Principal*
EMP: 2 EST: 2008
SALES (est): 130K Privately Held
SIC: 3469 Spinning metal for the trade

Monroe City
Knox County

(G-10188)
SHOUSE SAWMILL
4679 S State Road 241 (47557-7034)
PHONE..........................812 743-2017
Gerald Shouse, *Owner*
EMP: 9 EST: 2008

SALES (est): 1.2MM Privately Held
SIC: 2421 Sawmills & planing mills, general

(G-10189)
TRI-STATE PRINTING & EMB LLC
6250 S State Road 61 (47557-7103)
PHONE..........................812 743-2825
Burdetta Scott, *Principal*
EMP: 2 EST: 2014
SALES (est): 112.3K Privately Held
SIC: 2752 Commercial printing, litho-
graphic

Monroeville
Allen County

(G-10190)
AG PLUS INC
306 W South St (46773-9390)
PHONE..........................260 623-6121
Ron Roy, *Branch Mgr*
EMP: 3
SALES (corp-wide): 102.1MM Privately
Held
SIC: 5191 2041 5153 Fertilizers & agricul-
tural chemicals; flour & other grain mill
products; grain elevators
PA: Ag Plus, Inc.
401 N Main St
South Whitley IN 46787
260 723-5141

(G-10191)
**AMERICAN MITSUBA
CORPORATION**
Also Called: American Mtsuba Corp Ind Plant
21600 Monroeville Rd (46773-9623)
PHONE..........................989 779-4962
Mishel Ashtary, *Branch Mgr*
EMP: 190
SQ FT: 96,000
SALES (corp-wide): 3.6B Privately Held
WEB: www.cmellc.com
SIC: 3621 3714 Motors, electric; motor ve-
hicle parts & accessories
HQ: American Mitsuba Corporation
2945 Three Leaves Dr
Mount Pleasant MI 48858
989 779-4962

(G-10192)
CME LLC
21600 Monroeville Rd (46773-9623)
PHONE..........................260 623-3700
Fax: 260 623-3773
Marlene Dehner, *Manager*
Toshifumi Kohno,
▲ EMP: 261
SALES (est): 39.6MM Privately Held
WEB: www.cmellc.com
SIC: 3643 Current-carrying wiring devices

(G-10193)
**CUSTOM HARDWOOD
CABINETRY**
12504 Fackler Rd (46773-9538)
PHONE..........................260 623-3147
Matt Hunter, *Owner*
EMP: 2
SALES (est): 87.9K Privately Held
SIC: 2521 Cabinets, office: wood

(G-10194)
DUX SIGNAL KITS LLC
23132 Monroeville Rd (46773-9647)
PHONE..........................260 623-3017
Neil Ternet, *Mng Member*
EMP: 2
SALES: 470K Privately Held
SIC: 3669 7389 5063 Signaling appara-
tus, electric; ; signaling equipment, electri-
cal

(G-10195)
**GERARDOT PERFORMANCE
PRODUCTS**
108 W Barnhart St (46773-9392)
P.O. Box 223 (46773-0223)
PHONE..........................260 623-3048
Donald Gerardot, *Owner*
EMP: 5 EST: 1967

SALES: 500K **Privately Held**
SIC: 2399 Seat belts, automobile & aircraft

(G-10196)
KATHYS SEWING INC
10118 Grotrian Rd (46773-9580)
PHONE......................................260 623-6387
Katherine Sheehan, *Owner*
EMP: 3
SALES (est): 218.3K **Privately Held**
SIC: 2399 Fabricated textile products

(G-10197)
MONROEVILLE BOX PALLET & WOOD
Also Called: Freedom Lumber Company
20009 Monroeville Rd (46773-9589)
P.O. Box 505 (46773-0505)
PHONE......................................260 623-3128
Fax: 260 623-3183
Donald Witte, *CEO*
Eric Kissinger, *President*
Donald Green, *General Mgr*
EMP: 24
SQ FT: 44,000
SALES: 1.8MM **Privately Held**
SIC: 2448 2441 Pallets, wood; shipping
cases, wood: nailed or lock corner

(G-10198)
PRECAST SPECIALTIES INC
111 Utility Dr (46773-9315)
P.O. Box 452 (46773-0452)
PHONE......................................260 623-6131
Fax: 260 623-3019
William A Kriesel, *President*
Bill Hanford, *Project Mgr*
Danial Schuhler, *Finance Mgr*
Eric Schaekel, *Sales Staff*
EMP: 16
SQ FT: 12,000
SALES (est): 1MM **Privately Held**
WEB: www.precastspec.com
SIC: 3271 3272 Architectural concrete:
block, split, fluted, screen, etc.; concrete
products

(G-10199)
RNG PERFORMANCE LLC
24315 S County Line Rd E (46773-9521)
PHONE......................................260 602-5613
Todd Hoffman, *Owner*
Jenatte Hoffman, *Co-Owner*
EMP: 2 EST: 2011
SALES (est): 102.8K **Privately Held**
SIC: 3519 Parts & accessories, internal
combustion engines

(G-10200)
STENSLAND ENGINES INC
4933 Morgan Rd (46773-9729)
PHONE......................................260 623-6859
David Stensland, *Principal*
EMP: 3
SALES (est): 274.4K **Privately Held**
SIC: 3519 Internal combustion engines

Monrovia
Morgan County

(G-10201)
AIR-TECH INDUSTRIAL DESIGN
580 W Main St (46157-9547)
PHONE......................................317 797-1804
William R Nelson, *President*
EMP: 3
SALES: 3MM **Privately Held**
SIC: 3564 Air purification equipment

(G-10202)
BOB BELCHER
Also Called: Belcher Gravel
6624 W State Road 42 (46157-9395)
PHONE......................................317 996-3712
Bob Belcher, *Principal*
EMP: 3
SALES (est): 120K **Privately Held**
SIC: 1442 Construction sand & gravel

(G-10203)
FAT QUARTER ANNIES QUI
2975 W Crosscreek Dr (46157-8100)
PHONE......................................317 918-1481

EMP: 2
SALES (est): 77.4K **Privately Held**
SIC: 3131 Quarters

(G-10204)
LANGFORDS DELIVERY SERVICE
10 Nw Union Church Rd (46157-1000)
PHONE......................................317 996-3594
Vernon Langford, *President*
EMP: 2
SALES (est): 174.5K **Privately Held**
SIC: 5083 5261 2426 Landscaping equip-
ment; nurseries & garden centers; floor-
ing, hardwood

(G-10205)
PRO TECH AUTOMATION INC
8236 N Hall Rd (46157-9253)
PHONE......................................317 201-3875
David A Foxx, *President*
EMP: 7
SALES: 2MM **Privately Held**
SIC: 3496 Conveyor belts

(G-10206)
SCEPTER STEEL INC
380 Maple St (46157-9559)
PHONE......................................317 996-2103
Janet Mitchell, *President*
EMP: 12
SALES (est): 670K **Privately Held**
SIC: 3272 Concrete products

Monterey
Pulaski County

(G-10207)
K & B TRAILER SALES MFG
93 E 800 N (46960-9116)
PHONE......................................574 946-4382
Keith Bailey, *President*
Connie S Bailey, *Vice Pres*
EMP: 2
SALES: 194K **Privately Held**
SIC: 3523 7692 Trailers & wagons, farm;
welding repair

(G-10208)
PJMORT WOODWORKING
8835 S 1000 E (46960-9336)
PHONE......................................574 542-9680
EMP: 2
SALES (est): 125.5K **Privately Held**
SIC: 2431 Millwork

Montezuma
Parke County

(G-10209)
BIG INCH FABRICATORS CNSTR INC
6127 W Us Highway 36 (47862-8107)
P.O. Box 99 (47862-0099)
PHONE......................................765 245-9353
Fax: 765 245-9355
Douglas McCord, *President*
Blake Hartman, *Corp Secy*
George Brinkley, *Exec VP*
Brad Bhartman, *Manager*
Doug McCord, *Admin Sec*
EMP: 65
SQ FT: 45,000
SALES: 18.4MM **Privately Held**
WEB: www.biginch.net
SIC: 3498 Fabricated pipe & fittings

(G-10210)
NEWLINS WELDING & TANK MAINT
5360 W Us Highway 36 (47862)
P.O. Box 439 (47862-0439)
PHONE......................................765 245-2741
Jerry Newlin, *Owner*
EMP: 2
SALES (est): 369.2K **Privately Held**
SIC: 7699 7692 Aircraft & heavy equip-
ment repair services; welding repair

(G-10211)
TIMBERLAND RESOURCES INC
Also Called: Superior Hardwoods
6429 W 100 N (47862-8011)
PHONE......................................765 245-2634
Jack T Shannon Jr, *President*
James Garrard, *Vice Pres*
EMP: 25
SALES (est): 600.8K
SALES (corp-wide): 117.5MM **Privately Held**
SIC: 2421 Sawmills & planing mills, gen-
eral
PA: J.T. Shannon Lumber Company, Inc.
2200 Cole Rd
Horn Lake MS 38637
662 393-3765

(G-10212)
TRIVAEO LLC
4250 N River Rd (47862-8082)
PHONE......................................765 387-4451
Pat Graham,
Mark Graham,
Connie Helton,
EMP: 3 EST: 2016
SALES (est): 78.2K **Privately Held**
SIC: 7372 7389 Prepackaged software;
business oriented computer software;

Montgomery
Daviess County

(G-10213)
APEXX ENTERPRISES LLC
Also Called: Apexx Engineering
973 S 800 E (47558-5346)
PHONE......................................812 486-2443
Shad Truelove, *Partner*
EMP: 15 EST: 2013
SQ FT: 8,070
SALES (est): 1.2MM **Privately Held**
SIC: 3089 3479 3053 2821 Plastic &
fiberglass tanks; painting, coating & hot
dipping; packing, metallic; polystyrene
resins; vinyl resins

(G-10214)
BARBS HOMEMADE NOODLES
787 S 700 E (47558-5562)
PHONE......................................812 486-3762
Frank Grayber, *Partner*
EMP: 2
SALES (est): 91.6K **Privately Held**
SIC: 2098 Noodles (e.g. egg, plain &
water), dry

(G-10215)
BILL GRABER LOGGING LLC
6722 E 400 N (47558-5291)
PHONE......................................812 486-2709
William Graber, *Owner*
EMP: 3
SALES (est): 158.4K **Privately Held**
SIC: 2411 Logging

(G-10216)
CEDAR WOODWORKING
Also Called: Knapp Engraving
7932 E 625 N (47558-5085)
PHONE......................................812 486-2765
William Knapp, *Owner*
Darvin Knapp, *Owner*
EMP: 3 EST: 2008
SALES: 500K **Privately Held**
SIC: 2434 2759 Wood kitchen cabinets;
engraving

(G-10217)
COBLENTZ CABINET
8876 E 800 N (47558-5107)
PHONE......................................812 687-7525
Paul Coblentz, *Principal*
EMP: 2
SALES (est): 236K **Privately Held**
SIC: 2434 Wood kitchen cabinets

(G-10218)
COUNTRYSIDE PRINTING
7243 E 300 N (47558-5626)
PHONE......................................812 486-2454
Virgil Raber, *Principal*
EMP: 2

SALES (est): 154.3K **Privately Held**
SIC: 2759 Screen printing

(G-10219)
COUNTRYSIDE SAWMILL
8753 E 450 N (47558-5197)
PHONE......................................812 486-2991
Glenn Knepp, *Principal*
EMP: 3 EST: 2010
SALES (est): 216.8K **Privately Held**
SIC: 2421 Sawmills & planing mills, gen-
eral

(G-10220)
CUSTOM CABINETS & FURN LLC
4578 N 875 E (47558-5196)
PHONE......................................812 486-2503
Norman Graber,
Gary Graber,
EMP: 11
SALES: 2.5MM **Privately Held**
SIC: 5712 2434 Furniture stores; wood
kitchen cabinets

(G-10221)
CUSTOM TABLES & CABINETS
Also Called: Piece Vallet Cabinets
5127 E 300 N (47558-5714)
PHONE......................................812 486-3831
Kevin Wittmer, *Owner*
EMP: 2
SALES (est): 149.1K **Privately Held**
SIC: 2434 Wood kitchen cabinets

(G-10222)
DELBERT KEMP
3590 N 700 E (47558-5228)
PHONE......................................812 486-3325
Fax: 812 486-3272
Delbert Kemp,
Ruth Kemp,
EMP: 26
SALES (est): 1.9MM **Privately Held**
SIC: 1751 2521 Cabinet building & instal-
lation; cabinets, office: wood; bookcases,
office: wood; panel systems & partitions
(free-standing), office: wood

(G-10223)
E M WOODWORKING
6000 N 450 E (47558-5044)
PHONE......................................812 486-2696
Mervin Knepp, *Principal*
EMP: 8
SALES (est): 598.9K **Privately Held**
SIC: 2431 Millwork

(G-10224)
G & R WOODWORKING LLC
7747 N 775 E (47558-5099)
PHONE......................................812 687-7701
Glenn R Graber,
EMP: 8
SALES: 160K **Privately Held**
SIC: 2431 Millwork

(G-10225)
GRABER THERM-O-LOC WINDOWS
9058 E 500 N (47558-5171)
PHONE......................................812 486-3273
Delbert K Graber, *Partner*
Ben Graber, *Partner*
Mark Graber, *Partner*
EMP: 3 EST: 1990
SALES: 1.2MM **Privately Held**
SIC: 3211 Window glass, clear & colored

(G-10226)
GRABER WOODWORKS INC
5155 N 900 E (47558-5166)
PHONE......................................812 486-2861
Fax: 812 486-2861
Henry Graber, *President*
Dean Graber, *Corp Secy*
Wilmer Graber, *Vice Pres*
EMP: 9
SQ FT: 3,400
SALES: 300K **Privately Held**
SIC: 2511 2434 5211 Wood household
furniture; wood kitchen cabinets; cabinets,
kitchen

GEOGRAPHIC

(G-10227)
GREEN FAST CURE LLC
5461 E 300 N (47558-5749)
PHONE.................................812 486-2510
Mervin R Knepp, *Principal*
EMP: 3 **EST:** 2016
SALES (est): 173.8K **Privately Held**
SIC: 3567 Industrial furnaces & ovens

(G-10228)
HARDWOOD DOOR MFG LLC
5084 N 575 E (47558-5052)
PHONE.................................812 486-3313
Dallas Wagler, *Mng Member*
EMP: 8
SALES (est): 840.3K **Privately Held**
SIC: 2434 Wood kitchen cabinets

(G-10229)
K & K INDUSTRIES INC
8518 E 550 N (47558-5073)
PHONE.................................812 486-3281
Fax: 812 486-3284
Bonnita Knepp, *Corp Secy*
Jerry Stoll, *Vice Pres*
Verlin Knepp, *Executive*
▼ **EMP:** 100
SQ FT: 25,000
SALES (est): 24.6MM **Privately Held**
WEB: www.kkindustries.com
SIC: 2439 Trusses, wooden roof

(G-10230)
KNEPPS LOGGING BANDMILLING
5220 N 650 E (47558-5279)
PHONE.................................812 486-7721
EMP: 3
SALES (est): 220.7K **Privately Held**
SIC: 2411 Logging camps & contractors

(G-10231)
L AND D CUSTOM WOODWORKING
3610 N 900 E (47558-5205)
PHONE.................................812 486-2958
Leroy Wittmar, *Owner*
Darvin Wittmar, *Co-Owner*
EMP: 5
SALES (est): 499.7K **Privately Held**
SIC: 2499 Decorative wood & woodwork

(G-10232)
LARRY GRABER CABINETS
9407 E 500 N (47558-5167)
PHONE.................................812 486-2713
Ernest Smith, *Owner*
Larry Graber, *Owner*
EMP: 2
SALES: 150K **Privately Held**
SIC: 2517 Home entertainment unit cabinets, wood

(G-10233)
M & H WOODWORKING LLC
3591 N 775 E (47558-5220)
PHONE.................................812 486-2570
Jason Raber,
Martin Raber,
EMP: 3
SALES (est): 268.7K **Privately Held**
SIC: 1751 2499 Cabinet & finish carpentry; decorative wood & woodwork

(G-10234)
MARNER DOOR MANUFACTURING LLC
4254 N 525 E (47558-5025)
PHONE.................................812 486-3128
Lester Marner, *Mng Member*
David Marner,
EMP: 19
SQ FT: 200
SALES (est): 3.4MM **Privately Held**
SIC: 3442 Metal doors, sash & trim

(G-10235)
MERVIN KNEPPS MOLDING
6349 N 900 E (47558-5146)
PHONE.................................812 486-2971
Fax: 812 486-2971
Mervin Knepp, *Owner*
EMP: 4
SQ FT: 5,000

SALES (est): 366.1K **Privately Held**
SIC: 2431 Moldings, wood: unfinished & prefinished

(G-10236)
PAUL KNEPP SAWMILL INC
Also Called: Paul Knepp Saw Mill
3589 N 900 E (47558-5206)
PHONE.................................812 486-3773
Martha Knepp, *President*
EMP: 4
SALES (est): 434.4K **Privately Held**
SIC: 2448 Pallets, wood

(G-10237)
PEACE VALLEY CABINETS INC
5127 E 300 N (47558-5714)
PHONE.................................812 486-3831
Kevin Wittmer, *Principal*
EMP: 4
SALES (est): 338K **Privately Held**
SIC: 2434 Wood kitchen cabinets

(G-10238)
PRAIRIE CREEK PRTG & BK STR
Also Called: Prairie Creek Book Store
9309 E 800 N (47558-5110)
PHONE.................................812 636-7243
Amos Graver, *Owner*
EMP: 4 **EST:** 1996
SALES (est): 386.8K **Privately Held**
SIC: 2752 5942 Commercial printing, offset; book stores

(G-10239)
RABERS BUGGY SHOP LLC
7209 E 300 N (47558-5626)
PHONE.................................812 486-3789
Victor Raber, *Owner*
EMP: 6
SQ FT: 2,000
SALES (est): 750K **Privately Held**
SIC: 7692 3496 Welding repair; cages, wire

(G-10240)
RABERS WHL WORKS & BUGGY WORKS
7226 E 300 N (47558-5626)
PHONE.................................812 486-2786
Paul Raber, *Owner*
EMP: 8
SALES (est): 450K **Privately Held**
SIC: 2499 Spokes, wood

(G-10241)
SHEPHERDS LOFT
8008 E 625 N (47558-5084)
PHONE.................................812 486-2304
EMP: 2
SALES (est): 106.9K **Privately Held**
SIC: 3944 Craft & hobby kits & sets

(G-10242)
SOUTHERN INDIANA COLLAR CO
Also Called: Southern Indiana Collar Mfg Co
1692 N 725 E (47558-5653)
PHONE.................................812 486-3714
Marlon Ray Raber, *Partner*
Ken Raber, *Partner*
EMP: 3
SQ FT: 150
SALES (est): 150K **Privately Held**
SIC: 5941 3199 Saddlery & equestrian equipment; harness or harness parts

(G-10243)
STARLIGHT PRINTING
3792 N 525 E (47558-5024)
PHONE.................................812 486-3905
EMP: 2
SALES (est): 83.9K **Privately Held**
SIC: 2752 Commercial printing, lithographic

(G-10244)
SWARTZENTRUBER SAWMILL
5912 N 900 E (47558-5739)
PHONE.................................812 486-3350
Randy Swartzentrube, *Owner*
EMP: 3

SALES (est): 219.2K **Privately Held**
SIC: 2421 Sawmills & planing mills, general

(G-10245)
W & J SAWMILL LLC
9533 E 600 N (47558-5152)
PHONE.................................812 486-2719
Jonas Knepp, *President*
EMP: 3 **EST:** 2002
SALES (est): 252.3K **Privately Held**
SIC: 2421 Sawmills & planing mills, general

(G-10246)
W & W PALLET CO LLC
7799 E 300 N (47558-5632)
PHONE.................................812 486-3548
Vernon Wagler, *Owner*
EMP: 4
SALES (est): 265.2K **Privately Held**
SIC: 2448 Pallets, wood & wood with metal

(G-10247)
WAGLERS CUSTOM CABINETS
8170 E 200 N (47558-5639)
PHONE.................................812 486-2878
David Wagler, *Principal*
EMP: 2
SALES (est): 247.1K **Privately Held**
SIC: 2434 Wood kitchen cabinets

(G-10248)
WITTMER WOODWORKING LLC
4637 E 200 N (47558-5013)
PHONE.................................812 486-3115
Joseph Witwicke, *Mng Member*
Harold Wittmer, *Mng Member*
EMP: 8
SALES (est): 467.1K **Privately Held**
SIC: 2431 Woodwork, interior & ornamental

(G-10249)
YODERS CABINETS
5207 N 775 E (47558-5240)
PHONE.................................812 486-3826
Wayne Yoder, *Principal*
EMP: 2
SALES (est): 160.8K **Privately Held**
SIC: 2434 Wood kitchen cabinets

Monticello
White County

(G-10250)
5 DIAMOND X
10891 N Ravinia Blvd (47960-8107)
PHONE.................................574 601-8056
Doug Nelson, *President*
EMP: 2
SALES (est): 87.4K **Privately Held**
SIC: 2759 Publication printing

(G-10251)
ADKEV INC
1207 N 6th St (47960-1542)
PHONE.................................574 583-4420
Melissa Timmons, *Engineer*
Bill Cheever, *Project Engr*
Jeremy Kyser, *Manager*
EMP: 10
SALES (est): 2.3MM
SALES (corp-wide): 70.1MM **Privately Held**
SIC: 3089 Molding primary plastic; injection molding of plastics
PA: Adkev, Inc.
664 S Iroquois St
Goodland IN 47948
219 297-4484

(G-10252)
AFFORDABLE SCREEN PRINTING EMB
8262 N Kiger Dr (47960-7102)
PHONE.................................574 278-7885
Tina Frybort, *Owner*
EMP: 2
SALES (est): 137.4K **Privately Held**
SIC: 2752 Commercial printing, lithographic

(G-10253)
BALL CORPORATION
1104 N 6th St (47960-1555)
PHONE.................................574 583-9418
Matt Sol, *Safety Mgr*
Staci Davis, *Purch Agent*
Freddy Spencer, *Engineer*
Scott Lafond, *Electrical Engi*
Christine Craig, *CPA*
EMP: 11
SALES (corp-wide): 10.9B **Publicly Held**
SIC: 3499 Boxes for packing & shipping, metal
PA: Ball Corporation
10 Longs Peak Dr
Broomfield CO 80021
303 469-3131

(G-10254)
BALL METAL BEVERAGE CONT CORP
Also Called: Ball Metal Beverage Cont Div
501 N 6th St (47960-1840)
PHONE.................................574 583-9418
Ross Rittvreg, *Branch Mgr*
Emily McGuire, *Administration*
EMP: 200
SALES (corp-wide): 10.9B **Publicly Held**
SIC: 3411 Can lids & ends, metal
HQ: Ball Metal Beverage Container Corp.
9300 W 108th Cir
Westminster CO 80021

(G-10255)
BCBG MAX AZRIA GROUP LLC
1712 North Bch (47960)
PHONE.................................620 442-1111
EMP: 2
SALES (corp-wide): 979.1MM **Privately Held**
SIC: 2335 Women's, juniors' & misses' dresses
HQ: Bcbg Max Azria Group, Llc
2761 Fruitland Ave
Vernon CA 90058
323 589-2224

(G-10256)
BLASTED WORKS
214 N Main St (47960-2131)
PHONE.................................574 583-3211
Fax: 574 583-3307
Trina Jo Clerget, *Partner*
Stephen A Clerget, *Partner*
EMP: 3
SQ FT: 4,500
SALES: 390K **Privately Held**
SIC: 2752 7374 2789 7699 Commercial printing, offset; computer graphics service; trade binding services; photographic & optical goods equipment repair services

(G-10257)
CARTER SEPTIC TANK INC
1720 N Buckeye St (47960-1301)
PHONE.................................574 583-5796
Max K Van Meter, *President*
Margaret E Van Meter, *Corp Secy*
EMP: 5 **EST:** 1953
SALES (est): 280K **Privately Held**
SIC: 3272 Septic tanks, concrete

(G-10258)
COVERITE-CUSTOM COVERS
8593 N State Road 39 (47960-7216)
P.O. Box 4, Buffalo (47925-0004)
PHONE.................................574 278-7152
Donna McCormick, *Owner*
EMP: 2
SALES (est): 100K **Privately Held**
WEB: www.coverite.com
SIC: 2394 Canvas & related products

(G-10259)
DON ANDERSON
Also Called: Liberty Signs
10739 N 650 E (47960-7125)
PHONE.................................574 278-7243
Don Anderson, *Owner*
Anna Marie Anderson, *Co-Owner*
EMP: 2
SALES (est): 126.9K **Privately Held**
SIC: 3993 Signs & advertising specialties

▲ = Import ▼=Export
◆ =Import/Export

(G-10260)
DONALDSON COMPANY INC
303 N 6th St (47960-1859)
PHONE..................952 887-3131
Dave Page, *Principal*
EMP: 8
SALES (est): 1.1MM **Privately Held**
SIC: 3569 3564 Filters; blowers & fans

(G-10261)
EASTON TECHNICAL PRODUCTS INC
Also Called: True Flight Arrow Co
2709 S Freeman Rd (47960-7742)
P.O. Box 746 (47960-0746)
PHONE..................574 583-5131
Fax: 574 583-9271
John Gooding, *Manager*
EMP: 30
SALES (corp-wide): 321MM **Privately Held**
WEB: www.eastonarchery.com
SIC: 3949 Arrows, archery
HQ: Easton Technical Products, Inc.
  5040 W Harold Gatty Dr
  Salt Lake City UT 84116

(G-10262)
EMERSON INDUSTRIAL AUTOMATION
705 N 6th St (47960-1711)
PHONE..................574 583-9171
EMP: 2
SALES (est): 107.4K **Privately Held**
SIC: 3562 Ball & roller bearings

(G-10263)
GIRTZ INDUSTRIES INC
Also Called: Girtz Engineering
5262 N East Shafer Dr (47960-7313)
PHONE..................844 464-4789
Fax: 574 278-6221
David A Girtz, *President*
Jim Siffring, *VP Sales*
Elizabeth Girtz, *Admin Sec*
▲ **EMP:** 100
SQ FT: 50,000
SALES (est): 31.6MM **Privately Held**
WEB: www.girtz.com
SIC: 3444 Sheet metal specialties, not stamped

(G-10264)
HALSEN BROTHERS SHEET METAL
Also Called: Honeywell Authorized Dealer
300 Tioga Rd (47960-2459)
PHONE..................574 583-3358
Ronald Hansen, *President*
Ron Halsen, *President*
Randy Halsen, *Vice Pres*
EMP: 2
SQ FT: 2,000
SALES: 225K **Privately Held**
SIC: 3444 1711 Sheet metalwork; warm air heating & air conditioning contractor

(G-10265)
HOME NEWS ENTERPRISES LLC
Also Called: Herald Journal, The
114 S Main St (47960-2328)
P.O. Box 409 (47960-0409)
PHONE..................574 583-5121
Fax: 574 583-4241
EMP: 20
SALES (corp-wide): 60.8MM **Privately Held**
SIC: 2741 2791 2711 Misc Publishing Typesetting Services Newspapers-Publishing/Printing
PA: Home News Enterprises, L.L.C.
  333 2nd St
  Columbus IN 47201
  800 876-7811

(G-10266)
INDUSTRIAL PALLET CORPORATION
5091 S Stone Dr (47960-7668)
PHONE..................574 583-4800
EMP: 3 **EST:** 2007
SALES (est): 181.1K **Privately Held**
SIC: 2448 Mfg Wood Pallets/Skids

(G-10267)
JACOBS MFG LLC
806 N 1st St (47960)
PHONE..................574 583-3883
James Jacobs,
Rick Jacobs,
EMP: 3
SALES (est): 639.9K **Privately Held**
SIC: 3523 Farm machinery & equipment

(G-10268)
JORDAN MANUFACTURING CO INC (PA)
1200 S 6th St (47960-8200)
PHONE..................800 328-6522
David N Jordan, *President*
Patrick Jordan, *General Mgr*
David Wolfe, *Vice Pres*
George Dudum, *VP Opers*
Keith Lehocky, *Safety Dir*
◆ **EMP:** 210
SQ FT: 180,000
SALES (est): 132.5MM **Privately Held**
SIC: 2392 5021 Cushions & pillows; outdoor & lawn furniture

(G-10269)
MONSANTO COMPANY
306 N Main St (47960-2133)
PHONE..................574 583-0028
EMP: 8
SALES (corp-wide): 41.2B **Privately Held**
SIC: 2879 Agricultural chemicals
HQ: Monsanto Company
  800 N Lindbergh Blvd
  Saint Louis MO 63167
  314 694-1000

(G-10270)
MONTICELLO MACHINE CO INC
7779 E 175 N (47960-7484)
PHONE..................574 583-9537
EMP: 3
SALES (est): 150K **Privately Held**
SIC: 3599 Machine Shop

(G-10271)
MONTICELLO VAULT BURIAL CO
2304 N 750 E (47960-8738)
PHONE..................574 583-3206
Chester Wilson, *Owner*
EMP: 2
SALES (est): 185.3K **Privately Held**
SIC: 3272 Burial vaults, concrete or precast terrazzo

(G-10272)
MSCA LLC
303 N 6th St (47960-1859)
PHONE..................574 583-6220
Patrick Yoder, *Principal*
▲ **EMP:** 6
SALES (est): 585.9K **Privately Held**
SIC: 3089 Plastics products

(G-10273)
NEON BAY
5014 E Indiana Beach Rd (47960-1263)
PHONE..................574 583-6366
Darrel Carr, *Owner*
EMP: 3
SALES (est): 152.4K **Privately Held**
SIC: 2813 Neon

(G-10274)
NEWS REMINDER
114 S Main St (47960-2328)
P.O. Box 409 (47960-0409)
PHONE..................574 583-5121
Don Herd, *President*
EMP: 11
SALES (est): 370K **Privately Held**
SIC: 2711 Newspapers, publishing & printing

(G-10275)
OMNI LOOSELEAF INC
4087 E Monon Rd (47960-7161)
PHONE..................219 253-8020
Anna Kroyman, *President*
Jack Van Valkenburg, *Vice Pres*
EMP: 3
SALES (est): 125K **Privately Held**
SIC: 2782 Looseleaf binders & devices

(G-10276)
OUTDOOR ROOMSCAPES INC
11965 W 800 N (47960-8058)
PHONE..................574 965-2009
Michelle Schwindler, *President*
EMP: 2
SALES (est): 221.9K **Privately Held**
SIC: 2499 Kitchen, bathroom & household ware: wood

(G-10277)
OWENS MACHINE & WELDING
1110 N 6th St (47960-1555)
PHONE..................574 583-9566
Fax: 574 583-7440
Rudy Owens, *Owner*
EMP: 5
SQ FT: 8,100
SALES (est): 413K **Privately Held**
SIC: 7692 3444 Welding repair; sheet metalwork

(G-10278)
PATRIOT PORCELAIN LLC
114 Constitution Plz (47960-2113)
PHONE..................574 583-5128
L Dowal Dellinger, *Principal*
EMP: 2
SALES (est): 244.9K **Privately Held**
SIC: 3261 Vitreous plumbing fixtures

(G-10279)
PIMMLER HOLDINGS INC (PA)
3137 S Freeman Rd (47960-7793)
P.O. Box 705 (47960-0705)
PHONE..................574 583-8090
Thomas Pimmler, *Principal*
▲ **EMP:** 6
SALES (est): 1.6MM **Privately Held**
SIC: 3495 Wire springs

(G-10280)
POLYMER SCIENCE INC (PA)
Also Called: PSI
2577 S Freeman Rd (47960-7831)
PHONE..................574 583-3751
Fred E Ennis, *President*
Lois Shoup, *Controller*
Jordan Penn, *Mktg Coord*
Alan E Leighton, *Admin Sec*
▲ **EMP:** 40
SQ FT: 28,000
SALES: 5MM **Privately Held**
WEB: www.polymerscience.org
SIC: 3081 Unsupported plastics film & sheet

(G-10281)
RADICAL GRAPHICS & SIGN SP LLC
4805 E Honeycreek Ct (47960-1289)
PHONE..................574 870-8873
EMP: 3
SALES: 90K **Privately Held**
SIC: 3993 Mfg Signs/Advertising Specialties

(G-10282)
REGAL BELOIT AMERICA INC
705 N 6th St (47960-1711)
PHONE..................574 583-9171
Glenn Fischer, *Branch Mgr*
EMP: 250
SALES (corp-wide): 3.3B **Publicly Held**
WEB: www.kopflex.com
SIC: 3621 3644 Motors, electric; generators & sets, electric; electric conduits & fittings; electric outlet, switch & fuse boxes
HQ: Regal Beloit America, Inc.
  200 State St
  Beloit WI 53511
  608 364-8800

(G-10283)
RHON INC
802 N 1st St (47960-3205)
PHONE..................574 297-5217
Matt Duncan, *President*
EMP: 3
SALES: 200K **Privately Held**
SIC: 3356 Nonferrous rolling & drawing

(G-10284)
T & G GAMES INC
4900 N Boxman Pl (47960-7322)
PHONE..................574 297-5455
Ted Leuenberger, *President*
EMP: 2
SALES (est): 83K **Privately Held**
SIC: 3944 Games, toys & children's vehicles

(G-10285)
T & L SHARPENING INC
2663 S Freeman Rd (47960-7843)
P.O. Box 338 (47960-0338)
PHONE..................574 583-3868
Fax: 574 583-9250
Thomas E All, *President*
Melissa Payne, *Admin Sec*
EMP: 22 **EST:** 1978
SQ FT: 7,000
SALES (est): 2.6MM **Privately Held**
WEB: www.cutting-tools.com
SIC: 7699 3545 Professional instrument repair services; files, machine tool

(G-10286)
TWIN LAKES CANVAS INC
1103 N 6th St (47960-1547)
PHONE..................574 583-2000
Fax: 574 583-2003
Roger Mitchell, *President*
EMP: 4
SQ FT: 5,000
SALES (est): 398.1K **Privately Held**
SIC: 2394 Awnings, fabric: made from purchased materials

(G-10287)
UNIQUE GRAPHIC DESIGNS INC
Also Called: Embroidery Designs
1279 N State Road 39 (47960-7286)
PHONE..................574 583-7119
Fax: 574 583-7119
Denise Hood, *Owner*
EMP: 5 **EST:** 1996
SQ FT: 1,100
SALES (est): 200K **Privately Held**
SIC: 2395 2759 Embroidery & art needlework; screen printing

(G-10288)
WHYTE HORSE WINERY LLC
1510 S Airport Rd (47960-2701)
PHONE..................574 583-2345
Abbey Franks, *Manager*
EMP: 3
SALES (est): 331.6K **Privately Held**
WEB: www.whytehorsewinery.com
SIC: 2084 Wines

Montpelier
Blackford County

(G-10289)
BRC RUBBER & PLASTICS INC
623 W Monroe St (47359-1240)
PHONE..................765 728-8510
Fax: 765 728-8513
Don Newman, *Buyer*
Jerry Odom, *Manager*
EMP: 50
SALES (corp-wide): 171.4MM **Privately Held**
SIC: 3061 2822 Mechanical rubber goods; synthetic rubber
PA: Brc Rubber & Plastics, Inc.
  1029a W State Blvd
  Fort Wayne IN 46808
  260 693-2171

(G-10290)
EMHART TEKNOLOGIES LLC
Stanley Engineered Fastening
7345 N 400 E (47359-9646)
PHONE..................765 728-2433
Mark Grey, *Manager*
EMP: 120
SALES (corp-wide): 12.7B **Publicly Held**
WEB: www.helicoil.com
SIC: 3541 3452 5085 Machine tools, metal cutting type; bolts, nuts, rivets & washers; fasteners, industrial: nuts, bolts, screws, etc.

HQ: Emhart Teknologies Llc
480 Myrtle St
New Britain CT 06053
800 783-6427

(G-10291)
FBN CORPORATION
Also Called: Indiana Veneer
890 W Huntington St (47359-1294)
P.O. Box 115 (47359-0115)
PHONE.................................765 728-2438
Fax: 765 728-2439
Ed Mc Coin, *President*
EMP: 75
SALES (est): 8.4MM **Privately Held**
SIC: 2435 Hardwood veneer & plywood

(G-10292)
IRVING MATERIALS INC
5067 E Cummins Rd (47359-9653)
PHONE.................................765 728-5335
Fax: 765 728-8007
Joe Langel, *Branch Mgr*
EMP: 9
SALES (corp-wide): 800.6MM **Privately Held**
SIC: 3273 Ready-mixed concrete
PA: Irving Materials, Inc.
8032 N State Road 9
Greenfield IN 46140
317 326-3101

(G-10293)
MIDWEST VENEER PRODUCTS CO
6104 N Main Street Rd (47359-9601)
PHONE.................................765 728-2950
Fax: 765 728-3102
Dan Turner, *President*
Jeremy McCoin, *Vice Pres*
EMP: 27
SALES: 2MM **Privately Held**
SIC: 2435 Hardwood veneer & plywood

(G-10294)
SMITH CONSULTING INC
850 W Huntington St (47359-1294)
P.O. Box 159 (47359-0159)
PHONE.................................765 728-5980
Terry Smith, *President*
EMP: 32
SQ FT: 52,000
SALES (est): 6.3MM **Privately Held**
SIC: 2653 8742 Boxes, solid fiber: made from purchased materials; quality assurance consultant

---

Mooreland
Henry County

(G-10295)
KAREMAR PRODUCTIONS
6789 E State Road 36 (47360-9529)
PHONE.................................765 766-5117
Marlin Evans, *Owner*
EMP: 2
SALES (est): 178K **Privately Held**
SIC: 2759 7336 Visiting cards (including business): printing; commercial art & graphic design

---

Moores Hill
Dearborn County

(G-10296)
AIRGAS USA LLC
601 Front St (47032)
PHONE.................................812 537-4101
Steve Bentle, *Manager*
EMP: 5
SALES (corp-wide): 164.2MM **Privately Held**
SIC: 2813 Carbon dioxide
HQ: Airgas Usa, Llc
259 N Radnor Chester Rd # 100
Radnor PA 19087
610 687-5253

(G-10297)
APPALACHIAN LOG STRUCTURES
Also Called: Heritage Log Homes
10994 Chesterville Rd (47032-9258)
PHONE.................................812 744-5711
Anita Dyer, *Owner*
EMP: 2
SALES (est): 174.7K **Privately Held**
SIC: 2452 Log cabins, prefabricated, wood

(G-10298)
HARING CONTRACTORS INC
11231 State Road 350 (47032-9397)
PHONE.................................812 744-6870
Manfield Haring, *President*
Tony H Haring, *Vice Pres*
EMP: 3
SALES (est): 290K **Privately Held**
WEB: www.haringcontractors.net
SIC: 3296 Insulation: rock wool, slag & silica minerals

(G-10299)
TEAMAIR MRO LTD
12978 Josephs Field Ln (47032-9499)
PHONE.................................812 584-3733
EMP: 3
SALES (est): 252.8K **Privately Held**
SIC: 3724 Aircraft engines & engine parts

Mooresville
Morgan County

(G-10300)
ADVANCE AERO INC
135 E Harrison St (46158-1626)
PHONE.................................317 513-6071
Todd N Wilson, *President*
Joseph Johnson, *Technical Mgr*
Christine Wilson, *Office Mgr*
EMP: 25
SQ FT: 5,000
SALES (est): 1.9MM **Privately Held**
SIC: 3441 Fabricated structural metal

(G-10301)
AFFINIS GROUP LLC (PA)
1050 Indianapolis Rd (46158-1158)
P.O. Box 236 (46158-0236)
PHONE.................................317 831-3830
Fax: 317 834-4280
Adriene Standeford, *Sales Staff*
Brad Key, *Supervisor*
Robert E Mc Afee,
Stephen E Dowling,
Robert McAfee,
EMP: 4
SALES (est): 911.4K **Privately Held**
SIC: 2656 3089 Sanitary food containers; plastic kitchenware, tableware & houseware

(G-10302)
AMBASSADOR STEEL CORPORATION
149 Sycamore Ln (46158-7923)
PHONE.................................317 834-3434
Fax: 317 831-2456
Ron Latimer, *Plant Mgr*
John Pratt, *Sales Staff*
George Nicolich, *Contract Mgr*
Tony Gaskins, *Manager*
EMP: 30
SALES (corp-wide): 20.2B **Publicly Held**
WEB: www.ambassadorsteel.com
SIC: 1791 3449 3441 Structural steel erection; miscellaneous metalwork; fabricated structural metal
HQ: Ambassador Steel Corporation
1340 S Grandstaff Dr
Auburn IN 46706
260 925-5440

(G-10303)
BROWNS SIMPLY PRINTINGS
126 S Jefferson St (46158-1654)
PHONE.................................317 490-7493
Joshua A Brown, *Owner*
EMP: 2
SALES (est): 92.3K **Privately Held**
SIC: 2752 Commercial printing, lithographic

(G-10304)
CAPITAL ADHESIVES & PACKG CORP
1260 S Old State Road 67 (46158-8243)
PHONE.................................317 834-5415
Fax: 317 834-5425
Roger Wathen, *President*
Mark Angermeier, *Vice Pres*
Elaine Angermeier, *Treasurer*
Mike Payne, *Manager*
Natalie Wathen, *Admin Sec*
EMP: 12
SQ FT: 15,000
SALES (est): 5.7MM **Privately Held**
WEB: www.capitaladhesives.com
SIC: 2891 5085 5084 Adhesives; adhesives, tape & plasters; industrial machinery & equipment

(G-10305)
CARTER LEE BUILDING COMPONENT
Also Called: A Pro-Build Company
9028 N Old State Road 67 (46158-6366)
PHONE.................................317 834-5380
David Carter, *CEO*
Dale Kukowski, *President*
EMP: 90
SQ FT: 400,000
SALES (est): 9.2MM **Privately Held**
SIC: 2439 Trusses, wooden roof

(G-10306)
COUGAR BAG INC
3310 Hancel Cir (46158-8205)
PHONE.................................317 831-9720
Steve Holsapple, *President*
Rick Langdon, *Vice Pres*
EMP: 26
SQ FT: 7,000
SALES (est): 6.1MM **Privately Held**
SIC: 2673 Plastic & pliofilm bags

(G-10307)
DEFELICE ENGINEERING INC
7451 N Ridgeway Ln (46158-6687)
PHONE.................................317 834-2832
Brian V Defelice, *President*
Joann Hendriyx, *Corp Secy*
EMP: 2
SQ FT: 5,400
SALES (est): 334.8K **Privately Held**
WEB: www.firepan.com
SIC: 3544 Special dies & tools

(G-10308)
EQUIPMENT TECHNOLOGIES INC (PA)
Also Called: Et Sprayers
2201 Hancel Pkwy (46158-8297)
PHONE.................................800 861-2142
Fax: 317 834-4501
Matthew Hayes, *President*
Corey Bailey, *Inv Control Mgr*
Greg Long, *Design Engr*
Brent Stiers, *CFO*
Bria Lewellyn, *Supervisor*
◆ EMP: 26
SQ FT: 20,000
SALES (est): 8.3MM **Privately Held**
SIC: 3523 Sprayers & spraying machines, agricultural

(G-10309)
ET WORKS LLC (PA)
Also Called: Equipment Technologies
2201 Hancel Pkwy (46158-8297)
PHONE.................................317 834-4500
Justin Honegger, *Engineer*
Ryan Larsh, *Engineer*
Matthew Hayes,
EMP: 25
SALES (est): 11.5MM **Privately Held**
SIC: 3523 Sprayers & spraying machines, agricultural

(G-10310)
HILLTOP LEATHER
450 S Indiana St (46158-1710)
PHONE.................................317 831-4855
Tom Thompson, *Owner*
EMP: 2 EST: 2011
SALES (est): 131.1K **Privately Held**
SIC: 3199 Leather goods

(G-10311)
HOPKINS GRAVEL SAND & CONCRETE
540 State Road 267 (46158-8949)
P.O. Box 636 (46158-0636)
PHONE.................................317 831-2704
Fax: 317 831-2052
Jeremy Hopkins Jr, *President*
Jane Sisk, *Exec Dir*
EMP: 8
SQ FT: 500
SALES (est): 730K **Privately Held**
SIC: 1442 3273 Gravel mining; ready-mixed concrete

(G-10312)
HUMAN ELEMENT THERAPEUTICS
4601 E Viola Dr (46158-8281)
PHONE.................................317 446-4062
Robin Mills, *Principal*
EMP: 2
SALES (est): 74.4K **Privately Held**
SIC: 2819 Elements

(G-10313)
HYDRAULIC PRESS BRICK COMPANY
6618 N Tidewater Rd (46158)
PHONE.................................317 290-1140
Fax: 317 831-8975
Ira Smith, *Sales Mgr*
Stephen K Rowe, *Sales Mgr*
EMP: 24
SALES (corp-wide): 702.7MM **Privately Held**
WEB: www.hpbhaydite.com
SIC: 3295 1442 Minerals, ground or treated; construction sand & gravel
HQ: Hydraulic Press Brick Company Inc
3600 Woodview Trce # 300
Indianapolis IN 46268
317 290-1140

(G-10314)
INSIDE SYSTEMS
1053 E Jessup Way (46158-7259)
PHONE.................................317 831-3772
John Littlejohn, *Owner*
John Bradley, *Partner*
EMP: 2
SALES (est): 169.1K **Privately Held**
SIC: 3089 Plastic processing

(G-10315)
IRVING MATERIALS INC
Also Called: I M I
501 N Samuel Moore Pkwy (46158-1418)
PHONE.................................317 831-0224
Fax: 317 831-0225
Bobby Fox, *Site Mgr*
Gene Wiggiam, *Manager*
EMP: 10
SALES (corp-wide): 800.6MM **Privately Held**
SIC: 3273 Ready-mixed concrete
PA: Irving Materials, Inc.
8032 N State Road 9
Greenfield IN 46140
317 326-3101

(G-10316)
JACOBS MACHINE & TOOL CO INC
Also Called: Jmt
315 E Washington St (46158-1462)
P.O. Box 2 (46158-0002)
PHONE.................................317 831-2917
Janet Jacobs, *President*
James Jacobs, *General Mgr*
Michael Jacobs, *Treasurer*
EMP: 15
SQ FT: 13,800
SALES (est): 1.3MM **Privately Held**
WEB: www.jmt.com
SIC: 3544 Special dies & tools

(G-10317)
JOHN M WOOLEY LUMBER COMPANY
200 E South St (46158-1725)
P.O. Box 6 (46158-0006)
PHONE.................................317 831-2700
Fax: 317 831-8663

John S Wooley, *Branch Mgr*
EMP: 22
SALES (corp-wide): 6.8MM **Privately Held**
SIC: 2421 2426 2411 Kiln drying of lumber; hardwood dimension & flooring mills; logging
PA: John M Wooley Lumber Company Inc
1789 S Old State Road 67
Martinsville IN 46151
765 349-3299

(G-10318)
JOHNSON & JOHNSON
2100 Innovation Blvd (46158)
PHONE.................................317 539-8300
EMP: 3
SALES (corp-wide): 76.4B **Publicly Held**
SIC: 2676 Feminine hygiene paper products
PA: Johnson & Johnson
1 Johnson And Johnson Plz
New Brunswick NJ 08933
732 524-0400

(G-10319)
M D HOLDINGS LLC
Also Called: Saniserv
451 E County Line Rd (46158-1811)
P.O. Box 1089 (46158-5089)
PHONE.................................317 831-7030
Lynn Haddix, *Purch Agent*
Kevin Leap, *VP Finance*
Pam May, *Accountant*
Steve Dowling, *VP Sales*
Kim Waggoner, *Marketing Mgr*
▲ EMP: 4
SQ FT: 75,000
SALES (est): 911.4K **Privately Held**
WEB: www.saniserv.com
SIC: 3556 3589 5046 Ice cream manufacturing machinery; commercial cooking & foodwarming equipment; restaurant equipment & supplies
PA: Affinis Group Llc
1050 Indianapolis Rd
Mooresville IN 46158
317 831-3830

(G-10320)
MAINLINE CONVEYOR SYSTEMS INC
10970 N Holland Dr S (46158-7661)
P.O. Box 24 (46158-0024)
PHONE.................................317 831-2795
Fax: 317 831-2719
Roger D Brown, *President*
EMP: 10
SQ FT: 12,000
SALES (est): 1.7MM **Privately Held**
WEB: www.mainlineconveyor.com
SIC: 3535 5084 Conveyors & conveying equipment; industrial machinery & equipment

(G-10321)
MAJESTIC BLOCK AND BRICK INC
520 S Park Dr (46158-1757)
P.O. Box 99 (46158-0099)
PHONE.................................317 831-2455
Charles O Cross, *President*
William B Nunn, *Admin Sec*
EMP: 46
SALES (est): 6.2MM
SALES (corp-wide): 15.1MM **Privately Held**
WEB: www.majesticblockandbrick.com
SIC: 3271 Brick, concrete
PA: L. Thorn Company, Inc.
6000 Grant Line Rd
New Albany IN 47150
812 246-4461

(G-10322)
MESTEK INC
Linel
101 Linel Dr (46158-8254)
PHONE.................................317 831-5314
Fax: 317 831-9259
Rebecca Morris, *Controller*
EMP: 26
SALES (corp-wide): 678.1MM **Privately Held**
SIC: 3444 3479 Sheet metalwork; painting of metal products

PA: Mestek, Inc.
260 N Elm St
Westfield MA 01085
413 568-9571

(G-10323)
MOLEX LLC
1500 Hancel Pkwy (46158-8296)
PHONE.................................317 834-5600
Fax: 317 834-5611
Gene Hill, *Manager*
EMP: 30
SALES (corp-wide): 44.4B **Privately Held**
WEB: www.molex.com
SIC: 3669 3678 Emergency alarms; electronic connectors
HQ: Molex, Llc
2222 Wellington Ct
Lisle IL 60532
630 969-4550

(G-10324)
MOORESVILLE WELDING INC
220 E Washington St (46158-1459)
PHONE.................................317 831-2265
Fax: 317 831-2450
Jeff Allen, *President*
EMP: 7 EST: 1939
SQ FT: 14,000
SALES: 800K **Privately Held**
WEB: www.mooresvillewelding.com
SIC: 3713 3536 7692 3537 Truck beds; hoists; automotive welding; industrial trucks & tractors; farm machinery & equipment; sheet metalwork

(G-10325)
MOTORAMA AUTO CTR INC (PA)
Also Called: Motorama Kart Parts
10509 N Old State Road 67 (46158)
PHONE.................................317 831-0036
William L McLaughlin, *President*
EMP: 9
SQ FT: 25,000
SALES (est): 2MM **Privately Held**
WEB: www.mkpshop.com
SIC: 5521 3714 Automobiles, used cars only; motor vehicle parts & accessories

(G-10326)
MT OLIVE MANUFACTURING INC
3304 Hancel Cir (46158-8205)
PHONE.................................317 834-8525
Steven Paul Langley, *President*
Lisa Langley, *Vice Pres*
▲ EMP: 90
SQ FT: 48,000
SALES: 7MM
SALES (corp-wide): 185.5MM **Privately Held**
SIC: 2891 Sealing wax
HQ: Bremen Corporation
405 Industrial Dr
Bremen IN 46506
574 546-4238

(G-10327)
NATIONAL EXHAUST CLEANING INC
634 E State Road 42 (46158-6023)
PHONE.................................317 831-4750
Marcia Shepherd, *President*
EMP: 13
SQ FT: 14,000
SALES: 425K **Privately Held**
SIC: 3669 7349 Fire alarm apparatus, electric; air duct cleaning

(G-10328)
NICE-PAK PRODUCTS INC
1 Nice Pak Rd (46158-1398)
PHONE.................................845 365-1700
Fax: 317 831-6490
Herb Baer, *Exec VP*
Shawn Smith, *Vice Pres*
Travis Brown, *Transportation*
Betty Ball, *Buyer*
Ken Berg, *Sales Staff*
EMP: 550
SALES (corp-wide): 428.1MM **Privately Held**
WEB: www.nicepak.com
SIC: 2621 2392 Towels, tissues & napkins: paper & stock; household furnishings

PA: Nice-Pak Products, Inc.
2 Nice Pak Park
Orangeburg NY 10962
845 365-2772

(G-10329)
OLIVER MACHINE AND TOOL CORP
110 Industrial Dr (46158)
P.O. Box 1454, Martinsville (46151-0454)
PHONE.................................765 349-2271
Fax: 317 834-9056
Robert Green, *President*
Kerry Weaver, *Vice Pres*
Eric Strohmeyer, *Treasurer*
EMP: 10
SQ FT: 3,000
SALES: 2.9MM **Privately Held**
SIC: 3599 Machine shop, jobbing & repair

(G-10330)
OMEGA CO
12494 N Woodlawn Dr (46158-6178)
PHONE.................................317 831-4471
Michael A Kemp, *President*
EMP: 3
SALES (est): 224.8K **Privately Held**
SIC: 3999 Manufacturing industries

(G-10331)
OVERTON & SONS TL & DIE CO INC (PA)
Also Called: Overton Industries
1250 S Old State Road 67 (46158-8243)
P.O. Box 69 (46158-0069)
PHONE.................................317 831-4542
Fax: 317 831-7388
Steve Overton, *CEO*
Ron E Overton, *President*
Rick Overton, *Co-President*
Dale Bates, *Vice Pres*
Kevin Phillips, *Engineer*
EMP: 35
SALES (est): 18.1MM **Privately Held**
WEB: www.overtonind.com
SIC: 3544 7692 3545 Special dies & tools; welding repair; machine tool accessories

(G-10332)
OVERTON & SONS TL & DIE CO INC
1250 S Old State Road 67 (46158-8243)
PHONE.................................317 831-4542
Jamie Broyles, *Manager*
EMP: 10
SALES (corp-wide): 18.1MM **Privately Held**
WEB: www.overtonind.com
SIC: 3544 Special dies & tools
PA: Overton & Sons Tool & Die Co., Inc.
1250 S Old State Road 67
Mooresville IN 46158
317 831-4542

(G-10333)
OVERTON MOLD INC
1248 S Old State Road 67 (46158-8243)
P.O. Box 609 (46158-0609)
PHONE.................................317 831-9595
Ron Overton, *President*
Steve Overton, *Corp Secy*
Rick Overton, *Vice Pres*
Daryl Strahl, *Vice Pres*
EMP: 19
SQ FT: 10,000
SALES (est): 1.7MM **Privately Held**
SIC: 3544 Industrial molds

(G-10334)
PACMOORE PRODUCTS INC
100 Pacmoore Pkwy (46158-6195)
P.O. Box 397 (46158-0397)
PHONE.................................317 831-2666
William Moore, *Branch Mgr*
EMP: 30
SALES (corp-wide): 5.5MM **Privately Held**
WEB: www.pacmoore.com
SIC: 2046 Starch
PA: Pacmoore Products, Inc.
1844 Summer St
Hammond IN 46320

(G-10335)
PRODIGY GROUP INC
310 Indianapolis Rd Ste E (46158-2320)
PHONE.................................317 834-5480
Fax: 317 834-5490
Robert Brewington, *President*
EMP: 32
SQ FT: 20,000
SALES (est): 5.7MM **Privately Held**
WEB: www.prodigygroup.com
SIC: 3599 Machine shop, jobbing & repair

(G-10336)
REED RAYMOND TRUST
133 Justin Dr (46158-7644)
PHONE.................................317 831-7246
Sharon McCool, *Co-Owner*
EMP: 2
SALES (est): 91.8K **Privately Held**
SIC: 3523 Harvesters, fruit, vegetable, tobacco, etc.

(G-10337)
ROBERT J MATT
Also Called: Tackle Service Center
246 E Washington St (46158-1459)
PHONE.................................317 831-2400
Fax: 317 831-8500
Robert J Matt, *Owner*
EMP: 4
SQ FT: 4,000
SALES (est): 150K **Privately Held**
SIC: 7699 5941 5091 3949 Fishing equipment repair; bait & tackle; hunting equipment; fishing tackle; hunting equipment & supplies; sporting & athletic goods

(G-10338)
S EDWARDS INCORPORATED
Also Called: Ace Tool & Engineering Co
292 W Harrison St (46158-1633)
P.O. Box 326 (46158-0326)
PHONE.................................317 831-0261
Fax: 317 831-8798
Stephen A Edwards, *President*
Cheryl Edwards, *Owner*
Donald Barry, *General Mgr*
EMP: 6
SQ FT: 10,000
SALES (est): 973.5K **Privately Held**
SIC: 3599 Machine shop, jobbing & repair

(G-10339)
SANISERV
451 E County Line Rd (46158-1811)
P.O. Box 1089 (46158-5089)
PHONE.................................317 831-7030
Fax: 317 831-7036
Robert McAfee, *CEO*
EMP: 28
SALES (est): 4.7MM **Privately Held**
SIC: 2024 Dairy based frozen desserts

(G-10340)
SIGN FOR IT LLC
68 W Main St (46158-1660)
PHONE.................................317 834-4636
David Stinson,
EMP: 2
SALES (est): 182.7K **Privately Held**
SIC: 3993 Signs & advertising specialties

(G-10341)
SONNY SCAFFOLDS INC (PA)
319 Harlan Dr (46158-1359)
PHONE.................................317 831-3900
Charlotte Cosgrove, *President*
Richard Blake, *Vice Pres*
EMP: 14
SQ FT: 7,200
SALES (est): 1.4MM **Privately Held**
SIC: 3446 Scaffolds, mobile or stationary: metal

(G-10342)
SUN POLYMERS INTERNATIONAL INC
100 Sun Polymers Dr (46158-7549)
PHONE.................................317 834-6410
Charles C K Lee, *President*
EMP: 2
SALES (est): 102.2K **Privately Held**
SIC: 2821 Polyethylene resins

G
E
O
G
R
A
P
H
I
C

(G-10343)
TOA (USA) LLC
2000 Pleiades Dr (46158-7144)
PHONE.................................317 834-0522
Fax: 317 834-0654
Shinichi Iizuka, CEO
Junichiro Kondo, President
Bob Whyte, VP Opers
Daisuke Obayashi, Purchasing
Brenda Lanham, QC Mgr
◆ EMP: 292 EST: 2000
SQ FT: 440,000
SALES (est): 214.2MM Privately Held
SIC: 3714 Air brakes, motor vehicle

(G-10344)
TOP LOCK CORPORATION
319 Harlan Dr (46158-1359)
PHONE.................................317 831-2000
Eugene D Perry, President
EMP: 3
SALES (est): 392.3K Privately Held
SIC: 3429 1799 Locks or lock sets; scaf-
folding construction

(G-10345)
YARDARM MARINE PRODUCTS INC
2100 Hancel Pkwy (46158-8289)
P.O. Box 174, West Newton (46183-0174)
PHONE.................................317 831-4950
Paul J Delk, President
Pam Delk, Treasurer
EMP: 24
SQ FT: 5,000
SALES (est): 4.8MM Privately Held
SIC: 3443 3536 Metal parts; boat lifts

Morgantown
Morgan County

(G-10346)
03 CORP
6797 Morningstar Dr (46160-8335)
PHONE.................................812 597-0276
Barbra Witzke, President
Paul Witzke, Vice Pres
EMP: 2
SALES (est): 150.1K Privately Held
SIC: 2951 Concrete, asphaltic (not from re-
fineries)

(G-10347)
ALL 4U PRINTING LLC
Also Called: Sunpress South
6710 W 425 S (46160-8235)
PHONE.................................317 845-2955
Fax: 317 842-9504
Misty Slentz, President
EMP: 2
SALES: 50K Privately Held
WEB: www.sunpressinc.com
SIC: 2752 Commercial printing, offset

(G-10348)
ALL-PRO PUMP & REPAIR INC
7907 W 500 S (46160-9667)
PHONE.................................317 738-4203
Patrick Beach, President
EMP: 3
SALES: 320K Privately Held
SIC: 3561 Pumps & pumping equipment

(G-10349)
AMERICAN DOOR CONTROLS INC
51 W State Road 45 (46160-8928)
PHONE.................................812 988-4853
Martha Jessup, CEO
Frank Jessup, President
EMP: 2
SQ FT: 800
SALES: 130K Privately Held
WEB: www.amerdoor.com
SIC: 3699 Door opening & closing devices,
electrical

(G-10350)
CJ LOGGING LLC
2336 S Cnservation Clb Rd (46160-9370)
PHONE.................................812 360-0163
EMP: 2

SALES (est): 169.4K Privately Held
SIC: 2411 Logging

(G-10351)
D K TOOLS & ENGINEERING
6250 Spearsville Rd (46160-8723)
PHONE.................................812 325-4532
Donald D Kirts, Owner
EMP: 2 EST: 2001
SALES (est): 25K Privately Held
SIC: 3589 Service industry machinery

(G-10352)
HEALTHCARE DATA INC
Also Called: Health Probe
5693 S Bear Wallow Rd # 100
(46160-9315)
PHONE.................................812 342-9947
Douglas Darbro, President
Mary Jean Eichauer, Vice Pres
EMP: 10
SALES (est): 623.8K Privately Held
WEB: www.healthprobe.com
SIC: 7372 Prepackaged software

(G-10353)
HOOSIER TOOL & GRINDING INC
1382 N Fruitdale Rd (46160-8581)
P.O. Box 728, Nashville (47448-0728)
PHONE.................................812 597-0213
Fax: 812 597-0213
David Patterson, CEO
Mark Patterson, Vice Pres
EMP: 2
SALES (est): 400K Privately Held
SIC: 3599 Machine shop, jobbing & repair

(G-10354)
INDIAN CREEK OUTDOOR POWER LLC
320 E State Road 135 (46160-9735)
PHONE.................................812 597-3055
Sandra Shearer,
EMP: 2 EST: 2015
SALES (est): 57.6K Privately Held
SIC: 7538 7694 5088 Engine repair;
motor repair services; golf carts

(G-10355)
JUSTIN MOLLO
7890 Spearsville Rd (46160-9023)
PHONE.................................812 361-7694
Justin Mollo, Principal
EMP: 3
SALES (est): 189.4K Privately Held
SIC: 3471 Decorative plating & finishing of
formed products

(G-10356)
LAST ROUND COFFEE LLC
389 E Washington St (46160-9763)
PHONE.................................317 292-0500
Zach Butler,
EMP: 2
SALES (est): 62.3K Privately Held
SIC: 2095 Roasted coffee

(G-10357)
NJ LOGGING LLC
1825 W Three Story HI Rd (46160-9279)
PHONE.................................812 597-0782
Nina Law, Owner
EMP: 3
SALES (est): 293.2K Privately Held
SIC: 2411 Logging camps & contractors

(G-10358)
TDF OF INDIANA INC
7209 E Mahalasville Rd (46160-8322)
PHONE.................................812 597-4009
Allen Oden, President
EMP: 2
SALES: 100K Privately Held
SIC: 2511 Wood household furniture

Morocco
Newton County

(G-10359)
ACTION COOLING TOWERS INC
2649 S 500 W (47963-8048)
P.O. Box 480 (47963-0480)
PHONE.................................219 285-2660
Tim D Mangum, President
EMP: 5
SALES (est): 375.2K Privately Held
SIC: 2499 Cooling towers, wood or wood &
sheet metal combination

(G-10360)
AMISH ROBS TATTOOS LLC
106 S Main St (47963-8290)
PHONE.................................219 863-9727
Robert Talesky,
EMP: 2
SQ FT: 2,000
SALES (est): 107.5K Privately Held
SIC: 3231 7299 Stained glass: made from
purchased glass; tattoo parlor

(G-10361)
CKC TOOL INC
508 S Polk St (47963-8144)
PHONE.................................219 285-6415
Chris Schultz, Owner
EMP: 6
SALES: 600K Privately Held
SIC: 3089 Injection molded finished plastic
products

(G-10362)
CKC TOOL INC
511 S Lincoln St (47963-8014)
P.O. Box 209 (47963-0209)
PHONE.................................219 285-6415
Chris Schultz, President
EMP: 3
SQ FT: 5,500
SALES (est): 288.1K Privately Held
SIC: 3544 Special dies, tools, jigs & fix-
tures

(G-10363)
SIX SIGMA MOLD INC
511 S Lincoln St (47963-8014)
P.O. Box 660 (47963-0660)
PHONE.................................219 285-6539
Todd Metzinger, President
John D Rush, Admin Sec
EMP: 6
SQ FT: 17,000
SALES: 1.2MM Privately Held
SIC: 3544 Industrial molds

(G-10364)
SOUTHLAKE MACHINE CORP
112 N Polk St (47963-8297)
P.O. Box 487 (47963-0487)
PHONE.................................219 285-6150
Fax: 219 285-6151
Rex Clark, Owner
EMP: 7
SQ FT: 5,000
SALES (est): 968K Privately Held
SIC: 3547 7699 Steel rolling machinery;
industrial equipment services

Morristown
Shelby County

(G-10365)
APEX ELECTRIC & SIGN INC (PA)
500 N Range Line Rd (46161-9641)
P.O. Box 130, Maxwell (46154-0130)
PHONE.................................317 326-1325
Greg Heuer, Principal
EMP: 2 EST: 2010
SALES (est): 348.5K Privately Held
SIC: 3993 Signs & advertising specialties

(G-10366)
BUNGE NORTH AMERICA FOUNDATION
700 N Range Line Rd (46161-9643)
PHONE.................................765 763-7500
Brian Searfoss, Manager
EMP: 100 Privately Held
WEB: www.bungemarion.com
SIC: 2075 Soybean oil mills
HQ: Bunge North America Foundation
1391 Timberlk Mnr Pkwy # 31
Chesterfield MO 63017
314 872-3030

(G-10367)
CGS SERVICES INC
Also Called: Caldwell Gravel Sales Tm
2920 E Us Highway 52 (46161-9649)
P.O. Box 212 (46161-0212)
PHONE.................................765 763-6258
Fax: 765 763-6174
Paul Cadwell, CEO
Paul Caldwell, CEO
Dana Caldwell, President
Wanda Caldwell, Corp Secy
EMP: 3 EST: 1968
SQ FT: 1,700
SALES (est): 837.5K
SALES (corp-wide): 1.5B Publicly Held
WEB: www.cgsservices.com
SIC: 1442 4953 Gravel mining; sanitary
landfill operation
PA: Advanced Disposal Services, Inc.
90 Fort Wade Rd Ste 200
Ponte Vedra FL 32081
904 737-7900

(G-10368)
CRANEWERKS INC
511 N Range Line Rd (46161-9641)
PHONE.................................765 663-2909
Fax: 317 642-0520
Mark Thomas, President
EMP: 20
SQ FT: 7,500
SALES (est): 6.8MM Privately Held
WEB: www.cranewerks.net
SIC: 3536 Hoists

(G-10369)
FREUDENBERG-NOK GENERAL PARTNR
General Industries Division
487 W Main St (46161-9745)
P.O. Box 245 (46161-0245)
PHONE.................................765 763-7246
Fax: 765 763-6011
Stacy Flora, Enginr/R&D Mgr
EMP: 150
SQ FT: 45,000
SALES (corp-wide): 8.3B Privately Held
WEB: www.freudenberg-nok.com
SIC: 3053 3965 3714 3643 Gaskets, all
materials; oil seals, rubber; packing, rub-
ber; fasteners, buttons, needles & pins;
motor vehicle parts & accessories; cur-
rent-carrying wiring devices; mechanical
rubber goods
HQ: Freudenberg-Nok General Partnership
47774 W Anchor Ct
Plymouth MI 48170
734 451-0020

(G-10370)
FREUDENBERG-NOK GENERAL PARTNR
487 W Main St (46161-9745)
PHONE.................................765 763-7246
Fax: 317 392-1347
Tony Goanes, Manager
EMP: 120
SALES (corp-wide): 8.3B Privately Held
WEB: www.freudenberg-nok.com
SIC: 3053 5085 Gaskets, packing & seal-
ing devices; industrial supplies
HQ: Freudenberg-Nok General Partnership
47774 W Anchor Ct
Plymouth MI 48170
734 451-0020

(G-10371)
INTEGRITY BIO-FUELS LLC
780 E Industrial Dr (46161-9616)
PHONE.................................765 763-6020
Charles Whittington, President

John S Whittington, *Vice Pres*
John Whittington, *Vice Pres*
Guy Herrell, *Plant Mgr*
Kari Crowder, *Office Mgr*
EMP: 12
SQ FT: 55,000
SALES (est): 3.2MM **Privately Held**
WEB: www.integritybiofuels.com
SIC: 2911 Diesel fuels

(G-10372)
KBI INC
2618 E Us Highway 52 (46161-9802)
PHONE....................765 763-6114
Fax: 765 763-6073
Kenneth Klosterman, *Ch of Bd*
Bob Jung, *CFO*
EMP: 100
SQ FT: 25,000
SALES (est): 9.8MM
SALES (corp-wide): 207.2MM **Privately Held**
WEB: www.kbi.com
SIC: 2051 Buns, bread type: fresh or frozen
PA: Klosterman Baking Co.
4760 Paddock Rd
Cincinnati OH 45229
513 242-5667

(G-10373)
KICK OUT JAMS LLC
6559 E 1200 N (46161-9753)
PHONE....................765 763-0225
Sherri Dugger,
Randy Dugger,
EMP: 2
SALES (est): 75.9K **Privately Held**
SIC: 2033 Jams, jellies & preserves: packaged in cans, jars, etc.

(G-10374)
MARCUMS WELDING & STL PROC INC
454 E Main St (46161-9760)
PHONE....................765 763-7279
Charles J Marcum, *President*
Devin Cox, *Sales Staff*
EMP: 6
SALES (est): 1MM **Privately Held**
SIC: 3441 Fabricated structural metal

(G-10375)
PARK 100 FOODS INC
Also Called: Kettle Processed Foods
205 Central Pkwy (46161-9647)
PHONE....................765 763-6064
Fax: 765 763-7132
Will Copass, *Owner*
Cory Schornack, *Manager*
Mark Turney, *Manager*
EMP: 62
SALES (corp-wide): 95MM **Privately Held**
SIC: 2013 Frozen meats from purchased meat
PA: Park 100 Foods Inc
326 E Adams St
Tipton IN 46072
765 675-3480

(G-10376)
WOODS OF AMBER
632 S Washington St (46161-9771)
PHONE....................765 763-6926
Ronald Zellar, *Owner*
EMP: 2
SALES (est): 73.4K **Privately Held**
SIC: 2499 Carved & turned wood

Mount Pleasant
Perry County

(G-10377)
CASH LOGGING
20198 N State Road 66 (47520-5100)
PHONE....................812 843-5335
James Cash, *Owner*
EMP: 3
SALES: 120K **Privately Held**
SIC: 2411 Logging camps & contractors

Mount Summit
Henry County

(G-10378)
BIG ALS ATHLETICS
303 S Walnut (47361)
P.O. Box 218 (47361-0218)
PHONE....................765 836-5203
EMP: 3
SALES (est): 130K **Privately Held**
SIC: 3552 2396 Mfg Textile Machinery Mfg Auto/Apparel Trimming

(G-10379)
KAIROS SPECIALTY METALS CORP
404 W Main St (47361)
PHONE....................765 836-5540
John Deradoorian, *President*
EMP: 25
SALES (est): 108.3K **Privately Held**
SIC: 3444 Sheet metalwork

Mount Vernon
Posey County

(G-10380)
ADM MILLING CO
614 W 2nd St (47620-1706)
PHONE....................812 838-4445
Fax: 812 838-6602
Kim Banks, *Branch Mgr*
EMP: 100
SALES (corp-wide): 60.8B **Publicly Held**
WEB: www.admmilling.com
SIC: 2041 Grain mills (except rice)
HQ: Adm Milling Co.
8000 W 110th St Ste 300
Overland Park KS 66210
913 491-9400

(G-10381)
AIR LIQUIDE TOM UTLEY
721 W 6th St (47620-1635)
PHONE....................812 838-0599
EMP: 3 EST: 2008
SALES (est): 120K **Privately Held**
SIC: 1321 Natural Gas Liquids Production

(G-10382)
AIRGAS USA LLC
1101 Hwy 69 S (47620)
P.O. Box 330 (47620-0330)
PHONE....................812 838-8808
Mike Curtis, *Principal*
EMP: 25
SALES (corp-wide): 164.2MM **Privately Held**
SIC: 2813 Industrial gases
HQ: Airgas Usa, Llc
259 N Radnor Chester Rd # 100
Radnor PA 19087
610 687-5253

(G-10383)
ASTRAZENECA PHARMACEUTICALS LP
4601 Highway 62 E (47620-9682)
PHONE....................812 429-5000
Jeff Bottoms, *Branch Mgr*
EMP: 40
SALES (corp-wide): 22.4B **Privately Held**
WEB: www.bms.com
SIC: 2834 Pharmaceutical preparations
HQ: Astrazeneca Pharmaceuticals Lp
1 Medimmune Way
Gaithersburg MD 20878

(G-10384)
ATI INC (PA)
103 Brown St (47620-1425)
P.O. Box 686 (47620-0686)
PHONE....................812 431-5409
Kenneth Juncker, *Ch of Bd*
Duane Tiede, *President*
Steve Hannam, *Principal*
C Anthony Juncker, *Principal*
David L Juncker, *Admin Sec*
◆ EMP: 9 EST: 1997
SQ FT: 36,000

SALES (est): 1.9MM **Privately Held**
WEB: www.agtracks.com
SIC: 3545 3061 3829 Cutting tools for machine tools; automotive rubber goods (mechanical); meteorologic tracking systems

(G-10385)
AVENTINE RENEWABLE ENERGY
Also Called: Aventine Renewabie Fuels
7201 Port Rd (47620-8524)
PHONE....................812 838-9598
Mike Murray, *Engineer*
EMP: 2
SALES (est): 265.2K **Privately Held**
SIC: 2869 Ethanolamines

(G-10386)
BRISTOL-MYERS SQUIBB COMPANY
6400 William Keck Byp (47620-6929)
PHONE....................812 307-2000
Phil Campbell, *Director*
EMP: 130
SALES (corp-wide): 20.7B **Publicly Held**
WEB: www.bms.com
SIC: 2834 Pharmaceutical preparations
PA: Bristol-Myers Squibb Company
430 E 29th St Fl 14
New York NY 10016
212 546-4000

(G-10387)
BWXT NCLEAR OPRTIONS GROUP INC
1400 Old Highway 69 S (47620-8749)
PHONE....................812 838-1200
Michael Keene, *President*
Kathleen Mathew, *Opers Mgr*
Farrah Corbett, *Human Res Mgr*
Brad Winter, *Manager*
EMP: 151 **Publicly Held**
SIC: 3462 Nuclear power plant forgings, ferrous
HQ: Bwxt Nuclear Operations Group, Inc.
2016 Mount Athos Rd
Lynchburg VA 24504

(G-10388)
COUNTRYMARK REF LOGISTICS LLC
Also Called: Countrymark Cooperative
1200 Refinery Rd (47620-9265)
PHONE....................812 838-4341
Fax: 812 838-8196
Charles E Smith, *President*
Jon Lantz, *Vice Pres*
Terrill Needham, *Vice Pres*
Matt Smorch, *Vice Pres*
Pat Ward, *Vice Pres*
EMP: 100
SALES (est): 17.9MM
SALES (corp-wide): 216.4MM **Privately Held**
SIC: 2911 1382 1311 Petroleum refining; aerial geophysical exploration oil & gas; crude petroleum & natural gas production
PA: Countrymark Cooperative Holding Corporation
225 S East St Ste 144
Indianapolis IN 46202
800 808-3170

(G-10389)
COY OIL INC (PA)
7451 Sauerkraut Ln N (47620-8175)
P.O. Box 575 (47620-0575)
PHONE....................812 838-3146
Michael Cash, *President*
EMP: 5
SQ FT: 2,400
SALES (est): 825.2K **Privately Held**
SIC: 1311 1381 Crude petroleum production; natural gas production; spudding in oil & gas wells

(G-10390)
COY OIL INC
7451 Sauerkraut Ln N (47620-8175)
PHONE....................618 966-2126
Danny Stewart, *Manager*
EMP: 3

SALES (est): 151.4K
SALES (corp-wide): 825.2K **Privately Held**
SIC: 1381 Directional drilling oil & gas wells
PA: Coy Oil, Inc
7451 Sauerkraut Ln N
Mount Vernon IN 47620
812 838-3146

(G-10391)
CT PHOENIX OF INDIANA INC
1600 W 4th St (47620)
PHONE....................812 838-2414
Fax: 812 838-2427
Lawrence Tully, *President*
EMP: 10
SALES (est): 1.6MM **Privately Held**
SIC: 3089 Plastic processing

(G-10392)
FISCHER WOODWORKING INC
3190 Ford Rd N (47620-7333)
PHONE....................812 985-9488
Stan Fischer, *President*
EMP: 7
SQ FT: 10,000
SALES: 250K **Privately Held**
SIC: 2431 Woodwork, interior & ornamental

(G-10393)
GOTTMAN ELECTRIC CO INC
3350 Old Highway 62 (47620-6924)
P.O. Box 752 (47620-0752)
PHONE....................812 838-0037
Fax: 812 838-4828
Terry Gottman, *President*
Herschel E Gottman, *Exec VP*
EMP: 6
SQ FT: 6,000
SALES: 600K **Privately Held**
SIC: 1731 General electrical contractor; electric motor repair

(G-10394)
GREEN PLAINS INC
8999 W Franklin Rd (47620-9179)
PHONE....................812 985-7480
Dan Labhart, *Branch Mgr*
EMP: 50
SALES (corp-wide): 3.6B **Publicly Held**
SIC: 2869 Ethyl alcohol, ethanol
PA: Green Plains Inc.
1811 Aksarben Dr
Omaha NE 68106
402 884-8700

(G-10395)
INDIANA KY ILL INTERSTATE QUA
6508 Uebelhack Rd (47620-9746)
PHONE....................812 985-9966
Scott Braster, *President*
EMP: 2
SALES: 5.8K **Privately Held**
SIC: 3131 Quarters

(G-10396)
J & J WELDING INC
1114 W 4th St (47620-1688)
P.O. Box 579 (47620-0579)
PHONE....................812 838-4391
Dorothy Smith, *President*
Bryan Smith, *Vice Pres*
Timothy Smith, *Vice Pres*
Karen Baker, *Office Mgr*
Darren Saltzman, *Shareholder*
▲ EMP: 20
SQ FT: 11,250
SALES (est): 3.4MM **Privately Held**
SIC: 7692 3443 3599 3471 Welding repair; fabricated plate work (boiler shop); machine shop, jobbing & repair; plating & polishing; sheet metalwork

(G-10397)
JAMPLAST INC
6450 Leonard Rd N (47620-6986)
P.O. Box 504 (47620-0504)
PHONE....................812 838-8562
◆ EMP: 5
SALES (est): 855.8K **Privately Held**
SIC: 2821 Thermoplastic materials

(G-10398)
MATHESON TRI-GAS INC
1101 Holler Rd (47620)
PHONE..................................812 838-5518
Mike Curtis, *Manager*
EMP: 13
SALES (corp-wide): 34.9B **Privately Held**
WEB: www.mgindustries.com
SIC: 2813 5084 Industrial gases; nitrogen;
oxygen, compressed or liquefied; argon;
welding machinery & equipment; safety
equipment
HQ: Matheson Tri-Gas, Inc.
150 Allen Rd Ste 302
Basking Ridge NJ 07920
908 991-9200

(G-10399)
MAYHEW OIL & GAS LLC
Also Called: Mayhew Oil & Gas Development
6508 Uebelhack Rd (47620-9746)
P.O. Box 715 (47620-0715)
PHONE..................................812 985-9966
Don W Mayhew, *Owner*
EMP: 2
SALES (est): 252.1K **Privately Held**
SIC: 1311 Crude petroleum production;
natural gas production

(G-10400)
**MEAD JOHNSON & COMPANY
LLC**
Also Called: Mead Johnson Nutritionals
62 W State Rd (47620)
PHONE..................................812 429-5000
Philena Mead, *Branch Mgr*
EMP: 7
SALES (corp-wide): 15.2B **Privately Held**
SIC: 2834 Pharmaceutical preparations
HQ: Mead Johnson & Company, Llc
2400 W Lloyd Expy
Evansville IN 47712
812 429-5000

(G-10401)
MICHROCHEM LLC
Also Called: Mac Industrial Services
901 E 3rd St (47620-2109)
PHONE..................................812 838-1832
Michael Andrews, *Managing Prtnr*
EMP: 6
SALES (est): 791.2K **Privately Held**
SIC: 3589 High pressure cleaning equip-
ment

(G-10402)
**MORROWS MT VERNON ELC
MTR SVC**
Also Called: Morrows Electric Motor Service
214 W 2nd St (47620-1809)
P.O. Box 532 (47620-0532)
PHONE..................................812 838-5641
Fax: 812 838-6921
David Morrow, *President*
Kimberly Morrow, *Vice Pres*
EMP: 7
SQ FT: 5,000
SALES: 300K **Privately Held**
SIC: 7694 Armature rewinding shops

(G-10403)
**MT VERNON COAL TRANSFER
CO**
Alliance Resource Partners
3300 Bluff Rd (47620-8528)
P.O. Box 742 (47620-0742)
PHONE..................................812 838-5531
Fax: 812 838-3215
V F Mayer, *Branch Mgr*
EMP: 10
SALES (corp-wide): 1.8B **Publicly Held**
SIC: 1221 Bituminous coal & lignite-sur-
face mining
HQ: Mt Vernon Coal Transfer Co (Inc)
1717 S Boulder Ave
Tulsa OK 74119
918 295-7600

(G-10404)
**NEWS PUBLISHING COMPANY
LLC**
Also Called: Mt. Vernon Democrat
132 E 2nd St (47620-1805)
PHONE..................................812 838-4811
Fax: 812 838-3696
Angela Geralds, *Principal*
EMP: 5 **Privately Held**
WEB: www.leaderunion.com
SIC: 2759 8999 Commercial printing;
newspaper column writing
HQ: News Publishing Company, Llc
537 Main St
Tell City IN 47586
812 547-3424

(G-10405)
PRINTCRAFTERS INC
304 W 4th St (47620-1822)
P.O. Box 487 (47620-0487)
PHONE..................................812 838-4106
Fax: 812 838-5263
Harriette Alley, *President*
EMP: 5
SQ FT: 2,200
SALES (est): 340K **Privately Held**
SIC: 2752 2759 Commercial printing, off-
set; letterpress printing

(G-10406)
**RUSSELLS EXCVTG & SEPTIC
TANKS**
Also Called: Russell's Septic Tank Service
6800 Leonard Rd S (47620-8123)
P.O. Box 512 (47620-0512)
PHONE..................................812 838-2471
Fax: 812 838-4834
John Russell, *President*
Ruth Russell, *Corp Secy*
Jeffrey Russell, *Vice Pres*
EMP: 6
SALES (est): 980.1K **Privately Held**
SIC: 1794 1711 3272 Excavation & grad-
ing, building construction; septic system
construction; septic tanks, concrete

(G-10407)
**SABIC INNOVATIVE PLASTICS
MT V**
1 Lexan Ln (47620-9367)
PHONE..................................812 838-4385
Joseph Castrale, *President*
Sandeep Dhawan, *General Mgr*
Aliene Elkins, *Business Mgr*
Michael L Walsh, *Vice Pres*
Mike Walsh, *VP Mfg*
◆ EMP: 1342
SALES (est): 228.8MM **Privately Held**
WEB: www.sabic-ip.com
SIC: 2821 3087 3081 Plastics materials &
resins; custom compound purchased
resins; unsupported plastics film & sheet
HQ: Sabic Innovative Plastics Us Llc
2500 City W Blvd Ste 100
Houston TX 77042

(G-10408)
**SCHENK SONS WLDG & TREE
SVC IN**
11018 Altheide Rd (47620-9684)
PHONE..................................812 985-3954
Steve Schenk, *Owner*
EMP: 2 EST: 1997
SALES (est): 81.4K **Privately Held**
SIC: 0783 7692 Ornamental shrub & tree
services; welding repair

(G-10409)
STANDARD INDUSTRIES INC
Also Called: GAF Materials
901 Givens Rd (47620-8200)
PHONE..................................812 838-4861
Fax: 812 838-5074
Jon Houchins, *Plant Mgr*
Troy Utley, *Mfg Staff*
Henry Loper, *Purch Mgr*
Tj Jenkins, *QC Mgr*
Chad Chaddowell, *Engineer*
EMP: 119
SALES (corp-wide): 1.5B **Privately Held**
SIC: 2493 Insulation & roofing material, re-
constituted wood
HQ: Standard Industries Inc.
1 Campus Dr
Parsippany NJ 07054

(G-10410)
**TRON MECHANICAL
INCORPORATED**
Also Called: TMI Contractors
331 W 2nd St (47620-1801)
P.O. Box 691 (47620-0691)
PHONE..................................812 838-4715
Fax: 812 838-1461
Phillip R Wells, *President*
EMP: 120
SQ FT: 45,000
SALES: 16MM **Privately Held**
SIC: 1711 3441 Process piping contractor;
fabricated structural metal

(G-10411)
TWO RIVERS CAMPING CLUB I
623 W 7th St (47620-1637)
PHONE..................................812 838-3687
Joann Brass, *Owner*
EMP: 9
SALES (est): 412.5K **Privately Held**
SIC: 3792 Travel trailers & campers

(G-10412)
**UNITED MINERALS AND PRPTS
INC**
Also Called: Cimbar Performance Mineral
2700 Bluff Rd (47620-8521)
PHONE..................................812 838-5236
Paul Householder, *Manager*
EMP: 50
SALES (corp-wide): 29.3MM **Privately
Held**
SIC: 3295 2851 2822 2816 Minerals,
ground or treated; paints & allied prod-
ucts; synthetic rubber; inorganic pigments
PA: United Minerals And Properties, Inc.
49 Jackson Lake Rd Ste O
Chatsworth GA 30705
770 387-0319

(G-10413)
**VALERO RENEWABLE FUELS
CO LLC**
7201 Port Rd (47620-8524)
PHONE..................................812 833-3900
Travis Defrief, *Branch Mgr*
EMP: 35
SALES (corp-wide): 93.9B **Publicly Held**
SIC: 2869 Ethyl alcohol, ethanol
HQ: Valero Renewable Fuels Company, Llc
1 Valero Way
San Antonio TX 78249

(G-10414)
**WESTECH BUILDING
PRODUCTS INC**
7451 Highway 62 E (47620-9131)
PHONE..................................812 985-3628
John A Labuda, *Manager*
Kellie Shelton, *Supervisor*
◆ EMP: 29
SALES (est): 7MM **Privately Held**
SIC: 3275 Gypsum products

(G-10415)
ZELLER ELEVATOR CO
8875 Meinschein Rd (47620-9709)
PHONE..................................812 985-5888
L M Zeller, *Owner*
EMP: 8
SALES (est): 430K **Privately Held**
SIC: 1796 3534 Elevator installation &
conversion; elevators & moving stairways

Mulberry
Clinton County

(G-10416)
ALL AMERICAN AWARDS INC
11624 S Glick St (46058)
P.O. Box 646, Lafayette (47902-0646)
PHONE..................................765 296-4333
Fax: 765 296-4447
Leonard Herr, *President*
Mike Lueken, *Vice Pres*
R Kevin Sims, *Treasurer*
EMP: 8
SQ FT: 10,000
SALES (est): 720K **Privately Held**
SIC: 2796 Etching on copper, steel, wood
or rubber: printing plates

(G-10417)
GRINER ENGINEERING
515 W Jackson St (46058-9537)
P.O. Box 111 (46058-0111)
PHONE..................................765 296-2955
Fax: 765 296-2272
Stephen Griner, *Owner*
EMP: 2
SQ FT: 3,000
SALES: 150K **Privately Held**
SIC: 3714 Power transmission equipment,
motor vehicle

(G-10418)
**PUBLISHERS SOVEREIGN
GRACE**
307 S Glick St (46058-2229)
P.O. Box 491 (46058-0491)
PHONE..................................765 296-5538
Charles V Turner, *Principal*
EMP: 4
SALES (est): 215.9K **Privately Held**
SIC: 2741 Miscellaneous publishing

(G-10419)
RED BARN INDUSTRIES INC
5665 W County Road 700 N (46058-9408)
PHONE..................................765 379-3197
James H Schlatter, *President*
Penelope Schlatter, *Vice Pres*
EMP: 10 EST: 1995
SQ FT: 3,600
SALES: 600K **Privately Held**
SIC: 3621 Coils, for electric motors or gen-
erators

Muncie
Delaware County

(G-10420)
A-1 GRAPHICS INC
2500 W 7th St (47302-1692)
PHONE..................................765 289-1851
Fax: 765 289-0752
Mike Green, *President*
Jordan Green, *Sales Staff*
EMP: 7 EST: 1964
SQ FT: 6,900
SALES (est): 1.2MM **Privately Held**
SIC: 2791 2752 2675 Photocomposition,
for the printing trade; commercial printing,
offset; die-cut paper & board

(G-10421)
AAA GALVANIZING - JOLIET INC
Also Called: Azz Galvanizing - Muncie
2415 S Walnut St (47302-4143)
PHONE..................................765 289-3427
EMP: 49
SALES (corp-wide): 903.1MM **Publicly
Held**
SIC: 3479 Metal Coating And Allied Serv-
ices, Nsk
HQ: Aaa Galvanizing - Joliet, Inc.
625 Mills Rd
Joliet IL 60433
815 723-5000

(G-10422)
**ACADEMY OF MDEL
ARONAUTICS INC**
Also Called: A M A
5161 E Memorial Dr (47302-9252)
PHONE..................................765 287-1256
Fax: 765 289-4248
Bob Brown, *President*
Erin Dobbs, *Partner*
Gary Fitch, *Exec VP*
Elizabeth Helms, *Opers Staff*
Vicki Barkdull, *Controller*
EMP: 54
SQ FT: 25,000
SALES: 151.2K **Privately Held**
WEB: www.ezrc.com
SIC: 8699 2741 Personal interest organi-
zation; miscellaneous publishing

(G-10423)
ACE SIGN SYSTEMS INC
3621 W Royerton Rd (47304-9101)
PHONE..................................765 288-1000
Bob Jones, *President*
Russel Jones, *Treasurer*
EMP: 8
SQ FT: 12,000
SALES: 500K **Privately Held**
WEB: www.acesign.com
SIC: 3993 Signs, not made in custom sign
painting shops

(G-10424)
**ADVANCED SIGN & GRAPHICS
INC**
3939 E Mcgalliard Rd (47303-1500)
PHONE..................................765 284-8360
Dave Flannery, *President*
Gary Mader, *Vice Pres*
Brandon Flannery, *Finance Mgr*
Stephanie Wulff, *Office Mgr*
Gary J Mader, *Manager*
EMP: 13
SQ FT: 7,500
SALES (est): 1.2MM **Privately Held**
WEB: www.advancedsigns.com
SIC: 3993 Signs & advertising specialties;
neon signs; electric signs

(G-10425)
AFTERIMAGE GIS (PA)
808 E Cooper Rd (47303-9453)
PHONE..................................765 744-1346
Eric Shanayda, *Principal*
EMP: 5
SALES (est): 469.6K **Privately Held**
SIC: 2741 Miscellaneous publishing

(G-10426)
ALL STEEL CARPORTS INC
2200 N Granville Ave (47303-2165)
PHONE..................................765 284-0694
Ignaclo Chavez, *President*
Michael Burton, *Manager*
▲ EMP: 8
SALES (est): 2.2MM **Privately Held**
SIC: 3448 Buildings, portable: prefabri-
cated metal

(G-10427)
**ALL STEEL CRPRTS BUILDINGS
LLC**
2200 N Granville Ave (47303-2165)
PHONE..................................765 284-0694
Ignaclo Chavez, *President*
▲ EMP: 2
SALES (est): 190K **Privately Held**
SIC: 3448 Carports: prefabricated metal

(G-10428)
ALLIED ENTERPRISES INC
3228 W Kilgore Ave (47304-4908)
P.O. Box 267 (47308-0267)
PHONE..................................765 288-8849
Fax: 765 288-8864
John R Miller, *President*
Greg Miller, *Partner*
Barry Stinson, *Prdtn Mgr*
◆ EMP: 30
SQ FT: 28,000
SALES (est): 6.2MM **Privately Held**
SIC: 3714 5013 5088 5084 Motor vehicle
transmissions, drive assemblies & parts;
automotive supplies & parts; marine
propulsion machinery & equipment; en-
gines & transportation equipment; power
transmission equipment

(G-10429)
ALPHA WATER CONDITIONING
4021 N Broadway Ave Rear (47303-1047)
PHONE..................................765 281-8820
Fax: 765 287-0742
Bill Miller, *President*
EMP: 2
SALES (est): 133.2K **Privately Held**
SIC: 2899 Water treating compounds

(G-10430)
**AMERICAN MOBILE SOUND IND
LLC**
Also Called: AMS Pro Sound and
Lightingame
2418 W 7th St (47302-1600)
PHONE..................................765 288-1500
Slade S Member, *President*
EMP: 6 EST: 2001
SALES (est): 888.8K **Privately Held**
SIC: 3651 Amplifiers: radio, public address
or musical instrument

(G-10431)
ANNETTE BALFOUR
2201 E Memorial Dr Rear (47302-4673)
PHONE..................................765 286-1910
Annette Balfour, *Owner*
EMP: 2
SALES (est): 75K **Privately Held**
SIC: 7692 Welding repair

(G-10432)
**ARROWHEAD PLASTIC
ENGINEERING (PA)**
Also Called: Arrowhead Composites
2909 S Hoyt Ave (47302-3935)
P.O. Box 75, Eaton (47338-0075)
PHONE..................................765 286-0533
Fax: 765 286-1681
Thomas W Kishel, *President*
Jeff Miller, *Mfg Staff*
Monte Foist, *Engineer*
Clara McCoy, *Finance Mgr*
Mike Harrold, *Persnl Dir*
EMP: 50 EST: 1972
SQ FT: 35,000
SALES (est): 14.8MM **Privately Held**
WEB: www.arrowheadinc.com
SIC: 3089 Plastic processing

(G-10433)
ARTISAN TOOL & DIE INC
3805 W State Road 28 (47303-8902)
PHONE..................................765 288-6653
Fax: 765 286-1517
H Doug Mansfield, *President*
Chad Jones, *Foreman/Supr*
Alan Yoes, *Manager*
EMP: 20
SQ FT: 15,000
SALES (est): 3.5MM **Privately Held**
SIC: 3544 Industrial molds

(G-10434)
**AUL BROTHERS TOOL & DIE
INC**
9609 W Jackson St (47304-9654)
PHONE..................................765 759-5124
Fax: 765 759-6003
EMP: 14 EST: 1942
SQ FT: 11,000
SALES (est): 1.2MM **Privately Held**
SIC: 3469 3544 Mfg Metal Stampings Mfg
Dies/Tools/Jigs/Fixtures

(G-10435)
AUNTIE ANNES
3501 N Grnville Ave Ste 3 (47303)
PHONE..................................765 288-8077
Kermit Willer, *Owner*
EMP: 11 EST: 2001
SALES (est): 237.9K **Privately Held**
SIC: 5461 2052 Pretzels; pretzels

(G-10436)
**AUTOMATED LOGIC
CORPORATION**
Also Called: Automated Logic - Indiana
117 N High St (47305-1613)
PHONE..................................765 286-1993
Brian Brinkman, *Principal*
Mark Beals, *Technology*
EMP: 30
SALES (corp-wide): 59.8B **Publicly Held**
SIC: 3822 Temperature controls, automatic
HQ: Automated Logic Corporation
1150 Roberts Blvd Nw
Kennesaw GA 30144
770 429-3000

(G-10437)
BALL STATE UNIVERSITY
Also Called: Ball State Daily News
276 Park Journalism Bldg (47306-0001)
PHONE..................................765 285-8218
Joy Coleman, *Manager*
EMP: 5
SALES (corp-wide): 543.1MM **Privately
Held**
WEB: www.bsu.edu
SIC: 2711 8221 Newspapers; university
PA: Ball State University
2000 W University Ave
Muncie IN 47306
765 289-1241

(G-10438)
**BECKETT BRONZE COMPANY
INC (PA)**
401 W 23rd St (47302-5083)
P.O. Box 2425 (47307-0425)
PHONE..................................765 282-2261
Fax: 765 282-2268
Susan Herro, *President*
Stephen Dixon, *Vice Pres*
Trevor Kelley, *Opers Mgr*
Ray Logan, *Facilities Mgr*
Jerry Fair, *Foreman/Supr*
EMP: 25
SQ FT: 22,000
SALES (est): 12.9MM **Privately Held**
WEB: www.beckettbronze.com
SIC: 3451 3366 Screw machine products;
copper foundries

(G-10439)
**BECKETT BRONZE COMPANY
INC**
106 E 20th St (47302-5003)
P.O. Box 2425 (47307-0425)
PHONE..................................765 282-2261
Kay Dixon, *Branch Mgr*
EMP: 20
SALES (corp-wide): 12.9MM **Privately
Held**
WEB: www.beckettbronze.com
SIC: 3366 Bushings & bearings, bronze
(nonmachined)
PA: Beckett Bronze Company, Inc.
401 W 23rd St
Muncie IN 47302
765 282-2261

(G-10440)
BLONDIES COOKIES INC
3501 N Grnville Ave Ste 99 (47303)
PHONE..................................765 288-3872
Fax: 765 288-3872
Leslie Spydell, *Manager*
EMP: 7
SALES (corp-wide): 10.6MM **Privately
Held**
SIC: 2052 5149 Cookies; crackers, cook-
ies & bakery products
PA: Blondie's Cookies Inc
303 N Meridian St
Greentown IN 46936
765 628-3978

(G-10441)
BOOMERS
2627 S Walnut St (47302-5063)
PHONE..................................765 741-4031
EMP: 2
SALES (est): 114.8K **Privately Held**
SIC: 2899 Chemical preparations

(G-10442)
BOWMAN ART GLASS STUDIO
3929 W Kilgore Ave (47304-4813)
PHONE..................................765 281-4527
Richard Darmanin, *Principal*
EMP: 2
SALES (est): 144.4K **Privately Held**
SIC: 3231 Stained glass: made from pur-
chased glass

(G-10443)
**BRAND SHEET METAL WORKS
INC**
Also Called: Brand Restaurant Equipment
907 S Burlington Dr (47302-2899)
PHONE..................................765 284-5594
Fax: 765 284-2152
Michael B Brand, *President*

Alex M Brand, *Vice Pres*
Kathy Brand, *Admin Sec*
EMP: 7 EST: 1946
SQ FT: 12,500
SALES (est): 540K **Privately Held**
SIC: 3444 5046 7692 3351 Sheet metal
specialties, not stamped; restaurant sheet
metalwork; commercial cooking & food
service equipment; welding repair; copper
rolling & drawing

(G-10444)
**C & J PLATING & GRINDING
LLC**
411 E 3rd St (47302-2415)
PHONE..................................765 288-8728
Howard Larsen,
EMP: 4
SALES (est): 285.2K **Privately Held**
SIC: 1446 3471 Grinding sand mining;
plating & polishing

(G-10445)
CAMTOOL INC
3690 S Hoyt Ave (47302-4900)
PHONE..................................765 286-9725
Greg Haisley, *President*
EMP: 11
SQ FT: 10,000
SALES (est): 1.8MM **Privately Held**
WEB: www.camtoolinc.com
SIC: 3599 Machine shop, jobbing & repair

(G-10446)
COMCAST SPOTLIGHT MUNCIE
420 W Washington St (47305-1570)
PHONE..................................765 216-1728
EMP: 2
SALES (est): 120K **Privately Held**
SIC: 3648 Mfg Lighting Equipment

(G-10447)
**COMPLETE PROPERTY CARE
LLC**
806 W Jackson St (47305-1551)
P.O. Box 2443 (47307-0443)
PHONE..................................765 288-0890
Fax: 765 288-0899
Daniel Norton, *Mng Member*
Lance Norton, *Property Mgr*
Glenda Norton-Perry,
EMP: 8
SQ FT: 600
SALES (est): 300K **Privately Held**
WEB: www.completepropertycarellc.com
SIC: 7349 1389 6519 6531 Building
maintenance services; construction, re-
pair & dismantling services; real property
lessors; real estate brokers & agents; real
estate leasing & rentals; construction site
cleanup

(G-10448)
CONCANNONS PASTRY SHOP
620 N Walnut St (47305-1453)
PHONE..................................765 288-8551
Fax: 765 288-2395
J Michael Concannon, *Owner*
EMP: 21
SQ FT: 3,200
SALES: 680K **Privately Held**
SIC: 5461 2051 Cakes; bread, cake & re-
lated products

(G-10449)
COOL CAYENNE LLC
1701 W Jackson St (47303-4963)
PHONE..................................765 282-0977
Jon Bennett, *CEO*
EMP: 2
SALES (est): 168.7K **Privately Held**
WEB: www.coolcayenne.com
SIC: 2759 5651 Screen printing; family
clothing stores

(G-10450)
COVINGTON PRODUCTS INC
112 W Fuson Rd (47302-8601)
P.O. Box 2345 (47307-0345)
PHONE..................................765 282-6626
Fax: 765 282-6715
Jerry W Covington, *President*
Paul Covington, *Vice Pres*
EMP: 10 EST: 1967
SQ FT: 6,500

G
E
O
G
R
A
P
H
I
C

SALES (est): 1.5MM **Privately Held**
SIC: 3469 3544 Stamping metal for the trade; special dies & tools; die sets for metal stamping (presses)

(G-10451)
CS KERN INC
3401 S Hamilton Ave (47302-9115)
PHONE................................765 289-8600
C Steven Kern, *President*
Bart Dawson, *Admin Sec*
EMP: 34
SQ FT: 5,500
SALES (est): 4.9MM **Privately Held**
SIC: 2759 7336 Commercial printing; commercial art & graphic design

(G-10452)
CUTTING EDGE WIRE EDM INC
1800 W Mt Pleasant Blvd (47302-9559)
PHONE................................765 284-3820
Steven Cross, *President*
Rachel Cross, *Corp Secy*
EMP: 3
SQ FT: 2,000
SALES: 500K **Privately Held**
SIC: 3544 Special dies, tools, jigs & fixtures

(G-10453)
DARK STAR INC
Also Called: Dark Star Printing & Advg
1309 S Nebo Rd 400w (47304-4779)
PHONE................................765 759-4764
Fax: 765 759-8355
Kathy Spangler, *President*
Jeffrey Joe Spangler, *COO*
EMP: 12
SQ FT: 9,600
SALES: 735.2K **Privately Held**
SIC: 2396 7389 5199 Screen printing on fabric articles; embroidering of advertising on shirts, etc.; advertising specialties

(G-10454)
DAVID GONZALES
Also Called: Montezuma Jewelry
701 E Mcgalliard Rd (47303-2020)
PHONE................................765 284-6960
Fax: 765 282-7407
David Gonzales, *Owner*
EMP: 3
SQ FT: 900
SALES (est): 262.4K **Privately Held**
WEB: www.montezumajewelry.com
SIC: 3911 5944 Jewelry, precious metal; jewelry, precious stones & precious metals

(G-10455)
DEBBIES HANDMADE SOAP
1140 E County Road 500 S (47302-8709)
PHONE................................765 747-5090
Debbie Acree, *Principal*
EMP: 3
SALES (est): 213.4K **Privately Held**
SIC: 2079 Olive oil

(G-10456)
DELAWARE COUNTY HOME BLDRS INC
Also Called: Delaware County Mobile Homes
2411 N Dr Martin Luther (47303)
PHONE................................765 289-6328
Fax: 765 289-5010
Kevin D Steen, *President*
Jone A Steen, *Corp Secy*
EMP: 2 EST: 1982
SQ FT: 1,000
SALES (est): 278.2K **Privately Held**
SIC: 2452 5271 Modular homes, prefabricated, wood; mobile homes

(G-10457)
DELAWARE DYNAMICS LLC
700 S Mulberry St (47302-2356)
PHONE................................765 284-3335
Ryan A Haas,
▲ EMP: 89
SALES (est): 29.4MM **Privately Held**
SIC: 3312 Tool & die steel

(G-10458)
DELBERT M DAWSON & SON INC
Also Called: Dawson Sheet Metal
1405 W Kilgore Ave (47305-2134)
PHONE................................765 284-9711
Fax: 765 288-3279
Leon Van Ulzen, *President*
Albert Oliver, *Vice Pres*
EMP: 8 EST: 1926
SQ FT: 7,000
SALES: 220K **Privately Held**
SIC: 3441 3444 3599 Fabricated structural metal; sheet metalwork; machine shop, jobbing & repair

(G-10459)
DIAMOND PLASTICS CORPORATION
4100 Niles Rd (47302-9544)
P.O. Box 2447 (47307-0447)
PHONE................................765 287-9234
Fax: 765 287-9256
Kurt Van Laar, *Project Mgr*
Joe Dye, *Prdtn Mgr*
Michelle Quire, *Safety Mgr*
Peggy Duke, *Human Res Mgr*
David Dear, *Manager*
EMP: 55
SALES (corp-wide): 124.1MM **Privately Held**
WEB: www.dpcpipe.com
SIC: 3084 Plastics pipe
PA: Diamond Plastics Corporation
1212 Johnstown Rd
Grand Island NE 68803
765 287-9234

(G-10460)
DIRECT CONTROL SYSTEMS INC
4200 W County Road 750 N (47303-8936)
P.O. Box 267, Gaston (47342-0267)
PHONE................................765 282-7474
Fax: 765 282-5988
Randy Sayre, *President*
EMP: 8
SQ FT: 5,000
SALES: 500K **Privately Held**
WEB: www.direct-control.com
SIC: 3625 8711 3613 Electric controls & control accessories, industrial; electrical or electronic engineering; switchgear & switchboard apparatus

(G-10461)
DMI DISTRIBUTION INC
401 S Lincoln St (47302-2600)
P.O. Box 426, Winchester (47394-0426)
PHONE................................765 287-0035
EMP: 25
SALES (corp-wide): 27.9MM **Privately Held**
SIC: 2448 4225 Mfg Wood Pallets/Skids General Warehouse/Storage
PA: D M I Distribution, Inc.
990 Industrial Park Dr
Winchester IN 47394
765 584-3234

(G-10462)
DON CASE
3200 E County Road 350 N (47303-9263)
PHONE................................765 748-1325
EMP: 2
SALES (est): 85.9K **Privately Held**
SIC: 3523 Farm machinery & equipment

(G-10463)
DRIESSEN WATER INC
Also Called: Culligan
1509 N Wheeling Ave (47303-2880)
PHONE................................765 529-4905
James Ewing, *Manager*
EMP: 6
SALES (corp-wide): 44.8MM **Privately Held**
WEB: www.culliganmiami.com
SIC: 5999 7389 2899 Water purification equipment; water softener service; water treating compounds
PA: Driessen Water, Inc.
110 W Fremont St
Owatonna MN 55060
507 200-0820

(G-10464)
DRIVE PROCESS SERVICES INC
6017 W Hellis Dr (47304-3453)
PHONE................................765 741-9717
Susan Posocco, *President*
Raymond Posocco, *Vice Pres*
EMP: 2 EST: 1994
SALES: 250K **Privately Held**
SIC: 3511 Turbines & turbine generator sets

(G-10465)
E & B PAVING INC
4308 E County Road 350 N (47303-9142)
PHONE................................765 289-7131
Fax: 765 289-7214
Douglas Jump, *District Mgr*
Michael Shelley, *Plant Engr*
EMP: 12
SALES (corp-wide): 800.6MM **Privately Held**
SIC: 1611 2951 1771 Surfacing & paving; asphalt paving mixtures & blocks; blacktop (asphalt) work
HQ: E & B Paving, Inc.
286 W 300 N
Anderson IN 46012
765 643-5358

(G-10466)
EAGLE CNC MACHINING INC
801 W Riggin Rd (47303-6417)
PHONE................................765 289-2816
Greg Phillips, *President*
Nadine Phillips, *Vice Pres*
Gerald Phillips Jr, *Treasurer*
EMP: 11
SQ FT: 4,800
SALES (est): 1.5MM **Privately Held**
SIC: 3599 Machine & other job shop work; machine shop, jobbing & repair

(G-10467)
EATON EMTS
703 W 13th St (47302-7603)
PHONE................................765 587-4910
EMP: 2
SALES (est): 110K **Privately Held**
SIC: 3625 Relays And Industrial Controls, Nsk

(G-10468)
ELEGANT NEEDLEWORKS INC
7500 N Janna Dr (47303-9766)
PHONE................................765 284-9427
Masha Bawden, *President*
Linda Beurkhardt, *Admin Sec*
EMP: 2
SALES (est): 169.2K **Privately Held**
SIC: 2284 Needle & handicraft thread

(G-10469)
ELEMENTAL S A PROTECTION
509 N Forest Ave (47304-3816)
PHONE................................765 717-7325
Chadwick L Menning, *Administration*
EMP: 2
SALES (est): 74.4K **Privately Held**
SIC: 2819 Elements

(G-10470)
EXIDE TECHNOLOGIES
2601 W Mt Pleasant Blvd (47302-9102)
P.O. Box 2098 (47307-0098)
PHONE................................765 747-9980
Fax: 765 282-5461
Jeff Troutman, *Plant Mgr*
Steve Lynn, *Opers Staff*
Jeffrey Traupman, *QA Dir*
Daniel Henke, *Engineer*
Scott Davis, *Manager*
EMP: 130
SALES (corp-wide): 2.6B **Privately Held**
WEB: www.exideworld.com
SIC: 3691 3341 3339 Lead acid batteries (storage batteries); secondary nonferrous metals; primary nonferrous metals
PA: Exide Technologies (Inc.)
13000 Deerfield Pkwy # 200
Milton GA 30004
678 566-9000

(G-10471)
FEMYER DRAPERY SHOP
4409 W Burton Dr (47304-3538)
PHONE................................765 282-3398

Allen Femyer, *Owner*
EMP: 2
SALES (est): 82.5K **Privately Held**
SIC: 2391 Curtains & draperies

(G-10472)
FICKLE PEACH INC
117 E Charles St (47305-2413)
PHONE................................765 282-5211
Brion Fickle, *Owner*
EMP: 4
SALES (est): 413.5K **Privately Held**
SIC: 2599 Bar, restaurant & cafeteria furniture

(G-10473)
FRANKLIN STAMPING INDS INC
105 W Fuson Rd (47302-8601)
P.O. Box 2898 (47307-0898)
PHONE................................765 282-5138
Fax: 765 288-2783
Vicki Franklin, *President*
Sharon Franklin, *Vice Pres*
Walter Franklin, *Shareholder*
EMP: 13
SQ FT: 40,000
SALES (est): 2.6MM **Privately Held**
SIC: 3469 3544 Stamping metal for the trade; special dies & tools

(G-10474)
FRED JAY STEWART
Also Called: Stewart Trucking
4001 E Centennial Ave (47303-2653)
PHONE................................765 284-1386
Fax: 765 284-2728
EMP: 13
SALES (est): 950K **Privately Held**
SIC: 1442 4212 Construction Sand/Gravel Local Trucking Operator

(G-10475)
GAGAN PETROLEUM INC
5302 N Wheeling Ave (47304-5851)
PHONE................................765 254-1330
EMP: 2
SALES (est): 109K **Privately Held**
SIC: 1381 Oil/Gas Well Drilling

(G-10476)
GERDAU AMERISTEEL US INC
1810 S Macedonia Ave (47302-3669)
P.O. Box 2531 (47307-0531)
PHONE................................765 286-5454
Mike Barrett, *Manager*
EMP: 232 **Privately Held**
SIC: 3312 Hot-rolled iron & steel products; bars & bar shapes, steel, hot-rolled; structural shapes & pilings, steel
HQ: Gerdau Ameristeel Us Inc.
4221 W Boy Scout Blvd # 600
Tampa FL 33607
813 286-8383

(G-10477)
GKN AEROSPACE MUNCIE INC
Also Called: Sermatech-Aeroforge
3901 S Delaware Dr (47302-9549)
PHONE................................765 747-7147
Fax: 765 282-1372
Kevin Cummins, *CEO*
Jack Durham, *Purch Mgr*
EMP: 40
SALES: 16MM
SALES (corp-wide): 12.7B **Privately Held**
SIC: 3356 Titanium
PA: Gkn Limited
Po Box 55
Redditch WORCS B98 0
152 751-7715

(G-10478)
GRAPHIC PACKAGING INTL
301 S Butterfield Rd (47303-4317)
PHONE................................765 289-7391
EMP: 3
SALES (est): 213.4K **Privately Held**
SIC: 2631 Paperboard Mill

(G-10479)
GRAPHICS UNLIMITED
500 S Celia Ave B (47303-4616)
PHONE................................765 288-6816
Fax: 765 288-6816
Charles Chesney, *Owner*
EMP: 2

SQ FT: 1,000
SALES (est): 110K **Privately Held**
SIC: 2791 Typesetting

(G-10480)
H & H COMMERCIAL HEAT TREATING
2200 E 8th St (47302-3701)
P.O. Box 948 (47308-0948)
PHONE....................765 288-3618
Fax: 765 741-8234
Arthur D Hensley, *President*
Mary Hensley, *Corp Secy*
Brandon Hensley, *Vice Pres*
Tony Hensley, *Vice Pres*
EMP: 4 **EST:** 1940
SQ FT: 6,000
SALES: 220K **Privately Held**
SIC: 3398 Metal heat treating; annealing of metal; brazing (hardening) of metal; metal burning

(G-10481)
HAWKINS INC
4601 S Delaware Dr (47302-9177)
PHONE....................765 288-8930
Keith Uccello, *Branch Mgr*
EMP: 21
SALES (corp-wide): 504.1MM **Publicly Held**
SIC: 3312 Chemicals & other products derived from coking
PA: Hawkins, Inc.
2381 Rosegate
Roseville MN 55113
612 331-6910

(G-10482)
HAWKINS DARRYAL
Also Called: Hawkins Industrial Resource Co
1001 E 18th St (47302-4324)
P.O. Box 2631 (47307-0631)
PHONE....................765 282-6021
Darryal Hawkins, *Principal*
EMP: 3
SQ FT: 20,000
SALES: 500K **Privately Held**
SIC: 5084 3069 Industrial machinery & equipment; molded rubber products

(G-10483)
HAYLEX MANUFACTURING LLC
Also Called: Luick Quality Gage & Tool
4401 S Delaware Dr (47302-9400)
P.O. Box 2608 (47307-0608)
PHONE....................765 288-1818
Chris Flanagan, *President*
Marsha Clements, *Purch Agent*
Reese Steve, *Regl Sales Mgr*
Ellison Don, *Sales Staff*
Jeannie Flanagan, *Mng Member*
EMP: 21 **EST:** 2011
SQ FT: 62,000
SALES (est): 3.3MM **Privately Held**
WEB: www.luick.com
SIC: 3599 Machine shop, jobbing & repair

(G-10484)
HC FARMS
1010 E County Road 700 N (47303-9463)
PHONE....................765 289-9909
Jeff Hotmire, *Partner*
EMP: 4
SALES: 100K **Privately Held**
SIC: 3523 Driers (farm): grain, hay & seed

(G-10485)
HEARTHMARK LLC
Also Called: Jarden Home Brands
1501 E 9th St (47302-3600)
PHONE....................765 557-3000
Tod Lee, *Manager*
Ed McVay, *Manager*
EMP: 115
SALES (corp-wide): 14.7B **Publicly Held**
SIC: 3221 Food containers, glass
HQ: Hearthmark, Llc
9999 E 121st St
Fishers IN 46037

(G-10486)
HENKEL (DH)
3416 S Hoyt Ave (47302-2081)
PHONE....................765 284-5050
Dan Irvin, *President*
Derek Roesener, *CFO*

▲ **EMP:** 89
SALES (est): 21MM
SALES (corp-wide): 23.6B **Privately Held**
SIC: 3479 Coating of metals with plastic or resins
HQ: Henkel Us Operations Corporation
1 Henkel Way
Rocky Hill CT 06067
860 571-5100

(G-10487)
HIATT ENTERPRISES INC (PA)
Also Called: Hiatt Printing
1716 N Wheeling Ave Ste 1 (47303-1673)
PHONE....................765 289-7756
Chris Hiatt, *President*
David G Hiatt, *Vice Pres*
EMP: 20
SQ FT: 3,000
SALES (est): 2.7MM **Privately Held**
WEB: www.hiattprinting.com
SIC: 7334 2759 7389 2791 Photocopying & duplicating services; card printing & engraving, except greeting; invitations: printing; printing broker; typesetting; bookbinding & related work; commercial printing, lithographic

(G-10488)
HIATT ENTERPRISES INC
Also Called: Hiatt Printing
506 N Mckinley Ave (47303-3543)
PHONE....................765 289-2700
Chris Savage, *Manager*
EMP: 7
SALES (corp-wide): 2.7MM **Privately Held**
WEB: www.hiattprinting.com
SIC: 7334 2791 2789 2759 Photocopying & duplicating services; typesetting; bookbinding & related work; commercial printing; commercial printing, lithographic
PA: Hiatt Enterprises, Inc.
1716 N Wheeling Ave Ste 1
Muncie IN 47303
765 289-7756

(G-10489)
HITE WELDING & CHASSIS
1715 E 18th St (47302-4517)
PHONE....................765 741-0046
Charles Hite, *Owner*
EMP: 2
SALES (est): 70K **Privately Held**
WEB: www.hiteservices.com
SIC: 7692 Welding repair

(G-10490)
HONEYWELL INTERNATIONAL INC
201 E 18th St (47302-4124)
PHONE....................765 284-3300
Richard Clasby, *General Mgr*
EMP: 300
SALES (corp-wide): 40.5B **Publicly Held**
SIC: 3724 Aircraft engines & engine parts
PA: Honeywell International Inc.
115 Tabor Rd
Morris Plains NJ 07950
973 455-2000

(G-10491)
HOOSIER HORSE REVIEW LLC
7301 S County Road 400 W (47302-9770)
P.O. Box 493, Daleville (47334-0493)
PHONE....................765 212-1320
Tom Crouch,
EMP: 5
SALES (est): 357.3K **Privately Held**
SIC: 2759 Publication printing

(G-10492)
HORIZON ATOMTN FABRICATION LLC
3620 S Hoyt Ave (47302-4900)
PHONE....................765 896-9491
Kyle Combs,
Douglas Shreves,
EMP: 4
SALES (est): 577.6K **Privately Held**
SIC: 3569 General industrial machinery

(G-10493)
INDIANA BRIDGE-MIDWEST STL INC
1810 S Macedonia Ave (47302-3669)
PHONE....................765 288-1985
Fax: 765 288-1631
Chunilal H Gala, *President*
Christian Klink, *President*
Kishpaugh Jeff, *General Mgr*
Brad Debruler, *Engineer*
Ken Crismore, *Treasurer*
EMP: 56
SALES (est): 18.9MM **Privately Held**
SIC: 3441 Fabricated structural metal

(G-10494)
INDIANA NEWSPAPERS LLC
Muncie Star Press
345 S High St (47305-2326)
P.O. Box 2408 (47307-0408)
PHONE....................765 213-5700
Fax: 765 213-5703
Emith Smelser, *Manager*
Ron Daugherty, *Info Tech Dir*
EMP: 35
SALES (corp-wide): 3.1B **Publicly Held**
SIC: 2711 Newspapers, publishing & printing
HQ: Indiana Newspapers Llc
130 S Meridian St
Indianapolis IN 46225
317 444-4000

(G-10495)
IRVING MATERIALS INC
4304 E County Road 350 N (47303-9142)
PHONE....................765 836-4007
Fax: 765 836-4010
Fritz Ford, *Branch Mgr*
EMP: 6
SALES (corp-wide): 800.6MM **Privately Held**
SIC: 3273 Ready-mixed concrete
PA: Irving Materials, Inc.
8032 N State Road 9
Greenfield IN 46140
317 326-3101

(G-10496)
IRVING MATERIALS INC
4312 E County Road 350 N (47303-9142)
PHONE....................765 288-5566
Fax: 765 288-5574
Dennis Layman, *Manager*
Rock Shideler, *Executive*
EMP: 20
SALES (corp-wide): 800.6MM **Privately Held**
SIC: 3273 Ready-mixed concrete
PA: Irving Materials, Inc.
8032 N State Road 9
Greenfield IN 46140
317 326-3101

(G-10497)
IRVING MATERIALS INC
Also Called: I M I
4304 E County Road 350 N (47303-9142)
PHONE....................765 288-0288
Fax: 765 287-8465
Charlie Burke, *Exec Officer*
Lawrence Robinson, *Sales Staff*
Randy Tooley, *Manager*
EMP: 17
SALES (corp-wide): 800.6MM **Privately Held**
SIC: 3273 5032 Ready-mixed concrete; aggregate
PA: Irving Materials, Inc.
8032 N State Road 9
Greenfield IN 46140
317 326-3101

(G-10498)
J P WHITT INC
Also Called: Budget Blinds
827 S Tillotson Ave (47304-4500)
PHONE....................765 759-0521
Jeff Whittern, *President*
EMP: 2
SALES: 400K **Privately Held**
SIC: 2591 2431 Drapery hardware & blinds & shades; window blinds; blinds vertical; blinds (shutters), wood

(G-10499)
JD NORMAN INDUSTRIES INC
3301 W Mt Pleasant Blvd (47302-9103)
PHONE....................765 288-8098
Justin D Norman, *President*
EMP: 62
SALES (corp-wide): 183.7MM **Privately Held**
SIC: 3714 Transmission housings or parts, motor vehicle
PA: Jd Norman Industries, Inc.
787 W Belden Ave
Addison IL 60101
630 458-3700

(G-10500)
JEANNINE STASSEN
1217 W University Ave (47303-3657)
PHONE....................765 289-3756
Jeannine Stassen, *Principal*
EMP: 2 **EST:** 2010
SALES (est): 117.5K **Privately Held**
SIC: 2844 Perfumes & colognes

(G-10501)
JEREMY PARKER
Also Called: Squeeze Play
3501 N Grnvle Ave Ste 95 (47303)
PHONE....................765 284-5414
Jeremy Parker, *Owner*
EMP: 3
SALES (est): 213.4K **Privately Held**
SIC: 2759 Screen printing
PA: Jeremy Parker
194 W 600 N
Alexandria IN 46001

(G-10502)
KEIHIN AIRCON NORTH AMERICA
4400 N Superior Dr (47303-6436)
PHONE....................765 213-4915
Fax: 765 213-4930
Hiroshi Seikai, *Principal*
Robert Riddle, *Vice Pres*
Brian Kidd, *Mfg Spvr*
▲ **EMP:** 175
SALES (est): 30.6MM
SALES (corp-wide): 3.3B **Privately Held**
WEB: www.kac-inc.com
SIC: 3714 Air conditioner parts, motor vehicle
HQ: Keihin North America, Inc.
2701 Enterprise Dr # 100
Anderson IN 46013
765 298-6030

(G-10503)
KEN-BAR TOOL & ENGINEERING INC
Also Called: Comcast
3121 S Walnut St (47302-5693)
PHONE....................765 284-4408
Fax: 765 284-4441
Timothy D Hale, *President*
Kathy Church, *Admin Sec*
EMP: 34
SQ FT: 17,500
SALES (est): 7.1MM **Privately Held**
SIC: 3544 3545 Special dies & tools; jigs & fixtures; gauges (machine tool accessories)

(G-10504)
KEPPLER STEEL AND FABRICATING
1401 S Macedonia Ave (47302-3662)
PHONE....................765 289-1529
Fax: 765 284-2308
Jack Keppler Jr, *President*
Dan Keppler, *Vice Pres*
EMP: 10 **EST:** 1961
SQ FT: 20,000
SALES (est): 1.8MM **Privately Held**
SIC: 3441 Fabricated structural metal

(G-10505)
KIRBY RISK CORPORATION
Store 10
1619 S Walnut St (47302-3268)
PHONE....................765 254-5460
Fax: 765 286-7480
Gary A Latta, *Branch Mgr*
EMP: 16

SALES (corp-wide): 401.3MM **Privately Held**
WEB: www.kirbyrisk.com
SIC: **5063** 7694 Electrical supplies; rebuilding motors, except automotive
PA: Kirby Risk Corporation
1815 Sagamore Pkwy N
Lafayette IN 47904
765 448-4567

(G-10506)
LABEL TECH INC
2601 S Walnut St (47302-5063)
P.O. Box 2666 (47307-0666)
PHONE.................................765 747-1234
Fax: 765 747-1236
Kirk McShurley, *President*
Eric Heline, *Manager*
Jay McShurley, *Shareholder*
Josh Rodeffer, *Graphic Designe*
EMP: 20
SQ FT: 15,000
SALES (est): 3.5MM **Privately Held**
SIC: **2759** 5112 2761 2672 Labels & seals: printing; stationery & office supplies; manifold business forms; coated & laminated paper; packaging paper & plastics film, coated & laminated; labels, paper: made from purchased material

(G-10507)
LAKEMASTER INC
2407 S Walnut St (47302-4143)
P.O. Box 2462 (47307-0462)
PHONE.................................765 288-3718
Wayne C Willitzer, *President*
Carol Willitzer, *Vice Pres*
EMP: 20
SQ FT: 7,000
SALES (est): 4.4MM **Privately Held**
WEB: www.lakemasterinc.com
SIC: **3536** 3448 3441 3354 Hoists; prefabricated metal buildings; fabricated structural metal; aluminum extruded products; public building & related furniture; metal household furniture

(G-10508)
LAL ACQUISITION INC (PA)
Also Called: Lift-A-Loft
9501 S Center Rd (47302-9443)
P.O. Box 2645 (47307-0645)
PHONE.................................765 288-3691
Fax: 317 251-5885
Todd E Hunt, *President*
Brett Blood, *Vice Pres*
Dale Shrout, *Design Engr*
Jacquelyn Duggan, *CFO*
Jackie Duggan, *VP Finance*
▼ EMP: 50
SQ FT: 110,000
SALES (est): 9.2MM **Privately Held**
WEB: www.liftaloft.com
SIC: **3537** Trucks, tractors, loaders, carriers & similar equipment

(G-10509)
LARRY FLOWERS WHOLESALE
Also Called: Paper Products
2948 S Chippewa Ln (47302-5596)
PHONE.................................765 747-5156
Larry Flowers, *Owner*
EMP: 5
SALES (est): 33.4K **Privately Held**
SIC: **2679** 5992 Paper products, converted; flowers, fresh

(G-10510)
LEAR MANUFACTURING
Also Called: Lear Lawn & Garden
2204 N Wolfe St (47303-2437)
PHONE.................................765 282-6273
Fax: 765 282-6268
Richard Lear, *Owner*
EMP: 2
SQ FT: 1,300
SALES: 500K **Privately Held**
SIC: **3061** 5261 Mechanical rubber goods; lawn & garden equipment

(G-10511)
LEHI PROSTHETICS DENTAL LAB
1501 W Jackson St (47303-4943)
PHONE.................................765 288-4613
Fax: 765 288-3219

Lee W Hicks, *President*
EMP: 3
SQ FT: 3,400
SALES (est): 230K **Privately Held**
SIC: **3843** Dental equipment & supplies

(G-10512)
LIFT-A-LOFT MANUFACTURING INC
9501 S Center Rd (47302-9443)
P.O. Box 2645 (47307-0645)
PHONE.................................317 288-3691
Fax: 765 284-1023
Todd E Hunt, *President*
Jacquelyn S Duggan, *CFO*
EMP: 3
SQ FT: 110,000
SALES (est): 3.9MM
SALES (corp-wide): 9.2MM **Privately Held**
SIC: **3537** Lift trucks, industrial: fork, platform, straddle, etc.
PA: Lal Acquisition , Inc.
9501 S Center Rd
Muncie IN 47302
765 288-3691

(G-10513)
LOWERYS HOME MADE CANDIES
Also Called: Lowery's Candies
6255 W Kilgore Ave (47304-4731)
PHONE.................................765 288-7300
Fax: 765 747-9662
Donald H Brown, *CEO*
Michael Brown, *President*
Charles Good, *President*
Vicky Brown Good, *Corp Secy*
Sharon Brown Crecelius, *Vice Pres*
EMP: 30 EST: 1940
SALES (est): 1.7MM **Privately Held**
SIC: **5441** 2064 2066 Candy; candy & other confectionery products; chocolate & cocoa products

(G-10514)
MACHINE KEYS INC
309 N Timber Ridge Ct (47304-5772)
PHONE.................................765 228-4208
Daniel T Wickliffe, *Principal*
▲ EMP: 6
SALES (est): 611.8K **Privately Held**
SIC: **3452** Machine keys

(G-10515)
MAGNA POWERTRAIN AMERICA INC
Mpt Muncie
4701 S Cowan Rd (47302-9560)
P.O. Box 2950 (47307-0950)
PHONE.................................765 587-1300
Jamie Lopeman, *Purch Mgr*
Joe Barr, *Engineer*
David Boxell, *Engineer*
Sherry Gossett, *Human Res Mgr*
Dan Mills, *Branch Mgr*
EMP: 150
SALES (corp-wide): 38.9B **Privately Held**
SIC: **3714** Motor vehicle parts & accessories
HQ: Magna Powertrain Of America, Inc.
1870 Technology Dr
Troy MI 48083

(G-10516)
MAGNA POWERTRAIN AMERICA INC
Also Called: Mpt Muncie East
1400 W Fuson Rd (47302-8684)
P.O. Box 2778 (47307-0778)
PHONE.................................765 587-1300
Fax: 765 587-1404
Tom Haskett, *Senior Buyer*
Kevin Jessie, *Research*
Brian Atterson, *Engineer*
Tim Fry, *Branch Mgr*
EMP: 40
SALES (corp-wide): 38.9B **Privately Held**
SIC: **3714** Motor vehicle parts & accessories
HQ: Magna Powertrain Of America, Inc.
1870 Technology Dr
Troy MI 48083

(G-10517)
MAILROOM LLC
4801 N Wheeling Ave (47304-6512)
PHONE.................................765 254-0000
Shawn Phillips, *Principal*
EMP: 4
SALES (est): 397.9K **Privately Held**
SIC: **3444** Mail (post office) collection or storage boxes, sheet metal

(G-10518)
MATRIX TECHNOLOGIES INC
Also Called: Delaware Machinery
700 S Mulberry St (47302-2356)
PHONE.................................765 284-3335
Fax: 765 289-7185
Robert A Haas, *CEO*
EMP: 6
SQ FT: 8,000
SALES (est): 750K **Privately Held**
SIC: **3829** Measuring & controlling devices

(G-10519)
MCINTIRE CONCRETE
4701 W County Road 1000 N
(47303-9601)
PHONE.................................765 759-7111
Fax: 765 759-7120
Richard McIntire, *President*
Brad McIntire, *Vice Pres*
Becki Stuffel, *Office Mgr*
▲ EMP: 23 EST: 1997
SQ FT: 8,000
SALES (est): 4.6MM **Privately Held**
WEB: www.mcintireconcrete.com
SIC: **5211** 3273 Concrete & cinder block; ready-mixed concrete

(G-10520)
MID-CITY PLATING COMPANY INC
921 E Charles St (47305-2697)
P.O. Box 6 (47308-0006)
PHONE.................................765 289-2374
Fax: 765 289-2520
Anton Muzzarelli, *President*
Helen Muzzarelli, *Vice Pres*
Rodney Muzzarelli, *Treasurer*
Jerry Rollins, *Lab Dir*
Marsha Muzzarelli, *Admin Sec*
EMP: 50 EST: 1966
SQ FT: 70,000
SALES (est): 5.3MM **Privately Held**
WEB: www.mcplating.com
SIC: **3471** Electroplating of metals or formed products

(G-10521)
MID-WEST METAL PRODUCTS CO INC (PA)
Also Called: Mid-West Homes For Pets
3142 S Cowan Rd (47302-9106)
P.O. Box 1031 (47308-1031)
PHONE.................................888 741-1044
Fax: 765 741-3167
Steven M Smith, *CEO*
Kevin P Smith, *Vice Pres*
Bryan Brand, *Plant Mgr*
Don Rolland, *Purchasing*
Carl Rolssen, *CFO*
◆ EMP: 25
SQ FT: 120,000
SALES (est): 37.2MM **Privately Held**
WEB: www.midwestmetal.com
SIC: **3496** Miscellaneous fabricated wire products; grilles & grillework, woven wire; mesh, made from purchased wire; cages, wire

(G-10522)
MID-WEST METAL PRODUCTS CO INC
3500 S Hoyt Ave (47302-6419)
PHONE.................................765 741-3140
Fax: 765 741-3144
Ted Baker, *Branch Mgr*
EMP: 15
SALES (corp-wide): 37.2MM **Privately Held**
WEB: www.midwestmetal.com
SIC: **3315** 3599 Wire, steel: insulated or armored; machine shop, jobbing & repair

PA: Mid-West Metal Products Company, Inc.
3142 S Cowan Rd
Muncie IN 47302
888 741-1044

(G-10523)
MID-WEST METAL PRODUCTS CO INC
2100 W Mt Pleasant Blvd (47302-9101)
P.O. Box 1031 (47308-1031)
PHONE.................................765 741-3137
Fax: 765 741-3138
Ronald Smithson, *Prdtn Mgr*
Matt Aarbis, *Branch Mgr*
EMP: 70
SALES (corp-wide): 37.2MM **Privately Held**
WEB: www.midwestmetal.com
SIC: **3496** Cages, wire
PA: Mid-West Metal Products Company, Inc.
3142 S Cowan Rd
Muncie IN 47302
888 741-1044

(G-10524)
MIDDLETOWNE SOFTWARE LLC
2006 S Daly Ave (47302-2057)
PHONE.................................765 760-5007
Farouk E Chagla, *Principal*
EMP: 2
SALES (est): 100.5K **Privately Held**
SIC: **7372** Prepackaged software

(G-10525)
MOTORCRAFT INC
1219 S Walnut St (47302-3260)
P.O. Box 2006 (47307-0006)
PHONE.................................765 282-4272
Fax: 765 284-2990
John Maul, *President*
Kim Martin, *Principal*
Connie Maul, *Vice Pres*
EMP: 3
SQ FT: 2,000
SALES (est): 726.1K **Privately Held**
WEB: www.motorcraft.com
SIC: **5063** 5084 7694 Motors, electric; compressors, except air conditioning; electric motor repair

(G-10526)
MPT MUNCIE LLC
4701 S Cowan Rd (47302-9560)
PHONE.................................765 587-1300
Jake Hirsch, *President*
Thomas More, *Vice Pres*
▲ EMP: 35
SALES (est): 6.1MM
SALES (corp-wide): 38.9B **Privately Held**
SIC: **3714** Motor vehicle engines & parts
HQ: Magna Powertrain Usa, Inc.
1870 Technology Dr
Troy MI 48083
248 680-4900

(G-10527)
MUNCIE CABINET DISCOUNTERS
4205 N Wheeling Ave (47304-1202)
PHONE.................................765 216-7367
Greg Rawson, *President*
EMP: 2
SALES (est): 158.9K **Privately Held**
SIC: **2434** Wood kitchen cabinets

(G-10528)
MUNCIE CASTING CORP
1406 E 18th St (47302-4511)
P.O. Box 2328 (47307-0328)
PHONE.................................765 288-2611
Wayne Vest, *President*
Bob Buchert, *General Mgr*
Bob Buckert, *General Mgr*
Jim Cash, *Maint Spvr*
Janet Knott, *Purchasing*
EMP: 45
SQ FT: 53,000
SALES (est): 7.5MM **Privately Held**
SIC: **3543** 3365 3544 3322 Industrial patterns; aluminum & aluminum-based alloy castings; special dies, tools, jigs & fixtures; malleable iron foundries

▲ = Import ▼=Export
◆ =Import/Export

(G-10529)
MUNCIE METAL PRODUCTS
820 E Willard St (47302-3580)
PHONE.....................765 288-3421
James Wise, *Owner*
EMP: 3
SQ FT: 6,300
SALES: 200K **Privately Held**
SIC: 3599 Machine shop, jobbing & repair

(G-10530)
MUNCIE METAL SPINNING INC
1100 E 20th St (47302-5399)
PHONE.....................765 288-1937
Fax: 765 288-8901
Donald Ulrich, *President*
William Ulrich, *Treasurer*
Paul Ulrich, *Admin Sec*
EMP: 10
SQ FT: 55,000
SALES: 650K **Privately Held**
SIC: 3469 3446 Spinning metal for the trade; ornamental metal stampings; ornamental metalwork

(G-10531)
MUNCIE MOLD & ENGINEERING LLC
704 S Burlington Dr (47302-2826)
PHONE.....................765 282-0522
Fax: 765 282-4447
Kevin Malloy,
Mathew Malloy,
EMP: 7
SQ FT: 1,800
SALES (est): 835.3K **Privately Held**
SIC: 3544 Industrial molds

(G-10532)
MUNCIE NOVELTY COMPANY INC
Also Called: Indiana Ticket Company
9610 N State Road 67 (47303-9123)
P.O. Box 823 (47308-0823)
PHONE.....................765 288-8301
Fax: 765 288-3434
David Broyles, *President*
Joseph Broyles, *Corp Secy*
James Broyles, *Vice Pres*
Robert Broyles, *Vice Pres*
Connie Nauck, *Office Mgr*
EMP: 100 **EST:** 1936
SQ FT: 35,000
SALES (est): 23MM **Privately Held**
WEB: www.muncienovelty.com
SIC: 2791 2759 2752 Typesetting; schedule, ticket & tag printing & engraving; commercial printing, lithographic

(G-10533)
MUNCIE POWER PRODUCTS INC (HQ)
201 E Jackson St Ste 500 (47305-2838)
P.O. Box 548 (47308-0548)
PHONE.....................765 284-7721
Terry L Walker, *CEO*
Ray Chambers, *CEO*
Terry L Walker, *CEO*
Mitchell Miller, *Managing Dir*
Brian Maher, *Opers Mgr*
◆ **EMP:** 120 **EST:** 1935
SQ FT: 71,000
SALES (est): 82.9MM
SALES (corp-wide): 118MM **Privately Held**
WEB: www.munciepower.com
SIC: 3714 5013 Motor vehicle parts & accessories; motor vehicle supplies & new parts

(G-10534)
MUNCIE POWER PRODUCTS INC
1210 E Seymour St (47302-2568)
PHONE.....................765 896-9816
EMP: 2
SALES (corp-wide): 118MM **Privately Held**
SIC: 3714 Motor vehicle parts & accessories
HQ: Muncie Power Products, Inc.
201 E Jackson St Ste 500
Muncie IN 47305
765 284-7721

(G-10535)
MUNCIE PRECISION HARD CHROME
1001 E 18th St (47302-4324)
P.O. Box 2631 (47307-0631)
PHONE.....................765 288-2489
Fax: 765 288-2490
Darryal Hawkins, *President*
EMP: 5
SQ FT: 28,000
SALES (est): 360K **Privately Held**
SIC: 3471 7389 Chromium plating of metals or formed products; grinding, precision: commercial or industrial

(G-10536)
MUNCIE SAND & GRAVEL INC
Also Called: Schick Sand & Gravel
4210 E Mcgalliard Rd (47303-9172)
PHONE.....................765 282-6422
William Hood, *President*
Robert A Shick, *Manager*
EMP: 4
SALES (est): 410K **Privately Held**
SIC: 1442 Construction sand & gravel

(G-10537)
NASG INDIANA LLC
Also Called: North American Stamping Group
3401 W 8th St (47302-1912)
PHONE.....................765 381-4310
Brandon Jarrett, *Opers Mgr*
Chris Wagner, *Production*
Golden Hurd, *Mng Member*
Jason Trimble, *Manager*
EMP: 39
SALES (est): 10.1MM **Privately Held**
SIC: 3465 Automotive stampings

(G-10538)
NATIONAL HANDICAPPED WORKSHOP
5900 W Kilgore Ave (47304-4724)
PHONE.....................765 287-8331
Cheryl Guinn, *President*
Jake Guinn, *Vice Pres*
Dean Guinn, *Treasurer*
EMP: 80
SALES (est): 2.7MM **Privately Held**
SIC: 7389 2842 2841 5063 Telemarketing services; specialty cleaning, polishes & sanitation goods; soap & other detergents; light bulbs & related supplies

(G-10539)
NORMAL CITY MUSIC CO
2112 W Berwyn Rd (47304-3303)
PHONE.....................765 289-2041
Roger Macconnell, *Owner*
EMP: 2
SALES: 20K **Privately Held**
SIC: 3931 Musical instruments

(G-10540)
OSC HOLDINGS LLC
1150 W Kilgore Ave (47305-1588)
PHONE.....................765 751-7000
Wilbur R Davis, *President*
Ronald K Fauquher, *Senior VP*
David L Hahn, *Treasurer*
Donald J Engel, *Admin Sec*
EMP: 4
SALES (est): 548.1K **Privately Held**
SIC: 5045 7372 Computer peripheral equipment; computer software; prepackaged software

(G-10541)
OUTFITTER
1800 N Wheeling Ave (47303-1623)
PHONE.....................765 289-6456
Cary Malchow, *Owner*
EMP: 2
SQ FT: 2,000
SALES (est): 177.9K **Privately Held**
SIC: 2759 2395 Screen printing; embroidery & art needlework

(G-10542)
P-AMERICAS LLC
Also Called: Pepsico
2901 N Walnut St (47303-1964)
PHONE.....................765 289-0270
Fax: 765 286-3510
Dan Quinn, *Manager*

EMP: 34
SALES (corp-wide): 63.5B **Publicly Held**
SIC: 4225 5149 2086 General warehousing; soft drinks; carbonated beverages, nonalcoholic: bottled & canned
HQ: P-Americas Llc
1 Pepsi Way
Somers NY 10589
336 896-5740

(G-10543)
PARALOGICS LLC
301 S Batterfill Rd (47303)
PHONE.....................765 587-4618
EMP: 4
SALES (est): 338.9K **Privately Held**
SIC: 2911 2999 Mineral waxes, natural; waxes, petroleum: not produced in petroleum refineries

(G-10544)
PENGAD/WEST INC
Also Called: Pengad/Indy
1106 E Seymour St Ste A (47302-2592)
P.O. Box 1776 (47308-1776)
PHONE.....................765 286-3000
Fax: 765 287-1941
Greta Rutter, *Managing Dir*
James D Funkhouser, *Mfg Spvr*
EMP: 29
SALES (corp-wide): 6.9MM **Privately Held**
WEB: www.pengad.com
SIC: 2759 2796 2761 2752 Commercial printing; platemaking services; manifold business forms; commercial printing, lithographic
PA: Pengad/West, Inc.
55 Oak St
Bayonne NJ 07002
201 436-5625

(G-10545)
PETER AUSTIN CO
900 W 1st St (47305-2214)
P.O. Box 1147 (47308-1147)
PHONE.....................765 288-6397
Fax: 765 288-6397
Peter Austin, *Partner*
Adam Austin, *Partner*
EMP: 2 **EST:** 1902
SQ FT: 4,000
SALES: 100K **Privately Held**
SIC: 7694 7629 5085 Electric motor repair; tool repair, electric; tools

(G-10546)
PHILLIPS PATTERN & CASTING INC (PA)
801 W Riggin Rd (47303-6417)
PHONE.....................765 288-2319
Greg Phillips, *President*
Nadine E Phillips, *Vice Pres*
EMP: 15 **EST:** 1947
SQ FT: 26,000
SALES: 3MM **Privately Held**
WEB: www.phillipspatterns.com
SIC: 3365 3366 Aluminum & aluminum-based alloy castings; castings (except die): brass; castings (except die): bronze

(G-10547)
PRECISION MOLD & TOOL INC
2401 S Monroe St (47302-4200)
P.O. Box 42 (47308-0042)
PHONE.....................765 284-4415
Fax: 765 747-2714
Mark D Dunn, *President*
Bruce A Dunn, *Vice Pres*
Buford R Dunn, *Shareholder*
EMP: 11
SQ FT: 22,000
SALES (est): 1.4MM **Privately Held**
SIC: 3599 3544 Machine shop, jobbing & repair; industrial molds

(G-10548)
PREMIER LABEL COMPANY INC
1205 E Washington St (47305-2051)
PHONE.....................765 289-5000
Fax: 765 289-7481
Mark Ratliff, *President*
Susan Haynes, *Vice Pres*
Mark Dellinger, *Sales Mgr*
Lowell Pequignot, *Shareholder*
EMP: 10

SQ FT: 6,000
SALES: 1.5MM **Privately Held**
WEB: www.premierlabel.com
SIC: 2759 Flexographic printing; labels & seals: printing

(G-10549)
PROPELLERHEADS
4319 W Clara Ln (47304-5470)
PHONE.....................317 219-0408
EMP: 2
SALES (est): 82.5K **Privately Held**
SIC: 7372 Prepackaged software

(G-10550)
PROVISION PUBLISHING LLC
3141 E Shockley Rd (47302-8614)
PHONE.....................765 282-3928
Kimberly Conway, *Owner*
EMP: 2
SALES (est): 128.5K **Privately Held**
SIC: 2741 Miscellaneous publishing

(G-10551)
QUALITY PALLET
1000 E Seymour St (47302-2564)
PHONE.....................765 212-2215
EMP: 3
SALES (est): 129.4K **Privately Held**
SIC: 2448 Pallets, wood & wood with metal

(G-10552)
RABBONI BOOK PUBLISHING CO LLC
1100 N Saybrook Ln (47304-5057)
PHONE.....................765 254-9969
Josephine Blocher, *Principal*
EMP: 2
SALES (est): 59.2K **Privately Held**
SIC: 2741 Miscellaneous publishing

(G-10553)
RAMAR INDUSTRIES INC
6200 N Wheeling Ave (47304-9117)
PHONE.....................765 288-7319
Fax: 765 284-7445
Raymond E Weeks, *President*
Mark Wiley, *Corp Secy*
EMP: 2
SALES (est): 110K **Privately Held**
WEB: www.ramar.net
SIC: 3531 Backhoes

(G-10554)
REBER MACHINE & TOOL CO INC
1112 S Liberty St (47302-3141)
P.O. Box 2403 (47307-0403)
PHONE.....................765 288-0297
Fax: 765 288-3844
Neil Reber, *President*
Terry Reber, *Vice Pres*
Rick Dishman, *Plant Mgr*
Ernie Maxwell, *Purch Mgr*
Eric Dishman, *QC Mgr*
EMP: 40 **EST:** 1942
SQ FT: 60,000
SALES (est): 4MM **Privately Held**
WEB: www.rebermachine.com
SIC: 3544 3599 Jigs & fixtures; machine & other job shop work

(G-10555)
RED GOLD
3500 S Cowan Rd (47302-9555)
PHONE.....................765 254-1705
Jerry Kutche, *Owner*
Rachel Hunter, *Sales Staff*
EMP: 2
SALES (est): 96.5K **Privately Held**
SIC: 2099 Food preparations

(G-10556)
REEDS PLASTIC TOPS INC
2150 E Memorial Dr (47302-4670)
PHONE.....................765 282-1471
Fax: 765 288-7619
Ronald F Reed, *President*
Lisa Reed, *Admin Sec*
EMP: 7 **EST:** 1962
SQ FT: 45,000
SALES (est): 540K **Privately Held**
SIC: 2541 5031 3442 Counter & sink tops; molding, all materials; metal doors, sash & trim

(G-10557)
REGAL INC
Also Called: Regal Marketing
305 N Gray St (47303-4415)
PHONE.................................765 747-1155
Steve Nale, President
Richard Lee, Corp Secy
EMP: 2
SQ FT: 1,200
SALES (est): 110K Privately Held
SIC: 2389 5999 Men's miscellaneous accessories; trophies & plaques

(G-10558)
RELIANCE MACHINE COMPANY INC (PA)
4605 S Walnut St (47302-8532)
PHONE.................................765 284-0151
Richard Cardemon, CEO
Christopher Cardemon, President
Jammie Lynn Minniear, Vice Pres
EMP: 62
SQ FT: 80,000
SALES (est): 4.2MM Privately Held
WEB: www.cartec-naso.com
SIC: 3599 Machine shop, jobbing & repair

(G-10559)
ROCHESTER METAL PRODUCTS CORP
2100 N Granville Ave (47303-2153)
PHONE.................................765 288-6624
Robert E Kersey, Branch Mgr
EMP: 70
SALES (corp-wide): 87.7MM Privately
Held
SIC: 3524 Lawnmowers, residential: hand
or power
PA: Rochester Metal Products Corp.
616 Indiana Ave
Rochester IN 46975
574 223-3164

(G-10560)
SERA TECH BIOLOGICALS
1318 S Madison St (47302-3440)
PHONE.................................765 288-2699
Douglas Short, Manager
EMP: 2
SALES (est): 90.6K Privately Held
SIC: 2836 Biological products, except diagnostic

(G-10561)
SHELL ◉
2001 W Mcgalliard Rd (47304-2149)
PHONE.................................765 282-4635
Shane Neal, CEO
EMP: 2 EST: 2018
SALES (est): 81.9K Privately Held
SIC: 1311 Crude petroleum & natural gas

(G-10562)
SIGN PROS
3509 W County Road 400 N (47304-9040)
PHONE.................................765 289-2177
Fax: 765 289-5435
Rick Brinson, Principal
EMP: 2
SALES (est): 160.2K Privately Held
SIC: 3993 Signs & advertising specialties

(G-10563)
SINFLEX PAPER CO INC
301 S Butterfield Rd (47303-4317)
PHONE.................................765 789-6688
Fax: 765 789-6734
Matthew Burton, President
EMP: 30
SQ FT: 55,000
SALES: 8MM Privately Held
SIC: 2679 2653 Corrugated paper: made
from purchased material; sheets, corrugated: made from purchased materials

(G-10564)
SP HOLDINGS INC
Also Called: Smart Products
3401 N Commerce Dr (47303-1509)
PHONE.................................765 284-9545
Fax: 765 284-7270
Ken Hess, President
EMP: 10
SQ FT: 1,300

SALES (est): 2.2MM Privately Held
SIC: 3553 Bandsaws, woodworking

(G-10565)
SPARTECH LLC
1401 E Memorial Dr (47302-4402)
PHONE.................................765 281-5100
D Gorenc, Mfg Staff
Greg Bauer, Manager
EMP: 120
SALES (corp-wide): 1.4B Privately Held
SIC: 2821 Plastics materials & resins
PA: Spartech Llc
11650 Lkeside Crossing Ct
Saint Louis MO 63105
314 569-7400

(G-10566)
SPENCER PRINTING INC
4404 S Madison St (47302-5669)
P.O. Box 1701 (47308-1701)
PHONE.................................765 288-6111
Fax: 765 288-7277
Gary Watson, President
Richard Mikels, Treasurer
EMP: 8
SQ FT: 3,000
SALES (est): 1.2MM Privately Held
SIC: 2752 Commercial printing, offset

(G-10567)
STEVEN BLOCK
7805 N Tanglewood Ln (47304-9105)
PHONE.................................765 749-5394
Steven Block, Principal
EMP: 2
SALES (est): 211K Privately Held
SIC: 2431 Millwork

(G-10568)
TAURUS TECH & ENGRG LLC
Also Called: Taurus Tool & Engineering
5101 W County Road 400 S (47302-8984)
PHONE.................................765 282-2090
Fax: 765 282-1594
James McDonald, President
Dwayne Irelan, Prdtn Mgr
Jim Stout, Engineer
Jim McDonald, Mktg Dir
Debra Parrish-Keith, Office Mgr
EMP: 25
SQ FT: 22,760
SALES (est): 5.6MM Privately Held
WEB: www.taurustool.com
SIC: 3599 3544 3999 Machine shop, jobbing & repair; custom machinery; jigs &
fixtures; models, except toy

(G-10569)
TISHLER INDUSTRIES INC (PA)
Also Called: Ameristeel
1810 S Macedonia Ave (47302-3669)
PHONE.................................765 286-5454
Ravi Talwar, President
Mary Kay Guinn, President
Eleanor C Talwar, Admin Sec
EMP: 2
SQ FT: 8,000
SALES (est): 12.7MM Privately Held
WEB: www.tishlerindustries.com
SIC: 3443 Fabricated plate work (boiler
shop)

(G-10570)
TITLE TEN MANUFACTURING LLC
Also Called: Warrior Rack
401 W Willard St (47302-3152)
PHONE.................................765 388-2482
Robert Moore, CEO
EMP: 2
SALES (est): 145.6K Privately Held
SIC: 2542 Racks, merchandise display or
storage: except wood

(G-10571)
TODAYS SIGNS AND GRAPHICS
1804 N Wheeling Ave Ste 1 (47303-1699)
PHONE.................................765 288-4771
Fax: 765 288-4779
Jim Hathaway, Owner
Greg Hathaway, General Mgr
EMP: 4
SALES (est): 181.5K Privately Held
SIC: 3993 Signs & advertising specialties

(G-10572)
TOMKEN PLASTIC TECH INC
4601 N Superior Dr (47303-6430)
PHONE.................................765 284-2472
Fax: 765 284-1277
Randi Carmichael, President
Bruce Carmichael, Chairman
Kim Murdock, Vice Pres
Gary Buckles, Purchasing
Don Pike, QC Mgr
▼ EMP: 48 EST: 1960
SQ FT: 56,100
SALES (est): 11.3MM Privately Held
WEB: www.tomkentool.com
SIC: 3089 Injection molding of plastics

(G-10573)
TONNE WINERY
101 W Royerton Rd (47303-9382)
PHONE.................................765 896-9821
Kathy Simmons, Principal
EMP: 4
SALES (est): 317.6K Privately Held
SIC: 2084 Wines

(G-10574)
TOOL ROOM SERVICE
1403 S Liberty St (47302-3147)
PHONE.................................765 287-0062
Timothy Osborn, General Mgr
Angelic Lykins, Info Tech Mgr
EMP: 3 EST: 2016
SALES (est): 218.4K Privately Held
SIC: 3599 Machine shop, jobbing & repair

(G-10575)
TRI STATE OPTICAL INC
Also Called: Cunningham Optical One
1608 W Mcgalliard Rd (47304-2205)
PHONE.................................765 289-4475
Fax: 765 284-2806
Paula Schull, Manager
EMP: 24
SALES (corp-wide): 14.2MM Privately
Held
SIC: 5995 3851 Opticians; ophthalmic
goods
PA: Tri State Optical Inc
5233 Coldwater Rd
Fort Wayne IN 46825
260 482-1555

(G-10576)
UNITED HOME SUPPLY INC
Also Called: Kitchen & Baths By Untd HM
Sup
3600 N Everbrook Ln Ste C (47304-6371)
PHONE.................................765 288-2737
Fax: 765 288-5273
Gary L West, President
John West, Vice Pres
EMP: 6 EST: 1961
SQ FT: 18,000
SALES (est): 818.4K Privately Held
SIC: 2599 5211 Cabinets, factory; bathroom fixtures, equipment & supplies; cabinets, kitchen; counter tops

(G-10577)
VISION ASSOCIATES
1904 W Mcgalliard Rd (47304-2211)
PHONE.................................765 288-1575
Fax: 765 284-5486
Daniel Chalfant, Owner
EMP: 8
SALES (est): 470K Privately Held
SIC: 3851 Ophthalmic goods

(G-10578)
WALBURN SERVICE INC
Also Called: Walburn Kitchens
109 S Claypool Rd (47303-5130)
PHONE.................................765 289-3383
Fax: 765 289-3384
William T Walburn, President
Barbara Walburn, Corp Secy
William L Walburn, Vice Pres
▲ EMP: 3
SQ FT: 5,000
SALES (est): 327.6K Privately Held
SIC: 2434 Wood kitchen cabinets

(G-10579)
WALLYS LOCKSHOP
606 W 11th St (47302-3129)
PHONE.................................765 748-2282

Walter Beall, Owner
EMP: 2 EST: 2008
SALES (est): 132.9K Privately Held
SIC: 3429 Locks or lock sets

(G-10580)
WATERFIELD AUTOMOTIVE MCH SP
3600 S Meeker Ave (47302-9094)
PHONE.................................765 288-6262
Stan Waters, Partner
Laura Waters, Partner
EMP: 2
SQ FT: 3,500
SALES (est): 297.3K Privately Held
SIC: 3599 7539 Machine shop, jobbing &
repair; machine shop, automotive

(G-10581)
WEARLY MONUMENTS INC (PA)
4000 W Kilgore Ave (47304-4814)
PHONE.................................765 284-9796
Fax: 765 284-9820
Brian Whittaker, President
▲ EMP: 30 EST: 1899
SQ FT: 10,000
SALES (est): 5.3MM Privately Held
WEB: www.wearlymonuments.com
SIC: 5999 3281 Monuments, finished to
custom order; cut stone & stone products

(G-10582)
WELDORS INC
2702 S Monroe St (47302-5219)
PHONE.................................765 289-9074
Samuel Norris, President
Jana Norris, Treasurer
EMP: 3
SQ FT: 3,000
SALES (est): 75K Privately Held
SIC: 7692 Welding repair

(G-10583)
WHISLER CUSTOM LEATHER CO
1108 E Royerton Rd (47303-9440)
PHONE.................................765 212-8932
Connie Whisler, Principal
EMP: 2
SALES (est): 126.3K Privately Held
SIC: 3199 Leather goods

(G-10584)
WILHOITE MONUMENTS INC
4710 S Madison St (47302-5681)
PHONE.................................765 286-7423
Fax: 765 216-1643
James Wilhoite, President
Patricia Wilhoite, Corp Secy
▲ EMP: 5
SQ FT: 3,700
SALES: 400K Privately Held
SIC: 5999 3366 Monuments, finished to
custom order; bronze foundry

(G-10585)
WILSON HEARING AID CENTER
3716 N Wheeling Ave (47304-1766)
PHONE.................................765 747-4131
Chuck Wilson, Owner
EMP: 5
SQ FT: 2,600
SALES: 350K Privately Held
SIC: 3842 5999 Hearing aids; hearing aids

(G-10586)
WINE N VINE
1524 E Mcgalliard Rd (47303-2210)
PHONE.................................765 282-3300
Jeffrey Johnson, Owner
Bonnie Johnson, Co-Owner
EMP: 2
SALES (est): 151.1K Privately Held
SIC: 2084 5921 Wine cellars, bonded: engaged in blending wines; wine

(G-10587)
WITT INDUSTRIES INC
Muncie Division
2415 S Walnut St (47302-4143)
PHONE.................................765 289-3427
Fax: 765 286-0752
Joe Wendel, Manager
EMP: 35

2018 Harris Indiana
Industrial Directory

▲ = Import ▼=Export
◆ =Import/Export

SALES (corp-wide): 60.8MM **Privately Held**
WEB: www.witt.com
SIC: 3479 3547 Hot dip coating of metals or formed products; galvanizing lines (rolling mill equipment)
HQ: Witt Industries, Inc.
4600 N Masn Montgomery Rd
Mason OH 45040
513 871-5700

(G-10588)
WOOD TRUSS SYSTEMS INC
5600 W Shoreline Ter (47304-6097)
PHONE..................................765 751-9990
Jay Halteman, *President*
Robert Halteman, *Admin Sec*
Joe Halteman, *Admin Asst*
EMP: 4
SALES (est): 270K **Privately Held**
WEB: www.woodtrusssystems.com
SIC: 3541 Die sinking machines

(G-10589)
WT PRODUCTS INC
3005 W Woodbridge Dr (47304-1074)
PHONE..................................765 216-7998
Jeffrey Messersmith, *President*
EMP: 3
SALES (est): 241.1K **Privately Held**
SIC: 2399 Fabricated textile products

Munster
Lake County

(G-10590)
411 NEWSPAPER
1130 Camellia Dr (46321-3619)
PHONE..................................219 922-8846
Jackie Harris, *Principal*
EMP: 5
SALES (est): 203.9K **Privately Held**
SIC: 2711 Commercial printing & newspaper publishing combined; newspapers, publishing & printing

(G-10591)
A & M RUBBER STAMPS INC
424 Hickory Ln (46321-2322)
PHONE..................................219 836-0892
Gail Reno, *Principal*
EMP: 2
SALES (est): 122K **Privately Held**
SIC: 3953 Embossing seals & hand stamps

(G-10592)
A M MANUFACTURING CO INC
9200 Calumet Ave Ste Nw07 (46321-0047)
PHONE..................................219 472-7272
Mark Vandrunen, *President*
Claudia Kunis, *Admin Sec*
Holly Rentner, *Admin Sec*
▼ EMP: 32 EST: 1953
SQ FT: 25,000
SALES (est): 8.1MM **Privately Held**
WEB: www.ammfg.com
SIC: 3556 Bakery machinery

(G-10593)
ACCURATE PUBLISHING CO
8445 Manor Ave Apt 301 (46321-2288)
PHONE..................................219 836-1397
Dr Irma Langston, *Owner*
EMP: 2
SALES (est): 84K **Privately Held**
SIC: 2741 Miscellaneous publishing

(G-10594)
AM MANUFACTURING COMPANY IND
9200 Calumet Ave (46321-2885)
PHONE..................................800 342-6744
Claudia Kunis, *Owner*
EMP: 14
SALES (est): 1.9MM **Privately Held**
SIC: 3999 Barber & beauty shop equipment

(G-10595)
AMERICAN PRINTING
8208 Calumet Ave (46321-1704)
PHONE..................................219 836-5600

John Yerga, *Owner*
EMP: 2
SALES (est): 176.1K **Privately Held**
SIC: 2752 Commercial printing, offset

(G-10596)
ARCHITECTURAL ACCENTS INC
1547 Ridge Rd (46321-1930)
PHONE..................................219 922-9333
Fax: 219 922-9350
J Michael Harrigan, *President*
Nancy Harrigan, *Corp Secy*
EMP: 13
SQ FT: 10,000
SALES (est): 1.3MM **Privately Held**
SIC: 2434 2431 5031 Wood kitchen cabinets; mantels, wood; newel posts, wood; millwork

(G-10597)
AUTOMTION CTRL PANL SLTONS INC
514 Jenna Dr (46321-4233)
PHONE..................................219 961-8308
Ritesh Parikh, *President*
EMP: 10
SALES (est): 350K **Privately Held**
SIC: 3699 Electrical equipment & supplies

(G-10598)
AWAVE SOFTWARE LLC
1317 Macarthur Blvd (46321-3107)
PHONE..................................219 285-1852
David Michael Milan, *Administration*
EMP: 2
SALES (est): 136K **Privately Held**
SIC: 7372 Prepackaged software

(G-10599)
BYWAY BREWING COMPANY LLC
1939 Rosewood Ct (46321-5150)
PHONE..................................312 543-7639
Thomas Duszynski, *CFO*
David Toth, *Administration*
EMP: 2
SALES (est): 177.3K **Privately Held**
SIC: 2082 Malt beverages

(G-10600)
C & J K INDUSTRIES INC
230 Timrick Dr (46321-2139)
PHONE..................................219 746-5760
Loydd A Hayes, *President*
EMP: 2 EST: 2012
SALES (est): 124.1K **Privately Held**
SIC: 3999 Manufacturing industries

(G-10601)
COMMUNITY DIAGNOSTIC CENTER
Also Called: Community Healtcare System
10020 Don S Powers Dr (46321-4054)
PHONE..................................219 836-4599
Ronda McKay, *Vice Pres*
Rose Garcia, *Exec Dir*
Kimberly Harper, *Administration*
Linda Woodley, *Administration*
EMP: 4
SALES (est): 315.7K **Privately Held**
SIC: 3841 Diagnostic apparatus, medical

(G-10602)
CONTACT PRODUCTS INC
Also Called: Everett Charles Technologies
8736 Schreiber Dr (46321-2640)
PHONE..................................219 838-1911
David Vanloan, *President*
EMP: 33
SALES (est): 2.5MM **Privately Held**
SIC: 3825 Test equipment for electronic & electric measurement

(G-10603)
CROSSROADS SERVICES INC
9200 Calumet Ave Ste 6 (46321-0107)
PHONE..................................219 972-3631
Timothy M Riley, *President*
Tim Riley, *Principal*
EMP: 3
SALES (est): 967.6K **Privately Held**
SIC: 1389 Excavating slush pits & cellars

(G-10604)
GALAXY ARTS
Also Called: Galaxy Arts and Sciences
8748 Madison Ave (46321-2412)
PHONE..................................219 836-6033
Franklin D Darrington, *Owner*
EMP: 2
SALES (est): 75K **Privately Held**
WEB: www.galaxyarts.com
SIC: 7384 2542 Photofinish laboratories; fixtures: display, office or store: except wood

(G-10605)
HETTY INCORPORATED (PA)
Also Called: Miss Print
8244 Calumet Ave (46321-1704)
PHONE..................................219 836-2517
Rick Baltensberger, *Owner*
Nancy Lochivski, *Manager*
EMP: 6
SALES (est): 739.7K **Privately Held**
WEB: www.missprint.com
SIC: 2752 7336 2791 2789 Commercial printing, offset; graphic arts & related design; typesetting; bookbinding & related work

(G-10606)
HOOSIER PRINTING CO INC
8208 Calumet Ave (46321-1704)
PHONE..................................219 836-8877
Fax: 219 836-8912
John Yerga, *President*
EMP: 3
SQ FT: 3,600
SALES: 125K **Privately Held**
SIC: 2759 2791 Commercial printing; typesetting

(G-10607)
HOW PUBS USA
601 45th St (46321-2875)
PHONE..................................219 933-9251
Kristol Bill, *Principal*
EMP: 2
SALES (est): 62.9K **Privately Held**
SIC: 2711 Newspapers

(G-10608)
IDENTITY LOGIX LLC
Also Called: Identitylogix
10048 Wellington Ter (46321-4371)
PHONE..................................219 379-5560
Gus Kremmidas, *Principal*
Michael Hrobat, *Vice Pres*
EMP: 8
SALES (est): 477.5K **Privately Held**
SIC: 7372 Business oriented computer software

(G-10609)
IM IMPRESSED
9540 Fran Lin Pkwy (46321-3921)
PHONE..................................219 838-7959
Deleta Siuruek, *Owner*
Carl Siuruek, *Co-Owner*
EMP: 4
SALES: 150K **Privately Held**
SIC: 2759 Screen printing

(G-10610)
INTELLIGENT SOFTWARE INC
9609 Cypress Ave (46321-3417)
PHONE..................................219 923-6166
Fax: 219 923-2930
Paul Gordon, *President*
Curtis Blaine, *Vice Pres*
EMP: 5
SALES (est): 500.1K **Privately Held**
SIC: 7372 5734 Application computer software; business oriented computer software; educational computer software; home entertainment computer software; software, business & non-game

(G-10611)
JAMES J MAGINOT PRINTING
8720 Calumet Ave (46321-2527)
PHONE..................................219 836-5692
Fax: 219 836-1193
James Maginot, *Principal*
EMP: 2
SALES (est): 108.5K **Privately Held**
SIC: 2752 Commercial printing, lithographic

(G-10612)
LARGUS SPEEDY PRINT CORP
Also Called: Largus Printing
732 45th Ave (46321-2818)
PHONE..................................219 922-8414
Fax: 219 922-8474
Thomas Largus, *President*
Carol Largus, *Principal*
EMP: 20 EST: 1977
SALES (est): 3.3MM **Privately Held**
SIC: 2752 2791 2789 2759 Commercial printing, offset; typesetting; bookbinding & related work; commercial printing

(G-10613)
LEE ENTERPRISES INC TIMES
Also Called: Times, The
601 45th St (46321-2875)
PHONE..................................219 933-3200
Fax: 219 933-3325
William Howard, *President*
Daniel Riordan, *Editor*
Doug Ross, *Editor*
Judy Milne, *Controller*
Briseida Zacharias, *Regl Sales Mgr*
EMP: 22
SALES (est): 38.5K
SALES (corp-wide): 566.9MM **Publicly Held**
WEB: www.lee.net
SIC: 2711 Newspapers, publishing & printing; commercial printing & newspaper publishing combined
PA: Lee Enterprises, Incorporated
201 N Harrison St Ste 600
Davenport IA 52801
563 383-2100

(G-10614)
LEE PUBLICATIONS INC
601 45th St (46321-2875)
PHONE..................................219 933-9251
William V Monopoli, *Publisher*
Paul Mullamey, *Manager*
EMP: 100
SALES (corp-wide): 566.9MM **Publicly Held**
SIC: 2711 2791 2759 Newspapers, publishing & printing; typesetting; commercial printing
HQ: Lee Publications, Inc.
201 N Harrison St Ste 600
Davenport IA 52801
563 383-2100

(G-10615)
LITHOGRPHIC COMMUNICATIONS LLC
9701 Indiana Pkwy (46321-4003)
PHONE..................................219 924-9779
Fax: 219 924-3252
Richard Pietrzak, *CEO*
Christina Woo, *President*
Bill Hanyzewski, *Sales Mgr*
Ron Fjeldheim, *Manager*
Gerri Hanyzewski, *Admin Sec*
EMP: 50
SQ FT: 28,000
SALES (est): 9.4MM **Privately Held**
WEB: www.litho-com.com
SIC: 2752 Commercial printing, offset

(G-10616)
LITTLE GREEN APPLE
923 Ridge Rd Unit A (46321-1721)
PHONE..................................219 836-5025
Thomas K Carpenter, *Owner*
EMP: 2
SALES (est): 104K **Privately Held**
SIC: 3571 Personal computers (microcomputers)

(G-10617)
NWITIMESCOM
601 45th St (46321-2875)
PHONE..................................219 933-3200
Deb Anselm, *General Mgr*
Kerry Erickson, *Editor*
Chris Mallonee, *Opers Staff*
Veronica Magana, *Accounts Exec*
Lisa Tavoletti, *Accounts Exec*
EMP: 13
SALES (est): 703.8K **Privately Held**
SIC: 2711 Newspapers, publishing & printing

G
E
O
G
R
A
P
H
I
C

(G-10618)
OHARA SPORTS INC
9450 Calumet Ave (46321-2812)
PHONE..................................219 836-5554
William O'Hara, *Owner*
EMP: 8
SQ FT: 5,000
SALES (est): 764.8K Privately Held
SIC: 5941 5699 2261 Football equipment;
basketball equipment; baseball equip-
ment; soccer supplies; uniforms; screen
printing of cotton broadwoven fabrics

(G-10619)
**ON SITE MACHINING
CORPORATION**
1148 Park Dr (46321-2513)
PHONE..................................219 923-2292
Aleksander Desancic, *Principal*
EMP: 2
SALES (est): 111.9K Privately Held
SIC: 3599 Machine shop, jobbing & repair

(G-10620)
**ORTHOTIC PROSTHETIC
SPECIALIST**
625 Ridge Rd Ste D (46321-1695)
PHONE..................................219 836-8668
Joseph C Rooker, *Principal*
EMP: 2
SALES (est): 351.3K Privately Held
SIC: 3842 Limbs, artificial; prosthetic appli-
ances

(G-10621)
P-AMERICAS LLC
Also Called: Pepsico
9300 Calumet Ave (46321-2810)
PHONE..................................219 836-1800
Fax: 219 836-6314
Dave Williams, *Prdtn Mgr*
Matt Goldasic, *Maint Spvr*
Douglass Menacher, *Sales Staff*
Winston Wright, *Branch Mgr*
Antonio Pacheco, *Manager*
EMP: 200
SQ FT: 40,000
SALES (corp-wide): 63.5B Publicly Held
SIC: 2086 Carbonated soft drinks, bottled
& canned
HQ: P-Americas Llc
1 Pepsi Way
Somers NY 10589
336 896-5740

(G-10622)
PDA SOLUTIONS LLC
8840 Calumet Ave Ste 103 (46321-2546)
PHONE..................................219 629-4658
Shanu Kondamuri, *CEO*
Glenn Landmesser, *President*
EMP: 2
SALES (est): 99.9K Privately Held
SIC: 3845 Patient monitoring apparatus

(G-10623)
PEPSI BEVERAGES COMPANY
Also Called: Pepsico
9300 Calumet Ave (46321-2810)
PHONE..................................219 836-1800
Fax: 219 874-6146
Bob Gritzman, *Sales Dir*
Melody Harvey, *Marketing Staff*
Charles Thomas, *Branch Mgr*
Mark Jaske, *Manager*
Jose Rizo, *Supervisor*
EMP: 35
SALES (corp-wide): 63.5B Publicly Held
WEB: www.integratedesolutions.com
SIC: 2086 Carbonated soft drinks, bottled
& canned
HQ: Pepsi Beverages Company
110 S Byhalia Rd
Collierville TN 38017
901 853-5736

(G-10624)
**PINDER INSTRUMENTS
COMPANY INC**
Also Called: Pinder Industries
9751 Indiana Pkwy Ste A (46321-4061)
P.O. Box 4099, Hammond (46324-0099)
PHONE..................................219 924-7070
Fax: 219 924-6962
Walter Tokarz, *CEO*

William Tokarz, *President*
Van Brzycki, *Purch Dir*
EMP: 30 EST: 1953
SQ FT: 14,500
SALES (est): 4MM Privately Held
WEB: www.pinderindustries.com
SIC: 3672 3679 3822 3613 Printed circuit
boards; wiring boards; harness assem-
blies for electronic use: wire or cable;
temperature controls, automatic; panel &
distribution boards & other related appa-
ratus

(G-10625)
RADAR ASSOC CORP
1117 Melbrook Dr (46321-3007)
PHONE..................................219 838-8030
Barbara J Hannigan, *President*
Glenn Hannigan, *Treasurer*
EMP: 2
SALES (est): 192.3K Privately Held
SIC: 3812 Radar systems & equipment

(G-10626)
ROCKWELL AUTOMATION INC
225 45th St (46321-2848)
PHONE..................................219 924-3002
Michael Bohling, *Mfg Staff*
Beth Carpenter, *Buyer*
Michael Germick, *Technical Mgr*
Greg Kramer, *Engineer*
Theodore Maryonovich, *Engineer*
EMP: 50 Publicly Held
SIC: 3625 Control equipment, electric
PA: Rockwell Automation, Inc.
1201 S 2nd St
Milwaukee WI 53204

(G-10627)
**ROYAL BRUSH
MANUFACTURING INC**
Also Called: Royal & Langnickel Brush Mfg
515 45th St (46321-2813)
PHONE..................................219 660-4170
Fax: 219 660-4181
George Dovellos, *President*
Herrick Michael, *Vice Pres*
Gus Dovellos, *Treasurer*
Steve Taylor, *Sales Staff*
Mary Keane, *Mktg Dir*
◆ EMP: 50 EST: 1991
SQ FT: 38,000
SALES (est): 10.7MM Privately Held
WEB: www.royalbrush.com
SIC: 3991 Brushes, except paint & varnish

(G-10628)
RS2 TECHNOLOGIES LLC
400 Fisher St Ste G (46321-2358)
PHONE..................................877 682-3532
Douglas Robinson, *Mng Member*
Gary Staley,
Robert Sulek,
EMP: 19
SALES: 10MM Privately Held
WEB: www.rs2tech.com
SIC: 7372 3625 Prepackaged software;
electric controls & control accessories, in-
dustrial

(G-10629)
SPRIGATI LLC
8250 Baring Ave (46321-1409)
PHONE..................................219 484-9455
Ryan Lamb, *Principal*
EMP: 2
SALES (est): 91.3K Privately Held
SIC: 2033 Spaghetti & other pasta sauce:
packaged in cans, jars, etc.

(G-10630)
**STAR CASE MANUFACTURING
CO LLC**
648 Superior Ave (46321-4035)
PHONE..................................219 922-4440
Fax: 219 922-4442
Darren Eason, *President*
Christine Baumler, *Sales Staff*
▲ EMP: 50
SQ FT: 25,000
SALES (est): 7.4MM Privately Held
WEB: www.starcase.com
SIC: 2449 Wood containers

(G-10631)
TEAM SPIRIT
10429 Columbia Ave (46321-4017)
PHONE..................................219 924-6272
Kathleen Hulse, *Owner*
EMP: 3
SALES: 60K Privately Held
SIC: 2399 Military insignia, textile

(G-10632)
TEC-AIR LLC
9200 Calumet Ave Ste Nw1 (46321-0048)
PHONE..................................219 301-7084
Nagesh Palakurthi, *CEO*
Robert J McMurtry, *President*
Nancy Pearson, *CFO*
EMP: 100
SQ FT: 130,000
SALES: 16MM Privately Held
SIC: 3089 3469 Injection molded finished
plastic products; metal stampings
HQ: Angstrom Usa Llc
26980 Trolley Indus Dr
Taylor MI 48180
313 295-0100

(G-10633)
THREE FLOYDS BREWING LLC
9750 Indiana Pkwy (46321-4004)
PHONE..................................219 922-4425
Pat Niebling, *Human Res Mgr*
Nicholas Floyd, *Mng Member*
▲ EMP: 6
SQ FT: 30,000
SALES (est): 1.2MM Privately Held
SIC: 2082 Beer (alcoholic beverage)

(G-10634)
TWIN SPARROW PRESS
9833 Whitehall Gdn (46321-9130)
PHONE..................................917 331-5247
Philip Sidener, *Principal*
EMP: 2 EST: 2015
SALES (est): 62.9K Privately Held
SIC: 2711 Newspapers

(G-10635)
**TWISTED MTAL FBRICATION
SVCS I**
1331 Azalea Dr (46321-3707)
PHONE..................................219 923-8045
Thomas Montella, *Principal*
EMP: 2
SALES (est): 85.6K Privately Held
SIC: 3499 Fabricated metal products

(G-10636)
VANS IRON WORKS (PA)
1604 Mourning Dove Dr (46321-5144)
PHONE..................................219 934-1935
EMP: 5
SQ FT: 3,000
SALES (est): 1.2MM Privately Held
SIC: 3446 3496 Mfg Architectural Metal-
work Mfg Misc Fabricated Wire Products

(G-10637)
VEITSCH-RADEX AMERICA LLC
9245 Calumet Ave Ste 100 (46321-4178)
PHONE..................................219 237-2420
Michael Kuschinsky, *President*
EMP: 20
SALES (est): 1.1MM
SALES (corp-wide): 2.2B Privately Held
SIC: 3255 Foundry refractories, clay
HQ: Rhi Us Ltd.
3956 Virginia Ave
Cincinnati OH 45227

(G-10638)
VELKO HINGE INC
9325 Kennedy Ct (46321-2817)
PHONE..................................219 924-6363
Alina Jansen, *President*
Joe Mamone, *Purch Mgr*
Patti Gorgei, *Manager*
Glenn Van Til, *Info Tech Mgr*
EMP: 27
SQ FT: 34,500
SALES: 2.8MM Privately Held
WEB: www.velko.com
SIC: 3429 Manufactured hardware (gen-
eral)

Nabb
Clark County

(G-10639)
DEREELTECH LLC
9571 Barker Dr Bldg 3 (47147-7156)
PHONE..................................812 293-4786
James Nelson, *Manager*
EMP: 26
SQ FT: 254,000
SALES (corp-wide): 16MM Privately
Held
SIC: 3351 Copper rolling & drawing
PA: Dereeltech, L.L.C.
11111 N Scottsdale Rd # 230
Scottsdale AZ 85254
623 201-2793

(G-10640)
GINAS ESSENTIALS
7705 Carrol Rd (47147-9639)
PHONE..................................812 406-3276
Martin Baird, *Principal*
EMP: 2 EST: 2016
SALES (est): 96K Privately Held
SIC: 2841 Soap & other detergents

Napoleon
Ripley County

(G-10641)
NAPOLEON LUMBER CO
Us Hwy 421 S (47034)
PHONE..................................812 852-4545
Fax: 812 852-4949
Neal M Dean, *President*
EMP: 3
SQ FT: 1,500
SALES (est): 183K Privately Held
SIC: 2452 6519 Log cabins, prefabricated,
wood; prefabricated buildings, wood;
modular homes, prefabricated, wood;
farm land leasing

(G-10642)
SCHULER PRODUCTS CO
8968 N Us 421 (47034)
P.O. Box 166 (47034-0166)
PHONE..................................812 852-4419
Fax: 812 852-2299
John Peetz, *Owner*
EMP: 7 EST: 1962
SQ FT: 3,000
SALES: 850K Privately Held
SIC: 3429 Casket hardware

(G-10643)
**WAGNER TRUSS
MANUFACTURING**
9410 N Us 421 (47034)
P.O. Box 121 (47034-0121)
PHONE..................................812 852-2206
Joe Wagner, *President*
Janet Wagner, *Corp Secy*
EMP: 14 EST: 1993
SQ FT: 15,000
SALES: 1MM Privately Held
SIC: 2439 Trusses, wooden roof

Nappanee
Elkhart County

(G-10644)
**AG PROCESSING A
COOPERATIVE**
Also Called: Supersweet Farm Service
302 S Main St (46550-2528)
PHONE..................................574 773-4138
Fax: 574 773-5251
Bobby Gluck, *Manager*
EMP: 20
SALES (corp-wide): 3.4B Privately Held
WEB: www.agp.com
SIC: 2075 5191 Soybean oil, cake or
meal; animal feeds

▲ = Import ▼=Export
◆ =Import/Export

PA: Ag Processing Inc A Cooperative
12700 W Dodge Rd
Omaha NE 68154
402 496-7809

(G-10645)
ALPINE ENTERPRISES
12844 N 700 W (46550-9707)
P.O. Box 409 (46550-0409)
PHONE..................................574 773-5475
Kenneth Mullet, *General Mgr*
EMP: 5
SALES (est): 386.4K **Privately Held**
SIC: 2499 Decorative wood & woodwork

(G-10646)
ARCHER-DANIELS-MIDLAND COMPANY
Also Called: ADM
252 S Jackson St (46550-2113)
PHONE..................................574 773-4138
EMP: 25
SALES (corp-wide): 60.8B **Publicly Held**
SIC: 2041 Flour & other grain mill products
PA: Archer-Daniels-Midland Company
77 W Wacker Dr Ste 4600
Chicago IL 60601
312 634-8100

(G-10647)
ARCHER-DANIELS-MIDLAND COMPANY
Also Called: ADM
301 S Jackson St (46550-2721)
PHONE..................................574 773-4131
Michael Will, *Branch Mgr*
EMP: 20
SALES (corp-wide): 60.8B **Publicly Held**
WEB: www.admworld.com
SIC: 2041 5191 Flour & other grain mill products; feed
PA: Archer-Daniels-Midland Company
77 W Wacker Dr Ste 4600
Chicago IL 60601
312 634-8100

(G-10648)
ASCOT ENTERPRISES INC (PA)
Also Called: Imperial Fabrics
503 S Main St (46550-2531)
P.O. Box 165 (46550-0165)
PHONE..................................877 773-7751
Fax: 574 773-2529
Howard Yoder, *CEO*
Kenneth J Manning, *President*
Rob Greenlee, *General Mgr*
Dianne Fuller, *Purch Mgr*
Alan Sands, *CFO*
▲ **EMP:** 25
SQ FT: 12,000
SALES (est): 95.4MM **Privately Held**
WEB: www.ascotenterprises.com
SIC: 2391 2591 2392 Curtains, window: made from purchased materials; draperies, plastic & textile: from purchased materials; window shades; blinds vertical; venetian blinds; bedspreads & bed sets: made from purchased materials

(G-10649)
ASCOT ENTERPRISES INC
Also Called: Ascot Plant 10
1901 Cheyenne St (46550-9463)
PHONE..................................574 773-7751
Bev Conrad, *Manager*
EMP: 53
SALES (corp-wide): 95.4MM **Privately Held**
SIC: 2391 2591 Curtains, window: made from purchased materials; window shades
PA: Ascot Enterprises Inc
503 S Main St
Nappanee IN 46550
877 773-7751

(G-10650)
ASCOT ENTERPRISES INC
1901 Cheyenne St (46550-9463)
PHONE..................................574 773-3104
Bev Conrad, *Manager*
EMP: 53

SALES (corp-wide): 95.4MM **Privately Held**
SIC: 2391 2591 2392 Curtains & draperies; drapery hardware & blinds & shades; household furnishings
PA: Ascot Enterprises Inc
503 S Main St
Nappanee IN 46550
877 773-7751

(G-10651)
ATC TRAILERS HOLDINGS INC
306 S Nappanee St (46550-2540)
P.O. Box 396 (46550-0396)
PHONE..................................574 773-2440
Steven L Brenneman, *President*
Jeffrey Shenk, *Vice Pres*
Peter Gingerich, *CFO*
Jonathan Wenger, *Admin Sec*
EMP: 210
SQ FT: 80,000
SALES (est): 19.1MM **Privately Held**
SIC: 3715 Truck trailers

(G-10652)
BARKMAN CUSTOM WOODWORKING
30235 Us Highway 6 (46550-9469)
PHONE..................................574 773-9212
Sam Barkman, *President*
EMP: 11
SQ FT: 4,500
SALES (est): 1.7MM **Privately Held**
SIC: 2431 Moldings, wood: unfinished & prefinished

(G-10653)
BEER AND SLABAUGH INC
23965 Us Highway 6 (46550-3396)
PHONE..................................574 773-3413
Fax: 574 773-7635
Rodney Beer, *President*
Tracey Beer, *Corp Secy*
Barney Beer, *Vice Pres*
EMP: 35
SQ FT: 6,000
SALES (est): 5.5MM **Privately Held**
SIC: 1794 1623 1622 1442 Excavation & grading, building construction; sewer line construction; bridge construction; construction sand & gravel

(G-10654)
BORKHOLDER CORPORATION (PA)
Also Called: Borkholder Building Supply
786 Us Highway 6 (46550-9526)
P.O. Box 32 (46550-0032)
PHONE..................................574 773-4083
Fax: 574 773-2897
Freeman D Borkholder, *President*
Dwayne Borkholder, *Exec VP*
Brandon Myers, *Treasurer*
Paul Thiry, *Regl Sales Mgr*
Eric Gilbert, *Manager*
EMP: 50 **EST:** 1982
SQ FT: 25,000
SALES (est): 38.2MM **Privately Held**
WEB: www.borkholder.com
SIC: 5031 2511 Building materials, interior; building materials, exterior; wood bedroom furniture; kitchen & dining room furniture

(G-10655)
BORKHOLDER LAVON
Also Called: Lb Woodworking
492 Us Highway 6 (46550-9523)
PHONE..................................574 773-3714
Lavon Borkholder, *Owner*
EMP: 2
SALES (est): 730.7K **Privately Held**
SIC: 2431 Woodwork, interior & ornamental

(G-10656)
BOUNTHANHS EGG ROLLS
1415 Us Highway 6 (46550-9538)
PHONE..................................574 546-4276
Bounthanh Chiu, *Owner*
EMP: 4
SQ FT: 240
SALES (est): 260K **Privately Held**
SIC: 2038 Frozen specialties

(G-10657)
BRETHREN IN CHRIST MEDIA MINIS (PA)
Also Called: Evangel Press
69954 County Road 11 (46550-9420)
PHONE..................................574 773-3164
Fax: 574 773-5934
Darren Shaw, *Vice Pres*
▲ **EMP:** 9 **EST:** 1880
SQ FT: 22,500
SALES (est): 2.2MM **Privately Held**
WEB: www.evangelpress.com
SIC: 2731 Books: publishing & printing; pamphlets: publishing & printing

(G-10658)
CHALLENGER DOOR LLC (PA)
1205 E Lincoln St (46550-2240)
PHONE..................................574 773-0470
Irv Yoder, *VP Opers*
Lamar Chupp, *Safety Dir*
Myron Miller, *Prdtn Mgr*
Jimmy Faroh, *Production*
Brock Bales, *Purch Mgr*
EMP: 81
SALES (est): 28.9MM **Privately Held**
SIC: 3442 Shutters, door or window: metal

(G-10659)
CHALLENGER DOOR LLC
Also Called: Challenger Design
24785 Us Highway 6 (46550-9404)
PHONE..................................574 773-8200
Rich Moore, *Principal*
Joe Sheets, *Accounts Mgr*
Larry Shroyer, *Manager*
Jason Beer, *Associate*
EMP: 33
SALES (corp-wide): 28.9MM **Privately Held**
SIC: 2599 Cabinets, factory
PA: Challenger Door, Llc.
1205 E Lincoln St
Nappanee IN 46550
574 773-0470

(G-10660)
CHASE MANUFACTURING LLC
506 S Oakland Ave (46550-2327)
PHONE..................................574 546-4776
Zachary Nickell, *Mng Member*
EMP: 140
SALES (est): 19.4MM **Privately Held**
SIC: 2431 Millwork

(G-10661)
COMMERCIAL STRUCTURES CORP (PA)
655 N Tomahawk Trl (46550-9362)
PHONE..................................574 773-7931
Fax: 574 773-7933
David H Johnson, *President*
Melissa Henderson, *Controller*
Jack Lawrence, *Manager*
Eric Johnson, *Admin Sec*
EMP: 35
SQ FT: 40,000
SALES (est): 7.1MM **Privately Held**
WEB: www.comstruc.com
SIC: 2451 Mobile buildings: for commercial use

(G-10662)
CONSOLIDATED NUTRITION LC
301 S Jackson St (46550-2721)
PHONE..................................574 773-4131
Nina Adams, *Principal*
EMP: 2
SALES (est): 62.3K **Privately Held**
SIC: 2048 Prepared feeds

(G-10663)
COPPES-NAPPANEE COMPANY INC
Also Called: Coppes Nappanee Co
401 E Market St Ste Xx (46550-2154)
PHONE..................................574 773-0007
Fax: 574 773-2889
Dennis Mishler, *President*
Donald Dickey, *Vice Pres*
Richard Hamsher, *Vice Pres*
EMP: 15
SQ FT: 60,000

SALES: 1.2MM **Privately Held**
SIC: 2434 2541 2511 5211 Wood kitchen cabinets; vanities, bathroom: wood; cabinets, except refrigerated: show, display, etc.: wood; cabinets, lockers & shelving; wood household furniture; cabinets, kitchen

(G-10664)
COUNTRY CRAFTSMAN WDWKG LLC
8563 W 1100 N (46550-8628)
PHONE..................................574 773-4911
Gene L Miller, *Principal*
EMP: 2
SALES (est): 201.7K **Privately Held**
SIC: 2431 Millwork

(G-10665)
CRAFTECH BUILDING SYSTEMS INC
Also Called: HECKAMAN HOMES
2676 E Market St (46550-9397)
PHONE..................................574 773-4167
Fax: 574 773-2546
John Mahnken, *CEO*
Dale Klein, *Vice Pres*
Keith Manuel, *Vice Pres*
Scott Styers, *Vice Pres*
Stephen Burkins, *CFO*
EMP: 50
SQ FT: 180,000
SALES: 13.2MM **Privately Held**
WEB: www.heckamanhomes.com
SIC: 2452 Modular homes, prefabricated, wood

(G-10666)
DB POLISHING
6445 W 1350 N (46550-9709)
PHONE..................................574 518-2443
Katy Berger, *Office Mgr*
EMP: 3 **EST:** 2013
SALES (est): 190.9K **Privately Held**
SIC: 3471 Polishing, metals or formed products

(G-10667)
DH MACHINE INC
352 N Tomahawk Trl (46550-9049)
PHONE..................................574 773-9211
Delbert W Helmuth, *President*
Karl E Miller, *General Mgr*
Levi Helmuth, *Purch Mgr*
Karen Hofer, *CFO*
▲ **EMP:** 90
SQ FT: 69,000
SALES (est): 20.8MM **Privately Held**
SIC: 3441 Fabricated structural metal

(G-10668)
EZS CUSTOM WOODWORKING
Also Called: E Z'S Custom Woodworking
24314 County Road 46 (46550-9331)
PHONE..................................574 831-3078
Ezra Miller, *Owner*
EMP: 6
SALES (est): 338.7K **Privately Held**
SIC: 3714 Motor vehicle parts & accessories

(G-10669)
FAIRMONT HOMES LLC (DH)
Also Called: Friendship Homes Division
502 S Oakland Ave (46550-2332)
P.O. Box 27 (46550-0027)
PHONE..................................574 773-7941
Fax: 574 773-2185
Brian Cira, *President*
Nathan Yoder, *General Mgr*
Maison Neuve, *Vice Pres*
Steve Maisonneuve, *VP Opers*
Joshua Isbell, *Plant Supt*
EMP: 243
SQ FT: 900,000
SALES (est): 150.6MM
SALES (corp-wide): 773.8MM **Publicly Held**
WEB: www.fairmonthomes.com
SIC: 2451 Mobile homes, except recreational
HQ: Fairmont Homes, Llc
1001 N Central Ave Fl 8
Phoenix AZ 85004
574 773-7941

(G-10670)
FAIRMONT HOMES LLC
Century Homes
1961 E Market St (46550)
PHONE..................................574 773-2041
Jim Shea Jr, *Branch Mgr*
EMP: 5
SQ FT: 2,000
SALES (corp-wide): 773.8MM **Publicly Held**
WEB: www.fairmonthomes.com
SIC: 2451 5271 Mobile homes, except recreational; mobile homes
HQ: Fairmont Homes, Llc
502 S Oakland Ave
Nappanee IN 46550
574 773-7941

(G-10671)
G & W HERBS
10517 W 1100 N (46550-8770)
PHONE..................................574 646-2134
Gerald D Miller, *President*
Wanda Miller, *Vice Pres*
EMP: 2 EST: 1995
SALES: 30K **Privately Held**
SIC: 2833 5499 Vitamins, natural or synthetic: bulk, uncompounded; spices & herbs

(G-10672)
GEHL INDUSTRIES INC
9547 W 1050 N (46550-8623)
PHONE..................................574 773-7663
Rohman Lehman, *President*
Deborah Lehman, *Vice Pres*
EMP: 10
SALES (est): 1.3MM **Privately Held**
WEB: www.gehlindustries.com
SIC: 2521 Cabinets, office: wood

(G-10673)
GEM INDUSTRIES INC
1400 Northwood Dr (46550-1112)
PHONE..................................574 773-4513
Ernie Germann, *President*
EMP: 2 EST: 2000
SALES (est): 89.4K **Privately Held**
SIC: 3999 Manufacturing industries

(G-10674)
GRAVELTON MACHINE SHOP INC
23965 Us Highway 6 (46550-9106)
PHONE..................................574 773-3413
Harlan D Beer, *President*
EMP: 4
SALES (est): 513K **Privately Held**
SIC: 7699 7692 Industrial machinery & equipment repair; welding repair

(G-10675)
GRRREAT CREATIONS
Also Called: G C I
597 Shawnee St (46550-9052)
P.O. Box 231 (46550-0231)
PHONE..................................574 773-5331
Fax: 574 773-3543
Devon EBY, *Mng Member*
Hal Easley, *Manager*
Jim Reed,
EMP: 24
SQ FT: 6,000
SALES (est): 3.2MM **Privately Held**
WEB: www.grrreatcreations.com
SIC: 3429 Clamps, metal

(G-10676)
GULF STREAM COACH INC
Also Called: Gulf Stream Coach Plant 59
2404 E Market St (46550-9457)
PHONE..................................574 773-7761
EMP: 1064
SALES (corp-wide): 157.7MM **Privately Held**
SIC: 3716 Motor homes
PA: Gulf Stream Coach, Inc.
503 S Oakland Ave
Nappanee IN 46550
574 773-7761

(G-10677)
GULF STREAM COACH INC (PA)
Also Called: Yellowstone Rv
503 S Oakland Ave (46550-2328)
P.O. Box 1005 (46550-0905)
PHONE..................................574 773-7761
Fax: 574 773-5761
James F Shea Jr, *Ch of Bd*
Dan Shea, *President*
Brian Shea, *President*
Phil Savari, *Exec VP*
Tricia L Campbell, *Purch Agent*
▼ EMP: 125
SQ FT: 500,000
SALES (est): 157.7MM **Privately Held**
WEB: www.gulfstreamcoach.com
SIC: 3716 3792 3714 2451 Motor homes; recreational van conversion (self-propelled), factory basis; travel trailers & campers; house trailers, except as permanent dwellings; motor vehicle parts & accessories; mobile homes

(G-10678)
HEPTON WELDING LLC
9352 W Hepton Rd (46550-8702)
PHONE..................................800 570-4238
David Mast, *Mng Member*
Marietta Mast,
EMP: 6
SQ FT: 7,000
SALES (est): 889.4K **Privately Held**
SIC: 7692 Welding repair

(G-10679)
HERITAGE CONVERTION LLC
2112 Beech Rd (46550-9033)
PHONE..................................574 773-0750
EMP: 2 EST: 2009
SALES (est): 100K **Privately Held**
SIC: 3799 Mfg Transportation Equipment

(G-10680)
HILLTOP METAL FABRICATING LLC
71024 County Road 13 (46550-9126)
PHONE..................................574 773-4975
EMP: 7
SALES (est): 483.5K **Privately Held**
SIC: 3446 Gratings, tread: fabricated metal

(G-10681)
HILLTOP SPECIALTIES LLC
71024 County Road 13 (46550-9126)
PHONE..................................574 773-4975
Mel Lehman, *Manager*
EMP: 6 EST: 2003
SALES (est): 639.4K **Privately Held**
SIC: 3291 Steel wool

(G-10682)
HOCHSTETLER WELDING
7262 W 1350 N (46550-9782)
PHONE..................................574 773-0600
Brian E Hochstetler, *Principal*
EMP: 5
SALES (est): 283.8K **Privately Held**
SIC: 7692 Welding repair

(G-10683)
HOLIDAY HOUSE INC
1852 W Market St (46550-9065)
PHONE..................................574 773-9536
Dustin Lannan, *President*
EMP: 25
SALES (est): 607.8K **Privately Held**
SIC: 3999 Manufacturing industries

(G-10684)
HOOSIER POWDER COATING LLC
9583 W 1350 N (46550-8790)
PHONE..................................574 253-7737
James Faroh, *Principal*
EMP: 4
SALES (est): 460K **Privately Held**
SIC: 3479 Metal coating & allied service

(G-10685)
INTECH TRAILERS INC
1940 W Market St (46550-9045)
P.O. Box 486 (46550-0486)
PHONE..................................574 773-9536
Adam Maxwell, *President*
Tom Franko, *Treasurer*

▼ EMP: 56
SALES: 5.7MM **Privately Held**
SIC: 3715 Trailer bodies

(G-10686)
J&J MANUFACTURING
7663 W 800 N (46550-8727)
PHONE..................................574 646-2069
EMP: 2
SALES: 30K **Privately Held**
SIC: 3479 Painting Coating & Hot Dipping

(G-10687)
JATEX INC
551 Shawnee St (46550-9052)
P.O. Box 156, Bremen (46506-0156)
PHONE..................................574 773-5928
Fax: 574 773-3678
Phillip D Jacobs, *President*
Andrew Malstaff, *General Mgr*
Jodie Malstaff, *Controller*
EMP: 12
SQ FT: 4,160
SALES: 200K **Privately Held**
WEB: www.jatexinc.net
SIC: 3842 3599 Orthopedic appliances; machine shop, jobbing & repair

(G-10688)
JOHNS BUTCHER SHOP
158 N Main St (46550-1938)
PHONE..................................574 773-4632
Miller Russell, *Owner*
Nancy Miller, *Principal*
EMP: 5
SQ FT: 4,000
SALES (est): 548K **Privately Held**
SIC: 4222 2011 5421 Storage, frozen or refrigerated goods; meat packing plants; meat markets, including freezer provisioners

(G-10689)
KOUNTRY WOOD PRODUCTS LLC (PA)
352 Shawnee St (46550-9061)
PHONE..................................574 773-5673
Ola Yoder, *CEO*
Perry Miller, *President*
Virgil Yoder, *Vice Pres*
Dan Mains, *Safety Dir*
Howard Miller, *Prdtn Mgr*
EMP: 210
SQ FT: 270,000
SALES (est): 88.7MM **Privately Held**
SIC: 2434 5211 5031 Wood kitchen cabinets; cabinets, kitchen; kitchen cabinets

(G-10690)
L & L WOODWORKING LLC
13614 N 700 W (46550-9722)
PHONE..................................574 535-4613
Levi Schwartz, *Owner*
EMP: 3
SQ FT: 2,592
SALES (est): 159.7K **Privately Held**
SIC: 2431 Interior & ornamental woodwork & trim

(G-10691)
LEGACY WOOD CREATIONS LLC
24675 County Road 54 (46550-9433)
PHONE..................................574 773-4405
Andrew Miller, *Principal*
EMP: 4
SALES (est): 360.4K **Privately Held**
SIC: 2431 Millwork

(G-10692)
MARTINS BUGGY SHOP
24070 County Road 46 (46550-9331)
PHONE..................................574 831-3699
Leroy M Martin, *Owner*
EMP: 2
SALES (est): 321K **Privately Held**
SIC: 3799 Carriages, horse drawn

(G-10693)
MILLER HARDWOODS LLC
8760 W 1350 N (46550-8788)
PHONE..................................574 773-9371
Fax: 574 773-9371
Levi A Miller,
EMP: 2 EST: 1975

SALES (est): 277.7K **Privately Held**
SIC: 2421 Sawmills & planing mills, general

(G-10694)
MILLER MACHINE SHOP LLC
2028 Beech Rd (46550-9032)
PHONE..................................574 773-2900
Duane Miller, *Mng Member*
Joseph Helmugh,
EMP: 3
SALES (est): 325K **Privately Held**
SIC: 3599 Machine shop, jobbing & repair

(G-10695)
MILLER MFG CORP
901 E Lincoln St (46550-2145)
P.O. Box 72 (46550-0072)
PHONE..................................574 773-4136
Fax: 574 773-2070
Ronald Hestad, *President*
Daniel Poston, *Vice Pres*
Don Grayam, *Site Mgr*
Chris Weiler, *Manager*
EMP: 35 EST: 1952
SQ FT: 52,000
SALES (est): 6.7MM **Privately Held**
WEB: www.millermfgcorp.com
SIC: 3499 3714 3469 3444 Metal ladders; motor vehicle wheels & parts; metal stampings; sheet metalwork; fabricated plate work (boiler shop); fabricated structural metal

(G-10696)
MULLET CUSTOM INTERIORS LLC
106 3b Rd (46550-9558)
PHONE..................................574 773-9442
Ben J Mullet, *Mng Member*
Julie Hochstetler, *Mng Member*
EMP: 14
SALES (est): 977.7K **Privately Held**
WEB: www.mulletrivermodelworks.com
SIC: 2431 Moldings, wood: unfinished & prefinished

(G-10697)
NATURAL LIGHTING LLC
29618 County Road 146 (46550-9491)
PHONE..................................574 907-9457
EMP: 2
SALES (est): 138.7K **Privately Held**
SIC: 3648 Lighting equipment

(G-10698)
NC COATINGS LLC
30338 County Road 56 (46550-9105)
PHONE..................................574 213-4754
Loren Graber, *Principal*
EMP: 2
SALES (est): 69.9K **Privately Held**
SIC: 3479 Metal coating & allied service

(G-10699)
NEWMAR CORPORATION (PA)
355 Delaware St (46550-9453)
P.O. Box 30 (46550-0030)
PHONE..................................574 773-7791
Fax: 574 773-2381
Mahlon Miller, *President*
Matthew Miller, *President*
Richard Parks, *Principal*
Jay Kinney, *Business Mgr*
Kevin Bogan, *Vice Pres*
EMP: 920
SQ FT: 600,000
SALES (est): 293MM **Privately Held**
WEB: www.newmarcorp.com
SIC: 3716 3792 Motor homes; travel trailers & campers

(G-10700)
OMNIMAX INTERNATIONAL INC
Amerimax Building Products
2341 E Market St (46550-9306)
PHONE..................................574 848-7432
Mitchell B Lewis, *CEO*
EMP: 40
SALES (corp-wide): 821.3MM **Privately Held**
WEB: www.amerimaxbp.com
SIC: 3272 Building materials, except block or brick: concrete

▲ = Import ▼=Export
◆ =Import/Export

HQ: Omnimax International, Inc.
30 Technology Pkwy S # 400
Peachtree Corners GA 30092

(G-10701)
OMNIMAX INTERNATIONAL INC
Amerimax Building Products
2341 E Market St (46550-9306)
PHONE...................................574 773-7981
Mitchell B Lewis, *CEO*
EMP: 132
SALES (corp-wide): 821.3MM **Privately Held**
WEB: www.amerimaxbp.com
SIC: 3441 Fabricated structural metal
HQ: Omnimax International, Inc.
30 Technology Pkwy S # 400
Peachtree Corners GA 30092

(G-10702)
PAULS WELDING
7930 W 1000 N (46550-8795)
PHONE...................................574 646-2015
Paul H Miller, *President*
Paul Hershberger, *Project Mgr*
Paul Helmuth, *Opers Mgr*
Chris Heet, *Sales Staff*
Paul Miller, *Sales Executive*
EMP: 24 EST: 1979
SALES (est): 5.4MM **Privately Held**
WEB: www.paulswelding.net
SIC: 7699 3441 Farm machinery repair;
industrial machinery & equipment repair;
fabricated structural metal

(G-10703)
R & R CUSTOM WOODWORKING INC
30480 County Road 52 (46550-9472)
PHONE...................................574 773-5436
Fax: 574 773-5478
Raymond J Yoder, *President*
EMP: 20
SALES (est): 1.7MM **Privately Held**
SIC: 2434 2426 2499 Wood kitchen cabinets; furniture stock & parts, hardwood; decorative wood & woodwork

(G-10704)
RAPSURE INC
305 S Main St (46550-2527)
PHONE...................................574 773-2995
Fax: 574 773-2996
Mike Yoder, *President*
Tina Yoder, *Vice Pres*
EMP: 3
SQ FT: 3,600
SALES: 300K **Privately Held**
WEB: www.rapsureinc.com
SIC: 3799 Trailers & trailer equipment

(G-10705)
S & H CABINETS ✪
70932 County Road 3 (46550-8976)
PHONE...................................574 773-7465
Warren S Hochstetler, *Owner*
EMP: 4 EST: 2017
SALES (est): 346.8K **Privately Held**
SIC: 2434 Wood kitchen cabinets

(G-10706)
SLABAUGHS MEAT PROCESSING
72700 County Road 101 (46550-9444)
PHONE...................................574 773-0381
Mark Slabaugh, *Principal*
EMP: 3 EST: 2010
SALES (est): 183.1K **Privately Held**
SIC: 2011 Meat packing plants

(G-10707)
SULLIVAN GROUP INC
302 Dal Mar Way (46550-9202)
P.O. Box 167 (46550-0167)
PHONE...................................574 773-2108
Fax: 574 773-2001
Kerry Sullivan, *President*
Paula Sullivan, *Treasurer*
Mike Miller, *Creative Dir*
EMP: 15
SQ FT: 15,000
SALES (est): 2.4MM **Privately Held**
WEB: www.sullivansportswear.com
SIC: 2261 Screen printing of cotton broad-woven fabrics

(G-10708)
TEACH ENTERPRISES INC
Also Called: Quality Foam Designs
72377 Airline Dr (46550-9455)
P.O. Box 2207, Elkhart (46515-2207)
PHONE...................................574 773-3108
EMP: 25
SQ FT: 25,000
SALES (corp-wide): 21.8MM **Privately Held**
SIC: 3086 Plastic Foam Fabricator And Packaging Materials
PA: Teach Enterprises, Inc.
2600 S Nappanee St
Elkhart IN 46517
574 293-5547

(G-10709)
UFP NAPPANEE LLC
Also Called: Quality Hardwood Sales
493 Shawnee St (46550-9064)
PHONE...................................574 773-2505
EMP: 84
SALES (est): 8.5MM
SALES (corp-wide): 3.9B **Publicly Held**
SIC: 2499 2431 2452 Decorative wood & woodwork; furniture inlays (veneers); moldings & baseboards, ornamental & trim; panels & sections, prefabricated, wood
PA: Universal Forest Products, Inc.
2801 E Beltline Ave Ne
Grand Rapids MI 49525
616 364-6161

(G-10710)
WILLIAMSBURG FURNITURE INC (PA)
2096 Cheyenne St (46550-9464)
PHONE...................................800 582-8183
L G Feiler III, *President*
Julie Yoder, *Vice Pres*
Joseph Loving, *Treasurer*
Christopher G Walter, *Admin Sec*
▲ EMP: 102
SQ FT: 45,000
SALES (est): 16.2MM **Privately Held**
WEB: www.williamsburgfurniture.com
SIC: 2512 2515 Upholstered household furniture; mattresses & foundations

(G-10711)
YODER KITCHEN CORP (PA)
501 S Main St (46550-2531)
PHONE...................................574 773-3197
Fax: 574 773-2885
Shawn Yoder, *Owner*
Stephanie Yoder, *Corp Secy*
Dave Sleeth, *VP Mfg*
Terri Borkholder, *Purch Agent*
Mary Beth Spicher, *Purch Agent*
EMP: 25
SQ FT: 13,000
SALES (est): 4MM **Privately Held**
WEB: www.yoderkitchens.com
SIC: 2434 Wood kitchen cabinets; vanities, bathroom: wood

Nashville
Brown County

(G-10712)
AIM MEDIA INDIANA OPER LLC
Brown County Democrat
147 E Main St (47448-7008)
PHONE...................................812 988-2221
Sara Clifford, *Branch Mgr*
EMP: 5
SALES (corp-wide): 42.4MM **Privately Held**
SIC: 2711 Commercial printing & newspaper publishing combined
PA: Aim Media Indiana Operating, Llc
2980 N National Rd A
Columbus IN 47201
812 372-7811

(G-10713)
ANGLERS MANUFACTURING
217 Salt Creek Rd (47448-8694)
PHONE...................................812 988-8040
Mark Settles, *Principal*
EMP: 2 EST: 2007

SALES (est): 112.7K **Privately Held**
SIC: 3999 Manufacturing industries

(G-10714)
AVIONICS MOUNTS INC
4510 State Road 46 E (47448-8673)
PHONE...................................812 988-2949
Archie Johnson, *President*
EMP: 5
SALES (est): 97.4K **Privately Held**
SIC: 3444 Sheet metalwork

(G-10715)
BEAR WALLOW DISTILLERY
4484 Old State Road 46 (47448-8128)
PHONE...................................812 657-4923
EMP: 3 EST: 2015
SALES (est): 207.4K **Privately Held**
SIC: 2085 Distilled & blended liquors

(G-10716)
BROCKWOOD FARM
7867 Axsom Branch Rd (47448-9592)
PHONE...................................812 837-9607
Harry Hopkins, *Owner*
EMP: 2
SALES: 60K **Privately Held**
WEB: www.brockwoodfarm.com
SIC: 3589 6531 Sewer cleaning equipment, power; real estate agents & managers

(G-10717)
BROWN COUNTY DEMOCRAT INC
147 E Main St (47448-7008)
P.O. Box 277 (47448-0277)
PHONE...................................812 988-2221
Fax: 812 988-6502
EMP: 6
SQ FT: 1,800
SALES (est): 395.7K
SALES (corp-wide): 60.8MM **Privately Held**
SIC: 2711 Newspapers-Publishing/Printing
PA: Home News Enterprises, L.L.C.
333 2nd St
Columbus IN 47201
800 876-7811

(G-10718)
BROWN COUNTY WINE COMPANY (PA)
4520 State Road 46 E (47448-8673)
PHONE...................................812 988-6144
David Schrodt, *President*
Cynthia Schrodt, *Corp Secy*
EMP: 2
SALES: 525K **Privately Held**
SIC: 2084 5921 Wines; wine

(G-10719)
CANDY DISH INC
61 W Main St (47448-7082)
P.O. Box 392 (47448-0392)
PHONE...................................317 269-6262
Fax: 812 988-7606
Franklin C Miller, *President*
Judith J Miller, *Corp Secy*
EMP: 9
SALES (est): 1MM **Privately Held**
WEB: www.thecandydish.com
SIC: 2064 2033 5441 Candy & other confectionery products; jams, including imitation: packaged in cans, jars, etc.; jellies, edible, including imitation: in cans, jars, etc.; fruit butters: packaged in cans, jars, etc.; candy, nut & confectionery stores

(G-10720)
CEDAR CREEK WINERY
36 E Franklin St (47448-7004)
PHONE...................................812 988-1111
EMP: 2
SALES (est): 147K **Privately Held**
SIC: 5921 2084 Wine; wines

(G-10721)
CRYSTAL SOURCE (PA)
Also Called: Wishful Thinking
150 S Old School Way (47448-7033)
P.O. Box 573 (47448-0573)
PHONE...................................812 988-7009
Fax: 812 988-4423
Larry Jenkins, *President*

Sharon Jenkins, *Vice Pres*
EMP: 3
SQ FT: 1,240
SALES (est): 394.4K **Privately Held**
SIC: 5944 3911 5947 5999 Jewelry stores; jewelry, precious metal; gifts & novelties; rubber stamps

(G-10722)
DIE PROTECTION TECH LLC
6040 Crooked Creek Rd (47448-9464)
PHONE...................................812 837-9507
Greg Dickerson, *Principal*
EMP: 2
SALES (est): 137.1K **Privately Held**
SIC: 3544 Special dies & tools

(G-10723)
ELECTRIC METAL FAB INC
4889 Helmsburg Rd (47448-8896)
PHONE...................................812 988-9353
Fax: 812 988-7080
Amanda Chittum, *President*
Robert Chittum, *Vice Pres*
David Rost, *Vice Pres*
EMP: 16
SQ FT: 8,016
SALES (est): 4.9MM **Privately Held**
WEB: www.electricmetalfab.com
SIC: 3441 Fabricated structural metal

(G-10724)
EXTREME METAL FAB INC
4889 Helmsburg Rd (47448-8896)
PHONE...................................812 988-9353
David Sisson, *Principal*
EMP: 12
SALES (est): 879.5K **Privately Held**
SIC: 3499 Furniture parts, metal

(G-10725)
HEARTHSTONE OF INDIANA
3204 Helmsburg Rd (47448-7822)
PHONE...................................812 988-2127
Jeff McCabe, *Owner*
EMP: 3
SALES: 430K **Privately Held**
SIC: 2452 Log cabins, prefabricated, wood

(G-10726)
HELMSBURG SAWMILL INC
Also Called: Pool Enterprises
2230 State Road 45 (47448-8401)
P.O. Box 3, Helmsburg (47435-0003)
PHONE...................................812 988-6161
Bill Pool, *President*
Susan Pool, *Corp Secy*
Kevin S Pool, *Vice Pres*
EMP: 15
SALES: 300K **Privately Held**
SIC: 2421 2426 Lumber: rough, sawed or planed; hardwood dimension & flooring mills

(G-10727)
KNIGHTS WOODWORKING LLC
3991 State Road 46 W (47448-8632)
PHONE...................................812 988-2106
Fax: 812 988-2021
Don Knight,
Jason Knight,
EMP: 5
SALES (est): 674.7K **Privately Held**
SIC: 2449 Rectangular boxes & crates, wood

(G-10728)
LE AIR CO INC
1313 Timber Crest Rd (47448-8523)
PHONE...................................812 988-1313
Gary Napier, *President*
Trumbauer Jari N, *Vice Pres*
Bruce Trumbaure, *Vice Pres*
Vicki Napier, *Admin Sec*
EMP: 4
SALES (est): 100K **Privately Held**
SIC: 3446 Brasswork, ornamental: structural

(G-10729)
MERCANTILE STORE (PA)
Also Called: Mercantile 1
44 N Van Buren St (47448-7029)
P.O. Box 335 (47448-0335)
PHONE...................................812 988-6939
Clenna Perkins, *Owner*

EMP: 2
SQ FT: 1,000
SALES (est): 445.9K **Privately Held**
SIC: 5947 5699 2396 Gift shop; souvenirs; sports apparel; stamping fabric articles

(G-10730)
MOONSHINE LEATHER COMPANY INC
38 S Van Buren St (47448-7036)
P.O. Box 1652 (47448-1652)
PHONE.................................812 988-1326
Fax: 812 988-1326
Mike Kline, *President*
Russ Smith, *Manager*
EMP: 12
SALES: 500K **Privately Held**
WEB: www.moonshineleather.com
SIC: 3172 Personal leather goods

(G-10731)
MOUNTAIN MADE MUSIC INC
3315 Hoover Rd (47448-8553)
PHONE.................................812 988-8869
EMP: 2 EST: 1985
SQ FT: 1,300
SALES (est): 120K **Privately Held**
SIC: 5735 3931 Ret Music Store Mfg Musical Instruments

(G-10732)
PGS LLC (PA)
Also Called: Trilogy Gallery
120 E Main St (47448-7008)
PHONE.................................812 988-4030
Fax: 812 988-5573
Grant Stuart, *Owner*
EMP: 35
SQ FT: 2,800
SALES (est): 2.3MM **Privately Held**
WEB: www.bccrc.net
SIC: 5947 5999 2392 Gift shop; Christmas lights & decorations; banners; household furnishings

(G-10733)
PIT BULL LEATHER COMPANY INC
Also Called: Distinctive Creations
20 N Van Buren St (47448-7029)
P.O. Box 398 (47448-0398)
PHONE.................................812 988-6007
Gloria Dobbs, *President*
EMP: 2
SQ FT: 3,000
SALES (est): 225K **Privately Held**
WEB: www.pitbull-breed.com
SIC: 3172 Personal leather goods

(G-10734)
SCHUSTER GLASS STUDIO
3847 Mount Liberty Rd (47448-8817)
PHONE.................................812 988-7377
Ronald L Schuster, *Owner*
EMP: 5
SALES: 260K **Privately Held**
SIC: 3231 5947 Leaded glass; artcraft & carvings

(G-10735)
TWISTED WICK CANDLE CO
102 S Van Buren St (47448-7037)
P.O. Box 1249 (47448-1249)
PHONE.................................812 988-6123
Rich Scheve, *Principal*
EMP: 2
SALES (est): 101.8K **Privately Held**
SIC: 3999 Candles

(G-10736)
TYCO WELDING
6473 State Road 46 E (47448-8939)
PHONE.................................812 988-8770
Timothy Kelp, *Partner*
Roger Kelp, *Partner*
EMP: 2
SALES: 24K **Privately Held**
SIC: 7692 Welding repair

(G-10737)
VILLAGE CANDLEMAKER INC
157 S Van Buren St (47448-7037)
P.O. Box 1397 (47448-1397)
PHONE.................................812 988-7201

Barbara Parks, *President*
EMP: 6 EST: 1965
SQ FT: 1,500
SALES: 500K **Privately Held**
SIC: 5999 3999 Candle shops; candles

(G-10738)
WILKERSON LOGGING INC
4263 Hoover Rd (47448-8549)
PHONE.................................812 988-4960
Norman Wilkerson, *President*
Kenneth Wilkerson, *Vice Pres*
Robert Wilkerson, *Vice Pres*
Dale Wilkerson, *Shareholder*
EMP: 4
SALES (est): 280.6K **Privately Held**
SIC: 2411 Logging

(G-10739)
WILKERSON SAWMILL
5400 Hoover Rd (47448-8544)
PHONE.................................812 988-7436
Dale Wilkerson, *Partner*
Kenneth Wilkerson, *Partner*
Norman Wilkerson, *Partner*
Robert Wilkerson, *Partner*
Terren Wilkerson, *Partner*
EMP: 7
SALES (est): 826.5K **Privately Held**
SIC: 2421 Sawmills & planing mills, general

New Albany
Floyd County

(G-10740)
ACCUPRINT OF KENTUCKIANA INC
4101 Reas Ln (47150-2230)
PHONE.................................812 944-8603
Fax: 812 944-8605
Brian Branham, *President*
Leslie Reesor, *VP Sales*
EMP: 8
SALES (est): 1.2MM **Privately Held**
SIC: 2759 Commercial printing

(G-10741)
ADVANCE FABRICATORS INC
980 Progress Blvd (47150-2297)
PHONE.................................812 944-6941
Fax: 812 949-7053
Gary Ragsdale, *President*
Kimberly Ragsdale, *Corp Secy*
Frank Jones, *Project Mgr*
EMP: 28
SQ FT: 15,000
SALES (est): 7.8MM **Privately Held**
SIC: 3441 3535 Fabricated structural metal; conveyors & conveying equipment

(G-10742)
ALLTERRAIN PAVING & CNSTR LLC
2235 Corydon Pike (47150-6119)
PHONE.................................502 265-4731
John F Neace, *Mng Member*
Stephen L Triplett,
EMP: 20
SQ FT: 6,000
SALES: 4MM **Privately Held**
SIC: 2951 Asphalt paving mixtures & blocks

(G-10743)
AMERICAN BEVERAGE MARKETERS
810 Progress Blvd (47150-2257)
PHONE.................................812 944-3585
EMP: 2 EST: 2014
SALES (est): 266.9K **Privately Held**
SIC: 5149 2086 Groceries & related products; bottled & canned soft drinks

(G-10744)
AMERICAN MACHINE FABRICATION
1223 E 8th St (47150-3345)
PHONE.................................812 944-4136
Norbert Andres, *President*
EMP: 8
SQ FT: 4,000

SALES (est): 625.8K **Privately Held**
SIC: 7699 3441 7692 3444 Industrial machinery & equipment repair; fabricated structural metal; welding repair; sheet metalwork

(G-10745)
AQUA UTILITY SERVICES LLC
1829 E Spring St (47150-1651)
PHONE.................................812 284-9243
George Hughes Jr,
EMP: 8
SALES (est): 965.6K **Privately Held**
SIC: 4953 2842 ; disinfectants, household or industrial plant

(G-10746)
ARCHIBALD BROTHERS INTL INC
Also Called: Archibald Frozen Desserts
209 Quality Ave Ste 1 (47150-7256)
PHONE.................................812 941-8267
Edward Meyer, *CEO*
Corey Merz, *Vice Pres*
▲ EMP: 9
SQ FT: 3,000
SALES: 1.5MM **Privately Held**
SIC: 2024 Ices, flavored (frozen dessert)

(G-10747)
ASEMPAC INC
5300 Foundation Blvd (47150-9321)
PHONE.................................812 945-6303
Gary Parks, *President*
John R Slavsky Jr, *President*
Dave Morrison, *Vice Pres*
James M Greer, *Admin Sec*
▲ EMP: 25
SQ FT: 18,000
SALES (est): 1.5MM **Privately Held**
SIC: 7389 3479 7336 3993 Packaging & labeling services; engraving jewelry silverware, or metal; silk screen design; signs & advertising specialties; automotive & apparel trimmings

(G-10748)
ASPIRE INDUSTRIES
5329 Foundation Blvd (47150-9321)
PHONE.................................812 542-1561
Todd Dome, *President*
Virginia Morman, *Principal*
EMP: 12
SALES (est): 1.3MM **Privately Held**
SIC: 3999 Atomizers, toiletry

(G-10749)
B&W PACKAGING MFG LLC
4140 Capitol Dr (47150-2283)
PHONE.................................812 280-9578
Mark Wasdovich, *Principal*
Lisa Ellis, *Office Mgr*
EMP: 42 EST: 2013
SQ FT: 100,000
SALES: 9.4MM **Privately Held**
SIC: 2653 3086 Corrugated & solid fiber boxes; packaging & shipping materials, foamed plastic

(G-10750)
BARE METAL INC
4160 Capitol Dr (47150-2283)
PHONE.................................812 948-1313
Robert Burton, *President*
Debra Burton, *Vice Pres*
▲ EMP: 18
SQ FT: 28,000
SALES (est): 2.1MM **Privately Held**
WEB: www.baremetal.com
SIC: 3471 1799 Plating & polishing; paint & wallpaper stripping

(G-10751)
BETHLEHEM PACKG DIE CUTNG INC
802 E 8th St (47150-3264)
PHONE.................................812 282-8740
Fax: 812 282-8741
John C Denney, *President*
Vicky L Denney, *Vice Pres*
Marilyn Denney, *Office Mgr*
Roger Workman, *Maintence Staff*
EMP: 12
SQ FT: 35,000

SALES: 1.9MM **Privately Held**
WEB: www.bethpac.com
SIC: 2675 5199 Cardboard cut-outs, panels & foundations: die-cut; packaging materials

(G-10752)
BF SHAFFER CO
2712 Clearstream Ct (47150-5153)
PHONE.................................812 949-8356
Doris Shaffer, *Principal*
EMP: 2
SALES (est): 173.6K **Privately Held**
SIC: 3011 Tires & inner tubes

(G-10753)
BLUE GRASS CHEMICAL SPC LLC (PA)
895 Industrial Blvd (47150-2252)
PHONE.................................812 948-1115
Fax: 812 948-1561
Paul McCauley, *Exec VP*
Dan L Sparks, *Mng Member*
▲ EMP: 20
SQ FT: 31,500
SALES: 2.9MM **Privately Held**
SIC: 2899 3555 2869 Metal treating compounds; printing trades machinery; industrial organic chemicals

(G-10754)
BRUCE FOX INC (PA)
1909 Mcdonald Ln (47150-2498)
PHONE.................................812 945-3511
Fax: 812 945-0275
John R Slavsky, *Ch of Bd*
James M Greer, *President*
David H Morrison, *President*
Gary Parks, *COO*
Dave Miller, *Vice Pres*
▲ EMP: 129 EST: 1937
SQ FT: 50,000
SALES (est): 13.9MM **Privately Held**
WEB: www.brucefox.com
SIC: 3914 5094 Trophies; trophies

(G-10755)
BRYANT INDUSTRIES INC
Also Called: Industrial Machine & Tool
201b E 18th St (47150-1601)
PHONE.................................812 944-6010
Lonnie Bryant, *President*
Jerry Bryant, *Treasurer*
EMP: 10
SQ FT: 10,000
SALES (est): 760K **Privately Held**
SIC: 3599 3544 Machine shop, jobbing & repair; special dies, tools, jigs & fixtures

(G-10756)
C F SLATTERY STEEL FABRICATION
2101 Logan St (47150-3966)
PHONE.................................812 948-9167
EMP: 2 EST: 1937
SQ FT: 3,600
SALES: 150K **Privately Held**
SIC: 3441 5085 Steel Fabrication And Wholesales Welding Supplies

(G-10757)
CABINETS BY RICK INC
1630 Grant Line Rd (47150-3929)
PHONE.................................812 945-2220
Richard L Henson Jr, *President*
Patricia A Henson, *Admin Sec*
EMP: 4 EST: 1985
SQ FT: 9,600
SALES: 1MM **Privately Held**
WEB: www.cabinetsbyrick.com
SIC: 2434 Wood kitchen cabinets

(G-10758)
CHESTER POOL SYSTEMS INC
5311 Foundation Blvd (47150-9321)
PHONE.................................812 949-7333
▲ EMP: 31
SQ FT: 30,000
SALES: 7.5MM **Privately Held**
SIC: 3949 Mfg Sporting/Athletic Goods

(G-10759)
CHESTER POOL SYSTEMS INC
5311 Foundation Blvd (47150-9321)
PHONE.................................812 949-7333

Fax: 812 246-4260
Robert D Uhl, *President*
Greg Carnforth, *Vice Pres*
Eamon Kelly, *Engineer*
Robert Larson, *Accounts Mgr*
Pete Gumaelius, *Sales Staff*
EMP: 50
SQ FT: 44,000
SALES (est): 4.5MM Privately Held
WEB: www.chesterpools.com
SIC: 3949 1799 Swimming pools, except plastic; swimming pool construction

(G-10760)
CIMTECH INC
325 Park East Blvd (47150-7257)
PHONE..............................812 948-1472
Fax: 812 948-1436
Anne Pfeiffer, *CEO*
Chris Craig, *Vice Pres*
Shawn Grim, *Prdtn Mgr*
Frank Wethington, *Sales Mgr*
David Magula, *Admin Sec*
EMP: 38
SQ FT: 23,000
SALES (est): 7.1MM Privately Held
SIC: 3599 Machine shop, jobbing & repair

(G-10761)
CLARK FOODS INC (PA)
Also Called: American Beverage Marketers
810 Progress Blvd (47150-2257)
P.O. Box 347 (47151-0347)
PHONE..............................812 949-3075
George Wagner III, *President*
Robert Brigandi, *Vice Pres*
Bill Hinkebein, *Vice Pres*
William A Hinkebein, *Vice Pres*
Charles E Wagner, *Vice Pres*
◆ EMP: 52
SQ FT: 110,000
SALES (est): 35.9MM Privately Held
SIC: 5149 2086 Soft drinks; bottled & canned soft drinks

(G-10762)
CNHI LLC
Also Called: New Albany Tribune
318 Pearl St Ste 100 (47150-3450)
PHONE..............................812 944-6481
Fax: 812 949-6585
Shea V Hoy, *Publisher*
Steve Kozarovich, *Manager*
EMP: 40 Privately Held
WEB: www.clintonnc.com
SIC: 2711 2791 2752 Newspapers, publishing & printing; typesetting; commercial printing, lithographic
HQ: Cnhi, Llc
445 Dexter Ave
Montgomery AL 36104

(G-10763)
COFFEYS CUSTOM UPHOLSTERY
610 Silver St (47150-1739)
PHONE..............................812 948-8611
Fax: 812 948-8611
Jim Coffey, *Partner*
Gary Coffey, *Partner*
Mark Anthony Coffey, *Partner*
EMP: 4
SQ FT: 8,700
SALES (est): 200K Privately Held
SIC: 7641 5712 2512 Reupholstery; furniture stores; upholstered household furniture

(G-10764)
COMHAR LLC
3660 Security Pkwy (47150)
PHONE..............................812 399-2123
Robert Coffey,
EMP: 12
SQ FT: 5,300
SALES (est): 660K Privately Held
SIC: 3714 Air brakes, motor vehicle

(G-10765)
CONFORMA CLAD INC
501 Park East Blvd (47150-7252)
PHONE..............................812 948-2118
Fax: 812 945-6662
Tolleen Portada, *CEO*
Mike Harlan, *President*
Harrison B Horan, *President*

Benjamin Jacobson, *Director*
Timothy Whelan, *Admin Sec*
▲ EMP: 115
SALES (est): 12.7MM
SALES (corp-wide): 2.3B Publicly Held
WEB: www.conformaclad.com
SIC: 3479 Coating of metals & formed products
PA: Kennametal Inc.
600 Grant St Ste 5100
Pittsburgh PA 15219
412 248-8000

(G-10766)
CUSTOM PLYWOOD INC
Also Called: CPI AIRCRAFT INTERIORS
301 Quality Ave (47150-7264)
PHONE..............................812 944-7300
Fax: 812 944-7373
Roger Ledbetter, *President*
Doug Durham, *General Mgr*
Pat Hecker, *Human Resources*
Vickie Kidder, *Sales Staff*
DOT Wild, *Manager*
EMP: 79
SQ FT: 80,000
SALES (est): 14.6MM Privately Held
SIC: 2435 Hardwood plywood, prefinished

(G-10767)
CYCLONE ADG LLC
166 Mills Ln (47150-6601)
PHONE..............................520 403-2927
Scott Rollefstad, *Chief Engr*
Alberto Moore,
EMP: 2
SALES (est): 135.8K Privately Held
SIC: 3812 Aircraft/aerospace flight instruments & guidance systems

(G-10768)
DIMENSION PLYWOOD INC
Also Called: Architectural Plywood
415 Industrial Blvd (47150-2244)
PHONE..............................812 944-6491
Fax: 812 944-7421
Paul Horstman, *President*
EMP: 8
SALES (est): 1.7MM Privately Held
WEB: www.billkraemerveneers.com
SIC: 2435 5031 Plywood, hardwood or hardwood faced; veneer

(G-10769)
DISCOUNT LABELS LLC
Also Called: Labels Unlimited
4115 Profit Ct (47150-7207)
P.O. Box 709 (47151-0709)
PHONE..............................812 945-2617
Fax: 812 949-5239
Allen Conway, *President*
Mike Gore, *General Mgr*
Luckett Tim, *Vice Pres*
Andrew Turner, *Vice Pres*
Shawn Dailey, *Production*
▲ EMP: 3946
SALES (est): 50.8MM Publicly Held
WEB: www.dlabels.com
SIC: 2679 3069 5199 Labels, paper: made from purchased material; stationers' rubber sundries; advertising specialties
HQ: Cenveo Corporation
200 Frst Stamford Pl Fl 2
Stamford CT 06902
303 790-8023

(G-10770)
E M CUMMINGS VENEERS INC
601 E 4th St (47150-3312)
P.O. Box 49 (47151-0049)
PHONE..............................812 944-2269
Fax: 812 944-0212
Edward J Zoeller, *President*
Edward Zoeller, *Executive*
EMP: 20
SQ FT: 35,000
SALES (est): 4.3MM Privately Held
WEB: www.emcummingsveneer.com
SIC: 2435 Veneer stock, hardwood

(G-10771)
ELECTROMECHANICAL RES LABS
Also Called: Erl
2560 Charlestown Rd (47150-2557)
P.O. Box 1026 (47151-1026)
PHONE..............................812 948-8484
Fax: 812 944-8808
Dr Larry C Wilkins, *Principal*
Ron Monell, *Business Mgr*
EMP: 50 EST: 1970
SQ FT: 35,000
SALES: 22MM Privately Held
WEB: www.erlinc.net
SIC: 3625 Marine & navy auxiliary controls

(G-10772)
ERL PROPERTIES INC
Also Called: Law Valve of Texas
2560 Charlestown Rd (47150-2557)
PHONE..............................812 948-8484
Larry Wilkins, *President*
Jeff Liebert, *Principal*
EMP: 5 EST: 1997
SALES: 1MM Privately Held
WEB: www.erlproductions.com
SIC: 6512 2531 Nonresidential building operators; public building & related furniture

(G-10773)
ESAREY HARDWOOD CREATIONS LLC
534 Hoffman Dr (47150-7600)
PHONE..............................419 610-6486
Joseph Esarey, *Principal*
EMP: 2
SALES (est): 50.2K Privately Held
SIC: 2499 Wood products

(G-10774)
EXTREME QUALITY PRINTS
1938 E Oak St (47150-1728)
PHONE..............................812 987-7617
Shon Crowdus, *Principal*
EMP: 2
SALES (est): 83.9K Privately Held
SIC: 2752 Commercial printing, lithographic

(G-10775)
FALLS CITIES PRINTING INC
323 Vincennes St (47150-1622)
PHONE..............................812 949-9051
Fax: 812 949-9054
Phillip M Alles, *President*
EMP: 10
SQ FT: 16,000
SALES (est): 1.1MM Privately Held
WEB: www.fallscities.com
SIC: 2752 2761 Commercial printing, offset; manifold business forms

(G-10776)
FILTRATION TECH SYSTEMS LLC
4345 Security Pkwy (47150-9366)
PHONE..............................812 944-9368
Steve Wallace, *President*
Carl Wilson, *Sales Mgr*
EMP: 25
SQ FT: 34,000
SALES (est): 2.5MM Privately Held
WEB: www.filtrationtech.com
SIC: 3599 Machine shop, jobbing & repair

(G-10777)
FINE SIGNS AND GRAPHICS
802 E 8th St (47150-3264)
PHONE..............................812 944-7446
Kathy Copas, *Owner*
EMP: 3
SALES (est): 130K Privately Held
WEB: www.finesignsandgraphics.com
SIC: 3993 Signs & advertising specialties

(G-10778)
FIRE KING INTERNATIONAL LLC (HQ)
101 Security Pkwy (47150-9367)
PHONE..............................812 948-8400
Fax: 812 949-8837
Jim Poteet, *CEO*
Gary Weisman, *President*
Ed Carpenter, *COO*

William Wolf, *Exec VP*
Jones Jennifer, *Vice Pres*
◆ EMP: 41
SQ FT: 30,000
SALES (est): 35.3MM
SALES (corp-wide): 173.4MM Privately Held
WEB: www.fireking.com
SIC: 3499 5044 Locks, safe & vault: metal; vaults & safes
PA: Fki Security Group, Llc
101 Security Pkwy
New Albany IN 47150
812 948-8400

(G-10779)
FIRE KING INTERNATIONAL LLC
900 Park Pl (47150-2261)
PHONE..............................812 948-2795
Fax: 812 948-0437
Van G Carlisle, *President*
EMP: 20
SALES (corp-wide): 173.4MM Privately Held
WEB: www.fireking.com
SIC: 2522 5044 3499 3429 Filing boxes, cabinets & cases: except wood; vaults & safes; safes & vaults, metal; locks or lock sets
HQ: Fk Safety And Security, L.L.C
101 Security Pkwy
New Albany IN 47150
812 948-8400

(G-10780)
FIRE KING SECURITY PDTS LLC
111 Security Pkwy (47150-9366)
PHONE..............................812 948-8400
Jim Poteet, *CEO*
Michael Smith, *President*
Michael Lynch, *CFO*
William Whitehead, *Sales Staff*
Lloyd Jones, *Sales Executive*
◆ EMP: 114
SALES (est): 30.3MM
SALES (corp-wide): 173.4MM Privately Held
SIC: 5044 3499 2522 Vaults & safes; fire- or burglary-resistive products; office furniture, except wood
PA: Fki Security Group, Llc
101 Security Pkwy
New Albany IN 47150
812 948-8400

(G-10781)
FKI SECURITY GROUP LLC (PA)
Also Called: Fire King Security Group
101 Security Pkwy (47150-9366)
P.O. Box 559 (47151-0559)
PHONE..............................812 948-8400
Jim Poteet, *CEO*
Kimberley Field, *Vice Pres*
John Rhoads, *Vice Pres*
Doug Jones, *Electrical Engi*
Michael Lynch, *CFO*
◆ EMP: 363
SQ FT: 270,000
SALES (est): 173.4MM Privately Held
SIC: 3429 5044 3499 2522 Locks or lock sets; vaults & safes; safes & vaults, metal; filing boxes, cabinets & cases: except wood

(G-10782)
FLOYD COUNTY BREWING COMPANY L
129 W Main St (47150-5958)
PHONE..............................502 724-3202
Brian Hampton, *Administration*
EMP: 4 EST: 2015
SALES (est): 237.1K Privately Held
SIC: 2082 Malt beverages

(G-10783)
FOAM FABRICATORS INC
950 Progress Blvd (47150-2296)
PHONE..............................812 948-1696
Fax: 812 948-2450
James Hughes, *Manager*
EMP: 30
SQ FT: 30,000 Publicly Held
WEB: www.foamfabricators.com
SIC: 2821 3086 Polystyrene resins; plastics foam products

HQ: Foam Fabricators, Inc.
8722 E San Alberto Dr # 200
Scottsdale AZ 85258
480 607-7330

(G-10784)
FRANK H MONROE HTG & COOLG INC
Also Called: Honeywell Authorized Dealer
595 Industrial Blvd (47150-2246)
PHONE..........................812 945-2566
Fax: 812 945-4060
Frank H Monroe, *Ch of Bd*
Steve Laduke, *President*
Carla Johnson, *Corp Secy*
James Crosier, *Vice Pres*
EMP: 12
SQ FT: 16,000
SALES (est): 2.4MM **Privately Held**
WEB: www.frankhmonroe.com
SIC: 1711 3444 Warm air heating & air conditioning contractor; refrigeration contractor; sheet metalwork

(G-10785)
FUTURE MOLD INC
100 Galvin Way (47150-1500)
PHONE..........................812 941-8661
Fax: 812 941-8662
Christopher Poff, *President*
Jerry Mehling, *Vice Pres*
Marlin Andres, *Shareholder*
EMP: 17
SQ FT: 7,500
SALES (est): 2.8MM **Privately Held**
WEB: www.futuremold.com
SIC: 3544 3089 8711 Forms (molds), for foundry & plastics working machinery; industrial molds; injection molding of plastics; engineering services

(G-10786)
GEA INC
615 State St (47150-4733)
PHONE..........................812 944-1401
Andrea Haymaker, *Principal*
EMP: 2 EST: 2010
SALES (est): 181.5K **Privately Held**
SIC: 3713 Dump truck bodies

(G-10787)
GEORGES CUSTOM WOOD WORKING
1603 Beechwood Ave (47150-3936)
PHONE..........................812 944-3344
George Kreilein, *President*
EMP: 3
SQ FT: 5,000
SALES (est): 260.1K **Privately Held**
WEB: www.georgeswood.com
SIC: 2511 Lawn furniture: wood

(G-10788)
GLOBE MECHANICAL INC
20 W 7th St (47150-5912)
PHONE..........................812 949-2001
Fax: 812 949-2005
Marlin Andres, *President*
Bryan Kruer, *President*
Deanna Beville, *Admin Sec*
EMP: 99
SQ FT: 40,000
SALES: 55.4MM **Privately Held**
WEB: www.globemechanical.com
SIC: 3498 Tube fabricating (contract bending & shaping)

(G-10789)
GRAPHIC PACKAGING INTL INC
Also Called: Carton Craft
2549 Charlestown Rd Ste 1 (47150-2554)
PHONE..........................812 949-4393
Tim Daniel, *Manager*
EMP: 60 **Publicly Held**
SIC: 2653 Boxes, solid fiber: made from purchased materials
HQ: Graphic Packaging International, Llc
1500 Riveredge Pkwy # 100
Atlanta GA 30328

(G-10790)
GRAPHIC PACKAGING INTL INC
1502 Beeler St (47150-3160)
PHONE..........................812 948-1608
Tim Daniel, *Plant Mgr*
EMP: 40 **Publicly Held**

SIC: 2752 Commercial printing, lithographic
HQ: Graphic Packaging International, Llc
1500 Riveredge Pkwy # 100
Atlanta GA 30328

(G-10791)
GT COMPUTERS LLC
1006 State St (47150-4742)
PHONE..........................502 550-7490
Jesus Guerrero,
EMP: 3
SALES: 50K **Privately Held**
SIC: 3571 Computers, digital, analog or hybrid

(G-10792)
HARTFORD HEAT TREATMENT
37 W 5th St (47150-5910)
PHONE..........................812 725-8272
Mike Simmons, *VP Opers*
EMP: 3
SALES (est): 192.9K **Privately Held**
SIC: 3398 Metal heat treating

(G-10793)
HIM GENTLEMANS BOUTIQUE
314 Pearl St (47150-3418)
PHONE..........................812 924-7441
EMP: 2
SALES (est): 90.4K **Privately Held**
SIC: 2389 2321 3143 Men's miscellaneous accessories; men's & boys' dress shirts; dress shoes, men's

(G-10794)
HITACHI CABLE AMERICA INC
5301 Foundation Blvd (47150)
PHONE..........................812 945-9011
EMP: 235
SALES (corp-wide): 82.2B **Privately Held**
SIC: 3052 Rubber And Plastics Hose And Beltings, Ns
HQ: Hitachi Cable America Inc.
2 Manhattanville Rd # 301
Purchase NY 10577
914 694-9200

(G-10795)
HITACHI CABLE AMERICA INC
Automotive Products Division
5300 Grant Line Rd (47150-9335)
PHONE..........................812 945-9011
Fax: 812 945-9006
Jolene Yates, *Senior Buyer*
Troy Hickman, *Sales Dir*
Juan Carlos Chequer, *Branch Mgr*
EMP: 442
SALES (corp-wide): 87.9B **Privately Held**
SIC: 3643 Power line cable
HQ: Hitachi Cable America Inc.
2 Manhattanville Rd # 301
Purchase NY 10577
914 694-9200

(G-10796)
HITACHI CBLE AUTO PDTS USA INC (DH)
5300 Grant Line Rd (47150-9335)
PHONE..........................812 945-9011
▲ EMP: 150
SQ FT: 188,000
SALES (est): 26.3MM
SALES (corp-wide): 82.2B **Privately Held**
SIC: 3052 3492 3714 Rubber And Plastics Hose And Beltings, Ns
HQ: Hitachi Cable America Inc.
2 Manhattanville Rd # 301
Purchase NY 10577
914 694-9200

(G-10797)
HOOSIER DADDY WOODWORKS
1903 Depauw Ave (47150-2749)
PHONE..........................812 949-2801
Norma Condra, *Principal*
EMP: 2 EST: 2008
SALES (est): 152.6K **Privately Held**
SIC: 2431 Millwork

(G-10798)
HOOSIER WOODWORKING MCHY LLC
3306 Cobblers Ct (47150-9462)
PHONE..........................812 944-3302

Steve Meyer, *Principal*
Jason Neafus, *Principal*
EMP: 3
SALES (est): 1.6MM **Privately Held**
SIC: 3553 7389 Woodworking machinery;

(G-10799)
HOT STONE LLC
202 Pearl St (47150-3416)
PHONE..........................812 949-4969
EMP: 2
SALES (est): 154.5K **Privately Held**
SIC: 3446 Mfg Architectural Metalwork

(G-10800)
HUNCILMAN INC
2072 Mcdonald Ave (47150-3745)
PHONE..........................812 945-3544
Gordon L Huncilman, *President*
Jeff Huncilman, *Exec VP*
Jeffery A Huncilman, *Vice Pres*
EMP: 2
SQ FT: 42,000
SALES (est): 295K **Privately Held**
SIC: 3524 Lawnmowers, residential: hand or power

(G-10801)
IDEAL WOOD PRODUCTS
Also Called: Ideal Archtectural Doors Plywd
890 Central Ct (47150-7234)
PHONE..........................812 949-5181
Fax: 812 945-9256
Steven Morency, *President*
Rick Hayden, *Vice Pres*
Robert Ziegelmeier, *Vice Pres*
▲ EMP: 78
SQ FT: 85,000
SALES (est): 7.8MM **Privately Held**
WEB: www.idealdoor.net
SIC: 2431 2435 Doors, wood; hardwood veneer & plywood

(G-10802)
IMAGE VAULT LLC
101 Security Pkwy (47150-9366)
PHONE..........................812 948-8400
Jim Poteet, *CEO*
Shawn Kruger, *Vice Pres*
John Mobley, *Plant Mgr*
Angela Adkins, *Buyer*
Andrew Silvers, *Electrical Engi*
EMP: 9
SALES (est): 1.5MM
SALES (corp-wide): 173.4MM **Privately Held**
WEB: www.image-vault.com
SIC: 3699 3651 7371 Electrical equipment & supplies; household audio & video equipment; computer software systems analysis & design, custom
PA: Fki Security Group, Llc
101 Security Pkwy
New Albany IN 47150
812 948-8400

(G-10803)
IMI SOUTH LLC
1732 Lincoln Ave (47150-3959)
PHONE..........................812 945-6605
Fax: 812 949-4520
Mike Harman, *Branch Mgr*
EMP: 20
SALES (corp-wide): 800.6MM **Privately Held**
SIC: 3273 Ready-mixed concrete
HQ: Imi South, Llc
1440 Selinda Ave
Louisville KY 40213
502 456-6930

(G-10804)
IMPRESSIVE PRINTING
515 E Daisy Ln (47150-4446)
PHONE..........................812 913-1101
Ketra Taylor, *Principal*
EMP: 2
SALES (est): 105.9K **Privately Held**
SIC: 2752 Commercial printing, lithographic

(G-10805)
INDCO INC
4040 Earnings Way (47150-2275)
PHONE..........................812 945-4383
Fax: 812 944-9742

Mark Hennis, *President*
Kris Wilberding, *Vice Pres*
Jim Copler, *Purchasing*
Robin Whitmer, *Sales Staff*
Jacinda Maudlin, *Marketing Mgr*
▼ EMP: 8 EST: 1975
SQ FT: 11,000
SALES (est): 2.5MM **Privately Held**
WEB: www.indco.com
SIC: 3559 5084 3586 3531 Paint making machinery; chemical machinery & equipment; industrial machinery & equipment; measuring & dispensing pumps; construction machinery

(G-10806)
INDUS LLC (PA)
3050 Autumn Hill Trl (47150-9468)
PHONE..........................502 553-1770
Shivaprasad Dhanapal, *Mng Member*
EMP: 3
SQ FT: 1,000
SALES (est): 500K **Privately Held**
SIC: 3089 Molding primary plastic

(G-10807)
INTEGRITY SIGN SOLUTIONS INC
4302 Security Pkwy (47150-9374)
PHONE..........................502 233-8755
Melissa Hobbs, *President*
Michael Hobbs, *Vice Pres*
EMP: 5 EST: 2010
SQ FT: 16,000
SALES: 500K **Privately Held**
SIC: 5199 3993 Advertising specialties; signs & advertising specialties

(G-10808)
J & J PALLET CORP
2234 E Market St (47150-1508)
PHONE..........................812 948-9382
John C Jones, *Branch Mgr*
EMP: 30
SALES (corp-wide): 6.5MM **Privately Held**
SIC: 2448 Pallets, wood
PA: J & J Pallet Corp
2234 E Market St
New Albany IN 47150
812 944-8670

(G-10809)
J & J PALLET CORP (PA)
2234 E Market St (47150-1508)
P.O. Box 583 (47151-0583)
PHONE..........................812 944-8670
Fax: 812 944-8675
John C Jones, *President*
Susan Kelley, *Technology*
Susan Jackson, *Admin Sec*
EMP: 25 EST: 1972
SQ FT: 13,000
SALES (est): 6.5MM **Privately Held**
WEB: www.jjpallet.com
SIC: 2448 7699 Pallets, wood; pallet repair

(G-10810)
JONES POPCORN INC
Also Called: Clark's Snacks
125 Quality Ave (47150-2287)
P.O. Box 48 (47151-0048)
PHONE..........................812 941-8810
Fax: 812 941-8830
Ryan Jones, *President*
James Jones, *President*
Megan Heier, *QC Mgr*
Linda Jones, *Admin Sec*
EMP: 70
SQ FT: 80,000
SALES: 9MM **Privately Held**
WEB: www.clarksnacks.com
SIC: 2099 Popcorn, packaged: except already popped

(G-10811)
K & I HARD CHROME INC
1900 E Main St (47150-5798)
PHONE..........................812 948-1166
Fax: 812 948-1703
Robert A Eckerle, *President*
EMP: 21 EST: 1974
SQ FT: 32,000

▲ = Import ▼=Export
◆ =Import/Export

SALES: 1.6MM **Privately Held**
SIC: 3471 Electroplating of metals or
formed products

(G-10812)
KEEN SCREEN
3314 Grant Line Rd (47150-6411)
PHONE..................................812 945-5336
Jacob Boger, *Principal*
EMP: 3
SALES (est): 227.6K **Privately Held**
SIC: 2759 Screen printing

(G-10813)
KENNAMETAL INC
Also Called: Kennametal Consora Clad
501 Park East Blvd (47150-7252)
PHONE..................................812 948-2118
Brian Dickman, *Sales Engr*
Chad Juliot, *Marketing Staff*
Johnny Martin, *Branch Mgr*
EMP: 126
SALES (corp-wide): 2.3B **Publicly Held**
PA: Kennametal Inc.
    600 Grant St Ste 5100
    Pittsburgh PA 15219
    412 248-8000

(G-10814)
**KINGS-QLITY RSTRTION SVCS
LLC**
1818 E Market St (47150-1657)
PHONE..................................812 944-4347
Angela J King, *Mng Member*
EMP: 13 EST: 2008
SALES (est): 300.5K **Privately Held**
SIC: 1522 2842 7217 Residential con-
struction; specialty cleaning preparations;
carpet & upholstery cleaning

(G-10815)
L THORN COMPANY INC (PA)
6000 Grant Line Rd (47150-9622)
PHONE..................................812 246-4461
Fax: 812 246-2678
Mike Ludden, *President*
Kyle Ludden, *COO*
Gregory Bickel, *Vice Pres*
Robert Burgan, *Vice Pres*
Chris Cook, *Opers Mgr*
EMP: 20
SQ FT: 69,500
SALES (est): 15.1MM **Privately Held**
WEB: www.lthorn.com
SIC: 3272 5211 Concrete products, pre-
cast; brick

(G-10816)
LAGNAIPPE LLC
Also Called: PIP Printing
802 E 8th St (47150-3264)
PHONE..................................812 288-9291
Vicky Denney,
EMP: 7
SALES (est): 707.8K **Privately Held**
SIC: 2752 Commercial printing, offset

(G-10817)
**LANCASTER CUSTOM
CABINETS INC**
5301 Grant Line Rd (47150-9336)
PHONE..................................812 949-4750
Fax: 812 949-3166
Steve Lancaster, *President*
EMP: 3
SALES: 160K **Privately Held**
SIC: 2599 Cabinets, factory

(G-10818)
LOUISVILLE VENEER CORP
301 E Elm St (47150-3430)
PHONE..................................502 500-7176
Fax: 812 944-7170
Marc Quirici, *CEO*
Giuseppe Quirici, *President*
Richard Witt, *Controller*
▼ EMP: 6 EST: 1996
SQ FT: 45,000
SALES (est): 724.9K **Privately Held**
WEB: www.louisvilleveneer.com
SIC: 2435 Veneer stock, hardwood

(G-10819)
**LOZIER MACHINERY
INCORPORATED**
695 Industrial Blvd (47150-2248)
PHONE..................................812 945-2558
Eric R Lozier, *President*
EMP: 8
SALES (est): 570K **Privately Held**
WEB: www.loziermachinery.com
SIC: 3553 Woodworking machinery

(G-10820)
LSI WALLCOVERING INC (PA)
2073 Mcdonald Ave (47150-3759)
PHONE..................................502 458-1502
Philip J Tarullo, *President*
Edward Ernest, *COO*
Greg Bowling, *Admin Sec*
▲ EMP: 91 EST: 1978
SQ FT: 4,800
SALES (est): 23.4MM **Privately Held**
SIC: 2851 3999 Vinyl coatings, strippable;
feathers & feather products

(G-10821)
**LUKEMEIER INDUS MOLD &
MCH CO**
Also Called: Limmco Tool
4300 Security Pkwy (47150-9374)
PHONE..................................812 945-3375
Fax: 812 944-1848
Mary Lukemeier, *President*
Louis Lukemeier, *Corp Secy*
Melissa Scaggs, *CFO*
EMP: 20 EST: 1975
SQ FT: 21,000
SALES (est): 2.7MM **Privately Held**
SIC: 3089 3544 Injection molding of plas-
tics; special dies, tools, jigs & fixtures

(G-10822)
MARTIN INDUSTRIES
4235 Earnings Way (47150-7204)
PHONE..................................502 553-6599
Nancy Martin, *Principal*
EMP: 3 EST: 2009
SALES (est): 198.4K **Privately Held**
SIC: 3999 Manufacturing industries

(G-10823)
MATHES HOME CARE
1621 Charlestown Rd (47150-3339)
PHONE..................................812 944-2211
John Mathes, *Owner*
Joe Dones, *CFO*
EMP: 2
SALES (est): 88K **Privately Held**
SIC: 5999 3842 Medical apparatus & sup-
plies; wheelchairs

(G-10824)
MEDISHIELD
1598 Rector Ln (47150-1934)
PHONE..................................502 939-9903
EMP: 2
SALES (est): 86.6K **Privately Held**
SIC: 3845 Electromedical equipment

(G-10825)
MEILINK SAFE COMPANY
101 Security Pkwy (47150-9366)
P.O. Box 559 (47151-0559)
PHONE..................................812 941-0024
Fax: 812 941-0120
Van G Carlisle, *President*
Douglas J Voet, *Admin Sec*
EMP: 27
SALES (est): 233.5K
SALES (corp-wide): 173.4MM **Privately
Held**
WEB: www.fireking.com
SIC: 3499 5044 2522 5021 Safes &
vaults, metal; vaults & safes; filing boxes,
cabinets & cases: except wood; filing
units
HQ: Fk Safety And Security, L.L.C
    101 Security Pkwy
    New Albany IN 47150
    812 948-8400

(G-10826)
METAL DYNAMICS LTD
30 E 10th St (47150-5837)
PHONE..................................812 949-7998
Fax: 812 949-8187

Daniel Meyer, *President*
Myra Meyer, *Purchasing*
Don Lott, *Engineer*
▲ EMP: 20
SQ FT: 75,000
SALES (est): 3.1MM **Privately Held**
WEB: www.metaldynamicsltd.com
SIC: 2542 3441 3444 Cabinets: show,
display or storage: except wood; fabri-
cated structural metal; sheet metalwork

(G-10827)
**METAL SALES
MANUFACTURING CORP**
999 Park Pl (47150-7232)
PHONE..................................812 941-0041
Fax: 812 944-1418
Stewart Fourtney, *Branch Mgr*
EMP: 31
SALES (corp-wide): 425.1MM **Privately
Held**
SIC: 3449 3446 3444 2952 Miscella-
neous metalwork; architectural metal-
work; sheet metalwork; asphalt felts &
coatings
HQ: Metal Sales Manufacturing Corporation
    545 S 3rd St Ste 200
    Louisville KY 40202
    502 855-4300

(G-10828)
METALITE CORPORATION
1815 Troy St (47150-5775)
PHONE..................................812 944-6600
Fax: 812 944-8474
Marvin Friedman, *President*
Wane Friedman, *Vice Pres*
EMP: 70 EST: 1973
SQ FT: 200,000
SALES (est): 8.7MM **Privately Held**
SIC: 3645 3646 3648 Residential lighting
fixtures; commercial indusl & institutional
electric lighting fixtures; reflectors for
lighting equipment: metal

(G-10829)
MEYER ICE CREAM LLC
209 Quality Ave Ste 3 (47150-7256)
PHONE..................................812 941-8267
Corey Merz, *President*
EMP: 5 EST: 2015
SALES (est): 186.2K **Privately Held**
SIC: 2024 Ice cream & frozen desserts

(G-10830)
MIDWEST-TEK INC
4345 Security Pkwy (47150-9374)
PHONE..................................812 981-3551
Stephen R Wallace, *President*
Sheila Wallace, *Vice Pres*
EMP: 8
SALES (est): 1MM **Privately Held**
SIC: 3089 Injection molding of plastics

(G-10831)
MIKE MUGLER
Also Called: M & M Printing
3712 Dove Cir (47150-9702)
PHONE..................................812 945-4266
Mike Mugler, *Owner*
EMP: 2
SALES: 50K **Privately Held**
SIC: 2752 Commercial printing, litho-
graphic; commercial printing, offset

(G-10832)
MITCHELL VENEERS INC
4250 Earnings Way (47150-7203)
PHONE..................................812 941-9663
Stephen Mitchell, *President*
▼ EMP: 4
SALES (est): 1.9MM **Privately Held**
SIC: 2435 5031 Veneer stock, hardwood;
lumber: rough, dressed & finished

(G-10833)
NEXGEN MOLD & TOOL INC
4300 Security Pkwy (47150-9374)
P.O. Box 6747 (47151-6747)
PHONE..................................812 945-3375
John Lukes, *President*
Nichole Lukes, *Vice Pres*
Kevin Rose, *CFO*
Kevin Gancher, *Manager*
▼ EMP: 40
SQ FT: 26,000

SALES: 7MM **Privately Held**
WEB: www.nexgenmoldandtool.com
SIC: 3089 3544 Injection molded finished
plastic products; special dies, tools, jigs &
fixtures

(G-10834)
NVSD LLC
2235 Corydon Pike (47150-6119)
PHONE..................................502 561-0007
Darren Pavey, *General Mgr*
EMP: 2
SALES (est): 116K **Privately Held**
SIC: 3543 Foundry patternmaking

(G-10835)
**OHIO VALLEY CREATIVE ENRGY
INC**
626 Albany St (47150-5004)
PHONE..................................502 468-9787
Shane Corbin, *President*
EMP: 3
SALES (est): 171.9K **Privately Held**
SIC: 3269 Pottery products

(G-10836)
OHIO VALLEY DOOR CORP
2143 Willow St (47150-1520)
P.O. Box 84 (47151-0084)
PHONE..................................812 945-5285
Fax: 812 945-5730
Gerald F Brewer Sr, *Ch of Bd*
Gerald F Brewer Jr, *President*
Angela Taylor, *Corp Secy*
EMP: 22
SQ FT: 40,000
SALES (est): 4.7MM **Privately Held**
WEB: www.ohiovalleydoor.com
SIC: 2431 Doors, wood

(G-10837)
OLD CAPITAL PRINTING LLC
3314 Grant Line Rd Ste 3 (47150-6411)
P.O. Box 75, Crandall (47114-0075)
PHONE..................................812 946-9444
Elizabeth Mayne, *Administration*
EMP: 2 EST: 2014
SALES (est): 135.8K **Privately Held**
SIC: 2752 Commercial printing, litho-
graphic

(G-10838)
**PACKAGING LGSTICS
SLUTIONS LLC**
Also Called: Pls
3001 E Lobo Rdg (47150-9595)
PHONE..................................502 807-8346
John Moore,
EMP: 49
SQ FT: 58,000
SALES (est): 5.1MM **Privately Held**
SIC: 2653 Boxes, corrugated: made from
purchased materials

(G-10839)
PADGETT INC
901 E 4th St (47150-3328)
P.O. Box 1375 (47151-1375)
PHONE..................................812 945-2391
Fax: 812 948-0641
James R Padgett, *President*
Larry Brunson, *COO*
Beverly Padgett, *Vice Pres*
Robert J Padgett, *Vice Pres*
Steven Bush, *Project Mgr*
EMP: 160
SQ FT: 98,000
SALES (est): 11.4MM **Privately Held**
WEB: www.padgett-inc.com
SIC: 7349 1796 1791 3444 Building
maintenance, except repairs; machine
moving & rigging; structural steel erection;
sheet metalwork

(G-10840)
**PAYNE-SPARKMAN
MANUFACTURING**
2571 Roanoke Ave (47150-3724)
PHONE..................................812 944-4893
Fax: 812 944-1225
Steve Payne, *President*
Rich Mooney, *Electrical Engi*
Alex Dillion, *Sales Staff*
Coby Kraft, *Sales Staff*
Steve Steele, *Sales Staff*

G
E
O
G
R
A
P
H
I
C

▲ **EMP:** 15
SQ FT: 2,000
SALES (est): 2.4MM **Privately Held**
WEB: www.paynesparkman.com
SIC: 3674 Solid state electronic devices

(G-10841)
PERFUMERY
621 Park East Blvd (47150-7253)
PHONE............................812 777-0657
EMP: 3
SALES (est): 90K **Privately Held**
SIC: 2844 Perfumes & colognes

(G-10842)
PHASE THREE ELECTRIC INC
2115 E Market St (47150-1593)
PHONE............................812 945-9922
Fax: 812 945-3577
Harold Carey, *President*
Richard Haley, *Treasurer*
EMP: 6
SQ FT: 8,400
SALES (est): 1.3MM **Privately Held**
SIC: 7694 5063 Electric motor repair; motors, electric

(G-10843)
PHOTO SPECIALTIES
232 Maevi Dr (47150-4527)
PHONE............................812 944-5111
Francis Duerr Jr, *Owner*
EMP: 2
SALES (est): 84K **Privately Held**
SIC: 2759 Screen printing

(G-10844)
PILLSBURY COMPANY LLC
707 Pillsbury Ln (47150-2239)
PHONE............................812 944-8411
Fax: 812 949-1869
Dave Woolley, *Plant Mgr*
Moses Cordero, *Personnel*
David Woolley, *Manager*
EMP: 50
SALES (corp-wide): 15.7B **Publicly Held**
WEB: www.pillsbury.com
SIC: 2041 Flour mills, cereal (except rice); doughs, frozen or refrigerated
HQ: The Pillsbury Company Llc
　　1 General Mills Blvd
　　Minneapolis MN 55426

(G-10845)
PNC BANK NATIONAL ASSOCIATION
5170 Charlestown Rd Ste 1 (47150-8400)
PHONE............................812 948-4490
Fax: 812 948-4485
Carol Udell, *Branch Mgr*
EMP: 9
SALES (corp-wide): 18B **Publicly Held**
SIC: 3944 Banks, toy
HQ: Pnc Bank, National Association
　　222 Delaware Ave
　　Wilmington DE 19801
　　877 762-2000

(G-10846)
POLY GROUP LLC
Also Called: Nouvex
3000 Tech Ave Ste 2221 (47150)
PHONE............................812 590-4750
Craig Kalmer, *COO*
Thomas Hopkins, *Officer*
EMP: 6
SALES (est): 69K **Privately Held**
SIC: 2835 Microbiology & virology diagnostic products

(G-10847)
PPG INDUSTRIES INC
Also Called: PPG 4313
3314 Grant Line Rd Ste 1 (47150-6411)
PHONE............................812 944-4164
Jeff Branham, *Manager*
EMP: 24
SALES (corp-wide): 14.2B **Publicly Held**
WEB: www.ppg.com
SIC: 2851 Paints & allied products
PA: Ppg Industries, Inc.
　　1 Ppg Pl
　　Pittsburgh PA 15272
　　412 434-3131

(G-10848)
PRINTER PLUS
410 Pearl St (47150-3420)
PHONE............................812 945-5955
Fax: 812 945-5955
Warren Campbell, *Owner*
EMP: 4
SALES: 180K **Privately Held**
SIC: 2752 Commercial printing, offset

(G-10849)
PRINTING ALL STARS
802 E 8th St (47150-3264)
PHONE............................812 288-9291
EMP: 2
SALES (est): 202.6K **Privately Held**
SIC: 2752 Commercial printing, offset

(G-10850)
PTG SILICONES INC
827 Progress Blvd (47150-2256)
PHONE............................812 948-8719
Amy S Cahill, *CEO*
Brendan J Cahill, *President*
EMP: 3
SQ FT: 5,100
SALES (est): 711.1K **Privately Held**
WEB: www.ptgsilicones.com
SIC: 2822 3089 Silicone rubbers; injection molding of plastics

(G-10851)
QRS INC
Also Called: Riverside Recycle
1001 Floyd St (47150-5947)
P.O. Box 819 (47151-0819)
PHONE............................812 948-1323
Fax: 812 948-1326
Josh Carroll, *Manager*
EMP: 9
SALES (corp-wide): 14.8B **Publicly Held**
WEB: www.qrsrecycling.com
SIC: 4953 3341 2611 Recycling, waste materials; secondary nonferrous metals; pulp mills
HQ: Qrs, Inc.
　　357 Marshall Ave Ste 104
　　Saint Louis MO 63119
　　314 963-8000

(G-10852)
QUIKSET BOLLARD COMPANY
2234 E Market St (47150-1508)
P.O. Box 583 (47151-0583)
PHONE............................502 648-6734
Tony Perkins, *General Mgr*
EMP: 2
SALES (est): 175.5K **Privately Held**
SIC: 2097 Manufactured ice

(G-10853)
RAIL PROTECTION PLUS LLC
3913 Horne Ave (47150-9779)
PHONE............................812 399-1084
Edmund J Holt, *Principal*
EMP: 3
SALES: 150K **Privately Held**
SIC: 3715 Semitrailers for truck tractors

(G-10854)
RAUCH INC (PA)
845 Park Pl (47150-2262)
PHONE............................812 945-4063
Fax: 812 941-8820
Bettye R Dunham, *CEO*
Tony Euler, *Plant Mgr*
Kay Schuler, *Opers Mgr*
Danny McPheron, *CFO*
Deanne Byrd, *Human Res Dir*
EMP: 110
SQ FT: 45,000
SALES (est): 10.1MM **Privately Held**
SIC: 8331 7389 3599 Job training services; packaging & labeling services; machine shop, jobbing & repair

(G-10855)
RICHARDSON IMAGING SVCS INC
Also Called: Eagle Sign & Design
4239 Earnings Way (47150-7204)
PHONE............................888 561-0007
Glenn M Richardson, *President*
Joseph Bates, *Principal*
John Shircliffe,

EMP: 20
SQ FT: 35,000
SALES: 1.2MM
SALES (corp-wide): 7.7MM **Privately Held**
WEB: www.eaglesign.com
SIC: 3446 Architectural metalwork
PA: Richardson Imaging Services Inc
　　4105 Earnings Way
　　New Albany IN 47150
　　812 949-2422

(G-10856)
RITE WAY INDUSTRIES INC
4201 Reas Ln (47150-2232)
PHONE............................812 206-8665
Fax: 812 206-8329
Deborah Embry, *President*
Terry Williams, *Engineer*
Debbie Embry, *Treasurer*
Carmen Mills, *Sales Executive*
EMP: 30
SQ FT: 21,000
SALES (est): 6.2MM **Privately Held**
WEB: www.ritewayindustries.com
SIC: 3545 Cutting tools for machine tools

(G-10857)
RIVER CITY WINERY LLC
321 Pearl St (47150-3417)
PHONE............................812 945-9463
Melissa Humphrey, *Owner*
Tom Fox, *Pub Rel Staff*
EMP: 7 **EST:** 2008
SALES (est): 759.7K **Privately Held**
SIC: 2084 Wines

(G-10858)
ROBINSON LUMBER COMPANY INC
1750 Ormond Rd (47150-3784)
PHONE............................812 944-8020
Fax: 812 944-4242
Janet Babcock, *Office Mgr*
Jack Grace, *Branch Mgr*
David Furlong, *Maintence Staff*
EMP: 20
SALES (corp-wide): 25.8MM **Privately Held**
WEB: www.robinsonflooring.com
SIC: 2421 Sawmills & planing mills, general
PA: Robinson Lumber Company, Inc.
　　4000 Tchoupitoulas St
　　New Orleans LA
　　504 895-6377

(G-10859)
RONALDO DESIGNER JEWELRY INC (PA)
115 E Spring St Ste 102 (47150-3436)
P.O. Box 1604 (47151-1604)
PHONE............................812 972-7220
Ronnie E Needham, *President*
Michael J Scheser, *Exec VP*
Linda Needham, *CFO*
D Kevin Ryan, *General Counsel*
EMP: 60
SQ FT: 3,744
SALES (est): 6.4MM **Privately Held**
SIC: 5944 5094 3911 Jewelry, precious stones & precious metals; jewelry; jewelry, precious metal

(G-10860)
S & J PRECISION INC
4345 Security Pkwy (47150-9374)
PHONE............................812 944-9368
Sheila Wallace, *President*
Jerry Goodhue, *Purch Mgr*
Stephen R Wallace, *Admin Sec*
EMP: 25
SQ FT: 34,000
SALES (est): 5.5MM **Privately Held**
WEB: www.sandjprecision.com
SIC: 3599 Machine shop, jobbing & repair

(G-10861)
SENIOR PATHWAYS MAGAZINE LLC
115 Rossmoore Dr (47150-4528)
PHONE............................812 697-1750
Emily Anna, *Principal*
EMP: 3

SALES (est): 158.7K **Privately Held**
SIC: 2721 Periodicals

(G-10862)
SIGNS OF TIMES LLC
714 Mount Tabor Rd (47150-2213)
PHONE............................812 981-3000
Fax: 812 981-3981
Steve Hall,
EMP: 4
SALES (est): 367.4K **Privately Held**
SIC: 3993 Signs & advertising specialties

(G-10863)
SOUTHERN INDIANA BUS SOURCE
Also Called: News & Tribune
318 Pearl St Ste 100 (47150-3450)
PHONE............................812 206-6397
Fax: 812 945-6350
Janice Ashby, *Principal*
EMP: 4
SALES (est): 192.5K **Privately Held**
SIC: 2711 Newspapers

(G-10864)
SPAWN MATE INC
2049 Indiana Ave (47150-3748)
P.O. Box 1144 (47151-1144)
PHONE............................812 948-2174
Fax: 812 948-8811
Kathy Gahagen, *Plant Mgr*
Cathy Gahagen, *Branch Mgr*
EMP: 11
SALES (corp-wide): 20.1MM **Privately Held**
WEB: www.spawnmate.com
SIC: 2873 Fertilizers: natural (organic), except compost
PA: Spawn Mate, Inc.
　　260 Westgate Dr
　　Watsonville CA 95076
　　831 763-5300

(G-10865)
SPECTRUM
1608 Vance Ave (47150-3961)
PHONE............................812 941-6899
EMP: 2
SALES (est): 76.8K **Privately Held**
SIC: 2759 Commercial printing

(G-10866)
STEMWOOD CORP
2710 Grant Line Rd (47150-4051)
P.O. Box 1347 (47151-1347)
PHONE............................812 945-6646
Fax: 812 945-7549
David E Wunderlin, *President*
Dave Brumett, *VP Mfg*
Kris Johnson, *Manager*
EMP: 65
SQ FT: 180,000
SALES (est): 10.1MM **Privately Held**
SIC: 2435 2421 2426 Veneer stock, hardwood; lumber: rough, sawed or planed; hardwood dimension & flooring mills

(G-10867)
STEMWOOD MANUFACTURING LLC
2710 Grant Line Rd (47150-4051)
P.O. Box 1347 (47151-1347)
PHONE............................812 945-6646
David Wunderlin, *President*
Stephen Scott, *Principal*
Kristin Johnson, *Assistant VP*
Rodney Bramer, *Vice Pres*
David Brumett, *Vice Pres*
EMP: 25
SALES (est): 1.8MM **Privately Held**
SIC: 2421 Kiln drying of lumber

(G-10868)
STUMLERS MACHINE INC
222 E 4th St (47150-2941)
P.O. Box 87 (47151-0087)
PHONE............................812 944-2467
Fax: 812 944-5049
Roger Stumler, *President*
Mike Stumler, *Vice Pres*
EMP: 5
SQ FT: 3,100
SALES (est): 450K **Privately Held**
SIC: 3599 Machine & other job shop work

▲ = Import ▼=Export
◆ =Import/Export

(G-10869)
SUPERIOR VENEER & PLYWOOD LLC
1819 Dewey St (47150-5767)
PHONE....................................812 941-8850
Matt Gillion,
EMP: 2
SQ FT: 7,200
SALES (est): 257.3K **Privately Held**
WEB: www.superiorveneer.com
SIC: 2435 Hardwood veneer & plywood

(G-10870)
TECHNIDYNE CORPORATION (PA)
100 Quality Ave (47150-7222)
PHONE....................................812 948-2884
Fax: 812 945-6847
Stephen Jerome Popson, Ch of Bd
Michael T Popson, President
Thomas B Crawford, Vice Pres
Helen Popson, Vice Pres
Joyce Harris, Finance Mgr
EMP: 42
SQ FT: 28,000
SALES (est): 5.7MM **Privately Held**
WEB: www.technidyne.com
SIC: 3823 Industrial instrmnts msrmnt display/control process variable

(G-10871)
VENEER CURRY SALES LLC
1014 E 6th St (47150-3359)
PHONE....................................812 945-6623
Michael A Gray, Principal
EMP: 10
SALES (est): 1.3MM **Privately Held**
SIC: 2435 Hardwood veneer & plywood

(G-10872)
W AY-FM MEDIA GROUP INC
3211 Grant Line Rd Ste 1 (47150-2175)
P.O. Box 1043 (47151-1043)
PHONE....................................812 945-1043
Matthew Hahn, General Mgr
EMP: 6 EST: 2008
SALES (est): 434K **Privately Held**
SIC: 7313 3663 Radio advertising representative; radio receiver networks

(G-10873)
W M KELLEY CO INC
620 Durgee Rd (47150-8816)
PHONE....................................812 945-3529
Fax: 812 948-9971
Michael A Kelley, President
Frederick J Kelley, Admin Sec
EMP: 48 EST: 1968
SQ FT: 90,000
SALES (est): 16.3MM **Privately Held**
WEB: www.wmkelley.com
SIC: 3535 5084 Conveyors & conveying equipment; industrial machinery & equipment

(G-10874)
W-M LUMBER AND WOOD PDTS INC
1801 E Main St (47150-5782)
PHONE....................................812 944-6711
Fax: 812 944-1074
Robert W Marshall Sr, President
Robert Marshall Jr, Corp Secy
Lydia Hess, Vice Pres
EMP: 20
SQ FT: 30,000
SALES (est): 3.2MM **Privately Held**
WEB: www.palletsandmore.com
SIC: 2448 Skids, wood

(G-10875)
WORKFLOW SOLUTIONS LLC
Also Called: One Source Labs
2125 E Spring St (47150-1564)
PHONE....................................502 627-0257
Tracy M Brown,
EMP: 2 EST: 2012
SALES (est): 129.1K **Privately Held**
SIC: 2899 8099 7381 5199 ; physical examination & testing services; physical examination service, insurance; fingerprint service; first aid supplies

(G-10876)
YOLI INC
1404 Bell Ln Ste 1 (47150-7288)
PHONE....................................812 945-8530
Armando Banos, Branch Mgr
EMP: 21 **Privately Held**
SIC: 2099 5149 Seasonings & spices; spices & seasonings
PA: Yoli Inc.
4251 W 129th St
Alsip IL 60803

(G-10877)
YOUNG MACHINE CO INC
904 Industrial Blvd (47150-2255)
PHONE....................................812 944-5807
Fax: 812 944-3049
Larry E Young, President
Debbie Coats, Office Mgr
EMP: 12 EST: 1964
SQ FT: 10,000
SALES (est): 1.1MM **Privately Held**
SIC: 3599 Machine shop, jobbing & repair

New Carlisle
St. Joseph County

(G-10878)
ARCELORMITTAL KOTE INC (DH)
Also Called: I/N Tek & I/N Kote
30755 Edison Rd (46552-9728)
PHONE....................................574 654-1000
Fax: 574 654-1862
John Brett, President
Keith Howell, COO
Daniel G Mull, Exec VP
Neil Johlberg, Vice Pres
Patrick D Parker, Vice Pres
▲ **EMP:** 9
SQ FT: 300,000
SALES (est): 31.9MM **Privately Held**
SIC: 3479 3471 Galvanizing of iron, steel or end-formed products; electrolizing steel
HQ: Arcelormittal Usa Llc
1 S Dearborn St Ste 1800
Chicago IL 60603
312 346-0300

(G-10879)
AXIS MOLD INC
53450 Tamarack Rd (46552-9757)
PHONE....................................574 292-8904
Cole Boniface, President
EMP: 2
SALES (est): 182.1K **Privately Held**
SIC: 3544 Industrial molds

(G-10880)
CARRIS REELS INC
31977 Us Highway 20 (46552-8442)
PHONE....................................269 545-3400
Fax: 269 545-3401
EMP: 19
SALES (corp-wide): 81.3MM **Privately Held**
SIC: 2499 Mfg Wood Products
HQ: Carris Reels Inc
49 Main St
Proctor VT 05765
802 773-9111

(G-10881)
EDCOAT LIMITED PARTNERSHIP
30350 Edison Rd (46552-9728)
PHONE....................................574 654-9105
Fax: 574 654-9106
Gerry Degner, Partner
EMP: 40
SQ FT: 260,000
SALES (est): 5.9MM **Privately Held**
SIC: 3479 5051 Painting of metal products; painting, coating & hot dipping; metals service centers & offices

(G-10882)
FIVE STAR SHEETS LLC
54370 Smilax Rd (46552-9751)
PHONE....................................574 654-8058
Andrew JP Schaefer, President
Andy Schaefer, General Mgr
Derrick Andrzejewski, Superintendent
Scott T Swick, Vice Pres

Jay Butterfield, Plant Mgr
EMP: 100
SQ FT: 100,000
SALES (est): 50.7MM **Privately Held**
WEB: www.fivestarsheets.com
SIC: 2653 Boxes, corrugated: made from purchased materials

(G-10883)
I/N TEK LP
30755 Edison Rd (46552-9695)
PHONE....................................574 654-1000
Fax: 574 654-7878
Tom Kramer, Engineer
Gary V Asperen, Mng Member
John Franiak, Manager
▲ **EMP:** 250
SQ FT: 600,000
SALES (est): 112.2MM **Privately Held**
SIC: 3316 Strip steel, cold-rolled: from purchased hot-rolled
HQ: Arcelormittal Usa Llc
1 S Dearborn St Ste 1800
Chicago IL 60603
312 346-0300

(G-10884)
MIKE MAGIERA INC
8011 N 850 E (46552-9144)
PHONE....................................574 654-3044
Fax: 574 654-3044
Michael Magiera, President
Judy Lee Parmley, Admin Sec
EMP: 2
SQ FT: 7,000
SALES (est): 230.9K **Privately Held**
SIC: 3728 Aircraft parts & equipment

(G-10885)
MILES SYSTEMS MANUFACTURING
7385 N Walker Rd (46552-9328)
PHONE....................................574 988-0067
EMP: 2
SALES (est): 68.7K **Privately Held**
SIC: 3999 Manufacturing industries

(G-10886)
ROBERT BOSCH LLC
Also Called: Bosch Auto Proving Ground
32104 State Road 2 (46552-9605)
PHONE....................................574 654-4000
Robert G Schmidt, Principal
EMP: 60
SALES (corp-wide): 261.7MM **Privately Held**
WEB: www.boschservice.com
SIC: 3714 Motor vehicle parts & accessories
HQ: Robert Bosch Llc
2800 S 25th Ave
Broadview IL 60155
248 876-1000

(G-10887)
SUPERIOR MACHINE INC
33721 Early Rd (46552-8233)
PHONE....................................574 654-8243
Harry Dudeck Jr, President
EMP: 2
SALES (est): 208.3K **Privately Held**
SIC: 3599 Machine shop, jobbing & repair

(G-10888)
TEJAS TUBULAR PRODUCTS INC
31140 Edison Rd (46552-9729)
PHONE....................................574 249-0623
Richard Hyatte, Maintence Staff
EMP: 90
SALES (corp-wide): 247.8MM **Privately Held**
SIC: 3317 Steel pipe & tubes
PA: Tejas Tubular Products, Inc.
8799 North Loop E Ste 300
Houston TX 77029
281 822-3400

(G-10889)
UNIFRAX I LLC
54401 Smilax Rd (46552-9751)
PHONE....................................574 654-7100
Tom J Lord, Plant Mgr
Dave Allen, Manager
Jason Flagg, Manager
Lori Pallo, Personnel Assit

EMP: 150 **Publicly Held**
WEB: www.insulfrax.com
SIC: 3299 3296 Ceramic fiber; mineral wool
HQ: Unifrax I Llc
600 Rverwalk Pkwy Ste 120
Tonawanda NY 14150

New Castle
Henry County

(G-10890)
ALLEGHENY LUDLUM LLC
Also Called: ATI Allegheny Ludlum
516 W State Road 38 (47362-9786)
P.O. Box 309 (47362-0309)
PHONE....................................765 529-9570
Fax: 765 521-6492
Greg Counts, Manager
EMP: 144 **Publicly Held**
WEB: www.alleghenyludlum.com
SIC: 3312 3471 3398 3316 Stainless steel; hot-rolled iron & steel products; plating & polishing; metal heat treating; cold finishing of steel shapes
HQ: Allegheny Ludlum, Llc
1000 Six Ppg Pl
Pittsburgh PA 15222
412 394-2800

(G-10891)
AMERICAN KEEPER CORPORATION
3300 S Commerce Dr (47362-8706)
PHONE....................................765 521-2080
Hideki Sugiyama, President
David Alexander, General Mgr
▲ **EMP:** 32
SQ FT: 60,000
SALES (est): 6MM
SALES (corp-wide): 179.3MM **Privately Held**
SIC: 2396 Automotive & apparel trimmings
PA: Keeper Co.,Ltd.
2-4-36, Tsujidokandai
Fujisawa KNG 251-0
466 351-895

(G-10892)
ATLAS DOCK SYSTEMS INC
5363 W State Road 38 (47362-9195)
PHONE....................................317 714-3850
Brian Siefert, President
EMP: 6
SQ FT: 8,000
SALES (est): 882K **Privately Held**
WEB: www.atlasdock.com
SIC: 3732 Boat building & repairing

(G-10893)
BRYANT PRINTING
2601 Broad St (47362-3402)
PHONE....................................765 521-3379
Fax: 765 529-3349
Susanne McCutchen, Owner
EMP: 4
SQ FT: 800
SALES (est): 373.3K **Privately Held**
SIC: 2752 5943 Commercial printing, offset; office forms & supplies

(G-10894)
BUSTERS CEMENT PRODUCTS INC (PA)
3450 S Spiceland Rd (47362-9686)
PHONE....................................765 529-0287
Frank J Hayes, President
Steven Hayes, Vice Pres
Randall Hayes, Admin Sec
EMP: 10
SQ FT: 1,000
SALES (est): 733K **Privately Held**
SIC: 3273 3241 Ready-mixed concrete; cement, hydraulic

(G-10895)
C & C PALLETS AND LUMBER LLC
1611 S County Road 275 W (47362-9716)
PHONE....................................765 524-3214
Casey Polk, Mng Member
EMP: 4

SALES (est): 196.5K **Privately Held**
SIC: 2448 5211 4212 Pallets, wood; lumber products; local trucking, without storage

(G-10896)
CHASE ELECTRIC
1467 S County Road 250 E (47362-9577)
PHONE................................765 388-2183
Harry Chase, *Owner*
EMP: 2
SALES (est): 146.4K **Privately Held**
SIC: 3699 Electrical equipment & supplies

(G-10897)
COURIER-TIMES INC
Also Called: New Castle Courier Times
201 S 14th St (47362-3328)
PHONE................................765 529-1111
Fax: 765 529-1731
David Paxton, *Ch of Bd*
David Mathis, *VP Finance*
▲ EMP: 60
SQ FT: 17,000
SALES: 4MM
SALES (corp-wide): 318.6MM **Privately Held**
WEB: www.thecouriertimes.com
SIC: 2711 2791 2759 Newspapers, publishing & printing; typesetting; commercial printing
PA: Paxton Media Group, Llc
100 Television Ln
Paducah KY 42003
270 575-8630

(G-10898)
CROSS MODULAR SET INC
4429 N Prairie Rd (47362-9230)
PHONE................................765 836-1511
Weber Cross, *President*
Linda Cross, *Vice Pres*
EMP: 2
SALES (est): 132.4K **Privately Held**
SIC: 2452 Modular homes, prefabricated, wood

(G-10899)
CROWN EQUIPMENT CORPORATION
Also Called: Crown Lift Trucks
1817 I Ave (47362-2611)
PHONE................................765 520-2422
Lu Ann, *Branch Mgr*
EMP: 121
SALES (corp-wide): 3.1B **Privately Held**
SIC: 3537 Lift trucks, industrial: fork, platform, straddle, etc.
PA: Crown Equipment Corporation
44 S Washington St
New Bremen OH 45869
419 629-2311

(G-10900)
FERGYS CABINETS
2506 Grand Ave (47362-5301)
PHONE................................765 529-0116
Darrell Ferguson, *Owner*
EMP: 2
SALES (est): 125K **Privately Held**
SIC: 2434 5211 Wood kitchen cabinets; cabinets, kitchen

(G-10901)
FOAM RUBBER LLC
Also Called: Foam Rubber Products
2000 Troy Ave (47362-5364)
P.O. Box 525 (47362-0525)
PHONE................................765 521-2000
Fax: 765 521-2759
Don Cotleur, *General Mgr*
Lenny Tekippe, *General Mgr*
Terry Warrum, *CFO*
Mark Grogan, *Accounts Mgr*
Martin Gonzalez, *Officer*
▲ EMP: 225
SQ FT: 50,000
SALES (est): 52.4MM **Privately Held**
SIC: 3086 5199 Insulation or cushioning material, foamed plastic; foams & rubber

(G-10902)
FOUR STAR SCREEN PRINTING LLC
1379 N Cadiz Pike (47362-9742)
PHONE................................765 533-3006

Julia Miller, *Owner*
EMP: 2
SALES (est): 125.5K **Privately Held**
SIC: 2752 Commercial printing, lithographic

(G-10903)
GREDE LLC
Also Called: New Castle Foundry
2700 Plum St (47362-3045)
PHONE................................765 521-8000
Fax: 765 593-3202
Jeff Hipple, *Branch Mgr*
EMP: 200
SALES (corp-wide): 6.2B **Publicly Held**
WEB: www.grede.com
SIC: 3321 3714 3322 Gray & ductile iron foundries; motor vehicle parts & accessories; malleable iron foundries
HQ: Grede Llc
1 Towne Sq Ste 550
Southfield MI 48076

(G-10904)
HIBBING INTERNATIONAL FRICTION
2001 Troy Ave (47362-5365)
PHONE................................765 529-7001
Fax: 765 529-0727
James L Taylor Jr, *President*
EMP: 10
SQ FT: 21,000
SALES (est): 1.5MM **Privately Held**
WEB: www.hibbingfriction.com
SIC: 3499 5013 Friction material, made from powdered metal; automotive brakes

(G-10905)
HOOSIER WELDING
1726 S County Road 125 W (47362-8946)
PHONE................................765 521-4539
Jody Castle, *President*
Karen Castle, *Admin Sec*
EMP: 3
SALES (est): 130K **Privately Held**
SIC: 7692 Welding repair

(G-10906)
HORSE CIRCUIT NEWS INC
8098 E County Road 400 S (47362-9535)
PHONE................................800 537-3958
Fax: 765 332-2670
Jay Wicker, *President*
Elsie Flippo, *Admin Sec*
EMP: 2
SALES (est): 130.8K **Privately Held**
SIC: 2711 Newspapers: publishing only, not printed on site

(G-10907)
INTERNTIONAL PIPE CONS SLS LLC
900 New York Ave (47362-4423)
P.O. Box 366 (47362-0366)
PHONE................................765 388-2222
Tara Ryan, *CFO*
Tamara Blevins, *Mng Member*
EMP: 10
SALES (est): 3.5MM **Privately Held**
SIC: 3312 7389 Pipes & tubes;

(G-10908)
KARENS KOUNTRY KRAFTS
3916 Viking Trl (47362-8812)
PHONE................................765 238-2873
Karen Mitchell, *Principal*
EMP: 2
SALES (est): 62.3K **Privately Held**
SIC: 2022 Processed cheese

(G-10909)
KVK US TECHNOLOGIES INC
1016 S 25th St (47362-5367)
PHONE................................765 529-1100
Chad McClung, *President*
Kevin Winters, *Mfg Staff*
EMP: 2 EST: 2007
SQ FT: 26,000
SALES: 1.2MM **Privately Held**
SIC: 2821 Plastics materials & resins

(G-10910)
MAGNA MACHINE & TOOL CO INC
3722 N Messick Rd (47362-9315)
PHONE................................765 766-5388
Fax: 765 766-5300
Eugene Weaver, *President*
Michael Broyles, *Treasurer*
EMP: 45 EST: 1975
SQ FT: 26,000
SALES (est): 8.8MM **Privately Held**
WEB: www.magnamachine.com
SIC: 3599 Machine shop, jobbing & repair; custom machinery

(G-10911)
MARGISON GRAPHICS LLC
Also Called: Margison Sign Company
1813 S Memorial Dr (47362-1217)
PHONE................................765 529-8250
Fax: 765 529-8253
Bryant Margison, *Software Dev*
Debbie Margison,
▼ EMP: 3
SQ FT: 5,500
SALES (est): 324K **Privately Held**
SIC: 3993 Signs, not made in custom sign painting shops

(G-10912)
MD/LF INCORPORATED
Also Called: Organi Gro
187 S Denny Dr (47362-9138)
PHONE................................765 575-8130
Dave Denison, *President*
EMP: 6
SQ FT: 2,000
SALES (est): 597.5K **Privately Held**
SIC: 2875 Fertilizers, mixing only

(G-10913)
NEW CASTLE SAW MILL
2910 Outer Dr (47362-2068)
PHONE................................765 529-6635
Fax: 765 529-4528
Ronald Gross, *President*
EMP: 7
SALES (est): 610K **Privately Held**
SIC: 2421 5211 Sawmills & planing mills, general; lumber products

(G-10914)
OLSON RACE CARS
129 N 26th St (47362-3430)
PHONE................................765 529-6933
Herb Olson, *Owner*
EMP: 2
SALES (est): 138.5K **Privately Held**
SIC: 3711 5531 Automobile assembly, including specialty automobiles; speed shops, including race car supplies

(G-10915)
QUALITY FABRICATION IND INC
3174 S Commerce Dr (47362-8743)
P.O. Box 1110 (47362-7110)
PHONE................................765 529-9776
Fax: 765 529-9718
Howard Rader, *President*
Todd Rader, *Vice Pres*
Gary Brown, *Manager*
EMP: 18
SALES (est): 3.5MM **Privately Held**
SIC: 3441 Fabricated structural metal

(G-10916)
R&S SIGN DESIGN
Also Called: Visual Values
3963 S State Road 103 (47362-8701)
PHONE................................765 520-5594
Fax: 765 593-1262
Jim Howard, *Owner*
EMP: 3
SALES (est): 130K **Privately Held**
SIC: 3993 Signs & advertising specialties

(G-10917)
SCREEN PRINT EXPRESS INC
Also Called: Screen Printing
1107 Fleming St (47362-4236)
PHONE................................765 521-2727
Fax: 765 529-1059
Michael Dickins, *President*
EMP: 3
SQ FT: 2,300

SALES (est): 172.8K **Privately Held**
SIC: 2759 Screen printing

(G-10918)
SIDELINE GRAPHIX
319 Parkview Dr (47362-2972)
PHONE................................765 520-9042
Risa Bowers, *Owner*
Mark Bowers, *Co-Owner*
EMP: 2
SALES (est): 182.9K **Privately Held**
SIC: 2759 Screen printing

(G-10919)
THREAD CREATIONS INC
2004 S Memorial Dr (47362-1220)
PHONE................................765 521-3886
Fax: 765 521-0905
Sheri Stockton, *President*
Cheri Stockton, *President*
EMP: 2 EST: 1993
SALES (est): 114.6K **Privately Held**
SIC: 2395 2396 Embroidery products, except schiffli machine; screen printing on fabric articles

(G-10920)
TS TECH INDIANA LLC
3800 Brooks Dr (47362-8758)
PHONE................................765 465-4294
Masashi Sawada, *President*
Paul Giertz, *Safety Mgr*
Jason MA, *Treasurer*
Terry Kamphaus, *Manager*
Tetsuya Takahashi, *Admin Sec*
▲ EMP: 3
SALES (est): 10.6MM
SALES (corp-wide): 4.5B **Privately Held**
SIC: 2531 Seats, automobile
HQ: Ts Tech Americas, Inc.
8458 E Broad St
Reynoldsburg OH 43068
614 575-4100

(G-10921)
WESTERN PRODUCTS INDIANA INC
387 W State Road 38 (47362-9786)
P.O. Box 545 (47362-0545)
PHONE................................765 529-6230
Roger K Crowe, *President*
Charles Nelson, *Vice Pres*
Michelle Crabtree, *Office Mgr*
EMP: 15
SQ FT: 46,225
SALES (est): 3.4MM **Privately Held**
SIC: 3452 3429 Bolts, nuts, rivets & washers; manufactured hardware (general)

(G-10922)
WIMMER MFG INC
201 W County Road 100 S (47362-9769)
P.O. Box 43 (47362-0043)
PHONE................................765 465-9846
Kyle York, *Manager*
EMP: 12
SALES (est): 1MM **Privately Held**
SIC: 3999 Manufacturing industries

(G-10923)
WIMMER VAULTS INC
Also Called: Wimmer Burial Vaults
900 New York Ave (47362-4423)
P.O. Box 607 (47362-0607)
PHONE................................765 529-5702
Greg York, *President*
EMP: 9 EST: 1910
SQ FT: 10,000
SALES (est): 530K **Privately Held**
SIC: 3272 Burial vaults, concrete or precast terrazzo

New Harmony
Posey County

(G-10924)
CDG OPERATION LLC
6555 Griffin Rd (47631-9400)
PHONE................................812 682-3770
Dick Campbell, *Mng Member*
EMP: 12
SALES (est): 1MM **Privately Held**
SIC: 2911 Oils, fuel

▲ = Import ▼=Export
◆ =Import/Export

(G-10925)
POSEY COUNTY NEWS
801 North St (47631)
PHONE..................................812 682-3950
Donna Kohlmeyer, *Principal*
EMP: 5
SALES (est): 237.8K **Privately Held**
SIC: 2711 Job printing & newspaper publishing combined

New Haven
Allen County

(G-10926)
AFFORDABLE SOUNDS INC
10848 Rose Ave Ste 3 (46774-8912)
PHONE..................................260 493-7742
Fax: 260 493-7742
Brad Stanfield, *President*
EMP: 2
SALES (est): 168.4K **Privately Held**
SIC: 3842 Hearing aids

(G-10927)
ALEPH BET DOCUMENT CENTRE
13539 Old 24 E (46774-9006)
PHONE..................................260 749-2288
Samuel Wahli, *Principal*
EMP: 2
SALES (est): 223.3K **Privately Held**
SIC: 2752 Commercial printing, lithographic

(G-10928)
ALMET INC
300 Hartzell Rd (46774-1123)
P.O. Box 346 (46774-0346)
PHONE..................................260 493-1556
Fax: 260 493-1299
James R Greim, *Principal*
Joyce Nahrwold, *Corp Secy*
Thomas A Bada, *Vice Pres*
Gregory H Lynch, *Vice Pres*
EMP: 63 **EST:** 1969
SQ FT: 100,000
SALES (est): 16.2MM **Privately Held**
WEB: www.almet.com
SIC: 3441 Building components, structural steel; joists, open web steel; long-span series

(G-10929)
AMOS D GRABER & SONS
5229 Bruick Rd (46774-9760)
PHONE..................................260 749-0526
Amos D Graber Sr, *Owner*
EMP: 10
SALES: 495K **Privately Held**
SIC: 7699 7692 5661 Blacksmith shop; welding repair; shoe stores

(G-10930)
B S T ENTERPRISES INC
1900 Summit St (46774-9583)
P.O. Box 305 (46774-0305)
PHONE..................................260 493-4313
Fax: 260 493-4576
Barry K Stroh, *President*
Sharon Stroh, *Corp Secy*
EMP: 6
SQ FT: 14,000
SALES (est): 900K **Privately Held**
SIC: 3544 3599 Special dies, tools, jigs & fixtures; machine shop, jobbing & repair

(G-10931)
BOE KNOWS MOLD
488 Courtney Dr (46774-2626)
PHONE..................................260 760-7136
Robert McDowell, *Owner*
EMP: 2 **EST:** 2010
SALES (est): 138.3K **Privately Held**
SIC: 3544 Industrial molds

(G-10932)
BUCHAN LOGGING INC
Also Called: Buchan Saw Mill
2802 Ryan Rd (46774-9634)
PHONE..................................260 749-4697
Daniel Buchan, *President*
EMP: 10

SALES (est): 610K **Privately Held**
SIC: 2411 Logging camps & contractors

(G-10933)
CABLECRAFT MOTION CONTROLS LLC (PA)
2110 Summit St (46774-9524)
PHONE..................................260 749-5105
John Leech, *CEO*
Christopher Carmien,
▲ **EMP:** 251
SALES (est): 96.4MM **Privately Held**
SIC: 3315 3568 Steel wire & related products; power transmission equipment

(G-10934)
CHALLENGE TOOL & MFG INC
Also Called: Ctm
11725 Lincoln Hwy E (46774-9386)
P.O. Box 306 (46774-0306)
PHONE..................................260 749-9558
Fax: 260 749-6724
Larry Redmon, *President*
Gary Collins, *Vice Pres*
Colleen Fuelling, *Purch Dir*
Chris Kendall, *Engineer*
Howard Dager, *Human Res Dir*
EMP: 68 **EST:** 1968
SQ FT: 100,000
SALES (est): 14MM **Privately Held**
WEB: www.ctm-inc.com
SIC: 3631 Household cooking equipment

(G-10935)
CONTINENTAL DIAMOND TOOL CORP
1221 Hartzell St (46774-1418)
P.O. Box 126 (46774-0126)
PHONE..................................260 493-1294
Fax: 260 749-7326
Debra S Viggiano, *President*
Jennifer Fisher, *Purchasing*
Karl Zimmerman, *Sales Staff*
Jordan Donnelly, *Manager*
Raymond P Viggiano, *Admin Sec*
EMP: 42
SQ FT: 20,000
SALES (est): 9.6MM **Privately Held**
WEB: www.cdtusa.net
SIC: 3541 Machine tools, metal cutting type; saws, power (metalworking machinery); grinding machines, metalworking

(G-10936)
CSC-INDIANA LLC
2190 Summit St (46774-9524)
PHONE..................................708 625-3255
Mike Rubinstein, *CFO*
▲ **EMP:** 50
SQ FT: 250,000
SALES (est): 15.5MM **Privately Held**
SIC: 2653 Sheets, solid fiber: made from purchased materials

(G-10937)
CSD GROUP INC
Also Called: Custom Sound Designs
3003 Ryan Rd (46774-9347)
PHONE..................................260 918-3500
Doug Hood, *President*
EMP: 20
SQ FT: 1,500
SALES (est): 4.4MM **Privately Held**
SIC: 3651 5099 Audio electronic systems; sound reproducing equipment; video & audio equipment

(G-10938)
DENNIS ADAMS INC
Also Called: D & D Auto Detailing Sups
5108 N Webster Rd (46774-9706)
P.O. Box 143 (46774-0143)
PHONE..................................260 493-4829
Dennis Adams, *President*
EMP: 2
SALES: 103K **Privately Held**
SIC: 2842 Cleaning or polishing preparations

(G-10939)
EZ CUT TOOL LLC
110 Rose Ave (46774-1129)
PHONE..................................260 748-0732
Steven Michaels,
EMP: 4 **EST:** 2008

SALES (est): 714.1K **Privately Held**
SIC: 3541 Machine tools, metal cutting type

(G-10940)
GANAL CORPORATION
Also Called: New Haven Bakery
915 Lincoln Hwy E (46774-1424)
PHONE..................................260 749-2161
Fax: 260 749-4687
George Branning, *President*
Nancy Branning, *Admin Sec*
EMP: 8
SQ FT: 1,600
SALES (est): 414.2K **Privately Held**
SIC: 5461 2051 Bread; bread, cake & related products

(G-10941)
GLAZE TOOL AND ENGINEERING INC
1610 Summit St (46774-1522)
P.O. Box 267 (46774-0267)
PHONE..................................260 493-4557
Fax: 260 493-3489
E William Glaze, *President*
Barbara J Glaze, *Corp Secy*
E William Glaze Jr, *Vice Pres*
Greg Maxwell, *Engineer*
Tyson Biehl, *Manager*
EMP: 30
SQ FT: 18,000
SALES (est): 6.5MM **Privately Held**
WEB: www.glazetool.com
SIC: 3544 3569 3549 Industrial molds; assembly machines, non-metalworking; metalworking machinery

(G-10942)
HARTMAN BROTHERS HEAT & AC
535 Green St (46774-1470)
PHONE..................................260 493-4402
Fax: 260 493-4975
Richard Hartman, *President*
Arnold Hartman, *Principal*
Lester Hartman, *Corp Secy*
EMP: 18
SQ FT: 4,000
SALES (est): 3.6MM **Privately Held**
WEB: www.hartmanbrothers.com
SIC: 1711 1761 3444 Warm air heating & air conditioning contractor; sheet metalwork; sheet metalwork

(G-10943)
HINTON KEITH & HINTON TAMMY
442 Lincoln Hwy W (46774-2164)
PHONE..................................260 749-4867
EMP: 2
SALES (est): 100.6K **Privately Held**
SIC: 3949 Mfg Sporting/Athletic Goods

(G-10944)
ILF INDUSTRIES
9702 Greenmoor Dr (46774-1940)
PHONE..................................260 749-1931
David Menze, *Owner*
EMP: 2
SALES (est): 50.3K **Privately Held**
SIC: 2731 Pamphlets: publishing & printing

(G-10945)
JCR AUTOMATION INC
1426 Ryan Rd (46774-9635)
PHONE..................................260 749-6606
Rick Johnson, *President*
Paul Rush, *Business Mgr*
Carlo Renninger, *Vice Pres*
Ashley Lanier, *Purchasing*
Darrick Snyder, *Technology*
EMP: 12
SQ FT: 12,000
SALES (est): 1.3MM **Privately Held**
WEB: jcrautomation.com
SIC: 3549 Assembly machines, including robotic; marking machines, metalworking

(G-10946)
KILLER CAMAROS CUSTOM CAMARO
Also Called: Killer Car Customs
4762 Zelt Cv (46774-3143)
PHONE..................................260 255-2425

Debra Ferguson, *Owner*
EMP: 3 **EST:** 2011
SALES (est): 180K **Privately Held**
SIC: 3714 Instrument board assemblies, motor vehicle

(G-10947)
KWIK LOK CORPORATION INDIANA
1222 Ryan Rd (46774-9350)
P.O. Box 96 (46774-0096)
PHONE..................................260 493-1220
Fax: 260 493-4797
Jerry H Paxton, *President*
◆ **EMP:** 60 **EST:** 1960
SQ FT: 20,000
SALES (est): 16.1MM **Privately Held**
WEB: www.kwiklok.com
SIC: 3565 Packaging machinery
HQ: Kwik Lok Corporation
2712 S 16th Ave
Yakima WA 98903
509 248-4770

(G-10948)
MASON TOTAL PROPERTY CARE
3706 Norland Ln (46774-1959)
PHONE..................................260 385-3573
Angela Mason, *Principal*
EMP: 3
SALES (est): 108.8K **Privately Held**
SIC: 2851 0783 Paints & allied products; ornamental shrub & tree services

(G-10949)
NEW HAVEN TROPHIES & SHIRTS
710 Broadway St (46774-1602)
PHONE..................................260 749-0269
Fax: 260 749-2983
William Snyder, *President*
EMP: 5
SQ FT: 8,000
SALES (est): 420K **Privately Held**
SIC: 2759 5999 Screen printing; trophies & plaques

(G-10950)
NORMAN STEIN & ASSOCIATES
9520 Paulding Rd (46774-9693)
PHONE..................................260 749-5468
Norman Stein, *President*
Beverly Stein, *Vice Pres*
EMP: 13
SQ FT: 7,200
SALES (est): 1.9MM **Privately Held**
WEB: www.normanstein.com
SIC: 5088 3443 Tanks & tank components; tanks, standard or custom fabricated: metal plate

(G-10951)
PARKER-HANNIFIN CORPORATION
Also Called: Climate Systems Division
10801 Rose Ave (46774-9576)
PHONE..................................260 748-6000
Tim Louvar, *Senior Engr*
Adrian Clark, *Human Res Mgr*
Morgan Jarrett, *Sales Engr*
Darryl Miller, *Branch Mgr*
Mark Hunsberger, *Manager*
EMP: 600
SALES (corp-wide): 12B **Publicly Held**
WEB: www.parker.com
SIC: 3492 3585 3494 3429 Hose & tube fittings & assemblies, hydraulic/pneumatic; refrigeration & heating equipment; valves & pipe fittings; manufactured hardware (general)
PA: Parker-Hannifin Corporation
6035 Parkland Blvd
Cleveland OH 44124
216 896-3000

(G-10952)
PETER FRANKLIN JEWELERS INC (PA)
507 Broadway St (46774-1403)
PHONE..................................260 749-4315
Fax: 260 749-4315
Peter Franklin Ball, *President*
Alexa Thomas, *Sales Associate*
Jordan Wills, *Sales Associate*

G
E
O
G
R
A
P
H
I
C

Roger Tackett, *Branch Mgr*
EMP: 5
SQ FT: 800
SALES (est): 1.8MM **Privately Held**
WEB: www.peterfranklinjewelers.com
SIC: 3911 5944 Jewelry, precious metal; jewelry, precious stones & precious metals

(G-10953)
PETERS ENTERPRISES
Also Called: Peters Equipment
217 State Road 930 W (46774-2147)
PHONE......................260 493-6435
Ron Peters, *Owner*
Marylou Peters, *Co-Owner*
EMP: 3
SALES (est): 140.4K **Privately Held**
SIC: 3524 Lawn & garden tractors & equipment

(G-10954)
PRIORITY ELECTRONICS LLC
10104 Paulding Rd (46774-9363)
PHONE......................260 749-0143
Joseph Oberlin,
EMP: 4 **EST:** 2012
SALES (est): 660.2K **Privately Held**
SIC: 3679 7389 Harness assemblies for electronic use: wire or cable;

(G-10955)
S & S OPTICAL CO INC
416 Ann St (46774-1278)
PHONE......................260 749-9614
Fax: 260 749-5328
Richard Stein, *President*
Arno Stein, *Treasurer*
Suzanne Stein, *Admin Sec*
EMP: 16 **EST:** 1965
SQ FT: 14,000
SALES (est): 2MM **Privately Held**
SIC: 3229 3827 Pressed & blown glass; optical instruments & lenses

(G-10956)
S & W SWING SETS
17007 Doty Rd (46774-9726)
PHONE......................260 414-6200
Sam Schmucker, *Partner*
William Graver, *Partner*
EMP: 2 **EST:** 1989
SALES: 100K **Privately Held**
WEB: www.sandwswingset.com
SIC: 3949 5945 Playground equipment; hobby, toy & game shops

(G-10957)
SCHMUCKER WOODWORKING LLC
13131 Ehle Rd (46774-9753)
PHONE......................260 413-9784
Matthew Schmucker, *Mng Member*
EMP: 4 **EST:** 2014
SALES (est): 310.7K **Privately Held**
SIC: 2431 Millwork

(G-10958)
SDI LAFARGA LLC
Also Called: La Farga
1640 Ryan Rd (46774-9240)
PHONE......................260 748-6565
Jerry Evans, *Maint Spvr*
Derek Ham, *Engineer*
Thomas W Scrogham, *Finance*
Kandy White, *Sales Staff*
Kurt Breischaft,
▲ **EMP:** 56 **EST:** 2010
SALES (est): 22.3MM **Privately Held**
SIC: 3351 Copper & copper alloy sheet, strip, plate & products

(G-10959)
SUPERIOR ALUMINUM ALLOYS LLC
14214 Edgerton Rd (46774-9636)
PHONE......................260 749-7599
Fax: 260 749-7598
Denny Luma, *Principal*
Jeff Makofka, *Manager*
▼ **EMP:** 123 **EST:** 1997
SQ FT: 180,000

SALES (est): 40.4MM **Publicly Held**
WEB: www.superioraluminumalloys.com
SIC: 3341 5051 Aluminum smelting & refining (secondary); aluminum bars, rods, ingots, sheets, pipes, plates, etc.
HQ: Omnisource, Llc
7575 W Jefferson Blvd
Fort Wayne IN 46804
260 422-5541

(G-10960)
T N D PRINTING
Also Called: T & D Printing
514 Broadway St Ste 100 (46774-1487)
PHONE......................260 493-4949
Fax: 260 493-1918
Gary Swaidner, *Owner*
EMP: 4
SQ FT: 1,200
SALES: 225K **Privately Held**
SIC: 2759 Commercial printing

(G-10961)
TRINITY CSTM BUILT PALLETS LLC
12802 Irving Rd (46774-9489)
PHONE......................260 466-4625
Mitchel Thompson, *Administration*
EMP: 3
SALES (est): 145K **Privately Held**
SIC: 2448 Wood pallets & skids

(G-10962)
U B MACHINE INC
1615 Lincoln Hwy E (46774-1569)
P.O. Box 673 (46774-0673)
PHONE......................260 493-3381
Fax: 260 493-4663
Greg Urbine, *President*
Lori Case, *Office Mgr*
EMP: 20
SQ FT: 1,300
SALES (est): 2.6MM **Privately Held**
SIC: 3711 5531 3714 Chassis, motor vehicle; automotive & home supply stores; motor vehicle parts & accessories

New Market
Montgomery County

(G-10963)
JOE WOODROW
Also Called: New Market Welding
107 W Main St (47965-5004)
P.O. Box 312 (47965-0312)
PHONE......................765 866-0436
Fax: 765 866-0436
Joe Woodrow, *Owner*
Teresa Woodrow, *Co-Owner*
EMP: 4
SALES (est): 85.7K **Privately Held**
SIC: 7692 Welding repair

(G-10964)
MONUMENTAL STONE WORKS INC
105 S 3rd St (47965-5018)
P.O. Box 112 (47965-0112)
PHONE......................765 866-0658
Fax: 765 866-0719
Friederich Rademacher, *President*
EMP: 22
SQ FT: 5,000
SALES: 1MM **Privately Held**
SIC: 3272 Cast stone, concrete

New Palestine
Hancock County

(G-10965)
ACE SCREEN PRINTING LLC
4220 S 650 W (46163-9127)
PHONE......................317 861-7477
Kamafily Sissoko, *Principal*
EMP: 2
SALES (est): 92.3K **Privately Held**
SIC: 2752 Commercial printing, lithographic

(G-10966)
ALL STAR TURF MANAGEMENT LLC
7441 W Creekside Ct (46163-9557)
PHONE......................317 861-1234
Nathan C Johnson, *Principal*
EMP: 4
SALES (est): 286.1K **Privately Held**
SIC: 3523 Turf & grounds equipment

(G-10967)
ANASAZI INSTRUMENTS INC
23 S Westside Dr A (46163-1113)
PHONE......................317 861-7657
Craig H Bradley, *President*
Bill Beardon, *Vice Pres*
Christopher Tully, *Vice Pres*
Craig Bradley, *QC Mgr*
Tom Goldsmith, *Engineer*
EMP: 12
SQ FT: 8,000
SALES: 3.1MM **Privately Held**
SIC: 3826 Spectrometers

(G-10968)
BRANDYWINE VINYRD & WINERY LLC
8437 W 1200 N (46163-9300)
PHONE......................317 403-5669
Jennifer Baker, *Principal*
EMP: 4
SALES (est): 147.5K **Privately Held**
SIC: 2084 Wines

(G-10969)
CARTER CABINET CO INC
5839 S 600 W (46163-9519)
PHONE......................317 985-5782
Tom Carter, *Principal*
EMP: 2
SALES (est): 165.5K **Privately Held**
SIC: 2434 Wood kitchen cabinets

(G-10970)
HEIDENREICH WOODWORKING INC
4175 S Kelly Dr (46163-9060)
PHONE......................317 861-9331
Robert Heidenreich, *Principal*
EMP: 2
SALES (est): 155.3K **Privately Held**
SIC: 2431 Millwork

(G-10971)
INFORMA BUSINESS MEDIA INC
Also Called: American Trucker
4639 W Stonehaven Ln (46163-8657)
P.O. Box 603, Indianapolis (46206-0603)
PHONE......................317 233-1310
Ellen Rowlett, *Manager*
EMP: 30 **Privately Held**
SIC: 2721 Magazines: publishing only, not printed on site
HQ: Informa Business Media, Inc.
605 3rd Ave
New York NY 10158
212 204-4200

(G-10972)
INTEGRITY MACHINE SYSTEMS
22 S Westside Dr (46163-1113)
PHONE......................317 897-3338
Tom East, *Principal*
EMP: 24
SALES (est): 5.2MM **Privately Held**
SIC: 3541 Machine tools, metal cutting type

(G-10973)
T & S ENGINEERING LLC
34 N Depot St Ste B (46163-8685)
PHONE......................812 969-3860
Fax: 317 861-4241
Richard Thomas,
EMP: 4
SQ FT: 2,500
SALES: 140K **Privately Held**
SIC: 3599 Machine & other job shop work

(G-10974)
WISE PRINTING INC
3721 S Fallow Trl (46163-9129)
PHONE......................317 861-6220
David Wise, *Principal*
EMP: 2

SALES (est): 164.1K **Privately Held**
SIC: 2752 Commercial printing, lithographic

New Paris
Elkhart County

(G-10975)
BETTER WAY PARTNERS LLC
Also Called: Better Way Products
70891 County Road 23 (46553-9771)
PHONE......................574 831-3340
Fax: 574 831-3611
Roger Korenstra, *Mng Member*
Bruce Korenstra,
Andy Peachey, *Real Est Agnt*
Denise Scott, *Real Est Agnt*
EMP: 420
SQ FT: 71,000
SALES (est): 88.6MM
SALES (corp-wide): 1.6B **Publicly Held**
WEB: www.dockbox.com
SIC: 3089 Laminating of plastic
PA: Patrick Industries, Inc.
107 W Franklin St
Elkhart IN 46516
574 294-7511

(G-10976)
COUNTRY COMPACT
69594 County Road 117 (46553-9797)
PHONE......................574 831-6682
Enos Weaver, *Owner*
EMP: 3
SALES (est): 263.5K **Privately Held**
SIC: 3524 Lawn & garden tractors & equipment

(G-10977)
DENNIS POLK & ASSOCIATES INC
Also Called: Polk, Dennis Equipment
4916 N Sr 15 (46553)
P.O. Box 326, Leesburg (46538-0326)
PHONE......................574 831-3555
Dennis Polk, *President*
Pam Polk, *Corp Secy*
Jared Frantz, *Sales Staff*
▲ **EMP:** 8
SALES (est): 1.3MM **Privately Held**
SIC: 5083 2721 Agricultural machinery & equipment; magazines: publishing only, not printed on site

(G-10978)
ELKHART COUNTY GRAVEL INC (PA)
19242 Us Highway 6 (46553-9763)
PHONE......................574 831-2815
Fax: 574 831-2914
Barney C Beer, *President*
Tracey Beer, *Corp Secy*
Rodney D Beer, *Vice Pres*
EMP: 10
SQ FT: 1,500
SALES: 5.4MM **Privately Held**
SIC: 1442 Sand mining; gravel mining

(G-10979)
EXCHANGE PUBLISHING CORP
Also Called: Farmers Exchange
19401 Industrial Dr (46553-9714)
P.O. Box 45 (46553-0045)
PHONE......................574 831-2138
Fax: 574 831-2131
Steve Yeater, *President*
Matt Yeater, *Principal*
Jerry Goshert, *Editor*
Courtney Lipply, *Assoc Editor*
EMP: 20
SQ FT: 11,500
SALES (est): 682K **Privately Held**
SIC: 2711 Job printing & newspaper publishing combined

(G-10980)
FOAMITURE
19240 Tarman Rd (46553-9117)
PHONE......................574 831-4775
Robert Steury, *Principal*
EMP: 2

SALES (est): 121.7K **Privately Held**
SIC: 3999 Barber & beauty shop equipment

(G-10981)
HERES YOUR SIGN DIY WORKSHOP &
18808 County Road 46 (46553-9645)
PHONE..................................574 238-6369
Kimberly Neff, *Principal*
EMP: 2
SALES (est): 72.6K **Privately Held**
SIC: 3993 Signs & advertising specialties

(G-10982)
HI POINT MACHINE AND TOOL INC
19519 Industrial Dr 2 (46553-9636)
P.O. Box 9 (46553-0009)
PHONE..................................574 831-5361
Don Muhlnickel Jr, *President*
EMP: 3
SQ FT: 6,000
SALES (est): 344.8K **Privately Held**
SIC: 3599 Machine shop, jobbing & repair

(G-10983)
HOOSIER WOOD CREATIONS INC
19881 County Road 146 (46553-9657)
P.O. Box 831, Goshen (46527-0831)
PHONE..................................574 831-6330
Mark Eash, *President*
Willard Shetler, *Corp Secy*
Harry Hostetler, *Shareholder*
EMP: 60
SQ FT: 8,000
SALES (est): 6.3MM **Privately Held**
SIC: 2511 Wood household furniture

(G-10984)
HOOVER WELL DRILLING INC
20477 County Road 46 (46553-9609)
P.O. Box 187 (46553-0187)
PHONE..................................574 831-4901
William Hoover, *President*
EMP: 9
SALES (est): 1.1MM **Privately Held**
WEB: www.hoover.org
SIC: 1381 1781 Drilling oil & gas wells; water well drilling

(G-10985)
INDEPENDENT PROTECTION CO INC
Also Called: Turtle Top
67895 Industrial Dr (46553-9634)
PHONE..................................574 831-5680
Fax: 574 831-3407
Phil Tom, *Branch Mgr*
Timm Bledsoe, *Telecom Exec*
EMP: 60
SALES (corp-wide): 58.3MM **Privately Held**
WEB: www.ipclp.com
SIC: 3643 3792 3713 3711 Lightning protection equipment; travel trailers & campers; truck & bus bodies; motor vehicles & car bodies; van conversion; recreational van conversion (self-propelled), factory basis
PA: Independent Protection Company, Inc.
     1607 S Main St
     Goshen IN 46526
     574 533-4116

(G-10986)
ITERA LLC
19260 County Road 46 # 3 (46553-9660)
P.O. Box 110 (46553-0110)
PHONE..................................574 538-3838
Bostjan Jevsek, *Mng Member*
Vanesa Carlson,
EMP: 5
SQ FT: 10,000
SALES: 650K **Privately Held**
SIC: 2452 Modular homes, prefabricated, wood

(G-10987)
J W WOODWORKING INC
72057 County Road 17 (46553-9659)
PHONE..................................574 831-3033
Jim Wise, *President*
David Wise, *Shareholder*

EMP: 4
SQ FT: 10,000
SALES: 550K **Privately Held**
SIC: 2511 2431 2521 2541 Wood household furniture; kitchen & dining room furniture; staircases & stairs, wood; desks, office; wood; store & office display cases & fixtures

(G-10988)
KOUNTRY KRAFT WOOD PRODUCTS
68604 County Road 15 (46553-9786)
PHONE..................................574 831-6736
Fax: 574 831-6733
Elias Martin, *Owner*
EMP: 5
SALES (est): 50K **Privately Held**
SIC: 2511 Wood household furniture

(G-10989)
KREUTER MANUFACTURING CO INC (PA)
Also Called: KMC Controls
19476 Industrial Dr (46553-9714)
PHONE..................................574 831-4626
Fax: 574 831-4628
Jon Hilberg, *President*
Kent James, *President*
Gary Ganger, *COO*
Doug Miller, *Vice Pres*
Scott Taylor, *Vice Pres*
▲ EMP: 5
SQ FT: 77,000
SALES (est): 34.7MM **Privately Held**
SIC: 3625 Control equipment, electric

(G-10990)
MERCHANTS METALS LLC
71347 County Road 23 (46553-9145)
PHONE..................................574 831-4060
Fax: 574 831-3515
Tim Moore, *Plant Mgr*
Ernest Heimann, *Branch Mgr*
EMP: 70
SALES (corp-wide): 2.2B **Privately Held**
SIC: 3315 1799 Chain link fencing; fence construction
HQ: Merchants Metals Llc
     211 Perimeter Center Pkwy
     Atlanta GA 30346
     770 741-0300

(G-10991)
MIKE GROSS
68080 County Road 23 (46553-9707)
PHONE..................................574 529-2201
Mike Gross, *Principal*
EMP: 2 EST: 2016
SALES (est): 89.8K **Privately Held**
SIC: 2411 Logging

(G-10992)
ROLANDS PROCESSING
68417 County Road 15 (46553-9786)
PHONE..................................574 831-4301
Roland Martin, *Owner*
EMP: 3
SALES (est): 233.3K **Privately Held**
SIC: 2099 Food preparations

(G-10993)
ROTATIONAL MOLDING TECH INC
Also Called: Romotech
67742 County Road 23 # 1 (46553-9186)
PHONE..................................574 831-6450
Fax: 574 831-7450
Dave Smith, *President*
Marian Mantel, *Vice Pres*
Kevin Cox, *Safety Mgr*
Jim Wolfe, *Purch Mgr*
Diana Coleman, *Manager*
EMP: 60
SQ FT: 3,335,000
SALES (est): 11.5MM **Privately Held**
WEB: www.romotek.com
SIC: 3089 Molding primary plastic

(G-10994)
SMOKER CRAFT INC (PA)
68143 Clunette St (46553-3700)
P.O. Box 65 (46553-0065)
PHONE..................................574 831-2103
Fax: 574 831-7003

Douglas Smoker, *President*
Byron Smoker, *Vice Pres*
Ben Robbins, *Buyer*
Grace Spero, *Sales Staff*
Mark Peppel, *Manager*
▼ EMP: 475 EST: 1869
SQ FT: 500,000
SALES: 165MM **Privately Held**
WEB: www.smokercraft.com
SIC: 3732 5551 3731 Motorized boat, building & repairing; boat dealers; ferryboats, building & repairing

(G-10995)
STARCRAFT MARINE LLC
Also Called: Monark Marine
68143 Clunette St (46553-3700)
P.O. Box 65 (46553-0065)
PHONE..................................574 831-2103
Harold A Schrock, *President*
Joseph Blackburn,
Doug Smoker,
▼ EMP: 260
SQ FT: 280,000
SALES (est): 36.5MM **Privately Held**
WEB: www.starcraftmarine.com
SIC: 3732 Pontoons, except aircraft & inflatable; boats, fiberglass: building & repairing

(G-10996)
STEVE MITCHELL
Also Called: Precision Tool
69420 County Road 27 (46553-9739)
PHONE..................................574 831-4848
Fax: 574 831-4851
Steve Mitchell, *Owner*
EMP: 7
SQ FT: 4,000
SALES (est): 522.1K **Privately Held**
SIC: 3452 3599 Bolts, metal; machine shop, jobbing & repair

(G-10997)
SYLVAN MARINE INC (PA)
Also Called: Smoker Craft
68143 Clunette St (46553-3700)
P.O. Box 65 (46553-0065)
PHONE..................................574 831-2950
Doug Smoker, *President*
Peter Barrett, *Chief Mktg Ofcr*
Monir Elzalaki, *Manager*
▼ EMP: 400
SALES (est): 32.9MM **Privately Held**
WEB: www.sylvanmarine.com
SIC: 3732 Boat building & repairing

(G-10998)
T S MANUFACTURING
68563 County Road 17 (46553-9790)
PHONE..................................574 831-6647
Lenius Martin, *Principal*
EMP: 2
SALES (est): 170.9K **Privately Held**
SIC: 3999 Manufacturing industries

(G-10999)
TRAVEL LITE INC
71913 County Road 23 (46553-9770)
PHONE..................................574 831-3000
Larry Johns, *President*
Dustin Johns, *Vice Pres*
Lindsey Johns, *Sales Staff*
▼ EMP: 40 EST: 1998
SQ FT: 40,000
SALES: 5.9MM **Privately Held**
WEB: www.travellitecampers.com
SIC: 3715 Truck trailers

(G-11000)
VEADA INDUSTRIES INC
19240 Tarman Rd (46553-9117)
P.O. Box 26 (46553-0026)
PHONE..................................574 831-4775
Fax: 574 831-4609
Robert W Steury, *President*
Douglas V Steury, *Vice Pres*
Chris Hamadanchi, *Purch Mgr*
David Hartzler, *Accountant*
Rose Hochstetler, *Human Res Dir*
▼ EMP: 540
SQ FT: 100,000

SALES (est): 68.9MM **Privately Held**
WEB: www.veada.com
SIC: 2394 2531 3732 2392 Canvas & related products; tents: made from purchased materials; vehicle furniture; boat building & repairing; household furnishings

(G-11001)
WORLD MISSIONARY PRESS INC
19168 County Road 146 (46553-9225)
P.O. Box 120 (46553-0120)
PHONE..................................574 831-2111
Fax: 574 831-2161
Jay E Benson, *President*
Vicky R Benson, *Vice Pres*
Wes Culver, *Vice Pres*
Robert Moore, *Vice Pres*
Marie C Mack, *Treasurer*
▼ EMP: 46 EST: 1961
SQ FT: 30,344
SALES: 4.6MM **Privately Held**
WEB: www.wmpress.org
SIC: 2731 Books: publishing & printing

(G-11002)
YODERS CUSTOM SERVICE
Also Called: Yoder's Lockworks
18638 County Road 46 (46553-9105)
PHONE..................................574 831-4717
Weldon Yoder, *Owner*
EMP: 2
SALES (est): 130K **Privately Held**
SIC: 3873 Watches, clocks, watchcases & parts

New Point
Decatur County

(G-11003)
NEW POINT PRODUCTS INC
Also Called: New Point Products Martguild
8563 E State Rte 46 (47263)
PHONE..................................812 663-6311
Fax: 812 663-5530
Paul F Laugle, *President*
Cathy Laugle, *Admin Sec*
EMP: 9
SQ FT: 6,000
SALES (est): 1.2MM **Privately Held**
WEB: www.quotecastings.com
SIC: 3543 3544 3369 3366 Industrial patterns; special dies, tools, jigs & fixtures; nonferrous foundries; copper foundries; aluminum foundries

---

New Richmond
Montgomery County

(G-11004)
DAVRON FABRICATING
3873 W 750 N (47967-8018)
PHONE..................................765 339-7303
Ron Grana, *Partner*
Dave Green, *Partner*
EMP: 2
SALES (est): 93.6K **Privately Held**
SIC: 7692 Welding repair

New Ross
Montgomery County

(G-11005)
JJ MACHINE
8834 E 400 S (47968-8046)
PHONE..................................765 723-1511
Nancy Jones, *Owner*
EMP: 4
SQ FT: 12,000
SALES (est): 476.6K **Privately Held**
SIC: 3599 3544 Machine shop, jobbing & repair; special dies & tools

(G-11006)
WRIGHTS WOODWORKING
8862 E 500 S (47968-8037)
PHONE..................................765 723-1546

Joseph Wright, *Owner*
EMP: 2
SALES (est): 174.3K **Privately Held**
SIC: 2431 Millwork

New Salisbury
Harrison County

(G-11007)
AJS GYROS TO GO
441 Rocky Meadow Rd Ne (47161-8108)
PHONE..................................812 951-1715
Alison Hanover, *Principal*
EMP: 4
SALES (est): 244K **Privately Held**
SIC: 2024 Ice cream, bulk

(G-11008)
CUNNINGHAM PRINTING INC
Also Called: Allegra Print & Imaging
175 W Whiskey Run Rd Ne (47161-8804)
PHONE..................................812 347-2438
Tom Cunningham, *President*
EMP: 6
SQ FT: 2,500
SALES (est): 602.1K **Privately Held**
SIC: 2752 Commercial printing, offset

(G-11009)
ECO WATER OF SOUTHERN INDIANA
Also Called: Ecowater
7685 Highway 135 Ne (47161-7723)
P.O. Box 3585, Montrose CO (81402-3585)
PHONE..................................812 734-1407
Wayne Whalen, *Partner*
Teresa Boyd, *Partner*
Dennis Chandler, *Partner*
Deborah Halter-Chandler, *Partner*
EMP: 5
SALES (est): 400K **Privately Held**
SIC: 3589 Water treatment equipment, industrial

(G-11010)
REPUBLIC ETCHING CARVING
5925 Highway 135 Ne (47161-8128)
PHONE..................................812 366-8111
Alfred Wood, *Principal*
EMP: 2
SALES (est): 103.8K **Privately Held**
SIC: 2759 Commercial printing

(G-11011)
SCHMIDT CABINET CO INC
1355 Highway 64 Ne (47161-8434)
P.O. Box 68 (47161-0068)
PHONE..................................812 347-1031
Fax: 812 347-2440
John Calvin Schmidt, *President*
Jonni Bilaura, *Corp Secy*
Jeffery Schmidt, *Vice Pres*
Michael Schmidt, *Vice Pres*
EMP: 25 **EST:** 1959
SQ FT: 5,600
SALES (est): 4MM **Privately Held**
WEB: www.schmidt-cabinets.com
SIC: 2434 2511 Wood kitchen cabinets; wood household furniture

New Washington
Clark County

(G-11012)
LOGO DESIGNS INC
7619 Bthlehem New Wash Rd
(47162-9636)
PHONE..................................812 293-4750
Fax: 812 293-4493
EMP: 3
SALES (est): 160K **Privately Held**
SIC: 2396 Screen Printing Company

New Whiteland
Johnson County

(G-11013)
PREDATOR PERCUSSION LLC
1174 Dark Star Ct (46184-9239)
PHONE..................................317 919-7659
Michael Martin,
EMP: 2
SALES (est): 62.5K **Privately Held**
SIC: 3999 Manufacturing industries

(G-11014)
SPACEPORT EXPLRTION CENTRE INC
144 Tracy Ridge Blvd (46184-1065)
PHONE..................................765 606-1512
Brian Tanner, *Ch of Bd*
George Allison,
William Brown,
EMP: 4 **EST:** 2014
SQ FT: 5,000
SALES (est): 191.6K **Privately Held**
SIC: 3663 8299 8733 Space satellite communications equipment; educational services; research institute

Newberry
Greene County

(G-11015)
GRIFFIN INDUSTRIES LLC
7358 S Griffin Rd (47449-7044)
PHONE..................................812 659-3399
Fax: 812 659-9997
James Davis, *General Mgr*
Todd Ervin, *Plant Mgr*
Dustin Wendel, *Safety Mgr*
EMP: 42
SALES (corp-wide): 3.6B **Publicly Held**
WEB: www.griffinind.com
SIC: 2077 2048 Animal & marine fats & oils; prepared feeds
HQ: Griffin Industries Llc
4221 Alexandria Pike
Cold Spring KY 41076
859 781-2010

Newburgh
Warrick County

(G-11016)
A-1 WELDING & REPAIR
5077 New York Dr (47630-9131)
PHONE..................................812 853-9701
Susan Rich, *Owner*
EMP: 3
SALES (est): 184.3K **Privately Held**
SIC: 3441 Fabricated structural metal

(G-11017)
ACADEMY ENERGY GROUP LLC (PA)
106 State St Ste C (47630-1200)
PHONE..................................312 931-7443
William Morrison, *President*
Andy Lynch, *Exec VP*
Brian Schmidt, *Exec VP*
EMP: 4
SALES (est): 1.8MM **Privately Held**
SIC: 3699 5063 Electrical equipment & supplies; electrical apparatus & equipment

(G-11018)
ACCESS SOLUTIONS
8322 Lancaster Dr (47630-2708)
PHONE..................................812 490-6026
Anthony Christian,
EMP: 2
SALES (est): 220.3K **Privately Held**
SIC: 1442 Construction sand & gravel

(G-11019)
ALCOA WARRICK LLC
4400 W State Route 66 (47630-9140)
P.O. Box 10 (47629-0010)
PHONE..................................812 853-6111
Fax: 812 853-4048
Benjamin Kahrs, *CEO*
EMP: 6
SALES (corp-wide): 11.6B **Publicly Held**
SIC: 3355 Aluminum rolling & drawing
HQ: Alcoa Warrick Llc
201 Isabella St Ste 500
Pittsburgh PA 15212
412 553-4545

(G-11020)
ARCONIC INC
Alcoa
State Highway 66 (47630)
PHONE..................................812 853-6111
Fax: 812 853-4381
Jeff France, *Opers Staff*
Denise Summerville, *Production*
John Pracht, *Engineer*
Pam Meek, *Electrical Engi*
Adam Tieman, *Electrical Engi*
EMP: 408
SALES (corp-wide): 12.9B **Publicly Held**
SIC: 3334 3353 Primary aluminum; aluminum sheet, plate & foil
PA: Arconic Inc.
390 Park Ave Fl 12
New York NY 10022
212 836-2758

(G-11021)
ARCONIC INC
Also Called: Alcoa
2792 Laura Lynn Ln (47630-8919)
PHONE..................................412 553-4545
Fax: 412 553-4498
David Milbourne, *Vice Pres*
Melissa Miller, *Vice Pres*
Bruce Thompson, *Vice Pres*
Shelley Wheat, *Vice Pres*
Scott Zahorchak, *Vice Pres*
EMP: 385
SALES (corp-wide): 12.9B **Publicly Held**
SIC: 3334 3353 1099 Primary aluminum; aluminum sheet & strip; coils, sheet aluminum; plates, aluminum; foil, aluminum; bauxite mining
PA: Arconic Inc.
390 Park Ave Fl 12
New York NY 10022
212 836-2758

(G-11022)
ARCONIC INC
4700 Darlington Rd (47630-9708)
PHONE..................................812 842-3300
EMP: 2
SALES (est): 90.8K **Privately Held**
SIC: 3353 3444 Mfg Aluminum Sheet/Foil Mfg Sheet Metalwork

(G-11023)
CABINETS & COUNTERS INC
7000 Savannah Dr (47630-2181)
PHONE..................................812 858-3300
Fax: 812 858-3305
Jim Johnston, *President*
Jacqueline Johnston, *Vice Pres*
Simmons Heather, *Warehouse Mgr*
▲ **EMP:** 20
SQ FT: 6,000
SALES: 1MM **Privately Held**
SIC: 2541 2542 2821 Table or counter tops, plastic laminated; cabinets: show, display or storage: except wood; counters or counter display cases: except wood; plastics materials & resins

(G-11024)
CINDON INC
Also Called: American Hydraulic Hoses
8400 Golden Dr (47630-2589)
PHONE..................................812 853-5450
Fax: 812 853-6775
Celinda Sisco, *Owner*
EMP: 10
SALES (est): 593.3K **Privately Held**
SIC: 7699 3492 Construction equipment repair; hose & tube fittings & assemblies, hydraulic/pneumatic

(G-11025)
CLOUD DEFENSIVE LLC (PA)
717 Adams St (47630-1307)
PHONE..................................812 760-5017
Sean McCauley, *Principal*
Eric Small, *Principal*
EMP: 2
SALES (est): 337K **Privately Held**
SIC: 3949 3648 3643 5091 Shooting equipment & supplies, general; flashlights; electric switches; hunting equipment & supplies; firearms, sporting

(G-11026)
CUSTOM SIGN & ENGINEERI
5344 Vann Rd (47630-8481)
PHONE..................................812 401-1550
Fax: 812 401-1554
Scott Elpers, *Owner*
Allison Elpers, *Info Tech Mgr*
EMP: 2
SALES (est): 495.9K **Privately Held**
SIC: 3993 Electric signs

(G-11027)
ELLWOCKS AUTO PARTS RESTORAT
Also Called: Mopar Detail Connection
5820 Lisa Ln (47630-8822)
PHONE..................................812 962-4942
Chris Rutherford, *President*
EMP: 6 **EST:** 1978
SALES (est): 286.2K **Privately Held**
SIC: 3999 5092 Novelties, bric-a-brac & hobby kits; hobby goods

(G-11028)
FLIGHT INTEGRITY LLC
2111 Eaglewood Dr (47630-8697)
PHONE..................................812 455-6642
Patricia Cox, *Principal*
EMP: 2 **EST:** 2010
SALES (est): 128.6K **Privately Held**
SIC: 3699 Flight simulators (training aids), electronic

(G-11029)
G & M REBUILDERS INC
7140 Savannah Dr (47630-2183)
PHONE..................................812 858-9233
Fax: 812 858-8233
Charles Dillback, *President*
EMP: 4
SQ FT: 4,300
SALES (est): 485K **Privately Held**
SIC: 3621 7539 Motors & generators; electrical services

(G-11030)
H20 FACTORY
Also Called: H 20 Factory
7899 Bell Oaks Dr (47630-2579)
PHONE..................................812 858-1948
Elizabeth Hohler, *Owner*
EMP: 2 **EST:** 2001
SALES (est): 121.7K **Privately Held**
SIC: 3589 Water filters & softeners, household type

(G-11031)
HURST ENTERPRISE
7866 Owens Dr (47630-2625)
P.O. Box 5 (47629-0005)
PHONE..................................812 853-0901
Fax: 812 853-0966
Bill Hurst, *Principal*
EMP: 2 **EST:** 2008
SALES (est): 132.9K **Privately Held**
SIC: 3999 Manufacturing industries

(G-11032)
INTERNATIONAL FOOD TECH INC
8499 Spencer Dr (47630-8952)
P.O. Box 503 (47629-0503)
PHONE..................................812 853-9432
Joseph Greif, *President*
EMP: 2
SQ FT: 5,000
SALES: 400K **Privately Held**
SIC: 2023 Condensed, concentrated & evaporated milk products

(G-11033)
INTERRACHEM LLC
5722 Prospect Dr (47630-8306)
P.O. Box 727 (47629-0727)
PHONE....................................812 858-3147
Curtis R Ellis,
Brian Hallett,
Howard A Nevins,
EMP: 6
SALES (est): 254.1K Privately Held
SIC: 2899 Chemical preparations

(G-11034)
J PORTER MFG CO
8900 Woodland Dr (47630-2404)
PHONE....................................812 853-9395
John Porter, Owner
EMP: 2
SALES (est): 138.4K Privately Held
SIC: 3423 Hand & edge tools

(G-11035)
LIBERTY INDUSTRIES LC
Also Called: Tower Innovations
3266 Tower Rd (47630-8301)
PHONE....................................812 853-0595
Barbara Wortley, Mng Member
William Gates,
Bill Gates,
David Nicholson,
▼ EMP: 35
SALES (est): 8.8MM Privately Held
SIC: 3441 Fabricated structural metal

(G-11036)
LITTLE GREEN APPLE
8449 Bell Oaks Dr (47630-2582)
PHONE....................................812 853-8761
EMP: 2 EST: 2015
SALES (est): 92.7K Privately Held
SIC: 3571 Personal computers (microcomputers)

(G-11037)
LOZANO WLDG & FABRICATION LLC
8677 Hanover Dr (47630-9326)
PHONE....................................812 858-1379
Cesar Lozano, Principal
EMP: 2
SALES (est): 55.3K Privately Held
SIC: 3999 Manufacturing industries

(G-11038)
MAR KEL INC
Also Called: Mar-Kel Quick Print
4111 Merchant Dr (47630-2551)
PHONE....................................812 853-6133
Fax: 812 853-9522
Jerry Titzer, President
Margaret E Titzer, Corp Secy
Kevin Titzer, Vice Pres
EMP: 4
SQ FT: 1,580
SALES (est): 520.2K Privately Held
SIC: 2752 7334 2789 Commercial printing, offset; photocopying & duplicating services; bookbinding & related work

(G-11039)
MTCR SITE SERVICES LLC
6033 Vann Rd (47630-9676)
PHONE....................................812 598-6516
Holli D Bame,
EMP: 5 EST: 2015
SALES (est): 826.2K Privately Held
SIC: 3823 Fluidic devices, circuits & systems for process control

(G-11040)
PAYNE GEORGE A PETROLEUM ENGR
5844 Sharon Rd (47630-9537)
P.O. Box 743 (47629-0743)
PHONE....................................812 853-3813
George A Payne, Owner
EMP: 2
SALES: 100K Privately Held
SIC: 1311 1389 Crude petroleum production; natural gas production; oil consultants

(G-11041)
PERFECT SIGN LLC
1944 Lakes Edge Dr (47630-8020)
PHONE....................................812 518-6459
Steve Roelle, Administration
EMP: 2
SALES (est): 111.4K Privately Held
WEB: www.theperfectsign.com
SIC: 3993 Signs & advertising specialties

(G-11042)
PILLOW PALS INC
6566 Sharon Rd (47630-1939)
PHONE....................................812 853-8241
Brenda Rusche, President
Thomas J Rusche, Med Doctor
EMP: 4
SALES (est): 227.7K Privately Held
SIC: 2392 7389 Pillowcases: made from purchased materials;

(G-11043)
POWER SYSTEMS INNOVATIONS INC
3247 Commerce Dr (47630-8334)
PHONE....................................812 480-4380
Chris Kruckenberg, President
Alan Wolfinger, Vice Pres
▲ EMP: 7
SALES (est): 1.2MM Privately Held
SIC: 3679 Electronic components

(G-11044)
RALPH RANSOM VENEERS
Also Called: Ralph Ransom Logging
6599 Heathervale Ct (47630-9696)
PHONE....................................812 858-9956
Ralph Ransom, Owner
EMP: 5
SALES: 1.1MM Privately Held
SIC: 2411 Logging

(G-11045)
RED BULL NORTH AMERICA INC
7533 Chapel Hill Ct (47630-9640)
PHONE....................................216 401-3950
EMP: 3
SALES (corp-wide): 3.5B Privately Held
SIC: 2086 Bottled & canned soft drinks
HQ: Red Bull North America, Inc.
1740 Stewart St
Santa Monica CA 90404

(G-11046)
SCHNUCK MARKETS INC
Also Called: Schnucks
8301 Bell Oaks Dr (47630-2586)
PHONE....................................812 853-9505
Fax: 812 858-5739
Scott Berry, Manager
EMP: 150
SALES (corp-wide): 3.2B Privately Held
WEB: www.schnucks.com
SIC: 5411 5812 5912 5992 Supermarkets, chain; eating places; drug stores & proprietary stores; florists; cookies & crackers; bread, cake & related products
PA: Schnuck Markets, Inc.
11420 Lackland Rd
Saint Louis MO 63146
314 994-9900

(G-11047)
SEILER & SONS
5922 Seiler Rd (47630-8217)
PHONE....................................812 858-9598
Linda Seiler, Owner
EMP: 5
SALES (est): 313.5K Privately Held
SIC: 3441 Fabricated structural metal

(G-11048)
SHIRTAILS
4944 State Route 261 (47630-2856)
P.O. Box 146 (47629-0146)
PHONE....................................812 858-8605
Fax: 812 858-8605
EMP: 2
SQ FT: 900
SALES (est): 91K Privately Held
SIC: 2759 2395 5699 Screen Printing Embroidery And Ret Clothing

(G-11049)
SIGNS BY DESIGN
4133 Merchant Dr Ste 5 (47630-2530)
PHONE....................................812 853-7784
Fax: 812 853-6195
Andy Rentsch, Owner
Dave Miller, Co-Owner
EMP: 8
SQ FT: 3,000
SALES: 90K Privately Held
SIC: 3993 Signs, not made in custom sign painting shops

(G-11050)
SLEDGEHAMMER PRINTING
4956 State Route 261 (47630-2856)
PHONE....................................812 629-2160
EMP: 2
SALES (est): 83.9K Privately Held
SIC: 2752 Commercial printing, lithographic

(G-11051)
SMI MANUFACTURING INC
Also Called: SMI Marketing
7457 W State Route 66 (47630-2196)
PHONE....................................812 428-2794
Peter Schuck, President
Jean Schuck, Corp Secy
John Schuck, Vice Pres
▲ EMP: 5 EST: 1973
SQ FT: 7,500
SALES (est): 1MM Privately Held
WEB: www.smimanufacturing.com
SIC: 3714 Vacuum brakes, motor vehicle

(G-11052)
TREY EXPLORATION INC
2699 Sr 261 (47630)
P.O. Box 906 (47629-0906)
PHONE....................................812 858-3146
Fax: 812 490-5098
Howard Nevins, President
Andy Chwiss, Facilities Mgr
EMP: 4
SQ FT: 1,200
SALES (est): 125.9K Privately Held
SIC: 1382 1311 Oil & gas exploration services; crude petroleum production

(G-11053)
TRISTATE PLASTIC TOPS
4395 State Route 261 (47630-2655)
P.O. Box 803 (47629-0803)
PHONE....................................812 853-7827
Fax: 812 853-7827
Gordon Snider, Owner
EMP: 2
SQ FT: 3,500
SALES (est): 141.2K Privately Held
SIC: 1799 1751 2541 Counter top installation; cabinet building & installation; cabinet & finish carpentry; wood partitions & fixtures

(G-11054)
UNITED MINERALS
3699 Darlington Rd (47630-9779)
PHONE....................................812 842-0978
Red Faulkenberg, Manager
EMP: 2
SALES (est): 151.9K Privately Held
SIC: 6211 1481 Oil & gas lease brokers; nonmetallic mineral services

(G-11055)
VIBRONICS INC
10744 W Highway 662 (47630-8830)
P.O. Box 5488, Evansville (47716-5488)
PHONE....................................812 853-2300
Fax: 812 853-3354
John E Wiegand, President
Cindy Boyer, Officer
EMP: 8
SQ FT: 3,500
SALES (est): 550K Privately Held
WEB: www.vibronics.com
SIC: 1081 Metal mining services

Newport
Vermillion County

(G-11056)
NEWPORT PALLET INC
1888 S State Rd 63 (47966)
P.O. Box 279 (47966-0279)
PHONE....................................217 497-8220
Adam Winland, President
EMP: 8
SALES (est): 1.1MM Privately Held
SIC: 2448 Pallets, wood & wood with metal

Nineveh
Johnson County

(G-11057)
EDS TRADING POST INC
8012 S Nineveh Rd (46164-8906)
PHONE....................................317 933-4867
EMP: 4
SQ FT: 8,000
SALES (est): 34.4K Privately Held
SIC: 3484 5947 7841 5941 Mfg Small Arms Ret Gifts/Novelties Video Tape Rental Ret Sport Goods/Bicycles Truck Rental/Leasing

(G-11058)
TOYOTA
8192 Sweetwater Dr (46164-9147)
PHONE....................................317 755-4791
Dave Julius, Executive
EMP: 2
SALES (est): 87.2K Privately Held
SIC: 3711 Motor vehicles & car bodies

Noblesville
Hamilton County

(G-11059)
AMERICAN FABRICATED CARBIDE CO
1335 Pleasant St (46060-3616)
PHONE....................................317 773-5520
Fax: 317 776-0910
Charles Marshall, President
EMP: 6
SQ FT: 800
SALES: 200K Privately Held
SIC: 3599 Machine & other job shop work

(G-11060)
AMERICAN FEEDING SYSTEMS INC
15425 Endeavor Dr (46060-4921)
PHONE....................................317 773-5517
Fax: 317 773-6044
Robert Camp, President
Matt Mp, Vice Pres
Cory Camp, Engineer
Scot Finney, Design Engr
▲ EMP: 22
SQ FT: 16,000
SALES: 2.8MM Privately Held
WEB: www.americanfeeding.com
SIC: 3559

(G-11061)
BARLEY ISLAND BREWING CO
639 Conner St (46060-2532)
PHONE....................................317 770-5280
Fax: 317 770-5254
Jeff Eaton, Owner
EMP: 15
SALES (est): 1.2MM Privately Held
SIC: 2082 5812 5181 Beer (alcoholic beverage); eating places; beer & ale

(G-11062)
BASTINE POTTERY INC
16509 Cyntheanne Rd (46060-9651)
PHONE....................................317 776-0210
Sherri Bastine, President
EMP: 2
SQ FT: 7,533

G
E
O
G
R
A
P
H
I
C

SALES: 100K **Privately Held**
SIC: **3269** Kitchen & table articles, coarse earthenware; art & ornamental ware, pottery

(G-11063)
BATES TECHNOLOGIES LLC
14560 Bergen Blvd (46060-3364)
PHONE.................................317 841-2400
Ted L Bates, *CEO*
Daryll Day, *President*
Ralph Shannon, *Purchasing*
Keri Schmitt, *Manager*
Darrell Day, *Administration*
▲ EMP: 56
SQ FT: 25,000
SALES (est): 10.5MM **Privately Held**
WEB: www.batestech.com
SIC: **3545** Wheel turning equipment, diamond point or other; machine tool attachments & accessories
HQ: Lapmaster International, Llc
501 W Algonquin Rd Ste A
Mount Prospect IL 60056
224 659-7101

(G-11064)
BATTERIES PLUS
2640 Conner St (46060-3141)
PHONE.................................317 219-0007
Jay Norvell, *Principal*
EMP: 2
SALES (est): 120.8K **Privately Held**
SIC: **5531 5063 3691** Batteries, automotive & truck; batteries; storage batteries

(G-11065)
BEAVER GRAVEL CORPORATION
Also Called: Beaver Materials
16101 River Rd (46062-9567)
PHONE.................................317 773-0679
Fax: 317 773-0048
Allyn Beaver, *President*
John B Shank, *Corp Secy*
Gary Beaver, *Vice Pres*
Jerry Matlock, *CFO*
EMP: 60
SQ FT: 2,100
SALES (est): 9.8MM **Privately Held**
SIC: **1442 3273 3272** Gravel mining; ready-mixed concrete; concrete products

(G-11066)
BEAVER PRODUCTS INC
16101 River Rd (46062-9567)
PHONE.................................317 773-0679
Allyn Beaver, *Corp Secy*
R G Beaver, *Vice Pres*
EMP: 10
SQ FT: 2,100
SALES (est): 700K **Privately Held**
SIC: **3272** Concrete products, precast; wall & ceiling squares, concrete

(G-11067)
BENSHAW INC
235 Westchester Blvd (46062-7497)
PHONE.................................412 487-8235
EMP: 3
SALES (est): 128.3K **Privately Held**
SIC: **3625** Motor starters & controllers, electric

(G-11068)
BORGWARNER PDS ANDERSON LLC (HQ)
13975 Borgwarner Dr (46060-9421)
PHONE.................................765 778-6499
Tania Wingfield, *Vice Pres*
Kent Jones, *Human Res Mgr*
◆ EMP: 340
SALES (est): 1.3B
SALES (corp-wide): 9.8B **Publicly Held**
WEB: www.remy.net
SIC: **3714 3694 3625 3621** Motor vehicle parts & accessories; engine electrical equipment; relays & industrial controls; motors & generators; automotive supplies & parts
PA: Borgwarner Inc.
3850 Hamlin Rd
Auburn Hills MI 48326
248 754-9200

(G-11069)
BRAND WAVE INC
240 Yorkshire Cir (46060-3867)
PHONE.................................661 414-2115
EMP: 2
SALES (est): 97.7K **Privately Held**
SIC: **2752** Commercial printing, lithographic

(G-11070)
BRAND WAVE LLC
240 Yorkshire Cir (46060-3867)
PHONE.................................661 414-2115
Mike Conlon, *Principal*
EMP: 2
SALES (est): 132.1K **Privately Held**
SIC: **3993** Signs & advertising specialties

(G-11071)
BRAZING PREFORMS LLC
15402 Stony Creek Way (46060-4383)
PHONE.................................317 705-6455
Kevin Brandenburg, *Manager*
EMP: 6
SALES (est): 285.3K **Privately Held**
SIC: **7692** Brazing

(G-11072)
BREAKERS UNLIMITED INC
15241 Stony Creek Way (46060-4380)
PHONE.................................317 474-9431
Sam Dagenhart, *Manager*
EMP: 6
SALES (corp-wide): 9.7MM **Privately Held**
WEB: www.breakersunlimited.com
SIC: **3613** Switchgear & switchboard apparatus
PA: Breakers Unlimited, Inc.
15241 Stony Creek Way
Noblesville IN 46060
800 875-3294

(G-11073)
BULLDOG AWARD CO INC
Also Called: Lasting Impressions
777 Conner St (46060-2511)
P.O. Box 2018 (46061-2018)
PHONE.................................317 773-3379
Jeff Street, *Owner*
Michael Dimieri, *Personnel Exec*
EMP: 3
SQ FT: 2,400
SALES: 150K **Privately Held**
SIC: **5099 3993 3953** Rubber stamps; signs & advertising specialties; marking devices

(G-11074)
BURCO MOLDING INC
15015 Herriman Blvd (46060-4253)
PHONE.................................317 773-5699
Fax: 317 773-6003
Clovis E Burrow, *President*
Randy E Burrow, *Vice Pres*
Dennis Roudebush, *Sales Staff*
EMP: 58 EST: 1970
SQ FT: 34,000
SALES (est): 12.9MM **Privately Held**
WEB: www.burco-molding.com
SIC: **3089 3544** Injection molded finished plastic products; special dies, tools, jigs & fixtures

(G-11075)
BUTTERFIELD FOODS LLC
635 Westfield Rd (46060-1323)
PHONE.................................317 776-4775
Fax: 317 776-4784
Frank Violi, *Owner*
D G Elmore,
EMP: 120
SQ FT: 54,000
SALES: 20MM **Privately Held**
WEB: www.butterfield-foods.com
SIC: **2038 2099 2824** Soups, frozen; pizza, frozen; sandwiches, assembled & packaged: for wholesale market; protein fibers

(G-11076)
C & G SALSA COMPANY LLC
5282 E 156th St (46062-6827)
P.O. Box 6085, Fishers (46038-6085)
PHONE.................................317 569-9099
Charles Ferguson, *Mng Member*

Glenda S Ferguson,
EMP: 2
SALES (est): 207.9K **Privately Held**
SIC: **2099** Pasta, uncooked: packaged with other ingredients

(G-11077)
CABINET COTTAGE LLC
1111 Westfield Rd (46062-9277)
PHONE.................................317 369-0051
Jerry Berges, *Mng Member*
EMP: 3
SALES (est): 246.6K **Privately Held**
SIC: **2434** Wood kitchen cabinets

(G-11078)
CARROLL DISTRG & CNSTR SUP INC
20935 Cicero Rd (46060)
PHONE.................................317 984-2400
Dan Carroll, *Branch Mgr*
EMP: 4
SALES (corp-wide): 111.1MM **Privately Held**
SIC: **5082 3444** Contractors' materials; concrete forms, sheet metal
PA: Carroll Distributing & Construction Supply, Inc.
1502 E Main St
Ottumwa IA 52501
641 683-1888

(G-11079)
CHADS SIGNS INSTALLATIONS INC (PA)
Also Called: Csi Signs
555 Park 32 West Dr (46062-9452)
PHONE.................................317 867-2737
Chad Huff, *President*
Steven R Lloyd, *Principal*
EMP: 24
SALES (est): 3.5MM **Privately Held**
SIC: **3993** Electric signs

(G-11080)
CHEMTREX LLC
6315 Edenshall Ln (46062-4633)
PHONE.................................317 508-4223
Darrin T Hugill, *Owner*
Joe Warrender, *Co-Owner*
EMP: 3
SALES: 500K **Privately Held**
SIC: **3677** Filtration devices, electronic

(G-11081)
CIRCLE CITY LIGHTING INC
21570 Anchor Bay Dr (46062-6791)
PHONE.................................317 439-0824
Bryan Durr, *Officer*
EMP: 2
SALES (est): 150.7K **Privately Held**
SIC: **3648** Lighting equipment

(G-11082)
CIRCLE CITY SERVICES LTD
176 Logan St (46060-1437)
PHONE.................................317 770-6287
James Heck, *President*
EMP: 2 EST: 1999
SALES (est): 141.2K **Privately Held**
SIC: **2273** Mats & matting

(G-11083)
CJS STOP N GO
5855 E 211th St Ste 34 (46062-6876)
PHONE.................................317 877-0681
Chris Matchik, *Principal*
EMP: 2 EST: 2012
SALES (est): 206.5K **Privately Held**
SIC: **2911** Petroleum refining

(G-11084)
CONTROLLED AUTOMATION INC
15421 Stony Creek Way A (46060-4330)
PHONE.................................317 770-3870
Fax: 317 776-1280
Dean A Graham, *President*
Rhenda G Graham, *Admin Sec*
EMP: 18
SQ FT: 4,200
SALES (est): 2.9MM **Privately Held**
WEB: www.controlledautomationinc.com
SIC: **3613** Control panels, electric

(G-11085)
COUDEN WOODWORKS INC
23808 Couden Rd (46060-9784)
PHONE.................................317 370-0835
Mark Sterner, *Owner*
EMP: 2
SALES (est): 249.2K **Privately Held**
SIC: **2431** Millwork

(G-11086)
COUNTRY MOON WINERY LLC
16222 Prairie Baptist Rd (46060-9350)
PHONE.................................317 773-7942
Brian Harger, *Mng Member*
EMP: 2
SALES (est): 115.3K **Privately Held**
SIC: **2084 7299** Wines; facility rental & party planning services

(G-11087)
CREATIVE LDSCP & COMPOST CO
Also Called: Creative Ldscpg & Compost Co
18377 Deshane Ave (46060-8825)
PHONE.................................317 776-2909
Fax: 317 776-0153
Teri Haas, *President*
John Haas, *Vice Pres*
EMP: 3
SQ FT: 12,500
SALES (est): 370K **Privately Held**
SIC: **4953 2875 0782 0181** Non-hazardous waste disposal sites; compost; landscape contractors; shrubberies grown in field nurseries

(G-11088)
CRUSADERBIT SOFTWARE LLC
18493 Oakmont Dr (46062-7547)
PHONE.................................317 773-2317
Timothy T Trandel,
EMP: 2
SALES (est): 104.7K **Privately Held**
SIC: **7372** Prepackaged software

(G-11089)
D & D MOULDINGS & MILLWORK
15509 Stony Creek Way (46060-4386)
PHONE.................................317 770-5500
Fax: 317 770-5509
Michael L Dilk, *President*
Daniel S De Lay, *Vice Pres*
EMP: 17
SQ FT: 15,000
SALES (est): 2.8MM **Privately Held**
SIC: **2431** Doors & door parts & trim, wood

(G-11090)
DARLINGTON COOKIE COMPANY (PA)
Also Called: Darlington Farms
8001 E 196th St (46062-9091)
PHONE.................................800 754-2202
Phillip R Hockemeyer, *President*
EMP: 68
SQ FT: 2,200
SALES (est): 16.3MM **Privately Held**
SIC: **2052 5149** Cookies; crackers; cookies & bakery products

(G-11091)
DIAMOND HOOSIER
518 Sunset Dr (46060-1223)
PHONE.................................317 773-1411
Dave Jellison, *Owner*
EMP: 3
SALES (est): 160K **Privately Held**
SIC: **2721 7941** Periodicals; sports promotion

(G-11092)
DICKEY CONSUMER PRODUCTS INC
Also Called: DMD Pharmaceuticals
15268 Stony Creek Way # 100 (46060-4392)
P.O. Box 1055 (46061-1055)
PHONE.................................317 773-8330
Fax: 317 773-8660
David Dickey, *CEO*
Dawn Dickey, *Exec VP*
David Riddle, *CFO*
EMP: 14
SQ FT: 15,000

SALES (est): 1.2MM **Privately Held**
SIC: 2833 Medicinals & botanicals

(G-11093)
DIRECTED PHOTONICS INC
7178 Oakbay Dr (46062-9760)
PHONE.................................317 877-3142
Robert Marusa, *President*
EMP: 6
SALES: 774.5K **Privately Held**
SIC: 3699 Laser systems & equipment

(G-11094)
DIRECTIONAL BUSINESS INTELLIGE
149 Stony Creek Overlook (46060-5427)
PHONE.................................317 770-0805
Douglas Irving, *Principal*
EMP: 2
SALES (est): 110.2K **Privately Held**
SIC: 1381 Directional drilling oil & gas wells

(G-11095)
DISPENSIT
17555 Willow View Rd (46062-4394)
PHONE.................................317 776-8740
Jeff Beals, *Manager*
EMP: 2
SALES (est): 163K **Privately Held**
SIC: 3586 Measuring & dispensing pumps

(G-11096)
E & B PAVING INC
17042 Middletown Ave (46060-7157)
PHONE.................................317 781-1030
Fax: 317 781-1127
Dan Paddock, *Manager*
EMP: 16
SALES (corp-wide): 800.6MM **Privately Held**
SIC: 3273 Ready-mixed concrete
HQ: E & B Paving, Inc.
286 W 300 N
Anderson IN 46012
765 643-5358

(G-11097)
E & B PAVING INC
17042 Middletown Ave (46060-7157)
PHONE.................................317 773-4132
Fax: 317 773-4137
Matt Cisco, *Project Mgr*
Vince Kenney, *Project Mgr*
Larry Canterbury, *Manager*
EMP: 85
SALES (corp-wide): 800.6MM **Privately Held**
SIC: 1611 2951 3444 3272 Surfacing & paving; asphalt & asphaltic paving mixtures (not from refineries); sheet metalwork; concrete products
HQ: E & B Paving, Inc.
286 W 300 N
Anderson IN 46012
765 643-5358

(G-11098)
E & B PAVING INC
15215 River Rd (46062-9572)
PHONE.................................317 773-8216
P Durving, *Manager*
EMP: 3
SALES (corp-wide): 800.6MM **Privately Held**
SIC: 3273 Ready-mixed concrete
HQ: E & B Paving, Inc.
286 W 300 N
Anderson IN 46012
765 643-5358

(G-11099)
ELI LILLY AND CO
10871 Monarch Springs Ct (46060-8304)
PHONE.................................317 433-1244
Aubrey Hawkins, *Principal*
Chad Wolfe, *Research*
EMP: 2 EST: 2011
SALES (est): 136.7K **Privately Held**
SIC: 2834 Pharmaceutical preparations

(G-11100)
ENVISION EPOXY
16517 Anderson Way (46062-5502)
PHONE.................................317 448-3400
EMP: 3

(G-11101)
ET PRINTING ✪
746 Westfield Rd (46062-6902)
PHONE.................................317 219-7966
EMP: 2 EST: 2018
SALES (est): 83.9K **Privately Held**
SIC: 2752 Commercial printing, lithographic

(G-11102)
FEEDING CONCEPTS INC
15235 Herriman Blvd (46060-4230)
PHONE.................................317 773-2040
Fax: 317 773-1494
John Graham II, *President*
James Graham, *Engineer*
EMP: 15
SQ FT: 15,900
SALES (est): 3.4MM **Privately Held**
WEB: www.feedingconcepts.com
SIC: 3559

(G-11103)
FIELD RUBBER PRODUCTS INC
3211 Conner St (46060-2411)
PHONE.................................317 773-3787
Fax: 317 773-9285
John M Field, *President*
Michael Field, *President*
EMP: 12 EST: 1955
SQ FT: 30,000
SALES (est): 2.1MM **Privately Held**
WEB: www.fieldrubber.com
SIC: 3069 Molded rubber products

(G-11104)
FILSON EARTHWORK COMPANY
21785 Riverwood Ave (46062-9560)
P.O. Box 538 (46061-0538)
PHONE.................................317 774-3180
Greg Filson, *President*
EMP: 15
SALES (est): 2MM **Privately Held**
SIC: 1389 Excavating slush pits & cellars

(G-11105)
FOUNDRY SERVICES INC
10482 Winghaven Dr (46060-4464)
PHONE.................................317 955-8112
Fax: 317 955-8088
Douglas Weir, *President*
EMP: 115
SQ FT: 70,000
SALES (est): 17.2MM **Privately Held**
SIC: 3366 Castings (except die)

(G-11106)
FREDS DRIVEWAYS INC
1101 Westfield Rd (46062-5708)
PHONE.................................317 770-6094
Tina Hopkins, *President*
Fred Hopkins, *Vice Pres*
EMP: 2
SALES (est): 179K **Privately Held**
WEB: www.fredsdriveways.com
SIC: 2951 Concrete, asphaltic (not from refineries)

(G-11107)
FREW PROCESS GROUP LLC
15305 Stony Creek Way (46060-4382)
PHONE.................................317 565-5000
Kimberly Imbro, *Sales Associate*
Scott Young,
Roger McIninch,
EMP: 6
SQ FT: 10,000
SALES: 620K **Privately Held**
SIC: 5074 3491 3823 Heating equipment (hydronic); industrial valves; automatic regulating & control valves; magnetic flow meters, industrial process type; turbine flow meters, industrial process type

(G-11108)
GARED HOLDINGS LLC
Also Called: Gared Sports
9200 E 146th St Ste A (46060-4362)
PHONE.................................317 774-9840
Dimitrios Koukoulomatis, *CEO*
Carlos Castellon, *Vice Pres*
Marty Retter, *Plant Mgr*

Richard Gregor, *Project Mgr*
Dionne Malone, *Project Mgr*
◆ EMP: 110 EST: 1925
SQ FT: 3,500
SALES (est): 18.3MM **Privately Held**
WEB: www.garedsports.com
SIC: 3949 Sporting & athletic goods

(G-11109)
GASCO LLC
15305 Stony Creek Way (46060-4382)
PHONE.................................317 565-5000
Fax: 317 565-5010
Mike Smith, *Mng Member*
EMP: 2
SALES (est): 106.9K **Privately Held**
SIC: 3612 Generator voltage regulators

(G-11110)
GEM-ROSE CORP
597 Christian Ave (46060-3722)
P.O. Box 644 (46061-0644)
PHONE.................................317 773-6400
Fax: 317 773-2616
Roger Brown, *President*
Tammy Brown, *Vice Pres*
EMP: 5 EST: 1982
SQ FT: 15,000
SALES: 700K **Privately Held**
SIC: 3441 Fabricated structural metal

(G-11111)
GLOBAL ISOTOPES LLC (PA)
Also Called: Zevacor Molecular
14395 Bergen Blvd (46060-3305)
PHONE.................................317 578-1251
Kelli Lightfoot,
Bree Roenigk,
Ken Smithmier,
John Zehner,
EMP: 6 EST: 2012
SQ FT: 70,000
SALES: 9.5MM **Privately Held**
SIC: 2834 8742 3845 3559 Druggists' preparations (pharmaceuticals); management consulting services; electromedical equipment; pharmaceutical machinery

(G-11112)
GLOBAL USA INC
Also Called: Z-Athletic, Inc.
23044 State Road 37 N (46060-6958)
PHONE.................................317 219-5647
Jian Zhao, *President*
▲ EMP: 4 EST: 1993
SALES: 800K **Privately Held**
SIC: 3949 Sporting & athletic goods

(G-11113)
GREEN ILLUMINATING SYSTEMS INC
10330 Pleasant St Ste 600 (46060-3957)
P.O. Box 932 (46061-0932)
PHONE.................................317 869-7430
Thomas Treinen, *President*
EMP: 3
SALES: 3MM **Privately Held**
SIC: 3646 Commercial indusl & institutional electric lighting fixtures

(G-11114)
GREENCYCLE INC
2695 Cicero Rd (46060-1026)
PHONE.................................317 773-3350
Greg Hart, *Branch Mgr*
EMP: 2 **Privately Held**
SIC: 2875 4953 5261 Compost; sanitary landfill operation; lawn & garden supplies; top soil
PA: Greencycle, Inc
400 Central Ave Ste 115
Northfield IL 60093

(G-11115)
GUL FOR MEDIA DEVELOPMENT
15505 Wandering Way (46060-8009)
PHONE.................................317 726-9544
Segvan Johnson, *CEO*
EMP: 3
SALES (est): 123.2K **Privately Held**
SIC: 2836 Culture media

(G-11116)
H M C SCREEN PRINTING INC
954 Conner St (46060-2621)
PHONE.................................317 773-8532

Fax: 317 773-1172
Paul Howard, *President*
Tanya Howard, *Executive*
EMP: 13
SQ FT: 3,000
SALES (est): 1.6MM **Privately Held**
WEB: www.hmcscreenprinting.com
SIC: 2759 Screen printing

(G-11117)
HAGER INDUSTRIES INC
230 Riverwood Dr (46062-8841)
PHONE.................................317 219-6622
Myles Hager, *Principal*
EMP: 3 EST: 2008
SALES (est): 199.5K **Privately Held**
SIC: 3999 Manufacturing industries

(G-11118)
HANLON SOLUTIONS RESOURCE INC
3501 Conner St Ste X (46060-2492)
PHONE.................................317 776-4880
James D Hanlon, *President*
◆ EMP: 3
SALES: 400K **Privately Held**
SIC: 3589 High pressure cleaning equipment

(G-11119)
HARRELL FAMILY LLC
Also Called: Window Makeover
15525 Stony Creek Way (46060-4386)
PHONE.................................317 770-4550
EMP: 6
SALES (est): 865.1K **Privately Held**
SIC: 3531 3462 Subgraders (construction equipment); construction or mining equipment forgings, ferrous

(G-11120)
HELMER INC
Also Called: Helmer Scientific
14400 Bergen Blvd (46060-3307)
PHONE.................................317 773-9073
Fax: 317 773-9082
David Helmer, *Owner*
Lori Gabrek, *Vice Pres*
Troy Rector, *Vice Pres*
Jacob Eckert, *Opers Staff*
Andrea Sines, *Production*
EMP: 170
SQ FT: 32,000
SALES (est): 51.1MM **Privately Held**
WEB: www.helmerinc.com
SIC: 3841 3821 Blood transfusion equipment; autoclaves, laboratory

(G-11121)
HOLGIN TECHNOLOGIES LLC
15335 Endeavor Dr Ste 100 (46060-4943)
PHONE.................................317 774-5181
Alan McMullen, *Mng Member*
EMP: 10
SALES: 500K **Privately Held**
SIC: 3841 Surgical & medical instruments

(G-11122)
HUVER MANUFACTURING TECH LLC
Also Called: Hu/Man Tech
10210 Carmine Dr (46060-8379)
PHONE.................................317 460-8605
Aaron Huver,
EMP: 3
SALES (est): 258.4K **Privately Held**
SIC: 3499 Fabricated metal products

(G-11123)
IDI FABRICATION INC (PA)
14444 Herriman Blvd (46060-4900)
PHONE.................................317 776-6577
Scott Doll, *President*
Peter Jarosz, *Vice Pres*
Denis Pauze, *Engineer*
Mary Jarosz, *Human Resources*
Nicole Christman, *Manager*
▲ EMP: 80
SQ FT: 55,000
SALES: 26.3MM **Privately Held**
SIC: 3567 Induction & dielectric heating equipment

(G-11124)
IMAGE CONCEPTS INC ✪
6215 Buttonwood Dr (46062-9140)
PHONE...................................317 408-5558
Nancy Meers, *President*
EMP: 2 EST: 2017
SALES (est): 67K Privately Held
SIC: 2329 Men's & boys' clothing

(G-11125)
IN DUCTILE LLC
Also Called: Indiana Ductile
1600 S 8th St (46060-3739)
PHONE...................................317 776-8000
Fax: 317 776-8895
Roger L Mears,
Jack Kruse,
EMP: 25
SQ FT: 225,000
SALES (est): 4.6MM Privately Held
WEB: www.indianaductile.com
SIC: 3321 Ductile iron castings

(G-11126)
INDIANA ARTISAN INC
203 Surrey Hl (46062-9049)
PHONE...................................317 607-8715
Eric Freeman, *Principal*
EMP: 3
SALES (est): 214.6K Privately Held
SIC: 2084 Wines

(G-11127)
INDUSTRIAL DIELECTRICS INC
Also Called: IDI Composites International
407 S 7th St (46060-2708)
P.O. Box 357 (46061-0357)
PHONE...................................317 773-1766
Fax: 317 773-3877
Thomas K Merrell, *President*
Thomas Flood, *Vice Pres*
Dave Blake, *Mfg Staff*
Dale Silvernell, *Engineer*
Brad Yusiewicz, *Controller*
◆ EMP: 85
SQ FT: 100,000
SALES: 40.5MM
SALES (corp-wide): 187.5MM Privately Held
SIC: 2821 Molding compounds, plastics
PA: Industrial Dielectrics Holdings, Inc.
407 S 7th St
Noblesville IN 46060
317 773-1766

(G-11128)
INDUSTRIAL DLCTRICS HLDNGS INC (PA)
Also Called: IDI
407 S 7th St (46060-2708)
P.O. Box 357 (46061-0357)
PHONE...................................317 773-1766
Thomas K Merrell, *President*
John D Merrell, *Vice Pres*
Anibal Miranda, *Plant Mgr*
Monica Crawford, *Human Resources*
Connie Juskow, *Cust Mgr*
◆ EMP: 630 EST: 1966
SQ FT: 15,000
SALES (est): 187.5MM Privately Held
WEB: www.idiplastic.com
SIC: 2821 Plastics materials & resins

(G-11129)
INDY POWDER COATINGS LLC
10482 Winghaven Dr (46060-4464)
PHONE...................................317 236-7177
Fax: 317 236-7180
Sam Eidy, *CFO*
Harold Aubert, *Mng Member*
EMP: 18
SQ FT: 65,000
SALES (est): 2MM Privately Held
WEB: www.indypowdercoating.com
SIC: 3479 Coating of metals & formed
products

(G-11130)
INTEGRATORCOM INC
Also Called: Security Automation Systems
14670 Cumberland Rd (46060-8708)
PHONE...................................317 776-3500
Mark Bates, *COO*
EMP: 98
SQ FT: 19,000

SALES (est): 6.3MM Privately Held
WEB: www.integrator.com
SIC: 8711 3823 3613 Electrical or electronic engineering; industrial instrmnts
msrmnt display/control process variable;
switchgear & switchboard apparatus

(G-11131)
INTEGRITY HEARING (PA)
5628 Merritt Cir (46062-2202)
PHONE...................................317 882-9151
EMP: 2
SALES (est): 225.2K Privately Held
SIC: 5999 3842 Hearing aids; hearing aids

(G-11132)
IRVING MATERIALS INC
Also Called: I M I
17050 River Rd (46062-9566)
PHONE...................................317 770-1745
Fax: 317 326-4141
Prent Alfod, *Manager*
EMP: 10
SALES (corp-wide): 800.6MM Privately
Held
SIC: 3273 Ready-mixed concrete
PA: Irving Materials, Inc.
8032 N State Road 9
Greenfield IN 46140
317 326-3101

(G-11133)
IRVING MATERIALS INC
Also Called: I M I
12798 State Road 38 E (46060-8806)
PHONE...................................317 773-3640
Tim Burke, *Branch Mgr*
EMP: 26
SALES (corp-wide): 800.6MM Privately
Held
SIC: 3273 Ready-mixed concrete
PA: Irving Materials, Inc.
8032 N State Road 9
Greenfield IN 46140
317 326-3101

(G-11134)
JAM GRAPHICS INC
176 Logan St 314 (46060-1437)
PHONE...................................317 896-5662
John M Arrivo, *President*
Donna Arrivo, *Vice Pres*
EMP: 2
SALES: 1MM Privately Held
WEB: www.jamgraphics.net
SIC: 2759 Commercial printing

(G-11135)
JAMES WAFFORD
Also Called: Logan Street Signs and Banners
1720 S 10th St (46060-3835)
PHONE...................................317 773-7200
James Wafford, *Owner*
EMP: 3
SQ FT: 800
SALES (est): 311.6K Privately Held
SIC: 2759 3993 Visiting cards (including
business): printing; signs & advertising
specialties

(G-11136)
KELLEY GLOBAL BRANDS LLC ✪
Also Called: Klh Audio
984 Logan St Ste 301 (46060-2209)
PHONE...................................833 554-8326
David Kelley, *President*
John Kerns, *Vice Pres*
EMP: 8 EST: 2017
SALES (est): 319.7K Privately Held
SIC: 3651 Speaker systems

(G-11137)
KING SYSTEMS CORPORATION
Also Called: Ambu
15011 Herriman Blvd (46060-4253)
PHONE...................................317 776-6823
Fax: 317 776-6827
Steve Davis, *CEO*
Donnie Young, *Maint Spvr*
Andy Camp, *Mfg Staff*
Joanna Powell, *Production*
Sean Williams, *Production*
◆ EMP: 465 EST: 1977
SQ FT: 100,000

SALES (est): 136.7MM
SALES (corp-wide): 53.3MM Privately
Held
WEB: www.kingsystems.com
SIC: 3841 Surgical & medical instruments;
anesthesia apparatus
HQ: Ambu Inc.
6230 Old Dobbin Ln # 250
Columbia MD 21045
410 768-6464

(G-11138)
KIRBY MACHINE COMPANY LLC
1709 Cherry St (46060-3029)
PHONE...................................317 773-6700
EMP: 17
SALES: 500K Privately Held
WEB: www.kmcmold.com
SIC: 3312 Tool & die steel

(G-11139)
KITTERMAN MACHINE CO INC
87 S 8th St (46060-2605)
P.O. Box 277 (46061-0277)
PHONE...................................317 773-2283
Fax: 317 773-6326
Randy Burrow, *President*
Bud Sallee, *Opers Mgr*
EMP: 8 EST: 1951
SQ FT: 5,280
SALES (est): 912.7K Privately Held
SIC: 3544 3599 Industrial molds; machine
& other job shop work

(G-11140)
LAND ENTERPRISES
7116 Summer Oak Dr (46062-7488)
PHONE...................................317 774-9475
Gerald Beland, *Owner*
EMP: 2
SALES (est): 120K Privately Held
SIC: 3523 7389 Farm machinery & equip-
ment; business services

(G-11141)
LESLIE WEBBER MEDIA & PUBG LLC
6685 Braemar Ave N (46062-4107)
PHONE...................................317 774-0598
Leslie A Webber, *Principal*
EMP: 2
SALES (est): 87.6K Privately Held
SIC: 2741 Miscellaneous publishing

(G-11142)
LOWE MACHINE TOOLS LLC
7080 Willowleaf Ct (46062-8422)
PHONE...................................248 705-7562
Paul Lowe, *Mng Member*
EMP: 2
SALES (est): 126.7K Privately Held
SIC: 3545 Machine tool accessories

(G-11143)
MA-RI-AL CORP
Also Called: Beaver Readi-Mix
16101 River Rd (46062-9567)
PHONE...................................317 773-0679
Allyn Beaver, *President*
Gary Beaver, *Vice Pres*
EMP: 55
SQ FT: 3,500
SALES (est): 6.8MM Privately Held
SIC: 3273 Ready-mixed concrete

(G-11144)
MADISON RIVER INDUSTRIES LLC
16567 River Rd (46062-9566)
PHONE...................................317 472-6375
Cari Wright, *Administration*
EMP: 8
SALES (est): 873.6K Privately Held
SIC: 3999 Manufacturing industries

(G-11145)
MARIETTA MARTIN MATERIALS INC
Also Called: Noblesville Sand & Gravel
15215 River Rd (46062-9572)
PHONE...................................317 776-4460
Fax: 317 776-4469
Larry Kilday, *Branch Mgr*
EMP: 18 Publicly Held
WEB: www.martinmarietta.com

SIC: 1442 1422 1411 Construction sand
& gravel; crushed & broken limestone; dimension stone
PA: Martin Marietta Materials Inc
2710 Wycliff Rd
Raleigh NC 27607

(G-11146)
MARK LAMASTER
Also Called: Lamaster Radiation Consulting
16271 E 191st St (46060-9295)
P.O. Box 135, Lapel (46051-0135)
PHONE...................................765 534-4185
Mark Lamaster, *Owner*
Thelma Lamaster, *Co-Owner*
EMP: 2
SALES (est): 245.8K Privately Held
SIC: 3674 Radiation sensors

(G-11147)
MCI/SCREWDRIVER SYSTEMS INC
Also Called: Verizon Business
14800 Herriman Blvd (46060-4313)
P.O. Box 927 (46061-0927)
PHONE...................................317 776-1970
S Neal Graham, *President*
EMP: 10
SQ FT: 16,000
SALES (est): 920K Privately Held
WEB: www.mciscrewdrivers.com
SIC: 3599 Machine shop, jobbing & repair

(G-11148)
METRO PLASTICS TECH INC
17145 Metro Park Ct (46060-4051)
P.O. Box 1208 (46061-1208)
PHONE...................................317 776-0860
Fax: 317 773-4034
Lindsey R Hahn, *President*
Alice L Hahn, *Vice Pres*
Scott Adams, *Project Mgr*
Kellie Glass, *Prdtn Mgr*
Dawn Northcutt, *Controller*
▲ EMP: 80 EST: 1975
SQ FT: 50,000
SALES (est): 23.1MM Privately Held
SIC: 3089 Injection molding of plastics

(G-11149)
MEYER FOODS INC
18247 Pennington Rd (46060-8237)
PHONE...................................317 773-6594
Jeffery L Meyer, *Principal*
EMP: 6 EST: 2010
SALES (est): 32K Privately Held
SIC: 2099 Food preparations

(G-11150)
MICROCHIP TECHNOLOGY INC
9779 E 146th St Ste 130 (46060-4327)
PHONE...................................317 773-8323
Mike Pennington, *Manager*
EMP: 6
SALES (corp-wide): 3.9B Publicly Held
WEB: www.microchip.com
SIC: 3674 Semiconductors & related de-
vices
PA: Microchip Technology Inc
2355 W Chandler Blvd
Chandler AZ 85224
480 792-7200

(G-11151)
MINUTEMAN PRESS
746 Westfield Rd (46062-6902)
PHONE...................................317 316-0566
EMP: 2
SALES (est): 83.9K Privately Held
SIC: 2752 Commercial printing, litho-
graphic

(G-11152)
MO3D PRINTING LLC
19257 Pathway Pointe (46062-8299)
PHONE...................................317 345-0061
Justin Moe, *Principal*
EMP: 2
SALES (est): 97.8K Privately Held
SIC: 2752 Commercial printing, litho-
graphic

▲ = Import ▼=Export
◆ =Import/Export

(G-11153)
MOFFITT CONSULTING SERVICES
15365 Cherry Tree Rd (46062-9577)
PHONE..................................317 773-5570
Karen Moffitt, *Owner*
EMP: 2
SALES (est): 160.7K **Privately Held**
SIC: 3699 8742 Electronic training devices; administrative services consultant

(G-11154)
MOLEX LLC
10 S 9th St (46060-2630)
PHONE..................................317 770-4900
EMP: 3
SALES (corp-wide): 44.4B **Privately Held**
SIC: 3678 Electronic connectors
HQ: Molex, Llc
2222 Wellington Ct
Lisle IL 60532
630 969-4550

(G-11155)
MORRIS PRECISION INC
102 Lilac Ct (46062-9728)
PHONE..................................574 656-3089
Fax: 574 656-8708
EMP: 25
SALES: 3MM **Privately Held**
SIC: 3599 Mfg Industrial Machinery

(G-11156)
MORRIS PRECISION INC
102 Lilac Ct (46062-9728)
PHONE..................................574 656-8707
EMP: 15 EST: 1977
SQ FT: 11,000
SALES (est): 1.4MM **Privately Held**
SIC: 3599 Mfg Industrial Machinery

(G-11157)
NEON SAFETY GROUP LLC
6896 Carters Grove Dr (46062-7969)
PHONE..................................317 774-5144
Richard Deuschle, *Principal*
EMP: 2
SALES (est): 164.4K **Privately Held**
SIC: 2813 Neon

(G-11158)
NETSHAPE TECHNOLOGIES LLC (HQ)
Also Called: Mpp
14670 Cumberland Rd (46060-8708)
PHONE..................................812 248-9273
Fax: 812 248-9275
Dax Whitehouse, *CEO*
Ric Wrye, *COO*
▲ EMP: 30
SQ FT: 8,000
SALES (est): 162.4MM
SALES (corp-wide): 197.8MM **Privately Held**
WEB: www.netshapetech.com
SIC: 3339 Antimony refining (primary)
PA: Metal Powder Products, Llc
16855 Suthpark Dr Ste 100
Westfield IN 46074
317 805-3764

(G-11159)
NEXXT SPINE LLC
14425 Bergen Blvd Ste B (46060-3422)
PHONE..................................317 436-7801
Andrew Elsbury, *President*
Lori Davis, *Accountant*
Bill Del Russo, *VP Sales*
Lindsay Friend, *Admin Asst*
EMP: 12
SALES (est): 2.4MM **Privately Held**
SIC: 3841 Surgical & medical instruments; fixation appliances, internal

(G-11160)
NOBLE INDUSTRIES INC
17575 Presley Dr (46060-2477)
PHONE..................................317 773-1926
Fax: 317 776-2910
William Parker, *CEO*
Gregory Parker, *President*
Dee McKinney, *Corp Secy*
Steve Hurst, *Purch Mgr*
Brenda Parker Snyder, *VP Sls/Mktg*
EMP: 50 EST: 1970

SQ FT: 70,000
SALES (est): 13.6MM **Privately Held**
WEB: www.nobleindustries.com
SIC: 3444 Sheet metal specialties, not stamped

(G-11161)
NOBLESVILLE PACK & SHIP
199 N 9th St (46060-2212)
PHONE..................................317 776-6306
Abralin Dean, *Principal*
EMP: 2
SALES (est): 115.8K **Privately Held**
SIC: 7389 2621 Mailbox rental & related service; specialty or chemically treated papers

(G-11162)
ORBITAL INSTALLATION TECH LLC
9750 E 150 St Ste 1200 (46060-5583)
PHONE..................................317 774-3668
Denise Roberts, *Principal*
EMP: 2
SALES (est): 334.8K **Privately Held**
SIC: 3663

(G-11163)
P F APPLE LLC
19541 Heather Ln (46060-1162)
PHONE..................................317 773-8683
Paula Fenn, *Principal*
EMP: 2
SALES (est): 146.4K **Privately Held**
SIC: 3571 Personal computers (microcomputers)

(G-11164)
PAXXAL INC
14425 Bergen Blvd Ste A (46060-3422)
PHONE..................................317 296-7724
Ezzeldin El Massry, *President*
Abdulmajed Jalali, *President*
▲ EMP: 9
SQ FT: 20,000
SALES (est): 1.6MM **Privately Held**
SIC: 3089 Pallets, plastic

(G-11165)
PICKLED PEDALER
499 Banbury Rd (46062-9021)
PHONE..................................317 877-0624
Nicole Eliason, *Owner*
EMP: 2 EST: 2013
SALES (est): 142.1K **Privately Held**
SIC: 2035 Pickled fruits & vegetables

(G-11166)
PRODUCTIVITY RESOURCES INC
325 Pickwick Ct (46062-9071)
P.O. Box 15, Carmel (46082-0015)
PHONE..................................317 245-4040
Gayle Robinson, *President*
Greg Newkirk, *Consultant*
EMP: 5
SALES (est): 616K **Privately Held**
SIC: 3469 Capacitor or condenser cans & cases, stamped metal

(G-11167)
PSD AND MORE LLC (PA)
Also Called: Psd Concepts
15260 Herriman Blvd (46060-4224)
PHONE..................................317 770-4577
Jose Luis Contreras, *Mng Member*
Fernando Aguera,
EMP: 2 EST: 2010
SQ FT: 38,000
SALES: 400K **Privately Held**
SIC: 2541 Store & office display cases & fixtures

(G-11168)
QSP PRINTING INC
5920 E 161st St (46062-9265)
PHONE..................................317 773-0864
Alan D Weaver, *President*
EMP: 6
SQ FT: 2,800
SALES: 430K **Privately Held**
WEB: www.qspprinting.com
SIC: 2752 7334 Commercial printing, offset; photocopying & duplicating services

(G-11169)
R R FORREST COMPANY INC
Also Called: Aids To Navigation/Buoys
58 Chesterfield Dr (46060-3859)
PHONE..................................317 502-3286
EMP: 3
SALES (est): 169.7K **Privately Held**
SIC: 3089 Mfg And Distributor Of Buoys Aids To Nav

(G-11170)
RAIN SONG FARMS LLC
Also Called: Rain Song Winery
19539 Pilgrim Rd (46060-9440)
PHONE..................................317 640-4534
Carrie Taylor, *Owner*
Brian Taylor,
EMP: 2 EST: 2010
SQ FT: 3,000
SALES (est): 83.7K **Privately Held**
SIC: 2084 Wine cellars, bonded: engaged in blending wines

(G-11171)
RCS CONTRACTOR SUPPLIES INC
5000 Conner St (46060-2420)
P.O. Box 541 (46061-0541)
PHONE..................................317 773-6279
Donald Reynolds, *President*
Daris L Reynolds Sr, *Corp Secy*
Daris L Reynolds Jr, *Vice Pres*
EMP: 3
SALES (est): 660.4K **Privately Held**
WEB: www.rcs-supplies.com
SIC: 2675 Stencils & lettering materials: die-cut

(G-11172)
REALIZE INC
15515 Endeavor Dr (46060-4922)
PHONE..................................317 915-0295
Todd Reese, *President*
Tina Ryker, *Sales Mgr*
Jeff Costin, *Sales Staff*
EMP: 12
SQ FT: 2,400
SALES: 1.8MM **Privately Held**
WEB: www.realizeinc.com
SIC: 3999 Models, general, except toy

(G-11173)
REBEL DEVIL CUSTOMS
14164 E 239th St (46060-5571)
PHONE..................................303 921-7131
Michael C Johnson, *Owner*
▲ EMP: 4 EST: 2012
SQ FT: 1,440
SALES: 2K **Privately Held**
SIC: 3711 Motor vehicles & car bodies

(G-11174)
RED WING SHOE COMPANY INC
17017 Mercantile Blvd (46060-3941)
PHONE..................................317 219-6777
EMP: 2
SALES (est): 77.4K
SALES (corp-wide): 568.6MM **Privately Held**
SIC: 3143 Men's footwear, except athletic
PA: Red Wing Shoe Company, Inc.
314 Main St
Red Wing MN 55066
651 388-8211

(G-11175)
REVOLVER LLC
13904 Town Center Blvd # 800 (46060-4004)
PHONE..................................317 418-1824
Josh Trisler,
EMP: 3
SALES: 500K **Privately Held**
SIC: 2389 Apparel & accessories

(G-11176)
RF MANUFACTURING INC
1780 S 10th St (46060-3835)
PHONE..................................317 773-8610
Jeff Query, *President*
EMP: 9 EST: 2011
SALES: 1.4MM **Privately Held**
SIC: 3441 3599 7389 Fabricated structural metal; machine shop, jobbing & repair;

(G-11177)
ROWLAND PRINTING CO INC
Also Called: Image Builders/Rowland Prtg
199 N 9th St (46060-2212)
PHONE..................................317 773-1829
Dane Rowland, *President*
Dean Rowland, *Human Res Mgr*
Pat Lane, *Sales Staff*
John Lyon, *Marketing Staff*
Ted Rowland, *Exec Dir*
EMP: 16
SALES (est): 1.7MM **Privately Held**
WEB: www.rowlandprinting.com
SIC: 2752 2791 7311 2789 Commercial printing, offset; typesetting, computer controlled; advertising agencies; bookbinding & related work; commercial printing; newspapers

(G-11178)
RWB & ASSOCIATES LLC
Also Called: Fanattic-Bedz
16217 Stony Ridge Dr (46060-8068)
PHONE..................................317 219-6572
EMP: 2
SQ FT: 1,500
SALES (est): 140K **Privately Held**
SIC: 2511 8711 Mfg Wood Household Furniture Engineering Services

(G-11179)
SAM MOURON EQUIPMENT CO INC
15535 Stony Creek Way (46060-4386)
PHONE..................................317 776-1799
Fax: 317 776-1899
Kerry Creek, *President*
Mark Adams, *Vice Pres*
Dawn Ehrgott, *Office Mgr*
EMP: 15 EST: 1953
SQ FT: 23,000
SALES (est): 3.2MM **Privately Held**
SIC: 3444 Sheet metal specialties, not stamped

(G-11180)
SCHURZ COMMUNICATIONS INC
Also Called: Noblesville Daily Times, The
802 Mulberry St (46060-3408)
PHONE..................................317 773-9960
Fax: 317 770-5770
Terry L Coomer, *Branch Mgr*
EMP: 50
SALES (corp-wide): 882.7MM **Publicly Held**
WEB: www.schurz.com
SIC: 2711 Newspapers, publishing & printing
HQ: Schurz Communications, Inc.
1301 E Douglas Rd Ste 200
Mishawaka IN 46545
574 247-7237

(G-11181)
SCHWARTZS TRAILER SALES INC
117 Cicero Rd (46060-1402)
PHONE..................................317 773-2608
Fax: 317 773-7505
Glen Schwartz, *President*
Patricia Schwartz, *Corp Secy*
Pat Schwartz, *Vice Pres*
Brent Crandall, *Manager*
EMP: 6
SQ FT: 3,000
SALES (est): 680K **Privately Held**
SIC: 3715 5599 Truck trailers; utility trailers

(G-11182)
SHOOTING STARS SYNCHRO INC
21480 Candlewick Rd (46062-7616)
PHONE..................................317 710-1462
Cheryl Giannuzzi, *Principal*
EMP: 3 EST: 2008
SALES (est): 203.1K **Privately Held**
SIC: 3621 Synchros

(G-11183)
SIGN SER HOMES
50 N 9th St (46060-2203)
PHONE..................................317 214-8005
Sandra Chambers, *Manager*

G E O G R A P H I C

EMP: 2 EST: 2014
SALES (est): 86.4K **Privately Held**
SIC: 3993 Signs & advertising specialties

(G-11184)
SMC CORPORATION OF AMERICA (HQ)
10100 Smc Blvd (46060-8701)
P.O. Box 1880 (46061-1880)
PHONE...........................317 899-3182
Yoshiki Takada, *President*
Stephen Conners, *Principal*
Julie Dheehr, *Principal*
Brent Poe, *Principal*
William Ramsey, *Vice Pres*
▲ EMP: 350
SQ FT: 241,300
SALES (est): 305.1MM
SALES (corp-wide): 5.5B **Privately Held**
WEB: www.smcusa.com
SIC: 3625 3492 3491 3559 Actuators, industrial; control valves, fluid power; hydraulic & pneumatic; pressure valves & regulators, industrial; automotive related machinery; fluid power actuators, hydraulic or pneumatic; pneumatic relays, air-conditioning type; switches, pneumatic positioning remote
PA: Smc Corporation
4-14-1, Sotokanda
Chiyoda-Ku TKY 101-0
352 078-271

(G-11185)
SOULFUL SCENTS LLC
19388 Golden Meadow Way (46060-7515)
PHONE...........................317 319-8001
Renee P Barker, *Principal*
EMP: 2
SALES (est): 114.5K **Privately Held**
SIC: 2844 Toilet preparations

(G-11186)
SOUTHFIELD CORPORATION
15215 N River Ave (46060)
PHONE...........................317 773-5340
Tod True, *Manager*
EMP: 27
SALES (corp-wide): 285MM **Privately Held**
WEB: www.prairiegroup.com
SIC: 3273 Ready-mixed concrete
PA: Southfield Corporation
8995 W 95th St
Palos Hills IL 60465
708 344-1000

(G-11187)
SPECTRUM BRANDS INC
20975 Creek Rd (46060-9383)
PHONE...........................317 773-6627
Shanah Tran, *Branch Mgr*
EMP: 21
SALES (corp-wide): 5B **Publicly Held**
SIC: 3231 3499 3229 3564 Aquariums & reflectors, glass; aquarium accessories, metal; pressed & blown glass; blowers & fans; lighting equipment
HQ: Spectrum Brands, Inc.
3001 Deming Way
Middleton WI 53562
608 275-3340

(G-11188)
SPEEDWAY LLC
Also Called: Speedway Superamerica 3303
17645 Little Chicago Rd (46062-8906)
PHONE...........................317 867-3699
Jim Mason, *Manager*
EMP: 10 **Publicly Held**
WEB: www.speedwaynet.com
SIC: 1311 Crude petroleum production
HQ: Speedway Llc
500 Speedway Dr
Enon OH 45323
937 864-3000

(G-11189)
SPEEDWAY LLC
Also Called: Speedway Superamerica 3304
3150 Conner St (46060-2406)
PHONE...........................317 770-0225
Jennifer High, *Manager*
EMP: 10 **Publicly Held**
WEB: www.speedwaynet.com
SIC: 1311 Crude petroleum production

HQ: Speedway Llc
500 Speedway Dr
Enon OH 45323
937 864-3000

(G-11190)
STRAWTOWN POTTERY & ANTIQUES
12738 Strawtown Ave (46060-6971)
PHONE...........................317 984-5080
Matt Garrison, *President*
Diane Garrison, *Vice Pres*
EMP: 2
SALES (est): 148.9K **Privately Held**
SIC: 3269 5023 5719 5932 Art & ornamental ware, pottery; pottery; pottery; antiques

(G-11191)
T L E LLC
Also Called: Thread Letter Emblem
17039 Mercantile Blvd (46060-3941)
PHONE...........................317 257-1424
EMP: 3 EST: 1969
SALES (est): 170K **Privately Held**
SIC: 2395 Embroidery Services

(G-11192)
TEA UNWRAPPED LLC
15486 Herriman Blvd (46060-4215)
PHONE...........................317 558-8550
Cheryl E Watson, *President*
EMP: 2
SALES (est): 117.4K **Privately Held**
SIC: 2099 Sandwiches, assembled & packaged: for wholesale market

(G-11193)
TEC TRANSPORT LLC
20218 Cyntheanne Rd (46060-9331)
PHONE...........................765 534-3253
Carol J Sherrill,
EMP: 4
SALES (est): 298K **Privately Held**
SIC: 3715 Truck trailers

(G-11194)
THERAMETRIC TECHNOLOGIES INC
9880 Douglas Floyd Pkwy (46060-7900)
PHONE...........................317 565-8065
George K Stookey, *President*
Lisa Hoover, *Director*
EMP: 11
SQ FT: 2,100
SALES (est): 2.1MM **Privately Held**
WEB: www.therametric.com
SIC: 3829 Measuring & controlling devices

(G-11195)
TRAVELING BOOKBINDER INC
10712 Talisman Dr (46060-7630)
PHONE...........................317 441-4901
Jeffrey T Saxton, *President*
EMP: 2 EST: 1970
SALES (est): 169.6K **Privately Held**
SIC: 2732 Books: printing & binding

(G-11196)
TRIUNITY LLC
Also Called: Shear Line Golf
15209 Herriman Blvd (46060-4230)
PHONE...........................317 703-1147
George Doran Sr, *President*
EMP: 3
SQ FT: 2,300
SALES (est): 231K **Privately Held**
SIC: 3949 Golf equipment

(G-11197)
UNITED PARCEL SERVICE INC
Also Called: UPS
14350 Mundy Dr Ste 800 (46060-7229)
PHONE...........................317 776-9494
Fax: 317 776-9594
Jane Weaver, *Owner*
EMP: 4
SALES (corp-wide): 65.8B **Publicly Held**
WEB: www.ups.com
SIC: 7389 2752 2789 Notary publics; mailbox rental & related service; commercial printing, lithographic; binding only: books, pamphlets, magazines, etc.

PA: United Parcel Service, Inc.
55 Glenlake Pkwy
Atlanta GA 30328
404 828-6000

(G-11198)
UNIVERSAL BLOWER PAC INC
440 Park 32 West Dr (46062-9213)
PHONE...........................317 773-7256
Fax: 317 776-5086
Ray Fiechter, *President*
Fiechter Carol, *Admin Sec*
EMP: 21 EST: 1979
SQ FT: 15,000
SALES (est): 10.3MM **Privately Held**
WEB: www.universalblowerpac.com
SIC: 3564 Blowing fans: industrial or commercial

(G-11199)
VIBROMATIC COMPANY INC (PA)
1301 S 6th St (46060-3712)
P.O. Box 1358 (46061-1358)
PHONE...........................317 773-3885
Fax: 317 773-2342
Brad Graham, *Exec VP*
Terry Hawkins, *Director*
EMP: 34 EST: 1956
SQ FT: 35,000
SALES (est): 4.3MM **Privately Held**
WEB: www.vibromatic.net
SIC: 3559 3444 3829 ; hoppers, sheet metal; measuring & controlling devices

(G-11200)
YOUR WINDOW WASHER LLC
15566 Outside Trl (46060-8122)
PHONE...........................317 701-1710
EMP: 2
SALES (est): 106K **Privately Held**
SIC: 3556 Food products machinery

(G-11201)
ZR TACTICAL SOLUTIONS LLC
Also Called: Zrts
15223 Herriman Blvd Ste 4 (46060-4218)
PHONE...........................317 721-9787
Adam Hooker, *General Mgr*
EMP: 2
SALES (est): 178.5K **Privately Held**
SIC: 3489 Guns or gun parts, over 30 mm.

Norman
Jackson County

(G-11202)
BALDWIN LOGGING INC
11763 State Road 58 E (47264-8631)
PHONE...........................812 834-1040
Dennis Baldwin, *Manager*
EMP: 3
SALES (est): 254K **Privately Held**
SIC: 2411 Logging

(G-11203)
JUSTIN BLACKWELL
Also Called: Blackwell Limestone
7071 State Road 446 (47264-8685)
P.O. Box 209, Heltonville (47436-0209)
PHONE...........................812 834-6350
Justin Blackwell, *Owner*
EMP: 16
SALES (est): 1.6MM **Privately Held**
WEB: www.justinblackwell.com
SIC: 3281 Limestone, cut & shaped

(G-11204)
S&S MACHINERY REPAIR LLC
12807 W Us Highway 50 (47264-9766)
PHONE...........................812 521-2368
Beth Singer, *Principal*
EMP: 4
SALES (est): 639.1K **Privately Held**
SIC: 3541 Machine tool replacement & repair parts, metal cutting types

---

North Judson
Starke County

(G-11205)
A & S LOGGING INC
2340 E 800 S (46366-8465)
PHONE...........................574 896-3136
Cheyenne Allen, *Principal*
EMP: 3
SALES (est): 191K **Privately Held**
SIC: 2411 Logging

(G-11206)
AMERICAN OAK PRESERVING CO INC (PA)
Also Called: Starburst Sales
601 Mulberry St (46366-1044)
P.O. Box 187 (46366-0187)
PHONE...........................574 896-2171
Fax: 574 896-3055
Charles K Vorm, *President*
James Long, *Vice Pres*
Theresa Roy, *Engineer*
Kirsten Martin, *Treasurer*
James Johnston, *Human Res Mgr*
▲ EMP: 47 EST: 1915
SQ FT: 100,000
SALES (est): 9.8MM **Privately Held**
WEB: www.americanoak.net
SIC: 3999 Foliage, artificial & preserved; artificial trees & flowers

(G-11207)
C E KERSTING & SONS
6800 S 300 W (46366-8338)
P.O. Box 296 (46366-0296)
PHONE...........................574 896-2766
Fax: 574 896-3967
Charles Kersting Jr, *Partner*
Melvin Kersting, *Partner*
EMP: 3 EST: 1936
SQ FT: 10,000
SALES (est): 1.2MM **Privately Held**
SIC: 2448 2441 Pallets, wood; nailed wood boxes & shook

(G-11208)
CALLISONS INC
Also Called: I P Callison & Sons
7675 S 100 W (46366-8447)
PHONE...........................574 896-5074
Greg Allender, *Manager*
EMP: 3
SALES (corp-wide): 36.5MM **Privately Held**
WEB: www.ipcallison.com
SIC: 2087 Extracts, flavoring
PA: Callisons, Inc.
2400 Callison Rd Ne
Lacey WA 98516
360 412-3340

(G-11209)
CHESTER INC
Also Called: A B I Dept
6020 S 500 W (46366-8874)
PHONE...........................574 896-5600
Fax: 574 896-5622
Larry Holt, *Branch Mgr*
EMP: 20
SALES (corp-wide): 21.3MM **Privately Held**
WEB: www.chestertech.com
SIC: 5083 2096 Agricultural machinery & equipment; potato chips & similar snacks
PA: Chester Inc
555 Eastport Centre Dr A
Valparaiso IN 46383
219 465-7555

(G-11210)
COLD CRAFT BREWING LLC
Also Called: Bottle Neck Solutions
424 Lane St (46366-1226)
PHONE...........................314 712-0883
Mitch Fingerhut, *Branch Mgr*
EMP: 3
SALES (corp-wide): 1.1MM **Privately Held**
SIC: 2099 2095 Tea blending; roasted coffee

PA: Cold Craft Brewing Llc
104 Bronson St Ste 22
Santa Cruz CA 95062
314 712-0883

(G-11211)
EVELYN DOLLAHAN
Also Called: 4d Manufacturing
520 E 625 S (46366-8486)
PHONE..............................574 896-2971
Evelyn Dollahan, *Owner*
EMP: 4
SALES (est): 387.2K **Privately Held**
SIC: 3523 Cattle feeding, handling & watering equipment

(G-11212)
FINGERHUT BAKERY INC (PA)
119 Lane St (46366-1219)
PHONE..............................574 896-5937
Fax: 574 896-5114
Keith Fingerhut, *President*
EMP: 15
SALES (est): 765.3K **Privately Held**
SIC: 5461 2052 2051 Cakes; cookies & crackers; bread, cake & related products

(G-11213)
MAPPA MUNDI MAGAZINE
307 Lane St (46366-1222)
PHONE..............................574 896-4952
EMP: 2 **EST:** 2001
SALES (est): 100K **Privately Held**
SIC: 2721 Periodicals-Publishing/Printing

(G-11214)
THERMO PRODUCTS LLC (HQ)
5235 W State Road 10 # 5 (46366-8786)
P.O. Box 217 (46366-0217)
PHONE..............................574 896-2133
Fax: 574 896-5301
Allen A Kuehl, *President*
Dale Bowman, *COO*
Jim Archer, *Mfg Mgr*
Everett James, *Engineer*
Pam Derr, *Personnel*
EMP: 74 **EST:** 1946
SQ FT: 70,000
SALES (est): 16MM
SALES (corp-wide): 172.4MM **Publicly Held**
SIC: 3585 3433 Furnaces, warm air: electric; air conditioning units, complete: domestic or industrial; heating equipment, except electric
PA: Burnham Holdings, Inc.
1241 Harrisburg Ave
Lancaster PA 17603
717 390-7800

North Liberty
St. Joseph County

(G-11215)
HYDRO EXTRUSION NORTH AMER LLC
400 S Main St (46554-9639)
PHONE..............................888 935-5757
Randy Unrein, *Plant Mgr*
Kasondra Kaiser, *Buyer*
EMP: 170
SALES (corp-wide): 13.8B **Privately Held**
SIC: 3354 Aluminum extruded products
HQ: Hydro Extrusion North America, Llc
6250 N River Rd
Rosemont IL 60018
877 710-7272

(G-11216)
HYDRO EXTRUSION NORTH AMER LLC
400 S Main St (46554-9639)
PHONE..............................888 935-5757
Henry Boots, *Branch Mgr*
EMP: 300
SALES (corp-wide): 13.8B **Privately Held**
WEB: www.hydroaluminumna.com
SIC: 3354 3471 3444 Rods, extruded, aluminum; plating & polishing; sheet metalwork

HQ: Hydro Extrusion North America, Llc
6250 N River Rd
Rosemont IL 60018
877 710-7272

(G-11217)
INTEGRITECH MFG INC
67911 State Road 23 (46554-9714)
PHONE..............................574 656-3046
Kent D Morris, *Principal*
EMP: 3
SALES (est): 167.1K **Privately Held**
SIC: 3999 Manufacturing industries

(G-11218)
LONGHORN SAND AND GRAVEL LLC
30430 Osborne Rd (46554-9623)
PHONE..............................574 656-3231
EMP: 3
SALES (est): 333.4K **Privately Held**
SIC: 1442 Gravel mining

(G-11219)
R D LANEY FAMILY HONEY COMPANY
25725 New Rd (46554-9379)
PHONE..............................574 656-8701
Fax: 574 656-8603
Kay Laney, *Principal*
Dave Laney, *Chairman*
Linda Laney, *Vice Pres*
EMP: 6
SALES: 450K **Privately Held**
WEB: www.laneyhoney.com
SIC: 2099 5149 Honey, strained & bottled; honey

(G-11220)
RAPID RULE CO INC
69159 Pine Rd (46554-9397)
PHONE..............................574 784-2273
Fax: 574 784-8131
Douglas Seely III, *President*
EMP: 2
SALES (est): 150K **Privately Held**
SIC: 3423 Rules or rulers, metal

(G-11221)
SHOEMAKER WELDING CO
65508 State Road 23 (46554-9404)
PHONE..............................574 656-4412
Alan Shoemaker, *Owner*
EMP: 3
SQ FT: 3,000
SALES: 400K **Privately Held**
SIC: 3561 7692 Pumps & pumping equipment; welding repair

(G-11222)
SINGLE SOURCE INC
791 Industrial Pkwy (46554-9239)
PHONE..............................574 656-3400
Fax: 574 656-3322
Greg Singleton, *President*
Tom Moore, *Vice Pres*
Tanya Forester, *Office Mgr*
EMP: 15 **EST:** 2001
SQ FT: 8,600
SALES: 1.5MM **Privately Held**
SIC: 3599 Machine shop, jobbing & repair

(G-11223)
WOODS UNLIMITED INC
67850 Sycamore Rd (46554-9214)
PHONE..............................574 656-3382
Dean Shoue, *President*
John Shoue, *Vice Pres*
Janet Shoue, *Treasurer*
Ester Shoue, *Admin Sec*
EMP: 5
SALES (est): 402.8K **Privately Held**
SIC: 2499 2541 Kitchen, bathroom & household ware: wood; cabinets, except refrigerated: show, display, etc.: wood

---

North Manchester
Wabash County

(G-11224)
AIR FIXTURES INC
1108 N Sycamore St (46962-1151)
P.O. Box 147 (46962-0147)
PHONE..............................260 982-2169
Fax: 260 982-7839
Leon L Bazzoni, *President*
M B Bazzoni, *Vice Pres*
EMP: 15
SQ FT: 3,000
SALES (est): 1.4MM **Privately Held**
SIC: 3563 3494 Air & gas compressors including vacuum pumps; valves & pipe fittings

(G-11225)
BKB MANUFACTURING INC
607 S Wabash Rd (46962-8148)
P.O. Box 326 (46962-0326)
PHONE..............................260 982-8524
Fax: 260 982-1332
Josh Beery, *Plant Mgr*
EMP: 3
SALES (est): 240.9K **Privately Held**
SIC: 3999 Manufacturing industries

(G-11226)
CAM METAL FABRICATION LLC
911 W Main St (46962-1912)
PHONE..............................260 982-6280
Michael G Catenazzo,
▲ **EMP:** 8
SALES (est): 1.2MM **Privately Held**
SIC: 3441 Fabricated structural metal

(G-11227)
CUSTOM MAGNETICS INC (PA)
Also Called: James Electronics Div.
801 W Main St (46962-1452)
PHONE..............................773 463-6500
Fax: 260 982-4942
Kirti Shah, *President*
Raju Shah, *General Mgr*
Linda Reed, *Controller*
▲ **EMP:** 50 **EST:** 1974
SQ FT: 18,000
SALES (est): 10.7MM **Privately Held**
WEB: www.custommag.com
SIC: 3612 3613 3621 Specialty transformers; switchboard apparatus, except instruments; electronic coils, transformers & other inductors; motors & generators

(G-11228)
CUSTOM MAGNETICS INC
Also Called: James Electronics Div
801 W Main St (46962-1452)
PHONE..............................773 463-6500
Fax: 773 463-1504
Tito Chowdhury, *Branch Mgr*
EMP: 20
SALES (est): 2.5MM
SALES (corp-wide): 10.7MM **Privately Held**
WEB: www.custommag.com
SIC: 3677 Electronic transformers
PA: Custom Magnetics Inc
801 W Main St
North Manchester IN 46962
773 463-6500

(G-11229)
HEARTH GLOW INC
2234 E 1450 N (46962-8617)
PHONE..............................260 839-3205
Roger Presl, *President*
Kathryn Presl, *Corp Secy*
EMP: 9
SALES: 700K **Privately Held**
SIC: 2411 Fuel wood harvesting

(G-11230)
HF GROUP LLC
Heckman Bindery
1010 N Sycamore St (46962-1252)
P.O. Box 89 (46962-0089)
PHONE..............................260 982-2107
Fax: 260 982-1104
Virginia Aughinbaugh, *Human Res Mgr*

Jim Heckman, *Branch Mgr*
Cindy Knafel, *Info Tech Mgr*
EMP: 270
SALES (corp-wide): 28MM **Privately Held**
SIC: 2789 Bookbinding & related work
PA: Hf Group, Llc
8844 Mayfield Rd
Chesterland OH 44026
440 729-2445

(G-11231)
IN THE SPOTLIGHT LLC
3106 E 1450 N (46962-8511)
PHONE..............................260 519-1805
Linda Caldwell, *Principal*
EMP: 2
SALES (est): 157.5K **Privately Held**
SIC: 3648 Spotlights

(G-11232)
JOHNSON ENGRAVING & TROPHIES
1302 Beckley St (46962-2115)
P.O. Box 205 (46962-0205)
PHONE..............................260 982-7868
Fax: 260 982-6276
Jerry Johnson, *Owner*
Teresa Johnson, *Owner*
EMP: 2
SALES: 36K **Privately Held**
SIC: 3993 5999 3479 Signs & advertising specialties; trophies & plaques; etching on metals

(G-11233)
MANCHESTER NORTH NEWS JOURNAL
1306 State Road 114 W (46962-1944)
P.O. Box 368 (46962-0368)
PHONE..............................260 982-6383
Fax: 260 982-8233
Mike Rees, *President*
David Purvis-Fenker, *Editor*
Tim McLaughlin, *Manager*
EMP: 4 **EST:** 1966
SALES (est): 273.5K **Privately Held**
WEB: www.nmpaper.com
SIC: 2711 Commercial printing & newspaper publishing combined

(G-11234)
MANCHESTER TOOL & DIE INC
601 S Wabash Rd (46962-8148)
P.O. Box 326 (46962-0326)
PHONE..............................260 982-8524
Fax: 260 982-4575
Barry Blocher, *President*
Connie Burgess, *Opers Staff*
EMP: 95
SQ FT: 65,000
SALES (est): 17.4MM **Privately Held**
WEB: www.bkbmfg.com
SIC: 3599 Machine shop, jobbing & repair

(G-11235)
MANCHESTER TOOL AND DIE PLANT
405 Beckley St (46962-1440)
PHONE..............................260 982-0702
Josh Beery, *Manager*
EMP: 2
SALES (est): 176.9K **Privately Held**
SIC: 3544 Special dies & tools

(G-11236)
MM HOLDINGS I LLC
Also Called: Manchester Metals
205 Wabash Rd (46962-1418)
P.O. Box 345 (46962-0345)
PHONE..............................260 982-2191
David Boyd, *President*
EMP: 135
SQ FT: 100,000
SALES (est): 34.7MM
SALES (corp-wide): 0 **Privately Held**
SIC: 3321 Gray iron castings
HQ: The Electric Materials Company
50 S Washington St
North East PA 16428
814 725-9621

(G-11237)
NICHOLAS PRECISION WORKS LLC
1101 Taylor St (46962-8183)
P.O. Box 150 (46962-0150)
PHONE..........................260 306-3426
Anthony Andrew Nicholas, *President*
Ryan Alderfer, *Manager*
Daisy Ruth Nicholas,
James Allen Nicholas,
EMP: 7
SQ FT: 10,000
SALES: 1MM **Privately Held**
SIC: 3545 Cutting tools for machine tools

(G-11238)
NORTH MANCHESTER ETHANOL LLC
Also Called: Poet Brfnng- N Mnchster 24000
868 E 800 N (46962-8957)
P.O. Box 369 (46962-0369)
PHONE..........................260 774-3532
Steve Pittman, *General Mgr*
EMP: 3
SALES (est): 568K **Privately Held**
SIC: 2869 Ethyl alcohol, ethanol
PA: Poet, Llc
4615 N Lewis Ave
Sioux Falls SD 57104

(G-11239)
NOVAE CORP
11870 N 650 E (46962-8152)
PHONE..........................260 982-7075
Chris Storie, *Principal*
EMP: 36 **Privately Held**
SIC: 3524 Lawn & garden equipment
PA: Novae Corp.
1 Novae Pkwy
Markle IN 46770

(G-11240)
P & J SECTIONAL HOUSING
14385 N 200 E (46962-8619)
PHONE..........................260 982-7231
Jeff Walters, *Partner*
EMP: 2
SALES (est): 110.9K **Privately Held**
WEB: www.nmanchester.net
SIC: 1389 Construction, repair & dismantling services

(G-11241)
QUALITY HARDWOOD PRODUCTS INC
2234 E 1450 N (46962-8617)
PHONE..........................260 982-2043
Fax: 260 982-6595
Roger Presl, *President*
Kathryn Presl, *Treasurer*
EMP: 15
SQ FT: 5,000
SALES: 2MM **Privately Held**
SIC: 2421 2426 Custom sawmill; hardwood dimension & flooring mills

(G-11242)
ROTAM TOOL CORPORATION (PA)
11606 N State Road 15 (46962-8688)
PHONE..........................260 982-8318
Henry Becker, *President*
Gail Becker, *Treasurer*
EMP: 12
SQ FT: 20,000
SALES: 500K **Privately Held**
WEB: www.total-tote.com
SIC: 3599 3544 3469 Machine shop, jobbing & repair; special dies, tools, jigs & fixtures; metal stampings

(G-11243)
SCHULER PRECISION TOOL LLC
6177 W State Road 114 (46962-8600)
PHONE..........................260 982-2704
Fax: 260 982-6558
Ned Schuler, *President*
EMP: 9
SALES (est): 921.5K **Privately Held**
SIC: 7389 7692 3441 Grinding, precision: commercial or industrial; welding repair; fabricated structural metal

(G-11244)
SCHUTZ BROTHERS INC
1604 East St (46962-1090)
P.O. Box 300 (46962-0300)
PHONE..........................260 982-8581
Fax: 260 982-7911
Mitchell Schutz, *President*
Carol Snodgrass, *Web Dvlpr*
Sandra Jones, *Shareholder*
Penny Schutz, *Admin Sec*
EMP: 14 EST: 1946
SQ FT: 5,000
SALES (est): 2.2MM **Privately Held**
WEB: www.schutzbrothers.com
SIC: 5191 3199 Equestrian equipment; saddlery; harness equipment; equestrian related leather articles; saddles or parts; harness or harness parts

(G-11245)
STRAUSS VEAL FEEDS INC (PA)
600 Strauss Provimi Rd (46962-1393)
P.O. Box 149 (46962-0149)
PHONE..........................260 982-8611
Fax: 260 982-7653
David Grant, *President*
Donald Strauss, *Chairman*
Greg Martin, *Vice Pres*
▲ EMP: 30
SQ FT: 30,000
SALES (est): 16.4MM **Privately Held**
WEB: www.straussfeeds.com
SIC: 2048 Livestock feeds

(G-11246)
TOTAL TOTE INC
Also Called: Rotam Tooling
11606 N State Road 15 (46962-8688)
PHONE..........................260 982-8318
Fax: 260 982-6672
Henry Becker, *President*
Joe Fritz, *Manager*
EMP: 11
SQ FT: 4,000
SALES (est): 423K
SALES (corp-wide): 500K **Privately Held**
WEB: www.total-tote.com
SIC: 3599 Custom machinery; machine shop, jobbing & repair
PA: Rotam Tool Corporation
11606 N State Road 15
North Manchester IN 46962
260 982-8318

North Vernon
Jennings County

(G-11247)
ANNA DAISYS LLC
309 N State St (47265-1454)
PHONE..........................812 346-7623
Anna Smith, *Principal*
EMP: 2
SALES (est): 160.9K **Privately Held**
SIC: 2273 Carpets & rugs

(G-11248)
ATMOSPHERE ANNEALING LLC
1300 Indtl Dr (47265)
PHONE..........................812 346-1275
William Baxter, *Manager*
EMP: 30
SALES: 3.2MM
SALES (corp-wide): 35.7MM **Privately Held**
SIC: 3398 Annealing of metal
HQ: Atmosphere Annealing, Llc
209 W Mount Hope Ave # 2
Lansing MI 48910
517 485-5090

(G-11249)
CONCEPT TOOL & ENGINEERING
508 5th St (47265)
P.O. Box 1108 (47265-5108)
PHONE..........................812 352-0055
Tim Rickly, *President*
Micheal Deaton, *Superintendent*
Ed Kaufer, *Superintendent*
Don Matern, *Superintendent*
Montez Sutton, *Superintendent*
EMP: 6

SQ FT: 8,500
SALES: 600K **Privately Held**
SIC: 3089 Injection molding of plastics

(G-11250)
COWCO INC
3780 S State Highway 7 (47265-7995)
PHONE..........................812 346-8993
Michael Biehle, *President*
Edward Biehle, *Corp Secy*
Joe Biehle, *Manager*
▲ EMP: 3
SALES: 300K **Privately Held**
SIC: 3523 Farm machinery & equipment

(G-11251)
CULLMAN CASTING CORPORATION
3750 N County Road 75 W (47265-6004)
P.O. Box 894 (47265-0894)
PHONE..........................256 735-0900
Yoshihiko Ota, *Branch Mgr*
EMP: 6
SALES (corp-wide): 18.8B **Privately Held**
SIC: 3596 Weighing machines & apparatus
HQ: Cullman Casting Corporation
251 County Road 490
Cullman AL 35055

(G-11252)
DAVE OMARA PAVING INC (PA)
1100 E O And M Ave (47265-1319)
P.O. Box 423 (47265-0423)
PHONE..........................812 346-1214
Fax: 812 346-1216
Nancy O'Mara, *President*
Amy Hill, *Corp Secy*
Dan O'Mara, *Shareholder*
Dave O'Mara, *Shareholder*
Rob O'Mara, *Shareholder*
EMP: 2
SQ FT: 100
SALES (est): 1MM **Privately Held**
SIC: 2951 2952 Asphalt paving mixtures & blocks; asphalt felts & coatings

(G-11253)
DECATUR MOLD TOOL AND ENGRG
3330 N State Rd 7 (47265)
P.O. Box 387 (47265-0387)
PHONE..........................812 346-5188
Richard L Apsley, *President*
Rachel Apsley, *Corp Secy*
Larry Waltz, *Vice Pres*
Roger Robinette, *Project Mgr*
Kevin Alberring, *Engineer*
▲ EMP: 110
SQ FT: 87,000
SALES: 28MM **Privately Held**
WEB: www.decaturmold.com
SIC: 3089 3599 7699 Injection molded finished plastic products; electrical discharge machining (EDM); industrial machinery & equipment repair

(G-11254)
DECATUR PLASTIC PRODUCTS INC
655 Montrow Pkwy (47265-4908)
PHONE..........................812 352-6050
Junior Fields, *Branch Mgr*
EMP: 75
SALES (corp-wide): 56.5MM **Privately Held**
WEB: www.decaturplastics.com
SIC: 3999 Flocking metal products
PA: Decatur Plastic Products, Inc.
3250 N State Highway 7
North Vernon IN 47265
812 346-5159

(G-11255)
DECATUR PLASTIC PRODUCTS INC (PA)
Also Called: Dpp
3250 N State Highway 7 (47265-7490)
P.O. Box 1079 (47265-5079)
PHONE..........................812 346-5159
Fax: 812 346-5210
Yu Cha Riley, *Ch of Bd*
Gary Riley Sr, *Vice Ch Bd*
Robert Riley, *President*
Jeff Baker, *Business Mgr*
John Justice, *Plant Mgr*

▲ EMP: 190
SQ FT: 75,730
SALES (est): 56.5MM **Privately Held**
WEB: www.decaturplastics.com
SIC: 3089 Injection molding of plastics

(G-11256)
EBS LOGGING LLC
3600 E County Road 600 N (47265-8262)
PHONE..........................812 346-9248
Loretta Franklin, *Principal*
EMP: 2
SALES (est): 81.7K **Privately Held**
SIC: 2411 Logging

(G-11257)
ERLER INDUSTRIES INC (PA)
418 Stockwell St (47265-1464)
PHONE..........................812 346-4421
Fax: 812 346-1892
J Mark Erler, *President*
Linda Erler, *Admin Sec*
EMP: 100
SQ FT: 200,000
SALES (est): 22MM **Privately Held**
WEB: www.erler.com
SIC: 3479 Coating of metals & formed products

(G-11258)
GARR CUSTOM PALLETS INC ○
750 S Stonehenge (47265-6462)
PHONE..........................812 352-8887
Kelly S Pruitt, *Principal*
EMP: 3 EST: 2017
SALES (est): 141.8K **Privately Held**
SIC: 2448 Pallets, wood & wood with metal

(G-11259)
GERDAU MACSTEEL ATMOSPHERE ANN
1300 Industrial Dr (47265-4883)
P.O. Box 1049 (47265-5049)
PHONE..........................812 346-1275
William Baxter, *Manager*
EMP: 32 **Privately Held**
WEB: www.aaimac.com
SIC: 3398 Tempering of metal
HQ: Gerdau Macsteel Atmosphere Annealing
209 W Mount Hope Ave # 1
Lansing MI 48910
517 782-0415

(G-11260)
HANSON AGGREGATES MIDWEST LLC
610 S County Road 250 E (47265-7602)
PHONE..........................812 346-6100
Fax: 812 846-6558
Harold Trowbridge, *Manager*
EMP: 11
SALES (corp-wide): 20.3B **Privately Held**
SIC: 1422 Limestones, ground
HQ: Hanson Aggregates Midwest Llc
207 Old Harrods Creek Rd
Louisville KY 40223
502 244-7550

(G-11261)
HILEX POLY
1001 2nd St (47265-6518)
PHONE..........................812 346-1066
Rex Varn, *COO*
Danny Young, *Purch Mgr*
Chad Bembrick, *Engineer*
Chris Tamme, *Plant Engr*
EMP: 16
SALES (est): 2.9MM **Privately Held**
SIC: 2673 Plastic bags: made from purchased materials

(G-11262)
HOOSIER INDUSTRIAL ELECTRIC
Rodgers Park Dr (47265)
PHONE..........................812 346-2232
Fax: 812 346-2236
Stephen Blackburn Jr, *President*
Laurie Blackburn, *Principal*
Donald Chaille, *Vice Pres*
Steve Blackburn, *Foreman/Supr*
Cheryl Grunden, *Info Tech Mgr*
EMP: 15
SQ FT: 15,000

SALES (est): 2.4MM **Privately Held**
SIC: **1731** 5063 7694 General electrical contractor; motors, electric; electric motor repair

(G-11263)
INDIANA SOUTHERN MILLWORK INC (PA)
Also Called: Jonesville Desk
819 Buckeye St (47265-1623)
PHONE...............................812 346-6129
Fax: 812 346-5384
Jerry R Lowman, *President*
EMP: 25
SQ FT: 32,000
SALES (est): 1.5MM **Privately Held**
WEB: www.simillwork.com
SIC: **2521** 2431 2541 Wood office furniture; wood office filing cabinets & bookcases; millwork; wood partitions & fixtures

(G-11264)
INDIANA SOUTHERN MOLD CORP
2945 N State Highway 3 (47265-9252)
P.O. Box 119 (47265-0119)
PHONE...............................812 346-2622
Fax: 812 346-2625
Angela J Grindstaff, *President*
Daisy Rees, *Office Mgr*
▲ EMP: 20
SQ FT: 14,000
SALES (est): 3.4MM **Privately Held**
WEB: www.soindmoldcorp.com
SIC: **3544** Industrial molds

(G-11265)
INDUSTRIAL UTILITIES INC
3680 E County Road 450 S (47265-7762)
PHONE...............................812 346-4489
William E Blackburn, *President*
EMP: 2
SALES (est): 119.7K **Privately Held**
SIC: **3999** Cigarette filters

(G-11266)
INJECTION MOLD INC
134 E O And M Ave (47265-1125)
P.O. Box 443 (47265-0443)
PHONE...............................812 346-7002
Delbert A Vawter, *President*
EMP: 12
SQ FT: 8,300
SALES (est): 1.7MM **Privately Held**
SIC: **3544** Industrial molds

(G-11267)
LEES READY-MIX & TRUCKING INC (PA)
Also Called: Lee's Ready Mix
1100 W Jfk Dr (47265-4910)
P.O. Box 496 (47265-0496)
PHONE...............................812 346-9767
Debra Jo Brown, *President*
James Fear, *Treasurer*
EMP: 50 EST: 1971
SQ FT: 5,000
SALES (est): 9.7MM **Privately Held**
SIC: **3273** 4212 Ready-mixed concrete; local trucking, without storage

(G-11268)
MANAR INC
Also Called: C E W Enterprises
1050 W Jfk Dr (47265)
P.O. Box 1105 (47265-5105)
PHONE...............................812 346-2858
Fax: 812 346-2865
Richard Miller, *Branch Mgr*
EMP: 50
SALES (est): 8.4MM
SALES (corp-wide): 49.4MM **Privately Held**
WEB: www.manarinc.com
SIC: **3089** Injection molding of plastics
PA: Manar, Inc.
905 S Walnut St
Edinburgh IN 46124
812 526-2891

(G-11269)
MARTINREA INDUSTRIES INC
Also Called: North Vernon Division
505 Industrial Dr (47265-4887)
P.O. Box 927 (47265-0927)
PHONE...............................812 346-5750
Donald Smith, *Buyer*
Matt Horak, *Branch Mgr*
Jeremiah Hendern, *Program Mgr*
EMP: 225
SALES (corp-wide): 2.8B **Privately Held**
WEB: www.reedcitytool.com
SIC: **3317** 3714 Steel pipe & tubes; motor vehicle parts & accessories
HQ: Martinrea Industries, Inc.
10501 Mi State Road 52
Manchester MI 48158
734 428-2400

(G-11270)
MASCHINO INDUSTRIES INC
1405 S County Road 750 W (47265-6964)
P.O. Box 1, Hayden (47245-0001)
PHONE...............................812 346-3083
Lester Maschino, *President*
Kenny Maschino, *Vice Pres*
EMP: 5
SQ FT: 6,000
SALES (est): 500K **Privately Held**
SIC: **3599** Machine & other job shop work

(G-11271)
NORTH VERNON ELECTRIC INC
1511 E Buckeye St (47265-9796)
PHONE...............................812 392-2985
Fax: 812 346-3450
John L Lindsay, *President*
Kathy Kraemer, *Vice Pres*
EMP: 10
SQ FT: 4,300
SALES: 1MM **Privately Held**
SIC: **5063** 1731 7694 Electrical supplies; electrical work; electric motor repair

(G-11272)
NORTH VERNON PLAIN DLR & SUN
Also Called: North Vernon Sun
528 E O And M Ave (47265-1217)
P.O. Box 988 (47265-0988)
PHONE...............................812 346-3973
Fax: 812 346-8368
Barbara King, *President*
Susan King, *Corp Secy*
Madelon King, *Vice Pres*
EMP: 22
SQ FT: 4,500
SALES (est): 1.4MM **Privately Held**
WEB: www.northvernon.com
SIC: **2711** 7336 2791 2789 Job printing & newspaper publishing combined; commercial art & graphic design; typesetting; bookbinding & related work; commercial printing, lithographic

(G-11273)
NOVOLEX INC
1001 2nd St (47265-6518)
PHONE...............................812 346-1066
David Brooks, *Manager*
Karen Imes, *Manager*
Brian Crecelius, *Programmer Anys*
EMP: 200
SALES (corp-wide): 2.9B **Privately Held**
SIC: **2673** Plastic bags: made from purchased materials
HQ: Hilex Poly Co. Llc
101 E Carolina Ave
Hartsville SC 29550
843 857-4800

(G-11274)
ONSPOT OF NORTH AMERICA INC (HQ)
1075 Rodgers Park Dr (47265-5603)
P.O. Box 1077 (47265-5077)
PHONE...............................203 377-0777
Fax: 203 380-0441
Patrick D Freyer, *President*
Eric Jones, *Vice Pres*
Colin Chambless, *Manager*
Kapria Dilligard, *Manager*
EMP: 4
SQ FT: 2,500

SALES (est): 4.2MM
SALES (corp-wide): 355.7MM **Privately Held**
WEB: www.onspot.com
SIC: **3496** 5072 Tire chains; chains
PA: Vbg Group Ab (Publ)
Kungsgatan 57
Trollhattan 461 3
521 277-700

(G-11275)
ONSPOT OF NORTH AMERICA INC
Also Called: On Spot of North America
1075 Rodgers Park Dr (47265-5603)
P.O. Box 1077 (47265-5077)
PHONE...............................812 346-1719
Fax: 812 346-1819
Doris Short, *Manager*
EMP: 22
SQ FT: 20,000
SALES (corp-wide): 355.7MM **Privately Held**
WEB: www.onspot.com
SIC: **3496** 3714 3462 Tire chains; motor vehicle parts & accessories; iron & steel forgings
HQ: Onspot Of North America Inc.
1075 Rodgers Park Dr
North Vernon IN 47265
203 377-0777

(G-11276)
PATRIOT PACKAGING LLC
1002 Rodgers Park Dr (47265)
P.O. Box 131 (47265-0131)
PHONE...............................812 346-0700
Issaac Brown, *President*
EMP: 7
SALES (est): 1MM **Privately Held**
SIC: **3565** Packaging machinery

(G-11277)
PBM INDUSTRIES INC
Also Called: Poolguard
1150 J F K Dr (47265-4910)
P.O. Box 658 (47265-0658)
PHONE...............................812 346-2648
Fax: 812 346-2650
Merle Stoner, *President*
Dick Apsley, *Vice Pres*
Scott Hines, *Purch Agent*
Ben Stone, *Admin Sec*
▲ EMP: 25
SALES (est): 3.5MM **Privately Held**
WEB: www.poolguard.com
SIC: **3699** 1731 Security devices; electrical work

(G-11278)
PLASFINCO LLC
1060 Jfk Dr (47265)
P.O. Box 372 (47265-0372)
PHONE...............................812 346-3900
Fax: 812 346-3910
Kenton Rousch, *President*
Richard Miller, *Admin Sec*
EMP: 40
SQ FT: 8,000
SALES (est): 3.8MM **Privately Held**
WEB: www.plasfinco.com
SIC: **3479** 1721 Painting, coating & hot dipping; painting & paper hanging

(G-11279)
PROCOAT PRODUCTS INC
604 W Montrow Indus Pkwy (47265)
P.O. Box 657 (47265-0657)
PHONE...............................812 352-6083
James Messer, *President*
EMP: 7
SALES: 300K **Privately Held**
SIC: **3999** Manufacturing industries

(G-11280)
R & M TOOL ENGINEERING INC
2895 N State Highway 7 (47265-7188)
P.O. Box 156 (47265-0156)
PHONE...............................812 352-0240
Robert M Williams, *President*
Mark Williams, *Vice Pres*
Scarlet D Williams, *Financial Exec*
Scarlet Williams, *Office Mgr*
EMP: 11
SQ FT: 9,600

SALES (est): 1.7MM **Privately Held**
WEB: www.rmteinc.com
SIC: **3544** Special dies, tools, jigs & fixtures

(G-11281)
SET ENTERPRISES OF MI INC
1 Steel Way (47265-1243)
P.O. Box 117 (47265-0117)
PHONE...............................812 346-1700
Chuck Sudwischer, *Manager*
EMP: 10
SALES (corp-wide): 77.5MM **Privately Held**
WEB: www.michsteel.com
SIC: **3325** 5051 3316 3312 Steel foundries; metals service centers & offices; cold finishing of steel shapes; blast furnaces & steel mills
HQ: Set Enterprises Of Mi, Inc.
30500 Van Dyke Ave # 701
Warren MI 48093
586 573-3600

(G-11282)
SIT CAN HAPPEN LLC
130 N County Road 400 W (47265-7459)
PHONE...............................812 346-4188
Candice C McKing, *Principal*
EMP: 2 EST: 2007
SALES (est): 100K **Privately Held**
SIC: **3399** Primary metal products

(G-11283)
TEMPEST TOOL & MACHINE INC
7235 W Us Highway 50 (47265-7574)
PHONE...............................812 346-6464
Fax: 812 346-8616
William D Tempest, *President*
Dixie L Tempest, *Corp Secy*
EMP: 14
SQ FT: 13,750
SALES: 1.8MM **Privately Held**
WEB: www.tempesttool.com
SIC: **3599** Machine shop, jobbing & repair

(G-11284)
TOSMO AMERICA INC
819 Buckeye St (47265-1623)
PHONE...............................812 953-1481
Travis Campbell, *President*
Trent Miller, *Manager*
EMP: 15
SQ FT: 42,000
SALES: 1MM **Privately Held**
SIC: **3511** Turbines & turbine generator sets

(G-11285)
VERNON NORTH INDUSTRY CORP (HQ)
Also Called: Nvic
3750 N County Road 75 W (47265-6004)
P.O. Box 894 (47265-0894)
PHONE...............................812 346-8772
Fax: 812 346-3687
Jack Bodi, *President*
Mike Martin, *Safety Mgr*
Brad Tidd, *Purchasing*
Samuel Stewart, *Human Res Mgr*
Craig Rice, *Manager*
▲ EMP: 95
SQ FT: 160,000
SALES (est): 62MM
SALES (corp-wide): 18.8B **Privately Held**
WEB: www.nvic-cwt.com
SIC: **3321** Gray & ductile iron foundries
PA: Toyota Industries Corporation
2-1, Toyodacho
Kariya AIC 448-0
566 222-511

(G-11286)
WEBSTER WEST INC
Also Called: Webster West Packaging
1050 Rodgers Park Dr (47265-6428)
P.O. Box 888 (47265-0888)
PHONE...............................812 346-5666
Fax: 812 346-2900
William C Akers II, *President*
James F Akers, *Admin Sec*
EMP: 40
SQ FT: 124,000

SALES (est): 15.3MM **Privately Held**
WEB: www.websterwest.com
SIC: 2653 Boxes, corrugated: made from purchased materials

(G-11287)
WINDSTREAM TECHNOLOGIES INC
819 Buckeye St (47265-1623)
PHONE..............................812 953-1481
Dan Bates, *President*
Travis Campbell, *COO*
Daniel C Harris, *Exec VP*
Claudio Chami, *Vice Pres*
Chris Galazzi, *Vice Pres*
◆ **EMP:** 30
SALES (est): 9.1MM **Privately Held**
SIC: 3511 Turbines & turbine generator set units, complete

North Webster
Kosciusko County

(G-11288)
ABLE PRINTING & BUS SVCS LLC
740 S Main St (46555-7700)
P.O. Box 286 (46555-0286)
PHONE..............................574 834-7006
Fax: 574 834-4149
Connie Beery, *Owner*
Wayne Beery, *Owner*
Betty Miller, *Manager*
Constance J Beery,
EMP: 3
SQ FT: 3,000
SALES (est): 133.1K **Privately Held**
SIC: 5199 3861 Advertising specialties; printing equipment, photographic

(G-11289)
B THYSTRUP US CORPORATION
Also Called: Adventureglass
201 E Epworth Forest Rd (46555-9651)
P.O. Box 467 (46555-0467)
PHONE..............................574 834-2554
Fax: 574 834-2809
Dan Thystrup, *President*
Bo Thystrup, *Vice Pres*
EMP: 5
SALES (est): 1.1MM **Privately Held**
WEB: www.adventureglass.com
SIC: 5091 3229 Boats, canoes, watercrafts & equipment; glass fiber products

(G-11290)
CHEMATICS INC
Also Called: Chem-Elec
4519 N Sr13 (46555)
P.O. Box 293 (46555-0293)
PHONE..............................574 834-2406
Fax: 574 834-7427
William Woenker, *CEO*
Agnes Woenker, *Corp Secy*
Ed Woenker, *Sales/Mktg Dir*
EMP: 14
SQ FT: 10,000
SALES (est): 2.6MM **Privately Held**
WEB: www.chematics.com
SIC: 2835 Blood derivative diagnostic agents

(G-11291)
DEGOOD DMENSIONAL CONCEPTS INC
7815 N State Road 13 (46555-9609)
PHONE..............................574 834-5437
Fax: 574 834-5736
Scott Degood, *President*
Mary Degood, *Vice Pres*
EMP: 13 EST: 1997
SQ FT: 5,000
SALES (est): 2.5MM **Privately Held**
WEB: www.degooddc.com
SIC: 3599 Machine shop, jobbing & repair

(G-11292)
GROOVEMADE LLC
Also Called: Threads Embroidery
713 S Main St (46555)
PHONE..............................574 834-1138
Richard G Hicks, *Mng Member*
EMP: 2

SALES (est): 130K **Privately Held**
SIC: 2284 Embroidery thread

(G-11293)
INDIANA DIMENSIONAL PDTS LLC
Also Called: Idp
7224 N State Road 13 (46555-9602)
P.O. Box 271 (46555-0271)
PHONE..............................574 834-7681
Fax: 574 834-7392
Phlip Faccenda, *CEO*
Ernie Strichland Sr, *President*
Tonya Blanchard, *Vice Pres*
EMP: 75
SQ FT: 325,000
SALES (est): 8.6MM **Privately Held**
WEB: www.indianadimensional.com
SIC: 3993 3161 7336 Advertising novelties; displays & cutouts, window & lobby; sample cases; graphic arts & related design

(G-11294)
J C MFG INC (PA)
7248 N State Road 13 (46555-9602)
P.O. Box 340 (46555-0340)
PHONE..............................574 834-2881
Fax: 574 834-7307
Kim M Cripe, *President*
Joe Sparks, *Vice Pres*
Anne Pease, *Accountant*
EMP: 39
SQ FT: 1,500
SALES (est): 5.8MM **Privately Held**
WEB: www.jcpontoon.com
SIC: 3732 Pontoons, except aircraft & inflatable; non-motorized boat, building & repairing

(G-11295)
JRZ INDUSTRIES INC
133 S East St (46555)
P.O. Box 331, Warsaw (46581-0331)
PHONE..............................574 834-4543
Fax: 574 834-3699
Murray Rhodes, *President*
Joan Rhodes, *Corp Secy*
EMP: 3
SALES (est): 270K **Privately Held**
WEB: www.jrzmedia.com
SIC: 3714 Motor vehicle parts & accessories

(G-11296)
LASER GRAPHX INC
7196 N State Road 13 (46555-9701)
PHONE..............................574 834-4443
William Hackleman, *President*
Kris Hackleman, *Treasurer*
EMP: 4
SALES (est): 318.9K **Privately Held**
SIC: 3479 Engraving jewelry silverware, or metal

(G-11297)
NORTH WEBSTER CONSTRUCTION INC
Also Called: Pacemaker Buildings
7240 N State Road 13 (46555-9602)
P.O. Box 259 (46555-0259)
PHONE..............................574 834-4448
Toll Free:.............................888　-
Wayne O Schrock, *President*
Jack Brunetto, *Controller*
Carl Schrock, *Admin Sec*
EMP: 29 EST: 1975
SQ FT: 2,000
SALES (est): 4.4MM **Privately Held**
WEB: www.pacemakerbuildings.com
SIC: 1542 2439 Commercial & office building, new construction; farm building construction; trusses, wooden roof

(G-11298)
OPPORTUNITIES
6122 N 675 E (46555-9216)
PHONE..............................574 518-0606
Theodore Shoemaker, *Owner*
EMP: 2
SALES (est): 146.4K **Privately Held**
SIC: 2842 Specialty cleaning preparations

(G-11299)
PAULUS PLASTIC COMPANY INC
304 E George St (46555)
P.O. Box 223 (46555-0223)
PHONE..............................574 834-7663
Cecil H Paulus, *President*
Doris Paulus, *Officer*
EMP: 5
SQ FT: 7,000
SALES: 500K **Privately Held**
SIC: 5082 7542 3494 Construction & mining machinery; carwash, self-service; well adapters

(G-11300)
PRECISION WIRE INC
Also Called: Precision Wire Service
7493 E 800 N (46555-9607)
PHONE..............................574 834-7545
Fax: 574 834-5858
Jodi Mikesell, *President*
EMP: 7
SQ FT: 2,500
SALES (est): 640K **Privately Held**
SIC: 3679 Harness assemblies for electronic use: wire or cable

(G-11301)
SIGN GRAPHICS
7196 N State Road 13 (46555-9701)
PHONE..............................574 834-7100
Fax: 574 834-4443
William Hackleman, *Owner*
Christine Hackleman, *Principal*
EMP: 4
SQ FT: 4,800
SALES: 325K **Privately Held**
SIC: 3993 Signs & advertising specialties

(G-11302)
WEBSTER CUSTOM CANVAS INC
221 N Main St (46555)
P.O. Box 250 (46555-0250)
PHONE..............................574 834-4497
Fax: 574 834-4497
William Krumm Jr, *President*
Nancy Krumm, *Vice Pres*
EMP: 2
SQ FT: 11,000
SALES (est): 225.2K **Privately Held**
SIC: 2394 5551 1761 Awnings, fabric: made from purchased materials; boat dealers; roofing contractor

---

Notre Dame
St. Joseph County

(G-11303)
AVE MARIA PRESS INC
Also Called: SPIRITUAL BOOK ASSOCIATES
1865 Moreau Dr (46556)
PHONE..............................574 287-2831
Fax: 574 239-2904
Thomas J O'Hara, *President*
Frank J Cunningham, *President*
Michael Amodei, *Editor*
Anthony V Szakaly, *Chairman*
Mark Witbeck, *Treasurer*
▼ **EMP:** 58
SQ FT: 51,000
SALES: 3.8MM **Privately Held**
WEB: www.avemariapress.com
SIC: 2731 2752 Books: publishing & printing; commercial printing, offset

(G-11304)
UNIVERSITY NOTRE DAME DU LAC
Also Called: Observer, The
024 S Dinnina Hl (46556)
PHONE..............................574 631-7471
Chris Hine, *Principal*
Bill Dwyer, *Teacher*
EMP: 75
SALES (corp-wide): 1.1B **Privately Held**
WEB: www.nd.edu
SIC: 2711 8221 Newspapers, publishing & printing; university

PA: University Of Notre Dame Du Lac
805 Grace Hall
Notre Dame IN 46556
574 631-6401

(G-11305)
UNIVERSITY NOTRE DAME DU LAC
Also Called: Notre Dame Press
310 Flanner Hall Fl 3 (46556-4637)
PHONE..............................574 631-6346
Fax: 574 631-8148
Ann Bromley, *Sales Mgr*
Susan Roberts, *Marketing Staff*
Tracy Weber, *Manager*
Lisa Mackenzie, *Technology*
Barbara Hanrahan, *Director*
EMP: 15
SALES (corp-wide): 1.1B **Privately Held**
WEB: www.nd.edu
SIC: 2711 2721 2731 8221 Newspapers; periodicals; book publishing; university
PA: University Of Notre Dame Du Lac
805 Grace Hall
Notre Dame IN 46556
574 631-6401

Oakland City
Gibson County

(G-11306)
ARROW MINING INC (HQ)
1216 E County Road 900 S (47660-9055)
PHONE..............................270 683-4186
William B Murphy, *President*
EMP: 3
SQ FT: 2,200
SALES (est): 87.8MM **Privately Held**
SIC: 1221 Surface mining, bituminous

(G-11307)
ARROW MINING INC
Also Called: Triad Mining Co of Indiana
1216 E County Road 900 S (47660-9055)
PHONE..............................812 328-2117
Mike Howard, *Principal*
EMP: 48 **Privately Held**
SIC: 1221 Bituminous coal & lignite-surface mining
HQ: Arrow Mining, Inc.
1216 E County Road 900 S
Oakland City IN 47660
270 683-4186

(G-11308)
ARROW MINING INC
1216 E County Road 900 S (47660-9055)
PHONE..............................812 328-6154
Ronnie Thompson, *Manager*
EMP: 30 **Privately Held**
SIC: 1221 1241 Surface mining, bituminous; coal mining services
HQ: Arrow Mining, Inc.
1216 E County Road 900 S
Oakland City IN 47660
270 683-4186

(G-11309)
BRIDON-AMERICAN CORPORATION
Also Called: Bridon American Oakland
11698 E 200 S (47660-7627)
PHONE..............................812 749-3115
Fax: 812 749-4682
Andrew Dick, *Managing Dir*
Phil Young, *Manager*
EMP: 40
SALES (corp-wide): 744.8K **Privately Held**
WEB: www.bridonamerican.com
SIC: 3496 Woven wire products
HQ: Bridon-American Corporation
280 New Commerce Blvd
Hanover Township PA 18706
570 822-3349

(G-11310)
MORGAN EXCAVATING
5268 S 875 E (47660-8531)
PHONE..............................812 385-6036
David Morgan, *Partner*
Ryan Morgan, *Partner*
EMP: 3

SALES: 125K **Privately Held**
SIC: **1542** 1389 Nonresidential construction; oil field services

(G-11311)
PEABODY ENERGY CORPORATION
6280 S 1025 E (47660-7716)
PHONE..................................314 342-3400
Chad Wirthwein, *Branch Mgr*
EMP: 9
SALES (corp-wide): 5.1B **Publicly Held**
SIC: **1241** Coal mining services
PA: Peabody Energy Corporation
701 Market St
Saint Louis MO 63101
314 342-3400

(G-11312)
PEABODY ENERGY CORPORATION
6280 S And 1025 E (47660)
PHONE..................................812 795-4026
EMP: 98
SALES (corp-wide): 5.1B **Publicly Held**
SIC: **1221** Bituminous coal surface mining
PA: Peabody Energy Corporation
701 Market St
Saint Louis MO 63101
314 342-3400

(G-11313)
PEABODY MIDWEST MINING LLC
Also Called: Black Beauty Mining
6280 S 1025 E (47660-7716)
PHONE..................................812 795-0040
Fax: 812 795-0311
Doug Reynolds, *Manager*
EMP: 7
SALES (corp-wide): 5.1B **Publicly Held**
SIC: **1499** 1221 1241 Mineral abrasives mining; bituminous coal & lignite-surface mining; coal mining services
HQ: Peabody Midwest Mining Llc
566 Dickeyville Rd
Lynnville IN 47619

(G-11314)
ROYS DISPOSAL
924 E County Road 1150 S (47660-9027)
PHONE..................................812 721-3443
Phillip Roy, *Owner*
Juanita Roy, *Co-Owner*
EMP: 2 EST: 1975
SALES (est): 88.8K **Privately Held**
SIC: **3713** Garbage, refuse truck bodies

(G-11315)
SHAMROCK ENGINEERING INC
1020 W Morton St (47660-7617)
PHONE..................................812 867-0009
David Dunn, *President*
Laura-Lee M Dunn, *Vice Pres*
Carmille Cook, *Purchasing*
Greg Adams, *Engineer*
Jim English, *Engineer*
EMP: 32
SQ FT: 10,000
SALES (est): 8.8MM **Privately Held**
WEB: www.shamrockeng.com
SIC: **3569** Assembly machines, non-metalworking

(G-11316)
TRIAD MINING INC
1216 E County Road 900 S (47660-9055)
PHONE..................................812 328-2117
Fax: 812 328-6238
Ronnie Thompson, *CEO*
EMP: 12
SALES (est): 1.5MM **Privately Held**
SIC: **1241** Coal mining services

Oaktown
Knox County

(G-11317)
BLACK PANTHER MINING LLC
12661 N Agri Care Rd (47561-8086)
PHONE..................................812 745-2920
Donald R Blankenberger, *Mng Member*
EMP: 2

SALES (est): 210K **Privately Held**
SIC: **1241** Coal mining services

(G-11318)
GREEN FOREST SAWMILL LLC
407 W Main St (47561-5406)
PHONE..................................812 745-3335
Paige Nicol, *Owner*
EMP: 10
SALES (est): 1.1MM **Privately Held**
SIC: **2421** Sawmills & planing mills, general

Odon
Daviess County

(G-11319)
BAE SYSTEMS INC
209 E Walnut St (47562-1329)
PHONE..................................812 863-0514
Dana Chandler, *CEO*
EMP: 4
SALES (corp-wide): 24.2B **Privately Held**
SIC: **3812** 3721 Aircraft/aerospace flight instruments & guidance systems; nonmotorized & lighter-than-air aircraft
HQ: Bae Systems, Inc.
1101 Wilson Blvd Ste 2000
Arlington VA 22209

(G-11320)
BERRY GLOBAL INC
10485 E 1250 N (47562-5321)
PHONE..................................812 558-3510
EMP: 8 **Publicly Held**
SIC: **3089** Plastic containers, except foam
HQ: Berry Global, Inc.
101 Oakley St
Evansville IN 47710
812 424-2904

(G-11321)
COUNTRY VIEW FURN MFG & UPHL
8659 N 1000 E (47562-5634)
PHONE..................................812 636-5024
Viola Graber, *Managing Prtnr*
Henry Graber, *Partner*
EMP: 5
SQ FT: 3,200
SALES (est): 503.5K **Privately Held**
SIC: **2511** 2512 Wood household furniture; upholstered household furniture

(G-11322)
COUNTRY WOODWORKING LLC
7650 E 1000 N (47562-5034)
PHONE..................................812 636-6004
William G Wagler,
EMP: 3
SALES (est): 418.5K **Privately Held**
SIC: **2431** Millwork

(G-11323)
CUSTOM MOULDING
9061 E 875 N (47562-5195)
PHONE..................................812 636-7110
Fax: 812 636-7110
John D Graber, *Owner*
EMP: 3
SALES (est): 334.6K **Privately Held**
SIC: **2439** Trusses, wooden roof

(G-11324)
D&G TIMBER INC
21198 Us Highway 231 (47562-4804)
PHONE..................................812 486-3356
Fax: 812 486-3356
Dean Swartzentruber, *President*
Garry Swartzentruber, *Treasurer*
EMP: 30
SALES: 2.6MM **Privately Held**
SIC: **5031** 2448 2421 Pallets, wood; pallets, wood; lumber: rough, sawed or planed

(G-11325)
FLYNN SONS SAND & GRAVEL
11971 N Us Highway 231 (47562-5402)
PHONE..................................812 636-4400
Jeanna W Flynn, *Principal*
EMP: 2

SALES (est): 118.3K **Privately Held**
SIC: **1442** Construction sand & gravel

(G-11326)
GRABER
Also Called: Water Front Rabbitry
6608 E 1000 N (47562-5074)
PHONE..................................812 636-7699
Sheila Graber, *Owner*
EMP: 2 EST: 2011
SALES: 24K **Privately Held**
SIC: **2015** 7389 Rabbit, processed: frozen;

(G-11327)
GRABER MANUFACTURING
Also Called: Graber Manufacturing & Repair
Ct Rd 1050 N (47562)
PHONE..................................812 636-7725
Fax: 812 687-7264
Lester Graber, *Partner*
Mark Graber, *Partner*
Samuel Graber, *Partner*
Eli Wagler, *Partner*
EMP: 4
SALES (est): 410.1K **Privately Held**
SIC: **3524** 3714 3799 Carts or wagons for lawn & garden; axles, motor vehicle; carriages, horse drawn

(G-11328)
GRABER STEEL & FAB LLC
8528 N 900 E (47562-5194)
PHONE..................................812 636-8418
Fax: 812 636-7783
Nick M Graber, *Owner*
Nicholas M Graber,
EMP: 40 EST: 1972
SQ FT: 22,000
SALES: 6.2MM **Privately Held**
WEB: www.nickgraber.com
SIC: **3441** Fabricated structural metal

(G-11329)
GRABERS KOUNTRY KORNER
8902 N 900 E (47562-5186)
PHONE..................................812 636-4399
Fax: 812 636-8045
Stephen R Graber, *Owner*
EMP: 30
SQ FT: 25,000
SALES: 1MM **Privately Held**
WEB: www.donut-hill.com
SIC: **2051** 5149 5461 Cakes, pies & pastries; groceries & related products; bakeries

(G-11330)
GRABERS PORTABLE BAND MILL
10722 N 1000 E (47562-5223)
PHONE..................................812 636-4158
Steve Graber, *Principal*
EMP: 9 EST: 2008
SALES (est): 600K **Privately Held**
SIC: **2421** Sawmills & planing mills, general

(G-11331)
JIM GRABER LOGGING LLC
10514 N 1000 E (47562-5222)
PHONE..................................812 636-7000
Jim Graber, *Manager*
EMP: 6 EST: 2011
SALES (est): 561.6K **Privately Held**
SIC: **2411** Logging

(G-11332)
JOHN G WAGLER
9639 N 1150 E (47562-5379)
PHONE..................................812 709-1681
John G Wagler, *Principal*
EMP: 2
SALES (est): 209.6K **Privately Held**
SIC: **2431** Millwork

(G-11333)
LAKESIDE WOODWORKING
8024 N 775 E (47562-5138)
PHONE..................................812 687-7901
Leroy Graber, *Owner*
EMP: 4
SALES (est): 346.7K **Privately Held**
SIC: **2431** Millwork

(G-11334)
MAST WOODWORKING
9922 E 1000 N (47562-5218)
PHONE..................................812 636-7938
Mervin Mast, *Principal*
EMP: 2 EST: 2011
SALES (est): 173.7K **Privately Held**
SIC: **2431** Millwork

(G-11335)
MYERS ENTERPRISES INC
Also Called: Odon Journal
102 W Main St (47562-1306)
P.O. Box 307 (47562-0307)
PHONE..................................812 636-7350
Fax: 812 636-7359
John L Meyers, *President*
Sue Ann Myers, *Vice Pres*
EMP: 4 EST: 1964
SQ FT: 1,000
SALES (est): 283.5K **Privately Held**
SIC: **2711** Newspapers, publishing & printing

(G-11336)
N & R WOODWORKING LLC
10546 N 700 E (47562-5022)
PHONE..................................812 787-0644
Norman Wagler, *Principal*
EMP: 2
SALES (est): 140.5K **Privately Held**
SIC: **2431** Millwork

(G-11337)
ODON FEED AND GRAIN INC
500 S East St (47562-1554)
PHONE..................................812 636-7392
Ben Swartzentruber, *President*
Naomi Swartzentruber, *Corp Secy*
EMP: 8 EST: 1978
SQ FT: 2,000
SALES: 1MM **Privately Held**
SIC: **2048** Stock feeds, dry

(G-11338)
ODON MACHINE & MANUFACTURING
409 W Elnora St (47562-1015)
PHONE..................................812 636-7781
Fax: 812 636-7781
John W Jones, *Owner*
EMP: 3
SQ FT: 2,400
SALES: 170K **Privately Held**
SIC: **3599** Machine shop, jobbing & repair

(G-11339)
ROLLIN MINI BARNS LLC
6950 E 800 N (47562-5133)
PHONE..................................812 687-7581
Ron Stoll, *Principal*
EMP: 4
SALES (est): 470.7K **Privately Held**
SIC: **3448** Buildings, portable: prefabricated metal

(G-11340)
SHILOH CUSTOM WOODWORKS
9394 E 1000 N (47562-5221)
PHONE..................................812 636-0100
EMP: 4
SALES (est): 257.3K **Privately Held**
SIC: **2431** Millwork

(G-11341)
SMITH EXCAVATING
10122 E1400 N (47562)
PHONE..................................812 636-0054
John Smith, *Principal*
EMP: 3
SALES (est): 213.6K **Privately Held**
SIC: **3531** Construction machinery

(G-11342)
STOLLS WOODWORKING LLC
8779 N 1025 E (47562-4812)
PHONE..................................812 486-5117
John Stoll Jr, *Principal*
EMP: 5
SALES (est): 418.8K **Privately Held**
SIC: **2431** Millwork

(G-11343)
VERNON GREYBER
Also Called: Southern Indiana Vinyl Window
9808 E 1100 N (47562-5230)
PHONE..............................812 636-7880
Vernon Greyber, *Owner*
EMP: 4 EST: 1994
SALES: 800K **Privately Held**
SIC: 3231 Doors, glass: made from purchased glass

(G-11344)
WAGLER COMPETITION PDTS LLC
9612 N 675 E (47562-5073)
PHONE..............................812 486-9360
Jeremy Wagler, *Principal*
EMP: 4
SALES (est): 579.9K **Privately Held**
SIC: 3714 Motor vehicle parts & accessories

(G-11345)
WITTMER DISTRIBUTORS
11057 N 700 E (47562-5085)
PHONE..............................812 636-7786
John Wittmer, *Owner*
EMP: 3
SALES (est): 140K **Privately Held**
SIC: 2499 7389 Decorative wood & woodwork;

Oldenburg
Franklin County

(G-11346)
VILLAGE WORKSHOP INC
3047 Washington St (47036)
PHONE..............................812 933-1527
Brian Rennekamp, *President*
EMP: 2
SALES (est): 200K **Privately Held**
SIC: 2434 Wood kitchen cabinets

Orland
Steuben County

(G-11347)
COMMERCIAL PALLET RECYCL INC (PA)
5235 N State Road 327 (46776-9574)
P.O. Box 124, Hudson (46747-0124)
PHONE..............................260 829-1021
Melinda Squier, *President*
EMP: 10
SALES (est): 699.3K **Privately Held**
SIC: 2448 5031 Pallets, wood; pallets, wood

(G-11348)
CPG - OHIO LLC
9880 W Maple St (46776-5442)
PHONE..............................260 829-6721
Benzion Kaufman, *Administration*
EMP: 15
SALES (corp-wide): 8.8MM **Privately Held**
SIC: 2671 2673 Plastic film, coated or laminated for packaging; plastic bags: made from purchased materials
PA: Cpg - Ohio Llc
470 Northland Blvd
Cincinnati OH 45240
513 825-4800

(G-11349)
CRYSTAL VALLEY FARMS LLC (PA)
Also Called: Miller Meat Poultry
9622 W 350 N (46776-5468)
P.O. Box 239 (46776-0239)
PHONE..............................260 829-6550
Galen Miller, *Principal*
EMP: 560
SALES (est): 73.2MM **Privately Held**
SIC: 2015 Poultry slaughtering & processing

(G-11350)
CTA ACOUSTICS INC
9670 W Maple St (46776-5419)
PHONE..............................260 829-1030
James Pike, *Manager*
EMP: 224 **Privately Held**
SIC: 3714 Motor vehicle body components & frame
PA: Cta Acoustics, Inc.
25211 Dequindre Rd
Madison Heights MI 48071

(G-11351)
KAIN TOOL INC
9775 W Maple St (46776-5420)
P.O. Box 258 (46776-0258)
PHONE..............................260 829-6569
Rod Kain, *President*
Melody Kain, *Vice Pres*
Ryan L Kain, *Vice Pres*
Rodney Kain, *Mfg Staff*
EMP: 2
SALES (est): 373K **Privately Held**
SIC: 3544 Jigs & fixtures

(G-11352)
KEMCO INTERNATIONAL INC
9915 W Maple St (46776-5467)
P.O. Box 467 (46776-0467)
PHONE..............................260 829-1263
Rose Marie George, *President*
EMP: 15
SQ FT: 13,000
SALES (est): 2.7MM **Privately Held**
SIC: 2899 Chemical preparations

(G-11353)
MADSEN WIRE LLC
101 Madsen St (46776-5417)
PHONE..............................260 829-6561
Steve Cochran,
EMP: 30
SALES (est): 4.8MM **Privately Held**
SIC: 3315 Steel wire & related products

(G-11354)
NOBLE WIRE PRODUCTS INC
Also Called: Madsen Wire Products
101 Madsen St (46776-5417)
P.O. Box 1687, Noblesville (46061-1687)
PHONE..............................317 773-1926
Fax: 260 829-6652
Gregory Parker, *President*
Kasey Robinson, *Plant Mgr*
EMP: 9 EST: 2012
SALES (est): 41.6K **Privately Held**
SIC: 3496 Miscellaneous fabricated wire products

(G-11355)
PINE MANOR INC (HQ)
Also Called: Miller Poultry
9622 W 350 N (46776-5468)
P.O. Box 239 (46776-0239)
PHONE..............................800 532-4186
Fax: 574 533-6954
Galen Miller, *President*
Kevin Diehl, *Principal*
Ursula Miller, *Vice Pres*
John Sauder, *Vice Pres*
▲ EMP: 450
SALES (est): 79.5MM **Privately Held**
WEB: www.pine-manor.com
SIC: 2048 2015 0254 Poultry feeds; livestock feeds; poultry slaughtering & processing; chicken hatchery

(G-11356)
QUALITY CONVERTERS INC
Also Called: Q C I
9675 W Maple St (46776-5419)
P.O. Box 308 (46776-0308)
PHONE..............................260 829-6541
Fax: 260 829-6543
Cova Feltner, *President*
Dan Hamilton, *Plant Mgr*
EMP: 25
SQ FT: 31,800
SALES (est): 2.4MM **Privately Held**
WEB: www.qualityconvertersinc.com
SIC: 2396 3714 3429 Automotive trimmings, fabric; motor vehicle parts & accessories; manufactured hardware (general)

(G-11357)
RD SMITH MANUFACTURING INC
5990 N State Road 327 (46776-5436)
PHONE..............................260 829-6709
Fax: 260 829-6784
Roger Smith, *President*
EMP: 4
SQ FT: 6,000
SALES (est): 554.3K **Privately Held**
SIC: 3451 Screw machine products

(G-11358)
UCOM INC
9725 W Maple St (46776-5420)
P.O. Box 254 (46776-0254)
PHONE..............................260 829-1294
Fax: 260 829-1268
Russell Owens, *CEO*
Judy Olis, *Purchasing*
Linda Modert, *Sales Staff*
Jean Anderson, *Manager*
EMP: 10
SQ FT: 12,500
SALES (est): 2MM **Privately Held**
WEB: www.ucominc.com
SIC: 3643 Current-carrying wiring devices; electric connectors; electric switches

(G-11359)
UNIVERSAL PACKG SYSTEMS INC
Also Called: Paklab
9880 W Naples St (46776)
PHONE..............................260 829-6721
Tammy Detro, *Branch Mgr*
EMP: 388
SALES (corp-wide): 423.8MM **Privately Held**
SIC: 2844 3565 7389 2671 Cosmetic preparations; bottling machinery: filling, capping, labeling; packaging & labeling services; plastic film, coated or laminated for packaging
PA: Universal Packaging Systems, Inc.
380 Townline Rd Ste 130
Hauppauge NY 11788
631 543-2277

(G-11360)
YA-NVR-NO
8405 N 650 W (46776-9641)
PHONE..............................260 833-8883
Craig McKellar, *Principal*
EMP: 2
SALES (est): 184.6K **Privately Held**
SIC: 3993 Signs & advertising specialties

Orleans
Orange County

(G-11361)
COLEMAN SAWMILL SUPPLY
260 S 6th St (47452-9764)
P.O. Box 201 (47452-0201)
PHONE..............................812 865-4001
Stephen Coleman, *Owner*
EMP: 5
SALES (est): 672.9K **Privately Held**
SIC: 2421 Lumber: rough, sawed or planed

(G-11362)
HUDELSON SHARPENING & MCH SP
27 W Quarry Rd (47452-9281)
PHONE..............................812 865-3951
Fax: 812 865-3801
Daniel Hudelson, *Owner*
Sheila Morgan, *Manager*
EMP: 8
SQ FT: 8,500
SALES: 1MM **Privately Held**
SIC: 3599 Machine shop, jobbing & repair

(G-11363)
LANA HUDELSON
Also Called: Hudelson Fabrication
27 W Quarry Rd (47452-9281)
PHONE..............................812 865-3951
Lana Hudelson, *Owner*
EMP: 4

SALES: 400K **Privately Held**
SIC: 2431 3312 Brackets, wood; sheet or strip, steel, hot-rolled

(G-11364)
ORANGE CNTY WLDG & FABRICATION
6063 N County Road 200 E (47452-9174)
PHONE..............................812 653-5754
Heath Grissom, *Owner*
Mike Sampson, *Manager*
EMP: 5
SALES (est): 444.8K **Privately Held**
SIC: 3499 Fabricated metal products

(G-11365)
ORANGE COUNTY CONCRETE INC
409 E Jefferson St (47452-1511)
PHONE..............................812 865-2425
Fax: 812 865-2062
William Puckett, *President*
Wendy Sprigler, *Corp Secy*
Vance Elliott, *Vice Pres*
EMP: 6
SALES: 629.1K **Privately Held**
WEB: www.orangecountyconcrete.com
SIC: 3273 5211 Ready-mixed concrete; concrete & cinder block

(G-11366)
ORANGE COUNTY PROCESSING
5028 N State Road 37 (47452-9025)
PHONE..............................812 865-2028
Marvin Hammack, *Manager*
EMP: 10
SALES (est): 814.1K **Privately Held**
SIC: 2011 Meat packing plants

(G-11367)
PROFAB CUSTOM METAL WORKS INC
7040 N State Road 337 (47452-9175)
P.O. Box 300 (47452-0300)
PHONE..............................812 865-3999
James Shelby, *President*
EMP: 7 EST: 2007
SALES (est): 1.4MM **Privately Held**
SIC: 3441 Fabricated structural metal

(G-11368)
PROGRESS EXAMINER
233 S 2nd St (47452-1601)
P.O. Box 225 (47452-0225)
PHONE..............................812 865-3242
John F Noblitt, *Owner*
EMP: 4
SALES (est): 231.7K **Privately Held**
SIC: 2711 Newspapers, publishing & printing

(G-11369)
ROSES SQUARE DANCE ACC
448 E Liberty Rd (47452-1516)
PHONE..............................812 865-2821
Ralph Warren, *Owner*
Rose Warren, *Partner*
EMP: 2
SQ FT: 950
SALES (est): 121.2K **Privately Held**
SIC: 5699 2341 Square dance apparel; women's & children's undergarments

---

Osceola
St. Joseph County

(G-11370)
AVENUE INDUSTRIES INC
1453 3rd St (46561-2055)
PHONE..............................574 674-6971
Steve Watford, *Owner*
EMP: 4
SALES (est): 536.9K **Privately Held**
SIC: 3441 Fabricated structural metal

(G-11371)
BUSINESS ADVENTURES INC
1327 3rd St (46561-2053)
PHONE..............................574 674-9996
James W Gerber, *President*
Bonnie Gerber, *Treasurer*
Wayne Gerber, *Admin Sec*

EMP: 7
SQ FT: 5,000
SALES (est): 620K **Privately Held**
SIC: 3647 2759 7371 Motor vehicle lighting equipment; screen printing; custom computer programming services

(G-11372)
BUY BULK DISPLAYS LLC
1610 3rd St (46561-2054)
PHONE......................574 222-4378
Brandon Geisel,
EMP: 2
SQ FT: 10,000
SALES (est): 79.8K **Privately Held**
SIC: 3993 Signs & advertising specialties

(G-11373)
CALI NAIL
Also Called: Cali Nail Salon
941 Lincolnway W (46561-2014)
PHONE......................574 674-4126
Thong Nguyen, Owner
EMP: 5
SALES (est): 343.7K **Privately Held**
SIC: 3999 7231 Fingernails, artificial; manicurist, pedicurist

(G-11374)
CHAPMAN ENVIRONMENTAL CONTROLS
10463 Pleasant Valley Ct (46561-9336)
P.O. Box 288 (46561-0288)
PHONE......................574 674-8706
Frank Chapman, President
Penny Chapman, Corp Secy
EMP: 2
SALES (est): 75K **Privately Held**
SIC: 7389 3829 Air pollution measuring service; measuring & controlling devices

(G-11375)
CUSTOM DESIGN LAMINATES INC
Also Called: Focal Point Cabinetry
10055 Mckinley Hwy (46561-9751)
PHONE......................574 674-9174
Ralph R Erbe, President
Vance Erbe, Corp Secy
EMP: 15
SQ FT: 18,000
SALES: 2.3MM **Privately Held**
SIC: 1799 2541 2434 Counter top installation; table or counter tops, plastic laminated; wood kitchen cabinets

(G-11376)
FLAGS INTERNATIONAL INC
10845 Mckinley Hwy (46561-9199)
PHONE......................574 674-5125
Fax: 574 674-5134
William O'Keefe, President
EMP: 5 EST: 2016
SQ FT: 4,000
SALES (est): 142K **Privately Held**
SIC: 5999 2399 Banners, flags, decals & posters; emblems, badges & insignia

(G-11377)
HOMES & LIFESTYLES MAGAZINE
11859 Lincolnway (46561-1927)
PHONE......................574 674-6639
Fax: 574 674-7200
Fred Bradley, President
Cheryl Bradley, Treasurer
EMP: 50
SQ FT: 6,000
SALES (est): 4.9MM **Privately Held**
WEB: www.homes2see.com
SIC: 2721 Trade journals: publishing only, not printed on site

(G-11378)
INKME LLC
54732 Scrmento Meadows Dr (46561-8768)
PHONE......................574 520-1203
Rachel Clements, Principal
EMP: 2
SALES (est): 95.1K **Privately Held**
SIC: 2752 Commercial printing, lithographic

(G-11379)
JPE CONSULTING LLP
10451 Dunn Rd (46561-9033)
P.O. Box 282 (46561-0282)
PHONE......................574 675-9552
David Parker, Partner
Dan Elek, Partner
EMP: 2
SALES: 150K **Privately Held**
WEB: www.complyguard.com
SIC: 7372 7371 Prepackaged software; custom computer programming services

(G-11380)
LAFREE ENTERPRISES
11645 Mckinley Hwy (46561-9506)
PHONE......................574 674-5906
Daniel Lafree, Principal
EMP: 3 EST: 2001
SALES (est): 352K **Privately Held**
SIC: 3553 Woodworking machinery

(G-11381)
LEHUE MACHINE AND TOOL
55981 Wynnewood Dr (46561-9517)
PHONE......................574 329-5456
EMP: 5 EST: 2015
SALES (est): 217.9K **Privately Held**
SIC: 3544 Special dies, tools, jigs & fixtures

(G-11382)
MIDWEST PLASTICS COMPANY INC
401 Lincolnway W (46561-2637)
PHONE......................574 674-0161
Michael Malloy, Principal
EMP: 3
SALES (est): 256.2K **Privately Held**
SIC: 2611 Pulp manufactured from waste or recycled paper

(G-11383)
R B TOOL & MACHINERY CO
Also Called: Hollingsworth & Associates
10120 Glenwood Ave (46561-9446)
PHONE......................574 679-0082
Robert S Hollingsworth, Owner
EMP: 6
SALES: 1MM **Privately Held**
SIC: 5084 3561 3545 Industrial machine parts; pumps & pumping equipment; machine tool accessories

(G-11384)
ULTRA TECH RACING ENGINES
11301 Idlewood Dr (46561-9383)
PHONE......................574 674-6028
Norman Beerhorst, Owner
EMP: 2
SQ FT: 3,000
SALES: 300K **Privately Held**
SIC: 3519 5531 Gasoline engines; speed shops, including race car supplies

(G-11385)
US SIGNCRAFTERS INC
Also Called: U. S. Signcrafters
216 Lincolnway E (46561-2769)
PHONE......................574 674-5055
Fax: 574 674-5255
James G Kyle, CEO
Scott D Franko, President
Scott Franko, President
Jackie Wade, Office Mgr
Randy Whiteman, Consultant
EMP: 17
SQ FT: 7,500
SALES (est): 2.3MM **Privately Held**
WEB: www.ussigncrafters.com
SIC: 3993 1799 Electric signs; sign installation & maintenance

(G-11386)
VALLEY SHARPENING INC
102 Osceola Ave (46561-2208)
P.O. Box 125 (46561-0125)
PHONE......................574 674-9077
Fax: 574 674-9110
Kenneth Harlacher, President
Margaret Harlacher, Treasurer
EMP: 4
SQ FT: 15,000

SALES: 250K **Privately Held**
SIC: 7699 3425 Knife, saw & tool sharpening & repair; saws, hand: metalworking or woodworking

(G-11387)
VERTICAL POWER CO
10254 Jefferson Rd (46561-9552)
PHONE......................574 276-8094
EMP: 3
SALES (est): 217.3K **Privately Held**
SIC: 3841 Muscle exercise apparatus, ophthalmic

Osgood
Ripley County

(G-11388)
API AMERICAS INC
604 Railroad Ave (47037-7500)
PHONE......................812 689-6502
EMP: 2 **Privately Held**
SIC: 3497 Metal foil & leaf
HQ: Api Americas Inc.
3841 Greenway Cir
Lawrence KS 66046

(G-11389)
BEST METAL FINISHING INC
1050 Railroad Ave (47037-7507)
PHONE......................812 689-9950
Jeff Liter, President
EMP: 25
SALES (est): 2.9MM **Privately Held**
WEB: www.eni.com
SIC: 3471 Finishing, metals or formed products

(G-11390)
DOUBLE E ENTERPRISE INC
205 Western Ave (47037-1054)
PHONE......................812 689-0671
Michael Effing, President
EMP: 2
SQ FT: 11,000
SALES (est): 452.7K **Privately Held**
SIC: 3449 Miscellaneous metalwork

(G-11391)
HICKS FARMS
3871 W County Road 1050 N (47037-9213)
PHONE......................812 852-4055
Brad Hicks, Partner
EMP: 4
SALES: 400K **Privately Held**
SIC: 3523 Driers (farm): grain, hay & seed

(G-11392)
LASER MARKING TECHNOLOGIES
873 W County Road 600 N (47037-8649)
PHONE......................812 852-7999
Preston Davis, President
EMP: 5 EST: 1996
SALES (est): 410K **Privately Held**
WEB: www.lasermarking.com
SIC: 7389 2759 Engraving service; laser printing

(G-11393)
LAUGHERY VALLEY AG CO-OP INC (PA)
336 N Buckeye St (47037-1130)
P.O. Box 177 (47037-0177)
PHONE......................812 689-4401
Richard L Miller, CEO
EMP: 8 EST: 1928
SQ FT: 4,000
SALES (est): 21.4MM **Privately Held**
SIC: 5191 5172 5153 2875 Farm supplies; feed; seeds: field, garden & flower; fertilizer & fertilizer materials; petroleum products; grains; fertilizers, mixing only; prepared feeds; flour & other grain mill products

(G-11394)
SCHMALTZ READY MIX CONCRETE (PA)
Also Called: Laughery Gravel Co
705 Tanglewood Rd (47037-9013)
P.O. Box 159 (47037-0159)
PHONE......................812 689-5140
William L Schmaltz, Owner
EMP: 5
SALES (est): 1.1MM **Privately Held**
SIC: 1442 3273 Sand mining; gravel mining; ready-mixed concrete

(G-11395)
SIMON AND SONS
5802 N Us Highway 421 (47037-8901)
PHONE......................812 852-3636
Jim Simon, Owner
Cindy Simon, Co-Owner
EMP: 2
SALES (est): 122K **Privately Held**
SIC: 3011 Tire & inner tube materials & related products

(G-11396)
THOMAS & SKINNER INC
525 Western Ave (47037-1060)
PHONE......................812 689-4811
Fax: 812 689-4811
Bob Smith, Manager
EMP: 18
SALES (corp-wide): 81.5MM **Privately Held**
WEB: www.thomas-skinner.com
SIC: 3264 Magnets, permanent: ceramic or ferrite; ferrite & ferrite parts
PA: Thomas & Skinner Inc
1120 E 23rd St
Indianapolis IN 46205
317 923-2501

Ossian
Wells County

(G-11397)
BERNE APPAREL COMPANY (PA)
2501 E 850 N (46777-9365)
P.O. Box 530 (46777-0530)
PHONE......................260 622-1500
Ronald W Nussbaum, President
Richard E Honig, Vice Pres
Shannon Rose, Controller
Phil Gibson, Manager
Nick Rodriquez, Manager
▲ EMP: 30
SALES (est): 61.8MM **Privately Held**
WEB: www.berneapparel.com
SIC: 2326 2329 2339 2325 Work apparel, except uniforms; jackets, overall & work; overalls & coveralls; hunting coats & vests, men's; jackets (suede, leatherette, etc.), sport: men's & boys'; women's & misses' outerwear; men's & boys' trousers & slacks

(G-11398)
COTTONWOOD CORP (PA)
Also Called: Cottonwood Farm
1412 Evergreen Ct (46777-9090)
PHONE......................260 820-0415
Tim Ringger, President
Dale Gerber, Corp Secy
EMP: 3
SALES (est): 280.3K **Privately Held**
SIC: 2013 Prepared pork products from purchased pork

(G-11399)
GINGERBREAD HOUSE PUBLICATIONS
11216 N 500 E (46777-9728)
PHONE......................260 622-4868
Avis Hulvey, Owner
EMP: 3
SALES (est): 110K **Privately Held**
SIC: 2741 2731 Miscellaneous publishing; newsletter publishing; book publishing

(G-11400)
HAVEN MANUFACTURING IND INC
6935 N State Road 1 (46777-9650)
P.O. Box 551, Angola (46703-0551)
PHONE..................................260 622-4150
Leonard Feddema, *President*
Dave Leonard, *QC Mgr*
Jack Feddema, *Admin Sec*
EMP: 23 EST: 2011
SALES (est): 4.8MM **Privately Held**
SIC: 3545 3469 Cutting tools for machine tools; machine parts, stamped or pressed metal

(G-11401)
HEYERLYS BAKERY INC
Also Called: Heyerly Bakery
107 N Jefferson St (46777-1103)
P.O. Box 391 (46777-0391)
PHONE..................................260 622-4196
Ronald Heyerly, *President*
Galen Heyerly, *Vice Pres*
Lynn Heyerly, *Treasurer*
Stanley Heyerly, *Admin Sec*
EMP: 18
SQ FT: 3,000
SALES (est): 973.2K **Privately Held**
SIC: 5461 2052 2051 Bakeries; cookies & crackers; bread, cake & related products

(G-11402)
J R P MACHINE PRODUCTS LLP
420 Carol Ann Ln (46777-9100)
PHONE..................................260 622-4746
John R Perkins Jr, *Managing Prtnr*
Mark W Perkins, *Partner*
EMP: 7
SALES (est): 998.9K **Privately Held**
SIC: 3599 Machine shop, jobbing & repair

(G-11403)
LINDER OIL CO INC
820 Industrial Pkwy (46777-9122)
PHONE..................................260 622-4680
Fax: 260 622-4689
Robert J Marshall, *President*
Linda L Marshall, *Admin Sec*
EMP: 12
SQ FT: 8,000
SALES (est): 3.5MM **Privately Held**
SIC: 2992 Oils & greases, blending & compounding; cutting oils, blending: made from purchased materials

(G-11404)
MELCHING MACHINE INC
1630 Baker Dr (46777-9391)
PHONE..................................260 622-4315
Fax: 260 622-4361
Ted E Melching, *President*
Ryan Melching, *Vice Pres*
Susan Reynolds, *Purch Dir*
EMP: 35 EST: 1937
SQ FT: 24,000
SALES (est): 6.2MM **Privately Held**
WEB: www.melching.com
SIC: 3599 3544 7692 Machine shop, jobbing & repair; special dies, tools, jigs & fixtures; welding repair

(G-11405)
RETHCEIF ENTERPRISES LLC
Also Called: Rethceif Packaging
420 Industrial Pkwy (46777-9121)
PHONE..................................260 622-7200
Timothy Fiechter, *President*
Chris Honegger, *Vice Pres*
EMP: 14
SQ FT: 20,000
SALES (est): 4.1MM **Privately Held**
SIC: 3565 Packaging machinery

(G-11406)
ROEMBKE MFG & DESIGN INC (PA)
1580 Baker Dr (46777-9391)
PHONE..................................260 622-4135
John Roembke, *CEO*
Greg Roembke, *President*
Jim Berry, *Director*
Dave Jaskie, *Director*
Troy Smith, *Director*
EMP: 30 EST: 1976
SQ FT: 62,500

SALES (est): 6.2MM **Privately Held**
SIC: 3069 3544 Hard rubber & molded rubber products; special dies, tools, jigs & fixtures

(G-11407)
ROEMBKE MFG & DESIGN INC
Also Called: Custom Precision Components
1580 Baker Dr (46777-9391)
PHONE..................................260 622-4030
Fax: 260 622-6967
Marty Adams, *Manager*
EMP: 35
SALES (corp-wide): 6.2MM **Privately Held**
SIC: 3069 7692 Hard rubber & molded rubber products; welding repair
PA: Roembke Mfg & Design Inc
　1580 Baker Dr
　Ossian IN 46777
　260 622-4135

(G-11408)
SPECIAL K ALPACAS
10562 N Meridian Rd (46777-9351)
PHONE..................................260 638-4515
Kathleen Kowal, *Owner*
EMP: 2
SALES (est): 101.9K **Privately Held**
SIC: 2231 Alpacas, mohair: woven

(G-11409)
SUCCESS ENTRMT GROUP INTL INC
215 N Jefferson St (46777-9700)
PHONE..................................260 490-9990
Chris Hong, *CEO*
Steve Andrew Chen, *Ch of Bd*
Brian Kistler, *President*
Tony Chang, *COO*
Frank Tseng, *CFO*
EMP: 5 EST: 2013
SALES: 313K **Privately Held**
SIC: 3861 7384 Motion picture film; home movies, developing & processing

(G-11410)
SUCCESS HOLDING GROUP CORP USA
215 N Jefferson St (46777-9700)
PHONE..................................260 490-9990
Steve Andrew Chen, *President*
EMP: 3 EST: 2014
SALES (est): 138.6K **Privately Held**
SIC: 3861 7384 Motion picture film; home movies, developing & processing

(G-11411)
SUCCESS HOLDING GROUP INTL INC
215 N Jefferson St (46777-9700)
PHONE..................................260 450-1982
Chris Hong, *CEO*
Steve Andrew Chen, *Ch of Bd*
Brian Kistler, *President*
Y Tristan Kuo, *CFO*
EMP: 7
SALES (est): 88.1K **Privately Held**
SIC: 8331 2086 Job training & vocational rehabilitation services; bottled & canned soft drinks

(G-11412)
SURE-FLO SEAMLESS GUTTERS INC
9192 N 750 E (46777-9216)
PHONE..................................260 622-4372
Stanley Worthman, *Owner*
EMP: 3
SALES (est): 210K **Privately Held**
SIC: 1761 3444 Gutter & downspout contractor; gutters, sheet metal

(G-11413)
THERMTRON MFG INC
1625 Baker Dr (46777-9391)
PHONE..................................260 622-6000
Fax: 260 622-6002
Mike Gerber, *Principal*
EMP: 2
SALES (est): 117K **Privately Held**
SIC: 3999 Manufacturing industries

(G-11414)
TI GROUP AUTO SYSTEMS LLC
Also Called: Ossian Plant
1200 Baker Dr (46777-9106)
PHONE..................................260 622-7900
Paul Gauger, *Human Res Dir*
Harold Clinger, *Branch Mgr*
John Gunter, *Director*
EMP: 252
SALES (corp-wide): 4B **Privately Held**
WEB: www.tiautomotive.com
SIC: 3714 Motor vehicle parts & accessories
HQ: Ti Group Automotive Systems, Llc
　2020 Taylor Rd
　Auburn Hills MI 48326
　248 296-8000

(G-11415)
WELD DONE
Also Called: Weld-Done Shop
5945 E Us Highway 224 (46777-8950)
PHONE..................................260 597-7237
Fax: 260 597-7427
Denis Drayer, *Owner*
EMP: 4
SALES (est): 170.7K **Privately Held**
SIC: 7692 Welding repair

Otisco
Clark County

(G-11416)
CONCRETE LADY INC (PA)
4910 Highway 3 (47163-9402)
PHONE..................................812 256-2765
Fax: 812 256-2765
Peggy Woods, *President*
Carl Woods, *Vice Pres*
James Woods, *Director*
EMP: 21
SQ FT: 4,000
SALES (est): 1.7MM **Privately Held**
SIC: 3272 5947 Concrete products, precast; gift shop

Otterbein
Benton County

(G-11417)
BEST ELECTRIC MOTOR SERVICE
11430 E Us Hwy 52 (47970)
P.O. Box 547 (47970-0547)
PHONE..................................765 583-2408
Jeff Best, *Partner*
Doug Best, *Partner*
EMP: 4
SQ FT: 5,000
SALES (est): 270K **Privately Held**
SIC: 7694 7231 Armature rewinding shops; unisex hair salons

(G-11418)
HELENA AGRI-ENTERPRISES LLC
502 W Oxford St (47970)
PHONE..................................765 583-4458
Mike McCarty,
EMP: 2
SALES (corp-wide): 70.7B **Privately Held**
SIC: 5191 2819 Chemicals, agricultural; chemicals, high purity: refined from technical grade
HQ: Helena Agri-Enterprises, Llc
　255 Schilling Blvd # 300
　Collierville TN 38017
　901 761-0050

(G-11419)
KERKHOFF ASSOCIATES INC (PA)
Also Called: K A Components
21 W Oxford St (47970-8576)
P.O. Box 578 (47970-0578)
PHONE..................................765 583-4491
Fax: 765 583-4845
Timothy C Kerkhoff, *President*
Michael Kerkhoff, *Treasurer*
Julia Kerkhoff, *Admin Sec*

EMP: 20 EST: 1953
SQ FT: 2,400
SALES (est): 13.1MM **Privately Held**
SIC: 2439 2431 Trusses, except roof: laminated lumber; panel work, wood

(G-11420)
KNK BATTERY LLC
9117 E State Road 26 (47970-8062)
PHONE..................................765 426-2016
Shawn A Klemme, *Principal*
EMP: 3
SALES (est): 339.5K **Privately Held**
SIC: 3691 Storage batteries

(G-11421)
ROWE TRUCK EQUIPMENT INC (PA)
102 W 1st St (47970)
PHONE..................................765 583-4461
Fax: 765 583-2907
John C Rowe, *President*
Larry Wilcrout, *Vice Pres*
Ryan Deweese, *Controller*
Mark Batcheldor, *Sales Mgr*
Pattie Panfil, *Info Tech Mgr*
▲ EMP: 75
SQ FT: 175,000
SALES: 23MM **Privately Held**
WEB: www.rowetruck.com
SIC: 3713 Truck beds

Otwell
Pike County

(G-11422)
DUTCHTOWN HOMES
1011 N State Road 257 (47564-5418)
PHONE..................................812 354-2197
Shawn Wilson, *Owner*
EMP: 2
SALES (est): 149.9K **Privately Held**
SIC: 2451 Mobile homes

Owensburg
Greene County

(G-11423)
BRAY LOGGING
6399 E State Road 58 (47453-8259)
PHONE..................................812 863-7947
Christopher W Bray, *Principal*
EMP: 3
SALES (est): 222.6K **Privately Held**
SIC: 2411 Logging camps & contractors

(G-11424)
CARR LOGGING
9322 E State Road 58 (47453-8273)
PHONE..................................812 863-7585
Carl Carr, *Principal*
EMP: 3 EST: 2010
SALES (est): 239K **Privately Held**
SIC: 2411 Logging

(G-11425)
D & M SYSTEMS INC
6516 S Thomas Ct (47453-8288)
PHONE..................................812 327-2384
Millard Reeves, *President*
Tyler Reeves, *Vice Pres*
Toby Reeves, *Admin Sec*
EMP: 5
SQ FT: 261,360
SALES (est): 384.7K **Privately Held**
SIC: 1791 3441 Structural steel erection; fabricated structural metal

---

Owensville
Gibson County

(G-11426)
ABSOLUTE CUSTOM MACHINE LLC
5954 S 1075 W (47665-8915)
PHONE..................................812 724-2284
Erin Smith, *Principal*
EMP: 2 EST: 2016

▲ = Import ▼=Export
◆ =Import/Export

SALES (est): 89.6K **Privately Held**
SIC: 3599 Industrial machinery

(G-11427)
ANCHOR INDUSTRIES
9248 W 280 S (47665-8933)
PHONE.....................................812 664-0772
Faye Masterson, *Principal*
EMP: 2
SALES (est): 80.6K **Privately Held**
SIC: 3999 Manufacturing industries

(G-11428)
**KENNY DEWIG MEATS
SAUSAGE INC**
Also Called: Dewig Deer Processing
9208 W State Road 165 (47665-8750)
PHONE.....................................812 724-2333
Kenny Dewig, *President*
Tamara Dewig, *Vice Pres*
EMP: 4
SALES (est): 336K **Privately Held**
SIC: 2011 Meat packing plants

(G-11429)
**MONTGOMERY
MANUFACTURING CO**
202 S Main St (47665)
P.O. Box 38 (47665-0038)
PHONE.....................................812 724-2505
William Davis, *President*
Sibly Davis, *Treasurer*
EMP: 6 EST: 1935
SQ FT: 7,000
SALES: 250K **Privately Held**
SIC: 3873 Timers for industrial use, clockwork mechanism only

(G-11430)
**SUPERIOR AG RESOURCES
COOP INC**
504 S 2nd St (47665)
P.O. Box 247 (47665-0247)
PHONE.....................................812 724-4455
Wayne Scott, *Manager*
EMP: 8
SALES (corp-wide): 68.1MM **Privately Held**
SIC: 5191 2879 2875 0721 Fertilizers & agricultural chemicals; agricultural chemicals; fertilizers, mixing only; crop planting & protection
PA: Superior Ag Resources Cooperative, Inc.
901 N Main St
Huntingburg IN 47542
812 683-2809

Oxford
Benton County

(G-11431)
**DRUG PLASTICS AND GLASS
CO INC**
5 Bottle Dr (47971-8675)
PHONE.....................................765 385-0035
Fax: 765 385-0729
Darrin Bowman, *Manager*
Hung Nguyen, *Director*
Jennifer Lanie, *Executive*
EMP: 80
SALES (corp-wide): 166.9MM **Privately Held**
WEB: www.drugplastics.com
SIC: 3085 Plastics bottles
PA: Drug Plastics And Glass Company, Inc.
1 Bottle Dr
Boyertown PA 19512
610 367-5000

(G-11432)
LANDEC AG INC
201 N Michigan St (47971-8505)
PHONE.....................................765 385-1000
Dr Natarajan Balachalder, *Vice Pres*
EMP: 10
SALES (corp-wide): 524.2MM **Publicly Held**
WEB: www.landecag.com
SIC: 2879 Agricultural chemicals

HQ: Landec Ag, Inc.
201 N Michigan St
Oxford IN 47971

(G-11433)
LANDEC AG INC (HQ)
Also Called: Fielders Choice Direct
201 N Michigan St (47971-8505)
PHONE.....................................765 385-1000
Natarajan Balachander, *CEO*
William Gass, *Vice Pres*
Dennis Schlott, *Vice Pres*
Mike Godlove, *CFO*
EMP: 11
SALES (est): 2.8MM
SALES (corp-wide): 524.2MM **Publicly Held**
WEB: www.landecag.com
SIC: 2879 5153 Agricultural chemicals; corn
PA: Landec Corporation
5201 Great America Pkwy
Santa Clara CA 95054
650 306-1650

(G-11434)
**PLAY 2 WIN SCREENPRINTING
LLC**
8975 E 200 S (47971-8705)
PHONE.....................................765 426-0679
Robert Troy Watt, *Principal*
EMP: 2
SALES (est): 146.4K **Privately Held**
SIC: 2759 Screen printing

Palmyra
Harrison County

(G-11435)
BLUE RIVER FARM SUPPLY INC
14485 Greene St Ne (47164-8860)
PHONE.....................................812 364-6675
Fax: 812 364-6675
John Gammon Jr, *President*
EMP: 3
SQ FT: 7,000
SALES (est): 601.4K **Privately Held**
SIC: 5211 5191 2048 Lumber products; farm supplies; prepared feeds

(G-11436)
KIESLER MACHINE INC
Also Called: Kmi
13700 S Mrtn Mathis Rd Ne (47164-8768)
P.O. Box 357 (47164-0357)
PHONE.....................................812 364-6610
Fax: 812 364-6610
Garry Kiesler, *President*
Betty Keisler, *Admin Sec*
EMP: 7
SQ FT: 7,200
SALES: 200K **Privately Held**
SIC: 3599 Machine shop, jobbing & repair

(G-11437)
OWENS MACHINERY INC
1502 W Palmyra Lake Rd (47164-6704)
PHONE.....................................812 968-3285
Fax: 812 968-3642
Fredrick Owen, *President*
Kay Owen, *Treasurer*
J R Eckart, *Shareholder*
EMP: 7 EST: 1979
SQ FT: 14,080
SALES (est): 653.3K **Privately Held**
WEB: www.owensmachinery.com
SIC: 7389 3554 Relocation service; corrugating machines, paper

(G-11438)
PREFERRED POPCORN LLC
3055 W Bradford Rd Ne (47164-7935)
PHONE.....................................308 850-6631
EMP: 11
SALES (corp-wide): 50MM **Privately Held**
SIC: 2099 Popcorn, packaged: except already popped
PA: Preferred Popcorn, L.L.C.
1132 9th Rd
Chapman NE 68827
308 986-2526

(G-11439)
PRESTON FARMS LLC
3055 W Bradford Rd Ne (47164-7935)
PHONE.....................................812 364-6123
Charles Shacklette, *Principal*
EMP: 2 EST: 2016
SALES (est): 62.3K **Privately Held**
SIC: 2099 Food preparations

(G-11440)
QBC CATERING
2124 E County Line Rd S (47164-6966)
PHONE.....................................812 364-4293
Ron Smith, *Owner*
EMP: 2
SALES: 40K **Privately Held**
SIC: 2099 Food preparations

(G-11441)
SX4
3363 E Wetzel Rd (47164-6978)
PHONE.....................................812 967-2502
Steven Robbins, *Principal*
EMP: 2
SALES (est): 161K **Privately Held**
SIC: 3799 All terrain vehicles (ATV)

Paoli
Orange County

(G-11442)
ANDIS LOGGING INC
76 W County Road 550 S (47454-9416)
PHONE.....................................812 723-2357
Fax: 812 723-9912
Rob Andis, *President*
▼ EMP: 15
SALES (est): 1.1MM **Privately Held**
SIC: 2411 Logging camps & contractors

(G-11443)
B B CYCLES LLC
2547 N State Road 37 (47454-9446)
PHONE.....................................812 723-4265
Gina Burton, *Mng Member*
EMP: 7
SALES (est): 815.4K **Privately Held**
SIC: 3751 Motorcycles & related parts

(G-11444)
BENHAM SAWMILL LLC
150 W County Road 250 N (47454-9122)
P.O. Box 305 (47454-0305)
PHONE.....................................812 723-2644
Ronald Benham, *Administration*
EMP: 2
SALES (est): 132.9K **Privately Held**
SIC: 2421 Sawmills & planing mills, general

(G-11445)
BEST CHAIRS INCORPORATED
1700 W Willowcreek Rd (47454-9023)
PHONE.....................................812 367-1761
Fax: 812 723-9104
Steven M Wahl, *Branch Mgr*
EMP: 48
SALES (corp-wide): 250MM **Privately Held**
SIC: 2512 5712 Chairs: upholstered on wood frames; furniture stores
PA: Best Chairs Incorporated
1 Best Dr
Ferdinand IN 47532
812 367-1761

(G-11446)
CABINETMAKER INC
Also Called: Cabinetmaker, The
1714 E Owl Hollow Rd (47454-9085)
PHONE.....................................812 723-3461
Mary Barnard, *President*
Dale Barnard, *Vice Pres*
EMP: 2
SALES: 180K **Privately Held**
WEB: www.the-cabinetmaker.com
SIC: 2434 2511 2426 8331 Wood kitchen cabinets; wood household furniture; hardwood dimension & flooring mills; skill training center

(G-11447)
**CALCAR QUARRIES
INCORPORATED**
731 Ne Main St (47454-9237)
PHONE.....................................812 723-2109
Fax: 812 723-5314
Jerry Meadows, *President*
Mary Meadows, *Vice Pres*
Maxine Riester, *Admin Sec*
EMP: 15 EST: 1934
SQ FT: 1,000
SALES (est): 1.2MM **Privately Held**
SIC: 1422 2951 3274 Limestones, ground; asphalt & asphaltic paving mixtures (not from refineries); lime

(G-11448)
CAVE QUARRIES INC
1156 N County Road 425 W (47454-9002)
PHONE.....................................812 936-7743
Fax: 812 936-9631
Joe Knies, *Principal*
EMP: 7
SALES (est): 578.7K **Privately Held**
SIC: 1422 Crushed & broken limestone

(G-11449)
**ELLIOTT MANUFACTURING AND
FABR**
2302 W Coffee Dr N (47454-8816)
PHONE.....................................812 865-0516
EMP: 2
SALES (est): 138.1K **Privately Held**
SIC: 3999 Manufacturing industries

(G-11450)
**FLETCHER HEATING &
COOLING**
2049 W County Road 500 N (47454-9629)
P.O. Box 49 (47454-0049)
PHONE.....................................812 865-2984
Bill Fletcher, *Owner*
EMP: 3
SALES: 150K **Privately Held**
SIC: 1711 3585 Heating & air conditioning contractors; heating & air conditioning combination units

(G-11451)
G AND P ENTERPRISES IND INC
Also Called: Internal Honing Service
782 N Greenbriar Dr (47454-9667)
P.O. Box 111 (47454-0111)
PHONE.....................................812 723-3837
Fax: 812 723-5703
Jordan Beck, *Principal*
EMP: 9
SQ FT: 8,500
SALES (est): 2.7MM **Privately Held**
WEB: www.stevecole.com
SIC: 5051 3471 3599 Tubing, metal; chromium plating of metals or formed products; machine shop, jobbing & repair

(G-11452)
**HARMON HRMON UYSUGI
OPTMTRISTS (PA)**
488 W Hospital Rd Ste 1 (47454-8808)
PHONE.....................................812 723-4752
Fax: 812 723-4753
Eric Harmon, *Owner*
EMP: 10
SALES (est): 708.4K **Privately Held**
SIC: 8042 3851 Specialized optometrists; lenses, ophthalmic

(G-11453)
**INDIANA HANDLE COMPANY
INC**
Also Called: I H C
1514 W Main St (47454-1076)
P.O. Box 300 (47454-0300)
PHONE.....................................812 723-3159
Fax: 812 723-5630
Raymond L Farlow, *President*
R Edward Farlow, *Vice Pres*
Patricia Bridgewater, *Admin Sec*
EMP: 90 EST: 1932
SQ FT: 43,200
SALES (est): 9MM **Privately Held**
WEB: www.classicwoodproducts.com
SIC: 2426 Turnings, furniture: wood

(G-11454)
JASPER SEATING COMPANY INC
Also Called: Jasper Group
1352 W Hospital Rd (47454-9215)
PHONE....................812 723-1323
Chris Edwards, *Manager*
EMP: 56
SALES (est): 5MM
SALES (corp-wide): 228.8MM **Privately Held**
SIC: 2521 2522 Wood office furniture; office furniture, except wood
PA: Jasper Seating Company Inc
225 Clay St
Jasper IN 47546
812 482-3204

(G-11455)
LINER PRODUCTS LLC
1468 W Hospital Rd (47454-9215)
PHONE....................812 723-0244
Fax: 812 723-0405
Jeffrey Reynolds, *Mng Member*
Steven F Crooke,
Jerry W Fanska,
Patrick Schmidt,
EMP: 15
SALES: 18.8MM
SALES (corp-wide): 2.9B **Publicly Held**
SIC: 3084 Plastics pipe
HQ: Reynolds Construction, Llc.
4544 N State Road 37
Orleans IN 47452
812 865-3232

(G-11456)
MULZER CRUSHED STONE INC
3880 W Us Highway 150 (47454)
PHONE....................812 723-4137
Fax: 812 723-2469
Marvin Lynch, *Manager*
EMP: 17
SALES (corp-wide): 29.7B **Privately Held**
WEB: www.mulzer.com
SIC: 1422 Crushed & broken limestone
HQ: Mulzer Crushed Stone Inc
534 Mozart St
Tell City IN 47586
812 547-7921

(G-11457)
STANDS PHOTOGRAPHY
792 S Ridgecrest Ln (47454-9257)
PHONE....................812 723-3922
Don Stands, *Owner*
EMP: 2
SALES (est): 63K **Privately Held**
SIC: 7221 2759 Photographer, still or video; invitations: printing

Paragon
Morgan County

(G-11458)
J W JONES COMPANY LLC
Also Called: Rock Equipment
2468 S State Road 67 (46166-9502)
P.O. Box 64 (46166-0064)
PHONE....................765 537-2279
Liz Reuter, *Controller*
Stacey Ford, *Mktg Dir*
John W Jones, *Mng Member*
Michelle Phillips, *Analyst*
◆ **EMP:** 50
SALES (est): 16.4MM **Privately Held**
WEB: www.jwjonescompany.com
SIC: 3532 Rock crushing machinery, stationary

(G-11459)
JONES TRUCKING INC
2468 S State Road 67 (46166-9502)
P.O. Box 64 (46166-0064)
PHONE....................765 537-2279
John W Jones, *President*
EMP: 8
SALES (est): 800K **Privately Held**
SIC: 3532 Mining machinery

Paris Crossing
Jennings County

(G-11460)
PRECISION ENTERPRISES LLC
9775 S County Road 550 W (47270-9527)
PHONE....................812 873-6391
Les H Covey, *Principal*
EMP: 2
SALES (est): 142K **Privately Held**
SIC: 3599 Machine shop, jobbing & repair

(G-11461)
TOUCHDOWN FISHING LURES LLC
5975 W State Highway 250 (47270-9783)
PHONE....................812 873-8355
Leonard Hendrix, *Principal*
EMP: 2
SALES (est): 77.8K **Privately Held**
SIC: 3949 Bags, golf

Parker City
Randolph County

(G-11462)
COUNTY LINE COMPANIES LLC
3535 N Cross 800 E (47368)
PHONE....................866 959-7866
EMP: 2
SALES (est): 112.3K **Privately Held**
SIC: 3599 Amusement park equipment

(G-11463)
FPC FEED & MANUFACTURING
10727 W State Road 32 (47368-9307)
PHONE....................765 468-7768
Ferral Ford, *Owner*
EMP: 3
SALES: 250K **Privately Held**
SIC: 3523 Trailers & wagons, farm

(G-11464)
RELIABLE POLISHING CO
12517 W State Road 32 (47368-9397)
PHONE....................765 744-7824
EMP: 3 EST: 2010
SALES (est): 123.1K **Privately Held**
SIC: 3471 Polishing, metals or formed products

Patoka
Gibson County

(G-11465)
DENNIS K MARVELL
3700 W 250 N (47666-9249)
PHONE....................812 779-5107
Dennis Marvel, *Principal*
EMP: 3 EST: 2011
SALES (est): 258.9K **Privately Held**
SIC: 2411 Logging

(G-11466)
H & H MANUFACTURING INC
499 N 150 W (47666)
P.O. Box 12 (47666-0012)
PHONE....................812 664-3582
James Holzmeyer, *President*
Rick Hensley, *Vice Pres*
EMP: 5
SQ FT: 2,600
SALES: 500K **Privately Held**
SIC: 3462 Pump & compressor forgings, ferrous

Patriot
Switzerland County

(G-11467)
EAT DESSERT FIRST INC
10023 State Road 156 (47038-9674)
PHONE....................812 438-9600
Cindy Kerr, *President*
EMP: 7

SQ FT: 4,000
SALES (est): 1MM **Privately Held**
SIC: 2051 Bread, cake & related products

(G-11468)
HILLTOP BASIC RESOURCES INC
Also Called: Patriot Plant
14208 State Road 156 (47038-9836)
P.O. Box 157 (47038-0157)
PHONE....................812 594-2293
Fax: 812 594-2294
Roger Thayer, *Manager*
EMP: 40
SALES (corp-wide): 116.7MM **Privately Held**
WEB: www.hilltopbasicresources.com
SIC: 1442 Common sand mining; gravel mining
PA: Hilltop Basic Resources, Inc.
1 W 4th St Ste 1100
Cincinnati OH 45202
513 651-5000

(G-11469)
SWITZERLAND HILLS INC
Also Called: Swiss Caps
19091 Us Highway 250 (47038-9254)
PHONE....................812 594-2810
Fax: 812 594-2216
Anthony Gregory, *President*
Christie Gregory, *Vice Pres*
EMP: 35
SQ FT: 4,600
SALES (est): 5.5MM **Privately Held**
WEB: www.swisscaps.cc
SIC: 3792 5013 Pickup covers, canopies or caps; truck parts & accessories

Pekin
Washington County

(G-11470)
CENTURY GRAVE & VAULT SERVICE
2807 S Franklin School Rd (47165-8198)
PHONE....................812 967-2110
Carl Hudgens, *Owner*
EMP: 3
SALES (est): 272.3K **Privately Held**
SIC: 3272 Burial vaults, concrete or precast terrazzo

(G-11471)
CUSTOMER 1ST LLC (PA)
Also Called: Customer 1st Safes & Services
8899 E Daily Rd Lot 51 (47165-8964)
PHONE....................812 967-6727
Jack Hurst, *CEO*
Deb Gonika, *COO*
Jackie Hurst,
▲ **EMP:** 5
SALES (est): 472.6K **Privately Held**
SIC: 3499 7699 Safes & vaults, metal; locksmith shop

(G-11472)
FLEMING MACHINE WORKS INC
9934 S Fleming Rd (47165-8585)
PHONE....................812 967-4086
Lisa Fleming, *President*
EMP: 2
SALES (est): 160.5K **Privately Held**
SIC: 3599 Machine shop, jobbing & repair

(G-11473)
GREEN BANNER PUBLICATIONS INC (PA)
490 E State Road 60 (47165-7928)
P.O. Box 38 (47165-0038)
PHONE....................812 967-3176
Fax: 812 967-3194
Joseph V Green, *President*
Wanda A Green, *Corp Secy*
Jill B Green, *Vice Pres*
EMP: 25 EST: 1933
SQ FT: 4,400
SALES (est): 5.3MM **Privately Held**
SIC: 2711 2752 2791 2789 Newspapers, publishing & prinung; commercial printing, offset; typesetting; bookbinding & related work

(G-11474)
INDIANA ORDNANCE WORKS INC (PA)
11020 E Fitzpatrick Ln (47165-8437)
PHONE....................812 256-4478
Fax: 812 280-1796
Darwin B Harting, *President*
Robert Curts, *Exec VP*
Robert Reed, *Exec VP*
Lester Morgan, *Engineer*
David Hackel, *Treasurer*
EMP: 4
SQ FT: 61,000
SALES: 3.1MM **Privately Held**
SIC: 3489 Ordnance & accessories

(G-11475)
MARK MIDDLETON
5691 S Olive Branch Rd (47165-8241)
PHONE....................812 967-2853
Mark Middleton, *Owner*
Karen Middleton, *Co-Owner*
EMP: 3
SALES (est): 199.1K **Privately Held**
WEB: www.markmiddleton.com
SIC: 2421 Sawmills & planing mills, general

(G-11476)
MILLER WELDING & MECHANIC SVC
9556 Voyles Rd (47165-9618)
PHONE....................812 923-3359
Fax: 812 923-3359
Mark Miller, *President*
EMP: 2
SALES (est): 243K **Privately Held**
SIC: 3599 7692 Custom machinery; machine shop, jobbing & repair; welding repair

(G-11477)
MOULD-RITE INC
5885 E Old Pekin Rd (47165-7187)
P.O. Box 339 (47165-0339)
PHONE....................812 967-3200
Fax: 812 967-3252
David Robertson, *President*
Cherry Robertson, *General Mgr*
▲ **EMP:** 25
SQ FT: 16,000
SALES (est): 3.7MM **Privately Held**
WEB: www.mouldrite.com
SIC: 2426 Dimension, hardwood

(G-11478)
R C LASER INC
540 E State Road 60 (47165-7846)
PHONE....................812 923-1918
Fax: 812 923-1924
Charlie Hanson, *President*
William D Best, *Shareholder*
EMP: 8
SALES (est): 740K **Privately Held**
SIC: 3444 Sheet metalwork

(G-11479)
SCRAPBOOK NOOK
205 W State Road 60 (47165-7978)
PHONE....................812 967-3306
Linda Stewart, *Owner*
EMP: 4
SALES (est): 193.2K **Privately Held**
SIC: 2782 Scrapbooks

(G-11480)
WILLS ELECTRIC SERVICE INC
Also Called: Wills Electric Motor Serv
85 E Shorts Corner Rd (47165-8737)
PHONE....................812 883-5653
James Wills, *Owner*
Rosemary Wills, *Co-Owner*
EMP: 2
SALES (est): 130K **Privately Held**
SIC: 1731 7699 7694 Electrical work; pumps & pumping equipment repair; electric motor repair

(G-11481)
WORLEY LUMBER COMPANY INC
5803 E Hurst Rd (47165-7107)
P.O. Box 219 (47165-0219)
PHONE....................812 967-3521
Fax: 812 967-3551

Rick Lanham, *President*
Debrorah Lanham, *Corp Secy*
EMP: 14 EST: 1972
SQ FT: 15,000
SALES: 3MM **Privately Held**
SIC: 2421 Lumber: rough, sawed or planed

Pendleton
Madison County

(G-11482)
AIM MEDIA INDIANA OPER LLC
Times Post, The
126 W State St (46064-1034)
P.O. Box 9 (46064-0009)
PHONE..............................765 778-2324
John Senger, *Branch Mgr*
EMP: 2
SALES (corp-wide): 42.4MM **Privately Held**
SIC: 2711 Commercial printing & newspaper publishing combined
PA: Aim Media Indiana Operating, Llc
2980 N National Rd A
Columbus IN 47201
812 372-7811

(G-11483)
BALLANTRAE INC
Also Called: Delco Remy America
600 Corporation Dr (46064-8610)
PHONE..............................800 372-3555
Raj Sahah, *CFO*
EMP: 338
SALES (est): 185.3MM
SALES (corp-wide): 9.8B **Publicly Held**
SIC: 3714 3694 Motor vehicle engines & parts; engine electrical equipment
HQ: Borgwarner Pds (Anderson), L.L.C.
13975 Borgwarner Dr
Noblesville IN 46060

(G-11484)
BLACK SWAN VAPORS LLC
118 W State St (46064-1034)
PHONE..............................317 645-5210
William E Cecil, *Administration*
EMP: 6
SALES (est): 345.6K **Privately Held**
SIC: 5194 2131 5993 Smokeless tobacco; chewing tobacco; cigar store

(G-11485)
BORGWARNER PDS (INDIANA) INC (HQ)
600 Corporation Dr (46064-8610)
PHONE..............................800 372-3555
Ronald T Hundzinski, *President*
Kevin Quinn, *General Mgr*
Victor Polen, *COO*
David Krall, *Senior VP*
Shawn Pallagi, *Senior VP*
EMP: 4330 **EST:** 2014
SALES (est): 1.7B
SALES (corp-wide): 9.8B **Publicly Held**
SIC: 3694 3714 Battery charging alternators & generators; motor vehicle engines & parts; motor vehicle transmissions, drive assemblies & parts; motor vehicle electrical equipment
PA: Borgwarner Inc.
3850 Hamlin Rd
Auburn Hills MI 48326
248 754-9200

(G-11486)
BORGWARNER PDS ANDERSON LLC
600 Corporation Dr (46064-8610)
PHONE..............................765 778-6641
Jim Steel, *Branch Mgr*
EMP: 250
SALES (corp-wide): 9.8B **Publicly Held**
WEB: www.remy.net
SIC: 3714 Motor vehicle parts & accessories
HQ: Borgwarner Pds (Anderson), L.L.C.
13975 Borgwarner Dr
Noblesville IN 46060

(G-11487)
CAD/CAM TECHNOLOGIES INC
178 S Heritage Way (46064-8599)
P.O. Box 320 (46064-0320)
PHONE..............................765 778-2020
Fax: 765 778-3027
Randall Maynard, *President*
John Young, *Sales Engr*
EMP: 6
SQ FT: 1,500
SALES: 1,000K **Privately Held**
WEB: www.cad-camtech.com
SIC: 7372 8243 Prepackaged software; software training, computer

(G-11488)
ENGINERED REFR SHAPES SVCS LLC (PA)
Also Called: Erss
3370 W 1000 S (46064-9523)
P.O. Box 341 (46064-0341)
PHONE..............................765 778-8040
Garry E EBY,
EMP: 2
SQ FT: 17,500
SALES: 3.5MM **Privately Held**
SIC: 3823 8711 Refractometers, industrial process type; engineering services

(G-11489)
FLYOVER ENTERPRISES INC
1068 Chipmunk Ln (46064-9166)
PHONE..............................317 417-1747
John Perkins, *President*
Bryan Dixon, *Vice Pres*
Brad Holtz, *Vice Pres*
EMP: 3
SALES (est): 348.6K **Privately Held**
SIC: 3272 Building materials, except block or brick: concrete

(G-11490)
GO PRINT LLC
1260 W 700 S (46064-9118)
PHONE..............................765 778-1111
Jason Kistler, *Principal*
EMP: 6
SALES (est): 540K **Privately Held**
SIC: 2752 Commercial printing, lithographic

(G-11491)
JKL SOFTWARE
210 E Water St (46064-1047)
PHONE..............................765 778-3032
Kenneth U Lau DDS, *Principal*
EMP: 2
SALES (est): 122.7K **Privately Held**
WEB: www.jklsoftware.com
SIC: 7372 Business oriented computer software

(G-11492)
KENT MACHINE INC
8677 S State Road 9 (46064-9569)
PHONE..............................765 778-7777
Zane Kennedy, *President*
Harold Kennedy, *Treasurer*
Rob Amburn, *Sales Executive*
Nehersta Pierce, *Manager*
Sandra Kennedy, *Admin Sec*
EMP: 25
SQ FT: 17,000
SALES: 3MM **Privately Held**
WEB: www.kentmachine.com
SIC: 3544 Special dies & tools; jigs & fixtures

(G-11493)
MADISON COUNTY CABINETS INC
Also Called: MCC
9592 W 650 S (46064-9737)
Rural Route 9592 W 650 S (46064)
PHONE..............................765 778-4646
Fax: 765 778-3111
Russell Bowman, *President*
Larry Boone, *Corp Secy*
Daniel Bowman, *Vice Pres*
EMP: 16
SQ FT: 17,000
SALES: 1.9MM **Privately Held**
SIC: 2434 Wood kitchen cabinets

(G-11494)
MAGNEQUENCH INC
237 S Pendleton Ave Ste C (46064-1187)
PHONE..............................765 778-7809
Hong Zhang, *Ch of Bd*
Constantine Karayanno, *President*
Archibald Cox Jr, *President*
Gary Riley, *COO*
Shannon Song, *Senior VP*
▲ **EMP:** 1300
SALES (est): 137.9MM
SALES (corp-wide): 475.6MM **Publicly Held**
SIC: 3499 Magnets, permanent: metallic
HQ: Neo Performance Materials Ulc
121 King St W Suite 1740
Toronto ON M5H 3
416 367-8588

(G-11495)
MVP DUMPSTERS INC
8093 S 600 W (46064-8779)
PHONE..............................317 502-3155
Robert J Davis, *Principal*
EMP: 4 **EST:** 2016
SALES (est): 375.6K **Privately Held**
SIC: 3443 Dumpsters, garbage

(G-11496)
NEO MAGNEQUENCH DIST LLC
237 S Pendleton Ave (46064-1186)
PHONE..............................765 778-7809
James Herchenroeder, *Vice Pres*
EMP: 8 **EST:** 2016
SALES (est): 453K **Privately Held**
SIC: 3625 Control circuit devices, magnet & solid state

(G-11497)
NEWCO METALS INC (PA)
7268 S State Road 13 (46064-9565)
PHONE..............................317 485-7721
Fax: 317 485-6906
Chris Rasmussen, *President*
Kipp Barber, *Owner*
Steve Craver, *Senior VP*
Sarah Orpet, *Vice Pres*
Chris Ross, *Vice Pres*
EMP: 29
SQ FT: 5,000
SALES (est): 18.8MM **Privately Held**
WEB: www.newcometals.com
SIC: 5093 5051 3341 Nonferrous metals scrap; metals service centers & offices; secondary nonferrous metals

(G-11498)
OLD REMCO HOLDINGS LLC (HQ)
600 Corporation Dr (46064-8610)
PHONE..............................765 778-6499
John J Pittas, *President*
John Combes, *President*
John Mayfield, *President*
Mark R McFeely, *COO*
Michael L Gravelle, *Senior VP*
◆ **EMP:** 250
SALES (est): 2.2B
SALES (corp-wide): 9.8B **Publicly Held**
WEB: www.mmknopf.com
SIC: 3694 3714 Battery charging alternators & generators; motor vehicle engines & parts; motor vehicle transmissions, drive assemblies & parts; motor vehicle electrical equipment
PA: Borgwarner Inc.
3850 Hamlin Rd
Auburn Hills MI 48326
248 754-9200

(G-11499)
PENDLETON DOOR COMPANY
8680 S 750 W (46064-9757)
PHONE..............................765 778-4164
David Miller, *President*
EMP: 8
SQ FT: 2,400
SALES: 360K **Privately Held**
SIC: 2431 Doors, wood

(G-11500)
PENDLETON TIMES
Also Called: Lapell Post
6837 S State Road 67 (46064-9312)
P.O. Box 9 (46064-0009)
PHONE..............................765 778-2324

Fax: 765 778-7152
Andy Gruehr, *Owner*
Scott Slade, *Editor*
EMP: 7
SALES (est): 248.4K **Privately Held**
SIC: 2711 Newspapers, publishing & printing

(G-11501)
PROCYON PHARMACEUTICALS INC
206 Jh Walker Dr (46064-9377)
PHONE..............................765 778-9710
EMP: 2
SALES (est): 74.4K **Privately Held**
SIC: 2834 Pharmaceutical preparations

(G-11502)
REMAN HOLDINGS LLC (DH)
600 Corporation Dr (46064-8610)
PHONE..............................800 372-5131
Thomas Snyder, *President*
Susan Goldy, *Vice Pres*
Dave Stoll, *CFO*
Harold Sperlich,
EMP: 4
SALES (est): 108.9MM
SALES (corp-wide): 9.8B **Publicly Held**
SIC: 3714 3694 Motor vehicle engines & parts; battery charging alternators & generators

(G-11503)
REMY ELECTRIC MOTORS LLC
600 Corporation Dr (46064-8610)
PHONE..............................765 778-6466
John J Pittas,
Jeremiah J Shives,
EMP: 30
SALES (est): 1.8MM
SALES (corp-wide): 9.8B **Publicly Held**
SIC: 3621 3694 Starters, for motors; alternators, automotive
HQ: Old Remco Holdings, L.L.C.
600 Corporation Dr
Pendleton IN 46064

(G-11504)
REMY POWER PRODUCTS LLC
600 Corporation Dr (46064-8610)
PHONE..............................765 778-6499
David Nichols, *President*
Michael Caruso, *Treasurer*
EMP: 3000
SQ FT: 8,000
SALES: 150MM
SALES (corp-wide): 9.8B **Publicly Held**
SIC: 3625 3694 Motor starters & controllers, electric; starter, electric motor; alternators, automotive; motors, electric
HQ: Remy International Holdings, Inc.
600 Corporation Dr
Pendleton IN 46064

(G-11505)
SIGN AGE INC
8521 S State Road 9 (46064-9569)
PHONE..............................765 778-5254
Jeremy Adams, *President*
EMP: 3
SALES (est): 200K **Privately Held**
SIC: 3993 Signs & advertising specialties

(G-11506)
SO INDUSTRIES LLC ✪
4197 W 950 S (46064-9525)
PHONE..............................765 606-7596
Caleb Hardy, *Principal*
EMP: 2 **EST:** 2017
SALES (est): 74.6K **Privately Held**
SIC: 3999 Manufacturing industries

(G-11507)
TANGO ROMEO INDUSTRIES LLC
Also Called: Sarge's Shooting Bags
5567 S Cladwell Dr (46064-9593)
PHONE..............................765 623-1317
Anthony R Smith,
EMP: 2
SALES (est): 115.2K **Privately Held**
SIC: 3999 Manufacturing industries

G
E
O
G
R
A
P
H
I
C

(G-11508)
THREE LITTLE MONKEYS
129 S Pendleton Ave # 3 (46064-1183)
PHONE..........................765 778-9370
Heather Suarez, *Owner*
EMP: 3
SALES (est): 265.8K Privately Held
SIC: 2339 Maternity clothing

(G-11509)
TYLER TRUSS SYSTEMS INC
7883 W Fall Creek Dr (46064-8601)
PHONE..........................765 221-5050
Mark Dodd, *President*
EMP: 11
SALES (est): 456.7K Privately Held
SIC: 7929 2439 Entertainment service;
structural wood members

(G-11510)
VISHAY AMERICAS INC
555 S Pendleton Ave (46064-1329)
PHONE..........................765 778-4878
Anne Taylor, *Branch Mgr*
EMP: 2
SALES (corp-wide): 2.6B Publicly Held
SIC: 3676 Electronic resistors
HQ: Vishay Americas, Inc.
1 Greenwich Pl
Shelton CT 06484
203 452-5648

(G-11511)
WOLFE DIVERSIFIED INDS LLC (PA)
Also Called: Esc Promotions
9408 W Constellation Dr (46064-7511)
PHONE..........................765 683-9374
Dustin Close, *CFO*
David Orourke, *Sales Staff*
Chris Lyght, *Software Dev*
Joseph C Wolf,
Chad Wolfe,
EMP: 36
SQ FT: 4,000
SALES (est): 8.8MM Privately Held
SIC: 7372 Educational computer software

(G-11512)
WOOD MEDIC INC
9494 S 300 W (46064-9528)
P.O. Box 254 (46064-0254)
PHONE..........................765 778-4544
Lyndon Crumpacker, *President*
Mindy Crumpacker, *Admin Sec*
EMP: 5
SALES (est): 601.6K Privately Held
SIC: 2491 Wood preserving

Pennville
Jay County

(G-11513)
DYNO NOBEL INC
Also Called: Wampum Hardware
7860 W 400 N (47369-9488)
P.O. Box 352 (47369-0352)
PHONE..........................260 731-4431
Ron Bunch, *Branch Mgr*
EMP: 15 Privately Held
SIC: 2892 1629 Explosives; blasting con-
tractor, except building demolition
HQ: Dyno Nobel Inc.
2795 E Cottonwood Pkwy # 500
Salt Lake City UT 84121
801 364-4800

Peru
Miami County

(G-11514)
A&A SCREEN PRINTING
311 W 8th St (46970-1928)
PHONE..........................765 473-8783
Fax: 765 475-9311
Andrew Krisher, *Partner*
Anthony Krisher, *Partner*
EMP: 3 EST: 2001

SALES: 100K Privately Held
SIC: 2752 Commercial printing, lithographic

(G-11515)
AMERICAN STATIONERY CO
300 N Park Ave (46970-1701)
PHONE..........................765 473-4438
Michael Bakehorn, *President*
EMP: 2
SALES (est): 110K Privately Held
SIC: 2759 2679 Invitations: printing; sta-
tionery: printing; gift wrap; paper: made
from purchased material; novelties,
paper: made from purchased material

(G-11516)
ASC INC
Also Called: Fullfillment Center
N Miami Industrial Park (46970)
PHONE..........................765 472-5331
Melissa Pattison, *Manager*
EMP: 60
SALES (corp-wide): 48.1MM Privately
Held
WEB: www.merrimade.com
SIC: 2678 Stationery products
PA: Asc, Inc.
100 N Park Ave
Peru IN 46970
765 473-4438

(G-11517)
B & G SALES
421 Harrison Ave (46970-1146)
PHONE..........................765 473-7668
Betty Hall, *Owner*
EMP: 2 EST: 2013
SALES (est): 165.6K Privately Held
SIC: 1542 3272 Nonresidential construc-
tion; building materials, except block or
brick: concrete

(G-11518)
BRYAN STEAM LLC
Also Called: Bryan Boilers
783 Chili Ave (46970-1103)
PHONE..........................765 473-6651
Fax: 765 473-3074
Brian O'Toole, *President*
Beth Barker, *Vice Pres*
Kelly Stephens, *Plant Mgr*
Gene Musall, *Maint Spvr*
Ralph Lopez, *Purch Agent*
▲ EMP: 99
SQ FT: 195,000
SALES (est): 21.9MM
SALES (corp-wide): 172.4MM Publicly
Held
WEB: www.bryanboilers.com
SIC: 3433 Boilers, low-pressure heating:
steam or hot water
PA: Burnham Holdings, Inc.
1241 Harrisburg Ave
Lancaster PA 17603
717 390-7800

(G-11519)
CAPITAL CUSTOM SIGNS
1251 N Lancer St (46970-3642)
PHONE..........................765 689-7170
Michael Murray, *Owner*
Luisa Murray, *Co-Owner*
EMP: 2
SALES: 100K Privately Held
SIC: 3993 Signs & advertising specialties

(G-11520)
CDB SCREEN PRINTING INC
185 Madison Ave (46970-1044)
PHONE..........................765 472-4404
Cliff D Bakehorn, *President*
EMP: 6
SQ FT: 8,000
SALES: 180K Privately Held
WEB: www.bakehorn.com
SIC: 2759 Screen printing

(G-11521)
CERES SOLUTIONS COOP INC
6519 S State Road 19 (46970-7713)
PHONE..........................765 473-3922
Fax: 765 473-9233
Larry Easterday, *Branch Mgr*
EMP: 6

SALES (corp-wide): 331.8MM Privately
Held
SIC: 2875 Fertilizers, mixing only
PA: Ceres Solutions Cooperative Incorpo-
rated
2025 S Wabash St
Wabash IN 46992
800 992-3495

(G-11522)
CO-TRONICS INC
2935 W 100 N (46970-7587)
P.O. Box 1037, Logansport (46947-0937)
PHONE..........................574 722-3850
Ronald L Sink Jr, *President*
David Williams, *Vice Pres*
Diane Denny, *Admin Sec*
▲ EMP: 12 EST: 1961
SQ FT: 13,000
SALES (est): 3.1MM Privately Held
SIC: 3089 Molding primary plastic; thermo-
formed finished plastic products

(G-11523)
DAILY PERU TRIBUNE PUBG CO
Also Called: Peru Tribune
26 W 3rd St (46970-2155)
PHONE..........................765 473-6641
Fax: 765 472-4438
Fred Paxton, *President*
EMP: 45 EST: 1921
SQ FT: 8,000
SALES (est): 1.7MM
SALES (corp-wide): 318.6MM Privately
Held
WEB: www.perutribune.com
SIC: 2711 7371 Newspapers, publishing &
printing; custom computer programming
services
PA: Paxton Media Group, Llc
100 Television Ln
Paducah KY 42003
270 575-8630

(G-11524)
DORIS DRAPERY BOUTIQUE
68 N Broadway (46970-2238)
PHONE..........................765 472-5850
Doris Eliason-Wood, *Owner*
EMP: 7
SQ FT: 2,000
SALES (est): 514.8K Privately Held
SIC: 2391 1799 5231 5719 Draperies,
plastic & textile: from purchased materi-
als; drapery track installation; wallpaper;
venetian blinds; floor laying & floor work

(G-11525)
E & B PAVING INC
Cemetary Rd (46970)
PHONE..........................765 472-3626
Gary Stebbins, *Branch Mgr*
EMP: 2
SALES (corp-wide): 800.6MM Privately
Held
SIC: 3273 Ready-mixed concrete
HQ: E & B Paving, Inc.
286 W 300 N
Anderson IN 46012
765 643-5358

(G-11526)
EBERT MACHINE COMPANY INC
Also Called: Thrift Products Heating Spc
2177 S State Road 19 (46970-7473)
PHONE..........................765 473-3728
Fax: 765 473-3804
Joel Ebert, *President*
Rob Parnell, *Sales Mgr*
Anna Ebert, *Mktg Dir*
Weldon M Ebert, *Admin Sec*
EMP: 37
SQ FT: 21,000
SALES (est): 6.8MM Privately Held
WEB: www.ebertmachine.com
SIC: 3451 3639 Screw machine products;
hot water heaters, household

(G-11527)
FRED ANDERSON
Also Called: Anderson Machine Tool
4757 N 400 E (46970-8569)
PHONE..........................765 985-2099
Debra Anderson, *Owner*
EMP: 2

SALES: 80K Privately Held
SIC: 3599 3544 Machine shop, jobbing &
repair; special dies, tools, jigs & fixtures

(G-11528)
GJS HOME AND OFFICE FURNITURE
21 E Main St (46970-2210)
PHONE..........................765 472-2478
Gloria Hentgen, *Owner*
EMP: 3
SALES (est): 567.6K Privately Held
WEB: www.dawcoinc.com
SIC: 2522 Office furniture, except wood

(G-11529)
HERAEUS ELECTRO-NITE CO LLC
1025 Industrial Pkwy (46970-9590)
PHONE..........................765 473-8275
Fax: 765 473-4725
Jim Myers, *Manager*
David Bettencourt, *Director*
Sheila Hanover, *Planning*
Georgina Xu, *Analyst*
EMP: 130 Privately Held
WEB: www.electro-nite.com
SIC: 3823 3674 Temperature measure-
ment instruments, industrial; semiconduc-
tors & related devices
HQ: Heraeus Electro-Nite Co., Llc
541 S Industrial Dr
Hartland WI 53029
215 944-9000

(G-11530)
HOLLANDS DEER PROCESSING LLC
1848 W Lovers Lane Rd (46970-8775)
PHONE..........................765 472-5876
Chris Hollands, *Mng Member*
EMP: 10
SALES (est): 754.2K Privately Held
SIC: 2015 Poultry slaughtering & process-
ing

(G-11531)
IAS CORP
206 N Grant St (46970-1618)
PHONE..........................209 836-8610
Fax: 209 606-5119
Dan Westerlund, *Principal*
EMP: 3
SALES (est): 220.5K Privately Held
SIC: 3829 Measuring & controlling devices

(G-11532)
INTECH AUTOMATION SYSTEMS CORP
Also Called: I A S
206 N Grant St (46970-1618)
PHONE..........................209 836-8610
Fax: 925 606-5119
Dan Westerlund, *President*
Dianne Westerland, *Treasurer*
EMP: 7
SALES: 682.4K Privately Held
SIC: 3829 Thermocouples

(G-11533)
IRVING MATERIALS INC
Also Called: I M I
351 N 150 W (46970-7589)
PHONE..........................765 472-5370
Fax: 765 473-8357
Mike Maverick, *Manager*
EMP: 5
SALES (corp-wide): 800.6MM Privately
Held
SIC: 3273 Ready-mixed concrete
PA: Irving Materials, Inc.
8032 N State Road 9
Greenfield IN 46140
317 326-3101

(G-11534)
JOLENE D PAVEY
Also Called: Wilhelm AG Lime
4641 S 50 W (46970-7623)
PHONE..........................765 473-6171
Jolene D Pavey, *Principal*
EMP: 2
SALES (est): 159.1K Privately Held
SIC: 3274 Lime

(G-11535)
K&T PERFORMANCE ENGRG LLC
Also Called: American Performance Engrg
1975 N Lancer St (46970-3670)
PHONE...................................765 437-0185
Matt Thatcher, *Mng Member*
Larry Barnett,
EMP: 2
SQ FT: 6,000
SALES (est): 135.1K **Privately Held**
SIC: 8711 3599 Mechanical engineering;
machine shop, jobbing & repair

(G-11536)
LUFKIN INDUSTRIES INC
401 Blair Pike (46970-1505)
PHONE...................................765 472-2935
EMP: 8
SALES (est): 870K **Privately Held**
SIC: 3533 Mfg Oil/Gas Field Machinery

(G-11537)
MISSION ANNOUNCEMENT CO
100 N Park Ave (46970-1702)
PHONE...................................626 332-4084
Gerald Cohen, *President*
EMP: 40 EST: 1953
SQ FT: 30,000
SALES: 2MM **Privately Held**
SIC: 2759 Announcements: engraved

(G-11538)
MPI HOLDINGS INC
Also Called: Marburger Foods
3311 S State Road 19 (46970-7476)
PHONE...................................765 473-3086
John A Marburger, *President*
EMP: 225
SQ FT: 40,000
SALES (est): 22.6MM **Privately Held**
SIC: 2011 2013 Meat packing plants;
sausages & other prepared meats

(G-11539)
PERU HARDWOOD PRODUCTS INC
2678 N Mexico Rd (46970-8152)
PHONE...................................765 473-4844
Jon D Eisaman, *President*
Joseph Eisaman, *Corp Secy*
EMP: 15
SQ FT: 5,000
SALES: 1.4MM **Privately Held**
SIC: 2448 Pallets, wood

(G-11540)
PRECISION PULSE LLP
4995 E 550 S (46970-8956)
PHONE...................................765 472-6002
Troy Coblentz, *Principal*
EMP: 2
SALES (est): 117.7K **Privately Held**
SIC: 7692 Welding repair

(G-11541)
PRECISION STITCH INDIANA INC
404 W Canal St (46970-1878)
PHONE...................................765 473-6734
Fax: 765 473-8687
Phil Van Baalen, *President*
Stephanie Van Baalen, *Admin Sec*
EMP: 8
SQ FT: 4,000
SALES (est): 480.3K **Privately Held**
SIC: 2395 Embroidery & art needlework

(G-11542)
PROGRESS RAIL SERVICES CORP
588 W 7th St (46970-1880)
PHONE...................................765 472-2002
Keith Walls, *Branch Mgr*
EMP: 3
SALES (corp-wide): 45.4B **Publicly Held**
SIC: 3519 Internal combustion engines
HQ: Progress Rail Services Corporation
1600 Progress Dr
Albertville AL 35950
256 593-1260

(G-11543)
RADEL WOOD PRODUCTS INC
1630 W Logansport Rd (46970-3149)
PHONE...................................765 472-2940

Fax: 765 472-3013
Gerald Radel, *President*
Marie Radel, *Corp Secy*
EMP: 19
SQ FT: 3,000
SALES (est): 2.4MM **Privately Held**
SIC: 2434 Wood kitchen cabinets; vanities,
bathroom: wood

(G-11544)
REPROCOMM INC (PA)
Also Called: Modern Graphics
179 N Miami St (46970-2106)
PHONE...................................765 472-5700
Fax: 765 472-1299
James Clary, *President*
Terence L Lucterhand, *President*
David R Sattler, *President*
Ronald L Meyer, *Corp Secy*
Harry Rodkey, *Vice Pres*
EMP: 40 EST: 1963
SQ FT: 6,000
SALES (est): 15MM **Privately Held**
WEB: www.moderngraphics.com
SIC: 5111 2752 2791 2789 Printing &
writing paper; commercial printing, offset;
typesetting; bookbinding & related work;
commercial printing

(G-11545)
SMITHFIELD DIRECT LLC
3311 S State Road 19 (46970-7476)
PHONE...................................765 473-3086
Micheal Fritz, *Manager*
EMP: 30 **Privately Held**
SIC: 2011 Meat packing plants
HQ: Smithfield Direct, Llc
4225 Naperville Rd # 600
Lisle IL 60532

(G-11546)
SMITHFIELD FOODS
3311 S State Road 19 (46970-7476)
PHONE...................................765 473-3086
EMP: 3
SALES (est): 128.3K **Privately Held**
SIC: 3556 Food products machinery

(G-11547)
SNAVELYS MACHINE & MFG CO INC
Also Called: Snavely Machine
1070 Industrial Pkwy (46970-9589)
P.O. Box 1221 (46970-4221)
PHONE...................................765 473-8395
Fax: 765 473-3539
Joseph G Kinney, *President*
Mike Inderhees, *COO*
Tricia Crowe, *Purch Mgr*
Jason Amonepott, *CFO*
Jason Amonett, *CFO*
EMP: 140
SQ FT: 172,000
SALES (est): 15MM **Privately Held**
WEB: www.snavelymachine.com
SIC: 3599 Machine shop, jobbing & repair

(G-11548)
STANDARD FUSEE CORPORATION
Also Called: Orion Safety Products
3157 N 500 W (46970-7559)
PHONE...................................765 472-4375
Fax: 765 473-3254
Debbie Townsend, *Principal*
Rod Utter, *Plant Mgr*
EMP: 40
SALES (corp-wide): 20.2MM **Privately Held**
WEB: www.orionsignals.com
SIC: 2899 5047 3949 3842 Flares, fire-
works & similar preparations; medical &
hospital equipment; sporting & athletic
goods; surgical appliances & supplies;
switchgear & switchboard apparatus;
manufactured hardware (general)
PA: Standard Fusee Corporation
28320 Saint Michaels Rd
Easton MD 21601
410 822-0318

(G-11549)
STONE QUARY (PA)
Also Called: Rock Hollow Golf Club
350 N 150 W (46970-7589)
P.O. Box 187 (46970-0187)
PHONE...................................765 473-5578
Fax: 765 473-3048
Terry W Smith, *President*
Rebecca Smith, *Corp Secy*
Todd Smith, *Vice Pres*
EMP: 27
SALES (est): 1.9MM **Privately Held**
WEB: www.rockhollowgolf.com
SIC: 7992 1442 1422 Public golf courses;
sand mining; gravel mining; crushed &
broken limestone

(G-11550)
SUGAR CREEK CANDIES INC
1688 W Hoosier Blvd (46970-3600)
PHONE...................................765 681-1607
Jill P Wolfe, *President*
Harry Wolfe, *Treasurer*
EMP: 10
SALES (est): 370K **Privately Held**
SIC: 2064 Candy & other confectionery
products

(G-11551)
THRUSH CO INC
340 W 8th St (46970-1929)
P.O. Box 228 (46970-0228)
PHONE...................................765 472-3351
Julius P Marburger, *President*
Jeff Marburger, *Plant Mgr*
Sara M Marburger, *Admin Sec*
Leigh Denniston,
▲ EMP: 39
SQ FT: 60,000
SALES: 5.6MM **Privately Held**
WEB: www.thrushco.com
SIC: 3561 3443 Pumps & pumping equip-
ment; heat exchangers, condensers &
components

(G-11552)
TIP TO TAIL AEROSPACE LLC ✪
1697 W Hoosier Blvd 11 (46970-3600)
PHONE...................................765 437-6556
Andrew Boles, *Principal*
EMP: 2 EST: 2017
SALES (est): 170.8K **Privately Held**
SIC: 3721 Aircraft

(G-11553)
TRACY K HULLETT
Also Called: Hulletts Backhoe Service
268 W 3rd St (46970-1960)
PHONE...................................765 472-3349
Tracy K Hullett, *Principal*
EMP: 2 EST: 2012
SALES (est): 137.6K **Privately Held**
SIC: 3531 Backhoes

(G-11554)
VALVOLINE EXPRESS
318 W Main St (46970-1952)
PHONE...................................765 473-4891
John Riffle, *Manager*
EMP: 2
SALES (est): 99.4K **Privately Held**
SIC: 2741 Miscellaneous publishing

(G-11555)
VICKERY TAPE & LABEL CO INC
Also Called: Jl Vincent Enterprises
20 W Canal St (46970-2164)
PHONE...................................765 472-1974
Fax: 765 472-7354
Jim Vicent, *President*
Michael Gable, *Vice Pres*
Brandon Mitchell, *Vice Pres*
EMP: 10 EST: 1947
SQ FT: 12,000
SALES (est): 2MM **Privately Held**
WEB: www.vickerytape.com
SIC: 2672 Tape, pressure sensitive: made
from purchased materials; labels (un-
printed), gummed: made from purchased
materials

(G-11556)
WC REDMON CO INC
200 Harrison Ave (46970-1155)
P.O. Box 7 (46970-0007)
PHONE...................................765 473-6683

Fax: 765 473-6686
C Peter Redmon, *CEO*
Timothy Jackson, *COO*
Morris Kandy, *Opers Mgr*
Samuel Redmon, *CFO*
Lori V Gagnon, *VP Sales*
▲ EMP: 15 EST: 1920
SQ FT: 103,000
SALES (est): 3.5MM **Privately Held**
WEB: www.redmonusa.com
SIC: 2511 2499 5023 Nursery furniture:
wood; storage chests, household: wood;
novelty furniture: wood; whatnot shelves:
wood; hampers, laundry; decorative home
furnishings & supplies

(G-11557)
WESTERN REMAN INDUSTRIAL INC (DH)
Also Called: Wri
588 W 7th St (46970-1880)
PHONE...................................765 472-2002
Fax: 765 473-3850
Sean McGowan, *President*
Fred Knechtel, *Vice Pres*
Sheila Cannon, *Admin Sec*
▲ EMP: 9
SQ FT: 115,000
SALES (est): 28.4MM
SALES (corp-wide): 9.8B **Publicly Held**
SIC: 3714 Rebuilding engines & transmis-
sions, factory basis; motor vehicle en-
gines & parts

(G-11558)
WESTERN REMAN INDUSTRIAL LLC
588 W 7th St (46970-1880)
PHONE...................................765 472-2002
Sean McGowan, *Plant Mgr*
▲ EMP: 75
SALES (est): 8.4MM
SALES (corp-wide): 9.8B **Publicly Held**
SIC: 3743 Industrial locomotives & parts
HQ: Western Reman Industrial, Inc.
588 W 7th St
Peru IN 46970
765 472-2002

(G-11559)
WOODCREST MANUFACTURING INC (PA)
150 E Washington Ave (46970-1031)
P.O. Box 848 (46970-0848)
PHONE...................................765 472-4471
Fax: 765 472-5362
Walter B Woodhams, *President*
Mark L Woodhams, *President*
Sam Brown, *Purchasing*
Woodhams Dorothy, *Admin Sec*
▲ EMP: 100
SQ FT: 65,000
SALES (est): 20.5MM **Privately Held**
WEB: www.woodcrestmfg.com
SIC: 2511 Wood household furniture; juve-
nile furniture: wood; wood bedroom furni-
ture; dressers, household: wood

(G-11560)
WOODCREST MANUFACTURING INC
217 E Canal St (46970-2427)
PHONE...................................765 472-5361
Fax: 765 472-5363
Bruce White, *Manager*
EMP: 14
SALES (corp-wide): 20.5MM **Privately Held**
WEB: www.woodcrestmfg.com
SIC: 2511 2515 Wood household furniture;
mattresses & bedsprings
PA: Woodcrest Manufacturing Inc
150 E Washington Ave
Peru IN 46970
765 472-4471

Petersburg
Pike County

(G-11561)
BCBG MAX AZRIA GROUP LLC
215 S 9th St (47567-1539)
PHONE...................................620 694-4256

EMP: 2
SALES (corp-wide): 979.1MM **Privately Held**
SIC: 2335 Women's, juniors' & misses' dresses
HQ: Bcbg Max Azria Group, Llc
2761 Fruitland Ave
Vernon CA 90058
323 589-2224

(G-11562)
FOUR STAR FABRICATORS INC
810 S Industrial Park Dr (47567-8311)
P.O. Box 67 (47567-0067)
PHONE..............................812 354-9995
Fax: 812 354-3809
Kim Walhall, *CEO*
Tom Walthall, *President*
Larry Dick, *Vice Pres*
EMP: 75
SQ FT: 55,000
SALES (est): 29.2MM **Privately Held**
WEB: www.fourstarfab.com
SIC: 3441 3443 Building components, structural steel; fabricated plate work (boiler shop)

(G-11563)
FOUR STAR FIELD SERVICES
804 S Industrial Park Dr # 10 (47567-8311)
P.O. Box 67 (47567-0067)
PHONE..............................812 354-9995
Jesse Nickson, *Principal*
EMP: 7 **EST:** 2014
SALES (est): 709.4K **Privately Held**
SIC: 3315 Welded steel wire fabric

(G-11564)
FRED D MCCRARY
Also Called: McCrary, Fred D Oil Co
4295 W County Road 350 N (47567-8660)
PHONE..............................812 354-6520
Fred D McCrary, *Owner*
EMP: 5
SALES (est): 338.8K **Privately Held**
SIC: 1311 Crude petroleum & natural gas

(G-11565)
ONYETT WELDING & MACHINE INC
Also Called: Onyett, A.B. & Sons
409 N 8th St (47567-1121)
PHONE..............................812 582-2999
Fax: 812 354-9279
Jack Onyett, *President*
EMP: 2 **EST:** 1935
SALES (est): 259.3K **Privately Held**
SIC: 3523 7692 Farm machinery & equipment; welding repair

(G-11566)
PIKE COUNTY PUBLISHING CORP (PA)
Also Called: Press Dispatch
820 E Poplar St (47567-1258)
P.O. Box 68 (47567-0068)
PHONE..............................812 354-8500
Fax: 812 354-2014
Frank Heuring, *President*
John Heuring, *Manager*
EMP: 16
SQ FT: 2,100
SALES (est): 767.4K **Privately Held**
SIC: 2711 Newspapers: publishing only, not printed on site

(G-11567)
PIKE PUBLISHING
407 E Walnut St (47567-1443)
P.O. Box 353 (47567-0353)
PHONE..............................812 354-4701
Eric Gogel, *Principal*
EMP: 2
SALES (est): 59.2K **Privately Held**
SIC: 2741 Miscellaneous publishing

(G-11568)
SMGF LLC
Also Called: Onyett Fabricators
3377 N State Road 57 (47567-8048)
PHONE..............................812 354-8899
Jessica Elpers, *Manager*
EMP: 76
SQ FT: 28,000

SALES (est): 3MM **Privately Held**
SIC: 3542 3441 Machine tools, metal forming type; fabricated structural metal

(G-11569)
SOLAR SOURCES INC
625 N 9th St (47567-1166)
P.O. Box 7 (47567-0007)
PHONE..............................812 354-8776
Steven Cummins, *Plant Mgr*
Donald A Keller, *Manager*
Candice Bruns, *Admin Sec*
EMP: 87
SALES (corp-wide): 186.3MM **Privately Held**
WEB: www.solarsources.com
SIC: 1221 Strip mining, bituminous
PA: Solar Sources, Inc.
6755 Gray Rd
Indianapolis IN 46237
317 788-0084

(G-11570)
T & E WELDING INC
10 W Locust St (47567-1655)
PHONE..............................812 324-0140
Timothy Evans, *Principal*
EMP: 10 **EST:** 2008
SALES (est): 23MM **Privately Held**
SIC: 7692 Welding repair

(G-11571)
TRIAD WARSH PLANT SCALE HOUSE
4251 W County Road 125 S (47567-8797)
PHONE..............................812 385-0909
Fax: 812 385-0705
EMP: 2 **EST:** 2010
SALES (est): 100K **Privately Held**
SIC: 3648 Mfg Lighting Equipment

Pierceton
Kosciusko County

(G-11572)
HERMAN TOOL & MACHINE INC
Also Called: Hermans' Christmas Land
2 Arnolt Dr (46562-9640)
PHONE..............................574 594-5544
Fax: 574 594-5984
James Read Jr, *President*
EMP: 10 **EST:** 1967
SQ FT: 23,500
SALES (est): 1.1MM **Privately Held**
SIC: 3544 3446 5999 7692 Dies, plastics forming; extrusion dies; punches, forming & stamping; ornamental metalwork; Christmas lights & decorations; welding repair; machine tool accessories; sheet metalwork

(G-11573)
MIDWEST ROLL FORMING & MFG INC
Also Called: Omco
1 Arnolt Dr (46562-9641)
PHONE..............................574 594-2100
Fax: 574 594-2847
Gary Schuster, *CEO*
Len Parker, *Principal*
Andrew Kinkade, *Opers Mgr*
Jennie Skeens, *QC Mgr*
Lynn Darlage, *Engineer*
EMP: 150
SQ FT: 92,000
SALES (est): 52.4MM **Privately Held**
WEB: www.omcoform.com
SIC: 3444 Sheet metalwork
HQ: Ohio Moulding Corporation
30396 Lakeland Blvd
Wickliffe OH 44092
440 944-2100

(G-11574)
NORTHERN GASES AND SUPS INC (PA)
1426 S State Road 13 (46562-9759)
P.O. Box 417 (46562-0417)
PHONE..............................574 594-2104
Fax: 574 594-2104
E Marie Trump, *CEO*
Steven R Trump, *President*
Mary Bolinger, *Vice Pres*

Charles L Trump, *Admin Sec*
EMP: 12 **EST:** 1947
SQ FT: 10,500
SALES (est): 1.4MM **Privately Held**
SIC: 2813 5169 5084 5999 Acetylene; industrial gases; welding machinery & equipment; welding supplies; industrial supplies

(G-11575)
PARAGON MEDICAL INC
Also Called: Pierceton I&I
22 Pequignot Dr (46562-9088)
PHONE..............................574 594-2140
EMP: 4
SALES (corp-wide): 191.6MM **Privately Held**
SIC: 3089 3841 Plastic containers, except foam; thermoformed finished plastic products; surgical & medical instruments
PA: Paragon Medical, Inc.
8 Matchett Dr
Pierceton IN 46562
574 594-2140

(G-11576)
PARAGON MEDICAL INC (PA)
Also Called: Pierceton Case & Tray
8 Matchett Dr (46562-9075)
PHONE..............................574 594-2140
Fax: 574 594-2154
Tobias W Buck, *President*
Tom Lowe, *Business Mgr*
Gary Mc Gill, *COO*
Cory Colman, *Vice Pres*
Dan Owens, *Vice Pres*
▲ **EMP:** 268
SQ FT: 50,000
SALES (est): 191.6MM **Privately Held**
SIC: 3089 3841 7371 Plastic containers, except foam; thermoformed finished plastic products; surgical & medical instruments; computer software development & applications

(G-11577)
PIERCETON RUBBER PRODUCTS INC
3076 S 900 E (46562-9769)
PHONE..............................574 594-3002
Fax: 574 594-3018
John Burnau, *CEO*
Tammy Burneau, *Admin Sec*
EMP: 10
SQ FT: 30,000
SALES (est): 1.6MM **Privately Held**
WEB: www.dynacushion.com
SIC: 3069 Mats or matting, rubber

(G-11578)
S P X CORP
5 Arnolt Dr (46562-9641)
P.O. Box 710 (46562-0710)
PHONE..............................574 594-9681
Rob Hollacher, *President*
EMP: 6
SALES (est): 577.8K **Privately Held**
SIC: 3364 Nonferrous die-castings except aluminum

(G-11579)
SHILOH INDUSTRIES INC
5 Arnolt Dr (46562-9641)
PHONE..............................574 594-9681
Randy Kinsey, *Plant Mgr*
EMP: 19 **Publicly Held**
SIC: 3465 Automotive stampings
PA: Shiloh Industries, Inc.
880 Steel Dr
Valley City OH 44280

Pimento
Vigo County

(G-11580)
PEABODY MIDWEST MINING LLC
Also Called: Black Beauty Farmersburg
5526 E French Dr (47866-9543)
PHONE..............................812 495-6070
EMP: 200
SALES (corp-wide): 5.6B **Publicly Held**
SIC: 1221 Coal Mine

HQ: Peabody Midwest Mining, Llc
566 Dickeyville Rd
Lynnville IN 47619
812 434-8500

Pine Village
Warren County

(G-11581)
HOOKER CORNER WINERY LLC
444 W State Road 26 (47975-8057)
PHONE..............................765 585-1225
Jae A Brier, *Principal*
EMP: 2
SALES (est): 70.4K **Privately Held**
SIC: 2084 Wines

Pittsboro
Hendricks County

(G-11582)
AIRGAS USA LLC
8000 N County Road 225 E (46167-9094)
PHONE..............................317 892-5221
Shawn Riehle, *Manager*
EMP: 8
SALES (corp-wide): 164.2MM **Privately Held**
SIC: 2813 Industrial gases
HQ: Airgas Usa, Llc
259 N Radnor Chester Rd # 100
Radnor PA 19087
610 687-5253

(G-11583)
JOHNSON CONTROLS INC
314 Brixton Woods West Dr (46167-8950)
PHONE..............................317 917-5043
EMP: 60
SALES (corp-wide): 41.9B **Publicly Held**
SIC: 2531 3691 3822 8744 Mfg Public Building Furn Mfg Storage Batteries Mfg Environmntl Controls Facilities Support Svcs
PA: Johnson Controls, Inc.
5757 N Green Bay Ave
Milwaukee WI 53209
414 524-1200

(G-11584)
LACOPA INTERNATIONAL INC
5028 Hill Valley Dr (46167-9122)
PHONE..............................317 410-1483
Dan Linson, *President*
Beth Linson, *Corp Secy*
▼ **EMP:** 6
SALES: 3MM **Privately Held**
SIC: 3448 Prefabricated metal buildings

(G-11585)
MATHESON TRI-GAS INC
8000 N County Road 225 E (46167-9094)
PHONE..............................317 892-5221
Shawn Riehle, *Manager*
EMP: 8
SALES (corp-wide): 34.9B **Privately Held**
SIC: 2813 5084 Industrial gases; nitrogen; oxygen, compressed or liquefied; argon; welding machinery & equipment; safety equipment
HQ: Matheson Tri-Gas, Inc.
150 Allen Rd Ste 302
Basking Ridge NJ 07920
908 991-9200

(G-11586)
ROW PRINTING INC ✪
4406 Quail Creek Trce N (46167-8701)
PHONE..............................317 441-4301
Sandra Laycock, *Owner*
EMP: 2 **EST:** 2018
SALES (est): 83.9K **Privately Held**
SIC: 2752 Commercial printing, lithographic

(G-11587)
SEED & SATCHEL LLC ✪
4298 E County Road 1000 N (46167-9440)
PHONE..............................317 892-2557
Meagan Miller, *Principal*
EMP: 2 **EST:** 2017

▲ = Import ▼=Export
◆ =Import/Export

SALES (est): 77.4K **Privately Held**
SIC: 3161 Satchels

(G-11588)
STEEL DYNAMICS INC
Also Called: Engineered Bar Products Div
8000 N County Road 225 E (46167-9094)
PHONE.................................317 892-7000
David Olson, *Supervisor*
EMP: 369 **Publicly Held**
SIC: 3312 Plate, sheet & strip, except
coated products
PA: Steel Dynamics, Inc.
7575 W Jefferson Blvd
Fort Wayne IN 46804

(G-11589)
WARREN POWER ATTACHMENTS
4614 E County Road 1000 N (46167-9441)
PHONE.................................317 892-4737
Laura Warren, *Technology*
Aaron Warren,
Doug Warren,
EMP: 5
SQ FT: 18,000
SALES: 15MM **Privately Held**
WEB: www.warrenattachments.com
SIC: 3315 Welded steel wire fabric

Plainfield
Hendricks County

(G-11590)
ABRA AUTO BODY & GLASS LP
Also Called: ABRA Autobody & Glass
2170 E Main St (46168-1861)
PHONE.................................317 839-8940
Doug Russell, *Branch Mgr*
EMP: 22
SALES (corp-wide): 1.9B **Privately Held**
SIC: 7532 3713 3711 Body shop, automo-
tive; truck & bus bodies; automobile bod-
ies, passenger car, not including engine,
etc.
PA: Abra Auto Body & Glass Lp
7225 Northland Dr N # 110
Brooklyn Park MN 55428
888 872-2272

(G-11591)
AEL/SPAN LLC
Also Called: Delphi Pdts & Svc Solutions
6032 Gateway Dr (46168-7655)
PHONE.................................317 203-4602
Russell Hollen, *Supervisor*
EMP: 25 **Privately Held**
SIC: 3625 4225 Switches, electronic appli-
cations; general warehousing & storage
PA: Ael/Span, Llc
41775 Ecorse Rd Ste 100
Van Buren Twp MI 48111

(G-11592)
AMS PRODUCTIONS MACHINING INC
800 Andico Rd (46168-9659)
P.O. Box 376 (46168-0376)
PHONE.................................317 838-9273
John Anderson, *President*
Larry Bowen, *Vice Pres*
Bryan Burdine, *Vice Pres*
Robert Hines, *Vice Pres*
EMP: 50
SQ FT: 30,000
SALES: 3.9MM **Privately Held**
WEB: www.amsmachining.com
SIC: 3599 Machine shop, jobbing & repair

(G-11593)
APOTEX CORP
2516 Airwest Blvd (46168-7701)
PHONE.................................317 839-6550
Jim Roudebush, *Manager*
EMP: 25
SALES (corp-wide): 324.8MM **Privately Held**
SIC: 2836 Biological products, except diag-
nostic
HQ: Apotex Corp.
2400 N Commerce Pkwy # 400
Weston FL 33326

(G-11594)
ARTISANZ FABRICATION MCH LLC
2198 Reeves Rd (46168-7927)
PHONE.................................317 708-0228
John Gegner, *Sales Staff*
EMP: 7
SALES (est): 868.1K **Privately Held**
SIC: 2449 3021 3052 3081 Shipping
cases & drums, wood: wirebound & ply-
wood; overshoes, plastic; rubber & plas-
tics hose & beltings; plastic belting;
packing materials, plastic sheet

(G-11595)
BECTON DICKINSON AND COMPANY
2350 Reeves Rd (46168-7933)
PHONE.................................317 561-2900
Kara McKee, *Branch Mgr*
EMP: 429
SALES (corp-wide): 12B **Publicly Held**
SIC: 3841 Hypodermic needles & syringes
PA: Becton, Dickinson And Company
1 Becton Dr
Franklin Lakes NJ 07417
201 847-6800

(G-11596)
BELL AEROSPACE LLC
4510 Redcliff South Ln (46168-7572)
PHONE.................................904 505-4055
Justin Bell,
EMP: 2 EST: 2016
SALES (est): 86K **Privately Held**
SIC: 3721 Aircraft

(G-11597)
BRANGENE LLC
815 Walton Dr (46168-2237)
PHONE.................................317 203-9172
Robert Mount,
James Mount,
EMP: 2 EST: 2014
SALES (est): 120.3K **Privately Held**
SIC: 7372 7389 Business oriented com-
puter software;

(G-11598)
BUIS ENTERPRISES INC
Also Called: RPS Printing Services
6987 S County Road 750 E (46168-8679)
PHONE.................................317 839-7394
Thomas Buis, *President*
EMP: 27
SQ FT: 16,000
SALES (est): 3MM **Privately Held**
SIC: 2752 Commercial printing, offset

(G-11599)
CARRIAGE HOUSE WOODWORKING
1601 E Main St Ste 12 (46168-2807)
PHONE.................................317 406-3042
James A Barker, *President*
Rita Barker, *Admin Sec*
EMP: 2
SALES (est): 160K **Privately Held**
SIC: 2434 5712 Wood kitchen cabinets;
customized furniture & cabinets

(G-11600)
CHATEAU THOMAS WINERY INC (PA)
6291 Cambridge Way (46168-7905)
PHONE.................................317 837-9463
Fax: 317 837-8464
Dr Charles Thomas, *President*
Tom Tise, *General Mgr*
Jill Thomas, *Vice Pres*
Sheryl Gilmore, *Office Mgr*
Trina Sowers, *Office Mgr*
EMP: 35
SALES (est): 4.7MM **Privately Held**
WEB: www.chateauthomas.com
SIC: 2084 Wines

(G-11601)
COUNTY WEST SPORTS
1702 E Main St (46168-1849)
PHONE.................................317 839-4076
Fax: 317 839-5585
Jeffrey Hazelbaker, *Partner*
Janice Hazelbaker, *Partner*
EMP: 2

SQ FT: 1,200
SALES (est): 250.5K **Privately Held**
SIC: 5192 2759 Books, periodicals &
newspapers; screen printing

(G-11602)
COVIDIEN LP
Respiratory Solutions
2824 Airwest Blvd (46168-7700)
PHONE.................................317 837-8199
Doug Van Epps, *Manager*
EMP: 207 **Privately Held**
WEB: www.mallinckrodt.com
SIC: 3845 3999 3714 3841 Electromed-
ical apparatus; patient monitoring appara-
tus; wheelchair lifts; motor vehicle parts &
accessories; surgical & medical instru-
ments; industrial instrmnts msrmnt dis-
play/control process variable
HQ: Covidien Lp
15 Hampshire St
Mansfield MA 02048
508 261-8000

(G-11603)
CROWN EQUIPMENT CORPORATION
Also Called: Crown Lift Trucks
2495 E Perry Rd (46168-7620)
PHONE.................................317 875-7233
Jim Blanchard, *Manager*
EMP: 72
SALES (corp-wide): 3.1B **Privately Held**
SIC: 3537 Lift trucks, industrial: fork, plat-
form, straddle, etc.
PA: Crown Equipment Corporation
44 S Washington St
New Bremen OH 45869
419 629-2311

(G-11604)
DIGITAL EVOLUTION
Also Called: Superior Satellite
2028 Stafford Rd Ste D (46168-2197)
PHONE.................................317 839-7963
Shane Jeffers, *Owner*
EMP: 3
SALES (est): 200K **Privately Held**
SIC: 3651 Home entertainment equipment,
electronic

(G-11605)
DJO LLC
790 Columbia Rd (46168-7558)
PHONE.................................317 406-2000
Krysti Corona, *Admin Sec*
EMP: 8
SALES (corp-wide): 7.1B **Publicly Held**
SIC: 3842 Adhesive tape & plasters, med-
icated or non-medicated
HQ: Djo, Llc
10300 N Enterprise Dr
Mequon WI 53092
760 727-1283

(G-11606)
DONALDSON COMPANY INC
1251 S Perry Rd (46168-5689)
PHONE.................................317 838-5568
Tod E Carpenter, *CEO*
EMP: 2
SALES (est): 117.7K **Privately Held**
SIC: 3599 3569 3714 3564 Industrial ma-
chinery; general industrial machinery;
motor vehicle parts & accessories; blow-
ers & fans

(G-11607)
EARL R HAMILTON
Also Called: R&R Signs
312 Wayside Dr (46168-1781)
PHONE.................................317 838-9386
Earl R Hamilton, *Principal*
EMP: 2
SALES (est): 114.1K **Privately Held**
SIC: 3993 Signs & advertising specialties

(G-11608)
ELI LILLY AND COMPANY
Also Called: Elanco Animal Division
2222 Stanley Rd (46168-8400)
PHONE.................................317 433-3624
Faye Doyle, *Branch Mgr*
EMP: 14

SALES (corp-wide): 22.8B **Publicly Held**
WEB: www.lilly.com
SIC: 2834 Pharmaceutical preparations
PA: Eli Lilly And Company
Lilly Corporate Ctr
Indianapolis IN 46285
317 276-2000

(G-11609)
FEDEX OFFICE & PRINT SVCS INC
2245 E Main St Ste 190 (46168-2787)
PHONE.................................317 839-3896
Fax: 317 839-4201
Jeff Mize, *Branch Mgr*
EMP: 4
SALES (corp-wide): 65.4B **Publicly Held**
WEB: www.fedex.com
SIC: 2759 5099 7334 Commercial print-
ing; signs, except electric; photocopying &
duplicating services
HQ: Fedex Office And Print Services, Inc.
7900 Legacy Dr
Plano TX 75024
214 550-7000

(G-11610)
FORD MOTOR COMPANY
2675 Reeves Rd Ste 101 (46168-7937)
PHONE.................................317 837-2302
Tom Degiacomois, *Manager*
EMP: 52
SALES (corp-wide): 156.7B **Publicly Held**
SIC: 3711 3713 3714 6153 Automobile
assembly, including specialty automobiles; truck & bus bodies; motor vehicle
parts & accessories; financing of dealers
by motor vehicle manufacturers organ.;
buying of installment notes; financing: automobiles, furniture, etc., not a deposit
bank; automobile loans, including insurance; passenger car leasing
PA: Ford Motor Company
1 American Rd
Dearborn MI 48126
313 322-3000

(G-11611)
FOUR SEASON OIL INC
1237 American Ave (46168-3268)
PHONE.................................317 215-1214
Harjinder Badesha, *Principal*
EMP: 2
SALES (est): 90.1K **Privately Held**
SIC: 1311 Crude petroleum & natural gas

(G-11612)
GEORGE MARSHALL
648 S East St (46168-1414)
PHONE.................................317 839-6563
Marsha George-Wn-Bjhe, *Owner*
EMP: 2
SALES (est): 90K **Privately Held**
SIC: 3679 Electronic components

(G-11613)
HAPPY VALLEY SAND & GRAVEL INC
4232 E Us Highway 40 (46168-8189)
PHONE.................................317 839-6800
Gordon Potts, *President*
Kimberly Potts, *Corp Secy*
EMP: 4 EST: 1999
SALES (est): 380K **Privately Held**
SIC: 1442 Construction sand & gravel

(G-11614)
HEIDIPOPS GOURMET POPCORN LLC
2498 Futura Pkwy Ste 165 (46168-2620)
PHONE.................................317 863-0844
Russell A Greene,
Heidi Greene,
Russell Greene,
EMP: 2
SALES (est): 187.1K **Privately Held**
SIC: 2064 Popcorn balls or other treated
popcorn products

(G-11615)
HINES BINDERY SYSTEMS SERVICE
212 E Main St (46168-1115)
PHONE.................................317 839-6432

Fax: 317 839-7002
Ron Crabbe, *President*
Serena Phillips, *Admin Asst*
EMP: 9
SQ FT: 30,000
SALES (est): 1.5MM **Privately Held**
WEB: www.hinesbindery.com
SIC: 5999 2789 Business machines &
equipment; bookbinding & repairing:
trade, edition, library, etc.

(G-11616)
INDILABEL LLC
2198 Reeves Rd Ste 4c (46168-7928)
PHONE....................317 839-8814
Rick Bogdan, *Sales Staff*
Robert J Selge, *Mng Member*
EMP: 10
SQ FT: 20,000
SALES (est): 3.7MM **Privately Held**
WEB: www.indilabel.com
SIC: 2679 Labels, paper: made from pur-
chased material

(G-11617)
INTEGRITY MARKETING TEAM INC
4067 Cheltonham Ct (46168-9094)
PHONE....................317 517-0012
Donald Denman, *President*
Patti Denman, *Treasurer*
Christopher Denman, *Sales Mgr*
EMP: 3
SALES (est): 129.3K **Privately Held**
SIC: 6799 3613 Investors; switchgear &
switchgear accessories

(G-11618)
INTEGRITY RTTIONAL MOLDING LLC
701 N Carr Rd (46168-8828)
PHONE....................317 837-1101
Fax: 317 837-1982
Bill Delong, *President*
Garry Richarson, *Vice Pres*
Terry Stemple, *Vice Pres*
Brent Froelich, *Marketing Staff*
EMP: 20
SQ FT: 10,000
SALES (est): 6.9MM **Privately Held**
WEB: www.integrityrotational.com
SIC: 3089 Molding primary plastic

(G-11619)
INVACARE CORPORATION
1100 Whitaker Rd (46168-7636)
PHONE....................317 838-5500
Steve Wilson, *Branch Mgr*
EMP: 10
SALES (corp-wide): 966.5MM **Publicly Held**
WEB: www.invacare.com
SIC: 3842 Surgical appliances & supplies
PA: Invacare Corporation
1 Invacare Way
Elyria OH 44035
440 329-6000

(G-11620)
J ENNIS FABRICS INC (USA)
853 Columbia Rd Ste 125 (46168-7560)
PHONE....................877 953-6647
Eric Olsen, *President*
Lois Ennis, *Admin Sec*
◆ **EMP:** 6
SQ FT: 40,000
SALES (est): 685.7K **Privately Held**
SIC: 2394 5131 Canvas covers & drop
cloths; piece goods & notions

(G-11621)
JECO PLASTIC PRODUCTS LLC
885 Andico Rd (46168-9659)
P.O. Box 26 (46168-0026)
PHONE....................317 839-4943
Fax: 317 839-1209
Craig Carson, *CEO*
▼ **EMP:** 18
SQ FT: 37,000
SALES (est): 5.6MM **Privately Held**
WEB: www.jecoplastics.com
SIC: 3089 Molding primary plastic

(G-11622)
MADELYN HARWOOD INC
7454 Hawthorne Dr (46168-1888)
PHONE....................317 839-7890
Madeltn Harwood, *Principal*
EMP: 3
SALES (est): 180.4K **Privately Held**
SIC: 2491 Vehicle lumber, treated wood

(G-11623)
MASCOT TRUCK PARTS USA LLC
849 Whitaker Rd Ste D (46168-7529)
PHONE....................317 839-9525
Bill Statham, *President*
EMP: 90 EST: 2014
SQ FT: 3,500
SALES (est): 17.6MM **Privately Held**
SIC: 3714 Motor vehicle parts & acces-
sories

(G-11624)
MATRIX LABEL SYSTEMS INC
4692 S County Road 600 E (46168-8620)
PHONE....................317 839-1973
Gerald Perrill, *President*
Cindy Perrill, *Vice Pres*
▲ **EMP:** 46
SALES (est): 5.9MM **Privately Held**
SIC: 2759 Labels & seals: printing

(G-11625)
MAXIM PIPETTE SERVICE INC
4310 Saratoga Pkwy # 100 (46168-9207)
P.O. Box 387 (46168-0387)
PHONE....................877 536-2946
Mohammad Mahariq, *President*
EMP: 5
SALES (est): 483.4K **Privately Held**
SIC: 3823 Industrial flow & liquid measur-
ing instruments

(G-11626)
MEDTRONIC ○
2824 Airwest Blvd (46168-7700)
PHONE....................317 837-8664
EMP: 6 EST: 2017
SALES (est): 581.1K **Privately Held**
SIC: 3845 Electromedical equipment

(G-11627)
MERITOR INC
849 Whitaker Rd (46168-7529)
PHONE....................317 279-2180
Fax: 317 839-9786
James Smith, *Opers Staff*
Jeremy Crutchfield, *Engineer*
Brian Cavagnini, *Branch Mgr*
Christopher Vanaartsen, *Manager*
Todd Chirillo, *Director*
EMP: 8 **Publicly Held**
SIC: 3714 5013 Motor vehicle parts & ac-
cessories; automotive supplies & parts
PA: Meritor, Inc.
2135 W Maple Rd
Troy MI 48084

(G-11628)
MIDWEST ARCFT MCH & TL CO INC
204 N Mill St (46168-1142)
PHONE....................317 839-1515
Fax: 317 839-6863
John Fazli, *President*
Dawn Fazli, *CFO*
EMP: 25
SQ FT: 4,000
SALES (est): 5MM **Privately Held**
SIC: 3724 5088 Aircraft engines & engine
parts; aircraft equipment & supplies
PA: Wbh, Inc.
123 N Pine St
Indianapolis IN 46202

(G-11629)
NIAGARA BOTTLING LLC
1250 Whitaker Rd (46168-7616)
PHONE....................909 758-5313
EMP: 5
SALES (corp-wide): 330MM **Privately Held**
SIC: 2086 Water, pasteurized: packaged in
cans, bottles, etc.

PA: Niagara Bottling, Llc
2560 E Philadelphia St
Ontario CA 91761
909 230-5000

(G-11630)
NICE-PAK PRODUCTS INC
381 Airtech Pkwy (46168-7416)
PHONE....................317 839-0373
Mark Sands, *Branch Mgr*
EMP: 475
SALES (corp-wide): 428.1MM **Privately Held**
SIC: 2621 Sanitary tissue paper
PA: Nice-Pak Products, Inc.
2 Nice Pak Park
Orangeburg NY 10962
845 365-2772

(G-11631)
NSK CORPORATION
Also Called: NSK Corporation, Plainfield Wh
1581 Perry Rd Ste A (46168-7615)
PHONE....................317 837-8879
Ray Peters, *Manager*
EMP: 20
SALES (corp-wide): 9.5B **Privately Held**
SIC: 3562 Ball & roller bearings
HQ: Nsk Corporation
4200 Goss Rd
Ann Arbor MI 48105
734 913-7500

(G-11632)
OAK-RITE MFG CORP
701 N Carr Rd (46168-8828)
P.O. Box 380 (46168-0380)
PHONE....................317 839-2301
Fax: 317 839-2363
Tim Shaul, *President*
Jerry Steward, *Vice Pres*
EMP: 35 EST: 1962
SQ FT: 65,000
SALES (est): 2.2MM **Privately Held**
WEB: www.oakrite.com
SIC: 3442 3469 Moldings & trim, except
automobile; metal; metal stampings

(G-11633)
ORR PAVING INC
3442 S State Road 267 (46168-3012)
P.O. Box 249 (46168-0249)
PHONE....................317 839-4110
Robert Orr, *Principal*
EMP: 3
SALES (est): 300.4K **Privately Held**
SIC: 2951 Paving blocks

(G-11634)
PEAFIELD PRODUCTS INC
4692 S County Road 600 E (46168-8620)
PHONE....................317 839-8473
Gerald Perrill, *President*
EMP: 10
SALES (est): 900K **Privately Held**
SIC: 2672 2893 2796 Labels (unprinted),
gummed: made from purchased materi-
als; printing ink; platemaking services

(G-11635)
PEPITO MILLER BEV IMPORTS LLC
Also Called: P&M Beverage Imports
4188 Scioto Dr (46168-9092)
PHONE....................317 416-3215
Troy Pepito, *CEO*
Robert Miller, *Principal*
EMP: 2
SALES (est): 62.3K **Privately Held**
SIC: 2082 2084 Malt beverages; ale (alco-
holic beverage); wine coolers (beverages)

(G-11636)
PLAINFIELD SIGN GRAPHIC DESIGN
8285 E County Road 300 S (46168-8502)
PHONE....................317 839-9499
Fax: 317 839-0154
Lee Faulkner, *President*
Mike Watson, *Vice Pres*
EMP: 4
SQ FT: 2,500
SALES: 235K **Privately Held**
WEB: www.plainfieldsign.com
SIC: 3993 Signs & advertising specialties

(G-11637)
PROJECTED SOUND INC
469 Avon Ave (46168-1001)
PHONE....................317 839-4111
Fax: 317 839-2476
J Hilligoss, *President*
Richard Hilligoss, *Vice Pres*
Paul Stlaurent, *Treasurer*
▲ **EMP:** 25
SQ FT: 17,000
SALES (est): 3MM **Privately Held**
SIC: 3699 Electric sound equipment

(G-11638)
Q-EDGE CORPORATION
1581 Perry Rd Ste B (46168-7615)
PHONE....................317 203-6800
Mark Chien, *President*
▲ **EMP:** 49
SALES (est): 18.3MM **Privately Held**
SIC: 3571 Electronic computers

(G-11639)
R E FERGUSON & ASSOCIATES INC
Also Called: Creative Designs
7851 Quail Rdg S (46168-9395)
PHONE....................317 839-9311
EMP: 6
SQ FT: 24,000
SALES (est): 47.7K **Privately Held**
SIC: 3599 Design Assembly And Fabricat-
ing Services

(G-11640)
REGENT AEROSPACE CORPORATION
2501 E Perry Rd (46168-7621)
PHONE....................317 837-4000
Michael Lilley, *Vice Pres*
EMP: 7 **Privately Held**
SIC: 1799 3728 Renovation of aircraft in-
teriors; aircraft parts & equipment
PA: Regent Aerospace Corporation
28110 Harrison Pkwy
Valencia CA 91355

(G-11641)
ROLLS-ROYCE CORPORATION
Also Called: Rolls-Royce Liftfan Factory
758 Columbia Rd Ste 199 (46168-7585)
PHONE....................317 230-2000
EMP: 1158
SALES (corp-wide): 21.5B **Privately Held**
SIC: 3724 Aircraft engines & engine parts
HQ: Rolls-Royce Corporation
450 S Meridian St
Indianapolis IN 46225

(G-11642)
SAINT-GOBAIN ABRASIVES INC
1001 Perry Rd (46168-7639)
PHONE....................317 837-0700
Fax: 317 839-1442
Alan Freidman, *Manager*
EMP: 169
SALES (corp-wide): 213.5MM **Privately Held**
WEB: www.sgabrasives.com
SIC: 2834 Intravenous solutions
HQ: Saint-Gobain Abrasives, Inc.
1 New Bond St
Worcester MA 01606
508 795-5000

(G-11643)
SHAUGHNESSY-KNIEP-HAWE-PAPER
865 Perry Rd (46168-7638)
PHONE....................317 837-7041
Ed Kniep, *Manager*
EMP: 25
SALES (corp-wide): 896.8MM **Privately Held**
SIC: 2759 Commercial printing
HQ: Shaughnessy-Kniep-Hawe-Paper
Company
2355 Ball Dr
Saint Louis MO 63146
314 810-8100

▲ = Import ▼=Export
◆ =Import/Export

(G-11644)
SPEEDWAY LLC
Also Called: Speedway Superamerica 3338
3066 E Main St (46168-2722)
PHONE..............................317 838-5479
EMP: 10 **Publicly Held**
WEB: www.speedwaynet.com
SIC: 1311 Crude petroleum production
HQ: Speedway Llc
500 Speedway Dr
Enon OH 45323
937 864-3000

(G-11645)
STARKEN PRINTING CO INC
131 N Mill St (46168-1139)
PHONE..............................317 839-6852
Fax: 317 839-5857
Tom Wesseler, *President*
EMP: 4
SQ FT: 5,500
SALES (est): 570.3K **Privately Held**
SIC: 2752 Commercial printing, offset

(G-11646)
THERMAL STRUCTURES INC
2800 Airwest Blvd (46168-7700)
PHONE..............................951 736-9911
EMP: 60 **Publicly Held**
SIC: 3724 Aircraft engines & engine parts
HQ: Thermal Structures, Inc.
2362 Railroad St
Corona CA 92880
951 736-9911

(G-11647)
TKO ENTERPRISES INC
Also Called: T.K.O. Graphix
2751 Stafford Rd (46168-2198)
PHONE..............................317 271-1398
Fax: 317 271-5986
Thomas Taulman II, *CEO*
Denny Smith, *COO*
Chris Hurley, *Vice Pres*
Tom McClelland, *Vice Pres*
Michael K Smith, *Vice Pres*
EMP: 99
SQ FT: 50,000
SALES (est): 32.9MM **Privately Held**
WEB: www.tkographix.com
SIC: 2759 3993 2752 2396 Commercial
printing; signs & advertising specialties;
commercial printing, lithographic; automo-
tive & apparel trimmings

(G-11648)
TOBACCO ZONE INC
4306 Stillwater Way (46168-7707)
PHONE..............................317 268-6808
Lakhvir Singh, *Principal*
EMP: 4 EST: 2010
SALES (est): 302.7K **Privately Held**
SIC: 2869 Fuels

(G-11649)
UNIVERSAL SIGN GROUP INC
5083 Nicodemus Dr (46168-8442)
PHONE..............................317 697-1165
Sigmund Mirkowski, *Principal*
EMP: 2 EST: 2011
SALES (est): 124.5K **Privately Held**
SIC: 3993 Signs & advertising specialties

(G-11650)
WBH INC
Also Called: Midwest Aircraft
204 N Mill St (46168-1142)
PHONE..............................317 839-1515
Richard Lane, *Manager*
EMP: 15 **Privately Held**
WEB: www.aerospaceproducts.com
SIC: 3724 3728 Aircraft engines & engine
parts; aircraft parts & equipment
PA: Wbh, Inc.
123 N Pine St
Indianapolis IN 46202

(G-11651)
WHIRLPOOL CORPORATION
2801 Airwest Blvd (46168-7700)
PHONE..............................317 837-5300
Fax: 317 837-5300
Mark Deering, *Engineer*
Barry Parker, *Branch Mgr*
Kara Hegg, *Manager*
Stella Shultz, *Manager*

Jeff Burk, *Info Tech Dir*
EMP: 800
SALES (corp-wide): 21.2B **Publicly Held**
WEB: www.whirlpoolcorp.com
SIC: 3633 Laundry dryers, household or
coin-operated
PA: Whirlpool Corporation
2000 N M 63
Benton Harbor MI 49022
269 923-5000

(G-11652)
WINFIELD SOLUTIONS LLC
923 Whitaker Rd Ste G (46168-7407)
PHONE..............................317 838-3733
Troy Kesler, *Branch Mgr*
EMP: 3
SALES (corp-wide): 12.8B **Privately Held**
SIC: 5191 2048 8742 Chemicals, agricul-
tural; fertilizer & fertilizer materials; feed
concentrates; business consultant
HQ: Winfield Solutions, Llc
1080 County Road F W
Saint Paul MN 55126

(G-11653)
**ZEPPELIN COMMANDER PRESS
INC**
1026 Kirkwood Dr (46168-2216)
PHONE..............................317 839-9025
John M Miller, *President*
EMP: 2
SALES (est): 76.1K **Privately Held**
SIC: 2741 Miscellaneous publishing

Plainville
Daviess County

(G-11654)
C AND S MACHINE INC
19 Main St (47568-9612)
P.O. Box 39 (47568-0039)
PHONE..............................812 687-7203
Fax: 812 687-7203
Matthew Bellamy, *President*
EMP: 6 EST: 1994
SALES (est): 400K **Privately Held**
SIC: 3599 Machine shop, jobbing & repair

(G-11655)
TERRY EATON
2761 E 900 N (47568-5102)
PHONE..............................812 687-7579
Terry Eaton, *Principal*
EMP: 3
SALES (est): 193.8K **Privately Held**
SIC: 3625 Motor controls & accessories

(G-11656)
TMGG LLC
Also Called: Tri-Star Glove
714 5th St (47568-5243)
P.O. Box 90 (47568-0090)
PHONE..............................812 687-7444
Rodman Townsend Jr,
INA Grayber,
Eric Moll,
◆ EMP: 30
SQ FT: 30,000
SALES (est): 4.3MM **Privately Held**
WEB: www.tri-starglove.com
SIC: 2381 Fabric dress & work gloves

(G-11657)
WAGLER MINI BARN PRODUCTS
8972 N 550 E (47568-5155)
PHONE..............................812 687-7372
Kenneth Wagler, *General Ptnr*
EMP: 5
SALES (est): 630K **Privately Held**
SIC: 3448 2452 Prefabricated metal build-
ings; log cabins, prefabricated, wood

Pleasant Mills
Adams County

(G-11658)
TRAVEL HOME SOLUTIONS
2242 Mulberry St (46780)
PHONE..............................260 592-7628

Teresa Scare, *Owner*
EMP: 2
SALES: 70K **Privately Held**
SIC: 3711 Motor vehicles & car bodies

Plymouth
Marshall County

(G-11659)
3M COMPANY
2925 Gary Dr (46563-8889)
PHONE..............................574 948-8103
EMP: 324
SALES (corp-wide): 31.6B **Publicly Held**
SIC: 3841 Surgical instruments & appara-
tus
PA: 3m Company
3m Center
Saint Paul MN 55144
651 733-1110

(G-11660)
A SCHULMAN INC
1301 Flora St (46563-1344)
PHONE..............................574 935-5131
Fax: 574 935-5278
Karen Ray, *Branch Mgr*
EMP: 22
SQ FT: 25,000
SALES (corp-wide): 2.4B **Publicly Held**
WEB: www.ferro.com
SIC: 2851 2816 Lacquers, varnishes,
enamels & other coatings; inorganic pig-
ments
PA: A. Schulman, Inc.
3637 Ridgewood Rd
Fairlawn OH 44333
330 666-3751

(G-11661)
AAA GALVANIZING - JOLIET INC
Also Called: Azz Galvanizing Plymouth
2631 Jim Neu Dr (46563-3311)
PHONE..............................574 935-4500
Bob Shireman, *Plant Mgr*
Todd Bella, *Sales Mgr*
EMP: 49
SALES (corp-wide): 810.4MM **Publicly
Held**
SIC: 3479 Hot dip coating of metals or
formed products; coating of metals &
formed products
HQ: Aaa Galvanizing - Joliet, Inc.
625 Mills Rd
Joliet IL 60433

(G-11662)
AK INDUSTRIES INC
2055 Pidco Dr (46563-1374)
P.O. Box 640 (46563-0640)
PHONE..............................574 936-6022
Fax: 574 936-5811
John S Sabo, *President*
▲ EMP: 90
SQ FT: 50,000
SALES (est): 22.3MM **Privately Held**
WEB: www.akindustries.com
SIC: 3089 3272 Plastic & fiberglass tanks;
septic tanks, plastic; concrete products

(G-11663)
ALL POINTS TOOL & MFG
2743 Pioneer Dr (46563-6722)
P.O. Box 687 (46563-0687)
PHONE..............................574 935-3944
Fax: 574 935-3516
Jerry Firoky, *Partner*
Mike Cenetar, *Partner*
Krisha Drue, *Partner*
Leonard Kuzmicz, *Partner*
EMP: 4
SQ FT: 5,000
SALES (est): 579K **Privately Held**
WEB: www.allpointstool.com
SIC: 3599 Machine shop, jobbing & repair

(G-11664)
**AMERICAN CONTAINERS INC
(PA)**
2526 Western Ave (46563-1050)
PHONE..............................574 936-4068
Fax: 574 936-4036
Leonard Isban, *CEO*

Leonard D Isban, *CEO*
Michael Isban, *President*
Robert Calverley, *General Mgr*
Joan Isban, *Vice Pres*
▲ EMP: 65 EST: 1965
SQ FT: 70,000
SALES (est): 33.8MM **Privately Held**
WEB: www.acontainers.com
SIC: 2653 2671 2652 2631 Boxes, corru-
gated: made from purchased materials;
packaging paper & plastics film, coated &
laminated; setup paperboard boxes; pa-
perboard mills

(G-11665)
**AMERICAS BEST MILLWRK
SUPPLRS**
10605 Nutmeg Rd (46563-8545)
P.O. Box 177 (46563-0177)
PHONE..............................574 780-0066
Dana Rodeghero,
EMP: 7
SALES: 950K **Privately Held**
SIC: 2431 Millwork

(G-11666)
AMISH WOODWORKING LLC
8870 State Road 17 (46563-9479)
PHONE..............................574 941-4439
Don Green, *Principal*
EMP: 2
SALES (est): 185.2K **Privately Held**
SIC: 2431 Millwork

(G-11667)
ANGELINAS CIGARS
1906 N Oak Dr (46563-3495)
PHONE..............................574 935-5544
Alan Collins, *Owner*
EMP: 2
SALES (est): 74.7K **Privately Held**
SIC: 5812 2121 Eating places; cigars

(G-11668)
BAY VALLEY FOODS LLC
1430 Western Ave (46563-1030)
P.O. Box 19057, Green Bay WI (54307-
9057)
PHONE..............................574 936-4061
Tony Lenne, *Manager*
EMP: 150
SALES (corp-wide): 6.3B **Publicly Held**
SIC: 2033 2035 Canned fruits & special-
ties; pickles, sauces & salad dressings
HQ: Bay Valley Foods, Llc
3200 Riverside Dr Ste A
Green Bay WI 54301
800 558-4700

(G-11669)
BOMARKO INC (PA)
1955 N Oak Dr (46563-3493)
P.O. Box 1510 (46563-5510)
PHONE..............................574 936-9901
Fax: 574 936-5314
James D Azzar, *President*
Kenneth Akers, *Mfg Mgr*
Mark Wentzel, *QC Mgr*
Ron Stephens, *Engineer*
John Yeakey, *CFO*
◆ EMP: 110
SQ FT: 180,000
SALES (est): 46.2MM **Privately Held**
WEB: www.bomarko.com
SIC: 2671 Waxed paper: made from pur-
chased material; paper coated or lami-
nated for packaging

(G-11670)
BOWEN PRINTING INC
200 S Michigan St (46563-2238)
PHONE..............................574 936-3924
Fax: 574 936-3646
David Ruff, *President*
Alice Ruff, *Admin Sec*
EMP: 6
SQ FT: 4,800
SALES (est): 540K **Privately Held**
SIC: 2752 Lithographing on metal; letters,
circular or form: lithographed

(G-11671)
BOWMANS TIN SHOP INC
113 E Laporte St (46563-2119)
PHONE..............................574 936-3234
Fax: 574 936-3234

Hal Bowman, *President*
EMP: 3
SQ FT: 2,500
SALES: 350K **Privately Held**
SIC: 1711 3444 Warm air heating & air conditioning contractor; irrigation sprinkler system installation; sheet metalwork

(G-11672)
BPC MANUFACTURING OPERATION
1755 N Oak Dr (46563-3413)
PHONE..................................574 936-9894
Don Rodda, *Owner*
▲ **EMP:** 30
SALES (est): 4.1MM **Privately Held**
SIC: 2821 Plastics materials & resins

(G-11673)
BUFFINGTON ELECTRIC MOTORS
Also Called: Buffington Farm Service
2520 Lake Ave (46563-7845)
PHONE..................................574 935-5453
Michael Buffington, *President*
EMP: 2
SALES (est): 170.7K **Privately Held**
SIC: 7694 5083 7699 Rewinding stators; grain elevators equipment & supplies; farm machinery repair

(G-11674)
CNHI LLC
Also Called: Pilot News
214 N Michigan St (46563-2135)
P.O. Box 220 (46563-0220)
PHONE..................................574 936-3101
Jerry Bingle, *Business Mgr*
Greg Hildebrand, *Production*
Alan Hall, *Manager*
Cindy Stockton, *Director*
EMP: 25 **Privately Held**
WEB: www.clintonnc.com
SIC: 2711 Commercial printing & newspaper publishing combined
HQ: Cnhi, Llc
    445 Dexter Ave
    Montgomery AL 36104

(G-11675)
COCA COLA BTLG CO KOKOMO IND
Coca-Cola
1701 Pidco Dr (46563-1358)
PHONE..................................574 936-3220
Fax: 574 936-5414
Roger D Stiles, *Sales Mgr*
Francis Eloert, *Manager*
EMP: 20
SALES (est): 2.9MM
SALES (corp-wide): 2.2MM **Privately Held**
WEB: www.cckokomo.com
SIC: 2086 Bottled & canned soft drinks
PA: Coca Cola Bottling Co Kokomo Ind Inc
    2305 Davis Rd
    Kokomo IN 46901
    765 457-4421

(G-11676)
COMPLETE PRINTER INC
1920 Jim Neu Dr (46563-1396)
PHONE..................................574 936-9505
Pj Martin, *President*
EMP: 9 **EST:** 2013
SALES (est): 426.3K **Privately Held**
SIC: 2752 Commercial printing, offset

(G-11677)
CONCRETE PUMPING MICHIANA LLC
16200 Lincoln Hwy (46563-8033)
PHONE..................................574 936-2140
Lynn Springer, *Principal*
William Lawrence,
EMP: 9
SALES (est): 760K **Privately Held**
SIC: 3273 Ready-mixed concrete

(G-11678)
CULVER TOOL & ENGINEERING INC
Also Called: Cte Solutions
1901 Walter Glaub Dr (46563-1387)
P.O. Box 970 (46563-0970)
PHONE..................................574 935-9611
Fax: 574 935-9613
Wade Berger, *President*
David Winrotte, *President*
William Mc Queen, *Corp Secy*
Mark Morris, *Vice Pres*
EMP: 55 **EST:** 1955
SQ FT: 12,800
SALES (est): 7.7MM **Privately Held**
WEB: www.culvertool.com
SIC: 7389 3599 Metal cutting services; machine shop, jobbing & repair

(G-11679)
DANNY WEBB PLUMBING
Also Called: Webb, Danny Plumbing & Heating
18391 6th Rd (46563-8835)
PHONE..................................574 936-2746
Danny Webb, *Owner*
EMP: 2
SALES (est): 135.5K **Privately Held**
SIC: 1711 2842 Plumbing contractors; cleaning or polishing preparations

(G-11680)
DEAN FOODS CO
1430 Western Ave (46563-1030)
PHONE..................................214 303-3400
Dave Kreskai, *Principal*
EMP: 2 **EST:** 2016
SALES (est): 62.3K **Privately Held**
SIC: 2026 Fluid milk

(G-11681)
DURA-VENT CORP
1435 N Michigan St Ste 3 (46563-1100)
PHONE..................................574 936-2432
Fax: 574 936-2505
Gary J Scott, *President*
EMP: 9
SALES (est): 1.2MM **Privately Held**
SIC: 3052 Rubber & plastics hose & beltings

(G-11682)
EAGLE CRAFT INC
904 Markley Dr (46563-3201)
PHONE..................................574 936-3196
Fax: 574 936-3116
Charles Wicks, *President*
David Wicks, *Vice Pres*
EMP: 20
SQ FT: 53,000
SALES (est): 3.1MM **Privately Held**
SIC: 3792 3713 Pickup covers, canopies or caps; truck & bus bodies

(G-11683)
FARM INNOVATORS INC
2255 Walter Glaub Dr (46563-3435)
P.O. Box 546 (46563-0546)
PHONE..................................574 936-5096
Benjamin T Clark Sr, *Ch of Bd*
Benjamin T Clark Jr, *President*
Diane M Clark, *Corp Secy*
David Ward, *Vice Pres*
▲ **EMP:** 25
SQ FT: 38,000
SALES (est): 6.6MM **Privately Held**
WEB: www.farminnovators.com
SIC: 3567 3523 Electrical furnaces, ovens & heating devices, exc. induction; farm machinery & equipment

(G-11684)
FERRELLGAS LP
11867 Lincoln Hwy (46563-8684)
PHONE..................................574 936-2725
Rick O'Conner, *Manager*
EMP: 8 **Publicly Held**
SIC: 5984 2813 Liquefied petroleum gas, delivered to customers' premises; industrial gases
HQ: Ferrellgas, L.P.
    7500 College Blvd # 1000
    Overland Park KS 66210

(G-11685)
FLEXIBLE TECHNOLOGIES INC
HI Tech Duravent
1435 N Michigan St Ste 3 (46563-1100)
PHONE..................................574 936-2432
Victoria Carson, *Principal*
Tracy Campama, *Branch Mgr*
EMP: 32
SALES (corp-wide): 4.1B **Privately Held**
SIC: 3052 Rubber hose
HQ: Flexible Technologies, Inc.
    528 Carwellyn Rd
    Abbeville SC 29620
    864 366-5441

(G-11686)
FOIL LAMINATING INC
1000 Pidco Dr (46563-1367)
PHONE..................................574 935-3645
Fax: 574 936-5627
Donald T Kindt, *President*
James B Porter III, *President*
Barbara J Kindt, *Admin Sec*
EMP: 30
SQ FT: 60,000
SALES (est): 4.2MM **Privately Held**
WEB: www.foillaminating.com
SIC: 3497 3081 Foil, laminated to paper or other materials; plastic film & sheet

(G-11687)
GALAXY CONTAINER LLC
1001 Pidco Dr (46563-1368)
PHONE..................................574 936-6300
Kurt Wiesemes,
EMP: 6
SALES (est): 549.3K **Privately Held**
SIC: 2653 Boxes, corrugated: made from purchased materials

(G-11688)
HONEYWELL INTERNATIONAL INC
504 E Garro St (46563-2234)
PHONE..................................574 935-0200
Shawn Grobe, *Branch Mgr*
EMP: 699
SALES (corp-wide): 40.5B **Publicly Held**
SIC: 3724 Aircraft engines & engine parts
PA: Honeywell International Inc.
    115 Tabor Rd
    Morris Plains NJ 07950
    973 455-2000

(G-11689)
I E SIGNS & GRAPHICS LLC
1221 W Garro St (46563-2060)
PHONE..................................574 936-4652
EMP: 3
SALES (est): 280K **Privately Held**
SIC: 3577 Mfg Computer Peripheral Equipment

(G-11690)
INDIANA HEAT TRANSFER CORP
500 W Harrison St (46563-1399)
PHONE..................................574 936-3171
Fax: 574 935-8200
Daniel B Altman, *President*
E Richard Hite, *Admin Sec*
EMP: 213
SQ FT: 165,000
SALES (est): 48.5MM **Privately Held**
WEB: www.ihtc.net
SIC: 3714 Radiators & radiator shells & cores, motor vehicle

(G-11691)
INDIANA METAL STAMPING CO
500 W Harrison St (46563-1324)
PHONE..................................574 936-2964
Daniel Altman, *President*
EMP: 2
SALES (est): 94.6K **Privately Held**
SIC: 3469 Stamping metal for the trade

(G-11692)
INDIANA TECHNOLOGY AND MANUFAC
6100 Michigan Rd (46563-7798)
PHONE..................................574 936-2112
EMP: 2 **EST:** 2015
SALES (est): 167.4K **Privately Held**
SIC: 3599 Machine shop, jobbing & repair

(G-11693)
INDIANA TOOL & MFG CO INC
Also Called: Itamco Company
6100 Michigan Rd (46563-7798)
P.O. Box 399 (46563-0399)
PHONE..................................574 936-5548
Fax: 574 936-7224
Donald K Neidig, *CEO*
Noble L Neidig, *President*
Gary L Neidig, *Vice Pres*
Dorothy Neidig, *Admin Sec*
◆ **EMP:** 100 **EST:** 1955
SQ FT: 80,000
SALES (est): 27.9MM **Privately Held**
WEB: www.itamco.com
SIC: 3462 3545 Gear & chain forgings; machine tool attachments & accessories

(G-11694)
INDUSTRIAL TRANSMISSION EQP
Also Called: I T Equipment
2033 Western Ave (46563-1041)
P.O. Box 340 (46563-0340)
PHONE..................................574 936-3028
Fax: 574 935-4581
Dale R Poisel, *President*
Paula Poisel, *Vice Pres*
Ed Crousore, *Plant Mgr*
Alicia Blackford, *Purchasing*
Bob Crosby, *Sales Engr*
▲ **EMP:** 48
SQ FT: 35,000
SALES (est): 11.9MM **Privately Held**
WEB: www.itequipment.com
SIC: 3535 5084 3537 3443 Conveyors & conveying equipment; materials handling machinery; conveyor systems; industrial trucks & tractors; fabricated plate work (boiler shop); fabricated structural metal

(G-11695)
INTRST FORESTRY INC
Also Called: Interstate Forestry
10200 W County Line Rd (46563-9418)
PHONE..................................574 936-1284
Bill Carpenter, *Owner*
Gary Messer, *Principal*
EMP: 5
SALES (est): 670.1K **Privately Held**
SIC: 2421 Lumber: rough, sawed or planed

(G-11696)
IRECO METALS INC
1433 Western Ave (46563-1029)
PHONE..................................574 936-2146
John Oliver Jr, *Principal*
EMP: 2
SALES (est): 127.4K **Privately Held**
SIC: 2892 Explosives

(G-11697)
JOHNS WELDING AND FABRICATION
1203 N Michigan St (46563-1115)
PHONE..................................574 936-1702
John Cavinder, *Principal*
EMP: 2
SALES (est): 148.3K **Privately Held**
SIC: 1799 7692 Welding on site; welding repair

(G-11698)
KAY INDUSTRIES INC
7834 Queen Rd (46563-8818)
PHONE..................................574 236-6220
Fax: 574 936-8486
John Colage, *Branch Mgr*
EMP: 10
SQ FT: 2,000
SALES (corp-wide): 1.9MM **Privately Held**
WEB: www.kayind.com
SIC: 3621 3612 Phase or rotary converters (electrical equipment); transformers, except electric
PA: Kay Industries Inc
    7834 Queen Rd
    Plymouth IN 46563
    574 236-6220

(G-11699)
KAY INDUSTRIES INC (PA)
7834 Queen Rd (46563-8818)
P.O. Box 1323, South Bend (46624-1323)
PHONE..................................574 236-6220
Fax: 574 289-5932
Lawrence Katz, *President*
Greg Schroff, *General Mgr*
Aaron Katz, *Chairman*
EMP: 10
SQ FT: 10,000
SALES (est): 1.9MM **Privately Held**
WEB: www.kayind.com
SIC: 3621 Phase or rotary converters
(electrical equipment)

(G-11700)
LAFFERTY & LAFFERTY LLC
8923 8a Rd (46563-8919)
PHONE..................................574 935-4852
EMP: 2 EST: 2001
SALES (est): 110K **Privately Held**
SIC: 3999 Mfg Misc Products

(G-11701)
LASALLE BRISTOL CORPORATION
B P C Manufacturing
1755 N Oak Dr (46563-3413)
PHONE..................................574 936-9894
Fax: 574 936-9271
Don Rodda, *Manager*
EMP: 120
SQ FT: 57,000
SALES (corp-wide): 356.3MM **Privately Held**
WEB: www.lasallebristol.com
SIC: 5023 3432 Floor coverings; faucets & spigots, metal & plastic
HQ: Bristol Lasalle Corporation
601 County Road 17
Elkhart IN 46516
574 295-4400

(G-11702)
LEAR CORPORATION
2000 Walter Glaub Dr (46563-1386)
PHONE..................................574 935-3818
Dave McKee, *Manager*
EMP: 50
SALES (corp-wide): 20.4B **Publicly Held**
WEB: www.lear.com
SIC: 3714 Motor vehicle parts & accessories
PA: Lear Corporation
21557 Telegraph Rd
Southfield MI 48033
248 447-1500

(G-11703)
LIPPERT COMPONENTS MFG INC
Also Called: R V Window Manufacture
1101 N Oak Dr (46563-3415)
PHONE..................................574 935-5122
Fax: 574 935-5745
Kammy Wireman, *Branch Mgr*
EMP: 133
SALES (corp-wide): 2.1B **Publicly Held**
WEB: www.hehrintl.com
SIC: 3211 3714 3442 3231 Flat glass; motor vehicle parts & accessories; metal doors, sash & trim; products of purchased glass
HQ: Lippert Components Manufacturing, Inc.
3501 County Road 6 E
Elkhart IN 46514
574 535-1125

(G-11704)
MAAX INC
Also Called: Maax Aker Plastics
1001 N Oak Dr (46563-3416)
PHONE..................................574 936-3838
Fax: 574 936-9824
Christopher Perron, *Principal*
James Vanderweide, *Plant Mgr*
Olivier Guichard, *Materials Mgr*
Maria Fragoso, *Credit Mgr*
Robert Sauve, *Manager*
EMP: 21

SALES (corp-wide): 174.1MM **Privately Held**
SIC: 3088 3431 Tubs (bath, shower & laundry), plastic; shower stalls, fiberglass & plastic; metal sanitary ware
PA: Maax Bath Inc
160 Boul Saint-Joseph
Lachine QC H8S 2
514 844-4155

(G-11705)
MANUWAL SAWMILL INC
15771 14th Rd (46563-9331)
PHONE..................................574 936-8187
Dale Manuwal, *President*
EMP: 3
SQ FT: 5,760
SALES (est): 344.1K **Privately Held**
SIC: 2421 Sawmills & planing mills, general

(G-11706)
MILLENIUM SHEET METAL INC
6730 W County Line Rd (46563-8843)
PHONE..................................574 935-9101
Fax: 574 232-3653
John Drews, *President*
EMP: 15
SQ FT: 14,900
SALES (est): 1.2MM **Privately Held**
WEB: www.milleniumsm.com
SIC: 1711 3444 Ventilation & duct work contractor; sheet metalwork

(G-11707)
MO SIGNS LLC
1842 W Jefferson St (46563-8020)
PHONE..................................574 780-4075
EMP: 2 EST: 2011
SALES (est): 176.4K **Privately Held**
SIC: 3993 Signs & advertising specialties

(G-11708)
OASIS LIFESTYLE LLC
Also Called: Oasis Bath
1400 Pidco Dr (46563-1353)
P.O. Box 82 (46563-0082)
PHONE..................................574 948-0004
Mark Naylor, *President*
EMP: 28
SALES (est): 4.4MM **Privately Held**
SIC: 5719 3088 3842 Bath accessories; shower stalls, fiberglass & plastic; tubs (bath, shower & laundry), plastic; bathroom fixtures, plastic; whirlpool baths, hydrotherapy equipment

(G-11709)
PACTIV CORPORATION
1411 Pidco Dr (46563-1352)
PHONE..................................574 936-7065
James Burr, *Plant Mgr*
Chris Unruh, *Technology*
Dennis Hughes, *Systems Mgr*
EMP: 200
SQ FT: 30,000 **Privately Held**
WEB: www.pactiv.com
SIC: 3069 3081 2821 2671 Foam rubber; unsupported plastics film & sheet; plastics materials & resins; packaging paper & plastics film, coated & laminated
HQ: Pactiv Llc
1900 W Field Ct
Lake Forest IL 60045
847 482-2000

(G-11710)
PATTY PROCESSING INC
1955 N Oak Dr (46563-3412)
P.O. Box 1510 (46563-5510)
PHONE..................................574 936-9901
Geza Verik, *President*
Mark Lee, *Accountant*
Valerie Overmyer, *Human Res Mgr*
James Walker, *Info Tech Mgr*
▼ EMP: 250
SALES: 40MM **Privately Held**
WEB: www.bomarko.com
SIC: 2671 Paper coated or laminated for packaging

(G-11711)
PH INC
Also Called: Valmont Site Pro 1
2400 Walter Glaub Dr (46563-3434)
PHONE..................................877 467-4763

Myron C Noble, *Ch of Bd*
EMP: 23
SALES (corp-wide): 2.7B **Publicly Held**
SIC: 3441 3365 3369 Tower sections, radio & television transmission; aluminum & aluminum-based alloy castings; white metal castings (lead, tin, antimony), except die
HQ: Pirod Inc.
1545 Pidco Dr
Plymouth IN 46563
574 936-7221

(G-11712)
PIROD INC (HQ)
Also Called: Valmont Structures
1545 Pidco Dr (46563-1354)
P.O. Box 128 (46563-0128)
PHONE..................................574 936-7221
Fax: 574 936-6796
Myron C Noble, *President*
Mark C Jaksich, *CFO*
Clint Klingerman, *Marketing Staff*
R Andrew Massey, *Admin Sec*
◆ EMP: 13 EST: 1996
SQ FT: 230,000
SALES (est): 51.9MM
SALES (corp-wide): 2.7B **Publicly Held**
SIC: 3441 3365 3369 Tower sections, radio & television transmission; aluminum & aluminum-based alloy castings; white metal castings (lead, tin, antimony), except die
PA: Valmont Industries, Inc.
1 Valmont Plz Ste 500
Omaha NE 68154
402 963-1000

(G-11713)
PLYMOUTH FOUNDRY INC
523 W Harrison St (46563-1388)
P.O. Box 537 (46563-0537)
PHONE..................................574 936-2106
Fax: 574 936-5705
Sam C Schlosser, *President*
James D Bopp, *Vice Pres*
William F Schlosser, *Vice Pres*
EMP: 36 EST: 1931
SQ FT: 60,000
SALES (est): 9.6MM **Privately Held**
WEB: www.plymouthfoundry.com
SIC: 3321 3599 3322 Gray iron castings; ductile iron castings; machine shop, jobbing & repair; malleable iron foundries

(G-11714)
PLYMOUTH PDTS ACQUISITION INC
1800 Jim Neu Dr Ste 7 (46563-3306)
PHONE..................................574 936-4757
Fax: 574 936-8044
Don Wisniewski, *President*
▲ EMP: 6 EST: 1959
SQ FT: 10,000
SALES (est): 1MM **Privately Held**
WEB: www.plymouthproducts.com
SIC: 3545 Machine tool accessories

(G-11715)
PLYMOUTH READY MART INC
422 N Michigan St (46563-1738)
PHONE..................................574 936-5251
Jimmy Latis, *President*
EMP: 5 EST: 2001
SALES (est): 295K **Privately Held**
SIC: 5411 3273 Grocery stores; ready-mixed concrete

(G-11716)
PREGIS LLC
1411 Pidco Dr (46563-1352)
PHONE..................................574 936-7065
Ron Duerksen, *Branch Mgr*
EMP: 5
SALES (corp-wide): 4.8B **Privately Held**
WEB: www.motion-ind.com
SIC: 3086 Packaging & shipping materials, foamed plastic
HQ: Pregis Llc
1650 Lake Cook Rd Ste 400
Deerfield IL 60015
847 597-2200

(G-11717)
PRETZELS INC
2910 Commerce St (46563-8991)
PHONE..................................574 941-2201
EMP: 156
SALES (corp-wide): 78.3MM **Privately Held**
SIC: 5461 2099 Pretzels; food preparations
PA: Pretzels Inc
123 W Harvest Rd
Bluffton IN 46714
260 824-4838

(G-11718)
QUINTS WELDING
8888 King Rd (46563-9576)
PHONE..................................574 936-9138
Y Quint, *Principal*
EMP: 2
SALES (est): 84.3K **Privately Held**
SIC: 7692 Welding repair

(G-11719)
RBC PRCSION PDTS - PLYMUTH INC (DH)
2928 Gary Dr (46563-8897)
PHONE..................................574 935-3027
Michael J Hartnett, *President*
Thomas J Williams, *Principal*
Daniel A Bergeron, *Vice Pres*
Thomas C Crainer, *Vice Pres*
Richard J Edwards, *Vice Pres*
▲ EMP: 60
SQ FT: 32,000
SALES (est): 8.8MM
SALES (corp-wide): 674.9MM **Publicly Held**
SIC: 3562 3312 Ball & roller bearings; blast furnaces & steel mills
HQ: Roller Bearing Company Of America, Inc.
102 Willenbrock Rd
Oxford CT 06478
203 267-7001

(G-11720)
READY PAC FOODS INC
Also Called: Tanimura & Antle
2050 N Oak Dr (46563-3407)
PHONE..................................574 935-9800
Dan Correll, *Manager*
EMP: 300 **Privately Held**
SIC: 2099 5148 Salads, fresh or refrigerated; vegetables, fresh
HQ: Ready Pac Foods, Inc.
4401 Foxdale St
Irwindale CA 91706
626 856-8686

(G-11721)
REWARD INC
11040 4a Rd (46563-9563)
PHONE..................................574 936-7196
Fax: 574 936-6602
Richard Ward, *Ch of Bd*
Elfrieda Ward, *President*
EMP: 12
SQ FT: 10,000
SALES (est): 1.6MM **Privately Held**
WEB: www.rewardcvsprings.com
SIC: 3567 Heating units & devices, industrial: electric

(G-11722)
RIDGE IRON LLC ✪
1911 Western Ave (46563-1039)
PHONE..................................646 450-0092
Carson Garner, *Mng Member*
EMP: 6 EST: 2017
SALES (est): 175.4K **Privately Held**
SIC: 3999 5051 5999 Manufacturing industries; structural shapes, iron or steel; miscellaneous retail stores

(G-11723)
RODEGHERO ENTERPRISE
10605 Nutmeg Rd (46563-8545)
PHONE..................................574 935-0568
Dana Rodeghero, *Principal*
EMP: 4
SALES (est): 313.6K **Privately Held**
SIC: 2491 Structural lumber & timber, treated wood

(G-11724)
SATELLITE SOFTWARE
15231 12th Rd (46563-8132)
PHONE..................................574 842-3370
Pat Renneker, *President*
EMP: 2 EST: 2001
SALES (est): 167.7K **Privately Held**
SIC: 7372 Prepackaged software

(G-11725)
STONE QUARY
Also Called: Aggregate Service
10988 11th Rd (46563-9037)
PHONE..................................574 936-2975
Sue Drake, *Manager*
EMP: 7
SQ FT: 800
SALES (est): 224K
SALES (corp-wide): 1.9MM **Privately Held**
WEB: www.rockhollowgolf.com
SIC: 1442 Construction sand & gravel
PA: The Stone Quary
350 N 150 W
Peru IN 46970
765 473-5578

(G-11726)
SUPERB HORTICULTURE LLC
2811 Us Highway 31 (46563-9196)
PHONE..................................800 567-8264
Sam Erwin, *CEO*
▲ **EMP:** 12
SALES (est): 2.1MM **Privately Held**
SIC: 3523 Farm machinery & equipment

(G-11727)
THERMO CUBE INCORPORATED
2255 Walter Glaub Dr (46563-3435)
PHONE..................................574 936-5096
Benjamin T Clark Jr, *President*
EMP: 2 EST: 1999
SALES (est): 176.1K **Privately Held**
SIC: 3699 Electrical equipment & supplies

(G-11728)
TITUS INC
9887 6b Rd (46563-8913)
PHONE..................................574 936-3345
Fax: 574 936-3345
Thomas Read, *President*
EMP: 15
SQ FT: 17,400
SALES (est): 2.9MM **Privately Held**
WEB: www.titusinc.com
SIC: 7692 3599 3541 3446 Welding re-
pair; custom machinery; machine tools,
metal cutting type; architectural metal-
work; fabricated structural metal

(G-11729)
TITUS MFG LLC
7991 Lilac Rd (46563-9502)
PHONE..................................574 286-1928
EMP: 2
SALES (est): 89.2K **Privately Held**
SIC: 3999 Manufacturing industries

(G-11730)
TOWN & COUNTRY PRESS INC
1920 Jim Neu Dr (46563-1396)
P.O. Box 417 (46563-0417)
PHONE..................................574 936-9505
Fax: 574 936-5028
Philip Martin, *President*
Benjamin Martin, *Principal*
Sherrie Martin, *Corp Secy*
Philip Martin Jr, *Vice Pres*
EMP: 17
SQ FT: 10,000
SALES: 1.5MM **Privately Held**
SIC: 2752 2759 2791 Commercial print-
ing, offset; letterpress printing; typesetting

(G-11731)
TRADING POST
523 E Jefferson St (46563-1829)
PHONE..................................574 935-5460
Diana Harrell, *Owner*
EMP: 4
SALES (est): 184.9K **Privately Held**
SIC: 2711 Newspapers

(G-11732)
U S GRANULES CORPORATION
1433 Western Ave (46563-1098)
P.O. Box 130 (46563-0130)
PHONE..................................574 936-2146
John J Oliver, *President*
Joyce Klingerman, *Corp Secy*
James Faulstich, *Safety Mgr*
▲ **EMP:** 52
SALES (est): 13.5MM **Privately Held**
WEB: www.usgranules.com
SIC: 3399 Metal powders, pastes & flakes

(G-11733)
VALMONT INDUSTRIES INC
1545 Pidco Dr (46563-1354)
PHONE..................................574 935-3058
Sean Gallagher, *Vice Pres*
Scott Krouse, *Sales Dir*
Jennifer Gurtner, *Branch Mgr*
EMP: 5
SALES (corp-wide): 2.7B **Publicly Held**
SIC: 3441 Fabricated structural metal
PA: Valmont Industries, Inc.
1 Valmont Plz Ste 500
Omaha NE 68154
402 963-1000

(G-11734)
VIKING PAPER COMPANY
1001 Pidco Dr (46563-1368)
PHONE..................................574 936-6300
Fax: 574 936-1144
Robert Walker, *Vice Pres*
Ken Froeschke, *Opers Mgr*
EMP: 50
SALES (corp-wide): 19.9MM **Privately Held**
SIC: 5113 2631 Bags, paper & disposable
plastic; paperboard mills
PA: Viking Paper Company
5148 Stickney Ave
Toledo OH 43612
419 729-4951

(G-11735)
WESTROCK CP LLC
1100 Pidco Dr (46563-1347)
PHONE..................................574 936-2118
Fax: 574 936-7416
Owen Glock, *Branch Mgr*
EMP: 5
SALES (corp-wide): 14.8B **Publicly Held**
SIC: 4225 2674 2672 2671 General
warehousing & storage; bags: uncoated
paper & multiwall; coated & laminated
paper; packaging paper & plastics film,
coated & laminated; folding paperboard
boxes; paperboard mills
HQ: Westrock Cp, Llc
504 Thrasher St
Norcross GA 30071

(G-11736)
WESTROCK RKT COMPANY
1810 Pidco Dr (46563-1361)
PHONE..................................574 936-2118
Owen Glock, *Branch Mgr*
EMP: 14
SALES (corp-wide): 14.8B **Publicly Held**
SIC: 2653 Partitions, solid fiber: made from
purchased materials
HQ: Westrock Rkt Company
1000 Abernathy Rd Ste 125
Atlanta GA 30328
770 448-2193

(G-11737)
WIERS FLEET PARTNERS INC (PA)
2111 Jim Neu Dr (46563-3302)
PHONE..................................574 936-4076
Fax: 574 936-9301
Thomas Wiers, *President*
Carrie Wiers, *Corp Secy*
EMP: 17
SQ FT: 80,000
SALES (est): 1.6MM **Privately Held**
SIC: 3713 Truck bodies (motor vehicles)

(G-11738)
WITT GALVANIZING
2631 Jim Neu Dr (46563-3311)
PHONE..................................574 935-4500
R Harris, *Principal*
EMP: 6 EST: 2007

SALES (est): 768.2K **Privately Held**
SIC: 3479 Galvanizing of iron, steel or end-
formed products

(G-11739)
WITT INDUSTRIES INC
2631 Jim Neu Dr (46563-3311)
PHONE..................................574 935-4500
Fax: 574 935-3576
Philip Burner, *Manager*
EMP: 50
SALES (corp-wide): 60.8MM **Privately Held**
WEB: www.witt.com
SIC: 3479 Galvanizing of iron, steel or end-
formed products
HQ: Witt Industries, Inc.
4600 N Masn Montgomery Rd
Mason OH 45040
513 871-5700

(G-11740)
WORLD GRAFFIX LLC
14717 Lincoln Hwy (46563-8017)
PHONE..................................574 936-1927
Andrew Wright,
Patricia Wright,
EMP: 5
SALES: 80K **Privately Held**
WEB: www.worldgraffix.net
SIC: 7336 3993 Commercial art & graphic
design; signs & advertising specialties

(G-11741)
ZENTIS NORTH AMERICA LLC
2050 N Oak Dr (46563-3407)
PHONE..................................574 941-1100
Anne Cavanaugh, *Purch Agent*
Robert Knapp, *Plant Engr*
Margarita Carrillo, *VP Human Res*
Shelly Barra, *Manager*
James Sweeny, *Info Tech Mgr*
EMP: 300
SALES (corp-wide): 704.5MM **Privately Held**
SIC: 2033 Canned fruits & specialties
HQ: Zentis North America, Llc
1741 Tomlinson Rd
Philadelphia PA 19116
215 676-3900

(G-11742)
ZENTIS SWEET OVTIONS HOLDG LLC
2050 N Oak Dr (46563-3407)
PHONE..................................574 941-1100
Norbert Weichele, *CEO*
John Tordi, *Maintenance Dir*
Tanya Raasch, *Opers Mgr*
Michael Maciejack, *Prdtn Mgr*
John Snajkowski, *Opers Staff*
▲ **EMP:** 190
SALES (est): 62.1MM
SALES (corp-wide): 704.5MM **Privately Held**
SIC: 2033 2034 2037 Canned fruits &
specialties; dried & dehydrated fruits;
frozen fruits & vegetables
PA: Zentis Gmbh & Co. Kg
Julicher Str. 177
Aachen 52070
241 476-00

Poland
Owen County

(G-11743)
RON GLASSCOCK
Also Called: Signs of Times
3282 N County Road 700 E (47868-8217)
PHONE..................................812 986-2342
Ron Glasscock, *Owner*
EMP: 2
SALES (est): 78K **Privately Held**
SIC: 7336 3993 Creative services to ad-
vertisers, except writers; graphic arts &
related design; signs & advertising spe-
cialties

Poneto
Wells County

(G-11744)
ANDERSEN CORPORATION
219 W State Road 218 (46781-5430)
P.O. Box 116 (46781-0116)
PHONE..................................260 694-6861
Fax: 260 694-6701
William Wolf, *Principal*
EMP: 1217
SALES (corp-wide): 3B **Privately Held**
SIC: 2431 Windows, wood
PA: Andersen Corporation
100 4th Ave N
Bayport MN 55003
651 264-5150

(G-11745)
COUNTRY CABINETS
3900 W State Road 218 (46781-9747)
PHONE..................................260 694-6777
Fax: 260 694-6900
Ted Habegger, *Owner*
Jane Habegger, *Co-Owner*
EMP: 6
SALES: 425K **Privately Held**
SIC: 2434 2511 Wood kitchen cabinets;
wood household furniture

(G-11746)
HOOSIER ENGINEERING CO INC
7726 S Meridian Rd (46781-9510)
PHONE..................................260 694-6887
Steve Studebaker, *President*
EMP: 2 EST: 1997
SALES (est): 269.5K **Privately Held**
SIC: 3325 Steel foundries

Portage
Porter County

(G-11747)
A PLUS DATACOMM
3282 Roswell Dr (46368-5154)
PHONE..................................219 472-1644
Jose G Martinez, *Principal*
EMP: 2
SALES: 100K **Privately Held**
SIC: 3669 Communications equipment

(G-11748)
ADVANCED CONTROL PANELS INC
1845 Willowcreek Rd (46368-1323)
PHONE..................................219 763-4000
Abraham Peute, *President*
EMP: 10 EST: 2005
SQ FT: 1,500
SALES (est): 2.6MM **Privately Held**
SIC: 3613 Control panels, electric

(G-11749)
AQUESTIVE THERAPEUTICS
6465 Ameriplex Dr (46368-1389)
PHONE..................................219 762-4143
Keith Kendall, *Branch Mgr*
EMP: 139
SALES (corp-wide): 66.9MM **Publicly Held**
SIC: 2834 Pharmaceutical preparations
PA: Aquestive Therapeutics, Inc.
30 Technology Dr
Warren NJ 07059
908 941-1900

(G-11750)
BADGER DAYLIGHTING CORP
5597 Old Porter Rd Ste D (46368-6209)
PHONE..................................219 762-9177
EMP: 2
SALES (est): 142.9K **Privately Held**
SIC: 3648 Lighting equipment

(G-11751)
BETA STEEL CORP
6500 S Boundary Rd (46368-1334)
PHONE..................................219 787-0001
John Goodwin, *Principal*
Leslie Monteleone, *Human Res Mgr*

▲ = Import ▼=Export
◆ =Import/Export

EMP: 5
SALES (est): 133K **Privately Held**
SIC: 3312 Beehive coke oven products

(G-11752)
BUSINESS HEALTH
5715 Independence Ave (46368-3311)
PHONE..................................219 762-7105
Steve Padilla, *Owner*
EMP: 2
SALES (est): 15.5K **Privately Held**
SIC: 2899

(G-11753)
CALUMITE COMPANY LLC
1605 Adler Cir Ste I (46368-6414)
PHONE..................................219 787-8667
Fax: 219 787-9651
Mark Abraham, *Mng Member*
R W Hopkins Jr, *Mng Member*
EMP: 14
SALES (est): 4.4MM
SALES (corp-wide): 376.1MM **Privately Held**
WEB: www.calumitellc.com
SIC: 5099 3211 Containers: glass, metal or plastic; sheet glass; plate glass, polished & rough
PA: Edw. C. Levy Co.
  9300 Dix
  Dearborn MI 48120
  313 429-2200

(G-11754)
CAMACO PORTAGE MFG LLC
6515 Ameriplex Dr Ste B (46368-7714)
PHONE..................................248 657-0246
Jesus Tome, *General Mgr*
EMP: 3
SQ FT: 142,000
SALES (est): 125.5K
SALES (corp-wide): 535.7MM **Privately Held**
SIC: 3714 Motor vehicle body components & frame
HQ: Camaco, Llc
  37000 W 12 Mile Rd
  Farmington Hills MI 48331
  248 442-6800

(G-11755)
CARMEUSE LIME & STONE
165 Steel Dr (46368-1379)
PHONE..................................219 787-9190
EMP: 2
SALES (est): 359.6K **Privately Held**
SIC: 3274 Mfg Lime Products

(G-11756)
CHROME DEPOSIT CORPORATION (PA)
6640 Melton Rd (46368-1279)
PHONE..................................219 763-1571
Fax: 219 762-3370
Philip Court, *President*
G R Conley, *Vice Pres*
Ken Langfitt, *Vice Pres*
Lisa Woelk, *Admin Sec*
EMP: 45
SQ FT: 50,000
SALES (est): 23.7MM **Privately Held**
WEB: www.cdcportage.com
SIC: 3471 Chromium plating of metals or formed products; electroplating & plating

(G-11757)
CLANCYS OF PORTAGE
2542 Portage Mall (46368-3006)
PHONE..................................219 764-4995
Michelle Clancy, *President*
EMP: 12
SALES (est): 278K **Privately Held**
WEB: www.clancysofportage.com
SIC: 5812 5182 2599 American restaurant; liquor; bar, restaurant & cafeteria furniture

(G-11758)
CROWN ELEC SVCS & AUTOMTN INC (HQ)
Also Called: Crown E.S.A.
5960 Southport Rd (46368-6407)
PHONE..................................972 929-4700
Fax: 219 736-1636
Thomas B Adams, *President*
William English, *Vice Pres*

Bradly Hendrickson, *Vice Pres*
Miroslav Arsov, *Project Engr*
David Shanks, *Electrical Engi*
EMP: 97
SQ FT: 33,191
SALES (est): 14.5MM
SALES (corp-wide): 35.3MM **Privately Held**
SIC: 8711 3823 3594 Electrical or electronic engineering; industrial instrmnts msrmnt display/control process variable; fluid power pumps & motors
PA: Glenmount Global Solutions, Inc.
  805 Las Cimas Pkwy 440
  Austin TX 78746
  219 850-5167

(G-11759)
D & E AUTO ELECTRIC INC
5665 Old Porter Rd (46368-1137)
PHONE..................................219 763-3892
Fax: 219 762-2443
Edward Carda, *President*
Carol Carda, *Vice Pres*
Janice Carda, *Admin Sec*
EMP: 10
SQ FT: 3,200
SALES (est): 1.4MM **Privately Held**
SIC: 3621 3714 3694 3625 Starters, for motors; drive shafts, motor vehicle; alternators, automotive; relays & industrial controls

(G-11760)
ENTERTAINMENT EXPRESS
3460 Anthony Dr (46368-8004)
PHONE..................................219 763-3610
Kerry Kapica, *Owner*
EMP: 11
SALES (est): 390K **Privately Held**
WEB: www.entertainmentexpressdjs.com
SIC: 5947 7929 2759 Gifts & novelties; disc jockey service; invitation & stationery printing & engraving

(G-11761)
EXPRESS PRINTING & COPYING
Also Called: X-Press Printing
2554 Portage Mall (46368-3006)
PHONE..................................219 762-3508
Fax: 219 763-3439
David Capron Sr, *President*
Betty Sergent, *Manager*
EMP: 6
SQ FT: 3,000
SALES (est): 723K **Privately Held**
SIC: 2752 Commercial printing, offset

(G-11762)
FERALLOY CORPORATION
6755 Waterway Dr (46368-1383)
P.O. Box 1349, Granite City IL (62040-1349)
PHONE..................................219 787-9698
Fax: 219 787-6996
Don Wilke, *Engineer*
John Hirt, *Branch Mgr*
EMP: 60
SALES (corp-wide): 9.7B **Publicly Held**
WEB: www.feralloy.com
SIC: 5051 3316 Iron or steel flat products; cold finishing of steel shapes
HQ: Feralloy Corporation
  8755 W Higgins Rd Ste 970
  Chicago IL 60631
  503 286-8869

(G-11763)
FIVE STAR HYDRAULICS INC
1210 Crisman Rd (46368-1231)
PHONE..................................219 762-1619
Fax: 219 762-3938
Timothy Bowgren, *President*
Janiece Barrett, *Office Mgr*
▲ **EMP:** 31
SQ FT: 2,400
SALES (est): 6.4MM **Privately Held**
WEB: www.fivestarhydraulics.com
SIC: 7699 3593 Hydraulic equipment repair; fluid power cylinders & actuators

(G-11764)
FLOWSERVE CORPORATION
6675 Daniel Burnham Dr F (46368-1794)
PHONE..................................219 763-1000
Scott Ton, *Branch Mgr*

EMP: 9
SALES (corp-wide): 3.6B **Publicly Held**
SIC: 3561 Pumps & pumping equipment
PA: Flowserve Corporation
  5215 N Oconnor Blvd Connor
  Irving TX 75039
  972 443-6500

(G-11765)
GI PROPERTIES INC (PA)
Also Called: Correct Construction
6610 Melton Rd (46368-1236)
PHONE..................................219 763-1177
Paul K Graegin, *President*
Mike Singleton, *Facilities Mgr*
EMP: 5
SALES (est): 74.8MM **Privately Held**
SIC: 1623 3441 7353 Pipeline construction; fabricated structural metal; heavy construction equipment rental

(G-11766)
GLOBAL STONE PORTAGE LLC
6600 Us Highway 12 (46368-1276)
PHONE..................................219 787-9190
Richard Powers, *Manager*
EMP: 4
SALES (est): 207.9K **Privately Held**
SIC: 1422 5211 Crushed & broken limestone; lime & plaster

(G-11767)
GOODYEAR TIRE & RUBBER COMPANY
6791 Melton Rd (46368-1246)
PHONE..................................219 762-0651
Jason Klein, *Branch Mgr*
EMP: 2
SALES (corp-wide): 15.3B **Publicly Held**
SIC: 5014 3011 Tires & tubes; inner tubes, all types
PA: The Goodyear Tire & Rubber Company
  200 E Innovation Way
  Akron OH 44316
  330 796-2121

(G-11768)
GRAPHIC PACKAGING INTL LLC
Also Called: Altivity Packaging
5900 Carlson Ave (46368-1309)
PHONE..................................219 762-4855
Leslie Crouch, *Branch Mgr*
EMP: 53 **Publicly Held**
SIC: 2631 Container board
HQ: Graphic Packaging International, Llc
  1500 Riveredge Pkwy # 100
  Atlanta GA 30328

(G-11769)
GREEN PIPE & SUPPLY INC
46 Sunset Trl (46368-1004)
PHONE..................................219 762-1077
Fax: 219 762-7131
Fred T Green, *President*
Sarah J Green, *Corp Secy*
EMP: 3
SALES (est): 230K **Privately Held**
SIC: 3494 Valves & pipe fittings

(G-11770)
HAMILTON CANVAS INC
2305 Hamstrom Rd Ste F (46368-2274)
PHONE..................................219 763-1686
Rhonda Hamilton, *Owner*
EMP: 2 **EST:** 2006
SALES (est): 180.7K **Privately Held**
SIC: 2211 Canvas

(G-11771)
JGR ENTERPRISES LLC
6525 Daniel Burnham Dr D (46368-6412)
PHONE..................................586 264-3400
EMP: 2
SALES (est): 81.1K **Privately Held**
SIC: 2311 Tuxedos: made from purchased materials

(G-11772)
LANCES DRIVESHAFT & COMPONENTS
2076 Dombey Rd (46368-1441)
PHONE..................................219 762-2531
Fax: 219 762-2578
Lance Morris, *President*
EMP: 3

SQ FT: 1,600
SALES: 300K **Privately Held**
SIC: 7539 3714 Automotive repair shops; drive shafts, motor vehicle

(G-11773)
LEAR CORPORATION
6750 Daniel Burnham Dr A (46368-1869)
PHONE..................................219 764-5101
EMP: 6
SALES (corp-wide): 20.4B **Publicly Held**
SIC: 3714 Motor vehicle parts & accessories
PA: Lear Corporation
  21557 Telegraph Rd
  Southfield MI 48033
  248 447-1500

(G-11774)
LYNN BROS ELECTRIC INC
5685 Old Porter Rd (46368-1137)
PHONE..................................219 762-6386
Fax: 219 762-9458
Eric Lynn, *Principal*
EMP: 4 **EST:** 2011
SALES (est): 465.6K **Privately Held**
SIC: 3699 1731 Electrical equipment & supplies; electrical work

(G-11775)
MID-CONTINENT COAL AND COKE CO
1150 E Boundary Rd (46368-1154)
P.O. Box 602 (46368-0602)
PHONE..................................219 787-8171
Randy Sullivan, *Manager*
EMP: 40
SALES (corp-wide): 7.7MM **Privately Held**
WEB: www.midcontinentcoke.com
SIC: 3295 3312 Minerals, ground or treated; blast furnaces & steel mills
HQ: Mid-Continent Coal And Coke Company
  20600 Chagrin Blvd # 850
  Cleveland OH 44122
  216 283-5700

(G-11776)
MINTEQ SHAPES AND SERVICES INC
1789 Schiller St (46368-1226)
PHONE..................................219 762-4863
Carl Laib, *President*
▲ **EMP:** 10
SQ FT: 3,000
SALES (est): 4.6MM **Publicly Held**
WEB: www.mineralstech.com
SIC: 3297 Nonclay refractories
PA: Minerals Technologies Inc.
  622 3rd Ave Rm 3800
  New York NY 10017

(G-11777)
MISSISSIPPI LIME COMPANY
570 E Boundary Rd (46368-1127)
PHONE..................................800 437-5463
EMP: 4
SALES (corp-wide): 417MM **Privately Held**
SIC: 3274 Quicklime
HQ: Mississippi Lime Company
  3870 S Lindbergh Blvd # 200
  Saint Louis MO 63127
  314 543-6300

(G-11778)
MONOSOL LLC
1500 Louis Sullivan Dr (46368-6435)
PHONE..................................219 763-7589
Mark Wendorf, *Engineer*
Tim Boyle, *Manager*
EMP: 99
SALES (corp-wide): 4.6B **Privately Held**
SIC: 2671 3565 Plastic film, coated or laminated for packaging; packaging machinery
HQ: Monosol, Llc
  707 E 80th Pl Ste 301
  Merrillville IN 46410
  219 762-3165

(G-11779)
MONOSOL LLC
1701 County Line Rd (46368-1595)
PHONE..................................219 762-3165

Lisa Campbell, *Purchasing*
Kyle Kleinline, *Research*
Jon Knight, *Research*
Tom Ford, *Engineer*
Tim Boyle, *Branch Mgr*
EMP: 99
SALES (corp-wide): 4.6B **Privately Held**
SIC: 2671 Plastic film, coated or laminated for packaging
HQ: Monosol, Llc
    707 E 80th Pl Ste 301
    Merrillville IN 46410
    219 762-3165

(G-11780)
MOOSEIN INDUSTRIES LLC
1256 Camelot Mnr (46368-5336)
PHONE....................219 406-7306
Randall K Bolde,
EMP: 3
SALES (est): 257.9K **Privately Held**
SIC: 3999 Manufacturing industries

(G-11781)
NEO INDUSTRIES LLC
1775 Willowcreek Rd (46368-1324)
PHONE....................219 762-6075
EMP: 2 **Privately Held**
SIC: 3471 Plating & polishing
HQ: Neo Industries, Llc
    1400 E Angela Blvd
    South Bend IN 46617
    574 217-4078

(G-11782)
NEO INDUSTRIES (INDIANA) INC
1775 Willowcreek Rd (46368-1324)
PHONE....................219 762-6075
Fax: 219 762-5439
Kevin Walsh, *President*
Doug Johnson, *Admin Sec*
▲ **EMP:** 115
SALES (est): 12.1MM **Privately Held**
WEB: www.neoindustriesllc.com
SIC: 3471 Electroplating & plating
HQ: Neo Industries, Llc
    1400 E Angela Blvd
    South Bend IN 46617
    574 217-4078

(G-11783)
NEW PARADIGMS INDUSTRIAL ART
6520 Lakewood Ave (46368-2402)
PHONE....................219 762-4046
Scott Jackson, *President*
EMP: 2 EST: 2001
SALES (est): 126.3K **Privately Held**
SIC: 3471 Sand blasting of metal parts

(G-11784)
NLMK INDIANA LLC
6500 S Boundary Rd (46368-1334)
PHONE....................219 787-8200
Robert Miller, *President*
Alexander Tseitline, *Vice Pres*
Corinn Grossetti, *CFO*
Barb Weinman, *Sales Mgr*
John Dorsey, *Sales Staff*
▲ **EMP:** 380
SQ FT: 600,000
SALES (est): 139.1MM
SALES (corp-wide): 510MM **Privately Held**
WEB: www.betasteelcorp.com
SIC: 3312 Hot-rolled iron & steel products
HQ: Nlmk, Pao
    2 Pl. Metallurgov
    Lipetsk 39804

(G-11785)
NORTHERN TRANS & DIFFERENTIAL
6641 Melton Rd (46368-1235)
PHONE....................219 764-4009
Fax: 219 764-2839
Kevin Westerman, *Owner*
EMP: 2
SQ FT: 3,300
SALES (est): 349.8K **Privately Held**
SIC: 3714 7537 Differentials & parts, motor vehicle; motor vehicle transmissions, drive assemblies & parts; automotive transmission repair shops

(G-11786)
OZINGA BROS INC
Also Called: Ozinga Ready Mix
1575 Adler Cir Ste B (46368-6408)
PHONE....................219 949-9800
Fax: 219 949-2741
Donald Rapley, *President*
James A Ozinga, *President*
EMP: 100
SQ FT: 15,000
SALES (corp-wide): 269.8MM **Privately Held**
SIC: 3273 Ready-mixed concrete
PA: Ozinga Bros., Inc.
    19001 Old Lagrange Rd # 30
    Mokena IL 60448
    708 326-4200

(G-11787)
P R F
6737 Central Ave Ste D (46368-3273)
PHONE....................219 477-8660
Gerald Sampson, *Owner*
EMP: 2
SALES: 82K **Privately Held**
SIC: 3799 Trailers & trailer equipment

(G-11788)
PORTAGE CUSTOM WEAR LLC
2536 Portage Mall (46368-3006)
PHONE....................219 841-9070
Brandon Starr, *Administration*
EMP: 6
SALES (est): 594.4K **Privately Held**
SIC: 2759 Screen printing

(G-11789)
PSC MACHINING AND ENGRG INC
6672 Melton Rd (46368-1236)
PHONE....................219 764-4270
William Stockwell, *President*
Bill Stockwell, *General Mgr*
Ron Hough, *Corp Secy*
Jeannette Cappadora, *Office Mgr*
EMP: 18
SQ FT: 12,000
SALES (est): 3.7MM **Privately Held**
SIC: 3599 7692 3541 Machine shop, jobbing & repair; welding repair; machine tools, metal cutting type

(G-11790)
PYRO INDUSTRIAL SERVICES INC
6610 Shepherd Ave (46368-6400)
P.O. Box 237 (46368-0237)
PHONE....................219 787-5700
Fax: 219 787-0700
John L Carlson, *CEO*
Raymond W McMillan, *President*
Margaret K Warnke, *Corp Secy*
James R Harting, *Vice Pres*
Chris Carlson, *Supervisor*
EMP: 25 EST: 1975
SQ FT: 12,000
SALES (est): 5MM **Privately Held**
SIC: 1741 5085 3297 Refractory or acid brick masonry; refractory material; nonclay refractories

(G-11791)
RANDALL RENTS OF INDIANA INC
6480 Us Highway 20 (46368-1268)
PHONE....................219 763-1155
Randall Truckenbrodt, *President*
EMP: 10
SQ FT: 6,000
SALES (est): 1.8MM
SALES (corp-wide): 18MM **Privately Held**
SIC: 3531 7353 Construction machinery; heavy construction equipment rental
PA: Randall Industries, Inc.
    741 S Rte 83
    Elmhurst IL 60126
    630 833-9100

(G-11792)
SEA QUEST LURES INC
2141 Whippoorwill St (46368-1681)
PHONE....................219 762-4362
Richard Holm, *Principal*
EMP: 2

SALES (est): 146K **Privately Held**
SIC: 3949 Sporting & athletic goods

(G-11793)
SEDONA INC
3195 Willowcreek Rd (46368-4446)
PHONE....................219 764-9675
Sharon Garbertt, *Branch Mgr*
EMP: 6 **Privately Held**
SIC: 7372 Business oriented computer software
HQ: Sedona, Inc.
    612 Valley View Dr
    Moline IL 61265
    309 736-4104

(G-11794)
SIEMENS INDUSTRY INC
Also Called: Siemens Industrial Services
6625 Daniel Burnham Dr (46368-1698)
PHONE....................219 763-7927
Thomas Engel, *Manager*
EMP: 62
SALES (corp-wide): 97.7B **Privately Held**
WEB: www.sea.siemens.com
SIC: 3613 3823 3625 3621 Switchgear & switchgear accessories; industrial instrmnts msrmnt display/control process variable; relays & industrial controls; motors & generators; power transmission equipment
HQ: Siemens Industry, Inc.
    100 Technology Dr
    Alpharetta GA 30005
    770 740-3000

(G-11795)
SSSI INC
1865 Willowcreek Rd (46368-1323)
PHONE....................219 762-8901
EMP: 6
SALES (corp-wide): 177MM **Privately Held**
SIC: 3499 Aerosol valves, metal
PA: Sssi, Inc.
    2755a Park Ave
    Washington PA 15301
    724 743-5815

(G-11796)
STEEL TECHNOLOGIES LLC
5830 Southport Rd (46368-1289)
PHONE....................502 245-2110
Fax: 219 762-7520
Bill Horvath, *Manager*
EMP: 180
SQ FT: 60,000 **Privately Held**
WEB: www.steeltechnologies.com
SIC: 3316 3398 3312 Cold finishing of steel shapes; metal heat treating; blast furnaces & steel mills
HQ: Steel Technologies Llc
    700 N Hurstbourne Pkwy # 400
    Louisville KY 40222
    502 245-2110

(G-11797)
TEAM & CLUB SPORTING GOODS
6218 Old Porter Rd (46368-1620)
PHONE....................219 762-5477
Ralph A Messina, *Owner*
Ralph Messina, *Owner*
EMP: 6
SALES (est): 281.7K **Privately Held**
SIC: 3949 5091 Sporting & athletic goods; sporting & recreation goods

(G-11798)
TMS INTERNATIONAL LLC
1575 Adler Cir Ste E (46368-6408)
PHONE....................219 762-2176
EMP: 4 **Privately Held**
SIC: 3312 Blast furnaces & steel mills
HQ: Tms International, Llc
    12 Monongahela Ave
    Glassport PA 15045
    412 678-6141

(G-11799)
UNITED STATES STEEL CORP
Midwest Division
6300 Us Highway 12 (46368-1267)
P.O. Box 220 (46368-0220)
PHONE....................219 762-3131
Fax: 219 763-5515

John Guidan, *Opers-Prdtn-Mfg*
David Stobbe, *Manager*
Dave Suarez, *Planning*
EMP: 100
SALES (corp-wide): 12.2B **Publicly Held**
SIC: 3312 3471 3316 Sheet or strip, steel, hot-rolled; plating & polishing; cold finishing of steel shapes
PA: United States Steel Corp
    600 Grant St Ste 468
    Pittsburgh PA 15219
    412 433-1121

(G-11800)
USW LU 6103-07
1919 Willowcreek Rd (46368-1514)
PHONE....................219 762-4433
EMP: 2
SALES: 417K **Privately Held**
SIC: 3441 Fabricated structural metal

(G-11801)
WESTROCK CP LLC
5900 Carlson Ave (46368-1309)
PHONE....................219 762-4855
Les Crouch, *Manager*
EMP: 400
SALES (corp-wide): 14.8B **Publicly Held**
WEB: www.smurfit-stone.com
SIC: 2631 Paperboard mills
HQ: Westrock Cp, Llc
    504 Thrasher St
    Norcross GA 30071

(G-11802)
YONGLI AMERICA LLC
6625 Daniel Burnham Dr (46368-1698)
PHONE....................219 763-7920
Richard Garrity, *President*
EMP: 5
SQ FT: 18,000
SALES: 8MM **Privately Held**
SIC: 3496 Conveyor belts

Porter
Porter County

(G-11803)
CUSTOM FITZ LLC
10 Wagner Rd (46304-1748)
PHONE....................219 405-0896
EMP: 2
SALES (est): 102.7K **Privately Held**
SIC: 3999 Manufacturing industries

(G-11804)
CUSTOM TS & TROPHIES
30 E Burwell Dr (46304)
PHONE....................219 926-4174
Joe Mullet, *Partner*
Laurie Mullet, *Partner*
EMP: 2
SALES (est): 130K **Privately Held**
SIC: 3479 7336 Engraving jewelry silverware, or metal; silk screen design

(G-11805)
DMC DISTRIBUTION LLC
172 S 19th St (46304-1906)
PHONE....................219 926-6401
Devin Craven, *Principal*
EMP: 2
SALES (est): 118K **Privately Held**
SIC: 8748 3999 5961 4832 Educational consultant; education aids, devices & supplies; educational supplies & equipment, mail order; educational

(G-11806)
WORTHINGTON STEEL COMPANY
100 Worthington Dr (46304-8812)
PHONE....................219 929-4000
Fax: 219 929-4007
Dee Caskey, *Buyer*
Ryan Gilbride, *Buyer*
Don Hale, *Buyer*
Jenni Veenstra, *Buyer*
Rex Appel, *Engineer*
EMP: 175

▲ = Import ▼=Export
◆ =Import/Export

SALES (corp-wide): 3.5B **Publicly Held**
SIC: 3316 3471 3312 Cold finishing of
steel shapes; plating & polishing; blast
furnace & related products
HQ: The Worthington Steel Company
200 W Wlson Bridge Rd
Worthington OH 43085
614 438-3210

Portland
Jay County

(G-11807)
ACCELERATED CURING INC
304 E 100 N (47371-7646)
PHONE...................................260 726-3202
Fax: 260 726-3108
Robert Mc Cabe, *President*
EMP: 11
SQ FT: 30,000
SALES (est): 1.7MM **Privately Held**
WEB: www.acceleratedcuring.com
SIC: 3089 Plastic processing

(G-11808)
ALLEGHENY LUDLUM CORP
250 E Lafayette St (47371-1099)
PHONE...................................412 394-2800
Preston Costa, *Principal*
EMP: 2
SALES (est): 90.8K **Privately Held**
SIC: 3312 Blast furnaces & steel mills

(G-11809)
CARRERA MANUFACTURING INC
1000 N Morton St (47371-1631)
PHONE...................................260 726-9800
James D Hiester, *Principal*
EMP: 18
SALES (est): 4.4MM **Privately Held**
SIC: 3089 Injection molding of plastics

(G-11810)
CENTRAL COCA-COLA BTLG CO INC
1617 N Meridian St (47371-9301)
PHONE...................................260 726-7126
EMP: 2
SALES (corp-wide): 35.4B **Publicly Held**
SIC: 5149 2086 8741 Soft drinks; soft
drinks: packaged in cans, bottles, etc.;
management services
HQ: Central Coca-Cola Bottling Company,
Inc.
555 Taxter Rd Ste 550
Elmsford NY 10523
914 789-1100

(G-11811)
COCA-COLA BOTTLING CO PORTLAND
1617 N Meridian St (47371-9301)
PHONE...................................260 726-7126
Fax: 260 726-2385
Marvin J Herb, *Manager*
EMP: 83 EST: 1921
SQ FT: 92,000
SALES (est): 10.6MM **Privately Held**
SIC: 2086 Bottled & canned soft drinks

(G-11812)
COLLEGIATE PRIDE INC
Also Called: THE FALCON MINT
807 N Meridian St (47371-1126)
PHONE...................................260 726-7818
Fax: 260 726-7849
John Goodrich, *President*
EMP: 7
SALES (est): 510K **Privately Held**
WEB: www.falconmint.com
SIC: 3911 5944 Jewelry, precious metal;
jewelry stores

(G-11813)
COMMERCIAL ELECTRIC CO INC
Also Called: Pennville Custom Cabinetry
600 E Votaw St (47371-1610)
P.O. Box 1266 (47371-3266)
PHONE...................................260 726-9357
Fax: 260 726-7044

Mark S Goldman, *Chairman*
Doris Goldman, *Exec VP*
EMP: 25
SQ FT: 50,000
SALES (est): 3MM **Privately Held**
WEB: www.pennvillecabinetry.com
SIC: 2434 2511 Wood kitchen cabinets;
wood household furniture
PA: Commercial Electric Co Inc
2296 S Brookview Dr
Portland IN 47371

(G-11814)
D J INVESTMENTS INC
Also Called: Hearing Aid Outlet
111 W North St Ste C (47371-1153)
PHONE...................................260 726-7346
Dan Ahrens, *Branch Mgr*
EMP: 2
SALES (est): 74.2K
SALES (corp-wide): 540K **Privately Held**
SIC: 7349 3842 Building maintenance, ex-
cept repairs; hearing aids
PA: D J Investments Inc
0660 E 200 S
Hartford City IN 47348
765 348-4381

(G-11815)
DAYTON PROGRESS CORPORATION
1314 N Meridian St (47371-1029)
PHONE...................................260 726-6861
Fax: 260 726-6859
Sara Rhodehamel, *Purch Agent*
Ryan Myers, *Engineer*
Daniel Sharkey, *Branch Mgr*
EMP: 40
SALES (corp-wide): 2.2B **Privately Held**
WEB: www.daytonpunch.com
SIC: 3544 Punches, forming & stamping
HQ: Dayton Progress Corporation
500 Progress Rd
Dayton OH 45449
937 859-5111

(G-11816)
DISPLAY CRAFT
803 W Water St (47371-1753)
PHONE...................................260 726-4535
Fax: 260 726-4758
EMP: 5 EST: 1970
SQ FT: 3,000
SALES (est): 280K **Privately Held**
SIC: 2499 3089 3086 Mfg Wood Products
Mfg Plastic Products Mfg Plastic Foam
Products

(G-11817)
DONALD H & SUSAN K MINCH
2825 W 400 N (47371-8448)
PHONE...................................260 726-9486
Susan Minch, *Owner*
EMP: 2
SALES (est): 64.6K **Privately Held**
SIC: 3269 Art & ornamental ware, pottery

(G-11818)
ERNST CONCRETE
1125 W Water St (47371-1759)
PHONE...................................260 726-8282
John Ernst, *President*
EMP: 3
SALES (est): 286.1K **Privately Held**
SIC: 3273 Ready-mixed concrete

(G-11819)
FCC (INDIANA) INC
555 Industrial Park Dr (47371-9399)
PHONE...................................260 726-8023
Yoshitaka Saito, *President*
Jeff Bailey, *VP Admin*
▲ EMP: 742
SQ FT: 357,000
SALES: 313.8MM
SALES (corp-wide): 1.6B **Privately Held**
SIC: 3714 Clutches, motor vehicle
PA: F.C.C. Co., Ltd.
7000-36, Nakagawa, Hosoecho, Kita-
Ku
Hamamatsu SZO 431-1
535 232-400

(G-11820)
FCC (NORTH AMERICA) INC (HQ)
555 Industrial Dr (47371-9399)
PHONE...................................260 726-8023
Satoshi Makaya, *President*
EMP: 32
SALES: 544.1MM
SALES (corp-wide): 1.6B **Privately Held**
SIC: 3714 Transmissions, motor vehicle
PA: F.C.C. Co., Ltd.
7000-36, Nakagawa, Hosoecho, Kita-
Ku
Hamamatsu SZO 431-1
535 232-400

(G-11821)
FCC ADAMS
555 Industrial Dr (47371-9399)
PHONE...................................260 589-8555
EMP: 11
SALES (est): 4.2MM **Privately Held**
SIC: 3714 Motor vehicle parts & acces-
sories

(G-11822)
FISHER PACKING COMPANY
300 W Walnut St (47371-1810)
PHONE...................................260 726-7355
Fax: 260 726-7255
John Fisher, *President*
Janice Fisher, *Admin Sec*
EMP: 25
SQ FT: 8,000
SALES (est): 2.1MM **Privately Held**
SIC: 5421 5147 0751 2013 Meat mar-
kets, including freezer provisioners;
meats, fresh; slaughtering: custom live-
stock services; sausages & other pre-
pared meats

(G-11823)
FLAMESPRAY MACHINE SERVICE
237 E Votaw St (47371-1418)
PHONE...................................260 726-6236
Fax: 260 726-6234
Jack Batt, *President*
Kristie Batt, *Vice Pres*
EMP: 4
SALES (est): 100K **Privately Held**
SIC: 7699 3599 Industrial machinery &
equipment repair; machine shop, jobbing
& repair

(G-11824)
FULLENKAMP MACHINE & MFG INC
1507 N Meridian St (47371-9000)
PHONE...................................260 726-8345
Fax: 260 726-6112
Richard E Fullenkamp, *President*
EMP: 16
SQ FT: 20,000
SALES (est): 2.3MM **Privately Held**
WEB: www.fullenkampmachine.com
SIC: 3599 7692 Machine shop, jobbing &
repair; welding repair

(G-11825)
GRAPHIC PRINTING CO INC (PA)
Also Called: Commercial Review, The
309 W Main St (47371-1803)
P.O. Box 1049 (47371-3149)
PHONE...................................260 726-8141
Fax: 260 726-8143
John C Ronald, *President*
Stephen Ronald, *Shareholder*
EMP: 27 EST: 1946
SQ FT: 20,000
SALES (est): 2.3MM **Privately Held**
SIC: 2711 Commercial printing & newspa-
per publishing combined

(G-11826)
GREAZY PICKLE LLC
211 W Main St (47371-2124)
P.O. Box 128 (47371-0128)
PHONE...................................260 726-9200
Chris Grieshop, *Owner*
EMP: 5
SALES (est): 511.3K **Privately Held**
SIC: 2599 Bar, restaurant & cafeteria furni-
ture

(G-11827)
GREG MOSER ENGINEERING INC
Also Called: Moser Engineering
102 Performance Way (47371-9012)
PHONE...................................260 726-6689
Fax: 260 726-4159
Greg Moser, *President*
Jeff Geesaman, *Prdtn Mgr*
Bruce Hedges, *Controller*
Kip Hayden, *Sales Mgr*
EMP: 35
SQ FT: 50,000
SALES (est): 6.3MM **Privately Held**
WEB: www.moserengineering.com
SIC: 7539 3714 3444 Machine shop, au-
tomotive; motor vehicle parts & acces-
sories; sheet metalwork

(G-11828)
HOOSIER ALL-STARS INC
303 E Arch St (47371-1909)
PHONE...................................317 408-0513
EMP: 2
SALES (est): 113.8K **Privately Held**
SIC: 2721 Periodicals-Publishing/Printing

(G-11829)
J & P CUSTOM PLATING INC
807 N Meridian St (47371-1126)
P.O. Box 16 (47371-0016)
PHONE...................................260 726-9696
Fax: 260 726-9684
John B Goodrich, *President*
EMP: 6 EST: 1971
SQ FT: 2,400
SALES (est): 633.9K **Privately Held**
WEB: www.jpcustomplating.com
SIC: 3471 5531 Plating of metals or
formed products; automotive & home sup-
ply stores

(G-11830)
JAY MOBILE HOME ADDITIONS
2443 N 200 W (47371-7981)
PHONE...................................260 726-9274
Fax: 260 726-9095
Ray Riendeau, *President*
Diane Riendeau, *Corp Secy*
EMP: 6 EST: 1981
SALES (est): 360K **Privately Held**
SIC: 2451 Mobile homes, personal or pri-
vate use

(G-11831)
JOYCE/DAYTON CORP
Also Called: Portland Division
1621 N Meridian St (47371-9301)
PHONE...................................260 726-9361
Fax: 260 726-7993
Darry Rowles, *Engineer*
Mike Lakes, *Controller*
Gary Fulton, *Manager*
EMP: 60
SALES (corp-wide): 2.5B **Publicly Held**
SIC: 3569 3537 3462 Jack screws; indus-
trial trucks & tractors; iron & steel forgings
HQ: Joyce/Dayton Corp.
3300 S Dixie Dr Ste 101
Dayton OH 45439
937 294-6261

(G-11832)
JRDS INDUSTRIES
1700 N Meridian St (47371-9303)
PHONE...................................260 729-5037
Ken Fredericksen, *Principal*
Katherine Reynolds, *Production*
EMP: 2
SALES (est): 175.4K **Privately Held**
SIC: 3999 Manufacturing industries

(G-11833)
KABLE TOOL & ENGINEERING
530 E 300 N (47371-7917)
PHONE...................................260 726-9670
Jason Kable, *Owner*
EMP: 2
SALES (est): 179.7K **Privately Held**
SIC: 3469 Machine parts, stamped or
pressed metal

(G-11834)
LPI PAVING & EXCAVATING (PA)
1401 W Votaw St (47371-9501)
PHONE...................................260 726-9564
Fax: 260 726-2042
Bill Davis, *President*
EMP: 6
SQ FT: 6,000
SALES: 450K **Privately Held**
SIC: 1794 4212 1442 Excavation work;
dump truck haulage; gravel mining

(G-11835)
MARV KAHLIG & SONS INC
3229 S 500 E (47371-7182)
PHONE...................................260 335-2212
Marvin Kahlig, *President*
Jayne Kahlig, *Corp Secy*
EMP: 4
SALES: 100K **Privately Held**
SIC: 3259 Clay sewer & drainage pipe &
tile

(G-11836)
**MOTHERSON SUMI SYSTEMS
LIMITED**
700 Industrial Dr (47371-1156)
PHONE...................................260 726-6501
James Kennedy, *Manager*
EMP: 700
SALES (corp-wide): 1.1B **Privately Held**
WEB: www.stoneridge.com
SIC: 3714 3694 Automotive wiring har-
ness sets; engine electrical equipment
PA: Motherson Sumi Systems Limited
Sector-127, Plot No.1, 11th Floor
Noida UP 20130
120 667-9500

(G-11837)
MSSL WIRING SYSTEM INC
700 Industrial Dr (47371-1156)
PHONE...................................260 726-6501
Fax: 260 726-6286
Jim Kennedy, *Plant Mgr*
Larry Brinkley, *Purch Mgr*
Jim Hutchison, *Admin Mgr*
EMP: 37
SALES (corp-wide): 1.1B **Privately Held**
SIC: 3679 Harness assemblies for elec-
tronic use: wire or cable
HQ: Mssl Wiring System Inc.
8640 E Market St
Warren OH 44484
330 856-3366

(G-11838)
PERFORMANCE TOOL INC
103 Performance Dr (47371-9012)
PHONE...................................260 726-6572
Lon R Racster, *President*
Paul Reffitt, *Plant Mgr*
EMP: 17
SALES (est): 2.9MM **Privately Held**
WEB: www.performancetool.net
SIC: 3449 Miscellaneous metalwork

(G-11839)
PIER-MAC PLASTICS INC
1000 N Morton St (47371-1631)
PHONE...................................260 726-9844
Fax: 260 726-2041
Jim Hiester, *President*
Patricia A McCabe, *Admin Sec*
EMP: 40
SQ FT: 70,000
SALES (est): 7.9MM **Privately Held**
WEB: www.pier-macplastics.com
SIC: 3089 3449 Injection molding of plas-
tics; miscellaneous metalwork

(G-11840)
**POET BIOREFINING -
PORTLAND**
1542 S 200 W (47371-6244)
PHONE...................................260 726-7154
Fax: 260 726-6157
Audrey Muhlenkamp, *General Mgr*
EMP: 8
SALES (est): 131.8K **Privately Held**
SIC: 2869 Ethanolamines

(G-11841)
PREMIER ETHANOL LLC
Also Called: Poet Brfining- Portland 18200
1542 S 200 W (47371-6244)
PHONE...................................260 726-2681
Matt Tomano, *General Mgr*
Greg Noble,
EMP: 5
SALES (est): 1.7MM **Privately Held**
SIC: 2869 Ethyl alcohol, ethanol
PA: Poet, Llc
4615 N Lewis Ave
Sioux Falls SD 57104

(G-11842)
PREMIER ETHANOL LLC
Also Called: Poet Brfining- Portland 18200
1542 S 200 W (47371-6244)
PHONE...................................260 726-7154
Jeff Lautt, *CEO*
Matt Tomano, *General Mgr*
EMP: 5
SALES (est): 1MM **Privately Held**
SIC: 2869 Ethyl alcohol, ethanol
PA: Poet, Llc
4615 N Lewis Ave
Sioux Falls SD 57104

(G-11843)
PRIORITY PLASTICS INC (PA)
500 Industrial Dr (47371-9399)
PHONE...................................260 726-7000
Andrew Srenco, *President*
William P Negrini, *President*
Maury B Poscover, *Admin Sec*
▼ **EMP:** 90 EST: 2008
SALES (est): 37.7MM **Privately Held**
SIC: 3089 Tubs, plastic (containers)

(G-11844)
QUALTECH TOOL & ENGRG INC
103 Performance Dr (47371-9012)
PHONE...................................260 726-6572
Fax: 260 726-6597
Juliet Barber, *President*
Glynn Barber, *Vice Pres*
EMP: 22
SQ FT: 22,000
SALES (est): 2.3MM **Privately Held**
SIC: 3312 3545 3544 Tool & die steel &
alloys; machine tool accessories; special
dies, tools, jigs & fixtures

(G-11845)
RED GOLD INC
957 W 200 S (47371)
PHONE...................................260 726-8140
Doug Harris, *Agent*
Wanda Sanders, *CTO*
EMP: 2
SALES (corp-wide): 226MM **Privately
Held**
WEB: www.redgold.com
SIC: 2033 4783 Tomato products: pack-
aged in cans, jars, etc.; tomato sauce:
packaged in cans, jars, etc.; tomato
purees: packaged in cans, jars, etc.; con-
tainerization of goods for shipping
PA: Red Gold, Inc.
1500 Tomato Country Way
Elwood IN 46036
765 557-5500

(G-11846)
**SONOCO PRTECTIVE
SOLUTIONS INC**
1619 N Meridian St (47371-9301)
PHONE...................................260 726-9333
EMP: 2
SALES (corp-wide): 5B **Publicly Held**
SIC: 3086 Plastics foam products
HQ: Sonoco Protective Solutions, Inc.
1 N 2nd St
Hartsville SC 29550
843 383-7000

(G-11847)
**SONOCO PRTECTIVE
SOLUTIONS INC**
1619 N Meridian St (47371-9301)
PHONE...................................260 726-9333
Fax: 260 726-6667
Penny Hethcote, *Branch Mgr*
EMP: 86
SQ FT: 90,000

SALES (corp-wide): 5B **Publicly Held**
WEB: www.createccorp.com
SIC: 2821 3089 3714 Polystyrene resins;
molding primary plastic; motor vehicle
parts & accessories
HQ: Sonoco Protective Solutions, Inc.
1 N 2nd St
Hartsville SC 29550
843 383-7000

(G-11848)
**STONEHENGE CONCRETE &
GRAVEL**
1125 W Water St (47371-1759)
PHONE...................................260 726-8282
EMP: 3 EST: 1986
SALES (est): 170K **Privately Held**
SIC: 1442 Construction Sand/Gravel

(G-11849)
TDY INDUSTRIES LLC
Portland Forge
250 E Lafayette St (47371-1099)
P.O. Box 905 (47371-0905)
PHONE...................................260 726-8121
Fax: 260 726-8021
Patrick W Bennett, *President*
Joday Auker, *Administration*
EMP: 300
SQ FT: 200,000 **Publicly Held**
SIC: 3463 3462 Nonferrous forgings; iron
& steel forgings
HQ: Tdy Industries, Llc
1000 Six Ppg Pl
Pittsburgh PA 15222
412 394-2896

(G-11850)
**THANATOS MANUFACTURING
LLC**
4263 W 200 S (47371-7291)
PHONE...................................260 251-8498
Madison Valentine, *Administration*
EMP: 2
SALES (est): 53.3K **Privately Held**
SIC: 3999 Manufacturing industries

(G-11851)
TIPSY GLASS LLC
704 W Race St (47371-1341)
PHONE...................................260 251-0021
Audrey Muhlenkamp, *Principal*
EMP: 2
SALES (est): 68.6K **Privately Held**
SIC: 2084 Wines, brandy & brandy spirits

(G-11852)
TNT CONSTRUCTION
114 Jack Imel Ave (47371-3038)
PHONE...................................260 726-2643
Eric Trobridge, *Owner*
EMP: 8
SALES (est): 422.2K **Privately Held**
SIC: 2452 Prefabricated wood buildings

(G-11853)
**TRICOUNTY SURGICAL AND
ASSOC**
Also Called: Burgermeister, Herman MD
510b W Votaw St Ste B (47371-1322)
PHONE...................................260 726-2890
Fax: 260 726-3131
Herman Burgermeister MD, *President*
Allen Shepherd MD, *President*
EMP: 2
SALES (est): 304K **Privately Held**
SIC: 3841 Surgical & medical instruments

(G-11854)
TYSON FOODS INC
1355 W Tyson Rd (47371-7997)
PHONE...................................260 726-3118
Fax: 260 726-3329
Dee Farra, *Plant Mgr*
Troy Young, *Engineer*
Levi Fuller, *Project Engr*
Randy Colclasure, *Controller*
Lisa Barnett, *Human Res Dir*
EMP: 350
SALES (corp-wide): 38.2B **Publicly Held**
SIC: 2032 2096 2051 Mexican foods:
packaged in cans, jars, etc.; potato chips
& similar snacks; bread, cake & related
products

PA: Tyson Foods, Inc.
2200 W Don Tyson Pkwy
Springdale AR 72762
479 290-4000

(G-11855)
W & M MANUFACTURING INC
1000 N Morton St (47371-1631)
PHONE...................................260 726-9800
Jim Hiester, *President*
James Hiester, *Plant Mgr*
EMP: 140 EST: 1961
SQ FT: 90,000
SALES (est): 14.7MM **Privately Held**
WEB: www.wmmanufacturing.com
SIC: 3471 Plating of metals or formed
products

Poseyville
Posey County

(G-11856)
HOEHN PLASTICS INC
11481 W 925 S (47633-9637)
P.O. Box 248 (47633-0248)
PHONE...................................812 874-3646
Fax: 812 874-3144
Jason D Hoehn, *President*
Melissa Higgins, *Vice Pres*
Virgil Hogan, *Safety Dir*
Jane Snyder, *Personnel*
EMP: 68
SQ FT: 60,000
SALES (est): 14MM **Privately Held**
WEB: www.hoehnplastics.com
SIC: 2821 Plastics materials & resins

(G-11857)
INFINITY DRONES LLC
5700 High School Rd (47633-8861)
PHONE...................................812 457-7140
EMP: 2
SALES (est): 121.8K **Privately Held**
SIC: 3721 Motorized aircraft

(G-11858)
NIX BUS SALES INC
Hwy 165 N (47633)
P.O. Box 130 (47633-0130)
PHONE...................................812 464-2576
Fax: 812 874-3409
Larry Broerman, *President*
EMP: 23
SALES (est): 1.9MM **Privately Held**
SIC: 3711 Buses, all types, assembly of

(G-11859)
NIX EQUIPMENT LLC
160 W Main St (47633-9022)
PHONE...................................812 874-2231
Matthew Nix, *Principal*
EMP: 29
SALES (est): 1.1MM **Privately Held**
SIC: 3549 Metalworking machinery

(G-11860)
PC IMPRINTS
158b Lockwood St (47633-8606)
PHONE...................................812 622-0855
EMP: 2
SALES (est): 83.9K **Privately Held**
SIC: 2752 Commercial printing, litho-
graphic

(G-11861)
REEVES FEED & GRAIN LLC
96 N Walnut St (47633-9019)
PHONE...................................812 453-3313
Jeffrey C Reeves, *Mng Member*
Christine Reeves,
EMP: 4
SALES: 500K **Privately Held**
SIC: 2099 Food preparations

(G-11862)
WESTERN GREEN LLC
5401 St Wndl Cynthiana Rd (47633-9104)
PHONE...................................812 963-3373
Zach Snyder, *President*
EMP: 50

SALES (est): 1.5MM
SALES (corp-wide): 21.1MM **Privately Held**
SIC: 3272 Concrete products
PA: Western Excelsior Corporation
901 W Grand Ave
Mancos CO 81328
970 533-7412

Princeton
Gibson County

(G-11863)
ALTEK INC
1603 E Broadway St (47670-3110)
P.O. Box 262 (47670-0262)
PHONE..................................812 385-2561
Fax: 812 385-3633
Karl G Koch, *President*
Kelly Koch, *Vice Pres*
Robin Wise, *Office Mgr*
John Kemper, *Technical Staff*
EMP: 8
SQ FT: 5,400
SALES (est): 3.1MM **Privately Held**
WEB: www.altek.us
SIC: 7694 5063 7699 Electric motor re-
pair; motors, electric; pumps & pumping
equipment repair; tool repair services

(G-11864)
BEMR LLC
Also Called: RPM Tool
106 N 1st Ave (47670-1002)
PHONE..................................812 385-8509
Matthew Robbins, *Mng Member*
EMP: 3
SQ FT: 7,000
SALES: 350K **Privately Held**
WEB: www.rpmtool.com
SIC: 3469 Machine parts, stamped or
pressed metal

(G-11865)
BERRY GLOBAL INC
889 W Gach Rd (47670-9240)
PHONE..................................812 386-1525
EMP: 2 **Publicly Held**
SIC: 3089 3081 Bottle caps, molded plas-
tic; unsupported plastics film & sheet
HQ: Berry Global, Inc.
101 Oakley St
Evansville IN 47710
812 424-2904

(G-11866)
BPREX CLOSURES LLC
Also Called: Rexam
889 W Gach Rd (47670-9240)
PHONE..................................812 386-1525
Fax: 812 386-1528
Bob Fella, *Branch Mgr*
Robert Fella, *Manager*
EMP: 87 **Publicly Held**
SIC: 3089 2671 Bowl covers, plastic;
packaging paper & plastics film, coated &
laminated
HQ: Bprex Closures, Llc
101 Oakley St
Evansville IN 47710
812 424-2904

(G-11867)
BURT PRODUCTS INC
315 S West St (47670-2155)
PHONE..................................812 386-6890
Roger P Mizeur, *President*
Jane E Mizeur, *Treasurer*
EMP: 5
SQ FT: 6,600
SALES (est): 589.9K **Privately Held**
SIC: 3621 3613 Motors, electric; switches,
electric power except snap, push button,
etc.

(G-11868)
DIVERSITY-VUTEQ LLC
825 E 350 S (47670-9222)
PHONE..................................812 761-0210
Kazumasa Watanabe, *Ch of Bd*
Taro Fukuda, *President*
Chris Spence, *Mng Member*
▲ EMP: 153

SALES (est): 6.6MM **Privately Held**
SIC: 3089 Automotive parts, plastic

(G-11869)
ENGLER MACHINE & TOOL INC
1106 W 150 S (47670-9305)
PHONE..................................812 386-6254
Fax: 812 386-6268
Tim Engler, *President*
Tammy Engler, *Corp Secy*
EMP: 10
SQ FT: 10,000
SALES (est): 1.6MM **Privately Held**
WEB: www.englermachine.com
SIC: 5531 3519 Automobile & truck equip-
ment & parts; engines, diesel & semi-
diesel or dual-fuel

(G-11870)
ENOVAPREMIER LLC
858 E 350 S (47670-9222)
PHONE..................................812 385-0576
Erin Johnson, *Human Res Mgr*
Jim Schum, *Branch Mgr*
EMP: 75 **Privately Held**
WEB: www.enovapremier.com
SIC: 3089 3714 3011 Automotive parts,
plastic; motor vehicle parts & accessories;
motorcycle tires, pneumatic
PA: Enovapremier Llc
1630 Lyndon Farm Ct # 100
Louisville KY 40223

(G-11871)
FEDERAL ASSEMBLY INC
Also Called: F A I
115 S Hall St (47670-2021)
PHONE..................................812 386-7062
Fax: 812 358-7596
Chris R Holley, *President*
Melody D Prior, *President*
Hank Potter, *Manager*
EMP: 50
SQ FT: 16,500
SALES (est): 8.6MM **Privately Held**
WEB: www.federalassembly.com
SIC: 3569 Assembly machines, non-metal-
working

(G-11872)
FIRST PLACE TROPHIES
1595 E State Road 64 (47670-8827)
PHONE..................................812 385-3279
Fax: 812 386-7916
Phyllis Ernst, *Owner*
EMP: 3
SQ FT: 1,000
SALES (est): 180.3K **Privately Held**
WEB: www.firstplacetrophies.com
SIC: 5999 3993 Trophies & plaques; signs
& advertising specialties

(G-11873)
GIBSON COUNTY COAL LLC
2579 W Gibson Coal Rd (47670-8556)
PHONE..................................812 385-1816
Fax: 812 385-0130
Joseph W Craft,
EMP: 290
SQ FT: 7,000
SALES (est): 31.1MM
SALES (corp-wide): 1.8B **Publicly Held**
WEB: www.arlpbenefits.com
SIC: 1241 1221 Coal mining services; bi-
tuminous coal surface mining
HQ: Alliance Coal, Llc
1717 S Boulder Ave # 400
Tulsa OK 74119
918 295-7600

(G-11874)
HANSEN CORPORATION
901 S 1st St (47670-2369)
PHONE..................................812 385-3000
Mike Karsonovich, *President*
Erik Davis, *Engineer*
John Muncy, *Engineer*
Steve Sallee, *Engineer*
Kevin Slagle, *Engineer*
▲ EMP: 300
SQ FT: 135,000

SALES (est): 58.9MM
SALES (corp-wide): 130MM **Privately Held**
WEB: www.hansen-motor.com
SIC: 3621 3873 3566 Motors, electric;
timing motors, synchronous, electric;
sliprings, for motors or generators; frequency converters (electric generators);
watches, clocks, watchcases & parts;
speed changers, drives & gears
HQ: Electrocraft, Inc.
1 Progress Dr
Dover NH 03820
603 742-3330

(G-11875)
HIGHWAY MACHINE CO INC
Also Called: H M C
3010 S Old Us Highway 41 (47670-9206)
PHONE..................................812 385-3639
Fax: 812 385-5232
Robert J Smith III, *President*
Henry Smith, *Plant Mgr*
Bart McKee, *Purchasing*
Greg Kermode, *Engineer*
Steve Auberry, *Financial Exec*
◆ EMP: 45
SQ FT: 25,000
SALES (est): 14MM **Privately Held**
WEB: www.hmcgears.com
SIC: 3599 Machine shop, jobbing & repair

(G-11876)
HOLZMEYER DIE & MOLD MFG CORP
333 S 2nd Ave (47670-1067)
P.O. Box 610 (47670-0610)
PHONE..................................812 386-6015
Fax: 812 386-6070
Alan Holzmeyer, *President*
Ty Koelker, *President*
Mark Burns, *Vice Pres*
Gary Powers, *Vice Pres*
Angela Controller, *Controller*
EMP: 34 EST: 1980
SQ FT: 39,600
SALES: 6MM **Privately Held**
WEB: www.holzmeyer.com
SIC: 3089 Injection molding of plastics;
thermoformed finished plastic products

(G-11877)
MARK RUSSELL
610 E Christian St (47670-2752)
PHONE..................................812 386-8069
Merla Russell, *Owner*
Mark Russell, *Co-Owner*
EMP: 3
SALES (est): 170K **Privately Held**
WEB: www.russellindustries.com
SIC: 3679 Transducers, electrical

(G-11878)
MIDNITE GRAFIX
3437 S 125 E (47670-9214)
PHONE..................................812 386-9430
Lori Barrell, *Owner*
EMP: 3
SALES: 100K **Privately Held**
SIC: 2759 Screen printing

(G-11879)
NAAS INC
Also Called: Naas Heating and Cooling
200 Tennessee St (47670-3016)
PHONE..................................812 385-3578
Jim F Naas, *President*
Lisa Nass, *Corp Secy*
EMP: 15
SQ FT: 900
SALES (est): 1.5MM **Privately Held**
WEB: www.naas.com
SIC: 3273 1711 Ready-mixed concrete;
warm air heating & air conditioning con-
tractor

(G-11880)
NIDEC MOTOR CORPORATION
Also Called: Hurst Manufacturing Division
1551 E Broadway St (47670-3137)
PHONE..................................812 385-2564
Fax: 812 386-7504
Greg Davis, *Plant Mgr*
EMP: 85

SALES (corp-wide): 13.9B **Privately Held**
SIC: 3625 3594 Motor controls, electric;
fluid power pumps & motors
HQ: Nidec Motor Corporation
8050 West Florissant Ave
Saint Louis MO 63136

(G-11881)
PRINCETON PUBLISHING INC
Also Called: Princeton Daily Clarion
100 N Gibson St (47670-1855)
P.O. Box 30 (47670-0030)
PHONE..................................812 385-2525
Fax: 812 386-6199
Gary Blackburn, *President*
Mona J Brehm, *Corp Secy*
William Brehm, *Vice Pres*
EMP: 50
SQ FT: 10,000
SALES (est): 3MM
SALES (corp-wide): 224.9MM **Privately Held**
WEB: www.pdclarion.com
SIC: 2711 2752 2731 Commercial printing
& newspaper publishing combined; com-
mercial printing, lithographic; book pub-
lishing
PA: Brehm Communications, Inc.
16644 W Bernardo Dr # 300
San Diego CA 92127
858 451-6200

(G-11882)
SOUTHLAND CONTAINER CORP
Also Called: Milagro Packaging
Rr 1 Box 174 (47670)
PHONE..................................812 385-0774
Dave Kaat, *Owner*
EMP: 14
SALES (corp-wide): 1.2B **Privately Held**
WEB: www.concept-pkg.com
SIC: 2653 Boxes, corrugated: made from
purchased materials
PA: Southland Container Corporation
60 Fairview Church Rd
Spartanburg SC 29303
864 578-0085

(G-11883)
TBIN LLC
Also Called: Toyota Boshoku Indiana
1698 S 100 W (47670-9351)
PHONE..................................812 491-9100
Christopher P Felts,
EMP: 2 EST: 2007
SALES (est): 180K **Privately Held**
SIC: 3999 Barber & beauty shop equip-
ment

(G-11884)
TOYOTA BOSHOKU AMERICA INC
1698 S 100 W (47670-9351)
PHONE..................................812 385-2040
Shigetoshi Miyoshi, *CEO*
Takanichi Japan, *Principal*
Hiromi Harada, *Treasurer*
EMP: 10
SALES (est): 3MM **Privately Held**
SIC: 2531 Seats, automobile

(G-11885)
TOYOTA BOSHOKU AMERICA INC
1698 S 100 W (47670-9351)
PHONE..................................812 385-2040
Hiromi Harada, *Branch Mgr*
EMP: 23
SALES (corp-wide): 13.1B **Privately Held**
SIC: 3711 5013 Automobile assembly, in-
cluding specialty automobiles; automotive
trim
HQ: Toyota Boshoku America, Inc.
1360 Dolwick Dr Ste 125
Erlanger KY 41018
859 817-4000

(G-11886)
TOYOTA BOSHOKU INDIANA LLC
Also Called: Tisa
1698 S 100 W (47670-9351)
PHONE..................................812 491-9100
Brian Malinao, *President*
Jeff Willis, *Training Super*

(PA)=Parent Co (HQ)=Headquarters (DH)=Div Headquarters
✪ = New Business established in last 2 years

2018 Harris Indiana
Industrial Directory

445

GEOGRAPHIC

▲ **EMP:** 575
SQ FT: 200,000
SALES (est): 69.1MM
SALES (corp-wide): 13.1B **Privately Held**
WEB: www.tisa1.com
SIC: 2531 Seats, automobile
HQ: Toyota Boshoku America, Inc.
1360 Dolwick Dr Ste 125
Erlanger KY 41018
859 817-4000

(G-11887)
TOYOTA MOTOR MFG IND INC (DH)
4000 S Tulip Tree Dr (47670-2300)
P.O. Box 4000 (47670-4000)
PHONE..............................812 387-2266
Seizo Okamoto, *Ch of Bd*
Norm Bafunno, *President*
Tsutomu Kobayashi, *Corp Secy*
Chuck Klus, *Plant Engr Mgr*
Bill Dyer, *Human Res Mgr*
◆ **EMP:** 213
SALES (est): 848.4MM
SALES (corp-wide): 275.7B **Privately Held**
SIC: 3711 Truck & tractor truck assembly

(G-11888)
TRI STATE MONUMENT COMPANY
106 E Brumfield Ave (47670-1704)
PHONE..............................812 386-7303
Colvin Funeral Home, *Owner*
Mark Walter, *General Mgr*
EMP: 3
SALES: 100K **Privately Held**
SIC: 3272 Monuments & grave markers, except terrazo

(G-11889)
VUTEQ USA INC
819 E 350 S (47670-9222)
PHONE..............................812 385-2584
Erin Higginson, *Human Res Mgr*
Shuji Mapsuyama, *Branch Mgr*
David Hayden, *Supervisor*
EMP: 5
SALES (corp-wide): 439.7MM **Privately Held**
WEB: www.vuteqil.com
SIC: 3711 Automobile assembly, including specialty automobiles
HQ: Vuteq Usa, Inc.
100 Carley Dr
Georgetown KY 40324
502 863-6322

Quincy
Owen County

(G-11890)
HOOSIER MARINE
10151 N Us Highway 231 (47456-8551)
PHONE..............................812 879-5549
Andy Naanes, *Principal*
EMP: 2
SALES (est): 192.9K **Privately Held**
SIC: 3732 Boat building & repairing

(G-11891)
JOHN GARRISON WOODWORKING LLC
2951 Combes Rd (47456-8506)
PHONE..............................765 795-4681
John Garrison, *Principal*
EMP: 2 EST: 2010
SALES (est): 171.4K **Privately Held**
SIC: 2431 Millwork

Ramsey
Harrison County

(G-11892)
ALVIN J NIX
2820 Fairdale Rd Nw (47166-8408)
PHONE..............................812 347-2510
Alvin J Nix, *Principal*
EMP: 2

SALES (est): 160K **Privately Held**
SIC: 3715 Truck trailers

(G-11893)
KELLUM IMPRINTS INC
Also Called: Kellum Imprints & Trophies
1675 Highway 64 Nw (47166-8546)
PHONE..............................812 347-2546
Fax: 812 347-3803
Annissa J Reas, *President*
Annissa Reas, *President*
Joseph Kellum, *Vice Pres*
Ann Kellum, *Admin Sec*
EMP: 3
SALES (est): 242.8K **Privately Held**
SIC: 2395 Embroidery products, except schiffli machine

(G-11894)
RAMSEY POPCORN CO INC
5645 Clover Valley Rd Nw (47166-8252)
PHONE..............................812 347-2441
Fax: 812 347-3336
Wilfred E Sieg Jr, *President*
Steve Wetzel, *President*
Daniel R Sieg, *Vice Pres*
Melissa Carpenter, *Export Mgr*
Eric Sieg, *Treasurer*
▲ **EMP:** 35 EST: 1946
SQ FT: 30,000
SALES (est): 36.1MM **Privately Held**
WEB: www.ramseypopcorn.com
SIC: 5145 2099 Popcorn & supplies; popcorn, packaged: except already popped

(G-11895)
TYSON FOODS INC
495 Highway 64 Nw (47166-8534)
PHONE..............................812 347-2452
Fax: 812 347-2453
Troy Mason, *Business Mgr*
Jay Wall, *Manager*
EMP: 20
SALES (corp-wide): 38.2B **Publicly Held**
SIC: 2015 Poultry slaughtering & processing
PA: Tyson Foods, Inc.
2200 W Don Tyson Pkwy
Springdale AR 72762
479 290-4000

Redkey
Jay County

(G-11896)
BELL AQUACULTURE LLC (PA)
9885 W State Road 67 (47373-8900)
P.O. Box 2205, Minneapolis MN (55402-0205)
PHONE..............................765 369-3100
Brian Baldwin, *CEO*
Norman McCowan, *President*
Deb Snider, *Controller*
Shelli Brunson, *Manager*
EMP: 40
SALES (est): 9.9MM **Privately Held**
SIC: 2092 Fresh or frozen packaged fish

(G-11897)
FAB SOLUTIONS LLC
10135 W 800 S (47373-9236)
PHONE..............................765 744-2671
Ron Byers, *Senior Partner*
Brooke Byers, *Opers-Prdtn-Mfg*
Dillon Byers, *Manager*
EMP: 6
SQ FT: 4,000
SALES (est): 574K **Privately Held**
SIC: 3496 Miscellaneous fabricated wire products

(G-11898)
GARY DEVOSS
409 S Spencer St (47373-9293)
PHONE..............................765 369-2492
Gary Devoss, *CEO*
EMP: 2
SALES (est): 174.9K **Privately Held**
SIC: 3571 Electronic computers

(G-11899)
R N A INDUSTRIES CORP ✪
251 E Sheridan St (47373-9279)
P.O. Box 61 (47373-0061)
PHONE..............................765 288-4413
EMP: 2 EST: 2017
SALES (est): 100.7K **Privately Held**
SIC: 3999 Manufacturing industries

Reelsville
Putnam County

(G-11900)
C C COOK AND SON LBR CO INC
6236 W Us Highway 40 (46171-8809)
PHONE..............................765 672-4235
Fax: 765 672-4600
Richard R Cook, *President*
Charles H Cook, *Corp Secy*
EMP: 40
SQ FT: 40,000
SALES (est): 5.5MM **Privately Held**
SIC: 2448 2421 Pallets, wood; kiln drying of lumber

(G-11901)
FABSHOP
8732 W County Road 1075 S (46171-8875)
PHONE..............................317 549-1681
Nevil Algie, *Owner*
Nan Algie, *Co-Owner*
EMP: 2
SALES (est): 89K **Privately Held**
SIC: 3498 Tube fabricating (contract bending & shaping)

(G-11902)
KESTER LOGGING INC
5596 S County Road 625 W (46171-9620)
PHONE..............................765 672-8170
Jerry Kester, *President*
Mary Jane Kester, *Corp Secy*
EMP: 3
SALES (est): 750K **Privately Held**
SIC: 2411 Logging camps & contractors

(G-11903)
RELIABLE SEALANTS LLC
3382 W County Road 875 S (46171-9453)
PHONE..............................765 672-4455
Mary Giles, *Partner*
James Giles, *Partner*
EMP: 3
SALES (est): 500K **Privately Held**
SIC: 2891 Caulking compounds

Remington
Jasper County

(G-11904)
AMERICAN FIBERTECH CORPORATION (PA)
4 N New York St (47977-8000)
P.O. Box 220 (47977-0220)
PHONE..............................219 261-3586
Fax: 219 261-2211
Robin R Meister, *President*
Jay A Wiegand, *Corp Secy*
Rosemary Nagel, *Clerk*
EMP: 74
SQ FT: 36,160
SALES (est): 58.2MM **Privately Held**
WEB: www.ind-pallet-corp.com
SIC: 2448 Pallets, wood

(G-11905)
BUNGE NORTH AMERICA FOUNDATION
Also Called: Solae
413 N Cressy Ave (47977-8830)
P.O. Box 127 (47977-0127)
PHONE..............................219 261-2124
Eric Barber, *Production*
Chris Steindrenner, *Manager*
EMP: 40 **Privately Held**
WEB: www.bungemarion.com
SIC: 2075 Soybean protein concentrates & isolates

HQ: Bunge North America Foundation
1391 Timberlk Mnr Pkwy # 31
Chesterfield MO 63017
314 872-3030

(G-11906)
DUPONT
Also Called: Solae
600 Harrington St (47977-8881)
PHONE..............................219 261-2124
Dale Perman, *Plant Mgr*
◆ **EMP:** 60
SALES (est): 6.4MM **Privately Held**
SIC: 2075 Soybean oil mills

(G-11907)
IMPACT FORGE GROUP LLC
18325 S 580 W (47977-8601)
PHONE..............................219 261-2115
Barry Gaines, *Branch Mgr*
EMP: 165
SALES (corp-wide): 6.2B **Publicly Held**
SIC: 3462 Iron & steel forgings
HQ: Impact Forge Group, Llc
2805 Norcross Dr
Columbus IN 47201
812 342-4437

(G-11908)
IRVING MATERIALS INC
318 W South St (47977-8626)
P.O. Box 328 (47977-0328)
PHONE..............................219 261-2441
Fax: 219 866-7889
Jerry Cyr, *Branch Mgr*
EMP: 5
SQ FT: 750
SALES (corp-wide): 800.6MM **Privately Held**
SIC: 3273 Ready-mixed concrete
PA: Irving Materials, Inc.
8032 N State Road 9
Greenfield IN 46140
317 326-3101

(G-11909)
SOLAE LLC
413 N Cressy Ave (47977-8830)
PHONE..............................800 325-7108
EMP: 2
SALES (corp-wide): 62.4B **Publicly Held**
SIC: 2075 2076 Soybean oil mills; vegetable oil mills
HQ: Solae, Llc
4300 Duncan Ave
Saint Louis MO 63110
314 659-3000

(G-11910)
SOLAE LLC
413 N Cressy Ave (47977-8830)
PHONE..............................219 261-2124
Dale Perman, *Plant Mgr*
Eric Barber, *Engineer*
Rich Hall, *Maintence Staff*
EMP: 60
SALES (corp-wide): 62.4B **Publicly Held**
WEB: www.solae.com
SIC: 2075 Soybean protein concentrates & isolates
HQ: Solae, Llc
4300 Duncan Ave
Saint Louis MO 63110
314 659-3000

Rensselaer
Jasper County

(G-11911)
AIRODAPT LLC
809 E Stewart Dr (47978-3218)
PHONE..............................559 331-0156
Frank Airoso, *Mng Member*
Jolyne Airoso, *Mng Member*
EMP: 2
SALES (est): 103K **Privately Held**
SIC: 3423 7389 Carpenters' hand tools, except saws: levels, chisels, etc.;

(G-11912)
AMERICAN MELT BLOWN FILTRATION
1030 E Elm St (47978-2364)
PHONE..................................219 866-3500
Fred Geyer, *President*
Scott Lucero, *Vice Pres*
Stephanie Geyer, *Treasurer*
◆ EMP: 33 EST: 2011
SQ FT: 50,000
SALES (est): 8.7MM **Privately Held**
SIC: 2621 3589 5075 Milk filter disks; water filters & softeners, household type; air filters

(G-11913)
ARCHER-DANIELS-MIDLAND COMPANY
Also Called: ADM
1201 W State Road 114 (47978-7265)
PHONE..................................219 866-2810
EMP: 6
SALES (corp-wide): 60.8B **Publicly Held**
WEB: www.admworld.com
SIC: 2041 Flour & other grain mill products
PA: Archer-Daniels-Midland Company
77 W Wacker Dr Ste 4600
Chicago IL 60601
312 634-8100

(G-11914)
ARCHER-DANIELS-MIDLAND COMPANY
Also Called: ADM
9179 W State Road 14 (47978-8645)
PHONE..................................219 866-3939
Jeff Henady, *Manager*
EMP: 8
SALES (corp-wide): 60.8B **Publicly Held**
WEB: www.admworld.com
SIC: 2041 Flour & other grain mill products
PA: Archer-Daniels-Midland Company
77 W Wacker Dr Ste 4600
Chicago IL 60601
312 634-8100

(G-11915)
B & C MACHINING INC
Also Called: Hi-Tech Hydraulics
320 E Merritt St (47978-2060)
PHONE..................................219 924-5411
Fax: 219 924-6356
Jim Leibrand, *President*
Roman Zdonek, *Chairman*
Edward Moskalick, *Vice Pres*
EMP: 20
SQ FT: 9,800
SALES (est): 3.3MM **Privately Held**
SIC: 3599 7699 Machine shop, jobbing & repair; hydraulic equipment repair

(G-11916)
CAMPBELL PRINTING CO INC
125 N Van Rensselaer St (47978-2651)
PHONE..................................219 866-5913
William F Campbell, *President*
EMP: 4 EST: 1941
SQ FT: 2,200
SALES: 225K **Privately Held**
WEB: www.printing-by-campbell.com
SIC: 2752 2759 Commercial printing, offset; letterpress printing

(G-11917)
CHIEF INDUSTRIES INC
Chief Buildings Div
1225 E Maple St (47978-2120)
PHONE..................................219 866-4121
Fax: 219 866-4124
John Price, *Branch Mgr*
EMP: 146
SALES (corp-wide): 331.1MM **Privately Held**
WEB: www.chiefind.com
SIC: 3448 3441 3316 Buildings, portable: prefabricated metal; fabricated structural metal; cold finishing of steel shapes
PA: Chief Industries, Inc.
3942 W Old Highway 30
Grand Island NE 68803
308 389-7200

(G-11918)
CONAGRA BRANDS INC
Also Called: Golden Valley Microwave Foods
750 E Drexel Pkwy (47978-7294)
PHONE..................................740 387-2722
Ken Dobin, *Plant Mgr*
Jeff Stevens, *Branch Mgr*
EMP: 211
SALES (corp-wide): 7.9B **Publicly Held**
WEB: www.conagra.com
SIC: 2099 Popcorn, packaged: except already popped
PA: Conagra Brands, Inc.
222 Merchandise Mart Plz
Chicago IL 60654
312 549-5000

(G-11919)
CONAGRA BRANDS INC
Also Called: Hunt Wesson Foods
750 E Drexel Pkwy (47978-7294)
PHONE..................................219 866-3020
Fax: 219 866-3263
Kenneth Dobin, *Branch Mgr*
EMP: 227
SALES (corp-wide): 7.9B **Publicly Held**
WEB: www.conagra.com
SIC: 5149 2099 2096 Groceries & related products; food preparations; potato chips & similar snacks
PA: Conagra Brands, Inc.
222 Merchandise Mart Plz
Chicago IL 60654
312 549-5000

(G-11920)
DAVIS WATER SERVICES INC
Also Called: Davis Water Conditioning
4898 S 1000 W (47978-8835)
PHONE..................................219 394-2270
Michael L Davis, *President*
EMP: 3
SALES (est): 310K **Privately Held**
SIC: 3589 Sewage & water treatment equipment; water treatment equipment, industrial; water filters & softeners, household type

(G-11921)
DEZIGNS BY CINDY ZIESE
5270 W 300 N (47978-7488)
PHONE..................................219 819-8786
Cindy Ziese, *Owner*
EMP: 3
SALES (est): 160K **Privately Held**
SIC: 3993 Signs & advertising specialties; advertising artwork; advertising novelties; displays & cutouts, window & lobby

(G-11922)
FAIRYLAN LLC
7175 N 700 W (47978-7442)
PHONE..................................219 866-3077
Philip Richards,
EMP: 2
SALES (est): 84.3K **Privately Held**
SIC: 2741 Miscellaneous publishing

(G-11923)
FILTRATION PARTS INCORPORATED
513 N Melville St (47978-2369)
PHONE..................................704 661-8135
Fred Geyer, *President*
Stephanie Geyer, *Treasurer*
EMP: 10 EST: 2016
SALES (est): 433K **Privately Held**
SIC: 3089 3082 Fittings for pipe, plastic; tubes, unsupported plastic

(G-11924)
FYT FUELS LLC
1722 W 400 N (47978-8541)
PHONE..................................520 304-6451
Lawrence Sakin, *CEO*
David Bradley, *Ch of Bd*
Adam Siegel, *General Ptnr*
Larry Bruce, *CFO*
EMP: 4
SALES (est): 229.8K **Privately Held**
SIC: 2869 Industrial organic chemicals

(G-11925)
GENOVA PRODUCTS INC
Also Called: Rensselaer Products
1100 E Elm St (47978-2363)
PHONE..................................219 866-5136
Fax: 219 866-2142
Greg Biggs, *Plant Mgr*
Dave Barden, *Safety Mgr*
Barry Baker, *Branch Mgr*
EMP: 60
SQ FT: 7,500
SALES (corp-wide): 190.8MM **Privately Held**
WEB: www.genovaproducts.com
SIC: 3089 3084 Plastic processing; plastics pipe
PA: Genova Products, Inc.
7034 E Court St
Davison MI 48423
810 744-4500

(G-11926)
GENUINE MACHINE DESIGN INC
Also Called: G M D
509 E Drexel Pkwy (47978-7294)
PHONE..................................219 866-8060
Scott Vollmer, *President*
Phil Albrecht, *Vice Pres*
▼ EMP: 9
SQ FT: 12,000
SALES (est): 1.3MM **Privately Held**
WEB: www.gmdmachinery.com
SIC: 3599 Custom machinery

(G-11927)
HENSLEY CUSTOM CABINETRY
3281 E 400 N (47978-7330)
PHONE..................................219 843-5331
Kim Hensley, *Owner*
Robert Hensley, *Owner*
EMP: 3
SALES (est): 140K **Privately Held**
SIC: 2521 Cabinets, office: wood

(G-11928)
IROQUOIS BIO-ENERGY CO LLC (HQ)
751 W State Road 114 (47978-7362)
P.O. Box 218 (47978-0218)
PHONE..................................219 866-5990
Roger Boer, *Treasurer*
Stephanie Vanderhere, *Accountant*
Adam Barten, *Manager*
Shannan Wagner, *Info Tech Mgr*
Keith Gibson,
EMP: 9
SALES (est): 8.4MM **Privately Held**
SIC: 2869 Fuels

(G-11929)
JENNY LYNN SOAP COMPANY LLC
402 S Mckinley Ave (47978-2900)
PHONE..................................219 863-8243
Julie Evers, *Mng Member*
EMP: 3 EST: 2014
SALES (est): 159.1K **Privately Held**
SIC: 2841 Soap: granulated, liquid, cake, flaked or chip

(G-11930)
KANKAKEE VALLEY PUBLISHING CO
Also Called: Rensselaer Republican
117 N Van Rensselaer St (47978-2651)
PHONE..................................219 866-5111
Larry Perrotto, *President*
Gary Yount, *Principal*
J Michael Perrotto, *Vice Pres*
EMP: 161
SALES (est): 5.6MM **Privately Held**
WEB: www.rensselaerrepublican.com
SIC: 2711 2752 Commercial printing & newspaper publishing combined; commercial printing, lithographic
PA: Community Media Group Inc.
805 S Logan St
West Frankfort IL 62896

(G-11931)
LEGGETT & PLATT INCORPORATED
Also Called: Sealy Components
1132 N Cullen St (47978-2009)
P.O. Box 258 (47978-0258)
PHONE..................................219 866-7181
Fax: 219 866-3865
Ron Morgan, *Manager*
EMP: 300
SQ FT: 95,000
SALES (corp-wide): 3.9B **Publicly Held**
SIC: 2515 Box springs, assembled
PA: Leggett & Platt, Incorporated
1 Leggett Rd
Carthage MO 64836
417 358-8131

(G-11932)
MORRIS MACHINE & TOOL
828 N Scott St (47978-2158)
PHONE..................................219 866-3018
Russell Morris, *Owner*
EMP: 2
SALES (est): 139.8K **Privately Held**
SIC: 3599 7692 Machine shop, jobbing & repair; welding repair

(G-11933)
NEW NGC INC
Also Called: National Gypsum Company
1325 E Maple St (47978-2116)
PHONE..................................219 866-7570
Shane Bwhaley, *Plant Mgr*
David Holston, *Manager*
Randy Sopher, *Manager*
EMP: 92
SALES (corp-wide): 685.8MM **Privately Held**
SIC: 3275 Gypsum products; building board, gypsum; plaster & plasterboard, gypsum; wallboard, gypsum
HQ: New Ngc, Inc.
2001 Rexford Rd
Charlotte NC 28211

(G-11934)
OUTTADAWAY LLC
503 W Washington St (47978-2714)
PHONE..................................219 866-8885
Ned J Tonner, *Mng Member*
EMP: 2
SALES (est): 119K **Privately Held**
SIC: 3496 Miscellaneous fabricated wire products

(G-11935)
REINFORCEMENTS DESIGN
3195 1/2 W Clark St (47978-8893)
PHONE..................................219 866-8626
Fax: 219 866-8626
Rein Von Treger, *Owner*
EMP: 5
SALES: 250K **Privately Held**
SIC: 7336 3993 Graphic arts & related design; signs & advertising specialties

(G-11936)
RENSSELAER EAGLE VAULT CORP
Also Called: Rensselaer Septic Tanks
250 N Mckinley Ave (47978-2641)
P.O. Box 70 (47978-0070)
PHONE..................................219 866-5123
Eric Jackson, *Owner*
William C Jackson, *President*
EMP: 5
SQ FT: 2,000
SALES (est): 811.6K **Privately Held**
SIC: 5087 3272 Concrete burial vaults & boxes; monuments, concrete; septic tanks, concrete

(G-11937)
RENSSELAER PRINT CO
116 N Cullen St (47978-2644)
PHONE..................................219 866-5000
Morris Barlow, *Owner*
Pamela Barlow, *Co-Owner*
EMP: 2
SQ FT: 200
SALES (est): 208K **Privately Held**
SIC: 2752 Commercial printing, offset

G
E
O
G
R
A
P
H
I
C

(G-11938)
SIGNS OF SEASONS
2675 W Clark St (47978-8892)
PHONE.................................219 866-4507
Suzanne Gilmore, *Owner*
EMP: 2
SALES (est): 80K **Privately Held**
WEB: www.signsoftheseasons.com
SIC: 3993 Signs & advertising specialties

(G-11939)
SOUTHERN FUEL LLC
1250 N Mckinley Ave (47978-2068)
PHONE.................................219 689-3552
Derich Schultz, *Administration*
EMP: 3
SALES (est): 191.9K **Privately Held**
SIC: 2869 Fuels

(G-11940)
STARK TRUSS COMPANY INC
1317 N Owen St (47978-7532)
PHONE.................................219 866-2772
Fax: 219 866-2795
Craig Wagner, *Branch Mgr*
EMP: 90
SALES (corp-wide): 207.5MM **Privately Held**
WEB: www.starktruss.com
SIC: 2439 Trusses, wooden roof
PA: Stark Truss Company, Inc.
109 Miles Ave Sw
Canton OH 44710
330 478-2100

(G-11941)
TAG SOFTWARE
4093 N Us Highway 231 (47978-7564)
PHONE.................................219 866-3100
EMP: 2
SALES (est): 100K **Privately Held**
SIC: 7372 Prepackaged Software Services

(G-11942)
TALBERT MANUFACTURING INC (PA)
1628 W State Road 114 (47978-7266)
PHONE.................................219 866-7141
Fax: 219 866-5437
Andy Tanner, *President*
Bobbi Kaufman, *Vice Pres*
Greg Smith, *Vice Pres*
Shawn Capper, *Engineer*
Brian Sharp, *Controller*
EMP: 200 EST: 1957
SQ FT: 100,000
SALES (est): 49.3MM **Privately Held**
WEB: www.talbertmfg.com
SIC: 3715 Truck trailers

(G-11943)
TRUMAN RITCHIE
Also Called: Electric Motor Company
262 E 550 N (47978-8578)
PHONE.................................219 956-2211
Truman Ritchie, *Owner*
EMP: 2
SALES: 57K **Privately Held**
SIC: 7694 Electric motor repair

Reynolds
White County

(G-11944)
BUSCHMAN TANK CARS INC
601 E 2nd St (47980-8151)
P.O. Box 273 (47980-0273)
PHONE.................................219 984-5444
Richard Buschman, *President*
Beverly Buschman, *Corp Secy*
EMP: 2
SALES: 0 **Privately Held**
SIC: 3444 Culverts, sheet metal

(G-11945)
EXCEL CO-OP INC
Also Called: Fertilizer Plant
319 N Us Highway 421 (47980-8126)
P.O. Box 278 (47980-0278)
PHONE.................................219 984-5950
Jeff Ruemler, *Principal*
EMP: 9

SALES (corp-wide): 30.3MM **Privately Held**
WEB: www.excelco-op.com
SIC: 1479 Fertilizer mineral mining
PA: Excel Co-Op, Inc
5250 E Us Highway 36 # 1000
Avon IN 46123
317 745-4491

(G-11946)
MONSANTO COMPANY
371 N Diener Rd (47980-8010)
PHONE.................................574 870-0397
EMP: 62
SALES (corp-wide): 41.2B **Privately Held**
SIC: 2879 Agricultural chemicals
HQ: Monsanto Company
800 N Lindbergh Blvd
Saint Louis MO 63167
314 694-1000

(G-11947)
PERFECT PIG INC
332 W 100 N (47980-8051)
PHONE.................................219 984-5355
Brian Furrer, *Partner*
EMP: 3
SALES (est): 359.5K **Privately Held**
SIC: 2013 Pigs' feet, cooked & pickled: from purchased meat

(G-11948)
SCOTTS MIRACLE-GRO COMPANY
Also Called: Morning Song Wild Bird Feed
10 E 100 S (47980-8120)
PHONE.................................219 984-6110
Dan Medley, *Branch Mgr*
EMP: 58
SALES (corp-wide): 2.6B **Publicly Held**
WEB: www.scotts.com
SIC: 2873 2048 Fertilizers: natural (organic), except compost; prepared feeds
PA: The Scotts Miracle-Gro Company
14111 Scottslawn Rd
Marysville OH 43040
937 644-0011

(G-11949)
US MOLDERS INC
59 W 100 N (47980-8052)
PHONE.................................219 984-5058
Tim Hebble, *President*
Colleen Bowers, *Office Mgr*
EMP: 42
SQ FT: 50,000
SALES (est): 8.1MM **Privately Held**
SIC: 3089 Molding primary plastic; injection molding of plastics

Richland
Spencer County

(G-11950)
GOLDMAN MACHINE SERVICES
5233 W County Road 600 N (47634-9315)
PHONE.................................812 359-5440
Kenneth Goldman, *Owner*
EMP: 2 EST: 1994
SALES (est): 90K **Privately Held**
SIC: 3339 Beryllium metal

Richmond
Wayne County

(G-11951)
A PLUS SIGN AREA LTG SPCALISTS
920 Progress Dr (47374-8407)
PHONE.................................765 966-4857
Eddie Thompson, *Partner*
Jeff Thompson, *Partner*
EMP: 4 EST: 1996
SALES (est): 290K **Privately Held**
SIC: 3993 Signs & advertising specialties

(G-11952)
AHAUS TOOL & ENGINEERING INC
200 Industrial Pkwy (47374-3704)
P.O. Box 280 (47375-0280)
PHONE.................................765 962-3573
Fax: 765 962-3426
Kevin M Ahaus, *President*
Fredric A Ahaus, *Chairman*
Jeff Sheridan, *Vice Pres*
Jeffrey S Sheridan, *Vice Pres*
Marie Tilton, *Production*
▲ EMP: 90 EST: 1946
SQ FT: 65,000
SALES: 19.1MM **Privately Held**
WEB: www.ahaus.com
SIC: 3599 3544 Custom machinery; special dies & tools

(G-11953)
ANGIES PRINTING LLC
1751 Sheridan St (47374-1811)
PHONE.................................765 966-6237
Randy Sullivan, *Principal*
EMP: 2
SALES (est): 83.9K **Privately Held**
SIC: 2752 Commercial printing, lithographic

(G-11954)
APEX AG SOLUTIONS LLC
5532 Arba Pike (47374-9230)
PHONE.................................937 564-5421
Torey W Hunt, *Mng Member*
EMP: 14 EST: 2013
SALES: 2.1MM **Privately Held**
SIC: 1389 8711 Construction, repair & dismantling services; engineering services

(G-11955)
APLUS SIGNS
920 Progress Dr (47374-8407)
PHONE.................................765 966-4857
Fax: 765 962-4858
Jeff Thompson, *Principal*
EMP: 2
SALES (est): 236.1K **Privately Held**
SIC: 3993 Signs, not made in custom sign painting shops

(G-11956)
ASAHI TEC AMERICA CORPORATION
1757 Sheridan St (47374-1811)
PHONE.................................765 962-8399
Fax: 765 962-8353
Yoshihiko Okaeaki, *Vice Pres*
EMP: 9
SQ FT: 9,000
SALES (est): 1.4MM **Privately Held**
SIC: 3652 Compact laser discs, prerecorded

(G-11957)
AUGUSTIN PRTG & DESIGN SVCS (PA)
Also Called: Prinit Press
211 Nw 7th St (47374-4051)
PHONE.................................765 966-7130
Fax: 765 966-7131
Mike Gibbs, *Owner*
EMP: 5
SQ FT: 1,800
SALES (est): 265K **Privately Held**
WEB: www.prinitpress.com
SIC: 2752 2732 Commercial printing, offset; books: printing only; pamphlets: printing only, not published on site

(G-11958)
AUNT MILLIES
415 N 12th St (47374-3209)
PHONE.................................765 966-6691
Jon Rice, *Principal*
EMP: 2
SALES (est): 107.7K **Privately Held**
SIC: 2051 Bakery: wholesale or wholesale/retail combined

(G-11959)
B&F PLASTICS INC
540 N 8th St (47374-2304)
PHONE.................................765 962-6125
Fax: 765 962-7170
Bruce Upchurch, *President*

Bob Cramer, *Vice Pres*
Chris Smith, *Vice Pres*
Dave Cheek, *Plant Mgr*
Todd Suttle, *Plant Engr*
▼ EMP: 53
SQ FT: 20,000
SALES (est): 20MM **Privately Held**
WEB: www.bfplastics.com
SIC: 3081 Unsupported plastics film & sheet

(G-11960)
BARRETT PAVING MATERIALS INC
5834 Inke Rd (47374-9618)
PHONE.................................765 935-3060
Fax: 765 962-8446
Claude Seibel, *Manager*
EMP: 12
SQ FT: 2,000
SALES (corp-wide): 95.5MM **Privately Held**
WEB: www.barrettpaving.com
SIC: 1429 1422 5032 Igneous rock, crushed & broken-quarrying; crushed & broken limestone; stone, crushed or broken
HQ: Barrett Paving Materials Inc.
3 Becker Farm Rd Ste 307
Roseland NJ 07068
973 533-1001

(G-11961)
BELDEN 1993 LLC
Belden Division
2200 Us Highway 27 S (47374-7437)
PHONE.................................606 348-8433
Robert J Vokurka, *Branch Mgr*
EMP: 200
SALES (corp-wide): 2.3B **Publicly Held**
SIC: 3357 Nonferrous wiredrawing & insulating
HQ: Belden 1993 Llc
1 N Brentwood Blvd # 1500
Saint Louis MO 63105

(G-11962)
BELDEN INC
Also Called: Belden Cdt
350 Nw N St (47374-1828)
PHONE.................................765 962-7561
Donald Carter, *Engineer*
Brett Crawford, *Engineer*
Ruth Gray, *Engineer*
Scott Dillon, *Branch Mgr*
Jason Parker, *Manager*
EMP: 700
SALES (corp-wide): 2.3B **Publicly Held**
WEB: www.belden.com
SIC: 3357 3496 3315 Building wire & cable, nonferrous; miscellaneous fabricated wire products; steel wire & related products
PA: Belden Inc.
1 N Brentwood Blvd Fl 15
Saint Louis MO 63105
314 854-8000

(G-11963)
BELDEN WIRE & CABLE CO LLC
Also Called: Belden Cdt
2200 Us Highway 27 S (47374-7437)
PHONE.................................606 348-8433
Fax: 606 348-3499
Dale Parker, *Principal*
Harry Hubler, *Director*
Andy Brown, *Technician*
EMP: 325
SALES (corp-wide): 2.3B **Publicly Held**
WEB: www.belden.com
SIC: 3357 Communication wire
HQ: Belden Wire & Cable Company Llc
2200 Us Highway 27 S
Richmond IN 47374

(G-11964)
BERRY GLOBAL INC
630 Commerance Rd (47374)
PHONE.................................765 966-1414
Gary Teegarden, *Principal*
EMP: 2 **Publicly Held**
SIC: 3089 3081 Bottle caps, molded plastic; unsupported plastics film & sheet

HQ: Berry Global, Inc.
101 Oakley St
Evansville IN 47710
812 424-2904

(G-11965)
BERRY GLOBAL INC
630 Commerce Rd (47374-2600)
PHONE...................................765 962-4253
Gary Teegarden, *Manager*
EMP: 330 **Publicly Held**
WEB: www.6sens.com
SIC: 3089 3081 Bottle caps, molded plastic; unsupported plastics film & sheet
HQ: Berry Global, Inc.
101 Oakley St
Evansville IN 47710
812 424-2904

(G-11966)
BILLS PRINTING
1310 Nw 5th St (47374-1840)
PHONE...................................765 962-7674
Fax: 765 966-9835
William A Cole, *Owner*
EMP: 6
SALES: 500K **Privately Held**
WEB: www.billsprinting.com
SIC: 2752 Commercial printing, lithographic

(G-11967)
BOSTON TOOL COMPANY INC
800 S 9th St (47374-6236)
P.O. Box 1521 (47375-1521)
PHONE...................................765 935-6282
Fax: 765 935-7332
Suzanne A Meier, *President*
Adolph T Meier, *Vice Pres*
Adolf T Meier, *Admin Sec*
EMP: 16
SQ FT: 10,000
SALES (est): 1.1MM **Privately Held**
SIC: 3544 Special dies & tools

(G-11968)
BUMBLEBEE QUICK PRINT INC
211 Nw 7th St (47374-4051)
PHONE...................................765 962-0368
Fax: 765 965-9088
Kenneth Pust, *President*
Larry L Parker, *President*
Gayla Parker, *Corp Secy*
EMP: 5
SQ FT: 2,500
SALES (est): 515.1K **Privately Held**
SIC: 2752 Commercial printing, offset

(G-11969)
CHAMPION TARGET
232 Industrial Pkwy (47374-3704)
P.O. Box 1151 (47375-1151)
PHONE...................................765 966-7745
Fax: 765 966-7747
Tim Emmenegger, *President*
EMP: 30 **EST:** 2010
SALES (est): 576.3K **Privately Held**
SIC: 3255 Clay refractories

(G-11970)
CMJ & ASSOCIATES CORPORATION
160 Fort Wayne Ave (47374-3058)
PHONE...................................765 962-1947
Gregory L Dale, *President*
EMP: 8
SALES (est): 1.2MM **Privately Held**
SIC: 3496 Miscellaneous fabricated wire products

(G-11971)
COLOR-BOX LLC
1056 Industries Rd (47374-9769)
PHONE...................................765 983-7618
Tim Hous, *Principal*
EMP: 86
SALES (corp-wide): 44.4B **Privately Held**
SIC: 2653 Corrugated & solid fiber boxes
HQ: Color-Box Llc
623 S G St
Richmond IN 47374
765 966-7588

(G-11972)
COLOR-BOX LLC (DH)
Also Called: Georgia-Pacific
623 S G St (47374-6134)
PHONE...................................765 966-7588
Fax: 765 935-4243
James Hannan, *CEO*
Christian Fischer, *Exec VP*
Michael E Adams, *Senior VP*
Julie Brehm, *Senior VP*
Tye Darland, *Senior VP*
EMP: 100
SALES (est): 178.4MM
SALES (corp-wide): 44.4B **Privately Held**
WEB: www.georgia-pacific.com
SIC: 2653 Boxes, corrugated: made from purchased materials
HQ: Georgia-Pacific Llc
133 Peachtree St Nw
Atlanta GA 30303
404 652-4000

(G-11973)
CONTRACT INDUS TOOLING INC (PA)
Also Called: CIT
2351 Production Ct (47374-8408)
PHONE...................................765 966-1134
Kim Wuertemberger, *President*
Mike Catey, *Vice Pres*
Kim Brooks, *Manager*
Michael J Catey, *Admin Sec*
▲ **EMP:** 80
SQ FT: 118,000
SALES (est): 23MM **Privately Held**
WEB: www.c-i-t.com
SIC: 3599 Machine shop, jobbing & repair

(G-11974)
CREATEIT HLTHCARE SLUTIONS INC
814 E Main St Ste 3 (47374-4316)
PHONE...................................765 993-0988
Jamie Schnitzius, *CEO*
Jonathan Meade, *COO*
EMP: 3 **EST:** 2015
SQ FT: 200
SALES (est): 107.9K **Privately Held**
SIC: 7372 Business oriented computer software

(G-11975)
CUSTOM DIE CASTING INC
1134 Nw T St (47374-1454)
PHONE...................................765 935-3979
Fax: 765 935-6487
Kenneth W Zarbock Jr, *President*
EMP: 15
SQ FT: 12,000
SALES (est): 1.8MM **Privately Held**
WEB: www.custompartnet.com
SIC: 3363 3364 Aluminum die-castings; zinc & zinc-base alloy die-castings

(G-11976)
DAS BIG DAWG BREWHAUS LLC
3407 National Rd W (47374-4416)
PHONE...................................765 965-9463
Jeffrey Haist, *President*
Melanie Haist, *Owner*
Mike Miller, *Owner*
EMP: 9
SALES (est): 1MM **Privately Held**
SIC: 2082 Beer (alcoholic beverage)

(G-11977)
DICK BAUMGARTNERS BASKET
707 Beeson Rd (47374-9452)
PHONE...................................765 220-1767
Richard E Baumgartner, *President*
EMP: 32
SALES (est): 504.6K **Privately Held**
SIC: 7032 3949 Sporting camps; basketball equipment & supplies, general

(G-11978)
DWYER-WILBERT INC
Also Called: Dwyer-Wilbert Monument
1014 National Rd W (47374-5141)
PHONE...................................765 962-3605
Fax: 765 962-4223
William J Dwyer, *President*
Martha Dwyer, *Corp Secy*
EMP: 6

SQ FT: 6,500
SALES: 500K **Privately Held**
SIC: 3281 5999 Burial vaults, stone; monuments, finished to custom order

(G-11979)
E C T FRANKLIN CONTROL SYSTEMS
Also Called: Ect
1831 W Main St (47374-3821)
PHONE...................................765 939-2531
Fax: 765 939-2631
Harold Brown, *President*
EMP: 8
SALES (est): 161K **Privately Held**
SIC: 3625 Electric controls & control accessories, industrial

(G-11980)
ELDER GROUP INC
4251 W Industries Rd (47374-1385)
PHONE...................................765 966-7676
Fax: 765 966-7677
Gerald H Davis, *President*
Alan H Elder, *Chairman*
Joe Elleman, *Prdtn Mgr*
Gary Cox, *Design Engr*
Mark Harrington, *CFO*
EMP: 80
SQ FT: 125,000
SALES (est): 23.8MM **Privately Held**
WEB: www.reeloptions.com
SIC: 2655 3995 Reels (fiber), textile: made from purchased material; casket linings

(G-11981)
ELEVATOR EQUIPMENT CORPORATION
2230 Nw 12th St (47374-1471)
PHONE...................................765 966-7761
Fax: 765 966-7299
Jim Snyder, *Safety Mgr*
Kevin Antrim, *Sales Staff*
Jerry Benjamin, *Manager*
Rick Hooker, *Manager*
EMP: 52
SALES (corp-wide): 19.6MM **Privately Held**
WEB: www.eecovalves.com
SIC: 3534 3621 3594 3593 Elevators & moving stairways; motors & generators; fluid power pumps & motors; fluid power cylinders & actuators; miscellaneous fabricated wire products; fabricated structural metal
PA: Elevator Equipment Corporation
4035 Goodwin Ave
Los Angeles CA 90039
323 245-0147

(G-11982)
ENDURANCE METALS LLC
1300 Rose City Blvd (47374-9581)
PHONE...................................765 960-5834
Brandon C Searcy, *Mng Member*
Michael Tresten,
EMP: 4
SALES: 600K **Privately Held**
SIC: 3312 Stainless steel

(G-11983)
ENVIRO FINISHING OF INDIANA
511 Industrial Pkwy (47374-7941)
PHONE...................................765 966-8183
Fax: 765 966-8036
Robert Livesay, *President*
Doug Ullery, *Vice Pres*
Erika Wilson, *Assistant*
EMP: 10
SALES (est): 1.3MM **Privately Held**
WEB: www.envirofinishing.com
SIC: 2426 Hardwood dimension & flooring mills

(G-11984)
ENVIROTECH EXTRUSION INC
4810 Woodside Dr (47374-2634)
PHONE...................................765 966-8068
Fax: 765 964-4557
Jerry Martin, *President*
Jack Beilfuss Sr, *General Mgr*
Richard Ward, *Vice Pres*
Robert Shortle, *CFO*
▲ **EMP:** 50
SQ FT: 76,000

SALES (est): 8MM **Privately Held**
WEB: www.enviroext.com
SIC: 3061 2273 Mechanical rubber goods; carpets & rugs

(G-11985)
EXPRESS IMPRESSIONS PRTG LLC
1334 Fairacres Rd (47374-1110)
PHONE...................................765 966-2679
Fax: 765 965-1890
Sandy Smith, *Owner*
EMP: 4
SALES: 175K **Privately Held**
WEB: www.expressimpressions.com
SIC: 2752 7334 Commercial printing, lithographic; photocopying & duplicating services

(G-11986)
FEDERAL CARTRIDGE COMPANY
232 Industrial Pkwy (47374-3704)
PHONE...................................765 966-7745
Tim Emmenedder, *Manager*
Tim Emmenegger, *Manager*
EMP: 4
SALES (corp-wide): 2.3B **Publicly Held**
WEB: www.federalcartridge.com
SIC: 3949 Trap racks (clay targets)
HQ: Federal Cartridge Company
900 Bob Ehlen Dr
Anoka MN 55303
800 379-1732

(G-11987)
FEDERATED PUBLICATIONS INC
Also Called: Federated Publicators
1175 N A St (47374-3226)
PHONE...................................765 962-1575
EMP: 190
SALES (corp-wide): 3.1B **Publicly Held**
SIC: 2711 Newspapers: publishing only, not printed on site
HQ: Federated Publications Inc.
155 Van Buren St W
Battle Creek MI 49017
269 962-5394

(G-11988)
FRICKERS INC
3237 Chester Blvd (47374-1014)
PHONE...................................765 965-6655
Fax: 765 965-6184
Jamie Oler, *General Mgr*
Carie Outon, *General Mgr*
Renee Lattimore, *Regional Mgr*
Lisa Wackler, *Regional Mgr*
Matt Thatcher, *Manager*
EMP: 28 **EST:** 1997
SALES (est): 2.4MM **Privately Held**
SIC: 3965 5813 5812 Buttons & parts; drinking places; eating places

(G-11989)
GANNETT CO INC
Also Called: Palladium Item, The
1175 North Dr (47374)
PHONE...................................765 962-1575
Fax: 765 973-4570
Patrick Doyle, *Principal*
EMP: 160
SALES (corp-wide): 3.1B **Publicly Held**
SIC: 2711 Newspapers, publishing & printing
PA: Gannett Co., Inc.
7950 Jones Branch Dr
Mc Lean VA 22102
703 854-6000

(G-11990)
GRAFCOR INC
Also Called: Innomark Communications
601 Nw 5th St (47374-2972)
PHONE...................................765 966-7030
Fax: 765 966-5677
William Fair, *President*
Gary Boens, *Vice Pres*
Paul Molyneaux, *Vice Pres*
EMP: 22
SQ FT: 20,000
SALES (est): 3.1MM **Privately Held**
WEB: www.grafcor.com
SIC: 2752 Commercial printing, offset

(PA)=Parent Co (HQ)=Headquarters (DH)=Div Headquarters
✪ = New Business established in last 2 years

2018 Harris Indiana
Industrial Directory

449

GEOGRAPHIC

(G-11991)
GRANITE MARBLE & MORE INC
Also Called: Wholesale Stone Distribution
425 Nw K St (47374-2161)
PHONE......................................765 939-4846
Senthil P Muruganantham, *President*
Senthil Muruganantham, *Vice Pres*
▲ EMP: 5
SALES (est): 602.8K **Privately Held**
WEB: www.gmandmore.com
SIC: 3281 Granite, cut & shaped

(G-11992)
GROSS ROOFING SHEET METALS
1751 Sheridan St (47374-1811)
PHONE......................................765 965-0068
EMP: 2 EST: 2015
SALES (est): 117.3K **Privately Held**
SIC: 3444 Sheet metalwork

(G-11993)
H & P TOOL CO INC
610 S G St (47374-6135)
P.O. Box 486 (47375-0486)
PHONE......................................765 962-4504
Fax: 765 962-4506
George A Peters, *President*
Carolyn Peters, *Corp Secy*
Vickie Jackson, *Office Mgr*
EMP: 25
SQ FT: 25,000
SALES (est): 2.4MM **Privately Held**
WEB: www.hptoolco.com
SIC: 3545 3544 Tools & accessories for machine tools; jigs & fixtures

(G-11994)
HAGERSTOWN PLASTICS INC
621 S J St (47374-6139)
PHONE......................................765 939-3849
Debra Wilson, *President*
Darrell Rutledge, *President*
Leon Pasley Jr, *Vice Pres*
EMP: 3
SQ FT: 3,600
SALES: 1MM **Privately Held**
SIC: 3089 Injection molding of plastics

(G-11995)
HANGER PRSTHETCS & ORTHO INC
Also Called: Orpro Prosthetics & Orthotics
1200 Chester Blvd (47374-1905)
PHONE......................................765 966-5069
Vinit Asar, *CEO*
Carrie Melton, *Manager*
EMP: 3
SALES (corp-wide): 1B **Publicly Held**
SIC: 3842 5999 Limbs, artificial; orthopedic appliances; orthopedic & prosthesis applications
HQ: Hanger Prosthetics & Orthotics, Inc.
10910 Domain Dr Ste 300
Austin TX 78758
512 777-3800

(G-11996)
HILLS PET NUTRITION INC
Also Called: Hill's Pet Products
2859 Salisbury Rd N (47374-9737)
PHONE......................................765 966-4549
Chris Curtis, *Manager*
EMP: 187
SALES (corp-wide): 15.4B **Publicly Held**
SIC: 2047 Dog & cat food
HQ: Hill's Pet Nutrition, Inc.
400 Sw 8th Ave Ste 101
Topeka KS 66603
785 354-8523

(G-11997)
HILLS PET NUTRITION INC
2325 Union Pike (47374-9701)
P.O. Box 2146 (47375-2146)
PHONE......................................765 935-7071
Fax: 765 935-7275
Kathy Zaleha, *Plant Mgr*
Peggy Seward, *Receptionist*
EMP: 180
SALES (corp-wide): 15.4B **Publicly Held**
SIC: 2047 Dog & cat food

HQ: Hill's Pet Nutrition, Inc.
400 Sw 8th Ave Ste 101
Topeka KS 66603
785 354-8523

(G-11998)
HOLLAND COLOURS AMERICAS INC
1501 Progress Dr (47374-1486)
PHONE......................................765 935-0329
Fax: 765 966-3376
R Harmsen, *Principal*
Joseph Gleeson, *Sales Staff*
Gert Luiten, *Manager*
Pam Riggle, *Manager*
Primsam Patalinghug, *Technology*
▲ EMP: 85
SQ FT: 60,500
SALES (est): 34.7MM
SALES (corp-wide): 103.6MM **Privately Held**
SIC: 2865 Color pigments, organic
HQ: Holland Colours N.V.
Halvemaanweg 1
Apeldoorn 7323
553 680-700

(G-11999)
HOOSIER CONTAINER INC
1001 Indiana Ave (47374-2867)
P.O. Box 546 (47375-0546)
PHONE......................................765 966-2541
Fax: 765 962-3859
William Akers II, *President*
Michael Akey Jr, *Corp Secy*
James F Akers, *CFO*
Grayson Fitzhugh, *Shareholder*
EMP: 35
SQ FT: 78,000
SALES (est): 5.9MM **Privately Held**
WEB: www.hoosiercontainer.com
SIC: 2653 Boxes, corrugated: made from purchased materials; pads, corrugated: made from purchased materials

(G-12000)
HOOVEN - DAYTON CORP
165 Industrial Pkwy (47374-3702)
PHONE......................................765 935-3999
EMP: 28
SALES (corp-wide): 22MM **Privately Held**
SIC: 2679 2672 2671 2759 Converted Paper Products, Nec, Nsk
PA: The Hooven - Dayton Corp
511 Byers Rd
Miamisburg OH 45342
937 233-4473

(G-12001)
IMPERIAL PRODUCTS LLC
Also Called: Homeshield
451 Industrial Pkwy (47374-3709)
P.O. Box 368 (47375-0368)
PHONE......................................765 966-0322
Fax: 765 966-2403
David Petratis, *Principal*
Brent L Korb, *CFO*
Jairaj T Chetnani, *Treasurer*
Kevin P Delaney, *Admin Sec*
▲ EMP: 69
SQ FT: 90,000
SALES (est): 12.7MM **Publicly Held**
SIC: 3442 Window & door frames
PA: Quanex Building Products Corporation
1800 West Loop S Ste 1500
Houston TX 77027

(G-12002)
INX INTERNATIONAL INK CO
1056 Industries Rd (47374-9769)
PHONE......................................765 939-6625
Fax: 765 939-8556
Randy Robinson, *Manager*
EMP: 2
SALES (corp-wide): 1.4B **Privately Held**
SIC: 2893 Printing ink
HQ: Inx International Ink Co
150 N Martingale Rd # 700
Schaumburg IL 60173
630 382-1800

(G-12003)
IU EAST BUSINESS OFFICE
2325 Chester Blvd (47374-1220)
PHONE......................................765 973-8218

Kathryn Cruz-Uribe, *Chancellor*
David Frantz, *Manager*
Molly Vanderpool, *Hlthcr Dir*
EMP: 7
SALES (est): 534K **Privately Held**
SIC: 2761 Continuous forms, office & business

(G-12004)
J J LITES
4469 Webster Rd (47374-9530)
PHONE......................................765 966-3252
Mike Jenkins, *Vice Pres*
EMP: 2
SALES (est): 125K **Privately Held**
SIC: 3647 Automotive lighting fixtures

(G-12005)
JASON INCORPORATED
Also Called: Janesville Acoustics
3031 W Industries Rd (47374-1390)
PHONE......................................248 455-7919
Dave Cataldi, *Branch Mgr*
EMP: 7
SALES (corp-wide): 648.6MM **Publicly Held**
SIC: 3714 Motor vehicle parts & accessories
HQ: Jason Incorporated
833 E Michigan St Ste 900
Milwaukee WI 53202
414 277-9300

(G-12006)
JASON INCORPORATED
Sealeze
2350 Salisbury Rd N (47374-9726)
PHONE......................................800 787-7325
Fax: 804 271-3428
Doug Pollak, *Division Pres*
David Farmer, *Prdtn Mgr*
David Chrisman, *Engineer*
Angela Clarke, *Marketing Staff*
Sara Strube, *Marketing Staff*
EMP: 54
SQ FT: 5,000
SALES (corp-wide): 648.6MM **Publicly Held**
WEB: www.jasoninc.com
SIC: 3991 3442 Brushes, household or industrial; metal doors, sash & trim
HQ: Jason Incorporated
833 E Michigan St Ste 900
Milwaukee WI 53202
414 277-9300

(G-12007)
JASON INCORPORATED
Assembled Products Group
2350 Salisbury Rd N (47374-9726)
PHONE......................................847 215-1948
Steve Carolla, *Branch Mgr*
EMP: 200
SALES (corp-wide): 648.6MM **Publicly Held**
WEB: www.jasoninc.com
SIC: 3469 3699 Metal stampings; electrical equipment & supplies
HQ: Jason Incorporated
833 E Michigan St Ste 900
Milwaukee WI 53202
414 277-9300

(G-12008)
JM HUTTON & CO INC (PA)
Also Called: J M Hutton & Company
1501 S 8th St (47374-6907)
P.O. Box 129 (47375-0129)
PHONE......................................765 962-3591
Richard E Jeffers, *President*
Richard N Jeffers, *President*
◆ EMP: 80
SQ FT: 170,000
SALES: 19.2MM **Privately Held**
WEB: www.jmhutton.com
SIC: 3995 3469 Burial caskets; metal stampings

(G-12009)
JM HUTTON & CO INC
Also Called: JM Hutton & Company
1117 N E St (47374-3249)
P.O. Box 129 (47375-0129)
PHONE......................................765 962-3506
Fax: 765 966-0149
Richard N Jeffers, *President*

EMP: 44
SALES (corp-wide): 19.2MM **Privately Held**
WEB: www.jmhutton.com
SIC: 3995 Burial caskets
PA: J.M. Hutton & Co., Inc.
1501 S 8th St
Richmond IN 47374
765 962-3591

(G-12010)
JOHNS MANVILLE CORPORATION
814 Richmond Ave (47374-2896)
P.O. Box 428 (47375-0428)
PHONE......................................765 973-5200
Fax: 765 973-5373
Robert Stevens, *Plant Mgr*
Emerson Bungard, *Branch Mgr*
Dave Young, *Manager*
Anthony Persyn, *Senior Mgr*
EMP: 115
SALES (corp-wide): 242.1B **Publicly Held**
WEB: www.jm.com
SIC: 3296 Fiberglass insulation
HQ: Johns Manville Corporation
717 17th St Ste 800
Denver CO 80202
303 978-2000

(G-12011)
LAND OLAKES INC
505 N 4th St (47374-2358)
PHONE......................................765 962-9561
EMP: 15
SALES (corp-wide): 12.8B **Privately Held**
SIC: 2048 Prepared feeds
PA: Land O'lakes, Inc.
4001 Lexington Ave N
Arden Hills MN 55126
651 375-2222

(G-12012)
MACALLISTER MACHINERY CO INC
Also Called: Caterpillar Authorized Dealer
4791 E Main St (47374-2674)
PHONE......................................765 966-0759
Chad Brogan, *Branch Mgr*
EMP: 11
SALES (corp-wide): 1B **Publicly Held**
WEB: www.macallister.com
SIC: 7359 3541 5084 5082 Equipment rental & leasing; machine tools, metal cutting type; machine tools & accessories; construction & mining machinery; heavy construction equipment rental
PA: Macallister Machinery Co Inc
6300 Southeastern Ave
Indianapolis IN 46203
317 545-2151

(G-12013)
MAGAWS OF BOSTON
Also Called: Magaws of Boston The
5774 State Road 227 S (47374-9424)
PHONE......................................765 935-6170
William Magaw, *Principal*
EMP: 2 EST: 2009
SALES (est): 57.1K **Privately Held**
SIC: 8999 7389 3299 Sculptor's studio; ; architectural sculptures: gypsum, clay, papier mache, etc.

(G-12014)
MARTIN EKWLOR PHRMCUTICALS INC
Also Called: Vesco
2800 Southeast Pkwy (47374-5857)
P.O. Box 565 (47375-0565)
PHONE......................................765 962-4410
Fax: 765 966-5158
Ike Martin Ekwealor, *President*
Susan Ekwealor, *Vice Pres*
EMP: 15
SQ FT: 5,000
SALES (est): 1.5MM **Privately Held**
SIC: 2834 5122 Pharmaceutical preparations; pharmaceuticals

(G-12015)
MASTERBRAND CABINETS INC
1340 Rose City Blvd (47374-9581)
P.O. Box 1567 (47375-1567)
PHONE............................765 966-3940
Dan Colley, *Branch Mgr*
EMP: 360
SALES (corp-wide): 5.2B **Publicly Held**
WEB: www.mbcabinets.com
SIC: 2434 Wood kitchen cabinets
HQ: Masterbrand Cabinets, Inc.
1 Masterbrand Cabinets Dr
Jasper IN 47546
812 482-2527

(G-12016)
MEREDITHS INC
Also Called: Saver Systems
800 S 7th St (47374-6123)
PHONE............................765 966-5084
Fax: 765 935-4999
John Meredith, *President*
Nancy Freeman, *Marketing Staff*
▲ EMP: 25
SQ FT: 30,000
SALES (est): 6.2MM **Privately Held**
WEB: www.chimneyliner.com
SIC: 2899 Waterproofing compounds

(G-12017)
MICHAEL DARGIE
Also Called: Dargie Racing Engines
1700 Nw 11th St (47374-1419)
PHONE............................765 935-2241
Fax: 765 935-3779
Michael Dargie, *Owner*
EMP: 3 EST: 1997
SALES: 250K **Privately Held**
SIC: 3519 Gasoline engines

(G-12018)
MILSO INDUSTRIES INC
401 Industrial Pkwy (47374-3709)
PHONE............................765 966-8012
Fax: 765 935-6264
Dale Palmer, *Manager*
EMP: 100
SALES (corp-wide): 1.5B **Publicly Held**
SIC: 5087 3995 Caskets; burial caskets
HQ: Milso Industries Inc.
534 Union St
Brooklyn NY 11215
718 624-4593

(G-12019)
**MOSEY MANUFACTURING CO
INC (PA)**
262 Fort Wayne Ave (47374-2392)
PHONE............................765 983-8800
Fax: 765 966-4355
George N Mosey, *President*
Stephen A Mosey, *Exec VP*
Dan Kindley, *Vice Pres*
Kenneth L Mackey, *Vice Pres*
John Proctor, *Manager*
EMP: 27 EST: 1946
SQ FT: 40,000
SALES (est): 78.8MM **Privately Held**
WEB: www.moseymfg.com
SIC: 3541 Machine tools, metal cutting
type

(G-12020)
**MOSEY MANUFACTURING CO
INC**
Also Called: Mosey Plant II
1700 N F St (47374-2563)
PHONE............................765 983-8870
Fax: 765 935-0927
Ken Mackey, *Systems Mgr*
EMP: 175
SALES (corp-wide): 78.8MM **Privately
Held**
WEB: www.moseymfg.com
SIC: 3541 3714 Machine tools, metal cut-
ting type; motor vehicle transmissions,
drive assemblies & parts
PA: Mosey Manufacturing Co Inc
262 Fort Wayne Ave
Richmond IN 47374
765 983-8800

(G-12021)
**MOSEY MANUFACTURING CO
INC**
Machine Tool Innovators Div
534 N 17th St (47374-3333)
PHONE............................765 983-8870
Fax: 765 962-6338
Vince Johnson, *Manager*
EMP: 6
SALES (corp-wide): 78.8MM **Privately
Held**
WEB: www.moseymfg.com
SIC: 3541 Machine tools, metal cutting
type
PA: Mosey Manufacturing Co Inc
262 Fort Wayne Ave
Richmond IN 47374
765 983-8800

(G-12022)
**MOSEY MANUFACTURING CO
INC**
Also Called: Mosey Manufacturing Plant 7
1700 N F St (47374-2563)
PHONE............................765 983-8889
Fax: 765 983-8891
Jim Wilman, *Manager*
EMP: 65
SALES (corp-wide): 78.8MM **Privately
Held**
WEB: www.moseymfg.com
SIC: 3541 3714 3322 Machine tools,
metal cutting type; motor vehicle parts &
accessories; malleable iron foundries
PA: Mosey Manufacturing Co Inc
262 Fort Wayne Ave
Richmond IN 47374
765 983-8800

(G-12023)
NEW HOLLAND RICHMOND INC
3100 W Industries Rd (47374-1391)
P.O. Box 249, Centerville (47330-0249)
PHONE............................765 962-7724
Jessie Straeter, *CEO*
Melinda Straeter, *Admin Sec*
EMP: 2 EST: 2013
SALES (est): 405.2K **Privately Held**
SIC: 3523 Farm machinery & equipment

(G-12024)
NIXON TOOL CO INC
301 N 3rd St (47374-3005)
P.O. Box 1505 (47375-1505)
PHONE............................765 966-6608
Fax: 765 966-1987
Scott Nixon, *President*
Jan Liebert, *Purchasing*
Troy See, *QC Mgr*
Rose Burroughs, *Financial Exec*
EMP: 30
SQ FT: 15,000
SALES: 300K **Privately Held**
WEB: www.nixontool.com
SIC: 3599 3544 3545 Machine shop, job-
bing & repair; electrical discharge machin-
ing (EDM); jigs & fixtures; gauges
(machine tool accessories)

(G-12025)
**OERLIKON BALZERS COATING
USA**
1580 Progress Dr (47374-1485)
PHONE............................765 935-7424
Fax: 765 935-7631
Norman B Lawton, *President*
Scott Murray, *General Mgr*
Bradley L Lawton, *Exec VP*
Jeffrey L Lawton, *Vice Pres*
Boyd E Moilanen, *CFO*
EMP: 21
SALES (est): 4.8MM
SALES (corp-wide): 224.7MM **Privately
Held**
SIC: 2851 Coating, air curing
PA: Star Cutter Co.
23461 Industrial Park Dr
Farmington Hills MI 48335
248 474-8200

(G-12026)
OSBORN INTL
1400 Industries Rd (47374-1377)
PHONE............................765 965-3722
EMP: 5

SALES (est): 30.1K **Privately Held**
SIC: 3291 Buffing or polishing wheels,
abrasive or nonabrasive

(G-12027)
PAUST INC (PA)
Also Called: Paust Printers
14 N 10th St (47374-3142)
P.O. Box 1326 (47375-1326)
PHONE............................765 962-1507
Fax: 765 962-4997
Kenneth E Paust, *President*
Linda Paust, *Vice Pres*
EMP: 14
SQ FT: 14,500
SALES (est): 6.7MM **Privately Held**
WEB: www.paust.com
SIC: 5199 2752 Advertising specialties;
commercial printing, offset

(G-12028)
PETERSON SANKO CORP
505 Industrial Pkwy (47374-7941)
PHONE............................765 966-9656
Fax: 765 966-8684
Lisa Wolf, *Supervisor*
EMP: 2 EST: 2010
SALES (est): 181.5K **Privately Held**
SIC: 3714 Motor vehicle parts & acces-
sories

(G-12029)
PFRANK QUARTER HORSES
3921 Park Elwood Rd (47374-0600)
PHONE............................765 220-0257
EMP: 2
SALES (est): 77.4K **Privately Held**
SIC: 3131 Quarters

(G-12030)
PONTONE INDUSTRIES LLC
401 Industrial Pkwy (47374-3709)
PHONE............................765 966-8012
Harry Pontone,
Michael Pontone,
◆ EMP: 130
SALES (est): 8.8MM **Privately Held**
SIC: 3995 Burial caskets

(G-12031)
PRETTY BRILLIANT LLC
Also Called: Fbapower
822 E Main St (47374-4331)
PHONE............................765 277-2308
Chris Green, *Partner*
EMP: 7
SALES (est): 448.3K **Privately Held**
SIC: 4813 2741 ;

(G-12032)
**PRIMEX COLOR
COMPOUNDING**
1235 N F St (47374-2448)
PHONE............................800 222-5116
EMP: 2
SALES (corp-wide): 1.1B **Privately Held**
SIC: 2865 Dyes & pigments
HQ: Primex Color, Compounding & Addi-
tives Corporation
61 River Dr
Garfield NJ 07026
800 282-7933

(G-12033)
**PRIMEX DESIGN FABRICATION
CORP**
400 Industrial Pkwy (47374-3727)
PHONE............................765 935-2990
Fax: 765 966-2196
Mike Cramer, *President*
Debbie Robinson, *Draft/Design*
Joanie Clark, *Project Engr*
May Johnson, *Human Res Dir*
Cleve Campbell, *Manager*
▼ EMP: 90
SALES (est): 17.9MM
SALES (corp-wide): 1.1B **Privately Held**
WEB: www.woodruffcorp.com
SIC: 3089 Plastic containers, except foam
HQ: Primex Plastics Corporation
1235 N F St
Richmond IN 47374
765 966-7774

(G-12034)
**PRIMEX PLASTICS
CORPORATION (HQ)**
1235 N F St (47374-2448)
PHONE............................765 966-7774
Fax: 765 935-1083
Mike Cramer, *President*
Steve Cramer, *General Mgr*
Jeff Longsworth, *General Mgr*
Ray Van Walleghem, *General Mgr*
Matt Brunner, *Business Mgr*
▲ EMP: 500 EST: 1965
SQ FT: 1,000,000
SALES (est): 447.9MM
SALES (corp-wide): 1.1B **Privately Held**
WEB: www.primexplastics.com
SIC: 3081 2821 Plastic film & sheet; poly-
ethylene film; thermoplastic materials
PA: Icc Industries Inc.
460 Park Ave Fl 7
New York NY 10022
212 521-1700

(G-12035)
**PRODUCTIVITY FABRICATORS
INC**
2332 Flatley Rd (47374-1334)
PHONE............................765 966-2896
Jon R Odom, *President*
Connie Odom, *Vice Pres*
EMP: 10 EST: 1994
SQ FT: 40,000
SALES (est): 2.2MM **Privately Held**
WEB: www.cyberprofab.com
SIC: 3441 Building components, structural
steel

(G-12036)
PTC ALLIANCE CORPORATION
1480 Nw 11th St (47374-1469)
PHONE............................765 259-3334
Peter Whiting, *CEO*
Cary Hart, *President*
Tom Crowley, *CFO*
Dennis Smith, *Maintence Staff*
EMP: 20
SALES (est): 4MM **Privately Held**
SIC: 3317 Steel pipe & tubes

(G-12037)
**PTC TUBULAR PRODUCTS LLC
(HQ)**
1480 Nw 11th St (47374-1469)
PHONE............................765 259-3334
Kerry Hart, *Vice Pres*
Dave Mc Donald, *CFO*
EMP: 66
SALES (est): 33.6MM **Privately Held**
SIC: 3317 Steel pipe & tubes

(G-12038)
PURINA ANIMAL NUTRITION LLC
1759 Sheridan St (47374-1811)
P.O. Box 548 (47375-0548)
PHONE............................765 962-8547
Fax: 765 962-8169
Marty Ingemanfon, *Opers-Prdtn-Mfg*
EMP: 47
SALES (corp-wide): 12.8B **Privately Held**
WEB: www.landolakesidd.com
SIC: 2048 Stock feeds, dry; poultry feeds;
feed supplements
HQ: Purina Animal Nutrition Llc
1080 County Road F W
Shoreview MN 55126

(G-12039)
QUALITRONICS INC (PA)
1200 Nw O St (47374-1495)
PHONE............................765 966-2039
Fax: 765 962-4807
Chris Cornett, *CEO*
Jj Cornett, *Vice Pres*
Dennis Eaton, *Vice Pres*
EMP: 60
SQ FT: 24,000
SALES: 6MM **Privately Held**
WEB: www.qualitronicsinc.com
SIC: 3679 Harness assemblies for elec-
tronic use: wire or cable

(G-12040)
QUANEX HOMESHIELD LLC
451 Industrial Pkwy (47374-3709)
PHONE............................765 966-0322

Stephanie Rogers, *Production*
Tim Harris, *Technical Mgr*
Geoff Williams, *Engineer*
Kenneth Maurer, *Controller*
Willie Mullins, *Manager*
EMP: 69　**Publicly Held**
SIC: 3442 Window & door frames
HQ: Quanex Homeshield, Llc
　　311 W Coleman St
　　Rice Lake WI 54868
　　715 234-9061

(G-12041)
RECYCLING CENTER INC
630 S M St (47374-6842)
P.O. Box 2038 (47375-2038)
PHONE.................................765 966-8295
Fax: 765 966-0398
Jack Edelman, *President*
Debra Edelman, *Vice Pres*
EMP: 100
SQ FT: 25,000
SALES (est): 30.4MM　**Privately Held**
WEB: www.recyclingcenter.com
SIC: 5093 4953 3341 3231 Ferrous
　metal scrap & waste; refuse collection &
　disposal services; secondary nonferrous
　metals; products of purchased glass; pulp
　mills

(G-12042)
REEVES MANUFACTURING INC
1214 Sheridan St (47374-2125)
PHONE.................................765 935-3875
Fax: 765 935-4033
Dennis Frame, *President*
Deborah Reeves, *Corp Secy*
EMP: 7
SQ FT: 15,000
SALES (est): 827.6K　**Privately Held**
SIC: 3441 5051 3469 Fabricated struc-
　tural metal; iron & steel (ferrous) prod-
　ucts; metal stampings

(G-12043)
RICHMOND BAKING CO
520 N 6th St (47374-2353)
P.O. Box 698 (47375-0698)
PHONE.................................765 962-8535
Fax: 765 962-2253
James R Quigg, *CEO*
William M Quigg, *President*
Tim Kaatz, *Vice Pres*
Gerald Lady, *Vice Pres*
Jerry Lady, *Vice Pres*
EMP: 135　**EST:** 1902
SQ FT: 180,000
SALES (est): 49.3MM　**Privately Held**
WEB: www.richmondbaking.com
SIC: 2052 Cookies; crackers, dry; bakery
　products, dry

(G-12044)
RICHMOND BAKING GEORGIA INC
520 N 6th St (47374-2353)
P.O. Box 698 (47375-0698)
PHONE.................................765 962-8535
EMP: 3
SALES (est): 68.6K　**Privately Held**
SIC: 2052 Cookies & crackers

(G-12045)
RICHMOND CASTING COMPANY
1775 Rich Rd (47374-1479)
P.O. Box 1247 (47375-1247)
PHONE.................................765 935-4090
Fax: 765 935-2168
Gill McBride, *President*
Garry England, *Executive*
EMP: 35
SQ FT: 28,000
SALES (est): 7.9MM　**Privately Held**
WEB: www.richmondcasting.com
SIC: 3321 Gray iron castings; ductile iron
　castings

(G-12046)
RICHMOND PATTERN
301 N 3rd St (47374-3005)
PHONE.................................765 935-7342
Bruce Linginfelter, *Principal*
EMP: 2
SALES (est): 174.9K　**Privately Held**
WEB: www.richmondpattern.com
SIC: 3543 Industrial patterns

(G-12047)
ROMARK INDUSTRIES INC
1751 S 8th St (47374-6897)
P.O. Box 1423 (47375-1423)
PHONE.................................765 966-6211
Fax: 765 962-2628
Danny Sullivan, *President*
Patricia Sullivan, *Corp Secy*
EMP: 50
SQ FT: 50,000
SALES (est): 6.5MM　**Privately Held**
WEB: www.romark-ind.com
SIC: 3995 7261 Burial caskets; funeral
　service & crematories

(G-12048)
SHELL PACKAGING CORPORATION
Also Called: Flexcon
400 Industrial Pkwy (47374-3727)
PHONE.................................765 965-6861
Gordon Gaebel, *Engineer*
Pat Cullum, *Finance Mgr*
Kerry Madison, *Manager*
Anna Mennerick, *Manager*
Mike Duncan, *CTO*
EMP: 2
SALES (corp-wide): 14MM　**Privately Held**
WEB: www.flexcontainer.com
SIC: 2631 Packaging board
PA: Shell Packaging Corporation
　　200 Connell Dr Ste 1200
　　Berkeley Heights NJ 07922
　　908 871-7000

(G-12049)
SHELL PIPE LINE CORPORATION
1221 S 9th St (47374-6970)
PHONE.................................765 962-1329
Mack Kotta, *Owner*
EMP: 2
SALES (corp-wide): 305.1B　**Privately Held**
SIC: 2911 Gasoline
HQ: Shell Pipe Line Corporation
　　2 Shell Plz Ste 1160
　　Houston TX 77002
　　713 241-6161

(G-12050)
SILGAN WHITE CAP CORPORATION
1701 Williamsburg Pike (47374-1492)
P.O. Box 488 (47375-0488)
PHONE.................................765 983-9200
Jim Staijkowski, *Planning Mgr*
EMP: 200
SALES (corp-wide): 4B　**Publicly Held**
WEB: www.silganclosures.com
SIC: 3411 Metal cans
HQ: Silgan White Cap Corporation
　　4 Landmark Sq Ste 400
　　Stamford CT 06901

(G-12051)
SMITHFOODS RICHMOND INC
Also Called: Smith Dairy Wayne Division
1590 Nw 11th St (47374-1404)
P.O. Box 250 (47375-0250)
PHONE.................................330 683-8710
Fax: 765 935-2184
Nathan Schmid, *President*
Amy L Miller, *Treasurer*
Steve Schmid, *Admin Sec*
▲ **EMP:** 125　**EST:** 1921
SQ FT: 45,000
SALES (est): 45MM
SALES (corp-wide): 62.3MM　**Privately Held**
WEB: www.smithdairy.com
SIC: 2026 2023 Milk processing (pasteur-
　izing, homogenizing, bottling); ice cream
　mix, unfrozen: liquid or dry
PA: Smithfoods Inc.
　　1381 Dairy Ln
　　Orrville OH 44667
　　330 683-8710

(G-12052)
SPECIALTY ENTERPRISES INC
2931 Us Highway 35 N (47374-9707)
PHONE.................................765 935-4556
Fax: 765 962-1400

Gary Cummins, *President*
Mona Cummins, *Vice Pres*
EMP: 10
SALES (est): 1.5MM　**Privately Held**
SIC: 3995 Burial caskets

(G-12053)
SPRINT SPECTRUM LP
3721 E Main St (47374-3614)
PHONE.................................765 983-6991
Fax: 765 983-2244
Martina Clark, *Branch Mgr*
EMP: 7
SALES (corp-wide): 85.9B　**Publicly Held**
WEB: www.sprintpcs.com
SIC: 3661 Telephone sets, all types except
　cellular radio
HQ: Sprint Spectrum L.P.
　　6800 Sprint Pkwy
　　Overland Park KS 66251

(G-12054)
STAMP WORKS
121 S 5th St (47374-4222)
PHONE.................................765 962-5201
Fax: 765 966-4725
Richard Williams, *President*
EMP: 3
SALES: 50K　**Privately Held**
SIC: 3953 Embossing seals & hand
　stamps

(G-12055)
STOLLE TOOL INC
4693 Webster Rd (47374-9529)
PHONE.................................765 935-5185
Fax: 765 962-0594
Ronald E Stolle, *President*
Carol Sue Stolle, *Vice Pres*
EMP: 10
SQ FT: 6,300
SALES: 500K　**Privately Held**
SIC: 3544 7692 Special dies & tools;
　welding repair

(G-12056)
SUPERIOR OPRTING SOLUTIONS INC
4307 National Rd W (47374-4712)
PHONE.................................765 993-4094
David Marcelle Sams, *President*
EMP: 4
SALES: 100K　**Privately Held**
SIC: 3823 Industrial instrmnts msrmnt dis-
　play/control process variable

(G-12057)
TALE CHASER PUBLISHING INC
54 S 14th St (47374-5604)
PHONE.................................765 962-4309
Jack Humphrey, *Principal*
EMP: 2
SALES (est): 245.5K　**Privately Held**
SIC: 2741 Miscellaneous publishing

(G-12058)
TBK AMERICA INC
3700 W Industries Rd (47374-1386)
PHONE.................................765 962-0147
Takaaki Kishi, *President*
◆ **EMP:** 35
SQ FT: 60,000
SALES (est): 1.3MM
SALES (corp-wide): 410.3MM　**Privately Held**
SIC: 3561 Pumps & pumping equipment
PA: Tbk Co., Ltd.
　　4-21-1, Minaminaruse
　　Machida TKY 194-0
　　427 391-471

(G-12059)
TEAM GEAR PRINTING LLC
3451 Dorothy Ln (47374-6747)
PHONE.................................765 935-4748
Mark A Mendenhall, *Principal*
EMP: 2
SALES (est): 155.5K　**Privately Held**
SIC: 2752 Commercial printing, litho-
　graphic

(G-12060)
TEAM GEAR PRINTING LLC
4714 National Rd E (47374-3736)
PHONE.................................765 977-2995
Mark A Mendenhall, *Administration*

EMP: 4
SALES (est): 325.9K　**Privately Held**
SIC: 2752 Commercial printing, litho-
　graphic

(G-12061)
TERESA L POWELL CPA
321 Sw 1st St (47374-5303)
PHONE.................................765 962-1862
Myron Powell, *Owner*
EMP: 2
SALES (est): 156.4K　**Privately Held**
SIC: 3599 Industrial machinery

(G-12062)
TERRI LOGAN STUDIOS
2101 Reeveston Rd (47374-5752)
PHONE.................................765 966-7876
Terri Logan, *Owner*
EMP: 5
SALES (est): 313.6K　**Privately Held**
SIC: 3911 Jewelry, precious metal

(G-12063)
TERZ DESIGN AND IMPRINTING LLC
2305 Vi Post Rd (47374-9498)
PHONE.................................765 965-9762
Jon Christian Terzini, *Principal*
EMP: 2　**EST:** 2010
SALES (est): 166K　**Privately Held**
SIC: 2759 Imprinting

(G-12064)
TGC AUTO CARE PRODUCTS INC
421 S 33rd St (47374-6722)
PHONE.................................765 962-7725
Terry Christ, *President*
Marthea J Christ, *President*
EMP: 5
SQ FT: 6,000
SALES (est): 250K　**Privately Held**
SIC: 2842 5169 Degreasing solvent; spe-
　cialty cleaning & sanitation preparations

(G-12065)
THINKSHORTCUT PUBLISHING LLC
2695 Inke Rd (47374-9360)
PHONE.................................765 935-1127
Gary Arndts, *Owner*
EMP: 2
SALES (est): 98.6K　**Privately Held**
SIC: 2741 Miscellaneous publishing

(G-12066)
THOUSAND ONE INC
Also Called: Signgrafx & Engraving
1001 S E St (47374-6317)
P.O. Box 1502 (47375-1502)
PHONE.................................765 962-3636
Fax: 765 962-2575
Peggy North, *President*
Rollie North, *Vice Pres*
EMP: 6　**EST:** 1983
SALES (est): 490K　**Privately Held**
SIC: 3993 Signs & advertising specialties

(G-12067)
TIEDEMANN-BEVS INDUSTRIES LLC
Also Called: Tiedmann and Sons
4225 W Industries Rd (47374-1385)
PHONE.................................765 962-4914
Robert Galletly, *President*
Pam Soper, *General Mgr*
Peter Galletly, *Exec VP*
Peter W Galletly, *Exec VP*
Jose Sierra, *Opers Mgr*
◆ **EMP:** 44
SQ FT: 65,000
SALES: 16MM　**Privately Held**
WEB: www.bevsthreads.com
SIC: 5131 3995 Piece goods & other fab-
　rics; casket linings
PA: Strength Capital Partners, L.L.C.
　　350 N Old Woodwrd Ave # 100
　　Birmingham MI 48009

(G-12068)
TRANSCENDIA INC
Also Called: Seal Tran Div
300 Industrial Pkwy (47374-3706)
PHONE.................................765 935-1520

Fax: 765 935-4924
Larry Sturgis, *Purchasing*
Keith Badgeley, *Branch Mgr*
Dennis Backus, *Manager*
EMP: 150
SALES (corp-wide): 449.7MM **Privately
Held**
WEB: www.transilwrap.com
SIC: 3081 2891 2851 Polyvinyl film &
sheet; adhesives & sealants; paints & al-
lied products
PA: Transcendia, Inc.
9201 Belmont Ave
Franklin Park IL 60131
847 678-1800

(G-12069)
TRI DON LLC
5679 Park Elwood Rd (47374-9610)
PHONE..................................765 966-7300
Donald Delay, *Owner*
EMP: 2
SALES (est): 125.5K **Privately Held**
SIC: 3599 Industrial machinery

(G-12070)
TURNER PAVING COMPANY
1458 Nw 5th St (47374-1842)
PHONE..................................765 962-4408
Bary Barker, *Owner*
Gary Barker, *Manager*
EMP: 2
SALES (est): 110K **Privately Held**
SIC: 3531 Pavers

(G-12071)
U S AGGREGATES INC
6340 State Road 121 (47374-8602)
PHONE..................................765 966-8155
Larry Capps, *Manager*
EMP: 8
SALES (corp-wide): 248.2MM **Privately
Held**
WEB: www.usagg.com
SIC: 1442 Construction sand & gravel
HQ: U S Aggregates Inc
5400 W 86th St
Indianapolis IN 46268
317 872-6010

(G-12072)
VANDOR CORPORATION
Also Called: C.J. Boots Casket Company
4251 W Industries Rd (47374-1385)
PHONE..................................765 683-9760
EMP: 35
SALES (corp-wide): 2.6MM **Privately
Held**
SIC: 3995 5087 Burial caskets; caskets
PA: Vandor Corporation
4251 W Industries Rd
Richmond IN 47374
765 966-7676

(G-12073)
VET SIGNS LLC ✪
2171 State Route 227 N (47374)
PHONE..................................937 733-4727
Shaun Fudge, *Mng Member*
EMP: 2 EST: 2017
SALES (est): 85.6K **Privately Held**
SIC: 3499 3449 Fabricated metal prod-
ucts; miscellaneous metalwork

(G-12074)
**WAYNE MACHINE
MANUFACTURERS**
1747 S 5th St (47374-6823)
P.O. Box 427 (47375-0427)
PHONE..................................765 962-0459
Jeffrey Baker Sr, *President*
Art Reece, *Plant Mgr*
EMP: 6
SQ FT: 5,000
SALES (est): 1.3MM **Privately Held**
WEB: www.wayne-machine.com
SIC: 3599 Machine shop, jobbing & repair

(G-12075)
WESTERN-CULLEN-HAYES INC
120 N 3rd St (47374-3002)
P.O. Box 756 (47375-0756)
PHONE..................................765 962-0526
Fax: 765 966-5374
Ron McDaniel, *President*
Kevin Hertel, *General Mgr*

EMP: 28
SALES (est): 3.2MM
SALES (corp-wide): 16.8MM **Privately
Held**
SIC: 5084 3743 3312 Safety equipment;
railroad equipment; blast furnaces & steel
mills
PA: Western-Cullen-Hayes, Inc.
2700 W 36th Pl
Chicago IL 60632
773 254-9600

(G-12076)
**WINANDY GREENHOUSE
COMPANY**
2211 Peacock Rd (47374-3835)
PHONE..................................765 935-2111
Fax: 765 935-2110
Mike Winandy, *President*
Elizabeth Doherty, *Vice Pres*
Michael Doherty, *Vice Pres*
Brent Wilber, *Manager*
EMP: 30
SQ FT: 3,000
SALES (est): 7.4MM **Privately Held**
SIC: 3448 3231 Greenhouses: prefabri-
cated metal; products of purchased glass

(G-12077)
YAMAGUCHI MFG USA INC
1771 Sheridan St (47374-1811)
PHONE..................................765 973-9130
Kenzo Yamaguchi, *President*
Taizo Yamaguchi, *Director*
Yasuyuki Imai, *Admin Sec*
EMP: 3
SALES (est): 246.5K **Privately Held**
SIC: 3545 Precision tools, machinists'
PA: Yamagichi Manufacturing,Co.,Ltd.
292-69, Ashitaka
Numazu SZO 410-0
559 252-000

(G-12078)
YORK GROUP INC
Ambedco Stamping
620 S J St (47374-6140)
PHONE..................................765 966-1576
Fax: 765 935-0348
Scott Wright, *Manager*
EMP: 56
SQ FT: 80,000
SALES (corp-wide): 1.5B **Publicly Held**
WEB: www.yorkgrp.com
SIC: 3469 3995 Metal stampings; burial
caskets
HQ: The York Group Inc
2 N Shore Ctr
Pittsburgh PA 15212
412 995-1600

(G-12079)
YORK GROUP INC
Also Called: York Technology
1620 Rich Rd (47374-1435)
PHONE..................................765 966-0077
Fax: 765 935-5572
Don Birdsall, *Principal*
EMP: 4
SALES (corp-wide): 1.5B **Publicly Held**
WEB: www.yorkgrp.com
SIC: 3089 Injection molded finished plastic
products
HQ: The York Group Inc
2 N Shore Ctr
Pittsburgh PA 15212
412 995-1600

Ridgeville
Randolph County

(G-12080)
CARDEMON INC
Also Called: Car-TEC
108 W 2nd St (47380-1328)
PHONE..................................765 857-1000
Fax: 765 857-1000
Chris Cardemon, *President*
Jammie Minniear, *Treasurer*
EMP: 14
SQ FT: 30,000
SALES: 1.6MM **Privately Held**
SIC: 3599 Machine shop, jobbing & repair

(G-12081)
QUICK CLICK MARKETING INC
9270 N Us Highway 27 (47380-9161)
PHONE..................................765 857-2167
Donna Bickel, *Principal*
EMP: 5
SALES (est): 210K **Privately Held**
SIC: 2836 Culture media

(G-12082)
**RELIANCE MACHINE COMPANY
INC**
Also Called: Cartec Company
108 W 2nd St (47380-1328)
PHONE..................................765 857-1000
Joe Baker, *Plant Mgr*
EMP: 15
SALES (corp-wide): 4.2MM **Privately
Held**
WEB: www.cartec-naso.com
SIC: 3599 Machine shop, jobbing & repair
PA: Reliance Machine Company Inc
4605 S Walnut St
Muncie IN 47302
765 284-0151

(G-12083)
**UTILITY ACCESS SOLUTIONS
INC**
205 S Walnut St (47380-1331)
PHONE..................................765 744-6528
Joe Goodhew, *President*
EMP: 3
SALES (est): 138.1K
SALES (corp-wide): 747.7MM **Publicly
Held**
SIC: 1611 1442 General contractor, high-
way & street construction; construction
sand mining
HQ: Newpark Mats & Integrated Services
Llc
9320 Lkeside Blvd Ste 100
The Woodlands TX 77381
281 362-6800

Riley
Vigo County

(G-12084)
MAPLE-HUNTER DECALS
8075 St Rd 46 (47871)
P.O. Box 805 (47871-0805)
PHONE..................................812 894-9759
John Hunter, *Owner*
EMP: 2 EST: 2000
SALES: 45K **Privately Held**
SIC: 2759 Decals: printing

Rising Sun
Ohio County

(G-12085)
**ADVANCED MBILITY
SOLUTIONS LLC**
4669 Cass Union Rd (47040-9690)
PHONE..................................812 438-2338
Kim F Wagner, *Mng Member*
EMP: 6
SALES (est): 223K **Privately Held**
SIC: 8011 3841 Medical centers; medical
instruments & equipment, blood & bone
work

(G-12086)
**COMBUSTION AND SYSTEMS
INC**
116 N Walnut St (47040-1134)
P.O. Box 3705, Lawrenceburg (47025-
3705)
PHONE..................................859 814-8847
Cindy Wills, *President*
Dennis Steinbis, *Opers Mgr*
EMP: 6
SALES (est): 587.6K **Privately Held**
SIC: 2023 Powdered baby formula

(G-12087)
**DELPHOS HERALD OF INDIANA
INC**
Also Called: Ohio County News, The
235 Main St (47040-1224)
PHONE..................................812 438-2011
Tim Hillman, *Manager*
EMP: 2
SALES (corp-wide): 1.1MM **Privately
Held**
SIC: 2711 Newspapers: publishing only,
not printed on site
HQ: The Delphos Herald Of Indiana Inc
126 W High St
Lawrenceburg IN 47025
812 537-0063

(G-12088)
GROVE FOREST PRODUCTS
16423 N State Route 156 (47040-9399)
PHONE..................................812 432-3312
Fax: 812 432-3312
Kenneth Grove, *Owner*
EMP: 2
SALES (est): 150K **Privately Held**
SIC: 5211 2411 0811 Lumber products;
logging; timber tracts

(G-12089)
KENNETH FIEKERT
Also Called: Fiekert Homestead Wine
412 S High St (47040-1123)
PHONE..................................812 551-5122
Kenneth Fiekert, *Owner*
EMP: 4
SALES (est): 182.9K **Privately Held**
SIC: 2084 Wine cellars, bonded: engaged
in blending wines

(G-12090)
OMI INDUSTRIES INC
1300 Barbour Way (47040-8334)
PHONE..................................812 438-9218
Laura Haupert, *Research*
Jim Elwood, *Manager*
Ron Mulford, *Manager*
Steve Lattis, *Director*
EMP: 5
SALES (corp-wide): 17.2MM **Privately
Held**
WEB: www.odormanagement.com
SIC: 3822 5169 Auto controls regulating
residntl & coml environmt & applncs; aro-
matic chemicals
PA: Omi Industries, Inc.
1 Corporate Dr Ste 100
Lake Zurich IL 60047
847 304-9111

(G-12091)
REES HARPS INC
Also Called: Harps On Main
222 Main St (47040-1225)
PHONE..................................812 438-3032
Fax: 812 438-3089
William Rees, *CEO*
Garen Rees, *General Mgr*
Pamela Rees, *Vice Pres*
▲ EMP: 12 EST: 1976
SALES: 700K **Privately Held**
WEB: www.traditionalharps.com
SIC: 3931 5736 5099 Harps & parts; mu-
sical instrument stores; musical instru-
ments

(G-12092)
TRI STATE MOLD
7255 State Route 56 W (47040-9285)
PHONE..................................859 240-7643
Geoff Briceno, *Owner*
EMP: 2
SALES: 30K **Privately Held**
SIC: 3544 Industrial molds

Roachdale
Putnam County

(G-12093)
GLOBAL SONICS LLC
5 Big Walnut Acres (46172-9399)
P.O. Box 394, Danville (46122-0394)
PHONE..................................765 522-5548
Winford Adams,

G E O G R A P H I C

EMP: 3
SALES: 2.5MM **Privately Held**
WEB: www.globalsonics.com
SIC: 3699 Cleaning equipment, ultrasonic, except medical & dental

(G-12094)
NO-SAIL SPLASH GUARD CO INC
Also Called: Adcomm Bindery
10254 N Us Highway 231 (46172-9190)
PHONE................................765 522-2100
Fax: 765 522-2105
Charles E Phillips, *President*
EMP: 7
SALES (est): 911.5K **Privately Held**
SIC: 3069 2782 3993 Rubber automotive products; looseleaf binders & devices; signs & advertising specialties

(G-12095)
VALESCO MANUFACTURING INC (PA)
9875 N County Road 600 E (46172-9133)
PHONE................................765 522-2740
George Robertson, *President*
Craig Robertson, *Controller*
EMP: 2
SQ FT: 2,000
SALES (est): 732K **Privately Held**
SIC: 3523 Weeding machines, agricultural; hulling machinery, agricultural

(G-12096)
W ROBBINS & SONS INC
207 N West St (46172-9073)
P.O. Box 377 (46172-0377)
PHONE................................765 522-1736
Fax: 765 522-1736
William M Robbins, *President*
EMP: 2
SQ FT: 30,000
SALES (est): 120K **Privately Held**
SIC: 2732 2789 2759 2752 Books: printing & binding; bookbinding & related work; commercial printing; commercial printing, lithographic; book publishing

Roann
Wabash County

(G-12097)
NOMANCO TRAILERS
State Road 400 N (46974)
PHONE................................765 833-6711
Fax: 765 833-5711
Dave Schuler, *Owner*
Bertha Schuler, *Co-Owner*
EMP: 7
SQ FT: 12,000
SALES: 1.4MM **Privately Held**
WEB: www.nomanco.com
SIC: 3799 3537 Trailers & trailer equipment; industrial trucks & tractors

Roanoke
Huntington County

(G-12098)
ANDROID INDUSTRIES LLC
Also Called: Android Industries Fort Wayne
13004 Fogwell Pkwy (46783-8790)
PHONE................................260 672-0112
Dennis Donnay, *Plant Mgr*
EMP: 60
SALES (corp-wide): 485.2MM **Privately Held**
SIC: 3711 Motor vehicles & car bodies
PA: Android Industries, L.L.C.
2155 Executive Hills Dr
Auburn Hills MI 48326
248 454-0500

(G-12099)
BEHNING INC
Also Called: Craftsman Lithograph
287 N Main St (46783-1001)
P.O. Box 370 (46783-0370)
PHONE................................260 672-2663
Barbara Behning, *President*

Arthur Behning, *Treasurer*
Gertrude Behning, *Admin Sec*
EMP: 4
SQ FT: 1,900
SALES (est): 314.5K **Privately Held**
SIC: 2759 2771 Stationery: printing; greeting cards

(G-12100)
BRONZE BOW SOFTWARE INC
7717 Aboite Rd (46783-9649)
PHONE................................260 672-9516
Kurt Boller, *President*
Emily Boller, *Vice Pres*
EMP: 3
SALES (est): 218.1K **Privately Held**
WEB: www.bronzebow.com
SIC: 7372 Application computer software

(G-12101)
FOGWELL TECHNOLOGIES
10525 W Yoder Rd (46783-9613)
PHONE................................260 410-1898
Adam Fogwell, *Owner*
EMP: 3
SALES (est): 283.7K **Privately Held**
SIC: 3465 Automotive stampings

(G-12102)
GENERAL MOTORS LLC
12200 Lafayette Center Rd (46783-9628)
PHONE................................260 672-1224
Fax: 260 673-2755
Cathy Clegg, *COO*
William Muzzillo, *Mfg Mgr*
Robert Swanson, *Engineer*
Mark Gevaart, *Comms Mgr*
Jim Layton, *Info Tech Mgr*
EMP: 3900 **Publicly Held**
SIC: 3711 3713 Motor vehicles & car bodies; truck & bus bodies
HQ: General Motors Llc
300 Renaissance Ctr L1
Detroit MI 48243

(G-12103)
GILPIN CUSTOM WOODWORKING
10611 Coopers Hawk Trce (46783-8750)
PHONE................................260 413-6618
Trevor J Gilpin, *Owner*
EMP: 2
SALES (est): 85.2K **Privately Held**
SIC: 2431 Millwork

(G-12104)
INTRI-CUT TOOL COMPANY LLC
5130 E 900 N (46783-9705)
P.O. Box 710 (46783-0710)
PHONE................................260 672-9602
Fax: 260 672-1005
Trent Lehman, *Vice Pres*
J B Hoy,
EMP: 10
SQ FT: 3,500
SALES: 980K **Privately Held**
SIC: 3544 3599 Special dies, tools, jigs & fixtures; electrical discharge machining (EDM)

(G-12105)
JAMES DAVID INC
Also Called: Winco Printing & Gift Shop
11323 Nightingale Cv (46783-8798)
PHONE................................260 744-0579
Fax: 260 744-0579
James E Tolbert, *President*
Marilyn Tolbert, *Corp Secy*
EMP: 2
SQ FT: 3,125
SALES: 178K **Privately Held**
WEB: www.wincoprint.com
SIC: 2752 Commercial printing, offset

(G-12106)
OSTERHOLT CONSTRUCTION INC
Also Called: Osterholt Truss
6486 N Mayne Rd (46783-9150)
PHONE................................260 672-3493
Fax: 260 672-3584
Steven Osterholt, *President*
Janet Osterholt, *Admin Sec*
EMP: 6
SQ FT: 9,000

SALES: 450K **Privately Held**
SIC: 1761 2439 Roofing contractor; structural wood members

(G-12107)
ROANOKE WOODWORKING INC
7477 E State Road 114-92 (46783-9211)
PHONE................................260 672-8462
Fax: 260 672-9555
James Shuff, *President*
EMP: 4
SALES: 1.7MM **Privately Held**
SIC: 5211 2499 Cabinets, kitchen; kitchen, bathroom & household ware: wood

(G-12108)
TROVES
270 N Main St (46783-1001)
PHONE................................260 672-0878
Melani Wilson, *Principal*
EMP: 2
SALES (est): 81.7K **Privately Held**
SIC: 2389 7389 Men's miscellaneous accessories; apparel designers, commercial

(G-12109)
VERA BRADLEY INC
12420 Stonebridge Rd (46783-9300)
PHONE................................260 482-4673
EMP: 110
SALES (corp-wide): 454.6MM **Publicly Held**
SIC: 3171 Women's handbags & purses
PA: Vera Bradley, Inc.
12420 Stonebridge Rd
Roanoke IN 46783
877 708-8372

(G-12110)
VERA BRADLEY INC (PA)
12420 Stonebridge Rd (46783-9300)
PHONE................................877 708-8372
Robert J Hall, *Ch of Bd*
Robert Wallstrom, *President*
John Enwright, *CFO*
Beatrice Mac Cabe, *Ch Credit Ofcr*
Kevin Korney, *Chief Mktg Ofcr*
EMP: 285
SQ FT: 188,000
SALES: 454.6MM **Publicly Held**
SIC: 3171 3111 2392 2844 Women's handbags & purses; accessory products, leather; household furnishings; blankets, comforters & beddings; towels, dishcloths & dust cloths; toilet preparations

(G-12111)
VERA BRADLEY INTERNATIONAL LLC (HQ)
12420 Stonebridge Rd (46783-9300)
PHONE................................260 482-4673
Richard Baum, *Director*
EMP: 5 EST: 2006
SALES (est): 17.2MM
SALES (corp-wide): 454.6MM **Publicly Held**
SIC: 3171 5632 Women's handbags & purses; women's accessory & specialty stores; handbags
PA: Vera Bradley, Inc.
12420 Stonebridge Rd
Roanoke IN 46783
877 708-8372

(G-12112)
W & W GRAVEL CO INCORPORATED (PA)
8031 W County Line Rd S (46783-9301)
PHONE................................260 672-3591
Mark L Welker, *President*
EMP: 18
SQ FT: 1,000
SALES (est): 993.8K **Privately Held**
WEB: www.ontheball.com
SIC: 1442 Gravel mining

Rochester
Fulton County

(G-12113)
AD-VANCE MAGNETICS INC
625 Monroe St (46975-1426)
P.O. Box 69 (46975-0069)
PHONE................................574 223-3158
Fax: 574 223-2524
Richard D Vance, *President*
Kay Nixon, *Vice Pres*
EMP: 38
SQ FT: 32,000
SALES (est): 7.5MM **Privately Held**
WEB: www.advancemag.com
SIC: 3499 3444 3341 7389 Magnetic shields, metal; sheet metalwork; secondary nonferrous metals; metal cutting services

(G-12114)
AG TECHNOLOGIES INC
1268 E 100 S (46975-8036)
PHONE................................574 224-8324
James Straeter, *President*
EMP: 3
SALES (est): 180K **Privately Held**
SIC: 8731 2879 Commercial physical research; agricultural chemicals

(G-12115)
AKORI SOFTWARE
1510 Cardinal Cir (46975-2514)
PHONE................................574 595-5413
EMP: 2
SALES (est): 92K **Privately Held**
SIC: 7372 Prepackaged Software Services

(G-12116)
AQSEPTENCE GROUP INC
Also Called: Air Vac Sewer Systems
4217 N Old Us Highway 31 (46975-8321)
PHONE................................574 223-3980
Fax: 574 223-5566
Mark Jones, *Branch Mgr*
EMP: 75 **Privately Held**
WEB: www.airvac.com
SIC: 3589 Sewage & water treatment equipment
HQ: Aqseptence Group, Inc.
1950 Old Highway 8 Nw
New Brighton MN 55112
651 636-3900

(G-12117)
CAMCAR LLC
4366 N Old Us Highway 31 (46975-8322)
PHONE................................574 223-3131
Curt Moss, *Controller*
▲ EMP: 120 **Privately Held**
WEB: www.tfsi.textron.com
SIC: 3452 5072 Bolts, nuts, rivets & washers; bolts, nuts & screws
HQ: Camcar Llc
6125 18 Mile Rd
Sterling Heights MI 48314
586 254-3900

(G-12118)
COMPETITIVE DESIGNS INC
4477 Deere Trail Ct (46975-7104)
PHONE................................574 223-9406
Lloyd Jennings Jr, *President*
Judith Jennings, *Vice Pres*
EMP: 2
SALES (est): 128.2K **Privately Held**
SIC: 3799 7549 5531 Recreational vehicles; high performance auto repair & service; speed shops, including race car supplies

(G-12119)
CONTEGO INTERNATIONAL INC (PA)
1013 Arthur St (46975-2449)
P.O. Box 49 (46975-0049)
PHONE................................574 223-5989
Todd Beehler, *CEO*
Dan French, *COO*
Tony Scott, *Exec VP*
Richard Zhou, *Vice Pres*
John M Schwartz, *Director*
◆ EMP: 5

SQ FT: 2,000
SALES: 7.5MM **Privately Held**
SIC: **2851** Paints & allied products

(G-12120)
CULVERS PORT SIDE MARINA
1409 Wentzel St (46975-7661)
PHONE..................................574 223-5090
Glenn Bailey, *President*
EMP: 12 EST: 2008
SALES (est): 695.6K **Privately Held**
SIC: **5551** 4493 4491 3732 Motor boat dealers; marinas; docks, incl. buildings & facilities: operation & maintenance; boat building & repairing

(G-12121)
DEAN FOODS COMPANY
1700 N Old Us 31 (46975)
P.O. Box 642, Huntington (46750-0642)
PHONE..................................574 223-2141
Fax: 574 223-2544
Ken Graham, *Manager*
Jim Lanciotti,
EMP: 127 **Publicly Held**
SIC: **2026** Milk processing (pasteurizing, homogenizing, bottling)
PA: Dean Foods Company
2711 N Haskell Ave
Dallas TX 75204

(G-12122)
DELTA TOOL MANUFACTURING INC
1090 W 325 S (46975-7572)
PHONE..................................574 223-4863
Fax: 574 223-6387
Dan Hartman, *President*
Steve Whistler, *Treasurer*
▲ EMP: 6
SQ FT: 30,000
SALES: 1MM **Privately Held**
SIC: **3449** 3544 Miscellaneous metalwork; special dies & tools

(G-12123)
FBSA LLC
Also Called: Freedman Mobility Seating
7346 W 400 N (46975-8723)
PHONE..................................574 542-2001
Fax: 574 542-2019
Christy Nunes, *Managing Dir*
Peter Redding, *Sales Mgr*
Jay Schooler, *Sales Associate*
Craig Freedman,
EMP: 35
SQ FT: 117,000
SALES (est): 5.3MM **Privately Held**
WEB: www.braunseating.com
SIC: **2531** Vehicle furniture

(G-12124)
FLENAR MANUFACTURING LLC
2906 Ft Wayne Rd (46975-8616)
PHONE..................................574 893-4070
Brian Flenar, *Principal*
Matthew Flenar, *Principal*
EMP: 2
SALES (est): 230.3K **Privately Held**
SIC: **3599** Machine & other job shop work; machine shop, jobbing & repair

(G-12125)
FULTON CO R E M C
1448 W S R 14 (46975)
P.O. Box 230 (46975-0230)
PHONE..................................574 223-3156
Ron Jana, *President*
EMP: 2
SALES: 12.3MM **Privately Held**
SIC: **3634** Electric housewares & fans

(G-12126)
HARDESTY PRINTING CO INC (PA)
1218 N State Road 25 (46975-7551)
PHONE..................................574 223-4553
Fax: 574 223-2662
Francis D Hardesty, *President*
Randy Hardesty, *President*
Alice Hardesty, *Corp Secy*
Bill Hardesty, *Vice Pres*
Randall Hardesty, *Vice Pres*
EMP: 13

SALES (est): 1.7MM **Privately Held**
SIC: **2752** 2791 2789 Commercial printing, offset; typesetting; bookbinding & related work

(G-12127)
HEARTLAND FILLED MACHINE LLC
5176 State Road 110 (46975-9052)
PHONE..................................574 223-6931
John J Shirk,
EMP: 5
SALES: 400K **Privately Held**
SIC: **3569** 7699 Filters; industrial machinery & equipment repair

(G-12128)
HOFFMAN QUALITY GRAPHICS
2096 Sycamore Dr (46975-8180)
P.O. Box 821 (46975-0821)
PHONE..................................574 223-5738
Art Hoffman, *Owner*
EMP: 2
SALES (est): 159.8K **Privately Held**
SIC: **2752** Commercial printing, lithographic

(G-12129)
INNOVATIVE COMPOSITES LTD
5408 State St Ste 25 (46975)
PHONE..................................574 857-2224
Fax: 574 857-5004
Philip W Connolly, *President*
David Lobley, *General Mgr*
EMP: 12
SQ FT: 10,000
SALES: 1.5MM **Privately Held**
SIC: **2821** Plastics materials & resins

(G-12130)
JOBSITE TRAILER CORPORATION
Also Called: Jobsite Mobile Offices
1393 N Lucas St (46975-1156)
P.O. Box 288 (46975-0288)
PHONE..................................574 224-4000
Fax: 574 223-3224
James B Guthrie, *CEO*
EMP: 20
SQ FT: 40,000
SALES (est): 3.2MM **Privately Held**
WEB: www.jobsiteusa.net
SIC: **2451** 2452 3448 Mobile buildings: for commercial use; prefabricated buildings, wood; prefabricated metal buildings

(G-12131)
KUERT CONCRETE INC
Also Called: Rochester Concrete Plant
1101 W 13th St (46975-2509)
PHONE..................................574 223-2414
Fax: 574 223-5887
Kent Ganshorn, *Branch Mgr*
EMP: 5
SALES (corp-wide): 14.4MM **Privately Held**
SIC: **3273** Ready-mixed concrete
PA: Kuert Concrete Inc
3402 Lincoln Way W
South Bend IN 46628
574 232-9911

(G-12132)
LAU INDUSTRIES INC
510 N State Road 25 (46975-9776)
PHONE..................................574 223-3181
Fax: 574 223-3903
Scott Marquardt, *Manager*
EMP: 100 **Privately Held**
SIC: **3564** 3714 Ventilating fans: industrial or commercial; motor vehicle parts & accessories
HQ: Lau Industries, Inc.
4509 Springfield St
Dayton OH 45431
937 476-6500

(G-12133)
LAWRENCE SHIRKS
Also Called: Shirks Wood Products
4920 State Road 110 (46975-7001)
PHONE..................................574 223-5118
Lawrence Shirks, *Owner*
EMP: 3
SALES: 140K **Privately Held**
SIC: **2541** Wood partitions & fixtures

(G-12134)
LYNTECH ENGINEERING INC
6310 E State Road 14 (46975-8501)
P.O. Box 58 (46975-0058)
PHONE..................................574 224-2300
Fax: 574 224-2700
Jason Hudkins, *President*
Amanda Hudkins, *Vice Pres*
EMP: 6
SQ FT: 3,000
SALES (est): 1.6MM **Privately Held**
SIC: **3559** 8711 Automotive related machinery; machine tool design

(G-12135)
MACHINED CASTINGS SPC LLC
290 Blacketor Dr (46975-9090)
PHONE..................................574 223-5694
Fax: 574 223-3369
Monte Howard Hoffman,
Debora Dee Hoffman,
EMP: 10
SQ FT: 6,000
SALES (est): 1.8MM **Privately Held**
SIC: **3365** Machinery castings, aluminum

(G-12136)
MARSHALL ELECTRIC CORPORATION (PA)
425 N State Road 25 (46975-9700)
P.O. Box 909 (46975-0909)
PHONE..................................574 223-4367
John C Marrs, *President*
Ted Denton, *Vice Pres*
John McLochlin, *Warehouse Mgr*
Don Recupido, *Engineer*
Amy S Floor, *Treasurer*
◆ EMP: 15
SQ FT: 45,000
SALES (est): 19.5MM **Privately Held**
WEB: www.marshall-electric.com
SIC: **3677** Baluns

(G-12137)
MCGREWS WELL DRILLING INC
7413 S 125 W (46975-7554)
PHONE..................................574 857-3875
Robert McGrews, *President*
Keith McGrews, *Vice Pres*
Mellie McGrews, *Admin Sec*
EMP: 5
SALES (est): 200K **Privately Held**
SIC: **1381** 1781 5251 Service well drilling; water well drilling; pumps & pumping equipment

(G-12138)
MIDWEST SHEET METAL INC
2467 E 200 N (46975-7428)
P.O. Box 66 (46975-0066)
PHONE..................................574 223-3332
Fax: 574 223-5216
Ted R Richard Sr, *President*
EMP: 3
SQ FT: 5,200
SALES: 574K **Privately Held**
WEB: www.midwestductwork.com
SIC: **1711** 3444 Warm air heating & air conditioning contractor; ventilation & duct work contractor; sheet metalwork

(G-12139)
MODERN MATERIALS INC
435 N State Road 25 (46975-9700)
PHONE..................................574 223-4509
Fax: 574 223-4647
Brian Goodman, *President*
Matthew Horn, *Vice Pres*
▲ EMP: 27 EST: 1975
SQ FT: 87,000
SALES (est): 1.6MM **Privately Held**
WEB: www.modernmaterials.net
SIC: **3479** Coating of metals & formed products

(G-12140)
MODULAR BUILDERS INC
2756 Ft Wayne Rd (46975-8613)
P.O. Box 496, South Whitley (46787-0496)
PHONE..................................574 223-4934
Fax: 574 223-8779
Randal Fletcher, *President*
Jasper Dulin, *Vice Pres*
Simon Dragan, *Treasurer*
EMP: 30 EST: 1999
SQ FT: 30,000

SALES (est): 4.4MM **Privately Held**
WEB: www.modularbuilders.com
SIC: **2452** 2451 Prefabricated wood buildings; mobile homes, industrial or commercial use
PA: Whitley Manufacturing Co., Inc.
201 W 1st St
South Whitley IN 46787

(G-12141)
MURPHY ELECTRIC
4606 W 100 N (46975-7930)
PHONE..................................574 224-9473
EMP: 2
SALES (est): 154.4K **Privately Held**
SIC: **3699** Mfg Electrical Equipment/Supplies

(G-12142)
OLYMPIC FIBERGLASS INDUSTRIES
1235 E 4th St (46975-9104)
P.O. Box 920 (46975-0920)
PHONE..................................574 223-3101
Fax: 574 223-8560
William A Adams, *President*
Ardith Adams, *Corp Secy*
EMP: 55
SQ FT: 100,000
SALES (est): 5.3MM **Privately Held**
SIC: **3089** 3799 3431 Toilets, portable chemical: plastic; trailers & trailer equipment; metal sanitary ware

(G-12143)
PRAIRIE MILLS PRODUCTS LLC
401 E 4th St (46975-1105)
P.O. Box 97 (46975-0097)
PHONE..................................574 223-3177
John Cory, *President*
Tammi Richardson, *Human Resources*
EMP: 15
SQ FT: 100,000
SALES (est): 2.5MM **Privately Held**
SIC: **2041** Grain mills (except rice)

(G-12144)
RAMCO BUILDER AND SUPPLY LLC
Also Called: Ramco Supply
4572 N Old Us Highway 31 (46975-7387)
PHONE..................................574 223-7802
David Whitaker, *Prdtn Mgr*
Jake Frey, *Sales Staff*
Shanan Miller, *Sales Staff*
Keith Woods, *Sales Staff*
Marvin Ramer, *Mng Member*
EMP: 28
SQ FT: 12,000
SALES (est): 7.2MM **Privately Held**
SIC: **5211** 3444 Lumber products; metal roofing & roof drainage equipment

(G-12145)
ROCHESTER CEMENT PRODUCTS
2184 Sweetgum Rd (46975-7585)
PHONE..................................574 223-3917
Toll Free:..................................877 -
Fax: 574 224-3917
Thomas Grosvenor, *President*
EMP: 6
SALES (est): 400K **Privately Held**
WEB: www.rochestercement.com
SIC: **3272** 5084 Septic tanks, concrete; industrial machinery & equipment

(G-12146)
ROCHESTER HOMES INC (PA)
1345 N Lucas St (46975-1156)
P.O. Box 587 (46975-0587)
PHONE..................................574 223-4321
Fax: 765 689-9093
Kenny Anderson, *President*
Julie Anderson, *Vice Pres*
Alex Berlin, *VP Sales*
Brian Ungerer, *Executive Asst*
EMP: 125
SQ FT: 137,000
SALES (est): 32.4MM **Privately Held**
WEB: www.rochesterhomesinc.com
SIC: **2452** 2451 Modular homes, prefabricated, wood; mobile homes, personal or private use

(G-12147)
ROCHESTER MANUFACTURING LLC
2903 Ft Wayne Rd (46975-8616)
PHONE..................................574 224-2044
EMP: 2
SALES (est): 87.2K
SALES (corp-wide): 6.2B Publicly Held
SIC: 3714 Motor vehicle parts & accessories
HQ: American Axle & Manufacturing, Inc.
1 Dauch Dr
Detroit MI 48211

(G-12148)
ROCHESTER METAL PRODUCTS CORP (PA)
616 Indiana Ave (46975-1418)
P.O. Box 488 (46975-0488)
PHONE..................................574 223-3164
Fax: 574 223-2326
Robert E Kersey, President
Mike Yeargean, General Mgr
Greg Loving, Senior VP
Michael Boucher, Safety Dir
Buddy Rice, Project Engr
EMP: 340 EST: 1937
SQ FT: 200,000
SALES (est): 87.7MM Privately Held
WEB: www.rochestermetals.com
SIC: 3321 Gray iron castings; ductile iron castings

(G-12149)
ROCHESTER RTTIONAL MOLDING INC
Also Called: R R M
1952 E Lucas St (46975-8602)
P.O. Box 205 (46975-0205)
PHONE..................................574 223-8844
Fax: 574 223-8303
Marilyn Wade, President
Wayne Allen Wade, Vice Pres
Allen Wade, Director
Cara Shambarger, Admin Sec
▼ EMP: 17
SQ FT: 16,000
SALES (est): 4.3MM Privately Held
WEB: www.rrmplastics.com
SIC: 3089 Molding primary plastic

(G-12150)
RONALD CHILEEN FURNITURE
9369 Ohio St (46975-9775)
PHONE..................................574 542-4505
Ronald Chileen, Owner
EMP: 4
SALES (est): 141.7K Privately Held
SIC: 2434 5712 Wood kitchen cabinets; cabinet work, custom

(G-12151)
RONALD HOLLOWAY
Also Called: Holloway Electric Motor Svc
426 Main St (46975-1242)
PHONE..................................574 223-6825
Ronald Holloway, Owner
EMP: 4
SQ FT: 2,000
SALES: 150K Privately Held
SIC: 7694 Electric motor repair

(G-12152)
SCRAPWOOD SAWMILL
3488 S Wabash Rd (46975-7159)
PHONE..................................574 223-2725
Dan M Peters, Owner
EMP: 2
SALES (est): 106.8K Privately Held
SIC: 2421 Custom sawmill

(G-12153)
SENTINEL CORP
Also Called: Rochester Sentinel, The
118 E 8th St (46975-1508)
P.O. Box 260 (46975-0260)
PHONE..................................574 223-2111
Fax: 574 223-5782
Margery Overmyer, Treasurer
Sarah Wilson, Mng Member
EMP: 32
SQ FT: 17,000

SALES (est): 1.8MM Privately Held
WEB: www.rochsent.com
SIC: 2711 Commercial printing & newspaper publishing combined

(G-12154)
SHOPPING GUIDE NEWS INC
617 Main St (46975-1319)
P.O. Box 229 (46975-0229)
PHONE..................................574 223-5417
Fax: 574 223-8330
Barb Foster, President
Steve Foster, Vice Pres
EMP: 12 EST: 2000
SALES (est): 921.9K Privately Held
SIC: 2752 Commercial printing, lithographic

(G-12155)
SMITH MACHINE AND TOOL
3392 Wabash Ave (46975-7190)
PHONE..................................574 223-2318
Richard Smith, Owner
EMP: 6
SQ FT: 8,000
SALES (est): 441.6K Privately Held
SIC: 3544 Dies, plastics forming; forms (molds), for foundry & plastics working machinery

(G-12156)
TEAM PRIDE ATHLETIC AP CORP
2196 Sweetgum Rd (46975-7585)
PHONE..................................574 224-8326
Michael Barnett, President
Allen Farghing, Vice Pres
EMP: 5
SQ FT: 2,000
SALES (est): 894.5K Privately Held
WEB: www.teampdeathletics.com
SIC: 2759 Screen printing

(G-12157)
TOPP INDUSTRIES INCORPORATED
420 N State Road 25 (46975-9700)
P.O. Box 420 (46975-0420)
PHONE..................................574 223-3681
Fax: 574 223-6106
Kevin Birchmeyer, President
David Birchmeier, Vice Pres
EMP: 90
SQ FT: 37,000
SALES (est): 26.7MM Privately Held
WEB: www.toppindustries.com
SIC: 3089 Plastic hardware & building products

(G-12158)
TRUCK STYLIN UNLIMITED
Also Called: Truck Stylin & Collision
2123 Southway 31 (46975-8195)
PHONE..................................574 223-8800
Richard Smith, Owner
▲ EMP: 9
SALES (est): 861.7K Privately Held
SIC: 3479 5531 Painting, coating & hot dipping; truck equipment & parts

(G-12159)
VAN DUYNE BLOCK AND GRAVEL
2602 S 500 E (46975-8423)
PHONE..................................574 223-6656
Robert Macy, President
Carol Sue Macy, Treasurer
EMP: 3 EST: 1946
SQ FT: 8,000
SALES (est): 350.1K Privately Held
SIC: 3271 1442 4212 Blocks, concrete or cinder: standard; gravel mining; dump truck haulage

(G-12160)
WEARLYPOCOCK MONUMENTS
1229 Main St (46975-2038)
PHONE..................................574 223-2010
Chuck Pocock, Owner
EMP: 2
SALES (est): 111.5K Privately Held
SIC: 3272 Monuments & grave markers, except terrazo

(G-12161)
WILSON FERTILIZER & GRAIN INC (PA)
1827 E Lucas St (46975-7793)
P.O. Box 545 (46975-0545)
PHONE..................................574 223-3175
Fax: 574 224-2676
Terry Moore, President
EMP: 8
SQ FT: 5,000
SALES (est): 2.6MM Privately Held
SIC: 5191 5153 2875 2874 Animal feeds; seeds & bulbs; grains; fertilizers, mixing only; phosphatic fertilizers; prepared feeds

(G-12162)
WINNING EDGE OF ROCHESTER INC
221 Rouch Place Dr (46975-8013)
PHONE..................................574 223-6090
Fax: 574 223-4155
Bradly Good, President
EMP: 16
SQ FT: 8,800
SALES (est): 1.3MM Privately Held
WEB: www.thewinedge.com
SIC: 2396 5999 5941 5699 Screen printing on fabric articles; trophies & plaques; sporting goods & bicycle shops; uniforms; embroidery products, except schiffli machine

Rockport
Spencer County

(G-12163)
AIRGAS USA LLC
6500 N Us Highway 231 (47635-9061)
P.O. Box 425 (47635-0425)
PHONE..................................812 362-7593
Fax: 812 362-7637
Matt Gronseth, Branch Mgr
EMP: 9
SALES (corp-wide): 164.2MM Privately Held
SIC: 5169 5084 5085 2813 Industrial gases; gases, compressed & liquefied; carbon dioxide; dry ice; welding machinery & equipment; safety equipment; welding supplies; industrial gases; carbon dioxide; nitrous oxide; dry ice, carbon dioxide (solid); industrial inorganic chemicals; calcium carbide
HQ: Airgas Usa, Llc
259 N Radnor Chester Rd # 100
Radnor PA 19087
610 687-5253

(G-12164)
AK STEEL CORPORATION
Also Called: Rockport Works
6500 N Us Highway 231 (47635-9061)
PHONE..................................812 362-7317
Jamie Litherland, Project Mgr
Eric Petersen, Manager
Danny Lovell, Manager
Roger Murphy, Manager
EMP: 110 Publicly Held
WEB: www.ketnar.org
SIC: 3312 Stainless steel; sheet or strip, steel, hot-rolled; coated or plated products; sheet or strip, steel, cold-rolled: own hot-rolled
HQ: Ak Steel Corporation
9227 Centre Pointe Dr
West Chester OH 45069
513 425-4200

(G-12165)
ALIG LLC
6500 N Us Highway 231 (47635-9061)
P.O. Box 425 (47635-0425)
PHONE..................................812 362-7593
Matt Gronseth, General Mgr
EMP: 2
SALES (corp-wide): 164.2MM Privately Held
WEB: www.mgindustries.com
SIC: 2819 2813 Hydrogen sulfide; oxygen, compressed or liquefied

HQ: Alig Llc
2700 Post Oak Blvd
Houston TX 77056
212 626-4936

(G-12166)
BECKER ELEC
6500 N Us Highway 231 (47635-9061)
PHONE..................................812 362-9000
Dennis Boyd, Manager
EMP: 2 EST: 2007
SALES (est): 226.6K Privately Held
SIC: 3699 Electrical equipment & supplies

(G-12167)
DAWSON MACHINE SHOP INC
614 N State Road 161 (47635-8831)
PHONE..................................812 649-4777
Chris Dawson, President
Lori Dawson, Treasurer
EMP: 11 EST: 1998
SQ FT: 4,000
SALES: 1MM Privately Held
SIC: 3599 Machine shop, jobbing & repair

(G-12168)
HOOPLE COUNTRY KITCHENS INC
714 N 5th St (47635-1103)
PHONE..................................812 649-2351
Fax: 812 649-2836
David N Caskey, President
Denise A Caskey, Vice Pres
Franklin E Caskey, Treasurer
Katherine Caskey, Admin Sec
EMP: 20
SQ FT: 22,500
SALES (est): 2.8MM Privately Held
SIC: 2099 Salads, fresh or refrigerated

(G-12169)
MIDWEST GRAPHIX LLC
1540 S County Road 100 W D (47635-8643)
PHONE..................................812 649-2522
Joshua Allen, Principal
EMP: 3
SALES (est): 270.9K Privately Held
SIC: 3993 Signs & advertising specialties

(G-12170)
MULZER CRUSHED STONE INC
Also Called: Mulzer Crush Stone
411 Washington St (47635-1266)
PHONE..................................812 649-5055
Fax: 812 649-5056
Eric Miller, Purch Mgr
Jeff Champion, Marketing Staff
EMP: 25
SALES (corp-wide): 29.7B Privately Held
WEB: www.mulzer.com
SIC: 5032 1442 1422 Sand, construction; gravel; construction sand & gravel; crushed & broken limestone
HQ: Mulzer Crushed Stone Inc
534 Mozart St
Tell City IN 47586
812 547-7921

(G-12171)
NEWS PUBLISHING COMPANY LLC
Also Called: Spencer Cnty Journal-Democrat
541 Main St (47635-1429)
P.O. Box 6 (47635-0006)
PHONE..................................812 649-4440
Fax: 812 649-9197
Angela Geralds, Sales/Mktg Mgr
EMP: 2 Privately Held
WEB: www.leaderunion.com
SIC: 2711 2791 Newspapers: publishing only, not printed on site; typesetting
HQ: News Publishing Company, Llc
542 7th St
Tell City IN 47586
502 633-4334

(G-12172)
ROCKPORT ROLL SHOP LLC
6500 N Us Highway 231 (47635-9061)
P.O. Box 102 (47635-0102)
PHONE..................................812 362-6419
Douglas Major,
Dick Court,
EMP: 48
SQ FT: 86,000

SALES (est): 8.8MM **Privately Held**
SIC: 3355 Aluminum rolling & drawing

(G-12173)
SUPERIOR FABRICATION INC
1654 S County Road 200 W (47635-8223)
PHONE...................................812 649-2630
Fax: 812 649-4007
Curtis Drake, *President*
Dana Piper, *Accounts Mgr*
Charlotte Drake, *Admin Sec*
EMP: 13
SQ FT: 30,000
SALES (est): 2.5MM **Privately Held**
SIC: 3441 Fabricated structural metal

Rockville
Parke County

(G-12174)
C B PRINTING
792 N Us Highway 41 (47872-7091)
PHONE...................................765 569-0900
Catherine Brook, *Owner*
EMP: 2
SALES (est): 140.8K **Privately Held**
SIC: 2752 Commercial printing, litho-
graphic

(G-12175)
CITY WELDING & FABRICATION
255 N Dormeyer Ave (47872-8107)
P.O. Box 69 (47872-0069)
PHONE...................................765 569-5403
Fax: 765 569-6977
Andy Willhite, *Owner*
EMP: 9
SQ FT: 10,000
SALES (est): 1MM **Privately Held**
SIC: 1799 7692 3523 3444 Welding on
site; welding repair; farm machinery &
equipment; sheet metalwork

(G-12176)
JUDSON HARNESS & SADDLERY
4889 E 350 N (47872-8152)
PHONE...................................765 569-0918
Chris Herschberger, *Owner*
EMP: 3
SQ FT: 3,850
SALES: 215K **Privately Held**
SIC: 3199 5191 5941 Saddles or parts;
harness or harness parts; saddlery; sad-
dlery & equestrian equipment

(G-12177)
MICHAEL O BAIRD
Also Called: Baird Sawmill
4484 N Guion Rd (47872-8191)
PHONE...................................765 569-6721
Michael O Baird, *Owner*
EMP: 2
SALES (est): 211.7K **Privately Held**
SIC: 2421 Sawmills & planing mills, gen-
eral

(G-12178)
PARK COUNTY AGGREGATES LLC
5081 N State Road 59 (47872-8239)
P.O. Box 399, Montezuma (47862-0399)
PHONE...................................765 245-2344
Fax: 765 245-2257
Todd Crane,
EMP: 5
SALES (est): 316.8K **Privately Held**
SIC: 5032 3444 1629 Brick, stone & re-
lated material; culverts, sheet metal;
drainage system construction

(G-12179)
ROCKVILLE WOODWORKS
2282 N Marshall Rd (47872-7084)
PHONE...................................765 569-6483
EMP: 2
SALES (est): 167.1K **Privately Held**
SIC: 2431 Millwork

(G-12180)
SCOTT PET PRODUCTS INC (PA)
Also Called: T. E. Scott
1543 N Us Highway 41 (47872-7146)
P.O. Box 168 (47872-0168)
PHONE...................................765 569-4636
Fax: 765 569-4631
Michael R Bassett, *CEO*
James Stormer, *Exec VP*
Paul Hayden, *Admin Sec*
◆ EMP: 130
SQ FT: 140,000
SALES: 42.7MM **Privately Held**
WEB: www.scottpet.com
SIC: 5199 3199 5999 Pet supplies; dog
furnishings: collars, leashes, muzzles,
etc.: leather; pet supplies

(G-12181)
TINCHERS CREATIVE WOODWORKS
11206 E Ferndale Rd (47872-7930)
PHONE...................................765 344-0062
Guy Tincher, *Owner*
Theresa Tincher, *Co-Owner*
EMP: 2
SALES (est): 110.9K **Privately Held**
SIC: 2431 Woodwork, interior & ornamen-
tal

(G-12182)
TORCH NEWSPAPERS INC
Also Called: Parke County Sentinel
125 W High St (47872-1735)
P.O. Box 187 (47872-0187)
PHONE...................................765 569-2033
Fax: 765 569-1424
Mary Joan Harney, *President*
Robert Nash, *Vice Pres*
EMP: 8
SQ FT: 2,400
SALES (est): 552.2K **Privately Held**
SIC: 2711 Newspapers: publishing only,
not printed on site

(G-12183)
WALNUT ACRES SAWMILL LLC
6218 E 100 N (47872-8142)
PHONE...................................765 344-0027
Alvin King, *Principal*
EMP: 3
SALES (est): 195.1K **Privately Held**
SIC: 2421 Sawmills & planing mills, gen-
eral

Rolling Prairie
Laporte County

(G-12184)
CREATIVE SOLUTIONS
3606 E Us Highway 20 (46371-9561)
PHONE...................................219 778-4919
Joyce Blint, *Partner*
Pamela Fudlow, *Partner*
EMP: 2
SALES (est): 69.6K **Privately Held**
SIC: 2395 Embroidery products, except
schiffli machine

(G-12185)
FAST MANUFACTURING LLC
3956 E 800 N (46371-8877)
PHONE...................................219 778-8123
Catherine R Foreman, *Principal*
EMP: 8
SALES (est): 620.8K **Privately Held**
SIC: 3999 Manufacturing industries

(G-12186)
GRIMM MOLD & DIE CO INC
200 S Depot St (46371-7010)
P.O. Box 218 (46371-0218)
PHONE...................................219 778-4211
Fax: 219 778-4051
Timothy Grimm, *President*
Sheila Grimm, *Vice Pres*
EMP: 12
SQ FT: 10,000

SALES (est): 1.7MM **Privately Held**
SIC: 3599 3544 3545 Custom machinery;
dies, plastics forming; forms (molds), for
foundry & plastics working machinery;
machine tool accessories

(G-12187)
HARTLAND PRODUCTS INC
Also Called: Ken Co Hartland
5022 E Oaknoll Rd (46371-9667)
PHONE...................................219 778-9034
Fax: 219 778-9875
Kenneth Coates, *President*
EMP: 20
SALES (est): 2.2MM **Privately Held**
SIC: 3089 Injection molded finished plastic
products

(G-12188)
J AND G ENTERPRISES
5556 E 300 N (46371-9431)
PHONE...................................219 778-4319
Gilbert Bradburn, *Owner*
Janet Bradburn, *Owner*
EMP: 2
SALES (est): 50K **Privately Held**
SIC: 2434 Wood kitchen cabinets

(G-12189)
M AND G DIRT AND GRAVEL LLC
4203 N 600 E (46371-9690)
PHONE...................................219 778-9341
Matthew A Deutscher, *Principal*
EMP: 3
SALES (est): 120K **Privately Held**
SIC: 1442 Construction sand & gravel

(G-12190)
OTECH CORPORATION
Also Called: Otech
4744 E Oaknoll Rd (46371)
P.O. Box 116 (46371-0116)
PHONE...................................219 778-8001
Fax: 219 778-8007
Jack O'Donnell, *President*
Christine Stantz, *Controller*
Harold Sullivan, *Admin Sec*
▼ EMP: 60
SQ FT: 66,000
SALES (est): 35.1MM **Privately Held**
WEB: www.otechcompounds.com
SIC: 3089 Injection molding of plastics

(G-12191)
PRAIRIE SUN VINEYARD LLC
3131 N 700 E (46371-9423)
PHONE...................................219 741-5918
Edward H Keiley, *Owner*
EMP: 2
SALES (est): 67.3K **Privately Held**
SIC: 2084 Wines

(G-12192)
PRINT2PROMO GROUP INC
7592 E 400 N (46371-9486)
PHONE...................................219 778-4649
Barbara S Van Wynsberghe, *Owner*
EMP: 3
SALES (est): 224.5K **Privately Held**
SIC: 2752 Commercial printing, litho-
graphic

(G-12193)
PYRAMID EQUIPMENT (PA)
211 S Prairie St (46371-7012)
P.O. Box 127 (46371-0127)
PHONE...................................219 778-2591
Fax: 219 778-2592
David E Surma, *President*
Jon Paul Surma, *CFO*
Sandra L Surma, *Treasurer*
EMP: 10
SQ FT: 60,000
SALES (est): 2.1MM **Privately Held**
SIC: 7692 7538 5084 5531 Welding re-
pair; engine repair; industrial machinery &
equipment; trailer hitches, automotive;
garbage disposals; welding on site

(G-12194)
PYRAMID EQUIPMENT
8 S Depot St (46371-7028)
P.O. Box 127 (46371-0127)
PHONE...................................219 778-4253
Fax: 574 778-2592

Chris Surma, *Manager*
EMP: 4
SALES (corp-wide): 2.1MM **Privately Held**
SIC: 7692 Welding repair
PA: Pyramid Equipment
211 S Prairie St
Rolling Prairie IN 46371
219 778-2591

(G-12195)
WAX CONNECTIONS INC
3628 E Us Highway 20 (46371-9561)
PHONE...................................219 778-2325
Fax: 219 778-2325
Debora K Yergler, *President*
EMP: 5
SALES (est): 589K **Privately Held**
SIC: 3567 Industrial furnaces & ovens

Rome
Perry County

(G-12196)
DIANE DIXON
8172 Triplett Rd (47574-9631)
PHONE...................................812 836-4179
Diane Dixon, *Partner*
EMP: 2
SALES (est): 89.1K **Privately Held**
SIC: 3581 Automatic vending machines

Rome City
Noble County

(G-12197)
AGGREATE SYSTEMS (PA)
102 Industry Bnd (46784-1031)
PHONE...................................260 854-4711
Dick Siebert, *General Mgr*
EMP: 14
SALES: 7MM **Privately Held**
WEB: www.aggsystems.net
SIC: 3535 Conveyors & conveying equip-
ment

(G-12198)
AGGREATE SYSTEMS
106 Industry Bnd (46784-1031)
P.O. Box 235 (46784-0235)
PHONE...................................260 854-4711
Dick Sibert, *Branch Mgr*
EMP: 2
SALES (est): 508.8K
SALES (corp-wide): 7MM **Privately Held**
SIC: 3441 Building components, structural
steel
PA: Aggreate Systems
102 Industry Bnd
Rome City IN 46784
260 854-4711

(G-12199)
FRUITION INDUSTRIES LLC
105 Warrner Dr (46784-9326)
P.O. Box 416 (46784-0416)
PHONE...................................260 854-2325
EMP: 3
SALES (est): 258.3K **Privately Held**
SIC: 3999 Manufacturing industries

(G-12200)
ROME CY AREA YOUTH CTR BASBAL
705 Kelly Street Ext (46784-9686)
PHONE...................................260 854-4599
Steven Herendeen, *Commissioner*
EMP: 2
SALES (est): 84K **Privately Held**
SIC: 3949 Baseball equipment & supplies,
general

(G-12201)
WEST LAKES MARINE INC (PA)
Also Called: West Lakes Boat Mart
85 E Holiday Pt (46784-9748)
PHONE...................................260 854-2525
Fax: 260 854-3760
Richard Reynolds, *President*
Hugh B Reynolds, *Principal*

William Reynolds, *Vice Pres*
Mary L Reynolds, *Treasurer*
EMP: 10
SQ FT: 800
SALES (est) 5.4MM **Privately Held**
WEB: www.westlakesmarine.com
SIC: 5551 5541 4493 3732 Motor boat dealers; outboard motors; marine supplies; marine service station; marinas; boat building & repairing

Romney
Tippecanoe County

(G-12202)
ANDERSONS FERTILIZER SERVICE
527 W 1150 S (47981-9646)
P.O. Box 4 (47981-0004)
PHONE..................................765 538-3285
Fax: 765 538-2188
Richard D Anderson, *President*
Beth Miller, *Vice Pres*
EMP: 5
SQ FT: 2,000
SALES (est) 2.5MM **Privately Held**
SIC: 5191 2875 Fertilizer & fertilizer materials; chemicals, agricultural; fertilizers, mixing only

Rosedale
Parke County

(G-12203)
C MODESITT OIL PRODUCTION LLC
10807 S 625 W (47874-7309)
PHONE..................................812 249-0678
Charlene Modesitt, *Principal*
EMP: 3
SALES (est) 228K **Privately Held**
SIC: 1311 Crude petroleum & natural gas production

(G-12204)
JOE WADE CUSTOMS
324 N Main St (47874-9613)
PHONE..................................765 548-0333
Joe Wade, *Principal*
EMP: 2
SALES (est) 161.3K **Privately Held**
SIC: 3714 Propane conversion equipment, motor vehicle

(G-12205)
KT CAKES
13699 N Rock Run Ch Rd (47874-8002)
PHONE..................................812 442-6047
Carla Duis, *Owner*
EMP: 2
SALES (est) 89K **Privately Held**
SIC: 2051 Bakery: wholesale or wholesale/retail combined

(G-12206)
SUMMERLOT ENGINEERED PDTS INC
Also Called: S E P
11655 N Us Highway 41 (47874-9106)
P.O. Box 5216, Terre Haute (47805-0216)
PHONE..................................812 466-7266
Fax: 812 466-7269
Raymond L Summerlot, *CEO*
Adam Summerlot, *President*
Daniel Bell, *Mfg Mgr*
Daniel Miller, *Mfg Mgr*
Ashley Summerlot, *Finance*
EMP: 18 **EST:** 1970
SQ FT: 23,000
SALES: 5MM **Privately Held**
WEB: www.summerlot.com
SIC: 3535 5051 7692 3531 Bulk handling conveyor systems; steel; welding repair; construction machinery

(G-12207)
T AND T HYDRAULICS INC
7443 S 625 W (47874-7089)
PHONE..................................765 548-2355
Rick Trout, *President*

James Trout, *Vice Pres*
EMP: 3
SQ FT: 4,000
SALES: 300K **Privately Held**
SIC: 7699 3569 Hydraulic equipment repair; filters

(G-12208)
TAGHLEEF INDUSTRIES INC
Also Called: Aet Films
3600 E Head Ave (47874-9124)
P.O. Box 5038, Terre Haute (47805-0038)
PHONE..................................302 326-5500
Fax: 812 462-5006
John White, *Manager*
EMP: 603
SALES (corp-wide): 117MM **Privately Held**
WEB: www.appliedextrusion.com
SIC: 3081 3089 2671 Polypropylene film & sheet; plastic processing; packaging paper & plastics film, coated & laminated
HQ: Taghleef Industries Inc.
500 Creek View Rd Ste 301
Newark DE 19711
302 326-5500

Rossville
Clinton County

(G-12209)
B & L CUSTOM CABINETS INC
7427 N County Road 300 W (46065-7304)
PHONE..................................765 379-2471
Jesse L Longnecker, *President*
Julie Brubaker, *Shareholder*
Alexa Longnecker, *Shareholder*
Suzanne Longnecker, *Shareholder*
Todd Longnecker, *Shareholder*
EMP: 9
SQ FT: 10,000
SALES: 950K **Privately Held**
SIC: 2434 Wood kitchen cabinets

(G-12210)
CIRCLE R INDUSTRIES INC
5262 W 750 S (46065-9124)
PHONE..................................765 379-2768
Fax: 765 379-9887
Darrell Rinehart, *President*
Betty Rinehart, *Corp Secy*
EMP: 2
SALES: 100K **Privately Held**
SIC: 4212 1794 3441 7692 Local trucking, without storage; excavation work; fabricated structural metal; welding repair

(G-12211)
MAUREEN SHARP
153 N Gaddis St (46065-9435)
PHONE..................................765 379-3644
Maureen Sharp, *Principal*
EMP: 2
SALES (est) 107.9K **Privately Held**
SIC: 2789 Bookbinding & related work

Royal Center
Cass County

(G-12212)
CAMPBELLS WELDING & MACHINE
202 E Day St (46978-9019)
P.O. Box 477 (46978-0477)
PHONE..................................574 643-6705
Dale Campbell, *Owner*
EMP: 2
SALES (est) 70.7K **Privately Held**
SIC: 7692 Welding repair

(G-12213)
ROYAL CENTER LOCKER PLANT INC
104 S Chicago St (46978-7029)
P.O. Box 250 (46978-0250)
PHONE..................................574 643-3275
Fax: 574 643-3031
Steve Layer, *President*
Doris Knoll, *Branch Mgr*
EMP: 17 **EST:** 1971

SQ FT: 20,000
SALES (est) 768K **Privately Held**
SIC: 0751 5421 2013 2011 Slaughtering: custom livestock services; meat & fish markets; sausages & other prepared meats; meat packing plants

(G-12214)
ROYAL CENTER RECORD
120 Michael Ln (46978-9614)
PHONE..................................574 643-3165
Fax: 574 643-9440
Jeffrey Funk, *Owner*
Cathy Funk, *Co-Owner*
EMP: 2
SALES (est) 84K **Privately Held**
SIC: 2711 2752 Job printing & newspaper publishing combined; commercial printing, offset

(G-12215)
ROYAL TOOL & MOLDING INC
412 S Chicago St (46978-9088)
P.O. Box 566 (46978-0566)
PHONE..................................574 643-6800
Douglas Schroder, *President*
David Logan, *Vice Pres*
Theresa Schroder, *Treasurer*
EMP: 5
SQ FT: 3,500
SALES: 370K **Privately Held**
SIC: 3544 Industrial molds

(G-12216)
WHALLON MACHINERY INC
205 N Chicago St (46978-2101)
P.O. Box 429 (46978-0429)
PHONE..................................574 643-9561
Fax: 574 643-9218
Leslie Smith, *President*
Leslie G Smith, *President*
Michael K Wallon, *Vice Pres*
Brandi Jones, *Parts Mgr*
Karen Daulton, *Controller*
EMP: 50
SQ FT: 40,000
SALES (est) 12.5MM **Privately Held**
WEB: www.whallon.com
SIC: 3565 Bottling & canning machinery; canning machinery, food

Rushville
Rush County

(G-12217)
CHIEF METAL WORKS INC
1705 W Us Highway 52 (46173-8790)
PHONE..................................765 932-2134
Brad Pike, *President*
Shannon Phillips, *Admin Sec*
EMP: 2
SALES (est) 237.4K **Privately Held**
SIC: 3471 7692 3479 5599 Sand blasting of metal parts; welding repair; painting of metal products; utility trailers; farm machinery & equipment

(G-12218)
COMMUNITY HOLDINGS INDIANA INC
Also Called: Rushville Republican
315 N Main St (46173-1635)
P.O. Box 189 (46173-0189)
PHONE..................................765 932-2222
Fax: 765 932-4358
Kevin Green, *Branch Mgr*
EMP: 20
SQ FT: 30,000 **Privately Held**
WEB: www.clintonnc.com
SIC: 2711 Newspapers, publishing & printing
HQ: Community Holdings Of Indiana, Inc.
3500 Colonnade Pkwy # 600
Birmingham AL 35243

(G-12219)
EMERSON CLIMATE TECH INC
616 Conrad Harcourt Way (46173-1166)
PHONE..................................765 932-2956
EMP: 8
SALES (corp-wide): 15.2B **Publicly Held**
SIC: 3585 Condensers, refrigeration

HQ: Emerson Climate Technologies, Inc.
1675 Campbell Rd
Sidney OH 45365
937 498-3011

(G-12220)
EMERSON CLIMATE TECH INC
500 Conrad Harcourt Way (46173-1164)
PHONE..................................765 932-1902
Tom Zoskie, *Manager*
EMP: 300
SALES (corp-wide): 15.2B **Publicly Held**
WEB: www.copeland-corp.com
SIC: 3585 Condensers, refrigeration
HQ: Emerson Climate Technologies, Inc.
1675 Campbell Rd
Sidney OH 45365
937 498-3011

(G-12221)
FIELDS OUTDOOR ADVENTURES LLP
126 S Perkins St (46173-1933)
PHONE..................................765 932-3964
Mark Fields, *Manager*
EMP: 4
SALES (est) 200K **Privately Held**
SIC: 3949 Sporting & athletic goods

(G-12222)
GAINESCRAFT INC
Also Called: Moormann Bros Mfg Co
203 N Hannah St (46173-1737)
P.O. Box 125 (46173-0125)
PHONE..................................765 932-3590
Fax: 765 932-3594
Robert Gaines, *President*
Jamey L Gaines, *Vice Pres*
Angie Scott, *Admin Sec*
EMP: 5
SQ FT: 8,000
SALES (est) 765K **Privately Held**
SIC: 3823 Liquid level instruments, industrial process type

(G-12223)
INDIANA VECO MANUFACTURING
Also Called: Vibration Eliminator
1104 N Fort Wayne Rd (46173-7552)
PHONE..................................765 932-2858
Fax: 765 932-4673
Stewart Levey, *President*
Kirby Ammerman, *Principal*
Donald Warrick, *Vice Pres*
Kylie Turner, *Admin Sec*
EMP: 23 **EST:** 1950
SALES (est) 3.6MM
SALES (corp-wide): 6.3MM **Privately Held**
WEB: www.veco-ny.com
SIC: 3829 Measuring & controlling devices; vibration meters, analyzers & calibrators
PA: Vibration Eliminator Co., Inc.
15 Dixon Ave
Copiague NY 11726
631 841-4000

(G-12224)
INTAT PRECISION INC
2148 N State Road 3 (46173-9302)
P.O. Box 488 (46173-0488)
PHONE..................................765 932-5323
Fax: 765 932-3032
Donald Carson, *President*
Dave Payne, *CTO*
▲ **EMP:** 400
SQ FT: 400,000
SALES (est) 146.7MM
SALES (corp-wide): 36.6B **Privately Held**
WEB: www.intat.com
SIC: 3321 Ductile iron castings
HQ: Aisin Takaoka Co.,Ltd.
1, Tenno, Takaokashinmachi
Toyota AIC 473-0
565 541-123

(G-12225)
JLB INDUSTRIAL LLC
5066 S The Farm Rd (46173-7369)
PHONE..................................765 561-1751
Jade Brumfield, *Principal*
EMP: 6

▲ = Import ▼=Export
◆ =Import/Export

SALES (est): 427.8K **Privately Held**
SIC: 3443 3585 Boiler shop products: boilers, smokestacks, steel tanks; refrigeration & heating equipment

(G-12226)
KEITH ISON
Also Called: Vinyl Therm of Indiana
615 Conrad Harcourt Way (46173-1167)
PHONE....................................765 938-1460
Keith Ison, *Owner*
EMP: 4
SQ FT: 3,600
SALES: 180K **Privately Held**
SIC: 2431 Windows & window parts & trim, wood

(G-12227)
L&S SANITATION SERVICE
270 S 100 W (46173-7776)
PHONE....................................765 932-5410
Tracy Stanley, *Owner*
EMP: 6
SALES (est): 402.8K **Privately Held**
SIC: 2842 Drain pipe solvents or cleaners

(G-12228)
LEE MACHINE INC
505 E 11th St (46173-1316)
PHONE....................................765 932-3100
Jeff Lee, *Principal*
EMP: 3
SALES (est): 185.6K **Privately Held**
SIC: 3599 Machine shop, jobbing & repair

(G-12229)
MCCREARY CONCRETE PRODUCTS INC (PA)
810 N Fort Wayne Rd (46173-1427)
PHONE....................................765 932-3058
Fax: 765 932-2461
Chris Elbrecht, *President*
Mike Shumaker, *Vice Pres*
EMP: 5
SQ FT: 5,000
SALES (est): 3.8MM **Privately Held**
SIC: 3272 Concrete products, precast; manhole covers or frames, concrete; septic tanks, concrete

(G-12230)
MORTON BUILDINGS INC
1224 S State Road 3 (46173-8509)
PHONE....................................765 932-3979
Fax: 765 932-4785
Steve Bohman, *Managing Dir*
Steve Bohaman, *Manager*
EMP: 15
SALES (corp-wide): 492.6MM **Privately Held**
WEB: www.mortonbuildings.com
SIC: 3448 Buildings, portable: prefabricated metal
PA: Morton Buildings, Inc.
252 W Adams St
Morton IL 61550
800 447-7436

(G-12231)
PRT INC
Also Called: Prevention Response Technology
700 W 5th St (46173-1557)
PHONE....................................765 938-3333
Daniel Gehlhausen, *President*
Caroline Gehlhausen, *Corp Secy*
Kyle Gehlhausen, *Vice Pres*
EMP: 5
SALES (est): 771K **Privately Held**
SIC: 2899 Fire retardant chemicals

(G-12232)
SHAW MACHINING SERVICES I
1866 N 450 W (46173-8621)
PHONE....................................765 663-2732
Charles V Shaw, *Principal*
EMP: 2
SALES (est): 128.1K **Privately Held**
SIC: 3599 Machine shop, jobbing & repair

(G-12233)
SHELBY GRAVEL INC
982 S Flatrock River Rd (46173-7349)
PHONE....................................765 932-3292
Fax: 765 938-1104
Aaron Hale, *Manager*

EMP: 3
SALES (corp-wide): 55.5MM **Privately Held**
SIC: 3273 Ready-mixed concrete
PA: Shelby Gravel, Inc
157 E Rampart St
Shelbyville IN 46176
317 398-4485

(G-12234)
SMOKERS HOST 307
1510 N Main St (46173-1119)
PHONE....................................765 938-1877
Bill Sidman, *Principal*
EMP: 2
SALES (est): 174.3K **Privately Held**
SIC: 2111 Cigarettes

(G-12235)
STARKEY WELDING INC
Also Called: Star Weld
709 W 1st St (46173-1708)
PHONE....................................765 932-2005
Tim Starkey, *President*
Jane Starkey, *Admin Sec*
EMP: 6
SALES: 650K **Privately Held**
SIC: 7692 Welding repair

(G-12236)
TRANE US INC
1300 N Benjamin St (46173-1173)
P.O. Box 219 (46173-0219)
PHONE....................................765 932-7200
Fax: 765 932-5218
Vicki Laird, *Engineer*
Helen Pass, *Design Engr*
Amy Kissell, *Controller*
Greg Harcourt, *Branch Mgr*
EMP: 100 **Privately Held**
SIC: 3585 Refrigeration & heating equipment
HQ: Trane U.S. Inc.
3600 Pammel Creek Rd
La Crosse WI 54601
608 787-2000

(G-12237)
VIBRATION ELIMINATOR CO INC
Also Called: Veco Indiana Manufacturing
1104 N Fort Wayne Rd (46173-7552)
PHONE....................................765 932-2858
Dick McDonald, *Manager*
EMP: 25
SQ FT: 10,000
SALES (est): 1.5MM
SALES (corp-wide): 6.3MM **Privately Held**
WEB: www.veco-ny.com
SIC: 3714 Shock absorbers, motor vehicle
PA: Vibration Eliminator Co., Inc.
15 Dixon Ave
Copiague NY 11726
631 841-4000

Russellville
Putnam County

(G-12238)
ALBERTSON SEED SALES
3868 W County Road 1200 S
(46175-9603)
PHONE....................................765 267-0680
Jeff Albertson, *Principal*
EMP: 2
SALES (est): 62.3K **Privately Held**
SIC: 2074 Cottonseed oil mills

(G-12239)
ST CLAIR GROUP INC
Also Called: Metal Forming Industries
7903 W County Road 1325 N
(46175-5500)
PHONE....................................765 435-3091
Diane Fordice, *Plant Mgr*
EMP: 75
SQ FT: 16,000
SALES (corp-wide): 35MM **Privately Held**
SIC: 2819 Copper compounds or salts, inorganic

PA: St. Clair Group Inc.
101 W Main St
Lebanon IN 46052
317 339-6149

Russiaville
Howard County

(G-12240)
B&M MILLWRIGHT INC
2719 S 1280 W (46979-9766)
PHONE....................................765 883-8177
Richard Myers, *Principal*
EMP: 2
SALES (est): 173.3K **Privately Held**
SIC: 7692 Welding repair

(G-12241)
HOLLINGSWORTH SAWMILL INC
Also Called: HOLLINGSWORTH LUMBER
6810 W 400 S (46979-9702)
PHONE....................................765 883-5836
Fax: 765 883-7669
Hollingsworth Darin, *President*
Joel Hollingsworth, *Vice Pres*
Kaleb Hollingsworth, *Vice Pres*
Brenda Robertson, *Human Res Mgr*
Jack Eldridge, *Marketing Staff*
EMP: 17 EST: 1983
SQ FT: 50,000
SALES: 3.3MM **Privately Held**
WEB: www.hollingsworthlumber.com
SIC: 2421 5211 5031 Custom sawmill; lumber products; lumber: rough, dressed & finished

(G-12242)
IRON MEN INDUSTRIES INC
6086 W 250 S (46979-9506)
PHONE....................................574 596-2251
Chris Thayer, *Treasurer*
EMP: 2
SALES (est): 141.5K **Privately Held**
SIC: 3999 Manufacturing industries

(G-12243)
RICHARD MYERS MLLWRGHT
2719 S 1280 W (46979-9766)
PHONE....................................765 883-8177
Richard Myers, *Owner*
EMP: 7
SALES (est): 96.5K **Privately Held**
SIC: 7692 Welding repair

(G-12244)
UNLIMITED INK CUSTOM SCREEN
6239 W 250 S (46979-9506)
PHONE....................................765 889-3212
Jami Guge, *Principal*
EMP: 2 EST: 2015
SALES (est): 131K **Privately Held**
SIC: 2752 Commercial printing, lithographic

Saint Anthony
Dubois County

(G-12245)
ERNIES WELDING SHOP
3854 E 450 S (47575-9743)
PHONE....................................812 326-2600
Martha J Wehr, *Owner*
EMP: 4
SQ FT: 4,800
SALES (est): 255K **Privately Held**
SIC: 7692 Automotive welding

(G-12246)
INTERNATIONAL PAPER COMPANY
3565 E 550 S St Rt 6 (47575)
P.O. Box 37 (47575-0037)
PHONE....................................812 326-2125
EMP: 84
SALES (corp-wide): 21.7B **Publicly Held**
WEB: www.tin.com
SIC: 2653 Boxes, corrugated: made from purchased materials

PA: International Paper Company
6400 Poplar Ave
Memphis TN 38197
901 419-9000

(G-12247)
JASPER SEATING COMPANY INC
Also Called: Klem Hospitality
4582 S Cross St (47575-9639)
P.O. Box 231, Jasper (47547-0231)
PHONE....................................812 326-2361
Henry Jasper, *Manager*
EMP: 90
SALES (est): 7.7MM
SALES (corp-wide): 228.8MM **Privately Held**
SIC: 2521 Chairs, office: padded, upholstered or plain; wood
PA: Jasper Seating Company Inc
225 Clay St
Jasper IN 47546
812 482-3204

(G-12248)
P & R FARMS LLC
5195 E State Road 64 (47575-9613)
PHONE....................................812 326-2010
Patrick Lueken, *Mng Member*
EMP: 4 EST: 1983
SALES (est): 273.2K **Privately Held**
SIC: 2015 0252 5154 Egg processing; chicken eggs; cattle

(G-12249)
PHILIP REINISCH COMPANY LLC
5170 S 3rd St (47575-9732)
P.O. Box 127 (47575-0127)
PHONE....................................812 326-2626
Steve Hoffman, *President*
Stanford J Reinisch, *President*
Steven Hoffman, *Corp Secy*
Steven Reinisch, *Director*
▲ EMP: 150
SQ FT: 153,000
SALES (est): 12.6MM **Privately Held**
WEB: www.woodmaster.com
SIC: 2511 Wood household furniture

(G-12250)
U B KLEM FURNITURE CO INC
3861 E Schnellville Rd (47575-9633)
PHONE....................................812 326-2236
Fax: 812 326-2525
Urban J Klem Jr, *President*
U B Klem, *President*
Kathy Klem, *Corp Secy*
Kevin Lytle, *Engineer*
John Gossett, *Human Res Dir*
▲ EMP: 95
SQ FT: 110,000
SALES (est): 16.5MM **Privately Held**
WEB: www.ubklem.com
SIC: 2599 Restaurant furniture, wood or metal

Saint Croix
Perry County

(G-12251)
PHIL ETIENNES TIMBER HARVEST
Also Called: Phil Etienne Timber
25993 Saint Croix Rd (47576-9081)
PHONE....................................812 843-5132
Fax: 812 843-5362
Phil Etienne, *President*
Jo Ann Etienne, *Corp Secy*
Joann Etiennes, *Sales Executive*
EMP: 45
SALES (est): 7MM **Privately Held**
SIC: 2421 2426 Lumber: rough, sawed or planed; hardwood dimension & flooring mills

Saint Joe
Dekalb County

(G-12252)
BAKER METALWORKS
5843 County Road 59 (46785-9778)
PHONE..................................260 572-9353
EMP: 2
SALES (est): 133.7K Privately Held
SIC: 3441 Fabricated structural metal

(G-12253)
DELUXE SOAP COMPANY LLC
6031 State Road 1 (46785-9798)
P.O. Box 12517, Fort Wayne (46863-2517)
PHONE..................................260 422-5614
Matthew Henry, Mng Member
EMP: 2
SALES (est): 108.9K Privately Held
SIC: 2841 Soap: granulated, liquid, cake,
flaked or chip

(G-12254)
ECOVANTAGE LLC
6878 County Road 62 (46785-9717)
PHONE..................................260 337-0338
Carlyle Holman, Mng Member
EMP: 3
SALES (est): 600K Privately Held
SIC: 5031 2499 Lumber, plywood & mill-
work; fencing, docks & other outdoor
wood structural products

(G-12255)
**FIBERGLASS PDTS BOAT
REPAIRING**
311 Spencer St (46785)
PHONE..................................260 337-5636
Fax: 260 337-1274
EMP: 4
SALES (est): 270K Privately Held
SIC: 4493 1799 3732 Marina Operation
Trade Contractor Boatbuilding/Repairing

(G-12256)
**LIGHT HOUSE WOODWORKING
DBA**
5553 County Road 79a (46785-9736)
PHONE..................................260 704-0589
Durwin Miller, Principal
EMP: 2
SALES (est): 203.7K Privately Held
SIC: 2431 Millwork

(G-12257)
NUCOR CORPORATION
Also Called: Vulcraft Division
6610 County Rd 60 (46785)
P.O. Box 1000 (46785-1000)
PHONE..................................260 337-1800
Fax: 260 337-1801
Mark Johanningsmeier, Production
Stuart Grzenkowicz, Purch Mgr
David Findley, Engineer
Scott Bogan, Sales Associate
Shannon Phillips, Branch Mgr
EMP: 100
SALES (corp-wide): 20.2B Publicly Held
WEB: www.nucor.com
SIC: 3312 Blast furnaces & steel mills
PA: Nucor Corporation
1915 Rexford Rd Ste 400
Charlotte NC 28211
704 366-7000

(G-12258)
SECHLERS PICKLES INC (PA)
Also Called: Sechler's Fine Pickles
5686 State Rd 1 (46785)
P.O. Box 152 (46785-0152)
PHONE..................................260 337-5461
Fax: 260 337-5771
Max Troyer, President
▲ EMP: 32 EST: 1921
SQ FT: 58,000
SALES (est): 4.8MM Privately Held
WEB: www.sechlerspickles.com
SIC: 2035 Pickles, vinegar; pickled fruits &
vegetables

Saint John
Lake County

(G-12259)
**AMERICAN CMNTY BNK IND
MODEM 2**
Also Called: Schererville Branch
7880 Wicker Ave (46373-7601)
PHONE..................................219 627-3381
EMP: 2
SALES (est): 88.3K Privately Held
SIC: 3661 Modems

(G-12260)
BEVERLYS INCENSE
9214 Maple Ct (46373-9147)
P.O. Box 394 (46373-0394)
PHONE..................................219 558-2461
Valorie Doll-Rosinski, Owner
EMP: 2
SALES (est): 121.9K Privately Held
SIC: 2899 Incense

(G-12261)
COMPUMARK INDUSTRIES INC
9853 Northcote Ave (46373-9529)
P.O. Box 430 (46373-0430)
PHONE..................................219 365-0508
John Beatrice, President
EMP: 5
SALES (est): 402.9K Privately Held
WEB: www.compumark-ind.com
SIC: 7373 7378 7372 Computer systems
analysis & design; computer maintenance
& repair; utility computer software

(G-12262)
DIGITAL HELIUM LLC
9301 W 94th Pl (46373-8717)
P.O. Box 423 (46373-0423)
PHONE..................................219 365-4038
Matthew B Hanson, Owner
EMP: 3
SALES (est): 192K Privately Held
SIC: 2813 Helium

(G-12263)
**EAGLE CREEK MACHINING
COMPANY**
9680 Industrial Dr (46373-9475)
PHONE..................................219 365-3621
Blair W Haddle, Principal
EMP: 3
SALES (est): 304.4K Privately Held
SIC: 3599 Machine shop, jobbing & repair

(G-12264)
J DS BIG BOYS TOYS
13361 W 83rd Pl (46373-9170)
PHONE..................................219 365-7807
EMP: 2
SALES (est): 140K Privately Held
SIC: 3489 Mfg Ordnance/Accessories

(G-12265)
MIDWEST AEROSPACE LTD
9465 Joliet St (46373-9435)
PHONE..................................219 365-7250
Lou Giannini, President
Michael R Lippner, Principal
Joseph Grabas, Sls & Mktg Exec
Bill Hogan, CFO
Joseph Giannini, Executive
▲ EMP: 10
SQ FT: 4,000
SALES (est): 900K Privately Held
SIC: 3728 Aircraft parts & equipment

(G-12266)
**PERFORMANCE MINERALS
CORP (PA)**
Also Called: PMC
10220 Wicker Ave Ste 3s (46373-8400)
PHONE..................................219 365-8356
Stephen Gleason, President
▲ EMP: 8
SQ FT: 35,000
SALES (est): 5.6MM Privately Held
WEB: www.bentonite.com
SIC: 3295 Minerals, ground or otherwise
treated

(G-12267)
PERM INDUSTRIES INC
Also Called: Perm Machine & Tool Co
9660 Industrial Dr (46373-9475)
P.O. Box 660 (46373-0660)
PHONE..................................219 365-5000
Fax: 219 365-4847
Lee J Milazzo, President
▲ EMP: 25
SQ FT: 25,000
SALES (est): 3.9MM Privately Held
WEB: www.permmachine.com
SIC: 3544 Special dies & tools

(G-12268)
R & B FINE PRINTING INC
9720 Industrial Dr (46373-8881)
PHONE..................................219 365-9490
Fax: 219 365-9492
Ronald M Foltman Jr, President
EMP: 4
SQ FT: 3,000
SALES (est): 300K Privately Held
WEB: www.rbfineprinting.com
SIC: 2759 Commercial printing

(G-12269)
**RAW DESIGN AND
FABRICATION LLC**
8821 Mallard Ln (46373-8986)
PHONE..................................708 466-5835
Brian Chelgren,
EMP: 2
SALES (est): 62.5K Privately Held
SIC: 3999 Manufacturing industries

(G-12270)
SILENT WITNESS ENTERPRISES
9804 W Oakridge Dr (46373-9549)
PHONE..................................219 365-6660
Bill Anderson, President
EMP: 2
SALES (est): 88.3K Privately Held
SIC: 3699 Electrical equipment & supplies

(G-12271)
SM INDUSTRIES LLC
13701 Limerick Dr (46373-9676)
PHONE..................................219 613-5295
Patrick M Fagen, Administration
EMP: 2
SALES (est): 194.7K Privately Held
SIC: 3999 Manufacturing industries

(G-12272)
SMITHS MEDICAL ASD INC
12010 W 90th Ave (46373-9292)
PHONE..................................219 365-2376
EMP: 4
SALES (corp-wide): 4.1B Privately Held
SIC: 3841 Surgical & medical instruments
HQ: Smiths Medical Asd, Inc.
6000 Nathan Ln N Ste 100
Plymouth MN 55442
763 383-3000

(G-12273)
YAGER PALLET
9155 Calumet Ave (46373-9153)
PHONE..................................219 365-2766
Gerald Yager, Principal
EMP: 4
SALES (est): 308.4K Privately Held
SIC: 2448 Pallets, wood & wood with metal

Saint Meinrad
Spencer County

(G-12274)
AUTOMATED ROUTING INC
16920 N State Road 545 (47577-9631)
PHONE..................................812 357-2429
Fax: 812 357-7667
Barry Schaefer, President
David Schaeffer, Vice Pres
Scott Schaefer, Admin Sec
EMP: 135
SQ FT: 119,000
SALES (est): 22.6MM Privately Held
WEB: www.automatedrouting.com
SIC: 2499 Decorative wood & woodwork

(G-12275)
ST MEINRAD ARCHABBEY (PA)
Also Called: Carenotes
200 Hill Dr (47577-1301)
PHONE..................................812 357-6611
Fax: 812 357-8388
Rt Rev Justin Duvall, President
Jennifer Keller, Associate Dir
Kurt Stasiak, Admin Sec
EMP: 55 EST: 1854
SQ FT: 720,000
SALES: 30.5MM Privately Held
WEB: www.saintmeinrad.edu
SIC: 8221 2731 Theological seminary;
book publishing

(G-12276)
ST MEINRAD ARCHABBEY
Abbey Press
State Rte 545 (47577)
PHONE..................................812 357-6611
Gerald Wilhite, Manager
EMP: 220
SALES (corp-wide): 30.5MM Privately
Held
WEB: www.saintmeinrad.edu
SIC: 2752 2721 Commercial printing, litho-
graphic; magazines: publishing only, not
printed on site
PA: St Meinrad Archabbey
200 Hill Dr
Saint Meinrad IN 47577
812 357-6611

Saint Paul
Decatur County

(G-12277)
KITCHEN QUEEN LLC
58 W County Rd 650 N (47272)
PHONE..................................812 662-8399
Duane Miller, Mng Member
EMP: 4
SALES (est): 416.8K Privately Held
SIC: 3444 Flues & pipes, stove or furnace:
sheet metal

(G-12278)
KNEPPS CUSTOM WELDING
7586 N County Road 450 W (47272-9780)
PHONE..................................765 525-5130
Don Knepp, Owner
EMP: 2
SALES (est): 70.4K Privately Held
SIC: 7692 Welding repair

(G-12279)
**MYERS FROZEN FOOD
PROVISIONERS**
405 W Dorsey St (47272-9569)
P.O. Box 12 (47272-0012)
PHONE..................................765 525-6304
Fax: 765 525-9635
Robert A Myers, CEO
Anthony Myers, President
Mary Myers, Vice Pres
Mike Myers, Admin Sec
EMP: 8
SQ FT: 13,000
SALES (est): 1.5MM Privately Held
SIC: 5142 2011 Meat, frozen: packaged;
cured meats from meat slaughtered on
site

(G-12280)
SIGN MASTERS
207 S Taylor St (47272-9619)
PHONE..................................765 525-7446
Fax: 765 525-7447
Thomas Pike, Partner
Patty Pike, Partner
EMP: 2
SQ FT: 2,400
SALES: 100K Privately Held
SIC: 3993 Signs, not made in custom sign
painting shops

▲ = Import ▼=Export
◆ =Import/Export

Salem
Washington County

(G-12281)
ALLSPORTS
210 N Main St (47167-2031)
PHONE..............................812 883-3561
Robert Wall, *Principal*
EMP: 2
SALES (est): 119.3K **Privately Held**
SIC: 2759 Screen printing

(G-12282)
AMERICAN WEDGE COMPANY INC
215 Tarr Ave (47167-9202)
P.O. Box 275 (47167-0275)
PHONE..............................812 883-1086
Rick Graves, *President*
Phyllis Graves, *Manager*
EMP: 4
SALES: 250K **Privately Held**
SIC: 2499 Handles, wood

(G-12283)
ARMOR CLAD INC
6170 E State Road 56 (47167-7496)
P.O. Box 503 (47167-0503)
PHONE..............................812 883-8734
Glynn Sumner, *President*
EMP: 4 EST: 2010
SALES (est): 437.1K **Privately Held**
SIC: 2851 Shellac (protective coating)

(G-12284)
BAIRD HOME CORPORATION
Also Called: Baird Homes of Distinction
1401 W Mulberry St (47167-9452)
PHONE..............................812 883-1141
Fax: 812 883-1187
Charles Rickard, *Branch Mgr*
EMP: 6
SALES (corp-wide): 15.6MM **Privately Held**
SIC: 2392 Household furnishings
PA: Baird Home Corporation
3495 Us Highway 441
Fruitland Park FL 34731
352 787-2500

(G-12285)
CAMPBELL COBERT WOODCRAFT
621 E Rudder Rd (47167-7986)
PHONE..............................812 883-5399
Cobert Campbell, *Owner*
EMP: 5
SALES (est): 193.9K **Privately Held**
SIC: 1751 2512 Cabinet building & installation; upholstered household furniture

(G-12286)
FRANK MILLER LUMBER CO INC
7016 E Old 56 (47167-7408)
P.O. Box 192 (47167-0192)
PHONE..............................812 883-8077
Fax: 812 883-1785
Frank Miller, *Branch Mgr*
EMP: 30
SALES (est): 4MM
SALES (corp-wide): 35.5MM **Privately Held**
WEB: www.frankmiller.com
SIC: 2421 Lumber: rough, sawed or planed
PA: Frank Miller Lumber Co Inc
1690 Frank Miller Rd
Union City IN 47390
800 345-2643

(G-12287)
GEORGE VOYLES SAWMILL INC
Also Called: George Voyles Logging
4887 W Apple Ln (47167-8244)
PHONE..............................812 472-3968
George Voyles, *President*
Wilma Voyles, *Treasurer*
EMP: 24
SQ FT: 2,000
SALES: 1.2MM **Privately Held**
SIC: 2411 2426 2421 Logging; hardwood dimension & flooring mills; sawmills & planing mills, general

(G-12288)
GKN SINTER METALS LLC
198 S Imperial Dr (47167-6604)
PHONE..............................812 883-3381
Robert Allen, *Engineer*
Carl Campbell, *Engineer*
William Hamilton, *Engineer*
Daniel Hammontree, *Engineer*
Mac McKinley, *Engineer*
EMP: 240
SQ FT: 225,000
SALES (corp-wide): 12.7B **Privately Held**
SIC: 3499 3714 Friction material, made from powdered metal; motor vehicle parts & accessories
HQ: Gkn Sinter Metals, Llc
2200 N Opdyke Rd
Auburn Hills MI 48326
248 296-7832

(G-12289)
GREEN BANNER PUBLICATIONS INC
Also Called: Washington County Addition
105 E Walnut St (47167-2044)
PHONE..............................812 883-5555
EMP: 4
SALES (corp-wide): 5.3MM **Privately Held**
SIC: 2711 Newspapers
PA: Green Banner Publications Inc
490 E State Road 60
Pekin IN 47165
812 967-3176

(G-12290)
HANSON AGGREGATES EAST LLC
1510 W Market St (47167-9206)
PHONE..............................812 883-2191
Ken Howell, *Superintendent*
EMP: 13
SALES (corp-wide): 20.3B **Privately Held**
SIC: 3281 Cut stone & stone products
HQ: Hanson Aggregates East Llc
3131 Rdu Center Dr
Morrisville NC 27560
919 380-2500

(G-12291)
HILLCREST PALLETS
5445 W Kansas Church Rd (47167-8237)
PHONE..............................812 883-3636
Nelson Garber, *Partner*
Ella Mae Garber, *Partner*
Jesse Garber, *Partner*
EMP: 5
SALES (est): 876.1K **Privately Held**
SIC: 2448 Pallets, wood

(G-12292)
HOOSIER PRECAST LLC
200 Tarr Ave (47167-9202)
PHONE..............................812 883-4665
Fax: 812 883-4667
Christain Newkirk,
Christian Newkirk,
Bill Vonderay,
EMP: 10 EST: 1961
SQ FT: 12,000
SALES (est): 1.4MM **Privately Held**
SIC: 3272 Concrete products, precast

(G-12293)
HUNTERS RIDGE WINERY LLC
9945 E Garrison Hollow Rd (47167-6160)
PHONE..............................812 967-9463
Gregory Paul Ratliff, *President*
EMP: 2
SALES (est): 81.4K **Privately Held**
SIC: 2084 Wines, brandy & brandy spirits

(G-12294)
HUSQVRNA CNSMR OTDR PROD NA
Also Called: Peerless Gear
1555 S Jackson St (47167-9189)
PHONE..............................812 883-3575
Peter Klas, *Manager*
EMP: 180
SALES (corp-wide): 4.6B **Privately Held**
SIC: 3524 Lawn & garden equipment

HQ: Husqvarna Consumer Outdoor Products N.A., Inc.
9335 Harris Corners Pkwy P
Charlotte NC 28269
704 597-5000

(G-12295)
INTERNATIONAL WOOD INC
803 N Deer Run Rd (47167-6432)
PHONE..............................812 883-5778
Jerry Freel, *President*
Dean Calhoun, *Treasurer*
Gavin Freel, *Admin Sec*
▲ EMP: 40
SALES: 5.5MM **Privately Held**
SIC: 2421 Sawmills & planing mills, general; lumber: rough, sawed or planed

(G-12296)
JEANS EXTRUSIONS INC
201 Jeans Dr (47167-9200)
P.O. Box 307 (47167-0307)
PHONE..............................812 883-2581
Fax: 812 883-2585
Burl Jean, *President*
Vince Lewandowski, *General Mgr*
Carmelita Jean, *Corp Secy*
EMP: 155
SQ FT: 60,000
SALES (est): 23.8MM **Privately Held**
WEB: www.jeans-extrusions.com
SIC: 3053 Gaskets, all materials

(G-12297)
KIMBALL FURNITURE GROUP LLC
Also Called: Kimball Office
200 Kimball Blvd (47167-9682)
PHONE..............................812 883-1850
Jim Duncan, *Plant Mgr*
Russell Hobson, *Engineer*
Kathy Sigler, *Branch Mgr*
Karen Lechner, *Manager*
EMP: 140
SALES (corp-wide): 669.9MM **Publicly Held**
SIC: 2522 Office furniture, except wood
HQ: Kimball Furniture Group, Llc
1600 Royal St
Jasper IN 47549

(G-12298)
LANE QUICK
1304 S Jackson St (47167-9794)
PHONE..............................812 896-1890
Eddie Gilstrap, *Partner*
Gary Persinger, *Mng Member*
EMP: 3
SALES (est): 371.7K **Privately Held**
SIC: 2992 Lubricating oils & greases

(G-12299)
LEADER PUBLISHING CO OF SALEM
Also Called: Salem Leader, The
117 E Walnut St 119 (47167-2044)
PHONE..............................812 883-4446
Fax: 812 883-4446
EMP: 25
SQ FT: 4,500
SALES (est): 1.8MM **Privately Held**
SIC: 2711 2752 2791 2759 Newspapers-Publish/Print Lithographic Coml Print Typesetting Services Commercial Printing Misc Publishing

(G-12300)
MADE RITE MANUFACTURING INC
3967 E Sullivan Ln (47167-7724)
PHONE..............................812 967-2652
Lloyd Gray, *President*
Tricia Gray, *Admin Sec*
EMP: 7
SQ FT: 100
SALES: 400K **Privately Held**
WEB: www.maderitemfg.com
SIC: 3449 1799 Miscellaneous metalwork; welding on site

(G-12301)
MICHAEL L BAKER
8779 E New Phladelphia Rd (47167-6217)
PHONE..............................812 967-2160
Michael L Baker, *Owner*

EMP: 5
SALES (est): 316.3K **Privately Held**
SIC: 2411 Logging

(G-12302)
MILLERS SAW MILL
76 E Miller Sawmill Rd (47167-7946)
PHONE..............................812 883-5246
Cecil O Miller, *Owner*
EMP: 3
SALES (est): 156.8K **Privately Held**
SIC: 2421 Sawmills & planing mills, general

(G-12303)
PAYNTER MACHINE WORKS INC
1302 E Hackberry St (47167-9604)
PHONE..............................812 883-2808
Fax: 812 883-6669
William Paynter, *President*
Janet Paynter, *Treasurer*
EMP: 6 EST: 1946
SQ FT: 7,200
SALES (est): 807.2K **Privately Held**
SIC: 3599 Machine shop, jobbing & repair

(G-12304)
REDNECK MONSHINERS SIGNS T-SHI
2810 W Terry Ave (47167-6947)
PHONE..............................812 844-0694
Doyle Adams, *Principal*
EMP: 2
SALES (est): 76.9K **Privately Held**
SIC: 3993 Signs & advertising specialties

(G-12305)
SOUTHERN INDIANA SAWMILL LLC
3325 N Highland Rd (47167-8993)
PHONE..............................502 664-5723
Michael Beck, *Principal*
EMP: 2
SALES (est): 75.9K **Privately Held**
SIC: 2499 Wood products

(G-12306)
STINGEL ENTERPRISES INC
Also Called: Amtek Wholesale Signs
1002 Webb St (47167-9714)
PHONE..............................812 883-0054
Fax: 812 883-0255
John Stingel, *President*
Sharon Stingel, *Vice Pres*
Loretta Hall, *Cust Mgr*
Ben Morris, *Info Tech Mgr*
EMP: 17
SQ FT: 4,000
SALES (est): 1.9MM **Privately Held**
SIC: 3993 Signs & advertising specialties

(G-12307)
TECUMSEH PRODUCTS COMPANY
Also Called: Tecumseh Peerless Gear Mch Div
1555 S Jackson St (47167-9189)
PHONE..............................812 883-3575
Fax: 812 883-5316
Don Francis, *Div Sub Head*
Pete Klas, *Opers Mgr*
Roger Ingram, *Purch Mgr*
Doug Sanders, *QC Dir*
Gary Bowles, *Engineer*
EMP: 500
SQ FT: 165,000
SALES (corp-wide): 724.4MM **Privately Held**
WEB: www.tecumseh.com
SIC: 7537 3592 3568 3566 Automotive transmission repair shops; carburetors; power transmission equipment; speed changers, drives & gears; iron & steel forgings
HQ: Tecumseh Products Company Llc
5683 Hines Dr
Ann Arbor MI 48108
734 585-9500

(G-12308)
TERREL AUTOMOTIVE MACHINE INC
707 S Main St (47167-1041)
PHONE..............................812 883-3859
Fax: 812 883-3859

GEOGRAPHIC

Mark Hoke, *President*
Jennifer Hoke, *Admin Sec*
EMP: 3
SQ FT: 9,600
SALES (est): 200K **Privately Held**
SIC: 3599 Machine shop, jobbing & repair

San Pierre
Starke County

(G-12309)
M A STUDIO INC
Also Called: Memorial Arts Studio
3153 S 900 W (46374-9587)
PHONE...........................574 275-2200
Michael Anthony, *President*
EMP: 2
SALES (corp-wide): 1.8MM **Privately Held**
SIC: 2396 Veils & veiling: bridal, funeral, etc.
PA: M A Studio Inc.
　　605 Front St
　　Welaka FL 32193
　　574 275-2200

Sandford
Vigo County

(G-12310)
JAG METAL SPINNING INC
1022 Crawford St (47885)
PHONE...........................812 533-5501
Glen F Price, *President*
EMP: 7
SALES (est): 1.3MM **Privately Held**
SIC: 3469 Spinning metal for the trade

(G-12311)
SUES CUSTOM SHIRTS
4932 N Orchard Pl (47885-8863)
PHONE...........................812 535-4429
EMP: 2
SALES (est): 70K **Privately Held**
SIC: 2395 7389 Pleating/Stitching Services Business Services

Schererville
Lake County

(G-12312)
103 COLLECTION LLC
7402 Nature View Dr (46375)
PHONE...........................800 896-2945
Melinda Herron,
EMP: 2 EST: 2015
SALES (est): 87.5K **Privately Held**
SIC: 2844 7389 Shaving preparations; lotions, shaving; suntan lotions & oils;

(G-12313)
ACTEGA NORTH AMERICA INC
650 W 67th Pl (46375-1357)
PHONE...........................800 426-4657
EMP: 4 **Privately Held**
SIC: 2851 Lacquers, varnishes, enamels & other coatings
HQ: Actega North America, Inc.
　　950 S Chester Ave Ste B2
　　Delran NJ 08075
　　856 829-6300

(G-12314)
ALSIP PALLET COMPANY INC
1154 Thiel Dr (46375-3087)
PHONE...........................219 322-3288
Frank Jagiella, *Principal*
EMP: 4
SALES (est): 305.9K **Privately Held**
SIC: 2448 Pallets, wood

(G-12315)
AUTOMATION & CONTROL SVCS INC
2440 Ontario St (46375-2700)
PHONE...........................219 558-2060
Kristine Florkiewicz, *Vice Pres*
Kristy Hurst, *Purchasing*

Jonathan Bateman, *Engineer*
Roger Florkiewicz, *Incorporator*
EMP: 12
SQ FT: 10,500
SALES (est): 4.7MM **Privately Held**
SIC: 3625 Relays & industrial controls; control equipment, electric; electric controls & control accessories, industrial; industrial controls: push button, selector switches, pilot

(G-12316)
B E A LL INC
2401 Capri Dr (46375-2438)
P.O. Box 93 (46375-0093)
PHONE...........................219 322-5158
Mark Deall, *Director*
EMP: 2
SALES (est): 168.7K **Privately Held**
SIC: 2721 Periodicals

(G-12317)
BEACON HOUSE
7203 Starling Dr (46375-4441)
PHONE...........................219 756-2131
Salina Mohit, *Partner*
A Mohit, *Partner*
EMP: 2
SALES (est): 75.3K **Privately Held**
SIC: 2731 Books: publishing & printing

(G-12318)
BOFREBO INDUSTRIES INC
Also Called: Endustra Filter Manufacturers
1145 Birch Dr (46375-1334)
PHONE...........................219 322-1550
Fax: 219 322-5870
Robert E Geyer, *President*
Terry Yow, *Natl Sales Mgr*
Martha O Geyer, *Admin Sec*
▼ **EMP:** 49
SQ FT: 43,500
SALES (est): 11MM **Privately Held**
WEB: www.endustra.com
SIC: 3569 Filters, general line: industrial; filters

(G-12319)
D & F INDUSTRIES INC
315 Nottingham Ln (46375-1808)
PHONE...........................219 865-2926
EMP: 2
SALES (est): 110K **Privately Held**
SIC: 3999 Mfg Misc Products

(G-12320)
DEKKER LIGHTING
2142 Us Highway 41 (46375-2806)
PHONE...........................219 227-8520
EMP: 4 EST: 2011
SALES (est): 190K **Privately Held**
SIC: 3229 3648 Mfg Pressed/Blown Glass Mfg Lighting Equipment

(G-12321)
FERGUSON WATERWORKS
450 Kennedy Ave (46375-1235)
PHONE...........................219 440-5254
EMP: 2
SALES (est): 79.9K **Privately Held**
SIC: 3589 3432 Water treatment equipment, industrial; plumbing fixture fittings & trim

(G-12322)
HILLSIDE MOTOR SALES LLC
1212 W Us Highway 30 (46375-1557)
PHONE...........................219 322-7700
Sean Talic, *Manager*
EMP: 2
SALES (est): 254.4K **Privately Held**
SIC: 3621 Electric motor & generator parts

(G-12323)
HOFFMASTER ELECTRIC INC
1635 Hartley Dr (46375-2281)
PHONE...........................219 616-1313
David Hoffmaster, *President*
EMP: 2
SQ FT: 1,500
SALES: 750K **Privately Held**
SIC: 3612 3613 3644 Power & distribution transformers; control transformers; power transformers, electric; fuses & fuse equipment; electric outlet, switch & fuse boxes

(G-12324)
INDIANA TOWN PLANNER LLC
7654 Starling Dr (46375-3390)
PHONE...........................219 384-3555
Stacy Travis, *Administration*
EMP: 2
SALES (est): 84.3K **Privately Held**
SIC: 2741 Miscellaneous publishing

(G-12325)
JC TREEATIONS INC
842 Manistee Ave (46375-1290)
PHONE...........................219 322-2911
John Popp, *President*
Christine Popp, *Admin Sec*
EMP: 2
SALES (est): 50K **Privately Held**
SIC: 2431 Woodwork, interior & ornamental

(G-12326)
JOHNSON SALES CORP
1145 Birch Dr (46375-1334)
PHONE...........................219 322-9558
Robert E Geyer, *President*
EMP: 2
SALES (est): 342.9K **Privately Held**
SIC: 3822 Appliance controls except air-conditioning & refrigeration

(G-12327)
JOY SWEET CUPCAKES
7230 Bell St (46375-3530)
PHONE...........................219 276-3791
Sarah Harris, *President*
EMP: 3
SALES (est): 146.8K **Privately Held**
SIC: 2051 Pies, bakery: except frozen

(G-12328)
KATHY ZUCCARELLI
1314 Eagle Ridge Dr (46375-1360)
PHONE...........................219 865-4095
Katherine M Zuccarelli DDS, *Principal*
EMP: 2
SALES (est): 134.1K **Privately Held**
SIC: 3843 Enamels, dentists'

(G-12329)
KENNEDY METAL PRODUCTS INC
1050 Kennedy Ave (46375-1308)
PHONE...........................219 322-9388
Brian De St Jean, *President*
EMP: 15 EST: 2010
SALES (est): 6.7MM **Privately Held**
SIC: 3441 Fabricated structural metal

(G-12330)
LEONS FABRICATION INC
8850 Parrish Ave (46375-2437)
PHONE...........................219 365-5272
Fax: 219 365-4384
Timothy Grzych, *President*
Timothy Grzych, *President*
Cynthia Van Volkenburgh, *Vice Pres*
EMP: 10
SQ FT: 13,000
SALES (est): 1MM **Privately Held**
WEB: www.leonsfabrication.com
SIC: 7692 3446 3444 3443 Welding repair; architectural metalwork; sheet metalwork; fabricated plate work (boiler shop); fabricated structural metal; gray & ductile iron foundries

(G-12331)
LIBERATION
5308 Gull Dr (46375-4452)
PHONE...........................219 736-7329
Richard Howard III, *Principal*
EMP: 2
SALES (est): 96.1K **Privately Held**
SIC: 3312 Blast furnaces & steel mills

(G-12332)
LOCOLI INC (PA)
Also Called: St John Sports
1650 Us Highway 41 Ste E (46375-1773)
PHONE...........................219 365-3125
Fax: 219 365-3125
John Collet, *President*
Carol Collet, *Corp Secy*
EMP: 20
SQ FT: 12,000

SALES (est): 5.4MM **Privately Held**
SIC: 5699 5136 5137 2396 Sports apparel; sportswear, men's & boys'; sportswear, women's & children's; screen printing on fabric articles; embroidery & art needlework

(G-12333)
MASON CORPORATION
1049 Us Highway 41 (46375-1303)
P.O. Box 38 (46375-0038)
PHONE...........................219 865-8040
Fax: 219 322-3611
Todd Hofer, *President*
Mike Mason, *COO*
John Oliphant, *Purch Mgr*
Gail Guerrero, *Purch Agent*
Steve Oslizlo, *Plant Engr*
◆ **EMP:** 100 EST: 1950
SQ FT: 70,000
SALES (est): 25.4MM **Privately Held**
WEB: www.masoncorp.org
SIC: 2819 Tin (stannic/stannous) compounds or salts, inorganic

(G-12334)
MIDWEST AUTO REPAIR INC
Also Called: Midwest Tire & Auto Repair
1901 Lincolnwood Rd (46375-1886)
PHONE...........................219 322-0364
William R Jarvis, *President*
John Jarvis, *Admin Sec*
EMP: 24
SQ FT: 12,000
SALES (est): 3.2MM **Privately Held**
WEB: www.valpotire.com
SIC: 5014 5531 7538 Tires & tubes; automotive repair shops; automotive tires; general automotive repair shops; motor vehicle parts & accessories

(G-12335)
MIDWEST PIPECOATING INC
925 Kennedy Ave (46375-1325)
PHONE...........................219 322-4564
Fax: 219 322-2761
Laura Vangorp, *Superintendent*
Ken Andreoli, *Purchasing*
Steve Rodda, *QC Dir*
Tony Betz, *QC Mgr*
Christy Crowley, *Marketing Staff*
EMP: 100
SQ FT: 27,000
SALES (corp-wide): 158MM **Privately Held**
SIC: 1799 2851 Coating, caulking & weather, water & fireproofing; paints & allied products
HQ: Midwest Pipecoating, Inc.
　　7865 Jefferson Hwy
　　Maple Grove MN 55369
　　763 425-4167

(G-12336)
MY CHOICE RECYCLING INC
Also Called: Recycledgranite.com
1952 Us Hwy 41 Schrrville (46375)
PHONE...........................219 313-1388
Julie Rizzo, *Exec Dir*
EMP: 3 EST: 2008
SQ FT: 2,000
SALES (est): 235.5K **Privately Held**
SIC: 3281 Cut stone & stone products

(G-12337)
NAIL PRO
246 W Us Highway 30 (46375-1854)
PHONE...........................219 322-9220
Kenny Tran, *Owner*
EMP: 4
SALES (est): 412.1K **Privately Held**
SIC: 2844 Manicure preparations

(G-12338)
NECTOR MACHINE & FABRICATING
595 Kennedy Ave (46375-1236)
PHONE...........................219 322-6878
Fax: 219 865-3729
John Rakoczy, *President*
Jean Rakoczy, *Vice Pres*
EMP: 6
SQ FT: 14,000

SALES (est): 882.2K **Privately Held**
SIC: 3599 3499 7692 3444 Machine & other job shop work; machine bases, metal; welding repair; sheet metalwork

(G-12339)
NEOSPHERE ENERGY INC
1802 Robinhood Blvd Ste 4 (46375-1845)
PHONE..................................219 781-7893
James H Zappia, *President*
Michael Felgian, *CFO*
EMP: 100
SALES: 5MM **Privately Held**
SIC: 2869 Industrial organic chemicals

(G-12340)
NU-TEC INDUSTRIES INC
1319 Saint Andrews Dr (46375-2905)
PHONE..................................219 844-1233
Richard Ingram, *President*
Sylvester Lee Brown, *Vice Pres*
Diana Ingram, *Treasurer*
EMP: 20
SQ FT: 30,000
SALES (est): 2.2MM **Privately Held**
SIC: 2431 Doors, wood

(G-12341)
OGDEN WELDING SYSTEMS INC
372 Division St (46375-1223)
PHONE..................................219 322-5252
Fax: 219 865-1825
Jeffrey W Darnell, *President*
Gordon L Verbeek, *Senior VP*
Gordon Verbeek, *Opers Mgr*
Sandy Cielesz, *Production*
Jim Green, *Production*
◆ **EMP:** 40
SQ FT: 50,000
SALES (est): 19.4MM **Privately Held**
WEB: www.ogdenwelding.com
SIC: 5084 3699 3548 3537 Industrial machinery & equipment; electrical welding equipment; welding apparatus; industrial trucks & tractors

(G-12342)
PROGRESS GROUP INC
918 Kennedy Ave (46375-1326)
PHONE..................................219 322-3700
Fax: 219 865-8157
Steven M Desancic, *President*
EMP: 60
SQ FT: 59,200
SALES (est): 8.1MM **Privately Held**
SIC: 7699 3599 5251 Pumps & pumping equipment repair; machine shop, jobbing & repair; pumps & pumping equipment

(G-12343)
QUALITY PRINTING OF NW IND
Also Called: Minuteman Press
2315 Us Highway 41 (46375-2809)
PHONE..................................219 322-6677
Stephen Watson, *President*
Terry Watson, *Vice Pres*
EMP: 5
SALES (est): 827K **Privately Held**
SIC: 2752 2791 2789 2759 Commercial printing, offset; typesetting; bookbinding & related work; commercial printing

(G-12344)
RYCO ELECTRIC
710 65th St (46375-1309)
PHONE..................................219 319-0934
Richard W Dawson, *President*
EMP: 4
SALES (est): 117.6K **Privately Held**
SIC: 3699 Electrical equipment & supplies

(G-12345)
SITESUCCESS INC
521 Saint Andrews Dr (46375-2951)
PHONE..................................219 808-4076
Kristen Watson, *Principal*
EMP: 2
SALES (est): 122.1K **Privately Held**
SIC: 2741 Miscellaneous publishing

(G-12346)
SPARK MARKETING LLC
1112 Us Highway 41 # 102 (46375-1361)
P.O. Box 1113 (46375-5613)
PHONE..................................219 301-0071

Kristen Jurczak, *President*
EMP: 3
SALES (est): 243.3K **Privately Held**
SIC: 8742 2759 7389 3993 Marketing consulting services; letterpress & screen printing; embroidering of advertising on shirts, etc.; signs & advertising specialties; bus card advertising; distribution of advertising material or sample services

(G-12347)
SPEEDHOOK SPECIALISTS INC
2321 Deerpath Dr W (46375-2546)
P.O. Box 11215, Merrillville (46411-1215)
PHONE..................................877 773-4665
Andrew J Pratscher, *President*
EMP: 7
SALES (est): 400K **Privately Held**
WEB: www.speedhook.com
SIC: 3949 Fishing equipment

(G-12348)
THERMAL PRODUCT SOLUTIONS
1470 Mackinaw Pl (46375-1289)
PHONE..................................708 758-6530
Charles Lazzara, *Manager*
EMP: 2
SALES (est): 107.4K **Privately Held**
SIC: 3567 Industrial furnaces & ovens

(G-12349)
TMS INTERNATIONAL LLC
833 W Lincoln Hwy 310w (46375-1674)
PHONE..................................219 864-0044
EMP: 2 **Privately Held**
SIC: 3312 Blast furnaces & steel mills
HQ: Tms International, Llc
12 Monongahela Ave
Glassport PA 15045
412 678-6141

(G-12350)
UNITED MECHANICAL TECH INC
6808 Swan Ln (46375-4475)
PHONE..................................219 608-0717
Yvonne Andros, *President*
EMP: 2
SALES (est): 142.9K **Privately Held**
SIC: 3321 Gray & ductile iron foundries

(G-12351)
US METALS
833 W Lincoln Hwy (46375-1674)
PHONE..................................219 515-2756
EMP: 2
SALES (est): 97.7K **Privately Held**
SIC: 3432 Plumbing fixture fittings & trim

(G-12352)
WHOLEAF ALOE DISTRIBUTORS
46 Oak Ct (46375-1011)
PHONE..................................219 322-7217
Russell Crist, *Owner*
EMP: 6
SALES (est): 450.2K **Privately Held**
SIC: 2844 Face creams or lotions

(G-12353)
ZELS
7889 W Lincoln Hwy (46375)
PHONE..................................219 864-1011
Fax: 219 864-1312
Don Jeonake, *Partner*
EMP: 20
SALES (est): 1.9MM **Privately Held**
WEB: www.zels.com
SIC: 2013 5812 Roast beef from purchased meat; eating places

Schneider
Lake County

(G-12354)
E J BOGNAR INC
Also Called: Carb-Rite
23810 Highland St (46376-9757)
P.O. Box 175 (46376-0175)
PHONE..................................412 344-9900
Fax: 219 552-9114
Gene Cox, *Manager*
EMP: 14

SALES (corp-wide): 8MM **Privately Held**
WEB: www.ejbognar.com
SIC: 2819 3297 Industrial inorganic chemicals; nonclay refractories
PA: E.J. Bognar Incorporated
733 Washington Rd Fl 5
Pittsburgh PA 15228
412 344-9900

Scottsburg
Scott County

(G-12355)
AMERICAN PLASTIC MOLDING CORP
Also Called: A P M
965 S Elm St (47170-2173)
P.O. Box 480 (47170-0480)
PHONE..................................812 752-2292
Fax: 812 752-5155
Anne E Coates, *President*
▲ **EMP:** 110
SQ FT: 65,000
SALES (est): 35.6MM **Privately Held**
WEB: www.apmc.com
SIC: 3089 Injection molding of plastics

(G-12356)
FLEENOR SAWMILL INC
571 N State Road 39 (47170-4805)
PHONE..................................812 752-3594
Perry Fleenor, *President*
Dorothy Fleenor, *Treasurer*
EMP: 2
SALES (est): 228.4K **Privately Held**
SIC: 2421 Sawmills & planing mills, general

(G-12357)
GENESIS PLASTICS AND ENGRG LLC
640 N Wilson Rd (47170-7727)
P.O. Box 228 (47170-0228)
PHONE..................................812 752-6742
James Gladden, *President*
Larry Gladden, *Mfg Dir*
Wade Becht, *Engineer*
Cory Rough, *Engineer*
Vince Schroeder, *Sls & Mktg Exec*
▲ **EMP:** 110
SQ FT: 60,000
SALES (est): 25.8MM **Privately Held**
WEB: www.genesisllc.com
SIC: 3089 Injection molded finished plastic products

(G-12358)
GENPAK LLC
845 S Elm St (47170-2172)
PHONE..................................812 752-3111
Jerry Coomes, *Plant Engr*
Rich Rosenberg, *Director*
EMP: 150
SALES (corp-wide): 12.5B **Privately Held**
WEB: www.genpak.com
SIC: 3089 2656 Plastic containers, except foam; sanitary food containers
HQ: Genpak Llc
10601 Westlake Dr
Charlotte NC 28273
980 256-7729

(G-12359)
GREEN BANNER PUBLICATIONS INC
Also Called: Giveaway, The
730 N Gardner St (47170-1412)
P.O. Box 159 (47170-0159)
PHONE..................................812 752-3171
Joe Green, *Owner*
EMP: 6
SALES (corp-wide): 5.3MM **Privately Held**
SIC: 2711 Newspapers: publishing only, not printed on site
PA: Green Banner Publications Inc
490 E State Road 60
Pekin IN 47165
812 967-3176

(G-12360)
GREEN BANNER PUBLICATIONS INC
Also Called: Scott County Jurnl & Chronicle
183 E Mcclain Ave (47170-1845)
PHONE..................................812 752-3171
Joseph V Green, *Manager*
EMP: 6
SALES (corp-wide): 5.3MM **Privately Held**
SIC: 2711 Newspapers: publishing only, not printed on site
PA: Green Banner Publications Inc
490 E State Road 60
Pekin IN 47165
812 967-3176

(G-12361)
HS MACHINE WELDING
733 W Bellevue Ave (47170-6734)
PHONE..................................812 752-2825
John Collins, *Owner*
EMP: 2
SALES (est): 70K **Privately Held**
SIC: 7692 Welding repair

(G-12362)
ILPEA INDUSTRIES INC (HQ)
Also Called: Holm Industries
745 S Gardner St (47170-2178)
P.O. Box 450 (47170-0450)
PHONE..................................812 752-2526
Fax: 812 752-3563
Wayne Heverly, *President*
Romano Comper, *General Mgr*
Ken Chenoweth, *Vice Pres*
David McGill, *Vice Pres*
Kevin Pelton, *Prdtn Mgr*
▲ **EMP:** 66
SALES (est): 197.1MM **Privately Held**
WEB: www.holmindustries.com
SIC: 3053 3089 Gaskets, all materials; window frames & sash, plastic

(G-12363)
ILPEA INDUSTRIES INC
Jarrow Products Division
745 S Gardner St (47170-2178)
PHONE..................................812 752-2526
Charles Cruz, *Manager*
EMP: 90 **Privately Held**
WEB: www.holmindustries.com
SIC: 3053 3069 3585 3442 Gaskets, all materials; weather strip, sponge rubber; refrigeration & heating equipment; metal doors, sash & trim
HQ: Ilpea Industries, Inc.
745 S Gardner St
Scottsburg IN 47170
812 752-2526

(G-12364)
IMPERIAL MARBLE INCORPORATED
325 W Lovers Ln (47170-6729)
P.O. Box 194 (47170-0194)
PHONE..................................812 752-5384
Fax: 812 752-4897
Oakly Barker, *President*
Joe Wolf, *General Mgr*
Oakley Barker, *Admin Sec*
▲ **EMP:** 10 **EST:** 1973
SQ FT: 5,000
SALES (est): 1.2MM **Privately Held**
SIC: 3281 3949 3088 2821 Bathroom fixtures, cut stone; sporting & athletic goods; plastics plumbing fixtures; plastics materials & resins

(G-12365)
INDIANA BOTTLE COMPANY INC (PA)
300 W Lovers Ln (47170-6729)
PHONE..................................812 752-8700
Fax: 812 752-8702
David G Baker, *President*
David A Keener, *Corp Secy*
Mike McCarty, *Sales Mgr*
EMP: 38
SQ FT: 25,000
SALES (est): 8.1MM **Privately Held**
WEB: www.indianabottle.com
SIC: 3085 Plastics bottles

GEOGRAPHIC

(G-12366)
INSON TOOL & MACHINE INC
833 S Gardner St (47170-2179)
P.O. Box 673 (47170-0673)
PHONE..............................812 752-3754
David Ingalls, *President*
EMP: 5
SALES (est): 380K **Privately Held**
SIC: 3544 Special dies, tools, jigs & fixtures

(G-12367)
INTEGRTIVE PLYGRAPH TRNING LLC
1352 S Phillips Ln (47170-6959)
PHONE..............................812 595-2884
EMP: 2
SALES (est): 183.4K **Privately Held**
SIC: 3829 Polygraph devices

(G-12368)
IRVING MATERIALS INC
784 N Wilson Rd (47170-7728)
PHONE..............................812 883-4242
Fax: 812 883-8829
Bryan Gross, *Branch Mgr*
EMP: 3
SALES (corp-wide): 800.6MM **Privately Held**
SIC: 3273 Ready-mixed concrete
PA: Irving Materials, Inc.
   8032 N State Road 9
   Greenfield IN 46140
   317 326-3101

(G-12369)
JAR WELDING & MACHINE INC
1217 S Gardner St (47170-6777)
PHONE..............................812 752-6253
Joe Stewart, *President*
Jack Rose, *President*
Pat Rose, *Corp Secy*
EMP: 4
SQ FT: 10,000
SALES (est): 914.9K **Privately Held**
SIC: 5085 7692 Welding supplies; welding repair

(G-12370)
JOURNAL AND CHRONICLE INC
Also Called: J & C Printing Co
39 E Wardell St (47170-1831)
PHONE..............................812 752-5060
Pam Noble, *President*
EMP: 4
SALES (est): 250K **Privately Held**
SIC: 5943 2759 2791 2789 Office forms & supplies; commercial printing; typesetting; bookbinding & related work; commercial printing, lithographic

(G-12371)
KING INVESTMENTS INC
Also Called: Proseries Products
505 E Mcclain Ave (47170-1752)
PHONE..............................812 752-6000
Fax: 812 752-5746
Bill Sellers, *President*
EMP: 16
SQ FT: 9,100
SALES (est): 939.2K **Privately Held**
SIC: 7389 3599 Design, commercial & industrial; custom machinery

(G-12372)
MAJESTY ENTERPRISES INC
Also Called: Majesty Express
2068 S Jimtown Ln (47170-8025)
P.O. Box 833 (47170-0833)
PHONE..............................812 752-6446
Girdley Comes, *President*
EMP: 8
SALES (est): 800.7K **Privately Held**
SIC: 2391 7363 Curtains & draperies; truck driver services

(G-12373)
MAX POWDER COATING INC
1250 S Main St Bldg A (47170-6665)
PHONE..............................812 752-4200
Susan Hill, *Owner*
EMP: 7 EST: 2011
SALES (est): 624.2K **Privately Held**
SIC: 3479 Coating of metals & formed products

(G-12374)
MERRILL MANUFACTURING INC
1052 S Bond St (47170-6745)
PHONE..............................812 752-6688
Fax: 812 752-5688
Jeff Merrill, *President*
EMP: 10 EST: 1978
SQ FT: 27,000
SALES (est): 1.1MM **Privately Held**
SIC: 2511 Bedspring frames: wood

(G-12375)
MULTI-COLOR CORPORATION
Turfway
2281 S Us Highway 31 (47170-6754)
PHONE..............................812 752-0586
Tom Vogt, *Manager*
EMP: 30
SQ FT: 1,500
SALES (corp-wide): 1.3B **Publicly Held**
WEB: www.multicolorcorp.com
SIC: 2759 2796 2754 Labels & seals: printing; platemaking services; commercial printing, gravure
PA: Multi-Color Corporation
   4053 Clough Woods Dr
   Batavia OH 45103
   513 381-1480

(G-12376)
MULTI-COLOR CORPORATION
2281 S Us Highway 31 (47170-6754)
PHONE..............................812 752-3187
Fax: 812 752-3193
Frank Gerace, *Branch Mgr*
EMP: 140
SALES (corp-wide): 1.3B **Publicly Held**
WEB: www.multicolorcorp.com
SIC: 2752 2754 2759 2671 Commercial printing, offset; commercial printing, gravure; commercial printing; packaging paper & plastics film, coated & laminated
PA: Multi-Color Corporation
   4053 Clough Woods Dr
   Batavia OH 45103
   513 381-1480

(G-12377)
NEW HOPE SERVICES INC
Also Called: Kids Place
1642 W Mcclain Ave Ste 1 (47170-1161)
PHONE..............................812 752-4892
Fax: 812 752-4961
Steve Nauman, *Treasurer*
Ronald Sandbach, *CTO*
Scott Borden, *IT/INT Sup*
Jean Robbins, *Exec Dir*
Ashley Wells, *Director*
EMP: 40
SALES (corp-wide): 8.9MM **Privately Held**
WEB: www.newhopeservices.org
SIC: 2396 8322 8331 3993 Automotive & apparel trimmings; child related social services; sheltered workshop; signs & advertising specialties
PA: New Hope Services, Inc.
   725 Wall St
   Jeffersonville IN 47130
   812 288-8248

(G-12378)
RICHEYS MOLD AND TOOL INC
101 E Owen St (47170-1517)
PHONE..............................812 752-1059
Chris Richey, *Principal*
EMP: 2 EST: 2001
SALES (est): 170K **Privately Held**
SIC: 3544 Industrial molds

(G-12379)
SAMTEC INC
861 S Lake Rd S (47170-6837)
PHONE..............................812 517-6081
EMP: 5
SALES (corp-wide): 600MM **Privately Held**
SIC: 3699 Electrical equipment & supplies
PA: Samtec Inc
   520 Park East Blvd
   New Albany IN 47150
   812 944-6733

(G-12380)
SOUTHERN MOLD AND TOOL INC
915 S Elm St (47170-2173)
P.O. Box 160 (47170-0160)
PHONE..............................812 752-3333
Fax: 812 752-6266
Anne Coates, *President*
Randy La Naster, *Supervisor*
EMP: 7 EST: 1980
SQ FT: 5,000
SALES (est): 899.7K **Privately Held**
SIC: 3544 Forms (molds), for foundry & plastics working machinery

(G-12381)
SPANKYS PAINTBALL
2799 E State Road 356 (47170-6207)
PHONE..............................812 752-7375
Jeffrey Case, *Principal*
EMP: 2
SALES (est): 122.7K **Privately Held**
SIC: 3523 Farm machinery & equipment

(G-12382)
SPENCER LOGGING
5297 N State Road 39 (47170-5171)
PHONE..............................812 595-0987
Joe Spencer, *Owner*
Marilyn Spencer, *Co-Owner*
EMP: 2
SALES: 97K **Privately Held**
SIC: 2411 Logging

(G-12383)
STANLEY ALLEN
Also Called: Allen Machine & Tool
1176 Allen St (47170-1110)
PHONE..............................812 752-2720
Stanley Allen, *Owner*
EMP: 3
SQ FT: 3,600
SALES: 175K **Privately Held**
SIC: 3599 3544 Machine shop, jobbing & repair; special dies, tools, jigs & fixtures

(G-12384)
TOTAL CONCEPTS DESIGN INC
1054 S Taylor Mill Rd (47170-6908)
P.O. Box 6 (47170-0006)
PHONE..............................812 752-6534
Fax: 812 752-6534
Charles E Mayer, *President*
Arthur G Mayer, *Vice Pres*
Karen Mayer-Sebastian, *Purch Mgr*
Crystal D Mayer, *CFO*
Morgan Menaf, *Human Res Mgr*
EMP: 80
SQ FT: 40,000
SALES (est): 18.4MM **Privately Held**
WEB: www.totalconceptsofdesign.com
SIC: 3086 7692 3444 Packaging & shipping materials, foamed plastic; welding repair; sheet metalwork

(G-12385)
WAKELAM JOHN
Also Called: Wakelam Lumber Company
160 E State Road 356 (47170-6624)
PHONE..............................812 752-5243
John Wakelam, *Owner*
EMP: 8 EST: 1965
SQ FT: 20,000
SALES (est): 529.9K **Privately Held**
SIC: 2421 Sawmills & planing mills, general

Seelyville
Vigo County

(G-12386)
KELLOGG COMPANY
9445 Us Hwy 40 (47878)
PHONE..............................812 877-1588
Tim McGee, *Vice Pres*
EMP: 703
SALES (corp-wide): 12.9B **Publicly Held**
SIC: 2043 Cereal breakfast foods
PA: Kellogg Company
   1 Kellogg Sq
   Battle Creek MI 49017
   269 961-2000

Sellersburg
Clark County

(G-12387)
ALLIANCE ELECTRIC
1002 Industrial Blvd (47172-2000)
PHONE..............................812 590-3500
J Casner Wheelock, *Administration*
EMP: 2
SALES (est): 327.7K **Privately Held**
SIC: 3699 Electrical equipment & supplies

(G-12388)
APEX SALES & REPAIR LLC
7703 Locust Dr (47172-1853)
PHONE..............................812 248-9001
Aaron Ellis, *Mng Member*
EMP: 21
SALES (est): 3.3MM **Privately Held**
SIC: 3599 Machine shop, jobbing & repair

(G-12389)
BSBW CULTURED MARBLE INC
860 S Penn Ave (47172-1627)
P.O. Box 166 (47172-0166)
PHONE..............................812 246-5619
Dewey Daniel, *President*
Teresa Goospree, *Admin Sec*
EMP: 20
SALES (est): 2.2MM **Privately Held**
SIC: 3281 Cut stone & stone products

(G-12390)
C-LINE ENGINEERING INC
1001 Somerset Ct (47172-2812)
PHONE..............................812 246-4822
Fax: 812 246-2721
Evelyn Rita Schroder, *Corp Secy*
EMP: 5
SALES: 300K **Privately Held**
SIC: 3714 3711 Motor vehicle parts & accessories; chassis, motor vehicle

(G-12391)
CHAMPION WOOD PRODUCTS INC
840 S Penn Ave Ste A (47172-1671)
PHONE..............................812 282-9460
Fax: 812 283-0403
Andrew B Thurstone, *President*
Barbara A Lamb, *Vice Pres*
EMP: 88 EST: 1969
SQ FT: 20,000
SALES (est): 9.7MM **Privately Held**
SIC: 2499 2431 2426 Decorative wood & woodwork; moldings, wood: unfinished & prefinished; hardwood dimension & flooring mills

(G-12392)
ELEMENT ELITE TUMBLING
4601 Commerce Pass (47172-1357)
PHONE..............................502 751-5654
Helen Noel Rich, *Principal*
EMP: 2
SALES (est): 74.4K **Privately Held**
SIC: 2819 Elements

(G-12393)
ERNST CONCRETE ENTERPRISES
4710 Utica Sellersburg Rd (47172-9325)
PHONE..............................812 284-5205
Scott Elliott, *Manager*
EMP: 8
SALES (est): 626.4K **Privately Held**
SIC: 3273 Ready-mixed concrete

(G-12394)
FABCREATION
7412 Highway 31 E (47172-1944)
PHONE..............................812 246-6222
Douglas Pixley, *Owner*
EMP: 2
SALES (est): 59.9K **Privately Held**
SIC: 7699 8999 7692 Blacksmith shop; artist; welding repair

(G-12395)
HAAS CABINET CO INC (PA)
625 W Utica St (47172-1197)
PHONE..............................812 246-4431

▲ = Import ▼=Export
◆ =Import/Export

Fax: 800 338-6244
Jeffrey Todd Haas, *President*
Don C Haas, *Chairman*
Phillip Flora, *Vice Pres*
Bryant L Haas, *Vice Pres*
Thomas K Coats, *Admin Sec*
▲ EMP: 180 EST: 1939
SQ FT: 140,000
SALES (est): 48.7MM **Privately Held**
WEB: www.haascabinet.com
SIC: 2434 4213 4225 2511 Wood kitchen
cabinets; vanities, bathroom: wood; con-
tract haulers; general warehousing; wood
household furniture

(G-12396)
HANDSON (HQ)
4700 Utica Sellersburg Rd (47172-9325)
PHONE..................................812 246-4481
Fax: 812 246-4481
Robert Liter, *President*
John G Liter, *Vice Pres*
Mary Hillibrand, *Treasurer*
Susan Neill, *Admin Sec*
EMP: 15
SQ FT: 1,000
SALES (est): 2.8MM
SALES (corp-wide): 18.4MM **Privately
Held**
SIC: 1422 1442 Crushed & broken lime-
stone; construction sand & gravel
PA: Liter's, Inc.
5918 Haunz Ln
Louisville KY 40241
502 241-7637

(G-12397)
**HANSON AGGREGATES
MIDWEST LLC**
5417 State Rd 403 (47172)
PHONE..................................812 246-1942
JD Owsley, *Manager*
EMP: 25
SALES (corp-wide): 20.3B **Privately Held**
SIC: 1422 Crushed & broken limestone
HQ: Hanson Aggregates Midwest Llc
207 Old Harrods Creek Rd
Louisville KY 40223
502 244-7550

(G-12398)
**INTERACTIVE SURFACE TECH
LLC**
1511 Avco Blvd (47172-1875)
PHONE..................................812 246-0900
Lawrence Gorin,
EMP: 3
SALES (est): 276.9K **Privately Held**
SIC: 2671 Plastic film, coated or laminated
for packaging

(G-12399)
JKNK VENTURES INC
Also Called: Pro Laminators
1511 Avco Blvd (47172-1875)
P.O. Box 274 (47172-0274)
PHONE..................................812 246-0900
Fax: 812 246-1900
Karen Haywood, *President*
Jack Haywood, *Admin Sec*
EMP: 17
SQ FT: 12,000
SALES (est): 1.7MM **Privately Held**
WEB: www.prolaminators.com
SIC: 7389 2672 Laminating service;
coated & laminated paper

(G-12400)
LEHIGH CEMENT COMPANY LLC
301 Highway 31 (47172-1300)
PHONE..................................812 246-5472
EMP: 2
SALES (corp-wide): 20.3B **Privately Held**
SIC: 3241 Portland cement
HQ: Lehigh Cement Company Llc
300 E John Carpenter Fwy
Irving TX 75062
877 534-4442

(G-12401)
LEHIGH HANSON ECC INC
Hwy 31 (47172)
PHONE..................................812 246-5472
Fax: 812 246-2730
Paul Stewart, *Branch Mgr*
EMP: 266

SALES (corp-wide): 20.3B **Privately Held**
WEB: www.essroc.com
SIC: 3241 Cement, hydraulic
HQ: Lehigh Hanson Ecc, Inc.
3251 Bath Pike
Nazareth PA 18064
610 837-6725

(G-12402)
LEHIGH HANSON ECC INC
301 Highway 31 (47172-1300)
PHONE..................................812 246-7700
Fax: 812 246-7800
Paul Stewart, *Branch Mgr*
EMP: 250
SALES (corp-wide): 20.3B **Privately Held**
WEB: www.essroc.com
SIC: 3531 Batching plants, for aggregate
concrete & bulk cement; aerial work plat-
forms: hydraulic/elec. truck/carrier
mounted; automobile wrecker hoists
HQ: Lehigh Hanson Ecc, Inc.
3251 Bath Pike
Nazareth PA 18064
610 837-6725

(G-12403)
LIGHTUPTOYSCOM LLC (PA)
8512 Commerce Park Dr (47172-1353)
PHONE..................................812 246-1916
Christopher Kelly, *CEO*
Joshua Kelly, *President*
Renata Kelly, *COO*
Zach Barker, *Accountant*
EMP: 41
SQ FT: 10,000
SALES (est): 25.7MM **Privately Held**
SIC: 3944 Electronic games & toys

(G-12404)
MANITOWOC
2100 Future Dr (47172-1874)
PHONE..................................540 375-9300
Larry Scott, *Principal*
EMP: 12
SALES (est): 1.1MM **Privately Held**
SIC: 2086 Carbonated beverages, nonal-
coholic: bottled & canned

(G-12405)
**MANITOWOC BEVERAGE EQP
INC (HQ)**
Also Called: Flomatic International
2100 Future Dr (47172-1874)
PHONE..................................812 246-7000
Terry Growcock, *CEO*
Michael J Kachmer, *President*
T G Musial, *Vice Pres*
Tim Wood, *CFO*
C J Laurino, *Treasurer*
▲ EMP: 160
SQ FT: 150,000
SALES (est): 22.3MM
SALES (corp-wide): 1.4B **Publicly Held**
SIC: 3585 Ice making machinery; cold
drink dispensing equipment (not coin-op-
erated)
PA: Welbilt, Inc.
2227 Welbilt Blvd
Trinity FL 34655
727 375-7010

(G-12406)
**MANITOWOC BEVERAGE
SYSTEMS INC**
Also Called: M B S
2100 Future Dr (47172-1874)
PHONE..................................800 367-4233
John Barber, *CEO*
Terry D Growcock, *President*
Robert R Friedl, *Principal*
Glenn E Tellock, *Treasurer*
Errol D Flynn, *Admin Sec*
◆ EMP: 1400
SALES (est): 153.7MM
SALES (corp-wide): 1.4B **Publicly Held**
SIC: 3585 Soda fountain & beverage dis-
pensing equipment & parts
PA: Welbilt, Inc.
2227 Welbilt Blvd
Trinity FL 34655
727 375-7010

(G-12407)
**MASTER ELECTRIC SERVICE
LLC**
1233 Bringham Dr Ste A (47172-2037)
PHONE..................................812 246-3707
Mark Spear, *Owner*
EMP: 7
SALES (est): 1MM **Privately Held**
SIC: 3699 Electrical equipment & supplies

(G-12408)
**METAL SALES
MANUFACTURING CORP**
7800 Highway 60 (47172-1859)
PHONE..................................812 246-1866
Fax: 812 246-0829
Craig Mackin, *Principal*
Melissa Meredith, *Manager*
EMP: 30
SALES (corp-wide): 425.1MM **Privately
Held**
SIC: 3444 Sheet metalwork
HQ: Metal Sales Manufacturing Corporation
545 S 3rd St Ste 200
Louisville KY 40202
502 855-4300

(G-12409)
MULTIPLEX COMPANY INC (HQ)
2100 Future Dr (47172-1874)
PHONE..................................812 246-7000
Terry Growcock, *CEO*
J Walter Kisling III, *President*
Ray Uetrecht, *CFO*
◆ EMP: 8
SQ FT: 150,000
SALES (est): 22.1MM
SALES (corp-wide): 1.4B **Publicly Held**
WEB: www.servend.com
SIC: 3585 Cold drink dispensing equip-
ment (not coin-operated)
PA: Welbilt, Inc.
2227 Welbilt Blvd
Trinity FL 34655
727 375-7010

(G-12410)
OAKLEY INDUSTRIES LLC
Also Called: Axis Machine and Tool
1229 Bringham Dr Ste B (47172-2028)
PHONE..................................812 246-2600
Matt Oakley, *President*
Paul Harstrom, *General Mgr*
EMP: 4 EST: 2015
SALES (est): 271.9K **Privately Held**
SIC: 3599 Custom machinery

(G-12411)
OWINGS PATTERNS INC
3011 Progress Way (47172-2022)
PHONE..................................812 944-5577
Fax: 812 944-5644
Robert Owings, *President*
EMP: 15
SQ FT: 6,000
SALES (est): 4MM **Privately Held**
WEB: www.owingspatterns.com
SIC: 3543 Industrial patterns

(G-12412)
RICHARDS SCALE COMPANY
820 S Penn Ave (47172-1627)
P.O. Box S (47172-0417)
PHONE..................................812 246-3354
Fax: 812 246-2255
Dick Lachapell, *President*
Joy Goff, *Purch Dir*
Tom Best, *Sales Staff*
Dan Waddell, *Sales Staff*
▲ EMP: 6
SQ FT: 5,000
SALES (est): 1MM **Privately Held**
WEB: www.scalepro.com
SIC: 3596 Industrial scales; weighing ma-
chines & apparatus

(G-12413)
ROLLERBOAT INC
2810 Coopers Ln (47172-9535)
PHONE..................................512 931-3936
David Lee, *Principal*
F Jean Lee, *Principal*
EMP: 2 EST: 2012

SALES (est): 256.6K **Privately Held**
SIC: 3732 Non-motorized boat, building &
repairing

(G-12414)
**SELLERSBURG METALS &
WLDG CO**
1000 Service Dr (47172-1459)
P.O. Box 414 (47172-0414)
PHONE..................................812 248-0811
William Niemann, *President*
William Nieman, *President*
Karisa Harbin, *Corp Secy*
EMP: 10
SQ FT: 6,000
SALES (est): 1.7MM **Privately Held**
SIC: 3449 Miscellaneous metalwork

(G-12415)
SIDNEY & JANICE BOND
4400 Sunrise Ct (47172-9248)
PHONE..................................812 366-8160
Sidney Bond, *Principal*
EMP: 2
SALES (est): 145.9K **Privately Held**
SIC: 2452 8049 Log cabins, prefabricated,
wood; modular homes, prefabricated,
wood; physical therapist

(G-12416)
SIGNET CABINETRY INC
1400 Service Dr (47172-1461)
PHONE..................................812 248-0612
Stephen Brown, *President*
EMP: 4
SALES (est): 512.4K **Privately Held**
SIC: 2434 Wood kitchen cabinets

(G-12417)
SIGNET MILLWORK LLC
1400 Service Dr (47172-1461)
PHONE..................................812 248-0612
Steve Brown, *Mng Member*
Scott Gregor,
John Hunter,
EMP: 30 EST: 2013
SQ FT: 32,000
SALES (est): 3.5MM **Privately Held**
SIC: 2599 Cabinets, factory

(G-12418)
**SMALLWOOD CONSULTING
LLC**
7018 Plum Creek Dr (47172-8919)
PHONE..................................812 406-8040
Andrew Smallwood, *Principal*
EMP: 2
SALES (est): 34.2K **Privately Held**
SIC: 8748 2741 4813 7361 Business
consulting; ; ; executive placement; com-
puter software development & applica-
tions; marketing consulting services

(G-12419)
STEVEN A WILLIAMS
Also Called: Williams Backhoe Service
2922 Teakwood Landing Dr (47172-8500)
PHONE..................................812 664-3405
EMP: 2
SALES (est): 110K **Privately Held**
SIC: 3531 Mfg Construction Machinery

(G-12420)
SUPERIOR PRINT INC
840 S Indiana Ave (47172-1614)
P.O. Box 401 (47172-0401)
PHONE..................................812 246-6311
Fax: 812 246-4368
Charles Stewart, *Ch of Bd*
Dennis Amos, *President*
Mark Stewart, *President*
EMP: 30
SQ FT: 7,000
SALES (est): 6.9MM
SALES (corp-wide): 19.1MM **Privately
Held**
SIC: 2752 Commercial printing, offset
PA: Stewart Graphics, Inc.
1419 Fabricon Blvd
Jeffersonville IN 47130
812 283-0455

(G-12421)
VIVID LEDS INC
1108 Dora Dr (47172-8001)
P.O. Box 9 (47172-0009)
PHONE..............................800 974-3570
Michael Zeneri, CEO
EMP: 11 EST: 2010
SALES (est): 1.3MM Privately Held
WEB: www.vividleds.us
SIC: 3229 5063 Bulbs for electric lights;
light bulbs & related supplies

Selma
Delaware County

(G-12422)
CAST METALS TECHNOLOGY
11200 E State Road 32 (47383-9548)
PHONE..............................765 284-3888
EMP: 12
SALES (est): 656.8K Privately Held
SIC: 3599 Machine shop, jobbing & repair

(G-12423)
FDS NORTHWOOD LLC
2727 S County Road 762 E (47383-9708)
PHONE..............................765 289-2481
David Stanley, Principal
EMP: 2
SALES (est): 105.8K Privately Held
SIC: 2499 Wood products

(G-12424)
LEROY R SOLLARS
305 1/2 Rd N (47383)
PHONE..............................765 284-9417
Leroy R Sollars, Principal
EMP: 3
SALES (est): 170.9K Privately Held
SIC: 3572 Tape storage units, computer

(G-12425)
PERFECTION KITCHEN & BATH CTR
Also Called: Perfection Kitchen & Bath Ctr
10210 E Katie Ln (47383-9529)
PHONE..............................765 289-7594
Fax: 765 289-7594
Tom Yoder, President
Carolyn Yoder, Vice Pres
EMP: 2
SALES (est): 241.8K Privately Held
SIC: 2541 1799 Wood partitions & fixtures;
demountable partition installation

Seymour
Jackson County

(G-12426)
ACME SPORTS INC
800 E Tipton St (47274-3524)
P.O. Box 462 (47274-0462)
PHONE..............................812 522-4008
Joe Hardesty, President
Steve Hardesty, Owner
EMP: 2
SALES (est): 266.8K Privately Held
SIC: 3484 Guns (firearms) or gun parts, 30
mm. & below

(G-12427)
AIM MEDIA INDIANA OPER LLC
Tribune The
100 Saint Louis Ave (47274-2304)
PHONE..............................812 522-4871
Melissa Bane, Branch Mgr
EMP: 12
SALES (corp-wide): 42.4MM Privately
Held
SIC: 2711 Commercial printing & newspaper publishing combined
PA: Aim Media Indiana Operating, Llc
2980 N National Rd A
Columbus IN 47201
812 372-7811

(G-12428)
AISIN USA MFG INC (DH)
1700 E 4th Street Rd (47274-4309)
PHONE..............................812 523-1969

Fax: 812 523-1984
Tsukasa Ito, President
Dennis Putman, Vice Pres
Benjamin Wills, Engineer
Mike Held, Accounts Mgr
Takashi Tanaka, Admin Sec
▲ EMP: 277
SQ FT: 276,000
SALES (est): 216.8MM
SALES (corp-wide): 36.6B Privately Held
WEB: www.aisinusa.com
SIC: 3714 Motor vehicle engines & parts
HQ: Aisin Holdings Of America, Inc.
1665 E 4th Street Rd
Seymour IN 47274
812 524-8144

(G-12429)
ALTERRA PLASTICS LLC
2213 Killion Ave (47274-4305)
PHONE..............................812 271-1890
Saquib Toor, Mng Member
◆ EMP: 12
SQ FT: 100,000
SALES (est): 1.2MM Privately Held
SIC: 2821 Molding compounds, plastics

(G-12430)
AMERICAN EXPRESS TRAVEL
709 A Ave E (47274-3234)
PHONE..............................812 523-0106
Bill Baird, Manager
EMP: 150
SALES (corp-wide): 35.5B Publicly Held
WEB: www.astoriasoftware.com
SIC: 4724 7331 2752 Travel agencies; direct mail advertising services; commercial
printing, lithographic
HQ: American Express Travel Related
Services Company, Inc.,
200 Vesey St
New York NY 10285
212 640-2000

(G-12431)
B & H ELECTRIC AND SUPPLY INC (PA)
740 C Ave E (47274-3249)
P.O. Box 1005 (47274-1005)
PHONE..............................812 522-5607
Fax: 812 522-5313
Greg Hunt, President
EMP: 23
SALES (est): 6.2MM Privately Held
SIC: 3621 5063 7699 Motors, electric;
motors, electric; industrial equipment
services

(G-12432)
BARRY STUCKWISCH
Also Called: Barry Stuckwisch Mowing
1330 N State Road 11 (47274-8454)
PHONE..............................812 525-1052
Barry Stuckwisch, Owner
EMP: 4
SALES (est): 150.8K Privately Held
SIC: 3523 Grounds mowing equipment

(G-12433)
BLACKERBY & ASSOCIATES
444 Persimmon Dr (47274-8674)
PHONE..............................812 216-2370
Jerry Blackerby, Owner
EMP: 2
SALES (est): 93.9K Privately Held
SIC: 3544 Special dies, tools, jigs & fixtures

(G-12434)
BLEYS PROSTHETICS & ORTHOTICS
50 Hancock St (47274-4406)
PHONE..............................812 704-3894
William Bley Sr, Owner
EMP: 2
SALES (est): 150K Privately Held
SIC: 3842 Surgical appliances & supplies

(G-12435)
BRYANT PRODUCTS INC
816 F Ave E (47274-3269)
P.O. Box 1227 (47274-3827)
PHONE..............................812 522-5929
Fax: 812 523-1124
Gregg Bryant, President
Tim Bryant, Vice Pres

Scott Bryant, CFO
Scott E Bryant, CFO
EMP: 10
SQ FT: 25,000
SALES: 1.5MM Privately Held
SIC: 2439 7538 2449 2441 Trusses,
wooden roof; diesel engine repair: automotive; wood containers; nailed wood
boxes & shook

(G-12436)
C & T ENGINEERING INC
322 Thompson Rd (47274-3363)
PHONE..............................812 522-5854
Fax: 812 522-6024
Richard Troxell, President
Derick Troxell, Vice Pres
Jeffrey Prewitt, Admin Sec
EMP: 12
SQ FT: 6,700
SALES (est): 1.2MM Privately Held
WEB: www.ctengineeringinc.com
SIC: 3544 7699 Forms (molds), for
foundry & plastics working machinery;
plastics products repair

(G-12437)
CALCEAN LLC
2213 Killion Ave (47274-4305)
PHONE..............................812 672-4995
EMP: 2 EST: 2015
SALES (est): 213.6K Privately Held
SIC: 5052 3295 6211 Nonmetallic minerals & concentrate; minerals, ground or
otherwise treated; mineral leasing dealers

(G-12438)
COMPETITION TL ENGRG IINE INC
2600 Montgomery Dr (47274-8338)
PHONE..............................812 524-1991
Richard Findley, President
Jessie Wyatt, Corp Secy
EMP: 6
SQ FT: 9,000
SALES (est): 795.2K Privately Held
SIC: 3544 Special dies & tools

(G-12439)
CRANE HILL MACHINE INC
Also Called: Royalty
2476 E Us Highway 50 (47274-8697)
PHONE..............................812 358-3534
Fax: 812 358-2351
Marshall Royalty, President
EMP: 25
SQ FT: 37,000
SALES: 3MM Privately Held
SIC: 3599 Machine & other job shop work

(G-12440)
CROWN SUPPLY CO INC
1191 King Ave (47274-1822)
P.O. Box 206 (47274-0206)
PHONE..............................812 522-6987
Fax: 812 523-3100
Paul Personett, President
Gregory Personett, Vice Pres
Sharon Personett, Treasurer
EMP: 14
SQ FT: 16,500
SALES: 1MM Privately Held
SIC: 2541 2434 Table or counter tops,
plastic laminated; wood kitchen cabinets

(G-12441)
CUMMINS
845 A Ave E (47274-3236)
PHONE..............................812 524-6381
David Phillips, Mfg Dir
Frederick Williams, Buyer
Will Horn, Human Res Dir
Luwanna J Hallett, Human Resources
◆ EMP: 5
SALES (est): 574.6K Privately Held
SIC: 3519 Internal combustion engines

(G-12442)
CUMMINS INC
800 E 3rd St (47274-3906)
PHONE..............................812 522-9366
Fax: 812 523-0300
Kellie Mikesell, Safety Mgr
Louis Guretis, Buyer
Chuck Thompson, Engineer
Carl White, Engineer

Darren Wallman, Manager
EMP: 600
SALES (corp-wide): 20.4B Publicly Held
WEB: www.cummins.com
SIC: 3519 3621 3511 Engines, diesel &
semi-diesel or dual-fuel; motors & generators; turbines & turbine generator sets
PA: Cummins Inc.
500 Jackson St
Columbus IN 47201
812 377-5000

(G-12443)
DARLAGE INVESTMENTS LLC
860 F Ave E (47274-3269)
PHONE..............................812 522-5929
Adrienne Nicholson, Manager
EMP: 11
SALES (est): 423.1K Privately Held
SIC: 3999 Manufacturing industries

(G-12444)
DEER COUNTRY EQUIPMENT LLC
Also Called: John Deere Authorized Dealer
1250 W 2nd St (47274-2764)
P.O. Box 549 (47274-0549)
PHONE..............................812 522-1922
Thomas C Bryant, President
Richard L Apsley, Vice Pres
EMP: 25
SQ FT: 23,000
SALES (est): 3.3MM Privately Held
SIC: 5083 7699 5261 3524 Agricultural
machinery & equipment; agricultural
equipment repair services; lawn & garden
equipment; lawn & garden equipment

(G-12445)
DICKSONS INC
Also Called: Dicksons Inspirational Gifts
709 B Ave E (47274-3244)
P.O. Box 368 (47274-0368)
PHONE..............................812 522-1308
Fax: 812 522-1319
Thomas E Templeton, Ch of Bd
James M Potts, President
Sue Watt, Production
Vickie Marshall, Purch Agent
Todd Hubinger, Research
◆ EMP: 200
SQ FT: 220,000
SALES (est): 41.2MM
SALES (corp-wide): 162.5MM Privately
Held
WEB: www.dicksonsgifts.com
SIC: 3961 5049 Rosaries & small religious
articles, except precious metal; religious
supplies
PA: Templeton Coal Company, Inc.
701 Wabash Ave Ste 501
Terre Haute IN 47807
812 232-7037

(G-12446)
DOUGLAS K GRESHAM
1540 N County Road 900 W (47274-9479)
PHONE..............................812 445-3174
Douglas K Gresham, Owner
EMP: 2
SALES (est): 102.7K Privately Held
SIC: 2033 Barbecue sauce: packaged in
cans, jars, etc.

(G-12447)
ENERGY TWO INC
184 E County Road 800 N (47274-9188)
P.O. Box 213, Cortland (47228-0213)
PHONE..............................812 497-3113
Matt Tangman, CEO
Greg Marshall, Treasurer
Ruth Ann Hendrix, Admin Sec
EMP: 3
SALES: 1.1MM Privately Held
SIC: 2824 2836 Soybean fibers; biological
products, except diagnostic

(G-12448)
EXCEL MANUFACTURING INC
1705 E 4th Street Rd (47274-4310)
PHONE..............................812 523-6764
Fax: 812 522-4307
Delbert Kilgas, President
Brent Kilgas, Admin Sec
▲ EMP: 80
SQ FT: 60,000

SALES (est): 21.6MM **Privately Held**
WEB: www.excelmanufacturinginc.com
SIC: **3369** 3599 Nonferrous foundries; machine shop, jobbing & repair

(G-12449)
EXCEL TOOL INC
2020 1st Ave (47274-3396)
PHONE..................812 522-6880
Fax: 812 522-6524
Richard L Elmore, *President*
Jay Elmore, *Vice Pres*
Rod Boardman, *Engineer*
Craig Elmore, *Admin Sec*
EMP: 60
SQ FT: 55,000
SALES (est): 8.6MM **Privately Held**
WEB: www.exceleti.com
SIC: **3544** 3599 Dies & die holders for metal cutting, forming, die casting; industrial molds; machine shop, jobbing & repair

(G-12450)
FINDLEY FOSTER CORP
14 S County Road 1250 E (47274-9553)
PHONE..................812 524-7279
Eileen Foster, *President*
EMP: 9
SQ FT: 60,000
SALES (est): 803.8K **Privately Held**
SIC: **2448** 2441 Pallets, wood; skids, wood; nailed wood boxes & shook

(G-12451)
GRAESSLE-MERCER CO
100 N Pine St (47274-2142)
P.O. Box 288 (47274-0288)
PHONE..................812 522-5478
Fax: 812 522-1545
George G Graessle, *CEO*
Doris Graessle, *Treasurer*
EMP: 20 EST: 1904
SQ FT: 16,450
SALES (est): 3MM **Privately Held**
WEB: www.gmcprint.com
SIC: **2752** 2791 2789 2732 Commercial printing, offset; typesetting; bookbinding & related work; book printing

(G-12452)
HACKMAN CABINET CO
1156 Darcis Dr (47274-7662)
PHONE..................812 522-4118
Harold Jhackman, *Principal*
EMP: 2
SALES (est): 158.4K **Privately Held**
SIC: **2434** Wood kitchen cabinets

(G-12453)
HAWKINS MACHINE & TOOL INC
2166 N County Road 900 E (47274-9290)
PHONE..................812 522-5529
Timothy Hawkins, *Partner*
Sheila Hawkins, *Partner*
EMP: 2
SALES (est): 180K **Privately Held**
SIC: **3544** Special dies, tools, jigs & fixtures

(G-12454)
HICKMAN WILLIAMS & COMPANY
2083 Upper Heiskell Ct (47274-9618)
PHONE..................812 522-6293
EMP: 5
SALES (corp-wide): 190.1MM **Privately Held**
SIC: **3624** Carbon & graphite products
PA: Hickman, Williams & Company
250 E 5th St Ste 300
Cincinnati OH 45202
513 621-1946

(G-12455)
HIGH VALUE METAL INC
101 Blish St (47274-1701)
PHONE..................812 522-6468
Fax: 812 522-6468
Fred Maschino, *President*
Phylis Maschino, *Corp Secy*
EMP: 2
SALES: 25K **Privately Held**
SIC: **3449** Bars, concrete reinforcing: fabricated steel

(G-12456)
HOME PDTS INTL - N AMER INC
885 N Chestnut St (47274-1246)
PHONE..................773 890-1010
Fax: 812 522-4919
John Pugh, *Vice Pres*
EMP: 280
SALES (corp-wide): 501.4MM **Privately Held**
SIC: **3089** Organizers for closets, drawers, etc.: plastic
HQ: Home Products International - North America, Inc.
4501 W 47th St
Chicago IL 60632
773 890-1010

(G-12457)
I-FLY DRONES LLC
5269 E County Road 400 S (47274-9029)
PHONE..................812 524-3863
Andrew Markel, *Principal*
EMP: 2
SALES (est): 155.3K **Privately Held**
SIC: **3721** Motorized aircraft

(G-12458)
INDIANA TRUSS CO LLC
860 F Ave E (47274-3269)
PHONE..................812 522-5929
Scott E Bryant, *Principal*
EMP: 3 EST: 2011
SALES (est): 186.7K **Privately Held**
SIC: **2439** Structural wood members

(G-12459)
INTEGRITY MOLDING INC
2710 Montgomery Dr (47274-8305)
PHONE..................812 524-1243
Larry Bryant, *President*
EMP: 8
SALES (est): 250K **Privately Held**
WEB: www.integritymolding.com
SIC: **3089** Molding primary plastic

(G-12460)
J TEES
9389 N County Road 100 E (47274-9573)
PHONE..................812 524-9292
Scott Jackson, *Owner*
EMP: 2
SALES (est): 125K **Privately Held**
SIC: **2759** Screen printing

(G-12461)
JACKSON-JENNINGS LLC
103 Community Dr (47274-1955)
P.O. Box 304 (47274-0304)
PHONE..................812 522-4911
Robert Marley, *Principal*
EMP: 4
SALES (est): 1MM **Privately Held**
SIC: **1321** Liquefied petroleum gases (natural) production

(G-12462)
KENNEY ORTHOPEDICS SEYMOUR LLC (HQ)
629 E Tipton St (47274-3519)
PHONE..................812 271-1627
John M Kenney, *Mng Member*
Patrick Conley,
William Lester,
Thomas McIntosh,
Timothy C Ruth,
EMP: 5 EST: 2014
SALES: 1.2MM
SALES (corp-wide): 15MM **Privately Held**
SIC: **3842** Surgical appliances & supplies
PA: Kenney Ortho Group, Inc.
208 Normandy Ct
Nicholasville KY 40356
859 241-1015

(G-12463)
KEURIG DR PEPPER INC
Also Called: RC Canada Dry Bottling Company
1450 Schleter Rd (47274-3361)
PHONE..................812 522-3823
EMP: 98 **Publicly Held**
SIC: **2086** Soft drinks: packaged in cans, bottles, etc.

PA: Keurig Dr Pepper Inc.
5301 Legacy Dr
Plano TX 75024

(G-12464)
KING INDUSTRIAL CORPORATION
Also Called: Kinco
105 S Obrien St (47274-2437)
P.O. Box 372 (47274-0372)
PHONE..................812 522-3261
Fax: 812 522-7254
Mark King, *CEO*
EMP: 60
SQ FT: 30,000
SALES (est): 8MM **Privately Held**
WEB: www.kingind.com
SIC: **3544** Special dies & tools

(G-12465)
KREMERS URBAN PHRMCUTICALS INC (HQ)
Also Called: Lannett Company
1101 C Ave W (47274-3342)
PHONE..................812 523-5347
Arthur P Bedrosian, *CEO*
George Stevenson, *President*
John M ABT, *Vice Pres*
Xiu Xiu Cheng, *Vice Pres*
Kevin Smith, *Vice Pres*
▲ EMP: 153
SQ FT: 263,855
SALES (est): 111.2MM
SALES (corp-wide): 633.3MM **Publicly Held**
SIC: **2834** Tablets, pharmaceutical; syrups, pharmaceutical
PA: Lannett Company, Inc.
9000 State Rd
Philadelphia PA 19136
215 333-9000

(G-12466)
LEES READY-MIX & TRUCKING
Also Called: County Materials
1122 E 4th Street Rd (47274-1838)
P.O. Box 496, North Vernon (47265-0496)
PHONE..................812 522-7270
Ted Schultz, *Manager*
EMP: 8
SALES (corp-wide): 9.7MM **Privately Held**
SIC: **3273** 4212 Ready-mixed concrete; local trucking, without storage
PA: Lees Ready-Mix & Trucking Inc.
1100 W Jfk Dr
North Vernon IN 47265
812 346-9767

(G-12467)
LLOYD & MONA SULIVAN
Also Called: Stitch N Time
2169 N County Road 400 E (47274-8613)
PHONE..................812 522-9191
Lloyd Sulivan, *Partner*
Mona Sulivan, *Partner*
EMP: 2
SALES (est): 87.6K **Privately Held**
SIC: **2395** Embroidery & art needlework

(G-12468)
LOGGING
10680 W Seymour Rd (47274-9003)
PHONE..................812 216-3544
Brittney Anderson, *Principal*
EMP: 3
SALES (est): 98.8K **Privately Held**
SIC: **2411** Logging

(G-12469)
MAJESTIC CASKETS & URNS INC
2019 2nd Ave (47274-3213)
PHONE..................812 523-3630
Don Von Dielingen, *President*
EMP: 8
SALES (est): 973.5K **Privately Held**
SIC: **3995** Burial caskets

(G-12470)
MIDWEST SIGN COMPANY INC
819 N Obrien St (47274-1857)
PHONE..................317 931-9535
Mark Booher, *Principal*
EMP: 2 EST: 2010

SALES (est): 136.3K **Privately Held**
SIC: **3993** Signs & advertising specialties

(G-12471)
NEW VISION MANUFACTURING INC
835 E 10th St (47274-1302)
PHONE..................812 522-5585
Jack Matthews, *President*
Lora Fausett, *Admin Sec*
EMP: 8
SALES (est): 920.6K **Privately Held**
SIC: **3647** Locomotive & railroad car lights

(G-12472)
P-AMERICAS LLC
Also Called: Pepsico
1811 1st Ave (47274-3316)
PHONE..................812 522-3421
Fax: 812 522-3407
Thomas Levine, *Manager*
EMP: 32
SALES (corp-wide): 63.5B **Publicly Held**
SIC: **2086** 5149 4226 Soft drinks: packaged in cans, bottles, etc.; groceries & related products; special warehousing & storage
HQ: P-Americas Llc
1 Pepsi Way
Somers NY 10589
336 896-5740

(G-12473)
PACKAGING CORPORATION AMERICA
Also Called: Seymour Division
2200 D Ave E (47274-3259)
PHONE..................812 522-3100
Tommy Hines, *Safety Mgr*
Jim Patton, *Branch Mgr*
Kevin Lovelace, *Manager*
Curt Smith, *Manager*
EMP: 25
SALES (corp-wide): 6.4B **Publicly Held**
WEB: www.columbuscontainer.com
SIC: **2653** 3412 Boxes, corrugated: made from purchased materials; display items, solid fiber: made from purchased materials; metal barrels, drums & pails
PA: Packaging Corporation Of America
1955 W Field Ct
Lake Forest IL 60045
847 482-3000

(G-12474)
PD SUB LLC
Also Called: Jim Pharmatech
2223 Killion Ave (47274-4305)
PHONE..................812 524-0534
Jeff Dorries, *CFO*
David Sandilands, *CFO*
EMP: 50
SALES: 30.1MM
SALES (corp-wide): 23.1MM **Privately Held**
SIC: **2834** Pharmaceutical preparations
PA: Pd International Holdings, Llc
13161 Lakefront Dr
Earth City MO 63045
314 968-2376

(G-12475)
PHOENIX CUSTOM KITCHENS INC
Also Called: Buffington Custom Kitchens
6600 N Us Highway 31 (47274-8511)
PHONE..................812 523-1890
Fax: 812 522-6532
Ron Buffington, *President*
EMP: 4
SQ FT: 6,000
SALES: 300K **Privately Held**
SIC: **2434** Wood kitchen cabinets

(G-12476)
PRAIRIE GOLD RUSH
17390 S State Road 58 (47274-8321)
PHONE..................812 342-3608
Cheryl Delap, *Owner*
Ken Delap, *Co-Owner*
EMP: 2
SALES (est): 107.3K **Privately Held**
SIC: **2721** Periodicals: publishing only

G E O G R A P H I C

(G-12477)
PREMIER AG CO-OP INC (PA)
811 W 2nd St (47274-2711)
P.O. Box 304 (47274-0304)
PHONE..................................812 522-4911
Fax: 812 372-6801
Harold Cooper, *CEO*
James Geis, *President*
Dennis Stewart, *Vice Pres*
Bruce Morris, *Manager*
Bill Metz, *Admin Sec*
EMP: 20 **EST:** 1923
SQ FT: 5,000
SALES: 90.9MM **Privately Held**
SIC: 5153 5191 5172 5411 Grain eleva-
tors; farm supplies; petroleum brokers;
convenience stores; cooperage stock
products: staves, headings, hoops, etc.

(G-12478)
R R DONNELLEY & SONS COMPANY
709 A Ave E (47274-3234)
PHONE..................................812 523-1800
Mark A Angelson, *CEO*
EMP: 7
SALES (corp-wide): 6.9B **Publicly Held**
SIC: 2759 Commercial printing
PA: R. R. Donnelley & Sons Company
35 W Wacker Dr Ste 3650
Chicago IL 60601
312 326-8000

(G-12479)
RBS TEES CO
1102 Gaiser Dr (47274-3642)
PHONE..................................812 522-8675
Randy Brown, *Owner*
EMP: 2
SALES: 81K **Privately Held**
SIC: 2396 Screen printing on fabric articles

(G-12480)
RNS IMAGING INC
574 Lasher Dr (47274-1938)
PHONE..................................812 523-2435
Richard Stewart, *President*
EMP: 2
SALES (est): 188.8K **Privately Held**
SIC: 3829 Medical diagnostic systems, nu-
clear

(G-12481)
ROYALTY INVESTMENTS LLC
Also Called: Cranehill Mch & Fabrication
2476 E Us Highway 50 (47274-8697)
PHONE..................................812 358-3534
Marshall Royalty,
David W Burgess,
Erin Royalty,
EMP: 35
SQ FT: 70,000
SALES (est): 3.5MM **Privately Held**
WEB: www.cranehillmachine.com
SIC: 3599 Machine shop, jobbing & repair

(G-12482)
SCHNEIDERS WOOD SHOP INC
5910 N Us Highway 31 (47274-8514)
PHONE..................................812 522-4621
Fax: 812 522-4621
Irving R Schneider Jr, *President*
Gary Schneider, *Treasurer*
EMP: 3
SALES: 400K **Privately Held**
SIC: 2448 Pallets, wood

(G-12483)
SCHWARZ PHARMA
1101 C Ave W (47274-3342)
PHONE..................................812 523-3457
Fax: 812 523-1887
Carol Rorig, *Administration*
EMP: 3
SALES (est): 81.8K **Privately Held**
SIC: 2834 Pharmaceutical preparations

(G-12484)
SEXTON MELINDA
Also Called: Sexton & Associates
622 W 2nd St (47274-2126)
PHONE..................................812 522-4059
Melinda Sexton, *Owner*
Rusty Cauldwell, *Project Mgr*
Bryan May, *Web Dvlpr*

Brian Montiel, *Art Dir*
EMP: 3 **EST:** 1997
SALES (est): 224K **Privately Held**
SIC: 7311 3993 7336 Advertising consultant; signs & advertising specialties; commercial art & graphic design; creative
services to advertisers, except writers;
silk screen design

(G-12485)
SEYMOUR MANUFACTURING CO INC (HQ)
500 N Broadway St (47274-1793)
P.O. Box 248 (47274-0248)
PHONE..................................812 522-2900
Fax: 812 522-6109
Bill Henthorn, *CEO*
Berl Grant, *President*
Steven Fletcher, *Vice Pres*
Roger Hackman, *Vice Pres*
Richard V Redmond, *Treasurer*
▲ **EMP:** 110 **EST:** 1872
SQ FT: 210,000
SALES (est): 28.3MM **Privately Held**
WEB: www.seymourmfg.com
SIC: 3423 3429 Garden & farm tools, in-
cluding shovels; fireplace equipment,
hardware: andirons, grates, screens

(G-12486)
SEYMOUR PRECISION MACHINING
1733 1st Ave (47274-3383)
PHONE..................................812 524-1813
Keith Staley, *President*
Troy Gohimer, *Vice Pres*
Marsha Gohimer, *Treasurer*
Jenny Staley, *Admin Sec*
EMP: 7
SQ FT: 3,600
SALES: 900K **Privately Held**
SIC: 3599 Machine shop, jobbing & repair

(G-12487)
SEYMOUR TRBUNE A CAL LTD PRTNR
Also Called: Tribune, The
100 Saint Louis Ave (47274-2304)
P.O. Box 447 (47274-0447)
PHONE..................................812 522-4871
Fax: 812 522-3371
Richard Davis, *Principal*
Freedom N Inc, *General Ptnr*
R D Threshie Jr, *General Ptnr*
Zach Spicer, *Regional Mgr*
EMP: 37
SQ FT: 6,500
SALES (est): 1.9MM **Privately Held**
WEB: www.freedom.com
SIC: 2711 Newspapers, publishing & print-
ing

(G-12488)
SEYMOUR TUBING INC (DH)
1515 E 4th Street Rd (47274-4301)
PHONE..................................812 523-0842
Fax: 812 523-3648
Toru Nishikado, *President*
Yasutaka Nakano, *Treasurer*
Ken Nagai, *Admin Sec*
Yoshiharu Shibanuma, *Admin Sec*
▲ **EMP:** 325
SQ FT: 358,536
SALES (est): 72.8MM
SALES (corp-wide): 53.2B **Privately Held**
WEB: www.seymourtubing.com
SIC: 3312 Tubes, steel & iron
HQ: Nippon Steel & Sumikin Pipe Co., Ltd.
1-1-3, Yurakucho
Chiyoda-Ku TKY 100-0
367 580-275

(G-12489)
SILGAN PLASTICS CORPORATION
3779 N County Road 850 E (47274-9921)
PHONE..................................812 522-0900
EMP: 2
SALES (corp-wide): 4B **Publicly Held**
SIC: 3089 Plastic containers, except foam
HQ: Silgan Plastics Corporation
14515 North Outer 40 Rd # 210
Chesterfield MO 63017

(G-12490)
SILGAN PLASTICS LLC
3779 N County Road 850 E (47274-9281)
PHONE..................................812 522-0900
John Peters, *Opers Mgr*
Ron Johnson, *Human Resources*
Deanna Lawyer, *Human Resources*
Jim Burns, *Manager*
Jack Stephen, *Manager*
EMP: 180
SQ FT: 450,000
SALES (corp-wide): 4B **Publicly Held**
WEB: www.silganplastics.com
SIC: 3085 Plastics bottles
HQ: Silgan Plastics Llc
14515 North Outer 40 Rd # 210
Chesterfield MO 63017
800 274-5426

(G-12491)
SILGAN PLASTICS LLC
S O Brien St (47274)
PHONE..................................812 522-0900
Thomas Hendricks, *President*
EMP: 10
SALES (corp-wide): 4B **Publicly Held**
WEB: www.silganplastics.com
SIC: 3089 3085 Plastic containers, except
foam; plastics bottles
HQ: Silgan Plastics Llc
14515 North Outer 40 Rd # 210
Chesterfield MO 63017
800 274-5426

(G-12492)
SPACEGUARD INC
Also Called: Spaceguard Products
711 S Commerce Dr (47274-4023)
PHONE..................................812 523-3044
Fax: 812 523-3362
Edward Murphy, *Chairman*
Hauris Lewis, *Senior VP*
Eddie Murphy, *Vice Pres*
Matt Sipe, *QC Mgr*
Scott Jump, *Accounts Mgr*
▼ **EMP:** 40 **EST:** 1995
SQ FT: 55,000
SALES (est): 8.3MM **Privately Held**
WEB: www.spaceguardproducts.com
SIC: 3496 Mesh, made from purchased
wire; barbed wire, made from purchased
wire

(G-12493)
SPRAY SAND & GRAVEL INC (PA)
1635 Murray Hill Dr (47274-4806)
PHONE..................................812 523-8081
John R Schleibaum, *President*
Peggy Schleibaum, *Corp Secy*
EMP: 6
SALES (est): 989.7K **Privately Held**
SIC: 1442 Gravel mining

(G-12494)
SPRAY SAND & GRAVEL INC
6492 E State Road 258 (47274-9655)
P.O. Box 1104 (47274-3704)
PHONE..................................812 522-5417
Fax: 812 522-6860
Rick Schleibaum, *Owner*
EMP: 7
SALES (corp-wide): 989.7K **Privately Held**
SIC: 1442 Construction sand & gravel
PA: Spray Sand & Gravel, Inc
1635 Murray Hill Dr
Seymour IN 47274
812 523-8081

(G-12495)
STOGDILL SPORTS
1244 Hickory Hill Rd (47274-2620)
PHONE..................................812 524-7081
Howard Stogdill, *Owner*
EMP: 2 **EST:** 2000
SALES (est): 60K **Privately Held**
SIC: 2395 Embroidery products, except
schiffli machine

(G-12496)
THORMAX ENTERPRISES LLC
6976 Lydia Ln (47274-4812)
P.O. Box 683 (47274-0683)
PHONE..................................812 530-7744
Chad Whittymore, *Mng Member*

EMP: 1
SALES: 2.2MM **Privately Held**
SIC: 3317 3498 4225 Steel pipe & tubes;
fabricated pipe & fittings; miniwarehouse,
warehousing

(G-12497)
TRAVOMATIC CORP INDIANA DIV
2230 D Ave E (47274-3259)
P.O. Box 628 (47274-0628)
PHONE..................................812 522-8177
Fax: 812 522-9441
Carolyn Findley, *Principal*
EMP: 3
SALES (est): 289.2K **Privately Held**
SIC: 3085 Plastics bottles

(G-12498)
VALEO NORTH AMERICA INC
1231 A Ave N (47274-3364)
PHONE..................................248 619-8300
Steve Finlay, *Site Mgr*
Ricardo Munguia, *Purchasing*
Justin Butler, *QC Mgr*
Sanders Brott, *Engineer*
Graham Segal, *Engineer*
EMP: 656 **Privately Held**
SIC: 3641 Electric lamps
HQ: Valeo North America, Inc.
150 Stephenson Hwy
Troy MI 48083

(G-12499)
WELMER JEWELERS INC
106 S Chestnut St (47274-2302)
P.O. Box 488 (47274-0488)
PHONE..................................812 522-4082
Joseph L Welmer, *President*
Betty Welmer, *Corp Secy*
EMP: 2
SQ FT: 1,500
SALES: 120K **Privately Held**
SIC: 5944 7631 3911 Jewelry, precious
stones & precious metals; silverware;
watches; watch repair; jewel settings &
mountings, precious metal

(G-12500)
WICHMAN WOODWORKING INC
8305 N County Road 300 E (47274-9112)
PHONE..................................812 522-8450
Dale Wichman, *President*
EMP: 2
SALES: 125K **Privately Held**
SIC: 2431 Millwork

(G-12501)
WOODSONG PUBLISHING
5989 Spring Meadow Ln (47274-5505)
PHONE..................................812 528-0875
Larry Arrowood, *Principal*
EMP: 2
SALES (est): 59.2K **Privately Held**
SIC: 2741 Miscellaneous publishing

(G-12502)
WRIGHT IMPLEMENT I LLC
1250 W 2nd St (47274-2764)
PHONE..................................812 522-1922
Fax: 812 522-2086
EMP: 25
SALES (corp-wide): 14.9MM **Privately Held**
SIC: 5083 7699 5261 3524 Agricultural
machinery & equipment; agricultural
equipment repair services; lawn & garden
equipment; lawn & garden equipment
PA: Wright Implement I, Llc
3225 Carter Rd
Owensboro KY 42301
270 683-3606

Sharpsville
Tipton County

(G-12503)
AAA MUDJACKERS
5873 W 300 N (46068-9146)
PHONE..................................317 574-1990
David Mc Donald, *Principal*
EMP: 2

SALES (est): 262.5K **Privately Held**
SIC: **1389** 1771 Mud service, oil field drilling; concrete work

(G-12504)
CLAYHILL WIND & SOLAR LLC
3660 W 500 S (46068-9406)
PHONE.................................765 437-2395
R Rex Higgins,
Rebecca Higgins,
EMP: 2
SALES (est): 200K **Privately Held**
SIC: **3511** Turbines & turbine generator sets

(G-12505)
FUNCTIONAL DEVICES INC
101 Commerce Dr (46068-9412)
P.O. Box 437 (46068-0437)
PHONE.................................765 883-5538
Fax: 765 883-7505
Kenneth W Rittmann, *Ch of Bd*
Mark Fernandes, *President*
Karen Price, *Business Mgr*
Tony Stevenson, *Business Mgr*
Zach Adams, *Production*
▲ EMP: 2
SQ FT: 50,000
SALES (est): 727.1K **Privately Held**
WEB: www.functionaldevices.com
SIC: **3625** 3643 3823 Relays, for electronic use; current-carrying wiring devices; industrial instrmnts msrmnt display/control process variable

(G-12506)
HARMON BOATS INC
596 W Meridian St (46068-9581)
PHONE.................................765 963-5358
Toll Free:...877 -
Roger A Harmon, *President*
Roger Harmon, *President*
EMP: 9
SALES (est): 550K **Privately Held**
SIC: **3732** 7532 7699 4493 Boats, fiberglass: building & repairing; body shop, trucks; boat repair; boat yards, storage & incidental repair

(G-12507)
TIPTON ENGRG ELC MTR SVCS INC
159 W Vine St (46068-8927)
P.O. Box 76 (46068-0076)
PHONE.................................765 963-3380
Matt Braught, *President*
Jennifer Braught, *Treasurer*
EMP: 4
SQ FT: 7,500
SALES (est): 500K **Privately Held**
SIC: **7371** 7694 5063 Computer software systems analysis & design, custom; electric motor repair; motors, electric

Shelburn
Sullivan County

(G-12508)
NASH SHEET METAL CO
4295 E County Road 800 N (47879-8061)
PHONE.................................812 397-5306
Patrick L Nash, *Owner*
EMP: 3
SALES (est): 320.4K **Privately Held**
SIC: **3444** Ducts, sheet metal; ventilators, sheet metal

(G-12509)
ROYSTER CLARK CLOSED
2745 W State Road 48 (47879-8320)
PHONE.................................812 397-2617
Scamah Orm, *Principal*
EMP: 2
SALES (est): 101.8K **Privately Held**
SIC: **1479** Chemical & fertilizer mining

(G-12510)
SIGNALING SOLUTION INC
Also Called: Tssi
6274 N County Road 25 E (47879-8260)
P.O. Box 168, Westminster MD (21158-0168)
PHONE.................................812 533-1345

William Ataras, *President*
Colleen Ataras, *Admin Sec*
EMP: 5
SALES: 100K **Privately Held**
SIC: **3679** Electronic components

(G-12511)
SKY THUNDER LLC
6521 N Us Highway 41 (47879-8346)
PHONE.................................812 397-0102
M A Kimberling, *Mng Member*
▲ EMP: 40
SQ FT: 12,000
SALES: 3MM **Privately Held**
SIC: **2899** Flares, fireworks & similar preparations

(G-12512)
VW CO
6521 N Us Highway 41 (47879-8346)
PHONE.................................812 397-0102
Michael Kimberling, *Executive Asst*
EMP: 2
SALES (est): 236K **Privately Held**
SIC: **2899** Fireworks

(G-12513)
WHOLESALE DRAINAGE SUPPLY INC
8300 N Us Highway 41 (47879-8219)
PHONE.................................812 397-5100
Joe Frey, *President*
EMP: 6
SALES (est): 1MM **Privately Held**
SIC: **3272** Concrete products used to facilitate drainage

(G-12514)
WRIGHTS TIMBER PRODUCTS
201 S Hymera Church St (47879-8107)
PHONE.................................812 383-7138
Carl E Wright, *Owner*
EMP: 5
SALES (est): 217.1K **Privately Held**
SIC: **2411** Wood chips, produced in the field

Shelby
Lake County

(G-12515)
PROEDGE INC
23326 Shelby Rd (46377)
P.O. Box 201 (46377-0201)
PHONE.................................219 552-9550
Fax: 219 552-9596
Adelbert Bell, *President*
Kim Patterson, *Data Proc Staff*
Susan Bell, *Admin Sec*
Jessica France, *Clerk*
EMP: 25
SQ FT: 45,000
SALES (est): 3.6MM **Privately Held**
SIC: **4225** 2754 General warehousing & storage; commercial printing, gravure

(G-12516)
SQUARE 1 DESIGNS & SIGNS
23316 Shelby Rd (46377)
P.O. Box 163 (46377-0163)
PHONE.................................219 552-0079
Kathy Shelbourne, *Partner*
Grant Everman, *Partner*
EMP: 3
SALES (est): 338.6K **Privately Held**
WEB: www.sq1designs.com
SIC: **3993** Electric signs

Shelbyville
Shelby County

(G-12517)
A & H ENTERPRISES LLC
Also Called: Office Hub
60 E Washington St (46176-1351)
PHONE.................................317 398-3070
Shannon Huber, *Mng Member*
Scott Huber,
EMP: 8

SALES: 1.5MM **Privately Held**
SIC: **5943** 2754 7349 5712 Office forms & supplies; business form & card printing, gravure; building maintenance services; office furniture

(G-12518)
ATMOSPHERE DYNAMICS CORP
1107 Saint Joseph St (46176-3241)
PHONE.................................317 392-6262
Fax: 317 392-1778
John M Coffin, *President*
EMP: 3
SQ FT: 7,000
SALES (est): 300K **Privately Held**
WEB: www.atmospheredynamics.com
SIC: **2819** Catalysts, chemical

(G-12519)
BANKS MACHINE & ENGRG INC
Also Called: Capital Industries
1677 W 400 N (46176-8586)
PHONE.................................317 642-4980
Fax: 812 526-8807
Joseph P McKinley, *President*
Kent Colclazier, *Vice Pres*
Steve Halfaker, *Vice Pres*
Robert Schrock, *Engineer*
Dragan Stevanovic, *Sales Mgr*
▼ EMP: 60
SQ FT: 50,000
SALES (est): 15.1MM **Privately Held**
SIC: **3443** 3599 3535 3569 Fabricated plate work (boiler shop); machine & other job shop work; custom machinery; conveyors & conveying equipment; robots, assembly line: industrial & commercial; assembly machines, including robotic; industrial machinery & equipment; robots, industrial

(G-12520)
BARRINGTON PACKAGING SYSTEMS I
19 W South St (46176-2021)
PHONE.................................847 382-8066
EMP: 4 EST: 2014
SALES (est): 327.4K **Privately Held**
SIC: **2631** Container, packaging & boxboard

(G-12521)
BLUE RIVER PRINTING INC
55 E Washington St (46176-1350)
P.O. Box 211 (46176-0211)
PHONE.................................317 392-3676
Bryan K Gaffney, *President*
EMP: 6
SALES (est): 1.2MM **Privately Held**
SIC: **7334** 2759 Photocopying & duplicating services; commercial printing

(G-12522)
BLUE RIVER ROASTERS LLC
2138 Cherokee Dr (46176-3128)
PHONE.................................317 392-9668
Vicki L Jaussaud, *Principal*
EMP: 2 EST: 2013
SALES (est): 85K **Privately Held**
SIC: **2095** Roasted coffee

(G-12523)
BLUE RIVER STAMPING INC
600 Northridge Dr (46176-8929)
PHONE.................................317 395-5600
Shimana Matsuiosi, *President*
Hiriama Minoru, *Vice Pres*
Mitsutake Yanakita, *Vice Pres*
Gounami Kacuhiko, *Treasurer*
EMP: 80
SALES (est): 5.5MM
SALES (corp-wide): 1.9B **Privately Held**
WEB: www.pkusa.com
SIC: **3465** Automotive stampings
HQ: Pk U.S.A., Inc.
600 Northridge Dr
Shelbyville IN 46176
317 395-5500

(G-12524)
BRAZEWAY INC
1109 Lincoln St (46176-2349)
PHONE.................................317 392-2533
Fax: 317 392-2538
Todd Walterman, *Safety Dir*
Amber Dile, *Human Res Dir*

Dave Skrzypchak, *Branch Mgr*
Brandon Frey, *Manager*
EMP: 55
SALES (corp-wide): 218MM **Privately Held**
WEB: www.brazeway.com
SIC: **3354** 3444 Aluminum extruded products; sheet metalwork
PA: Brazeway, Inc.
2711 E Maumee St
Adrian MI 49221
517 265-2121

(G-12525)
BREWER MACHINE & MFG INC
1501 Miller Ave (46176-3136)
P.O. Box 985 (46176-3985)
PHONE.................................317 398-3505
Fax: 317 398-3234
Darren Brewer, *President*
Anthony Winkler, *Corp Secy*
Randy Moorhead, *Vice Pres*
Vicky Isley, *Admin Sec*
EMP: 30
SQ FT: 54,000
SALES (est): 6.1MM **Privately Held**
WEB: www.brewermachine.com
SIC: **3599** 3842 Machine shop, jobbing & repair; welders' hoods

(G-12526)
CENTRAL COCA-COLA BTLG CO INC
405 N Harrison St (46176-1303)
PHONE.................................800 241-2653
EMP: 2
SALES (corp-wide): 35.4B **Publicly Held**
SIC: **5149** 2086 8741 Soft drinks; soft drinks: packaged in cans, bottles, etc.; management services
HQ: Central Coca-Cola Bottling Company, Inc.
555 Taxter Rd Ste 550
Elmsford NY 10523
914 789-1100

(G-12527)
CNC MACHINE INC
1380 N 450 W (46176-9019)
PHONE.................................317 835-4575
Fax: 317 835-1711
Charley Crum, *President*
Becky Crum, *Admin Sec*
EMP: 5
SQ FT: 5,200
SALES (est): 611K **Privately Held**
SIC: **3599** Machine shop, jobbing & repair

(G-12528)
CUSTOM COATINGS
2446 N Michigan Rd (46176-9726)
P.O. Box 192 (46176-0192)
PHONE.................................317 392-7908
Fax: 317 392-1724
Dennis Metz, *Manager*
EMP: 4
SALES (est): 430.9K **Privately Held**
SIC: **3479** Painting, coating & hot dipping

(G-12529)
CUSTOM MACHINING INC (PA)
1204 Hale Rd (46176-2371)
P.O. Box 192 (46176-0192)
PHONE.................................317 392-2328
Darrell Mollenkopf, *President*
Patricia Mollenkopf, *Corp Secy*
Sara Goedde, *Office Mgr*
Lisa Lay, *Office Admin*
EMP: 25 EST: 1938
SALES (est): 3.7MM **Privately Held**
WEB: www.custommachininginc.com
SIC: **3541** 3554 Grinding machines, metalworking; coating & finishing machinery, paper

(G-12530)
DRILLING & TRENCHING SUP INC
Also Called: Drilling World
860 Elston Dr (46176-1823)
PHONE.................................317 825-0919
Karen Arnett, *Branch Mgr*
EMP: 11

SALES (corp-wide): 9.2MM **Privately Held**
SIC: 3545 Drilling machine attachments & accessories
PA: Drilling & Trenching Supply, Incorporated
1458 Mariani Ct
Tracy CA 95376
510 895-1650

(G-12531)
DUNHAM RUBBER BELTING CORP
245 Northridge Dr (46176-8521)
PHONE..................................317 604-5313
EMP: 2
SALES (est): 77.4K **Privately Held**
SIC: 3052 Rubber belting

(G-12532)
ENBI GLOBAL INC (PA)
1703 Mccall Dr (46176-9783)
PHONE..................................317 395-7324
Scott Saunders, *Principal*
Bill Nieboer, *VP Opers*
Darren Kraft, *Engineer*
Mark Jaworski, *Design Engr*
Greg Rochford, *Human Res Mgr*
EMP: 11
SALES (est): 6.8MM **Privately Held**
SIC: 3547 Rolling mill machinery; finishing equipment, rolling mill

(G-12533)
ENBI INDIANA INC (PA)
1703 Mccall Dr (46176-9783)
PHONE..................................317 398-3267
James Maulucci, *President*
Jim Maulucci, *Plant Mgr*
Mark Jaworski, *Design Engr*
Kevin Stephens, *Controller*
Greg Rochford, *Human Res Mgr*
▲ **EMP:** 125 **EST:** 1992
SQ FT: 50,000
SALES (est): 44.9MM **Privately Held**
SIC: 3069 Printers' rolls & blankets: rubber or rubberized fabric

(G-12534)
FREUDENBERG-NOK GENERAL PARTNR
Rubber Products Division
1700 Miller Ave (46176-3114)
P.O. Box 38 (46176-0038)
PHONE..................................317 421-3400
Fax: 317 392-3406
Jon Dolan, *Manager*
EMP: 215
SALES (corp-wide): 8.3B **Privately Held**
WEB: www.freudenberg-nok.com
SIC: 3053 5085 3714 Oil seals, rubber; packing, rubber; gaskets; motor vehicle parts & accessories
HQ: Freudenberg-Nok General Partnership
47774 W Anchor Ct
Plymouth MI 48170
734 451-0020

(G-12535)
FREUDENBERG-NOK GENERAL PARTNR
Also Called: Freduenberg-Nok Sealing Tech
877 Miller Ave Ste B (46176-2309)
PHONE..................................734 354-5504
Joe Diale, *Branch Mgr*
EMP: 20
SALES (corp-wide): 8.3B **Privately Held**
SIC: 2821 3714 3053 3061 Plastics materials & resins; motor vehicle parts & accessories; gaskets, packing & sealing devices; mechanical rubber goods
HQ: Freudenberg-Nok General Partnership
47774 W Anchor Ct
Plymouth MI 48170
734 451-0020

(G-12536)
GD COX INC
Also Called: Sports Locker Room
105 S Harrison St (46176-1343)
PHONE..................................317 398-0035
Fax: 317 398-0041
Gary Cox, *President*
Diana Cox, *Vice Pres*
EMP: 5

SQ FT: 3,500
SALES (est): 460K **Privately Held**
SIC: 2759 7389 Screen printing; embroidering of advertising on shirts, etc.

(G-12537)
HUBER BROTHERS INC
3955 N 100 W (46176-9416)
PHONE..................................317 392-1566
Fax: 317 392-0422
John T Huber, *President*
James Huber, *Vice Pres*
EMP: 9 **EST:** 1970
SQ FT: 25,000
SALES (est): 1.1MM **Privately Held**
WEB: www.huberbrothers.com
SIC: 3479 1721 Painting of metal products; commercial painting

(G-12538)
INDIANA PRECISION FORGE LLC
Also Called: I P F
302 Northbrook Dr (46176-9305)
PHONE..................................317 421-0102
Norihito Kuntani, *President*
Rodney Anspaugh, *Principal*
Yashkik Nakahara,
Takashi Iwaguchi,
▲ **EMP:** 75 **EST:** 1996
SQ FT: 85,000
SALES (est): 16.1MM
SALES (corp-wide): 53.2B **Privately Held**
WEB: www.ipfllc.com
SIC: 3714 Motor vehicle brake systems & parts; motor vehicle body components & frame
HQ: Nippon Steel & Sumikin Precision Forge, Inc.
1, Nittocho
Handa AIC
569 221-811

(G-12539)
INSTALLED BUILDING PDTS LLC
Also Called: B C I
886 W Mausoleum Rd (46176-9719)
PHONE..................................317 398-3216
Ted Pike, *Manager*
EMP: 6
SQ FT: 6,600
SALES (corp-wide): 1.1B **Publicly Held**
WEB: www.dwdcpa.com
SIC: 1742 3357 Insulation, buildings; non-ferrous wiredrawing & insulating
HQ: Installed Building Products Llc
495 S High St Ste 50
Columbus OH 43215
614 221-3399

(G-12540)
J & L TOOL & MACHINE INC
1441 Miller Ave (46176-3134)
P.O. Box 367 (46176-0367)
PHONE..................................317 398-6281
Fax: 317 392-4267
Kathy Callahan, *President*
Robert Landwerlen, *Vice Pres*
Dennis Ashwill, *Opers Mgr*
Rick Walton, *Technology*
Debbie Sommerfield, *Administration*
EMP: 14
SQ FT: 22,000
SALES (est): 2.6MM **Privately Held**
WEB: www.jltool.com
SIC: 3599 Machine shop, jobbing & repair

(G-12541)
JEFFERSON HOMEBUILDERS INC
Also Called: Culpeper Wood Preservers
701 W Mausoleum Rd (46176-9720)
P.O. Box 260 (46176-0260)
PHONE..................................317 398-0874
Fax: 317 398-4825
Jay Macy, *Vice Pres*
Jim Poweoo, *Branch Mgr*
EMP: 37
SALES (corp-wide): 71.6MM **Privately Held**
WEB: www.culpeperwood.com
SIC: 2491 2861 Structural lumber & timber, treated wood; gum & wood chemicals

PA: Jefferson Homebuilders, Inc.
501 N Main St
Culpeper VA 22701
540 825-5898

(G-12542)
KASCO MFG CO INC
170 W 600 N (46176-9737)
PHONE..................................317 398-7973
Fax: 317 398-2107
P Phil Kaster, *President*
Danette Kaster, *CFO*
Freda P Kaster, *Admin Sec*
EMP: 27 **EST:** 1965
SQ FT: 16,000
SALES (est): 5.5MM **Privately Held**
WEB: www.kascomfg.com
SIC: 3523 Farm machinery & equipment; planting, haying, harvesting & processing machinery; fertilizing machinery, farm; spreaders, fertilizer

(G-12543)
KIRBY RISK CORPORATION
Also Called: Arco Electric Products
2325 E Michigan Rd (46176-1896)
PHONE..................................317 398-9713
Fax: 317 398-2655
Hal Pike, *Manager*
EMP: 13
SALES (corp-wide): 401.3MM **Privately Held**
WEB: www.kirbyrisk.com
SIC: 3469 3675 Capacitor or condenser cans & cases, stamped metal; electronic capacitors
PA: Kirby Risk Corporation
1815 Sagamore Pkwy N
Lafayette IN 47904
765 448-4567

(G-12544)
KN PLATECH AMERICA CORPORATION
1755 Mccall Dr (46176-9783)
PHONE..................................317 392-7707
Hiroaki Koga, *President*
Takayuki Masuda, *Principal*
Mark Haler, *Opers Mgr*
Wally Blake, *QC Mgr*
Randie Danhauer, *Human Res Mgr*
▲ **EMP:** 2
SALES (est): 526.6K **Privately Held**
SIC: 3089 Blow molded finished plastic products

(G-12545)
KNAUF INSULATION INC
240 Elizabeth St (46176-1420)
PHONE..................................317 421-3341
Bob Claxton, *President*
Jason Hoke, *Engineer*
EMP: 288
SALES (corp-wide): 6.8B **Privately Held**
SIC: 3296 Fiberglass insulation
HQ: Knauf Insulation, Inc.
1 Knauf Dr
Shelbyville IN 46176
317 398-4434

(G-12546)
KNAUF INSULATION INC
400 Walker St (46176-1680)
PHONE..................................317 398-4434
Bob Knecht, *Branch Mgr*
EMP: 400
SALES (corp-wide): 6.8B **Privately Held**
WEB: www.knaufusa.com
SIC: 3296 Fiberglass insulation
HQ: Knauf Insulation, Inc.
1 Knauf Dr
Shelbyville IN 46176
317 398-4434

(G-12547)
KNAUF INSULATION INC (HQ)
1 Knauf Dr (46176-8626)
PHONE..................................317 398-4434
Christopher Griffin, *CEO*
Ian Boland, *Area Mgr*
Jeffery Brisley, *Senior VP*
Jeff Brisley, *Vice Pres*
Glenn Brower, *Vice Pres*
◆ **EMP:** 150

SALES (est): 460.4MM
SALES (corp-wide): 6.8B **Privately Held**
WEB: www.knaufusa.com
SIC: 3296 Fiberglass insulation
PA: Gebr. Knauf Kg
Am Bahnhof 7
Iphofen 97346
932 331-0

(G-12548)
LACAP CONTAINER CORP
521 One Half E Hndrcks St (46176)
PHONE..................................317 835-4282
Fax: 317 398-8328
Jerry L Caplinger, *President*
Roy Knopp, *Vice Pres*
Joy Caplinger, *Admin Sec*
EMP: 6
SQ FT: 11,500
SALES: 1MM **Privately Held**
WEB: www.lacapcontainer.com
SIC: 2653 Boxes, corrugated: made from purchased materials

(G-12549)
LUNA PRESS PRODUCTIONS LLC
118 S Harrison St (46176-1344)
PHONE..................................317 398-8895
EMP: 2
SALES (est): 78K **Privately Held**
SIC: 2741 Misc Publishing

(G-12550)
MAKUTA TECHNICS INC
2155 Intelliplex Dr (46176-8538)
PHONE..................................317 642-0001
Elmer Kaplan, *Ch of Bd*
Stuart P Kaplan, *President*
EMP: 17
SQ FT: 11,000
SALES (est): 3.4MM **Privately Held**
WEB: www.makuta.com
SIC: 3089 3714 3544 2821 Plastic processing; motor vehicle parts & accessories; special dies, tools, jigs & fixtures; plastics materials & resins

(G-12551)
MARK CONCRETE PRODUCTS INC
1126 Miller Ave (46176-2358)
PHONE..................................317 398-8616
James Ross, *President*
Sharon Ross, *Treasurer*
EMP: 8
SQ FT: 20,000
SALES: 593.9K **Privately Held**
SIC: 3272 5999 4225 Burial vaults, concrete or precast terrazzo; septic tanks, concrete; concrete products, precast; monuments, finished to custom order; warehousing, self-storage

(G-12552)
NAI PRINT SOLUTIONS
168 W Hendricks St (46176-2004)
PHONE..................................317 392-1207
EMP: 2
SALES (est): 83.9K **Privately Held**
SIC: 2752 Commercial printing, lithographic

(G-12553)
NCI GROUP INC
Also Called: Metal Building Components Mbci
1780 Mccall Dr (46176-9783)
P.O. Box 657 (46176-0657)
PHONE..................................317 392-3536
Fax: 317 392-1111
Robert Fordham, *Plant Supt*
Bill Craft, *Plant Mgr*
EMP: 50
SALES (corp-wide): 1.7B **Publicly Held**
SIC: 3448 3444 Prefabricated metal components; metal roofing & roof drainage equipment
HQ: Nci Group, Inc.
10943 N Sam Huston Pkwy W
Houston TX 77064
281 897-7788

▲ = Import ▼=Export
◆ =Import/Export

(G-12554)
NEXT PRODUCTS LLC
2201 E Michigan Rd (46176-1821)
P.O. Box 310 (46176-0310)
PHONE..................................317 392-4701
William J Williams,
◆ **EMP:** 15
SALES (est): 1.5MM **Privately Held**
SIC: 3993 Signs & advertising specialties

(G-12555)
NIPPON STEEL & SUMIKIN
400 Northbrook Dr (46176-5511)
PHONE..................................219 228-0110
Kimura Hadeoki, *President*
Keita Maruishi, *CFO*
Junichi Hiwatashi, *CTO*
EMP: 4 **EST:** 2016
SALES (est): 161K **Privately Held**
SIC: 3315 Steel wire & related products

(G-12556)
PIERCY MACHINE CO INC
945 W 300 S (46176-9604)
PHONE..................................317 398-9296
Sandra Piercy, *President*
Gaylon M Piercy, *Vice Pres*
EMP: 4
SALES: 260K **Privately Held**
WEB: www.piercymachine.net
SIC: 3599 3544 Machine shop, jobbing &
repair; special dies, tools, jigs & fixtures

(G-12557)
PILKINGTON NORTH AMERICA INC
Also Called: Shelbyville Plant
300 Northridge Dr (46176-8954)
PHONE..................................317 392-7000
Daniel Eckstein, *Human Res Dir*
Dan Robinson, *Manager*
Tom Burke, *Info Tech Mgr*
EMP: 550
SALES (corp-wide): 5.6B **Privately Held**
WEB: www.low-eglass.com
SIC: 3211 3231 Flat glass; products of
purchased glass
HQ: Pilkington North America, Inc.
811 Madison Ave Fl 1
Toledo OH 43604
614 802-7027

(G-12558)
PK USA INC (HQ)
600 Northridge Dr (46176-8929)
PHONE..................................317 395-5500
Fax: 317 395-5501
Kazuhiko Onami, *President*
Satoshi Moritoki, *Principal*
Mori Toki, *Vice Pres*
Tim Grimes, *Engineer*
Yoichiro Miura, *Sales Staff*
▲ **EMP:** 325
SQ FT: 240,000
SALES (est): 126.4MM
SALES (corp-wide): 1.9B **Privately Held**
WEB: www.pkusa.com
SIC: 3465 3089 3714 3429 Body parts,
automobile: stamped metal; injection
molding of plastics; motor vehicle engines
& parts; furniture builders' & other house-
hold hardware
PA: Press Kogyo Co., Ltd.
1-1-1, Shiohama, Kawasaki-Ku
Kawasaki KNG 210-0
442 662-581

(G-12559)
PLASTIC MOLDINGS COMPANY LLC
Also Called: PMC
1451 Miller Ave (46176-3134)
PHONE..................................317 392-4139
Fax: 317 392-4309
Jed Morris, *Manager*
EMP: 150
SALES (corp-wide): 32.2MM **Privately Held**
WEB: www.plasticmoldings.com
SIC: 3089 Injection molding of plastics
PA: Plastic Moldings Company, Llc.
9825 Kenwood Rd Ste 302
Blue Ash OH 45242
513 921-5040

(G-12560)
PRECISN FBRCTN OF SHLBYVLE INC
7340 E State Road 44 (46176-9106)
PHONE..................................765 544-2204
Kyle Ketchum, *Principal*
EMP: 4
SALES (est): 448.1K **Privately Held**
SIC: 3444 Sheet metalwork

(G-12561)
PRINT IT WEAR IT INC
679 Brentwood Dr (46176-9572)
PHONE..................................317 946-1456
Michelle L Robbins, *Owner*
EMP: 2
SALES (est): 90.5K **Privately Held**
SIC: 2752 Commercial printing, litho-
graphic

(G-12562)
RISCO PRODUCTS INC
1344 N Michigan Rd (46176-9754)
PHONE..................................317 392-6150
Scott Luie, *President*
Rich Clark, *Vice Pres*
▲ **EMP:** 2
SALES (est): 165K **Privately Held**
SIC: 3499 Safe deposit boxes or chests,
metal; safes & vaults, metal

(G-12563)
ROB NOLLEY INC
Also Called: Tubesock, Inc.
1110 Fallway Ct (46176-3600)
P.O. Box 26 (46176-0026)
PHONE..................................317 825-5211
Robert Nolley, *President*
EMP: 4
SALES (est): 290K **Privately Held**
SIC: 7372 7373 7374 7376 Prepackaged
software; computer integrated systems
design; data processing & preparation;
computer facilities management; com-
puter maintenance & repair;

(G-12564)
RUSH JAW COMPANY THE INC
6870 W 100 S (46176-9024)
PHONE..................................317 729-5095
Glenn D Rush, *President*
Cathy Rush, *Admin Sec*
EMP: 4
SQ FT: 6,000
SALES: 700K **Privately Held**
SIC: 3545 3599 Chucks: drill, lathe or
magnetic (machine tool accessories); ma-
chine shop, jobbing & repair

(G-12565)
RYOBI DIE CASTING (USA) INC (HQ)
800 W Mausoleum Rd (46176-9719)
PHONE..................................317 398-3398
Fax: 317 398-2873
Takashi Yokoyama, *CEO*
Thomas L Johnson, *President*
Hideki Tanyfuji, *Vice Pres*
Harley Sheets, *Plant Mgr*
George Umeda, *Plant Mgr*
▲ **EMP:** 593
SQ FT: 582,509
SALES (est): 219.8MM
SALES (corp-wide): 2.3B **Privately Held**
WEB: www.ryobidiecasting.com
SIC: 3714 3444 3365 3363 Transmission
housings or parts, motor vehicle; sheet
metalwork; aluminum foundries; alu-
minum die-castings
PA: Ryobi Limited
762, Mesakicho
Fuchu HIR 726-0
847 411-111

(G-12566)
SELCO ENGINEERING INC
1677 W 400 N (46176-8586)
PHONE..................................317 297-1888
Fax: 317 297-4553
Stephan A Sellers, *President*
Kent R Colclazier, *Vice Pres*
Kent Colclazier, *Vice Pres*
Jeff Johnson, *Project Engr*
Dan Miller, *Project Engr*
EMP: 20

SQ FT: 18,000
SALES (est): 3.2MM **Privately Held**
WEB: www.selcoeng.com
SIC: 8711 3599 Industrial engineers; cus-
tom machinery

(G-12567)
SHELBY GRAVEL INC (PA)
Also Called: Shelby Materials
157 E Rampart St (46176-9499)
P.O. Box 242 (46176-0242)
PHONE..................................317 398-4485
Fax: 317 398-2727
Philip E Haehl, *President*
Allen Miracle, *Business Mgr*
Greg Wertz, *Corp Secy*
Matt Haehl, *Vice Pres*
Richard H Haehl, *Vice Pres*
EMP: 30
SQ FT: 5,000
SALES (est): 55.5MM **Privately Held**
SIC: 3273 1442 Ready-mixed concrete;
common sand mining; gravel mining

(G-12568)
SHELBYVILLE NEWSPAPERS INC
Also Called: Extra, The
123 E Washington St (46176-1463)
P.O. Box 750 (46176-0750)
PHONE..................................317 398-6631
Fax: 317 398-0194
Paul Mahoney, *President*
EMP: 67 **EST:** 1947
SQ FT: 10,000
SALES (est): 3.3MM **Privately Held**
WEB: www.shelbynews.com
SIC: 2711 2752 Commercial printing &
newspaper publishing combined; com-
mercial printing, offset

(G-12569)
SIGNS MORE
628 Highpointe Blvd (46176-2200)
PHONE..................................317 392-9184
Holly Simpson, *Owner*
EMP: 2 **EST:** 2010
SALES (est): 15.8K **Privately Held**
SIC: 3993 Signs, not made in custom sign
painting shops

(G-12570)
SQUARE 1 DSIGN MANUFACTURE INC
1 Clark Rd (46176-1867)
P.O. Box 998, Franklin (46131-0998)
PHONE..................................866 647-7771
Sean Hubbard, *CEO*
EMP: 13
SQ FT: 1,800
SALES (est): 3.9MM **Privately Held**
SIC: 3531 3599 5082 5084 Construction
machinery; custom machinery; construc-
tion & mining machinery; sawmill machin-
ery & equipment; woodworking machinery

(G-12571)
STAGE DOOR GRAPHICS
207 S Harrison St (46176-2159)
P.O. Box 277 (46176-0277)
PHONE..................................317 398-9011
Fax: 317 392-4247
Richard Delaney, *Owner*
EMP: 5
SQ FT: 1,600
SALES (est): 260K **Privately Held**
SIC: 2752 2759 Commercial printing, off-
set; commercial printing

(G-12572)
STERLING FORMULATIONS LLC
1402 S Nor St (46176)
PHONE..................................317 490-0823
Vince Plowman, *Vice Pres*
William Selkirk,
▲ **EMP:** 4
SQ FT: 10,000
SALES (est): 654.3K **Privately Held**
SIC: 2899 Chemical preparations

(G-12573)
TAYLOR COMMUNICATIONS INC
1750 Miller Ave (46176-3114)
PHONE..................................317 392-3235
Fax: 317 398-2078
Mark Pohovey, *Plant Mgr*

John Smith, *Safety Mgr*
Greg Schofield, *Manager*
EMP: 97
SALES (corp-wide): 3.5B **Privately Held**
WEB: www.stdreg.com
SIC: 2759 2761 Business forms: printing;
manifold business forms
HQ: Taylor Communications, Inc.
4205 S 96th St
Omaha NE 68127
402 898-6422

(G-12574)
TEN CATE ENBI INC (INDIANA)
1703 Mccall Dr (46176-9783)
PHONE..................................317 398-3267
Daniel Brady, *Vice Pres*
J Lee Mc Neeley, *Admin Sec*
EMP: 120
SQ FT: 55,000
SALES (est): 12.7MM **Privately Held**
WEB: www.tencate-enbi.com
SIC: 3069 3312 Molded rubber products;
blast furnaces & steel mills
PA: Platinum Equity, Llc
360 N Crescent Dr Bldg S
Beverly Hills CA 90210

(G-12575)
THERMO TRANSFER INC
1601 Miller Ave (46176-3138)
PHONE..................................317 398-3503
Fax: 317 398-3548
Narendra P Jhala, *President*
Sondra Jhala, *Vice Pres*
EMP: 12
SQ FT: 17,000
SALES: 3.2MM **Privately Held**
WEB: www.thermotransferinc.com
SIC: 3567 Fuel-fired furnaces & ovens

(G-12576)
TIPPECANOE PRESS INC
230 N Knightstown Rd (46176-8906)
PHONE..................................317 392-1207
Fax: 317 398-0741
Gregory Wickizer, *President*
EMP: 11 **EST:** 1924
SQ FT: 27,000
SALES (est): 1.5MM **Privately Held**
SIC: 2752 5943 2759 2789 Commercial
printing, offset; office forms & supplies;
letterpress printing; bookbinding & related
work; manifold business forms; coated &
laminated paper

(G-12577)
TORAY RESIN COMPANY
821 W Mausoleum Rd (46176-9719)
PHONE..................................317 398-7833
Delight Owu, *Engineer*
Fred Hourigan, *Electrical Engi*
Jeffrey Scott, *Sales Staff*
Mark Barton, *Manager*
Sandy McColley, *Executive*
EMP: 65
SALES (corp-wide): 20.6B **Privately Held**
SIC: 2821 Plastics materials & resins
HQ: Toray Resin Company
2800 Livernois Rd D115
Troy MI 48083
248 269-8800

(G-12578)
TRIUMPH CONTROLS LLC
1960 N Michigan Rd (46176-9384)
PHONE..................................317 421-8760
Fax: 317 392-1963
Dave Tiles, *Branch Mgr*
EMP: 13 **Publicly Held**
WEB: www.triumph-controls.com
SIC: 3812 Aircraft control instruments
HQ: Triumph Controls, Llc
205 Church Rd
North Wales PA 19454

(G-12579)
TRIUMPH GROUP OPERATIONS INC
850 Elston Dr (46176-1823)
PHONE..................................317 392-5000
Jim Mason, *Branch Mgr*
EMP: 2 **Publicly Held**
SIC: 3444 Sheet metalwork

HQ: The Triumph Group Operations Inc
899 Cassatt Rd Ste 210
Berwyn PA 19312

(G-12580)
TRIUMPH THERMAL SYSTEMS INC
1960 N Michigan Rd (46176-9384)
PHONE.................................419 273-1192
David Rasor, *Branch Mgr*
Cris Rickle, *Manager*
EMP: 3 **Publicly Held**
WEB: www.triumph-thermal.com
SIC: 3728 Aircraft parts & equipment
HQ: Triumph Thermal Systems, Llc
200 Railroad St
Forest OH 45843
419 273-2511

(G-12581)
V I P TOOLING INC
739 E Franklin St (46176-1608)
PHONE.................................317 398-0753
Fax: 317 398-7912
Paul R Nolting, *President*
Kelby Graham, *Engineer*
Karen Scott, *Manager*
EMP: 19
SQ FT: 50,000
SALES: 2.3MM **Privately Held**
WEB: www.viptooling.com
SIC: 3545 Precision tools, machinists'; cutting tools for machine tools

(G-12582)
VERNON SHARP
Also Called: Sharp's Woodshop
2202 W Mckay Rd (46176-9069)
PHONE.................................317 398-0631
Fax: 317 392-9488
Vernon Sharp, *Owner*
EMP: 4
SQ FT: 3,000
SALES (est): 240.7K Privately Held
SIC: 2499 Decorative wood & woodwork

(G-12583)
W A P LLC
Also Called: Pure Flow Airdog
705 W Mausoleum Rd (46176-9720)
PHONE.................................317 421-3180
Fax: 317 421-3190
Wayne Michael Farr, *General Mgr*
Clifford Strachman, *Exec Dir*
EMP: 40
SQ FT: 30,000
SALES (est): 652.1K
SALES (corp-wide): 6.7MM **Privately Held**
WEB: www.wellmanautomotive.com
SIC: 3519 Parts & accessories, internal combustion engines
PA: Shares Inc
1611 S Miller St
Shelbyville IN 46176
317 398-8218

(G-12584)
WAP INC
Also Called: Diesel Rx Products
705 W Mausoleum Rd (46176-9720)
P.O. Box 441014, Indianapolis (46244-1014)
PHONE.................................877 421-3187
David E Duba, *President*
EMP: 5
SALES (est): 912.9K **Privately Held**
SIC: 3519 Parts & accessories, internal combustion engines

(G-12585)
WILLIAMS PLASTICS LLC
2201 E Michigan Rd (46176-1821)
P.O. Box 212 (46176-0212)
PHONE.................................317 398-1630
Fax: 317 398-3561
William J Williams, *President*
Rick Owen, *Exec VP*
Pam Brown, *Vice Pres*
Clay Williams, *Vice Pres*
Mike Gobel, *Plant Mgr*
▲ **EMP:** 160
SQ FT: 165,000

SALES (est): 38MM **Privately Held**
WEB: www.williamsindustries.com
SIC: 3089 2759 2752 Injection molding of plastics; decals: printing; screen printing; commercial printing, offset

(G-12586)
YUSHIRO MANUFACTURING AMER INC
Also Called: Yuma
783 W Mausoleum Rd (46176-9720)
P.O. Box 217 (46176-0217)
PHONE.................................317 398-9862
Aisaku Ota, *CEO*
Masahisa Hirobe, *President*
Kaz Takakura, *Principal*
Shingo Kikuchi, *Vice Pres*
Dwane L Rice, *Treasurer*
▲ **EMP:** 38
SQ FT: 54,800
SALES: 33MM
SALES (corp-wide): 296.2MM **Privately Held**
WEB: www.yumaind.com
SIC: 2992 2899 2842 2841 Rust arresting compounds, animal or vegetable oil base; chemical preparations; specialty cleaning, polishes & sanitation goods; soap & other detergents
PA: Yushiro Chemical Industry Co., Ltd.
2-34-16, Chidori
Ota-Ku TKY 146-0
337 506-761

Sheridan
Hamilton County

(G-12587)
ABZ CORP
4310 W State Road 38 (46069-9639)
PHONE.................................317 758-2699
Pam Powell, *President*
▲ **EMP:** 2
SALES (est): 299.1K **Privately Held**
SIC: 3496 Miscellaneous fabricated wire products

(G-12588)
CHERRYTREE FARMS LLC
4310 W State Road 38 (46069-9639)
P.O. Box 108 (46069-0108)
PHONE.................................317 758-4495
John Corbett, *Partner*
EMP: 10
SALES: 1.4MM **Privately Held**
WEB: www.cherrytreefarms.com
SIC: 2011 Pork products from pork slaughtered on site

(G-12589)
EMC PRECISION MACHINING II LLC
701 S Main St (46069-1340)
PHONE.................................317 758-4451
Jack Zeman,
EMP: 77
SALES (corp-wide): 13.9MM **Privately Held**
SIC: 3451 Screw machine products
PA: Emc Precision Machining Ii, Llc
145 Northrup St
Elyria OH 44035
440 365-4171

(G-12590)
HUBS CHUB INC
Also Called: Hubs-Chub
2451 W 246th St (46069-9332)
PHONE.................................317 758-5494
Fax: 317 758-5494
Philip L Yeater, *President*
EMP: 15
SQ FT: 2,400
SALES: 400K **Privately Held**
WEB: www.mtbr.com
SIC: 3949 Fishing equipment

(G-12591)
JBS UNITED INC
4310 W State Road 38 (46069-9639)
PHONE.................................800 382-9909
EMP: 10
SQ FT: 4,500

SALES (corp-wide): 130.9MM **Privately Held**
SIC: 2048 5153 Mfg Prepared Feeds Whol Grain/Field Beans
PA: Jbs United, Inc.
4310 W State Road 38
Sheridan IN 46069
317 758-4495

(G-12592)
JBS UNITED INC
322 S Main St (46069-1113)
PHONE.................................317 758-2609
Howard Thomas, *Vice Pres*
John M Corbett, *Exec Dir*
John Corbett,
EMP: 25
SALES (est): 1.8MM **Privately Held**
SIC: 2048 Prepared feeds

(G-12593)
JBS UNITED ANIMAL HLTH II LLC
322 S Main St (46069-1113)
PHONE.................................317 758-2616
Joseph S Duffey, *
EMP: 15
SALES (est): 1.2MM **Privately Held**
SIC: 2834 Pharmaceutical preparations

(G-12594)
JBS UNITED TRADING INC
4310 W State Road 38 (46069-9639)
PHONE.................................317 758-4495
John M Corbett, *Chairman*
EMP: 2 **EST:** 2012
SALES (est): 80.9K **Privately Held**
SIC: 2048 Prepared feeds

(G-12595)
KNOTHOLE WOODWORKS LLC
3852 W State Road 38 (46069-9603)
PHONE.................................317 600-8151
Bryan Essex, *Owner*
EMP: 2 **EST:** 2011
SALES (est): 174.3K **Privately Held**
SIC: 2431 Millwork

(G-12596)
REEDER & KLINE MACHINE CO INC
501 W 261st St (46069-9219)
PHONE.................................317 846-6591
Fax: 317 846-9409
Lawrence C Sparks III, *President*
David Cole, *Corp Secy*
EMP: 40 **EST:** 1947
SQ FT: 100,000
SALES (est): 593.4K **Privately Held**
WEB: www.reederkline.com
SIC: 3599 3541 Machine shop, jobbing & repair; machine tools, metal cutting type

(G-12597)
ROCKWELL DIVERSIFIED WOODWORKS
26715 Dunbar Rd (46069-9316)
PHONE.................................317 758-4797
EMP: 2 **EST:** 2007
SALES (est): 142.9K **Privately Held**
SIC: 2431 Millwork

(G-12598)
SHERIDAN MANUFACTURING CO INC
508 S Main St (46069-1337)
PHONE.................................317 758-6000
Fax: 317 758-0811
Jim Newby, *President*
Larry Newby, *Corp Secy*
EMP: 4
SQ FT: 3,000
SALES (est): 536.9K **Privately Held**
SIC: 3599 Machine shop, jobbing & repair

(G-12599)
UNITED ANIMAL HEALTH INC (PA)
322 S Main St (46069-1113)
P.O. Box 108 (46069-0108)
PHONE.................................317 758-4495
John B Swisher, *CEO*
Donald E Orr Jr, *President*
John Corbett, *Principal*
John L McGraw, *Vice Pres*

Douglas M Webel, *Vice Pres*
▼ **EMP:** 52
SQ FT: 5,000
SALES (est): 139.7MM **Privately Held**
WEB: www.jbsunited.com
SIC: 2048 5153 0213 Livestock feeds; grains; hog feedlot

(G-12600)
UNITED ANIMAL HEALTH INC
Also Called: Phytex
4310 W State Road 38 (46069-9639)
PHONE.................................207 771-0965
Donald E Orr, *Branch Mgr*
EMP: 10
SALES (corp-wide): 139.7MM **Privately Held**
SIC: 2048 5153 0213 Livestock feeds; grains; hog feedlot
PA: United Animal Health, Inc.
322 S Main St
Sheridan IN 46069
317 758-4495

(G-12601)
WALLACE GRAIN CO INC
604 S Main St (46069-1339)
P.O. Box 109 (46069-0109)
PHONE.................................317 758-4434
Fax: 317 758-4435
Craig Wallace, *President*
Jamie Mossburg, *General Mgr*
Chris Wallace, *Vice Pres*
EMP: 14
SQ FT: 37,000
SALES (est): 4MM **Privately Held**
SIC: 5191 5153 2048 2041 Feed; grains; prepared feeds; flour & other grain mill products

---

Shipshewana
Lagrange County

(G-12602)
ALL RVS MANUFACTURING INC
1055 N 625 W (46565-8564)
PHONE.................................574 538-1559
Merle Schmucker, *CEO*
Kalynn Schmucker, *Admin Sec*
EMP: 2
SALES (est): 270.7K **Privately Held**
SIC: 3999 Atomizers, toiletry

(G-12603)
AMERICAN RELIANCE INDS CO
860 N Tuscany Dr (46565-9181)
P.O. Box 246 (46565-0246)
PHONE.................................260 768-4704
Fax: 260 768-4983
Curt L Riegsecker, *President*
John Jantzi, *President*
Larry J Chupp, *Vice Pres*
Larry Chupp, *Vice Pres*
Dee Bellows, *Inv Control Mgr*
EMP: 20 **EST:** 2001
SQ FT: 10,000
SALES (est): 4.5MM **Privately Held**
WEB: www.legacysleepers.com
SIC: 3713 Truck cabs for motor vehicles

(G-12604)
AURORA SERVICES INC
7155 N 675 W (46565-9743)
P.O. Box 744 (46565-0744)
PHONE.................................260 463-4901
Daniel Byler, *President*
Dawn Byler, *Vice Pres*
EMP: 3 **EST:** 2001
SALES (est): 250K **Privately Held**
SIC: 2711 Newspapers

(G-12605)
B HONEY & CANDLES
2260 N 1000 W (46565-9011)
PHONE.................................574 642-1145
EMP: 2
SALES (est): 75.6K **Privately Held**
SIC: 3999 Candles

(G-12606)
BEECHYS MOLDING PLUS
1365 N 500 W (46565-9708)
PHONE.................................260 768-7030

David W Beechy, *Principal*
EMP: 5
SALES (est): 456K **Privately Held**
SIC: 3089 Molding primary plastic

(G-12607)
CANVAS SHOP LLC
850 Taylor Dr (46565-8536)
PHONE...................................260 768-7755
Fax: 260 768-7766
Mike Unternahrer, *Owner*
EMP: 3 EST: 1996
SQ FT: 6,000
SALES (est): 297.4K **Privately Held**
WEB: www.thecanvashop.com
SIC: 2394 Awnings, fabric: made from purchased materials

(G-12608)
CNC LASER INC
3408 N 915 W (46565-9605)
PHONE...................................260 562-3953
Fax: 260 562-3953
Robert S Bowen, *President*
EMP: 2
SALES (est): 233.1K **Privately Held**
SIC: 3699 Laser systems & equipment

(G-12609)
CRESTVIEW WOODWORKING LLC
6510 W 450 N (46565-8995)
PHONE...................................260 768-4707
Duane Miller, *Principal*
EMP: 2 EST: 2010
SALES (est): 105.1K **Privately Held**
SIC: 2431 Millwork

(G-12610)
D L MILLER WOODWORKING
5345 N 400 W (46565-8525)
PHONE...................................260 562-9329
D L Miller, *Principal*
EMP: 6
SALES (est): 742.3K **Privately Held**
SIC: 2431 Millwork

(G-12611)
DAVIS HEZAKIH CORP
Also Called: Davis Hotel
255 E Main St (46565-1301)
PHONE...................................260 768-7300
Alvin Miller, *President*
Elsie Miller, *Vice Pres*
EMP: 16
SQ FT: 5,600
SALES (est): 890K **Privately Held**
SIC: 3499 Fire- or burglary-resistive products

(G-12612)
DOUBLE EAGLE INDUSTRIES INC
775 N 740 W (46565-9113)
PHONE...................................260 768-4121
Fax: 260 768-4123
Raymond S Miller, *President*
Rocky Miller, *Exec VP*
Mark Woodworth, *Vice Pres*
EMP: 35
SQ FT: 46,750
SALES (est): 4.7MM **Privately Held**
WEB: www.doubleeagleind.com
SIC: 3713 3621 Truck bodies & parts; generator sets: gasoline, diesel or dual-fuel

(G-12613)
ERVINS MILLWORK SHOP LLC
8645 W 100 S (46565-9472)
PHONE...................................260 768-3222
Ervin S Bontrager, *Owner*
EMP: 7
SALES (est): 852.9K **Privately Held**
SIC: 2426 Hardwood dimension & flooring mills

(G-12614)
FAIRVIEW WOODWORKING
8655 W 100 S (46565-9472)
PHONE...................................260 768-3255
Leroy Bontrager, *Principal*
EMP: 4 EST: 2008
SALES (est): 290.8K **Privately Held**
SIC: 2431 Millwork

(G-12615)
G & B DIRECTIONAL BORING LLC
2620 N 850 W (46565-9767)
PHONE...................................574 538-8132
Enos L Gingerich, *Administration*
EMP: 4 EST: 2015
SALES (est): 373.4K **Privately Held**
SIC: 1381 Directional drilling oil & gas wells

(G-12616)
HIGHLAND RIDGE RV INC
Also Called: Open Range Rv
3195 N State Road 5 (46565-9313)
P.O. Box 460, Middlebury (46540-0460)
PHONE...................................260 768-7771
Randall Graber, *President*
Geoff Hoffman, *Purch Mgr*
Russ Yeo, *QC Mgr*
Gareth Troyer, *Engineer*
Todd Slaubaugh, *Design Engr*
EMP: 330
SALES (est): 62.6MM
SALES (corp-wide): 7.2B **Publicly Held**
SIC: 5561 3799 3792 Campers (pickup coaches) for mounting on trucks; recreational vehicles; camping trailers & chassis
HQ: Jayco, Inc.
903 S Main St
Middlebury IN 46540
574 825-5861

(G-12617)
HILLTOP MACHINE SHOP LLC
10515 W Us Highway 20 (46565-9814)
PHONE...................................260 768-9196
David Yoder,
Samuel F Yoder,
EMP: 6
SALES (est): 440K **Privately Held**
SIC: 3599 Machine shop, jobbing & repair

(G-12618)
INSTANT RAIN IRRIGATION LLC
5420 W 450 N (46565-9808)
PHONE...................................260 336-1237
Kevin Schrock, *Principal*
EMP: 2
SALES (est): 293.9K **Privately Held**
SIC: 2752 Commercial printing, lithographic

(G-12619)
INTEGRITY PALLET LLC
9385 W 750 N (46565-8998)
PHONE...................................574 612-2119
George Etchason, *Principal*
EMP: 3
SALES (est): 128.1K **Privately Held**
SIC: 2448 Wood pallets & skids

(G-12620)
INTEGRITY WOODCRAFTING
4285 N 500 W (46565-9712)
PHONE...................................260 562-2067
EMP: 2
SALES (est): 85.2K **Privately Held**
SIC: 2431 Millwork

(G-12621)
INTERSTATE TRUSS LLC
4875 N 675 W (46565-9774)
PHONE...................................260 463-6124
Andrew Lambright, *Mng Member*
EMP: 5
SALES (est): 246.4K **Privately Held**
SIC: 2439 Structural wood members

(G-12622)
JC REFRIGERATION LLC
6495 W 200 N (46565-8982)
PHONE...................................260 768-4067
Harley Lambright,
Carolyn Lambright,
▼ EMP: 3
SALES (est): 359.8K **Privately Held**
SIC: 7623 3632 Refrigerator repair service; household refrigerators & freezers

(G-12623)
JOJOS PRETZELS
205 N Harrison St (46565)
P.O. Box 728 (46565-0728)
PHONE...................................260 768-7759
Levi King, *Owner*
EMP: 12 EST: 1990
SALES (est): 858.9K **Privately Held**
SIC: 2052 5812 Pretzels; eating places

(G-12624)
KZRV LP
985 N 900 W (46565-9139)
PHONE...................................260 768-4016
Tonja Zook Nicholas, *Partner*
Trista Nunemaker, *Partner*
Daryl E Zook, *General Ptnr*
Art Kalb, *District Mgr*
Kurt Walker, *Plant Mgr*
◆ EMP: 300 EST: 1972
SQ FT: 414,225
SALES (est): 54.9MM
SALES (corp-wide): 7.2B **Publicly Held**
WEB: www.kz-rv.com
SIC: 3792 Trailer coaches, automobile
PA: Thor Industries, Inc.
601 E Beardsley Ave
Elkhart IN 46514
574 970-7460

(G-12625)
L & C WELDING LLC
11705 W 300 S (46565-8631)
PHONE...................................260 593-3410
Larry Miller, *Administration*
EMP: 2 EST: 2009
SALES (est): 89.2K **Privately Held**
SIC: 7692 Welding repair

(G-12626)
L & N WOODWORKING
2240 N 925 W (46565-9135)
PHONE...................................260 768-7008
Leroy Cambright, *Principal*
EMP: 4
SALES (est): 398.3K **Privately Held**
SIC: 2431 Millwork

(G-12627)
L A M B WOODWORKING
5510 W 200 N (46565-9226)
PHONE...................................260 768-7992
Lavern Beechy, *Owner*
EMP: 4
SALES (est): 370.4K **Privately Held**
SIC: 2431 Millwork

(G-12628)
LAKEPARK INDUSTRIES IND INC
750 E Middlebury St (46565-8801)
P.O. Box 729 (46565-0729)
PHONE...................................260 768-7411
Fax: 260 768-4746
James Hoyt, *President*
Lloyd A Miller, *Corp Secy*
Steve Heffner, *Buyer*
EMP: 53
SQ FT: 198,000
SALES (est): 620K **Privately Held**
SIC: 3465 3714 3469 Automotive stampings; motor vehicle parts & accessories; metal stampings
PA: Midway Products Group, Inc.
1 Lyman E Hoyt Dr
Monroe MI 48161

(G-12629)
LAMBRIGHT COUNTRY CHIMES L L C
8340 Us High Way 20 (46565)
PHONE...................................260 768-9138
Orley Lambright, *Mng Member*
EMP: 3 EST: 2008
SALES (est): 277.2K **Privately Held**
SIC: 3999 Wind chimes

(G-12630)
LEGENDARY DESIGNS INC
2685 N 850 W (46565-9767)
P.O. Box 70 (46565-0070)
PHONE...................................260 768-9170
Leon Yoder, *President*
Jason Pletcher, *Prdtn Mgr*
EMP: 4 EST: 1996

SALES (est): 350.6K **Privately Held**
WEB: www.legendarydesigns.com
SIC: 3993 Signs, not made in custom sign painting shops

(G-12631)
LIVIN LITE CORP
Also Called: Livin' Lite Rv
985 N 900 W (46565-9139)
PHONE...................................574 862-2228
Fax: 574 862-2202
Scott Tuttle, *President*
EMP: 35 EST: 2001
SQ FT: 32,000
SALES (est): 7.2MM **Privately Held**
SIC: 3792 Travel trailers & campers

(G-12632)
MASTER PIECE KRAFTS LLC
4875 N 675 W (46565-9774)
PHONE...................................260 768-4330
Adam Yoder, *Owner*
EMP: 3
SALES (est): 254.8K **Privately Held**
SIC: 1751 2499 Carpentry work; decorative wood & woodwork

(G-12633)
MILLER CARRIAGE CO
3035 N 850 W (46565-8942)
PHONE...................................260 768-4553
John Miller, *Owner*
EMP: 6 EST: 1971
SQ FT: 9,600
SALES (est): 480K **Privately Held**
SIC: 3799 Horse trailers, except fifth-wheel type

(G-12634)
MILLER MILLING INC
700 E North Village Dr (46565)
P.O. Box 526 (46565-0526)
PHONE...................................260 768-9171
Floyd Miller, *President*
EMP: 8
SQ FT: 7,200
SALES (est): 590K **Privately Held**
WEB: www.millermilling.com
SIC: 2426 Frames for upholstered furniture, wood

(G-12635)
MILLER STEEL FABRICATORS
3235 N 675 W (46565-8604)
PHONE...................................260 768-7321
Raymond M Miller, *Owner*
Marlene M Miller, *Owner*
EMP: 2
SALES (est): 194.3K **Privately Held**
SIC: 3441 Fabricated structural metal

(G-12636)
MILLERS CUSTOM CABINETS
8170 W State Road 120 (46565-8928)
PHONE...................................260 768-7830
Homer Miller, *Principal*
EMP: 2
SALES (est): 100K **Privately Held**
SIC: 2434 Wood kitchen cabinets

(G-12637)
MK MFG LLC
8895 W 250 N (46565-9618)
PHONE...................................260 768-4678
Michael Yoder, *President*
EMP: 2
SALES (est): 80.6K **Privately Held**
SIC: 3999 Manufacturing industries

(G-12638)
MUDD-OX INC
8525 W 750 N (46565-9294)
PHONE...................................260 768-7221
Matthew Oxender, *President*
EMP: 10
SQ FT: 2,050
SALES (est): 1.7MM **Privately Held**
WEB: www.muddox.net
SIC: 3799 Recreational vehicles

(G-12639)
NEWBURY FARM & LOGGING LLC
3650 N 1150 W (46565-9644)
PHONE...................................574 825-9969

Gary Schrock, *Principal*
EMP: 3
SALES (est): 170K **Privately Held**
SIC: 2411 Logging

(G-12640)
OXBO INTERNATIONAL CORPORATION
10605 W 750 N (46565-9585)
PHONE..................................260 768-3217
Fax: 260 768-3219
Jerry Yoder, *Manager*
EMP: 4
SALES (corp-wide): 231.3MM **Privately Held**
SIC: 3523 Farm machinery & equipment
HQ: Oxbo International Corporation
7275 Batavia Byron Rd
Byron NY 14422
585 548-2665

(G-12641)
PALLET ONE OF INDIANA INC
5345 W 200 N (46565-9228)
PHONE..................................260 768-4021
Vance K Maultsby Jr, *CEO*
Howe Wallace, *CEO*
EMP: 70
SALES (est): 9.1MM
SALES (corp-wide): 403.3MM **Privately Held**
WEB: www.palex.com
SIC: 2448 2426 Pallets, wood; lumber, hardwood dimension
PA: Palletone, Inc
6001 Foxtrot Ave
Bartow FL 33830
863 533-1147

(G-12642)
PALLETONE INDIANA TRNSP LLC
5345 W 200 N (46565-9228)
PHONE..................................260 768-4021
Ted Grubbs, *Principal*
EMP: 11 EST: 2016
SALES (est): 1.4MM **Privately Held**
SIC: 2448 Pallets, wood

(G-12643)
PETER STONE COMPANY
805 E North Village Dr (46565-8651)
P.O. Box 88 (46565-0088)
PHONE..................................260 768-9150
Fax: 260 768-9125
Peter Stone, *President*
Charles Matthews, *Principal*
▲ **EMP:** 25 EST: 1996
SALES (est): 1.5MM **Privately Held**
WEB: www.stonehorses.com
SIC: 3944 7371 Hobby horses; computer software development & applications

(G-12644)
PRINT PLACE INC
8100 W Us Highway 20 B (46565-9169)
PHONE..................................260 768-7878
Fax: 260 768-7068
Aaron Speltis, *President*
Aaron Stoltzfus, *Principal*
EMP: 2
SALES (est): 241.3K **Privately Held**
WEB: www.printplaceindiana.com
SIC: 2752 Commercial printing, offset

(G-12645)
QUALITY FENCE LTD
6450 W 275 N (46565-9103)
PHONE..................................260 768-4986
Mervin Yoder, *President*
Edna Yoder, *Vice Pres*
EMP: 3
SALES: 500K **Privately Held**
SIC: 1799 2499 2448 Fence construction; fencing, wood; pallets, wood

(G-12646)
RED WAGON
255 N Harrison St Ste 206 (46565)
P.O. Box 5 (46565-0005)
PHONE..................................260 768-3090
Heidi Stolppsus, *Owner*
EMP: 2

SALES (est): 56K **Privately Held**
SIC: 3942 3944 5092 Dolls & stuffed toys; games, toys & children's vehicles; toys & hobby goods & supplies

(G-12647)
RIDLEY USA INC
Also Called: Hubbard Feeds
135 Main St (46565)
P.O. Box 156 (46565-0156)
PHONE..................................260 768-4103
Fax: 260 768-4529
Jim Long, *Branch Mgr*
EMP: 24
SALES (corp-wide): 1.2B **Privately Held**
WEB: www.hubbardfeeds.net
SIC: 2048 Livestock feeds
HQ: Ridley Usa Inc.
111 W Cherry St Ste 500
Mankato MN 56001
507 388-9400

(G-12648)
RODEX MACHINING
7400 W 650 N (46565-9244)
PHONE..................................260 768-4844
Fax: 260 768-7455
Eli Mast, *Owner*
EMP: 2
SALES (est): 81.5K **Privately Held**
SIC: 3599 Machine shop, jobbing & repair

(G-12649)
SHIPSHEWANA BREAD BOX CORP
Also Called: Bread Box Bake Shop
140 One Half N Morton St (46565)
P.O. Box 775 (46565-0775)
PHONE..................................260 768-4629
David Scherger, *President*
Margaret Scherger, *Vice Pres*
EMP: 25
SALES (est): 1MM **Privately Held**
WEB: www.shipshewanabakery.com
SIC: 5461 2052 2051 Bread; cookies & crackers; bread, cake & related products

(G-12650)
SLABACH LOGGING LLC
7615 W 200 N (46565-9210)
PHONE..................................260 768-4644
Melvin Slabach, *Principal*
EMP: 3
SALES (est): 363.2K **Privately Held**
SIC: 2411 Logging camps & contractors

(G-12651)
STATE LINE WOODWORKING
6520 N 675 W (46565-8559)
PHONE..................................260 768-4577
Steven Miller, *Principal*
EMP: 2
SALES (est): 221.7K **Privately Held**
SIC: 2431 Millwork

(G-12652)
STATELINE WOODTURNINGS LLC
7005 W 650 N (46565-9778)
PHONE..................................260 768-4507
Jerry Yoder,
EMP: 2
SQ FT: 6,000
SALES (est): 265.9K **Privately Held**
SIC: 2426 Hardwood dimension & flooring mills

(G-12653)
STONEY ACRES WOODWORKING LLC
2685 S 1000 W (46565-8617)
PHONE..................................260 768-4367
Levi Lee Beachy,
EMP: 9
SALES (est): 1.2MM **Privately Held**
SIC: 2431 Millwork

(G-12654)
STREAMSIDE WOODSHOP LLC
2275 N 925 W (46565-9135)
PHONE..................................260 768-7887
Merl Stoltzfus,
Ruby Stoltzfus,
EMP: 2

SALES: 550K **Privately Held**
SIC: 2511 Wood bedroom furniture

(G-12655)
VALLEY LINE WOOD PRODUCTS LLC
2935 N 500 W (46565-9235)
PHONE..................................260 768-7807
Alton Bontreger, *Principal*
▲ **EMP:** 8 EST: 1998
SALES (est): 1.2MM **Privately Held**
SIC: 2514 Household furniture: upholstered on metal frames

(G-12656)
VAN GO INC
7187 N 1150 W (46565-9619)
P.O. Box 12, Wakarusa (46573-0012)
PHONE..................................574 862-2807
EMP: 6
SQ FT: 3,500
SALES (est): 340K **Privately Held**
SIC: 2431 Mfg Woodwork

(G-12657)
WELLSPRING COMPONENTS LLC
1085 N 850 W (46565-9123)
PHONE..................................260 768-7336
Norman R Yoder,
EMP: 8
SQ FT: 12,000
SALES (est): 2MM **Privately Held**
SIC: 3714 3493 3799 Motor vehicle parts & accessories; steel springs, except wire; carriages, horse drawn

(G-12658)
WEST POINT WOODWORKING LLC
6565 W 200 N (46565-9222)
PHONE..................................260 768-4750
Mose Miller,
EMP: 9 EST: 2001
SALES (est): 980.4K **Privately Held**
SIC: 2431 Millwork

(G-12659)
WINGARDS SALES LLC
3715 N State Road 5 (46565-9007)
PHONE..................................260 768-7961
David Wingard,
Denny Troyer,
Sam Wingard,
Velda Wingard,
EMP: 4
SQ FT: 5,000
SALES (est): 689.4K **Privately Held**
SIC: 3365 2511 Aluminum & aluminum-based alloy castings; wood lawn & garden furniture

(G-12660)
YODERS MEATS INC
Also Called: Yoder's Meat Shop
435 S Van Buren St (46565-9176)
PHONE..................................260 768-4715
Robert Yoder, *President*
Perry A Yoder, *Vice Pres*
Rosanna R Yoder, *Admin Sec*
EMP: 9
SALES (est): 1.1MM **Privately Held**
WEB: www.yodersmeatshoppe.com
SIC: 0751 5812 5421 2013 Slaughtering: custom livestock services; restaurant, family: independent; meat markets, including freezer provisioners; sausages & other prepared meats; meat packing plants

Shirley
Henry County

(G-12661)
CONTACT FABRICATORS IND INC
4449 N County Road 950 W (47384-9657)
PHONE..................................765 779-4125
Fax: 765 779-0023
Randall J Russell, *President*
Garland Frederick, *Vice Pres*
EMP: 5

SQ FT: 3,500
SALES: 750K **Privately Held**
SIC: 3643 Contacts, electrical

(G-12662)
SHIRLEY FOODS INC
505 Walnut St (47384-1229)
P.O. Box 457 (47384-0457)
PHONE..................................765 738-6511
Fax: 765 738-6881
Gary Toth, *President*
Brian Toth, *Vice Pres*
Juanita Toth, *Treasurer*
EMP: 10
SQ FT: 8,000
SALES: 220K **Privately Held**
SIC: 2099 Tortillas, fresh or refrigerated

(G-12663)
TECH CASTINGS LLC
1102 South St (47384-1227)
P.O. Box 332 (47384-0332)
PHONE..................................765 535-4100
Jeff Lantz, *President*
EMP: 25
SQ FT: 25,000
SALES (est): 4.9MM **Privately Held**
SIC: 3369 Aerospace castings, nonferrous: except aluminum; castings, except die-castings, precision

Shoals
Martin County

(G-12664)
BOONDOCKS LOGGING LLC ✪
12471 Sanders Ln (47581-7485)
PHONE..................................812 247-3363
James Carpenter, *Owner*
EMP: 2 EST: 2017
SALES (est): 81.7K **Privately Held**
SIC: 2411 Logging

(G-12665)
COUNTRY PINES INC
Also Called: Country Pines Printing
11013 Country Pines Rd (47581-7239)
PHONE..................................812 247-3315
Fax: 812 247-3962
Wilma Albright, *President*
Melvin Albright, *Vice Pres*
Eloise Hay Cox, *Treasurer*
EMP: 10
SQ FT: 3,000
SALES (est): 1.7MM **Privately Held**
SIC: 2752 2791 Commercial printing, offset; typesetting

(G-12666)
GYPSUM EXPRESS LTD
9720 Us Highway 50 (47581-7260)
PHONE..................................812 247-2648
Joseph Dawkins, *Terminal Mgr*
Tim Strahley, *Branch Mgr*
Raymond Ruiz, *Info Tech Mgr*
EMP: 2
SALES (corp-wide): 124.8MM **Privately Held**
SIC: 3537 Trucks: freight, baggage, etc.: industrial, except mining
PA: Gypsum Express Ltd.
8280 Sixty Rd
Baldwinsville NY 13027
315 638-2201

(G-12667)
NEW NGC INC
Also Called: National Gypsum Co
9720 Us Highway 50 (47581-7260)
PHONE..................................812 247-2424
Terri Gammon, *Safety Mgr*
Charles Newell, *Branch Mgr*
EMP: 120
SALES (corp-wide): 685.8MM **Privately Held**
WEB: www.natgyp.com
SIC: 3275 Wallboard, gypsum
HQ: New Ngc, Inc.
2001 Rexford Rd
Charlotte NC 28211

▲ = Import ▼=Export
◆ =Import/Export

(G-12668)
OLD PATHS TRACT SOCIETY INC
11298 Old Paths Ln (47581-7234)
PHONE..................812 247-2560
Fax: 812 247-2476
Kenneth Montgomery, *President*
Stanley Montgomery, *Vice Pres*
Bryan Montgomery, *Supervisor*
Jerald Montgomery, *Admin Sec*
EMP: 19 **EST:** 1937
SQ FT: 12,800
SALES: 542.5K **Privately Held**
SIC: 8661 2731 Non-church religious organizations; pamphlets: publishing & printing

(G-12669)
SHOALS NEWS
311 High St (47581-5502)
P.O. Box 240 (47581-0240)
PHONE..................812 247-2828
Fax: 812 247-2243
Stephen Deckard, *Owner*
EMP: 2
SQ FT: 1,875
SALES (est): 135K **Privately Held**
SIC: 2711 Newspapers: publishing only, not printed on site

(G-12670)
TEDROWS WOOD PRODUCTS INC
7910 Coal Hollow Rd (47581-7334)
P.O. Box 561 (47581-0561)
PHONE..................812 247-2260
Fax: 812 247-2265
Mark Tedrow, *Vice Pres*
Brian Tedrow, *Treasurer*
Bob Tedrow, *Admin Sec*
EMP: 10
SQ FT: 7,500
SALES (est): 1.3MM **Privately Held**
SIC: 2426 Furniture dimension stock, hardwood

(G-12671)
UNITED STATES GYPSUM COMPANY
12802 Deep Cut Lake Rd (47581-7746)
P.O. Box 1377 (47581-1377)
PHONE..................812 247-2101
Fax: 812 247-2371
Pat Vogef, *Branch Mgr*
EMP: 212
SALES (corp-wide): 3.2B **Publicly Held**
WEB: www.usg.com
SIC: 3275 Gypsum products
HQ: United States Gypsum Company Inc
550 W Adams St Ste 1300
Chicago IL 60661
312 606-4000

(G-12672)
UNITED STATES GYPSUM COMPANY
8754 E State Road 450 (47581-7552)
P.O. Box 1377 (47581-1377)
PHONE..................812 388-6866
Pat McFarland, *Principal*
John Jones, *Plant Mgr*
Michaeldiana French, *Foreman/Supr*
Jeff Ralph, *Foreman/Supr*
Jerry Sidebottom, *Foreman/Supr*
EMP: 117
SALES (corp-wide): 3.2B **Publicly Held**
SIC: 3275 Gypsum products
HQ: United States Gypsum Company Inc
550 W Adams St Ste 1300
Chicago IL 60661
312 606-4000

(G-12673)
WHITE RIVER OUTFITTERS LLC
314 Main St (47581-5507)
P.O. Box 812 (47581-0812)
PHONE..................812 787-0921
Cody Roush, *Principal*
EMP: 4 **EST:** 2011
SALES (est): 366K **Privately Held**
SIC: 3949 Sporting & athletic goods

Sidney
Kosciusko County

(G-12674)
INNOVATIVE METALWORKS LLC
106 S Main St (46562-8910)
PHONE..................260 839-0295
Justin Dobeurn, *Owner*
EMP: 2
SALES (est): 278.8K **Privately Held**
SIC: 7692 Welding repair

Silver Lake
Kosciusko County

(G-12675)
COUNTRY WELDING LLC
11706 S 600 W (46982-9243)
PHONE..................260 352-2938
Clarence Boring,
EMP: 2
SALES: 25K **Privately Held**
SIC: 7692 Welding repair

(G-12676)
CUSTOM MARBLE UNLIMITED
10379 S Roosevelt St (46982-9174)
PHONE..................574 594-2948
Greg Helton, *President*
Joellen Helton, *Vice Pres*
EMP: 2
SALES: 55K **Privately Held**
SIC: 2493 Marbleboard (stone face hard board)

(G-12677)
PAR-KAN COMPANY LLC
2915 W 900 S (46982-9300)
PHONE..................260 352-2141
Steve Parker, *CEO*
David Caldwell, *President*
Kenneth Moudy, *Corp Secy*
Rick Burton, *CFO*
◆ **EMP:** 100
SQ FT: 220,000
SALES (est): 26.4MM **Privately Held**
WEB: www.par-kan.com
SIC: 3537 3523 3443 Stands, ground servicing aircraft; trailers & wagons, farm; dumpsters, garbage; hoppers, metal plate

(G-12678)
PIERCETON WELDING & FABG
9730 S State Road 15 (46982-9132)
P.O. Box 126 (46982-0126)
PHONE..................260 352-0106
Fax: 260 352-0107
Rick Craft, *Executive Asst*
EMP: 5
SALES (est): 266.7K **Privately Held**
SIC: 7692 Welding repair

(G-12679)
ROH CUSTOM CABINETRY LLC
6784 W Stat Rd 114 Lot 21 (46982)
PHONE..................260 802-1158
Ryan Harshman, *Principal*
EMP: 2
SALES (est): 84.7K **Privately Held**
SIC: 2434 Wood kitchen cabinets

(G-12680)
SPEEDWAY SAND & GRAVEL INC
2896 S 1600 E (46982-8511)
PHONE..................574 893-7355
Bob Roth, *Principal*
EMP: 2
SALES (est): 111.3K **Privately Held**
SIC: 1442 Construction sand & gravel

(G-12681)
SPLENDOR BOATS LLC
9526 S State Road 15 (46982-9131)
PHONE..................260 352-2835
Brandon Coward, *Sales Staff*
Darren Parker, *Programmer Anys*
Adam Heckaman,
Andrew Heckaman,
Amy Parker,

EMP: 17
SQ FT: 52,400
SALES (est): 3.2MM **Privately Held**
WEB: www.splendorboats.com
SIC: 3089 3732 3714 5551 Plastic processing; boats, fiberglass: building & repairing; motor vehicle parts & accessories; boat dealers

(G-12682)
WABASH VALLEY MANUFACTURING
505 E Main St (46982-8943)
P.O. Box 5 (46982-0005)
PHONE..................260 352-2102
Fax: 260 352-2160
Gene Moriarty, *President*
Daniel Denoble, *Vice Pres*
Vincent Tortorici, *CFO*
Peggi Benson, *Accounting Mgr*
Aneala Bays, *Human Res Dir*
▲ **EMP:** 165
SQ FT: 250,000
SALES (est): 33.5MM **Privately Held**
SIC: 2514 3444 3441 2851 Metal lawn & garden furniture; sheet metalwork; fabricated structural metal; paints & allied products

---

Sims
Grant County

(G-12683)
PIPE CREEK JR
6377 W 600 S (46986-9773)
PHONE..................765 922-7991
Ron Lewis, *Principal*
EMP: 7
SALES (est): 311K **Privately Held**
SIC: 1429 Crushed & broken stone

Solsberry
Greene County

(G-12684)
HENRY HOLSTERS LLC
1604 State Ferry Rd (47459-7007)
PHONE..................812 369-2266
Andrew Henry,
EMP: 2 **EST:** 2008
SALES: 150K **Privately Held**
SIC: 2821 Plastics materials & resins

(G-12685)
HUDSON CONCRETE PRODUCTS INC
Also Called: Hudson Sales & Service
10017 E New Ln (47459-7151)
P.O. Box 24 (47459-0024)
PHONE..................812 825-2917
Fax: 812 825-2917
John V Hudson, *President*
Freeda B Hudson, *Vice Pres*
EMP: 7
SQ FT: 3,600
SALES: 678K **Privately Held**
SIC: 3272 5261 Septic tanks, concrete; lawn & garden equipment

(G-12686)
KIRBY TOOL AND DIE INC
2716 N Pierce Dr (47459-6037)
PHONE..................812 369-7779
Amy Lynn Kirby, *CEO*
EMP: 2
SALES (est): 130K **Privately Held**
SIC: 3441 Fabricated structural metal

(G-12687)
RICKS CUSTOM SHEET METAL LLC
13089 E Newton Dr (47459-8381)
PHONE..................812 825-3959
Ricky Anderson, *Principal*
EMP: 2
SALES (est): 145.8K **Privately Held**
SIC: 3444 Sheet metalwork

South Bend
St. Joseph County

(G-12688)
3BTECH INC
Also Called: 3b Tech Computers
3431 Wm Richards Dr B (46628-9477)
PHONE..................574 233-0508
Johnny Zhu, *CEO*
Jianqing Zhu, *President*
▲ **EMP:** 20
SQ FT: 58,000
SALES: 15MM **Privately Held**
WEB: www.3btech.net
SIC: 5734 3571 Computer & software stores; electronic computers

(G-12689)
A-1 DOOR SPECIALTIES INC
212 Ullery St Ste 3 (46637-3358)
PHONE..................260 749-1635
Shawn Rafferty, *Manager*
EMP: 2
SALES (corp-wide): 1MM **Privately Held**
WEB: www.a-1door.com
SIC: 1751 5211 3429 Window & door installation & erection; door & window products; door locks, bolts & checks
PA: A-1 Door Specialties, Inc
2216 Wayne Haven St Ste A
Fort Wayne IN 46803
260 749-1635

(G-12690)
AAA CABINET GUY LLC
60822 Greenridge Ct (46614-9744)
PHONE..................574 299-9371
Randall L Figg, *Principal*
EMP: 2
SALES (est): 120K **Privately Held**
SIC: 2434 Wood kitchen cabinets

(G-12691)
AAA TOOL AND DIE COMPANY INC (PA)
25101 Cleveland Rd (46628-9734)
PHONE..................574 246-1222
Fax: 574 246-1220
John Shirrell, *President*
Susanne Shirrell, *Corp Secy*
EMP: 17 **EST:** 1961
SQ FT: 20,000
SALES (est): 3.2MM **Privately Held**
SIC: 3544 Special dies & tools; jigs & fixtures

(G-12692)
ABRO INDUSTRIES INC (PA)
3580 Blackthorn Ct (46628-6158)
P.O. Box 1174 (46624-1174)
PHONE..................574 232-8289
Fax: 574 232-8295
Peter F Baranay, *CEO*
Tim Demarais, *Vice Pres*
Daniel C Pease, *Vice Pres*
Nancy Baranay, *Treasurer*
Ashley Schmitt Reed, *Controller*
◆ **EMP:** 30
SQ FT: 14,000
SALES (est): 43.2MM **Privately Held**
WEB: www.abro.com
SIC: 5085 5099 5013 3563 Adhesives, tape & plasters; fire extinguishers; safety equipment & supplies; motor vehicle supplies & new parts; body repair or paint shop supplies, automotive; air & gas compressors; specialty cleaning, polishes & sanitation goods; coated & laminated paper

(G-12693)
ABTREX INDUSTRIES INC
Also Called: Indiana Division
59640 Market St (46614-4021)
PHONE..................574 234-7773
Fax: 574 288-6180
Keith Byars, *President*
EMP: 40
SQ FT: 21,000

SALES (corp-wide): 18.4MM **Privately Held**
WEB: www.abtrex.com
SIC: **3443** 3564 3444 Tanks, lined: metal plate; blowers & fans; sheet metalwork
PA: Abtrex Industries, Inc.
28530 Reynolds St
Inkster MI 48141
734 728-0550

(G-12694)
ACTION MACHINE INC
1847 Prairie Ave (46613-1444)
PHONE..................................574 287-9650
Fax: 574 232-8727
Roger Klinedinst, *President*
Terry Munger, *Vice Pres*
Diana Zeigner, *Marketing Staff*
Bob Guzman, *Manager*
Tim Klinedinst, *Supervisor*
▲ EMP: 16
SQ FT: 12,000
SALES: 3.6MM **Privately Held**
WEB: www.actionmachineinc.com
SIC: **3599** 5013 3714 Machine shop, jobbing & repair; automotive supplies & parts; motor vehicle parts & accessories

(G-12695)
ADMIRAL PETROLEUM COMPANY
52394 Ind St Rte 933 (46637-3813)
PHONE..................................574 272-2051
Vanessa Young, *Branch Mgr*
EMP: 6
SALES (corp-wide): 1B **Privately Held**
SIC: **2911** Petroleum refining
HQ: Admiral Petroleum Company
1410 Commwl Dr Ste 202
Wilmington NC 28403
616 837-6218

(G-12696)
AIR TECHNOLOGY INC
5706 S Bridgeton Ln (46614-6317)
PHONE..................................574 231-0579
James C Short, *President*
▲ EMP: 1
SALES: 1MM **Privately Held**
WEB: www.airtechnologyinc.com
SIC: **3585** Humidifiers & dehumidifiers

(G-12697)
ALPHA BAKING CO INC
Also Called: Kreamo Bakers
1910 Lincoln Way W (46628-2622)
PHONE..................................574 234-0188
Fax: 574 287-1839
Larry K Mitchell, *Manager*
EMP: 15
SQ FT: 50,000
SALES (corp-wide): 228.8MM **Privately Held**
WEB: www.alphabaking.com
SIC: **2051** 4225 Bakery: wholesale or wholesale/retail combined; general warehousing & storage
PA: Alpha Baking Co., Inc.
5001 W Polk St
Chicago IL 60644
773 261-6000

(G-12698)
ALTAPURE LLC
1400 E Angela Blvd # 102 (46617-1365)
PHONE..................................574 485-2145
Carl L Ricciardi,
EMP: 6
SALES (est): 855.7K **Privately Held**
SIC: **2842** Sanitation preparations, disinfectants & deodorants

(G-12699)
AM GENERAL HOLDINGS LLC (HQ)
105 N Niles Ave (46617-2705)
P.O. Box 7025 (46634-7025)
PHONE..................................574 237-6222
Charles M Hall, *President*
Howard Glaser, *President*
John Ulrich, *COO*
Daniel J Dell'orto, *Exec VP*
Thomas R Douglas, *Senior VP*
EMP: 19

SALES: 488.7MM **Privately Held**
SIC: **3714** 3711 8711 Motor vehicle parts & accessories; military motor vehicle assembly; engineering services

(G-12700)
AM GENERAL LLC
Also Called: AM General Commercial
105 N Niles Ave (46617-2705)
P.O. Box 7025 (46634-7025)
PHONE..................................574 235-7326
Andrew Hove, *President*
Howard Glaser, *President*
Daniel Dell'orto, *Exec VP*
Robert Whalen, *Administration*
EMP: 99
SALES (est): 1.6MM **Privately Held**
SIC: **8711** 3711 3714 Engineering services; motor vehicles & car bodies; automobile assembly, including specialty automobiles; transmissions, motor vehicle; motor vehicle body components & frame

(G-12701)
AM GENERAL LLC
105 N Niles Ave (46617-2705)
PHONE..................................574 257-4268
Adare Fritz, *Manager*
Radu Dimian, *Manager*
Tina Woods, *Manager*
EMP: 630 **Privately Held**
WEB: www.amgmil.com
SIC: **3711** Motor vehicles & car bodies
HQ: Am General Llc
105 N Niles Ave
South Bend IN 46617
574 237-6222

(G-12702)
AM GENERAL LLC
711 W Chippewa Ave (46614-3711)
PHONE..................................574 258-6699
James Bryant, *Plant Mgr*
EMP: 325
SQ FT: 185,000 **Privately Held**
WEB: www.amgmil.com
SIC: **3711** 3714 Military motor vehicle assembly; motor vehicle parts & accessories
HQ: Am General Llc
105 N Niles Ave
South Bend IN 46617
574 237-6222

(G-12703)
AMERICAN BOTTLING COMPANY
4610 S Burnett Dr (46614-3822)
PHONE..................................574 291-9000
Bob Shannon, *Manager*
EMP: 38
SQ FT: 6,000 **Publicly Held**
WEB: www.cs-americas.com
SIC: **5149** 2086 Soft drinks; bottled & canned soft drinks
HQ: The American Bottling Company
5301 Legacy Dr
Plano TX 75024

(G-12704)
AMERICAN GREEN TECHNOLOGY INC (HQ)
52129 Ind St Rte 933 (46637-3847)
PHONE..................................269 340-9975
Danny Bogar, *CEO*
Jason Green, *President*
Linda Lee, *Exec VP*
Gordon Norquist, *Exec VP*
Charles Weiser, *Exec VP*
▲ EMP: 16
SALES (est): 14.2MM
SALES (corp-wide): 1.6B **Privately Held**
SIC: **5063** 3564 Lighting fixtures, commercial & industrial; air purification equipment
PA: Ushio Inc.
1-6-5, Marunouchi
Chiyoda-Ku TKY 100-0
356 571-000

(G-12705)
AMERICAN REPROGRAPHICS CO LLC
Also Called: Sbd Reprographics
1303 Northside Blvd (46615-3922)
PHONE..................................574 287-2944
Mark Tallarico, *General Mgr*
EMP: 6
SALES (corp-wide): 394.5MM **Publicly Held**
SIC: **2759** Commercial printing
HQ: American Reprographics Company, L.L.C.
1981 N Broadway Ste 385
Walnut Creek CA 94596
925 949-5100

(G-12706)
AMERICAN SANDBLASTING
57375 Allen St (46619)
PHONE..................................574 233-1384
Joe Kuharic, *Owner*
EMP: 2
SALES (est): 111.8K **Privately Held**
SIC: **3471** Cleaning, polishing & finishing

(G-12707)
ANGELS WINGS EXPEDITED
1246 Echo Dr (46614-2142)
PHONE..................................574 339-3038
Asher Ray, *President*
EMP: 10
SALES: 1.1MM **Privately Held**
SIC: **3715** Truck trailers

(G-12708)
APOLLO PRECISION MACHINING INC
4085 Ralph Jones Dr (46628-9465)
PHONE..................................574 271-1197
Fax: 574 271-1251
Joe Mankowski, *President*
EMP: 20
SQ FT: 20,000
SALES (est): 3.4MM **Privately Held**
WEB: www.apollopm.com
SIC: **3599** Machine shop, jobbing & repair

(G-12709)
APOLLO PRTG & GRAPHICS CTR INC
731 S Michigan St (46601-3101)
PHONE..................................574 287-3707
Fax: 574 288-5373
Gus Koucouthakis Jr, *President*
Janet Koucouthakis, *Vice Pres*
EMP: 20
SQ FT: 12,000
SALES: 2.3MM **Privately Held**
WEB: www.apolloprinting.com
SIC: **2759** Letterpress printing; thermography

(G-12710)
APOTHECARYS OINTMENT LLC
2630 Prairie Ave (46614-4270)
PHONE..................................574 930-6662
Valerie Jones, *Owner*
EMP: 2
SALES (est): 74.4K **Privately Held**
SIC: **2834** Ointments

(G-12711)
AROUND CAMPUS LLC
319 Lamonte Ter (46616-1316)
PHONE..................................574 360-6571
Patricia A Kepschull, *Principal*
EMP: 2
SALES (est): 160.5K **Privately Held**
SIC: **3648** Decorative area lighting fixtures

(G-12712)
ASPHALT ENGINEERS INC
59755 Market St (46614-4024)
PHONE..................................574 289-5557
Fax: 574 289-5558
EMP: 30 EST: 1972
SQ FT: 3,000
SALES: 1.5MM **Privately Held**
SIC: **1771** 2951 Concrete Contractor Mfg Asphalt Mixtures/Blocks

(G-12713)
ASTAR INC
645 Wilber St (46628-2358)
P.O. Box 3566 (46619-0566)
PHONE..................................574 234-2137
Fax: 574 232-1913
Sidney Moore Jr, *President*
Dorothy Moore, *Corp Secy*
EMP: 40
SQ FT: 40,000
SALES (est): 7.3MM **Privately Held**
WEB: www.astar.com
SIC: **3089** 3544 Injection molding of plastics; forms (molds), for foundry & plastics working machinery

(G-12714)
ATTCO MACHINE PRODUCTS INC
2411 Foundation Dr (46628-4391)
PHONE..................................574 234-1063
Richard Verwilst, *President*
Ken La Pace, *Plant Mgr*
EMP: 47 EST: 1962
SQ FT: 26,500
SALES (est): 9.1MM **Privately Held**
WEB: www.attco.com
SIC: **3728** 3769 3812 Aircraft parts & equipment; guided missile & space vehicle parts & auxiliary equipment; missile guidance systems & equipment

(G-12715)
AUCILLA INCORPORATED
3333 N Kenmore St (46628-4375)
PHONE..................................574 234-9036
Fax: 574 234-9057
EMP: 30 EST: 1977
SQ FT: 56,000
SALES (est): 6.4MM **Privately Held**
SIC: **3089** Mfg Plastic Products

(G-12716)
AUNALYTICS INC
460 Stull St Ste 100 (46601-3311)
PHONE..................................574 307-9230
Nitesh Chawla, *President*
Dave Cieslak, *COO*
Tracy D Graham, *CFO*
EMP: 3 EST: 2011
SALES (est): 73.5K
SALES (corp-wide): 627.1K **Privately Held**
SIC: **7371** 7372 7374 8748 Computer software systems analysis & design, custom; business oriented computer software; data processing & preparation; business consulting
PA: Data Realty Llc
460 Stull St Ste 100
South Bend IN 46601
574 307-9230

(G-12717)
AUTO EXTRAS INC
1400 S Main St (46613-2206)
PHONE..................................574 855-2370
James Cretacci, *Principal*
EMP: 6
SALES (est): 346.4K **Privately Held**
SIC: **3465** Body parts, automobile: stamped metal

(G-12718)
AUTOSEM INC
1701 S Main St (46613-2211)
PHONE..................................574 288-8866
Fax: 574 288-6227
Terri Califano, *President*
Terri Calisano, *Financial Exec*
▲ EMP: 17
SQ FT: 30,000
SALES: 1.5MM **Privately Held**
WEB: www.autosem.com
SIC: **3679** 3674 Electronic circuits; semiconductors & related devices

(G-12719)
AVARROTES LULIANA
1601 S Walnut St (46613-1437)
PHONE..................................574 232-6803
Maria Garcia, *Owner*
Guadalupe Garcia, *Co-Owner*
EMP: 2

SALES (est): 122.1K **Privately Held**
SIC: **2032** Mexican foods: packaged in cans, jars, etc.

(G-12720)
BAMAR PLASTICS INC
1702 Robinson St (46613-3490)
PHONE..................................574 234-4066
Fax: 574 234-1849
Barry A Lee, *President*
James McVay, *Vice Pres*
EMP: 30 EST: 1978
SQ FT: 35,000
SALES (est): 6.5MM **Privately Held**
WEB: www.bamarplastics.com
SIC: **3089** Injection molding of plastics

(G-12721)
BARRY SEAT COVER & AUTO GLASS
1924 S Michigan St (46613-2398)
PHONE..................................574 288-4603
Fax: 574 288-4722
Greg Barth, *President*
Gary Barth, *Vice Pres*
EMP: 12 EST: 1945
SALES (est): 1MM **Privately Held**
SIC: **7532** 7536 7538 3714 Upholstery & trim shop, automotive; paint shop, automotive; automotive glass replacement shops; general automotive repair shops; motor vehicle parts & accessories

(G-12722)
BERTRAND PRODUCTS INC
2323 Foundation Dr (46628-4326)
P.O. Box 3786 (46619-0786)
PHONE..................................574 234-4181
Paul Bonin, *President*
Deborah Bonin, *Admin Sec*
EMP: 33 EST: 1953
SQ FT: 44,000
SALES: 4.3MM **Privately Held**
WEB: www.bertrandproducts.net
SIC: **3728** Aircraft assemblies, subassemblies & parts

(G-12723)
BLUDOT INC
4335 Meghan Beeler Ct (46628-8416)
PHONE..................................574 277-2306
Fax: 574 277-3785
W Scott Blue, *President*
▲ EMP: 6
SQ FT: 17,900
SALES (est): 1MM **Privately Held**
WEB: www.bludotinc.com
SIC: **3714** 3568 Motor vehicle brake systems & parts; power transmission equipment

(G-12724)
BLUEFIN SOFTWARE LLC
105 E Jefferson Blvd # 800 (46601-1917)
PHONE..................................574 643-1091
Tanya Stankovich, *Vice Pres*
EMP: 2 EST: 2010
SALES (est): 120K **Privately Held**
SIC: **7372** Prepackaged software

(G-12725)
BRITER PRODUCTS INC
1901 N Bendix Dr (46628-1603)
PHONE..................................574 386-8167
Babulal Lalwani, *CEO*
Avanti Lalwani, *Vice Pres*
EMP: 5
SALES (est): 216.3K **Privately Held**
SIC: **3499** Metal ladders

(G-12726)
BRUSH STROKES INC
19320 Haviland Dr (46637-2016)
PHONE..................................800 272-2307
Charles Bennett, *President*
Linda Bennett, *Treasurer*
EMP: 3
SALES (est): 119.1K **Privately Held**
SIC: **2741** 8412 Art copy & poster publishing; museums & art galleries

(G-12727)
BURKHART ADVERTISING INC (PA)
1335 Mishawaka Ave (46615-2275)
P.O. Box 536 (46624-0536)
PHONE..................................574 233-2101
Fax: 574 236-1953
Janette Burkhart Miller, *Ch of Bd*
Charles B Miller, *President*
Sara Miller, *Vice Pres*
Nancy Seidler, *Project Mgr*
Bill Erdman, *Prdtn Mgr*
EMP: 15
SQ FT: 7,000
SALES (est): 16.7MM **Privately Held**
WEB: www.burkhartadv.com
SIC: **7312** 3993 Billboard advertising; electric signs; neon signs

(G-12728)
BURKHART ADVERTISING INC
1247 Mishawaka Ave (46615-1127)
P.O. Box 536 (46624-0536)
PHONE..................................574 234-4444
Fax: 574 287-7078
Maurie Vanbruaene, *Opers Mgr*
Robert Kraabel, *Manager*
EMP: 19
SALES (corp-wide): 16.7MM **Privately Held**
WEB: www.burkhartadv.com
SIC: **3993** 1799 7312 3444 Signs, not made in custom sign painting shops; sign installation & maintenance; outdoor advertising services; sheet metalwork
PA: Burkhart Advertising Inc.
1335 Mishawaka Ave
South Bend IN 46615
574 233-2101

(G-12729)
BWT LLC
802 Fellows St (46601-3121)
PHONE..................................574 232-3338
Carl Spezio, *Branch Mgr*
EMP: 25 **Privately Held**
SIC: **3398** Metal heat treating
HQ: Bwt Llc
201 Brookfield Pkwy
Greenville SC 29607

(G-12730)
C E M PRINTING & SPECIALITIES
50750 Marie Ct (46637-2317)
PHONE..................................269 684-6998
Edward Mollis, *President*
Charles Mollis, *Vice Pres*
EMP: 2
SALES: 100K **Privately Held**
SIC: **7389** 2759 Printing broker; commercial printing

(G-12731)
C M GRINDING INC
55643 Fairview Ave (46628-1199)
PHONE..................................574 234-6812
Fax: 574 233-8739
Calvis Mayfield, *President*
Adrienne Mayfield, *Admin Sec*
EMP: 10
SQ FT: 6,600
SALES (est): 1.4MM **Privately Held**
SIC: **3599** Grinding castings for the trade

(G-12732)
CENTRAL COCA-COLA BTLG CO INC
1400 W Ireland Rd (46614)
PHONE..................................574 291-1511
Fax: 574 291-1929
Jeff Stroisnki, *Branch Mgr*
EMP: 50
SALES (corp-wide): 35.4B **Publicly Held**
WEB: www.cocacola.com
SIC: **2086** Bottled & canned soft drinks
HQ: Central Coca-Cola Bottling Company, Inc.
555 Taxter Rd Ste 550
Elmsford NY 10523
914 789-1100

(G-12733)
CENTRAL STATES FABRICATING
3015 N Kenmore St (46628-4307)
PHONE..................................574 288-5607
Fax: 574 293-1342
Michael Cocanower, *President*
Ellen Cocanower, *Corp Secy*
Clyde Cocanower, *Vice Pres*
EMP: 14 EST: 1972
SQ FT: 18,000
SALES (est): 2.7MM **Privately Held**
SIC: **3441** 3599 Fabricated structural metal; machine shop, jobbing & repair

(G-12734)
CHASE PLASTIC SERVICES INC
5245 Dylan Dr (46628-6501)
PHONE..................................574 239-4090
Allen Ardeuini, *Co-Owner*
EMP: 15 **Privately Held**
SIC: **3087** Custom compound purchased resins
PA: Chase Plastic Services, Inc.
6467 Waldon Center Dr # 200
Clarkston MI 48346

(G-12735)
CLAEYS CANDY INC
525 S Taylor St (46601-2744)
P.O. Box 1535 (46634-1535)
PHONE..................................574 287-1818
Fax: 574 287-4184
Gregg Claeys, *President*
Michael Machallieck, *Corp Secy*
Donald H Claeys, *Vice Pres*
Brian Machallieck, *Vice Pres*
EMP: 19 EST: 1919
SQ FT: 40,000
SALES (est): 3.8MM **Privately Held**
WEB: www.claeyscandy.com
SIC: **2064** 2066 Candy & other confectionery products; chocolate

(G-12736)
CLEAN-SEAL INC
20900 Ireland Rd (46614-3823)
P.O. Box 2919 (46680-2919)
PHONE..................................574 299-1888
Ronald Moore, *President*
Chris Moore, *Corp Secy*
Bill Dawson, *Vice Pres*
Brandi Nelson, *Regl Sales Mgr*
Linda Sellers, *Regl Sales Mgr*
EMP: 48
SQ FT: 90,000
SALES (est): 8.7MM **Privately Held**
WEB: www.cleangrip.net
SIC: **3052** 5085 Hose, pneumatic: rubber or rubberized fabric; gaskets & seals; springs

(G-12737)
CLP TOWNE INC
Also Called: Towne Air Freight
24805 Us Highway 20 (46628-5911)
PHONE..................................574 233-3183
Philip D Cardinal, *Terminal Mgr*
Ed Murphy, *Manager*
EMP: 8
SALES (corp-wide): 1.1B **Publicly Held**
WEB: www.towneair.com
SIC: **3537** Trucks: freight, baggage, etc.: industrial, except mining
HQ: Clp Towne Inc.
24805 Us Highway 20
South Bend IN 46628
574 233-3183

(G-12738)
COLLIERS GLASSBLOCK INC
Also Called: Collier's Glass Block Windows
824 Park Ave (46616-1338)
P.O. Box 4574 (46634-4574)
PHONE..................................574 288-8682
Fax: 574 288-9460
Casey Collier, *President*
Susann Collier, *Treasurer*
EMP: 3
SALES (est): 219K **Privately Held**
WEB: www.colliersjs.com
SIC: **3229** Blocks & bricks, glass

(G-12739)
COMBINED TECHNOLOGIES INC
3620 W Mcgill St (46628-4369)
PHONE..................................574 251-4968
Dave Sult, *Branch Mgr*
EMP: 40
SALES (corp-wide): 4MM **Privately Held**
WEB: www.ctipack.com
SIC: **2631** 2657 2653 Container, packaging & boxboard; folding paperboard boxes; corrugated & solid fiber boxes
PA: Combined Technologies, Inc.
732 Florsheim Dr Ste 14
Libertyville IL 60048
847 968-4855

(G-12740)
CONTAINER SERVICE CORP
2811 Viridian Dr (46628-4360)
PHONE..................................574 232-7474
Fax: 574 232-8061
Michael D Harrison, *President*
Deborah Harrison, *Vice Pres*
John Sade, *Vice Pres*
Lee Galvan, *Plant Mgr*
Brian Gamble, *Purchasing*
EMP: 68 EST: 1966
SQ FT: 100,000
SALES (est): 15.7MM **Privately Held**
WEB: www.containerservicecorp.com
SIC: **2653** Boxes, corrugated: made from purchased materials

(G-12741)
CONTINENTAL CARBONIC PDTS INC
4075 Ralph Jones Dr (46628-9465)
PHONE..................................574 273-2800
Fax: 574 271-0532
Ty Munger, *Manager*
EMP: 2
SALES (corp-wide): 34.9B **Privately Held**
WEB: www.ccpidryice.com
SIC: **2813** 5169 Dry ice, carbon dioxide (solid); dry ice
HQ: Continental Carbonic Products, Inc.
3985 E Harrison Ave
Decatur IL 62526
217 428-2068

(G-12742)
CONTROL DEVELOPMENT INC
2633 Foundation Dr (46628-4332)
PHONE..................................574 288-7338
Fax: 574 288-7339
Terrance Kinney, *President*
Promit Das, *Vice Pres*
Dave Waggoner, *Software Engr*
EMP: 10
SQ FT: 8,000
SALES (est): 2.2MM **Privately Held**
WEB: www.controldevelopment.com
SIC: **3827** Optical instruments & apparatus; optical test & inspection equipment

(G-12743)
CSPINE INC
3501 Miller Dr (46634)
PHONE..................................574 936-7893
Charles Schneckenburger, *President*
Troy Walters, *Vice Pres*
Dave Baughman, *Shareholder*
Scott Beehler, *Shareholder*
Richard Holt, *Shareholder*
EMP: 5
SQ FT: 4,200
SALES: 800K **Privately Held**
SIC: **3841** Surgical & medical instruments

(G-12744)
CUPPRINT LLC
635 S Lafayette Blvd (46601-2219)
P.O. Box 181, Notre Dame (46556-0181)
PHONE..................................574 323-5250
Richard A Nussbaum II,
EMP: 6
SALES (est): 291.2K **Privately Held**
SIC: **2741** Business service newsletters: publishing & printing
PA: Huhtamaki Cupprint Limited
Ballymaley Business Park
Ennis

G
E
O
G
R
A
P
H
I
C

(G-12745)
CURTIS PRODUCTS INC (PA)
401 N Bendix Dr (46628-1744)
PHONE....................................574 289-4891
Fax: 574 232-9589
David Fheckaman, *President*
John R Heckaman, *Vice Pres*
Jon Heckaman, *Vice Pres*
Aaron Mattix, *Project Mgr*
Vince Zmudzinski, *Opers Mgr*
EMP: 45
SQ FT: 180,000
SALES (est): 36.9MM **Privately Held**
SIC: 3498 Tube fabricating (contract bending & shaping)

(G-12746)
CURTIS PRODUCTS INC
722 Carroll St (46601-3111)
PHONE....................................574 289-4891
David Heckaman, *President*
EMP: 155
SALES (corp-wide): 36.9MM **Privately Held**
SIC: 3498 Fabricated pipe & fittings
PA: Curtis Products Inc
401 N Bendix Dr
South Bend IN 46628
574 289-4891

(G-12747)
CUSTOM HONING INC
24840 Us Highway 20 (46628-5912)
PHONE....................................574 233-2846
Fax: 574 232-9345
Stephen P Keiler, *President*
EMP: 9
SQ FT: 23,000
SALES (est): 1.3MM **Privately Held**
WEB: www.customhoning.com
SIC: 3599 Machine shop, jobbing & repair; tubing, flexible metallic

(G-12748)
CUSTOM MACHINE MFR LLC
4111 Technology Dr (46628-9751)
PHONE....................................574 251-0292
Fax: 574 251-0294
Stephen A Johnson,
Tim Barkley,
Adam Faulkner,
EMP: 42 EST: 1999
SQ FT: 35,000
SALES (est): 8.7MM **Privately Held**
SIC: 3531 Construction machinery

(G-12749)
CUSTOM MILLWORK & DISPLAY LLC
1607 S Main St (46613-2209)
PHONE....................................574 289-9772
Fax: 574 289-9772
Jerrel Mead,
Carroll Mead,
Charles Sausman,
EMP: 9 EST: 2000
SQ FT: 10,000
SALES (est): 918.9K **Privately Held**
SIC: 2431 2531 2521 2511 Woodwork, interior & ornamental; public building & related furniture; wood office furniture; wood household furniture; structural wood members; hardwood dimension & flooring mills

(G-12750)
CUSTOM MILLWORK & DISPLAY INC
2102 W Washington St # 1 (46628-2001)
PHONE....................................574 289-4000
Jerrel Mead, *President*
Joe Welker, *Vice Pres*
David Welker, *Treasurer*
Kelle Welker, *Admin Sec*
EMP: 13
SALES (est): 1.8MM **Privately Held**
WEB: www.fancywoodwork.com
SIC: 2431 Millwork

(G-12751)
DERBY INC
Also Called: Derby Industries
24350 State Road 23 (46614-9696)
PHONE....................................574 233-4500
Fax: 574 288-4550

David M Karafa, *CEO*
Andrew S Karafa, *CEO*
Andrew J Karafa, *President*
Ken Chrzan, *Partner*
Kenneth Chrzan, *Vice Pres*
◆ EMP: 65 EST: 1975
SQ FT: 42,000
SALES (est): 11.5MM **Privately Held**
WEB: www.derbyinc.com
SIC: 2515 3161 Mattresses, innerspring or box spring; cases, carrying; musical instrument cases; camera carrying bags

(G-12752)
DOCKSIDE
1835 Lincoln Way E (46613-3422)
PHONE....................................574 400-0848
Jason Gobokowiecze, *President*
EMP: 5
SALES (est): 216.4K **Privately Held**
SIC: 2082 Malt beverages

(G-12753)
DURAMOLD CASTINGS INC
1901 N Bendix Dr (46628-1603)
P.O. Box 424, Mishawaka (46546-0424)
PHONE....................................574 251-1111
Fax: 574 251-0372
Bob A Lalwani, *President*
K B Lalwani, *Admin Sec*
▲ EMP: 25
SQ FT: 8,800
SALES (est): 6.4MM **Privately Held**
SIC: 3369 Castings, except die-castings, precision

(G-12754)
DWYER INSTRUMENTS INC
6850 Enterprise Dr (46628-8474)
PHONE....................................219 879-8868
EMP: 5
SALES (corp-wide): 100MM **Privately Held**
SIC: 3823 Industrial instrmnts msrmnt display/control process variable
PA: Dwyer Instruments Inc
102 Indiana Highway 212
Michigan City IN 46360
219 879-8868

(G-12755)
EATON CORPORATION
2930 Foundation Dr (46628-4337)
PHONE....................................574 283-5004
Bill Armstrong, *Branch Mgr*
Ichaya Dhungel, *Manager*
Bryan Fiscus, *Manager*
Carlos Vega, *Manager*
EMP: 217 **Privately Held**
SIC: 3625 Motor controls & accessories
HQ: Eaton Corporation
1000 Eaton Blvd
Cleveland OH 44122
440 523-5000

(G-12756)
EATON CORPORATION
2930 Foundation Dr (46628-4337)
PHONE....................................574 288-4446
Fax: 574 233-2589
John Oneal, *Principal*
EMP: 100 **Privately Held**
WEB: www.eaton.com
SIC: 3462 3715 3568 3537 Automotive forgings, ferrous: crankshaft, engine, axle, etc.; truck trailers; power transmission equipment; industrial trucks & tractors
HQ: Eaton Corporation
1000 Eaton Blvd
Cleveland OH 44122
440 523-5000

(G-12757)
ECHOSTAR CORPORATION
3725 Cleveland Road Ext (46628-8461)
PHONE....................................574 271-0595
EMP: 20
SALES (corp-wide): 3.1B **Publicly Held**
SIC: 3663 Mfg Satellite Television Equipment
PA: Echostar Corporation
100 Inverness Ter E # 200
Englewood CO 80112
303 706-4000

(G-12758)
ED STUMP ASSEMBLY INC
Also Called: E S A I
60856 Us 31 S (46614-5190)
PHONE....................................574 291-0058
Edward Stump, *President*
Sherry Stump, *Admin Sec*
EMP: 2 EST: 1962
SQ FT: 1,500
SALES: 330K **Privately Held**
SIC: 3911 Jewelry, precious metal

(G-12759)
EICHSTEDT MANUFACTURING INC
23020 Ireland Rd (46614-4414)
PHONE....................................574 288-8881
Fax: 574 288-2777
Robert W Eichstedt Jr, *President*
Mark Eichstedt, *Vice Pres*
EMP: 5 EST: 1959
SQ FT: 5,000
SALES (est): 576.2K **Privately Held**
SIC: 3083 Plastic finished products, laminated

(G-12760)
ELKHART PLASTICS INC (PA)
Also Called: Portland Plastics
3300 N Kenmore St (46628-4314)
PHONE....................................574 232-8066
Jack Welter, *CEO*
Frank Ermeti, *Vice Pres*
Chuck Huston, *Vice Pres*
Todd Outman, *Vice Pres*
Tyler Winright, *Plant Mgr*
EMP: 58
SQ FT: 65,000
SALES (est): 135.7MM **Privately Held**
SIC: 3089 Plastic containers, except foam; plastic processing

(G-12761)
ELKHART PLASTICS INC
3300 N Kenmore St (46628-4314)
PHONE....................................574 232-8066
Jack Welter, *President*
EMP: 58
SALES (corp-wide): 135.7MM **Privately Held**
SIC: 3089 Plastic processing
PA: Elkhart Plastics, Inc.
3300 N Kenmore St
South Bend IN 46628
574 232-8066

(G-12762)
EM BLACK OXIDE
3702 W Sample St Ste 4052 (46619-2963)
PHONE....................................574 233-4933
Kaginielg Tenddrenda, *Owner*
EMP: 2
SALES (est): 160.8K **Privately Held**
SIC: 3479 Metal coating & allied service

(G-12763)
ENDEAVOR MACHINED PRODUCTS INC
1705 N Bendix Dr (46628-1601)
PHONE....................................574 232-1940
James Duszynski, *President*
Martin Mitchell, *Vice Pres*
Terry Sulich, *Vice Pres*
EMP: 6 EST: 2009
SALES (est): 971.3K **Privately Held**
SIC: 3599 Machine shop, jobbing & repair

(G-12764)
ENGEL MANUFACTURING CO INC
411 W Indiana Ave (46613-2017)
PHONE....................................574 232-3800
Fax: 574 232-4311
Stephen J Engel, *President*
Pam Trinkley, *Office Mgr*
EMP: 5
SQ FT: 1,500
SALES (est): 540K **Privately Held**
WEB: www.engelmfg.com
SIC: 3599 Machine shop, jobbing & repair

(G-12765)
ENVIRONMENTAL TECHNOLOGY INC
Also Called: Environment Tech of Fort Wayne
1850 N Sheridan St (46628-1525)
PHONE....................................574 233-1202
Thad M Jones, *President*
Kathy Schrader, *Vice Pres*
Robert Tax, *Software Engr*
Nancy Watson, *Associate*
EMP: 26
SQ FT: 35,000
SALES (est): 5.8MM **Privately Held**
WEB: www.networketi.com
SIC: 3823 3674 3625 3577 Temperature measurement instruments, industrial; pressure measurement instruments, industrial; industrial process measurement equipment; semiconductors & related devices; relays & industrial controls; computer peripheral equipment

(G-12766)
ENYART ELECTRIC MOTOR SERVICE
1313 Prairie Ave (46613-1603)
PHONE....................................574 288-4731
Fax: 574 282-4860
Richard Holm, *President*
Rich Siri, *President*
Kith Walorsai, *Vice Pres*
EMP: 8
SQ FT: 3,500
SALES (est): 1.6MM **Privately Held**
SIC: 7694 5063 Electric motor repair; motors, electric

(G-12767)
EVS LTD
3702 W Sample St (46619-2947)
P.O. Box 1363 (46624-1363)
PHONE....................................574 233-5707
Michael L Harmon, *President*
James Decraene, *Vice Pres*
EMP: 15
SQ FT: 6,000
SALES (est): 2.5MM **Privately Held**
WEB: www.evsltd.com
SIC: 3944 Child restraint seats, automotive

(G-12768)
EXPANDED METALS CO IND LLC
1400 Riverside Dr (46616-1600)
PHONE....................................574 287-6471
Fax: 574 287-6511
David Lerman, *Ch of Bd*
Mike Lanciotti, *Manager*
Gerald Lerman, *Vice Pres*
James Lerman, *Vice Pres*
Michael Lerman, *Vice Pres*
EMP: 30 EST: 1998
SQ FT: 160,000
SALES: 5MM **Privately Held**
WEB: www.steelwarehouse.com
SIC: 3317 3339 Welded pipe & tubes; primary nonferrous metals
HQ: Steel Warehouse Company Llc
2722 Tucker Dr
South Bend IN 46619
574 236-5100

(G-12769)
EXPRESS PRESS INDIANA INC (PA)
325 N Dixie Way (46637-3311)
PHONE....................................574 277-3355
Fax: 574 271-8502
Brian Clauser, *President*
Mike Schaefer, *Vice Pres*
Dave Kytta, *Director*
EMP: 30 EST: 1977
SALES (est): 4.4MM **Privately Held**
WEB: www.express-press.com
SIC: 2752 2796 2791 2789 Commercial printing, offset; platemaking services; typesetting; bookbinding & related work

(G-12770)
EXPRESS PRESS INDIANA INC
Also Called: Express Press 4
3505 W Mcgill St (46628-4352)
PHONE....................................219 874-2223
Fax: 219 879-4247
Janet Beck, *Branch Mgr*
EMP: 4

SALES (corp-wide): 4.4MM **Privately Held**
WEB: www.express-press.com
SIC: 2752 Commercial printing, offset
PA: Express Press Of Indiana Incorporated
325 N Dixie Way
South Bend IN 46637
574 277-3355

(G-12771)
F S G INC
222 E Walter St (46614-2641)
PHONE.................................574 291-5998
Wayne Farrington, *President*
EMP: 3
SQ FT: 3,400
SALES: 75K **Privately Held**
SIC: 3599 Machine shop, jobbing & repair

(G-12772)
FAST SIGNS
Also Called: Fastsigns
2411 Mishawaka Ave (46615-2144)
PHONE.................................574 254-0545
Tom Sloma, *Owner*
EMP: 5
SALES (est): 306.2K **Privately Held**
SIC: 3993 Signs & advertising specialties

(G-12773)
FAULKENS FLOORCOVER
2045 N Meade St (46628-3154)
PHONE.................................574 300-4260
Derrick Faulkens, *Owner*
EMP: 10
SALES (est): 550K **Privately Held**
SIC: 5713 5031 2273 5023 Floor cover-
ing stores; building materials, interior;
floor coverings, textile fiber; floor cover-
ings; floor cushion & padding

(G-12774)
FDC GRAPHICS FILMS INC
3820 Wlliam Richardson Dr (46628-9795)
PHONE.................................574 273-4400
Fax: 574 271-3597
Judith A Eck, *Principal*
George Marsh, *Vice Pres*
▲ EMP: 70
SQ FT: 45,000
SALES (est): 29.1MM **Privately Held**
WEB: www.fdcfilms.com
SIC: 2824 Vinyl fibers

(G-12775)
FEDERAL-MOGUL LLC
5435 Dylan Dr Ste 200 (46628-7002)
PHONE.................................574 271-0274
Randall Heideman, *Branch Mgr*
EMP: 6
SALES (corp-wide): 21.7B **Publicly Held**
SIC: 3462 3559 3694 3812 Automotive &
internal combustion engine forgings; railroad, construction & mining forgings; degreasing machines, automotive &
industrial; automotive electrical equipment; acceleration indicators & systems
components, aerospace; computer logic
modules
HQ: Federal-Mogul Llc
27300 W 11 Mile Rd # 101
Southfield MI 48034

(G-12776)
FEDERAL-MOGUL POWERTRAIN LLC
Also Called: Federal Mogul
3605 W Cleveland Road Ext (46628-9779)
PHONE.................................574 271-5954
Mark Tripsa, *Manager*
EMP: 460
SALES (corp-wide): 21.7B **Publicly Held**
SIC: 3053 3592 Gaskets & sealing de-
vices; pistons & piston rings
HQ: Federal-Mogul Powertrain Llc
26555 Northwestern Hwy
Southfield MI 48033

(G-12777)
FEDEX OFFICE & PRINT SVCS INC
2202 S Bend Ave Ste C (46635-1664)
PHONE.................................574 271-0398
EMP: 40

SALES (corp-wide): 47.4B **Publicly Held**
SIC: 7334 2791 2789 Photocopying Serv-
ices Typesetting Services
Bookbinding/Related Work
HQ: Fedex Office And Print Services, Inc.
7900 Legacy Dr
Dallas TX 75024
214 550-7000

(G-12778)
FERGUSON EQUIPMENT INC
25170 Edison Rd (46628-5615)
PHONE.................................574 234-4303
Fax: 574 234-4368
Melvin Burdue, *President*
Evelyn Ferguson, *Corp Secy*
Sherri Burdue, *Vice Pres*
EMP: 12 EST: 1965
SQ FT: 10,000
SALES (est): 2MM **Privately Held**
SIC: 3542 3493 Machine tools, metal
forming type; steel springs, except wire;
automobile springs

(G-12779)
FISERV MRTG SERVICING SYSTEMS (HQ)
Also Called: Mortgageserv
3575 Moreau Ct 2 (46628-4320)
PHONE.................................574 282-3300
Tom Glamin, *President*
Joan Sinnessy, *CFO*
EMP: 200
SQ FT: 34,000
SALES (est): 14.2MM
SALES (corp-wide): 5.7B **Publicly Held**
SIC: 7374 7375 7372 8744 Data pro-
cessing service; on-line data base infor-
mation retrieval; business oriented
computer software; facilities support serv-
ices; computer integrated systems de-
sign; custom computer programming
services
PA: Fiserv, Inc.
255 Fiserv Dr
Brookfield WI 53045
262 879-5000

(G-12780)
FISHING ABILITIES INC
22770 Adams Rd (46628-9221)
PHONE.................................574 273-0842
Daniel Badur, *Principal*
EMP: 2 EST: 2010
SALES (est): 131.6K **Privately Held**
SIC: 3949 Sporting & athletic goods

(G-12781)
FLORA RACING
3319 W Sample St (46619-3050)
PHONE.................................574 233-0642
Fax: 574 232-8381
Jeff Flora, *Owner*
EMP: 2 EST: 1994
SALES (est): 164.4K **Privately Held**
SIC: 3714 Motor vehicle body components
& frame

(G-12782)
FRANK W MARTINEZ
54555 Pine Rd (46628-5628)
PHONE.................................574 232-6081
Frank W Martinez, *Owner*
EMP: 2
SALES (est): 210.2K **Privately Held**
SIC: 3599 Machine shop, jobbing & repair

(G-12783)
FRANKS MACHINE SHOP TOOL & DIE
24133 State Road 2 (46619-5517)
PHONE.................................574 288-6899
Frank Szocs, *Owner*
EMP: 3 EST: 2000
SALES (est): 291.4K **Privately Held**
SIC: 3599 Machine shop, jobbing & repair

(G-12784)
FULTON INDUSTRIES INC (PA)
100 E Wayne St Ste 320 (46601-2351)
PHONE.................................574 968-3222
John D Razzano, *President*
▲ EMP: 30
SQ FT: 73,500
SALES (est): 58.8MM **Privately Held**
SIC: 3599 Machine shop, jobbing & repair

(G-12785)
G & N WAREHOUSE & PACKAGING
209 College St (46628-2198)
P.O. Box 3158 (46619-0158)
PHONE.................................574 234-3717
Michael Wells, *President*
Robert Walker, *Vice Pres*
David Wells, *Admin Sec*
EMP: 7
SQ FT: 37,000
SALES: 500K **Privately Held**
SIC: 3599 7692 3444 Machine shop, job-
bing & repair; custom machinery; welding
repair; sheet metalwork

(G-12786)
G T A DRUM INC
1410 Napier St (46601-2639)
PHONE.................................574 288-3459
Yatish J Joshi, *President*
EMP: 4
SALES (est): 384.1K **Privately Held**
SIC: 3069 Fuel tanks, collapsible: rubber-
ized fabric

(G-12787)
GENERAL MCH & SAW CO OF IND
Also Called: General Machine & Saw Co Ind
3636 Gagnon St (46628-4365)
PHONE.................................574 232-6077
Fax: 574 232-1510
Joseph Murphy, *President*
EMP: 14
SALES (est): 2.3MM **Privately Held**
SIC: 3312 Primary finished or semifinished
shapes

(G-12788)
GENERAL SHEET METAL WORKS INC (PA)
Also Called: General Stamping & Metalworks
25101 Cleveland Rd (46628-9734)
PHONE.................................574 288-0611
Fax: 574 288-0647
John Axelberg, *President*
Taylor Lewis Axelburg, *COO*
Seth Doolen, *Engineer*
Matt Wilfing, *Design Engr*
John Ryal, *CFO*
EMP: 27 EST: 1922
SQ FT: 80,000
SALES (est): 40.7MM **Privately Held**
WEB: www.generalsheetmetalworks.com
SIC: 7692 3469 3444 1799 Welding re-
pair; metal stampings; sheet metalwork;
welding on site

(G-12789)
GENERAL TRANSMISSION PDTS LLC
105 N Niles Ave (46617-2705)
PHONE.................................574 284-2917
Marilyn Harris,
EMP: 15
SALES (est): 1.8MM **Privately Held**
WEB: www.amgmil.com
SIC: 3612 Transmission & distribution volt-
age regulators
HQ: Am General Llc
105 N Niles Ave
South Bend IN 46617
574 237-6222

(G-12790)
GRAND MASTER LLC
1619 Miami St (46613-2849)
PHONE.................................574 288-8273
Christopher Szajko, *Principal*
EMP: 2
SALES (est): 117.9K **Privately Held**
SIC: 3663 Studio equipment, radio & tele-
vision broadcasting

(G-12791)
GRYPHON PRINT STUDIO
3702 W Sample St (46619-2947)
PHONE.................................574 514-1644
Steven Estes, *Principal*
EMP: 2
SALES (est): 159.9K **Privately Held**
SIC: 2752 Commercial printing, litho-
graphic

(G-12792)
GTA CONTAINERS INC
4201 Linden Ave (46619-1744)
PHONE.................................574 288-3459
Yatish Joshi, *Manager*
EMP: 18
SALES (est): 1.5MM
SALES (corp-wide): 7.3MM **Privately Held**
WEB: www.gtacontainers.com
SIC: 3069 Fuel tanks, collapsible: rubber-
ized fabric
PA: Gta Containers, Inc.
4201 Linden Ave
South Bend IN 46619
574 288-3459

(G-12793)
GTA CONTAINERS INC (PA)
4201 Linden Ave (46619-1744)
PHONE.................................574 288-3459
Fax: 574 289-6060
Yatish Joshi, *President*
Simon Addicott, *Vice Pres*
Glenda G Lamont, *Vice Pres*
David Brown, *Senior Engr*
Glenda Lamont, *CFO*
▲ EMP: 28
SQ FT: 25,000
SALES (est): 7.3MM **Privately Held**
WEB: www.gtacontainers.com
SIC: 3069 2394 3443 5113 Fuel tanks,
collapsible: rubberized fabric; tarpaulins,
fabric: made from purchased materials;
industrial vessels, tanks & containers;
boxes & containers

(G-12794)
HATCH PRINTS
901 N Saint Peter St (46617-1542)
PHONE.................................312 952-1908
Katrina Harrington, *Principal*
EMP: 2
SALES (est): 83.9K **Privately Held**
SIC: 2752 Commercial printing, litho-
graphic

(G-12795)
HEADCO INDUSTRIES INC
Also Called: Bearing Headquarters Co
1625 Commerce Dr (46628-1502)
PHONE.................................574 288-4471
Fax: 574 288-8938
Bill Jones, *Manager*
EMP: 7
SALES (corp-wide): 162.5MM **Privately Held**
WEB: www.his-tech.com
SIC: 5085 5084 3599 Bearings, bushings,
wheels & gears; bearings; sprockets; hy-
draulic systems equipment & supplies;
machine shop, jobbing & repair
PA: Headco Industries, Inc.
2601 Parkes Dr
Broadview IL 60155
708 681-4400

(G-12796)
HERAEUS
1822 Se Macgregor Rd (46614-3557)
PHONE.................................574 299-1862
EMP: 2
SALES (est): 207K **Privately Held**
SIC: 3843 Dental equipment & supplies

(G-12797)
HERAEUS KULZER LLC (MITSUI)
300 Heraeus Dr (46614-2557)
PHONE.................................574 299-5466
Michael Bellovich, *Human Res Mgr*
Shannon Barbour, *Accounts Mgr*
Leonard Lucchese, *Manager*
Christopher Holden,
Kira Geiss,
▲ EMP: 65
SQ FT: 70,000
SALES: 73.4MM
SALES (corp-wide): 12.4B **Privately Held**
WEB: www.heraeus-kulzer-us.com
SIC: 3843 Dental equipment & supplies
PA: Mitsui Chemicals,Inc.
1-5-2, Higashishimbashi
Minato-Ku TKY 105-0
362 532-100

(G-12798)
HERAUS KULZER INC
4315 S Lafayette Blvd (46614-2517)
PHONE....................................574 291-0661
Fax: 574 291-0791
Kerry Connelly, *CEO*
EMP: 12
SALES (est): 2.1MM **Privately Held**
SIC: 3843 Dental equipment & supplies

(G-12799)
HONEYWELL INTERNATIONAL INC
3520 Westmoor St (46628-1373)
P.O. Box 10 (46624-0010)
PHONE....................................574 231-2000
Kevin Gill, *Human Res Mgr*
Gretchen Nieb, *Branch Mgr*
EMP: 4
SALES (corp-wide): 40.5B **Publicly Held**
WEB: www.honeywell.com
SIC: 3728 3494 Aircraft parts & equipment; valves & pipe fittings
PA: Honeywell International Inc.
　　115 Tabor Rd
　　Morris Plains NJ 07950
　　973 455-2000

(G-12800)
HONEYWELL INTERNATIONAL INC
3520 Westmoor St (46628-1373)
PHONE....................................574 231-3000
Mary Beth McGarvey, *President*
EMP: 700
SALES (corp-wide): 40.5B **Publicly Held**
WEB: www.honeywell.com
SIC: 3724 Aircraft engines & engine parts
PA: Honeywell International Inc.
　　115 Tabor Rd
　　Morris Plains NJ 07950
　　973 455-2000

(G-12801)
HONEYWELL INTERNATIONAL INC
3520 Westmoor St (46628-1373)
P.O. Box 1795 (46634-1795)
PHONE....................................574 231-3000
Brian Harker, *Branch Mgr*
EMP: 4
SALES (corp-wide): 40.5B **Publicly Held**
WEB: www.honeywell.com
SIC: 3724 Aircraft engines & engine parts
PA: Honeywell International Inc.
　　115 Tabor Rd
　　Morris Plains NJ 07950
　　973 455-2000

(G-12802)
HOOSIER SPRING CO INC
4604 S Burnett Dr (46614-3822)
PHONE....................................574 291-7550
Fax: 574 299-0846
Gregory M Suth, *President*
Robert Suth, *Vice Pres*
Robert J Canter, *Treasurer*
▼ EMP: 108 EST: 1954
SQ FT: 36,000
SALES: 15.5MM **Privately Held**
WEB: www.hoosierspring.com
SIC: 3495 Precision springs

(G-12803)
HOOSIER TANK AND MFG INC
1710 N Sheridan St (46628-1523)
PHONE....................................574 232-8368
Fax: 574 233-7189
Thomas R Kinnucan Jr, *President*
Jason Welsch, *General Mgr*
William R Welsch Jr, *Vice Pres*
Alex Welsch, *Purch Mgr*
Ron Commons, *QC Mgr*
EMP: 90
SQ FT: 80,000
SALES (est): 19.1MM **Privately Held**
WEB: www.hoosiertank.com
SIC: 3443 3469 Tanks, standard or custom fabricated: metal plate; metal stampings

(G-12804)
HORIZON GLOBAL AMERICAS INC
3310 Wlliam Richardson Dr (46628-9747)
PHONE....................................517 767-4142
John Matuszewski, *Branch Mgr*
Michael Bristow, *Manager*
EMP: 242
SALES (corp-wide): 892.9MM **Publicly Held**
SIC: 3714 Motor vehicle brake systems & parts
HQ: Horizon Global Americas Inc.
　　47912 Halyard Dr Ste 100
　　Plymouth MI 48170
　　734 656-3000

(G-12805)
HOT SHOT MULTIMEDIA ENTPS LLC
Also Called: Hot Shot USA
1610 Hilltop Dr (46614-1515)
PHONE....................................317 537-7527
Jeffrey Weber Jr, *Exec Dir*
EMP: 3
SALES (est): 110K **Privately Held**
SIC: 8999 7372 Personal services; prepackaged software

(G-12806)
HUBBELL INCORPORATED DELAWARE (HQ)
Also Called: Hubbell Raco Division
3902 W Sample St (46619-2933)
P.O. Box 4002 (46634-4002)
PHONE....................................574 234-7151
Fax: 574 283-4244
Timothy H Powers, *President*
Gary N Amato, *President*
Jean Schroeder, *Warehouse Mgr*
Richard Nixon, *Purch Agent*
Beverly Kiebel, *Buyer*
▲ EMP: 484 EST: 1933
SQ FT: 350,000
SALES (est): 310.5MM
SALES (corp-wide): 3.6B **Publicly Held**
WEB: www.racoinc.com
SIC: 3644 3699 3613 Outlet boxes (electric wiring devices); electrical equipment & supplies; switchgear & switchboard apparatus
PA: Hubbell Incorporated
　　40 Waterview Dr
　　Shelton CT 06484
　　475 882-4000

(G-12807)
IES SUBSIDIARY HOLDINGS INC
1125 S Walnut St (46619-4303)
PHONE....................................330 830-3500
William Johnson, *Project Mgr*
John Senese, *Manager*
Bill Crawford, *Manager*
William Hoffman, *Info Tech Mgr*
Kira Armstrong, *Administration*
EMP: 12 **Publicly Held**
WEB: www.magnetech.com
SIC: 3264 7694 3621 Magnets, permanent: ceramic or ferrite; armature rewinding shops; motors & generators
HQ: Ies Subsidiary Holdings, Inc
　　5433 Westheimer Rd # 500
　　Houston TX 77056
　　713 860-1500

(G-12808)
IMAGINEERING ENTERPRISES INC
Also Called: Imagineering Finishing Tech
3722 Foundation Ct (46628-4361)
PHONE....................................574 287-0642
Fax: 574 807-8846
F James Hammer, *President*
Robert Bator, *Manager*
EMP: 25
SQ FT: 56,000
SALES (est): 2.1MM
SALES (corp-wide): 20.7MM **Privately Held**
SIC: 3479 8711 Coating of metals & formed products; engineering services
PA: Imagineering Enterprises Inc
　　1302 W Sample St
　　South Bend IN 46619
　　574 287-2941

(G-12809)
IMAGINEERING ENTERPRISES INC (PA)
Also Called: Imagineering Finishing Tech
1302 W Sample St (46619-3895)
PHONE....................................574 287-2941
F James Hammer, *President*
Sandy Cochran, *General Mgr*
Mathew Huff, *COO*
Michelle M Hammer, *Exec VP*
Butch Funkhouser, *Plant Mgr*
▲ EMP: 130
SQ FT: 33,000
SALES (est): 20.7MM **Privately Held**
WEB: www.imagineering-inc.com
SIC: 3479 8711 Coating of metals & formed products; engineering services

(G-12810)
INDIANA INTEGRATED CIRCUITS IN
1400 E Angela Blvd (46617-1364)
PHONE....................................574 217-4612
Jason Kulick, *Principal*
Ursula Mahl, *Research*
Alan Isaacson, *VP Bus Dvlpt*
Carlos Ortega, *Technician*
EMP: 3
SALES (est): 329.8K **Privately Held**
SIC: 3679 Electronic circuits

(G-12811)
INDIANA WHISKEY CO
1115 W Sample St (46619-3829)
PHONE....................................574 339-1737
Charles Florance, *President*
Braden Weldy, *Officer*
EMP: 3
SQ FT: 4,500
SALES (est): 311.9K **Privately Held**
SIC: 2085 Distilled & blended liquors

(G-12812)
INDUSTRIAL METAL-FAB INC
2806 W Sample St (46619-3299)
PHONE....................................574 288-8368
Fax: 574 288-8360
Mark E Beaudway, *President*
Ken Klockow, *QC Mgr*
Monte C Beaudway, *Admin Sec*
▲ EMP: 30
SQ FT: 65,000
SALES (est): 7.2MM **Privately Held**
WEB: www.imfonline.com
SIC: 3443 3599 3441 Fabricated plate work (boiler shop); machine shop, jobbing & repair; fabricated structural metal

(G-12813)
INOVATEUS SOLAR LLC
19890 State Line Rd (46637-1553)
PHONE....................................574 485-1400
Tj Kanczuzewski, *President*
Lindsey Foley, *CFO*
Mike Pound, *Risk Mgmt Dir*
▼ EMP: 30
SALES (est): 20.7MM **Privately Held**
SIC: 5211 3433 Solar heating equipment; solar heaters & collectors

(G-12814)
INSTY-PRINTS OF SOUTH BEND
129 S Lafayette Blvd (46601-1518)
PHONE....................................574 289-6977
Fax: 574 289-6980
Cosimo Rulli, *Owner*
Ronald Goodwin, *General Mgr*
Jeremy Protsman, *Production*
EMP: 5
SQ FT: 1,000
SALES (est): 531.9K **Privately Held**
WEB: www.instysb.com
SIC: 2752 2789 Commercial printing, offset; bookbinding & related work

(G-12815)
INTEGRITY CUSTOM CONCEPTS LLC
244 S Olive St Ste S (46619-2108)
PHONE....................................574 252-2366
Becky Pontius, *CEO*
Will Moore, *Vice Pres*
Andrew Braun, *Natl Sales Mgr*
EMP: 4

SALES: 325K **Privately Held**
SIC: 2821 Polyvinyl chloride resins (PVC)

(G-12816)
INTERNATIONAL BAKERS SERVICES
1902 N Sheridan St (46628-1592)
PHONE....................................574 287-7111
William Busse Jr, *President*
Thomas E Coomes, *Vice Pres*
EMP: 29 EST: 1946
SQ FT: 25,000
SALES (est): 4.9MM **Privately Held**
WEB: www.internationalbakers.com
SIC: 2087 Flavoring extracts & syrups

(G-12817)
INTERNATIONAL BRAKE INDS INC
4300 Quality Dr (46628-9665)
PHONE....................................419 905-7468
Fax: 419 224-1696
Char Silver, *Principal*
EMP: 24 **Privately Held**
SIC: 3713 3714 Truck & bus bodies; motor vehicle brake systems & parts
HQ: International Brake Industries, Inc.
　　1840 Mccullough St
　　Lima OH 45801
　　419 227-4421

(G-12818)
INTERPLASTIC CORPORATION
Also Called: Molding Products Division
1545 S Olive St (46619-4295)
PHONE....................................574 234-1105
Fax: 574 234-6686
Troy Wade, *General Mgr*
Timothy Simko, *Opers Mgr*
Gary Held, *Systems Mgr*
Diane Richardson, *Director*
EMP: 40
SALES (corp-wide): 302.9MM **Privately Held**
WEB: www.interplastic.com
SIC: 2821 Plastics materials & resins
PA: Interplastic Corporation
　　1225 Willow Lake Blvd
　　Saint Paul MN 55110
　　651 481-6860

(G-12819)
IRONCRAFT CO INC
Also Called: A1 Iron & Aluminum Co
50655 Ind St Rte 933 (46637-2053)
PHONE....................................574 272-0866
Fax: 574 272-0816
Bruce L Calvert, *President*
Beatrice Calvert, *Corp Secy*
EMP: 5 EST: 1945
SALES (est): 516K **Privately Held**
SIC: 3446 Fences or posts, ornamental iron or steel; railings, prefabricated metal; stairs, staircases, stair treads: prefabricated metal

(G-12820)
J F JELENKO CO
300 Heraeus Dr (46614-2557)
PHONE....................................914 273-8600
Christian Brutzer, *Principal*
EMP: 2
SALES (est): 134.1K **Privately Held**
SIC: 3843 Dental equipment & supplies

(G-12821)
J-I-T DISTRIBUTING INC
4111 Technology Dr (46628-9751)
PHONE....................................574 251-0292
Stephen A Johnson, *President*
Tim Barkley, *Vice Pres*
Randy Chudzicki, *Sales Staff*
EMP: 65
SQ FT: 40,000
SALES (est): 8.3MM **Privately Held**
WEB: www.cmmbuilt.com
SIC: 3569 Robots, assembly line: industrial & commercial

(G-12822)
JKP PRINTING INC
1701 Linden Ave (46628-2346)
PHONE....................................574 246-1650
Evelyn O'Neal, *President*
Janice Kimbrough, *President*
EMP: 3

▲ = Import ▼=Export
◆ =Import/Export

SQ FT: 900
SALES (est): 310.7K Privately Held
SIC: 2752 Commercial printing, offset

(G-12823)
JMS ENGINEERED PLASTICS INC
52275 State Road 933 (46637-3849)
P.O. Box 1557 (46634-1557)
PHONE.....................574 277-3228
David M Martinez, *CEO*
EMP: 75
SALES: 8.1MM Privately Held
SIC: 3089 8711 Automotive parts, plastic; building construction consultant

(G-12824)
JMS MOLD & ENGINEERING CO INC
50941 Ind St Rte 933 (46637-2057)
PHONE.....................574 272-0198
Fax: 574 272-8601
Ronald Scope, *President*
EMP: 13 EST: 1967
SALES (est): 1.3MM Privately Held
SIC: 3544 Industrial molds; forms (molds), for foundry & plastics working machinery

(G-12825)
JOURNEYMAN TOOL & MOLD INC
3601 Gagnon St (46628-4366)
PHONE.....................574 237-1880
Fax: 574 237-1882
Michael Meyer, *President*
Tammi Meyer, *Vice Pres*
EMP: 5
SQ FT: 5,200
SALES: 500K Privately Held
SIC: 3544 Industrial molds

(G-12826)
JUST INK LLC
1657 Commerce Dr Ste 9b (46628-1593)
PHONE.....................800 948-7671
Shalonda Morgan,
Roy Morgan,
EMP: 2
SALES (est): 80.6K Privately Held
SIC: 2759 Letterpress & screen printing

(G-12827)
K RA INTERNATIONAL LLC
3300 W Sample St Ste 1206 (46619-3079)
PHONE.....................574 258-7151
Hari Agarwal, *Manager*
EMP: 2
SALES (est): 108.9K Privately Held
SIC: 3679 Electronic components

(G-12828)
KILL-N-EM INC
Also Called: Carother's Printing Company
2118 Franklin St (46613-2120)
PHONE.....................574 233-6655
Fax: 574 234-5419
Thomas E Podemski, *Principal*
Carol Podemski, *Principal*
Lynda Podemski, *Accounts Mgr*
Keith T Podemski, *Representative*
EMP: 5
SQ FT: 4,800
SALES: 300K Privately Held
SIC: 2752 Commercial printing, offset

(G-12829)
KOKOKU WIRE INDUSTRIES CORP
406 Manitou Pl (46616-1325)
PHONE.....................574 287-5610
Kevin Hughes, *President*
EMP: 35
SQ FT: 200,000
SALES (est): 5.1MM Privately Held
SIC: 3315 Wire, steel: insulated or armored

(G-12830)
KROGER CO
1217 E Ireland Rd (46614-3497)
PHONE.....................574 291-0740
Fax: 574 299-4320
Alf Pesce, *Manager*
EMP: 103

SALES (corp-wide): 122.6B Publicly Held
WEB: www.kroger.com
SIC: 5411 5912 5992 5812 Supermarkets, chain; drug stores; florists; eating places; meat & fish markets; bread, cake & related products
PA: The Kroger Co
    1014 Vine St Ste 1000
    Cincinnati OH 45202
    513 762-4000

(G-12831)
KUERT CONCRETE INC (PA)
3402 Lincoln Way W (46628-1455)
PHONE.....................574 232-9911
Fax: 574 232-9977
Steve Fidler, *President*
Tim Miller, *Vice Pres*
Jim Sellers, *QC Mgr*
Ron Ericson, *CFO*
Kent Ganshorn, *Manager*
EMP: 45 EST: 1927
SQ FT: 10,000
SALES (est): 14.4MM Privately Held
WEB: www.kuert.com
SIC: 3273 5032 Ready-mixed concrete; concrete building products

(G-12832)
KUHARIC ENTERPRISES
57890 Crumstown Hwy (46619-9646)
PHONE.....................574 288-9410
John Kuharic, *Partner*
Christine Kuharic, *Partner*
EMP: 2
SALES (est): 167.8K Privately Held
SIC: 0191 4151 0711 3443 General farms, primarily crop; school buses; lime spreading services; culverts, metal plate

(G-12833)
KW MAINTENANCE SERVICES LLC
Also Called: Koontz-Wagner Maintenance Svcs
3801 Voorde Dr Ste B (46628-1643)
PHONE.....................574 232-2051
Paul M Witek, *President*
EMP: 42
SALES (est): 4.2MM
SALES (corp-wide): 40MM Privately Held
SIC: 7694 Electric motor repair
PA: Kw Services, Llc
    3801 Voorde Dr Ste B
    South Bend IN 46628
    574 232-2051

(G-12834)
L C TYPESETTING COMPANY INC
2611 S Main St (46614-1017)
PHONE.....................574 232-4700
Fax: 574 232-5541
Garrett Swanson, *President*
◆ EMP: 4
SQ FT: 1,000
SALES (est): 313.8K Privately Held
SIC: 2791 2759 Typesetting; commercial printing

(G-12835)
LANEY SOFTWARE CO
17144 Moonlite Dr (46614-9115)
PHONE.....................260 312-0759
Michael Laney, *Principal*
EMP: 2
SALES (est): 167.9K Privately Held
WEB: www.lsoftware.biz
SIC: 7372 Prepackaged software

(G-12836)
LASALLES LANDING VINEYARD LLC
51739 Lilac Rd (46628-9782)
PHONE.....................574 277-2711
David Sabato, *Principal*
EMP: 2
SALES (est): 129K Privately Held
SIC: 2084 Wines, brandy & brandy spirits

(G-12837)
LEBERMUTH COMPANY INC (PA)
Also Called: American Home Fragrance
4004 Technology Dr (46628-9745)
P.O. Box 4103 (46634-4103)
PHONE.....................574 259-7000
Fax: 574 258-7450
Robert Brown, *President*
Alan Brown, *COO*
▲ EMP: 57
SQ FT: 100,000
SALES (est): 16.7MM Privately Held
WEB: www.lebermuth.com
SIC: 2899 5149 5169 Incense; organic & diet foods; flavourings & fragrances; essential oils

(G-12838)
LECO CORPORATION
Also Called: Flight Dept
4100 Lathrop St (46628-6103)
PHONE.....................574 288-9017
Fax: 574 289-9039
Phil Rollins, *Branch Mgr*
EMP: 3
SALES (corp-wide): 204.9MM Privately Held
WEB: www.pier33.com
SIC: 3821 4493 3826 3825 Laboratory apparatus, except heating & measuring; chemical laboratory apparatus; boat yards, storage & incidental repair; marine basins; analytical instruments; instruments to measure electricity; industrial instrmnts msrmnt display/control process variable; porcelain electrical supplies
PA: Leco Corporation
    3000 Lakeview Ave
    Saint Joseph MI 49085
    269 983-5531

(G-12839)
LINDE LLC
3809 W Calvert St (46613-1020)
PHONE.....................574 234-4887
James Copenhaver, *Transptn Dir*
Tom Sulvinsky, *Branch Mgr*
EMP: 9
SALES (corp-wide): 20.1B Privately Held
SIC: 5169 2813 Industrial gases; industrial gases
HQ: Linde Llc
    200 Somerset Corporate Bl
    Bridgewater NJ 08807
    908 464-8100

(G-12840)
LIPPERT COMPONENTS INC
1280 S Olive St (46619-4208)
PHONE.....................574 312-6654
EMP: 10
SALES (corp-wide): 2.1B Publicly Held
SIC: 3711 Chassis, motor vehicle
HQ: Lippert Components, Inc.
    3501 County Road 6 E
    Elkhart IN 46514
    800 551-9149

(G-12841)
LIPPERT COMPONENTS INC
1902 W Sample St (46619-3622)
PHONE.....................574 535-1125
EMP: 60
SALES (corp-wide): 2.1B Publicly Held
SIC: 3711 Chassis, motor vehicle
HQ: Lippert Components, Inc.
    3501 County Road 6 E
    Elkhart IN 46514
    800 551-9149

(G-12842)
LJT TEXAS LLC (DH)
Also Called: Lock Joint Tube Texas
515 W Ireland Rd (46614-3805)
PHONE.....................800 257-6859
David L Lerman, *CEO*
Ted Lerman, *President*
Michael Lerman, *Vice Pres*
Sean Ryan, *Production*
Ingrid Horne, *Sales Staff*
EMP: 47
SALES (est): 18.3MM Privately Held
SIC: 3317 Tubes, wrought: welded or lock joint

HQ: Steel Warehouse Company Llc
    2722 Tucker Dr
    South Bend IN 46619
    574 236-5100

(G-12843)
LOCK JOINT TUBE LLC (DH)
Also Called: L J T
515 W Ireland Rd (46614-3805)
PHONE.....................574 299-5326
Fax: 574 299-3460
David Lerman, *CEO*
Ted Lerman, *President*
Teresa Rhoades, *QC Mgr*
Shane Forslund, *Accountant*
Darryl Johnson, *Sales Staff*
▲ EMP: 200
SQ FT: 295,000
SALES (est): 43.8MM Privately Held
WEB: www.ljtube.com
SIC: 3317 Welded pipe & tubes; tubes, wrought: welded or lock joint
HQ: Steel Warehouse Company Llc
    2722 Tucker Dr
    South Bend IN 46619
    574 236-5100

(G-12844)
LOGISTICK INC
19880 State Line Rd (46637-1545)
PHONE.....................800 758-5840
Ashley Brickley, *President*
EMP: 9
SQ FT: 8,000
SALES (est): 1.9MM Privately Held
WEB: www.logistick.com
SIC: 3799 2679 Trailers & trailer equipment; pallet spacers, fiber: made from purchased material

(G-12845)
LUDWICK GRAPHICS INC (PA)
1312 Honan Dr (46614-2174)
PHONE.....................574 233-2165
Fax: 574 288-7735
Robert B Ludwick, *President*
James Ludwick, *Vice Pres*
Rob Ludwick, *Sales Staff*
Ann Farkas, *Admin Sec*
EMP: 12 EST: 1920
SQ FT: 18,000
SALES: 2MM Privately Held
WEB: www.ludwickgraphics.com
SIC: 2752 2796 2791 2789 Commercial printing, offset; platemaking services; typesetting; bookbinding & related work

(G-12846)
MACHINING SOLUTIONS
942 S 27th St (46615-1724)
PHONE.....................574 292-3227
Jason Szabo, *Owner*
EMP: 2
SALES (est): 100K Privately Held
SIC: 3552 Textile machinery

(G-12847)
MACK TOOL & ENGINEERING INC
2820 Viridian Dr (46628-4359)
PHONE.....................574 233-8424
Fax: 574 233-1849
Melvin W Hartz, *CEO*
Paul Hartz, *President*
Kevin Jacobs, *General Mgr*
David Talcott, *Vice Pres*
Rob Saltzman, *Purch Mgr*
EMP: 50
SQ FT: 27,000
SALES (est): 1.8MM Privately Held
WEB: www.macktool.com
SIC: 3728 Aircraft parts & equipment

(G-12848)
MAGNETS R US INC
63300 State Road 331 (46614-9498)
PHONE.....................574 633-0061
Larry Frank, *President*
▲ EMP: 2
SALES (est): 222.5K Privately Held
SIC: 3499 Magnets, permanent: metallic

(G-12849)
MAHOGANY SCENTS
53154 Bracken Fern Dr (46637-4583)
PHONE.....................574 271-1364

G
E
O
G
R
A
P
H
I
C

John Beard, *Owner*
EMP: 3 **EST:** 2015
SALES: 265.6K **Privately Held**
SIC: 2844 Toilet preparations

(G-12850)
MAITLAND ENGINEERING INC
2713 Foundation Dr (46628-4334)
PHONE...................................574 287-0155
Fax: 574 287-0180
Patricia Clark, *President*
Scott Cripe, *COO*
Matt Wilcoxson, *Info Tech Mgr*
Chris Kleva, *Director*
EMP: 46
SQ FT: 15,000
SALES: 6MM **Privately Held**
WEB: www.maitlandengineering.com
SIC: 3842 3599 Implants, surgical; machine shop, jobbing & repair

(G-12851)
MANUFACTURING TECHNOLOGY INC (PA)
1702 W Washington St (46628-2061)
P.O. Box 3059 (46619-0059)
PHONE...................................574 230-0258
Fax: 574 233-9489
Robert C Adams II, *President*
Michael Skinner, *President*
Glyn Jones, *Managing Prtnr*
Doug Wait, *General Mgr*
Daniel C Adams, *Vice Pres*
▼ **EMP:** 140
SQ FT: 65,000
SALES: 46.9MM **Privately Held**
WEB: www.mtiwelding.com
SIC: 3548 7692 Welding apparatus; welding repair

(G-12852)
MANUFACTURING TECHNOLOGY INC
402 N Sheridan St (46619-1416)
P.O. Box 3059 (46619-0059)
PHONE...................................574 233-9490
Michael Lainan, *Branch Mgr*
EMP: 25
SQ FT: 114,000
SALES (corp-wide): 46.9MM **Privately Held**
SIC: 3548 Welding apparatus
PA: Manufacturing Technology, Inc.
1702 W Washington St
South Bend IN 46628
574 230-0258

(G-12853)
MASTER METAL MACHINING INC
Also Called: Master Metal Engineering
4520 S Burnett Dr (46614-3820)
PHONE...................................574 299-0222
Brian Pyszka, *President*
Gary Ray, *Prdtn Mgr*
Barbara Dull, *QC Mgr*
Chet Pierce, *Engineer*
Tom Cleveland, *Financial Exec*
EMP: 75
SQ FT: 25,000
SALES (est): 13.1MM **Privately Held**
WEB: www.mastermetal.net
SIC: 3599 Machine shop, jobbing & repair

(G-12854)
MASTERBILT INCORPORATED
325 S Walnut St (46601-2653)
P.O. Box 3715 (46619-0715)
PHONE...................................574 287-6567
Fax: 574 288-7680
Robert Michalk, *President*
Lawrence Kowalewski, *Vice Pres*
Jim Young, *QC Mgr*
▲ **EMP:** 10
SQ FT: 9,900
SALES (est): 1MM **Privately Held**
WEB: www.masterbilt-inc.com
SIC: 3599 Machine shop, jobbing & repair

(G-12855)
MAURER ENVIRONMENTAL DRILLING
51711 Emmons Rd (46637-2804)
PHONE...................................574 272-7524
Fax: 574 272-6651

Rob Maurer, *President*
EMP: 2
SALES: 130K **Privately Held**
SIC: 1381 Drilling water intake wells

(G-12856)
MAUTZ PAINT FACTORY
1201 S Main St (46601-3339)
PHONE...................................574 289-2497
Fax: 574 289-2497
Sherwin Williams, *Manager*
Kevin Varney, *Systs Prg Mgr*
EMP: 4
SALES (est): 264.7K **Privately Held**
SIC: 2851 5198 Paints & allied products; paints

(G-12857)
MCCAFFERY SIGN DESIGNS
1310 S Main St Ste 2 (46601-3358)
PHONE...................................574 232-9991
Fax: 574 232-9997
James McCaffery, *President*
EMP: 4
SALES: 375K **Privately Held**
SIC: 3993 Signs & advertising specialties

(G-12858)
MCCORMICK & COMPANY INC
3425 Lathrop St (46628-4393)
PHONE...................................574 234-8101
Mike Calhoun, *Branch Mgr*
EMP: 95
SQ FT: 50,000
SALES (corp-wide): 4.8B **Publicly Held**
WEB: www.mccormick.com
SIC: 2099 Seasonings & spices
PA: Mccormick & Company Incorporated
18 Loveton Cir
Sparks MD 21152
410 771-7301

(G-12859)
MEDITATION COMPANY
830 Oak Ridge Dr (46617-2219)
PHONE...................................574 217-3157
Melvin Ward, *Principal*
EMP: 2
SALES (est): 57.2K **Privately Held**
SIC: 5091 3949 7999 5137 Sporting & recreation goods; sporting & athletic goods; instruction schools, camps & services; sportswear, women's & children's; men's & boys' sportswear & work clothing

(G-12860)
METALSTAMP INC
24545 State Road 23 (46614-9699)
PHONE...................................574 232-5997
Fax: 574 234-4198
Ernest Zeller, *President*
Daniel Fuchs, *Corp Secy*
Richard Zeller, *Vice Pres*
Pat Trimboli, *QC Mgr*
Steven Zeller, *Controller*
EMP: 70
SQ FT: 100,000
SALES (est): 15MM **Privately Held**
SIC: 3469 Machine parts, stamped or pressed metal

(G-12861)
MICHIANA PALLET RECYCLE INC
55022 Pear Rd (46628-4509)
PHONE...................................574 232-8566
Fax: 574 232-8218
Jim Knapp, *President*
EMP: 5
SQ FT: 15,000
SALES (est): 470K **Privately Held**
SIC: 2448 Pallets, wood

(G-12862)
MICROSCREEN LLC
1106 High St (46601-3705)
PHONE...................................574 232-4358
Fax: 574 234-7496
Holly Wallace, *General Mgr*
Mark Lowdermilk,
EMP: 23
SALES (est): 4.2MM **Privately Held**
WEB: www.microscreen.com
SIC: 3674 Semiconductors & related devices

(G-12863)
MIDWEST ORTHOTIC SERVICES LLC (PA)
Also Called: Midwest Orthotic and Tech Ctr
17530 Dugdale Dr (46635-1583)
PHONE...................................574 233-3352
Bernie Veldman,
Pam Veldman
EMP: 90
SQ FT: 9,000
SALES (est): 14MM **Privately Held**
SIC: 3842 Braces, orthopedic; orthopedic appliances

(G-12864)
MITO-CRAFT INC
Also Called: Graphie-Tees
505 S Logan St (46615-2419)
PHONE...................................574 287-4555
Lynn A Rodriquez, *President*
John Rodriquez, *Corp Secy*
Andrea Kaiser, *Vice Pres*
EMP: 8 **EST:** 1957
SQ FT: 6,000
SALES (est): 721.2K **Privately Held**
WEB: www.graphietees.com
SIC: 2759 2752 2672 2396 Screen printing; commercial printing, lithographic; coated & laminated paper; automotive & apparel trimmings

(G-12865)
MOSSBERG & COMPANY INC (PA)
301 E Sample St (46601-3547)
PHONE...................................574 289-9253
Fax: 574 289-6622
James W Hillman, *President*
William Knight, *Vice Pres*
Alan Gall, *Opers Mgr*
Ricky Reynolds, *Senior Buyer*
David Kelsey, *QA Dir*
EMP: 136 **EST:** 1930
SQ FT: 80,000
SALES (est): 32.9MM **Privately Held**
SIC: 2752 2759 Commercial printing, offset; letterpress printing

(G-12866)
MOSSBERG & COMPANY INC
4100 Technology Dr (46628-9772)
PHONE...................................574 236-1094
EMP: 2
SALES (corp-wide): 32.9MM **Privately Held**
SIC: 2752 Commercial printing, lithographic
PA: Mossberg & Company Inc
301 E Sample St
South Bend IN 46601
574 289-9253

(G-12867)
MRC TECHNOLOGY INC
1901 S Lafayette Blvd (46613-2123)
PHONE...................................574 232-9057
Fax: 574 232-9173
Andrew J Zaderej, *President*
George Zaderej, *Vice Pres*
EMP: 10
SQ FT: 7,000
SALES: 1MM **Privately Held**
SIC: 3629 3621 3625 5013 Battery chargers, rectifying or nonrotating; starters, for motors; electric controls & control accessories, industrial; automotive servicing equipment

(G-12868)
NATIONAL CONSOLIDATED CORP
Also Called: Natcon
25855 State Road 2 (46619-4736)
PHONE...................................574 289-7885
Fax: 574 288-3450
James Kilbourne, *President*
Carol Kilbourne, *Admin Sec*
EMP: 12 **EST:** 1974
SQ FT: 11,800
SALES (est): 4.2MM **Privately Held**
SIC: 5084 3451 Hydraulic systems equipment & supplies; machine tools & metalworking machinery; tool & die makers' equipment; screw machine products

(G-12869)
NELLO CAPITAL INC (PA)
105 E Jefferson Blvd (46601-1922)
PHONE...................................574 288-3632
Daniel Ianello, *President*
Robert Rumpler, *Vice Pres*
Kevin Brisson, *CFO*
EMP: 4
SQ FT: 10,000
SALES (est): 15.9MM **Privately Held**
SIC: 3663 Airborne radio communications equipment

(G-12870)
NELLO INC (HQ)
Also Called: Nello Corporation
1201 S Sheridan St (46619-2941)
P.O. Box 1960 (46634-1960)
PHONE...................................574 288-3632
Fax: 574 288-5860
Dan Ianello, *President*
Bob Rumpler, *Vice Pres*
Jim Smart, *Warehouse Mgr*
Kevin Brisson, *CFO*
Bradd Grwinski, *Human Res Mgr*
▼ **EMP:** 12
SQ FT: 95,000
SALES (est): 30.6MM
SALES (corp-wide): 15.9MM **Privately Held**
WEB: www.nelloinc.com
SIC: 3441 Fabricated structural metal
PA: Nello Capital, Inc.
105 E Jefferson Blvd
South Bend IN 46601
574 288-3632

(G-12871)
NEO INDUSTRIES LLC (HQ)
1400 E Angela Blvd (46617-1364)
PHONE...................................574 217-4078
Michael Quig, *President*
Linda Haines, *Finance Spvr*
EMP: 14 **EST:** 1998
SALES (est): 31.8MM **Privately Held**
SIC: 3471 Plating of metals or formed products

(G-12872)
NERP LLC
58016 Crumstown Hwy (46619-9646)
PHONE...................................574 303-6377
Mathew Napieralski,
Frances Napieralski,
EMP: 2
SALES (est): 213.8K **Privately Held**
SIC: 3714 Motor vehicle brake systems & parts

(G-12873)
NEW CARBON COMPANY LLC (PA)
Also Called: Carbon's Golden Malted
4101 Wlliam Richardson Dr (46628-9485)
P.O. Box 129, Concordville PA (19331-0128)
PHONE...................................574 247-2270
Fax: 574 247-2280
Rich Cleaver, *Senior VP*
Charlie Frank, *Vice Pres*
Moses Kyles, *Purchasing*
Joseph Crowley, *Treasurer*
Billy Mills, *Sales Mgr*
◆ **EMP:** 1
SQ FT: 37,800
SALES: 50MM **Privately Held**
WEB: www.newcarbon.com
SIC: 2045 2041 5149 Pancake mixes, prepared: from purchased flour; flour & other grain mill products; flour

(G-12874)
NEW NELLO OPERATING CO LLC
1201 S Sheridan St (46619-2941)
PHONE...................................574 288-3632
Dan Ianello, *President*
EMP: 125
SALES (est): 4MM **Privately Held**
SIC: 3441 Fabricated structural metal

(G-12875)
NICHOLLS PRINTING
1219 Mishawaka Ave (46615-1127)
PHONE...................................574 233-1388

▲ = Import ▼=Export
◆ =Import/Export

EMP: 2 EST: 1923
SQ FT: 1,500
SALES: 40K Privately Held
SIC: 2759 2752 Contract Printing

(G-12876)
NORRES NORTH AMERICA INC
2520 Foundation Dr (46628-4329)
PHONE.....................................855 667-7370
Burkhard Mollen, CEO
EMP: 8
SALES (est): 181.7K Privately Held
SIC: 3312 Pipes & tubes

(G-12877)
NORTH AMERICAN SIGNS INC (PA)
Also Called: Site Enhancement Services
3601 Lathrop St (46628-6108)
P.O. Box 30 (46624-0030)
PHONE.....................................574 234-5252
Fax: 574 237-6166
Noel H Yarger, Ch of Bd
John Yarger, President
Dick Whitteberry, COO
Sarah Barker, Project Mgr
Alan Eiker, Project Mgr
EMP: 80
SQ FT: 51,000
SALES (est): 15MM Privately Held
WEB: www.northamericansigns.com
SIC: 3993 Electric signs; advertising artwork; neon signs

(G-12878)
NORTHERN BRACE CO INC (PA)
Also Called: Northern Brace Nthrn Prsthtics
610 N Michigan St Ste 104 (46601-1078)
PHONE.....................................574 233-4221
Fax: 574 233-3966
Timothy S West, President
EMP: 2
SALES (est): 257.6K Privately Held
SIC: 3842 5999 Orthopedic appliances; orthopedic & prosthesis applications

(G-12879)
NORTHERN INDIANA ORDNANCE CO
Also Called: M & K Services
60161 Mayflower Rd (46614-9320)
PHONE.....................................574 289-5938
John B Mumford, President
Rosanne Kroen, Corp Secy
James T Mumford, Vice Pres
EMP: 4
SQ FT: 700
SALES (est): 400K Privately Held
SIC: 8742 8734 3482 5932 Industry specialist consultants; testing laboratories; small arms ammunition; antiques; handyman service

(G-12880)
NORTHERN PROSTHETICS INC
610 N Michigan St Ste 104 (46601-1078)
PHONE.....................................574 233-2459
Kelly L West, President
Timothy West, Vice Pres
Laura Macfarline, Office Mgr
EMP: 2
SALES (est): 150.1K Privately Held
SIC: 3842 5999 Prosthetic appliances; artificial limbs

(G-12881)
OCTAPHARMA PLASMA INC
2102 S Michigan St (46613-2320)
PHONE.....................................574 234-9568
Toni Mogerman, President
EMP: 5
SALES (corp-wide): 1.4B Privately Held
SIC: 2836 Plasmas
HQ: Octapharma Plasma, Inc.
10644 Westlake Dr
Charlotte NC 28273
704 654-4600

(G-12882)
ODYSSIAN TECHNOLOGY LLC
511 E Colfax Ave (46617-2715)
PHONE.....................................574 257-7555
Susan Bennett,
Barton Bennett,
EMP: 6
SQ FT: 6,100

SALES (est): 549.9K Privately Held
WEB: www.odyssian.com
SIC: 8711 6794 8734 3643 Engineering services; patent owners & lessors; testing laboratories; current-carrying wiring devices; aircraft parts & equipment

(G-12883)
OMICRON BIOCHEMICALS INC
115 S Hill St (46617-2701)
PHONE.....................................574 287-6910
Anthony S Serianni, President
Shikai Zhao, COO
Qingfeng Pan, Research
▼ EMP: 11
SALES (est): 1.7MM Privately Held
WEB: www.omicronbio.com
SIC: 2819 2869 Chemicals, reagent grade: refined from technical grade; industrial organic chemicals

(G-12884)
OUTSOURCE TECHNOLOGIES INC
1832 N Kenmore St (46628-1610)
PHONE.....................................574 233-1303
Sylvester Klusczinski, President
Susan Klusczinski, Corp Secy
▲ EMP: 25
SQ FT: 12,000
SALES (est): 3MM Privately Held
SIC: 3089 3499 Plastic hardware & building products; metal household articles

(G-12885)
OVERGAARDS ARTCRAFT PRINTERS
2213 S Michigan St (46613-2321)
PHONE.....................................574 234-8464
Fax: 574 287-5037
Thomas Overgaard, President
EMP: 2
SQ FT: 3,000
SALES: 330K Privately Held
SIC: 2752 2759 2791 2789 Commercial printing, offset; letterpress printing; typesetting; bookbinding & related work

(G-12886)
P J MARKETING SERVICES INC
20950 Ireland Rd (46614-3823)
PHONE.....................................574 259-8843
▲ EMP: 7 EST: 1984
SALES (est): 1.1MM Privately Held
SIC: 5199 2396 2395 Whol Nondurable Goods Mfg Auto/Apparel Trimming Pleating/Stitching Services

(G-12887)
PALACIO TROPICAL
2012 W Western Ave (46619-3524)
PHONE.....................................574 289-0742
EMP: 2
SALES (est): 125.4K Privately Held
SIC: 2679 Mfg Converted Paper Products

(G-12888)
PATS CLEANING SERVICE ROB
18840 Darden Rd (46637-4009)
PHONE.....................................574 272-3067
Patricia Robinson, Owner
Larry Robinson, Owner
EMP: 2
SALES (est): 146.3K Privately Held
SIC: 3589 Commercial cleaning equipment

(G-12889)
PEERLESS MACHINERY INC
4406 Technology Dr (46628-9700)
PHONE.....................................574 210-5990
Gannon Clark, President
Ron Nitowski, Vice Pres
EMP: 2
SALES (est): 140.1K Privately Held
SIC: 7699 3541 Industrial machinery & equipment repair; machine tools, metal cutting type

(G-12890)
PEPSI BEVERAGE COMPANY
5435 Dylan Dr (46628-7003)
PHONE.....................................574 271-0633
EMP: 2

SALES (est): 55.1K Privately Held
SIC: 5149 2086 Cooking oils & shortenings; bottled & canned soft drinks

(G-12891)
PERFECTION MOLD & TOOL INC
1116 Mishawaka Ave (46615-1126)
PHONE.....................................574 292-0824
Patrick Moon, President
EMP: 6 EST: 1998
SALES (est): 664.5K Privately Held
WEB: www.moldshop.net
SIC: 3544 Special dies & tools

(G-12892)
PFIZER INC
6879 Entp Dr Ste 500 (46628)
PHONE.....................................574 232-9927
Leon Bertschy, Manager
EMP: 11
SALES (corp-wide): 52.5B Publicly Held
WEB: www.pfizer.com
SIC: 2834 Pharmaceutical preparations
PA: Pfizer Inc.
235 E 42nd St
New York NY 10017
212 733-2323

(G-12893)
PGI MFG LLC (PA)
Also Called: Fulton Industries
100 E Wayne St Ste 320 (46601-2351)
PHONE.....................................574 968-3222
John Razzano, President
Dave Razzano,
EMP: 69
SQ FT: 1,500
SALES (est): 37.6MM Privately Held
SIC: 3599 Machine shop, jobbing & repair

(G-12894)
PHOENIX DRUM DRYER INC
1531 Kemble Ave (46613-1831)
PHONE.....................................574 251-9040
Michael Vance, President
EMP: 12
SALES (est): 1.7MM Privately Held
SIC: 3412 Metal barrels, drums & pails

(G-12895)
PHOENIX ENGINEERING & MFG INC
1531 Kemble Ave (46613-1831)
PHONE.....................................574 251-9040
Michael Vance, President
Marilyn Vance, Treasurer
EMP: 3
SQ FT: 4,500
SALES: 560K Privately Held
SIC: 3537 Cradles, drum

(G-12896)
PIONEER METAL FINISHING LLC
2424 Foundation Dr (46628-4327)
PHONE.....................................574 287-7239
Robert Pyle, President
EMP: 75
SALES (corp-wide): 93MM Privately Held
SIC: 3471 Finishing, metals or formed products; anodizing (plating) of metals or formed products
PA: Pioneer Metal Finishing, Llc
480 Pilgrim Way Ste 1400
Green Bay WI 54304
877 721-1100

(G-12897)
PLASTIC MOLDING MFG INC
5102 Dylan Dr (46628-6500)
PHONE.....................................574 234-9036
Richard McKenney, President
EMP: 30
SALES (est): 140.1K Privately Held
SIC: 3089 Injection molding of plastics
PA: Plastic Molding Mfg, Inc.
34 Tower St
Hudson MA 01749

(G-12898)
PLASTICS FABG & DISTRG LLC
219 E Tutt St (46601-3126)
PHONE.....................................574 233-7527
John Pask, Owner
EMP: 2 EST: 1984

SALES (est): 369.6K Privately Held
SIC: 3089 Injection molding of plastics; plastic processing

(G-12899)
PMG INCORPORATED
5534 Colonial Ln (46614-6212)
PHONE.....................................574 291-3805
Chris Cummings, President
Joe Sorocco, Partner
EMP: 2
SALES (est): 130K Privately Held
SIC: 3678 Electronic connectors

(G-12900)
POINT MACHINE PRODUCTS INC
621 S Scott St (46601-2823)
PHONE.....................................574 289-2429
Donald V Lamont, President
Glenda Lamont, Corp Secy
EMP: 5
SQ FT: 3,600
SALES (est): 320K Privately Held
SIC: 3599 Machine shop, jobbing & repair

(G-12901)
PORTER CASE INC
3718 W Western Ave (46619-2839)
P.O. Box 3971 (46619-0971)
PHONE.....................................574 289-2616
Fax: 574 289-2747
Gary Pond, President
Ralph Reeves, Sales Dir
▲ EMP: 6
SQ FT: 6,000
SALES: 43.9K Privately Held
WEB: www.portercase.com
SIC: 3161 Clothing & apparel carrying cases; traveling bags; cases, carrying

(G-12902)
PRECISION MILLWORK & PLAS INC
Also Called: Precision Mill Work & Plastics
3311 Wliam Richardson Dr (46628-9747)
PHONE.....................................574 243-8720
Fax: 574 243-8718
Larry Shoemaker, President
Diane Shoemaker, Corp Secy
EMP: 25
SQ FT: 20,000
SALES (est): 4.4MM Privately Held
WEB: www.precisionmillwork.net
SIC: 2542 2541 Fixtures, store: except wood; counters or counter display cases: except wood; fixtures: display, office or store: except wood; store fixtures, wood; counters or counter display cases, wood; display fixtures, wood

(G-12903)
PRINT MANAGEMENT SOLUTIONS
1833 Hass Dr (46635-2043)
PHONE.....................................574 234-7269
Thomas Gorski, Principal
EMP: 2
SALES (est): 140K Privately Held
SIC: 2752 Commercial printing, lithographic

(G-12904)
PRINT MY MERCH LLC
3702 W Sample St Ste 1103 (46619-2947)
PHONE.....................................574 323-5541
EMP: 2 EST: 2015
SALES (est): 83.9K Privately Held
SIC: 2752 Lithographic Commercial Printing

(G-12905)
PRO-TOTE SYSTEM INC
Also Called: D&A Transportation
1705 S Olive St (46613-1120)
P.O. Box 3966 (46619-0966)
PHONE.....................................574 287-6006
Lori K Gesto, President
EMP: 11
SQ FT: 15,000
SALES: 2MM Privately Held
WEB: www.protote.com
SIC: 3531 Automobile wrecker hoists

(G-12906)
PROFORMA PRINT PROMO GROUP
3702 W Sample St (46619-2947)
PHONE..................................574 931-2941
EMP: 2 Privately Held
SIC: 2752 Commercial printing, lithographic

(G-12907)
PSI MOLDED PLASTICS IND INC
Also Called: Plastic Solutions, Inc.
3615 Voorde Dr (46628-1644)
PHONE..................................574 288-2100
Fax: 574 237-0077
Daniel Millf, *President*
Steve Schmidt, *General Mgr*
Roberto Flores, *Principal*
David Jastrzembski, *Vice Pres*
Christopher J Lee, *Vice Pres*
◆ EMP: 180
SQ FT: 100,000
SALES: 24MM
SALES (corp-wide): 103.2MM Privately Held
WEB: www.plasticsolutions.com
SIC: 3089 Injection molding of plastics
PA: Psi Molded Plastics, Inc.
    4900 Highway 501
    Myrtle Beach SC 29579
    843 347-4218

(G-12908)
Q S I INC
Also Called: Qsi Printers and Mailers
3024 Mishawaka Ave (46615-2398)
PHONE..................................574 282-1200
Fax: 574 282-2844
Susan P Carrico, *President*
Rachel Thomas, *MIS Mgr*
EMP: 20 EST: 1970
SQ FT: 17,000
SALES (est): 3.1MM Privately Held
WEB: www.qsibillers.com
SIC: 2752 7331 2791 Commercial printing, offset; mailing service; typesetting

(G-12909)
QUALITY MOLDED PRODUCTS INC
Also Called: SPI Industries
19850 State Line Rd (46637-1545)
PHONE..................................574 272-3733
Fax: 574 272-7626
John W Doster I, *CEO*
James Doster, *President*
Ed Trapp, *General Mgr*
Susan M Doster, *Corp Secy*
John Townsend, *VP Opers*
▲ EMP: 55
SQ FT: 44,000
SALES: 9.5MM Privately Held
WEB: www.moldedparts.com
SIC: 3089 Injection molding of plastics

(G-12910)
R 2 DIAGNOSTICS INC
1801 Commerce Dr (46628-1562)
PHONE..................................574 288-4377
Michael J Morris, *President*
Marc Goldford, *Director*
EMP: 6
SALES (est): 836.6K Privately Held
WEB: www.r2diagnostics.com
SIC: 3841 2835 Diagnostic apparatus, medical; in vitro & in vivo diagnostic substances

(G-12911)
R K C INSTRUMENT
4245 Meghan Beeler Ct (46628-8418)
PHONE..................................574 273-6099
Fax: 574 247-9657
Teru Hochi, *President*
Dave Wolverton, *Manager*
EMP: 10
SALES (est): 1MM Privately Held
WEB: www.rkcinst.com
SIC: 3825 Instruments to measure electricity

(G-12912)
R M MFG HOUSING SVC
1001 S Mayflower Rd L (46619-3923)
PHONE..................................574 288-5207

M P Fletcher, *Principal*
EMP: 2
SALES (est): 124.8K Privately Held
SIC: 3999 Manufacturing industries

(G-12913)
RADECKI GALLERIES INC
721 E Jefferson Blvd (46617-2902)
PHONE..................................574 287-0266
Fax: 574 287-4875
Ronald Radecki, *President*
Adell Radecki, *Corp Secy*
EMP: 5
SQ FT: 5,000
SALES (est): 415.9K Privately Held
SIC: 2499 8999 5932 Picture frame molding, finished; art restoration; antiques

(G-12914)
REDDINGTON DESIGN INC
4221 Ralph Jones Ct (46628-9794)
PHONE..................................574 272-0790
Fax: 574 272-0807
Randal Redding, *President*
Renee Hums, *Vice Pres*
▲ EMP: 6
SQ FT: 1,800
SALES (est): 750K Privately Held
WEB: www.reddingtondesign.com
SIC: 3993 Signs & advertising specialties

(G-12915)
RIETH-RILEY CNSTR CO INC
25200 State Road 23 (46614-9501)
PHONE..................................574 288-8321
Fax: 574 522-5748
John Yadon, *Systems Mgr*
EMP: 30
SALES (corp-wide): 226.8MM Privately Held
WEB: www.reithriley.com
SIC: 1771 2951 Concrete work; asphalt paving mixtures & blocks
PA: Rieth-Riley Construction Co., Inc.
    3626 Elkhart Rd
    Goshen IN 46526
    574 875-5183

(G-12916)
RINK PRINTING COMPANY INC
Also Called: Rink Riverside Printing
814 S Main St (46601-3008)
PHONE..................................574 232-7935
Fax: 574 288-2115
Michael S Rink, *President*
Joseph Castenando, *Exec VP*
June Belew, *Vice Pres*
Joseph Castenand, *Vice Pres*
Steve Sayre, *Purchasing*
EMP: 30 EST: 1958
SQ FT: 55,000
SALES: 4.7MM Privately Held
WEB: www.rinkprinting.com
SIC: 2752 2759 2791 2789 Offset & photolithographic printing; commercial printing, offset; letterpress printing; typesetting; bookbinding & related work; die-cut paper & board

(G-12917)
RISING IMPROVEMENTS LLC
17526 Douglas Rd Lot 9 (46635-1733)
PHONE..................................608 295-8301
Robert L Miller Sr, *Administration*
EMP: 2 EST: 2016
SALES (est): 91.8K Privately Held
SIC: 3842 Wheelchairs

(G-12918)
ROUND 2 LLC
4073 Meghan Beeler Ct (46628-8410)
PHONE..................................574 243-3000
Thomas Lowe,
▲ EMP: 18
SQ FT: 10,000
SALES (est): 3.2MM Privately Held
SIC: 3944 Toy trains, airplanes & automobiles

(G-12919)
ROWAN INDUSTRIES LLC
52555 Kenilworth Rd (46637-3016)
PHONE..................................574 302-1203
Martin A Couch, *President*
EMP: 2

SALES (est): 104.5K Privately Held
SIC: 3999 Manufacturing industries

(G-12920)
ROYAL ADHESIVES & SEALANTS LLC (HQ)
Also Called: Royal Elastomers
2001 W Washington St (46628-2032)
PHONE..................................574 246-5000
Fax: 574 246-5425
Ted Clark, *President*
Richard Foukes, *President*
Mark S Masters, *President*
Timothy O'Neil, *General Mgr*
Steven De Jesus, *Regional Mgr*
◆ EMP: 100
SALES (est): 478.9MM
SALES (corp-wide): 2.3B Publicly Held
WEB: www.royaladhesives.com
SIC: 2891 7389 8711 Adhesives & sealants; packaging & labeling services; building construction consultant
PA: H.B. Fuller Company
    1200 Willow Lake Blvd
    Saint Paul MN 55110
    651 236-5900

(G-12921)
ROYAL ADHESIVES & SEALANTS LLC
Royal Elastomers
2001 W Washington St (46628-2032)
PHONE..................................574 246-5000
Gordon Wall, *Opers Staff*
EMP: 40
SQ FT: 60,000
SALES (corp-wide): 2.3B Publicly Held
WEB: www.royaladhesives.com
SIC: 3586 2891 2821 2822 Measuring & dispensing pumps; epoxy adhesives; epoxy resins; urea resins; elastomers, nonvulcanizable (plastics); synthetic rubber
HQ: Royal Adhesives And Sealants Llc
    2001 W Washington St
    South Bend IN 46628
    574 246-5000

(G-12922)
ROYAL HOLDINGS INC
2001 W Washington St (46628-2032)
PHONE..................................574 246-5000
Ted Clark, *CEO*
Randy Greenlee, *Vice Pres*
Steve Zens, *Vice Pres*
Pam Patterson, *Purchasing*
Steve Fushi, *Engineer*
EMP: 107
SALES (est): 165.1MM
SALES (corp-wide): 352MM Privately Held
SIC: 2891 Adhesives & sealants
PA: Arsenal Capital Partners Lp
    100 Park Ave Fl 31
    New York NY 10017
    212 771-1717

(G-12923)
RPM MACHINERY LLC
3953 Ralph Jones Dr (46628-9792)
PHONE..................................574 271-0800
Fax: 574 271-0889
Kenny Ringle, *Parts Mgr*
Craig Goad, *CFO*
Jay Courtney, *Manager*
EMP: 12
SALES (corp-wide): 21.1MM Privately Held
WEB: www.macrent.net
SIC: 5531 3599 Truck equipment & parts; machine shop, jobbing & repair
PA: Rpm Machinery, Llc
    3911 Limestone Dr
    Fort Wayne IN 46809
    260 747-1561

(G-12924)
RUBBER SHOP INC
Also Called: Royal Rubber Company
500 W Chippewa Ave (46614-3708)
P.O. Box 2375 (46680-2375)
PHONE..................................574 291-6440
Fax: 574 291-0437
Victor M Grabovez, *President*
Claire Grabovez, *Vice Pres*
Leigh Anne Roberts, *Controller*

EMP: 5 EST: 1946
SQ FT: 30,000
SALES (est): 803.1K Privately Held
WEB: www.royalrubber.com
SIC: 3061 3053 3052 3011 Mechanical rubber goods; gaskets, packing & sealing devices; rubber & plastics hose & beltings; tires & inner tubes

(G-12925)
SAMPCO INC
Also Called: Sampco of Indiana
915 W Ireland Rd (46614-3842)
PHONE..................................413 442-4043
Fax: 574 299-1891
Dennis Boo, *Manager*
EMP: 110
SALES (corp-wide): 72.2MM Privately Held
SIC: 2599 7389 3993 2952 Boards: planning, display, notice; design, commercial & industrial; signs & advertising specialties; asphalt felts & coatings; distribution of advertising material or sample services
PA: Sampco, Inc.
    56 Downing Pkwy
    Pittsfield MA 01201
    413 442-4043

(G-12926)
SAN MAR
54555 Pine Rd (46628-5628)
PHONE..................................574 286-6884
Fax: 574 232-3225
EMP: 3
SALES (est): 18.7K Privately Held
SIC: 3599 Industrial machinery

(G-12927)
SANMAR TOOL & MANUFACTURING
54555 Pine Rd (46628-5628)
PHONE..................................574 232-6081
Frank Martinez, *President*
Sandy Martinez, *Vice Pres*
EMP: 4
SALES (est): 462.2K Privately Held
SIC: 3544 0752 Special dies, tools, jigs & fixtures; boarding services, kennels

(G-12928)
SC SUPPLY COMPANY LLC
1908 Portage Ave (46616-2031)
P.O. Box 11531 (46634-0531)
PHONE..................................574 287-0252
Susan Caldwell, *President*
EMP: 3
SALES: 1.2MM Privately Held
WEB: www.scsupplyco.com
SIC: 3669 Traffic signals, electric

(G-12929)
SCHAFER INDUSTRIES INC (PA)
Also Called: Schafer Gear Works-South Bend
4701 Nimtz Pkwy (46628-6151)
PHONE..................................574 234-4116
Fax: 574 234-4115
Bipin Doshi, *President*
Chuck Tate, *General Mgr*
Glenn Duncan, *Principal*
Stan Blenke, *Exec VP*
Stanley Blenke, *Vice Pres*
▲ EMP: 100 EST: 2000
SQ FT: 100,000
SALES (est): 34MM Privately Held
WEB: www.schafergear.com
SIC: 3499 3462 Fire- or burglary-resistive products; gears, forged steel

(G-12930)
SCHURZ COMMUNICATIONS INC
225 W Colfax Ave (46626-1000)
PHONE..................................574 235-6496
David Ray, *Manager*
Jeff Wesolowski, *Manager*
Ian Wilson, *Manager*
Judy Kovacs, *Clerk*
EMP: 500
SALES (corp-wide): 882.7MM Publicly Held
SIC: 2711 Commercial printing & newspaper publishing combined

▲ = Import ▼=Export
◆ =Import/Export

HQ: Schurz Communications, Inc.
1301 E Douglas Rd Ste 200
Mishawaka IN 46545
574 247-7237

(G-12931)
SEGURA PUBLISHING COMPANY
1045 W Washington St (46601-1434)
PHONE..................................574 631-3143
Joseph Segura, *President*
Joe Segura, *Master*
EMP: 3 EST: 1981
SALES (est): 220K Privately Held
WEB: www.segura.com
SIC: 2796 Etching on copper, steel, wood or rubber: printing plates

(G-12932)
SHAKOUR INDUSTRIES INC
Also Called: South Bend Metal Products Co
4550 S Burnett Dr (46614-3820)
PHONE..................................574 289-0100
Fax: 574 289-0101
Gabriel R Shakour, *President*
Michelle Shakour, *Admin Sec*
EMP: 6 EST: 1953
SQ FT: 4,800
SALES: 350K Privately Held
SIC: 3469 3544 2759 2796 Metal stampings; industrial molds; laser printing; engraving platemaking services; engraving on copper, steel, wood or rubber: printing plates

(G-12933)
SIBLEY MACHINE & FOUNDRY CORP
206 E Tutt St (46601-3127)
PHONE..................................574 232-2910
Fax: 574 232-2910
William H Voll Jr, *President*
Ann Voll, *Executive*
EMP: 20
SQ FT: 50,000
SALES (est): 3.3MM Privately Held
WEB: www.castandmachine.com
SIC: 3599 Machine shop, jobbing & repair

(G-12934)
SIERRA MACHINE
26378 Lakeview Dr (46619-4588)
PHONE..................................574 232-5694
Jerry Coon, *Principal*
EMP: 3
SALES (est): 140K Privately Held
SIC: 3451 Screw machine products

(G-12935)
SIGN CREATIONS LLC
55234 Holmes Rd (46628-4912)
PHONE..................................574 855-1246
Timothy Grontkowski, *Principal*
EMP: 3
SALES (est): 187.7K Privately Held
SIC: 3993 Signs & advertising specialties

(G-12936)
SIGN DEALS DELIVERED
19355 Sundale Dr (46614-5846)
PHONE..................................574 276-7404
Anjie Brenda, *Principal*
EMP: 2
SALES (est): 136.3K Privately Held
SIC: 3993 Signs & advertising specialties

(G-12937)
SIMEOC LLC
18125 Chipstead Dr (46637-4424)
PHONE..................................240 210-5685
Cynthia Nikolai, *Mng Member*
Gregory Madey, *Mng Member*
EMP: 2
SALES (est): 43.6K Privately Held
SIC: 7372 Application computer software

(G-12938)
SKY KING UNLIMITED INC
50571 Indiana Sr 533 (46637)
PHONE..................................574 271-9170
Ron Carabbia, *Principal*
EMP: 11 Privately Held
SIC: 2899 Fireworks

PA: Sky King Unlimited, Inc.
7350 S Us Highway 1
Port Saint Lucie FL

(G-12939)
SLATILE ROOFING AND SHTMTL CO
1703 S Ironwood Dr Ste A (46613-3499)
PHONE..................................574 233-7485
Fax: 574 233-7531
Gerald E Longerot, *President*
Ann C Longerot, *Corp Secy*
Ken Hoy, *Project Mgr*
Joshua Longerot, *Project Mgr*
Robert Davis, *Safety Mgr*
EMP: 30
SQ FT: 27,000
SALES (est): 5.3MM Privately Held
SIC: 1761 3444 1741 Roofing contractor; sheet metalwork; sheet metalwork; tuck-pointing or restoration

(G-12940)
SOMMERS GRAPHICS INC
Also Called: Sommers Graphics Group
60750 Greenridge Ct (46614-9744)
PHONE..................................574 282-2000
Fax: 574 287-1111
Stephen Sommers, *President*
Susan Sommers, *Admin Sec*
David L Patton Jr, *Representative*
EMP: 19
SQ FT: 25,000
SALES: 2.2MM Privately Held
SIC: 2752 Commercial printing, lithographic; commercial printing, offset; photolithographic printing

(G-12941)
SOUTH BEND BREW WERKS LLC
216 S Michigan St (46601-2002)
PHONE..................................801 209-2987
EMP: 3
SALES (est): 280.9K Privately Held
SIC: 2082 Malt beverages

(G-12942)
SOUTH BEND CHOCOLATE CO INC (PA)
3300 W Sample St Ste 110 (46619-3077)
P.O. Box 4104 (46634-4104)
PHONE..................................574 233-2577
Mark Tarner, *President*
S Eric Marshall, *Principal*
Julie Tarner, *Corp Secy*
Justin Weidner, *Plant Mgr*
Sherri Huffer, *Store Mgr*
▲ EMP: 12
SQ FT: 50,000
SALES (est): 61.7MM Privately Held
WEB: www.sbchocolate.com
SIC: 5149 2066 5441 5812 Chocolate; chocolate; candy; cafe

(G-12943)
SOUTH BEND ETHANOL LLC
3201 W Calvert St (46613-1010)
PHONE..................................574 703-3360
EMP: 3
SALES (est): 200K Privately Held
SIC: 1311 Natural gas production

(G-12944)
SOUTH BEND FORM TOOL CO INC
408 W Indiana Ave (46613-2093)
PHONE..................................574 289-2441
Fax: 574 289-3330
Herb Eggers, *President*
Lori Eggers, *Vice Pres*
Amy Cavazos, *Admin Sec*
EMP: 23
SQ FT: 15,600
SALES (est): 4.2MM Privately Held
WEB: www.sbform.com
SIC: 3544 Dies & die holders for metal cutting, forming, die casting; jigs & fixtures

(G-12945)
SOUTH BEND SMOKE TIME INC
1841 S Bend Ave (46637-5637)
PHONE..................................574 318-4837
Janpal Singh, *Principal*
EMP: 2

SALES (est): 170.8K Privately Held
SIC: 2111 Cigarettes

(G-12946)
SOUTH BEND TRIBUNE CORP (DH)
225 W Colfax Ave (46626-1001)
PHONE..................................574 235-6161
Fax: 574 235-6091
David C Ray, *President*
Kimberly D Wilson, *President*
Steven Funk, *Vice Pres*
Mark Hocker, *Treasurer*
Cheryl J Morey, *Admin Sec*
EMP: 500
SQ FT: 80,000
SALES (est): 54.8MM
SALES (corp-wide): 882.7MM Publicly Held
WEB: www.sbtinfo.com
SIC: 2711 Commercial printing & newspaper publishing combined
HQ: Schurz Communications, Inc.
1301 E Douglas Rd Ste 200
Mishawaka IN 46545
574 247-7237

(G-12947)
SOUTH BEND WOODWORKS LLC
707 S Scott St (46601-2825)
PHONE..................................574 232-8875
Michael Linddurg, *Mng Member*
EMP: 15
SALES (est): 871.6K Privately Held
SIC: 2431 Millwork

(G-12948)
SPECIALTY PRODUCTS & POLYMERS
50869 Hawthorne Meadow Dr (46628-1863)
PHONE..................................269 684-5931
Rick Ray, *CEO*
EMP: 2
SALES (est): 146.1K Privately Held
SIC: 3069 Molded rubber products

(G-12949)
SPIN-CAST PLASTICS INC
3300 N Kenmore St (46628-4374)
PHONE..................................574 232-8066
Fax: 574 232-6036
Robert R Latek, *Vice Pres*
▲ EMP: 90 EST: 1968
SQ FT: 80,000
SALES (est): 11MM
SALES (corp-wide): 3.6B Publicly Held
WEB: www.energyabsorption.com
SIC: 3089 Injection molded finished plastic products
HQ: Energy Absorption Systems, Inc.
70 W Madison St Ste 350
Chicago IL 60602
312 467-6750

(G-12950)
SSD CONTROL TECHNOLOGY INC
1801 S Main St (46613-2221)
PHONE..................................574 289-5942
Fax: 574 289-5984
Steve Estes, *President*
Dave Konieczny, *Vice Pres*
Lowell Tully, *Vice Pres*
EMP: 32
SQ FT: 23,500
SALES (est): 6.5MM Privately Held
WEB: www.ifweld.com
SIC: 3599 5084 1799 Custom machinery; machine tools & accessories; welding on site

(G-12951)
ST AUGUSTINES PRESS INC (PA)
17917 Killington Way (46614-9773)
P.O. Box 2285 (46680-2285)
PHONE..................................574 291-3500
Bruce Fingerhut, *President*
A J Freddoso, *Treasurer*
Laila Fingerhut, *Bd of Directors*
EMP: 2

SALES: 427.2K Privately Held
WEB: www.staugustine.net
SIC: 2731 Books: publishing only

(G-12952)
STAFFORD CONSTRUCTION INC
111 Cherry St (46601-2604)
PHONE..................................574 287-9696
Charles E Stafford, *President*
EMP: 3
SALES (est): 212.6K Privately Held
SIC: 2759 Commercial printing

(G-12953)
STAMPRINT INC
2609 S Main St (46614-1017)
PHONE..................................574 233-3900
Fax: 574 233-9550
Darren Hanson, *President*
Steve Sommers, *CFO*
Jill Hanson, *Manager*
EMP: 7 EST: 1965
SQ FT: 10,000
SALES (est): 580K Privately Held
WEB: www.stamprint.net
SIC: 2791 7334 2759 2789 Typesetting; photocopying & duplicating services; commercial printing; bookbinding & related work; commercial printing, offset

(G-12954)
STAR NOVA US LLC (PA)
3702 W Sample St (46619-2947)
PHONE..................................269 830-5802
Patrick L Magliozzo, *President*
Bin Ren, *President*
Patrick Magliozzi, *Project Mgr*
EMP: 9
SALES (est): 797K Privately Held
SIC: 2542 Racks, merchandise display or storage: except wood

(G-12955)
STEEL STORAGE INC
1408 Elwood Ave Ste A (46628-2757)
PHONE..................................574 282-2618
Fax: 574 282-2621
Frank Prusinski, *President*
EMP: 20
SQ FT: 25,000
SALES (est): 3.3MM Privately Held
WEB: www.steelstorage.net
SIC: 3443 5051 Metal parts; steel

(G-12956)
STEEL WAREHOUSE OF OHIO LLC
2722 Tucker Dr (46619-4292)
PHONE..................................574 236-5100
EMP: 2
SALES (est): 264.2K Privately Held
SIC: 3312 Blast Furnaces And Steel Mills

(G-12957)
STRATEGIC MFG & SUP INC ✪
Also Called: SMS
59661 Moonbeam Ct (46614-9608)
PHONE..................................574 643-1050
Jonathan Cochran, *President*
EMP: 6 EST: 2017
SALES (est): 198K Privately Held
SIC: 3999 Manufacturing industries

(G-12958)
STRESCORE INC
24445 State Road 23 (46614-9540)
P.O. Box 270 (46624-0270)
PHONE..................................574 233-1117
Fax: 574 288-0050
Ralph M Hass, *President*
John S Reihl, *Vice Pres*
Betty Hensley, *Bookkeeper*
▲ EMP: 50
SQ FT: 2,000
SALES (est): 9MM Privately Held
WEB: www.strescore.com
SIC: 3272 Prestressed concrete products

(G-12959)
STUMP HOME SPECIALTIES MFG INC
2220 S Main St (46613-2316)
PHONE..................................574 291-0050
Fax: 574 299-0683
Arthur Stump, *President*

Louise Stump, *Corp Secy*
EMP: 3 **EST:** 1959
SQ FT: 15,000
SALES (est): 190K **Privately Held**
WEB: www.stumphomespecialties.com
SIC: 2511 Wood household furniture

(G-12960)
SUGARPASTE
Also Called: Crystal Colors
2211 S Michigan St (46613-2321)
PHONE..............................574 276-8703
Elizabeth Parvu, *Owner*
Ron Parvu, *Co-Owner*
EMP: 2
SALES: 100K **Privately Held**
WEB: www.sugarpaste.com
SIC: 2087 Food colorings

(G-12961)
SUMMIT LLC
Also Called: AlphaGraphics
201 N Main St (46601-1216)
PHONE..............................574 287-7468
Fax: 574 287-8054
Pat Welch, *Mng Member*
EMP: 8
SQ FT: 2,600
SALES (est): 1.3MM **Privately Held**
SIC: 2752 Commercial printing, offset

(G-12962)
SURESTEP LLC
17530 Dugdale Dr (46635-1583)
PHONE..............................574 233-3352
Bernie Veldman,
EMP: 50
SALES (est): 4.7MM **Privately Held**
SIC: 3842 Surgical appliances & supplies

(G-12963)
SUZUKI GARPHYTTAN CORP
Also Called: GARPHYTTAN WIRE
4404 Nimtz Pkwy (46628-4317)
PHONE..............................574 232-8800
Fax: 574 232-2565
Kirk Manning, *President*
James Tomei, *VP Opers*
Dave Rogers, *Opers Mgr*
Sue Brown, *Purch Mgr*
Steve Williams, *Purchasing*
▲ **EMP:** 65
SQ FT: 120,000
SALES: 54MM
SALES (corp-wide): 53.2B **Privately Held**
SIC: 3495 Precision springs
HQ: Suzuki Garphyttan Ab
Bruksvagen 3
Garphyttan 719 4
192 951-00

(G-12964)
SYSCON INTERNATIONAL INC
Also Called: Syscon-Plantstar
1108 High St (46601-3796)
PHONE..............................574 232-3900
Fax: 574 287-5916
Townsend Thomas, *President*
Magaret Thomas, *Vice Pres*
EMP: 200
SQ FT: 125,000
SALES (est): 13MM **Privately Held**
WEB: www.syscon-intl.com
SIC: 3823 Industrial instrmnts msrmnt display/control process variable; analyzers, industrial process type; data loggers, industrial process type; temperature measurement instruments, industrial

(G-12965)
SYSTEMS & SERVICES OF MICHIANA (PA)
Also Called: Express Press
3505 W Mcgill St (46628-4352)
PHONE..............................574 273-1111
Fax: 574 273-3250
Brian Clauser, *President*
Norman L Wiggers, *President*
Sandra Clauser, *Admin Sec*
EMP: 5 **EST:** 1977
SALES (est): 2.2MM **Privately Held**
SIC: 5112 2752 Office supplies; office filing supplies; business forms; commercial printing, offset

(G-12966)
SYSTEMS & SERVICES OF MICHIANA
Also Called: Systems and Services
325 N Dixie Way Ste 300 (46637-3311)
PHONE..............................574 277-3355
Mark D Schaffer, *Branch Mgr*
EMP: 5
SALES (est): 347.5K
SALES (corp-wide): 2.2MM **Privately Held**
SIC: 5112 2752 Office supplies; commercial printing, offset
PA: Systems & Services Of Michiana Inc
3505 W Mcgill St
South Bend IN 46628
574 273-1111

(G-12967)
TDC LOGGING LLC
24890 Edison Rd (46628-4974)
PHONE..............................574 289-4243
Rose Calhoun, *Principal*
EMP: 2
SALES (est): 131.7K **Privately Held**
SIC: 2411 Logging

(G-12968)
THERM-O-LITE LLC
Also Called: Thermolite Windows System
3502 W Sample St (46619-2921)
PHONE..............................574 234-4004
Fax: 574 234-4005
Richard S Champlin, *President*
Mark Neilson, *Corp Secy*
William Harper, *Treasurer*
EMP: 8 **EST:** 1979
SQ FT: 15,000
SALES (est): 1.8MM **Privately Held**
WEB: www.thermolitewindows.com
SIC: 2431 Windows & window parts & trim, wood; doors & door parts & trim, wood

(G-12969)
THREE STAR ELECTRIC INC
52620 Helmen Ave (46637-3216)
PHONE..............................574 272-3136
William Winland Sr, *President*
Daniel Collins, *Vice Pres*
EMP: 5
SQ FT: 7,500
SALES (est): 342.6K **Privately Held**
SIC: 1731 7694 5999 General electrical contractor; electric motor repair; motors, electric

(G-12970)
TIMKEN COMPANY
3502 W Sample St (46619-2921)
PHONE..............................574 288-7188
Nick Stewart, *Branch Mgr*
EMP: 289
SALES (corp-wide): 3B **Publicly Held**
SIC: 3562 Ball & roller bearings
PA: The Timken Company
4500 Mount Pleasant St Nw
North Canton OH 44720
234 262-3000

(G-12971)
TIMKEN COMPANY
Also Called: Timken Furnaces Agency
3010 Mishawaka Ave (46615-2348)
PHONE..............................574 287-1566
John S Campbell, *Branch Mgr*
EMP: 163
SALES (corp-wide): 3B **Publicly Held**
SIC: 3562 Ball & roller bearings
PA: The Timken Company
4500 Mount Pleasant St Nw
North Canton OH 44720
234 262-3000

(G-12972)
TIRE RACK INC (PA)
Also Called: Tire Rack, The
7101 Vorden Pkwy (46628-8422)
PHONE..............................888 541-1777
Michael A Joines, *President*
William Strutner, *Editor*
Thomas F Veldman, *Chairman*
Matthew E Edmonds, *Vice Pres*
Mark P Veldman, *Vice Pres*
◆ **EMP:** 400
SQ FT: 530,000

SALES (est): 1.3B **Privately Held**
SIC: 5014 3714 Automobile tires & tubes; motor vehicle wheels & parts

(G-12973)
TK FINISHING
3702 W Sample St Ste 4045 (46619-2976)
PHONE..............................574 233-1617
Margaret Tenderenda, *Principal*
EMP: 3
SALES (est): 213.3K **Privately Held**
SIC: 3471 Finishing, metals or formed products

(G-12974)
TOMS INTERIOR WINDOWS LLC
3702 W Sample St Ste 1133 (46619-2964)
PHONE..............................574 233-0799
Jeff Tom,
EMP: 3
SALES (est): 415.7K **Privately Held**
SIC: 2431 Storm windows, wood

(G-12975)
TOYO SEIKO NORTH AMERICA INC
3507 N Olive Rd Ste E (46628-8468)
PHONE..............................574 288-2000
Yoshihiro Watanzabe, *CEO*
EMP: 6
SALES (est): 782.4K **Privately Held**
SIC: 3398 Shot peening (treating steel to reduce fatigue)

(G-12976)
TRANE US INC
3725 Cleveland Rd Ste 300 (46628-8470)
PHONE..............................574 282-4880
Dave Sommer, *Branch Mgr*
EMP: 20 **Privately Held**
SIC: 3585 Refrigeration & heating equipment
HQ: Trane U.S. Inc.
3600 Pammel Creek Rd
La Crosse WI 54601
608 787-2000

(G-12977)
TRANSFORMATION INDUSTRIES LLC
615 Cushing St (46616-1117)
PHONE..............................574 457-9320
Kory Lantz, *Principal*
EMP: 2
SALES (est): 111.7K **Privately Held**
SIC: 3999 Manufacturing industries

(G-12978)
TRC MFG INC
17460 Fleetwood Ln (46635-1365)
PHONE..............................574 262-9299
Martin L Borton, *Ch of Bd*
Jim Hite, *President*
EMP: 23
SQ FT: 40,000
SALES (est): 3.4MM **Privately Held**
SIC: 3799 Recreational vehicles

(G-12979)
TRIANGLE MACHINE INC
3702 W Sample St Ste 1125 (46619-2977)
PHONE..............................574 246-0165
Long T Lam, *President*
MAI Tran, *Admin Sec*
EMP: 7
SQ FT: 1,800
SALES (est): 700K **Privately Held**
SIC: 3599 Machine shop, jobbing & repair

(G-12980)
ULTRA MONTANE ASSOCIATES INC
Also Called: MICHAEL JONES
206 Marquette Ave (46617-1111)
PHONE..............................574 289-9786
Fax: 574 289-1461
Michael Jones, *President*
E Michael Jones, *President*
Marc Brammer, *Vice Pres*
Ruth Jones, *Admin Sec*
EMP: 4
SALES (est): 197.6K **Privately Held**
WEB: www.culturewars.com
SIC: 2721 Magazines: publishing only, not printed on site

(G-12981)
UNITED COATINGS TECH INC
1011 S Main St (46601-3335)
PHONE..............................574 287-4774
Mark Huffer, *President*
Matthew Culp, *Sales Staff*
Kurt Rimelspach, *Manager*
▲ **EMP:** 15
SQ FT: 36,000
SALES (est): 3.2MM **Privately Held**
WEB: www.unitedcoatingstechnologies.com
SIC: 2851 Paints & paint additives

(G-12982)
VALAD MCHNING CNTRLESS GRNDING
Also Called: Kaley Centerless Grinding
2825 S Main St (46614-1021)
PHONE..............................574 291-5541
Fax: 574 291-5857
Michael Boyle, *President*
EMP: 2
SQ FT: 3,000
SALES (est): 170K **Privately Held**
SIC: 3599 Machine shop, jobbing & repair

(G-12983)
VALUE PRODUCTION INC
2629 Foundation Dr (46628-4332)
PHONE..............................574 246-1913
Nevin Siqueira, *President*
Steven Hartz, *Vice Pres*
EMP: 32
SQ FT: 15,000
SALES (est): 1.2MM **Privately Held**
WEB: www.valueprod.com
SIC: 3728 3812 Aircraft parts & equipment; defense systems & equipment

(G-12984)
VALUE TOOL & ENGINEERING INC (PA)
2629 Foundation Dr (46628-4332)
PHONE..............................574 246-1913
Steven Hartz, *President*
EMP: 52
SQ FT: 30,000
SALES (est): 13.6MM **Privately Held**
WEB: www.valuetooleng.com
SIC: 3599 Machine shop, jobbing & repair

(G-12985)
W J HAGERTY & SONS LTD INC
3801 Linden Ave (46619-1844)
P.O. Box 1496 (46624-1496)
PHONE..............................574 288-4991
M Patrick Hagerty, *Ch of Bd*
Debra Hagerty, *President*
Shelley Meszaros, *Vice Pres*
Batalis Dmydro, *Engineer*
Maryhelene Thurber, *VP Sales*
◆ **EMP:** 45 **EST:** 1895
SQ FT: 57,000
SALES (est): 10.3MM **Privately Held**
WEB: www.hagerty-polish.com
SIC: 2842 Cleaning or polishing preparations; specialty cleaning preparations; polishing preparations & related products

(G-12986)
WALNUT STREET HARDWOODS
25490 Trunk Trl (46619-9653)
PHONE..............................574 287-1023
Wayne Calhoun, *President*
EMP: 28
SALES (est): 3.2MM **Privately Held**
WEB: www.walnut-street.com
SIC: 2421 Sawmills & planing mills, general

(G-12987)
WALSH & KELLY INC
24358 State Road 23 (46614-9697)
PHONE..............................219 924-5900
Gary Piclyk, *Principal*
Kevin Kelly, *Branch Mgr*
EMP: 60
SALES (corp-wide): 21.7MM **Privately Held**
SIC: 2951 1611 1771 Asphalt & asphaltic paving mixtures (not from refineries); surfacing & paving; concrete work

▲ = Import ▼=Export
◆ =Import/Export

PA: Walsh & Kelly Inc
1700 E Main St
Griffith IN 46319
219 924-5900

(G-12988)
WATCON INC (PA)
2215 S Main St (46613-2315)
P.O. Box 2829 (46680-2829)
PHONE..................................574 287-3397
Fax: 574 287-2427
George A Resnik Jr, *President*
Timothy Henthorn, *Vice Pres*
Thomas Resnik, *Vice Pres*
Mary Jensen, *Manager*
Millie Spicer, *Manager*
EMP: 10 EST: 1947
SQ FT: 16,000
SALES (est): 2MM **Privately Held**
WEB: www.watcon-inc.com
SIC: 2899 3589 7389 Water treating com-
pounds; water treatment equipment, in-
dustrial; inspection & testing services

(G-12989)
WDMI INC
715 W Ireland Rd (46614-3809)
PHONE..................................574 291-7100
Fax: 574 291-7171
Chuck Houin, *Manager*
EMP: 25
SALES (corp-wide): 10.4MM **Privately
Held**
WEB: www.transit-mix.com
SIC: 3273 Ready-mixed concrete
PA: Wdmi, Inc.
2341 W Jefferson St
Plymouth IN 46563

(G-12990)
**WHEEL HORSE SALES &
SERVICE**
51465 Ind Ste Rte 933 (46637-1617)
PHONE..................................574 272-4242
James Bernath, *President*
EMP: 12
SALES: 1MM **Privately Held**
SIC: 3524 Lawn & garden equipment

(G-12991)
**WILLIAMSBURG FURNITURE
INC**
3300 W Sample St (46619-3079)
PHONE..................................574 387-5691
Alejeandra Garcia, *President*
EMP: 3
SALES (est): 180.2K **Privately Held**
SIC: 2512 2515 Upholstered household
furniture; mattresses & foundations
PA: Williamsburg Furniture, Inc.
2096 Cheyenne St
Nappanee IN 46550

(G-12992)
WOODS ENTERPRISES
26795 State Road 2 (46619-9795)
PHONE..................................574 232-7449
Carl Woods, *Owner*
EMP: 2
SALES: 60K **Privately Held**
SIC: 0811 2431 2395 2396 Tree farm; in-
terior & ornamental woodwork & trim; em-
broidery & art needlework; screen printing
on fabric articles

(G-12993)
YODER SOFTWARE INC
1121 N Notre Dame Ave (46617-1342)
PHONE..................................574 302-6232
John Yoder, *President*
Michael Seelinger, *Vice Pres*
EMP: 2
SALES (est): 72.9K **Privately Held**
SIC: 7372 Prepackaged software

South Milford
Lagrange County

(G-12994)
**TRI-STATE HARDWOOD
COMPANY**
7050 S State Rd 3 (46786)
P.O. Box 213 (46786-0213)
PHONE..................................260 351-3111
Fax: 260 351-2228
Robert G Lewis, *President*
Denver Calhoun, *President*
Donnie Howard, *Admin Sec*
▼ EMP: 30
SQ FT: 28,000
SALES: 10.1MM **Privately Held**
WEB: www.tristatehardwood.com
SIC: 2421 Sawmills & planing mills, gen-
eral; planing mill, independent; except
millwork; kiln drying of lumber

(G-12995)
WIBLE LUMBER INC
7155 S State Rte 3 (46786)
P.O. Box 7 (46786-0007)
PHONE..................................260 351-2441
Fax: 260 351-3777
David Wible, *President*
Scott Butler, *Accounts Mgr*
EMP: 35
SQ FT: 40,000
SALES (est): 6.7MM **Privately Held**
WEB: www.wiblelumber.com
SIC: 2431 2435 Millwork; hardwood ve-
neer & plywood

South Whitley
Whitley County

(G-12996)
AG PLUS INC (PA)
401 N Main St (46787-1250)
P.O. Box 306 (46787-0306)
PHONE..................................260 723-5141
Jeff Mize, *CEO*
Kent Hoffman, *Chairman*
Stanley Studebaker, *Corp Secy*
Dan Bacon, *Vice Pres*
EMP: 24 EST: 1912
SQ FT: 5,000
SALES (est): 102.1MM **Privately Held**
WEB: www.agplusinc.com
SIC: 5191 2041 5153 Fertilizer & fertilizer
materials; animal feeds; feed; flour &
other grain mill products; grain elevators

(G-12997)
DWYER INSTRUMENTS INC
367 W 1st St (46787-1258)
P.O. Box 373, Michigan City (46361-0373)
PHONE..................................260 723-5138
Fax: 260 723-6229
Dock Craig, *Manager*
EMP: 80
SQ FT: 10,000
SALES (corp-wide): 100MM **Privately
Held**
WEB: www.dwyer-inst.com
SIC: 3823 3825 3824 3545 Pressure
measurement instruments, industrial; in-
struments to measure electricity; fluid me-
ters & counting devices; machine tool
accessories
PA: Dwyer Instruments Inc
102 Indiana Highway 212
Michigan City IN 46360
219 879-8868

(G-12998)
ECOJACKS LLC
Also Called: Lumber WD Furn Mg Sell WD
Flrg
503 E Broad St (46787-1017)
PHONE..................................574 306-0414
Brian Mack, *Mng Member*
Austin Brenneman,
EMP: 3 EST: 2011

(G-12999)
FOX PRODUCTS CORPORATION
6110 S State Road 5 (46787-9770)
P.O. Box 347 (46787-0347)
PHONE..................................260 723-4888
Fax: 260 723-6188
Alan H Fox, *President*
Pamela M Fox, *Corp Secy*
Cara Greulich, *Human Res Mgr*
▲ EMP: 130 EST: 1949
SQ FT: 50,000
SALES (est): 20.1MM **Privately Held**
WEB: www.foxproducts.com
SIC: 3931 5736 Bassoons; oboes & Eng-
lish horns; musical instrument stores

(G-13000)
**JOHNSON BROS S WHITLEY
SIGN CO**
Also Called: Johnson Brothers Sign Co .
304 N Calhoun St (46787-1344)
PHONE..................................260 723-5161
Hal Howard, *President*
Bill Howard, *President*
Tim Grant, *Vice Pres*
Les Cripe, *Treasurer*
EMP: 19 EST: 1929
SQ FT: 10,000
SALES: 1MM **Privately Held**
SIC: 3993 7629 Electric signs; neon signs;
electrical repair shops

(G-13001)
KUCKUCK TRANSPORT LLC
2165 S 625 W (46787-9651)
PHONE..................................260 609-0316
Ricky Kuckuck,
Brenna Kuckuck,
Jarrod Kuckuck,
EMP: 8
SALES: 1MM **Privately Held**
SIC: 3715 Truck trailers

(G-13002)
**NUTRITIONAL RESEARCH
ASSOC (PA)**
Also Called: Whitley Feeds Div
407 E Broad St (46787-1001)
P.O. Box 354 (46787-0354)
PHONE..................................260 723-4931
Fax: 260 723-6297
Barbar Pook, *President*
Albert O Germann II,
EMP: 10
SQ FT: 6,000
SALES: 979K **Privately Held**
SIC: 5191 2833 2834 2077 Animal feeds;
vegetable oils, medicinal grade: refined or
concentrated; vitamins, natural or syn-
thetic: bulk, uncompounded; pharmaceuti-
cal preparations; animal & marine fats &
oils; prepared feeds; dog & cat food

(G-13003)
SOLID ROCK GBC
213 Reed St (46787-1265)
PHONE..................................260 723-4806
Tonya Swenson, *Principal*
EMP: 2
SALES (est): 90.7K **Privately Held**
SIC: 2653 Corrugated & solid fiber boxes

(G-13004)
**SOUTH WHTLY TRBNE PRCTN
NEWS**
113 S State St (46787-1390)
PHONE..................................260 723-4771
Fax: 260 723-4771
John Trannter, *Manager*
EMP: 4
SALES (est): 170K **Privately Held**
SIC: 2711 Newspapers

(G-13005)
STEVE REIFF INC (PA)
Also Called: Farmland Lumber
5650 W 800 S (46787-9764)
PHONE..................................260 723-4360
Fax: 260 723-6558

SALES: 250K **Privately Held**
SIC: 2426 2431 2521 2511 Lumber,
hardwood dimension; floor baseboards,
wood; wood office furniture; wood household furniture

Steven Reiff, *President*
Doug Reiff, *Vice Pres*
Stan Reiff, *Vice Pres*
Doris Reiff, *Treasurer*
EMP: 51
SQ FT: 9,300
SALES (est): 5.7MM **Privately Held**
SIC: 3471 7532 3479 Sand blasting of
metal parts; truck painting & lettering;
painting of metal products

(G-13006)
STUMP PRINTING CO INC
Also Called: Stump's
101 Carroll Rd (46787-1139)
P.O. Box 305 (46787-0305)
PHONE..................................260 723-5171
Fax: 260 723-6976
Dan Haight, *CEO*
Wendy Moyle, *Exec VP*
Jeanice Croy, *CFO*
▲ EMP: 185
SALES (est): 93.5MM **Privately Held**
WEB: www.stumpsparty.com
SIC: 5199 2679 5961 2759 Novelties,
paper; novelties, paper: made from pur-
chased material; catalog sales; commer-
cial printing

(G-13007)
SUPERIOR PRECISION INC
602 Hathaway Dr (46787-1234)
PHONE..................................260 229-3871
Fax: 260 723-5778
Tony Starkey, *President*
EMP: 15
SQ FT: 22,500
SALES (est): 920K **Privately Held**
WEB: www.sprecision.com
SIC: 3541 Vertical turning & boring ma-
chines (metalworking)

(G-13008)
SYNERGY FEEDS LLC
401 N Main St (46787-1250)
P.O. Box 306 (46787-0306)
PHONE..................................260 723-5141
Jeff Mize, *Principal*
EMP: 20
SALES (est): 5.2MM **Privately Held**
SIC: 2048 5191 Bone meal, prepared as
animal feed; animal feeds

(G-13009)
WHITLEY EVERGREEN INC (HQ)
201 W 1st St (46787-1256)
P.O. Box 496 (46787-0496)
PHONE..................................260 723-5131
Fax: 260 723-6949
Barry Gossett, *Ch of Bd*
Simon Dragan, *President*
Randall Holler, *Vice Pres*
Bob Jones, *Vice Pres*
Dan Lipinski, *Vice Pres*
EMP: 86
SQ FT: 75,000
SALES (est): 31.3MM **Privately Held**
SIC: 2451 Mobile buildings: for commercial
use

(G-13010)
**WHITLEY WELDING & FABG &
REPR**
7700 S State Road 5 (46787-9765)
PHONE..................................260 723-5111
Fax: 260 723-5111
Bill Jenkins, *President*
Brian Jennings, *Vice Pres*
EMP: 3
SALES: 600K **Privately Held**
SIC: 7692 Welding repair

Speedway
Marion County

(G-13011)
CONTAINMED INC (PA)
1404 Main St (46224-6526)
PHONE..................................317 487-8800
Cary Bettenhausen, *President*
Tyler Deal, *COO*
Todd Bettenhausen, *Vice Pres*
EMP: 22

SALES (est): 4.8MM **Privately Held**
SIC: 3999 Barber & beauty shop equipment

(G-13012)
DALLARA LLC
Also Called: Dallara Indycar Factory
1201 Main St (46224-6533)
PHONE................................317 388-5400
Andrea Pontremoli, *CEO*
Stefano Deponti, *General Mgr*
Gary Weiss, *Accounting Mgr*
Sam Garrett, *Senior Mgr*
Lisa Johnson, *Admin Asst*
EMP: 13
SALES (est): 3.6MM
SALES (corp-wide): 322.9K **Privately Held**
SIC: 3714 Motor vehicle parts & accessories
PA: Partecipazioni Dallara Spa
Via Guglielmo Marconi 8
Varano De' Melegari PR
052 555-0711

(G-13013)
DALLARA RESEARCH CENTER LLC
1201 Main St Ste B (46224-6533)
PHONE................................317 388-5416
Stefano Deponti, *CEO*
Kyle Schwab, *Administration*
EMP: 3 EST: 2014
SALES: 1.5MM
SALES (corp-wide): 475.3K **Privately Held**
SIC: 7372 Prepackaged software
PA: Dallara Usa Holding, Inc.
1201 Main St Ste B
Speedway IN 46224
317 388-5400

(G-13014)
DALLARA USA HOLDING INC (PA)
1201 Main St Ste B (46224-6533)
PHONE................................317 388-5400
Stefano Deponti, *Admin Sec*
EMP: 3
SALES (est): 475.3K **Privately Held**
SIC: 6719 7372 Personal holding companies, except banks; prepackaged software

(G-13015)
OMR NORTH AMERICA INC
4755 Gilman St (46224-6981)
PHONE................................317 956-9509
Matthew Conrad, *President*
EMP: 10
SALES (est): 478.7K
SALES (corp-wide): 14.4MM **Privately Held**
SIC: 3465 Body parts, automobile: stamped metal
PA: Omr Holding Spa
Via Vittor Pisani 16
Milano MI 20124
030 213-501

(G-13016)
WB REFRACTORY SERVICE INC
5342 Maplewood Dr (46224-3328)
PHONE................................317 450-7386
Loyd Wallace, *President*
EMP: 7
SALES (est): 494.8K **Privately Held**
SIC: 3255 Foundry refractories, clay

Spencer
Owen County

(G-13017)
BABBS SUPERMARKET INC
Also Called: Babbs Super-Value
459 W Morgan St (47460-1221)
P.O. Box 620 (47460-0620)
PHONE................................812 829-2231
Fax: 812 829-4231
Robert W Babbs, *President*
EMP: 82
SQ FT: 22,000

SALES: 11.4MM **Privately Held**
SIC: 5411 2051 Grocery stores, independent; bread, cake & related products

(G-13018)
BOSTON SCIENTIFIC CORPORATION
780 Brookside Dr (47460-1021)
PHONE................................812 829-4877
Fax: 812 829-4870
Bruce Fisher, *General Mgr*
Ryan Ralston, *Project Mgr*
Brian Sills, *Opers Mgr*
Mike Darling, *Facilities Mgr*
Deborah Newforth, *Opers Staff*
EMP: 1000
SALES (corp-wide): 9B **Publicly Held**
WEB: www.bsci.com
SIC: 3841 Surgical & medical instruments
PA: Boston Scientific Corporation
300 Boston Scientific Way
Marlborough MA 01752
508 683-4000

(G-13019)
CHECKERED RACING & CHROME LLC
2221 N Srd St (47460)
PHONE................................812 275-2875
Eddie Pierce, *Mng Member*
Jason Hiter,
EMP: 10
SQ FT: 8,000
SALES: 1.3MM **Privately Held**
SIC: 3711 Chassis, motor vehicle

(G-13020)
COOK INCORPORATED
Also Called: Cook Urological
1100 W Morgan St (47460-9426)
PHONE................................812 829-4891
Nate Myers, *General Mgr*
Debbie Farley, *Buyer*
Beth Bartholomew, *QC Mgr*
Steven Stickels, *Engineer*
Mike Kalb, *Finance*
EMP: 550
SALES (corp-wide): 980.1MM **Privately Held**
SIC: 3841 Surgical & medical instruments
HQ: Cook Incorporated
750 N Daniels Way
Bloomington IN 47404
812 339-2235

(G-13021)
CORE RESOURCES LLC
150 S Montgomery St (47460-1740)
PHONE................................812 829-2240
Fax: 812 829-2260
David Detraz, *Owner*
EMP: 7
SALES (est): 1MM **Privately Held**
SIC: 3499 Fabricated metal products

(G-13022)
CRESCENDO INC
Also Called: Winner's Circle
56 E Jefferson St (47460-1705)
PHONE................................812 829-4759
Fax: 812 829-4741
Marilyn Keith, *President*
Joe Keith, *Treasurer*
EMP: 3
SQ FT: 5,500
SALES: 240K **Privately Held**
SIC: 5091 5941 2791 2752 Sporting & recreation goods; sporting goods & bicycle shops; typesetting; commercial printing, lithographic; automotive & apparel trimmings; pleating & stitching

(G-13023)
EAGLE NEST WORKSHOP
3230 Pheasant Ln (47460-5902)
PHONE................................812 876-3215
Greg Hoffman, *Owner*
EMP: 2
SALES (est): 79K **Privately Held**
SIC: 2511 Wood household furniture

(G-13024)
EVANS ADHESIVE CORPORATION
7140 State Highway 246 (47460-6412)
PHONE................................812 859-4245
Carla McCracken, *Principal*
EMP: 3
SALES (est): 123.2K **Privately Held**
SIC: 2891 Adhesives

(G-13025)
FENDER 4 STAR MEATS PROCESSING
Also Called: Fender 4 Star Meat Processing
1494 Rocky Hill Rd (47460-5598)
PHONE................................812 829-3240
Lewis Fender, *President*
Janice Fender, *Treasurer*
Steve Fender, *Admin Sec*
EMP: 7
SQ FT: 5,000
SALES: 200K **Privately Held**
SIC: 2011 Meat packing plants

(G-13026)
FINZER ROLLER INC
Also Called: Finzer Roller Indiana
650 W Market St (47460-1132)
PHONE................................812 829-1455
Fax: 812 829-1457
David M Finzer, *President*
Martin Finzer, *Vice Pres*
Lee Barnes, *Plant Mgr*
Clay Klepper, *Technical Staff*
EMP: 24
SQ FT: 20,000
SALES (est): 3.7MM
SALES (corp-wide): 25.6MM **Privately Held**
WEB: www.finzerroller.com
SIC: 3069 3061 Roll coverings, rubber; mechanical rubber goods
PA: Finzer Roller, Inc.
129 Rawls Rd
Des Plaines IL 60018
847 390-6200

(G-13027)
FRANKLINS MERCANTILE
7115 Kimberly Ln (47460-5872)
PHONE................................812 876-0426
Kathleen Franklins, *Owner*
EMP: 3
SALES (est): 180K **Privately Held**
SIC: 5411 2038 Grocery stores; pizza, frozen

(G-13028)
INDIANA HARDWOOD SPECIALISTS
4341 N Us Highway 231 (47460-6669)
PHONE................................812 829-4866
Fax: 812 829-4860
Thomas G Derleth, *President*
Tom Derleth, *Executive*
Ronda Derleth, *Admin Sec*
EMP: 43
SQ FT: 30,000
SALES (est): 5.3MM **Privately Held**
WEB: www.indianahardwoodspec.com
SIC: 2426 Flooring, hardwood

(G-13029)
IONIC CUT STONE INC
1201 Kelley Farm Dr (47460-7046)
P.O. Box 409 (47460-0409)
PHONE................................812 829-3416
Fax: 812 829-3468
Franklin Bault, *President*
Debra Bault, *Vice Pres*
EMP: 9
SALES (est): 1.3MM **Privately Held**
SIC: 3281 5032 Cut stone & stone products; limestone, cut & shaped; limestone

(G-13030)
MARK PARMENTER
Also Called: White Rver Fndry/Creative Arts
358 S East St (47460-1814)
PHONE................................812 829-6583
Mark Parmenter, *Owner*
▲ EMP: 5
SALES (est): 426.8K **Privately Held**
WEB: www.whiteriverfoundry.com
SIC: 3366 Bronze foundry

(G-13031)
OWEN LEADER INC
114 E Franklin St (47460-1818)
P.O. Box 22 (47460-0022)
PHONE................................812 829-3936
Fax: 812 829-4666
John Gillaspy, *President*
Adriana Gillaspy, *Corp Secy*
Tom Douglas, *Vice Pres*
EMP: 5 EST: 1969
SQ FT: 8,000
SALES (est): 246.1K **Privately Held**
SIC: 2711 Newspapers: publishing only, not printed on site

(G-13032)
OWEN VALLEY WINERY LLC
491 Timber Ridge Rd (47460-5980)
PHONE................................812 828-0883
Preston D Leaderbrand,
Anthonny Leaderbrand,
EMP: 2
SALES (est): 150K **Privately Held**
SIC: 2084 Wines

(G-13033)
PRESTON LEADERBRAND ✪
491 Timber Ridge Rd (47460-5980)
PHONE................................812 828-0883
Preston Leaderbrand, *Owner*
EMP: 13 EST: 2017
SALES (est): 366.4K **Privately Held**
SIC: 2084 Wines

(G-13034)
QUALITY SURFACES INC
2087 Franklin Rd (47460-5038)
PHONE................................812 876-5838
Fax: 812 876-5842
Monte Job, *President*
Sky Job, *Vice Pres*
Jeff Hamilton, *Plant Mgr*
Carl Landis, *Facilities Mgr*
EMP: 20
SALES (est): 3.3MM **Privately Held**
WEB: www.qualitysurfaces.com
SIC: 2541 3281 1799 Counter & sink tops; cut stone & stone products; counter top installation

(G-13035)
R E CASEBEER & SONS INC
661 W Market St (47460-1131)
P.O. Box 130 (47460-0130)
PHONE................................812 829-3284
Fax: 812 829-0874
R Keith Casebeer, *President*
Robert Casebeer, *Vice Pres*
Kevin B Casebeer, *Treasurer*
EMP: 8 EST: 1952
SALES (est): 1.6MM **Privately Held**
SIC: 2421 6552 2426 2411 Sawmills & planing mills, general; land subdividers & developers, commercial; hardwood dimension & flooring mills; logging

(G-13036)
SKID ROW WOOD PRODUCTS INC
2270 Wood Dr (47460-6853)
PHONE................................812 828-0349
Fax: 812 828-0354
Steve Watkins, *President*
EMP: 19
SALES (est): 2.2MM **Privately Held**
SIC: 2448 Pallets, wood

(G-13037)
SPENCER EVENING WORLD (PA)
114 E Franklin St (47460-1877)
P.O. Box 226 (47460-0226)
PHONE................................812 829-2255
John Gillaspy, *President*
Philip L Gillaspy, *Principal*
Thomas B Gillaspy, *Principal*
EMP: 60
SQ FT: 13,400
SALES (est): 7.2MM **Privately Held**
WEB: www.spencereveningworld.com
SIC: 2752 2711 2791 Commercial printing, offset; commercial printing & newspaper publishing combined; typesetting

(G-13038)
STAMPING SPECIALTY CO INC
State Roads 46 & 43 (47460)
P.O. Box 539 (47460-0539)
PHONE..............................812 829-0760
Fax: 812 829-0766
Scott Barrier, *President*
EMP: 5 EST: 1945
SQ FT: 4,000
SALES: 400K **Privately Held**
WEB: www.stampingspecialty.com
SIC: 3599 Custom machinery

(G-13039)
STELLO PRODUCTS INC
840 W Hillside Ave (47460-1117)
P.O. Box 89 (47460-0089)
PHONE..............................812 829-2246
Fax: 812 829-6053
Todd Zellers, *President*
Debbie Jordan, *Treasurer*
Ambur Summerlot, *Treasurer*
Nannett Edwards, *Admin Sec*
EMP: 12
SQ FT: 18,000
SALES: 1.8MM **Privately Held**
WEB: www.stelloproducts.com
SIC: 3993 Signs, not made in custom sign
painting shops

(G-13040)
STEPHEN G MORROW INC
Also Called: Steve's Automotive Center
2632 Schooling Rd (47460-5155)
P.O. Box 352 (47460-0352)
PHONE..............................812 876-7837
Stephen Morrow, *President*
EMP: 5
SALES (est): 354.1K **Privately Held**
SIC: 3714 Transmissions, motor vehicle

(G-13041)
**VANCE PRODUCTS
INCORPORATED**
Also Called: Cook Urological
1100 W Morgan St (47460-9426)
PHONE..............................812 829-4891
Fax: 812 829-1801
Pete Yonkman, *President*
Fredrick Roemer, *Vice Pres*
Rick Stines, *Facilities Mgr*
Randall Wrightsman, *Engineer*
John R Kamstra, *Treasurer*
EMP: 330 EST: 1977
SQ FT: 45,000
SALES (est): 64.7MM
SALES (corp-wide): 980.1MM **Privately
Held**
WEB: www.cookuro.com
SIC: 3841 Surgical & medical instruments;
catheters; needles, suture
PA: Cook Group Incorporated
750 N Daniels Way
Bloomington IN 47404
812 339-2235

Spencerville
Allen County

(G-13042)
AGRI - TRADERS & REPAIR LLC
16702 Campbell Rd (46788-9641)
PHONE..............................260 238-4225
Lorn Lengagher, *Mng Member*
Aaron Lengagher,
▲ EMP: 5 EST: 2006
SALES: 700K **Privately Held**
SIC: 3715 Trailer bodies

(G-13043)
AGRITRADERS MFG INC
16702 Campbell Rd (46788-9641)
PHONE..............................260 238-4225
Robert Pfister, *President*
EMP: 8
SALES (est): 800K **Privately Held**
SIC: 3715 Truck trailers

(G-13044)
CAMPBELL ROAD SAWMILL
17127 Campbell Rd (46788-9641)
PHONE..............................260 238-4252
John R Graber, *Owner*

EMP: 5
SALES (est): 758.7K **Privately Held**
SIC: 2421 Sawmills & planing mills, gen-
eral

(G-13045)
DEEP THREE INC
Also Called: Stealth Furniture
17607 Rupert Rd (46788-9660)
PHONE..............................260 705-2283
Lee Hershberger, *President*
Michelle Hershberger, *Vice Pres*
EMP: 3
SALES (est): 123.8K **Privately Held**
SIC: 3089 7389 Plastics products;

(G-13046)
FLEETWOOD MOTOR HOMES
17728 Lochner Rd (46788-9241)
PHONE..............................260 627-6800
EMP: 2 EST: 2011
SALES (est): 180K **Privately Held**
SIC: 3716 Mfg Motor Homes

(G-13047)
GRABER LUMBER LP
17528 Cuba Rd (46788-9629)
PHONE..............................260 238-4124
Neil Graber, *Partner*
Jason Graber, *Partner*
EMP: 40 EST: 2001
SALES (est): 6.7MM **Privately Held**
SIC: 2411 7389 Logging camps & contrac-
tors;

(G-13048)
**HULL PRECISION MACHINING
INC**
6974 State Road 1 (46788-9431)
P.O. Box 113 (46788-0113)
PHONE..............................260 238-4372
Fax: 260 238-4379
Clarence Hull, *President*
Jetteree W Hull, *Corp Secy*
EMP: 5
SALES: 400K **Privately Held**
SIC: 3599 Machine shop, jobbing & repair

(G-13049)
KRAFFT GRAVEL INC (PA)
6031 County Road 68 (46788-9409)
PHONE..............................260 238-4653
Gerald Krafft, *President*
Jennie Krafft, *Vice Pres*
Beverly Krafft, *Admin Sec*
EMP: 5
SALES (est): 485.7K **Privately Held**
SIC: 1442 4212 Construction sand mining;
gravel mining; local trucking, without stor-
age

(G-13050)
**RHINEHART DEVELOPMENT
CORP**
Also Called: Calf-Teria
5345 County Road 68 (46788-9719)
PHONE..............................260 238-4442
Fax: 260 238-4447
Phillip R Rhinehart, *President*
Elizabeth Rorick, *Project Mgr*
Tom Diehl, *Sales Mgr*
Philip Rhinehart, *Sales Executive*
Mike Gamble, *Manager*
EMP: 20
SQ FT: 30,000
SALES (est): 4.7MM **Privately Held**
SIC: 3469 3523 Stamping metal for the
trade; barn, silo, poultry, dairy & livestock
machinery; poultry brooders, feeders &
waterers; dairy equipment (farm)

(G-13051)
RHINEHART FINISHING LLC
5345 County Road 68 (46788-9719)
PHONE..............................260 238-4442
Kendra McDaniel, *Business Mgr*
Don McDaniel, *Vice Pres*
John Minnich, *Plant Mgr*
Katie Dove, *Human Res Mgr*
Perry Jackson, *Manager*
EMP: 75
SQ FT: 85,000
SALES (est): 9.1MM **Privately Held**
SIC: 3471 Finishing, metals or formed
products

(G-13052)
TIMBER LINE CRATING LP
17501 Campbell Rd (46788-9640)
PHONE..............................260 238-3075
John Schwartz, *Partner*
EMP: 12
SALES (est): 1.4MM **Privately Held**
SIC: 2449 Berry crates, wood: wirebound

Spiceland
Henry County

(G-13053)
**AMERICAN BOTTLING
COMPANY**
6083 State Rd (47385)
PHONE..............................765 987-7800
Ed Cole, *Manager*
EMP: 30 **Publicly Held**
SIC: 2086 Soft drinks: packaged in cans,
bottles, etc.
HQ: The American Bottling Company
5301 Legacy Dr
Plano TX 75024

(G-13054)
DRAPER INC (PA)
411 S Pearl St (47385-9637)
P.O. Box 425 (47385-0425)
PHONE..............................765 987-7999
Fax: 765 987-7142
John D Pidgeon, *President*
Terry Coffey, *President*
Todd Garner, *Regional Mgr*
Ross Rhoades, *Regional Mgr*
Michael D Broome, *Vice Pres*
◆ EMP: 277
SQ FT: 462,000
SALES (est): 130.2MM **Privately Held**
SIC: 3861 2591 3651 Photographic
equipment & supplies; drapery hardware
& blinds & shades; household audio &
video equipment

(G-13055)
HALCOMB WELDING LLC
8017 S Mill Rd (47385-9751)
PHONE..............................765 345-7156
Scott Halcomb, *Principal*
EMP: 2
SALES (est): 77.5K **Privately Held**
SIC: 7692 Welding repair

(G-13056)
MR FUEL
140 Holwager Dr (47385-9639)
PHONE..............................317 531-0891
EMP: 4
SALES (est): 389.9K **Privately Held**
SIC: 2869 Fuels

(G-13057)
PUNJAB EMPIRE INC
5809 S State Road 3 (47385-9633)
PHONE..............................765 987-8786
Benny Khera, *Mng Member*
EMP: 3
SALES (est): 152.9K **Privately Held**
SIC: 3421 Table & food cutlery, including
butchers'

(G-13058)
**SPICELAND WOOD PRODUCTS
INC**
609 S Pearl St (47385-9766)
P.O. Box 406 (47385-0406)
PHONE..............................765 987-8156
Fax: 765 987-7608
Rob Davis, *Owner*
EMP: 16
SQ FT: 19,000
SALES (est): 1.5MM **Privately Held**
WEB: www.spicelandwood.com
SIC: 2434 Wood kitchen cabinets

Springport
Henry County

(G-13059)
IRVING MATERIALS INC
Also Called: i M I
1078 E Luray Rd (47386-9715)
PHONE..............................765 755-3447
Fax: 765 755-3208
Kevin Gibson, *Branch Mgr*
EMP: 5
SALES (corp-wide): 800.6MM **Privately
Held**
SIC: 3273 Ready-mixed concrete
PA: Irving Materials, Inc.
8032 N State Road 9
Greenfield IN 46140
317 326-3101

Springville
Lawrence County

(G-13060)
BENS QUARRY LLC
303 E Ingram Rd (47462-9416)
PHONE..............................812 824-3730
Ben Ingram, *Mng Member*
EMP: 2
SALES (est): 380.7K **Privately Held**
SIC: 1429 Boulder, crushed & broken-
quarrying

(G-13061)
CLARKS CNC LLC
1718 S Jackson Pike (47462-6262)
PHONE..............................812 508-1773
Monty Clark, *Owner*
EMP: 4 EST: 2016
SALES (est): 194K **Privately Held**
SIC: 3545 Measuring tools & machines,
machinists' metalworking type

(G-13062)
**D & M TOOL CORPORATION
(HQ)**
699 Washboard Rd (47462-5180)
PHONE..............................812 279-8882
Fax: 812 279-6676
John Lucas, *CEO*
Bill Gilbert, *President*
Ansel Deckard Jr, *Chairman*
Bill Maddox, *Vice Pres*
Timothy Deckard, *Info Tech Mgr*
EMP: 25 EST: 1970
SQ FT: 28,000
SALES: 2MM
SALES (corp-wide): 15.9MM **Privately
Held**
WEB: www.spcmfg.com
SIC: 3089 Injection molding of plastics
PA: Specialty Manufacturers, Inc.
2410 Executive Dr Ste 201
Indianapolis IN
317 241-1111

(G-13063)
EMBREE MACHINE INC
1435 Greer Ln (47462-5046)
PHONE..............................812 275-5729
Patrick Embree II, *President*
Pat Embree, *Sales Staff*
EMP: 5
SQ FT: 1,100
SALES: 75K **Privately Held**
SIC: 3599 Machine shop, jobbing & repair

(G-13064)
**INTEGRITY DEFENSE SERVICES
INC ✪**
1463 S State Road 45 (47462-6343)
PHONE..............................812 675-4913
David W Burkett, *President*
Kristin R Schnarr, *COO*
Richard N Speer Jr, *CFO*
Derrick Held, *Manager*
EMP: 14 EST: 2017
SQ FT: 40,640

SALES (est): 1.9MM **Privately Held**
SIC: 3731 3728 7699 Military ships, building & repairing; military aircraft equipment & armament; fire control (military) equipment repair

(G-13065)
MILLERS QUICK PRODUCTION
6581 State Road 54 W (47462-5143)
P.O. Box 148 (47462-0148)
PHONE..............................812 278-8374
Kent Miller, *Owner*
EMP: 3
SALES (est): 89.6K **Privately Held**
SIC: 3549 Wiredrawing & fabricating machinery & equipment, ex. die

(G-13066)
PLASTICS RESEARCH AND DEV INC
Also Called: Prd
747 Washboard Rd (47462-5181)
PHONE..............................812 279-8885
John Lucas, *CEO*
John Passanisi, *President*
Connie Robinson, *Buyer*
Russell Coolidge, *Engineer*
John Black, *Manager*
▲ EMP: 29
SALES (est): 1.9MM
SALES (corp-wide): 15.9MM **Privately Held**
WEB: www.prd-inc.com
SIC: 3544 3089 Special dies, tools, jigs & fixtures; injection molded finished plastic products
HQ: D & M Tool Corporation
699 Washboard Rd
Springville IN 47462
812 279-8882

(G-13067)
ROBERT L YOUNG
Also Called: Circle Y Farms
4436 S Young Dr (47462-6414)
PHONE..............................812 863-4475
Robert L Young, *Owner*
EMP: 4
SALES (est): 295.8K **Privately Held**
SIC: 0211 2411 Beef cattle feedlots; logging

(G-13068)
ROGERS GROUP INC
Also Called: Sieboldt Quarry
938 Sieboldt Quarry Rd (47462-5353)
PHONE..............................812 275-7860
Fax: 812 275-7776
Danny Powell, *Manager*
EMP: 17
SALES (corp-wide): 1B **Privately Held**
WEB: www.rogersgroupinc.com
SIC: 1442 Gravel mining
PA: Rogers Group, Inc.
421 Great Circle Rd
Nashville TN 37228
615 242-0585

Star City
Pulaski County

(G-13069)
ALAN DAILY
7300 S 600 E (46985-9075)
PHONE..............................574 595-6253
Alan Daily, *Owner*
Darline Daily, *Co-Owner*
EMP: 2
SALES (est): 134.3K **Privately Held**
SIC: 2711 Newspapers, publishing & printing

(G-13070)
ROUDEBUSH COMPANY INCORPORATED
583 S State Rd 119 (46985)
P.O. Box 348 (46985-0348)
PHONE..............................574 595-7115
Fax: 574 595-7196
Scott Roudebush, *President*
Clara Roudebush, *Admin Sec*
▲ EMP: 3
SQ FT: 3,000

SALES (est): 329.3K **Privately Held**
SIC: 2511 5712 5961 2499 Wood household furniture; furniture stores; furniture & furnishings, mail order; decorative wood & woodwork

State Line
Warren County

(G-13071)
ARCHER-DANIELS-MIDLAND COMPANY
Also Called: ADM
7979 S 1100 W (47982)
PHONE..............................765 793-2512
Nathan Suttles, *Manager*
EMP: 5
SALES (corp-wide): 60.8B **Publicly Held**
WEB: www.admworld.com
SIC: 2041 Flour & other grain mill products
PA: Archer-Daniels-Midland Company
77 W Wacker Dr Ste 4600
Chicago IL 60601
312 634-8100

Staunton
Clay County

(G-13072)
MINOR PRODUCTS COMPANY INC
Staunton Rd N (47881)
P.O. Box 146 (47881-0146)
PHONE..............................812 448-3611
Bradley D Minor, *President*
EMP: 8
SALES (est): 704.9K **Privately Held**
SIC: 2449 Boxes, wood: wirebound

Stendal
Pike County

(G-13073)
AUSTIN POWDER COMPANY
8146 S Old St Rd Rt 64 Hw (47585)
P.O. Box 19 (47585-0019)
PHONE..............................812 536-2885
Jeffrey Perry, *Manager*
EMP: 5
SALES (corp-wide): 566.9MM **Privately Held**
SIC: 2892 Explosives
HQ: Austin Powder Company
25800 Science Park Dr # 300
Cleveland OH 44122
216 464-2400

(G-13074)
HEFLIN HFLIN OIL GAS PRODUCERS
9823 S County Road 800 E (47585-8833)
PHONE..............................812 536-3464
A T Heflin, *Principal*
EMP: 3 EST: 2001
SALES (est): 144.7K **Privately Held**
SIC: 1311 Crude petroleum & natural gas

Stinesville
Monroe County

(G-13075)
BIG CREEK LLC
8248 Main St (47464)
PHONE..............................812 876-0835
David Edgeworth,
EMP: 10
SALES: 1.5MM **Privately Held**
WEB: www.bigcreek.net
SIC: 1422 Limestones, ground

Stockwell
Tippecanoe County

(G-13076)
CLASSIC ENGRAVING
7522 S 775 E (47983)
P.O. Box 156 (47983-0156)
PHONE..............................765 523-3355
Patricia Jewell, *Partner*
Andrea Huber, *Partner*
EMP: 2
SALES (est): 209.3K **Privately Held**
SIC: 2759 Engraving

Stroh
Lagrange County

(G-13077)
HAYWARD & SAMS LLP
Also Called: Stroh Fixit Shop
4250 E 1175 S (46789)
P.O. Box 190 (46789-0190)
PHONE..............................260 351-4166
Mark Hayward, *Managing Prtnr*
David Sams, *Partner*
EMP: 5
SALES (est): 823.8K **Privately Held**
SIC: 7699 1711 3561 Lawn mower repair shop; heating & air conditioning contractors; pumps, domestic: water or sump

Sullivan
Sullivan County

(G-13078)
ALLOMATIC PRODUCTS COMPANY (DH)
609 E Chaney St (47882-7452)
P.O. Box 267 (47882-0267)
PHONE..............................800 686-4729
Fax: 812 268-0417
David Coolidge, *President*
Martha Slopsema, *Vice Pres*
Curtis T Short, *CFO*
John Shell, *Treasurer*
Kaila Taufique, *Sales Associate*
▲ EMP: 162
SQ FT: 170,000
SALES (est): 20.5MM **Privately Held**
WEB: www.allomatic.com
SIC: 3714 Motor vehicle transmissions, drive assemblies & parts

(G-13079)
ARCHER-DANIELS-MIDLAND COMPANY
ADM
323 N Holloway St (47882-1340)
PHONE..............................812 268-4334
Matthew Briscoe, *Branch Mgr*
EMP: 12
SALES (corp-wide): 60.8B **Publicly Held**
WEB: www.admworld.com
SIC: 2041 Flour & other grain mill products
PA: Archer-Daniels-Midland Company
77 W Wacker Dr Ste 4600
Chicago IL 60601
312 634-8100

(G-13080)
ATLAS ENERGY INDIANA LLC
32 S Court St Ste F (47882-1510)
PHONE..............................812 268-4900
Warren Hanks,
EMP: 6
SALES (est): 652.5K **Privately Held**
SIC: 1311 Natural gas production

(G-13081)
DODD SAW MILLS INC
85 E County Road 450 N (47882-7542)
PHONE..............................812 268-4811
Fax: 812 268-4766
Louis Glascock, *President*
Tom Harrison, *COO*
Donna Glascock, *Admin Sec*
EMP: 35

SQ FT: 50,000
SALES: 7MM **Privately Held**
WEB: www.doddsawmill.com
SIC: 2448 Pallets, wood

(G-13082)
DODD WOOD PRODUCTS INC
85 E County Road 450 N (47882-7542)
PHONE..............................812 268-0798
Louise Classcock, *President*
Donna Classcock, *Corp Secy*
EMP: 40
SALES: 2.5MM **Privately Held**
SIC: 2421 Sawmills & planing mills, general

(G-13083)
GRAYSVILLE MFG INC
4391 N County Road 875 W (47882-7141)
PHONE..............................812 382-4616
Scott W Snyder, *Principal*
EMP: 2 EST: 2016
SALES (est): 129.3K **Privately Held**
SIC: 3999 Manufacturing industries

(G-13084)
KELK PUBLISHING LLC
249 W Washington St (47882-1433)
P.O. Box 130 (47882-0130)
PHONE..............................812 268-6356
Gillian Kelk, *President*
EMP: 3
SALES (est): 109.1K **Privately Held**
SIC: 2741 Miscellaneous publishing

(G-13085)
KENS TOOL & DESIGN
2437 N Section St (47882-7522)
PHONE..............................812 268-6653
Ken Plummer, *Owner*
Dan Plummer, *Co-Owner*
▲ EMP: 10
SALES: 500K **Privately Held**
SIC: 3599 Machine shop, jobbing & repair

(G-13086)
MCCAMMON ENGINEERING CORP
1863 W County Road 500 S (47882-7772)
PHONE..............................812 356-4455
Fax: 812 398-4407
Brent Mc Cammon, *President*
EMP: 5
SQ FT: 7,200
SALES: 150K **Privately Held**
WEB: www.mccammonengineering.com
SIC: 3069 3087 Molded rubber products; custom compound purchased resins

(G-13087)
MEIER WINERY & VINYARD LLC
4251 N State Road 63 (47882-7581)
PHONE..............................812 382-4220
Pamela A Meier, *Administration*
EMP: 2 EST: 2016
SALES (est): 73.3K **Privately Held**
SIC: 2084 Wines, brandy & brandy spirits

(G-13088)
MONTRO COMPANY
240 E Depot St (47882-1346)
PHONE..............................812 268-4390
Tony Trotter, *Owner*
EMP: 3
SALES (est): 217.7K **Privately Held**
SIC: 3365 Aluminum & aluminum-based alloy castings

(G-13089)
NORTH AMERICAN LATEX CORP
49 Industrial Park Dr (47882-7521)
PHONE..............................812 268-6608
Fax: 812 268-3865
Nelson Ellis, *President*
Kevin Beard, *Vice Pres*
J Bradley Stewart, *Vice Pres*
Bruce R Wolfe, *Admin Sec*
EMP: 62
SQ FT: 60,000
SALES (est): 9.5MM **Privately Held**
SIC: 3069 Medical & laboratory rubber sundries & related products; atomizer bulbs, rubber; air-supported rubber structures

▲ = Import ▼=Export
◆ =Import/Export

(G-13090)
PIERCE OIL CO INC
Also Called: Sullivan Daily Times
115 W Jackson St (47882-1505)
P.O. Box 130 (47882-0130)
PHONE....................812 268-6356
Fax: 812 268-3110
Nancy P Gettinger, *President*
Sarah J Geitz, *Corp Secy*
Tom P Gettinger, *Vice Pres*
EMP: 19
SQ FT: 5,800
SALES (est): 1.2MM **Privately Held**
WEB: www.pierceoil.com
SIC: 2711 2791 2759 Commercial printing
& newspaper publishing combined; type-
setting; commercial printing

(G-13091)
PULSE ENERGY
3137 N Old 41 (47882-9233)
PHONE....................812 268-6700
Bryan Anderson, *Principal*
EMP: 2 EST: 2007
SALES (est): 99.8K **Privately Held**
SIC: 1389 Oil consultants

(G-13092)
RAYBESTOS POWERTRAIN
110 Industrial Park Dr (47882-7520)
P.O. Box 227 (47882-0227)
PHONE....................812 268-1370
David Ramsey, *Info Tech Mgr*
EMP: 4
SALES (est): 653.7K **Privately Held**
SIC: 3714 Motor vehicle parts & acces-
sories

(G-13093)
RAYBESTOS POWERTRAIN LLC
312 S St Clair St (47882-7497)
PHONE....................812 268-1211
David Coolidge, *Branch Mgr*
Waynetta Hodges, *Supervisor*
EMP: 22 **Privately Held**
WEB: www.raybestospowertrain.com
SIC: 3714 Motor vehicle engines & parts
HQ: Raybestos Powertrain, Llc
711 Tech Dr
Crawfordsville IN 47933

(G-13094)
SALESMAN SAWMILL INC
3396 N County Road 550 W (47882-7577)
PHONE....................812 382-9154
James Salesman, *President*
EMP: 7
SALES (est): 672.8K **Privately Held**
SIC: 2421 Sawmills & planing mills, gen-
eral

(G-13095)
STEEL WORKS WELDING INC
2768 S County Road 100 W (47882-7857)
PHONE....................812 268-0334
L Neal Alexander, *President*
EMP: 10
SALES: 300K **Privately Held**
SIC: 7692 Welding repair

(G-13096)
SULLIVAN IMI
939 S Section St (47882-7834)
PHONE....................812 268-3306
Fax: 812 268-3308
EMP: 3 EST: 2012
SALES (est): 198.5K **Privately Held**
SIC: 3273 Ready-mixed concrete

(G-13097)
VALLEY TILE CORPORATION
2437 N Section St (47882-7522)
PHONE....................812 268-3328
Kenn Plummer, *President*
Dennis Long, *Vice Pres*
Dan Plummer, *Vice Pres*
Jeff Long, *Treasurer*
EMP: 4 EST: 1998
SQ FT: 36,000
SALES (est): 688.5K **Privately Held**
SIC: 3069 Tile, rubber

(G-13098)
VEAD DODD SAWMILL INC
165 E County Road 300 N (47882-7561)
PHONE....................812 268-4486

Fax: 812 268-0515
Marilyn Dodd, *President*
John Dodd, *President*
Tom Harrisonh, *President*
Debra Harrison, *Treasurer*
Darda Drew, *Admin Sec*
EMP: 16
SQ FT: 3,000
SALES: 1.3MM **Privately Held**
SIC: 2421 2426 Lumber: rough, sawed or
planed; hardwood dimension & flooring
mills

Summitville
Madison County

(G-13099)
I C MATTRESSES & MORE LLC
1525 W 1850 N (46070-9229)
PHONE....................765 635-7239
Marcia Parker,
EMP: 2
SALES (est): 170.4K **Privately Held**
SIC: 2515 Mattresses, containing felt, foam
rubber, urethane, etc.

(G-13100)
PANNELL & SON WELDING INC
207 N Summit St (46070-9325)
PHONE....................765 948-3606
Mark Pannell, *President*
EMP: 5
SALES: 328K **Privately Held**
SIC: 3545 7692 Machine tool accessories;
welding repair

(G-13101)
PRAISEWORTHY PRESS LLC
151 W Indiana St (46070-9762)
PHONE....................765 536-2077
Laura Matney,
Bart Matney,
EMP: 3
SALES: 230K **Privately Held**
SIC: 2741 Miscellaneous publishing

(G-13102)
R & R ENGINEERING CO INC
Also Called: U-Bolts Engineering
801 S Main St (46070-8900)
P.O. Box 428 (46070-0428)
PHONE....................765 536-2331
Fax: 765 358-3957
Ralph Amos, *President*
Carey Fisher, *General Mgr*
Janet Amos, *Vice Pres*
Paul Dent, *Sales Staff*
Scott Amos, *Executive*
▲ EMP: 46
SQ FT: 300,000
SALES (est): 9.7MM **Privately Held**
WEB: www.randrengineering.com
SIC: 3452 3496 Bolts, metal; miscella-
neous fabricated wire products

(G-13103)
ROBERT ATKINS (PA)
Also Called: A&M Tool & Die
303 E North Main St (46070-9318)
P.O. Box 445 (46070-0445)
PHONE....................765 536-4164
Fax: 765 536-4663
Robert Atkins, *Owner*
EMP: 4
SQ FT: 5,000
SALES (est): 900K **Privately Held**
SIC: 3544 3465 Special dies, tools, jigs &
fixtures; automotive stampings

(G-13104)
ROOKIES UNLIMITED INC
103 South Mnr (46070)
P.O. Box 96 (46070-0096)
PHONE....................765 536-2726
Steve Horn, *President*
EMP: 6 EST: 2008
SQ FT: 9,000
SALES (est): 385K **Privately Held**
SIC: 3993 7389 2759 5941 Signs & ad-
vertising specialties; embroidering of ad-
vertising on shirts, etc.; screen printing;
specialty sport supplies

(G-13105)
SPIRITBUILDING PUBLISHING
15591 N State Road 9 (46070-9622)
PHONE....................765 623-2238
Ivan Benson, *Principal*
EMP: 8
SALES (est): 611.5K **Privately Held**
SIC: 2741 Miscellaneous publishing

(G-13106)
SUPER SEAL INC
548 E 1800 N (46070-9063)
PHONE....................765 639-4993
Bret Nicholson, *President*
EMP: 10
SALES: 190K **Privately Held**
SIC: 1799 1721 2951 1611 Parking lot
maintenance; pavement marking contrac-
tor; asphalt paving mixtures & blocks; sur-
facing & paving

(G-13107)
TCS CABINETS
557 E 1450 N (46070-9390)
PHONE....................765 208-5350
Scott Rowland, *Principal*
EMP: 4
SALES (est): 238K **Privately Held**
SIC: 2434 Wood kitchen cabinets

(G-13108)
TUBULAR ENGRG & SLS CO INC
107 S Main St (46070-9711)
P.O. Box 235 (46070-0235)
PHONE....................765 536-2225
Fax: 765 536-2828
Roy H Grant, *President*
EMP: 15
SALES (est): 1.2MM **Privately Held**
SIC: 3429 3496 Furniture builders' & other
household hardware; miscellaneous fabri-
cated wire products

Sunman
Ripley County

(G-13109)
CELEBRATE SEASON
957 N Meridian St (47041-7771)
P.O. Box 188 (47041-0188)
PHONE....................609 261-5200
Daryl Mills, *Branch Mgr*
EMP: 11
SALES (corp-wide): 855.6K **Privately
Held**
SIC: 2771 Greeting cards
PA: Celebrate The Season
1725 Roe Crest Dr
North Mankato MN

(G-13110)
DEUFOL SUNMAN INC (HQ)
Also Called: J&J Packaging
924 S Meridian St (47041-8498)
PHONE....................812 623-1140
Fax: 812 623-1167
Robert Leitgabel, *President*
Glenn Weber, *Admin Sec*
Amber Flowers, *Planning*
Phyllis Moser, *Representative*
▲ EMP: 8
SQ FT: 200,000
SALES (est): 45.2MM
SALES (corp-wide): 339.2MM **Privately
Held**
WEB: www.jjpackaging.com
SIC: 2631 Container, packaging &
boxboard
PA: Deufol Se
Johannes-Gutenberg-Str. 3-5
Hofheim Am Taunus 65719
612 250-00

(G-13111)
**GOODS ON TARGET SPORTING
INC**
8663 E Hoff Rd (47041-7864)
PHONE....................812 623-2300
Fax: 812 623-2347
Leon Kersey, *President*
Rebecca Kersey, *Treasurer*
EMP: 6
SQ FT: 12,000

SALES: 2MM **Privately Held**
WEB: www.ontargetpolaris.com
SIC: 3799 5941 5611 All terrain vehicles
(ATV); sporting goods & bicycle shops;
clothing, sportswear, men's & boys'

(G-13112)
HOOKER DEER DRAG CO LLC
27499 Lawrenceville Rd (47041-9683)
PHONE....................812 623-2706
Steve Huster,
EMP: 2
SALES (est): 88.1K **Privately Held**
SIC: 3949 Sporting & athletic goods

(G-13113)
K2M PRINTING
5250 E State Road 48 (47041-8708)
PHONE....................812 623-3040
EMP: 2
SALES (est): 83.9K **Privately Held**
SIC: 2752 Commercial printing, litho-
graphic

(G-13114)
MCPHERSONS (US) INC
957 N Meridian St (47041-7771)
P.O. Box 188 (47041-0188)
PHONE....................812 623-2225
Fax: 812 623-4117
Darryl Mills, *General Mgr*
Kyle Brock, *Principal*
Penny Hartman, *Principal*
Waverly Jutzi, *Principal*
Kenny Schuman, *Principal*
EMP: 200
SALES (est): 22.5MM
SALES (corp-wide): 3.5B **Privately Held**
WEB: www.masterpiece-studio.com
SIC: 2771 Greeting cards
HQ: The Occasions Group Inc
1750 Tower Blvd
North Mankato MN 56003
800 296-9029

(G-13115)
**MS & J QUALITY SCREW MCH
PDTS**
8925 E County Road 1000 N (47041-8065)
PHONE....................812 623-3002
Fax: 812 623-3120
Michael Czerniak, *President*
Becky Horstman, *Admin Asst*
EMP: 13
SALES: 1MM **Privately Held**
WEB: www.msandj.com
SIC: 3451 Screw machine products

(G-13116)
SAMCO INC
19992 N Manchester Rd (47041-8766)
PHONE....................812 926-4282
Barb Hanlin, *Manager*
EMP: 3
SALES (corp-wide): 839.8K **Privately
Held**
SIC: 3589 5084 Water purification equip-
ment, household type; pollution control
equipment, air (environmental)
PA: Samco Inc
5599 Kugler Mill Rd
Cincinnati OH

(G-13117)
SELECT GOURMET POPCORN
9632 N County Road 800 E (47041-7711)
PHONE....................812 212-2202
EMP: 2
SALES (est): 75.9K **Privately Held**
SIC: 2099 Popcorn, packaged: except al-
ready popped

(G-13118)
SKY FIRE GROUP LLC
21868 Lake Tambo Rd (47041-9022)
PHONE....................812 623-8980
K Koumoutsos, *Mng Member*
Konstantine Koumoutsos, *Mng Member*
EMP: 9 EST: 2008
SALES: 600K **Privately Held**
SIC: 2899 Fireworks

G
E
O
G
R
A
P
H
I
C

(G-13119)
SUNMAN ENGINEERING INC
131 W Washington St (47041-7706)
P.O. Box 397 (47041-0397)
PHONE.................................812 623-4072
Fax: 812 623-4495
Michael Thomas, *President*
EMP: 4
SQ FT: 1,500
SALES (est): 423.4K **Privately Held**
SIC: 3599 Machine shop, jobbing & repair

(G-13120)
TRIMBLE COMBUSTION SYSTEMS INC
215 Nieman St Ste 2 (47041-8931)
P.O. Box 191 (47041-0191)
PHONE.................................812 623-4545
Patrick W Trimble, *President*
Lori A Trimble, *Vice Pres*
EMP: 5
SQ FT: 2,500
SALES (est): 747.7K **Privately Held**
WEB: www.trimblecombustion.com
SIC: 3433 Gas burners, industrial

(G-13121)
WIRE-TEK INC
234 Industrial Dr (47041-7790)
PHONE.................................812 623-8300
Greg Hauck, *President*
EMP: 8 EST: 1970
SQ FT: 30,000
SALES (est): 1.7MM **Privately Held**
SIC: 3496 Miscellaneous fabricated wire products

(G-13122)
WOLFE ENGINEERED PLASTICS LLC
215 Nieman St (47041-8931)
P.O. Box 518 (47041-0518)
PHONE.................................812 623-8403
Kelly L Wolfe, *President*
▲ EMP: 3
SQ FT: 4,500
SALES (est): 563K **Privately Held**
WEB: www.weplastics.com
SIC: 5031 3952 Composite board products, woodboard; boards, drawing, artists'

Swayzee
Grant County

(G-13123)
HIGH NOTE PUBLISHING
571 S 1400 E34 (46986-9732)
P.O. Box 455 (46986-0455)
PHONE.................................765 313-1699
Jeremey Johnson, *Principal*
EMP: 2
SALES (est): 101.7K **Privately Held**
SIC: 2741 Miscellaneous publishing

(G-13124)
IRVING MATERIALS INC
I M I
6377 W 600 S (46986-9773)
PHONE.................................765 922-7991
Ray Rich, *Branch Mgr*
EMP: 15
SALES (corp-wide): 800.6MM **Privately Held**
SIC: 3273 Ready-mixed concrete
PA: Irving Materials, Inc.
8032 N State Road 9
Greenfield IN 46140
317 326-3101

(G-13125)
IRVING MATERIALS INC
Also Called: I M I
6455 W 600 S (46986-9773)
PHONE.................................765 922-7931
Joseph Frazier, *Manager*
EMP: 9
SALES (corp-wide): 800.6MM **Privately Held**
SIC: 3273 Ready-mixed concrete
PA: Irving Materials, Inc.
8032 N State Road 9
Greenfield IN 46140
317 326-3101

Switz City
Greene County

(G-13126)
REEDS RFI INC
248 N 475 W (47465-7035)
PHONE.................................812 659-2872
Charles Reed, *Principal*
Tamba Reed, *Vice Pres*
EMP: 2 EST: 2016
SALES (est): 90.2K **Privately Held**
SIC: 3812 4225 7629 7622 Antennas, radar or communications; general warehousing & storage; electronic equipment repair; intercommunication equipment repair

(G-13127)
TOM SPENCER CONCRETE PRODUCTS
Road 600 W St Rd (47465)
P.O. Box 147 (47465-0147)
PHONE.................................812 659-2318
Fax: 812 659-2318
Thomas G Spencer, *President*
Beth Spencer, *Corp Secy*
EMP: 10 EST: 1979
SALES (est): 1.3MM **Privately Held**
SIC: 3272 Concrete stuctural support & building material

Syracuse
Kosciusko County

(G-13128)
AARON ASPHALT MAINTENANCE SEAL
9031 E Circle Dr S (46567-7561)
PHONE.................................574 528-6370
EMP: 3 EST: 2000
SALES (est): 200K **Privately Held**
SIC: 2951 Mfg Asphalt Mixtures/Blocks

(G-13129)
BAYVIEW ESTATES
400 S Harkless Dr (46567-2011)
PHONE.................................574 457-4136
Larry Nelson, *Owner*
Lyn Tolson, *Principal*
EMP: 2
SALES (est): 206.2K **Privately Held**
SIC: 2451 Mobile homes

(G-13130)
COLBIN TOOL COMPANY INC
1021 N Indiana Ave (46567-1016)
PHONE.................................574 457-3184
Fax: 574 457-3184
Don Strouse, *President*
Dave Blanchard, *Vice Pres*
Sally Strouse, *Treasurer*
Richard Williamson, *Shareholder*
EMP: 35
SQ FT: 18,500
SALES (est): 6.8MM **Privately Held**
WEB: www.colbintool.com
SIC: 3446 3714 3469 Railings, prefabricated metal; motor vehicle parts & accessories; metal stampings

(G-13131)
G M S I INC
6521 E Cornelius Rd (46567-9767)
P.O. Box 189 (46567-0189)
PHONE.................................574 457-4646
Carolyn Anderson, *President*
Russel Anderson, *Vice Pres*
EMP: 5
SALES (est): 475.6K **Privately Held**
WEB: www.transcriptionlabels.com
SIC: 2679 Tags & labels, paper

(G-13132)
GROSS & SONS LUMBER AND VENEER
8516 E 1250 N (46567-8298)
PHONE.................................574 457-5214
Charles Gross, *Owner*

EMP: 2
SALES (est): 99K **Privately Held**
SIC: 2421 5211 Sawmills & planing mills, general; lumber products

(G-13133)
HELMUTH QUALITY POWER SYSTEM
100 S Huntington St (46567-1515)
PHONE.................................574 457-2002
Helmuth Howard, *Principal*
EMP: 2 EST: 2015
SALES (est): 141.7K **Privately Held**
SIC: 3569 Generators: steam, liquid oxygen or nitrogen

(G-13134)
HIGHWATER MARINE LLC
Godfrey Marine Syracuse
300 E Chicago St (46567-1624)
PHONE.................................574 457-2082
Fax: 574 457-4278
Ted Hegge, *Manager*
EMP: 85 **Privately Held**
WEB: www.sanpanboats.com
SIC: 3732 Boat building & repairing
PA: Highwater Marine Llc
4500 Middlebury St
Elkhart IN 46516

(G-13135)
IMAGE GROUP INC
4598 E 1200 N (46567-7833)
PHONE.................................574 457-3111
Fax: 574 457-3114
James E Plummer Sr, *President*
Eleanor J Plummer, *Treasurer*
EMP: 29 EST: 1959
SALES (est): 4.2MM **Privately Held**
SIC: 2752 3993 2789 Offset & photolithographic printing; signs & advertising specialties; bookbinding & related work

(G-13136)
JP INCORPORATED - INDIANA
Also Called: Jasper Plastics Solutions
501 W Railroad Ave (46567-1568)
PHONE.................................574 457-2062
Roger Korenstra, *CEO*
Sam Korenstra, *President*
Bruce Korenstra, *Corp Secy*
EMP: 300
SQ FT: 163,000
SALES (est): 76.8MM **Privately Held**
SIC: 2821 Plastics materials & resins

(G-13137)
LAKE TOOL & DIE INC
1009 W Brooklyn St (46567-1433)
P.O. Box 190, North Webster (46555-0190)
PHONE.................................574 457-8274
Gloria Herman, *President*
Greg Herman, *Principal*
EMP: 5
SALES (est): 792.4K **Privately Held**
SIC: 3544 Special dies, tools, jigs & fixtures

(G-13138)
NATIONAL PRODUCTS INC
201 E Medusa St (46567-1337)
PHONE.................................574 457-4565
Fax: 574 457-5456
Everardo Ganz, *President*
Dale R Ganz, *Admin Sec*
EMP: 14
SQ FT: 6,240
SALES (est): 6.4MM **Privately Held**
WEB: www.nationalproducts.net
SIC: 5031 2421 Plywood; lumber: rough, dressed & finished; custom sawmill

(G-13139)
PARKER-HANNIFIN CORPORATION
Also Called: Engineered Seals Division
501 S Sycamore St (46567-1529)
PHONE.................................574 528-9400
Fax: 574 528-9640
Dave Hone, *General Mgr*
Doug Lue, *General Mgr*
Ed Kent, *Regional Mgr*
Stacey Bailey, *QC Mgr*
Greg Dunn, *Engineer*
EMP: 200

SALES (corp-wide): 12B **Publicly Held**
WEB: www.parker.com
SIC: 3061 3594 Mechanical rubber goods; fluid power pumps & motors
PA: Parker-Hannifin Corporation
6035 Parkland Blvd
Cleveland OH 44124
216 896-3000

(G-13140)
POLY-WOOD LLC
1001 W Brooklyn St (46567-1433)
PHONE.................................574 457-3284
Fax: 574 457-4723
Doug Rassi, *President*
Rus Munn, *General Mgr*
Scott Carrington, *Engineer*
Anji Metzler, *Sales Mgr*
Bryce Glock, *Accounts Mgr*
◆ EMP: 100
SQ FT: 166,422
SALES (est): 29MM **Privately Held**
WEB: www.polywoodinc.com
SIC: 2514 3821 Metal household furniture; laboratory apparatus & furniture

(G-13141)
ROCHESTER HEAT TREATING CO
8039 E Cherokee Rd (46567-8759)
PHONE.................................574 224-4328
Fax: 574 224-4329
George T Hardie, *President*
EMP: 9
SQ FT: 65,000
SALES: 1MM **Privately Held**
SIC: 3398 Metal heat treating

(G-13142)
RODESWOOD LLC
14852 County Road 50 (46567-9299)
PHONE.................................574 457-4496
Fax: 574 658-3331
Enos Rodes, *Mng Member*
EMP: 2
SALES (est): 204K **Privately Held**
SIC: 2511 2431 2451 1751 Wood household furniture; moldings & baseboards, ornamental & trim; mobile homes, industrial or commercial use; carpentry work

(G-13143)
ROGERS ELECTRO-MATICS INC
405 W Chicago St (46567-1506)
P.O. Box 186 (46567-0186)
PHONE.................................574 457-2305
Fax: 574 457-3170
Robert W Haller, *President*
EMP: 15
SQ FT: 7,500
SALES (est): 3.5MM **Privately Held**
WEB: www.rogerselectromatics.com
SIC: 3679 Electronic circuits

(G-13144)
STEVES PALLETS INC
12661 N Pleasant Grove Rd (46567-9708)
P.O. Box 415 (46567-0415)
PHONE.................................574 457-3620
Steven R Sturgill, *President*
EMP: 11
SALES (est): 1.3MM **Privately Held**
SIC: 2448 Pallets, wood & wood with metal

(G-13145)
SUPERIOR TRUSS & COMPONENTS
72298 State Road 13 (46567-9236)
PHONE.................................574 457-8925
Fax: 574 457-8937
EMP: 4
SALES (est): 272.9K **Privately Held**
SIC: 2439 Mfg Structural Wood Members

(G-13146)
SWISS PERFECTION LLC
100 S Huntington St (46567-1515)
PHONE.................................574 457-4457
Fax: 260 692-6290
Roy Schwartz, *President*
EMP: 10
SQ FT: 15,000
SALES (est): 2MM **Privately Held**
WEB: www.swissperfection.com
SIC: 3523 Barn, silo, poultry, dairy & livestock machinery

(G-13147)
SYRACUSE GLASS INC
1107 S Huntington St D (46567-1979)
PHONE...................................574 457-5516
Pat Eakins, *President*
Valerie Eakins, *Admin Sec*
EMP: 3
SQ FT: 2,900
SALES (est): 420.5K **Privately Held**
SIC: 1793 3442 Glass & glazing work;
metal doors, sash & trim

(G-13148)
T-N-T PERFORMANCE MCH SP LLC
210 E Maple Grove St (46567-1705)
PHONE...................................574 457-5056
Timothy Bowling, *Principal*
EMP: 2
SALES (est): 98.6K **Privately Held**
SIC: 3599 Machine shop, jobbing & repair

(G-13149)
THOMAS STRICKLER
Also Called: Tesco
6749 E Cornelius Rd (46567-9769)
PHONE...................................574 457-2473
Thomas Strickler, *Owner*
EMP: 3
SALES (est): 108.4K **Privately Held**
WEB: www.thomasstrickler.com
SIC: 3999 Manufacturing industries

(G-13150)
THOMSON INDUSTRIES INC
1209 Shore Ln (46567-2160)
PHONE...................................574 529-2496
Thomas Hodgson, *Principal*
EMP: 2
SALES (est): 151.5K **Privately Held**
SIC: 3999 Manufacturing industries

(G-13151)
TRANTER GRAPHICS INC
Also Called: 500 Line
8094 N State Road 13 (46567-7206)
P.O. Box 338 (46567-0338)
PHONE...................................574 834-2626
Tammy C Tranter, *President*
C Patrick Tranter, *Chairman*
M Jennelle Dohan, *Vice Pres*
Jenelle Tranter, *VP Mktg*
Janelle Michel, *Mktg Coord*
EMP: 95
SQ FT: 52,000
SALES (est): 16.1MM **Privately Held**
SIC: 2759 7336 Flexographic printing; silk
screen design

(G-13152)
WAWASEE ALUMINUM WORKS INC
Also Called: Polar Kraft Boats
300 E Chicago St (46567-1624)
PHONE...................................574 457-2082
Andy Cripe, *President*
Susan Cripe, *CFO*
EMP: 42
SALES (est): 2.5MM **Privately Held**
SIC: 3732 Motorized boat, building & re-
pairing

(G-13153)
WAYSEEKER LLC
9521 N Koher Rd E (46567-8331)
PHONE...................................574 529-0199
Karl Keiper, *Administration*
EMP: 2 **EST:** 2011
SALES (est): 98.8K **Privately Held**
SIC: 2732 Books: printing only

(G-13154)
WILLIAM D DARR
5416 E 950 N (46567-7616)
PHONE...................................574 518-0453
Will Darr, *Owner*
EMP: 2
SALES (est): 201.4K **Privately Held**
SIC: 3699 Electrical equipment & supplies

Tell City
Perry County

(G-13155)
ATHLETIC AVENUE & MORE INC
802 31st St (47586-2610)
PHONE...................................812 547-7655
Fax: 812 547-5550
Dennis Litherland, *President*
Joe Litherland, *Admin Sec*
EMP: 7
SALES (est): 640K **Privately Held**
SIC: 5941 3993 Sporting goods & bicycle
shops; signs & advertising specialties

(G-13156)
ATTC MANUFACTURING INC
10455 State Road 37 (47586-8322)
PHONE...................................812 547-5060
Hideaki Ando, *President*
Yoshiharu Higuchi, *President*
Mack Sawada, *Corp Secy*
Richard Texas, *Prdtn Mgr*
Rockie Riley, *Maint Spvr*
▲ **EMP:** 281
SQ FT: 160,000
SALES (est): 72.8MM
SALES (corp-wide): 36.6B **Privately Held**
WEB: www.attcmanufacturing.com
SIC: 3714 Motor vehicle parts & acces-
sories
HQ: Aisin Takaoka Co.,Ltd.
1, Tenno, Takaokashinmachi
Toyota AIC 473-0
565 541-123

(G-13157)
C&C DEER PROCESSING
5515 Advantage Rd (47586-9259)
PHONE...................................812 836-2323
Cindy Scherzinger, *Principal*
EMP: 2
SALES (est): 89.9K **Privately Held**
SIC: 2011 Meat packing plants

(G-13158)
CHARLES E WATTS
Also Called: Catholic Church School Market
42 Zurich Way (47586-2032)
PHONE...................................812 547-8516
Fax: 812 547-6582
Charles E Watts, *Owner*
EMP: 2
SALES (est): 298.4K **Privately Held**
SIC: 7311 2752 Advertising agencies; post
cards, picture: lithographed

(G-13159)
DONS AUTOMOTIVE AND MACHINE
1047 6th St (47586-2323)
PHONE...................................812 547-6292
Fax: 812 547-5107
Donald Froehlich, *Owner*
EMP: 4
SALES (est): 544.5K **Privately Held**
SIC: 7538 3599 General automotive repair
shops; machine shop, jobbing & repair

(G-13160)
ETTENSOHN & COMPANY LLC
9018 State Road 237 (47586-8569)
PHONE...................................812 547-5491
Joe Ettensohn, *CEO*
EMP: 8
SQ FT: 17,000
SALES (est): 673.1K **Privately Held**
SIC: 1521 2431 1751 New construction,
single-family houses; millwork; planing
mill, millwork; cabinet & finish carpentry

(G-13161)
FINE GUYS INC
Also Called: Logos
1001 Main St (47586-2305)
PHONE...................................812 547-8630
Zac Heartz, *Mng Member*
EMP: 4
SALES (est): 360.8K **Privately Held**
SIC: 3993 Signs & advertising specialties

(G-13162)
FIREHOUSE PRINTING LLC
711 Humboldt St (47586-2265)
PHONE...................................812 547-3109
Christopher Cail, *Administration*
EMP: 4
SALES (est): 21.1K **Privately Held**
SIC: 2752 Commercial printing, litho-
graphic

(G-13163)
FRETINA CORP
2001 Main St (47586-1388)
P.O. Box 39 (47586-0039)
PHONE...................................812 547-6471
Jonathan Smith, *President*
Tina Smith, *Vice Pres*
Lahna Fisher, *Treasurer*
EMP: 10
SALES (est): 570K **Privately Held**
SIC: 8741 1241 Management services;
coal mining services

(G-13164)
INDUSTRIAL MACHINE
1645 Main St (47586-1361)
P.O. Box 532 (47586-0532)
PHONE...................................812 547-5656
Bill Burnette, *Owner*
EMP: 6
SALES (est): 349.7K **Privately Held**
SIC: 3599 Machine shop, jobbing & repair

(G-13165)
LASHER LUMBER INC
15147 State Road 145 (47586-8525)
PHONE...................................812 836-2618
David Lasher, *Owner*
EMP: 7
SALES (est): 720K **Privately Held**
SIC: 2421 Sawmills & planing mills, gen-
eral

(G-13166)
MICHAEL DEOM PROFESSIONAL
9394 Abner Rd (47586-9021)
PHONE...................................812 836-2206
Michael Deom, *Principal*
EMP: 6
SALES (est): 314.6K **Privately Held**
SIC: 2411 Logging camps & contractors

(G-13167)
MULZER CRUSHED STONE INC (DH)
Also Called: Tell City Concrete Supply
534 Mozart St (47586-2446)
P.O. Box 249 (47586-0249)
PHONE...................................812 547-7921
Fax: 812 547-6757
Kenneth Mulzer Jr, *President*
Jon Goldsberry, *General Mgr*
Brian Peters, *Safety Dir*
Matthew Bunner, *Safety Mgr*
Elton Harding, *Purchasing*
EMP: 20 **EST:** 1939
SQ FT: 3,600
SALES (est): 479.7MM
SALES (corp-wide): 29.7B **Privately Held**
WEB: www.mulzer.com
SIC: 1422 3273 5191 5085 Crushed &
broken limestone; ready-mixed concrete;
limestone, agricultural; industrial supplies
HQ: Crh Americas, Inc.
3 Glenlake Pkwy Ste 12
Sandy Springs GA 30328
770 804-3363

(G-13168)
MULZER CRUSHED STONE INC
Also Called: Stone Sand & Concrete Sales
3rd Lafayette St (47586)
P.O. Box 249 (47586-0249)
PHONE...................................812 547-3467
Fax: 812 547-1415
Natalie Maasberg, *Marketing Staff*
Edward Hagedorn, *Manager*
EMP: 20
SALES (corp-wide): 29.7B **Privately Held**
WEB: www.mulzer.com
SIC: 5032 3273 Stone, crushed or broken;
ready-mixed concrete

HQ: Mulzer Crushed Stone Inc
534 Mozart St
Tell City IN 47586
812 547-7921

(G-13169)
NEWS PUBLISHING COMPANY LLC (DH)
Also Called: Perry County News
537 Main St (47586-2210)
P.O. Box 309 (47586-0309)
PHONE...................................812 547-3424
Fax: 812 547-2847
Mark Eisenlohr, *President*
EMP: 17 **EST:** 2015
SALES (est): 1.2MM **Privately Held**
WEB: www.leaderunion.com
SIC: 2711 Commercial printing & newspa-
per publishing combined
HQ: Landmark Community Newspapers,
Llc
601 Taylorsville Rd
Shelbyville KY 40065
502 633-4334

(G-13170)
NEWS PUBLISHING COMPANY LLC (DH)
542 7th St (47586)
PHONE...................................502 633-4334
Michael Abernathey, *President*
Louis F Ryan, *Admin Sec*
Gary D Miller, *Asst Sec*
EMP: 3
SQ FT: 5,600
SALES (est): 280.3K **Privately Held**
WEB: www.pioneernews.net
SIC: 2711 Newspapers: publishing only,
not printed on site
HQ: Landmark Community Newspapers,
Llc
601 Taylorsville Rd
Shelbyville KY 40065
502 633-4334

(G-13171)
PARKER-HANNIFIN CORPORATION
Process Advnced Filtration Div
2002 Main St (47586-1391)
PHONE...................................812 547-4710
Jennifer Bolen, *Buyer*
Rene Kreisle, *Human Res Mgr*
Travis Reiff, *Manager*
Carlo King, *Manager*
EMP: 100
SQ FT: 80,000
SALES (corp-wide): 12B **Publicly Held**
WEB: www.parker.com
SIC: 3594 Fluid power pumps & motors
PA: Parker-Hannifin Corporation
6035 Parkland Blvd
Cleveland OH 44124
216 896-3000

(G-13172)
PARKER-HANNIFIN CORPORATION
2002 Main St (47586-1391)
PHONE...................................608 824-0500
Donald E Washkewicz, *Ch of Bd*
EMP: 18
SALES (corp-wide): 12B **Publicly Held**
SIC: 3821 3561 Laboratory apparatus &
furniture; pumps & pumping equipment
PA: Parker-Hannifin Corporation
6035 Parkland Blvd
Cleveland OH 44124
216 896-3000

(G-13173)
RUDYS FOOD & FUEL LLC
9780 W State Road 66 (47586-8580)
PHONE...................................812 547-2530
Dianna Rudolph, *Owner*
EMP: 2
SALES (est): 211.3K **Privately Held**
SIC: 2869 Fuels

(G-13174)
WAUPACA FOUNDRY INC
9856 State Hwy 66 (47586)
PHONE...................................812 547-0700
Fax: 812 547-0725
Gary Gigante, *President*

Dan Goble, *Purch Agent*
Shelby Applegate, *QC Mgr*
David Litherland, *Project Engr*
Brian Hammack, *Maintence Staff*
EMP: 923
SALES (corp-wide): 87.9B **Privately Held**
SIC: 3321 Gray iron castings
HQ: Waupaca Foundry, Inc.
1955 Brunner Dr
Waupaca WI 54981
715 258-6611

(G-13175)
WEBB WHEEL PRODUCTS INC
9840 W State Route 66 (47586)
PHONE................812 548-0477
Kent Finkbiner, *Branch Mgr*
EMP: 177
SALES (corp-wide): 242.1B **Publicly Held**
SIC: 3714 Motor vehicle parts & accessories
HQ: Webb Wheel Products, Inc.
2310 Industrial Dr Sw
Cullman AL 35055
256 739-6660

(G-13176)
WG S GLOBAL SERVICES
9856 W State Road 66 (47586-8581)
PHONE................810 239-4947
EMP: 2
SALES (est): 169K **Privately Held**
SIC: 3599 Machine shop, jobbing & repair

(G-13177)
WGS GLOBAL SERVICES LC
840 5th St (47586-2424)
PHONE................812 548-4446
Ghaffan M Saab, *Branch Mgr*
Joshua Bostrom, *Manager*
EMP: 237 **Privately Held**
SIC: 3711 Automobile assembly, including specialty automobiles
PA: Wgs Global Services, L.C.
6350 Taylor Dr
Flint MI 48507

Templeton
Benton County

(G-13178)
LAMINATING SPECIALTIES INC IND
5833 E Old Us Highway 52 (47986-4700)
PHONE................765 385-0023
Fax: 765 385-0024
John Brost, *President*
Allen Adwell, *Corp Secy*
EMP: 7
SALES (est): 532.6K **Privately Held**
SIC: 7389 2789 Laminating service; bookbinding & related work; trade binding services

Tennyson
Warrick County

(G-13179)
DON DETZER LLC
12859 N County Road 125 W (47637-9437)
PHONE................812 362-7599
Don Detzer, *Principal*
EMP: 4
SALES (est): 521.2K **Privately Held**
SIC: 3569 Filters

(G-13180)
PIGEON SWITCH POTTERY
1896 Pigeon Switch (47637)
P.O. Box 196 (47637-0196)
PHONE................812 567-4124
Penny Williams, *Owner*
EMP: 2
SALES (est): 104K **Privately Held**
SIC: 3269 Pottery products

(G-13181)
TAMARACK PETROLEUM COMPANY INC
2611 E Kelly Rd (47637-9205)
PHONE................812 567-4023
Howard Peacock, *Manager*
EMP: 7
SALES (corp-wide): 5.9MM **Privately Held**
SIC: 1311 Crude petroleum & natural gas
PA: Tamarack Petroleum Company, Inc.
777 E Wisconsin Ave # 1920
Milwaukee WI 53202
414 276-4885

(G-13182)
TRIPLE H TOOL CO
7677 Folsomville Rd (47637-7257)
PHONE................812 567-4600
Fax: 812 567-4603
Donald Hunt, *Owner*
Wanda Hunt, *Co-Owner*
EMP: 2
SQ FT: 1,200
SALES (est): 154.8K **Privately Held**
SIC: 3544 Industrial molds

(G-13183)
YOUR FACE OUR PLACE PRINT SHOP
3877 State Road 161 N (47637-9003)
PHONE................812 567-4510
John Maltby, *Partner*
Karen Maltby, *Partner*
EMP: 2
SALES (est): 142K **Privately Held**
SIC: 2752 Commercial printing, lithographic

Terre Haute
Vigo County

(G-13184)
A H EMERY COMPANY
Also Called: Emery Winslow Scale Co.
4530 N 25th St (47805-2513)
PHONE................812 466-5265
Judy Torphy, *Purchasing*
William Fischer, *Branch Mgr*
EMP: 47
SALES (est): 7.9MM
SALES (corp-wide): 14MM **Privately Held**
SIC: 3596 Industrial scales; railroad track scales; truck (motor vehicle) scales; weighing machines & apparatus
PA: The A H Emery Company
73 Cogwheel Ln
Seymour CT 06483
203 881-9333

(G-13185)
A P MACHINE & TOOL INC
1301 Elm St (47807-2194)
PHONE................812 232-4939
Fax: 812 232-3579
Andre G Ponsot, *President*
Antionette Ponsot, *Vice Pres*
EMP: 10 EST: 1966
SQ FT: 11,000
SALES (est): 1.4MM **Privately Held**
SIC: 3599 Machine shop, jobbing & repair

(G-13186)
ACE SIGN COMPANY INC
1140 3rd Ave (47807-1544)
PHONE................812 232-4206
Fax: 812 232-4206
Jeffrey Bose, *President*
EMP: 8
SALES (est): 590K **Privately Held**
SIC: 3993 Signs & advertising specialties

(G-13187)
ADVANCED LIMB WOUND CARE
303 S 14th St (47807-4019)
PHONE................812 232-0957
John Trench, *Principal*
EMP: 3
SALES (est): 234.4K **Privately Held**
SIC: 3842 Limbs, artificial

(G-13188)
ADVICS MANUFACTURING IND LLC
Also Called: ABI
10550 James Adams St (47802-9294)
PHONE................812 298-1617
Atsushi Takenaga, *President*
Kazuza Tsukamoto, *Treasurer*
Ryoichi Koizumi, *Mng Member*
Tetsuya Saida, *Admin Sec*
▲ **EMP:** 400
SQ FT: 150,000
SALES (est): 104.3MM
SALES (corp-wide): 36.6B **Privately Held**
WEB: www.aisinbrake.com
SIC: 3714 Air brakes, motor vehicle
HQ: Advics North America, Inc.
1650 Kingsview Dr
Lebanon OH 45036
513 696-5450

(G-13189)
AIDAN INDUSTRIES INCORPORATED
8539 E Sunset Ave (47805-7951)
PHONE................812 239-2803
Richard Whitlock, *President*
EMP: 2 EST: 2012
SALES (est): 112.3K **Privately Held**
SIC: 3999 Manufacturing industries

(G-13190)
ALL AMERICAN TENT & AWNING INC
Also Called: Ace Sign & Awning
1140 3rd Ave (47807-1544)
PHONE................812 232-4220
Fax: 812 232-4220
Russell Ferrell, *President*
Jeffrey Bose, *Vice Pres*
EMP: 15
SQ FT: 7,000
SALES (est): 1.2MM **Privately Held**
WEB: www.acesignawning.com
SIC: 3993 3444 7359 Signs & advertising specialties; awnings & canopies; tent & tarpaulin rental

(G-13191)
ALL STATE MANUFACTURING CO INC
Also Called: Allstate Mfg
4024 2nd Pkwy (47804-4243)
PHONE................812 466-2276
Fax: 812 466-7570
Rudy Stakeman, *CEO*
Peggy Thomas, *Manager*
EMP: 10
SQ FT: 90,000
SALES (est): 2.1MM **Privately Held**
WEB: www.allstatemfg.com
SIC: 2522 Cabinets, office: except wood

(G-13192)
ALWAYS SUN TANNING CENTER (PA)
1420 N 25th St (47803-1065)
PHONE................812 238-2786
Cathy Sweat, *Owner*
EMP: 5
SALES (est): 626.5K **Privately Held**
SIC: 3648 7299 Sun tanning equipment, incl. tanning beds; tanning salon

(G-13193)
AMPACET CORPORATION
3701 N Fruitridge Ave (47804-4263)
P.O. Box 5357 (47805-0357)
PHONE................812 466-5231
Fax: 812 466-6926
George Hiland, *Purchasing*
EMP: 157
SALES (corp-wide): 632.6MM **Privately Held**
WEB: www.ampacet.com
SIC: 2821 2851 5169 2865 Plastics materials & resins; paints & allied products; synthetic resins, rubber & plastic materials; color pigments, organic
PA: Ampacet Corporation
660 White Plains Rd # 360
Tarrytown NY 10591
914 631-6600

(G-13194)
AMPACET CORPORATION
Also Called: Ampacet Research & Development
3801 N Fruitridge Ave (47804-1771)
P.O. Box 5086 (47805-0086)
PHONE................812 466-9828
Fax: 812 466-6796
Prakash Patel, *Manager*
EMP: 42
SALES (corp-wide): 632.6MM **Privately Held**
WEB: www.ampacet.com
SIC: 8733 8731 2851 Research institute; commercial physical research; paints & allied products
PA: Ampacet Corporation
660 White Plains Rd # 360
Tarrytown NY 10591
914 631-6600

(G-13195)
ASSOCIATED LABEL INC
8402 E Davis Ave (47805-9739)
P.O. Box 339, Seelyville (47878-0339)
PHONE................812 877-3682
Fax: 812 877-3788
Brian Grayless, *President*
Darrell Bland, *Vice Pres*
Brent Grayless, *Treasurer*
EMP: 4
SQ FT: 3,500
SALES (est): 568.4K **Privately Held**
SIC: 2679 Labels, paper: made from purchased material

(G-13196)
B B & H SIGNS INCORPORATED
Also Called: Sign Express
2212 S 3rd St (47802-3047)
PHONE................812 235-1340
Fax: 812 235-1340
Fred Huber, *President*
EMP: 2
SQ FT: 3,000
SALES: 300K **Privately Held**
SIC: 3993 7532 Signs, not made in custom sign painting shops; truck painting & lettering

(G-13197)
BANE-WELKER EQUIPMENT LLC
Also Called: Kubota Authorized Dealer
300 W Margaret Dr (47802-3789)
PHONE................812 234-2627
Fax: 812 232-2240
Mark Fruits, *Parts Mgr*
Patricia Minnis, *Treasurer*
Michael Romack, *Sales Executive*
Joseph Minnis, *Branch Mgr*
EMP: 13
SALES (corp-wide): 51.5MM **Privately Held**
SIC: 3524 5083 Grass catchers, lawn mower; farm & garden machinery
PA: Bane-Welker Equipment, Llc
33 E 700 S
Ladoga IN 47954
765 866-0494

(G-13198)
BEMIS COMPANY INC
Bemis North America
1350 N Fruitridge Ave (47804-4218)
P.O. Box 905 (47808-0905)
PHONE................812 466-2213
Fax: 812 460-6370
Michael Clark, *Engineer*
Steven E White, *Engineer*
Clayton Bettenbrock, *Project Engr*
Carol Stearman, *Accounting Dir*
Tamara Shake, *Asst Controller*
EMP: 100
SALES (corp-wide): 4B **Publicly Held**
WEB: www.bemis.com
SIC: 3081 Polyethylene film; packing materials, plastic sheet
PA: Bemis Company, Inc.
2301 Industrial Dr
Neenah WI 54956
920 527-5000

(G-13199)
BENCHMARK INC (PA)
Also Called: Benchmark Fabricated Steel
4149 4th Pkwy (47804-4262)
PHONE................................812 238-0659
Fax: 812 238-2171
Edward T Hazledine, *President*
Eric Adame, *General Mgr*
Mark Sellers, *General Mgr*
Bill Anderson, *Vice Pres*
Dale Arnett, *Vice Pres*
EMP: 3
SQ FT: 24,000
SALES (est): 1.9MM **Privately Held**
SIC: 3441 Building components, structural steel

(G-13200)
BENCHMARK INC
Also Called: Benchmark Fabricated Steel
4149 4th Pkwy (47804-4262)
PHONE................................812 238-2691
Edward T Hazledine, *Branch Mgr*
EMP: 15
SALES (corp-wide): 1.9MM **Privately Held**
SIC: 3448 Prefabricated metal buildings
PA: Benchmark Inc
4149 4th Pkwy
Terre Haute IN 47804
812 238-0659

(G-13201)
BIBLES FOR BLIND & VISUALLY
3228 E Rose Hill Ave (47805-1228)
PHONE................................812 466-3134
Keith Reedy, *Owner*
EMP: 9
SALES: 109.5K **Privately Held**
SIC: 2731 5942 Book publishing; books, religious

(G-13202)
BIG PICTURE DATA IMAGING LLC
608 N 13th St (47807-2114)
PHONE................................812 235-0202
Fax: 812 235-0255
Tim Wells,
Todd Mankin,
Chuck Studey,
EMP: 3
SQ FT: 1,100
SALES (est): 199.6K **Privately Held**
SIC: 2759 7379 7374 Screen printing; data processing consultant; computer graphics service

(G-13203)
BLACK DOG VINEYARD INC
7622 N Meneely St (47805-7909)
PHONE................................812 877-1933
Kevin A Hoolehan, *Principal*
EMP: 2
SALES (est): 109.4K **Privately Held**
SIC: 2084 Wines, brandy & brandy spirits

(G-13204)
BOOMERANG BAY LLC
530 Farrington St (47807-5095)
PHONE................................812 236-2027
Robert Lavanne, *Mng Member*
EMP: 2
SALES (est): 121.2K **Privately Held**
SIC: 2087 Cocktail mixes, nonalcoholic

(G-13205)
CARD CALENDAR PUBLISHING LLC
2500 Prairieton Rd (47802-1946)
PHONE................................812 234-5999
John F Card,
EMP: 4
SALES (est): 330K **Privately Held**
SIC: 2741 Miscellaneous publishing

(G-13206)
CENTER FOR DIAGNOSTIC IMAGING
4313 S 7th St (47802-4365)
PHONE................................812 234-0555
Fax: 812 478-1185
Adrian Lauer, *President*
Owen Lauer, *Mng Member*
EMP: 18 **EST:** 1994

SALES (est): 1.1MM **Privately Held**
WEB: www.indianamri.com
SIC: 8071 3829 X-ray laboratory, including dental; medical diagnostic systems, nuclear

(G-13207)
CENTRAL BRACE & LIMB CO INC
500 E Springhill Dr Ste G (47802-4439)
PHONE................................812 232-2145
Fax: 812 232-1416
Jan Gunnett, *Manager*
EMP: 2
SALES (est): 160.7K
SALES (corp-wide): 4MM **Privately Held**
SIC: 3842 5999 Braces, orthopedic; limbs, artificial; orthopedic & prosthesis applications
PA: Central Brace & Limb Co Inc
1901 N Capitol Ave
Indianapolis IN 46202
317 925-4296

(G-13208)
CENTRAL COCA-COLA BTLG CO INC
924 Lafayette Ave (47804-2930)
PHONE................................812 232-9543
EMP: 88
SALES (corp-wide): 35.4B **Publicly Held**
SIC: 2086 Bottled & canned soft drinks
HQ: Central Coca-Cola Bottling Company, Inc.
555 Taxter Rd Ste 550
Elmsford NY 10523
914 789-1100

(G-13209)
CERTAINTEED CORPORATION
1001 W Industrial Dr (47802-7506)
PHONE................................812 645-0400
Jeff Heffner, *Branch Mgr*
EMP: 8
SALES (corp-wide): 213.5MM **Privately Held**
WEB: www.certainteed.net
SIC: 3255 Fire clay blocks, bricks, tile or special shapes
HQ: Certainteed Corporation
20 Moores Rd
Malvern PA 19355
610 893-5000

(G-13210)
CHEETAH BUILDING PRODUCTS
4600 N 13th St (47805-1602)
PHONE................................812 466-1234
H Baton, *Owner*
EMP: 2
SALES (est): 91.3K **Privately Held**
SIC: 3272 Concrete products

(G-13211)
CLABBER GIRL CORPORATION
900 Wabash Ave (47807-3208)
P.O. Box 150 (47808-0150)
PHONE................................812 232-9446
Gary L Morris, *President*
Mark D Miles, *Principal*
Eric Gloe, *Vice Pres*
W Curtis Brighton, *Admin Sec*
◆ EMP: 100
SALES (est): 17.8MM
SALES (corp-wide): 43.7MM **Privately Held**
WEB: www.bakewithlove.com
SIC: 2099 2046 2045 Baking powder; corn starch; prepared flour mixes & doughs
PA: Hulman & Company
900 Wabash Ave
Terre Haute IN 47807
812 232-9446

(G-13212)
CLEAR VIEW CSTM WINDOWS DOORS
9630 E Us Highway 40 (47803-9224)
PHONE................................812 877-1000
Kelly McGinty, *President*
EMP: 5
SQ FT: 1,010

SALES (est): 595.9K **Privately Held**
SIC: 2431 Window frames, wood; door frames, wood

(G-13213)
COLONIAL BAKING CO INC
660 N 1st St (47807-1916)
PHONE................................812 232-4466
Glen Brock, *Manager*
EMP: 2
SALES (est): 98.3K **Privately Held**
SIC: 2051 Bread, cake & related products

(G-13214)
COLUMBIAN HOME PRODUCTS LLC
1600 Beech St (47804-3200)
PHONE................................812 238-5044
Fax: 812 238-5041
Doug Kellam, *Branch Mgr*
Gary Heath, *Manager*
Jim Hewitt, *Manager*
EMP: 24
SALES (corp-wide): 46.7MM **Privately Held**
WEB: www.columbianhp.com
SIC: 3469 Cooking ware, porcelain enameled
PA: Columbian Home Products, Llc
404 N Rand Rd
North Barrington IL 60010
847 307-8600

(G-13215)
COMPUTER SOLUTIONS SYSTEMS CO
Also Called: Cs Technology
19 S 6th St Ste 900 (47807-3534)
PHONE................................812 235-9008
Fax: 812 235-5544
Nicholas Mahurin, *President*
EMP: 11
SQ FT: 8,500
SALES (est): 2MM **Privately Held**
WEB: www.csnetwork.net
SIC: 3571 5734 7376 Electronic computers; modems, monitors, terminals & disk drives; computers; computer facilities management

(G-13216)
COMPUTRAIN LEARNING CENTER INC
530 Farrington St (47807-5095)
PHONE................................812 235-7419
Fax: 812 235-3937
Ron L Harrison, *President*
EMP: 13
SALES (est): 680K **Privately Held**
WEB: www.ctconsultinggroup.com
SIC: 8243 7379 7372 Software training, computer; computer related maintenance services; computer related consulting services; application computer software

(G-13217)
COUNTRY BARN CANDLES LLC
9835 Sable Ridge Ln (47802-9697)
PHONE................................812 299-2929
Jill Truelove, *Administration*
EMP: 2
SALES (est): 96.2K **Privately Held**
SIC: 3999 Candles

(G-13218)
COUNTRY CABIN LLC
5125 S Us Highway 41 (47802-4789)
PHONE................................812 232-4635
Kelly Rost,
EMP: 4
SALES (est): 296.3K **Privately Held**
SIC: 5023 3944 Decorating supplies; craft & hobby kits & sets

(G-13219)
CROSSROADS DOOR & HARDWARE INC
1301 Eagle St (47807-2731)
PHONE................................812 234-9751
Michael Jones, *President*
Mike Jones, *Parts Mgr*
Joseph Harazin, *CFO*
Mark A Sellers, *Manager*
EMP: 7
SQ FT: 14,000

SALES: 2.4MM **Privately Held**
WEB: www.crossroadsdoor.com
SIC: 3442 3429 Metal doors, sash & trim; manufactured hardware (general)

(G-13220)
CULTOR FOOD SCIENCE
100 Pfizer Dr (47802-8019)
PHONE................................812 299-6700
Fax: 812 299-9196
Lloyd Driggers, *Principal*
Rhonda Milner, *Info Tech Mgr*
EMP: 4
SALES (est): 262.2K **Privately Held**
SIC: 2087 Flavoring extracts & syrups

(G-13221)
D&D AUTOMATION INC
1207 E Dallas Dr (47802-8682)
PHONE................................812 299-1045
Fax: 812 299-3902
David Decker, *President*
Billy McCarter, *Prdtn Mgr*
Mike Decker, *Treasurer*
EMP: 9
SQ FT: 8,500
SALES (est): 743K **Privately Held**
WEB: www.ddautomation.com
SIC: 3599 3544 7699 Machine shop, jobbing & repair; forms (molds), for foundry & plastics working machinery; industrial machinery & equipment repair

(G-13222)
DANISCO USA INC
11 W Litesse Dr (47802-8036)
PHONE................................812 299-6700
Ryan Loftus, *Engineer*
EMP: 9
SALES (corp-wide): 62.4B **Publicly Held**
SIC: 2099 Food preparations
HQ: Danisco Usa Inc.
4 New Century Pkwy
New Century KS 66031
913 764-8100

(G-13223)
DATA LABEL INC (PA)
1000 Spruce St (47807-2195)
PHONE................................812 232-0408
Fax: 812 232-0408
George Snyder, *President*
Karen Jackson, *General Mgr*
Marlin Bartley, *Vice Pres*
Kurt Kahl, *Vice Pres*
Michael Riggs, *Vice Pres*
▼ EMP: 150
SQ FT: 78,675
SALES (est): 33.8MM **Privately Held**
WEB: www.datalabel.net
SIC: 2754 Labels: gravure printing

(G-13224)
DEDE TOOL & MACHINE INC
799 W Springhill Dr (47802-8760)
P.O. Box 10126 (47801-0126)
PHONE................................812 232-7365
Fax: 812 478-2152
Daniel Farmer, *President*
Dan Farmer, *Executive*
EMP: 8
SQ FT: 8,000
SALES (est): 1.1MM **Privately Held**
WEB: www.dedetool.com
SIC: 3599 Machine shop, jobbing & repair

(G-13225)
DRONE WORKS LLC
933 S 5th St Apt 3 (47807-5026)
PHONE................................812 917-4691
Christopher Garner, *Principal*
EMP: 2
SALES (est): 102.7K **Privately Held**
SIC: 3721 Motorized aircraft

(G-13226)
E I DU PONT DE NEMOURS & CO
Also Called: Dupont Nutrition & Health
11 W Litesse Dr (47802-8036)
PHONE................................812 299-6700
Gary Reid, *Branch Mgr*
EMP: 4
SALES (corp-wide): 62.4B **Publicly Held**
SIC: 2099 Food preparations

GEOGRAPHIC

HQ: E. I. Du Pont De Nemours And Company
974 Centre Rd
Wilmington DE 19805
302 774-1000

(G-13227)
E I DU PONT DE NEMOURS & CO
11 W Litesse Dr (47802-8036)
PHONE...............................812 299-6700
EMP: 2
SALES (corp-wide): 62.4B **Publicly Held**
SIC: 2879 Agricultural chemicals
HQ: E. I. Du Pont De Nemours And Company
974 Centre Rd
Wilmington DE 19805
302 774-1000

(G-13228)
E I DU PONT DE NEMOURS & CO
Also Called: Danisco USA
33 W Litesse Dr (47802-8036)
P.O. Box 8266 (47808)
PHONE...............................812 299-6700
Bruce Milner, *Prdtn Mgr*
Lloyd Driggers, *Manager*
Mark Middleton, *Manager*
EMP: 80
SALES (corp-wide): 62.4B **Publicly Held**
SIC: 2819 Industrial inorganic chemicals
HQ: E. I. Du Pont De Nemours And Company
974 Centre Rd
Wilmington DE 19805
302 774-1000

(G-13229)
EAST 40 SPORTS APPAREL INC
215 Deming Ln (47803-2082)
PHONE...............................812 877-3695
Fax: 812 877-3695
Patricia Gard, *President*
James Gard, *Treasurer*
EMP: 3
SQ FT: 3,000
SALES: 225K **Privately Held**
SIC: 7336 5941 2396 Silk screen design; sporting goods & bicycle shops; automotive & apparel trimmings

(G-13230)
EBC LLC
1075 Crawford St (47807-4907)
PHONE...............................812 234-4111
John Nugent, *President*
Tony Ellis, *Treasurer*
◆ EMP: 25
SQ FT: 150,000
SALES (est): 5.7MM **Privately Held**
WEB: www.ebcsteelbuildings.com
SIC: 3441 Fabricated structural metal

(G-13231)
ELI LILLY
1445 S 1st St (47802-1910)
PHONE...............................812 242-5900
Robert Crile, *Manager*
Les Miller, *Manager*
David Shore, *Senior Mgr*
Andrea Gregory, *Executive Asst*
Lora Khoury, *Admin Asst*
EMP: 5
SALES (est): 414.3K **Privately Held**
SIC: 2834 Pharmaceutical preparations

(G-13232)
ENMAC LLC
13200 S Us Highway 41 (47802-9139)
P.O. Box 141, Pimento (47866-0141)
PHONE...............................812 298-8711
Curtis Dodine, *Owner*
EMP: 6
SALES (est): 901.7K **Privately Held**
SIC: 3421 Table & food cutlery, including butchers'

(G-13233)
F T MOORE AND SONS INC
3648 E Broadlands Ave (47805-1058)
PHONE...............................812 466-3762
Martin D Moore, *President*
EMP: 6
SALES (est): 564.6K **Privately Held**
SIC: 7692 1799 Welding repair; welding on site

(G-13234)
FAVRES GUN SHOP
Also Called: Favre Gunshop
520 N 42nd St (47803-1122)
PHONE...............................812 235-0198
Danny Favre, *Owner*
EMP: 2
SALES (est): 123.5K **Privately Held**
SIC: 3484 7699 Guns (firearms) or gun parts, 30 mm. & below; gun services

(G-13235)
FORSYTH BROTHERS CONCRETE PDTS (PA)
4500 N Fruitridge St (47805-2360)
PHONE...............................812 466-4080
Fax: 812 466-9812
Jeffrey A Bell, *President*
Lydia Dalton, *Admin Sec*
EMP: 6 EST: 1907
SQ FT: 13,200
SALES (est): 1MM **Privately Held**
SIC: 3272 5074 Burial vaults, concrete or precast terrazzo; septic tanks, concrete; plumbing fittings & supplies

(G-13236)
FRITO-LAY NORTH AMERICA INC
6541 State Road 42 (47803-9220)
PHONE...............................812 877-2425
Fax: 812 877-7356
Brad Reynolds, *Principal*
EMP: 160
SALES (corp-wide): 63.5B **Publicly Held**
SIC: 2096 Potato chips & similar snacks
HQ: Frito-Lay North America, Inc.
7701 Legacy Dr
Plano TX 75024

(G-13237)
FUTUREX INDUSTRIES INC
10000 S Carlisle St (47802-8693)
PHONE...............................812 299-5708
Fax: 812 299-2342
Tami Davies, *Sales Staff*
Brandon Vest, *Manager*
EMP: 65
SALES (corp-wide): 89.5MM **Privately Held**
WEB: www.futurexind.com
SIC: 3081 2865 Plastic film & sheet; polyethylene film; styrene
PA: Futurex Industries, Inc.
80 E Smith St
Bloomingdale IN 47832
765 498-3900

(G-13238)
GARTLAND FOUNDRY COMPANY INC
330 Grant St (47802-3063)
P.O. Box 2008 (47802-0008)
PHONE...............................812 232-0226
Fax: 812 232-7569
Bill Grimes, *President*
William Grimes, *President*
Don Powell, *Vice Pres*
Mark Nelson, *Human Res Dir*
Ken Stanton, *Manager*
▲ EMP: 110 EST: 1902
SQ FT: 100,000
SALES (est): 41.6MM **Privately Held**
WEB: www.gartlandfoundry.com
SIC: 3321 Gray iron castings

(G-13239)
GENESCO INC
Also Called: Lids
3401 S Us Highway 41 A13b (47802-4154)
PHONE...............................812 234-9722
Jake Deering, *Manager*
EMP: 2
SALES (corp-wide): 2.9B **Publicly Held**
WEB: www.genesco.com
SIC: 2353 Hats & caps
PA: Genesco Inc.
1415 Murfreesboro Pike
Nashville TN 37217
615 367-7000

(G-13240)
GLAS-COL LLC
711 Hulman St (47802-1629)
PHONE...............................812 235-6167

Paul Adams, *Treasurer*
EMP: 74
SALES (est): 9.6MM
SALES (corp-wide): 162.5MM **Privately Held**
SIC: 3281 Cut stone & stone products
PA: Templeton Coal Company, Inc.
701 Wabash Ave Ste 501
Terre Haute IN 47807
812 232-7037

(G-13241)
GOETZ PRINTING
Also Called: Goetz Printing & Copy Center
415 Barton Ave (47803-2138)
PHONE...............................812 243-2086
Fax: 812 232-6504
John Mullican, *Owner*
EMP: 11
SQ FT: 10,000
SALES (est): 1.2MM **Privately Held**
WEB: www.goetzprinting.com
SIC: 2752 2791 2789 Commercial printing, offset; typesetting; bookbinding & related work

(G-13242)
GOLDEN FRAME INC
509 E Voorhees St (47802-3058)
PHONE...............................812 232-0048
Fax: 812 234-2403
Todd Stokes, *President*
Sally Stokes, *Vice Pres*
EMP: 2
SQ FT: 2,200
SALES: 72K **Privately Held**
SIC: 7699 3479 5999 5231 Picture framing, custom; etching & engraving; trophies & plaques; glass, leaded or stained

(G-13243)
GRAPHIC FX INC
1130 Walnut St (47807-3823)
PHONE...............................812 234-0000
Fax: 812 234-4014
Chad McKay, *President*
EMP: 13
SQ FT: 9,000
SALES: 800K **Privately Held**
WEB: www.gfxsp.com
SIC: 2759 5699 7389 3949 Promotional printing; screen printing; customized clothing & apparel; advertising, promotional & trade show services; team sports equipment

(G-13244)
HANGER PRSTHETCS & ORTHO INC
4142 S 7th St (47802-4123)
PHONE...............................812 235-6451
Fax: 812 231-0141
Rick Wells, *Manager*
EMP: 3
SALES (corp-wide): 1B **Publicly Held**
SIC: 3842 Prosthetic appliances
HQ: Hanger Prosthetics & Orthotics, Inc.
10910 Domain Dr Ste 300
Austin TX 78758
512 777-3800

(G-13245)
HAPCO REBUILDERS INC
129 N 2nd St (47807-2908)
PHONE...............................812 232-2550
William J Groth, *President*
EMP: 2
SALES: 120K **Privately Held**
SIC: 3714 Camshafts, motor vehicle; crankshaft assemblies, motor vehicle

(G-13246)
HEARTLAND STEEL PROCESSING LLC
455 W Industrial Dr (47802-9266)
PHONE...............................812 299-4157
Mark D Millett, *President*
Gary Lowe, *Maint Spvr*
Lynn Woolever, *Maint Spvr*
Roberto Bohrer, *Opers Staff*
Gary Sinders, *Engineer*
▲ EMP: 200
SQ FT: 800,000

SALES (est): 100MM **Publicly Held**
SIC: 3316 3312 Cold-rolled strip or wire; iron & steel: galvanized, pipes, plates, sheets, etc.
PA: Steel Dynamics, Inc.
7575 W Jefferson Blvd
Fort Wayne IN 46804

(G-13247)
HONEY CREEK MACHINE INC
1537 W Harlan Dr (47802-9771)
PHONE...............................812 299-5255
Danny Kerr, *Mng Member*
EMP: 20
SQ FT: 28,400
SALES (est): 4.7MM **Privately Held**
SIC: 3559 Plastics working machinery; metal finishing equipment for plating, etc.

(G-13248)
HOOSIER FIBERGLASS INDUSTRIES
2011 S 3rd St (47802-3042)
PHONE...............................812 232-5027
Fax: 812 234-3320
Lyndon Tucker, *President*
EMP: 16 EST: 1958
SQ FT: 60,000
SALES (est): 1.4MM **Privately Held**
SIC: 3089 3081 Thermoformed finished plastic products; unsupported plastics film & sheet

(G-13249)
HORNER INDUSTRIAL SERVICES INC
3601 Scherer Rd (47804-4265)
PHONE...............................812 466-5281
Phil Horner, *Principal*
EMP: 4
SALES (corp-wide): 46.7MM **Privately Held**
SIC: 3625 7694 7699 7629 Electric controls & control accessories, industrial; electric motor repair; pumps & pumping equipment repair; electrical equipment repair, high voltage
PA: Horner Industrial Services, Inc.
1521 E Washington St
Indianapolis IN 46201
317 639-4261

(G-13250)
HULMAN & COMPANY (PA)
Also Called: Clabber Girl
900 Wabash Ave (47807-3208)
P.O. Box 150 (47808-0150)
PHONE...............................812 232-9446
Fax: 812 478-7180
Mary H George, *Ch of Bd*
Jeffery G Belskus, *President*
Gary Morris, *Vice Pres*
Jeffrey G Belskus, *CFO*
W Curtis Brighton, *Admin Sec*
▼ EMP: 120
SQ FT: 200,000
SALES (est): 43.7MM **Privately Held**
WEB: www.bakewithlove.com
SIC: 2099 Baking powder

(G-13251)
HUX OIL CORP
5451 Riley Rd (47802-8875)
P.O. Box 1027, Riley (47871-1027)
PHONE...............................812 894-2096
Fax: 812 894-2097
Cynthia S Martin, *President*
Alice Prothero, *COO*
Alice K Prothero, *Admin Sec*
EMP: 6
SQ FT: 2,500
SALES: 1.5MM **Privately Held**
SIC: 1311 Crude petroleum production

(G-13252)
HYDRITE CHEMICAL CO
2400 Erie Canal Rd (47802-3975)
PHONE...............................812 232-5411
Fax: 812 232-1148
Val Kizik, *Branch Mgr*
Derek Stewart, *Manager*
Brian Rindfleisch, *Programmer Anys*
EMP: 30

▲ = Import ▼=Export
◆ =Import/Export

SALES (corp-wide): 1B **Privately Held**
WEB: www.hydrite.com
SIC: 2819 5169 2899 Industrial inorganic chemicals; chemicals & allied products; chemical preparations
PA: Hydrite Chemical Co.
300 N Patrick Blvd Fl 2
Brookfield WI 53045
262 792-1450

(G-13253)
I2R
711 Hulman St (47802-1629)
P.O. Box 2128 (47802-0128)
PHONE..................................812 235-6167
Steve Sterrett, *Principal*
EMP: 4 EST: 2010
SALES (est): 337.7K **Privately Held**
SIC: 3821 Laboratory apparatus & furniture

(G-13254)
IMPRINT IT ALL
1419 S 25th St (47803-2927)
PHONE..................................812 234-0024
Fax: 812 234-0003
Paul Williams, *Owner*
EMP: 3
SALES (est): 260K **Privately Held**
SIC: 2759 Screen printing

(G-13255)
INDIANA SCALE COMPANY INC
1607 Maple Ave (47804-3234)
PHONE..................................812 232-0893
Fax: 812 232-6876
Fred Herrmann, *President*
▲ EMP: 14
SQ FT: 35,000
SALES: 3.3MM **Privately Held**
SIC: 3596 5046 8741 Industrial scales; scales, except laboratory; management services

(G-13256)
INDUSTRIAL MAINT ENGRG INC
Also Called: Ais Gauging
5350 N 13th St (47805-1615)
PHONE..................................812 466-5478
John Young Jr, *President*
Stephen Herrmann, *Vice Pres*
Glenn A Wrightsman, *Vice Pres*
Megan Gord, *Office Mgr*
EMP: 7
SALES (est): 1.1MM **Privately Held**
SIC: 2819 Aluminum compounds

(G-13257)
INDYBAKE PRODUCTS LLC
Also Called: Kellogg's Snacks
9445 E Us Highway 40 (47803-9218)
PHONE..................................812 877-1588
Fax: 812 877-9816
Ronald Westman, *Mng Member*
Pauline Westman,
EMP: 90
SQ FT: 100,000
SALES (est): 9.4MM **Privately Held**
SIC: 2045 2052 Prepared flour mixes & doughs; cookies & crackers

(G-13258)
INTERNATIONAL LABEL MFG LLC
1925 S 13th St (47802-2411)
P.O. Box 6129 (47802-6129)
PHONE..................................812 235-5071
Fax: 812 232-3402
Lisa Gonzales, *Vice Pres*
Michelle Naugle, *Sales Staff*
Anna Wetnight,
Laurie Taylor,
Kris Toney, *Associate*
EMP: 13
SQ FT: 40,000
SALES: 2.8MM **Privately Held**
WEB: www.internationallabelmfg.com
SIC: 2752 2759 2761 Commercial printing, offset; labels & seals: printing; manifold business forms

(G-13259)
INTERNATIONAL PAPER COMPANY
320 S 25th St Ste 2 (47803-2232)
PHONE..................................800 643-7244
Doug Roberts, *Branch Mgr*

EMP: 27
SALES (corp-wide): 21.7B **Publicly Held**
WEB: www.internationalpaper.com
SIC: 2621 2672 2611 2653 Paper mills; printing paper; text paper; bristols; coated & laminated paper; pulp mills; boxes, corrugated: made from purchased materials; food containers (liquid tight), including milk cartons; cartons, milk: made from purchased material; container, packaging & boxboard; container board; packaging board
PA: International Paper Company
6400 Poplar Ave
Memphis TN 38197
901 419-9000

(G-13260)
JADCORE LLC
Also Called: Premier Compounding
300 N Fruitridge Ave A (47803-1330)
PHONE..................................812 234-2724
Fax: 812 232-4203
David C Doti, *President*
David Doti, *Vice Pres*
Chuck Wells, *Plant Mgr*
Larry Drake, *Maint Spvr*
Terry Frandsen, *CFO*
◆ EMP: 200
SQ FT: 680,000
SALES (est): 79.6MM **Privately Held**
WEB: www.jadcore.com
SIC: 3089 4225 5162 4212 Plastic containers, except foam; general warehousing; plastics materials & basic shapes; local trucking, without storage; bags: plastic, laminated & coated

(G-13261)
JONES & SONS INC
3527 Erie Canal Rd (47802-9115)
PHONE..................................812 299-2287
Fax: 812 298-8107
Kurt Jones, *Manager*
EMP: 23
SALES (corp-wide): 20.3MM **Privately Held**
SIC: 3273 5083 3272 1711 Ready-mixed concrete; landscaping equipment; concrete products, precast; septic system construction
PA: Jones & Sons, Inc.
1262 S State Road 57
Washington IN 47501
812 254-4731

(G-13262)
JONES FABRICATION & MACHINING
5600 N Us Highway 41 (47805-9303)
PHONE..................................812 466-2237
Ronald Miller, *President*
Jeff Kackley, *General Mgr*
Bryan Kaufman, *Admin Sec*
EMP: 39
SALES (est): 9.1MM **Privately Held**
SIC: 3541 Milling machines

(G-13263)
JWS MACHINE INC
501 S Airport St (47803-9705)
PHONE..................................812 917-5571
Fax: 812 442-1998
Jeff Stark, *CEO*
Eric Stark, *COO*
Andy Frye, *Engineer*
Lori L Stark, *CFO*
Lori Stark, *CFO*
EMP: 47
SQ FT: 88,000
SALES (est): 8.3MM **Privately Held**
SIC: 3599 Machine shop, jobbing & repair

(G-13264)
KBSHIMMER BATH AND BODY INC
2820 S State Road 63 (47802-8798)
PHONE..................................317 979-2307
Jason Rose, *President*
Christina Rose, *Vice Pres*
EMP: 2
SALES (est): 221.2K **Privately Held**
SIC: 2844 Cosmetic preparations

(G-13265)
KELLY METAL PRODUCTS INC
1415 E Pugh Dr (47802-3978)
PHONE..................................812 232-1221
Fax: 812 232-2815
Lawrence Kelly, *President*
Susan Kelly, *Corp Secy*
Robert J Kelly, *Vice Pres*
EMP: 8
SQ FT: 10,000
SALES: 669.5K **Privately Held**
WEB: www.kellymetalproducts.net
SIC: 3599 5051 Machine & other job shop work; steel

(G-13266)
KLEPTZ ALUMINUM INC
Also Called: Kleptz Aluminum & Vinyl Pdts
1135 Poplar St (47807-4597)
PHONE..................................812 238-2946
Fax: 812 238-2145
Frank A Kleptz, *President*
David Kleptz, *Treasurer*
EMP: 9 EST: 1960
SQ FT: 50,000
SALES (est): 2.1MM **Privately Held**
SIC: 5031 5211 3442 Building materials, exterior; doors; windows; doors, storm: wood or metal; windows, storm: wood or metal; siding; metal doors, sash & trim

(G-13267)
KOSTYO WOODWORKING INC
3399 Fort Harrison Rd (47804-1758)
PHONE..................................812 466-7350
Steve Kostyo, *President*
EMP: 5
SQ FT: 6,000
SALES (est): 712.9K **Privately Held**
SIC: 2431 1799 1751 Millwork; counter top installation; cabinet & finish carpentry
PA: Specialty Bottlers Inc
2155 N 13th St # 57
Terre Haute IN

(G-13268)
KUSTOM KILNS 5 LLC
1400 E Polymer Dr (47802-9202)
PHONE..................................260 820-3636
EMP: 2
SALES (est): 270K **Privately Held**
SIC: 3559 Mfg Misc Industry Machinery

(G-13269)
LAMARVIS INDUSTRIES LLC
1429 S 13th 1/2 St (47802-1407)
PHONE..................................317 797-0483
EMP: 2
SALES (est): 84.3K **Privately Held**
SIC: 3999 Manufacturing industries

(G-13270)
LAMI-CRAFTS INC
2806 S 7th St (47802-3888)
PHONE..................................812 232-3012
Fax: 812 232-3012
Michael Burk, *President*
EMP: 5 EST: 1963
SQ FT: 5,000
SALES: 300K **Privately Held**
SIC: 2434 1751 Wood kitchen cabinets; counter & sink tops

(G-13271)
LAMINATED TOPS OF TERRE HAUTE
700 N 5th St (47807-1906)
PHONE..................................812 235-2920
Fax: 812 232-1763
Margaret Ann Lemont, *Owner*
EMP: 4
SQ FT: 8,000
SALES: 2.5MM **Privately Held**
WEB: www.laminatedtops.com
SIC: 2521 5211 1799 Cabinets, office: wood; tables, office: wood; cabinets, kitchen; counter top installation

(G-13272)
LARRY H POOLE
Also Called: Gear Up Awards
7826 E Rose Hill Ave (47805-9703)
PHONE..................................812 466-9345
Larry H Poole, *Owner*
EMP: 2

SALES (est): 80K **Privately Held**
SIC: 3479 5999 Engraving jewelry silverware, or metal; trophies & plaques

(G-13273)
LAWRENCO STEEL INC
4000 E Evans Ave (47805-9548)
PHONE..................................812 466-7115
Fax: 812 466-7915
Scott A Lawrence, *President*
EMP: 7
SQ FT: 20,000
SALES (est): 990K **Privately Held**
SIC: 3441 Fabricated structural metal

(G-13274)
LENEX STEEL COMPANY
2325 S 6th St (47802-3018)
PHONE..................................317 818-1622
Fax: 812 232-8322
Kevin Williams, *Purchasing*
Mark Phillips, *Branch Mgr*
EMP: 41
SALES (corp-wide): 9.1MM **Privately Held**
SIC: 5051 3444 Steel; sheet metalwork
PA: Lenex Steel Company
450 E 96th St Ste 100
Indianapolis IN 46240
317 818-1622

(G-13275)
LINDE GAS NORTH AMERICA LLC
834 S 10th St (47807-4901)
PHONE..................................888 345-0894
JP Deaton, *Manager*
EMP: 7
SALES (corp-wide): 20.1B **Privately Held**
SIC: 3829 Breathalyzers
HQ: Linde Gas North America Llc
200 Somerset Corp Blvd # 7000
Bridgewater NJ 08807

(G-13276)
LSC COMMUNICATIONS INC
200 Hulman St (47802-1042)
PHONE..................................812 234-1585
Greg Ruddell, *Branch Mgr*
EMP: 2
SALES (corp-wide): 3.6B **Publicly Held**
SIC: 2732 Book printing
PA: Lsc Communications, Inc.
191 N Wacker Dr Ste 1400
Chicago IL 60606
773 272-9200

(G-13277)
MACHINE TOOL SERVICE INC
117 Elm St (47807-1998)
PHONE..................................812 232-1912
Fax: 812 232-5664
Forrest Jim Perry, *President*
Samuel Hoar, *Vice Pres*
Brad Perry, *Director*
Bruce Hines, *Admin Sec*
EMP: 14 EST: 1965
SQ FT: 20,000
SALES: 1MM **Privately Held**
WEB: www.machinetoolservice.com
SIC: 3599 5084 Machine shop, jobbing & repair; industrial machinery & equipment

(G-13278)
MAHER SUPPLY INC
Also Called: Maher Cnstr Roofg & Siding
910 N 10th St (47807-1525)
PHONE..................................812 234-7699
Thomas R Maher, *President*
Marcia Maher, *Admin Sec*
EMP: 30
SQ FT: 60,000
SALES: 2MM **Privately Held**
WEB: www.maher-northside.com
SIC: 5211 1761 3442 1521 Lumber & other building materials; roofing contractor; siding contractor; storm doors or windows, metal; shutters, door or window: metal; general remodeling, single-family houses

(G-13279)
MARY DUNCAN
Also Called: Embroidery Express
601 W Honey Creek Dr (47802-2218)
PHONE..................................812 238-3637

Fax: 812 917-4103
Mary Duncan, *Owner*
EMP: 11
SQ FT: 4,000
SALES (est): 390K **Privately Held**
SIC: 2395 Embroidery products, except schiffli machine

(G-13280)
MASCHINO WOODWORKS
739 N Forest Dr (47803-4216)
PHONE.....................................812 230-7428
Craig Maschino, *Principal*
EMP: 2
SALES (est): 165.5K **Privately Held**
SIC: 2431 Millwork

(G-13281)
MBC CEREAL FINES INC
9748 S Carlisle St (47802-9625)
PHONE.....................................812 299-2191
Fax: 812 299-9866
Bary Cown, *President*
Donald J Cowan, *President*
Cheryl Mercker, *Corp Secy*
Barry Cowan, *Vice Pres*
EMP: 9
SQ FT: 6,000
SALES: 1.8MM **Privately Held**
SIC: 3999 Pet supplies

(G-13282)
MENARD INC
Also Called: Midwest Manufacturing
4600 N 13th St (47805-1602)
PHONE.....................................812 466-1234
EMP: 668
SALES (corp-wide): 13B **Privately Held**
SIC: 2499 2421 3444 3271 Fencing, wood; building & structural materials, wood; roof deck, sheet metal; blocks, concrete: landscape or retaining wall; design services
PA: Menard, Inc.
    5101 Menard Dr
    Eau Claire WI 54703
    715 876-5911

(G-13283)
MERIDIAN BRICK LLC
5601 E Price Dr (47802-8527)
PHONE.....................................812 894-2454
Greg Camp, *Manager*
EMP: 29
SALES (corp-wide): 441MM **Privately Held**
WEB: www.boralbricks.com
SIC: 3251 Brick & structural clay tile
PA: Meridian Brick Llc
    6455 Shiloh Rd D
    Alpharetta GA 30005
    770 645-4500

(G-13284)
MERVIS INDUSTRIES INC
Also Called: Goodman & Wolfe
830 S 13th St (47807)
PHONE.....................................812 232-1251
Fax: 812 234-9066
Cindy Lewis, *Opers Mgr*
Brian Munk, *Safety Mgr*
Tom Haley, *Branch Mgr*
EMP: 15
SALES (corp-wide): 161.2MM **Privately Held**
SIC: 5093 3341 4953 Metal scrap & waste materials; secondary nonferrous metals; recycling, waste materials
PA: Mervis Industries, Inc.
    3295 E Main St Ste C
    Danville IL 61834
    217 442-5300

(G-13285)
MIDWEST PRINTING
1925 S 13th St (47802-2411)
P.O. Box 6125 (47802-6125)
PHONE.....................................812 238-1641
Cecilia Meyers, *President*
EMP: 2
SALES (est): 288.2K **Privately Held**
SIC: 2752 Commercial printing, lithographic

(G-13286)
MIKRO FURNITURE
Also Called: Welcome Friends
7975 E Chandler Ave (47803-7700)
PHONE.....................................812 877-9550
Michael D Roe, *Owner*
EMP: 2
SALES: 90K **Privately Held**
SIC: 2426 Hardwood dimension & flooring mills

(G-13287)
MODERN WELDING & BOILER WORKS
3500 Plum St (47803-1133)
P.O. Box 3106 (47803-0106)
PHONE.....................................812 232-5039
Fax: 812 232-6386
Terry Sanders, *President*
Chris Sanders, *Vice Pres*
EMP: 2
SQ FT: 52,000
SALES (est): 287.9K **Privately Held**
SIC: 3441 Fabricated structural metal

(G-13288)
N E W INTERSTATE CONCRETE INC
2223 E Margaret Dr (47802-3338)
PHONE.....................................812 234-5983
Fax: 812 232-2380
N Cameron White, *President*
Preston White, *Vice Pres*
Pam White, *Treasurer*
Michelle Naimola-Hunter, *Info Tech Mgr*
EMP: 10
SQ FT: 9,500
SALES (est): 2MM **Privately Held**
SIC: 3273 Ready-mixed concrete

(G-13289)
NEOTERIC INCORPORATED
Also Called: Neoteric Hovercraft
1649 Tippecanoe St (47807-2345)
PHONE.....................................812 234-1120
Fax: 812 234-3217
Christopher Fitzgerald, *President*
Jerry Hay, *Director*
Dennis Meng, *Director*
Steven Songer, *Director*
Barbara R Johnson, *Admin Sec*
▲ EMP: 11
SQ FT: 10,000
SALES: 1.7MM **Privately Held**
WEB: www.neoterichovercraft.com
SIC: 3732 Boat building & repairing

(G-13290)
NEWSPAPER HOLDING INC
Also Called: Tribune Star
222 S 7th St (47807-3601)
P.O. Box 149 (47808)
PHONE.....................................812 231-4200
Fax: 812 231-4321
Jeremiah Turner, *Principal*
EMP: 56 **Privately Held**
WEB: www.clintonnc.com
SIC: 2711 Newspapers: publishing only, not printed on site
HQ: Newspaper Holding, Inc.
    425 Locust St
    Johnstown PA 15901
    814 532-5102

(G-13291)
NOVELIS CORPORATION
5901 N 13th St (47805-1695)
P.O. Box 1607 (47808)
PHONE.....................................812 462-2287
Stan Miles, *Plant Mgr*
Joe Wright, *Opers Mgr*
Chris Koszewski, *Opers-Prdtn-Mfg*
Clay Cooke, *Engineer*
Wayne Jeffers, *Engineer*
EMP: 250
SALES (corp-wide): 6.7B **Privately Held**
SIC: 3353 3444 5051 Aluminum sheet & strip; foil, aluminum; sheet metalwork; aluminum bars, rods, ingots, sheets, pipes, plates, etc.
HQ: Novelis Corporation
    3560 Lenox Rd Ne Ste 2000
    Atlanta GA 30326
    404 760-4000

(G-13292)
NRK INC
1126 S 13th St (47802-1410)
PHONE.....................................812 232-1800
Randy Keyes, *President*
Amy K Land, *Admin Sec*
EMP: 45
SQ FT: 10,000
SALES (est): 7.9MM **Privately Held**
WEB: www.nrkinc.com
SIC: 1731 3699 General electrical contractor; security control equipment & systems

(G-13293)
NUMERICAL CONCEPTS INC
4040 1st Pkwy (47804-4298)
PHONE.....................................812 466-5261
Fax: 812 466-1663
Nancy Seidel Jones, *President*
Steve Turner, *Plant Mgr*
Randy Butrum, *QC Mgr*
Paul White, *Manager*
EMP: 85
SQ FT: 76,000
SALES (est): 19.6MM **Privately Held**
WEB: www.numericalconcepts.com
SIC: 3555 3599 Printing trades machinery; machine shop, jobbing & repair

(G-13294)
OHIO TRANSMISSION CORPORATION
Also Called: Otp Industrial Solutions
1502 Lafayette Ave (47804-2504)
PHONE.....................................812 466-2734
Fax: 812 466-2831
Rod Garing, *Branch Mgr*
Brett Brown, *Manager*
EMP: 8 **Privately Held**
WEB: www.otpnet.com
SIC: 7629 3561 3536 Electrical repair shops; pumps & pumping equipment; hoists, cranes & monorails
HQ: Ohio Transmission Corporation
    1900 Jetway Blvd
    Columbus OH 43219
    614 342-6247

(G-13295)
P & M FABRICATION
2820 S Center St (47802-3842)
PHONE.....................................812 232-7640
Melvin Ennen, *Owner*
EMP: 2
SALES (est): 52.8K **Privately Held**
SIC: 3999 Manufacturing industries

(G-13296)
PARTY CASK
Also Called: Party Cask Southeast
1652 S 25th St (47803-3623)
PHONE.....................................812 234-3008
Don Thompson, *Owner*
EMP: 2
SALES (est): 262K **Privately Held**
SIC: 5921 2086 Liquor stores; bottled & canned soft drinks

(G-13297)
PATRICK & SHARON HOCTOR
Also Called: Animal Finders Guide
13469 S Trueblood Pl (47802-9195)
P.O. Box 99, Prairie Creek (47869-0099)
PHONE.....................................812 898-2678
Fax: 812 898-2013
Patrick Hoctor, *Owner*
Sharon Hoctor, *Co-Owner*
EMP: 3
SQ FT: 1,540
SALES (est): 99K **Privately Held**
SIC: 0752 5154 2711 5074 Breeding services, pet & animal specialties (not horses); livestock; newspapers, publishing & printing; stoves, wood burning; masonry & other stonework

(G-13298)
PATRIOT LABEL INC
9192 E Us Highway 40 (47803)
PHONE.....................................812 877-1611
Jack Kirchner, *President*
EMP: 4
SALES (est): 450K **Privately Held**
SIC: 2679 Tags & labels, paper

(G-13299)
PEACE LOVE CUPCAKES
3833 N 25th St (47805-2936)
PHONE.....................................812 239-1591
Rhonda Noe, *Principal*
EMP: 4
SALES (est): 181.9K **Privately Held**
SIC: 2051 Bread, cake & related products

(G-13300)
PEACE VALLEY CABINETS INC
1111 E Royse Dr (47802-4173)
PHONE.....................................812 238-5134
Scott Mundell, *Principal*
EMP: 2
SALES (est): 222.3K **Privately Held**
SIC: 2434 Wood kitchen cabinets

(G-13301)
PFIZER INC
411 E Dallas Dr (47802-8035)
PHONE.....................................212 733-2323
Fax: 812 299-6007
Ed Grey, *Opers-Prdtn-Mfg*
Julie Harpenau, *Human Res Dir*
Mr C Hutz, *Persnl Mgr*
Dennis West, *Senior Mgr*
Jeff Hamilton, *Info Tech Mgr*
EMP: 600
SALES (corp-wide): 52.5B **Publicly Held**
WEB: www.pfizer.com
SIC: 2833 2834 2865 8731 Medicinals & botanicals; pharmaceutical preparations; biological stains; commercial physical research
PA: Pfizer Inc.
    235 E 42nd St
    New York NY 10017
    212 733-2323

(G-13302)
PHOENIX COLOR CORP
200 Hulman St (47802-1042)
PHONE.....................................812 234-1585
EMP: 90 **Publicly Held**
SIC: 2752 Commercial printing, offset
HQ: Phoenix Color Corp.
    18249 Phoenix Rd
    Hagerstown MD 21742
    301 733-0018

(G-13303)
PHOENIX COLOR CORP
Also Called: M L X Graphics
200 Hulman St (47802-1042)
PHONE.....................................812 238-1551
Fax: 812 235-2926
Brian Brough, *Manager*
EMP: 10
SQ FT: 2,900 **Publicly Held**
WEB: www.moorelangen.com
SIC: 2752 Commercial printing, offset
HQ: Phoenix Color Corp.
    18249 Phoenix Rd
    Hagerstown MD 21742
    301 733-0018

(G-13304)
PLM HOLDINGS INC
3956 S State Road 63 (47802-8747)
P.O. Box 10038 (47801-0038)
PHONE.....................................812 232-0624
Fax: 812 234-2087
Percy L Mossbarger, *President*
William N Mossbarger, *Admin Sec*
EMP: 45
SQ FT: 8,000
SALES (est): 7MM
SALES (corp-wide): 12.4MM **Privately Held**
SIC: 2421 Sawmills & planing mills, general
PA: Maley & Wertz Inc.
    900 E Columbia St
    Evansville IN 47711
    812 425-3358

(G-13305)
POLYONE CORPORATION
3915 1st Pkwy (47804-4234)
PHONE.....................................812 466-5116
EMP: 7 **Publicly Held**
SIC: 2821 3087 Thermoplastic materials; custom compound purchased resins

▲ = Import ▼=Export
◆ =Import/Export

PA: Polyone Corporation
33587 Walker Rd
Avon Lake OH 44012

(G-13306)
PPG INDUSTRIES INC
Also Called: PPG 4378
1700 Wabash Ave (47807-3323)
PHONE..................................812 232-0672
Lisa Dashiell, *Branch Mgr*
EMP: 24
SALES (corp-wide): 14.2B **Publicly Held**
WEB: www.ppg.com
SIC: 2851 Paints & allied products
PA: Ppg Industries, Inc.
1 Ppg Pl
Pittsburgh PA 15272
412 434-3131

(G-13307)
PRAIRIE GROUP
Also Called: Perry Material Sales
5222 E Margaret Dr (47803-9319)
PHONE..................................812 877-9886
Fax: 812 877-6230
Tom Plant, *Manager*
EMP: 20
SALES (est): 2MM **Privately Held**
SIC: 3273 5211 Ready-mixed concrete;
brick

(G-13308)
**PRECISION LABEL
INCORPORATED**
8890 E Davis Ave (47805-7964)
P.O. Box 397, Seelyville (47878-0397)
PHONE..................................812 877-3811
Fax: 812 877-4824
Randall Bland, *President*
Darrell Bland, *Vice Pres*
EMP: 11
SQ FT: 6,000
SALES (est): 1.6MM **Privately Held**
SIC: 2672 2759 Labels (unprinted),
gummed: made from purchased materi-
als; commercial printing

(G-13309)
PRESSTIME GRAPHICS INC
1016 Poplar St (47807-3820)
PHONE..................................812 234-3815
Fax: 812 234-4131
Joseph Selliken, *President*
Paul Akers, *Vice Pres*
Cathy Fox, *Vice Pres*
Marsha Hay, *Sales Staff*
Steve Linn, *Marketing Staff*
EMP: 20
SQ FT: 14,800
SALES (est): 2.9MM **Privately Held**
WEB: www.presstime.com
SIC: 2752 7331 2791 2789 Commercial
printing, offset; direct mail advertising
services; typesetting; bookbinding & re-
lated work; commercial printing

(G-13310)
**PRODUCTION MACHINING
COMPANY**
4850 N 13th St (47805-1600)
PHONE..................................812 466-2885
Fax: 812 466-2885
Thomas J Haverkamp, *President*
EMP: 7
SQ FT: 10,000
SALES (est): 918K **Privately Held**
SIC: 3451 Screw machine products

(G-13311)
PROX COMPANY INC
1179 E Garden Dr S (47802-9360)
PHONE..................................812 232-4324
Fax: 812 232-4325
EMP: 15 EST: 1875
SQ FT: 35,000
SALES: 1.5MM **Privately Held**
SIC: 3532 3568 3462 3312 Mfg Mining
Machinery Mfg Power Transmsn Equip
Mfg Iron/Steel Forgings Blast Furnace-
Steel Work

(G-13312)
**PRUETT MANUFACTURING CO
INC**
3953 Trey Cir (47803-3583)
PHONE..................................812 234-9497
Fax: 812 232-5245
Shirley A Pruett, *President*
Peggy Evans, *Corp Secy*
Tom Barnett Exec, *Vice Pres*
EMP: 18
SQ FT: 26,000
SALES: 2MM **Privately Held**
WEB: www.pruettmanufacturing.com
SIC: 3469 7692 3568 3471 Stamping
metal for the trade; welding repair; power
transmission equipment; plating & polish-
ing; fabricated plate work (boiler shop)

(G-13313)
QUICK PANIC RELEASE LLC
2216 Dutch Ln (47802-2754)
PHONE..................................812 841-5733
Jeff Bensinger, *Mng Member*
EMP: 2
SALES (est): 87.1K **Privately Held**
SIC: 3699 Security devices

(G-13314)
RACO INDUSTRIES LLC
1607 Maple Ave (47804-3234)
PHONE..................................812 232-3676
Greg Morris, *Design Engr*
EMP: 2
SALES (est): 85.9K **Privately Held**
SIC: 3596 Scales & balances, except labo-
ratory

(G-13315)
**RANKIN PUMP AND SUPPLY CO
INC**
130 N 11th St (47807-2796)
PHONE..................................812 238-2535
Fax: 812 238-2536
Thomas G Rankin Jr, *President*
EMP: 8
SQ FT: 6,000
SALES (est): 1.3MM **Privately Held**
WEB: www.rankinecowater.com
SIC: 3561 5084 5051 5085 Pumps &
pumping equipment; pumps & pumping
equipment; cable, wire; industrial fittings;
pumps & pumping equipment repair

(G-13316)
RECOGNITION PLUS
25 S 6th St (47807-3510)
PHONE..................................812 232-2372
Fax: 812 235-7717
Jim Pendergast, *President*
EMP: 6 EST: 1944
SQ FT: 12,000
SALES (est): 680K **Privately Held**
SIC: 5999 3993 Trophies & plaques; signs
& advertising specialties

(G-13317)
RECONSERVE OF INDIANA
1150 E Harlan Dr (47802-9147)
PHONE..................................310 458-1574
Frank Renderknecht, *Plant Mgr*
EMP: 8
SALES (est): 934.2K **Privately Held**
SIC: 2048 Livestock feeds

(G-13318)
REFRESHMENT SERVICES INC
Pepsico
3875 4th Pkwy (47804-4256)
PHONE..................................812 466-0602
Fax: 812 466-0503
Gloria Chambers, *Manager*
EMP: 50
SALES (corp-wide): 88.8MM **Privately
Held**
SIC: 5962 2086 Merchandising machine
operators; carbonated beverages, nonal-
coholic: bottled & canned
PA: Refreshment Services, Inc.
1121 Locust St
Quincy IL 62301
217 223-8600

(G-13319)
REYNOLDS & CO INC
1916 S 25th St (47802-2799)
PHONE..................................812 232-5313
Fax: 812 232-5311
Gerald S Reynolds, *President*
Kevin Collenbaugh, *Vice Pres*
Jean Reynolds, *Admin Sec*
EMP: 21 EST: 1946
SQ FT: 17,000
SALES (est): 3.8MM **Privately Held**
WEB: www.reynoldsandco.com
SIC: 3599 7699 Custom machinery; indus-
trial machinery & equipment repair

(G-13320)
REYNOLDS NORTH
1025 N Fruitridge Ave (47804-1770)
PHONE..................................812 235-5313
Tom Albright, *General Mgr*
Gerry Reynolds, *Principal*
EMP: 2
SALES (est): 150.5K **Privately Held**
SIC: 3599 Machine shop, jobbing & repair

(G-13321)
RK MACHINE INC
Also Called: A-1 Machine
3170 N 25th St (47804-1610)
PHONE..................................812 466-0550
Fax: 812 466-0549
Ronald C Miller Jr, *President*
Karey Miller, *General Mgr*
EMP: 19
SQ FT: 15,000
SALES (est): 3.4MM **Privately Held**
SIC: 3599 Machine shop, jobbing & repair

(G-13322)
S & G EXCAVATING INC (PA)
545 E Margaret Dr (47802-3795)
PHONE..................................812 234-4848
Fax: 812 234-4858
Kenneth E Steiner Jr, *President*
Jack D Steiner, *Corp Secy*
EMP: 60 EST: 1956
SQ FT: 2,000
SALES (est): 16.9MM **Privately Held**
SIC: 1429 1442 1794 Trap rock, crushed
& broken-quarrying; construction sand &
gravel; excavation work

(G-13323)
S & T FULFILLMENT LLC
351 S Airport St (47803-9705)
P.O. Box 2244 (47802-0244)
PHONE..................................812 466-4900
Thomas J Lee,
Shermannah C Lee,
▲ EMP: 19
SALES (est): 3.1MM **Privately Held**
SIC: 3953 Marking devices

(G-13324)
SHENANGO LLC
1200 College Ave (47802-1496)
PHONE..................................812 235-2058
Bob Staley, *VP Opers*
Jeremy Hartle, *Opers Mgr*
R Dixon Hayes,
Robert Staley,
EMP: 14
SQ FT: 12,000
SALES (est): 2.4MM **Privately Held**
SIC: 3325 Alloy steel castings, except in-
vestment

(G-13325)
**SHERWOOD-TEMPLETON COAL
CO INC**
701 Wabash Ave Ste 501 (47807-3219)
PHONE..................................812 232-7037
Thomas E Templeton, *President*
David J Wulf, *Vice Pres*
Tomas W Thomas, *Treasurer*
Thomas W Higgins, *Director*
Andrew Myers, *Director*
EMP: 7 EST: 1929
SQ FT: 4,000
SALES (est): 1MM
SALES (corp-wide): 162.5MM **Privately
Held**
WEB: www.glascol.com
SIC: 3567 Heating units & devices, indus-
trial: electric

PA: Templeton Coal Company, Inc.
701 Wabash Ave Ste 501
Terre Haute IN 47807
812 232-7037

(G-13326)
SIGNCENTER INC
333 N Fruitridge Ave (47803-1329)
PHONE..................................812 232-4994
Fax: 812 232-1420
John B Criss, *President*
Helene C Steppe, *Corp Secy*
EMP: 5
SQ FT: 8,300
SALES: 676.9K **Privately Held**
WEB: www.thesigncenter.com
SIC: 3993 1799 Electric signs; sign instal-
lation & maintenance

(G-13327)
SIMMA SOFTWARE INC
5940 S Ernest St (47802-8114)
PHONE..................................812 418-0526
Thomas Simma Jr, *President*
EMP: 2
SALES (est): 198.6K **Privately Held**
SIC: 7372 Business oriented computer
software

(G-13328)
SIMPLE TO ELEGANT
1601 S 3rd St (47802-1013)
P.O. Box 3693 (47803-0693)
PHONE..................................812 234-8700
Jeanette Winchester, *Owner*
EMP: 6
SALES (est): 450.7K **Privately Held**
WEB: www.simpletoelegant.com
SIC: 2335 7299 Wedding gowns &
dresses; miscellaneous personal service

(G-13329)
SMITH SMALL ENGINE SERVICE
Also Called: Smith's Small Engines
1515 N 25th St (47803-1076)
PHONE..................................812 232-1318
James Smith, *Owner*
EMP: 4
SQ FT: 6,000
SALES (est): 429.1K **Privately Held**
WEB: www.smithsse.com
SIC: 3599 7699 3469 Machine shop, job-
bing & repair; engine repair & replace-
ment, non-automotive; lawn mower repair
shop; metal stampings

(G-13330)
**SMITHS AROSPC COMPONENTS
HAUTE**
333 S 3rd St (47807-3410)
PHONE..................................812 235-5210
James Donohue, *Plant Mgr*
EMP: 3 EST: 2008
SALES (est): 291.3K **Privately Held**
SIC: 3724 Aircraft engines & engine parts

(G-13331)
SOIL-MAX INC
1201 S 1st St (47802-1907)
PHONE..................................888 764-5629
Al Myers, *President*
Lynda Bell, *Vice Pres*
Brian Dewey, *Manager*
Michael Kane, *Manager*
▼ EMP: 34
SALES (est): 7.2MM **Privately Held**
WEB: www.soilmax.com
SIC: 3523 Plows, agricultural: disc, mold-
board, chisel, listers, etc.
PA: Ag Leader Technology, Inc.
2202 S Riverside Dr
Ames IA 50010

(G-13332)
**SONY CORPORATION OF
AMERICA**
1800 N Fruitridge Ave (47804-1780)
PHONE..................................812 462-8726
Pamela Kar, *Principal*
EMP: 2
SALES (est): 97.2K **Privately Held**
SIC: 3695 Magnetic & optical recording
media

(G-13333)
SONY DADC US INC
3181 N Fruitridge Ave (47804-1700)
PHONE......................................812 462-8116
James M Frische, *President*
EMP: 27
SALES (corp-wide): 80.1B **Privately Held**
SIC: 3695 Optical disks & tape, blank
HQ: Sony Dadc Us Inc.
　　1800 N Fruitridge Ave
　　Terre Haute IN 47804
　　812 462-8100

(G-13334)
SONY DADC US INC (DH)
1800 N Fruitridge Ave (47804-1780)
P.O. Box 3710 (47803-0710)
PHONE......................................812 462-8100
Fax: 812 462-8866
David Rubenstein, *President*
Michael Frey, *President*
Warren Maccaroni, *Vice Pres*
Wallace R Page, *Treasurer*
▲ EMP: 1100
SQ FT: 250,000
SALES (est): 303MM
SALES (corp-wide): 80.1B **Privately Held**
SIC: 3695 3652 3651 3577 Optical disks
& tape, blank; compact laser discs, prere-
corded; household audio & video equip-
ment; computer peripheral equipment;
computer storage devices
HQ: Sony Corporation Of America
　　25 Madison Ave Fl 27
　　New York NY 10010
　　212 833-8000

(G-13335)
SONY DADC US INC
1600 N Fruitridge Ave (47804-1792)
PHONE......................................812 462-8784
EMP: 386
SALES (corp-wide): 80.1B **Privately Held**
SIC: 3695 Optical disks & tape, blank
HQ: Sony Dadc Us Inc.
　　1800 N Fruitridge Ave
　　Terre Haute IN 47804
　　812 462-8100

(G-13336)
**SOUDER POWER WASHING
LLC**
7425 E Troy Ct (47802-9565)
PHONE......................................812 894-2544
William A Kirchner, *Principal*
EMP: 2
SALES (est): 177.6K **Privately Held**
SIC: 3633 Washing machines, household:
including coin-operated

(G-13337)
SPARKLE POOLS INC
2225 N 25th St (47804-3698)
PHONE......................................812 232-1292
Fax: 812 232-5725
Thomas Sedletzeck, *President*
Marti Trimble, *Treasurer*
EMP: 15 EST: 1966
SQ FT: 4,500
SALES (est): 1MM **Privately Held**
WEB: www.sparklepoolsonline.com
SIC: 1799 3949 5091 5999 Swimming
pool construction; swimming pools, plas-
tic; swimming pools, equipment & sup-
plies; swimming pool chemicals,
equipment & supplies

(G-13338)
**SPECIALTY RIM SUPPLY INC
(PA)**
500 S 9th St (47807-4420)
PHONE......................................812 234-3002
Richard Cuvelier, *CEO*
Kevin Bishop, *President*
Willie Bryant, *Plant Mgr*
Stephanie Griffin, *CFO*
Shawn Mc Nair, *Controller*
▼ EMP: 5
SALES (est): 1MM **Privately Held**
SIC: 3465 Body parts, automobile:
stamped metal

(G-13339)
SPECTACULAR SOIREES
2270 Ohio Blvd (47803-2162)
PHONE......................................812 841-4311
Janice Board, *Principal*
EMP: 5
SALES (est): 427.6K **Privately Held**
SIC: 2335 Wedding gowns & dresses

(G-13340)
SPECTRUM INDUSTRY
500 8th Ave (47804-4072)
P.O. Box 4323 (47804-0323)
PHONE......................................812 231-8355
Mary Clark, *Principal*
EMP: 2
SALES (est): 197.9K **Privately Held**
SIC: 3825 Spectrum analyzers

(G-13341)
SPENCE/BANKS INC (PA)
Also Called: Automated Fuels
700 N 1st St (47807-1923)
P.O. Box 2009 (47802-0009)
PHONE......................................812 234-3538
Fax: 812 234-2658
James D Owen, *President*
Tye Jefferies, *Manager*
EMP: 14 EST: 1979
SQ FT: 3,800
SALES: 11MM **Privately Held**
WEB: www.spencebanks.com
SIC: 2992 5172 5983 Lubricating oils; pe-
troleum products; fuel oil dealers

(G-13342)
SPRINGHILL WHOLESALE INC
1430 E Springhill Dr (47802-4366)
PHONE......................................812 299-2181
Fax: 812 299-1435
Kenneth W Figg, *President*
Georgia Figg, *Vice Pres*
Bob Nicoson, *Vice Pres*
Gary Figg, *Treasurer*
Mike Figg, *Admin Sec*
EMP: 26
SQ FT: 24,000
SALES: 2MM **Privately Held**
WEB: www.springhillwhsle.com
SIC: 2752 5699 5136 5651 Transfers,
decalcomania or dry: lithographed; T-
shirts, custom printed; shirts, men's &
boys'; family clothing stores; women's &
children's clothing

(G-13343)
SQUARE DONUTS INC
935 Wabash Ave (47807-3229)
PHONE......................................812 232-6463
Richard A Comer, *President*
Patricia Comer, *Treasurer*
Deninne Helton, *Manager*
EMP: 6 EST: 1954
SALES (est): 680.5K **Privately Held**
SIC: 2051 5461 Doughnuts, except
frozen; bakery: wholesale or
wholesale/retail combined; doughnuts

(G-13344)
STELLA JONES
2901 Ohio Blvd (47803-2239)
PHONE......................................812 232-2316
Stella Jones, *Principal*
EMP: 5
SALES (est): 728.5K **Privately Held**
SIC: 3743 Railroad equipment

(G-13345)
SUN CHEMICAL CORPORATION
1350 N Fruitridge Ave (47804-1716)
PHONE......................................812 235-8031
Fax: 812 466-9126
Rod Yamamoto, *COO*
Bruce Wilson, *Purch Mgr*
Charles Davidson, *Engineer*
William Murer, *Controller*
Mari Idland, *Human Res Dir*
EMP: 2
SALES (corp-wide): 7B **Privately Held**
WEB: www.sunchemical.com
SIC: 2893 Printing ink
HQ: Sun Chemical Corporation
　　35 Waterview Blvd Ste 100
　　Parsippany NJ 07054
　　973 404-6000

(G-13346)
SUNRISE COAL LLC (PA)
1183 E Canvasback Dr (47802-5304)
PHONE......................................812 299-2800
Fax: 812 398-2210
Brent K Bilsland, *President*
Lawrence D Martin, *President*
Ronald E Laswell, *Vice Pres*
Heather L Tryon, *CFO*
Henry K Bilsland,
EMP: 154
SQ FT: 1,500
SALES (est): 57.6MM **Privately Held**
SIC: 1222 Bituminous coal-underground
mining

(G-13347)
SYCAMORE COAL INC
Also Called: Vectren Fuels, Inc.
1183 E Canvasback Dr (47802-5304)
PHONE......................................812 491-4000
Fax: 812 491-4027
Carl Chapman, *President*
EMP: 1
SALES (est): 2.3MM
SALES (corp-wide): 57.6MM **Privately
Held**
SIC: 1241 Coal mining services
PA: Sunrise Coal, Llc
　　1183 E Canvasback Dr
　　Terre Haute IN 47802
　　812 299-2800

(G-13348)
TANGENT RAIL PRODUCTS INC
2901 Ohio Blvd Ste 252 (47803-2248)
PHONE......................................412 325-0202
Celeste Frazee, *Branch Mgr*
EMP: 28 **Privately Held**
SIC: 2491 3743 Wood preserving; railroad
equipment
HQ: Tangent Rail Products, Inc.
　　101 W Station Square Dr # 600
　　Pittsburgh PA 15219
　　412 325-0202

(G-13349)
TECHNICOTE INC
3200 N 25th St (47804-1602)
PHONE......................................812 466-9844
Fax: 812 466-5419
Tim Mundy, *Manager*
EMP: 75
SALES (corp-wide): 78.2MM **Privately
Held**
WEB: www.technicote.com
SIC: 2891 2851 Adhesives; paints & allied
products
PA: Technicote, Inc.
　　222 Mound Ave
　　Miamisburg OH 45342
　　800 358-4448

(G-13350)
**TEMPLETON COAL COMPANY
INC (PA)**
Also Called: Glas-Col Div
701 Wabash Ave Ste 501 (47807-3293)
P.O. Box 2128 (47802-0128)
PHONE......................................812 232-7037
Fax: 812 232-3752
Thomas E Templeton, *CEO*
Tomas Thomas, *Corp Secy*
Tom Thomas, *Treasurer*
Karen Elliott, *Accounting Mgr*
Jenny Samm, *Sales Staff*
EMP: 8 EST: 1920
SQ FT: 4,000
SALES (est): 162.5MM **Privately Held**
WEB: www.glascol.com
SIC: 5074 3567 3961 5049 Plumbing fit-
tings & supplies; heating equipment (hy-
dronic); heating units & devices,
industrial: electric; rosaries & small reli-
gious articles, except precious metal; reli-
gious supplies; injection molded finished
plastic products

(G-13351)
**TEMPLETON COAL COMPANY
INC**
Glas-Col Apparatus Division
711 Hulman St (47802-1629)
P.O. Box 2128 (47802-0128)
PHONE......................................812 232-7037

Fax: 812 234-6975
Tim Voll, *Design Engr*
Cathy Hopkins, *Accountant*
Jim Jacso, *Marketing Mgr*
Steve Sterredt, *Mng Member*
EMP: 90
SQ FT: 44,000
SALES (corp-wide): 162.5MM **Privately
Held**
WEB: www.glascol.com
SIC: 3585 3826 3821 3531 Heating
equipment, complete; analytical instru-
ments; laboratory apparatus & furniture;
construction machinery
PA: Templeton Coal Company, Inc.
　　701 Wabash Ave Ste 501
　　Terre Haute IN 47807
　　812 232-7037

(G-13352)
**TERRE HAUTE COCA-COLA
BTLG CO**
924 Lafayette Ave (47804-2930)
PHONE......................................812 232-9543
Fax: 812 232-8468
Barry Powell, *General Mgr*
EMP: 60 EST: 1983
SALES (est): 6.6MM **Privately Held**
SIC: 2086 Bottled & canned soft drinks

(G-13353)
**TERRE HAUTE WILBERT
BURIAL VLT**
509 E Preston St (47802-3576)
PHONE......................................812 235-0339
Fax: 812 232-0470
Timothy A Puttmann, *President*
▲ EMP: 12 EST: 1957
SQ FT: 13,800
SALES (est): 1.9MM **Privately Held**
SIC: 3272 3281 Burial vaults, concrete or
precast terrazzo; monuments, cut stone
(not finishing or lettering only)

(G-13354)
THIS & THAT PRODUCTS
3784 Hotel St (47802-8893)
PHONE......................................812 299-2688
Bob Dillion, *Owner*
EMP: 2
SALES (est): 77K **Privately Held**
SIC: 2499 Woodenware, kitchen & house-
hold

(G-13355)
TINAS CERAMICS & THINGS
1001 N 3rd St (47807-1829)
PHONE......................................812 917-4190
EMP: 2
SALES (est): 89.5K **Privately Held**
SIC: 3269 Pottery products

(G-13356)
TREDEGAR CORPORATION
Tredegar Film Products Div
3400 Fort Harrison Rd (47804-1799)
P.O. Box 1072 (47808)
PHONE......................................812 466-0266
Fax: 812 466-0225
Jim Sullivan, *Plant Mgr*
Chris Ladd, *Safety Mgr*
Donna Westerfield, *Purch Agent*
James Edington, *Engineer*
Michael Fisher, *Engineer*
EMP: 80
SALES (corp-wide): 1B **Publicly Held**
WEB: www.tredegar.com
SIC: 3354 3089 3081 Aluminum extruded
products; plastic processing; polyethylene
film
PA: Tredegar Corporation
　　1100 Boulders Pkwy # 200
　　North Chesterfield VA 23225
　　804 330-1000

(G-13357)
TRH SOFTWARE INC
1503 7th Ave (47807-1217)
PHONE......................................812 264-2428
Terry R Higgins, *Principal*
EMP: 2 EST: 2008
SALES (est): 101.8K **Privately Held**
SIC: 7372 Prepackaged software

▲ = Import ▼=Export
◆ =Import/Export

(G-13358)
TRI AEROSPACE LLC
1055 S Hunt St (47803-9702)
PHONE..................................812 872-2400
Fax: 812 877-3330
Robert Abernathy, *General Mgr*
Linda Carrithers, *Purch Mgr*
Brian Sydney, *Engineer*
David Abrams, *Marketing Mgr*
R Laurence Cross, *Manager*
EMP: 37
SQ FT: 27,000
SALES (est): 8.8MM Privately Held
WEB: www.triaerospace.com
SIC: 3724 3728 3714 3511 Aircraft en-
gines & engine parts; aircraft parts &
equipment; motor vehicle parts & acces-
sories; turbines & turbine generator sets;
screw machine products; machine shop,
jobbing & repair

(G-13359)
TURBINES INC
7303 Maynard Wheeler Ln (47803-9561)
PHONE..................................812 877-2587
James M Mills, *President*
Peggy Mills, *Treasurer*
EMP: 20
SQ FT: 13,200
SALES (est): 4.2MM Privately Held
WEB: www.turbinesinc.com
SIC: 4581 5088 3724 Aircraft cleaning &
janitorial service; transportation equip-
ment & supplies; aircraft engines & en-
gine parts

(G-13360)
VALLEY PRESS TC
629 S 9th St (47807-4421)
PHONE..................................812 234-8030
Toll Free:..................................888 -
Fax: 812 235-4230
Allan Thompson, *President*
Sharon Cupp, *Corp Secy*
EMP: 13
SQ FT: 5,000
SALES (est): 1.4MM Privately Held
WEB: www.valleypress.com
SIC: 7331 2752 Direct mail advertising
services; commercial printing, offset

(G-13361)
VCO INC
Also Called: Logo Connxtion
1210 Wabash Ave (47807-3312)
PHONE..................................812 235-3540
Toll Free:..................................877 -
Doug Lemond, *President*
Angie Lemond, *Vice Pres*
EMP: 6
SALES (est): 534.3K Privately Held
WEB: www.vco-edusa.net
SIC: 2395 Embroidery products, except
schiffli machine; embroidery & art needle-
work

(G-13362)
VIGO MACHINE SHOP INC
3920 Locust St (47803-1337)
PHONE..................................812 235-8393
Gary P Michl, *President*
Pat Michl, *Principal*
EMP: 25
SQ FT: 24,000
SALES (est): 6.6MM Privately Held
SIC: 3599 Machine shop, jobbing & repair

(G-13363)
VOGES MACHINE
Also Called: Voges Machine Shop
4876 W Kennett Dr (47802-9823)
PHONE..................................812 299-1546
David Voges, *Owner*
EMP: 3
SALES: 300K Privately Held
SIC: 3599 Machine shop, jobbing & repair

(G-13364)
VOGES RESTORATION AND WDWKG
5696 W Cantrell Dr (47802-9440)
PHONE..................................812 299-1546
David Voges, *Owner*
EMP: 4

SALES: 88K Privately Held
SIC: 2499 3449 Applicators, wood; miscellaneous metalwork

(G-13365)
WABASH VALLEY MAGAZINE
721 Wabash Ave Ste 411 (47807-3203)
PHONE..................................812 231-4294
Eric Weeks, *Principal*
EMP: 3
SALES (est): 282K Privately Held
SIC: 2721 Periodicals

(G-13366)
WABASH VALLEY MOTOR & MCH INC
3909 N Fruitridge Ave (47805-2350)
P.O. Box 5221 (47805-0221)
PHONE..................................812 466-7400
Lee Shippley, *President*
Greg Sutliff, *Sales Staff*
Jim Everhart, *Admin Sec*
EMP: 6
SQ FT: 10,000
SALES (est): 3.2MM Privately Held
SIC: 5063 7694 Motors, electric; electric
motor repair

(G-13367)
WABASH VALLEY PACKAGING CORP
1303 E Industrial Dr (47802-9275)
PHONE..................................812 299-7181
Ward M Hubbard, *President*
Curtis W Stephens, *Vice Pres*
EMP: 10
SALES (est): 2.1MM Privately Held
WEB: www.wabashvalleypkg.com
SIC: 2653 Boxes, corrugated: made from
purchased materials

(G-13368)
WESTFIELD STEEL INC
3345 Fort Harrison Rd (47804-1758)
PHONE..................................812 466-3500
Charles F Prine, *Branch Mgr*
EMP: 30
SALES (est): 3.1MM
SALES (corp-wide): 140.5MM Privately
Held
WEB: www.westfieldsteel.com
SIC: 5051 3441 Steel; fabricated structural
metal
PA: Westfield Steel Inc
530 W State Road 32
Westfield IN 46074
317 896-5587

(G-13369)
WHEELS IN SKY
1026 Monterey Ave (47803-2767)
PHONE..................................812 249-8233
Mike Wheeler, *Principal*
EMP: 2
SALES (est): 139.6K Privately Held
SIC: 3312 Blast furnaces & steel mills

(G-13370)
WINSLOW SCALE COMPANY
4530 N 25th St (47805-2513)
PHONE..................................812 466-5265
Fax: 812 466-1046
Walter Young, *CEO*
William K Fischer, *President*
EMP: 58
SQ FT: 80,000
SALES (est): 8.9MM
SALES (corp-wide): 14MM Privately
Held
WEB: www.emerywinslow.com
SIC: 3596 Industrial scales
PA: The A H Emery Company
73 Cogwheel Ln
Seymour CT 06483
203 881-9333

(G-13371)
WOODBURN GRAPHICS INC
25 S 6th St (47807-3510)
P.O. Box 9299 (47808-9299)
PHONE..................................812 232-0323
Fax: 812 232-2733
Marilyn Pendergast, *President*
James Pendergast, *Exec VP*
Curt Pendergast, *CFO*
Michael Pendergast, *Controller*

EMP: 43 EST: 1902
SQ FT: 62,000
SALES (est): 7MM Privately Held
WEB: www.woodburngraphics.com
SIC: 2752 2791 2789 2761 Commercial
printing, offset; typesetting; bookbinding &
related work; manifold business forms;
commercial printing

(G-13372)
X-TREME LAZER TAG
844 W Johnson Dr (47802-4189)
PHONE..................................812 238-8412
Gerry Modesitt, *Owner*
EMP: 7
SALES (est): 720.6K Privately Held
SIC: 3699 Laser systems & equipment

(G-13373)
YANKEE CANDLE COMPANY INC
3401 S Us Highway 41 E14 (47802-4146)
PHONE..................................812 234-1717
Denise Maris, *Manager*
EMP: 9
SALES (corp-wide): 14.7B Publicly Held
SIC: 5999 5199 3999 Candle shops; can-
dles; barber & beauty shop equipment
HQ: The Yankee Candle Company Inc
16 Yankee Candle Way
South Deerfield MA 01373
413 665-8306

(G-13374)
YANKEE STEEL INC
431 N 14th St (47807-2208)
PHONE..................................812 232-5353
David Atlogic, *President*
Sharon Atlogic, *Corp Secy*
EMP: 5
SQ FT: 9,600
SALES (est): 778.6K Privately Held
SIC: 3441 1799 Fabricated structural
metal; welding on site

Thorntown
Boone County

(G-13375)
HINTZ EQUIPMENT INC
1091 N Terrace Rd (46071-9525)
PHONE..................................765 362-6115
Robert Kelsey, *President*
Maria Kelsey, *Treasurer*
EMP: 3
SQ FT: 1,200
SALES: 200K Privately Held
SIC: 3589 5084 7699 Sewer cleaning
equipment, power; industrial machinery &
equipment; sewer cleaning & rodding

(G-13376)
J & J WOODCRAFTERS
2416 N State Road 75 (46071-9235)
PHONE..................................765 436-2466
John Dieterline, *Owner*
EMP: 3
SALES: 200K Privately Held
SIC: 2511 2517 Wood bedroom furniture;
wood desks, bookcases & magazine
racks; home entertainment unit cabinets,
wood; radio cabinets & cases, wood;
stereo cabinets, wood; television cabinets, wood

(G-13377)
PERDUE FARMS INC
4586 N Us Highway 52 (46071-9287)
PHONE..................................765 436-7990
Fax: 765 436-7919
Michael Maroney, *Manager*
EMP: 100
SALES (corp-wide): 5.5B Privately Held
WEB: www.perdue.com
SIC: 2015 Chicken slaughtering & process-
ing; turkey processing & slaughtering
PA: Perdue Farms Inc.
31149 Old Ocean City Rd
Salisbury MD 21804
410 543-3000

(G-13378)
STALCOP LLC (PA)
Also Called: Stalcop Cold US
1217 W Main St (46071-8986)
PHONE..................................765 436-7926
Fax: 765 436-2179
Ron St Clair, *Partner*
Dave Riddle, *CFO*
▲ EMP: 75 EST: 1994
SQ FT: 60,000
SALES (est): 25.7MM Privately Held
WEB: www.stalcop.com
SIC: 3444 3366 3354 3316 Sheet metal-
work; copper foundries; aluminum ex-
truded products; cold finishing of steel
shapes

(G-13379)
U S AGGREGATES INC
6990 N 875 W (46071-8957)
PHONE..................................765 436-7665
Fax: 765 436-2539
William Kaelin, *Manager*
EMP: 8
SALES (corp-wide): 248.2MM Privately
Held
WEB: www.usagg.com
SIC: 1422 Crushed & broken limestone
HQ: U S Aggregates Inc
5400 W 86th St
Indianapolis IN 46268
317 872-6010

Tippecanoe
Marshall County

(G-13380)
A J COIL INC
20015 Apple Rd (46570-9763)
PHONE..................................574 353-7174
Fax: 574 353-7174
Rachel Banghart, *President*
Russell Yazel, *Vice Pres*
EMP: 5
SALES (est): 691.5K Privately Held
SIC: 3495 Wire springs

(G-13381)
GEN ENTERPRISES
Also Called: Singles Ministry, The
3500 18b Rd (46570-9799)
PHONE..................................574 498-6777
Robert Grigsby, *Owner*
EMP: 2
SALES (est): 157.6K Privately Held
SIC: 2673 2759 Bags: plastic, laminated &
coated; publication printing

(G-13382)
HENSLEY FABRICATING & EQP CO
Also Called: Hensley Hydra-Haulers
17624 State Road 331 (46570-9750)
PHONE..................................574 498-6514
Fax: 574 498-6525
Paul Hensley, *Ch of Bd*
Gregory L Hensley, *President*
Beatrice Hensley, *Corp Secy*
Pam Pennington, *Shareholder*
Paula Poisel, *Shareholder*
▼ EMP: 40 EST: 1963
SQ FT: 37,000
SALES (est): 11.4MM Privately Held
WEB: www.hensleyfab.com
SIC: 3443 Tanks, standard or custom fabri-
cated: metal plate

(G-13383)
LEE E NORRIS CNSTR & GRN CO (PA)
Also Called: B.N.W. Industries
7930 N 700 E (46570-9613)
PHONE..................................574 353-7855
Dan Norris, *President*
Chuck Norris, *Project Mgr*
Aaron Norris, *Admin Sec*
▲ EMP: 1
SQ FT: 32,000
SALES (est): 2.2MM Privately Held
WEB: www.belt-o-matic.com
SIC: 3523 Driers (farm): grain, hay & seed

(G-13384)
NICORR LLC
1260 20th Rd (46570-9764)
P.O. Box 176 (46570-0176)
PHONE..............................574 353-1700
Jeff Unterbrink, *Manager*
Jerry Faulkner,
EMP: 9
SQ FT: 5,000
SALES (est): 1.3MM **Privately Held**
SIC: 3444 Metal flooring & siding

(G-13385)
NORRIS THERMAL TECH INC
7930 N 700 E (46570-9613)
PHONE..............................574 353-7855
W Woelfer, *Manager*
◆ EMP: 2
SALES (est): 433.2K **Privately Held**
SIC: 3556 Food products machinery

(G-13386)
PREMIER TRUSS & LUMBER COMPANY
18140 State Road 331 (46570-9747)
PHONE..............................574 498-6022
Toll Free:.................................877 -
Larrie Kreft, *President*
Rodney Kreft, *Vice Pres*
EMP: 12
SALES (est): 2MM **Privately Held**
SIC: 2439 Trusses, wooden roof

Tipton
Tipton County

(G-13387)
APPLE GROUP INC
122 N East St (46072-1740)
PHONE..............................765 675-4777
Fax: 765 675-7422
Judith Burton, *President*
Ed Burton, *Corp Secy*
Christopher Beasley, *Engineer*
EMP: 20
SQ FT: 15,000
SALES (est): 1.3MM **Privately Held**
WEB: www.applegroup.com
SIC: 2396 2395 5199 Fabric printing & stamping; screen printing on fabric articles; embroidery & art needlework; advertising specialties

(G-13388)
ATKISSON ENTERPRISES INC
Also Called: Progress Tool & Die Shop
632 Mill St (46072-1052)
PHONE..............................765 675-7593
Fax: 765 675-7538
Michael Atkisson, *President*
Jaime Atkisson, *Corp Secy*
EMP: 12 EST: 1967
SQ FT: 25,000
SALES (est): 1.7MM **Privately Held**
SIC: 3544 3469 Special dies & tools; metal stampings

(G-13389)
BOTTCHER AMERICA CORPORATION
717 Industrial Dr (46072-1071)
PHONE..............................765 675-4449
Fax: 765 675-4111
Jeff Hoover, *Manager*
EMP: 35
SALES (corp-wide): 243.6MM **Privately Held**
WEB: www.digitalrollers.com
SIC: 5084 2796 Printing trades machinery, equipment & supplies; platemaking services
HQ: Bottcher America Corporation
4600 Mercedes Dr
Belcamp MD 21017
410 273-7000

(G-13390)
DC COATERS INC
550 Industrial Dr (46072-8463)
PHONE..............................765 675-6006
Fax: 765 675-6110
Dennis Cook, *President*
Max Mc Neal, *Corp Secy*

Stephen Gill, *Exec VP*
Linda Cook, *Vice Pres*
Bob Johnson, *Plant Mgr*
EMP: 35
SALES (est): 5MM **Privately Held**
WEB: www.dccoaters.com
SIC: 3479 1721 Coating of metals & formed products; painting & paper hanging

(G-13391)
FRANCO CORPORATION
600 Industrial Dr (46072-8429)
PHONE..............................765 675-6691
Fax: 765 675-3874
Thomas H Hammonds, *President*
EMP: 3 EST: 1980
SQ FT: 10,000
SALES (est): 409.7K **Privately Held**
SIC: 2891 Sealing compounds, synthetic rubber or plastic; sealing wax

(G-13392)
INTEGRITY EDM LLC
641 Cleveland St (46072-1132)
PHONE..............................317 333-7630
Dave Langenkamp, *General Mgr*
Jacob Newlin, *Purchasing*
Steve Parent, *Purchasing*
Roy Proffitt, *QC Mgr*
Mark Jennings, *Engineer*
EMP: 15
SQ FT: 2,500
SALES (est): 8.8MM **Privately Held**
WEB: www.integrityedm.com
SIC: 3724 Aircraft engines & engine parts

(G-13393)
INTERNATIONAL PAPER COMPANY
815 Industrial Dr (46072-1067)
PHONE..............................765 675-6732
Fax: 765 675-6595
Gary Schmidt, *General Mgr*
EMP: 161
SALES (corp-wide): 21.7B **Publicly Held**
SIC: 2621 Paper mills
PA: International Paper Company
6400 Poplar Ave
Memphis TN 38197
901 419-9000

(G-13394)
IRVING MATERIALS INC
Also Called: I M I
929 E Jefferson St (46072-9497)
PHONE..............................765 675-6327
Fax: 765 675-3577
May Buch, *Branch Mgr*
EMP: 4
SALES (corp-wide): 800.6MM **Privately Held**
SIC: 3273 Ready-mixed concrete
PA: Irving Materials, Inc.
8032 N State Road 9
Greenfield IN 46140
317 326-3101

(G-13395)
LEX TOOLING LLC
604 Berryman Pike (46072-8596)
PHONE..............................765 675-6301
Fax: 765 675-9686
Joseph Tucker, *Mng Member*
EMP: 3
SQ FT: 2,400
SALES (est): 339.6K **Privately Held**
WEB: www.lextooling.com
SIC: 3544 Special dies, tools, jigs & fixtures

(G-13396)
M U HOLDINGS INC
815 W Jefferson St Bldg 4 (46072-1860)
PHONE..............................765 675-8054
Janusz J Jaworski, *President*
▲ EMP: 12
SALES (est): 1.6MM **Privately Held**
SIC: 1411 Granite dimension stone

(G-13397)
MANIER WELDING & FABRICATIONS
859 Market Rd (46072-8413)
PHONE..............................765 675-6078
Fax: 765 675-6089

Mark Manier, *Owner*
EMP: 3 EST: 1997
SQ FT: 8,400
SALES (est): 405K **Privately Held**
SIC: 7692 Welding repair

(G-13398)
MCCORMICK PRINTING IMPRESSIONS
618 Oak St (46072-1142)
PHONE..............................765 675-9556
Fax: 765 675-9558
Kevin McCormick, *President*
Mary Frances Fernung, *Vice Pres*
Mary Fernung, *Vice Pres*
Chris McCormick, *Manager*
EMP: 7
SQ FT: 6,500
SALES (est): 500K **Privately Held**
WEB: www.mccormackprinting.com
SIC: 2759 Screen printing

(G-13399)
MCCREARY CONCRETE PRODUCTS INC
875 Industrial Dr (46072-1067)
PHONE..............................317 844-5157
Chris Elbrecht, *Branch Mgr*
EMP: 7
SALES (est): 809.5K
SALES (corp-wide): 3.8MM **Privately Held**
SIC: 3272 Concrete products, precast
PA: Mccreary Concrete Products, Inc.
810 N Fort Wayne Rd
Rushville IN 46173
765 932-3058

(G-13400)
PARK 100 FOODS INC (PA)
326 E Adams St (46072-2001)
PHONE..............................765 675-3480
Fax: 765 675-3474
Gary Meade, *President*
Sami Signorino, *President*
Jim Washburn, *Chairman*
David Alves, *Vice Pres*
Rob McConnell, *Maintenance Dir*
▲ EMP: 80
SQ FT: 45,000
SALES (est): 95MM **Privately Held**
WEB: www.park100foods.com
SIC: 2013 2032 2035 Frozen meats from purchased meat; cooked meats from purchased meat; soups, except seafood: packaged in cans, jars, etc.; pickles, sauces & salad dressings

(G-13401)
PLAKES TOOLING INC
881 S 725 W (46072-8782)
PHONE..............................765 963-2745
Cassandra Plake, *President*
Jack Plake, *President*
EMP: 3
SALES (est): 121K **Privately Held**
SIC: 3599 Machine shop, jobbing & repair

(G-13402)
RAY BROTHERS NOBLE CANNING CO
1361 S 500 E (46072-8556)
PHONE..............................765 552-9432
Fax: 765 675-7400
Mark Noble, *President*
Ray Noble, *Chairman*
Brenda Noble, *Admin Sec*
EMP: 50 EST: 1925
SQ FT: 87,000
SALES: 4.5MM **Privately Held**
SIC: 2033 Tomato products: packaged in cans, jars, etc.

(G-13403)
REAL IMAGE LLC
501 N Main St (46072-1320)
PHONE..............................765 675-7325
Paige Hoover,
EMP: 2
SALES: 100K **Privately Held**
SIC: 2395 Embroidery & art needlework

(G-13404)
RENEWED PERFORMANCE COMPANY
1095 Development Dr (46072-1070)
P.O. Box 196 (46072-0196)
PHONE..............................765 675-7586
Fax: 765 675-7589
Christopher A Palabrica, *President*
Christopher Palabrica, *General Mgr*
Elfie R Palabrica, *Shareholder*
EMP: 10
SQ FT: 24,000
SALES (est): 10MM **Privately Held**
SIC: 3711 Fire department vehicles (motor vehicles), assembly of

(G-13405)
SORENSEN CUSTOM CABINETS
21 E 400 S (46072-9289)
PHONE..............................765 292-2225
Kris Sorensen, *Owner*
Mary Sorensen, *Principal*
EMP: 6 EST: 1975
SQ FT: 5,000
SALES (est): 250K **Privately Held**
SIC: 2434 Wood kitchen cabinets

(G-13406)
STEEL PARTS CORPORATION
801 Berryman Pike (46072-8492)
P.O. Box 700 (46072-0700)
PHONE..............................765 675-2191
Fax: 765 675-4232
Dr James E Ashton, *Ch of Bd*
John Riggle, *President*
Richard L Fagan, *COO*
Ron Cook, *Vice Pres*
Jeff Frost, *Plant Mgr*
EMP: 300
SQ FT: 235,000
SALES (est): 41.4MM
SALES (corp-wide): 205.8MM **Privately Held**
SIC: 3465 3594 3568 3469 Automotive stampings; fluid power pumps & motors; power transmission equipment; metal stampings; manufactured hardware (general)
PA: Resilience Capital Partners Llc
25101 Chagrin Blvd # 350
Cleveland OH 44122
216 292-0200

(G-13407)
STEEL PARTS MANUFACTURING INC (HQ)
801 Berryman Pike (46072-8492)
P.O. Box 700 (46072-0700)
PHONE..............................765 675-2191
Robert W Potokar, *President*
John F Riggle, *Vice Pres*
Jeff Frost, *Plant Mgr*
Melvin Ogden, *QC Mgr*
Kevin W Bliss, *CFO*
EMP: 44
SALES (est): 46.9MM **Privately Held**
SIC: 3714 Transmissions, motor vehicle

(G-13408)
TEMPLE-INLAND INC
815 Industrial Dr (46072-1067)
PHONE..............................765 675-6732
Linda Burnham, *Safety Mgr*
William Kraft, *Maintence Staff*
EMP: 6
SALES (est): 65.9K **Privately Held**
SIC: 8661 2653 Temples; corrugated & solid fiber boxes

(G-13409)
TRUSS PARTNERS LLC
Also Called: Truss Manufacturing Company
840 S 550 W (46072-8434)
P.O. Box 702, Zionsville (46077-0702)
PHONE..............................765 675-5700
Fax: 317 896-3776
Chris Weintraut,
Tom Weintraut,
EMP: 100
SQ FT: 55,000
SALES (est): 10.3MM **Privately Held**
WEB: www.tmctruss.com
SIC: 2439 Trusses, wooden roof

Topeka
Lagrange County

(G-13410)
A JS FURNITURE LLC
5355 W 400 S (46571-9043)
PHONE...........................574 642-1273
Alvin Beechy Jr, *Mng Member*
EMP: 4
SALES: 600K **Privately Held**
SIC: 2426 5021 Furniture dimension
stock, hardwood; furniture

(G-13411)
ASCOT ENTERPRISES INC
129 Roy St (46571)
PHONE...........................260 593-3733
Cory Manning, *Manager*
EMP: 90
SALES (corp-wide): 95.4MM **Privately Held**
WEB: www.ascotenterprises.com
SIC: 2391 Curtains & draperies
PA: Ascot Enterprises Inc
503 S Main St
Nappanee IN 46550
877 773-7751

(G-13412)
CHAMPION HOME BUILDERS INC
308 Sheridian Dr (46571)
P.O. Box 95 (46571-0095)
PHONE...........................260 593-2962
Fax: 260 593-3404
Jayson Kayna, *Manager*
EMP: 350
SQ FT: 70,000
SALES (corp-wide): 236.5MM **Publicly Held**
SIC: 2451 Mobile homes
HQ: Champion Home Builders, Inc.
755 W Big Beaver Rd # 1000
Troy MI 48084
248 614-8200

(G-13413)
CONNECTION LLC
211 W Lake St (46571)
PHONE...........................260 593-3999
Ernesto Saucedo, *Project Mgr*
David Buskirk, *Engineer*
Robert Doyle, *Senior Engr*
Doretta Yoter, *Mng Member*
Nancy Amor,
EMP: 3
SALES: 250K **Privately Held**
SIC: 2721 Magazines: publishing only, not
printed on site

(G-13414)
COOPER-STANDARD AUTOMOTIVE INC
324 Morrow St (46571-9076)
PHONE...........................260 593-2156
Ruby Crider, *Branch Mgr*
EMP: 176
SALES (corp-wide): 3.6B **Publicly Held**
WEB: www.cooperstandard.com
SIC: 3443 Heat exchangers, condensers &
components
HQ: Cooper-Standard Automotive Inc.
39550 Orchard Hill Pl
Novi MI 48375
248 596-5900

(G-13415)
D & E WORKSHOP
9680 W 700 S (46571-9134)
PHONE...........................260 593-0195
Daniel Lehman, *Owner*
EMP: 7
SALES (est): 824.9K **Privately Held**
SIC: 2511 Rockers, except upholstered:
wood

(G-13416)
D A HOCHSTETLER & SONS LLP
4165 S 500 W (46571-9546)
PHONE...........................574 642-1144
Albert L Hochstetler, *Principal*

Daniel A Hochstetler, *Principal*
Ivan J Hochstetler, *Principal*
EMP: 12 **EST:** 1950
SQ FT: 10,000
SALES (est): 1.5MM **Privately Held**
SIC: 3544 3523 3441 3594 Special dies
& tools; farm machinery & equipment;
fabricated structural metal; fluid power
pumps & motors; sheet metalwork

(G-13417)
DS CORP
Also Called: Rossroads Rv
1115 W Lake St (46571-9787)
P.O. Box 2000, Goshen (46527-2000)
PHONE...........................260 593-3850
Duane Rheinheimer, *President*
▲ **EMP:** 150
SQ FT: 33,000
SALES (est): 24.8MM
SALES (corp-wide): 7.2B **Publicly Held**
WEB: www.thorindustries.com
SIC: 3716 3792 Motor homes; travel trailers & campers
PA: Thor Industries, Inc.
601 E Beardsley Ave
Elkhart IN 46514
574 970-7460

(G-13418)
FOREST RIVER CHEROKEE INC
402 Lehman Ave (46571-9456)
PHONE...........................260 593-2566
John Quake, *Manager*
Joe Luther, *Manager*
Mark Steele, *Manager*
Kayla Fugate, *Receptionist*
Sue Vicary, *Receptionist*
EMP: 2
SALES (est): 248.5K **Privately Held**
SIC: 3792 Travel trailers & campers

(G-13419)
FOUR WOODS LAMINATING INC (PA)
7550 W 500 S (46571-9444)
PHONE...........................260 593-2246
Glen Yoder, *President*
Wayne Miller, *Vice Pres*
Glen Riegsecker, *Treasurer*
EMP: 50
SALES (est): 4.2MM **Privately Held**
SIC: 1751 3714 2431 Cabinet & finish
carpentry; motor vehicle parts & accessories; millwork

(G-13420)
GENERAL FABR
Also Called: General Fabrication
7360 S State Road 5 (46571-9714)
P.O. Box 665 (46571-0665)
PHONE...........................260 593-3858
Elmer Sheperd, *Owner*
EMP: 2
SALES (est): 160.8K **Privately Held**
SIC: 3441 Fabricated structural metal

(G-13421)
HONEYVILLE METAL INC
Also Called: Hmi Machinery
4200 S 900 W (46571-9142)
PHONE...........................800 593-8377
Fax: 260 593-2486
Mark Hochstetler, *President*
Ora Hochstetler, *Chairman*
Ivan Birky, *Senior VP*
Melvin Gingerich, *Vice Pres*
Tim Miller, *Design Engr*
EMP: 67 **EST:** 1951
SQ FT: 137,000
SALES (est): 23.3MM **Privately Held**
SIC: 3523 3564 Farm machinery & equipment; dust or fume collecting equipment,
industrial

(G-13422)
HOOSIER BUGGY SHOP
5245 S 600 W (46571-9549)
PHONE...........................260 593-2192
Maynard Hochstetler, *Owner*
EMP: 4 **EST:** 1960
SQ FT: 5,700
SALES (est): 200K **Privately Held**
SIC: 3799 7699 Carriages, horse drawn;
horse drawn vehicle repair

(G-13423)
LAMBRIGHT WOODWORKING LLC
7785 W 300 S (46571-9752)
PHONE...........................260 593-2721
Fax: 260 593-2721
Cletus Lambright, *General Mgr*
EMP: 24
SQ FT: 12,900
SALES (est): 1.9MM **Privately Held**
SIC: 2434 2511 5712 2431 Wood kitchen
cabinets; wood household furniture; furniture stores; doors & door parts & trim,
wood; wood partitions & fixtures

(G-13424)
NEW STYLE OF CROSSROADS LLC
9585 W 700 S (46571-9130)
PHONE...........................260 593-3800
Leroy Yoeder, *Owner*
EMP: 12
SQ FT: 8,600
SALES (est): 1.4MM **Privately Held**
SIC: 2431 Moldings, wood: unfinished &
prefinished

(G-13425)
NISHIKAWA COOPER LLC (DH)
Also Called: Nisco
324 Morrow St (46571-9076)
PHONE...........................260 593-2156
Fax: 260 593-2037
Futoshi Higashida, *President*
Chad Klopfenstein, *Vice Pres*
Michael Talaga, *Vice Pres*
Tony Baker, *Plant Mgr*
Ensign Matt, *Project Mgr*
▲ **EMP:** 452
SQ FT: 250,000
SALES (est): 205.8MM
SALES (corp-wide): 903.4MM **Privately Held**
SIC: 3069 Weather strip, sponge rubber
HQ: Nishikawa Of America Inc
324 Morrow St
Topeka IN 46571
260 593-2156

(G-13426)
NISHIKAWA OF AMERICA INC (HQ)
324 Morrow St (46571-9076)
PHONE...........................260 593-2156
Bunji Yamamoti, *President*
Jol Vanatti, *Partner*
Bill Burga, *Vice Pres*
▲ **EMP:** 6
SALES (est): 205.8MM
SALES (corp-wide): 903.4MM **Privately Held**
SIC: 3069 Weather strip, sponge rubber
PA: Nishikawa Rubber Co.,Ltd.
2-2-8, Misasamachi, Nishi-Ku
Hiroshima HIR 733-0
822 379-371

(G-13427)
PERFORMANCE COATINGS SPC LLC
7030 W 665 S (46571-9745)
PHONE...........................574 606-8153
Amie Ernsberger, *Administration*
EMP: 2
SALES (est): 89.1K **Privately Held**
SIC: 3479 Metal coating & allied service

(G-13428)
S & H METAL PRODUCTS INC
122 Redman Dr (46571-9786)
P.O. Box 35 (46571-0035)
PHONE...........................260 593-2565
Fax: 260 593-2583
Freeman J Helmuth, *President*
Tina M Helmuth, *Admin Sec*
EMP: 22
SQ FT: 31,000
SALES (est): 4.1MM **Privately Held**
SIC: 3714 3444 Motor vehicle body components & frame; ducts, sheet metal

(G-13429)
SNAX IN PAX INC
204 Hawpatch Dr (46571-9472)
PHONE...........................260 593-3066

Bill Huggins, *President*
Ruby Huggins, *Corp Secy*
EMP: 23
SQ FT: 30,000
SALES (est): 11.7MM **Privately Held**
WEB: www.snaxinpax.com
SIC: 5145 2038 Snack foods; snacks, including onion rings, cheese sticks, etc.

(G-13430)
SUN RISE METAL SHOP
3070 W 350 S (46571-8946)
Rural Route 2 Box 104 (46571)
PHONE...........................260 463-4026
Enos A Kuhns, *Owner*
EMP: 3
SQ FT: 3,120
SALES (est): 181.5K **Privately Held**
SIC: 3523 5231 5074 5191 Cattle feeding, handling & watering equipment; hog
feeding, handling & watering equipment;
paint; plumbing & hydronic heating supplies; farm supplies

(G-13431)
TOWER ADVERTISING PRODUCTS INC (PA)
Also Called: Tower Ribbons
1015 W Lake St (46571-9611)
P.O. Box 540 (46571-0540)
PHONE...........................260 593-2103
Fax: 260 593-2107
C Craig Miller, *President*
Mary Sue Miller, *Treasurer*
Richard Smith, *Sales Mgr*
▲ **EMP:** 80
SQ FT: 40,000
SALES (est): 14.6MM **Privately Held**
SIC: 2241 5094 3993 Ribbons; trophies;
signs & advertising specialties

(G-13432)
WOODSIDE CUSTOM CANVAS LLC
9305 W 650 S (46571-9443)
PHONE...........................260 593-2420
Dale Miller,
Carol Miller,
EMP: 2 **EST:** 2011
SALES (est): 76.9K **Privately Held**
SIC: 2394 Canvas awnings & canopies

(G-13433)
YODERS & SONS REPAIR SHOP
6035 W 800 S (46571-9563)
PHONE...........................260 593-2727
Perry Yoder, *Owner*
EMP: 2
SALES (est): 152.4K **Privately Held**
SIC: 7692 Welding repair

Trafalgar
Johnson County

(G-13434)
BESSE VENEERS INC
718 E Park St (46181-8745)
PHONE...........................906 428-3113
John Besse, *President*
EMP: 24
SALES (est): 1.4MM **Privately Held**
SIC: 2435 Hardwood veneer & plywood

(G-13435)
DRONEYE IMAGING LLC
5127 S 200 W (46181-9110)
PHONE...........................317 878-4065
Brian Pfaehler, *Principal*
EMP: 2
SALES (est): 137K **Privately Held**
SIC: 3721 Motorized aircraft

(G-13436)
INDIANA ARCHITECTURAL PLYWOOD (PA)
750 E Park St (46181-8745)
P.O. Box 39 (46181-0039)
PHONE...........................317 878-4822
Fax: 317 878-4897
Horst Michaelis, *CEO*
James A Moreland, *President*
Robin Stovall, *Traffic Mgr*
Lance Lindsay, *Purch Agent*

Frank Michaelis, *Purchasing*
▲ **EMP:** 40
SQ FT: 55,000
SALES (est): 7.7MM **Privately Held**
WEB: www.iaplywood.com
SIC: 2435 2431 3429 2511 Plywood, hardwood or hardwood faced; doors & door parts & trim, wood; panel work, wood; manufactured hardware (general); wood household furniture

(G-13437)
RING-CO LLC
8402 S 250 W (46181-9260)
PHONE..............................317 641-7050
Patricia Ringer,
EMP: 4
SALES (est): 302.6K **Privately Held**
SIC: 3711 Truck & tractor truck assembly

(G-13438)
SIGNATURE FORMULATIONS LLC
3 Trafalgar Sq (46181-9515)
PHONE..............................317 878-4086
Irma Jobst,
EMP: 8
SALES (est): 1.3MM **Privately Held**
SIC: 2844 Hair preparations, including shampoos

(G-13439)
TOWNSEND SALES INC
4141 S 25 W (46181-8913)
PHONE..............................317 736-4047
Fax: 317 736-4558
Kenneth Townsend, *President*
Rosemae Townsend, *Corp Secy*
Lee Townsend, *Vice Pres*
EMP: 8
SQ FT: 2,000
SALES: 1.4MM **Privately Held**
WEB: www.townsendsales.com
SIC: 5083 3523 Livestock equipment; farm machinery & equipment

Trail Creek
Laporte County

(G-13440)
ALPHA-PURE CORPORATION
251 N Roeske Ave (46360-5072)
P.O. Box 471229, Charlotte NC (28247-1229)
PHONE..............................877 645-7676
▲ **EMP:** 9
SALES (est): 1MM **Privately Held**
SIC: 3569 Filters

(G-13441)
FIBER BOND CORPORATION
Also Called: Fiberbond
110 Menke Rd (46360-6596)
PHONE..............................219 879-4541
Fax: 219 874-7502
Barre Seid, *Ch of Bd*
Daniel Dobbins, *President*
John Marienau, *President*
Rick White, *Manager*
Cheryl Dudek, *Administration*
▲ **EMP:** 130
SQ FT: 200,000
SALES (est): 27.8MM **Privately Held**
WEB: www.fiberbond.net
SIC: 2297 Bonded-fiber fabrics, except felt

(G-13442)
SENTINEL ALARM INC
2815 E Michigan Blvd (46360-5398)
PHONE..............................219 874-6051
Ken Stokes, *President*
EMP: 6 **EST:** 1977
SQ FT: 10,000
SALES (est): 530K **Privately Held**
WEB: www.sentinelalarm.com
SIC: 1731 3669 Fire detection & burglar alarm systems specialization; burglar alarm apparatus, electric; fire alarm apparatus, electric

(G-13443)
T R BULGER INC
3123 E Michigan Blvd (46360-6523)
PHONE..............................219 879-8525
Fax: 219 879-1066
Thomas R Bulger, *President*
EMP: 9
SQ FT: 5,600
SALES (est): 993.5K **Privately Held**
SIC: 1711 8711 3444 Heating & air conditioning contractors; refrigeration contractor; heating & ventilation engineering; furnace casings, sheet metal; ventilators, sheet metal

(G-13444)
WEBER SIGN SERVICE INC
320 Trail St (46360-6446)
PHONE..............................219 872-5060
William P Weber, *President*
Kathleen Weber, *Admin Sec*
EMP: 5
SQ FT: 3,600
SALES (est): 513.8K **Privately Held**
SIC: 3993 7312 Signs, not made in custom sign painting shops; outdoor advertising services

Troy
Spencer County

(G-13445)
AMERICAN COLLOID COMPANY
11645 State Road 545 (47588-9036)
PHONE..............................812 547-3567
Tracey Coyle, *Plant Mgr*
EMP: 5 **Publicly Held**
WEB: www.colloid.com
SIC: 1459 2899 Bentonite mining; chemical preparations
HQ: American Colloid Company
2870 Forbs Ave
Hoffman Estates IL 60192

(G-13446)
CONSOLIDATED RECYCLING CO INC (PA)
11210 Solomon Rd (47588-9029)
P.O. Box 3642, Evansville (47735-3642)
PHONE..............................812 547-7951
Paul K Carson, *President*
Michael Sturgeon, *CFO*
David Carson, *Treasurer*
David E Carson, *Admin Sec*
EMP: 30 **EST:** 1979
SQ FT: 12,000
SALES (est): 9.3MM **Privately Held**
SIC: 2899 Oil treating compounds

(G-13447)
POLYFREEZE LLC
11210 Solomon Rd (47588-9029)
PHONE..............................812 547-7951
Dave Carson, *CEO*
EMP: 10
SALES (est): 1.4MM **Privately Held**
SIC: 2899 Oil treating compounds

(G-13448)
TROY MEGGITT INC (HQ)
Also Called: Meggitt Control Systems
3 Industrial Dr (47588)
P.O. Box 40 (47588-0040)
PHONE..............................812 547-7071
Stephen Young, *CEO*
Jennifer Land, *Accountant*
Val Yeomans, *Administration*
EMP: 95
SQ FT: 125,000
SALES (est): 20.9MM
SALES (corp-wide): 2.6B **Privately Held**
WEB: www.stewartwarnersw.com
SIC: 3443 3433 7699 5088 Heat exchangers, condensers & components; heating equipment, except electric; aircraft flight instrument repair; aircraft engines & engine parts
PA: Meggitt Plc
Atlantic House, Aviation Park West
Christchurch BH23
120 259-7597

(G-13449)
WAUPACA PALLET
11225 Solomon Rd (47588-9029)
PHONE..............................812 547-1565
EMP: 4
SALES (est): 248.1K **Privately Held**
SIC: 2448 Wood pallets & skids

Twelve Mile
Cass County

(G-13450)
FIELD CONSTRUCTION
5222 E County Road 650 N (46988-9530)
PHONE..............................574 664-2010
John Field, *Owner*
EMP: 8
SALES (est): 310.9K **Privately Held**
WEB: www.fieldconstruction.com
SIC: 1389 Construction, repair & dismantling services

Underwood
Scott County

(G-13451)
MC CUSTOM CABINETS INC
2157 W Salem Rd (47177-6713)
PHONE..............................502 641-1528
Michael B Allgood, *President*
Clara Allgood, *Admin Sec*
EMP: 2 **EST:** 2010
SALES (est): 233.4K **Privately Held**
SIC: 2434 Wood kitchen cabinets

Union City
Randolph County

(G-13452)
APPLEGATE LIVESTOCK EQP INC (HQ)
902 S State Road 32 (47390-9153)
P.O. Box 151 (47390-0151)
PHONE..............................765 964-3715
Gary Anderson, *President*
Duane Brim, *General Mgr*
Paul Franzmann, *Vice Pres*
Jim Lewis, *Materials Mgr*
Aaron Applegate, *Sales Mgr*
▲ **EMP:** 65
SQ FT: 131,500
SALES (est): 28.7MM
SALES (corp-wide): 591.3MM **Privately Held**
WEB: www.applegatesteel.com
SIC: 3523 3317 Barn, silo, poultry, dairy & livestock machinery; cattle feeding, handling & watering equipment; welded pipe & tubes
PA: Ag Growth International Inc
198 Commerce Dr
Winnipeg MB R3P 0
204 489-1855

(G-13453)
B & M STEEL & WELDING INC
Also Called: B&M Steel Fabrication
1251 S Jackson Pike (47390-8316)
P.O. Box 405 (47390-0405)
PHONE..............................765 964-5868
Fax: 765 964-6956
Steve Rader, *President*
Todd Rader, *General Mgr*
EMP: 8
SQ FT: 6,000
SALES (est): 1.7MM **Privately Held**
SIC: 3441 Fabricated structural metal

(G-13454)
CARDINAL ETHANOL LLC
1554 N County Rd 600 E (47390)
PHONE..............................765 964-3137
Robert John Davis, *Ch of Bd*
Thomas E Chalfant, *Vice Ch Bd*
Jeff Painter, *President*
Jeremey Herlyn, *Plant Mgr*
Justin McElhany, *Maint Spvr*
EMP: 55

SALES: 228.5MM **Privately Held**
SIC: 2869 2085 Ethyl alcohol, ethanol; distillers' dried grains & solubles & alcohol

(G-13455)
FRANK MILLER LUMBER CO INC (PA)
1690 Frank Miller Rd (47390-8446)
PHONE..............................800 345-2643
Fax: 765 964-6618
Steven P James, *President*
Martha M Mathias, *COO*
Joann Johnson, *Vice Pres*
Joellen Johnston, *CFO*
Tina M Root, *Treasurer*
▼ **EMP:** 150 **EST:** 1903
SQ FT: 2,000
SALES (est): 35.5MM **Privately Held**
WEB: www.frankmiller.com
SIC: 2426 2421 Hardwood dimension & flooring mills; custom sawmill

(G-13456)
GARVER MANUFACTURING INC
224 N Columbia St (47390-1432)
P.O. Box 306 (47390-0306)
PHONE..............................765 964-5828
Fax: 765 964-5828
Michael Read, *President*
Alberta Read, *Corp Secy*
Fredrick Read, *Vice Pres*
EMP: 3
SQ FT: 10,000
SALES (est): 370.3K **Privately Held**
SIC: 3523 Dairy equipment (farm)

(G-13457)
HUB CITY STL & FABRICATION LLC
4487 S Arba Pike (47390-8528)
PHONE..............................260 760-0370
Kevin Kerns,
David Stewart,
EMP: 3
SALES: 950K **Privately Held**
SIC: 3444 Sheet metalwork

(G-13458)
NICKS AUTOMOTIVE INC
2741 N 700 E (47390-9131)
P.O. Box 403 (47390-0403)
PHONE..............................765 964-6843
Fax: 765 964-3837
Nick McOwen, *President*
Nick Mc Eowen, *President*
EMP: 10
SQ FT: 5,000
SALES (est): 1.6MM **Privately Held**
SIC: 7532 5531 3312 Body shop, automotive; truck equipment & parts; blast furnaces & steel mills

(G-13459)
PEPCON CONCRETE INC
1567 Frank Miller Rd (47390-8999)
PHONE..............................765 964-6572
Fax: 765 964-6572
Larry Grimes, *Plant Mgr*
EMP: 3
SALES (est): 200.9K **Privately Held**
SIC: 3273 Ready-mixed concrete

(G-13460)
REIT-PRICE MFG CO INCORPORATED
522 W Chestnut St (47390-1308)
PHONE..............................765 964-3252
Fax: 765 964-5343
Roger L Stewart, *President*
EMP: 5 **EST:** 1900
SQ FT: 10,000
SALES (est): 855K **Privately Held**
WEB: www.reitprice.com
SIC: 2392 3991 Mops, floor & dust; brooms & brushes

(G-13461)
SYNERGY SOFTWARE GROUP INC
814 W Oak St (47390-1234)
PHONE..............................765 229-4003
Kyle Walters, *Principal*
EMP: 2
SALES (est): 56.5K **Privately Held**
SIC: 7372 Prepackaged software

(G-13462)
UNIFLEX RELAY SYSTEMS LLC
526 W Division St (47390-1007)
PHONE..................................765 232-4675
Linda D Wilcox, *Exec Dir*
EMP: 3
SALES (est): 246.8K **Privately Held**
SIC: 3931 Musical instruments

Union Mills
Laporte County

(G-13463)
HOT STAMPING & PRINTING
Also Called: D&D Manufacturing
6601 W 900 S (46382-9623)
PHONE..................................219 767-2429
Fax: 574 767-2429
John Doll Jr, *Owner*
EMP: 3
SQ FT: 3,000
SALES (est): 217.1K **Privately Held**
SIC: 3089 Novelties, plastic

(G-13464)
MONSANTO COMPANY
10201 S 700 W (46382-9523)
PHONE..................................219 733-2938
EMP: 167
SALES (corp-wide): 41.2B **Privately Held**
SIC: 2879 Agricultural chemicals
HQ: Monsanto Company
     800 N Lindbergh Blvd
     Saint Louis MO 63167
     314 694-1000

(G-13465)
THERMO-CYCLER INDUSTRIES INC (PA)
111 E Hamilton St (46382-9702)
P.O. Box 22 (46382-0022)
PHONE..................................219 767-2990
Fax: 219 767-2991
Gregory Kelver, *President*
Dena Eaton, *Purchasing*
EMP: 8
SALES (est): 2.9MM **Privately Held**
WEB: www.thermocycler.com
SIC: 5075 3564 Warm air heating equipment & supplies; ventilating equipment & supplies; ventilating fans: industrial or commercial

Uniondale
Wells County

(G-13466)
TGM MANUFACTURING INC
Also Called: Gilberts Machine
5980 N 400 W (46791-9736)
PHONE..................................260 758-3055
Fax: 260 758-3055
Terry Gilbert, *President*
Todd Gehring, *Vice Pres*
▲ EMP: 10
SQ FT: 4,000
SALES (est): 1.6MM **Privately Held**
SIC: 3599 Machine shop, jobbing & repair

Universal
Vermillion County

(G-13467)
HOG SLAT INCORPORATED
Also Called: Parking Bumper Company
18506 S Rangeline Rd (47884)
P.O. Box 181 (47884-0181)
PHONE..................................765 828-0828
Fax: 765 828-8717
David Swalls, *Controller*
April Kenkins, *Manager*
EMP: 14
SALES (corp-wide): 635.6MM **Privately Held**
WEB: www.hogslat.com
SIC: 3523 3272 Hog feeding, handling & watering equipment; concrete products

PA: Hog Slat, Incorporated
     206 Fayetteville St
     Newton Grove NC 28366
     800 949-4647

Upland
Grant County

(G-13468)
AVIS INDUSTRIAL CORPORATION (PA)
1909 S Main St (46989)
P.O. Box 548 (46989-0548)
PHONE..................................765 998-8100
Fax: 765 998-8111
Leland E Boren, *CEO*
Michelle W Patishall, *CFO*
Angela M Darlington, *Admin Sec*
▲ EMP: 25 EST: 1983
SQ FT: 23,000
SALES (est): 319.4MM **Privately Held**
WEB: www.avisindustrial.com
SIC: 3429 3462 3312 3531 Locks or lock sets; iron & steel forgings; tubes, steel & iron; construction machinery; cranes, locomotive; fuel pumps, motor vehicle; baling machines, for scrap metal, paper or similar material

(G-13469)
DE WITT TOOL & DIE INC
10040 E 500 S (46989-9434)
PHONE..................................765 998-7320
Fax: 765 998-7320
J Daniel Dewitt II, *President*
EMP: 4
SQ FT: 3,600
SALES: 160K **Privately Held**
SIC: 3544 3599 Special dies & tools; jigs & fixtures; machine & other job shop work; electrical discharge machining (EDM)

(G-13470)
FOOD & FUEL UPLAND
280 N Main St (46989-9180)
PHONE..................................765 998-0840
EMP: 5
SALES (est): 395.7K **Privately Held**
SIC: 2869 Fuels

(G-13471)
HORSE N AROUND ANIMAL & TACK
7288 S 825 E (46989-9718)
P.O. Box 525 (46989-0525)
PHONE..................................765 618-2032
Tim Rumler, *Owner*
Melissa Rumler, *Co-Owner*
EMP: 2
SALES: 5K **Privately Held**
SIC: 3111 Bridle leather

(G-13472)
PIERCE COMPANY INC (HQ)
35 N 8th St (46989)
P.O. Box 548 (46989-0548)
PHONE..................................765 998-8100
Fax: 765 998-3348
Leland E Boren, *President*
Tracee L Pennington, *Treasurer*
Angela M Taylor, *Admin Sec*
▲ EMP: 29
SQ FT: 185,000
SALES (est): 65.7MM
SALES (corp-wide): 319.4MM **Privately Held**
WEB: www.thepiercecompany.com
SIC: 3714 Motor vehicle parts & accessories; fuel pipes, motor vehicle; water pump, motor vehicle; governors, motor vehicle
PA: Avis Industrial Corporation
     1909 S Main St
     Upland IN 46989
     765 998-8100

(G-13473)
ROSS MACHINING
8855 E 500 S (46989-9463)
PHONE..................................765 998-2400
Fax: 765 998-2401
Ross Malonek, *Owner*

EMP: 2
SALES (est): 254.7K **Privately Held**
SIC: 3599 Machine shop, jobbing & repair

(G-13474)
UPLAND STOP & GO LLC
7175 E 600 S (46989-9331)
PHONE..................................765 998-0840
Aaron Cardale, *Principal*
EMP: 5
SALES (est): 350.1K **Privately Held**
SIC: 2911 Petroleum refining

(G-13475)
UPLAND VILLAGE LAUNDRY LLC
87 E Berry Ave (46989-9144)
P.O. Box 255 (46989-0255)
PHONE..................................765 998-1260
Lois D Jones,
EMP: 2
SALES (est): 25K **Privately Held**
SIC: 3582 Dryers, laundry: commercial, including coin-operated

Urbana
Wabash County

(G-13476)
CYCLONE MANUFACTURING CO INC
151 N Washington St (46990-9539)
P.O. Box 67 (46990-0067)
PHONE..................................260 774-3311
Fax: 260 774-3416
Daniel E Speicher III, *President*
EMP: 15 EST: 1868
SQ FT: 40,000
SALES (est): 3.4MM **Privately Held**
SIC: 3444 Sheet metal specialties, not stamped

(G-13477)
KALENBORN ABRESIST CORPORATION (HQ)
5541 N State Road 13 (46990-9548)
P.O. Box 38 (46990-0038)
PHONE..................................800 348-0717
Fax: 260 774-8188
Craig Frendewey, *President*
Norm Cornell, *Foreman/Supr*
Robert Tayloe, *QC Mgr*
Troy Ray, *Treasurer*
Russ Bauer, *Sales Mgr*
▲ EMP: 42 EST: 1977
SQ FT: 30,000
SALES: 13MM
SALES (corp-wide): 47.9MM **Privately Held**
WEB: www.abresist.com
SIC: 3444 3317 Pipe, sheet metal; steel pipe & tubes
PA: Kalenborn International Gmbh & Co.Kg
     Asbacher Str. 50
     VettelschoB 53560
     264 518-0

Vallonia
Jackson County

(G-13478)
WILDSIDE SIGNS
10207 N State Road 135 (47281-8048)
PHONE..................................812 358-3849
Mason Fleetwood, *Owner*
EMP: 2
SALES (est): 77.5K **Privately Held**
SIC: 3993 Signs & advertising specialties

Valparaiso
Porter County

(G-13479)
A & A MANUFACTURING CO INC
Gortrac Division
386 E State Road 2 (46383-9701)
PHONE..................................219 462-0822

Keith Powell, *Branch Mgr*
EMP: 100
SQ FT: 12,600
SALES (corp-wide): 1.7B **Privately Held**
WEB: www.aandamfg.com
SIC: 3599 Flexible metal hose, tubing & bellows
HQ: Dynatect Manufacturing, Inc.
     2300 S Calhoun Rd
     New Berlin WI 53151
     262 786-1500

(G-13480)
A DINE TECH INC
1609 Woodbine Dr (46383-8603)
PHONE..................................219 464-4764
John Christos, *President*
EMP: 3
SQ FT: 2,487
SALES: 100K **Privately Held**
SIC: 7372 Business oriented computer software

(G-13481)
A TO Z SIGN SHOP
55 Us Highway 30 Bldg B (46383)
PHONE..................................219 462-7489
Jack Adams, *Partner*
Ted Zoumis, *Partner*
EMP: 2
SALES: 100K **Privately Held**
SIC: 3993 Signs & advertising specialties

(G-13482)
ABIGAILS BAKING COMPANY LLC
557 Chestnut St (46385-4603)
PHONE..................................219 299-1785
EMP: 8
SALES (est): 829.4K **Privately Held**
SIC: 2051 Bread, cake & related products

(G-13483)
ABSOGRAPH SIGN CO
125 Windridge Rd (46385-6045)
PHONE..................................630 940-4093
Melissa West, *Principal*
EMP: 2
SALES (est): 161.9K **Privately Held**
SIC: 3993 Signs & advertising specialties

(G-13484)
ADVANCED PROTECTIVE TECH LLC
Also Called: Kbs Coatings
1101 Cumberland Xing # 180 (46383-2356)
PHONE..................................877 548-9323
Jim Krolak, *Vice Pres*
Ben Bonkoski, *Opers Mgr*
EMP: 7
SALES (est): 710K **Privately Held**
SIC: 2851 Paints & paint additives

(G-13485)
AERO MACHINE LLC
1251 Transport Dr Ste A (46383-8476)
PHONE..................................219 548-0490
Fax: 219 548-0382
Tom Jaeger, *President*
Don Freeman, *Vice Pres*
EMP: 32
SQ FT: 35,000
SALES (est): 5.6MM **Privately Held**
SIC: 3599 Machine shop, jobbing & repair

(G-13486)
AFTERMATH CIDERY AND WINERY
454 Greenwich St (46383-6532)
PHONE..................................219 299-8463
EMP: 2
SALES (est): 75.4K **Privately Held**
SIC: 2084 Wines, brandy & brandy spirits

(G-13487)
AGRATI - PARK FOREST LLC
4001 Redbow Dr (46383-5963)
PHONE..................................219 531-2202
Shishoni Welch, *Auditor*
Eugene Anderson, *Branch Mgr*
Gene Anderson, *Manager*
Brandon Davidson, *Supervisor*
EMP: 40

SALES (corp-wide): 927.2K **Privately Held**
WEB: www.contmid.com
SIC: **3452** Bolts, metal; screws, metal
HQ: Agrati - Park Forest, Llc
    24000 S Western Ave
    Park Forest IL 60466
    708 228-5193

(G-13488)
AJS BELTS
215 Sauk Trl (46385-7931)
PHONE.....................................219 628-0074
John Barbossa, *Principal*
▲ EMP: 2
SALES (est): 181.2K **Privately Held**
SIC: **3949** Sporting & athletic goods

(G-13489)
ALS ENVIROMENTAL
2400 Cumberland Dr (46383-2502)
PHONE.....................................219 299-8127
EMP: 3
SALES (est): 186.5K **Privately Held**
SIC: **2869** Laboratory chemicals, organic

(G-13490)
AM STABILIZERS CORPORATION
705 Silhavy Rd (46383-4463)
PHONE.....................................219 844-3980
Benjamin Labovitz, *President*
Lou Ann Robinson, *Accounting Mgr*
◆ EMP: 1
SALES (est): 6.7MM
SALES (corp-wide): 2.2B **Privately Held**
SIC: **2821** Polyvinyl chloride resins (PVC)
HQ: Amfine Chemical Corporation
    777 Perrace Ave Ste 602b
    Hasbrouck Heights NJ 07604

(G-13491)
AMERICAN FIRE COMPANY
2603 Oakwood Dr (46383-2223)
P.O. Box 1264 (46384-1264)
PHONE.....................................219 840-0630
Michael Brettin, *Principal*
EMP: 4
SALES (est): 746K **Privately Held**
SIC: **5063** 1731 7382 3669 Fire alarm systems; fire detection & burglar alarm systems specialization; fire alarm maintenance & monitoring; fire alarm apparatus, electric

(G-13492)
AMERICAN MEDICAL & DNTL EQP LL
3201 Parker Dr (46383-2467)
PHONE.....................................219 628-2928
Matthew Welter, *Principal*
EMP: 2
SALES (est): 86.6K **Privately Held**
SIC: **3843** Dental equipment

(G-13493)
ANDERSON WINERY AND VINEYARD
430 E Us Highway 6 (46383-9746)
PHONE.....................................219 464-4936
Denna Fyock, *President*
David Lundstrom, *President*
EMP: 5
SALES: 225K **Privately Held**
SIC: **2084** Wines, brandy & brandy spirits

(G-13494)
AOC LLC
2552 Industrial Dr (46383-9507)
PHONE.....................................219 465-4384
Craig Juel, *Manager*
EMP: 90
SALES (corp-wide): 290.6MM **Privately Held**
WEB: www.aoc-resins.com
SIC: **2295** 2851 2821 Plastic coated yarns or fabrics; paints & allied products; plastics materials & resins
HQ: Aoc, Llc
    955 Highway 57
    Collierville TN 38017

(G-13495)
APPLIED BIOMEDICAL TECHNO
4205 Victoria Dr (46383-2061)
PHONE.....................................219 465-2079
Bill Ruff, *Owner*
EMP: 2
SALES (est): 20K **Privately Held**
SIC: **3671** Picture tube reprocessing

(G-13496)
AQUA SPA
2505 Laporte Ave Ste 119 (46383-6995)
PHONE.....................................219 548-4772
EMP: 2
SALES (est): 94K **Privately Held**
SIC: **2844** Toilet Preparations

(G-13497)
ARCH WOOD PROTECTION INC
2852 Raystone Dr (46383-0616)
PHONE.....................................219 464-3949
Lauri Findling, *Plant Mgr*
Jim Bentincksmith, *Manager*
Lauri Finding, *Manager*
EMP: 12
SQ FT: 11,250
SALES (corp-wide): 5.1B **Privately Held**
SIC: **2819** 2899 2861 Industrial inorganic chemicals; chemical preparations; gum & wood chemicals
HQ: Arch Wood Protection, Inc.
    5660 New Northside Dr
    Atlanta GA 30328
    678 627-2000

(G-13498)
ARTEMIS INTL SOLUTIONS CORP
2600 Roosevelt Rd (46383-0970)
PHONE.....................................708 665-3155
Amy Rouse-Ho, *Branch Mgr*
EMP: 2
SALES (est): 56.5K **Privately Held**
SIC: **7372** Prepackaged software
HQ: Artemis International Solutions Corporation
    401 Congress Ave Ste 2650
    Austin TX 78701
    512 201-8222

(G-13499)
ASAP SIGN & LIGHTING MAINT
276 W State Road 130 (46385-8706)
PHONE.....................................219 464-8865
Harry O Keehn, *President*
Mabel Keehn, *Corp Secy*
EMP: 3
SQ FT: 2,000
SALES (est): 200K **Privately Held**
SIC: **3993** Signs & advertising specialties

(G-13500)
AVIATION FUEL GROUP LLC
159 Brockton Pl (46385-8056)
PHONE.....................................219 462-6081
Richard Dimarco Esq, *Bd of Directors*
EMP: 3
SALES (est): 175.4K **Privately Held**
SIC: **2869** Fuels

(G-13501)
AWARDS AMERICA
397 E Us Highway 30 (46383-9554)
PHONE.....................................219 462-7903
Donna North, *Owner*
EMP: 20
SQ FT: 12,000
SALES (est): 1.8MM **Privately Held**
SIC: **2399** 3999 Emblems, badges & insignia: from purchased materials; plaques, picture, laminated; identification badges & insignia

(G-13502)
BACH TECH INC
67 S 500 W (46385-9036)
PHONE.....................................219 531-7424
Jeff Reidenbach, *President*
EMP: 2
SQ FT: 2,672
SALES: 500K **Privately Held**
SIC: **3579** Mailing, letter handling & addressing machines

(G-13503)
BARNETT INDUSTRIAL INC
3012 Grand Trunk Rd (46383-9145)
PHONE.....................................219 814-7500
Robert Edward Barnett, *President*
EMP: 10 EST: 2008
SQ FT: 8,500
SALES (est): 1.3MM **Privately Held**
SIC: **3499** Machine bases, metal

(G-13504)
BATH & BODY WORKS LLC
2410 Laporte Ave Ste 140 (46383-6969)
PHONE.....................................219 531-2146
Meridith Bradford, *Manager*
EMP: 40
SALES (corp-wide): 12.6B **Publicly Held**
WEB: www.bath-and-body.com
SIC: **5999** 2844 Perfumes & colognes; toilet preparations
HQ: Bath & Body Works, Llc
    7 Limited Pkwy E
    Reynoldsburg OH 43068

(G-13505)
BATH GALLERY SHOWROOM
709 Morthland Dr (46383-6409)
PHONE.....................................219 531-2150
Jack Hodurek, *President*
EMP: 2
SALES (est): 146.4K **Privately Held**
SIC: **3432** 5074 Plumbing fixture fittings & trim; plumbing fittings & supplies

(G-13506)
BAUM CABINETRY LLC
4 Spectacle Dr (46383-1053)
PHONE.....................................219 575-6309
Joseph Drew, *Owner*
EMP: 2
SALES (est): 198K **Privately Held**
SIC: **2434** Wood kitchen cabinets

(G-13507)
BAXTER DESIGN & ADVERTISING
656 Franklin St (46383-6427)
PHONE.....................................219 464-9237
Sue Baxter, *Owner*
EMP: 2
SALES (est): 236.8K **Privately Held**
SIC: **7311** 2721 Advertising consultant; periodicals

(G-13508)
BEULAH INC
808 N 360 W (46385-7912)
P.O. Box 1516 (46384-1516)
PHONE.....................................219 309-5635
Fax: 219 764-7795
Sheila Nevill, *President*
David Nevill, *Vice Pres*
Marilyn Thomsen, *Director*
EMP: 8
SALES (est): 903.8K **Privately Held**
WEB: www.beulahinc.com
SIC: **3542** Machine tools, metal forming type

(G-13509)
BIRD PUBLISHING COMPANY
1600 Edgewater Beach Rd (46383-1185)
PHONE.....................................219 462-6330
Charles Bird, *Owner*
Hannah Bird, *Co-Owner*
EMP: 2
SALES (est): 53.2K **Privately Held**
SIC: **2731** 7812 Book publishing; video tape production

(G-13510)
BLYTHES SPORT SHOP INC
2810 Calumet Ave (46383-2606)
PHONE.....................................219 476-0026
Fax: 219 477-4829
Michael Blythe, *Vice Pres*
Kathy Mackenzie, *Engineer*
EMP: 25
SQ FT: 11,000
SALES (corp-wide): 5.6MM **Privately Held**
SIC: **5941** 2396 Firearms; automotive & apparel trimmings

PA: Blythes Sport Shop Inc
    138 N Broad St
    Griffith IN 46319
    219 924-4403

(G-13511)
BOARDWORKS INC
1203 Formula Dr (46383-4342)
PHONE.....................................219 464-8111
Fax: 219 464-9716
Robert P Klett, *President*
EMP: 3
SQ FT: 2,000
SALES (est): 340K **Privately Held**
WEB: www.boardworks.com
SIC: **2541** 2519 Table or counter tops, plastic laminated; fiberglass furniture, household: padded or plain

(G-13512)
BOY-CONN PRINTERS INC
803 Glendale Blvd (46383-3718)
P.O. Box 1083 (46384-1083)
PHONE.....................................219 462-2665
Fax: 219 477-4760
Gary Connors, *President*
Susan Connors, *Vice Pres*
EMP: 4
SQ FT: 3,500
SALES (est): 297K **Privately Held**
SIC: **2752** Commercial printing, offset

(G-13513)
BREWHOUSE SUPPLIES LLC
1555 W Lincolnway Ste 102 (46385-3801)
PHONE.....................................219 286-7285
Jeffery L Blade,
Amanda Blade,
EMP: 2 EST: 2013
SALES (est): 134.1K **Privately Held**
SIC: **2084** Wines

(G-13514)
BROWNS DAIRY INC (PA)
Also Called: Valpo Velvet Shoppe
57 Monroe St (46383-5535)
PHONE.....................................219 464-4141
Mike Brown, *President*
Mark Brown, *Vice Pres*
Elizabeth Brown, *Treasurer*
Sue Cain, *Admin Sec*
EMP: 15
SQ FT: 10,000
SALES (est): 1.1MM **Privately Held**
SIC: **2024** 5812 Ice cream, bulk; ice cream stands or dairy bars

(G-13515)
BRQ QUICKPRINT INC
Also Called: Quick Print
1310 Lincolnway (46383-5824)
PHONE.....................................219 464-1070
Fax: 219 477-4740
Bonnie Hontz, *President*
Rod L Hontz, *CFO*
EMP: 3
SQ FT: 2,500
SALES: 291.3K **Privately Held**
WEB: www.brqquickprint.com
SIC: **2752** Commercial printing, offset; color lithography

(G-13516)
BRYSON C TOOTHAKER
45 Tayside St (46385-9281)
PHONE.....................................219 462-9179
EMP: 2 EST: 2012
SALES (est): 120K **Privately Held**
SIC: **2752** Lithographic Commercial Printing

(G-13517)
BWAY CORPORATION
4002 Montdale Park Dr (46383-0606)
PHONE.....................................219 462-8915
Cheri Jabaay, *Purch Agent*
Ronald Brockway, *Branch Mgr*
Mark Peracki, *Maintence Staff*
Jeff Saucier, *Maintence Staff*
EMP: 70
SALES (corp-wide): 787.1MM **Privately Held**
SIC: **3411** 3499 Metal cans; ammunition boxes, metal

HQ: Bway Corporation
8607 Roberts Dr Ste 250
Atlanta GA 30350

(G-13518)
C MILLIGAN INVESTMENTS LLC
1208 Pine Creek Rd (46383-7203)
PHONE....................................219 241-5811
Carolyn A Milligan, *Mng Member*
EMP: 5
SALES (est): 341.3K **Privately Held**
SIC: 1311 Oil shale mining

(G-13519)
CASE WEINKAUFF
671 E 100 S (46383-9516)
PHONE....................................219 733-9484
Case Weinkauff, *Principal*
EMP: 2
SALES (est): 302.9K **Privately Held**
SIC: 3523 Farm machinery & equipment

(G-13520)
CATHAY INDUSTRIES (USA) INC (HQ)
Also Called: Cathay Pigments
4901 Evans Ave (46383-8383)
PHONE....................................219 531-5359
Kevin Miles, *President*
Melanie Marshall, *Chairman*
▲ EMP: 45
SQ FT: 77,000
SALES: 35MM **Privately Held**
SIC: 2816 Color pigments; iron oxide pig-
ments (ochers, siennas, umbers)
PA: Cathay Industries Asia Pacific Limited
Rm 901a 9/F Chinachem Golden
Plaza
Tsim Sha Tsui KLN
272 122-57

(G-13521)
CERAMIX 101
908 Roosevelt Rd Ste C (46383-4376)
PHONE....................................219 531-6536
Julie Reynolds, *Principal*
EMP: 3
SALES (est): 280.1K **Privately Held**
SIC: 3795 Tanks & tank components

(G-13522)
CHICAGO AUTOMATED LABELING
44 N 450 E (46383-9310)
PHONE....................................219 531-0646
Fax: 219 462-8315
Mark Walker, *President*
Ken Walker, *Vice Pres*
EMP: 12
SQ FT: 5,200
SALES (est): 2.4MM **Privately Held**
WEB: www.chicagoautolabel.com
SIC: 3565 Packaging machinery

(G-13523)
COUNTERFITTERS INC
359 Franklin St Ste C (46383-5432)
PHONE....................................219 531-0848
Fax: 219 531-0848
Darrell Mech, *President*
EMP: 2
SALES: 450K **Privately Held**
SIC: 5211 2434 Cabinets, kitchen; wood
kitchen cabinets

(G-13524)
CRISMAN SAND CO INC
251 Indiana Ave (46383-5582)
PHONE....................................219 762-2619
Craig Vincent, *President*
John Magurean, *Corp Secy*
Eric Hein, *Manager*
EMP: 8 EST: 1924
SALES (est): 730.5K **Privately Held**
SIC: 1442 Sand mining

(G-13525)
CUSTOM MACHINING SERVICES INC
Also Called: Custom Crimp
326 N 400 E (46383-9704)
PHONE....................................219 462-6128
Fax: 219 464-2773
Jack L Thompson, *President*
Joe Intagliata, *Vice Pres*

Mary Ann Thompson, *Admin Sec*
◆ EMP: 45 EST: 1931
SQ FT: 28,000
SALES (est): 8.3MM **Privately Held**
WEB: www.customcrimp.com
SIC: 3599 7692 Machine shop, jobbing &
repair; welding repair

(G-13526)
CUSTOM QLTING PLLOW CSHION SVC
102 Harmel Dr (46383-5928)
PHONE....................................219 464-7316
Curt Bielski, *Owner*
EMP: 5
SALES: 79K **Privately Held**
WEB: www.sewhat.com
SIC: 2211 5949 Draperies & drapery fab-
rics, cotton; sewing, needlework & piece
goods

(G-13527)
D-J PRINTING SPECIALISTS INC
Also Called: American Speedy Printing
2600 Roosevelt Rd 200-4 (46383-0970)
PHONE....................................219 465-1164
Fax: 219 462-4606
Phyllis Grutz, *President*
EMP: 3
SQ FT: 1,728
SALES: 250K **Privately Held**
SIC: 2759 Commercial printing

(G-13528)
DEUTSCH LLC
1753 Crestview Dr (46383-6647)
PHONE....................................219 464-1557
Richard R Deutsch, *President*
EMP: 3
SALES (est): 166.3K **Privately Held**
SIC: 3594 Motors: hydraulic, fluid power or
air

(G-13529)
DUNE RIDGE WINERY LLC
1903 Cheyenne Cir (46383-7031)
PHONE....................................219 548-4605
Kathy Holevinsky, *Principal*
EMP: 2
SALES (est): 90K **Privately Held**
SIC: 2084 Wines

(G-13530)
DUNELAND SPECIALTIES INC
2005 Calumet Ave (46383-2705)
PHONE....................................219 464-1616
Charlotte Brechner, *President*
Ronald E Brechner, *Corp Secy*
EMP: 2
SALES (est): 100K **Privately Held**
WEB: www.dunelandspecialties.com
SIC: 5947 5199 2752 Gift, novelty & sou-
venir shop; advertising specialties; com-
mercial printing, lithographic

(G-13531)
DYNATECT MANUFACTURING INC
386 E State Road 2 (46383-9701)
PHONE....................................219 465-1898
EMP: 7
SALES (est): 517.7K **Privately Held**
SIC: 3999 Barber & beauty shop equip-
ment

(G-13532)
EL POPULAR SAUSAGE FACTORY LLC
555 Eastport Centre Dr (46383-2911)
P.O. Box 2237 (46384-2237)
PHONE....................................219 476-7040
Pete Peuquet, *President*
Drew Peuquet, *Vice Pres*
Jennifer Ritchie, *Purchasing*
Kevin McGuffey, *Treasurer*
Edward Garza, *Mng Member*
EMP: 7
SQ FT: 9,000
SALES (est): 773.8K **Privately Held**
SIC: 2013 Sausages & other prepared
meats

(G-13533)
ELEGAN GRAPHICS
5905 Murvihill Rd (46383-8376)
PHONE....................................219 462-9921
Chuck Williams, *Principal*
EMP: 2
SALES (est): 154.6K **Privately Held**
SIC: 2759 Screen printing

(G-13534)
ELEGAN SPORTSWEAR INC
Also Called: Elegan Customwear
212 Lincolnway (46383-5691)
PHONE....................................219 464-8416
Fax: 219 464-3977
Charles Williams, *President*
Luther Williams, *Corp Secy*
Craig Gall, *Vice Pres*
EMP: 15
SQ FT: 12,000
SALES: 3MM **Privately Held**
SIC: 2395 2396 Embroidery products, ex-
cept schiffli machine; screen printing on
fabric articles

(G-13535)
ELITE CRETE SYSTEMS INC (PA)
1151 Transport Dr (46383-8491)
PHONE....................................219 465-7671
Ken Freestone, *President*
Thomas Gladden, *Research*
Kathy Paxton, *CFO*
Mario Nicasio, *Technical Staff*
Jeff Sherer, *Director*
◆ EMP: 25
SQ FT: 125,000
SALES: 20MM **Privately Held**
WEB: www.elitecrete.com
SIC: 2295 Resin or plastic coated fabrics

(G-13536)
EMBROIDME
2254 Morthland Dr (46385-5372)
PHONE....................................219 465-1400
Fax: 219 465-1422
Tony Miccllche, *Principal*
EMP: 2 EST: 2007
SALES (est): 74.4K **Privately Held**
SIC: 5949 5947 5942 2759 Sewing,
needlework & piece goods; gift, novelty &
souvenir shop; book stores; screen print-
ing

(G-13537)
EMERSON ELECTRIC CO
2300 Evans Ave (46383-4054)
PHONE....................................219 465-2411
Mark Horst, *VP Human Res*
EMP: 4
SALES (corp-wide): 15.2B **Publicly Held**
SIC: 3823 Industrial instrmnts msrmnt dis-
play/control process variable
PA: Emerson Electric Co.
8000 West Florissant Ave
Saint Louis MO 63136
314 553-2000

(G-13538)
EXCEL MACHINE TECHNOLOGIES INC
405 Elm St (46383-3620)
PHONE....................................219 548-0708
David L Defries, *President*
Kathleen Defries, *Vice Pres*
EMP: 17
SQ FT: 120,000
SALES (est): 3MM **Privately Held**
WEB: www.excelmachine.com
SIC: 3599 Machine shop, jobbing & repair

(G-13539)
FAIRWAY LASER SYSTEMS INC
950 Transport Dr (46383)
PHONE....................................219 462-6892
EMP: 4
SQ FT: 1,600
SALES (est): 557.3K **Privately Held**
SIC: 3699 Mfg Electrical Equipment/Sup-
plies

(G-13540)
FASHION FLOORING AND LTG INC
2510 Beech St (46383-4097)
PHONE....................................219 531-5667
Fax: 219 531-4319
Walter W Carter, *President*
Walter Carter, *President*
Jean Carter, *Vice Pres*
EMP: 7
SQ FT: 12,700
SALES: 2.2MM **Privately Held**
SIC: 5713 3645 Carpets; residential light-
ing fixtures

(G-13541)
FASTENER EQUIPMENT CORPORATION
1150 Loudermilk Ln (46383-8475)
PHONE....................................708 957-5100
Le Roy Loudermilk, *President*
John Ewing, *Director*
▲ EMP: 6
SQ FT: 30,000
SALES (est): 1.2MM **Privately Held**
WEB: www.fastenerequipmentcorp.com
SIC: 5084 3545 Machine tools & metal-
working machinery; machine tool attach-
ments & accessories

(G-13542)
FEDEX OFFICE & PRINT SVCS INC
2505 Laporte Ave Ste 115 (46383-6995)
PHONE....................................219 462-6270
Fax: 219 462-6715
EMP: 4
SALES (corp-wide): 65.4B **Publicly Held**
WEB: www.fedex.com
SIC: 2759 5099 7334 Commercial print-
ing; signs, except electric; photocopying &
duplicating services
HQ: Fedex Office And Print Services, Inc.
7900 Legacy Dr
Plano TX 75024
214 550-7000

(G-13543)
FIGURE EIGHT BREWING LLC
150 Washington St (46383-5507)
PHONE....................................219 477-2000
Tom Uban, *Mng Member*
EMP: 27
SQ FT: 12,000
SALES (est): 3.9MM **Privately Held**
SIC: 2082 Beer (alcoholic beverage)

(G-13544)
FROZEN GARDEN LLC
315 E 316 N Ste C (46383-8467)
PHONE....................................219 286-3578
Allyson Straka,
EMP: 10
SALES: 200K **Privately Held**
SIC: 2037 Frozen fruits & vegetables

(G-13545)
G F M S INDUSTRIES
166 Wessex Ct (46385-7711)
PHONE....................................219 464-1445
Norman Smith, *Principal*
EMP: 2
SALES (est): 113.2K **Privately Held**
SIC: 3999 Manufacturing industries

(G-13546)
GARY ELECTRIC MOTOR SERVICE CO
393 E Us Highway 30 (46383-9554)
PHONE....................................219 884-6555
Fax: 219 884-3577
Randal Massena, *President*
Frank Kantroski, *Vice Pres*
EMP: 12
SQ FT: 35,000
SALES: 7MM **Privately Held**
SIC: 7694 Electric motor repair

(G-13547)
GAST SIGN CO
499 W Us Highway 30 (46385-9218)
PHONE....................................219 759-4336
Joseph Gast, *Owner*
EMP: 3

SALES (est): 195.8K **Privately Held**
SIC: 3993 Signs & advertising specialties

(G-13548)
GLOBAL ENERGY RESOURCES LLC
Also Called: Ger
5206 Garden Gtwy (46383-1002)
PHONE..................................219 712-2556
Joseph Smolar,
EMP: 3 **EST:** 2008
SQ FT: 4,000
SALES (est): 370K **Privately Held**
SIC: 2869 Industrial organic chemicals

(G-13549)
GNOME INDUSTRIES INC
808 N 360 W Rear (46385-7912)
PHONE..................................219 764-3337
EMP: 2 **EST:** 2011
SALES (est): 130K **Privately Held**
SIC: 3999 Mfg Misc Products

(G-13550)
GOATEE SHIRT PRINTING
1039 N 200 W (46385-8517)
PHONE..................................219 916-2443
Megan Sexton, *Principal*
EMP: 2 **EST:** 2016
SALES (est): 110.1K **Privately Held**
SIC: 2752 Commercial printing, lithographic

(G-13551)
GOURMET EXPRESS
1256 Morthland Dr (46385-6250)
PHONE..................................219 921-9927
Carol Herbrand, *Owner*
EMP: 4
SALES (est): 313.3K **Privately Held**
SIC: 2741 Miscellaneous publishing

(G-13552)
GRID ELEMENT SLED
460 Bond Ave Ste D (46385-4202)
PHONE..................................219 462-2687
Nathan Walker, *Principal*
EMP: 2
SALES (est): 74.4K **Privately Held**
SIC: 2819 Elements

(G-13553)
GRID ELEMENTS
20 Tower Rd (46385-9282)
PHONE..................................219 615-9683
Jennifer Walker, *Principal*
EMP: 2
SALES (est): 83.9K **Privately Held**
SIC: 2819 Elements

(G-13554)
HARDWOODS BY BILL LLC
2450 Honelee Ct (46385-8096)
PHONE..................................219 465-5346
William Stocky, *Principal*
EMP: 2 **EST:** 2014
SALES (est): 67.5K **Privately Held**
SIC: 2499 Wood products

(G-13555)
HEAT WAGONS INC
Also Called: WOOD KOVERS
342 N 400 E (46383-9704)
PHONE..................................219 464-8818
John Walsh, *President*
John Barney, *Vice Pres*
John Leurck, *Vice Pres*
Jim Santay, *Marketing Staff*
Brad Lundgren, *Director*
▲ **EMP:** 10
SQ FT: 24,000
SALES: 5.5MM **Privately Held**
WEB: www.heatwagon.com
SIC: 3433 3567 7359 Space heaters, except electric; industrial furnaces & ovens; equipment rental & leasing

(G-13556)
HOME RUN LLC
Also Called: Hoosier Bat Company
312 N 325 E Ste B (46383-6965)
P.O. Box 432 (46384-0432)
PHONE..................................219 531-1006
Dave Cook, *Mng Member*
EMP: 4 **EST:** 1991

SQ FT: 6,000
SALES: 250K **Privately Held**
WEB: www.hoosierbat.com
SIC: 3949 Baseball equipment & supplies, general

(G-13557)
HOOSIER FIRE EQUIPMENT INC (PA)
4009 Montdale Park Dr (46383-0607)
PHONE..................................219 462-1707
Fax: 219 464-0283
Nick Swartz, *President*
Cindy Swartz, *Corp Secy*
Timothy Swartz, *Sales Mgr*
Taylor Chitwood, *Director*
EMP: 20
SQ FT: 15,500
SALES (est): 3.5MM **Privately Held**
SIC: 5087 3561 5084 5063 Firefighting equipment; pumps & pumping equipment; industrial machinery & equipment; electrical apparatus & equipment; motor vehicle supplies & new parts

(G-13558)
I E M C
Also Called: Industrial Elec Maint Co
1150 Lincolnway Ste 1 (46385-5800)
PHONE..................................219 464-2890
Bryant Mitol, *Owner*
EMP: 3
SQ FT: 1,000
SALES (est): 250K **Privately Held**
SIC: 7629 3663 Electrical equipment repair services; radio & TV communications equipment

(G-13559)
IDEAL SIGN CORP
507 N 325 W (46385-8717)
P.O. Box 1302 (46384-1302)
PHONE..................................219 406-2092
Jamie Bartok, *Principal*
EMP: 2
SALES (est): 132.5K **Privately Held**
SIC: 3993 Signs & advertising specialties

(G-13560)
INNOVATIVE RESCUE SYSTEMS INC
Also Called: Amkus Rescue Systems
4201 Montdale Dr (46383)
PHONE..................................219 548-1028
Kyle Smith, *President*
James Cunningham, *CFO*
EMP: 2
SALES (est): 113.4K **Privately Held**
SIC: 3546 Power-driven handtools

(G-13561)
IRONGATE V LLC
214 Edgewood Dr (46385-7382)
PHONE..................................219 464-8704
Thomas Krafft, *Principal*
EMP: 2
SALES (est): 111.3K **Privately Held**
SIC: 2082 Malt beverages

(G-13562)
J V C MACHINING
766 N 500 E (46383-9733)
PHONE..................................219 462-0363
John V Cortez, *Principal*
EMP: 2
SQ FT: 3,096
SALES (est): 118.8K **Privately Held**
SIC: 3599 Machine shop, jobbing & repair

(G-13563)
JEMARKEL HEALTH-TECH LLC
2701 Beech St Ste R (46383-6001)
PHONE..................................219 548-5881
Fax: 219 548-5891
Thomas E Brandt,
▲ **EMP:** 12
SALES (est): 950.7K **Privately Held**
SIC: 3841 Muscle exercise apparatus, ophthalmic

(G-13564)
JM MACHINE
354 W Division Rd (46385-9049)
PHONE..................................219 464-4477
Jim Cane, *Owner*

EMP: 2
SALES (est): 77.5K **Privately Held**
SIC: 3469 Machine parts, stamped or pressed metal

(G-13565)
KELLER LOGGING LLC ✪
210 W 375 S (46385-9623)
P.O. Box 9 (46384-0009)
PHONE..................................219 309-0379
Ben Keller, *President*
EMP: 2 **EST:** 2017
SALES (est): 83.3K **Privately Held**
SIC: 2411 Logging

(G-13566)
KELLER MACHINE & WELDING INC
5705 Murvihill Rd (46383-6313)
PHONE..................................219 464-4915
Fax: 219 462-5245
Daniel S Keller, *President*
Daniel Keller, *President*
EMP: 32
SQ FT: 1,200
SALES (est): 5.4MM **Privately Held**
SIC: 3441 3599 Fabricated structural metal; custom machinery

(G-13567)
KOBALTEC LLC
1450 Clark Rd (46385-9811)
PHONE..................................219 462-1483
Matthew Berg, *CEO*
Brittany Taroli, *CFO*
▲ **EMP:** 5
SQ FT: 10,000
SALES (est): 265.8K **Privately Held**
SIC: 3492 Hose & tube fittings & assemblies, hydraulic/pneumatic

(G-13568)
LABTEST EQUIPMENT COMPANY
72 Timber Dr (46385-9685)
PHONE..................................219 462-3300
James Mattel, *Owner*
EMP: 83
SQ FT: 2,238
SALES: 30MM **Privately Held**
SIC: 3826 Analytical instruments

(G-13569)
LAKE CABLE OF INDIANA LLC
2700 Evans Ave (46383-4440)
PHONE..................................847 238-3000
Emile Tohme, *President*
Mary Oziemkowski, *CFO*
William L Runzel,
EMP: 103
SQ FT: 126,000
SALES (est): 35.6MM **Privately Held**
SIC: 3496 Miscellaneous fabricated wire products

(G-13570)
LANDGREBE MANUFACTURING INC
208 N 250 W (46385-9242)
PHONE..................................219 462-9587
Fax: 219 477-2001
George Landgrebe, *President*
Beth Landgrebe, *Vice Pres*
EMP: 3
SQ FT: 8,500
SALES: 500K **Privately Held**
WEB: www.towtrailer.com
SIC: 3537 3799 Dollies (hand or power trucks), industrial except mining; aircraft engine cradles; platforms, stands, tables, pallets & similar equipment; towing bars & systems; automobile trailer chassis; trailers & trailer equipment

(G-13571)
LANGENWLTER CRPT DYG VLPARAISO
185 Wexford Rd (46385-8038)
PHONE..................................219 531-7601
Arthur Snow, *Owner*
Susan Snow, *Owner*
EMP: 2
SALES (est): 82.1K **Privately Held**
SIC: 2273 Dyeing & finishing of tufted rugs & carpets

(G-13572)
LAPIS SERVICES INC
1101 Cumberland Xing (46383-2356)
PHONE..................................219 464-9131
Jere Brigg, *President*
Mary Kwiatkowski, *CFO*
EMP: 3
SALES (est): 660K **Privately Held**
SIC: 3444 8999 Sheet metalwork; services

(G-13573)
LASER SYSTEMS
104 Billings St Ste A (46383-3601)
PHONE..................................219 465-1155
Drew Watson, *President*
EMP: 3
SALES (est): 242.1K **Privately Held**
SIC: 3861 Toners, prepared photographic (not made in chemical plants)

(G-13574)
LEE PUBLICATIONS INC
Also Called: Howard Pblctions Vidette Times
1111 Glendale Blvd (46383-3724)
PHONE..................................219 462-5151
Don Asher, *Branch Mgr*
EMP: 50
SALES (corp-wide): 566.9MM **Publicly Held**
SIC: 2711 Newspapers, publishing & printing
HQ: Lee Publications, Inc.
201 N Harrison St Ste 600
Davenport IA 52801
563 383-2100

(G-13575)
LEGACY VULCAN LLC
Also Called: Whitcomb Yard
4105 Montdale Park Dr (46383-0608)
PHONE..................................219 465-3066
Gary Whitcomb, *Manager*
EMP: 23 **Publicly Held**
WEB: www.vulcanmaterials.com
SIC: 1422 Crushed & broken limestone
HQ: Legacy Vulcan, Llc
1200 Urban Center Dr
Vestavia AL 35242
205 298-3000

(G-13576)
LEGACY VULCAN LLC
Also Called: Ralston Yard
651 Axe Ave (46383-6479)
PHONE..................................219 462-5832
Nan Ralston, *President*
EMP: 30 **Publicly Held**
WEB: www.vulcanmaterials.com
SIC: 3272 Concrete products
HQ: Legacy Vulcan, Llc
1200 Urban Center Dr
Vestavia AL 35242
205 298-3000

(G-13577)
LITKO AEROSYSTEMS INC
316 E 316 N Ste 6 (46383-6993)
PHONE..................................219 462-9295
Kenneth R Litko, *President*
▼ **EMP:** 5
SQ FT: 2,100
SALES (est): 597.4K **Privately Held**
WEB: www.litkoaero.com
SIC: 3999 Miniatures

(G-13578)
M AND B FABRICATING LLC
826 N 360 W (46385-7912)
PHONE..................................219 762-5032
Ryan Mathas, *Mng Member*
EMP: 12
SALES (est): 1.5MM **Privately Held**
SIC: 3441 Fabricated structural metal

(G-13579)
MCGILL MANUFACTURING CO INC
2300 Evans Ave (46383-4054)
PHONE..................................219 465-2200
Fax: 219 465-2290
Tony Pajk, *President*
Joe Hofferth, *Manager*
◆ **EMP:** 510 **EST:** 1905
SQ FT: 200,000

▲ = Import ▼=Export
◆ =Import/Export

SALES (est): 112.7MM
SALES (corp-wide): 3.3B **Publicly Held**
WEB: www.emerson-ept.com
SIC: **3562** Ball & roller bearings; roller
bearings & parts
HQ: Regal Beloit America, Inc.
200 State St
Beloit WI 53511
608 364-8800

(G-13580)
MECHANICAL PARTS & SVCS INC
Also Called: Mpsi
304 Burlington Beach Rd (46383-1939)
P.O. Box 4030, Carmel (46082-4030)
PHONE............................219 670-1986
David E Baldea, *President*
Nancy J Baldea, *Admin Sec*
▲ EMP: 3
SALES (est): 391.7K **Privately Held**
SIC: **3824** Mechanical counters

(G-13581)
MORIN CORP
302 Elmhurst Ave (46385-4515)
PHONE............................219 465-8334
Jim White, *CEO*
EMP: 2
SALES (est): 94.5K **Privately Held**
SIC: **3444** Sheet metalwork

(G-13582)
MR COPYRITE
308 Lincolnway (46383-5609)
PHONE............................219 462-1108
Fax: 219 462-1109
Diane Price, *Owner*
EMP: 3 EST: 1974
SALES (est): 252.3K **Privately Held**
SIC: **2752** Commercial printing, offset

(G-13583)
N-OVATIONS INC
506 Franklin St (46383-4251)
PHONE............................219 464-0441
Robert K Kirkpatrick, *Principal*
EMP: 3
SALES (est): 210.7K **Privately Held**
SIC: **3821** Clinical laboratory instruments,
except medical & dental

(G-13584)
NAGYS WINERY LLC
109 Shorewood Dr (46385-8067)
PHONE............................219 331-0588
David Nagy, *Owner*
EMP: 2
SALES (est): 67.3K **Privately Held**
SIC: **2084** Wines

(G-13585)
NARROW GATE PUBLISHING LLC
113 Shorewood Dr (46385-8067)
PHONE............................219 464-8579
Monica J Kerr, *Owner*
EMP: 2
SALES (est): 44.3K **Privately Held**
SIC: **2741** Miscellaneous publishing

(G-13586)
NATIONAL EQUIPMENT INC
Also Called: Enduring Graphics
358 Harrison Blvd (46383-3414)
PHONE............................219 462-1205
Wayne Cobb, *President*
Edward Cobb, *Vice Pres*
EMP: 7
SALES (est): 770K **Privately Held**
SIC: **3523 5083** Farm machinery & equip-
ment; agricultural machinery & equipment

(G-13587)
NEW ELEMENTS LLC
212 Morthland Dr (46383-6221)
PHONE............................219 465-1389
Justine Goodwin, *Administration*
EMP: 2
SALES (est): 75.1K **Privately Held**
SIC: **2819** Elements

(G-13588)
NGH RETAIL LLC
315 E 316 N Ste A (46383-8467)
PHONE............................219 476-0772
Mark A Laursen,
▲ EMP: 3
SALES (est): 813.3K **Privately Held**
SIC: **5999 3724** Engines & parts, air-
cooled; aircraft engines & engine parts

(G-13589)
NGH RETAIL LLC
301 W 550 N (46385-8715)
PHONE............................219 476-0772
Mark Laursen, *President*
Debbie Laursen, *General Mgr*
▲ EMP: 5
SALES (est): 340K **Privately Held**
SIC: **3433** Heating equipment, except elec-
tric

(G-13590)
NISOURCE INC
2755 Raystone Dr (46383-9565)
PHONE............................877 647-5990
Philip Pack, *Principal*
Stephen P Smith, *Exec VP*
Violet G Sistovaris, *Senior VP*
Vern Vannostran Jr, *Project Mgr*
Caroline Rosenbaum, *Admin Asst*
EMP: 7
SALES (est): 640K **Privately Held**
SIC: **1321** Natural gas liquids

(G-13591)
NOODLE SHOP CO - COLORADO INC
71 Silhavy Rd Ste 101 (46383-4493)
PHONE............................219 548-0921
EMP: 4
SALES (est): 136K **Privately Held**
SIC: **2098** Noodles (e.g. egg, plain &
water), dry

(G-13592)
NORTH AMERICA PACKAGING CORP
Also Called: Southcorp Packaging North
Amer
4002 Montdale Park Dr (46383-0606)
PHONE............................219 462-8915
Jeff Nicolee, *Branch Mgr*
EMP: 108
SALES (corp-wide): 787.1MM **Privately
Held**
WEB: www.nampac.com
SIC: **3089** Pails, plastic
HQ: North America Packaging Corp
1515 W 22nd St Ste 550
Oak Brook IL 60523
630 203-4100

(G-13593)
NORTH STAR STONE INC
312 N 325 E (46383-6964)
PHONE............................219 464-7272
Fax: 219 477-0033
Mary C Andrews, *President*
Chris Andrews, *Vice Pres*
EMP: 27
SALES (est): 5.3MM **Privately Held**
SIC: **3271** Architectural concrete: block,
split, fluted, screen, etc.

(G-13594)
OLYMPUS MANUFACTURING SYSTEMS
4703 N Calumet Ave (46383-1611)
PHONE............................219 465-1520
Stylianos Shepard, *President*
Sharon Shepard, *Treasurer*
EMP: 5
SQ FT: 1,200
SALES: 800K **Privately Held**
SIC: **3542** Machine tools, metal forming
type

(G-13595)
OMNITECH SYSTEMS INC
450 Campbell St Ste 2 (46385-6299)
PHONE............................219 531-5532
Fax: 219 464-0380
Jon Barrett, *President*
Keldon S Pickering, *Vice Pres*
Joi Rodriguez, *Research*

Jon D Barrett, *Director*
EMP: 40
SQ FT: 10,000
SALES: 6MM **Privately Held**
SIC: **3841** Surgical & medical instruments

(G-13596)
OWENS CORNING SALES LLC
2552 Industrial Dr (46383-9507)
PHONE............................219 465-4324
Fax: 219 465-4360
Craig Gule, *Manager*
EMP: 78 **Publicly Held**
WEB: www.owenscorning.com
SIC: **3296** Mineral wool
HQ: Owens Corning Sales, Llc
1 Owens Corning Pkwy
Toledo OH 43659
419 248-8000

(G-13597)
PERMA LUBRICATION
2503 Chicago St Ste A (46383-5863)
PHONE............................219 531-9155
Fax: 219 477-6444
Garland Bridgewater, *President*
Jeff Seymour, *Regl Sales Mgr*
EMP: 6
SALES (est): 105.4K **Privately Held**
SIC: **3569** Lubricating equipment

(G-13598)
PERMA-GREEN SUPREME INC
5609 Murvihill Rd (46383-6315)
PHONE............................219 548-3801
Fax: 219 476-7113
Thomas F Jessen, *President*
Thomas Jessen, *Admin Sec*
EMP: 25
SQ FT: 30,000
SALES (est): 5.3MM **Privately Held**
WEB: www.ride-onspreader.com
SIC: **3559** Chemical machinery & equip-
ment

(G-13599)
POWDER PROCESSING & TECH LLC
5103 Evans Ave (46383-8387)
PHONE............................219 462-4141
Regina Hofferth, *Buyer*
Michael Ruffin, *Engineer*
John J Kaziow, *Mng Member*
Bradley Monton, *Manager*
Errol Menke,
▲ EMP: 42
SALES (est): 11.7MM **Privately Held**
WEB: www.ppctechnology.com
SIC: **3399** Powder, metal

(G-13600)
POWDERTECH CORP
5103 Evans Ave (46383-8387)
PHONE............................219 462-4141
Fax: 219 462-0376
Ken Bartelt, *President*
Toshio Honjo, *Exec VP*
Masao Ogawa, *Admin Sec*
▲ EMP: 60
SQ FT: 200,000
SALES: 10MM
SALES (corp-wide): 102.7MM **Privately
Held**
SIC: **3399** Iron, powdered
PA: Powdertech Co., Ltd.
217, Toyofuta
Kashiwa CHI 277-0
471 455-751

(G-13601)
PRATT (JET CORR) INC
Also Called: Pratt Industries USA
3155 S State Road 49 (46383-7831)
PHONE............................219 548-9191
Fax: 219 476-0275
Robert Young, *General Mgr*
Rob Yarger, *Maint Spvr*
Pam Ratcliff, *Purchasing*
Brad Mossner, *Controller*
EMP: 300
SALES (corp-wide): 2.1B **Privately Held**
SIC: **2653** Boxes, corrugated: made from
purchased materials; sheets, solid fiber:
made from purchased materials

HQ: Pratt (Jet Corr), Inc.
1800 Sarasot Bus Pkwy Ne B
Conyers GA 30013
770 929-1300

(G-13602)
PRATT PAPER (IN) LLC
3050 Anthony Pratt Dr (46383-0032)
PHONE............................219 477-1040
Jay Henessey, *General Mgr*
EMP: 21
SALES (corp-wide): 2.1B **Privately Held**
SIC: **2621** Paper mills
HQ: Pratt Paper (In), Llc
1800 Sarasot Bus Pkwy Ne C
Conyers GA 30013
770 918-5678

(G-13603)
Q AIR INC
4008 Murvihill Rd (46383)
PHONE............................219 476-7048
Steve Qualizza, *President*
EMP: 2
SALES (est): 306K **Privately Held**
SIC: **3728** Aircraft parts & equipment

(G-13604)
QUALITY TOOL & MACHINE CO
393 S State Road 49 (46383-7858)
PHONE............................219 464-2411
Robert Malackowski, *Owner*
EMP: 4 EST: 1967
SQ FT: 5,000
SALES (est): 421K **Privately Held**
SIC: **3599** Machine shop, jobbing & repair

(G-13605)
QUANTUM COVERS LLC
1313 Peachtree Dr (46383-4027)
PHONE............................219 307-0893
Cynthia Treble, *President*
EMP: 3 EST: 2013
SALES (est): 179.2K **Privately Held**
SIC: **3572** Computer storage devices

(G-13606)
R F EXPRESS CORP
2601 Vale Park Rd (46383-2737)
PHONE............................219 510-5193
Zlata Krcma, *President*
Jan Krcma, *Vice Pres*
◆ EMP: 2
SALES (est): 337.2K **Privately Held**
SIC: **3826** Gas testing apparatus; instru-
ments measuring magnetic & electrical
properties

(G-13607)
REGAL BELOIT AMERICA INC
Also Called: McGill Manufacturing Company
2300 Evans Ave (46383-4054)
PHONE............................219 465-2200
Jim Johnson, *Branch Mgr*
EMP: 200
SALES (corp-wide): 3.3B **Publicly Held**
SIC: **3562** Ball & roller bearings
HQ: Regal Beloit America, Inc.
200 State St
Beloit WI 53511
608 364-8800

(G-13608)
REGAL BELOIT AMERICA INC
Also Called: Rollway Bearing
2300 Evans Ave (46383-4054)
PHONE............................219 465-2200
Fax: 219 465-2205
Allen Davis, *Manager*
EMP: 22
SALES (corp-wide): 3.3B **Publicly Held**
WEB: www.kopflex.com
SIC: **3562** Ball & roller bearings
HQ: Regal Beloit America, Inc.
200 State St
Beloit WI 53511
608 364-8800

(G-13609)
ROBERT W SHEFFER
4411 Evans Ave (46383-8407)
PHONE............................219 464-2095
Robert Sheffer, *Principal*
EMP: 2 EST: 2007
SALES (est): 143.9K **Privately Held**
SIC: **2499** Decorative wood & woodwork

G
E
O
G
R
A
P
H
I
C

(G-13610)
RON EATON
333 E 600 N (46383-9724)
PHONE..................................219 464-1607
Ron Eaton, *Principal*
EMP: 3
SALES (est): 183.3K **Privately Held**
SIC: 3625 Motor controls & accessories

(G-13611)
SALT CREEK HARVEST LLC
314 W 700 N (46385-8403)
PHONE..................................708 927-5569
Noel Pol, *Partner*
Patricia Melanie Beauchamp, *Principal*
EMP: 2 EST: 2012
SALES (est): 144.7K **Privately Held**
SIC: 2426 5193 0252 Lumber, hardwood
dimension; flowers & nursery stock;
chicken eggs

(G-13612)
SALT CREEK WOODWORKS
2755 Heavilin Rd (46385-7399)
PHONE..................................219 730-7553
EMP: 2
SALES (est): 85.2K **Privately Held**
SIC: 2431 Millwork

(G-13613)
SEISMIC VISION LLC
967 Misty Glen Dr (46385-8870)
PHONE..................................219 548-8704
Jay Phalora,
EMP: 2
SALES (est): 144.8K **Privately Held**
SIC: 1382 Seismograph surveys

(G-13614)
**SEPARATION TECHNOLOGIES
INC**
463 E Us Highway 30 # 4 (46383-9564)
PHONE..................................219 548-5814
Deborah J Lamb, *President*
EMP: 2
SQ FT: 2,000
SALES (est): 282.8K **Privately Held**
WEB: www.separationtechnologies.com
SIC: 3677 5084 Filtration devices, elec-
tronic; chemical process equipment

(G-13615)
SHERRY PRINT SOLUTIONS INC
66 E 602 N (46383-9124)
PHONE..................................708 255-5457
EMP: 2
SALES (est): 89.4K **Privately Held**
SIC: 2752 Commercial printing, litho-
graphic

(G-13616)
**SHINABARGAR CUSTOM
STAIRS**
176 Goodview Dr (46385-9611)
PHONE..................................219 462-1735
Gene Shinabargar, *Owner*
Jane Shinabargar, *Co-Owner*
EMP: 3
SALES (est): 215.5K **Privately Held**
SIC: 2431 Staircases & stairs, wood

(G-13617)
SHOREMET LLC
3601 Enterprise Ave (46383-8318)
PHONE..................................219 390-3336
Danny Mislenkov, *President*
EMP: 11
SALES (est): 1.3MM **Privately Held**
SIC: 2819 Industrial inorganic chemicals

(G-13618)
SIGN WRITE SIGNS LLC
1451 Joliet Rd (46385-5407)
PHONE..................................219 477-3840
Fax: 219 464-7583
Thomas Steindler,
Barbara Steindle,
EMP: 6
SQ FT: 5,600
SALES (est): 633.2K **Privately Held**
SIC: 3993 1799 Signs & advertising spe-
cialties; sign installation & maintenance

(G-13619)
SIGNWORKS
2003 Calumet Ave (46383-2705)
PHONE..................................219 462-5353
Fax: 219 531-0367
Jay Fredrick, *Owner*
EMP: 2
SALES (est): 181.4K **Privately Held**
SIC: 3993 Signs, not made in custom sign
painting shops

(G-13620)
SMITH READY MIX INC (PA)
251 Lincolnway (46383-5525)
P.O. Box 489 (46384-0489)
PHONE..................................219 462-3191
Fax: 219 465-4025
Douglas Smith, *President*
Paul Manoski, *Vice Pres*
Byron Smith III, *Treasurer*
David P Smith, *Admin Sec*
EMP: 15 EST: 1949
SQ FT: 11,000
SALES: 12.7MM **Privately Held**
WEB: www.smithreadymix.com
SIC: 3273 Ready-mixed concrete

(G-13621)
SMITH READY MIX INC
251 Lincolnway (46383-5525)
PHONE..................................219 374-5581
EMP: 10
SALES (corp-wide): 12.7MM **Privately
Held**
SIC: 3273 Mfg Ready Mix Concrete
PA: Smith Ready Mix, Inc.
251 Lincolnway
Valparaiso IN 46383
219 462-3191

(G-13622)
SOFTWARE SNEAK
259 Indiana Ave (46383-5573)
PHONE..................................219 510-5894
EMP: 2
SALES (est): 56.5K **Privately Held**
SIC: 7372 Prepackaged software

(G-13623)
SPECIALTY FOOD GROUP LLC
463 E Us Highway 30 (46383-9564)
PHONE..................................219 531-2142
Bill Karris, *Branch Mgr*
EMP: 14
SALES (corp-wide): 49.2MM **Privately
Held**
SIC: 2096 Corn chips & other corn-based
snacks
HQ: Specialty Food Group, L.L.C.
6905 Nw 25th St
Miami FL 33122

(G-13624)
**STEELCO INDUSTRIAL
LUBRICANTS**
Also Called: Quality Pdts Northwestern Ind
358 Ruge St (46385-6266)
P.O. Box 136 (46384-0136)
PHONE..................................219 462-0333
Fax: 219 462-4800
Donald Lee, *President*
C A Max, *Vice Pres*
EMP: 3
SQ FT: 1,000
SALES (est): 280K **Privately Held**
SIC: 2911 5085 Greases, lubricating; in-
dustrial supplies

(G-13625)
SUPREME SIGNS
265 Springhill Dr (46385-8888)
PHONE..................................219 384-0198
Raymond Wlodarski, *Principal*
EMP: 3 EST: 2008
SALES (est): 285K **Privately Held**
SIC: 3993 Signs & advertising specialties

(G-13626)
TASK FORCE TIPS INC (PA)
3701 Innovation Way (46383-8395)
PHONE..................................219 462-6161
Stewart G McMillan, *President*
Alicia Spagna, *President*
Nathan Calabrese, *Vice Pres*
Rod Carringer, *Vice Pres*

Philip Gerace, *Vice Pres*
▲ EMP: 195
SQ FT: 175,000
SALES (est): 38MM **Privately Held**
SIC: 3429 3569 Nozzles, fire fighting; fire-
fighting apparatus & related equipment

(G-13627)
TASK FORCE TIPS INC
Also Called: Production Dynamics
3701 Innovation Way (46383-8395)
PHONE..................................219 462-6161
Fax: 219 462-0318
Pat Jarosak, *Engineer*
Michael Mayer, *Engineer*
Bob Allen, *Manager*
EMP: 10
SALES (corp-wide): 38MM **Privately
Held**
SIC: 3429 3599 Nozzles, fire fighting; ma-
chine shop, jobbing & repair
PA: Task Force Tips Inc
3701 Innovation Way
Valparaiso IN 46383
219 462-6161

(G-13628)
**THORGREN TOOL & MOLDING
CO**
1100 Evans Ave (46383-3717)
PHONE..................................219 462-1801
Fax: 219 462-7941
Robert G Thorgren Jr, *President*
Francisco Avila, *General Mgr*
Rob Thorgren, *Plant Supt*
Kevin Szirovecz, *Controller*
Gerardo Gallegos, *Manager*
▲ EMP: 96 EST: 1943
SQ FT: 100,000
SALES (est): 22.2MM **Privately Held**
WEB: www.thorgren.com
SIC: 3089 3544 2221 Injection molding of
plastics; special dies, tools, jigs & fixtures;
broadwoven fabric mills, manmade

(G-13629)
TOP DESIGN CNC INC
41 N 400 E (46383-0618)
PHONE..................................219 662-2915
Michael Pavlo, *President*
Chris Pavlo, *Vice Pres*
EMP: 5
SQ FT: 1,500
SALES (est): 250K **Privately Held**
SIC: 2599 3131 Cabinets, factory; coun-
ters

(G-13630)
UFS CORPORATION
330 N 400 E (46383-9704)
PHONE..................................219 464-2027
Fax: 219 464-8646
H Frederick Hess III, *President*
Julia F Hess, *Corp Secy*
Julia Hess, *CPA*
▲ EMP: 11
SQ FT: 6,000
SALES (est): 2.5MM **Privately Held**
WEB: www.ufsc.com
SIC: 3559 Paint making machinery

(G-13631)
UGN INC
2252 Industrial Dr (46383-9511)
PHONE..................................219 464-7813
Fax: 219 477-1028
Mike Alonzo, *Project Engr*
Tom Woods, *Branch Mgr*
EMP: 200
SALES (corp-wide): 2.2B **Privately Held**
WEB: www.ugn.com
SIC: 3714 Motor vehicle parts & acces-
sories
HQ: G N U Inc
18410 Crossing Dr Ste C
Tinley Park IL 60487
773 437-2400

(G-13632)
UNION ELECTRIC STEEL CORP
3702 Montdale Dr (46383)
P.O. Box 29 (46384-0029)
PHONE..................................219 464-1031
Fax: 219 464-7499
Barry Allison, *Safety Mgr*
Barry Kahot, *Manager*

EMP: 110
SALES (corp-wide): 432.4MM **Publicly
Held**
WEB: www.uniones.com
SIC: 3325 3462 3312 Rolling mill rolls,
cast steel; iron & steel forgings; blast fur-
naces & steel mills
HQ: Union Electric Steel Corporation
726 Bell Ave
Carnegie PA 15106
412 429-7655

(G-13633)
**UNITED MACHINE
CORPORATION**
753 Axe Ave (46383-6477)
PHONE..................................219 548-8050
Robert Kotynski, *President*
EMP: 25
SQ FT: 30,000
SALES (est): 3.6MM **Privately Held**
WEB: www.unitedmachinecorp.com
SIC: 3599 3542 7629 Machine shop, job-
bing & repair; machine tools, metal form-
ing type; electrical repair shops

(G-13634)
VALPARAISO FIRE FIGHTERS
2065 Cumberland Dr (46383)
PHONE..................................219 462-5291
Chad Dutz, *Chief*
Scott Arnold, *Chief*
EMP: 68 **Privately Held**
SIC: 9224 3711 Fire department, not in-
cluding volunteer; ambulances (motor ve-
hicles), assembly of

(G-13635)
VITAL SIGNS
4411 Evans Ave Ste D (46383-8411)
PHONE..................................219 548-1605
Steve Jacobs, *Owner*
EMP: 3
SALES (est): 228.5K **Privately Held**
SIC: 3993 Signs, not made in custom sign
painting shops

(G-13636)
**WEGENER STEEL AND
FABRICATING**
906 Evans Ave (46383-3797)
PHONE..................................219 462-3911
Fax: 219 462-8377
Ed Cobb, *President*
EMP: 9 EST: 1944
SQ FT: 21,000
SALES (est): 6.1MM **Privately Held**
WEB: www.wegenersteel.com
SIC: 5051 3324 Steel; steel investment
foundries

(G-13637)
WILLIAM H SADLIER INC
4405 Blair Ln (46383-9166)
PHONE..................................219 465-0453
Mike Collins, *Principal*
EMP: 2
SALES (est): 73.3K **Privately Held**
SIC: 2731 Book publishing

(G-13638)
X-L BOX INC
1035 N State Road 149 (46385-8518)
PHONE..................................219 763-3736
Fax: 219 763-3386
James G Kyle, *President*
Christopher Peres, *Vice Pres*
EMP: 40
SQ FT: 12,000
SALES (est): 5.8MM **Privately Held**
SIC: 2448 7699 Pallets, wood; pallet re-
pair

Van Buren
Grant County

(G-13639)
DIAMOND FOODS LLC
4943 N 900 E (46991-9744)
PHONE..................................209 467-6000
EMP: 11

SALES (corp-wide): 566.9MM **Privately Held**
SIC: 2068 Salted & roasted nuts & seeds
PA: Diamond Foods, Llc
1050 Diamond St
Stockton CA 95205
209 467-6000

(G-13640)
MILL CREEK CUSTOM DELUXE BOX
3815 N 900 E (46991-9749)
PHONE.....................................765 934-3901
Larry E Pattison, *Owner*
EMP: 7
SALES (est): 897.7K **Privately Held**
SIC: 2631 Cardboard

(G-13641)
MODERN MACHINE & TOOL INC
106 W Main St (46991-7013)
P.O. Box 318 (46991-0318)
PHONE.....................................765 934-3110
Fax: 765 934-2133
Darroll Korporal, *President*
EMP: 9
SALES (est): 1.3MM **Privately Held**
SIC: 3599 Machine shop, jobbing & repair

Veedersburg
Fountain County

(G-13642)
CHOWNINGS JEWELERS
Also Called: Chowning Jewelers
115 E 2nd St (47987-1403)
PHONE.....................................765 294-4476
Larry Chowning, *Owner*
Jeff Chowning, *Manager*
EMP: 2
SQ FT: 3,000
SALES (est): 64K **Privately Held**
SIC: 7631 3915 Jewelry repair services; jewel cutting, drilling, polishing, recutting or setting

(G-13643)
FLEX-N-GATE CORPORATION
Also Called: Masterguard
1200 E 8th St (47987-8316)
PHONE.....................................765 294-3050
Fax: 765 294-3059
Ken Medlin, *Plant Mgr*
David Moody, *Plant Mgr*
Rita Brown, *Buyer*
Linda Cooper, *Buyer*
JD Troy, *Electrical Engi*
EMP: 1400
SALES (corp-wide): 3.3B **Privately Held**
WEB: www.flex-n-gate.com
SIC: 3714 Motor vehicle parts & accessories
PA: Flex-N-Gate Corporation
1306 E University Ave
Urbana IL 61802
217 384-6600

(G-13644)
KRUPP GERLACH COMPANY
1291 E 8th St (47987-8316)
PHONE.....................................765 294-0045
Fax: 765 294-0008
Bruce Lutes, *Principal*
▲ EMP: 2
SALES (est): 240.8K **Privately Held**
SIC: 3312 Forgings, iron & steel

(G-13645)
PAYTONS BARBECUE
119 E Washington St (47987-1551)
PHONE.....................................765 294-2716
Fax: 765 294-0434
Marylin Payton, *Owner*
EMP: 7
SQ FT: 4,000
SALES: 460K **Privately Held**
SIC: 2013 2099 Prepared pork products from purchased pork; prepared beef products from purchased beef; food preparations

(G-13646)
STERLING SALES AND ENGINEERING
324 S Sterling Ave (47987-8210)
P.O. Box 164 (47987-0164)
PHONE.....................................765 376-0454
Robert Gross, *President*
Scott Bratcher, *Treasurer*
Kathleen Gross, *Admin Sec*
EMP: 2
SALES: 420K **Privately Held**
SIC: 5051 3366 Foundry products; brass foundry; castings (except die): brass; castings (except die): copper & copper-base alloy

(G-13647)
THYSSENKRUPP CRANKSHAFT CO LLC
1291 E 8th St (47987-8316)
PHONE.....................................765 294-0045
Bruce Lutes, *Plant Mgr*
EMP: 75
SALES (corp-wide): 48.7B **Privately Held**
SIC: 3462 Iron & steel forgings
HQ: Thyssenkrupp Crankshaft Company Llc
1000 Lynch Rd
Danville IL 61834

(G-13648)
WRIB MANUFACTURING INC
110 E Jackson St (47987-1520)
P.O. Box 246 (47987-0246)
PHONE.....................................765 294-2841
Fax: 217 446-9800
Joshua Rubin, *President*
Jeff Rubin, *Corp Secy*
EMP: 3 EST: 1977
SALES (est): 697K **Privately Held**
WEB: www.wribmfg.com
SIC: 3559 7692 3441 3325 Foundry machinery & equipment; welding repair; fabricated structural metal; steel foundries; fabricated plate work (boiler shop); heating equipment, except electric

Velpen
Pike County

(G-13649)
LOUANNA STILWELL
6451 S County Road 1075 E (47590-8847)
PHONE.....................................812 631-0647
Louanna Stilwell, *Principal*
EMP: 3
SALES (est): 138.5K **Privately Held**
SIC: 2411 Logging

(G-13650)
WRAITH ARMS RESOLUTIONS LLC
9602 E 475s (47590-9626)
PHONE.....................................812 380-1208
Jesse Smith, *CEO*
EMP: 3
SALES (est): 214.7K **Privately Held**
SIC: 3484 Guns (firearms) or gun parts, 30 mm. & below

Vernon
Jennings County

(G-13651)
LONE STAR TOOL & DIE WELD
432 4th St (47282)
PHONE.....................................812 346-9681
John Raymer, *Owner*
EMP: 2
SALES (est): 166.8K **Privately Held**
SIC: 3544 Special dies & tools

(G-13652)
QUALITY MOLD & ENGINEERING
230 N State Highways 3/7 (47282)
P.O. Box 202 (47282-0202)
PHONE.....................................812 346-6577
Fax: 812 346-3045

Stephen Day, *President*
EMP: 7
SQ FT: 3,000
SALES (est): 941.6K **Privately Held**
SIC: 3544 Industrial molds

Versailles
Ripley County

(G-13653)
ELGIN FASTENER GROUP LLC
1415 S Benham Rd (47042-8411)
PHONE.....................................812 689-8917
EMP: 3
SALES (corp-wide): 70MM **Privately Held**
SIC: 3399 3452 Metal fasteners; bolts, metal
HQ: Elgin Fastener Group, Llc
10217 Brecksville Rd # 101
Brecksville OH 44141

(G-13654)
HANSON AGGREGATES MIDWEST LLC
606 W County Road 300 S (47042-9152)
PHONE.....................................812 689-5017
Neal Allen, *Manager*
EMP: 14
SALES (corp-wide): 20.3B **Privately Held**
SIC: 1422 Limestones, ground
HQ: Hanson Aggregates Midwest Llc
207 Old Harrods Creek Rd
Louisville KY 40223
502 244-7550

(G-13655)
MADISON ELECTRONICS INC
475 S Tanglewood Rd (47042-9574)
P.O. Box 2 (47042-0002)
PHONE.....................................812 689-4204
Fax: 812 689-6259
Tony Grida, *President*
EMP: 15
SQ FT: 15,500
SALES (est): 2.3MM **Privately Held**
SIC: 3672 3679 Circuit boards, television & radio printed; harness assemblies for electronic use: wire or cable

(G-13656)
MIRRUS CORPORATION INC
225 N Us Highway 421 (47042)
PHONE.....................................812 689-1411
Fax: 812 689-1512
Russell Stenger, *President*
EMP: 32
SQ FT: 10,000
SALES: 900K **Privately Held**
WEB: www.mirruscorp.com
SIC: 5013 3711 Automotive engines & engine parts; automobile assembly, including specialty automobiles

(G-13657)
RIPLEY PUBLISHING CO INC
Also Called: Osgood Journal
115 S Washington St (47042-8016)
P.O. Box 158 (47042-0158)
PHONE.....................................812 689-6364
Linda Chandler, *President*
Gene Demaree, *President*
Dorothy Craig, *Corp Secy*
Jo Jean Demaree, *Vice Pres*
EMP: 13
SALES (est): 819.7K **Privately Held**
WEB: www.ripleynews.com
SIC: 2711 Newspapers: publishing only, not printed on site

(G-13658)
T & M PRECISION INC
1861 S Us Highway 421 (47042-8302)
PHONE.....................................513 253-2274
Mary Gutman, *Branch Mgr*
EMP: 3 **Privately Held**
SIC: 3599 Machine shop, jobbing & repair
PA: T & M Precision, Inc.
1861 S Us Highway 421
Versailles IN 47042

(G-13659)
T & M PRECISION INC (PA)
Also Called: Gutman, Anthony & Mary
1861 S Us Highway 421 (47042-8302)
PHONE.....................................812 689-5769
Anthony Gutman, *Owner*
Mary Gutman, *Co-Owner*
EMP: 5
SALES (est): 363K **Privately Held**
SIC: 3599 Custom machinery; machine shop, jobbing & repair

Vevay
Switzerland County

(G-13660)
BESI MANUFACTURING INC
503 Vineyard St (47043-1050)
PHONE.....................................812 427-4114
Fax: 812 427-3291
Gary Pavy, *Manager*
EMP: 18
SALES (corp-wide): 11.9MM **Privately Held**
WEB: www.besi-inc.com
SIC: 3711 Buses, all types, assembly of
PA: Besi Manufacturing Inc
9087 Sutton Pl
West Chester OH 45011
513 874-0232

(G-13661)
CROSS COUNTRY HARDWOODS LLC
Also Called: Hardwood Flooring
10071 Bill Peelman Rd (47043-2659)
PHONE.....................................812 571-4226
Nathan E Miller, *President*
Betty Miller, *Vice Pres*
EMP: 12
SQ FT: 2,200
SALES (est): 871.1K **Privately Held**
SIC: 2426 Flooring, hardwood

(G-13662)
CUSTOM BUILT CABINETS AND
8587 Elmo Rayles Rd (47043-9623)
PHONE.....................................812 427-9733
Raymond Byler, *Owner*
EMP: 4
SALES (est): 224K **Privately Held**
SIC: 2434 Wood kitchen cabinets

(G-13663)
FERRY STREET WOODWORKS
319 Ferry St (47043-1103)
PHONE.....................................812 427-9663
EMP: 2 EST: 2011
SALES (est): 175.9K **Privately Held**
SIC: 2431 Millwork

(G-13664)
HERITAGE LOG HOMES
10648 Stevens Rd (47043-2809)
PHONE.....................................812 427-2591
Tony Fisher, *Principal*
EMP: 2
SALES (est): 200.2K **Privately Held**
WEB: www.heritagehomestore.com
SIC: 2452 Log cabins, prefabricated, wood

(G-13665)
SPIRAL-FAB INC
10034 E State Road 156 (47043-2718)
PHONE.....................................812 427-3006
Fax: 812 427-2000
Renee A Gregg, *President*
Bill Gregg, *Vice Pres*
William J Gregg, *Vice Pres*
EMP: 5
SQ FT: 4,000
SALES (est): 965.6K **Privately Held**
WEB: www.spiral-fab.com
SIC: 3312 Wire products, steel or iron

(G-13666)
SWISS ALPS PRINTING INC
Also Called: Swiss Alps Printing & Off Sups
108 W Pike St (47043-1132)
PHONE.....................................812 427-3844
Fax: 812 427-3404
Tonya Krall, *President*
EMP: 3

SQ FT: 2,000
SALES: 200K **Privately Held**
SIC: 2752 Commercial printing, offset

(G-13667)
VEVAY NEWSPAPERS INC
111 W Market St (47043-1159)
P.O. Box 157 (47043-0157)
PHONE....................................812 427-2311
Fax: 812 427-2793
Jane W Jacobs, *President*
Don R Wallis Sr, *Treasurer*
EMP: 6 EST: 1959
SALES (est): 368.5K **Privately Held**
SIC: 2711 Newspapers: publishing only,
   not printed on site

Vincennes
Knox County

(G-13668)
BABB LUMBER COMPANY INC
700 Fulton Glass Rd (47591-3634)
PHONE....................................812 886-0551
Fax: 812 886-0284
EMP: 16
SALES (corp-wide): 17.6MM **Privately
Held**
SIC: 2421 2491 Sawmills And Planing
   Mills, General
PA: Babb Lumber Company, Inc.
   6652 Highway 41
   Ringgold GA 30736
   706 935-2411

(G-13669)
BIRDEYE INC
Also Called: Waggway Tool
483 N Mount Zion Rd (47591-9683)
PHONE....................................812 886-0598
Craig Waggoner, *President*
Jamie Waggoner, *Admin Sec*
EMP: 10
SALES: 10MM **Privately Held**
WEB: www.birdeye.com
SIC: 3531 Construction machinery

(G-13670)
C & S FAMILY INC
Also Called: Riley Equipment
2205 S Old Decker Rd (47591-6114)
P.O. Box 435 (47591-0435)
PHONE....................................812 886-5500
Fax: 812 886-5515
Riley Charles G, *President*
Shelly J Newton, *Principal*
Guy Lankford, *Safety Mgr*
Cheryl Sorgius, *Accountant*
Brett Andricks, *Manager*
▼ EMP: 50
SQ FT: 110,000
SALES (est): 19.1MM **Privately Held**
WEB: www.rileyequipment.com
SIC: 3535 Bulk handling conveyor systems

(G-13671)
C&S SOLUTIONS
2064 N Old Highway 41 (47591-8926)
P.O. Box 33 (47591-0033)
PHONE....................................812 895-0048
Steven E Howder, *Principal*
EMP: 5
SALES (est): 427.9K **Privately Held**
SIC: 7372 Prepackaged software

(G-13672)
CELESTIAL CANDLE
138 E 17th St (47591-4300)
PHONE....................................812 886-4819
D M Sprinkle, *Principal*
EMP: 2
SALES (est): 211.6K **Privately Held**
SIC: 3999 Candles

(G-13673)
CERAN INC
2000 Chestnut St (47591-1760)
PHONE....................................812 882-2680
Dale Biehl, *Owner*
Tim Kiger, *General Mgr*
Chris Copp, *Manager*
Johnna Hoalt, *Manager*
Randy Evans, *Info Tech Mgr*

EMP: 7 EST: 2015
SALES (est): 77.1K **Privately Held**
SIC: 3211 Flat glass

(G-13674)
DIAMOND III INC
4298 E Bristol Dr (47591-6598)
PHONE....................................812 882-6269
Lewis O Pohl, *President*
Carolyn Pohl, *Corp Secy*
On Wells, *Legal Staff*
EMP: 3 EST: 1981
SALES (est): 282.4K **Privately Held**
SIC: 1381 Drilling oil & gas wells

(G-13675)
ELEMENTS
4 N 2nd St (47591-1215)
PHONE....................................812 881-9400
EMP: 2
SALES (est): 74.4K **Privately Held**
SIC: 2819 Elements

(G-13676)
ENERGY DRILLING LLC
1290 N State Road 67 (47591-8011)
PHONE....................................618 943-5314
Donald E Jones Jr, *Mng Member*
EMP: 4 EST: 2011
SALES (est): 233.5K **Privately Held**
SIC: 1381 Drilling oil & gas wells

(G-13677)
EWING PRINTING COMPANY INC
516 Vigo St (47591-1145)
P.O. Box 537 (47591-0537)
PHONE....................................812 882-2415
Fax: 812 886-6912
Jim Zeigler, *President*
Jerry Zeigler, *Vice Pres*
Elizabeth Fleck, *Graphic Designe*
Hannah Swank, *Graphic Designe*
EMP: 12 EST: 1961
SALES (est): 2.4MM **Privately Held**
WEB: www.ewingprinting.com
SIC: 2752 2796 2791 2789 Commercial
   printing, offset; platemaking services;
   typesetting; bookbinding & related work;
   commercial printing

(G-13678)
EXCELL USA INC
1065 E Beckes Ln (47591-8029)
PHONE....................................812 895-1687
Fax: 812 895-1831
Tatstya Acawa, *CEO*
Tatsuya Nakagawa, *President*
Motohiro Abe, *Vice Pres*
Mokoto Yamaguchi, *Vice Pres*
▲ EMP: 100
SQ FT: 40,000
SALES (est): 21.1MM
SALES (corp-wide): 67.4MM **Privately
Held**
WEB: www.excellusa.com
SIC: 3069 Floor coverings, rubber; flooring,
   rubber: tile or sheet
PA: Excell Corporation
   1-3-19, Yaesu
   Chuo-Ku TKY 103-0
   332 815-311

(G-13679)
EXPRESS SIGN & NEON LLC
119 S 15th St (47591-5421)
PHONE....................................812 882-0104
Brian Phillips, *Owner*
EMP: 5
SALES (est): 572.1K **Privately Held**
SIC: 3993 Neon signs

(G-13680)
FARBEST FOODS
3672 S Keller Rd (47591-7620)
P.O. Box 1400 (47591-7400)
PHONE....................................812 886-2125
Ted J Seger, *Principal*
Marc Maynard, *Vice Pres*
EMP: 2
SALES (est): 385.9K **Privately Held**
SIC: 5144 2015 Poultry & poultry prod-
   ucts; poultry slaughtering & processing

(G-13681)
FIA-INDIANA
3320 S Keller Rd (47591-7630)
PHONE....................................812 895-4700
Hiroharu Murahashi, *Principal*
Andrew Willis, *Prdtn Mgr*
Zane Duckworth, *Manager*
Dave Turpin, *Senior Mgr*
Steve Yochum, *Senior Mgr*
EMP: 4
SALES (est): 318.3K **Privately Held**
SIC: 3999 Manufacturing industries

(G-13682)
FORD SAWMILLS INC
2019 E Old Terre Haute Rd (47591-6825)
PHONE....................................812 324-2134
Fax: 812 882-5843
David Ford, *President*
Emily Ridgley, *Vice Pres*
John Ford, *Director*
EMP: 35
SQ FT: 64,000
SALES (est): 5.2MM **Privately Held**
SIC: 2448 2426 Pallets, wood; hardwood
   dimension & flooring mills

(G-13683)
FUTABA INDIANA AMERICA CORP
3320 S Keller Rd (47591-7630)
PHONE....................................812 895-4700
Hiroharu Murahashi, *President*
Yasuyoshi Shirai, *Principal*
Jamie Taylor, *Engineer*
Hiroshi Ishikawa, *Treasurer*
Darren Youngblood, *Manager*
▲ EMP: 500
SQ FT: 400,000
SALES (est): 114MM
SALES (corp-wide): 4.1B **Privately Held**
WEB: www.futabaindiana.com
SIC: 3089 3465 2396 Automotive parts,
   plastic; body parts, automobile: stamped
   metal; automotive & apparel trimmings
HQ: Fic America Corp.
   485 E Lies Rd
   Carol Stream IL 60188

(G-13684)
HURRICANE DITCHER COMPANY INC
2425 S Cathlinette Rd (47591-5572)
PHONE....................................812 886-9663
Fax: 812 886-0530
John L Snyder, *President*
Paul M Snyder, *Corp Secy*
Virgina Snyder, *Vice Pres*
Daniel Weil, *Info Tech Mgr*
EMP: 15
SQ FT: 14,450
SALES (est): 3.8MM **Privately Held**
WEB: www.hurricane-ditcher.com
SIC: 3531 3523 Entrenching machines;
   farm machinery & equipment

(G-13685)
INDIANA NEWSPAPERS LLC
Also Called: Vincennes Sun-Commercial
702 Main St (47591-2910)
P.O. Box 396 (47591-0396)
PHONE....................................812 886-9955
Fax: 812 885-2235
Vicky Palmer, *Principal*
Paula Rupprecht, *Principal*
Michael E Quayle, *Branch Mgr*
EMP: 65
SALES (corp-wide): 3.1B **Publicly Held**
SIC: 2711 2791 2752 Newspapers, pub-
   lishing & printing; typesetting; commercial
   printing, lithographic
HQ: Indiana Newspapers Llc
   130 S Meridian St
   Indianapolis IN 46225
   317 444-4000

(G-13686)
JAY C FOOD 84
1400 Washington Ave (47591-2256)
PHONE....................................812 886-9311
Jess Hendershot, *Manager*
EMP: 3
SALES (est): 123.1K **Privately Held**
SIC: 2051 Cakes, bakery: except frozen

(G-13687)
JONES & SONS INC
784 S 6th Street Rd (47591-9246)
P.O. Box 671 (47591-0671)
PHONE....................................812 882-2957
Fax: 812 886-0308
Aaron Alrnes, *Branch Mgr*
EMP: 33
SALES (corp-wide): 20.3MM **Privately
Held**
WEB: www.jonesandsons.com
SIC: 3273 5032 3446 3272 Ready-mixed
   concrete; stone, crushed or broken; con-
   crete & cinder block; architectural metal-
   work; concrete products
PA: Jones & Sons, Inc.
   1262 S State Road 57
   Washington IN 47501
   812 254-4731

(G-13688)
KARRAN USA
1291 E Ramsey Rd (47591-6299)
P.O. Box 667 (47591-0667)
PHONE....................................410 975-0128
Todd Donovan, *Principal*
Brook Fuller, *Opers Mgr*
▲ EMP: 3 EST: 2013
SALES (est): 160K **Privately Held**
SIC: 3131 3261 Boot & shoe accessories;
   sinks, vitreous china

(G-13689)
KNOX COUNTY ASSOCIATION (PA)
Also Called: KCARC Formerly: Knox
2525 N 6th St (47591-2405)
PHONE....................................812 886-4312
Fax: 812 882-4985
Michael R Carney, *President*
Diana Gratzek, *General Mgr*
Mary Shidler, *Mfg Mgr*
Tina Carie, *Human Resources*
Michael R Caney, *Exec Dir*
EMP: 100
SALES: 15.3MM **Privately Held**
SIC: 2521 7032 Wood office furniture;
   sporting & recreational camps

(G-13690)
LEWIS BROTHERS BAKERIES INC
Also Called: Lewis Bakeries
2792 S Old Decker Rd (47591-7603)
PHONE....................................812 886-6533
Fax: 812 886-6921
Carl Finfrock, *General Mgr*
Michael Kafoure, *General Mgr*
Dan Seyer, *Plant Mgr*
John Sanders, *Safety Mgr*
Randy Bottoms, *Manager*
EMP: 175
SQ FT: 4,000
SALES (corp-wide): 473.3MM **Privately
Held**
WEB: www.lewisbakeries.net
SIC: 5149 2053 2051 Bakery products;
   frozen bakery products, except bread;
   bread, cake & related products
PA: Lewis Brothers Bakeries Inc
   500 N Fulton Ave
   Evansville IN 47710
   812 425-4642

(G-13691)
M & D DRAPERIES
2022 Jackson Dr (47591-5921)
PHONE....................................812 886-4608
Ruth Bard, *Principal*
EMP: 3
SALES (est): 127.1K **Privately Held**
SIC: 2391 Curtains & draperies

(G-13692)
MIDWEST FAST STRUCTURES LLC
2341 S Old Decker Rd (47591-6122)
PHONE....................................812 886-3060
Rex Alton, *President*
EMP: 2
SQ FT: 36,000
SALES: 3MM **Privately Held**
SIC: 2452 Prefabricated wood buildings

(G-13693)
MILLER MACHINE & WELDING
2610 S Old Decker Rd (47591-7604)
PHONE.................................812 882-7566
Fax: 812 882-9775
Rick Miller, *Owner*
EMP: 6
SQ FT: 10,000
SALES (est): 673K **Privately Held**
SIC: 7692 3599 Welding repair; machine shop, jobbing & repair

(G-13694)
PACKAGING CORPORATION AMERICA
Pca/Vincennes 390
408 E Saint Clair St (47591-2364)
P.O. Box 786 (47591-0786)
PHONE.................................812 882-7631
Fax: 812 882-7880
Lisa Williams, *Mktg Dir*
Bob Muffat, *Manager*
Chris Haynes, *Manager*
Deidre Martin, *Executive*
EMP: 106
SALES (corp-wide): 6.4B **Publicly Held**
WEB: www.packagingcorp.com
SIC: 2653 Boxes, corrugated: made from purchased materials
PA: Packaging Corporation Of America
1955 W Field Ct
Lake Forest IL 60045
847 482-3000

(G-13695)
PEABODY MIDWEST MINING LLC
Air Quality 1 (47591)
PHONE.................................812 743-9292
EMP: 3
SALES (corp-wide): 5.6B **Publicly Held**
SIC: 1241 Coal Mining Services
HQ: Peabody Midwest Mining, Llc
566 Dickeyville Rd
Lynnville IN 47619
812 434-8500

(G-13696)
PERDUE FARMS INC
500 Perdue Rd (47591-9373)
PHONE.................................812 886-0593
Fax: 812 886-9835
John Snyder, *Manager*
EMP: 26
SALES (corp-wide): 5.5B **Privately Held**
WEB: www.perdue.com
SIC: 2015 Poultry slaughtering & processing
PA: Perdue Farms Inc.
31149 Old Ocean City Rd
Salisbury MD 21804
410 543-3000

(G-13697)
PIONEER OIL COMPANY INC
Also Called: Don Jones Oil Company
400 Main St (47591-2020)
P.O. Box 237 (47591-0237)
PHONE.................................812 494-2800
Donald E Jones Jr, *President*
Debra L Jones, *Corp Secy*
Brent Jones, *Vice Pres*
Mark Jones, *Vice Pres*
Jenna Sibert, *Vice Pres*
EMP: 16
SQ FT: 15,600
SALES (est): 4MM **Privately Held**
SIC: 1382 Oil & gas exploration services

(G-13698)
PIONEER OILFIELD SERVICES LLC
1290 N State Road 67 (47591-8011)
P.O. Box 237 (47591-0237)
PHONE.................................812 882-0999
Donald E Jones Jr, *President*
Mark Jones, *President*
Brent Jones, *Vice Pres*
EMP: 60
SALES (est): 5.6MM **Privately Held**
SIC: 1389 Oil field services

(G-13699)
PPG INDUSTRIES INC
Also Called: PPG 4379
417 Main St (47591-2006)
PHONE.................................812 882-0440
Bill Swain, *Branch Mgr*
William Swain, *Manager*
EMP: 24
SALES (corp-wide): 14.2B **Publicly Held**
WEB: www.ppg.com
SIC: 2851 Paints & allied products
PA: Ppg Industries, Inc.
1 Ppg Pl
Pittsburgh PA 15272
412 434-3131

(G-13700)
RESTORCO INC
1202 Barnett St (47591-4424)
P.O. Box 807 (47591-0807)
PHONE.................................812 882-3987
EMP: 10 EST: 1997
SALES (est): 1.2MM **Privately Held**
SIC: 2843 Mfg Surface Active Agents

(G-13701)
REX ALTON & COMPANIES INC
Also Called: Rex Alton Trucking
2341 S Old Decker Rd (47591-6122)
PHONE.................................812 882-8519
Fax: 812 882-8624
Rex Alton, *President*
Rita Alton, *Corp Secy*
EMP: 22
SQ FT: 32,000
SALES (est): 2.3MM **Privately Held**
WEB: www.rexaltoncompanies.com
SIC: 1771 1442 4212 1721 Concrete work; construction sand & gravel; local trucking, without storage; industrial painting; exterior cleaning, including sandblasting; building components, structural steel

(G-13702)
RICHARD E LEONARD LLC
2101 Mckinley Ave (47591-5937)
PHONE.................................812 882-7343
Richard Leonard, *Principal*
EMP: 2
SALES (est): 113.3K **Privately Held**
SIC: 2741 Miscellaneous publishing

(G-13703)
ROGERS GROUP INC
Also Called: Knox City Sand & Gravel
1200 S 6th Street Rd (47591-9382)
P.O. Box 943 (47591-0943)
PHONE.................................812 882-3640
Fax: 812 886-5908
Maurice Holscher, *President*
EMP: 35
SALES (corp-wide): 1B **Privately Held**
WEB: www.rogersgroupinc.com
SIC: 2951 1771 3274 2875 Asphalt & asphaltic paving mixtures (not from refineries); blacktop (asphalt) work; lime; fertilizers, mixing only; construction sand & gravel
PA: Rogers Group, Inc.
421 Great Circle Rd
Nashville TN 37228
615 242-0585

(G-13704)
S HUCK FOOD AND FUEL
2816 N 6th St (47591-3627)
PHONE.................................812 886-4323
Fax: 812 886-4323
Christina Neal, *Principal*
EMP: 5
SALES (est): 242.5K **Privately Held**
SIC: 2869 Fuels

(G-13705)
SCHOTT GEMTRON CORPORATION
Schott Hometech North America
2000 Chestnut St (47591-1760)
PHONE.................................812 882-2680
Fax: 812 886-5784
Philip Kolvenbach, *Opers Mgr*
Tammy Adams, *Controller*
Jennifer Chansler, *Financial Exec*
Dale Biehl, *Manager*
EMP: 500
SQ FT: 275,000 **Privately Held**
WEB: www.gemtron.com
SIC: 3231 Tempered glass: made from purchased glass; mirrored glass
HQ: Schott Gemtron Corporation
615 Highway 68
Sweetwater TN 37874
423 337-3522

(G-13706)
SLICERS
2715 Washington Ave (47591-3657)
PHONE.................................812 255-0655
Mark E Melton, *Principal*
EMP: 2
SALES (est): 152.5K **Privately Held**
SIC: 3799 Recreational vehicles

(G-13707)
SPP INC
Also Called: Screen Printing Plus
1001 Main St (47591-2915)
P.O. Box 1565 (47591-7565)
PHONE.................................812 882-6203
Fax: 812 882-6210
EMP: 10
SQ FT: 5,000
SALES (est): 500K **Privately Held**
SIC: 2759 3993 2396 2395 Commercial Printing Mfg Signs/Ad Specialties Mfg Auto/Apparel Trim Pleating/Stitching Svcs

(G-13708)
SUNRISE ENERGY LLC
1290 N State Road 67 (47591-8011)
P.O. Box 237 (47591-0237)
PHONE.................................812 886-9990
Donald Jones, *President*
Don Jones, *Owner*
EMP: 5
SALES (est): 354.7K **Privately Held**
SIC: 1389 Oil & gas wells: building, repairing & dismantling

(G-13709)
TABCO BUSINESS FORMS INC
638 Broadway St (47591-2028)
P.O. Box 434 (47591-0434)
PHONE.................................812 882-2836
Brad Pilyeu, *President*
Mary Clark, *Manager*
EMP: 4 EST: 1959
SQ FT: 7,000
SALES (est): 307.4K
SALES (corp-wide): 15.8MM **Privately Held**
WEB: www.kramac.com
SIC: 2752 2791 2789 2759 Commercial printing, offset; typesetting; bookbinding & related work; commercial printing
PA: Tabco Business Forms, Inc.
1100 S State Road 46
Terre Haute IN 47803
812 232-4660

(G-13710)
TRI STATE PRINTING & EMBROIDER
24 N 1st St (47591-1211)
PHONE.................................812 316-0094
Burdetta Scott, *President*
EMP: 5
SALES (est): 225K **Privately Held**
SIC: 2752 Commercial printing, lithographic

(G-13711)
VINCENNES SUN COMMERCIAL
702 Main St (47591-2910)
P.O. Box 396 (47591-0396)
PHONE.................................812 886-9955
Fax: 812 886-2002
EMP: 60
SALES (est): 2.4MM **Privately Held**
SIC: 2711 Newspapers-Publishing/Printing

(G-13712)
VINCENNES WELDING CO INC
923 N 13th St (47591-4721)
PHONE.................................812 882-9682
Fax: 812 882-5593
Bruce Cooper, *President*
EMP: 12 EST: 1912
SQ FT: 5,000

SALES (est): 550K **Privately Held**
SIC: 7692 3599 3441 Welding repair; machine shop, jobbing & repair; fabricated structural metal

(G-13713)
WABASH STEEL LLC
2007 Oliphant Dr (47591-1763)
P.O. Box 117 (47591-0117)
PHONE.................................317 818-1622
Keith Sullivan, *Project Mgr*
Bill Burgett,
Lori Gillette,
EMP: 5
SQ FT: 220,000
SALES (est): 9.1MM **Privately Held**
WEB: www.kokosing-inc.com
SIC: 3441 Bridge sections, prefabricated highway; bridge sections, prefabricated railway
PA: Lenex Steel Company
450 E 96th St Ste 100
Indianapolis IN 46240
317 818-1622

(G-13714)
WABASH VALLEY PUBLISHING LLC
611 N 7th St (47591-3101)
P.O. Box 131 (47591-0131)
PHONE.................................812 494-2152
Mary Daniel-Evans, *Administration*
EMP: 4 EST: 2016
SALES (est): 76.2K **Privately Held**
SIC: 2711 Newspapers

(G-13715)
WAG-WAY TOOL INCORPORATED
483 N Mount Zion Rd (47591-9683)
PHONE.................................812 886-0598
Fax: 812 886-0226
Craig Waggoner, *President*
EMP: 10
SQ FT: 18,000
SALES (est): 3MM **Privately Held**
SIC: 3531 Buckets, excavating: clamshell, concrete, dragline, etc.

(G-13716)
WARREN HOMES INC
Also Called: Gallery of Kitchens
2807 Adams Meyer Ln (47591-3600)
PHONE.................................812 882-1059
Douglas Warren, *President*
Brent Kehl, *Admin Sec*
EMP: 4
SALES: 55MM **Privately Held**
SIC: 2514 Kitchen cabinets: metal

(G-13717)
WILBERT SEXTON CORPORATION
426 S 15th St (47591-5409)
PHONE.................................812 882-3555
Jay Foreman, *Manager*
EMP: 4
SALES (corp-wide): 1.4MM **Privately Held**
WEB: www.meighendemers.com
SIC: 3272 Concrete products
PA: Wilbert Sexton Corporation
1908 W Allen St
Bloomington IN 47403
812 336-6469

(G-13718)
WINDY KNOLL WINERY
845 N Atkinson Rd (47591-9687)
PHONE.................................812 726-1600
Rick Lesser, *President*
Gwen Leser, *Partner*
EMP: 3
SALES (est): 269.4K **Privately Held**
WEB: www.windyknollwinery.com
SIC: 2084 Wines

Wabash
Wabash County

(G-13719)
ADVANCED BTRY CHARGER SVC LLC
650 Valley Brook Ln (46992-2026)
PHONE.................................260 563-3909
Bruce Richman, *Principal*
EMP: 3
SALES (est): 163.4K **Privately Held**
SIC: 3691 Storage batteries

(G-13720)
AL-FE HEAT TREATING INC
200 Wedcor Ave (46992-4200)
PHONE.................................260 563-8321
Fax: 260 563-8919
Dan Anderson, *VP Opers*
Dan Andersen, *Manager*
EMP: 40
SALES (corp-wide): 45.5MM **Privately Held**
WEB: www.al-fe.com
SIC: 3398 Metal heat treating
PA: Al-Fe Heat Treating Inc
  6920 Pointe Inverness Way # 140
  Fort Wayne IN 46804
  260 747-9422

(G-13721)
B WALTER & COMPANY INC
655 Factory St (46992-3213)
P.O. Box 278 (46992-0278)
PHONE.................................260 563-2181
Fax: 260 563-6301
Arthur Jasen, *CEO*
Kyle McCoart, *Engineer*
Thomas Frank, *CFO*
▲ EMP: 20 EST: 1887
SQ FT: 80,474
SALES (est): 4.2MM **Privately Held**
WEB: www.bwalter.com
SIC: 3469 3452 Stamping metal for the trade; bolts, nuts, rivets & washers

(G-13722)
BULLDOG BATTERY CORPORATION (PA)
Also Called: Precision Battery Fabrication
98 E Canal St (46992-3104)
P.O. Box 766 (46992-0766)
PHONE.................................260 563-0551
Fax: 260 563-8245
Norman L Benjamin, *President*
Regina M Thompson, *Principal*
Teresa King, *Opers Mgr*
Thomas Wagner, *CFO*
Doug Mays, *Controller*
◆ EMP: 120
SQ FT: 120,000
SALES (est): 27.4MM **Privately Held**
SIC: 3691 Storage batteries

(G-13723)
CUSTOM CARTON INC
3758 W Old 24 (46992-7779)
PHONE.................................260 563-7411
Fax: 260 563-7412
Margret Marquardt, *President*
Allan Marquardt, *Corp Secy*
EMP: 10 EST: 1966
SQ FT: 23,000
SALES (est): 1.8MM **Privately Held**
SIC: 2657 7389 Folding paperboard boxes; packaging & labeling services

(G-13724)
DIVERSIFIED COATING & FABG INC
3406 W 50 N (46992-8687)
PHONE.................................260 563-2858
Tyann D Leland, *President*
Mark A Milam, *Admin Sec*
EMP: 22
SALES: 2.2MM **Privately Held**
SIC: 1799 3441 Coating of metal structures at construction site; fabricated structural metal

(G-13725)
DS PRODUCTS INC
Also Called: Global Precision Parts
202 Wedcor Ave (46992-4200)
PHONE.................................260 563-9030
Todd Kriegel, *President*
David Kreigel, *Chairman*
Yolanada Von Lehmden, *Controller*
Yolanda Vonlehmden, *Controller*
Byron Bechtold, *Manager*
▲ EMP: 60
SQ FT: 48,000
SALES (est): 7.9MM **Privately Held**
SIC: 3451 Screw machine products

(G-13726)
E & S METAL INC
3673 W Old 24 (46992-8408)
PHONE.................................260 563-7714
James Enser, *President*
EMP: 10
SQ FT: 30,000
SALES (est): 730K **Privately Held**
SIC: 3559 3356 7692 3567 Foundry machinery & equipment; lead & zinc; welding repair; industrial furnaces & ovens; blowers & fans; sheet metalwork

(G-13727)
FRED S CARVER INC (DH)
1569 Morris St (46992-3538)
PHONE.................................260 563-7577
Fax: 260 563-7625
James E Holbrook, *President*
Jeffery A Deplanty, *Corp Secy*
Beth Gillespie, *Vice Pres*
Michael P Santoni, *Vice Pres*
Kimberly Oneal, *Info Tech Mgr*
▲ EMP: 7
SALES (est): 1.1MM
SALES (corp-wide): 1.4B **Privately Held**
WEB: www.carverpress.com
SIC: 3542 Presses: hydraulic & pneumatic, mechanical & manual; pressing machines
HQ: Sterling, Inc.
  2900 S 160th St
  New Berlin WI 53151
  414 354-0970

(G-13728)
HAYNES HONEY LLC
1269 E 500 S (46992-7962)
PHONE.................................260 563-6397
Shirley Haynes, *Owner*
EMP: 2
SALES (est): 99.5K **Privately Held**
SIC: 3999 Beekeepers' supplies

(G-13729)
HELFIN SHEET METAL INC
1965 S Wabash St (46992-4122)
P.O. Box 543 (46992-0543)
PHONE.................................260 563-2417
Fax: 260 569-1134
John Helfin, *President*
Linda Helfin, *Vice Pres*
EMP: 2
SALES (est): 327.3K **Privately Held**
SIC: 3444 7692 Sheet metalwork; welding repair

(G-13730)
HIPSHER TOOL & DIE INC
1593 S State Road 115 (46992-8380)
PHONE.................................260 563-4143
Fax: 260 563-0288
Jerry Hipsher, *Vice Pres*
Bruce Gerber, *Sales Staff*
Daniel Hipsher, *Manager*
Julie Hook Dahl, *Admin Sec*
EMP: 16 EST: 1946
SQ FT: 39,000
SALES (est): 1.7MM **Privately Held**
WEB: www.hipshertool.com
SIC: 3544 Special dies & tools

(G-13731)
HOOSIER JIFFY PRINT
675 Stitt St (46992-2211)
PHONE.................................260 563-8715
Fax: 260 563-0514
Rob Wilson, *President*
EMP: 4 EST: 1976
SQ FT: 4,000

SALES (est): 401.3K **Privately Held**
WEB: www.yourscrapbooksite.com
SIC: 2759 2752 Letterpress printing; commercial printing, offset

(G-13732)
HOT OFF PRESS
832 Manchester Ave (46992-1422)
PHONE.................................260 591-8331
Lisa Ulrey, *Administration*
EMP: 2
SALES (est): 55K **Privately Held**
SIC: 2741 Miscellaneous publishing

(G-13733)
LAP CSTM EMB GRMENT PRTG LLC
2472 E State Road 524 (46992-9045)
PHONE.................................260 782-0762
David Pefley, *Principal*
EMP: 2
SALES (est): 168.2K **Privately Held**
SIC: 2752 Commercial printing, lithographic

(G-13734)
M F Y DESIGNS INC
1051 N State Road 15 (46992-8631)
PHONE.................................260 563-6662
Fax: 260 569-0705
Rebecca J Long, *President*
EMP: 3
SALES (est): 234.5K **Privately Held**
SIC: 3993 Signs & advertising specialties

(G-13735)
M M CONVERTING INC
3758 W Old 24 (46992-7779)
PHONE.................................260 563-7411
Alan L Marquardt, *President*
EMP: 4 EST: 2007
SALES (est): 180.5K **Privately Held**
SIC: 3999 Pads, permanent waving

(G-13736)
MAFCOTE WABASH PAPER COATING
301 Wedcor Ave (46992-4202)
PHONE.................................260 563-4181
Fax: 260 563-2724
Daryl Evans, *Vice Pres*
EMP: 3
SALES (est): 132.8K **Privately Held**
SIC: 2611 Pulp mills, chemical & semi-chemical processing

(G-13737)
MARTIN YALE INDUSTRIES LLC
251 Wedcor Ave (46992-4201)
PHONE.................................260 563-0641
Greg German, *President*
Desiree Harnish, *Manager*
◆ EMP: 129
SQ FT: 140,000
SALES (est): 24.7MM **Privately Held**
WEB: www.martinyale.com
SIC: 3579 Paper cutters, trimmers & punches
PA: Lv2 Equity Partners, Llc
  2013 W Wackerly St # 200
  Midland MI 48640
  989 631-2687

(G-13738)
METAL SOURCE LLC
1733 S Wabash St (46992-4119)
P.O. Box 238 (46992-0238)
PHONE.................................260 563-8833
Benjamin Gebhart, *President*
Chris Lochner, *Vice Pres*
Jason Stanley, *Materials Mgr*
Marcus Olson, *Controller*
Max Mattern, *Manager*
▲ EMP: 50 EST: 1998
SQ FT: 9,000
SALES (est): 17.1MM **Privately Held**
SIC: 3356 Zinc & zinc alloy bars, plates, sheets, etc.; zinc & zinc alloy: rolling, drawing or extruding

(G-13739)
MIDWESTERN PALLET SERVICE INC
Also Called: MPS
3632 W Old 24 (46992-8408)
PHONE.................................260 563-1526
Fax: 260 563-6436
Robert E Velasquez, *President*
Sheeri Bachman, *Admin Sec*
EMP: 4
SQ FT: 3,200
SALES: 350K **Privately Held**
SIC: 2448 Pallets, wood; skids, wood; cargo containers, wood

(G-13740)
MILLINER PRINTING COMPANY INC
425 S Wabash St (46992-3325)
P.O. Box 282 (46992-0282)
PHONE.................................260 563-5717
Fax: 260 563-0866
Tim Eslava, *President*
EMP: 5
SQ FT: 4,500
SALES: 400K **Privately Held**
SIC: 2752 Commercial printing, offset

(G-13741)
MORTON BUILDINGS INC
1873 S State Rte 115 (46992)
P.O. Box 564 (46992-0564)
PHONE.................................260 563-2118
Fax: 260 563-2119
David Mc Vicker, *Manager*
Dave McVicker, *Manager*
EMP: 10
SALES (corp-wide): 492.6MM **Privately Held**
WEB: www.mortonbuildings.com
SIC: 5039 3448 2452 Prefabricated structures; prefabricated metal buildings; prefabricated wood buildings
PA: Morton Buildings, Inc.
  252 W Adams St
  Morton IL 61550
  800 447-7436

(G-13742)
MOSIERS TARPS
4021 S State Road 15 (46992-9014)
PHONE.................................260 563-3332
Fax: 260 563-1814
Jeffrey Mosier, *Owner*
Jim Schlemmer, *Office Mgr*
EMP: 7
SQ FT: 5,000
SALES (est): 620.7K **Privately Held**
SIC: 2394 7532 Tarpaulins, fabric: made from purchased materials; tops (canvas or plastic), installation or repair: automotive

(G-13743)
OLD RAS INC
4525 W Old 24 (46992-8357)
PHONE.................................260 563-7461
EMP: 5
SALES (corp-wide): 375MM **Privately Held**
SIC: 3334 Primary aluminum
HQ: Old Ras, Inc.

  Beachwood OH 44122

(G-13744)
OLYMPIA BUSINESS SYSTEMS INC
Also Called: Intimus International NA
251 Wedcor Ave (46992-4201)
P.O. Box 357 (46992-0357)
PHONE.................................800 225-5644
Javier Ortiz De Zarate, *CEO*
EMP: 10
SALES (est): 2.6MM
SALES (corp-wide): 177.3MM **Publicly Held**
WEB: www.gsashredders.com
SIC: 3589 Shredders, industrial & commercial
HQ: Wedcor Holdings, Inc.
  251 Wedcor Ave
  Wabash IN 46992
  260 563-0641

(G-13745)
OWENS CORNING SALES LLC
Also Called: Owens Corning Sales Therm
3711 Mill St (46992-7778)
PHONE..........................260 563-2111
EMP: 4 Publicly Held
SIC: 3296 Fiberglass insulation
HQ: Owens Corning Sales, Llc
1 Owens Corning Pkwy
Toledo OH 43659
419 248-8000

(G-13746)
PAPER OF WABASH COUNTY INC
606 N State Road 13 (46992-7735)
P.O. Box 603 (46992-0603)
PHONE..........................260 563-8326
Wayne Rees, President
Mike Rees, Exec VP
Julie Freegan, Admin Sec
Mona Rees, Admin Sec
Melinda Roberts, Graphic Designe
EMP: 35
SQ FT: 5,000
SALES (est): 2.2MM Privately Held
SIC: 2711 Commercial printing & newspaper publishing combined; job printing & newspaper publishing combined

(G-13747)
PAPERWORKS INDUSTRIES INC
Also Called: Smurfit Stone Container
455 Factory St (46992-3212)
P.O. Box 217 (46992-0217)
PHONE..........................260 563-3102
Fax: 260 569-3404
Richard Townley, General Mgr
John Henry, Project Mgr
Jerry Conley, Supervisor
Steve Zellers, Supervisor
EMP: 225
SALES (corp-wide): 13.3B Privately Held
SIC: 2631 Folding boxboard
HQ: Paperworks Industries, Inc.
40 Monument Rd Ste 200
Bala Cynwyd PA 19004

(G-13748)
PAPERWORKS INDUSTRIES INC
455 Factory St (46992-3212)
P.O. Box 217 (46992-0217)
PHONE..........................260 569-3352
Fred J Kalakay, Principal
EMP: 7
SALES (corp-wide): 13.3B Privately Held
SIC: 2631 Paperboard mills
HQ: Paperworks Industries, Inc.
40 Monument Rd Ste 200
Bala Cynwyd PA 19004

(G-13749)
PETTIT PRINTING INC
789 S Carroll St (46992-3210)
P.O. Box 704 (46992-0704)
PHONE..........................260 563-2346
Fax: 260 563-1325
Gregory Pettit, President
Gabriele Pettit, Vice Pres
Greg Pettit, Vice Pres
EMP: 6
SQ FT: 2,600
SALES: 500K Privately Held
WEB: www.pettitprinting.com
SIC: 2752 Commercial printing, offset

(G-13750)
POLY PLASTICS LTD
Also Called: Pbs Company
98 E Canal St (46992-3104)
P.O. Box 766 (46992-0766)
PHONE..........................260 569-9088
Norman Benjamin, President
EMP: 10
SALES (est): 1.2MM Privately Held
SIC: 2671 Plastic film, coated or laminated for packaging

(G-13751)
PRECISION BATTERY FABRICAT
375 Wedcor Ave (46992-4202)
PHONE..........................260 563-5138
Fax: 260 563-8618
Norman Benjamin, Principal
EMP: 2

SALES (est): 186.5K Privately Held
SIC: 3315 Steel wire & related products

(G-13752)
REAL ALLOY RECYCLING LLC
4525 W Old 24 (46992-8357)
PHONE..........................262 637-9858
Daniel Rangel, Principal
EMP: 55
SQ FT: 160,000
SALES (corp-wide): 64.5MM Privately Held
SIC: 3341 Secondary nonferrous metals
HQ: Real Alloy Recycling, Llc
3700 Park East Dr Ste 300
Beachwood OH
216 755-8900

(G-13753)
REAL ALLOY RECYCLING LLC
305 Dimension Ave (46992-4131)
P.O. Box 747 (46992-0747)
PHONE..........................260 563-2409
Terrance J Hogan, Manager
EMP: 23
SALES (corp-wide): 64.5MM Privately Held
SIC: 3341 Aluminum smelting & refining (secondary)
HQ: Real Alloy Recycling, Llc
3700 Park East Dr Ste 300
Beachwood OH
216 755-8900

(G-13754)
S & J CREATIVE DESIGN LLC
6037 E 450 S (46992-9180)
PHONE..........................765 251-0110
Steven Mitchell,
EMP: 2
SALES (est): 87.2K Privately Held
SIC: 3999 Manufacturing industries

(G-13755)
SHERMS MARINE
8662 S 400 W (46992-9291)
PHONE..........................260 563-8051
Sherman Truss, Owner
EMP: 3
SALES (est): 121.4K Privately Held
SIC: 5551 3732 Motor boat dealers; non-motorized boat, building & repairing

(G-13756)
SMITH WELDING & REPAIR SERVICE
1605 S Baumbauer Rd (46992-9124)
PHONE..........................260 563-0710
EMP: 2
SALES (est): 70K Privately Held
SIC: 7692 Welding Repair

(G-13757)
TAS WELDING & GRAN SERVICES LL
5459 W Old 24 (46992-8358)
PHONE..........................765 210-4274
Tim Sparks, President
EMP: 8
SALES (est): 758.8K Privately Held
SIC: 7692 Welding repair

(G-13758)
THERMAFIBER INC (HQ)
3711 Mill St (46992-7778)
PHONE..........................260 563-2111
Charles E Dana, President
Gregory Greenberg, Vice Pres
David Rabuano, Vice Pres
Douglas E Mays, CFO
Gregory Lamastus, Treasurer
◆ EMP: 93
SQ FT: 3,000
SALES (est): 34.6MM Publicly Held
SIC: 3296 Fiberglass insulation

(G-13759)
TRU-CUT MACHINE & TOOL INC
Also Called: Statzer C Mark
556 E Baumbauer Rd Lot 41 (46992-9306)
PHONE..........................260 569-1802
Fax: 260 563-1883
Mark Statzer, President
Clista Statzer, Corp Secy
EMP: 3

SQ FT: 55,000
SALES: 140K Privately Held
SIC: 3542 Machine tools, metal forming type

(G-13760)
UNITED TOOL COMPANY INC
838 Lafontaine Ave (46992-4107)
P.O. Box 242 (46992-0242)
PHONE..........................260 563-3143
Fax: 260 563-5759
Michael R Bechtol, President
Deborah Bechtol, Corp Secy
Debra Bechtol, Corp Secy
Troy Poland, Vice Pres
EMP: 14 EST: 1966
SQ FT: 12,000
SALES: 1.2MM Privately Held
SIC: 3599 7692 Machine shop, jobbing & repair; welding repair

(G-13761)
WABASH CASTINGS INC
3837 Mill St (46992-7838)
PHONE..........................260 563-8371
Robert Hollacher, President
John Young, CFO
EMP: 175
SQ FT: 175,000
SALES: 15MM Privately Held
SIC: 3365 Aluminum foundries

(G-13762)
WABASH INSTRUMENT CORP
300 Olive St (46992-2526)
PHONE..........................260 563-8406
Fax: 260 563-8400
Shethar Davis, President
J Douglas Craig, Corp Secy
EMP: 15
SQ FT: 30,000
SALES (est): 2.6MM Privately Held
WEB: www.winsco.com
SIC: 3821 Physics laboratory apparatus

(G-13763)
WABASH METAL PRODUCTS INC (DH)
Also Called: Wabash Mpi
1569 Morris St (46992-3538)
P.O. Box 298 (46992-0298)
PHONE..........................260 563-1184
Fax: 260 563-1396
Bruce Freeman, President
James E Holbrook, President
Jeffery A Deplanty, Corp Secy
Tom Breslin, COO
Gary Burton, QC Mgr
◆ EMP: 85 EST: 1974
SQ FT: 35,000
SALES (est): 15.3MM
SALES (corp-wide): 1.4B Privately Held
WEB: www.wabashmpi.com
SIC: 3542 Presses: hydraulic & pneumatic, mechanical & manual
HQ: Sterling, Inc.
2900 S 160th St
New Berlin WI 53151
414 354-0970

(G-13764)
WABASH PLAIN DEALER
123 W Canal St (46992-3042)
PHONE..........................260 563-2131
Fax: 260 563-0816
J Fred Paxton, President
EMP: 35
SQ FT: 15,000
SALES (est): 1.2MM
SALES (corp-wide): 318.6MM Privately Held
WEB: www.wabashplaindealer.com
SIC: 2711 2752 Commercial printing & newspaper publishing combined; commercial printing, lithographic
PA: Paxton Media Group, Llc
100 Television Ln
Paducah KY 42003
270 575-8630

(G-13765)
WABASH VALLEY TOOL & ENGRG
1253 S State Road 115 (46992-9241)
PHONE..........................260 563-7690
Fax: 260 563-7690

Laureen D Deeter, President
EMP: 2
SQ FT: 1,200
SALES: 95K Privately Held
SIC: 3544 Special dies, tools, jigs & fixtures

(G-13766)
WABASH WELDING SERVICES INC (PA)
150 Smith St (46992-3322)
P.O. Box 241 (46992-0241)
PHONE..........................260 563-2363
Fax: 260 563-0321
Thomas C Ehret, President
Teresa Ehret, Vice Pres
EMP: 20 EST: 1975
SQ FT: 15,000
SALES: 1.5MM Privately Held
SIC: 1796 3441 Millwright; fabricated structural metal

(G-13767)
WEST PLAINS DISTRIBUTION LLC
Also Called: Kentner Creek
1600 S Olive St (46992)
PHONE..........................260 563-9500
Will Woodward,
EMP: 2
SALES (est): 66K Privately Held
SIC: 1442 Gravel mining

(G-13768)
WEST PLAINS MINING LLC
6601 W Old 24 (46992-1421)
P.O. Box 584 (46992-0584)
PHONE..........................260 563-9500
Tim Langley, Sales Mgr
William A Woodward, Mng Member
EMP: 40
SALES (est): 577.5K Privately Held
SIC: 1422 Limestones, ground

(G-13769)
ZOOMERS RV OF INDIANA LLC
1090 Manchester Ave (46992-1638)
PHONE..........................260 414-1978
Michael Kurtz, Principal
EMP: 2 EST: 2016
SALES (est): 188.6K Privately Held
SIC: 3716 Motor homes

Wadesville
Posey County

(G-13770)
ARTISAN SHEET METAL CORP
1101 Rexing Rd (47638-9128)
PHONE..........................812 422-7393
Fax: 812 425-7151
Michael R Embry, President
Kathy M Embry, Corp Secy
EMP: 6
SQ FT: 5,000
SALES: 400K Privately Held
SIC: 1761 3446 3444 Architectural sheet metal work; architectural metalwork; sheet metalwork

(G-13771)
AZTEC PRINTING INC (PA)
9800 Highway 66 (47638-9011)
PHONE..........................812 422-1462
Fax: 812 425-7928
Joyce Gumbrell, President
EMP: 6 EST: 1962
SQ FT: 2,500
SALES: 336.9K Privately Held
SIC: 2752 Commercial printing, offset

(G-13772)
HERITAGE CABINETS LLC
11911 Winery Rd (47638-9602)
PHONE..........................812 963-3435
Paul A Elpers, Principal
EMP: 2
SALES (est): 218.7K Privately Held
SIC: 2434 Wood kitchen cabinets

(G-13773)
MSK MOLD INC
2591 Juanita Ave (47638-9751)
PHONE....................................812 985-5457
Scott Allen Pate, *President*
Lisa Pate, *Vice Pres*
EMP: 4
SALES: 200K Privately Held
SIC: 3544 Industrial molds

(G-13774)
PARKER EXPLORATION &
PRODUCTIO
2940 Donner Rd (47638-9057)
PHONE....................................812 673-4017
Delwin Parker, *Principal*
EMP: 2
SALES (est): 227.3K Privately Held
SIC: 3824 Production counters

Wakarusa
Elkhart County

(G-13775)
DWYER INSTRUMENTS INC
55 Ward St (46573-9588)
PHONE....................................574 862-2590
Doug Sowder, *Branch Mgr*
EMP: 90
SQ FT: 1,800
SALES (corp-wide): 100MM Privately
Held
WEB: www.dwyer-inst.com
SIC: 3823 Industrial instrmnts msrmnt dis-
play/control process variable
PA: Dwyer Instruments Inc
102 Indiana Highway 212
Michigan City IN 46360
219 879-8868

(G-13776)
ECOM PUBLISHING INC
Also Called: Wakarusa Tribune
114 S Elkhart St (46573-2016)
P.O. Box 507 (46573-0507)
PHONE....................................574 862-2179
Nancy Nich, *President*
Al Nich, *Shareholder*
EMP: 3
SQ FT: 1,200
SALES (est): 140K Privately Held
SIC: 2711 Newspapers

(G-13777)
FREIGHTLINER CSTM CHASSIS
CORP
66540 State Road 19 (46573-9597)
PHONE....................................260 517-9678
EMP: 3
SALES (est): 205K
SALES (corp-wide): 193.7B Privately
Held
SIC: 3711 Truck tractors for highway use,
assembly of
HQ: Freightliner Custom Chassis Corpora-
tion
552 Hyatt St
Gaffney SC 29341

(G-13778)
HAHN ENTERPRISES INC
Also Called: Weldy Enterprises
911 E Waterford St (46573-9560)
PHONE....................................574 862-4491
Fax: 574 862-2122
Don Hahn, *President*
Darren Hahn, *Vice Pres*
Linda Hahn, *Admin Sec*
EMP: 9 EST: 1971
SQ FT: 15,000
SALES (est): 3.4MM Privately Held
WEB: www.weldyenterprises.com
SIC: 5083 3523 Farm & garden machin-
ery; farm machinery & equipment; cattle
feeding, handling & watering equipment;
haying machines: mowers, rakes, stack-
ers, etc.; hog feeding, handling & water-
ing equipment

(G-13779)
J & N STONE INC
905 E Waterford St (46573-9560)
P.O. Box 442 (46573-0442)
PHONE....................................574 862-4251
Fax: 574 862-2944
Lengacher Sr Jack W, *President*
Nadine K Lengacher, *Corp Secy*
Jack Lengacher Jr, *Senior VP*
Jeff Lengacher, *Vice Pres*
Jamie Lengacher, *CFO*
EMP: 130 EST: 1973
SQ FT: 155,000
SALES (est): 20.5MM Privately Held
SIC: 3281 Cut stone & stone products

(G-13780)
J JESSE INC
Also Called: Jessco
904 Nelsons Pkwy (46573-9580)
P.O. Box 503 (46573-0503)
PHONE....................................574 862-4538
Fax: 574 862-2636
Jack Jesse, *President*
Carolyn Jesse, *Corp Secy*
EMP: 11
SQ FT: 4,000
SALES (est): 1.4MM Privately Held
SIC: 2541 2821 2511 Store & office dis-
play cases & fixtures; plastics materials &
resins; wood household furniture

(G-13781)
KAEB SALES INC
27481 County Road 40 (46573-9709)
PHONE....................................574 862-2777
Craig Coon, *Manager*
EMP: 12
SALES (corp-wide): 10MM Privately
Held
SIC: 3556 Dairy & milk machinery
PA: Kaeb Sales, Inc.
484 N State Route 49
Cissna Park IL 60924
815 457-2649

(G-13782)
LIQUID TECHNOLOGIES
ELKHART
208 N Elkhart St (46573-9729)
PHONE....................................574 596-1883
Mark Clickovich, *Owner*
EMP: 2
SALES (est): 92.2K Privately Held
SIC: 2851 Paints & allied products

(G-13783)
LUE MANUFACTURING INC
27667 County Road 40 (46573-9709)
PHONE....................................574 862-4249
Fax: 574 862-4912
Steven R Gongwer, *President*
EMP: 16
SQ FT: 15,000
SALES: 1.2MM Privately Held
SIC: 2541 Table or counter tops, plastic
laminated

(G-13784)
LYCRO PRODUCTS CO INC
66557 State Road 19 (46573-9799)
PHONE....................................574 862-4981
Fax: 574 862-3983
Gregory Schoen, *President*
EMP: 45 EST: 1970
SQ FT: 55,000
SALES (est): 8.5MM Privately Held
SIC: 3599 Machine & other job shop work

(G-13785)
MARTIN WELDING SHOP
27585 County Road 40 (46573-9709)
PHONE....................................574 862-2578
Mervin Martin, *Owner*
EMP: 2
SALES (est): 94.9K Privately Held
SIC: 7692 Welding repair

(G-13786)
MERVIN M BURKHOLDER
26253 County Road 42 (46573-9711)
PHONE....................................574 862-4144
Mervin M Burkholder, *Principal*
EMP: 5

SALES (est): 203.4K Privately Held
SIC: 7692 Welding repair

(G-13787)
MICHIANA COLUMN & TRUSS
LLC
611 E Waterford St (46573-9557)
PHONE....................................574 862-2828
Ronald R Martin,
Loren Martin,
Sheldon Weaver,
EMP: 5
SALES (est): 570K Privately Held
SIC: 2493 Reconstituted wood products

(G-13788)
MICHIANA COLUMN & TRUSS
LLC
611 E Waterford St (46573-9557)
PHONE....................................574 862-2828
Ronald R Martin,
Loren Martin,
Shelton Weaver,
EMP: 10
SQ FT: 12,000
SALES (est): 1.4MM Privately Held
SIC: 2439 Trusses, wooden roof

(G-13789)
PERFORMANCE TECHNOLOGY
INC
65251 State Road 19 (46573-9310)
P.O. Box 461 (46573-0461)
PHONE....................................574 862-2116
Fax: 574 862-4897
James Mikel, *President*
Neil Hannewyk, *Vice Pres*
M Sherman Drew, *Treasurer*
Tina Mikel Sect, *Manager*
Tina Mikel, *Admin Sec*
EMP: 9
SQ FT: 7,850
SALES (est): 1.4MM Privately Held
SIC: 3714 7538 Motor vehicle engines &
parts; engine rebuilding: automotive

(G-13790)
PRIME TIME MANUFACTURING
66149 State Road 19 (46573-9327)
P.O. Box 3030, Elkhart (46515-3030)
PHONE....................................574 862-3001
Jeff Rank, *Principal*
EMP: 2
SALES (est): 246.8K Privately Held
SIC: 3999 Manufacturing industries

(G-13791)
PROVIDENT TOOL & DIE INC
Also Called: Turnomat
66100 State Road 19 (46573-9330)
P.O. Box 214 (46573-0214)
PHONE....................................574 862-1233
Fax: 574 862-1233
Craig Henkler, *President*
EMP: 7
SQ FT: 4,000
SALES: 500K Privately Held
WEB: www.providenttool.com
SIC: 3599 Machine shop, jobbing & repair

(G-13792)
REM INDUSTRIES INC
902 Nelsons Pkwy (46573-9580)
P.O. Box 408 (46573-0408)
PHONE....................................574 862-2127
Robert Miller, *President*
Jason Miller, *President*
EMP: 28 EST: 1991
SQ FT: 10,000
SALES (est): 3.8MM Privately Held
WEB: www.rem-ind.com
SIC: 3429 5712 2531 2511 Furniture
hardware; furniture stores; public building
& related furniture; wood household furni-
ture

(G-13793)
RICHMONDS FEED SERVICE INC
704 E Waterford St (46573-9562)
PHONE....................................574 862-2984
David Rchmond, *President*
Jane Richmond, *Corp Secy*
Jenny Neely, *Manager*
EMP: 4
SQ FT: 8,000

SALES (est): 403.7K Privately Held
SIC: 2048 Livestock feeds

(G-13794)
RIGHT ANGLE STL &
FABRICATION
29508 County Road 38 (46573-9705)
P.O. Box 559 (46573-0559)
PHONE....................................574 862-2432
Carl E Cook, *President*
EMP: 2
SALES (est): 505.6K Privately Held
SIC: 3441 Expansion joints (structural
shapes), iron or steel

(G-13795)
SCHROCK AGGREGATE
COMPANY INC (HQ)
111 Industrial Dr (46573-8513)
PHONE....................................574 862-4167
David L Schrock, *President*
Diana Schrock, *Admin Sec*
EMP: 1
SALES (est): 3.4MM
SALES (corp-wide): 2.2MM Privately
Held
SIC: 2951 3272 1442 Paving mixtures;
paving materials, prefabricated concrete;
gravel mining
PA: Schrock Excavating, Inc
111 Industrial Dr
Wakarusa IN 46573
574 862-4167

(G-13796)
SCHROCK EXCAVATING INC
(PA)
111 Industrial Dr (46573-8513)
P.O. Box 473, Bremen (46506-0473)
PHONE....................................574 862-4167
Fax: 574 862-4066
David L Schrock, *President*
Diana Schrock, *Corp Secy*
EMP: 39
SQ FT: 26,000
SALES (est): 2.2MM Privately Held
WEB: www.schrockexcavating.com
SIC: 1794 1771 1795 2951 Excavation
work; driveway, parking lot & blacktop
contractors; demolition, buildings & other
structures; paving mixtures; gravel mining

(G-13797)
WAKARUSA AG LLC
711 E Waterford St (46573-9558)
PHONE....................................574 862-1163
Frank Martin, *Administration*
EMP: 7 EST: 2014
SALES (est): 111.8K Privately Held
SIC: 5083 3531 5012 Tractors, agricul-
tural; tractors, construction; truck tractors

Waldron
Shelby County

(G-13798)
FLAT ROCK FURNITURE INC
(PA)
1424 Miller Ave (46182)
PHONE....................................317 398-1501
Fax: 765 525-5296
Vance A McQueen, *President*
Vance Mc Queen, *Benefits Mgr*
Christine Brammer, *Sales Staff*
Alicia Knecht, *Executive*
EMP: 20
SQ FT: 16,500
SALES (est): 4.4MM Privately Held
WEB: www.flatrockhickory.com
SIC: 2511 Wood household furniture

(G-13799)
HEWITT MANUFACTURING
COMPANY
5365 S 600 E (46182-9559)
P.O. Box 262 (46182-0262)
PHONE....................................765 525-9829
Donald G Hewitt, *Owner*
Gene Hewitt, *Human Res Mgr*
EMP: 10
SQ FT: 6,000

SALES (est): 92.9K **Privately Held**
WEB: www.hewittmfg.com
SIC: 3496 Miscellaneous fabricated wire products

(G-13800)
LARRY ATWOOD
Also Called: Atwood Concrete Construction
6597 S 250 E (46182-9736)
PHONE.................................765 525-6851
Larry Atwood, *Owner*
EMP: 3
SALES (est): 424.5K **Privately Held**
SIC: 5032 3444 Concrete & cinder building products; concrete forms, sheet metal

Walkerton
St. Joseph County

(G-13801)
AMERICAN ROLLER COMPANY LLC
Also Called: Walkerton Plant
201 Industrial Park Dr (46574-1069)
PHONE.................................574 586-3101
Fax: 574 586-7059
Marc Lugabihl, *Maint Spvr*
Nick Jerkovic, *Engineer*
Chris Stouffer, *Branch Mgr*
Steve Russell, *Info Tech Mgr*
EMP: 50
SALES (corp-wide): 102MM **Privately Held**
WEB: www.americanroller.com
SIC: 3069 Rubber rolls & roll coverings
PA: American Roller Company, Llc
1440 13th Ave
Union Grove WI 53182
262 878-8665

(G-13802)
FREEHOLD GAMES LLC
69080 Sycamore Rd (46574-9744)
PHONE.................................574 656-9031
Charles Bucklew,
Jason Grinblat,
EMP: 2 EST: 2013
SALES (est): 142.8K **Privately Held**
SIC: 7372 7389 Home entertainment computer software;

(G-13803)
INDIANIAN WOODCRAFTS
Also Called: Indianian Wood Crafts
72099 Spruce Rd (46574-8708)
PHONE.................................574 586-3741
Jon M Pairitz, *Owner*
EMP: 3
SALES (est): 210.8K **Privately Held**
SIC: 2511 1751 Wood household furniture; cabinet & finish carpentry

(G-13804)
JUNOLL INDUSTRIES
27045 Tyler Rd (46574-8719)
PHONE.................................574 586-2719
EMP: 2
SALES (est): 79K **Privately Held**
SIC: 3999 Mfg Misc Products

(G-13805)
LOG LIFESTYLES INC
72300 Walkerton Trl (46574-8710)
PHONE.................................574 850-6158
William Flaugher, *President*
EMP: 3
SALES (est): 184K **Privately Held**
SIC: 2411 Logging

(G-13806)
MODERN DOOR CORPORATION
1300 Virginia St (46574-1073)
PHONE.................................574 586-3117
Fax: 574 586-7782
Garry L Matz, *President*
Gary Sokol, *Plant Engr*
Thomas R Blend, *CFO*
▲ EMP: 100 EST: 1977
SQ FT: 150,000

SALES (est): 27.8MM
SALES (corp-wide): 28.1MM **Privately Held**
WEB: www.plyco.com
SIC: 3442 3444 Garage doors, overhead: metal; sheet metalwork
PA: Plyco Corporation
500 Industrial Dr
Elkhart Lake WI 53020
920 876-3611

(G-13807)
NORTHERN WOOD PRODUCTS INC
3573 Thorn Rd (46574-8227)
PHONE.................................574 586-3068
Fax: 574 586-3068
Richard Maher, *President*
June Maher, *Corp Secy*
EMP: 9
SALES: 460K **Privately Held**
SIC: 2411 Logging camps & contractors

(G-13808)
POLYGON COMPANY (PA)
103 Industrial Park Dr (46574-1068)
P.O. Box 176 (46574-0176)
PHONE.................................574 586-3145
Fax: 574 586-7336
James Shobert, *CEO*
Timothy Shobert, *President*
Jim Davis, *Division Mgr*
Fadorsen Bob, *Vice Pres*
Scott Farrisee, *Vice Pres*
▲ EMP: 245 EST: 1950
SALES (est): 75.6MM **Privately Held**
WEB: www.polygoncompany.com
SIC: 3082 Unsupported plastics profile shapes

(G-13809)
POLYGON COMPANY
Tenesse St (46574)
P.O. Box 176 (46574-0176)
PHONE.................................574 586-3145
Kent Deal, *Manager*
EMP: 55
SALES (corp-wide): 75.6MM **Privately Held**
WEB: www.polygoncompany.com
SIC: 3082 Unsupported plastics profile shapes
PA: Polygon Company
103 Industrial Park Dr
Walkerton IN 46574
574 586-3145

(G-13810)
ROSS ENGINEERING & MACHINE
70100 Stephens St (46574-1243)
PHONE.................................574 586-7791
Fax: 574 586-7087
Eric Morris, *Principal*
EMP: 21
SQ FT: 6,500
SALES: 2MM **Privately Held**
SIC: 3544 Special dies & tools

(G-13811)
TWIN MAPLE TOOL INC
324 Liberty St (46574-1246)
P.O. Box 13 (46574-0013)
PHONE.................................574 586-7500
Robert Rudecki, *President*
EMP: 10
SQ FT: 10,000
SALES: 353.7K **Privately Held**
SIC: 3544 3469 3465 Special dies, tools, jigs & fixtures; special dies & tools; jigs & fixtures; industrial molds; metal stampings; automotive stampings

(G-13812)
ULTRA MANUFACTURING INC
648 Stephens St (46574-1264)
P.O. Box 28 (46574-0028)
PHONE.................................574 586-2320
Michael Austin, *President*
Tammy Austin, *Co-Owner*
Adam Gilpin, *Opers Staff*
Josh Rizek, *QC Mgr*
EMP: 25
SQ FT: 12,000

SALES: 2.2MM
SALES (corp-wide): 4MM **Privately Held**
WEB: www.ultramfg1.com
SIC: 3469 Machine parts, stamped or pressed metal
PA: Austin & Austin, Inc.
59632 Timberwood Ln
Goshen IN 46528
574 586-2320

(G-13813)
WALKERTON TOOL & DIE INC
106 Industrial Park Dr (46574-1065)
P.O. Box 58 (46574-0058)
PHONE.................................574 586-3162
Fax: 574 586-2755
Scott Rizek, *President*
Harold Rizek, *Treasurer*
EMP: 30
SQ FT: 17,000
SALES (est): 4.5MM **Privately Held**
WEB: www.walkertontool.com
SIC: 2759 3544 3599 3549 Publication printing; card printing & engraving, except greeting; special dies & tools; jigs & fixtures; machine shop, jobbing & repair; metalworking machinery

(G-13814)
WARNKE ASSOCIATES INC
8401 N Tippecanoe Dr (46574-8147)
PHONE.................................574 586-3331
Paul M Warnke, *President*
EMP: 3
SALES (est): 27.2K **Privately Held**
SIC: 3089 Corrugated panels, plastic

Walton
Cass County

(G-13815)
CONNER SAWMILL INC
Also Called: Conner Saw Mill
300 North St (46994-4177)
P.O. Box 308 (46994-0308)
PHONE.................................574 626-3227
Fax: 574 626-2106
Eldon Conner, *President*
Jean Conner, *Corp Secy*
EMP: 15 EST: 1964
SQ FT: 7,000
SALES (est): 1.5MM **Privately Held**
SIC: 2448 2421 2449 Pallets, wood; custom sawmill; wood containers

(G-13816)
MUEHLHAUSEN SPRING COMPANY
602 Michele Ln (46994-4172)
P.O. Box 261 (46994-0261)
PHONE.................................574 626-2351
EMP: 4
SALES (est): 148.4K **Privately Held**
SIC: 3493 Mfg Steel Springs-Nonwire

(G-13817)
TERICK SALES
Also Called: Terick Sales & Service
3519 E County Road 800 S (46994-9246)
PHONE.................................574 626-3173
Rick Canfield, *Owner*
Teri Canfield, *Owner*
EMP: 2 EST: 1987
SALES (est): 157K **Privately Held**
SIC: 3699 Electronic training devices

(G-13818)
WALTON INDUSTRIAL PARK INC
Also Called: IRONMONGER SPRING DIVISION
7585 S Us Hwy 35 (46994)
P.O. Box 318 (46994-0318)
PHONE.................................574 626-2929
Fax: 574 626-2452
Jo Ellen Ironmonger, *President*
Steven Ironmonger, *Vice Pres*
Crystal Slldck, *Treasurer*
EMP: 12
SQ FT: 18,000
SALES: 1.3MM **Privately Held**
SIC: 3495 7389 3679 Precision springs; bicycle assembly service; harness assemblies for electronic use: wire or cable

Wanatah
Laporte County

(G-13819)
AMERICA CORN CUTTER
9203 Twin Acres Dr (46390-9415)
PHONE.................................219 733-0855
Carol Bunton-Benkie, *Owner*
EMP: 2 EST: 2007
SALES (est): 132.1K **Privately Held**
SIC: 3999 Manufacturing industries

(G-13820)
ASL TECHNOLOGIES LLC
10525 W Us Highway 30 3d (46390-9412)
PHONE.................................219 733-2777
David Bickford,
EMP: 7
SQ FT: 4,500
SALES: 1.5MM **Privately Held**
WEB: www.aslfilter.com
SIC: 3569 Filters

(G-13821)
B PLUS ENTERPRISES INC
122 S Illinois St (46390-9998)
P.O. Box 75 (46390-0075)
PHONE.................................219 733-9404
Fax: 219 733-9409
Phillipe E Boule, *President*
EMP: 5
SQ FT: 5,000
SALES: 60K **Privately Held**
SIC: 3089 Molding primary plastic

(G-13822)
COMMTINEO LLC
Also Called: Comtineo
10525 W Us Highway 30 4c (46390-9411)
P.O. Box 1536, Valparaiso (46384-1536)
PHONE.................................219 476-3667
Kevin Babich, *CEO*
EMP: 13
SQ FT: 9,600
SALES: 1.7MM **Privately Held**
SIC: 8741 1731 4812 1623 Business management; electrical work; radio telephone communication; transmitting tower (telecommunication) construction; microwave communication equipment; telecommunications consultant

(G-13823)
CONTINNTAL CRPNTRY CMPNNTS LLC
9702 W Us Highway 30 (46390-9538)
PHONE.................................219 369-4839
Justin Wright, *Owner*
EMP: 40 EST: 2011
SQ FT: 16,500
SALES (est): 6MM **Privately Held**
SIC: 1751 2439 2452 Carpentry work; structural wood members; trusses, wooden roof; prefabricated wood buildings; panels & sections, prefabricated, wood

(G-13824)
INSULATION SPECIALTIES OF AMER
1095 Kabert Dr (46390-9633)
P.O. Box 10 (46390-0010)
PHONE.................................219 733-2502
Fax: 219 733-2300
Monie Parker, *President*
Don Sommers, *Vice Pres*
Robert Peacock, *Treasurer*
EMP: 38
SQ FT: 30,000
SALES (est): 6.1MM **Privately Held**
WEB: www.insulationspecialties.com
SIC: 3299 3297 3296 3264 Ceramic fiber; nonclay refractories; mineral wool; porcelain electrical supplies

(G-13825)
STEINDLER SIGNS
105 Koselke St (46390-9577)
P.O. Box 285 (46390-0285)
PHONE.................................219 733-2551
Tom Steindler Jr, *Owner*
Jessica Parks, *Accounts Mgr*
Bob Wszolek, *Graphic Designe*

EMP: 3
SALES (est): 389.3K **Privately Held**
SIC: 3993 Electric signs

(G-13826)
TESLA WIRELESS COMPANY LLC
10525 W Us Highway 30 4c (46390-9411)
P.O. Box 1415, Valparaiso (46384-1415)
PHONE......................................219 363-7922
Kevin Babich, *President*
EMP: 5
SQ FT: 4,800
SALES: 400K **Privately Held**
SIC: 3568 Power transmission equipment

(G-13827)
W KENDALL & SONS INC (PA)
10270 W Us Highway 30 (46390-9542)
P.O. Box 9 (46390-0009)
PHONE......................................219 733-2412
Fax: 219 733-2032
Gary Rice, *President*
Scott Rice, *Treasurer*
Wayne Rice, *Shareholder*
EMP: 9
SQ FT: 25,000
SALES (est): 1.3MM **Privately Held**
WEB: www.wkendall.com
SIC: 3471 3479 Sand blasting of metal
　parts; painting, coating & hot dipping

Warren
Huntington County

(G-13828)
DUGHERTY INC
609 E 1st St (46792-9647)
PHONE......................................260 375-2010
EMP: 15
SALES (est): 696.2K **Privately Held**
SIC: 3523 Mfg Farm Machinery/Equipment

(G-13829)
ECOLAB INC
2847 E 600 S (46792-9426)
P.O. Box 462 (46792-0462)
PHONE......................................260 375-4710
Fax: 260 375-4716
Chris Lewe, *Manager*
EMP: 13
SALES (corp-wide): 13.8B **Publicly Held**
WEB: www.ecolab.com
SIC: 2841 Soap & other detergents
PA: Ecolab Inc.
　1 Ecolab Pl
　Saint Paul MN 55102
　800 232-6522

(G-13830)
GEMINI OIL LLC
1323 W 600 S (46792-9747)
PHONE......................................260 571-8388
Dennis Wiles, *Mng Member*
Steven Wiles,
EMP: 7
SALES: 400K **Privately Held**
SIC: 1382 Oil & gas exploration services

(G-13831)
HY-LINE NORTH AMERICA LLC
1029 Mill Site Dr (46792-9605)
PHONE......................................260 375-3041
Fax: 260 375-2179
Curt Schmidt, *Manager*
EMP: 40
SALES (corp-wide): 2.5B **Privately Held**
WEB: www.hyline.com
SIC: 0254 2015 Chicken hatchery; poultry
　slaughtering & processing
HQ: Hy-Line North America, Llc
　1755 West Lakes Pkwy A
　West Des Moines IA 50266
　515 225-6030

(G-13832)
SALAMONIE MILLS INC
525 N Wayne St (46792)
PHONE......................................260 375-2200
Fax: 260 375-2814
Kevin Grayer, *President*
Don McDaniels, *Vice Pres*
Wendell Jackson, *Admin Sec*

EMP: 14
SQ FT: 1,200
SALES (est): 7.2MM **Privately Held**
SIC: 5191 5153 2041 Feed; grain eleva-
　tors; flour & other grain mill products

(G-13833)
SATURN WHEEL COMPANY INC
507 E 9th St (46792-9269)
P.O. Box 610 (46792-0610)
PHONE......................................260 375-4720
Mike Haggerty, *President*
Roger McClellan, *COO*
Stacy Haggerty, *Vice Pres*
Fred McCracken, *CFO*
EMP: 69
SQ FT: 36,000
SALES: 6MM **Privately Held**
SIC: 3471 Coloring & finishing of aluminum
　or formed products

Warsaw
Kosciusko County

(G-13834)
AARDVARK GRAPHICS
Also Called: Branded By Jdh
4121 Deer Run N (46582-6908)
PHONE......................................574 267-4799
Jack Harrell, *Owner*
EMP: 2
SALES: 21K **Privately Held**
SIC: 2759 Screen printing

(G-13835)
ACEYS TROPHIES & AWARDS
301 S Scott St (46580-4502)
PHONE......................................574 267-1426
Chuck Lisenbee, *Owner*
EMP: 2
SALES (est): 99K **Privately Held**
SIC: 5999 3479 Trophies & plaques; etch-
　ing on metals

(G-13836)
AKZO NOBEL COATINGS INC
1102 Leiter Dr (46580-2475)
PHONE......................................574 372-2000
Deanna Cripe, *Buyer*
EMP: 17
SALES (corp-wide): 11.3B **Privately Held**
SIC: 2819 2821 Industrial inorganic chem-
　icals; plastics materials & resins
HQ: Akzo Nobel Coatings Inc.
　8220 Mohawk Dr
　Strongsville OH 44136
　440 297-5100

(G-13837)
ALPHA MANUFACTURING AND DESIGN
2070 N Cessna Rd (46582-6420)
PHONE......................................574 267-2171
Ben Garden, *Owner*
Nick Brandt, *General Mgr*
EMP: 25
SQ FT: 18,000
SALES (est): 489.8K **Privately Held**
SIC: 3841 Surgical & medical instruments

(G-13838)
AMERI KAN
1919 E Center St (46580-2296)
PHONE......................................574 533-7032
EMP: 2
SALES (est): 73.4K **Privately Held**
SIC: 3411 Metal cans

(G-13839)
APPLIED THERMAL TECH INC
2169 N 100 E (46582-7872)
PHONE......................................574 269-7116
Fax: 574 269-7906
Miroslav Bradican, *President*
Charles V Zichichi, *Vice Pres*
Robert Gunow Jr, *CFO*
Jay Slone, *Sales Executive*
Rebecca Aspinwall, *Manager*
EMP: 20
SQ FT: 8,000
SALES (est): 5.4MM **Privately Held**
SIC: 3398 Metal heat treating

(G-13840)
ASPHALT MATERIALS INC
2820 Durbin St (46580-3883)
PHONE......................................574 267-5076
Joe Nuncy, *Branch Mgr*
EMP: 16
SALES (corp-wide): 248.2MM **Privately Held**
SIC: 2951 Asphalt & asphaltic paving mix-
　tures (not from refineries)
PA: Asphalt Materials, Inc.
　5400 W 86th St
　Indianapolis IN 46268
　317 872-6010

(G-13841)
BABSCO SUPPLY INC
Also Called: Babsco Electric
2361 N Shelby Dr (46580-2164)
PHONE......................................574 267-8999
Fax: 574 267-2106
Joe Hammond, *Principal*
EMP: 5
SALES (est): 502.7K
SALES (corp-wide): 10MM **Privately Held**
WEB: www.babsco.com
SIC: 5063 3699 Electrical supplies; light-
　ing fixtures; electrical equipment & sup-
　plies
PA: Babsco Supply, Inc.
　2410 S Main St
　Elkhart IN 46517
　574 293-0631

(G-13842)
BARTEL PRINTING COMPANY INC
310 Cedar St (46580-3026)
PHONE......................................574 267-7421
Fax: 574 267-2021
Penny Bartel, *President*
Murray Bartel, *Vice Pres*
John Miller, *Administration*
EMP: 8 EST: 1970
SQ FT: 3,000
SALES: 2MM **Privately Held**
SIC: 2752 2759 Commercial printing, off-
　set; commercial printing

(G-13843)
BEACHWOOD LUMBER CO INC
Also Called: Beachwood Manufacturing
7878 W Old Road 30 (46580-8367)
PHONE......................................574 858-9325
Toll Free:......................................866　-
Fax: 574 858-2171
Dan Burns, *President*
EMP: 12
SQ FT: 2,000
SALES: 926.1K **Privately Held**
SIC: 2439 Trusses, except roof: laminated
　lumber; trusses, wooden roof

(G-13844)
BILTZ SIGNS
5843 E Mckenna Rd (46582-8027)
PHONE......................................574 594-2703
Ray Biltz, *Principal*
EMP: 2
SALES (est): 102.8K **Privately Held**
SIC: 3993 Signs & advertising specialties

(G-13845)
BIOMET INC (HQ)
Also Called: Zimmer Biomet
345 E Main St (46580-2746)
P.O. Box 587 (46581-0587)
PHONE......................................574 267-6639
Fax: 574 267-8137
Thomas R Allen, *President*
Taylor Erickson, *President*
Bradley Tandy, *Senior VP*
Robin T Barney, *Senior VP*
Adam R Johnson, *Senior VP*
◆ EMP: 950 EST: 1977
SQ FT: 769,333

SALES (est): 1.9B
SALES (corp-wide): 7.8B **Publicly Held**
WEB: www.biomet.com
SIC: 3842 3841 3845 Orthopedic appli-
　ances; supports: abdominal, ankle, arch,
　kneecap, etc.; surgical appliances & sup-
　plies; implants, surgical; surgical & med-
　ical instruments; medical instruments &
　equipment, blood & bone work; surgical
　instruments & apparatus; suction therapy
　apparatus; electromedical equipment;
　electromedical apparatus; ultrasonic med-
　ical equipment, except cleaning
PA: Zimmer Biomet Holdings, Inc.
　345 E Main St
　Warsaw IN 46580
　574 267-6131

(G-13846)
BIOMET BIOLOGICS LLC
56 E Bell Dr (46582-6924)
P.O. Box 587 (46581-0587)
PHONE......................................574 267-2038
Stuart Kleopfer,
EMP: 40
SALES (est): 5.2MM
SALES (corp-wide): 7.8B **Publicly Held**
WEB: www.biomet.com
SIC: 3842 Surgical appliances & supplies
HQ: Biomet, Inc.
　345 E Main St
　Warsaw IN 46580
　574 267-6639

(G-13847)
BIOMET EUROPE LTD
56 E Bell Dr (46582-6924)
PHONE......................................574 267-2038
Jeffrey R Binder, *President*
EMP: 8
SALES (est): 703K
SALES (corp-wide): 7.8B **Publicly Held**
SIC: 3842 3841 3845 Implants, surgical;
　supports: abdominal, ankle, arch,
　kneecap, etc.; surgical appliances & sup-
　plies; medical instruments & equipment,
　blood & bone work; surgical instruments
　& apparatus; suction therapy apparatus;
　electromedical apparatus; ultrasonic med-
　ical equipment, except cleaning
HQ: Biomet, Inc.
　345 E Main St
　Warsaw IN 46580
　574 267-6639

(G-13848)
BIOMET INC
737 N Detroit St (46580-2910)
PHONE......................................574 372-6999
Nelson Cabrera, *Administration*
EMP: 3 EST: 2011
SALES (est): 488.1K **Privately Held**
SIC: 5047 3841 Medical & hospital equip-
　ment; surgical & medical instruments

(G-13849)
BIOMET ORTHOPEDICS LLC
56 E Bell Dr (46582-6924)
P.O. Box 587 (46581-0587)
PHONE......................................574 267-6639
Fax: 574 627-8137
Jeffrey R Binder, *President*
Debra Neilson, *Manager*
Jacqueline K Huber, *Admin Sec*
EMP: 2500
SALES (est): 228.8MM
SALES (corp-wide): 7.8B **Publicly Held**
WEB: www.discoveryelbow.com
SIC: 3842 Implants, surgical
PA: Zimmer Biomet Holdings, Inc.
　345 E Main St
　Warsaw IN 46580
　574 267-6131

(G-13850)
BIOMET SPORTS MEDICINE LLC
56 E Bell Dr (46582-6924)
P.O. Box 587 (46581-0587)
PHONE......................................574 267-6639
Fax: 574 372-1718
David A Nolan Jr, *President*
Kevin Stone, *Vice Pres*
Michael T Hodges, *Treasurer*
Bradley J Tandy, *Admin Sec*
EMP: 90

▲ = Import ▼=Export
◆ =Import/Export

SQ FT: 36,000
SALES (est): 11.2MM
SALES (corp-wide): 7.8B **Publicly Held**
WEB: www.arthrotek.com
SIC: 3841 Surgical & medical instruments
HQ: Biomet, Inc.
345 E Main St
Warsaw IN 46580
574 267-6639

(G-13851)
BORNEMANN PRODUCTS INC
2562 Walton Blvd (46582-6522)
PHONE..................................574 546-2881
Tom Jackson, *Principal*
EMP: 2
SALES (est): 162.4K **Privately Held**
SIC: 3714 Motor vehicle parts & accessories

(G-13852)
BUHRT ENGINEERING & CNSTR
27 E 250 N (46582-6956)
PHONE..................................574 267-3720
Dennis R Buhrt, *President*
Janice L Buhrt, *Admin Sec*
EMP: 25
SQ FT: 25,000
SALES (est): 6.9MM **Privately Held**
WEB: www.buhrt.com
SIC: 3444 1791 7699 3537 Sheet metalwork; iron work, structural; industrial equipment services; industrial trucks & tractors; fabricated plate work (boiler shop); fabricated structural metal

(G-13853)
CARDINAL SERVICES INC INDIANA (PA)
504 N Bay Dr (46580-4627)
PHONE..................................574 267-3823
N Jane Greene, *President*
Randy Hall, *Vice Pres*
Leanne Ford, *CFO*
Ray Hunsberger, *Admin Sec*
EMP: 75 EST: 1954
SQ FT: 44,600
SALES: 20.8MM **Privately Held**
SIC: 8331 8361 4131 3523 Job training services; vocational rehabilitation agency; rehabilitation center, residential: health care incidental; intercity & rural bus transportation; barn, silo, poultry, dairy & livestock machinery; motor vehicle parts & accessories

(G-13854)
CARDINAL SERVICES INC INDIANA
Also Called: CCI Contract Manufacturing
1770 E Smith St (46580-4659)
PHONE..................................574 371-1305
Fax: 574 267-7329
Jay Tate, *General Mgr*
EMP: 50
SQ FT: 45,000
SALES (corp-wide): 20.8MM **Privately Held**
SIC: 3569 Assembly machines, non-metalworking
PA: Cardinal Services Inc Of Indiana
504 N Bay Dr
Warsaw IN 46580
574 267-3823

(G-13855)
CARDINAL SERVICES INC INDIANA
Also Called: CCI Big Boy Products
504 N Bay Dr (46580-4627)
PHONE..................................574 267-3823
Fax: 574 267-6200
Mark Randall, *Branch Mgr*
EMP: 25
SALES (corp-wide): 20.8MM **Privately Held**
SIC: 3714 Trailer hitches, motor vehicle
PA: Cardinal Services Inc Of Indiana
504 N Bay Dr
Warsaw IN 46580
574 267-3823

(G-13856)
CIGARETTES PLUS
843 N Lake St (46580-2551)
PHONE..................................574 267-3166
Wade Frauhiger, *Owner*
EMP: 2
SALES (est): 169.7K **Privately Held**
SIC: 3999 Cigarette & cigar products & accessories

(G-13857)
CIRCLE M SPRING INC
930 Executive Dr (46580-8535)
PHONE..................................574 267-2883
Thadd Mellott, *President*
Dena Mellott, *Admin Sec*
▲ EMP: 35
SALES (est): 3.2MM **Privately Held**
WEB: www.circlemspring.com
SIC: 3841 3495 Surgical & medical instruments; wire springs

(G-13858)
CNC CONCEPTS INC
3019 S County Farm Rd (46580-8240)
PHONE..................................574 269-2301
Stephen S Kline, *Principal*
EMP: 2
SALES (est): 138.1K **Privately Held**
SIC: 3599 Machine shop, jobbing & repair

(G-13859)
CONCEPTS IN STONE & TILE INC
118 N Buffalo St (46580-2728)
PHONE..................................574 267-4712
David McHose, *President*
Kimberly McHose, *Corp Secy*
EMP: 3
SALES (est): 337K **Privately Held**
SIC: 3281 1743 Curbing, granite or stone; tile installation, ceramic

(G-13860)
CRYSTAL LAKE LLC (PA)
4217 W Old Road 30 (46580-6842)
P.O. Box 220, Atwood (46502-0220)
PHONE..................................574 267-3101
Diane Lancaster, *Accounts Mgr*
Ron Truex,
EMP: 1
SQ FT: 10,000
SALES (est): 10.7MM **Privately Held**
SIC: 2015 Eggs, processed: frozen; egg albumen

(G-13861)
CRYSTAL LAKE LLC
6500 W Crystal Lake Rd (46580-8986)
P.O. Box 220, Atwood (46502-0220)
PHONE..................................574 858-2514
Ron Truex, *Manager*
EMP: 74
SQ FT: 56,341
SALES (corp-wide): 10.7MM **Privately Held**
SIC: 2015 2038 Egg processing; eggs, processed: frozen; frozen specialties
PA: Crystal Lake Llc
4217 W Old Road 30
Warsaw IN 46580
574 267-3101

(G-13862)
CXR COMPANY INC
2599 N Fox Farm Rd (46580-6536)
P.O. Box 1114 (46581-1114)
PHONE..................................574 269-6020
Fax: 574 269-7140
Barbara Calhan, *CEO*
Cassandra Stewart, *President*
Paula Zeigler, *Vice Pres*
EMP: 12
SQ FT: 8,000
SALES (est): 922K **Privately Held**
WEB: www.cxrcompany.com
SIC: 3844 7699 X-ray apparatus & tubes; X-ray equipment repair

(G-13863)
DEPUY MITEK LLC
700 Orthopaedic Dr (46582-3900)
PHONE..................................574 267-8143
EMP: 3

SALES (corp-wide): 76.4B **Publicly Held**
SIC: 3841 Surgical & medical instruments
HQ: Depuy Mitek, Llc
325 Paramount Dr
Raynham MA 02767
508 880-8100

(G-13864)
DEPUY PRODUCTS INC (HQ)
700 Orthopaedic Dr (46582-3900)
PHONE..................................574 267-8143
Fax: 574 267-7196
Andrew Ekdahl, *President*
Peter Batesko III, *Treasurer*
Lori Morel, *Finance*
Gordon Ummerson, *VP Mktg*
Scott R Ryan, *Admin Sec*
EMP: 47
SALES (est): 1.4B
SALES (corp-wide): 76.4B **Publicly Held**
SIC: 3842 Surgical appliances & supplies
PA: Johnson & Johnson
1 Johnson And Johnson Plz
New Brunswick NJ 08933
732 524-0400

(G-13865)
DEPUY SYNTHES INC (DH)
Also Called: Synthes USA
700 Orthopaedic Dr (46582-3900)
PHONE..................................574 267-8143
Fax: 610 695-2475
Michel Orsinger, *CEO*
▲ EMP: 277
SQ FT: 15,000
SALES (est): 1.4B
SALES (corp-wide): 76.4B **Publicly Held**
SIC: 3841 Medical instruments & equipment, blood & bone work
HQ: Depuy Products Inc
700 Orthopaedic Dr
Warsaw IN 46582
574 267-8143

(G-13866)
DEPUY SYNTHES SALES INC
Depuy Synthes Jint Rcnstrction
700 Orthopaedic Dr (46582-3900)
PHONE..................................574 267-8143
EMP: 10
SALES (corp-wide): 76.4B **Publicly Held**
SIC: 3842 Surgical appliances & supplies
HQ: Depuy Synthes Sales Inc
325 Paramount Dr
Raynham MA 02767
508 880-8100

(G-13867)
DMP INDUSTRIES LLC ✪
1411 E Springhill Rd (46580-1815)
PHONE..................................260 413-6701
April Isch, *Owner*
EMP: 2 EST: 2017
SALES (est): 100.5K **Privately Held**
SIC: 3999 Manufacturing industries

(G-13868)
EGG INNOVATIONS LLC (PA)
4799 W 100 N (46580-8997)
P.O. Box 1275 (46581-1275)
PHONE..................................574 267-7545
John Brunnquell, *President*
Charlie Flood, *Vice Pres*
Steve Hagopian, *Vice Pres*
John Hornbostel, *Vice Pres*
Wes Larue, *Vice Pres*
EMP: 4
SQ FT: 5,000
SALES: 40MM **Privately Held**
WEB: www.egginnovations.com
SIC: 2015 2048 Egg processing; prepared feeds

(G-13869)
ELIGIUS INDUSTRIES LLC
728 Dogwood Ln (46582-1905)
PHONE..................................574 267-5313
EMP: 2 EST: 2009
SALES (est): 71K **Privately Held**
SIC: 3999 Mfg Misc Products

(G-13870)
ELKHART COUNTY GRAVEL INC
2042 W 300 N (46582-8312)
PHONE..................................574 831-2815
Stacy Jackson, *Manager*

EMP: 5
SALES (corp-wide): 5.4MM **Privately Held**
SIC: 1442 Sand mining; gravel mining
PA: Elkhart County Gravel Inc
19242 Us Highway 6
New Paris IN 46553
574 831-2815

(G-13871)
ELMOS
1900 Plaza Dr (46580-1207)
PHONE..................................574 371-2050
Jeryl Leamon, *Manager*
EMP: 2
SALES (est): 154.3K **Privately Held**
SIC: 3578 Automatic teller machines (ATM)

(G-13872)
ELYSIAN COMPANY LLC
110 E Center St (46580-2840)
PHONE..................................574 267-2259
Elise Lauren Wright, *President*
EMP: 2
SALES (est): 171.2K **Privately Held**
SIC: 2335 Women's, juniors' & misses' dresses

(G-13873)
ENPAK LLC
939 E Pound Dr N (46582-6943)
PHONE..................................574 268-7273
Marlene Mulero-Betances, *President*
Rick Rivera, *Vice Pres*
EMP: 4
SALES (est): 335.9K **Privately Held**
SIC: 7389 3569 8742 ; robots, assembly line: industrial & commercial; management consulting services

(G-13874)
FANCIL ROBERT WELDING SVC LLC
Also Called: Fancil Welding Service
721 S Buffalo St (46580-4312)
PHONE..................................574 267-8627
Robert Fancil, *President*
Jerry Fancil, *Vice Pres*
EMP: 3
SALES (est): 213.7K **Privately Held**
SIC: 7692 Welding repair

(G-13875)
FLEXAUST COMPANY INC
1605 W Center St (46580-2405)
PHONE..................................574 371-3248
Richard Meyer, *Branch Mgr*
EMP: 5
SALES (corp-wide): 177.3MM **Privately Held**
SIC: 3599 Hose, flexible metallic
HQ: Flexaust Company Inc
1200 Prospect St Ste 325
La Jolla CA 92037
619 232-8429

(G-13876)
FLEXAUST INC (DH)
1510 Armstrong Rd (46580-2402)
P.O. Box 4275 (46581-4275)
PHONE..................................574 267-7909
Fax: 574 267-4665
Richard Meyer, *President*
Michael Harvey, *Vice Pres*
Mike Obrien, *Vice Pres*
Eddie Huff, *Opers Mgr*
Steve Norton, *Safety Mgr*
◆ EMP: 127
SQ FT: 106,000
SALES (est): 52.7MM
SALES (corp-wide): 177.3MM **Privately Held**
WEB: www.flexhaust.com
SIC: 3052 Rubber & plastics hose & beltings
HQ: Flexaust Company Inc
1200 Prospect St Ste 325
La Jolla CA 92037
619 232-8429

(G-13877)
FLINT GROUP US LLC
Also Called: Flint Ink North America Div
3025 E Old Road 30 (46582-8078)
P.O. Box 287 (46581-0287)
PHONE..................................574 269-4603

Roger Cook, *Production*
Kent Blackford, *Manager*
Ken Blackford, *Manager*
EMP: 27
SALES (corp-wide): 3.5B **Privately Held**
WEB: www.flintink.com
SIC: 2893 Printing ink
PA: Flint Group Us Llc
14909 N Beck Rd
Plymouth MI 48170
734 781-4600

(G-13878)
FRONTLINE MFG INC
Also Called: Front Line Manufacturing
2466 W 200 N (46580-8320)
PHONE............................574 269-6751
Fax: 574 269-5430
Marty White, *Manager*
EMP: 100 **Privately Held**
SIC: 3088 Plastics plumbing fixtures
PA: Frontline Mfg., Inc.
2446 N 200 W
Warsaw IN 46580

(G-13879)
FRONTLINE MFG INC (PA)
2446 N 200 W (46580-8308)
P.O. Box 916 (46581-0916)
PHONE............................574 453-2902
Fax: 574 453-2904
Ray Doss, *Owner*
Paul Carter, *Engineer*
Karl Schmucker, *Admin Sec*
EMP: 100
SQ FT: 45,000
SALES (est): 20.4MM **Privately Held**
SIC: 3088 Shower stalls, fiberglass & plastic; tubs (bath, shower & laundry), plastic

(G-13880)
G & S JOHNSON OUTDOORS LLC
Also Called: Albertson's Sports Shop
3400 E Us Highway 30 (46580-6713)
PHONE............................574 267-3891
Kirk Johnson, *Mng Member*
Gary Johnson, *Mng Member*
EMP: 4
SALES (est): 650K **Privately Held**
SIC: 5941 3949 Sporting goods & bicycle shops; sporting & athletic goods

(G-13881)
GI TAPE & LABEL
701 N Union St (46580-2661)
PHONE............................574 269-2836
Fax: 574 267-5460
Jerry Irvine, *Owner*
EMP: 5
SQ FT: 5,000
SALES (est): 600.2K **Privately Held**
SIC: 2679 Tags & labels, paper

(G-13882)
GOON JONN
Also Called: Lake Area Promotional Spc
107 E Market St (46580-2807)
PHONE............................574 306-2927
John Goon, *Owner*
Tina Goon, *Co-Owner*
EMP: 2
SALES (est): 168.5K **Privately Held**
SIC: 2754 Imprinting, gravure

(G-13883)
GRABER RONALD D YODER &
Also Called: D and R Custom Logging
1515 Fox Farm Rd (46580-2136)
PHONE............................574 268-9512
Ronald Yoder, *Partner*
David Graber, *Partner*
EMP: 2
SALES (est): 190K **Privately Held**
SIC: 2411 Logging

(G-13884)
GRACE MANUFACTURING INC
1500 W Center St (46580-2410)
P.O. Box 856 (46581-0856)
PHONE............................574 267-8000
Fax: 574 269-1775
Nancy Hoeppner, *Ch of Bd*
Dan Hoeppner, *President*
Rhonda Hoeppner, *Corp Secy*
Robert Hoeppner, *Director*

EMP: 15
SQ FT: 11,200
SALES (est): 1.1MM **Privately Held**
WEB: www.grace-mfg.com
SIC: 3499 3429 Metal household articles; furniture parts, metal; manufactured hardware (general)

(G-13885)
GRAYCRAFT SIGNS PLUS INC
3304 Lake City Hwy (46580-3923)
PHONE............................574 269-3780
Scott Gray, *Branch Mgr*
EMP: 2
SALES (est): 72.6K **Privately Held**
SIC: 3993 Signs & advertising specialties
PA: Graycraft Signs Plus Inc.
2428 Getz Rd
Fort Wayne IN 46804

(G-13886)
GREATBATCH LTD
Also Called: Greatbatch Medical
265 E Bell Dr Ste A (46582-9301)
PHONE............................260 755-7484
EMP: 10
SALES (corp-wide): 1.4B **Publicly Held**
SIC: 3675 3692 3691 Electronic capacitors; primary batteries, dry & wet; storage batteries
HQ: Greatbatch Ltd.
10000 Wehrle Dr
Clarence NY 14031
612 331-6750

(G-13887)
H PROTO DEVELOPMENT INC
Also Called: Old Fashion Woods
332 N 300 E (46582-6600)
PHONE............................574 267-6372
James Holbrook, *President*
Deana Holbrook, *Vice Pres*
EMP: 4
SALES (est): 260K **Privately Held**
SIC: 3599 Machine shop, jobbing & repair

(G-13888)
HAND INDUSTRIES INC
Also Called: Acorn Ridge Highlands
315 S Hand Ave (46582-2596)
PHONE............................574 267-3525
Terry E Hand, *CEO*
John G Hand, *President*
William F Hand, *Chairman*
Leon Horn, *Admin Sec*
EMP: 20
SQ FT: 19,000
SALES (est): 2.5MM **Privately Held**
WEB: www.avshop.com
SIC: 3471 3499 0212 Cleaning, polishing & finishing; novelties & giftware, including trophies; beef cattle except feedlots

(G-13889)
HARDESTY PRINTING CO INC
411 W Market St (46580-2832)
PHONE............................574 267-7591
Fax: 574 267-4267
Frank Hardesty, *Branch Mgr*
EMP: 11
SALES (est): 1.4MM
SALES (corp-wide): 1.7MM **Privately Held**
SIC: 2752 2791 2789 Commercial printing, offset; typesetting; bookbinding & related work
PA: Hardesty Printing Co Inc
1218 N State Road 25
Rochester IN 46975
574 223-4553

(G-13890)
HOLLI HELMS
Also Called: Helms Enterprise
1 Ems B37 Ln Lot 46 (46582-9714)
PHONE............................574 253-8923
Holli Helms, *Principal*
EMP: 5
SALES (est): 141.8K **Privately Held**
SIC: 7372 Business oriented computer software

(G-13891)
HUGH K EAGAN
Also Called: Allegra Print & Imaging
201 W Center St (46580-2816)
PHONE............................574 269-5411
Hugh K Eagan, *Owner*
EMP: 2 **EST:** 2010
SALES (est): 181.3K **Privately Held**
SIC: 2752 Commercial printing, offset

(G-13892)
INDIANA VAC-FORM
Also Called: Easterwood
2030 N Boeing Rd (46582-7860)
PHONE............................574 269-1725
Fax: 574 269-2723
Greg Wood, *President*
Donald Robinson, *President*
Donna Robinson, *Corp Secy*
Chris Hubner, *Director*
▲ **EMP:** 17
SQ FT: 45,000
SALES (est): 3.1MM **Privately Held**
WEB: www.invacform.com
SIC: 3089 Thermoformed finished plastic products; plastic processing

(G-13893)
INSTRUMENTAL MACHINE & DEV INC
Also Called: IMD
2098 N Pound Dr W (46582-6550)
PHONE............................574 267-7713
Fax: 574 267-2551
Todd Speicher, *President*
Rick Henderson, *Maint Spvr*
EMP: 70
SQ FT: 12,000
SALES (est): 11.3MM **Privately Held**
WEB: www.instrumentalmachine.com
SIC: 3599 Machine shop, jobbing & repair

(G-13894)
INTUITIVE SOFTWARE LLC
1015 Logan St (46580-4273)
PHONE............................574 268-8239
Michael Aleman, *Owner*
EMP: 2
SALES (est): 98.1K **Privately Held**
SIC: 7372 Prepackaged software

(G-13895)
JENCO ENGINEERING INC
27 E 250 N (46582-6956)
PHONE............................574 267-4608
Fax: 574 267-4303
Dennis Buhrt, *President*
EMP: 2
SALES (est): 249.7K **Privately Held**
SIC: 3569 3599 General industrial machinery; industrial machinery

(G-13896)
KESTERS ELECTRIC MOTOR SERVICE
1408 Armstrong Rd (46582-2420)
PHONE............................574 269-2889
Thurl Kester, *Owner*
EMP: 2 **EST:** 1955
SALES (est): 226K **Privately Held**
SIC: 7694 Electric motor repair

(G-13897)
KEYSTONE DESIGNS INC
3606 E Us Highway 30 (46580-6712)
PHONE............................574 269-5531
Fax: 574 453-2909
Deanna Hicks, *President*
Richard G Hicks, *Principal*
EMP: 45
SQ FT: 3,500
SALES (est): 7.1MM **Privately Held**
SIC: 2541 Counter & sink tops

(G-13898)
KMC CORPORATION
602 Leiter Dr (46580-2461)
PHONE............................574 267-7033
Fax: 574 269-5497
Richard L Grover, *President*
EMP: 60
SQ FT: 50,000
SALES (est): 6.4MM **Privately Held**
SIC: 2512 2515 Upholstered household furniture; mattresses & bedsprings

(G-13899)
KUERT CONCRETE INC
155 W 600 N (46582-7790)
PHONE............................574 453-3993
Greg Towner, *Exec VP*
Mark Walker, *Director*
EMP: 12
SALES (corp-wide): 14.4MM **Privately Held**
WEB: www.kuert.com
SIC: 3273 Ready-mixed concrete
PA: Kuert Concrete Inc
3402 Lincoln Way W
South Bend IN 46628
574 232-9911

(G-13900)
LAKELAND TECHNOLOGY INC
Also Called: B&M Instruments
542 E 200 N (46582-7857)
PHONE............................574 267-1503
Fax: 574 269-6133
Mark Workman, *President*
Ray Hollett, *Manager*
Danny Moon, *Prgrmr*
EMP: 25
SQ FT: 4,000
SALES: 5MM **Privately Held**
WEB: www.bminstruments.com
SIC: 3599 Machine shop, jobbing & repair

(G-13901)
LASER PLUS
3950 N Blue Heron Dr (46582-7778)
PHONE............................574 269-1246
Jon Schutz, *Owner*
EMP: 5
SALES (est): 351.5K **Privately Held**
WEB: www.laserplus.net
SIC: 3577 Printers, computer

(G-13902)
LSC COMMUNICATIONS US LLC
2801 W Old Road 30 (46580-8783)
P.O. Box 837 (46581-0837)
PHONE............................574 267-7101
Thomas Patrick, *Safety Mgr*
EMP: 6
SALES (corp-wide): 3.6B **Publicly Held**
SIC: 2752 Commercial printing, lithographic
HQ: Lsc Communications Us, Llc
191 N Wacker Dr Ste 1400
Chicago IL 60606
844 572-5720

(G-13903)
MARINE MOORING INC
3404 N 600 E (46582-8030)
PHONE............................574 594-5787
Fax: 574 594-2857
Randall P Pollen, *President*
Donna J Pollen, *Vice Pres*
▲ **EMP:** 40
SQ FT: 8,000
SALES (est): 5.2MM **Privately Held**
WEB: www.marinemoorings.com
SIC: 2394 Canvas & related products; canopies, fabric: made from purchased materials; tents: made from purchased materials

(G-13904)
MAVRON INC
152 S Zimmer Rd (46580-2369)
PHONE............................574 267-3044
Fax: 574 267-4826
Sheal Dirck, *President*
Ronald L Dirck, *Chairman*
Nancy Dirck, *Corp Secy*
Danial Zuniga, *Senior VP*
▼ **EMP:** 17
SQ FT: 40,000
SALES: 3.1MM **Privately Held**
WEB: www.mavron.com
SIC: 3713 Specialty motor vehicle bodies

(G-13905)
MAXCARE ORTHTICS PRSTHTICS LLC
3159 E Center Street Ext (46582-3901)
PHONE............................574 267-5852
Mark Haines,
Christine Haines,
EMP: 3

SALES (est): 310.3K **Privately Held**
SIC: 3842 Prosthetic appliances; limbs, artificial; braces, elastic; braces, orthopedic

(G-13906)
MEAGAN INC
Also Called: J & B Pallet
711 S Buffalo St (46580-4312)
PHONE....................574 267-8626
James Marsillet, *President*
James R Marsillett Sr, *President*
Mary A Marsillett, *CFO*
EMP: 11
SQ FT: 4,800
SALES (est): 1.6MM **Privately Held**
SIC: 2448 Pallets, wood; pallets, wood & wood with metal

(G-13907)
MED-CUT INC
Also Called: Instru-Med
727 N Detroit St (46580-2910)
PHONE....................574 269-1982
Daniel M Carteaux, *President*
Cathy J Miller, *Corp Secy*
Mitch Miller, *VP Opers*
Art Cunliffe, *Purch Mgr*
H Anthony Miller Jr, *Admin Sec*
EMP: 55
SQ FT: 30,000
SALES (est): 9.9MM **Privately Held**
WEB: www.instru-med.com
SIC: 3841 Surgical & medical instruments

(G-13908)
MEDICAL DEVICE BUS SVCS INC (HQ)
700 Orthopaedic Dr (46582-3994)
P.O. Box 988 (46581-0988)
PHONE....................574 267-8143
Ciro Romer, *President*
Larry Williamson, *Exec VP*
Brian Nichols, *QC Mgr*
Steve Bell, *Engineer*
Bill Walton, *Engineer*
▲ EMP: 1200
SQ FT: 400,000
SALES (est): 360MM
SALES (corp-wide): 76.4B **Publicly Held**
SIC: 3842 Surgical appliances & supplies
PA: Johnson & Johnson
1 Johnson And Johnson Plz
New Brunswick NJ 08933
732 524-0400

(G-13909)
MEDTRNIC SOFAMOR DANEK USA INC
2500 Silveus Xing (46582-8598)
PHONE....................574 267-6826
Keister Ronald, *Senior Buyer*
Diana Butterfield, *Human Res Dir*
Dean Zentz, *Branch Mgr*
Schumacher Ryan, *Senior Mgr*
EMP: 5 **Privately Held**
WEB: www.mysinustools.com
SIC: 3842 Implants, surgical
HQ: Medtronic Sofamor Danek Usa, Inc.
1800 Pyramid Pl
Memphis TN 38132
901 396-3133

(G-13910)
MEGAN INC
711 S Buffalo St (46580-4312)
PHONE....................574 267-8626
Mary Marsillett, *President*
EMP: 17
SQ FT: 55,000
SALES: 2.2MM **Privately Held**
SIC: 2448 Skids, wood

(G-13911)
MILESTONE AV TECHNOLOGIES LLC
Also Called: Da-Lite
3100 N Detroit St (46582-2288)
PHONE....................574 267-8101
Melissa Kroll, *Partner*
Joe Davis, *Sales Staff*
Ilya Sirotin, *Sales Staff*
EMP: 415

SALES (corp-wide): 20.7MM **Privately Held**
SIC: 3861 Screens, projection; projectors, still or motion picture, silent or sound; tripods, camera & projector
HQ: Milestone Av Technologies Llc
6436 City West Pkwy
Eden Prairie MN 55344
866 977-3901

(G-13912)
NEULL INCORPORATED
4002 N State Road 15 (46582-7751)
P.O. Box 55 (46581-0055)
PHONE....................574 267-5575
Fax: 574 267-3938
Stephanie Coble, *Branch Mgr*
EMP: 3
SALES (est): 235.1K **Privately Held**
SIC: 3842 Orthopedic appliances

(G-13913)
NEW DALTON FOUNDRY LLC (PA)
1900 E Jefferson St (46580-3761)
PHONE....................574 267-8111
Steven Shaffer,
EMP: 3
SALES (est): 94MM **Privately Held**
SIC: 3321 Gray iron castings

(G-13914)
NEXTREMITY SOLUTIONS INC
210 N Buffalo St (46580-2730)
PHONE....................732 383-7901
Nick A Deeter, *CEO*
Rod K Mayer, *President*
Isaac C Mensah, *COO*
Frank A Patton, *CFO*
EMP: 2
SALES (est): 403.1K **Privately Held**
SIC: 8731 3841 Medical research, commercial; surgical & medical instruments

(G-13915)
NGINSTRUMENTS INC
Also Called: Avalign Cutting Tools Division
4643 N State Road 15 (46582-7789)
P.O. Box 767 (46581-0767)
PHONE....................574 268-2112
Fax: 574 268-0253
Whittaker Include, *President*
Timothy M Nicholas, *Vice Pres*
Angela Davis, *Engineer*
Mark Delaney, *Engineer*
Richard Franco, *Treasurer*
EMP: 78
SALES (est): 16.6MM **Privately Held**
WEB: www.nginstruments.com
SIC: 3841 Surgical & medical instruments
PA: Avalign Technologies, Inc.
2275 Half Day Rd Ste 126
Bannockburn IL 60015

(G-13916)
NORTHERN INDIANA TRUSS
2208 N 500 W (46580-6527)
PHONE....................574 858-0505
Jay A Hostetler, *Principal*
EMP: 3 EST: 2015
SALES (est): 185.6K **Privately Held**
SIC: 2439 Structural wood members

(G-13917)
OFFICIAL SPORTS INTL INC
4120 Corridor Dr (46582-6998)
PHONE....................574 269-1404
Fax: 574 269-7653
Mary Lou Tobin, *President*
Lynn Tobin, *General Mgr*
Paul Tobin, *Vice Pres*
Kris Huffman, *Buyer*
▲ EMP: 15
SQ FT: 5,000
SALES (est): 1.4MM **Privately Held**
WEB: www.officialsports.com
SIC: 3949 2329 2339 5961 Soccer equipment & supplies; men's & boys' athletic uniforms; uniforms, athletic; women's, misses' & juniors'; fitness & sporting goods, mail order; clothing, mail order (except women's); women's apparel, mail order

(G-13918)
ORTHOPEDIATRICS CORP
2850 Frontier Dr (46582-7001)
PHONE....................574 268-6379
Terry D Schlotterback, *Ch of Bd*
Mark C Throdahl, *President*
David R Bailey, *Exec VP*
Gregory A Odle, *Exec VP*
Fred L Hite, *CFO*
EMP: 62
SQ FT: 13,000
SALES (est): 45.6MM **Privately Held**
WEB: www.orthopediatrics.sb.siliconmtn.com
SIC: 3842 5999 Surgical appliances & supplies; orthopedic appliances; orthopedic & prosthesis applications

(G-13919)
ORTHOPEDIATRICS US DIST
2850 Frontier Dr (46582-7001)
PHONE....................574 268-6379
Mark Throdahl, *President*
Fred Hite, *CFO*
EMP: 75
SQ FT: 3,000
SALES (est): 4.3MM **Privately Held**
SIC: 3842 Surgical appliances & supplies

(G-13920)
OSBORN MANUFACTURING CORP
960 N Lake St (46580-2528)
P.O. Box 1650 (46581-1650)
PHONE....................574 267-6156
Fax: 574 267-6527
Vivian Kelly, *President*
Jerry Kelly, *Vice Pres*
Scott Kelly, *Vice Pres*
Aimee Kintzel, *Vice Pres*
EMP: 10
SQ FT: 22,000
SALES (est): 1.5MM **Privately Held**
WEB: www.osbornmfg.com
SIC: 3423 3089 Hand & edge tools; thermoformed finished plastic products

(G-13921)
OUTDOOR INDUSTRIES
221 S Hand Ave (46580-2515)
PHONE....................574 551-5936
EMP: 2
SALES (est): 170.1K **Privately Held**
SIC: 3999 Manufacturing industries

(G-13922)
PANDORA PRINTING ✪
1831 Rosemont Ave (46580-2344)
PHONE....................574 551-9624
Fernando Malagon, *Principal*
EMP: 2 EST: 2018
SALES (est): 83.9K **Privately Held**
SIC: 2752 Commercial printing, lithographic

(G-13923)
PAPERS INC
114 W Market St (46580-2812)
PHONE....................574 269-2932
Margarett Smith, *Manager*
EMP: 6
SALES (est): 305.5K
SALES (corp-wide): 47.6MM **Privately Held**
WEB: www.the-papers.com
SIC: 2711 Newspapers: publishing only, not printed on site
PA: The Papers Inc
206 S Main St
Milford IN 46542
574 658-4111

(G-13924)
PELICAN BAY SOLUTIONS LLC
126 E Deerwood Ct (46582-6919)
PHONE....................574 268-4456
Toby Farling,
EMP: 2
SALES (est): 67K **Privately Held**
SIC: 2741 Guides: publishing & printing

(G-13925)
PENDRY COATINGS LLC
1119 Seymour Midwest Dr (46580-1215)
PHONE....................574 268-2956

George Pendry, *Vice Pres*
EMP: 3
SALES (est): 51.9K **Privately Held**
SIC: 2851 5169 Coating, air curing; chemicals & allied products
PA: Seymour Midwest Llc
2666 S Country Club Rd
Warsaw IN 46580

(G-13926)
PERFECTION BAKERIES INC
Also Called: Aunt Millie's Bakeries
2557 E Us Highway 30 (46580-7128)
PHONE....................574 269-9706
Dave Dunham, *Manager*
EMP: 7
SALES (corp-wide): 515.3MM **Privately Held**
WEB: www.perfectionpastries.com
SIC: 2051 Bakery: wholesale or wholesale/retail combined
PA: Perfection Bakeries, Inc.
350 Pearl St
Fort Wayne IN 46802
260 424-8245

(G-13927)
POLYONE CORPORATION
Also Called: Spartech Plastics
3454 N Detroit St (46582-2284)
P.O. Box 958 (46581-0958)
PHONE....................574 267-1100
Julie A McAlindon, *Opers-Prdtn-Mfg*
EMP: 160 **Publicly Held**
SIC: 2821 Plastics materials & resins
PA: Polyone Corporation
33587 Walker Rd
Avon Lake OH 44012

(G-13928)
PRECISION MEDICAL TECH INC
2059 N Pound Dr W (46582-6546)
PHONE....................574 267-6385
Kurt Kamholz, *President*
Ryan Thornburgh, *Business Mgr*
James Eastwood, *Engineer*
Jeff Forker, *Engineer*
Jeff Thornburgh, *Treasurer*
EMP: 35
SQ FT: 6,000
SALES (est): 6.7MM **Privately Held**
WEB: www.premedtec.com
SIC: 3842 Orthopedic appliances

(G-13929)
PREMIER CONCEPTS INC
2371 N Rainbow Dr (46582-6718)
PHONE....................574 269-7570
Raymond Doss, *President*
EMP: 5
SALES (est): 480K **Privately Held**
SIC: 3469 Kitchen fixtures & equipment: metal, except cast aluminum

(G-13930)
PVA UNLIMITED INC
2234 E Hendricks St (46580-3734)
PHONE....................574 269-2782
Fax: 574 269-2756
Bob South, *Manager*
EMP: 2
SALES (est): 261.9K **Privately Held**
SIC: 3423 Garden & farm tools, including shovels

(G-13931)
R R DONNELLEY & SONS COMPANY
Also Called: Warsaw Mfg Div
2801 W Old Road 30 (46580-8783)
PHONE....................574 267-7101
Fax: 574 267-9482
Steve Shingledecker, *Engineer*
Grant McGuire, *Sales/Mktg Mgr*
EMP: 920
SQ FT: 800,000
SALES (corp-wide): 6.9B **Publicly Held**
WEB: www.rrdonnelley.com
SIC: 2759 Commercial printing
PA: R. R. Donnelley & Sons Company
35 W Wacker Dr Ste 3650
Chicago IL 60601
312 326-8000

GEOGRAPHIC

(G-13932)
RAYCO STEEL PROCESS INC
207 S Lincoln St (46580-3771)
P.O. Box 1016 (46581-1016)
PHONE...................................574 267-7676
Fax: 574 267-6460
Jim Rooney, *President*
Deb Pilther, *Shareholder*
Sharon Swartz, *Admin Sec*
EMP: 11
SQ FT: 10,000
SALES (est): 1.8MM **Privately Held**
WEB: www.raycotools.com
SIC: 3842 3599 Orthopedic appliances;
machine shop, jobbing & repair

(G-13933)
RAYMOND TRUEX
5383 W 400 N (46582-8505)
PHONE...................................574 858-2260
Tina Truex, *Principal*
EMP: 3
SALES (est): 159.2K **Privately Held**
SIC: 2395 Embroidery products, except
schiffli machine

(G-13934)
RBK DEVELOPMENT INC
Also Called: Superior Wood Products
1058 W 400 N (46582-7038)
PHONE...................................574 267-5879
Fax: 574 269-3488
Gale Schaffer, *President*
Bruce Korenstra, *Corp Secy*
EMP: 32
SQ FT: 35,000
SALES (est): 4.6MM **Privately Held**
SIC: 2434 2517 2541 2511 Wood kitchen
cabinets; home entertainment unit cabi-
nets, wood; wood partitions & fixtures;
wood household furniture

(G-13935)
RIEPEN LLC
Also Called: Danco Anodizing
2450 Deelyn Dr (46580-8500)
P.O. Box 2050 (46581-2050)
PHONE...................................574 269-5900
Fax: 574 269-5966
Sherri V Scherer, *General Ptnr*
Jesse Armenta, *Engineer*
Keenan Yates, *Supervisor*
David Tatge,
Lisa E Tatge,
EMP: 83
SALES (est): 8.7MM **Privately Held**
SIC: 3471 Anodizing (plating) of metals or
formed products

(G-13936)
RMI HOLDINGS LLC
Also Called: R M I
4130 Corridor Dr (46582-6998)
PHONE...................................317 214-7076
Jim Evans, *Principal*
EMP: 28
SALES (est): 3.1MM **Privately Held**
WEB: www.rickmantool.com
SIC: 3842 3841 Orthopedic appliances;
surgical & medical instruments

(G-13937)
SEMMATERIALS LP
2820 Durbin St (46580-3883)
PHONE...................................574 267-5076
Jason Conrad, *Branch Mgr*
EMP: 7
SQ FT: 720
SALES (corp-wide): 2B **Publicly Held**
WEB: www.semgroup.com
SIC: 2951 Asphalt paving mixtures &
blocks
HQ: Semmaterials, L.P.
6520 S Yale Ave Ste 700
Tulsa OK 74136
918 524-8100

(G-13938)
SEYMOUR MIDWEST LLC (PA)
2666 S Country Club Rd (46580-7408)
P.O. Box 1674 (46581-1674)
PHONE...................................574 267-7875
Fax: 574 267-8508
Bill Henthorn, *President*
Daniel E Miller, *Vice Pres*
▲ EMP: 93

SQ FT: 18,000
SALES (est): 61.4MM **Privately Held**
WEB: www.midwestrake.com
SIC: 3423 Garden & farm tools, including
shovels

(G-13939)
SEYMOUR MIDWEST LLC
Also Called: PVA Unlimited
2234 E Hendricks St (46580-3734)
P.O. Box 1552 (46581-1552)
PHONE...................................574 269-2782
Bob South, *Mng Member*
EMP: 4 **Privately Held**
WEB: www.midwestrake.com
SIC: 3081 3069 Polyvinyl film & sheet;
sponge rubber & sponge rubber products
PA: Seymour Midwest Llc
2666 S Country Club Rd
Warsaw IN 46580

(G-13940)
SJG ENTERPRISES INC
Also Called: Graycraft Signs Plus
3304 Lake City Hwy (46580-3923)
PHONE...................................574 269-4806
Fax: 574 269-4806
Scott Gray, *President*
Jody Bowers, *Supervisor*
EMP: 4
SALES (est): 560.2K **Privately Held**
SIC: 3993 Signs, not made in custom sign
painting shops

(G-13941)
SJS COMPONENTS LLC
6778 S State Road 13 (46580-8648)
PHONE...................................260 578-0192
Scott Brown, *Mng Member*
EMP: 3
SALES (est): 120K **Privately Held**
SIC: 2541 Wood partitions & fixtures

(G-13942)
SPECIALTY MACHINE STAMPING
Also Called: Specialty Machines
3890 N 300 W (46582-8528)
PHONE...................................574 658-3350
Fax: 574 658-3979
Frederick Kalinowski, *President*
Earl Berkey, *Manager*
EMP: 2
SQ FT: 6,000
SALES (est): 58.5K **Privately Held**
SIC: 3599 Machine shop, jobbing & repair

(G-13943)
SUPER CAR WASH OF WARSAW
Also Called: JG Grinestoppers
2223 E Center St (46580-3719)
PHONE...................................574 269-6922
Jim Gast, *President*
EMP: 10 EST: 1996
SALES (est): 1.1MM **Privately Held**
SIC: 3589 7542 Car washing machinery;
carwashes

(G-13944)
SUPPER WASH
2233 E Center St (46580-3719)
P.O. Box 1849 (46581-1849)
PHONE...................................574 269-2233
Jim Gast, *Owner*
EMP: 7
SALES (est): 270K **Privately Held**
SIC: 3589 Car washing machinery

(G-13945)
SURFACE ENHANCEMENT
Also Called: Warsaw Electropolishing
125 W 250 N (46582-7864)
PHONE...................................574 269-1366
Fax: 574 269-1193
Earl H Kline, *Owner*
Cheri A Kline, *Principal*
EMP: 6
SQ FT: 4,000
SALES (est): 633.5K **Privately Held**
WEB: www.showoffstainless.com
SIC: 3599 3471 Machine shop, jobbing &
repair; polishing, metals or formed prod-
ucts

(G-13946)
SUSIES SANDBAR
1360 W Center St (46580-2468)
PHONE...................................574 269-5355
Donald Radabaugh Jr, *Director*
EMP: 4
SALES (est): 394.7K **Privately Held**
SIC: 2599 Bar, restaurant & cafeteria furni-
ture

(G-13947)
SYMMETRY MEDICAL INC
486 W 350 N (46582-7744)
PHONE...................................574 267-8700
Fax: 574 267-1871
Anita Bolinger, *Senior Buyer*
Jeff Foster, *QC Mgr*
Greg Neher, *Engineer*
Sibyl Nelson, *Controller*
Brinda Whitaker, *Manager*
EMP: 130
SALES (corp-wide): 871.2MM **Privately Held**
SIC: 3841 Surgical instruments & appara-
tus
HQ: Symmetry Medical Inc.
3724 N State Road 15
Warsaw IN 46582

(G-13948)
SYMMETRY MEDICAL INC (HQ)
3724 N State Road 15 (46582-7000)
PHONE...................................574 268-2252
William Dow, *CEO*
Robert S Rutledge, *President*
Chris Cummins, *Senior VP*
Andrew J Miclot, *Senior VP*
David J Golde, *Vice Pres*
▲ EMP: 9
SQ FT: 15,800
SALES (est): 191.3MM
SALES (corp-wide): 871.2MM **Privately Held**
WEB: www.symmetrymedical.com
SIC: 3841 3842 Surgical & medical instru-
ments; orthopedic appliances
PA: Tecomet Inc.
115 Eames St
Wilmington MA 01887
978 642-2400

(G-13949)
SYMMETRY MEDICAL MFG INC
Also Called: Jet Engineering
3724 N State Road 15 (46582-7000)
PHONE...................................574 371-2284
Bryan Lair, *General Mgr*
Kim Clark, *Vice Pres*
Michelle Senior, *Purch Mgr*
Jason Vanderreyden, *Admin Asst*
▲ EMP: 70
SQ FT: 42,000
SALES (est): 29.7MM
SALES (corp-wide): 871.2MM **Privately Held**
SIC: 3369 3469 3463 Titanium castings,
except die-casting; metal stampings; non-
ferrous forgings
HQ: Symmetry Medical Inc.
3724 N State Road 15
Warsaw IN 46582

(G-13950)
SYMMETRY NEW BEDFORD RE LLC
3724 N State Road 15 (46582-7000)
PHONE...................................574 268-2252
EMP: 4 EST: 2013
SALES (est): 189.3K
SALES (corp-wide): 871.2MM **Privately Held**
SIC: 3841 Surgical & medical instruments
HQ: Symmetry Medical Inc.
3724 N State Road 15
Warsaw IN 46582

(G-13951)
TEXMO PRCISION CASTINGS US INC
Also Called: Medcast
596 E 200 N (46582-7857)
PHONE...................................574 269-1368
Fax: 574 269-6442
Satish Patel, *President*
Milind Ranadive, *Admin Sec*

▲ EMP: 60
SQ FT: 30,000
SALES (est): 16.3MM **Privately Held**
SIC: 3324 3823 Commercial investment
castings, ferrous; absorption analyzers:
infrared, X-ray, etc.: industrial

(G-13952)
TILI LLC
Also Called: Arby's
1980 N Detroit St (46580-2222)
PHONE...................................574 267-6995
Christopher Polk,
EMP: 2 EST: 2014
SALES (est): 62.3K **Privately Held**
SIC: 2099 Ready-to-eat meals, salads &
sandwiches

(G-13953)
TORNIER INC
100 Capital Dr Ste 201 (46582-6704)
PHONE...................................574 268-0861
EMP: 7
SALES (corp-wide): 744.9MM **Privately Held**
WEB: www.tornier.com
SIC: 3842 5999 Implants, surgical; ortho-
pedic & prosthesis applications
HQ: Tornier, Inc.
10801 Nesbitt Ave S
Bloomington MN 55437

(G-13954)
TRIPLE INC
610 E Bell Dr (46582-9337)
P.O. Box 1865 (46581-1865)
PHONE...................................574 267-1450
Fax: 574 267-8097
Yung-Kun Lu, *President*
▲ EMP: 5
SALES (est): 605K **Privately Held**
SIC: 3842 5047 Orthopedic appliances;
orthopedic equipment & supplies

(G-13955)
ULTREXX INC
Also Called: Symmetry Medical
3724 N State Road 15 (46582-7000)
PHONE...................................260 897-2680
Fax: 260 897-3884
EMP: 150
SALES (est): 25.6MM **Privately Held**
SIC: 3599 Machine Shop

(G-13956)
UNION TOOL CORP
1144 N Detroit St (46580-2917)
P.O. Box 935 (46581-0935)
PHONE...................................574 267-3211
Fax: 574 267-5703
Michael T Simpson, *President*
Chuck T Simpson, *Co-President*
Mervin Jones, *Plant Mgr*
Lisa Joy, *Data Proc Staff*
▼ EMP: 32
SQ FT: 37,000
SALES (est): 8MM **Privately Held**
WEB: www.uniontoolcorp.com
SIC: 3599 3559 Custom machinery; metal
finishing equipment for plating, etc.

(G-13957)
VAN EXPLORER COMPANY INC (PA)
Also Called: Explorer Sport Trucks
2749 N Fox Farm Rd (46580-6547)
P.O. Box 4527 (46581-4527)
PHONE...................................574 267-7666
Fax: 574 269-3628
Robert Kesler, *Ch of Bd*
Steve Kesler, *President*
Gary Cowan, *General Mgr*
Darlene Perkins, *General Mgr*
Doris Kesler, *Corp Secy*
◆ EMP: 25 EST: 1980
SQ FT: 140,000
SALES (est): 26MM **Privately Held**
WEB: www.explorervan.com
SIC: 3716 Recreational van conversion
(self-propelled), factory basis

(G-13958)
WARSAW CHEMICAL COMPANY INC
390 Argonne Rd (46580-3884)
P.O. Box 858 (46581-0858)
PHONE..........................574 267-3251
Fax: 574 267-3884
Kenneth E Bucher, *President*
Dino Pellegrene, *Regional Mgr*
Vic Gamble, *Vice Pres*
Michelle Spangle, *Purch Agent*
Leigh Utter, *Purch Agent*
EMP: 85
SQ FT: 200,000
SALES: 22.9MM **Privately Held**
WEB: www.warsaw-chem.com
SIC: 5169 2842 2891 2841 Industrial chemicals; cleaning or polishing preparations; adhesives & sealants; soap & other detergents; alkalies & chlorine

(G-13959)
WARSAW COIL CO INC
1809 W Winona Ave (46580-2351)
P.O. Box 1057 (46581-1057)
PHONE..........................574 267-6041
Fax: 574 269-6715
Thomas Joyner, *President*
Diane Doran, *Corp Secy*
Bradley C Joyner, *Vice Pres*
▲ EMP: 100 EST: 1954
SQ FT: 55,000
SALES (est): 17.3MM **Privately Held**
WEB: www.warsawcoil.com
SIC: 3677 Electronic coils, transformers & other inductors

(G-13960)
WARSAW CUSTOM CABINET (PA)
1697 W 350 S (46580-8201)
PHONE..........................574 267-5794
Paul F Mundinger, *Owner*
Vivian Mundinger, *Co-Owner*
EMP: 3
SQ FT: 3,500
SALES (est): 301.1K **Privately Held**
SIC: 2434 Wood kitchen cabinets; vanities, bathroom: wood

(G-13961)
WARSAW CUT GLASS COMPANY INC
505 S Detroit St (46580-4406)
P.O. Box 1322 (46581-1322)
PHONE..........................574 267-6581
Fax: 574 267-6581
Randolph Kirkendall, *President*
Linda Kirkendall, *Vice Pres*
EMP: 8
SQ FT: 4,000
SALES (est): 570K **Privately Held**
SIC: 3231 5719 Cut & engraved glassware: made from purchased glass; glassware

(G-13962)
WARSAW FOUNDRY COMPANY INC
1212 N Detroit St (46580-2919)
P.O. Box 227 (46581-0227)
PHONE..........................574 267-8772
Fax: 574 269-6238
John W Petro, *President*
Mike Petro, *Corp Secy*
John Petro, *Vice Pres*
EMP: 60
SALES (est): 10.6MM **Privately Held**
WEB: www.warsawfoundryco.com
SIC: 3321 1446 2431 Gray iron castings; molding sand mining; moldings, wood: unfinished & prefinished

(G-13963)
WARSAW ORTHOPEDIC INC
Also Called: Sofamor/Danek Group Mfg Div
2500 Silveus Xing (46582-8598)
P.O. Box 1157 (46581-1157)
PHONE..........................901 396-3133
Gene Sponseller, *President*
William Reynolds, *Vice Pres*
J Mark Merrill, *Treasurer*
Richard Duerr, *Admin Sec*
EMP: 175 EST: 1951
SQ FT: 80,000
SALES (est): 26K **Privately Held**
SIC: 3842 Implants, surgical; prosthetic appliances
HQ: Medtronic Sofamor Danek Usa, Inc.
1800 Pyramid Pl
Memphis TN 38132
901 396-3133

(G-13964)
WHITE MACHINE INC
1903 White Industrial Dr (46580-2370)
PHONE..........................574 267-5895
John White, *President*
EMP: 3 EST: 1961
SQ FT: 2,000
SALES: 185K **Privately Held**
SIC: 3599 Machine shop, jobbing & repair

(G-13965)
WILDMAN BUSINESS GROUP LLC
Also Called: Wildman Corporate Apparel
800 S Buffalo St (46580-4710)
PHONE..........................866 369-1552
Fax: 574 269-1070
Josh Wildman, *CEO*
Brent Wildman, *President*
Steve Bryant, *COO*
EMP: 168 EST: 1952
SQ FT: 55,000
SALES (est): 20.3MM **Privately Held**
WEB: www.wildmanuniform.com
SIC: 7218 7213 5087 5199 Industrial uniform supply; linen supply, non-clothing; janitors' supplies; first aid supplies; screen printing; embroidery products, except schiffli machine

(G-13966)
WILDMAN CORPORATE APPAREL LTD
800 S Buffalo St Ste 1 (46580-4710)
PHONE..........................574 269-7266
Brent Wildman, *President*
Karen Wildman, *Vice Pres*
EMP: 11
SQ FT: 4,000
SALES (est): 1.1MM **Privately Held**
WEB: www.signetexpressions.com
SIC: 2395 Embroidery & art needlework

(G-13967)
WILEY YOUNG & ASSOCIATES
Also Called: Zimmer Medwest
121 W Market St Ste B (46580-2866)
PHONE..........................574 269-7006
Fred J Rowland, *Principal*
EMP: 8
SALES (est): 1MM **Privately Held**
SIC: 3842 Prosthetic appliances

(G-13968)
WINONA PVD COATINGS LLC
1180 Polk Dr (46582-8602)
P.O. Box 1856 (46581-1856)
PHONE..........................574 269-3255
Jamie T Visker, *CEO*
Larry Beals, *Vice Pres*
Kirk Sobecki, *Vice Pres*
Tonja Busch, *QC Mgr*
Fred Fribley,
▲ EMP: 45
SQ FT: 68,000
SALES (est): 16.9MM **Privately Held**
SIC: 3479 Coating of metals & formed products

(G-13969)
WORTH TAX AND FINANCIAL SVC
Also Called: Jackson Hewitt Tax Service
3201 E Center Street Ext (46582-3907)
P.O. Box 725, Winona Lake (46590-0725)
PHONE..........................574 267-4687
Beverly Worth, *Owner*
EMP: 5
SQ FT: 5,700 **Privately Held**
SIC: 7291 8299 2731 6282 Tax return preparation services; educational services; books: publishing only; investment advice; exercise salon

(G-13970)
XYZ MACHINING INC
5141 W 100 S (46580-8962)
PHONE..........................574 269-5541
Steve Kline, *President*
Tim Norman, *President*
EMP: 2
SALES: 500K **Privately Held**
WEB: www.xyzmachining.com
SIC: 3599 Machine shop, jobbing & repair

(G-13971)
ZIMMER INC (HQ)
Also Called: Z Hotel
1800 W Center St (46580-2304)
P.O. Box 708 (46581-0708)
PHONE..........................330 343-8801
Fax: 574 372-4402
David C Dvorak, *President*
James T Crines, *CFO*
◆ EMP: 500
SQ FT: 108,000
SALES (est): 664.3MM
SALES (corp-wide): 7.8B **Publicly Held**
WEB: www.zimmer.com
SIC: 3842 Orthopedic appliances; implants, surgical; surgical appliances & supplies
PA: Zimmer Biomet Holdings, Inc.
345 E Main St
Warsaw IN 46580
574 267-6131

(G-13972)
ZIMMER INC
1800 W Center St (46580-2304)
PHONE..........................574 268-3100
EMP: 3
SALES (corp-wide): 7.8B **Publicly Held**
SIC: 3842 Orthopedic appliances; implants, surgical; surgical appliances & supplies
HQ: Zimmer, Inc.
1800 W Center St
Warsaw IN 46580
330 343-8801

(G-13973)
ZIMMER INC
1113 W Lake St (46580-2532)
PHONE..........................574 371-1557
EMP: 3
SALES (corp-wide): 7.8B **Publicly Held**
SIC: 3842 Orthopedic appliances; implants, surgical; surgical appliances & supplies
HQ: Zimmer, Inc.
1800 W Center St
Warsaw IN 46580
330 343-8801

(G-13974)
ZIMMER INC
1777 W Center St (46580-2303)
PHONE..........................574 267-6131
Carolyn Stidham, *Branch Mgr*
EMP: 5
SALES (corp-wide): 7.8B **Publicly Held**
SIC: 3842 Orthopedic appliances
HQ: Zimmer, Inc.
1800 W Center St
Warsaw IN 46580
330 343-8801

(G-13975)
ZIMMER BIOMET HOLDINGS INC (PA)
345 E Main St (46580-2746)
PHONE..........................574 267-6131
Fax: 574 372-4446
Larry C Glasscock, *Ch of Bd*
Bryan C Hanson, *President*
Aure Bruneau, *President*
Robert D Delp, *President*
Katarzyna Mazur-Hofsaess, *President*
EMP: 257 EST: 1927
SQ FT: 115,000
SALES: 7.8B **Publicly Held**
SIC: 3842 Surgical appliances & supplies; orthopedic appliances; implants, surgical

(G-13976)
ZIMMER PRODUCTION INC
345 E Main St (46580-2746)
PHONE..........................574 267-6131
Keneth R Coonce, *President*

James T Crines, *Vice Pres*
EMP: 2
SALES (est): 137K
SALES (corp-wide): 7.8B **Publicly Held**
SIC: 3842 Orthopedic appliances
PA: Zimmer Biomet Holdings, Inc.
345 E Main St
Warsaw IN 46580
574 267-6131

(G-13977)
ZIMMER US INC
Also Called: Zimmer Biomet
1800 W Center St (46580-2304)
P.O. Box 708 (46581-0708)
PHONE..........................574 267-6131
Jeffery McCaulley, *President*
Joseph A Cucolo, *President*
David C Dvorak, *President*
James T Crines, *CFO*
EMP: 77
SALES (est): 14.8MM
SALES (corp-wide): 7.8B **Publicly Held**
SIC: 3842 Orthopedic appliances
PA: Zimmer Biomet Holdings, Inc.
345 E Main St
Warsaw IN 46580
574 267-6131

Washington
Daviess County

(G-13978)
B & D ELECTRIC INC
413 W Van Trees St (47501-2597)
PHONE..........................812 254-2122
Fax: 812 254-2122
Tony D Blessinger, *President*
Greg P Hauser, *Vice Pres*
Greg Hauser, *Info Tech Mgr*
Jackie Daily, *Admin Sec*
EMP: 15 EST: 1961
SQ FT: 6,000
SALES: 4.7MM **Privately Held**
WEB: www.bdelectric.com
SIC: 1731 7694 General electrical contractor; electric motor repair

(G-13979)
DESTINATION YACHTS INC
2610 S 140 W (47501-8076)
PHONE..........................812 254-8800
Fax: 812 486-2771
Sheldon T Graber, *President*
EMP: 17
SQ FT: 16,000
SALES (est): 3.2MM **Privately Held**
WEB: www.destinationyachts.com
SIC: 3732 Houseboats, building & repairing

(G-13980)
DIGITAL SOLUTIONS
402 S State Road 57 (47501-4027)
PHONE..........................812 257-0333
Dan Leigh, *Principal*
EMP: 3 EST: 2011
SALES (est): 227.7K **Privately Held**
SIC: 3663 Space satellite communications equipment

(G-13981)
DOUGLAS P TERRELL
Also Called: D Terrell & Company
1289 S State Road 57 (47501-4367)
PHONE..........................812 254-1976
Doug Terrell, *Owner*
EMP: 2
SALES: 200K **Privately Held**
SIC: 2759 Commercial printing

(G-13982)
FRESH START INC
113 N Industrial Park Rd (47501-7747)
PHONE..........................812 254-3398
Fax: 812 254-3398
Tim Weaver, *President*
EMP: 15
SALES: 450K **Privately Held**
SIC: 8361 2511 8322 8661 Residential care; wood lawn & garden furniture; alcoholism counseling, nontreatment; miscellaneous denomination church

G
E
O
G
R
A
P
H
I
C

(G-13983)
GRAIN PROCESSING
CORPORATION
1443 S 300 W (47501-7410)
PHONE...................................812 257-0480
Fax: 812 257-2749
Brad Quigley, *Manager*
EMP: 15
SALES (corp-wide): 637MM **Privately Held**
WEB: www.gpcequipment.com
SIC: 2869 2085 2046 Grain alcohol, industrial; grain alcohol for beverage purposes; corn starch; corn oil, refined
HQ: Grain Processing Corporation
1600 Oregon St
Muscatine IA 52761
563 264-4265

(G-13984)
GREEN STEAK PULLING INC
1312 E 200 N (47501-7669)
PHONE...................................812 254-6858
Steve Boyd, *President*
EMP: 2
SALES (est): 149.7K **Privately Held**
SIC: 3537 Tractors, used in plants, docks, terminals, etc.: industrial

(G-13985)
GWALTNEY DRILLING INC
101 Se 3rd St (47501-3208)
P.O. Box 520 (47501-0520)
PHONE...................................812 254-5085
Michael Crouch, *President*
Michael V Crouch, *President*
Dave Osman, *Vice Pres*
EMP: 1 EST: 1950
SQ FT: 3,000
SALES: 2.2MM
SALES (corp-wide): 16MM **Privately Held**
SIC: 1381 Drilling oil & gas wells
HQ: Natural Gas Processors Inc
107 Se 3rd St
Washington IN
812 254-5087

(G-13986)
HOOSIER READY MIX LLC
1115 S 300 W (47501-8217)
PHONE...................................812 254-7625
Joseph Knepp, *Principal*
Stacy Culver, *Mng Member*
EMP: 10
SALES: 2MM **Privately Held**
SIC: 3273 Ready-mixed concrete

(G-13987)
IRVING MATERIALS INC
Also Called: I M I
611 W Main St (47501-2510)
PHONE...................................812 254-0820
Dustin Bowersock, *Plant Mgr*
Brad Wagler, *Branch Mgr*
EMP: 3
SALES (corp-wide): 800.6MM **Privately Held**
SIC: 3273 5032 Ready-mixed concrete; concrete building products
PA: Irving Materials, Inc.
8032 N State Road 9
Greenfield IN 46140
317 326-3101

(G-13988)
JONES & SONS INC (PA)
1262 S State Road 57 (47501-4366)
P.O. Box 2357 (47501-0997)
PHONE...................................812 254-4731
Fax: 812 254-3293
Darrell Jones, *President*
Marsha Jones-Bauer, *Corp Secy*
Bert Marcus Jones, *Vice Pres*
Mike Healy, *CFO*
Susan Orr, *Credit Mgr*
EMP: 35
SQ FT: 10,000
SALES: 20.3MM **Privately Held**
WEB: www.jonesandsons.com
SIC: 3273 3271 Ready-mixed concrete; blocks, concrete or cinder: standard

(G-13989)
JONES ENGINEERING INC
897 W 150 S (47501-7371)
PHONE...................................812 254-6456
Fax: 812 254-4022
Sam Jones, *President*
Madonna Jones, *Corp Secy*
Jeff Jones, *Vice Pres*
EMP: 3
SQ FT: 7,000
SALES: 500K **Privately Held**
SIC: 3621 Motors & generators

(G-13990)
MATHESON TRI-GAS INC
1285 S 300 W (47501-8207)
PHONE...................................812 257-0470
Bill Haywood, *Manager*
EMP: 15
SALES (corp-wide): 34.9B **Privately Held**
SIC: 2813 5084 Industrial gases; nitrogen; oxygen, compressed or liquefied; argon; welding machinery & equipment; safety equipment
HQ: Matheson Tri-Gas, Inc.
150 Allen Rd Ste 302
Basking Ridge NJ 07920
908 991-9200

(G-13991)
MEMERING FARMS
3867 N State Road 57 (47501-7582)
PHONE...................................812 254-8170
Gary Memering, *Partner*
Scott Arthur, *Partner*
EMP: 3
SALES (est): 354.9K **Privately Held**
SIC: 3523 Driers (farm): grain, hay & seed

(G-13992)
NASCO INDUSTRIES INC
3 Ne 21st St (47501-3111)
P.O. Box 427 (47501-0427)
PHONE...................................812 254-7393
Fax: 812 254-6476
Todd N Smith, *President*
Neil A Smith, *Chairman*
Dave Wildridge, *Opers Mgr*
Zack Smith, *Purchasing*
Patty Kelsey, *Engineer*
▲ EMP: 120 EST: 1979
SQ FT: 56,000
SALES (est): 22.2MM **Privately Held**
WEB: www.nascoinc.com
SIC: 2385 Waterproof outerwear

(G-13993)
NEWSPAPER HOLDING INC
Also Called: Washington Times Herald
102 E Van Trees St (47501-2943)
P.O. Box 471 (47501-0471)
PHONE...................................812 254-0480
Fax: 812 254-7517
Roger Pratt, *President*
Ron Smith, *Manager*
EMP: 30 **Privately Held**
WEB: www.clintonnc.com
SIC: 2711 Newspapers: publishing only, not printed on site
HQ: Newspaper Holding, Inc.
425 Locust St
Johnstown PA 15901
814 532-5102

(G-13994)
OLON INDUSTRIES INC (US)
2510 E National Hwy (47501-9597)
P.O. Box 669 (47501-0669)
PHONE...................................812 254-0427
Frank Guratzsch, *Principal*
Susan Doherty, *Manager*
EMP: 15
SALES (corp-wide): 23.3MM **Privately Held**
SIC: 3429 2431 2426 Furniture hardware; millwork; hardwood dimension & flooring mills
HQ: Olon Industries Inc. (Us)
411 Union St
Geneva IL 60134
630 232-4705

(G-13995)
OLON INDUSTRIES INC (US)
2510 E National Hwy (47501-9597)
PHONE...................................812 254-6718

Guratzsch Frank, *Branch Mgr*
EMP: 5
SALES (corp-wide): 23.3MM **Privately Held**
SIC: 3083 Laminated plastic sheets
HQ: Olon Industries Inc. (Us)
411 Union St
Geneva IL 60134
630 232-4705

(G-13996)
P J J T DISTRIBUTORS INC
501 N Meridian St (47501-2013)
P.O. Box 633 (47501-0633)
PHONE...................................812 254-2218
Fax: 812 254-7942
Mary Lynne Portee, *President*
Lynne Portee, *Corp Secy*
EMP: 12
SALES (est): 1.1MM **Privately Held**
SIC: 2721 8748 Magazines: publishing only, not printed on site; publishing consultant

(G-13997)
PEABODY MIDWEST MINING
LLC
Also Called: Standard Coal Lab
1281 S 300 W (47501-8207)
PHONE...................................812 254-7714
Melody Cockerham, *Manager*
EMP: 3
SALES (corp-wide): 5.1B **Publicly Held**
SIC: 1221 Bituminous coal surface mining
HQ: Peabody Midwest Mining Llc
566 Dickeyville Rd
Lynnville IN 47619

(G-13998)
PERDUE FARMS INC
65 S 200 W (47501-3482)
P.O. Box 539 (47501-0539)
PHONE...................................812 254-8500
Fax: 812 254-3738
Sabrina Englehart, *Facilities Mgr*
Tom Schaffer, *Manager*
Nicole Larkey, *Manager*
Jerome Kutche, *Maintence Staff*
EMP: 60
SALES (corp-wide): 5.5B **Privately Held**
WEB: www.perdue.com
SIC: 2015 Poultry slaughtering & processing
PA: Perdue Farms Inc.
31149 Old Ocean City Rd
Salisbury MD 21804
410 543-3000

(G-13999)
PERDUE FARMS INC
Also Called: Oak Tree Experimental Farm
100 W 400 N (47501)
PHONE...................................757 787-5210
Bruce Roberts, *Branch Mgr*
EMP: 197
SALES (corp-wide): 5.5B **Privately Held**
SIC: 2015 Poultry slaughtering & processing
PA: Perdue Farms Inc.
31149 Old Ocean City Rd
Salisbury MD 21804
410 543-3000

(G-14000)
PRECIBALL USA
219 E Main St Ste 4x (47501-2990)
PHONE...................................812 257-5555
Savanna Georgia,
EMP: 2
SALES (est): 58.3K **Privately Held**
SIC: 3999 Bristles, dressing of

(G-14001)
RAPAR INC
705 W National Hwy (47501-3330)
PHONE...................................812 254-9886
Mellisa Williams, *Owner*
EMP: 5
SALES (est): 297.8K **Privately Held**
SIC: 2599 7389 Bar, restaurant & cafeteria furniture;

(G-14002)
RESCOM MANAGEMENT
SYSTEMS INC
3625 W 450 S (47501-7454)
P.O. Box 348 (47501-0348)
PHONE...................................812 254-5641
Daniel Jones, *CEO*
Tracy Lee Jones, *Vice Pres*
EMP: 25
SQ FT: 4,000
SALES (est): 3.1MM **Privately Held**
SIC: 7692 8748 Welding repair; safety training service

(G-14003)
SOUTHERN INDIANA CHEMICAL
(PA)
Also Called: Pete's Peaches
358 E 900 N (47501-7256)
PHONE...................................812 687-7118
Pete Slowik, *President*
EMP: 3
SALES (est): 1MM **Privately Held**
SIC: 0175 2879 Peach orchard; agricultural chemicals

(G-14004)
TROY STUART
Also Called: Source Hospitality Mfg Group
1 Fountain View Est # 2 (47501-9590)
PHONE...................................812 887-0403
Troy D Stuart, *Owner*
EMP: 2
SALES (est): 120K **Privately Held**
SIC: 2599 Hotel furniture

(G-14005)
TYSON FRESH MEATS INC
Also Called: I B P
Rr 3 (47501)
PHONE...................................812 486-2800
Robert Peterson, *Branch Mgr*
EMP: 40
SALES (corp-wide): 38.2B **Publicly Held**
SIC: 2013 Sausages & other prepared meats
HQ: Tyson Fresh Meats, Inc.
800 Stevens Port Dr
Dakota Dunes SD 57049
605 235-2061

(G-14006)
WALLYS CONSTRUCTION
1279 S 3t (47501)
PHONE...................................812 254-4154
Wallace Knapp, *Principal*
EMP: 5
SALES (est): 292.7K **Privately Held**
SIC: 1389 Construction, repair & dismantling services

(G-14007)
WILLIAMS BROS HEALTH CARE
INC
7 Williams Brothers Dr (47501-4535)
PHONE...................................812 257-2505
Charles C Williams, *President*
EMP: 40 EST: 1998
SALES (est): 7.2MM
SALES (corp-wide): 88.6MM **Privately Held**
SIC: 5912 7352 5999 5169 Drug stores & proprietary stores; medical equipment rental; telephone & communication equipment; oxygen; hospital equipment & furniture; wheelchair lifts
PA: Williams Bros. Health Care Pharmacy, Inc.
10 Williams Brothers Dr
Washington IN 47501
812 254-2497

(G-14008)
WILLIAMS BROS HEALTH CARE
PHA (PA)
10 Williams Brothers Dr (47501-4535)
P.O. Box 271 (47501-0271)
PHONE...................................812 254-2497
Fax: 812 254-7857
Charles C Williams, *Exec VP*
Jeffrey W Williams, *Vice Pres*
Mark Williams, *Admin Sec*
EMP: 110

SALES (est): 88.6MM **Privately Held**
SIC: **5047** 7352 5999 5169 Medical
equipment & supplies; hospital equipment
& furniture; medical equipment rental;
telephone & communication equipment;
oxygen; wheelchair lifts

Waterloo
Dekalb County

(G-14009)
1ST ATTACK ENGINEERING INC
2730 County Road 47 (46793-9723)
PHONE...................................260 837-2435
Jeffrey Cook, *President*
Jody Cook, *Vice Pres*
EMP: 4
SALES (est): 654.1K **Privately Held**
SIC: **3711** Fire department vehicles (motor
vehicles), assembly of

(G-14010)
CHARLESTON METAL
PRODUCTS INC (PA)
350 Grant St (46793-9442)
PHONE...................................260 837-8211
Fax: 260 837-8101
G William Tucker Sr, *CEO*
George William Tucker Sr, *President*
George Davis, *Plant Mgr*
Jason Brown, *QC Mgr*
Bill Essman, *Engineer*
▲ EMP: 113 EST: 1946
SQ FT: 124,000
SALES: 20.5MM **Privately Held**
WEB: www.charlestonmetal.com
SIC: **3451** Screw machine products

(G-14011)
CHARLESTON METAL
PRODUCTS INC
Also Called: H & N Machine Division of
350 Grant St (46793-9442)
PHONE...................................260 837-8211
Fax: 765 284-2286
Jeff Dragoo, *Opers-Prdtn-Mfg*
EMP: 20
SALES (corp-wide): 20.5MM **Privately
Held**
WEB: www.charlestonmetal.com
SIC: **3599** 3541 3451 Machine shop, job-
bing & repair; machine tools, metal cutting
type; screw machine products
PA: Charleston Metal Products Inc
350 Grant St
Waterloo IN 46793
260 837-8211

(G-14012)
COUNTRY STONE
Also Called: Wilhelm Gravel
2280 County Road 27 (46793-9413)
P.O. Box 1160, Milan IL (61264-1160)
PHONE...................................260 837-7134
Ron Bjustrom, *President*
Chris Albright, *General Mgr*
▲ EMP: 25
SQ FT: 340
SALES (est): 2.5MM **Privately Held**
SIC: **1442** Construction sand & gravel;
common sand mining; gravel mining;
sand mining

(G-14013)
ELSIE MANUFACTURING CO INC
600 W Maple St (46793-9547)
P.O. Box 97 (46793-0097)
PHONE...................................260 837-8841
Brian Ruegsegger, *President*
Tyler Ruegsegger, *Engineer*
Sandra Shipe, *Treasurer*
EMP: 9 EST: 1947
SQ FT: 5,000
SALES (est): 1.4MM **Privately Held**
WEB: www.elsiemfg.com
SIC: **3443** 3452 Fabricated plate work
(boiler shop); bolts, nuts, rivets & washers

(G-14014)
HEARTLAND CASTINGS INC
675 E Union St (46793)
P.O. Box 37 (46793-0037)
PHONE...................................260 837-8311

Jordan Pfister, *Owner*
EMP: 20
SQ FT: 36,000
SALES: 1.3MM **Privately Held**
SIC: **3369** Zinc & zinc-base alloy castings,
except die-castings

(G-14015)
INDIANA U BOLTS INC
300 E Railroad St (46793)
PHONE...................................317 870-1940
Fax: 260 868-2173
Dan Dickerhoof, *President*
Damian Dickerhoof, *Vice Pres*
Darrin Dickerhoof, *Vice Pres*
Rose Dickerhoof, *CFO*
▲ EMP: 40 EST: 1963
SQ FT: 75,000
SALES (est): 645.5K **Privately Held**
WEB: www.rodsin.com
SIC: **3462** 3429 3452 3444 Automotive
forgings, ferrous; crankshaft, engine, axle,
etc.; metal fasteners; bolts, nuts, rivets &
washers; sheet metalwork; nonferrous
rolling & drawing

(G-14016)
KCMA & SERVICES LLC
1954 County Road 43 (46793-9708)
PHONE...................................260 645-0885
Brian Walker,
EMP: 2 EST: 2012
SALES (est): 160.9K **Privately Held**
SIC: **2099** 3625 8299 Maple syrup; motor
controls & accessories; educational serv-
ices

(G-14017)
LOCKWOOD WELDING INC
2450 County Road 32 (46793-9423)
PHONE...................................260 925-2086
Ken Lockwood, *President*
EMP: 5
SALES: 375K **Privately Held**
SIC: **7692** Welding repair

(G-14018)
MERRITT SAND AND GRAVEL
INC (PA)
2007 County Road 39 (46793-9788)
PHONE...................................260 665-2513
Fax: 260 665-2350
John E Merritt, *President*
Stuart Wilson, *Treasurer*
EMP: 10
SQ FT: 2,300
SALES (est): 3MM **Privately Held**
WEB: www.merrittsand.com
SIC: **5211** 1442 Sand & gravel; sand min-
ing; gravel & pebble mining

(G-14019)
NUCOR CORPORATION
Nucor Building Systems
305 Industrial Pkwy (46793-9498)
PHONE...................................260 837-7891
Fax: 260 837-7384
Ray P E, *General Mgr*
Johanna Threm, *General Mgr*
Stacey Fisher, *Prdtn Mgr*
Todd Lindler, *Prdtn Mgr*
Dirk Stauffer, *Safety Mgr*
EMP: 100
SALES (corp-wide): 20.2B **Publicly Held**
WEB: www.nucor.com
SIC: **3312** Blast furnaces & steel mills
PA: Nucor Corporation
1915 Rexford Rd Ste 400
Charlotte NC 28211
704 366-7000

(G-14020)
NUCOR CORPORATION
Also Called: Nucor Building Systems
305 Industrial Pkwy (46793-9498)
PHONE...................................260 837-7891
Johanna Threm, *General Mgr*
EMP: 141
SALES (corp-wide): 20.2B **Publicly Held**
SIC: **3312** Blast furnaces & steel mills
PA: Nucor Corporation
1915 Rexford Rd Ste 400
Charlotte NC 28211
704 366-7000

(G-14021)
R & D CONCRETE PRODUCTS
OF IND
2397 County Road 27 (46793-9373)
PHONE...................................260 837-6511
Ronald D Bjustrom, *President*
EMP: 10
SALES (est): 1.3MM **Privately Held**
SIC: **3271** Concrete block & brick

(G-14022)
R P WAKEFIELD COMPANY INC
600 W Maple St (46793-9547)
P.O. Box 97 (46793-0097)
PHONE...................................260 837-8841
Brian Ruegsegger, *President*
Sandra Rhoads, *Corp Secy*
Robert Simon, *Vice Pres*
EMP: 25 EST: 1953
SQ FT: 60,000
SALES (est): 3.4MM **Privately Held**
WEB: www.rpwakefield.com
SIC: **2431** Mantels, wood; moldings, wood:
unfinished & prefinished; panel work,
wood

(G-14023)
RICHARD SQUIER PALLETS INC
2522 Us Highway 6 (46793-9414)
P.O. Box 668 (46793-0668)
PHONE...................................260 281-2434
Fax: 260 281-2428
Richard Squier Jr, *President*
EMP: 25
SQ FT: 40,000
SALES (est): 3.9MM **Privately Held**
SIC: **2448** Pallets, wood

(G-14024)
STAR TECHNOLOGY INC
200 Executive Dr (46793-9448)
PHONE...................................260 837-7833
Fax: 260 837-7834
Joe Zimmermanm, *President*
Donn R Starkey, *President*
Melissa Eshbach, *Opers Mgr*
Jill Exford, *Prdtn Mgr*
Gary Teagardin, *Sales Mgr*
◆ EMP: 23
SQ FT: 13,000
SALES (est): 7MM **Privately Held**
WEB: www.star-technology.com
SIC: **2821** Epoxy resins; polyurethane
resins; thermosetting materials; acrylic
resins

(G-14025)
WATERLOO PRESS INC
415 W Railroad St (46793-9614)
PHONE...................................260 837-3781
Fax: 260 837-6701
Maurice Stafford, *President*
Mike Stafford, *Vice Pres*
EMP: 8
SQ FT: 4,000
SALES (est): 1.1MM **Privately Held**
WEB: www.waterloopress.com
SIC: **2759** Flexographic printing

(G-14026)
WHOLISTIC GARDENS
4840 County Road 4 (46793-9770)
PHONE...................................260 573-1088
Michael Moor, *President*
Ellen Moor, *Vice Pres*
EMP: 2 EST: 2013
SQ FT: 1,280
SALES: 20K **Privately Held**
SIC: **2023** Dietary supplements, dairy &
non-dairy based

(G-14027)
WILHELM GRAVEL CO INC
Also Called: Country Stones and The Gravel
2280 County Road 27 (46793-9413)
P.O. Box 1160, Milan IL (61264-1160)
PHONE...................................260 837-6511
Ron Bjustrom, *President*
Jeff Wilhelm, *Plant Mgr*
EMP: 26
SQ FT: 2,500
SALES (est): 2.4MM **Privately Held**
SIC: **1442** Gravel mining

Waveland
Montgomery County

(G-14028)
JOSEPH FISHER
6492 E 850 N (47989-7514)
PHONE...................................765 435-7231
Joseph Fisher, *Owner*
EMP: 2
SALES (est): 141.4K **Privately Held**
SIC: **2221** Comforters & quilts, manmade
fiber & silk

Wawaka
Noble County

(G-14029)
B & J SPECIALTY INC (PA)
7919 N 100 E (46794-9734)
PHONE...................................260 761-5011
Fax: 260 347-9480
John Wicker, *President*
Scott Sizemore, *Foreman/Supr*
John Halderman, *QC Mgr*
Robert Weeks, *Engineer*
Earl Thompson, *Design Engr*
▲ EMP: 70
SQ FT: 29,000
SALES: 14MM **Privately Held**
WEB: www.bjspecialtyinc.com
SIC: **3599** Machine shop, jobbing & repair

(G-14030)
BASELINE TOOL CO INC
8458 N Baseline Rd (46794-9736)
PHONE...................................260 761-4932
Fax: 260 761-2104
Clayton Morr, *President*
Carolyn Morr, *Corp Secy*
EMP: 18
SQ FT: 11,840
SALES: 1.8MM **Privately Held**
WEB: www.baselinetool.com
SIC: **3543** 7629 Foundry patternmaking;
electrical repair shops

(G-14031)
BERKEY MACHINE
CORPORATION
7037a N Triplett St (46794-9799)
PHONE...................................260 761-4002
Fax: 260 761-2902
Dennis Berkey, *President*
Doug Allen, *President*
Amy Allen, *Corp Secy*
EMP: 5
SQ FT: 5,000
SALES: 300K **Privately Held**
SIC: **3544** 3545 Special dies, tools, jigs &
fixtures; machine tool accessories

(G-14032)
FRICK SERVICES INC (PA)
3154 Depot St (46794)
PHONE...................................260 761-3311
Fax: 260 761-3112
Louise R Frick, *Corp Secy*
Dan Frick, *Exec VP*
▲ EMP: 30
SQ FT: 3,000
SALES (est): 88.6MM **Privately Held**
SIC: **5191** 5153 5261 4221 Fertilizer &
fertilizer materials; grains; fertilizer; farm
product warehousing & storage; prepared
feeds; trucking, except local

(G-14033)
METALCRAFT INC
3330 W Us Highway 6 (46794-9750)
P.O. Box 57 (46794-0057)
PHONE...................................260 761-3001
Fax: 260 761-3513
John Muholland, *President*
Tim Gage, *Vice Pres*
EMP: 10
SQ FT: 18,000
SALES (est): 2.7MM **Privately Held**
WEB: www.metalcft.com
SIC: **3444** Metal housings, enclosures,
casings & other containers

G
E
O
G
R
A
P
H
I
C

West Baden Springs
Orange County

(G-14034)
MARK MORIN LOGGING
757 N Walnut St (47469-7722)
P.O. Box 127 (47469-0127)
PHONE...................................812 327-4917
Mark A Morin, *President*
EMP: 3
SALES (est): 174.4K **Privately Held**
SIC: 2411 Logging

(G-14035)
MWF LLC
8228 W State Road 56 (47469-9414)
P.O. Box 207 (47469-0207)
PHONE...................................812 936-5303
Scott May,
EMP: 8
SALES (est): 1.6MM **Privately Held**
SIC: 3087 Custom compound purchased resins

(G-14036)
TC PRINTING & MORE LLC
8304 W Us Highway 150 (47469-9400)
PHONE...................................812 936-3069
EMP: 2
SALES (est): 68K **Privately Held**
SIC: 2759 Commercial Printing

West College Corner
Union County

(G-14037)
RONS GENERAL REPAIR
403 Ramsey St (47003)
PHONE...................................765 732-3805
George Clinton, *Owner*
EMP: 3
SALES (est): 138.8K **Privately Held**
SIC: 7692 Welding repair

(G-14038)
UC INK LLC
6549 S Kirker Rd (47003-9366)
PHONE...................................765 220-5502
Mary Joe Rydell,
Rachel Rude,
EMP: 2
SALES: 40K **Privately Held**
SIC: 2261 Screen printing of cotton broad-woven fabrics

West Harrison
Dearborn County

(G-14039)
HOGAN STAMPING LLC
305 Maple St (47060-1016)
PHONE...................................812 656-8222
Fax: 812 656-8444
Robert Howeler,
EMP: 12
SALES (est): 1.4MM **Privately Held**
SIC: 3353 Aluminum sheet, plate & foil

(G-14040)
M-TECH MACHINE PRODUCTS
27755 Daugherty Ln Ste A (47060-9600)
PHONE...................................812 637-3500
Fax: 812 637-3545
Michael Hamonds, *Owner*
EMP: 4
SQ FT: 2,200
SALES (est): 293.3K **Privately Held**
SIC: 3599 Machine shop, jobbing & repair

(G-14041)
NORTHBEND PATTERN WORKS INC
28080 Ziegler Blvd (47060)
P.O. Box 160, Harrison OH (45030-0160)
PHONE...................................812 637-3000
Dale L Ziegler, *President*
Nancy Ziegler, *Vice Pres*
EMP: 29
SQ FT: 35,000
SALES (est): 4.7MM **Privately Held**
SIC: 3543 Industrial patterns

(G-14042)
ROBINSON INTERNATIONAL INC
2147 Seeley Rd (47060-9020)
PHONE...................................812 637-0678
EMP: 2
SALES (est): 150K **Privately Held**
SIC: 2899 8999 Real Estate/Construction/Process Engineering

(G-14043)
SHELBY PRODUCTS CORPORATION
Also Called: Stoneybrook Wood Products
27687 Ste Rte 1 (47060)
PHONE...................................317 398-4870
D G Elmore, *President*
Chuck Woods, *General Mgr*
EMP: 4
SQ FT: 7,500
SALES (est): 239.7K **Privately Held**
SIC: 7353 7699 3524 2439 Heavy construction equipment rental; aircraft & heavy equipment repair services; lawn & garden equipment; timbers, structural: laminated lumber; garden machinery & equipment; timber products, rough

(G-14044)
WALTS WELDING & FABRICATING
5664 Bischoff Hill Rd (47060-9467)
PHONE...................................812 637-5338
Rick Walter, *Owner*
EMP: 3
SALES (est): 194.8K **Privately Held**
SIC: 7692 Welding repair

West Lafayette
Tippecanoe County

(G-14045)
A L S INC
3730 Westlake Ct (47906-8612)
PHONE...................................765 497-4750
Thomas F Lampe, *President*
Sandria A Lampe, *Corp Secy*
▲ EMP: 50
SQ FT: 10,000
SALES (est): 3.7MM **Privately Held**
SIC: 5147 2013 2011 Meats & meat products; sausages & other prepared meats; meat packing plants

(G-14046)
ADRANOS ENERGETICS LLC
137 Prophet Dr (47906-1235)
PHONE...................................208 539-2439
Brandon Terry, *Chief Engr*
Christopher Stoker,
EMP: 3
SALES (est): 156.7K **Privately Held**
SIC: 3764 Guided missile & space vehicle propulsion unit parts

(G-14047)
ADRANOS RDX LLC
137 Prophet Dr (47906-1235)
PHONE...................................208 539-2439
EMP: 3
SALES (est): 123.2K **Privately Held**
SIC: 2892 Explosives

(G-14048)
AKINA INC
3495 Kent Ave Ste M200 (47906-4181)
PHONE...................................765 464-0501
Fax: 765 464-0820
Kinam Park, *President*
Sarah Skidmore, *Development*
Marietta Smith, *Accounts Mgr*
John Garner, *Manager*
EMP: 10
SQ FT: 5,000
SALES (est): 1.4MM **Privately Held**
WEB: www.akinainc.com
SIC: 2834 Pharmaceutical preparations

(G-14049)
AMRI SSCI LLC
3065 Kent Ave (47906-1076)
PHONE...................................765 463-0112
Fax: 765 497-2649
William S Marth, *President*
EMP: 90
SQ FT: 48,800
SALES (est): 19.3MM
SALES (corp-wide): 113.5MM **Privately Held**
SIC: 2834 Pharmaceutical preparations
HQ: Albany Molecular Research, Inc.
26 Corporate Cir
Albany NY 12203

(G-14050)
ANIMATED DYNAMICS INC
1281 Win Hentschel Blvd (47906-4182)
PHONE...................................765 418-5359
John Turek, *Principal*
David D Nolte,
EMP: 2
SALES (est): 252.7K **Privately Held**
SIC: 3826 Analytical instruments

(G-14051)
AZLAND INC
345 Burnetts Rd Ste 300 (47906-9761)
PHONE...................................765 429-6200
Brian Vorst, *President*
Darryl Hatke, *Vice Pres*
EMP: 4
SALES (est): 362.5K **Privately Held**
SIC: 3523 Farm machinery & equipment

(G-14052)
BEV REXAM CAN AMERICAS INC
4750 Swisher Rd (47906-9782)
PHONE...................................773 399-3000
Stephen Howell, *Principal*
EMP: 2
SALES (est): 73.4K **Privately Held**
SIC: 3411 Metal cans

(G-14053)
BIOANALYTICAL SYSTEMS INC (PA)
Also Called: Basi
2701 Kent Ave (47906-1350)
PHONE...................................765 463-4527
Fax: 765 497-1102
Larry S Boulet, *Ch of Bd*
Jacqueline M Lemke, *President*
Philip A Downing, *Senior VP*
James S Bourdage, *Vice Pres*
James Bourdage, *Vice Pres*
EMP: 157
SQ FT: 120,000
SALES: 24.2MM **Publicly Held**
WEB: www.bioanalytical.com
SIC: 8731 3841 Medical research, commercial; surgical & medical instruments; diagnostic apparatus, medical

(G-14054)
BIOKORF LLC
1008 Ravinia Rd (47906-2327)
PHONE...................................765 727-0782
Andrew Otte,
Teresa Carvajal,
Rodolfo Pinal,
EMP: 2
SALES (est): 128K **Privately Held**
SIC: 2834 2899 8731 Tablets, pharmaceutical; gelatin: edible, technical, photographic or pharmaceutical; medical research, commercial

(G-14055)
BIOSCIENCE VACCINES INC
1425 Innovation Pl (47906-1000)
PHONE...................................765 464-5890
Anthony Hubbard, *Vice Pres*
EMP: 6
SALES (est): 676.6K **Privately Held**
SIC: 2836 Biological products, except diagnostic

(G-14056)
CARGILL INCORPORATED
1281 Win Hentschel Blvd (47906-4182)
PHONE...................................217 253-3389
Fax: 217 253-4741
Doug Childers, *Manager*
EMP: 20
SALES (corp-wide): 88.8B **Privately Held**
WEB: www.cargill.com
SIC: 2048 Prepared feeds
PA: Cargill, Incorporated
15407 Mcginty Rd W
Wayzata MN 55391
952 742-7575

(G-14057)
CHEMTURA CORPORATION
5268 Grapevine Dr (47906-9044)
PHONE...................................765 497-6782
EMP: 105
SALES (corp-wide): 1.7B **Publicly Held**
SIC: 2869 8731 Mfg Industrial Organic Chemicals Commercial Physical Research
PA: Chemtura Corporation
1818 Market St Ste 3700
Philadelphia PA 06762
203 573-2000

(G-14058)
CHROMCRAFT REVINGTON INC (DH)
1330 Win Hentschel Blvd (47906-4149)
PHONE...................................662 562-8203
Ronald H Butler, *CEO*
E Michael Hanna, *Senior VP*
James M La Neve, *CFO*
▲ EMP: 50
SQ FT: 4,500
SALES (est): 44MM
SALES (corp-wide): 70.7MM **Privately Held**
WEB: www.chromcraftrevington.com
SIC: 2511 2512 2521 2531 Wood household furniture; upholstered household furniture; wood office furniture; public building & related furniture
HQ: Sport-Haley, Inc.
200 Union Blvd Ste 400
Lakewood CO 80228
303 320-8800

(G-14059)
CHYALL PHARMACEUTICAL
1281 Win Hentschel Blvd (47906-4182)
PHONE...................................765 237-3391
Leonard J Chyall, *President*
EMP: 3
SALES (est): 223K **Privately Held**
SIC: 2834 Pharmaceutical preparations

(G-14060)
CONTROL SOLUTIONS
221 Timbercrest Rd (47906-8504)
PHONE...................................765 313-1984
Rodney Winebrenner, *Principal*
EMP: 3 EST: 2010
SALES (est): 268.2K **Privately Held**
SIC: 3625 Relays & industrial controls

(G-14061)
COX JOHN
Also Called: Spaulding Products and Mfg Co
140 Tamiami Ct (47906-1205)
PHONE...................................765 463-6396
John Cox, *Owner*
EMP: 2
SALES: 50K **Privately Held**
SIC: 3559 2653 Automotive maintenance equipment; display items, corrugated: made from purchased materials

(G-14062)
CREATIVE CONSTRUCTION PUBG
2720 S River Rd (47906-4347)
PHONE...................................765 743-9704
Wesley G Crawford, *President*
Bonnie L Crawford, *CFO*
EMP: 2
SALES (est): 217K **Privately Held**
SIC: 2721 Trade journals: publishing only, not printed on site

(G-14063)
DAYTON-PHOENIX GROUP INC (HQ)
Also Called: DPG
4750 Swisher Rd (47906-9782)
PHONE...................................765 742-4410

▲ = Import ▼=Export
◆ =Import/Export

Fax: 765 583-4109
Gale Cooken, *CEO*
Rebecca Ferguson, *Sales Staff*
Shannon McGrew, *Supervisor*
EMP: 61 **EST:** 1954
SQ FT: 36,000
SALES (est): 11.7MM **Privately Held**
WEB: www.dynohm.com
SIC: 3625 3676 Resistors & resistor units; electronic resistors

(G-14064)
DOW AGROSCIENCE
1281 Win Hentschel Blvd (47906-4182)
PHONE....................765 743-0015
EMP: 2
SALES (est): 159.4K **Privately Held**
SIC: 2879 Agricultural chemicals

(G-14065)
EFIL PHARMACEUTICALS CORP
3706 Litchfield Pl (47906-8738)
PHONE....................765 491-7247
Kee-Hong Kim, *CEO*
EMP: 2
SALES (est): 74.4K **Privately Held**
SIC: 2833 Medicinal chemicals

(G-14066)
ENDOCYTE INC
3000 Kent Ave Ste A1-100 (47906-1075)
PHONE....................765 463-7175
Fax: 765 463-9271
John C Aplin, *Ch of Bd*
Michael A Sherman, *President*
Michael T Andriole, *CFO*
Beth A Taylor, *Controller*
Katherine K Parker, *VP Human Res*
EMP: 78
SQ FT: 25,400
SALES: 70K **Privately Held**
WEB: www.endocyte.com
SIC: 2834 Pharmaceutical preparations

(G-14067)
FLIR DETECTION INC
Also Called: Flir Systems
3000 Kent Ave (47906-1075)
PHONE....................765 775-1701
Carlo Diciolla, *Manager*
EMP: 12
SALES (corp-wide): 1.8B **Publicly Held**
SIC: 3812 Search & detection systems & instruments
HQ: Flir Detection, Inc.
1024 S Innovation Way
Stillwater OK 74074
703 678-2111

(G-14068)
GH PRODUCTS INC
3917 Sunnycroft Pl (47906-8817)
PHONE....................619 208-4823
Eli Weinstein, *Principal*
EMP: 5
SALES: 950K **Privately Held**
SIC: 3663 Radio & TV communications equipment

(G-14069)
GLCC LAUREL LLC
1 Geddes Way (47906-5394)
PHONE....................765 497-6100
Robert Wood, *President*
Billie S Flaherty, *Vice Pres*
Arthur C Fullerton, *Admin Sec*
EMP: 200
SALES (est): 17.9MM
SALES (corp-wide): 11.4B **Privately Held**
WEB: www.cromptoncorp.com
SIC: 2819 Bromine, elemental
HQ: Lanxess Solutions Us Inc.
199 Benson Rd
Middlebury CT 06762
203 573-2000

(G-14070)
GOLDSTONE JEWELRY INC
3617 Montclair St (47906-8607)
PHONE....................765 742-1975
Fax: 765 742-0470
Brenda Canaan, *President*
Brenda Kirleis, *President*
EMP: 2

SALES (est): 270K **Privately Held**
SIC: 5944 3911 7631 Jewelry, precious stones & precious metals; jewelry, precious metal; jewelry repair services

(G-14071)
GOOSE BUMPS LLC
187 Turnberry Ct (47906-8749)
PHONE....................765 491-2142
Tom Long, *Principal*
EMP: 2
SALES (est): 118.2K **Privately Held**
SIC: 3999 Pet supplies

(G-14072)
GRIFFIN ANALYTICAL TECH LLC
3000 Kent Ave Ste E1 (47906-1075)
PHONE....................765 775-1701
Dennis Barket, *General Mgr*
Bonnie Ahlgrim, *Office Mgr*
William A Sundermeier, *Mng Member*
Chelsea Pardue, *Administration*
EMP: 43
SALES (est): 50.6K **Privately Held**
WEB: www.griffinanalytical.com
SIC: 3826 Analytical instruments

(G-14073)
GROWING CHILD
2336 Northwestern Ave (47906-1806)
P.O. Box 2505 (47996-2505)
PHONE....................765 464-0920
Dennis Dunn, *President*
EMP: 2
SALES (est): 147.8K **Privately Held**
SIC: 2711 2721 Newspapers, publishing & printing; periodicals: publishing only; periodicals: publishing & printing

(G-14074)
HASSER ENTERPRISES INC
8023 Us Highway 52 W (47906-9457)
PHONE....................765 583-1444
Melvin Hasser, *President*
Linda Hasser, *Admin Sec*
EMP: 3
SQ FT: 11,000
SALES: 800K **Privately Held**
SIC: 3469 Metal stampings

(G-14075)
I NOODLES
111 N Chauncey Ave (47906-3003)
PHONE....................765 447-2288
EMP: 3
SALES (est): 91.3K **Privately Held**
SIC: 2098 Macaroni & spaghetti

(G-14076)
IN SPACE LLC
3495 Kent Ave Ste G100 (47906-4172)
PHONE....................765 775-2107
Amy Austin, *Office Mgr*
Bill Anderson, *Director*
Benjamin Austin,
William Anderson,
Stephen Heister,
EMP: 5
SALES: 380K **Privately Held**
SIC: 8711 3764 Consulting engineer; guided missile & space vehicle propulsion unit parts

(G-14077)
INDIANA MANUFACTURING INST
1105 Challenger Ave (47906-1168)
PHONE....................765 494-4935
EMP: 2 **EST:** 2016
SALES (est): 156.2K **Privately Held**
SIC: 3999 Barber & beauty shop equipment

(G-14078)
IRVING MATERIALS INC
Also Called: I M I
301 Ahlers Dr (47906-5992)
PHONE....................765 743-3806
Fax: 765 743-8304
Bob Johnson, *Branch Mgr*
EMP: 35
SQ FT: 3,000
SALES (corp-wide): 800.6MM **Privately Held**
SIC: 3273 Ready-mixed concrete

PA: Irving Materials, Inc.
8032 N State Road 9
Greenfield IN 46140
317 326-3101

(G-14079)
KYLIN THERAPEUTICS INC
3000 Kent Ave (47906-1075)
PHONE....................765 412-6661
Eric Davis, *Principal*
EMP: 5
SALES: 1,000K **Privately Held**
SIC: 2834 Pharmaceutical preparations

(G-14080)
LACTOR LLC
3221 Covington St (47906-1189)
PHONE....................765 496-6838
Azza Ahmed, *Principal*
Jeffrey Brewer, *Principal*
Elisha Hollandbeck, *Admin Asst*
EMP: 2
SALES (est): 56.5K **Privately Held**
SIC: 7372 Application computer software

(G-14081)
LAFAYETTE MARKETING INC
Also Called: Tree Pro
3180 W 250 N (47906-5143)
PHONE....................765 474-5374
Fax: 765 463-3157
Tom Mills, *President*
Donna Mills, *Corp Secy*
▲ **EMP:** 20
SQ FT: 36,000
SALES (est): 4.5MM **Privately Held**
SIC: 3524 Lawn & garden tractors & equipment

(G-14082)
LAFAYETTE VENETIAN BLIND INC (PA)
Also Called: Lafayette Interior Fashions
3000 Klondike Rd (47906-5210)
P.O. Box 2838 (47996-2838)
PHONE....................765 464-2500
Fax: 765 423-2402
Joseph N Morgan, *President*
Rebecca Dexter, *Managing Prtnr*
Dennis Morgan, *Corp Secy*
Greg Jones, *Buyer*
Mark Lowe-Massi, *Natl Sales Mgr*
▲ **EMP:** 850
SQ FT: 300,000
SALES (est): 165MM **Privately Held**
WEB: www.lafvb.com
SIC: 2591 2391 Window blinds; venetian blinds; mini blinds; blinds vertical; draperies, plastic & textile: from purchased materials

(G-14083)
LODOS THERANOSTICS LLC
132 Vigo Ct (47906-1171)
PHONE....................765 427-2492
You-Yeon Won, *CEO*
Younjae Kim, *CFO*
EMP: 2
SALES (est): 103.8K **Privately Held**
SIC: 2834 Solutions, pharmaceutical

(G-14084)
M4 SCIENCES LLC
1800 Woodland Ave (47906-2274)
PHONE....................765 479-6215
James B Mann, *CEO*
Brian Gootee, *COO*
Phil Fassnacht, *VP Sales*
Gootee Brian, *Director*
EMP: 5
SALES (est): 771.9K **Privately Held**
WEB: www.m4sciences.com
SIC: 3545 Machine tool accessories

(G-14085)
MIFTEK CORPORATION
1231 Cumberland Ave (47906-1358)
Drawer 292 Park L (47906)
PHONE....................765 491-3848
Joseph Robinson, *President*
Masanobu Yamamoto, *Vice Pres*
EMP: 2
SALES (est): 221.5K **Privately Held**
SIC: 3841 Diagnostic apparatus, medical

(G-14086)
MOBILE ENERLYTICS LLC
1281 Win Hentschel Blvd (47906-4182)
PHONE....................765 464-6909
Yu Hu, *Principal*
EMP: 2 **EST:** 2014
SALES (est): 131.6K **Privately Held**
SIC: 7372 Application computer software

(G-14087)
MOBILE LIMB & BRACE INC
2041 Klondike Rd (47906-5122)
P.O. Box 1437, Windermere FL (34786-1437)
PHONE....................765 463-4100
Greg Decamp, *President*
Darci Decamp, *Vice Pres*
EMP: 3
SQ FT: 1,800
SALES: 150K **Privately Held**
WEB: www.mobilelimbandbrace.com
SIC: 3842 Limbs, artificial

(G-14088)
MR-LINK LLC ✪
3024 Benton St (47906-1130)
PHONE....................765 476-3185
Zhongming Liu, *President*
Ranajay Mandal, *Vice Pres*
EMP: 2 **EST:** 2017
SALES (est): 98.4K **Privately Held**
SIC: 3845 Electromedical equipment

(G-14089)
NATUREGENIC INC (PA)
1281 Win Hentschel Blvd (47906-4182)
PHONE....................765 807-5525
Miyoung Kim, *CEO*
Sunghwa Choe, *Founder*
Young Chan Myung, *Development*
Jihon Choe, *Treasurer*
EMP: 6
SALES (est): 456.5K **Privately Held**
SIC: 2834 8731 Proprietary drug products; agricultural research; biotechnical research, commercial; natural resource research

(G-14090)
NEON GLASSWORKS LLC
3330 Crawford St (47906-1182)
PHONE....................765 497-1135
Dan Gadbery, *Principal*
EMP: 2
SALES (est): 129.1K **Privately Held**
SIC: 2813 Neon

(G-14091)
OPEN CANVAS LLC
103 N University St (47906-2829)
PHONE....................317 908-6524
Richard Roberson, *Owner*
EMP: 4
SALES (est): 75K **Privately Held**
SIC: 2211 Canvas

(G-14092)
PAPAYAN INDUSTRIES
906 Rose St (47906-2442)
PHONE....................765 387-7274
Jack O'Reilly, *Owner*
EMP: 2
SALES (est): 87K **Privately Held**
SIC: 3999 Manufacturing industries

(G-14093)
PAPER STREET PRESS
1841 King Eider Dr (47906-6508)
PHONE....................765 894-0027
EMP: 2
SALES (est): 81.8K **Privately Held**
SIC: 2741 Miscellaneous publishing

(G-14094)
PHYTOPTION LLC
3495 Kent Ave Ste P100 (47906-4179)
PHONE....................765 490-7738
Jingmin Zhang, *General Mgr*
EMP: 2
SALES (est): 168.8K **Privately Held**
SIC: 2834 Pharmaceutical preparations

(G-14095)
POWER PLACE PRODUCTS INC
4840 Us Highway 231 N (47906-9298)
PHONE...................................765 583-2333
EMP: 7
SALES (est): 682.9K Privately Held
SIC: 3949 Mfg Sporting/Athletic Goods

(G-14096)
PREDICTIVE WEAR LLC
1401 Shining Armor Ln (47906-5474)
PHONE...................................765 464-4891
Matthew Albaugh, Manager
Pablo Argote, Manager
Sriram Boppana,
Michael Drakopoulos,
Orlando Hoilett,
EMP: 11
SALES (est): 408.3K Privately Held
SIC: 3841 3845 8082 Surgical & medical
instruments; diagnostic apparatus, med-
ical; automated blood & body fluid analyz-
ers, except laboratory; patient monitoring
apparatus; home health care services

(G-14097)
PROAXIS INC
Also Called: Excenart
345 Burnetts Rd (47906-9761)
PHONE...................................765 742-4200
Fax: 765 742-4211
Beth Vorst, CEO
Brian Vorst, President
Darryl Hatke, Vice Pres
EMP: 49
SQ FT: 70,000
SALES (est): 13.5MM Privately Held
WEB: www.proaxisinc.com
SIC: 3444 3312 Sheet metalwork; struc-
tural shapes & pilings, steel

(G-14098)
PURDUE GMP CENTER LLC
Also Called: Chao Center, The
3070 Kent Ave (47906-1075)
PHONE...................................765 464-8414
Joseph B Hornett,
EMP: 18
SALES (est): 4MM Privately Held
SIC: 2834 Pharmaceutical preparations

(G-14099)
PURDUE STUDENT PUBG
FOUNDATION
Also Called: Purdue Exponent, The
460 Northwestern Ave (47906-2966)
P.O. Box 2506 (47996-2506)
PHONE...................................765 743-1111
Fax: 765 743-6087
Patrick Kuhnle, Publisher
Spencer Bailey, Advt Staff
EMP: 36
SQ FT: 22,500
SALES: 3.6MM Privately Held
WEB: www.purdueexponent.net
SIC: 2711 Commercial printing & newspa-
per publishing combined; newspapers,
publishing & printing

(G-14100)
R DREW & CO INC
Also Called: Clay Critters
4866 N 9th Street Rd (47906-9762)
PHONE...................................765 420-7232
Fax: 765 423-4546
Rebecca Bollinger, President
▼ EMP: 19
SQ FT: 1,500
SALES (est): 2.2MM Privately Held
WEB: www.claycritters.com
SIC: 3269 4724 Figures: pottery, china,
earthenware & stoneware; travel agen-
cies

(G-14101)
RESEARCH MACHINING
SERVICES
694 S Russell St (47907-2121)
PHONE...................................765 494-3710
EMP: 2 EST: 2008
SALES (est): 193.3K Privately Held
SIC: 3599 Machine shop, jobbing & repair

(G-14102)
RETTIG ENTERPRISES INC
1950 E 800 N (47906-9009)
PHONE...................................765 567-2441
Don Rettig, President
Vicki Rettig, Corp Secy
Mark Rettig, Vice Pres
Judith Rettig, Director
EMP: 6 EST: 1937
SQ FT: 3,000
SALES: 285K Privately Held
SIC: 3446 5261 Architectural metalwork;
lawn & garden equipment

(G-14103)
RHODES AMPLIFICATION LLC
4209 State Road 43 N (47906-5749)
P.O. Box 2143 (47996-2143)
PHONE...................................765 775-5100
Kyle Rhodes, President
EMP: 2
SALES (est): 171.6K Privately Held
SIC: 3651 Amplifiers: radio, public address
or musical instrument

(G-14104)
ROLLS-ROYCE CORPORATION
1801 Newman Rd (47906-4510)
PHONE...................................317 230-8515
Hal Raines, Branch Mgr
EMP: 3
SALES (corp-wide): 21.5B Privately Held
SIC: 3724 3443 3462 3731 Aircraft engines & engine parts; industrial vessels,
tanks & containers; nuclear power plant
forgings, ferrous; submarines, building &
repairing; railroad locomotives & parts,
electric or nonelectric; yachts, building &
repairing
HQ: Rolls-Royce Corporation
450 S Meridian St
Indianapolis IN 46225

(G-14105)
SAVRAN TECHNOLOGIES LLC
2533 Yeoman Ln (47906-0617)
PHONE...................................765 409-2050
Cagri Savran, President
EMP: 4 EST: 2015
SALES (est): 90K Privately Held
SIC: 2835 In vitro diagnostics

(G-14106)
SCAGGS MOTO DESIGNS
4909 Leicester Way (47906-8643)
PHONE...................................765 426-2526
EMP: 2
SALES (est): 112.3K Privately Held
SIC: 3999 Manufacturing industries

(G-14107)
SMARTGAIT LLC
3000 Kent Ave Ste C2-108 (47906-1075)
PHONE...................................765 404-0726
Babak Ziaie, Principal
EMP: 3
SALES (est): 187.6K Privately Held
SIC: 3826 7373 7375 Analytical instru-
ments; systems software development
services; information retrieval services;
data base information retrieval

(G-14108)
SOIL DYNAMICS INSTRUMENTS
INC
3309 Elkhart St (47906-1161)
PHONE...................................765 497-0511
Vincent P Drnevich, President
Roxanne Drnevich, Corp Secy
EMP: 2
SALES (est): 200K Privately Held
SIC: 3821 Laboratory apparatus & furniture

(G-14109)
SPEAK MODALITIES LLC
6137 Naschette Pkwy (47906-5778)
PHONE...................................765 742-4252
Michael Zentner, Mng Member
EMP: 3
SALES (est): 145.9K Privately Held
SIC: 7372 Educational computer software

(G-14110)
SPENSA TECHNOLOGIES INC
Also Called: Spensatech
1281 Win Hentschel Blvd (47906-4182)
PHONE...................................765 588-3592
Johnny Park, President
Michael Shepard, COO
Jason Tennenhouse, Vice Pres
Lisa Park, Prdtn Mgr
Chad Aeschliman, Engineer
EMP: 31
SALES: 390K
SALES (corp-wide): 3.2MM Privately
Held
SIC: 3822 8731 7371 Hardware for envi-
ronmental regulators; computer (hard-
ware) development; computer software
development & applications
HQ: Dtn, Llc
11400 Rupp Dr
Burnsville MN 55337
402 390-2328

(G-14111)
SWIFT FUELS LLC
1435 Win Hentschel Blvd # 205
(47906-4152)
PHONE...................................765 464-8336
Chris Dacosta, CEO
Rob Broin, Chairman
Don Bower, Vice Pres
Jon Ziulkowski, Vice Pres
Joel Dykstra, CFO
◆ EMP: 9 EST: 2012
SALES: 800K Privately Held
SIC: 2869 5172 Fuels; fuel oil

(G-14112)
TERAGRAPHICS INK LLC
204 E Pine Ave (47906-4881)
PHONE...................................765 430-2863
Raul Renz, Administration
EMP: 6
SALES (est): 249.8K Privately Held
SIC: 2711 Commercial printing & newspa-
per publishing combined

(G-14113)
THERMPHYSCAL PRPTS RES
LAB INC
Also Called: Tprl
3080 Kent Ave (47906-1075)
PHONE...................................765 463-1581
Thomas Goerz, President
Robert Larsen, Vice Pres
David Taylor, Mktg Dir
EMP: 4
SQ FT: 10,500
SALES: 500K Privately Held
WEB: www.tprl.com
SIC: 8734 3823 Product testing laboratory,
safety or performance; industrial instrmnts
msrmnt display/control process variable

(G-14114)
ULTIMATE SPORTS INC
Also Called: USI
820 Hillcrest Rd (47906-2354)
PHONE...................................765 423-2984
Fax: 765 742-7258
Kevin Metheny, President
Pamela Metheny, Vice Pres
EMP: 2
SQ FT: 30,000
SALES (est): 288.8K Privately Held
WEB: www.usi-skis.com
SIC: 3714 Motor vehicle parts & acces-
sories

(G-14115)
WABASH ENVIRONMENTAL
PDTS LLC
120 Burke Ct (47906-1801)
P.O. Box 2258, Lafayette (47996-2258)
PHONE...................................765 464-3440
Dan Bauer, Sales Mgr
EMP: 4
SALES (est): 514.4K Privately Held
SIC: 3564 Air cleaning systems

(G-14116)
WABASH PRINTING COMPANY
3776 Campus Suites Blvd # 222
(47906-0942)
PHONE...................................765 650-1701
Logan Chapin, Principal
EMP: 2
SALES (est): 92.3K Privately Held
SIC: 2752 Commercial printing, litho-
graphic

(G-14117)
WELL INK
360 Brown St (47906-3243)
PHONE...................................765 743-3413
EMP: 2
SALES (est): 155.9K Privately Held
SIC: 2752 Commercial printing, litho-
graphic

(G-14118)
ZS SYSTEMS LLC
3339 Cardigan Ct (47906-8722)
PHONE...................................765 586-2738
Sergey Zakharov,
▲ EMP: 2
SQ FT: 1,000
SALES (est): 317.1K Privately Held
SIC: 3823 Industrial instrmnts msrmnt dis-
play/control process variable

West Lebanon
Warren County

(G-14119)
DYNA-FAB CORPORATION
3893 S State Road 263 (47991-8005)
PHONE...................................765 893-4423
Fax: 765 893-4035
John Rew, Vice Pres
EMP: 28
SQ FT: 30,000
SALES (est): 6.8MM Privately Held
WEB: www.dyna-fab.org
SIC: 3531 3444 3443 Backhoes, tractors,
cranes, plows & similar equipment; sheet
metalwork; fabricated plate work (boiler
shop)

(G-14120)
GILLUM MACHINE & TOOL INC
3365 W State Road 28 (47991-8077)
PHONE...................................765 893-4426
Fax: 765 893-4543
Jack P Gillum, President
Dan Gillum, Vice Pres
Mary I Gillum, Treasurer
Debby Beckett, Admin Sec
EMP: 11
SQ FT: 7,500
SALES: 100K Privately Held
SIC: 3599 7692 3544 Machine shop, job-
bing & repair; welding repair; special dies,
tools, jigs & fixtures

(G-14121)
INTERSTATE METALS LLC
3454 W State Road 28 (47991-8077)
PHONE...................................765 893-4449
Patrick Cole, Partner
Pj Stoll, Partner
EMP: 10
SALES (est): 892.6K Privately Held
SIC: 3449 Miscellaneous metalwork

(G-14122)
TRU-FLEX LLC (HQ)
Also Called: Custom-Flex
2391 S State Road 263 (47991-8132)
PHONE...................................765 893-4403
Fax: 765 893-4114
Gregg Notestine, CEO
Kathy Ward, CFO
▲ EMP: 107
SALES (est): 41.9MM
SALES (corp-wide): 417MM Privately
Held
SIC: 3714 3499 Motor vehicle parts & ac-
cessories; fire- or burglary-resistive prod-
ucts
PA: Hbm Holdings Company
101 S Hanley Rd Ste 1050
Saint Louis MO 63105
314 376-2540

▲ = Import ▼=Export
◆ =Import/Export

West Terre Haute
Vigo County

(G-14123)
CUSTOM KILN WORKS
4400 W Concannon Ave (47885-9679)
PHONE...................................812 535-3561
EMP: 4 EST: 2012
SALES (est): 300K **Privately Held**
SIC: 3559 Mfg Misc Industry Machinery

(G-14124)
DEER RIDGEWOOD CRAFT LLC
5330 Yuma Rd (47885-8523)
PHONE...................................812 535-3744
Wade Biggs, *Mng Member*
Larry Biggs,
Carolyn Biggs,
Leticia Fiddler,
EMP: 4
SALES (est): 160.3K **Privately Held**
SIC: 7641 2499 Antique furniture repair & restoration; trophy bases, wood

(G-14125)
KRAFT N KREATIONS
4589 S Robinson Pl (47885-8979)
PHONE...................................812 243-1754
Kylee M Fervida, *Owner*
EMP: 2
SALES (est): 62.3K **Privately Held**
SIC: 2022 Processed cheese

(G-14126)
MARION TOOL & DIE INC (PA)
Also Called: Marion Manufacturing
1126 W National Ave (47885-1336)
PHONE...................................812 533-9800
Fax: 812 533-9801
Tamara Marion, *President*
Leonard N Marion, *Vice Pres*
Timothy M Marion, *Vice Pres*
Shane Turner, *Director*
Cassie J Marion, *Admin Sec*
▲ EMP: 57
SQ FT: 20,000
SALES (est): 22.6MM **Privately Held**
WEB: www.mariontool.com
SIC: 3545 Precision tools, machinists'

(G-14127)
MID-WEST OIL COMPANY INC
Also Called: Express Mart
15 E National Ave (47885-1444)
PHONE...................................812 533-1227
Brandi Newburn, *Manager*
EMP: 3
SALES (corp-wide): 2.1MM **Privately Held**
WEB: www.midwestoilgas.com
SIC: 1321 Liquefied petroleum gases (natural) production
PA: Mid-West Oil Company Inc
301 S 3rd St
Terre Haute IN 47807
812 232-7020

(G-14128)
QUALITY COUNCIL OF INDIANA
Also Called: Qci
602 W Paris Ave (47885-1124)
PHONE...................................812 533-4215
Fax: 812 533-4216
Bill Wortman, *President*
Odis Pittman, *Web Dvlpr*
Diana Magnetti, *Administration*
EMP: 8
SALES (est): 1.4MM **Privately Held**
WEB: www.qualityacademy.com
SIC: 7372 Publishers' computer software

(G-14129)
SG SOLUTIONS LLC
444 W Sandford Ave (47885-8200)
PHONE...................................812 535-6000
Steven Chichester, *Mng Member*
Rick Koons,
◆ EMP: 50
SALES (est): 7.6MM **Privately Held**
SIC: 1311 Coal gasification

(G-14130)
SYCAMORE WINERY LLC
3980 N Gosnell Pl (47885-9267)
PHONE...................................812 243-0565
Sarah Pigg, *President*
Daniel Pigg,
EMP: 2
SALES (est): 80.4K **Privately Held**
SIC: 2084 Wines, brandy & brandy spirits

Westfield
Hamilton County

(G-14131)
1GLOBAL DS LLC
1225 Emerald Viking Ct (46074-7620)
PHONE...................................765 413-2211
Kim Arbuckle, *President*
EMP: 15
SALES (est): 1.2MM **Privately Held**
SIC: 3993 7389 Signs & advertising specialties;

(G-14132)
ABSOLUTE STONE POLSG REPR LLC
Also Called: Granite and Marble
3801 Crest Point Dr (46062-6541)
PHONE...................................317 709-9539
Brian Gately,
EMP: 2
SALES (est): 139K **Privately Held**
SIC: 3281 Cut stone & stone products

(G-14133)
ACORN WOODWORKS
16116 Ditch Rd (46074-9639)
P.O. Box 468 (46074-0468)
PHONE...................................317 867-4377
David R Sochar, *Owner*
EMP: 5
SALES (est): 363.7K **Privately Held**
SIC: 2499 Decorative wood & woodwork

(G-14134)
ALLI MEDICAL LLC
36 E Rowan Run (46074-9750)
P.O. Box 643 (46074-0643)
PHONE...................................317 625-4535
Nicola Booth,
EMP: 2
SALES (est): 174.9K **Privately Held**
SIC: 3842 5047 3841 Ligatures, medical; instruments, surgical & medical; surgical & medical instruments

(G-14135)
AMERICAN INTEGRATED MFG CO
629 E Columbine Ln (46074-8733)
PHONE...................................317 445-2056
Bret McCauley, *President*
EMP: 5
SALES (est): 349.3K **Privately Held**
SIC: 3549 Metalworking machinery

(G-14136)
AMERICAN VETERAN GROUP LLC
17020 Emerald Green Cir (46074-9155)
PHONE...................................317 600-4749
Jennifer Reinking, *Manager*
Jerry Warner,
EMP: 2
SALES (est): 110K **Privately Held**
SIC: 2759 3841 3842 5084 Commercial printing; surgical & medical instruments; surgical appliances & supplies; industrial machinery & equipment; management consulting services

(G-14137)
AUTOMATIC POOL COVERS INC
17397 Oak Ridge Rd (46074-7833)
PHONE...................................317 579-2000
Michael J Shebek, *President*
Katherine Shebek, *Corp Secy*
Todd Freeman, *Senior VP*
Mike Shadoan, *Vice Pres*
Brian Garrett, *Design Engr*
▲ EMP: 35
SQ FT: 30,000

SALES (est): 7.8MM **Privately Held**
WEB: www.apcmidwest.com
SIC: 5999 3561 5091 Swimming pool chemicals, equipment & supplies; swimming pools, hot tubs & sauna equipment & supplies; pumps & pumping equipment; swimming pools, equipment & supplies

(G-14138)
BALL SYSTEMS INC
16469 Southpark Dr (46074-8435)
PHONE...................................317 804-2330
Fax: 317 848-0207
Patrick Turley, *President*
Andrew Caine, *Vice Pres*
EMP: 27
SQ FT: 8,500
SALES (est): 7.5MM **Privately Held**
WEB: www.ballsystems.com
SIC: 3825 3612 Test equipment for electronic & electrical circuits; engine electrical test equipment; transformers, except electric

(G-14139)
BRALLAN PRESS LLC
2102 E 161st St (46074-9434)
PHONE...................................317 525-4335
Mark Strange, *Administration*
EMP: 4
SALES (est): 78.8K **Privately Held**
SIC: 2741 Miscellaneous publishing

(G-14140)
C & S SANDBLASTING & WLDG LLC
17623 Washington St (46074-9105)
PHONE...................................317 867-6341
Charles Stalanaker,
EMP: 5
SALES: 700K **Privately Held**
SIC: 7692 1799 Welding repair; sandblasting of building exteriors

(G-14141)
CAVE & COMPANY PRINTING
104 W Main St (46074-9480)
PHONE...................................317 896-5337
Fax: 317 896-5680
Donald Cave, *President*
Barbara Cave, *Corp Secy*
Kim Floor, *Vice Pres*
EMP: 8
SQ FT: 3,200
SALES (est): 850K **Privately Held**
WEB: www.caveprinting.com
SIC: 2752 Commercial printing, offset

(G-14142)
CENTURA SOLID SURFACING INC
3525 W State Road 32 (46074-9363)
PHONE...................................317 867-5555
Ronald Maurer, *President*
Jean Maurer, *Vice Pres*
EMP: 15
SQ FT: 100,000
SALES (est): 1.2MM **Privately Held**
SIC: 1799 3281 Counter top installation; cut stone & stone products

(G-14143)
CENTURY MARBLE CO INC
3525 W State Road 32 (46074-9363)
PHONE...................................317 867-5555
Fax: 317 867-0740
Ronald Maurer, *President*
Benjamin A Maurer, *President*
Jean Maurer, *Corp Secy*
EMP: 40
SQ FT: 100,000
SALES (est): 6MM **Privately Held**
SIC: 3281 Furniture, cut stone; household articles, except furniture: cut stone

(G-14144)
COGNEX CORPORATION
804 Allen Ct (46074-9323)
PHONE...................................317 867-5079
EMP: 2
SALES (corp-wide): 747.9MM **Publicly Held**
SIC: 3823 Industrial instrmnts msrmnt display/control process variable

PA: Cognex Corporation
1 Vision Dr
Natick MA 01760
508 650-3000

(G-14145)
CORRUGATED PACKAGING SYSTEMS
17435 Tiller Ct (46074-9082)
PHONE...................................317 848-0000
Heather Wyant, *Principal*
EMP: 6
SALES (est): 882K **Privately Held**
SIC: 2653 Corrugated & solid fiber boxes

(G-14146)
COVER CARE LLC
Also Called: Automtic Pool Cver Prfssionals
17397 Oak Ridge Rd # 100 (46074-7833)
PHONE...................................513 297-4094
Curtis J Greene, *Manager*
EMP: 5
SALES (est): 219.5K **Privately Held**
SIC: 3949 Swimming pools, plastic

(G-14147)
CPS INC
Also Called: Corporate Packaging Solutions
17435 Tiller Ct (46074-9082)
PHONE...................................317 804-2300
Jason Ray, *President*
EMP: 2
SALES (est): 452.8K **Privately Held**
SIC: 2679 Corrugated paper: made from purchased material

(G-14148)
CREATIVE MCHNING CONCEPTS INC
17018 Westfield Park Rd (46074-9303)
PHONE...................................317 896-9250
Fax: 317 896-5928
John Bailey, *President*
John A Huser Jr, *Vice Pres*
EMP: 6
SQ FT: 10,500
SALES: 1MM **Privately Held**
SIC: 3599 Machine shop, jobbing & repair

(G-14149)
CRETACEOUS CURES
15541 Wildflower Ln (46074-9780)
PHONE...................................317 379-7744
Scott Babbitt, *President*
Stafford Babbitt, *Vice Pres*
EMP: 4
SALES (est): 156.7K **Privately Held**
SIC: 2834 Drugs affecting parasitic & infective diseases

(G-14150)
CROSSBOW GROUP INC
16356 Trace Blvd N (46074-8445)
PHONE...................................317 603-0406
Gerald Kramer, *Principal*
EMP: 2 EST: 2010
SALES (est): 146.9K **Privately Held**
SIC: 3949 Crossbows

(G-14151)
CURTIS DYNA-FOG LTD
Also Called: B&G Curtis Dyna-Fog
525 Park St (46074-9409)
P.O. Box 297 (46074-0297)
PHONE...................................317 896-2561
Conrad D Mc Ginnis, *President*
Dennis Roudebush, *Vice Pres*
Thomas W Ditlinger, *Treasurer*
John Stowe, *Shareholder*
Gary Myers, *Admin Sec*
◆ EMP: 65 EST: 1946
SQ FT: 80,000
SALES (est): 18.3MM **Privately Held**
WEB: www.dynafog.com
SIC: 3559 3545 Chemical machinery & equipment; machine tool attachments & accessories

(G-14152)
CUSTOM CAST STONE INC
734 E 169th St (46074-7902)
PHONE...................................317 896-1700
Fax: 317 896-1701
James Kent Grubaugh, *President*
Bruce R Lyon, *Vice Pres*

G E O G R A P H I C

Jeff M Marshall, *Manager*
EMP: 53
SQ FT: 20,000
SALES (est): 10.7MM **Privately Held**
WEB: www.customcaststone.com
SIC: 3272 Cast stone, concrete

(G-14153)
CUSTOM WOODWORKS INC
17440 Westfield Park Rd (46074-9537)
PHONE.................................317 867-2929
Tom Harris, *President*
EMP: 5
SALES: 700K **Privately Held**
SIC: 2499 Decorative wood & woodwork

(G-14154)
D&G PUBLISHING INC
17336 Tilbury Way (46074-2239)
PHONE.................................317 531-8678
Jeffrey L Duncan, *Principal*
EMP: 2
SALES (est): 148.6K **Privately Held**
SIC: 2741 Miscellaneous publishing

(G-14155)
DAJAC INC
17406 Tiller Ct Ste 600 (46074-0180)
PHONE.................................317 608-0500
David G Novak, *Principal*
Terri M Novak, *Corp Secy*
Steve Trent, *Sales Staff*
Terri Novak, *Admin Sec*
EMP: 7
SALES (est): 673K **Privately Held**
SIC: 3647 7389 Headlights (fixtures), vehicular;

(G-14156)
DAMALAK PRINTING INC
Also Called: Cave & Co. Printing
104 W Main St (46074-9480)
PHONE.................................317 896-5337
Laurie L Damalak, *President*
Troy A Damalak, *Vice Pres*
EMP: 5
SALES (est): 604.8K **Privately Held**
SIC: 2752 Commercial printing, lithographic

(G-14157)
DAVIS TOOL & MACHINE INC
19224 Eagletown Rd (46074-9228)
PHONE.................................317 896-9278
Fax: 317 896-2181
Steven Davis, *President*
Mary Ann Davis, *Admin Sec*
EMP: 15
SQ FT: 12,000
SALES (est): 1.9MM **Privately Held**
SIC: 3599 7692 Custom machinery; machine shop, jobbing & repair; welding repair

(G-14158)
DEPTH PLUS DESIGN LLC
505 Birch St (46074-9484)
PHONE.................................317 370-0532
Zebulun Wood, *Principal*
Terry Million,
Tyler Tetzloff,
EMP: 3
SALES (est): 125.1K **Privately Held**
SIC: 7379 5092 7371 7372 ; video games; computer software development & applications; application computer software

(G-14159)
DESHAZO LLC
1022 Kendall Ct Ste 2 (46074-9558)
PHONE.................................317 867-7677
Ray Lacey, *Principal*
Kelly Marshall, *Office Mgr*
EMP: 54
SALES (corp-wide): 93.5MM **Privately Held**
WEB: www.deshazo.com
SIC: 3536 Hoists, cranes & monorails
PA: Deshazo, Llc
200 Kilsby Cir
Bessemer AL 35022
205 664-2006

(G-14160)
DOTTED LIME RESALE LLC
4232 Zachary Ln (46062-0005)
PHONE.................................317 908-3905
Elena Vaughner, *Principal*
EMP: 2
SALES (est): 182.8K **Privately Held**
SIC: 3274 Lime

(G-14161)
DURAMARK TECHNOLOGIES INC
16450 Southpark Dr (46074-8396)
PHONE.................................317 867-5700
Brian Singleton, *President*
Steve Diller, *Vice Pres*
Bill Bussick, *Mng Member*
EMP: 60
SQ FT: 18,000
SALES: 3.4MM **Privately Held**
WEB: www.duramarktechnologies.com
SIC: 2752 Decals, lithographed

(G-14162)
ENOISE CONTROL INC
129 Penn St (46074-9544)
PHONE.................................317 774-1900
Jeffrey S Unger, *President*
Elizabeth Murdock, *Info Tech Mgr*
EMP: 3
SQ FT: 2,600
SALES (est): 2MM **Privately Held**
WEB: www.enoisecontrol.com
SIC: 3625 Noise control equipment

(G-14163)
ENTERPRISE MARKING PRODUCTS
17450 Tiller Ct (46074-9082)
PHONE.................................317 867-7600
EMP: 15
SQ FT: 12,500
SALES (est): 2.5MM **Privately Held**
SIC: 2679 Mfg Labels

(G-14164)
FURNACE DESIGN TECHNOLOGY LLC
Also Called: Russell Distributing
16903 Spring Mill Rd (46074-8359)
PHONE.................................317 896-5506
Roger Russell, *Mng Member*
Ron Russell,
EMP: 2
SQ FT: 5,000
SALES: 340K **Privately Held**
SIC: 3567 Fuel-fired furnaces & ovens

(G-14165)
GLOBAL PACKAGING LLC
16707 Southpark Dr (46074-8078)
PHONE.................................317 896-2089
Mike Haragan, *Sales Mgr*
J R Spitznogle,
EMP: 30
SALES (est): 6.6MM **Privately Held**
WEB: www.globalpackaging.net
SIC: 2099 Chili pepper or powder

(G-14166)
GRAND JUNCTION BREWERY
1189 E 181st St (46074-8926)
PHONE.................................317 804-9583
Jon Knight, *Owner*
EMP: 2
SALES (est): 62.3K **Privately Held**
SIC: 2082 Malt beverages

(G-14167)
GREEN APPLE ACTIVE LLC ◆
17304 Tilbury Way (46074-2239)
PHONE.................................910 585-1151
Michelle Petrowski, *President*
EMP: 2 **EST:** 2018
SALES (est): 85.9K **Privately Held**
SIC: 3571 Personal computers (microcomputers)

(G-14168)
GS SALES INC
2802 Pyrenean Pl (46074-5411)
PHONE.................................317 595-6750
Fax: 317 595-6755
George Southard, *Owner*
EMP: 2

(G-14169)
INDIANA MILLS & MANUFACTURING (PA)
Also Called: Immi
18881 Immi Way (46074-3001)
PHONE.................................317 896-9531
Fax: 317 896-2142
Larry Gray, *CEO*
James R Anthony, *President*
Kevin Tribbett, *General Mgr*
Nick Awabdy, *Vice Pres*
Norman Gould, *Vice Pres*
▲ **EMP:** 500 **EST:** 1961
SQ FT: 250,000
SALES (est): 231.3MM **Privately Held**
WEB: www.imminet.com
SIC: 3714 Motor vehicle parts & accessories

(G-14170)
INFRARED LAB SYSTEMS LLC
17408 Tiller Ct Ste 1900 (46074-8521)
PHONE.................................317 896-1565
Craig L Denney, *Owner*
Diane Denney, *Admin Asst*
EMP: 12
SALES (est): 2MM **Privately Held**
SIC: 3826 Analytical instruments

(G-14171)
INNOVATIVE CORP
Also Called: Innovative Home Offices
17401 Tiller Ct Ste H (46074-8967)
PHONE.................................317 804-5977
Christopher Radseck, *President*
John Lustig, *Vice Pres*
EMP: 26
SQ FT: 14,000
SALES (est): 4.2MM **Privately Held**
SIC: 3089 2517 2434 5211 Organizers for closets, drawers, etc.: plastic; wood television & radio cabinets; wood kitchen cabinets; closets, interiors & accessories; cabinet & finish carpentry

(G-14172)
KAN JAM LLC
17401 Tiller Ct Ste A (46074-8967)
P.O. Box 864, Getzville NY (14068-0864)
PHONE.................................317 804-9129
Mitch Rubin,
Charles Sciandra,
EMP: 2
SALES (est): 328.7K
SALES (corp-wide): 21MM **Privately Held**
SIC: 3944 Darts & dart games
PA: Ws Tailgating, Llc
17401 Tiller Ct Ste A
Westfield IN 46074
317 804-9129

(G-14173)
KP HOLDINGS LLC
2000 E 196th St (46074-3801)
PHONE.................................317 867-0234
John Ball, *President*
Gregory Griffin, *Vice Pres*
Mike Bance, *VP Finance*
Kristie Haneline, *Admin Sec*
EMP: 430
SQ FT: 110,000
SALES (est): 21.3MM **Privately Held**
SIC: 3714 Motor vehicle parts & accessories

(G-14174)
LOGO USA CORPORATION (PA)
320 Parkway Cir (46074-9306)
PHONE.................................317 867-8518
Fax: 317 867-8514
George Sanburn, *President*
Kim Sanburn, *Corp Secy*
Angie Sanburn, *Vice Pres*
EMP: 15
SQ FT: 10,000
SALES (est): 1.3MM **Privately Held**
SIC: 2396 Screen printing on fabric articles

(G-14175)
MAXIM INTEGRATED PRODUCTS INC
16848 Southpark Dr (46074-8131)
PHONE.................................252 227-7202
Fax: 317 399-2726
EMP: 5
SALES (corp-wide): 2.3B **Publicly Held**
SIC: 3674 Microcircuits, integrated (semiconductor)
PA: Maxim Integrated Products, Inc.
160 Rio Robles
San Jose CA 95134
408 601-1000

(G-14176)
MERCS MINIATURES LLC
Also Called: Megacon Games
46 W Clear Lake Ln (46074-8158)
P.O. Box 30 (46074-0030)
PHONE.................................765 661-6724
Keith David Lowe,
EMP: 3
SALES: 300K **Privately Held**
SIC: 3999 7389 Miniatures;

(G-14177)
MOTION ENGINEERING COMPANY INC
Also Called: M E C
17338 Wstfeld Pk Rd Ste 4 (46074)
P.O. Box 427 (46074-0427)
PHONE.................................317 804-7990
Ronald D Jones, *President*
Judy K Jones, *Vice Pres*
EMP: 5
SQ FT: 2,000
SALES (est): 1.9MM **Privately Held**
WEB: www.highspeedimaging.com
SIC: 5065 7359 7812 3827 Video equipment, electronic; equipment rental & leasing; motion picture & video production; magnifying instruments, optical; motion picture cameras, equipment & supplies

(G-14178)
PORTER SYSTEMS INC
Also Called: Porter Engineered Systems
2000 E 196th St (46074-3801)
PHONE.................................317 867-0234
EMP: 2
SALES (est): 88.3K **Privately Held**
SIC: 3694 Mfg Engine Electrical Equipment

(G-14179)
PORTER SYSTEMS INC
Also Called: Porter Engineered Systems
2000 E 196th St (46074-3801)
PHONE.................................317 867-0234
EMP: 45
SALES (est): 3.4MM **Privately Held**
SIC: 3441 Fabricated structural metal; expansion joints (structural shapes), iron or steel

(G-14180)
PPG INDUSTRIES INC
Also Called: PPG 4371
3132 E State Road 32 (46074-8730)
PHONE.................................317 867-5934
Steve Taylor, *Manager*
EMP: 24
SALES (corp-wide): 14.2B **Publicly Held**
WEB: www.ppg.com
SIC: 2851 Paints & allied products
PA: Ppg Industries, Inc.
1 Ppg Pl
Pittsburgh PA 15272
412 434-3131

(G-14181)
PREMIUM SRFC FBRICATION OF IND
17401 Tiller Ct Ste D (46074-8967)
P.O. Box 945 (46074-0945)
PHONE.................................317 867-1013
Fax: 317 867-0712
Ronald Gennaro, *President*
Cheryl Gennaro, *Admin Sec*
EMP: 20
SQ FT: 4,000
SALES (est): 2.1MM **Privately Held**
WEB: www.premiumsurface.com
SIC: 2541 Counter & sink tops

▲ = Import ▼=Export
◆ =Import/Export

(G-14182)
R J HANLON COMPANY INC (PA)
17408 Tiller Ct Ste 600 (46074-8517)
PHONE..................................317 867-2900
Robert J Hanlon, *President*
Kathleen C Hanlon, *Treasurer*
Anthony Parisi, *Asst Sec*
EMP: 49 **EST:** 1976
SQ FT: 8,000
SALES (est): 9.1MM **Privately Held**
WEB: www.rjhanlon.com
SIC: 2394 Cloth, drop (fabric): made from purchased materials; liners & covers, fabric: made from purchased materials

(G-14183)
RELATIONAL INTELLIGENCE LLC
14948 Annabel Ct (46074-2219)
PHONE..................................317 669-8900
Tim A Gardner, *Principal*
EMP: 2
SALES (est): 158.1K **Privately Held**
SIC: 7372 Prepackaged software

(G-14184)
REVERE INDUSTRIES LLC (PA)
16855 Suthpark Dr Ste 100 (46074)
PHONE..................................317 580-2420
James R Hamelink, *CEO*
Sean Black, *President*
Danny Neff, *General Mgr*
Ben James, *COO*
James R Crews Jr, *Vice Pres*
EMP: 4
SALES: 245.4MM **Privately Held**
SIC: 3089 3399 3363 3497 Injection molding of plastics; aluminum atomized powder; aluminum die-castings; metal foil & leaf

(G-14185)
ROBINSON INDUSTRIES INC
Also Called: Frakes Electric Company
17111 Westfield Park Rd (46074-9537)
PHONE..................................317 867-3214
Fax: 317 867-3217
Richard Robinson, *President*
Carolyn Robinson, *Corp Secy*
EMP: 22
SQ FT: 4,000
SALES (est): 3.8MM **Privately Held**
WEB: www.frakesindustrial.com
SIC: 7694 5084 5063 5251 Electric motor repair; pumps & pumping equipment; motors, electric; pumps & pumping equipment; motors, electric

(G-14186)
ROBINSON INDUSTRIES INC
Also Called: Frakes Industrial Sales & Svc
17111 Westfield Park Rd (46074-9537)
PHONE..................................317 867-3214
Richard J Robinson, *President*
Carolyn A Robinson, *Admin Sec*
EMP: 22
SALES (est): 4.1MM **Privately Held**
SIC: 7694 5084 5063 5251 Armature rewinding shops; industrial machinery & equipment; electrical apparatus & equipment; hardware

(G-14187)
SCREEN PRINTING SUPER STORE
17408 Tiller Ct Ste 100 (46074-8510)
PHONE..................................317 804-9904
Bubba Thomas, *Manager*
EMP: 2
SALES (est): 166K **Privately Held**
SIC: 2759 Screen printing

(G-14188)
SHELBY GRAVEL INC
17701 Spring Mill Rd (46074-9232)
PHONE..................................317 804-8100
EMP: 31
SALES (corp-wide): 55.5MM **Privately Held**
SIC: 5211 3273 Cement; ready-mixed concrete
PA: Shelby Gravel, Inc
157 E Rampart St
Shelbyville IN 46176
317 398-4485

(G-14189)
SILICIS TECHNOLOGIES INC
17225 Westfield Park Rd (46074-9537)
PHONE..................................317 896-5044
Michael Stigler, *CEO*
EMP: 35
SQ FT: 36,000
SALES (est): 3.3MM **Privately Held**
SIC: 3812 8731 Aircraft/aerospace flight instruments & guidance systems; electronic research

(G-14190)
STANDARD LOCKNUT LLC
1045 E 169th St (46074-9630)
P.O. Box 780 (46074-0780)
PHONE..................................317 399-2230
Fax: 317 867-4231
Ollie Martins, *President*
Richard Goddard, *COO*
Ed Wetzel, *CFO*
Trisha Beaty, *Accountant*
Marti Jensen, *Accountant*
▲ **EMP:** 155 **EST:** 1941
SQ FT: 125,000
SALES (est): 62.9MM **Privately Held**
WEB: www.stdlocknut.com
SIC: 3562 3451 3541 3452 Roller bearings & parts; screw machine products; machine tools, metal cutting type; bolts, nuts, rivets & washers

(G-14191)
SUGAR CODED SOFTWARE LLC
16743 Ashley Blvd Apt C (46074-8689)
PHONE..................................858 652-0797
Tyler Sugar, *Owner*
EMP: 2
SALES (est): 64.2K **Privately Held**
SIC: 7372 Prepackaged software

(G-14192)
SUN POWER TECHNOLOGIES LLC
17406 Tiller Ct Ste 900 (46074-8987)
PHONE..................................317 399-8113
Brett Reinhardt,
Roger Fox,
EMP: 2
SQ FT: 1,200
SALES (est): 240K **Privately Held**
WEB: www.sunpowertech.com
SIC: 3699 Electrical equipment & supplies

(G-14193)
SYNERMED INTERNATIONAL INC
17408 Tiller Ct Ste 1900 (46074-8521)
PHONE..................................317 896-1565
Jerry Denney, *President*
EMP: 6
SALES (est): 931.3K **Privately Held**
WEB: www.synermedinc.com
SIC: 2835 In vitro diagnostics

(G-14194)
THOMAS & BETTS CORP
16577 Brookhollow Dr (46062-7150)
PHONE..................................901 252-8000
Todd Smith, *District Mgr*
EMP: 2
SALES (est): 104.1K **Privately Held**
SIC: 3643 Current-carrying wiring devices

(G-14195)
UN SEEN PRESS CO
Also Called: Un Seen Tesh
17272 Futch Way (46074-8801)
PHONE..................................317 867-5594
Nicole Kobrowsky, *CEO*
Michael Kabrowsky, *CFO*
EMP: 3
SALES (est): 206.4K **Privately Held**
WEB: www.kobrowski.com
SIC: 2741 Miscellaneous publishing

(G-14196)
UNIFORM HOOD LACE INC
18881 Immi Way Ste B (46074-3001)
PHONE..................................317 896-9555
Fax: 317 867-0641
James R Anthony, *President*
Anthony M Schelonka, *CFO*
EMP: 6
SQ FT: 6,100

SALES (est): 665.5K **Privately Held**
WEB: www.uniformhoodlace.com
SIC: 3053 Packing materials; gaskets, all materials

(G-14197)
UPPER LEVEL NETWORKS
16545 Southpark Dr (46074-8347)
PHONE..................................317 863-0955
Gregory S Paton, *President*
EMP: 3
SALES (est): 281.2K **Privately Held**
SIC: 3131 Uppers

(G-14198)
VICAIR AMERICA LLC ✪
16461 Chalet Cir (46074-8781)
PHONE..................................317 281-0809
David Hartley, *CEO*
Max Rogmans,
EMP: 3 **EST:** 2017
SALES (est): 117.4K **Privately Held**
SIC: 3841 Surgical & medical instruments

(G-14199)
VOEGE PRECISION MCH PDTS LLC
Also Called: Voege Precision Machine Pdts
17808 Commerce Dr (46074-9089)
PHONE..................................317 867-4699
John Voege,
Alana Voege,
EMP: 6 **EST:** 1999
SQ FT: 6,000
SALES: 240K **Privately Held**
SIC: 3599 Machine shop, jobbing & repair

(G-14200)
WEAS ENGINEERING INC
17297 Oak Ridge Rd (46074-7907)
P.O. Box 550 (46074-0550)
PHONE..................................317 867-4477
Fax: 317 867-1040
W Andrew Weas Sr, *President*
Randy McDaniel, *Area Mgr*
Tyler Morton, *Area Mgr*
Hannelore Weas, *Corp Secy*
Greg Wannemuehler, *Vice Pres*
EMP: 15
SALES (est): 4.6MM **Privately Held**
SIC: 2899 Water treating compounds

(G-14201)
WESTFIELD DONUTS
212 E Main St (46074-9347)
P.O. Box 649 (46074-0649)
PHONE..................................317 896-5856
James Hicks, *Owner*
EMP: 2
SALES (est): 75.7K **Privately Held**
SIC: 5461 2051 Doughnuts; doughnuts, except frozen

(G-14202)
WHOLESALE HRDWOOD INTRIORS INC
Also Called: W H I
17715 Commerce Dr Ste 300 (46074-8972)
PHONE..................................317 867-3660
Keith Bell, *Branch Mgr*
EMP: 14
SALES (corp-wide): 16.8MM **Privately Held**
SIC: 2861 2435 Hardwood distillates; plywood, hardwood or hardwood faced
PA: Wholesale Hardwood Interiors, Inc.
1030 Campbellsville Byp
Campbellsville KY 42718
270 789-1323

(G-14203)
WOLFIES GRILL 5 LLC
Also Called: Italian House On Park, The
219 Park St (46074-9407)
PHONE..................................317 804-5619
EMP: 4
SALES (est): 100.4K **Privately Held**
SIC: 2084 Wines

Westpoint
Tippecanoe County

(G-14204)
ARBORAMERICA INC
7852 W 200 S (47992-9362)
PHONE..................................765 572-1212
Javier Arregui, *CEO*
Jason Cook, *Opers Mgr*
Walter Beineke, *Engineer*
EMP: 7
SALES (est): 719.7K **Privately Held**
SIC: 0783 0851 2411 Ornamental shrub & tree services; forestry services; logging

(G-14205)
FREED MACHINING & TOOL INC
6033 W 800 S (47992-9262)
PHONE..................................765 538-3019
Micheal Freed, *President*
Holly Freed, *Vice Pres*
EMP: 3
SALES: 200K **Privately Held**
SIC: 3599 Machine shop, jobbing & repair

(G-14206)
INNOVATIVE EQUIPMENT INC
Also Called: Its
9227 W 600 S (47992-9247)
PHONE..................................765 572-2367
Chris Sims, *President*
EMP: 4
SALES: 240K **Privately Held**
WEB:
www.innovativetransportsolutions.com
SIC: 3799 Transportation equipment

(G-14207)
ROOF MASTERS PLUS
7800 W 650 S (47992-9327)
PHONE..................................765 572-1321
Mike Freeman, *Owner*
EMP: 2
SALES: 227K **Privately Held**
SIC: 1761 3444 Roofing contractor; metal roofing & roof drainage equipment

Westport
Decatur County

(G-14208)
AMCOR PHRM PACKG USA INC
1108 N State Road 3 (47283-9513)
PHONE..................................812 591-2332
Chuck Bendixen, *Manager*
EMP: 140
SALES (corp-wide): 9.1B **Privately Held**
WEB: www.alcanpackaging.com
SIC: 3221 Vials, glass
HQ: Amcor Pharmaceutical Packaging Usa, Llc
625 Sharp St N
Millville NJ 08332
856 327-1540

(G-14209)
CROSSPOWER LLC
1268 E County Road 1000 S (47283-9125)
PHONE..................................812 591-2009
Ron Moore,
Diana Moore,
EMP: 2
SALES (est): 152K **Privately Held**
SIC: 3542 Machine tools, metal forming type

(G-14210)
NIPRO PHRMPCKGING AMRICAS CORP
1108 N State Road 3 (47283-9104)
PHONE..................................812 591-2332
Bob Chtatham, *Branch Mgr*
EMP: 9
SALES (corp-wide): 3.7B **Privately Held**
SIC: 3221 Vials, glass
HQ: Nipro Pharmapackaging Americas Corp.
1200 N 10th St
Millville NJ 08332

(G-14211)
SARDINIA MACHINE
12337 S State Road 3 (47283-9353)
PHONE.................................812 591-2091
Fax: 812 591-2091
Ron Pyles, *Partner*
Fritz Reichel, *General Ptnr*
EMP: 6
SQ FT: 9,000
SALES (est): 777.6K Privately Held
SIC: 3599 Machine shop, jobbing & repair

(G-14212)
WINCHESTER STEEL
10622 S County Road 100 W
(47283-9770)
PHONE.................................812 591-2071
Roberta Cruser, *Owner*
Phillip Cruser, *Principal*
EMP: 2
SALES (est): 100.4K Privately Held
SIC: 3324 Steel investment foundries

Westville
Laporte County

(G-14213)
APPEL-OLSON LLC
942 N 651 E (46391-9649)
PHONE.................................219 926-6679
Damien Appel, *Owner*
EMP: 2
SALES (est): 85.9K Privately Held
SIC: 3571 Personal computers (microcomputers)

(G-14214)
BUCHANAN IRON WORKS INC
103 Greenway St (46391-8502)
P.O. Box 823 (46391-0823)
PHONE.................................219 785-4480
Fax: 219 785-4480
Kim Buchanan, *President*
Jan Buchanan, *Vice Pres*
EMP: 5
SQ FT: 8,000
SALES (est): 987.1K Privately Held
SIC: 3441 7692 Fabricated structural metal; welding repair

(G-14215)
DELUXE HOMES
1888 S Rolling Meadows Dr (46391-3409)
PHONE.................................219 256-1701
EMP: 2 EST: 2015
SALES (est): 122.5K Privately Held
SIC: 2782 Checkbooks

(G-14216)
G G B INC
7512 S 800 W (46391-9734)
PHONE.................................219 733-2897
Greg Bekavac, *President*
EMP: 3 EST: 1994
SALES: 30K Privately Held
SIC: 3677 Coil windings, electronic

(G-14217)
HEADS FIRST
Also Called: Heads 1st
7 Plain St (46391-8400)
PHONE.................................219 785-4100
James McMahon, *Manager*
EMP: 4
SALES (est): 583.3K Privately Held
SIC: 3714 7699 Motor vehicle engines & parts; professional instrument repair services

(G-14218)
HUNTS MAINTENANCE INC
107 Greenway St (46391-8500)
PHONE.................................219 785-2333
Paul Shafer, *Principal*
EMP: 6
SALES (est): 60.8K Privately Held
SIC: 4953 3443 1794 Rubbish collection & disposal; dumpsters, garbage; excavation work

(G-14219)
IMERYS STEELCASTING USA INC
620 E Us Highway 6 (46391-9405)
PHONE.................................219 921-1012
Neal Hiemstra, *Manager*
EMP: 3
SALES (corp-wide): 2.6MM Privately Held
WEB: www.stollberg.com
SIC: 3399 Powder, metal
HQ: Imerys Steelcasting Usa, Inc.
   4111 Witmer Rd
   Niagara Falls NY 14305
   716 278-1634

(G-14220)
NORTHWEST FARM FERTILIZERS
4725 S Us Highway 421 (46391)
PHONE.................................219 785-2331
Fax: 574 785-2116
Kevin Hannon, *Manager*
EMP: 7 EST: 1928
SALES (est): 1.4MM Privately Held
SIC: 5153 5191 2875 Grain elevators; farm supplies; fertilizers, mixing only

(G-14221)
WAR - LLC- WESTVILLE PRTG
Also Called: Slater Publishing Co
361 W Main St (46391-9356)
P.O. Box 617 (46391-0617)
PHONE.................................219 785-2821
Fax: 574 785-2821
Robert Warth, *President*
Carol Warth, *Corp Secy*
Scott Warth, *Vice Pres*
EMP: 6
SQ FT: 9,500
SALES (est): 275K Privately Held
SIC: 2759 2791 2789 2752 Commercial printing; typesetting; bookbinding & related work; commercial printing, lithographic

Wheatfield
Jasper County

(G-14222)
GEORGIA-PACIFIC LLC
604 Na Sandifer Rd (46392)
P.O. Box 159 (46392-0159)
PHONE.................................219 776-0069
Curt Riggen, *Branch Mgr*
EMP: 2
SALES (corp-wide): 44.4B Privately Held
WEB: www.gp.com
SIC: 2679 Corrugated paper: made from purchased material
HQ: Georgia-Pacific Llc
   133 Peachtree St Nw
   Atlanta GA 30303
   404 652-4000

(G-14223)
GEORGIA-PACIFIC LLC
484 E 1400 N (46392-8817)
PHONE.................................219 956-3100
Steve Ivers, *Engineer*
Eric Kimlinger, *Human Res Mgr*
Mark Harris, *Manager*
EMP: 110
SALES (corp-wide): 44.4B Privately Held
WEB: www.gp.com
SIC: 2431 3275 Millwork; gypsum products
HQ: Georgia-Pacific Llc
   133 Peachtree St Nw
   Atlanta GA 30303
   404 652-4000

(G-14224)
HARVS WELDING INC
8700 N 400 W (46392-9695)
PHONE.................................219 345-5959
Fax: 219 987-4949
Harvey Kamminga, *President*
Norma Kamminga, *Corp Secy*
EMP: 2
SALES (est): 294.7K Privately Held
SIC: 7692 Automotive welding

(G-14225)
IN-PRINT ❂
886 E 900 N (46392-8229)
PHONE.................................219 956-3001
EMP: 2 EST: 2017
SALES (est): 92.3K Privately Held
SIC: 2752 Commercial printing, lithographic

(G-14226)
JP CUSTOM CABINETRY INC
13467 Whippoorwill Ln (46392-7439)
PHONE.................................219 956-3587
Jeremy Peterson, *President*
EMP: 2
SALES: 30K Privately Held
SIC: 2434 Wood kitchen cabinets

(G-14227)
KANKAKEE VALLEY STEEL INC
12632 N 400 E (46392-9239)
P.O. Box 277 (46392-0277)
PHONE.................................219 828-4011
Mark Forszt, *President*
EMP: 2
SALES (est): 169.8K Privately Held
SIC: 3312 Hot-rolled iron & steel products

(G-14228)
OZINGA BROS INC
Also Called: Ozinga Ready Mix
11607 N State Road 49 (46392-8217)
PHONE.................................219 956-3418
Fax: 219 956-3416
Daryl Sculley, *Manager*
EMP: 12
SALES (corp-wide): 269.8MM Privately Held
SIC: 3273 Ready-mixed concrete
PA: Ozinga Bros., Inc.
   19001 Old Lagrange Rd # 30
   Mokena IL 60448
   708 326-4200

(G-14229)
R D-N-P DRILLING INC
3759 W 900 N (46392-9717)
PHONE.................................219 956-3481
Karen Eger, *President*
Paul Eger, *Vice Pres*
Vicki Eger, *Admin Sec*
EMP: 9
SALES: 1.1MM Privately Held
WEB: www.rdnpdrilling.com
SIC: 1241 Test boring, anthracite mining

(G-14230)
RUSTIC N CHIC LLC
1917 W 1100 N (46392-9655)
PHONE.................................219 987-4957
Brook Caldanaro-Wright,
EMP: 3
SALES (est): 183.2K Privately Held
SIC: 3081 2395 Vinyl film & sheet; embroidery & art needlework

Wheatland
Knox County

(G-14231)
CYPRESS SPRINGS ENTERPRISES
11536 E Lucky Point Rd (47597-8231)
PHONE.................................812 743-8888
Alan Smith, *President*
Kyle Bledsoe, *Branch Mgr*
EMP: 5
SALES (est): 714.2K Privately Held
SIC: 3761 3769 3812 Guided missiles & space vehicles; guided missile & space vehicle parts & aux eqpt, rsch & dev; defense systems & equipment; missile guidance systems & equipment; space vehicle guidance systems & equipment

(G-14232)
PEABODY MIDWEST MINING LLC
Also Called: Black Beauty Air Qulty 1 Mine
Se 610 E And Se 700 S S 7 (47597)
PHONE.................................812 743-2910
EMP: 218
SALES (corp-wide): 5.6B Publicly Held
SIC: 1221 1222 Bituminous Coal Mining
HQ: Peabody Midwest Mining, Llc
   566 Dickeyville Rd
   Lynnville IN 47619
   812 434-8500

Whiteland
Johnson County

(G-14233)
A & M INNOVATIONS LLC
37 Erins Ct (46184-9670)
PHONE.................................317 306-6118
Anita Hill, *Administration*
EMP: 2
SALES (est): 100.3K Privately Held
SIC: 2759 Screen printing

(G-14234)
CAD & MACHINING SERVICES INC
Also Called: CMS
521 Williamson St (46184-1643)
PHONE.................................317 535-1067
Fax: 317 535-1179
John Meyer, *President*
Teena Hunsberger,
EMP: 11 EST: 1993
SQ FT: 7,500
SALES (est): 1.7MM Privately Held
SIC: 3599 Machine & other job shop work

(G-14235)
CELLOFOAM NORTH AMERICA INC
Also Called: Indiana Division
150 Crossroads Dr (46184-9778)
PHONE.................................317 535-9008
Fax: 317 535-5211
Mark Slade, *Manager*
EMP: 91
SALES (corp-wide): 119.7MM Privately Held
WEB: www.cellofoam.com
SIC: 2821 3086 Polystyrene resins; plastics foam products
PA: Cellofoam North America Inc.
   1917 Rockdale Indstrl Blv
   Conyers GA 30012
   770 929-3688

(G-14236)
CERTA CRAFT INC
140 Crossroads Dr (46184-9778)
PHONE.................................317 535-0226
Emil Kernel III, *President*
EMP: 7
SALES (est): 847K Privately Held
SIC: 3599 Machine shop, jobbing & repair

(G-14237)
CRYSTAL GRAPHICS INC
530 Main St (46184-1517)
PHONE.................................317 535-9202
Richard Ashbrook, *President*
Crystal Ashbrook, *Vice Pres*
EMP: 6
SQ FT: 2,500
SALES (est): 630K Privately Held
SIC: 2752 Commercial printing, offset

(G-14238)
GLIDDEN RACING ENGINES
5026 N Graham Rd (46184-9306)
P.O. Box 236 (46184-0236)
PHONE.................................317 535-5225
Bill Glidden, *Owner*
Shanon Springer, *Manager*
EMP: 2
SALES (est): 212.2K Privately Held
SIC: 3519 Internal combustion engines

(G-14239)
HUBBARD INC
6774 N Us Highway 31 (46184-9552)
PHONE.................................317 535-1926
Phillip Hubbard Jr, *President*
EMP: 2
SALES: 750K Privately Held
SIC: 1731 3536 Electrical work; hoists, cranes & monorails

▲ = Import ▼=Export
◆ =Import/Export

(G-14240)
ICI AMERICAS INC ✪
43 N Us Highway 31 (46184-1545)
PHONE..................................317 535-5626
Denzel Marten, *Manager*
EMP: 2 EST: 2017
SALES (est): 74.4K **Privately Held**
SIC: 2821 Plastics materials & resins

(G-14241)
IRVING MATERIALS INC
Also Called: I M I
600 Tracy Rd (46184-9698)
PHONE..................................317 535-7566
Jean Wiggins, *Manager*
EMP: 9
SALES (corp-wide): 800.6MM **Privately Held**
SIC: 3273 Ready-mixed concrete
PA: Irving Materials, Inc.
8032 N State Road 9
Greenfield IN 46140
317 326-3101

(G-14242)
LEISTNER AQUATIC SERVICES INC
6237 N 25 W (46184-9542)
PHONE..................................317 535-6099
Keith Leistner, *President*
EMP: 5
SALES: 300K **Privately Held**
SIC: 1629 7389 7999 3589 Pond construction; water softener service; fishing lakes & piers, operation; sewage & water treatment equipment; swimming pool filter & water conditioning systems; boats, canoes, watercrafts & equipment

(G-14243)
PRINTWORKS INC
655 Tracy Rd (46184-9698)
PHONE..................................317 535-1250
Jeff Helton, *President*
Nancy Helton, *Corp Secy*
EMP: 7
SQ FT: 5,500
SALES (est): 1MM **Privately Held**
SIC: 2752 Commercial printing, offset

(G-14244)
RAYBURN AUTOMOTIVE INC
4725 N Graham Rd (46184-9331)
PHONE..................................317 535-8232
Fax: 317 535-8492
Carl J Rayburn, *President*
EMP: 7
SALES: 400K **Privately Held**
SIC: 3711 3714 Automobile assembly, including specialty automobiles; motor vehicle engines & parts

(G-14245)
SANDPAPER STUDIO LLC
6403 N 300 E (46184-9725)
PHONE..................................317 435-7479
Torrey Dawley, *Principal*
EMP: 3
SALES (est): 184.6K **Privately Held**
SIC: 3291 Sandpaper

(G-14246)
SOLID SURFACE CRAFTSMEN INC
100 Crossroads Dr Ste D (46184-9782)
PHONE..................................317 535-2333
Fax: 317 247-5990
Randy Davis, *President*
EMP: 4
SQ FT: 4,600
SALES (est): 483.6K **Privately Held**
SIC: 2542 2821 2541 Counters or counter display cases: except wood; plastics materials & resins; wood partitions & fixtures

(G-14247)
WALLS LAWN & GARDEN INC
Also Called: Wall's Enterprises
201 N Us Highway 31 (46184-1461)
P.O. Box 235 (46184-0235)
PHONE..................................317 535-9059
Fax: 317 535-9871
Gregg Wall, *President*
Aubrey Wall, *Vice Pres*
Jerie Wall, *Vice Pres*
Wayne Wall, *Vice Pres*
EMP: 8
SQ FT: 4,000
SALES (est): 437.7K **Privately Held**
WEB: www.wallaceenterprisesinc.com
SIC: 0782 0782 3999 Lawn & garden services; custom pulverizing & grinding of plastic materials

(G-14248)
WOODWORKING BY RICH
119 Ardmoor Dr (46184-1429)
PHONE..................................317 535-5750
Mark Rich, *Principal*
EMP: 3 EST: 2010
SALES (est): 352.7K **Privately Held**
SIC: 2431 Millwork

Whitestown
Boone County

(G-14249)
BEL-MAR PRODUCTS CORPORATION
5 E Pierce St (46075-9380)
PHONE..................................317 769-3262
Fax: 317 769-3262
Quinton Elrod, *President*
Steve Elrod, *Vice Pres*
Mary Lou Elrod, *Treasurer*
EMP: 8 EST: 1945
SQ FT: 10,000
SALES (est): 1MM **Privately Held**
WEB: www.belmarproducts.com
SIC: 3724 3599 3545 7692 Aircraft engines & engine parts; machine shop, jobbing & repair; tools & accessories for machine tools; welding repair; special dies, tools, jigs & fixtures

(G-14250)
CEMEX MATERIALS LLC
4360 Whitelick Dr (46075-9376)
PHONE..................................317 769-5801
Rob Davoren, *Branch Mgr*
EMP: 27 **Privately Held**
WEB: www.rinkermaterials.com
SIC: 3273 Ready-mixed concrete
HQ: Cemex Materials, Llc
1501 Belvedere Rd
West Palm Beach FL 33406
561 833-5555

(G-14251)
CUMMINS MIDWEST REGIONAL DIST (PA)
4820 S Indianapolis Rd (46075-9533)
PHONE..................................901 302-8143
Tom Linebarger, *CEO*
Dana Crockett, *Manager*
EMP: 99 EST: 2016
SQ FT: 160,000
SALES (est): 6.9MM **Privately Held**
SIC: 3714 Motor vehicle parts & accessories

(G-14252)
DAIMLER TRUCKS NORTH AMER LLC
4140 Anson Blvd (46075-4492)
PHONE..................................317 769-8500
EMP: 2
SALES (corp-wide): 193.7B **Privately Held**
SIC: 3711 Motor vehicles & car bodies
HQ: Daimler Trucks North America Llc
4555 N Channel Ave
Portland OR 97217
503 745-8000

(G-14253)
GREENCYCLE OF INDIANA INC
4227 S Perry Worth Rd (46075-9398)
PHONE..................................317 769-5668
Mike Braher, *General Mgr*
John Repenning, *Vice Pres*
EMP: 4 **Privately Held**
SIC: 2499 Mulch or sawdust products, wood; mulch, wood & bark
HQ: Greencycle Of Indiana, Inc
400 Central Ave Ste 115
Northfield IL 60093

(G-14254)
HYDRO CONDUIT OF TEXAS LP
Also Called: Whitestown - Precast
4360 Whitelick Dr (46075-9376)
PHONE..................................317 769-2261
Wayne Terhune, *Manager*
EMP: 6 **Privately Held**
WEB: www.prestressservices.com
SIC: 3272 Concrete products
HQ: Hydro Conduit Of Texas, Lp
6560 Langfield Rd 3-H
Houston TX 77092

(G-14255)
INDIANA INDUSTRIAL SVCS LLC (PA)
5294 Performance Way (46075-8812)
PHONE..................................317 769-6099
Fax: 317 769-5520
Jerry Cunningham, *President*
Bruce Cunningham, *Vice Pres*
Kate Hamilton, *Vice Pres*
Ron Smalling, *Warehouse Mgr*
Jeremy Hamilton, *Manager*
▼ EMP: 110
SQ FT: 23,000
SALES (est): 23.4MM **Privately Held**
WEB: www.indianaindustrial.net
SIC: 1796 7692 Installing building equipment; machinery installation; welding repair

(G-14256)
MEYER INDUSTRIES INC
Also Called: Vault Plant, The
6851 S Indianapolis Rd (46075-9515)
P.O. Box 411, Zionsville (46077-0411)
PHONE..................................317 769-3497
Fred Meyer, *Branch Mgr*
EMP: 5
SALES (corp-wide): 137K **Privately Held**
SIC: 3272 5087 Burial vaults, concrete or precast terrazzo; concrete burial vaults & boxes
PA: Meyer Industries Inc
10 W Market St Ste 800
Indianapolis IN

(G-14257)
PITNEY BOWES INC
5490 Industrial Ct (46075-8808)
PHONE..................................317 769-8300
Gary McGuire, *Branch Mgr*
EMP: 7
SALES (corp-wide): 3.5B **Publicly Held**
SIC: 3579 Canceling machinery, post office
PA: Pitney Bowes Inc.
3001 Summer St Ste 3
Stamford CT 06905
203 356-5000

(G-14258)
PITNEY BOWES INC
5490 Industrial Ct (46075-8808)
PHONE..................................317 769-8300
Mark Patrie, *Manager*
EMP: 100
SALES (corp-wide): 3.5B **Publicly Held**
SIC: 3579 7359 Postage meters; business machine & electronic equipment rental services
PA: Pitney Bowes Inc.
3001 Summer St Ste 3
Stamford CT 06905
203 356-5000

(G-14259)
PRECAST SOLUTIONS INC
Also Called: Cgm
6145 S Indianapolis Rd (46075-9526)
PHONE..................................317 545-6557
John R Davis III, *CEO*
EMP: 15
SQ FT: 10,000
SALES (est): 1.2MM **Privately Held**
WEB: www.cgmmfg.com
SIC: 3275 3273 Gypsum products; ready-mixed concrete

(G-14260)
R W MACHINE INCORPORATED
3463 S 500 E (46075-9555)
PHONE..................................317 769-6798
Ronald A Wing, *President*
EMP: 2

SALES (est): 137.5K **Privately Held**
SIC: 3511 Steam engines

(G-14261)
SANDERS PRE-CAST CONCRETE
6051 S Indianapolis Rd (46075-9527)
PHONE..................................317 769-5503
Mark Sanders, *President*
Devon Moon, *CFO*
Michael Turpin, *CFO*
Austin Sanders, *Manager*
Belinda Cripe, *Admin Sec*
EMP: 30 EST: 1998
SALES (est): 8.3MM **Privately Held**
SIC: 3272 Concrete products, precast

(G-14262)
SOFTWARE SALES INCORPORATED
3370 S 450 E (46075-9707)
PHONE..................................317 258-7442
Brad Schweibold, *Principal*
EMP: 2
SALES (est): 159.4K **Privately Held**
SIC: 7372 Prepackaged software

(G-14263)
TANK CONSTRUCTION & SERVICE CO
Also Called: Tmr Group
6145 S Indianapolis Rd (46075-9526)
PHONE..................................317 509-6294
Thomas Riddle, *President*
EMP: 10
SALES (est): 823.2K **Privately Held**
SIC: 7699 1791 1731 3443 Tank repair; storage tanks, metal: erection; electrical work; fabricated plate work (boiler shop); fabricated structural metal; petroleum storage tanks, pumping & draining

(G-14264)
TRIM-A-DOOR
4036 Perry Blvd (46075-9709)
PHONE..................................317 769-8746
Sherry Crabb, *Manager*
EMP: 4 EST: 2015
SALES (est): 151K **Privately Held**
SIC: 5031 2431 Door frames, all materials; doors & door parts & trim, wood

(G-14265)
WSG MANUFACTURING LLC
4485 S Perry Worth Rd (46075-8804)
PHONE..................................765 934-2101
Brian Hamilton, *Administration*
EMP: 6
SALES (est): 91.3K **Privately Held**
SIC: 2064 Popcorn balls or other treated popcorn products

Whiting
Lake County

(G-14266)
ALMOST FAMOUS PRINTING
1309 119th St (46394-1625)
PHONE..................................219 793-6388
Keely Schalk, *Principal*
EMP: 2 EST: 2007
SALES (est): 119.3K **Privately Held**
SIC: 2759 Screen printing

(G-14267)
ANALYTICALAB INC (PA)
1404 119th St Ste A (46394-1734)
PHONE..................................219 473-9777
Mary Lordsburg, *President*
Joy Stevens, *Corp Secy*
EMP: 5 EST: 1999
SALES (est): 300K **Privately Held**
SIC: 3823 Analyzers, industrial process type

(G-14268)
B P SECURITY
2815 Indianapolis Blvd (46394-2197)
PHONE..................................219 473-3700
Kristine Curtis, *Manager*
EMP: 3

SALES: 61K Privately Held
SIC: 2911 Petroleum refining

(G-14269)
BAKER PETROLITE LLC
2831 Indian Airforce Blvd (46394)
PHONE..............................219 473-5329
Ken Ross, *Manager*
EMP: 8
SALES (corp-wide): 122B Publicly Held
WEB: www.bakerpetrolite.com
SIC: 2899 Chemical preparations
HQ: Baker Petrolite Llc
    12645 W Airport Blvd
    Sugar Land TX 77478
    281 276-5400

(G-14270)
BIZIK MASONRY CORPORATION
2435 Indianapolis Blvd (46394-2164)
PHONE..............................219 659-1348
Charlotte Bizik, *President*
James Bizik, *Vice Pres*
EMP: 2
SQ FT: 1,500
SALES (est): 184.9K Privately Held
SIC: 1793 3231 Glass & glazing work;
    products of purchased glass

(G-14271)
MEDEGEN HOLDINGS LLC
648 114th St (46394-1006)
PHONE..............................219 473-1674
EMP: 2
SALES (est): 77.4K Privately Held
SIC: 3069 Fabricated rubber products

(G-14272)
OXBOW CARBON & MINERALS
2815 Indianapolis Blvd (46394-2197)
PHONE..............................219 473-0359
Lonnie Griffith, *Principal*
EMP: 3
SALES (est): 253K Privately Held
SIC: 2911 Petroleum refining

(G-14273)
POLYJOHN ENTERPRISES CORP (PA)
Also Called: Sinks N More
2500 Gaspar Ave (46394-2176)
PHONE..............................219 659-1152
Fax: 219 659-0625
Michael S Cooper, *President*
Ken Cooper, *Vice Pres*
Robert Pully, *Mfg Mgr*
Edith Murray, *Purch Mgr*
Vaughan Smith, *Plant Engr*
◆ EMP: 100
SQ FT: 35,000
SALES (est): 36.4MM Privately Held
WEB: www.polyjohn.com
SIC: 3089 Toilets, portable chemical: plastic

(G-14274)
PRAXAIR INC
166 Indiana 130 (46394)
P.O. Box 712 (46394-0712)
PHONE..............................219 398-3777
Rose Kendall, *Principal*
Ed Jurasevich, *Plant Mgr*
EMP: 12
SALES (corp-wide): 11.4B Publicly Held
SIC: 2813 Industrial gases
PA: Praxair, Inc.
    10 Riverview Dr
    Danbury CT 06810
    203 837-2000

(G-14275)
REGION SIGNS INC
1345 119th St (46394-1627)
PHONE..............................219 473-1616
Carolyn Sarvanidin, *CEO*
EMP: 10
SALES (est): 1.2MM Privately Held
WEB: www.regionsigns.com
SIC: 3993 5099 Signs, not made in custom sign painting shops; safety equipment & supplies

(G-14276)
WALLETS BELTS & STUFF LLC
2042 Schrage Ave (46394-2041)
PHONE..............................219 218-3576

EMP: 2
SALES (est): 110.1K Privately Held
SIC: 3172 Wallets

(G-14277)
WHITING CLEAN ENERGY INC
2155 Standard Ave (46394-2201)
PHONE..............................219 473-0653
Erika Harding, *President*
Richard Moroney, *President*
Cameron Eveland, *General Mgr*
Dale Bell, *District Mgr*
Steven Bray, *Vice Pres*
EMP: 28
SALES (est): 5.9MM
SALES (corp-wide): 240.2B Privately Held
SIC: 3612 Transformers, except electric
HQ: Bp Alternative Energy North America Inc.
    700 Louisiana St Ste 3300
    Houston TX 77002

(G-14278)
WHITING METALS LLC
2230 Indianapolis Blvd (46394-1956)
P.O. Box 482 (46394-0482)
PHONE..............................219 659-6955
Alexander Gross, *Mng Member*
Jeffrey Condon,
Condon Jeffrey,
EMP: 8 EST: 2009
SALES (est): 1.2MM Privately Held
SIC: 3339 Primary nonferrous metals

Wilkinson
Hancock County

(G-14279)
MAINS ENTERPRISES INC
9762 N Nashville Rd (46186-9729)
PHONE..............................765 425-0162
Bill Mains, *President*
Brandon Blackwell, *Vice Pres*
EMP: 2
SALES (est): 162.9K Privately Held
SIC: 3479 7389 Engraving jewelry silverware, or metal; engraving service

(G-14280)
RAIL SCALE INC
5303 N 800 E (46186-9765)
PHONE..............................317 339-6486
EMP: 2 EST: 2011
SALES (est): 150.5K Privately Held
SIC: 3825 Instruments to measure electricity

Williams
Lawrence County

(G-14281)
B M P LOGGING LLC
11202 Swamp Lake Rd (47470-8023)
PHONE..............................812 272-2149
EMP: 3 EST: 2011
SALES (est): 175.9K Privately Held
SIC: 2411 Logging

(G-14282)
INDIAN CREEK QUARRIES LLC
12587 Mount Olive Rd (47470-8038)
PHONE..............................812 388-5622
Sheldon Graber,
EMP: 8
SALES (est): 865.8K Privately Held
SIC: 1422 Crushed & broken limestone

Williamsburg
Wayne County

(G-14283)
BROADCAST CONNECTION INC
2164 W New Garden Rd (47393-9769)
PHONE..............................765 847-2519
EMP: 2 EST: 2008

SALES (est): 120K Privately Held
SIC: 3663 Mfg Radio/Tv Communication Equipment

(G-14284)
RUSTIC ACRES WOODWORKS
4600 W New Garden Rd (47393-9751)
PHONE..............................765 886-5699
David Fisher, *Principal*
EMP: 2
SALES (est): 154.2K Privately Held
SIC: 2431 Millwork

(G-14285)
WILLIAMS COMPANIES INC
6690 W Davis Meyers Rd (47393-9712)
PHONE..............................765 886-6149
John Williams, *General Mgr*
EMP: 2
SALES (corp-wide): 8B Publicly Held
WEB: www.williams.com
SIC: 2911 Gases & liquefied petroleum gases
PA: The Williams Companies Inc
    1 Williams Ctr
    Tulsa OK 74172
    918 573-2000

Williamsport
Warren County

(G-14286)
ACCUBURN WILLIAMSPORT INC
304 W Washington St (47993-1078)
P.O. Box 35 (47993-0035)
PHONE..............................765 762-1100
Fax: 765 762-2982
Marcus McGowen, *President*
EMP: 14
SQ FT: 37,000
SALES: 3.5MM Privately Held
SIC: 3441 Fabricated structural metal; fabricated structural metal for bridges; fabricated structural metal for ships

(G-14287)
BRITTON VAULT CO DOUGLAS
3486 W 400 S (47993-8283)
P.O. Box 333, West Lebanon (47991-0333)
PHONE..............................765 893-4071
Douglas Britton, *President*
EMP: 3
SALES (est): 181.6K Privately Held
SIC: 3272 Burial vaults, concrete or precast terrazzo

(G-14288)
CRYOGENIC SUPPORT SYSTEMS INC
Also Called: Kaniewski & Odle Trckg & Repr
1903 W State Road 63 (47993-8063)
PHONE..............................765 764-4961
Dave Kaniewski, *President*
EMP: 2
SQ FT: 7,200
SALES: 500K Privately Held
SIC: 3441 Fabricated structural metal

(G-14289)
D H GRAVEL COMPANY
7794 S State Road 263 (47993-8271)
PHONE..............................765 893-4914
James Salts, *Principal*
EMP: 3 EST: 2008
SALES (est): 180.1K Privately Held
SIC: 1442 Construction sand & gravel

(G-14290)
GINGER OLIVIAE PUBLISHING LLC
303 S 2nd St (47993-1342)
PHONE..............................765 762-3132
Julie A Gritten, *Principal*
EMP: 3
SALES (est): 83.7K Privately Held
SIC: 2711 Newspapers

(G-14291)
HOSE TECHNOLOGY INC
2520 E Us Hwy 41 (47993)
P.O. Box 206 (47993-0206)
PHONE..............................765 762-5501
Trajan Trajanovski, *President*
Gene McGowen, *President*
Gloria J McGowen, *Admin Sec*
EMP: 20
SALES (est): 3.5MM
SALES (corp-wide): 436.8MM Privately Held
WEB: www.hosetechnology.com
SIC: 3599 Hose, flexible metallic
HQ: Kuriyama Of America, Inc.
    360 E State Pkwy
    Schaumburg IL 60173
    847 755-0360

(G-14292)
INDIANA PRECISION PLASTICS INC
701 State Road 28 E (47993-1071)
PHONE..............................765 762-2452
Fax: 765 762-2453
Tony Sciotto, *Ch of Bd*
Samuel Lombard, *President*
Pattsy Johnson, *Treasurer*
EMP: 12
SQ FT: 20,000
SALES: 1.5MM Privately Held
WEB: www.indianaprecisionplastics.com
SIC: 3089 Injection molding of plastics

(G-14293)
KURI TEC MANUFACTURING INC
2600 E Us Hwy 41 (47993)
P.O. Box 220 (47993-0220)
PHONE..............................765 764-6000
Fax: 765 764-6001
Trajan Trajanovski, *President*
Nathan Rosswurm, *Engineer*
Fred Bobzien, *Treasurer*
EMP: 22
SALES (est): 4.1MM
SALES (corp-wide): 436.8MM Privately Held
WEB: www.kuriyama.com
SIC: 3084 Plastics pipe
HQ: Kuriyama Of America, Inc.
    360 E State Pkwy
    Schaumburg IL 60173
    847 755-0360

(G-14294)
PIONEER ELECTRIC
107 Fall St (47993-1307)
PHONE..............................765 762-2000
Michael Rennick, *Owner*
EMP: 2
SALES (est): 147.3K Privately Held
SIC: 3699 Electrical equipment & supplies

(G-14295)
PRAIRIES EDGE MACHINING INC
4920 W Division Rd (47993-8408)
PHONE..............................765 986-2222
Vincent J Silver, *President*
EMP: 3
SALES: 150K Privately Held
SIC: 3599 Machine shop, jobbing & repair

(G-14296)
ROGERS GROUP INC
Also Called: Interstate Gravel
3255 W 650 S (47993-8212)
PHONE..............................765 893-4463
Fax: 765 893-4970
Sandy Williams, *Branch Mgr*
EMP: 12
SQ FT: 1,500
SALES (corp-wide): 1B Privately Held
WEB: www.rogersgroupinc.com
SIC: 5032 1442 Gravel; sand, construction; construction sand & gravel
PA: Rogers Group, Inc.
    421 Great Circle Rd
    Nashville TN 37228
    615 242-0585

▲ = Import ▼=Export
◆ =Import/Export

(G-14297)
ROGERS GROUP INC
Also Called: Wabash Sand & Gravel
429 W Washington St (47993-1366)
PHONE................................765 762-2660
EMP: 14
SALES (corp-wide): 1.3B Privately Held
SIC: 1442 Construction Sand/Gravel
PA: Rogers Group, Inc.
421 Great Circle Rd
Nashville TN 37228
615 242-0585

(G-14298)
TMF CENTER INC
105 Slauter Ln (47993-1088)
PHONE................................765 762-3800
Lloyd Gowen, Manager
EMP: 182
SALES (corp-wide): 30.9MM Privately
Held
SIC: 3531 Construction machinery attach-
ments
PA: Tmf Center, Inc.
300 W Washington St
Williamsport IN 47993
765 762-1000

(G-14299)
TMF CENTER INC (PA)
300 W Washington St (47993-1078)
PHONE................................765 762-1000
Fax: 765 762-0100
Andy Van Meter, President
Lori Van Meter, Corp Secy
JD Green, Plant Mgr
Lloyd McGowen, CFO
Lori V Meter, Treasurer
EMP: 18
SQ FT: 250,000
SALES (est): 30.9MM Privately Held
WEB: www.tmfcenter.com
SIC: 3531 Construction machinery attach-
ments

(G-14300)
WILLIAMSPORT TIRE MART LLC
18 Front St (47993-1133)
PHONE................................765 762-6315
Jeff Houchens,
EMP: 4
SALES: 50K Privately Held
SIC: 3011 Tires & inner tubes

Winamac
Pulaski County

(G-14301)
BRAUN CORPORATION (DH)
Also Called: Braun Lift
631 W 11th St (46996-1245)
P.O. Box 310 (46996-0310)
PHONE................................574 946-6153
Fax: 574 946-7935
Nick Gutwein, CEO
Matt Beck, Area Mgr
Justin White, Area Mgr
Kevin B McMahon, Exec VP
Jeff Ruff, Exec VP
▼ EMP: 500
SQ FT: 500,000
SALES (est): 153.6MM
SALES (corp-wide): 9.3B Privately Held
WEB: www.entervan.com
SIC: 3999 Wheelchair lifts

(G-14302)
BRAUN CORPORATION
627 W 11th St (46996-1245)
P.O. Box 310 (46996-0310)
PHONE................................574 946-7413
Frank Smith, Manager
EMP: 500
SALES (corp-wide): 9.3B Privately Held
WEB: www.entervan.com
SIC: 3534 3842 Elevators & moving stair-
ways; surgical appliances & supplies
HQ: The Braun Corporation
631 W 11th St
Winamac IN 46996
574 946-6153

(G-14303)
BRAUN MOTOR WORKS INC
(PA)
Also Called: Legend Valley Products
144 S 100 W (46996-7711)
P.O. Box 7 (46996-0007)
PHONE................................574 205-0102
Fax: 574 542-2132
Ralph Braun, CEO
▲ EMP: 7
SALES (est): 3.7MM Privately Held
WEB: www.obrienmfg.com
SIC: 5084 3713 Compaction equipment;
cleaning equipment, high pressure, sand
or steam; processing & packaging equip-
ment; truck & bus bodies

(G-14304)
GALBREATH LLC (HQ)
480 E 150 S (46996-7768)
P.O. Box 220 (46996-0220)
PHONE................................219 946-6631
Fax: 574 946-4579
Nick Franiak, Chief Engr
Larry Harvey, VP Finance
John Defenbaugh,
◆ EMP: 130
SQ FT: 250,000
SALES (est): 45.5MM
SALES (corp-wide): 574.7MM Privately
Held
SIC: 3443 3523 Industrial vessels, tanks &
containers; planting, haying, harvesting &
processing machinery
PA: Wastequip, Llc
6525 Morrison Blvd # 300
Charlotte NC 28211
704 366-7140

(G-14305)
GALBREATH LLC
480 E 150 S (46996-7768)
PHONE................................574 946-6631
Rob Girton, Planning Mgr
EMP: 100
SALES (corp-wide): 574.7MM Privately
Held
SIC: 3443 Fabricated plate work (boiler
shop)
HQ: Galbreath Llc
480 E 150 S
Winamac IN 46996
219 946-6631

(G-14306)
GALFAB LLC (PA)
612 W 11th St (46996-1211)
PHONE................................574 946-7767
Fax: 574 946-7994
Jerome Samson, CEO
Benjamin Scheiner, Vice Pres
Perry Frakes, Plant Mgr
Randy Sommers, Prdtn Mgr
Pam Creech, Buyer
EMP: 66
SALES (est): 12.5MM Privately Held
WEB: www.galfab.com
SIC: 3537 3443 3536 3531 Industrial
trucks & tractors; dumpsters, garbage;
hoists, cranes & monorails; construction
machinery

(G-14307)
HEALEY CUSTOM CABINETRY
LLC
802 N Us Highway 35 (46996-8000)
PHONE................................574 946-4000
Belinda Healey, Principal
EMP: 2 EST: 2014
SALES (est): 237K Privately Held
SIC: 2434 Wood kitchen cabinets

(G-14308)
IRVING MATERIALS INC
1132 S Us Highway 35 (46996-7746)
P.O. Box 458 (46996-0458)
PHONE................................574 946-3754
Fax: 574 946-6701
George Scheffer, Manager
EMP: 10
SALES (corp-wide): 800.6MM Privately
Held
SIC: 3273 Ready-mixed concrete

PA: Irving Materials, Inc.
8032 N State Road 9
Greenfield IN 46140
317 326-3101

(G-14309)
KEVIN KOLISH CORP
Also Called: Protective Coatings
436 N Monticello St (46996-1328)
PHONE................................574 946-3238
Fax: 574 946-3238
Kevin Kolish, President
EMP: 5
SQ FT: 6,000
SALES (est): 467.5K Privately Held
SIC: 3479 Coating of metals & formed
products

(G-14310)
LINK RENTAL COMPANY INC
Also Called: Linkster's
103 E Pearl St (46996-1310)
P.O. Box 158 (46996-0158)
PHONE................................574 946-7373
Mary Sue Link, President
EMP: 4
SALES (est): 380K Privately Held
SIC: 5084 2121 Compaction equipment;
cigars

(G-14311)
MANDALA SCREEN PRINTING
INC
950 E 250 N (46996-8512)
PHONE................................574 946-6290
Greg Hildebrandt, President
EMP: 2 EST: 1976
SALES: 200K Privately Held
SIC: 2759 Decals: printing

(G-14312)
METAL FAB ENGINEERING INC
9341 S State Road 39 (46996-7726)
PHONE................................574 278-7150
Fax: 574 278-3350
Leslie Ezra, President
EMP: 16 EST: 1950
SQ FT: 22,000
SALES (est): 4.3MM Privately Held
WEB: www.metalfabengineering.com
SIC: 3469 3499 3465 Stamping metal for
the trade; novelties & specialties, metal;
body parts, automobile: stamped metal

(G-14313)
ORTMAN MEAT PROCESSING
INC
2035 S State Road 119 (46996-8553)
PHONE................................574 946-7113
Jim Ortman, President
Mary Ortman, Admin Sec
EMP: 4
SALES (est): 355.1K Privately Held
SIC: 2011 Meat packing plants

(G-14314)
PLYMOUTH TUBE COMPANY
Also Called: Winamac Cold Draw
572 W State Road 14 (46996-8873)
P.O. Box 278 (46996-0278)
PHONE................................574 946-6191
Fax: 574 946-3678
Kyle Kroening, General Mgr
EMP: 200
SALES (corp-wide): 277.4MM Privately
Held
WEB: www.plymouth.com
SIC: 3317 3354 3498 3341 Steel pipe &
tubes; aluminum extruded products; fabri-
cated pipe & fittings; secondary nonfer-
rous metals; cold finishing of steel
shapes; blast furnaces & steel mills
PA: Plymouth Tube Company
29w 150 Warrenville Rd
Warrenville IL 60555
630 393-3550

(G-14315)
PLYMOUTH TUBE COMPANY
Winamac Hot
572 W State Road 14 (46996-8873)
PHONE................................574 946-3125
Gavin Ford, Manager
EMP: 98

SALES (corp-wide): 277.4MM Privately
Held
WEB: www.plymouth.com
SIC: 3317 Tubes, seamless steel; tubes,
wrought: welded or lock joint
PA: Plymouth Tube Company
29w 150 Warrenville Rd
Warrenville IL 60555
630 393-3550

(G-14316)
PLYMOUTH TUBE COMPANY
Also Called: Plymouth Tube Co CARbn&ally
572 W State Road 14 (46996-8873)
PHONE................................574 946-6657
Fax: 574 946-7220
Don Van Pelt, President
Chris Krohn, Production
EMP: 116
SALES (corp-wide): 277.4MM Privately
Held
WEB: www.plymouth.com
SIC: 3317 Tubes, wrought: welded or lock
joint
PA: Plymouth Tube Company
29w 150 Warrenville Rd
Warrenville IL 60555
630 393-3550

(G-14317)
PULASKI COUNTY PRESS INC
114 W Main St (46996-1208)
P.O. Box 19 (46996-0019)
PHONE................................574 946-6628
John Haley, President
Carolyn Haley-Majors, Treasurer
Beth Grund, Sales Staff
Elizabeth Haley, Admin Sec
EMP: 9
SQ FT: 7,000
SALES (est): 578.3K Privately Held
WEB: www.pulaskijournal.com
SIC: 2711 2752 Newspapers: publishing
only, not printed on site; commercial print-
ing, offset

(G-14318)
R & D MACHINE SHOP INC
935 N Us Highway 35 (46996-8001)
PHONE................................574 946-6109
Donald Rife, Partner
EMP: 2
SALES (est): 128.4K Privately Held
SIC: 3599 Machine shop, jobbing & repair

(G-14319)
R & S WELDING & FABRICATING
961 W 25 S (46996-7672)
PHONE................................574 946-6816
Fax: 574 946-6815
Robert Rosenbaum, President
Susan Rosenbaum, Vice Pres
EMP: 5
SQ FT: 8,000
SALES (est): 380K Privately Held
WEB: www.rswelding.com
SIC: 1799 3599 7692 Welding on site;
machine shop, jobbing & repair; welding
repair

(G-14320)
S & S PRECAST INC
840 W 25 S (46996)
P.O. Box 138 (46996-0138)
PHONE................................574 946-4123
Clara Schmicker, President
Jim Paulsen, Division Mgr
Susan Shinn, Corp Secy
Bill Vires, Supervisor
EMP: 20
SQ FT: 7,500
SALES (est): 3.2MM Privately Held
WEB: www.sandsprecast.com
SIC: 3272 Concrete products, precast

(G-14321)
S&F MANUFACTURING INC
Also Called: Krystil Klear Filtration
9449 S 550 W (46996-8463)
PHONE................................574 278-7865
Fax: 574 278-7115
Fred J Geyer, President
EMP: 64
SALES (est): 12.6MM Privately Held
SIC: 3569 Filter elements, fluid, hydraulic
line

(G-14322)
THOMAS P KASTEN
Also Called: T & D Property Specialist
4620 N Us Highway 35 (46996-8037)
PHONE................................574 806-4663
Thomas P Kasten, *Owner*
EMP: 2
SALES (est): 125.6K **Privately Held**
SIC: 3585 Heating & air conditioning combination units

(G-14323)
WASTEQUIP MFG
461 E Rosser Rd (46996-8928)
PHONE................................574 946-6631
Robert Rasmussen, *President*
JP McLaughlin, *Manager*
▲ **EMP:** 34
SALES (est): 1.4MM **Privately Held**
SIC: 3549 Metalworking machinery

Winchester
Randolph County

(G-14324)
ALUMINUM FOUNDRIES INC
1036 N Old Highway 27 (47394-8571)
P.O. Box 69 (47394-0069)
PHONE................................765 584-6501
Fax: 765 584-1544
Russell C Symmes, *President*
Steven Bailey, *Vice Pres*
Jean Laughman, *Controller*
EMP: 115 **EST:** 1945
SALES (est): 12.2MM **Privately Held**
WEB: www.aluminumfoundries.com
SIC: 3365 3363 3544 3369 Aluminum & aluminum-based alloy castings; aluminum die-castings; industrial molds; nonferrous foundries

(G-14325)
ANCHOR GLASS CONTAINER CORP
603 E North St (47394-1717)
PHONE................................765 584-6101
Fax: 765 584-3523
Gary Jarrett, *Branch Mgr*
EMP: 416
SALES (corp-wide): 264.1K **Privately Held**
WEB: www.anchorglass.com
SIC: 3221 3229 Packers' ware (containers), glass; pressed & blown glass
HQ: Anchor Glass Container Corporation
　　401 E Jackson St Ste 1100
　　Tampa FL 33602

(G-14326)
CCM INDUSTRIES INC
610 N 100 E (47394-8302)
PHONE................................765 545-0597
Kevin Cook, *Principal*
EMP: 2
SALES (est): 101.8K **Privately Held**
SIC: 3999 Manufacturing industries

(G-14327)
CM TECH
1036 N Old Highway 27 (47394-8571)
PHONE................................765 584-6501
Russell Symmes, *CEO*
EMP: 2
SALES (est): 90.8K **Privately Held**
SIC: 3325 Steel foundries

(G-14328)
ELEYS WOODWORKING
3602 W 200 N (47394-8919)
PHONE................................765 584-3531
David Eley, *Principal*
EMP: 4
SALES (est): 375.6K **Privately Held**
SIC: 2431 Millwork

(G-14329)
ERNEST ENTERPRISES INC
1041 N Old Highway 27 (47394-8571)
PHONE................................765 584-5700
James A Ernest, *President*
EMP: 3
SALES (est): 205.3K **Privately Held**
SIC: 3273 Ready-mixed concrete

(G-14330)
FUTURE SIGNS SALES & SERVICE
709 S Main St (47394-2147)
P.O. Box 211 (47394-0211)
PHONE................................765 749-5180
Dan McKnight, *Principal*
EMP: 3 **EST:** 2009
SALES (est): 226K **Privately Held**
SIC: 3993 Signs & advertising specialties

(G-14331)
HYDROJET SIGNS
Also Called: Hydrojet Signs and Fabricating
707 N Co Rd 400 E (47394)
P.O. Box 537 (47394-0537)
PHONE................................765 584-2125
Leslie Isenberger, *Owner*
EMP: 9
SALES (est): 216.7K **Privately Held**
SIC: 3993 Signs & advertising specialties

(G-14332)
INDIANA MARUJUN LLC
Also Called: I M L
200 Inks Dr (47394-9454)
PHONE................................765 584-7639
Ryoji Takagi, *President*
Atsushi Watanabe, *President*
Mike Goddard, *Vice Pres*
John Pleiman, *Vice Pres*
Mary Anderson, *Purchasing*
▲ **EMP:** 40 **EST:** 1999
SQ FT: 182,500
SALES (est): 17.5MM **Privately Held**
SIC: 3714 Motor vehicle parts & accessories

(G-14333)
JABRA SIGNS & GRAPHICS
406 S Brown St (47394-2203)
PHONE................................765 584-7100
Richard Sanders, *Owner*
EMP: 3
SALES (est): 166.3K **Privately Held**
SIC: 3993 Signs & advertising specialties

(G-14334)
JD NORMAN INDUSTRIES INC
1099 Rainbow Dr (47394-8286)
PHONE................................765 584-6069
Mike Coulter, *Branch Mgr*
EMP: 30
SALES (corp-wide): 183.7MM **Privately Held**
SIC: 3714 3544 Transmission housings or parts, motor vehicle; special dies & tools
PA: Jd Norman Industries, Inc.
　　787 W Belden Ave
　　Addison IL 60101
　　630 458-3700

(G-14335)
KMC ENTERPRISES INC
1094 N Old Highway 27 (47394-8571)
P.O. Box 186 (47394-0186)
PHONE................................765 584-1533
Keith Covert, *President*
Jim Covert, *Treasurer*
EMP: 6
SALES (est): 824.8K **Privately Held**
SIC: 3469 Machine parts, stamped or pressed metal

(G-14336)
MARKSMEN TOOL & DIE INC
230 N Jackson St (47394-1405)
PHONE................................765 584-3600
Rick Mosier, *President*
EMP: 3
SALES: 100K **Privately Held**
SIC: 3544 Special dies, tools, jigs & fixtures

(G-14337)
MAUL TECHNOLOGY CO
300 W Martin St (47394-1012)
P.O. Box 310 (47394-0310)
PHONE................................765 584-2101
Steven J Smith, *President*
Beverly Edwards, *CFO*
EMP: 25
SQ FT: 40,000

SALES (est): 8MM
SALES (corp-wide): 29.2B **Publicly Held**
SIC: 3229 Pressed & blown glass
HQ: Vhc Ltd.
　　300 W Martin St
　　Winchester IN 47394
　　765 584-2101

(G-14338)
NEWS-GAZETTE
224 W Franklin St (47394-1808)
P.O. Box 429 (47394-0429)
PHONE................................765 584-4501
Fax: 765 584-3066
Larry Perrato, *President*
Ricky Williams, *Vice Pres*
Vicki Delhaye, *Graphic Designe*
EMP: 19
SQ FT: 5,000
SALES (est): 1MM **Privately Held**
WEB: www.winchesternewsgazette.com
SIC: 2711 Job printing & newspaper publishing combined

(G-14339)
OMEGA ENTERPRISES INC
732 W Washington St (47394-1425)
P.O. Box 514 (47394-0514)
PHONE................................765 584-1990
Fax: 765 584-2157
Jim Jarrett, *President*
Mary Jarrett, *Admin Sec*
EMP: 22
SALES (est): 3.9MM **Privately Held**
SIC: 3544 Industrial molds

(G-14340)
S P R ATHLETICS LLC
4662 N 100 E (47394-8330)
PHONE................................419 308-2732
Sean Richardson, *Principal*
EMP: 2
SALES (est): 119.8K **Privately Held**
SIC: 3949 Sporting & athletic goods

(G-14341)
STALLION SPORTSWEAR INC (PA)
117 S Main St (47394-1822)
PHONE................................765 584-5097
Fax: 765 584-1075
Philip J Tharp, *President*
Lisa Tharp, *Corp Secy*
Jay Tharp, *Vice Pres*
EMP: 20
SQ FT: 20,500
SALES (est): 1.4MM **Privately Held**
SIC: 2329 2339 5699 2396 Men's & boys' sportswear & athletic clothing; sportswear, women's; sports apparel; automotive & apparel trimmings; men's & boys' furnishings

(G-14342)
TOA WINCHESTER LLC
200 Inks Dr (47394-9454)
PHONE................................765 584-7639
Shinichi Iizuka, *CEO*
Mikio Yoshida, *President*
EMP: 300
SQ FT: 450,000
SALES (est): 6.7MM **Privately Held**
SIC: 3465 Automotive stampings

(G-14343)
VHC LTD (HQ)
Also Called: Maul Technology
300 W Martin St (47394-1012)
P.O. Box 310 (47394-0310)
PHONE................................765 584-2101
Fax: 765 584-1452
James Pike, *Ch of Bd*
Steven J Smith, *President*
Beverly Edwards, *CFO*
▲ **EMP:** 35 **EST:** 1952
SQ FT: 120,000
SALES (est): 8MM
SALES (corp-wide): 29.2B **Publicly Held**
WEB: www.maultechnology.com
SIC: 3559 Glass making machinery: blowing, molding, forming, etc.
PA: Cerberus Capital Management, L.P.
　　875 3rd Ave
　　New York NY 10022
　　212 891-2100

(G-14344)
WICKS PIE
217 Se Greenville Ave (47394-1714)
PHONE................................765 584-8401
Mike Wickersham, *President*
Duane Wickersham, *Chairman*
EMP: 6
SQ FT: 6,000
SALES (est): 338.8K **Privately Held**
SIC: 2064 Fruits: candied, crystallized, or glazed

(G-14345)
WICKS PIES INC
217 Se Greenville Ave (47394-1714)
P.O. Box 268 (47394-0268)
PHONE................................765 584-8401
Michael D Wickersham, *Ch of Bd*
Rob Kelly, *Principal*
Clark G Loney, *Corp Secy*
EMP: 50
SQ FT: 35,000
SALES (est): 8.4MM **Privately Held**
WEB: www.wickspies.com
SIC: 2053 Frozen bakery products, except bread; pies, bakery: frozen

Windfall
Tipton County

(G-14346)
B TRUCKING & BACKHOE INC
3491 E 700 N (46076-9346)
PHONE................................765 437-5960
Tony Browning, *Owner*
EMP: 2
SALES (est): 187.1K **Privately Held**
SIC: 3531 Backhoes

(G-14347)
CHEGAR MANUFACTURING CO INC
951 N Independence St (46076-9213)
P.O. Box 338 (46076-0338)
PHONE................................765 945-7444
Fax: 765 945-7594
Mark McClelland, *President*
EMP: 22 **EST:** 1973
SQ FT: 10,000
SALES (est): 3.8MM **Privately Held**
SIC: 3443 Fabricated plate work (boiler shop)

(G-14348)
MONSANTO COMPANY
908 N Independence St (46076-9213)
P.O. Box 367 (46076-0367)
PHONE................................317 945-7121
Thomas Boller, *Opers Spvr*
Donn Cummings, *Branch Mgr*
EMP: 25
SALES (corp-wide): 41.2B **Privately Held**
WEB: www.monsanto.com
SIC: 2879 Agricultural chemicals
HQ: Monsanto Company
　　800 N Lindbergh Blvd
　　Saint Louis MO 63167
　　314 694-1000

Winona Lake
Kosciusko County

(G-14349)
ABC INDUSTRIES INC (PA)
301 Kings Hwy (46590-1132)
P.O. Box 77, Warsaw (46581-0077)
PHONE................................800 426-0921
Fax: 574 267-2045
Steven Fleagle, *President*
William R Linnemeier, *Vice Pres*
Daren Maierle, *Manager*
Keri Goldwood, *Clerk*
Troy Burns, *Associate*
▲ **EMP:** 85
SQ FT: 85,000
SALES: 32MM **Privately Held**
WEB: www.abc-industries.net
SIC: 1711 3089 5199 Ventilation & duct work contractor; reinforcing mesh, plastic; packaging materials

▲ = Import ▼=Export
◆ =Import/Export

(G-14350)
LAKE HOUSE
720 E Canal St (46590-1070)
PHONE..................................574 265-6945
Jake England, *Principal*
EMP: 4
SALES (est): 335.3K **Privately Held**
SIC: 3949 Surfboards

(G-14351)
LITTLE CRICKET LETTERPRESS
702 Chestnut Ave (46590-1314)
PHONE..................................317 762-2044
Steve Beeson, *Owner*
EMP: 2
SALES (est): 70.9K **Privately Held**
SIC: 2759 Letterpress printing

(G-14352)
OLD GUY WOODCRAFTERS LLC
1312 Freedom Pkwy (46590-5794)
PHONE..................................574 527-9044
Philip W Barkey, *President*
EMP: 2
SALES (est): 129.9K **Privately Held**
SIC: 2511 Wood household furniture

(G-14353)
PICKSLAYS WOODWORKING
1313 Wooster Rd (46590-5721)
PHONE..................................530 388-8697
EMP: 2
SALES (est): 118.2K **Privately Held**
SIC: 2431 Millwork

(G-14354)
WARSAW CUSTOM CABINET
904 Chestnut Ave (46590-1316)
PHONE..................................574 267-5794
Timothy P Mundinger, *Branch Mgr*
EMP: 3
SALES (est): 170.1K
SALES (corp-wide): 301.1K **Privately Held**
SIC: 2434 Wood kitchen cabinets
PA: Warsaw Custom Cabinet
1697 W 350 S
Warsaw IN 46580
574 267-5794

(G-14355)
WHITMAN PUBLICATIONS INC
401 Kings Hwy (46590-1133)
PHONE..................................574 268-2062
Wendall Whitman, *President*
Julie Kline, *Admin Sec*
EMP: 3
SALES (est): 142.2K **Privately Held**
SIC: 2731 Book publishing

(G-14356)
WORKROOM INC
204 13th St (46590-1311)
PHONE..................................574 269-6624
Rhonda Raber, *President*
EMP: 2 EST: 1997
SALES (est): 100.2K **Privately Held**
SIC: 2399 Fabricated textile products

Winslow
Pike County

(G-14357)
MILLS CUSTOM POWDER COATING
1444 E County Road 475 S (47598-8487)
PHONE..................................812 766-0308
Jason Mills, *Principal*
EMP: 2 EST: 2013
SALES (est): 160.1K **Privately Held**
SIC: 3479 Coating of metals & formed products

(G-14358)
RAILWORKS WOOD PRODUCTS INC
3818 S County Road 50 E (47598-8866)
PHONE..................................812 789-5331
Fax: 812 789-5335
Bill Donley, *Principal*
EMP: 2 EST: 2010

SALES (est): 117.3K **Privately Held**
SIC: 2491 Wood preserving

(G-14359)
SISSON STEEL INC
739 S State Road 61 (47598-8453)
PHONE..................................812 354-8701
Jim Gaskins, *President*
Stephanie Gaskins-Mcguire, *Principal*
Greg Mullins, *Principal*
Cindy Gaskins, *Corp Secy*
Emily J Mullins, *Treasurer*
EMP: 17
SQ FT: 16,000
SALES (est): 4.7MM **Privately Held**
SIC: 3441 3446 3444 3443 Building components, structural steel; architectural metalwork; sheet metalwork; fabricated plate work (boiler shop)

(G-14360)
STELLA-JONES CORPORATION
3818 S County Road 50 E (47598-8866)
PHONE..................................812 789-5331
Steve Bashan, *Branch Mgr*
EMP: 19 **Privately Held**
SIC: 2491 Wood preserving; railroad cross bridges & switch ties, treated wood
HQ: Stella-Jones Corporation
1000 Cliffmine Rd Ste 500
Pittsburgh PA 15275

(G-14361)
TANGENT RAIL PRODUCTS INC
3818 S County Road 50 E (47598-8866)
PHONE..................................812 789-5331
Steve Basham, *Branch Mgr*
EMP: 30 **Privately Held**
SIC: 2421 Outdoor wood structural products; railroad ties, sawed
HQ: Tangent Rail Products, Inc.
101 W Station Square Dr # 600
Pittsburgh PA 15219
412 325-0202

Wolcott
White County

(G-14362)
CIVES CORPORATION
Also Called: Cives Steel Company
337 N 700 W (47995-8204)
PHONE..................................219 279-4000
Fax: 219 279-4001
Benjammine Merkling, *Project Mgr*
Richard Connelly, *Branch Mgr*
EMP: 120
SALES (corp-wide): 651.3MM **Privately Held**
WEB: www.cives.com
SIC: 3441 Building components, structural steel
PA: Cives Corporation
3700 Mansell Rd Ste 500
Alpharetta GA 30022
770 993-4424

(G-14363)
DWYER INSTRUMENTS INC
204 E Sherry Ln (47995-8329)
PHONE..................................219 279-2031
Fax: 219 279-2363
Jeff Nelson, *Branch Mgr*
Barabra Gross, *IT/INT Sup*
EMP: 120
SALES (corp-wide): 100MM **Privately Held**
SIC: 3823 Industrial instrmnts msrmnt display/control process variable; pressure measurement instruments, industrial; pressure gauges, dial & digital; manometers, industrial process type
PA: Dwyer Instruments Inc
102 Indiana Highway 212
Michigan City IN 46360
219 879-8868

(G-14364)
H & B PORK INC
6032 N 1200 E (47995-8500)
PHONE..................................219 261-3053
Harold Waibel, *President*
Bruce Waibel, *Corp Secy*
EMP: 4

SALES (est): 365.1K **Privately Held**
SIC: 2011 Pork products from pork slaughtered on site

(G-14365)
INDIANA RIBBON INC (PA)
106 N 2nd St (47995-8326)
P.O. Box 355 (47995-0355)
PHONE..................................219 279-2112
Fax: 219 279-3174
Joseph Hickman, *President*
David Hickman, *Vice Pres*
Jane Johnson, *Treasurer*
▲ EMP: 32
SQ FT: 150,000
SALES (est): 7MM **Privately Held**
WEB: www.inrib.com
SIC: 2655 2241 5949 2631 Spools, fiber: made from purchased material; ribbons; notions, including trim; paperboard mills; automotive & apparel trimmings

(G-14366)
INDIANA RIBBON INC
106 N 2nd St (47995-8326)
P.O. Box 355 (47995-0355)
PHONE..................................219 279-2112
Joseph Hickman, *President*
EMP: 50
SALES (corp-wide): 7MM **Privately Held**
WEB: www.inrib.com
SIC: 2655 4225 Spools, fiber: made from purchased material; general warehousing & storage
PA: Indiana Ribbon Inc
106 N 2nd St
Wolcott IN 47995
219 279-2112

(G-14367)
NEW WOLCOTT ENTERPRISE
125 W Market St (47995-8130)
P.O. Box 78 (47995-0078)
PHONE..................................219 279-2167
Fax: 219 279-2167
Barbara Lawson, *Owner*
EMP: 2
SALES (est): 129.8K **Privately Held**
SIC: 2711 Newspapers: publishing only, not printed on site

Wolcottville
Lagrange County

(G-14368)
BITTERSWEET LLC
2250 W 550 S (46795-9503)
PHONE..................................574 642-1184
Samira Panjaki, *Principal*
EMP: 2 EST: 2013
SALES (est): 127K **Privately Held**
SIC: 2431 Millwork

(G-14369)
BRAUN WITTE PATTERN WORKS INC
4705 S 050 E (46795-9015)
PHONE..................................260 463-8210
EMP: 2
SALES (est): 130K **Privately Held**
SIC: 3553 3543 Mfg Woodworking Machinery Mfg Industrial Patterns

(G-14370)
D AND E SURPLUS LLC
4205 S 900 E (46795-9729)
PHONE..................................260 351-3200
Derek Lower, *Principal*
EMP: 9
SALES (est): 745.9K **Privately Held**
SIC: 2421 Building & structural materials, wood

(G-14371)
HEADLANDS LTD
Also Called: Herrero Printing Co
9125 E 480 S (46795-8713)
PHONE..................................260 426-9884
Fax: 260 424-4507
Diana J Hensch, *President*
William Worrell, *Vice Pres*
EMP: 2
SQ FT: 3,500

SALES: 350K **Privately Held**
SIC: 2759 Labels & seals: printing; letterpress printing

(G-14372)
HEARTLAND TABLE PADS LLC
401 N Main St (46795-9209)
PHONE..................................888 487-2377
Zoran Unger, *Mng Member*
Gary Hill,
EMP: 6
SALES (est): 728K **Privately Held**
SIC: 3292 Table pads & padding, asbestos

(G-14373)
L W WOODWORKING LLC
4635 S 200 W (46795-9508)
PHONE..................................260 463-8938
Lester A Beechy, *Principal*
EMP: 4
SALES (est): 372.6K **Privately Held**
SIC: 2431 Millwork

(G-14374)
MATRIX MANUFACTURING INC
4935 S 300 E (46795-9240)
PHONE..................................260 854-4659
Fax: 260 854-4659
George Tetzloff, *President*
Rob Hanselman, *Vice Pres*
EMP: 8
SQ FT: 15,000
SALES (est): 1.6MM **Privately Held**
SIC: 3444 3544 Sheet metal specialties, not stamped; special dies & tools

(G-14375)
NEWMAN LOGGING INC
6340 E 700 S (46795-8880)
PHONE..................................260 351-3550
Bruce R Newman, *Principal*
EMP: 6
SALES (est): 417K **Privately Held**
SIC: 2411 Logging camps & contractors

(G-14376)
SCHWARTZ WOODWORKING LLC
7240 S 075 W B (46795-9500)
PHONE..................................260 854-9457
Marvin Schwartz,
EMP: 2
SALES (est): 190K **Privately Held**
SIC: 2431 Millwork

(G-14377)
VINYL CREATOR
11889 N Angling Rd-57 (46795-9618)
PHONE..................................260 318-5133
EMP: 2
SALES (est): 149.7K **Privately Held**
SIC: 2759 Commercial printing

(G-14378)
WOODSIDE WOODWORKS
4795 S 200 W (46795-9508)
PHONE..................................260 499-3220
Lavern Bontrager, *Owner*
EMP: 4
SALES (est): 400.6K **Privately Held**
SIC: 2431 Millwork

Wolflake
Noble County

(G-14379)
GROUP DEKKO INC
1075 S Washington St (46796)
P.O. Box 35 (46796-0035)
PHONE..................................260 635-2134
Lee Hastings, *Manager*
EMP: 53
SALES (corp-wide): 2.5B **Publicly Held**
SIC: 3585 3699 3694 Parts for heating, cooling & refrigerating equipment; electrical equipment & supplies; engine electrical equipment
HQ: Group Dekko, Inc.
2505 Dekko Dr
Garrett IN 46738

G
E
O
G
R
A
P
H
I
C

Woodburn
Allen County

(G-14380)
BF GOODRICH TIRE
MANUFACTURING
18906 Old 24 (46797-9048)
P.O. Box 277 (46797-0277)
PHONE....................................260 493-8100
Fax: 260 493-8205
EMP: 3
SALES (est): 359K **Privately Held**
SIC: 5014 3999 Automobile tires & tubes;
atomizers, toiletry

(G-14381)
BUDGET SALES INC
17606 Notestine Rd (46797-9766)
PHONE....................................260 657-5185
Gary Schwartz, *President*
EMP: 2
SALES (est): 333.9K **Privately Held**
SIC: 3429 Manufactured hardware (gen-
eral)

(G-14382)
CUMMINS ENGINE SERVICE
20329 Notestine Rd (46797-9791)
PHONE....................................260 657-1436
Daniel L Cummins, *Owner*
EMP: 3
SALES (est): 351.6K **Privately Held**
SIC: 3519 Internal combustion engines

(G-14383)
HANSON AGGREGATES
MIDWEST LLC
22821 Dawkins Rd (46797-9520)
P.O. Box 32, Paulding OH (45879-0032)
PHONE....................................419 399-4846
Bruce Rowley, *Manager*
EMP: 7
SALES (corp-wide): 20.3B **Privately Held**
SIC: 1422 5032 Limestones, ground; lime-
stone
HQ: Hanson Aggregates Midwest Llc
207 Old Harrods Creek Rd
Louisville KY 40223
502 244-7550

(G-14384)
HORIZON VINYL WINDOWS INC
7434 Brush College Rd (46797-9474)
PHONE....................................260 632-0207
Steve L Mast, *CEO*
EMP: 3
SALES: 300K **Privately Held**
SIC: 2591 Window blinds

(G-14385)
KENN FELD GROUP LLC (PA)
4724 N State Road 101 (46797-9690)
PHONE....................................260 632-4242
Ralph Thieme, *Principal*
EMP: 18
SALES (est): 1.6MM **Privately Held**
SIC: 3531 Excavators: cable, clamshell,
crane, derrick, dragline, etc.

(G-14386)
MICHELIN NORTH AMERICA INC
Also Called: BF Goodrich
18906 Old 24 (46797-9048)
P.O. Box 277 (46797-0277)
PHONE....................................260 493-8100
Bill Elks, *Branch Mgr*
Randy Hayden, *Manager*
Don Weimer, *Info Tech Mgr*
Tom Beesley, *Data Admn*
Robert Hastings, *Maintence Staff*
EMP: 1335
SALES (corp-wide): 803.2MM **Privately
Held**
WEB: www.michelin-us.com
SIC: 3011 Automobile tires, pneumatic
HQ: Michelin North America, Inc.
1 Parkway S
Greenville SC 29615
864 458-5000

(G-14387)
MIDWEST TILE AND CONCRETE
PDTS (PA)
4309 Webster Rd (46797-9571)
PHONE....................................260 749-5173
Fax: 260 493-2477
Terry Hamlin, *President*
Joseph Schaeffer, *Corp Secy*
Jim Menzie, *Opers Mgr*
Dane Adams, *Controller*
Ryan Hartup, *Sales Staff*
EMP: 2
SQ FT: 7,000
SALES (est): 6.7MM **Privately Held**
SIC: 3272 5032 Septic tanks, concrete;
sewer pipe, clay

(G-14388)
MIDWEST TILE AND CONCRETE
PDTS
Also Called: Midwest Tile & Concrete Pdts
4309 Webster Rd (46797-9571)
PHONE....................................260 749-5173
Fax: 260 478-6738
Linda Ohlwine, *Manager*
EMP: 2
SALES (est): 224.7K
SALES (corp-wide): 6.7MM **Privately
Held**
SIC: 3272 Concrete products
PA: Midwest Tile And Concrete Products
Inc
4309 Webster Rd
Woodburn IN 46797
260 749-5173

(G-14389)
MJS CONCRETE
19427 Notestine Rd (46797-9672)
PHONE....................................260 341-5640
Steve Schmucker, *Principal*
EMP: 2
SALES (est): 91.3K **Privately Held**
SIC: 3272 Concrete products

(G-14390)
SPECIAL PRODUCT SERVICES
INC
22416 Front St (46797-9682)
P.O. Box 95 (46797-0095)
PHONE....................................260 632-1302
Fax: 260 632-4056
Janice Ehle, *President*
Lynn Ehle, *General Mgr*
EMP: 10
SQ FT: 10,000
SALES (est): 1.1MM **Privately Held**
WEB: www.specialproductservices.com
SIC: 3089 Thermoformed finished plastic
products

(G-14391)
WATTRE INC
9301 Roberts Rd (46797-9758)
PHONE....................................260 657-3701
Curtis Graber, *President*
Julia Graber, *Treasurer*
EMP: 5
SALES (est): 641.2K **Privately Held**
WEB: www.customsounddesigns.com
SIC: 3679 Electronic loads & power sup-
plies

(G-14392)
WOODBURN DIAMOND DIE CO
INC (PA)
23012 Tile Mill Rd (46797-9644)
P.O. Box 155 (46797-0155)
PHONE....................................260 632-4217
Fax: 260 632-4388
Farver Rex C, *President*
Jane E Farver, *Corp Secy*
Chris Farver, *Vice Pres*
Mike Blough, *QC Mgr*
Deb Hamilton, *QC Mgr*
▲ EMP: 82 EST: 1958
SQ FT: 21,000
SALES (est): 12.1MM **Privately Held**
WEB: www.woodburndd.com
SIC: 3544 3915 3291 Diamond dies, met-
alworking; jewelers' materials & lapidary
work; abrasive products

Worthington
Greene County

(G-14393)
BUNGE NORTH AMERICA INC
7383 N 100 W (47471-6310)
PHONE....................................812 875-3113
Wade Ellis, *General Mgr*
EMP: 48 **Privately Held**
SIC: 2041 Corn flour
HQ: Bunge North America, Inc.
1391 Tmberlake Manor Pkwy
Chesterfield MO 63017
314 292-2000

(G-14394)
DMP LLC
2868 W 325 N (47471-5149)
PHONE....................................812 699-0086
Dia Serach, *CEO*
Mike Gallagher, *Marketing Staff*
EMP: 2
SALES (est): 160.9K **Privately Held**
SIC: 1541 3949 2819 Food products
manufacturing or packing plant construc-
tion; team sports equipment; inorganic
metal compounds or salts

(G-14395)
OWEN COUNTY PALLET
9628 Stahl Rd (47471-6265)
PHONE....................................812 859-4617
Samuel Hochetler, *Owner*
EMP: 4
SALES: 500K **Privately Held**
SIC: 2448 7389 Pallets, wood & wood with
metal;

Wyatt
St. Joseph County

(G-14396)
BADLANDS PICK UP VAN ACC
SALV
Also Called: Badlands Accessories Salvage
66521 State Rd 331 (46595)
PHONE....................................574 633-2156
Gunther Bardan, *Owner*
EMP: 2
SALES (est): 162.6K **Privately Held**
WEB: www.badlandsjournal.com
SIC: 3711 Trucks, pickup, assembly of

Yoder
Allen County

(G-14397)
DEDICATED SOFTWARE
Also Called: Affordable Computer Repair
6018 Hamilton Rd (46798-9787)
PHONE....................................260 341-4166
Don Huguenard, *Owner*
EMP: 2 EST: 1983
SALES (est): 133.7K **Privately Held**
WEB: www.dedicatedsoftware.net
SIC: 7372 Prepackaged software

(G-14398)
HGC CUSTOM CHROME
17507 Wayne St (46798-9521)
PHONE....................................260 447-4731
John Hoffmeier, *Principal*
EMP: 4 EST: 2012
SALES (est): 254.7K **Privately Held**
SIC: 7532 3471 Body shop, automotive;
electroplating & plating

(G-14399)
PLEASANT INDUSTRIES INC
6045 Hamilton Rd (46798-9787)
PHONE....................................260 638-4699
J Lynn French, *President*
Vicky French, *Treasurer*
EMP: 5 EST: 2001
SQ FT: 2,000
SALES (est): 410K **Privately Held**
SIC: 3599 Machine shop, jobbing & repair

Yorktown
Delaware County

(G-14400)
A & W FIREARMS
8400 W County Road 400 S (47396-9500)
PHONE....................................765 716-6856
Adam Harrod, *Partner*
Wendy Harrod, *Partner*
EMP: 4
SALES (est): 159.9K **Privately Held**
SIC: 5941 7389 3482 3489 Firearms;
ammunition; ; small arms ammunition;
cartridges, 30 mm. & below; guns or gun
parts, over 30 mm.; firearms & ammuni-
tion, except sporting; firearms, except
sporting

(G-14401)
AUL IN THE FAMILY TOOL AND
DIE
Also Called: Aftco Manufacturing
9801 W Jackson St (47396-9657)
PHONE....................................765 759-5161
Fax: 765 759-6733
Staci Corle, *Ch of Bd*
Adrian Aul, *Ch of Bd*
Mark Aul, *President*
EMP: 4 EST: 1964
SQ FT: 5,000
SALES: 1.5MM **Privately Held**
SIC: 3544 Special dies & tools

(G-14402)
BBS CELEBRATION CENTER
1019 S Yorkchester Dr (47396-9396)
PHONE....................................765 730-6575
Barbara Baker, *Owner*
EMP: 2
SALES (est): 129.6K **Privately Held**
SIC: 3999 5199 5947 Manufacturing in-
dustries; gifts & novelties; gifts & novel-
ties; balloon shops

(G-14403)
DAKOTA ENGINEERING INC
Also Called: Fabcomp
2401 N Executive Park Dr (47396-9806)
PHONE....................................317 546-8460
Fax: 317 546-8467
Alan Jones Jr, *President*
Stephen Murray, *Treasurer*
▲ EMP: 22
SQ FT: 18,000
SALES (est): 4.2MM **Privately Held**
WEB: www.dakotaengineering.com
SIC: 3599 Machine shop, jobbing & repair

(G-14404)
G & T DISTRIBUTION
9108 W Sutherland Ave (47396-1642)
PHONE....................................765 759-8611
George Doll, *Owner*
EMP: 2 EST: 2000
SALES (est): 130K **Privately Held**
SIC: 3699 Electrical equipment & supplies

(G-14405)
HOLLOWAY VINYL SIGNS GRAP
4100 S Native Ct (47396-9124)
PHONE....................................765 717-1581
William Holloway, *Principal*
EMP: 3
SALES (est): 197.4K **Privately Held**
SIC: 3993 Signs & advertising specialties

(G-14406)
INDUSTRIES LLC
13501 W River Valley Rd (47396-9407)
PHONE....................................765 759-5577
EMP: 2 EST: 2007
SALES (est): 85K **Privately Held**
SIC: 3999 Mfg Misc Products

(G-14407)
MIASA AUTOMOTIVE LLC
2101 S West St (47396-1148)
PHONE....................................765 751-9967
Richard Hill, *General Mgr*
Christopher Bering, *CFO*
Joaquin Echarte, *Mng Member*
▲ EMP: 22

SALES (est): 7.1MM **Privately Held**
SIC: 3714 Power transmission equipment, motor vehicle

(G-14408)
MURSIX CORPORATION
Also Called: Twoson Tool Company
2401 N Executive Park Dr (47396-9806)
P.O. Box 591, Muncie (47308-0591)
PHONE..................................765 282-2221
Fax: 765 289-2255
Steve Murray, *Ch of Bd*
Todd A Murray, *President*
Karen Beard, *Vice Pres*
Shawn Cummings, *Project Mgr*
Terry Simmons, *Project Mgr*
▲ EMP: 200
SQ FT: 85,000
SALES (est): 63.9MM **Privately Held**
SIC: 3469 3679 Stamping metal for the trade; harness assemblies for electronic use: wire or cable

(G-14409)
OLETA PUBLISHING CO INC
3009 S Sugar Maple St (47396-9441)
P.O. Box 7187, Fishers (46038-7187)
PHONE..................................765 730-7195
Jonathan Newby, *President*
EMP: 2
SALES (est): 120K **Privately Held**
SIC: 2741 Catalogs: publishing & printing

(G-14410)
PRINTING CREATIONS INC
2410 S Vine St (47396-1516)
PHONE..................................765 759-9679
Fax: 765 759-8773
Carolyn A Grieves, *President*
Michael Grieves, *Vice Pres*
EMP: 3
SQ FT: 2,600
SALES (est): 369.2K **Privately Held**
WEB: www.printingcreations.com
SIC: 2752 7311 8743 Commercial printing, offset; advertising agencies; public relations services

(G-14411)
R & L DIE CO INC
4801 S County Road 700 W (47396-9406)
PHONE..................................765 759-6880
EMP: 2
SALES (est): 133.9K **Privately Held**
SIC: 3544 Special dies & tools

(G-14412)
TFX PLATING COMPANY LLC
2401 N Executive Park Dr (47396-9806)
PHONE..................................765 289-2436
Todd Murray, *Mng Member*
Brad Murray,
Stephen F Murray,
EMP: 8
SQ FT: 10,000
SALES (est): 995.5K **Privately Held**
WEB: www.tfxplating.com
SIC: 3471 Electroplating of metals or formed products

Zanesville
Allen County

(G-14413)
LENGERICH MEATS INC
3095 W Van Horn St (46799)
PHONE..................................260 638-4123
Jim Strephen, *President*
William Stephan, *Principal*
Richard Keiffer, *Treasurer*
EMP: 20
SALES (est): 1.1MM **Privately Held**
SIC: 2011 0751 5421 Meat packing plants; slaughtering: custom livestock services; meat & fish markets

Zionsville
Boone County

(G-14414)
4 KIDS BOOKS
4450 Weston Pointe Dr # 120 (46077-7207)
PHONE..................................317 733-8710
Cynthia Thompson, *Owner*
EMP: 13
SALES (est): 1.2MM **Privately Held**
SIC: 3944 Books, toy: picture & cutout

(G-14415)
A SIGN-BY-DESIGN INC
4725 W 106th St (46077-8761)
P.O. Box 691 (46077-0691)
PHONE..................................317 876-7900
Beverly Miller, *President*
Charles Miller, *Vice Pres*
EMP: 30
SQ FT: 12,000
SALES (est): 4.1MM **Privately Held**
WEB: www.asignbydesign.com
SIC: 3993 Electric signs

(G-14416)
AMERICAN LABEL PRODUCTS INC
4949 W 106th St (46077-8717)
P.O. Box 488 (46077-0488)
PHONE..................................317 873-9850
Michelle Misterka, *President*
Matt Misterka, *Manager*
EMP: 3
SQ FT: 3,000
SALES (est): 544.8K **Privately Held**
WEB: www.americanlabelproducts.com
SIC: 2672 Adhesive papers, labels or tapes: from purchased material

(G-14417)
ANYPRINT LLC
6546 Yorkshire Cir (46077-9147)
PHONE..................................317 402-5979
Jody Ashley, *Principal*
EMP: 2 EST: 2015
SALES (est): 140.3K **Privately Held**
SIC: 2752 Commercial printing, lithographic

(G-14418)
APPLIED MATERIAL SOLUTIONS LLC
3610 Mossy Rock Dr (46077-5504)
PHONE..................................317 769-3829
Chris Hammond, *Principal*
EMP: 2
SALES (est): 126.9K **Privately Held**
SIC: 3559 Semiconductor manufacturing machinery

(G-14419)
B HAPPY PEANUT BUTTER LLC
340 Raintree Dr (46077-2016)
PHONE..................................317 733-3831
Jonathan Weed, *Owner*
EMP: 2
SALES (est): 165.6K **Privately Held**
SIC: 2099 Peanut butter

(G-14420)
BCBG MAX AZRIA GROUP LLC
2325 Aberdeen Blvd (46077)
PHONE..................................913 631-0090
EMP: 2
SALES (corp-wide): 979.1MM **Privately Held**
SIC: 2335 Women's, juniors' & misses' dresses
HQ: Bcbg Max Azria Group, Llc
2761 Fruitland Ave
Vernon CA 90058
323 589-2224

(G-14421)
BCD & ASSOCIATES
10830 Bennett Pkwy Ste G (46077-1188)
PHONE..................................317 873-5394
Fax: 317 873-1416
Duane Durkos, *Owner*
EMP: 5

SQ FT: 2,500
SALES: 350K **Privately Held**
WEB: www.bcdandassociates.com
SIC: 3841 3599 Diagnostic apparatus, medical; custom machinery

(G-14422)
BENTZ TRANSPORT PRODUCTS INC
3943 Weston Pointe Dr (46077-8584)
PHONE..................................260 622-9100
Keith Bentz, *President*
EMP: 15
SQ FT: 45,000
SALES: 4.5MM **Privately Held**
WEB: www.bentzusa.com
SIC: 3713 3714 Truck bodies & parts; truck cabs for motor vehicles; motor vehicle parts & accessories

(G-14423)
BOILERS & MORE INC
8639 W 96th St (46077-8432)
PHONE..................................317 873-2007
David Ratliff, *Principal*
EMP: 4
SALES (est): 717.5K **Privately Held**
SIC: 3443 8748 Boilers: industrial, power, or marine; environmental consultant

(G-14424)
CALAVERA TOOL WORKS LLC
9823 Buttondown Ln (46077-8132)
PHONE..................................765 481-6775
Michael Williams, *Principal*
EMP: 2
SALES (est): 98.6K **Privately Held**
SIC: 3599 Machine shop, jobbing & repair

(G-14425)
CELESTIAL DESIGNS LLC
80 N First St (46077-1544)
PHONE..................................317 733-3110
Fax: 317 733-0110
Kathy Tonetti, *Owner*
Karen Maier, *Office Mgr*
EMP: 2
SALES (est): 120K **Privately Held**
WEB: www.shopcelestialdesigns.com
SIC: 7389 5699 5199 5162 Sewing contractor; customized clothing & apparel; advertising specialties; plastics materials; screen printing; emblems, embroidered

(G-14426)
CHEMIGEN INC
6584 Regents Park Dr (46077-7306)
PHONE..................................317 902-6630
Greg Merrell, *CEO*
Brian Johnstone, *COO*
EMP: 4
SALES (est): 32.6K **Privately Held**
SIC: 2834 Pharmaceutical preparations

(G-14427)
CLEAR SOFTWARE LLC
10 S Main St (46077-1518)
PHONE..................................317 732-8831
Jonathan Gilman, *CEO*
Adam Kosecki, *Vice Pres*
Brad Deveau, *Manager*
Scott Woodall, *Manager*
Joyce Carpenter, *Director*
EMP: 5
SALES (est): 402.6K **Privately Held**
SIC: 7372 Business oriented computer software

(G-14428)
COMPOST BINS PRO
10000 Fox Trce (46077-9790)
PHONE..................................317 873-0555
David Norris, *Principal*
EMP: 3
SALES (est): 187.5K **Privately Held**
SIC: 2875 Compost

(G-14429)
DEGLER MKTG & MAILING SVCS
8930 Cooper Rd (46077-8493)
PHONE..................................317 873-5550
Ward Degler, *Owner*
Jeanne Degler, *Partner*
EMP: 23

SALES: 750K **Privately Held**
SIC: 7331 7311 2741 Direct mail advertising services; advertising agencies; catalogs: publishing & printing

(G-14430)
DELTA MICROINVERTER LLC
6779 Woodcliff Cir (46077-9173)
PHONE..................................317 274-5935
Joseph Trebley, *Manager*
EMP: 3 EST: 2014
SALES (est): 159K **Privately Held**
SIC: 3629 Inverters, nonrotating: electrical

(G-14431)
FANIMATION INC
Also Called: Wind Deco
10983 Bennett Pkwy (46077-9187)
PHONE..................................317 733-4113
Tom Frampton, *CEO*
Nathan Frampton, *President*
Ed Frampton, *Vice Pres*
Heidi Watson, *Purch Agent*
Jay Boughner, *Controller*
◆ EMP: 45
SQ FT: 16,000
SALES: 36MM **Privately Held**
WEB: www.fanimation.com
SIC: 3634 Ceiling fans

(G-14432)
FINLEY CREEK VINEYARDS LLC ✪
795 S Us 421 (46077-4216)
PHONE..................................317 769-5483
EMP: 2 EST: 2017
SALES (est): 62.3K **Privately Held**
SIC: 2084 Wines

(G-14433)
GAMEFACE INC
1555 W Oak St Ste 100 (46077-1959)
P.O. Box 342 (46077-0342)
PHONE..................................317 363-8855
Stacy Smallwood, *President*
Richard Calkins, *Vice Pres*
▲ EMP: 4
SQ FT: 1,200
SALES: 367.5K **Privately Held**
SIC: 3949 Sporting & athletic goods

(G-14434)
GOOD IMPRESSIONS PRINTING INC
170 W Hawthorne St (46077-1617)
PHONE..................................317 873-6809
Fax: 317 873-5222
EMP: 3
SQ FT: 1,200
SALES (est): 331.9K **Privately Held**
SIC: 2752 Quick And Commerical Printing

(G-14435)
GRAVEL CONVEYORS INC (PA)
5005 W 106th St (46077-9228)
PHONE..................................317 873-8686
Fax: 317 873-9431
Michael Pettijohn, *President*
Joe A Pettijohn, *Vice Pres*
Ronald Pettijohn, *Admin Sec*
EMP: 15
SALES (est): 5.6MM **Privately Held**
SIC: 3535 4212 3713 3594 Conveyors & conveying equipment; dump truck haulage; truck & bus bodies; fluid power pumps & motors

(G-14436)
GREEN APPLE UTILITIES LLC ✪
1475 W Oak St Unit 5063 (46077-2037)
PHONE..................................440 278-0183
EMP: 2 EST: 2018
SALES (est): 85.9K **Privately Held**
SIC: 3571 Personal computers (microcomputers)

(G-14437)
GVS FILTER TECHNOLOGY INC
4522 Winterspring Cres (46077-9276)
PHONE..................................317 442-3925
Hugh Chilton, *Principal*
Chris Schoonover, *Vice Pres*
EMP: 2

GEOGRAPHIC

SALES (est): 204K **Privately Held**
SIC: 3569 Filters

(G-14438)
HOPWOOD CELLARS
12 E Cedar St (46077-1501)
PHONE..................................317 873-4099
Ron Hopwood, *Principal*
EMP: 9
SALES (est): 908K **Privately Held**
SIC: 2084 Wines

(G-14439)
INDY MEDICAL SUPPLIES LLC
650 S 800 E (46077-9716)
PHONE..................................866 744-9013
Harry Coleman, *President*
Bonita Webster, *Vice Pres*
EMP: 5
SALES (est): 765.7K **Privately Held**
SIC: 5047 2836 Medical equipment & supplies; electro-medical equipment; veterinary biological products

(G-14440)
JENSEN PUBLICATIONS INC
7333 Fox Hollow Rdg (46077-8206)
PHONE..................................317 514-8864
Chris Jensen, *Principal*
EMP: 4 EST: 2011
SALES (est): 222.9K **Privately Held**
SIC: 2741 Miscellaneous publishing

(G-14441)
JERRY L FUELLING
8470 E 300 S (46077-8696)
PHONE..................................317 709-6978
Jerry L Fuelling, *Principal*
EMP: 3
SALES (est): 222.4K **Privately Held**
SIC: 2869 Fuels

(G-14442)
JEZROC METALWORKS LLC
205 S 1100 E (46077-8505)
PHONE..................................317 417-1132
Matt Quanrud, *Owner*
EMP: 4 EST: 2010
SALES (est): 591K **Privately Held**
SIC: 3441 Fabricated structural metal

(G-14443)
JOHNSON SAFE COMPANY
8750 E 200 S (46077-8796)
PHONE..................................317 876-7233
Fax: 317 876-7233
Jeffrey D Johnson, *Owner*
EMP: 4
SQ FT: 3,000
SALES (est): 190K **Privately Held**
SIC: 5999 3499 Vaults & safes; safes & vaults, metal

(G-14444)
KIDS WORLD PRODUCTIONS INC
11551 Willow Bend Dr (46077-7717)
PHONE..................................317 674-6090
Don M Newman, *President*
Stacy Johnson, *Vice Pres*
Troy Holder, *Admin Sec*
▲ EMP: 4
SALES (est): 292.4K **Privately Held**
SIC: 2731 5999 Book publishing; toiletries, cosmetics & perfumes

(G-14445)
KING TUT INC
4720 Pebblepointe Pass (46077-8950)
P.O. Box 314 (46077-0314)
PHONE..................................317 938-9907
Amardeep Singh, *Principal*
EMP: 5
SALES (est): 90.9K **Privately Held**
SIC: 2711 Newspapers

(G-14446)
MAG SOFTWARE INC
49 Boone Vlg Ste 275 (46077-1231)
PHONE..................................317 755-4080
Mickey James, *President*
Gary James, *General Mgr*
EMP: 2
SALES: 40K **Privately Held**
SIC: 7372 Application computer software

(G-14447)
MGTC INC (DH)
11541 Trail Ridge Pl (46077-9726)
PHONE..................................317 780-0609
Thomas J Wilson, *President*
Theresa Mason, *Vice Pres*
Robert D Wilson, *Vice Pres*
Tony Pounds, *Plant Mgr*
Carol Totten, *Prdtn Mgr*
▲ EMP: 48
SQ FT: 25,000
SALES (est): 16.7MM
SALES (corp-wide): 313.3MM **Publicly Held**
WEB: www.motionwear.com
SIC: 2339 Sportswear, women's
HQ: Fila U.S.A., Inc.
930 Ridgebrook Rd Ste 200
Sparks MD 21152
410 773-3000

(G-14448)
MGTC INC
Also Called: Kimber Creek Limited
11541 Trail Ridge Pl (46077-9726)
PHONE..................................317 873-8697
Thomas J Wilson, *President*
EMP: 3
SALES (est): 274.3K **Privately Held**
SIC: 3089 Automotive parts, plastic

(G-14449)
MID WEST DIGITAL EXPRESS INC
Also Called: Corporate Printing
10815 Deandra Dr (46077-9253)
PHONE..................................317 733-1214
Fax: 317 733-1215
Joseph Matly, *President*
EMP: 14
SQ FT: 8,000
SALES (est): 4.4MM **Privately Held**
WEB: www.corpprinting.com
SIC: 2752 7336 Commercial printing, offset; graphic arts & related design

(G-14450)
NAPTOWN ETCHING
7313 Mayflower Park Dr (46077-7903)
PHONE..................................317 733-8776
Tony Hughes, *Owner*
EMP: 2 EST: 2015
SALES (est): 48K **Privately Held**
SIC: 3229 Pressed & blown glass

(G-14451)
NITTO INC
Also Called: Nistem
10505 Bennett Pkwy 300 (46077-7847)
PHONE..................................317 879-2840
Mak Sakuraeda, *Manager*
EMP: 2
SALES (corp-wide): 8B **Privately Held**
SIC: 3053 5085 Gaskets, packing & sealing devices; gaskets & seals
HQ: Nitto, Inc.
809 Principal Ct
Chesapeake VA 23320
757 436-5540

(G-14452)
NOEL STUDIO INC
75 N Main St (46077-1547)
P.O. Box 248 (46077-0248)
PHONE..................................317 297-1117
Nancy Noel, *President*
▼ EMP: 12
SQ FT: 6,500
SALES (est): 1MM **Privately Held**
WEB: www.nanoel.com
SIC: 2741 5199 5999 Posters: publishing only, not printed on site; art copy: publishing only, not printed on site; art goods; art dealers

(G-14453)
NPP PACKAGING GRAPHICS
610 White Oak Ct (46077-9049)
PHONE..................................317 522-2010
Dave Norton, *Vice Pres*
EMP: 2
SALES (est): 173.9K **Privately Held**
SIC: 2759 Commercial printing

(G-14454)
P413 CORPORATION
Also Called: UPS Store 6991
7163 Whitestown Pkwy (46077-7626)
PHONE..................................317 769-0679
Donald Barrett, *President*
EMP: 3
SQ FT: 1,580
SALES: 300K **Privately Held**
SIC: 7389 2759 Courier or messenger service; commercial printing

(G-14455)
PERFECT SEATING LLC
10730 Bennett Pkwy A (46077-8180)
PHONE..................................317 733-1284
EMP: 10
SQ FT: 5,400
SALES (est): 840K **Privately Held**
SIC: 2211 Cotton Broadwoven Fabric Mill

(G-14456)
PIENIADZE INC
Also Called: Game Face Brands
1555 W Oak St Ste 100 (46077-1959)
P.O. Box 342 (46077-0342)
PHONE..................................888 226-6241
Stacy Smallwood, *President*
Richard Calkins, *Vice Pres*
EMP: 3
SQ FT: 1,200
SALES: 487K **Privately Held**
SIC: 2844 3949 Toilet preparations; arrows, archery

(G-14457)
POSTERS 2 PRINTS LLC
9389 Timberwolf Ln (46077-8322)
PHONE..................................317 769-3784
Michael Slate, *Principal*
EMP: 2
SALES (est): 110K **Privately Held**
SIC: 2752 Commercial printing, lithographic

(G-14458)
RABBIT LANE LLC
1765 Continental Dr (46077-8755)
PHONE..................................317 733-8380
Alex J Varas, *Principal*
EMP: 3
SALES (est): 196.8K **Privately Held**
SIC: 2066 Chocolate

(G-14459)
REDMAN INDUSTRIES LLC
6696 E Stonegate Dr (46077-8196)
PHONE..................................317 768-3004
Michael Redman, *Owner*
EMP: 2
SALES (est): 77K **Privately Held**
SIC: 3999 Manufacturing industries

(G-14460)
REMCO PRODUCTS CORPORATION
Also Called: Poly Pro Tools
4735 W 106th St (46077-8761)
P.O. Box 698 (46077-0698)
PHONE..................................317 876-9856
Fax: 317 876-9858
Mike Garrison, *President*
Dan Buckley, *Business Mgr*
Travis Clark, *Business Mgr*
Eric Perez, *Business Mgr*
Cary Wagner, *Accounting Mgr*
▲ EMP: 19
SQ FT: 27,000
SALES (est): 4.6MM **Privately Held**
WEB: www.remcoproducts.com
SIC: 3089 Plastic containers, except foam; tubs, plastic (containers); plastic processing

(G-14461)
SELVINS MARBLE & GRAN SP LLC
10806 Deandra Dr (46077-9240)
PHONE..................................317 370-4237
Selvin Cordero, *President*
EMP: 3
SQ FT: 2,900
SALES (est): 185.2K **Privately Held**
SIC: 3281 Curbing, granite or stone

(G-14462)
SHARP WRAPS LLC
1664 Williams Way (46077-1184)
PHONE..................................317 989-8447
Joshua D Sharp,
EMP: 2
SALES (est): 90.8K **Privately Held**
SIC: 3713 Specialty motor vehicle bodies

(G-14463)
SIGHTWAVEOPTICS
4139 Creekside Pass (46077-9288)
PHONE..................................317 513-8322
EMP: 2
SALES (est): 110K **Privately Held**
SIC: 3827 Mfg Optical Instruments/Lenses

(G-14464)
SOMER INC
Also Called: Somer Dental Laboratories
11707 N Michigan Rd (46077-9325)
P.O. Box 250 (46077-0250)
PHONE..................................317 873-1111
Fax: 317 873-1124
Larry Sowinski, *President*
Keith Spencer, *Treasurer*
EMP: 32
SQ FT: 14,700
SALES (est): 2.5MM **Privately Held**
WEB: www.somer.com
SIC: 8072 8021 3843 3842 Crown & bridge production; offices & clinics of dentists; dental equipment & supplies; surgical appliances & supplies

(G-14465)
SPORTSMANIA SALES INC
260 S First St Ste 4 (46077-1602)
PHONE..................................317 873-5501
Bob Rogers, *President*
Sandra Rogers, *Corp Secy*
EMP: 4
SQ FT: 1,400
SALES (est): 325.6K **Privately Held**
SIC: 2395 5699 Emblems, embroidered; T-shirts, custom printed

(G-14466)
STENIDY INDUSTRIES INC
10305 Cottonwood Ct (46077-8388)
PHONE..................................317 873-5343
Stephen L Kessel, *President*
Stephen Kessel, *Principal*
Elaine Kessel, *Admin Sec*
EMP: 2
SQ FT: 1,500
SALES (est): 300.4K **Privately Held**
SIC: 2821 Molding compounds, plastics

(G-14467)
TAFT AVIATION PROPERTY LLC
11329 E State Road 32 (46077-9757)
PHONE..................................317 769-4487
Mark Montgomery, *Mng Member*
EMP: 3
SALES (est): 212.3K **Privately Held**
SIC: 3728 Refueling equipment for use in flight, airplane

(G-14468)
TEN POINT TRIM CORP
4750 Nw Plaza West Dr (46077-9181)
PHONE..................................317 875-5424
Fax: 317 337-0580
Thomas J Sampsell, *President*
Shelly S Williams, *Exec VP*
Thomas L McNulty, *Vice Pres*
Tom McNulty, *Vice Pres*
Charlie Williamson, *Plant Mgr*
EMP: 40
SQ FT: 70,000
SALES (est): 15.9MM **Privately Held**
WEB: www.tenpointtrim.com
SIC: 3444 3449 3316 Forming machine work, sheet metal; miscellaneous metalwork; cold finishing of steel shapes

(G-14469)
TINTS & PRINTS BY TIERNEY LLC
4211 Honeysuckle Ln (46077-8536)
PHONE..................................317 769-5895
Tierney Williams, *Owner*
EMP: 2 EST: 2011

SALES (est): 111.1K **Privately Held**
SIC: **2752** Commercial printing, lithographic

(G-14470)
VILLAGE CUSTOM EMBROIDERY INC
80 N First St (46077-1544)
PHONE..................................317 733-3110
Karen P Maier, *President*
EMP: 3
SALES (est): 389.5K **Privately Held**
WEB: www.villagecustomembroidery.com
SIC: **2395** Embroidery & art needlework

(G-14471)
WOODGRAIN CONSTRUCTION INC
3380 S 875 E (46077-9527)
PHONE..................................317 873-5608
Tom Harvard, *President*
Scott Staser, *Vice Pres*
EMP: 8
SALES (est): 630K **Privately Held**
SIC: **2491** Piles, foundation & marine construction: treated wood

(G-14472)
XEROX CORPORATION
4545 Northwestern Dr (46077-7834)
PHONE..................................317 471-4220
John Robinson, *President*
EMP: 7
SALES (corp-wide): 10.2B **Publicly Held**
WEB: www.xerox.com
SIC: **3861** Photographic equipment & supplies
PA: Xerox Corporation
201 Merritt 7
Norwalk CT 06851
203 968-3000

(G-14473)
ZIONSVILLE CUSTOM CABINETS
10830 Bennett Pkwy Ste E (46077-1188)
PHONE..................................317 339-0380
EMP: 2
SALES (est): 164.4K **Privately Held**
SIC: **2434** Wood kitchen cabinets

(G-14474)
ZIONSVILLE TOWING INC
4901 W 106th St (46077-8717)
PHONE..................................317 873-4550
John Imel, *President*
Steve Imel, *President*
EMP: 5
SQ FT: 5,000
SALES: 100K **Privately Held**
SIC: **7699** 7549 5261 7692 Lawn mower repair shop; towing service, automotive; nurseries & garden centers; welding repair

(G-14475)
ZOGMAN ENTERPRISES INC
Also Called: Good Impressions Printing
170 W Hawthorne St (46077-1617)
PHONE..................................317 873-6809
Charles Herzog, *President*
Dennis Disman, *Vice Pres*
EMP: 3
SALES: 300K **Privately Held**
SIC: **2752** Commercial printing, offset

SIC INDEX

SIC NO	PRODUCT

A

3291 Abrasive Prdts
2891 Adhesives & Sealants
3563 Air & Gas Compressors
3585 Air Conditioning & Heating Eqpt
3721 Aircraft
3724 Aircraft Engines & Engine Parts
3728 Aircraft Parts & Eqpt, NEC
2812 Alkalies & Chlorine
3363 Aluminum Die Castings
3354 Aluminum Extruded Prdts
3365 Aluminum Foundries
3355 Aluminum Rolling & Drawing, NEC
3353 Aluminum Sheet, Plate & Foil
3483 Ammunition, Large
3826 Analytical Instruments
2077 Animal, Marine Fats & Oils
2389 Apparel & Accessories, NEC
3446 Architectural & Ornamental Metal Work
7694 Armature Rewinding Shops
3292 Asbestos products
2952 Asphalt Felts & Coatings
3822 Automatic Temperature Controls
3581 Automatic Vending Machines
3465 Automotive Stampings
2396 Automotive Trimmings, Apparel Findings, Related Prdts

B

2673 Bags: Plastics, Laminated & Coated
2674 Bags: Uncoated Paper & Multiwall
3562 Ball & Roller Bearings
2836 Biological Prdts, Exc Diagnostic Substances
1221 Bituminous Coal & Lignite: Surface Mining
1222 Bituminous Coal: Underground Mining
2782 Blankbooks & Looseleaf Binders
3312 Blast Furnaces, Coke Ovens, Steel & Rolling Mills
3564 Blowers & Fans
3732 Boat Building & Repairing
3452 Bolts, Nuts, Screws, Rivets & Washers
2732 Book Printing, Not Publishing
2789 Bookbinding
2731 Books: Publishing & Printing
3131 Boot & Shoe Cut Stock & Findings
2051 Bread, Bakery Prdts Exc Cookies & Crackers
3251 Brick & Structural Clay Tile
3991 Brooms & Brushes
3995 Burial Caskets
2021 Butter

C

3578 Calculating & Accounting Eqpt
2064 Candy & Confectionery Prdts
2033 Canned Fruits, Vegetables & Preserves
2032 Canned Specialties
2394 Canvas Prdts
3624 Carbon & Graphite Prdts
2895 Carbon Black
3955 Carbon Paper & Inked Ribbons
3592 Carburetors, Pistons, Rings & Valves
2273 Carpets & Rugs
2823 Cellulosic Man-Made Fibers
3241 Cement, Hydraulic
3253 Ceramic Tile
2043 Cereal Breakfast Foods
2022 Cheese
1479 Chemical & Fertilizer Mining
2899 Chemical Preparations, NEC
2361 Children's & Infants' Dresses & Blouses
3261 China Plumbing Fixtures & Fittings
2066 Chocolate & Cocoa Prdts
2111 Cigarettes
2121 Cigars
3255 Clay Refractories
1459 Clay, Ceramic & Refractory Minerals, NEC
1241 Coal Mining Svcs
3479 Coating & Engraving, NEC
2095 Coffee
3316 Cold Rolled Steel Sheet, Strip & Bars
3582 Commercial Laundry, Dry Clean & Pressing Mchs
2759 Commercial Printing
2754 Commercial Printing: Gravure
2752 Commercial Printing: Lithographic
3646 Commercial, Indl & Institutional Lighting Fixtures

3669 Communications Eqpt, NEC
3577 Computer Peripheral Eqpt, NEC
3572 Computer Storage Devices
3575 Computer Terminals
3271 Concrete Block & Brick
3272 Concrete Prdts
3531 Construction Machinery & Eqpt
1442 Construction Sand & Gravel
2679 Converted Paper Prdts, NEC
3535 Conveyors & Eqpt
2052 Cookies & Crackers
3366 Copper Foundries
2298 Cordage & Twine
2653 Corrugated & Solid Fiber Boxes
3961 Costume Jewelry & Novelties
2261 Cotton Fabric Finishers
2211 Cotton, Woven Fabric
2074 Cottonseed Oil Mills
3466 Crowns & Closures
1311 Crude Petroleum & Natural Gas
1422 Crushed & Broken Limestone
1429 Crushed & Broken Stone, NEC
3643 Current-Carrying Wiring Devices
2391 Curtains & Draperies
3087 Custom Compounding Of Purchased Plastic Resins
3281 Cut Stone Prdts
3421 Cutlery
2865 Cyclic-Crudes, Intermediates, Dyes & Org Pigments

D

3843 Dental Eqpt & Splys
2835 Diagnostic Substances
2675 Die-Cut Paper & Board
3544 Dies, Tools, Jigs, Fixtures & Indl Molds
1411 Dimension Stone
2047 Dog & Cat Food
3942 Dolls & Stuffed Toys
2591 Drapery Hardware, Window Blinds & Shades
2381 Dress & Work Gloves
2034 Dried Fruits, Vegetables & Soup
1381 Drilling Oil & Gas Wells

E

3634 Electric Household Appliances
3641 Electric Lamps
3694 Electrical Eqpt For Internal Combustion Engines
3629 Electrical Indl Apparatus, NEC
3699 Electrical Machinery, Eqpt & Splys, NEC
3845 Electromedical & Electrotherapeutic Apparatus
3675 Electronic Capacitors
3677 Electronic Coils & Transformers
3679 Electronic Components, NEC
3571 Electronic Computers
3678 Electronic Connectors
3676 Electronic Resistors
3471 Electroplating, Plating, Polishing, Anodizing & Coloring
3534 Elevators & Moving Stairways
3431 Enameled Iron & Metal Sanitary Ware
2677 Envelopes
2892 Explosives

F

2241 Fabric Mills, Cotton, Wool, Silk & Man-Made
3499 Fabricated Metal Prdts, NEC
3498 Fabricated Pipe & Pipe Fittings
3443 Fabricated Plate Work
3069 Fabricated Rubber Prdts, NEC
3441 Fabricated Structural Steel
2399 Fabricated Textile Prdts, NEC
2295 Fabrics Coated Not Rubberized
2297 Fabrics, Nonwoven
3523 Farm Machinery & Eqpt
3965 Fasteners, Buttons, Needles & Pins
2875 Fertilizers, Mixing Only
2655 Fiber Cans, Tubes & Drums
2091 Fish & Seafoods, Canned & Cured
2092 Fish & Seafoods, Fresh & Frozen
3211 Flat Glass
2087 Flavoring Extracts & Syrups
2045 Flour, Blended & Prepared
2041 Flour, Grain Milling
3824 Fluid Meters & Counters
3593 Fluid Power Cylinders & Actuators
3594 Fluid Power Pumps & Motors

3492 Fluid Power Valves & Hose Fittings
2657 Folding Paperboard Boxes
3556 Food Prdts Machinery
2099 Food Preparations, NEC
3149 Footwear, NEC
2053 Frozen Bakery Prdts
2037 Frozen Fruits, Juices & Vegetables
2038 Frozen Specialties
2371 Fur Goods
2599 Furniture & Fixtures, NEC

G

3944 Games, Toys & Children's Vehicles
3524 Garden, Lawn Tractors & Eqpt
3053 Gaskets, Packing & Sealing Devices
2369 Girls' & Infants' Outerwear, NEC
3221 Glass Containers
3231 Glass Prdts Made Of Purchased Glass
3321 Gray Iron Foundries
2771 Greeting Card Publishing
3769 Guided Missile/Space Vehicle Parts & Eqpt, NEC
3764 Guided Missile/Space Vehicle Propulsion Units & parts
3761 Guided Missiles & Space Vehicles
2861 Gum & Wood Chemicals
3275 Gypsum Prdts

H

3423 Hand & Edge Tools
3425 Hand Saws & Saw Blades
3171 Handbags & Purses
3429 Hardware, NEC
2426 Hardwood Dimension & Flooring Mills
2435 Hardwood Veneer & Plywood
2353 Hats, Caps & Millinery
3433 Heating Eqpt
3536 Hoists, Cranes & Monorails
2252 Hosiery, Except Women's
2392 House furnishings: Textile
3639 Household Appliances, NEC
3651 Household Audio & Video Eqpt
3631 Household Cooking Eqpt
2519 Household Furniture, NEC
3633 Household Laundry Eqpt
3632 Household Refrigerators & Freezers
3635 Household Vacuum Cleaners

I

2097 Ice
2024 Ice Cream
2819 Indl Inorganic Chemicals, NEC
3823 Indl Instruments For Meas, Display & Control
3569 Indl Machinery & Eqpt, NEC
3567 Indl Process Furnaces & Ovens
3537 Indl Trucks, Tractors, Trailers & Stackers
2813 Industrial Gases
2869 Industrial Organic Chemicals, NEC
3543 Industrial Patterns
1446 Industrial Sand
3491 Industrial Valves
2816 Inorganic Pigments
3825 Instrs For Measuring & Testing Electricity
3519 Internal Combustion Engines, NEC
3462 Iron & Steel Forgings
1011 Iron Ores

J

3915 Jewelers Findings & Lapidary Work
3911 Jewelry: Precious Metal

K

1455 Kaolin & Ball Clay
2253 Knit Outerwear Mills
2259 Knitting Mills, NEC

L

3821 Laboratory Apparatus & Furniture
3952 Lead Pencils, Crayons & Artist's Mtrls
2386 Leather & Sheep Lined Clothing
3151 Leather Gloves & Mittens
3199 Leather Goods, NEC
3111 Leather Tanning & Finishing
3648 Lighting Eqpt, NEC
3274 Lime
3996 Linoleum & Hard Surface Floor Coverings, NEC
2085 Liquors, Distilled, Rectified & Blended

S I C

SIC NO	PRODUCT
2411	Logging
2992	Lubricating Oils & Greases
3161	Luggage

M

SIC NO	PRODUCT
2098	Macaroni, Spaghetti & Noodles
3545	Machine Tool Access
3541	Machine Tools: Cutting
3542	Machine Tools: Forming
3599	Machinery & Eqpt, Indl & Commercial, NEC
3322	Malleable Iron Foundries
2082	Malt Beverages
2761	Manifold Business Forms
3999	Manufacturing Industries, NEC
3953	Marking Devices
2515	Mattresses & Bedsprings
3829	Measuring & Controlling Devices, NEC
3586	Measuring & Dispensing Pumps
2011	Meat Packing Plants
3568	Mechanical Power Transmission Eqpt, NEC
2833	Medicinal Chemicals & Botanical Prdts
2329	Men's & Boys' Clothing, NEC
2323	Men's & Boys' Neckwear
2325	Men's & Boys' Separate Trousers & Casual Slacks
2321	Men's & Boys' Shirts
2311	Men's & Boys' Suits, Coats & Overcoats
2322	Men's & Boys' Underwear & Nightwear
2326	Men's & Boys' Work Clothing
3143	Men's Footwear, Exc Athletic
3412	Metal Barrels, Drums, Kegs & Pails
3411	Metal Cans
3442	Metal Doors, Sash, Frames, Molding & Trim
3497	Metal Foil & Leaf
3398	Metal Heat Treating
2514	Metal Household Furniture
1081	Metal Mining Svcs
1099	Metal Ores, NEC
3469	Metal Stampings, NEC
3549	Metalworking Machinery, NEC
2026	Milk
2023	Milk, Condensed & Evaporated
2431	Millwork
3296	Mineral Wool
3295	Minerals & Earths: Ground Or Treated
3532	Mining Machinery & Eqpt
3496	Misc Fabricated Wire Prdts
2741	Misc Publishing
3449	Misc Structural Metal Work
1499	Miscellaneous Nonmetallic Mining
2451	Mobile Homes
3061	Molded, Extruded & Lathe-Cut Rubber Mechanical Goods
3716	Motor Homes
3714	Motor Vehicle Parts & Access
3711	Motor Vehicles & Car Bodies
3751	Motorcycles, Bicycles & Parts
3621	Motors & Generators
3931	Musical Instruments

N

SIC NO	PRODUCT
1321	Natural Gas Liquids
2711	Newspapers: Publishing & Printing
2873	Nitrogenous Fertilizers
3297	Nonclay Refractories
3644	Noncurrent-Carrying Wiring Devices
3364	Nonferrous Die Castings, Exc Aluminum
3463	Nonferrous Forgings
3369	Nonferrous Foundries: Castings, NEC
3357	Nonferrous Wire Drawing
3299	Nonmetallic Mineral Prdts, NEC
1481	Nonmetallic Minerals Svcs, Except Fuels

O

SIC NO	PRODUCT
2522	Office Furniture, Except Wood
3579	Office Machines, NEC
1382	Oil & Gas Field Exploration Svcs
1389	Oil & Gas Field Svcs, NEC
3533	Oil Field Machinery & Eqpt
3851	Ophthalmic Goods
3827	Optical Instruments
3489	Ordnance & Access, NEC
3842	Orthopedic, Prosthetic & Surgical Appliances/Splys

P

SIC NO	PRODUCT
3565	Packaging Machinery
2851	Paints, Varnishes, Lacquers, Enamels

SIC NO	PRODUCT
2671	Paper Coating & Laminating for Packaging
2672	Paper Coating & Laminating, Exc for Packaging
3554	Paper Inds Machinery
2621	Paper Mills
2631	Paperboard Mills
2542	Partitions & Fixtures, Except Wood
2951	Paving Mixtures & Blocks
2844	Perfumes, Cosmetics & Toilet Preparations
2721	Periodicals: Publishing & Printing
3172	Personal Leather Goods
2879	Pesticides & Agricultural Chemicals, NEC
2911	Petroleum Refining
2834	Pharmaceuticals
3652	Phonograph Records & Magnetic Tape
2874	Phosphatic Fertilizers
3861	Photographic Eqpt & Splys
2035	Pickled Fruits, Vegetables, Sauces & Dressings
3085	Plastic Bottles
3086	Plastic Foam Prdts
3083	Plastic Laminated Plate & Sheet
3084	Plastic Pipe
3088	Plastic Plumbing Fixtures
3089	Plastic Prdts
3082	Plastic Unsupported Profile Shapes
3081	Plastic Unsupported Sheet & Film
2821	Plastics, Mtrls & Nonvulcanizable Elastomers
2796	Platemaking & Related Svcs
2395	Pleating & Stitching For The Trade
3432	Plumbing Fixture Fittings & Trim, Brass
3264	Porcelain Electrical Splys
2096	Potato Chips & Similar Prdts
3269	Pottery Prdts, NEC
2015	Poultry Slaughtering, Dressing & Processing
3546	Power Hand Tools
3612	Power, Distribution & Specialty Transformers
3448	Prefabricated Metal Buildings & Cmpnts
2452	Prefabricated Wood Buildings & Cmpnts
7372	Prepackaged Software
2048	Prepared Feeds For Animals & Fowls
3229	Pressed & Blown Glassware, NEC
3692	Primary Batteries: Dry & Wet
3399	Primary Metal Prdts, NEC
3339	Primary Nonferrous Metals, NEC
3334	Primary Production Of Aluminum
3331	Primary Smelting & Refining Of Copper
3672	Printed Circuit Boards
2893	Printing Ink
3555	Printing Trades Machinery & Eqpt
2999	Products Of Petroleum & Coal, NEC
2531	Public Building & Related Furniture
2611	Pulp Mills
3561	Pumps & Pumping Eqpt

R

SIC NO	PRODUCT
3663	Radio & T V Communications, Systs & Eqpt, Broadcast/Studio
3671	Radio & T V Receiving Electron Tubes
3743	Railroad Eqpt
3273	Ready-Mixed Concrete
2493	Reconstituted Wood Prdts
3695	Recording Media
3625	Relays & Indl Controls
3645	Residential Lighting Fixtures
2384	Robes & Dressing Gowns
3547	Rolling Mill Machinery & Eqpt
3351	Rolling, Drawing & Extruding Of Copper
3356	Rolling, Drawing-Extruding Of Nonferrous Metals
3021	Rubber & Plastic Footwear
3052	Rubber & Plastic Hose & Belting

S

SIC NO	PRODUCT
2068	Salted & Roasted Nuts & Seeds
2656	Sanitary Food Containers
2676	Sanitary Paper Prdts
2013	Sausages & Meat Prdts
2421	Saw & Planing Mills
3596	Scales & Balances, Exc Laboratory
3451	Screw Machine Prdts
3812	Search, Detection, Navigation & Guidance Systs & Instrs
3341	Secondary Smelting & Refining Of Nonferrous Metals
3674	Semiconductors
3589	Service Ind Machines, NEC
2652	Set-Up Paperboard Boxes
3444	Sheet Metal Work
3731	Shipbuilding & Repairing
2079	Shortening, Oils & Margarine

SIC NO	PRODUCT
3993	Signs & Advertising Displays
2262	Silk & Man-Made Fabric Finishers
2221	Silk & Man-Made Fiber
3914	Silverware, Plated & Stainless Steel Ware
3484	Small Arms
3482	Small Arms Ammunition
2841	Soap & Detergents
2086	Soft Drinks
2436	Softwood Veneer & Plywood
2075	Soybean Oil Mills
2842	Spec Cleaning, Polishing & Sanitation Preparations
3559	Special Ind Machinery, NEC
2429	Special Prdt Sawmills, NEC
3566	Speed Changers, Drives & Gears
3949	Sporting & Athletic Goods, NEC
2678	Stationery Prdts
3511	Steam, Gas & Hydraulic Turbines & Engines
3325	Steel Foundries, NEC
3324	Steel Investment Foundries
3317	Steel Pipe & Tubes
3493	Steel Springs, Except Wire
3315	Steel Wire Drawing & Nails & Spikes
3691	Storage Batteries
3259	Structural Clay Prdts, NEC
2439	Structural Wood Members, NEC
2843	Surface Active & Finishing Agents, Sulfonated Oils
3841	Surgical & Medical Instrs & Apparatus
3613	Switchgear & Switchboard Apparatus
2824	Synthetic Organic Fibers, Exc Cellulosic
2822	Synthetic Rubber (Vulcanizable Elastomers)

T

SIC NO	PRODUCT
3795	Tanks & Tank Components
3661	Telephone & Telegraph Apparatus
2393	Textile Bags
2269	Textile Finishers, NEC
2299	Textile Goods, NEC
3552	Textile Machinery
2284	Thread Mills
2296	Tire Cord & Fabric
3011	Tires & Inner Tubes
2141	Tobacco Stemming & Redrying
2131	Tobacco, Chewing & Snuff
3799	Transportation Eqpt, NEC
3792	Travel Trailers & Campers
3713	Truck & Bus Bodies
3715	Truck Trailers
2791	Typesetting

V

SIC NO	PRODUCT
3494	Valves & Pipe Fittings, NEC
2076	Vegetable Oil Mills
3647	Vehicular Lighting Eqpt

W

SIC NO	PRODUCT
3873	Watch & Clock Devices & Parts
2385	Waterproof Outerwear
3548	Welding Apparatus
7692	Welding Repair
2046	Wet Corn Milling
2084	Wine & Brandy
3495	Wire Springs
2335	Women's & Misses' Dresses
2339	Women's & Misses' Outerwear, NEC
2341	Women's, Misses' & Children's Underwear & Nightwear
2441	Wood Boxes
2449	Wood Containers, NEC
2511	Wood Household Furniture
2512	Wood Household Furniture, Upholstered
2434	Wood Kitchen Cabinets
2521	Wood Office Furniture
2448	Wood Pallets & Skids
2499	Wood Prdts, NEC
2491	Wood Preserving
2517	Wood T V, Radio, Phono & Sewing Cabinets
2541	Wood, Office & Store Fixtures
3553	Woodworking Machinery
2231	Wool, Woven Fabric

X

SIC NO	PRODUCT
3844	X-ray Apparatus & Tubes

Y

SIC NO	PRODUCT
2281	Yarn Spinning Mills
2282	Yarn Texturizing, Throwing, Twisting & Winding Mills

Standard Industrial Classification Numerical Index

SIC NO	PRODUCT

10 METAL MINING

1011 Iron Ores
1081 Metal Mining Svcs
1099 Metal Ores, NEC

12 COAL MINING

1221 Bituminous Coal & Lignite: Surface Mining
1222 Bituminous Coal: Underground Mining
1241 Coal Mining Svcs

13 OIL AND GAS EXTRACTION

1311 Crude Petroleum & Natural Gas
1321 Natural Gas Liquids
1381 Drilling Oil & Gas Wells
1382 Oil & Gas Field Exploration Svcs
1389 Oil & Gas Field Svcs, NEC

14 MINING AND QUARRYING OF NONMETALLIC MINERALS, EXCEPT FUELS

1411 Dimension Stone
1422 Crushed & Broken Limestone
1429 Crushed & Broken Stone, NEC
1442 Construction Sand & Gravel
1446 Industrial Sand
1455 Kaolin & Ball Clay
1459 Clay, Ceramic & Refractory Minerals, NEC
1479 Chemical & Fertilizer Mining
1481 Nonmetallic Minerals Svcs, Except Fuels
1499 Miscellaneous Nonmetallic Mining

20 FOOD AND KINDRED PRODUCTS

2011 Meat Packing Plants
2013 Sausages & Meat Prdts
2015 Poultry Slaughtering, Dressing & Processing
2021 Butter
2022 Cheese
2023 Milk, Condensed & Evaporated
2024 Ice Cream
2026 Milk
2032 Canned Specialties
2033 Canned Fruits, Vegetables & Preserves
2034 Dried Fruits, Vegetables & Soup
2035 Pickled Fruits, Vegetables, Sauces & Dressings
2037 Frozen Fruits, Juices & Vegetables
2038 Frozen Specialties
2041 Flour, Grain Milling
2043 Cereal Breakfast Foods
2045 Flour, Blended & Prepared
2046 Wet Corn Milling
2047 Dog & Cat Food
2048 Prepared Feeds For Animals & Fowls
2051 Bread, Bakery Prdts Exc Cookies & Crackers
2052 Cookies & Crackers
2053 Frozen Bakery Prdts
2064 Candy & Confectionery Prdts
2066 Chocolate & Cocoa Prdts
2068 Salted & Roasted Nuts & Seeds
2074 Cottonseed Oil Mills
2075 Soybean Oil Mills
2076 Vegetable Oil Mills
2077 Animal, Marine Fats & Oils
2079 Shortening, Oils & Margarine
2082 Malt Beverages
2084 Wine & Brandy
2085 Liquors, Distilled, Rectified & Blended
2086 Soft Drinks
2087 Flavoring Extracts & Syrups
2091 Fish & Seafoods, Canned & Cured
2092 Fish & Seafoods, Fresh & Frozen
2095 Coffee
2096 Potato Chips & Similar Prdts
2097 Ice
2098 Macaroni, Spaghetti & Noodles
2099 Food Preparations, NEC

21 TOBACCO PRODUCTS

2111 Cigarettes
2121 Cigars
2131 Tobacco, Chewing & Snuff
2141 Tobacco Stemming & Redrying

22 TEXTILE MILL PRODUCTS

2211 Cotton, Woven Fabric
2221 Silk & Man-Made Fiber
2231 Wool, Woven Fabric
2241 Fabric Mills, Cotton, Wool, Silk & Man-Made

2252 Hosiery, Except Women's
2253 Knit Outerwear Mills
2259 Knitting Mills, NEC
2261 Cotton Fabric Finishers
2262 Silk & Man-Made Fabric Finishers
2269 Textile Finishers, NEC
2273 Carpets & Rugs
2281 Yarn Spinning Mills
2282 Yarn Texturizing, Throwing, Twisting & Winding Mills
2284 Thread Mills
2295 Fabrics Coated Not Rubberized
2296 Tire Cord & Fabric
2297 Fabrics, Nonwoven
2298 Cordage & Twine
2299 Textile Goods, NEC

23 APPAREL AND OTHER FINISHED PRODUCTS MADE FROM FABRICS AND SIMILAR MATERIAL

2311 Men's & Boys' Suits, Coats & Overcoats
2321 Men's & Boys' Shirts
2322 Men's & Boys' Underwear & Nightwear
2323 Men's & Boys' Neckwear
2325 Men's & Boys' Separate Trousers & Casual Slacks
2326 Men's & Boys' Work Clothing
2329 Men's & Boys' Clothing, NEC
2335 Women's & Misses' Dresses
2339 Women's & Misses' Outerwear, NEC
2341 Women's, Misses' & Children's Underwear & Nightwear
2353 Hats, Caps & Millinery
2361 Children's & Infants' Dresses & Blouses
2369 Girls' & Infants' Outerwear, NEC
2371 Fur Goods
2381 Dress & Work Gloves
2384 Robes & Dressing Gowns
2385 Waterproof Outerwear
2386 Leather & Sheep Lined Clothing
2389 Apparel & Accessories, NEC
2391 Curtains & Draperies
2392 House furnishings: Textile
2393 Textile Bags
2394 Canvas Prdts
2395 Pleating & Stitching For The Trade
2396 Automotive Trimmings, Apparel Findings, Related Prdts
2399 Fabricated Textile Prdts, NEC

24 LUMBER AND WOOD PRODUCTS, EXCEPT FURNITURE

2411 Logging
2421 Saw & Planing Mills
2426 Hardwood Dimension & Flooring Mills
2429 Special Prdt Sawmills, NEC
2431 Millwork
2434 Wood Kitchen Cabinets
2435 Hardwood Veneer & Plywood
2436 Softwood Veneer & Plywood
2439 Structural Wood Members, NEC
2441 Wood Boxes
2448 Wood Pallets & Skids
2449 Wood Containers, NEC
2451 Mobile Homes
2452 Prefabricated Wood Buildings & Cmpnts
2491 Wood Preserving
2493 Reconstituted Wood Prdts
2499 Wood Prdts, NEC

25 FURNITURE AND FIXTURES

2511 Wood Household Furniture
2512 Wood Household Furniture, Upholstered
2514 Metal Household Furniture
2515 Mattresses & Bedsprings
2517 Wood T V, Radio, Phono & Sewing Cabinets
2519 Household Furniture, NEC
2521 Wood Office Furniture
2522 Office Furniture, Except Wood
2531 Public Building & Related Furniture
2541 Wood, Office & Store Fixtures
2542 Partitions & Fixtures, Except Wood
2591 Drapery Hardware, Window Blinds & Shades
2599 Furniture & Fixtures, NEC

26 PAPER AND ALLIED PRODUCTS

2611 Pulp Mills
2621 Paper Mills
2631 Paperboard Mills
2652 Set-Up Paperboard Boxes

2653 Corrugated & Solid Fiber Boxes
2655 Fiber Cans, Tubes & Drums
2656 Sanitary Food Containers
2657 Folding Paperboard Boxes
2671 Paper Coating & Laminating for Packaging
2672 Paper Coating & Laminating, Exc for Packaging
2673 Bags: Plastics, Laminated & Coated
2674 Bags: Uncoated Paper & Multiwall
2675 Die-Cut Paper & Board
2676 Sanitary Paper Prdts
2677 Envelopes
2678 Stationery Prdts
2679 Converted Paper Prdts, NEC

27 PRINTING, PUBLISHING, AND ALLIED INDUSTRIES

2711 Newspapers: Publishing & Printing
2721 Periodicals: Publishing & Printing
2731 Books: Publishing & Printing
2732 Book Printing, Not Publishing
2741 Misc Publishing
2752 Commercial Printing: Lithographic
2754 Commercial Printing: Gravure
2759 Commercial Printing
2761 Manifold Business Forms
2771 Greeting Card Publishing
2782 Blankbooks & Looseleaf Binders
2789 Bookbinding
2791 Typesetting
2796 Platemaking & Related Svcs

28 CHEMICALS AND ALLIED PRODUCTS

2812 Alkalies & Chlorine
2813 Industrial Gases
2816 Inorganic Pigments
2819 Indl Inorganic Chemicals, NEC
2821 Plastics, Mtrls & Nonvulcanizable Elastomers
2822 Synthetic Rubber (Vulcanizable Elastomers)
2823 Cellulosic Man-Made Fibers
2824 Synthetic Organic Fibers, Exc Cellulosic
2833 Medicinal Chemicals & Botanical Prdts
2834 Pharmaceuticals
2835 Diagnostic Substances
2836 Biological Prdts, Exc Diagnostic Substances
2841 Soap & Detergents
2842 Spec Cleaning, Polishing & Sanitation Preparations
2843 Surface Active & Finishing Agents, Sulfonated Oils
2844 Perfumes, Cosmetics & Toilet Preparations
2851 Paints, Varnishes, Lacquers, Enamels
2861 Gum & Wood Chemicals
2865 Cyclic-Crudes, Intermediates, Dyes & Org Pigments
2869 Industrial Organic Chemicals, NEC
2873 Nitrogenous Fertilizers
2874 Phosphatic Fertilizers
2875 Fertilizers, Mixing Only
2879 Pesticides & Agricultural Chemicals, NEC
2891 Adhesives & Sealants
2892 Explosives
2893 Printing Ink
2895 Carbon Black
2899 Chemical Preparations, NEC

29 PETROLEUM REFINING AND RELATED INDUSTRIES

2911 Petroleum Refining
2951 Paving Mixtures & Blocks
2952 Asphalt Felts & Coatings
2992 Lubricating Oils & Greases
2999 Products Of Petroleum & Coal, NEC

30 RUBBER AND MISCELLANEOUS PLASTICS PRODUCTS

3011 Tires & Inner Tubes
3021 Rubber & Plastic Footwear
3052 Rubber & Plastic Hose & Belting
3053 Gaskets, Packing & Sealing Devices
3061 Molded, Extruded & Lathe-Cut Rubber Mechanical Goods
3069 Fabricated Rubber Prdts, NEC
3081 Plastic Unsupported Sheet & Film
3082 Plastic Unsupported Profile Shapes
3083 Plastic Laminated Plate & Sheet
3084 Plastic Pipe
3085 Plastic Bottles
3086 Plastic Foam Prdts
3087 Custom Compounding Of Purchased Plastic Resins
3088 Plastic Plumbing Fixtures

S I C

SIC NO	PRODUCT

3089 Plastic Prdts

31 LEATHER AND LEATHER PRODUCTS

3111 Leather Tanning & Finishing
3131 Boot & Shoe Cut Stock & Findings
3143 Men's Footwear, Exc Athletic
3149 Footwear, NEC
3151 Leather Gloves & Mittens
3161 Luggage
3171 Handbags & Purses
3172 Personal Leather Goods
3199 Leather Goods, NEC

32 STONE, CLAY, GLASS, AND CONCRETE PRODUCTS

3211 Flat Glass
3221 Glass Containers
3229 Pressed & Blown Glassware, NEC
3231 Glass Prdts Made Of Purchased Glass
3241 Cement, Hydraulic
3251 Brick & Structural Clay Tile
3253 Ceramic Tile
3255 Clay Refractories
3259 Structural Clay Prdts, NEC
3261 China Plumbing Fixtures & Fittings
3264 Porcelain Electrical Splys
3269 Pottery Prdts, NEC
3271 Concrete Block & Brick
3272 Concrete Prdts
3273 Ready-Mixed Concrete
3274 Lime
3275 Gypsum Prdts
3281 Cut Stone Prdts
3291 Abrasive Prdts
3292 Asbestos products
3295 Minerals & Earths: Ground Or Treated
3296 Mineral Wool
3297 Nonclay Refractories
3299 Nonmetallic Mineral Prdts, NEC

33 PRIMARY METAL INDUSTRIES

3312 Blast Furnaces, Coke Ovens, Steel & Rolling Mills
3315 Steel Wire Drawing & Nails & Spikes
3316 Cold Rolled Steel Sheet, Strip & Bars
3317 Steel Pipe & Tubes
3321 Gray Iron Foundries
3322 Malleable Iron Foundries
3324 Steel Investment Foundries
3325 Steel Foundries, NEC
3331 Primary Smelting & Refining Of Copper
3334 Primary Production Of Aluminum
3339 Primary Nonferrous Metals, NEC
3341 Secondary Smelting & Refining Of Nonferrous Metals
3351 Rolling, Drawing & Extruding Of Copper
3353 Aluminum Sheet, Plate & Foil
3354 Aluminum Extruded Prdts
3355 Aluminum Rolling & Drawing, NEC
3356 Rolling, Drawing-Extruding Of Nonferrous Metals
3357 Nonferrous Wire Drawing
3363 Aluminum Die Castings
3364 Nonferrous Die Castings, Exc Aluminum
3365 Aluminum Foundries
3366 Copper Foundries
3369 Nonferrous Foundries: Castings, NEC
3398 Metal Heat Treating
3399 Primary Metal Prdts, NEC

34 FABRICATED METAL PRODUCTS, EXCEPT MACHINERY AND TRANSPORTATION EQUIPMENT

3411 Metal Cans
3412 Metal Barrels, Drums, Kegs & Pails
3421 Cutlery
3423 Hand & Edge Tools
3425 Hand Saws & Saw Blades
3429 Hardware, NEC
3431 Enameled Iron & Metal Sanitary Ware
3432 Plumbing Fixture Fittings & Trim, Brass
3433 Heating Eqpt
3441 Fabricated Structural Steel
3442 Metal Doors, Sash, Frames, Molding & Trim
3443 Fabricated Plate Work
3444 Sheet Metal Work
3446 Architectural & Ornamental Metal Work
3448 Prefabricated Metal Buildings & Cmpnts
3449 Misc Structural Metal Work
3451 Screw Machine Prdts
3452 Bolts, Nuts, Screws, Rivets & Washers
3462 Iron & Steel Forgings
3463 Nonferrous Forgings
3465 Automotive Stampings

3466 Crowns & Closures
3469 Metal Stampings, NEC
3471 Electroplating, Plating, Polishing, Anodizing & Coloring
3479 Coating & Engraving, NEC
3482 Small Arms Ammunition
3483 Ammunition, Large
3484 Small Arms
3489 Ordnance & Access, NEC
3491 Industrial Valves
3492 Fluid Power Valves & Hose Fittings
3493 Steel Springs, Except Wire
3494 Valves & Pipe Fittings, NEC
3495 Wire Springs
3496 Misc Fabricated Wire Prdts
3497 Metal Foil & Leaf
3498 Fabricated Pipe & Pipe Fittings
3499 Fabricated Metal Prdts, NEC

35 INDUSTRIAL AND COMMERCIAL MACHINERY AND COMPUTER EQUIPMENT

3511 Steam, Gas & Hydraulic Turbines & Engines
3519 Internal Combustion Engines, NEC
3523 Farm Machinery & Eqpt
3524 Garden, Lawn Tractors & Eqpt
3531 Construction Machinery & Eqpt
3532 Mining Machinery & Eqpt
3533 Oil Field Machinery & Eqpt
3534 Elevators & Moving Stairways
3535 Conveyors & Eqpt
3536 Hoists, Cranes & Monorails
3537 Indl Trucks, Tractors, Trailers & Stackers
3541 Machine Tools: Cutting
3542 Machine Tools: Forming
3543 Industrial Patterns
3544 Dies, Tools, Jigs, Fixtures & Indl Molds
3545 Machine Tool Access
3546 Power Hand Tools
3547 Rolling Mill Machinery & Eqpt
3548 Welding Apparatus
3549 Metalworking Machinery, NEC
3552 Textile Machinery
3553 Woodworking Machinery
3554 Paper Inds Machinery
3555 Printing Trades Machinery & Eqpt
3556 Food Prdts Machinery
3559 Special Ind Machinery, NEC
3561 Pumps & Pumping Eqpt
3562 Ball & Roller Bearings
3563 Air & Gas Compressors
3564 Blowers & Fans
3565 Packaging Machinery
3566 Speed Changers, Drives & Gears
3567 Indl Process Furnaces & Ovens
3568 Mechanical Power Transmission Eqpt, NEC
3569 Indl Machinery & Eqpt, NEC
3571 Electronic Computers
3572 Computer Storage Devices
3575 Computer Terminals
3577 Computer Peripheral Eqpt, NEC
3578 Calculating & Accounting Eqpt
3579 Office Machines, NEC
3581 Automatic Vending Machines
3582 Commercial Laundry, Dry Clean & Pressing Mchs
3585 Air Conditioning & Heating Eqpt
3586 Measuring & Dispensing Pumps
3589 Service Ind Machines, NEC
3592 Carburetors, Pistons, Rings & Valves
3593 Fluid Power Cylinders & Actuators
3594 Fluid Power Pumps & Motors
3596 Scales & Balances, Exc Laboratory
3599 Machinery & Eqpt, Indl & Commercial, NEC

36 ELECTRONIC AND OTHER ELECTRICAL EQUIPMENT AND COMPONENTS, EXCEPT COMPUTER

3612 Power, Distribution & Specialty Transformers
3613 Switchgear & Switchboard Apparatus
3621 Motors & Generators
3624 Carbon & Graphite Prdts
3625 Relays & Indl Controls
3629 Electrical Indl Apparatus, NEC
3631 Household Cooking Eqpt
3632 Household Refrigerators & Freezers
3633 Household Laundry Eqpt
3634 Electric Household Appliances
3635 Household Vacuum Cleaners
3639 Household Appliances, NEC
3641 Electric Lamps
3643 Current-Carrying Wiring Devices
3644 Noncurrent-Carrying Wiring Devices

3645 Residential Lighting Fixtures
3646 Commercial, Indl & Institutional Lighting Fixtures
3647 Vehicular Lighting Eqpt
3648 Lighting Eqpt, NEC
3651 Household Audio & Video Eqpt
3652 Phonograph Records & Magnetic Tape
3661 Telephone & Telegraph Apparatus
3663 Radio & T V Communications, Systs & Eqpt, Broadcast/Studio
3669 Communications Eqpt, NEC
3671 Radio & T V Receiving Electron Tubes
3672 Printed Circuit Boards
3674 Semiconductors
3675 Electronic Capacitors
3676 Electronic Resistors
3677 Electronic Coils & Transformers
3678 Electronic Connectors
3679 Electronic Components, NEC
3691 Storage Batteries
3692 Primary Batteries: Dry & Wet
3694 Electrical Eqpt For Internal Combustion Engines
3695 Recording Media
3699 Electrical Machinery, Eqpt & Splys, NEC

37 TRANSPORTATION EQUIPMENT

3711 Motor Vehicles & Car Bodies
3713 Truck & Bus Bodies
3714 Motor Vehicle Parts & Access
3715 Truck Trailers
3716 Motor Homes
3721 Aircraft
3724 Aircraft Engines & Engine Parts
3728 Aircraft Parts & Eqpt, NEC
3731 Shipbuilding & Repairing
3732 Boat Building & Repairing
3743 Railroad Eqpt
3751 Motorcycles, Bicycles & Parts
3761 Guided Missiles & Space Vehicles
3764 Guided Missile/Space Vehicle Propulsion Units & parts
3769 Guided Missile/Space Vehicle Parts & Eqpt, NEC
3792 Travel Trailers & Campers
3795 Tanks & Tank Components
3799 Transportation Eqpt, NEC

38 MEASURING, ANALYZING AND CONTROLLING INSTRUMENTS; PHOTOGRAPHIC, MEDICAL AN

3812 Search, Detection, Navigation & Guidance Systs & Instrs
3821 Laboratory Apparatus & Furniture
3822 Automatic Temperature Controls
3823 Indl Instruments For Meas, Display & Control
3824 Fluid Meters & Counters
3825 Instrs For Measuring & Testing Electricity
3826 Analytical Instruments
3827 Optical Instruments
3829 Measuring & Controlling Devices, NEC
3841 Surgical & Medical Instrs & Apparatus
3842 Orthopedic, Prosthetic & Surgical Appliances/Splys
3843 Dental Eqpt & Splys
3844 X-ray Apparatus & Tubes
3845 Electromedical & Electrotherapeutic Apparatus
3851 Ophthalmic Goods
3861 Photographic Eqpt & Splys
3873 Watch & Clock Devices & Parts

39 MISCELLANEOUS MANUFACTURING INDUSTRIES

3911 Jewelry: Precious Metal
3914 Silverware, Plated & Stainless Steel Ware
3915 Jewelers Findings & Lapidary Work
3931 Musical Instruments
3942 Dolls & Stuffed Toys
3944 Games, Toys & Children's Vehicles
3949 Sporting & Athletic Goods, NEC
3952 Lead Pencils, Crayons & Artist's Mtrls
3953 Marking Devices
3955 Carbon Paper & Inked Ribbons
3961 Costume Jewelry & Novelties
3965 Fasteners, Buttons, Needles & Pins
3991 Brooms & Brushes
3993 Signs & Advertising Displays
3995 Burial Caskets
3996 Linoleum & Hard Surface Floor Coverings, NEC
3999 Manufacturing Industries, NEC

73 BUSINESS SERVICES

7372 Prepackaged Software

76 MISCELLANEOUS REPAIR SERVICES

7692 Welding Repair
7694 Armature Rewinding Shops

SIC SECTION

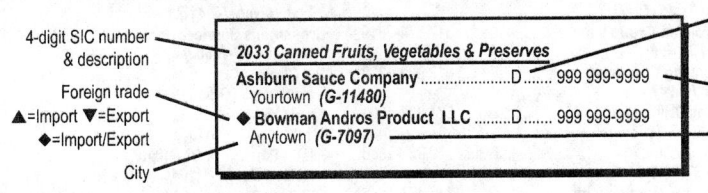
10 METAL MINING

1011 Iron Ores

◆ **Arcelormittal Holdings LLC** ....D 219 399-1200
East Chicago **(G-2516)**

◆ **Arcelormittal Minorca Mine Inc** ....G 219 399-1200
East Chicago **(G-2518)**

1081 Metal Mining Svcs

Better Metal Systems LLC ....G 219 290-2539
Hammond **(G-5851)**

Diamond Mining Lead ....G 317 340-7760
Indianapolis **(G-6740)**

James F Reilly 3 Ent ....G 574 277-8267
Mishawaka **(G-10058)**

P M I LLC ....G 812 374-3856
Edinburgh **(G-2619)**

Postle Aluminum Company LLC ....E 574 389-0800
Elkhart **(G-3104)**

Turner Contracting Inc ....D 812 834-5954
Bedford **(G-586)**

Vibronics Inc ....G 812 853-2300
Newburgh **(G-11055)**

1099 Metal Ores, NEC

Arconic Inc ....B 412 553-4545
Newburgh **(G-11021)**

General Steel ....G 317 251-9583
Indianapolis **(G-6999)**

12 COAL MINING

1221 Bituminous Coal & Lignite: Surface Mining

ANR Pipeline Company ....G 260 463-3342
Lagrange **(G-9031)**

Arrow Mining Inc ....G 270 683-4186
Oakland City **(G-11306)**

Arrow Mining Inc ....E 812 328-2117
Oakland City **(G-11307)**

Arrow Mining Inc ....E 812 328-6154
Oakland City **(G-11308)**

Colony Bay Cond Owners ....G 260 436-4764
Fort Wayne **(G-4167)**

Eagle River Coal LLC ....G 618 252-0490
Evansville **(G-3471)**

Foertsch Construction Co Inc ....D 812 529-8211
Lamar **(G-9099)**

Gibson County Coal LLC ....B 812 385-1816
Princeton **(G-11873)**

Hickman Williams & Company ....F 708 656-8818
La Porte **(G-8764)**

Mt Vernon Coal Transfer Co ....F 812 838-5531
Mount Vernon **(G-10403)**

Peabody Bear Run Mining LLC ....A 812 659-7126
Evansville **(G-3666)**

Peabody Energy Corporation ....D 812 795-4026
Oakland City **(G-11312)**

Peabody Midwest Mining LLC ....C 812 743-2910
Wheatland **(G-14232)**

Peabody Midwest Mining LLC ....C 812 644-7323
Cannelburg **(G-1285)**

Peabody Midwest Mining LLC ....C 812 495-6070
Pimento **(G-11580)**

Peabody Midwest Mining LLC ....E 812 434-8500
Lynnville **(G-9436)**

Peabody Midwest Mining LLC ....G 812 254-7714
Washington **(G-13997)**

Peabody Midwest Mining LLC ....C 812 782-3209
Francisco **(G-4817)**

Peabody Midwest Mining LLC ....G 812 795-0040
Oakland City **(G-11313)**

Peabody Wild Boar Mining LLC ....G 812 434-8500
Lynnville **(G-9437)**

Rogers Group Inc ....D 812 332-6341
Bloomington **(G-815)**

Sandy Little Coal Co Inc ....G 812 529-8216
Evanston **(G-3325)**

▲ **Solar Sources Inc** ....F 317 788-0084
Indianapolis **(G-7960)**

Solar Sources Inc ....D 812 354-8776
Petersburg **(G-11569)**

Vigo Coaf Inc ....B 812 759-8446
Evansville **(G-3800)**

Vigo Coal Operating Co Inc ....C 812 759-8446
Evansville **(G-3801)**

1222 Bituminous Coal: Underground Mining

Peabody Midwest Mining LLC ....C 812 743-2910
Wheatland **(G-14232)**

Peabody Midwest Mining LLC ....E 812 434-8500
Lynnville **(G-9436)**

Solar Sources Underground LLC ....G 317 788-0084
Indianapolis **(G-7961)**

Sunrise Coal LLC ....C 812 299-2800
Terre Haute **(G-13346)**

Sunrise Coal LLC ....C 812 398-2200
Carlisle **(G-1297)**

1241 Coal Mining Svcs

Al Perry Enterprises Inc ....G 812 867-7727
Evansville **(G-3347)**

Arrow Mining Inc ....E 812 328-6154
Oakland City **(G-11308)**

B B Mining Inc ....G 812 845-2717
Cynthiana **(G-2329)**

Black Panther Mining LLC ....G 812 745-2920
Oaktown **(G-11317)**

▲ **English Resources Inc** ....G 812 423-6716
Evansville **(G-3479)**

ERC Mining Indiana Corp ....G 812 665-9780
Jasonville **(G-8234)**

Fretina Corp ....F 812 547-6471
Tell City **(G-13163)**

Gibson County Coal LLC ....B 812 385-1816
Princeton **(G-11873)**

Kq Servicing LLC ....G 812 486-9244
Loogootee **(G-9388)**

Paringa Resources Limited ....G 314 422-4150
Evansville **(G-3663)**

Peabody Energy Corporation ....G 314 342-3400
Oakland City **(G-11311)**

Peabody Midwest Mining LLC ....G 812 743-9292
Vincennes **(G-13695)**

Peabody Midwest Mining LLC ....E 812 434-8500
Lynnville **(G-9436)**

Peabody Midwest Mining LLC ....G 812 795-0040
Oakland City **(G-11313)**

Pittman Mine Service LLC ....E 812 847-2340
Linton **(G-9311)**

R D-N-P Drilling Inc ....G 219 956-3481
Wheatfield **(G-14229)**

Rogers Group Inc ....E 812 333-6324
Bloomington **(G-816)**

Stone Coal Services LLC ....G 812 455-8215
Evansville **(G-3752)**

Sun Energy Group LLC ....F 812 683-1178
Huntingburg **(G-6180)**

Sycamore Coal Inc ....G 812 491-4000
Terre Haute **(G-13347)**

Triad Mining Inc ....F 812 328-2117
Oakland City **(G-11316)**

Vectren Corporation ....A 812 491-4000
Evansville **(G-3794)**

Vectren Corporation ....E 812 424-6411
Evansville **(G-3795)**

13 OIL AND GAS EXTRACTION

1311 Crude Petroleum & Natural Gas

ANR Pipeline Company ....G 260 463-3342
Lagrange **(G-9031)**

Atlas Energy Indiana LLC ....G 812 268-4900
Sullivan **(G-13080)**

Avon Carbon Capture RES Assoc ....G 317 753-8829
Avon **(G-430)**

B N Oil LLC ....G 859 816-2244
Lawrenceburg **(G-9132)**

Barger Engineering Inc ....G 812 476-3077
Evansville **(G-3370)**

Briggs Exploration Prod Co LLC ....G 812 249-0564
Evansville **(G-3401)**

C Milligan Investments LLC ....G 219 241-5811
Valparaiso **(G-13518)**

C Modesitt Oil Production LLC ....G 812 249-0678
Rosedale **(G-12203)**

Carlton West Oil Company LLC ....G 812 375-9689
Columbus **(G-1867)**

Ceres Solutions LLP ....G 765 477-6542
Lafayette **(G-8874)**

Common Sense Producing LLC ....G 317 622-1682
Greenfield **(G-5515)**

Core Minerals Operating Co Inc ....G 812 759-6950
Evansville **(G-3430)**

Countrymark Coop Holdg Corp ....E 800 808-3170
Indianapolis **(G-6676)**

Countrymark Ref Logistics LLC ....D 812 838-4341
Mount Vernon **(G-10388)**

Coy Oil Inc ....G 812 838-3146
Mount Vernon **(G-10389)**

Four Season Oil Inc ....G 317 215-1214
Plainfield **(G-11611)**

Fred D McCrary ....G 812 354-6520
Petersburg **(G-11564)**

Gallagher Drilling Inc ....E 812 477-6746
Evansville **(G-3514)**

Green Cow Power LLC ....G 219 984-5915
Goshen **(G-5229)**

Heflin Hflin Oil Gas Producers ....G 812 536-3464
Stendal **(G-13074)**

Hux Oil Corp ....G 812 894-2096
Terre Haute **(G-13251)**

Iam Petroleum Inc ....G 260 625-9951
Columbia City **(G-1793)**

Imperial Petroleum Inc ....G 812 867-1433
Evansville **(G-3549)**

James Mobile Oil Change ....G 219 455-5321
Crown Point **(G-2266)**

K S Oil Corp ....G 812 453-3026
Evansville **(G-3581)**

Lassus Bros Oil Inc ....G 260 625-4003
Fort Wayne **(G-4424)**

Mannon L Walters Inc ....F 812 867-5946
Evansville **(G-3613)**

Mayhew Oil & Gas LLC ....G 812 985-9966
Mount Vernon **(G-10399)**

Moore Engineering & Prod Co ....F 812 479-1051
Evansville **(G-3636)**

Employee Codes: A=Over 500 employees, B=251-500
C=101-250, D=51-100, E=20-50, F=10-19, G=2-9

2018 Harris Indiana
Industrial Directory

547

S I C

Nickolick Development ....G......812 422-8526
Evansville (G-3644)

Paul E Potts ....G......812 354-3241
Hazleton (G-6010)

Payne George A Petroleum Engr ....G......812 853-3813
Newburgh (G-11040)

Robinson Engineering & Oil Co ....F......812 477-1575
Evansville (G-3707)

Ryan Oil Co LLC ....G......812 422-4168
Evansville (G-3713)

Sater Enterprises ....G......812 477-1529
Evansville (G-3714)

◆ Sg Solutions LLC ....E......812 535-6000
West Terre Haute (G-14129)

Shell ....G......765 282-4635
Muncie (G-10561)

South Bend Ethanol LLC ....G......574 703-3360
South Bend (G-12043)

Speedway LLC ....F......765 827-0321
Connersville (G-2071)

Speedway LLC ....F......317 867-3699
Noblesville (G-11188)

Speedway LLC ....F......317 838-5479
Plainfield (G-11644)

Speedway LLC ....G......219 929-1054
Chesterton (G-1631)

Speedway LLC ....F......317 770-0225
Noblesville (G-11189)

Speedway LLC ....F......317 783-6361
Indianapolis (G-7974)

Strategic Talent LLC ....G......317 489-4000
Indianapolis (G-8011)

Tamarack Petroleum Company Inc ......G......812 567-4023
Tennyson (G-13181)

Trey Exploration Inc ....G......812 858-3146
Newburgh (G-11052)

Universal Operating Inc ....G......812 477 1584
Evansville (G-3789)

Viannos Village Cretan Oil ....G......219 513-6720
Highland (G-6058)

Vickery Drilling Co ....G......812 473-4671
Evansville (G-3798)

1321 Natural Gas Liquids

Air Liquide Tom Utley ....G......812 838-0599
Mount Vernon (G-10381)

Citizens By-Products Coal Co ....F......317 927-4738
Indianapolis (G-6613)

Daylight Engineering Inc ....G......812 983-2518
Elberfeld (G-2633)

Excel Co-Op Inc ....G......574 967-4166
Flora (G-3995)

Jackson-Jennings LLC ....G......812 522-4911
Seymour (G-12461)

Mid-West Oil Company Inc ....G......812 533-1227
West Terre Haute (G-14127)

Nisource Inc ....G......877 647-5990
Valparaiso (G-13590)

Semstream LP ....G......765 482-8105
Lebanon (G-9222)

1381 Drilling Oil & Gas Wells

Armstrong Drilling Inc ....G......765 455-2445
Burlington (G-1209)

Beechler Well Drlg & Pump Svc ....G......317 849-2535
Fishers (G-3877)

Bkb Petroleum Inc ....G......574 389-8159
Elkhart (G-2725)

Countrymark Coop Holdg Corp ....E......812 759-6962
Evansville (G-3433)

Coy Oil Inc ....G......618 966-2126
Mount Vernon (G-10390)

Coy Oil Inc ....G......812 838-1206
Mount Vernon (G-10389)

Diamond III Inc ....G......812 882-6269
Vincennes (G-13674)

Directional Business Intellige ....G......317 770-0805
Noblesville (G-11094)

Directional Drilling Co LLC ....G......812 208-3392
Farmersburg (G-3837)

Energy Drilling LLC ....G......618 943-5314
Vincennes (G-13676)

Energy Inc ....G......765 948-3504
Alexandria (G-41)

G & B Directional Boring LLC ....G......574 538-8132
Shipshewana (G-12615)

Gagan Petroleum Inc ....G......765 254-1330
Muncie (G-10475)

Gallagher Drilling Inc ....E......812 477-6746
Evansville (G-3514)

Gwaltney Drilling Inc ....G......812 254-5085
Washington (G-13985)

Hamilton Bros Inc ....F......317 241-2571
Indianapolis (G-7067)

Hindi Petroleum Group II Inc ....G......317 574-0619
Carmel (G-1405)

Hoosier Drilling Contrs Inc ....F......812 689-1260
Madison (G-9470)

Hoover Well Drilling Inc ....G......574 831-4901
New Paris (G-10984)

Hydro-Exc Inc ....E......219 922-9886
Griffith (G-5778)

Indiana Drilling Company Inc ....G......812 477-1575
Evansville (G-3551)

John Remmler Well Drilling ....G......812 663-8178
Greensburg (G-5616)

Magnum Drilling Svcs Inc ....G......812 985-3981
Evansville (G-3611)

Maurer Environmental Drilling ....G......574 272-7524
South Bend (G-12855)

McGrews Well Drilling Inc ....G......574 857-3875
Rochester (G-12137)

Michael R Harris ....G......812 425-9411
Evansville (G-3625)

Midwest Energy Partners LLC ....G......317 600-3235
Indianapolis (G-7505)

Sr Petroleum Inc ....G......574 383-5879
Granger (G-5439)

Universal Operating Inc ....G......812 477-1584
Evansville (G-3789)

US Oilfield Company LLC ....E......888 584-7565
Carmel (G-1505)

Vickery Drilling Co ....G......812 473-4671
Evansville (G-3798)

1382 Oil & Gas Field Exploration Svcs

Barger Engineering Inc ....G......812 476-3077
Evansville (G-3370)

Breitburn Operating LP ....G......812 738-3338
Corydon (G-2091)

Countrymark Coop Holdg Corp ....E......800 808-3170
Indianapolis (G-6676)

Countrymark Ref Logistics LLC ....D......812 838-4341
Mount Vernon (G-10388)

Enviropeel USA ....G......317 631-9100
Indianapolis (G-6873)

Gemini Oil LLC ....G......260 571-8388
Warren (G-13830)

Hansford Co ....G......317 255-4756
Indianapolis (G-7070)

Imperial Petroleum Inc ....G......812 867-1433
Evansville (G-3549)

Legacy Resources Co LP ....G......317 328-5660
Indianapolis (G-7394)

Michael R Harris ....G......812 425-9411
Evansville (G-3625)

Mid Central Land & Exploration ....G......812 476-9393
Carmel (G-1440)

Pioneer Oil Company Inc ....F......812 494-2800
Vincennes (G-13697)

Plymouth Oil and Gas Inc ....G......574 875-4808
Goshen (G-5311)

Seismic Vision LLC ....G......219 548-8704
Valparaiso (G-13613)

Silver Petroleum Corp ....G......260 824-2220
Bluffton (G-891)

Trey Exploration Inc ....G......812 858-3146
Newburgh (G-11052)

Vickery Drilling Co ....G......812 473-4671
Evansville (G-3798)

1389 Oil & Gas Field Svcs, NEC

AAA Mudjackers ....G......317 574-1990
Sharpsville (G-12503)

Abari Properties Development ....G......317 721-9230
Indianapolis (G-6306)

All-Phase Construction Co LLC ....G......317 345-7057
Fishers (G-3869)

Apex AG Solutions LLC ....F......937 564-5421
Richmond (G-11954)

ARS Nebraska LLC ....E......765 832-5210
Clinton (G-1713)

Breitburn Operating LP ....G......812 738-3338
Corydon (G-2091)

Bst Corp ....G......812 925-7911
Boonville (G-909)

Central Ind Oil Co ....G......317 253-1131
Indianapolis (G-6583)

Centre Township ....E......765 482-1729
Lebanon (G-9173)

Complete Property Care LLC ....G......765 288-0890
Muncie (G-10447)

Core Laboratories LP ....F......260 312-0455
Fort Wayne (G-4178)

Crossroads Services Inc ....G......219 972-3631
Munster (G-10603)

E Z Choice ....G......219 852-4281
Hammond (G-5873)

Field Construction ....G......574 664-2010
Twelve Mile (G-13450)

Filson Earthwork Company ....F......317 774-3180
Noblesville (G-11104)

G E Kerr Companies Inc ....G......417 426-5504
Kokomo (G-8627)

Gallagher Drilling Inc ....E......812 477-6746
Evansville (G-3514)

Gas City B & K Inc ....G......765 674-9651
Gas City (G-5125)

Hellweg Holdings LLC ....G......317 909-6764
McCordsville (G-9669)

Helvie & Sons Inc ....G......765 674-1372
Marion (G-9530)

Imperial Petroleum Inc ....G......812 867-1433
Evansville (G-3549)

Indiana Petroleum Contractors ....G......812 477-1575
Evansville (G-3552)

Jay Costas Companies Inc ....G......219 663-4364
Crown Point (G-2267)

Johnson Eh Construction LLC ....G......812 344-8450
Columbus (G-1952)

Jtm Home & Building ....G......219 690-1445
Lowell (G-9411)

K S Oil Corp ....G......812 453-3026
Evansville (G-3581)

Ken Tex Crude Producers Inc ....G......812 723-2108
Lafayette (G-8938)

Lucas Oil Pro Plling Prmotions ....G......812 246-3350
Charlestown (G-1572)

Matrix Nac ....F......219 931-6600
Hammond (G-5914)

Morgan Excavating ....G......812 385-6036
Oakland City (G-11310)

Oilfield Research Inc ....G......812 424-2907
Evansville (G-3653)

Onsite Construction Services ....E......312 723-8060
Chesterton (G-1625)

P & J Sectional Housing ....G......260 982-7231
North Manchester (G-11240)

Panhandle Eastrn Pipe Line LP ....E......317 873-2410
Indianapolis (G-7649)

Payne George A Petroleum Engr ....G......812 853-3813
Newburgh (G-11040)

Pinnacle Oil Trading LLC ....G......317 875-9465
Indianapolis (G-7697)

Pioneer Oilfield Services LLC ....D......812 882-0999
Vincennes (G-13698)

Pulse Energy ....G......812 268-6700
Sullivan (G-13091)

Quick Well Service Inc ....G......812 426-1924
Evansville (G-3692)

RC Enterprise LLC ....G......317 225-6747
Indianapolis (G-7823)

Ricker Oil Company Inc ....E......317 780-1777
Indianapolis (G-7841)

Rodgers Enterprises LLC ....G......765 396-3143
Eaton (G-2588)

Rs Used Oil Services Inc ....F......866 778-7336
Carmel (G-1473)

Saybolt LP ....G......812 282-7242
Clarksville (G-1695)

Siswd Processing ....G......812 574-4080
Madison (G-9495)

Specialized Services Inc ....G......317 485-8561
Fortville (G-4782)

Sunrise Energy LLC ....G......812 886-9990
Vincennes (G-13708)

Tradebe Environmental Svcs LLC ....G......800 388-7242
Merrillville (G-9759)

Tradebe GP ....G......800 388-7242
East Chicago (G-2572)

Tradebe Industrial Svcs LLC ....E......800 388-7242
East Chicago (G-2573)

United Oil Corp ....G......260 489-3511
Fort Wayne (G-4716)

US Oilfield Company LLC ....E......888 584-7565
Carmel (G-1505)

Valley Scale Company LLC ....F......812 282-5269
Clarksville (G-1699)

Wallys Construction ....G......812 254-4154
Washington (G-14006)

14 MINING AND QUARRYING OF NONMETALLIC MINERALS, EXCEPT FUELS

1411 Dimension Stone

B G Hoadley Quarries Inc ....E 812 332-1447
  Bloomington *(G-671)*

B G Hoadley Quarries Inc ....E 812 332-1447
  Bloomington *(G-672)*

Demotte Decorative Stone Inc ....G 219 987-5461
  Demotte *(G-2434)*

▲ Elliott Stone Co Inc ....E 812 275-5556
  Bedford *(G-540)*

Garrity Stone Inc ....G 317 546-0893
  Indianapolis *(G-6985)*

Independent Limestone Co LLC ......E 812 824-4951
  Bloomington *(G-744)*

▲ Indiana Lmstone Acqisition LLC ...D ... 812 275-3341
  Bloomington *(G-745)*

Indiana Quarriers & Carvers ....F ... 812 935-8383
  Gosport *(G-5351)*

▼ Indiana Stone Works ....E ... 812 279-0448
  Bedford *(G-553)*

Legacy Vulcan LLC ....F ... 219 696-5467
  Lowell *(G-9414)*

▲ M U Holdings Inc ....F ... 765 675-8054
  Tipton *(G-13396)*

Marietta Martin Materials Inc ....F ... 317 776-4460
  Noblesville *(G-11145)*

Martin Mretta Magnesia Spc LLC ....E ... 765 795-3536
  Cloverdale *(G-1729)*

Rush County Stone Co Inc ....G ... 765 629-2211
  Milroy *(G-9985)*

Stone Center of Indiana LLC ....E ... 317 849-9100
  Indianapolis *(G-8009)*

Tremain Ceramic Tile & Flr Cvg ....E ... 317 542-1491
  Indianapolis *(G-8093)*

1422 Crushed & Broken Limestone

3d Stone Inc ....E ... 812 824-5805
  Bloomington *(G-651)*

Aggrock Quarries Inc ....E ... 812 246-2582
  Charlestown *(G-1557)*

Barrett Paving Materials Inc ....F ... 765 935-3060
  Richmond *(G-11960)*

Big Creek LLC ....F ... 812 876-0835
  Stinesville *(G-13075)*

Calcar Quarries Incorporated ....F ... 812 723-2109
  Paoli *(G-11447)*

Carmeuse Lime Inc ....E ... 219 949-1450
  Gary *(G-5033)*

Cave Quarries Inc ....G ... 812 936-7743
  Paoli *(G-11448)*

Corydon Stone & Asphalt Inc ....E ... 812 738-2216
  Corydon *(G-2096)*

Francesville Vulcan Materials ....E ... 219 567-9155
  Francesville *(G-4812)*

Global Stone Portage LLC ....G ... 219 787-9190
  Portage *(G-11766)*

Handson ....F ... 812 246-4481
  Sellersburg *(G-12396)*

Hanson Aggregates Midwest LLC .....E ... 812 246-1942
  Sellersburg *(G-12397)*

Hanson Aggregates Midwest LLC .....G ... 419 399-4846
  Woodburn *(G-14383)*

Hanson Aggregates Midwest LLC .....F ... 812 689-5017
  Versailles *(G-13654)*

Hanson Aggregates Midwest LLC .....D ... 260 747-3105
  Fort Wayne *(G-4320)*

Hanson Aggregates Midwest LLC .....F ... 812 889-2120
  Lexington *(G-9251)*

Hanson Aggregates Midwest LLC .....F ... 812 346-6100
  North Vernon *(G-11260)*

Hanson Aggregates Midwest LLC .....F ... 765 653-7205
  Cloverdale *(G-1726)*

Hanson Aggrgates Southeast Inc .....D ... 317 788-4086
  Indianapolis *(G-7072)*

Harris Stone Service Inc ....F ... 765 522-6241
  Bainbridge *(G-477)*

Indian Creek Quarries LLC ....G ... 812 388-5622
  Williams *(G-14282)*

John S Davis Inc ....F ... 812 347-2707
  Depauw *(G-2457)*

Kellers Limestone Service ....F ... 219 326-1688
  La Porte *(G-8776)*

Legacy Vulcan LLC ....E ... 219 465-3066
  Valparaiso *(G-13575)*

Marietta Martin Materials Inc ....F ... 765 459-3194
  Kokomo *(G-8663)*

Marietta Martin Materials Inc ....F ... 317 789-4020
  Indianapolis *(G-7455)*

Marietta Martin Materials Inc ....F ... 317 776-4460
  Noblesville *(G-11145)*

Martin Marietta Materials Inc ....E ... 317 846-8540
  Indianapolis *(G-6272)*

Meshberger Stone Inc ....F ... 812 579-5241
  Columbus *(G-1971)*

Meshberger Stone Inc ....G ... 765 525-6442
  Flat Rock *(G-3991)*

Mulzer Crushed Stone Inc ....E ... 812 365-2145
  English *(G-3316)*

Mulzer Crushed Stone Inc ....E ... 812 547-7921
  Tell City *(G-13167)*

Mulzer Crushed Stone Inc ....E ... 812 723-4137
  Paoli *(G-11456)*

Mulzer Crushed Stone Inc ....E ... 812 547-7921
  Evansville *(G-3642)*

Mulzer Crushed Stone Inc ....E ... 812 937-2442
  Dale *(G-2332)*

Mulzer Crushed Stone Inc ....E ... 812 256-3346
  Charlestown *(G-1574)*

Mulzer Crushed Stone Inc ....E ... 812 649-5055
  Rockport *(G-12170)*

Nalc LLC ....E ... 502 548-9590
  Cloverdale *(G-1732)*

▲ New Point Stone Co Inc ....F ... 812 663-2021
  Greensburg *(G-5627)*

New Point Stone Co Inc ....F ... 812 852-4225
  Batesville *(G-512)*

New Point Stone Co Inc ....F ... 765 698-2227
  Laurel *(G-9128)*

New Point Stone Co Inc ....F ... 812 663-2422
  Greensburg *(G-5628)*

Paul H Rohe Co Inc ....F ... 812 926-1471
  Aurora *(G-384)*

Robertson Crushed Stone Inc ....F ... 812 633-4881
  Milltown *(G-9976)*

Rock Creek Stone LLC ....G ... 260 694-6880
  Bluffton *(G-890)*

Rogers Group Inc ....E ... 812 333-8560
  Bloomington *(G-813)*

Rogers Group Inc ....E ... 219 474-5125
  Kentland *(G-8523)*

Seminole Stone Inc ....F ... 812 634-7115
  Jasper *(G-8305)*

Stone Quary ....E ... 765 473-5578
  Peru *(G-11549)*

Stone Street Quarries Inc ....E ... 260 639-6511
  Hoagland *(G-6067)*

U S Aggregates Inc ....G ... 765 436-7665
  Thorntown *(G-13379)*

U S Aggregates Inc ....E ... 765 564-2282
  Delphi *(G-2430)*

West Plains Mining LLC ....E ... 260 563-9500
  Wabash *(G-13768)*

1429 Crushed & Broken Stone, NEC

Barrett Paving Materials Inc ....F ... 765 935-3060
  Richmond *(G-11960)*

Bens Quarry LLC ....G ... 812 824-3730
  Springville *(G-13060)*

Hanson Aggrgates Southeast Inc .....D ... 317 788-4086
  Indianapolis *(G-7072)*

Johnson Materials ....G ... 812 373-9044
  Columbus *(G-1953)*

Mulzer Crushed Stone Inc ....C ... 812 739-4777
  Leavenworth *(G-9165)*

New Point Stone Co Inc ....F ... 812 663-2422
  Greensburg *(G-5628)*

Pipe Creek Jr ....G ... 765 922-7991
  Sims *(G-12683)*

S & G Excavating Inc ....D ... 812 234-4848
  Terre Haute *(G-13322)*

1442 Construction Sand & Gravel

Access Solutions ....G ... 812 490-6026
  Newburgh *(G-11018)*

Asphalt Materials Inc ....B ... 317 872-6010
  Indianapolis *(G-6426)*

Asphalt Materials Inc ....G ... 317 875-4670
  Indianapolis *(G-6428)*

Beaver Gravel Corporation ....D ... 317 773-0679
  Noblesville *(G-11065)*

Beer and Slabaugh Inc ....E ... 574 773-3413
  Nappanee *(G-10653)*

Bob Belcher ....G ... 317 996-3712
  Monrovia *(G-10202)*

Brookfield Sand & Gravel Inc ....E ... 317 835-2235
  Fairland *(G-3821)*

Cgs Services Inc ....G ... 765 763-6258
  Morristown *(G-10367)*

Corydon Stone & Asphalt Inc ....E ... 812 738-2216
  Corydon *(G-2096)*

Country Estates ....G ... 812 925-6443
  Boonville *(G-913)*

▲ Country Stone ....E ... 260 837-7134
  Waterloo *(G-14012)*

Crisman Sand Co Inc ....G ... 219 762-2619
  Valparaiso *(G-13524)*

D H Gravel Company ....G ... 765 893-4914
  Williamsport *(G-14289)*

Elkhart County Gravel Inc ....F ... 574 831-2815
  New Paris *(G-10978)*

Elkhart County Gravel Inc ....F ... 574 831-2815
  Warsaw *(G-13870)*

Elkhart County Gravel Inc ....F ... 574 825-7913
  Middlebury *(G-9883)*

Flynn Sons Sand & Gravel ....G ... 812 636-4400
  Odon *(G-11325)*

Fred Jay Stewart ....F ... 765 284-1386
  Muncie *(G-10474)*

Gibson County Sand & Grav Inc ....G ... 812 851-5800
  Haubstadt *(G-6001)*

Gravel Doctor Indianapolis LLC ....G ... 317 399-4585
  Indianapolis *(G-7037)*

Hagerstown Gravel & Cnstr ....F ... 765 489-4812
  Hagerstown *(G-5806)*

Handson ....F ... 812 246-4481
  Sellersburg *(G-12396)*

Hanson Aggrgates Southeast Inc .....D ... 317 788-4086
  Indianapolis *(G-7072)*

Happy Valley Sand & Gravel Inc ....G ... 317 839-6800
  Plainfield *(G-11613)*

Harrison Hauling Inc ....G ... 574 862-3196
  Goshen *(G-5235)*

Harrison Sand and Gravel Co ....F ... 812 663-2021
  Greensburg *(G-5606)*

Henschen Sand and Gravel ....G ... 260 367-2636
  Howe *(G-6126)*

Hilltop Basic Resources Inc ....E ... 812 594-2293
  Patriot *(G-11468)*

Hopkins Gravel Sand & Concrete ......G ... 317 831-2704
  Mooresville *(G-10311)*

Hydraulic Press Brick Company ....E ... 317 290-1140
  Mooresville *(G-10313)*

Illiana Remedial Action Inc ....G ... 219 844-4862
  Hammond *(G-5898)*

Irving Materials Inc ....F ... 574 653-2749
  Huntington *(G-6218)*

Irving Materials Inc ....G ... 765 922-7285
  Marion *(G-9534)*

Irving Materials Inc ....F ... 765 778-4760
  Anderson *(G-123)*

Krafft Gravel Inc ....G ... 260 238-4653
  Spencerville *(G-13049)*

La Fontaine Gravel Inc ....G ... 765 981-4849
  La Fontaine *(G-8724)*

Lafarge North America Inc ....G ... 219 378-1193
  East Chicago *(G-2547)*

Lake County Sand & Gravel LLC ....G ... 219 988-4540
  Merrillville *(G-9725)*

Lees Ready-Mix & Trucking Inc ....F ... 812 372-1800
  Columbus *(G-1958)*

Legacy Vulcan LLC ....F ... 219 567-9155
  Francesville *(G-4814)*

Legacy Vulcan LLC ....G ... 219 253-6686
  Monon *(G-10176)*

Longhorn Sand and Gravel LLC ....G ... 574 656-3231
  North Liberty *(G-11218)*

Longhorn Sand and Gravel LLC ....G ... 574 532-2788
  Mishawaka *(G-10071)*

LPI Paving & Excavating ....G ... 260 726-9564
  Portland *(G-11834)*

M and G Dirt and Gravel LLC ....G ... 219 778-9341
  Rolling Prairie *(G-12189)*

Marietta Martin Materials Inc ....F ... 317 776-4460
  Noblesville *(G-11145)*

Marietta Martin Materials Inc ....G ... 317 831-7391
  Martinsville *(G-9622)*

Mauckport Sand & Gravel ....G ... 812 732-8800
  Mauckport *(G-9655)*

Merritt Sand and Gravel Inc ....F ... 260 665-2513
  Waterloo *(G-14018)*

Michele L Gravel ....G ... 317 889-0521
  Indianapolis *(G-7496)*

Mulzer Crushed Stone Inc ....E ... 812 649-5055
  Rockport *(G-12170)*

S
I
C

Muncie Sand & Gravel Inc ....G........ 765 282-6422
Muncie (G-10536)

Nugent Sand Company ....G........ 812 372-7508
Columbus (G-1983)

Old Dutch Sand Co Inc ....G........ 219 938-7020
Gary (G-5080)

Paddack Brothers Inc ....F........ 765 659-4777
Frankfort (G-4849)

Paul H Rohe Co Inc ....F........ 812 926-1471
Aurora (G-384)

Phend and Brown Inc ....E........ 574 658-4166
Milford (G-9961)

Quikrete Companies Inc ....E........ 317 251-2281
Indianapolis (G-7805)

Rex Alton & Companies Inc ....E........ 812 882-8519
Vincennes (G-13701)

Rinker Materials Corp ....G........ 317 353-2118
Indianapolis (G-7846)

Rogers Group Inc ....G........ 765 342-9655
Martinsville (G-9634)

Rogers Group Inc ....G........ 765 342-6898
Martinsville (G-9635)

Rogers Group Inc ....E........ 812 824-8565
Bloomington (G-814)

Rogers Group Inc ....E........ 812 849-3530
Mitchell (G-10170)

Rogers Group Inc ....F........ 765 762-2660
Williamsport (G-14297)

Rogers Group Inc ....F........ 812 275-7860
Springville (G-13068)

Rogers Group Inc ....G........ 765 893-4463
Williamsport (G-14296)

Rogers Group Inc ....E........ 812 882-3640
Vincennes (G-13703)

Rogers Group Inc ....E........ 812 333-6324
Bloomington (G-816)

Roskovenski Sand & Gravel Inc ....G........ 765 832-6748
Clinton (G-1719)

S & G Excavating Inc ....D........ 812 234-4848
Terre Haute (G-13322)

Schmaltz Ready Mix Concrete ....G........ 812 689-5140
Osgood (G-11394)

Schrock Aggregate Company Inc ....G........ 574 862-4167
Wakarusa (G-13795)

Schrock Excavating Inc ....E........ 574 862-4167
Wakarusa (G-13796)

Shelby Gravel Inc ....E........ 317 398-4485
Shelbyville (G-12567)

Shelby Gravel Inc ....F........ 812 526-2731
Edinburgh (G-2628)

Shelby Gravel Inc ....F........ 317 738-3445
Franklin (G-4929)

Southfield Corporation ....E........ 812 824-1355
Bloomington (G-829)

Speedway Sand & Gravel Inc ....G........ 574 893-7355
Silver Lake (G-12680)

Spray Sand & Gravel Inc ....G........ 812 523-8081
Seymour (G-12493)

Spray Sand & Gravel Inc ....G........ 812 522-5417
Seymour (G-12494)

Stafford Gravel Inc ....F........ 260 868-2503
Butler (G-1243)

Stone Quary ....G........ 574 936-2975
Plymouth (G-11725)

Stone Quary ....E........ 765 473-5578
Peru (G-11549)

Stonehenge Concrete & Gravel ....G........ 260 726-8282
Portland (G-11848)

Sugar Creek Gravel & Stone ....G........ 765 362-1646
Crawfordsville (G-2199)

Todd L Wise ....G........ 260 799-4828
Albion (G-36)

U S Aggregates Inc ....G........ 765 966-8155
Richmond (G-12071)

▲ U S Aggregates Inc ....G........ 317 872-6010
Indianapolis (G-8120)

U S Aggregates Inc ....F........ 765 362-2500
Crawfordsville (G-2202)

U S Aggregates Inc ....G........ 765 564-2580
Delphi (G-2429)

U S Aggregates Inc ....E........ 765 564-2282
Delphi (G-2430)

Utility Access Solutions Inc ....G........ 765 744-6528
Ridgeville (G-12083)

Van Duyne Block and Gravel ....G........ 574 223-6656
Rochester (G-12159)

W & W Gravel Co Incorporated ....F........ 260 672-3591
Roanoke (G-12112)

Wallace Construction Inc ....F........ 317 422-5356
Martinsville (G-9647)

West Plains Distribution LLC ....G........ 260 563-9500
Wabash (G-13767)

White River Gravel Company Inc ....G........ 317 834-6818
Indianapolis (G-8192)

Wilhelm Gravel Co Inc ....E........ 260 837-6511
Waterloo (G-14027)

Zimmerman-Newcomer Gravel ....G........ 574 658-4063
Milford (G-9967)

1446 Industrial Sand

3M Indianapolis ....G........ 317 692-3000
Indianapolis (G-6289)

C & J Plating & Grinding LLC ....G........ 765 288-8728
Muncie (G-10444)

Millburn Peat Company Inc ....E........ 219 362-7025
La Porte (G-8794)

Warsaw Foundry Company Inc ....D........ 574 267-8772
Warsaw (G-13962)

1455 Kaolin & Ball Clay

Unimin Corporation ....G........ 812 683-2179
Huntingburg (G-6183)

1459 Clay, Ceramic & Refractory Minerals, NEC

American Colloid Company ....G........ 812 547-3567
Troy (G-13445)

1479 Chemical & Fertilizer Mining

Excel Co-Op Inc ....G........ 219 984-5950
Reynolds (G-11945)

Royster Clark Closed ....G........ 812 397-2617
Shelburn (G-12509)

Wild Boar Mine ....G........ 812 922-1015
Lynnville (G-9438)

1481 Nonmetallic Minerals Svcs, Except Fuels

243 Quarry ....G........ 765 653-4100
Cloverdale (G-1723)

Imine Corporation ....G........ 877 464-6388
Indianapolis (G-7165)

United Minerals ....G........ 812 842-0978
Newburgh (G-11054)

1499 Miscellaneous Nonmetallic Mining

Classic Rock Face Block Inc ....G........ 260 704-3113
Fort Wayne (G-4160)

Goh A&C Inc ....E........ 812 738-2217
Corydon (G-2099)

Hanson Agrigoods Midwest Inc ....F........ 317 635-9048
Cloverdale (G-1727)

Millburn Peat Company Inc ....E........ 219 362-7025
La Porte (G-8794)

Peabody Midwest Mining LLC ....G........ 812 795-0040
Oakland City (G-11313)

20 FOOD AND KINDRED PRODUCTS

2011 Meat Packing Plants

▲ A L S Inc ....E........ 765 497-4750
West Lafayette (G-14045)

Bains Packing and Rfrgn ....F........ 260 244-5209
Columbia City (G-1765)

Berne Locker Storage ....G........ 260 589-2806
Berne (G-608)

Beutler Meat Processing Co ....F........ 765 742-7285
Lafayette (G-8860)

Bob Evans Farms Inc ....G........ 317 846-3261
Carmel (G-1319)

Brook Locker Plant ....G........ 219 275-2611
Brook (G-1098)

Butcher Block ....F........ 219 696-9111
Lowell (G-9401)

C&C Deer Processing ....G........ 812 836-2323
Tell City (G-13157)

Cannelburg Processing Plant ....G........ 812 486-3223
Cannelburg (G-1283)

Cargill Incorporated ....B........ 402 533-4227
Hammond (G-5858)

Cherrytree Farms LLC ....F........ 317 758-4495
Sheridan (G-12588)

Dewig Bros Meats ....G........ 812 768-6208
Haubstadt (G-5998)

Dewig Bros Packing Co Inc ....E........ 812 768-6208
Haubstadt (G-5999)

Drews Deer Processing ....G........ 812 279-6246
Mitchell (G-10162)

Fender 4 Star Meats Processing ....G........ 812 829-3240
Spencer (G-13025)

Ferdinand Processing Inc ....G........ 812 367-2073
Ferdinand (G-3850)

Foods Peer ....G........ 317 735-4283
Indianapolis (G-6946)

Griffin Industries LLC ....E........ 812 379-9528
Columbus (G-1935)

H & B Pork Inc ....G........ 219 261-3053
Wolcott (G-14364)

H P Schmitt Packing Co Inc ....G........ 260 724-3146
Decatur (G-2384)

Hilltop Processing Inc ....G........ 812 544-2174
Lamar (G-9100)

Hobart Locker & Meat Pkg Co ....G........ 219 942-5952
Crown Point (G-2257)

Hrr Enterprises Inc ....E........ 219 362-9050
La Porte (G-8768)

▼ Indiana Packers Corporation ....A........ 765 564-3680
Delphi (G-2422)

Jemdd LLC ....E........ 260 768-4156
Lagrange (G-9049)

Johns Butcher Shop ....G........ 574 773-4632
Nappanee (G-10688)

K W Deer Processing ....G........ 812 824-2492
Bloomington (G-756)

Kane-Miller Corp ....E........ 219 362-9050
La Porte (G-8775)

Kenny Dewig Meats Sausage Inc ....G........ 812 724-2333
Owensville (G-11428)

Lengerich Meats Inc ....E........ 260 638-4123
Zanesville (G-14413)

▲ Manley Meats Inc ....E........ 260 592-7313
Decatur (G-2392)

▲ Mariah Foods Corp ....C........ 812 378-3366
Columbus (G-1967)

Merkley & Sons Inc ....E........ 812 482-7020
Jasper (G-8295)

Milan Food Bank ....G........ 812 654-3682
Milan (G-9945)

Monon Meat Packing Company ....G........ 219 253-6363
Monon (G-10177)

Moody Meats ....G........ 317 272-4533
Avon (G-455)

Mpi Holdings Inc ....C........ 765 473-3086
Peru (G-11538)

Myers Frozen Food Provisioners ....G........ 765 525-6304
Saint Paul (G-12279)

Old Hoosier Meats ....G........ 574 825-2940
Middlebury (G-9913)

Onu Acre LLC ....G........ 765 565-1355
Carthage (G-1515)

Orange County Processing ....F........ 812 865-2028
Orleans (G-11366)

Ortman Meat Processing Inc ....G........ 574 946-7113
Winamac (G-14313)

Parretts Meat Proc & Catrg ....F........ 574 967-3711
Flora (G-4001)

Pates Slaughtering & Proc ....G........ 812 866-4710
Hanover (G-5963)

Rihm Inc ....G........ 765 478-3426
Cambridge City (G-1260)

Royal Center Locker Plant Inc ....F........ 574 643-3275
Royal Center (G-12213)

Ruwaldt Packing Co Inc ....E........ 219 942-2911
Hobart (G-6093)

Sander Processing ....E........ 812 481-0044
Celestine (G-1537)

Slabaughs Meat Processing ....G........ 574 773-0381
Nappanee (G-10706)

Smithfield Direct LLC ....G........ 812 867-6644
Evansville (G-3738)

Smithfield Direct LLC ....E........ 765 473-3086
Peru (G-11545)

Smithland Butchering Co Inc ....G........ 317 729-5398
Elizabethtown (G-2651)

Tyson Foods Inc ....A........ 574 753-6121
Logansport (G-9373)

Tyson Fresh Meats Inc ....B........ 574 753-6134
Logansport (G-9374)

Uselman Packing Co ....G........ 765 832-2112
Clinton (G-1722)

W & W Locker ....G........ 260 344-3400
Andrews (G-185)

Wilsons Locker & Proc Plant ....G........ 812 358-2632
Brownstown (G-1194)

Yoders Meats Inc ....G........ 260 768-4715
Shipshewana (G-12660)

2013 Sausages & Meat Prdts

▲ A L S Inc ....E 765 497-4750
West Lafayette (G-14045)
Big B Distributors Inc ....F 812 425-5235
Evansville (G-3384)
Butcher Block..F 219 696-9111
Lowell (G-9401)
Conagra Brands Inc ....B 402 240-5000
Indianapolis (G-6645)
Cosmos Superior Foods LLC ....G 317 975-2747
Carmel (G-1345)
Cottonwood Corp.....................................G 260 820-0415
Ossian (G-11398)
Cottonwood Corp.....................................G 260 565-3185
Craigville (G-2121)
El Popular Sausage Factory LLC ....G 219 476-7040
Valparaiso (G-13532)
Farm Boy Meats of Evansville ....C 812 425-5231
Evansville (G-3498)
Fisher Packing Company ....E 260 726-7355
Portland (G-11822)
Grabill Country Meat 1 Inc ....F 260 627-3691
Grabill (G-5369)
Grandma Hams Farm LLC ....G 317 253-0635
Indianapolis (G-7035)
Hillshire Brands Company ....B 260 456-4802
Fort Wayne (G-4335)
Hilltop Processing Inc ....G 812 544-2174
Lamar (G-9100)
▼ Indiana Packers Corporation ....A 765 564-3680
Delphi (G-2422)
Jemdd LLC ....E 260 768-4156
Lagrange (G-9049)
Klemms Meat Market ....G 317 632-1963
Indianapolis (G-7357)
▲ Manley Meats Inc ....E 260 592-7313
Decatur (G-2392)
Merkley & Sons Inc ....E 812 482-7020
Jasper (G-8295)
Millers Locker Plant ....G 765 234-2381
Crawfordsville (G-2175)
▲ Monogram Frozen Foods LLC ....C 574 848-0344
Bristol (G-1072)
Mpi Holdings Inc ....C 765 473-3086
Peru (G-11538)
Park 100 Foods Inc ....E 317 549-4545
Indianapolis (G-7656)
▲ Park 100 Foods Inc ....D 765 675-3480
Tipton (G-13400)
Park 100 Foods Inc ....D 765 763-6064
Morristown (G-10375)
Parretts Meat Proc & Catrg ....F 574 967-3711
Flora (G-4001)
Pates Slaughtering & Proc......................G 812 866-4710
Hanover (G-5963)
Paytons Barbecue....................................G 765 294-2716
Veedersburg (G-13645)
Perfect Pig Inc ....G 219 984-5355
Reynolds (G-11947)
Plumrose USA Inc....................................C 574 295-8190
Elkhart (G-3100)
Rihm Inc ....G 765 478-3426
Cambridge City (G-1260)
Royal Center Locker Plant Inc ....F 574 643-3275
Royal Center (G-12213)
Rubicon Foods LLC ....F 317 826-8793
Indianapolis (G-7872)
Ruwaldt Packing Co Inc ....E 219 942-2911
Hobart (G-6093)
Saint Adrian Meats Sausage LLC...........G 317 403-3305
Lebanon (G-9221)
Sander Processing ....E 812 481-0044
Celestine (G-1537)
Tyson Foods Inc......................................A 574 753-6121
Logansport (G-9373)
Tyson Fresh Meats Inc ....E 812 486-2800
Washington (G-14005)
Wilsons Locker & Proc Plant...................G 812 358-2632
Brownstown (G-1194)
Wolfs Bar B Q Inc....................................D 812 424-8891
Evansville (G-3814)
Yoders Meats Inc.....................................G 260 768-4715
Shipshewana (G-12660)
Zels...E 219 864-1011
Schererville (G-12353)

2015 Poultry Slaughtering, Dressing & Processing

Cargill Incorporated................................B 402 533-4227
Hammond (G-5858)

Crystal Lake LLC......................................G 574 267-3101
Warsaw (G-13860)
Crystal Lake LLC......................................D 574 858-2514
Warsaw (G-13861)
Crystal Valley Farms LLC ....A 260 829-6550
Orland (G-11349)
◆ Culver Duck Farms Inc ....G 574 825-9537
Middlebury (G-9880)
Egg Innovations LLC ....G 574 267-7545
Warsaw (G-13868)
Farbest Farms Inc ....F 812 481-1034
Huntingburg (G-6164)
Farbest Foods ....G 812 886-2125
Vincennes (G-13680)
Farbest Foods Inc ....A 812 683-4200
Huntingburg (G-6165)
Farbest Foods Intl Inc ....G 812 683-4200
Huntingburg (G-6166)
Graber ....G 812 636-7699
Odon (G-11326)
Hollands Deer Processing LLC ....F 765 472-5876
Peru (G-11530)
Hy-Line North America LLC ....E 260 375-3041
Warren (G-13831)
Lambrights Inc ....D 260 463-2178
Lagrange (G-9056)
◆ Maple Leaf Inc ....B 574 453-4455
Leesburg (G-9238)
Maple Leaf Farms Inc ....G 574 658-4121
Milford (G-9958)
◆ Maple Leaf Farms Inc ....G 574 453-4500
Milford (G-9957)
▲ Midwest Poultry Services LP ....F 574 353-7232
Mentone (G-9689)
P & R Farms LLC ....G 812 326-2010
Saint Anthony (G-12248)
Perdue Farms Inc ....D 812 254-8500
Washington (G-13998)
Perdue Farms Inc ....G 812 886-0593
Vincennes (G-13696)
Perdue Farms Inc ....D 765 436-7990
Thorntown (G-13377)
Perdue Farms Inc ....F 757 787-5210
Washington (G-13999)
Perdue Farms Inc ....G 765 325-2997
Lebanon (G-9214)
▲ Pine Manor Inc ....B 800 532-4186
Orland (G-11355)
Pletchers Poultry Processing ....G 574 831-2329
Goshen (G-5310)
Rose Acre Farms Inc ....D 219 253-6681
Monon (G-10178)
Tyson Foods Inc......................................E 812 347-2452
Ramsey (G-11895)
Tyson Foods Inc......................................A 812 738-3219
Corydon (G-2114)

2021 Butter

Conagra Brands Inc ....B 317 329-3700
Indianapolis (G-6646)
Dairy Farmers America Inc ....D 574 533-3141
Goshen (G-5196)
Dillman Farm Incorporated ....G 812 825-5525
Bloomington (G-713)
Tulip Tree Creamery LLC ....G 317 331-5469
Indianapolis (G-8112)

2022 Cheese

Capriole Inc ....G 812 923-9408
Greenville (G-5647)
Dream Kraft LLC ....G 317 545-2988
Indianapolis (G-6766)
Foremost Farms USA Cooperative ....G 317 842-7755
Indianapolis (G-6949)
Graham Cheese Corporation ....E 812 692-5237
Elnora (G-3289)
▲ Huber Orchards Inc ....E 812 923-9463
Borden (G-930)
Karens Kountry Krafts..............................G 765 238-2873
New Castle (G-10908)
Kitchen Krafts ....G 765 458-6858
Liberty (G-9262)
Kraft N Kreations ....G 812 243-1754
West Terre Haute (G-14125)
Kroger Limited Partnership II ....D 765 364-5200
Crawfordsville (G-2166)
Middlebury Cheese Company LLC..........E 574 825-9511
Middlebury (G-9906)
Tulip Tree Creamery LLC.........................G 317 331-5469
Indianapolis (G-8112)

2023 Milk, Condensed & Evaporated

Baird Ice Cream Co..................................G 812 283-3345
Clarksville (G-1673)
Capricorn Foods LLC ....G 219 670-1872
Merrillville (G-9707)
Combustion and Systems Inc.................G 859 814-8847
Rising Sun (G-12086)
Dairy Farmers America Inc ....G 574 533-3141
Goshen (G-5196)
International Food Tech Inc ....G 812 853-9432
Newburgh (G-11032)
Nestle Usa Inc ....C 765 778-6000
Anderson (G-144)
▲ Smithfoods Richmond Inc ....G 330 683-8710
Richmond (G-12051)
▲ Vesta Pharmaceuticals Inc ....E 317 895-9000
Indianapolis (G-8158)
Vitamorph Labs LLC ....G 219 237-0174
Highland (G-6059)
Wholistic Gardens ....G 260 573-1088
Waterloo (G-14026)

2024 Ice Cream

AJS Gyros To Go ....G 812 951-1715
New Salisbury (G-11007)
▲ Archibald Brothers Intl Inc ....G 812 941-8267
New Albany (G-10746)
Bonnie Doon Ice Cream Corp ....F 574 255-9841
Mishawaka (G-10011)
Brics ....G 317 257-5757
Indianapolis (G-6507)
Browns Dairy Inc......................................G 219 464-4141
Valparaiso (G-13514)
Buckner Inc ....F 317 570-0533
Indianapolis (G-6520)
Cloverleaf Farms Dairy ....G 219 938-5140
Gary (G-5038)
Ice Cream On Wheels Inc ....G 800 884-9793
Griffith (G-5779)
Ice Cream Specialties Inc.......................D 765 474-2989
Lafayette (G-8919)
La Michoacana ....G 574 293-9799
Elkhart (G-2980)
Meyer Ice Cream LLC ....G 812 941-8267
New Albany (G-10829)
Mishawaka Frozen Custard.....................E 574 255-8000
Mishawaka (G-10092)
National Ice Corp ....G 317 887-9446
Indianapolis (G-7572)
Nestle Dreyers Ice Cream Co ....C 260 483-3102
Fort Wayne (G-4497)
Penguin Enterprises LLC ....G 812 333-0475
Bloomington (G-797)
Ritters Frozen Custard Inc ....G 317 859-1038
Greenwood (G-5739)
Saniserv...E 317 831-7030
Mooresville (G-10339)
Suiza Dairy Group LLC............................C 260 724-2136
Decatur (G-2407)

2026 Milk

Conagra Dairy Foods Company ....B 317 329-3700
Indianapolis (G-6647)
Dairy Farmers America Inc ....D 574 533-3141
Goshen (G-5196)
Dean Foods Co...G 214 303-3400
Plymouth (G-11680)
Dean Foods Company ....C 574 223-2141
Rochester (G-12121)
East Side Jersey Dairy Inc ....G 812 536-2207
Holland (G-6105)
East Side Jersey Dairy Inc ....E 765 649-1261
Anderson (G-104)
Instantwhip-Indianapolis Inc...................F 317 899-1533
Indianapolis (G-7244)
Jacobs & Brichford LLC...........................G 765 692-0056
Connersville (G-2057)
Jujuberry LLC ....G 765 673-0058
Marion (G-9539)
Prairie Farms Dairy Inc ....D 765 649-1261
Anderson (G-154)
Royal Food Products Inc ....D 317 782-2660
Indianapolis (G-7865)
▲ Smithfoods Richmond Inc ....C 330 683-8710
Richmond (G-12051)
Suiza Dairy Group LLC............................D 260 355-2273
Huntington (G-6254)
Swissland Milk Company Inc..................G 260 589-2761
Berne (G-628)

Urban Swirl ....G....... 574 387-4035
Granger *(G-5448)*

Yogurtz ....G....... 317 853-6600
Carmel *(G-1511)*

2032 Canned Specialties

Avarrotes Luliana ....G....... 574 232-6803
South Bend *(G-12719)*

Eden Foods Inc ....E....... 765 396-3344
Eaton *(G-2583)*

El Popular Inc ....F....... 219 397-3728
East Chicago *(G-2526)*

Frito-Lay North America Inc ....B....... 765 659-1831
Frankfort *(G-4834)*

H & H Partnership Inc ....G....... 765 513-4739
Kokomo *(G-8634)*

▼ Mead Johnson & Company LLC ......B....... 812 429-5000
Evansville *(G-3620)*

▲ Morgan Foods Inc ....A....... 812 794-1170
Austin *(G-398)*

Park 100 Foods Inc ....E....... 317 549-4545
Indianapolis *(G-7656)*

▲ Park 100 Foods Inc ....D....... 765 675-3480
Tipton *(G-13400)*

Tyson Foods Inc ....B....... 260 726-3118
Portland *(G-11854)*

Vitamins Inc ....E....... 219 879-7356
Michigan City *(G-9859)*

2033 Canned Fruits, Vegetables & Preserves

Bay Valley Foods LLC ....C....... 574 936-4061
Plymouth *(G-11668)*

▲ Caj Food Products Inc ....F....... 888 524-6882
Fishers *(G-3884)*

Candy Dish Inc ....G....... 317 269-6262
Nashville *(G-10719)*

Conagra Brands Inc ....F....... 765 563-3182
Brookston *(G-1103)*

Dillman Farm Incorporated ....G....... 812 825-5525
Bloomington *(G-713)*

Douglas K Gresham ....G....... 812 445-3174
Seymour *(G-12446)*

Dutch Kettle LLC ....F....... 574 546-4033
Bremen *(G-997)*

Eden Foods Inc ....E....... 765 396-3344
Eaton *(G-2583)*

Holic LLC ....F....... 765 444-8115
Middletown *(G-9936)*

Kick Out Jams LLC ....G....... 765 763-0225
Morristown *(G-10373)*

Millers Mill ....G....... 574 825-2010
Middlebury *(G-9908)*

Milroy Canning Company ....G....... 765 629-2221
Milroy *(G-9983)*

Nestle Usa Inc ....C....... 765 778-6000
Anderson *(G-144)*

New Business Corporation ....G....... 219 886-2700
Gary *(G-5079)*

Ray Brothers Noble Canning Co ....E....... 765 552-9432
Tipton *(G-13402)*

Red Gold Inc ....G....... 260 726-8140
Portland *(G-11845)*

Red Gold Inc ....C....... 260 368-9017
Geneva *(G-5138)*

Sprigati LLC ....G....... 219 484-9455
Munster *(G-10629)*

Zentis North America LLC ....B....... 574 941-1100
Plymouth *(G-11741)*

▲ Zentis Sweet Ovtions Holdg LLC .....C....... 574 941-1100
Plymouth *(G-11742)*

2034 Dried Fruits, Vegetables & Soup

Williams West & Witts Pdts Co ....G....... 219 879-8236
Michigan City *(G-9860)*

▲ Zentis Sweet Ovtions Holdg LLC .....C....... 574 941-1100
Plymouth *(G-11742)*

2035 Pickled Fruits, Vegetables, Sauces & Dressings

Bay Valley Foods LLC ....C....... 574 936-4061
Plymouth *(G-11668)*

Big B Distributors Inc ....F....... 812 425-5235
Evansville *(G-3384)*

Food Specialties Inc ....G....... 317 271-0862
Indianapolis *(G-6945)*

Grafton Peek Incorporated ....E....... 317 557-8377
Greenwood *(G-5698)*

Indiana Pickle Company LLC ....G....... 317 698-7292
Indianapolis *(G-7189)*

▲ Kolossos Inc ....G....... 312 952-6991
Long Beach *(G-9377)*

Lava Lips ....G....... 317 965-6629
Indianapolis *(G-7386)*

Park 100 Foods Inc ....E....... 317 549-4545
Indianapolis *(G-7656)*

▲ Park 100 Foods Inc ....D....... 765 675-3480
Tipton *(G-13400)*

Pickle Bites ....G....... 219 902-6315
Hammond *(G-5927)*

Pickled Pedaler ....G....... 317 877-0624
Noblesville *(G-11165)*

Red Gold Inc ....C....... 260 368-9017
Geneva *(G-5138)*

Richards Restaurant Inc ....F....... 260 997-6823
Bryant *(G-1201)*

Rickles Pickles ....G....... 260 495-9024
Fremont *(G-4974)*

Royal Food Products Inc ....F....... 317 782-2660
Indianapolis *(G-7865)*

▲ Sechlers Pickles Inc ....C....... 260 337-5461
Saint Joe *(G-12258)*

Van Schouwen Farms ....G....... 219 696-0877
Hebron *(G-6023)*

2037 Frozen Fruits, Juices & Vegetables

▲ Caj Food Products Inc ....F....... 888 524-6882
Fishers *(G-3884)*

Fox Smoothies LLC ....G....... 812 333-3051
Bloomington *(G-726)*

Frozen Garden LLC ....F....... 219 286-3578
Valparaiso *(G-13544)*

Hawaiian Smoothie LLC ....G....... 317 598-1730
Fishers *(G-3923)*

Hawaiian Smoothie LLC ....G....... 317 881-7290
Greenwood *(G-5702)*

▲ Zentis Sweet Ovtions Holdg LLC .....C....... 574 941-1100
Plymouth *(G-11742)*

2038 Frozen Specialties

Bimbo Bakeries Usa Inc ....E....... 812 678-3471
Dubois *(G-2475)*

Bounthanhs Egg Rolls ....G....... 574 546-4276
Nappanee *(G-10656)*

Butterfield Foods LLC ....C....... 317 776-4775
Noblesville *(G-11075)*

Conagra Brands Inc ....B....... 402 240-5000
Indianapolis *(G-6645)*

Crystal Lake LLC ....D....... 574 858-2514
Warsaw *(G-13861)*

Franklins Mercantile ....G....... 812 876-0426
Spencer *(G-13027)*

Grabill Country Meat 1 Inc ....F....... 260 627-3691
Grabill *(G-5369)*

Schwans Home Service Inc ....E....... 317 882-6624
Greenwood *(G-5748)*

Snax In Pax Inc ....E....... 260 593-3066
Topeka *(G-13429)*

2041 Flour, Grain Milling

ADM Milling Co ....D....... 812 838-4445
Mount Vernon *(G-10380)*

ADM Milling Co ....E....... 317 783-3321
Beech Grove *(G-591)*

AG Plus Inc ....E....... 260 723-5141
South Whitley *(G-12996)*

AG Plus Inc ....G....... 260 623-6121
Monroeville *(G-10190)*

AG Processing A Cooperative ....G....... 574 831-2292
Goshen *(G-5168)*

▼ Agricor Inc ....D....... 765 662-0606
Marion *(G-9507)*

Archer-Daniels-Midland Company ....G....... 219 297-4582
Goodland *(G-5157)*

Archer-Daniels-Midland Company ....G....... 317 783-3321
Beech Grove *(G-592)*

Archer-Daniels-Midland Company ....E....... 574 773-4138
Nappanee *(G-10646)*

Archer-Daniels-Midland Company ....E....... 574 773-4131
Nappanee *(G-10647)*

Archer-Daniels-Midland Company ....G....... 260 824-0079
Bluffton *(G-864)*

Archer-Daniels-Midland Company ....F....... 317 784-2200
Indianapolis *(G-6415)*

Archer-Daniels-Midland Company ....G....... 219 866-2810
Rensselaer *(G-11913)*

Archer-Daniels-Midland Company ....E....... 260 728-8000
Decatur *(G-2369)*

Archer-Daniels-Midland Company ....G....... 812 424-3581
Evansville *(G-3363)*

Archer-Daniels-Midland Company ....G....... 765 762-6763
Attica *(G-296)*

Archer-Daniels-Midland Company ....G....... 219 866-3939
Rensselaer *(G-11914)*

Archer-Daniels-Midland Company ....G....... 765 793-2512
State Line *(G-13071)*

Archer-Daniels-Midland Company ....G....... 765 523-3286
Frankfort *(G-4818)*

Archer-Daniels-Midland Company ....C....... 765 362-2965
Crawfordsville *(G-2134)*

Archer-Daniels-Midland Company ....F....... 812 268-4334
Sullivan *(G-13079)*

Big Brick House Bakery LLP ....B....... 260 563-1071
Fort Wayne *(G-4107)*

Bundy Bros & Sons Inc ....B....... 812 966-2551
Medora *(G-9681)*

Bunge North America Inc ....E....... 812 875-3113
Worthington *(G-14393)*

Cargill Incorporated ....G....... 574 353-7621
Mentone *(G-9685)*

Cargill Dry Corn Ingredients Inc ....G....... 317 632-1481
Indianapolis *(G-6555)*

Clunette Elevator Co Inc ....F....... 574 858-2281
Leesburg *(G-9234)*

Crust N More Inc ....F....... 317 890-7878
Indianapolis *(G-6701)*

Dillman Farm Incorporated ....G....... 812 825-5525
Bloomington *(G-713)*

Kerry Inc ....C....... 812 464-9151
Evansville *(G-3586)*

Kerry Inc ....E....... 812 464-9151
Evansville *(G-3587)*

Laughery Valley AG Co-Op Inc ....G....... 812 689-4401
Osgood *(G-11393)*

▲ Martinsville Milling Co Inc ....G....... 317 253-2581
Indianapolis *(G-7461)*

◆ New Carbon Company LLC ....G....... 574 247-2270
South Bend *(G-12873)*

Nunn Milling Company Inc ....E....... 812 425-3303
Evansville *(G-3649)*

Pillsbury Company LLC ....E....... 812 944-8411
New Albany *(G-10844)*

Prairie Mills Products LLC ....F....... 574 223-3177
Rochester *(G-12143)*

Prinova Solutions ....F....... 219 879-7356
Michigan City *(G-9829)*

Rico Aroma LLC ....G....... 765 471-1700
Lafayette *(G-8992)*

Roy Umbarger and Sons Inc ....F....... 317 422-5195
Bargersville *(G-486)*

Salamonie Mills Inc ....F....... 260 375-2200
Warren *(G-13832)*

Tribine Industries LLC ....G....... 316 282-8011
Logansport *(G-9371)*

Vitamins Inc ....E....... 219 879-7356
Michigan City *(G-9859)*

Wallace Grain Co Inc ....F....... 317 758-4434
Sheridan *(G-12601)*

2043 Cereal Breakfast Foods

General Mills Inc ....D....... 317 509-3709
Fishers *(G-3916)*

Kellogg Company ....A....... 812 877-1588
Seelyville *(G-12386)*

Loutsa Inc ....F....... 317 273-0123
Indianapolis *(G-7420)*

2045 Flour, Blended & Prepared

◆ Clabber Girl Corporation ....D....... 812 232-9446
Terre Haute *(G-13211)*

Donuts N Coffee Inc ....G....... 812 376-2796
Columbus *(G-1908)*

▲ Harlan Bakeries LLC ....G....... 317 272-3600
Avon *(G-443)*

▲ Harlan Bakeries-Avon LLC ....B....... 317 272-3600
Avon *(G-444)*

Indybake Products LLC ....D....... 812 877-1588
Terre Haute *(G-13257)*

◆ New Carbon Company LLC ....G....... 574 247-2270
South Bend *(G-12873)*

2046 Wet Corn Milling

APM&co Inc ....G&o.... 317 409-5639
Lewisville *(G-9248)*

Cargill Incorporated ....B....... 402 533-4227
Hammond *(G-5858)*

◆ Clabber Girl Corporation ....D....... 812 232-9446
Terre Haute *(G-13211)*

Colorcon Inc ....E....... 317 545-6211
Indianapolis *(G-6633)*

Enjoy Life Natural Brands LLC ....F 773 632-2163
Jeffersonville *(G-8356)*
Grain Processing Corporation ....F 812 257-0480
Washington *(G-13983)*
Ingredion Incorporated ....F 317 295-4122
Indianapolis *(G-7229)*
Ingredion Incorporated ....D 317 635-4455
Indianapolis *(G-7231)*
Pacmoore Products Inc ....E 317 831-2666
Mooresville *(G-10334)*
Tate Lyle Ingrdnts Amricas LLC ....B 765 474-5474
Lafayette *(G-9007)*
Tate Lyle Ingrdnts Amricas LLC ....D 765 448-7123
Lafayette *(G-9008)*

2047 Dog & Cat Food

Bench & Field Pet Foods LLC ....G 800 525-4802
Mishawaka *(G-10007)*
Bhj Usa Inc ....E 574 722-3933
Logansport *(G-9324)*
▲ Canines Choice Inc ....G 765 662-2633
Marion *(G-9514)*
Eagle Pet Products Inc ....D 574 259-7834
Mishawaka *(G-10038)*
Hills Pet Nutrition Inc ....C 765 966-4549
Richmond *(G-11996)*
Hills Pet Nutrition Inc ....C 765 935-7071
Richmond *(G-11997)*
Macor ....E 574 255-2658
Mishawaka *(G-10072)*
Nestle Usa Inc ....C 765 778-6000
Anderson *(G-144)*
Nutritional Research Assoc ....F 260 723-4931
South Whitley *(G-13002)*
Trio Milling Inc ....G 765 795-4088
Cloverdale *(G-1740)*
United Pet Foods Inc ....F 574 674-5981
Elkhart *(G-3233)*
Wellpet LLC ....D 574 259-7834
Mishawaka *(G-10150)*

2048 Prepared Feeds For Animals & Fowls

Archer-Daniels-Midland Company ....G 574 831-2292
Goshen *(G-5171)*
Birds Nest Inc ....G 574 247-0201
Granger *(G-5394)*
Blue River Farm Supply Inc ....G 812 364-6675
Palmyra *(G-11435)*
Bristow Milling Co LLC ....G 812 843-5176
Bristow *(G-1094)*
Bundy Bros & Sons Inc ....F 812 966-2551
Medora *(G-9681)*
Cargill Incorporated ....G 574 353-7621
Mentone *(G-9685)*
Cargill Incorporated ....G 574 353-7623
Mentone *(G-9686)*
Cargill Incorporated ....E 217 253-3389
West Lafayette *(G-14056)*
Cargill Incorporated ....B 402 533-4227
Hammond *(G-5858)*
Cargill Dry Corn Ingrdents Inc ....D 317 632-1481
Indianapolis *(G-6555)*
Consolidated Nutrition Lc ....G 574 773-4131
Nappanee *(G-10662)*
Egg Innovations LLC ....G 574 267-7545
Warsaw *(G-13868)*
▲ Envigo Rms Inc ....C 317 806-6080
Indianapolis *(G-6871)*
Envigo Rms Inc ....G 317 806-6080
Greenfield *(G-5530)*
Excel Coop Inc ....G 574 967-3943
Brookston *(G-1104)*
Flinn Farms Bedford Seed Inc ....G 812 279-4136
Bedford *(G-542)*
▲ Frick Services Inc ....E 260 761-3311
Wawaka *(G-14032)*
Griffin Industries LLC ....E 812 659-3399
Newberry *(G-11015)*
Griffin Industries LLC ....E 812 379-9528
Columbus *(G-1935)*
Gro-Tec Inc ....F 765 853-1246
Modoc *(G-10173)*
Harvest Land Co-Op Inc ....F 765 489-4141
Hagerstown *(G-5807)*
HMS Zoo Diets Inc ....G 260 824-5157
Bluffton *(G-877)*
Hog Slat Incorporated ....E 574 967-4145
Camden *(G-1274)*
Hunter Nutrition Inc ....G 765 563-1003
Brookston *(G-1105)*

Innovative Concepts Group ....G 317 408-0292
Indianapolis *(G-7236)*
Jbs United Inc ....F 800 382-9909
Sheridan *(G-12591)*
Jbs United Inc ....E 317 758-2609
Sheridan *(G-12592)*
Jbs United Trading Inc ....E 317 758-4495
Sheridan *(G-12594)*
Jfs Milling Inc ....E 812 324-2022
Bruceville *(G-1197)*
Kent Nutrition Group Inc ....E 574 722-5368
Logansport *(G-9345)*
Lambrights Inc ....D 260 463-2178
Lagrange *(G-9056)*
Land OLakes Inc ....F 765 962-9561
Richmond *(G-12011)*
Laughery Valley AG Co-Op Inc ....G 812 689-4401
Osgood *(G-11393)*
Lowes Pellets and Grain Inc ....G 812 663-7863
Greensburg *(G-5621)*
Mark Hackman ....G 812 522-8257
Brownstown *(G-1190)*
▼ Matam Corp ....G 317 264-9908
Indianapolis *(G-7465)*
▲ Micronutrients USA LLC ....D 317 486-5880
Indianapolis *(G-7500)*
Novartis Animal Health US Inc ....G 317 276-2348
Greenfield *(G-5562)*
Nutritional Research Assoc ....F 260 723-4931
South Whitley *(G-13002)*
Odon Feed and Grain Inc ....G 812 636-7392
Odon *(G-11337)*
▲ Pine Manor Inc ....B 800 532-4186
Orland *(G-11355)*
Purina Animal Nutrition LLC ....E 765 962-8547
Richmond *(G-12038)*
Purina Animal Nutrition LLC ....E 765 659-4791
Frankfort *(G-4852)*
Purina Animal Nutrition LLC ....E 812 424-5501
Evansville *(G-3690)*
Purina Animal Nutrition LLC ....E 574 658-4137
Milford *(G-9962)*
Purina Mills LLC ....E 812 424-5501
Evansville *(G-3691)*
Purina Mills LLC ....E 574 658-4137
Milford *(G-9963)*
Reconserve of Indiana ....G 310 458-1574
Terre Haute *(G-13317)*
Regal Mills Odon ....G 812 295-2299
Loogootee *(G-9393)*
Richmonds Feed Service Inc ....G 574 862-2984
Wakarusa *(G-13793)*
Ridley USA Inc ....E 260 768-4103
Shipshewana *(G-12647)*
Sappers Market and Greenhouses ....G 219 942-4995
Hobart *(G-6094)*
Scotts Miracle-Gro Company ....D 219 984-6110
Reynolds *(G-11948)*
▲ Strauss Veal Feeds Inc ....E 260 982-8611
North Manchester *(G-11245)*
Super Blend Inc ....G 260 463-7486
Lagrange *(G-9069)*
Synergy Feeds LLC ....E 260 723-5141
South Whitley *(G-13008)*
▼ United Animal Health Inc ....D 317 758-4495
Sheridan *(G-12599)*
United Animal Health Inc ....E 207 771-0965
Sheridan *(G-12600)*
United Feeds ....G 317 627-5637
Carmel *(G-1504)*
Wallace Grain Co Inc ....F 317 758-4434
Sheridan *(G-12601)*
Wanafeed Corporation ....G 317 862-4032
Indianapolis *(G-8178)*
Wilson Fertilizer & Grain Inc ....G 574 223-3175
Rochester *(G-12161)*
Winfield Solutions LLC ....G 317 838-3733
Plainfield *(G-11652)*

2051 Bread, Bakery Prdts Exc Cookies & Crackers

Abigails Baking Company LLC ....G 219 299-1785
Valparaiso *(G-13482)*
Achaemenian Shahpur ....G 812 331-1317
Bloomington *(G-656)*
Almiras Bakery ....E 219 844-4334
Hammond *(G-5839)*
Alpha Baking Co Inc ....F 574 234-0188
South Bend *(G-12697)*

Alpha Baking Co Inc ....C 219 324-7440
La Porte *(G-8730)*
Aunt Millies ....G 765 966-6691
Richmond *(G-11958)*
B&B Goodiez ....G 765 338-6833
Connersville *(G-2039)*
Babbs Supermarket Inc ....D 812 829-2231
Spencer *(G-13017)*
Backdoor Baking Company LLC ....G 317 927-7275
Indianapolis *(G-6452)*
Bimbo Bakeries Usa Inc ....E 219 844-0465
Hammond *(G-5853)*
Bimbo Bakeries Usa Inc ....E 317 273-0444
Indianapolis *(G-6475)*
Bimbo Bakeries Usa Inc ....E 812 479-6934
Evansville *(G-3385)*
Brunos Breads LLC ....G 219 883-5126
Gary *(G-5031)*
Buehler Foods Inc ....C 812 467-7255
Evansville *(G-3404)*
Cake Bake Shop Inc ....G 317 257-2253
Indianapolis *(G-6533)*
Colonial Baking Co Inc ....G 812 232-4466
Terre Haute *(G-13213)*
Concannons Pastry Shop ....G 765 288-8551
Muncie *(G-10448)*
Confectionery Products Mfg Inc ....G 317 269-7363
Indianapolis *(G-6649)*
Craftmark Bakery LLC ....F 317 548-3929
Indianapolis *(G-6685)*
Dawn Food Products Inc ....C 800 333-3296
Crown Point *(G-2244)*
Donut Bank Inc ....E 812 426-0011
Evansville *(G-3462)*
Eat Dessert First Inc ....G 812 438-9600
Patriot *(G-11467)*
Enjoy Life Natural Brands LLC ....F 773 632-2163
Jeffersonville *(G-8356)*
Fingerhut Bakery Inc ....F 574 896-5937
North Judson *(G-11212)*
Fountain Acres Foods ....F 765 847-1897
Fountain City *(G-4786)*
Ganal Corporation ....G 260 749-2161
New Haven *(G-10940)*
Georgetown Donuts ....G 260 493-6719
Fort Wayne *(G-4299)*
Grabers Kountry Korner ....E 812 636-4399
Odon *(G-11329)*
Gutierrez Mexican Bakery & Mkt ....G 574 534-9979
Goshen *(G-5232)*
▲ Harlan Bakeries LLC ....G 317 272-3600
Avon *(G-443)*
▲ Harlan Bakeries-Avon LLC ....B 317 272-3600
Avon *(G-444)*
Hartford Bakery Inc ....B 812 425-4642
Evansville *(G-3533)*
Hearthside Food Solutions LLC ....B 219 878-1522
Michigan City *(G-9802)*
Heyerlys Bakery Inc ....F 260 622-4196
Ossian *(G-11401)*
Holsum of Fort Wayne Inc ....C 260 456-2130
Fort Wayne *(G-4337)*
Holsum of Fort Wayne Inc ....C 219 362-4561
La Porte *(G-8766)*
Indiana Baking Co ....F 260 483-5997
Fort Wayne *(G-4362)*
Irish Cupcakes Inc ....G 574 289-8669
Elkhart *(G-2939)*
Jay C Food 84 ....G 812 886-9311
Vincennes *(G-13686)*
Jennys Backery ....G 260 447-9592
Fort Wayne *(G-4393)*
Joy Sweet Cupcakes ....G 219 276-3791
Schererville *(G-12327)*
Just Desserts Inc ....F 317 872-2253
Indianapolis *(G-7323)*
Kbi Inc ....D 765 763-6114
Morristown *(G-10372)*
Klosterman Baking Co ....E 317 359-5545
Indianapolis *(G-7361)*
Kristens Homemade Delight ....G 765 566-2200
Burlington *(G-1211)*
Kroger Co ....D 574 294-6092
Elkhart *(G-2975)*
Kroger Co ....G 574 291-0740
South Bend *(G-12830)*
Kt Cakes ....G 812 442-6047
Rosedale *(G-12205)*
Lakeshore Foods Corp ....C 219 362-8513
La Porte *(G-8785)*

▲ Lewis Brothers Bakeries Inc............C 812 425-4642
Evansville *(G-3600)*

Lewis Brothers Bakeries Inc............C 812 886-6533
Vincennes *(G-13690)*

Lou Mary Donuts Inc............F 765 474-9131
Lafayette *(G-8960)*

Maplehurst Bakeries LLC............C 317 858-9000
Greenwood *(G-5723)*

▲ Maplehurst Bakeries LLC............C 317 858-9000
Brownsburg *(G-1160)*

Mel Rhon Inc............G 574 546-4559
Bremen *(G-1010)*

Moms Homemade Pies Co LLC............G 765 453-4417
Kokomo *(G-8669)*

Moores Pie Shop Inc............G 765 457-2428
Kokomo *(G-8672)*

Mr Mhammads Sweet-Bean Snacks............G 317 519-0728
Indianapolis *(G-7553)*

Neeta Sweet Cupcakes n Minis............G 574 286-7032
Granger *(G-5426)*

New Horizons Baking Company............D 260 495-7055
Fremont *(G-4970)*

Omg Cupcakes & Sweets LLC............G 317 281-7926
Indianapolis *(G-7619)*

Pasteleria Gresil LLC............G 317 299-8801
Indianapolis *(G-7659)*

Peace Love Cupcakes............G 812 239-1591
Terre Haute *(G-13299)*

▼ Perfection Bakeries Inc............G 260 424-8245
Fort Wayne *(G-4524)*

Perfection Bakeries Inc............D 260 483-5481
Fort Wayne *(G-4525)*

Perfection Bakeries Inc............G 574 269-9706
Warsaw *(G-13926)*

Pinch of Sugar............G 812 476-7650
Evansville *(G-3671)*

Richards Bakery............F 260 424-4012
Fort Wayne *(G-4592)*

Ricker Oil Company Inc............D 317 920-0850
Indianapolis *(G-7842)*

Schnuck Markets Inc............C 812 853-9505
Newburgh *(G-11046)*

Scholars Inn Bakehouse............G 812 331-6029
Bloomington *(G-822)*

Shipshewana Bread Box Corp............E 260 768-4629
Shipshewana *(G-12649)*

Square Donuts Inc............G 812 232-6463
Terre Haute *(G-13343)*

Strauss Bakeries Inc............D 574 293-9027
Elkhart *(G-3194)*

Sugar Spice Cupcake Event Plg............G 260 610-5103
Fort Wayne *(G-4659)*

Sweet Art Inc............G 317 787-3647
Indianapolis *(G-8026)*

Sweet LLC............G 812 455-0886
Evansville *(G-3755)*

Sweet N Sassy Cupcakes............G 317 652-6132
Indianapolis *(G-8027)*

Toms Donuts of Auburn LLC............G 260 927-1224
Auburn *(G-362)*

Torti Products Inc............G 219 730-2071
Highland *(G-6057)*

Tyson Foods Inc............B 260 726-3118
Portland *(G-11854)*

United Pies of Elkhart Inc............G 574 294-3419
Elkhart *(G-3234)*

Westfield Donuts............G 317 896-5856
Westfield *(G-14201)*

Weston Foods Us Inc............A 317 858-9000
Brownsburg *(G-1176)*

2052 Cookies & Crackers

Almiras Bakery............E 219 844-4334
Hammond *(G-5839)*

Aunt Beths Products Inc............G 574 259-6244
Mishawaka *(G-10000)*

Auntie Annes............F 765 288-8077
Muncie *(G-10435)*

Auntie Annes............G 574 271-8740
Mishawaka *(G-10001)*

Blondies Cookies Inc............F 765 628-3978
Greentown *(G-5644)*

Blondies Cookies Inc............G 765 288-3872
Muncie *(G-10440)*

Buehler Foods Inc............G 812 467-7255
Evansville *(G-3404)*

Clif Bar & Company............G 510 596-6451
Indianapolis *(G-6620)*

Darlington Cookie Company............D 800 754-2202
Noblesville *(G-11090)*

Fingerhut Bakery Inc............F 574 896-5937
North Judson *(G-11212)*

Grace Island Spcalty Foods Inc............G 260 357-3336
Garrett *(G-5006)*

Hartzells Homemade Ice Cream............F 812 332-3502
Bloomington *(G-738)*

Hearthside Food Solutions LLC............B 219 878-1522
Michigan City *(G-9802)*

Heaven Sent Gurmet Cookies Inc............G 219 980-1066
Gary *(G-5062)*

Heyerlys Bakery Inc............F 260 622-4196
Ossian *(G-11401)*

Indybake Products LLC............D 812 877-1588
Terre Haute *(G-13257)*

Jojos Pretzels............F 260 768-7759
Shipshewana *(G-12623)*

Las Perlas Tapatias Inc............G 765 447-0601
Lafayette *(G-8956)*

Mike-Sells West Virginia Inc............G 317 241-7422
Indianapolis *(G-7516)*

▼ Pretzels Inc............C 260 824-4838
Bluffton *(G-886)*

Richmond Baking Co............C 765 962-8535
Richmond *(G-12043)*

Richmond Baking Georgia Inc............C 765 962-8535
Richmond *(G-12044)*

Schnuck Markets Inc............C 812 853-9505
Newburgh *(G-11046)*

Shipshewana Bread Box Corp............E 260 768-4629
Shipshewana *(G-12649)*

Strauss Bakeries Inc............D 574 293-9027
Elkhart *(G-3194)*

Victorian House Scones LLC............G 765 742-2709
Lafayette *(G-9015)*

Weston Foods Us Inc............A 317 858-9000
Brownsburg *(G-1176)*

2053 Frozen Bakery Prdts

Alpha Baking Co Inc............C 219 324-7440
La Porte *(G-8730)*

Labraid Inc............G 219 754-2501
La Crosse *(G-8721)*

Lewis Brothers Bakeries Inc............C 812 886-6533
Vincennes *(G-13690)*

Moores Pie Shop Inc............G 765 457-2428
Kokomo *(G-8672)*

Printer Zink Inc............G 765 644-3959
Anderson *(G-156)*

United Pies of Elkhart Inc............G 574 294-3419
Elkhart *(G-3234)*

Wicks Pies Inc............E 765 584-8401
Winchester *(G-14345)*

2064 Candy & Confectionery Prdts

Abbotts Candy and Gifts Inc............E 765 489-4442
Hagerstown *(G-5801)*

◆ Albanese Conf Group Inc............C 219 942-1877
Merrillville *(G-9693)*

Albanese Conf Group Inc............G 219 738-2333
Merrillville *(G-9694)*

▲ American Licorice Company............E 510 487-5500
La Porte *(G-8731)*

American Licorice Company............C 219 362-5790
La Porte *(G-8732)*

Bosphorus Breakfast Hookah Bar............G 317 624-1700
Indianapolis *(G-6497)*

Brookes Candy Co............G 765 665-3646
Clinton *(G-1715)*

Candies Inc............F 260 747-7514
Fort Wayne *(G-4138)*

Candy Dish Inc............G 317 269-6262
Nashville *(G-10719)*

◆ CK Products LLC............D 260 484-2517
Fort Wayne *(G-4154)*

Claeys Candy Inc............F 574 287-1818
South Bend *(G-12735)*

Copper Kettle Fudge LLC............G 260 417-1036
Fort Wayne *(G-4174)*

David M Pszonka............G 219 988-2235
Hebron *(G-6011)*

▲ Debrand Inc............D 260 969-8333
Fort Wayne *(G-4203)*

Donaldsons Chocolates Inc............F 765 482-3334
Lebanon *(G-9181)*

Dulceria Garza Inc............G 219 397-1062
East Chicago *(G-2525)*

Goods Candies............G 765 785-6776
Kennard *(G-8516)*

Heidipops Gourmet Popcorn LLC............G 317 863-0844
Plainfield *(G-11614)*

Libs Mike & Choclat Fctry LLC............G 812 424-8750
Evansville *(G-3601)*

Lowerys Home Made Candies............E 765 288-7300
Muncie *(G-10513)*

Nestle Usa Inc............C 765 778-6000
Anderson *(G-144)*

Old World Fudge & Cds Dogs LLC............G 260 610-2249
Columbia City *(G-1815)*

Olympia Candy Kitchen............F 574 533-5040
Goshen *(G-5301)*

Queen City Candy LLC............G 812 537-5203
Greendale *(G-5494)*

Schimpff Confectionery............F 812 283-8367
Jeffersonville *(G-8423)*

Stephen Libs Candy Co Inc............F 812 473-0048
Evansville *(G-3748)*

Sugar Creek Candies Inc............F 765 681-1607
Peru *(G-11550)*

Sweet Properties LLC............G 812 283-8367
Jeffersonville *(G-8431)*

Ugo Bars LLC............G 812 322-3499
Bloomington *(G-850)*

Whiskey Business............G 317 823-5078
Indianapolis *(G-8191)*

Wicks Pie............G 765 584-8401
Winchester *(G-14344)*

Wsg Manufacturing LLC............G 765 934-2101
Whitestown *(G-14265)*

▲ Zachary Confections Inc............C 765 659-4751
Frankfort *(G-4861)*

2066 Chocolate & Cocoa Prdts

Abbotts Candy and Gifts Inc............E 765 489-4442
Hagerstown *(G-5801)*

Candies Inc............F 260 747-7514
Fort Wayne *(G-4138)*

Claeys Candy Inc............F 574 287-1818
South Bend *(G-12735)*

▲ Debrand Inc............D 260 969-8333
Fort Wayne *(G-4203)*

Donaldsons Chocolates Inc............F 765 482-3334
Lebanon *(G-9181)*

LLC Tipton Mills............G 716 825-4422
Columbus *(G-1964)*

Lowerys Home Made Candies............E 765 288-7300
Muncie *(G-10513)*

Olympia Candy Kitchen............F 574 533-5040
Goshen *(G-5301)*

Rabbit Lane LLC............G 317 733-8380
Zionsville *(G-14458)*

▲ South Bend Chocolate Co Inc............F 574 233-2577
South Bend *(G-12942)*

Stephen Libs Candy Co Inc............F 812 473-0048
Evansville *(G-3748)*

Sweet Things Inc............F 317 872-8720
Indianapolis *(G-8028)*

2068 Salted & Roasted Nuts & Seeds

Diamond Foods LLC............F 209 467-6000
Van Buren *(G-13639)*

Lgin LLC............G 260 562-2233
Howe *(G-6127)*

Stephen Libs Candy Co Inc............F 812 473-0048
Evansville *(G-3748)*

2074 Cottonseed Oil Mills

Albertson Seed Sales............G 765 267-0680
Russellville *(G-12238)*

2075 Soybean Oil Mills

AG Processing A Cooperative............E 574 773-4138
Nappanee *(G-10644)*

Bunge North America Inc............D 260 724-2101
Decatur *(G-2372)*

Bunge North America Foundation............E 219 261-2124
Remington *(G-11905)*

Bunge North America Foundation............G 765 763-7500
Morristown *(G-10366)*

Cargill Incorporated............E 765 423-4302
Lafayette *(G-8866)*

Cargill Incorporated............B 402 533-4227
Hammond *(G-5858)*

◆ Dupont............D 219 261-2124
Remington *(G-11906)*

Mothersoy Inc............G 812 424-5357
Evansville *(G-3639)*

◆ Solae............G 260 724-2101
Decatur *(G-2405)*

Solae LLC ....G...... 800 325-7108
Remington (G-11909)

Solae LLC ....D...... 219 261-2124
Remington (G-11910)

2076 Vegetable Oil Mills

Catchrs LLC ....G...... 310 902-9723
Indianapolis (G-6567)

Skinny and Company LLC ....F...... 888 865-4278
Indianapolis (G-7950)

Solae LLC ....G...... 800 325-7108
Remington (G-11909)

2077 Animal, Marine Fats & Oils

American Reusable Energy LLC ....G...... 317 965-2604
Greenwood (G-5666)

Bunge North America Inc ....D...... 260 724-2101
Decatur (G-2372)

Darling Ingredients Inc ....E...... 317 784-4486
Indianapolis (G-6727)

Geo Pfaus Sons Company Inc ....E...... 800 732-8645
Jeffersonville (G-8369)

Griffin Industries LLC ....E...... 812 659-3399
Newberry (G-11015)

Griffin Industries LLC ....E...... 812 379-9528
Columbus (G-1935)

Hrr Enterprises Inc ....E...... 219 362-9050
La Porte (G-8768)

Kane-Miller Corp ....E...... 219 362-9050
La Porte (G-8775)

Nutritional Research Assoc ....F...... 260 723-4931
South Whitley (G-13002)

Standard Fertilizer Company ....F...... 812 663-8391
Greensburg (G-5634)

2079 Shortening, Oils & Margarine

Bunge North America Inc ....D...... 260 724-2101
Decatur (G-2372)

Cargill Incorporated ....E...... 765 423-4302
Lafayette (G-8866)

Debbies Handmade Soap ....G...... 765 747-5090
Muncie (G-10455)

Northern Indiana Oil LLC ....G...... 765 749-3791
Indianapolis (G-7593)

Olive Leaf LLC ....G...... 812 323-3073
Bloomington (G-786)

Olive Mill ....G...... 317 574-9200
Carmel (G-1445)

2082 Malt Beverages

Barley Island Brewing Co ....F...... 317 770-5280
Noblesville (G-11061)

Beer Baron LLC ....G...... 317 735-2706
Indianapolis (G-6466)

Best Beers LLC ....G...... 812 332-1234
Bloomington (G-681)

Brick Road Brewery Corp ....G...... 219 362-7623
La Porte (G-8742)

Byway Brewing Company LLC ....G...... 312 543-7639
Munster (G-10599)

Calumet Breweries Inc ....E...... 219 845-2242
Hammond (G-5856)

Chapmans Cider Company LLC ....G...... 260 444-1194
Angola (G-202)

Crankshaft Brewing Co ....G...... 317 939-0138
Brownsburg (G-1146)

Daredevil Brewing Co ....G...... 317 512-2202
Indianapolis (G-6726)

Das Big Dawg Brewhaus LLC ....G...... 765 965-9463
Richmond (G-11976)

Dockside ....G...... 574 400-0848
South Bend (G-12752)

Drinkgp LLC ....G...... 317 410-4748
Indianapolis (G-6767)

Figure Eight Brewing LLC ....E...... 219 477-2000
Valparaiso (G-13543)

Floyd County Brewing Company L ......G...... 502 724-3202
New Albany (G-10782)

Grand Junction Brewery ....G...... 317 804-9583
Westfield (G-14166)

Indiana City Brewing LLC ....F...... 317 643-1103
Indianapolis (G-7177)

Irongate V LLC ....G...... 219 464-8704
Valparaiso (G-13561)

Laotto Brewing LLC ....G...... 260 897-3152
Avilla (G-413)

Lennies Inc ....D...... 812 323-2112
Bloomington (G-765)

Mishawaka Brewing Company ....E...... 574 256-9993
Granger (G-5423)

Oaken Barrel Brewing Co Inc ....E...... 317 887-2287
Greenwood (G-5730)

Pepito Miller Bev Imports LLC ....G...... 317 416-3215
Plainfield (G-11635)

Power House Brewing Co ....G...... 812 343-1302
Columbus (G-1998)

Round Town Brewery LLC ....G...... 317 657-6397
Indianapolis (G-7864)

South Bend Brew Werks LLC ....G...... 801 209-2987
South Bend (G-12941)

▲ Sun King Brewing Company LLC ....G...... 317 602-3702
Indianapolis (G-8017)

Tavistock Restaurants LLC ....D...... 317 488-1230
Indianapolis (G-8040)

▲ Terrance Smith Distributing ....D...... 765 644-3396
Anderson (G-175)

The Tap ....F...... 812 486-9795
Bloomington (G-839)

Thieme and Wagner Brewing Co ....G...... 765 477-0667
Lafayette (G-9010)

▲ Three Floyds Brewing LLC ....G...... 219 922-4425
Munster (G-10633)

Turonis Forget ME Not Inn ....E...... 812 477-7500
Evansville (G-3779)

Under Staircase Brewing Co LLC ....G...... 260 580-2586
Fort Wayne (G-4713)

Upland Brewing Company ....G...... 317 602-3931
Indianapolis (G-8131)

Upland Brewing Company Inc ....E...... 812 330-7421
Bloomington (G-851)

Wasser Brewing Company LLC ....G...... 765 653-3240
Greencastle (G-5481)

Windmill Brewing ....G...... 219 440-2189
Dyer (G-2512)

2084 Wine & Brandy

Aftermath Cidery and Winery ....G...... 219 299-8463
Valparaiso (G-13486)

Ajll LLC ....G...... 812 477-3611
Evansville (G-3346)

Ancient Cellars ....G...... 503 437-4827
Indianapolis (G-6399)

Anderson Winery and Vineyard ....G...... 219 464-4936
Valparaiso (G-13493)

At The Barn Winery ....G...... 513 310-8810
Lawrenceburg (G-9131)

Bacchus Winery Golf Vinyrd LLC ....G...... 574 732-4663
Logansport (G-9323)

Belgian Horse Winery LLC ....G...... 765 779-3002
Middletown (G-9933)

Best Vineyards ....G...... 812 969-9463
Elizabeth (G-2642)

Black Dog Vineyard Inc ....G...... 812 877-1933
Terre Haute (G-13203)

Brandywine Vinyrd & Winery LLC ....G...... 317 403-5669
New Palestine (G-10968)

Brewhouse Supplies LLC ....G...... 219 286-7285
Valparaiso (G-13513)

Brown County Wine Company ....G...... 812 988-6144
Nashville (G-10718)

Brumate LLC ....G...... 317 474-7352
Indianapolis (G-6515)

Butler Vineyards ....G...... 219 929-1400
Chesterton (G-1597)

Butler Vineyards ....G...... 812 332-6660
Bloomington (G-692)

Carousel Winery ....G...... 812 849-1005
Mitchell (G-10158)

Cedar Creek Winery ....G...... 765 342-9000
Martinsville (G-9597)

Cedar Creek Winery ....G...... 812 988-1111
Nashville (G-10720)

Cellar Masters LLC ....E...... 317 817-9473
Indianapolis (G-6574)

Chateau Thomas Winery Inc ....E...... 317 837-9463
Plainfield (G-11600)

Cherry Hill Vineyard LLC ....G...... 317 846-5170
Carmel (G-1337)

Copia Vineyards and Winery LLC ....G...... 805 835-6094
Indianapolis (G-6664)

Country Hritg Wnery Vinyrd Inc ....F...... 260 637-2980
Laotto (G-9105)

Country Moon Winery LLC ....G...... 317 773-7942
Noblesville (G-11086)

Daniels Vineyard LLC ....G...... 317 894-6860
Greenfield (G-5519)

Dune Ridge Winery LLC ....G...... 219 548-4605
Valparaiso (G-13529)

Durm Vineyard Inc ....G...... 317 862-9463
Indianapolis (G-6771)

Easley Enterprises Inc ....E...... 317 636-4516
Indianapolis (G-6789)

Ertel Cellars Winery Inc ....E...... 812 933-1500
Batesville (G-500)

Family Vineyard ....G...... 812 322-1720
Indianapolis (G-6904)

Finley Creek Vineyards LLC ....G...... 317 769-5483
Zionsville (G-14432)

Fruit Hills Winery Orchrd LLC ....G...... 574 848-9463
Bristol (G-1061)

Ghost Trail Winery LLC ....G...... 317 387-0052
Indianapolis (G-7004)

Graybull Organic Wines Inc ....G...... 317 797-2186
Indianapolis (G-7039)

Harmony Winery ....G...... 317 585-9463
Fishers (G-3922)

Hartland Winery LLC ....G...... 260 587-3316
Ashley (G-286)

Harvest Moon Winery LLC ....G...... 317 258-4615
McCordsville (G-9668)

Heagy Vineyards LLC ....G...... 317 752-4484
Carmel (G-1401)

Home - Little Creek Winery ....G...... 812 319-3951
Evansville (G-3539)

Hooker Corner Winery LLC ....G...... 765 585-1225
Pine Village (G-11581)

Hoosier Crush Corp ....G...... 765 292-6375
Atlanta (G-295)

Hopwood Cellars ....G...... 317 873-4099
Zionsville (G-14438)

Hotel Tango Whiskey Inc ....E...... 317 653-1806
Indianapolis (G-7135)

▲ Huber Orchards Inc ....E...... 812 923-9463
Borden (G-930)

Huckleberry Winery ....G...... 317 850-4445
Bargersville (G-483)

Hunters Ridge Winery LLC ....G...... 812 967-9463
Salem (G-12293)

Indiana Artisan Inc ....G...... 317 607-8715
Noblesville (G-11126)

▲ Indiana Wholesale Wine Lq Co ....G...... 317 667-0231
Indianapolis (G-7197)

James Lake Vineyard Inc ....G...... 260 495-9463
Fremont (G-4963)

Jeter Winery Inc ....G...... 317 862-9193
Indianapolis (G-7302)

John King ....G...... 317 801-3080
Indianapolis (G-7307)

Kenneth Fiekert ....G...... 812 551-5122
Rising Sun (G-12089)

Laker Winery LLC ....G...... 812 934-4633
Batesville (G-508)

Lane Byler Winery ....G...... 260 920-4377
Auburn (G-341)

Lanthier Winery & Restaurant ....F...... 812 273-2409
Madison (G-9477)

Lasalles Landing Vineyard LLC ....G...... 574 277-2711
South Bend (G-12836)

Madison Vineyards Inc ....G...... 812 273-6500
Madison (G-9484)

Mallow Run LLC ....G...... 317 422-1556
Bargersville (G-484)

Meier Winery & Vinyard LLC ....G...... 812 382-4220
Sullivan (G-13087)

Melissa King ....G...... 219 989-1497
Hammond (G-5915)

Mystique Winery and Vinyrd LLC ....G...... 812 922-5612
Lynnville (G-9435)

Nagys Winery LLC ....G...... 219 331-0588
Valparaiso (G-13584)

Oak Hill Winery LLC ....G...... 765 395-3632
Converse (G-2081)

▲ Oliver Wine Company Inc ....D...... 812 822-0466
Bloomington (G-787)

Owen Valley Winery LLC ....G...... 812 828-0883
Spencer (G-13032)

Peace Water Winery ....G...... 317 810-1330
Carmel (G-1449)

Pepito Miller Bev Imports LLC ....G...... 317 416-3215
Plainfield (G-11635)

Pfeiffer Winery & Vineyard ....G...... 812 952-2650
Corydon (G-2108)

Poco A Poco LLC ....G...... 317 443-5753
Leo (G-9245)

Prairie Sun Vineyard LLC ....G...... 219 741-5918
Rolling Prairie (G-12191)

Preston Leaderbrand ....F...... 812 828-0883
Spencer (G-13033)

◆ PRI-Pak Inc ....C...... 812 260-2291
Greendale **(G-5493)**

Prp Wine International ....G...... 317 288-0005
Indianapolis **(G-7784)**

Rain Song Farms LLC ....G...... 317 640-4534
Noblesville **(G-11170)**

Red Gate Farms Inc ....G...... 812 277-9750
Bedford **(G-573)**

Rick Black Associates LLC ....G...... 765 838-3498
Lafayette **(G-8991)**

River City Winery ....G...... 317 868-8223
Franklin **(G-4927)**

River City Winery LLC ....G...... 812 945-9463
New Albany **(G-10857)**

S L Thomas Family Winery Inc ...G...... 812 273-3755
Madison **(G-9494)**

Shady Creek Vineyard ....G...... 219 874-9463
Michigan City **(G-9843)**

Shady Frog Winery LLC ....G...... 317 366-3370
Bargersville **(G-487)**

Simmons Winery & Farm Market ...G...... 812 546-0091
Columbus **(G-2015)**

Stoney Creek Winery ....G...... 574 642-4454
Millersburg **(G-9975)**

Sutter Home Winery ....G...... 317 848-3003
Carmel **(G-1486)**

Sycamore Winery LLC ....G...... 812 243-0565
West Terre Haute **(G-14130)**

Thomas Chateau Winery ....G...... 812 339-9463
Bloomington **(G-840)**

Tipsy Glass LLC ....G...... 260 251-0021
Portland **(G-11851)**

Tonne Winery ....G...... 765 896-9821
Muncie **(G-10573)**

Traders Point Winery ....G...... 317 879-9463
Indianapolis **(G-8088)**

Twin Willows LLC ....G...... 812 497-0254
Freetown **(G-4950)**

Two Ees Winery ....G...... 260 672-2000
Huntington **(G-6257)**

Victorias Vineyard ....G...... 765 348-3070
Hartford City **(G-5996)**

Vineyard Fishery Products LLC .....G...... 317 902-0753
Indianapolis **(G-8164)**

Whyte Horse Winery LLC ....G...... 574 583-2345
Monticello **(G-10288)**

Windy Knoll Winery ....G...... 812 726-1600
Vincennes **(G-13718)**

Wine and Canvas Dev LLC ....G...... 317 914-2806
Columbus **(G-2035)**

Wine N Vine ....G...... 765 282-3300
Muncie **(G-10586)**

Winzerwald Winery LLC ....G...... 812 357-7000
Bristow **(G-1096)**

Winzerwald Winery LLC ....G...... 812 357-7000
Bristow **(G-1097)**

Wolfies Grill 5 LLC ....G...... 317 804-5619
Westfield **(G-14203)**

Workers In Vineyard Inc ....G...... 317 245-7256
Indianapolis **(G-8215)**

2085 Liquors, Distilled, Rectified & Blended

Bear Wallow Distillery ....G...... 812 657-4923
Nashville **(G-10715)**

Blue Marble Cocktails Inc ....E...... 888 400-3090
Indianapolis **(G-6486)**

Cardinal Ethanol LLC ....D...... 765 964-3137
Union City **(G-13454)**

▲ Cardinal Spirits LLC ....E...... 812 202-6789
Bloomington **(G-695)**

Easley Enterprises Inc ....E...... 317 636-4516
Indianapolis **(G-6789)**

Grain Processing Corporation ....F...... 812 257-0480
Washington **(G-13983)**

Heartland Distillers LLC ....G...... 317 598-9775
Indianapolis **(G-7084)**

Indiana Whiskey Co ....G...... 574 339-1737
South Bend **(G-12811)**

Joseph & Jones LLC ....G...... 317 691-0328
Indianapolis **(G-7312)**

Mgpi Processing Inc ....F...... 812 532-4100
Greendale **(G-5491)**

Old Fort Distillery Inc ....G...... 260 705-5128
Grabill **(G-5381)**

◆ PRI-Pak Inc ....C...... 812 260-2291
Greendale **(G-5493)**

Royal Inc ....F...... 812 424-4925
Evansville **(G-3711)**

Three Rivers Distilling Co LLC ......G...... 260 745-9355
Fort Wayne **(G-4684)**

Virtuoso Distillers LLC ....G...... 574 876-4450
Mishawaka **(G-10147)**

West Fork Whiskey Co ....G...... 812 583-9797
Indianapolis **(G-8185)**

2086 Soft Drinks

▲ Ahf Industries Inc ....C...... 812 936-9988
French Lick **(G-4984)**

American Beverage Marketers ....G...... 812 944-3585
New Albany **(G-10743)**

American Bottling Company ....E...... 260 484-4177
Fort Wayne **(G-4068)**

American Bottling Company ....E...... 765 987-7800
Spiceland **(G-13053)**

American Bottling Company ....E...... 574 291-9000
South Bend **(G-12703)**

American Water Works Co Inc ......G...... 765 362-3940
Crawfordsville **(G-2133)**

Angel Falls Water Company ....G...... 812 939-9107
Clay City **(G-1701)**

Battery Xpress ....G...... 765 759-2288
Indianapolis **(G-6458)**

▼ Capitol Source Network ....G...... 260 248-9747
Columbia City **(G-1771)**

Central Coca-Cola Btlg Co Inc ......E...... 765 423-5668
Lafayette **(G-8873)**

Central Coca-Cola Btlg Co Inc ......D...... 765 642-9951
Anderson **(G-82)**

Central Coca-Cola Btlg Co Inc ......D...... 812 232-9543
Terre Haute **(G-13208)**

Central Coca-Cola Btlg Co Inc ......E...... 317 398-0129
Indianapolis **(G-6580)**

Central Coca-Cola Btlg Co Inc ......E...... 574 291-1511
South Bend **(G-12732)**

Central Coca-Cola Btlg Co Inc ......C...... 260 478-2978
Fort Wayne **(G-4142)**

Central Coca-Cola Btlg Co Inc ......G...... 317 243-3771
Indianapolis **(G-6581)**

Central Coca-Cola Btlg Co Inc ......G...... 812 482-7475
Jasper **(G-8241)**

Central Coca-Cola Btlg Co Inc ......G...... 800 241-2653
Bloomington **(G-699)**

Central Coca-Cola Btlg Co Inc ......G...... 260 726-7126
Portland **(G-11810)**

Central Coca-Cola Btlg Co Inc ......G...... 800 241-2653
Shelbyville **(G-12526)**

Circle City Sonorans LLC ....G...... 317 401-9787
Indianapolis **(G-6609)**

◆ Clark Foods Inc ....D...... 812 949-3075
New Albany **(G-10761)**

▲ Coca Cola Btlg Co Kokomo Ind ...D...... 765 457-4421
Kokomo **(G-8607)**

Coca Cola Btlg Co Kokomo Ind .....E...... 574 936-3220
Plymouth **(G-11675)**

Coca-Cola Bottling Co Cnsld ....D...... 812 228-3200
Evansville **(G-3421)**

Coca-Cola Bottling Co Inc ....E...... 812 376-3381
Columbus **(G-1873)**

Coca-Cola Bottling Co Portland .....D...... 260 726-7126
Portland **(G-11811)**

Dads Root Beer Company LLC ......G...... 812 482-5352
Jasper **(G-8243)**

Dr Pepper Bottling Co ....G...... 765 647-3576
Brookville **(G-1113)**

Dr Pepper Bottling Company ....G...... 812 332-1200
Bloomington **(G-716)**

Dr Pepper Snapple Group I ....G...... 260 484-4177
Fort Wayne **(G-4220)**

Glacier Bottling Company LLC ....G...... 574 293-0357
Elkhart **(G-2880)**

Ice River Springs Kentland LLC .....E...... 219 474-6300
Kentland **(G-8521)**

Indianapolis Gatorade ....G...... 317 821-6400
Indianapolis **(G-7199)**

Interactions Inc ....D...... 574 722-6207
Logansport **(G-9341)**

JC Distributers Inc ....G...... 502 276-6311
Jeffersonville **(G-8382)**

Keurig Dr Pepper Inc ....D...... 812 522-3823
Seymour **(G-12463)**

Manitowoc ....F...... 540 375-9300
Sellersburg **(G-12404)**

Niagara Bottling LLC ....G...... 909 758-5313
Plainfield **(G-11629)**

P-Americas LLC ....C...... 219 836-1800
Munster **(G-10621)**

P-Americas LLC ....G...... 812 794-4455
Austin **(G-399)**

P-Americas LLC ....E...... 812 522-3421
Seymour **(G-12472)**

P-Americas LLC ....C...... 317 876-6800
Indianapolis **(G-7644)**

P-Americas LLC ....E...... 765 647-3576
Brookville **(G-1124)**

P-Americas LLC ....C...... 812 332-1200
Bloomington **(G-794)**

P-Americas LLC ....E...... 765 289-0270
Muncie **(G-10542)**

Party Cask ....G...... 812 234-3008
Terre Haute **(G-13296)**

Pepsi Beverage Company ....G...... 574 271-0633
South Bend **(G-12890)**

Pepsi Beverages Company ....E...... 219 836-1800
Munster **(G-10623)**

Pepsi Bottling Ventures LLC ....D...... 765 659-7313
Frankfort **(G-4850)**

Pepsi-Cola ....G...... 812 634-1844
Jasper **(G-8300)**

Pepsi-Cola Metro Btlg Co Inc ....E...... 812 332-1200
Bloomington **(G-798)**

Pepsico ....F...... 317 334-0153
Indianapolis **(G-7671)**

▲ Pepsico ....E...... 317 821-6400
Indianapolis **(G-7672)**

Pepsico Inc ....F...... 260 579-3461
Fort Wayne **(G-4522)**

◆ PRI-Pak Inc ....C...... 812 260-2291
Greendale **(G-5493)**

Qtg Pepsi Co Larry Davi ....G...... 317 830-4020
Indianapolis **(G-7794)**

Quaker Oats Company ....G...... 317 821-6442
Indianapolis **(G-7795)**

Red Bull North America Inc ....G...... 216 401-3950
Newburgh **(G-11045)**

Refreshment Services Inc ....G...... 812 466-0602
Terre Haute **(G-13318)**

Royal Crown Bottling Corp ....C...... 812 424-7978
Evansville **(G-3710)**

Shepherd Distributing ....G...... 317 991-3877
Indianapolis **(G-7932)**

Snapple Beverage Corp ....G...... 812 424-7978
Evansville **(G-3739)**

Success Holding Group Intl Inc ......G...... 260 450-1982
Ossian **(G-11411)**

Swanel Inc ....D...... 219 932-7676
Hammond **(G-5947)**

Terre Haute Coca-Cola Btlg Co .....D...... 812 232-9543
Terre Haute **(G-13352)**

▲ Vin Elite Imports Inc ....G...... 317 264-9250
Indianapolis **(G-8163)**

2087 Flavoring Extracts & Syrups

Boomerang Bay LLC ....G...... 812 236-2027
Terre Haute **(G-13204)**

C A Derr & Company ....G...... 812 897-2920
Boonville **(G-911)**

Callisons Inc ....G...... 574 896-5074
North Judson **(G-11208)**

Central Coca-Cola Btlg Co Inc ......E...... 317 243-3771
Indianapolis **(G-6581)**

Cultor Food Science ....G...... 812 299-6700
Terre Haute **(G-13220)**

▲ Dairychem Laboratories Inc ......F...... 317 849-8400
Fishers **(G-3897)**

International Bakers Services ....E...... 574 287-7111
South Bend **(G-12816)**

Moseley Laboratories Inc ....E...... 317 866-8460
Greenfield **(G-5560)**

North Street Companies LLC ....G...... 317 457-4520
Greenfield **(G-5561)**

Savor Flavor LLC ....G...... 812 667-1030
Dillsboro **(G-2472)**

Sugarpaste ....G...... 574 276-8703
South Bend **(G-12960)**

Tate Lyle Ingrdnts Amricas LLC .....B...... 765 474-5474
Lafayette **(G-9007)**

Vitamins Inc ....E...... 219 879-7356
Michigan City **(G-9859)**

William Leman Co ....E...... 574 546-2371
Bremen **(G-1033)**

2091 Fish & Seafoods, Canned & Cured

Midwest Caviar LLC ....G...... 812 338-3610
English **(G-3315)**

2092 Fish & Seafoods, Fresh & Frozen

Bell Aquaculture LLC ....E...... 765 369-3100
Redkey **(G-11896)**

Collins Caviar Company ....G...... 269 231-5100
Michigan City **(G-9775)**

H & H Partnership Inc............G....... 765 513-4739
Kokomo *(G-8634)*
Ohio Valley Caviar............G....... 812 338-4367
English *(G-3317)*

2095 Coffee

Blue River Roasters LLC............G....... 317 392-9668
Shelbyville *(G-12522)*
Cadillac Coffee Company............E....... 260 489-6281
Fort Wayne *(G-4133)*
Cold Craft Brewing LLC............G....... 314 712-0883
North Judson *(G-11210)*
▲ Darrins Coffee Company............F....... 317 732-5037
Clermont *(G-1711)*
Farmer Bros Co............G....... 812 424-3309
Evansville *(G-3499)*
Harvest Cafe Coffee & Tea LLC............G....... 317 585-9162
Indianapolis *(G-7079)*
Hoosier Roaster Llc............G....... 574 257-1415
Mishawaka *(G-10051)*
Java Roaster............G....... 765 742-2037
Lafayette *(G-8930)*
Last Round Coffee LLC............G....... 317 292-0500
Morgantown *(G-10356)*
Suncoast Coffee Inc............E....... 317 251-3198
Indianapolis *(G-8018)*
Tjs Roaster............G....... 812 985-9615
Evansville *(G-3765)*

2096 Potato Chips & Similar Prdts

Candy Cents Vending Inc............G....... 317 378-9197
Indianapolis *(G-6546)*
Chester Inc............E....... 574 896-5600
North Judson *(G-11209)*
Conagra Brands Inc............C....... 219 866-3020
Rensselaer *(G-11919)*
Frito-Lay North America Inc............B....... 765 659-1831
Frankfort *(G-4834)*
Frito-Lay North America Inc............C....... 765 471-1833
Lafayette *(G-8901)*
Frito-Lay North America Inc............C....... 812 877-2425
Terre Haute *(G-13236)*
Frito-Lay North America Inc............E....... 765 659-4517
Frankfort *(G-4835)*
Grace Island Spcalty Foods Inc............G....... 260 357-3336
Garrett *(G-5006)*
Inventure Foods Inc............E....... 260 824-2800
Bluffton *(G-879)*
▲ Magic Company............E....... 260 747-1502
Fort Wayne *(G-4449)*
Mike-Sells West Virginia Inc............F....... 317 241-7422
Indianapolis *(G-7516)*
Monogram Comfort Foods LLC............D....... 574 848-0344
Bristol *(G-1071)*
Poore Brothers - Bluffton LLC............B....... 260 824-2800
Bluffton *(G-885)*
Specialty Food Group LLC............F....... 219 531-2142
Valparaiso *(G-13623)*
Tyson Foods Inc............B....... 260 726-3118
Portland *(G-11854)*

2097 Ice

Airgas Inc............E....... 317 632-7106
Indianapolis *(G-6354)*
Arctic Ice Express Inc............E....... 812 333-0423
Bloomington *(G-664)*
Bryant Ice Co Inc............G....... 765 459-4543
Kokomo *(G-8602)*
Celebration Ice LLC............G....... 812 634-9801
Jasper *(G-8240)*
Cosner Ice Company Inc............E....... 812 279-8930
Bedford *(G-535)*
Home City Ice Company............E....... 317 638-0437
Indianapolis *(G-7112)*
Home City Ice Company............E....... 317 926-2451
Indianapolis *(G-7113)*
Home City Ice Company............E....... 765 762-6096
Attica *(G-305)*
Home City Ice Company............E....... 219 661-8369
Crown Point *(G-2258)*
Home City Ice Company............E....... 317 926-2451
Indianapolis *(G-7114)*
Quikset Bollard Company............G....... 502 648-6734
New Albany *(G-10852)*
Slip Harris Company LLC............G....... 812 923-5674
Greenville *(G-5654)*
Superior Ice Co Inc............F....... 812 847-4312
Linton *(G-9314)*
United States Cold Storage Inc............E....... 765 482-2653
Lebanon *(G-9231)*

2098 Macaroni, Spaghetti & Noodles

Barbs Homemade Noodles............G....... 812 486-3762
Montgomery *(G-10214)*
Essenhaus Inc............B....... 574 825-6790
Middlebury *(G-9885)*
Harringtons Noodles Inc............G....... 574 546-3861
Bremen *(G-1002)*
I Noodles............G....... 765 447-2288
West Lafayette *(G-14075)*
Noodle Alley............G....... 574 258-1889
Mishawaka *(G-10096)*
Noodle Shop Co - Colorado Inc............G....... 219 548-0921
Valparaiso *(G-13591)*
Sandra Rice Noodle............G....... 317 823-8323
Indianapolis *(G-7893)*

2099 Food Preparations, NEC

Adrian Orchards Inc............G....... 317 784-0550
Indianapolis *(G-6329)*
◆ Ameriqual Group LLC............A....... 812 867-1300
Evansville *(G-3353)*
Ameriqual Group LLC............E....... 812 867-1444
Evansville *(G-3354)*
Amish Country Popcorn Inc............E....... 260 589-8513
Berne *(G-607)*
Atkins Nutritionals Inc............G....... 317 622-4154
Greenfield *(G-5504)*
B Happy Peanut Butter LLC............G....... 317 733-3831
Zionsville *(G-14419)*
Big Brick House Bakery LLP............G....... 260 563-1071
Fort Wayne *(G-4107)*
Butterfield Foods LLC............C....... 317 776-4775
Noblesville *(G-11075)*
C & G Salsa Company LLC............G....... 317 569-9099
Noblesville *(G-11076)*
Calhoun St Soup Salad Spirits............G....... 260 456-7005
Fort Wayne *(G-4134)*
Cbfc LLC............F....... 317 352-0444
Indianapolis *(G-6569)*
Ciderleaf Tea Company Inc............G....... 812 375-1937
Columbus *(G-1870)*
◆ Clabber Girl Corporation............D....... 812 232-9446
Terre Haute *(G-13211)*
Cold Craft Brewing LLC............G....... 314 712-0883
North Judson *(G-11210)*
Conagra Brands Inc............C....... 317 329-3700
Indianapolis *(G-6644)*
Conagra Brands Inc............B....... 402 240-5000
Indianapolis *(G-6645)*
Conagra Brands Inc............C....... 740 387-2722
Rensselaer *(G-11918)*
Conagra Brands Inc............C....... 219 866-3020
Rensselaer *(G-11919)*
Danisco USA Inc............G....... 812 299-6700
Terre Haute *(G-13222)*
Deep Pockets Foods LLC............G....... 317 815-4898
Carmel *(G-1354)*
Dole............G....... 812 576-2186
Guilford *(G-5798)*
E I Du Pont De Nemours & Co............G....... 812 299-6700
Terre Haute *(G-13226)*
Eiseles Honey LLC............G....... 317 896-5830
Indianapolis *(G-6817)*
Entree Vous Greenwood............G....... 317 881-0800
Greenwood *(G-5691)*
Frito-Lay North America Inc............B....... 765 659-1831
Frankfort *(G-4834)*
Frito-Lay North America Inc............E....... 765 659-4517
Frankfort *(G-4835)*
G and G Peppers LLC............E....... 765 358-4519
Gaston *(G-5132)*
Global Packaging LLC............E....... 317 896-2089
Westfield *(G-14165)*
Gonzalez International Inc............G....... 317 558-3700
Carmel *(G-1387)*
Harris Sugar Bush LLC............G....... 765 653-5108
Greencastle *(G-5460)*
Harvey Hinklemeyers............G....... 765 452-1942
Kokomo *(G-8636)*
Hoople Country Kitchens Inc............E....... 812 649-2351
Rockport *(G-12168)*
▼ Hulman & Company............C....... 812 232-9446
Terre Haute *(G-13250)*
I Love Salad LLC............G....... 317 688-7512
Indianapolis *(G-7154)*
Jones Popcorn Inc............D....... 812 941-8810
New Albany *(G-10810)*
Kcma & Services LLC............G....... 260 645-0885
Waterloo *(G-14016)*
Kerry Inc............C....... 812 464-9151
Evansville *(G-3586)*
Keywest LLC............G....... 317 821-8419
Indianapolis *(G-7347)*
LLC Black Jewell............G....... 800 948-2302
Columbus *(G-1963)*
Lm Sugarbush LLC............G....... 812 967-4491
Borden *(G-935)*
▲ Magic Company............E....... 260 747-1502
Fort Wayne *(G-4449)*
Maple Acres............G....... 260 636-2073
Avilla *(G-414)*
McCormick & Company Inc............D....... 574 234-8101
South Bend *(G-12858)*
▼ Mead Johnson & Company LLC............B....... 812 429-5000
Evansville *(G-3620)*
Meyer Foods Inc............G....... 317 773-6594
Noblesville *(G-11149)*
MI Tierra............G....... 812 376-0668
Columbus *(G-1973)*
Mike-Sells West Virginia Inc............F....... 317 241-7422
Indianapolis *(G-7516)*
Millers Mill............G....... 574 825-2010
Middlebury *(G-9908)*
Mishawaka Food Pantry Inc............G....... 574 220-6213
Mishawaka *(G-10091)*
Natural Answers............G....... 219 922-3663
Highland *(G-6052)*
◆ O-M Distributors Inc............E....... 219 853-1900
Hammond *(G-5924)*
Paytons Barbecue............G....... 765 294-2716
Veedersburg *(G-13645)*
Peanut Butter and Jelly............G....... 317 205-9211
Indianapolis *(G-7667)*
Pgp International Inc............G....... 812 867-5129
Evansville *(G-3668)*
Poore Brothers - Bluffton LLC............B....... 260 824-2800
Bluffton *(G-885)*
Pop Tique Popcorn............G....... 260 459-3767
Fort Wayne *(G-4539)*
Preferred Popcorn LLC............F....... 308 850-6631
Palmyra *(G-11438)*
Preston Farms LLC............G....... 812 364-6123
Palmyra *(G-11439)*
Pretzels Inc............C....... 574 941-2201
Plymouth *(G-11717)*
▼ Pretzels Inc............C....... 260 824-4838
Bluffton *(G-886)*
Pro Foods America Inc............G....... 317 826-8526
Indianapolis *(G-7766)*
Qbc Catering............G....... 812 364-4293
Palmyra *(G-11440)*
R D Laney Family Honey Company............G....... 574 656-8701
North Liberty *(G-11219)*
▲ Ramsey Popcorn Co Inc............E....... 812 347-2441
Ramsey *(G-11894)*
Ready Pac Foods Inc............B....... 574 935-9800
Plymouth *(G-11720)*
Red Gold............G....... 765 254-1705
Muncie *(G-10555)*
Red Tortilla Inc............G....... 260 403-2681
Fort Wayne *(G-4584)*
Reeves Feed & Grain LLC............G....... 812 453-3313
Poseyville *(G-11861)*
Reidco Inc............E....... 812 358-3000
Brownstown *(G-1191)*
Rolands Processing............G....... 574 831-4301
New Paris *(G-10992)*
Select Gourmet Popcorn............G....... 812 212-2202
Sunman *(G-13117)*
Shirley Foods Inc............F....... 765 738-6511
Shirley *(G-12662)*
▲ Skjodt-Brrett Cntract Pckg LLC............B....... 765 482-6856
Lebanon *(G-9224)*
Tailgaters Inc............G....... 812 827-3600
Huntingburg *(G-6181)*
Tc Heartland LLC............C....... 317 876-7121
Indianapolis *(G-8041)*
▼ Tc Heartland LLC............B....... 317 566-9750
Carmel *(G-1487)*
Tea Unwrapped LLC............G....... 317 558-8550
Noblesville *(G-11192)*
Thyme In Kitchen LLC............G....... 812 624-0344
Evansville *(G-3763)*
Tili LLC............G....... 574 267-6995
Warsaw *(G-13952)*
Tipton Mills Foods LLC............G....... 812 372-0900
Columbus *(G-2021)*
Todd Couch Regional Office............F....... 312 863-2520
Fishers *(G-3977)*

S I C

Tordilleria Del Valle ....G 765 654-9590
Frankfort (G-4857)

Torti Products Inc ....G 219 730-2071
Highland (G-6057)

Treehugger Maple Syrup LLC ....G 765 698-3728
Laurel (G-9129)

Vitality Bowls ....G 317 581-9496
Carmel (G-1506)

Vivolac Cultures Corporation ....E 317 866-9528
Greenfield (G-5583)

Williams West & Witts Pdts Co ....G 219 879-8236
Michigan City (G-9860)

Yoli Inc ....E 812 945-8530
New Albany (G-10876)

21 TOBACCO PRODUCTS

2111 Cigarettes

Big Red Liquors Inc ....G 812 339-9552
Bloomington (G-683)

Fast Lane Foods Inc ....F 219 879-3300
Michigan City (G-9792)

Smoker Friendly ....G 812 556-0244
Jasper (G-8309)

Smokers Host 307 ....G 765 938-1877
Rushville (G-12234)

South Bend Smoke Time Inc ....G 574 318-4837
South Bend (G-12945)

2121 Cigars

Angelinas Cigars ....G 574 935-5544
Plymouth (G-11667)

Bob Low Discount Tobacco ....G 765 868-9713
Kokomo (G-8600)

Link Rental Company Inc ....G 574 946-7373
Winamac (G-14310)

▼ National Cigar Corporation ....E 765 659-3326
Frankfort (G-4842)

2131 Tobacco, Chewing & Snuff

Black Swan Vapors LLC ....G 317 645-5210
Pendleton (G-11484)

La Porte Smokes and Beverages ....G 219 575-7754
La Porte (G-8783)

2141 Tobacco Stemming & Redrying

Kraft Heinz Foods Company ....E 260 347-1300
Kendallville (G-8489)

22 TEXTILE MILL PRODUCTS

2211 Cotton, Woven Fabric

Anippe ....G 317 979-1110
Fishers (G-3872)

Artsy Canvas ....G 855 206-9045
Indianapolis (G-6423)

Autumn Interiors ....G 317 894-1494
Indianapolis (G-6447)

Columbus Canvas LLC ....G 812 376-9414
Columbus (G-1874)

Covers of Indiana Inc ....G 317 244-0291
Indianapolis (G-6680)

Custom Cut Canvas LLC ....G 260 221-3000
Ligonier (G-9280)

Custom Qlting Pllow Cshion Svc ....G 219 464-7316
Valparaiso (G-13526)

Dean Boslers ....G 812 476-8787
Evansville (G-3455)

▲ Down-Lite International Inc ....G 513 229-3696
Middletown (G-9934)

Hamilton Canvas Inc ....G 219 763-1686
Portage (G-11770)

House of Bluez ....G 812 401-2583
Evansville (G-3543)

Kleidoscope Quilting ....G 812 932-3264
Batesville (G-507)

Majestic Drapieries ....G 574 259-3080
Mishawaka (G-10073)

Maloney Group Inc ....F 812 285-7400
Jeffersonville (G-8395)

Millers Custom Care Candes ....G 574 658-4976
Milford (G-9960)

▲ Mpr Corporation ....E 574 848-5100
Bristol (G-1073)

Onu Acre LLC ....G 765 565-1355
Carthage (G-1515)

Open Canvas LLC ....G 317 908-6524
West Lafayette (G-14091)

Panel Solutions Inc ....F 574 295-0222
Elkhart (G-3072)

Perfect Seating LLC ....F 317 733-1284
Zionsville (G-14455)

Ping Custom Drapery Workroom ....G 317 984-3251
Cicero (G-1665)

▲ Pyro Shield Inc ....F 219 661-8600
Crown Point (G-2290)

Scaggs Lrgent Scrnprinting LLC ....G 765 362-5477
Crawfordsville (G-2195)

Trinity Guardion ....F 812 932-2600
Batesville (G-521)

Whitetower Collection LLC ....G 847 826-0927
Lafayette (G-9024)

Wine & Canvas South Bend LLC ....G 574 807-1562
Elkhart (G-3263)

Wine and Canvas Dev LLC ....F 317 345-1567
Indianapolis (G-8204)

Wnc of Dayton LLC ....G 937 999-8868
Indianapolis (G-8207)

Zig-Zag Crnr Qilts Baskets LLC ....G 317 326-3115
Greenfield (G-5586)

2221 Silk & Man-Made Fiber

Altec Engineering Inc ....E 574 293-1965
Elkhart (G-2679)

Custom Sewing Service ....G 812 428-7015
Evansville (G-3451)

Goldshield Fiber Glass Inc ....C 260 728-2476
Decatur (G-2382)

Hard Surface Fabrications Inc ....G 574 259-4843
Mishawaka (G-10048)

Joseph Fisher ....G 765 435-7231
Waveland (G-14028)

Kabert Industries Inc ....D 765 874-2335
Lynn (G-9428)

Kabert Industries Inc ....G 765 874-1300
Lynn (G-9429)

M C L Window Coverings Inc ....F 317 577-2670
Fishers (G-3942)

Raine Inc ....F 765 622-7687
Anderson (G-157)

Sampson Fiberglass Inc ....E 574 255-4356
Mishawaka (G-10120)

Slipcover Xpress Inc ....G 260 482-7177
Fort Wayne (G-4631)

Structural Composites Ind Inc ....D 260 894-4083
Ligonier (G-9296)

▲ Thorgren Tool & Molding Co ....D 219 462-1801
Valparaiso (G-13628)

2231 Wool, Woven Fabric

Alpaca Holler LLC ....G 513 544-6866
Guilford (G-5796)

Blumenau Alpacas ....G 219 713-6171
Lowell (G-9400)

Cornerstone Woods Alpaca LLC ....G 574 546-4179
Bremen (G-993)

Duneland Alpacas Ltd ....G 219 877-4417
Michigan City (G-9784)

Kds Industries LLC ....G 574 333-2720
Elkhart (G-2957)

Pendleton Woolen Mills Inc ....D 219 879-0326
Michigan City (G-9828)

RB Concepts ....G 317 735-2172
Bloomington (G-808)

Special K Alpacas ....G 260 638-4515
Ossian (G-11408)

2241 Fabric Mills, Cotton, Wool, Silk & Man-Made

▲ Indiana Ribbon Inc ....E 219 279-2112
Wolcott (G-14365)

Leap Frogz Screenprinting EMB ....G 317 786-2441
Indianapolis (G-7390)

Masson M Ross Co Inc ....F 317 632-8021
Indianapolis (G-7464)

Permawick Company Inc ....F 812 376-0703
Columbus (G-1993)

Round Two Begins Corporation ....G 574 825-9800
Middlebury (G-9917)

▲ Tower Advertising Products Inc ....D 260 593-2103
Topeka (G-13431)

Web Industries Fort Wayne Inc ....E 260 432-0027
Fort Wayne (G-4750)

2252 Hosiery, Except Women's

▲ Fbf Originals Inc ....G 765 349-7474
Martinsville (G-9603)

▲ For Bare Feet Inc ....C 765 349-7474
Martinsville (G-9606)

Just Standout LLC ....G 317 531-6956
Indianapolis (G-7325)

Simply Socks Yarn Company ....G 260 416-2397
Fort Wayne (G-4628)

Socks For The Homeless Inc ....F 317 568-3942
Indianapolis (G-7957)

Standout Socks ....G 317 531-6950
Indianapolis (G-7990)

2253 Knit Outerwear Mills

Dyer Signwerks Inc ....G 219 322-7722
Dyer (G-2495)

Mammoth Hats Inc ....F 812 849-2772
Mitchell (G-10166)

Professional Gifting Inc ....F 317 257-3466
Indianapolis (G-7771)

She Lettered ....G 317 844-4555
Indianapolis (G-7924)

Speechlesstees LLC ....G 260 417-9394
Fort Wayne (G-4639)

Zip-A-Tee Shirt Inc ....G 219 879-5556
Michigan City (G-9863)

2259 Knitting Mills, NEC

McHenry Manufacturing Inc ....F 260 824-8146
Bluffton (G-881)

2261 Cotton Fabric Finishers

A D I Screen Printing ....G 765 457-8580
Kokomo (G-8589)

Action Embroidery Inc ....G 850 626-1796
Jeffersonville (G-8319)

Chattin Walter R Cotton ....G 812 254-5031
Columbus (G-1869)

▲ Concept Prints Inc ....F 317 290-1222
Indianapolis (G-6648)

Gad-A-Bout Screenprinting Inc ....G 765 855-5681
Centerville (G-1542)

Graphic22 Inc ....G 219 921-5409
Chesterton (G-1608)

OHara Sports Inc ....G 219 836-5554
Munster (G-10618)

Sullivan Group Inc ....F 574 773-2108
Nappanee (G-10707)

UC Ink LLC ....G 765 220-5502
West College Corner (G-14038)

2262 Silk & Man-Made Fabric Finishers

Apparel Promotions Inc ....G 574 294-7165
Elkhart (G-2694)

▲ Classic Products Corp ....E 260 484-2695
Fort Wayne (G-4159)

Graphic22 Inc ....G 219 921-5409
Chesterton (G-1608)

▲ Main Event Mdsg Group LLC ....F 317 570-8900
Indianapolis (G-7442)

Spectrum Marketing ....G 765 643-5566
Anderson (G-168)

2269 Textile Finishers, NEC

Graphic22 Inc ....G 219 921-5409
Chesterton (G-1608)

Tt2 LLC ....G 260 438-4575
Fort Wayne (G-4707)

2273 Carpets & Rugs

Advanced Services LLC ....F 317 780-6909
Indianapolis (G-6336)

Anna Daisys LLC ....G 812 346-7623
North Vernon (G-11247)

Circle City Services Ltd ....G 317 770-6287
Noblesville (G-11082)

▲ Envirotech Extrusion Inc ....E 765 966-8068
Richmond (G-11984)

Faulkens Floorcover ....F 574 300-4260
South Bend (G-12773)

Indiana Rug Company ....G 574 252-4653
Mishawaka (G-10053)

▲ Jpc LLC ....F 574 293-8030
Elkhart (G-2951)

Langenwlter Crpt Dyg Vlparaiso ....G 219 531-7601
Valparaiso (G-13571)

Manta Rugs ....G 765 869-5940
Boswell (G-940)

Mountville Mats ....G 574 753-8858
Logansport (G-9355)

Recreation Insites LLC .... G 317 578-0588
Fishers *(G-3961)*

Todd K Hockemeyer Inc .... G 260 639-3591
Fort Wayne *(G-4689)*

2281 Yarn Spinning Mills

Three Points Alpaca Farm LLC .... G 812 363-3876
Batesville *(G-520)*

2282 Yarn Texturizing, Throwing, Twisting & Winding Mills

BP Wind Energy North Amer Inc .... G 765 884-1000
Fowler *(G-4797)*

2284 Thread Mills

Elegant Needleworks Inc .... G 765 284-9427
Muncie *(G-10468)*

Groovemade LLC .... G 574 834-1138
North Webster *(G-11292)*

2295 Fabrics Coated Not Rubberized

American Elkhart LLC .... G 574 293-0333
Elkhart *(G-2683)*

Aoc LLC .... D 219 465-4384
Valparaiso *(G-13494)*

Apparel Promotions Inc .... G 574 294-7165
Elkhart *(G-2694)*

C M I Enterprises Inc .... D 305 685-9651
Elkhart *(G-2744)*

Clear Edge Filtration Inc .... G 219 306-7339
Crown Point *(G-2235)*

D K Enterprises LLC .... G 260 356-9011
Huntington *(G-6200)*

◆ Elite Crete Systems Inc .... E 219 465-7671
Valparaiso *(G-13535)*

Ferrill-Fisher Incorporated .... G 812 935-9000
Bloomington *(G-724)*

ISI Inc .... F 317 631-7980
Indianapolis *(G-7275)*

▲ Mpr Corporation .... E 574 848-5100
Bristol *(G-1073)*

Patrick Industries Inc .... C 574 255-9692
Mishawaka *(G-10100)*

Pmw Holdings LLC .... G 317 339-4685
Indianapolis *(G-7703)*

Sirmax North America Inc .... E 765 639-0300
Anderson *(G-167)*

2296 Tire Cord & Fabric

▲ Muhlen Sohn Industries LP .... F 765 640-9674
Anderson *(G-140)*

2297 Fabrics, Nonwoven

Carver Non-Woven Tech LLC .... C 260 627-0033
Fremont *(G-4954)*

▲ Fiber Bond Corporation .... C 219 879-4541
Trail Creek *(G-13441)*

Midwest Nonwovens Indiana LLC .... E 317 241-8956
Indianapolis *(G-7508)*

Vita Nonwovens LLC .... E 260 747-0990
Fort Wayne *(G-4729)*

2298 Cordage & Twine

Apollo North America Inc .... G 317 573-0777
Carmel *(G-1312)*

C-Cat Inc .... F 317 568-2899
Indianapolis *(G-6531)*

▲ Hessville Cable & Sling Co .... E 773 768-8181
Gary *(G-5064)*

Kentuckiana Wire Rope & Supply .... F 812 282-3667
Jeffersonville *(G-8386)*

▲ Sandin Mfg Inc .... D 219 872-2253
Michigan City *(G-9839)*

2299 Textile Goods, NEC

3w Enterprises LLC .... G 847 366-6555
Elkhart *(G-2654)*

Abercrombie Textiles I LLC .... G 574 825-9800
Middlebury *(G-9867)*

▲ Anokhi International Inc .... G 260 750-0418
Fort Wayne *(G-4077)*

Blocksom & Co .... E 219 878-4458
Michigan City *(G-9771)*

Blush Salon Boutique .... G 317 523-1635
Fishers *(G-3881)*

East Heat Wood Pellets LLC .... G 317 638-4840
Indianapolis *(G-6790)*

Ruby Enterprises Inc .... G 765 649-2060
Anderson *(G-164)*

Tippmann Products LLC .... G 260 438-7946
Fort Wayne *(G-4685)*

◆ Wolf Corporation .... E 260 749-9393
Fort Wayne *(G-4760)*

23 APPAREL AND OTHER FINISHED PRODUCTS MADE FROM FABRICS AND SIMILAR MATERIAL

2311 Men's & Boys' Suits, Coats & Overcoats

▲ Ashley Worldwide Inc .... G 574 259-2481
Granger *(G-5390)*

Formal Affairs Tuxedo Shop .... G 574 875-6654
Elkhart *(G-2868)*

Hearts Rmned Lifestyle Cir LLC .... G 800 807-0485
Gary *(G-5061)*

Jgr Enterprises LLC .... G 586 264-3400
Portage *(G-11771)*

Raine Inc .... F 765 622-7687
Anderson *(G-157)*

Sugar Tree Incorporated .... G 260 417-3362
Fort Wayne *(G-4660)*

2321 Men's & Boys' Shirts

European Concepts LLC .... G 888 797-9005
Fort Wayne *(G-4250)*

Him Gentlemans Boutique .... G 812 924-7441
New Albany *(G-10793)*

Hoogies Sports House Inc .... G 574 533-9875
Goshen *(G-5238)*

Stallion Sportswear Inc .... E 765 584-5097
Winchester *(G-14341)*

2322 Men's & Boys' Underwear & Nightwear

Krazy Klothes Ltd .... G 317 687-8310
Indianapolis *(G-7368)*

2323 Men's & Boys' Neckwear

Sycamore Enterprises Inc .... G 812 491-0901
Evansville *(G-3756)*

2325 Men's & Boys' Separate Trousers & Casual Slacks

▲ Berne Apparel Company .... E 260 622-1500
Ossian *(G-11397)*

2326 Men's & Boys' Work Clothing

▲ Berne Apparel Company .... E 260 622-1500
Ossian *(G-11397)*

Dance Sophisticates .... E 317 634-7728
Indianapolis *(G-6725)*

Gohn Bros Manufacturing Co .... G 574 825-2400
Middlebury *(G-9889)*

Steel Grip Inc .... D 765 397-3344
Kingman *(G-8533)*

2329 Men's & Boys' Clothing, NEC

Adidas North America Inc .... F 219 878-5822
Michigan City *(G-9764)*

▲ Berne Apparel Company .... E 260 622-1500
Ossian *(G-11397)*

CJS Mens Wear .... G 260 436-4788
Fort Wayne *(G-4153)*

Designs 4 U Inc .... G 765 793-3026
Covington *(G-2118)*

Fashion City .... G 260 744-6753
Fort Wayne *(G-4256)*

▲ H3 Sportgear LLC .... G 317 595-7500
Fishers *(G-3920)*

Image Concepts Inc .... G 317 408-5558
Noblesville *(G-11124)*

◆ Indiana Knitwear Corporation .... E 317 462-4413
Greenfield *(G-5540)*

Jcs Enterprises Inc .... G 812 284-4827
Clarksville *(G-1688)*

▲ Official Sports Intl Inc .... F 574 269-1404
Warsaw *(G-13917)*

Sports Licensed Division .... A 317 895-7000
Indianapolis *(G-7977)*

Stallion Sportswear Inc .... E 765 584-5097
Winchester *(G-14341)*

Vf Outdoor LLC .... F 317 843-9419
Indianapolis *(G-8159)*

2335 Women's & Misses' Dresses

Bcbg Max Azria Group LLC .... G 319 753-0437
Fort Wayne *(G-4102)*

Bcbg Max Azria Group LLC .... G 515 964-7355
Fishers *(G-3875)*

Bcbg Max Azria Group LLC .... G 515 993-4753
Evansville *(G-3371)*

Bcbg Max Azria Group LLC .... G 574 289-3937
Albion *(G-16)*

Bcbg Max Azria Group LLC .... G 620 694-4256
Petersburg *(G-11561)*

Bcbg Max Azria Group LLC .... G 620 442-1111
Monticello *(G-10255)*

Bcbg Max Azria Group LLC .... G 641 872-1842
Fort Wayne *(G-4103)*

Bcbg Max Azria Group LLC .... G 712 243-1965
Fort Wayne *(G-4104)*

Bcbg Max Azria Group LLC .... G 712 277-3937
Merrillville *(G-9700)*

Bcbg Max Azria Group LLC .... G 913 631-0090
Zionsville *(G-14420)*

Elysian Company LLC .... G 574 267-2259
Warsaw *(G-13872)*

Mark Heister Design Inc .... G 312 527-0422
La Porte *(G-8789)*

Simple To Elegant .... G 812 234-8700
Terre Haute *(G-13328)*

Spectacular Soirees .... G 812 841-4311
Terre Haute *(G-13339)*

Sugar Tree Incorporated .... G 260 417-3362
Fort Wayne *(G-4660)*

2339 Women's & Misses' Outerwear, NEC

▲ Berne Apparel Company .... E 260 622-1500
Ossian *(G-11397)*

Best Friends Inc .... G 765 985-3872
Denver *(G-2453)*

Brighton Collectibles LLC .... E 317 580-0912
Indianapolis *(G-6510)*

CM Reed LLC .... G 517 546-4100
Greendale *(G-5485)*

Dance Sophisticates .... E 317 634-7728
Indianapolis *(G-6725)*

Designs 4 U Inc .... G 765 793-3026
Covington *(G-2118)*

▲ H3 Sportgear LLC .... G 317 595-7500
Fishers *(G-3920)*

Hair Huggers LLC .... G 317 776-9977
Fishers *(G-3921)*

Hidinghilda LLC .... G 260 760-7093
Fort Wayne *(G-4332)*

Hoogies Sports House Inc .... G 574 533-9875
Goshen *(G-5238)*

▲ Maingate Inc .... D 317 243-2000
Indianapolis *(G-7444)*

Mgtc Inc .... G 317 786-1693
Indianapolis *(G-7494)*

▲ Mgtc Inc .... E 317 780-0609
Zionsville *(G-14447)*

Motionwear LLC .... G 317 780-4182
Indianapolis *(G-7547)*

▲ Official Sports Intl Inc .... F 574 269-1404
Warsaw *(G-13917)*

Pariah .... G 317 250-0612
Indianapolis *(G-7655)*

Sports Licensed Division .... A 317 895-7000
Indianapolis *(G-7977)*

Stallion Sportswear Inc .... E 765 584-5097
Winchester *(G-14341)*

Sycamore Enterprises Inc .... G 812 491-0901
Evansville *(G-3756)*

Three Little Monkeys .... G 765 778-9370
Pendleton *(G-11508)*

2341 Women's, Misses' & Children's Underwear & Nightwear

Krazy Klothes Ltd .... G 317 687-8310
Indianapolis *(G-7368)*

Roses Square Dance Acc .... G 812 865-2821
Orleans *(G-11369)*

2353 Hats, Caps & Millinery

Comfycaps By Cindy .... G 269 683-6881
Elkhart *(G-2764)*

Genesco Inc .... G 812 234-9722
Terre Haute *(G-13239)*

Lids Corporation .... G 260 471-4287
Fort Wayne *(G-4434)*

S I C

Mad Hatters Unlimited ....G...... 219 852-6011
Hammond (G-5910)
Mammoth Hats Inc ....F...... 812 849-2772
Mitchell (G-10166)

2361 Children's & Infants' Dresses & Blouses
Aleo Inc ....G...... 317 324-8583
Fishers (G-3868)

2369 Girls' & Infants' Outerwear, NEC
◆ Indiana Knitwear Corporation ....E...... 317 462-4413
Greenfield (G-5540)
Rittenhouse Square ....G...... 260 824-4200
Bluffton (G-889)

2371 Fur Goods
Yannis Furs Inc ....G...... 317 580-0914
Indianapolis (G-8224)

2381 Dress & Work Gloves
Glove Corporation ....D...... 501 362-2437
Alexandria (G-43)
Setser Fabricating LLC ....G...... 812 546-2169
Columbus (G-2012)
Steel Grip Inc ....D...... 765 397-3344
Kingman (G-8533)
▲ Tmgg LLC ....E...... 812 687-7444
Plainville (G-11656)

2384 Robes & Dressing Gowns
Wells Robe Sales & Rental ....G...... 317 542-9062
Indianapolis (G-8183)

2385 Waterproof Outerwear
Ie Products Mad Dasher Inc ....E...... 260 747-0545
Fort Wayne (G-4357)
▲ Nasco Industries Inc ....C...... 812 254-7393
Washington (G-13992)

2386 Leather & Sheep Lined Clothing
Clinton Harness Shop ....G...... 574 533-9797
Goshen (G-5189)
Hilltop Leather ....G...... 317 508-3404
Martinsville (G-9612)

2389 Apparel & Accessories, NEC
◆ Celebration Creations Inc ....E...... 800 762-8286
Indianapolis (G-6573)
Dance Sophisticates ....E...... 317 634-7728
Indianapolis (G-6725)
Death Studios ....G...... 219 362-4321
La Porte (G-8750)
Designs 4 U Inc ....G...... 765 793-3026
Covington (G-2118)
Fall Creek Corporation ....G...... 765 482-1861
Lebanon (G-9182)
Five Star Fabulous LLC ....G...... 260 579-3401
Fort Wayne (G-4264)
Gary Muslim Center ....G...... 219 885-3018
Gary (G-5051)
▼ Ghost Forge L T D ....G...... 765 362-8654
Crawfordsville (G-2154)
Giggling Wenches Handcrafts ....G...... 765 482-9776
Lebanon (G-9183)
Golden Pride Hair Company LLC ....G...... 812 777-9604
Indianapolis (G-7020)
Higgins Dyan ....G...... 812 876-0754
Ellettsville (G-3281)
Him Gentlemans Boutique ....G...... 812 924-7441
New Albany (G-10793)
Knotts and Frye Inc ....G...... 317 925-6406
Indianapolis (G-7362)
Moose Lodge ....G...... 219 362-2446
La Porte (G-8798)
Nebo Ridge Enterprises LLC ....G...... 317 471-1089
Carmel (G-1441)
Pdb II Inc ....G...... 219 865-1888
Dyer (G-2507)
Precise Title Inc ....G...... 219 987-2286
Demotte (G-2445)
Regal Inc ....G...... 765 747-1155
Muncie (G-10557)
Revolver LLC ....G...... 317 418-1824
Noblesville (G-11175)
Rittenhouse Square ....G...... 260 824-4200
Bluffton (G-889)
▲ Rivars Inc ....E...... 765 789-6119
Indianapolis (G-7847)

Troves ....G...... 260 672-0878
Roanoke (G-12108)
Urserys LLC ....G...... 619 206-1761
Gary (G-5113)

2391 Curtains & Draperies
Artisan Interiors Inc ....E...... 574 825-9494
Middlebury (G-9873)
▲ Ascot Enterprises Inc ....E...... 877 773-7751
Nappanee (G-10648)
Ascot Enterprises Inc ....D...... 260 593-3733
Topeka (G-13411)
Ascot Enterprises Inc ....E...... 574 773-7751
Nappanee (G-10649)
Ascot Enterprises Inc ....E...... 574 773-3104
Nappanee (G-10650)
Custom Draperies of Indiana ....G...... 219 924-2500
Hammond (G-5867)
Custom Drapery Service Inc ....G...... 317 587-1518
Indianapolis (G-6712)
Doris Drapery Boutique ....G...... 765 472-5850
Peru (G-11524)
F & R Draperies ....G...... 812 284-4682
Clarksville (G-1680)
Femyer Drapery Shop ....G...... 765 282-3398
Muncie (G-10471)
Foremost Flexible Fabricating ....G...... 812 663-4756
Greensburg (G-5600)
Greenwood Draperie Corp ....G...... 317 882-0130
Greenwood (G-5699)
Industrial Sewing Machine Co ....G...... 812 425-2255
Evansville (G-3558)
▲ Lafayette Venetian Blind Inc ....A...... 765 464-2500
West Lafayette (G-14082)
M & D Draperies ....G...... 812 886-4608
Vincennes (G-13691)
Majesty Enterprises Inc ....G...... 812 752-6446
Scottsburg (G-12372)
Mar-Co Packaging Inc ....G...... 765 564-3979
Delphi (G-2423)
Merin Interiors Indianapolis ....G...... 317 251-6603
Indianapolis (G-7482)
Mill End Drapery Inc ....G...... 317 257-4800
Indianapolis (G-7518)
Mm Window Fashions ....G...... 317 585-4933
Fishers (G-3947)
Northwest Interiors Inc ....G...... 574 294-2326
Elkhart (G-3067)
Quality Drapery Corporation ....E...... 765 481-2370
Lebanon (G-9218)
Queen Ann Custom Drapies ....G...... 317 802-6130
Carmel (G-1460)
Silk Mountain Creation ....G...... 317 815-1660
Carmel (G-1481)

2392 House furnishings: Textile
Arden Companies LLC ....D...... 260 747-1657
Fort Wayne (G-4089)
Artisan Interiors Inc ....E...... 574 825-9494
Middlebury (G-9873)
▲ Ascot Enterprises Inc ....E...... 877 773-7751
Nappanee (G-10648)
Ascot Enterprises Inc ....D...... 574 773-3104
Nappanee (G-10650)
Bags By Brenda ....G...... 765 779-4287
Markleville (G-9585)
Baird Home Corporation ....G...... 812 883-1141
Salem (G-12284)
Barrett Manufacturing Inc ....G...... 812 753-5808
Fort Branch (G-4026)
Blanket Hog ....G...... 219 308-9532
Crown Point (G-2228)
Bleu Rooster Designs ....G...... 317 845-0889
Fishers (G-3880)
Crash Beds LLC ....G...... 317 601-4436
Greenwood (G-5677)
Evansville Assn For The Blind ....C...... 812 422-1181
Evansville (G-3482)
▲ Inhabit Inc ....G...... 317 636-1699
Indianapolis (G-7233)
◆ Jordan Manufacturing Co Inc ....C...... 800 328-6522
Monticello (G-10268)
Keter North America LLC ....G...... 765 298-6800
Anderson (G-129)
Nice-Pak Products Inc ....A...... 845 365-1700
Mooresville (G-10328)
Ohio Table Pad of Indiana ....E...... 260 463-2139
Lagrange (G-9062)
Pgs LLC ....E...... 812 988-4030
Nashville (G-10732)

Pillow Pals Inc ....G...... 812 853-8241
Newburgh (G-11042)
Quilt Designs Inc ....G...... 574 534-2502
Elkhart (G-3132)
R&D Investment Holdings Inc ....E...... 260 749-1301
Fort Wayne (G-4575)
Regency Pad Corp ....D...... 731 587-9596
Evansville (G-3702)
Reit-Price Mfg Co Incorporated ....G...... 765 964-3252
Union City (G-13460)
Rhyne & Associates Inc ....F...... 317 786-4459
Indianapolis (G-7838)
▼ Veada Industries Inc ....A...... 574 831-4775
New Paris (G-11000)
Vera Bradley Inc ....B...... 877 708-8372
Roanoke (G-12110)
▲ Virtus Inc ....E...... 812 932-0131
Batesville (G-523)

2393 Textile Bags
Meese Inc ....D...... 812 273-1008
Madison (G-9485)
Raine Inc ....F...... 765 622-7687
Anderson (G-157)
Ts2 Tctical Spec-Solutions Inc ....G...... 765 437-3650
Bedford (G-585)

2394 Canvas Prdts
AK Supply Inc ....F...... 317 895-0410
Indianapolis (G-6358)
Angola Canvas Co Inc ....F...... 260 665-9913
Angola (G-191)
Beverly Tent & Awning Co ....G...... 219 931-3723
Hammond (G-5852)
Blessing Enterprises Inc ....F...... 219 736-9800
Merrillville (G-9702)
Canvas Shop LLC ....G...... 260 768-7755
Shipshewana (G-12607)
Cool Planet LLC ....G...... 317 927-9000
Indianapolis (G-6662)
Cork Medical LLC ....G...... 317 361-4651
Indianapolis (G-6667)
Coverite-Custom Covers ....G...... 574 278-7152
Monticello (G-10258)
Dometic Corporation ....B...... 260 463-7657
Lagrange (G-9037)
Fort Wayne Awning Co Inc ....G...... 260 478-1636
Fort Wayne (G-4269)
▲ Gosport Manufacturing Co Inc ......G...... 812 879-4224
Gosport (G-5350)
▲ Gta Containers Inc ....E...... 574 288-3459
South Bend (G-12793)
Hare Canvas Products ....G...... 260 758-8800
Markle (G-9577)
Indianapolis Marine Co ....F...... 317 545-4646
Indianapolis (G-7202)
◆ J Ennis Fabrics Inc (usa) ....G...... 877 953-6647
Plainfield (G-11620)
Lafayette Tent & Awning Co ....E...... 765 742-4277
Lafayette (G-8951)
Larrys Canvas Cleaning ....G...... 260 463-2220
Lagrange (G-9057)
Lomont Holdings Co Inc ....E...... 800 545-9023
Angola (G-228)
▲ Marine Mooring Inc ....E...... 574 594-5787
Warsaw (G-13903)
Marion Tent & Awning Co ....G...... 765 664-7722
Marion (G-9546)
Meese Inc ....D...... 812 273-1008
Madison (G-9485)
Miller Canvas Shop ....G...... 574 658-3563
Milford (G-9959)
Montgomery Tent & Awning Co ....F...... 317 357-9759
Indianapolis (G-7538)
Mosiers Tarps ....G...... 260 563-3332
Wabash (G-13742)
R J Hanlon Company Inc ....E...... 317 867-2900
Westfield (G-14182)
Shade By Design Inc ....G...... 317 602-3513
Indianapolis (G-7920)
T J Snuggles Inc ....E...... 574 546-4404
Bremen (G-1028)
T K Sales & Service ....G...... 219 962-8982
Gary (G-5104)
◆ Transhield Inc ....E...... 574 742-4333
Elkhart (G-3222)
Twin Lakes Canvas Inc ....G...... 574 583-2000
Monticello (G-10286)
▼ Veada Industries Inc ....A...... 574 831-4775
New Paris (G-11000)

Vessell Trim Co ....F...... 812 424-2963
  Evansville (G-3797)
Webster Custom Canvas Inc ....G...... 574 834-4497
  North Webster (G-11302)
Woodside Custom Canvas LLC..........G...... 260 593-2420
  Topeka (G-13432)

2395 Pleating & Stitching For The Trade

2 Bears LLC ....G...... 317 375-1634
  Indianapolis (G-6284)
A B C Embroidery Inc ....G...... 260 636-7311
  Albion (G-14)
A D I Screen Printing ....G...... 765 457-8580
  Kokomo (G-8589)
A Time To Stitch Inc......................G...... 812 422-5968
  Evansville (G-3330)
▲ A-1 Awards Inc ....F...... 317 546-9000
  Indianapolis (G-6301)
Abracadabra Graphics ....G...... 812 336-1971
  Bloomington (G-654)
Advantage Embroidery Inc ....G...... 765 471-0188
  Bringhurst (G-1037)
After Hours Embroidery ....G...... 812 926-9355
  Aurora (G-368)
Apparel Promotions Inc ....G...... 574 294-7165
  Elkhart (G-2694)
Apple Group Inc ....E...... 765 675-4777
  Tipton (G-13387)
Arizona Sport Shirts Inc ....E...... 317 481-2160
  Indianapolis (G-6419)
Avon Sports Apparel Corp ....G...... 317 887-2673
  Greenwood (G-5668)
Baron Embroidery Corp ....G...... 260 484-8700
  Auburn (G-316)
Barrett Manufacturing Inc ....G...... 812 753-5808
  Fort Branch (G-4026)
Bears Den EMB & More LLC ....G...... 260 724-4070
  Decatur (G-2370)
▲ Burston Marketing Inc ....F...... 574 262-4005
  Elkhart (G-2739)
Celestial Designs LLC ....G...... 317 733-3110
  Zionsville (G-14425)
Charles Coons............................G...... 765 362-6509
  Crawfordsville (G-2138)
Cindys In Stitches ....G...... 317 841-1408
  Fishers (G-3890)
▲ Classic Products Corp ....E...... 260 484-2695
  Fort Wayne (G-4159)
CLC Embroidery LLC.....................G...... 219 395-9600
  Chesterton (G-1600)
Coaches Connection Inc ....G...... 260 356-0400
  Huntington (G-6198)
Columbus Embroidery ....G...... 812 273-0860
  Madison (G-9454)
Company Pride Shirts LLC ....G...... 812 526-5700
  Edinburgh (G-2601)
▲ Concept Prints Inc ....F...... 317 290-1222
  Indianapolis (G-6648)
Connies Satin Stitch ....G...... 219 942-1887
  Hobart (G-6077)
Corporate Shirts Direct Inc ....G...... 317 474-6033
  Franklin (G-4877)
Country Stitches Embroidery ....G...... 219 324-7625
  La Porte (G-8746)
Cowpokes Inc..............................E...... 765 642-3911
  Anderson (G-91)
Creative Embroidery Designs ....G...... 812 479-8280
  Evansville (G-3438)
Creative Solutions ....G...... 219 778-4919
  Rolling Prairie (G-12184)
Crescendo Inc ....G...... 812 829-4759
  Spencer (G-13022)
Custom Imprint Corporation ....E...... 800 378-3397
  Merrillville (G-9709)
D & J Custom Embroidery ....G...... 219 874-9061
  Michigan City (G-9779)
Dave Turner ....G...... 765 674-3360
  Gas City (G-5122)
Digistitch...................................G...... 574 538-3960
  Goshen (G-5199)
▲ Dkm Embroidery Inc ....G...... 260 471-4070
  Fort Wayne (G-4215)
Dugout ....G...... 765 642-8528
  Anderson (G-100)
Elegan Sportswear Inc ....F...... 219 464-8416
  Valparaiso (G-13534)
Embroidery N Things Inc ....G...... 317 859-8963
  Bargersville (G-482)
Embroidery Nation........................G...... 574 967-3928
  Flora (G-3994)

Embroidery Plus Inc ....G...... 317 243-3445
  Indianapolis (G-6848)
Embroidery Solutions U S ....G...... 812 923-9152
  Greenville (G-5649)
Favor It Promotions Inc ....F...... 317 733-1112
  Carmel (G-1379)
Four Season Sports Inc ....G...... 812 279-0384
  Bedford (G-543)
Freckles Graphics Inc ....F...... 765 448-4692
  Lafayette (G-8900)
Gettelfinger Holdings LLC ....G...... 812 923-9065
  Floyds Knobs (G-4012)
Giraffe X Graphics Inc ....G...... 317 546-4944
  Indianapolis (G-7007)
Golden Threads ....G...... 765 557-7801
  Elwood (G-3299)
Graphic22 Inc ....G...... 219 921-5409
  Chesterton (G-1608)
HWH Embroidery Inc ....G...... 317 895-0201
  Indianapolis (G-7149)
Imperial Designs ....G...... 765 985-2712
  Denver (G-2454)
Imperial Trophy & Awards Co ....G...... 260 432-8161
  Fort Wayne (G-4361)
J N P Custom Designs Inc ....G...... 317 253-2198
  Indianapolis (G-7289)
Jasper EMB & Screen Prtg..............G...... 812 482-4787
  Jasper (G-8260)
Jer-Maur Corporation ....G...... 812 384-8290
  Bloomfield (G-640)
Just Monograms LLC ....G...... 812 827-3693
  Jasper (G-8269)
Kellum Imprints Inc ....G...... 812 347-2546
  Ramsey (G-11893)
Kerham Inc ....E...... 260 483-5444
  Fort Wayne (G-4409)
Lavender Patch Fabr Quilts LLC ....G...... 574 848-0011
  Bristol (G-1066)
Lloyd & Mona Sulivan ....G...... 812 522-9191
  Seymour (G-12467)
Locoli Inc ....E...... 219 365-3125
  Schererville (G-12332)
Logo Boys Inc ....G...... 574 256-6844
  Mishawaka (G-10070)
▲ Maingate Inc ....D...... 317 243-2000
  Indianapolis (G-7444)
Marie S Embroidery ....G...... 219 931-2561
  Hammond (G-5912)
Mary Duncan ....F...... 812 238-3637
  Terre Haute (G-13279)
McBeth Designs Inc ....G...... 317 848-7313
  Carmel (G-1435)
McKinneys Embroidery & Sup Co........G...... 317 984-9039
  Arcadia (G-265)
National Athletic Sportswear ....F...... 260 436-2248
  Fort Wayne (G-4490)
Outfitter ....G...... 765 289-6456
  Muncie (G-10541)
▲ P J Marketing Services Inc...........G...... 574 259-8843
  South Bend (G-12886)
P Js Custom Embroidering LLC ....G...... 219 787-9161
  Chesterton (G-1627)
Paige Marschall ....G...... 574 277-1631
  Granger (G-5428)
Perdue Printed Products Inc ....G...... 260 456-7575
  Fort Wayne (G-4523)
Precision Stitch Indiana Inc ....G...... 765 473-6734
  Peru (G-11541)
Profit Finders Incorporated..............F...... 317 251-7792
  Indianapolis (G-7773)
Progressive Design Apparel Inc ....E...... 317 293-5888
  Indianapolis (G-7775)
Pumpkinvine Quilting Inc ....G...... 574 825-1151
  Middlebury (G-9916)
Quilt Designs Inc..........................G...... 574 534-2502
  Elkhart (G-3132)
Quilt Expressions ....G...... 317 913-1916
  Fishers (G-3960)
Quilters Garden ....G...... 812 539-4939
  Lawrenceburg (G-9154)
Ram Graphics Inc ....E...... 765 724-7783
  Alexandria (G-48)
Raymond Truex ....G...... 574 858-2260
  Warsaw (G-13933)
Real Image Llc ....G...... 765 675-7325
  Tipton (G-13403)
Rensew Inc ....G...... 574 257-0665
  Mishawaka (G-10116)
Robert Burkhart ....G...... 219 448-0365
  Alexandria (G-52)

Rustic N Chic LLC.........................G...... 219 987-4957
  Wheatfield (G-14230)
Safety Vehicle Emblem Inc ....F...... 317 885-7565
  Indianapolis (G-7884)
Select Embroidery/Top It Off ....F...... 812 337-8049
  Bloomington (G-823)
Sew Unique Inc ....G...... 317 257-0503
  Indianapolis (G-7918)
Shilling Sales Inc ....E...... 260 426-2626
  Fort Wayne (G-4621)
Shirtails ....G...... 812 858-8605
  Newburgh (G-11048)
Shirts N Things S N T Graphics..........G...... 317 271-3515
  Indianapolis (G-7935)
Spectrum Marketing ....G...... 765 643-5566
  Anderson (G-168)
Sportsmania Sales Inc. ....G...... 317 873-5501
  Zionsville (G-14465)
Spp Inc ....F...... 812 882-6203
  Vincennes (G-13707)
◆ Stoffel Seals Corporation ....E...... 845 353-3800
  Angola (G-248)
Stogdill Sports ....G...... 812 524-7081
  Seymour (G-12495)
Sues Custom Shirts.......................G...... 812 535-4429
  Sandford (G-12311)
T L E LLC ....G...... 317 257-1424
  Noblesville (G-11191)
Thread Creations Inc ....G...... 765 521-3886
  New Castle (G-10919)
Topstitch Inc ....F...... 574 293-6633
  Elkhart (G-3220)
Unique Graphic Designs Inc ....G...... 574 583-7119
  Monticello (G-10287)
Vco Inc ....G...... 812 235-3540
  Terre Haute (G-13361)
Vickers Graphics Inc ....G...... 765 868-4646
  Kokomo (G-8712)
Village Custom Embroidery Inc ....G...... 317 733-3110
  Zionsville (G-14470)
Wanda Harrington ....G...... 765 642-1628
  Anderson (G-182)
Wasu Inc ....G...... 765 448-4450
  Lafayette (G-9022)
Wildman Business Group LLC ....C...... 866 369-1552
  Warsaw (G-13965)
Wildman Corporate Apparel Ltd ....F...... 574 269-7266
  Warsaw (G-13966)
Winning Edge of Rochester Inc ....F...... 574 223-6090
  Rochester (G-12162)
Winters Assoc Prmtnal Pdts Inc ....F...... 812 330-7000
  Bloomington (G-858)
Woods Enterprises ....G...... 574 232-7449
  South Bend (G-12992)
Zig-Zag Crnr Qilts Baskets LLC..........G...... 317 326-3115
  Greenfield (G-5586)

2396 Automotive Trimmings, Apparel Findings, Related Prdts

A New Company Inc ....G...... 574 293-9088
  Elkhart (G-2658)
▲ A-1 Awards Inc ....F...... 317 546-9000
  Indianapolis (G-6301)
Ad Vision Graphics Inc....................G...... 812 476-4932
  Evansville (G-3343)
▲ American Keeper Corporation ....E...... 765 521-2080
  New Castle (G-10891)
Apple Group Inc ....E...... 765 675-4777
  Tipton (G-13387)
Arizona Sport Shirts Inc ....E...... 317 481-2160
  Indianapolis (G-6419)
▲ Asempac Inc ....E...... 812 945-6303
  New Albany (G-10747)
Athletic Edge Inc..........................F...... 260 489-6613
  Fort Wayne (G-4095)
▲ Berry Plastics Ik LLC ....D...... 641 648-5047
  Evansville (G-3379)
Big Als Athletics ....G...... 765 836-5203
  Mount Summit (G-10378)
Blythes Sport Shop Inc ....E...... 219 476-0026
  Valparaiso (G-13510)
▲ Burston Marketing Inc ....F...... 574 262-4005
  Elkhart (G-2739)
Charles Coons.............................G...... 765 362-6509
  Crawfordsville (G-2138)
Chicago Color Graphics ....G...... 312 856-1433
  Hammond (G-5860)
Coaches Connection Inc ....G...... 260 356-0400
  Huntington (G-6198)

Codybro LLC ....G....... 765 827-5441
　Connersville (G-2044)

Crescendo Inc ....G....... 812 829-4759
　Spencer (G-13022)

Cross Printwear Inc ....F....... 317 293-1776
　Indianapolis (G-6694)

Custom Imprint Corporation ......E....... 800 378-3397
　Merrillville (G-9709)

D S E Inc ....E....... 812 376-0310
　Columbus (G-1904)

Dance World Bazaar Corporation ....G....... 812 663-7679
　Greensburg (G-5598)

Dark Star Inc ....F....... 765 759-4764
　Muncie (G-10453)

Dave Turner ....G....... 765 674-3360
　Gas City (G-5122)

Diverse Sales Solutions LLC ......G....... 317 514-2403
　Indianapolis (G-6747)

East 40 Sports Apparel Inc ....G....... 812 877-3695
　Terre Haute (G-13229)

Elegan Sportswear Inc ....F....... 219 464-8416
　Valparaiso (G-13534)

F Robert Gardner Co Inc ....G....... 317 634-2333
　Indianapolis (G-6900)

Fiedeke Vinyl Coverings Inc ......F....... 574 534-3408
　Goshen (G-5214)

Flag & Banner Company Inc ....F....... 317 299-4880
　Indianapolis (G-6931)

▲ Futaba Indiana America Corp ....B....... 812 895-4700
　Vincennes (G-13683)

Game Plan Graphics LLC ....G....... 812 663-3238
　Greensburg (G-5602)

Geckos ....G....... 765 762-0822
　Attica (G-301)

Graphix Unlimited Inc ....E....... 574 546-3770
　Bremen (G-1000)

Greensburg Printing Co Inc ....G....... 812 663-8265
　Greensburg (G-5604)

Greenwood Models Inc ....G....... 317 859-2988
　Greenwood (G-5700)

Imperial Trophy & Awards Co ....G....... 260 432-8161
　Fort Wayne (G-4361)

▲ Indiana Ribbon Inc ....E....... 219 279-2112
　Wolcott (G-14365)

Jasper EMB & Screen Prtg ....G....... 812 482-4787
　Jasper (G-8260)

JAT Inc LLC ....G....... 317 201-3684
　Indianapolis (G-7298)

Jer-Maur Corporation ....G....... 812 384-8290
　Bloomfield (G-640)

Kennyleeholmescom ....G....... 574 612-2526
　Elkhart (G-2961)

Kerham Inc ....E....... 260 483-5444
　Fort Wayne (G-4409)

▼ Kewanna Screen Printing Inc ....G....... 574 653-2683
　Kewanna (G-8526)

Locoli Inc ....E....... 219 365-3125
　Schererville (G-12332)

Logo Designs Inc ....G....... 812 293-4750
　New Washington (G-11012)

Logo USA Corporation ....F....... 317 867-8518
　Westfield (G-14174)

Logos Express Inc ....G....... 317 272-1200
　Lebanon (G-9201)

Lomont Holdings Co Inc ....E....... 800 545-9023
　Angola (G-228)

M A Studio Inc ....G....... 574 275-2200
　San Pierre (G-12309)

Mac Designs ....G....... 317 580-9390
　Carmel (G-1431)

▲ Maingate Inc ....D....... 317 243-2000
　Indianapolis (G-7444)

Masco Corporation of Indiana ....D....... 317 848-1812
　Indianapolis (G-7463)

Mercantile Store ....G....... 812 988-6939
　Nashville (G-10729)

Mito-Craft Inc ....G....... 574 287-4555
　South Bend (G-12864)

Modern Muscle Car Factory Inc ....G....... 574 329-6390
　Elkhart (G-3044)

New Hope Services Inc ....E....... 812 752-4892
　Scottsburg (G-12377)

New Hope Services Inc ....E....... 812 288-8248
　Jeffersonville (G-8403)

▲ P J Marketing Services Inc ....G....... 574 259-8843
　South Bend (G-12886)

Plastimatic Arts Corp ....E....... 574 254-9000
　Mishawaka (G-10104)

Precision Multi Media ....G....... 765 359-0466
　Crawfordsville (G-2188)

Printing Plus Inc........................G....... 317 574-1313
　Carmel (G-1455)

Progressive Design Apparel Inc ....E....... 317 293-5888
　Indianapolis (G-7775)

Quality Converters Inc ....E....... 260 829-6541
　Orland (G-11356)

Ram Graphics Inc ....G....... 765 724-7783
　Alexandria (G-48)

Rbs Tees Co ....G....... 812 522-8675
　Seymour (G-12479)

Robert Burkhart ....G....... 219 448-0365
　Alexandria (G-52)

Safety Vehicle Emblem Inc ....F....... 317 885-7565
　Indianapolis (G-7884)

Select Embroidery/Top It Off ....G....... 812 337-8049
　Bloomington (G-823)

Shirts N Things S N T Graphics ....G....... 317 271-3515
　Indianapolis (G-7935)

Sir Graphics Inc ....G....... 574 272-9330
　Granger (G-5436)

Specialty Shoppe ....G....... 574 772-7873
　Knox (G-8582)

Spectrum Marketing ....G....... 765 643-5566
　Anderson (G-168)

▲ SPI Binding Co Inc ....F....... 765 794-4992
　Darlington (G-2361)

Sport Form Inc ....G....... 260 589-2200
　Berne (G-625)

Sportscenter Inc ....G....... 260 436-6198
　Fort Wayne (G-4642)

Spp Inc ....F....... 812 882-6203
　Vincennes (G-13707)

Stallion Sportswear Inc ....E....... 765 584-5097
　Winchester (G-14341)

Star Quality Awards Inc ....G....... 812 273-1740
　Madison (G-9496)

Stines Printing ....G....... 260 356-5994
　Huntington (G-6253)

Sycamore Enterprises Inc ....G....... 812 491-0901
　Evansville (G-3756)

Thread Creations Inc ....G....... 765 521-3886
　New Castle (G-10919)

Tko Enterprises Inc ....D....... 317 271-1398
　Plainfield (G-11647)

Travis Britton ....G....... 317 762-6018
　Indianapolis (G-8092)

Winning Edge of Rochester Inc ....F....... 574 223-6090
　Rochester (G-12162)

Winters Assoc Prmtnal Pdts Inc ....F....... 812 330-7000
　Bloomington (G-858)

Woods Enterprises ....G....... 574 232-7449
　South Bend (G-12992)

2399 Fabricated Textile Prdts, NEC

American Orthpdics Prosthetics ....G....... 765 447-0111
　Lafayette (G-8851)

Art Ovation ....G....... 317 769-4301
　Brownsburg (G-1135)

Awards America ....E....... 219 462-7903
　Valparaiso (G-13501)

▲ Carcapsule USA Inc ....G....... 219 945-9493
　Hobart (G-6073)

Country Sewing ....G....... 260 347-9733
　Kendallville (G-8467)

Eastern Banner Supply Corp ....G....... 812 448-2222
　Brazil (G-960)

Edna B LLC ....G....... 574 271-4300
　Granger (G-5403)

Expo Designers Co Inc ....E....... 317 784-5610
　Indianapolis (G-6896)

◆ Fabri-Tech Inc ....E....... 317 849-7755
　McCordsville (G-9666)

Flags International Inc ....G....... 574 674-5125
　Osceola (G-11376)

Frazier Products ....F....... 317 781-9781
　Indianapolis (G-6961)

Gerardot Performance Products ....G....... 260 623-3048
　Monroeville (G-10195)

Happy Headgear LLC ....G....... 574 892-5792
　Argos (G-274)

Indiana Fabric Solutions Inc ....E....... 812 279-0255
　Bedford (G-551)

Indiana Skydiving Center ....E....... 765 659-5557
　Frankfort (G-4837)

Jack House LLC ....G....... 251 990-5960
　Converse (G-2079)

Kathys Sewing Inc ....G....... 260 623-6387
　Monroeville (G-10196)

Lakestreet Enterprises LLC ....G....... 260 768-7991
　Lagrange (G-9055)

Rubber & Gasket Co Amer Inc .....G....... 260 432-9070
　Fort Wayne (G-4597)

▲ Shield Restraint Systems Inc ....C....... 574 266-8330
　Elkhart (G-3167)

Smiths TAC Shack ....G....... 765 345-5590
　Knightstown (G-8560)

Summit Seating Inc ....F....... 574 264-9636
　Elkhart (G-3198)

Team Spirit ....G....... 219 924-6272
　Munster (G-10631)

Widows Walk ....G....... 812 285-8850
　Clarksville (G-1700)

Wiseguys Seating & Accessry Co ....G....... 574 294-6030
　Elkhart (G-3264)

Wolf Technical Engineering LLC ....G....... 800 783-9653
　Indianapolis (G-8209)

Workroom Inc ....G....... 574 269-6624
　Winona Lake (G-14356)

Wt Products Inc ....G....... 765 216-7998
　Muncie (G-10589)

24 LUMBER AND WOOD PRODUCTS, EXCEPT FURNITURE

2411 Logging

A & A Logging ....G....... 502 553-4132
　Henryville (G-6031)

A & S Logging Inc ....G....... 574 896-3136
　North Judson (G-11205)

Albert Ransom Logging Inc ....G....... 812 567-2012
　Dale (G-2330)

▼ Andis Logging Inc ....F....... 812 723-2357
　Paoli (G-11442)

Anthony D Etienne Logging ....G....... 812 843-5872
　Magnet (G-9502)

Arboramerica Inc ....G....... 765 572-1212
　Westpoint (G-14204)

Artys Logging ....G....... 812 969-3124
　Elizabeth (G-2641)

B M P Logging LLC ....G....... 812 272-2149
　Williams (G-14281)

Baldwin Logging Inc ....G....... 812 834-1040
　Norman (G-11202)

Bill Graber Logging LLC ....G....... 812 486-2709
　Montgomery (G-10215)

Blackwood Solutions Inc ....G....... 812 824-6728
　Bloomington (G-684)

Blue River Timber LLC ....G....... 812 291-0411
　Evansville (G-3387)

Boondocks Logging LLC ....G....... 812 247-3363
　Shoals (G-12664)

Bray Logging ....G....... 812 863-7947
　Owensburg (G-11423)

Brocks Incorporated ....G....... 765 721-3068
　Bainbridge (G-473)

Buchan Logging Inc ....G....... 260 728-2136
　Decatur (G-2371)

Buchan Logging Inc ....F....... 260 749-4697
　New Haven (G-10932)

Burton Lumber Co Inc ....F....... 812 866-4438
　Lexington (G-9249)

Campbell Logging ....G....... 812 972-6280
　Birdseye (G-634)

Cannon Timber LLC ....G....... 219 754-1088
　La Crosse (G-8719)

Carr Logging ....G....... 812 863-7585
　Owensburg (G-11424)

Carvers Logging LLP ....G....... 812 732-4932
　Mauckport (G-9653)

Cash Logging ....G....... 812 843-5335
　Mount Pleasant (G-10377)

Charles Kolb Logging ....G....... 765 458-7766
　Liberty (G-9258)

Charles Kolb Sons Logging ....G....... 765 647-4309
　Brookville (G-1112)

Christman Logging ....G....... 502 525-2649
　Madison (G-9449)

CJ Logging LLC ....G....... 812 360-0163
　Morgantown (G-10350)

Coffman Logging ....G....... 812 732-4857
　Corydon (G-2094)

D Timber Inc ....G....... 219 374-8085
　Crown Point (G-2242)

Daniel Griffin ....G....... 765 492-3257
　Cayuga (G-1518)

Daniel Skaggs & Company ....G....... 765 342-0071
　Martinsville (G-9600)

Delmar Knepp Logging ....G....... 812 486-2565
　Loogootee (G-9381)

Dennis Etiennes Logging Inc...........G....... 812 843-4518
Cannelton (G-1289)
Dennis K Marvell...........G....... 812 779-5107
Patoka (G-11465)
Duncan Logging Inc...........G....... 812 564-2488
Coalmont (G-1745)
Dwight Smith Logging...........G....... 812 834-5546
Heltonville (G-6026)
Ebs Logging LLC...........G....... 812 346-9248
North Vernon (G-11256)
Ferree Logging LLC...........G....... 812 786-1676
Corydon (G-2098)
First Choice Forestry & Log...........G....... 574 271-9425
Granger (G-5407)
George Voyles Sawmill Inc...........E....... 812 472-3968
Salem (G-12287)
Graber Lumber LP...........E....... 260 238-4124
Spencerville (G-13047)
Graber Ronald D Yoder &...........G....... 574 268-9512
Warsaw (G-13883)
Griffin Logging LLC...........G....... 765 592-5701
Mecca (G-9678)
Grove Forest Products...........G....... 812 432-3312
Rising Sun (G-12088)
Hartman Logging...........G....... 765 653-3889
Greencastle (G-5461)
Hearth Glow Inc...........G....... 260 839-3205
North Manchester (G-11229)
Ice Logging LLC...........G....... 312 860-0897
Chesterfield (G-1587)
Indiana Logging Company Corp...........G....... 765 523-2616
Lafayette (G-8921)
J Robert Switzer...........G....... 765 474-1307
Lafayette (G-8927)
Jeff Halls Logging Inc...........G....... 812 941-8020
Floyds Knobs (G-4015)
Jim Graber Logging LLC...........G....... 812 636-7000
Odon (G-11331)
Jim Rhodes Logging...........G....... 812 739-4221
English (G-3313)
John M Wooley Lumber Company...........E....... 317 831-2700
Mooresville (G-10317)
Joseph M Schmidt...........G....... 260 223-3498
Decatur (G-2387)
Kaho Brothers Inc...........G....... 812 659-2901
Lyons (G-9439)
Keith Bixler...........G....... 812 866-1637
Lexington (G-9252)
Keller Logging LLC...........G....... 219 309-0379
Valparaiso (G-13565)
Kester Logging Inc...........G....... 765 672-8170
Reelsville (G-11902)
Kinser Timber Products Inc...........G....... 812 876-4775
Gosport (G-5352)
Knepp Logging...........G....... 812 486-3741
Loogootee (G-9387)
Knepps Logging Bandmilling...........G....... 812 486-7721
Montgomery (G-10230)
Lake States Veneer Inc...........G....... 260 244-4767
Columbia City (G-1806)
Log Lifestyles Inc...........G....... 574 850-6158
Walkerton (G-13805)
Loggers Incorporated...........E....... 812 939-2797
Clay City (G-1704)
Logging...........G....... 812 216-3544
Seymour (G-12468)
Louanna Stilwell...........G....... 812 631-0647
Velpen (G-13649)
Mark Morin Logging...........G....... 812 327-4917
West Baden Springs (G-14034)
Maurice Lukens Jr...........G....... 765 345-2971
Knightstown (G-8555)
Michael Deom Professional...........G....... 812 836-2206
Tell City (G-13166)
Michael L Baker...........G....... 812 967-2160
Salem (G-12301)
Michael Skaggs...........G....... 812 732-8809
Mauckport (G-9656)
Midwest Logging & Veneer...........G....... 765 342-2774
Martinsville (G-9626)
Mike Gross...........G....... 574 529-2201
New Paris (G-10991)
Napoleon Hardwood Lbr Co Inc...........E....... 812 852-4090
Greensburg (G-5626)
Newbury Farm & Logging LLC...........G....... 574 825-9969
Shipshewana (G-12639)
Newman Logging Inc...........G....... 260 351-3550
Wolcottville (G-14375)
NJ Logging LLC...........G....... 812 597-0782
Morgantown (G-10357)

Northern Wood Products Inc...........G....... 574 586-3068
Walkerton (G-13807)
Ohio River Veneer LLC...........F....... 812 824-7928
Bloomington (G-784)
Paul Marshall and Son Log...........G....... 260 724-2852
Decatur (G-2398)
Pingleton Sawmill Inc...........E....... 765 653-2878
Greencastle (G-5473)
Poplar Log Homes Inc...........G....... 765 342-9910
Martinsville (G-9633)
R E Casebeer & Sons Inc...........G....... 812 829-3284
Spencer (G-13035)
Ralph Ransom Veneers...........G....... 812 858-9956
Newburgh (G-11044)
Rasche Bro Logging...........G....... 812 357-7782
Ferdinand (G-3862)
Richard Greg Etienne Logging...........G....... 812 843-5132
Derby (G-2462)
Robert L Young...........G....... 812 863-4475
Springville (G-13067)
Rodney Sloan Logging...........G....... 812 934-5321
Batesville (G-518)
Ronald Lee Allen...........G....... 812 644-7649
Loogootee (G-9394)
Ronald Wright Logging LLC...........G....... 812 338-2665
English (G-3319)
Rural Land Inc...........G....... 812 843-4518
Cannelton (G-1291)
Slabach Logging LLC...........G....... 260 768-4644
Shipshewana (G-12650)
Specialties Co LLC...........F....... 260 432-3973
Fort Wayne (G-4638)
Spencer Logging...........G....... 812 595-0987
Scottsburg (G-12382)
Tdc Logging LLC...........G....... 574 289-4243
South Bend (G-12967)
Tri-State Forest Products Inc...........F....... 317 328-1850
Indianapolis (G-8096)
Universal Forest Products Indi...........C....... 574 273-6326
Granger (G-5447)
Walton Logging...........G....... 812 365-9635
Marengo (G-9505)
Waninger Knneth Sons Log Tmber...........F....... 812 357-5200
Fulda (G-4992)
Weaver Logging...........G....... 260 589-9985
Berne (G-629)
White Oak Land & Timber LLC...........G....... 812 482-5102
Jasper (G-8314)
Wilkerson Logging Inc...........G....... 812 988-4960
Nashville (G-10738)
William Browning...........G....... 765 647-6397
Brookville (G-1132)
William S Bane...........G....... 812 358-5790
Brownstown (G-1193)
Williams Bros Logging LLC...........G....... 270 547-0266
Mauckport (G-9659)
Wrights Timber Products...........G....... 812 383-7138
Shelburn (G-12514)

2421 Saw & Planing Mills

Adkins Sawmill Inc...........G....... 812 849-4036
Mitchell (G-10154)
Arbor Industries Inc...........E....... 574 825-2375
Middlebury (G-9872)
B & B Sawmill Inc...........G....... 812 834-5072
Bedford (G-530)
Babb Lumber Company Inc...........F....... 812 886-0551
Vincennes (G-13668)
Baxter Lumber LLC...........F....... 812 873-6868
Deputy (G-2459)
Benham Sawmill LLC...........G....... 812 723-2644
Paoli (G-11444)
Better Built Barns Inc...........G....... 812 477-2001
Evansville (G-3382)
Burton Lumber Co Inc...........F....... 812 866-4438
Lexington (G-9249)
Byler Sawmill...........G....... 812 577-5761
Bennington (G-605)
C & L Lumber Inc...........G....... 812 536-2171
Huntingburg (G-6152)
C C Cook and Son Lbr Co Inc...........E....... 765 672-4235
Reelsville (G-11900)
Campbell Road Sawmill...........G....... 260 238-4252
Spencerville (G-13044)
Cedar Creek Sawmill LLC...........E....... 260 627-3985
Grabill (G-5359)
Chisholm Lumber & Sup Co Inc...........E....... 317 547-3535
Indianapolis (G-6601)
Classic Baluster LLC...........F....... 765 344-1619
Brazil (G-957)

Coleman Sawmill Supply...........G....... 812 865-4001
Orleans (G-11361)
Conner Sawmill Inc...........F....... 574 626-3227
Walton (G-13815)
Coomer & Sons Sawmill & Pallet...........D....... 765 659-2846
Frankfort (G-4824)
Countryside Sawmill...........G....... 812 486-2991
Montgomery (G-10219)
Crone Lumber Co Inc...........E....... 765 342-1160
Martinsville (G-9599)
Crookedstick Sawmill LLC...........G....... 317 714-8930
Coatesville (G-1748)
D and E Surplus LLC...........G....... 260 351-3200
Wolcottville (G-14370)
D&G Timber Inc...........E....... 812 486-3356
Odon (G-11324)
Deer Run Sawmill LLC...........G....... 812 732-4608
Mauckport (G-9654)
Dehart Pallet & Lumber Co...........F....... 812 794-2974
Austin (G-396)
Dmray Sawmill Inc...........G....... 812 723-1109
Hardinsburg (G-5964)
Dodd Wood Products Inc...........E....... 812 268-0798
Sullivan (G-13082)
Eastern Red Cedar Products LLC...........G....... 812 365-2495
Marengo (G-9504)
Fleenor Sawmill Inc...........E....... 812 752-3594
Scottsburg (G-12356)
Flodders Sawmill...........G....... 765 628-0280
Greentown (G-5645)
Forest Products Group Inc...........E....... 765 659-1807
Frankfort (G-4832)
Forest Products Mfg Co...........E....... 812 482-5625
Jasper (G-8251)
Frank Miller Lumber Co Inc...........E....... 812 883-8077
Salem (G-12286)
▼ Frank Miller Lumber Co Inc...........C....... 800 345-2643
Union City (G-13455)
George Voyles Sawmill Inc...........E....... 812 472-3968
Salem (G-12287)
Grabers Portable Band Mill...........G....... 812 636-4158
Odon (G-11330)
Great Lakes Forest Pdts Inc...........E....... 574 389-9663
Elkhart (G-2897)
Great Lakes Forest Pdts Inc...........D....... 574 389-9663
Elkhart (G-2898)
Green Forest Sawmill LLC...........E....... 812 745-3335
Oaktown (G-11318)
Gross & Sons Lumber and Veneer...........G....... 574 457-5214
Syracuse (G-13132)
Helmsburg Sawmill Inc...........F....... 812 988-6161
Nashville (G-10726)
Herbert S Sawmill...........G....... 812 663-9347
Greensburg (G-5607)
Hites Hardwood Lumber Corp...........F....... 574 278-7783
Buffalo (G-1203)
Hollingsworth Sawmill Inc...........F....... 765 883-5836
Russiaville (G-12241)
Homestead Properties Inc...........G....... 812 866-4415
Deputy (G-2460)
Hope Hardwoods Inc...........F....... 812 546-4427
Hope (G-6114)
Indiana Southern Hardwoods...........E....... 812 326-2053
Huntingburg (G-6171)
Indiana Wood Products Inc...........D....... 574 825-2129
Middlebury (G-9893)
▲ International Wood Inc...........E....... 812 883-5778
Salem (G-12295)
Intrst Forestry Inc...........G....... 574 936-1284
Plymouth (G-11695)
J M McCormick...........G....... 317 874-4444
Indianapolis (G-7288)
Jackson Brothers Lumber Co...........F....... 812 847-7812
Linton (G-9308)
John M Wooley Lumber Company...........E....... 317 831-2700
Mooresville (G-10317)
Kinser Timber Products Inc...........G....... 812 876-4775
Gosport (G-5352)
Kinsers Hardwood...........G....... 812 834-5568
Heltonville (G-6027)
Koetter Woodworking...........F....... 812 923-8875
Borden (G-933)
Lasher Lumber Inc...........G....... 812 836-2618
Tell City (G-13165)
Ledgewood & Sons Sawmill...........G....... 812 939-8212
Coal City (G-1742)
Loggers Incorporated...........E....... 812 939-2797
Clay City (G-1704)
Mann Road Sawmill Inc...........G....... 765 342-2700
Martinsville (G-9621)

Manuwal Sawmill Inc ....G.... 574 936-8187
Plymouth *(G-11705)*
Mark Middleton ....G.... 812 967-2853
Pekin *(G-11475)*
Maurice Lukens Jr ....G.... 765 345-2971
Knightstown *(G-8555)*
Menard Inc ....A.... 812 466-1234
Terre Haute *(G-13282)*
Michael O Baird ....G.... 765 569-6721
Rockville *(G-12177)*
Miller Custom Forest Products ....G.... 765 478-3057
Connersville *(G-2064)*
Miller Hardwoods LLC ....G.... 574 773-9371
Nappanee *(G-10693)*
Millers Saw Mill ....G.... 812 883-5246
Salem *(G-12302)*
Millwork Specialties Co Inc ....G.... 219 362-2960
La Porte *(G-8795)*
Modular Green Systems LLC ....G.... 260 547-4121
Craigville *(G-2123)*
Napoleon Hardwood Lbr Co Inc ....E.... 812 852-4090
Greensburg *(G-5626)*
National Products Inc ....F.... 574 457-4565
Syracuse *(G-13138)*
New Castle Saw Mill ....G.... 765 529-6635
New Castle *(G-10913)*
Norstam Veneers Inc ....D.... 812 732-4391
Mauckport *(G-9658)*
North Central Ind Shavings LLC ....G.... 765 395-3875
Converse *(G-2080)*
Oldenburg Pallet Inc ....G.... 812 933-0568
Batesville *(G-513)*
ONeal Wood Products Inc ....G.... 765 342-2709
Martinsville *(G-9631)*
Phil Etiennes Timber Harvest ....E.... 812 843-5132
Saint Croix *(G-12251)*
Pike Lumber Company Inc ....E.... 574 893-4511
Carbon *(G-1293)*
Pingleton Sawmill Inc ....E.... 765 653-2878
Greencastle *(G-5473)*
PLM Holdings Inc ....E.... 812 232-0624
Terre Haute *(G-13304)*
Quality Hardwood Products Inc ....F.... 260 982-2043
North Manchester *(G-11241)*
R & M Enterprises ....G.... 765 795-6395
Indianapolis *(G-7806)*
R Booe & Son Hardwoods Inc ....E.... 812 835-2663
Centerpoint *(G-1540)*
R E Casebeer & Sons Inc ....G.... 812 829-3284
Spencer *(G-13035)*
Randall Lowe & Sons Sawmill ....F.... 812 936-2254
French Lick *(G-4988)*
Robinson Lumber Company Inc ....E.... 812 944-8020
New Albany *(G-10858)*
Rodney Sloan Logging ....G.... 812 934-5321
Batesville *(G-518)*
Ronald Wright Logging LLC ....G.... 812 338-2665
English *(G-3319)*
Salesman Sawmill Inc ....G.... 812 382-9154
Sullivan *(G-13094)*
Sanders Saw Mill Inc ....F.... 812 738-4793
Corydon *(G-2111)*
Scrapwood Sawmill ....G.... 574 223-2725
Rochester *(G-12152)*
Shouse Sawmill ....G.... 812 743-2017
Monroe City *(G-10188)*
Speer Ron Sawmill & Lumber Co ....G.... 812 834-5515
Bedford *(G-579)*
Stemwood Corp ....D.... 812 945-6646
New Albany *(G-10866)*
Stemwood Manufacturing LLC ....E.... 812 945-6646
New Albany *(G-10867)*
Stillions Saw Mill ....G.... 812 824-6542
Bloomington *(G-832)*
Swartzentruber Sawmill ....G.... 812 486-3350
Montgomery *(G-10244)*
Tangent Rail Products Inc ....E.... 812 789-5331
Winslow *(G-14361)*
Terry L Ray ....G.... 765 342-3180
Martinsville *(G-9641)*
Timberland Resources Inc ....E.... 765 245-2634
Montezuma *(G-10211)*
Tree City Saw Mill ....G.... 812 663-6363
Greensburg *(G-5638)*
▼ Tri-State Hardwood Company ....E.... 260 351-3111
South Milford *(G-12994)*
Ufp Granger LLC ....E.... 574 277-7670
Granger *(G-5445)*
Universal Forest Products Inc ....E.... 574 277-7670
Granger *(G-5446)*
Universal Forest Products Indi ....C.... 574 273-6326
Granger *(G-5447)*
Vead Dodd Sawmill Inc ....F.... 812 268-4486
Sullivan *(G-13098)*
W & J Sawmill Llc ....G.... 812 486-2719
Montgomery *(G-10245)*
Wakelam John ....G.... 812 752-5243
Scottsburg *(G-12385)*
Walnut Acres Sawmill LLC ....G.... 765 344-0027
Rockville *(G-12183)*
Walnut Street Hardwoods ....E.... 574 287-1023
South Bend *(G-12986)*
Werner Sawmill Inc ....E.... 812 482-7565
Jasper *(G-8313)*
Wilkerson Sawmill ....G.... 812 988-7436
Nashville *(G-10739)*
▲ Woodparts International Corp ....F.... 574 293-0566
Elkhart *(G-3266)*
Worley Lumber Company Inc ....F.... 812 967-3521
Pekin *(G-11481)*

2426 Hardwood Dimension & Flooring Mills

A JS Furniture LLC ....G.... 574 642-1273
Topeka *(G-13410)*
A New Covenant Woodwork LLC ....G.... 812 737-2929
Laconia *(G-8835)*
Als Woodcraft Inc ....F.... 812 967-4458
Borden *(G-927)*
Auto Wood Restoration ....G.... 219 797-3775
Hanna *(G-5958)*
Brown Ridge Studio ....G.... 812 335-0643
Bloomington *(G-690)*
Burton Lumber Co Inc ....F.... 812 866-4438
Lexington *(G-9249)*
Cabinetmaker Inc ....G.... 812 723-3461
Paoli *(G-11446)*
Champion Wood Products Inc ....D.... 812 282-9460
Sellersburg *(G-12391)*
Chisholm Lumber & Sup Co Inc ....E.... 317 547-3535
Indianapolis *(G-6601)*
Cross Country Hardwoods LLC ....F.... 812 571-4226
Vevay *(G-13661)*
Custom Millwork & Display LLC ....G.... 574 289-9772
South Bend *(G-12749)*
Dehart Pallet & Lumber Co ....F.... 812 794-2974
Austin *(G-396)*
Digital Carvings LLC ....G.... 812 269-6123
Ellettsville *(G-3278)*
Dmi Furniture Inc ....F.... 812 683-4035
Huntingburg *(G-6156)*
Dutch Made Inc ....G.... 260 657-3331
Harlan *(G-5970)*
Ecojacks LLC ....G.... 574 306-0414
South Whitley *(G-12998)*
Enviro Finishing of Indiana ....F.... 765 966-8183
Richmond *(G-11983)*
Ervins Millwork Shop LLC ....G.... 260 768-3222
Shipshewana *(G-12613)*
Floortech ....G.... 317 887-6825
Indianapolis *(G-6939)*
Ford Sawmills Inc ....E.... 812 324-2134
Vincennes *(G-13682)*
Forest Products Group Inc ....E.... 765 659-1807
Frankfort *(G-4832)*
Forest Products Mfg Co ....E.... 812 482-5625
Jasper *(G-8251)*
▼ Frank Miller Lumber Co Inc ....C.... 800 345-2643
Union City *(G-13455)*
George Voyles Sawmill Inc ....E.... 812 472-3968
Salem *(G-12287)*
Graber Furniture ....G.... 812 295-4939
Loogootee *(G-9383)*
Helmsburg Sawmill Inc ....F.... 812 988-6161
Nashville *(G-10726)*
Herbert S Sawmill ....F.... 812 663-9347
Greensburg *(G-5607)*
Heritage Hardwoods KY Inc ....D.... 812 288-5855
Jeffersonville *(G-8372)*
▲ Holmes & Company Inc ....E.... 260 244-6149
Columbia City *(G-1790)*
Homestead Properties Inc ....F.... 812 866-4415
Deputy *(G-2460)*
Hoosier Hrdwood Rclamation LLC ....G.... 765 299-6507
Crawfordsville *(G-2159)*
Indiana Handle Company Inc ....D.... 812 723-3159
Paoli *(G-11453)*
Indiana Hardwood Specialists ....E.... 812 829-4866
Spencer *(G-13028)*
Indiana Wood Products Inc ....D.... 574 825-2129
Middlebury *(G-9893)*
Jackson Brothers Lumber Co ....F.... 812 847-7812
Linton *(G-9308)*
James A Andrew Inc ....G.... 765 269-9807
Lafayette *(G-8929)*
Jeff Hury Hardwood Floors Pntg ....G.... 812 204-8650
Evansville *(G-3574)*
John M Wooley Lumber Company ....E.... 317 831-2700
Mooresville *(G-10317)*
Kentucky Wood Floors LLC ....E.... 812 256-2164
Borden *(G-932)*
Kentucky-Indiana Lumber Co Inc ....E.... 812 464-2428
Evansville *(G-3584)*
Kinsers Hardwood ....G.... 812 834-5568
Heltonville *(G-6027)*
Knies Sawmill Inc ....G.... 812 683-3402
Huntingburg *(G-6173)*
Langfords Delivery Service ....G.... 317 996-3594
Monrovia *(G-10204)*
Maurice Lukens Jr ....G.... 765 345-2971
Knightstown *(G-8555)*
Midwest Cnstr Components ....G.... 765 654-8719
Frankfort *(G-4841)*
Mikro Furniture ....G.... 812 877-9550
Terre Haute *(G-13286)*
Miller Milling Inc ....G.... 260 768-9171
Shipshewana *(G-12634)*
Mo-Wood Products Inc ....G.... 812 482-5625
Jasper *(G-8296)*
▲ Mould-Rite Inc ....E.... 812 967-3200
Pekin *(G-11477)*
Napoleon Hardwood Lbr Co Inc ....E.... 812 852-4090
Greensburg *(G-5626)*
Norstam Veneers Inc ....D.... 812 732-4391
Mauckport *(G-9658)*
Olon Industries Inc (us) ....F.... 812 256-6400
Jeffersonville *(G-8408)*
Olon Industries Inc (us) ....F.... 812 254-0427
Washington *(G-13994)*
Pallet One of Indiana Inc ....D.... 260 768-4021
Shipshewana *(G-12641)*
Phil Etiennes Timber Harvest ....E.... 812 843-5132
Saint Croix *(G-12251)*
Pike Lumber Company Inc ....E.... 574 893-4511
Carbon *(G-1293)*
Pingleton Sawmill Inc ....E.... 765 653-2878
Greencastle *(G-5473)*
Prized Possession ....G.... 317 842-1498
Indianapolis *(G-7762)*
Quality Hardwood Products Inc ....F.... 260 982-2043
North Manchester *(G-11241)*
R & R Custom Woodworking Inc ....E.... 574 773-5436
Nappanee *(G-10703)*
R E Casebeer & Sons Inc ....G.... 812 829-3284
Spencer *(G-13035)*
Randall Lowe & Sons Sawmill ....F.... 812 936-2254
French Lick *(G-4988)*
Rice Flooring ....G.... 574 830-5147
Elkhart *(G-3145)*
Rogers Group Inc ....E.... 812 333-6324
Bloomington *(G-816)*
Rwh Woodworking ....G.... 317 714-5179
Greenfield *(G-5570)*
Salt Creek Harvest LLC ....G.... 708 927-5569
Valparaiso *(G-13611)*
▲ Santarossa Mosaic Tile Co Inc ....C.... 317 632-9494
Indianapolis *(G-7895)*
Stateline Woodturnings LLC ....G.... 260 768-4507
Shipshewana *(G-12652)*
Stemwood Corp ....D.... 812 945-6646
New Albany *(G-10866)*
Swartzndrber Hrdwood Creat LLC ....E.... 574 534-2502
Goshen *(G-5337)*
Tedrows Wood Products Inc ....F.... 812 247-2260
Shoals *(G-12670)*
Universal Forest Products Indi ....C.... 574 273-6326
Granger *(G-5447)*
Vead Dodd Sawmill Inc ....F.... 812 268-4486
Sullivan *(G-13098)*
Weberdings Carving Shop Inc ....F.... 812 934-3710
Batesville *(G-524)*
Werner Sawmill Inc ....E.... 812 482-7565
Jasper *(G-8313)*

2429 Special Prdt Sawmills, NEC

L M Woodworking ....G.... 574 534-9177
Goshen *(G-5260)*
Premier AG Co-Op Inc ....E.... 812 522-4911
Seymour *(G-12477)*

2431 Millwork

Company	Location	Code	Phone
A & M Woodworking	Millersburg *(G-9968)*	G	574 642-4555
A&J Woodworking LLC	Goshen *(G-5162)*	G	574 642-4551
Alberding Woodworking Inc	Decatur *(G-2365)*	E	260 728-9526
▲ Alexandria Mw LLC	La Porte *(G-8729)*	G	219 324-9541
AMC Acquisition Corporation	Elkhart *(G-2681)*	D	215 572-0738
American Heritage Shutters	Indianapolis *(G-6388)*	G	317 598-6908
Americas Best Millwrk Supplrs	Plymouth *(G-11665)*	G	574 780-0066
Amish Hills Woodworking and MA	Goshen *(G-5170)*	G	574 875-3558
Amish Woodworking LLC	Plymouth *(G-11666)*	G	574 941-4439
Andersen Corporation	Poneto *(G-11744)*	A	260 694-6861
Antreasian Design Inc	Indianapolis *(G-6404)*	F	317 546-3234
Architectural Accents Inc	Munster *(G-10596)*	F	219 922-9333
Barkman Custom Woodworking	Nappanee *(G-10652)*	F	574 773-9212
Beaver Mouldings LLC	Lagrange *(G-9033)*	G	260 463-4822
Bittersweet LLC	Wolcottville *(G-14368)*	G	574 642-1184
Borkholder Lavon	Nappanee *(G-10655)*	G	574 773-3714
Borkholder Wood Products	Bremen *(G-984)*	G	574 546-2613
Branik Inc	Fort Wayne *(G-4117)*	G	260 467-1808
Bratco Inc	Holland *(G-6104)*	G	812 536-4071
Burkes Garden Wood Pdts LLC	Brazil *(G-955)*	F	765 344-1724
Burks Door & Sash Inc	Carmel *(G-1324)*	F	317 844-2484
Bwt Custom Woodworking LLC	Jasper *(G-8239)*	G	812 634-1800
By-Pass Paint Shop Inc	Elkhart *(G-2740)*	F	574 264-5334
Byler Family Wood Working	Goshen *(G-5183)*	G	574 825-3339
C&A Woodworking Inc	Elkhart *(G-2745)*	G	574 875-1273
C&M Woodworking LLC	Leo *(G-9240)*	G	260 403-4555
Cac Wall Panels LP	Harlan *(G-5967)*	G	260 437-4003
Cana Inc	Elkhart *(G-2748)*	D	574 266-6566
Cash & Carry Lumber Co Inc	Daleville *(G-2337)*	F	765 378-7575
Center Line Wood Works Inc	Fishers *(G-3887)*	G	317 770-9486
Centerline Woodworking	Lagrange *(G-9034)*	G	260 768-4116
Central Ind Mulding Mllwk Inc	Indianapolis *(G-6582)*	F	317 568-1639
Central Indiana Woodworkers	Indianapolis *(G-6584)*	G	317 407-9228
Central Overhead Door	Lowell *(G-9402)*	G	219 696-1566
Champion Wood Products Inc	Sellersburg *(G-12391)*	D	812 282-9460
Chase Manufacturing LLC	Nappanee *(G-10660)*	C	574 546-4776
Childress Corporation	Fishers *(G-3889)*	G	317 774-8571
Chisholm Lumber & Sup Co Inc	Indianapolis *(G-6601)*	E	317 547-3535
Chris Schwartz	Grabill *(G-5360)*	G	260 615-9574
Circle City Woodworking	Indianapolis *(G-6610)*	G	765 637-6687
Clark Millworks	Angola *(G-203)*	G	260 665-1270
Clear View Cstm Windows Doors	Terre Haute *(G-13212)*	G	812 877-1000
Clinton Custom Wood Turning	Goshen *(G-5188)*	G	574 535-0543
Cns Custom Woodworks Inc	Columbus *(G-1872)*	G	812 350-2431
Complete Lumber Inc	Evansville *(G-3426)*	F	812 473-6400
Concord Realstate Corp	Lafayette *(G-8876)*	F	765 423-5555
Cornerstone Mill Work	Garrett *(G-4998)*	G	260 357-0754
Cornerstone Moulding Inc	Bremen *(G-992)*	E	574 546-4249
Couden Woodworks Inc	Noblesville *(G-11085)*	G	317 370-0835
Country Craftsman Wdwkg LLC	Nappanee *(G-10664)*	G	574 773-4911
Country Woodworking LLC	Odon *(G-11322)*	G	812 636-6004
Crestview Woodworking LLC	Shipshewana *(G-12609)*	G	260 768-4707
Custom Door Manufacturing	Loogootee *(G-9380)*	G	812 636-3667
Custom Draperies of Indiana	Hammond *(G-5867)*	G	219 924-2500
Custom Interior Dynamics LLC	Indianapolis *(G-6714)*	F	317 632-0477
Custom Millwork & Display LLC	South Bend *(G-12749)*	G	574 289-9772
Custom Millwork & Display Inc	South Bend *(G-12750)*	F	574 289-4000
Custom Wood Finishing	Millersburg *(G-9969)*	G	574 642-1213
Custom Woodworking	Bloomington *(G-709)*	G	812 339-6601
Custom Woodworking	Evansville *(G-3452)*	G	812 422-6786
D & D Mouldings & Millwork	Noblesville *(G-11089)*	F	317 770-5500
D L Miller Woodworking	Shipshewana *(G-12610)*	G	260 562-9329
Daniel Bontrager	Goshen *(G-5198)*	G	574 825-5656
Diverse Woodworking LLC	Georgetown *(G-5143)*	G	812 366-3000
Dobbins Interior Woodworks	Dillsboro *(G-2466)*	G	812 221-0058
Doors & Drawers Inc	Goshen *(G-5203)*	F	574 533-3509
Double L Woodworking L L C	Goshen *(G-5204)*	F	260 768-3155
Dovetail Woodworks	Brazil *(G-959)*	G	812 448-8832
Dr Restorations Inc	Clermont *(G-1712)*	G	317 646-7150
Dubois Wood Products Inc	Huntingburg *(G-6159)*	E	812 683-5105
Dutch Made Inc	Harlan *(G-5970)*	G	260 657-3331
Dutchcraft Corporation	Lagrange *(G-9039)*	G	260 463-8366
E M Woodworking	Montgomery *(G-10223)*	G	812 486-2696
Earthwise Woodworks LLC	Greenwood *(G-5684)*	G	317 887-0142
Eckhart Woodworking Inc	Monroe *(G-10181)*	E	260 692-6218
Ecojacks LLC	South Whitley *(G-12998)*	G	574 306-0414
Ed Lloyd Co	Columbus *(G-1917)*	G	812 342-2505
Eleys Woodworking	Winchester *(G-14328)*	G	765 584-3531
Englehardt Custom Woodworking	Evansville *(G-3478)*	G	812 425-9282
Ettensohn & Company LLC	Tell City *(G-13160)*	G	812 547-5491
Expert Woodworks	Lake Village *(G-9082)*	G	219 345-2705
Fairview Woodworking	Shipshewana *(G-12614)*	G	260 768-3255
Faske Wood Moulding Inc	Borden *(G-929)*	F	812 923-5601
Ferry Street Woodworks	Vevay *(G-13663)*	G	812 427-9663
Finish Design Woodworking Inc	Jeffersonville *(G-8360)*	E	812 284-9240
Fischer Woodcraft Inc	Beech Grove *(G-594)*	G	317 627-6035
Fischer Woodworking Inc	Mount Vernon *(G-10392)*	G	812 985-9488
Flp Woodworks	Fort Wayne *(G-4268)*	G	260 424-3904
Forest Products Group Inc	Frankfort *(G-4832)*	E	765 659-1807
Four Woods Laminating Inc	Topeka *(G-13419)*	E	260 593-2246
Fourth Shift Inc	Indianapolis *(G-6952)*	F	317 567-3072
Franks Woodworking	Anderson *(G-107)*	G	765 378-0424
G & R Woodworking LLC	Montgomery *(G-10224)*	G	812 687-7701
G & S Rural Woodworking	Hartford City *(G-5980)*	G	765 348-7781
Garyrae Inc	Mishawaka *(G-10045)*	F	574 255-7141
Genesis Products Inc	Elkhart *(G-2878)*	E	574 266-8293
▲ Genesis Products LLC	Elkhart *(G-2879)*	C	877 266-8292
Georgia-Pacific LLC	Wheatfield *(G-14223)*	C	219 956-3100
Gilpin Custom Woodworking	Roanoke *(G-12103)*	G	260 413-6618
Grabill Cabinet Company Inc	Grabill *(G-5368)*	C	877 472-2782
Guereca Woodworking	Decatur *(G-2383)*	G	260 724-3994
Gutter One Supply	Indianapolis *(G-7060)*	G	317 872-1257
Guys Wood N Things	Holton *(G-6107)*	G	812 689-0433
Heidenreich Woodworking Inc	New Palestine *(G-10970)*	G	317 861-9331
Hickory Valley Woodworking LLC	Loogootee *(G-9385)*	G	812 486-2857
Hilltop Woodworking	Madison *(G-9468)*	G	812 689-3462
Hiltys Woodwork	Fort Wayne *(G-4336)*	G	260 627-2905
Hoosier Custom Woodworking	Millersburg *(G-9970)*	G	574 642-3764
Hoosier Daddy Woodworks	New Albany *(G-10797)*	G	812 949-2801
Hoosier Interior Doors Inc	Goshen *(G-5241)*	G	574 534-3072
Hoosier Wood Works	Bloomington *(G-742)*	G	812 325-9823
Hrh Door Corp	Evansville *(G-3544)*	G	812 479-5680
Hudec Construction Company	Griffith *(G-5777)*	E	219 922-9811
Hurst Jeff Custom Woodworking	Ferdinand *(G-3853)*	G	812 367-1430
▲ Ideal Wood Products	New Albany *(G-10801)*	D	812 949-5181
▲ Indiana Architectural Plywood	Trafalgar *(G-13436)*	E	317 878-4822
▲ Indiana Dimension Inc	Logansport *(G-9340)*	D	574 739-2319
Indiana Lumber Inc	Bloomington *(G-746)*	G	812 837-9493
Indiana Southern Millwork Inc	North Vernon *(G-11263)*	E	812 346-6129
Indianapolis Wdwkg Intl LLC	Fishers *(G-3929)*	E	317 841-7800
Integrity Woodcrafting	Shipshewana *(G-12620)*	G	260 562-2067
Interior Fixs & Mllwk Co Inc	Knightsville *(G-8561)*	G	812 446-0933
▲ Irvine Shade & Door Inc	Elkhart *(G-2940)*	D	574 522-1446
Ivy Woodworks LLC	Indianapolis *(G-7278)*	G	317 842-4085
J P Whitt Inc	Muncie *(G-10498)*	G	765 759-0521
J W Woodworking Inc	New Paris *(G-10987)*	G	574 831-3033
Jackson Brothers Lumber Co	Linton *(G-9308)*	F	812 847-7812
James G Henager	Elberfeld *(G-2636)*	G	812 795-2230
JC Treeations Inc	Schererville *(G-12325)*	G	219 322-2911
John G Wagler	Odon *(G-11332)*	G	812 709-1681
John Garrison Woodworking LLC	Quincy *(G-11891)*	G	765 795-4681
John Gebhart Woodworkings	Cayuga *(G-1521)*	G	765 492-3898
John Pater Design Fabrication	Aurora *(G-381)*	F	812 926-4845
Jrs Wood Shop	Kingman *(G-8532)*	G	765 498-2663

S I C

K Lash & Son Inc G 260 347-3660
Kendallville *(G-8482)*
Keith Ison G 765 938-1460
Rushville *(G-12226)*
Kentucky-Indiana Lumber Co Inc E 812 464-2428
Evansville *(G-3584)*
Kerkhoff Associates Inc E 765 583-4491
Otterbein *(G-11419)*
Key Millwork Inc G 260 426-6501
Fort Wayne *(G-4410)*
Kh Woodworking G 317 702-5094
Greenfield *(G-5548)*
Kitchen Konnection Inc G 812 277-0393
Bedford *(G-557)*
Kleeman Cabinetry G 812 926-0428
Aurora *(G-382)*
▲ **Knapke & Sons Inc** E 260 639-0112
Hoagland *(G-6065)*
Knothole Woodworks LLC G 317 600-8151
Sheridan *(G-12595)*
▲ **Koetter Woodworking Inc** B 812 923-8875
Borden *(G-934)*
Kostyo Woodworking Inc G 812 466-7350
Terre Haute *(G-13267)*
Kraigs Custom Woodworking G 574 904-7501
Mishawaka *(G-10066)*
Kuntry Lumber and Farm Sup Ltd E 260 463-3242
Lagrange *(G-9051)*
L & L Woodworking LLC G 574 535-4613
Nappanee *(G-10690)*
L & N Woodworking G 260 768-7008
Shipshewana *(G-12626)*
L A M B Woodworking G 260 768-7992
Shipshewana *(G-12627)*
L W Woodworking LLC G 260 463-8938
Wolcottville *(G-14373)*
Lakeside Woodworking G 812 687-7901
Odon *(G-11333)*
Lakeview Woodworking G 574 642-1335
Goshen *(G-5262)*
Lambright Woodworking LLC E 260 593-2721
Topeka *(G-13423)*
Lana Hudelson G 812 865-3951
Orleans *(G-11363)*
Larkin Woodworks G 765 795-5332
Cloverdale *(G-1728)*
▲ **Larry Robertson Associates** E 812 537-4090
Indianapolis *(G-7381)*
Legacy Wood Creations LLC G 574 773-4405
Nappanee *(G-10691)*
Light House Woodworking DBA G 260 704-0589
Saint Joe *(G-12256)*
Ligonier Woodworking G 260 894-9969
Ligonier *(G-9289)*
Lockerbie Square Cab Co Inc G 317 635-1134
Indianapolis *(G-7413)*
Loggers Incorporated E 812 939-2797
Clay City *(G-1704)*
Louisiana-Pacific Corporation D 574 825-5845
Middlebury *(G-9905)*
M & M Trim Inc G 317 791-7009
Indianapolis *(G-7430)*
Maple City Woodworking Corp D 574 642-3342
Goshen *(G-5279)*
Maple Leaf Woodworking G 260 768-8166
Lagrange *(G-9059)*
Marquise Enterprises Ltd G 317 578-3400
Indianapolis *(G-7458)*
Marvelous Woodworking LLC G 317 679-5890
Lebanon *(G-9203)*
Maschino Woodworks G 812 230-7428
Terre Haute *(G-13280)*
Mast Woodworking G 812 636-7938
Odon *(G-11334)*
Mdl Woodworking LLC G 260 242-1824
Fort Wayne *(G-4463)*
Menard Inc E 260 441-0406
Fort Wayne *(G-4465)*
Mervin Knepps Molding G 812 486-2971
Montgomery *(G-10235)*
▲ **Middlebury Hardwood Pdts Inc** C 574 825-9524
Middlebury *(G-9907)*
Midwest Custom Woodworking G 574 349-1645
Lagrange *(G-9061)*
Mikes Creative Woodworks LLC G 502 649-3665
Charlestown *(G-1573)*
Miller Door & Trim Inc G 574 533-8141
Goshen *(G-5294)*
Mishawaka Door LLC G 574 259-2822
Mishawaka *(G-10090)*

Miter Craft Inc G 317 462-3621
Greenfield *(G-5555)*
Molargik Woodworking Inc G 260 357-6625
Garrett *(G-5016)*
Monroe Wood Works G 317 979-0964
Indianapolis *(G-7537)*
Mountjoy Wooding G 317 897-6792
Indianapolis *(G-7550)*
Mullet Custom Interiors LLC F 574 773-9442
Nappanee *(G-10696)*
N & R Woodworking Llc G 812 787-0644
Odon *(G-11336)*
Nalleys Woodworking G 812 923-1299
Greenville *(G-5651)*
Napoleon Hardwood Lbr Co Inc E 812 852-4090
Greensburg *(G-5626)*
New Style of Crossroads LLC F 260 593-3800
Topeka *(G-13424)*
◆ **Nickell Moulding Company Inc** C 574 295-5223
Elkhart *(G-3063)*
Nov Oak Woodworking G 812 422-1973
Evansville *(G-3647)*
Nu-TEC Industries Inc E 219 844-1233
Schererville *(G-12340)*
Ohio Valley Door Corp E 812 945-5285
New Albany *(G-10836)*
Olon Industries Inc (us) F 812 254-0427
Washington *(G-13994)*
Omega National Products LLC C 574 295-5353
Elkhart *(G-3068)*
Owen Woodworking G 317 331-6936
Danville *(G-2354)*
Patrick Industries Inc C 574 293-1521
Elkhart *(G-3082)*
Pendleton Door Company G 765 778-4164
Pendleton *(G-11499)*
Philip Konrad & Sons Inc F 574 772-3966
Knox *(G-8576)*
Pickslays Woodworking G 530 388-8697
Winona Lake *(G-14353)*
Pinnacle Woodworking LLC G 765 345-2301
Knightstown *(G-8559)*
PJmort Woodworking G 574 542-9680
Monterey *(G-10208)*
Power Plant Service Inc E 260 432-6716
Fort Wayne *(G-4542)*
▼ **Pro-Form Plastics Inc** E 812 522-4433
Crothersville *(G-2220)*
PTG Inc G 317 892-4625
Brownsburg *(G-1165)*
R P Wakefield Company Inc E 260 837-8841
Waterloo *(G-14022)*
Real Wood Works G 812 277-1462
Bedford *(G-571)*
Redlin Custom Woodworking LLC G 317 578-1852
Fishers *(G-3962)*
Riddle Ridge Woodworks G 812 596-4503
English *(G-3318)*
Ro Vic Wood Products Inc E 812 283-9199
Jeffersonville *(G-8420)*
▲ **Robert Weed Plywood Corp** B 574 848-7631
Bristol *(G-1081)*
Rockville Woodworks G 765 569-6483
Rockville *(G-12179)*
Rockwell Diversified Woodworks G 317 758-4797
Sheridan *(G-12597)*
Rodeswood LLC G 574 457-4496
Syracuse *(G-13142)*
Rogers Group Inc E 812 333-6324
Bloomington *(G-816)*
Rst Custom Woodworking LL G 317 602-2490
Indianapolis *(G-7870)*
Rustic Acres Woodworks G 765 886-5699
Williamsburg *(G-14284)*
Salt Creek Woodworks G 219 730-7553
Valparaiso *(G-13612)*
Samswoodworking G 574 772-6482
Knox *(G-8580)*
Schindler Woodwork G 513 314-5943
Cedar Grove *(G-1522)*
Schlabach Hardwoods G 574 642-1157
Goshen *(G-5320)*
Schmucker Woodworking LLC G 260 413-9784
New Haven *(G-10957)*
Schwartz Woodworking G 260 593-3193
Millersburg *(G-9973)*
Schwartz Woodworking LLC G 260 854-9457
Wolcottville *(G-14376)*
Scp Building Products LLC G 574 772-2955
Knox *(G-8581)*

Shamrock Cabinets Inc E 812 482-7969
Jasper *(G-8308)*
Shiloh Custom Woodworks G 812 636-0100
Odon *(G-11340)*
Shinabargar Custom Stairs G 219 462-1735
Valparaiso *(G-13616)*
Signature Industries Inc G 260 350-3688
Lagrange *(G-9064)*
Sorg Millwork G 260 639-3223
Fort Wayne *(G-4637)*
South Bend Woodworks LLC F 574 232-8875
South Bend *(G-12947)*
Spectrum Finishing LLC E 260 463-7300
Lagrange *(G-9066)*
State Line Woodworking G 260 768-4577
Shipshewana *(G-12651)*
Stephens Woodworking G 812 487-2818
Guilford *(G-5799)*
Steven Block G 765 749-5394
Muncie *(G-10567)*
Stock Building Supply LLC E 260 490-0616
Fort Wayne *(G-4650)*
Stolls Woodworking LLC G 812 486-5117
Odon *(G-11342)*
Stoney Acres Woodworking LLC G 260 768-4367
Shipshewana *(G-12653)*
Swiss Woodworking & Sales G 260 849-9669
Berne *(G-627)*
Tartan Properties LLC G 317 714-7337
Indianapolis *(G-8037)*
Tarter Woodworking LLC G 765 349-4193
Martinsville *(G-9640)*
Therm-O-Lite LLC G 574 234-4004
South Bend *(G-12968)*
Timothy J Troyer G 574 546-1115
Bremen *(G-1029)*
Tinchers Creative Woodworks G 765 344-0062
Rockville *(G-12181)*
Toms Interior Windows LLC G 574 233-0799
South Bend *(G-12974)*
Trim-A-Door G 317 769-8746
Whitestown *(G-14264)*
▲ **Tru-Cut Inc** E 765 683-9920
Anderson *(G-179)*
Ubelhor Construction Inc F 812 357-2220
Bristow *(G-1095)*
Ufp Nappanee LLC D 574 773-2505
Nappanee *(G-10709)*
Universal Door Carrier Inc G 317 241-3447
Indianapolis *(G-8129)*
Universal Forest Products Indi C 574 273-6326
Granger *(G-5447)*
Van Go Inc G 574 862-2807
Shipshewana *(G-12656)*
Verns Woodworking G 574 773-7930
Bremen *(G-1031)*
W & M Woodworking G 260 854-3126
Lagrange *(G-9071)*
Wagler Woodworking G 812 486-6357
Loogootee *(G-9397)*
Walnut Lane Woodworking G 574 633-2114
Bremen *(G-1032)*
Warsaw Foundry Company Inc D 574 267-8772
Warsaw *(G-13962)*
▲ **Waynedale Mill Inc** F 260 436-7100
Fort Wayne *(G-4746)*
Weaver Woodworking G 260 565-3647
Bluffton *(G-897)*
Weberdings Carving Shop Inc F 812 934-3710
Batesville *(G-524)*
West Point Woodworking LLC G 260 768-4750
Shipshewana *(G-12658)*
White Aspen Woodworking LLC G 765 471-4962
Lafayette *(G-9023)*
Whites Woodworks G 765 341-6678
Martinsville *(G-9648)*
Wible Lumber Inc E 260 351-2441
South Milford *(G-12995)*
Wichman Woodworking Inc G 812 522-8450
Seymour *(G-12500)*
Wildwood Millwork LLC G 574 535-9104
Goshen *(G-5346)*
Wilmes Window Mfg Co Inc E 812 275-7575
Ferdinand *(G-3864)*
Wittmer Woodworking LLC G 812 486-3115
Montgomery *(G-10248)*
Wood Creations Inc G 574 522-7765
Elkhart *(G-3265)*
Wood Spc By Fehrenbacher Inc E 812 963-9414
Evansville *(G-3815)*

Wood Specialists LLC ....G...... 219 779-9026
  Crown Point (G-2322)
◆ Wood-Mizer Holdings Inc...............C...... 317 271-1542
  Indianapolis (G-8212)
Woodland Ridge Woodworking...........G...... 812 821-8032
  Ellettsville (G-3285)
Woods Enterprises ....G...... 574 232-7449
  South Bend (G-12992)
Woodside Woodworks ....G...... 260 499-3220
  Wolcottville (G-14378)
Woodworking By Rich ....G...... 317 535-5750
  Whiteland (G-14248)
Woodwright Door & Trim Inc ....G...... 574 522-1667
  Elkhart (G-3267)
Wrights Woodworking ....G...... 765 723-1546
  New Ross (G-11006)
Yellow Dog Woodworking LLC ....G...... 502 817-9395
  Greenville (G-5656)
Yoder Woodworking ....G...... 574 825-0402
  Middlebury (G-9929)

2434 Wood Kitchen Cabinets

AAA Cabinet Guy LLC ....G...... 574 299-9371
  South Bend (G-12690)
Academy Inc....................................G...... 574 293-7113
  Elkhart (G-2663)
Acme Cabinets Corp.........................G...... 219 924-1800
  Griffith (G-5760)
Advanced Cabinet Systems Inc...........D...... 765 677-8000
  Marion (G-9506)
Aldridge Cabinets ....G...... 812 873-6723
  Deputy (G-2458)
All About Organizing ....G...... 513 238-8157
  Lawrenceburg (G-9130)
American Woodmark Corporation ....B...... 765 677-1690
  Gas City (G-5118)
Americas Cabinet Co of Ind ....G...... 317 788-9533
  Greenfield (G-5500)
Architectural Accents Inc..................F...... 219 922-9333
  Munster (G-10596)
Aristoline Cabinet Inc ....E...... 260 482-9719
  Fort Wayne (G-4090)
B & L Custom Cabinets Inc................G...... 765 379-2471
  Rossville (G-12209)
Baum Cabinetry LLC ....G...... 219 575-6309
  Valparaiso (G-13506)
Beebe Cabinet Co Inc ....F...... 574 293-3580
  Elkhart (G-2720)
Bremtown Fine Cstm Cbnetry Inc ....D...... 574 546-2781
  Bremen (G-988)
Brookwood Cabinet Company Inc ....F...... 260 749-5012
  Fort Wayne (G-4123)
Burns Cabinets and Disp Inc..............G...... 260 897-2219
  Avilla (G-401)
C & R Woodworks ....G...... 317 422-9603
  Martinsville (G-9596)
Cabinet & Countertop Solutio ....G...... 219 775-3540
  Crown Point (G-2232)
Cabinet Cottage LLC ....G...... 317 369-0051
  Noblesville (G-11077)
Cabinet Crafters Corp.......................G...... 765 724-7074
  Alexandria (G-37)
Cabinetmaker Inc ....G...... 812 723-3461
  Paoli (G-11446)
Cabinetry Green LLC ....G...... 317 842-1550
  Fishers (G-3883)
Cabinetry Ideas Inc ....G...... 317 722-1300
  Indianapolis (G-6532)
Cabinets By Gentry..........................G...... 765 378-7900
  Anderson (G-80)
Cabinets By Rick Inc ....G...... 812 945-2220
  New Albany (G-10757)
Carriage House Woodworking............G...... 317 406-3042
  Plainfield (G-11599)
Carter Cabinet Co Inc ....G...... 317 985-5782
  New Palestine (G-10969)
Cassini - D & D Mfg Inc....................G...... 765 449-7992
  Lafayette (G-8870)
Cedar Woodworking ....G...... 812 486-2765
  Montgomery (G-10216)
Coblentz Cabinet..............................G...... 812 687-7525
  Montgomery (G-10217)
Columbus Cstm Cbinets Furn LLC .....G...... 812 379-9411
  Columbus (G-1875)
Commercial Electric Co Inc ....E...... 260 726-9357
  Portland (G-11813)
Coppes-Nappanee Company Inc..........F...... 574 773-0007
  Nappanee (G-10663)
Corbetts Custom Cabinetry LLC ....G...... 812 670-6211
  Jeffersonville (G-8346)

Corner Cabinet................................G...... 317 859-6336
  Greenwood (G-5676)
Cornerstone Cabinetry LLC ....G...... 574 250-2690
  Granger (G-5397)
Counterfitters Inc ....G...... 219 531-0848
  Valparaiso (G-13523)
Countertop Connections Inc...............G...... 317 822-9858
  Franklin (G-4878)
Countertops & More ....G...... 317 346-0111
  Franklin (G-4879)
Country Cabinets ....G...... 260 694-6777
  Poneto (G-11745)
Country View Cabinets LLC................G...... 574 825-3150
  Goshen (G-5193)
Countryside Cabinetry LLC ....G...... 765 597-2391
  Marshall (G-9590)
County Line Cabinetry LLC.................G...... 574 642-1202
  Middlebury (G-9879)
Crossrads Cntrtops Cbnetry LLC.........G...... 317 908-9254
  Indianapolis (G-6696)
Crown Cab & Counter Top Inc ....F...... 219 663-2725
  Crown Point (G-2238)
Crown Supply Co Inc ....F...... 812 522-6987
  Seymour (G-12440)
Custom Built Cabinets and ....G...... 812 427-9733
  Vevay (G-13662)
Custom Cabinet & Millwork ....G...... 219 696-9827
  Lowell (G-9403)
Custom Cabinets & Furn LLC ....F...... 812 486-2503
  Montgomery (G-10220)
Custom Design Laminates Inc............F...... 574 674-9174
  Osceola (G-11375)
Custom Tables & Cabinets.................G...... 812 486-3831
  Montgomery (G-10221)
Dan Goode Cabinet...........................G...... 317 541-9878
  Indianapolis (G-6724)
Daugherty Cabinets ....G...... 574 272-9205
  Granger (G-5400)
Doors & Drawers Inc.........................F...... 574 533-3509
  Goshen (G-5203)
Double T Manufacturing Corp ....F...... 574 262-1340
  Elkhart (G-2799)
Douglas Dye and Associates..............G...... 317 844-1709
  Carmel (G-1362)
DS Woods Custom Cabinets...............G...... 260 692-6565
  Decatur (G-2376)
Dutch Made Inc ....C...... 260 657-3311
  Grabill (G-5363)
Dutch Made Inc ....G...... 260 657-3331
  Harlan (G-5970)
E & S Wood Creations LLC ....F...... 260 768-3033
  Lagrange (G-9040)
Eds Wood Craft ....G...... 812 768-6617
  Haubstadt (G-6000)
Elko Inc ....E...... 812 473-8400
  Evansville (G-3473)
Evia Custom Cabinets LLC ....G...... 317 987-5504
  Carmel (G-1376)
▲ Fehrenbacher Cabinets Inc ....E...... 812 963-3377
  Evansville (G-3502)
Fergys Cabinets ....G...... 765 529-0116
  New Castle (G-10900)
Finish Alternatives ....G...... 317 440-2899
  Indianapolis (G-6922)
Fusion Wood Products LLC ....G...... 574 389-0307
  Elkhart (G-2872)
Gentrys Cabinet Inc ....G...... 765 643-6611
  Anderson (G-109)
Graber Cabinetry LLC........................E...... 260 627-2243
  Grabill (G-5366)
Graber Furniture ....G...... 812 295-4939
  Loogootee (G-9383)
Graber Woodworks Inc.......................G...... 812 486-2861
  Montgomery (G-10226)
Grabill Cabinet Company Inc..............C...... 877 472-2782
  Grabill (G-5368)
Grabill Woodworking Specialty ....G...... 260 627-5982
  Grabill (G-5371)
▲ Granitech ....E...... 574 674-6988
  Elkhart (G-2893)
▲ H-C Liquidating Corp ....A...... 574 535-9300
  Goshen (G-5233)
▲ Haas Cabinet Co Inc ....C...... 812 246-4431
  Sellersburg (G-12395)
Hackman Cabinet Co ....G...... 812 522-4118
  Seymour (G-12452)
Hardwood Door Mfg LLC....................G...... 812 486-3313
  Montgomery (G-10228)
Harlan Cabinets Inc ....D...... 260 657-5154
  Harlan (G-5972)

Healey Custom Cabinetry LLC ....G...... 574 946-4000
  Winamac (G-14307)
Herb Rahman & Sons Inc ....G...... 812 367-2513
  Ferdinand (G-3852)
Heritage Cabinets LLC ....G...... 812 963-3435
  Wadesville (G-13772)
Heritage Fine Furn & Cabinetry ....G...... 812 205-5437
  Evansville (G-3538)
Houck Industries Inc ....E...... 812 663-5675
  Greensburg (G-5614)
Hurst Custom Cabinets Inc ....G...... 812 683-3378
  Huntingburg (G-6170)
Independent Cabinets ....G...... 502 594-6026
  Memphis (G-9683)
Innovative Corp................................E...... 317 804-5977
  Westfield (G-14171)
Interior Fixs & Mllwk Co Inc ....G...... 812 446-0933
  Knightsville (G-8561)
J & J Cabinets ....G...... 219 374-6816
  Cedar Lake (G-1530)
J and G Enterprises ....G...... 219 778-4319
  Rolling Prairie (G-12188)
J G Cabinet & Counter Inc ....G...... 260 723-4275
  Larwill (G-9123)
J Miller Cabinetry Inc........................G...... 260 691-2032
  Columbia City (G-1800)
James G Henager..............................G...... 812 795-2230
  Elberfeld (G-2636)
Jds Pugh Cabinets Inc ....F...... 317 835-2910
  Fairland (G-3822)
John Pater Design Fabrication ....F...... 812 926-4845
  Aurora (G-381)
Johnny Bontrager ....G...... 260 463-8912
  Lagrange (G-9050)
Johnny Graber Woodworking................G...... 260 466-4957
  Grabill (G-5376)
Johns Fine Cabinetry ....G...... 765 296-2388
  Colburn (G-1753)
JP Custom Cabinetry Inc ....G...... 219 956-3587
  Wheatfield (G-14226)
Jrs Custom Cabinets Co ....E...... 219 696-7205
  Lowell (G-9410)
Kelwood Designs LLC Cabinetry ....G...... 574 862-2472
  Goshen (G-5251)
Kitchen Jewels Inc ....E...... 812 482-9663
  Jasper (G-8286)
Kitchen Kompact Inc ....C...... 812 282-6681
  Jeffersonville (G-8390)
Kitchen Konnection Inc......................G...... 812 277-0393
  Bedford (G-557)
Kline Cabinet Makers LLC..................F...... 317 326-3049
  Maxwell (G-9662)
Kokomo Cabinetry ....G...... 765 457-2385
  Kokomo (G-8652)
Kountry Wood Products LLC...............C...... 574 773-5673
  Nappanee (G-10689)
Kramer Furn & Cab Makers Inc ....F...... 812 526-2711
  Edinburgh (G-2615)
Lambright Woodworking LLC...............E...... 260 593-2721
  Topeka (G-13423)
Lami-Crafts Inc................................G...... 812 232-3012
  Terre Haute (G-13270)
Laminique Inc..................................E...... 765 482-4222
  Lebanon (G-9197)
Leroy E Doty Cabinet Shop.................G...... 219 663-1139
  Crown Point (G-2275)
Lockerbie Square Cab Co Inc ....G...... 317 635-1134
  Indianapolis (G-7413)
Madison Cabinets Inc........................G...... 260 639-3915
  Hoagland (G-6066)
Madison County Cabinets Inc..............F...... 765 778-4646
  Pendleton (G-11493)
Marcotte Cabinets ....G...... 574 520-1342
  Granger (G-5419)
Martinson Cabinet Shop ....G...... 219 926-1566
  Chesterton (G-1619)
Masterbrand Cabinets Inc ....G...... 812 482-2527
  Jasper (G-8290)
Masterbrand Cabinets Inc ....B...... 765 966-3940
  Richmond (G-12015)
▲ Masterbrand Cabinets Inc ....B...... 812 482-2527
  Jasper (G-8291)
Masterbrand Cabinets Inc ....G...... 574 535-9300
  Goshen (G-5282)
Masterbrand Cabinets Inc ....D...... 812 482-2527
  Celestine (G-1536)
Masterbrand Cabinets Inc ....C...... 812 482-2513
  Jasper (G-8292)
Masterbrand Cabinets Inc...................A...... 812 367-1104
  Ferdinand (G-3858)

Masterbrand Cabinets Inc ....C 812 482-2527
Huntingburg *(G-6175)*
Masterbrand Cabinets Inc ....B 256 362-5530
Jasper *(G-8293)*
Mc Custom Cabinets Inc ....G 502 641-1528
Underwood *(G-13451)*
McKinney & Sell Inc ....G 877 665-3300
Bourbon *(G-945)*
Meyer Custom Woodworking Inc ....G 812 695-2021
Dubois *(G-2477)*
Michiana Cabinet & Refacing LL ....G 574 277-0801
Granger *(G-5420)*
Milestone Cabinetry ....G 219 947-0600
Merrillville *(G-9735)*
Miller Cabinetry & Furn LLC ....G 260 657-5052
Grabill *(G-5380)*
Miller Maid Cabinets Inc ....F 317 786-0418
Indianapolis *(G-7520)*
Millers Custom Cabinets ....G 260 768-7830
Shipshewana *(G-12636)*
Mouron & Company Inc ....F 317 243-7955
Indianapolis *(G-7551)*
Muncie Cabinet Discounters ....G 765 216-7367
Muncie *(G-10527)*
Myers Cabinet Company ....G 765 342-7781
Martinsville *(G-9628)*
N & K Cabinet Inc ....G 765 552-6997
Elwood *(G-3308)*
Orchard Lane Cabinets ....G 574 825-7568
Goshen *(G-5302)*
Oxford Cabinet Company LLC ....G 765 223-2101
Liberty *(G-9269)*
Patrick Industries Inc ....E 574 293-1521
Elkhart *(G-3084)*
Paynes Fine Cabrinetry ....G 765 589-9176
Lafayette *(G-8978)*
Peace Valley Cabinets Inc ....G 812 238-5134
Terre Haute *(G-13300)*
Peace Valley Cabinets Inc ....G 812 486-3831
Montgomery *(G-10237)*
Philip Konrad & Sons Inc ....F 574 772-3966
Knox *(G-8576)*
Phoenix Custom Kitchens Inc ....G 812 523-1890
Seymour *(G-12475)*
Plastic Line Manufacturing ....E 219 769-8022
Merrillville *(G-9747)*
Pumpkin Patch Market Inc ....G 574 825-3312
Middlebury *(G-9915)*
R & R Custom Woodworking Inc ....E 574 773-5436
Nappanee *(G-10703)*
Rabb & Howe Cabinet Top Co ....F 317 926-6442
Indianapolis *(G-7811)*
Radel Wood Products Inc ....F 765 472-2940
Peru *(G-11543)*
Rainbow Design Inc ....E 260 593-2856
Lagrange *(G-9063)*
Rbk Development Inc ....E 574 267-5879
Warsaw *(G-13934)*
Rmg Cabinet ....G 219 712-6129
Hammond *(G-5935)*
Rogers Cabinetry ....G 574 664-9931
Logansport *(G-9362)*
Roh Custom Cabinetry LLC ....G 260 802-1158
Silver Lake *(G-12679)*
Ronald Chileen Furniture ....G 574 542-4505
Rochester *(G-12150)*
Rush County Wood Products ....G 765 629-0603
Milroy *(G-9986)*
S & H Cabinets ....G 574 773-7465
Nappanee *(G-10705)*
Saco Industries Inc ....B 219 690-9900
Lowell *(G-9422)*
Schmidt Cabinet Co Inc ....E 812 347-1031
New Salisbury *(G-11011)*
Schrock Cabinet ....G 812 482-2527
Jasper *(G-8304)*
Shamrock Cabinets Inc ....E 812 482-7969
Jasper *(G-8308)*
Signet Cabinetry Inc ....G 812 248-0612
Sellersburg *(G-12416)*
Sims Cabinet Co Inc ....E 317 634-1747
Indianapolis *(G-7948)*
Sorensen Custom Cabinets ....G 765 292-2225
Tipton *(G-13405)*
Spiceland Wood Products Inc ....F 765 987-8156
Spiceland *(G-13058)*
Steves Cabinets & More ....G 765 296-9419
Colburn *(G-1754)*
Strohbeck Cabinet Install ....G 812 923-5013
Floyds Knobs *(G-4019)*
Superior Laminating Inc ....F 574 361-7266
Goshen *(G-5331)*
TCS Cabinets ....G 765 208-5350
Summitville *(G-13107)*
Trillium Cabinet Company Inc ....G 317 471-8870
Indianapolis *(G-8100)*
Twin Spires Cabinetry LLC ....G 502 644-4183
Jeffersonville *(G-8436)*
Vans Cabinet Shop ....G 574 658-9625
Milford *(G-9966)*
Village Workshop Inc ....G 812 933-1527
Oldenburg *(G-11346)*
Waglers Custom Cabinets ....G 812 486-2878
Montgomery *(G-10247)*
▲ Walburn Service Inc ....G 765 289-3383
Muncie *(G-10578)*
▲ Walters Cabinet Shop ....G 765 452-9634
Kokomo *(G-8714)*
Warsaw Custom Cabinet ....G 574 267-5794
Winona Lake *(G-14354)*
Warsaw Custom Cabinet ....G 574 267-5794
Warsaw *(G-13960)*
William A Kadar ....G 219 884-7404
Gary *(G-5116)*
William R Arvin ....G 812 486-5255
Loogootee *(G-9398)*
Wisemans Custom Cabinets Inc ....G 812 678-3601
Dubois *(G-2478)*
Yoder Kitchen Corp ....E 574 773-3197
Nappanee *(G-10711)*
Yoders Cabinets ....G 812 486-3826
Montgomery *(G-10249)*
Zinn Kitchens Inc ....E 574 967-4179
Bringhurst *(G-1039)*
Zionsville Custom Cabinets ....G 317 339-0380
Zionsville *(G-14473)*

2435 Hardwood Veneer & Plywood

◆ Amos-Hill Associates Inc ....C 812 526-2671
Edinburgh *(G-2595)*
Besse Veneers Inc ....E 906 428-3113
Trafalgar *(G-13434)*
Carlisle Veneers Inc ....E 812 398-2225
Carlisle *(G-1296)*
Chisholm Lumber & Sup Co Inc ....E 317 547-3535
Indianapolis *(G-6601)*
Custom Plywood Inc ....D 812 944-7300
New Albany *(G-10766)*
▲ Danzer Services Inc ....G 812 526-2601
Edinburgh *(G-2603)*
Danzer Veneer Americas Inc ....F 812 526-6789
Edinburgh *(G-2604)*
◆ David R Webb Company Inc ....B 812 526-2601
Edinburgh *(G-2605)*
Dimension Plywood Inc ....G 812 944-6491
New Albany *(G-10768)*
E M Cummings Veneers Inc ....E 812 944-2269
New Albany *(G-10770)*
FBN Corporation ....D 765 728-2438
Montpelier *(G-10291)*
▲ Flexible Materials Inc ....D 812 280-7000
Jeffersonville *(G-8361)*
Flexible Materials Inc ....D 812 280-9578
Jeffersonville *(G-8362)*
Flexible Materials Inc ....G 812 948-7786
Floyds Knobs *(G-4010)*
▲ Form Wood Industries Inc ....E 812 284-3676
Jeffersonville *(G-8363)*
▲ Heitink Veneers Incorporated ....E 812 336-6436
Bloomington *(G-739)*
Heritage Hardwoods KY Inc ....D 812 288-5855
Jeffersonville *(G-8372)*
Heritage Unlimited LLC ....F 574 538-8021
Goshen *(G-5237)*
Hoehn Hardwoods ....G 812 968-3242
Corydon *(G-2101)*
▲ Ideal Wood Products ....D 812 949-5181
New Albany *(G-10801)*
▲ Indiana Architectural Plywood ....E 317 878-4822
Trafalgar *(G-13436)*
▼ Indiana Veneers Corp ....D 317 926-2458
Indianapolis *(G-7196)*
Jasper Veneer Inc ....E 812 482-4245
Jasper *(G-8265)*
Kimball Furniture Group LLC ....D 812 482-8401
Jasper *(G-8278)*
▼ Louisville Veneer Corp ....G 502 500-7176
New Albany *(G-10818)*
▲ Marwood Inc ....F 812 288-8344
Jeffersonville *(G-8398)*
Midwest Veneer Products Co ....E 765 728-2950
Montpelier *(G-10293)*
▼ Miller Veneers Inc ....C 317 638-2326
Indianapolis *(G-7521)*
▼ Mitchell Veneers Inc ....G 812 941-9663
New Albany *(G-10832)*
Norstam Veneers Inc ....D 812 732-4391
Mauckport *(G-9658)*
Patrick Industries Inc ....D 574 522-7710
Elkhart *(G-3081)*
Patrick Industries Inc ....C 574 294-7511
Elkhart *(G-3080)*
▲ Robert Weed Plywood Corp ....B 574 848-7631
Bristol *(G-1081)*
Rwp West LLC ....G 208 549-2410
Bristol *(G-1083)*
Sexton Plywood & Veneer Co ....G 812 454-0488
Evansville *(G-3725)*
Sims-Lohman Inc ....G 317 467-0710
Greenfield *(G-5574)*
Stemwood Corp ....D 812 945-6646
New Albany *(G-10866)*
Superior Veneer & Plywood LLC ....G 812 941-8850
New Albany *(G-10869)*
Universal Forest Products Indi ....C 574 273-6326
Granger *(G-5447)*
Veneer Curry Sales LLC ....F 812 945-6623
New Albany *(G-10871)*
Wholesale Hrdwood Intriors Inc ....F 317 867-3660
Westfield *(G-14202)*
Wible Lumber Inc ....E 260 351-2441
South Milford *(G-12995)*

2436 Softwood Veneer & Plywood

Douglas Dye and Associates ....G 317 844-1709
Carmel *(G-1362)*
▲ HI Tech Veneer LLC ....E 812 284-9775
Jeffersonville *(G-8373)*
▲ JDC Veneers Inc ....D 812 284-9775
Jeffersonville *(G-8384)*
Kimball Furniture Group LLC ....D 812 482-8401
Jasper *(G-8278)*

2439 Structural Wood Members, NEC

Beachwood Lumber Co Inc ....F 574 858-9325
Warsaw *(G-13843)*
▲ Brenco LLC ....G 219 844-9570
Hammond *(G-5854)*
Bryant Products Inc ....F 812 522-5929
Seymour *(G-12435)*
Carter Lee Building Component ....D 317 834-5380
Mooresville *(G-10305)*
Carter-Lee Building Components ....E 317 639-5431
Indianapolis *(G-6561)*
Classic Truss WD Cmponents Inc ....E 812 944-5821
Clarksville *(G-1678)*
Composite Designs Inc ....G 574 453-2902
Leesburg *(G-9235)*
Continntal Crpntry Cmpnnts LLC ....E 219 369-4839
Wanatah *(G-13823)*
Custom Millwork & Display LLC ....G 574 289-9772
South Bend *(G-12749)*
Custom Moulding ....G 812 636-7110
Odon *(G-11323)*
Daviess County Metal Sales ....D 812 486-4299
Cannelburg *(G-1284)*
Georgetown Truss Company Inc ....E 812 951-2647
Georgetown *(G-5145)*
Ghk Truss LLC ....E 812 282-6600
Clarksville *(G-1681)*
Indiana Truss Co LLC ....G 812 522-5929
Seymour *(G-12458)*
Interstate Truss LLC ....G 260 463-6124
Shipshewana *(G-12621)*
James G Henager ....G 812 795-2230
Elberfeld *(G-2636)*
▼ K & K Industries Inc ....D 812 486-3281
Montgomery *(G-10229)*
Kentucky-Indiana Lumber Co Inc ....E 812 464-2428
Evansville *(G-3584)*
Kerkhoff Associates Inc ....E 765 583-4491
Otterbein *(G-11419)*
Madison Truss Company ....G 812 273-5482
Madison *(G-9483)*
Martin Truss Manufacturing ....G 574 862-4457
Elkhart *(G-3021)*
Meadors & Assoc Inc ....G 317 736-6944
Franklin *(G-4906)*
Michiana Column & Truss LLC ....F 574 862-2828
Wakarusa *(G-13788)*

North Webster Construction Inc ... E ... 574 834-4448
North Webster *(G-11297)*
Northern Indiana Truss ... G ... 574 858-0505
Warsaw *(G-13916)*
Osterholt Construction Inc ... G ... 260 672-3493
Roanoke *(G-12106)*
Premier Truss & Lumber Company ... F ... 574 498-6022
Tippecanoe *(G-13386)*
Shelby Products Corporation ... G ... 317 398-4870
West Harrison *(G-14043)*
Stark Truss Company Inc ... D ... 219 866-2772
Rensselaer *(G-11940)*
Superior Truss & Components ... G ... 574 457-8925
Syracuse *(G-13145)*
Superior Truss & Panel Inc ... E ... 708 339-1200
Gary *(G-5103)*
Truss Partners LLC ... D ... 765 675-5700
Tipton *(G-13409)*
Truss Systems Inc ... F ... 812 897-3064
Boonville *(G-923)*
Trusslink ... G ... 219 362-3968
La Porte *(G-8832)*
Tyler Truss Systems Inc ... F ... 765 221-5050
Pendleton *(G-11509)*
Ufp Granger LLC ... E ... 574 277-7670
Granger *(G-5445)*
Wagner Truss Manufacturing ... F ... 812 852-2206
Napoleon *(G-10643)*
White Water Truss Llc ... G ... 765 489-6261
Hagerstown *(G-5816)*

2441 Wood Boxes

A S M Inc ... G ... 260 724-8220
Decatur *(G-2363)*
American Fibertech Corporation ... E ... 219 261-3586
Clarks Hill *(G-1670)*
Ash-Lin Inc ... F ... 317 861-1540
Fountaintown *(G-4789)*
Bryant Products Inc ... F ... 812 522-5929
Seymour *(G-12435)*
C & C Mailbox Products ... G ... 765 358-4880
Gaston *(G-5130)*
C E Kersting & Sons ... G ... 574 896-2766
North Judson *(G-11207)*
Douglas Industries LLC ... G ... 260 327-3692
Larwill *(G-9121)*
F & F Contracting ... G ... 574 867-4471
Grovertown *(G-5795)*
Findley Foster Corp ... G ... 812 524-7279
Seymour *(G-12450)*
Hoosier Box and Skid Inc ... G ... 574 256-2111
Mishawaka *(G-10050)*
Indiana Wood Products Inc ... D ... 574 825-2129
Middlebury *(G-9893)*
▼ Industrial Woodkraft Inc ... E ... 812 897-4893
Boonville *(G-914)*
JR Grber Sons Fmly Ltd Prtnr ... G ... 260 657-1071
Grabill *(G-5377)*
Leclere Manufacturing Inc ... G ... 812 683-5627
Jasper *(G-8287)*
Meyer Custom Woodworking Inc ... G ... 812 695-2021
Dubois *(G-2477)*
Monroeville Box Pallet & Wood ... E ... 260 623-3128
Monroeville *(G-10197)*
Whitakerr Dalemon ... G ... 812 738-2396
Corydon *(G-2116)*

2448 Wood Pallets & Skids

A Pallet Company ... G ... 317 687-9020
Indianapolis *(G-6299)*
A S M Inc ... G ... 260 724-8220
Decatur *(G-2363)*
A-1 Pallet Co Inc Clarksville ... E ... 812 288-6339
Clarksville *(G-1671)*
A-1 Pallet Co Inc Clarksville ... G ... 812 288-6339
Clarksville *(G-1672)*
A1 Pallet Liquidators ... G ... 765 356-4020
Anderson *(G-57)*
A1 Pallets Inc ... G ... 812 425-0381
Evansville *(G-3331)*
Alsip Pallet Company Inc ... G ... 219 322-3288
Schererville *(G-12314)*
American Fibertech Corporation ... D ... 219 261-3586
Remington *(G-11904)*
American Fibertech Corporation ... E ... 219 261-3586
Clarks Hill *(G-1670)*
American Pallet & Recycl Inc ... G ... 219 322-4391
Dyer *(G-2492)*
Anthony Wayne Rehabilitation C ... D ... 260 744-6145
Fort Wayne *(G-4078)*
Ash-Lin Inc ... F ... 317 861-1540
Fountaintown *(G-4789)*
Axtrom Industries ... E ... 812 859-4873
Freedom *(G-4946)*
B & B Pallet ... G ...
Clinton *(G-1714)*
Barks Lumber Co Inc ... G ... 812 732-4680
Central *(G-1545)*
Basiloid Products Corp ... E ... 812 692-5511
Elnora *(G-3286)*
Billy D Snider ... G ... 765 795-6426
Cloverdale *(G-1724)*
Bravo Trailers LLC ... D ... 574 848-7500
Bristol *(G-1049)*
Bristol Pallet ... G ... 574 862-1862
Goshen *(G-5179)*
Buckingham Pallets Inc ... F ... 317 846-8601
Carmel *(G-1323)*
Burton Lumber Co Inc ... F ... 812 866-4438
Lexington *(G-9249)*
C & C Pallets and Lumber LLC ... G ... 765 524-3214
New Castle *(G-10895)*
C C Cook and Son Lbr Co Inc ... E ... 765 672-4235
Reelsville *(G-11900)*
C E Kersting & Sons ... G ... 574 896-2766
North Judson *(G-11207)*
Calumet Pallet Company Inc ... D ... 219 932-4550
Michigan City *(G-9772)*
Chep (usa) Inc ... E ... 317 780-0700
Indianapolis *(G-6598)*
Columbus Pallet Corporation ... G ... 812 372-7272
Columbus *(G-1880)*
Commercial Pallet Recycl Inc ... F ... 260 829-1021
Orland *(G-11347)*
Conner Sawmill Inc ... F ... 574 626-3227
Walton *(G-13815)*
Coomer & Sons Sawmill & Pallet ... D ... 765 659-2846
Frankfort *(G-4824)*
Corr-Wood Manufacturing Inc ... E ... 812 867-0700
Evansville *(G-3431)*
D and S Pallet ... G ... 765 866-7263
Crawfordsville *(G-2148)*
D&G Timber Inc ... E ... 812 486-3356
Odon *(G-11324)*
Danwood Industries ... G ... 219 369-1484
La Porte *(G-8749)*
Dehart Pallet & Lumber Co ... F ... 812 794-2974
Austin *(G-396)*
Dmi Distribution Inc ... E ... 765 287-0035
Muncie *(G-10461)*
Dodd Saw Mills Inc ... E ... 812 268-4811
Sullivan *(G-13081)*
Duro Inc ... G ... 574 293-6860
Elkhart *(G-2804)*
Duro Recycling Inc ... E ... 574 522-2572
Elkhart *(G-2805)*
Ernest A Cooper ... E ... 812 284-0436
Jeffersonville *(G-8357)*
Evansville Pallets ... G ... 812 550-0199
Evansville *(G-3489)*
F & F Contracting ... G ... 574 867-4471
Grovertown *(G-5795)*
Findley Foster Corp ... G ... 812 524-7279
Seymour *(G-12450)*
Ford Sawmills Inc ... E ... 812 324-2134
Vincennes *(G-13682)*
Fowler Ridge IV Wind Farm LLC ... G ... 765 884-1029
Fowler *(G-4800)*
Garr Custom Pallets Inc ... G ... 812 352-8887
North Vernon *(G-11258)*
Gonzalez Pallets ... G ... 317 644-1242
Indianapolis *(G-7023)*
Graber Box & Pallet Fmly Lmt P ... E ... 260 657-5657
Grabill *(G-5365)*
Green Stream Company ... D ... 574 293-1949
Elkhart *(G-2899)*
Greene County Pallet Inc ... F ... 812 384-8362
Bloomfield *(G-638)*
H & A Products Inc ... F ... 574 226-0079
Elkhart *(G-2902)*
H & M Bay Inc ... G ... 410 463-5430
Fort Wayne *(G-4312)*
Hagemier Products ... G ... 812 526-0377
Franklin *(G-4894)*
Hillcrest Pallets ... G ... 812 883-3636
Salem *(G-12291)*
Hoosier Box and Skid Inc ... G ... 574 256-2111
Mishawaka *(G-10050)*
Hoosier Pallet ... G ... 765 629-2899
Milroy *(G-9981)*
Indiana Pallet Co Inc ... E ... 219 398-4223
East Chicago *(G-2539)*
Indiana Wood Products Inc ... D ... 574 825-2129
Middlebury *(G-9893)*
Industrial Lumber Products Inc ... G ... 219 324-7697
La Porte *(G-8770)*
Industrial Pallet Corporation ... G ... 574 583-4800
Monticello *(G-10266)*
▼ Industrial Woodkraft Inc ... E ... 812 897-4893
Boonville *(G-914)*
Indy Pallet Company Inc ... G ... 317 843-0452
Carmel *(G-1413)*
Integrity Pallet LLC ... G ... 574 612-2119
Shipshewana *(G-12619)*
J & J Pallet Corp ... E ... 812 948-9382
New Albany *(G-10808)*
J & J Pallet Corp ... E ... 812 944-8670
New Albany *(G-10809)*
J & J Pallet Corp ... E ... 812 288-4487
Clarksville *(G-1687)*
Jennings County Pallets Inc ... E ... 812 458-6288
Butlerville *(G-1248)*
Jennings County Pallets Inc ... E ... 812 458-6288
Butlerville *(G-1249)*
JR Grber Sons Fmly Ltd Prtnr ... G ... 260 657-1071
Grabill *(G-5377)*
K & S Pallet Inc ... F ... 260 422-1264
Fort Wayne *(G-4402)*
K J Pallets ... G ... 812 342-6476
Columbus *(G-1954)*
Kamps Inc ... E ... 317 634-8360
Indianapolis *(G-7332)*
Kerst Pallet ... G ... 765 585-3026
Attica *(G-306)*
Kevin Coomer Pallet Co ... G ... 765 324-2294
Colfax *(G-1756)*
Leclere Manufacturing Inc ... G ... 812 683-5627
Jasper *(G-8287)*
Lemler Pallet Inc ... G ... 574 646-2707
Bourbon *(G-944)*
Lovett Pallet Recycling LLC ... D ... 317 638-4840
Indianapolis *(G-7421)*
M M Paltech Inc ... G ... 219 932-5308
Hammond *(G-5909)*
Meagan Inc ... F ... 574 267-8626
Warsaw *(G-13906)*
Megan Inc ... F ... 574 267-8626
Warsaw *(G-13910)*
Michiana Pallet Recycle Inc ... G ... 574 232-8566
South Bend *(G-12861)*
Midwestern Pallet Service Inc ... G ... 260 563-1526
Wabash *(G-13739)*
Millwood Box & Pallet ... G ... 765 628-7330
Kokomo *(G-8667)*
Milroy Pallet Inc ... G ... 765 629-2919
Milroy *(G-9984)*
Monroeville Box Pallet & Wood ... E ... 260 623-3128
Monroeville *(G-10197)*
Myers Wood Products ... G ... 765 597-2147
Bloomingdale *(G-649)*
Napoleon Hardwood Lbr Co Inc ... E ... 812 852-4090
Greensburg *(G-5626)*
Neumayr Lumber Co Inc ... F ... 765 764-4148
Attica *(G-308)*
Newport Pallet Inc ... G ... 217 497-8220
Newport *(G-11056)*
Newport Pallet Inc ... E ... 765 505-9463
Hillsdale *(G-6061)*
North Central Pallets Inc ... E ... 574 892-6142
Argos *(G-276)*
Oldenburg Pallet Inc ... G ... 812 933-0568
Batesville *(G-513)*
Owen County Pallet ... G ... 812 859-4617
Worthington *(G-14395)*
Pallet Builder Inc ... F ... 765 948-3345
Fairmount *(G-3834)*
Pallet One of Indiana Inc ... D ... 260 768-4021
Shipshewana *(G-12641)*
Pallet Recyclers LLC ... G ... 812 402-0095
Evansville *(G-3661)*
Palletone Indiana Trnsp LLC ... F ... 260 768-4021
Shipshewana *(G-12642)*
Pallets Viveros LLC ... G ... 765 307-0112
Crawfordsville *(G-2182)*
Paul Knepp Sawmill Inc ... G ... 812 486-3773
Montgomery *(G-10236)*
Peru Hardwood Products Inc ... F ... 765 473-4844
Peru *(G-11539)*
Phoenix Pallet Inc ... F ... 574 262-0458
Elkhart *(G-3094)*

S I C

Powell Systems Inc ....G...... 765 884-0613
Fowler **(G-4804)**

Powell Systems Inc ....E...... 765 884-0980
Fowler **(G-4805)**

Premier Lumber Company ....F...... 219 801-6018
Chesterton **(G-1628)**

Pro Pallet LLC ....G...... 219 292-3389
Gary **(G-5087)**

Quality Fence Ltd ....G...... 260 768-4986
Shipshewana **(G-12645)**

Quality Pallet ....E...... 765 348-4840
Hartford City **(G-5989)**

Quality Pallet ....G...... 765 212-2215
Muncie **(G-10551)**

Quality Pallets Inc ....G...... 812 873-6818
Commiskey **(G-2036)**

R & E Pallet Inc ....G...... 219 873-9671
Michigan City **(G-9833)**

Richard Squier Pallets Inc ....E...... 260 281-2434
Waterloo **(G-14023)**

Ridg-U-Rak Inc ....G...... 574 273-8036
Granger **(G-5431)**

Rs Pallet Inc ....G...... 574 596-8777
Bristol **(G-1082)**

Satco Inc ....E...... 317 856-0301
Indianapolis **(G-7896)**

Schneiders Wood Shop Inc ....G...... 812 522-4621
Seymour **(G-12482)**

Schwartzville Pallet ....E...... 260 244-4144
Columbia City **(G-1834)**

Servants Inc ....E...... 812 634-2201
Jasper **(G-8307)**

Servants Inc ....D...... 812 634-2201
Jasper **(G-8306)**

Skid Row Wood Products Inc ....F...... 812 828-0349
Spencer **(G-13036)**

Sparkman Mfg Inc ....G...... 812 873-6052
Commiskey **(G-2037)**

Steves Pallets ....G...... 260 856-2047
Cromwell **(G-2211)**

Steves Pallets Inc ....F...... 574 457-3620
Syracuse **(G-13144)**

Tc Pallets & Peddler Sweet LLC ....G...... 812 283-1090
Jeffersonville **(G-8433)**

Trinity Cstm Built Pallets LLC ....G...... 260 466-4625
New Haven **(G-10961)**

Ufp Granger LLC ....E...... 574 277-7670
Granger **(G-5445)**

Vest Pallet Co ....G...... 812 839-6247
Canaan **(G-1282)**

Vision IV Inc ....E...... 812 423-0119
Evansville **(G-3804)**

W & W Pallet Co LLC ....G...... 812 486-3548
Montgomery **(G-10246)**

W-M Lumber and Wood Pdts Inc ....E...... 812 944-6711
New Albany **(G-10874)**

Waupaca Pallet ....G...... 812 547-1565
Troy **(G-13449)**

Whitakerr Dalemon ....G...... 812 738-2396
Corydon **(G-2116)**

X-L Box Inc ....E...... 219 763-3736
Valparaiso **(G-13638)**

Yager Pallet ....G...... 219 365-2766
Saint John **(G-12273)**

Yoder & Sons Pallets ....G...... 260 625-2835
Columbia City **(G-1848)**

2449 Wood Containers, NEC

A S M Inc ....G...... 260 724-8220
Decatur **(G-2363)**

A-1 Pallet Co Inc Clarksville ....G...... 812 288-6339
Clarksville **(G-1672)**

American Fibertech Corporation ....E...... 219 261-3586
Clarks Hill **(G-1670)**

Anthony Wayne Rehabilitation C ....D...... 260 744-6145
Fort Wayne **(G-4078)**

Artisanz Fabrication Mch LLC ....G...... 317 708-0228
Plainfield **(G-11594)**

Bryant Products Inc ....F...... 812 522-5929
Seymour **(G-12435)**

Case Indy Products Inc ....G...... 317 677-0200
Indianapolis **(G-6563)**

▲ CH Ellis Co Inc ....G...... 317 636-3351
Indianapolis **(G-6592)**

Conner Sawmill Inc ....F...... 574 626-3227
Walton **(G-13815)**

Corr-Wood Manufacturing Inc ....E...... 812 867-0700
Evansville **(G-3431)**

F & F Contracting ....G...... 574 867-4471
Grovertown **(G-5795)**

Gordon Lumber Company ....G...... 219 924-0500
Griffith **(G-5774)**

Indiana Southern Hardwoods ....E...... 812 326-2053
Huntingburg **(G-6171)**

▼ Industrial Woodkraft Inc ....E...... 812 897-4893
Boonville **(G-914)**

J R Graber & Sons Inc ....E...... 260 657-5620
Grabill **(G-5375)**

Knights Woodworking LLC ....G...... 812 988-2106
Nashville **(G-10727)**

Minor Products Company Inc ....G...... 812 448-3611
Staunton **(G-13072)**

▲ Star Case Manufacturing Co LLC .....E...... 219 922-4440
Munster **(G-10630)**

Timber Line Crating LP ....F...... 260 238-3075
Spencerville **(G-13052)**

W & M Enterprises Inc ....E...... 812 537-4656
Lawrenceburg **(G-9161)**

Zehrhaus Inc ....G...... 260 486-3198
Fort Wayne **(G-4764)**

2451 Mobile Homes

Accent Complex Inc ....G...... 574 522-2368
Elkhart **(G-2664)**

Bayview Estates ....G...... 574 457-4136
Syracuse **(G-13129)**

Champion Home Builders Inc ....B...... 260 593-2962
Topeka **(G-13412)**

Clayton Homes Inc ....G...... 260 553-5500
Garrett **(G-4997)**

Clayton Homes Inc ....G...... 812 423-4052
Evansville **(G-3419)**

Commercial Structures Corp ....E...... 574 773-7931
Nappanee **(G-10661)**

Commercial Structures Corp ....G...... 574 773-7931
Goshen **(G-5191)**

Commodore Corporation ....C...... 574 534-3067
Goshen **(G-5192)**

Dutchtown Homes ....G...... 812 354-2197
Otwell **(G-11422)**

Fairmont Homes LLC ....C...... 574 773-7941
Nappanee **(G-10669)**

Fairmont Homes LLC ....G...... 574 773-2041
Nappanee **(G-10670)**

Fr Chinook LLC ....G...... 317 356-1666
Indianapolis **(G-6955)**

▼ Gulf Stream Coach Inc ....C...... 574 773-7761
Nappanee **(G-10677)**

Heritage Financial Group Inc ....D...... 574 522-8000
Elkhart **(G-2914)**

Hi-Tech Housing Inc ....D...... 574 848-5593
Bristol **(G-1062)**

Home Phone Inc ....G...... 812 280-3657
Jeffersonville **(G-8375)**

Jay Mobile Home Additions ....G...... 260 726-9274
Portland **(G-11830)**

Jobsite Trailer Corporation ....E...... 574 224-4000
Rochester **(G-12130)**

Kropf Industries Inc ....E...... 574 533-2171
Goshen **(G-5258)**

Lcf Enterprises LLC ....G...... 260 483-3248
Fort Wayne **(G-4428)**

Liberty Homes Inc ....D...... 574 533-0438
Goshen **(G-5265)**

Lippert Components Inc ....E...... 574 535-1125
Goshen **(G-5271)**

Lippert Components Inc ....D...... 574 535-1125
Goshen **(G-5268)**

Mark-Line Industries LLC ....C...... 574 825-5851
Bristol **(G-1068)**

Modular Builders Inc ....E...... 574 223-4934
Rochester **(G-12140)**

Rev Recreation Group Inc ....E...... 260 728-9564
Decatur **(G-2401)**

Rev Recreation Group Inc ....C...... 260 724-4217
Decatur **(G-2403)**

Rochester Homes Inc ....C...... 574 223-4321
Rochester **(G-12146)**

Rodeswood LLC ....G...... 574 457-4496
Syracuse **(G-13142)**

Skyline Champion Corporation ....B...... 574 294-6521
Elkhart **(G-3175)**

Skyline Corporation ....G...... 574 848-7621
Bristol **(G-1087)**

Skyline Homes Inc ....C...... 574 294-6521
Elkhart **(G-3176)**

Thornes Homes Inc ....G...... 812 275-4656
Bedford **(G-584)**

◆ Tyson Corporation ....E...... 317 241-8396
Indianapolis **(G-8119)**

Whitley Evergreen Inc ....D...... 260 723-5131
South Whitley **(G-13009)**

Woodland Park Inc ....D...... 574 825-2104
Middlebury **(G-9927)**

Zieman Manufacturing Company ....G...... 574 522-5202
Goshen **(G-5347)**

2452 Prefabricated Wood Buildings & Cmpnts

(ebs Composites) Engineered Bo ....F...... 574 266-3471
Elkhart **(G-2653)**

Affordable Luxury Homes Inc ....D...... 260 758-2141
Markle **(G-9575)**

All American Group Inc ....B...... 574 262-0123
Elkhart **(G-2676)**

◆ All American Group Inc ....G...... 574 262-0123
Elkhart **(G-2674)**

All American Homes LLC ....G...... 574 266-3044
Elkhart **(G-2677)**

All American Homes Indiana LLC ....B...... 260 724-9171
Decatur **(G-2366)**

Appalachian Log HMS Fultn Elc ....G...... 260 356-5431
Huntington **(G-6186)**

Appalachian Log Structures ....G...... 812 744-5711
Moores Hill **(G-10297)**

Burns Construction Inc ....E...... 574 382-2315
Macy **(G-9440)**

Burnside Enterprises ....G...... 765 664-4032
Marion **(G-9513)**

Classic Buildings Inc ....E...... 812 944-5821
Clarksville **(G-1677)**

Colluci Construction-Log Homes ....G...... 812 843-5607
English **(G-3312)**

Continntal Crpntry Cmpnnts LLC ....E...... 219 369-4839
Wanatah **(G-13823)**

Country Charm ....G...... 765 572-2588
Attica **(G-299)**

Craftech Building Systems Inc ....E...... 574 773-4167
Nappanee **(G-10665)**

Cross Modular Set Inc ....G...... 765 836-1511
New Castle **(G-10898)**

Custom Built Barns Inc ....G...... 765 457-9037
Kokomo **(G-8610)**

Delaware County Home Bldrs Inc ....G...... 765 289-6328
Muncie **(G-10456)**

E & L Construction Inc ....G...... 765 525-7081
Manilla **(G-9503)**

Edna Troyer ....G...... 260 894-4405
Ligonier **(G-9281)**

Expedition Log Homes ....G...... 219 663-5555
Crown Point **(G-2252)**

Hearthstone of Indiana ....G...... 812 988-2127
Nashville **(G-10725)**

Heritage Log Homes ....G...... 812 427-2591
Vevay **(G-13664)**

Heston Log Homes Inc ....G...... 219 778-4074
La Porte **(G-8763)**

Hi-Tech Housing Inc ....D...... 574 848-5593
Bristol **(G-1062)**

Homette Corporation ....G...... 574 294-6521
Elkhart **(G-2919)**

Itera LLC ....G...... 574 538-3838
New Paris **(G-10986)**

Jobsite Trailer Corporation ....E...... 574 224-4000
Rochester **(G-12130)**

Landmark Home & Land Co Inc ....G...... 219 874-4065
Michigan City **(G-9808)**

Lauer Log Homes ....G...... 260 486-7010
Fort Wayne **(G-4426)**

Light House Homes Center ....F...... 765 448-4502
Lafayette **(G-8957)**

Mbsi Holdings LLC ....G...... 574 295-1214
Elkhart **(G-3023)**

Midwest Fast Structures LLC ....G...... 812 886-3060
Vincennes **(G-13692)**

Miller Brothers Builders Inc ....E...... 574 533-8602
Goshen **(G-5293)**

Modular Builders Inc ....E...... 574 223-4934
Rochester **(G-12140)**

Morton Buildings Inc ....F...... 260 563-2118
Wabash **(G-13741)**

Mosier Pallet & Lumber Co ....G...... 812 366-4817
Corydon **(G-2105)**

Napoleon Lumber Co ....G...... 812 852-4545
Napoleon **(G-10641)**

Neubau Contracting ....G...... 970 406-8084
Bloomington **(G-779)**

New Castle Modular Inc ....F...... 765 521-0788
Indianapolis **(G-7584)**

Omega National Products LLC ....C 574 295-5353
Elkhart (G-3068)
Premier Strctres Acqsition Inc ....D 574 522-4011
Elkhart (G-3113)
Rochester Homes Inc ....C 574 223-4321
Rochester (G-12146)
Sidney & Janice Bond ....G 812 366-8160
Sellersburg (G-12415)
Skyline Champion Corporation ....B 574 294-6521
Elkhart (G-3175)
TNT Construction ....G 260 726-2643
Portland (G-11852)
Travis C and Jan B Page ....G 812 398-5507
Carlisle (G-1298)
Tri-State Homes and Garages ....G 812 867-2411
Evansville (G-3773)
Tuff Shed ....G 317 481-8388
Indianapolis (G-8111)
Ufp Nappanee LLC ....D 574 773-2505
Nappanee (G-10709)
Wagler Mini Barn Products ....G 812 687-7372
Plainville (G-11657)
Woodland Manufacturing & Sup ....F 317 271-2266
Avon (G-472)

2491 Wood Preserving

Babb Lumber Company Inc ....F 812 886-0551
Vincennes (G-13668)
Birch Wood ....G 260 432-0011
Fort Wayne (G-4110)
Bridgewell Resources LLC ....G 812 285-1811
Jeffersonville (G-8331)
Chinet Company ....G 219 989-7040
Hammond (G-5861)
▲ Frederick Tool Corp ....E 574 295-6700
Elkhart (G-2870)
Hampels Woodland Products ....G 574 293-2124
Elkhart (G-2906)
Jefferson Homebuilders Inc ....E 317 398-0874
Shelbyville (G-12541)
Kustom Kilms LLC ....G 317 512-5813
Columbus (G-1956)
Madelyn Harwood Inc ....G 317 839-7890
Plainfield (G-11622)
Preserving Past ....G 574 835-0833
Elkhart (G-3115)
Pumpkin Patch Market Inc ....G 574 825-3312
Middlebury (G-9915)
Railworks Wood Products Inc ....G 812 789-5331
Winslow (G-14358)
Rodeghero Enterprise ....G 574 935-0568
Plymouth (G-11723)
Steinkamp Warehouses Inc ....E 812 683-3860
Huntingburg (G-6179)
Stella-Jones Corporation ....F 812 789-5331
Winslow (G-14360)
Tangent Rail Products Inc ....E 412 325-0202
Terre Haute (G-13348)
Universal Forest Products Indi ....C 574 273-6326
Granger (G-5447)
Wood Medic Inc ....G 765 778-4544
Pendleton (G-11512)
Woodgrain Construction Inc ....G 317 873-5608
Zionsville (G-14471)

2493 Reconstituted Wood Prdts

Custom Marble Unlimited ....G 574 594-2948
Silver Lake (G-12676)
Good Earth Compost LLC ....G 812 824-7928
Bloomington (G-732)
Greif Inc ....G 219 746-3753
Lowell (G-9407)
Kay Company Inc ....E 765 659-3388
Frankfort (G-4840)
Michiana Column & Truss LLC ....G 574 862-2828
Wakarusa (G-13787)
Midwest Bc ....G 219 369-4839
La Porte (G-8793)
▲ Midwest Products Co Inc ....D 219 942-1134
Hobart (G-6092)
Patrick Industries Inc ....C 574 294-7511
Elkhart (G-3080)
Patrick Industries Inc ....E 574 294-5758
Elkhart (G-3083)
Standard Industries Inc ....C 812 838-4861
Mount Vernon (G-10409)
Standard Industries Inc ....C 219 872-1111
Michigan City (G-9847)

2499 Wood Prdts, NEC

A S M Inc ....G 260 724-8220
Decatur (G-2363)
Acorn Woodworks ....G 317 867-4377
Westfield (G-14133)
Action Cooling Towers Inc ....G 219 285-2660
Morocco (G-10359)
Alpine Enterprises ....G 574 773-5475
Nappanee (G-10645)
American Wedge Company Inc ....G 812 883-1086
Salem (G-12282)
Automated Routing Inc ....C 812 357-2429
Saint Meinrad (G-12274)
▲ Bendix Mc II ....G 260 356-9720
Huntington (G-6192)
Buckaroos Inc ....F 317 899-9100
Indianapolis (G-6518)
Carris Reels Inc ....F 269 545-3400
New Carlisle (G-10880)
Champion Wood Products Inc ....D 812 282-9460
Sellersburg (G-12391)
Cin-Nan Treasures ....G 574 533-6593
Goshen (G-5187)
Clm Pallet Recycling Inc ....G 317 485-4080
Fortville (G-4770)
Corr-Wood Manufacturing Inc ....E 812 867-0700
Evansville (G-3431)
County Line Woodworking ....G 574 935-7107
Bremen (G-994)
Custom Woodworks Inc ....G 317 867-2929
Westfield (G-14153)
Daed Toolworks ....G 317 861-7419
Greenfield (G-5518)
Daramic LLC ....C 812 738-8274
Corydon (G-2097)
Deer Ridgewood Craft LLC ....G 812 535-3744
West Terre Haute (G-14124)
Detweilers Cabinet Shop ....G 765 629-2698
Milroy (G-9979)
Display Craft ....G 260 726-4535
Portland (G-11816)
Dutch Country Woodworking Inc ....G 260 499-4847
Lagrange (G-9038)
Dynamic Designs Scottys ....G 219 809-7268
Michigan City (G-9787)
Earl Chupp ....G 574 372-8400
Etna Green (G-3320)
Earth First Kentuckiana Inc ....G 812 248-0712
Charlestown (G-1565)
Earth First Kentuckiana Inc ....G 812 923-1227
Greenville (G-5648)
Ecovantage LLC ....G 260 337-0338
Saint Joe (G-12254)
Editions Ltd Gallery Fine Arts ....G 317 466-9940
Indianapolis (G-6806)
Esarey Hardwood Creations LLC ....G 419 610-6486
New Albany (G-10773)
FDS Northwood LLC ....G 765 289-2481
Selma (G-12423)
Fort Wayne Box & Pallet LLC ....G 260 409-4067
Fort Wayne (G-4270)
G & J ....G 765 457-9889
Kokomo (G-8626)
Gessner Woodworking ....G 812 389-2594
Celestine (G-1535)
Gibbs Susie Framing & Art ....G 765 428-2434
Lafayette (G-8907)
Grabill Woodworking Specialty ....G 260 627-5982
Grabill (G-5371)
Green Thumb of Indiana Inc ....G 260 897-2319
Avilla (G-405)
Greencycle of Indiana Inc ....G 317 780-8175
Indianapolis (G-7043)
Greencycle of Indiana Inc ....G 317 769-5668
Whitestown (G-14253)
Handle With Care Packaging ....G 812 250-1920
Evansville (G-3530)
Handle With Kare LLC ....G 260 420-1698
Fort Wayne (G-4317)
Hardwoods By Bill LLC ....G 219 465-5346
Valparaiso (G-13554)
Hartley J Company Inc ....G 812 376-9708
Columbus (G-1938)
Hilltop Wood Working ....F 270 604-1962
Madison (G-9467)
Hjj Inc ....G 219 362-4421
La Porte (G-8765)
J M Woodworking Co Inc ....G 260 627-8362
Grabill (G-5374)

J R Newby ....G 765 664-3501
Marion (G-9537)
Jolar Enterprises ....G 574 875-8369
Elkhart (G-2950)
Jt-Fencing LLC ....G 765 323-8591
Lafayette (G-8934)
Koetter Woodworking ....F 812 923-8875
Borden (G-933)
L and D Custom Woodworking ....G 812 486-2958
Montgomery (G-10231)
Landmark Wood Products Inc ....F 812 338-2641
English (G-3314)
Lillsun Manufacturing Co Inc ....G 260 356-6514
Huntington (G-6223)
M & H Woodworking LLC ....G 812 486-2570
Montgomery (G-10233)
Marc Woodworking Inc ....D 317 635-9663
Indianapolis (G-7451)
Master Piece Krafts LLC ....G 260 768-4330
Shipshewana (G-12632)
Menard Inc ....A 812 466-1234
Terre Haute (G-13282)
Meyer Mill Oak Woodcrafters ....G 317 462-1413
Greenfield (G-5550)
Millers Woodnthings Inc ....F 574 825-2996
Middlebury (G-9911)
Mj Finishing ....G 574 646-2080
Bremen (G-1011)
MJB Wood Group Inc ....G 574 295-5228
Elkhart (G-3043)
Moores Country Wood Crafting ....F 317 984-3326
Arcadia (G-266)
Mossberg Industries Inc ....D 260 357-5141
Garrett (G-5018)
Natures Woodshop LLC ....G 317 691-1462
Indianapolis (G-7577)
North Woods Village ....G 574 247-1866
Mishawaka (G-10097)
Omega National Products LLC ....C 574 295-5353
Elkhart (G-3068)
Ostler Enterprises Inc ....G 765 656-1275
Frankfort (G-4847)
Outdoor Roomscapes Inc ....G 574 965-2009
Monticello (G-10276)
Patrick Industries Inc ....E 574 294-5758
Elkhart (G-3083)
Patrick Industries Inc ....D 574 522-6100
Elkhart (G-3086)
Pfortune Art & Design Inc ....G 317 872-4123
Indianapolis (G-7681)
Pgc Mulch LLC ....G 812 455-0700
Evansville (G-3667)
Pioneer Cane & Handle Co ....G 812 859-4415
Clay City (G-1705)
Pumpkin Patch Market Inc ....G 574 825-3312
Middlebury (G-9915)
Quality Fence Ltd ....G 260 768-4986
Shipshewana (G-12645)
R & R Custom Woodworking Inc ....E 574 773-5436
Nappanee (G-10703)
Rabers Whl Works & Buggy Works ....G 812 486-2786
Montgomery (G-10240)
Radecki Galleries Inc ....G 574 287-0266
South Bend (G-12913)
Reising Son Originals ....G 812 437-1831
Evansville (G-3703)
Riegseckers Woodworks Inc ....G 574 642-3504
Goshen (G-5318)
Roanoke Woodworking Inc ....G 260 672-8462
Roanoke (G-12107)
Robert W Sheffer ....G 219 464-2095
Valparaiso (G-13609)
▲ Roudebush Company Incorporated ...G 574 595-7115
Star City (G-13070)
Rpf Inc ....G 317 727-6386
Boggstown (G-902)
Sac Acquisition LLC ....G 317 575-1795
Indianapolis (G-7883)
Schmuckers Wood Shop ....G 260 485-1434
Fort Wayne (G-4609)
Schug Awards LLC ....G 765 447-0002
Lafayette (G-8996)
Serie Hardwoods Inc ....G 765 275-2321
Attica (G-309)
Sharon Sperry ....G 219 736-0121
Merrillville (G-9753)
Southern Indiana Sawmill LLC ....G 502 664-5723
Salem (G-12305)
Stitch N Frame ....G 260 478-1301
Fort Wayne (G-4649)

This & That Products ....G....... 812 299-2688
Terre Haute (G-13354)

Touchwood Trans Inc ....G....... 317 941-0009
Indianapolis (G-8083)

Ufp Nappanee LLC ....D....... 574 773-2505
Nappanee (G-10709)

Urban Logging Company LLC ....F....... 317 710-4070
Indianapolis (G-8133)

Vernon Sharp ....G....... 317 398-0631
Shelbyville (G-12582)

Voges Restoration and Wdwkg ....G....... 812 299-1546
Terre Haute (G-13364)

W & S Woodworking ....G....... 812 486-3673
Loogootee (G-9396)

▲ WC Redmon Co Inc ....F....... 765 473-6683
Peru (G-11556)

Weberdings Carving Shop Inc ....F....... 812 934-3710
Batesville (G-524)

Wildwood Floral Co LLC ....G....... 916 220-4900
Indianapolis (G-8197)

Wittmer Distributors ....G....... 812 636-7786
Odon (G-11345)

Woodhollow LLC ....G....... 219 384-2802
Highland (G-6060)

Woodland Lbor Rltons Cnsulting ....G....... 219 879-6095
Michigan City (G-9861)

Woodland Restoration LLC ....G....... 219 509-3078
Hebron (G-6025)

Woods of Amber ....G....... 765 763-6926
Morristown (G-10376)

Woods Unlimited Inc ....G....... 574 656-3382
North Liberty (G-11223)

Yb Normal Custom Wood Working ....G....... 260 338-2003
Huntertown (G-6149)

25 FURNITURE AND FIXTURES

2511 Wood Household Furniture

A L E Enterprises ....G....... 317 856-2981
Indianapolis (G-6297)

A S M Inc ....G....... 260 724-8220
Decatur (G-2363)

Able Woodcrafters LLC ....G....... 317 915-1225
Indianapolis (G-6311)

Als Woodcraft Inc ....F....... 812 967-4458
Borden (G-927)

Antreasian Design Inc ....F....... 317 546-3234
Indianapolis (G-6404)

Barry A Wilcox ....G....... 260 495-3677
Fremont (G-4951)

▼ Bedder Way Company Inc ....E....... 317 783-5105
Indianapolis (G-6463)

Beebe Cabinet Co Inc ....F....... 574 293-3580
Elkhart (G-2720)

Best Chairs Incorporated ....D....... 812 367-1761
Cannelton (G-1287)

Borkholder Corporation ....E....... 574 773-4083
Nappanee (G-10654)

Cabinetmaker Inc ....G....... 812 723-3461
Paoli (G-11446)

▲ Chromcraft Revington Inc ....E....... 662 562-8203
West Lafayette (G-14058)

Commercial Electric Co Inc ....E....... 260 726-9357
Portland (G-11813)

Coppes-Nappanee Company Inc ....F....... 574 773-0007
Nappanee (G-10663)

Cosco Inc ....A....... 812 372-0141
Columbus (G-1883)

Country Cabinets ....G....... 260 694-6777
Poneto (G-11745)

Country View Furn Mfg & Uphl ....G....... 812 636-5024
Odon (G-11321)

Country Woodshop LLC ....E....... 574 642-3681
Goshen (G-5194)

Custom Built Barns Inc ....G....... 765 457-9037
Kokomo (G-8610)

Custom Millwork & Display LLC ....G....... 574 289-9772
South Bend (G-12749)

▲ Custom Wood Products Inc ....D....... 574 522-3300
Elkhart (G-2784)

D & E Workshop ....G....... 260 593-0195
Topeka (G-13415)

Dmi Furniture Inc ....F....... 812 683-4035
Huntingburg (G-6156)

Dmi Furniture Inc ....G....... 812 683-2123
Huntingburg (G-6155)

Dorel Home Furnishings Inc ....B....... 812 372-0141
Columbus (G-1909)

▲ Dorel USA Inc ....D....... 812 372-0141
Columbus (G-1914)

Douglas Dye and Associates ....G....... 317 844-1709
Carmel (G-1362)

Dubois Wood Products Inc ....C....... 812 683-3613
Huntingburg (G-6158)

Dubois Wood Products Inc ....E....... 812 683-5105
Huntingburg (G-6159)

E & S Wood Creations LLC ....F....... 260 768-3033
Lagrange (G-9040)

Eagle Nest Workshop ....G....... 812 876-3215
Spencer (G-13023)

Ecojacks LLC ....G....... 574 306-0414
South Whitley (G-12998)

Ed Lloyd Co ....G....... 812 342-2505
Columbus (G-1917)

Edna Troyer ....G....... 260 894-4405
Ligonier (G-9281)

Efurnituremax LLC ....G....... 317 697-9504
Indianapolis (G-6811)

F & N Woodworking LLC ....F....... 260 463-8938
Lagrange (G-9041)

▲ Fehrenbacher Cabinets Inc ....E....... 812 963-3377
Evansville (G-3502)

Flat Rock Furniture Inc ....E....... 317 398-1501
Waldron (G-13798)

Fresh Start Inc ....G....... 812 254-3398
Washington (G-13982)

Georges Custom Wood Working ....G....... 812 944-3344
New Albany (G-10787)

Gloria J Burnworth ....G....... 765 366-3950
Attica (G-302)

Graber Manufacturing LLC ....G....... 260 657-3400
Grabill (G-5367)

Graber Woodworks Inc ....G....... 812 486-2861
Montgomery (G-10226)

Grabill Cabinet Company Inc ....C....... 877 472-2782
Grabill (G-5368)

▲ Haas Cabinet Co Inc ....E....... 812 246-4431
Sellersburg (G-12395)

Hackney Home Furnishings Inc ....E....... 317 895-4300
Indianapolis (G-7065)

▲ Heartwood Manufacturing Inc ....E....... 812 933-0388
Batesville (G-503)

Heritage Fine Furn & Cabinetry ....G....... 812 205-5437
Evansville (G-3538)

Hickory Furniture Designs Inc ....F....... 765 642-0700
Anderson (G-114)

Home & Lawn Services ....G....... 260 633-9155
Fort Wayne (G-4338)

Homestead Primitives Inc ....G....... 812 782-3521
Francisco (G-4816)

Hoosier Wood Creations Inc ....D....... 574 831-6330
New Paris (G-10983)

▲ Indiana Architectural Plywood ....E....... 317 878-4822
Trafalgar (G-13436)

Indianian Woodcrafts ....G....... 574 586-3741
Walkerton (G-13803)

J & J Woodcrafters ....G....... 765 436-2466
Thorntown (G-13376)

J Jesse Inc ....F....... 574 862-4538
Wakarusa (G-13780)

J Miller Cabinetry Inc ....G....... 260 691-2032
Columbia City (G-1800)

J W Woodworking Inc ....G....... 574 831-3033
New Paris (G-10987)

Jason Randall Designs ....G....... 317 319-6747
Kokomo (G-8650)

▲ Jasper Chair Company Inc ....D....... 812 482-5239
Jasper (G-8255)

Jds Pugh Cabinets Inc ....F....... 317 835-2910
Fairland (G-3822)

Johnny Bontrager ....G....... 260 463-8912
Lagrange (G-9050)

Kasnak Restorations Inc ....G....... 317 852-9770
Brownsburg (G-1159)

◆ Kimball International Inc ....B....... 812 482-1600
Jasper (G-8282)

Kountry Kraft Wood Products ....G....... 574 831-6736
New Paris (G-10988)

Kramer Furn & Cab Makers Inc ....F....... 812 526-2711
Edinburgh (G-2615)

L R Nisley & Sons ....F....... 574 642-1245
Goshen (G-5261)

Lambright Woodworking LLC ....E....... 260 593-2721
Topeka (G-13423)

Leibering Dimension Inc ....E....... 812 367-2971
Ferdinand (G-3856)

Lockerbie Square Cab Co Inc ....G....... 317 635-1134
Indianapolis (G-7413)

Madison Cabinets Inc ....G....... 260 639-3915
Hoagland (G-6066)

Martins Wood Works ....G....... 574 862-4080
Goshen (G-5281)

Merrill Manufacturing Inc ....F....... 812 752-6688
Scottsburg (G-12374)

▲ Middlebury Hardwood Pdts Inc ....C....... 574 825-9524
Middlebury (G-9907)

Millers Woodnthings Inc ....F....... 574 825-2996
Middlebury (G-9911)

Mission Woodworking Inc ....E....... 574 848-5697
Bristol (G-1069)

Mobel Incorporated ....C....... 812 367-1214
Ferdinand (G-3859)

Moores Country Wood Crafting ....F....... 317 984-3326
Arcadia (G-266)

▲ Numark Industries Company Ltd ......F....... 317 718-2502
Avon (G-459)

Oak Lief ....G....... 765 642-9010
Anderson (G-147)

Oeding Corporation ....G....... 812 367-1271
Ferdinand (G-3860)

▲ Ofs Brands Holdings Inc ....A....... 800 521-5381
Huntingburg (G-6177)

Old Barn Creations LLC ....G....... 219 324-2553
La Porte (G-8801)

Old Guy Woodcrafters LLC ....G....... 574 527-9044
Winona Lake (G-14352)

Out of Sight Screen Co Inc ....G....... 317 430-1705
Indianapolis (G-7638)

Patrick Industries Inc ....E....... 574 293-1521
Elkhart (G-3084)

▲ Philip Reinisch Company Llc ....C....... 812 326-2626
Saint Anthony (G-12249)

Progressive Woodcraft LLC ....G....... 574 546-9010
Bremen (G-1017)

Prolam Products Inc ....D....... 812 867-1662
Evansville (G-3687)

Ramer Chair Co ....G....... 574 862-4179
Goshen (G-5316)

Rbk Development Inc ....E....... 574 267-5879
Warsaw (G-13934)

REM Industries Inc ....E....... 574 862-2127
Wakarusa (G-13792)

Rentown Cabinets ....G....... 574 546-2569
Bremen (G-1020)

Ro Vic Wood Products Inc ....E....... 812 283-9199
Jeffersonville (G-8420)

Rodeswood LLC ....G....... 574 457-4496
Syracuse (G-13142)

▲ Roudebush Company Incorporated .G....... 574 595-7115
Star City (G-13070)

Rwb & Associates LLC ....G....... 317 219-6572
Noblesville (G-11178)

Sampler Inc ....F....... 765 663-2233
Homer (G-6109)

Schmidt Cabinet Co Inc ....E....... 812 347-1031
New Salisbury (G-11011)

Shamrock Cabinets Inc ....E....... 812 482-7969
Jasper (G-8308)

Streamside Woodshop LLC ....G....... 260 768-7887
Shipshewana (G-12654)

Stump Home Specialties Mfg Inc ....G....... 574 291-0050
South Bend (G-12959)

Superior Woodcrafts LLC ....G....... 260 357-3743
Garrett (G-5023)

Swartzndrber Hrdwood Creat LLC ....E....... 574 534-2502
Goshen (G-5337)

Swings N Things ....G....... 260 336-8811
Lagrange (G-9070)

Tdf of Indiana Inc ....G....... 812 597-4009
Morgantown (G-10358)

Thomasville Furniture Inds Inc ....G....... 336 476-2175
Hammond (G-5950)

Timber Creek Design Co Inc ....F....... 317 297-5336
Indianapolis (G-8075)

▲ Walters Cabinet Shop ....G....... 765 452-9634
Kokomo (G-8714)

▲ WC Redmon Co Inc ....F....... 765 473-6683
Peru (G-11556)

Weberdings Carving Shop Inc ....F....... 812 934-3710
Batesville (G-524)

William A Kadar ....G....... 219 884-7404
Gary (G-5116)

Wingards Sales LLC ....G....... 260 768-7961
Shipshewana (G-12659)

Woodcrafters LLC ....G....... 765 469-5103
Denver (G-2455)

▲ Woodcrest Manufacturing Inc ....D....... 765 472-4471
Peru (G-11559)

Woodcrest Manufacturing Inc ....F....... 765 472-5361
Peru (G-11560)

Wooden Concept Inc ....G....... 317 293-3137
Indianapolis (G-8213)

2512 Wood Household Furniture, Upholstered

Aaron Company Incorporated ....F 219 838-0852
Gary (G-5026)
◆ Best Chairs Incorporated ....A 812 367-1761
Ferdinand (G-3846)
Best Chairs Incorporated ....E 812 367-1761
Paoli (G-11445)
Best Chairs Incorporated ....D 812 367-1761
Cannelton (G-1287)
Campbell Cobert Woodcraft ....G....... 812 883-5399
Salem (G-12285)
▲ Chromcraft Revington Inc ....E 662 562-8203
West Lafayette (G-14058)
Coffeys Custom Upholstery ....G....... 812 948-8611
New Albany (G-10763)
Country View Furn Mfg & Uphl ....G....... 812 636-5024
Odon (G-11321)
▲ Custom Wood Products Inc ....D 574 522-3300
Elkhart (G-2784)
Design Works Inc ....G....... 317 815-8619
Fishers (G-3899)
Furniture Sales & Marketing ....G....... 317 849-1508
Indianapolis (G-6970)
▼ Home Reserve LLC ....F 260 969-6939
Fort Wayne (G-4339)
▲ Jasper Chair Company Inc ....D 812 482-5239
Jasper (G-8255)
◆ Kimball International Inc ....B 812 482-1600
Jasper (G-8282)
KMC Corporation ....D 574 267-7033
Warsaw (G-13898)
Mastercraft Inc ....C 260 463-8702
Lagrange (G-9060)
Peggy Williams ....G....... 765 724-3862
Alexandria (G-47)
▲ Seating Technology Inc ....C 574 971-4100
Goshen (G-5322)
Shelby Westside Upholstering ....G....... 317 631-8911
Indianapolis (G-7931)
▲ Smith Brothers Berne Inc................B 260 589-2131
Berne (G-623)
Sylvia Kay Hartley ....G....... 317 984-3424
Arcadia (G-270)
Transformations By Wieland Inc ....D 800 440-9337
Fort Wayne (G-4698)
Vans TV & Appliance Inc ....F 260 927-8267
Auburn (G-366)
Williamsburg Furniture Inc ....G....... 574 387-5691
South Bend (G-12991)
▲ Williamsburg Furniture Inc ....C 800 582-8183
Nappanee (G-10710)

2514 Metal Household Furniture

▲ Austin-Westran LLC........................C 815 234-2811
Indianapolis (G-6441)
Best Chairs Incorporated ....D 812 367-1761
Cannelton (G-1287)
Bo-Mar Industries Inc ....E 317 899-1240
Indianapolis (G-6491)
Cosco Inc ....A 812 372-0141
Columbus (G-1883)
Delta Excell Incorporated ....E 765 642-0288
Anderson (G-93)
▲ Dorel USA Inc ....D 812 372-0141
Columbus (G-1914)
Flambeau Inc ....C 812 372-4899
Columbus (G-1931)
Hoosier Wallbeds Inc ....G....... 812 926-0055
Aurora (G-379)
Lakemaster Inc ....E 765 288-3718
Muncie (G-10507)
Mastercraft Inc ....C 260 463-8702
Lagrange (G-9060)
Mehringer Metal Design LLC ....G....... 812 634-6100
Jasper (G-8294)
Mouron & Company Inc ....F 317 243-7955
Indianapolis (G-7551)
▲ Pinnacle Seating Inc ....G....... 574 522-2636
Elkhart (G-3096)
◆ Poly-Wood LLC...............................D 574 457-3284
Syracuse (G-13140)
Prolam Products Inc ....D 812 867-1662
Evansville (G-3687)
▲ Seating Technology Inc ....C 574 971-4100
Goshen (G-5322)

Stainless Steel Kitchens ....G....... 574 272-2530
Granger (G-5440)
▲ Valley Line Wood Products LLC ......G....... 260 768-7807
Shipshewana (G-12655)
▲ Wabash Valley Manufacturing ....C 260 352-2102
Silver Lake (G-12682)
Warren Homes Inc ....G....... 812 882-1059
Vincennes (G-13716)

2515 Mattresses & Bedsprings

◆ Derby Inc ....D 574 233-4500
South Bend (G-12751)
Elkhart Bedding Co Inc ....F 574 293-6200
Elkhart (G-2820)
Firesmoke Org ....G....... 317 690-2542
Indianapolis (G-6923)
Futon Factory Inc ....F 317 549-8639
Indianapolis (G-6971)
Holder Bedding Inc ....G....... 765 642-1256
Anderson (G-115)
Holder Bedding Inc ....G....... 765 447-7907
Lafayette (G-8916)
I C Mattresses & More LLC ....G....... 765 635-7239
Summitville (G-13099)
Kimalco Inc ....G....... 812 463-3105
Evansville (G-3589)
KMC Corporation ....D 574 267-7033
Warsaw (G-13898)
Leggett & Platt Incorporated................B 219 866-7181
Rensselaer (G-11931)
Leggett & Platt Incorporated................D 219 766-2261
Kouts (G-8717)
Leggett & Platt Incorporated................C 260 347-2600
Kendallville (G-8490)
Loewenstein Furniture Inc ....G....... 800 521-5381
Huntingburg (G-6174)
Mastercraft Inc ....C 260 463-8702
Lagrange (G-9060)
May and Co Inc ....E 317 236-6500
Greenwood (G-5724)
▲ Seating Technology Inc ....C 574 971-4100
Goshen (G-5322)
Sleepmadecom LLC ....C 662 350-0999
Evansville (G-3734)
Solotat Industries LLC ....G....... 574 320-1436
Elkhart (G-3180)
Superior Mattress Inc ....G....... 812 422-5761
Evansville (G-3754)
Vans TV & Appliance Inc ....F 260 927-8267
Auburn (G-366)
Williamsburg Furniture Inc ....G....... 574 387-5691
South Bend (G-12991)
▲ Williamsburg Furniture Inc ....C 800 582-8183
Nappanee (G-10710)
◆ Wolf Corporation ....E 260 749-9393
Fort Wayne (G-4760)
Woodcrest Manufacturing Inc ....F 765 472-5361
Peru (G-11560)

2517 Wood T V, Radio, Phono & Sewing Cabinets

Eds Wood Craft ....G....... 812 768-6617
Haubstadt (G-6000)
▲ Fehrenbacher Cabinets Inc ....E 812 963-3377
Evansville (G-3502)
Graber Cabinetry LLC..........................E 260 627-2243
Grabill (G-5366)
Heather Sound Amplification ....G....... 574 255-6100
Mishawaka (G-10049)
Innovative Corp ....E 317 804-5977
Westfield (G-14171)
J & J Woodcrafters ....G....... 765 436-2466
Thorntown (G-13376)
◆ Kimball International Inc ....B 812 482-1600
Jasper (G-8282)
Larry Graber Cabinets ....G....... 812 486-2713
Montgomery (G-10232)
Madison Cabinets Inc ....G....... 260 639-3915
Hoagland (G-6066)
Rbk Development Inc ....E 574 267-5879
Warsaw (G-13934)
Sew Creative Threads LLC ....G....... 574 266-7397
Elkhart (G-3163)
Shamrock Cabinets Inc ....E 812 482-7969
Jasper (G-8308)
Timberline Woodworking Inc ....G....... 219 766-2733
Kouts (G-8718)
▲ Walters Cabinet Shop ....G....... 765 452-9634
Kokomo (G-8714)

William A Kadar..................................G....... 219 884-7404
Gary (G-5116)

2519 Household Furniture, NEC

▲ Aristocrat Inc ....G....... 812 634-0460
Jasper (G-8236)
Beachfront Furniture ....F 574 875-0817
Elkhart (G-2719)
Boardworks Inc ....G....... 219 464-8111
Valparaiso (G-13511)
Columbus Cstm Cbinets Furn LLC ......G....... 812 379-9411
Columbus (G-1875)
▲ Dimensions Furniture Inc................F 317 218-0025
Carmel (G-1361)
Ditto Sales Inc ....G....... 812 424-4098
Evansville (G-3460)
Ed and Daves Wood Chips LLC ....G....... 574 699-1263
Galveston (G-4994)
Keter North America LLC ....G....... 765 298-6800
Anderson (G-129)
Laminique Inc ....E 765 482-4222
Lebanon (G-9197)
Loewenstein Furniture Inc ....G....... 800 521-5381
Huntingburg (G-6174)
Midwest Cabinet Solutions Inc ....F 765 664-3938
Marion (G-9547)
Myers Designs Inc ....G....... 317 955-2450
Logansport (G-9356)
Resin Partners Inc ....D 765 724-7761
Alexandria (G-51)
Useful Home Products LLC ....G....... 765 459-0095
Kokomo (G-8711)
Weaver Fine Cabinets Furniture............G....... 812 342-4833
Columbus (G-2031)

2521 Wood Office Furniture

A L E Enterprises ....G....... 317 856-2981
Indianapolis (G-6297)
Antreasian Design Inc ....F 317 546-3234
Indianapolis (G-6404)
Aynes Upholstery LLC ....G....... 812 829-1321
Freedom (G-4947)
Beebe Cabinet Co Inc ....F 574 293-3580
Elkhart (G-2720)
▲ Chromcraft Revington Inc ....E 662 562-8203
West Lafayette (G-14058)
Custom Hardwood Cabinetry ....G....... 260 623-3147
Monroeville (G-10193)
Custom Millwork & Display LLC...........G....... 574 289-9772
South Bend (G-12749)
▲ Custom Wood Products Inc ....D 574 522-3300
Elkhart (G-2784)
Dbisp LLC...F 317 222-1671
Indianapolis (G-6729)
Delbert Kemp ....E 812 486-3325
Montgomery (G-10222)
Dmi Furniture Inc ....G....... 812 683-2123
Huntingburg (G-6155)
Double T Manufacturing Corp ....F 574 262-1340
Elkhart (G-2799)
Dubois Wood Realty Inc ....C 812 683-3613
Huntingburg (G-6160)
Ecojacks LLC ....G....... 574 306-0414
South Whitley (G-12998)
Eds Wood Craft ....G....... 812 768-6617
Haubstadt (G-6000)
◆ Environmental Products Inc ....F 219 393-3446
Kingsbury (G-8537)
Gehl Industries Inc ....F 574 773-7663
Nappanee (G-10672)
Graber Cabinetry LLC..........................E 260 627-2243
Grabill (G-5366)
Great American Desk Co Inc ....F 574 293-3591
Elkhart (G-2896)
Hensley Custom Cabinetry ....G....... 219 843-5331
Rensselaer (G-11927)
Indiana Furniture Inds Inc ....C 812 678-2396
Dubois (G-2476)
Indiana Southern Millwork Inc ....G....... 812 346-6129
North Vernon (G-11263)
▲ Izzy Plus ....G....... 574 821-1200
Middlebury (G-9895)
J W Woodworking Inc ....G....... 574 831-3033
New Paris (G-10987)
▲ Jasper Chair Company Inc ....D 812 482-5239
Jasper (G-8255)
Jasper Desk Company Inc ....F 812 482-4132
Jasper (G-8256)
Jasper Desk Company Inc ....D 812 482-6827
Jasper (G-8257)

▲ Jasper Seating Company Inc ....A 812 482-3204
Jasper *(G-8264)*

Jasper Seating Company Inc ......D 812 936-9977
French Lick *(G-4987)*

Jasper Seating Company Inc ......D 812 326-2361
Saint Anthony *(G-12247)*

Jasper Seating Company Inc ......D 812 723-1323
Paoli *(G-11454)*

Jofco Inc ....C 812 482-5154
Jasper *(G-8268)*

◆ Jofco Inc ....C 812 482-5154
Jasper *(G-8267)*

Johnco Corp ....G 317 576-4417
Indianapolis *(G-7308)*

Jsj Furniture Corporation ......C 574 825-5871
Middlebury *(G-9899)*

◆ Kimball Furniture Group LLC ....C 812 482-1600
Jasper *(G-8279)*

◆ Kimball International Inc ....B 812 482-1600
Jasper *(G-8282)*

Knox County Association ....G 812 886-4312
Vincennes *(G-13689)*

Laminated Tops of Terre Haute ....G 812 235-2920
Terre Haute *(G-13271)*

Leroy E Doty Cabinet Shop ....G 219 663-1139
Crown Point *(G-2275)*

Millmade Inc ....G 812 424-7778
Evansville *(G-3629)*

Mouron & Company Inc ....F 317 243-7955
Indianapolis *(G-7551)*

◆ National Office Furniture Inc ....C 812 482-1600
Jasper *(G-8298)*

▲ Ofs Brands Holdings Inc ....A 800 521-5381
Huntingburg *(G-6177)*

Rabb & Howe Cabinet Top Co ......F 317 926-6442
Indianapolis *(G-7811)*

Shamrock Cabinets Inc ....E 812 482-7969
Jasper *(G-8308)*

Steffy Wood Products Inc ....E 260 665-8016
Angola *(G-246)*

Swartzndrber Hrdwood Creat LLC ....E 574 534-2502
Goshen *(G-5337)*

2522 Office Furniture, Except Wood

All State Manufacturing Co Inc ....F 812 466-2276
Terre Haute *(G-13191)*

Apollo Outdoor Cstm Design Inc ....F 317 718-2502
Avon *(G-428)*

Deerwood Group ....G 219 866-5521
Monon *(G-10175)*

◆ Environmental Products Inc ....F 219 393-3446
Kingsbury *(G-8537)*

F D Ramsey & Co Inc ....F 219 362-2452
La Porte *(G-8757)*

Fire King International LLC ....E 812 948-2795
New Albany *(G-10779)*

◆ Fire King Security Pdts LLC ....C 812 948-8400
New Albany *(G-10780)*

◆ Fki Security Group LLC ....B 812 948-8400
New Albany *(G-10781)*

Genesis Products Inc ....E 574 262-4054
Elkhart *(G-2877)*

Gjs Home and Office Furniture ....G 765 472-2478
Peru *(G-11528)*

▲ Global ....G 317 494-6174
Franklin *(G-4889)*

Great American Desk Co Inc ....F 574 293-3591
Elkhart *(G-2896)*

Growth Principals LLC ....G 812 320-1574
Bloomington *(G-735)*

▲ Jasper Chair Company Inc ......D 812 482-5239
Jasper *(G-8255)*

Jasper Seating Company Inc ......D 812 723-1323
Paoli *(G-11454)*

▲ Jasper Seating Company Inc ....A 812 482-3204
Jasper *(G-8264)*

Jsj Furniture Corporation ....C 574 825-5871
Middlebury *(G-9899)*

Kimball Furniture Group LLC ....G 812 482-8517
Jasper *(G-8276)*

Kimball Furniture Group LLC ....B 812 634-3526
Jasper *(G-8277)*

Kimball Furniture Group LLC ....C 812 883-1850
Salem *(G-12297)*

◆ Kimball Furniture Group LLC ....C 812 482-1600
Jasper *(G-8279)*

◆ Kimball International Inc ....B 812 482-1600
Jasper *(G-8282)*

▲ Kimball National Office F ....G 812 634-3356
Jasper *(G-8283)*

Kimball Office Inc ....F 812 634-3220
Jasper *(G-8284)*

▲ Kimball Office Inc ....B 812 482-1600
Jasper *(G-8285)*

Kramer Furn & Cab Makers Inc ....F 812 526-2711
Edinburgh *(G-2615)*

Lui Plus ....G 812 309-9350
Indianapolis *(G-7425)*

Meilink Safe Company ....E 812 941-0024
New Albany *(G-10825)*

▲ Modernfold Inc ....C 800 869-9685
Greenfield *(G-5557)*

Office Furniture Warehouse Inc ....G 317 872-6477
Indianapolis *(G-7611)*

▲ Ofs Brands Holdings Inc ....A 800 521-5381
Huntingburg *(G-6177)*

▲ Pinnacle Seating Inc ....G 574 522-2636
Elkhart *(G-3096)*

Pulley-Kellam Co Inc ....E 260 356-6326
Huntington *(G-6240)*

Trendway Corporation ....F 317 870-3269
Indianapolis *(G-8094)*

Unique Global Solutions LLC ....G 765 779-5030
Anderson *(G-180)*

2531 Public Building & Related Furniture

Advanced Assembly LLC ....F 260 244-1700
Columbia City *(G-1761)*

▲ Chromcraft Revington Inc ....E 662 562-8203
West Lafayette *(G-14058)*

Cinematic Captioning Systems ....G 317 862-3418
Indianapolis *(G-6606)*

Clayton Dant Corporation ....G 317 842-2420
Fishers *(G-3891)*

County of Steuben ....G 260 833-2401
Angola *(G-205)*

Custom Millwork & Display LLC ....G 574 289-9772
South Bend *(G-12749)*

▲ Custom Wood Products Inc ......D 574 522-3300
Elkhart *(G-2784)*

Erl Properties Inc ....E 812 948-8484
New Albany *(G-10772)*

Fbsa LLC ....E 574 542-2001
Rochester *(G-12123)*

Fiberglass Engrg & Design Inc ....G 317 293-0002
Indianapolis *(G-6918)*

Finish Design Woodworking Inc ....E 812 284-9240
Jeffersonville *(G-8360)*

Fisher & Company Incorporated ....C 586 746-2000
Evansville *(G-3505)*

H John Enterprise Inc ....E 574 293-6008
Elkhart *(G-2903)*

Integrated Mfg & Assembly LLC ....B 260 244-1700
Columbia City *(G-1797)*

▲ Jasper Chair Company Inc ......D 812 482-5239
Jasper *(G-8255)*

▲ Jasper Seating Company Inc ....A 812 482-3204
Jasper *(G-8264)*

Johnson Controls Inc ......D 317 917-5043
Pittsboro *(G-11583)*

Johnson Controls Inc ......D 260 347-0500
Kendallville *(G-8481)*

Johnson Controls Inc ......D 219 736-7105
Crown Point *(G-2269)*

Johnson Controls Inc ......D 260 485-9999
Fort Wayne *(G-4398)*

Johnson Controls Inc ......C 260 479-4400
Fort Wayne *(G-4399)*

Johnson Controls Inc ......F 812 868-1374
Evansville *(G-3578)*

Jsj Furniture Corporation ......C 256 768-2871
Middlebury *(G-9898)*

Lakemaster Inc ....E 765 288-3718
Muncie *(G-10507)*

Lear Corporation ....B 219 852-0014
Hammond *(G-5907)*

Lippert Components Inc ....F 574 534-8177
Goshen *(G-5266)*

Lippert Components Inc ......D 574 534-2163
Goshen *(G-5270)*

Lippert Components Inc ....E 574 295-8166
Elkhart *(G-3001)*

▼ National Rcreation Systems Inc ....E 260 482-6023
Fort Wayne *(G-4491)*

▲ Nhk Seating of America Inc ....E 765 659-4781
Frankfort *(G-4844)*

Norco Industries Inc ....C 574 262-3400
Elkhart *(G-3065)*

▲ Nvb Playgrounds Inc ....G 317 826-2777
Indianapolis *(G-7607)*

Pauls Seating Inc ....G 574 522-0630
Elkhart *(G-3093)*

Preferred Seating Company LLC ....G 317 782-3323
Indianapolis *(G-7740)*

R&D Investment Holdings Inc ....E 260 749-1301
Fort Wayne *(G-4575)*

Recreation Insites LLC ....G 317 578-0588
Fishers *(G-3961)*

Recycle Design Inc ....G 765 374-0316
Anderson *(G-159)*

REM Industries Inc ....E 574 862-2127
Wakarusa *(G-13792)*

Sauder Woodworking Co ....G 800 537-1530
Grabill *(G-5384)*

Superior Seating Inc ....E 574 389-9011
Elkhart *(G-3200)*

T F S Inc ....G 260 422-5896
Fort Wayne *(G-4672)*

Tls By Design ....F 765 683-1971
Indianapolis *(G-8077)*

Toyota Boshoku America Inc ....E 812 385-2040
Princeton *(G-11884)*

▲ Toyota Boshoku Indiana LLC ....A 812 491-9100
Princeton *(G-11886)*

▲ Transportation Tech Inds ....E 812 962-5000
Evansville *(G-3769)*

▲ TS Tech Indiana LLC ....G 765 465-4294
New Castle *(G-10920)*

▼ Veada Industries Inc ....A 574 831-4775
New Paris *(G-11000)*

Weberdings Carving Shop Inc ....F 812 934-3710
Batesville *(G-524)*

Wolf Technical Engineering LLC ....G 800 783-9653
Indianapolis *(G-8209)*

2541 Wood, Office & Store Fixtures

A L Brewster Plywood Inc ....G 765 378-1040
Chesterfield *(G-1586)*

▼ American Stonecast Pdts Inc ....F 574 206-0097
Elkhart *(G-2686)*

Beebe Cabinet Co Inc ....F 574 293-3580
Elkhart *(G-2720)*

Boardworks Inc ....G 219 464-8111
Valparaiso *(G-13511)*

Bright Ideas LLC ....G 574 295-5533
Elkhart *(G-2735)*

▲ Cabinets & Counters Inc ....E 812 858-3300
Newburgh *(G-11023)*

Carmel Countertops Inc ....G 317 843-0331
Carmel *(G-1330)*

Classic Cabinetry ....G 317 823-1853
Indianapolis *(G-6617)*

Coppes-Nappanee Company Inc ....F 574 773-0007
Nappanee *(G-10663)*

Counter Design Co Inc ....E 812 477-1243
Evansville *(G-3432)*

Countertop Connections Inc ....G 317 822-9858
Franklin *(G-4878)*

Crown Cab & Counter Top Inc ....F 219 663-2725
Crown Point *(G-2238)*

Crown Supply Co Inc ....F 812 522-6987
Seymour *(G-12440)*

Custom Counters Inc ....G 812 546-0052
Columbus *(G-1903)*

Custom Design Laminates Inc ....F 574 674-9174
Osceola *(G-11375)*

Deem & Loureiro Inc ....G 770 652-9871
Indianapolis *(G-6731)*

Double T Manufacturing Corp ....F 574 262-1340
Elkhart *(G-2799)*

Eash LLC ....F 574 295-4450
Elkhart *(G-2811)*

Eds Wood Craft ....G 812 768-6617
Haubstadt *(G-6000)*

Elko Inc ....E 812 473-8400
Evansville *(G-3473)*

▼ Ell Enterprises Inc ....G 317 783-7838
Indianapolis *(G-6841)*

Euronique Inc ....E 812 983-3337
Elberfeld *(G-2634)*

▲ Fehrenbacher Cabinets Inc ....E 812 963-3377
Evansville *(G-3502)*

Fisher Specialties Inc ....G 260 385-8251
Harlan *(G-5971)*

Franks Wood Shop ....G 317 738-2039
Franklin *(G-4887)*

Freedom Valley Cabinets ....G 812 875-2509
Freedom *(G-4948)*

Garyrae Inc ....F 574 255-7141
Mishawaka *(G-10045)*

Gotokiosk LLC ....G...... 800 206-0177
Monroe (G-10182)
Graber Cabinetry LLC..........................E...... 260 627-2243
Grabill (G-5366)
H & S Custom Countertops Inc ....G...... 812 422-6314
Evansville (G-3526)
▲ Horizon Terra Incorporated ....D...... 812 280-0000
Jeffersonville (G-8377)
Indiana Southern Millwork Inc ....E...... 812 346-6129
North Vernon (G-11263)
▲ Interior Design Surfaces Inc ....E...... 317 829-3970
Carmel (G-1417)
J G Bowers Inc ....E...... 765 677-1000
Marion (G-9536)
J Jesse Inc ....F...... 574 862-4538
Wakarusa (G-13780)
J W Woodworking Inc ....G...... 574 831-3033
New Paris (G-10987)
▲ JC Moag Corporation ....D...... 812 284-8400
Jeffersonville (G-8383)
Jensen Cabinet Inc ....E...... 260 456-2131
Fort Wayne (G-4394)
Jurgen Associates Inc ....G...... 317 786-3513
Indianapolis (G-7322)
Keystone Designs Inc ....E...... 574 269-5531
Warsaw (G-13897)
Kline Cabinet Makers LLC ....F...... 317 326-3049
Maxwell (G-9662)
Lambright Woodworking LLC ....E...... 260 593-2721
Topeka (G-13423)
Lami-Crafts Inc ....G...... 812 232-3012
Terre Haute (G-13270)
Laminated Tops of Central Ind ....E...... 812 824-6299
Bloomington (G-763)
Laminique Inc ....E...... 765 482-4222
Lebanon (G-9197)
Lawrence Shirks ....G...... 574 223-5118
Rochester (G-12133)
Lue Manufacturing Inc ....F...... 574 862-4249
Wakarusa (G-13783)
Mica Shop Inc ....E...... 574 533-1102
Goshen (G-5287)
Michiana Laminated Products ....F...... 260 562-2871
Howe (G-6129)
▲ Middlebury Hardwood Pdts Inc ....C...... 574 825-9524
Middlebury (G-9907)
Millwood Custom Cabinets ....G...... 574 646-3009
Etna Green (G-3322)
Mishawaka Whse & Distrg LLC ....G...... 574 259-6011
Mishawaka (G-10093)
Mission Woodworking Inc ....E...... 574 848-5697
Bristol (G-1069)
Molargik Woodworking Inc ....G...... 260 357-6625
Garrett (G-5016)
Mouron & Company Inc ....F...... 317 243-7955
Indianapolis (G-7551)
Newlett Inc ....D...... 574 294-8899
Elkhart (G-3061)
▲ Our Country Home Entps Inc ....D...... 260 657-5605
Harlan (G-5974)
Patrick Industries Inc ....E...... 574 294-5758
Elkhart (G-3083)
Patrick Industries Inc ....E...... 574 293-1521
Elkhart (G-3084)
Perfection Kitchen & Bath Ctr ....G...... 765 289-7594
Selma (G-12425)
Plastic Line Manufacturing ....E...... 219 769-8022
Merrillville (G-9747)
Platinum Display Group ....G...... 317 731-5026
Indianapolis (G-7701)
Precision Millwork & Plas Inc ....E...... 574 243-8720
South Bend (G-12902)
▲ Precision Stone Works ....F...... 812 683-1102
Huntingburg (G-6178)
Premier Kitchen & Bath Inc...................G...... 574 294-6805
Elkhart (G-3111)
Premium Srfc Fbrication of Ind ....E...... 317 867-1013
Westfield (G-14181)
Prolam Products Inc ....D...... 812 867-1662
Evansville (G-3687)
Psd and More LLC ....G...... 317 770-4577
Noblesville (G-11167)
Ptf Cabinets & Tops LLC ....G...... 317 786-4367
Indianapolis (G-7787)
Quality Surfaces Inc ....E...... 812 876-5838
Spencer (G-13034)
Rabb & Howe Cabinet Top Co ....F...... 317 926-6442
Indianapolis (G-7811)
Rbk Development Inc ....E...... 574 267-5879
Warsaw (G-13934)

Reeds Plastic Tops Inc ....G...... 765 282-1471
Muncie (G-10556)
Sims Cabinet Co Inc ....E...... 317 634-1747
Indianapolis (G-7948)
SJS Components LLC ....G...... 260 578-0192
Warsaw (G-13941)
Solid Surface Craftsmen Inc ....G...... 317 535-2333
Whiteland (G-14246)
Timberline Woodworking Inc ....G...... 219 766-2733
Kouts (G-8718)
Tremain Ceramic Tile & Flr Cvg ....E...... 317 542-1491
Indianapolis (G-8093)
Tristate Plastic Tops ....G...... 812 853-7827
Newburgh (G-11053)
Wagners Plasti Craft Co ....G...... 260 627-3147
Fort Wayne (G-4731)
▲ Walters Cabinet Shop ....G...... 765 452-9634
Kokomo (G-8714)
Wert Fixture & Display Inc ....G...... 317 577-0905
Indianapolis (G-8184)
▼ Wood Technologies LLC ....E...... 260 627-8858
Grabill (G-5385)
Woods Unlimited Inc ....G...... 574 656-3382
North Liberty (G-11223)
Zehrhaus Inc ....G...... 260 486-3198
Fort Wayne (G-4764)

2542 Partitions & Fixtures, Except Wood

▼ A & A Sheet Metal Products ....D...... 219 326-1288
La Porte (G-8725)
Burns Cabinets and Disp Inc ....G...... 260 897-2219
Avilla (G-401)
▲ Cabinets & Counters Inc ....E...... 812 858-3300
Newburgh (G-11023)
Carr Metal Products Inc ....C...... 317 542-0691
Indianapolis (G-6558)
Cottom Automated Bus Soluti ....G...... 317 853-6531
Carmel (G-1346)
Creative Industries Inc ....F...... 317 248-1102
Indianapolis (G-6688)
Crown Cab & Counter Top Inc ....F...... 219 663-2725
Crown Point (G-2238)
▲ Deflecto LLC ....B...... 317 849-9555
Indianapolis (G-6732)
Elkhart Brass Manufacturing Co ....F...... 800 346-0250
Elkhart (G-2822)
Flambeau Inc ....C...... 812 372-4899
Columbus (G-1931)
Galaxy Arts ....G...... 219 836-6033
Munster (G-10604)
Georg Utz Inc ....E...... 812 526-2240
Edinburgh (G-2612)
Hitzer Inc ....E...... 260 589-8536
Berne (G-617)
Idx Corporation ....C...... 812 280-0000
Jeffersonville (G-8379)
Leggett & Platt Incorporated ....C...... 574 825-9561
Middlebury (G-9902)
▲ Metal Dynamics Ltd ....E...... 812 949-7998
New Albany (G-10826)
▲ Modernfold Inc ....C...... 800 869-9685
Greenfield (G-5557)
Organized Living Inc ....C...... 812 334-8839
Bloomington (G-791)
Patrick Industries Inc ....E...... 574 293-1521
Elkhart (G-3084)
Plastic Line Manufacturing ....E...... 219 769-8022
Merrillville (G-9747)
Precision Millwork & Plas Inc ....E...... 574 243-8720
South Bend (G-12902)
R Concepts Industries Inc ....D...... 574 295-6641
Elkhart (G-3135)
Shamrock Cabinets Inc ....E...... 812 482-7969
Jasper (G-8308)
Solid Surface Craftsmen Inc ....G...... 317 535-2333
Whiteland (G-14246)
Star Nova US LLC ....G...... 269 830-5802
South Bend (G-12954)
Tamwall Inc ....F...... 317 546-5055
Indianapolis (G-8034)
Title Ten Manufacturing LLC ....G...... 765 388-2482
Muncie (G-10570)
▲ Tru-Form Steel & Wire Inc ....E...... 765 348-5001
Hartford City (G-5993)
Wick - Fab Inc ....E...... 260 897-3303
Avilla (G-421)
William A Kadar ....G...... 219 884-7404
Gary (G-5116)

2591 Drapery Hardware, Window Blinds & Shades

A-1 Shade Co ....G...... 317 247-6447
Indianapolis (G-6303)
▲ Ascot Enterprises Inc ....E...... 877 773-7751
Nappanee (G-10648)
Ascot Enterprises Inc ....D...... 574 773-7751
Nappanee (G-10649)
Ascot Enterprises Inc ....D...... 574 773-3104
Nappanee (G-10650)
Beauti Pleat Draperies Inc ....G...... 317 887-1728
Greenwood (G-5669)
Continental Express ....G...... 574 294-5684
Elkhart (G-2770)
Custom Blind Co ....G...... 812 867-9280
Evansville (G-3449)
Custom Draperies of Indiana ....G...... 219 924-2500
Hammond (G-5867)
◆ Draper Inc ....B...... 765 987-7999
Spiceland (G-13054)
Greenwood Draperie Corp ....G...... 317 882-0130
Greenwood (G-5699)
Horizon Vinyl Windows Inc ....G...... 260 632-0207
Woodburn (G-14384)
▲ Irvine Shade & Door Inc ....G...... 574 522-1446
Elkhart (G-2940)
J P Whitt Inc ....G...... 765 759-0521
Muncie (G-10498)
▲ Lafayette Venetian Blind Inc ....A...... 765 464-2500
West Lafayette (G-14082)
Leeps Supply Co ....G...... 219 696-9511
Lowell (G-9413)
Merin Interiors Indianapolis ....G...... 317 251-6603
Indianapolis (G-7482)
Midwest Blind & Shade Co ....G...... 574 271-0770
Mishawaka (G-10085)
Mill End Drapery Inc ....G...... 317 257-4800
Indianapolis (G-7518)
Mitchell Fabrics Inc ....E...... 309 674-8631
Lafayette (G-8971)
▲ Oxford House Incorporated ....D...... 765 884-3265
Fowler (G-4803)
United Services Inc ....G...... 812 989-3320
Clarksville (G-1698)
▲ United Shade LLC ....D...... 574 262-0954
Elkhart (G-3236)
Vertical Plus Mri America LLC ....G...... 574 257-4674
Mishawaka (G-10146)
Vertical Sale ....G...... 260 438-4299
Fort Wayne (G-4726)
Vertical Vision Inc ....G...... 812 432-3763
Dillsboro (G-2474)

2599 Furniture & Fixtures, NEC

Affordable Furniture ....G...... 317 881-7726
Greenwood (G-5662)
American Natural Resources LLC ....F...... 219 922-6444
Griffith (G-5762)
Blue Collar ....G...... 260 359-8030
Huntington (G-6194)
Bollock Interprises Inc ....F...... 765 448-6000
Lafayette (G-8864)
Brass Ring ....G...... 317 635-7464
Indianapolis (G-6504)
Brick ....G...... 812 522-8636
Jonesville (G-8447)
Challenger Door Llc ....E...... 574 773-8200
Nappanee (G-10659)
◆ Champion Manufacturing Inc ....D...... 574 295-6893
Elkhart (G-2754)
Clancys of Portage ....F...... 219 764-4995
Portage (G-11757)
Concept Cabinet Shop ....G...... 317 272-7430
Avon (G-437)
Country Corner Woodworks LLC ....G...... 574 825-6782
Middlebury (G-9878)
Country Mill Cabinet Co Inc ....F...... 260 693-9289
Laotto (G-9106)
Creative Cabinet Designs ....G...... 812 637-3300
Lawrenceburg (G-9135)
Creative Woodworks LLC ....G...... 260 450-1742
Fort Wayne (G-4187)
Deerwood Group ....G...... 219 866-5521
Monon (G-10175)
Fickle Peach Inc ....G...... 765 282-5211
Muncie (G-10472)
Flat Rock ....G...... 219 852-5262
Hammond (G-5880)
Greazy Pickle LLC ....G...... 260 726-9200
Portland (G-11826)

S
I
C

Growlers ....G...... 219 924-0245
   Highland *(G-6048)*

▲ Hanco Inc ....E...... 800 968-6655
   Carmel *(G-1393)*

Joseph Lee ....G...... 317 931-9446
   Greenwood *(G-5710)*

Kci Crane Pro Services ....G...... 812 479-0488
   Evansville *(G-3582)*

Kimball Hospitality Inc ....F...... 812 482-8090
   Jasper *(G-8280)*

▲ Kimball Hospitality Inc ....D...... 812 482-8090
   Jasper *(G-8281)*

Knu LLC ....D...... 812 367-2068
   Ferdinand *(G-3855)*

Lancaster Custom Cabinets Inc ....G...... 812 949-4750
   New Albany *(G-10817)*

Longs Landing of Bedford ....G...... 812 278-8986
   Bedford *(G-560)*

Magnetic Concepts Corporation ....F...... 317 580-4021
   Carmel *(G-1433)*

Medreco Inc ....G...... 765 458-7444
   Liberty *(G-9265)*

Mulligans Sports Pub ....G...... 765 868-8230
   Kokomo *(G-8674)*

No Sag ....F...... 260 347-2600
   Kendallville *(G-8500)*

▲ Ofs Brands Holdings Inc ....A...... 800 521-5381
   Huntingburg *(G-6177)*

Rabb & Howe Cabinet Top Co .....F...... 317 926-6442
   Indianapolis *(G-7811)*

Rapar Inc ....G...... 812 254-9886
   Washington *(G-14001)*

Richeson Contracting Inc ....E...... 317 889-5995
   Indianapolis *(G-7840)*

S & R Concessions LLC ....F...... 260 570-3247
   Auburn *(G-351)*

Sampco Inc ....C...... 413 442-4043
   South Bend *(G-12925)*

Signet Millwork LLC ....E...... 812 248-0612
   Sellersburg *(G-12417)*

Susies Sandbar ....G...... 574 269-5355
   Warsaw *(G-13946)*

T F S Inc ....G...... 260 422-5896
   Fort Wayne *(G-4672)*

The Tap ....F...... 812 486-9795
   Bloomington *(G-839)*

Top Design Cnc Inc ....G...... 219 662-2915
   Valparaiso *(G-13629)*

Troy Stuart ....G...... 812 887-0403
   Washington *(G-14004)*

▲ U B Klem Furniture Co Inc ....D...... 812 326-2236
   Saint Anthony *(G-12250)*

United Cabinet Corporation Nit ....G...... 812 482-2561
   Jasper *(G-8312)*

United Home Supply Inc ....G...... 765 288-2737
   Muncie *(G-10576)*

Willie and Associates Inc ....G...... 219 662-9046
   Crown Point *(G-2320)*

Wittrock Enterprises LLC ....E...... 812 222-0373
   Greensburg *(G-5642)*

Zoom Seating ....G...... 574 825-3368
   Middlebury *(G-9932)*

26 PAPER AND ALLIED PRODUCTS

2611 Pulp Mills

Exeon Processors LLC ....E...... 765 674-2266
   Jonesboro *(G-8444)*

International Paper Company ....E...... 800 643-7244
   Terre Haute *(G-13259)*

International Paper Company ....C...... 317 510-6410
   Indianapolis *(G-7257)*

Jeda Equipment Services Inc .....Ga...... 317 842-9377
   Fishers *(G-3933)*

Mafcote Wabash Paper Coating ....G...... 260 563-4181
   Wabash *(G-13736)*

Midwest Plastics Company Inc ....G...... 574 674-0161
   Osceola *(G-11382)*

Parrish of Indiana Inc ....G...... 317 859-0934
   Indianapolis *(G-7657)*

Qrs Inc ....G...... 812 948-1323
   New Albany *(G-10851)*

Recycling Center Inc ....D...... 765 966-8295
   Richmond *(G-12041)*

Recycling Works Inc ....F...... 574 293-3751
   Elkhart *(G-3141)*

Starke County Recycling Inc ....F...... 574 772-2594
   Knox *(G-8584)*

2621 Paper Mills

Alliance Sheets LLC ....E...... 574 622-6020
   Bristol *(G-1042)*

◆ American Melt Blown Filtration ....E...... 219 866-3500
   Rensselaer *(G-11912)*

Bristol Myers ....G...... 812 428-1927
   Evansville *(G-3403)*

C D Ventures Inc ....G...... 765 482-9179
   Lebanon *(G-9171)*

Codybro LLC ....G...... 765 827-5441
   Connersville *(G-2044)*

E&S Wallcovering ....G...... 812 256-6668
   Charlestown *(G-1564)*

Goodwill Inds of Centl Ind ....E...... 317 587-0281
   Carmel *(G-1388)*

Gypsy Moon Ragdolls Inc ....G...... 260 589-2852
   Berne *(G-615)*

Harper Direct LLC ....B...... 214 245-5026
   Greendale *(G-5488)*

Huhtamaki Inc ....C...... 219 972-4264
   Hammond *(G-5896)*

Inland Paper Board & Packaging ....G...... 317 879-9710
   Indianapolis *(G-7234)*

International Paper Company ....G...... 317 871-6999
   Indianapolis *(G-7255)*

International Paper Company ....F...... 317 481-4000
   Indianapolis *(G-7256)*

International Paper Company ....C...... 317 510-6410
   Indianapolis *(G-7257)*

International Paper Company ....C...... 765 675-6732
   Tipton *(G-13393)*

International Paper Company ....F...... 317 715-9080
   Indianapolis *(G-7258)*

International Paper Company ....C...... 260 747-9111
   Fort Wayne *(G-4380)*

International Paper Company ....E...... 800 643-7244
   Terre Haute *(G-13259)*

International Paper Company ....C...... 219 844-6509
   Hammond *(G-5901)*

Lsc Communications Us LLC ......G...... 765 362-1300
   Crawfordsville *(G-2169)*

Mann Distribution Inc ....G...... 317 293-6785
   Indianapolis *(G-7449)*

New-Indy Hartford City LLC ....D...... 765 348-5440
   Hartford City *(G-5986)*

New-Indy Hartford City LLC ....F...... 260 347-4739
   Kendallville *(G-8499)*

Nice-Pak Products Inc ....A...... 845 365-1700
   Mooresville *(G-10328)*

Nice-Pak Products Inc ....B...... 317 839-0373
   Plainfield *(G-11630)*

Noblesville Pack & Ship ....G...... 317 776-6306
   Noblesville *(G-11161)*

▲ Panel Solutions Inc ....F...... 574 389-8494
   Elkhart *(G-3071)*

Pratt Paper (in) LLC ....E...... 219 477-1040
   Valparaiso *(G-13602)*

Roi Marketing Company ....G...... 317 644-0797
   Indianapolis *(G-7855)*

Royal Imprints Inc ....G...... 800 894-3151
   Ligonier *(G-9294)*

◆ Space Kraft ....F...... 317 871-6999
   Indianapolis *(G-7966)*

Supremex Midwest Inc ....D...... 317 253-4321
   Indianapolis *(G-8023)*

Supremex Midwest Inc ....E...... 317 253-4321
   Indianapolis *(G-8024)*

Temple Inland ....G...... 765 362-1074
   Crawfordsville *(G-2201)*

Twinrocker Hand Made Paper Inc ....G...... 765 563-3119
   Brookston *(G-1109)*

2631 Paperboard Mills

▲ American Containers Inc ....D...... 574 936-4068
   Plymouth *(G-11664)*

Arrow Container LLC ....D...... 317 882-6444
   Indianapolis *(G-6421)*

Artistic Carton Company ....E...... 260 925-6060
   Auburn *(G-312)*

Barrington Packaging Systems I ....G...... 847 382-8066
   Shelbyville *(G-12520)*

Clondalkin Pharma & Healthcare ....C...... 812 464-2461
   Evansville *(G-3420)*

Combined Technologies Inc ....E...... 574 251-4968
   South Bend *(G-12739)*

▲ Deufol Sunman Inc ....G...... 812 623-1140
   Sunman *(G-13110)*

Graphic Packaging Intl ....G...... 765 289-7391
   Muncie *(G-10478)*

Graphic Packaging Intl LLC ....B...... 260 347-7612
   Kendallville *(G-8476)*

Graphic Packaging Intl LLC ....D...... 219 762-4855
   Portage *(G-11768)*

Guy Cardboard ....G...... 812 989-4809
   Elizabeth *(G-2644)*

▲ Indiana Ribbon Inc ....E...... 219 279-2112
   Wolcott *(G-14365)*

International Paper Company ....G...... 765 359-0107
   Crawfordsville *(G-2162)*

International Paper Company ....C...... 317 510-6410
   Indianapolis *(G-7257)*

International Paper Company ....E...... 800 643-7244
   Terre Haute *(G-13259)*

Jenson Industries Inc ....G...... 317 871-0122
   Indianapolis *(G-7301)*

◆ Michigan City Paper Box Co .....D...... 219 872-8383
   Michigan City *(G-9817)*

Mill Creek Custom Deluxe Box .....G...... 765 934-3901
   Van Buren *(G-13640)*

Paperworks Industries Inc ....C...... 260 563-3102
   Wabash *(G-13747)*

Paperworks Industries Inc ....C...... 260 569-3352
   Wabash *(G-13748)*

PSC Industries Inc ....E...... 812 425-9071
   Evansville *(G-3688)*

Shell Packaging Corporation ....G...... 765 965-6861
   Richmond *(G-12048)*

Sonoco Products Company ....C...... 812 526-5511
   Edinburgh *(G-2629)*

Sonoco Products Company ....D...... 574 893-4521
   Akron *(G-7)*

Viking Paper Company ....E...... 574 936-6300
   Plymouth *(G-11734)*

Westrock Cp LLC ....E...... 574 936-2118
   Plymouth *(G-11735)*

Westrock CP LLC ....B...... 219 762-4855
   Portage *(G-11801)*

Westrock CP LLC ....E...... 574 296-2817
   Elkhart *(G-3258)*

Westrock Rkt Company ....D...... 765 396-3317
   Eaton *(G-2590)*

Westrock Rkt Company ....C...... 812 372-8873
   Columbus *(G-2033)*

2652 Set-Up Paperboard Boxes

▲ American Containers Inc ....D...... 574 936-4068
   Plymouth *(G-11664)*

Artistic Carton Company ....E...... 260 925-6060
   Auburn *(G-312)*

Barger Packaging Corporation .....D...... 574 389-1860
   Elkhart *(G-2715)*

▲ Dgp Intelsius LLC ....D...... 317 452-4006
   Indianapolis *(G-6738)*

Jessup Paper Box LLC ....E...... 765 588-9137
   Lafayette *(G-8931)*

Pathfinder Services Inc ....E...... 260 356-0500
   Huntington *(G-6236)*

Reddi-Pac Inc ....E...... 574 266-6933
   Elkhart *(G-3142)*

2653 Corrugated & Solid Fiber Boxes

▲ American Containers Inc ....D...... 574 936-4068
   Plymouth *(G-11664)*

B&W Packaging Mfg LLC ....E...... 812 280-9578
   New Albany *(G-10749)*

Buckeye Corrugated Inc ....D...... 330 576-0590
   Indianapolis *(G-6519)*

Capitol City Container Corp ....E...... 317 875-0290
   Indianapolis *(G-6549)*

Cardinal Container Corp ....E...... 317 898-2715
   Indianapolis *(G-6551)*

Color-Box LLC ....D...... 765 983-7618
   Richmond *(G-11971)*

Color-Box LLC ....D...... 765 966-7588
   Richmond *(G-11972)*

Combined Technologies Inc ....E...... 574 251-4968
   South Bend *(G-12739)*

Container Service Corp ....D...... 574 232-7474
   South Bend *(G-12740)*

Corrugated Packaging Systems ....G...... 317 848-0000
   Westfield *(G-14145)*

Cox John ....G...... 765 463-6396
   West Lafayette *(G-14061)*

CRA-Wal Inc ....D...... 317 856-3701
   Indianapolis *(G-6683)*

▲ Csc-Indiana LLC ....E...... 708 625-3255
   New Haven *(G-10936)*

Custom Packaging Inc ....F...... 317 876-9559
   Indianapolis *(G-6717)*

F & F Contracting...............................G......574 867-4471
Grovertown (G-5795)
Five Star Sheets LLC..........................D......574 654-8058
New Carlisle (G-10882)
Freedom Corrugated LLC.....................G......317 290-1140
Indianapolis (G-6963)
Galaxy Container LLC..........................E......574 936-6300
Plymouth (G-11687)
Graphic Packaging Intl Inc...................D......812 949-4393
New Albany (G-10789)
▲ Hamilton Exhibits LLC......................E......317 898-9300
Indianapolis (G-7068)
Hoosier Container Inc..........................E......765 966-2541
Richmond (G-11999)
Indiana Box Company...........................E......260 356-9660
Huntington (G-6215)
Indiana Box Company...........................E......317 462-7743
Greenfield (G-5539)
Innovative Packaging Assoc Inc..........F......260 356-6577
Huntington (G-6217)
International Paper Company.................C......260 868-2151
Butler (G-1232)
International Paper Company.................D......765 364-5342
Crawfordsville (G-2161)
International Paper Company.................D......812 326-2125
Saint Anthony (G-12246)
International Paper Company.................E......317 875-4101
Indianapolis (G-7259)
International Paper Company.................G......765 492-3341
Cayuga (G-1520)
International Paper Company.................D......317 390-3300
Indianapolis (G-7260)
International Paper Company.................D......317 510-6410
Indianapolis (G-7257)
International Paper Company.................E......800 643-7244
Terre Haute (G-13259)
▲ Jamil Packaging Corporation.............C......574 256-2600
Mishawaka (G-10059)
Kelly Box and Packaging Corp.............D......260 432-4570
Fort Wayne (G-4407)
Lacap Container Corp...........................G......317 835-4282
Shelbyville (G-12548)
Marion Paper Box Company..................F......765 664-6435
Marion (G-9544)
Met Pak Specialties Inc.......................F......260 420-2217
Fort Wayne (G-4467)
Midland Plastics Co Division................F......317 352-7785
Indianapolis (G-7503)
Northern Box Company Inc...................E......574 264-2161
Elkhart (G-3066)
Northern Indiana Packg Co Inc............F......260 356-9660
Huntington (G-6232)
Nova Packaging Group Inc...................E......765 651-2600
Marion (G-9548)
Orora North America............................E......317 879-4628
Indianapolis (G-7631)
Packaging Corporation America...........C......812 882-7631
Vincennes (G-13694)
Packaging Corporation America...........B......812 376-9301
Columbus (G-1989)
Packaging Corporation America...........E......812 526-5919
Edinburgh (G-2620)
Packaging Corporation America...........D......765 674-9781
Gas City (G-5126)
Packaging Corporation America...........G......317 247-0193
Indianapolis (G-7646)
Packaging Corporation America...........E......812 522-3100
Seymour (G-12473)
Packaging Corporation America...........G......812 482-4598
Jasper (G-8299)
Packaging Lgstics Slutions LLC...........E......502 807-8346
New Albany (G-10838)
Packaging Logic Inc.............................E......219 326-1350
La Porte (G-8803)
PCA Suthern Ind Corrugated LLC........G......812 376-9301
Columbus (G-1991)
Powell Systems Inc.............................G......765 884-0613
Fowler (G-4804)
Pratt (jet Corr) Inc..............................B......219 548-9191
Valparaiso (G-13601)
Pyramid Paper Products Inc.................E......812 372-0288
Columbus (G-2002)
Royal Box Group LLC...........................G......317 462-7743
Greenfield (G-5568)
Royal Box Group LLC...........................D......765 728-2416
Huntington (G-6244)
Servants Inc...D......812 634-2201
Jasper (G-8306)
Servants Inc...G......812 634-2201
Jasper (G-8307)

Sinflex Paper Co Inc............................E......765 789-6688
Muncie (G-10563)
Sisco Corporation................................D......812 422-2090
Evansville (G-3733)
Smith Consulting Inc...........................E......765 728-5980
Montpelier (G-10294)
Solid Rock Gbc....................................G......260 723-4806
South Whitley (G-13003)
Southland Container Corp....................F......812 385-0774
Princeton (G-11882)
Temple-Inland Inc.................................G......765 675-6732
Tipton (G-13408)
Tre Paper Co Inc..................................E......765 649-2536
Anderson (G-178)
Wabash Valley Packaging Corp............F......812 299-7181
Terre Haute (G-13367)
Webster West Inc.................................E......812 346-5666
North Vernon (G-11286)
Welch Packaging LLC...........................D......574 295-2460
Elkhart (G-3255)
▲ Welch Packaging Group Inc...............G......574 295-2460
Elkhart (G-3256)
Welch Packaging Marion LLC...............D......765 651-2600
Marion (G-9572)
Westrock Cp LLC..................................E......574 772-5545
Knox (G-8587)
Westrock Cp LLC..................................C......812 372-8873
Columbus (G-2032)
Westrock Cp LLC..................................C......574 256-0318
Mishawaka (G-10151)
Westrock CP LLC..................................E......574 296-2817
Elkhart (G-3258)
Westrock Rkt Company.........................F......574 936-2118
Plymouth (G-11736)

2655 Fiber Cans, Tubes & Drums

Charmaran Corporation.........................F......260 347-3347
Kendallville (G-8463)
Cornerstone Expediting LLC..................G......317 893-2891
Indianapolis (G-6670)
Elder Group Inc...................................D......765 966-7676
Richmond (G-11980)
▲ Indiana Ribbon Inc...........................E......219 279-2112
Wolcott (G-14365)
Indiana Ribbon Inc...............................E......219 279-2112
Wolcott (G-14366)
Jt Composites LLC...............................G......317 297-9520
Indianapolis (G-7320)
Mach 1 Paper and Poly Pdts Inc..........G......574 522-4500
Elkhart (G-3012)
Phenix Tube Corp.................................G......260 424-3734
Fort Wayne (G-4528)
Precision Products Group Inc...............E......260 484-4111
Fort Wayne (G-4552)
Precision Products Group Inc...............C......301 474-3100
Indianapolis (G-6277)
▲ Precision Products Group Inc.............B......330 698-4711
Indianapolis (G-6276)
Star Packaging Company Inc................G......317 357-3707
Indianapolis (G-7997)
Stone Industrial Inc.............................C......301 474-3100
Fort Wayne (G-4652)
▲ Tube Fabrication Inds Inc..................E......574 753-6377
Logansport (G-9372)

2656 Sanitary Food Containers

Affinis Group LLC.................................G......317 831-3830
Mooresville (G-10301)
Divine Grace Homecare.........................G......219 290-5911
Gary (G-5041)
Genpak LLC...C......812 752-3111
Scottsburg (G-12358)
Howe House Ltd Editions Inc................G......765 742-6831
Lafayette (G-8918)
Huhtamaki Inc......................................B......765 664-2330
Marion (G-9532)
International Paper Company.................C......317 510-6410
Indianapolis (G-7257)
International Paper Company.................E......800 643-7244
Terre Haute (G-13259)
Lucky Straw Inc...................................E......219 397-9910
East Chicago (G-2551)

2657 Folding Paperboard Boxes

Artistic Carton Company......................E......260 925-6060
Auburn (G-312)
Barger Packaging Corporation..............D......574 389-1860
Elkhart (G-2715)
Combined Technologies Inc..................E......574 251-4968
South Bend (G-12739)

Custom Carton Inc...............................F......260 563-7411
Wabash (G-13723)
Glaze Mfg Co.......................................F......574 612-1401
Elkhart (G-2881)
▲ Indiana Carton Company Inc.............D......574 546-3848
Bremen (G-1004)
Tre Paper Co Inc..................................E......765 649-2536
Anderson (G-178)
Westrock Cp LLC..................................G......574 936-2118
Plymouth (G-11735)

2671 Paper Coating & Laminating for Packaging

3M Company...B......765 348-3200
Hartford City (G-5976)
Accu-Label Inc.....................................E......260 482-5223
Fort Wayne (G-4036)
▲ American Containers Inc...................D......574 936-4068
Plymouth (G-11664)
◆ Bomarko Inc......................................C......574 936-9901
Plymouth (G-11669)
Bprex Closures LLC..............................D......812 386-1525
Princeton (G-11866)
Cpg - Ohio LLC.....................................F......260 829-6721
Orland (G-11348)
Crichlow Industries Inc.........................G......317 925-5178
Indianapolis (G-6692)
Custom Packaging Inc..........................F......317 876-9559
Indianapolis (G-6717)
Eagle Packaging Inc............................G......260 281-2333
Goshen (G-5208)
Flexible Materials Inc...........................D......812 280-9578
Jeffersonville (G-8362)
G & T Industries of Indiana.................E......812 634-2252
Jasper (G-8253)
Hooven - Dayton Corp.........................E......765 935-3999
Richmond (G-12000)
Huhtamaki Inc......................................C......219 972-4264
Hammond (G-5896)
▲ Innovative Energy Inc......................E......219 696-3639
Lowell (G-9409)
Interactive Surface Tech LLC...............G......812 246-0900
Sellersburg (G-12398)
Label Tech Inc.....................................E......765 747-1234
Muncie (G-10506)
LDI Ltd LLC..F......317 237-5400
Indianapolis (G-7388)
▲ Monosol LLC.....................................F......219 762-3165
Merrillville (G-9741)
Monosol LLC..D......219 763-7589
Portage (G-11778)
Monosol LLC..E......219 324-9459
La Porte (G-8797)
Monosol LLC..D......219 762-3165
Portage (G-11779)
Multi-Color Corporation........................C......812 752-3187
Scottsburg (G-12376)
NP Converters Inc................................E......812 448-2555
Brazil (G-973)
Pactiv Corporation...............................C......574 936-7065
Plymouth (G-11709)
▼ Patty Processing Inc........................C......574 936-9901
Plymouth (G-11710)
Poly Plastics Ltd..................................F......260 569-9088
Wabash (G-13750)
PSC Industries Inc...............................E......812 425-9071
Evansville (G-3688)
Sabert Corporation..............................G......260 747-3149
Fort Wayne (G-4600)
Sonoco Products Company....................C......812 526-5511
Edinburgh (G-2629)
◆ Stoffel Seals Corporation..................E......845 353-3800
Angola (G-248)
Taghleef Industries Inc........................A......302 326-5500
Rosedale (G-12208)
Universal Package LLC..........................F......812 937-3605
Dale (G-2335)
Universal Packg Systems Inc................B......260 829-6721
Orland (G-11359)
Vista Grphic Cmmunications LLC..........F......317 898-2000
Indianapolis (G-8166)
Vti Packaging Specialties.....................E......574 277-4119
Granger (G-5449)
Westrock Cp LLC..................................G......574 936-2118
Plymouth (G-11735)

2672 Paper Coating & Laminating, Exc for Packaging

3M Company	B	765 348-3200
Hartford City *(G-5976)*		
3M Company	B	317 692-6666
Indianapolis *(G-6288)*		
◆ Abro Industries Inc	E	574 232-8289
South Bend *(G-12692)*		
Accu-Label Inc	E	260 482-5223
Fort Wayne *(G-4036)*		
Adhesive Products Inc	G	317 899-0565
Indianapolis *(G-6325)*		
American Label Products Inc	G	317 873-9850
Zionsville *(G-14416)*		
Avery Dennison Corporation	G	765 221-9277
Anderson *(G-71)*		
Avery Dennison Corporation	C	260 481-4500
Fort Wayne *(G-4098)*		
Avery Dennison Corporation	G	219 696-7777
Lowell *(G-9399)*		
Avery Dennison Corporation	D	317 462-1988
Greenfield *(G-5505)*		
◆ Covalnce Spcialty Coatings LLC	E	812 424-2904
Evansville *(G-3435)*		
Daubert Vci Inc	E	574 772-9310
Knox *(G-8564)*		
F Robert Gardner Co Inc	E	317 634-2333
Indianapolis *(G-6900)*		
Fedex Office & Print Svcs Inc	E	317 337-2679
Indianapolis *(G-6912)*		
Gindor Inc	G	574 642-4004
Goshen *(G-5225)*		
HI Tech Label Inc	F	765 659-1800
Frankfort *(G-4836)*		
Hooven - Dayton Corp	E	765 935-3999
Richmond *(G-12000)*		
International Paper Company	E	800 643-7244
Terre Haute *(G-13259)*		
Jknk Ventures Inc	F	812 246-0900
Sellersburg *(G-12399)*		
L & L Press Inc	F	765 664-3162
Marion *(G-9541)*		
Label Tech Inc	E	765 747-1234
Muncie *(G-10506)*		
Lambel Corporation	F	317 849-6828
Indianapolis *(G-7377)*		
Lamco Finishers Inc	E	317 471-1010
Indianapolis *(G-7379)*		
▲ Marian Worldwide Inc	D	317 638-6525
Indianapolis *(G-7454)*		
Mito-Craft Inc	G	574 287-4555
South Bend *(G-12864)*		
Morgan Adhesives Company LLC	D	812 342-2004
Columbus *(G-1976)*		
NP Converters Inc	E	812 448-2555
Brazil *(G-973)*		
Peafield Products Inc	F	317 839-8473
Plainfield *(G-11634)*		
Precision Label Incorporated	F	812 877-3811
Terre Haute *(G-13308)*		
▲ Quality Engineered Products	E	574 294-6943
Elkhart *(G-3127)*		
R R Donnelley & Sons Company	B	260 624-2350
Angola *(G-242)*		
Specialty Adhesive Film Co	E	812 926-0156
Aurora *(G-387)*		
Standard Label Co	E	574 522-3548
Elkhart *(G-3187)*		
Tippecanoe Press Inc	F	317 392-1207
Shelbyville *(G-12576)*		
Vickery Tape & Label Co Inc	F	765 472-1974
Peru *(G-11555)*		
Westrock Cp LLC	G	574 936-2118
Plymouth *(G-11735)*		

2673 Bags: Plastics, Laminated & Coated

Adec Inc	C	574 848-7451
Bristol *(G-1040)*		
All-Flex Inc	G	812 949-8898
Georgetown *(G-5140)*		
▼ Berry Global Group Inc	F	812 424-2904
Evansville *(G-3377)*		
Cougar Bag Inc	E	317 831-9720
Mooresville *(G-10306)*		
Cpg - Ohio LLC	F	260 829-6721
Orland *(G-11348)*		
D and M Enterprises LLC	F	260 483-4008
Fort Wayne *(G-4197)*		
Eagle Industries Inc	F	812 282-1393
Jeffersonville *(G-8353)*		

Essentra Packaging US Inc	F	317 328-7355
Indianapolis *(G-6877)*		
Gen Enterprises	G	574 498-6777
Tippecanoe *(G-13381)*		
▲ Grrk Holdings Inc	E	317 872-0172
Indianapolis *(G-7053)*		
Hilex Poly	F	812 346-1066
North Vernon *(G-11261)*		
◆ Jadcore LLC	C	812 234-2724
Terre Haute *(G-13260)*		
Novipax LLC	D	201 791-7600
Indianapolis *(G-7601)*		
Novolex Inc	C	812 346-1066
North Vernon *(G-11273)*		
Printpack Inc	B	812 663-5091
Greensburg *(G-5629)*		
Putnam Plastics Inc	E	765 795-6102
Cloverdale *(G-1735)*		
Universal Transparent Bag Co	G	317 634-6425
Indianapolis *(G-8130)*		
Witham Machine	G	317 835-2076
Boggstown *(G-903)*		

2674 Bags: Uncoated Paper & Multiwall

▼ Lesac Corporation	E	219 879-3215
Michigan City *(G-9810)*		
Westrock Cp LLC	G	574 936-2118
Plymouth *(G-11735)*		

2675 Die-Cut Paper & Board

A-1 Graphics Inc	G	765 289-1851
Muncie *(G-10420)*		
AK Tool and Die	G	574 286-9010
Mishawaka *(G-9992)*		
American Steel Rule Die Inc	G	574 262-3437
Elkhart *(G-2685)*		
Bethlehem Packg Die Cutng Inc	F	812 282-8740
New Albany *(G-10751)*		
Bruce Payne	G	260 492-2259
Fort Wayne *(G-4124)*		
C & W Inkd	F	317 352-1000
Indianapolis *(G-6527)*		
Graphix Unlimited Inc	E	574 546-3770
Bremen *(G-1000)*		
▲ Harcourt Industries Inc	E	765 629-2625
Milroy *(G-9980)*		
Millcraft Paper Company	E	317 240-3500
Indianapolis *(G-7519)*		
Rcs Contractor Supplies Inc	G	317 773-6279
Noblesville *(G-11171)*		
Rink Printing Company Inc	E	574 232-7935
South Bend *(G-12916)*		
▼ Ross-Gage Inc	D	317 283-2323
Indianapolis *(G-7863)*		
Shirley Engraving Co Inc	F	317 634-4084
Indianapolis *(G-7934)*		
Tre Paper Co Inc	E	765 649-2536
Anderson *(G-178)*		
Triangle Printing Inc	G	317 786-3488
Indianapolis *(G-8098)*		
Westrock Rkt Company	C	812 372-8873
Columbus *(G-2033)*		

2676 Sanitary Paper Prdts

Bobby Little Creations	G	219 313-5102
Crown Point *(G-2229)*		
Johnson & Johnson	G	732 524-0400
Fishers *(G-3935)*		
Johnson & Johnson	G	317 539-8300
Mooresville *(G-10318)*		

2677 Envelopes

BSC Vntres Acquisition Sub LLC	D	260 665-7521
Angola *(G-198)*		
Cenveo Inc	D	317 791-5250
Indianapolis *(G-6588)*		
Double Envelope Corp	G	260 434-0500
Fort Wayne *(G-4219)*		
Envelope Service Inc	E	260 432-6277
Fort Wayne *(G-4237)*		
Westrock Mwv LLC	C	317 787-3361
Indianapolis *(G-8187)*		

2678 Stationery Prdts

Altstadt Business Forms Inc	F	812 425-3393
Evansville *(G-3349)*		
Asc Inc	D	765 472-5331
Peru *(G-11516)*		

Avery Dennison Corporation	D	219 696-7777
Lowell *(G-9399)*		

2679 Converted Paper Prdts, NEC

American Stationery Co	G	765 473-4438
Peru *(G-11515)*		
▲ Applied Coating Converting LLC	G	260 436-4455
Fort Wayne *(G-4082)*		
Associated Label Inc	G	812 877-3682
Terre Haute *(G-13195)*		
Avery Dennison Corporation	D	219 696-7777
Lowell *(G-9399)*		
Chronotrack Systems Corp	G	314 406-7243
Evansville *(G-3417)*		
Cps Inc	G	317 804-2300
Westfield *(G-14147)*		
▲ Discount Labels LLC	A	812 945-2617
New Albany *(G-10769)*		
Enterprise Marking Products	F	317 867-7600
Westfield *(G-14163)*		
Flutes Inc	D	317 870-6010
Indianapolis *(G-6941)*		
G M S I Inc	G	574 457-4646
Syracuse *(G-13131)*		
Georgia-Pacific LLC	G	219 776-0069
Wheatfield *(G-14222)*		
GI Tape & Label	G	574 269-2836
Warsaw *(G-13881)*		
HI Tech Label Inc	F	765 659-1800
Frankfort *(G-4836)*		
Hoosier Wallbeds Incorporated	G	812 747-7154
Lawrenceburg *(G-9145)*		
Hooven - Dayton Corp	E	765 935-3999
Richmond *(G-12000)*		
Indilabel LLC	F	317 839-8814
Plainfield *(G-11616)*		
Interpak Inc	G	765 482-9179
Lebanon *(G-9192)*		
John Wallace Builder Inc	G	765 447-3614
Lafayette *(G-8933)*		
Label Tech Inc	E	765 747-1234
Muncie *(G-10506)*		
Larry Flowers Wholesale	G	765 747-5156
Muncie *(G-10509)*		
Logistick Inc	G	800 758-5840
South Bend *(G-12844)*		
Mach 1 Paper and Poly Pdts Inc	G	574 522-4500
Elkhart *(G-3012)*		
Manchester Industries Inc VA	E	765 489-4521
Hagerstown *(G-5808)*		
Palacio Tropical	G	574 289-0742
South Bend *(G-12887)*		
Patriot Label Inc	G	812 877-1611
Terre Haute *(G-13298)*		
◆ Reflectix Inc	D	765 533-4332
Markleville *(G-9589)*		
Schwarz Partners LP	G	317 290-1140
Indianapolis *(G-7904)*		
Sheets LLC	G	317 290-1140
Indianapolis *(G-7927)*		
Shelf Tag Supply Corporation	G	317 580-4030
Carmel *(G-1479)*		
Signode Industrial Group LLC	E	574 266-6933
Elkhart *(G-3171)*		
Sinflex Paper Co Inc	E	765 789-6688
Muncie *(G-10563)*		
▲ Stump Printing Co Inc	C	260 723-5171
South Whitley *(G-13006)*		
▲ Urban Forest Products Llc	G	219 697-2900
Brook *(G-1100)*		
▲ Web Industries Dallas Inc	E	260 432-0027
Fort Wayne *(G-4749)*		
Westrock Rkt Company	C	812 372-8873
Columbus *(G-2033)*		

27 PRINTING, PUBLISHING, AND ALLIED INDUSTRIES

2711 Newspapers: Publishing & Printing

411 Newspaper	G	219 922-8846
Munster *(G-10590)*		
Aim Media Indiana Oper LLC	E	317 462-5528
Greenfield *(G-5497)*		
Aim Media Indiana Oper LLC	D	812 372-7811
Columbus *(G-1852)*		
Aim Media Indiana Oper LLC	F	812 522-4871
Seymour *(G-12427)*		
Aim Media Indiana Oper LLC	G	812 988-2221
Nashville *(G-10712)*		

Aim Media Indiana Oper LLC ... G ... 812 358-2111
Brownstown *(G-1179)*
Aim Media Indiana Oper LLC ... G ... 765 778-2324
Pendleton *(G-11482)*
Aim Media Indiana Oper LLC ... G ... 317 462-5528
Greenfield *(G-5498)*
Aim Media Indiana Oper LLC ... G ... 812 736-7101
Franklin *(G-4864)*
Aim Media Indiana Oper LLC ... E ... 317 462-5528
Greenfield *(G-5499)*
Aim Media Indiana Oper LLC ... D ... 812 372-7811
Columbus *(G-1851)*
Aim Media Indiana Oper LLC ... E ... 317 736-7101
Franklin *(G-4863)*
Alan Daily ... G ... 574 595-6253
Star City *(G-13069)*
All Printing and Publications ... E ... 260 636-2727
Albion *(G-15)*
Allen C Terhune & Associates ... G ... 765 948-4164
Fairmount *(G-3828)*
Alymat Publishing LLC ... G ... 812 933-9940
Batesville *(G-490)*
American Classifieds ... E ... 317 782-8111
Indianapolis *(G-6386)*
American Senior Homecare ... F ... 317 849-4968
Indianapolis *(G-6390)*
Aurora Services Inc ... G ... 260 463-4901
Shipshewana *(G-12604)*
Ball State University ... G ... 765 285-8218
Muncie *(G-10437)*
Beacon Publishing Co Inc ... G ... 812 637-0660
Lawrenceburg *(G-9134)*
Benton Review Newspaper ... G ... 765 884-1902
Fowler *(G-4795)*
Berne Tri Weekly News Inc ... G ... 260 589-2101
Berne *(G-609)*
Beverly G Inc ... G ... 812 401-1819
Evansville *(G-3383)*
Big E Publications Inc ... G ... 317 485-4097
Fortville *(G-4768)*
Brown County Democrat Inc ... G ... 812 988-2221
Nashville *(G-10717)*
Carroll Papers Inc ... G ... 574 967-4135
Flora *(G-3993)*
Carroll Papers Inc ... G ... 765 564-2222
Delphi *(G-2416)*
Catholic Moment ... G ... 765 742-2050
Lafayette *(G-8872)*
Catholic Press of Evansville ... G ... 812 424-5536
Evansville *(G-3414)*
Chesterton Tribune Inc ... F ... 219 926-1131
Chesterton *(G-1599)*
Chicken Scratch LLC ... G ... 260 486-9800
Fort Wayne *(G-4147)*
Ckmt Associates Inc ... E ... 219 924-2820
Hammond *(G-5863)*
Cliff A Ostermeyer ... G ... 615 361-7902
Indianapolis *(G-6621)*
Cnhi LLC ... E ... 574 936-3101
Plymouth *(G-11674)*
Cnhi LLC ... E ... 812 944-6481
New Albany *(G-10762)*
Colormax Digital Imaging Inc ... E ... 812 477-3805
Evansville *(G-3422)*
Community Holdings Indiana Inc ... F ... 765 622-1212
Anderson *(G-88)*
Community Holdings Indiana Inc ... F ... 574 722-5000
Logansport *(G-9332)*
Community Holdings Indiana Inc ... F ... 317 272-5800
Avon *(G-436)*
Community Holdings Indiana Inc ... G ... 812 934-4343
Batesville *(G-497)*
Community Holdings Indiana Inc ... E ... 765 932-2222
Rushville *(G-12218)*
Community Holdings Indiana Inc ... E ... 765 482-4650
Lebanon *(G-9175)*
Community Holdings Indiana Inc ... F ... 765 459-3121
Kokomo *(G-8608)*
Community Holdings Indiana Inc ... G ... 317 873-6397
Lebanon *(G-9176)*
Community Holdings Indiana Inc ... E ... 812 663-3111
Greensburg *(G-5594)*
Community Papers Inc ... G ... 317 241-7363
Indianapolis *(G-6639)*
Courier Printing Co Allen Cnty ... G ... 260 627-2728
Grabill *(G-5362)*
▲ Courier-Times Inc ... D ... 765 529-1111
New Castle *(G-10897)*
Criterion Press Inc ... F ... 317 236-1570
Indianapolis *(G-6693)*

Daily Peru Tribune Pubg Co ... E ... 765 473-6641
Peru *(G-11523)*
Decatur Publishing Co Inc ... E ... 260 724-2121
Decatur *(G-2374)*
Delphos Herald of Indiana ... E ... 812 537-0063
Lawrenceburg *(G-9137)*
Delphos Herald of Indiana Inc ... E ... 812 537-0063
Lawrenceburg *(G-9138)*
Delphos Herald of Indiana Inc ... G ... 812 438-2011
Rising Sun *(G-12087)*
Dubois County Free Press LLC ... G ... 812 639-9651
Huntingburg *(G-6157)*
Duboisspencer Counties Pubg ... F ... 812 367-2041
Ferdinand *(G-3848)*
Ecom Publishing Inc ... G ... 574 862-2179
Wakarusa *(G-13776)*
El Mexicano Inc ... G ... 260 456-6843
Fort Wayne *(G-4233)*
Elephant Enterprises ... G ... 248 366-5383
Hammond *(G-5878)*
Elwood Publishing Co Inc ... E ... 765 552-3355
Elwood *(G-3298)*
Elwood Publishing Co Inc ... G ... 765 724-4469
Alexandria *(G-40)*
Evansville Courier Co ... B ... 812 464-7500
Evansville *(G-3485)*
Exchange Publishing Corp ... E ... 574 831-2138
New Paris *(G-10979)*
Fairmount News ... G ... 765 948-4164
Fairmount *(G-3831)*
Federated Publications Inc ... C ... 765 962-1575
Richmond *(G-11987)*
Fort Wayne Newspapers Inc ... B ... 260 461-8444
Fort Wayne *(G-4277)*
Fountain County Neighbor ... G ... 765 762-2411
Attica *(G-300)*
Frankfort Newspaper ... G ... 859 254-2385
Frankfort *(G-4833)*
Franklin Township Civic League ... G ... 317 862-1774
Indianapolis *(G-6960)*
Ft Wayne Reader ... G ... 260 420-8580
Fort Wayne *(G-4289)*
Gannett Co Inc ... C ... 765 423-5512
Lafayette *(G-8902)*
Gannett Co Inc ... C ... 765 962-1575
Richmond *(G-11989)*
Gannett Co Inc ... G ... 765 423-5511
Lafayette *(G-8903)*
George P Stewart Printing Co ... E ... 317 924-5143
Indianapolis *(G-7002)*
Ginger Oliviae Publishing LLC ... G ... 765 762-3132
Williamsport *(G-14290)*
Granger Gazette ... G ... 574 277-2679
Granger *(G-5410)*
Graphic Printing Co Inc ... G ... 765 768-6022
Dunkirk *(G-2484)*
Graphic Printing Co Inc ... E ... 260 726-8141
Portland *(G-11825)*
Green Banner Publications Inc ... E ... 812 967-3176
Pekin *(G-11473)*
Green Banner Publications Inc ... G ... 812 752-3171
Scottsburg *(G-12359)*
Green Banner Publications Inc ... G ... 812 752-3171
Scottsburg *(G-12360)*
Green Banner Publications Inc ... G ... 812 883-5555
Salem *(G-12289)*
Growing Child ... G ... 765 464-0920
West Lafayette *(G-14073)*
Guide Book Publishing ... G ... 317 259-0599
Indianapolis *(G-7057)*
Hamilton News Inc ... G ... 260 488-3780
Fort Wayne *(G-4315)*
Harrison Cnty Democrate ... G ... 812 734-0560
Corydon *(G-2100)*
Hartford City News Times ... C ... 765 348-0110
Hartford City *(G-5982)*
Hendricks County Flyer ... G ... 317 272-5800
Avon *(G-447)*
Hielo Services LLC ... G ... 219 973-1952
Hobart *(G-6080)*
Home News Enterprises LLC ... E ... 812 342-1056
Columbus *(G-1940)*
Home News Enterprises LLC ... E ... 574 583-5121
Monticello *(G-10265)*
Hoosier Times Inc ... C ... 812 331-4270
Bloomington *(G-741)*
Hoosier Times Inc ... E ... 765 342-3311
Martinsville *(G-9613)*
Hoosier Times Inc ... E ... 812 275-3372
Bedford *(G-548)*

Hoosier Times Inc ... F ... 812 332-4401
Beech Grove *(G-596)*
Horizon Publications Inc ... E ... 260 244-5153
Columbia City *(G-1791)*
Horse Circuit News Inc ... G ... 800 537-3958
New Castle *(G-10906)*
How Pubs USA ... G ... 219 933-9251
Munster *(G-10607)*
Huntington County Tab Inc ... F ... 260 356-1107
Huntington *(G-6211)*
IBJ Book Publishing LLC ... G ... 317 564-9924
Carmel *(G-1409)*
IBJ Corporation ... D ... 317 634-6200
Indianapolis *(G-7156)*
Indiana News Media LLC ... G ... 812 546-4940
Hope *(G-6116)*
Indiana Newspapers LLC ... A ... 317 444-4000
Indianapolis *(G-7186)*
Indiana Newspapers LLC ... D ... 812 886-9955
Vincennes *(G-13685)*
Indiana Newspapers LLC ... F ... 317 444-3800
Indianapolis *(G-7187)*
Indiana Newspapers LLC ... E ... 765 213-5700
Muncie *(G-10494)*
Indiana University Bloomington ... F ... 812 855-2816
Bloomington *(G-748)*
Info Publishing Impact LLC ... G ... 317 912-3642
Fishers *(G-3931)*
J Aime Music Publishing LLC ... G ... 574 772-2934
Knox *(G-8569)*
Jackson County Banner ... F ... 812 358-2111
Brownstown *(G-1189)*
Janis Buhl ... G ... 765 478-5448
Cambridge City *(G-1258)*
Journal Gazette Foundation ... G ... 260 424-5257
Fort Wayne *(G-4400)*
Journal Publishing Co Inc ... G ... 812 876-2254
Ellettsville *(G-3282)*
Kaiser Press LLC ... G ... 317 619-7092
Indianapolis *(G-7329)*
Kankakee Valley Post News ... G ... 219 987-5111
Demotte *(G-2441)*
Kankakee Valley Publishing Co ... C ... 219 866-5111
Rensselaer *(G-11930)*
Kaspar Broadcasting Co Inc ... E ... 765 659-3338
Frankfort *(G-4839)*
Kendalville Mall ... G ... 260 897-2697
Avilla *(G-411)*
Kentuckiana Publishing ... G ... 812 273-2259
Madison *(G-9475)*
King Tut Inc ... G ... 317 938-9907
Zionsville *(G-14445)*
Knightstown Banner LLC ... E ... 765 345-2292
Knightstown *(G-8554)*
Kpc Media Group Inc ... C ... 260 347-0400
Kendallville *(G-8488)*
Kpc Media Group Inc ... E ... 260 925-2611
Auburn *(G-339)*
Kpc Media Group Inc ... G ... 678 645-0000
Angola *(G-227)*
Kpc Media Group Inc ... E ... 260 426-2640
Fort Wayne *(G-4415)*
La Grange Publishing Co Inc ... F ... 260 463-3243
Lagrange *(G-9052)*
La Ola Latino Americana ... F ... 317 822-0345
Indianapolis *(G-7372)*
La Voz De Indiana Inc ... G ... 317 423-0957
Indianapolis *(G-7373)*
Lagrange Publishing Co Inc ... F ... 260 463-2166
Lagrange *(G-9053)*
Leader Publishing Co of Salem ... E ... 812 883-4446
Salem *(G-12299)*
Lebanon Reporter ... F ... 765 482-4650
Lebanon *(G-9200)*
Lee Enterprises Inc Times ... E ... 219 933-3200
Munster *(G-10613)*
Lee Publications Inc ... E ... 219 462-5151
Valparaiso *(G-13574)*
Lee Publications Inc ... D ... 219 933-9251
Munster *(G-10614)*
Liberty Herald ... G ... 765 458-5114
Liberty *(G-9264)*
Life Path Numerology Center ... G ... 317 638-9752
Indianapolis *(G-7404)*
Loogootee Tribune Inc ... G ... 812 295-2500
Loogootee *(G-9389)*
Madison Courier ... E ... 812 265-3641
Madison *(G-9479)*
Manchester North News Journal ... G ... 260 982-6383
North Manchester *(G-11233)*

S
I
C

Mayhill Publications Inc ....E 765 345-5133
  Knightstown (G-8556)

Mexicano Newsletter ....G 260 704-0682
  Fort Wayne (G-4469)

Midcountry Media Inc ....D 765 345-5133
  Knightstown (G-8557)

Monster House Press ....G 440 364-4548
  Bloomington (G-775)

Montgomery & Associates Inc ....F 219 879-0088
  Michigan City (G-9821)

My Daily Wedding Deals LLC ....G 812 603-6149
  Indianapolis (G-7563)

Myers Enterprises Inc ....G 812 636-7350
  Odon (G-11335)

New Wolcott Enterprise ....G 219 279-2167
  Wolcott (G-14367)

News and Tribune ....G 812 206-2168
  Jeffersonville (G-8404)

News Banner Publications Inc .....E 260 824-0224
  Bluffton (G-883)

▲ News Dispatch ....G 219 874-7211
  Michigan City (G-9823)

News Examiner Circulation Dept ....G 765 825-2914
  Connersville (G-2066)

News Publishing Company LLC ....F 812 547-3424
  Tell City (G-13169)

News Publishing Company LLC ....G 502 633-4334
  Tell City (G-13170)

News Publishing Company LLC ....G 812 649-4440
  Rockport (G-12171)

News Publishing Company Inc ....G 260 461-8444
  Fort Wayne (G-4503)

News Reminder ....F 574 583-5121
  Monticello (G-10274)

News-Gazette ....F 765 584-4501
  Winchester (G-14338)

Newspaper Holding Inc ....D 812 231-4200
  Terre Haute (G-13290)

Newspaper Holding Inc ....G 812 254-0480
  Washington (G-13993)

Newton County Enterprises Inc ....G 219 474-5532
  Kentland (G-8522)

North Vernon Plain Dlr & Sun ....E 812 346-3973
  North Vernon (G-11272)

Northwest News & Printing ....G 260 637-9003
  Fort Wayne (G-4506)

Nuvo Inc ....E 317 254-2400
  Indianapolis (G-7605)

Nwitimescom ....F 219 933-3200
  Munster (G-10617)

Odb Inc ....G 260 673-0062
  Fort Wayne (G-4508)

Owen Leader Inc ....G 812 829-3936
  Spencer (G-13031)

Paper of Montgomery County ....G 765 361-8888
  Crawfordsville (G-2183)

Paper of Wabash County Inc ....E 260 563-8326
  Wabash (G-13746)

Papers Inc ....G 574 534-2591
  Goshen (G-5305)

Papers Inc ....G 574 269-2932
  Warsaw (G-13923)

Pathfinder Communications Corp ....E 574 295-2500
  Elkhart (G-3077)

Patrick & Sharon Hoctor ....G 812 898-2678
  Terre Haute (G-13297)

Paxton Media Group LLC ....E 765 664-5111
  Marion (G-9550)

Pendleton Times ....G 765 778-2324
  Pendleton (G-11500)

Pierce Oil Co Inc ....F 812 268-6356
  Sullivan (G-13090)

Pike County Publishing Corp ....F 812 354-8500
  Petersburg (G-11566)

Pilcher Publishing Co Inc ....G 219 696-7711
  Lowell (G-9419)

Posey County News ....G 812 682-3950
  New Harmony (G-10925)

Princeton Publishing Inc ....G 812 385-2525
  Princeton (G-11881)

Printers Group ....G 317 835-7720
  Fairland (G-3826)

Progress Examiner ....G 812 865-3242
  Orleans (G-11368)

Pulaski County Press Inc ....G 574 946-6628
  Winamac (G-14317)

Purdue Student Pubg Foundation ....E 765 743-1111
  West Lafayette (G-14099)

R R Donnelley Inc ....F 317 631-2203
  Indianapolis (G-7810)

Rapt Pen LLC ....G 317 547-8113
  Indianapolis (G-7817)

Region Communications Inc ....G 219 662-8888
  Crown Point (G-2294)

Republic Inc ....E 812 342-8028
  Columbus (G-2006)

Republican ....G 317 745-2777
  Danville (G-2356)

Ripley Publishing Co Inc ....F 812 689-6364
  Versailles (G-13657)

Rowland Printing Co Inc ....F 317 773-1829
  Noblesville (G-11177)

Royal Center Record ....G 574 643-3165
  Royal Center (G-12214)

Russ Print Shop ....F 219 996-3142
  Hebron (G-6022)

Russ Publishing ....F 812 847-4487
  Linton (G-9313)

Schurz Communications Inc ....B 574 235-6496
  South Bend (G-12930)

Schurz Communications Inc ....G 317 773-9960
  Noblesville (G-11180)

Schurz Communications Inc ....F 574 247-7237
  Mishawaka (G-10121)

Sentinel Corp ....G 574 223-2111
  Rochester (G-12153)

Service Publication Inc ....G 219 845-4445
  Hammond (G-5938)

Seymour Trbune A Cal Ltd Prtnr ....E 812 522-4871
  Seymour (G-12487)

Shelbyville Newspapers Inc ....D 317 398-6631
  Shelbyville (G-12568)

Shoals News ....G 812 247-2828
  Shoals (G-12669)

Snark Publishing LLC ....G 574 256-1027
  Mishawaka (G-10129)

Sommer Letter Company LLC ....G 260 414-6686
  Huntertown (G-6147)

South Bend Tribune ....G 574 971-5651
  Goshen (G-5324)

South Bend Tribune Corp ....B 574 235-6161
  South Bend (G-12946)

South Gibson Star-Times Inc ....F 812 753-3553
  Fort Branch (G-4029)

South Whtly Trbne Prctn News ....G 260 723-4771
  South Whitley (G-13004)

Southern Indiana Bus Source ....G 812 206-6397
  New Albany (G-10863)

Southsider ....G 317 781-0023
  Indianapolis (G-7964)

Special Ideas Incorporated ....G 812 834-5691
  Heltonville (G-6028)

Spectrum Print & Marketing ....G 317 908-7471
  Avon (G-467)

Spencer Evening World ....D 812 829-2255
  Spencer (G-13037)

Spencer Evening World ....G 765 795-4438
  Cloverdale (G-1738)

Sports Chronicle LLC ....G 317 353-9365
  Indianapolis (G-7975)

Sports Hotline ....G 765 664-8732
  Marion (G-9564)

Springs Valley Publishing Co ....G 812 936-9630
  French Lick (G-4989)

Teragraphics Ink LLC ....G 765 430-2863
  West Lafayette (G-14112)

The Findlay Publishing Co ....G 812 222-8000
  Batesville (G-559)

Thrify Nickel Wnt ADS Evansvil ....E 812 428-8484
  Evansville (G-3761)

Times ....E 765 296-3622
  Frankfort (G-4856)

Times Leader Publications LLC ....F 317 300-8782
  Indianapolis (G-8076)

Topics Newspapers Inc ....D 888 357-7827
  Fishers (G-3978)

Torch Newspapers Inc ....G 765 569-2033
  Rockville (G-12182)

Townepost LLC ....G 317 288-7101
  Indianapolis (G-8085)

Trading Post ....G 574 935-5460
  Plymouth (G-11731)

Triple Crown Media LLC ....D 574 533-2151
  Goshen (G-5342)

Trustees Indiana University ....B 812 855-0763
  Bloomington (G-846)

▲ Truth Publishing Company Inc ....C 574 294-1661
  Elkhart (G-3227)

Truth Publishing Company Inc ....E 765 653-5151
  Greencastle (G-5480)

Turkey Roost Publishing LLC ....G 402 972-6388
  Hardinsburg (G-5965)

Twice Daily LLC ....G 812 484-5417
  Evansville (G-3780)

Twin City Journal Reporter ....G 765 674-0070
  Gas City (G-5127)

Twin Sparrow Press ....G 917 331-5247
  Munster (G-10634)

University Notre Dame Du Lac ....D 574 631-7471
  Notre Dame (G-11304)

University Notre Dame Du Lac ....F 574 631-6346
  Notre Dame (G-11305)

USA Today ....G 212 715-2188
  Fishers (G-3982)

Vevay Newspapers Inc ....G 812 427-2311
  Vevay (G-13667)

Vincennes Sun Commercial ....D 812 886-9955
  Vincennes (G-13711)

Wabash Plain Dealer ....E 260 563-2131
  Wabash (G-13764)

Wabash Valley Publishing LLC ....G 812 494-2152
  Vincennes (G-13714)

▲ Warrick Publishing Co Inc ....E 812 897-2330
  Boonville (G-924)

Waynedale News Inc ....G 260 747-4535
  Fort Wayne (G-4747)

Western Wayne News ....G 765 478-5448
  Cambridge City (G-1262)

Whitewater Publications Inc ....E 765 647-4221
  Brookville (G-1131)

2721 Periodicals: Publishing & Printing

1632 Inc ....G 219 398-4155
  East Chicago (G-2514)

American Chiropractor Mag Inc ....E 260 471-4090
  Fort Wayne (G-4069)

American Graphics Group ....G 260 589-3117
  Berne (G-606)

American School Health Assn ....G 703 506-7675
  Bloomington (G-660)

Americas Coml Trnsp RES Co LLC .....F 812 379-2085
  Columbus (G-1854)

Ameriforce Media LLC ....G 812 961-9478
  Bloomington (G-661)

Apartment Assn of Fort Wayne ....G 260 482-2916
  Fort Wayne (G-4080)

Athletes Management & Service ....G 317 925-8200
  Indianapolis (G-6437)

B E A L I Inc ....G 219 322-5158
  Schererville (G-12316)

Baxter Design & Advertising ....G 219 464-9237
  Valparaiso (G-13507)

Bloom Magazine ....G 812 323-8959
  Bloomington (G-685)

Bonnier Corporation ....G 317 231-5862
  Indianapolis (G-6495)

Brent Croxton Inc ....G 317 846-7591
  Carmel (G-1322)

Brian Bex Report Inc ....G 765 489-5566
  Hagerstown (G-5804)

Christian Sound & Song Inc ....G 574 294-2893
  Elkhart (G-2756)

Compucomics ....G 812 876-1480
  Ellettsville (G-3275)

Connection LLC ....G 260 593-3999
  Topeka (G-13413)

Cr Publications ....G 219 931-6700
  Hammond (G-5866)

Creative Construction Pubg ....G 765 743-9704
  West Lafayette (G-14062)

▲ Dennis Polk & Associates Inc ....G 574 831-3555
  New Paris (G-10977)

Diamond Hoosier ....G 317 773-1411
  Noblesville (G-11091)

Don R Kill Publishing Inc ....G 574 271-9381
  Granger (G-5402)

Donnie Michaels Kicks ....G 765 457-4083
  Kokomo (G-8617)

Eco Partners Inc ....G 317 450-3346
  Carmel (G-1367)

Emmis Communications Corp ....D 317 266-0100
  Indianapolis (G-6854)

Emmis Operating Company ....E 317 266-0100
  Indianapolis (G-6855)

Emmis Publishing LP ....E 317 266-0100
  Indianapolis (G-6856)

Emmis Publishing Corporation ....G 317 266-0100
  Indianapolis (G-6857)

Emp of Evansville ....F 812 962-1309
  Evansville (G-3476)

Endowment Development Services ......F 317 542-9829
Indianapolis (G-6861)
Fort Wayne Newspapers Inc ....B 260 461-8444
Fort Wayne (G-4277)
Galbe Magazine LLC ....G 248 742-5231
Indianapolis (G-6265)
Greencastle Offset Inc ....G 765 653-4026
Greencastle (G-5458)
Growing Child ....G 765 464-0920
West Lafayette (G-14073)
◆ Herff Jones LLC ....C 800 419-5462
Indianapolis (G-7092)
Homes & Lifestyles Magazine ....E 574 674-6639
Osceola (G-11377)
Hoosier All-Stars Inc ....G 317 408-0513
Portland (G-11828)
Horizon Publishing Company LLC ....E 219 852-3200
Hammond (G-5895)
Inari Information Services ....G 812 331-2298
Bloomington (G-743)
Indiana Business Magazine ....G 317 692-1200
Indianapolis (G-7176)
Indiana State Medical Assn ....E 317 261-2060
Indianapolis (G-7192)
Indy Metro Woman Magazine ....G 317 843-1344
Indianapolis (G-7218)
Indy Sports Preview Program ....E 317 259-0570
Indianapolis (G-7222)
Informa Business Media Inc ....E 317 233-1310
New Palestine (G-10971)
International English Inc ....G 260 868-2670
Butler (G-1231)
It Factor Publications Inc ....E 219 228-8424
Highland (G-6050)
Kamrex Inc ....E 317 204-3779
Avon (G-452)
Limelight Publishing ....G 765 448-4461
Lafayette (G-8958)
Linear Publishing Corp ....G 317 722-8500
Indianapolis (G-7407)
Literature Sales ....G 219 873-3093
Michigan City (G-9812)
Lsc Communications Us LLC ....G 765 362-1300
Crawfordsville (G-2169)
Magazine Fulfillment Corp ....E 219 874-4245
Michigan City (G-9814)
Mappa Mundi Magazine ....G 574 896-4952
North Judson (G-11213)
Market Place Publications ....G 219 769-7733
Merrillville (G-9730)
Mennonite Inc Inc ....G 574 535-6050
Goshen (G-5286)
Michiana Business Publications ....G 260 497-0433
Fort Wayne (G-4470)
Michiana Executive Journal ....E 574 256-6666
Mishawaka (G-10080)
Midcountry Media Inc ....D 765 345-5133
Knightstown (G-8557)
Muzfeed Inc ....G 815 252-7676
Fort Wayne (G-4487)
National Retail Hardware Assn ....E 317 290-0338
Indianapolis (G-7576)
Omega One Connect Inc ....G 317 626-3445
Indianapolis (G-7618)
P J J T Distributors Inc ....F 812 254-2218
Washington (G-13996)
Pages Editorial Services Inc ....F 765 674-4212
Marion (G-9549)
Pearson Education Inc ....C 765 483-6500
Lebanon (G-9211)
Pearson Education Inc ....C 765 483-6738
Lebanon (G-9212)
Prairie Gold Rush ....G 812 342-3608
Seymour (G-12476)
Quarterly Group ....G 812 526-5600
Columbus (G-2005)
Raven Communications Inc ....G 317 576-9889
Indianapolis (G-7818)
Rick Singleton ....E 574 259-5555
Mishawaka (G-10117)
Roann Publishers ....G 574 831-2795
Goshen (G-5319)
Rough Notes Company Inc ....E 800 428-4384
Carmel (G-1470)
Rough Notes Company Inc ....E 317 582-1600
Carmel (G-1471)
Saturday Evening Post Soc Inc ....D 317 634-1100
Indianapolis (G-7898)
Senior Pathways Magazine LLC ....G 812 697-1750
New Albany (G-10861)
Servaas Inc ....G 317 633-2020
Indianapolis (G-7914)
Society For Ethnmusicology Inc ....G 812 855-6672
Bloomington (G-827)
St Meinrad Archabbey ....C 812 357-6611
Saint Meinrad (G-12276)
Stork News Northwest Indiana ....G 219 405-0499
Chesterton (G-1633)
Stork News Northwest Indiana ....G 219 808-5221
Hobart (G-6097)
Tl Enterprises LLC ....F 574 262-4706
Elkhart (G-3218)
Towne Post Network Inc ....G 317 288-7101
Indianapolis (G-8084)
Trustees Indiana University ....G 812 856-4186
Bloomington (G-845)
Trustees Indiana University ....G 812 855-3439
Bloomington (G-847)
Tucker Publishing Group Inc ....F 812 426-2115
Evansville (G-3778)
Ultra Montane Associates Inc ....G 574 289-9786
South Bend (G-12980)
Un Communications Group Inc ....E 317 844-8622
Carmel (G-1503)
United Brethren In Christ ....F 260 356-2312
Huntington (G-6258)
United Media Group Inc ....G 260 436-7417
Fort Wayne (G-4715)
University Notre Dame Du Lac ....F 574 631-6346
Notre Dame (G-11305)
USA Travel Magazine ....G 317 834-3683
Martinsville (G-9646)
Wabash Valley Magazine ....G 812 231-4294
Terre Haute (G-13365)
Whitetail Heartbeat ....G 260 336-1052
Middlebury (G-9925)

2731 Books: Publishing & Printing

AM Publishing Inc ....G 317 806-0001
Fishers (G-3870)
Aom Bookshop ....G 317 493-8095
Indianapolis (G-6405)
Athentic Inc ....F 219 362-8508
La Porte (G-8735)
▼ Author Solutions LLC ....B 812 339-6000
Bloomington (G-667)
▼ Ave Maria Press Inc ....D 574 287-2831
Notre Dame (G-11303)
Beacon House ....G 219 756-2131
Schererville (G-12317)
Beeman Jorgensen Inc ....G 317 841-7677
Indianapolis (G-6465)
Bibles For Blind & Visually ....G 812 466-3134
Terre Haute (G-13201)
Bird Publishing Company ....G 219 462-6330
Valparaiso (G-13509)
Bittinger Writings Inc ....G 317 846-9136
Carmel (G-1317)
Black Books Publishing Inc ....G 260 225-7479
Fort Wayne (G-4111)
▲ Brethren In Christ Media Minis ....G 574 773-3164
Nappanee (G-10657)
Bright Corp ....E 765 642-3114
Anderson (G-77)
Clinical Drug Information LLC ....G 317 735-5300
Indianapolis (G-6622)
Corby Publishing LP ....G 574 229-1107
Lakeville (G-9094)
Cr Publications ....G 219 931-6700
Hammond (G-5866)
Distance Learning Systems Ind ....E 888 955-3276
Greenwood (G-5681)
Fideli Publishing ....G 888 343-3542
Martinsville (G-9604)
Freight Trnsp RES Assoc Inc ....F 888 988-1699
Bloomington (G-727)
Frugal Times ....G 317 326-4165
Greenfield (G-5532)
Get Published Inc ....B 812 334-5279
Bloomington (G-731)
Gingerbread House Publications ....G 260 622-4868
Ossian (G-11399)
Glue + Paper Workshop LLC ....G 773 275-8935
Beverly Shores (G-630)
Hachette Book Group Inc ....C 765 483-9900
Lebanon (G-9185)
Hackett Publishing Company ....E 317 635-9250
Indianapolis (G-7063)
Hackett Publishing Company ....F 317 635-9250
Indianapolis (G-7064)
Harpercollins Publishers LLC ....D 219 324-4880
La Porte (G-8760)
Hawthorne Publishing ....G 317 867-5183
Carmel (G-1400)
Herff Jones LLC ....E 317 612-3400
Indianapolis (G-7089)
Herff Jones Yearbooks ....G 717 334-9123
Indianapolis (G-7094)
Horizon Publishing Company LLC ....E 219 852-3200
Hammond (G-5895)
Houghton Mifflin Harcourt Co ....G 317 359-5585
Indianapolis (G-7137)
Houghton Mifflin Harcourt Pubg ....C 317 359-5585
Indianapolis (G-7138)
Ilf Industries ....G 260 749-1931
New Haven (G-10944)
▼ Iuniverse Inc ....D 812 330-2909
Bloomington (G-752)
Kamrex Inc ....E 317 204-3779
Avon (G-452)
Kaplan Inc ....D 317 872-7220
Indianapolis (G-7333)
▲ Kids World Productions Inc ....G 317 674-6090
Zionsville (G-14444)
Lakota Language Consortium ....F 888 525-6828
Bloomington (G-762)
Main1media LLC ....G 317 841-7000
Indianapolis (G-7443)
National Federation of ....E 317 972-6900
Indianapolis (G-7571)
No-Load Fund Investor Inc ....G 317 571-1471
Carmel (G-1443)
Norlightspresscom ....G 812 675-8054
Bedford (G-566)
Old Paths Tract Society Inc ....F 812 247-2560
Shoals (G-12668)
Our Little Books LLC ....G 812 987-2475
Jeffersonville (G-8410)
Palibrio ....G 812 671-9757
Bloomington (G-795)
Pearson Education Inc ....E 317 428-3049
Indianapolis (G-7668)
Pearson Education Inc ....E 317 715-2150
Indianapolis (G-7669)
Penguin Random House LLC ....G 800 672-7836
Lebanon (G-9213)
Penguin Random House LLC ....C 765 362-5125
Crawfordsville (G-2184)
Princeton Publishing Inc ....E 812 385-2525
Princeton (G-11881)
Random House Inc ....G 410 386-7717
Crawfordsville (G-2191)
Regulations Update Svcs LLC ....G 812 334-4020
Bloomington (G-809)
Russel Warfield Inc ....G 317 243-7650
Indianapolis (G-7873)
Sacred Selections ....G 260 347-3758
Kendallville (G-8509)
Sewing Connection L L C ....G 317 745-1501
Avon (G-466)
Solution Tree Inc ....C 812 336-7700
Bloomington (G-828)
St Augustines Press Inc ....G 574 291-3500
South Bend (G-12951)
St Meinrad Archabbey ....D 812 357-6611
Saint Meinrad (G-12275)
Studio Indiana ....G 812 332-5073
Bloomington (G-833)
Three Cups LLC ....G 317 633-8082
Indianapolis (G-8070)
▲ Tom Doherty Company Inc ....G 317 352-8200
Indianapolis (G-8079)
Trafford Holdings Ltd ....G 888 232-4444
Bloomington (G-843)
Trustees Indiana University ....B 812 855-0763
Bloomington (G-846)
United Methodist Pubg Hse ....C 812 654-1325
Milan (G-9947)
University Notre Dame Du Lac ....F 574 631-6346
Notre Dame (G-11305)
University of Evansville ....G 812 479-2963
Evansville (G-3790)
◆ Voice of God Recordings Inc ....D 812 246-2137
Jeffersonville (G-8439)
W Robbins & Sons Inc ....G 765 522-1736
Roachdale (G-12096)
Wesleyan Church Corporation ....D 317 774-7900
Fishers (G-3984)
Whitman Publications Inc ....G 574 268-2062
Winona Lake (G-14355)

S I C

Wiley Publishing Inc .... B 317 842-2032
Indianapolis *(G-8198)*

William H Sadlier Inc .... G 219 465-0453
Valparaiso *(G-13637)*

▼ World Missionary Press Inc .... E 574 831-2111
New Paris *(G-11001)*

Worth Tax and Financial Svc .... G 574 267-4687
Warsaw *(G-13969)*

▲ Xlibris Corporation .... D 812 671-9162
Bloomington *(G-861)*

2732 Book Printing, Not Publishing

Augustin Prtg & Design Svcs .... G 765 966-7130
Richmond *(G-11957)*

Biblical Enterprises LLC .... G 812 391-0071
Bloomington *(G-682)*

Burkert-Walton Inc .... G 812 425-7157
Evansville *(G-3405)*

Codybro LLC .... G 765 827-5441
Connersville *(G-2044)*

Collier Pubg & Consulting .... E 317 513-8176
Indianapolis *(G-6632)*

▲ Courier Kendallville Inc .... E 260 347-3044
Kendallville *(G-8469)*

▲ Franklin Publishing Inc .... G 800 634-1993
Greenwood *(G-5696)*

Graessle-Mercer Co .... E 812 522-5478
Seymour *(G-12451)*

Herff Jones LLC .... G 317 612-3400
Indianapolis *(G-7089)*

Lsc Communications Inc .... G 812 234-1585
Terre Haute *(G-13276)*

Lsc Communications Us LLC .... G 765 362-1300
Crawfordsville *(G-2169)*

Mitchell-Fleming Printing Inc .... F 317 462-5467
Greenfield *(G-5554)*

Priority Printing LLC .... G 317 241-4234
Indianapolis *(G-7761)*

RR Donnelley & Sons Company ..... A 765 362-1300
Crawfordsville *(G-2194)*

▲ Solema USA Inc .... G 765 361-0806
Crawfordsville *(G-2196)*

Traveling Bookbinder Inc .... G 317 441-4901
Noblesville *(G-11195)*

W Robbins & Sons Inc .... G 765 522-1736
Roachdale *(G-12036)*

Wayseeker LLC .... G 574 529-0199
Syracuse *(G-13153)*

2741 Misc Publishing

124 Publishing LLC .... G 574 784-0046
Lakeville *(G-9092)*

200 Express .... G 260 833-2125
Angola *(G-186)*

39 Degrees North LLC .... F 855 447-3939
Bloomington *(G-650)*

Academy of Mdel Aronautics Inc ... D 765 287-1256
Muncie *(G-10422)*

Accurate Publishing Co .... G 219 836-1397
Munster *(G-10593)*

Advertiser Inc .... G 260 824-4770
Bluffton *(G-862)*

Advertising Communications Gro ... E 317 843-2523
Carmel *(G-1304)*

Afterimage Gis .... G 765 744-1346
Muncie *(G-10425)*

Aim Media Indiana Oper LLC .... D 812 372-7811
Columbus *(G-1851)*

Aj Express Broker Service .... G 812 866-1380
Madison *(G-9441)*

Alacheri Publishing LLC .... G 317 755-6670
Indianapolis *(G-6359)*

American Classifieds .... E 317 782-8111
Indianapolis *(G-6386)*

Ancient Faith Ministries .... G 219 728-6786
Chesterton *(G-1593)*

Annabella Publications LLC .... G 219 663-4244
Crown Point *(G-2226)*

App Factor .... G 219 229-1039
Chesterton *(G-1594)*

Arson Press .... G 812 345-3527
Bloomington *(G-666)*

Artistic Expressions Pubg .... G 317 502-6213
Gas City *(G-5119)*

AT&T Corp .... C 317 347-2163
Indianapolis *(G-6434)*

Athena Arts & Graphics Inc .... G 317 876-8916
Indianapolis *(G-6436)*

Athentic Inc .... F 219 362-8508
La Porte *(G-8735)*

Automobile Dealers Assn of Ind .... G 317 635-1441
Indianapolis *(G-6446)*

Barr None Music Publishers/Lea .... G 502 413-5443
Borden *(G-928)*

Batch Small Press LLC .... G 317 410-8923
Indianapolis *(G-6457)*

Bc Publications Inc .... G 765 334-8277
Carthage *(G-1512)*

Bittersweet Publishing .... G 317 640-3943
Fishers *(G-3879)*

Blue Guardian Publishing Co .... G 317 506-0763
Indianapolis *(G-6485)*

Bradford Press .... G 574 876-3601
Mishawaka *(G-10013)*

Brallan Press LLC .... G 317 525-4335
Westfield *(G-14139)*

Brallan Press LLC .... G 765 337-7909
Indianapolis *(G-6501)*

Brasilia Press Inc .... G 574 262-9700
Elkhart *(G-2732)*

Bright Corp .... E 765 642-3114
Anderson *(G-77)*

Brighter Dayz Publishing LLC .... G 317 793-1364
Indianapolis *(G-6509)*

Broccoli Press LLC .... G 317 815-4687
Fishers *(G-3882)*

Brush Strokes Inc .... G 800 272-2307
South Bend *(G-12726)*

Buchanan Publishing .... G 317 546-4524
Indianapolis *(G-6517)*

Buddy Eugene Publishing LLC ...... G 574 223-6048
Akron *(G-3)*

Caine Publishing LLC .... G 312 215-5253
Long Beach *(G-9376)*

Card Calendar Publishing LLC ...... G 812 234-5999
Terre Haute *(G-13205)*

Cardinal Publishers Group .... G 317 846-8190
Carmel *(G-1329)*

Carl Hugness Publishing .... G 812 273-2472
Madison *(G-9447)*

Cheyenne Enterprises LLC .... G 317 253-7795
Indianapolis *(G-6599)*

Cola Voce Music Inc .... G 317 466-0624
Indianapolis *(G-6630)*

Collective Press Inc .... G 812 325-1385
Bloomington *(G-701)*

College Network Inc .... G 800 395-3276
Indianapolis *(G-6631)*

Creative Publishing Concep .... G 317 844-3549
Carmel *(G-1347)*

Criterion Press Inc .... F 317 236-1570
Indianapolis *(G-6693)*

Crown Point Shopping News .... G 219 663-4212
Crown Point *(G-2241)*

Crown Training & Development ...... E 219 947-0845
Merrillville *(G-9708)*

Cupprint LLC .... G 574 323-5250
South Bend *(G-12744)*

Current Publishing LLC .... G 317 489-4444
Carmel *(G-1351)*

D&G Publishing Inc .... G 317 531-8678
Westfield *(G-14154)*

Degler Mktg & Mailing Svcs .... E 317 873-5550
Zionsville *(G-14429)*

Dow Theory Forecasts Inc .... E 219 931-6480
Hammond *(G-5872)*

Dungan Aerial Services Inc .... G 765 827-1355
Connersville *(G-2047)*

East Fork Studio & Press Inc .... G 765 458-6103
Brownsville *(G-1195)*

Echo Publications .... G 219 696-3756
Lowell *(G-9405)*

Education Connection Pubg LLC .... G 317 876-3355
Indianapolis *(G-6808)*

El Mexicano Inc .... G 260 456-6843
Fort Wayne *(G-4233)*

El Puente LLC .... G 574 533-9082
Goshen *(G-5211)*

Endowment Development Services ... F 317 542-9829
Indianapolis *(G-6861)*

Exploding Brain Press .... G 219 393-0796
Michigan City *(G-9789)*

Express Motors .... G 812 437-9495
Evansville *(G-3497)*

Fairylan LLC .... G 219 866-3077
Rensselaer *(G-11922)*

First Databank Inc .... G 317 571-7200
Indianapolis *(G-6926)*

Fish Factory .... G 219 929-9375
Chesterton *(G-1606)*

Flying Turtle Publishing LLC .... G 219 221-8488
Hammond *(G-5881)*

Fourth Freedom Forum Inc .... F 574 534-3402
Goshen *(G-5221)*

Full Press LLC .... G 260 433-7731
Fort Wayne *(G-4290)*

Gaunt Family LLC .... G 812 473-3167
Evansville *(G-3516)*

Gingerbread House Publications .... G 260 622-4868
Ossian *(G-11399)*

Gourmet Express .... G 219 921-9927
Valparaiso *(G-13551)*

Gypsum Express Ltd .... D 219 987-2181
Demotte *(G-2439)*

Gyrewide Publications & Bad .... G 765 721-7676
Greencastle *(G-5459)*

Harrison Macdonald & Sons .... F 765 742-9012
Lafayette *(G-8911)*

Harry B Higley & Sons Inc .... G 219 558-8183
Dyer *(G-2501)*

Hart Publishers Inc .... G 260 672-8978
Huntington *(G-6208)*

Harvard Business Publishing .... G 317 815-8232
Carmel *(G-1395)*

Hatfield Publications LLC .... G 317 581-9804
Carmel *(G-1398)*

Herff Jones LLC .... G 317 612-3400
Indianapolis *(G-7089)*

◆ Herff Jones LLC .... C 800 419-5462
Indianapolis *(G-7092)*

Heron Blue Publications LLC .... G 317 696-0674
Carmel *(G-1403)*

High Note Publishing .... G 765 313-1699
Swayzee *(G-13123)*

Home News Enterprises LLC .... E 574 583-5121
Monticello *(G-10265)*

Horizon Management Services ...... E 219 852-3200
Hammond *(G-5894)*

Hot Off Press .... G 260 591-8331
Wabash *(G-13732)*

Image House Inc .... F 219 947-0800
Crown Point *(G-2260)*

Imagination Publications LLC .... G 574 256-6666
Mishawaka *(G-10052)*

Indiana Town Planner LLC .... G 219 384-3555
Schererville *(G-12324)*

Ingroup .... G 317 817-9997
Indianapolis *(G-7232)*

International Code Council Inc .... G 317 879-1677
Indianapolis *(G-7252)*

Jensen Publications Inc .... G 317 514-8864
Zionsville *(G-14440)*

Job Scholar LLC .... G 419 564-9574
Huntington *(G-6221)*

Jossey-Bass Publishers .... G 877 762-2974
Indianapolis *(G-7313)*

Journal Publishing Co Inc .... G 812 876-2254
Ellettsville *(G-3282)*

Journeymann Precision Press .... G 260 724-6934
Decatur *(G-2388)*

Joyful Noise Recordings LLC .... G 317 632-3220
Indianapolis *(G-7316)*

Kelk Publishing LLC .... G 812 268-6356
Sullivan *(G-13084)*

Ketch Publishing .... G 812 327-0072
Bloomington *(G-758)*

Kids At Heart Publishing LLC .... G 765 478-5773
Cambridge City *(G-1259)*

Kiel Media LLC .... G 219 544-2060
La Crosse *(G-8720)*

Kokomo Press LLC .... G 317 575-9903
Carmel *(G-1424)*

Laptop Publishing LLC .... G 317 379-5716
Carmel *(G-1426)*

Lcas Inc .... G 541 219-0229
Hobart *(G-6088)*

Leader Publishing Co of Salem ..... E 812 883-4446
Salem *(G-12299)*

Leslie Webber Media & Pubg LLC ... G 317 774-0598
Noblesville *(G-11141)*

Lighthouse Publ Ministries .... G 260 209-6948
Fort Wayne *(G-4436)*

Lime City Press LLC .... G 260 344-3435
Huntington *(G-6225)*

Little I Publications LLC .... G 317 467-9297
Greenfield *(G-5549)*

Logansport Pharos Press .... G 574 753-4169
Logansport *(G-9351)*

Luna Press Productions LLC .... G 317 398-8895
Shelbyville *(G-12549)*

Macs Express Inc ....G...... 765 865-9700
  Kokomo (G-8662)
Martin Brown Publishers LLC..........G...... 765 459-8258
  Kokomo (G-8664)
McCrory Publishing ....G...... 260 485-1812
  Fort Wayne (G-4460)
McMillan Express ....G...... 260 447-7648
  Fort Wayne (G-4461)
Measure Press Inc ....G...... 812 473-0361
  Evansville (G-3621)
Mining Media Inc ....G...... 317 802-7116
  Indianapolis (G-7524)
Momaki Publishing LLC ....G...... 847 454-4641
  Merrillville (G-9740)
MT Publishing Company Inc ....G...... 812 468-8022
  Evansville (G-3640)
Mud Creek Publishing Inc ....G...... 317 577-9659
  Indianapolis (G-7556)
My County Publishing LLC ....G...... 765 630-8221
  Greencastle (G-5469)
Narrow Gate Publishing LLC ....G...... 219 464-8579
  Valparaiso (G-13585)
Nationwide Publishing Company ....G...... 260 312-3924
  Fort Wayne (G-4492)
New Philosopher Prss ....G...... 406 992-5791
  Bloomington (G-780)
New Readers Press ....G...... 317 514-6515
  Avon (G-457)
News Banner Publications Inc..........E...... 260 824-0224
  Bluffton (G-883)
▼ Noel Studio Inc.............................F...... 317 297-1117
  Zionsville (G-14452)
Novels By Nellotie ....G...... 812 583-1196
  Mitchell (G-10168)
Oleta Publishing Co Inc....................G...... 765 730-7195
  Yorktown (G-14409)
Paper Street Press ....G...... 765 894-0027
  West Lafayette (G-14093)
PCA Publishing Inc ....G...... 317 658-2055
  Indianapolis (G-7666)
Pelican Bay Solutions LLC ....G...... 574 268-4456
  Warsaw (G-13924)
Penlines Publishing LLC ....G...... 219 884-2632
  Gary (G-5084)
Pentera Group Inc ....F...... 317 543-2055
  Indianapolis (G-7670)
Pike Publishing ....G...... 812 354-4701
  Petersburg (G-11567)
Porchlight Group Inc ....G...... 317 804-1166
  Fishers (G-3954)
Portals of Light Inc ....G...... 765 981-2651
  Marion (G-9554)
Praise Gathering Music Group ....F...... 765 640-4428
  Anderson (G-155)
Praiseworthy Press LLC ....G...... 765 536-2077
  Summitville (G-13101)
Precisely Write Inc ....G...... 317 585-7701
  Indianapolis (G-7730)
Press Control Systems.....................G...... 317 887-1369
  Greenwood (G-5737)
Pretty Brilliant Press ....G...... 765 277-2308
  Richmond (G-12031)
Provision Publishing LLC ....G...... 765 282-3928
  Muncie (G-10550)
Pubco Inc.......................................F...... 219 874-4245
  Michigan City (G-9830)
Publishers Consulting Corp ....E...... 219 874-4245
  Michigan City (G-9831)
Publishers Sovereign Grace.............G...... 765 296-5538
  Mulberry (G-10418)
Purple Door Press............................G...... 219 690-1046
  Lowell (G-9421)
Rabboni Book Publishing Co LLC ......G...... 765 254-9969
  Muncie (G-10552)
Red Lark Press Inc ....G...... 260 224-7974
  Huntington (G-6243)
Rewind..G...... 812 361-0411
  Bloomington (G-810)
Richard E Leonard LLC ....G...... 812 882-7343
  Vincennes (G-13702)
Riebel Roque Inc.............................G...... 317 849-3680
  Indianapolis (G-7844)
Rol Publications ....G...... 812 366-4154
  Greenville (G-5653)
Rosswyvern Press LLC ....G...... 859 421-0864
  Clarksville (G-1694)
Rough Notes Company Inc ....E...... 317 582-1600
  Carmel (G-1471)
▲ Round World Products Inc............F...... 317 257-7352
  Carmel (G-1472)

Russ Print Shop ....F...... 219 996-3142
  Hebron (G-6022)
Rust Publishing In LLC ....G...... 765 653-5151
  Greencastle (G-5477)
Rutkowski & Associates Inc ....G...... 812 476-4520
  Evansville (G-3712)
Ryobi Press Parts ....G...... 800 901-3304
  Carmel (G-1474)
Sams Technical Publishing LLC.........F...... 317 396-9850
  Indianapolis (G-7889)
▲ Sand Dune Publishing Compa........G...... 219 938-7118
  Gary (G-5095)
Scalable Press ....G...... 510 396-5226
  Indianapolis (G-7900)
Schatzi Press ....G...... 317 335-2335
  McCordsville (G-9675)
Scher Maihem Publishing Ltd...........G...... 260 897-2697
  Auburn (G-352)
Scribe Publications Inc ....G...... 219 791-9254
  Merrillville (G-9752)
Scurvy Palace Publishing LLC ....G...... 317 809-4591
  Martinsville (G-9637)
Service Publication Inc....................G...... 219 845-4445
  Hammond (G-5938)
Sitesuccess Inc................................G...... 219 808-4076
  Schererville (G-12345)
Skyward Publishing LLC ....G...... 317 791-2212
  Indianapolis (G-7951)
Smallwood Consulting LLC ....G...... 812 406-8040
  Sellersburg (G-12418)
Spiritbuilding Publishing ....G...... 765 623-2238
  Summitville (G-13105)
Tacair Publications ....G...... 260 429-7975
  Churubusco (G-1658)
Tale Chaser Publishing Inc ....G...... 765 962-4309
  Indianapolis (G-12057)
▲ Tanglewood Publishing Inc...........G...... 812 877-9488
  Indianapolis (G-8035)
Taught It LLC ....G...... 317 469-4120
  Indianapolis (G-8039)
Tendre Press LLC ....G...... 812 606-9563
  Bloomington (G-837)
Testimony Publications LLC ....G...... 812 602-3031
  Evansville (G-3758)
Thinkshortcut Publishing LLC...........G...... 765 935-1127
  Richmond (G-12065)
Thm Publishing Sacramento LLC.......G...... 317 810-1340
  Carmel (G-1495)
Thomson Reuters Corporation ....G...... 317 570-9387
  Fishers (G-3976)
Thrify Nickel Wnt ADS Evansvil ....E...... 812 428-8484
  Evansville (G-3761)
Thunder Rolls Express ....G...... 812 667-5111
  Canaan (G-1281)
Timothy Reed Carry ME Mus Pubg ......G...... 812 322-7187
  Bloomington (G-842)
▲ Tom Doherty Company Inc............G...... 317 352-8200
  Indianapolis (G-8079)
Triangle Publishing ....G...... 765 677-2544
  Marion (G-9567)
True Stories Publishing Co LLC ....G...... 765 425-8224
  Indianapolis (G-8103)
Trustees Indiana University ....E...... 812 855-4848
  Bloomington (G-848)
Un Communications Group Inc ....E...... 317 844-8622
  Carmel (G-1503)
Un Seen Press Co ....G...... 317 867-5594
  Westfield (G-14195)
United Media Group Inc ....G...... 260 436-7417
  Fort Wayne (G-4715)
Valvoline Express ....G...... 765 473-4891
  Peru (G-11554)
Vintage Publishing LLC.....................G...... 812 719-7200
  Evansville (G-3803)
Wamingo Publishing LLP ....G...... 317 443-1326
  Indianapolis (G-8177)
Washington 2 Mount Publi ....G...... 812 332-1600
  Bloomington (G-853)
Wiggins Press LLC ....G...... 574 273-1769
  Granger (G-5452)
Williams Woods Pubg Svcs LLC ....G...... 317 270-0976
  Indianapolis (G-8201)
Willowgreen Inc...............................G...... 260 490-2222
  Fort Wayne (G-4756)
Woodsong Publishing ....G...... 812 528-0875
  Seymour (G-12501)
Worth Publications LLC.....................G...... 219 808-4001
  Crown Point (G-2323)
Wth Publications Inc........................G...... 574 646-2007
  Bourbon (G-951)

X Press Storage LLC ....G...... 219 942-1227
  Hobart (G-6102)
Yellow Door Publishing LLC ....G...... 574 256-5797
  Mishawaka (G-10152)
Zeppelin Commander Press Inc ....G...... 317 839-9025
  Plainfield (G-11653)

2752 Commercial Printing: Lithographic

2fresh Prints LLC.............................G...... 317 947-7164
  Indianapolis (G-6286)
2sweet Printing Service LLC ....G...... 317 476-4402
  Indianapolis (G-6287)
323ink LLC......................................G...... 812 282-3620
  Jeffersonville (G-8316)
3d Printing & Prototyping LLC ....G...... 317 319-8515
  Greenwood (G-5657)
A&A Screen Printing.........................G...... 765 473-8783
  Peru (G-11514)
A-1 Graphics Inc ....G...... 765 289-1851
  Muncie (G-10420)
A-1 Letter Shop Inc ....G...... 317 632-7212
  Indianapolis (G-6302)
AC Printing Inc ....G...... 708 418-9100
  Highland (G-6034)
Accent Complex Inc.........................G...... 574 522-2368
  Elkhart (G-2664)
Acclaim Graphics Inc ....G...... 812 424-5035
  Evansville (G-3334)
Accu-Label Inc ....E...... 260 482-5223
  Fort Wayne (G-4036)
Ace Screen Printing LLC ....G...... 317 861-7477
  New Palestine (G-10965)
Ad Craft Printers Incorporated ....G...... 219 942-9799
  Merrillville (G-9692)
Ad Plex-Rhodes Inc ....G...... 812 256-3396
  Charlestown (G-1556)
Advanced Print Solutions LLC ....G...... 513 405-3452
  Brookville (G-1110)
▲ Advantage Direct365 Corp ....E...... 260 490-1961
  Fort Wayne (G-4047)
Affordable Footwear & T-Shrt ....G...... 260 702-5134
  Fort Wayne (G-4049)
Affordable Screen Printing EMB ....G...... 574 278-7885
  Monticello (G-10252)
AG Apparel and Screen Prtg LLC ....G...... 260 483-3817
  Fort Wayne (G-4050)
AG Printing Specialists LLC ....G...... 866 445-6824
  Lafayette (G-8848)
Ah Printing Service..........................G...... 219 933-7686
  Hammond (G-5837)
Aim Media Indiana Oper LLC ....E...... 317 736-7101
  Franklin (G-4863)
Aim Media Indiana Oper LLC ....E...... 317 462-5528
  Greenfield (G-5497)
Aleph Bet Document Centre ....G...... 260 749-2288
  New Haven (G-10927)
All 4u Printing LLC...........................G...... 317 845-2955
  Morgantown (G-10347)
All American Screen Prtg LLC ....G...... 765 914-7600
  Hagerstown (G-5802)
All Printing and Publications ....E...... 260 636-2727
  Albion (G-15)
Allen C Terhune & Associates ....G...... 765 948-4164
  Fairmount (G-3828)
Allison Payment Systems LLC ....C...... 317 808-2400
  Indianapolis (G-6370)
Almighty Business Cards LLC ....G...... 260 615-4663
  Fort Wayne (G-4063)
Altstadt Business Forms Inc ....F...... 812 425-3393
  Evansville (G-3349)
American Express Travel ....G...... 812 523-0106
  Seymour (G-12430)
American Intl Mfg Slutions LLP..........G...... 317 443-5778
  Carmel (G-1310)
American Printing.............................G...... 219 836-5600
  Munster (G-10595)
American Printing Company...............F...... 574 533-5399
  Goshen (G-5169)
Anchor Enterprises ....G...... 812 282-7220
  Jeffersonville (G-8326)
Angies Printing LLC ....G...... 765 966-6237
  Richmond (G-11953)
Anyprint LLC....................................G...... 317 402-5979
  Zionsville (G-14417)
Apparel Design Group ....G...... 812 339-3355
  Bloomington (G-662)
Apple Press Inc ....G...... 317 253-7752
  Indianapolis (G-6409)
Athena Arts & Graphics Inc ....G...... 317 876-8916
  Indianapolis (G-6436)

Augustin Prtg & Design Svcs ....G....... 765 966-7130
Richmond *(G-11957)*

Avalon Enterprises Inc ....G....... 317 894-8666
Indianapolis *(G-6448)*

▼ Ave Maria Press Inc ....D....... 574 287-2831
Notre Dame *(G-11303)*

Aztec Printing Inc ....G....... 812 422-1462
Wadesville *(G-13771)*

B-Hive Printing ....G....... 812 897-3905
Boonville *(G-908)*

Bartel Printing Company Inc ....G....... 574 267-7421
Warsaw *(G-13842)*

Baugh Enterprises Inc ....F....... 812 334-8189
Bloomington *(G-674)*

Baxter Printing Inc ....G....... 219 923-1999
Highland *(G-6037)*

Beast Custom Athletic Printing ....G....... 765 610-6802
Fairmount *(G-3830)*

Benitos Printing ....G....... 812 282-4855
Jeffersonville *(G-8329)*

Bhar Printing Inc ....G....... 317 899-1020
Indianapolis *(G-6472)*

Biela Printing ....G....... 219 874-8094
Michigan City *(G-9768)*

Bills Printing ....G....... 765 962-7674
Richmond *(G-11966)*

Bizcard ....G....... 317 436-8649
Indianapolis *(G-6480)*

Blasted Works ....G....... 574 583-3211
Monticello *(G-10256)*

Bloomington Discount Prtg Inc ....G....... 812 332-9789
Bloomington *(G-688)*

Blue Creek Trail Map Co ....G....... 765 455-9867
Kokomo *(G-8599)*

Blue Print Specialties Inc ....G....... 765 742-6976
Lafayette *(G-8862)*

Bobs Quick Copy Shop ....G....... 765 457-9160
Kokomo *(G-8601)*

Bowen Printing Inc ....G....... 574 936-3924
Plymouth *(G-11670)*

Boy-Conn Printers Inc ....G....... 219 462-2665
Valparaiso *(G-13512)*

Brainstorm Print LLC ....G....... 317 466-1600
Indianapolis *(G-6500)*

Brand Prtg & Photo-Litho Co ....G....... 317 921-4095
Indianapolis *(G-6503)*

Brand Wave Inc ....G....... 661 414-2115
Noblesville *(G-11069)*

Bright Corp ....E....... 765 642-3114
Anderson *(G-77)*

Brinkman Press Inc ....G....... 317 722-0305
Indianapolis *(G-6511)*

Broadway Press ....G....... 765 644-8813
Anderson *(G-78)*

Browns Simply Printings ....G....... 317 490-7493
Mooresville *(G-10303)*

Brq Quickprint Inc ....G....... 219 464-1070
Valparaiso *(G-13515)*

Bryant Printing ....G....... 765 521-3379
New Castle *(G-10893)*

Bryson C Toothaker ....G....... 219 462-9179
Valparaiso *(G-13516)*

Budget Printing Centers Inc ....G....... 812 282-8832
Jeffersonville *(G-8334)*

Buis Enterprises Inc ....E....... 317 839-7394
Plainfield *(G-11598)*

Bumblebee Quick Print Inc ....G....... 765 962-0368
Richmond *(G-11968)*

Burkert-Walton Inc ....G....... 812 425-7157
Evansville *(G-3405)*

Business Art & Design Inc ....G....... 317 782-9108
Beech Grove *(G-593)*

C B Printing ....G....... 765 569-0900
Rockville *(G-12174)*

C J P Corporation ....G....... 219 924-1685
Highland *(G-6040)*

Campbell Printing Co Inc ....G....... 219 866-5913
Rensselaer *(G-11916)*

Carlton Ventures Inc ....G....... 317 637-2590
Indianapolis *(G-6556)*

Casino Printing For Less ....G....... 765 742-0000
Lafayette *(G-8869)*

Cause Printing Company ....G....... 260 224-3515
Huntington *(G-6197)*

Cave & Company Printing ....G....... 317 896-5337
Westfield *(G-14141)*

Cave Company Printing Inc ....G....... 812 863-4333
Bloomfield *(G-637)*

Cecils Printing & Office Sups ....G....... 812 683-4416
Huntingburg *(G-6153)*

Chameleon Lifestyles LLC ....G....... 317 468-3246
Greenfield *(G-5514)*

Charles E Watts ....G....... 812 547-8516
Tell City *(G-13158)*

Chicago Color Graphics ....G....... 312 856-1433
Hammond *(G-5860)*

▲ Chromasource Inc ....G....... 260 420-3000
Columbia City *(G-1772)*

Circle Printing LLC ....G....... 812 663-7367
Greensburg *(G-5593)*

CJ Printing ....G....... 219 924-1685
Hammond *(G-5862)*

Ckmt Associates Inc ....E....... 219 924-2820
Hammond *(G-5863)*

Clarke American Checks Inc ....C....... 812 283-9598
Jeffersonville *(G-8339)*

Classic Graphics Inc ....F....... 260 482-3487
Fort Wayne *(G-4156)*

Clondalkin Pharma & Healthcare ....C....... 317 328-7355
Indianapolis *(G-6623)*

Clondalkin Pharma & Healthcare ....C....... 812 464-2461
Evansville *(G-3420)*

Cnhi LLC ....E....... 812 944-6481
New Albany *(G-10762)*

Coaches Connection Inc ....G....... 260 356-0400
Huntington *(G-6198)*

Colormax Digital Imaging Inc ....E....... 812 477-3805
Evansville *(G-3422)*

▲ Colwell Inc ....C....... 260 347-1981
Kendallville *(G-8464)*

Colwell Inc ....C....... 260 347-1981
Kendallville *(G-8465)*

Commercial Print Shop Inc ....G....... 260 724-3722
Decatur *(G-2373)*

Commercial Printing of Lagro ....G....... 260 782-2421
Lagro *(G-9072)*

Community Holdings Indiana Inc ....F....... 574 722-5000
Logansport *(G-9332)*

Community Holdings Indiana Inc ....E....... 765 482-4650
Lebanon *(G-9175)*

Community Holdings Indiana Inc ....F....... 765 459-3121
Kokomo *(G-8608)*

Community Holdings Indiana Inc ....E....... 812 663-3111
Greensburg *(G-5594)*

Complete Printer Inc ....G....... 574 936-9505
Plymouth *(G-11676)*

Complete Prtg Solutions Inc ....G....... 812 285-9200
Jeffersonville *(G-8343)*

Consolidated Printing Svcs Inc ....F....... 765 468-6033
Farmland *(G-3841)*

Copy Solutions Inc ....G....... 260 436-2679
Fort Wayne *(G-4175)*

Copy-Print Shop Inc ....E....... 765 447-6868
Lafayette *(G-8877)*

Copymat Service Inc ....G....... 765 743-5995
Lafayette *(G-8878)*

Cornerstone Business Prtg LLC ....G....... 574 642-4060
Middlebury *(G-9877)*

Country Pines Inc ....F....... 812 247-3315
Shoals *(G-12665)*

Courier Communications LLC ....B....... 260 347-3044
Kendallville *(G-8468)*

Courier Printing Co Allen Cnty ....G....... 260 627-2728
Grabill *(G-5362)*

CPC ....G....... 812 358-5010
Brownstown *(G-1184)*

Craigs Printing Co ....G....... 812 358-5010
Brownstown *(G-1185)*

Creative Computer Services ....G....... 317 729-5779
Franklin *(G-4880)*

Creative Concept Ventures Inc ....G....... 812 282-9442
Jeffersonville *(G-8348)*

Creative Impressions Inc ....F....... 317 244-9842
Indianapolis *(G-6687)*

Crescendo Inc ....G....... 812 829-4759
Spencer *(G-13022)*

Crossroads Imprints Inc ....G....... 765 482-2931
Lebanon *(G-9177)*

Crystal Graphics Inc ....G....... 317 535-9202
Whiteland *(G-14237)*

Cunningham Printing Inc ....G....... 812 347-2438
New Salisbury *(G-11008)*

▲ Custom Forms Inc ....G....... 765 463-6162
Lafayette *(G-8884)*

D & E Printing Company Inc ....G....... 317 852-9048
Brownsburg *(G-1147)*

D & M Printing Inc ....G....... 812 847-4837
Linton *(G-9306)*

Damalak Printing Inc ....G....... 317 896-5337
Westfield *(G-14156)*

Data Print Initiatives LLC ....G....... 260 489-2665
Fort Wayne *(G-4200)*

Delp Printing & Mailing Inc ....E....... 317 872-9744
Indianapolis *(G-6733)*

Delphos Herald of Indiana Inc ....E....... 812 537-0063
Lawrenceburg *(G-9138)*

Digital Printing Incorporated ....F....... 812 265-2205
Madison *(G-9457)*

Digital Reprographics Inc ....G....... 260 483-8066
Fort Wayne *(G-4210)*

Dirty Squeegee Screen Prtg LLC ....G....... 574 358-0003
Middlebury *(G-9882)*

Diverse Sales Solutions LLC ....G....... 317 514-2403
Indianapolis *(G-6747)*

Diversfied Cmmunications Group ....F....... 317 755-3191
Indianapolis *(G-6749)*

Diversity Press LLC ....G....... 317 241-4234
Indianapolis *(G-6751)*

Dla Document Services ....G....... 812 854-1465
Crane *(G-2125)*

Doerr Printing Co ....G....... 317 568-0135
Indianapolis *(G-6756)*

Don Michiel Prints LLC ....G....... 812 550-7767
Evansville *(G-3461)*

Dove Printing Services ....G....... 317 843-8222
Indianapolis *(G-6761)*

Dps Printing ....G....... 260 503-9681
Columbia City *(G-1780)*

Drs Graphix Group Inc ....G....... 317 569-1855
Indianapolis *(G-6768)*

Duley Press Inc ....E....... 574 259-5203
Mishawaka *(G-10037)*

Duneland Specialties Inc ....G....... 219 464-1616
Valparaiso *(G-13530)*

Duramark Technologies Inc ....D....... 317 867-5700
Westfield *(G-14161)*

Dynamark Graphics Group Inc ....G....... 317 569-1855
Indianapolis *(G-6774)*

Dynamark Graphics Group Inc ....F....... 317 328-2565
Indianapolis *(G-6776)*

Dynamark Graphics Group Inc ....G....... 317 634-2963
Indianapolis *(G-6777)*

Dynamark Graphics Group Inc ....G....... 317 328-2555
Indianapolis *(G-6775)*

E James Dant ....G....... 812 476-2271
Evansville *(G-3469)*

Economy Offset Printers Inc ....G....... 574 534-6270
Goshen *(G-5210)*

Ed Sons Inc ....F....... 317 897-8821
Indianapolis *(G-6803)*

Elite Printing Inc ....G....... 317 781-9701
Indianapolis *(G-6839)*

Elite Printing Inc ....G....... 317 257-2744
Indianapolis *(G-6840)*

Em Printing & Embroidery LLC ....G....... 812 373-0082
Columbus *(G-1919)*

Envelope Service Inc ....E....... 260 432-6277
Fort Wayne *(G-4237)*

Envision Graphics Inc ....G....... 260 925-2266
Auburn *(G-329)*

▲ EP Graphics Inc ....C....... 877 589-2145
Berne *(G-613)*

Epi Printers Inc ....D....... 317 579-4870
Indianapolis *(G-6875)*

Espich Printing Inc ....G....... 260 244-0132
Columbia City *(G-1784)*

Et Printing ....G....... 317 219-7966
Noblesville *(G-11101)*

Evansville Bindery Inc ....G....... 812 423-2222
Evansville *(G-3483)*

Evansville Lithograph Co Inc ....G....... 812 477-0506
Evansville *(G-3486)*

Evansville Print Specialist ....G....... 812 423-5831
Evansville *(G-3490)*

Ewing Printing Company Inc ....F....... 812 882-2415
Vincennes *(G-13677)*

Excel Business Printing Inc ....G....... 317 259-1075
Indianapolis *(G-6891)*

Excell Color Graphics Inc ....E....... 260 482-2720
Fort Wayne *(G-4251)*

Express Impressions Prtg LLC ....G....... 765 966-2679
Richmond *(G-11985)*

Express Press Indiana Inc ....E....... 574 277-3355
South Bend *(G-12769)*

Express Press Indiana Inc ....G....... 219 874-2223
South Bend *(G-12770)*

Express Printing & Copying ....G....... 219 762-3508
Portage *(G-11761)*

Extreme Quality Prints ....G....... 812 987-7617
New Albany *(G-10774)*

F Robert Gardner Co Inc	G	317 634-2333	
Indianapolis *(G-6900)*			
Falls Cities Printing Inc	F	812 949-9051	
New Albany *(G-10775)*			
Fanstand Prints	G	317 579-9413	
Fishers *(G-3911)*			
Faris Mailing Inc	F	317 246-3315	
Indianapolis *(G-6905)*			
Fast Print Incorporated	G	260 484-5487	
Fort Wayne *(G-4257)*			
Faulkenberg Printing Co Inc	F	317 638-1359	
Franklin *(G-4886)*			
Fedex Office & Print Svcs Inc	E	317 631-6862	
Indianapolis *(G-6908)*			
Fedex Office & Print Svcs Inc	F	317 974-0378	
Indianapolis *(G-6909)*			
Fedex Office & Print Svcs Inc	F	317 917-1529	
Indianapolis *(G-6910)*			
Fedex Office & Print Svcs Inc	F	765 449-4950	
Lafayette *(G-8897)*			
Fehring F N & Son Printers	G	219 933-0439	
Hammond *(G-5879)*			
Fineline Graphics Incorporated	D	317 872-4490	
Indianapolis *(G-6921)*			
Firehouse Printing LLC	G	812 547-3109	
Tell City *(G-13162)*			
First Quality Printing Inc	G	317 506-8633	
Indianapolis *(G-6927)*			
First Quality Printing Center	G	317 546-5531	
Indianapolis *(G-6928)*			
Fiserv Inc	B	317 576-6700	
Indianapolis *(G-6929)*			
Forget ME Not Printing Ltd	G	317 508-7401	
Indianapolis *(G-6950)*			
Fort Wayne Printing Co Inc	F	260 471-7744	
Fort Wayne *(G-4280)*			
Four Part Inc	G	219 926-7777	
Chesterton *(G-1607)*			
Four Star Printing	G	765 620-9728	
Frankton *(G-4943)*			
Four Star Screen Printing LLC	G	765 533-3006	
New Castle *(G-10902)*			
Franklin Barry Gallery	G	317 822-8455	
Indianapolis *(G-6959)*			
Friends of Third World Inc	G	260 422-6821	
Fort Wayne *(G-4288)*			
Froggy Print LLC	G	317 965-7954	
Bloomington *(G-728)*			
Gannett Co Inc	C	765 423-5512	
Lafayette *(G-8902)*			
Garrett Printing & Graphics	G	812 422-6005	
Evansville *(G-3515)*			
Gary Printing Inc	G	219 886-1767	
Gary *(G-5052)*			
Get Printing Inc	G	574 533-6827	
Goshen *(G-5224)*			
Giles Agency Incorporated	G	317 842-5546	
Indianapolis *(G-7005)*			
Go Print LLC	G	765 778-1111	
Pendleton *(G-11490)*			
Goatee Shirt Printing	G	219 916-2443	
Valparaiso *(G-13550)*			
Goetz Printing	F	812 243-2086	
Terre Haute *(G-13241)*			
Good Impressions Printing Inc	G	317 873-6809	
Zionsville *(G-14434)*			
Goodprint LLC	G	201 926-0133	
Indianapolis *(G-7025)*			
Gospel Echoes Team Association	G	574 533-0221	
Goshen *(G-5228)*			
Grace Amazing Graphics	G	812 737-2841	
Laconia *(G-8836)*			
Grace Digital Printing	G	317 903-6172	
Indianapolis *(G-7032)*			
Gracies Paw Prints	G	317 910-9969	
Fishers *(G-3918)*			
Graessle-Mercer Co	E	812 522-5478	
Seymour *(G-12451)*			
Grafcor Inc	E	765 966-7030	
Richmond *(G-11990)*			
Granger Gazette	G	574 277-2679	
Granger *(G-5410)*			
Graphic Arts & Publ Svcs	G	574 294-1770	
Elkhart *(G-2894)*			
Graphic Expressions	G	219 663-2085	
Merrillville *(G-9717)*			
Graphic Expressions Inc	G	317 577-9622	
Fishers *(G-3919)*			
Graphic Menus Inc	F	765 396-3003	
Eaton *(G-2584)*			

Graphic Packaging Intl Inc	E	812 948-1608	
New Albany *(G-10790)*			
Graphicorp	G	317 867-3099	
Indianapolis *(G-7036)*			
Green Banner Publications Inc	E	812 967-3176	
Pekin *(G-11473)*			
Greencastle Offset Inc	G	765 653-4026	
Greencastle *(G-5458)*			
Greenline Screen Printing	G	317 572-1155	
Indianapolis *(G-7045)*			
Greensburg Printing Co Inc	G	812 663-8265	
Greensburg *(G-5604)*			
Gryphon Print Studio	G	574 514-1644	
South Bend *(G-12791)*			
Hager Inc	G	260 483-7075	
Fort Wayne *(G-4314)*			
Hardesty Printing Co Inc	F	574 223-4553	
Rochester *(G-12126)*			
Hardesty Printing Co Inc	G	574 267-7591	
Warsaw *(G-13889)*			
Hardingpoorman Inc	C	317 876-3355	
Indianapolis *(G-7074)*			
Hardingpoorman Group Inc	G	317 876-3355	
Indianapolis *(G-7075)*			
Harmony Press Inc	E	800 525-3742	
Bourbon *(G-943)*			
Hartford City News Times	C	765 348-0110	
Hartford City *(G-5982)*			
Hatch Prints	G	312 952-1908	
South Bend *(G-12794)*			
Haywood Printing Co Inc	E	765 742-4085	
Lafayette *(G-8912)*			
Heckley Printing	G	260 434-1370	
Fort Wayne *(G-4330)*			
Hennessey Montage Prints	G	317 841-7562	
Carmel *(G-1402)*			
Herff Jones LLC	E	317 612-3400	
Indianapolis *(G-7089)*			
Heron Printing Co Inc	G	317 865-0007	
Indianapolis *(G-7097)*			
Hetty Incorporated	G	219 836-2517	
Munster *(G-10605)*			
Hetty Incorporated	G	219 933-0833	
Hammond *(G-5892)*			
Hiatt Enterprises Inc	G	765 289-2700	
Muncie *(G-10488)*			
Hiatt Enterprises Inc	E	765 289-7756	
Muncie *(G-10487)*			
Highway Press Inc	G	812 283-6462	
Jeffersonville *(G-8374)*			
Hinen Printing Co	G	260 248-8984	
Columbia City *(G-1789)*			
Hoffman Quality Graphics	G	574 223-5738	
Rochester *(G-12128)*			
Home News Enterprises LLC	E	812 342-1056	
Columbus *(G-1940)*			
Hoosier Jiffy Print	G	260 563-8715	
Wabash *(G-13731)*			
Hoosier Press Inc	G	765 649-3716	
Anderson *(G-116)*			
Hoosier Reproduction Services	G	765 664-3162	
Marion *(G-9531)*			
Hoosier Times Inc	E	812 275-3372	
Bedford *(G-548)*			
Hoosier Times Inc	C	812 331-4270	
Bloomington *(G-741)*			
Horoho Printing Company Inc	G	765 452-8862	
Kokomo *(G-8640)*			
Howard Print Shop	G	765 453-6161	
Kokomo *(G-8641)*			
Huelseman Printing Co	G	765 647-3947	
Brookville *(G-1117)*			
Hugh K Eagan	G	574 269-5411	
Warsaw *(G-13891)*			
Humphrey Printing Co	G	317 241-6049	
Indianapolis *(G-7144)*			
Humphrey Printing Company Inc	F	765 452-0093	
Crown Point *(G-2259)*			
Ijs Custom Printing LLC	G	219 769-2050	
Merrillville *(G-9721)*			
Image Group Inc	E	574 457-3111	
Syracuse *(G-13135)*			
Image House Inc	F	219 947-0800	
Crown Point *(G-2260)*			
Impression Printing	G	765 342-6977	
Martinsville *(G-9614)*			
Impressions LLC	G	765 490-2575	
Lafayette *(G-8920)*			
Impressive Printing	G	812 913-1101	
New Albany *(G-10804)*			

In-Print	G	219 956-3001	
Wheatfield *(G-14225)*			
Indiana Newspapers LLC	A	317 444-4000	
Indianapolis *(G-7186)*			
Indiana Newspapers LLC	D	812 886-9955	
Vincennes *(G-13685)*			
Indigo Printing & Graphics	G	260 432-1320	
Huntertown *(G-6140)*			
Indy Color Printing LLC	G	317 371-8829	
Indianapolis *(G-7213)*			
Infinity Printing Promoti	G	317 332-4811	
Fishers *(G-3930)*			
Ink Spot	G	260 482-4492	
Fort Wayne *(G-4370)*			
Ink Spot Tattoo	G	260 244-0025	
Columbia City *(G-1796)*			
Ink Well Business Center	G	812 476-9147	
Evansville *(G-3560)*			
Inkme LLC	G	574 520-1203	
Osceola *(G-11378)*			
Inline Shirt Printing LLC	G	765 647-6356	
Brookville *(G-1118)*			
Innerprint Inc	G	317 509-6511	
McCordsville *(G-9670)*			
Instant Auto Finance Inc	G	260 483-9000	
Fort Wayne *(G-4374)*			
Instant Memorabilia Inc	G	219 661-8942	
Crown Point *(G-2263)*			
Instant Rain Irrigation LLC	G	260 336-1237	
Shipshewana *(G-12618)*			
Instant Refund Tax Service	G	317 536-1689	
Indianapolis *(G-7243)*			
Instant Warehouse	G	765 342-3430	
Martinsville *(G-9616)*			
Insty-Prints	G	317 788-1504	
Indianapolis *(G-7245)*			
Insty-Prints of South Bend	G	574 289-6977	
South Bend *(G-12814)*			
International Label Mfg LLC	F	812 235-5071	
Terre Haute *(G-13258)*			
J & J Printing Co	G	765 642-6642	
Anderson *(G-124)*			
J&J Sprts Screen Prtg Sprit Wr	G	812 909-2686	
Evansville *(G-3570)*			
J4 Printing LLC	G	260 417-5382	
Fort Wayne *(G-4389)*			
Jackson Group Inc	C	317 791-9000	
Indianapolis *(G-7294)*			
Jam Printing Inc	G	765 649-9292	
Anderson *(G-125)*			
James David Inc	G	260 744-0579	
Roanoke *(G-12105)*			
James J Maginot Printing	G	219 836-5692	
Munster *(G-10611)*			
JC Printing	G	574 721-9000	
Logansport *(G-9343)*			
Jem Printing Inc	G	812 376-9264	
Columbus *(G-1951)*			
Jk Graphics Inc	G	219 374-5930	
Cedar Lake *(G-1531)*			
Jkp Printing Inc	G	574 246-1650	
South Bend *(G-12822)*			
Journal and Chronicle Inc	G	812 752-5060	
Scottsburg *(G-12370)*			
JP Ownership Group Inc	D	317 791-1122	
Indianapolis *(G-7317)*			
K Irpcheadstart Program	G	219 345-2011	
Demotte *(G-2440)*			
K V S Inc	G	260 925-0525	
Auburn *(G-338)*			
K2m Printing	G	812 623-3040	
Sunman *(G-13113)*			
Kalems Enterprises Inc	G	317 399-1645	
Indianapolis *(G-7330)*			
Kankakee Valley Publishing Co	C	219 866-5111	
Rensselaer *(G-11930)*			
Kasting Printing Service	G	317 881-9411	
Indianapolis *(G-7334)*			
Kc Designs	G	812 876-4020	
Bloomington *(G-757)*			
Kelley Pagels Enterprises LLC	F	219 872-8552	
Michigan City *(G-9806)*			
Kellmark Corporation	E	574 264-9695	
Elkhart *(G-2958)*			
Kile Enterprises Inc	F	317 844-6629	
Carmel *(G-1423)*			
Kill-N-Em Inc	G	574 233-6655	
South Bend *(G-12828)*			
Kinkos Inc	G	765 449-4950	
Lafayette *(G-8939)*			

Kozs Quality Printing Inc ....G....... 219 696-6711
Lowell (G-9412)
Kpc Media Group Inc ....C....... 260 347-0400
Kendallville (G-8488)
Kpc Media Group Inc ....E....... 260 426-2640
Fort Wayne (G-4415)
L & L Press Inc ....F....... 765 664-3162
Marion (G-9541)
La Grange Publishing Co Inc ....F....... 260 463-3243
Lagrange (G-9052)
Lagnaippe LLC ....G....... 812 288-9291
New Albany (G-10816)
Lagwana Printing Inc ....E....... 260 463-4901
Lagrange (G-9054)
Langley Fine Art Prints ....G....... 219 872-0087
Long Beach (G-9378)
LAp Cstm EMB Grment Prtg LLC ....G....... 260 782-0762
Wabash (G-13733)
Largus Speedy Print Corp ....E....... 219 922-8414
Munster (G-10612)
Leader Publishing Co of Salem ....E....... 812 883-4446
Salem (G-12299)
Legacy Screen Printing Promoti ....G....... 219 262-4000
Chesterton (G-1618)
Legacy Screen Prtg Prmtons LLC ....G....... 219 262-4000
Michigan City (G-9809)
Lincoln Printing Corporation ....E....... 260 424-5200
Fort Wayne (G-4437)
Link Printing Services LLC ....G....... 317 826-9852
Indianapolis (G-7408)
▲ Litho Press Inc ....E....... 317 634-6468
Indianapolis (G-7409)
Lithogrphic Communications LLC ....E....... 219 924-9779
Munster (G-10615)
Lithotone Inc ....E....... 574 294-5521
Elkhart (G-3004)
Livings Graphics Inc ....G....... 574 264-4114
Elkhart (G-3006)
Loudon Printing Co Inc ....G....... 574 967-3944
Flora (G-3998)
Lsc Communications Us LLC ....G....... 574 267-7101
Warsaw (G-13902)
Lsc Communications Us LLC ....C....... 812 256-3396
Charlestown (G-1571)
Lucas Bus Forms & Swift Prtg ....G....... 260 482-7644
Fort Wayne (G-4443)
Ludwick Graphics Inc ....F....... 574 233-2165
South Bend (G-12845)
M M Printing Plus ....G....... 574 658-9345
Milford (G-9956)
Maco Press Inc ....G....... 317 846-5754
Carmel (G-1432)
Maco Reprograhics LLC ....G....... 812 464-8108
Evansville (G-3608)
Madison Courier ....E....... 812 265-3641
Madison (G-9479)
Maple Leaf Graphics Inc ....G....... 317 410-0321
Carmel (G-1434)
Mapleleaf Printing Co Inc ....G....... 574 534-7790
Goshen (G-5280)
Mar Kel Inc ....G....... 812 853-6133
Newburgh (G-11038)
Margins Printing LLC ....G....... 773 981-4251
Gary (G-5074)
Masco Corporation of Indiana ....D....... 317 848-1812
Indianapolis (G-7463)
Maury Boyd & Associates Inc ....F....... 317 849-6110
Indianapolis (G-7469)
Maximum Screen Printing ....G....... 502 802-4652
Jeffersonville (G-8399)
MD Laird Inc ....G....... 317 842-6338
Indianapolis (G-7473)
▲ Messenger LLC ....E....... 260 925-1700
Auburn (G-343)
Metropolitan Printing Svcs LLC ....E....... 812 332-7279
Bloomington (G-771)
Mf Printing LLC ....G....... 317 462-6895
Greenfield (G-5551)
Mid America Print Council ....G....... 765 463-3971
Lafayette (G-8968)
Mid West Digital Express Inc ....F....... 317 733-1214
Zionsville (G-14449)
Midwest Color Printing LLC ....G....... 812 822-2947
Bloomington (G-772)
Midwest Empire LLC ....G....... 317 786-7446
Indianapolis (G-7504)
Midwest Printing ....G....... 812 238-1641
Terre Haute (G-13285)
Mik Mocha Prints LLC ....G....... 812 376-8891
Columbus (G-1974)

Mike Mugler ....G....... 812 945-4266
New Albany (G-10831)
Miles Printing Corporation ....F....... 317 870-6115
Indianapolis (G-7517)
Miller Rainbow Printing Inc ....E....... 812 275-3355
Bedford (G-565)
Milliner Printing Company Inc ....G....... 260 563-5717
Wabash (G-13740)
Minute Print It Inc ....G....... 765 482-9019
Lebanon (G-9206)
Minuteman Press ....G....... 317 209-1677
Indianapolis (G-7525)
Minuteman Press ....G....... 317 316-0566
Noblesville (G-11151)
Mitchell-Fleming Printing Inc ....F....... 317 462-5467
Greenfield (G-5554)
Mito-Craft Inc ....G....... 574 287-4555
South Bend (G-12864)
Mo3d Printing LLC ....G....... 317 345-0061
Noblesville (G-11152)
Moan Racing Products LLC ....G....... 317 644-3100
Greenfield (G-5556)
Modern Printing Co ....G....... 260 347-1679
Kendallville (G-8495)
Moeller Printing Co Inc ....E....... 317 353-2224
Indianapolis (G-7533)
Montgomery & Associates Inc ....F....... 219 879-0088
Michigan City (G-9821)
Mooney Copy Service Inc ....G....... 812 423-6626
Evansville (G-3635)
Moreton Printing Co ....G....... 812 926-1692
Aurora (G-383)
Morris Printing Company Inc ....G....... 317 639-5553
Indianapolis (G-7545)
Mossberg & Company Inc ....C....... 574 289-9253
South Bend (G-12865)
Mossberg & Company Inc ....G....... 574 236-1094
South Bend (G-12866)
Movie Poster Print ....G....... 812 679-7301
Columbus (G-1977)
MPS Printing Inc ....G....... 812 273-4446
Madison (G-9489)
Mr Copy Inc ....G....... 812 334-2679
Bloomington (G-776)
Mr Copyrite ....G....... 219 462-1108
Valparaiso (G-13582)
Multi Packaging Solutions Inc ....B....... 317 241-2020
Indianapolis (G-7558)
Multi-Color Corporation ....C....... 812 752-3187
Scottsburg (G-12376)
Muncie Novelty Company Inc ....D....... 765 288-8301
Muncie (G-10532)
Nai Print Solutions ....G....... 317 392-1207
Shelbyville (G-12552)
ND Prints ....G .....
Indianapolis (G-7581)
Nea LLC ....G....... 574 295-0024
Elkhart (G-3059)
New Image Prtg & Design Inc ....F....... 260 969-0410
Fort Wayne (G-4500)
Newcomb Printing Services Inc ....G....... 219 874-3201
Michigan City (G-9763)
News Banner Publications Inc ....E....... 260 824-0224
Bluffton (G-883)
Newsletter Express Ltd ....G....... 317 876-8916
Indianapolis (G-7586)
Nicholls Printing ....G....... 574 233-1388
South Bend (G-12875)
Nicholson & Sons Printing Inc ....F....... 812 283-1200
Jeffersonville (G-8405)
Nielsen Company ....G....... 812 889-3493
Lexington (G-9254)
North Vernon Plain Dlr & Sun ....E....... 812 346-3973
North Vernon (G-11272)
Nova Graphics Inc ....F....... 317 577-6682
Indianapolis (G-7599)
Nussmeier Engraving Co ....E....... 812 425-1339
Evansville (G-3650)
Nwi Print & Mail LLC ....G....... 219 916-1358
Dyer (G-2505)
Oce Corporate Printing Div ....G....... 260 436-7395
Fort Wayne (G-4507)
Offset House Inc ....F....... 317 849-5155
Indianapolis (G-7612)
Offset One Inc ....F....... 260 456-8828
Fort Wayne (G-4509)
Old Capital Printing LLC ....G....... 812 946-9444
New Albany (G-10837)
Optimum System Products Inc ....F....... 812 289-1905
Marysville (G-9650)

Oswalt Menu Company Inc ....G....... 317 257-8039
Indianapolis (G-7636)
Ovation Communications Inc ....G....... 812 401-9100
Evansville (G-3659)
Overgaards Artcraft Printers ....G....... 574 234-8464
South Bend (G-12885)
Pack Printing ....G....... 317 437-9779
Indianapolis (G-7645)
Panda Prints ....G....... 574 322-1050
Bristol (G-1075)
Pandora Printing ....G....... 574 551-9624
Warsaw (G-13922)
Par Digital Imaging ....G....... 317 787-3330
Indianapolis (G-7652)
Pats Custom Printing and EMB ....G....... 765 456-1532
Kokomo (G-8678)
Paust Inc ....F....... 765 962-1507
Richmond (G-12027)
PC Imprints ....G....... 812 622-0855
Poseyville (G-11860)
Peerless Printing Corp ....F....... 765 664-8341
Marion (G-9553)
Pengad/West Inc ....E....... 765 286-3000
Muncie (G-10544)
Pentzer Printing Inc ....F....... 812 372-2896
Columbus (G-1992)
Perdue Printed Products Inc ....G....... 260 456-7575
Fort Wayne (G-4523)
Perfect Impressions Printing ....G....... 317 923-1756
Indianapolis (G-7674)
Pettit Printing Inc ....G....... 260 563-2346
Wabash (G-13749)
Phoenix Color Corp ....D....... 812 234-1585
Terre Haute (G-13302)
Phoenix Color Corp ....F....... 812 238-1551
Terre Haute (G-13303)
Pickle Prints LLC ....G....... 317 344-2495
Carmel (G-1450)
Picture Perfect Printing ....G....... 765 482-4241
Lebanon (G-9217)
Pinpoint Printer ....G....... 812 577-0630
Aurora (G-385)
PIP Printing ....G....... 317 843-5755
Carmel (G-1451)
Plastic Cardz ....G....... 260 440-1964
Fort Wayne (G-4532)
Plastic Cardz LLC ....G....... 260 431-6380
Fort Wayne (G-4533)
Posters 2 Prints LLC ....G....... 317 769-3784
Zionsville (G-14457)
Posters 2 Prints LLC ....F....... 800 598-5837
Indianapolis (G-7709)
Posters2prints LLC ....G....... 317 414-8972
Indianapolis (G-7710)
Prairie Creek Prtg & Bk Str ....G....... 812 636-7243
Montgomery (G-10238)
Precision Print LLC ....G....... 765 789-8799
Albany (G-12)
Preferred Print ....G....... 317 371-8829
Indianapolis (G-7739)
Premier Prints ....G....... 812 987-1129
Jeffersonville (G-8416)
Presstime Graphics Inc ....E....... 812 234-3815
Terre Haute (G-13309)
Prestige Printing Inc ....F....... 812 372-2500
Columbus (G-2000)
Pretty In Prints LLC ....G....... 317 252-3672
Indianapolis (G-7744)
Princeton Publishing Inc ....E....... 812 385-2525
Princeton (G-11881)
Print and Save LLP ....G....... 317 567-1459
Indianapolis (G-7748)
Print Center Inc ....G....... 219 874-9683
Long Beach (G-9379)
Print Ideas ....G....... 317 299-8766
Indianapolis (G-7749)
Print It Wear It Inc ....G....... 317 946-1456
Shelbyville (G-12561)
Print Management Solutions ....G....... 574 234-7269
South Bend (G-12903)
Print My Merch LLC ....G....... 574 323-5541
South Bend (G-12904)
Print My Merch LLC ....G....... 765 269-6772
Mishawaka (G-10108)
Print Place Inc ....G....... 260 768-7878
Shipshewana (G-12644)
Print Sharp Enterprises Inc ....G....... 317 899-2754
Indianapolis (G-7750)
Print Source Corporation ....G....... 260 589-2842
Bluffton (G-887)

Print Works of Lafayette Inc ....G...... 765 446-9735
Lafayette *(G-8983)*

Print2promo Group Inc......................G...... 219 778-4649
Rolling Prairie *(G-12192)*

Printcraft Press Inc ....G...... 765 457-2141
Kokomo *(G-8686)*

Printcrafters Inc ....G...... 812 838-4106
Mount Vernon *(G-10405)*

Printec Solutions Inc ....G...... 317 289-6510
Indianapolis *(G-7751)*

Printed By Erik Inc ....G...... 574 295-1203
Elkhart *(G-3116)*

Printer Plus ....G...... 812 945-5955
New Albany *(G-10848)*

Printer Zink Inc ....D...... 765 644-3959
Anderson *(G-156)*

Printing All Stars ....G...... 812 288-9291
New Albany *(G-10849)*

Printing Center Inc ....G...... 317 545-8518
Indianapolis *(G-7753)*

Printing Company LLC ....G...... 812 367-2668
Ferdinand *(G-3861)*

Printing Concepts Inc ....G...... 317 899-2754
Indianapolis *(G-7754)*

Printing Creations Inc ....G...... 765 759-9679
Yorktown *(G-14410)*

Printing Emporium Inc ....G...... 574 256-0059
Mishawaka *(G-10109)*

Printing In Time Inc ....G...... 502 807-3545
Elizabeth *(G-2645)*

◆ Printing Inc Louisville KY ....E...... 502 368-6555
Jeffersonville *(G-8417)*

Printing Partners Inc.........................D...... 317 635-2282
Indianapolis *(G-7755)*

Printing Partners East Inc ....G...... 317 356-2522
Indianapolis *(G-7756)*

Printing Phantom ....G...... 765 719-2097
Greencastle *(G-5474)*

Printing Place Inc-Photos Plus...........F...... 260 665-8444
Angola *(G-239)*

Printing Plus Inc ....G...... 317 574-1313
Carmel *(G-1455)*

Printing Solutions ....G...... 812 923-0756
Floyds Knobs *(G-4017)*

Printpack Inc ....G...... 812 334-5500
Bloomington *(G-802)*

Printworks Inc ....G...... 317 535-1250
Whiteland *(G-14243)*

Priority Press Inc ....G...... 317 240-0103
Indianapolis *(G-7760)*

Priority Printing LLC ....G...... 317 241-4234
Indianapolis *(G-7761)*

Pro Prints...G...... 812 932-3800
Batesville *(G-515)*

Proforma Premier Printing ....G...... 317 842-9181
Indianapolis *(G-7774)*

Proforma Print Promo Group............G...... 574 931-2941
South Bend *(G-12906)*

Progressive Printing Co Inc ....G...... 765 653-3814
Greencastle *(G-5475)*

Pubco Inc..F...... 219 874-4245
Michigan City *(G-9830)*

Publishers Consulting Corp ....E...... 219 874-4245
Michigan City *(G-9831)*

Pulaski County Press Inc ....G...... 574 946-6628
Winamac *(G-14317)*

Pussob Apparel & Printing LLC ....G...... 574 229-5795
Elkhart *(G-3123)*

Q Graphics Inc ....F...... 765 564-2314
Delphi *(G-2426)*

Q S I Inc...E...... 574 282-1200
South Bend *(G-12908)*

Qsp Printing Inc ....G...... 317 773-0864
Noblesville *(G-11168)*

Quad/Graphics Inc.............................B...... 260 748-5300
Fort Wayne *(G-4567)*

Quality Graphics Corp ....G...... 219 845-7084
Hammond *(G-5929)*

Quality Printing of NW Ind ....G...... 219 322-6677
Schererville *(G-12343)*

Quantumgraphix LLC ....G...... 317 819-0009
Indianapolis *(G-6279)*

Rainbow Printing LLC ....F...... 812 275-3372
Bedford *(G-569)*

Randall Corp......................................G...... 812 425-7122
Evansville *(G-3695)*

Rasure Prints ....G...... 812 454-6222
Evansville *(G-3696)*

Red Line Graphics Incorporated ....E...... 317 591-9400
Indianapolis *(G-7825)*

Regal Printing Inc ....G...... 317 844-1723
Carmel *(G-1464)*

Rensselaer Print Co...........................G...... 219 866-5000
Rensselaer *(G-11937)*

Reprocomm Inc ....F...... 765 423-2578
Lafayette *(G-8990)*

Reprocomm Inc ....E...... 765 472-5700
Peru *(G-11544)*

Rewright Printing ....G...... 219 513-8133
Highland *(G-6054)*

Rhr Corporation ....G...... 317 788-1504
Indianapolis *(G-7837)*

Richards Printery ....G...... 812 406-0295
Greenville *(G-5652)*

Riden Inc ....G...... 219 362-5511
La Porte *(G-8812)*

Rigdon Incorporated..........................G...... 765 393-2283
Anderson *(G-163)*

Rink Printing Company Inc ....E...... 574 232-7935
South Bend *(G-12916)*

Riverside Printing Co ....G...... 812 275-1950
Bedford *(G-574)*

Rock Hard Stones Custom ....G...... 219 613-0112
Merrillville *(G-9750)*

Ronnie Elmore Jr ....G...... 765 719-1681
Cloverdale *(G-1736)*

Row Printing ....G...... 317 796-3289
Brownsburg *(G-1167)*

Row Printing Inc ....G...... 317 441-4301
Pittsboro *(G-11586)*

Rowland Printing Co Inc ....F...... 317 773-1829
Noblesville *(G-11177)*

Royal Center Record ....G...... 574 643-3165
Royal Center *(G-12214)*

Rrc Corporation ....F...... 317 687-8325
Indianapolis *(G-7869)*

Running Around Screen Printing ....G...... 260 248-1216
Columbia City *(G-1832)*

Russ Print Shop ....F...... 219 996-3142
Hebron *(G-6022)*

Schutte Lithography Inc ....E...... 812 469-3500
Evansville *(G-3717)*

Scott Printing LLC ....G...... 812 306-7477
Evansville *(G-3718)*

Service Graphics Inc ....D...... 317 471-8246
Indianapolis *(G-7917)*

▲ Service Printers Inc ....E...... 574 266-6710
Elkhart *(G-3162)*

Shackelford Graphics ....G...... 317 783-3582
Indianapolis *(G-7919)*

Sharp Printing Services Inc ....G...... 317 842-5159
Fishers *(G-3969)*

Sharp Shirt Printing LLC ....G...... 260 413-9346
Fort Wayne *(G-4620)*

Shearer Printing Service Inc ....E...... 765 457-3274
Kokomo *(G-8695)*

Shelbyville Newspapers Inc ....D...... 317 398-6631
Shelbyville *(G-12568)*

Sherry Print Solutions Inc ....G...... 708 255-5457
Valparaiso *(G-13615)*

Shirley Engraving Co Inc ....F...... 317 634-4084
Indianapolis *(G-7934)*

Shopping Guide News Inc ....F...... 574 223-5417
Rochester *(G-12154)*

Sledgehammer Printing ....G...... 812 629-2160
Newburgh *(G-11050)*

Small Town Printers LLC ....G...... 812 596-1536
Elizabeth *(G-2647)*

Smith & Butterfield Co Inc ....F...... 812 422-3261
Evansville *(G-3735)*

Smith & Butterfield Co Inc ....E...... 812 422-3261
Evansville *(G-3736)*

Smith Business Supply Inc ....G...... 765 654-4442
Frankfort *(G-4853)*

Smitson Cmmnications Group LLC ......G...... 317 876-8916
Indianapolis *(G-7953)*

Solutions For Print LLC ....G...... 812 584-2701
Fountaintown *(G-4793)*

Sommers Graphics Inc ....F...... 574 282-2000
South Bend *(G-12940)*

Sound & Graphics..............................G...... 219 963-7293
Lake Station *(G-9077)*

Spectrum Press Inc ....E...... 812 335-1945
Bloomington *(G-831)*

Spencer Evening World......................D...... 812 829-2255
Spencer *(G-13037)*

Spencer Evening World......................G...... 765 795-4438
Cloverdale *(G-1738)*

Spencer Printing Inc ....G...... 765 288-6111
Muncie *(G-10566)*

Springhill Wholesale Inc ....E...... 812 299-2181
Terre Haute *(G-13342)*

Springs Valley Publishing Co ....G...... 812 936-9630
French Lick *(G-4989)*

St Clair Press ....G...... 317 612-9100
Indianapolis *(G-7980)*

St Meinrad Archabbey ....C...... 812 357-6611
Saint Meinrad *(G-12276)*

Stage Door Graphics ....G...... 317 398-9011
Shelbyville *(G-12571)*

Stamprint Inc ....G...... 574 233-3900
South Bend *(G-12953)*

Starken Printing Co Inc ....G...... 317 839-6852
Plainfield *(G-11645)*

Starlight Printing ....G...... 812 486-3905
Montgomery *(G-10243)*

Stines Printing ....G...... 260 356-5994
Huntington *(G-6253)*

Summit LLC ....G...... 574 287-7468
South Bend *(G-12961)*

Superior Print Inc ....E...... 812 246-6311
Sellersburg *(G-12420)*

Swiss Alps Printing Inc ....G...... 812 427-3844
Vevay *(G-13666)*

Sycamore Services Inc ....F...... 317 745-5456
Avon *(G-468)*

Systems & Services of Michiana ....G...... 574 273-1111
South Bend *(G-12965)*

Systems & Services of Michiana ....G...... 574 277-3355
South Bend *(G-12966)*

T-Flyerz Printing and Prom LLC ....G...... 260 729-7392
Bryant *(G-1202)*

Tabco Business Forms Inc ....G...... 812 882-2836
Vincennes *(G-13709)*

Target Printing Inc ....G...... 260 744-6038
Fort Wayne *(G-4675)*

Tatman Inc ....E...... 765 825-2164
Connersville *(G-2075)*

Tc Printing ....G...... 812 865-5127
French Lick *(G-4990)*

Tdk Graphics Inc ....F...... 219 663-7799
Crown Point *(G-2312)*

Team Gear Printing LLC ....G...... 765 935-4748
Richmond *(G-12059)*

Team Gear Printing LLC ....G...... 765 977-2995
Richmond *(G-12060)*

Tek Print LLC ....G...... 812 336-2525
Bedford *(G-583)*

Templeton Myers Inc ....E...... 317 898-6688
Indianapolis *(G-8053)*

▲ Tfi Inc ....F...... 317 290-1333
Indianapolis *(G-8055)*

The Office Sup of Southern Ind ....G...... 812 283-5523
Jeffersonville *(G-8434)*

This That EMB Screen Prtg LLC ....G...... 317 541-8548
Indianapolis *(G-8062)*

Thomas E Slade Inc ....F...... 812 471-7100
Evansville *(G-3760)*

Thompson Printing Service Inc ....G...... 317 783-7448
Indianapolis *(G-8068)*

Times...E...... 765 296-3622
Frankfort *(G-4856)*

Tints & Prints By Tierney LLC ....G...... 317 769-5895
Zionsville *(G-14469)*

Tippecanoe Press Inc ....F...... 317 392-1207
Shelbyville *(G-12576)*

Tko Enterprises Inc...........................D...... 317 271-1398
Plainfield *(G-11647)*

Tonya Gerhardt ....G...... 260 434-1370
Fort Wayne *(G-4691)*

Town & Country Industries Inc ....E...... 219 712-0893
Crown Point *(G-2316)*

Town & Country Press Inc ....F...... 574 936-9505
Plymouth *(G-11730)*

Town Country Printing ....G...... 765 452-0093
Kokomo *(G-8709)*

Tri State Printing & Embroider............G...... 812 316-0094
Vincennes *(G-13710)*

Tri-State Printing & EMB LLC ....G...... 812 743-2825
Monroe City *(G-10189)*

Triangle Printing Inc ....G...... 317 786-3488
Indianapolis *(G-8098)*

Triple Crown Media LLC ....D...... 574 533-2151
Goshen *(G-5342)*

Truth Publishing Company Inc ....E...... 765 653-5151
Greencastle *(G-5480)*

Twin Prints Inc..................................G...... 765 742-8656
Lafayette *(G-9014)*

Two B Enterprises Inc ....F...... 260 245-0119
Fort Wayne *(G-4711)*

S
I
C

Un Communications Group Inc ....E 317 844-8622
  Carmel (G-1503)
United Hero Apparel Printing ....G 812 306-1998
  Evansville (G-3787)
United Parcel Service Inc ....G 317 776-9494
  Noblesville (G-11197)
Unlimited Ink Custom Screen ....G 765 889-3212
  Russiaville (G-12244)
UPS Store 5219 ....G 219 750-9597
  Merrillville (G-9760)
Upside Prints Corporation ....F 812 319-4883
  Evansville (G-3791)
Upside Prints Corporation ....G 812 205-7374
  Bedford (G-588)
V & P Printing ....G 260 495-3741
  Fremont (G-4978)
Valley Press Tc ....F 812 234-8030
  Terre Haute (G-13360)
Vdk Printing LLC ....G 260 602-8212
  Fort Wayne (G-4724)
Visions Printing Inc ....G 317 960-2322
  Indianapolis (G-8165)
◆ Voice of God Recordings Inc ....D 812 246-2137
  Jeffersonville (G-8439)
Vomela ....G 574 522-6016
  Elkhart (G-3251)
W Robbins & Sons Inc ....G 765 522-1736
  Roachdale (G-12096)
W/S Packaging Group Inc ....G 317 578-4454
  Indianapolis (G-8173)
Wabash Plain Dealer ....E 260 563-2131
  Wabash (G-13764)
Wabash Printing Company ....G 765 650-1701
  West Lafayette (G-14116)
WAr - LLC- Westville Prtg ....G 219 785-2821
  Westville (G-14221)
Wayne Press Incorporated ....G 260 744-3022
  Fort Wayne (G-4743)
Well Ink ....G 765 743-3413
  West Lafayette (G-14117)
Whitewater Publications Inc ....E 765 647-4221
  Brookville (G-1131)
Wilkes Printing Inc ....G 812 847-0005
  Linton (G-9315)
▲ Williams Plastics LLC ....C 317 398-1630
  Shelbyville (G-12585)
Willis Curtis Genie Jr ....G 317 377-4711
  Indianapolis (G-8202)
Wise Business Forms Inc ....C 260 489-1561
  Fort Wayne (G-4759)
Wise Printing Inc ....G 317 861-6220
  New Palestine (G-10974)
Wise Printing Inc ....G 317 351-9477
  Indianapolis (G-8206)
Wolf Printing LLC ....G 317 577-1771
  Indianapolis (G-8208)
Woodburn Graphics Inc ....E 812 232-0323
  Terre Haute (G-13371)
Woodfield Printing Inc ....G 317 848-2000
  Indianapolis (G-6283)
Woods Printing Company Inc ....F 812 536-2261
  Holland (G-6106)
Wraco Enterprises Inc ....G 812 339-3987
  Bloomington (G-859)
Writeguard Business Systems ....G 317 849-7292
  Indianapolis (G-8219)
Xl Graphics Inc ....F 317 738-3434
  Franklin (G-4942)
Yahweh Design and Printing ....G 765 874-1003
  Lynn (G-9433)
Your Face Our Place Print Shop ....G 812 567-4510
  Tennyson (G-13183)
Zogman Enterprises Inc ....G 317 873-6809
  Zionsville (G-14475)

2754 Commercial Printing: Gravure

A & H Enterprises LLC ....G 317 398-3070
  Shelbyville (G-12517)
Acclaim Graphics Inc ....G 812 424-5035
  Evansville (G-3334)
Classic Media LLC ....G 260 482-3487
  Fort Wayne (G-4157)
▼ Data Label Inc ....C 812 232-0408
  Terre Haute (G-13223)
Edward ONeil Associates ....G 317 244-5400
  Indianapolis (G-6810)
Enterprise Marking Pdts Inc ....E 317 867-7600
  Fishers (G-3906)
Gary Printing Inc ....G 219 886-1767
  Gary (G-5052)

Goon Jonn ....G 574 306-2927
  Warsaw (G-13882)
Gulsad Inc ....G 317 541-1940
  Indianapolis (G-7059)
Mid America Coop Education ....G 317 726-6910
  Indianapolis (G-7502)
Multi-Color Corporation ....G 812 752-3187
  Scottsburg (G-12376)
Multi-Color Corporation ....E 812 752-0586
  Scottsburg (G-12375)
Nussmeier Engraving Co ....E 812 425-1339
  Evansville (G-3650)
Proedge Inc ....E 219 552-9550
  Shelby (G-12515)
Scott Culbertson ....G 260 357-6430
  Garrett (G-5022)
Stien Designs & Graphics Inc ....G 260 347-9136
  Kendallville (G-8511)
Viking Business Products Inc ....G 260 489-7787
  Fort Wayne (G-4727)
Westwood Paper Co ....G 317 843-1212
  Carmel (G-1509)

2759 Commercial Printing

5 Diamond X ....G 574 601-8056
  Monticello (G-10250)
A & E Screen Printing ....G 574 875-4488
  Elkhart (G-2655)
A & M Innovations LLC ....G 317 306-6118
  Whiteland (G-14233)
A Mayes Ing Inc ....G 317 925-5777
  Indianapolis (G-6298)
A Plus Images I N C ....G 317 405-8955
  Indianapolis (G-6300)
Aardvark Graphics ....G 574 267-4799
  Warsaw (G-13834)
Abracadabra Graphics ....G 812 336-1971
  Bloomington (G-654)
Acclaim Graphics Inc ....G 812 424-5035
  Evansville (G-3334)
Accu-Label Inc ....E 260 482-5223
  Fort Wayne (G-4036)
Accuprint of Kentuckiana Inc ....G 812 944-8603
  New Albany (G-10740)
Achievers Institute LLC ....G 812 278-8785
  Bedford (G-527)
Adams Smith ....G 219 661-2812
  Crown Point (G-2222)
Advantex Inc ....G 812 339-6479
  Bloomington (G-658)
After Hours Embroidery ....G 812 926-9355
  Aurora (G-368)
Allsports ....G 812 883-3561
  Salem (G-12281)
Almost Famous Printing ....G 219 793-6388
  Whiting (G-14266)
Altstadt Business Forms Inc ....F 812 425-3393
  Evansville (G-3349)
American Printing Indiana LLC ....E 765 825-7600
  Anderson (G-64)
American Reprographics Co LLC ....G 574 287-2944
  South Bend (G-12705)
American Stationery Co ....G 765 473-4438
  Peru (G-11515)
American Veteran Group LLC ....G 317 600-4749
  Westfield (G-14136)
Anchor Enterprises ....G 812 282-7220
  Jeffersonville (G-8326)
Andresen Graphic Processors ....F 317 291-7071
  Brownsburg (G-1133)
Anthony Wayne Rehabilitation C ....E 317 972-1000
  Edinburgh (G-2601)
Apollo Prtg & Graphics Ctr Inc ....E 574 287-3707
  South Bend (G-12709)
Apparel Design Group ....G 812 339-3355
  Bloomington (G-662)
B and R Engraving Inc ....G 317 894-3599
  Greenfield (G-5506)
B-Hive Printing ....G 812 897-3905
  Boonville (G-908)
Bartel Printing Company Inc ....G 574 267-7421
  Warsaw (G-13842)
Baxter Printing Inc ....G 219 923-1999
  Highland (G-6037)
Behning Inc ....G 260 672-2663
  Roanoke (G-12099)
Bell Graphics and Design LLC ....G 765 827-5441
  Connersville (G-2040)
Bennett Printing ....G 812 966-2917
  Medora (G-9680)

Bev Can Printers Llc ....G 219 617-6181
  La Porte (G-8738)
Bex Screen Printing Inc ....G 317 791-0375
  Indianapolis (G-6470)
Big Picture Data Imaging LLC ....G 812 235-0202
  Terre Haute (G-13202)
Bill Baldwins Screenprinting ....G 317 881-2712
  Greenwood (G-5670)
Bills Industries LLC ....G 765 629-0227
  Milroy (G-9977)
Bloomington Discount Prtg Inc ....G 812 332-9789
  Bloomington (G-688)
Blue Octopus Printing Company ....G 317 247-1997
  Indianapolis (G-6487)
Blue River Printing Inc ....G 317 392-3676
  Shelbyville (G-12521)
Blue River Services Inc ....C 812 738-2437
  Corydon (G-2090)
Bm Creations Inc ....G 219 922-8935
  Griffith (G-5767)
Brand Prtg & Photo-Litho Co ....G 317 921-4095
  Indianapolis (G-6503)
Bredensteiner & Assoc Inc ....G 317 921-2226
  Indianapolis (G-6505)
Brenmeer LLC ....G 260 267-0249
  Fort Wayne (G-4120)
Bruce Payne ....G 260 492-2259
  Fort Wayne (G-4124)
BT Management Inc ....G 219 794-9546
  Merrillville (G-9705)
Burkert-Walton Inc ....G 812 425-7157
  Evansville (G-3405)
Business Adventures Inc ....G 574 674-9996
  Osceola (G-11371)
C E M Printing & Specialities ....G 269 684-6898
  South Bend (G-12730)
C R Graphics ....G 317 881-6192
  Greenwood (G-5673)
Campbell Printing Co Inc ....G 219 866-5913
  Rensselaer (G-11916)
Cause Printing Company ....G 765 573-3330
  Marion (G-9516)
Ccmp Inc ....E 219 922-8935
  Griffith (G-5769)
CD Grafix LLC ....G 812 945-4443
  Clarksville (G-1675)
Cdb Screen Printing Inc ....G 765 472-4404
  Peru (G-11520)
Cecils Printing & Office Sups ....G 812 683-4416
  Huntingburg (G-6153)
Cedar Woodworking ....G 812 486-2765
  Montgomery (G-10216)
Celestial Designs LLC ....G 317 733-3110
  Zionsville (G-14425)
Clarke American Checks Inc ....G 812 283-9598
  Jeffersonville (G-8340)
Clarke American Checks Inc ....C 812 283-9598
  Jeffersonville (G-8339)
Classic Engraving ....G 765 523-3355
  Stockwell (G-13076)
Classic Graphics Inc ....F 260 482-3487
  Fort Wayne (G-4156)
Clondalkin Pharma & Healthcare ....C 317 328-7355
  Indianapolis (G-6623)
Clover Printing LLC ....G 260 657-3003
  Harlan (G-5968)
Coaches Connection Inc ....G 260 356-0400
  Huntington (G-6198)
Commercial Print Shop Inc ....G 260 724-3722
  Decatur (G-2373)
Company Pride Shirts LLC ....G 812 526-5700
  Edinburgh (G-2601)
Consolidated Printing Svcs Inc ....F 765 468-6033
  Farmland (G-3841)
Cool Cayenne LLC ....G 765 282-0977
  Muncie (G-10449)
Countryside Printing ....G 812 486-2454
  Montgomery (G-10218)
County West Sports ....G 317 839-4076
  Plainfield (G-11601)
Courier Printing Co Allen Cnty ....G 260 627-2728
  Grabill (G-5362)
▲ Courier-Times Inc ....D 765 529-1111
  New Castle (G-10897)
Cozy Cat Inc ....G 765 463-1254
  Lafayette (G-8879)
Craigs Printing Co ....G 812 358-5010
  Brownstown (G-1185)
Crider Holcomb Partnership LLC ....G 812 279-2200
  Bedford (G-536)

Criterion Press Inc	F	317 236-1570	
Indianapolis (G-6693)			
Crossing Creations	G	812 587-0212	
Columbus (G-1885)			
Cs Kern Inc	E	765 289-8600	
Muncie (G-10451)			
Custom Art Screen Printing	F	260 456-3909	
Fort Wayne (G-4193)			
Custom Candy Wrappers Company	G	574 247-0756	
Granger (G-5399)			
Custom Packaging Inc	F	317 876-9559	
Indianapolis (G-6717)			
D S E Inc	E	812 376-0310	
Columbus (G-1904)			
D-J Printing Specialists Inc	G	219 465-1164	
Valparaiso (G-13527)			
Dance World Bazaar Corporation	G	812 663-7679	
Greensburg (G-5598)			
Daniel Korb Laundry Company	D	812 425-6121	
Evansville (G-3453)			
David Indus Process PDT Co	G	317 577-0351	
Fishers (G-3898)			
Dec-O-Art Inc	E	574 294-6451	
Elkhart (G-2791)			
Design Media Connections LLC	G	317 819-2022	
Indianapolis (G-6735)			
Dimensional Imprinting Inc	G	260 417-0202	
Milton (G-9987)			
Distinct Images Inc	F	317 613-4413	
Indianapolis (G-6744)			
Docutech Document Service	G	219 690-3038	
Lowell (G-9404)			
Doerr Printing Co	G	317 568-0135	
Indianapolis (G-6756)			
Dog Ear Publishing	G	317 228-3656	
Indianapolis (G-6757)			
Douglas P Terrell	G	812 254-1976	
Washington (G-13981)			
E James Dant	G	812 476-2271	
Evansville (G-3468)			
E James Dant	G	812 476-2271	
Evansville (G-3469)			
Ed Sons Inc	F	317 897-8821	
Indianapolis (G-6803)			
El Shaddai Inc	G	260 359-9080	
Huntington (G-6203)			
Elegan Graphics	G	219 462-9921	
Valparaiso (G-13533)			
Elengas Customwear	G	317 577-1677	
Fishers (G-3902)			
Embroidme	G	219 465-1400	
Valparaiso (G-13536)			
Engraving and Stamp Center Inc	G	812 336-0606	
Bloomington (G-720)			
Entertainment Express	F	219 763-3610	
Portage (G-11760)			
Evansville Bindery Inc	G	812 423-2222	
Evansville (G-3483)			
Evansville Print Specialist	G	812 423-5831	
Evansville (G-3490)			
Ewing Printing Company Inc	F	812 882-2415	
Vincennes (G-13677)			
Excell Color Graphics Inc	E	260 482-2720	
Fort Wayne (G-4251)			
F Robert Gardner Co Inc	G	317 634-2333	
Indianapolis (G-6900)			
Faith Walkers	G	219 873-1900	
Michigan City (G-9791)			
Faulkenberg Printing Co Inc	F	317 638-1359	
Franklin (G-4886)			
Fedex Office & Print Svcs Inc	G	219 462-6270	
Valparaiso (G-13542)			
Fedex Office & Print Svcs Inc	G	317 839-3896	
Plainfield (G-11609)			
Fedex Office & Print Svcs Inc	F	317 251-2406	
Indianapolis (G-6914)			
Fehring F N & Son Printers	G	219 933-0439	
Hammond (G-5879)			
First Class Printing	G	317 808-2222	
Indianapolis (G-6925)			
Fiserv Inc	B	317 576-6700	
Indianapolis (G-6929)			
Formal Affairs Tuxedo Shop	G	574 875-6654	
Elkhart (G-2868)			
Fort Wayne Newspapers Inc	B	260 461-8444	
Fort Wayne (G-4277)			
Freckles Graphics Inc	F	765 448-4692	
Lafayette (G-8900)			
Full Color Direct LLC	G	317 538-4500	
Indianapolis (G-6968)			

Game Face Graphix LLC	G	317 340-0973	
Camby (G-1267)			
Gary Printing Inc	G	219 886-1767	
Gary (G-5052)			
Gd Cox Inc	G	317 398-0035	
Shelbyville (G-12536)			
Gen Enterprises	G	574 498-6777	
Tippecanoe (G-13381)			
Gettelfinger Holdings LLC	G	812 923-9065	
Floyds Knobs (G-4012)			
Giraffe X Graphics Inc	G	317 546-4944	
Indianapolis (G-7007)			
Goldden Corporation	F	765 423-4366	
Lafayette (G-8908)			
Goldleaf Promotional Products	G	317 202-2754	
Indianapolis (G-7022)			
▲ Goose Graphics L L C	G	260 563-4516	
Fort Wayne (G-4301)			
Graphic Fx Inc	F	812 234-0000	
Terre Haute (G-13243)			
Graphic Menus Inc	G	765 396-3003	
Eaton (G-2584)			
Graphic Ventures Inc	G	812 288-6093	
Clarksville (G-1683)			
Graphic Visions	G	812 331-7446	
Bloomington (G-733)			
Graphic22 Inc	G	219 921-5409	
Chesterton (G-1608)			
Graphics Lab Uv Printing Inc	F	765 457-5784	
Kokomo (G-8632)			
Graphix Unlimited Inc	E	574 546-3770	
Bremen (G-1000)			
Greensburg Printing Co Inc	G	812 663-8265	
Greensburg (G-5604)			
H M C Screen Printing Inc	F	317 773-8532	
Noblesville (G-11116)			
▲ Harcourt Industries Inc	E	765 629-2625	
Milroy (G-9980)			
Harmony Press Inc	E	800 525-3742	
Bourbon (G-943)			
Hartley J Company Inc	G	812 376-9708	
Columbus (G-1938)			
Haywood Printing Co Inc	E	765 742-4085	
Lafayette (G-8912)			
Headlands Ltd	G	260 426-9884	
Wolcottville (G-14371)			
Herff Jones Yearbooks	G	717 334-9123	
Indianapolis (G-7094)			
HI Tech Label Inc	F	765 659-1800	
Frankfort (G-4836)			
Hiatt Enterprises Inc	E	765 289-7756	
Muncie (G-10487)			
Hiatt Enterprises Inc	E	765 289-2700	
Muncie (G-10488)			
High End Concepts Inc	F	317 630-9901	
Indianapolis (G-7106)			
Highway Press Inc	G	812 283-6462	
Jeffersonville (G-8374)			
Hinen Printing Co.	G	260 248-8984	
Columbia City (G-1789)			
Hoosier Horse Review LLC	G	765 212-1320	
Muncie (G-10491)			
Hoosier Jiffy Print	G	260 563-8715	
Wabash (G-13731)			
Hoosier Printing Co Inc	G	219 836-8877	
Munster (G-10606)			
Hooven - Dayton Corp	E	765 935-3999	
Richmond (G-12000)			
Hot Cake	G	317 889-2253	
Indianapolis (G-7132)			
Hot Off Press	G	317 253-5987	
Indianapolis (G-7133)			
Hunt and Sons Memorial LLC	G	317 745-0940	
Danville (G-2348)			
Idenitee	G	317 462-4606	
Greenfield (G-5537)			
IM Impressed	G	219 838-7959	
Munster (G-10609)			
Imagination Graphics	G	812 423-6503	
Evansville (G-3547)			
Imprint It All	G	812 234-0024	
Terre Haute (G-13254)			
In Business For Life Inc	G	317 691-6169	
Carmel (G-1411)			
Indiana Letterpress LLC	G	574 967-0154	
Flora (G-3997)			
Industrial Graphic Design	G	260 856-2110	
Cromwell (G-2209)			
Inner City Sports TS	G	812 402-4143	
Evansville (G-3561)			

International Label Mfg LLC	F	812 235-5071	
Terre Haute (G-13258)			
J N P Custom Designs Inc	G	317 253-2198	
Indianapolis (G-7289)			
J Tees	G	812 524-9292	
Seymour (G-12460)			
J Y Design & Print Inc	G	260 357-3759	
Garrett (G-5014)			
Jac Jmr Inc	G	219 663-6700	
Crown Point (G-2264)			
Jam Graphics Inc	G	317 896-5662	
Noblesville (G-11134)			
James Wafford	G	317 773-7200	
Noblesville (G-11135)			
JB Graphics Inc	G	317 819-0008	
Carmel (G-1419)			
JC Printing & Mailing	G	765 742-6829	
Colburn (G-1752)			
Jer-Maur Corporation	G	812 384-8290	
Bloomfield (G-640)			
Jeremy Parker	G	765 284-5414	
Muncie (G-10501)			
Joans T-Shirt Printing LLC	G	812 934-2616	
Batesville (G-506)			
Jones & Webb Associates Inc	G	317 236-9755	
Indianapolis (G-7311)			
Journal and Chronicle Inc	G	812 752-5060	
Scottsburg (G-12370)			
Jt Printing LLC	G	317 271-7700	
Avon (G-451)			
Just Ink LLC	G	800 948-7671	
South Bend (G-12826)			
Karemar Productions	G	765 766-5117	
Mooreland (G-10295)			
Kays Graphics Inc.	G	317 236-9755	
Indianapolis (G-7335)			
Keefer Graphic Imaging Inc	G	260 426-7500	
Columbia City (G-1803)			
Keefer Printing Company Inc	G	260 424-4543	
Fort Wayne (G-4405)			
Keen Screen	G	812 945-5336	
New Albany (G-10812)			
Kelley Pagels Enterprises LLC	F	219 872-8552	
Michigan City (G-9806)			
Kennyleeholmescom	G	574 612-2526	
Elkhart (G-2961)			
▼ Kewanna Screen Printing Inc	G	574 653-2683	
Kewanna (G-8526)			
Kingery Group Inc	E	317 823-9585	
Indianapolis (G-7354)			
Kirchoff Custom Sports	G	812 434-0355	
Evansville (G-3592)			
Kissel Printers Inc.	G	812 424-5333	
Evansville (G-3593)			
Knoy Apparel	G	765 448-1031	
Lafayette (G-8945)			
Kozs Quality Printing Inc	G	219 696-6711	
Lowell (G-9412)			
L & L Press Inc	F	765 664-3162	
Marion (G-9541)			
◆ L C Typesetting Company Inc	G	574 232-4700	
South Bend (G-12834)			
La Grange Publishing Co Inc	F	260 463-3243	
Lagrange (G-9052)			
Label Logic Inc	E	574 266-6007	
Elkhart (G-2981)			
Label Tech Inc	E	765 747-1234	
Muncie (G-10506)			
Laconia Laser Engraving	G	812 786-3641	
Laconia (G-8837)			
Lambel Corporation	F	317 849-6828	
Indianapolis (G-7377)			
Lamco Finishers Inc	E	317 471-1010	
Indianapolis (G-7379)			
Languell Printing Inc	G	317 889-3545	
Greenwood (G-5717)			
Largus Speedy Print Corp	E	219 922-8414	
Munster (G-10612)			
Laser Marking Technologies	G	812 852-7999	
Osgood (G-11392)			
Leader Publishing Co of Salem	E	812 883-4446	
Salem (G-12299)			
Leap Frogz Screenprinting EMB	G	317 786-2441	
Indianapolis (G-7390)			
Lee Publications Inc	D	219 933-9251	
Munster (G-10614)			
▲ Liberty Book & Bb Manufactures	E	317 633-1450	
Indianapolis (G-7402)			
Light & Ink Corp	G	812 421-1400	
Evansville (G-3602)			

S
I
C

Lightning Printing	G	765 362-5999	
Crawfordsville (G-2168)			
Lincoln Printing Corporation	E	260 424-5200	
Fort Wayne (G-4437)			
Little Cricket Letterpress	G	317 762-2044	
Winona Lake (G-14351)			
▲ M Nelson & Associates Inc	G	317 228-1422	
Carmel (G-1430)			
Maco Press Inc	G	317 846-5754	
Carmel (G-1432)			
Mandala Screen Printing Inc	G	574 946-6290	
Winamac (G-14311)			
Maple-Hunter Decals	G	812 894-9759	
Riley (G-12084)			
Marie S Embroidery	G	219 931-2561	
Hammond (G-5912)			
Marketing Services Group Inc	B	317 381-2268	
Indianapolis (G-7456)			
Masco Corporation of Indiana	D	317 848-1812	
Indianapolis (G-7463)			
▲ Matrix Label Systems Inc	E	317 839-1973	
Plainfield (G-11624)			
Matrix Photo Laboratories Inc	F	317 635-4756	
Indianapolis (G-7467)			
McCormick Printing Impressions	G	765 675-9556	
Tipton (G-13398)			
Midnite Grafix	G	812 386-9430	
Princeton (G-11878)			
Midwest Graphics Inc	G	317 780-4600	
Indianapolis (G-7506)			
Minds Eye Graphics Inc	F	260 724-2050	
Decatur (G-2396)			
Minuteman Press	G	317 209-1677	
Indianapolis (G-7525)			
Mission Announcement Co	E	626 332-4084	
Peru (G-11537)			
Mito-Craft Inc	G	574 287-4555	
South Bend (G-12864)			
Moeller Printing Co Inc	G	317 353-2224	
Indianapolis (G-7533)			
Mooney Copy Service Inc	G	812 423-6626	
Evansville (G-3635)			
Moose Lake Products Co	F	260 432-2768	
Fort Wayne (G-4480)			
Mossberg & Company Inc	C	574 289-9253	
South Bend (G-12865)			
▲ MPS Indianapolis Inc	C	317 241-2020	
Indianapolis (G-7552)			
MPS Printing Inc	G	812 273-4446	
Madison (G-9489)			
Mr BS Sports & Design	G	260 347-4830	
Kendallville (G-8497)			
Multi Packaging Solutions Inc	B	317 241-2020	
Indianapolis (G-7558)			
Multi-Color Corporation	E	812 752-0586	
Scottsburg (G-12375)			
Multi-Color Corporation	C	812 752-3187	
Scottsburg (G-12376)			
Muncie Novelty Company Inc	D	765 288-8301	
Muncie (G-10532)			
New Haven Trophies & Shirts	G	260 749-0269	
New Haven (G-10949)			
New Process Graphics LLC	E	260 489-1700	
Fort Wayne (G-4502)			
News Publishing Company LLC	G	812 838-4811	
Mount Vernon (G-10404)			
Newton Business Forms	G	812 256-5399	
Charlestown (G-1575)			
Nicholls Printing	G	574 233-1388	
South Bend (G-12875)			
Nickprint Inc	G	317 489-3033	
Carmel (G-1442)			
Nielsen Enterprises Inc	G	574 277-3748	
Granger (G-5427)			
North Enterprises Inc	G	765 362-4410	
Crawfordsville (G-2179)			
Notables	G	765 649-1648	
Anderson (G-146)			
Npp Packaging Graphics	G	317 522-2010	
Zionsville (G-14453)			
Nussmeier Engraving Co	E	812 425-1339	
Evansville (G-3650)			
Offset House Inc	F	317 849-5155	
Indianapolis (G-7612)			
Offset One Inc	F	260 456-8828	
Fort Wayne (G-4509)			
◆ Omnisource Marketing Group Inc	E	317 575-3300	
Indianapolis (G-7620)			
Ooshirts Inc	G	317 246-9083	
Indianapolis (G-7624)			

Outfitter	G	765 289-6456	
Muncie (G-10541)			
Overgaards Artcraft Printers	G	574 234-8464	
South Bend (G-12885)			
P413 Corporation	G	317 769-0679	
Zionsville (G-14454)			
Panther Graphics LLC	G	317 223-3845	
Indianapolis (G-7650)			
Paper Tigers Inc	G	317 573-9040	
Indianapolis (G-7651)			
Paragon Printing Center Inc	G	574 533-5835	
Goshen (G-5306)			
Paramount Printing Ltd Inc	G	219 980-0445	
Gary (G-5083)			
Parlor City Trophy & Apparel	G	260 824-0216	
Bluffton (G-884)			
Pearson Printing Company	G	765 664-8769	
Marion (G-9551)			
Pengad/West Inc	F	765 286-3000	
Muncie (G-10544)			
Pentzer Printing Inc	F	812 372-2896	
Columbus (G-1992)			
Perdue Printed Products Inc	G	260 456-7575	
Fort Wayne (G-4523)			
Perfect Plastic Printing Corp	G	317 888-9447	
Greenwood (G-5731)			
Perrys Country Store	G	260 693-0084	
Churubusco (G-1655)			
Phantom Neon LLC	G	765 362-2221	
Crawfordsville (G-2186)			
Pheonix Inc	G	765 489-3030	
Hagerstown (G-5811)			
Phil Irwin Advertising Inc	F	317 547-5117	
Indianapolis (G-7683)			
Phillips Diversified Services	G	260 248-2975	
Columbia City (G-1818)			
Photo Screen Service Inc	G	317 636-7712	
Indianapolis (G-7688)			
Photo Specialties	G	812 944-5111	
New Albany (G-10843)			
Pierce Oil Co Inc	F	812 268-6356	
Sullivan (G-13090)			
Planks Printing Service Inc	G	574 533-1739	
Goshen (G-5309)			
Plastimatic Arts Corp	E	574 254-9000	
Mishawaka (G-10104)			
Play 2 Win Screenprinting LLC	G	765 426-0679	
Oxford (G-11434)			
Portage Custom Wear LLC	G	219 841-9070	
Portage (G-11788)			
Ppi Acquisition LLC	F	765 674-8627	
Marion (G-9555)			
Pratt Visual Solutions Company	E	800 428-7728	
Indianapolis (G-7720)			
Precision Label Incorporated	F	812 877-3811	
Terre Haute (G-13308)			
Preferred Enterprises Inc	G	765 457-0637	
Kokomo (G-8684)			
Premier Label Company Inc	F	765 289-5000	
Muncie (G-10548)			
Premier Print & Svcs Group Inc	F	574 273-2525	
Granger (G-5429)			
Premier Printing	G	765 459-8339	
Kokomo (G-8685)			
Premiere Advertising	G	317 722-2400	
Indianapolis (G-7742)			
Presstime Graphics Inc	E	812 234-3815	
Terre Haute (G-13309)			
Prince Manufacturing Corp	E	260 357-4484	
Garrett (G-5020)			
Printcrafters Inc	G	812 838-4106	
Mount Vernon (G-10405)			
Printers Express Inc	G	765 348-0069	
Hartford City (G-5988)			
Printing Partners Inc	D	317 635-2282	
Indianapolis (G-7755)			
Printing Place Inc-Photos Plus	F	260 665-8444	
Angola (G-239)			
Printing Services Inc	G	317 300-0363	
Indianapolis (G-7757)			
Printpack Inc	B	812 663-5091	
Greensburg (G-5629)			
Printwerk Graphics & Design	G	219 322-7722	
Dyer (G-2508)			
Priority Press Inc	E	317 241-4234	
Indianapolis (G-7759)			
Priority Press Inc	G	317 240-0103	
Indianapolis (G-7760)			
Priority Press Inc	G	317 848-9695	
Indianapolis (G-6278)			

Prn Graphics LLC	G	317 426-3545	
Indianapolis (G-7763)			
Prn Incorporated	G	317 624-4401	
Indianapolis (G-7764)			
Professional Print Brokers	G	260 824-2328	
Bluffton (G-888)			
Progressive Printing Co Inc	G	765 653-3814	
Greencastle (G-5475)			
Prototype Systems Inc	E	317 634-3040	
Carmel (G-1458)			
Quality Imagination Corp	G	317 753-0042	
Indianapolis (G-7797)			
Quality Printing of NW Ind	G	219 322-6677	
Schererville (G-12343)			
R & B Fine Printing Inc	G	219 365-9490	
Saint John (G-12268)			
R R Donnelley & Sons Company	A	574 267-7101	
Warsaw (G-13931)			
R R Donnelley & Sons Company	G	812 523-1800	
Seymour (G-12478)			
Rayco Marketing	G	574 293-8416	
Elkhart (G-3139)			
Raymond Little Print Shop	G	317 246-9083	
Indianapolis (G-7820)			
Regal Publications LLC	G	260 693-0698	
Churubusco (G-1656)			
Reprocomm Inc	E	765 472-5700	
Peru (G-11544)			
Republic Etching Carving	G	812 366-8111	
New Salisbury (G-11010)			
Rink Printing Company Inc	E	574 232-7935	
South Bend (G-12916)			
Rivera Screenprinting	G	812 663-0816	
Burney (G-1213)			
Riverside Printing Co	G	812 275-1950	
Bedford (G-574)			
Rock Garden Engraving	G	765 647-3357	
Brookville (G-1125)			
Rogers Marketing & Printing	G	317 838-7203	
Avon (G-465)			
Romanart Inc	G	219 736-9150	
Merrillville (G-9751)			
Rookies Unlimited Inc	G	765 536-2726	
Summitville (G-13104)			
Rowland Printing Co Inc	F	317 773-1829	
Noblesville (G-11177)			
Rubenstein LLC	G	317 946-2752	
Indianapolis (G-7871)			
Sampan Screen Print New Image	G	812 282-8499	
Jeffersonville (G-8422)			
Schutte Lithography Inc	E	812 469-3500	
Evansville (G-3717)			
Screen Art Advertising Co Inc	G	260 483-6514	
Fort Wayne (G-4611)			
Screen Print Express Inc	G	765 521-2727	
New Castle (G-10917)			
Screen Printing Super Store	G	317 804-9904	
Westfield (G-14187)			
Screenprint Special Tees LLC	G	317 396-0349	
Indianapolis (G-7906)			
Selby Publishing & Printing	G	765 453-5417	
Kokomo (G-8693)			
Service Graphics Inc	D	317 471-8246	
Indianapolis (G-7917)			
Shadow Custom Graphics	G	317 481-9710	
Indianapolis (G-7921)			
Shadow Graphix Inc	G	317 481-9710	
Indianapolis (G-7922)			
Shakour Industries Inc	G	574 289-0100	
South Bend (G-12932)			
Shaughnessy-Kniep-Hawe-paper	E	317 837-7041	
Plainfield (G-11643)			
Shirley Engraving Co Inc	F	317 634-4084	
Indianapolis (G-7934)			
Shirt Shack	G	812 550-0158	
Evansville (G-3726)			
Shirtails	G	812 858-8605	
Newburgh (G-11048)			
Sideline Graphix	G	765 520-9042	
New Castle (G-10918)			
Simplified Imaging LLC	G	219 663-5122	
Crown Point (G-2305)			
Sir Graphics Inc	G	574 272-9330	
Granger (G-5436)			
Sonoco Products Company	C	812 526-5511	
Edinburg (G-2629)			
South Bend Screen Process Inc	G	574 254-9000	
Mishawaka (G-10133)			
Southwest Grafix and AP Inc	F	812 425-5104	
Evansville (G-3740)			

Spark Marketing LLC......................G......219 301-0071
Schererville (G-12346)
Spectrum...G......812 923-7830
Georgetown (G-5153)
Spectrum...G......812 941-6899
New Albany (G-10865)
Spencer Evening World...................G......765 795-4438
Cloverdale (G-1738)
Sports Screen Impact....................G......812 926-9355
Aurora (G-389)
Sports Unlimited Printed AP...........G......574 772-4239
Knox (G-8583)
Spp Inc...F......812 882-6203
Vincennes (G-13707)
Stafford Construction Inc................G......574 287-9696
South Bend (G-12952)
Stage Door Graphics......................G......317 398-9011
Shelbyville (G-12571)
Stamprint Inc.................................G......574 233-3900
South Bend (G-12953)
Standout Creations LLC.................G......765 203-9110
Anderson (G-170)
Stands Photography.......................G......812 723-3922
Paoli (G-11457)
Stines Printing...............................G......260 356-5994
Huntington (G-6253)
◆ Stoffel Seals Corporation............E......845 353-3800
Angola (G-248)
Storm Graphics Inc.......................G......812 402-5202
Evansville (G-3753)
Stranco Inc....................................F......219 874-5221
Michigan City (G-9848)
Studio Printers..............................G......574 772-0900
Knox (G-8585)
▲ Stump Printing Co Inc...............C......260 723-5171
South Whitley (G-13006)
Syzygy Media Inc..........................G......317 509-8987
McCordsville (G-9677)
T N D Printing...............................G......260 493-4949
New Haven (G-10960)
T Productions Inc..........................F......574 257-8610
Mishawaka (G-10139)
Tabco Business Forms Inc.............G......812 882-2836
Vincennes (G-13709)
Tatman Inc....................................E......765 825-2164
Connersville (G-2075)
Taylor Communications Inc...........D......317 392-3235
Shelbyville (G-12573)
Tc Printing & More LLC.................G......812 936-3069
West Baden Springs (G-14036)
Team Image LLC...........................E......317 468-0802
Greenfield (G-5579)
Team Image LLC...........................E......317 477-7468
Greenfield (G-5580)
Team Pride Athletic AP Corp..........G......574 224-8326
Rochester (G-12156)
TEC Photography..........................G......812 332-9847
Bloomington (G-836)
Teeki Hut Custom Tees Inc...........G......317 205-3589
Indianapolis (G-8052)
Terz Design and Imprinting LLC.....G......765 965-9762
Richmond (G-12063)
Thermography Indianapolis LLC.....G......317 370-5111
Indianapolis (G-8059)
Thermovision Thermography..........G......317 306-6622
Indianapolis (G-8060)
Thomas E Slade Inc......................F......812 471-7100
Evansville (G-3760)
Thoughts Are Things.....................G......317 585-8053
Indianapolis (G-8069)
Tippecanoe Press Inc....................F......317 392-1207
Shelbyville (G-12576)
Tko Enterprises Inc.......................D......317 271-1398
Plainfield (G-11647)
Tma Enterprises Inc......................G......317 272-0694
Avon (G-469)
To a Tee Inc..................................G......317 757-8842
Indianapolis (G-8078)
Topstitch Inc.................................F......574 293-6633
Elkhart (G-3220)
Town & Country Press Inc.............F......574 936-9505
Plymouth (G-11730)
Trademark Screen Printing............G......317 885-3258
Greenwood (G-5755)
Tranter Graphics Inc.....................D......574 834-2626
Syracuse (G-13151)
Travis Britton.................................G......317 762-6018
Indianapolis (G-8092)
Tribune Showprint Inc...................G......574 943-3281
Earl Park (G-2513)

Trident Engraving Inc....................G......812 282-2098
Jeffersonville (G-8435)
Trinity Cmmnications Group Inc.....G......260 484-1029
Fort Wayne (G-4704)
Triple Crown Media LLC................D......574 533-2151
Goshen (G-5342)
Un Communications Group Inc......E......317 844-8622
Carmel (G-1503)
Unique Graphic Designs Inc..........G......574 583-7119
Monticello (G-10287)
Useful Products LLC.....................E......877 304-9036
Goodland (G-5161)
V & P Printing...............................G......260 495-3741
Fremont (G-4978)
▲ Valley Screen Process Co Inc....D......574 256-0901
Mishawaka (G-10144)
Varsity Sports Inc.........................G......219 987-7200
Demotte (G-2451)
Vickers Graphics Inc.....................G......765 868-4646
Kokomo (G-8712)
Vinyl Creator................................G......260 318-5133
Wolcottville (G-14377)
W Robbins & Sons Inc..................G......765 522-1736
Roachdale (G-12096)
Walkerton Tool & Die Inc..............E......574 586-3162
Walkerton (G-13813)
WAr - LLC- Westville Prtg..............G......219 785-2821
Westville (G-14221)
Warren Printing Services LLC........F......812 738-6508
Corydon (G-2115)
Waterloo Press Inc........................G......260 837-3781
Waterloo (G-14025)
Wayne Press Incorporated.............G......260 744-3022
Fort Wayne (G-4743)
Whitewater Publications Inc...........E......765 647-4221
Brookville (G-1131)
Wildman Business Group LLC........C......866 369-1552
Warsaw (G-13965)
▲ Williams Plastics LLC................C......317 398-1630
Shelbyville (G-12585)
Williams Printing Inc.....................G......765 468-6033
Farmland (G-3844)
Wilson Enterprises Inc...................G......765 362-1089
Crawfordsville (G-2205)
Wilson Printing.............................G......317 745-5868
Danville (G-2358)
Wise Business Forms Inc...............C......260 489-1561
Fort Wayne (G-4759)
Woodburn Graphics Inc.................E......812 232-0323
Terre Haute (G-13371)
Woodfield Printing Inc...................G......317 848-2000
Indianapolis (G-6283)
Writeguard Business Systems........G......317 849-7292
Indianapolis (G-8219)
X Printwear Inc..............................F......812 336-0700
Bloomington (G-860)
XI Graphics Inc.............................F......317 738-3434
Franklin (G-4942)
Xtreme Graphics............................G......812 989-6948
Jeffersonville (G-8443)

2761 Manifold Business Forms

Altstadt Business Forms Inc...........F......812 425-3393
Evansville (G-3349)
Anchor Enterprises..........................G......812 282-7220
Jeffersonville (G-8326)
Cornelius Printed Products Inc........E......317 923-1340
Indianapolis (G-6668)
E James Dant.................................G......812 476-2271
Evansville (G-3469)
Falls Cities Printing Inc..................F......812 949-9051
New Albany (G-10775)
Highland Computer Forms Inc........E......260 665-6268
Angola (G-219)
International Label Mfg LLC.............F......812 235-5071
Terre Haute (G-13258)
Iu East Business Office..................G......765 973-8218
Richmond (G-12003)
Label Tech Inc..............................E......765 747-1234
Muncie (G-10506)
Lincoln Printing Corporation...........E......260 424-5200
Fort Wayne (G-4437)
NP Converters Inc.........................E......812 448-2555
Brazil (G-973)
Pengad/West Inc...........................E......765 286-3000
Muncie (G-10544)
Printegra Corp..............................D......317 328-0022
Indianapolis (G-7752)
R R Donnelley & Sons Company.....B......260 624-2350
Angola (G-242)

Stewart Graphics Inc.....................E......812 283-0455
Jeffersonville (G-8430)
Taylor Communications Inc............D......317 392-3235
Shelbyville (G-12573)
Tippecanoe Press Inc....................F......317 392-1207
Shelbyville (G-12576)
Wise Business Forms Inc...............C......260 489-1561
Fort Wayne (G-4759)
Woodburn Graphics Inc.................E......812 232-0323
Terre Haute (G-13371)
Writeguard Business Systems.........G......317 849-7292
Indianapolis (G-8219)

2771 Greeting Card Publishing

Behning Inc....................................G......260 672-2663
Roanoke (G-12099)
Celebrate Season...........................F......609 261-5200
Sunman (G-13109)
Kellmark Corporation.....................E......574 264-9695
Elkhart (G-2958)
McPhersons (us) Inc......................E......812 623-2225
Sunman (G-13114)
Nussmeier Engraving Co...............E......812 425-1339
Evansville (G-3650)

2782 Blankbooks & Looseleaf Binders

Aom Bookshop...............................G......317 493-8095
Indianapolis (G-6405)
Clarke American Checks Inc...........C......812 283-9598
Jeffersonville (G-8338)
Clarke American Checks Inc...........C......812 283-9598
Jeffersonville (G-8339)
Codybro LLC.................................G......765 827-5441
Connersville (G-2044)
Deluxe Homes...............................G......219 256-1701
Westville (G-14215)
Eckhart & Company Inc.................E......317 347-2665
Indianapolis (G-6799)
Futurex Industries Inc...................E......765 498-8900
Bloomingdale (G-648)
▲ Harcourt Industries Inc.............E......765 629-2625
Milroy (G-9980)
Lamco Finishers Inc......................E......317 471-1010
Indianapolis (G-7379)
Leed Selling Tools Corp.................C......812 482-7888
Ireland (G-8229)
Leed Selling Tools Corp.................C......812 867-4340
Evansville (G-3599)
No-Sail Splash Guard Co Inc..........G......765 522-2100
Roachdale (G-12094)
Nussmeier Engraving Co...............E......812 425-1339
Evansville (G-3650)
Omni Looseleaf Inc.......................G......219 253-8020
Monticello (G-10275)
Printegra Corp..............................D......317 328-0022
Indianapolis (G-7752)
Raine Inc......................................F......765 622-7687
Anderson (G-157)
Scrapbook Nook............................E......812 967-3306
Pekin (G-11479)
▲ SPI Binding Co Inc...................E......765 794-4992
Darlington (G-2361)
Writeguard Business Systems........G......317 849-7292
Indianapolis (G-8219)

2789 Bookbinding

▲ A-1 Awards Inc........................F......317 546-9000
Indianapolis (G-6301)
Acclaim Graphics Inc....................G......812 424-5035
Evansville (G-3334)
Athena Arts & Graphics Inc...........G......317 876-8916
Indianapolis (G-6436)
Baxter Printing Inc........................G......219 923-1999
Highland (G-6037)
Blasted Works...............................G......574 583-3211
Monticello (G-10256)
Brand Prtg & Photo-Litho Co..........G......317 921-4095
Indianapolis (G-6503)
C & W Inkd....................................F......317 352-1000
Indianapolis (G-6527)
C J P Corporation..........................G......219 924-1685
Highland (G-6040)
Cecils Printing & Office Sups.........G......812 683-4416
Huntingburg (G-6153)
▲ Centennial Bindery LLC............E......812 472-4655
Clarksville (G-1676)
Ckmt Associates Inc......................E......219 924-2820
Hammond (G-5863)
Clarke American Checks Inc...........C......812 283-9598
Jeffersonville (G-8339)

S
I
C

Classic Graphics Inc ....F 260 482-3487
Fort Wayne *(G-4156)*

Consolidated Printing Svcs Inc ....F ... 765 468-6033
Farmland *(G-3841)*

Courier Printing Co Allen Cnty ....G 260 627-2728
Grabill *(G-5362)*

Creative Concept Ventures Inc ....G ... 812 282-9442
Jeffersonville *(G-8348)*

Crossrads Rhbilitation Ctr Inc ....C ... 317 897-7320
Indianapolis *(G-6697)*

Digital Printing Incorporated ....F ... 812 265-2205
Madison *(G-9457)*

Doerr Printing Co ....G ... 317 568-0135
Indianapolis *(G-6756)*

Dynamark Graphics Group Inc ....G ... 317 634-2963
Indianapolis *(G-6777)*

Dynamark Graphics Group Inc ....E ... 317 328-2555
Indianapolis *(G-6775)*

Eckhart & Company Inc ....G ... 317 347-2665
Indianapolis *(G-6799)*

Ed Sons Inc ....F ... 317 897-8821
Indianapolis *(G-6803)*

Elkhart Binding Inc ....G ... 574 522-5455
Elkhart *(G-2821)*

Epi Printers Inc ....D ... 317 579-4870
Indianapolis *(G-6875)*

Evansville Bindery Inc ....G ... 812 423-2222
Evansville *(G-3483)*

Ewing Printing Company Inc ....F ... 812 882-2415
Vincennes *(G-13677)*

Express Bindings ....G ... 317 269-8114
Indianapolis *(G-6897)*

Express Press Indiana Inc ....E ... 574 277-3355
South Bend *(G-12769)*

Faulkenberg Printing Co Inc ....F ... 317 638-1359
Franklin *(G-4886)*

Faulkners Bindery ....F ... 765 292-2285
Atlanta *(G-294)*

Fedex Office & Print Svcs Inc ....E ... 317 631-6862
Indianapolis *(G-6908)*

Fedex Office & Print Svcs Inc ....E ... 317 849-9683
Indianapolis *(G-6911)*

Fedex Office & Print Svcs Inc ....E ... 574 271-0398
South Bend *(G-12777)*

Fedex Office & Print Svcs Inc ....E ... 317 337-2679
Indianapolis *(G-6912)*

Fedex Office & Print Svcs Inc ....G ... 317 295-1063
Indianapolis *(G-6913)*

Fedex Office & Print Svcs Inc ....F ... 317 251-2406
Indianapolis *(G-6914)*

Fedex Office & Print Svcs Inc ....E ... 317 885-6480
Indianapolis *(G-6915)*

Fedex Office & Print Svcs Inc ....F ... 765 449-4950
Lafayette *(G-8897)*

Goetz Printing ....F ... 812 243-2086
Terre Haute *(G-13241)*

Graessle-Mercer Co ....E ... 812 522-5478
Seymour *(G-12451)*

Granger Gazette ....G ... 574 277-2679
Granger *(G-5410)*

Green Banner Publications Inc ....E ... 812 967-3176
Pekin *(G-11473)*

Greencastle Offset Inc ....G ... 765 653-4026
Greencastle *(G-5458)*

Greensburg Printing Co Inc ....G ... 812 663-8265
Greensburg *(G-5604)*

Hager Inc ....G ... 260 483-7075
Fort Wayne *(G-4314)*

Hardesty Printing Co Inc ....F ... 574 223-4553
Rochester *(G-12126)*

Hardesty Printing Co Inc ....F ... 574 267-7591
Warsaw *(G-13889)*

Hetty Incorporated ....G ... 219 836-2517
Munster *(G-10605)*

Hetty Incorporated ....G ... 219 933-0833
Hammond *(G-5892)*

Hf Group LLC ....B ... 260 982-2107
North Manchester *(G-11230)*

Hiatt Enterprises Inc ....G ... 765 289-2700
Muncie *(G-10488)*

Hiatt Enterprises Inc ....E ... 765 289-7756
Muncie *(G-10487)*

Hinen Printing Co ....G ... 260 248-8984
Columbia City *(G-1789)*

Hines Bindery Systems Service ....G ... 317 839-6432
Plainfield *(G-11615)*

Howard Print Shop ....G ... 765 453-6161
Kokomo *(G-8641)*

Image Group Inc ....E ... 574 457-3111
Syracuse *(G-13135)*

Infobind Systems Inc ....G ... 260 248-4989
Fort Wayne *(G-4369)*

Insty-Prints of South Bend ....G ... 574 289-6977
South Bend *(G-12814)*

Journal and Chronicle Inc ....G ... 812 752-5060
Scottsburg *(G-12370)*

Kays Graphics Inc ....G ... 317 236-9755
Indianapolis *(G-7335)*

L & L Press Inc ....F ... 765 664-3162
Marion *(G-9541)*

La Grange Publishing Co Inc ....G ... 260 463-3243
Lagrange *(G-9052)*

Lamco Finishers Inc ....E ... 317 471-1010
Indianapolis *(G-6756)*

Laminating Specialties Inc Ind ....G ... 765 385-0023
Templeton *(G-13178)*

Largus Speedy Print Corp ....E ... 219 922-8414
Munster *(G-10612)*

Leed Selling Tools Corp ....E ... 812 867-4340
Evansville *(G-3599)*

▲ Liberty Book & Bb Manufactures ....E ... 317 633-1450
Indianapolis *(G-7402)*

Lincoln Printing Corporation ....G ... 260 424-5200
Fort Wayne *(G-4437)*

Ludwick Graphics Inc ....G ... 574 233-2165
South Bend *(G-12845)*

Mar Kel Inc ....G ... 812 853-6133
Newburgh *(G-11038)*

Masco Corporation of Indiana ....D ... 317 848-1812
Indianapolis *(G-7463)*

Maureen Sharp ....G ... 765 379-3644
Rossville *(G-12211)*

Maury Boyd & Associates Inc ....F ... 317 849-6110
Indianapolis *(G-7469)*

Millcraft Paper Company ....E ... 317 240-3500
Indianapolis *(G-7519)*

Miller Rainbow Printing Inc ....G ... 812 275-3355
Bedford *(G-565)*

Mitchell-Fleming Printing Inc ....F ... 317 462-5467
Greenfield *(G-5554)*

Montgomery & Associates Inc ....F ... 219 879-0088
Michigan City *(G-9821)*

National Lib Bindery Co of Ind ....G ... 317 636-5606
Indianapolis *(G-7573)*

North Vernon Plain Dlr & Sun ....E ... 812 346-3973
North Vernon *(G-11272)*

Offset House Inc ....F ... 317 849-5155
Indianapolis *(G-7612)*

Offset One Inc ....F ... 260 456-8828
Fort Wayne *(G-4509)*

Overgaards Artcraft Printers ....G ... 574 234-8464
South Bend *(G-12885)*

PIP Printing ....G ... 317 843-5755
Carmel *(G-1451)*

Plastimatic Arts Corp ....E ... 574 254-9000
Mishawaka *(G-10104)*

Presstime Graphics Inc ....E ... 812 234-3815
Terre Haute *(G-13309)*

Printer Zink Inc ....D ... 765 644-3959
Anderson *(G-156)*

Printing Place Inc-Photos Plus ....F ... 260 665-8444
Angola *(G-239)*

Progressive Printing Co Inc ....G ... 765 653-3814
Greencastle *(G-5475)*

Quality Printing of NW Ind ....G ... 219 322-6677
Schererville *(G-12343)*

Reprocomm Inc ....F ... 765 423-2578
Lafayette *(G-8990)*

Reprocomm Inc ....E ... 765 472-5700
Peru *(G-11544)*

Rhr Corporation ....G ... 317 788-1504
Indianapolis *(G-7837)*

Riden Inc ....G ... 219 362-5511
La Porte *(G-8812)*

Rink Printing Company Inc ....E ... 574 232-7935
South Bend *(G-12916)*

Rise Inc ....E ... 260 665-9408
Angola *(G-243)*

Rowland Printing Co Inc ....F ... 317 773-1829
Noblesville *(G-11177)*

RR Donnelley & Sons Company ....A ... 765 362-1300
Crawfordsville *(G-2194)*

Schutte Lithography Inc ....G ... 812 469-3500
Evansville *(G-3717)*

Service Graphics Inc ....D ... 317 471-8246
Indianapolis *(G-7917)*

▲ Service Printers Inc ....E ... 574 266-6710
Elkhart *(G-3162)*

Spectrum Press Inc ....E ... 812 335-1945
Bloomington *(G-831)*

▲ SPI Binding Co Inc ....E ... 765 794-4992
Darlington *(G-2361)*

Stamprint Inc ....G ... 574 233-3900
South Bend *(G-12953)*

Stines Printing ....G ... 260 356-5994
Huntington *(G-6253)*

▲ Superior Sample Co Inc ....E ... 260 894-3136
Ligonier *(G-9297)*

Tabco Business Forms Inc ....G ... 812 882-2836
Vincennes *(G-13709)*

Tatman Inc ....F ... 765 825-2164
Connersville *(G-2075)*

Thomas E Slade Inc ....F ... 812 471-7100
Evansville *(G-3760)*

Tippecanoe Press Inc ....F ... 317 392-1207
Shelbyville *(G-12576)*

United Parcel Service Inc ....G ... 317 776-9494
Noblesville *(G-11197)*

◆ Voice of God Recordings Inc ....D ... 812 246-2137
Jeffersonville *(G-8439)*

W Robbins & Sons Inc ....G ... 765 522-1736
Roachdale *(G-12096)*

WAr - LLC- Westville Prtg ....G ... 219 785-2821
Westville *(G-14221)*

Whitewater Publications Inc ....E ... 765 647-4221
Brookville *(G-1131)*

Woodburn Graphics Inc ....E ... 812 232-0323
Terre Haute *(G-13371)*

2791 Typesetting

A-1 Graphics Inc ....G ... 765 289-1851
Muncie *(G-10420)*

Acclaim Graphics Inc ....G ... 812 424-5035
Evansville *(G-3334)*

Aim Media Indiana Oper LLC ....E ... 317 462-5528
Greenfield *(G-5497)*

Annual Reports Inc ....G ... 317 736-8838
Franklin *(G-4868)*

Athena Arts & Graphics Inc ....G ... 317 876-8916
Indianapolis *(G-6436)*

Brand Prtg & Photo-Litho Co ....G ... 317 921-4095
Indianapolis *(G-6503)*

BSC Vntres Acquisition Sub LLC ....D ... 260 665-7521
Angola *(G-198)*

C J P Corporation ....G ... 219 924-1685
Highland *(G-6040)*

Cecils Printing & Office Sups ....G ... 812 683-4416
Huntingburg *(G-6153)*

Ckmt Associates Inc ....E ... 219 924-2820
Hammond *(G-5863)*

Clarke American Checks Inc ....C ... 812 283-9598
Jeffersonville *(G-8339)*

Classic Graphics Inc ....F ... 260 482-3487
Fort Wayne *(G-4156)*

Clondalkin Pharma & Healthcare ....C ... 317 328-7355
Indianapolis *(G-6623)*

Cnhi LLC ....E ... 812 944-6481
New Albany *(G-10762)*

Community Holdings Indiana Inc ....E ... 765 482-4650
Lebanon *(G-9175)*

Community Holdings Indiana Inc ....F ... 765 459-3121
Kokomo *(G-8608)*

Community Holdings Indiana Inc ....E ... 812 663-3111
Greensburg *(G-5594)*

Community Papers Inc ....G ... 317 241-7363
Indianapolis *(G-6639)*

Composition LLC ....G ... 317 979-7214
Fishers *(G-3892)*

Consolidated Printing Svcs Inc ....F ... 765 468-6033
Farmland *(G-3841)*

Copyfire Typesetting Inc ....G ... 317 894-0408
Indianapolis *(G-6665)*

Copymat Service Inc ....G ... 765 743-5995
Lafayette *(G-8878)*

Country Pines Inc ....F ... 812 247-3315
Shoals *(G-12665)*

Courier Printing Co Allen Cnty ....G ... 260 627-2728
Grabill *(G-5362)*

▲ Courier-Times Inc ....D ... 765 529-1111
New Castle *(G-10897)*

Coy & Associates ....G ... 317 787-5089
Indianapolis *(G-6682)*

Creative Concept Ventures Inc ....G ... 812 282-9442
Jeffersonville *(G-8348)*

Crescendo Inc ....G ... 812 829-4759
Spencer *(G-13022)*

D & M Printing Inc ....G ... 812 847-4837
Linton *(G-9306)*

Digital Printing Incorporated ....F ... 812 265-2205
Madison *(G-9457)*

Doerr Printing Co ....G...... 317 568-0135
Indianapolis *(G-6756)*

Dynamark Graphics Group Inc ....G...... 317 634-2963
Indianapolis *(G-6777)*

Dynamark Graphics Group Inc ....E...... 317 328-2555
Indianapolis *(G-6775)*

Ed Sons Inc ....F...... 317 897-8821
Indianapolis *(G-6803)*

Evansville Bindery Inc........................G...... 812 423-2222
Evansville *(G-3483)*

Evansville Courier Co ....B...... 812 464-7500
Evansville *(G-3485)*

Ewing Printing Company Inc ....F...... 812 882-2415
Vincennes *(G-13677)*

Excell Color Graphics Inc ....E...... 260 482-2720
Fort Wayne *(G-4251)*

Express Press Indiana Inc ....E...... 574 277-3355
South Bend *(G-12769)*

Fedex Office & Print Svcs Inc ....E...... 317 631-6862
Indianapolis *(G-6908)*

Fedex Office & Print Svcs Inc ....E...... 317 849-9683
Indianapolis *(G-6911)*

Fedex Office & Print Svcs Inc ....E...... 574 271-0398
South Bend *(G-12777)*

Fedex Office & Print Svcs Inc ....E...... 317 337-2679
Indianapolis *(G-6912)*

Fedex Office & Print Svcs Inc ....G...... 317 295-1063
Indianapolis *(G-6913)*

Fedex Office & Print Svcs Inc ....F...... 317 251-2406
Indianapolis *(G-6914)*

Fedex Office & Print Svcs Inc ....E...... 317 885-6480
Indianapolis *(G-6914)*

Fedex Office & Print Svcs Inc ....F...... 765 449-4950
Lafayette *(G-8897)*

Fineline Digital Group Inc ....E...... 317 872-4490
Indianapolis *(G-6920)*

Fineline Graphics Incorporated ....D...... 317 872-4490
Indianapolis *(G-6921)*

First Quality Printing Inc ....G...... 317 506-8633
Indianapolis *(G-6927)*

Fort Wayne Printing Co Inc..................F...... 260 471-7744
Fort Wayne *(G-4280)*

Gary Printing Inc ....G...... 219 886-1767
Gary *(G-5052)*

Goetz Printing ....F...... 812 243-2086
Terre Haute *(G-13241)*

Graessle-Mercer Co ....E...... 812 522-5478
Seymour *(G-12451)*

Granger Gazette ....G...... 574 277-2679
Granger *(G-5410)*

Graphics Unlimited ....G...... 765 288-6816
Muncie *(G-10479)*

Green Banner Publications Inc.............E...... 812 967-3176
Pekin *(G-11473)*

Greensburg Printing Co Inc..................G...... 812 663-8265
Greensburg *(G-5604)*

Hager Inc..G...... 260 483-7075
Fort Wayne *(G-4314)*

Hardesty Printing Co Inc ....F...... 574 223-4553
Rochester *(G-12126)*

Hardesty Printing Co Inc ....F...... 574 267-7591
Warsaw *(G-13889)*

Hetty Incorporated..............................G...... 219 836-2517
Munster *(G-10605)*

Hetty Incorporated..............................G...... 219 933-0833
Hammond *(G-5892)*

Hiatt Enterprises Inc ....G...... 765 289-2700
Muncie *(G-10488)*

Hiatt Enterprises Inc ....E...... 765 289-7756
Muncie *(G-10487)*

Hinen Printing Co.................................G...... 260 248-8984
Columbia City *(G-1789)*

Home News Enterprises LLC................E...... 574 583-5121
Monticello *(G-10265)*

Hoosier Printing Co Inc ....G...... 219 836-8877
Munster *(G-10606)*

Hoosier Times Inc ....C...... 812 331-4270
Bloomington *(G-741)*

Howard Print Shop...............................G...... 765 453-6161
Kokomo *(G-8641)*

Indiana Newspapers LLC......................D...... 812 886-9955
Vincennes *(G-13685)*

Journal and Chronicle Inc ....C...... 812 752-5060
Scottsburg *(G-12370)*

Kpc Media Group Inc ....C...... 260 347-0400
Kendallville *(G-8488)*

Kpc Media Group Inc ....E...... 260 426-2640
Fort Wayne *(G-4415)*

L & L Press Inc ....F...... 765 664-3162
Marion *(G-9541)*

◆ L C Typesetting Company Inc ....G...... 574 232-4700
South Bend *(G-12834)*

La Grange Publishing Co Inc...............F...... 260 463-3243
Lagrange *(G-9052)*

Largus Speedy Print Corp.....................E...... 219 922-8414
Munster *(G-10612)*

Leader Publishing Co of Salem ....E...... 812 883-4446
Salem *(G-12299)*

Lee Publications Inc ....D...... 219 933-9251
Munster *(G-10614)*

Lincoln Printing Corporation ....E...... 260 424-5200
Fort Wayne *(G-4437)*

Ludwick Graphics Inc..........................F...... 574 233-2165
South Bend *(G-12845)*

▲ M Nelson & Associates Inc ....G...... 317 228-1422
Carmel *(G-1430)*

Maury Boyd & Associates Inc...............F...... 317 849-6110
Indianapolis *(G-7469)*

Miller Rainbow Printing Inc..................E...... 812 275-3355
Bedford *(G-565)*

Minute Print It Inc...............................G...... 765 482-9019
Lebanon *(G-9206)*

Muncie Novelty Company Inc ....D...... 765 288-8301
Muncie *(G-10532)*

News Publishing Company LLC............G...... 812 649-4440
Rockport *(G-12171)*

North Vernon Plain Dlr & Sun ....E...... 812 346-3973
North Vernon *(G-11272)*

Nussmeier Engraving Co ....F...... 812 425-1339
Evansville *(G-3650)*

Offset House Inc ....F...... 317 849-5155
Indianapolis *(G-7612)*

Offset One Inc ....F...... 260 456-8828
Fort Wayne *(G-4509)*

Overgaards Artcraft Printers ....G...... 574 234-8464
South Bend *(G-12885)*

Pierce Oil Co Inc ....F...... 812 268-6356
Sullivan *(G-13090)*

PIP Printing..G...... 317 843-5755
Carmel *(G-1451)*

Presstime Graphics Inc ....E...... 812 234-3815
Terre Haute *(G-13309)*

Printing Emporium Inc ....G...... 574 256-0059
Mishawaka *(G-10109)*

Printing Place Inc-Photos Plus............F...... 260 665-8444
Angola *(G-239)*

Priority Printing LLC............................G...... 317 241-4234
Indianapolis *(G-7761)*

Progressive Printing Co Inc..................G...... 765 653-3814
Greencastle *(G-5475)*

Pubco Inc ....F...... 219 874-4245
Michigan City *(G-9830)*

Publishers Consulting Corp ....E...... 219 874-4245
Michigan City *(G-9831)*

Q Graphics Inc ....G...... 574 967-3733
Flora *(G-4002)*

Q S I Inc..E...... 574 282-1200
South Bend *(G-12908)*

Quality Printing of NW Ind ....G...... 219 322-6677
Schererville *(G-12343)*

Quality Typesetting ....F...... 317 787-4466
Indianapolis *(G-7802)*

Regal Printing Inc ....G...... 317 844-1723
Carmel *(G-1464)*

Reprocomm Inc ....E...... 765 472-5700
Peru *(G-11544)*

Rhr Corporation ....G...... 317 788-1504
Indianapolis *(G-7837)*

Riden Inc ....G...... 219 362-5511
La Porte *(G-8812)*

Rink Printing Company Inc ....E...... 574 232-7935
South Bend *(G-12916)*

Rowland Printing Co Inc ....F...... 317 773-1829
Noblesville *(G-11177)*

Rrc Corporation ....F...... 317 687-8325
Indianapolis *(G-7869)*

Russ Print Shop ....F...... 219 996-3142
Hebron *(G-6022)*

▲ Service Printers Inc ....E...... 574 266-6710
Elkhart *(G-3162)*

Shirley Engraving Co Inc ....F...... 317 634-4084
Indianapolis *(G-7934)*

Spectrum Press Inc ....E...... 812 335-1945
Bloomington *(G-831)*

Spencer Evening World.........................D...... 812 829-2255
Spencer *(G-13037)*

Stamprint Inc ....F...... 574 233-3900
South Bend *(G-12953)*

Stines Printing....................................G...... 260 356-5994
Huntington *(G-6253)*

Tabco Business Forms Inc ....G...... 812 882-2836
Vincennes *(G-13709)*

Tatman Inc ....E...... 765 825-2164
Connersville *(G-2075)*

Thomas E Slade Inc............................F...... 812 471-7100
Evansville *(G-3760)*

Times..G...... 765 296-3622
Frankfort *(G-4856)*

Town & Country Press Inc ....F...... 574 936-9505
Plymouth *(G-11730)*

Triple Crown Media LLC ....D...... 574 533-2151
Goshen *(G-5342)*

Truth Publishing Company Inc ....E...... 765 653-5151
Greencastle *(G-5480)*

◆ Voice of God Recordings Inc.............D...... 812 246-2137
Jeffersonville *(G-8439)*

WAr - LLC- Westville Prtg......................G...... 219 785-2821
Westville *(G-14221)*

Woodburn Graphics Inc ....E...... 812 232-0323
Terre Haute *(G-13371)*

Writeguard Business Systems ....G...... 317 849-7292
Indianapolis *(G-8219)*

Xl Graphics Inc...................................F...... 317 738-3434
Franklin *(G-4942)*

2796 Platemaking & Related Svcs

Accucraft Imaging Inc ....G...... 219 933-3007
Hammond *(G-5834)*

All American Awards Inc ....G...... 765 296-4333
Mulberry *(G-10416)*

Bottcher America Corporation ....E...... 765 675-4449
Tipton *(G-13389)*

C & J Corporation ....G...... 574 255-6793
Mishawaka *(G-10015)*

Cecils Printing & Office Sups ....G...... 812 683-4416
Huntingburg *(G-6153)*

Crichlow Industries Inc ....G...... 317 925-5178
Indianapolis *(G-6692)*

▲ Cylicron LLC....................................D...... 812 283-4600
Jeffersonville *(G-8349)*

Diverse Sales Solutions LLC ....G...... 317 514-2403
Indianapolis *(G-6747)*

Dynamic Dies Inc ....E...... 317 247-4706
Indianapolis *(G-6778)*

Evantek Manufacturing Inds LLC ....E...... 812 437-9100
Evansville *(G-3493)*

Ewing Printing Company Inc ....F...... 812 882-2415
Vincennes *(G-13677)*

Excell Color Graphics Inc ....E...... 260 482-2720
Fort Wayne *(G-4251)*

Express Press Indiana Inc ....E...... 574 277-3355
South Bend *(G-12769)*

Fedex Office & Print Svcs Inc ....F...... 765 449-4950
Lafayette *(G-8897)*

Gary Printing Inc ....G...... 219 886-1767
Gary *(G-5052)*

▲ Grandview Aluminum Products........E...... 812 649-2569
Grandview *(G-5387)*

Graphik Mechanix Inc.........................G...... 260 426-7001
Fort Wayne *(G-4303)*

Its Personal Laser Engraving ....G...... 812 934-6657
Batesville *(G-505)*

Kik Custom Products Inc ....E...... 574 295-0000
Elkhart *(G-2968)*

Ludwick Graphics Inc..........................F...... 574 233-2165
South Bend *(G-12845)*

▲ M Nelson & Associates Inc ....G...... 317 228-1422
Carmel *(G-1430)*

Maury Boyd & Associates Inc...............F...... 317 849-6110
Indianapolis *(G-7469)*

Multi-Color Corporation ....E...... 812 752-0586
Scottsburg *(G-12375)*

Peafield Products Inc ....F...... 317 839-8473
Plainfield *(G-11634)*

Pengad/West Inc ....E...... 765 286-3000
Muncie *(G-10544)*

Rotation Dynamics Corporation ....E...... 219 325-8808
La Porte *(G-8813)*

Segura Publishing Company ....G...... 574 631-3143
South Bend *(G-12931)*

Shakour Industries Inc ....G...... 574 289-0100
South Bend *(G-12932)*

Shirley Engraving Co Inc ....F...... 317 634-4084
Indianapolis *(G-7934)*

28 CHEMICALS AND ALLIED PRODUCTS

2812 Alkalies & Chlorine

Eco Services Operations Corp ....E 219 932-7651
Hammond (G-5874)

▲ Hf Chlor-Alkali LLC ....E 317 591-0000
Indianapolis (G-7098)

Jci Jones Chemicals Inc ....F 317 787-8382
Beech Grove (G-599)

Kik Custom Products Inc ....E 574 295-0000
Elkhart (G-2968)

▲ Ulrich Chemical Inc ....D 317 898-8632
Indianapolis (G-8125)

Warsaw Chemical Company Inc ....D 574 267-3251
Warsaw (G-13958)

2813 Industrial Gases

A G A Gas Inc ....E 317 783-2331
Indianapolis (G-6295)

Air Products and Chemicals Inc ....E 260 868-9145
Butler (G-1221)

Air Products and Chemicals Inc ....E 219 787-9551
Chesterton (G-1591)

Airgas Inc ....E 317 632-7106
Indianapolis (G-6354)

Airgas Inc ....G 812 376-9155
Greenwood (G-5664)

Airgas Usa LLC ....E 812 838-8808
Mount Vernon (G-10382)

Airgas Usa LLC ....F 317 783-2331
Indianapolis (G-6356)

Airgas Usa LLC ....G 812 537-4101
Moores Hill (G-10296)

Airgas Usa LLC ....G 317 892-5221
Pittsboro (G-11582)

Airgas Usa LLC ....F 260 749-9576
Fort Wayne (G-4051)

Airgas Usa LLC ....G 317 248-8072
Indianapolis (G-6355)

Airgas Usa LLC ....E 812 474-0440
Evansville (G-3345)

Airgas Usa LLC ....G 812 362-7593
Rockport (G-12163)

Alig LLC ....G 812 362-7593
Rockport (G-12165)

Continental Carbonic Pdts Inc ....G 574 273-2800
South Bend (G-12741)

Digital Helium LLC ....G 219 365-4038
Saint John (G-12262)

Ferrellgas LP ....G 574 936-2725
Plymouth (G-11684)

Indiana Oxygen Company Inc ....D 317 290-0003
Indianapolis (G-7188)

Jt Composites LLC ....G 317 297-9520
Indianapolis (G-7320)

▲ Kik Aerosol Socal LLC ....C 626 363-6200
Elkhart (G-2966)

Linde Gas North America LLC ....F 219 989-9304
Hammond (G-5908)

Linde LLC ....D 219 324-0498
La Porte (G-8786)

Linde LLC ....G 574 234-4887
South Bend (G-12839)

Matheson Tri-Gas Inc ....F 812 838-5518
Mount Vernon (G-10398)

Matheson Tri-Gas Inc ....F 812 257-0470
Washington (G-13990)

Matheson Tri-Gas Inc ....G 317 892-5221
Pittsboro (G-11585)

Neon Bay ....G 574 583-6366
Monticello (G-10273)

Neon Glassworks LLC ....G 765 497-1135
West Lafayette (G-14090)

Neon Safety Group LLC ....G 317 774-5144
Noblesville (G-11157)

Northern Gases and Sups Inc ....F 574 594-2551
Pierceton (G-11574)

Petrogas International Corp ....G 260 484-0859
Auburn (G-347)

Praxair Inc ....F 219 398-3777
Whiting (G-14274)

Praxair Inc ....E 765 456-1128
Kokomo (G-8683)

Praxair Inc ....F 219 949-8407
Gary (G-5085)

Praxair Inc ....G 317 240-2500
Indianapolis (G-7721)

Praxair Inc ....C 219 398-3700
East Chicago (G-2562)

Praxair Inc ....E 219 326-7808
La Porte (G-8805)

Praxair Inc ....F 219 397-6940
East Chicago (G-2563)

Praxair Inc ....E 765 447-8171
Lafayette (G-8982)

Praxair Inc ....E 812 537-2898
Lawrenceburg (G-9153)

Praxair Distribution Inc ....G 317 481-4550
Indianapolis (G-7722)

Praxair Distribution Inc ....G 260 423-4468
Fort Wayne (G-4546)

Praxair Distribution Inc ....E 317 481-4550
Indianapolis (G-7723)

Weaver Air Products LLC ....G 317 848-4420
Carmel (G-1508)

2816 Inorganic Pigments

A Schulman Inc ....E 574 935-5131
Plymouth (G-11660)

Altair Nanotechnologies Inc ....A 317 333-7617
Anderson (G-60)

▲ Cathay Industries (usa) Inc ....G 219 531-5359
Valparaiso (G-13520)

Hammond Group Inc ....E 219 933-1560
Hammond (G-5885)

▲ Kibbechem Inc ....E 574 266-1234
Elkhart (G-2964)

Old Jim Customs LLC ....G 812 431-1460
Evansville (G-3654)

Silberline Mfg Co Inc ....C 260 728-2111
Decatur (G-2404)

United Minerals and Prpts Inc ....E 812 838-5236
Mount Vernon (G-10412)

2819 Indl Inorganic Chemicals, NEC

Airgas Usa LLC ....G 812 362-7593
Rockport (G-12163)

Akzo Nobel Coatings Inc ....F 574 372-2000
Warsaw (G-13836)

Alig LLC ....G 812 362-7593
Rockport (G-12165)

Allen Industries Inc ....G 317 595-0730
Indianapolis (G-6368)

▲ Amalgamated Incorporated ....G 260 489-2549
Fort Wayne (G-4065)

Arch Wood Protection Inc ....F 219 464-3949
Valparaiso (G-13497)

Astec Corp ....G 317 872-7550
Indianapolis (G-6432)

Atmosphere Dynamics Corp ....G 317 392-6262
Shelbyville (G-12518)

Catalyst Services Inc ....E 219 972-7803
Griffith (G-5768)

Central Indiana Ethanol LLC ....D 765 384-4001
Marion (G-9517)

Craft Laboratories Inc ....F 260 432-9467
Fort Wayne (G-4183)

Criterion Catalysts & Tech LP ....C 219 874-6211
Michigan City (G-9776)

▲ Crown Technology Inc ....E 317 845-0045
Indianapolis (G-6700)

Crystal Healing Elements ....G 312 623-1764
Fishers (G-3896)

Dallas Group of America Inc ....D 812 283-6675
Jeffersonville (G-8350)

▲ Davies-Imperial Coatings Inc ....E 219 933-0877
Hammond (G-5869)

Distinctive Elements ....G 260 704-2464
Fort Wayne (G-4213)

Dmp LLC ....G 812 699-0086
Worthington (G-14394)

Dover Chemical Corporation ....E 219 852-0042
Hammond (G-5871)

Dpa Investments Inc ....G 219 873-0914
Michigan City (G-9783)

E I Du Pont De Nemours & Co ....F 812 299-6700
Terre Haute (G-13228)

E J Bognar Inc ....F 412 344-9900
Schneider (G-12354)

Eco Services Operations Corp ....E 219 932-7651
Hammond (G-5874)

Element Armament LLC ....G 317 442-7924
Bargersville (G-480)

Element Elite Tumbling ....G 502 751-5654
Sellersburg (G-12392)

Element Homes ....G 219 310-2505
Crown Point (G-2249)

Element of Fun Travel ....G 317 435-9185
Demotte (G-2436)

Element Pro Services LLC ....G 574 271-5259
Granger (G-5404)

Elemental Inc ....G 812 684-8036
Huntingburg (G-6162)

Elemental S A Protection ....G 765 717-7325
Muncie (G-10469)

Elements ....G 812 881-9400
Vincennes (G-13675)

Elements Elearning LLC ....G 317 986-2113
Indianapolis (G-6820)

Esm Group Inc ....F 219 393-5502
Kingsbury (G-8538)

Gac Chemical Corporation ....G 317 917-0319
Indianapolis (G-6978)

▲ Geo Specialty Chemicals Inc ....G 765 448-9412
Lafayette (G-8906)

Giles Chemical Corporation ....G 812 537-4852
Greendale (G-5486)

Giles Manufacturing Company ....G 812 537-4852
Greendale (G-5487)

Gill Carbide Saw & TI Svc LLC ....G 317 698-6787
Martinsville (G-9609)

Glcc Laurel LLC ....C 765 497-6100
West Lafayette (G-14069)

Grid Element Sled ....G 219 462-2687
Valparaiso (G-13552)

Grid Elements ....G 219 615-9683
Valparaiso (G-13553)

◆ Hammond Group Inc ....E 219 931-9360
Hammond (G-5884)

Healing Elements LLC ....G 260 355-7181
Fort Wayne (G-4326)

Helena Agri-Enterprises LLC ....G 765 583-4458
Otterbein (G-11418)

Helena Agri-Enterprises LLC ....G 765 869-5518
Ambia (G-55)

Helena Agri-Enterprises LLC ....F 812 654-3177
Dillsboro (G-2467)

Human Element Therapeutics ....G 317 446-4062
Mooresville (G-10312)

Hydrite Chemical Co ....E 812 232-5411
Terre Haute (G-13252)

Indiana Oxide Corporation ....F 812 446-2525
Brazil (G-965)

Industrial Maint Engrg Inc ....G 812 466-5478
Terre Haute (G-13256)

Industrial Water MGT Inc ....G 317 889-0836
Greenwood (G-5706)

J 2 Systems and Supply LLC ....G 317 602-3940
Indianapolis (G-7281)

Jci Jones Chemicals Inc ....F 317 787-8382
Beech Grove (G-599)

Karyn K Cleveland ....G 317 698-6787
Martinsville (G-9619)

Kem Krest Corporation ....F 574 389-2650
Elkhart (G-2959)

Kennametal Inc ....G 219 362-1000
La Porte (G-8780)

Kml Inc ....E 260 897-3723
Laotto (G-9111)

◆ Mason Corporation ....D 219 865-8040
Schererville (G-12333)

▼ Metals and Additives LLC ....F 317 290-5007
Indianapolis (G-7490)

Metals and Additives Corp Inc ....E 812 446-2525
Brazil (G-969)

Metalworking Lubricants Co ....G 317 269-2444
Indianapolis (G-7491)

Nanolayer Technologies LLC ....F 260 414-4458
Fort Wayne (G-4489)

New Elements LLC ....G 219 465-1389
Valparaiso (G-13587)

Nochar Inc ....G 317 613-3046
Indianapolis (G-7589)

▼ Omicron Biochemicals Inc ....F 574 287-6910
South Bend (G-12883)

Perimeter Solutions LP ....G 219 933-1560
Hammond (G-5926)

PQ Corporation ....E 812 288-7186
Clarksville (G-1690)

Prosco Inc ....G 317 353-2920
Indianapolis (G-7779)

Reactor Services Intl Inc ....E 219 924-0507
Griffith (G-5789)

Reagent Chemical & RES Inc ....D 574 772-3271
Knox (G-8577)

Reagent Chemical & RES Inc ....F 574 772-7424
Knox (G-8578)

Remedium Services Group LLC .... F 317 660-6868
Carmel *(G-1467)*

Shoremet LLC .... F 219 390-3336
Valparaiso *(G-13617)*

St Clair Group Inc .... D 765 435-3091
Russellville *(G-12239)*

Substrate Treatments Lubr Inc .... G 574 258-0904
Mishawaka *(G-10137)*

Theraptic Elmnts By Lori Myers .... G 765 480-2525
Logansport *(G-9369)*

V Global Holdings LLC .... A 317 247-8141
Indianapolis *(G-8142)*

W R Grace & Co - Conn .... E 219 398-2040
East Chicago *(G-2580)*

▲ Waterstone Technology .... E 317 644-0862
Carmel *(G-1507)*

Wayne Chemical Inc .... E 260 432-1120
Fort Wayne *(G-4739)*

2821 Plastics, Mtrls & Nonvulcanizable Elastomers

A Schulman Inc .... G 812 253-5238
Evansville *(G-3329)*

Advance Prtective Coatings Inc .... G 317 228-0123
Indianapolis *(G-6330)*

Aearo Technologies LLC .... C 317 692-6666
Indianapolis *(G-6342)*

Akzo Nobel Coatings Inc .... F 574 372-2000
Warsaw *(G-13836)*

◆ Alterra Plastics LLC .... F 812 271-1890
Seymour *(G-12429)*

◆ AM Stabilizers Corporation .... G 219 844-3980
Valparaiso *(G-13490)*

Ameri-Kart Corp .... D 225 642-7874
Bristol *(G-1043)*

▲ Ameri-Kart Corp .... C 574 848-7462
Bristol *(G-1044)*

Ampacet Corporation .... C 812 466-5231
Terre Haute *(G-13193)*

Aoc LLC .... D 219 465-4384
Valparaiso *(G-13494)*

Apexx Enterprises LLC .... F 812 486-2443
Montgomery *(G-10213)*

Atc Plastics LLC .... G 317 469-7552
Indianapolis *(G-6435)*

▼ B C C Products Inc .... F 317 494-6420
Franklin *(G-4870)*

Bd Medical Development Inc .... G 219 310-8551
Crown Point *(G-2227)*

Best Formed Plastics LLC .... E 574 293-6128
Elkhart *(G-2722)*

▲ Bpc Manufacturing Operation .... E 574 936-9894
Plymouth *(G-11672)*

▲ Cabinets & Counters Inc .... E 812 858-3300
Newburgh *(G-11023)*

Cellofoam North America Inc .... D 317 535-9008
Whiteland *(G-14235)*

Cellofoam North America Inc .... F 317 535-0826
Greenwood *(G-5674)*

Chemtrusion Inc .... G 812 280-2910
Jeffersonville *(G-8336)*

Com-Tech Plastics Inc .... F 812 423-8270
Evansville *(G-3424)*

▲ Createc Corporation .... E 317 566-0022
Indianapolis *(G-6686)*

▲ Crossroads Sourcing Group Ltd .... F 847 940-4123
Carmel *(G-1348)*

▲ Double H Manufacturing Corp .... D 765 664-9090
Marion *(G-9521)*

DSM Engineering Plastics Inc .... F 812 435-7500
Evansville *(G-3463)*

DSM Engineering Plastics Inc .... G 812 435-7638
Evansville *(G-3464)*

◆ DSM Engineering Plastics Inc .... C 248 530-5500
Evansville *(G-3465)*

▲ Echo Engrg & Prod Sups Inc .... E 317 876-8848
Indianapolis *(G-6798)*

Efficient Plastics Solutions .... G 574 965-4690
Delphi *(G-2420)*

▲ Encom Inc .... G 812 421-7700
Evansville *(G-3477)*

Evoqua Water Technologies LLC .... E 317 280-4251
Indianapolis *(G-6885)*

Excista Corporation .... G 734 224-3652
Fishers *(G-3908)*

Foam Fabricators Inc .... E 812 948-1696
New Albany *(G-10783)*

Foamcraft Inc .... D 574 534-4343
Goshen *(G-5216)*

Freudenberg-Nok General Partnr .... E 734 354-5504
Shelbyville *(G-12535)*

G & T Industries of Indiana .... E 812 634-2252
Jasper *(G-8253)*

▲ Gaska Tape Inc .... D 574 294-5431
Elkhart *(G-2875)*

Graber Cabinetry LLC .... E 260 627-2243
Grabill *(G-5366)*

Grace W R & Co-Co .... G 317 876-4100
Indianapolis *(G-7033)*

Green Plus Plastics LLC .... G 931 510-0525
Indianapolis *(G-7042)*

▲ Green Tree Plastics LLC .... F 812 402-4127
Evansville *(G-3524)*

Henry Holsters LLC .... G 812 369-2266
Solsberry *(G-12684)*

Hoehn Plastics Inc .... D 812 874-3646
Poseyville *(G-11856)*

ICI Americas Inc .... G 317 535-5626
Whiteland *(G-14240)*

ICO Polymers North America Inc .... G 219 392-3375
East Chicago *(G-2535)*

▲ Imperial Marble Incorporated .... F 812 752-5384
Scottsburg *(G-12364)*

◆ Industrial Dielectrics Inc .... G 317 773-1766
Noblesville *(G-11127)*

◆ Industrial Dlctrics Hldngs Inc .... A 317 773-1766
Noblesville *(G-11128)*

◆ Industrial Plastics Group LLC .... E 812 831-4053
Evansville *(G-3556)*

Indy Rapid 3d LLC .... G 812 243-4175
Indianapolis *(G-7221)*

Injection Plastics .... G 574 784-2070
Lapaz *(G-9118)*

Innovative Composites Ltd .... F 574 857-2224
Rochester *(G-12129)*

Integral Technologies Inc .... G 812 550-1770
Evansville *(G-3562)*

Integrity Custom Concepts LLC .... G 574 252-2366
South Bend *(G-12815)*

Interplastic Corporation .... E 574 234-1105
South Bend *(G-12818)*

Interplastic Corporation .... G 574 259-1505
Mishawaka *(G-10054)*

Ip Moulding Inc .... D 574 825-5845
Middlebury *(G-9894)*

J Jesse Inc .... F 574 862-4538
Wakarusa *(G-13780)*

◆ Jamplast Inc .... G 812 838-8562
Mount Vernon *(G-10397)*

Jp Incorporated - Indiana .... B 574 457-2062
Syracuse *(G-13136)*

Kvk US Technologies Inc .... G 765 529-1100
New Castle *(G-10909)*

Leepoxy Plastics Inc .... G 260 747-7411
Fort Wayne *(G-4430)*

Lucent Polymers Inc .... G 812 492-7214
Evansville *(G-3606)*

Makuta Technics Inc .... F 317 642-0001
Shelbyville *(G-12550)*

Martin Holding Company LLC .... D 812 401-9988
Evansville *(G-3614)*

Matrix Tool Inc .... F 574 259-3093
Mishawaka *(G-10075)*

Matrixx Group Incorporated .... G 812 421-3600
Evansville *(G-3616)*

Matrixx Group Incorporated .... G 812 421-3600
Evansville *(G-3617)*

Matrixx Group Incorporated .... C 812 423-5218
Evansville *(G-3618)*

Monument Chemical LLC .... F 317 223-2630
Indianapolis *(G-7539)*

Nova Polymers Incorporated .... E 812 476-0339
Evansville *(G-3648)*

▲ Omni Plastics LLC .... D 812 422-0888
Evansville *(G-3655)*

Pactiv Corporation .... C 574 936-7065
Plymouth *(G-11709)*

Pmw Holdings LLC .... G 317 339-4685
Indianapolis *(G-7703)*

Polyfusion LLC .... G 260 624-7659
Angola *(G-237)*

Polymod Technologies Inc .... F 260 436-1322
Fort Wayne *(G-4538)*

Polyone Corporation .... C 574 267-1100
Warsaw *(G-13927)*

Polyone Corporation .... G 812 466-5116
Terre Haute *(G-13305)*

Precision Colors LLC .... F 260 969-6402
Fort Wayne *(G-4547)*

▲ Primex Plastics Corporation .... B 765 966-7774
Richmond *(G-12034)*

Process Systems & Services .... G 812 427-2331
Florence *(G-4004)*

Quadrant Epp Usa Inc .... D 260 479-4700
Fort Wayne *(G-4568)*

Quadrant Epp Usa Inc .... C 260 479-4100
Fort Wayne *(G-4569)*

Replas of Texas Inc .... G 812 421-3600
Evansville *(G-3704)*

Rim Molding and Engrg Inc .... F 574 294-1932
Elkhart *(G-3146)*

Royal Adhesives & Sealants LLC .... E 574 246-5000
South Bend *(G-12921)*

Sabic Innovative Plas US LLC .... D 812 372-0197
Columbus *(G-2010)*

◆ Sabic Innovative Plastics Mt V .... A 812 838-4385
Mount Vernon *(G-10407)*

Schulman .... G 812 253-5238
Evansville *(G-3716)*

Shaw Polymers LLC .... F 219 779-9450
Crown Point *(G-2303)*

Solid Surface Craftsmen Inc .... G 317 535-2333
Whiteland *(G-14246)*

Sonoco Prtective Solutions Inc .... D 260 726-9333
Portland *(G-11847)*

Spartech LLC .... C 765 281-5100
Muncie *(G-10565)*

◆ Star Technology Inc .... E 260 837-7833
Waterloo *(G-14024)*

Stenidy Industries Inc .... G 317 873-5343
Zionsville *(G-14466)*

Sun Polymers International Inc .... G 317 834-6410
Mooresville *(G-10342)*

Teknor Apex Co .... G 812 246-3357
Charlestown *(G-1583)*

Toray Resin Company .... D 317 398-7833
Shelbyville *(G-12577)*

▲ Triangle Rubber Co LLC .... C 574 533-3118
Goshen *(G-5340)*

Triangle Rubber Co LLC .... E 574 533-3118
Goshen *(G-5341)*

V Global Holdings LLC .... A 317 247-8141
Indianapolis *(G-8142)*

Vahala Foam Inc .... D 574 293-1287
Elkhart *(G-3240)*

Venture Indus .... G 765 348-5780
Hartford City *(G-5995)*

▲ Vidal Plastics LLC .... G 812 431-8075
Evansville *(G-3799)*

2822 Synthetic Rubber (Vulcanizable Elastomers)

BRC Rubber & Plastics Inc .... E 765 728-8510
Montpelier *(G-10289)*

Coleman Cable LLC .... C 765 449-7227
Lafayette *(G-8875)*

Exactseal Inc .... G 317 559-2220
Indianapolis *(G-6889)*

Fiber Technologies LLC .... G 812 569-4641
Bloomington *(G-725)*

▲ Gdc Inc .... C 574 533-3128
Goshen *(G-5222)*

ICO Polymers North America Inc .... G 219 392-3375
East Chicago *(G-2536)*

Iris Rubber Company Inc .... F 317 984-3561
Cicero *(G-1662)*

Parker-Hannifin Corporation .... D 574 533-1111
Goshen *(G-5307)*

PTG Silicones Inc .... G 812 948-8719
New Albany *(G-10850)*

Royal Adhesives & Sealants LLC .... E 574 246-5000
South Bend *(G-12921)*

Sealwrap Systems LLC .... G 317 462-3310
Greenfield *(G-5572)*

◆ T & M Rubber Inc .... E 574 533-3173
Goshen *(G-5338)*

▲ Triangle Rubber Co LLC .... C 574 533-3118
Goshen *(G-5340)*

United Minerals and Prpts Inc .... E 812 838-5236
Mount Vernon *(G-10412)*

2823 Cellulosic Man-Made Fibers

Applied Composites Engrg Inc .... E 317 243-4225
Indianapolis *(G-6411)*

Huhtamaki Inc .... C 219 972-4264
Hammond *(G-5896)*

2824 Synthetic Organic Fibers, Exc Cellulosic

Butterfield Foods LLC ....C 317 776-4775
Noblesville (G-11075)
Debra Schneider ....G 317 420-9360
Arcadia (G-263)
Energy Two Inc ....G 812 497-3113
Seymour (G-12447)
▲ Fdc Graphics Films Inc ....D 574 273-4400
South Bend (G-12774)
Indy Composite Works Inc ....E 317 280-9766
Indianapolis (G-7214)
Quadrant Epp Usa Inc ....D 260 479-4700
Fort Wayne (G-4568)
Quadrant Epp Usa Inc ....C 260 479-4100
Fort Wayne (G-4569)

2833 Medicinal Chemicals & Botanical Prdts

Acell Inc ....F 765 464-8198
Lafayette (G-8845)
Animalsink ....G 317 496-8467
Brownsburg (G-1134)
Cgenetech Inc ....G 317 295-1925
Indianapolis (G-6591)
Developmental Natural Res ....G 317 543-4886
Indianapolis (G-6737)
Dickey Consumer Products Inc ....F 317 773-8330
Noblesville (G-11092)
Efil Pharmaceuticals Corp ....G 765 491-7247
West Lafayette (G-14065)
G & W Herbs ....G 574 646-2134
Nappanee (G-10671)
◆ Indiana Botanic Gardens Inc ....C 219 947-4040
Hobart (G-6081)
Medtric LLC ....G 765 586-8228
Lafayette (G-8965)
Nuaxon Bioscience Inc ....G 812 762-4400
Bloomington (G-782)
Nutritional Research Assoc ....F 260 723-4931
South Whitley (G-13002)
Oza Compound Products ....G 260 483-0406
Fort Wayne (G-4515)
Pfizer Inc ....A 212 733-2323
Terre Haute (G-13301)
Pragmatics Inc ....G 574 295-7908
Elkhart (G-3106)
Vertellus Intgrted Pyrdnes LLC ....C 317 247-8141
Indianapolis (G-8154)
Vitamins Inc ....E 219 879-7356
Michigan City (G-9859)
◆ VSI Acquisition Corp ....C 317 247-8141
Indianapolis (G-8170)

2834 Pharmaceuticals

Abbott Laboratories ....E 317 356-5478
Indianapolis (G-6309)
▲ Accra-Pac Inc ....D 574 295-0000
Elkhart (G-2665)
Accra-Pac Inc ....D 905 660-0444
Elkhart (G-2666)
Acura Pharmaceutical Tech ....G 574 842-3305
Culver (G-2324)
Akina Inc ....F 765 464-0501
West Lafayette (G-14048)
Amri Ssci LLC ....D 765 463-0112
West Lafayette (G-14049)
Apothecarys Ointment LLC ....G 574 930-6662
South Bend (G-12710)
▲ Applied Laboratories Inc ....D 812 372-2607
Columbus (G-1856)
Aquestive Therapeutics ....C 219 762-4143
Portage (G-11749)
Areva Pharmaceuticals Inc ....F 855 853-4760
Georgetown (G-5141)
▲ Artemis International Inc ....G 260 436-6899
Fort Wayne (G-4092)
Assembly Biosciences Inc ....D 317 210-9311
Carmel (G-1316)
Astrazeneca Pharmaceuticals LP ....E 812 429-5000
Mount Vernon (G-10383)
Baxter Phrm Solutions ....G 812 355-5289
Bloomington (G-677)
▲ Baxter Phrm Solutions LLC ....D 812 333-0887
Bloomington (G-678)
Bayer Healthcare LLC ....F 574 252-4734
Mishawaka (G-10004)
Bayer Healthcare LLC ....C 574 252-4735
Mishawaka (G-10005)
Bayer Healthcare LLC ....D 574 255-3327
Elkhart (G-2717)
Biokorf LLC ....G 765 727-0782
West Lafayette (G-14054)
Birkat Adonai LLC ....G 219 221-9810
Elizabeth (G-2643)
Bloom Pharmaceutical ....G 260 615-2633
Fort Wayne (G-4113)
Briovarx ....F 812 256-8600
Jeffersonville (G-8333)
Bristol-Myers Squibb Company ....D 260 432-2764
Fort Wayne (G-4121)
Bristol-Myers Squibb Company ....C 812 307-2000
Mount Vernon (G-10386)
Brogan Pharmaceuticals LLC ....F 219 644-3693
Crown Point (G-2231)
Cardinal Health 414 LLC ....D 317 981-4100
Indianapolis (G-6552)
Catalent Indiana LLC ....B 812 355-6746
Bloomington (G-697)
Century Pharmaceuticals Inc ....F 317 849-4210
Indianapolis (G-6586)
Chemigen Inc ....G 317 902-6630
Zionsville (G-14426)
Chyall Pharmaceutical ....G 765 237-3391
West Lafayette (G-14059)
Colorcon Inc ....E 317 545-6211
Indianapolis (G-6633)
Colorcon Inc ....G 317 545-6211
Indianapolis (G-6634)
Colorcon Inc ....G 317 545-6211
Indianapolis (G-6635)
Cretaceous Cures ....G 317 379-7744
Westfield (G-14149)
Crosswind Pharmaceuticals LLC ....G 317 436-8522
Indianapolis (G-6698)
Crown Bioscience Indiana Inc ....G 317 872-6001
Indianapolis (G-6699)
Diabco Life Sciences LLC ....G 317 697-9988
Carmel (G-1359)
Elan Corp PLC ....G 317 442-1502
Fishers (G-3901)
▲ Elanco US Inc ....C 877 352-6261
Greenfield (G-5523)
Eli Lilly ....G 812 242-5900
Terre Haute (G-13231)
Eli Lilly and Co ....G 317 433-1244
Noblesville (G-11099)
Eli Lilly and Company ....A 317 276-2000
Indianapolis (G-6822)
Eli Lilly and Company ....F 317 276-2000
Indianapolis (G-6823)
Eli Lilly and Company ....C 317 748-1622
Fishers (G-3903)
Eli Lilly and Company ....F 317 276-2000
Indianapolis (G-6824)
Eli Lilly and Company ....F 317 277-1079
Indianapolis (G-6825)
Eli Lilly and Company ....F 317 276-7907
Indianapolis (G-6826)
Eli Lilly and Company ....G 317 276-2000
Indianapolis (G-6827)
Eli Lilly and Company ....G 317 651-7790
Indianapolis (G-6828)
Eli Lilly and Company ....F 317 276-2000
Indianapolis (G-6829)
Eli Lilly and Company ....E 317 277-0147
Indianapolis (G-6830)
Eli Lilly and Company ....F 317 276-2000
Greenfield (G-5524)
Eli Lilly and Company ....F 317 433-3624
Plainfield (G-11608)
Eli Lilly and Company ....F 317 276-7907
Indianapolis (G-6831)
Eli Lilly and Company ....F 317 276-5925
Indianapolis (G-6832)
Eli Lilly and Company ....F 317 276-2000
Indianapolis (G-6833)
Eli Lilly and Company ....G 317 276-2118
Indianapolis (G-6834)
Eli Lilly and Company ....F 317 276-2000
Indianapolis (G-6835)
Eli Lilly International Corp ....F 317 276-2000
Indianapolis (G-6836)
Emphymab Biotech LLC ....G 317 274-5935
Indianapolis (G-6858)
Endocyte Inc ....D 765 463-7175
West Lafayette (G-14066)
Energy Delivery Solutions LLC ....G 502 271-8753
Jeffersonville (G-8354)
Exelead Inc ....C 317 347-2800
Indianapolis (G-6893)
Fenwick Pharma LLC ....G 765 296-7443
Lafayette (G-8898)
Fisher Clinical Services Inc ....D 317 277-0337
Indianapolis (G-6930)
Genoa Healthcare LLC ....G 219 427-1837
Gary (G-5054)
Giles Manufacturing Company ....G 812 537-4852
Greendale (G-5487)
Global Isotopes LLC ....G 317 578-1251
Noblesville (G-11111)
▲ Hawthorne Products Inc ....G 765 768-6585
Dunkirk (G-2485)
Horizon Biotechnologies LLC ....G 317 534-2540
Greenwood (G-5703)
Ips-Integrated Prj Svcs LLC ....G 317 247-1200
Indianapolis (G-7266)
Jbs United Animal Hlth II LLC ....F 317 758-2616
Sheridan (G-12593)
Kemiron Great Lakes LLC ....E 219 397-2646
East Chicago (G-2543)
Komodo Pharmaceuticals Inc ....E 317 485-0023
Fortville (G-4781)
Kp Pharmaceutical Tech Inc ....E 812 330-8121
Bloomington (G-760)
▲ Kremers Urban Phrmcuticals Inc ....C 812 523-5347
Seymour (G-12465)
Kylin Therapeutics Inc ....G 765 412-6661
West Lafayette (G-14079)
Lexington Pharmaceuticals ....G 317 870-0370
Indianapolis (G-7400)
Loaded Pharmaceuticals Inc ....G 317 300-1996
Indianapolis (G-7412)
Lodos Theranostics LLC ....G 765 427-2492
West Lafayette (G-14083)
Martin Ekwlor Phrmcuticals Inc ....F 765 962-4410
Richmond (G-12014)
Mattox & Moore Inc ....G 317 632-7534
Indianapolis (G-7468)
Mead Johnson & Company LLC ....G 812 429-5000
Mount Vernon (G-10400)
▼ Mead Johnson & Company LLC ....B 812 429-5000
Evansville (G-3620)
Med-Rep Inc ....F 317 574-0497
Carmel (G-1436)
Merck Sharp & Dohme Corp ....F 317 286-3038
Indianapolis (G-7481)
Merrill Corporation ....F 574 255-2988
Mishawaka (G-10078)
Muroplex Therapeutics Inc ....G 317 502-0545
Indianapolis (G-7560)
Naturegenic Inc ....G 765 807-5525
West Lafayette (G-14089)
Noah Worcester Derm Society ....G 317 257-5907
Indianapolis (G-7588)
Northwind Pharmaceuticals LLC ....G 800 722-0772
Indianapolis (G-7597)
Novartis Corporation ....G 317 852-3839
Brownsburg (G-1161)
Nutritional Research Assoc ....F 260 723-4931
South Whitley (G-13002)
OH Pharmaceutical Co Ltd ....G 219 644-3239
Crown Point (G-2281)
Pd Sub LLC ....E 812 524-0534
Seymour (G-12474)
Pfizer Inc ....F 574 232-9927
South Bend (G-12892)
Pfizer Inc ....A 212 733-2323
Terre Haute (G-13301)
Pharma Form Finders LLC ....G 317 362-1191
Fishers (G-3950)
Phytoption LLC ....G 765 490-7738
West Lafayette (G-14094)
Procyon Pharmaceuticals Inc ....G 765 778-9710
Pendleton (G-11501)
Purdue Gmp Center LLC ....F 765 464-8414
West Lafayette (G-14098)
R2 Pharma LLC ....G 317 810-6205
Carmel (G-1461)
Relevo Inc ....G 317 644-0099
Carmel (G-1465)
Rph On Call LLC ....E 317 622-4800
Greenfield (G-5569)
Saint-Gobain Abrasives Inc ....C 317 837-0700
Plainfield (G-11642)
Sanofi US Services Inc ....E 317 228-5750
Indianapolis (G-7894)
Schwarz Pharma ....G 812 523-3457
Seymour (G-12483)

Somersaults LLC ....G 317 747-7496
Fishers *(G-3990)*
Sysgenomics LLC ....G 574 302-5396
Granger *(G-5442)*
Vesta Ingredients Inc ....G 317 895-9000
Indianapolis *(G-8157)*
Vita Vet Laboratories Inc ....G 765 662-9398
Marion *(G-9571)*
Vitamins Inc ....E 219 879-7356
Michigan City *(G-9859)*
Windsor Wartcare ....G 574 266-6555
Elkhart *(G-3262)*
Writt Sales & Supply Co Inc ....G 317 356-5478
Indianapolis *(G-8220)*

2835 Diagnostic Substances

Agdia Inc ....D 574 264-2014
Elkhart *(G-2671)*
▼ Archaeasolutions Inc ....G 770 487-5303
Evansville *(G-3362)*
Ascensia Diabetes Care US Inc ....E 201 875-8066
Mishawaka *(G-9998)*
Cardinal Health 414 LLC ....D 317 981-4100
Indianapolis *(G-6552)*
Chematics Inc ....F 574 834-2406
North Webster *(G-11290)*
Companion Diagnostics Inc ....G 860 227-9028
Indianapolis *(G-6640)*
Core Biologic LLC ....G 888 390-8838
Fort Wayne *(G-4177)*
Intervention Diagnostics Inc ....G 317 432-6091
Indianapolis *(G-7263)*
Microworks Inc ....G 219 661-8620
Crown Point *(G-2278)*
Poly Group LLC ....G 812 590-4750
New Albany *(G-10846)*
Pragmatics Inc ....G 574 295-7908
Elkhart *(G-3106)*
R 2 Diagnostics Inc ....G 574 288-4377
South Bend *(G-12910)*
◆ Roche Diagnostics Corporation ....A 800 428-5076
Indianapolis *(G-7851)*
Savran Technologies LLC ....G 765 409-2050
West Lafayette *(G-14105)*
Stanbio Laboratory LP ....F 830 249-0772
Elkhart *(G-3186)*
Strand Diagnostics LLC ....E 317 455-2100
Indianapolis *(G-8010)*
Synermed International Inc ....G 317 896-1565
Westfield *(G-14193)*
Sysgenomics LLC ....G 574 302-5396
Granger *(G-5442)*
Uridynamics Inc ....F 317 915-7896
Indianapolis *(G-8135)*

2836 Biological Prdts, Exc Diagnostic Substances

Apotex Corp ....E 317 839-6550
Plainfield *(G-11593)*
Baxter Heathcare Plasma Center ....G 260 451-8119
Fort Wayne *(G-4101)*
Biolife Plasma Services LP ....G 574 264-7204
Elkhart *(G-2724)*
Biosafe Engineering LLC ....E 317 858-8099
Indianapolis *(G-6477)*
Bioscience Vaccines Inc ....G 765 464-5890
West Lafayette *(G-14055)*
Corebiologic LLC ....G 260 437-0353
Fort Wayne *(G-4180)*
Csl Plasma Inc ....G 260 454-5083
Fort Wayne *(G-4191)*
Csl Plasma Inc ....G 317 688-5852
Indianapolis *(G-6703)*
Csl Plasma Inc ....D 317 352-9157
Indianapolis *(G-6704)*
Ctp Corporation ....D 317 787-5747
Greenwood *(G-5680)*
Culture Media LLC ....G 317 966-0847
Carmel *(G-1350)*
Energy Two Inc ....G 812 497-3133
Seymour *(G-12447)*
▲ Envigo Rms Inc ....C 317 806-6080
Indianapolis *(G-6871)*
Envigo Rms Inc ....G 317 806-6080
Greenfield *(G-5530)*
Extranet Talent ....G 317 362-0140
Indianapolis *(G-6898)*
Gul For Media Development ....G 317 726-9544
Noblesville *(G-11115)*

Harlan Development Company ....G 317 352-1583
Indianapolis *(G-7076)*
Indy Medical Supplies LLC ....G 866 744-9013
Zionsville *(G-14439)*
Indycoast Partners LLC ....G 317 454-1050
Carmel *(G-1414)*
Micrology Laboratories Llc ....G 574 533-3351
Goshen *(G-5289)*
Nerx Biosciences Inc ....F 317 251-7408
Indianapolis *(G-7583)*
Octapharma Plasma Inc ....G 574 234-9568
South Bend *(G-12881)*
Quick Click Marketing Inc ....G 765 857-2167
Ridgeville *(G-12081)*
Sera Tech Biologicals ....F 765 288-2699
Muncie *(G-10560)*
Vasmo Inc ....F 317 549-3722
Indianapolis *(G-8149)*

2841 Soap & Detergents

Aperion Care ....G 219 874-5211
Michigan City *(G-9766)*
Brulin Holding Company Inc ....E 317 923-3211
Indianapolis *(G-6513)*
Brulin Holding Company Inc ....D 317 923-3211
Indianapolis *(G-6514)*
◆ Circle - Prosco Inc ....D 812 339-3653
Bloomington *(G-700)*
Craft Laboratories Inc ....F 260 432-9467
Fort Wayne *(G-4183)*
Deluxe Soap Company LLC ....G 260 422-5614
Saint Joe *(G-12253)*
Earth Drops Handcrafted Soaps ....G 812 336-2491
Bloomington *(G-718)*
Ecolab Inc ....E 317 816-0983
Carmel *(G-1368)*
Ecolab Inc ....F 260 375-4710
Warren *(G-13829)*
Ecolab Inc ....D 260 359-3280
Huntington *(G-6202)*
Ginas Essentials ....G 812 406-3276
Nabb *(G-10640)*
Harts Handmade Naturals LLC ....G 317 407-9988
Greenwood *(G-5701)*
▲ Holloway House Inc ....E 317 485-4272
Fortville *(G-4779)*
J 2 Systems and Supply LLC ....G 317 602-3940
Indianapolis *(G-7281)*
Jeffreys Good Soap LLC ....G 219 926-3447
Chesterton *(G-1615)*
Jenny Lynn Soap Company LLC ....G 219 863-8243
Rensselaer *(G-11929)*
Lather Up LLC ....G 260 638-4978
Markle *(G-9579)*
Lush ....G 317 842-5874
Indianapolis *(G-7427)*
Metalworking Lubricants Co ....E 317 269-2444
Indianapolis *(G-7491)*
National Handicapped Workshop ....D 765 287-8331
Muncie *(G-10538)*
Paradigm Industries Inc ....G 317 574-8590
Carmel *(G-1448)*
Past & Present Soap & Snd LLC ....G 812 852-4328
Batesville *(G-514)*
◆ Phoenix Brands LLC ....F 203 975-0319
Indianapolis *(G-7685)*
Phoenix Brands LLC ....D 317 231-8044
Indianapolis *(G-7686)*
Soapy Soap Company ....G 812 575-0005
Bloomington *(G-826)*
Tall Cotton Marketing LLC ....G 312 320-5862
La Porte *(G-8825)*
Unilever United States Inc ....E 219 659-3200
Hammond *(G-5953)*
▲ Vintage Chemical Enterprises ....G 260 745-7272
Fort Wayne *(G-4728)*
Warsaw Chemical Company Inc ....D 574 267-3251
Warsaw *(G-13958)*
Wayne Concepts Mfg Inc ....G 260 482-8615
Fort Wayne *(G-4740)*
Wills-Stockton Acres LLC ....G 765 366-7307
Crawfordsville *(G-2204)*
▲ Yushiro Manufacturing Amer Inc ....E 317 398-9862
Shelbyville *(G-12586)*

2842 Spec Cleaning, Polishing & Sanitation Preparations

3M Company ....B 317 692-6666
Indianapolis *(G-6288)*

◆ Abro Industries Inc ....E 574 232-8289
South Bend *(G-12692)*
All Metal Polishing ....G 219 980-3011
Merrillville *(G-9695)*
Altapure LLC ....G 574 485-2145
South Bend *(G-12698)*
American Hydro Systems Inc ....F 866 357-5063
Fort Wayne *(G-4071)*
Andersons Agriculture Group LP ....F 765 564-6135
Delphi *(G-2414)*
Aqua Utility Services LLC ....G 812 284-9243
New Albany *(G-10745)*
Arden Companies LLC ....D 260 747-1657
Fort Wayne *(G-4089)*
Astec Corp ....G 317 872-7550
Indianapolis *(G-6432)*
B & S Products Corp ....G 574 537-0770
Goshen *(G-5175)*
Bane-Clene Corp ....E 317 546-5448
Indianapolis *(G-6455)*
▼ Blitz Manufacturing Co Ind ....G 812 284-2548
Jeffersonville *(G-8330)*
Blue Ribbon Products Inc ....G 317 972-7970
Indianapolis *(G-6489)*
Brulin Holding Company Inc ....E 317 923-3211
Indianapolis *(G-6513)*
Brulin Holding Company Inc ....D 317 923-3211
Indianapolis *(G-6514)*
Camco Manufacturing Inc ....F 574 264-1491
Elkhart *(G-2747)*
Carestone Inc ....E 219 853-0600
Hammond *(G-5857)*
Carmel Process Solutions Inc ....G 317 705-0217
Carmel *(G-1331)*
Craft Laboratories Inc ....F 260 432-9467
Fort Wayne *(G-4183)*
Custom Bottling & Packg Inc ....E 877 401-7195
Ashley *(G-285)*
Danny Webb Plumbing ....G 574 936-2746
Plymouth *(G-11679)*
Dennis Adams Inc ....G 260 493-4829
New Haven *(G-10938)*
Dry Inc ....F 503 977-9204
Fort Wayne *(G-4222)*
◆ Dynaloy LLC ....F 317 788-5694
Indianapolis *(G-6773)*
Ecolab Inc ....D 260 359-3280
Huntington *(G-6202)*
Elie Cleaning Services LLC ....F 317 983-3388
Indianapolis *(G-6837)*
Elkhart Metal Polishing Inc ....G 574 206-0666
Elkhart *(G-2826)*
▼ F B C Inc ....G 574 848-5288
Bristol *(G-1059)*
First Image ....G 219 791-9900
Merrillville *(G-9715)*
▲ Gillis Company ....G 574 273-9086
Granger *(G-5409)*
Global Ozone Innovations LLC ....G 574 294-5797
Elkhart *(G-2886)*
▲ Holloway House Inc ....E 317 485-4272
Fortville *(G-4779)*
Ideal Inc ....G 765 457-6222
Kokomo *(G-8643)*
Iron Out Inc ....E 800 654-0791
Fort Wayne *(G-4383)*
J 2 Systems and Supply LLC ....G 317 602-3940
Indianapolis *(G-7281)*
Kik Custom Products ....C 574 294-8695
Elkhart *(G-2967)*
Kings-Qlity Rstrtion Svcs LLC ....F 812 944-4347
New Albany *(G-10814)*
Kleen-Rite Supply Inc ....F 812 422-7483
Evansville *(G-3594)*
Kuhn & Sons Inc ....E 812 424-8268
Evansville *(G-3597)*
L&S Sanitation Service ....G 765 932-5410
Rushville *(G-12227)*
Metalworking Lubricants Co ....E 317 269-2444
Indianapolis *(G-7491)*
Modrak Products Company Inc ....F 219 838-0308
Gary *(G-5078)*
National Handicapped Workshop ....D 765 287-8331
Muncie *(G-10538)*
National Products LLC ....C 219 393-5536
Kingsbury *(G-8543)*
NCH Corporation ....E 317 899-3660
Indianapolis *(G-7579)*
Online Packaging Incorporated ....E 219 872-0925
Michigan City *(G-9825)*

S
I
C

Opportunities ....G....... 574 518-0606
North Webster *(G-11298)*

Parts Cleaning Tech LLC ....G....... 317 241-9379
Indianapolis *(G-7658)*

Powerclean Inc ....E....... 260 483-1375
Fort Wayne *(G-4543)*

Prosco Inc ....G....... 317 353-2920
Indianapolis *(G-7779)*

Reeders Cleaners ....F....... 812 945-4833
Clarksville *(G-1692)*

Relevo Labs LLC ....G....... 317 900-6949
Carmel *(G-1466)*

Rexford Rand Corp ....E....... 219 872-5561
Michigan City *(G-9834)*

Servaas Inc ....G....... 317 633-2020
Indianapolis *(G-7914)*

▲ Servaas Laboratories Inc ....E....... 317 636-7760
Indianapolis *(G-7915)*

Smart Systems ....G....... 800 348-0823
Mishawaka *(G-10126)*

Steritech-Usa Inc ....G....... 260 745-7272
Fort Wayne *(G-4647)*

Tate Soaps & Surfactants Inc ....G....... 765 868-4488
Kokomo *(G-8707)*

Tgc Auto Care Products Inc ....G....... 765 962-7725
Richmond *(G-12064)*

Valley Sanitation ....G....... 574 893-7070
Akron *(G-9)*

◆ W J Hagerty & Sons Ltd Inc ....E....... 574 288-4991
South Bend *(G-12985)*

Warsaw Chemical Company Inc .....D....... 574 267-3251
Warsaw *(G-13958)*

Wayne Chemical Inc ....E....... 260 432-1120
Fort Wayne *(G-4739)*

▲ Yushiro Manufacturing Amer Inc ......E....... 317 398-9862
Shelbyville *(G-12586)*

2843 Surface Active & Finishing Agents, Sulfonated Oils

▼ Classic Chemical Corp ....G....... 812 934-3289
Indianapolis *(G-6618)*

D S E Inc ....E....... 812 376-0310
Columbus *(G-1904)*

Restorco Inc ....F....... 812 882-3987
Vincennes *(G-13700)*

2844 Perfumes, Cosmetics & Toilet Preparations

103 Collection LLC ....G....... 800 896-2945
Schererville *(G-12312)*

All Occasions Gift Shop LLC ....G....... 513 314-5693
Metamora *(G-9762)*

Allen Industries Inc ....G....... 317 595-0730
Indianapolis *(G-6368)*

Ambre Blends ....G....... 317 257-0202
Indianapolis *(G-6381)*

▲ Annie Oakley Enterprises Inc ......F....... 260 894-7100
Ligonier *(G-9276)*

Aqua Spa ....G....... 219 548-4772
Valparaiso *(G-13496)*

Bath & Body Works LLC ....E....... 219 531-2146
Valparaiso *(G-13504)*

Bath & Body Works LLC ....F....... 317 468-0834
Greenfield *(G-5508)*

Bath & Body Works LLC ....E....... 317 209-1517
Avon *(G-432)*

Century Pharmaceuticals Inc ....E....... 317 849-4210
Indianapolis *(G-6586)*

Champagne Lipstick ....G....... 317 691-6045
Carmel *(G-1335)*

Classique Hair Style ....G....... 317 738-2104
Franklin *(G-4876)*

Conopco Inc ....G....... 219 659-3200
Hammond *(G-5864)*

Dentisse Inc ....G....... 260 444-3046
Fort Wayne *(G-4208)*

Desirable Scents ....G....... 317 504-4976
Lafayette *(G-8888)*

Di Cologne Group ....G....... 260 616-0158
Fort Wayne *(G-4209)*

Energy Delivery Solutions LLC ....G....... 502 271-8753
Jeffersonville *(G-8354)*

French Tips ....G....... 812 923-9055
Floyds Knobs *(G-4011)*

Hair Associates LLC ....F....... 317 844-7207
Carmel *(G-1392)*

Indiana Nanotech LLC ....G....... 317 385-1578
Indianapolis *(G-7185)*

Jeannine Stassen ....G....... 765 289-3756
Muncie *(G-10500)*

Kbshimmer Bath and Body Inc ....G....... 317 979-2307
Terre Haute *(G-13264)*

Kenra Professional LLC ....F....... 317 356-6491
Indianapolis *(G-7343)*

Kims Scrub Connection LLC ....G....... 812 867-1237
Evansville *(G-3590)*

Kin Naturals LLC ....G....... 219 213-9516
Highland *(G-6051)*

Kissy Face Lipstick LLC ....G....... 260 797-5024
Fort Wayne *(G-4411)*

Komun Scents ....G....... 317 308-0714
Indianapolis *(G-7365)*

Magnolia Products LLC ....G....... 812 306-8638
Evansville *(G-3610)*

Mahogany Scents ....G....... 574 271-1364
South Bend *(G-12849)*

▲ Malibu Wellness Inc ....E....... 317 624-7560
Indianapolis *(G-7447)*

▲ Mansfield - King LLC ....D....... 317 788-0750
Indianapolis *(G-7450)*

▲ Maverick Packaging Inc ....E....... 574 264-2891
Elkhart *(G-3022)*

Med-Rep Inc ....F....... 317 574-0497
Carmel *(G-1436)*

Nail Pro ....G....... 219 322-9220
Schererville *(G-12337)*

National Notification Ctr LLC ....G....... 317 613-6060
Indianapolis *(G-7574)*

North Coast Organics LLC ....G....... 260 246-0289
Fort Wayne *(G-4505)*

Oil Palace Limited ....G....... 317 679-9187
Indianapolis *(G-7613)*

Perfumery ....E....... 812 777-0657
New Albany *(G-10841)*

Pieniadze Inc ....G....... 888 226-6241
Zionsville *(G-14456)*

Pink Lipstick and Company ....G....... 317 992-6818
Indianapolis *(G-7692)*

Prairie Scents LLC ....G....... 765 361-6908
Crawfordsville *(G-2187)*

Relevo Inc ....G....... 317 644-0099
Carmel *(G-1465)*

Relevo Labs LLC ....G....... 317 900-6949
Carmel *(G-1466)*

Signature Formulations LLC ....G....... 317 878-4086
Trafalgar *(G-13438)*

Sincerely Different LLC ....G....... 574 292-1727
Granger *(G-5435)*

Soapy Soap Company ....G....... 812 575-0005
Bloomington *(G-826)*

Soulful Scents LLC ....G....... 317 319-8001
Noblesville *(G-11185)*

Star Nail ....G....... 765 453-0743
Kokomo *(G-8700)*

Universal Packg Systems Inc ....B....... 260 829-6721
Orland *(G-11359)*

Vera Bradley Inc ....B....... 877 708-8372
Roanoke *(G-12110)*

Wholeaf Aloe Distributors ....G....... 219 322-7217
Schererville *(G-12352)*

William Roam LLC ....G....... 317 356-2715
Indianapolis *(G-8199)*

Wonder Nail LLC ....G....... 317 462-8404
Greenfield *(G-5585)*

2851 Paints, Varnishes, Lacquers, Enamels

A F Wolke Co Inc ....G....... 812 738-4141
Corydon *(G-2086)*

A Schulman Inc ....E....... 574 935-5131
Plymouth *(G-11660)*

Aci Construction Company Inc ....F....... 317 549-1833
Indianapolis *(G-6317)*

Actega North America Inc ....G....... 800 426-4657
Schererville *(G-12313)*

Advanced Protective Tech LLC ....G....... 877 548-9323
Valparaiso *(G-13484)*

Ampacet Corporation ....C....... 812 466-5231
Terre Haute *(G-13193)*

Ampacet Corporation ....E....... 812 466-9828
Terre Haute *(G-13194)*

Aoc LLC ....D....... 219 465-4384
Valparaiso *(G-13494)*

Armor Clad Inc ....G....... 812 883-8734
Salem *(G-12283)*

▼ B C C Products Inc ....F....... 317 494-6420
Franklin *(G-4870)*

Baril Coatings Usa LLC ....F....... 260 665-8431
Angola *(G-197)*

Bender Wholesale Distributors ....F....... 574 264-4409
Elkhart *(G-2721)*

Bloomington Concret Surfaces ....G....... 812 345-0011
Bloomington *(G-686)*

Bondline Adhesives Inc ....F....... 812 423-4651
Evansville *(G-3390)*

Chad Simons ....G....... 219 405-1620
Chesterton *(G-1598)*

Chemicals Solvents & Lubr ....G....... 260 484-2000
Fort Wayne *(G-4145)*

Columbus Paint Supply ....G....... 812 375-1118
Columbus *(G-1879)*

◆ Contego International Inc ....G....... 574 223-5989
Rochester *(G-12119)*

Cornerstone Industries Corp ....D....... 317 852-6522
Brownsburg *(G-1145)*

Cp Inc ....E....... 765 825-4111
Connersville *(G-2045)*

D S E Inc ....E....... 812 376-0310
Columbus *(G-1904)*

▲ Davies-Imperial Coatings Inc ......G....... 219 933-0877
Hammond *(G-5869)*

Dist Council 91 ....G....... 812 962-9191
Evansville *(G-3459)*

Hammond Group Inc ....G....... 219 933-1560
Hammond *(G-5885)*

◆ IVc Industrial Coatings Inc ....C....... 812 442-5080
Brazil *(G-966)*

J D Petro and Associates Inc ....G....... 317 736-6566
Franklin *(G-4902)*

Lambert Asphlting Slcating Inc ....G....... 317 985-8061
Indianapolis *(G-7378)*

Liquid Technologies Elkhart ....G....... 574 596-1883
Wakarusa *(G-13782)*

▲ LSI Wallcovering Inc ....D....... 502 458-1502
New Albany *(G-10820)*

▲ Margco International LLC ....G....... 317 568-4274
Indianapolis *(G-7452)*

Mason Total Property Care ....G....... 260 385-3573
New Haven *(G-10948)*

Mautz Paint Factory ....G....... 574 289-2497
South Bend *(G-12856)*

Midwest Pipecoating Inc ....D....... 219 322-4564
Schererville *(G-12335)*

▲ Nanochem Technologies LLC ....E....... 574 970-2436
Elkhart *(G-3057)*

Ncp Coatings Inc ....G....... 574 255-9678
Mishawaka *(G-10094)*

Oerlikon Balzers Coating USA ....E....... 765 935-7424
Richmond *(G-12025)*

Pendry Coatings LLC ....G....... 574 268-2956
Warsaw *(G-13925)*

Phaze One LLC ....G....... 812 634-9545
Jasper *(G-8301)*

Pinder Polyurethane & Plas Inc ....G....... 219 397-8248
East Chicago *(G-2559)*

PPG Industries ....G....... 812 867-6601
Evansville *(G-3681)*

PPG Industries Inc ....E....... 317 745-0427
Avon *(G-462)*

PPG Industries Inc ....G....... 317 849-2340
Indianapolis *(G-7714)*

PPG Industries Inc ....E....... 317 267-0511
Indianapolis *(G-7715)*

PPG Industries Inc ....G....... 812 424-4774
Evansville *(G-3682)*

PPG Industries Inc ....E....... 812 473-0339
Evansville *(G-3683)*

PPG Industries Inc ....E....... 317 897-3836
Indianapolis *(G-7716)*

PPG Industries Inc ....E....... 317 577-2344
Fishers *(G-3956)*

PPG Industries Inc ....G....... 260 373-2373
Fort Wayne *(G-4545)*

PPG Industries Inc ....G....... 317 598-9448
Fishers *(G-3957)*

PPG Industries Inc ....G....... 812 285-0546
Jeffersonville *(G-8415)*

PPG Industries Inc ....G....... 317 787-9393
Indianapolis *(G-7717)*

PPG Industries Inc ....E....... 317 870-0345
Carmel *(G-1454)*

PPG Industries Inc ....G....... 812 944-4164
New Albany *(G-10847)*

PPG Industries Inc ....G....... 317 251-9494
Indianapolis *(G-7718)*

PPG Industries Inc ....E....... 317 546-5714
Indianapolis *(G-7719)*

PPG Industries Inc ....E....... 812 232-0672
Terre Haute *(G-13306)*

PPG Industries Inc ...... E 812 882-0440
Vincennes (G-13699)
PPG Industries Inc ...... E 317 867-5934
Westfield (G-14180)
Quality Coatings Inc ...... F 812 925-3314
Chandler (G-1553)
Randy Gehlhausen ...... G 812 327-4454
Bloomington (G-807)
▲ Red Spot Paint & Varnish Co ...... B 812 428-9100
Evansville (G-3697)
Red Spot Paint & Varnish Co ...... E 812 428-9100
Evansville (G-3698)
Red Spot Paint & Varnish Co ...... B 812 428-9100
Evansville (G-3699)
Redspot Paint and Varnish Co ...... C 812 428-9100
Evansville (G-3700)
Sansher Corporation ...... G 260 484-2000
Fort Wayne (G-4606)
▲ Silcotec Inc ...... F 219 324-4411
La Porte (G-8821)
Snow Management Group ...... G 574 252-5253
Mishawaka (G-10130)
Sonoco Products Company ...... C 812 526-5511
Edinburgh (G-2629)
T&T Coatings Inc ...... G 317 408-3752
Camby (G-1269)
Technicote Inc ...... D 812 466-9844
Terre Haute (G-13349)
Testworth Laboratories Inc ...... F 260 244-5137
Columbia City (G-1840)
Timber Ox Inc ...... G 317 758-5942
Cicero (G-1669)
Tnemec Company Inc ...... G 317 884-1806
Greenwood (G-5753)
Transcendia Inc ...... C 765 935-1520
Richmond (G-12068)
▲ United Coatings Tech Inc ...... F 574 287-4774
South Bend (G-12981)
United Minerals and Prpts Inc ...... E 812 838-5236
Mount Vernon (G-10412)
Van Zandt Enterprises Inc ...... E 812 423-3511
Evansville (G-3792)
▼ Vitracoat America Inc ...... F 574 262-2188
Elkhart (G-3249)
▲ Wabash Valley Manufacturing ...... C 260 352-2102
Silver Lake (G-12682)
Wayne Metal Protection Company ...... E 260 492-2529
Fort Wayne (G-4742)
▼ Weatherall Indiana Inc ...... F 812 256-3378
Charlestown (G-1585)
Winslow-Browning Inc ...... E 765 458-5157
Liberty (G-9273)
Woodys Paint Spot Ltd ...... G 574 255-0348
Bremen (G-1034)
▲ Worwag Coatings LLC ...... E 765 447-2137
Lafayette (G-9026)

2861 Gum & Wood Chemicals

Arch Wood Protection Inc ...... F 219 464-3949
Valparaiso (G-13497)
▲ Artemis International Inc ...... G 260 436-6899
Fort Wayne (G-4092)
Jefferson Homebuilders Inc ...... E 317 398-0874
Shelbyville (G-12541)
Pag Holdings Inc ...... G 814 446-2525
Brazil (G-974)
◆ Pag Holdings Inc ...... G 317 290-5006
Indianapolis (G-7648)
Wholesale Hrdwood Intriors Inc ...... F 317 867-3660
Westfield (G-14202)

2865 Cyclic-Crudes, Intermediates, Dyes & Org Pigments

Ampacet Corporation ...... C 812 466-5231
Terre Haute (G-13193)
Eco Services Operations Corp ...... E 219 932-7651
Hammond (G-5874)
▲ Futurex Industries Inc ...... C 765 498-3900
Bloomingdale (G-647)
Futurex Industries Inc ...... D 812 299-5708
Terre Haute (G-13237)
Hammond Group Inc ...... E 219 933-1560
Hammond (G-5885)
▲ Holland Colours Americas Inc ...... D 765 935-0329
Richmond (G-11998)
▲ Kibbechem Inc ...... E 574 266-1234
Elkhart (G-2964)
Pfizer Inc ...... A 212 733-2323
Terre Haute (G-13301)

Primex Color Compounding ...... G 800 222-5116
Richmond (G-12032)
Styrene Solutions LLC ...... G 574 876-4610
Elkhart (G-3195)
▼ VSI Liquidating Inc ...... E 317 247-8141
Indianapolis (G-8171)

2869 Industrial Organic Chemicals, NEC

▲ Aerchem LLC ...... G 812 334-9996
Bloomington (G-659)
Als Enviromental ...... G 219 299-8127
Valparaiso (G-13489)
Alternative Fuel Solutions LLC ...... G 260 224-1965
Huntington (G-6185)
Ambandash ...... G 260 415-1709
Fort Wayne (G-4067)
AMP Americas LLC ...... G 312 300-6700
Fair Oaks (G-87)
Andersons Clymers Ethanol LLC ...... G 574 722-2627
Logansport (G-9322)
Aventine Renewable Energy ...... G 812 838-9598
Mount Vernon (G-10385)
Aviation Fuel Group LLC ...... G 219 462-6081
Valparaiso (G-13500)
Beckman Coulter Inc ...... D 317 471-8029
Indianapolis (G-6460)
▲ Blue Grass Chemical Spc LLC ...... E 812 948-1115
New Albany (G-10753)
Brown & Brown Fuel ...... G 219 984-5173
Chalmers (G-1546)
Cardinal Ethanol LLC ...... D 765 964-3137
Union City (G-13454)
Cheli Fuel ...... G 317 377-1480
Indianapolis (G-6596)
Chemtura Corporation ...... C 765 497-6782
West Lafayette (G-14057)
▼ Classic Chemical Corp ...... G 812 934-3289
Indianapolis (G-6618)
Coeus Technology Inc ...... G 765 203-2304
Anderson (G-87)
Countrymark Ref Logistics LLC ...... G 800 808-3170
Indianapolis (G-6677)
Defrukuscn LLC ...... G 219 718-2128
Highland (G-6042)
Dover Chemical Corporation ...... E 219 852-0042
Hammond (G-5871)
Dow Silicones Corporation ...... F 260 347-5813
Kendallville (G-8474)
Eco Services Operations Corp ...... E 219 932-7651
Hammond (G-5874)
Elwood Fuel and Cigs LLC ...... G 317 244-5744
Indianapolis (G-6845)
Energy Quest Inc ...... G 317 827-9212
Indianapolis (G-6865)
◆ Enzyme Solutions Inc ...... F 260 553-9100
Garrett (G-5004)
Enzyme Solutions Inc ...... G 800 523-1323
Fort Wayne (G-4239)
Evonik Corporation ...... A 765 477-4300
Lafayette (G-8894)
Food & Fuel Upland ...... G 765 998-0840
Upland (G-13470)
Fountain Food and Fueling ...... G 765 847-5257
Fountain City (G-4787)
Fuel Prfmce Enhancement LLC ...... G 317 979-2316
Indianapolis (G-6966)
Fyt Fuels LLC ...... G 520 304-6451
Rensselaer (G-11924)
Gary Vehicle Maintenance-Fuel ...... G 219 881-0219
Gary (G-5053)
▲ Gdc Inc ...... C 574 533-3128
Goshen (G-5222)
Global Energy Resources LLC ...... G 219 712-2556
Valparaiso (G-13548)
Grain Processing Corporation ...... F 812 257-0480
Washington (G-13983)
Green Plains Bluffton LLC ...... D 260 846-0011
Bluffton (G-876)
Green Plains Inc ...... E 812 985-7480
Mount Vernon (G-10394)
Harvest Fuels LLC ...... G 832 895-6621
Carmel (G-1396)
Hoosier Ethanol Energy LLC ...... G 260 407-6161
Fort Wayne (G-4343)
Hoosier Penn Oil Co Inc ...... G 812 284-9433
Jeffersonville (G-8376)
Hucks Food Fuel ...... G 812 683-5566
Huntingburg (G-6168)
Iroquois Bio-Energy Co LLC ...... G 219 866-5990
Rensselaer (G-11928)

Jerry L Fuelling ...... G 317 709-6978
Zionsville (G-14441)
Louis Dreyfus Co AG Inds LLC ...... E 574 566-2100
Claypool (G-1706)
Midwest Bio-Products Inc ...... G 765 793-3426
Covington (G-2119)
Mirteq Holdings Inc ...... G 260 490-3706
Fort Wayne (G-4478)
Momentive Performance Mtls Inc ...... D 260 357-2000
Garrett (G-5017)
Mr Fuel ...... G 317 531-0891
Spiceland (G-13056)
Neosphere Energy Inc ...... G 219 781-7893
Schererville (G-12339)
North Manchester Ethanol LLC ...... G 260 774-3532
North Manchester (G-11238)
Ohio Valley Fuel Injection ...... G 812 987-5857
Charlestown (G-1578)
Old Copper Still Distlg Co LLC ...... G 812 342-0765
Columbus (G-1985)
▼ Omicron Biochemicals Inc ...... F 574 287-6910
South Bend (G-12883)
Org Chem Group LLC ...... D 812 464-4446
Evansville (G-3656)
Owens Fuel Center ...... G 260 358-1211
Huntington (G-6234)
Poet Biorefining - Portland ...... G 260 726-7154
Portland (G-11840)
Poet Brfining - Cloverdale LLC ...... D 765 795-3235
Cloverdale (G-1734)
Premier Ethanol LLC ...... G 260 726-2681
Portland (G-11841)
Premier Ethanol LLC ...... G 260 726-7154
Portland (G-11842)
Racing Fuel Ignite ...... G 765 733-0833
Marion (G-9558)
Rudys Food & Fuel LLC ...... G 812 547-2530
Tell City (G-13173)
Ryan Fuelling ...... G 260 403-6450
Fort Wayne (G-4599)
S Huck Food and Fuel ...... G 812 886-4323
Vincennes (G-13704)
Southern Fuel LLC ...... G 219 689-3552
Rensselaer (G-11939)
Super Hicksgas Fuel ...... G 219 345-2656
Demotte (G-2449)
◆ Swift Fuels LLC ...... G 765 464-8336
West Lafayette (G-14111)
Tobacco Zone Inc ...... G 317 268-6808
Plainfield (G-11648)
Top Fuel Crossfit ...... G 219 281-7001
Crown Point (G-2315)
▲ Triangle Rubber Co LLC ...... C 574 533-3118
Goshen (G-5340)
Ultimate Ethanol LLC ...... G 765 724-4384
Alexandria (G-54)
Valero Renewable Fuels Co LLC ...... E 812 833-3900
Mount Vernon (G-10413)
Vertellus Holdings LLC ...... G 317 247-8141
Indianapolis (G-8153)
Vertellus LLC ...... E 317 247-8141
Indianapolis (G-8155)
Vertellus Sbh Holdings LLC ...... E 317 247-8141
Indianapolis (G-8156)
Warrior Oil Service Inc ...... F 317 738-9777
Franklin (G-4940)

2873 Nitrogenous Fertilizers

Andersons Agriculture Group LP ...... E 574 626-2522
Galveston (G-4993)
Andersons Agriculture Group LP ...... F 574 753-4974
Logansport (G-9321)
Co-Alliance LLP ...... G 765 659-2596
Frankfort (G-4822)
◆ Knox Fertilizer Company Inc ...... G 574 772-6275
Knox (G-8570)
Scotts Company LLC ...... E 317 596-7830
Fishers (G-3968)
Scotts Company LLC ...... E 219 663-3830
Crown Point (G-2302)
Scotts Miracle-Gro Company ...... D 219 984-6110
Reynolds (G-11948)
Spawn Mate Inc ...... F 812 948-2174
New Albany (G-10864)
Ureas Music Group LLC ...... G 317 426-3103
Indianapolis (G-8134)

2874 Phosphatic Fertilizers

Andersons Agriculture Group LP ...... F 574 753-4974
Logansport (G-9321)

S I C

Andersons Agriculture Group LP ... E ... 574 626-2522
Galveston *(G-4993)*
Wilson Fertilizer & Grain Inc ... G ... 574 223-3175
Rochester *(G-12161)*

2875 Fertilizers, Mixing Only

Agbest Cooperative Inc ... G ... 765 358-3388
Gaston *(G-5129)*
Andersons Agriculture Group LP ... F ... 574 753-4974
Logansport *(G-9321)*
Andersons Agriculture Group LP ... E ... 574 626-2522
Galveston *(G-4993)*
Andersons Fertilizer Service ... G ... 765 538-3285
Romney *(G-12202)*
Bundy Bros & Sons Inc ... F ... 812 966-2551
Medora *(G-9681)*
Ceres Solutions Coop Inc ... G ... 765 473-3922
Peru *(G-11521)*
City of Fort Wayne ... G ... 260 749-8040
Fort Wayne *(G-4151)*
Clunette Elevator Co Inc ... F ... 574 858-2281
Leesburg *(G-9234)*
Co-Alliance LLP ... G ... 765 249-2233
Michigantown *(G-9864)*
Co-Alliance LLP ... G ... 765 659-3420
Frankfort *(G-4823)*
◆ **Co-Alliance Ltd Lblty Partnr** ... D ... 317 745-4491
Avon *(G-435)*
Compost Bins Pro ... G ... 317 873-0555
Zionsville *(G-14428)*
Creative Ldscp & Compost Co ... G ... 317 776-2909
Noblesville *(G-11087)*
Earth Mama Compost ... G ... 317 759-4589
Indianapolis *(G-6787)*
Elvin L Nuest Sales and Servic ... G ... 219 863-5216
Francesville *(G-4811)*
Green Thumb of Indiana Inc ... G ... 260 897-2319
Avilla *(G-405)*
Greencycle Inc ... G ... 317 773-3350
Noblesville *(G-11114)*
Harvest Land Co-Op Inc ... G ... 317 861-5080
Fountaintown *(G-4791)*
Harvest Land Co-Op Inc ... F ... 765 489-4141
Hagerstown *(G-5807)*
Kova Fertilizer Inc ... E ... 812 663-5081
Greensburg *(G-5620)*
Laughery Valley AG Co-Op Inc ... G ... 812 689-4401
Osgood *(G-11393)*
Lesco Inc ... G ... 317 876-7968
Indianapolis *(G-7398)*
Md/Lf Incorporated ... G ... 765 575-8130
New Castle *(G-10912)*
Miles Farm Supply LLC ... F ... 812 359-4463
Boonville *(G-917)*
Millburn Peat Company Inc ... E ... 219 362-7025
La Porte *(G-8794)*
Nachurs Alpine Solutions Corp ... G ... 812 738-1333
Corydon *(G-2106)*
Northwest Farm Fertilizers ... G ... 219 785-2331
Westville *(G-14220)*
Ostler Enterprises Inc ... G ... 765 656-1275
Frankfort *(G-4847)*
Rogers Group Inc ... E ... 812 882-3640
Vincennes *(G-13703)*
Roy Umbarger and Sons Inc ... F ... 317 422-5195
Bargersville *(G-486)*
Superior AG Resources Coop Inc ... G ... 812 724-4455
Owensville *(G-11430)*
Wilson Fertilizer & Grain Inc ... G ... 574 223-3175
Rochester *(G-12161)*

2879 Pesticides & Agricultural Chemicals, NEC

AG Technologies Inc ... G ... 574 224-8324
Rochester *(G-12114)*
Alpha Systems LLC ... F ... 574 295-5206
Elkhart *(G-2678)*
Dow Agroscience ... G ... 765 743-0015
West Lafayette *(G-14064)*
Dow Agrosciences LLC ... G ... 317 252-5602
Indianapolis *(G-6762)*
◆ **Dow Agrosciences LLC** ... A ... 317 337-3000
Indianapolis *(G-6763)*
Dupont 9 Building Company LLC ... G ... 260 432-4913
Fort Wayne *(G-4225)*
Dupont and Tonkel Partners LLC ... G ... 260 444-2264
Fort Wayne *(G-4226)*
Dupont Commons LLC ... G ... 260 637-3215
Fort Wayne *(G-4227)*
Dupont Orthodontics ... G ... 260 490-3554
Fort Wayne *(G-4228)*
E I Du Pont De Nemours & Co ... G ... 812 299-6700
Terre Haute *(G-13227)*
Eli Lilly International Corp ... F ... 317 276-2000
Indianapolis *(G-6836)*
Harvest Land Co-Op Inc ... F ... 765 489-4141
Hagerstown *(G-5807)*
Helena Agri-Enterprises LLC ... G ... 260 565-3196
Craigville *(G-2122)*
Helena Agri-Enterprises LLC ... E ... 574 268-4762
Huntington *(G-6209)*
Hub States Corporation ... G ... 317 816-9955
Carmel *(G-1408)*
Kep Chem Inc ... G ... 574 739-0501
Logansport *(G-9346)*
King-Tuesley Enterprises Inc ... E ... 800 428-3266
Indianapolis *(G-7353)*
Koch Industries Inc ... G ... 260 356-7191
Huntington *(G-6222)*
Landec Ag Inc ... F ... 765 385-1000
Oxford *(G-11432)*
Landec Ag Inc ... F ... 765 385-1000
Oxford *(G-11433)*
Midwest AG Fly Services Inc ... G ... 812 275-5579
Bedford *(G-564)*
Monsanto ... G ... 260 341-3227
Farmland *(G-3843)*
Monsanto Company ... D ... 574 870-0397
Reynolds *(G-11946)*
Monsanto Company ... C ... 219 733-2938
Union Mills *(G-13464)*
Monsanto Company ... G ... 574 583-0028
Monticello *(G-10269)*
Monsanto Company ... E ... 317 945-7121
Windfall *(G-14348)*
Monsanto Cotton ... G ... 229 759-0035
Evansville *(G-3634)*
▼ **Mycogen Corporation** ... F ... 317 337-3000
Indianapolis *(G-7565)*
Mycogen Crop Protection Inc ... E ... 317 337-3000
Indianapolis *(G-7566)*
Prime Source LLC ... G ... 812 867-8921
Evansville *(G-3685)*
Roy Umbarger and Sons Inc ... F ... 317 422-5195
Bargersville *(G-486)*
▲ **Sepro Corporation** ... E ... 317 580-8282
Carmel *(G-1478)*
Southern Indiana Chemical ... G ... 812 687-7118
Washington *(G-14003)*
Superior AG Resources Coop Inc ... G ... 812 724-4455
Owensville *(G-11430)*
V Global Holdings LLC ... A ... 317 247-8141
Indianapolis *(G-8142)*

2891 Adhesives & Sealants

3M Company ... B ... 317 692-6666
Indianapolis *(G-6288)*
Ace Extrusion LLC ... G ... 812 463-5230
Evansville *(G-3338)*
Ace Extrusion LLC ... D ... 812 463-5230
Evansville *(G-3340)*
Adhesive Solutions Company LLC ... G ... 260 691-0304
Columbia City *(G-1760)*
Alpha Systems LLC ... F ... 574 295-5206
Elkhart *(G-2678)*
Baril Coatings ... F ... 260 665-8431
Angola *(G-196)*
Big Dog Adhesives LLC ... G ... 574 299-6768
Elkhart *(G-2723)*
Bondline Adhesives Inc ... F ... 812 423-4651
Evansville *(G-3390)*
Capital Adhesives & Packg Corp ... F ... 317 834-5415
Mooresville *(G-10304)*
Cast Products LP ... D ... 574 255-9619
Mishawaka *(G-10017)*
▲ **Cast Products LP** ... E ... 574 294-2684
Elkhart *(G-2751)*
Chem Tech Inc ... F ... 574 848-1001
Bristol *(G-1052)*
Coleman Cable LLC ... C ... 765 449-7227
Lafayette *(G-8875)*
Colorimetric Inc ... E ... 574 255-9619
Mishawaka *(G-10019)*
▼ **Covalnce Spcalty Adhesives LLC** ... B ... 812 424-2904
Evansville *(G-3434)*
Custom Building Products Inc ... D ... 765 656-0234
Frankfort *(G-4827)*
▲ **Davies-Imperial Coatings Inc** ... E ... 219 933-0877
Hammond *(G-5869)*
▲ **Dehco Inc** ... D ... 574 294-2684
Elkhart *(G-2792)*
Evans Adhesive Corporation ... G ... 812 859-4245
Spencer *(G-13024)*
Flexible Materials Inc ... D ... 812 280-9578
Jeffersonville *(G-8362)*
Franco Corporation ... G ... 765 675-6691
Tipton *(G-13391)*
▲ **Gdc Inc** ... C ... 574 533-3128
Goshen *(G-5222)*
Glueboss Adhesive Company LLC ... G ... 855 458-2677
Elkhart *(G-2888)*
Harvey Adhesives Inc ... G ... 877 547-5558
Carmel *(G-1397)*
Hco Holding I Corporation ... E ... 317 248-1344
Indianapolis *(G-7081)*
▲ **Heartland Adhesives Inc** ... G ... 219 310-8645
Crown Point *(G-2256)*
Industrial Adhesives Indiana ... G ... 317 271-2100
Indianapolis *(G-7206)*
Iron Out Inc ... E ... 800 654-0791
Fort Wayne *(G-4383)*
▲ **Koch Enterprises Inc** ... G ... 812 465-9800
Evansville *(G-3596)*
Laticrete International Inc ... G ... 317 298-8510
Indianapolis *(G-7384)*
Lomont Holdings Co Inc ... E ... 800 545-9023
Angola *(G-228)*
Lord Corporation ... D ... 317 259-4161
Indianapolis *(G-7418)*
▲ **Marian Worldwide Inc** ... D ... 317 638-6525
Indianapolis *(G-7454)*
Morgan Adhesives Company LLC ... D ... 812 342-2004
Columbus *(G-1976)*
▲ **Mt Olive Manufacturing Inc** ... D ... 317 834-8525
Mooresville *(G-10326)*
Multiseal Inc ... C ... 812 428-3422
Evansville *(G-3641)*
▲ **Parr Corp** ... G ... 574 264-9614
Elkhart *(G-3075)*
Parr Technologies LLC ... F ... 574 264-9614
Elkhart *(G-3076)*
Parson Adhesives Inc ... E ... 812 401-7277
Evansville *(G-3664)*
Patrick Industries Inc ... C ... 574 294-7511
Elkhart *(G-3080)*
PPG Architectural Finishes Inc ... G ... 765 447-9334
Lafayette *(G-8981)*
PPG Architectural Finishes Inc ... G ... 317 787-9393
Indianapolis *(G-7713)*
PRC - Desoto International Inc ... E ... 317 290-1600
Indianapolis *(G-7728)*
PSC Industries Inc ... E ... 317 547-5439
Indianapolis *(G-7785)*
Red Cloud Adhesives Inc ... G ... 219 331-3239
Crown Point *(G-2292)*
Reliable Sealants LLC ... G ... 765 672-4455
Reelsville *(G-11903)*
◆ **Royal Adhesives & Sealants LLC** ... D ... 574 246-5000
South Bend *(G-12920)*
Royal Adhesives & Sealants LLC ... E ... 574 246-5000
South Bend *(G-12921)*
Royal Holdings Inc ... C ... 574 246-5000
South Bend *(G-12922)*
Sealcorpusa Inc ... E ... 866 868-0791
Evansville *(G-3720)*
Specialty Adhesive Film Co ... E ... 812 926-0156
Aurora *(G-387)*
Technicote Inc ... D ... 812 466-9844
Terre Haute *(G-13349)*
Testworth Laboratories Inc ... F ... 260 244-5137
Columbia City *(G-1840)*
Transcendia Inc ... C ... 765 935-1520
Richmond *(G-12068)*
Trellborg Sling Sltions US Inc ... C ... 260 748-5895
Fort Wayne *(G-4699)*
◆ **Tyden Group Holdings Corp** ... F ... 740 420-6777
Angola *(G-253)*
▲ **Uniseal Inc** ... C ... 812 425-1361
Evansville *(G-3784)*
Uniseal Inc ... G ... 812 425-1361
Evansville *(G-3785)*
Warsaw Chemical Company Inc ... D ... 574 267-3251
Warsaw *(G-13958)*
▼ **Weatherall Indiana Inc** ... F ... 812 256-3378
Charlestown *(G-1585)*

2892 Explosives

Adranos Rdx LLC ... G ... 208 539-2439
West Lafayette *(G-14047)*

Austin Powder Company ....G....... 812 536-2885
Stendal (G-13073)
Austin Powder Company ....F....... 812 342-1237
Columbus (G-1857)
Dyno Nobel Inc ....G....... 219 253-2525
Indianapolis (G-6780)
Dyno Nobel Inc ....F....... 260 731-4431
Pennville (G-11513)
Dyno Nobel Inc ....E....... 859 278-4770
Evansville (G-3467)
Ireco Metals Inc ....G....... 574 936-2146
Plymouth (G-11696)
Midland Powder LLC ....G....... 812 402-4070
Evansville (G-3627)
Mine Equipment Mill Supply Co ....D....... 812 402-4070
Evansville (G-3630)
Orica USA Inc ....F....... 812 256-7800
Jeffersonville (G-8409)

2893 Printing Ink

Braden Sutphin Ink Co ....G....... 317 352-8781
Indianapolis (G-6499)
Brand Prtg & Photo-Litho Co ....G....... 317 921-4095
Indianapolis (G-6503)
Budget Inks LLC ....G....... 877 636-4657
Angola (G-199)
CP Group Inc ....G....... 765 551-7768
Lafayette (G-8880)
Craftsnmoregalore LLC ....G....... 574 303-2231
Logansport (G-9333)
Enviro Ink ....G....... 260 748-0636
Fort Wayne (G-4238)
Flint Group US LLC ....E....... 317 471-8435
Indianapolis (G-6936)
Flint Group US LLC ....E....... 317 870-4422
Indianapolis (G-6937)
Flint Group US LLC ....E....... 574 269-4603
Warsaw (G-13877)
Industrial Organic Inks Inc ....G....... 219 878-0613
Chesterton (G-1614)
INX International Ink Co ....G....... 765 939-6625
Richmond (G-12002)
Nor-Cote International Inc ....G....... 800 488-9180
Crawfordsville (G-2176)
▲ Nor-Cote International Inc ....E....... 765 230-7252
Crawfordsville (G-2177)
Nor-Cote International Inc ....E....... 765 362-9180
Crawfordsville (G-2178)
Peafield Products Inc ....F....... 317 839-8473
Plainfield (G-11634)
Stamp N Scrap Ink Corp ....G....... 219 440-7239
Dyer (G-2510)
Sun Chemical Corporation ....D....... 765 659-6000
Frankfort (G-4854)
Sun Chemical Corporation ....G....... 812 235-8031
Terre Haute (G-13345)

2895 Carbon Black

Dean Co Inc ....G....... 317 891-2518
Greenfield (G-5520)

2899 Chemical Preparations, NEC

Addenda Corporation ....G....... 317 290-5007
Indianapolis (G-6324)
Agri Processing Services LLC ....G....... 765 860-5108
Carmel (G-1306)
Alebro LLC ....G....... 317 876-9212
Indianapolis (G-6360)
Alpha Water Conditioning ....G....... 765 281-8820
Muncie (G-10429)
American Colloid Company ....G....... 812 547-3567
Troy (G-13445)
Andersons Agriculture Group LP ....E....... 574 626-2522
Galveston (G-4993)
Arch Wood Protection Inc ....F....... 219 464-3949
Valparaiso (G-13497)
Astbury Water Technology Inc ....E....... 260 668-8900
Angola (G-194)
◆ Asterion LLC ....E....... 317 875-0051
Indianapolis (G-6433)
Bada Boom Fireworks LLC ....G....... 219 472-6700
Gary (G-5029)
Baker Petrolite LLC ....G....... 219 473-5329
Whiting (G-14269)
Bangs Laboratories Inc ....F....... 317 570-7020
Fishers (G-3873)
▲ Bell Pyrotechnics Incorporated ......G....... 812 859-3888
Bowling Green (G-952)
Beverlys Incense ....G....... 219 558-2461
Saint John (G-12260)

Biodyne-Midwest LLC ....F....... 888 970-0955
Fort Wayne (G-4108)
Biokorf LLC ....G....... 765 727-0782
West Lafayette (G-14054)
▲ Blue Grass Chemical Spc LLC ....E....... 812 948-1115
New Albany (G-10753)
Boomers ....G....... 765 741-4031
Muncie (G-10441)
Business Health ....G....... 219 762-7105
Portage (G-11752)
Camco Manufacturing Inc ....F....... 574 264-1491
Elkhart (G-2747)
Consolidated Recycling Co Inc ....E....... 812 547-7951
Troy (G-13446)
Craig Hydraulic Enterprises ....G....... 812 432-5108
Dillsboro (G-2464)
▲ Crown Technology Inc ....E....... 317 845-0045
Indianapolis (G-6700)
Custom Building Products Inc ....D....... 765 656-0234
Frankfort (G-4827)
Dannys Fireworks ....F....... 219 324-5757
La Porte (G-8748)
Driessen Water Inc ....G....... 765 529-4905
Muncie (G-10463)
Dumor Water Specialists Inc ....E....... 574 522-9500
Elkhart (G-2802)
Earthwise Plastics Inc ....E....... 765 673-0308
Gas City (G-5123)
Eco Services Operations Corp ....E....... 219 932-7651
Hammond (G-5874)
Es Deicing ....G....... 260 422-2020
Fort Wayne (G-4242)
Esm Group Inc ....F....... 219 393-5502
Kingsbury (G-8538)
Flexible Marketing Group ....G....... 574 296-0941
Elkhart (G-2855)
Gabriel Products Inc ....G....... 502 291-5388
Jeffersonville (G-8366)
Genchem International LLC ....G....... 317 574-4970
Carmel (G-1384)
Giles Chemical Corporation ....G....... 812 537-4852
Greendale (G-5486)
Harsco Corporation ....E....... 219 397-0200
East Chicago (G-2532)
Hydrite Chemical Co ....E....... 812 232-5411
Terre Haute (G-13252)
I N C O M Wholesale Supply ....G....... 574 722-2442
Logansport (G-9339)
Incense Incense ....G....... 317 544-9444
Danville (G-2349)
Innovative Chemical Resources ....G....... 317 695-6001
Indianapolis (G-7235)
Intense Incense ....G....... 765 457-3602
Kokomo (G-8647)
Interrachem LLC ....G....... 812 858-3147
Newburgh (G-11033)
Iron Out Inc ....E....... 800 654-0791
Fort Wayne (G-4383)
Jackson Hewitt Tax Service ....C....... 574 255-2200
Mishawaka (G-10057)
▲ Johnny Lemas ....G....... 260 833-8850
Angola (G-222)
Kaplan Enterprises Inc ....G....... 219 933-7993
Hammond (G-5904)
Kemco International Inc ....F....... 260 829-1263
Orland (G-11352)
Kemira Water Solutions Inc ....E....... 219 397-2646
East Chicago (G-2541)
Kemira Water Solutions Inc ....E....... 219 397-2646
East Chicago (G-2542)
Kenra Professional LLC ....E....... 317 356-6491
Indianapolis (G-7343)
▲ Kibbechem Inc ....E....... 574 266-1234
Elkhart (G-2964)
Klinge Enameling Company Inc ....G....... 317 359-8291
Indianapolis (G-7359)
Kyles Incense LLC ....G....... 219 682-4278
Merrillville (G-9724)
Le Kem of Indiana Inc ....G....... 812 932-5536
Batesville (G-509)
▲ Lebermuth Company Inc ....D....... 574 259-7000
South Bend (G-12837)
Lehigh Hanson Ecc Inc ....C....... 574 753-5121
Logansport (G-9348)
▲ Lynch Fireworks Display Inc ....G....... 812 537-1750
Greendale (G-5490)
Magnifiscents ....G....... 317 549-3880
Indianapolis (G-7440)
Mark & Jessies Firework Shack ....G....... 812 372-3855
Columbus (G-1968)

◆ Melrose Pyrotechnics Inc ....G....... 219 393-5522
Kingsbury (G-8542)
▲ Merediths Inc ....E....... 765 966-5084
Richmond (G-12016)
Metals and Additives Corp Inc ....E....... 812 446-2525
Brazil (G-969)
Metalworking Lubricants Co ....E....... 317 269-2444
Indianapolis (G-7491)
Millennial Fireworks ....G....... 812 732-5126
Mauckport (G-9657)
Miller Chemical Tech & MGT Inc ....G....... 317 560-5437
Franklin (G-4909)
Ncp Coatings Inc ....G....... 574 255-9678
Mishawaka (G-10094)
Nochar Inc ....G....... 317 613-3046
Indianapolis (G-7589)
▲ Patriotic Fireworks Inc ....G....... 317 381-0529
Indianapolis (G-7662)
Ploog Engineering Co Inc ....G....... 219 663-2854
Crown Point (G-2284)
Polyfreeze LLC ....F....... 812 547-7951
Troy (G-13447)
Polyfusion LLC ....E....... 260 624-7659
Angola (G-238)
Prosco Inc ....G....... 317 353-2920
Indianapolis (G-7779)
Prt Inc ....G....... 765 938-3333
Rushville (G-12231)
Pyrotechnic Productions Inc ....E....... 812 448-8196
Brazil (G-976)
Quaker Chemical Corp ....G....... 765 668-2441
Marion (G-9557)
Ricca Chemical Company LLC ....F....... 812 932-1161
Batesville (G-517)
Robinson International Inc ....G....... 812 637-0678
West Harrison (G-14042)
Sanco Industries Inc ....G....... 260 467-1791
Fort Wayne (G-4603)
Sanco Industries Inc ....E....... 260 426-6281
Fort Wayne (G-4604)
Schindler Electric Inc ....E....... 317 858-8215
Brownsburg (G-1168)
Scp Holdings Inc ....G....... 260 925-2588
Auburn (G-354)
Sharyls Hair With Flare ....G....... 765 885-5121
Fowler (G-4806)
Sky Fire Group LLC ....G....... 812 623-8980
Sunman (G-13118)
Sky King Unlimited Inc ....F....... 574 271-9170
South Bend (G-12938)
▲ Sky Thunder LLC ....E....... 812 397-0102
Shelburn (G-12511)
Standard Fusee Corporation ....E....... 765 472-4375
Peru (G-11548)
▲ Sterling Formulations LLC ....G....... 317 490-0823
Shelbyville (G-12572)
Summit Brands ....G....... 260 483-2519
Fort Wayne (G-4661)
Superior Manufacturing Div Mag ....G....... 260 456-3596
Fort Wayne (G-4668)
Total Cleaning Solutions LLC ....G....... 260 471-7761
Fort Wayne (G-4694)
United States Mineral Pdts Co ....D....... 260 356-2040
Huntington (G-6259)
Universal Services Inc ....G....... 219 397-4373
East Chicago (G-2577)
▲ Univertical LLC ....D....... 260 665-1500
Angola (G-255)
Univertical Semicdtr Pdts Inc ....G....... 260 665-1500
Angola (G-257)
Vw Co ....G....... 812 397-0102
Shelburn (G-12512)
◆ Warsaw Black Oxide Inc ....E....... 574 491-2975
Burket (G-1208)
Watcon Inc ....F....... 574 287-3397
South Bend (G-12988)
Water Sciences ....G....... 260 485-4655
Fort Wayne (G-4737)
Wax Shield ....G....... 317 831-1349
Camby (G-1270)
Weas Engineering Inc ....F....... 317 867-4477
Westfield (G-14200)
Workflow Solutions LLC ....G....... 502 627-0257
New Albany (G-10875)
▲ Yushiro Manufacturing Amer Inc ......E....... 317 398-9862
Shelbyville (G-12586)

S I C

29 PETROLEUM REFINING AND RELATED INDUSTRIES

2911 Petroleum Refining

Admiral Petroleum Company ....G 574 272-2051
South Bend (G-12695)

Advance Energy LLC ....G 312 665-0022
Hobart (G-6068)

Airgas Inc ....E 317 632-7106
Indianapolis (G-6354)

American Petroleum ....G 269 223-4135
Middlebury (G-9870)

B P Security ....G 219 473-3700
Whiting (G-14268)

Calumet Finance Corp ....G 317 328-5660
Indianapolis (G-6534)

Calumet Gp LLC ....F 317 328-5660
Indianapolis (G-6535)

Calumet International Inc ....G 317 328-5660
Indianapolis (G-6536)

▼ Calumet Karns City Ref LLC ....D 317 328-5660
Indianapolis (G-6537)

▲ Calumet Missouri LLC ....E 318 795-3800
Indianapolis (G-6538)

◆ Calumet Refining LLC ....G 317 328-5660
Indianapolis (G-6540)

Calumet Shreveport Llc ....D 317 328-5660
Indianapolis (G-6541)

▼ Calumet Spclty Pdts Prtners LP ....B 317 328-5660
Indianapolis (G-6542)

Cdg Operation LLC ....F 812 682-3770
New Harmony (G-10924)

Cjs Stop N Go ....G 317 877-0681
Noblesville (G-11083)

Countrymark Coop Holdg Corp ....E 800 808-3170
Indianapolis (G-6676)

Countrymark Ref Logistics LLC ....D 812 838-4341
Mount Vernon (G-10388)

Don Hartman Oil Co Inc ....G 765 643-5026
Anderson (G-98)

Emerald Cast Rnewable Fuel LLC ....G 765 942-5019
Ladoga (G-8840)

Fuel Recovery Service Inc ....G 317 372-3029
Indianapolis (G-6967)

HK Petroleum Ltd ....G 229 366-1313
Madison (G-9469)

Hometown Energy ....G 812 663-3391
Greensburg (G-5611)

Illinois Lubricants LLC ....G 260 436-2444
Fort Wayne (G-4358)

Imperial Petroleum Inc ....G 812 867-1433
Evansville (G-3549)

Integrity Bio-Fuels LLC ....F 765 763-6020
Morristown (G-10371)

Jpt Enterprises Inc ....G 260 672-1605
Fort Wayne (G-4401)

Keil Chemical Corporation ....D 219 931-2630
Hammond (G-5905)

Mid-Town Petro Acquisition LLC ....E 219 728-4110
Chesterton (G-1621)

Oxbow Carbon & Minerals ....G 219 473-0359
Whiting (G-14272)

Paralogics LLC ....G 765 587-4618
Muncie (G-10543)

Petroleum Solutions Inc ....G 574 546-2133
Bremen (G-1016)

Residual Pays Daily ....G 260 267-1617
Fort Wayne (G-4588)

Shell Pipe Line Corporation ....G 765 962-1329
Richmond (G-12049)

Steelco Industrial Lubricants ....G 219 462-0333
Valparaiso (G-13624)

Superior Oil Company Inc ....E 574 264-0161
Elkhart (G-3199)

Universal Services Inc ....G 219 397-4373
East Chicago (G-2577)

Upland Stop & Go LLC ....G 765 998-0840
Upland (G-13474)

Williams Companies Inc ....G 765 886-6149
Williamsburg (G-14285)

2951 Paving Mixtures & Blocks

03 Corp ....G 812 597-0276
Morgantown (G-10346)

Aaron Asphalt Maintenance Seal ....G 574 528-6370
Syracuse (G-13128)

Allterrain Paving & Cnstr LLC ....E 502 265-4731
New Albany (G-10742)

Asphalt Cutbacks Inc ....F 219 398-4230
East Chicago (G-2521)

Asphalt Engineers Inc ....E 574 289-5557
South Bend (G-12712)

Asphalt Materials Inc ....F 574 267-5076
Warsaw (G-13840)

Asphalt Materials Inc ....B 317 872-6010
Indianapolis (G-6426)

Asphalt Materials Inc ....E 317 243-8304
Indianapolis (G-6427)

Asphalt Materials Inc ....E 317 875-4670
Indianapolis (G-6428)

Asphalt Materials Inc ....E 317 872-5580
Indianapolis (G-6429)

Babcock Paving Inc ....G 219 987-5450
Demotte (G-2431)

Bowman Brothers Inc ....F 317 253-6043
Indianapolis (G-6498)

Calcar Quarries Incorporated ....F 812 723-2109
Paoli (G-11447)

Concrete & Asphalt Recycl Inc ....F 574 237-1928
Mishawaka (G-10021)

Corydon Stone & Asphalt Inc ....E 812 738-2216
Corydon (G-2096)

Dave OMara Paving Inc ....G 812 346-1214
North Vernon (G-11252)

DC Construction Services Inc ....E 317 577-0276
Indianapolis (G-6730)

Dynamic Landscapes LLC ....E 317 409-3487
Indianapolis (G-6779)

E & B Paving Inc ....E 765 643-5358
Anderson (G-101)

E & B Paving Inc ....E 765 674-5848
Marion (G-9522)

E & B Paving Inc ....F 765 289-7131
Muncie (G-10465)

E & B Paving Inc ....D 317 773-4132
Noblesville (G-11097)

F E Harding Paving Co Inc ....F 317 846-7401
Indianapolis (G-6899)

Freds Driveways Inc ....G 317 770-6094
Noblesville (G-11106)

Globe Asphalt Paving Co Inc ....E 317 568-4344
Indianapolis (G-7015)

Goh Con Inc ....E 812 282-1349
Clarksville (G-1682)

Hco Holding I Corporation ....E 317 248-1344
Indianapolis (G-7081)

Heritage Asphalt LLC ....G 317 872-6010
Indianapolis (G-7095)

Hotmix Inc ....G 812 926-1471
Aurora (G-380)

Hotmix Inc ....G 812 663-2020
Greensburg (G-5613)

Irving Materials Inc ....D 317 326-3101
Greenfield (G-5542)

Lafarge North America Inc ....G 219 378-1193
East Chicago (G-2547)

Laketon Refining Corporation ....E 260 982-0703
Laketon (G-9090)

Milestone Contractors LP ....C 765 772-7500
Lafayette (G-8970)

Milestone Contractors LP ....E 812 579-5248
Columbus (G-1975)

Monument Chemical LLC ....F 317 223-2630
Indianapolis (G-7539)

Niblock Excavating Inc ....D 574 848-4437
Bristol (G-1074)

Niblock Excavating Inc ....F 260 248-2100
Columbia City (G-1812)

Orr Paving Inc ....G 317 839-4110
Plainfield (G-11633)

Parsleys Seal Coating Inc ....G 812 876-5450
Ellettsville (G-3283)

Paul H Rohe Co Inc ....F 812 926-1471
Aurora (G-384)

Pavement Coatings Inc ....F 812 424-3400
Evansville (G-3665)

Rieth-Riley Cnstr Co Inc ....D 765 447-2324
Lafayette (G-8993)

Rieth-Riley Cnstr Co Inc ....E 574 288-8321
South Bend (G-12915)

Rieth-Riley Cnstr Co Inc ....C 574 875-5183
Gary (G-5093)

Rogers Group Inc ....E 812 882-3640
Vincennes (G-13703)

Rogers Group Inc ....G 812 333-8550
Bloomington (G-817)

Rogers Group Inc ....G 765 342-6898
Martinsville (G-9635)

Schrock Aggregate Company Inc ....G 574 862-4167
Wakarusa (G-13795)

Schrock Excavating Inc ....E 574 862-4167
Wakarusa (G-13796)

Scotts Grant County Asp Inc ....G 765 664-2754
Marion (G-9561)

Semmaterials LP ....G 574 267-5076
Warsaw (G-13937)

Super Seal Inc ....F 765 639-4993
Summitville (G-13106)

Triangle Asphalt Paving Corp ....E 765 482-5701
Lebanon (G-9229)

Valley Asphalt Corporation ....E 812 926-1471
Aurora (G-392)

Wallace Construction Inc ....F 317 422-5356
Martinsville (G-9647)

Walsh & Kelly Inc ....D 219 924-5900
South Bend (G-12987)

Walters Development LLC ....G 260 747-7531
Fort Wayne (G-4734)

2952 Asphalt Felts & Coatings

American Wholesalers Inc ....E 812 464-8781
Evansville (G-3351)

Architectural Metal Roofg Sup ....G 812 423-5257
Evansville (G-3364)

Asphalt Cutbacks Inc ....F 219 398-4230
East Chicago (G-2521)

Bituminous Materials & Sup LP ....G 317 228-8203
Indianapolis (G-6479)

Central States Mfg Inc ....D 219 879-4770
Michigan City (G-9773)

Dave OMara Paving Inc ....G 812 346-1214
North Vernon (G-11252)

Fibrosan USA ....G 574 612-4736
Elkhart (G-2849)

Fosbel Inc ....G 219 883-4479
Gary (G-5048)

Green Tek LLC ....G 317 294-1614
Carmel (G-1390)

Hco Holding I Corporation ....E 317 248-1344
Indianapolis (G-7081)

K Tech Specialty Coatings Inc ....F 260 587-3888
Ashley (G-287)

Metal Sales Manufacturing Corp ....E 812 941-0041
New Albany (G-10827)

Polar Seal Inc ....G 260 356-2369
Huntington (G-6239)

Pro-Mark Bldg Solutions LLC ....F 812 798-1178
Linton (G-9312)

Sampco Inc ....C 413 442-4043
South Bend (G-12925)

Schmidt Contracting Inc ....F 812 482-3923
Jasper (G-8303)

Standard Industries Inc ....C 219 872-1111
Michigan City (G-9847)

Thermoseal Co Ed Munoz Inc ....G 812 428-3343
Evansville (G-3759)

Triangle Asphalt Paving Corp ....E 765 482-5701
Lebanon (G-9229)

2992 Lubricating Oils & Greases

Allegheny Petroleum Pdts Co ....E 812 897-0760
Boonville (G-906)

Calumet Operating LLC ....F 317 328-5660
Indianapolis (G-6539)

Crescent Oil Company Inc ....G 317 634-1415
Indianapolis (G-6691)

▼ F B C Inc ....E 574 848-5288
Bristol (G-1059)

Golden Trngle Lbrcant Svcs LLC ....G 317 875-9465
Indianapolis (G-7021)

Hartland Distillations Inc ....F 812 464-4446
Evansville (G-3534)

Hill & Griffith Company ....E 317 241-9233
Indianapolis (G-7108)

◆ Idemitsu Lubricants Amer Corp ....D 812 284-3300
Jeffersonville (G-8378)

Illinois Lubricants LLC ....G 260 436-2444
Fort Wayne (G-4358)

J 2 Systems and Supply LLC ....G 317 602-3940
Indianapolis (G-7281)

Keil Chemical Corporation ....D 219 931-2630
Hammond (G-5905)

Klotz Special Formula Products ....F 260 490-0489
Fort Wayne (G-4412)

Lane Quick ....G 812 896-1890
Salem (G-12298)

Linder Oil Co Inc ....F 260 622-4680
Ossian (G-11403)

Metalloid Corporation ....E 260 356-3200
  Huntington *(G-6229)*

Metalworking Lubricants Co ....E 317 269-2444
  Indianapolis *(G-7491)*

Michiana Elkhart Inc ....G 574 206-0620
  Elkhart *(G-3030)*

Oil Technology Inc ....E 219 322-2724
  Dyer *(G-2506)*

Packaging Group Corp ....E 219 879-2500
  Michigan City *(G-9826)*

Permawick Company Inc ....F 812 376-0703
  Columbus *(G-1993)*

Petrochoice Holdings Inc ....E 317 634-7300
  Indianapolis *(G-7680)*

Petroleum Solutions Inc ....G 574 546-2133
  Bremen *(G-1016)*

Pinnacle Oil Holdings LLC ....F 317 875-9465
  Indianapolis *(G-7695)*

Pinnacle Oil Holdings LLC ....E 317 875-9465
  Indianapolis *(G-7696)*

Shalee Oils LLC ....G 765 329-4057
  Hartford City *(G-5990)*

Spence/Banks Inc ....F 812 234-3538
  Terre Haute *(G-13341)*

Tj Performance LLC ....G 765 580-0481
  Brownsville *(G-1196)*

Warrior Oil Service Inc ....F 317 738-9777
  Franklin *(G-4940)*

▲ Yushiro Manufacturing Amer Inc ......E 317 398-9862
  Shelbyville *(G-12586)*

2999 Products Of Petroleum & Coal, NEC

American Pellet Supply LLC ....F 812 398-2225
  Carlisle *(G-1295)*

Calumet Superior LLC ....C 317 328-5660
  Indianapolis *(G-6543)*

Paralogics LLC ....G 765 587-4618
  Muncie *(G-10543)*

30 RUBBER AND MISCELLANEOUS PLASTICS PRODUCTS

3011 Tires & Inner Tubes

BF Shaffer Co ....G 812 949-8356
  New Albany *(G-10752)*

Enovapremier LLC ....D 812 385-0576
  Princeton *(G-11870)*

Goodyear Tire & Rubber Company ....G 219 762-0651
  Portage *(G-11767)*

Hammer Industries Inc ....F 812 422-6953
  Evansville *(G-3529)*

▼ Hoosier Racing Tire Corp ....D 574 784-3409
  Lakeville *(G-9096)*

Michelin North America Inc ....A 260 493-8100
  Woodburn *(G-14386)*

Rubber Shop Inc ....G 574 291-6440
  South Bend *(G-12924)*

Simon and Sons ....G 812 852-3636
  Osgood *(G-11395)*

Williamsport Tire Mart LLC ....G 765 762-6315
  Williamsport *(G-14300)*

3021 Rubber & Plastic Footwear

Adidas Group ....G 317 895-7000
  Indianapolis *(G-6326)*

Artisanz Fabrication Mch LLC ....G 317 708-0228
  Plainfield *(G-11594)*

Nike Inc ....E 219 879-1320
  Michigan City *(G-9824)*

Piro Shoes LLC ....F 888 849-0916
  Fishers *(G-3951)*

Wise Industries Inc (del) ....G 219 947-5333
  Hobart *(G-6101)*

3052 Rubber & Plastic Hose & Belting

Artisanz Fabrication Mch LLC ....G 317 708-0228
  Plainfield *(G-11594)*

Clean-Seal Inc ....E 574 299-1888
  South Bend *(G-12736)*

Coupled Products LLC ....B 260 248-3200
  Columbia City *(G-1776)*

▲ Dunham Rubber & Belting Corp ....E 317 888-3002
  Greenwood *(G-5683)*

Dunham Rubber & Belting Corp ....G 800 876-5340
  Fort Wayne *(G-4224)*

Dunham Rubber Belting Corp ....G 317 604-5313
  Shelbyville *(G-12531)*

Dura-Vent Corp ....G 574 936-2432
  Plymouth *(G-11681)*

Exactseal Inc ....G 317 559-2220
  Indianapolis *(G-6889)*

◆ Flexaust Inc ....C 574 267-7909
  Warsaw *(G-13876)*

Flexible Technologies Inc ....E 574 936-2432
  Plymouth *(G-11685)*

▲ General Rbr Plas of Evansville ....E 812 464-5153
  Evansville *(G-3517)*

Hitachi Cable America Inc ....C 812 945-9011
  New Albany *(G-10794)*

▲ Hitachi Cble Auto Pdts USA Inc ....C 812 945-9011
  New Albany *(G-10796)*

▲ Kilgore Manufacturing Co Inc ....D 260 248-2002
  Columbia City *(G-1804)*

Mulhern Belting Inc ....G 219 879-2385
  Michigan City *(G-9822)*

Nova Flex Group ....F 317 334-1444
  Indianapolis *(G-7598)*

Quadrant Epp Usa Inc ....D 260 479-4700
  Fort Wayne *(G-4568)*

Quadrant Epp Usa Inc ....C 260 479-4100
  Fort Wayne *(G-4569)*

Radiator Specialty Company ....E 574 546-5606
  Bremen *(G-1018)*

Rubber Shop Inc ....G 574 291-6440
  South Bend *(G-12924)*

S & R Welding Inc ....G 317 710-0360
  Indianapolis *(G-7877)*

▲ Slb Corporation ....G 574 255-9774
  Mishawaka *(G-10125)*

Tri-State Hydraulics Indus Sup ....G 812 537-3485
  Greendale *(G-5495)*

3053 Gaskets, Packing & Sealing Devices

Aearo Technologies LLC ....C 317 692-6666
  Indianapolis *(G-6342)*

Apexx Enterprises LLC ....F 812 486-2443
  Montgomery *(G-10213)*

Barger Packaging Inc ....G 888 525-2845
  Elkhart *(G-2714)*

▲ Bonar Inc ....D 260 636-7430
  Albion *(G-17)*

BRC Rubber & Plastics Inc ....D 260 827-0871
  Bluffton *(G-869)*

BRC Rubber & Plastics Inc ....C 260 693-2171
  Hartford City *(G-5978)*

▲ BRC Rubber & Plastics Inc ....C 260 693-2171
  Fort Wayne *(G-4118)*

BRC Rubber & Plastics Inc ....C 260 894-4121
  Ligonier *(G-9278)*

BRC Rubber & Plastics Inc ....D 260 203-5300
  Fort Wayne *(G-4119)*

Breiner Company Inc ....F 317 272-2521
  Avon *(G-434)*

C&C Polo Enterprises Inc ....C 317 577-8266
  Indianapolis *(G-6529)*

▲ Cannon Fabrication Company ....F 765 629-2277
  Milroy *(G-9978)*

Cedar Creek Studios Inc ....G 260 627-7320
  Leo *(G-9241)*

EMT Industries Inc ....E 574 533-1273
  Granger *(G-5406)*

Essential Sealing Products Inc ....G 219 787-8711
  Chesterton *(G-1604)*

Exactseal Inc ....G 317 559-2220
  Indianapolis *(G-6889)*

Federal-Mogul Powertrain LLC ....B 574 271-5954
  South Bend *(G-12776)*

Fellwocks Automotive ....G 812 867-3658
  Evansville *(G-3503)*

Freudenberg-Nok General Partnr ....C 317 421-3400
  Shelbyville *(G-12534)*

Freudenberg-Nok General Partnr ....C 765 763-7246
  Morristown *(G-10369)*

Freudenberg-Nok General Partnr ....C 765 763-7246
  Morristown *(G-10370)*

Freudenberg-Nok General Partnr ....E 734 354-5504
  Shelbyville *(G-12535)*

▲ Gaska Tape Inc ....D 574 294-5431
  Elkhart *(G-2875)*

▲ General Rbr Plas of Evansville ....E 812 464-5153
  Evansville *(G-3517)*

Gindor Inc ....G 574 642-4004
  Goshen *(G-5225)*

Griffith Rbr Mills of Garrett ....E 260 357-0876
  Garrett *(G-5008)*

HI Tech Foam Products Inc ....G 317 614-1515
  Indianapolis *(G-7102)*

▲ Hi-Tech Foam Products LLC ....E 270 684-8331
  Indianapolis *(G-7105)*

▲ Hoosier Gasket Corporation ....D 317 545-2000
  Indianapolis *(G-7121)*

▲ Ilpea Industries Inc ....D 812 752-2526
  Scottsburg *(G-12362)*

Ilpea Industries Inc ....D 812 752-2526
  Scottsburg *(G-12363)*

Iris Rubber Company Inc ....F 317 984-3561
  Cicero *(G-1662)*

Jeans Extrusions Inc ....C 812 883-2581
  Salem *(G-12296)*

Knox Enterprises Inc ....C 317 714-3073
  Indianapolis *(G-7363)*

▲ Marian Worldwide Inc ....D 317 638-6525
  Indianapolis *(G-7454)*

Metallic Seals Inc ....C 317 780-0773
  Indianapolis *(G-7489)*

▲ Midwest Gasket Corporation ....E 765 629-2221
  Milroy *(G-9982)*

Nitto Inc ....C 317 879-2840
  Zionsville *(G-14451)*

Parker-Hannifin Corporation.................D 574 533-1111
  Goshen *(G-5307)*

Parker-Hannifin Corporation.................C 260 894-7125
  Ligonier *(G-9292)*

▼ Press-Seal Gasket Corporation ....C 260 436-0521
  Fort Wayne *(G-4557)*

Rubber Shop Inc ....G 574 291-6440
  South Bend *(G-12924)*

▲ Seal Products LLC ....C 260 436-5628
  Fort Wayne *(G-4612)*

◆ T & M Rubber Inc ....G 574 533-3173
  Goshen *(G-5338)*

▲ Tfco Incorporated ....G 219 324-4166
  La Porte *(G-8830)*

Trellborg Sling Prfiles US Inc ....E 330 995-5125
  Bristol *(G-1090)*

▲ Triangle Rubber Co LLC ....C 574 533-3118
  Goshen *(G-5340)*

▼ Trifab & Construction Inc ....G 219 845-1300
  Hammond *(G-5952)*

Uniform Hood Lace Inc ....G 317 896-9555
  Westfield *(G-14196)*

3061 Molded, Extruded & Lathe-Cut Rubber Mechanical Goods

Ace Extrusion LLC ....E 812 868-8640
  Evansville *(G-3339)*

◆ Ati Inc ....G 812 431-5409
  Mount Vernon *(G-10384)*

Bluffton Rubber....................................G 260 824-4501
  Bluffton *(G-868)*

BRC Rubber & Plastics Inc ....D 260 827-0871
  Bluffton *(G-869)*

BRC Rubber & Plastics Inc ....C 260 693-2171
  Churubusco *(G-1643)*

▲ BRC Rubber & Plastics Inc ....C 260 693-2171
  Fort Wayne *(G-4118)*

BRC Rubber & Plastics Inc ....C 260 894-4121
  Ligonier *(G-9278)*

BRC Rubber & Plastics Inc ....D 260 203-5300
  Fort Wayne *(G-4119)*

BRC Rubber & Plastics Inc ....C 260 693-2171
  Hartford City *(G-5978)*

BRC Rubber & Plastics Inc ....E 765 728-8510
  Montpelier *(G-10289)*

Coleman Cable LLC ....C 765 449-7227
  Lafayette *(G-8875)*

Cooper-Standard Automotive Inc...........B 260 925-0700
  Auburn *(G-322)*

Cooper-Standard Automotive Inc...........B 260 925-0700
  Auburn *(G-324)*

EMT Industries Inc ....E 574 533-1273
  Granger *(G-5406)*

Engineered Rubber & Plastics...............F 574 254-1405
  Mishawaka *(G-10041)*

▲ Envirotech Extrusion Inc ....E 765 966-8068
  Richmond *(G-11984)*

Fellwocks Automotive ....G 812 867-3658
  Evansville *(G-3503)*

Finzer Roller Inc ....E 812 829-1455
  Spencer *(G-13026)*

Freudenberg-Nok General Partnr ....E 734 354-5504
  Shelbyville *(G-12535)*

Freudenberg-Nok General Partnr ....C 765 763-7246
  Morristown *(G-10369)*

▲ Griffith Rbr Mills of Garrett ....E 260 357-3125
  Garrett *(G-5007)*

Iris Rubber Company Inc ....F 317 984-3561
Cicero **(G-1662)**

▲ Jasper Rubber Products Inc ....A 812 482-3242
Jasper **(G-8263)**

Lear Manufacturing ....G 765 282-6273
Muncie **(G-10510)**

Parker-Hannifin Corporation ....C 574 528-9400
Syracuse **(G-13139)**

Parker-Hannifin Corporation ....D 574 533-1111
Goshen **(G-5307)**

Rd Rubber Products Inc ....G 260 357-3571
Garrett **(G-5021)**

Rubber Shop Inc ....G 574 291-6440
South Bend **(G-12924)**

▲ South Bend Modern Molding Inc ......D 574 255-0711
Mishawaka **(G-10132)**

◆ T & M Rubber Inc ....G 574 533-3173
Goshen **(G-5338)**

▲ Triangle Rubber Co LLC ....C 574 533-3118
Goshen **(G-5340)**

Viking Inc ....E 260 244-6141
Columbia City **(G-1845)**

Western Consolidated Tech Inc ....D 260 495-9866
Fremont **(G-4982)**

3069 Fabricated Rubber Prdts, NEC

Acme Masking Company Inc ....E 317 272-6202
Avon **(G-425)**

Aeropro Holdings LLC ....G 317 849-9555
Indianapolis **(G-6349)**

American Roller Company LLC ....E 574 586-3101
Walkerton **(G-13801)**

Boyd Corporation ....F 574 389-1878
Elkhart **(G-2731)**

BRC Rubber & Plastics Inc ....D 260 827-0871
Bluffton **(G-869)**

Central Rubber & Plastics Inc ....G 574 534-6411
Goshen **(G-5185)**

Daramic LLC ....C 812 738-8274
Corydon **(G-2097)**

▲ Discount Labels LLC ....A 812 945-2617
New Albany **(G-10769)**

DSM Coating Resins Inc ....F 765 659-4721
Frankfort **(G-4829)**

E Industries Inc ....G 574 522-7550
Elkhart **(G-2808)**

Eis Fibercoating Inc ....E 574 722-5192
Logansport **(G-9334)**

▲ Enbi Indiana Inc ....C 317 398-3267
Shelbyville **(G-12533)**

Engraving and Stamp Center Inc ......G 812 336-0606
Bloomington **(G-720)**

Exactseal Inc ....G 317 559-2220
Indianapolis **(G-6889)**

▲ Excell Usa Inc ....D 812 895-1687
Vincennes **(G-13678)**

▲ Exemplary Foam Inc ....E 574 295-8888
Elkhart **(G-2841)**

Field Rubber Products Inc ....F 317 773-3787
Noblesville **(G-11103)**

Finzer Roller Inc ....E 812 829-1455
Spencer **(G-13026)**

Fluid Handling Technology Inc ....G 317 216-9629
Indianapolis **(G-6940)**

Foamcraft Inc ....G 574 534-4343
Goshen **(G-5216)**

Fuel Bladder Distributors Inc ....G 317 852-9156
Brownsburg **(G-1151)**

G T A Drum Inc ....G 574 288-3459
South Bend **(G-12786)**

▲ Gdc Inc ....C 574 533-3128
Goshen **(G-5222)**

General Furniture & Bedg Pdts ....G 317 849-2670
Indianapolis **(G-6997)**

Goodtime Manufacturing LLC ....G 317 876-3661
Indianapolis **(G-7026)**

Gorilla Plastic Rbr Group LLC ....G 317 635-9616
Indianapolis **(G-7029)**

Griffith Rbr Mills of Garrett ....F 260 357-0876
Garrett **(G-5008)**

Gta Containers Inc ....F 574 288-3459
South Bend **(G-12792)**

▲ Gta Containers Inc ....E 574 288-3459
South Bend **(G-12793)**

H A King Co Inc ....F 260 482-6376
Fort Wayne **(G-4313)**

Hawkins Darryal ....G 765 282-6021
Muncie **(G-10482)**

▲ Hi-Tech Foam Products LLC ....E 270 684-8331
Indianapolis **(G-7105)**

Ilpea Industries Inc ....D 812 752-2526
Scottsburg **(G-12363)**

Indiana Factory Outlet Marine ....G 260 799-4764
Larwill **(G-9122)**

Indiana Spray Foam ....G 219 696-6100
Lowell **(G-9408)**

Indianapolis Industrial Pdts ....G 317 359-3078
Indianapolis **(G-7201)**

Infinity Performance Inc ....E 317 479-1017
Indianapolis **(G-7227)**

Ink Angel Inc ....G 574 534-4415
Goshen **(G-5245)**

Innocor Foam Tech - Acp Inc ....F 574 294-7694
Elkhart **(G-2935)**

Iris Rubber Company Inc ....F 317 984-3561
Cicero **(G-1662)**

▲ Jpc LLC ....F 574 293-8030
Elkhart **(G-2951)**

Klh Holding Corporation ....F 317 634-3976
Indianapolis **(G-7358)**

Knox Enterprises Inc ....G 317 714-3073
Indianapolis **(G-7363)**

Larry G Byrd ....F 765 458-7285
Liberty **(G-9263)**

McCammon Engineering Corp ....G 812 356-4455
Sullivan **(G-13086)**

Medegen Holdings LLC ....G 219 473-1674
Whiting **(G-14271)**

Midwest Rubber Products Inc ....G 317 237-4037
Indianapolis **(G-7511)**

Midwest Rubber Sales Inc ....G 765 468-7105
Farmland **(G-3842)**

Nishikawa Cooper LLC ....C 260 593-2156
Fort Wayne **(G-4504)**

▲ Nishikawa Cooper LLC ....B 260 593-2156
Topeka **(G-13425)**

Nishikawa Cooper LLC ....A 574 546-5938
Bremen **(G-1012)**

▲ Nishikawa of America Inc ....D 260 593-2156
Topeka **(G-13426)**

No-Sail Splash Guard Co Inc ....G 765 522-2100
Roachdale **(G-12094)**

North American Latex Corp ....D 812 268-6608
Sullivan **(G-13089)**

Pactiv Corporation ....C 574 936-7065
Plymouth **(G-11709)**

Phoenix Closures Inc ....D 765 658-1800
Greencastle **(G-5472)**

Pierceton Rubber Products Inc ....F 574 594-3002
Pierceton **(G-11577)**

Protective Coatings Inc ....E 260 424-2900
Fort Wayne **(G-4563)**

Recreation Insites LLC ....G 317 578-0588
Fishers **(G-3961)**

Robco Engineered Rubber Pdts ....F 260 248-2888
Columbia City **(G-1829)**

Roembke Mfg & Design Inc ....E 260 622-4135
Ossian **(G-11406)**

Roembke Mfg & Design Inc ....E 260 622-4030
Ossian **(G-11407)**

▲ Schachtpfister Inc ....G 260 356-9775
Huntington **(G-6246)**

Servaas Inc ....G 317 633-2020
Indianapolis **(G-7914)**

Seymour Midwest LLC ....G 574 269-2782
Warsaw **(G-13939)**

▲ South Bend Modern Molding Inc ......D 574 255-0711
Mishawaka **(G-10132)**

Specialty Products & Polymers ....G 269 684-5931
South Bend **(G-12948)**

Sperry & Rice LLC ....E 765 647-4141
Brookville **(G-1126)**

Td Consulting LLC ....G 260 925-3089
Auburn **(G-360)**

Ten Cate Enbi Inc (indiana) ....C 317 398-3267
Shelbyville **(G-12574)**

Unique Tape Manufacturing LLC ....G 219 617-4204
Chesterton **(G-1637)**

Valley Tile Corporation ....G 812 268-3328
Sullivan **(G-13097)**

◆ Vestil Manufacturing Corp ....B 260 665-7586
Angola **(G-258)**

3081 Plastic Unsupported Sheet & Film

▲ American Renolit Corporation ....C 219 324-6886
La Porte **(G-8733)**

Artisanz Fabrication Mch LLC ....G 317 708-0228
Plainfield **(G-11594)**

Avery Dennison Corporation ....D 219 696-7777
Lowell **(G-9399)**

Azimuth Custom Extrusions LLC ....E 812 423-6180
Evansville **(G-3368)**

▼ B&F Plastics Inc ....D 765 962-6125
Richmond **(G-11959)**

▲ Bcw Diversified Inc ....E 765 644-2033
Anderson **(G-73)**

Bemis Company Inc ....D 812 466-2213
Terre Haute **(G-13198)**

Berry Global Inc ....G 812 334-7090
Bloomington **(G-679)**

Berry Global Inc ....G 812 386-1525
Princeton **(G-11865)**

Berry Global Inc ....G 765 966-1414
Richmond **(G-11964)**

Berry Global Inc ....E 812 867-6671
Evansville **(G-3375)**

Berry Global Inc ....B 765 962-4253
Richmond **(G-11965)**

◆ Berry Global Inc ....A 812 424-2904
Evansville **(G-3376)**

▼ Berry Global Group Inc ....E 812 424-2904
Evansville **(G-3377)**

Custom Covers Inc ....G 765 481-7800
Lebanon **(G-9178)**

D and M Enterprises LLC ....F 260 483-4008
Fort Wayne **(G-4197)**

Foil Laminating Inc ....E 574 935-3645
Plymouth **(G-11686)**

Futurex Industries Inc ....E 812 299-5708
Terre Haute **(G-13237)**

Futurex Industries Inc ....G 765 597-2221
Marshall **(G-9591)**

▲ Futurex Industries Inc ....C 765 498-3900
Bloomingdale **(G-647)**

Futurex Industries Inc ....E 765 498-8900
Bloomingdale **(G-648)**

Hoosier Fiberglass Industries ....F 812 232-5027
Terre Haute **(G-13248)**

Ie Products Mad Dasher Inc ....E 260 747-0545
Fort Wayne **(G-4357)**

Jack Laurie Coml Floors Inc ....G 317 569-2095
Indianapolis **(G-7293)**

▲ Mirwec Film Incorporated ....F 812 331-7194
Bloomington **(G-773)**

Pactiv Corporation ....C 574 936-7065
Plymouth **(G-11709)**

Petoskey Plastics Inc ....C 765 348-9808
Hartford City **(G-5987)**

Piedmont Plastics Inc ....G 317 947-4500
Indianapolis **(G-7689)**

▲ Polymer Science Inc ....E 574 583-3751
Monticello **(G-10280)**

▲ Primex Plastics Corporation ....B 765 966-7774
Richmond **(G-12034)**

Printpack Inc ....B 812 663-5091
Greensburg **(G-5629)**

Rustic N Chic LLC ....G 219 987-4957
Wheatfield **(G-14230)**

◆ Sabic Innovative Plastics Mt V ....A 812 838-4385
Mount Vernon **(G-10407)**

Seymour Midwest LLC ....G 574 269-2782
Warsaw **(G-13939)**

Sonoco Products Company ....C 812 526-5511
Edinburgh **(G-2629)**

Specialty Adhesive Film Co ....E 812 926-0156
Aurora **(G-387)**

Taghleef Industries Inc ....A 302 326-5500
Rosedale **(G-12208)**

Transcendia Inc ....C 765 935-1520
Richmond **(G-12068)**

Tredegar Corporation ....D 812 466-0266
Terre Haute **(G-13356)**

3082 Plastic Unsupported Profile Shapes

▲ 3d Parts Mfg LLC ....G 317 860-6941
Anderson **(G-56)**

Filtration Parts Incorporated ....F 704 661-8135
Rensselaer **(G-11923)**

▲ Polygon Company ....C 574 586-3145
Walkerton **(G-13808)**

Polygon Company ....D 574 586-3145
Walkerton **(G-13809)**

Precision Products Group Inc ....C 301 474-3100
Indianapolis **(G-6277)**

▲ Precision Products Group Inc ....B 330 698-4711
Indianapolis **(G-6276)**

Prolon Inc ....E 574 522-8900
Elkhart **(G-3119)**

Quadrant Epp Usa Inc ....D 260 479-4700
Fort Wayne **(G-4568)**

Quadrant Epp Usa Inc ....C 260 479-4100
  Fort Wayne *(G-4569)*
S H Leggitt Company ....G 574 264-0230
  Elkhart *(G-3152)*
▲ Sabin Corporation ....C 812 323-4500
  Bloomington *(G-820)*
▲ Specialty Manufacturing of Ind......E 812 256-4633
  Charlestown *(G-1581)*
Stone Industrial Inc....................C 301 474-3100
  Fort Wayne *(G-4652)*
▲ Stratikore ....G 574 807-0028
  La Porte *(G-8824)*

3083 Plastic Laminated Plate & Sheet

Ameri-Kart Corp ....D 225 642-7874
  Bristol *(G-1043)*
◆ American Art Clay Co Inc...........C 317 243-0066
  Indianapolis *(G-6385)*
Applied Composites Engrg Inc ......E 317 243-4225
  Indianapolis *(G-6411)*
▼ Berry Global Group Inc ....F 812 424-2904
  Evansville *(G-3377)*
Brownsburg Custom Cabinets ......G 317 271-1887
  Indianapolis *(G-6512)*
DSM Engineering Plastics Inc ......F 812 435-7500
  Evansville *(G-3463)*
◆ DSM Engineering Plastics Inc.......C 248 530-5500
  Evansville *(G-3465)*
Eichstedt Manufacturing Inc........G 574 288-8881
  South Bend *(G-12759)*
Elko Inc ....E 812 473-8400
  Evansville *(G-3473)*
F Robert Gardner Co Inc ....G 317 634-2333
  Indianapolis *(G-6900)*
Flexible Materials Inc ....D 812 280-9578
  Jeffersonville *(G-8362)*
General Fabricators Inc ....G 317 787-9354
  Indianapolis *(G-6996)*
Hancor Inc ....E 812 443-2080
  Brazil *(G-964)*
Hartson-Kennedy Cabinet Top Co ...B 765 668-8144
  Marion *(G-9529)*
Heywood Williams Inc ....G 574 295-8400
  Elkhart *(G-2915)*
▲ Jaeger-Ntek Sling Slutions Inc ......D 219 324-1111
  La Porte *(G-8774)*
Lockerbie Square Cab Co Inc ....G 317 635-1134
  Indianapolis *(G-7413)*
▲ Marian Worldwide Inc ....D 317 638-6525
  Indianapolis *(G-7454)*
Midwest Cabinet Solutions Inc ......F 765 664-3938
  Marion *(G-9547)*
Miller Waste Mills Inc ....E 507 454-6900
  Indianapolis *(G-7522)*
Olon Industries Inc (us)..............G 812 254-6718
  Washington *(G-13995)*
▲ Omni Plastics LLC ....D 812 422-0888
  Evansville *(G-3655)*
Pioneer Plastics Corporation........D 574 264-0702
  Elkhart *(G-3097)*
Plasticraft-Complete Acrylics ....G 765 610-9502
  Anderson *(G-153)*
Positron Corporation ....E 574 295-8777
  Elkhart *(G-3103)*
Sabic Innovative Plas US LLC ......D 812 372-0197
  Columbus *(G-2010)*
▲ Sabin Corporation ....C 812 323-4500
  Bloomington *(G-820)*
Shade Techniques LLC ....G 765 396-9903
  Eaton *(G-2589)*
Sims Cabinet Co Inc ....E 317 634-1747
  Indianapolis *(G-7948)*
Sonoco Products Company ....C 812 526-5511
  Edinburgh *(G-2629)*
Thrust Industries Inc ....F 812 437-3643
  Evansville *(G-3762)*
▲ Triangle Rubber Co LLC ....C 574 533-3118
  Goshen *(G-5340)*

3084 Plastic Pipe

Ace Extrusion LLC....................G 812 463-5230
  Evansville *(G-3338)*
Ace Extrusion LLC....................D 812 463-5230
  Evansville *(G-3340)*
Advanced Drainage Systems Inc ....F 812 443-2080
  Brazil *(G-953)*
Corrosion Technologies Inc..........G 317 894-0627
  Greenfield *(G-5516)*
▲ Cresline Plastic Pipe Co Inc..........E 812 428-9300
  Evansville *(G-3442)*

Cresline-Northwest LLC ....E 812 428-9300
  Evansville *(G-3443)*
Cresline-West Inc ....E 812 428-9300
  Evansville *(G-3444)*
Diamond Plastics Corporation ....D 765 287-9234
  Muncie *(G-10459)*
Genova Products Inc ....D 219 866-5136
  Rensselaer *(G-11925)*
Hancor Inc ....E 812 443-2080
  Brazil *(G-964)*
Kuri TEC Manufacturing Inc ....E 765 764-6000
  Williamsport *(G-14293)*
Liner Products LLC ....F 812 723-0244
  Paoli *(G-11455)*
Nibco Inc ....C 812 256-8500
  Charlestown *(G-1576)*
Pipeconx ....G 800 443-9081
  Evansville *(G-3672)*
Uniseal Inc ....G 812 425-1361
  Evansville *(G-3785)*

3085 Plastic Bottles

▲ Ahf Industries Inc....................C 812 936-9988
  French Lick *(G-4984)*
▼ Berry Global Group Inc ....F 812 424-2904
  Evansville *(G-3377)*
Drug Plastics and Glass Co Inc......D 765 385-0035
  Oxford *(G-11431)*
Indiana Bottle Company Inc..........E 812 752-8700
  Scottsburg *(G-12365)*
North America Packaging Corp........C 317 291-2396
  Indianapolis *(G-7591)*
Poly-Tainer Inc ....C 317 883-2072
  Greenwood *(G-5734)*
Polycon Industries Inc................C 219 738-1000
  Merrillville *(G-9748)*
◆ Setco LLC ....B 812 424-2904
  Evansville *(G-3724)*
Silgan Plastics LLC....................D 260 894-3118
  Ligonier *(G-9295)*
Silgan Plastics LLC....................C 812 522-0900
  Seymour *(G-12490)*
Silgan Plastics LLC....................F 812 522-0900
  Seymour *(G-12491)*
▲ Specialty Manufacturing of Ind......E 812 256-4633
  Charlestown *(G-1581)*
Travomatic Corp Indiana Div ....G 812 522-8177
  Seymour *(G-12497)*

3086 Plastic Foam Prdts

Abbp LLC................................G 812 402-5966
  Evansville *(G-3332)*
Ace Extrusion LLC.....................G 812 463-5230
  Evansville *(G-3338)*
Ace Extrusion LLC.....................D 812 463-5230
  Evansville *(G-3340)*
Aearo Technologies LLC...............C 317 692-6666
  Indianapolis *(G-6342)*
American Whitetail Inc ....F 812 937-7185
  Ferdinand *(G-3845)*
B&W Packaging Mfg LLC ....E 812 280-9578
  New Albany *(G-10749)*
Barger Packaging Corporation........D 574 389-1860
  Elkhart *(G-2715)*
▲ Bremen Corporation ....A 574 546-4238
  Bremen *(G-987)*
Carpenter Co ....B 574 522-2800
  Elkhart *(G-2750)*
Carpenter Co ....E 812 367-2211
  Ferdinand *(G-3847)*
Cellofoam North America Inc.........D 317 535-9008
  Whiteland *(G-14235)*
▲ Century Foam Inc....................E 574 293-5547
  Elkhart *(G-2753)*
▲ Createc Corporation ....E 317 566-0022
  Indianapolis *(G-6686)*
Creative Foam Corporation...........E 574 546-4238
  Bremen *(G-995)*
Cryovac Inc ....C 317 876-4100
  Indianapolis *(G-6702)*
Display Craft ....G 260 726-4535
  Portland *(G-11816)*
▲ Efp LLC ....D 574 295-4690
  Elkhart *(G-2814)*
Elliott Co of Indianapolis ....F 317 291-1213
  Indianapolis *(G-6842)*
Foam Fabricators Inc ....E 812 948-1696
  New Albany *(G-10783)*
▲ Foam Rubber LLC ....C 765 521-2000
  New Castle *(G-10901)*

▲ Foamcraft Inc ....C 317 545-3626
  Indianapolis *(G-6943)*
Foamcraft Inc ....D 574 293-8569
  Elkhart *(G-2860)*
Foamcraft Inc ....E 812 849-3350
  Mitchell *(G-10163)*
Foamcraft Inc ....D 574 534-4343
  Goshen *(G-5216)*
Fostek ....F 540 587-5870
  Mishawaka *(G-10044)*
Fxi Inc ....C 260 747-7485
  Fort Wayne *(G-4291)*
Fxi Inc ....C 260 925-1073
  Auburn *(G-333)*
G & T Industries Inc ....E 812 634-2252
  Jasper *(G-8252)*
▲ Gaska Tape Inc ....D 574 294-5431
  Elkhart *(G-2875)*
▲ Gdc Inc ....C 574 533-3128
  Goshen *(G-5222)*
▲ Hi-Tech Foam Products LLC.........E 270 684-8331
  Indianapolis *(G-7105)*
Innovative Packaging Assoc Inc ....F 260 356-6577
  Huntington *(G-6217)*
▲ Johnson Plastics & Sup Co Inc ......E 812 424-5554
  Evansville *(G-3579)*
▲ Kibbechem Inc ....E 574 266-1234
  Elkhart *(G-2964)*
Knox Enterprises Inc..................E 317 714-3073
  Indianapolis *(G-7363)*
Latham Manufacturing Corp...........C 260 459-4115
  Fort Wayne *(G-4425)*
Lifoam Industries LLC ....E 410 889-1023
  Fishers *(G-3939)*
M & C LLC ....G 812 482-7447
  Jasper *(G-8288)*
▼ Molded Foam LLC ....D 574 848-1500
  Bristol *(G-1070)*
Mossberg Industries Inc...............D 260 357-5141
  Garrett *(G-5018)*
Opflex Solutions Inc ....D 800 568-7036
  Indianapolis *(G-7627)*
Opflex Technologies LLC ....C 317 731-6123
  Indianapolis *(G-7628)*
Opflex Technologies LLC ....E 518 568-7036
  Indianapolis *(G-7629)*
▲ Perry Foam Products Inc ....E 765 474-3404
  Lafayette *(G-8980)*
Pregis LLC..............................G 574 936-7065
  Plymouth *(G-11716)*
PSC Industries Inc ....E 812 425-9071
  Evansville *(G-3688)*
Pyramid Paper Products Inc ....E 812 372-0288
  Columbus *(G-2002)*
◆ Rau Creations ....G 317 774-8789
  Carmel *(G-1463)*
Residue West Inc ....E 731 587-9596
  (G-3705)
Security Paks Intl LLC.................F 317 536-2662
  Carmel *(G-1477)*
Sevenoks Inc ....G 800 523-8715
  La Porte *(G-8818)*
Solotat Industries LLC.................G 574 320-1436
  Elkhart *(G-3180)*
Sonoco Prtective Solutions Inc ....G 260 726-9333
  Portland *(G-11846)*
Teach Enterprises Inc.................E 574 773-3108
  Nappanee *(G-10708)*
Total Concepts Design Inc ....D 812 752-6534
  Scottsburg *(G-12384)*
Tp/Elm Acquisition Sbusid Inc ....D 260 728-2161
  Decatur *(G-2408)*
Unique-Prescotech Inc ....E 479 646-2973
  Evansville *(G-3783)*
US Foam Corporation..................G 260 456-4998
  Fort Wayne *(G-4720)*
Useful Products LLC ....E 877 304-9036
  Goodland *(G-5161)*
Vahala Foam Inc.......................D 574 293-1287
  Elkhart *(G-3240)*
▲ Worldwide Foam Ltd ....G 574 968-8268
  Elkhart *(G-3269)*

3087 Custom Compounding Of Purchased Plastic Resins

▼ B C C Products Inc ....F 317 494-6420
  Franklin *(G-4870)*
Chase Plastic Services Inc............F 574 239-4090
  South Bend *(G-12734)*

Color Master Inc ....D........ 260 868-2320
Butler *(G-1226)*

Com-Tech Plastics Inc ....F........ 812 423-8270
Evansville *(G-3424)*

Crosspoint Polymer Tech LLC ....D........ 812 426-1350
Evansville *(G-3445)*

DSM Engineering Plastics Inc ....F........ 812 435-7500
Evansville *(G-3463)*

◆ DSM Engineering Plastics Inc ....C........ 248 530-5500
Evansville *(G-3465)*

▲ Enviroplas Inc ....D........ 812 868-0808
Evansville *(G-3480)*

▲ Matrixx-Qtr Inc ....D........ 812 429-0901
Evansville *(G-3619)*

McCammon Engineering Corp ....G........ 812 356-4455
Sullivan *(G-13086)*

Miller Waste Mills Inc ....E........ 507 454-6900
Indianapolis *(G-7522)*

Mwf LLC ....G........ 812 936-5303
West Baden Springs *(G-14035)*

Pmw Holdings LLC ....G........ 317 339-4685
Indianapolis *(G-7703)*

Polyone Corporation ....G........ 812 466-5116
Terre Haute *(G-13305)*

Polyram Compounds LLC ....G........ 703 439-7945
Evansville *(G-3679)*

◆ Sabic Innovative Plastics Mt V ......A........ 812 838-4385
Mount Vernon *(G-10407)*

Testworth Laboratories Inc ....F........ 260 244-5137
Columbia City *(G-1840)*

3088 Plastic Plumbing Fixtures

Altec Engineering Inc ....E........ 574 293-1965
Elkhart *(G-2679)*

Black Tie Manufacturing Inc ....G........ 574 971-6034
Elkhart *(G-2726)*

Frontline Mfg Inc ....D........ 574 269-6751
Warsaw *(G-13878)*

Frontline Mfg Inc ....D........ 574 453-2902
Warsaw *(G-13879)*

◆ Geberit Manufacturing Inc ....E........ 219 879-4466
Michigan City *(G-9797)*

▲ Hotel Vanities Intl LLC ....F........ 317 787-2330
Indianapolis *(G-7136)*

▲ Imperial Marble Incorporated ....F........ 812 752-5384
Scottsburg *(G-12364)*

Maax Inc ....E........ 574 936-3838
Plymouth *(G-11704)*

Nibco Inc ....C........ 574 296-1240
Goshen *(G-5298)*

Oasis Lifestyle LLC ....E........ 574 948-0004
Plymouth *(G-11708)*

▲ Royal Spa Corporation ....D........ 317 781-0828
Indianapolis *(G-7867)*

Ultra/Glas of Lakeville Inc ....F........ 574 784-8958
Lakeville *(G-9098)*

3089 Plastic Prdts

A Mayes Ing Inc ....G........ 317 925-5777
Indianapolis *(G-6298)*

▲ ABC Industries Inc ....D........ 800 426-0921
Winona Lake *(G-14349)*

ABI Plastics LLC ....G........ 574 294-1700
Elkhart *(G-2662)*

Accelerated Curing Inc ....F........ 260 726-3202
Portland *(G-11807)*

Accu-Mold LLC ....E........ 269 323-0388
Mishawaka *(G-9989)*

◆ Ace Mobility Inc ....G........ 317 241-2444
Indianapolis *(G-6316)*

Adkev Inc ....F........ 574 583-4420
Monticello *(G-10251)*

Affinis Group LLC ....G........ 317 831-3830
Mooresville *(G-10301)*

▲ AK Industries Inc ....D........ 574 936-6022
Plymouth *(G-11662)*

Akka Plastics Inc ....E........ 812 849-9256
Mitchell *(G-10155)*

All Amrcan Shtter Cmpnents LLC ......G........ 260 639-0112
Hoagland *(G-6062)*

Allin Plastics Engraving ....G........ 219 972-2223
Hammond *(G-5838)*

Altec Engineering Inc ....E........ 574 293-1965
Elkhart *(G-2679)*

Amcor Rigid Plastics Usa LLC ....D........ 317 736-4313
Franklin *(G-4867)*

▲ Ameri-Kart Corp ....C........ 574 848-7462
Bristol *(G-1044)*

▲ American Plastic Molding Corp ......C........ 812 752-2292
Scottsburg *(G-12355)*

American Window and Glass Inc ......C........ 812 464-9400
Evansville *(G-3352)*

Anderson Products ....G........ 765 794-4242
Darlington *(G-2359)*

▲ Anderson Products Incorporated ....D........ 574 293-5574
Elkhart *(G-2692)*

Apexx Enterprises LLC ....F........ 812 486-2443
Montgomery *(G-10213)*

Apr Plastic Fabricating Inc ....E........ 206 482-8523
Fort Wayne *(G-4085)*

Apr Plastic Fabricating Inc ....E........ 260 482-8523
Fort Wayne *(G-4086)*

Aptimise Composites LLC ....E........ 260 484-3139
Fort Wayne *(G-4088)*

AR Tee Enterprises Inc ....G........ 574 848-5543
Bristol *(G-1046)*

Arrowhead Plastic Engineering ....E........ 765 286-0533
Muncie *(G-10432)*

Arrowhead Plastic Engineering ....F........ 765 396-9113
Eaton *(G-2581)*

▼ Artek Inc ....E........ 260 484-4222
Fort Wayne *(G-4091)*

▼ Ashley Industrial Molding Inc ....C........ 260 587-9155
Ashley *(G-283)*

Ashley Industrial Molding Inc ....G........ 260 349-1982
Kendallville *(G-8456)*

Assmann Corporation America ....E........ 260 357-3181
Garrett *(G-4995)*

Associated Materials LLC ....G........ 260 451-9072
Fort Wayne *(G-4094)*

Astar Inc ....E........ 574 234-2137
South Bend *(G-12713)*

Auburn Hardwood Molding ....E........ 260 925-5959
Auburn *(G-314)*

Aucilla Incorporated ....E........ 574 234-9036
South Bend *(G-12715)*

B D Custom Manufacturing Inc ....F........ 574 848-0925
Bristol *(G-1047)*

B Plus Enterprises Inc ....G........ 219 733-9404
Wanatah *(G-13821)*

▲ B&B Molders LLC ....D........ 574 259-7838
Mishawaka *(G-10003)*

▲ B&J International LLC ....G........ 260 854-2215
Kendallville *(G-8459)*

Bamar Plastics Inc ....E........ 574 234-4066
South Bend *(G-12720)*

Beach Mold & Tool Inc ....G........ 502 649-9915
Jeffersonville *(G-8328)*

Bee Window Incorporated ....C........ 317 283-8522
Fishers *(G-3876)*

Beechys Molding Plus ....G........ 260 768-7030
Shipshewana *(G-12606)*

Beemak Plastics Inc ....G........ 317 841-4398
Indianapolis *(G-6464)*

Bender Mold & Machine Inc ....F........ 574 255-5176
Mishawaka *(G-10008)*

Bender Products Inc ....E........ 574 255-5350
Mishawaka *(G-10009)*

Berry Film Products Co Inc ....G........ 812 306-2690
Evansville *(G-3374)*

Berry Global Inc ....G........ 812 334-7090
Bloomington *(G-679)*

Berry Global Inc ....G........ 812 424-2904
Bloomington *(G-680)*

Berry Global Inc ....G........ 812 558-3510
Odon *(G-11320)*

Berry Global Inc ....G........ 812 386-1525
Princeton *(G-11865)*

Berry Global Inc ....G........ 765 966-1414
Richmond *(G-11964)*

Berry Global Inc ....E........ 812 867-6671
Evansville *(G-3375)*

Berry Global Inc ....B........ 765 962-4253
Richmond *(G-11965)*

◆ Berry Global Inc ....A........ 812 424-2904
Evansville *(G-3376)*

▼ Berry Global Group Inc ....F........ 812 424-2904
Evansville *(G-3377)*

Berry Plastics Group Inc ....G........ 812 424-2904
Evansville *(G-3378)*

▲ Berry Plastics Ik LLC ....D........ 641 648-5047
Evansville *(G-3379)*

Berry Plastics Opco Inc ....G........ 812 402-2903
Evansville *(G-3380)*

Berry Plastics Opco Inc ....E........ 812 424-2904
Evansville *(G-3381)*

Better Way Partners LLC ....B........ 574 831-3340
New Paris *(G-10975)*

Bhar Incorporated ....G........ 260 749-5168
Fort Wayne *(G-4106)*

Bk International LLC ....G........ 260 639-0112
Hoagland *(G-6063)*

BP Parallel LLC ....G........ 812 424-2904
Evansville *(G-3395)*

▼ Bprex Closure Systems LLC ....G........ 812 424-2904
Evansville *(G-3396)*

Bprex Closures LLC ....D........ 812 424-2904
Evansville *(G-3397)*

Bprex Closures LLC ....D........ 812 424-2904
Evansville *(G-3398)*

Bprex Closures LLC ....B........ 812 867-6671
Evansville *(G-3399)*

Bprex Closures LLC ....D........ 812 386-1525
Princeton *(G-11866)*

Bremen Composites LLC ....E........ 574 546-3791
Bremen *(G-986)*

▲ Brianza USA Corp ....G........ 574 855-9520
Elkhart *(G-2733)*

Buckhorn Inc ....D........ 260 824-0997
Bluffton *(G-870)*

Burco Molding Inc ....D........ 317 773-5699
Noblesville *(G-11074)*

▲ Butler-Macdonald Inc ....D........ 317 872-5115
Indianapolis *(G-6523)*

Bway Corporation ....F........ 317 297-4638
Indianapolis *(G-6525)*

▲ Calico Precision Molding LLC ....E........ 260 484-4500
Fort Wayne *(G-4135)*

Caplas Neptune LLC ....C........ 812 424-2904
Evansville *(G-3410)*

Captive Holdings LLC ....C........ 812 424-2904
Evansville *(G-3411)*

◆ Captive Plastics Inc ....C........ 812 424-2904
Evansville *(G-3412)*

Carr Metal Products Inc ....C........ 317 542-0691
Indianapolis *(G-6558)*

Carrera Manufacturing Inc ....F........ 260 726-9800
Portland *(G-11809)*

Cedar Creek Studios Inc ....G........ 260 627-7320
Leo *(G-9241)*

Central Packaging Inc ....C........ 260 436-7225
Fort Wayne *(G-4143)*

▲ Challenge Plastic Products Inc ......F........ 812 526-0582
Edinburgh *(G-2599)*

Ckc Tool Inc ....G........ 219 285-6415
Morocco *(G-10361)*

Closure Systems Intl Inc ....B........ 765 364-6300
Crawfordsville *(G-2141)*

CMS Technologies Inc ....G........ 219 395-8272
Chesterton *(G-1601)*

▲ Co-Tronics Inc ....F........ 574 722-3850
Peru *(G-11522)*

Color Master Inc ....D........ 260 868-2320
Butler *(G-1226)*

Com-Tech Plastics Inc ....D........ 812 421-3600
Evansville *(G-3423)*

Composites Syndicate LLC ....E........ 260 484-3139
Fort Wayne *(G-4172)*

Concept Tool & Engineering ....G........ 812 352-0055
North Vernon *(G-11249)*

Continental Strl Plas Inc ....C........ 260 355-4011
Huntington *(G-6199)*

◆ Cor-A-Vent Inc ....F........ 574 255-1910
Mishawaka *(G-10023)*

Cor-A-Vent Inc ....E........ 574 258-6161
Mishawaka *(G-10024)*

▲ CPI Card Group - Indiana Inc ....C........ 260 424-4920
Fort Wayne *(G-4182)*

▲ Cpx Inc ....D........ 219 474-5280
Kentland *(G-8519)*

Craddock Finishing Corporation ......E........ 812 425-2691
Evansville *(G-3436)*

Crane Composites ....G........ 574 295-9391
Elkhart *(G-2775)*

Crane Composites Inc ....D........ 815 467-8600
Goshen *(G-5195)*

▲ Crawford Industries LLC ....C........ 800 428-0840
Crawfordsville *(G-2144)*

Crescent Plastics Inc ....D........ 812 428-9305
Evansville *(G-3439)*

Crescent Plastics Inc ....D........ 812 428-9300
Evansville *(G-3440)*

Crescent-Cresline-Wabash Plast ......G........ 812 428-9300
Evansville *(G-3441)*

CT Phoenix of Indiana Inc ....F........ 812 838-2414
Mount Vernon *(G-10391)*

Custom Plastics LLC ....F........ 574 259-2340
Mishawaka *(G-10028)*

Custom Urethanes Inc ....G........ 219 924-1644
Highland *(G-6041)*

D & M Tool Corporation...................E...... 812 279-8882
Springville (G-13062)

D M Sales & Engineering Inc...............E...... 317 783-5493
Indianapolis (G-6722)

D&W Fine Pack LLC.........................B...... 260 432-3027
Fort Wayne (G-4198)

▲ DA Inc.....................................E...... 812 503-2302
Charlestown (G-1562)

▲ Decatur Mold Tool and Engrg.........C...... 812 346-5188
North Vernon (G-11253)

▲ Decatur Plastic Products Inc..........C...... 812 346-5159
North Vernon (G-11255)

Deep Three Inc............................G...... 260 705-2283
Spencerville (G-13045)

▲ Deflecto LLC.............................B...... 317 849-9555
Indianapolis (G-6732)

Dexterous Mold and Tool Inc...............E...... 812 422-8046
Evansville (G-3457)

Diamond Manufacturing Company........E...... 219 874-2374
Michigan City (G-9782)

▲ Digger Specialties Inc.................D...... 574 546-5999
Bremen (G-996)

Display Craft...............................G...... 260 726-4535
Portland (G-11816)

▲ Diversity-Vuteq LLC....................C...... 812 761-0210
Princeton (G-11868)

Dorel Juvenile Group Inc..................G...... 812 372-0141
Columbus (G-1911)

Dorel Juvenile Group Inc..................G...... 812 372-0141
Columbus (G-1913)

Drug Plastics Closures Inc................D...... 812 526-0555
Edinburgh (G-2608)

Eckco Inc..................................G...... 574 257-0299
Mishawaka (G-10039)

Eis Fibercoating Inc.......................E...... 574 722-5192
Logansport (G-9334)

Electro Transfer Systems Inc..............D...... 574 234-0600
Mishawaka (G-10040)

Elkcases Inc...............................E...... 574 295-7700
Elkhart (G-2819)

▲ Elkhart Cases Inc.......................E...... 574 295-7700
Elkhart (G-2823)

Elkhart Plastics Inc.......................E...... 574 389-9911
Elkhart (G-2827)

Elkhart Plastics Inc.......................D...... 574 232-8066
South Bend (G-12760)

Elkhart Plastics Inc.......................E...... 574 370-1079
Michigan City (G-9788)

Elkhart Plastics Inc.......................D...... 574 232-8066
South Bend (G-12761)

Elkhart Plastics Inc.......................C...... 574 825-9797
Middlebury (G-9884)

Engineered Rubber & Plastics...........F...... 574 254-1405
Mishawaka (G-10041)

Engrave Inc................................F...... 812 537-8693
Lawrenceburg (G-9140)

Enovapremier LLC.........................D...... 812 385-0576
Princeton (G-11870)

Exhibit A Plastics LLC.....................E...... 765 386-6702
Coatesville (G-1749)

Exo-S US LLC.............................B...... 260 562-4131
Howe (G-6123)

Exo-S US LLC.............................C...... 260 562-4100
Howe (G-6124)

◆ Exo-S US LLC...........................C...... 260 562-4100
Howe (G-6125)

Exton Inc..................................D...... 574 533-0447
Goshen (G-5212)

▲ Fairview Fittings & Mfg................G...... 574 206-8884
Elkhart (G-2843)

▲ Fas Plastic Enterprises Inc...........D...... 812 265-2928
Hanover (G-5960)

Fiberglas & Plastic Fabg..................E...... 317 549-1779
Indianapolis (G-6917)

▼ Fibertech Inc............................D...... 812 983-2642
Elberfeld (G-2635)

Filtration Parts Incorporated..............F...... 704 661-8135
Rensselaer (G-11923)

First Metals & Plastics Inc................E...... 812 379-4400
Columbus (G-1930)

First Place Trophy Inc.....................G...... 574 293-6147
Elkhart (G-2850)

Flair Molded Plastics Inc..................D...... 812 425-6155
Evansville (G-3508)

Flambeau Inc..............................C...... 812 372-4899
Columbus (G-1931)

Flexseals Manufacturing LLC..............G...... 574 293-0333
Elkhart (G-2856)

Flw Plastics Inc...........................E...... 812 546-0050
Hope (G-6112)

Focus Mold & Machine Inc.................G...... 812 422-9627
Evansville (G-3511)

Form/TEC Plastics Incorporated..........E...... 765 342-2300
Martinsville (G-9608)

▲ Fort Wayne Plastics Inc...............C...... 260 432-2520
Fort Wayne (G-4278)

Fred Smith Store Fixtures Inc..............E...... 812 347-2363
Depauw (G-2456)

▲ Futaba Indiana America Corp..........B...... 812 895-4700
Vincennes (G-13683)

Future Mold Inc............................F...... 812 941-8661
New Albany (G-10785)

Futurex Industries Inc......................E...... 765 498-8900
Bloomingdale (G-648)

General Fabricators Inc....................G...... 317 787-9354
Indianapolis (G-6996)

▲ Genesis Molding Inc...................D...... 574 256-9271
Mishawaka (G-10046)

▲ Genesis Plastics and Engrg LLC......C...... 812 752-6742
Scottsburg (G-12357)

Genesis Plastics Solutions LLC...........G...... 812 283-4435
Jeffersonville (G-8368)

▲ Genesis Plastics Welding Inc.........E...... 317 485-7887
Fortville (G-4776)

Genova Products Inc.......................D...... 219 866-5136
Rensselaer (G-11925)

Genpak LLC................................C...... 812 752-3111
Scottsburg (G-12358)

Global Plastics Inc........................D...... 317 299-2345
Indianapolis (G-7012)

Graber Manufacturing LLC.................G...... 260 657-3400
Grabill (G-5367)

Grafco Industries Ltd Partnr...............G...... 812 424-2904
Evansville (G-3522)

Graham Packaging Company LP...........D...... 812 868-8012
Evansville (G-3523)

▲ Green Leaf Inc..........................C...... 812 877-1546
Fontanet (G-4024)

Green Plus Plastics LLC...................G...... 317 672-2410
Indianapolis (G-7041)

Greenville Technology Inc..................F...... 765 221-7576
Anderson (G-113)

▲ Group Dekko Inc........................D...... 260 357-3621
Garrett (G-5009)

▲ Grrk Holdings Inc.......................E...... 317 872-0172
Indianapolis (G-7053)

H & W Molders............................G...... 812 423-9340
Evansville (G-3527)

▲ H A P Industries Inc....................G...... 765 948-3385
Jonesboro (G-8445)

H and H 3d Plastics Inc....................G...... 812 699-0379
Linton (G-9307)

H W Molders...............................G...... 812 423-3552
Evansville (G-3528)

Hagerstown Plastics Inc....................G...... 765 939-3849
Richmond (G-11994)

Hancor Inc.................................E...... 812 443-2080
Brazil (G-964)

Hart Plastics Inc...........................E...... 574 264-7060
Elkhart (G-2909)

Hartland Products Inc......................E...... 219 778-9034
Rolling Prairie (G-12187)

Helfrich Engineering Inc....................G...... 812 985-3118
Evansville (G-3537)

Holzmeyer Die & Mold Mfg Corp..........E...... 812 386-6015
Princeton (G-11876)

▲ Home Guard Industries Inc............D...... 260 627-6060
Grabill (G-5372)

Home Pdts Intl - N Amer Inc...............B...... 773 890-1010
Seymour (G-12456)

Hoosier Badge & Trophies Inc.............G...... 317 257-4441
Indianapolis (G-7120)

▲ Hoosier Custom Plastics LLC..........E...... 574 772-2120
Knox (G-8567)

Hoosier Fiberglass Industries..............G...... 812 232-5027
Terre Haute (G-13248)

Hoosier Pride Plastics Inc..................E...... 260 497-7080
Fort Wayne (G-4345)

Hopper Development Inc....................F...... 574 753-6621
Logansport (G-9336)

Hot Stamping & Printing....................G...... 219 767-2429
Union Mills (G-13463)

Ie Products Mad Dasher Inc................E...... 260 747-0545
Fort Wayne (G-4357)

Illinois Tool Works Inc......................C...... 260 347-8040
Kendallville (G-8480)

▲ Ilpea Industries Inc.....................D...... 812 752-2526
Scottsburg (G-12362)

▲ Indiana Plastics Inc....................E...... 574 294-3253
Elkhart (G-2932)

Indiana Precision Plastics Inc..............F...... 765 762-2452
Williamsport (G-14292)

▲ Indiana Vac-Form.......................F...... 574 269-1725
Warsaw (G-13892)

Indus LLC..................................G...... 502 553-1770
New Albany (G-10806)

Indy Parts Inc..............................G...... 317 243-7171
Indianapolis (G-7219)

Injection Plastic & Mfg Co..................F...... 574 784-2070
Lapaz (G-9117)

Innovative Corp............................E...... 317 804-5977
Westfield (G-14171)

Innovative Mold & Machine Inc............G...... 317 634-1177
Indianapolis (G-7238)

Inside Systems.............................G...... 317 831-3772
Mooresville (G-10314)

Integer Holdings Corporation...............C...... 317 454-8800
Indianapolis (G-7246)

Integrity Molding Inc.......................G...... 812 524-1243
Seymour (G-12459)

Integrity Rttional Molding LLC..............E...... 317 837-1101
Plainfield (G-11618)

Interactive Engineering Inc.................G...... 574 272-5851
Granger (G-5415)

▲ Irvine Shade & Door Inc...............D...... 574 522-1446
Elkhart (G-2940)

J H J Inc...................................G...... 574 256-6966
Mishawaka (G-10055)

J Plus Products Inc........................G...... 317 660-1003
Carmel (G-1418)

◆ Jadcore LLC.............................C...... 812 234-2724
Terre Haute (G-13260)

▼ Jeco Plastic Products LLC..............F...... 317 839-4943
Plainfield (G-11621)

Jet Technologies Inc.......................G...... 574 264-3613
Elkhart (G-2948)

JMS Engineered Plastics Inc...............D...... 574 277-3228
South Bend (G-12823)

Jones Machine & Tool Inc..................E...... 812 364-4588
Fredericksburg (G-4945)

▲ K&M Indiana LLC.......................C...... 812 256-3351
Charlestown (G-1569)

Kautex Inc.................................B...... 937 238-8096
Avilla (G-409)

Kenco Plastics Inc.........................F...... 219 324-6621
La Porte (G-8777)

Kenco Plastics Inc.........................F...... 219 362-7565
La Porte (G-8778)

Kenco Plastics Inc.........................F...... 219 326-5501
La Porte (G-8779)

Kendrion (mishawaka) LLC.................E...... 574 257-2422
Mishawaka (G-10063)

Kerr Group LLC............................D...... 812 424-2904
Evansville (G-3585)

Keusch Glass Inc..........................F...... 812 482-2566
Jasper (G-8271)

▲ Khorporate Holdings Inc...............C...... 260 357-3365
Laotto (G-9110)

▲ Kibbechem Inc..........................E...... 574 266-1234
Elkhart (G-2964)

Kimball Electronics Inc.....................E...... 317 357-3175
Indianapolis (G-7350)

Kimball Electronics Inc.....................D...... 317 545-5383
Indianapolis (G-7351)

▲ Kn Platech America Corporation......E...... 317 392-7707
Shelbyville (G-12544)

Kyle Machine & Tool Inc....................E...... 317 736-4743
Franklin (G-4904)

Laird Plastics Inc..........................G...... 317 890-1808
Indianapolis (G-7375)

◆ Lasalle Bristol Corporation............C...... 574 295-4400
Elkhart (G-2985)

Lepark Mold & Tool........................C...... 574 262-0518
Elkhart (G-2995)

Letica Corporation.........................C...... 248 652-0557
Fremont (G-4966)

Life Management Inc.......................G...... 260 747-7408
Fort Wayne (G-4435)

▲ Lighthouse Industries Inc..............E...... 219 879-1550
Michigan City (G-9811)

▲ Lincoln Industries Inc..................E...... 812 897-0715
Boonville (G-915)

Link Engineering LLC......................G...... 765 457-1166
Kokomo (G-8659)

▲ Lorentson Manufacturing Co..........E...... 765 452-4425
Kokomo (G-8660)

Lukemeier Indus Mold & Mch Co.........E...... 812 945-3375
New Albany (G-10821)

M&M Performance Inc......................G...... 574 536-6103
Goshen (G-5276)

S
I
C

Madillion Plastics Inc ....G...... 574 293-4434
Elkhart *(G-3014)*

Makuta Technics Inc ....F....... 317 642-0001
Shelbyville *(G-12550)*

◆ Manar Inc ....C....... 812 526-2891
Edinburgh *(G-2617)*

Manar Inc ....E....... 812 346-2858
North Vernon *(G-11268)*

Marco Plastics Inc ....F....... 812 333-0062
Bloomington *(G-769)*

Mary Jonas ....F....... 317 500-0600
Indianapolis *(G-7462)*

Mayco International LLC ....F....... 765 348-5780
Hartford City *(G-5984)*

Meese Inc ....D...... 812 273-1008
Madison *(G-9485)*

▲ Metro Plastics Tech Inc ....D...... 317 776-0860
Noblesville *(G-11148)*

▲ Meyer Plastics Inc ....D...... 317 259-4131
Indianapolis *(G-7493)*

Meyer Plastics Inc ....G...... 765 447-2195
Lafayette *(G-8967)*

Mgtc Inc ....G...... 317 873-8697
Zionsville *(G-14448)*

Mide Products LLC ....G...... 574 333-5906
Goshen *(G-5290)*

Midwest Rotational Molding LLC ....F...... 574 294-6891
Elkhart *(G-3040)*

Midwest-Tek Inc ....G...... 812 981-3551
New Albany *(G-10830)*

Mike H Inc ....G...... 574 262-0518
Elkhart *(G-3041)*

▲ Models LLC ....E....... 765 676-6700
Lebanon *(G-9207)*

Mossberg Industries Inc ....D...... 260 357-5141
Garrett *(G-5018)*

▲ Msca LLC ....G...... 574 583-6220
Monticello *(G-10272)*

MTA Technology LLC ....F....... 765 447-2221
Lafayette *(G-8973)*

▲ Mullinix Packages Inc ....C....... 260 747-3149
Fort Wayne *(G-4483)*

▲ Mytex Polymers US Corp ....E....... 812 280-2900
Jeffersonville *(G-8402)*

Neptune Flotation LLC ....F....... 317 588-3600
Indianapolis *(G-6274)*

New Market Plastics Inc ....F....... 317 758-5494
Ladoga *(G-8841)*

▼ Nexgen Mold & Tool Inc ....E....... 812 945-3375
New Albany *(G-10833)*

Nibco Inc ....E....... 812 256-8500
Charlestown *(G-1576)*

Nibco Inc ....C....... 574 296-1240
Goshen *(G-5298)*

Nibco Inc ....F....... 812 256-8500
Charlestown *(G-1577)*

◆ Nibco Inc ....B....... 574 295-3000
Elkhart *(G-3062)*

North America Packaging Corp ....C....... 219 462-8915
Valparaiso *(G-13592)*

▲ North American Extrusn & Assem ...E....... 260 636-3336
Albion *(G-30)*

Norton Packaging Inc ....E....... 574 867-6002
Hamlet *(G-5831)*

▲ Nyloncraft Inc ....B....... 574 256-1521
Mishawaka *(G-10098)*

Odyssey Machine Inc ....G...... 812 951-1160
Georgetown *(G-5151)*

Olympic Fiberglass Industries ....D...... 574 223-3101
Rochester *(G-12142)*

Omni Technologies Inc ....D...... 812 537-4102
Greendale *(G-5492)*

Osborn Manufacturing Corp ....F....... 574 267-6156
Warsaw *(G-13920)*

▼ OTech Corporation ....D...... 219 778-8001
Rolling Prairie *(G-12190)*

▲ Outsource Technologies Inc ......E....... 574 233-1303
South Bend *(G-12884)*

Panolam Industries Inc ....E....... 574 264-0702
Elkhart *(G-3073)*

Paragon Medical Inc ....G...... 574 594-2140
Pierceton *(G-11575)*

▲ Paragon Medical Inc ....G...... 574 594-2140
Pierceton *(G-11576)*

Paramount Plastics Inc ....E....... 574 264-2143
Elkhart *(G-3074)*

Patrick Industries Inc ....E....... 574 293-1521
Elkhart *(G-3084)*

Patrick Industries Inc ....C....... 574 294-8828
Elkhart *(G-3088)*

Patrick Industries Inc ....C....... 574 546-5222
Bremen *(G-1014)*

Patrick Industries Inc ....D...... 260 665-6112
Angola *(G-235)*

Paul Tirotta ....F....... 574 255-4101
Mishawaka *(G-10102)*

▲ Paxxal Inc ....G...... 317 296-7724
Noblesville *(G-11164)*

Pent Assemblies ....D...... 260 347-5828
Kendallville *(G-8501)*

▲ Pent Plastics Inc ....C....... 260 897-3775
Kendallville *(G-8502)*

▲ Penz Products Inc ....E....... 574 255-4736
Mishawaka *(G-10103)*

Perfect Manufacturing LLC ....E....... 317 924-5284
Indianapolis *(G-7675)*

Perfect Pallets Inc ....D...... 888 553-5559
Indianapolis *(G-7676)*

Permalatt Products Inc ....G...... 574 546-6311
Bremen *(G-1015)*

Phoenix Closures Inc ....D...... 765 658-1800
Greencastle *(G-5472)*

Pier-Mac Plastics Inc ....E....... 260 726-9844
Portland *(G-11839)*

◆ Pk USA Inc ....F....... 317 395-5500
Shelbyville *(G-12558)*

Plas-Tech Molding & Design Inc ....F....... 260 761-3006
Brimfield *(G-1036)*

Plastic Components Inc ....E....... 574 264-7514
Elkhart *(G-3099)*

Plastic Extrusions Company ....G...... 812 479-3232
Evansville *(G-3674)*

Plastic Molding Mfg Inc ....E....... 574 234-9036
South Bend *(G-12897)*

Plastic Moldings Company Llc ....C....... 317 392-4139
Shelbyville *(G-12559)*

Plastic Package LLC ....F....... 916 921-3399
La Porte *(G-8804)*

Plastic Processors Inc ....D...... 260 488-3999
Hamilton *(G-5827)*

Plastics Fabg & Distrg LLC ....G...... 574 233-7527
South Bend *(G-12898)*

▲ Plastics Research and Dev Inc ......E....... 812 279-8885
Springville *(G-13066)*

▼ Pliant Corp International ....G...... 812 424-2904
Evansville *(G-3675)*

Pliant International LLC ....G...... 812 424-2904
Evansville *(G-3676)*

Pliant Packaging Canada LLC ....G...... 812 424-2904
Evansville *(G-3677)*

▲ Poly HI Solidur Inc ....B....... 260 479-4100
Fort Wayne *(G-4537)*

◆ Poly-Seal LLC ....A....... 812 306-2573
Evansville *(G-3678)*

Polycon Industries Inc ....E....... 219 738-1000
Merrillville *(G-9748)*

Polygon ....G...... 317 240-1130
Indianapolis *(G-7705)*

◆ Polyjohn Enterprises Corp ....D...... 219 659-1152
Whiting *(G-14273)*

Polymer Equipment Co Inc ....G...... 765 855-3448
Centerville *(G-1543)*

Poppy Co ....G...... 317 442-2491
Brownsburg *(G-1164)*

PRC - Desoto International Inc ....F....... 317 290-1600
Indianapolis *(G-7728)*

Precision Plastics Indiana Inc ....C....... 260 244-6114
Columbia City *(G-1819)*

Precision Products Group Inc ....C....... 301 474-3100
Indianapolis *(G-6277)*

Premier Fiberglass Co Inc ....E....... 574 264-5457
Elkhart *(G-3110)*

▼ Primex Design Fabrication Corp ......D...... 765 935-2990
Richmond *(G-12033)*

▼ Priority Plastics Inc ....D...... 260 726-7000
Portland *(G-11843)*

▼ Pro-Form Plastics Inc ....E....... 812 522-4433
Crothersville *(G-2220)*

Prodigy Mold & Tool Inc ....E....... 812 753-3029
Haubstadt *(G-6004)*

▲ Production Plastic Molding ....G...... 317 872-4669
Indianapolis *(G-7769)*

▲ Progressive Plastics Inc ....F....... 765 552-2004
Elwood *(G-3310)*

Prolon Inc ....E....... 574 522-8900
Elkhart *(G-3119)*

◆ PSI Molded Plastics Ind Inc ......C....... 574 288-2100
South Bend *(G-12907)*

PTG Silicones Inc ....G...... 812 948-8719
New Albany *(G-10850)*

Puck Supply & Machine LLC ....F....... 574 293-3333
Elkhart *(G-3122)*

Pyramid Plastic Group Inc ....G...... 260 327-3145
Larwill *(G-9124)*

Quad 4 Plastics Inc ....E....... 574 293-8660
Elkhart *(G-3126)*

▲ Quality Molded Products Inc ......D...... 574 272-3733
South Bend *(G-12909)*

▲ Quality Plastics and Engrg Inc ......E....... 574 262-2621
Elkhart *(G-3128)*

R & R Plastics Inc ....D...... 219 393-5505
Kingsbury *(G-8545)*

R & R Technologies LLC ....E....... 812 526-2655
Edinburgh *(G-2623)*

R R Forrest Company Inc ....G...... 317 502-3286
Noblesville *(G-11169)*

R3 Composites Corp ....D...... 260 627-0033
Grabill *(G-5383)*

Ram North America Inc ....F....... 317 984-1971
Arcadia *(G-268)*

Red Star Contract Mfg Inc ....G...... 260 327-3145
Larwill *(G-9125)*

▲ Remco Products Corporation ......F....... 317 876-9856
Zionsville *(G-14460)*

Reschcor Inc ....E....... 574 295-2413
Bristol *(G-1079)*

Reschcor Inc ....E....... 574 295-2413
Elkhart *(G-3143)*

▲ Resin Partners Inc ....C....... 765 298-6800
Anderson *(G-161)*

Revere Industries LLC ....E....... 317 580-2420
Westfield *(G-14184)*

Revere Plastics Systems LLC ....G...... 812 670-2240
Jeffersonville *(G-8419)*

▼ Richardson Molding LLC ....C....... 812 342-0139
Columbus *(G-2008)*

Richardson Molding LLC ....G...... 317 787-9463
Indianapolis *(G-7839)*

▲ Rieke Corporation ....B....... 260 925-3700
Auburn *(G-349)*

River Valley Plastics Inc ....E....... 574 262-5221
Elkhart *(G-3148)*

Rix Products Inc ....G...... 812 426-1749
Evansville *(G-3706)*

▼ Rochester Rttional Molding Inc ......F....... 574 223-8844
Rochester *(G-12149)*

Roi Marketing Company ....G...... 317 644-0797
Indianapolis *(G-7855)*

Rotational Molding Tech Inc ....D...... 574 831-6450
New Paris *(G-10993)*

Royal Outdoor Products Inc ....C....... 574 658-9442
Milford *(G-9964)*

▲ Royer Corporation ....D...... 800 457-8997
Madison *(G-9493)*

▲ Sabin Corporation ....C....... 812 323-4500
Bloomington *(G-820)*

Sanko Gosei Tech USA Inc ....E....... 260 749-5168
Fort Wayne *(G-4605)*

Schlabach Window & Glass LLC ....G...... 765 628-2024
Kokomo *(G-8691)*

Shadowhouse Jiu-Jitsu Inc ....E....... 219 873-4556
La Porte *(G-8819)*

Silgan Plastics Corporation ....G...... 812 522-0900
Seymour *(G-12489)*

Silgan Plastics LLC ....F....... 812 522-0900
Seymour *(G-12491)*

Smiths Enterprises Inc ....G...... 765 378-6267
Chesterfield *(G-1589)*

Sonoco Prtective Solutions Inc ....D...... 260 726-9333
Portland *(G-11847)*

Southern Indiana Plastics Inc ....E....... 812 280-7474
Jeffersonville *(G-8425)*

Special Product Services Inc ....F....... 260 632-1302
Woodburn *(G-14390)*

▲ Spencer Industries Inc ....C....... 812 937-4561
Dale *(G-2333)*

▲ Spin-Cast Plastics Inc ....D...... 574 232-8066
South Bend *(G-12949)*

Splendor Boats LLC ....F....... 260 352-2835
Silver Lake *(G-12681)*

▲ Srg Global Trim Inc ....A....... 812 473-6200
Evansville *(G-3745)*

Standard Plastic Corp ....F....... 260 824-0214
Bluffton *(G-893)*

Starquest Products LLC ....G...... 574 537-0486
Goshen *(G-5330)*

▼ Sterling Berry Corporation ....G...... 812 424-2904
Evansville *(G-3749)*

Stien Designs & Graphics Inc ....G...... 260 347-9136
Kendallville *(G-8511)*

◆ Stoffel Seals Corporation ....E 845 353-3800
  Angola (G-248)
▼ Syndicate Sales Inc ....B 765 457-7277
  Kokomo (G-8704)
Taghleef Industries Inc ....A 302 326-5500
  Rosedale (G-12208)
▲ Tasus Corporation ....C 812 333-6500
  Bloomington (G-834)
TEC-Air LLC ....D 219 301-7084
  Munster (G-10632)
Tech Group North America Inc ....C 765 650-2300
  Frankfort (G-4855)
▲ Tecnoplast Usa LLC ....G 317 769-4929
  Anderson (G-174)
Tedco Inc ....G 765 489-5807
  Hagerstown (G-5815)
Tekmodo Structures LLC ....G 574 970-5800
  Elkhart (G-3210)
Templeton Coal Company Inc ....G 812 232-7037
  Terre Haute (G-13350)
Therma-Tru Corp ....F 260 868-5811
  Butler (G-1245)
Thermform Engineered Qulty LLC ......F 260 495-9842
  Fremont (G-4977)
▲ Thorgren Tool & Molding Co ....D 219 462-1801
  Valparaiso (G-13628)
Thrust Industries Inc ....F 812 437-3643
  Evansville (G-3762)
Tj Maintenance LLC ....G 219 776-8427
  Lake Village (G-9088)
▼ Tomken Plastic Tech Inc ....E 765 284-2472
  Muncie (G-10572)
Topp Industries Incorporated ....D 574 223-3681
  Rochester (G-12157)
Tredegar Corporation ....D 812 466-0266
  Terre Haute (G-13356)
▲ Trellborg Sling Sltions US Inc ......E 260 749-9631
  Fort Wayne (G-4700)
Trim-Lok Inc ....G 574 227-1143
  Elkhart (G-3223)
Trivalence Technologies LLC ....G 800 209-2517
  Evansville (G-3776)
▲ Tru-Form Steel & Wire Inc ....E 765 348-5001
  Hartford City (G-5993)
Tru-Form Steel & Wire Inc ....E 765 348-5001
  Hartford City (G-5994)
▲ Tulox Plastics Corporation ....C 765 664-5155
  Marion (G-9568)
US Molders Inc ....E 219 984-5058
  Reynolds (G-11949)
V N C Inc ....F 219 696-5031
  Lowell (G-9425)
Vee Engineering Inc ....G 765 778-7895
  Anderson (G-181)
Vee Engineering Inc ....D 260 424-6635
  Fort Wayne (G-4725)
Vixen Composites LLC ....F 574 970-1224
  Elkhart (G-3250)
Vytec Inc ....E 574 277-4295
  Granger (G-5450)
▲ Wabash Plastics Inc ....B 812 428-9300
  Evansville (G-3806)
Wabash Plastics Inc ....E 812 867-2447
  Evansville (G-3807)
Warnke Associates Inc ....G 574 586-3331
  Walkerton (G-13814)
Waste 1 ....G 765 477-9138
  Lafayette (G-9021)
Webco Inc ....G 260 244-4233
  Columbia City (G-1847)
Western Consolidated Tech Inc ....D 260 495-9866
  Fremont (G-4982)
▲ Williams Plastics LLC ....C 317 398-1630
  Shelbyville (G-12585)
Wilmes Window Mfg Co Inc ....E 812 275-7575
  Ferdinand (G-3864)
Wunder Co Inc ....F 219 962-8573
  Lake Station (G-9081)
Yanfeng US Automotive ....C 260 347-0500
  Kendallville (G-8515)
York Group Inc ....G 765 966-0077
  Richmond (G-12079)
ZF North America Inc ....B 765 429-1984
  Lafayette (G-9028)

31 LEATHER AND LEATHER PRODUCTS

3111 Leather Tanning & Finishing

Clinton Harness Shop ....G 574 533-9797
  Goshen (G-5189)
Color Glo ....G 812 926-2639
  Aurora (G-375)
▲ Fbf Originals Inc ....G 765 349-7474
  Martinsville (G-9603)
Horse N Around Animal & Tack ....G 765 618-2032
  Upland (G-13471)
▲ Liberty Book & Bb Manufactures ....E 317 633-1450
  Indianapolis (G-7402)
Royal Acres Equestrian Center ....G 219 874-7519
  Michigan City (G-9836)
Vera Bradley Inc ....B 877 708-8372
  Roanoke (G-12110)

3131 Boot & Shoe Cut Stock & Findings

Air Feet LLC ....G 317 441-1817
  Greenwood (G-5663)
Comfort Quarters Conversions ....G 574 262-3701
  Elkhart (G-2763)
Fat Quarter Annies Qui ....G 317 918-1481
  Monrovia (G-10203)
Indiana KY III Interstate Qua ....G 812 985-9966
  Mount Vernon (G-10395)
▲ Karran USA ....G 410 975-0128
  Vincennes (G-13688)
Pfrank Quarter Horses ....G 765 220-0257
  Richmond (G-12029)
Simple Quarters LLC ....G 812 216-8602
  Cicero (G-1667)
Suke Inc ....G 219 689-0321
  Crown Point (G-2311)
Top Design Cnc Inc ....G 219 662-2915
  Valparaiso (G-13629)
Upper Level Networks ....G 317 863-0955
  Westfield (G-14197)
Upper Level Sports LLC ....G 317 681-3754
  Indianapolis (G-8132)

3143 Men's Footwear, Exc Athletic

Him Gentlemans Boutique ....G 812 924-7441
  New Albany (G-10793)
Red Wing Shoe Company Inc ....G 317 219-6777
  Noblesville (G-11174)

3149 Footwear, NEC

Carl Dyers Original Moccasins ....G 812 667-5442
  Friendship (G-4991)
Integrated Orthotic Lab Inc ....G 317 852-4640
  Brownsburg (G-1156)
Marios Athletic Zone ....G 219 845-1800
  Hammond (G-5913)
Onfield Apparel Group LLC ....G 317 895-7249
  Indianapolis (G-7622)

3151 Leather Gloves & Mittens

5m Poultry LLC ....G 812 890-5558
  Carlisle (G-1294)
Glove Corporation ....D 501 362-2437
  Alexandria (G-43)

3161 Luggage

American Tourister ....G 812 526-0344
  Edinburgh (G-2594)
C H Ellis LLC ....E 317 636-3351
  Indianapolis (G-6528)
Carr Metal Products Inc ....C 317 542-0691
  Indianapolis (G-6558)
▲ CH Ellis Co Inc ....E 317 636-3351
  Indianapolis (G-6592)
▲ Cinda B USA LLC ....G 260 469-0803
  Fort Wayne (G-4150)
◆ Derby Inc ....D 574 233-4500
  South Bend (G-12751)
Ds Wood Products Inc ....G 574 642-3855
  Goshen (G-5205)
Elkcases Inc ....E 574 295-7700
  Elkhart (G-2819)
▲ Humes & Berg Mfg Co Inc ....G 219 391-5880
  East Chicago (G-2534)
Indiana Dimensional Pdts LLC ....D 574 834-7681
  North Webster (G-11293)

L M Products Inc ....E 765 643-3802
  Anderson (G-132)
Leed Selling Tools Corp ....C 812 482-7888
  Ireland (G-8229)
Markley Enterprise Inc ....D 574 295-4195
  Elkhart (G-3018)
◆ MTS Products Corp ....E 574 295-3142
  Elkhart (G-3054)
MTS Products Corp ....F 574 295-3142
  Elkhart (G-3055)
One Stop Travel Shop Inc ....G 812 339-9496
  Bloomington (G-789)
Oxford Industries Inc ....G 317 569-0866
  Indianapolis (G-7640)
▲ Porter Case Inc ....G 574 289-2616
  South Bend (G-12901)
Raine Inc ....F 765 622-7687
  Anderson (G-157)
Seed & Satchel LLC ....G 317 892-2557
  Pittsboro (G-11587)
Skirt & Satchel ....G 812 727-0292
  Bloomington (G-824)
▲ Td Innovations ....G 530 477-9780
  Bloomington (G-835)
▲ Tetrafab Corporation ....E 812 258-0000
  Floyds Knobs (G-4021)
Traveling Satchel LLC ....G 317 502-3241
  Indianapolis (G-8091)

3171 Handbags & Purses

Amanda Elizabeth LLC ....G 602 317-9633
  Fort Wayne (G-4066)
Aubry Lane LLC ....G 317 644-6372
  Indianapolis (G-6439)
CM Reed LLC ....G 517 546-4100
  Greendale (G-5485)
Maloney Group Inc ....F 812 285-7400
  Jeffersonville (G-8395)
Vera Bradley Inc ....E 219 878-1093
  Michigan City (G-9858)
Vera Bradley Inc ....C 260 482-4673
  Roanoke (G-12109)
Vera Bradley Inc ....B 877 708-8372
  Roanoke (G-12110)
Vera Bradley International LLC ....G 260 482-4673
  Roanoke (G-12111)

3172 Personal Leather Goods

Long Leather Works LLC ....G 812 336-5309
  Bloomington (G-767)
Maloney Group Inc ....F 812 285-7400
  Jeffersonville (G-8395)
Moonshine Leather Company Inc ....F 812 988-1326
  Nashville (G-10730)
Pit Bull Leather Company Inc ....G 812 988-6007
  Nashville (G-10733)
Sleepy Hollow Leather Inc ....G 219 926-1071
  Chesterton (G-1630)
Wallets Belts & Stuff LLC ....G 219 218-3576
  Whiting (G-14276)

3199 Leather Goods, NEC

Campbell Pet Company ....G 812 692-5208
  Elnora (G-3287)
Daltech Enterprises Inc ....G 260 527-4590
  Fremont (G-4957)
De Masqu Productions Ltd ....G 812 556-0061
  Jasper (G-8244)
Fast Holster LLC ....G 317 727-5243
  Indianapolis (G-6264)
Hilltop Leather ....G 317 831-4855
  Mooresville (G-10310)
Indy Holsters LLC ....G 317 370-7451
  Brownsburg (G-1152)
Judson Harness & Saddlery ....G 765 569-0918
  Rockville (G-12176)
L M Products Inc ....E 765 643-3802
  Anderson (G-132)
Mad Hatters Unlimited ....G 219 852-6011
  Hammond (G-5910)
Midwest Leather & Vinyl ....G 574 266-1700
  Elkhart (G-3039)
Sand Designs Inc ....G 574 293-5791
  Elkhart (G-3155)
Schutz Brothers Inc ....F 260 982-8581
  North Manchester (G-11244)
◆ Scott Pet Products Inc ....C 765 569-4636
  Rockville (G-12180)
Southern Indiana Collar Co ....G 812 486-3714
  Montgomery (G-10242)

Whisler Custom Leather Co...............G........ 765 212-8932
Muncie (G-10583)

32 STONE, CLAY, GLASS, AND CONCRETE PRODUCTS

3211 Flat Glass

Calumite Company LLC..............F...... 219 787-8667
Portage (G-11753)
Capitol City Glass Inc...............G...... 317 635-2556
Indianapolis (G-6550)
Carlex Glass America LLC.............B...... 260 925-5656
Auburn (G-320)
Carlex Indiana Assembly ....E...... 765 471-9399
Lafayette (G-8867)
Ceran Inc...................................G...... 812 882-2680
Vincennes (G-13673)
▲ Cleer Vision Tempered GL LLC ....E...... 574 262-0449
Elkhart (G-2758)
Fox Studios Inc ....F...... 317 253-0135
Indianapolis (G-6953)
Graber Therm-O-Loc Windows.........G...... 812 486-3273
Montgomery (G-10225)
Guardian Industries LLC ....G...... 812 422-6987
Evansville (G-3525)
Indiana Bevel Inc.........................G...... 317 596-0001
Fishers (G-3928)
Indy Glass Center Inc ....F...... 317 591-5000
Indianapolis (G-7217)
Lippert Components Mfg Inc ....C...... 574 935-5122
Plymouth (G-11703)
Mr Tintz ....G...... 219 844-5500
Hammond (G-5919)
Pilkington North America Inc ....E...... 317 346-0621
Franklin (G-4920)
Pilkington North America Inc ....A...... 317 392-7000
Shelbyville (G-12557)
Tint Unlimited ....G...... 812 402-6102
Evansville (G-3764)
Wallar Additions Inc.....................E...... 574 262-1989
Elkhart (G-3253)
Wilmes Window Mfg Co Inc ....E...... 812 275-7575
Ferdinand (G-3864)

3221 Glass Containers

Amcor Phrm Packg USA Inc...........C...... 812 591-2332
Westport (G-14208)
Anchor Glass Container Corp ....B...... 765 584-6101
Winchester (G-14325)
Anchor Glass Container Corp ....B...... 812 537-1655
Greendale (G-5482)
Ardagh Glass Inc ....F...... 765 651-1260
Marion (G-9508)
Ardagh Glass Inc ....G...... 765 768-7891
Dunkirk (G-2483)
Ardagh Glass Inc ....G...... 765 662-1172
Marion (G-9509)
◆ Ardagh Glass Inc ....B...... 317 558-1002
Indianapolis (G-6418)
Hearthmark LLC ....G...... 765 557-3000
Muncie (G-10485)
◆ Hearthmark LLC ....C...... 765 557-3000
Fishers (G-3924)
Nipro Phrmpckging Amricas Corp ...G...... 812 591-2332
Westport (G-14210)
Verallia North America..................G...... 765 768-7891
Dunkirk (G-2490)

3229 Pressed & Blown Glassware, NEC

Anchor Glass Container Corp ....B...... 765 584-6101
Winchester (G-14325)
▲ Apollo Design Technology Inc.........D...... 260 497-9191
Fort Wayne (G-4081)
B Thystrup US Corporation ....G...... 574 834-2554
North Webster (G-11289)
Cedar Shack ....G...... 219 682-5531
Cedar Lake (G-1527)
Colliers Glassblock Inc ....G...... 574 288-8682
South Bend (G-12738)
Creations In Glass ....G...... 219 326-7941
La Porte (G-8747)
Dekker Lighting ....G...... 219 227-8520
Schererville (G-12320)
Diversified Ophthalmics Inc...........F...... 317 780-1677
Indianapolis (G-6750)
G K Optical Company Inc ....E...... 317 881-2585
Indianapolis (G-6975)
General Signals Inc.......................F...... 812 474-4256
Evansville (G-3518)

Global Composites Inc ....C...... 574 522-9956
Elkhart (G-2883)
Hh Rellim Inc ....G...... 812 662-9944
Greensburg (G-5609)
Inspired Fire Glass Studio & G............G...... 765 474-1981
Lafayette (G-8925)
L D Barger Wholesale Neon Inc..........G...... 765 643-4506
Anderson (G-131)
Map of Easton ....G...... 574 293-0966
Elkhart (G-3017)
Maul Technology Co ....E...... 765 584-2101
Winchester (G-14337)
Naptown Etching ....G...... 317 733-8776
Zionsville (G-14450)
▲ Northern Indiana Manufacturing ....E...... 574 342-2105
Bourbon (G-946)
Palmetto Planters LLC ....G...... 765 396-4446
Eaton (G-2587)
Pyrotek Incorporated ....E...... 260 248-4141
Columbia City (G-1820)
S & S Optical Co Inc ....G...... 260 749-9614
New Haven (G-10955)
Spectrum Brands Inc....................E...... 317 773-6627
Noblesville (G-11187)
Stability America Inc.....................G...... 574 642-3029
Goshen (G-5326)
Talon Products LLC ....F...... 574 218-0100
Bristol (G-1089)
V & H Fiberglass Repair ....G...... 574 772-4920
Knox (G-8586)
Vivid Leds Inc ....F...... 800 974-3570
Sellersburg (G-12421)
Zimmerman Art Glass Company ....G...... 812 738-2206
Corydon (G-2117)

3231 Glass Prdts Made Of Purchased Glass

A New Company Inc ....F...... 574 293-9088
Elkhart (G-2658)
American Window and Glass Inc ....C...... 812 464-9400
Evansville (G-3352)
Amish Robs Tattoos LLC ....G...... 219 863-9727
Morocco (G-10360)
Bizik Masonry Corporation ....G...... 219 659-1348
Whiting (G-14270)
Bowman Art Glass Studio ....G...... 765 281-4527
Muncie (G-10442)
Cardinal Glass Industries Inc ....E...... 260 495-4105
Fremont (G-4953)
Carlex Glass America LLC ....B...... 260 925-5656
Auburn (G-320)
Carlex Glass America LLC ....B...... 260 894-7750
Ligonier (G-9279)
Cleer Vision Windows Inc ....F...... 574 262-0449
Elkhart (G-2759)
Cleer Vision Windows Inc ....F...... 574 262-0449
Elkhart (G-2760)
Creative Industries Inc ....F...... 317 248-1102
Indianapolis (G-6688)
▲ Crown Industries Inc ....E...... 219 791-9930
Crown Point (G-2239)
▲ D & W Inc ....D...... 574 264-9674
Elkhart (G-2785)
Dewilde Glass Inc ....G...... 765 742-0229
Lafayette (G-8890)
Etching Industries Corporation ....E...... 317 591-3500
Indianapolis (G-6882)
Faries-Mcmeekan Inc....................E...... 574 293-3526
Elkhart (G-2845)
▲ Floralcraft Distributors ....E...... 574 262-2639
Elkhart (G-2858)
Fox Studios Inc ....F...... 317 253-0135
Indianapolis (G-6953)
Gardner Glass Products Inc ....F...... 317 464-0881
Indianapolis (G-6984)
Glass Surgeons ....G...... 219 374-2500
Cedar Lake (G-1528)
Great Panes Glass Co ....G...... 260 426-0203
Fort Wayne (G-4306)
◆ Grote Industries Inc ....A...... 812 273-2121
Madison (G-9463)
Grote Industries LLC ....A...... 812 265-8273
Madison (G-9464)
Hartford TEC Glass Co Inc ....E...... 765 348-1282
Hartford City (G-5983)
Hector Engineering Co ....G...... 812 876-5274
Ellettsville (G-3280)
Indy Glass Center Inc ....F...... 317 591-5000
Indianapolis (G-7217)
▲ International Steel Company ....D...... 812 425-3311
Evansville (G-3565)

▲ JC Moag Corporation ....D...... 812 284-8400
Jeffersonville (G-8383)
Kaleidoscope Inc ....G...... 765 423-1951
Lafayette (G-8936)
Kinro Manufacturing Inc ....C...... 574 535-1125
Elkhart (G-2970)
◆ Kokomo Opalescent Glass Co ....E...... 765 457-8136
Kokomo (G-8654)
▲ Larry Robertson Associates ....E...... 812 537-4090
Indianapolis (G-7381)
Lippert Components Mfg Inc ....C...... 574 935-5122
Plymouth (G-11703)
▲ Middletown Enterprises Inc ....E...... 765 348-3100
Hartford City (G-5985)
Mominee Studios Inc ....G...... 812 473-1691
Evansville (G-3633)
Moores Country Wood Crafting ....F...... 317 984-3326
Arcadia (G-266)
Moss L Glass Co Inc ....F...... 765 642-4946
Indianapolis (G-7546)
Oldcastle Buildingenvelope Inc ....C...... 317 876-1155
Indianapolis (G-7616)
Oldcastle Buildingenvelope Inc ....D...... 317 876-1155
Indianapolis (G-7617)
Omega National Products LLC ....C...... 574 295-5353
Elkhart (G-3068)
Parsing Laser Designs LLC ....G...... 317 677-4316
Avon (G-460)
Pilkington North America Inc ....A...... 317 392-7000
Shelbyville (G-12557)
Pittsburgh Glass Works LLC ....B...... 812 867-6601
Evansville (G-3673)
Rainbows Stained Glass ....G...... 812 265-0030
Madison (G-9491)
▲ Ramco Engineering Inc ....G...... 574 266-1455
Elkhart (G-3136)
Recycling Center Inc ....D...... 765 966-8295
Richmond (G-12041)
Recycling Works Inc ....F...... 574 293-3751
Elkhart (G-3141)
Safelite Glass Corp ....G...... 260 423-2477
Fort Wayne (G-4601)
Schott Gemtron Corporation ....B...... 812 882-2680
Vincennes (G-13705)
Schuster Glass Studio....................G...... 812 988-7377
Nashville (G-10734)
▲ Sherwood Industries Inc ....E...... 574 262-2639
Elkhart (G-3166)
Spectrum Brands Inc....................E...... 317 773-6627
Noblesville (G-11187)
◆ State Wide Aluminum Inc ....D...... 574 262-2594
Elkhart (G-3191)
Taylor Made Group Holdings Inc ....C...... 260 347-1368
Kendallville (G-8512)
Vernon Greyber ....G...... 812 636-7880
Odon (G-11343)
Warsaw Cut Glass Company Inc ....G...... 574 267-6581
Warsaw (G-13961)
Whitaker Glass & Mirror LLC ....G...... 765 482-1500
Lebanon (G-9232)
Winandy Greenhouse Company............E...... 765 935-2111
Richmond (G-12076)

3241 Cement, Hydraulic

Busters Cement Products Inc.............F...... 765 529-0287
New Castle (G-10894)
Buzzi Unicem USA Inc....................E...... 317 780-9860
Indianapolis (G-6524)
Essroc Corp.................................G...... 317 351-9910
Indianapolis (G-6879)
Irving Materials Inc ....F...... 765 922-7285
Marion (G-9534)
Lafarge North America Inc ....G...... 219 378-1193
East Chicago (G-2547)
Lehigh Cement Company LLC............G...... 877 534-4442
Logansport (G-9347)
Lehigh Cement Company LLC............G...... 812 246-5472
Sellersburg (G-12400)
Lehigh Cement Company LLC............G...... 812 849-2191
Mitchell (G-10165)
Lehigh Hanson Ecc Inc ....C...... 574 753-5121
Logansport (G-9348)
Lehigh Hanson Ecc Inc ....G...... 812 246-5472
Sellersburg (G-12401)
Light House Homes Center ....F...... 765 448-4502
Lafayette (G-8957)
▲ Lone Star Industries Inc ....D...... 317 706-3314
Indianapolis (G-6271)
Lone Star Industries Inc ....G...... 574 674-8873
Elkhart (G-3007)

Lone Star Industries Inc...............G...... 260 482-4559
Fort Wayne (G-4440)
Lone Star Industries Inc...............G...... 317 780-9860
Indianapolis (G-7416)

3251 Brick & Structural Clay Tile

▲ Ceramica Inc...............F...... 317 546-0087
Indianapolis (G-6589)
Meridian Brick LLC...............E...... 812 894-2454
Terre Haute (G-13283)
▲ Santarossa Mosaic Tile Co Inc........C...... 317 632-9494
Indianapolis (G-7895)

3253 Ceramic Tile

▲ Laticrete International Inc..............G...... 317 298-8510
Indianapolis (G-7383)
Universal Export Partnr LLC..............G...... 219 939-9529
Gary (G-5112)

3255 Clay Refractories

Bmi Refractory Services Inc...............G...... 219 885-2209
Gary (G-5030)
Can-Clay Corp...............E...... 812 547-3461
Cannelton (G-1288)
Certainteed Corporation...............G...... 812 645-0400
Terre Haute (G-13209)
Champion Target...............E...... 765 966-7745
Richmond (G-11969)
Dvs Refractories LLC...............G...... 219 886-2004
Gary (G-5042)
Grefco Minerals Inc...............F...... 765 362-6000
Crawfordsville (G-2155)
◆ Hale Industries Inc...............E...... 317 577-0337
Fortville (G-4778)
Harbisonwalker Intl Inc...............G...... 219 881-4440
Gary (G-5057)
Harbisonwalker Intl Inc...............D...... 219 883-3335
Gary (G-5058)
Ht Enterprises Inc...............G...... 765 794-4174
Crawfordsville (G-2160)
Quikrete Companies Inc...............E...... 317 251-2281
Indianapolis (G-7805)
Refractory Specialists LLC...............G...... 260 969-1099
Fort Wayne (G-4585)
Thermal Ceramics Inc...............E...... 574 296-3500
Elkhart (G-3212)
Veitsch-Radex America LLC...............E...... 219 237-2420
Munster (G-10637)
Wb Refractory Service Inc...............G...... 317 450-7386
Speedway (G-13016)

3259 Structural Clay Prdts, NEC

Can-Clay Corp...............E...... 812 547-3461
Cannelton (G-1288)
Marv Kahlig & Sons Inc...............G...... 260 335-2212
Portland (G-11835)
Stone Artisans Ltd...............G...... 317 362-0107
Indianapolis (G-8008)

3261 China Plumbing Fixtures & Fittings

A Create Space Inc...............G...... 317 254-2600
Indianapolis (G-6294)
Bootz Manufacturing Company...............D...... 812 425-4646
Evansville (G-3393)
E-Z Sweep & Rake LLC...............G...... 574 533-2083
Goshen (G-5207)
▲ Interglobal Way Network LLC...............G...... 574 971-4490
Elkhart (G-2938)
▲ Josam Company...............D...... 219 872-5531
Michigan City (G-9805)
▲ Karran USA...............G...... 410 975-0128
Vincennes (G-13688)
Leeps Supply Co Inc...............D...... 219 756-5337
Merrillville (G-9726)
Patriot Porcelain LLC...............G...... 574 583-5128
Monticello (G-10278)

3264 Porcelain Electrical Splys

Ies Subsidiary Holdings Inc...............F...... 330 830-3500
South Bend (G-12807)
Ies Subsidiary Holdings Inc...............D...... 219 937-0100
Hammond (G-5897)
Insulation Specialties of Amer...............E...... 219 733-2502
Wanatah (G-13824)
Leco Corporation...............G...... 574 288-9017
South Bend (G-12838)
Thomas & Skinner Inc...............F...... 812 689-4811
Osgood (G-11396)

3269 Pottery Prdts, NEC

Bastine Pottery Inc...............G...... 317 776-0210
Noblesville (G-11062)
Daramic LLC...............C...... 812 738-8274
Corydon (G-2097)
Davis Vachon Artworks...............G...... 260 489-9160
Fort Wayne (G-4201)
Donald H & Susan K Minch...............G...... 260 726-9486
Portland (G-11817)
Grateful Heart Enterprises LLC...............G...... 765 838-2266
Lafayette (G-8910)
Molded Acstcal Pdts Easton Inc...............C...... 574 968-3124
Granger (G-5424)
Ohio Valley Creative Enrgy Inc...............G...... 502 468-9787
New Albany (G-10835)
Pigeon Switch Pottery...............G...... 812 567-4124
Tennyson (G-13180)
▼ R Drew & Co Inc...............F...... 765 420-7232
West Lafayette (G-14100)
Reiberg Ceramics...............G...... 317 283-8441
Indianapolis (G-7828)
Schmidt Marken Designs...............G...... 219 785-4238
La Porte (G-8816)
Sissys Ceramics...............G...... 951 550-7728
Elkhart (G-3173)
Stoneware 3...............G...... 812 696-2679
Farmersburg (G-3838)
Strawtown Pottery & Antiques...............G...... 317 984-5080
Noblesville (G-11190)
Tinas Ceramics & Things...............G...... 812 917-4190
Terre Haute (G-13355)
Yellow Banks Clay Company Inc...............F...... 812 567-4703
Dale (G-2336)

3271 Concrete Block & Brick

Camilles Studio...............G...... 219 365-5902
Cedar Lake (G-1526)
Cash Concrete Products Inc...............F...... 765 653-4007
Greencastle (G-5454)
Crown Brick & Supply Inc...............E...... 219 663-7880
Crown Point (G-2237)
Devening Block Inc...............G...... 812 372-4458
Columbus (G-1907)
Dubois Cnty Block & Brick Inc...............F...... 812 482-6293
Jasper (G-8247)
Engineered Products Inc...............G...... 219 662-2080
Crown Point (G-2250)
Evansville Block Co Inc...............F...... 812 422-2864
Evansville (G-3484)
Gary W Martin...............G...... 812 926-0935
Aurora (G-377)
▲ Hessit Works Inc...............G...... 812 829-6246
Freedom (G-4949)
Irving Materials Inc...............D...... 317 326-3101
Greenfield (G-5542)
Jones & Sons Inc...............E...... 812 254-4731
Washington (G-13988)
Lafarge North America Inc...............G...... 219 378-1193
East Chicago (G-2547)
Majestic Block & Supply Inc...............G...... 317 842-6602
Fishers (G-3943)
Majestic Block and Brick Inc...............E...... 317 831-2455
Mooresville (G-10321)
Menard Inc...............A...... 812 466-1234
Terre Haute (G-13282)
North Star Stone Inc...............E...... 219 464-7272
Valparaiso (G-13593)
Northfield Block Company...............G...... 800 424-0190
Indianapolis (G-7594)
Precast Specialties Inc...............F...... 260 623-6131
Monroeville (G-10198)
R & D Concrete Products of Ind...............F...... 260 837-6511
Waterloo (G-14021)
Shelby Gravel Inc...............F...... 317 738-3445
Franklin (G-4929)
Slaters Concrete Products...............G...... 260 347-0164
Kendallville (G-8510)
Slon Inc...............F...... 765 884-1792
Fowler (G-4807)
Southfield Corporation...............E...... 812 824-1355
Bloomington (G-829)
St Henry Tile Co Inc...............E...... 260 589-2880
Berne (G-626)
Stotlar Hill LLC...............G...... 260 497-0808
Fort Wayne (G-4654)
Van Duyne Block and Gravel...............G...... 574 223-6656
Rochester (G-12159)
W Martin Gary...............G...... 812 926-0935
Aurora (G-393)

3272 Concrete Prdts

55 Monument Cir Level Off LLC...............G...... 317 423-9472
Indianapolis (G-6292)
Accucast Industries...............F...... 219 929-1137
Chesterton (G-1590)
Ace Extrusion LLC...............E...... 812 436-4840
Evansville (G-3341)
▲ AK Industries Inc...............D...... 574 936-6022
Plymouth (G-11662)
Akron Concrete Products Inc...............F...... 574 893-4841
Akron (G-1)
Alberding Woodworking Inc...............G...... 260 728-9526
Decatur (G-2365)
Anderson Memorial Park...............F...... 765 643-3211
Anderson (G-65)
Arrow Vault Co Inc...............G...... 765 742-1704
Lafayette (G-8853)
B & G Sales...............G...... 765 473-7668
Peru (G-11517)
Beaver Gravel Corporation...............D...... 317 773-0679
Noblesville (G-11065)
Beaver Products Inc...............F...... 317 773-0679
Noblesville (G-11066)
Beyond Monumental...............G...... 317 454-8519
Indianapolis (G-6471)
Bill Walters Concrete Inc...............F...... 574 259-0056
Mishawaka (G-10010)
Brim Concrete Inc...............G...... 765 564-4975
Delphi (G-2415)
Britton Vault Co Douglas...............G...... 765 893-4071
Williamsport (G-14287)
Calumet Wilbert Vault Co Inc...............F...... 219 980-1173
Gary (G-5032)
Carter Septic Tank Inc...............G...... 574 583-5796
Monticello (G-10257)
Carters Concrete Block Inc...............E...... 574 722-2644
Logansport (G-9330)
Cash Concrete Products Inc...............F...... 765 653-4007
Greencastle (G-5454)
Century Concrete Inc...............G...... 765 739-6210
Bainbridge (G-474)
Century Grave & Vault Service...............G...... 812 967-2110
Pekin (G-11470)
Cheetah Building Products...............G...... 812 466-1234
Terre Haute (G-13210)
Columbus Vault Co...............G...... 812 372-3210
Columbus (G-1882)
Community Vault Inc...............G...... 574 255-3033
Mishawaka (G-10020)
Concrete Lady Inc...............E...... 812 256-2765
Otisco (G-11416)
Concrete Supply LLC...............E...... 812 474-6715
Evansville (G-3427)
County Materials Corp...............G...... 317 262-4920
Indianapolis (G-6678)
County Materials Corp...............E...... 317 323-6000
Maxwell (G-9660)
Creed & Dyer Precast Inc...............G...... 574 784-3361
Lakeville (G-9095)
Crenshaw Paving Inc...............G...... 765 249-2342
Michigantown (G-9865)
Custom Cast Stone Inc...............D...... 317 896-1700
Westfield (G-14152)
Dyer Vault Company Inc...............F...... 219 865-2521
Dyer (G-2496)
Dynamic Composites LLC...............G...... 260 625-8686
Columbia City (G-1781)
E & B Paving Inc...............D...... 317 773-4132
Noblesville (G-11097)
Eaton Septic Tank Company...............G...... 765 396-3275
Eaton (G-2582)
Edgewood Corporation Indiana...............E...... 317 786-9208
Carmel (G-1369)
Envision Epoxy...............G...... 317 448-3400
Noblesville (G-11100)
Erie-Haven Inc...............D...... 260 478-1674
Fort Wayne (G-4241)
Farmer Tank Incorporated...............G...... 574 264-4625
Elkhart (G-2846)
Flyover Enterprises Inc...............G...... 317 417-1747
Pendleton (G-11489)
Forsyth Brothers Concrete Pdts...............G...... 812 466-4080
Terre Haute (G-13235)
Fred Weber Inc...............F...... 317 262-4920
Indianapolis (G-6962)
Game Vault...............G...... 317 209-7795
Indianapolis (G-6980)
Grable Burial Vault Services...............G...... 574 753-4514
Logansport (G-9335)

Hanson Aggregates East LLC	F	260 490-9006	
Fort Wayne (G-4319)			
Hanson Pipe Precast	G	219 873-9509	
Michigan City (G-9800)			
Harris Burial Services	G	812 939-3605	
Clay City (G-1702)			
Harris Pre Cast Inc	G	219 362-2457	
La Porte (G-8761)			
Hd Supply Construction Supply	F	260 471-7619	
Fort Wayne (G-4325)			
▲ Hessit Works Inc	G	812 829-6246	
Freedom (G-4949)			
Hi-Tech Concrete Inc	G	765 477-5550	
Lafayette (G-8914)			
Hog Slat Incorporated	G	765 828-0828	
Universal (G-13467)			
Holman Septic Tank Sls Redymix	F	812 689-1913	
Holton (G-6108)			
Homeowners Equity & Rlty Corp	G	219 981-1700	
Gary (G-5066)			
Hoosier Precast LLC	F	812 883-4665	
Salem (G-12292)			
Horn Pre-Cast Inc	F	812 372-4458	
Columbus (G-1943)			
Howard & Sons Cement Products	G	574 293-1906	
Elkhart (G-2922)			
Hudson Concrete Products Inc	G	812 825-2917	
Solsberry (G-12685)			
Hydro Conduit of Texas LP	G	317 769-2261	
Whitestown (G-14254)			
Illinois Tool Works Inc	D	219 874-4217	
Michigan City (G-9803)			
Independent Concrete Pipe Co	E	419 841-3361	
Indianapolis (G-7170)			
Independent Concrete Pipe Co	E	800 875-4920	
Indianapolis (G-7171)			
Independent Concrete Pipe Co	E	317 262-4920	
Indianapolis (G-7172)			
Independent Concrete Pipe Co	E	317 262-4920	
Indianapolis (G-7173)			
Independent Concrete Pipe Co	E	317 262-4920	
Indianapolis (G-7174)			
Independent Concrete Pipe Co	E	317 326-2600	
Maxwell (G-9661)			
Indiana Barrier Wall LLC	G	260 747-5777	
Fort Wayne (G-4363)			
Indiana Precast Inc	E	812 372-7771	
Columbus (G-1946)			
Jones & Sons Inc	E	812 299-2287	
Terre Haute (G-13261)			
Jones & Sons Inc	E	812 882-2957	
Vincennes (G-13687)			
Kerr Concrete Pipe Co	G	317 569-9949	
Carmel (G-1422)			
Kreig De Vault	G	317 238-6234	
Indianapolis (G-7369)			
L Thorn Company Inc	E	812 246-4461	
New Albany (G-10815)			
Lafarge North America Inc	G	219 378-1193	
East Chicago (G-2547)			
Lebanon Berg Vault Co Inc	G	765 482-0302	
Lebanon (G-9198)			
Legacy Vulcan LLC	E	219 987-3040	
Demotte (G-2443)			
Legacy Vulcan LLC	F	574 293-1536	
Elkhart (G-2993)			
Legacy Vulcan LLC	E	219 462-5832	
Valparaiso (G-13576)			
Lowell Concrete Products Inc	E	219 696-3339	
Lowell (G-9415)			
M & W Concrete Pipe & Supply	E	812 426-2871	
Evansville (G-3607)			
Mark Concrete Products Inc	G	317 398-8616	
Shelbyville (G-12551)			
Martinsville Vault Company	G	765 342-4576	
Martinsville (G-9623)			
Maso Inc	F	260 432-3568	
Fort Wayne (G-4454)			
McCreary Concrete Products Inc	G	765 932-3058	
Rushville (G-12229)			
McCreary Concrete Products Inc	G	317 844-5157	
Tipton (G-13399)			
Meyer Industries Inc	G	317 769-3497	
Whitestown (G-14256)			
Midwest Tile and Concrete Pdts	G	260 749-5173	
Woodburn (G-14387)			
Midwest Tile and Concrete Pdts	G	260 749-5173	
Woodburn (G-14388)			
Minnick Concrete Products Inc	E	260 432-5031	
Fort Wayne (G-4477)			

Mjs Concrete	G	260 341-5640	
Woodburn (G-14389)			
Monticello Vault Burial Co	G	574 583-3206	
Monticello (G-10271)			
Monument Construction Inc	G	317 472-0271	
Indianapolis (G-7540)			
Monument Lighthouse Chart	G	317 657-0160	
Indianapolis (G-7541)			
Monumental Stone Works Inc	E	765 866-0658	
New Market (G-10964)			
Odon Vault Co	F	812 636-7386	
Bloomington (G-783)			
▲ Oldcastle Apg Midwest Inc	A	317 786-0971	
Indianapolis (G-7615)			
Omnimax International Inc	E	574 848-7432	
Nappanee (G-10700)			
Plaster Shak	G	317 881-6518	
Greenwood (G-5733)			
Precast Specialties Inc	F	260 623-6131	
Monroeville (G-10198)			
Prestress Services Inc	C	260 724-7117	
Decatur (G-2399)			
Quality Tank Trucks & Eqp Inc	G	317 635-0000	
Indianapolis (G-7801)			
Quality Vault Company	F	812 336-8127	
Bloomington (G-803)			
Quikrete Companies Inc	E	317 251-2281	
Indianapolis (G-7805)			
Ram North America Inc	G	317 984-1971	
Arcadia (G-268)			
Rensselaer Eagle Vault Corp	G	219 866-5123	
Rensselaer (G-11936)			
Rinker Materials	G	317 241-8237	
Indianapolis (G-7845)			
Rochester Cement Products	G	574 223-3917	
Rochester (G-12145)			
Rogers Group Inc	G	765 342-6898	
Martinsville (G-9635)			
Roofing & Insulation Sup Inc	G	317 547-4373	
Indianapolis (G-7861)			
Rosskovenski Concrete & Rdymx	G	765 832-6103	
Clinton (G-1720)			
Russells Excvtg & Septic Tanks	G	812 838-2471	
Mount Vernon (G-10406)			
S & M Precast Inc	G	812 294-3703	
Henryville (G-6032)			
S & S Precast Inc	E	574 946-4123	
Winamac (G-14320)			
◆ S S M Inc	G	317 357-4552	
Indianapolis (G-7880)			
Sanders Pre-Cast Concrete	G	317 769-5503	
Whitestown (G-14261)			
Scepter Steel Inc	F	317 996-2103	
Monrovia (G-10206)			
Schrock Aggregate Company Inc	G	574 862-4167	
Wakarusa (G-13795)			
Slon Inc	F	765 884-1792	
Fowler (G-4807)			
Southern Indiana Supply Inc	G	812 482-2267	
Jasper (G-8311)			
St Regis Culvert Inc	G	317 353-8065	
Indianapolis (G-7982)			
Stephenson Block Inc	G	574 264-6660	
Elkhart (G-3193)			
▲ Strescore Inc	E	574 233-1117	
South Bend (G-12958)			
Superior Vault Co Inc	F	812 256-5545	
Charlestown (G-1582)			
Superior Vault Co Inc	G	812 539-1830	
Aurora (G-391)			
▲ Terre Haute Wilbert Burial Vlt	F	812 235-0339	
Terre Haute (G-13353)			
Terrys Sewer Service	G	219 756-5238	
Merrillville (G-9758)			
Tom Spencer Concrete Products	F	812 659-2318	
Switz City (G-13127)			
Trenwa Inc	G	812 427-2217	
Florence (G-4005)			
Tretter Boeglin Inc	G	812 683-4598	
Huntingburg (G-6182)			
Tri State Monument Company	G	812 386-7303	
Princeton (G-11888)			
Van Gard Vault Co Inc	G	219 980-6233	
Gary (G-5114)			
Van Gard Vault Co Inc	E	219 949-7723	
Gary (G-5115)			
Vandivier Tudor Monuments	G	317 736-5292	
Franklin (G-4938)			
Vault	G	317 784-4000	
Beech Grove (G-604)			

Vertex Building Materials LLC	G	765 547-1883	
Brookville (G-1129)			
Wayne Burial Vault Company	G	317 357-4656	
Indianapolis (G-8179)			
Wearlypocock Monuments	G	574 223-2010	
Rochester (G-12160)			
Western Green LLC	E	812 963-3373	
Poseyville (G-11862)			
Wholesale Drainage Supply Inc	G	812 397-5100	
Shelburn (G-12513)			
Wicker Gallery	G	219 942-0783	
Hobart (G-6100)			
▲ Wilbert Burial Vault Co Inc	F	317 547-1387	
Indianapolis (G-8195)			
Wilbert Burial Vault Co Inc	E	812 753-3601	
Fort Branch (G-4030)			
Wilbert Sexton Corporation	G	812 882-3555	
Vincennes (G-13717)			
Wilbert Sexton Corporation	G	812 336-6469	
Bloomington (G-854)			
Wilbert Sexton Corporation	G	812 372-3210	
Columbus (G-2034)			
Wilson Burial Vault Inc	G	260 356-5722	
Huntington (G-6261)			
Wimmer Vaults Inc	G	765 529-5702	
New Castle (G-10923)			
Yoders Monuments Inc	G	260 768-7934	
Middlebury (G-9930)			

3273 Ready-Mixed Concrete

A & T Concrete Supply Inc	E	812 753-4252	
Fort Branch (G-4025)			
Aggregate Industries - Mwr Inc	E	260 665-2052	
Angola (G-189)			
All-Rite Ready Mix Inc	F	812 926-0920	
Aurora (G-369)			
Attica Ready Mixed Concrete	E	765 762-2424	
Attica (G-297)			
Beaver Gravel Corporation	D	317 773-0679	
Noblesville (G-11065)			
Brim Concrete Inc	G	765 564-4975	
Delphi (G-2415)			
Busters Cement Products Inc	F	765 529-0287	
New Castle (G-10894)			
Cash Concrete Products Inc	F	765 653-4007	
Greencastle (G-5454)			
Cash Concrete Products Inc	F	765 653-4887	
Greencastle (G-5455)			
Cemex	G	317 351-9912	
Indianapolis (G-6575)			
Cemex Materials LLC	E	317 891-7500	
Greenfield (G-5512)			
Cemex Materials LLC	E	317 891-3015	
Indianapolis (G-6576)			
Cemex Materials LLC	E	317 891-3015	
Greenfield (G-5513)			
Cemex Materials LLC	E	317 769-5801	
Whitestown (G-14250)			
Center Concrete Inc	G	800 453-4224	
Butler (G-1224)			
Central Concrete Supply LLC	F	812 481-2331	
Jasper (G-8242)			
Concrete Pumping Michiana LLC	G	574 936-2140	
Plymouth (G-11677)			
Concrete Supply LLC	G	812 474-6715	
Evansville (G-3427)			
Crawford County Concrete	G	812 739-2707	
Leavenworth (G-9163)			
E & B Paving Inc	F	260 356-0828	
Huntington (G-6201)			
E & B Paving Inc	G	765 472-3626	
Peru (G-11525)			
E & B Paving Inc	G	317 781-1030	
Noblesville (G-11096)			
E & B Paving Inc	G	317 773-8216	
Noblesville (G-11098)			
Eagle Ready-Mix Inc	E	574 642-4455	
Goshen (G-5209)			
Erie Haven Inc	G	260 665-2052	
Angola (G-212)			
Erie-Haven Inc	D	260 478-1674	
Fort Wayne (G-4241)			
Erie-Haven Inc	E	260 353-1133	
Bluffton (G-874)			
Erie-Haven Inc	G	260 478-1674	
Auburn (G-330)			
Ernest Enterprises Inc	G	765 584-5700	
Winchester (G-14329)			
Ernst Concrete	G	260 726-8282	
Portland (G-11818)			

Ernst Concrete Enterprises .... G .... 812 284-5205 Sellersburg (G-12393)	Irving Materials Inc .... G ...... 765 472-5370 Peru (G-11533)	Ozinga Bros Inc .... F ...... 219 956-3418 Wheatfield (G-14228)	
Harrison Concrete .... G .... 812 275-6682 Bedford (G-547)	Irving Materials Inc .... G ...... 765 675-6327 Tipton (G-13394)	Ozinga Bros Inc .... F ...... 574 546-2550 Bremen (G-1013)	
Hoosier Ready Mix LLC .... F .... 812 254-7625 Washington (G-13986)	Irving Materials Inc .... F ...... 765 922-7285 Marion (G-9534)	Ozinga Bros Inc .... E ...... 574 642-4455 Goshen (G-5303)	
Hopkins Gravel Sand & Concrete....... G .... 317 831-2704 Mooresville (G-10311)	Irving Materials Inc .... F ...... 765 674-2271 Marion (G-9535)	Ozinga Bros Inc .... D ...... 574 971-8239 Goshen (G-5304)	
Im Indiana Holdings Inc .... G .... 260 478-1674 Fort Wayne (G-4359)	Irving Materials Inc .... E ...... 812 333-8530 Bloomington (G-751)	Ozinga Bros Inc .... D ...... 219 949-9800 Portage (G-11786)	
IMI Bloomfield .... G .... 812 384-0045 Bloomfield (G-639)	Irving Materials Inc .... G ...... 317 535-7566 Whiteland (G-14241)	Ozinga Bros Inc .... E ...... 219 662-0925 Crown Point (G-2282)	
IMI South LLC .... E .... 812 945-6605 New Albany (G-10803)	Irving Materials Inc .... F ...... 317 872-0152 Indianapolis (G-7269)	Ozinga Indiana Rdymx Con Inc ...... F ...... 219 949-9800 Gary (G-5082)	
IMI South LLC .... G .... 812 273-1428 Madison (G-9472)	Irving Materials Inc .... G ...... 317 843-2944 Indianapolis (G-7270)	Pepcon Concrete Inc .... G ...... 765 964-6572 Union City (G-13459)	
IMI South LLC .... G .... 812 738-4173 Corydon (G-2103)	Irving Materials Inc .... F ...... 317 783-3381 Indianapolis (G-7271)	Plymouth Ready Mart Inc .... G ...... 574 936-5251 Plymouth (G-11715)	
IMI South LLC .... G .... 812 284-9732 Clarksville (G-1686)	Irving Materials Inc .... G ...... 574 722-3420 Logansport (G-9342)	Prairie Group .... E ...... 812 877-9886 Terre Haute (G-13307)	
IMI Southwest Inc .... E .... 812 424-3554 Evansville (G-3548)	Irving Materials Inc .... G ...... 317 243-7391 Indianapolis (G-7272)	Precast Solutions Inc .... F ...... 317 545-6557 Whitestown (G-14259)	
Interstate Block Corporation .... G .... 812 273-1742 Madison (G-9473)	Irving Materials Inc .... G ...... 317 831-0224 Mooresville (G-10315)	Primed & Ready LLC .... G ...... 317 694-2028 Indianapolis (G-7747)	
Irving Materials Inc .... D .... 317 326-3101 Greenfield (G-5542)	Irving Materials Inc .... F ...... 317 899-2187 Indianapolis (G-7273)	Purdy Concrete Inc .... E ...... 765 477-7687 Lafayette (G-8984)	
Irving Materials Inc .... F .... 812 424-3551 Evansville (G-3567)	Irving Materials Inc .... G ...... 765 647-6533 Brookville (G-1119)	Purdy Materials Inc .... F ...... 765 474-8993 Lafayette (G-8985)	
Irving Materials Inc .... G .... 765 825-2581 Connersville (G-2056)	Irving Materials Inc .... F ...... 260 356-7214 Huntington (G-6219)	Quikrete Companies Inc .... E ...... 317 251-2281 Indianapolis (G-7805)	
Irving Materials Inc .... G .... 765 644-8819 Anderson (G-122)	Jack Mix .... G ...... 812 923-8679 Floyds Knobs (G-4014)	Raver Ready Mix Concrete LLC...... G ...... 812 662-7900 Greensburg (G-5631)	
Irving Materials Inc .... F .... 317 770-1745 Noblesville (G-11132)	Jones & Sons Inc .... E ...... 812 254-4731 Washington (G-13988)	Rosskovenski Concrete & Rdymx.... G ...... 765 832-6103 Clinton (G-1720)	
Irving Materials Inc .... E .... 317 773-3640 Noblesville (G-11133)	Jones & Sons Inc .... E ...... 812 882-2957 Vincennes (G-13687)	Sagamore Ready Mix .... G ...... 317 573-5410 Indianapolis (G-6280)	
Irving Materials Inc .... E .... 317 335-2121 Fishers (G-3989)	Jones & Sons Inc .... E ...... 812 299-2287 Terre Haute (G-13261)	Sagamore Ready-Mix LLC .... D ...... 317 783-3768 Indianapolis (G-7886)	
Irving Materials Inc .... E .... 317 784-5433 Indianapolis (G-7268)	Kentucky Concrete Indiana LLC...... E ...... 812 282-6671 Jeffersonville (G-8388)	Sagamore Ready-Mix LLC .... E ...... 317 570-6201 Fishers (G-3967)	
Irving Materials Inc .... F .... 765 654-5333 Frankfort (G-4838)	Keystone Concrete Inc .... E ...... 260 693-6437 Churubusco (G-1653)	Schmaltz Ready Mix Concrete .... G ...... 812 689-5140 Osgood (G-11394)	
Irving Materials Inc .... G .... 765 482-5620 Lebanon (G-9193)	Kuert Concrete Inc .... E ...... 574 232-9911 South Bend (G-12831)	Shelby Gravel Inc .... E ...... 317 398-4485 Shelbyville (G-12567)	
Irving Materials Inc .... G .... 765 342-3369 Martinsville (G-9618)	Kuert Concrete Inc .... F ...... 574 293-0430 Goshen (G-5259)	Shelby Gravel Inc .... F ...... 317 738-3445 Franklin (G-4929)	
Irving Materials Inc .... G .... 812 254-0820 Washington (G-13987)	Kuert Concrete Inc .... G ...... 574 223-2414 Rochester (G-12131)	Shelby Gravel Inc .... E ...... 317 784-6678 Indianapolis (G-7929)	
Irving Materials Inc .... G .... 765 836-4007 Muncie (G-10495)	Kuert Concrete Inc .... F ...... 574 453-3993 Warsaw (G-13899)	Shelby Gravel Inc .... G ...... 765 932-3292 Rushville (G-12233)	
Irving Materials Inc .... E .... 765 288-5566 Muncie (G-10496)	Lafarge North America Inc .... G ...... 219 378-1193 East Chicago (G-2547)	Shelby Gravel Inc .... E ...... 317 804-8100 Westfield (G-14188)	
Irving Materials Inc .... G .... 765 755-3447 Springport (G-13059)	Lake George Material & Sup Co ...... G ...... 219 942-1912 Hobart (G-6087)	Shelby Gravel Inc .... G ...... 317 216-7556 Indianapolis (G-7930)	
Irving Materials Inc .... F .... 260 824-3428 Bluffton (G-880)	Lees Ready-Mix & Trucking .... G ...... 812 522-7270 Seymour (G-12466)	Smith Ready Mix Inc .... F ...... 219 462-3191 Valparaiso (G-13620)	
Irving Materials Inc .... F .... 765 288-0288 Muncie (G-10497)	Lees Ready-Mix & Trucking Inc ...... G ...... 812 346-9767 North Vernon (G-11267)	Smith Ready Mix Inc .... G ...... 219 374-5581 Cedar Lake (G-1533)	
Irving Materials Inc .... G .... 765 478-4914 Cambridge City (G-1257)	Lees Ready-Mix & Trucking Inc ...... F ...... 812 372-1800 Columbus (G-1958)	Smith Ready Mix Inc .... F ...... 219 874-6219 Michigan City (G-9844)	
Irving Materials Inc .... F .... 574 946-3754 Winamac (G-14308)	Lehigh Cement Company LLC........ C ...... 812 849-2191 Mitchell (G-10165)	Smith Ready Mix Inc .... F ...... 219 374-5581 Valparaiso (G-13621)	
Irving Materials Inc .... G .... 812 883-4242 Scottsburg (G-12368)	Lehigh Cement Company LLC........ G ...... 877 534-4442 Logansport (G-9347)	Southfield Corporation .... E ...... 812 824-1355 Bloomington (G-829)	
Irving Materials Inc .... F .... 812 683-4444 Huntingburg (G-6172)	Lewis Jerry Cnstr & Excvtg .... G ...... 765 653-2800 Greencastle (G-5467)	Southfield Corporation .... E ...... 317 773-5340 Noblesville (G-11186)	
Irving Materials Inc .... G .... 765 362-6904 Crawfordsville (G-2163)	▲ Lone Star Industries Inc .... D ...... 317 706-3314 Indianapolis (G-6271)	Speedway Redi Mix Inc .... G ...... 260 496-8877 Fort Wayne (G-4641)	
Irving Materials Inc .... E .... 765 423-2533 Lafayette (G-8926)	Ma-Ri-Al Corp .... D ...... 317 773-0679 Noblesville (G-11143)	Speedway Redi Mix Inc .... G ...... 765 671-1020 Marion (G-9563)	
Irving Materials Inc .... E .... 765 743-3806 West Lafayette (G-14078)	▲ McIntire Concrete .... E ...... 765 759-7111 Muncie (G-10519)	Speedway Redi Mix Inc .... G ...... 260 244-7205 Columbia City (G-1836)	
Irving Materials Inc .... G .... 219 261-2441 Remington (G-11908)	Mendoza Mexican Mix .... G ...... 219 791-9034 Merrillville (G-9731)	Speedway Redi Mix Inc .... G ...... 260 356-5600 Huntington (G-6250)	
Irving Materials Inc .... F .... 765 922-7991 Swayzee (G-13124)	Mendozas Inc .... G ...... 219 791-9034 Merrillville (G-9732)	Speedway Redi Mix Inc .... G ...... 260 665-5999 Angola (G-244)	
Irving Materials Inc .... G .... 765 552-5041 Elwood (G-3300)	Meuth Construction Supply Inc....... F ...... 812 424-8554 Evansville (G-3624)	Spurlino Mtls Indianapolis LLC ...... E ...... 765 339-4055 Linden (G-9305)	
Irving Materials Inc .... G .... 765 728-5335 Montpelier (G-10292)	Mulzer Crushed Stone Inc .... E ...... 812 547-7921 Tell City (G-13167)	St Henry Tile Co Inc .... E ...... 260 589-2880 Berne (G-626)	
Irving Materials Inc .... G .... 812 275-7450 Bedford (G-554)	Mulzer Crushed Stone Inc .... E ...... 812 547-3467 Tell City (G-13168)	Sullivan IMI .... G ...... 812 268-3306 Sullivan (G-13096)	
Irving Materials Inc .... F .... 765 452-4044 Kokomo (G-8649)	N E W Interstate Concrete Inc .... E ...... 812 234-5983 Terre Haute (G-13288)	Van Keppel Redi-Mix Inc .... F ...... 219 987-2811 Demotte (G-2450)	
Irving Materials Inc .... G .... 765 922-7931 Swayzee (G-13125)	Naas Inc .... F ...... 812 385-3578 Princeton (G-11879)	Wdmi Inc .... E ...... 574 291-7100 South Bend (G-12989)	
Irving Materials Inc .... G .... 317 888-0157 Greenwood (G-5708)	Ohio Valley Ready Mix Inc .... E ...... 812 282-6671 Jeffersonville (G-8407)	Wdmi Inc .... F ...... 765 868-9646 Kokomo (G-8715)	
Irving Materials Inc .... F .... 765 778-4760 Anderson (G-123)	Orange County Concrete Inc .... G ...... 812 865-2425 Orleans (G-11365)	Zimco Materials Inc .... E ...... 219 883-0870 Gary (G-5117)	

3274 Lime

Calcar Quarries Incorporated .... F 812 723-2109
Paoli *(G-11447)*

Carmeuse Lime Inc .... D 773 221-9400
Gary *(G-5034)*

Carmeuse Lime & Stone .... G 219 787-9190
Portage *(G-11755)*

Dotted Lime Resale LLC .... G 317 908-3905
Westfield *(G-14160)*

Hanson Aggregates Midwest LLC .... F 812 889-2120
Lexington *(G-9251)*

Harris Stone Service Inc .... F 765 522-6241
Bainbridge *(G-477)*

Jolene D Pavey .... G 765 473-6171
Peru *(G-11534)*

Meshberger Stone Inc .... F 812 579-5241
Columbus *(G-1971)*

Mississippi Lime Company 800 437-5463
Portage *(G-11777)*

Mulzer Crushed Stone Inc .... E 812 365-2145
English *(G-3316)*

New Point Stone Co Inc .... F 812 663-2422
Greensburg *(G-5628)*

Rogers Group Inc .... G 765 342-6898
Martinsville *(G-9635)*

Rogers Group Inc .... E 219 474-5125
Kentland *(G-8523)*

Rogers Group Inc .... E 812 882-3640
Vincennes *(G-13703)*

Rogers Group Inc .... E 812 849-3530
Mitchell *(G-10170)*

Rush County Stone Co Inc .... E 765 629-2211
Milroy *(G-9985)*

Twisted Lime Bartending .... G 317 607-6836
Indianapolis *(G-8118)*

3275 Gypsum Prdts

Esco Industries Inc .... E 574 522-4500
Elkhart *(G-2837)*

Georgia-Pacific LLC .... C 219 956-3100
Wheatfield *(G-14223)*

New Ngc Inc .... C 812 247-2424
Shoals *(G-12667)*

New Ngc Inc .... D 219 866-7570
Rensselaer *(G-11933)*

New Ngc Inc 765 828-0898
Clinton *(G-1718)*

Patrick Industries Inc .... E 574 294-7511
Elkhart *(G-3080)*

Patrick Industries Inc .... C 574 534-5300
Goshen *(G-5308)*

Patrick Industries Inc .... F 574 295-9660
Elkhart *(G-3090)*

Patrick Industries Inc .... D 574 294-1975
Elkhart *(G-3091)*

Precast Solutions Inc .... F 317 545-6557
Whitestown *(G-14259)*

United States Gypsum Company .... C 812 247-2101
Shoals *(G-12671)*

United States Gypsum Company .... E 812 388-6866
Shoals *(G-12672)*

United States Gypsum Company 219 392-4600
East Chicago *(G-2575)*

◆ Westech Building Products Inc .... E 812 985-3628
Mount Vernon *(G-10414)*

3281 Cut Stone Prdts

3d Stone Purchaser Inc .... E 812 824-5805
Bloomington *(G-652)*

Absolute Stone Polsg Repr LLC .... G 317 709-9539
Westfield *(G-14132)*

Accent Limestone & Carving Inc .... G 812 876-7040
Bloomington *(G-655)*

Architectural Stone Sales Inc .... G 812 279-2421
Bedford *(G-529)*

Artistic Stone Company Inc .... G 812 256-2890
Charlestown *(G-1558)*

Aurora Casket Company LLC .... B 800 457-1111
Aurora *(G-370)*

Bedford Limestone Suppliers .... E 812 279-9120
Bedford *(G-532)*

Bedford Stonecrafters Inc .... G 812 275-2646
Bedford *(G-534)*

Bsbw Cultured Marble Inc .... E 812 246-5619
Sellersburg *(G-12389)*

Bybee Stone Company Inc .... D 812 876-2215
Ellettsville *(G-3272)*

C & H Stone Co Inc .... E 812 336-2560
Bloomington *(G-694)*

Cassini - D & D Mfg Inc .... G 765 449-7992
Lafayette *(G-8870)*

Centura Solid Surfacing Inc .... F 317 867-5555
Westfield *(G-14142)*

Century Marble Co Inc .... E 317 867-5555
Westfield *(G-14143)*

▲ Ceramica Inc .... F 317 546-0087
Indianapolis *(G-6589)*

Classic Kitchen & Granite .... G 317 575-8883
Carmel *(G-1340)*

Concepts In Stone & Tile Inc .... G 574 267-4712
Warsaw *(G-13859)*

Coronado Stone Inc .... E 812 284-2845
Jeffersonville *(G-8347)*

▲ Dreamwork Stones LLC .... F 317 709-2202
Carmel *(G-1363)*

Dwyer-Wilbert Inc .... G 765 962-3605
Richmond *(G-11978)*

Edw C Levy Co .... E 765 364-9251
Crawfordsville *(G-2151)*

▲ Elliott Stone Co Inc .... G 812 275-5556
Bedford *(G-540)*

Evans Limestone Co .... E 812 279-9744
Bedford *(G-541)*

Glas-Col LLC .... D 812 235-6167
Terre Haute *(G-13240)*

Granite Innovations Inc .... G 219 690-1081
Hebron *(G-6013)*

▲ Granite Marble & More Inc .... G 765 939-4846
Richmond *(G-11991)*

▲ Granitech .... E 574 674-6988
Elkhart *(G-2893)*

Hanson Aggregates East LLC .... F 812 883-2191
Salem *(G-12290)*

Hanson Aggregates Midwest LLC .... F 812 889-2120
Lexington *(G-9251)*

▲ Imperial Marble Incorporated .... F 812 752-5384
Scottsburg *(G-12364)*

Indiana Cut Stone Inc .... E 812 275-0264
Bedford *(G-550)*

▲ Indiana Lmstone Acqisition LLC .... D 812 275-3341
Bloomington *(G-745)*

▼ Indiana Stone Works .... E 812 279-0448
Bedford *(G-553)*

Indianapolis Granite & MBL Inc .... G 317 259-4478
Indianapolis *(G-7200)*

▲ Interior Design Surfaces Inc .... G 317 829-3970
Carmel *(G-1417)*

Ionic Cut Stone Inc .... G 812 829-3416
Spencer *(G-13029)*

J & N Stone Inc .... C 574 862-4251
Wakarusa *(G-13779)*

J & N Stone Inc .... F 260 627-2404
Grabill *(G-5373)*

John Ley Monument Sales Inc .... G 260 347-7346
Avilla *(G-408)*

Justin Blackwell .... F 812 834-6350
Norman *(G-11203)*

Kopelov Cut Stone Inc .... G 812 675-0099
Bedford *(G-558)*

Liberty Cut Stone Inc .... G 812 935-5515
Gosport *(G-5353)*

▲ Majestic Marble Imports Inc .... F 317 237-4400
Indianapolis *(G-7445)*

▲ Marstone Products Ltd .... G 800 466-7465
Fairland *(G-3824)*

Michael and Sons Incorporated .... F 812 876-4736
Bloomfield *(G-644)*

Midwest Calcium Carbonates LLC .... E 217 222-1800
Cloverdale *(G-1731)*

My Choice Recycling Inc .... G 219 313-1388
Schererville *(G-12336)*

New Point Stone Co Inc .... F 765 698-2227
Laurel *(G-9128)*

Ohio River Trading Co .... G 765 653-4100
Cloverdale *(G-1733)*

Poyser Kelshaw Group LLC .... G 317 571-8493
Carmel *(G-1453)*

Quality Surfaces Inc .... G 812 876-5838
Spencer *(G-13034)*

Roman Marblene Company Inc .... F 812 738-1367
Corydon *(G-2110)*

Rush County Stone Co Inc .... G 765 629-2211
Milroy *(G-9985)*

Selvins Marble & Gran Sp LLC .... G 317 370-4237
Zionsville *(G-14461)*

Simple Cremations Burials LLC .... G 765 592-6226
Clinton *(G-1721)*

Slon Inc .... F 765 884-1792
Fowler *(G-4807)*

Stone Artisans Ltd .... G 317 362-0107
Indianapolis *(G-8008)*

Stone Center of Indiana LLC .... E 317 849-9100
Indianapolis *(G-8009)*

Stone Street Quarries Inc .... E 260 639-6511
Hoagland *(G-6067)*

Superior Canopy Corporation .... E 260 488-4065
Hamilton *(G-5829)*

▲ Terre Haute Wilbert Burial Vlt .... F 812 235-0339
Terre Haute *(G-13353)*

Texacon Cut Stone LLC .... G 812 824-3211
Bloomington *(G-838)*

Thomas Monuments Inc .... G 317 244-6525
Indianapolis *(G-8065)*

Tremain Ceramic Tile & Flr Cvg .... E 317 542-1491
Indianapolis *(G-8093)*

Unimin Corporation .... G 812 683-2179
Huntingburg *(G-6183)*

▲ Wearly Monuments Inc .... E 765 284-9796
Muncie *(G-10581)*

Wilbert Sexton Corporation .... G 812 334-0883
Bloomington *(G-855)*

3291 Abrasive Prdts

3M Company .... B 765 348-3200
Hartford City *(G-5976)*

3M Company .... B 317 692-6666
Indianapolis *(G-6288)*

Abrasive Products LLC .... G 317 423-3957
Indianapolis *(G-6312)*

Advanced Cutting Systems Inc .... E 260 423-3394
Fort Wayne *(G-4043)*

Andersons Agriculture Group LP .... F 765 564-6135
Delphi *(G-2414)*

▼ Calumet Abrasives Co Inc .... E 219 844-2695
Hammond *(G-5855)*

Chance Abrasives .... G 219 871-0977
Michigan City *(G-9774)*

Drake Corporation .... E 812 683-2101
Jasper *(G-8246)*

G & S Super Abrasives Inc .... E 260 665-5562
Angola *(G-215)*

Harsco Corporation .... F 219 944-6250
Gary *(G-5060)*

Hi-Perfrmnce Sperabrasives Inc .... G 317 899-1050
Indianapolis *(G-7104)*

Hilltop Specialties LLC .... G 574 773-4975
Nappanee *(G-10681)*

Mjp & Company LLC .... G 317 631-7263
Indianapolis *(G-7529)*

Osborn Intl .... G 765 965-3722
Richmond *(G-12026)*

Reed Minerals .... G 219 944-6250
Gary *(G-5089)*

Royer Enterprises Inc .... F 260 359-0689
Huntington *(G-6245)*

▲ Sandpaper America Inc .... G 317 631-7263
Indianapolis *(G-7892)*

Sandpaper Studio LLC .... G 317 435-7479
Whiteland *(G-14245)*

Sandusky Abrasive Wheel Co .... E 219 879-6601
Michigan City *(G-9840)*

▲ Woodburn Diamond Die Co Inc .... D 260 632-4217
Woodburn *(G-14392)*

3292 Asbestos products

Heartland Table Pads LLC .... G 888 487-2377
Wolcottville *(G-14372)*

3295 Minerals & Earths: Ground Or Treated

◆ American Art Clay Co Inc .... C 317 243-0066
Indianapolis *(G-6385)*

Beemsterboer Slag Corp .... E 219 931-7462
Hammond *(G-5848)*

Beemsterboer Slag Corp .... D 219 392-1930
East Chicago *(G-2522)*

Beemsterboer Slag Corp .... E 219 931-7462
Hammond *(G-5849)*

Butler Mill Service Company .... E 260 625-4930
Columbia City *(G-1769)*

Butler Mill Service Company .... E 260 868-5123
Butler *(G-1223)*

Calcean LLC .... E 812 672-4995
Seymour *(G-12437)*

Edw C Levy Co .... E 765 364-9251
Crawfordsville *(G-2151)*

Harsco Corporation .... F 219 944-6250
Gary *(G-5060)*

Hydraulic Press Brick Company .... E 317 290-1140
Mooresville *(G-10313)*

Hydraulic Press Brick Company ....E 317 290-1140
  Indianapolis (G-7150)
Irving Materials Inc ....F 765 922-7285
  Marion (G-9534)
Metal Services LLC ....G 219 787-1514
  Burns Harbor (G-1217)
Mid-Continent Coal and Coke Co ....E 219 787-8171
  Portage (G-11775)
▲ Performance Minerals Corp ....G 219 365-8356
  Saint John (G-12266)
Phoenix Services LLC ....E 219 397-0650
  East Chicago (G-2557)
Rogers Group Inc ....E 812 849-3530
  Mitchell (G-10170)
South Shore Slag LLC ....F 219 881-6544
  Hammond (G-5943)
Suez Wts Usa Inc ....G 219 397-0554
  East Chicago (G-2569)
Tms International LLC ....G 219 397-6550
  East Chicago (G-2571)
Unimin Corporation ....E 812 683-2179
  Huntington (G-6183)
United Minerals and Prpts Inc ....E 812 838-5236
  Mount Vernon (G-10412)

3296 Mineral Wool

Aearo Technologies LLC ....C 317 692-6666
  Indianapolis (G-6342)
▲ Anderson Products Incorporated .....D 574 293-5574
  Elkhart (G-2692)
Global Composites Inc ....G 574 522-0475
  Elkhart (G-2884)
Haring Contractors Inc ....G 812 744-6870
  Moores Hill (G-10298)
Hy-TEC Fiberglass Inc ....G 260 489-6601
  Fort Wayne (G-4352)
Insul-Coustic Corporation ....E 260 420-1480
  Fort Wayne (G-4376)
Insulation Fabricators Inc ....D 219 845-2008
  Hammond (G-5900)
Insulation Specialties of Amer ....E 219 733-2502
  Wanatah (G-13824)
Johns Manville Corporation ....C 765 973-5200
  Richmond (G-12010)
Johns Manville Corporation ....E 574 546-4666
  Bremen (G-1006)
Knauf Insulation Inc ....B 317 421-3341
  Shelbyville (G-12545)
Knauf Insulation Inc ....B 317 398-4434
  Shelbyville (G-12546)
◆ Knauf Insulation Inc ....B 317 398-4434
  Shelbyville (G-12547)
Molded Acstcal Pdts Easton Inc ....E 610 253-7135
  Elkhart (G-3045)
Owens Corning Sales LLC ....C 765 647-4131
  Brookville (G-1122)
Owens Corning Sales LLC ....E 765 647-2857
  Brookville (G-1123)
Owens Corning Sales LLC ....G 260 563-2111
  Wabash (G-13745)
Owens Corning Sales LLC ....E 219 465-4324
  Valparaiso (G-13596)
Owens Corning Sales LLC ....E 260 665-7318
  Angola (G-233)
PSC Industries Inc ....E 317 547-5439
  Indianapolis (G-7785)
◆ Thermafiber Inc ....D 260 563-2111
  Wabash (G-13758)
Unifrax I LLC ....C 574 654-7100
  New Carlisle (G-10889)
Unique-Prescotech Inc ....E 479 646-2973
  Evansville (G-3783)
United States Mineral Pdts Co ....D 260 356-2040
  Huntington (G-6259)

3297 Nonclay Refractories

E J Bognar Inc ....F 412 344-9900
  Schneider (G-12354)
Harbisonwalker Intl Inc ....D 219 883-3335
  Gary (G-5058)
Hill & Griffith Company ....E 317 241-9233
  Indianapolis (G-7108)
Insulation Specialties of Amer ....E 219 733-2502
  Wanatah (G-13824)
▲ J W Hicks Inc ....E 219 736-2212
  Merrillville (G-9723)
Magneco/Metrel Inc ....F 219 885-4190
  Gary (G-5073)
Minteq International Inc ....G 219 397-5978
  East Chicago (G-2553)

Minteq International Inc ....C 219 886-9555
  Gary (G-5077)
▲ Minteq Shapes and Services Inc .....F 219 762-4863
  Portage (G-11776)
One Eight Seven Incorporated ....G 219 886-2060
  Gary (G-5081)
Pyro Industrial Services Inc ....E 219 787-5700
  Portage (G-11790)
▲ Refractory Service Corporation ....E 219 397-7108
  East Chicago (G-2567)
Refractory Service Corporation ....E 219 853-0885
  Hammond (G-5932)
Resco Products Inc ....D 219 844-7830
  Hammond (G-5933)
Servsteel Inc ....E 219 736-6030
  Gary (G-5096)
Simko Sons Indus Refractories ....F 219 933-9100
  Hammond (G-5941)

3299 Nonmetallic Mineral Prdts, NEC

C & E Exteriors Inc ....G 317 984-5463
  Arcadia (G-261)
Double E Distributing Co Inc ....G 812 334-2220
  Bloomington (G-715)
Insulation Specialties of Amer ....E 219 733-2502
  Wanatah (G-13824)
Magaws of Boston ....G 765 935-6170
  Richmond (G-12013)
Nf Friction Composites Inc ....G 414 365-1550
  Logansport (G-9359)
Plaster Shak ....G 317 881-6518
  Greenwood (G-5733)
Thermal Ceramics Inc ....E 574 296-3500
  Elkhart (G-3212)
Unifrax I LLC ....C 574 654-7100
  New Carlisle (G-10889)

33 PRIMARY METAL INDUSTRIES

3312 Blast Furnaces, Coke Ovens, Steel & Rolling Mills

101 Tool & Die LLC ....G 260 203-2981
  Fort Wayne (G-4031)
▲ 3d Parts Mfg LLC ....G 317 860-6941
  Anderson (G-56)
▲ Act Systems International LLC ....F 812 437-4609
  Evansville (G-3342)
Advanced Engineering Inc ....F 260 356-8077
  Huntington (G-6184)
AK Steel Corporation ....C 812 362-7317
  Rockport (G-12164)
Allegheny Ludlum LLC ....C 765 529-9570
  New Castle (G-10890)
Allegheny Ludlum Corp ....G 412 394-2800
  Portland (G-11808)
Allied Tube & Conduit Corp ....E 765 459-8811
  Kokomo (G-8590)
Alro Steel Corporation ....D 260 749-1829
  Fort Wayne (G-4064)
◆ Arcelormittal Burns Harbor LLC ......A 219 787-2120
  Burns Harbor (G-1214)
◆ Arcelormittal Holdings LLC ....D 219 399-1200
  East Chicago (G-2516)
▲ Arcelormittal Indiana Hbr LLC ....A 219 399-1200
  East Chicago (G-2517)
Arcelormittal USA LLC ....D 219 787-2120
  Chesterton (G-1595)
Arcelormittal USA LLC ....A 312 899-3400
  East Chicago (G-2519)
Arcelormittal USA LLC ....C 219 399-6500
  East Chicago (G-2520)
Armco ....G 219 981-8864
  Merrillville (G-9698)
▲ ATI ....G 317 238-3073
  Indianapolis (G-6438)
▲ Avis Industrial Corporation ....E 765 998-8100
  Upland (G-13468)
Bahr Bros Mfg Inc ....E 765 664-6235
  Marion (G-9512)
Barsteel Corporation ....G 219 650-7100
  Merrillville (G-9699)
Best Tires & Wheels ....G 317 306-3379
  Franklin (G-4872)
Beta Steel Corp ....G 219 787-0001
  Portage (G-11751)
Black Plate Catering ....G 317 634-8030
  Indianapolis (G-6483)
Brownstown Qlty TI Automtn LLC ....F 812 358-9059
  Brownstown (G-1180)

By The Sword Inc ....F 877 433-9368
  Huntingburg (G-6151)
C & G Tool Inc ....E 812 524-7061
  Jonesville (G-8448)
Chicago Flame Hardening Co ....E 773 768-3608
  East Chicago (G-2524)
Chicago Steel Ltd Partnership ....G 219 949-1111
  Gary (G-5037)
Citizens Energy Group ....D 317 261-8794
  Indianapolis (G-6614)
Classic Industries Inc ....G 812 421-4006
  Evansville (G-3418)
CPM Acquisition Corp ....D 765 362-2600
  Crawfordsville (G-2142)
Daechang Seat Co Ltd USA ....F 317 755-3663
  Indianapolis (G-6723)
▲ Delaware Dynamics LLC ....G 765 284-3335
  Muncie (G-10457)
Dietrich Industries Inc ....C 219 931-3741
  Hammond (G-5870)
Dynamic Holdings LLC ....G 260 969-3500
  Fort Wayne (G-4230)
Elkhart Steel Service Inc ....E 574 262-2552
  Elkhart (G-2830)
Endurance Metals LLC ....G 765 960-5834
  Richmond (G-11982)
General Mch & Saw Co of Ind ....F 574 232-6077
  South Bend (G-12787)
Gerdau Ameristeel US Inc ....C 765 286-5454
  Muncie (G-10476)
Gregs Tool & Machine ....G 812 373-9329
  Columbus (G-1934)
Hawkins Inc ....E 765 288-8930
  Muncie (G-10481)
▲ Heartland Steel Processing LLC ......C 812 299-4157
  Terre Haute (G-13246)
Hebron Ventures North America ....G 260 437-7733
  Fort Wayne (G-4329)
Heidtman Steel Products Inc ....C 419 691-4646
  Butler (G-1229)
Hoosier Metal Products Inc ....G 812 372-5151
  Columbus (G-1941)
Hoosier Wheel LLC ....G 812 421-6900
  Evansville (G-3541)
Hynes Kokomo LLC ....G 330 799-3221
  Kokomo (G-8642)
▲ Indiana Harbor Coke Company LP ...C 219 397-5769
  East Chicago (G-2538)
Indiana Steel Fabricating Inc ....F 765 742-1031
  Lafayette (G-8922)
Indiana Tool Inc ....F 765 825-7117
  Connersville (G-2055)
Industrial Steel Cnstr Inc ....C 219 885-5610
  Gary (G-5069)
Insight Equity Holdings LLC ....A 219 378-1930
  East Chicago (G-2540)
Interntional Pipe Cons Sls LLC ....F 765 388-2222
  New Castle (G-10907)
Isg Burns Harbor Services LLC ....F 219 787-2120
  Burns Harbor (G-1215)
Kammerer Inc ....G 260 349-9098
  Kendallville (G-8484)
Kankakee Valley Steel Inc ....G 219 828-4011
  Wheatfield (G-14227)
Kanoff Enterprises ....G 574 575-6787
  Mishawaka (G-10062)
Kirby Machine Company LLC ....F 317 773-6700
  Noblesville (G-11138)
Kretler Tool & Engineering ....G 260 897-2662
  Avilla (G-412)
▲ Krupp Gerlach Company ....G 765 294-0045
  Veedersburg (G-13644)
L B Foster Company ....G 260 244-2887
  Columbia City (G-1805)
Lana Hudelson ....E 812 865-3951
  Orleans (G-11363)
Leed Thermal Processing Inc ....G 317 637-5102
  Indianapolis (G-7393)
Liberation ....G 219 736-7329
  Schererville (G-12331)
LTV Steel Co ....G 219 391-2076
  East Chicago (G-2550)
Mc Metalcraft Inc ....G 574 259-8101
  Mishawaka (G-10076)
McCombs and Son Company ....G 765 825-4581
  Connersville (G-2063)
▲ Meriwether Tool & Engineering ....F 260 744-6955
  Fort Wayne (G-4466)
Mid-Continent Coal and Coke Co ....E 219 787-8171
  Portage (G-11775)

Employee Codes: A=Over 500 employees, B=251-500
C=101-250, D=51-100, E=20-50, F=10-19, G=2-9   2018 Harris Indiana
Industrial Directory   615

S I C

Midwest Metal Products Inc...............E...... 219 879-8595
Michigan City *(G-9819)*

Midwest Tube Mills Inc....................D...... 812 265-1553
Madison *(G-9487)*

Mitchell Industries Inc...................F...... 812 849-4931
Mitchell *(G-10167)*

Mittal Steel USA...........................C...... 219 787-2113
Chesterton *(G-1622)*

▲ Nachi America Inc.......................C...... 317 535-5527
Greenwood *(G-5726)*

National Material LP.......................219 397-5088
East Chicago *(G-2554)*

Nelson Acquisition LLC...................D...... 574 753-6377
Logansport *(G-9358)*

Niagara Lasalle Corporation..............E...... 800 262-2558
Hammond *(G-5921)*

Nicks Automotive Inc......................F...... 765 964-6843
Union City *(G-13458)*

▲ Nlmk Indiana LLC.......................B...... 219 787-8200
Portage *(G-11784)*

▲ Nonferrous Products Inc...............E...... 317 738-2558
Franklin *(G-4914)*

Norres North America Inc.................G...... 855 667-7370
South Bend *(G-12876)*

▲ Ntk Precision Axle Corporation........B...... 765 656-1000
Frankfort *(G-4846)*

Nucor Cold Finish.........................G...... 219 937-1442
Crown Point *(G-2280)*

Nucor Corporation.........................D...... 260 337-1800
Saint Joe *(G-12257)*

Nucor Corporation.........................D...... 260 837-7891
Waterloo *(G-14019)*

Nucor Corporation.........................A...... 765 364-1323
Crawfordsville *(G-2180)*

Nucor Corporation.........................C...... 260 837-7891
Waterloo *(G-14020)*

Nucor Steel Corp..........................E...... 765 364-1323
Crawfordsville *(G-2181)*

Omnisource Holdings LLC.................G...... 260 969-3500
Fort Wayne *(G-4511)*

Pace Tool and Engineering Inc...........G...... 812 373-9885
Columbus *(G-1988)*

Parker-Hannifin Corporation..............E...... 260 587-9102
Ashley *(G-289)*

Parker-Hannifin Corporation..............C...... 260 636-2104
Albion *(G-32)*

Phoenix Services LLC......................D...... 219 399-7808
East Chicago *(G-2558)*

Pizo Operating Company LLC..............E...... 317 243-0811
Indianapolis *(G-7699)*

Plymouth Tube Company....................C...... 574 946-6191
Winamac *(G-14314)*

Proaxis Inc................................E...... 765 742-4200
West Lafayette *(G-14097)*

Progress Rail Services Corp..............C...... 219 397-5326
East Chicago *(G-2565)*

Prox Company Inc.........................F...... 812 232-4324
Terre Haute *(G-13311)*

Qualtech Tool & Engrg Inc................C...... 260 726-6572
Portland *(G-11844)*

▲ Rbc Prcsion Pdts - Plymuth Inc.......D...... 574 935-3027
Plymouth *(G-11719)*

Resource Ventures LLC....................G...... 260 432-9177
Fort Wayne *(G-4589)*

Resource Ventures II LLC.................G...... 260 969-3500
Fort Wayne *(G-4590)*

▲ Ryerson Tull Inc.......................D...... 219 764-3500
Burns Harbor *(G-1219)*

S W Industries Inc........................F...... 317 788-4221
Indianapolis *(G-7882)*

Schwartz Wheel Co.........................G...... 574 546-0101
Bremen *(G-1022)*

Set Enterprises of Mi Inc................F...... 812 346-1700
North Vernon *(G-11281)*

▲ Seymour Tubing Inc.....................B...... 812 523-0842
Seymour *(G-12488)*

▲ Shetlers Famous Staineless............G...... 260 368-9069
Geneva *(G-5139)*

Specialty Stainless......................C...... 317 337-9800
Indianapolis *(G-7968)*

Spiral-Fab Inc............................G...... 812 427-3006
Vevay *(G-13665)*

Sssi Inc...................................D...... 219 880-0818
Gary *(G-5101)*

Steel Dynamics Inc........................A...... 260 248-2600
Columbia City *(G-1837)*

Steel Dynamics Inc........................A...... 260 868-8000
Butler *(G-1244)*

Steel Dynamics Inc........................D...... 812 218-1490
Jeffersonville *(G-8428)*

Steel Dynamics Inc........................B...... 317 892-7000
Pittsboro *(G-11588)*

◆ Steel Dynamics Inc.....................B...... 260 969-3500
Fort Wayne *(G-4646)*

Steel Structural Products LLC............F...... 812 670-4195
Jeffersonville *(G-8429)*

Steel Technologies LLC....................C...... 765 362-3110
Crawfordsville *(G-2197)*

Steel Technologies LLC....................C...... 502 245-2110
Portage *(G-11796)*

Steel Warehouse of Ohio LLC..............G...... 574 236-5100
South Bend *(G-12956)*

Structural Source.........................G...... 260 489-0035
Fort Wayne *(G-4657)*

Swi..B...... 812 342-2409
Columbus *(G-2019)*

Ten Cate Enbi Inc (indiana)..............C...... 317 398-3267
Shelbyville *(G-12574)*

Tms International LLC.....................G...... 219 881-0266
Gary *(G-5106)*

Tms International LLC.....................G...... 219 762-2176
Portage *(G-11798)*

Tms International LLC.....................G...... 219 864-0044
Schererville *(G-12349)*

Tms International LLC.....................G...... 219 885-7491
Gary *(G-5107)*

Tms International LLC.....................G...... 219 881-0155
East Chicago *(G-2570)*

Union Electric Steel Corp................C...... 219 464-1031
Valparaiso *(G-13632)*

United Machine & Design Inc..............E...... 812 442-7468
Brazil *(G-980)*

United States Steel Corp.................D...... 219 762-3131
Portage *(G-11799)*

United States Steel Corp.................B...... 219 391-2045
East Chicago *(G-2576)*

United States Steel Corp.................G...... 219 888-2000
Gary *(G-5111)*

◆ Valbruna Slater Stainless Inc.........C...... 260 434-2800
Fort Wayne *(G-4722)*

Vicksmetal Armco Associates..............E...... 765 659-5555
Frankfort *(G-4858)*

Western-Cullen-Hayes Inc.................E...... 765 962-0526
Richmond *(G-12075)*

Wheels In Sky.............................G...... 812 249-8233
Terre Haute *(G-13369)*

Windsor Steel Inc.........................E...... 574 294-1060
Elkhart *(G-3261)*

Worthington Steel Company................C...... 219 929-4000
Porter *(G-11806)*

3315 Steel Wire Drawing & Nails & Spikes

▲ 1st Source Products Inc...............F...... 812 288-7466
Jeffersonville *(G-8315)*

▲ A-1 Wire Tech Inc......................D...... 815 226-0477
Elkhart *(G-2660)*

▲ Accel International......................F...... 260 897-9990
Avilla *(G-400)*

Belden Inc................................A...... 765 962-7561
Richmond *(G-11962)*

Best Weld Inc.............................F...... 765 641-7720
Anderson *(G-74)*

▲ Cablecraft Motion Controls LLC........B...... 260 749-5105
New Haven *(G-10933)*

Carico Enterprises LLC....................G...... 765 384-4451
Marion *(G-9515)*

E H Baare Corporation.....................G...... 765 778-7895
Anderson *(G-103)*

Essex Group Inc...........................C...... 260 424-1708
Fort Wayne *(G-4248)*

Essex Group Inc...........................D...... 260 248-5500
Columbia City *(G-1785)*

Fort Wayne Metals Res Pdts...............E...... 260 747-4154
Fort Wayne *(G-4273)*

▲ Fort Wayne Metals Res Pdts............C...... 260 747-4154
Fort Wayne *(G-4274)*

Fort Wayne Metals RES Pdts...............F...... 260 747-4154
Fort Wayne *(G-4275)*

Four Star Field Services..................G...... 812 354-9995
Petersburg *(G-11563)*

Fuzion Products LLC.......................G...... 317 536-0745
Indianapolis *(G-6973)*

▲ Group Dekko Inc........................D...... 260 357-3621
Garrett *(G-5009)*

Hammond Steel Components LLC.............G...... 630 816-1343
Hammond *(G-5888)*

Ifc Fence LLC.............................G...... 219 977-4000
Gary *(G-5067)*

Innovative Fabrication LLC...............D...... 317 215-5988
Indianapolis *(G-7237)*

Kingsford Products Inc....................G...... 740 862-4450
Decatur *(G-2389)*

Kokoku Wire Industries Corp..............E...... 574 287-5610
South Bend *(G-12829)*

Madsen Wire LLC...........................E...... 260 829-6561
Orland *(G-11353)*

Mayfield-Glenn Group Inc.................F...... 219 393-7117
Kingsbury *(G-8541)*

Merchants Metals Inc......................F...... 317 783-7678
Indianapolis *(G-7480)*

Merchants Metals LLC......................G...... 574 831-4060
New Paris *(G-10990)*

▼ Metal Technologies Auburn LLC.........B...... 260 925-4717
Auburn *(G-344)*

Mid-West Metal Products Co Inc...........F...... 765 741-3140
Muncie *(G-10522)*

▲ Midwest Bale Ties Inc..................F...... 765 364-0113
Crawfordsville *(G-2172)*

Nippon Steel & Sumikin....................G...... 219 228-0110
Shelbyville *(G-12555)*

Precision Battery Fabricat...............G...... 260 563-5138
Wabash *(G-13751)*

Pwt Group LLC.............................E...... 260 490-6477
Fort Wayne *(G-4565)*

REA Magnet Wire Company Inc..............B...... 765 477-8000
Lafayette *(G-8989)*

S & J Manufacturing LLC...................G...... 812 662-6640
Greensburg *(G-5632)*

▲ Sanlo Inc..............................D...... 219 879-0241
Michigan City *(G-9841)*

▲ Shivom Jay Steels Intl LLC............G...... 574 271-7222
Granger *(G-5434)*

Suggs Custom Design Solutions............G...... 574 549-2174
Elkhart *(G-3197)*

▲ Tru-Form Steel & Wire Inc.............E...... 765 348-5001
Hartford City *(G-5993)*

Truckpro LLC..............................F...... 765 482-6525
Lebanon *(G-9230)*

Tway Company Incorporated................E...... 317 636-2591
Indianapolis *(G-8116)*

Warren Power Attachments..................G...... 317 892-4737
Pittsboro *(G-11589)*

Wolfpack Chassis LLC......................E...... 260 349-1887
Kendallville *(G-8514)*

3316 Cold Rolled Steel Sheet, Strip & Bars

Allegheny Ludlum LLC......................C...... 765 529-9570
New Castle *(G-10890)*

Arcelormittal USA LLC.....................D...... 219 787-2120
Chesterton *(G-1595)*

Chief Industries Inc......................C...... 219 866-4121
Rensselaer *(G-11917)*

Dietrich Industries Inc...................C...... 219 931-3741
Hammond *(G-5870)*

Feralloy Corporation......................D...... 219 787-9698
Portage *(G-11762)*

▲ Heartland Steel Processing LLC........C...... 812 299-4157
Terre Haute *(G-13246)*

Heidtman Steel Products Inc..............C...... 419 691-4646
Butler *(G-1229)*

▲ I/N Tek LP.............................C...... 574 654-1000
New Carlisle *(G-10883)*

Illiana Steel Inc.........................E...... 219 397-3250
East Chicago *(G-2537)*

Mill Steel Co.............................C...... 765 622-4545
Anderson *(G-136)*

Niagara Lasalle Corporation..............E...... 800 262-2558
Hammond *(G-5921)*

▲ Niagara Lasalle Corporation...........C...... 219 853-6000
Hammond *(G-5922)*

Nucor Corporation.........................A...... 765 364-1323
Crawfordsville *(G-2180)*

Ohio River Metal Services Inc............C...... 812 282-4770
Jeffersonville *(G-8406)*

Plateplus Inc.............................D...... 219 392-3400
East Chicago *(G-2560)*

Plymouth Tube Company....................C...... 574 946-6191
Winamac *(G-14314)*

Quanex Corp Lasalle Steel Div............G...... 219 853-6202
Hammond *(G-5930)*

▲ Ryerson Tull Inc.......................D...... 219 764-3500
Burns Harbor *(G-1219)*

Set Enterprises of Mi Inc................F...... 812 346-1700
North Vernon *(G-11281)*

▲ Stalcop LLC............................D...... 765 436-7926
Thorntown *(G-13378)*

◆ Steel Dynamics Inc.....................B...... 260 969-3500
Fort Wayne *(G-4646)*

Steel Technologies LLC ....C 502 245-2110
Portage (G-11796)
Steel Technologies LLC ....D 812 663-9704
Greensburg (G-5635)
Steel Technologies LLC ....C 765 362-3110
Crawfordsville (G-2197)
Ten Point Trim Corp ....E 317 875-5424
Zionsville (G-14468)
United States Steel Corp ....D 219 762-3131
Portage (G-11799)
Ward Forging Co Inc ....G 812 923-7463
Floyds Knobs (G-4023)
Worthington Steel Company ....C 219 929-4000
Porter (G-11806)

3317 Steel Pipe & Tubes

37 Pipe & Supply LLC ....G 812 275-5676
Bedford (G-526)
Advanced Drainage Systems ....G 317 917-7960
Indianapolis (G-6333)
AK Tube LLC ....G 317 736-8888
Franklin (G-4866)
AK Tube LLC ....F 812 341-3200
Columbus (G-1853)
Allied Tube & Conduit Corp ....C 812 265-9255
Madison (G-9443)
American Hydroformers Inc ....F 260 428-2660
Fort Wayne (G-4072)
▲ Applegate Livestock Eqp Inc ....D 765 964-3715
Union City (G-13452)
◆ Bock Industries Inc ....D 574 295-8070
Elkhart (G-2729)
Century Tube LLC ....C 812 265-9255
Madison (G-9448)
E & H Tubing Inc ....E 812 358-3894
Brownstown (G-1186)
E & H Tubing Inc ....E 812 358-3894
Brownstown (G-1187)
Expanded Metals Co Ind LLC ....E 574 287-6471
South Bend (G-12768)
Hd Mechanical Inc ....G 219 924-6050
Griffith (G-5776)
▼ Indiana Tube Corporation ....B 812 467-7155
Evansville (G-3553)
▲ Kalenborn Abresist Corporation ......E 800 348-0717
Urbana (G-13477)
Ljt Texas LLC ....E 800 257-6859
South Bend (G-12842)
▲ Lock Joint Tube LLC ....C 574 299-5326
South Bend (G-12843)
Martinrea Industries Inc ....C 812 346-5750
North Vernon (G-11269)
Midwest Steel & Tube LLC ....E 219 398-2200
East Chicago (G-2552)
Moyers Inc ....E 574 264-3119
Elkhart (G-3052)
Napier & Napier ....G 765 580-9116
Liberty (G-9266)
▲ Paragon Tube Corporation ....E 260 424-1266
Fort Wayne (G-4520)
Perch Tree Inc ....G 630 450-4591
Fishers (G-3949)
Phoenix Specialities Ltd ....G 219 345-5812
Lake Village (G-9084)
Plymouth Tube Company ....C 574 946-6191
Winamac (G-14314)
Plymouth Tube Company ....G 574 653-2575
Kewanna (G-8527)
Plymouth Tube Company ....D 574 946-3125
Winamac (G-14315)
Plymouth Tube Company ....C 574 946-6657
Winamac (G-14316)
Ptc Alliance Corporation ....E 765 259-3334
Richmond (G-12036)
Ptc Tubular Products LLC ....D 765 259-3334
Richmond (G-12037)
Schuyler Corp ....F 574 533-2597
Goshen (G-5321)
Specialty Steel Works Inc ....G 877 289-2277
Hammond (G-5946)
Steuben Fabg & Engrg Inc ....G 260 665-3001
Angola (G-247)
Tejas Tubular Products Inc ....D 574 249-0623
New Carlisle (G-10888)
Thormax Enterprises LLC ....G 812 530-7744
Seymour (G-12496)
Tube Processing Corp ....C 317 782-9486
Indianapolis (G-8108)

3321 Gray Iron Foundries

37 Pipe & Supply LLC ....G 812 275-5676
Bedford (G-526)
Accucast Inc ....G 317 849-5521
Indianapolis (G-6314)
Accurate Castings Inc ....D 219 393-3122
La Porte (G-8726)
Akron Foundry Inc ....D 574 893-4548
Akron (G-2)
Atlas Foundry Company Inc ....C 765 662-2525
Marion (G-9510)
Bahr Bros Mfg Inc ....E 765 664-6235
Marion (G-9512)
Bremen Castings Inc ....C 574 546-2411
Bremen (G-985)
Ce Systems Inc ....E 812 372-8234
Columbus (G-1868)
Ej Usa Inc ....F 765 744-1184
Indianapolis (G-6818)
▲ Gartland Foundry Company Inc ......C 812 232-0226
Terre Haute (G-13238)
Grede LLC ....C 765 521-8000
New Castle (G-10903)
In Ductile LLC ....E 317 776-8000
Noblesville (G-11125)
▲ Intat Precision Inc ....C 765 932-5323
Rushville (G-12224)
J A Smit Inc ....G 812 424-8141
Evansville (G-3568)
Jkr Inc ....F 260 665-1067
Angola (G-221)
La Porte Technologies LLC ....F 219 362-1000
La Porte (G-8784)
Leons Fabrication Inc ....F 219 365-5272
Schererville (G-12330)
Metal Technologies Inc Alabama ....D 260 925-4717
Auburn (G-345)
◆ Metal Technologies Indiana Inc ....C 260 925-4717
Auburn (G-346)
Mm Holdings I LLC ....C 260 982-2191
North Manchester (G-11236)
▲ Navistar Cmponent Holdings LLC ....B 317 352-4500
Indianapolis (G-7578)
New Dalton Foundry LLC ....G 574 267-8111
Warsaw (G-13913)
Plymouth Foundry Inc ....E 574 936-2106
Plymouth (G-11713)
Precision Gage LLC ....E 260 925-4717
Auburn (G-348)
Richmond Casting Company ....E 765 935-4090
Richmond (G-12045)
Rochester Metal Products Corp ....B 574 223-3164
Rochester (G-12148)
▲ Transportation Tech Inds ....F 812 962-5000
Evansville (G-3769)
United Mechanical Tech Inc ....G 219 608-0717
Schererville (G-12350)
▲ Vernon North Industry Corp ....D 812 346-8772
North Vernon (G-11285)
Warsaw Foundry Company Inc ....D 574 267-8772
Warsaw (G-13962)
Waupaca Foundry Inc ....A 812 547-0700
Tell City (G-13174)
West Allis Gray Iron ....D 260 925-4717
Auburn (G-367)

3322 Malleable Iron Foundries

Accurate Castings Inc ....D 219 393-3122
La Porte (G-8726)
Ce Systems Inc ....E 812 372-8234
Columbus (G-1868)
Ewing Light Metals Co Inc ....F 317 926-4591
Indianapolis (G-6886)
Grede LLC ....C 765 521-8000
New Castle (G-10903)
Mosey Manufacturing Co Inc ....D 765 983-8889
Richmond (G-12022)
Muncie Casting Corp ....E 765 288-2611
Muncie (G-10528)
Plymouth Foundry Inc ....E 574 936-2106
Plymouth (G-11713)
Wirco Inc ....C 260 897-3768
Avilla (G-422)

3324 Steel Investment Foundries

▲ Aero Metals Inc ....B 219 326-1976
La Porte (G-8727)
Howmet Castings & Services Inc ....A 219 326-7400
La Porte (G-8767)

3325 Steel Foundries, NEC

Arcelormittal USA LLC ....D 219 787-2120
Chesterton (G-1595)
Bahr Bros Mfg Inc ....E 765 664-6235
Marion (G-9512)
CM Tech ....G 765 584-6501
Winchester (G-14327)
FCA US LLC ....A 765 454-0018
Kokomo (G-8624)
▲ Harrison Steel Castings Co ....A 765 762-2481
Attica (G-303)
Hoosier Engineering Co Inc ....G 260 694-6887
Poneto (G-11746)
▲ IBC US Holdings Inc ....G 317 738-2558
Franklin (G-4898)
Jec Steel Company ....G 574 326-3829
Elkhart (G-2946)
▲ Metaldyne Bsm LLC ....D 260 495-4315
Fremont (G-4968)
Set Enterprises of Mi Inc ....F 812 346-1700
North Vernon (G-11281)
Shenango LLC ....F 812 235-2058
Terre Haute (G-13324)
Southland Metals Inc ....G 574 252-4441
Mishawaka (G-10134)
Stanley Fastening Systems LP ....D 317 398-0761
Greenfield (G-5578)
Tupy American Foundry Corp ....G 317 859-0066
Greenwood (G-5757)
Union Electric Steel Corp ....C 219 464-1031
Valparaiso (G-13632)
United States Steel Corp ....B 219 888-2000
Gary (G-5111)
United States Steel Corp ....B 219 391-2045
East Chicago (G-2576)
West Allis Gray Iron ....D 260 925-4717
Auburn (G-367)
Wrib Manufacturing Inc ....G 765 294-2841
Veedersburg (G-13648)

3331 Primary Smelting & Refining Of Copper

▲ Univertical LLC ....D 260 665-1500
Angola (G-255)

3334 Primary Production Of Aluminum

Arconic Inc ....B 812 853-6111
Newburgh (G-11020)
Arconic Inc ....B 412 553-4545
Newburgh (G-11021)
◆ Closure Systems Intl Inc ....C 317 390-5000
Indianapolis (G-6624)
Closure Systems Intl Inc ....C 317 390-5000
Crawfordsville (G-2140)
Closure Systems Intl Inc ....B 765 364-6300
Crawfordsville (G-2141)
G&L Machine ....G 260 488-2100
Hamilton (G-5822)
Industrial Sales & Supply Inc ....F 317 240-0560
Indianapolis (G-7209)
Kingsford Products Inc ....G 740 862-4450
Decatur (G-2389)
▲ Nanshn Amrc Adv Alum Tech LLC ..C 765 838-8645
Lafayette (G-8974)
Old Ras Inc ....G 260 563-7461
Wabash (G-13743)
Scepter Inc ....D 812 735-2500
Bicknell (G-633)

3339 Primary Nonferrous Metals, NEC

Dallas Group of America Inc ....D 812 283-6675
Jeffersonville (G-8350)
Eco-Bat America LLC ....C 317 247-1303
Indianapolis (G-6801)
Exide Technologies ....C 765 747-9980
Muncie (G-10470)
Expanded Metals Co Ind LLC ....E 574 287-6471
South Bend (G-12768)
Goldman Machine Services ....G 812 359-5440
Richland (G-11950)

▲ J & T Marine Specialists Inc ....G 317 890-9444
Indianapolis (G-7280)
▲ Texmo Prcision Castings US Inc ......D 574 269-1368
Warsaw (G-13951)
Wegener Steel and Fabricating ....G 219 462-3911
Valparaiso (G-13636)
Winchester Steel ....G 812 591-2071
Westport (G-14212)

S
I
C

▲ Netshape Technologies LLC ....E 812 248-9273
Noblesville *(G-11158)*

Univertical Holdings Inc ....G 260 665-1500
Angola *(G-254)*

Whiting Metals LLC ....G 219 659-6955
Whiting *(G-14278)*

3341 Secondary Smelting & Refining Of Non-ferrous Metals

Ad-Vance Magnetics Inc ....E 574 223-3158
Rochester *(G-12113)*

▲ Advanced Magnesium Alloys Corp ..E 765 643-5873
Anderson *(G-59)*

All Pro Shearing Inc ....F 317 691-1005
Indianapolis *(G-6367)*

▲ Aluminum Conversion Inc ....G 260 856-2180
Cromwell *(G-2207)*

American Scrap Processing Inc ....D 219 398-1444
East Chicago *(G-2515)*

AMG Resources Corporation ....F 219 949-8150
Gary *(G-5028)*

Eco-Bat America LLC ....C 317 247-1303
Indianapolis *(G-6801)*

Exide Technologies ....C 765 747-9980
Muncie *(G-10470)*

Haynes International Inc ....A 219 326-8530
La Porte *(G-8762)*

Howmet Castings & Services Inc ....A 219 326-7400
La Porte *(G-8767)*

Induction Iron Incorporated ....F 813 969-3300
Evansville *(G-3554)*

▼ J Trockman & Sons Inc ....E 812 425-5271
Evansville *(G-3569)*

Joe W Morgan Inc ....D 812 423-5914
Evansville *(G-3575)*

Kendallville Iron & Metal Inc ....E 260 347-1958
Kendallville *(G-8486)*

▲ Koch Enterprises Inc ....G 812 465-9800
Evansville *(G-3596)*

Loeb-Lorman Metals Inc ....G 574 892-5063
Argos *(G-275)*

Mervis Industries Inc ....F 812 232-1251
Terre Haute *(G-13284)*

Mervis Industries Inc ....D 765 454-5800
Kokomo *(G-8665)*

Metal Spinners Inc ....F 260 665-2158
Angola *(G-229)*

▲ Nanshn Amrc Adv Alum Tech LLC ..C 765 838-8645
Lafayette *(G-8974)*

Newco Metals Inc ....G 765 644-6649
Anderson *(G-145)*

Newco Metals Inc ....E 317 485-7721
Pendleton *(G-11497)*

P & H Iron & Supply Inc ....F 219 853-0240
Hammond *(G-5925)*

Plymouth Tube Company ....C 574 946-6191
Winamac *(G-14314)*

Porter County Ir & Met Recycle ....F 219 996-7630
Hebron *(G-6020)*

Qrs Inc ....G 812 948-1323
New Albany *(G-10851)*

Real Alloy Recycling LLC ....D 262 637-9858
Wabash *(G-13752)*

Real Alloy Recycling LLC ....D 260 563-2409
Wabash *(G-13753)*

Recovery Technologies LLC ....E 260 745-3902
Fort Wayne *(G-4583)*

Recycling Center Inc ....D 765 966-8295
Richmond *(G-12041)*

Recycling Services Indiana Inc ....E 812 279-8114
Bedford *(G-572)*

Recycling Works Inc ....F 574 293-3751
Elkhart *(G-3141)*

S W Industries Inc ....F 317 788-4221
Indianapolis *(G-7882)*

Scepter Inc ....D 812 735-2500
Bicknell *(G-633)*

Special Metals Corporation ....E 574 262-3451
Elkhart *(G-3183)*

▼ Superior Aluminum Alloys LLC ....C 260 749-7599
New Haven *(G-10959)*

▲ Transmetco Corporation ....F 260 355-0089
Huntington *(G-6255)*

Versatile Processing Group Inc ....G 317 577-8930
Indianapolis *(G-8152)*

Winski Brothers Inc ....F 765 654-5323
Frankfort *(G-4860)*

3351 Rolling, Drawing & Extruding Of Copper

▲ Alconex Specialty Products ....D 260 744-3446
Fort Wayne *(G-4056)*

Brand Sheet Metal Works Inc ....G 765 284-5594
Muncie *(G-10443)*

Cerro Wire LLC ....D 812 793-2929
Crothersville *(G-2217)*

Dereeltech LLC ....E 812 293-4786
Nabb *(G-10639)*

E M F Corp ....D 260 488-2479
Hamilton *(G-5821)*

Essex Group Inc ....B 260 461-4000
Fort Wayne *(G-4244)*

International Wire Group Inc ....D 574 546-4680
Bremen *(G-1005)*

▲ Lake Copper Conductors LLC ....F 847 238-3000
Elkhart *(G-2983)*

REA Magnet Wire Company Inc ....B 765 477-8000
Lafayette *(G-8989)*

▲ Sdi Lafarga LLC ....D 260 748-6565
New Haven *(G-10958)*

3353 Aluminum Sheet, Plate & Foil

Alcoa Inc ....C 765 447-1707
Lafayette *(G-8849)*

Arconic Inc ....G 812 842-3300
Newburgh *(G-11022)*

Arconic Inc ....C 317 241-9393
Indianapolis *(G-6416)*

Arconic Inc ....B 812 853-6111
Newburgh *(G-11020)*

Arconic Inc ....B 412 553-4545
Newburgh *(G-11021)*

Closure Systems Intl Inc ....D 765 364-6300
Crawfordsville *(G-2139)*

Copper Brass Sale ....G 574 295-3100
Elkhart *(G-2773)*

Hogan Stamping LLC ....F 812 656-8222
West Harrison *(G-14039)*

Jupiter Aluminum Corporation ....E 219 932-3322
Fairland *(G-3823)*

▲ Jupiter Aluminum Corporation ....C 219 932-3322
Hammond *(G-5903)*

Lawrence Industries Inc ....G 260 432-9693
Fort Wayne *(G-4427)*

Novelis Corporation ....C 812 462-2287
Terre Haute *(G-13291)*

Overton & Sons TI & Die Co Inc ....E 317 736-7700
Franklin *(G-4918)*

Summit Manufacturing Corp ....E 260 428-2600
Fort Wayne *(G-4665)*

Taylor Made Enterprises ....G 765 653-8481
Greencastle *(G-5479)*

V N C Inc ....F 219 696-5031
Lowell *(G-9425)*

3354 Aluminum Extruded Prdts

◆ 80/20 Inc ....B 260 248-8030
Columbia City *(G-1757)*

▲ Alconex Specialty Products ....D 260 744-3446
Fort Wayne *(G-4056)*

Alexandria Extrusion Company ....E 317 545-1221
Indianapolis *(G-6363)*

▲ Alexin LLC ....D 260 353-3100
Bluffton *(G-863)*

Aluminum Extrusions ....G 574 206-0100
Elkhart *(G-2680)*

Arconic Inc ....A 765 771-3600
Lafayette *(G-8852)*

Bon L Manufacturing Company ....C 815 351-6802
Kentland *(G-8517)*

Brazeway Inc ....D 317 392-2533
Shelbyville *(G-12524)*

Dyna Technology Inc ....G 219 663-2920
Crown Point *(G-2247)*

Hautau Tube Cutoff Systems LLC ....F 765 647-1600
Brookville *(G-1116)*

Hoosier Trim Products LLC ....E 317 271-4007
Indianapolis *(G-7125)*

Hydro Extruder LLC ....D 765 825-1141
Connersville *(G-2053)*

Hydro Extruder LLC ....C 574 262-2667
Elkhart *(G-2926)*

Hydro Extrusion North Amer LLC ....C 888 935-5757
North Liberty *(G-11215)*

Hydro Extrusion North Amer LLC ....B 888 935-5757
North Liberty *(G-11216)*

Indalex Inc ....G 765 457-1117
Kokomo *(G-8645)*

▼ Indiana Gratings Inc ....F 765 342-7191
Martinsville *(G-9615)*

▲ Jupiter Aluminum Corporation ....C 219 932-3322
Hammond *(G-5903)*

Kinro Manufacturing Inc ....C 574 533-8337
Goshen *(G-5257)*

Lakemaster Inc ....E 765 288-3718
Muncie *(G-10507)*

McKinney Corporation ....E 765 448-4800
Lafayette *(G-8964)*

Napier & Napier ....G 765 580-9116
Liberty *(G-9266)*

Omnimax International Inc ....C 574 294-8576
Elkhart *(G-3070)*

Parco Incorporated ....E 260 451-0810
Fort Wayne *(G-4521)*

Patrick Aluminum Inc ....G 574 262-1907
Elkhart *(G-3079)*

Patrick Industries Inc ....G 574 255-9692
Mishawaka *(G-10101)*

Plymouth Tube Company ....C 574 946-6191
Winamac *(G-14314)*

▲ Stalcop LLC ....D 765 436-7926
Thorntown *(G-13378)*

Torsion Plastics LLC ....F 330 552-2184
Evansville *(G-3767)*

Tredegar Corporation ....D 812 466-0266
Terre Haute *(G-13356)*

3355 Aluminum Rolling & Drawing, NEC

A/C Fabricating Corp ....E 574 534-1415
Goshen *(G-5163)*

Alcoa Warrick LLC ....G 812 853-6111
Newburgh *(G-11019)*

▲ Alconex Specialty Products ....D 260 744-3446
Fort Wayne *(G-4056)*

Alconex Specialty Products ....G 260 744-3446
Fort Wayne *(G-4057)*

Gerard ....G 219 924-6388
Highland *(G-6046)*

Highmark Technologies LLC ....E 260 483-0012
Fort Wayne *(G-4334)*

▲ Postle Operating LLC ....E 574 389-0800
Elkhart *(G-3105)*

REA Magnet Wire Company Inc ....B 765 477-8000
Lafayette *(G-8989)*

Revere Industries ....G 317 638-1521
Indianapolis *(G-7835)*

Rockport Roll Shop LLc ....E 812 362-6419
Rockport *(G-12172)*

Spectra Metal Sales Inc ....G 317 822-8291
Indianapolis *(G-7973)*

3356 Rolling, Drawing-Extruding Of Nonferrous Metals

Arcelormittal USA LLC ....D 219 787-2120
Chesterton *(G-1595)*

Demotte Manufacturing Inc ....G 219 987-6196
Demotte *(G-2435)*

Dnm Converters & Cores ....G 502 599-5225
Clarksville *(G-1679)*

E & S Metal Inc ....F 260 563-7714
Wabash *(G-13726)*

Eco-Bat America LLC ....C 317 247-1303
Indianapolis *(G-6801)*

Ed Nickels ....G 219 887-6128
Merrillville *(G-9712)*

GKN Aerospace Muncie Inc ....E 765 747-7147
Muncie *(G-10477)*

Hammond Group Inc ....E 219 845-0031
Hammond *(G-5886)*

▲ Hammond Lead Products Llc ....G 219 931-9360
Hammond *(G-5887)*

Haynes International Inc ....A 765 457-3790
Kokomo *(G-8637)*

Haynes International Inc ....C 219 326-8530
La Porte *(G-8762)*

Haynes International Inc ....A 765 456-6000
Kokomo *(G-8638)*

Huntington Alloys Corporation ....E 574 262-3451
Elkhart *(G-2923)*

▲ Indiana U Bolts Inc ....E 317 870-1940
Waterloo *(G-14015)*

▲ Metal Source LLC ....E 260 563-8833
Wabash *(G-13738)*

Metals and Additives Corp Inc ....E 812 446-2525
Brazil *(G-969)*

Mi-Tech Tungsten Metals LLC ....D 317 549-4290
Indianapolis *(G-7495)*

Murrays Tin Cup ....G....... 260 349-1002
  Kendallville *(G-8498)*

Patricia J Nickels Inc ....G....... 502 489-4358
  Charlestown *(G-1579)*

Rhon Inc ....G....... 574 297-5217
  Monticello *(G-10283)*

Special Metals Corporation...........E....... 574 262-3451
  Elkhart *(G-3183)*

TI Group Auto Systems LLC ....C....... 260 587-6100
  Ashley *(G-291)*

Titanium Eagles Nutrition ....G....... 219 781-6018
  Lake Station *(G-9079)*

Titanium LLC ....G....... 765 236-6906
  Kokomo *(G-8708)*

Titanium Rails Nutrition LLC ....G....... 219 940-3704
  Hobart *(G-6099)*

▲ Tube Processing Corp ....B....... 317 787-1321
  Indianapolis *(G-8107)*

Tube Processing Corp ....G....... 317 264-7760
  Indianapolis *(G-8109)*

3357 Nonferrous Wire Drawing

▲ Accel International ....F....... 260 897-9990
  Avilla *(G-400)*

▲ Alconex Specialty Products.......D....... 260 744-3446
  Fort Wayne *(G-4056)*

◆ Almega/Tru-Flex Inc ....E....... 574 546-2113
  Bremen *(G-982)*

Belden 1993 LLC...........................C....... 606 348-8433
  Richmond *(G-11961)*

Belden Inc ....A....... 765 962-7561
  Richmond *(G-11962)*

Belden Inc ....C....... 317 818-6300
  Indianapolis *(G-6262)*

Belden Wire & Cable Co LLC ....B....... 606 348-8433
  Richmond *(G-11963)*

Cerro Wire LLC.............................D....... 812 793-2929
  Crothersville *(G-2217)*

Elektrisola Incorporated ....G....... 317 375-8192
  Indianapolis *(G-6819)*

▲ Essex Group Inc ....C....... 260 461-4000
  Fort Wayne *(G-4243)*

Essex Group Inc ....B....... 260 461-4000
  Fort Wayne *(G-4244)*

Essex Group Inc ....C....... 260 461-4183
  Fort Wayne *(G-4245)*

Essex Group Inc ....G....... 260 461-4994
  Fort Wayne *(G-4246)*

Essex Group Inc ....D....... 260 248-5500
  Columbia City *(G-1785)*

Essex Group Inc ....G....... 260 248-5500
  Columbia City *(G-1786)*

Essex Group Inc ....G....... 704 598-0222
  Fort Wayne *(G-4247)*

Essex Group Inc ....E....... 317 738-4365
  Franklin *(G-4885)*

General Cable Industries Inc ....E....... 317 271-8447
  Indianapolis *(G-6993)*

General Cable Industries Inc ....B....... 765 664-2321
  Marion *(G-9524)*

General Cable Industries Inc ....C....... 317 271-8447
  Indianapolis *(G-6994)*

Indy Wiring Services LLC ....G....... 317 371-7044
  Brownsburg *(G-1155)*

Installed Building Pdts LLC ....G....... 317 398-3216
  Shelbyville *(G-12539)*

International Wire Group Inc..........D....... 574 546-4680
  Bremen *(G-1005)*

Latch Gard Co Inc ....G....... 574 862-2373
  Elkhart *(G-2986)*

Precision Utilities Group Inc...........C....... 260 485-8300
  Fort Wayne *(G-4553)*

REA Magnet Wire Company Inc .....B....... 260 421-5400
  Fort Wayne *(G-4580)*

REA Magnet Wire Company Inc .....B....... 765 477-8000
  Lafayette *(G-8989)*

▲ Sanlo Inc ....D....... 219 879-0241
  Michigan City *(G-9841)*

▲ Telamon Corporation ....C....... 317 818-6888
  Carmel *(G-1488)*

Wire America Inc ....E....... 260 969-1700
  Fort Wayne *(G-4758)*

3363 Aluminum Die Castings

Aluminum Foundries Inc ....C....... 765 584-6501
  Winchester *(G-14324)*

▲ Batesville Products Inc ....D....... 513 381-2057
  Lawrenceburg *(G-9133)*

Custom Die Casting Inc..................F....... 765 935-3979
  Richmond *(G-11975)*

▲ Enkei America Moldings Inc ....G....... 812 373-7000
  Columbus *(G-1921)*

FCA US LLC ....A....... 765 454-1005
  Kokomo *(G-8625)*

General Aluminum Mfg Company ...C....... 260 495-2600
  Fremont *(G-4960)*

General Motors LLC.......................A....... 812 379-7360
  Bedford *(G-545)*

George Koch Sons MGT Inc ....G....... 812 422-3257
  Evansville *(G-3520)*

▲ Grandview Aluminum Products.......E....... 812 649-2569
  Grandview *(G-5387)*

Hill & Griffith Company ....E....... 317 241-9233
  Indianapolis *(G-7108)*

Kitchen-Quip Inc ....E....... 260 837-8311
  Kendallville *(G-8487)*

▲ Koch Enterprises Inc ....G....... 812 465-9800
  Evansville *(G-3596)*

▲ Littler Diecast A Brahm Corp ....D....... 765 789-4456
  Albany *(G-11)*

▲ Madison Precision Products Inc ......B....... 812 273-4702
  Madison *(G-9481)*

Noblitt International Corp...............G....... 812 372-9969
  Columbus *(G-1981)*

Revere Industries LLC ....G....... 317 580-2420
  Westfield *(G-14184)*

▲ Ryobi Die Casting (usa) Inc ....A....... 317 398-3398
  Shelbyville *(G-12565)*

Shiloh Industries Inc.....................E....... 260 925-4711
  Auburn *(G-356)*

◆ SUs Cast Products Inc ....D....... 574 753-4111
  Logansport *(G-9367)*

▲ Whb International Inc ....G....... 317 820-3001
  Indianapolis *(G-8188)*

3364 Nonferrous Die Castings, Exc Aluminum

▲ Aero Metals Inc........................B....... 219 326-1976
  La Porte *(G-8727)*

Brooks Langeloh ....G....... 219 691-3577
  Columbia City *(G-1768)*

Custom Die Casting Inc..................F....... 765 935-3979
  Richmond *(G-11975)*

Hill & Griffith Company ....E....... 317 241-9233
  Indianapolis *(G-7108)*

▼ Indiana Gratings Inc ....F....... 765 342-7191
  Martinsville *(G-9615)*

S P X Corp ....G....... 574 594-9681
  Pierceton *(G-11578)*

3365 Aluminum Foundries

AAA-Gpc Holdings LLC...................D....... 260 668-1468
  Angola *(G-187)*

Aluminum Foundries Inc................C....... 765 584-6501
  Winchester *(G-14324)*

Ashley Aluminum Foundry Inc ....G....... 812 793-2654
  Crothersville *(G-2215)*

Batesville Products Inc ....D....... 812 926-4230
  Aurora *(G-373)*

Busche Performance Group Inc ......C....... 260 636-7030
  Avilla *(G-402)*

Ce Systems Inc ....E....... 812 372-8234
  Columbus *(G-1868)*

Dillon Pattern Works Inc ....F....... 765 642-3549
  Anderson *(G-95)*

Dualtech Inc.................................E....... 317 738-9043
  Franklin *(G-4882)*

▲ Enkei America Inc ....A....... 812 373-7000
  Columbus *(G-1920)*

Ewing Light Metals Co Inc ....F....... 317 926-4591
  Indianapolis *(G-6886)*

FCA US LLC ....A....... 765 454-0018
  Kokomo *(G-8624)*

FCA US LLC ....A....... 765 454-1005
  Kokomo *(G-8625)*

Flextech Corporation ....G....... 574 271-9797
  Elkhart *(G-2857)*

Foley Pattern Company Inc............E....... 260 925-4113
  Auburn *(G-332)*

General Aluminum Mfg Company ...D....... 260 356-3900
  Huntington *(G-6206)*

General Aluminum Mfg Company ...C....... 260 495-2600
  Fremont *(G-4960)*

▲ Global ....G....... 317 494-6174
  Franklin *(G-4889)*

▲ Grandview Aluminum Products.......E....... 812 649-2569
  Grandview *(G-5387)*

Indiana Refractories Inc ....E....... 260 426-3286
  Fort Wayne *(G-4365)*

Kessington LLC.............................D....... 574 266-4500
  Elkhart *(G-2962)*

Machined Castings Spc LLC ....F....... 574 223-5694
  Rochester *(G-12135)*

▲ Madison Precision Products Inc ......B....... 812 273-4702
  Madison *(G-9481)*

Mahoney Foundries Inc..................D....... 260 347-1768
  Kendallville *(G-8493)*

▲ Metaldyne Bsm LLC ....D....... 260 495-4315
  Fremont *(G-4968)*

Montro Company ....G....... 812 268-4390
  Sullivan *(G-13088)*

Muncie Casting Corp ....E....... 765 288-2611
  Muncie *(G-10528)*

New Point Products Inc..................G....... 812 663-6311
  New Point *(G-11003)*

Ph Inc ....E....... 877 467-4763
  Plymouth *(G-11711)*

Phillips Pattern & Casting Inc.........F....... 765 288-2319
  Muncie *(G-10546)*

◆ Pirod Inc ....F....... 574 936-7221
  Plymouth *(G-11712)*

▲ Ryobi Die Casting (usa) Inc ....A....... 317 398-3398
  Shelbyville *(G-12565)*

Shipston Alum Tech Intl Inc ....C....... 317 738-0282
  Franklin *(G-4930)*

Shipston Alum Tech Intl LLC ....C....... 317 738-0282
  Franklin *(G-4931)*

Shipston Aluminum Tech Ind Inc ....C....... 317 738-0282
  Franklin *(G-4932)*

◆ SUs Cast Products Inc ....D....... 574 753-4111
  Logansport *(G-9367)*

▲ Vice Bros Pattern Shop & Fndry.......G....... 260 782-2585
  Lagro *(G-9073)*

Wabash Castings Inc ....C....... 260 563-8371
  Wabash *(G-13761)*

▲ Ward Corporation ....C....... 260 426-8700
  Fort Wayne *(G-4735)*

Wingards Sales LLC ....G....... 260 768-7961
  Shipshewana *(G-12659)*

3366 Copper Foundries

A Raymond Tinnerman Auto Inc ......C....... 574 722-5168
  Logansport *(G-9319)*

Ashley Aluminum Foundry Inc ....G....... 812 793-2654
  Crothersville *(G-2215)*

Beckett Bronze Company Inc ....E....... 765 282-2261
  Muncie *(G-10439)*

Beckett Bronze Company Inc ....E....... 765 282-2261
  Muncie *(G-10438)*

Complete Drives Inc ....F....... 260 489-6033
  Fort Wayne *(G-4171)*

Crosbie Foundry Co Inc ....G....... 574 262-1502
  Elkhart *(G-2777)*

Cunningham Pattern & Engrg Inc ....F....... 812 379-9571
  Columbus *(G-1902)*

Demotte Manufacturing Inc............G....... 219 987-6196
  Demotte *(G-2435)*

Ewing Light Metals Co Inc ....F....... 317 926-4591
  Indianapolis *(G-6886)*

Foundry Services Inc.....................C....... 317 955-8112
  Noblesville *(G-11105)*

▲ Grandview Aluminum Products.......E....... 812 649-2569
  Grandview *(G-5387)*

Leon R Dixon ....G....... 317 545-1956
  Indianapolis *(G-7397)*

▲ LFD Bearings LLC.....................G....... 574 245-0375
  Elkhart *(G-2996)*

Mahoney Foundries Inc..................D....... 260 347-1768
  Kendallville *(G-8493)*

▲ Mark Parmenter ....G....... 812 829-6583
  Spencer *(G-13030)*

Netshape Technologies LLC ....C....... 812 755-4501
  Campbellsburg *(G-1278)*

New Point Products Inc..................G....... 812 663-6311
  New Point *(G-11003)*

Parker-Hannifin Corporation..........C....... 260 636-2104
  Albion *(G-32)*

Phillips Pattern & Casting Inc.........F....... 765 288-2319
  Muncie *(G-10546)*

Poyser Kelshaw Group LLC.............G....... 317 571-8493
  Carmel *(G-1453)*

▲ Stalcop LLC ....D....... 765 436-7926
  Thorntown *(G-13378)*

Sterling Sales and Engineering ......G....... 765 376-0454
  Veedersburg *(G-13646)*

▲ Wilhoite Monuments Inc.............G....... 765 286-7423
  Muncie *(G-10584)*

▲ Yamaha Marine Precision Propel ...E....... 317 545-9080
  Indianapolis *(G-8223)*

Employee Codes: A=Over 500 employees, B=251-500
C=101-250, D=51-100, E=20-50, F=10-19, G=2-9   2018 Harris Indiana
Industrial Directory   619

3369 Nonferrous Foundries: Castings, NEC

Accurate Castings Inc ....D....... 219 393-3122
La Porte *(G-8726)*
Aluminum Foundries Inc ....C....... 765 584-6501
Winchester *(G-14324)*
▼ **ATI Casting Service LLC** ....E....... 219 362-1000
La Porte *(G-8736)*
Batesville Products Inc ....D....... 812 926-4230
Aurora *(G-373)*
▲ **Batesville Products Inc** ....D....... 513 381-2057
Lawrenceburg *(G-9133)*
Crosbie Foundry Co Inc ....E....... 574 262-1502
Elkhart *(G-2777)*
▲ **Duramold Castings Inc** ....E....... 574 251-1111
South Bend *(G-12753)*
Ewing Light Metals Co Inc ....E....... 317 926-4591
Indianapolis *(G-6886)*
▲ **Excel Manufacturing Inc** ....D....... 812 523-6764
Seymour *(G-12448)*
General Products Corporation ....C....... 260 668-1440
Angola *(G-217)*
Heartland Castings Inc ....E....... 260 837-8311
Waterloo *(G-14014)*
Howmet Castings & Services Inc ...A....... 219 326-7400
La Porte *(G-8767)*
Kitchen-Quip Inc ....E....... 260 837-8311
Kendallville *(G-8487)*
New Point Products Inc ....G....... 812 663-6311
New Point *(G-11003)*
▲ **Nonferrous Products Inc** ....E....... 317 738-2558
Franklin *(G-4914)*
▲ **Orthodontic Design and Prod** ...E....... 760 734-3995
Franklin *(G-4917)*
Ph Inc ....G....... 877 467-4763
Plymouth *(G-11711)*
◆ **Pirod Inc** ....F....... 574 936-7221
Plymouth *(G-11712)*
▲ **Symmetry Medical Mfg Inc** ......D....... 574 371-2284
Warsaw *(G-13949)*
Tdy Industries LLC ....C....... 219 362-1000
La Porte *(G-8827)*
Tech Castings LLC ....E....... 765 535-4100
Shirley *(G-12663)*
▲ **Ward Corporation** ....C....... 260 426-8700
Fort Wayne *(G-4735)*

3398 Metal Heat Treating

A Raymond Tinnerman Auto Inc ...C....... 574 722-5168
Logansport *(G-9319)*
▲ **Advanced Ntrding Solutions LLC** ...F....... 812 932-1010
Batesville *(G-489)*
Al Fe Heat Treating-Ohio Inc ......E....... 260 747-9422
Fort Wayne *(G-4053)*
Al-Fe Heat Treating Inc ....D....... 260 747-9422
Fort Wayne *(G-4054)*
Al-Fe Heat Treating Inc ....F....... 888 747-2533
Fort Wayne *(G-4055)*
Al-Fe Heat Treating Inc ....E....... 260 563-8321
Wabash *(G-13720)*
Albany Metal Treating Inc ....D....... 765 789-6470
Albany *(G-10)*
Allegheny Ludlum LLC ....E....... 765 529-9570
New Castle *(G-10890)*
Applied Thermal Tech Inc ....E....... 574 269-7116
Warsaw *(G-13839)*
Atmosphere Annealing LLC ....E....... 812 346-1275
North Vernon *(G-11248)*
▲ **B&J Rocket America Inc** ....E....... 574 825-5802
Middlebury *(G-9874)*
Bodycote Thermal Proc Inc ....E....... 812 662-0500
Greensburg *(G-5591)*
Bodycote Thermal Proc Inc ....D....... 260 423-1691
Fort Wayne *(G-4115)*
Bodycote Thermal Proc Inc ....E....... 574 295-2491
Elkhart *(G-2730)*
Bodycote Thermal Proc Inc ....E....... 317 924-4321
Indianapolis *(G-6493)*
Boyd Machine & Repair Co Inc ....E....... 260 635-2195
Kimmell *(G-8529)*
Bwt LLC ....E....... 574 232-3338
South Bend *(G-12729)*
Chicago Flame Hardening Co ....E....... 773 768-3608
East Chicago *(G-2524)*
Circle City Heat Treating Inc ....F....... 317 638-2252
Indianapolis *(G-6607)*
D & D Industries Inc ....G....... 219 844-5600
Hammond *(G-5868)*
Dependable Metal Treating Inc ....F....... 260 347-5744
Kendallville *(G-8473)*

Electro Seal Corporation ....G....... 219 926-8606
Chesterton *(G-1603)*
Estes Designs ....G....... 317 899-5556
Indianapolis *(G-6881)*
▲ **Exotic Metal Treating Inc** ....F....... 317 784-8565
Indianapolis *(G-6895)*
Gerdau Macsteel Inc ....E....... 260 356-9520
Huntington *(G-6207)*
Gerdau Macsteel Atmosphere Ann ...E....... 812 346-1275
North Vernon *(G-11259)*
H & H Commercial Heat Treating ...G....... 765 288-3618
Muncie *(G-10480)*
Hartford Heat Treatment ....E....... 812 725-8272
New Albany *(G-10792)*
Honeycomb Products Inc ....E....... 317 787-9351
Indianapolis *(G-7115)*
HTI ....E....... 574 722-2814
Logansport *(G-9337)*
Indiana Metal Treating Inc ....E....... 317 636-2421
Indianapolis *(G-7183)*
Learman Electronic Tool Assoc ....E....... 574 226-0420
Elkhart *(G-2991)*
Leed Thermal Processing Inc ......G....... 317 637-5102
Indianapolis *(G-7393)*
McLaughlin Services LLC ....F....... 260 897-4328
Avilla *(G-415)*
Metal Improvement Company LLC ...G....... 317 875-6030
Indianapolis *(G-7487)*
Mp Steel Indiana LLC ....E....... 260 347-1203
Kendallville *(G-8496)*
Niagara Lasalle Corporation ....E....... 800 262-2558
Hammond *(G-5921)*
Nitrex Inc ....E....... 317 346-7700
Franklin *(G-4913)*
▲ **Northern Indiana Manufacturing** ...E....... 574 342-2105
Bourbon *(G-946)*
Precision Heat Treating Corp ....E....... 260 749-5125
Fort Wayne *(G-4550)*
Quality Steel Treating Co Inc ......E....... 317 357-8691
Indianapolis *(G-7799)*
Rochester Heat Treating Co ....G....... 574 224-4328
Syracuse *(G-13141)*
◆ **Rogers Engineering and Mfg Co** ...E....... 765 478-5444
Cambridge City *(G-1261)*
Saran Industries LLC ....D....... 317 897-2170
Kokomo *(G-8690)*
Saran Industries LLC ....D....... 317 897-2170
Bloomington *(G-821)*
Simpson Alloy Services Inc ....E....... 812 969-2766
Elizabeth *(G-2646)*
Sinden Racing Service Inc ....F....... 317 243-7171
Indianapolis *(G-7949)*
Steel Technologies LLC ....C....... 502 245-2110
Portage *(G-11796)*
Sturm Heat Treating Inc ....F....... 317 357-2368
Indianapolis *(G-8014)*
Tool Dynamics LLC ....G....... 812 379-4243
Columbus *(G-2022)*
Toyo Seiko North America Inc ......G....... 574 288-2000
South Bend *(G-12975)*
Tri-State Metals Inc ....E....... 219 397-0470
East Chicago *(G-2574)*
Ward Corporation ....E....... 260 489-2281
Fort Wayne *(G-4736)*

3399 Primary Metal Prdts, NEC

Algalco LLC ....G....... 317 361-2787
Indianapolis *(G-6365)*
Creative Powder Coatings LLC .....D....... 260 489-3580
Fort Wayne *(G-4186)*
Elgin Fastener Group LLC ....G....... 812 689-8917
Versailles *(G-13653)*
▲ **Golden Beam Metals LLC** ....C....... 317 806-2750
Indianapolis *(G-7019)*
Hawk Precision Components Inc ....E....... 812 755-4501
Campbellsburg *(G-1277)*
▼ **Hope Powder Coat Inc** ....E....... 812 546-5555
Hope *(G-6115)*
Imerys Steelcasting Usa Inc ....G....... 219 921-1012
Westville *(G-14219)*
Intermetco Processing Inc ....E....... 812 423-5914
Evansville *(G-3564)*
▲ **ITW Gema** ....E....... 317 298-5000
Indianapolis *(G-7277)*
Jag Metal Solutions Inc ....G....... 765 445-4459
Knightstown *(G-8552)*
Jbs Powder Coating LLC ....E....... 812 952-1204
Lanesville *(G-9101)*
Keywest Metal ....G....... 219 513-8429
Griffith *(G-5781)*

Keywest Metal ....G....... 219 654-4063
Hobart *(G-6084)*
Netshape Technologies LLC ....C....... 812 755-4501
Campbellsburg *(G-1278)*
Newjac Inc ....D....... 765 483-2190
Lebanon *(G-9209)*
◆ **Omnisource LLC** ....C....... 260 422-5541
Fort Wayne *(G-4510)*
▲ **Powder Processing & Tech LLC** ...E....... 219 462-4141
Valparaiso *(G-13599)*
▲ **Powdertech Corp** ....E....... 219 462-4141
Valparaiso *(G-13600)*
Pro-Kote Indy ....E....... 317 872-0001
Indianapolis *(G-7767)*
Revere Industries LLC ....G....... 317 580-2420
Westfield *(G-14184)*
Shelton Powder Coating LLC ....E....... 574 323-8369
Granger *(G-5433)*
Sit Can Happen LLC ....G....... 812 346-4188
North Vernon *(G-11282)*
Ssw International Inc ....E....... 219 763-1199
Burns Harbor *(G-1220)*
TEC-Tool Inc ....G....... 812 526-3158
Indianapolis *(G-8044)*
Trinity Metals LLC ....G....... 317 358-8265
Indianapolis *(G-8101)*
◆ **Trinity Metals LLC** ....G....... 317 358-8265
Indianapolis *(G-8102)*
▲ **U S Granules Corporation** ....D....... 574 936-2146
Plymouth *(G-11732)*
Wendell Denton ....G....... 317 736-8397
Franklin *(G-4941)*

34 FABRICATED METAL PRODUCTS, EXCEPT MACHINERY AND TRANSPORTATION EQUIPMENT

3411 Metal Cans

Ameri Kan ....G....... 574 533-7032
Warsaw *(G-13838)*
Ball Inc ....F....... 317 736-8236
Franklin *(G-4871)*
Ball Metal Beverage Cont Corp ....C....... 574 583-9418
Monticello *(G-10254)*
Bev Rexam Can Americas Inc ....G....... 773 399-3000
West Lafayette *(G-14052)*
Bway Corporation ....D....... 219 462-8915
Valparaiso *(G-13517)*
Crown Cork & Seal Usa Inc ....D....... 765 362-3200
Crawfordsville *(G-2146)*
Norton Packaging Inc ....E....... 574 867-6002
Hamlet *(G-5831)*
Powell Systems Inc ....G....... 765 884-0613
Fowler *(G-4804)*
R & M Welding & Fabricating Sp ...G....... 812 295-9130
Loogootee *(G-9392)*
Red Gold LP ....F....... 765 754-8750
Alexandria *(G-49)*
Silgan Containers Mfg Corp ....F....... 219 362-7002
La Porte *(G-8822)*
Silgan Containers Mfg Corp ....D....... 219 845-1500
Hammond *(G-5939)*
Silgan Containers Mfg Corp ....D....... 219 362-7002
La Porte *(G-8823)*
Silgan White Cap Corporation ......C....... 812 425-6222
Evansville *(G-3731)*
Silgan White Cap Corporation ......C....... 765 983-9200
Richmond *(G-12050)*

3412 Metal Barrels, Drums, Kegs & Pails

Anthony Wayne Rehabilitation C ...D....... 260 744-6145
Fort Wayne *(G-4078)*
Container Life Cycle MGT LLC ......D....... 317 357-9853
Indianapolis *(G-6653)*
North America Packaging Corp ......C....... 317 291-2396
Indianapolis *(G-7591)*
Nova Packaging Group Inc ....E....... 765 651-2600
Marion *(G-9548)*
OBryan Barrel Company Inc ....E....... 812 479-6741
Evansville *(G-3651)*
Packaging Corporation America ....E....... 812 522-3100
Seymour *(G-12473)*
Phoenix Drum Dryer Inc ....F....... 574 251-9040
South Bend *(G-12894)*
Powell Systems Inc ....G....... 765 884-0613
Fowler *(G-4804)*
Powell Systems Inc ....E....... 765 884-0980
Fowler *(G-4805)*

▲ Tru-Form Steel & Wire Inc...............E...... 765 348-5001
Hartford City (G-5993)

3421 Cutlery

▲ Allen-Davis Enterprises Inc............G...... 574 303-2173
Mishawaka (G-9993)

▲ Andys Global Inc..........................G...... 317 595-8825
Indianapolis (G-6401)

Becks...G...... 765 566-3900
Burlington (G-1210)

Bemcor Inc.....................................F...... 219 937-1600
Hammond (G-5850)

Ceg & Supply LLC..........................G...... 317 435-6398
Martinsville (G-9598)

Enmac LLC......................................G...... 812 298-8711
Terre Haute (G-13232)

Harry & Izzys Northside LLC...........G...... 317 915-8045
Indianapolis (G-7078)

Hayabusa LLC................................G...... 317 594-1188
Indianapolis (G-7080)

Pettigrew.......................................G...... 260 868-2032
Butler (G-1238)

Punjab Empire Inc..........................G...... 765 987-8786
Spiceland (G-13057)

Rush Hour Station..........................G...... 812 323-7874
Bloomington (G-819)

◆ Samco Group Inc.........................G...... 219 872-4413
Michigan City (G-9838)

Sushiya-US.....................................G...... 260 444-4263
Fort Wayne (G-4669)

Vogel Brothers Corporation.............D...... 812 376-2775
Columbus (G-2030)

3423 Hand & Edge Tools

Airodapt LLC..................................G...... 559 331-0156
Rensselaer (G-11911)

AK Tool and Die..............................G...... 574 286-9010
Mishawaka (G-9992)

Atlas Die LLC..................................D...... 574 295-0277
Elkhart (G-2700)

▲ Bloomfield Mfg Co Inc.................E...... 812 384-4441
Bloomfield (G-635)

◆ Brinly-Hardy Company.................D...... 812 218-7200
Jeffersonville (G-8332)

▲ BT&f LLC.....................................G...... 574 272-6128
Granger (G-5395)

C-L Building & Leasing Inc...............G...... 574 293-8959
Elkhart (G-2746)

Carpenter Co Inc.............................E...... 317 297-2900
Indianapolis (G-6557)

▲ CJ Automotive Indiana LLC...........C...... 260 868-2147
Butler (G-1225)

D & D Manufacturing Inc.................G...... 812 432-3294
Dillsboro (G-2465)

▲ Frederick Tool Corp.....................E...... 574 295-6700
Elkhart (G-2870)

Hogen Industries Inc Indiana...........E...... 317 591-5070
Indianapolis (G-7111)

Ideal Pro Cnc Inc............................F...... 260 693-1954
Churubusco (G-1652)

Illiana Grinding Machining Inc..........G...... 219 884-5828
Merrillville (G-9722)

Indiana Precision Tooling Inc...........F...... 812 667-5141
Dillsboro (G-2468)

Indy Stud Welding..........................G...... 317 416-3617
Indianapolis (G-7223)

J Porter Mfg Co...............................G...... 812 853-9395
Newburgh (G-11034)

James W Hager................................G...... 765 643-0188
Alexandria (G-46)

▲ Josam Company..........................D...... 219 872-5531
Michigan City (G-9805)

Kaiser Tool Company Inc.................E...... 260 484-3620
Fort Wayne (G-4403)

Laidig Inc.......................................E...... 574 256-0204
Mishawaka (G-10067)

Master Manufacturing Company.......E...... 812 425-1561
Evansville (G-3615)

Mid-West Spring Mfg Co..................D...... 574 353-1409
Mentone (G-9688)

Nestor Sales LLC............................G...... 574 295-5535
Elkhart (G-3060)

Osborn Manufacturing Corp.............F...... 574 267-6156
Warsaw (G-13920)

Perry Products Inc..........................G...... 260 668-7860
Angola (G-236)

▼ Pro-Form Plastics Inc..................E...... 812 522-4433
Crothersville (G-2220)

PVA Unlimited Inc...........................G...... 574 269-2782
Warsaw (G-13930)

Rapid Rule Co Inc............................G...... 574 784-2273
North Liberty (G-11220)

Rich Manufacturing Inc...................G...... 765 436-2744
Lebanon (G-9220)

▲ Seymour Manufacturing Co Inc.....C...... 812 522-2900
Seymour (G-12485)

▲ Seymour Midwest LLC..................D...... 574 267-7875
Warsaw (G-13938)

Stalter Glass Inc............................G...... 574 825-2225
Middlebury (G-9920)

Stone Artisans Ltd..........................G...... 317 362-0107
Indianapolis (G-8008)

3425 Hand Saws & Saw Blades

Archer Products Inc........................G...... 317 899-0700
Indianapolis (G-6414)

Drake Corporation...........................E...... 812 683-2101
Jasper (G-8246)

Tsb LLC..G...... 812 314-8331
Edinburgh (G-2630)

Valley Sharpening Inc......................G...... 574 674-9077
Osceola (G-11386)

◆ Wood-Mizer Holdings Inc.............C...... 317 271-1542
Indianapolis (G-8212)

3429 Hardware, NEC

A Raymond Tinnerman Auto Inc.......C...... 574 722-5168
Logansport (G-9319)

A-1 Door Specialties Inc..................G...... 260 749-1635
South Bend (G-12689)

Allegion Public Ltd Company............F...... 317 810-3700
Carmel (G-1307)

Allegion S&S Holding Co Inc............B...... 317 810-3700
Carmel (G-1308)

▲ American Flame Inc....................D...... 260 459-1703
Fort Wayne (G-4070)

Assurance Locking Systems LLC......G...... 317 786-8724
Indianapolis (G-6430)

▲ Avis Industrial Corporation..........E...... 765 998-8100
Upland (G-13468)

▲ Batesville Products Inc...............D...... 513 381-2057
Lawrenceburg (G-9133)

▲ Bloomfield Mfg Co Inc.................E...... 812 384-4441
Bloomfield (G-635)

▲ Bottom Line Management Inc........F...... 812 944-7388
Clarksville (G-1674)

Budget Sales Inc.............................G...... 260 657-5185
Woodburn (G-14381)

Christopher Miller...........................G...... 812 442-0949
Brazil (G-956)

Creek Chassis Inc...........................G...... 317 247-4480
Indianapolis (G-6690)

Crossroads Door & Hardware Inc......G...... 812 234-9751
Terre Haute (G-13219)

Dorma...G...... 317 468-6742
Greenfield (G-5521)

Dormakaba USA Inc.........................A...... 317 806-4605
Indianapolis (G-6758)

◆ EJ Brooks Company......................D...... 260 624-4800
Angola (G-210)

Elkhart Hinge Co Inc........................F...... 574 293-2841
Elkhart (G-2825)

▼ Epco Products Inc........................E...... 260 747-8888
Fort Wayne (G-4240)

◆ Fabri-Tech Inc.............................E...... 317 849-7755
McCordsville (G-9666)

Fiedeke Vinyl Coverings Inc.............F...... 574 534-3408
Goshen (G-5214)

Fire King International LLC...............E...... 812 948-2795
New Albany (G-10779)

◆ Fki Security Group LLC.................B...... 812 948-8400
New Albany (G-10781)

▲ Frascio International LLC.............G...... 317 663-0030
Carmel (G-1382)

▲ Frederick Tool Corp.....................E...... 574 295-6700
Elkhart (G-2870)

▼ Geneva Manufacturing Inc...........E...... 260 368-7555
Geneva (G-5136)

Gibson Brothers Welding Inc...........F...... 765 948-5775
Fairmount (G-3832)

Grace Manufacturing Inc.................F...... 574 267-8000
Warsaw (G-13884)

Grrreat Creations...........................E...... 574 773-5331
Nappanee (G-10675)

▲ Guardian Ind Inc.........................E...... 219 874-5248
Michigan City (G-9799)

Hart Plastics Inc.............................E...... 574 264-7060
Elkhart (G-2909)

Hingecraft Corporation....................F...... 574 293-6543
Elkhart (G-2917)

Holland Metal Fab Inc.....................F...... 574 522-1434
Elkhart (G-2918)

Houck Industries Inc........................E...... 812 663-5675
Greensburg (G-5614)

Illinois Tool Works Inc....................D...... 219 874-4217
Michigan City (G-9803)

▲ Indiana Architectural Plywood......E...... 317 878-4822
Trafalgar (G-13436)

Indiana Custom Trucks LLC..............E...... 260 463-3244
Lagrange (G-9046)

▲ Indiana U Bolts Inc.....................E...... 317 870-1940
Waterloo (G-14015)

J Game Ventures LLC......................G...... 812 241-7096
Brownsburg (G-1157)

▲ JM Fittings LLC...........................D...... 260 747-9200
Fort Wayne (G-4396)

Kautex Inc......................................B...... 937 238-8096
Avilla (G-409)

Key Made Now.................................G...... 317 664-8582
Indianapolis (G-7344)

Keys R US.......................................G...... 317 616-0267
Indianapolis (G-7346)

L & S Lumber...................................G...... 765 886-1452
Greens Fork (G-5587)

L & W Engineering Inc.....................G...... 574 825-5351
Middlebury (G-9900)

◆ L E Johnson Products Inc.............D...... 574 293-5664
Elkhart (G-2977)

L E Johnson Products Inc.................E...... 574 293-5664
Elkhart (G-2978)

Latch Gard Co Inc...........................G...... 574 862-2373
Elkhart (G-2986)

Modern Forge Companies LLC..........A...... 708 388-1806
Merrillville (G-9738)

▲ Oak Security Group LLC...............F...... 317 585-9830
Indianapolis (G-7608)

Olon Industries Inc (us)...................F...... 812 254-0427
Washington (G-13994)

▲ Osr Inc.......................................E...... 812 342-7642
Columbus (G-1987)

Parker-Hannifin Corporation............A...... 260 748-6000
New Haven (G-10951)

▲ Pk USA Inc..................................B...... 317 395-5500
Shelbyville (G-12558)

Pridgeon & Clay Inc........................C...... 317 738-4885
Franklin (G-4923)

▲ Qmp Inc......................................G...... 574 262-1575
Elkhart (G-3124)

Quality Converters Inc....................E...... 260 829-6541
Orland (G-11356)

R & R Regulators Inc.......................F...... 574 522-5846
Elkhart (G-3134)

R&D Investment Holdings Inc...........E...... 260 749-1301
Fort Wayne (G-4575)

▲ Reelcraft Industries Inc...............C...... 855 634-9109
Columbia City (G-1824)

REM Industries Inc..........................E...... 574 862-2127
Wakarusa (G-13792)

▲ S C Pryor Inc..............................E...... 317 352-1281
Indianapolis (G-7878)

Samaron Corp.................................E...... 574 970-7070
Elkhart (G-3154)

Schuler Products Co........................G...... 812 852-4419
Napoleon (G-10642)

▲ Seymour Manufacturing Co Inc.....C...... 812 522-2900
Seymour (G-12485)

▲ Slb Corporation...........................F...... 574 255-9774
Mishawaka (G-10125)

Sparks Belting Company Inc............G...... 800 451-4537
Hammond (G-5945)

Sportcrafters Inc............................G...... 574 243-4994
Granger (G-5438)

Standard Fusee Corporation............E...... 765 472-4375
Peru (G-11548)

Stanley Security Solutions Inc.........E...... 317 598-0421
Indianapolis (G-7991)

Stanley Security Solutions Inc.........E...... 678 533-3846
Indianapolis (G-7992)

Stanley Security Solutions Inc.........G...... 317 849-2250
Indianapolis (G-7993)

Steel Parts Corporation...................B...... 765 675-2191
Tipton (G-13406)

Sur-Loc Inc....................................F...... 260 495-4065
Fremont (G-4975)

▲ Task Force Tips Inc.....................C...... 219 462-6161
Valparaiso (G-13626)

Task Force Tips Inc.........................F...... 219 462-6161
Valparaiso (G-13627)

Terry Liquidation III Inc...................E...... 219 362-3557
La Porte (G-8829)

Top Lock Corporation ....G....... 317 831-2000
Mooresville (G-10344)

Tri-State Hydraulics Indus Sup ....G....... 812 537-3485
Greendale (G-5495)

Tubular Engrg & Sls Co Inc..........F....... 765 536-2225
Summitville (G-13108)

▲ Ultra-Fab Products Inc ....F....... 574 294-7571
Elkhart (G-3231)

Universal Consolidated Methods ....E....... 260 637-2575
Fort Wayne (G-4719)

Velko Hinge Inc ....E....... 219 924-6363
Munster (G-10638)

Viking Inc ....E....... 260 244-6141
Columbia City (G-1845)

▲ Von Duprin LLC ....B....... 317 429-2866
Indianapolis (G-8168)

Von Duprin LLC ....G....... 317 899-2760
Indianapolis (G-8169)

W S F Fire Store ....E....... 812 421-3826
Evansville (G-3805)

Wallys Lockshop ....G....... 765 748-2282
Muncie (G-10579)

Ward Industries Inc...................F....... 574 825-2548
Middlebury (G-9923)

Western Products Indiana Inc ....F....... 765 529-6230
New Castle (G-10921)

Yoder Woodworking Inc ....G....... 574 546-5100
Bremen (G-1035)

3431 Enameled Iron & Metal Sanitary Ware

▲ Bootz Manufacturing Co LLC ....E....... 812 423-5401
Evansville (G-3391)

Bootz Manufacturing Co LLC ....G....... 812 423-5019
Evansville (G-3392)

Bootz Manufacturing Company ....D....... 812 425-4646
Evansville (G-3393)

▲ H A P Industries Inc ....G....... 765 948-3385
Jonesboro (G-8445)

▲ Josam Company ....D....... 219 872-5531
Michigan City (G-9805)

LCI Industries ....D....... 574 535-1125
Elkhart (G-2989)

Maax Inc ....E....... 574 936-3838
Plymouth (G-11704)

Olympic Fiberglass Industries........D....... 574 223-3101
Rochester (G-12142)

▲ Satellite Shelters ....E....... 574 350-2150
Bristol (G-1084)

Shank Brothers Inc ....F....... 260 744-4802
Fort Wayne (G-4618)

Stanley Oliver Products LLC ....G....... 260 499-3506
Lagrange (G-9068)

▼ T S F Co Inc ....G....... 812 985-2630
Evansville (G-3757)

Tiffany Marble of Indianapolis ....G....... 317 894-9141
Greenfield (G-5581)

3432 Plumbing Fixture Fittings & Trim, Brass

Ashley F Ward Inc ....E....... 574 294-1502
Elkhart (G-2696)

Ashley F Ward Inc ....E....... 219 879-4177
Michigan City (G-9767)

Barry Company Inc ....G....... 812 333-1850
Bloomington (G-673)

Bath Gallery Showroom ....G....... 219 531-2150
Valparaiso (G-13505)

Bootz Manufacturing Company........D....... 812 425-4646
Evansville (G-3393)

Buckaroos Inc ....F....... 317 899-9100
Indianapolis (G-6518)

Cloudburst Lawn Sprinkler Syst ....F....... 260 492-8400
Fort Wayne (G-4162)

Delta Faucet Company ....G....... 812 663-4433
Greensburg (G-5599)

▲ Eca Enterprises Inc ....E....... 812 526-6734
Edinburgh (G-2610)

Ferguson ....G....... 317 254-5965
Indianapolis (G-6916)

Ferguson Waterworks ....G....... 219 440-5254
Schererville (G-12321)

◆ Geberit Manufacturing Inc ....E....... 219 879-4466
Michigan City (G-9797)

▲ Josam Company ....D....... 219 872-5531
Michigan City (G-9805)

Lasalle Bristol Corporation ....C....... 574 936-9894
Plymouth (G-11701)

Lee Supply Corp ....G....... 812 333-4343
Bloomington (G-764)

LGS Plumbing Inc ....E....... 219 663-2177
Crown Point (G-2276)

◆ Masco Corporation of Indiana ....B....... 317 848-1812
Indianapolis (G-6273)

Nibco Inc ....C....... 574 296-1240
Goshen (G-5298)

Parker-Hannifin Corporation ....C....... 260 636-2104
Albion (G-32)

Rex Byers Htg & Coolg Systems ....F....... 765 459-8858
Kokomo (G-8689)

Schmidt Contracting Inc ....F....... 812 482-3923
Jasper (G-8303)

Siteone Landscape Supply LLC ....G....... 219 769-2351
Merrillville (G-9754)

St Regis Culvert Inc ....F....... 317 353-8065
Indianapolis (G-7982)

Stanley Oliver Products LLC ....G....... 260 499-3506
Lagrange (G-9068)

US Metals ....G....... 219 515-2756
Schererville (G-12351)

3433 Heating Eqpt

Allied Boiler & Welding Co ....G....... 317 272-4820
Avon (G-426)

▲ Bryan Steam LLC ....D....... 765 473-6651
Peru (G-11518)

Carrier Corporation ....D....... 317 243-0851
Indianapolis (G-6559)

Fives N Amercn Combustn Inc ....G....... 219 662-9600
Crown Point (G-2254)

Gmp Holdings LLC ....G....... 317 353-6580
Indianapolis (G-7016)

◆ Hale Industries Inc ....E....... 317 577-0337
Fortville (G-4778)

▲ Heat Wagons Inc ....F....... 219 464-8818
Valparaiso (G-13555)

Hitzer Inc ....E....... 260 589-8536
Berne (G-617)

▼ Inovateus Solar LLC ....E....... 574 485-1400
South Bend (G-12813)

▲ Marley-Wylain Company ....C....... 630 560-3703
Michigan City (G-9815)

Marley-Wylain Company ....G....... 219 879-6561
Michigan City (G-9816)

▲ Ngh Retail LLC ....G....... 219 476-0772
Valparaiso (G-13589)

Oesterling Chimney Sweep Inc ....G....... 812 372-3512
Columbus (G-1984)

▲ Our Country Home Entps Inc ....D....... 260 657-5605
Harlan (G-5974)

▲ Purolator Pdts A Filtration Co ....C....... 866 925-2247
Jeffersonville (G-8418)

Quanex Heat Treat ....E....... 260 356-9520
Huntington (G-6241)

Schmidt Contracting Inc ....F....... 812 482-3923
Jasper (G-8303)

Solar America Solutions LLC ....G....... 317 688-8581
Indianapolis (G-7959)

Southwark Metal Mfg Co ....G....... 317 823-5300
Indianapolis (G-7965)

Temptek Inc ....E....... 317 887-6352
Greenwood (G-5752)

Thermo Products LLC ....G....... 574 896-2133
North Judson (G-11214)

Trimble Combustion Systems Inc ....G....... 812 623-4545
Sunman (G-13120)

Troy Meggitt Inc ....D....... 812 547-7071
Troy (G-13448)

▲ Wayne/Scott Fetzer Company ....E....... 260 425-9200
Fort Wayne (G-4745)

Wrib Manufacturing Inc ....G....... 765 294-2841
Veedersburg (G-13648)

3441 Fabricated Structural Steel

99 Nufab Rebar LLC..................D....... 260 572-1315
Auburn (G-311)

A & B Fabricating & Maint Inc ....F....... 574 353-1012
Mentone (G-9684)

A & D Constructors Inc ....C....... 812 428-3708
Evansville (G-3328)

A-1 Welding & Repair ....G....... 812 853-9701
Newburgh (G-11016)

Accuburn Williamsport Inc ....F....... 765 762-1100
Williamsport (G-14286)

Advance Aero Inc ....G....... 317 513-6071
Mooresville (G-10300)

Advance Fabricators Inc ....E....... 812 944-6941
New Albany (G-10741)

Advanced Systems Intgrtion LLC ....F....... 260 447-5555
Fort Wayne (G-4045)

Aeromotive Mfg Inc ....G....... 765 552-0668
Elwood (G-3293)

Afc Industries Inc ....E....... 574 264-1987
Elkhart (G-2670)

Aggreate Systems ....G....... 260 854-4711
Rome City (G-12198)

Ajem Welding ....G....... 812 595-3541
Austin (G-394)

All City Metal Craft Inc ....G....... 317 782-9340
Indianapolis (G-6366)

Allen Fabricators Inc ....F....... 260 458-0008
Fort Wayne (G-4059)

Almet Inc ....D....... 260 493-1556
New Haven (G-10928)

Alum-Elec Structures Inc ....G....... 260 347-9362
Kendallville (G-8453)

Aluminum Wldg & Mch Works Inc ....G....... 219 787-8066
Chesterton (G-1592)

Ambassador Steel Corporation ....E....... 317 834-3434
Mooresville (G-10302)

American Fabricating ....G....... 812 897-0900
Boonville (G-907)

American Fabricators Inc ....G....... 219 844-4744
Hammond (G-5840)

American Machine Fabrication ....G....... 812 944-4136
New Albany (G-10744)

Amerimax Fabricated Products ....G....... 574 389-8960
Bristol (G-1045)

Anthony Wayne Rehabilitation C ....D....... 260 744-6145
Fort Wayne (G-4078)

Avenue Industries Inc ....G....... 574 674-6971
Osceola (G-11370)

Awol Metal Contorsion LLC ....G....... 260 909-0411
Kendallville (G-8457)

B & M Steel & Welding Inc ....G....... 765 964-5868
Union City (G-13453)

B C Welding Inc........................G....... 574 272-9008
Granger (G-5392)

Baker Metalworks ....G....... 260 572-9353
Saint Joe (G-12252)

Bedford Crane LLC ....E....... 812 275-4411
Bedford (G-531)

Benchmark Inc ....G....... 812 238-0659
Terre Haute (G-13199)

Blackhawk Millwright & Rigging ....G....... 765 662-7922
Kokomo (G-8598)

Bralin Laser Services Inc ....E....... 260 357-6511
Auburn (G-318)

Buchanan Iron Works Inc ....G....... 219 785-4480
Westville (G-14214)

Buhrt Engineering & Cnstr.............E....... 574 267-3720
Warsaw (G-13852)

Builders Iron Works Inc...............E....... 574 254-1553
Mishawaka (G-10014)

C & C Iron Inc ....E....... 219 769-2511
Merrillville (G-9706)

C & P Engineering & Mfg..............E....... 765 825-4293
Connersville (G-2042)

C F Slattery Steel Fabrication ....G....... 812 948-9167
New Albany (G-10756)

C Fabco/L Inc ....E....... 219 785-4181
La Porte (G-8743)

▲ CAM Metal Fabrication LLC ....G....... 260 982-6280
North Manchester (G-11226)

Centerline Studio ....G....... 317 423-3220
Indianapolis (G-6577)

Central Illinois Steel Company ....G....... 219 882-1026
Gary (G-5035)

Central States Fabricating ....F....... 574 288-5607
South Bend (G-12733)

Central States Mfg Inc ....D....... 219 879-4770
Michigan City (G-9773)

Century Steel Fabricating Inc ....F....... 317 834-1295
Camby (G-1265)

Chicago Specialty Steel Corp ....E....... 219 922-8888
Griffith (G-5771)

Chief Industries Inc....................C....... 219 866-4121
Rensselaer (G-11917)

Circle R Industries Inc ....G....... 765 379-2768
Rossville (G-12210)

Cives Corporation ....C....... 219 279-4000
Wolcott (G-14362)

▲ CJ Automotive Indiana LLC ....C....... 260 868-2147
Butler (G-1225)

Coffee Lomont & Moyer Inc ....F....... 260 422-7825
Fort Wayne (G-4166)

Craig Welding and Mfg Inc ....E....... 574 353-7912
Mentone (G-9687)

Crossrads Rhbilitation Ctr Inc ....C....... 317 897-7320
Indianapolis (G-6697)

Crown Mtal Fbricators Erectors ....G....... 219 661-8277
Crown Point (G-2240)

Cryogenic Support Systems Inc.........G....... 765 764-4961
Williamsport (G-14288)
▲ Crystal Industries Inc.........E....... 574 264-6166
Elkhart (G-2779)
Custom Steel Technologies LLC.........G....... 812 546-2299
Hope (G-6111)
Cutting Edge Craftsmen LLC.........G....... 317 757-6975
Indianapolis (G-6718)
Cyclone Shop Inc.........G....... 812 683-2887
Huntingburg (G-6154)
D & M Systems Inc.........G....... 812 327-2384
Owensburg (G-11425)
D A Hochstetler & Sons LLP.........F....... 574 642-1144
Topeka (G-13416)
Deco Corporation.........E....... 812 342-4767
Columbus (G-1906)
Deister Machine Company Inc.........C....... 260 422-0354
Fort Wayne (G-4207)
Delbert M Dawson & Son Inc.........G....... 765 284-9711
Muncie (G-10458)
Delphi Body Works.........F....... 765 564-2212
Delphi (G-2417)
▲ DH Machine Inc.........D....... 574 773-9211
Nappanee (G-10667)
Die-Mensional Metal Stamping.........F....... 812 265-3946
Madison (G-9456)
Diversified Coating & Fabg Inc.........E....... 260 563-2858
Wabash (G-13724)
DL Schwartz Co LLC.........G....... 260 692-1464
Berne (G-612)
Dpc Inc.........E....... 765 564-3752
Delphi (G-2419)
Dx 4 LLC.........F....... 260 410-3749
Fort Wayne (G-4229)
Dynamic Industrial Group LLC.........G....... 574 295-5525
Elkhart (G-2806)
▼ Dynamic Metals LLC.........D....... 574 262-2497
Elkhart (G-2807)
◆ Ebc LLC.........E....... 812 234-4111
Terre Haute (G-13230)
Edgewood Metal Fab LLC.........G....... 574 546-5947
Bremen (G-998)
Electric Metal Fab Inc.........F....... 812 988-9353
Nashville (G-10723)
Elevator Equipment Corporation.........D....... 765 966-7761
Richmond (G-11981)
Elixir Industries.........E....... 574 294-5685
Elkhart (G-2817)
Elixir Industries.........D....... 574 294-5685
Elkhart (G-2818)
Emergency Radio Service LLC.........E....... 317 821-0422
Ligonier (G-9282)
Engineered Conveyors Inc.........F....... 765 459-4545
Kokomo (G-8621)
▲ Ernstberger Enterprises Inc.........D....... 812 282-0488
Jeffersonville (G-8358)
Ers Holding Company Inc.........E....... 260 894-4145
Ligonier (G-9283)
Ers Tower LLC.........E....... 260 894-4145
Ligonier (G-9284)
Eta Fabrication Inc.........F....... 260 897-3711
Avilla (G-404)
Euclid Machine & Tool Inc.........E....... 219 397-1374
East Chicago (G-2528)
Evans Metal Products Co Inc.........F....... 574 264-2166
Elkhart (G-2838)
Fab-Tech Industries.........G....... 765 478-4191
Cambridge City (G-1256)
Fabricated Metals Corp.........F....... 219 734-6896
Chesterton (G-1605)
Fabricated Metals Corp.........F....... 219 871-0230
Michigan City (G-9790)
Fabricated Steel Corporation.........G....... 317 899-0012
Indianapolis (G-6901)
Farm Fab.........G....... 574 862-4775
Goshen (G-5213)
Fasttimes Fabrication Cus.........G....... 574 858-9222
Etna Green (G-3321)
First Metals & Plastics Inc.........E....... 812 379-4400
Columbus (G-1930)
Four Star Fabricators Inc.........D....... 812 354-9995
Petersburg (G-11562)
Ftr Trnsportation Intelligence.........G....... 888 988-1699
Bloomington (G-729)
Gannon Mtal Fbrcators Erectors.........G....... 219 398-0299
East Chicago (G-2529)
Gary Bridge and Iron Co Inc.........G....... 219 884-3792
Gary (G-5049)
Gary Earl.........G....... 812 279-6780
Bedford (G-544)

Gary Ratcliff.........G....... 765 538-3170
Lafayette (G-8905)
Geiger & Peters Inc.........D....... 317 322-7740
Indianapolis (G-6989)
Gem-Rose Corp.........G....... 317 773-6400
Noblesville (G-11110)
General Fabr.........G....... 260 593-3858
Topeka (G-13420)
Gl Properties Inc.........G....... 219 763-1177
Portage (G-11765)
Graber Steel & Fab LLC.........E....... 812 636-8418
Odon (G-11328)
Grant County Steel Inc.........F....... 765 668-7547
Marion (G-9527)
Greensgroomer Worldwide Inc.........G....... 317 388-0695
Indianapolis (G-7046)
Griffith Machine & Fabricating.........G....... 219 980-8855
Gary (G-5055)
Halo Metalworks Inc.........F....... 317 481-0100
Indianapolis (G-7066)
Hamilton Iron Works Inc.........G....... 574 533-3784
Goshen (G-5234)
Hammond Group Inc.........E....... 219 845-0031
Hammond (G-5886)
Harpring Steel Inc.........G....... 812 256-6326
Charlestown (G-1568)
Harris Rebar Nufab LLC.........D....... 260 925-5440
Auburn (G-334)
Heidtman Steel Products Inc.........C....... 419 691-4646
Butler (G-1229)
Helgeson Steel Inc.........F....... 574 293-5576
Elkhart (G-2912)
Horner Industrial Services Inc.........F....... 317 634-7165
Indianapolis (G-7129)
Huntington Sheet Metal Inc.........F....... 260 356-9011
Huntington (G-6212)
Igh Steel Fabrication Inc.........G....... 765 482-7534
Lebanon (G-9190)
▲ Imperial Stamping Corporation.........D....... 574 294-3780
Elkhart (G-2930)
In-Fab Inc.........G....... 812 279-8144
Bedford (G-549)
Indiana Bridge-Midwest Stl Inc.........D....... 765 288-1985
Muncie (G-10493)
▼ Indiana Gratings Inc.........F....... 765 342-7191
Martinsville (G-9615)
Indiana Steel & Engrg Inc.........E....... 812 275-3363
Bedford (G-552)
Indiana Steel Fabricating Inc.........E....... 317 247-4545
Indianapolis (G-7193)
Indiana Steel Fabricating Inc.........F....... 765 742-1031
Lafayette (G-8922)
▲ Indianapolis Fabrications LLC.........F....... 317 600-3522
Indianapolis (G-7198)
Industrial Contrs Skanska Inc.........E....... 812 423-7832
Evansville (G-3555)
▲ Industrial Metal-Fab Inc.........E....... 574 288-8368
South Bend (G-12812)
Industrial Steel Cnstr Inc.........C....... 219 885-5610
Gary (G-5069)
▲ Industrial Transmission Eqp.........E....... 574 936-3028
Plymouth (G-11694)
International Metals Proc Inc.........E....... 317 895-4141
Indianapolis (G-7254)
J A Smit Inc.........G....... 812 424-8141
Evansville (G-3568)
J Coffey Metal Masters Inc.........D....... 317 780-1864
Indianapolis (G-7284)
J L Squared Inc.........G....... 317 354-1513
Indianapolis (G-7287)
JD Metal Concepts Inc.........G....... 812 342-9111
Columbus (G-1950)
Jerico Metal Specialties Inc.........F....... 812 339-3182
Bloomington (G-755)
Jezroc Metalworks LLC.........G....... 317 417-1132
Zionsville (G-14442)
JL Walter & Associates Inc.........E....... 317 524-3600
Indianapolis (G-7306)
Just For Granite.........G....... 317 842-8255
Indianapolis (G-7324)
K-K Tool and Design Inc.........E....... 260 758-2940
Markle (G-9578)
Kammerer Dynamics Inc.........F....... 260 349-9098
Kendallville (G-8483)
Kammerer Inc.........G....... 260 347-0389
Kendallville (G-8485)
Keller Machine & Welding Inc.........E....... 219 464-4915
Valparaiso (G-13566)
Kenley Corporation.........G....... 765 825-7150
Connersville (G-2061)

Kennedy Metal Products Inc.........F....... 219 322-9388
Schererville (G-12329)
Keppler Steel and Fabricating.........F....... 765 289-1529
Muncie (G-10504)
Kirby Tool and Die Inc.........G....... 812 369-7779
Solsberry (G-12686)
Kokomo Metal Fabricators Inc.........G....... 765 459-8173
Kokomo (G-8653)
L & W Engineering Inc.........D....... 574 825-5351
Middlebury (G-9900)
Lacay Fabrication and Mfg Inc.........E....... 574 288-4678
Elkhart (G-2982)
Lakemaster Inc.........E....... 765 288-3718
Muncie (G-10507)
▲ Lawrence Cnty Fabrication Corp.........E....... 812 849-0124
Mitchell (G-10164)
Lawrenco Steel Inc.........G....... 812 466-7115
Terre Haute (G-13273)
Leons Fabrication Inc.........F....... 219 365-5272
Schererville (G-12330)
▼ Liberty Industries LC.........E....... 812 853-0595
Newburgh (G-11035)
Lippert Components Inc.........G....... 574 537-8900
Goshen (G-5269)
◆ M & S Steel Corp.........E....... 260 357-5184
Garrett (G-5015)
M and B Fabricating LLC.........F....... 219 762-5032
Valparaiso (G-13578)
Marcums Welding & Stl Proc Inc.........G....... 765 763-7279
Morristown (G-10374)
Marine Builders Inc.........D....... 812 283-7932
Jeffersonville (G-8396)
Marion Metal Products Inc.........E....... 765 662-8333
Marion (G-9543)
Marion Steel Fabrication Inc.........E....... 765 664-1478
Marion (G-9545)
▲ Marson International LLC.........E....... 574 295-4222
Elkhart (G-3020)
▲ Metal Dynamics Ltd.........E....... 812 949-7998
New Albany (G-10826)
Metal Masters Inc.........G....... 812 421-9162
Evansville (G-3623)
Metal Solutions Inc.........F....... 317 781-6734
Indianapolis (G-7488)
Metal Technologies Inc.........E....... 812 384-9800
Bloomfield (G-642)
▲ Metal Technologies Inc.........D....... 812 384-9800
Bloomfield (G-643)
▲ Metaltec Inc.........G....... 219 362-9811
La Porte (G-8792)
Metfab Inc.........G....... 317 322-0385
Indianapolis (G-7492)
Micrometl Indianapolis.........G....... 317 524-5400
Indianapolis (G-7499)
Miller Mfg Corp.........E....... 574 773-4136
Nappanee (G-10695)
Miller Steel Fabricators.........G....... 260 768-7321
Shipshewana (G-12635)
Modern Welding & Boiler Works.........G....... 812 232-5039
Terre Haute (G-13287)
Mofab Inc.........E....... 765 649-1288
Anderson (G-138)
Morse Metal Fab Inc.........E....... 574 674-6237
Granger (G-5425)
Munster Steel Co Inc.........E....... 219 924-5198
Hammond (G-5920)
▼ Nello Inc.........F....... 574 288-3632
South Bend (G-12870)
▼ New Mllennium Bldg Systems LLC.........G....... 260 969-3500
Fort Wayne (G-4501)
New Mllennium Bldg Systems LLC.........C....... 260 868-6000
Butler (G-1236)
New Nello Operating Co LLC.........C....... 574 288-3632
South Bend (G-12874)
Noble County Welding Inc.........F....... 260 897-4082
Avilla (G-416)
Northwest Alum Fabricators Inc.........G....... 219 844-4354
Hammond (G-5923)
Omnimax International Inc.........C....... 574 773-7981
Nappanee (G-10701)
▼ Ottenweller Co Inc.........C....... 260 484-3166
Fort Wayne (G-4513)
P & E Products.........G....... 765 969-2644
Connersville (G-2067)
P H Drew Incorporated.........E....... 317 297-5152
Indianapolis (G-7643)
Paden Engineering Co Inc.........G....... 812 546-4447
Hope (G-6117)
Pauls Welding.........E....... 574 646-2015
Nappanee (G-10702)

S I C

▲ Penz Products Inc ....E....... 574 255-4736
Mishawaka (G-10103)

Ph Inc ....E....... 877 467-4763
Plymouth (G-11711)

Phoenix Specialties Ltd ....G....... 219 345-5812
Lake Village (G-9085)

◆ Pirod Inc ....F....... 574 936-7221
Plymouth (G-11712)

Porter Systems Inc ....E....... 317 867-0234
Westfield (G-14179)

Precision Fabrication Inc ....E....... 260 422-4448
Fort Wayne (G-4549)

Precision Surveillance Corp ....E....... 219 397-4295
East Chicago (G-2564)

Preferred Tank & Tower Inc ....G....... 270 826-7950
Evansville (G-3684)

Prestress Services Inc ....C....... 260 724-7117
Decatur (G-2399)

Productivity Fabricators Inc ....F....... 765 966-2896
Richmond (G-12035)

Profab Custom Metal Works Inc ....G....... 812 865-3999
Orleans (G-11367)

Prokuma Incorporated ....G....... 812 461-1681
Evansville (G-3686)

Quality Fabrication Ind Inc ....F....... 765 529-9776
New Castle (G-10915)

Quikcut Incorporated ....E....... 260 447-8090
Fort Wayne (G-4573)

R Concepts Industries Inc ....D....... 574 295-6641
Elkhart (G-3135)

Rcr Metal Fab LLC ....G....... 219 923-9104
Griffith (G-5788)

Reeves Manufacturing Inc ....G....... 765 935-3875
Richmond (G-12042)

Refax Inc ....C....... 219 977-0414
Gary (G-5090)

Refax Wear Products Inc ....G....... 219 977-0414
Gary (G-5091)

Rex Alton & Companies Inc ....E....... 812 882-8519
Vincennes (G-13701)

Rf Manufacturing Inc ....G....... 317 773-8610
Noblesville (G-11176)

Right Angle Stl & Fabrication ....G....... 574 862-2432
Wakarusa (G-13794)

Robert D Meadows ....G....... 812 797-8294
Bedford (G-575)

San Jo Steel Inc ....F....... 317 888-6227
Greenwood (G-5747)

Sanbar of Indiana Inc ....G....... 317 375-6220
Indianapolis (G-7890)

Schmidt Contracting Inc ....F....... 812 482-3923
Jasper (G-8303)

Schuler Precision Tool LLC ....G....... 260 982-2704
North Manchester (G-11243)

Scott Steel Services Inc ....G....... 219 663-4740
Crown Point (G-2301)

Seiler & Sons ....G....... 812 858-9598
Newburgh (G-11047)

Service Steel Framing Inc ....F....... 260 868-5853
Butler (G-1239)

Sigma Steel Inc ....E....... 812 275-4489
Bedford (G-578)

Simko Industrial Fabricators ....E....... 219 933-9100
Hammond (G-5940)

Sinden Racing Service Inc ....F....... 317 243-7171
Indianapolis (G-7949)

Sisson Steel Inc ....F....... 812 354-8701
Winslow (G-14359)

Smco Inc ....E....... 574 295-1482
Elkhart (G-3178)

Smgf LLC ....D....... 812 354-8899
Petersburg (G-11568)

SMS Group Inc ....E....... 219 880-0256
Gary (G-5099)

Snyder & Co Inc ....G....... 765 447-3452
Lafayette (G-9000)

Special Fabrication Services ....G....... 812 384-5384
Elnora (G-3292)

Specialty Process Eqp Ctrl Inc ....G....... 812 473-8528
Evansville (G-3743)

Spreuer & Son Inc ....F....... 260 463-3513
Lagrange (G-9067)

Staab Sheet Metal Inc ....G....... 317 241-2553
Indianapolis (G-7983)

Stahl Equipment Inc ....E....... 812 925-3341
Chandler (G-1554)

Steel Services Inc ....G....... 317 783-5255
Indianapolis (G-7999)

Steel Tank & Fabricating Corp ....E....... 260 248-8971
Columbia City (G-1838)

Steeltech Partners LLC ....G....... 812 849-0124
Mitchell (G-10172)

Stephens Fabrication Inc ....E....... 765 459-9770
Kokomo (G-8701)

Stevens Ironworks Inc ....E....... 219 987-6332
Demotte (G-2448)

Stone City Ironworks Inc ....E....... 812 279-3023
Bedford (G-581)

Structural Iron & Fab Inc ....G....... 260 758-2273
Markle (G-9582)

Superior Equipment & Mfg ....G....... 260 925-0152
Auburn (G-359)

Superior Fabrication Inc ....F....... 812 649-2630
Rockport (G-12173)

Superior Layout ....G....... 812 371-1709
Columbus (G-2018)

Swager Communications Inc ....E....... 260 495-2515
Fremont (G-4976)

Swan Real Estate Mgmt Inc ....G....... 765 664-1478
Marion (G-9565)

Tank Construction & Service Co ....F....... 317 509-6294
Whitestown (G-14263)

TC Burton Enterprises LLC ....G....... 317 446-8776
Fishers (G-3972)

Thomas Cubit Inc ....G....... 219 933-0566
Hammond (G-5949)

Titan Metal Spinning Inc ....G....... 260 665-1067
Angola (G-251)

Titus Inc ....F....... 574 936-3345
Plymouth (G-11728)

Trade Line Fabricating Inc ....E....... 812 637-1444
Lawrenceburg (G-9159)

Tri-State Mechanical Inc ....F....... 260 471-0345
Fort Wayne (G-4702)

Triton Metal Products Inc ....G....... 260 488-1800
Hamilton (G-5830)

Tron Mechanical Incorporated ....C....... 812 838-4715
Mount Vernon (G-10410)

Tru-Form Steel & Wire Inc ....E....... 765 348-5001
Hartford City (G-5994)

▲ Tru-Form Steel & Wire Inc ....E....... 765 348-5001
Hartford City (G-5993)

Tube Processing Corp ....C....... 317 782-9486
Indianapolis (G-8108)

Tuttle Aluminum Intl Inc ....E....... 317 842-2420
Fishers (G-3980)

United States Steel Corp ....B....... 219 888-2000
Gary (G-5111)

Universal Door Carrier Inc ....G....... 317 241-3447
Indianapolis (G-8129)

Usw Lu 6103-07 ....G....... 219 762-4433
Portage (G-11800)

Valmont Industries Inc ....G....... 574 935-3058
Plymouth (G-11733)

Valmont Industries Inc ....D....... 574 295-6942
Elkhart (G-3242)

Vandergriff & Associates Inc ....G....... 812 422-6033
Evansville (G-3793)

Vans Industrial Inc ....E....... 219 931-4881
Hammond (G-5954)

Varied Products Indiana Inc ....F....... 219 763-2526
Chesterton (G-1640)

Vidimos Inc ....D....... 219 397-2728
East Chicago (G-2579)

Vincennes Welding Co Inc ....F....... 812 882-9682
Vincennes (G-13712)

Wabash Steel LLC ....G....... 317 818-1622
Vincennes (G-13713)

▲ Wabash Valley Manufacturing ....C....... 260 352-2102
Silver Lake (G-12682)

Wabash Welding Services Inc ....E....... 260 563-2363
Wabash (G-13766)

Westfield Steel Inc ....E....... 812 466-3500
Terre Haute (G-13368)

Westlund Concepts ....F....... 317 819-0611
Lapel (G-9120)

Wick - Fab Inc ....E....... 260 897-3303
Avilla (G-421)

Wings N Things Fabrication ....G....... 260 432-2992
Fort Wayne (G-4757)

Wiw Inc ....E....... 219 663-7900
Crown Point (G-2321)

Wrib Manufacturing Inc ....G....... 765 294-2841
Veedersburg (G-13648)

Yankee Steel Inc ....G....... 812 232-5353
Terre Haute (G-13374)

Zieman Manufacturing Company ....G....... 574 522-5202
Goshen (G-5347)

3442 Metal Doors, Sash, Frames, Molding & Trim

▼ A & A Sheet Metal Products ....D....... 219 326-1288
La Porte (G-8725)

All-Weather Products Inc ....G....... 812 867-6403
Evansville (G-3348)

American Window and Glass Inc ....C....... 812 464-9400
Evansville (G-3352)

Assa Abloy Door Group LLC ....F....... 800 826-2617
Elkhart (G-2697)

Ceco Metal Doors and Frames ....G....... 317 787-3455
Indianapolis (G-6572)

Challenger Door Llc ....D....... 574 773-0470
Nappanee (G-10658)

Champion of Evansville LLC ....F....... 812 424-2456
Evansville (G-3416)

Champion Opco LLC ....E....... 260 271-4076
Fort Wayne (G-4144)

Classee Vinyl Windows LLC ....G....... 574 825-7863
Middlebury (G-9875)

Cleer Vision Windows Inc ....F....... 574 262-0449
Elkhart (G-2759)

Cleer Vision Windows Inc ....F....... 574 262-0449
Elkhart (G-2760)

Crossroads Door & Hardware Inc ....G....... 812 234-9751
Terre Haute (G-13219)

Dexter Axle Company ....C....... 574 295-7888
Bristol (G-1054)

Door Service Supply ....G....... 317 496-0391
Greenwood (G-5682)

Elixir Industries ....D....... 574 294-5685
Elkhart (G-2818)

Evansville Metal Products Inc ....D....... 812 423-5632
Evansville (G-3487)

Global Building Products LLC ....E....... 574 296-6868
Elkhart (G-2882)

▲ Home Guard Industries Inc ....D....... 260 627-6060
Grabill (G-5372)

Hrh Door Corp ....G....... 812 479-5680
Evansville (G-3544)

Ilpea Industries Inc ....D....... 812 752-2526
Scottsburg (G-12363)

▲ Imperial Products LLC ....D....... 765 966-0322
Richmond (G-12001)

▲ International Steel Company ....D....... 812 425-3311
Evansville (G-3565)

IRD Group Inc ....E....... 812 425-3311
Evansville (G-3566)

Jason Incorporated ....D....... 800 787-7325
Richmond (G-12006)

Jeld-Wen Inc ....C....... 260 894-7111
Ligonier (G-9288)

Kinro Manufacturing Inc ....C....... 574 535-1125
Elkhart (G-2969)

Kinro Manufacturing Inc ....C....... 574 535-1125
Elkhart (G-2970)

▲ Kinro Manufacturing Inc ....E....... 574 535-1125
Elkhart (G-2971)

Kinro Manufacturing Inc ....D....... 574 535-1125
Elkhart (G-2972)

Kinro Manufacturing Inc ....G....... 574 533-8337
Goshen (G-5257)

Kitty Mac Inc ....G....... 888 549-0783
Indianapolis (G-7356)

Kleptz Aluminum Inc ....G....... 812 238-2946
Terre Haute (G-13266)

Lansing Building Products Inc ....G....... 765 448-4363
Lafayette (G-8955)

LCI Industries ....C....... 574 535-1125
Elkhart (G-2989)

Lippert Components Mfg Inc ....C....... 574 935-5122
Plymouth (G-11703)

Maher Supply Inc ....E....... 812 234-7699
Terre Haute (G-13278)

Marner Door Manufacturing LLC ....F....... 812 486-3128
Montgomery (G-10234)

Meridian Metalform Inc ....G....... 812 422-1524
Evansville (G-3622)

Midwest Pre-Finishing Inc ....G....... 260 728-9487
Decatur (G-2395)

▲ Modern Door Corporation ....D....... 574 586-3117
Walkerton (G-13806)

Multiple Resource Solution ....G....... 317 862-2584
Indianapolis (G-7559)

Oak-Rite Mfg Corp ....E....... 317 839-2301
Plainfield (G-11632)

Quanex Homeshield LLC ....D....... 765 966-0322
Richmond (G-12040)

Reeds Plastic Tops Inc ....G....... 765 282-1471
Muncie (G-10556)

Southeastern Aluminum Pdts Inc ......F 904 781-8200
Carmel *(G-1483)*
Sun Control Center LLC ......F 260 490-9902
Fort Wayne *(G-4666)*
Syracuse Glass Inc ......G 574 457-5516
Syracuse *(G-13147)*
Therma-Tru Corp ......E 260 868-5811
Butler *(G-1246)*
Trim-A-Seal of Indiana Inc ......F 219 883-2180
Gary *(G-5109)*
Universal Door Carrier Inc ......G 317 241-3447
Indianapolis *(G-8129)*
Wilmes Window Mfg Co Inc ......E 812 275-7575
Ferdinand *(G-3864)*
▲ **Worldwide Door Cmpnnts Ind Inc** ......G 219 992-9225
Lake Village *(G-9089)*

3443 Fabricated Plate Work

A & B Fabricating & Maint Inc ......F 574 353-1012
Mentone *(G-9684)*
Abtrex Industries Inc ......E 574 234-7773
South Bend *(G-12693)*
Ace Welding and Machine Inc ......G 812 379-9625
Columbus *(G-1849)*
Advantage Engineering Inc ......D 317 887-0729
Greenwood *(G-5660)*
Aearo Technologies LLC ......C 317 692-6666
Indianapolis *(G-6342)*
Allied Boiler & Welding Co ......G 317 272-4820
Avon *(G-426)*
▼ **Alloy Custom Products LLC** ......D 765 564-4684
Lafayette *(G-8850)*
Aluminum Wldg & Mch Works Inc ......G 219 787-8066
Chesterton *(G-1592)*
◆ **Asphalt Equipment Company Inc** ......G 260 672-3004
Fort Wayne *(G-4093)*
Axis Unlimited LLC ......G 574 370-8923
Elkhart *(G-2708)*
▼ **Banks Machine & Engrg Inc** ......D 317 642-4980
Shelbyville *(G-12519)*
▲ **Batesville Products Inc** ......D 513 381-2057
Lawrenceburg *(G-9133)*
Boilers & More Inc ......G 317 873-2007
Zionsville *(G-14423)*
Buhrt Engineering & Cnstr ......E 574 267-3720
Warsaw *(G-13852)*
Bulk Truck & Transport Service ......E 812 866-2155
Hanover *(G-5959)*
Caliente LLC ......E 260 426-3800
Fort Wayne *(G-4137)*
Carmel Engineering Inc ......F 765 279-8955
Kirklin *(G-8547)*
Carr Metal Products Inc ......C 317 542-0691
Indianapolis *(G-6558)*
Chegar Manufacturing Co Inc ......E 765 945-7444
Windfall *(G-14347)*
Codeweld Inc ......G 317 784-4140
Indianapolis *(G-6629)*
Coffee Lomont & Moyer Inc ......F 260 422-7825
Fort Wayne *(G-4166)*
Contech Engnered Solutions LLC ......G 317 407-4914
Fishers *(G-3893)*
Contech Engnered Solutions LLC ......F 317 842-7766
Indianapolis *(G-6655)*
Contech Engnered Solutions LLC ......E 812 849-3933
Mitchell *(G-10159)*
Contech Engnered Solutions LLC ......E 812 849-3933
Mitchell *(G-10160)*
Cooper-Standard Automotive Inc ......C 260 593-2156
Topeka *(G-13414)*
Cooper-Standard Automotive Inc ......C 574 546-5938
Bremen *(G-991)*
Creative Craftsmen Inc ......E 812 423-2844
Evansville *(G-3437)*
Croy Machine & Fabrication ......G 260 565-3682
Bluffton *(G-871)*
◆ **Ctb Inc** ......A 574 658-4191
Milford *(G-9952)*
Ctb Inc ......G 574 658-9323
Milford *(G-9953)*
Ctb Inc ......G 574 658-4191
Milford *(G-9954)*
◆ **CTB MN Investment Co Inc** ......E 574 658-4191
Milford *(G-9955)*
Dennis Manufacturing Inc ......G 812 755-4891
Campbellsburg *(G-1276)*
Dietrich Industries Inc ......C 219 931-3741
Hammond *(G-5870)*
Don R Fruchey Inc ......E 260 493-3626
Fort Wayne *(G-4218)*
Dpc Inc ......E 765 564-3752
Delphi *(G-2419)*
▲ **Dragon ESP Ltd** ......D 574 893-1569
Akron *(G-4)*
Dyna-Fab Corporation ......E 765 893-4423
West Lebanon *(G-14119)*
E-Tank Ltd ......F 317 296-0510
Indianapolis *(G-6783)*
Elsie Manufacturing Co Inc ......G 260 837-8841
Waterloo *(G-14013)*
Erapsco ......G 260 248-3524
Columbia City *(G-1783)*
Estes Waste Solutions LLC ......G 812 283-6400
Jeffersonville *(G-8359)*
F D Ramsey & Co Inc ......F 219 362-2452
La Porte *(G-8757)*
Fabstar Inc ......F 765 230-0261
Cayuga *(G-1519)*
Four Star Fabricators Inc ......D 812 354-9995
Petersburg *(G-11562)*
◆ **Galbreath LLC** ......C 219 946-6631
Winamac *(G-14304)*
Galbreath LLC ......D 574 946-6631
Winamac *(G-14305)*
Galfab LLC ......D 574 946-7767
Winamac *(G-14306)*
Gldn Rule Truss & Metal Sales ......G 812 866-1800
Lexington *(G-9250)*
Goudy Brothers Boiler Co Inc ......E 765 459-4416
Kokomo *(G-8631)*
Grabill Truss Incorporated ......G 260 627-0933
Grabill *(G-5370)*
Grant County Steel Inc ......F 765 668-7547
Marion *(G-9527)*
Greenfield Feeders Inc ......F 317 462-6363
Greenfield *(G-5534)*
▲ **Gta Containers Inc** ......E 574 288-3459
South Bend *(G-12793)*
◆ **Hale Industries Inc** ......E 317 577-0337
Fortville *(G-4778)*
▲ **Heat Exchanger Design Inc** ......E 317 917-1566
Indianapolis *(G-7086)*
▼ **Hensley Fabricating & Eqp Co** ......E 574 498-6514
Tippecanoe *(G-13382)*
Hmt LLC ......F 219 736-9901
Merrillville *(G-9720)*
Hoosier Tank and Mfg Inc ......D 574 232-8368
South Bend *(G-12803)*
Hunts Maintenance Inc ......G 219 785-2333
Westville *(G-14218)*
Industrial Contrs Skanska Inc ......E 812 423-7832
Evansville *(G-3555)*
▲ **Industrial Metal-Fab Inc** ......E 574 288-8368
South Bend *(G-12812)*
Industrial Steel Cnstr Inc ......C 219 885-5610
Gary *(G-5069)*
▲ **Industrial Transmission Eqp** ......E 574 936-3028
Plymouth *(G-11694)*
Ira Preservation Partners ......G 317 722-0710
Indianapolis *(G-7267)*
▲ **J & J Welding Inc** ......E 812 838-4391
Mount Vernon *(G-10396)*
J A Smit Inc ......G 812 424-8141
Evansville *(G-3568)*
Jiffy Lube ......F 317 882-5823
Greenwood *(G-5709)*
Jlb Industrial LLC ......G 765 561-1751
Rushville *(G-12225)*
Kammerer Inc ......G 260 347-0389
Kendallville *(G-8485)*
Kennedy Tank & Mfg Co ......C 317 787-1311
Indianapolis *(G-7342)*
Kokomo Metal Fabricators Inc ......G 765 459-8173
Kokomo *(G-8653)*
Kuharic Enterprises ......G 574 288-9410
South Bend *(G-12832)*
Lagrange Products Inc ......C 260 495-3025
Fremont *(G-4965)*
Lakeview Engineered Pdts Inc ......G 260 432-3479
Fort Wayne *(G-4422)*
Leons Fabrication Inc ......F 219 365-5272
Schererville *(G-12330)*
Lippert Components Inc ......D 574 535-1125
Goshen *(G-5268)*
Lynn Tool Company Inc ......G 765 874-2471
Lynn *(G-9430)*
◆ **M & S Steel Corp** ......E 260 357-5184
Garrett *(G-5015)*
M A C Corporation ......D 317 545-3341
Indianapolis *(G-7432)*
Madden Manufacturing Inc ......F 574 295-4292
Elkhart *(G-3013)*
Manchester Tank & Equipment Co ......D 812 275-5931
Bedford *(G-561)*
Manchester Tank & Equipment Co ......C 574 295-8200
Elkhart *(G-3016)*
Manitex International Inc ......C 574 772-5380
Knox *(G-8573)*
Manitex Sabre Inc ......D 574 772-5380
Knox *(G-8574)*
Marion Steel Fabrication Inc ......E 765 664-1478
Marion *(G-9545)*
Materials Processing Inc ......G 317 803-3010
Indianapolis *(G-7466)*
McWane Inc ......G 574 534-9328
Goshen *(G-5283)*
◆ **Metal Technologies Indiana Inc** ......C 260 925-4717
Auburn *(G-346)*
Miller Mfg Corp ......E 574 773-4136
Nappanee *(G-10695)*
Mitek Usa Inc ......D 219 924-3835
Griffith *(G-5786)*
Moon Fabricating Corp ......E 765 459-4194
Kokomo *(G-8670)*
Mvp Dumpsters Inc ......G 317 502-3155
Pendleton *(G-11495)*
Norman Stein & Associates ......F 260 749-5468
New Haven *(G-10950)*
▼ **Ottenweller Co Inc** ......C 260 484-3166
Fort Wayne *(G-4513)*
◆ **Par-Kan Company LLC** ......D 260 352-2141
Silver Lake *(G-12677)*
Parker-Hannifin Corporation ......E 219 297-3182
Goodland *(G-5160)*
Pb Metal Works ......G 765 489-1311
Hagerstown *(G-5810)*
Penway Inc ......E 812 526-2645
Edinburgh *(G-2621)*
Phoenix Fbrcators Erectors LLC ......C 317 271-7002
Avon *(G-461)*
Precision Cryogenic Systems ......F 317 273-2800
Indianapolis *(G-7733)*
Pruett Manufacturing Co Inc ......F 812 234-9497
Terre Haute *(G-13312)*
Quick Tanks Inc ......E 260 347-3850
Kendallville *(G-8503)*
Quick Tanks Inc ......G 260 347-3850
Kendallville *(G-8504)*
Quikcut Incorporated ......E 260 447-3880
Fort Wayne *(G-4574)*
◆ **Rogers Engineering and Mfg Co** ......E 765 478-5444
Cambridge City *(G-1261)*
Rolls-Royce Corporation ......G 317 230-8515
West Lafayette *(G-14104)*
▲ **Rolls-Royce Corporation** ......A 317 230-2000
Indianapolis *(G-7858)*
Royal Stamping Inc ......F 260 925-3312
Auburn *(G-350)*
Rugged Steel Works LLC ......F 260 444-4241
Fort Wayne *(G-4598)*
Sigma Steel Inc ......E 812 275-4489
Bedford *(G-578)*
Sisson Steel Inc ......F 812 354-8701
Winslow *(G-14359)*
◆ **Small Parts Inc** ......B 574 753-6323
Logansport *(G-9364)*
SMS Group Inc ......E 219 880-0256
Gary *(G-5099)*
Snyder & Co Inc ......G 765 447-3452
Lafayette *(G-9000)*
Spreuer & Son Inc ......F 260 463-3513
Lagrange *(G-9067)*
SPX Corporation ......C 812 849-5647
Mitchell *(G-10171)*
SPX Corporation ......C 219 879-6561
Michigan City *(G-9846)*
SPX Corporation ......C 704 752-4400
Angola *(G-245)*
Stahl Equipment Inc ......E 812 925-3341
Chandler *(G-1554)*
Steel Storage Inc ......E 574 282-2618
South Bend *(G-12955)*
Steel Tank & Fabricating Corp ......E 260 248-8971
Columbia City *(G-1838)*
Sterling Boiler and Mech LLC ......A 812 479-5447
Evansville *(G-3750)*
Stewart Warner South Wind ......G 812 547-7071
Indianapolis *(G-8005)*
Summit Manufacturing Corp ......E 260 428-2600
Fort Wayne *(G-4665)*

SIC

Sun Engineering Inc ....E 219 962-1191
Lake Station *(G-9078)*

T J B Inc ....G 219 293-8030
Elkhart *(G-3202)*

Tank Construction & Service Co ......F 317 509-6294
Whitestown *(G-14263)*

Temptek Inc ....G 317 887-6352
Greenwood *(G-5752)*

Thermodynamic Process Ctrl LLC ....G 317 780-5743
Indianapolis *(G-8058)*

▲ Thrush Co Inc ....E 765 472-3351
Peru *(G-11551)*

Tishler Industries Inc ....G 765 286-5454
Muncie *(G-10569)*

Tj Maintenance LLC ....G 219 776-8427
Lake Village *(G-9088)*

Troy Meggitt Inc ....D 812 547-7071
Troy *(G-13448)*

Twincorp Inc ....E 812 934-9226
Batesville *(G-522)*

Varied Products Indiana Inc ....F 219 763-2526
Chesterton *(G-1640)*

Versatile Metal Works LLC ....F 765 754-7470
Frankton *(G-4944)*

Wayne Metals LLC ....G 260 758-3121
Markle *(G-9584)*

▲ Wessels Company ....D 317 888-9800
Greenwood *(G-5759)*

Wrib Manufacturing Inc ....G 765 294-2841
Veedersburg *(G-13648)*

Yardarm Marine Products Inc ....E 317 831-4950
Mooresville *(G-10345)*

3444 Sheet Metal Work

37 Pipe & Supply LLC ....G 812 275-5676
Bedford *(G-526)*

3c Coman Ltd ....G 317 650-5156
Fortville *(G-4766)*

A & B Fabricating & Maint Inc ....F 574 353-1012
Mentone *(G-9684)*

▲ A S C Industries Inc ....E 574 264-1987
Elkhart *(G-2659)*

Abell Engineering & Mfg ....F 317 687-1174
Indianapolis *(G-6310)*

Abtrex Industries Inc ....E 574 234-7773
South Bend *(G-12693)*

Ace Welding and Machine Inc ....G 812 379-9625
Columbus *(G-1849)*

Ad-Vance Magnetics Inc ....E 574 223-3158
Rochester *(G-12113)*

▲ Advanced Mtlwrking Prctces LLC ....G 317 337-0441
Carmel *(G-1303)*

Advantage Manufacturing ....G 317 237-4289
Indianapolis *(G-6339)*

Aearo Technologies LLC ....C 317 692-6666
Indianapolis *(G-6342)*

All American Tent & Awning Inc ....F 812 232-4220
Terre Haute *(G-13190)*

All N One ....G 219 226-9263
Crown Point *(G-2224)*

Alro Steel Corporation ....E 317 781-3800
Indianapolis *(G-6378)*

Ameri-Kart Corp ....D 225 642-7874
Bristol *(G-1043)*

American Machine Fabrication ....G 812 944-4136
New Albany *(G-10744)*

AMS of Indiana Inc ....E 574 293-5526
Elkhart *(G-2689)*

Applied Metals & Mch Works Inc ......E 260 424-4834
Fort Wayne *(G-4083)*

Arconic Inc ....G 812 842-3300
Newburgh *(G-11022)*

Artisan Sheet Metal Corp ....G 812 422-7393
Wadesville *(G-13770)*

Atco-Gary Metal Tech LLC ....G 219 885-3232
Griffith *(G-5763)*

▲ Austin-Westran LLC ....E 815 234-2811
Indianapolis *(G-6441)*

Auto Truck Group LLC ....F 260 356-1610
Huntington *(G-6188)*

Avionics Mounts Inc ....G 812 988-2949
Nashville *(G-10714)*

▲ Awningtec Usa Incorporated ....E 812 734-0423
Corydon *(G-2088)*

▲ B&J Rocket America Inc ....E 574 825-5802
Middlebury *(G-9874)*

Ba Romines Sheet Metal Inc ....E 260 657-5500
Harlan *(G-5966)*

Bearcat Corp ....E 574 533-0448
Goshen *(G-5177)*

Benthall Bros Inc ....E 800 488-5995
Evansville *(G-3372)*

Blume Metal Sales LLC ....G 765 490-0600
Brookston *(G-1101)*

Bo-Mar Industries Inc ....E 317 899-1240
Indianapolis *(G-6491)*

Bon L Manufacturing Company ....G 815 351-6802
Kentland *(G-8517)*

Bowmans Tin Shop Inc ....G 574 936-3234
Plymouth *(G-11671)*

Brackett Heating & AC ....E 812 476-1138
Evansville *(G-3400)*

Brand Sheet Metal Works Inc ....G 765 284-5594
Muncie *(G-10443)*

Brazeway Inc ....D 317 392-2533
Shelbyville *(G-12524)*

Bright Sheet Metal Company Inc ....C 317 291-7600
Indianapolis *(G-6508)*

Buckaroos Inc ....F 317 899-9100
Indianapolis *(G-6518)*

Buhrt Engineering & Cnstr ....G 574 267-3720
Warsaw *(G-13852)*

Burkhart Advertising Inc ....F 574 234-4444
South Bend *(G-12728)*

Buschman Tank Cars Inc ....G 219 984-5444
Reynolds *(G-11944)*

C & C Mailbox Products ....G 765 358-4880
Gaston *(G-5130)*

C & K United Shtmtl & Mech ....G 812 423-5090
Evansville *(G-3407)*

C & L Sheet Metal LLC ....G 812 449-9126
Evansville *(G-3408)*

C & P Engineering & Mfg ....E 765 825-4293
Connersville *(G-2042)*

C&F Fabricating LLC ....G 765 362-5922
Crawfordsville *(G-2136)*

Campbell Ventilation Inc ....F 317 636-7211
Indianapolis *(G-6545)*

Cardinal Manufacturing Co Inc ....F 317 283-4175
Indianapolis *(G-6553)*

Carr Metal Products Inc ....C 317 542-0691
Indianapolis *(G-6558)*

Carroll Distrg & Cnstr Sup Inc ....G 317 984-2400
Noblesville *(G-11078)*

Cartesian Corp ....E 765 742-0293
Lafayette *(G-8868)*

Central States Mfg Inc ....D 219 879-4770
Michigan City *(G-9773)*

Centurion Industries Inc ....D 260 357-6665
Garrett *(G-4996)*

Champion of Evansville LLC ....F 812 424-2456
Evansville *(G-3416)*

Champion Opco LLC ....E 260 271-4076
Fort Wayne *(G-4144)*

Charmaran Corporation ....F 260 347-3347
Kendallville *(G-8463)*

Chisholm Lumber & Sup Co Inc ....E 317 547-3535
Indianapolis *(G-6601)*

Citadel Architectural Pdts Inc ....E 317 894-9400
Indianapolis *(G-6612)*

City Welding & Fabrication ....G 765 569-5403
Rockville *(G-12175)*

Cline Brothers Welding ....G 812 738-3537
Corydon *(G-2093)*

Clover Sheet Metal Company ....E 574 293-5912
Elkhart *(G-2761)*

CMa Supply Co Fort Wayne Inc ....F 260 471-9000
Fort Wayne *(G-4164)*

Cmg Inc ....G 317 890-1999
Indianapolis *(G-6626)*

Coffee Lomont & Moyer Inc ....F 260 422-7825
Fort Wayne *(G-4166)*

Columbus Engineering Inc ....E 812 342-1231
Columbus *(G-1876)*

Conover Custom Fabrication Inc ....F 317 784-1904
Indianapolis *(G-6652)*

Contech Engnered Solutions LLC ......E 812 849-3933
Mitchell *(G-10160)*

Continental Industries Inc ....D 574 262-4511
Elkhart *(G-2771)*

Creative Craftsmen Inc ....E 812 423-2844
Evansville *(G-3437)*

Cyclone Manufacturing Co Inc ....F 260 774-3311
Urbana *(G-13476)*

D & V Precision Sheetmetal ....E 317 462-2601
Greenfield *(G-3430)*

D A Hochstetler & Sons LLP ....F 574 642-1144
Topeka *(G-13416)*

Davids Inc ....F 812 376-6870
Columbus *(G-1905)*

Daviess County Metal Sales ....D 812 486-4299
Cannelburg *(G-1284)*

Deister Machine Company Inc ....C 260 422-0354
Fort Wayne *(G-4207)*

Delbert M Dawson & Son Inc ....G 765 284-9711
Muncie *(G-10458)*

Dexter Axle Company ....C 574 295-7888
Bristol *(G-1054)*

Die-Mensional Metal Stamping ....F 812 265-3946
Madison *(G-9456)*

Dietrich Industries Inc ....C 219 931-3741
Hammond *(G-5870)*

Ditech Inc ....D 812 526-0850
Edinburgh *(G-2607)*

Dpc Inc ....E 765 564-3752
Delphi *(G-2419)*

Dyna-Fab Corporation ....G 765 893-4423
West Lebanon *(G-14119)*

E & B Paving Inc ....D 317 773-4132
Noblesville *(G-11097)*

E & R Fabricating Inc ....G 812 275-0388
Bedford *(G-539)*

E & S Metal Inc ....E 260 563-7714
Wabash *(G-13726)*

E Fab Incorporated ....G 317 786-9593
Indianapolis *(G-6782)*

E H Baare Corporation ....G 765 778-7895
Anderson *(G-103)*

Eagle Magnetic Company Inc ....E 317 297-1030
Indianapolis *(G-6786)*

Edwards Steel Inc ....G 317 462-9451
Greenfield *(G-5522)*

Elixir Industries ....D 574 294-5685
Elkhart *(G-2818)*

Erny Sheet Metal Inc ....F 812 482-1044
Jasper *(G-8250)*

Estes Design and Manufacturing ....D 317 899-2203
Indianapolis *(G-6880)*

Eta Fabrication Inc ....E 260 897-3711
Avilla *(G-404)*

Exact Sheet Metal & Skylights ....E 219 670-3520
Crown Point *(G-2251)*

F D Ramsey & Co Inc ....E 219 362-2452
La Porte *(G-8757)*

F R Sheet Metal Co Inc ....G 219 949-2290
Gary *(G-5045)*

Flexco Products Inc ....C 574 294-2502
Elkhart *(G-2852)*

Fort Wayne Fabrication ....G 260 459-8848
Fort Wayne *(G-4272)*

Frank H Monroe Htg & Coolg Inc ....F 812 945-2566
New Albany *(G-10784)*

Freudenberg-Nok General Partnr ....B 260 894-7183
Ligonier *(G-9285)*

G & G Metal Spinners Inc ....E 317 923-3225
Indianapolis *(G-6974)*

G & N Warehouse & Packaging ....G 574 234-3717
South Bend *(G-12785)*

▲ Gammons Metal & Mfg Co Inc ....D 317 546-7091
Indianapolis *(G-6982)*

Gary Metal Mfg LLC ....G 219 885-3232
Gary *(G-5050)*

General Crafts Corp ....G 574 533-1936
Goshen *(G-5223)*

General Motors LLC ....B 765 668-2000
Marion *(G-9525)*

General Sheet Metal Works Inc ....E 574 288-0611
South Bend *(G-12788)*

▲ Girtz Industries Inc ....D 844 464-4789
Monticello *(G-10263)*

Gleason Corporation ....C 574 533-1141
Goshen *(G-5226)*

Goudy Brothers Boiler Co Inc ....E 765 459-4416
Kokomo *(G-8631)*

Grant County Steel Inc ....F 765 668-7547
Marion *(G-9527)*

Greenfield Feeders Inc ....F 317 462-6363
Greenfield *(G-5534)*

Greenwood Models Inc ....G 317 859-2988
Greenwood *(G-5700)*

Greg Moser Engineering Inc ....E 260 726-6689
Portland *(G-11827)*

Gross Roofing Sheet Metals ....G 765 965-0068
Richmond *(G-11992)*

Gsp-2700 LLC ....G 219 885-3232
Gary *(G-5056)*

H & H Home Improvement Inc ....G 812 288-8700
Clarksville *(G-1684)*

H & H Metal Products Inc ....F 812 256-0444
Charlestown *(G-1567)*

H & H Sheet Metal Inc .... F 317 787-0883	**L L Welding** .... G 765 565-6006	**Mooresville Welding Inc** .... G 317 831-2265
Beech Grove *(G-595)*	Carthage *(G-1514)*	Mooresville *(G-10324)*
Hallett Enterprises Inc .... G 317 495-7800	**Lake Air Balance** .... G 219 988-2449	**Morin Corp** .... G 219 465-8334
Crawfordsville *(G-2157)*	Hebron *(G-6015)*	Valparaiso *(G-13581)*
Halsen Brothers Sheet Metal ... G 574 583-3358	**Lapis Services Inc** .... G 219 464-9131	**Morse Metal Fab Inc** .... E 574 674-6237
Monticello *(G-10264)*	Valparaiso *(G-13572)*	Granger *(G-5425)*
Hartman Brothers Heat & AC .... F 260 493-4402	**Larry Atwood** .... G 765 525-6851	**Mossman Metal Works** .... G 765 676-6055
New Haven *(G-10942)*	Waldron *(G-13800)*	Lebanon *(G-9208)*
Heidtman Steel Products Inc ..... C 419 691-4646	**Lauck Manufacturing Co Inc** ..... F 317 787-6269	**Moyers Inc** .... E 574 264-3119
Butler *(G-1229)*	Indianapolis *(G-7385)*	Elkhart *(G-3052)*
Helfin Steel Metal Inc .... G 260 563-2417	**Lenex Steel Company** .... E 317 818-1622	**Mssh Inc** .... G 812 663-2180
Wabash *(G-13729)*	Terre Haute *(G-13274)*	Greensburg *(G-5624)*
Helming Bros Inc .... G 812 634-9797	**Leons Fabrication Inc** .... F 219 365-5272	**Napier & Napier** .... G 765 580-9116
Jasper *(G-8254)*	Schererville *(G-12330)*	Liberty *(G-9266)*
Herman Tool & Machine Inc ..... F 574 594-5544	**Lippert Components Inc** .... G 800 551-9149	**Nash Sheet Metal Co** .... G 812 397-5306
Pierceton *(G-11572)*	Elkhart *(G-2999)*	Shelburn *(G-12508)*
Hogen Industries Inc Indiana .... E 317 591-5070	**Lippert Components Inc** .... D 574 535-1125	**Nci Group Inc** .... G 317 392-3536
Indianapolis *(G-7111)*	Goshen *(G-5268)*	Shelbyville *(G-12553)*
Holbrook Manufacturing Inc ..... E 317 736-9387	**Lippert Components Inc** .... D 574 294-6852	**Nector Machine & Fabricating** ... G 219 322-6878
Franklin *(G-4896)*	Elkhart *(G-3000)*	Schererville *(G-12338)*
Horner Industrial Services Inc ... F 317 634-7165	**Lippert Components Inc** .... E 574 535-1125	**New England Sheets LLC** .... E 978 487-2500
Indianapolis *(G-7129)*	Goshen *(G-5272)*	Indianapolis *(G-7585)*
Hub City Stl & Fabrication LLC ... G 260 760-0370	**Lippert Components Inc** .... D 574 849-0869	**Nicorr LLC** .... G 574 353-1700
Union City *(G-13457)*	Goshen *(G-5273)*	Tippecanoe *(G-13384)*
Huntington Sheet Metal Inc ..... D 260 356-9011	**Lippert Components Inc** .... C 574 971-4320	**Noble Industries Inc** .... E 317 773-1926
Huntington *(G-6213)*	Goshen *(G-5275)*	Noblesville *(G-11160)*
Hy-Flex Corporation .... E 765 571-5125	**Lippert Components Inc** .... D 574 312-7445	**North American Manufacturing** ... E 765 948-3337
Knightstown *(G-8551)*	Middlebury *(G-9904)*	Fairmount *(G-3833)*
Hydro Extrusion North Amer LLC ... B 888 935-5757	**Loyal Mfg Corp** .... F 317 359-3185	**Novelis Corporation** .... C 812 462-2287
North Liberty *(G-11216)*	Indianapolis *(G-7422)*	Terre Haute *(G-13291)*
Imh Fabrication Inc .... F 317 252-5566	**M & S Indus Met Fbricators Inc** ... D 260 356-0300	**Omnimax International Inc** .... E 574 294-8576
Indianapolis *(G-7163)*	Huntington *(G-6226)*	Elkhart *(G-3070)*
Imh Fabrication Inc .... F 317 252-5566	**M T M Machining Inc** .... F 219 872-8677	**Original Tractor Cab Co Inc** ..... E 765 663-2214
Indianapolis *(G-7164)*	Michigan City *(G-9813)*	Arlington *(G-282)*
▼ **Independent Protection Co Inc** ... C 574 533-4116	**Mailroom LLC** .... G 765 254-0000	▼ **Ottenweller Co Inc** .... C 260 484-3166
Goshen *(G-5242)*	Muncie *(G-10517)*	Fort Wayne *(G-4513)*
▼ **Indiana Gratings Inc** .... F 765 342-7191	▲ **Major Tool and Machine Inc** ... B 317 636-6433	**Owens Machine & Welding** .... G 574 583-9566
Martinsville *(G-9615)*	Indianapolis *(G-7446)*	Monticello *(G-10277)*
Indiana Model Company Inc ..... D 317 787-6358	**Marion Steel Fabrication Inc** ... G 765 664-1478	**Padgett Inc** .... C 812 945-2391
Indianapolis *(G-7184)*	Marion *(G-9545)*	New Albany *(G-10839)*
Indiana Steel & Engrg Inc .... E 812 275-3363	**Marion Tent & Awning Co** .... G 765 664-7722	**Palmor Products Inc** .... E 800 872-2822
Bedford *(G-552)*	Marion *(G-9546)*	Lebanon *(G-9210)*
▲ **Indiana U Bolts Inc** .... E 317 870-1940	**Maron Products Incorporated** ... D 574 259-1971	**Paniccia Heating & Cooling** ..... G 219 872-2198
Waterloo *(G-14015)*	Mishawaka *(G-10074)*	Michigan City *(G-9827)*
Industrial Contrs Skanska Inc ... E 812 423-7832	**Martin Spouting Inc** .... G 260 485-5703	**Park County Aggregates LLC** ... G 765 245-2344
Evansville *(G-3555)*	Fort Wayne *(G-4453)*	Rockville *(G-12178)*
Industrial Steel Cnstr Inc .... C 219 885-5610	**Mary Jonas** .... F 317 500-0600	**Patrick Industries Inc** .... D 574 294-5959
Gary *(G-5069)*	Indianapolis *(G-7462)*	Elkhart *(G-3087)*
▲ **Italmac USA Inc** .... G 574 243-0217	**Matrix Manufacturing Inc** .... G 260 854-4659	**Peri Formwork Systems Inc** ..... F 317 390-0062
Granger *(G-5416)*	Wolcottville *(G-14374)*	Indianapolis *(G-7678)*
J & J Repair .... G 574 831-3075	**Mc Bride & Son Welding & Engrg** ... G 260 724-3534	**Pinnacle Equipment Company Inc** ... G 317 259-1180
Goshen *(G-5246)*	Decatur *(G-2393)*	Indianapolis *(G-7693)*
▲ **J & J Welding Inc** .... E 812 838-4391	**McD Machine Incorporated** ...... G 812 339-1240	**Powell Systems Inc** .... G 765 884-0613
Mount Vernon *(G-10396)*	Bloomington *(G-770)*	Fowler *(G-4804)*
J T D Spiral Inc .... G 260 497-1300	**Meese Inc** .... D 812 273-1008	**Poynter Sheet Metal Inc** .... B 317 893-1193
Fort Wayne *(G-4387)*	Madison *(G-9485)*	Greenwood *(G-5735)*
Jack Frost LLC .... E 812 477-7244	**Menard Inc** .... A 812 466-1234	**Precision Racg Components LLC** ... F 317 248-4764
Evansville *(G-3571)*	Terre Haute *(G-13282)*	Indianapolis *(G-7735)*
Jack Howard .... G 317 788-7643	**Mestek Inc** .... E 317 831-5314	**Precisn Fbrctn of Shlbyvle Inc** ... G 765 544-2204
Indianapolis *(G-7292)*	Mooresville *(G-10322)*	Shelbyville *(G-12560)*
JO Mory Inc .... E 260 897-3541	**Metal Art Inc** .... G 765 354-4571	**Proaxis Inc** .... G 765 742-4200
Avilla *(G-407)*	Middletown *(G-9938)*	West Lafayette *(G-14097)*
Joe Tricker .... G 630 759-0251	▲ **Metal Dynamics Ltd** .... E 812 949-7998	**Professional Fabricators Inc** ..... G 260 665-2555
Fishers *(G-3934)*	New Albany *(G-10826)*	Angola *(G-240)*
Johns Architectural Media .... G 630 450-7539	**Metal Sales Manufacturing Corp** ... E 812 246-1866	**PSI Group Inc** .... G 317 297-3211
Dyer *(G-2502)*	Sellersburg *(G-12408)*	Indianapolis *(G-7786)*
▲ **Josam Company** .... D 219 872-5531	**Metal Sales Manufacturing Corp** ... E 812 941-0041	**Pulley-Kellam Co Inc** .... E 260 356-6326
Michigan City *(G-9805)*	New Albany *(G-10827)*	Huntington *(G-6240)*
K-K Tool and Design Inc .... E 260 758-2940	**Metalcraft Inc** .... F 260 761-3001	**Quality Galvanized Pdts Inc** ..... G 574 848-5151
Markle *(G-9578)*	Wawaka *(G-14033)*	Bristol *(G-1076)*
Kairos Specialty Metals Corp ... E 765 836-5540	**Micro Metl Corporation** .... C 800 662-4822	**R & M Welding & Fabricating Sp** ... G 812 295-9130
Mount Summit *(G-10379)*	Indianapolis *(G-7497)*	Loogootee *(G-9392)*
▲ **Kalenborn Abresist Corporation** ... E 800 348-0717	**Microform Inc** .... G 574 522-9851	**R & R Manufacturing** .... G 260 244-5621
Urbana *(G-13477)*	Elkhart *(G-3035)*	Columbia City *(G-1823)*
Kammerer Inc .... G 260 347-0389	**Mid America Powered Vehicles** ... G 812 925-7745	**R & R Tool Manufacturing Inc** ... E 219 362-1681
Kendallville *(G-8485)*	Chandler *(G-1551)*	La Porte *(G-8810)*
Key Sheet Metal Inc .... G 317 546-7151	**Midwest Roll Forming & Mfg Inc** ... G 574 594-2100	**R C Laser Inc** .... E 812 923-1918
Indianapolis *(G-7345)*	Pierceton *(G-11573)*	Pekin *(G-11478)*
Kitchen Queen LLC .... G 812 662-8399	**Midwest Sheet Metal Inc** .... G 574 223-3332	**R Concepts Industries Inc** .... D 574 295-6641
Saint Paul *(G-12277)*	Rochester *(G-12138)*	Elkhart *(G-3135)*
Knox Inc .... F 260 665-6617	**Millenium Sheet Metal Inc** .... F 574 935-9101	**Ramco Builder and Supply LLC** ... E 574 223-7802
Angola *(G-226)*	Plymouth *(G-11706)*	Rochester *(G-12144)*
Koester Metals Inc .... E 260 495-1818	**Miller Mfg Corp** .... E 574 773-4136	**Rance Aluminum Fabrication** ... G 574 266-9028
Fremont *(G-4964)*	Nappanee *(G-10695)*	Elkhart *(G-3137)*
Kokomo Metal Fabricators Inc ... G 765 459-8173	▲ **Models LLC** .... E 765 676-6700	**Ricks Custom Sheet Metal LLC** ... G 812 825-3959
Kokomo *(G-8653)*	Lebanon *(G-9207)*	Solsberry *(G-12687)*
Koomler & Sons Inc .... F 260 482-7641	▲ **Modern Door Corporation** ..... D 574 586-3117	**Rite-Way Steel Inc** .... G 574 262-3465
Fort Wayne *(G-4414)*	Walkerton *(G-13806)*	Elkhart *(G-3147)*
L & W Engineering Inc .... D 574 825-5351	**Moore Metal Works & A/C L L C** ... G 812 422-9473	**River Valley Sheet Metal Inc** .... E 574 259-2538
Middlebury *(G-9900)*	Evansville *(G-3638)*	Mishawaka *(G-10118)*

S
I
C

◆ **Rogers Engineering and Mfg Co**.......E....... 765 478-5444
Cambridge City *(G-1261)*
Roof Masters Plus.......G....... 765 572-1321
Westpoint *(G-14207)*
▲ **Ryobi Die Casting (usa) Inc**.......A....... 317 398-3398
Shelbyville *(G-12565)*
S & H Metal Products Inc.......E....... 260 593-2565
Topeka *(G-13428)*
Sam Mouron Equipment Co Inc.......F....... 317 776-1799
Noblesville *(G-11179)*
Sanbar of Indiana Inc.......G....... 317 375-6220
Indianapolis *(G-7890)*
Schuster Sheet Metal Inc.......G....... 574 293-4802
Elkhart *(G-3159)*
Scotia Corporation.......E....... 260 479-8800
Fort Wayne *(G-4610)*
Sheet Metal Models Inc.......F....... 317 783-1303
Indianapolis *(G-7925)*
Sheet Metal Services Inc.......F....... 219 924-1206
Highland *(G-6055)*
Sheet Mtl Wkrs Local No 20.......F....... 317 541-0050
Indianapolis *(G-7926)*
Sigma Steel Inc.......E....... 812 275-4489
Bedford *(G-578)*
Signdoc Identity LLC.......G....... 317 247-9670
Indianapolis *(G-7946)*
Sisson Steel Inc.......F....... 812 354-8701
Winslow *(G-14359)*
Slabaugh Metal Fab.......E....... 574 546-2882
Bremen *(G-1024)*
Slabaugh Metal Fab LLC.......G....... 574 342-0554
Bourbon *(G-948)*
Slate Mechanical Inc.......F....... 765 452-9611
Kokomo *(G-8697)*
Slatile Roofing and Shtmtl Co.......E....... 574 233-7485
South Bend *(G-12939)*
Snodgrass Sheet Metal.......F....... 317 783-3181
Indianapolis *(G-7955)*
Snyder & Co Inc.......G....... 765 447-3452
Lafayette *(G-9000)*
Southwark Metal Mfg Co.......C....... 317 823-5300
Indianapolis *(G-7965)*
Spreuer & Son Inc.......F....... 260 463-3513
Lagrange *(G-9067)*
Stadry Enclosure Co.......G....... 812 284-2244
Jeffersonville *(G-8427)*
Stahl Equipment Inc.......E....... 812 925-3341
Chandler *(G-1554)*
▲ **Stalcop LLC**.......D....... 765 436-7926
Thorntown *(G-13378)*
◆ **State Wide Aluminum Inc**.......D....... 574 262-2594
Elkhart *(G-3191)*
Steel Tank & Fabricating Corp.......E....... 260 248-8971
Columbia City *(G-1838)*
Styled Rite Company Inc.......G....... 219 931-9844
Gary *(G-5102)*
Summit Manufacturing Corp.......E....... 260 428-2600
Fort Wayne *(G-4665)*
Superior Canopy Corporation.......E....... 260 488-4065
Hamilton *(G-5829)*
Sur-Loc Inc.......F....... 260 495-4065
Fremont *(G-4975)*
Sure-Flo Seamless Gutters Inc.......G....... 260 622-4372
Ossian *(G-11412)*
T R Bulger Inc.......G....... 219 879-8525
Trail Creek *(G-13443)*
Tarpenning-Lafollette Co Inc.......E....... 317 780-1500
Indianapolis *(G-8036)*
Ten Point Trim Corp.......E....... 317 875-5424
Zionsville *(G-14468)*
Thomas Cubit Inc.......G....... 219 933-0566
Hammond *(G-5949)*
Thomco Inc.......G....... 317 359-3539
Indianapolis *(G-8067)*
Total Concepts Design Inc.......D....... 812 752-6534
Scottsburg *(G-12384)*
Trade Line Fabricating Inc.......E....... 812 637-1444
Lawrenceburg *(G-9159)*
Trim-A-Seal of Indiana Inc.......F....... 219 883-2180
Gary *(G-5109)*
Triple J Ironworks Inc.......G....... 765 544-9152
Carthage *(G-1517)*
Triumph Group Operations Inc.......G....... 317 392-5000
Shelbyville *(G-12579)*
Tube Processing Corp.......C....... 317 782-9486
Indianapolis *(G-8108)*
▲ **Tube Processing Corp**.......B....... 317 787-1321
Indianapolis *(G-8107)*
Tube Processing Corp.......C....... 317 264-7760
Indianapolis *(G-8109)*

U S Sheet Metal and Roofing Co.......G....... 812 425-2428
Evansville *(G-3781)*
Universal Metalcraft Inc.......E....... 260 547-4457
Decatur *(G-2411)*
V N C Inc.......F....... 219 696-5031
Lowell *(G-9425)*
Vibromatic Company Inc.......E....... 317 773-3885
Noblesville *(G-11199)*
Vindhurst Sheet Metal LLC.......F....... 812 422-0143
Evansville *(G-3802)*
Vogler Copperworks LLC.......G....... 812 630-9010
Haubstadt *(G-6007)*
W & W Fabricating Inc.......G....... 765 362-2182
Crawfordsville *(G-2203)*
▲ **Wabash Valley Manufacturing**.......C....... 260 352-2102
Silver Lake *(G-12682)*
Wait Industries LLC.......G....... 574 347-4320
Granger *(G-5451)*
Wick - Fab Inc.......E....... 260 897-3303
Avilla *(G-421)*
Wiley Metal Fabricating Inc.......C....... 765 671-7865
Marion *(G-9573)*
Wiley Metal Fabricating Inc.......D....... 765 674-9707
Marion *(G-9574)*
Williams Tool & Machine Corp.......F....... 765 676-5859
Jamestown *(G-8233)*
Wilmes Window Mfg Co Inc.......E....... 812 275-7575
Ferdinand *(G-3864)*
Zimmer Metal Sales LLC.......G....... 574 862-1800
Goshen *(G-5348)*
Zimmer Welding Co.......G....... 317 632-5212
Indianapolis *(G-8226)*

3446 Architectural & Ornamental Metal Work

▼ **ABI Attachments Inc**.......E....... 877 788-7253
Mishawaka *(G-9988)*
All City Metal Craft Inc.......G....... 317 782-9340
Indianapolis *(G-6366)*
American Stair Corporation Inc.......D....... 815 886-9600
Hammond *(G-5841)*
Artisan Sheet Metal Corp.......G....... 812 422-7393
Wadesville *(G-13770)*
B & L Sheet Metal & Roofing.......F....... 812 332-4309
Bloomington *(G-670)*
Backyard Company.......G....... 317 727-0298
Indianapolis *(G-6453)*
Builders Iron Works Inc.......E....... 574 254-1553
Mishawaka *(G-10014)*
Centrum Force Fabrication.......G....... 574 295-5367
Goshen *(G-5186)*
Coffee Lomont & Moyer Inc.......F....... 260 422-7825
Fort Wayne *(G-4166)*
Colbin Tool Company Inc.......E....... 574 457-3183
Syracuse *(G-13130)*
Continental Industries Inc.......D....... 574 262-4511
Elkhart *(G-2771)*
Custom Interior Dynamics LLC.......F....... 317 632-0477
Indianapolis *(G-6714)*
Davids Inc.......F....... 812 376-6870
Columbus *(G-1905)*
De Vols Ornamental Iron.......G....... 765 482-1171
Lebanon *(G-9180)*
Decor Ironworks Inc.......G....... 219 865-1222
Dyer *(G-2493)*
Dormakaba USA Inc.......A....... 317 806-4605
Indianapolis *(G-6758)*
Dpc Inc.......E....... 765 564-3752
Delphi *(G-2419)*
E & H Bridge & Grating Inc.......G....... 812 277-8343
Bedford *(G-538)*
Evans Metal Products Co Inc.......F....... 574 264-2166
Elkhart *(G-2838)*
F W A Decks & Fencing.......G....... 219 865-3275
Dyer *(G-2498)*
Flag & Banner Company Inc.......F....... 317 299-4880
Indianapolis *(G-6931)*
G & N Fabrications LLC.......G....... 317 698-9539
Carmel *(G-1383)*
▲ **Gammons Metal & Mfg Co Inc**.......D....... 317 546-7091
Indianapolis *(G-6982)*
General Crafts Corp.......G....... 574 533-1936
Goshen *(G-5223)*
▲ **Gilpin Inc**.......E....... 260 724-9155
Decatur *(G-2381)*
Goudy Brothers Boiler Co Inc.......E....... 765 459-4416
Kokomo *(G-8631)*
Hamilton Iron Works Inc.......G....... 574 533-3784
Goshen *(G-5234)*
Hampton Ironworks Inc.......G....... 219 929-6448
Chesterton *(G-1611)*

Herman Tool & Machine Inc.......F....... 574 594-5544
Pierceton *(G-11572)*
Hgmc Supply Inc.......F....... 317 351-9500
Indianapolis *(G-7101)*
Hilltop Metal Fabricating LLC.......G....... 574 773-4975
Nappanee *(G-10680)*
Hot Stone LLC.......G....... 812 949-4969
New Albany *(G-10799)*
▲ **Imperial Stamping Corporation**.......D....... 574 294-3780
Elkhart *(G-2930)*
Imperial Trophy & Awards Co.......G....... 260 432-8161
Fort Wayne *(G-4361)*
▼ **Independent Protection Co Inc**.......C....... 574 533-4116
Goshen *(G-5242)*
▼ **Indiana Gratings Inc**.......F....... 765 342-7191
Martinsville *(G-9615)*
Industrial Contrs Skanska Inc.......E....... 812 423-7832
Evansville *(G-3555)*
Ironcraft Co Inc.......G....... 574 272-0866
South Bend *(G-12819)*
J A Smit Inc.......G....... 812 424-8141
Evansville *(G-3568)*
Jones & Sons Inc.......E....... 812 882-2957
Vincennes *(G-13687)*
K & K Fence Inc.......E....... 317 359-5425
Indianapolis *(G-7326)*
Kawneer Company Inc.......E....... 317 882-2314
Greenwood *(G-5712)*
Le Air Co Inc.......G....... 812 988-1313
Nashville *(G-10728)*
Leons Fabrication Inc.......F....... 219 365-5272
Schererville *(G-12330)*
Liquidspring LLC.......G....... 765 474-7816
Lafayette *(G-8959)*
Metal Sales Manufacturing Corp.......E....... 812 941-0041
New Albany *(G-10827)*
Mofab Inc.......G....... 765 649-1288
Anderson *(G-139)*
Mofab Inc.......E....... 765 649-1288
Anderson *(G-138)*
Muncie Metal Spinning Inc.......F....... 765 288-1937
Muncie *(G-10530)*
Open Gate LLC.......G....... 765 734-1314
Anderson *(G-148)*
Original Tractor Cab Co Inc.......E....... 765 663-2214
Arlington *(G-282)*
Ornamental Iron Works.......G....... 219 988-4929
Merrillville *(G-9743)*
Paragon Manufacturing Inc.......F....... 260 665-1492
Angola *(G-234)*
Parkers Custom Ironworks LLC.......G....... 812 897-3007
Boonville *(G-920)*
Power Train Corp Fort Wayne.......F....... 317 241-9393
Indianapolis *(G-7712)*
Reese Forge Orna Ironwork.......G....... 219 775-1039
Lake Village *(G-9086)*
Refax Wear Products Inc.......G....... 219 977-0414
Gary *(G-5091)*
Reiss Orna & Structurall Pdts.......E....... 317 925-2371
Indianapolis *(G-7830)*
Rettig Enterprises Inc.......G....... 765 567-2441
West Lafayette *(G-14102)*
Richardson Imaging Svcs Inc.......E....... 888 561-0007
New Albany *(G-10855)*
Rock Run Industries LLC.......E....... 574 361-0848
Millersburg *(G-9972)*
◆ **S S M Inc**.......G....... 317 357-4552
Indianapolis *(G-7880)*
San Jo Steel Inc.......F....... 317 888-6227
Greenwood *(G-5747)*
Schouten Metal Craft Inc.......G....... 317 546-2639
Indianapolis *(G-7903)*
Sharps Baton Mfg Corp.......G....... 574 214-9389
Elkhart *(G-3164)*
Sigma Steel Inc.......E....... 812 275-4489
Bedford *(G-578)*
Signature Metals Inc.......G....... 317 335-2207
McCordsville *(G-9676)*
Sisson Steel Inc.......F....... 812 354-8701
Winslow *(G-14359)*
Sonny Scaffolds Inc.......F....... 317 831-3900
Mooresville *(G-10341)*
Stevens Ironworks Inc.......E....... 219 987-6332
Demotte *(G-2448)*
Sugar Creek Fabricators Inc.......G....... 765 361-0891
Crawfordsville *(G-2198)*
Titus Inc.......F....... 574 936-3345
Plymouth *(G-11728)*
Upright Iron Works Inc.......G....... 219 922-1994
Griffith *(G-5794)*

Vans Iron Works ....G 219 934-1935
Munster *(G-10636)*

Ward Industries Inc...............................F 574 825-2548
Middlebury *(G-9923)*

Wiw Inc..E 219 663-7900
Crown Point *(G-2321)*

3448 Prefabricated Metal Buildings & Cmpnts

(ebs Composites) Engineered Bo ....F 574 266-3471
Elkhart *(G-2653)*

All American Homes LLC ....G 260 724-7391
Decatur *(G-2367)*

▲ All Steel Carports Inc.......................G 765 284-0694
Muncie *(G-10426)*

▲ All Steel Crprts Buildings LLC..........G 765 284-0694
Muncie *(G-10427)*

◆ Asphalt Equipment Company Inc .....G 260 672-3004
Fort Wayne *(G-4093)*

B & A Cnstr & Design Inc ....F 812 683-4600
Huntingburg *(G-6150)*

Benchmark Inc ....F 812 238-2691
Terre Haute *(G-13200)*

Biologics Modular LLC.........................G 317 456-9191
Brownsburg *(G-1137)*

Burns Construction Inc ....E 574 382-2315
Macy *(G-9440)*

Carter-Lee Building Components.........E 317 639-5431
Indianapolis *(G-6561)*

Central States Mfg Inc ....D 219 879-4770
Michigan City *(G-9773)*

Chief Industries Inc.............................C 219 866-4121
Rensselaer *(G-11917)*

Classic Buildings Inc...........................E 812 944-5821
Clarksville *(G-1677)*

◆ CTB MN Investment Co Inc ....E 574 658-4191
Milford *(G-9955)*

Falcon Metal Fabrication Inc................F 317 255-9365
Indianapolis *(G-6902)*

Five Starr Inc ....G 812 367-1554
Ferdinand *(G-3851)*

Full Metal Solutions LLC ....G 812 725-9660
Jeffersonville *(G-8365)*

Jobsite Trailer Corporation ....E 574 224-4000
Rochester *(G-12130)*

▼ Lacopa International Inc ....G 317 410-1483
Pittsboro *(G-11584)*

Laidig Inc ....E 574 256-0204
Mishawaka *(G-10067)*

Lakemaster Inc.....................................E 765 288-3718
Muncie *(G-10507)*

Maurer Constructors Inc ....G 812 236-5950
Brazil *(G-968)*

Metal Resources Inc ....G 219 886-2710
Gary *(G-5075)*

Miller Brothers Builders Inc ....E 574 533-8602
Goshen *(G-5293)*

Mobile Mini Inc ....G 260 749-6611
Fort Wayne *(G-4479)*

Mobile Mini Inc ....F 317 782-1513
Indianapolis *(G-7532)*

Mor/Ryde International Inc....................D 574 293-1581
Elkhart *(G-3047)*

Morton Buildings Inc ....F 765 932-3979
Rushville *(G-12230)*

Morton Buildings Inc ....F 260 563-2118
Wabash *(G-13741)*

Nci Group Inc ....E 317 392-3536
Shelbyville *(G-12553)*

Pathfinder Amramp LLC.......................G 260 356-0500
Huntington *(G-6235)*

Rollin Mini Barns LLC..........................G 812 687-7581
Odon *(G-11339)*

Sigma Steel Inc ....E 812 275-4489
Bedford *(G-578)*

▲ T & S Equipment Company ....C 260 665-9521
Angola *(G-249)*

Wagler Mini Barn Products ....G 812 687-7372
Plainville *(G-11657)*

Winandy Greenhouse Company...........E 765 935-2111
Richmond *(G-12076)*

Woodland Manufacturing & Sup ....F 317 271-2266
Avon *(G-472)*

Yoders Quality Barns............................G 260 565-4122
Bluffton *(G-898)*

3449 Misc Structural Metal Work

Alexander Screw Products Inc ....E 317 898-5313
Indianapolis *(G-6362)*

Aluminum Wldg & Mch Works Inc.........G 219 787-8066
Chesterton *(G-1592)*

Ambassador Steel Corporation ....E 317 834-3434
Mooresville *(G-10302)*

Circle City Rebar LLC...........................F 317 917-8566
Indianapolis *(G-6608)*

CMa Steel & Fabrication Inc.................G 260 207-9000
Fort Wayne *(G-4163)*

Coffee Lomont & Moyer Inc ....F 260 422-7825
Fort Wayne *(G-4166)*

Custom Secure Handles LLC................G 812 764-4948
Greensburg *(G-5597)*

▲ Delta Tool Manufacturing Inc..........G 574 223-4863
Rochester *(G-12122)*

Double E Enterprise Inc ....G 812 689-0671
Osgood *(G-11390)*

Edge Manufacturing Inc ....E 260 827-0482
Bluffton *(G-873)*

Engineered Rubber & Plastics..............F 574 254-1405
Mishawaka *(G-10041)*

Ertl Fabricating Inc ....F 765 393-1376
Anderson *(G-106)*

▼ Fabtration LLC ....F 812 989-6730
Georgetown *(G-5144)*

General Crafts Corp ....G 574 533-1936
Goshen *(G-5223)*

H & R Industrial LLC ....D 765 868-8408
Kokomo *(G-8635)*

High Value Metal Inc ....G 812 522-6468
Seymour *(G-12455)*

Hoosier Trim Products LLC ....E 317 271-4007
Indianapolis *(G-7125)*

Induction Iron Incorporated ....F 813 969-3300
Evansville *(G-3554)*

Interstate Metals LLC...........................F 765 893-4449
West Lebanon *(G-14121)*

Ironhorse Detailing Inc ....G 812 939-3300
Clay City *(G-1703)*

J & F Steel Corporation ....G 219 764-3500
Burns Harbor *(G-1216)*

K and S Farm and Machine Shop.........F 812 663-8567
Greensburg *(G-5617)*

Made Rite Manufacturing Inc................G 812 967-2652
Salem *(G-12300)*

McD Machine Incorporated ....G 812 339-1240
Bloomington *(G-770)*

Metal Sales Manufacturing Corp ....E 812 941-0041
New Albany *(G-10827)*

Metal Spinners Inc ....F 260 665-2158
Angola *(G-229)*

Metal Technology of Indiana.................E 765 482-1100
Lebanon *(G-9205)*

Millmark Enterprises Inc ....F 574 389-9904
Elkhart *(G-3042)*

Mor/Ryde International Inc....................D 574 293-1581
Elkhart *(G-3048)*

Mor/Ryde International Inc....................D 574 293-1581
Elkhart *(G-3049)*

Performance Tool Inc ....F 260 726-6572
Portland *(G-11838)*

Pier-Mac Plastics Inc ....E 260 726-9844
Portland *(G-11839)*

Qfs Holdings LLC.................................G 317 634-2543
Indianapolis *(G-7792)*

Rebar Corp of Indiana..........................G 260 471-2002
Fort Wayne *(G-4581)*

Roll Forming Corporation ....D 812 284-0650
Jeffersonville *(G-8421)*

Sellersburg Metals & Wldg Co ....F 812 248-0811
Sellersburg *(G-12414)*

Sherman Enterprises.............................G 260 636-6225
Albion *(G-35)*

Sigma Steel Inc ....E 812 275-4489
Bedford *(G-578)*

Stolz Structural Inc ....E 812 983-4720
Elberfeld *(G-2638)*

Superior Coatings Inc..........................G 574 546-0591
Bremen *(G-1027)*

Ten Point Trim Corp ....E 317 875-5424
Zionsville *(G-14468)*

Trivett Contracting Inc ....E 317 539-5150
Clayton *(G-1708)*

Trulite GL Alum Solutions LLC ....D 317 273-0646
Indianapolis *(G-8104)*

◆ United Roll Forming Corp.................E 574 294-2800
Elkhart *(G-3235)*

US Metals Inc.......................................G 219 398-1350
East Chicago *(G-2578)*

Vet Signs LLC......................................G 937 733-4727
Richmond *(G-12073)*

Voges Restoration and Wdwkg ....G 812 299-1546
Terre Haute *(G-13364)*

Wayne Steel Supply Inc ....E 260 489-6249
Fort Wayne *(G-4744)*

3451 Screw Machine Prdts

Aegis Sales & Engineering Inc ....F 260 483-4160
Fort Wayne *(G-4048)*

Alexander Screw Products Inc ....E 317 898-5313
Indianapolis *(G-6362)*

Ashley F Ward Inc ....F 574 294-1502
Elkhart *(G-2696)*

Ashley F Ward Inc ....E 219 879-4177
Michigan City *(G-9767)*

Auburn Manufacturing Inc ....F 260 925-8651
Auburn *(G-315)*

Auspro Manufacturing Co Inc...............G 574 264-3705
Elkhart *(G-2707)*

Beckett Bronze Company Inc ....F 765 282-2261
Muncie *(G-10438)*

▲ Charleston Metal Products Inc ....C 260 837-8211
Waterloo *(G-14010)*

Charleston Metal Products Inc ....E 260 837-8211
Waterloo *(G-14011)*

Demotte Manufacturing Inc..................E 219 987-6196
Demotte *(G-2435)*

▲ Ds Products Inc ....D 260 563-9030
Wabash *(G-13725)*

Dual Machine Corporation ....F 317 921-9850
Indianapolis *(G-6769)*

Ebert Machine Company Inc.................E 765 473-3728
Peru *(G-11526)*

EMC Precision Machining II LLC ....D 317 758-4451
Sheridan *(G-12589)*

▼ Epco Products Inc ....E 260 747-8888
Fort Wayne *(G-4240)*

Exactifab ....G 812 420-2723
Brazil *(G-961)*

F & F Screw Machine Products ....E 574 293-0362
Elkhart *(G-2842)*

Fitech Inc ....E 513 398-1414
Michigan City *(G-9794)*

Gapco Inc...G 317 787-6440
Indianapolis *(G-6983)*

Guardian Tech Group Ind LLC..............G 765 364-0863
Crawfordsville *(G-2156)*

H & E Machined Specialties..................F 260 424-2527
Fort Wayne *(G-4311)*

Ham Enterprises Machine Co ....G 765 342-7966
Martinsville *(G-9611)*

Hy-Matic Mfg Inc ....G 260 347-3651
Kendallville *(G-8479)*

Jerden Industries Inc............................E 812 332-1762
Bloomington *(G-754)*

Jessen Manufacturing Co Inc...............D 574 295-3836
Elkhart *(G-2947)*

Jrp Machine Co ....G 317 955-1905
Indianapolis *(G-7318)*

Kent Brenneke.....................................G 260 446-5383
Harlan *(G-5973)*

▲ Madison Tool and Die Inc ....E 812 273-2250
Madison *(G-9482)*

▲ Mid America Screw Products...........F 574 294-6905
Elkhart *(G-3036)*

Mitchel & Scott Machine Co.................B 317 639-5331
Indianapolis *(G-7526)*

▲ Mitchel Group Incorporated ....C 317 639-5331
Indianapolis *(G-7527)*

Ms & J Quality Screw Mch Pdts............F 812 623-3002
Sunman *(G-13115)*

Multitech Swiss Machining LLC ....G 260 894-4180
Ligonier *(G-9290)*

National Consolidated Corp..................F 574 289-7885
South Bend *(G-12868)*

Newsom Industries Inc.........................F 812 372-2844
Columbus *(G-1980)*

▲ Northern Indiana Manufacturing ......F 574 342-2105
Bourbon *(G-946)*

Precision Piece Parts Inc ....D 574 255-3185
Mishawaka *(G-10107)*

Prodigy Mold & Tool Inc ....E 812 753-3029
Haubstadt *(G-6004)*

Production Machining Company ....G 812 466-2885
Terre Haute *(G-13310)*

▲ RCO-Reed Corporation ....E 317 736-8014
Franklin *(G-4925)*

RD Smith Manufacturing Inc................G 260 829-6709
Orland *(G-11357)*

RTC..G 260 503-9770
Columbia City *(G-1831)*

S H Leggitt Company .... G 574 264-0230
 Elkhart **(G-3152)**

Sierra Machine .... G 574 232-5694
 South Bend **(G-12934)**

▲ Standard Locknut LLC .... C 317 399-2230
 Westfield **(G-14190)**

Terry Liquidation III Inc .... E 219 362-3557
 La Porte **(G-8829)**

Tri Aerospace LLC .... E 812 872-2400
 Terre Haute **(G-13358)**

Whitcraft Enterprises Inc .... F 260 422-6518
 Fort Wayne **(G-4753)**

Winn Machine Inc .... G 219 324-2978
 La Porte **(G-8833)**

3452 Bolts, Nuts, Screws, Rivets & Washers

Agrati - Park Forest LLC .... E 219 531-2202
 Valparaiso **(G-13487)**

Ashley F Ward Inc .... E 219 879-4177
 Michigan City **(G-9767)**

B K & M Inc .... G 219 924-0184
 Griffith **(G-5764)**

▲ B Walter & Company Inc .... E 260 563-2181
 Wabash **(G-13721)**

▲ Blush & Bobby Pins .... C 317 789-5166
 Carmel **(G-1318)**

▲ Bollhoff Inc .... E 260 347-3903
 Kendallville **(G-8461)**

▲ Camcar LLC .... C 574 223-3131
 Rochester **(G-12117)**

Cold Heading Co .... D 260 495-7003
 Fremont **(G-4955)**

Cold Heading Co .... G 260 587-3231
 Hudson **(G-6132)**

Cold Heading Co .... D 260 495-4222
 Fremont **(G-4956)**

Crystal Clear Inc .... G 317 753-5393
 Greenwood **(G-5678)**

Demotte Manufacturing Inc .... G 219 987-6196
 Demotte **(G-2435)**

Elgin Fastener Group LLC .... E 812 689-8917
 Versailles **(G-13653)**

Elsie Manufacturing Co Inc .... C 260 837-8841
 Waterloo **(G-14013)**

Emhart Teknologies LLC .... C 765 728-2433
 Montpelier **(G-10290)**

Enterkin Manufacturing Co Inc ...... E 317 462-4477
 Greenfield **(G-5529)**

▲ Fontana Fasteners Inc .... C 765 654-0477
 Frankfort **(G-4831)**

G4 Tool and Technology Inc .... F 574 970-0844
 Elkhart **(G-2874)**

▲ Hoosier Gasket Corporation ...... D 317 545-2000
 Indianapolis **(G-7121)**

▲ Imperial Stamping Corporation ... D 574 294-3780
 Elkhart **(G-2930)**

▲ Indiana Automotive Fas Inc .... B 317 467-0100
 Greenfield **(G-5538)**

▲ Indiana U Bolts Inc .... E 317 870-1940
 Waterloo **(G-14015)**

Kent Brenneke .... G 260 446-5383
 Harlan **(G-5973)**

▲ Key Fasteners Corp .... D 260 589-2626
 Berne **(G-619)**

▲ Machine Keys Inc .... G 765 228-4208
 Muncie **(G-10514)**

▲ McCoy Bolt Works Inc .... D 260 482-4476
 Fort Wayne **(G-4459)**

Mr Pin Shi Peter Lee .... G 574 264-9754
 Elkhart **(G-3053)**

Norco Industries Inc .... C 574 262-3400
 Elkhart **(G-3065)**

NSK Corporation .... C 765 458-5000
 Liberty **(G-9267)**

NSK Precision America Inc .... C 317 738-5000
 Franklin **(G-4916)**

Philip Pins .... G 219 769-1059
 Merrillville **(G-9745)**

Pin Point Av LLC .... G 317 750-3120
 Indianapolis **(G-7691)**

Pin-Up Curls LLC .... G 260 241-5871
 Fort Wayne **(G-4530)**

Pinup Curls Salon .... G 260 267-9659
 Fort Wayne **(G-4531)**

▲ R & R Engineering Co Inc .... E 765 536-2331
 Summitville **(G-13102)**

Rbc Prcision Pdts - Bremen Inc ..... F 574 546-4455
 Bremen **(G-1019)**

Rohder Machine & Tool Inc .... F 219 663-3697
 Crown Point **(G-2297)**

Rose Engineering Co Inc .... G 317 788-4446
 Indianapolis **(G-7862)**

Royal Pin Leisure Centers Inc ...... E 317 881-8686
 Greenwood **(G-5744)**

Standard Die Supply of Indiana ..... E 317 236-6200
 Indianapolis **(G-7989)**

▲ Standard Locknut LLC .... C 317 399-2230
 Westfield **(G-14190)**

Stanley Fastening Systems LP ...... D 317 398-0761
 Greenfield **(G-5578)**

Steve Mitchell .... G 574 831-4848
 New Paris **(G-10996)**

▲ Sunright America Inc .... C 812 342-3430
 Columbus **(G-2017)**

Western Products Indiana Inc .... F 765 529-6230
 New Castle **(G-10921)**

3462 Iron & Steel Forgings

▲ Accugear Inc .... C 260 497-6600
 Fort Wayne **(G-4037)**

Ashley F Ward Inc .... E 219 879-4177
 Michigan City **(G-9767)**

Autoform Tool & Mfg LLC .... C 260 624-2014
 Angola **(G-195)**

▲ Avis Industrial Corporation .... E 765 998-8100
 Upland **(G-13468)**

Beachy Machine Shop LLC .... G 765 452-9051
 Kokomo **(G-8597)**

Bwxt Nclear Oprtions Group Inc .... G 812 838-1200
 Mount Vernon **(G-10387)**

Custom Blacksmith Shop .... G 765 292-2745
 Atlanta **(G-293)**

Deister Concentrator LLC .... E 260 747-2700
 Fort Wayne **(G-4204)**

▲ Diamond Chain Company Inc ..... C 800 872-4246
 Indianapolis **(G-6739)**

Eaton Corporation .... D 574 288-4446
 South Bend **(G-12756)**

Emco Gears Inc .... G 317 243-3836
 Indianapolis **(G-6852)**

▲ Fairfield Manufacturing Co Inc ... A 765 772-4000
 Lafayette **(G-8896)**

Federal-Mogul LLC .... G 574 271-0274
 South Bend **(G-12775)**

Flexible Concepts Inc .... D 574 296-0941
 Elkhart **(G-2854)**

Fountaintown Forge Inc .... E 317 861-5403
 Fountaintown **(G-4790)**

General Products Corporation .... C 260 668-1440
 Angola **(G-217)**

H & H Manufacturing Inc .... G 812 664-3582
 Patoka **(G-11466)**

Hammer Time Forge .... G 812 448-2171
 Brazil **(G-963)**

Harrell Family LLC .... G 317 770-4550
 Noblesville **(G-11119)**

Horneco Fabrication Inc .... G 260 672-2064
 Fort Wayne **(G-4347)**

▲ Impact Forge Group LLC .... G 812 342-4437
 Columbus **(G-1944)**

Impact Forge Group LLC .... G 812 342-5527
 Columbus **(G-1945)**

Impact Forge Group LLC .... C 219 261-2115
 Remington **(G-11907)**

◆ Indiana Tool & Mfg Co Inc .... D 574 936-5548
 Plymouth **(G-11693)**

▲ Indiana U Bolts Inc .... E 317 870-1940
 Waterloo **(G-14015)**

Joyce/Dayton Corp .... D 260 726-9361
 Portland **(G-11831)**

Kanoff Enterprises .... G 574 575-6787
 Mishawaka **(G-10062)**

▲ Metaldyne Bsm LLC .... D 260 495-4315
 Fremont **(G-4968)**

▲ Modern Drop Forge Company LLC .B 708 489-4208
 Merrillville **(G-9737)**

Modern Forge Indiana LLC .... F 219 945-5945
 Merrillville **(G-9739)**

Mtr Machining Concept Inc .... G 260 587-3381
 Ashley **(G-288)**

▲ Nagakura Engrg Works Co Inc ... G 812 375-1382
 Columbus **(G-1978)**

Netshape Technologies LLC .... C 812 755-4501
 Campbellsburg **(G-1278)**

◆ Omnisource LLC .... C 260 422-5541
 Fort Wayne **(G-4510)**

Onspot of North America Inc .... E 812 346-1719
 North Vernon **(G-11275)**

▲ Patriot Products LLC .... F 317 736-8007
 Franklin **(G-4919)**

▲ Poseidon Barge Ltd .... D 260 422-8767
 Fort Wayne **(G-4541)**

Prox Company Inc .... F 812 232-4324
 Terre Haute **(G-13311)**

Quality Connections of Indiana ..... G 812 279-5852
 Bedford **(G-568)**

Rolls-Royce Corporation .... C 317 230-8515
 West Lafayette **(G-14104)**

▲ Rolls-Royce Corporation .... A 317 230-2000
 Indianapolis **(G-7858)**

▲ Schafer Industries Inc .... D 574 234-4116
 South Bend **(G-12929)**

Servaas Inc .... G 317 633-2020
 Indianapolis **(G-7914)**

Tdy Industries LLC .... B 260 726-8121
 Portland **(G-11849)**

Tecumseh Products Company .... E 812 883-3575
 Salem **(G-12307)**

Thyssenkrupp Crankshaft Co LLC .. D 765 294-0045
 Veedersburg **(G-13647)**

Ty Bowells Farrier Service .... E 812 537-3990
 Greendale **(G-5496)**

Union Electric Steel Corp .... C 219 464-1031
 Valparaiso **(G-13632)**

3463 Nonferrous Forgings

Autoform Tool & Mfg LLC .... C 260 624-2014
 Angola **(G-195)**

CMI Pgi Holdings LLC .... B 812 377-5000
 Columbus **(G-1871)**

Fountaintown Forge Inc .... E 317 861-5403
 Fountaintown **(G-4790)**

▲ Impact Forge Group LLC .... G 812 342-4437
 Columbus **(G-1944)**

▲ JM Fittings LLC .... D 260 747-9200
 Fort Wayne **(G-4396)**

Parker-Hannifin Corporation .... C 260 636-2104
 Albion **(G-32)**

▲ Symmetry Medical Mfg Inc .... D 574 371-2284
 Warsaw **(G-13949)**

Tdy Industries LLC .... B 260 726-8121
 Portland **(G-11849)**

Terrecorp Inc .... F 317 951-8325
 Indianapolis **(G-8054)**

3465 Automotive Stampings

Afco Performance Group LLC .... G 812 897-0900
 Boonville **(G-905)**

Auto Extras Inc .... G 574 855-2370
 South Bend **(G-12717)**

Benteler Automotive Corp .... C 574 534-1499
 Goshen **(G-5178)**

Blue River Stamping Inc .... D 317 395-5600
 Shelbyville **(G-12523)**

Body Panels Co .... F 812 962-6262
 Evansville **(G-3388)**

Fenders Inc .... G 574 293-3717
 Elkhart **(G-2847)**

Flex-N-Gate Corporation .... C 260 665-8288
 Angola **(G-214)**

Fogwell Technologies .... G 260 410-1898
 Roanoke **(G-12101)**

Fukai Toyotetsu Indiana Corp .... F 765 676-4800
 Jamestown **(G-8230)**

▲ Futaba Indiana America Corp ..... B 812 895-4700
 Vincennes **(G-13683)**

General Motors LLC .... B 765 668-2000
 Marion **(G-9525)**

▲ Heritage Products Inc .... G 765 364-9002
 Crawfordsville **(G-2158)**

Impressive Stamping & Mfg Co ..... G 260 824-2610
 Bluffton **(G-878)**

Kousei USA Inc .... G 812 373-7315
 Columbus **(G-1955)**

Lakepark Industries Ind Inc .... D 260 768-7411
 Shipshewana **(G-12628)**

Lcm Realty IV LLC .... G 574 312-6182
 Goshen **(G-5264)**

Lift .... G 812 394-5438
 Fairbanks **(G-3818)**

Lime City Manufacturing Co .... E 260 356-6826
 Huntington **(G-6224)**

Metal Fab Engineering Inc .... G 574 278-7150
 Winamac **(G-14312)**

Mpi Products LLC .... B 574 772-3850
 Knox **(G-8575)**

Multimactic New Haven LLC .... D 260 868-1067
 Butler **(G-1234)**

▲ Multimatic Indiana Inc .... C 260 868-1000
 Butler **(G-1235)**

Multimatic New Haven LLC ....G....... 260 868-1067
  Fort Wayne (G-4484)
Nasg Indiana LLC ....E....... 765 381-4310
  Muncie (G-10537)
Omr North America Inc ....F....... 317 956-9509
  Speedway (G-13015)
Patrick Custom Carbon ....G....... 815 721-5150
  Brownsburg (G-1162)
▲ Pk USA Inc ....B....... 317 395-5500
  Shelbyville (G-12558)
Pridgeon & Clay Inc ....C....... 317 738-4885
  Franklin (G-4923)
Pro-Tech Tool & Engineering ....G....... 765 258-3613
  Frankfort (G-4851)
Robert Atkins ....G....... 765 536-4164
  Summitville (G-13103)
Sacoma International Llc ....D....... 812 526-5600
  Edinburgh (G-2626)
Sermershiems Fiberglass Inc ....G....... 812 424-4701
  Evansville (G-3723)
Shiloh Industries Inc. ....F....... 574 594-9681
  Pierceton (G-11579)
▼ Specialty Rim Supply Inc ....G....... 812 234-3002
  Terre Haute (G-13338)
Steel Parts Corporation ....B....... 765 675-2191
  Tipton (G-13406)
Techna Fit of Indiana ....G....... 317 350-2153
  Brownsburg (G-1173)
The Pro Shear Corporation Corp ....G....... 260 408-1010
  Fort Wayne (G-4681)
TOA Winchester LLC ....B....... 765 584-7639
  Winchester (G-14342)
Tower Automotive Operations ....C....... 260 925-5113
  Auburn (G-363)
Tru-Form Metal Products Inc ....F....... 574 266-8020
  Elkhart (G-3225)
Twin Maple Tool Inc ....F....... 574 586-7500
  Walkerton (G-13811)

3466 Crowns & Closures

Charmaran Corporation ....F....... 260 347-3347
  Kendallville (G-8463)
Drug Plastics Closures Inc ....D....... 812 526-0555
  Edinburgh (G-2608)
▲ Rieke Corporation ....B....... 260 925-3700
  Auburn (G-349)

3469 Metal Stampings, NEC

A Raymond Tinnerman Auto Inc ....C....... 574 722-5168
  Logansport (G-9319)
Accu-Tool Inc ....G....... 260 248-4529
  Columbia City (G-1758)
Advanced Metal Fabricators Inc..........F....... 574 259-1263
  Mishawaka (G-9991)
Ameri-Tek Manufacturing Inc...............F....... 574 753-8058
  Logansport (G-9320)
Ark Model and Stampings Inc..............F....... 317 549-3394
  Indianapolis (G-6420)
ATI Products Inc. ....G....... 260 358-9254
  Huntington (G-6187)
Atkisson Enterprises Inc......................F....... 765 675-7593
  Tipton (G-13388)
Aul Brothers Tool & Die Inc ....F....... 765 759-5124
  Muncie (G-10434)
▲ Austin Tri-Hawk Automotive Inc ....C....... 812 794-0062
  Austin (G-395)
▲ B Walter & Company Inc ....E....... 260 563-2181
  Wabash (G-13721)
▲ B&J International LLC ....G....... 260 854-2215
  Kendallville (G-8459)
▲ B&J Rocket America Inc..................E....... 574 825-5802
  Middlebury (G-9874)
▲ Batesville Tool & Die Inc ....C....... 812 934-5616
  Batesville (G-494)
Bemr LLC ....G....... 812 385-8509
  Princeton (G-11864)
Btd Manufacturing Inc ....G....... 812 934-5616
  Batesville (G-495)
C E R Metal Marking Corp ....G....... 219 924-9710
  Highland (G-6039)
▲ Capco LLC ....D....... 812 375-1700
  Columbus (G-1866)
Carr Metal Products Inc.......................C....... 317 542-0691
  Indianapolis (G-6558)
Charmaran Corporation ....F....... 260 347-3347
  Kendallville (G-8463)
Cnc Industries Inc...............................D....... 260 490-5700
  Fort Wayne (G-4165)
Colbin Tool Company Inc ....E....... 574 457-3183
  Syracuse (G-13130)

Columbian Home Products LLC...........E....... 812 238-5041
  Terre Haute (G-13214)
Computer Technology ....G....... 812 283-5094
  Jeffersonville (G-8344)
Countryside Tool ....G....... 260 357-3839
  Garrett (G-4999)
Covington Products Inc ....F....... 765 282-6626
  Muncie (G-10450)
Crichlow Industries Inc ....G....... 317 925-5178
  Indianapolis (G-6692)
Crossrads Rhbilitation Ctr Inc ....G....... 317 897-7320
  Indianapolis (G-6697)
Da-Mar Industries Inc ....F....... 260 347-1662
  Kendallville (G-8471)
Diamond Manufacturing Company ....E....... 219 874-2374
  Michigan City (G-9782)
Die-Mensional Metal Stamping ....F....... 812 265-3946
  Madison (G-9456)
Dietech Corporation ....G....... 260 724-8946
  Decatur (G-2375)
Dixie Metal Spinning Corp ....G....... 317 541-1330
  Indianapolis (G-6753)
▲ Domar Machine & Tool Inc ....G....... 574 295-8791
  Elkhart (G-2798)
Dwyer Instruments Inc ....E....... 219 393-5250
  La Porte (G-8752)
Eaton Corporation ....C....... 260 925-3800
  Auburn (G-328)
Elixir Industries ....E....... 574 294-5685
  Elkhart (G-2816)
Elixir Industries ....E....... 574 294-5685
  Elkhart (G-2817)
Elixir Industries ....D....... 574 294-5685
  Elkhart (G-2818)
▼ Epco Products Inc ....E....... 260 747-8888
  Fort Wayne (G-4240)
Evansville Metal Products Inc ....D....... 812 423-5632
  Evansville (G-3487)
Express Motor Vehicle ADM LLC ....G....... 812 909-0116
  Evansville (G-3496)
▲ Fayette Tool and Engineering ....F....... 765 825-7518
  Connersville (G-2048)
▲ Ffesar Inc.......................................F....... 812 378-4220
  McCordsville (G-9667)
Flambeau Inc.......................................C....... 812 372-4899
  Columbus (G-1931)
▲ Form Wood Industries Inc. ....E....... 812 284-3676
  Jeffersonville (G-8363)
Franklin Stamping Inds Inc ....F....... 765 282-5138
  Muncie (G-10473)
Galloway Fabricating ....G....... 574 453-3802
  Leesburg (G-9236)
▲ Gammons Metal & Mfg Co Inc ....D....... 317 546-7091
  Indianapolis (G-6982)
General Devices Co Inc ....E....... 317 897-7000
  Indianapolis (G-6995)
General Motors LLC.............................B....... 765 668-2000
  Marion (G-9525)
General Sheet Metal Works Inc ....E....... 574 288-0611
  South Bend (G-12788)
▲ Group Dekko Inc ....D....... 260 357-3621
  Garrett (G-5009)
Gt Stamping Inc ....D....... 574 533-4108
  Goshen (G-5231)
◆ H D Williams Co...............................G....... 812 372-6476
  Columbus (G-1936)
H P Products Corporation ....G....... 812 331-8793
  Bloomington (G-736)
Harold Precision Products Inc..............E....... 765 348-2710
  Hartford City (G-5981)
Hasser Enterprises Inc........................G....... 765 583-1444
  West Lafayette (G-14074)
Haven Manufacturing Ind Inc...............E....... 260 622-4150
  Ossian (G-11400)
▲ Hoosier Stamping LLC ....G....... 812 993-2040
  Chandler (G-1549)
▲ Hoosier Stamping & Mfg Corp ....E....... 812 426-2778
  Evansville (G-3540)
Hoosier Tank and Mfg Inc ....D....... 574 232-8368
  South Bend (G-12803)
Hoosier Trim Products LLC ....E....... 317 271-4007
  Indianapolis (G-7125)
Hopper Development Inc.......................F....... 574 753-6621
  Logansport (G-9336)
Humphrey Tool Coinc ....G....... 574 753-3853
  Logansport (G-9338)
Imh Fabrication Inc ....F....... 317 252-5566
  Indianapolis (G-7163)
Imh Fabrication Inc.............................F....... 317 252-5566
  Indianapolis (G-7164)

▲ Imperial Stamping Corporation ....D....... 574 294-3780
  Elkhart (G-2930)
Impressive Stamping & Mfg Co ....G....... 260 824-2610
  Bluffton (G-878)
Indiana Fine Blanking..........................G....... 574 772-3850
  Knox (G-8568)
Indiana Metal Stamping Co ....G....... 574 936-2964
  Plymouth (G-11691)
▲ Indianapolis Metal Spinning Co........F....... 317 273-7440
  Indianapolis (G-7203)
Irwin Hodson Group Indiana LLC ....G....... 260 482-8052
  Fort Wayne (G-4384)
J & K Associates ....G....... 317 255-3588
  Indianapolis (G-7279)
Jag Metal Spinning Inc ....G....... 812 533-5501
  Sandford (G-12310)
Jam-Ko Engineering Company ....F....... 574 294-7684
  Elkhart (G-2944)
Jason Incorporated ....C....... 847 215-1948
  Richmond (G-12007)
◆ JM Hutton & Co Inc ....G....... 765 962-3591
  Richmond (G-12008)
JM Machine..G....... 219 464-4477
  Valparaiso (G-13564)
Johnson Controls Inc ....D....... 260 489-6104
  Fort Wayne (G-4397)
Kable Tool & Engineering ....G....... 260 726-9670
  Portland (G-11833)
Kimball Electronics Inc ....D....... 317 545-5383
  Indianapolis (G-7351)
Kirby Risk Corporation ....C....... 317 398-9713
  Shelbyville (G-12543)
KMC Enterprises Inc. ....G....... 765 584-1533
  Winchester (G-14335)
Koester Metals Inc ....E....... 260 495-1818
  Fremont (G-4964)
Krukemeier Machine and Tool Co ....F....... 317 784-7042
  Beech Grove (G-600)
L H Stamping Corporation ....D....... 260 432-5563
  Fort Wayne (G-4421)
Lakepark Industries Ind Inc ....D....... 260 768-7411
  Shipshewana (G-12628)
Lauck Manufacturing Co Inc.................F....... 317 787-6269
  Indianapolis (G-7385)
LH Industries Corp ....B....... 260 432-5563
  Fort Wayne (G-4431)
Lime City Manufacturing Co ....G....... 260 356-6826
  Huntington (G-6224)
Lippert Components Inc........................E....... 574 535-1125
  Goshen (G-5272)
Lippert Components Inc........................C....... 800 551-9149
  Elkhart (G-2999)
Lippert Components Inc........................G....... 574 535-1125
  Goshen (G-5268)
Lippert Components Inc........................D....... 574 294-6852
  Elkhart (G-3000)
Lippert Components Inc........................D....... 574 849-0869
  Goshen (G-5273)
Lippert Components Inc........................C....... 574 971-4320
  Goshen (G-5275)
Lippert Components Inc........................C....... 574 312-7445
  Middlebury (G-9904)
Logan Stampings Inc...........................E....... 574 722-3101
  Logansport (G-9349)
▲ Long Item Development Corp ....G....... 317 844-9491
  Carmel (G-1427)
Lynn Tool Company Inc........................G....... 765 874-2471
  Lynn (G-9430)
MA Metal Co Inc ....E....... 812 526-2666
  Columbus (G-1966)
▼ Mac Machine & Metal Works Inc.......E....... 765 825-5873
  Connersville (G-2062)
Maron Products Incorporated...............D....... 574 259-1971
  Mishawaka (G-10074)
Master Manufacturing Company ....E....... 812 425-1561
  Evansville (G-3615)
Mc Metalcraft Inc.................................G....... 574 259-8101
  Mishawaka (G-10076)
Mc Metalcraft Inc.................................D....... 574 259-8101
  Mishawaka (G-10077)
Metal Fab Engineering Inc ....F....... 574 278-7150
  Winamac (G-14312)
Metal Spinners Inc ....F....... 260 665-2158
  Angola (G-229)
Metal Spinners Inc ....E....... 260 665-7741
  Angola (G-230)
Metalstamp Inc.....................................D....... 574 232-5997
  South Bend (G-12860)
Mid-West Spring Mfg Co ....D....... 574 353-1409
  Mentone (G-9688)

Mier Products Inc................E....... 765 457-0223
Kokomo (G-8666)

Miller Mfg Corp................E....... 574 773-4136
Nappanee (G-10695)

Monroe Custom Utility Bodies........D....... 317 894-8684
Greenfield (G-5558)

Mpi Products LLC................B....... 574 772-3850
Knox (G-8575)

Muncie Metal Spinning Inc........F....... 765 288-1937
Muncie (G-10530)

▲ Mursix Corporation................C....... 765 282-2221
Yorktown (G-14408)

New Process Steel LP................E....... 260 868-1445
Butler (G-1237)

Oak-Rite Mfg Corp................E....... 317 839-2301
Plainfield (G-11632)

P & A Machine Inc................E....... 317 634-3673
Indianapolis (G-7641)

▲ Pent Plastics Inc................C....... 260 897-3775
Kendallville (G-8502)

▼ Perfecto Tool & Engineering Co....E....... 765 644-2821
Anderson (G-150)

Precision Stamping Inc................E....... 574 522-8987
Elkhart (G-3109)

Premier Concepts Inc................G....... 574 269-7570
Warsaw (G-13929)

Productivity Resources Inc........G....... 317 245-4040
Noblesville (G-11166)

Pruett Manufacturing Co Inc........G....... 812 234-9497
Terre Haute (G-13312)

▲ Qmp Inc................E....... 574 262-1575
Elkhart (G-3124)

Quality Die Set Corp................E....... 574 967-4411
Logansport (G-9361)

R & R Tool Manufacturing Inc........E....... 219 362-1681
La Porte (G-8810)

R Concepts Industries Inc........D....... 574 295-6641
Elkhart (G-3135)

RBM Manufacturing Inc................G....... 765 364-6933
Crawfordsville (G-2192)

Ready Machine Tool & Die Corp....E....... 765 825-3108
Connersville (G-2070)

Reeves Manufacturing Inc........G....... 765 935-3875
Richmond (G-12042)

Rhinehart Development Corp........E....... 260 238-4442
Spencerville (G-13050)

Rotam Tool Corporation................F....... 260 982-8318
North Manchester (G-11242)

Royal Stamping Inc................F....... 260 925-3312
Auburn (G-350)

Samco Inc................E....... 812 279-8131
Bedford (G-576)

Sha-Do Corp................G....... 574 848-9296
Bristol (G-1085)

Shakour Industries Inc................E....... 574 289-0100
South Bend (G-12932)

Small Parts Inc................B....... 574 739-6236
Logansport (G-9365)

Smith Small Engine Service........G....... 812 232-1318
Terre Haute (G-13329)

Stamina Metal Products Inc........G....... 574 534-7410
Goshen (G-5327)

Steel Parts Corporation................B....... 765 675-2191
Tipton (G-13406)

Steelmaster Machine & TI Corp....F....... 574 825-7670
Middlebury (G-9922)

Stone City Products Inc................D....... 812 275-3373
Bedford (G-582)

Swiss Metal Spinning Co................G....... 260 692-1401
Monroe (G-10187)

▲ Symmetry Medical Mfg Inc........D....... 574 371-2284
Warsaw (G-13949)

TEC-Air LLC................D....... 219 301-7084
Munster (G-10632)

Titan Manufacturing Co................G....... 219 662-7238
Crown Point (G-2314)

Trivector Manufacturing Inc........E....... 260 637-0141
Fort Wayne (G-4706)

▲ Tube Processing Corp................B....... 317 787-1321
Indianapolis (G-8107)

Tube Processing Corp................C....... 317 264-7760
Indianapolis (G-8109)

Twin Maple Tool Inc................F....... 574 586-7500
Walkerton (G-13811)

Ultra Manufacturing Inc................E....... 574 586-2320
Walkerton (G-13812)

Valley Tool & Die Stampings........E....... 574 722-4566
Logansport (G-9375)

Versatile Fabrication LLC................G....... 574 293-8504
Elkhart (G-3244)

Wayne Manufacturing Corp................E....... 260 637-5586
Laotto (G-9115)

Webber Manufacturing Company........E....... 317 357-8681
Indianapolis (G-8181)

Wenzel Acquisition Inc................G....... 260 495-9898
Fremont (G-4979)

Wenzel Metal Spinning Inc........D....... 260 495-9898
Fremont (G-4980)

Wenzel Metal Spinning Inc Ind........D....... 260 495-9898
Fremont (G-4981)

York Group Inc................C....... 765 966-1576
Richmond (G-12078)

ZF North America Inc................C....... 765 429-1678
Lafayette (G-9027)

ZF North America Inc................B....... 765 429-1984
Lafayette (G-9028)

Zojila LLC................G....... 765 404-3767
Lafayette (G-9029)

3471 Electroplating, Plating, Polishing, Anodizing & Coloring

502 Mold Polishing LLC................G....... 502 436-0239
Greenville (G-5646)

A Raymond Tinnerman Auto Inc........C....... 574 722-5168
Logansport (G-9319)

Aacoa Inc................C....... 574 262-4685
Elkhart (G-2661)

Abrasive Processing & Tech LLC........F....... 317 485-5157
Fortville (G-4767)

Albany Metal Treating Inc................D....... 765 789-6470
Albany (G-10)

Allegheny Ludlum LLC................C....... 765 529-9570
New Castle (G-10890)

American Sandblasting................G....... 574 233-1384
South Bend (G-12706)

Anderson Silver Plating Co........C....... 574 294-6447
Elkhart (G-2693)

▲ Arcelormittal Kote Inc................G....... 574 654-1000
New Carlisle (G-10878)

B-D Industries Inc................F....... 574 295-1420
Elkhart (G-2712)

▲ Bare Metal Inc................F....... 812 948-1313
New Albany (G-10750)

▲ Batesville Products Inc................D....... 513 381-2057
Lawrenceburg (G-9133)

Beemsterboer Slag Corp................E....... 219 931-7462
Hammond (G-5849)

Best Metal Finishing Inc................E....... 812 689-9950
Osgood (G-11389)

Better Metal Systems LLC................G....... 888 958-5945
Highland (G-6038)

▼ Blitz Manufacturing Co Ind........D....... 812 284-2548
Jeffersonville (G-8330)

Bon L Manufacturing Company........C....... 815 351-6802
Kentland (G-8517)

Brunswick Corporation................C....... 260 459-8200
Fort Wayne (G-4125)

C & J Plating & Grinding LLC........G....... 765 288-8728
Muncie (G-10444)

C & R Plating Corp................G....... 586 755-4900
Columbia City (G-1770)

▲ Ceramica Inc................F....... 317 546-0087
Indianapolis (G-6589)

Chief Metal Works Inc................G....... 765 932-2134
Rushville (G-12217)

Chrome Deposit Corporation........E....... 219 763-1571
Portage (G-11756)

Circle City Heat Treating Inc........F....... 317 638-2252
Indianapolis (G-6607)

Commercial Finishing Corp........E....... 317 267-0377
Indianapolis (G-6637)

Complete Finish Inc................F....... 260 587-3588
Ashley (G-284)

Crown Coatings LLC................G....... 317 482-2766
Fortville (G-4771)

Custom Polish & Chrome................G....... 260 665-7448
Angola (G-206)

Db Polishing................G....... 574 518-2443
Nappanee (G-10666)

Dekalb Metal Finishing Inc................E....... 260 925-1820
Auburn (G-327)

Deuxfreres LLC................D....... 317 241-7600
Indianapolis (G-6736)

Diamond Manufacturing Company........E....... 219 874-2374
Michigan City (G-9782)

DOT America Inc................F....... 260 244-5700
Columbia City (G-1779)

Doug Wilcox................G....... 812 476-1957
Lynnville (G-9434)

Electro-Spec Inc................D....... 317 738-9199
Franklin (G-4883)

Elkhart Plating Corp................F....... 574 294-1800
Elkhart (G-2828)

Emi LLC................E....... 812 437-9100
Evansville (G-3475)

Franke Plating Works Inc................D....... 260 422-8477
Fort Wayne (G-4284)

G and P Enterprises Ind Inc........G....... 812 723-3837
Paoli (G-11451)

Hand Industries Inc................E....... 574 267-3525
Warsaw (G-13888)

Heidtman Steel Products Inc........C....... 419 691-4646
Butler (G-1229)

Hgc Custom Chrome................G....... 260 447-4731
Yoder (G-14398)

Huthone LLC................G....... 260 248-2384
Columbia City (G-1792)

Hydro Extrusion North Amer LLC........B....... 888 935-5757
North Liberty (G-11216)

Industrial Anodizing Co Inc........E....... 317 637-4641
Indianapolis (G-7207)

Industrial Contrs Skanska Inc........E....... 812 423-7832
Evansville (G-3555)

Industrial Plating Inc................D....... 765 447-5036
Lafayette (G-8924)

▲ Industrial Research Inc................B....... 812 401-2333
Evansville (G-3557)

Indy Metal Finishing Co................E....... 317 858-5353
Brownsburg (G-1153)

▲ J & J Welding Inc................E....... 812 838-4391
Mount Vernon (G-10396)

J & L Dimensional Services Inc........E....... 219 325-3588
La Porte (G-8773)

J & P Custom Plating Inc................G....... 260 726-9696
Portland (G-11829)

Justin Mollo................G....... 812 361-7694
Morgantown (G-10355)

K & I Hard Chrome Inc................E....... 812 948-1166
New Albany (G-10811)

Kadet Products Inc................E....... 765 552-7341
Elwood (G-3303)

Keystone Automotive Inds Inc........C....... 574 206-1421
Elkhart (G-2963)

Klinge Enameling Company Inc........E....... 317 359-8291
Indianapolis (G-7359)

Kromet America Inc................E....... 812 346-5117
Lafayette (G-8946)

Lambert Metal Finishing Inc........G....... 260 493-0529
Fort Wayne (G-4423)

Linden Machine Shop LLC................G....... 765 339-7244
Linden (G-9304)

Madison Plating Inc................F....... 812 273-2211
Madison (G-9480)

McDowell Enterprises Inc................E....... 574 293-1042
Elkhart (G-3024)

Metal Finishing Co Inc................G....... 317 546-9004
Indianapolis (G-7486)

Michiana Metal Finishing Inc........G....... 574 206-0666
Elkhart (G-3033)

Mid-City Plating Company Inc........E....... 765 289-2374
Muncie (G-10520)

Midwest Surface Prep LLC................G....... 317 726-1336
Indianapolis (G-7513)

Miller Plating & Metal Finishi........G....... 812 424-3837
Evansville (G-3628)

Mpp Inc................E....... 260 422-5426
Fort Wayne (G-4482)

Muncie Precision Hard Chrome........G....... 765 288-2489
Muncie (G-10535)

Napier & Napier................G....... 765 580-9116
Liberty (G-9266)

National Material LP................C....... 219 397-5088
East Chicago (G-2554)

Neo Industries LLC................F....... 574 217-4078
South Bend (G-12871)

Neo Industries LLC................G....... 219 762-6075
Portage (G-11781)

▲ Neo Industries (indiana) Inc........C....... 219 762-6075
Portage (G-11782)

New Paradigms Industrial Art........G....... 219 762-4046
Portage (G-11783)

P & H LLC................G....... 765 654-5291
Frankfort (G-4848)

P & J Industries Inc................E....... 260 894-7143
Ligonier (G-9291)

Performance Powder Coating........G....... 765 438-5224
Kokomo (G-8680)

Pioneer Metal Finishing LLC................D....... 574 287-7239
South Bend (G-12896)

Poiry Partners LLC ....E 260 424-1030
Fort Wayne (G-4535)
Praxair Surface Tech Inc ....C 317 240-2544
Indianapolis (G-7726)
Precision Buffing and Polsg ....G 574 262-3430
Elkhart (G-3107)
Precision Polishing & Buffing ....G 317 352-0165
Indianapolis (G-7734)
Precoat Metals Corp ....C 317 462-7761
Greenfield (G-5565)
Pro Tech Metal Finishing ....E 260 894-4011
Ligonier (G-9293)
Professional Metal Refinishing ....G 260 436-2828
Fort Wayne (G-4562)
Progressive Plating Company ....E 317 923-2413
Indianapolis (G-7776)
Pruett Manufacturing Co Inc ....F 812 234-9497
Terre Haute (G-13312)
Quick Turn Anodizing LLC ....G 877 716-1150
Edinburgh (G-2622)
R & S Plating Inc ....G 317 925-2396
Indianapolis (G-7807)
Reckon Plating Inc ....E 260 744-4339
Fort Wayne (G-4582)
Reliable Polishing Co ....G 765 744-7824
Parker City (G-11464)
Rhinehart Finishing LLC ....D 260 238-4442
Spencerville (G-13051)
Riepen LLC ....D 574 269-5900
Warsaw (G-13935)
Roll Coater Inc ....G 317 652-1102
Indianapolis (G-7856)
Saturn Wheel Company Inc ....D 260 375-4720
Warren (G-13833)
Schaffsteins Truck Clean LLC ....F 812 464-2424
Evansville (G-3715)
Seleco Inc ....E 317 872-4148
Indianapolis (G-7908)
Southside Plating Works Inc ....G 219 293-5508
Elkhart (G-3182)
Steve Reiff Inc ....D 260 723-4360
South Whitley (G-13005)
▲ Sumco LLC ....D 317 241-7600
Indianapolis (G-8015)
▲ Superior Metal Tech LLC ....D 317 897-9850
Indianapolis (G-8022)
Surface Enhancement ....G 574 269-1366
Warsaw (G-13945)
T & J Plating Inc ....G 765 664-9669
Marion (G-9566)
Ternet Metal Finishing Inc ....G 260 897-3903
Avilla (G-419)
Tfx Plating Company LLC ....G 765 289-2436
Yorktown (G-14412)
Thorntons Welding ....G 812 332-8564
Bloomington (G-841)
Tk Finishing ....G 574 233-1617
South Bend (G-12973)
▲ Transportation Tech Inds ....F 812 962-5000
Evansville (G-3769)
Triplex Plating Inc ....E 219 874-3209
Michigan City (G-9855)
United States Steel Corp ....D 219 762-3131
Portage (G-11799)
W & M Manufacturing Inc ....C 260 726-9800
Portland (G-11855)
W Kendall & Sons Inc ....G 219 733-2412
Wanatah (G-13827)
Wayne Black Oxide Inc ....G 260 484-0280
Fort Wayne (G-4738)
Wayne Metal Protection Company ....E 260 492-2529
Fort Wayne (G-4742)
Whitlocks Pressure Wash ....F 765 825-5868
Connersville (G-2078)
Worthington Steel Company ....C 219 929-4000
Porter (G-11806)
Wrr Inc ....C 317 577-1149
Indianapolis (G-8221)
Yellow Dog Anodizing ....G 574 343-2247
Elkhart (G-3271)

3479 Coating & Engraving, NEC

AAA Galvanizing - Joliet Inc ....D 260 488-4477
Hamilton (G-5818)
AAA Galvanizing - Joliet Inc ....E 765 289-3427
Muncie (G-10421)
AAA Galvanizing - Joliet Inc ....E 574 935-4500
Plymouth (G-11661)
Accent Coatings LLC ....G 317 712-0017
Fishers (G-3865)
Aceys Trophies & Awards ....G 574 267-1426
Warsaw (G-13835)
Acme Coatings Inc ....G 317 272-6202
Avon (G-424)
Advanced Finishing Corporation ....G 317 335-2210
McCordsville (G-9664)
Alliance Coating LLC ....G 574 772-3372
Knox (G-8562)
▲ Alocit USA ....G 317 631-9111
Indianapolis (G-6377)
American Metal Coatings Inc ....F 765 608-2100
Anderson (G-61)
▲ Angola Wire Products Inc ....C 260 665-9447
Angola (G-192)
Apexx Enterprises LLC ....F 812 486-2443
Montgomery (G-10213)
Applied Metals & Mch Works Inc ....E 260 424-4834
Fort Wayne (G-4083)
▲ Arcelormittal Kote Inc ....G 574 654-1000
New Carlisle (G-10878)
Arrow Powder Coating LLC ....E 317 822-8002
Indianapolis (G-6422)
▲ Asempac Inc ....E 812 945-6303
New Albany (G-10747)
B-D Industries Inc ....F 574 295-1420
Elkhart (G-2712)
Beacon Industries Inc ....E 812 526-0100
Edinburgh (G-2596)
Blackfoot Powder Coating ....G 812 531-9315
Brazil (G-954)
Carmel Traphies Plus ....G 317 844-3770
Carmel (G-1332)
Carrara Industries Inc ....G 765 643-3430
Anderson (G-81)
Chemcoaters LLC ....E 219 977-1929
Gary (G-5036)
Chief Metal Works Inc ....G 765 932-2134
Rushville (G-12217)
Commercial Coatings Assoc LLC ....G 812 483-5130
Evansville (G-3425)
Commercial Finishing Corp ....E 317 267-0377
Indianapolis (G-6637)
▲ Conforma Clad Inc ....C 812 948-2118
New Albany (G-10765)
Craddock Finishing Corporation ....E 812 425-2691
Evansville (G-3436)
Creative Finishing ....G 812 591-8111
Greensburg (G-5595)
Creative Liquid Coatings Inc ....C 260 349-1862
Kendallville (G-8470)
▲ Creative Liquid Coatings Inc ....A 260 349-1862
Fort Wayne (G-4185)
Crichlow Industries Inc ....G 317 925-5178
Indianapolis (G-6692)
Crossroads Galvanizing LLC ....F 765 421-6741
Lafayette (G-8883)
Crown Group Co ....D 260 432-6900
Fort Wayne (G-4190)
Cunningham Quality Painting ....G 317 925-8852
Indianapolis (G-6711)
Custom Coating Inc ....E 260 925-0623
Auburn (G-325)
Custom Coatings ....G 317 392-7908
Shelbyville (G-12528)
Custom TS & Trophies ....G 219 926-4174
Porter (G-11804)
D & S Industries Inc ....F 574 848-7144
Bristol (G-1053)
D S E Inc ....E 812 376-0310
Columbus (G-1904)
DC Coaters Inc ....E 765 675-6006
Tipton (G-13390)
Dd Stoops Laser Engraving ....G 765 868-4999
Kokomo (G-8611)
Dearborn Coatings LLC ....G 513 600-9580
Lawrenceburg (G-9136)
Denver Stone ....E 317 244-5889
Indianapolis (G-6734)
Diamond Manufacturing Company ....E 219 874-2374
Michigan City (G-9782)
Edcoat Limited Partnership ....E 574 654-9105
New Carlisle (G-10881)
▼ Electric Coating Tech LLC ....E 219 378-1930
East Chicago (G-2527)
Electro-Coat Technologies ....E 574 266-7356
Elkhart (G-2815)
Elite Protective Coatings ....G 317 476-1712
Greenwood (G-5685)
Em Black Oxide ....G 574 233-4933
South Bend (G-12762)
Erler Industries Inc ....D 812 346-4421
North Vernon (G-11257)
Evansville Metal Products Inc ....D 812 423-5632
Evansville (G-3487)
Fasi Coatings LLC ....G 219 985-0788
Gary (G-5046)
Fremont Coatings Div ....G 260 495-4445
Fremont (G-4959)
French International Coatings ....G 574 505-0774
Akron (G-5)
Gale Enameling Co Inc ....G 317 839-7474
Indianapolis (G-6979)
▲ Gammons Metal & Mfg Co Inc ....D 317 546-7091
Indianapolis (G-6982)
Garrett Products ....G 260 357-5988
Garrett (G-5005)
Gateway Galvinizing Inc ....E 812 284-5241
Jeffersonville (G-8367)
Genesis Products Inc ....E 574 266-8293
Elkhart (G-2878)
Golden Frame Inc ....G 812 232-0048
Terre Haute (G-13242)
▲ Group Dekko Inc ....D 260 357-3621
Garrett (G-5009)
Harmon Coatings LLC ....G 317 326-4298
Greenfield (G-5536)
▲ Henkel ....D 765 284-5050
Muncie (G-10486)
▲ Holscher Products Inc ....E 765 884-8021
Fowler (G-4801)
Hoosier Badge & Trophies Inc ....G 317 257-4441
Indianapolis (G-7120)
Hoosier Powder Coating LLC ....G 574 253-7737
Nappanee (G-10684)
Huber Brothers Inc ....G 317 392-1566
Shelbyville (G-12537)
▲ IBC Coatings Technologies Ltd ....E 317 418-3725
Lebanon (G-9188)
IBC Materials & Tech LLC ....F 765 482-9802
Lebanon (G-9189)
Ideal Coatings LLC ....G 574 358-0182
Middlebury (G-9891)
Imagineering Enterprises Inc ....E 574 287-0642
South Bend (G-12808)
▲ Imagineering Enterprises Inc ....C 574 287-2941
South Bend (G-12809)
Imagineering Enterprises Inc ....F 317 635-8565
Indianapolis (G-7162)
Indiana Galvanizing LLC ....E 574 822-9102
Middlebury (G-9892)
Indy Powder Coating Inc ....G 317 244-2231
Indianapolis (G-7220)
Indy Powder Coatings LLC ....F 317 236-7177
Noblesville (G-11129)
Intratek Inc ....G 260 484-3377
Fort Wayne (G-4381)
▲ Itsuwa Usa LLC ....F 812 375-0323
Columbus (G-1949)
J&J Manufacturing ....G 574 646-2069
Nappanee (G-10686)
Jah Coatings LLC ....G 317 550-7169
Indianapolis (G-7296)
JM Christian LLC ....G 317 460-0984
Chesterton (G-1616)
Job Shop Coating Inc ....E 317 462-9714
Greenfield (G-5544)
Johnson Engraving & Trophies ....G 260 982-7868
North Manchester (G-11232)
Jupiter Aluminum Corporation ....E 219 932-3322
Fairland (G-3823)
▲ Keco Engineered Coatings Inc ....F 317 356-7279
Indianapolis (G-7338)
◆ Kennametal Stellite LP ....D 574 534-9532
Goshen (G-5253)
Kevin Kolish Corp ....G 574 946-3238
Winamac (G-14309)
Khamis Fine Jewelers Inc ....G 317 841-8440
Indianapolis (G-7348)
Klinge Enameling Company Inc ....E 317 359-8291
Indianapolis (G-7359)
Lansing Metallizing & Grinding ....G 219 931-1785
Hammond (G-5906)
Larry H Poole ....G 812 466-9345
Terre Haute (G-13272)
Laser Graphx Inc ....G 574 834-4443
North Webster (G-11296)
Lein Corporation ....E 765 674-6950
Marion (G-9542)
M S Powder Coating ....G 260 356-0300
Huntington (G-6227)

S I C

Mains Enterprises Inc ....G...... 765 425-0162
  Wilkinson *(G-14279)*
Make It Black Seal Coating ....G...... 219 629-6230
  Hobart *(G-6090)*
Max Powder Coating Inc ....G...... 812 752-4200
  Scottsburg *(G-12373)*
Mays+red Spot Coatings LLC ......G...... 317 558-2024
  Indianapolis *(G-7470)*
McNeil Coatings Consultants ......G...... 317 885-1557
  Greenwood *(G-5725)*
Mestek Inc ....E...... 317 831-5314
  Mooresville *(G-10322)*
Metal Improvement Company LLC ......E...... 260 495-4445
  Fremont *(G-4967)*
Metalized Coatings LLC ....G...... 219 851-0683
  La Porte *(G-8791)*
Midwest Custom Finishing Inc .....F...... 219 874-0099
  Michigan City *(G-9818)*
Midwest Custom Finishing Inc .....G...... 574 258-0099
  Mishawaka *(G-10086)*
Midwest Wheelcoaters LLC ....G...... 219 874-0099
  Michigan City *(G-9820)*
Mills Custom Powder Coating ......G...... 812 766-0308
  Winslow *(G-14357)*
▲ Modern Materials Inc ....E...... 574 223-4509
  Rochester *(G-12139)*
Modern Powder Coating LLC ....G...... 765 342-7039
  Martinsville *(G-9627)*
Momentive Performance Mtls Inc ......D...... 260 357-2000
  Garrett *(G-5017)*
Natural Coating Systems ....G...... 765 642-2464
  Anderson *(G-143)*
NC Coatings LLC ....G...... 574 213-4754
  Nappanee *(G-10698)*
Nda Energized Coatings ....G...... 260 499-0307
  Elkhart *(G-3058)*
Northern Ind Indus Catings LLC ......G...... 574 893-4621
  Akron *(G-6)*
Panacea Paints & Coatings Inc ......G...... 260 728-4222
  Decatur *(G-2397)*
Parsing Laser Designs LLC ....G...... 317 677-4316
  Avon *(G-460)*
Performance Coatings Spc LLC ......G...... 574 606-8153
  Topeka *(G-13427)*
Plasfinco LLC ....E...... 812 346-3900
  North Vernon *(G-11278)*
Powdercoil Technologies LLC ....G...... 708 634-2343
  Crown Point *(G-2288)*
Praxair Surface Tech Inc ....C...... 317 240-2500
  Indianapolis *(G-7724)*
◆ Praxair Surface Tech Inc ....C...... 317 240-2500
  Indianapolis *(G-7725)*
Praxair Surface Tech Inc ....G...... 317 240-2192
  Indianapolis *(G-7727)*
▲ Precoat Metals Corp ....E...... 317 462-7761
  Greenfield *(G-5564)*
Precoat Metals Corp ....D...... 219 393-3561
  La Porte *(G-8807)*
Precoat Metals Corp ....C...... 317 462-7761
  Greenfield *(G-5565)*
Premier Cstm Coatings LLC Ind ......G...... 317 557-7841
  Greenwood *(G-5736)*
Prince Manufacturing Corp ....E...... 260 357-4484
  Garrett *(G-5020)*
Procoat Inc ....G...... 317 263-5071
  Indianapolis *(G-7768)*
Professional Bowling Ball Svc .....G...... 317 786-4329
  Indianapolis *(G-7770)*
Pyramid Metallizing Inc ....G...... 219 879-9967
  Michigan City *(G-9832)*
Quality Pnt Prstned Fnshes Inc ......G...... 574 294-6944
  Elkhart *(G-3129)*
Quick Tanks Inc ....E...... 260 347-3850
  Kendallville *(G-8503)*
Quick Turn Anodizing LLC ....G...... 877 716-1150
  Edinburgh *(G-2622)*
Quickblades ....G...... 260 359-2072
  Huntington *(G-6242)*
Red Spot Paint & Varnish Co ....B...... 812 428-9100
  Evansville *(G-3699)*
Reed Contracting Company ....F...... 765 452-2638
  Kokomo *(G-8687)*
▲ Rightway Fasteners Inc ....C...... 812 342-2700
  Columbus *(G-2009)*
S T Praxair Technology Inc ....G...... 317 240-2500
  Indianapolis *(G-7881)*
Schafer Powder Coating Inc ....E...... 317 228-9987
  Carmel *(G-1475)*
Seavac USA LLC ....G...... 260 747-7123
  Fort Wayne *(G-4614)*

Secorp Inc ....G...... 219 874-5010
  Michigan City *(G-9842)*
Sermatech Intl Canada Corp ....G...... 317 240-2500
  Indianapolis *(G-7913)*
Sp3 ....E...... 260 547-4150
  Decatur *(G-2406)*
▲ Specialty Coating Systems Inc ......F...... 317 451-8549
  Indianapolis *(G-7967)*
Specialty Coatings LLC ....G...... 812 431-3375
  Evansville *(G-3742)*
Specialty Indus Coatings Corp ......G...... 574 784-3711
  Lakeville *(G-9097)*
Star Quality Awards Inc ....G...... 812 273-1740
  Madison *(G-9496)*
Steel Dynamics Inc ....D...... 812 218-1490
  Jeffersonville *(G-8428)*
Steve Reiff Inc ....G...... 260 723-4360
  South Whitley *(G-13005)*
▲ Superior Metal Tech LLC ....D...... 317 897-9850
  Indianapolis *(G-8022)*
T G R Inc ....F...... 765 452-8225
  Kokomo *(G-8705)*
Tri State Powder Coating LLC ......G...... 812 425-7010
  Evansville *(G-3771)*
▲ Truck Stylin Unlimited ....G...... 574 223-8800
  Rochester *(G-12158)*
TW Performance Coatings LLC ......G...... 317 331-8664
  Indianapolis *(G-8115)*
Twin Coatings & Finishes ....G...... 317 557-0633
  Indianapolis *(G-8117)*
Unique Specialty Services LLC ......G...... 219 395-8898
  Chesterton *(G-1636)*
Universal Coatings LLC ....G...... 574 520-3403
  Elkhart *(G-3237)*
Van Westrum Corporation ....G...... 317 926-3200
  Indianapolis *(G-8146)*
W Kendall & Sons Inc ....G...... 219 733-2412
  Wanatah *(G-13827)*
▲ Winona Powder Coating Inc ......D...... 574 267-8311
  Etna Green *(G-3324)*
▲ Winona Pvd Coatings LLC ....E...... 574 269-3255
  Warsaw *(G-13968)*
Witt Galvanizing ....G...... 574 935-4500
  Plymouth *(G-11738)*
Witt Industries Inc ....E...... 765 289-3427
  Muncie *(G-10587)*
Witt Industries Inc ....E...... 574 935-4500
  Plymouth *(G-11739)*
Wright Coatings Corporation ....G...... 317 937-6768
  Indianapolis *(G-8218)*

3482 Small Arms Ammunition

A & W Firearms ....G...... 765 716-6856
  Yorktown *(G-14400)*
Blythes Sport Shop Inc ....F...... 219 924-4403
  Griffith *(G-5766)*
Flexible Marketing Group ....G...... 574 296-0941
  Elkhart *(G-2855)*
Northern Indiana Ordnance Co ......G...... 574 289-5938
  South Bend *(G-12879)*
Solotat Industries LLC ....G...... 574 320-1436
  Elkhart *(G-3180)*
Sons of Thunder ....G...... 812 897-4908
  Boonville *(G-922)*

3483 Ammunition, Large

Flexible Marketing Group ....G...... 574 296-0941
  Elkhart *(G-2855)*
▲ Military Facilities ....G...... 812 854-1762
  Crane *(G-2129)*

3484 Small Arms

Acme Sports Inc ....G...... 812 522-4008
  Seymour *(G-12426)*
BCI Defense LLC ....G...... 574 546-2411
  Bremen *(G-983)*
Blythes Sport Shop Inc ....F...... 219 924-4403
  Griffith *(G-5766)*
CF Gunworks LLC ....G...... 317 538-1122
  Frankfort *(G-4821)*
Eds Trading Post Inc ....G...... 317 933-4867
  Nineveh *(G-11057)*
Enterprise MGT Solutions LLC ......G...... 219 545-8544
  Merrillville *(G-9713)*
Favres Gun Shop ....G...... 812 235-0198
  Terre Haute *(G-13234)*
Headstamp Fine Brass LLC ....G...... 812 212-8326
  Batesville *(G-502)*
Namacle LLC ....G...... 574 320-1436
  Elkhart *(G-3056)*

Patriot Arms ....G...... 812 859-4293
  Coal City *(G-1743)*
Rajo Guns Corp ....G...... 812 422-6945
  Evansville *(G-3694)*
Red Bull Armory LLC ....G...... 757 287-7738
  Mitchell *(G-10169)*
Solotat Industries LLC ....G...... 574 320-1436
  Elkhart *(G-3180)*
Suppress TEC LLC ....G...... 812 453-5813
  Elberfeld *(G-2640)*
Wraith Arms Resolutions LLC ......G...... 812 380-1208
  Velpen *(G-13650)*

3489 Ordnance & Access, NEC

A & W Firearms ....G...... 765 716-6856
  Yorktown *(G-14400)*
Allied Mfg Partners Inc ....G...... 260 428-2670
  Fort Wayne *(G-4062)*
Indiana Ordnance Works Inc ....G...... 812 256-4478
  Pekin *(G-11474)*
J DS Big Boys Toys ....G...... 219 365-7807
  Saint John *(G-12264)*
Prototech Enterprises Inc ....G...... 317 250-9644
  Carmel *(G-1457)*
Raytheon Company ....A...... 260 429-6000
  Fort Wayne *(G-4576)*
Zr Tactical Solutions LLC ....G...... 317 721-9787
  Noblesville *(G-11201)*

3491 Industrial Valves

AMG LLC ....E...... 317 329-4004
  Indianapolis *(G-6397)*
Fitch Inc ....G...... 260 637-0835
  Huntertown *(G-6138)*
Flosource Inc ....E...... 765 342-1360
  Martinsville *(G-9605)*
Frew Process Group LLC ....G...... 317 565-5000
  Noblesville *(G-11107)*
Gould Solenoid Valve Co ....F...... 317 547-5289
  Indianapolis *(G-7030)*
Henry Pratt Company LLC ....F...... 219 931-0405
  Hammond *(G-5891)*
Hoffman Sls & Specialty Co Inc ......G...... 317 846-6428
  Carmel *(G-1406)*
J D Gould Company Inc ....F...... 317 542-1876
  Indianapolis *(G-7285)*
▲ Nexus Valve Inc ....E...... 317 257-6050
  Fishers *(G-3948)*
◆ Nibco Inc ....B...... 574 295-3000
  Elkhart *(G-3062)*
Parker-Hannifin Corporation ....C...... 260 636-2104
  Albion *(G-32)*
Proportion-Air Inc ....D...... 317 335-2602
  McCordsville *(G-9674)*
S H Leggitt Company ....G...... 574 264-0230
  Elkhart *(G-3152)*
Shoemaker Inc ....F...... 260 625-4321
  Fort Wayne *(G-4622)*
▲ SMC Corporation of America ......B...... 317 899-3182
  Noblesville *(G-11184)*
▲ Specilzed Cmpnent Prts Ltd LLC ......C...... 260 925-2588
  Auburn *(G-357)*
TEC Inc ....G...... 765 827-3868
  Connersville *(G-2076)*
U S Valves Inc ....G...... 812 476-6662
  Evansville *(G-3782)*

3492 Fluid Power Valves & Hose Fittings

Cindon Inc ....F...... 812 853-5450
  Newburgh *(G-11024)*
Coupled Products LLC ....B...... 260 248-3200
  Columbia City *(G-1776)*
Daman Products Company Inc ......D...... 574 259-7841
  Mishawaka *(G-10030)*
Dependable Rubber Industrial ......G...... 765 447-5654
  Lafayette *(G-8887)*
▲ Hitachi Cble Auto Pdts USA Inc ......C...... 812 945-9011
  New Albany *(G-10796)*
Hydro Systems Mfg Inc ....G...... 260 436-4476
  Fort Wayne *(G-4353)*
Innovtive Hydrlic Slutions LLC ......G...... 317 252-0120
  Indianapolis *(G-7239)*
▲ JM Fittings LLC ....D...... 260 747-9200
  Fort Wayne *(G-4396)*
▲ Kilgore Manufacturing Co Inc ......D...... 260 248-2002
  Columbia City *(G-1804)*
▲ Kobaltec LLC ....G...... 219 462-1483
  Valparaiso *(G-13567)*
M & M Svc Stn Eqp Spcalist Inc ......G...... 317 347-8001
  Indianapolis *(G-7429)*

Macallister Machinery Co Inc......D.......260 483-6469
Fort Wayne *(G-4447)*
Mary Jonas......F.......317 500-0600
Indianapolis *(G-7462)*
Noble Composites Inc......C.......574 533-1462
Goshen *(G-5299)*
▲ Nrp Jones LLC......G.......219 362-4508
La Porte *(G-8800)*
P H C Industries Inc......G.......260 423-9461
Fort Wayne *(G-4516)*
Parker-Hannifin Corporation......A.......260 748-6000
New Haven *(G-10951)*
Proportion-Air Inc......D.......317 335-2602
McCordsville *(G-9674)*
▼ R P S Hydraulics Sales & Svc......E.......219 845-5526
Hammond *(G-5931)*
▲ Slb Corporation......F.......574 255-9774
Mishawaka *(G-10125)*
▲ SMC Corporation of America......B.......317 899-3182
Noblesville *(G-11184)*
▲ Techna-Fit Inc......G.......317 350-2153
Brownsburg *(G-1174)*
▲ Terry Liquidation III Inc......D.......219 362-9908
La Porte *(G-8828)*
Tri-State Hydraulics Indus Sup......G.......812 537-3485
Greendale *(G-5495)*

3493 Steel Springs, Except Wire

Cargo Systems Inc......G.......574 264-1600
Elkhart *(G-2749)*
Ferguson Equipment Inc......F.......574 234-4303
South Bend *(G-12778)*
Kokomo Spring Company Inc......F.......765 459-5156
Kokomo *(G-8656)*
M-3 and Associates Inc......E.......574 294-3988
Elkhart *(G-3010)*
Matthew Warren Inc......G.......574 722-8200
Logansport *(G-9354)*
Muehlhausen Spring Company......G.......574 626-2351
Walton *(G-13816)*
Muehlhausen Spring Company......G.......574 859-2481
Flora *(G-4000)*
Myers Spring Co Inc......E.......574 753-5105
Logansport *(G-9357)*
Pepka Spring Company Inc......F.......765 459-3114
Kokomo *(G-8679)*
▲ Precision Products Group Inc......B.......330 698-4711
Indianapolis *(G-6276)*
Preferred Metal Services Inc......G.......219 988-2386
Crown Point *(G-2289)*
Valley Tool & Die Stampings......E.......574 722-4566
Logansport *(G-9375)*
Wellspring Components LLC......G.......260 768-7336
Shipshewana *(G-12657)*
Winamac Coil Spring Inc......C.......574 653-2186
Kewanna *(G-8528)*

3494 Valves & Pipe Fittings, NEC

Air Fixtures Inc......F.......260 982-2169
North Manchester *(G-11224)*
Ashley F Ward Inc......E.......574 294-1502
Elkhart *(G-2696)*
Ashley F Ward Inc......E.......219 879-4177
Michigan City *(G-9767)*
Coupled Products LLC......B.......260 248-3200
Columbia City *(G-1776)*
Elkhart Products Corporation......C.......260 368-7246
Geneva *(G-5135)*
▼ Epco Products Inc......E.......260 747-8888
Fort Wayne *(G-4240)*
Green Pipe & Supply Inc......G.......219 762-1077
Portage *(G-11769)*
Hancor Inc......E.......812 443-2080
Brazil *(G-964)*
Honeywell International Inc......G.......574 231-2000
South Bend *(G-12799)*
Hy-Matic Mfg Inc......E.......260 347-3651
Kendallville *(G-8479)*
Indiana Seal......G.......317 841-3547
Indianapolis *(G-7190)*
▲ JM Fittings LLC......D.......260 747-9200
Fort Wayne *(G-4396)*
Madden Manufacturing Inc......F.......574 295-4292
Elkhart *(G-3013)*
◆ Nibco Inc......B.......574 295-3000
Elkhart *(G-3062)*
Parker-Hannifin Corporation......A.......260 748-6000
New Haven *(G-10951)*
Paulus Plastic Company Inc......G.......574 834-7663
North Webster *(G-11299)*

PHD Inc......C.......260 356-0120
Huntington *(G-6238)*
▼ R P S Hydraulics Sales & Svc......E.......219 845-5526
Hammond *(G-5931)*
Strahman Holdings Inc......G.......317 818-5030
Indianapolis *(G-6281)*
Strataflo Products Inc......F.......260 482-4366
Fort Wayne *(G-4655)*

3495 Wire Springs

A J Coil Inc......G.......574 353-7174
Tippecanoe *(G-13380)*
A Raymond Tinnerman Auto Inc......C.......574 722-5168
Logansport *(G-9319)*
▲ Barber Manufacturing Co Inc......D.......765 643-6905
Anderson *(G-72)*
▲ Circle M Spring Inc......E.......574 267-2883
Warsaw *(G-13857)*
▼ Hoosier Spring Co Inc......G.......574 291-7550
South Bend *(G-12802)*
Integrated Systems Management......G.......765 565-6108
Carthage *(G-1513)*
Leggett & Platt Incorporated......E.......260 347-2600
Kendallville *(G-8490)*
Mid-West Spring Mfg Co......G.......574 353-1409
Mentone *(G-9688)*
Myers Spring Co Inc......E.......574 753-5105
Logansport *(G-9357)*
Pepka Spring Company Inc......F.......765 459-3114
Kokomo *(G-8679)*
▲ Pimmler Holdings Inc......G.......574 583-8090
Monticello *(G-10279)*
▲ Precision Products Group Inc......B.......330 698-4711
Indianapolis *(G-6276)*
▲ Suzuki Garphyttan Corp......D.......574 232-8800
South Bend *(G-12963)*
United Air Works Inc......G.......317 576-0040
Indianapolis *(G-8127)*
Valley Tool & Die Stampings......E.......574 722-4566
Logansport *(G-9375)*
Walton Industrial Park Inc......F.......574 626-2929
Walton *(G-13818)*
Winamac Coil Spring Inc......C.......574 653-2186
Kewanna *(G-8528)*

3496 Misc Fabricated Wire Prdts

▲ Abz Corp......G.......317 758-2699
Sheridan *(G-12587)*
▲ Accel International......F.......260 897-9990
Avilla *(G-400)*
Accent Wire Products......G.......765 628-3587
Greentown *(G-5643)*
American Wire Rope & Sling of......G.......877 634-2545
Indianapolis *(G-6392)*
▲ Angola Wire Products Inc......C.......260 665-9447
Angola *(G-192)*
Angola Wire Products Inc......E.......260 665-3061
Angola *(G-193)*
Beal Systems Inc......G.......260 693-0772
Laotto *(G-9104)*
Belden Inc......A.......765 962-7561
Richmond *(G-11962)*
Bender Products Inc......E.......574 255-5350
Mishawaka *(G-10009)*
Benthall Bros Inc......G.......800 488-5995
Evansville *(G-3372)*
◆ Breyden Products Inc......E.......260 244-2995
Columbia City *(G-1767)*
Bridon-American Corporation......E.......812 749-3115
Oakland City *(G-11309)*
Cmj & Associates Corporation......G.......765 962-1947
Richmond *(G-11970)*
Commercial Group Lifting Pdts......G.......219 944-7200
Gary *(G-5039)*
▲ Dekko Acquisition Parent Inc......G.......260 347-0700
Kendallville *(G-8472)*
Elevator Equipment Corporation......D.......765 966-7761
Richmond *(G-11981)*
Essex Group Inc......D.......260 248-5500
Columbia City *(G-1785)*
F D Ramsey & Co Inc......F.......219 362-2452
La Porte *(G-8757)*
Fab Solutions LLC......G.......765 744-2671
Redkey *(G-11897)*
Fix & Sons Manufacturing Inc......F.......765 724-4041
Alexandria *(G-42)*
▲ General Cage LLC......E.......765 552-5039
Anderson *(G-108)*
Grc Enterprises Inc......E.......219 932-2220
East Chicago *(G-2530)*

Group Dekko Holdings Inc......G.......260 347-0700
Garrett *(G-5011)*
▲ Hessville Cable & Sling Co......E.......773 768-8181
Gary *(G-5064)*
Hewitt Manufacturing Company......F.......765 525-9829
Waldron *(G-13799)*
Indiana Wire Products Inc......F.......812 663-7441
Greensburg *(G-5615)*
Kentuckiana Wire Rope & Supply......F.......812 282-3667
Jeffersonville *(G-8386)*
Kewanna Metal Specialties Inc......D.......574 653-2554
Kewanna *(G-8525)*
▲ Khorporate Holdings Inc......C.......260 357-3365
Laotto *(G-9110)*
Kingsford Products Inc......G.......740 862-4450
Decatur *(G-2389)*
▲ Lafayette Wire Products Inc......D.......765 474-7896
Lafayette *(G-8952)*
Lake Cable of Indiana LLC......C.......847 238-3000
Valparaiso *(G-13569)*
Lauck Manufacturing Co Inc......F.......317 787-6269
Indianapolis *(G-7385)*
Macpactor Inc......G.......502 643-7845
Jeffersonville *(G-8393)*
Meese Inc......G.......812 273-1008
Madison *(G-9485)*
◆ Mid-West Metal Products Co Inc......E.......888 741-1044
Muncie *(G-10521)*
Mid-West Metal Products Co Inc......D.......765 741-3137
Muncie *(G-10523)*
Mid-West Spring Mfg Co......G.......574 353-1409
Mentone *(G-9688)*
Myers Spring Co Inc......E.......574 753-5105
Logansport *(G-9357)*
Noble Wire Products Inc......G.......317 773-1926
Orland *(G-11354)*
Onspot of North America Inc......G.......203 377-0777
North Vernon *(G-11274)*
Onspot of North America Inc......E.......812 346-1719
North Vernon *(G-11275)*
Organized Living Inc......C.......812 334-8839
Bloomington *(G-791)*
Outtadaway LLC......G.......219 866-8885
Rensselaer *(G-11934)*
▲ Precision Products Group Inc......B.......330 698-4711
Indianapolis *(G-6276)*
Pro Tech Automation Inc......G.......317 201-3875
Monrovia *(G-10205)*
Pwt Group LLC......E.......260 490-6477
Fort Wayne *(G-4565)*
▲ R & R Engineering Co Inc......E.......765 536-2331
Summitville *(G-13102)*
Rabers Buggy Shop LLC......G.......812 486-3789
Montgomery *(G-10239)*
▲ Reelcraft Industries Inc......C.......855 634-9109
Columbia City *(G-1824)*
S & S Industry & Manufacturing......F.......219 963-0213
Lake Station *(G-9076)*
▲ Sanlo Inc......D.......219 879-0241
Michigan City *(G-9841)*
▼ Spaceguard Inc......E.......812 523-3044
Seymour *(G-12492)*
Stanley Fastening Systems LP......D.......317 398-0761
Greenfield *(G-5578)*
Tubular Engrg & Sls Co Inc......F.......765 536-2225
Summitville *(G-13108)*
Valley Tool & Die Stampings......E.......574 722-4566
Logansport *(G-9375)*
Vans Iron Works......G.......219 934-1935
Munster *(G-10636)*
Winamac Coil Spring Inc......C.......574 653-2186
Kewanna *(G-8528)*
Wirco Inc......C.......260 897-3768
Avilla *(G-422)*
Wire-Tek Inc......G.......812 623-8300
Sunman *(G-13121)*
Yongli America LLC......G.......219 763-7920
Portage *(G-11802)*

3497 Metal Foil & Leaf

API Americas Inc......G.......812 689-6502
Osgood *(G-11388)*
Avery Dennison Corporation......D.......219 696-7777
Lowell *(G-9399)*
Foil Laminating Inc......E.......574 935-3645
Plymouth *(G-11686)*
Revere Industries LLC......G.......317 580-2420
Westfield *(G-14184)*

S I C

3498 Fabricated Pipe & Pipe Fittings

▲ A S C Industries Inc ....E 574 264-1987
Elkhart (G-2659)

A/C Fabricating Corp ....E 574 534-1415
Goshen (G-5163)

Allied Tube & Conduit Corp ....E 765 459-8811
Kokomo (G-8590)

Allied Tube & Conduit Corp ....C 812 265-9255
Madison (G-9443)

▲ B&J Rocket America Inc ....E 574 825-5802
Middlebury (G-9874)

Barry Company Inc ....E 317 578-2486
Fishers (G-3874)

Big Inch Fabricators Cnstr Inc ....D 765 245-9353
Montezuma (G-10209)

Cal Pipe Manufacturing Inc ....E 219 844-6800
Hobart (G-6070)

Calpipe Industries LLC ....E 219 844-6800
Hobart (G-6071)

Curtis Products Inc ....E 574 289-4891
South Bend (G-12745)

Curtis Products Inc ....C 574 289-4891
South Bend (G-12746)

▲ Elkhart Products Corporation ....B 574 264-3181
Elkhart (G-2829)

Fabshop ....G 317 549-1681
Reelsville (G-11901)

Globe Mechanical Inc ....D 812 949-2001
New Albany (G-10788)

Green Lake Tube LLC ....G 219 397-0495
East Chicago (G-2531)

▲ Green Leaf Inc ....G 812 877-1546
Fontanet (G-4024)

Hd Mechanical Inc ....G 219 924-6050
Griffith (G-5776)

Industrial Tube Components Inc ....G 317 431-2188
Lizton (G-9316)

Indy Tube Fabrication LLC ....G 317 883-2000
Franklin (G-4900)

Jae Enterprises Inc ....E 260 747-0568
Fort Wayne (G-4391)

Jae Enterprises Inc ....G 260 489-6249
Fort Wayne (G-4392)

▲ JM Fittings LLC ....D 260 747-9200
Fort Wayne (G-4396)

Johnson Controls ....C 317 826-2130
Indianapolis (G-7309)

Kautex Inc ....B 937 238-8096
Avilla (G-409)

Klene Pipe Structures Inc ....G 812 663-6445
Greensburg (G-5619)

L & W Engineering Inc ....G 574 825-5351
Middlebury (G-9900)

Nelson Global Products Inc ....D 608 719-1752
Fort Wayne (G-4493)

Parker-Hannifin Corporation ....E 260 587-9102
Ashley (G-289)

Plymouth Tube Company ....C 574 946-6191
Winamac (G-14314)

Porter County Fabricators ....G 219 663-4665
Crown Point (G-2287)

Precision Products Group Inc ....E 260 484-4111
Fort Wayne (G-4552)

Quality Hydraulic & Mch Svc ....G 317 892-2596
Danville (G-2355)

Russells Tube Forming Inc ....E 317 241-4072
Indianapolis (G-7874)

Scot Industries Inc ....F 608 778-2251
Auburn (G-353)

Southwark Metal Mfg Co ....G 317 823-5300
Indianapolis (G-7965)

St Regis Culvert Inc ....F 317 353-8065
Indianapolis (G-7982)

Staples Pipe & Muffler ....G 812 522-3569
Butlerville (G-1251)

Steuben Fabg & Engrg Inc ....G 260 665-3001
Angola (G-247)

Tb Plastic Extrusions Michiana ....E 574 266-7409
Elkhart (G-3206)

▲ Tcb Enterprises LLC ....F 574 522-3971
Elkhart (G-3207)

▲ Technifab Products Inc ....D 812 442-0520
Brazil (G-979)

Thormax Enterprises LLC ....G 812 530-7744
Seymour (G-12496)

Tube Processing Corp ....C 317 787-5747
Indianapolis (G-8106)

▲ Tube Processing Corp ....B 317 787-1321
Indianapolis (G-8107)

Tube Processing Corp ....C 317 782-9486
Indianapolis (G-8108)

Tube Processing Corp ....C 317 264-7760
Indianapolis (G-8109)

Tube Processing Corp ....C 317 787-1321
Indianapolis (G-8110)

Uniseal Inc ....G 812 425-1361
Evansville (G-3785)

▲ Whipp In Holdings LLC ....C 260 478-2363
Fort Wayne (G-4752)

3499 Fabricated Metal Prdts, NEC

4board LLC ....G 317 997-3354
Indianapolis (G-6291)

A & T Metal Fabricators LLC ....G 219 949-5066
Gary (G-5025)

Ad-Vance Magnetics Inc ....E 574 223-3158
Rochester (G-12113)

Agi International Inc ....F 317 536-2415
Indianapolis (G-6352)

▲ Aisin Chemical Indiana LLC ....E 812 793-2888
Crothersville (G-2213)

Amrosia Metal Fabrication Inc ....G 812 425-5707
Evansville (G-3356)

Assa Abloy Door Group LLC ....F 800 826-2617
Elkhart (G-2697)

B6 Manufacturing LLC ....G 317 549-4290
Indianapolis (G-6451)

Ball Corporation ....F 574 583-9418
Monticello (G-10253)

Barnett Industrial Inc ....F 219 814-7500
Valparaiso (G-13503)

Briter Products Inc ....G 574 386-8167
South Bend (G-12725)

Bway Corporation ....D 219 462-8915
Valparaiso (G-13517)

▲ Classic Trophy Co ....F 260 483-1161
Fort Wayne (G-4161)

Core Resources LLC ....G 812 829-2240
Spencer (G-13021)

Custom Metal Fabrication LLC ....G 574 257-8851
Mishawaka (G-10027)

▲ Customer 1st LLC ....G 812 967-6727
Pekin (G-11471)

Davis Hezakih Corp ....F 260 768-7300
Shipshewana (G-12611)

▲ Ditto Sales Inc ....E 812 482-3043
Jasper (G-8245)

Dubose Strapping Inc ....G 765 361-0000
Crawfordsville (G-2150)

E & H Bridge & Grating Inc ....G 812 277-8343
Bedford (G-538)

E&P Technologies LLC ....G 317 828-8482
Carmel (G-1366)

Etching Industries Corporation ....E 317 591-3500
Indianapolis (G-6882)

Extreme Metal Fab Inc ....F 812 988-9353
Nashville (G-10724)

Fabtron Corporation ....G 260 925-9553
Auburn (G-331)

◆ Fire King International LLC ....F 812 948-8400
New Albany (G-10778)

Fire King International LLC ....E 812 948-2795
New Albany (G-10779)

◆ Fire King Security Pdts LLC ....C 812 948-8400
New Albany (G-10780)

◆ Fki Security Group LLC ....B 812 948-8400
New Albany (G-10781)

Flexible Marketing Group ....G 574 296-0941
Elkhart (G-2855)

GKN Sinter Metals LLC ....C 812 883-3381
Salem (G-12288)

Gleason Corporation ....C 574 533-1141
Goshen (G-5226)

Grace Manufacturing Inc ....F 574 267-8000
Warsaw (G-13884)

◆ H & H Sales Company Inc ....F 260 637-3177
Huntertown (G-6139)

Hammer Industries Inc ....E 812 422-6953
Evansville (G-3529)

Hand Industries Inc ....E 574 267-3525
Warsaw (G-13888)

Hg Metal Fabrication ....G 317 491-3381
Indianapolis (G-7099)

Hibbing International Friction ....F 765 529-7001
New Castle (G-10904)

▲ Hosetract Industries Ltd ....F 260 489-8828
Fort Wayne (G-4349)

Huver Manufacturing Tech LLC ....G 317 460-8605
Noblesville (G-11122)

Illinois Tool Works Inc ....C 260 347-8040
Kendallville (G-8480)

Indy Aerospace Inc ....G 817 521-6508
Indianapolis (G-7212)

Innovative 3d Mfg LLC ....G 317 560-5080
Franklin (G-4901)

JC Metal Fabrication ....G 574 340-1109
Mishawaka (G-10061)

Johnson Safe Company ....G 317 876-7233
Zionsville (G-14443)

JRS Custom Fabrication ....G 765 676-4170
Jamestown (G-8231)

K C Creations ....G 937 748-8181
Indianapolis (G-7327)

Keener Corporation ....E 765 825-2100
Connersville (G-2059)

▲ Kiel NA LLC ....F 574 293-3600
Elkhart (G-2965)

Kimball Electronics Inc ....D 317 545-5383
Indianapolis (G-7351)

L & W Engineering Inc ....G 574 825-5351
Middlebury (G-9900)

▲ Liftco Inc ....E 574 266-5551
Elkhart (G-2997)

▲ Magnequench Inc ....A 765 778-7809
Pendleton (G-11494)

▲ Magnets R US Inc ....G 574 633-0061
South Bend (G-12848)

Meilink Safe Company ....E 812 941-0024
New Albany (G-10825)

Metal Fab Engineering Inc ....F 574 278-7150
Winamac (G-14312)

Michiana Metal Fabricatio ....G 574 256-9010
Mishawaka (G-10083)

Midwest Indus Met Fbrction Inc ....E 260 356-5262
Huntington (G-6230)

Midwest Industrial Metal ....G 260 358-0373
Huntington (G-6231)

Miller Mfg Corp ....E 574 773-4136
Nappanee (G-10695)

Mossberg Industries Inc ....D 260 357-5141
Garrett (G-5018)

Moyers Inc ....E 574 264-3119
Elkhart (G-3052)

Ms Manufacturing LLC ....E 812 442-7468
Brazil (G-972)

Murpac of Fort Wayne LLC ....G 260 424-2299
Fort Wayne (G-4485)

Nector Machine & Fabricating ....G 219 322-6878
Schererville (G-12338)

Nst Campbellsburg Inc ....G 812 755-4501
Campbellsburg (G-1279)

Orange Cnty Wldg & Fabrication ....G 812 653-5754
Orleans (G-11364)

▲ Outsource Technologies Inc ....E 574 233-1303
South Bend (G-12884)

▲ Phoenix Safe International LLC ....G 765 483-0954
Lebanon (G-9216)

Professional Bowling Ball Svc ....G 317 786-4329
Indianapolis (G-7770)

▲ Reelcraft Industries Inc ....C 855 634-9109
Columbia City (G-1824)

▲ Risco Products Inc ....G 317 392-6150
Shelbyville (G-12562)

◆ Rko Enterprises LLC ....G 812 273-8813
Madison (G-9492)

Rowe Conveyor LLC ....G 317 602-1024
Greenwood (G-5743)

▲ S C Pryor Inc ....E 317 352-1281
Indianapolis (G-7878)

▲ Schafer Industries Inc ....D 574 234-4116
South Bend (G-12929)

Shrock Manufacturing Inc ....E 574 264-4126
Elkhart (G-3168)

Smokers Iron Works ....G 574 674-6683
Elkhart (G-3179)

Spectrum Brands Inc ....E 317 773-6627
Noblesville (G-11187)

Sssi Inc ....G 219 762-8901
Portage (G-11795)

Stulls Mch & Fabrication Inc ....G 765 942-2717
Ladoga (G-8843)

Thomas & Skinner Inc ....B 317 923-2501
Indianapolis (G-8063)

Tic Toc Trophy Shop Inc ....G 574 893-4234
Akron (G-8)

Timothy White ....G 765 689-8270
Bunker Hill (G-1207)

Trophies & Awards Inc ....G 260 925-4672
Auburn (G-365)

▲ Tru-Flex LLC.....................................C...... 765 893-4403
West Lebanon (G-14122)

Tuff Stuff Sales and Svc Inc..............G...... 765 354-4151
Middletown (G-9943)

Tungsten Company LLC........................G...... 317 788-6732
Indianapolis (G-8113)

Tusca 2...G...... 812 876-2857
Bloomington (G-849)

Twisted Mtal Fbrication Svcs I...........G...... 219 923-8045
Munster (G-10635)

Vet Signs LLC....................................G...... 937 733-4727
Richmond (G-12073)

Youniquely Yours................................G...... 219 942-1489
Hobart (G-6103)

35 INDUSTRIAL AND COMMERCIAL MACHINERY AND COMPUTER EQUIPMENT

3511 Steam, Gas & Hydraulic Turbines & Engines

Allison Transmission Inc.....................C...... 317 821-5104
Indianapolis (G-6376)

Auxilius Heavy Industries LLC ....E...... 765 885-5099
Fowler (G-4794)

Clayhill Wind & Solar LLC...................G...... 765 437-2395
Sharpsville (G-12504)

Cummins Inc.......................................A...... 812 522-9366
Seymour (G-12442)

Design Engineering.............................F...... 219 926-2170
Chesterton (G-1602)

Drive Process Services Inc.................G...... 765 741-9717
Muncie (G-10464)

Falcon Manufacturing LLC..................F...... 317 884-3600
Columbus (G-1922)

General Electric Company ....D...... 812 933-0700
Batesville (G-501)

Glenwood M Brown Co LLC.................G...... 260 710-4428
Laotto (G-9108)

▲ Integrated Energy Technologies......E...... 812 421-7810
Evansville (G-3563)

Mantech Manifold................................G...... 260 479-2383
Fort Wayne (G-4452)

Power Wall Systems LLC.....................G...... 317 348-1260
Fishers (G-3955)

Prime Tech Inc....................................G...... 317 715-1162
Indianapolis (G-7746)

R W Machine Incorporated..................G...... 317 769-6798
Whitestown (G-14260)

Rolls-Royce PLC.................................G...... 317 306-2441
Martinsville (G-9636)

Siemens Energy Inc............................G...... 317 677-1340
Indianapolis (G-7936)

Tab Technologies.................................G...... 765 482-7561
Lebanon (G-9227)

Tosmo America Inc..............................F...... 812 953-1481
North Vernon (G-11284)

Tri Aerospace LLC...............................E...... 812 872-2400
Terre Haute (G-13358)

◆ Windstream Technologies Inc...........E...... 812 953-1481
North Vernon (G-11287)

3519 Internal Combustion Engines, NEC

Bes Racing Engines Inc ....F...... 812 576-2371
Guilford (G-5797)

Brunswick Corporation ....C...... 260 459-8200
Fort Wayne (G-4125)

Carlson Motorsports............................G...... 765 339-4407
Linden (G-9303)

Ccts Technology Group Inc ....G...... 305 209-5743
Indianapolis (G-6570)

Champion Racing Engines ....G...... 317 335-2491
McCordsville (G-9665)

▲ Cosworth LLC..................................D...... 844 278-6941
Indianapolis (G-6673)

◆ Cummins...G...... 812 524-6381
Seymour (G-12441)

Cummins - Allison Corp ....G...... 317 872-6244
Indianapolis (G-6705)

◆ Cummins Americas Inc.....................G...... 812 377-5000
Columbus (G-1886)

Cummins Crosspoint LLC.....................E...... 317 244-7251
Indianapolis (G-6707)

Cummins Crosspoint LLC.....................E...... 574 252-2154
Mishawaka (G-10026)

Cummins Crosspoint LLC.....................G...... 317 484-2146
Indianapolis (G-6708)

Cummins Crosspoint LLC.....................E...... 260 482-3691
Fort Wayne (G-4192)

Cummins Crosspoint LLC.....................E...... 812 867-4400
Evansville (G-3447)

Cummins Crosspoint LLC.....................E...... 317 243-7979
Indianapolis (G-6706)

Cummins Dist Holdco Inc.....................F...... 812 377-5000
Columbus (G-1888)

Cummins Emission Solutions Inc........E...... 608 987-3206
Columbus (G-1889)

◆ Cummins Engine Holding Co Inc.......F...... 812 377-5000
Columbus (G-1890)

Cummins Engine Service.....................G...... 260 657-1436
Woodburn (G-14382)

Cummins Inc.......................................B...... 812 377-5000
Columbus (G-1891)

Cummins Inc.......................................B...... 812 377-0150
Columbus (G-1892)

Cummins Inc.......................................B...... 812 377-6072
Columbus (G-1893)

Cummins Inc.......................................E...... 812 377-8601
Columbus (G-1894)

Cummins Inc.......................................E...... 812 377-2932
Columbus (G-1895)

Cummins Inc.......................................E...... 812 374-4774
Columbus (G-1897)

Cummins Inc.......................................G...... 317 244-7251
Indianapolis (G-6709)

Cummins Inc.......................................G...... 317 610-2493
Indianapolis (G-6710)

Cummins Inc.......................................A...... 812 522-9366
Seymour (G-12442)

Cummins Inc.......................................B...... 812 377-7000
Columbus (G-1899)

Cummins Inc.......................................E...... 812 524-6455
Columbus (G-1896)

Cummins Power Generation Inc...........E...... 574 262-4611
Elkhart (G-2783)

Cummins Power Generation Inc...........F...... 812 377-5000
Columbus (G-1900)

Cummins Repair Inc.............................G...... 260 632-4800
Harlan (G-5969)

Cummins-Scania Xpi Mfg LLC..............G...... 812 377-5000
Columbus (G-1901)

Engineered Machined Pdts Inc............C...... 317 462-8894
Greenfield (G-5528)

Engler Machine & Tool Inc ....F...... 812 386-6254
Princeton (G-11869)

Enhancement Power Products..............G...... 317 359-3461
Indianapolis (G-6870)

Ertl Enterprises Inc.............................F...... 765 622-9900
Anderson (G-105)

FCA US LLC..A...... 765 454-0018
Kokomo (G-8624)

Glidden Racing Engines.......................G...... 317 535-5225
Whiteland (G-14238)

Jolliff Diesel Service...........................G...... 812 692-5725
Elnora (G-3290)

▲ Lingenfelter Prfmce Engrg Inc...........E...... 260 724-2552
Decatur (G-2390)

Michael Dargie....................................G...... 765 935-2241
Richmond (G-12017)

Mitchell Smith Racing..........................G...... 765 640-0237
Anderson (G-137)

Power Investments Inc.........................F...... 317 738-2117
Franklin (G-4921)

Powerhouse Engines LLC.....................B...... 765 576-1418
Lynn (G-9431)

Price Motor Sport Engineering.............G...... 812 546-4220
Hope (G-6118)

Progress Rail Services Corp.................G...... 765 472-2002
Peru (G-11542)

Rng Performance LLC..........................G...... 260 602-5613
Monroeville (G-10199)

Stensland Engines Inc..........................G...... 260 623-6859
Monroeville (G-10200)

Ultra Tech Racing Engines...................G...... 574 674-6028
Osceola (G-11384)

W A P LLC..E...... 317 421-3180
Shelbyville (G-12583)

Wap Inc..G...... 877 421-3187
Shelbyville (G-12584)

3523 Farm Machinery & Eqpt

All Star Turf Management LLC.............G...... 317 861-1234
New Palestine (G-10966)

Andersons Agriculture Group LP.........F...... 765 564-6135
Delphi (G-2414)

▲ Applegate Livestock Eqp Inc ....D...... 765 964-3715
Union City (G-13452)

◆ AT Ferrell Company Inc ....E...... 260 824-3400
Bluffton (G-865)

Azland Inc..G...... 765 429-6200
West Lafayette (G-14051)

Barry Stuckwisch.................................G...... 812 525-1052
Seymour (G-12432)

BP Alternative Energy NA Inc..............G...... 765 884-1000
Fowler (G-4796)

▲ California Pellet Mill Company ....G...... 765 362-2600
Crawfordsville (G-2137)

Cardinal Services Inc Indiana..............D...... 574 267-3823
Warsaw (G-13853)

Carter Manufacturing Company ....G...... 765 563-3666
Brookston (G-1102)

Case and Quart Inc.............................G...... 260 368-7808
Geneva (G-5134)

▲ Case New Holland LLC....................F...... 765 482-5446
Lebanon (G-9172)

Case Show Homes LLC........................G...... 317 669-6202
Carmel (G-1334)

Case Weinkauff...................................G...... 219 733-9484
Valparaiso (G-13519)

CD & Ws Bordner Entps Inc.................G...... 765 268-2120
Cutler (G-2328)

Chief Metal Works Inc.........................G...... 765 932-2134
Rushville (G-12217)

City Welding & Fabrication ....G...... 765 569-5403
Rockville (G-12175)

Cnh Industrial America LLC.................C...... 765 482-5409
Lebanon (G-9174)

Commercial Star Inc............................F...... 765 386-2800
Coatesville (G-1747)

Coram USA LLC...................................F...... 260 451-8200
Fort Wayne (G-4176)

Cornelius Manufacturing Inc ....D...... 812 636-4319
Elnora (G-3288)

▲ Cowco Inc.......................................G...... 812 346-8993
North Vernon (G-11250)

CPM Acquisition Corp ....D...... 765 362-2600
Crawfordsville (G-2142)

Ctb Inc...E...... 574 658-4191
Milford (G-9951)

◆ Ctb Inc..A...... 574 658-4191
Milford (G-9952)

Ctb Inc...G...... 765 654-8517
Frankfort (G-4825)

CTB MN Investment Co Inc ....E...... 765 654-8517
Frankfort (G-4826)

◆ CTB MN Investment Co Inc ....E...... 574 658-4191
Milford (G-9955)

Custom Case Place LLC.......................G...... 260 715-1413
Fort Wayne (G-4194)

D A Hochstetler & Sons LLP ....F...... 574 642-1144
Topeka (G-13416)

Davern Machine Shop..........................G...... 765 505-1051
Dana (G-2342)

Delphi Products Co Inc........................F...... 800 382-7903
Delphi (G-2418)

Don Case..G...... 765 748-1325
Muncie (G-10462)

Dpc Inc..G...... 765 564-3752
Delphi (G-2419)

Dugherty Inc.......................................F...... 260 375-2010
Warren (G-13828)

Dwd Miller Inc....................................G...... 812 853-8497
Chandler (G-1548)

◆ Earthway Products Inc......................D...... 574 848-7491
Bristol (G-1058)

◆ Equipment Technologies Inc.............E...... 800 861-2142
Mooresville (G-10308)

Ernest Heighway..................................G...... 765 847-2865
Fountain City (G-4785)

Et Works LLC......................................E...... 317 834-4500
Mooresville (G-10309)

Evelyn Dollahan..................................G...... 574 896-2971
North Judson (G-11211)

▲ Farm Innovators Inc.........................E...... 574 936-5096
Plymouth (G-11683)

Fix & Sons Manufacturing Inc ....F...... 765 724-4041
Alexandria (G-42)

Fpc Feed & Manufacturing...................G...... 765 468-7768
Parker City (G-11463)

Frazier Products.................................F...... 317 781-9781
Indianapolis (G-6961)

◆ Galbreath LLC.................................C...... 219 946-6631
Winamac (G-14304)

Garver Manufacturing Inc ....G...... 765 964-5828
Union City (G-13456)

▲ Gator Cases Inc...............................F...... 260 627-8070
Columbia City (G-1787)

S
I
C

Gvm Inc..........G....... 765 689-5010
Bunker Hill *(G-1206)*
Hahn Enterprises Inc..........G....... 574 862-4491
Wakarusa *(G-13778)*
Haines Engineering..........G....... 260 589-3388
Berne *(G-616)*
Hampton Equipment LLC..........G....... 260 740-8704
Fort Wayne *(G-4316)*
Hc Farms..........G....... 765 289-9909
Muncie *(G-10484)*
▲ Headsight Inc..........G....... 574 546-5022
Bremen *(G-1003)*
Hicks Farms..........G....... 812 852-4055
Osgood *(G-11391)*
Hog Slat Incorporated..........F....... 765 828-0828
Universal *(G-13467)*
Hog Slat Incorporated..........E....... 574 967-4145
Camden *(G-1274)*
Honeyville Metal Inc..........D....... 800 593-8377
Topeka *(G-13421)*
Hurricane Ditcher Company Inc..........F....... 812 886-9663
Vincennes *(G-13684)*
International A I Inc..........G....... 812 824-2473
Bloomington *(G-750)*
Jacobs Mfg LLC..........G....... 574 583-3883
Monticello *(G-10267)*
Jl Manfcturing Fabrication Inc..........G....... 260 589-3723
Berne *(G-618)*
K & B Trailer Sales Mfg..........G....... 574 946-4382
Monterey *(G-10207)*
Kasco Mfg Co Inc..........E....... 317 398-7973
Shelbyville *(G-12542)*
Kenneth Fuhrman..........G....... 812 482-4612
Jasper *(G-8270)*
Laidig Inc..........E....... 574 256-0204
Mishawaka *(G-10067)*
Land Enterprises..........G....... 317 774-9475
Noblesville *(G-11140)*
▲ Lee E Norris Cnstr & Grn Co..........G....... 574 353-7855
Tippecanoe *(G-13383)*
Madison Manufacturing Inc..........E....... 574 633-4433
Bremen *(G-1009)*
Memering Farms..........G....... 812 254-8170
Washington *(G-13991)*
Millers Windmill Service..........G....... 574 825-2877
Middlebury *(G-9910)*
Mooresville Welding Inc..........G....... 317 831-2265
Mooresville *(G-10324)*
Mssh Inc..........G....... 812 663-2180
Greensburg *(G-5624)*
National Equipment Inc..........G....... 219 462-1205
Valparaiso *(G-13586)*
New Holland Richmond Inc..........G....... 765 962-7724
Richmond *(G-12023)*
Nichols Mfg Co Inc..........F....... 219 696-8577
Lowell *(G-9418)*
Onyett Welding & Machine Inc..........G....... 812 582-2999
Petersburg *(G-11565)*
Original Tractor Cab Co Inc..........E....... 765 663-2214
Arlington *(G-282)*
Oxbo International Corporation..........G....... 260 768-3217
Shipshewana *(G-12640)*
◆ Par-Kan Company LLC..........D....... 260 352-2141
Silver Lake *(G-12677)*
Red Case LLC..........G....... 317 250-5538
Beech Grove *(G-603)*
Reed Raymond Trust..........G....... 317 831-7246
Mooresville *(G-10336)*
Rhinehart Development Corp..........E....... 260 238-4442
Spencerville *(G-13050)*
Richard Young..........G....... 812 546-5208
Columbus *(G-2007)*
Robertson Machine Co Inc..........G....... 317 881-9405
Greenwood *(G-5741)*
Shelby Engineering Co Inc..........E....... 317 784-1135
Indianapolis *(G-7928)*
Snooks Land Holding Inc..........G....... 812 876-4540
Ellettsville *(G-3284)*
▼ Soil-Max Inc..........E....... 888 764-5629
Terre Haute *(G-13331)*
Spankys Paintball..........G....... 812 752-7375
Scottsburg *(G-12381)*
Specialty Welding & Machine..........G....... 812 969-2139
Elizabeth *(G-2649)*
Stan Clamme..........G....... 765 348-0008
Hartford City *(G-5991)*
Sun Rise Metal Shop..........G....... 260 463-4026
Topeka *(G-13430)*
▲ Superb Horticulture LLC..........F....... 800 567-8264
Plymouth *(G-11726)*
Swiss Perfection LLC..........F....... 574 457-4457
Syracuse *(G-13146)*
Townsend Sales Inc..........G....... 317 736-4047
Trafalgar *(G-13439)*
Valesco Manufacturing Inc..........G....... 765 522-2740
Roachdale *(G-12095)*
Valesco Manufacturing Inc..........G....... 812 636-6001
Loogootee *(G-9395)*
Wood Lighter Cases LLC..........G....... 812 969-3908
Elizabeth *(G-2650)*
Wright Brothers Implements LLC..........G....... 812 967-3029
Borden *(G-938)*
Writers of Vision..........G....... 812 239-6347
Farmersburg *(G-3839)*
Ziggity Systems Inc..........E....... 574 825-5849
Middlebury *(G-9931)*

3524 Garden, Lawn Tractors & Eqpt

American Gardenworks Inc..........F....... 765 869-4033
Boswell *(G-939)*
American Lawn Mower..........G....... 800 633-1501
Indianapolis *(G-6389)*
Bane-Welker Equipment LLC..........F....... 812 234-2627
Terre Haute *(G-13197)*
Brian J Spilman..........G....... 765 663-2860
Arlington *(G-281)*
◆ Brinly-Hardy Company..........D....... 812 218-7200
Jeffersonville *(G-8332)*
Country Compact..........G....... 574 831-6682
New Paris *(G-10976)*
Deer Country Equipment LLC..........E....... 812 522-1922
Seymour *(G-12444)*
Discount Power Equipment..........G....... 765 642-0040
Anderson *(G-96)*
Egenolf Enterprise Inc..........G....... 317 501-5069
Indianapolis *(G-6813)*
Forest Commodities Inc..........G....... 765 349-3291
Martinsville *(G-9607)*
Graber Manufacturing..........G....... 812 636-7725
Odon *(G-11327)*
▲ Great States Corporation..........E....... 317 392-3615
Indianapolis *(G-7040)*
Huncilman Inc..........G....... 812 945-3544
New Albany *(G-10800)*
Husqvrna Cnsmr Otdr Prod NA..........C....... 812 883-3575
Salem *(G-12294)*
Jacobsen Prof Lawn Care Inc..........F....... 765 246-7737
Coatesville *(G-1750)*
▲ Lafayette Marketing Inc..........E....... 765 474-5374
West Lafayette *(G-14081)*
Lastec LLC..........F....... 317 892-4444
Lizton *(G-9317)*
Magic Circle Corporation..........C....... 765 246-7737
Coatesville *(G-1751)*
Mtd Products Inc..........B....... 317 986-2042
Indianapolis *(G-7555)*
Novae Corp..........E....... 260 982-7075
North Manchester *(G-11239)*
▲ Novae Corp..........D....... 260 758-9800
Markle *(G-9581)*
Original Tractor Cab Co Inc..........E....... 765 663-2214
Arlington *(G-282)*
Palmor Products Inc..........E....... 800 872-2822
Lebanon *(G-9210)*
Peters Enterprises..........G....... 260 493-6435
New Haven *(G-10953)*
Rich Manufacturing Inc..........G....... 765 436-2744
Lebanon *(G-9220)*
Rochester Metal Products Corp..........D....... 765 288-6624
Muncie *(G-10559)*
S Phillippe Lawn & Landscape..........G....... 765 724-2020
Alexandria *(G-53)*
Schaefers Indiana Turf Corp..........G....... 260 489-3391
Fort Wayne *(G-4607)*
Shelby Products Corporation..........G....... 317 398-4870
West Harrison *(G-14043)*
Talon Terra LLC..........G....... 219 393-1400
La Porte *(G-8826)*
Trudel Family Ltd Partnership..........G....... 260 627-5626
Leo *(G-9246)*
Wheel Horse Sales & Service..........F....... 574 272-4242
South Bend *(G-12990)*
Wood-Mizer Holdings Inc..........D....... 317 892-4444
Lizton *(G-9318)*
◆ Wood-Mizer Holdings Inc..........C....... 317 271-1542
Indianapolis *(G-8212)*
Wright Implement I LLC..........E....... 812 522-1922
Seymour *(G-12502)*

3531 Construction Machinery & Eqpt

A & T Construction and Excvtg..........G....... 219 314-2439
Cedar Lake *(G-1524)*
AF Ohab Company Inc..........E....... 317 225-4740
Indianapolis *(G-6350)*
Altec Industries Inc..........C....... 317 872-3460
Indianapolis *(G-6379)*
▲ AMA Usa Inc..........G....... 317 329-6590
Indianapolis *(G-6380)*
Ameribridge LLC..........D....... 317 826-2000
Indianapolis *(G-6384)*
American Industrial Corp..........E....... 317 859-9900
Greenwood *(G-5665)*
▼ Asphalt Drum Mixers Inc..........E....... 260 637-5729
Huntertown *(G-6134)*
◆ Asphalt Equipment Company Inc..........G....... 260 672-3004
Fort Wayne *(G-4093)*
▲ Avis Industrial Corporation..........E....... 765 998-8100
Upland *(G-13468)*
B Trucking & Backhoe Inc..........G....... 765 437-5960
Windfall *(G-14346)*
Biggerstaff & Son Excavating..........G....... 317 784-6034
Indianapolis *(G-6474)*
Birdeye Inc..........F....... 812 886-0598
Vincennes *(G-13669)*
Boarder Magic By J & A..........G....... 317 545-4401
Indianapolis *(G-6492)*
Brooks Construction Co Inc..........E....... 260 478-1990
Fort Wayne *(G-4122)*
Caterpillar Inc..........C....... 765 448-5000
Lafayette *(G-8871)*
▲ Caterpillar Inc..........D....... 630 743-4094
Greenfield *(G-5511)*
Chads LLC..........G....... 812 323-7377
Ellettsville *(G-3273)*
Colby L Stanger..........G....... 574 536-5835
Goshen *(G-5190)*
Commercial Star Inc..........F....... 765 386-2800
Coatesville *(G-1747)*
Coneqtec Corp..........F....... 812 446-4055
Carbon *(G-1292)*
County of Lagrange..........E....... 260 499-6353
Lagrange *(G-9035)*
Critser Companies Inc..........G....... 219 663-0052
Crown Point *(G-2236)*
Crusher Parts Direct LLC..........G....... 812 822-1463
Bloomington *(G-708)*
Custom Machine Mfr LLC..........E....... 574 251-0292
South Bend *(G-12748)*
Dyna-Fab Corporation..........E....... 765 893-4423
West Lebanon *(G-14119)*
Galfab LLC..........D....... 574 946-7767
Winamac *(G-14306)*
Harding Materials Inc..........G....... 317 846-7401
Indianapolis *(G-7073)*
Harrell Family LLC..........G....... 317 770-4550
Noblesville *(G-11119)*
Highland Park Services Inc..........G....... 317 954-0456
Indianapolis *(G-7107)*
Hughes Paving Company Inc..........F....... 812 678-2126
French Lick *(G-4986)*
Hurricane Ditcher Company Inc..........F....... 812 886-9663
Vincennes *(G-13684)*
▼ Indco Inc..........G....... 812 945-4383
New Albany *(G-10805)*
J & J Stables..........G....... 812 279-2581
Bedford *(G-555)*
Jeda Equipment Services Inc..........G....... 317 842-9377
Fishers *(G-3933)*
▲ Jeffboat LLC..........C....... 812 288-0200
Jeffersonville *(G-8385)*
▲ Jinnings Equipment LLC..........G....... 260 447-4343
Fort Wayne *(G-4395)*
▲ Joyce Consulting LLC..........G....... 317 577-8504
Indianapolis *(G-7315)*
Kenn Feld Group LLC..........F....... 260 632-4242
Woodburn *(G-14385)*
Kentuckiana Machine & Tool..........G....... 502 301-9005
Lanesville *(G-9102)*
▲ Keystone Engrg & Mfg Corp..........G....... 317 271-6192
Avon *(G-453)*
Konecranes Inc..........F....... 219 661-9602
Crown Point *(G-2272)*
Lehigh Hanson Ecc Inc..........C....... 812 246-7700
Sellersburg *(G-12402)*
Lindas Gone Buggie..........G....... 219 299-0174
Hobart *(G-6089)*
Linkel Company..........G....... 812 934-5190
Batesville *(G-510)*

Maddock Construction Eqp LLC ....E 812 349-3000
  Bloomington *(G-768)*
Marshall Companies Indiana ....G 317 769-2666
  Lebanon *(G-9202)*
▲ Maximum Spndle Utilization Inc ......E 812 526-8250
  Edinburgh *(G-2618)*
Mears Machine Corp ....D 317 745-0656
  Danville *(G-2353)*
▲ Mortar Net Usa Ltd..........................G 800 664-6638
  Burns Harbor *(G-1218)*
My-Te Products Inc ....F 317 897-9880
  Indianapolis *(G-7564)*
Nobbe Concrete Products Inc ....G 765 647-4017
  Brookville *(G-1121)*
Paver Rescue Inc ....G 317 259-4880
  Indianapolis *(G-7664)*
Premier Hydraulic Augers Inc............E 260 456-8518
  Fort Wayne *(G-4555)*
Pro-Tote System Inc ....F 574 287-6006
  South Bend *(G-12905)*
Ramar Industries Inc ....G 765 288-7319
  Muncie *(G-10553)*
Randall Rents of Indiana Inc...............F 219 763-1155
  Portage *(G-11791)*
Smith Excavating ....G 812 636-0054
  Odon *(G-11341)*
Speedway Cnstr Pdts Corp..................G 260 203-9806
  Fort Wayne *(G-4640)*
Square 1 Dsign Manufacture Inc ....F 866 647-7771
  Shelbyville *(G-12570)*
Stedman Machine Company ....D 812 926-0038
  Aurora *(G-390)*
Steven A Williams ....G 812 664-3405
  Sellersburg *(G-12419)*
Summerlot Engineered Pdts Inc...........F 812 466-7266
  Rosedale *(G-12206)*
Templeton Coal Company Inc..............D 812 232-7037
  Terre Haute *(G-13351)*
Terex Corporation ....G 574 342-0086
  Bourbon *(G-949)*
Terex Corporation ....C 260 497-0728
  Fort Wayne *(G-4678)*
Tmf Center Inc ....C 765 762-3800
  Williamsport *(G-14298)*
Tmf Center Inc ....F 765 762-1000
  Williamsport *(G-14299)*
Tracy K Hullett..................................G 765 472-3349
  Peru *(G-11553)*
Turner Paving Company......................G 765 962-4408
  Richmond *(G-12070)*
Vires Backhoe and Dumptruc..............G 812 595-1630
  Deputy *(G-2461)*
Wag-Way Tool Incorporated ....F 812 886-0598
  Vincennes *(G-13715)*
Wakarusa Ag LLC ....G 574 862-1163
  Wakarusa *(G-13797)*
Wick - Fab Inc ....E 260 897-3303
  Avilla *(G-421)*

3532 Mining Machinery & Eqpt

▼ Aggregate Mfg Intl LLC...................E 812 278-9670
  Bedford *(G-528)*
Claymore Tools Inc ....G 574 255-6483
  Mishawaka *(G-10018)*
▼ Deister Machine Company Inc..........C 260 426-7495
  Fort Wayne *(G-4205)*
Deister Machine Company Inc..............F 260 426-7495
  Fort Wayne *(G-4206)*
Deister Machine Company Inc..............C 260 422-0354
  Fort Wayne *(G-4207)*
◆ J W Jones Company LLC ....G 765 537-2279
  Paragon *(G-11458)*
Jones Trucking Inc ....G 765 537-2279
  Paragon *(G-11459)*
▲ Keystone Engrg & Mfg Corp ....G 317 271-6192
  Avon *(G-453)*
Pillar Innovations LLC.......................G 812 474-9080
  Evansville *(G-3670)*
Prox Company Inc ....F 812 232-4324
  Terre Haute *(G-13311)*
Quality Systems LLC........................F 317 326-4660
  Indianapolis *(G-7800)*
Stedman Machine Company Inc...........D 812 926-0038
  Aurora *(G-390)*
United Conveyor Corporation...............E 574 256-0091
  Mishawaka *(G-10142)*

3533 Oil Field Machinery & Eqpt

Daylight Engineering Inc.....................G 812 983-2518
  Elberfeld *(G-2633)*

▲ Diedrich Drill Inc ....E 219 326-7788
  La Porte *(G-8751)*
Dilden Bros Inc.................................F 765 742-1717
  Lafayette *(G-8891)*
Emquip Corporation ....G 317 849-3977
  Indianapolis *(G-6860)*
Evergreen Drilling LLC.......................G 812 961-7701
  Evansville *(G-3494)*
Gesco Group LLC ....G 260 747-5088
  Fort Wayne *(G-4300)*
▲ Laibe Corporation ....D 317 231-2250
  Indianapolis *(G-7374)*
Llama Corporation ....G 888 701-7432
  Decatur *(G-2391)*
◆ Lucas Oil Racing Inc ....F 812 738-1147
  Corydon *(G-2104)*
Lufkin Industries Inc..........................G 765 472-2935
  Peru *(G-11536)*
▲ Mobile Drill Operating Co LLC ....E 317 260-8108
  Indianapolis *(G-7531)*
National Oilwell Varco Inc ....G 317 897-3099
  Indianapolis *(G-7575)*
▲ Nrp Jones LLC ....D 219 362-4508
  La Porte *(G-8800)*
Rose-Wall Mfg Inc ....G 317 894-4497
  Greenfield *(G-5567)*
Systems Engineering and Sls Co.........G 260 422-1671
  Fort Wayne *(G-4671)*

3534 Elevators & Moving Stairways

Braun Corporation ....B 574 946-7413
  Winamac *(G-14302)*
Convertastep LLC.............................G 260 969-8645
  Markle *(G-9576)*
Elevator Equipment Corporation..........D 765 966-7761
  Richmond *(G-11981)*
Elevator One LLC ....G 317 634-8001
  Indianapolis *(G-6821)*
Haines Engineering ....G 260 589-3388
  Berne *(G-616)*
Otis Elevator Company ....G 812 331-5605
  Bloomington *(G-793)*
Otis Elevator Company ....E 812 471-9770
  Evansville *(G-3658)*
▲ TEC Hoist LLC ....F 708 598-2300
  Griffith *(G-5791)*
Zeller Elevator Co ....G 812 985-5888
  Mount Vernon *(G-10415)*

3535 Conveyors & Eqpt

▲ 1st Source Products Inc ....E 812 288-7466
  Jeffersonville *(G-8315)*
Accu-Tech Automation Inc..................F 317 352-1490
  Indianapolis *(G-6313)*
Advance Fabricators Inc ....E 812 944-6941
  New Albany *(G-10741)*
Aggreate Systems.............................F 260 854-4711
  Rome City *(G-12197)*
Air Equipment & Engrg Inc ....E 765 349-9259
  Martinsville *(G-9594)*
▼ Banks Machine & Engrg Inc............D 317 642-4980
  Shelbyville *(G-12519)*
Berendsen Inc ....G 812 423-6468
  Evansville *(G-3373)*
Butterworth Industries Inc ....E 765 677-6725
  Gas City *(G-5121)*
C & P Engineering & Mfg.....................E 765 825-4293
  Connersville *(G-2042)*
▼ C & S Family Inc ....E 812 886-5500
  Vincennes *(G-13670)*
C T C Corporation ....G 812 849-2500
  Mitchell *(G-10156)*
C&M Conveyor Inc.............................C 812 849-5647
  Mitchell *(G-10157)*
Carman Industries Inc ....E 812 288-4710
  Jeffersonville *(G-8335)*
CPM Conveyor LLC ....G 765 918-5190
  Crawfordsville *(G-2143)*
Ctb Inc...E 765 654-8517
  Frankfort *(G-4825)*
CTB MN Investment Co Inc ....E 765 654-8517
  Frankfort *(G-4826)*
▲ Direct Conveyors LLC.....................E 317 346-7777
  Franklin *(G-4881)*
Fabricated Steel Corporation...............G 317 899-0012
  Indianapolis *(G-6901)*
Frontier Engineering ....G 317 823-6885
  Indianapolis *(G-6965)*
General Material Handling Co...............G 317 888-5735
  Indianapolis *(G-6998)*

George Koch Sons LLC......................C 812 465-9600
  Evansville *(G-3519)*
Gravel Conveyors Inc ....F 317 873-8686
  Zionsville *(G-14435)*
H & H Design & Tool Inc......................G 765 886-6199
  Economy *(G-2591)*
▼ Halo LLC ....D 317 575-9992
  Indianapolis *(G-6266)*
Hillenbrand Inc ....C 812 934-7500
  Batesville *(G-504)*
◆ Hirata Corporation of America ....E 317 856-8600
  Indianapolis *(G-7109)*
▲ Industrial Transmission Eqp ....E 574 936-3028
  Plymouth *(G-11694)*
Iron Bull Mfg LLC ....G 765 597-2480
  Marshall *(G-9592)*
▲ Keener Corporation ....E 765 825-2100
  Connersville *(G-2058)*
Keener Corporation ....D 765 825-2711
  Connersville *(G-2060)*
◆ Koehler Welding Supply Inc ....E 812 574-4103
  Madison *(G-9476)*
M Pro LLC..G 765 459-4750
  Kokomo *(G-8661)*
Mainline Conveyor Systems Inc ....F 317 831-2795
  Mooresville *(G-10320)*
Martin Grgory Cnvyor Engrg LLC ....G 812 923-9814
  Georgetown *(G-5149)*
McClamroch AG LLC ....G 765 362-4495
  Crawfordsville *(G-2171)*
▲ McGinty Conveyors Inc ....G 317 240-4315
  Indianapolis *(G-7472)*
Mid-State Automation Inc....................G 765 795-5500
  Cloverdale *(G-1730)*
Omni-Tron Tooling & Engrg ....G 574 262-2083
  Elkhart *(G-3069)*
Pia Automation US Inc ....C 812 474-3126
  Evansville *(G-3669)*
Prime Conveyor Inc ....E 219 736-1994
  Merrillville *(G-9749)*
Pro Epuipment Service.......................G 317 322-7858
  Indianapolis *(G-7765)*
▲ Production Hdlg Systems Inc............F 317 738-0485
  Franklin *(G-4924)*
Rowe Conveyor LLC...........................G 317 602-1024
  Greenwood *(G-5743)*
▼ Sager Metal Strip Company LLC .....E 219 874-3609
  Michigan City *(G-9837)*
▼ Screw Conveyor Corporation ....E 219 931-1450
  Hammond *(G-5936)*
Screw Conveyor Pacific Corp...............E 219 931-1450
  Hammond *(G-5937)*
▲ Shuttleworth LLC............................D 260 356-8500
  Huntington *(G-6248)*
Smock Material Handling Co ....F 317 890-3200
  Indianapolis *(G-7954)*
Sparks Belting Company Inc ....G 800 451-4537
  Hammond *(G-5945)*
Stahl Equipment Inc ....E 812 925-3341
  Chandler *(G-1554)*
Summerlot Engineered Pdts Inc...........F 812 466-7266
  Rosedale *(G-12206)*
Systec Corporation ....D 317 890-9230
  Indianapolis *(G-8031)*
United Conveyor Corporation...............E 574 256-0091
  Mishawaka *(G-10142)*
▼ Vestil Manufacturing Corp ....B 260 665-7586
  Angola *(G-258)*
Vibcon Corp......................................F 317 984-3543
  Arcadia *(G-271)*
W M Kelley Co Inc ....E 812 945-3529
  New Albany *(G-10873)*
Webber Manufacturing Company.........E 317 357-8681
  Indianapolis *(G-8181)*

3536 Hoists, Cranes & Monorails

Cranewerks Inc ....E 765 663-2909
  Morristown *(G-10368)*
Dearborn Crane and Engrg Co ....E 574 259-2444
  Mishawaka *(G-10035)*
Deatons Waterfront Svcs LLC ....F 317 336-7180
  Fortville *(G-4773)*
Deshazo LLC ....D 317 867-7677
  Westfield *(G-14159)*
Diamond Construction Svcs LLC..........G 513 314-3609
  Aurora *(G-376)*
Galfab LLC ....D 574 946-7767
  Winamac *(G-14306)*
Hoosier Crane Service Company ....E 574 523-2945
  Elkhart *(G-2920)*

Hubbard Inc ....G....... 317 535-1926
Whiteland (G-14239)

Indiana Steel & Engrg Inc ....E....... 812 275-3363
Bedford (G-552)

J V Crane & Engineering Inc ....E....... 219 942-8566
Hobart (G-6082)

Konecranes ....F....... 317 546-8122
Indianapolis (G-7366)

Lakemaster Inc ....E....... 765 288-3718
Muncie (G-10507)

Mooresville Welding Inc 317 831-2265
Mooresville (G-10324)

Ohio Transmission Corporation ....G....... 812 466-2734
Terre Haute (G-13294)

Royal ARC Welding Company ....E....... 260 587-3711
Ashley (G-290)

T & M Equipment Company Inc ...E....... 219 942-2299
Merrillville (G-9755)

T & M Equipment Company Inc ...F....... 317 293-9255
Indianapolis (G-8032)

▲ TEC Hoist LLC ....F....... 708 598-2300
Griffith (G-5791)

US Crane & Hoist Inc ....G....... 219 963-1400
Lake Station (G-9080)

Yardarm Marine Products Inc ....E....... 317 831-4950
Mooresville (G-10345)

3537 Indl Trucks, Tractors, Trailers & Stackers

All Borders Expediting LLC ....G....... 260 459-1434
Fort Wayne (G-4058)

AM General LLC ....A....... 574 258-7523
Mishawaka (G-9995)

▲ Ameri-Kart Corp ....C....... 574 848-7462
Bristol (G-1044)

American Industrial McHy Inc ....F....... 219 755-4090
Merrillville (G-9697)

▲ American Truck Company LLC ....F....... 260 969-4510
Fort Wayne (G-4074)

Arctrans LLC ....F....... 317 231-1620
Indianapolis (G-6417)

Basiloid Products Corp ....E....... 812 692-5511
Elnora (G-3286)

Bemcor Inc ....F....... 219 937-1600
Hammond (G-5850)

Buhrt Engineering & Cnstr ....E....... 574 267-3720
Warsaw (G-13852)

Clp Towne Inc ....G....... 574 233-3183
South Bend (G-12737)

Converto Mfg Co Inc ....G....... 765 478-3205
Cambridge City (G-1254)

Crown Equipment Corporation ....E....... 812 477-5511
Evansville (G-3446)

Crown Equipment Corporation ....D....... 574 293-1264
Elkhart (G-2778)

Crown Equipment Corporation ....C....... 765 520-2422
New Castle (G-10899)

Crown Equipment Corporation ....D....... 260 484-0055
Fort Wayne (G-4189)

Crown Equipment Corporation ....B....... 765 653-4240
Greencastle (G-5456)

Crown Equipment Corporation ....D....... 317 875-7233
Plainfield (G-11603)

Deco Corporation ....E....... 812 342-4767
Columbus (G-1906)

Diversified Qulty Svcs Ind LLC ....G....... 765 644-7712
Anderson (G-97)

Eaton Corporation ....E....... 260 925-3800
Auburn (G-328)

Eaton Corporation ....D....... 574 288-4446
South Bend (G-12756)

Elpers Truck Equipment LLC ....F....... 812 423-5787
Evansville (G-3474)

Extreme Trailer Service LLC ....G....... 812 406-1984
Charlestown (G-1566)

Fuentes Distributing ....G....... 219 808-2147
Hammond (G-5882)

Galfab LLC ....D....... 574 946-7767
Winamac (G-14306)

▲ Gleason Industrial Pdts Inc ....C....... 574 533-1141
Goshen (G-5227)

Great Dane LLC ....A....... 812 443-4711
Brazil (G-962)

Green Steak Pulling Inc ....G....... 812 254-6858
Washington (G-13984)

Gypsum Express Ltd ....G....... 812 247-2648
Shoals (G-12666)

◆ Hirata Corporation of America ....E....... 317 856-8600
Indianapolis (G-7109)

Hoist Liftruck Mfg LLC ....B....... 708 552-2722
East Chicago (G-2533)

Hy-TEC Fiberglass Inc ....G....... 260 489-6601
Fort Wayne (G-4352)

▲ Industrial Transmission Eqp ....E....... 574 936-3028
Plymouth (G-11694)

JD Materials ....G....... 219 662-1418
Crown Point (G-2268)

Joyce/Dayton Corp ....D....... 260 726-9361
Portland (G-11831)

Kokomo Truck Store ....G....... 765 459-5118
Kokomo (G-8657)

▲ Lafayette Wire Products Inc ....D....... 765 474-7896
Lafayette (G-8952)

Laidig Inc ....E....... 574 256-0204
Mishawaka (G-10067)

▼ Lal Acquisition Inc ....E....... 765 288-3691
Muncie (G-10508)

Landgrebe Manufacturing Inc ....G....... 219 462-9587
Valparaiso (G-13570)

Lift-A-Loft Manufacturing Inc ....G....... 317 288-3691
Muncie (G-10512)

▲ Major Tool and Machine Inc ....B....... 317 636-6433
Indianapolis (G-7446)

Michiana Forklift Inc ....G....... 574 326-3702
Elkhart (G-3031)

Mooresville Welding Inc ....G....... 317 831-2265
Mooresville (G-10324)

N-Complete Inc ....G....... 765 649-2244
Anderson (G-141)

Nelson J Hochstetler ....G....... 260 499-0315
Howe (G-6130)

Nomanco Trailers ....G....... 765 833-6711
Roann (G-12097)

◆ Ogden Welding Systems Inc ....E....... 219 322-5252
Schererville (G-12341)

◆ Par-Kan Company LLC ....D....... 260 352-2141
Silver Lake (G-12677)

Phoenix Engineering & Mfg Inc ....F....... 574 251-9040
South Bend (G-12895)

Pierce Tracy ....G....... 765 748-2361
Anderson (G-152)

Powell Systems Inc ....G....... 765 884-0980
Fowler (G-4805)

Powell Systems Inc ....G....... 765 884-0613
Fowler (G-4804)

Rance Aluminum Fabrication ....E....... 574 266-9028
Elkhart (G-3137)

Robert Dietrick Co Inc ....G....... 260 244-4668
Columbia City (G-1830)

Rowe Conveyor LLC ....G....... 317 602-1024
Greenwood (G-5743)

Ruben Martinez ....G....... 574 735-0803
Logansport (G-9363)

Selking International Inc ....G....... 574 522-2001
Elkhart (G-3161)

Selking International Inc ....E....... 260 482-3000
Fort Wayne (G-4615)

Southlake Lift Truck ....G....... 219 962-4695
Gary (G-5100)

Stahl Equipment Inc ....E....... 812 925-3341
Chandler (G-1554)

▲ Sto-Away Power Crane Inc ....G....... 219 942-9797
Crown Point (G-2310)

Storageworks Inc ....G....... 317 577-3511
Fishers (G-3971)

Supreme Corporation Georgia ....G....... 574 228-4130
Goshen (G-5335)

◆ Supreme Industries Inc ....D....... 574 642-3070
Goshen (G-5336)

Tk Sales and Marketing LLC ....G....... 812 430-5103
Evansville (G-3766)

▲ Toyoshima Indiana Inc ....F....... 317 638-3511
Indianapolis (G-8086)

◆ Toyota Industrial Eqp Mfg Inc ....B....... 812 342-0060
Columbus (G-2024)

Two Sticks Inc ....G....... 219 926-7910
Chesterton (G-1635)

Vermette Machine Company Inc ....F....... 219 931-5406
Hammond (G-5955)

W & M Enterprises Inc ....E....... 812 537-4656
Lawrenceburg (G-9161)

Wiese Holding Company ....F....... 317 241-8600
Indianapolis (G-8194)

3541 Machine Tools: Cutting

Accutech Mold & Machine Inc ....C....... 260 471-6102
Fort Wayne (G-4038)

American Tool Service Inc ....E....... 260 493-6351
Fort Wayne (G-4073)

American Tool Service Inc ....F....... 317 782-3551
Indianapolis (G-6391)

API International Inc ....F....... 317 894-1100
Greenfield (G-5502)

Bailey Tools & Supply Inc ....G....... 502 635-6348
Evansville (G-3369)

Butler Tool & Design Inc ....E....... 219 297-4531
Goodland (G-5158)

Capital Machine Company Inc ....F....... 317 638-6661
Indianapolis (G-6548)

Charleston Metal Products Inc ....E....... 260 837-8211
Waterloo (G-14011)

Claymore Tools Inc ....G....... 574 255-6483
Mishawaka (G-10018)

Continental Diamond Tool Corp ....E....... 260 493-1294
New Haven (G-10935)

Creative Tool Inc ....G....... 260 338-1222
Huntertown (G-6136)

Custom Machining Inc ....E....... 317 392-2328
Shelbyville (G-12529)

Cut-Pro Indexable Tooling LLC ....E....... 260 668-2400
Angola (G-207)

Cyberia Ltd ....G....... 317 721-2582
Indianapolis (G-6719)

Danubius Machine Inc ....G....... 219 662-7787
Crown Point (G-2243)

Dmg Mori Usa Inc ....G....... 317 913-0978
Indianapolis (G-6755)

Drake Corporation ....E....... 812 683-2101
Jasper (G-8246)

Eagle Precision Machining Inc ....E....... 260 637-4649
Huntertown (G-6137)

EDM Specialties Inc ....G....... 317 856-4700
Indianapolis (G-6807)

Emhart Teknologies LLC ....C....... 765 728-2433
Montpelier (G-10290)

▼ Epco Products Inc ....E....... 260 747-8888
Fort Wayne (G-4240)

Express Machine ....G....... 812 719-5979
Cannelton (G-1290)

EZ Cut Tool LLC ....G....... 260 748-0732
New Haven (G-10939)

G & G Millwright Service LLC ....G....... 260 571-4908
La Fontaine (G-8722)

G & S Super Abrasives Inc ....G....... 260 665-5562
Angola (G-215)

▲ Grinding and Polsg McHy Corp ....F....... 317 898-0750
Indianapolis (G-7050)

Hautau Tube Cutoff Systems LLC ....F....... 765 647-1600
Brookville (G-1116)

Hoosier Spline Broach Corp ....E....... 765 452-8273
Kokomo (G-8639)

Hy-Tech Machining Systems LLC ....F....... 765 649-6852
Anderson (G-118)

Indiana Hand Piece Repair ....G....... 260 436-0765
Fort Wayne (G-4364)

Indiana Oxygen Company Inc ....G....... 765 662-8700
Marion (G-9533)

Integrity Machine Systems ....E....... 317 897-3338
New Palestine (G-10972)

Jones Fabrication & Machining ....E....... 812 466-2237
Terre Haute (G-13262)

Kaiser Tool Company Inc ....E....... 260 484-3620
Fort Wayne (G-4403)

Kennedy Enterprises Inc ....E....... 765 724-2225
Anderson (G-128)

Landrums Mch Tl Repr & Svcs ....G....... 574 256-0312
Mishawaka (G-10068)

Loughmiller Mch Tl Design Inc ....E....... 812 295-3903
Loogootee (G-9390)

Macallister Machinery Co Inc ....F....... 765 966-0759
Richmond (G-9390)

Maxwell Milling Indiana Inc ....G....... 765 489-3506
Hagerstown (G-5809)

Micro Tool & Machine Co Inc ....G....... 574 272-9141
Granger (G-5421)

Micro-Precision Operations ....E....... 260 589-2136
Berne (G-620)

Midstates Tool & Die and Engrg ....E....... 574 264-3521
Elkhart (G-3037)

Midwest Mfg Resources Inc ....G....... 317 821-9872
Indianapolis (G-7507)

Miko-Hone Machine Co Inc ....G....... 574 642-4701
Goshen (G-5291)

Modern Die Systems Inc ....E....... 765 552-3145
Elwood (G-3307)

Mosey Manufacturing Co Inc ....F....... 765 983-8800
Richmond (G-12019)

Mosey Manufacturing Co Inc ....D....... 765 768-7462
Dunkirk (G-2486)

Mosey Manufacturing Co Inc ....D 765 552-3504
Dunkirk (G-2487)
Mosey Manufacturing Co Inc ....C 765 983-8870
Richmond (G-12020)
Mosey Manufacturing Co Inc ....C 765 983-8870
Richmond (G-12021)
Mosey Manufacturing Co Inc ....D 765 983-8889
Richmond (G-12022)
◆ Nap Asset Holdings Ltd ....D 812 482-2000
Jasper (G-8297)
Neuhaus Industrial Machining I ....G 260 710-2845
Fort Wayne (G-4498)
Peerless Machinery Inc ....G 574 210-5990
South Bend (G-12889)
Precision Abrasive Machinery ....G 765 378-3315
Daleville (G-2341)
Prototype Baker Engineering ....G 574 266-7223
Elkhart (G-3120)
PSc Machining and Engrg Inc ....F 219 764-4270
Portage (G-11789)
Pt Services Inc ....G 574 970-0512
Elkhart (G-3121)
Qig LLC ....E 260 244-3591
Columbia City (G-1821)
Qig LLC ....E 260 244-3591
Columbia City (G-1822)
Reeder & Kline Machine Co Inc ....E 317 846-6591
Sheridan (G-12596)
Roeder Industries ....G 812 654-3322
Milan (G-9946)
Rx Honing Machine Corp ....G 574 259-1606
Mishawaka (G-10119)
S&S Machinery Repair LLC ....G 812 521-2368
Norman (G-11204)
Solomon M Eicher ....G 812 289-1252
Marysville (G-9651)
Specialty Tool LLC ....F 260 493-6351
Indianapolis (G-7969)
Spindle-Tech Inc ....G 812 926-1114
Aurora (G-388)
▲ Standard Locknut LLC ....C 317 399-2230
Westfield (G-14190)
Station 21 American Drill ....G 219 661-0021
Crown Point (G-2309)
Stedman Machine Company ....D 812 926-0038
Aurora (G-390)
Superior Precision Inc ....F 260 229-3871
South Whitley (G-13007)
Tascon Corp ....E 317 547-6127
Indianapolis (G-8038)
◆ Thermwood Corporation ....D 812 937-4476
Dale (G-2334)
Titus Inc ....F 574 936-3345
Plymouth (G-11728)
TSA America LLC ....G 317 915-1950
Indianapolis (G-8105)
Versatile Metal Works LLC ....F 765 754-7470
Frankton (G-4944)
Whitesell Prcsion Cmpnents Inc ....C 812 282-4014
Jeffersonville (G-8442)
Wood Truss Systems Inc ....G 765 751-9990
Muncie (G-10588)
Wood-Mizer LLC ....G 317 271-1542
Indianapolis (G-8211)
Wyrco LLC ....G 317 691-2832
Fishers (G-3986)
Ynot Metal Inc ....G 517 617-6039
Angola (G-260)
▲ Zps America LLC ....E 317 452-4030
Indianapolis (G-8228)
Ztmt Inc ....G 502 296-4032
Georgetown (G-5155)

3542 Machine Tools: Forming

▲ A & M Systems Inc ....F 574 522-5000
Elkhart (G-2656)
A & M Tool Inc ....G 812 934-6533
Batesville (G-488)
A/C Fabricating Corp ....E 574 534-1415
Goshen (G-5163)
AAA-Gpc Holdings LLC ....D 260 668-1468
Angola (G-187)
Applied Metals & Mch Works Inc ....E 260 424-4834
Fort Wayne (G-4083)
Beatty International Inc ....E 219 931-3000
Hammond (G-5846)
Beatty Machine & Mfg Co ....E 219 931-3000
Hammond (G-5847)
Bemcor Inc ....F 219 937-1600
Hammond (G-5850)

Beulah Inc ....G 219 309-5635
Valparaiso (G-13508)
Black Equipment Company South ....G 812 477-6481
Evansville (G-3386)
Crosspower LLC ....G 812 591-2009
Westport (G-14209)
Davis Machine & Tool Inc ....F 812 526-2674
Edinburgh (G-2606)
Die-Mensional Metal Stamping ....F 812 265-3946
Madison (G-9456)
Egenolf Machine Inc ....G 317 787-5301
Indianapolis (G-6814)
Ferguson Equipment Inc ....F 574 234-4303
South Bend (G-12778)
Fortville Automotive Sup Inc ....G 317 485-5114
Fortville (G-4774)
▲ Frech U S A Inc ....F 219 874-2812
Michigan City (G-9795)
▲ Fred S Carver Inc ....F 260 563-7577
Wabash (G-13727)
Fulk Inc ....G 260 338-1012
Laotto (G-9107)
G & G Metal Spinners Inc ....E 317 923-3225
Indianapolis (G-6974)
▲ Hkn International LLC ....G 317 243-5959
Indianapolis (G-7110)
Idra North America Inc ....G 765 459-0085
Kokomo (G-8644)
Independent Rail Corporation ....E 317 780-8480
Indianapolis (G-7175)
Klueg Tool & Machine Inc ....G 812 867-5702
Evansville (G-3595)
▲ M R S Printing Erectors Inc ....G 317 888-1314
Greenwood (G-5722)
Mishawaka LLC ....G 574 259-1981
Mishawaka (G-10089)
▲ Nachi America Inc ....C 317 535-5527
Greenwood (G-5726)
Olympus Manufacturing Systems ....G 219 465-1520
Valparaiso (G-13594)
Plant Engineering Services Inc ....G 260 281-2917
Corunna (G-2085)
Precision Industries Corp ....F 574 522-2626
Elkhart (G-3108)
Quality Die Set Corp ....E 574 967-4411
Logansport (G-9361)
Rickie Allan Pease ....G 260 244-7579
Columbia City (G-1827)
Roadhog Inc ....E 317 858-7050
Brownsburg (G-1166)
Roeder Industries ....G 812 654-3322
Milan (G-9946)
▲ Sapp Inc ....F 317 512-8353
Edinburgh (G-2627)
Smgf LLC ....D 812 354-8899
Petersburg (G-11568)
Sullivan Engineered Services ....G 812 294-1724
Henryville (G-6033)
Toolmasters Inc ....G 574 256-1881
Mishawaka (G-10140)
Tru-Cut Machine & Tool Inc ....G 260 569-1802
Wabash (G-13759)
United Machine Corporation ....E 219 548-8050
Valparaiso (G-13633)
Versatile Metal Works LLC ....F 765 754-7470
Frankton (G-4944)
◆ Wabash Metal Products Inc ....D 260 563-1184
Wabash (G-13763)

3543 Industrial Patterns

Baseline Tool Co Inc ....F 260 761-4932
Wawaka (G-14030)
Bidwhist Industries ....G 219 879-2508
La Porte (G-8739)
Braun Witte Pattern Works Inc ....G 260 463-8210
Wolcottville (G-14369)
Charles Bane ....G 765 855-5100
Centerville (G-1541)
Cindys Crossstitch & Patterns ....G 317 410-0764
Indianapolis (G-6605)
▲ Core-Tech Inc ....D 260 748-4477
Fort Wayne (G-4179)
Cunningham Pattern & Engrg Inc ....F 812 379-9571
Columbus (G-1902)
D R Pattern Inc ....G 260 868-5585
Butler (G-1227)
Dillon Pattern Works Inc ....F 765 642-3549
Anderson (G-95)
Diversified Pattern & Engrg Co ....E 260 897-3771
Avilla (G-403)

Foley Pattern Company Inc ....E 260 925-4113
Auburn (G-332)
Hopper Development Inc ....F 574 753-6621
Logansport (G-9336)
K & K Inc ....F 574 266-8040
Elkhart (G-2953)
Maxwell Engineering Inc ....G 260 745-4991
Fort Wayne (G-4458)
Muncie Casting Corp ....E 765 288-2611
Muncie (G-10528)
New Point Products Inc ....G 812 663-6311
New Point (G-11003)
Northbend Pattern Works Inc ....E 812 637-3000
West Harrison (G-14041)
Northside Pattern Works Inc ....G 317 290-0501
Indianapolis (G-7595)
Nvsd LLC ....G 502 561-0007
New Albany (G-10834)
Ooten Pattern Works ....G 317 244-7348
Indianapolis (G-7625)
Owings Patterns Inc ....F 812 944-5577
Sellersburg (G-12411)
Peerless Pattern & Machine Co ....G 765 477-7719
Lafayette (G-8979)
Richmond Pattern ....G 765 935-7342
Richmond (G-12046)
Shells Inc ....D 574 342-2673
Bourbon (G-947)
Standard Pattern Company Inc ....G 260 456-4870
Fort Wayne (G-4644)
Weberdings Carving Shop Inc ....E 812 934-3710
Batesville (G-524)

3544 Dies, Tools, Jigs, Fixtures & Indl Molds

A & A Custom Automation Inc ....D 812 464-3650
Evansville (G-3327)
AAA Tool and Die Company Inc ....F 574 246-1222
South Bend (G-12691)
Accu-Mold LLC ....E 269 323-0388
Mishawaka (G-9989)
Accurate Tool & Engineering ....G 812 963-6677
Evansville (G-3335)
Accutech Mold & Machine Inc ....E 260 471-6102
Fort Wayne (G-4038)
Acme Masking Company Inc ....E 317 272-6202
Avon (G-425)
▲ Acro Engineering Inc ....E 812 663-6236
Greensburg (G-5588)
Admar Mold & Engineering Inc ....G 574 848-7085
Bristol (G-1041)
Advanced Mold & Engineering ....F 812 342-9000
Columbus (G-1850)
Advanced Products Tech Inc ....G 765 827-1166
Connersville (G-2038)
▲ Ahaus Tool & Engineering Inc ....D 765 962-3573
Richmond (G-11952)
Ajax Tool Inc ....E 260 747-7482
Fort Wayne (G-4052)
Al-Ex Inc ....G 574 206-0100
Elkhart (G-2673)
Allegiance Tool & Die Inc ....E 574 277-1819
Granger (G-5389)
Allied Steel Rule Dies Inc ....F 317 634-9835
Indianapolis (G-6369)
Aluminum Foundries Inc ....C 765 584-6501
Winchester (G-14324)
Ameri-Tek Manufacturing Inc ....F 574 753-8058
Logansport (G-9320)
American Steel Rule Die Inc ....G 574 262-3437
Elkhart (G-2685)
Apex Tool and Manufacturing ....F 812 425-8121
Evansville (G-3358)
Applied Composites Engrg Inc ....E 317 243-4225
Indianapolis (G-6411)
AR Tee Enterprises Inc ....G 574 848-5543
Bristol (G-1046)
Ark Model and Stampings Inc ....F 317 549-3394
Indianapolis (G-6420)
Artisan Tool & Die Inc ....G 765 288-6653
Muncie (G-10433)
Asbestos Abatement & Mold ....G 317 783-0350
Indianapolis (G-6425)
Astar Inc ....G 574 234-2137
South Bend (G-12713)
Atkisson Enterprises Inc ....F 765 675-7593
Tipton (G-13388)
Atlas Die LLC ....D 574 295-0277
Elkhart (G-2700)
Atlas Die Inc ....E 574 295-0050
Elkhart (G-2701)

S I C

Aul Brothers Tool & Die Inc ....F 765 759-5124
Muncie (G-10434)

Aul In The Family Tool and Die ....G 765 759-5161
Yorktown (G-14401)

Axis Mold Inc ....G 574 292-8904
New Carlisle (G-10879)

B & B Engineering Inc ....G 765 566-3460
Bringhurst (G-1038)

B & D Manufacturing Inc ....G 765 452-2761
Kokomo (G-8595)

B B & H Tool of Columbus Inc ....F 812 372-3707
Columbus (G-1858)

B M C Marketing Corp ....G 260 693-2193
Churubusco (G-1642)

B S T Enterprises Inc ....G 260 493-4313
New Haven (G-10930)

▲ B&J Rocket America Inc ....E 574 825-5802
Middlebury (G-9874)

B/C Precision Tool Inc ....G 812 577-0642
Greendale (G-5483)

▲ Batesville Products Inc ....D 513 381-2057
Lawrenceburg (G-9133)

▲ Batesville Tool & Die Inc ....C 812 934-5616
Batesville (G-494)

Beckys Die Cutting Inc ....G 260 467-1714
Fort Wayne (G-4105)

Bel-Mar Products Corporation ....G 317 769-3262
Whitestown (G-14249)

▲ Bell Machine Company Inc ....F 765 654-5225
Frankfort (G-4819)

Bennett Tool & Die Inc ....G 317 422-5140
Bargersville (G-478)

Berkey Machine Corporation ....G 260 761-4002
Wawaka (G-14031)

Bettner Wire Coating Dyes Inc ....F 812 372-2732
Columbus (G-1859)

Blackerby & Associates ....G 812 216-2370
Seymour (G-12433)

Blessing Tool & Die Inc ....G 574 875-1982
Elkhart (G-2727)

Boe Knows Mold ....D 260 760-7136
New Haven (G-10931)

Boston Tool Company Inc ....F 765 935-6282
Richmond (G-11967)

Bristol Tool and Die Inc ....F 574 848-5354
Bristol (G-1050)

Broken Mold Customs Inc ....G 219 863-1008
Demotte (G-2433)

Brownstown Qulty TI Design Inc ....F 812 358-4593
Brownstown (G-1181)

Bryan Machine Service Inc ....G 260 356-5530
Huntington (G-6195)

Bryant Industries Inc ....F 812 944-6010
New Albany (G-10755)

Btd Manufacturing Inc ....G 812 934-5616
Batesville (G-495)

Budco Tool and Die ....G 574 522-4004
Elkhart (G-2736)

Burco Molding Inc ....D 317 773-5699
Noblesville (G-11074)

Butler Tool & Design Inc ....F 219 297-4531
Goodland (G-5158)

C & A Tool Engineering Inc ....B 260 693-2167
Churubusco (G-1644)

C & A Tool Engineering Inc ....C 260 693-2167
Churubusco (G-1645)

C & A Tool Engineering Inc ....G 260 693-2167
Churubusco (G-1646)

C & A Tool Engineering Inc ....G 260 693-2167
Churubusco (G-1647)

C & T Tool Engineering Inc ....G 260 693-2167
Churubusco (G-1648)

C & A Tool Engineering Inc ....E 260 693-2167
Auburn (G-319)

C & A Tool Engineering Inc ....D 260 693-2167
Churubusco (G-1649)

C & A Tool Engineering Inc ....G 260 693-2167
Churubusco (G-1650)

C & T Engineering Inc. ....F 812 522-5854
Seymour (G-12436)

C-Way Tool and Die Inc ....G 812 256-6341
Charlestown (G-1559)

Center Line Mold & Tool Inc ....F 812 526-0970
Edinburgh (G-2598)

Century Tool & Engineering ....G 317 685-0942
Indianapolis (G-6587)

Chesterfield Tool & Engrg Inc ....E 765 378-5101
Daleville (G-2338)

Ckc Tool Inc ....G 219 285-6415
Morocco (G-10362)

CL Tech Inc ....G 812 526-0995
Edinburgh (G-2600)

Classic Die Services Inc ....E 260 748-6907
Fort Wayne (G-4155)

Classic Products Corp ....G 260 748-6907
Fort Wayne (G-4158)

Claymore Tools Inc ....G 574 255-6483
Mishawaka (G-10018)

Clifty Engineering and Tool Co ....C 812 273-3272
Madison (G-9452)

Collins Tool & Die Inc ....G 812 273-4765
Madison (G-9453)

Competition TI Engrg line Inc ....G 812 524-1991
Seymour (G-12438)

◆ Constellation Mold Inc ....F 812 424-5338
Evansville (G-3429)

Corydon Machine & Tool Co Inc ....E 812 738-3107
Corydon (G-2095)

Covington Products Inc ....F 765 282-6626
Muncie (G-10450)

CPM Acquisition Corp ....D 765 362-2600
Crawfordsville (G-2142)

Creative Tool and Machining ....F 812 378-3562
Columbus (G-1884)

Custom Engineering Inc ....G 812 424-3879
Evansville (G-3450)

Custom Gage & Tool Co Inc ....G 317 547-8257
Indianapolis (G-6713)

Cutting Edge Wire EDM Inc ....G 765 284-3820
Muncie (G-10452)

D & E Machine Inc ....G 765 653-8919
Greencastle (G-5457)

D & J Tool Co Inc ....G 260 636-2682
Albion (G-22)

D & S Machine Inc ....G 317 826-2900
Indianapolis (G-6720)

D 1 Mold & Tool LLC ....F 765 378-0693
Alexandria (G-39)

D A Hochstetler & Sons LLP ....F 574 642-1144
Topeka (G-13416)

D&D Automation Inc ....G 812 299-1045
Terre Haute (G-13221)

Davis Machine & Tool Inc ....F 812 526-2674
Edinburgh (G-2606)

Dayton Progress Corporation ....E 260 726-6861
Portland (G-11815)

De Witt Tool & Die Inc ....G 765 998-7320
Upland (G-13469)

Dedrick Tool & Die Inc ....G 260 824-3334
Bluffton (G-872)

Defelice Engineering Inc ....G 317 834-2832
Mooresville (G-10307)

▲ Delta Tool Manufacturing Inc ....G 574 223-4863
Rochester (G-12122)

Design & Mfg Solutions LLC ....F 765 478-9393
Cambridge City (G-1255)

Die Protection Tech LLC ....G 812 837-9507
Nashville (G-10722)

Die-Rite Machine and Tool Corp ....G 574 522-2366
Elkhart (G-2797)

Dieco of Indiana Inc ....F 765 825-4151
Connersville (G-2046)

Dietech Corporation ....G 260 724-8946
Decatur (G-2375)

Diversified Tools & Machine ....G 260 489-0272
Fort Wayne (G-4214)

DOE Run Tooling Inc ....G 812 265-3057
Madison (G-9458)

Drp Mold Inc ....G 765 349-3355
Martinsville (G-9602)

▲ Dwd Industries LLC ....E 260 728-9272
Decatur (G-2377)

Dwd Industries LLC ....G 260 639-3254
Hoagland (G-6064)

dwg Design Services Corp ....G 812 372-0864
Columbus (G-1915)

Dynamic Dies Inc ....E 317 247-4706
Indianapolis (G-6778)

E F M Corporation ....D 812 372-4421
Columbus (G-1916)

Earthchain Magnetic Pro ....G 317 803-8034
Indianapolis (G-6788)

Ecm Photo Tooling Inc ....E 574 264-4433
Elkhart (G-2813)

Elkhart Tool and Die Inc ....E 574 295-8500
Elkhart (G-2832)

Engrave Inc ....F 812 537-8693
Lawrenceburg (G-9140)

Epw LLC ....D 574 293-5090
Elkhart (G-2836)

Esteves-Dwd LLC ....D 260 728-9272
Decatur (G-2378)

Evansville Tool & Die Inc ....F 812 422-7101
Evansville (G-3492)

Evart Engineering Co Inc ....F 765 354-2232
Middletown (G-9935)

Excel Tool Inc ....D 812 522-6880
Seymour (G-12449)

Facet Engineering ....G 317 745-5070
Danville (G-2346)

▲ Fayette Tool and Engineering ....D 765 825-7518
Connersville (G-2048)

▲ Flare Inc ....G 260 490-1101
Fort Wayne (G-4265)

Focus Mold & Machine Inc ....G 812 422-9627
Evansville (G-3511)

Foil Die International Inc ....G 260 359-9011
Huntington (G-6204)

Foil Form Inc ....G 260 359-9011
Huntington (G-6205)

Fort Wayne Mold & Engrg Inc ....E 260 747-9168
Fort Wayne (G-4276)

▲ Fort Wayne Wire Die Inc ....C 260 747-1681
Fort Wayne (G-4281)

Fort Wayne Wire Die Inc ....G 260 747-1681
Fort Wayne (G-4282)

Franklin Stamping Inds Inc ....F 765 282-5138
Muncie (G-10473)

Fred Anderson ....G 765 985-2099
Peru (G-11527)

Future Mold Inc ....F 812 941-8661
New Albany (G-10785)

Future Tool & Engineering Co ....F 812 376-8699
Columbus (G-1932)

G C G Industries Inc ....E 260 482-7454
Fort Wayne (G-4292)

▲ Gammons Metal & Mfg Co Inc .....D 317 546-7091
Indianapolis (G-6982)

General Motors LLC ....B 765 668-2000
Marion (G-9525)

Gillum Machine & Tool Inc ....F 765 893-4426
West Lebanon (G-14120)

Glaze Tool and Engineering Inc ....E 260 493-4557
New Haven (G-10941)

Global Mold Solutions Inc ....E 574 259-6262
Mishawaka (G-10047)

Global Plastics Inc ....D 317 299-2345
Indianapolis (G-7012)

Granite Engineering & Tool Co ....F 812 375-9077
Columbus (G-1933)

Greenwood Tool & Die Co Inc ....G 219 924-9663
Griffith (G-5775)

Grimm Mold & Die Co Inc ....F 219 778-4211
Rolling Prairie (G-12186)

Grotrian Tool & Die ....G 260 894-3558
Ligonier (G-9286)

◆ Gta Enterprises Inc ....E 260 478-7800
Fort Wayne (G-4309)

Guardian Mold Prevent Corp ....G 708 878-5788
Dyer (G-2499)

◆ Gvs Technologies LLC ....F 574 293-0974
Elkhart (G-2901)

H & H Design & Tool Inc ....G 765 886-6199
Economy (G-2591)

H & M Tool & Die Inc ....F 812 663-8252
Greensburg (G-5605)

H & P Tool Co Inc ....E 765 962-4504
Richmond (G-11993)

Hanover Machine & Tool Inc ....G 812 265-6265
Hanover (G-5961)

Hawkins Machine & Tool Inc ....G 812 522-5529
Seymour (G-12453)

Heritage Tool and Die Inc ....G 260 359-8121
Huntington (G-6210)

Heritage Wire Die Inc ....G 260 728-9300
Decatur (G-2385)

Herman Tool & Machine Inc ....F 574 594-5544
Pierceton (G-11572)

Hermetic Coil Co Inc ....E 812 735-2400
Bicknell (G-631)

Hermetic Coil Co Inc ....E 812 735-2401
Bicknell (G-632)

Highland Machine Tool Inc ....G 812 923-8884
Floyds Knobs (G-4013)

Hipsher Tool & Die Inc ....F 260 563-4143
Wabash (G-13730)

Hook Development Inc ....G 260 432-7771
Fort Wayne (G-4341)

Hoosier Manufacturing LLC ....G 260 493-9990
Fort Wayne (G-4344)

◆ Hoosier Tool & Die Co Inc ... D ... 812 376-8286
Columbus *(G-1942)*
Hoosier Toolmaking & Engrg Inc ... G ... 260 493-9990
Fort Wayne *(G-4346)*
Hopper Development Inc ... F ... 574 753-6621
Logansport *(G-9336)*
Humphrey Tool Coinc ... G ... 574 753-3853
Logansport *(G-9338)*
Huntington Tool & Die Inc ... F ... 260 356-5940
Huntington *(G-6214)*
Huth Tool & Machine Corp ... G ... 260 749-9411
Fort Wayne *(G-4351)*
I T D Inc ... G ... 765 825-0151
Connersville *(G-2054)*
IAm Aw Tl Die Makers LL 229 ... G ... 574 333-5955
Elkhart *(G-2927)*
Indiana Model Company Inc ... D ... 317 787-6358
Indianapolis *(G-7184)*
▲ Indiana Southern Mold Corp ... E ... 812 346-2622
North Vernon *(G-11264)*
Indiana Steel Rule Die Inc ... G ... 317 352-9859
Indianapolis *(G-7194)*
Industrial Engineering Inc ... D ... 260 478-1514
Fort Wayne *(G-4367)*
▲ Industrial Tool & Die Corp ... F ... 812 424-9971
Evansville *(G-3559)*
Injection Mold Inc ... F ... 812 346-7002
North Vernon *(G-11266)*
Injection Plastic & Mfg Co ... F ... 574 784-2070
Lapaz *(G-9117)*
Inson Tool & Machine Inc ... G ... 812 752-3754
Scottsburg *(G-12366)*
Intri-Cut Tool Company LLC ... F ... 260 672-9602
Roanoke *(G-12104)*
▲ J B Tool Die & Engineering Co ... C ... 260 483-9586
Fort Wayne *(G-4386)*
J O Wolf Tool & Die Inc ... G ... 260 672-2605
Huntington *(G-6220)*
J P Corporation ... G ... 317 783-1000
Beech Grove *(G-598)*
J W Model & Engineering Inc ... G ... 317 788-7471
Indianapolis *(G-7290)*
Jacobs Machine & Tool Co Inc ... F ... 317 831-2917
Mooresville *(G-10316)*
Jam-Ko Engineering Company ... F ... 574 294-7684
Elkhart *(G-2944)*
James E Barnhizer ... G ... 765 458-9344
Liberty *(G-9261)*
JD Norman Industries Inc ... E ... 765 584-6069
Winchester *(G-14334)*
Jj Machine ... G ... 765 723-1511
New Ross *(G-11005)*
JMS Mold & Engineering Co Inc ... F ... 574 272-0198
South Bend *(G-12824)*
Jones Machine & Tool Inc ... E ... 812 364-4588
Fredericksburg *(G-4945)*
Journeyman Tool & Mold Inc ... G ... 574 237-1880
South Bend *(G-12825)*
Jus Rite Engineering Inc ... E ... 574 522-9600
Elkhart *(G-2952)*
K & K Inc ... F ... 574 266-8040
Elkhart *(G-2953)*
K & M Tool & Die Inc ... G ... 765 482-9464
Lebanon *(G-9194)*
K C Machine Inc ... G ... 574 293-1822
Elkhart *(G-2954)*
K Mold and Engineering Inc ... F ... 574 272-5858
Granger *(G-5417)*
K-K Tool and Design Inc ... E ... 260 758-2940
Markle *(G-9578)*
Kain Tool Inc ... G ... 260 829-6569
Orland *(G-11351)*
Kc Engineering Inc ... G ... 317 352-9742
Indianapolis *(G-7337)*
Keller Tool ... G ... 812 873-7344
Butlerville *(G-1250)*
Ken-Bar Tool & Engineering Inc ... E ... 765 284-4408
Muncie *(G-10503)*
Kent Machine Inc ... E ... 765 778-7777
Pendleton *(G-11492)*
Kimball Electronics Inc ... D ... 317 545-5383
Indianapolis *(G-7351)*
King Industrial Corporation ... D ... 812 522-3261
Seymour *(G-12464)*
Kitterman Machine Co Inc ... G ... 317 773-2283
Noblesville *(G-11139)*
▲ Knox Tool & Die Inc ... G ... 574 255-1256
Mishawaka *(G-10064)*
Kortzendorf Machine & Tool ... F ... 317 783-5449
Indianapolis *(G-7367)*

Kronmiller Machine & Tool ... G ... 260 436-1355
Fort Wayne *(G-4416)*
▲ Kruis Mold & Engineering Inc ... F ... 574 293-4613
Elkhart *(G-2976)*
Krukemeier Machine and Tool Co ... F ... 317 784-7042
Beech Grove *(G-600)*
L & L Engineering Co Inc ... G ... 317 786-6886
Beech Grove *(G-601)*
▲ L H Carbide Corporation ... C ... 260 432-5563
Fort Wayne *(G-4419)*
Laff or Die Productions ... G ... 219 942-3790
Hobart *(G-6086)*
Lake Tool & Die Inc ... G ... 574 457-8274
Syracuse *(G-13137)*
Lb Mold Inc ... E ... 812 526-2030
Edinburgh *(G-2616)*
Le Hue Machine & Tool Co Inc ... G ... 574 255-8404
Mishawaka *(G-10069)*
Lehue Machine and Tool ... G ... 574 329-5456
Osceola *(G-11381)*
Lex Tooling LLC ... G ... 765 675-6301
Tipton *(G-13395)*
LH Industries Corp ... B ... 260 432-5563
Fort Wayne *(G-4431)*
Liberty Tool and Engineering ... G ... 765 354-9550
Middletown *(G-9937)*
Lone Star Tool & Die Weld ... G ... 812 346-9681
Vernon *(G-13651)*
▲ Lorentson Manufacturing Co ... E ... 765 452-4425
Kokomo *(G-8660)*
Loughmiller Mch Tl Design Inc ... E ... 812 295-3903
Loogootee *(G-9390)*
Lukemeier Indus Mold & Mch Co ... E ... 812 945-3375
New Albany *(G-10821)*
M & R Pattern Inc ... G ... 219 778-4675
La Porte *(G-8788)*
M&M Machines ... G ... 260 349-1922
Kendallville *(G-8492)*
▼ Mac Machine & Metal Works Inc ... E ... 765 825-5873
Connersville *(G-2062)*
Machining Center Inc ... F ... 317 787-1965
Indianapolis *(G-7435)*
▲ Madison Tool and Die Inc ... D ... 812 273-2250
Madison *(G-9482)*
▲ Major Tool and Machine Inc ... B ... 317 636-6433
Indianapolis *(G-7446)*
Makuta Technics Inc ... F ... 317 642-0001
Shelbyville *(G-12550)*
Manchester Tool and Die Plant ... G ... 260 982-0702
North Manchester *(G-11235)*
Mark Tool & Die Inc ... F ... 765 533-4932
Markleville *(G-9588)*
Marksmen Tool & Die Inc ... G ... 765 584-3600
Winchester *(G-14336)*
▲ Matchless Machine & Tool Co ... E ... 765 342-4550
Martinsville *(G-9624)*
Matrix Manufacturing Inc ... G ... 260 854-4659
Wolcottville *(G-14374)*
Matrix Tool Inc ... F ... 574 259-3093
Mishawaka *(G-10075)*
Maxwell Engineering Inc ... G ... 260 745-4991
Fort Wayne *(G-4458)*
McGinn Tool & Engineering Co ... F ... 317 736-5512
Franklin *(G-4905)*
▲ Mdl Mold Die Components Inc ... G ... 812 373-0021
Columbus *(G-1970)*
Meck Die Inc ... G ... 574 262-5441
Elkhart *(G-3026)*
Melching Machine Inc ... E ... 260 622-4315
Ossian *(G-11404)*
Merit Tool & Manufacturing Inc ... F ... 765 396-9566
Eaton *(G-2586)*
Meyer Engineering Inc ... F ... 812 663-6535
Greensburg *(G-5623)*
▲ Michiana Global Mold Inc ... F ... 574 259-6262
Mishawaka *(G-10081)*
Michiana Metal Fabrication ... G ... 574 256-9010
Elkhart *(G-3032)*
▲ Michiana Plastics Inc ... E ... 574 259-6262
Mishawaka *(G-10084)*
Micro Tool & Machine Co Inc ... G ... 574 272-9141
Granger *(G-5421)*
Midwest Mold Remediation ... G ... 502 386-6559
Jeffersonville *(G-8401)*
Midwest Remediation ... E ... 317 826-0940
Indianapolis *(G-7510)*
Midwest Stl Rule Cutng Die Inc ... E ... 317 780-4600
Indianapolis *(G-7512)*
Midwest Tool & Die Corp ... E ... 260 483-4282
Fort Wayne *(G-4474)*

Millennium Tool Inc ... E ... 812 273-1566
Madison *(G-9488)*
Modern Die Systems Inc ... E ... 765 552-3145
Elwood *(G-3307)*
Modern Drop Forge Company ... F ... 708 388-1806
Merrillville *(G-9736)*
▲ Modern Drop Forge Company LLC ... B ... 708 489-4208
Merrillville *(G-9737)*
Mold Busters LLC ... G ... 812 989-0008
Floyds Knobs *(G-4016)*
Mold Removal Team of Hammond ... G ... 219 554-9719
Hammond *(G-5917)*
Mold Service Inc ... G ... 260 868-2920
Butler *(G-1233)*
Mold Stoppers of Indiana ... G ... 812 325-1609
Bloomington *(G-774)*
Moonlight Mold & Machine Inc ... G ... 765 868-9860
Kokomo *(G-8671)*
Morris Mold and Machine Co ... G ... 317 923-6653
Indianapolis *(G-7544)*
Msk Mold Inc ... G ... 812 985-5457
Wadesville *(G-13773)*
Muncie Casting Corp ... E ... 765 288-2611
Muncie *(G-10528)*
Muncie Mold & Engineering LLC ... G ... 765 282-0522
Muncie *(G-10531)*
My Pneumatic Tools and Service ... G ... 317 364-3324
Greensburg *(G-5625)*
New Die Concepts Inc ... G ... 260 420-9504
Fort Wayne *(G-4499)*
New Point Products Inc ... G ... 812 663-6311
New Point *(G-11003)*
▼ Nexgen Mold & Tool Inc ... E ... 812 945-3375
New Albany *(G-10833)*
Nixon Tool Co Inc ... E ... 765 966-6608
Richmond *(G-12024)*
Northern Tool and Die ... G ... 260 495-7314
Fremont *(G-4971)*
Northside Machine & Tool Inc ... F ... 765 654-4538
Frankfort *(G-4845)*
Northside Machining Inc ... G ... 812 683-3500
Huntingburg *(G-6176)*
O & R Precision Grinding Inc ... E ... 260 368-9394
Geneva *(G-5137)*
Omega Enterprises Inc ... E ... 765 584-1990
Winchester *(G-14339)*
Overton & Sons Tl & Die Co Inc ... E ... 317 831-4542
Mooresville *(G-10331)*
Overton & Sons Tl & Die Co Inc ... F ... 317 831-4542
Mooresville *(G-10332)*
Overton & Sons Tl & Die Co Inc ... E ... 317 736-7700
Franklin *(G-4918)*
Overton Mold Inc ... F ... 317 831-9595
Mooresville *(G-10333)*
P & H Engineering Inc ... G ... 765 676-6323
Jamestown *(G-8232)*
Paradise Machine & Tool Corp ... G ... 317 247-4606
Indianapolis *(G-7653)*
Parker-Hannifin Corporation ... D ... 574 533-1111
Goshen *(G-5307)*
PDQ Tooling LLC ... F ... 260 244-2984
Columbia City *(G-1816)*
Perfection Mold & Tool Inc ... G ... 574 292-0824
South Bend *(G-12891)*
▼ Perfecto Tool & Engineering Co ... E ... 765 644-2821
Anderson *(G-150)*
▲ Perm Industries Inc ... E ... 219 365-5000
Saint John *(G-12267)*
Piercy Machine Co Inc ... G ... 317 398-9296
Shelbyville *(G-12556)*
Pinnacle Tool Inc ... G ... 812 336-5000
Bloomington *(G-799)*
▲ Plastics Research and Dev Inc ... E ... 812 279-8885
Springville *(G-13066)*
Ploog Engineering Co Inc ... G ... 219 663-2854
Crown Point *(G-2284)*
▲ Precise Tooling Solutions Inc ... D ... 812 378-0247
Columbus *(G-1999)*
Precision Die Technologies ... E ... 260 482-5001
Fort Wayne *(G-4548)*
Precision Mold & Tool Inc ... F ... 765 284-4415
Muncie *(G-10547)*
Precision Plastics Indiana Inc ... C ... 260 244-6114
Columbia City *(G-1819)*
Precision Tubes Inc ... G ... 317 783-2339
Indianapolis *(G-7738)*
Precision Welding Corporation ... G ... 260 637-5514
Huntertown *(G-6144)*
▼ Premier Consulting Inc ... F ... 260 496-9300
Fort Wayne *(G-4554)*

Premier Mold ....G...... 574 293-2846
Elkhart (G-3112)

Pro Tool & Engineering Inc ....F...... 574 256-5911
Mishawaka (G-10110)

Progressive Tool & Machine ....G...... 812 346-1837
Columbus (G-2001)

Proton Mold Tool Inc ....G...... 812 923-7263
Floyds Knobs (G-4018)

Pt Tool Machine 219 275-3633
Brook (G-1099)

▲ Qmp Inc ....E...... 574 262-1575
Elkhart (G-3124)

Qualidie Corp ....F...... 317 632-6845
Indianapolis (G-7796)

Quality Die Set Corp ....E...... 574 967-4411
Logansport (G-9361)

Quality Machine & Tool Inc ....G...... 574 534-5664
Goshen (G-5314)

Quality Mold & Engineering ....G...... 812 346-6577
Vernon (G-13652)

Quality Steel & Aluminium ....G...... 574 294-7221
Elkhart (G-3131)

Quality Tool Co Inc ....F...... 260 484-0187
Fort Wayne (G-4572)

Quality Tool Design Inc ....G...... 765 377-4055
Connersville (G-2069)

Qualtech Tool & Engrg Inc ....E...... 260 726-6572
Portland (G-11844)

R & D Mold & Engineering Inc ....G...... 574 257-1070
Mishawaka (G-10113)

R & L Die Co Inc ....G...... 765 759-6880
Yorktown (G-14411)

R & M Tool Engineering Inc ....F...... 812 352-0240
North Vernon (G-11280)

R S E Tool and Die Inc ....F...... 574 848-7966
Bristol (G-1077)

Ready Machine Tool & Die Corp ....E...... 765 825-3108
Connersville (G-2070)

Reber Machine & Tool Co Inc ....G...... 765 288-0297
Muncie (G-10554)

Richeys Mold and Tool Inc.................G...... 812 752-1059
Scottsburg (G-12378)

River Valley Plastics Inc ....E...... 574 262-5221
Elkhart (G-3148)

Robert Atkins ....G...... 765 536-4164
Summitville (G-13103)

Roembke Mfg & Design Inc ....E...... 260 622-4135
Ossian (G-11406)

Ross Engineering & Machine ....E...... 574 586-7791
Walkerton (G-13810)

Rotam Tool Corporation ....F...... 260 982-8318
North Manchester (G-11242)

Royal Tool & Molding Inc ....G...... 574 643-6800
Royal Center (G-12215)

Royer Enterprises Inc ....F...... 260 359-0689
Huntington (G-6245)

Ruco Inc ....E...... 574 262-4110
Elkhart (G-3151)

Sanmar Tool & Manufacturing ....G...... 574 232-6081
South Bend (G-12927)

◆ Setco LLC ....B...... 812 424-2904
Evansville (G-3724)

Shakour Industries Inc ....G...... 574 289-0100
South Bend (G-12932)

Six Sigma Mold Inc ....G...... 219 285-6539
Morocco (G-10363)

Slick Engineering Industries...............G...... 765 354-2822
Middletown (G-9941)

Smith Machine and Tool ....G...... 574 223-2318
Rochester (G-12155)

South Bend Form Tool Co Inc ....E...... 574 289-2441
South Bend (G-12944)

Southern Mold and Tool Inc ....G...... 812 752-3333
Scottsburg (G-12380)

Specialty Engrg TI & Die LLC ....G...... 260 356-2678
Huntington (G-6249)

Specialty Tool & Die Company ....F...... 765 452-9209
Kokomo (G-8698)

Specialty Tooling Inc ....F...... 812 464-8521
Evansville (G-3744)

Stag Tool ....G...... 812 876-3281
Gosport (G-5355)

Stamets Tool & Engineering ....G...... 260 925-1382
Auburn (G-358)

Stamina Metal Products Inc ....G...... 574 534-7410
Goshen (G-5327)

Standard Die Supply of Indiana ....E...... 317 236-6200
Indianapolis (G-7989)

Stanley Allen 812 752-2720
Scottsburg (G-12383)

Star Tool & Die Inc ....F...... 574 264-3815
Elkhart (G-3189)

Ste Inc 260 358-9254
Huntington (G-6252)

Stolle Tool Inc ....F...... 765 935-5185
Richmond (G-12055)

Superior Tool & Die Company ....E...... 574 293-2591
Elkhart (G-3201)

T & L Tool & Die II Co Inc ....G...... 574 722-6246
Logansport (G-9368)

T & T Tool & Stamping Inc ....G...... 765 789-4670
Albany (G-13)

Taurus Tech & Engrg LLC ....E...... 765 282-2090
Muncie (G-10568)

▲ Thorgren Tool & Molding Co ....D...... 219 462-1801
Valparaiso (G-13628)

▲ Tmak Inc ....E...... 219 874-7661
Michigan City (G-9853)

Toolcraft LLC ....E...... 260 749-0454
Fort Wayne (G-4692)

Toolmasters Inc.................................G...... 574 256-1881
Mishawaka (G-10140)

▼ Tree City Tool & Engrg Co Inc..........D...... 812 663-4196
Greensburg (G-5639)

Tri State Mold ....G...... 859 240-7643
Rising Sun (G-12092)

Triple H Tool Co.................................G...... 812 567-4600
Tennyson (G-13182)

Triplet Tool and Die Co Inc ....E...... 812 867-2494
Evansville (G-3775)

▲ Triplex Industries Inc ....F...... 574 256-9253
Mishawaka (G-10141)

Tuff Tool Inc ....G...... 262 612-8300
Fort Wayne (G-4708)

Twin Maple Tool Inc ....G...... 574 586-7500
Walkerton (G-13811)

Unique-Prescotech Inc ....E...... 479 646-2973
Evansville (G-3783)

United Tool & Engineering Inc ....E...... 574 259-1953
Mishawaka (G-10143)

Universal Tool & Engrg Co ....D...... 317 842-8999
Fishers (G-3981)

Valley Tool & Die Stampings ....E...... 574 722-4566
Logansport (G-9375)

Vision Machine Works Inc ....F...... 574 259-6500
Mishawaka (G-10148)

W W G Inc ....G...... 317 783-6413
Indianapolis (G-8172)

Wabash Valley Tool & Engrg ....G...... 260 563-7690
Wabash (G-13765)

Walkerton Tool & Die Inc ....E...... 574 586-3162
Walkerton (G-13813)

▲ Ward Corporation ....C...... 260 426-8700
Fort Wayne (G-4735)

Ward Corporation ....E...... 260 489-2281
Fort Wayne (G-4736)

Wcm Tool & Machine Inc ....G...... 812 422-2315
Evansville (G-3810)

Werrco Inc ....G...... 812 358-8665
Brownstown (G-1192)

Western Consolidated Tech Inc ....D...... 260 495-9866
Fremont (G-4982)

Wilhite Industries Inc.........................G...... 812 853-8771
Boonville (G-925)

Wirco Inc ....C...... 260 897-3768
Avilla (G-422)

▲ Woodburn Diamond Die Co Inc ....D...... 260 632-4217
Woodburn (G-14392)

Wynn Wire Die Services Inc ....G...... 260 471-1395
Fort Wayne (G-4762)

3545 Machine Tool Access

A & A Machine Service Inc ....G...... 317 745-7367
Avon (G-423)

Advanced Prtctive Slutions LLC ....G...... 765 720-9574
Coatesville (G-1746)

Advent Precision Inc ....G...... 317 908-6937
Indianapolis (G-6340)

▲ Aeromet Industries Inc ....D...... 219 924-7442
Griffith (G-5761)

Astro Cutting Tools ....F...... 765 478-3662
Cambridge City (G-1253)

◆ Ati Inc ....G...... 812 431-5409
Mount Vernon (G-10384)

B & W Specialized Drilling ....G...... 219 746-9463
Highland (G-6036)

▲ Bates Technologies LLC ....D...... 317 841-2400
Noblesville (G-11063)

Bel-Mar Products Corporation............G...... 317 769-3262
Whitestown (G-14249)

Berkey Machine Corporation ....G...... 260 761-4002
Wawaka (G-14031)

Beverly Industrial Service ....F...... 812 667-5047
Dillsboro (G-2463)

Bristol Tool and Die Inc ....F...... 574 848-5354
Bristol (G-1050)

Butler Tool & Design Inc ....F...... 219 297-4531
Goodland (G-5158)

C & A Tool Engineering Inc ....B...... 260 693-2167
Churubusco (G-1644)

C & A Tool Engineering Inc ....E...... 260 693-2167
Auburn (G-319)

C-Way Tool and Die Inc ....G...... 812 256-6341
Charlestown (G-1559)

Capital Machine Company Inc ....F...... 317 638-6661
Indianapolis (G-6548)

Century Tool & Engineering ....G...... 317 685-0942
Indianapolis (G-6587)

Chesterfield Tool & Engrg Inc ....E...... 765 378-5101
Daleville (G-2338)

Chucks Stace-Allen Inc ....E...... 317 632-2401
Indianapolis (G-6604)

Clarks Cnc LLC ....G...... 812 508-1773
Springville (G-13061)

Claymore Tools Inc ....G...... 574 255-6483
Mishawaka (G-10018)

▲ Continental Enterprises Inc ....E...... 260 447-7000
Fort Wayne (G-4173)

◆ Curtis Dyna-Fog Ltd ....D...... 317 896-2561
Westfield (G-14151)

Custom Gage & Tool Co Inc ....G...... 317 547-8257
Indianapolis (G-6713)

Davis Tool and Gage Company ....G...... 317 852-5400
Brownsburg (G-1148)

Diamond Stone Technologies Inc ......F...... 812 276-6043
Bedford (G-537)

Dimensions In Tooling Inc ....F...... 574 273-1505
Granger (G-5401)

Drake Corporation ....F...... 636 464-5070
Indianapolis (G-6765)

Drake Corporation ....E...... 812 683-2101
Jasper (G-8246)

Drilling & Trenching Sup Inc ....F...... 317 825-0919
Shelbyville (G-12530)

Dwyer Instruments Inc ....D...... 260 723-5138
South Whitley (G-12997)

▲ E-Collar Technologies Inc ....E...... 260 357-0051
Garrett (G-5002)

Fairfield Manufacturing Co Inc ....E...... 765 772-4547
Lafayette (G-8895)

▲ Fastener Equipment Corporation.....G...... 708 957-5100
Valparaiso (G-13541)

Feddema Industries Inc ....F...... 260 665-6463
Angola (G-213)

▲ Frederick Tool Corp ....E...... 574 295-6700
Elkhart (G-2870)

Frontier Additive Mfg LLC ....G...... 765 413-5568
Crawfordsville (G-2153)

Fuhrman Precision Services ....G...... 260 728-9600
Decatur (G-2379)

G & S Super Abrasives Inc ....G...... 260 665-5562
Angola (G-215)

General Aluminum Mfg Company ....C...... 260 495-2600
Fremont (G-4960)

General Crafts Corp ....G...... 574 533-1936
Goshen (G-5223)

Global Cutting Solutions ....F...... 812 683-5808
Huntingburg (G-6167)

Grimm Mold & Die Co Inc ....F...... 219 778-4211
Rolling Prairie (G-12186)

H & P Tool Co Inc ....E...... 765 962-4504
Richmond (G-11993)

Harford Industries Inc ....G...... 219 929-6455
Chesterton (G-1612)

Haven Manufacturing Ind Inc ....E...... 260 622-4150
Ossian (G-11400)

Herman Tool & Machine Inc ....F...... 574 594-5544
Pierceton (G-11572)

Hoosier Spline Broach Corp ....E...... 765 452-8273
Kokomo (G-8639)

◆ Hoosier Tool & Die Co Inc ....D...... 812 376-8286
Columbus (G-1942)

Indiana Precision Tooling Inc ....F...... 812 667-5141
Dillsboro (G-2468)

◆ Indiana Tool & Mfg Co Inc ....D...... 574 936-5548
Plymouth (G-11693)

Industrial Sales & Supply Inc.............F...... 317 240-0560
Indianapolis (G-7209)

Jones Machine & Tool Inc ....E...... 812 364-4588
Fredericksburg (G-4945)

K-K Tool and Design Inc ....E 260 758-2940
Markle *(G-9578)*

Kaiser Tool Company Inc ....E 260 484-3620
Fort Wayne *(G-4403)*

Ken-Bar Tool & Engineering Inc ....E 765 284-4408
Muncie *(G-10503)*

Kennametal Inc ....C 812 948-2118
New Albany *(G-10813)*

Kennametal Inc ....C 574 534-2585
Goshen *(G-5252)*

Kennametal Inc ....C 317 696-8798
Indianapolis *(G-7341)*

Kent Brenneke ....G 260 446-5383
Harlan *(G-5973)*

Klueg Tool & Machine Inc ....G 812 867-5702
Evansville *(G-3595)*

Krukemeier Machine and Tool Co ....F 317 784-7042
Beech Grove *(G-600)*

KTI Cutting Tools Inc ....G 260 749-1465
Fort Wayne *(G-4418)*

Liberty Tool and Engineering ....G 765 354-9550
Middletown *(G-9937)*

▲ Logansport Machine Co Inc ....E 574 735-0225
Logansport *(G-9350)*

Longbow Machining LLC ....G 812 599-6728
Lexington *(G-9253)*

Lotec Inc ....E 574 294-1506
Elkhart *(G-3008)*

Loughmiller Mch TI Design Inc ....E 812 295-3903
Loogootee *(G-9390)*

Lowe Machine Tools LLC ....G 248 705-7562
Noblesville *(G-11142)*

M4 Sciences LLC ....G 765 479-6215
West Lafayette *(G-14084)*

▲ Marion Tool & Die Inc ....D 812 533-9800
West Terre Haute *(G-14126)*

Merit Tool & Manufacturing Inc ....F 765 396-9566
Eaton *(G-2586)*

Micro-Precision Operations ....E 260 589-2136
Berne *(G-620)*

Morris Mold and Machine Co ....G 317 923-6653
Indianapolis *(G-7544)*

▲ Nachi America Inc ....C 317 535-5527
Greenwood *(G-5726)*

Nachi Tool America Inc ....F 317 535-0320
Greenwood *(G-5728)*

◆ Nap Asset Holdings Ltd ....G 812 482-2000
Jasper *(G-8297)*

Netshape Technologies LLC ....C 812 755-4501
Campbellsburg *(G-1278)*

Nicholas Precision Works LLC ....G 260 306-3426
North Manchester *(G-11237)*

Nixon Tool Co Inc ....E 765 966-6608
Richmond *(G-12024)*

Oak View Tooling Inc ....F 260 244-7677
Columbia City *(G-1814)*

Overton & Sons TI & Die Co Inc ....E 317 736-7700
Franklin *(G-4918)*

Overton & Sons TI & Die Co Inc ....E 317 831-4542
Mooresville *(G-10331)*

Pannell & Son Welding Inc ....G 765 948-3606
Summitville *(G-13100)*

▲ Plymouth Pdts Acquisition Inc ....E 574 936-4757
Plymouth *(G-11714)*

Precision Cams Inc ....E 317 631-9100
Indianapolis *(G-7731)*

Precision Cams Inc ....G 317 780-0117
Indianapolis *(G-7732)*

Precision Tubes Inc ....G 317 783-2339
Indianapolis *(G-7738)*

Progressive Tool & Machine ....G 812 346-1837
Columbus *(G-2001)*

Qualtech Tool & Engrg Inc ....E 260 726-6572
Portland *(G-11844)*

R B Tool & Machinery Co ....G 574 679-0082
Osceola *(G-11383)*

Rite Way Industries Inc ....E 812 206-8665
New Albany *(G-10856)*

Riverside Tool Corp ....E 574 522-6798
Elkhart *(G-3149)*

▲ Rusach International Inc ....F 317 638-0298
Hope *(G-6119)*

Rush Jaw Company The Inc ....G 317 729-5095
Shelbyville *(G-12564)*

S-B Capable Concepts LLC ....G 812 420-2565
Brazil *(G-977)*

▲ Sapp Inc ....F 317 512-8353
Edinburgh *(G-2627)*

Scg Acquisition Company LLC ....E 574 294-1506
Elkhart *(G-3157)*

Scheidler Machine Incorporated ....G 812 662-6555
Greensburg *(G-5633)*

Slick Engineering Industries ....G 765 354-2822
Middletown *(G-9941)*

Specialty Tool LLC ....F 260 493-6351
Indianapolis *(G-7969)*

Spectrum Services Inc ....G 574 272-7605
Granger *(G-5437)*

Stapert Tool & Machine Co Inc ....G 317 787-2387
Indianapolis *(G-7995)*

Superior Tool & Die Company ....E 574 293-2591
Elkhart *(G-3201)*

Swiss Labs Machine & Engrg Inc ....G 317 346-6190
Franklin *(G-4935)*

T & L Sharpening Inc ....E 574 583-3868
Monticello *(G-10285)*

Tascon Corp ....E 317 547-6127
Indianapolis *(G-8038)*

Thomas L Wehr ....G 317 835-7824
Fairland *(G-3827)*

Toolcraft LLC ....E 260 749-0454
Fort Wayne *(G-4692)*

▲ Tri-State Industries Inc ....D 219 933-1710
Hammond *(G-5951)*

▲ Tsune America LLC ....F 812 378-9875
Edinburgh *(G-2631)*

V I P Tooling Inc ....F 317 398-0753
Shelbyville *(G-12581)*

▲ W F Meyers Company Inc ....E 812 275-4485
Bedford *(G-589)*

Ward Forging Co Inc ....E 812 923-7463
Floyds Knobs *(G-4023)*

Wbh Inc ....F 317 269-1510
Indianapolis *(G-8180)*

Whitney Tool Company Inc ....E 812 275-4491
Bedford *(G-590)*

Yamaguchi Mfg Usa Inc ....G 765 973-9130
Richmond *(G-12077)*

▲ Zps America LLC ....E 317 452-4030
Indianapolis *(G-8228)*

3546 Power Hand Tools

Beckler Power Equipment ....G 260 356-1188
Huntington *(G-6190)*

Black & Decker (us) Inc ....G 317 241-1200
Indianapolis *(G-6481)*

Bolttech Mannings Inc ....F 219 310-8389
Crown Point *(G-2230)*

Claymore Tools Inc ....G 574 255-6483
Mishawaka *(G-10018)*

▲ Diedrich Drill Inc ....E 219 326-7788
La Porte *(G-8751)*

Drake Corporation ....F 636 464-5070
Indianapolis *(G-6765)*

▲ Frederick Tool Corp ....E 574 295-6700
Elkhart *(G-2870)*

Illinois Tool Works Inc ....D 219 874-4217
Michigan City *(G-9803)*

Innovative Rescue Systems Inc ....G 219 548-1028
Valparaiso *(G-13560)*

James W Hager ....F 765 643-0188
Alexandria *(G-46)*

Key Sheet Metal Inc ....G 317 546-7151
Indianapolis *(G-7345)*

Stanley Fastening Systems LP ....D 317 398-0761
Greenfield *(G-5578)*

Steam Specialties Inc ....G 317 849-5601
Fishers *(G-3970)*

◆ Tippmann Sports LLC ....D 800 533-4831
Fort Wayne *(G-4686)*

Tippmann Sports LLC ....F 260 749-6022
Fort Wayne *(G-4687)*

3547 Rolling Mill Machinery & Eqpt

AAA-Gpc Holdings LLC ....D 260 668-1468
Angola *(G-187)*

▲ Amerifab Inc ....D 317 231-0100
Indianapolis *(G-6393)*

Enbi Global Inc ....F 317 395-7324
Shelbyville *(G-12532)*

Fab-Tech Industries ....G 765 478-4191
Cambridge City *(G-1256)*

Hoosier Roll Shop Services LLC ....F 219 844-8077
Hammond *(G-5893)*

Mae of America Inc ....G 765 561-4539
Indianapolis *(G-7436)*

Overton & Sons TI & Die Co Inc ....E 317 736-7700
Franklin *(G-4918)*

Premier Components LLC ....G 219 776-9372
Hebron *(G-6021)*

Southlake Machine Corp ....G 219 285-6150
Morocco *(G-10364)*

Systems Contracting Corp ....F 765 361-2991
Crawfordsville *(G-2200)*

Witt Industries Inc ....E 765 289-3427
Muncie *(G-10587)*

3548 Welding Apparatus

Best Equipment & Welding Co ....E 317 271-8652
Indianapolis *(G-6468)*

Bryant Machining & Welding LLC ....G 260 997-6059
Bryant *(G-1199)*

Coleman Cable LLC ....C 765 449-7227
Lafayette *(G-8875)*

▲ GC Fuller Mfg Co Inc ....F 812 539-2831
Lawrenceburg *(G-9144)*

Ken Anliker ....G 219 984-5676
Chalmers *(G-1547)*

Kennametal Inc ....C 574 534-2585
Goshen *(G-5252)*

▼ Manufacturing Technology Inc ....C 574 230-0258
South Bend *(G-12851)*

Manufacturing Technology Inc ....E 574 233-9490
South Bend *(G-12852)*

◆ Ogden Welding Systems Inc ....E 219 322-5252
Schererville *(G-12341)*

◆ Praxair Surface Tech Inc ....C 317 240-2500
Indianapolis *(G-7725)*

S T Praxair Technology Inc ....G 317 240-2500
Indianapolis *(G-7881)*

Schmucker Welding ....G 574 773-0456
Bremen *(G-1021)*

Star Metal Products ....E 317 631-5902
Indianapolis *(G-7996)*

Topspeed ....G 260 665-8889
Angola *(G-252)*

▲ Tri-State Industries Inc ....D 219 933-1710
Hammond *(G-5951)*

United Industrial & Wldg LLC ....G 812 526-4050
Columbus *(G-2028)*

3549 Metalworking Machinery, NEC

Aam-Equipco Inc ....G 574 272-8886
Granger *(G-5388)*

Abell Tool Co Inc ....G 317 887-0021
Greenwood *(G-5658)*

American Integrated Mfg Co ....G 317 445-2056
Westfield *(G-14135)*

▼ Banks Machine & Engrg Inc ....D 317 642-4980
Shelbyville *(G-12519)*

Brown Advanced Mfg LLC ....G 574 209-2003
Bremen *(G-989)*

Da-Mar Industries Inc ....F 260 347-1662
Kendallville *(G-8471)*

Dual Machine & Tool Co Inc ....G 812 256-2202
Charlestown *(G-1563)*

Dubois Machine Co Inc ....E 812 482-3644
Jasper *(G-8249)*

Finite Filtation Company ....G 219 789-8084
Crown Point *(G-2253)*

▲ Gary Machinery LLC ....E 219 980-5700
Griffith *(G-5773)*

George Koch Sons LLC ....C 812 465-9600
Evansville *(G-3519)*

Glaze Tool and Engineering Inc ....E 260 493-4557
New Haven *(G-10941)*

▲ Grinding and Polsg McHy Corp ....F 317 898-0750
Indianapolis *(G-7050)*

HI Def Machining LLC ....G 812 493-9943
Madison *(G-9465)*

Hy-Tech Machining Systems LLC ....F 765 649-6852
Anderson *(G-118)*

Illinois Tool Works Inc ....E 317 298-5000
Indianapolis *(G-7160)*

Innovative Mold & Machine Inc ....G 317 634-1177
Indianapolis *(G-7238)*

Jcr Automation Inc ....F 260 749-6606
New Haven *(G-10945)*

JI Manfcturing Fabrication Inc ....G 260 589-3723
Berne *(G-618)*

Jpg Machine & Tool LLC ....G 812 265-4512
Madison *(G-9474)*

Larrys Tls Hydraulic Jack Svcs ....G 317 243-8666
Indianapolis *(G-7382)*

McBroom Electric Co Inc ....D 317 926-3451
Indianapolis *(G-7471)*

▲ Meriwether Tool & Engineering ....F 260 744-6955
Fort Wayne *(G-4466)*

Micro-Precision Operations ....E 260 589-2136
Berne *(G-620)*

Midwest Precision Machining ....G...... 260 459-6866
Fort Wayne (G-4473)

Millers Quick Production ....G...... 812 278-8374
Springville (G-13065)

Modern Die Systems Inc ....E...... 765 552-3145
Elwood (G-3307)

Nix Equipment LLC ....E...... 812 874-2231
Poseyville (G-11859)

Pia Automation US Inc ....C...... 812 474-3126
Evansville (G-3669)

Precision Automation Co Inc ....E...... 812 283-7963
Clarksville (G-1691)

Quality Industrial Supplies ....F...... 219 324-2654
La Porte (G-8808)

Stulls Machining Center Inc ....G...... 765 942-2717
Ladoga (G-8842)

▲ Tube Form Solutions LLC ....G...... 574 295-5041
Elkhart (G-3228)

Tube Form Solutions LLC ....E...... 574 266-5230
Elkhart (G-3229)

Walkerton Tool & Die Inc ....G...... 574 586-3162
Walkerton (G-13813)

▲ Wastequip Mfg ....G...... 574 946-6631
Winamac (G-14323)

Wge Equipment Solutions LLC ....G...... 260 636-7218
Fort Wayne (G-4751)

3552 Textile Machinery

Advanced Products Tech Inc ....G...... 765 827-1166
Connersville (G-2038)

Big Als Athletics ....G...... 765 836-5203
Mount Summit (G-10378)

Custom Tees ....G...... 765 449-4893
Lafayette (G-8885)

Leap Frogz Screanprinting EMB ....G...... 317 786-2441
Indianapolis (G-7390)

Logo Zone Inc ....G...... 574 753-7569
Logansport (G-9352)

Machining Solutions ....G...... 574 292-3227
South Bend (G-12846)

Moores Inc ....G...... 574 533-6089
Goshen (G-5297)

3553 Woodworking Machinery

Braun Witte Pattern Works Inc ....G...... 260 463-8210
Wolcottville (G-14369)

Capital Machine Company Inc ....F...... 317 638-6661
Indianapolis (G-6548)

Core Wood Components LLC ....G...... 574 370-4457
Elkhart (G-2774)

Dubois Machine Co Inc ....E...... 812 482-3644
Jasper (G-8249)

Gr Huber Enterprises Inc ....G...... 574 293-7113
Elkhart (G-2892)

▲ Grinding and Polsg McHy Corp ....F...... 317 898-0750
Indianapolis (G-7050)

Hoosier Woodworking McHy LLC ....G...... 812 944-3302
New Albany (G-10798)

Indiana Flame Service ....E...... 219 787-7129
Chesterton (G-1613)

Lafree Enterprises ....G...... 574 674-5906
Osceola (G-11380)

Lozier Machinery Incorporated...........G...... 812 945-2558
New Albany (G-10819)

Nobbe Concrete Products Inc ....G...... 765 647-4017
Brookville (G-1121)

Northtech Machine LLC......................G...... 812 967-7400
Borden (G-936)

▲ PDQ Workholding LLC ....G...... 260 244-2919
Columbia City (G-1817)

Sandman Products LLC ....G...... 574 264-7700
Elkhart (G-3156)

Scheumann Cabinet Co.......................G...... 260 747-3509
Fort Wayne (G-4608)

Sp Holdings Inc ....F...... 765 284-9545
Muncie (G-10564)

◆ Veneer Services LLC ....F...... 317 346-0711
Indianapolis (G-8150)

◆ Wood-Mizer Holdings Inc ....F...... 317 271-1542
Indianapolis (G-8212)

3554 Paper Inds Machinery

Bahr Bros Mfg Inc ....E...... 765 664-6235
Marion (G-9512)

C & W Inkd ....F...... 317 352-1000
Indianapolis (G-6527)

Corrquest Automation Inc ....G...... 812 596-0049
Crandall (G-2124)

Custom Machining Inc ....E...... 317 392-2328
Shelbyville (G-12529)

Dovey Corporation ....F...... 765 649-2576
Anderson (G-99)

GTW Enterprises Inc ....E...... 219 362-2278
La Porte (G-8759)

◆ Haire Machine Corporation ....E...... 219 947-4545
Merrillville (G-9718)

Hoosier Shred ....G...... 317 915-7473
Indianapolis (G-7123)

Indiana Fiber Works............................G...... 317 524-5711
Indianapolis (G-7179)

▲ Jennerjahn Machine Inc ....E...... 765 998-2733
Matthews (G-9652)

Owens Machinery Inc ....G...... 812 968-3285
Palmyra (G-11437)

◆ Peerless Machine & Tool Corp ....D...... 765 662-2586
Marion (G-9552)

RPC Machinery Inc ....G...... 765 458-5655
Liberty (G-9271)

Stickle Steam Specialties Co ....F...... 317 636-6563
Indianapolis (G-8007)

3555 Printing Trades Machinery & Eqpt

Acutech LLC ....F...... 574 262-8228
Elkhart (G-2667)

▲ Blue Grass Chemical Spc LLC ....E...... 812 948-1115
New Albany (G-10753)

Egenolf Machine Inc ....D...... 317 787-5301
Indianapolis (G-6814)

Indiana Imprint LLC ....G...... 812 704-2773
Jeffersonville (G-8380)

Kbc Machine ....G...... 317 446-6163
Greenfield (G-5546)

Nea LLC ....G...... 574 295-0024
Elkhart (G-3059)

Numerical Concepts Inc ....D...... 812 466-5261
Terre Haute (G-13293)

Parsing Laser Designs LLC ....G...... 317 677-4316
Avon (G-460)

▲ Perfecta USA ....E...... 317 862-7371
Indianapolis (G-7677)

▲ Precision Rubber Plate Co Inc ....D...... 317 783-3226
Indianapolis (G-7737)

Rotation Dynamics Corporation ....E...... 219 325-8808
La Porte (G-8813)

◆ Scheffer International Inc ....E...... 219 736-6200
Crown Point (G-2299)

3556 Food Prdts Machinery

▼ A M Manufacturing Co Inc ....E...... 219 472-7272
Munster (G-10592)

Carmel Engineering Inc ....F...... 765 279-8955
Kirklin (G-8547)

Carmel Process Solutions Inc ....G...... 317 705-0217
Carmel (G-1331)

Centrifuge Support & Sups LLC..........G...... 317 830-6141
Camby (G-1264)

◆ CTB MN Investment Co Inc ....E...... 574 658-4191
Milford (G-9955)

▲ Flavor Burst Co LLP ....F...... 317 745-2952
Danville (G-2347)

Hinsdale Farms Ltd ....G...... 574 848-0344
Bristol (G-1063)

Intek Manufacturing LLC ....G...... 260 637-4100
Fort Wayne (G-4378)

JMS Electronics Corporation ....G...... 574 522-0246
Elkhart (G-2949)

Kaeb Sales Inc ....F...... 574 862-2777
Wakarusa (G-13781)

Kitchen-Quip Inc ....E...... 260 837-8311
Kendallville (G-8487)

▲ M D Holdings LLC ....G...... 317 831-7030
Mooresville (G-10319)

Metzger Dairy Inc ....F...... 260 564-5445
Kimmell (G-8531)

Mssh Inc ....G...... 812 663-2180
Greensburg (G-5624)

◆ Norris Thermal Tech Inc ....G...... 574 353-7855
Tippecanoe (G-13385)

◆ Reading Bakery Systems Ta ....F...... 317 337-0000
Indianapolis (G-7824)

Romculinary LLC ....G...... 630 235-3338
Indianapolis (G-7859)

Roost ....F...... 317 842-3735
Fishers (G-3964)

Rota Skipper Corporation ....F...... 708 331-0660
Crown Point (G-2298)

Smithfield Foods ....G...... 765 473-3086
Peru (G-11546)

Stutz Products Corp ....G...... 765 348-2510
Hartford City (G-5992)

Tgf Enterprises LLC............................G...... 440 840-9704
Indianapolis (G-8056)

Urschel Air Leasing LLC ....G...... 219 464-4811
Chesterton (G-1638)

◆ Urschel Laboratories Inc ....B...... 219 464-4811
Chesterton (G-1639)

▼ Willow Way LLC ....G...... 765 886-4640
Hagerstown (G-5817)

Your Window Washer LLC ....G...... 317 701-1710
Noblesville (G-11200)

3559 Special Ind Machinery, NEC

Al-Fe Systems Inc ....F...... 260 483-4411
Columbia City (G-1763)

▲ Alliance Winding Equipment ....D...... 260 478-2200
Fort Wayne (G-4061)

◆ American Art Clay Co Inc ....C...... 317 243-0066
Indianapolis (G-6385)

▲ American Feeding Systems Inc ....E...... 317 773-5517
Noblesville (G-11060)

AMI Industries Inc ....E...... 989 786-3755
Angola (G-190)

Amt Parts International Corp ....E...... 260 490-0223
Fort Wayne (G-4075)

Anatolia Group Ltd Partnership ....G...... 203 343-7808
Indianapolis (G-6398)

Anodizing Technologies Inc ....G...... 317 253-5725
Indianapolis (G-6402)

Applied Material Solutions LLC ....G...... 317 769-3829
Zionsville (G-14418)

Automatic Fastner Tools ....G...... 317 784-4111
Indianapolis (G-6444)

Cardinal Metal Finishing LLC ....C...... 866 585-8024
Kokomo (G-8604)

▼ Chuck Bivens Services Inc ....F...... 260 747-6195
Fort Wayne (G-4149)

City of Anderson ....G...... 765 648-6715
Anderson (G-86)

Computer Age Engineering Inc ....E...... 765 674-8551
Marion (G-9518)

Cox John ....G...... 765 463-6396
West Lafayette (G-14061)

CPM Acquisition Corp ....D...... 765 362-2600
Crawfordsville (G-2142)

◆ Curtis Dyna-Fog Ltd ....D...... 317 896-2561
Westfield (G-14151)

Custom Kiln Works ....G...... 812 535-3561
West Terre Haute (G-14123)

D W Stewart ....G...... 260 463-2607
Lagrange (G-9036)

Dubois Machine Co Inc ....E...... 812 482-3644
Jasper (G-8249)

E & R Manufacturing Company ....G...... 765 279-8826
Kirklin (G-8548)

E & S Metal Inc ....F...... 260 563-7714
Wabash (G-13726)

Eagle Consulting Inc ....G...... 317 590-0485
Indianapolis (G-6785)

▲ Engineered Steel Concepts Inc ....F...... 219 924-9056
Highland (G-6045)

Federal-Mogul LLC ....G...... 260 497-5563
Fort Wayne (G-4261)

Federal-Mogul LLC ....G...... 574 271-0274
South Bend (G-12775)

Feeding Concepts Inc.........................G...... 317 773-2040
Noblesville (G-11102)

First Gear Inc ....F...... 260 490-3238
Fort Wayne (G-4263)

Frontier Engineering ....G...... 317 823-6885
Indianapolis (G-6965)

Gabriel Intl Group LLC ....G...... 812 537-5400
Lawrenceburg (G-9143)

Global Isotopes LLC ....G...... 317 578-1251
Noblesville (G-11111)

Globaltech Manufacturing L ....G...... 317 571-1910
Carmel (G-1386)

H C Schumacher Machine Co Inc ....G...... 317 787-9361
Indianapolis (G-7062)

Hermetic Coil Co Inc ....E...... 812 735-2400
Bicknell (G-631)

Honey Creek Machine Inc ....G...... 812 299-5255
Terre Haute (G-13247)

Hoosier Feeder Company Inc ....G...... 765 445-3333
Knightstown (G-8550)

Hoosier Shred Llc ....G...... 317 989-9333
Indianapolis (G-7124)

Illinois Tool Works Inc ....E...... 317 390-5940
Indianapolis (G-7159)

▼ Indco Inc ....G...... 812 945-4383
New Albany (G-10805)

Integra Certified Document ....G 574 295-4611
   Elkhart *(G-2936)*
International Cryogenics Inc ....F 317 297-4777
   Indianapolis *(G-7253)*
J & J Engineering Inc ....F 317 462-2309
   Greenfield *(G-5543)*
Kenco Plastics Inc ....F 219 324-6621
   La Porte *(G-8777)*
▲ Koch Enterprises Inc ....G 812 465-9800
   Evansville *(G-3596)*
Kustom Kilns 5 LLC ....G 260 820-3636
   Terre Haute *(G-13268)*
Lindas ....G 812 265-0099
   Hanover *(G-5962)*
Lyntech Engineering Inc ....G 574 224-2300
   Rochester *(G-12134)*
Majestic Tool Inc ....G 812 426-0332
   Evansville *(G-3612)*
Merriman Steel and Equipment ....G 812 849-2784
   Bedford *(G-562)*
▲ Metal Technologies Inc ....D 812 384-9800
   Bloomfield *(G-643)*
Mid-State Automation Inc ....G 765 795-5500
   Cloverdale *(G-1730)*
Moorfeed Acquisition LLC ....F 317 545-7171
   Indianapolis *(G-7542)*
Moorfeed Corporation ....E 317 545-7171
   Greenfield *(G-5559)*
◆ Mvo Usa Inc ....F 317 585-5785
   Indianapolis *(G-7562)*
◆ Peerless Machine & Tool Corp ....D 765 662-2586
   Marion *(G-9552)*
Perma-Green Supreme Inc ....E 219 548-3801
   Valparaiso *(G-13598)*
Pgp Corp ....D 812 285-7700
   Jeffersonville *(G-8413)*
Plating Products Inc ....G 775 241-0416
   Kokomo *(G-8682)*
PSI Repair Services Inc ....G 812 485-5575
   Evansville *(G-3689)*
Reynoldsrussell Entps LLC ....G 317 431-5886
   Anderson *(G-162)*
Roland International Co LLC ....G 319 400-1106
   Carmel *(G-1469)*
Safety-Kleen Systems Inc ....F 219 397-1131
   East Chicago *(G-2568)*
Shanxi-Indiana LLC ....G 219 885-2209
   Gary *(G-5097)*
▲ Shar Systems Inc ....E 260 432-5312
   Fort Wayne *(G-4619)*
Sinden Racing Service Inc ....F 317 243-7171
   Indianapolis *(G-7949)*
▲ SMC Corporation of America ....B 317 899-3182
   Noblesville *(G-11184)*
Specialized Services Inc ....G 317 485-8561
   Fortville *(G-4782)*
Sugarcube Systems Inc ....G 765 543-6709
   Lafayette *(G-9005)*
Summit Foundry Systems Inc ....F 260 749-7740
   Fort Wayne *(G-4663)*
Summit Industrial Technologies ....G 260 494-3461
   Fort Wayne *(G-4664)*
Systems Engineering and Sls Co ....G 260 422-1671
   Fort Wayne *(G-4671)*
Tamco Manufacturing Co ....G 574 294-1909
   Elkhart *(G-3205)*
▲ Technifab Products Inc ....D 812 442-0520
   Brazil *(G-979)*
Toco Inc ....G 317 627-8854
   Greenwood *(G-5754)*
Trimax Machine LLC ....G 812 887-9281
   Bruceville *(G-1198)*
Triplet Tool and Die Co Inc ....E 812 867-2494
   Evansville *(G-3775)*
▲ UFS Corporation ....F 219 464-2027
   Valparaiso *(G-13630)*
▼ Union Tool Corp ....E 574 267-3211
   Warsaw *(G-13956)*
Univertical LLC ....E 260 665-1500
   Angola *(G-256)*
Vauterbuilt Inc ....G 219 712-2384
   Hebron *(G-6024)*
▲ Vhc Ltd ....E 765 584-2101
   Winchester *(G-14343)*
Vibcon Corp ....F 317 984-3543
   Arcadia *(G-271)*
Vibracoustic North America L P ....C 260 894-7199
   Ligonier *(G-9301)*
▲ Vibration Control Tech LLC ....G 260 894-7199
   Ligonier *(G-9302)*

Vibromatic Company Inc ....E 317 773-3885
   Noblesville *(G-11199)*
Wayne Chemical Inc ....E 260 432-1120
   Fort Wayne *(G-4739)*
Wrib Manufacturing Inc ....G 765 294-2841
   Veedersburg *(G-13648)*
◆ Wurk Metal Products Inc ....F 317 828-0170
   Clayton *(G-1710)*

3561 Pumps & Pumping Eqpt

3w Enterprises LLC ....G 847 366-6555
   Elkhart *(G-2654)*
All-Pro Pump & Repair Inc ....G 317 738-4203
   Morgantown *(G-10348)*
Autoform Tool & Mfg LLC ....C 260 624-2014
   Angola *(G-195)*
▲ Automatic Pool Covers Inc ....E 317 579-2000
   Westfield *(G-14137)*
Bradley Innovation Group LLC ....G 765 942-7127
   Ladoga *(G-8838)*
▲ Dura Products Inc ....F 855 502-3872
   Arcadia *(G-264)*
E C Schleyer Pump Co Inc ....G 765 643-3334
   Anderson *(G-102)*
FL Smidth ....G 812 402-9210
   Evansville *(G-3507)*
Flickinger Industries Inc ....E 260 432-4527
   Fort Wayne *(G-4267)*
◆ Flint & Walling Inc ....C 260 347-1781
   Kendallville *(G-8475)*
Flowserve Corporation ....E 219 763-1000
   Portage *(G-11764)*
◆ Franklin Electric Co Inc ....B 260 824-2900
   Fort Wayne *(G-4285)*
Grundfos Pumps Mfg Corp ....F 317 925-9661
   Indianapolis *(G-7055)*
Hayward & Sams LLP ....G 260 351-4166
   Stroh *(G-13077)*
Hayward Tyler Inc ....G 812 867-2848
   Evansville *(G-3536)*
Hoosier Fire Equipment Inc ....E 219 462-1707
   Valparaiso *(G-13557)*
Hy-Flex Corporation ....C 765 571-5125
   Knightstown *(G-8551)*
Madden Manufacturing Inc ....F 574 295-4292
   Elkhart *(G-3013)*
Mantra Enterprise LLC ....E 201 428-8709
   Fishers *(G-3944)*
Met-Pro Technologies LLC ....E 317 293-2930
   Indianapolis *(G-7485)*
Netshape Technologies LLC ....C 812 755-4501
   Campbellsburg *(G-1278)*
Ohio Transmission Corporation ....G 812 466-2734
   Terre Haute *(G-13294)*
Parker-Hannifin Corporation ....C 260 636-2104
   Albion *(G-32)*
Parker-Hannifin Corporation ....F 608 824-0500
   Tell City *(G-13172)*
PHD Inc ....C 260 356-0120
   Huntington *(G-6238)*
Pump Meter Solutions ....E 317 984-7867
   Arcadia *(G-267)*
R B Tool & Machinery Co ....G 574 679-0082
   Osceola *(G-11383)*
▼ R P S Hydraulics Sales & Svc ....E 219 845-5526
   Hammond *(G-5931)*
Rankin Pump and Supply Co Inc ....G 812 238-2535
   Terre Haute *(G-13315)*
Roland International Co LLC ....G 319 400-1106
   Carmel *(G-1469)*
Shoemaker Welding Co ....G 574 656-4412
   North Liberty *(G-11221)*
▲ Specialty Manufacturing of Ind ....E 812 256-4633
   Charlestown *(G-1581)*
◆ Sterling Fluid Systems USA LLC ......C 317 925-9661
   Indianapolis *(G-8003)*
◆ Tbk America Inc ....E 765 962-0147
   Richmond *(G-12058)*
▲ Thrush Co Inc ....E 765 472-3351
   Peru *(G-11551)*
Tuthill Corporation ....C 260 747-7529
   Fort Wayne *(G-4709)*
◆ Tuthill Corporation ....G 260 747-7529
   Fort Wayne *(G-4710)*
Wee Engineer Inc ....F 765 449-4280
   Dayton *(G-2362)*

3562 Ball & Roller Bearings

Bearing Service Company PA ....G 773 734-5132
   Griffith *(G-5765)*

Casters In Motion USA Ltd LLC ....G 812 437-4627
   Evansville *(G-3413)*
Emerson Industrial Automation ....G 574 583-9171
   Monticello *(G-10262)*
◆ McGill Manufacturing Co Inc ....A 219 465-2200
   Valparaiso *(G-13579)*
◆ Nachi Technology Inc ....C 317 535-5000
   Greenwood *(G-5727)*
NSK Corporation ....E 317 837-8879
   Plainfield *(G-11631)*
NSK Corporation ....C 765 458-5000
   Liberty *(G-9267)*
▲ NSK Precision America Inc ....G 317 738-5000
   Franklin *(G-4915)*
NSK Precision America Inc ....C 317 738-5000
   Franklin *(G-4916)*
▲ Rbc Prcsion Pdts - Plymuth Inc ....C 574 935-3027
   Plymouth *(G-11719)*
Regal Beloit America Inc ....C 219 465-2200
   Valparaiso *(G-13607)*
Regal Beloit America Inc ....E 219 465-2200
   Valparaiso *(G-13608)*
▲ Standard Locknut LLC ....C 317 399-2230
   Westfield *(G-14190)*
Timken Company ....B 574 288-7188
   South Bend *(G-12970)*
Timken Company ....C 574 287-1566
   South Bend *(G-12971)*

3563 Air & Gas Compressors

ABB Flexible Automation Inc ....E 317 876-9090
   Indianapolis *(G-6307)*
◆ Abro Industries Inc ....E 574 232-8289
   South Bend *(G-12692)*
Air Fixtures Inc ....F 260 982-2169
   North Manchester *(G-11224)*
◆ Boss Industries LLC ....E 219 324-7776
   La Porte *(G-8740)*
▲ Brama Inc ....E 317 786-7770
   Indianapolis *(G-6502)*
▲ Cook Compression Inc ....A 502 515-6900
   Jeffersonville *(G-8345)*
Custom Compressor Svcs Corp ....G 219 879-4966
   Michigan City *(G-9777)*
▲ Dekker Vacuum Technologies Inc ....E 219 861-0661
   Michigan City *(G-9781)*
◆ Howden Roots LLC ....C 765 827-9200
   Connersville *(G-2052)*
◆ K Grimmer Industries Inc ....E 317 736-3800
   Leo *(G-9243)*
▲ Kobelco Cmpsr Mfg Ind Inc ....D 574 295-3145
   Elkhart *(G-2973)*
Magnum Venus Products Inc ....F 727 573-2955
   Goshen *(G-5277)*
Midwest Finishing Systems Inc ....E 574 257-0099
   Mishawaka *(G-10087)*
◆ Praxair Surface Tech Inc ....C 317 240-2500
   Indianapolis *(G-7725)*
Precisionair LLC ....G 219 380-9267
   La Porte *(G-8806)*
◆ Sullair LLC ....B 219 879-5451
   Michigan City *(G-9849)*
▲ Sullivan-Palatek Inc ....D 219 874-2497
   Michigan City *(G-9850)*
Systems Engineering and Sls Co ....G 260 422-1671
   Fort Wayne *(G-4671)*
Three Rivers Comprsd AR Sstms ....G 260 248-8908
   Columbia City *(G-1841)*
Ultra Elec Precsion Air & Land ....G 260 327-4112
   Columbia City *(G-1843)*
▲ Vanair Manufacturing Inc ....C 219 879-5100
   Michigan City *(G-9857)*
Wee Engineer Inc ....F 765 449-4280
   Dayton *(G-2362)*

3564 Blowers & Fans

3-T Corp ....G 812 424-7878
   Evansville *(G-3326)*
Abtrex Industries Inc ....E 574 234-7773
   South Bend *(G-12693)*
▲ Aero-Flo Industries Inc ....G 219 393-3555
   La Porte *(G-8728)*
Air-Tech Industrial Design ....G 317 797-1804
   Monrovia *(G-10201)*
Airjet Inc ....D 574 264-0123
   Elkhart *(G-2672)*
American Air Filter Co Inc ....D 888 223-2003
   Lebanon *(G-9167)*
▲ American Green Technology Inc ....F 269 340-9975
   South Bend *(G-12704)*

◆ Blocksom & Co ....G 219 878-4455
   Michigan City *(G-9770)*

Blocksom & Co ....G 219 878-4458
   Michigan City *(G-9771)*

Buck & Company Inc ....G 574 292-0874
   Granger *(G-5396)*

◆ Clarcor Air Filtration Pdts ....D 502 969-2304
   Jeffersonville *(G-8337)*

Cor-A-Vent Inc ....E 574 258-6161
   Mishawaka *(G-10024)*

◆ CTB MN Investment Co Inc ....G 574 658-4191
   Milford *(G-9955)*

Dexter Axle Company ....C 574 295-7888
   Bristol *(G-1054)*

Donaldson Company Inc ....G 812 637-9200
   Lawrenceburg *(G-9139)*

Donaldson Company Inc ....B 765 659-4766
   Frankfort *(G-4828)*

Donaldson Company Inc ....G 952 887-3131
   Monticello *(G-10260)*

Donaldson Company Inc ....G 317 838-5568
   Plainfield *(G-11606)*

E & S Metal Inc ....F 260 563-7714
   Wabash *(G-13726)*

Electro Painters Inc ....G 317 875-8816
   Carmel *(G-1370)*

Eta Fabrication Inc ....F 260 897-3711
   Avilla *(G-404)*

F D Ramsey & Co Inc ....E 219 362-2452
   La Porte *(G-8757)*

Fan-Tastic Vent ....G 800 521-0298
   Elkhart *(G-2844)*

Gbi Air Systems Inc ....G 574 272-0600
   Granger *(G-5408)*

Gsi Group Inc ....E 317 787-3047
   Indianapolis *(G-7056)*

Honeyville Metal Inc ....D 800 593-8377
   Topeka *(G-13421)*

Horner Industrial Services Inc ....F 317 634-7165
   Indianapolis *(G-7129)*

◆ Howden Roots LLC ....C 765 827-9200
   Connersville *(G-2052)*

Iaire LLC ....G 317 806-2750
   Indianapolis *(G-7155)*

Kabert Industries Inc ....D 765 874-2335
   Lynn *(G-9428)*

Lau Industries Inc ....D 574 223-3181
   Rochester *(G-12132)*

Mechanovent Corporation ....G 219 326-1767
   La Porte *(G-8790)*

New York Blower Company ....C 217 347-3233
   La Porte *(G-8799)*

Pro Clean LLC ....G 574 867-1000
   Hamlet *(G-5832)*

▲ Purolator Pdts A Filtration Co ....C 866 925-2247
   Jeffersonville *(G-8418)*

Spectrum Brands Inc ....E 317 773-6627
   Noblesville *(G-11187)*

Terronics Development Corp ....G 765 552-0808
   Elwood *(G-3311)*

Thermo-Cycler Industries Inc ....G 219 767-2990
   Union Mills *(G-13465)*

U S Air Filtration Inc ....G 260 486-7399
   Fort Wayne *(G-4712)*

Universal Blower Pac Inc ....E 317 773-7256
   Noblesville *(G-11198)*

Wabash Environmental Pdts LLC .....G 765 464-3440
   West Lafayette *(G-14115)*

Wicks Air Filter Service Inc ....G 260 426-1782
   Fort Wayne *(G-4755)*

3565 Packaging Machinery

Blasdel Enterprises Inc ....F 812 663-3213
   Greensburg *(G-5590)*

Chicago Automated Labeling ....F 219 531-0646
   Valparaiso *(G-13522)*

◆ Closure Systems Intl Inc ....C 317 390-5000
   Indianapolis *(G-6624)*

▼ E-Pak Machinery Inc ....G 219 393-5541
   La Porte *(G-8753)*

Elf Machinery LLC ....C 219 393-5541
   La Porte *(G-8755)*

▲ Grrk Holdings Inc ....E 317 872-0172
   Indianapolis *(G-7053)*

Huhtamaki Inc ....B 765 664-2330
   Marion *(G-9532)*

◆ Kwik Lok Corporation Indiana ....D 260 493-1220
   New Haven *(G-10947)*

◆ Lindal North America Inc ....D 812 657-7142
   Columbus *(G-1962)*

▼ Liquid Packaging Solutions Inc ......E 219 393-3600
   La Porte *(G-8787)*

Monosol LLC ....D 219 763-7589
   Portage *(G-11778)*

Morgan Adhesives Company LLC .....D 812 342-2004
   Columbus *(G-1976)*

Patriot Packaging LLC ....G 812 346-0700
   North Vernon *(G-11276)*

Powell Systems Inc ....E 765 884-0980
   Fowler *(G-4805)*

Precision Automation Co Inc ....E 812 283-7963
   Clarksville *(G-1691)*

Rethceif Enterprises LLC ....F 260 622-7200
   Ossian *(G-11405)*

Universal Packg Systems Inc ....B 260 829-6721
   Orland *(G-11359)*

Webber Manufacturing Company .....E 317 357-8681
   Indianapolis *(G-8181)*

Whallon Machinery Inc ....E 574 643-9561
   Royal Center *(G-12216)*

3566 Speed Changers, Drives & Gears

▲ Aisin Drivetrain Inc ....C 812 793-2427
   Crothersville *(G-2214)*

An-Mar Wiring Systems Inc ....F 574 255-5523
   Mishawaka *(G-9996)*

▲ Auburn Gear LLC ....C 260 925-3200
   Auburn *(G-313)*

Champ Torque Converters Inc ....G 812 424-2602
   Evansville *(G-3415)*

▲ Hansen Corporation ....B 812 385-3000
   Princeton *(G-11874)*

Mitsubsh Trbchrgr & Engn AM In ....G 317 346-5291
   Franklin *(G-4912)*

Moore Machine & Gear Inc ....E 812 963-3074
   Evansville *(G-3637)*

Netshape Technologies LLC ....E 812 755-4501
   Campbellsburg *(G-1278)*

Png Speed and Custom Ctr LLC ....G 317 858-1919
   Brownsburg *(G-1163)*

Quad Plus LLC ....E 219 844-9214
   Hammond *(G-5928)*

State Gear Company Inc ....F 317 634-3521
   Indianapolis *(G-7998)*

▲ Sterling Electric Inc ....E 317 872-0471
   Indianapolis *(G-8001)*

Tecumseh Products Company ....B 812 883-3575
   Salem *(G-12307)*

United Precision Gear Co Inc ....G 317 784-4665
   Indianapolis *(G-8128)*

▲ Vanair Manufacturing Inc ....C 219 879-5100
   Michigan City *(G-9857)*

3567 Indl Process Furnaces & Ovens

Ajax Tocco Magnethermic Corp ....G 317 352-9880
   Indianapolis *(G-6357)*

Al-Fe Systems Inc ....F 260 483-4411
   Columbia City *(G-1763)*

▲ Austin-Westran LLC ....C 815 234-2811
   Indianapolis *(G-6441)*

Blasdel Enterprises Inc ....F 812 663-3213
   Greensburg *(G-5590)*

Brouillette Heating & Cooling ....G 765 884-0176
   Fowler *(G-4798)*

▲ Contour Hardening Inc ....E 888 867-2184
   Indianapolis *(G-6660)*

E & S Metal Inc ....F 260 563-7714
   Wabash *(G-13726)*

▲ Farm Innovators Inc ....E 574 936-5096
   Plymouth *(G-11683)*

Furnace Design Technology LLC ....G 317 896-5506
   Westfield *(G-14164)*

George Koch Sons LLC ....C 812 465-9600
   Evansville *(G-3519)*

Gillespie Mrrell Gen Contg LLC ....G 765 618-4084
   Marion *(G-9526)*

Green Fast Cure LLC ....G 812 486-2510
   Montgomery *(G-10227)*

▲ Heat Wagons Inc ....G 219 464-8818
   Valparaiso *(G-13555)*

Hoosier Metal Polish Inc ....F 219 474-6011
   Kentland *(G-8520)*

▲ IDI Fabrication Inc ....D 317 776-6577
   Noblesville *(G-11123)*

Industrial Combustn Engineers ....E 219 949-5066
   Gary *(G-5068)*

Infrared Technologies LLC ....G 317 326-2019
   Greenfield *(G-5541)*

Light Beam Technologies Inc ....G 260 635-2195
   Kimmell *(G-8530)*

Midwest Finishing Systems Inc ....E 574 257-0099
   Mishawaka *(G-10087)*

Ndiana Warm Floors Inc ....G 260 668-8836
   Angola *(G-232)*

Pac Corporation ....G 260 637-8792
   Fort Wayne *(G-4517)*

Power Plant Service Inc ....E 260 432-6716
   Fort Wayne *(G-4542)*

R & K Incinerator Inc ....G 260 565-3214
   Decatur *(G-2400)*

Reward Inc ....F 574 936-7196
   Plymouth *(G-11721)*

◆ Rogers Engineering and Mfg Co .....E 765 478-5444
   Cambridge City *(G-1261)*

Sherwood-Templeton Coal Co Inc ....G 812 232-7037
   Terre Haute *(G-13325)*

Templeton Coal Company Inc ....G 812 232-7037
   Terre Haute *(G-13350)*

Thermal Product Solutions ....G 708 758-6530
   Schererville *(G-12348)*

Thermal Tech & Temp Inc ....G 219 808-1258
   Crown Point *(G-2313)*

Thermo Transfer Inc ....F 317 398-3503
   Shelbyville *(G-12575)*

Universal Door Carrier Inc ....G 317 241-3447
   Indianapolis *(G-8129)*

W C Grant Company Incorporated ....F 260 484-6688
   Markle *(G-9583)*

Wax Connections Inc ....G 219 778-2325
   Rolling Prairie *(G-12195)*

3568 Mechanical Power Transmission Eqpt, NEC

Advanced Bearing Materials LLC ......E 812 663-3401
   Greensburg *(G-5589)*

▲ Aisin Drivetrain Inc ....C 812 793-2427
   Crothersville *(G-2214)*

◆ Allied Enterprises Inc ....E 765 288-8849
   Muncie *(G-10428)*

▲ Auburn Gear LLC ....C 260 925-3200
   Auburn *(G-313)*

Bearing Service Company PA ....G 773 734-5132
   Griffith *(G-5765)*

▲ Bludot Inc ....G 574 277-2306
   South Bend *(G-12723)*

▲ Cablecraft Motion Controls LLC ......B 260 749-5105
   New Haven *(G-10933)*

Drake Corporation ....E 812 683-2101
   Jasper *(G-8246)*

Eaton Corporation ....C 260 925-3800
   Auburn *(G-328)*

Eaton Corporation ....D 574 288-4446
   South Bend *(G-12756)*

Eaton Corporation ....F 317 704-2520
   Indianapolis *(G-6796)*

Fairfield Manufacturing Co Inc ....C 765 772-4547
   Lafayette *(G-8895)*

Fort Wayne Clutch Inc ....F 260 484-8505
   Fort Wayne *(G-4271)*

Friskney Gear & Machine Corp ....G 260 281-2200
   Corunna *(G-2084)*

Guardian Couplings LLC ....G 219 874-5248
   Michigan City *(G-9798)*

▲ Guardian Ind Inc ....G 219 874-5248
   Michigan City *(G-9799)*

▲ Ktr Corporation ....E 219 872-9100
   Michigan City *(G-9807)*

Millennium Supply Inc ....G 765 764-7000
   Attica *(G-307)*

▲ Nachi America Inc ....C 317 535-5527
   Greenwood *(G-5726)*

NSK Corporation ....B 765 458-5000
   Liberty *(G-9267)*

NSK Precision America Inc ....C 317 738-5000
   Franklin *(G-4916)*

Odin Corporation of Delaware ....G 317 849-3770
   Indianapolis *(G-7610)*

Parker-Hannifin Corporation ....G 260 894-7125
   Ligonier *(G-9292)*

Prox Company Inc ....F 812 232-4324
   Terre Haute *(G-13311)*

Pruett Manufacturing Co Inc ....F 812 234-9497
   Terre Haute *(G-13312)*

Rexnord Industries LLC ....B 865 220-7700
   Avon *(G-463)*

Rexnord Industries LLC ....D 317 273-5500
   Avon *(G-464)*

▲ Sanlo Inc ....D 219 879-0241
   Michigan City *(G-9841)*

Siemens Industry Inc...................D....... 219 763-7927
  Portage *(G-11794)*

Sparks Belting Company Inc..........G....... 800 451-4537
  Hammond *(G-5945)*

▲ Star Engineering & Mch Co Inc ....E....... 260 824-4825
  Bluffton *(G-894)*

Steel Parts Corporation.................B....... 765 675-2191
  Tipton *(G-13406)*

Tecumseh Products Company ....B....... 812 883-3575
  Salem *(G-12307)*

Tesla Wireless Company LLC...............G....... 219 363-7922
  Wanatah *(G-13826)*

Uniseal Inc........................G....... 812 425-1361
  Evansville *(G-3785)*

3569 Indl Machinery & Eqpt, NEC

ABB Flexible Automation Inc...............E....... 317 876-9090
  Indianapolis *(G-6307)*

▼ Action Filtration Inc ....G....... 812 546-6262
  Hope *(G-6110)*

Adaptek Systems Inc ....E....... 260 637-8660
  Fort Wayne *(G-4041)*

Agi International Inc ....F....... 317 536-2415
  Indianapolis *(G-6352)*

▲ Alpha-Pure Corporation ....G....... 877 645-7676
  Trail Creek *(G-13440)*

Amatrol Inc ....C....... 812 288-8285
  Jeffersonville *(G-8322)*

Arbuckle Industries Inc ....G....... 317 835-7489
  Fairland *(G-3819)*

Asl Technologies LLC ....G....... 219 733-2777
  Wanatah *(G-13820)*

▲ Avis Industrial Corporation ....E....... 765 998-8100
  Upland *(G-13468)*

▼ Banks Machine & Engrg Inc...........D....... 317 642-4980
  Shelbyville *(G-12519)*

Beatty International Inc ....E....... 219 931-3000
  Hammond *(G-5846)*

Bemcor Inc ....F....... 219 937-1600
  Hammond *(G-5850)*

Best Machine Co Inc.................G....... 765 827-0250
  Connersville *(G-2041)*

▼ Bofrebo Industries Inc............G....... 219 322-1550
  Schererville *(G-12318)*

▲ Boyer Machine & Tool Co Inc...........E....... 812 379-9581
  Columbus *(G-1861)*

◆ Burgess Enterprises LLC ....G....... 260 615-5194
  Albion *(G-18)*

C&S Machinery Inc ....G....... 812 937-2160
  Dale *(G-2331)*

Cardinal Services Inc Indiana..............E....... 574 371-1305
  Warsaw *(G-13854)*

Centrifuge Chicago Corporation ....G....... 219 852-5200
  Hammond *(G-5859)*

Clear Decision Filtration Inc ......F....... 219 567-2008
  Francesville *(G-4809)*

Cpp Filter Corporation.................G....... 765 446-8416
  Lafayette *(G-8881)*

Don Detzer LLC ....G....... 812 362-7599
  Tennyson *(G-13179)*

Donaldson Company Inc ....G....... 952 887-3131
  Monticello *(G-10260)*

Donaldson Company Inc ....G....... 317 838-5568
  Plainfield *(G-11606)*

Duesenburg Inc........................G....... 260 496-9650
  Fort Wayne *(G-4223)*

▲ East Chicago Machine Tool Sls ....D....... 219 663-4525
  Crown Point *(G-2248)*

Enpak LLC ....G....... 574 268-7273
  Warsaw *(G-13873)*

Enviro Filtration Inc ....G....... 815 469-2871
  Gary *(G-5044)*

Esco Technologies Inc ....G....... 317 346-0393
  Franklin *(G-4884)*

F D Deskins Company Inc ....G....... 317 284-4014
  Fishers *(G-3909)*

Faztech LLC ....G....... 812 327-0926
  Bloomington *(G-723)*

Federal Assembly Inc ....G....... 812 386-7062
  Princeton *(G-11871)*

Filters Plus ....G....... 812 430-0347
  Evansville *(G-3504)*

Filtration Plus Inc ....E....... 219 879-0663
  Michigan City *(G-9793)*

Glaze Tool and Engineering Inc............E....... 260 493-4557
  New Haven *(G-10941)*

GLS Machining & Design LLC ....G....... 765 754-8248
  Alexandria *(G-44)*

Guardian Fire Systems Inc................F....... 317 752-2768
  Fortville *(G-4777)*

Gvs Filter Technology Inc ....G....... 317 442-3925
  Zionsville *(G-14437)*

Heartland Filled Machine LLC...........G....... 574 223-6931
  Rochester *(G-12127)*

Helmuth Quality Power System...........G....... 574 457-2002
  Syracuse *(G-13133)*

Homer Banes........................G....... 765 449-8551
  Lafayette *(G-8917)*

Hook Industrial Sales Inc ....D....... 260 432-9441
  Fort Wayne *(G-4342)*

Horizon Atomtn Fabrication LLC...........G....... 765 896-9491
  Muncie *(G-10492)*

▲ Hy-Pro Corporation ....D....... 317 849-3535
  Anderson *(G-117)*

Hy-Tech Machining Systems LLC........F....... 765 649-6852
  Anderson *(G-118)*

Hydro Fire Protection Inc ....E....... 317 780-6980
  Indianapolis *(G-7151)*

▲ Industrial Mint Wldg Machining ....E....... 219 393-5531
  Kingsbury *(G-8539)*

J-I-T Distributing Inc...................D....... 574 251-0292
  South Bend *(G-12821)*

Jenco Engineering Inc..................G....... 574 267-4608
  Warsaw *(G-13895)*

Joyce/Dayton Corp ....D....... 260 726-9361
  Portland *(G-11831)*

Leasenet Incorporated ....G....... 317 575-4098
  Indianapolis *(G-7392)*

▼ Lesac Corporation ....E....... 219 879-3215
  Michigan City *(G-9810)*

Lube-Line Corporation ....G....... 260 637-3779
  Fort Wayne *(G-4442)*

Maxim Automation Inc ....G....... 317 418-9561
  Fishers *(G-3945)*

Melrose Group LLC ....G....... 317 437-6784
  Indianapolis *(G-7477)*

Midwest Fabrication LLC ....G....... 574 276-5041
  Granger *(G-5422)*

▲ Nachi America Inc ....C....... 317 535-5527
  Greenwood *(G-5726)*

Nichols Operating LLC ....G....... 812 753-3600
  Fort Branch *(G-4028)*

Perma Lubrication ....G....... 219 531-9155
  Valparaiso *(G-13597)*

Perma Lubrication ....G....... 317 241-0797
  Indianapolis *(G-7679)*

▲ Phoenix Assembly LLC ....D....... 317 884-3600
  Greenwood *(G-5732)*

▲ Phoenix Assembly Indiana LLC.........E....... 317 884-3600
  Columbus *(G-1995)*

Pillar Innovations LLC ....G....... 812 474-9080
  Evansville *(G-3670)*

Pittsfield Products Inc ....D....... 260 488-2124
  Hamilton *(G-5826)*

Power Drives Inc ....G....... 812 344-4351
  Columbus *(G-1997)*

Rosedale Filters LLC ....G....... 219 879-4700
  Michigan City *(G-9835)*

S&F Manufacturing Inc..................D....... 574 278-7865
  Winamac *(G-14321)*

Separation By Design Inc ....G....... 812 424-1239
  Evansville *(G-3722)*

Shamrock Engineering Inc................E....... 812 867-0009
  Oakland City *(G-11315)*

Spencer Machine and TI Co Inc.........E....... 812 282-6300
  Jeffersonville *(G-8426)*

SRK Filters LLC.........................G....... 765 647-9962
  Cedar Grove *(G-1523)*

Star Automation Inc ....G....... 812 475-9947
  Evansville *(G-3747)*

◆ Sullair LLC ....B....... 219 879-5451
  Michigan City *(G-9849)*

Summit Manufacturing Corp..........G....... 317 823-2848
  Indianapolis *(G-8016)*

Systems Engineering and Sls Co........G....... 260 422-1671
  Fort Wayne *(G-4671)*

T and T Hydraulics Inc ....G....... 765 548-2355
  Rosedale *(G-12207)*

▲ Task Force Tips Inc...................C....... 219 462-6161
  Valparaiso *(G-13626)*

Thomas L Wehr ....G....... 317 835-7824
  Fairland *(G-3827)*

Tier 1 Medical LLC ....G....... 317 316-7871
  Carmel *(G-1497)*

U S Filter ....G....... 317 280-4251
  Indianapolis *(G-8121)*

U S Filter Distribution ....G....... 317 271-1463
  Indianapolis *(G-8122)*

United States Filter ....G....... 812 471-0414
  Evansville *(G-3788)*

▲ US Centrifuge Systems LLC ....F....... 317 299-2020
  Indianapolis *(G-8136)*

▲ US Innovation Group Inc ....F....... 800 899-2040
  Indianapolis *(G-8137)*

Via Development Corp..................E....... 888 225-5842
  Marion *(G-9570)*

Wall Control Services Inc ....G....... 260 450-6411
  Fort Wayne *(G-4733)*

Webber Manufacturing Company........E....... 317 357-8681
  Indianapolis *(G-8181)*

3571 Electronic Computers

▲ 3btech Inc ....E....... 574 233-0508
  South Bend *(G-12688)*

A Is For Apple Learning Center ....G....... 219 629-3514
  Hammond *(G-5833)*

Alpha Prime Computers ....G....... 260 347-4800
  Kendallville *(G-8452)*

Appel-Olson LLC ....G....... 219 926-6679
  Westville *(G-14213)*

Apple American Group ....G....... 317 889-1167
  Greenwood *(G-5667)*

Apple American Language Inst ....G....... 812 867-7239
  Evansville *(G-3359)*

Apple Blossom Floral ....G....... 765 649-2480
  Anderson *(G-68)*

Apple Cyber LLC ....G....... 812 822-1341
  Bloomington *(G-663)*

Apple III LLC ....G....... 317 691-2869
  Carmel *(G-1313)*

Apple Inc...............................G....... 812 342-4225
  Columbus *(G-1855)*

Apple Ly Ever After Inc ....G....... 219 838-9397
  Highland *(G-6035)*

Apple Terrace LLC ....G....... 260 347-9400
  Kendallville *(G-8454)*

Bad Apple Macs LLC ....G....... 812 274-0469
  Madison *(G-9445)*

Bull Hn Info Systems Inc ....E....... 317 686-5500
  Indianapolis *(G-6521)*

C & K Enterprises Inc ....E....... 260 624-3123
  Angola *(G-201)*

Computer Solutions Systems Co ....F....... 812 235-9008
  Terre Haute *(G-13215)*

Country Club Computer ....G....... 317 271-4000
  Indianapolis *(G-6675)*

Creative Logic Equipment Corp ....G....... 317 271-1100
  Indianapolis *(G-6689)*

Custom Mtal Fnshng-Indiana LLC........G....... 765 489-4089
  Hagerstown *(G-5805)*

Dcs Car Audio ....G....... 812 437-8488
  Evansville *(G-3454)*

Ewireless LLC ....G....... 317 536-0400
  Indianapolis *(G-6887)*

Fletchs Apple Lane ....G....... 317 489-2697
  Indianapolis *(G-6934)*

Futuretek..............................G....... 317 631-0098
  Indianapolis *(G-6972)*

Gary Devoss ....G....... 765 369-2492
  Redkey *(G-11898)*

Green Apple Active LLC ....G....... 910 585-1151
  Westfield *(G-14167)*

Green Apple Active LLC ....G....... 317 698-1032
  Carmel *(G-1389)*

Green Apple Utilities Llc ....G....... 440 278-0183
  Zionsville *(G-14436)*

Greenfield Coffee Company.............G....... 317 498-9568
  Greenfield *(G-5533)*

Gregory & Appel ....G....... 317 823-0131
  Indianapolis *(G-7047)*

Gt Computers LLC ....G....... 502 550-7490
  New Albany *(G-10791)*

Happy Apple Educational Svcs ....G....... 765 338-9293
  Connersville *(G-2050)*

Hewlett-Packard Co ....G....... 765 534-4468
  Lapel *(G-9119)*

HP Inc...................................D....... 317 566-6200
  Indianapolis *(G-6268)*

HP Inc...................................A....... 317 334-3400
  Indianapolis *(G-7141)*

Indy Web Inc ....G....... 317 356-3622
  Indianapolis *(G-7224)*

Jacyl Technology Inc ....G....... 260 471-6067
  Fort Wayne *(G-4390)*

Kimball Electronics Inc ....B....... 812 634-4200
  Jasper *(G-8272)*

◆ Kimball Electronics Group LLC........A....... 812 634-4000
  Jasper *(G-8273)*

L5 Solutions LLC ....G....... 317 436-1044
  Indianapolis *(G-7371)*

S I C

Little Green Apple ....G....... 219 836-5025
Munster *(G-10616)*
Little Green Apple ....G....... 317 272-1168
Avon *(G-454)*
Little Green Apple ....G....... 812 853-8761
Newburgh *(G-11036)*
Little Green Apple Hallmark ....G....... 219 661-0420
Crown Point *(G-2277)*
Milani Custom Homes LLC ....G....... 219 455-5804
Merrillville *(G-9734)*
Oracle America Inc ....E....... 317 581-0078
Carmel *(G-1447)*
P F Apple LLC ....G....... 317 773-8683
Noblesville *(G-11163)*
Packetvac LLC ....G....... 317 414-6137
Indianapolis *(G-7647)*
PC Max Inc ....G....... 812 337-0630
Bloomington *(G-796)*
Prevail Design Systems LLC ....G....... 260 245-1245
Huntertown *(G-6145)*
▲ **Q-Edge Corporation** ....E....... 317 203-6800
Plainfield *(G-11638)*
Riddell Technologies LLC ....G....... 219 213-9602
Crown Point *(G-2296)*
Road Apple Psychotherapy ....G....... 574 230-3449
Knox *(G-8579)*

3572 Computer Storage Devices

EMC Corporation ....E....... 317 706-8600
Indianapolis *(G-6849)*
EMC Projects ....G....... 317 420-8005
Indianapolis *(G-6850)*
Emc2 ....G....... 317 435-8021
Indianapolis *(G-6851)*
Integrity Qntum Innvations LLC ....G....... 765 537-9037
Martinsville *(G-9617)*
Leroy R Sollars ....G....... 765 284-9417
Selma *(G-12424)*
Quantum 7 Group LLC ....G....... 812 824-9378
Bloomington *(G-804)*
Quantum Covers LLC ....G....... 219 307-0893
Valparaiso *(G-13605)*
Quantum Creative LLC ....G....... 812 381-2586
Bloomington *(G-805)*
Quantum Tech USA ....G....... 360 400-0905
Bloomington *(G-806)*
Quantumtech LLC ....G....... 786 512-0827
Indianapolis *(G-7803)*
R B Annis Instruments Inc ....G....... 765 848-1621
Greencastle *(G-5476)*
Scale Computing Inc ....E....... 317 856-9959
Indianapolis *(G-7901)*
▲ **Sony Dadc US Inc** ....A....... 812 462-8100
Terre Haute *(G-13334)*
Techknowledgey Inc ....G....... 574 971-4267
Goshen *(G-5339)*

3575 Computer Terminals

Bowmar LLC ....E....... 260 747-3121
Fort Wayne *(G-4116)*
C & P Distributing LLC ....E....... 574 256-1138
Mishawaka *(G-10016)*
Main Street Computers ....G....... 574 772-7890
Knox *(G-8572)*
Server Partners LLC ....G....... 317 917-2000
Indianapolis *(G-7916)*
Tempest Technical Sales Inc ....F....... 317 844-9236
Carmel *(G-1492)*

3577 Computer Peripheral Eqpt, NEC

Bull Hn Info Systems Inc ....E....... 317 686-5500
Indianapolis *(G-6521)*
C & G Labeling ....G....... 317 396-2953
Indianapolis *(G-6526)*
◆ **Carson Manufacturing Co Inc** ....F....... 317 257-3191
Indianapolis *(G-6560)*
Cisco Systems Inc ....E....... 317 816-5200
Carmel *(G-1339)*
Clovis LLC ....G....... 812 944-4791
Floyds Knobs *(G-4009)*
Environmental Technology Inc ....E....... 574 233-1202
South Bend *(G-12765)*
I E Signs & Graphics LLC ....G....... 574 936-4652
Plymouth *(G-11689)*
Impact Cnc LLC ....C....... 260 244-5511
Columbia City *(G-1794)*
La Zee Tek ....G....... 260 351-3274
Hudson *(G-6133)*
Laser Plus ....G....... 574 269-1246
Warsaw *(G-13901)*
Marteck Inc ....E....... 317 824-0240
Indianapolis *(G-7459)*
Motorola Inc ....G....... 765 455-5100
Kokomo *(G-8673)*
Ncs Pearson Inc ....D....... 317 297-0259
Indianapolis *(G-7580)*
Paradise Ink Inc ....G....... 812 402-4465
Evansville *(G-3662)*
PC Max Inc ....G....... 812 337-0630
Bloomington *(G-796)*
Printmaster LLC ....G....... 260 459-1900
Fort Wayne *(G-4561)*
Record / Play Tek Inc ....G....... 574 848-5233
Bristol *(G-1078)*
Scott Billman ....G....... 317 293-9921
Indianapolis *(G-7905)*
▲ **Sony Dadc US Inc** ....A....... 812 462-8100
Terre Haute *(G-13334)*
Syntag Rfld ....G....... 317 685-5292
Indianapolis *(G-8030)*
T n Z Technology LLC ....G....... 812 438-1205
Dillsboro *(G-2473)*
Whyte Haus ....G....... 260 484-5666
Fort Wayne *(G-4754)*
Xerox Corporation ....G....... 765 778-6249
Anderson *(G-183)*

3578 Calculating & Accounting Eqpt

Chase N Corydon ....F....... 812 738-3032
Corydon *(G-2092)*
Chase Southport Emerson ....G....... 317 266-7470
Indianapolis *(G-6594)*
Elmos ....G....... 574 371-2050
Warsaw *(G-13871)*
Fairfield Gas Way ....G....... 260 744-2186
Fort Wayne *(G-4253)*
Front End Digital Inc ....G....... 317 652-6134
Fishers *(G-3914)*
James R McNutt ....G....... 317 899-6955
Indianapolis *(G-7297)*
▲ **Jay Retail Systems LLC** ....G....... 574 842-2313
Culver *(G-2325)*
▲ **Standard Change-Makers Inc** ....C....... 317 899-6955
Indianapolis *(G-7987)*
Standard Change-Makers Inc ....F....... 317 899-6955
Indianapolis *(G-7988)*
Woundvision ....G....... 317 775-6054
Indianapolis *(G-8217)*

3579 Office Machines, NEC

Bach Tech Inc ....G....... 219 531-7424
Valparaiso *(G-13502)*
Bastian Automation Engrg LLC ....D....... 317 467-2583
Greenfield *(G-5507)*
Escalade Incorporated ....D....... 812 467-4449
Evansville *(G-3481)*
Glander ....G....... 317 889-1039
Greenwood *(G-5697)*
◆ **Martin Yale Industries LLC** ....C....... 260 563-0641
Wabash *(G-13737)*
Oce Copiers ....G....... 812 479-0000
Evansville *(G-3652)*
Pitney Bowes Inc ....G....... 317 769-8300
Whitestown *(G-14257)*
Pitney Bowes Inc ....E....... 260 436-7395
Indianapolis *(G-7698)*
Pitney Bowes Inc ....D....... 317 769-8300
Whitestown *(G-14258)*
Vernon A Stevens ....G....... 812 626-0010
Evansville *(G-3796)*
Voter Registration ....G....... 219 755-3795
Crown Point *(G-2319)*

3581 Automatic Vending Machines

Brashear ....G....... 219 778-2422
La Porte *(G-8741)*
Diane Dixon ....G....... 812 836-4179
Rome *(G-12196)*
▲ **Standard Change-Makers Inc** ....C....... 317 899-6955
Indianapolis *(G-7987)*
Window Man Inc ....G....... 317 755-3207
Indianapolis *(G-8203)*

3582 Commercial Laundry, Dry Clean & Pressing Mchs

Brian T Klem ....G....... 812 342-4080
Columbus *(G-1862)*
Chucks Cleaners ....G....... 260 488-3362
Hamilton *(G-5820)*
Commercial Laundry Equipment ....G....... 317 856-1234
Indianapolis *(G-6638)*
Donald L Gard ....G....... 219 663-7945
Crown Point *(G-2246)*
Hansford Prevent LLC ....G....... 317 985-2346
Indianapolis *(G-7071)*
Moores Inc ....G....... 574 533-6089
Goshen *(G-5297)*
Randolph Carpet-Tile Cleaning ....G....... 317 401-2300
Cicero *(G-1666)*
Steam Specialties Inc ....G....... 317 849-5601
Fishers *(G-3970)*
Upland Village Laundry LLC ....G....... 765 998-1260
Upland *(G-13475)*
W C Grant Company Incorporated ....F....... 260 484-6688
Markle *(G-9583)*

3585 Air Conditioning & Heating Eqpt

Advantage Engineering Inc ....D....... 317 887-0729
Greenwood *(G-5660)*
Air Systems Compents LP ....G....... 765 483-5841
Lebanon *(G-9166)*
Air Tech Comfort Systems ....G....... 219 663-9778
Cedar Lake *(G-1525)*
▲ **Air Technology Inc** ....G....... 574 231-0579
South Bend *(G-12696)*
Caliente LLC ....E....... 260 426-3800
Fort Wayne *(G-4137)*
Carrier Corporation ....D....... 317 243-0851
Indianapolis *(G-6559)*
Continental Carbonic Pdts Inc ....G....... 317 784-3311
Indianapolis *(G-6656)*
Crosspoint Power and Rfrgn LLC ....E....... 317 240-1967
Indianapolis *(G-6695)*
Crown Products & Services Inc ....G....... 317 564-4799
Carmel *(G-1349)*
Delivery Concepts Inc ....E....... 574 522-3981
Elkhart *(G-2793)*
Dometic Corporation ....B....... 260 463-7657
Lagrange *(G-9037)*
Duncan Service Company ....G....... 765 452-6799
Kokomo *(G-8618)*
Duncan Supply Co Inc ....G....... 765 446-0105
Lafayette *(G-8892)*
Elliott-Williams Company Inc ....D....... 317 453-2295
Indianapolis *(G-6843)*
Emerson Climate Tech Inc ....G....... 765 932-2956
Rushville *(G-12219)*
Emerson Climate Tech Inc ....G....... 937 498-3671
Greenfield *(G-5525)*
Emerson Climate Tech Inc ....B....... 765 932-1902
Rushville *(G-12220)*
Emerson Climate Tech Inc ....C....... 317 968-4250
Greenfield *(G-5526)*
Evansville Metal Products Inc ....E....... 812 421-6589
Evansville *(G-3488)*
Evansville Metal Products Inc ....D....... 812 423-5632
Evansville *(G-3487)*
Fletcher Heating & Cooling ....G....... 812 865-2984
Paoli *(G-11450)*
Flex-Tech Inc ....F....... 317 546-0183
Indianapolis *(G-6935)*
▲ **Flow Center Products Inc** ....G....... 765 364-9460
Crawfordsville *(G-2152)*
▲ **Geo-Flo Products Corporation** ....F....... 812 275-8513
Bedford *(G-546)*
Grayson Thermal Systems Corp ....C....... 317 739-3290
Franklin *(G-4893)*
Griffen Plmbng-Heating-Cooling ....E....... 574 295-2440
Elkhart *(G-2900)*
▲ **Grinon Industries LLC** ....E....... 317 388-5100
Indianapolis *(G-7051)*
Group Dekko Inc ....D....... 260 635-2134
Wolflake *(G-14379)*
Hrezo Industrial Eqp & Engrg ....F....... 812 537-4700
Greendale *(G-5489)*
Ilpea Industries Inc ....D....... 812 752-2526
Scottsburg *(G-12363)*
Industrial Combustn Engineers ....E....... 219 949-5066
Gary *(G-5068)*
Jlb Industrial LLC ....G....... 765 561-1751
Rushville *(G-12225)*
Lennox Ind Production Lxud 240 ....G....... 317 253-0353
Indianapolis *(G-7395)*
Lennox Lir Lennox Inds Intl ....G....... 317 334-1339
Indianapolis *(G-7396)*
Lute Supply ....G....... 260 480-2441
Fort Wayne *(G-4444)*
Madden Manufacturing Inc ....F....... 574 295-4292
Elkhart *(G-3013)*

▲ Manitowoc Beverage Eqp Inc .... C 812 246-7000
    Sellersburg *(G-12405)*

◆ Manitowoc Beverage Systems Inc .... A .. 800 367-4233
    Sellersburg *(G-12406)*

MD Moxie LLC .... E 260 347-1203
    Kendallville *(G-8494)*

◆ Mitsubishi Heavy Industries .... C ... 317 346-5000
    Franklin *(G-4911)*

Mitsubishi Heavy Industries .... E ... 714 960-3785
    Franklin *(G-4910)*

Mr Heat Inc .... G 219 345-5629
    Demotte *(G-2444)*

◆ Multiplex Company Inc .... G 812 246-7000
    Sellersburg *(G-12409)*

Parker-Hannifin Corporation .... A ... 260 748-6000
    New Haven *(G-10951)*

▼ Polar King International Inc .... E ... 260 428-2530
    Fort Wayne *(G-4536)*

▲ Proair LLC .... D 574 264-5494
    Elkhart *(G-3117)*

Proair LLC .... F 574 264-5494
    Elkhart *(G-3118)*

Qsens Equipment Solutions LLC .... G ... 317 443-6167
    Indianapolis *(G-7793)*

Ram Services Rfrgn & Mech .... G ... 317 679-8541
    Indianapolis *(G-7815)*

Redi/Controls Inc .... G 317 494-6600
    Franklin *(G-4926)*

Refrigeration Package Corp .... G ... 812 867-0900
    Evansville *(G-3701)*

Rheem Sales Company Inc .... G ... 479 648-4900
    Indianapolis *(G-7836)*

Stanton & Associates Inc .... G 574 247-5522
    Granger *(G-5441)*

Stewart Warner South Wind .... G ... 812 547-7071
    Indianapolis *(G-8005)*

Superior Distribution .... G 618 242-5560
    Indianapolis *(G-8021)*

◆ Supreme Corporation .... A 574 642-4888
    Goshen *(G-5332)*

Supreme Corporation .... B ... 260 894-9191
    Ligonier *(G-9298)*

Templeton Coal Company Inc .... D ... 812 232-7037
    Terre Haute *(G-13351)*

Thermo Products LLC .... D 574 896-2133
    North Judson *(G-11214)*

Thomas P Kasten .... G 574 806-4663
    Winamac *(G-14322)*

◆ Toyota Industries N Amer Inc .... B ... 812 341-3810
    Columbus *(G-2025)*

Trane US Inc .... D 812 421-8725
    Evansville *(G-3768)*

Trane US Inc .... G 317 255-8777
    Indianapolis *(G-8090)*

Trane US Inc .... E 574 282-4880
    South Bend *(G-12976)*

Trane US Inc .... E 260 489-0884
    Fort Wayne *(G-4697)*

Trane US Inc .... D 765 932-7200
    Rushville *(G-12236)*

▲ Twin Air Products Inc .... G 574 295-1129
    Elkhart *(G-3230)*

Validated Custom Solutions LLC .... G ... 317 259-7604
    Indianapolis *(G-8145)*

Washburn Heating & AC .... G 574 825-7697
    Middlebury *(G-9924)*

Webber Manufacturing Company .... E ... 317 357-8681
    Indianapolis *(G-8181)*

Whirlpool Corporation .... C 812 426-4000
    Evansville *(G-3811)*

3586 Measuring & Dispensing Pumps

Chemical Control Systems Inc .... G ... 219 465-5103
    Griffith *(G-5770)*

Cortex Safety Technologies LLC .... G ... 317 414-5607
    Carmel *(G-1344)*

Dispensit .... G 317 776-8740
    Noblesville *(G-11095)*

▼ Indco Inc .... G 812 945-4383
    New Albany *(G-10805)*

Madden Manufacturing Inc .... F ... 574 295-4292
    Elkhart *(G-3013)*

Rj Fuel Services Inc .... G 812 350-2897
    Edinburgh *(G-2625)*

Royal Adhesives & Sealants LLC .... E ... 574 246-5000
    South Bend *(G-12921)*

Separation By Design Inc .... G ... 812 424-1239
    Evansville *(G-3722)*

3589 Service Ind Machines, NEC

A&M Commercial Cleaning LLC .... G ... 765 720-3737
    Greencastle *(G-5453)*

Accutemp Products Inc .... D 260 493-0415
    Fort Wayne *(G-4039)*

Algaewheel Inc .... G 317 582-1400
    Indianapolis *(G-6364)*

American Hydro Systems Inc .... F ... 866 357-5063
    Fort Wayne *(G-4071)*

◆ American Melt Blown Filtration .... E ... 219 866-3500
    Rensselaer *(G-11912)*

Aqseptence Group Inc .... D 574 223-3980
    Rochester *(G-12116)*

Aqua Blast Corp .... F 260 728-4433
    Decatur *(G-2368)*

Astbury Water Technology Inc .... D ... 317 328-7153
    Indianapolis *(G-6431)*

Avon Mobile Wash .... G 317 517-1890
    Avon *(G-431)*

▲ Bio-Response Solutions Inc .... G ... 317 386-3500
    Danville *(G-2343)*

▲ Bottom Line Management Inc .... F ... 812 944-7388
    Clarksville *(G-1674)*

Brockwood Farm .... G 812 837-9607
    Nashville *(G-10716)*

▲ Canature USA Inc .... G 877 771-6789
    Carmel *(G-1326)*

▲ Canature Watergroup Usa Inc .... G ... 877 771-6789
    Carmel *(G-1327)*

Chem-Aqua .... G 317 899-3660
    Indianapolis *(G-6597)*

Chemical Control Systems Inc .... G ... 219 465-5103
    Griffith *(G-5770)*

City of Anderson .... D 765 648-6560
    Anderson *(G-85)*

City of Columbia City .... G ... 260 248-5118
    Columbia City *(G-1773)*

Clover Industrial Services LLC .... E ... 317 879-5001
    Indianapolis *(G-6625)*

Clute Enterprises Inc .... G 260 413-0810
    Huntertown *(G-6135)*

Commercial Star Inc .... F 765 386-2800
    Coatesville *(G-1747)*

Crestwood Equity Partners LP .... G ... 812 265-3313
    Madison *(G-9455)*

D K Tools & Engineering .... G 812 325-4532
    Morgantown *(G-10351)*

Davis Water Services Inc .... G ... 219 394-2270
    Rensselaer *(G-11920)*

▲ East Chicago Machine Tool Sls .... D ... 219 663-4525
    Crown Point *(G-2248)*

Eco Water of Southern Indiana .... G ... 812 734-1407
    New Salisbury *(G-11009)*

Environmental Management & Dev .... G ... 765 874-1539
    Lynn *(G-9426)*

Evoqua Water Technologies LLC .... G ... 317 280-4255
    Indianapolis *(G-6884)*

Ferguson Waterworks .... G 219 440-5254
    Schererville *(G-12321)*

Flora Wastewater Treatment .... G ... 574 967-3005
    Flora *(G-3996)*

Forecast Sales Inc .... G 317 829-0147
    Indianapolis *(G-6948)*

Freije Treatment Systems Inc .... E ... 888 766-7258
    Fishers *(G-3913)*

Freije Treatment Systems Inc .... G ... 317 508-3848
    Indianapolis *(G-6964)*

Global Water Technologies Inc .... G ... 317 452-4488
    Indianapolis *(G-7013)*

H20 Factory .... G 812 858-1948
    Newburgh *(G-11030)*

◆ Hanlon Solutions Resource Inc .... G ... 317 776-4880
    Noblesville *(G-11118)*

▼ Hawk Enterprises Elkhart Inc .... F ... 574 264-6772
    Elkhart *(G-2911)*

Hintz Equipment Inc .... G 765 362-6115
    Thorntown *(G-13375)*

Hoosier Truck & Trailer Srv .... G ... 317 887-4887
    Indianapolis *(G-7126)*

Hose & Go .... G 574 295-7800
    Elkhart *(G-2921)*

Indiana Concession Supply LLC .... F ... 317 353-1667
    Indianapolis *(G-7178)*

Industrial Services Group Inc .... F ... 317 334-0921
    Indianapolis *(G-7210)*

Jatech Scientific Inc .... G 765 345-2085
    Knightstown *(G-8553)*

Kelley Cadillac LLC .... G 260 434-4646
    Fort Wayne *(G-4406)*

Kemtune Inc .... G 260 745-0722
    Fort Wayne *(G-4408)*

Kendle Custom Inc .... G 812 985-5917
    Evansville *(G-3583)*

Kessco Water LLC .... G 765 362-3890
    Crawfordsville *(G-2165)*

Kirklin Waste Water Treatment .... G ... 765 279-5251
    Kirklin *(G-8549)*

Laserwash .... G 765 359-0582
    Crawfordsville *(G-2167)*

Leach & Sons WaterCare .... G ... 317 248-8954
    Danville *(G-2351)*

Leistner Aquatic Services Inc .... G ... 317 535-6099
    Whiteland *(G-14242)*

Leslie-Fisher Engineering Inc .... G ... 765 457-7796
    Kokomo *(G-8658)*

▼ Lonn Manufacturing Inc .... G 317 897-1440
    Indianapolis *(G-7417)*

▲ M D Holdings LLC .... G 317 831-7030
    Mooresville *(G-10319)*

Markle Water Treatment Plant .... G ... 260 758-3482
    Markle *(G-9580)*

Meister Cook LLC .... G 260 399-6692
    Fort Wayne *(G-4464)*

Michiana Carwash Systems LLC .... G ... 574 320-2331
    Goshen *(G-5288)*

Michrochem LLC .... G 812 838-1832
    Mount Vernon *(G-10401)*

Mid State Water Treatment .... G ... 765 884-1220
    Fowler *(G-4802)*

▲ Mohawk Laboratories .... G 317 899-3660
    Indianapolis *(G-7534)*

New Aqua LLC .... D 317 272-3000
    Avon *(G-456)*

Olympia Business Systems Inc .... F ... 800 225-5644
    Wabash *(G-13744)*

On The Go Portble Wtr Sftnr LL .... F ... 260 482-9614
    Bloomington *(G-788)*

Onion Enterprises Inc .... G 317 762-6007
    Indianapolis *(G-7623)*

Pats Cleaning Service Rob .... G ... 574 272-3067
    South Bend *(G-12888)*

Precision Chemical LLC .... G 317 570-1538
    Fishers *(G-3958)*

Pressure Systems Inc .... F 317 755-3050
    Indianapolis *(G-7743)*

Proshred Indianapolis Inc .... F 317 578-3650
    Indianapolis *(G-7780)*

Puritan Water Conditioning .... F ... 765 362-6340
    Crawfordsville *(G-2189)*

Samco Inc .... G 812 926-4282
    Sunman *(G-13116)*

SDP Manufacturing Inc .... F 765 768-5000
    Dunkirk *(G-2488)*

SSP Technologies Inc .... G 888 548-4668
    Chesterton *(G-1632)*

Stop & Shred .... G 260 483-6200
    Fort Wayne *(G-4653)*

Super Car Wash of Warsaw .... F ... 574 269-6922
    Warsaw *(G-13943)*

Supper Wash .... G 574 269-2233
    Warsaw *(G-13944)*

Taggarts Custom Sndblst LLC .... G ... 765 825-4584
    Connersville *(G-2074)*

Technical Water Treatment Inc .... G ... 574 277-1949
    Granger *(G-5444)*

Thermodyne Food Service Pdts .... E ... 260 428-2535
    Fort Wayne *(G-4682)*

▲ Thomas Green LLC .... G 317 337-0000
    Indianapolis *(G-8064)*

True Chem Inc .... G 317 769-2701
    Greenwood *(G-5756)*

US Water Systems Inc .... F 317 209-0889
    Indianapolis *(G-8138)*

Wall Control Services Inc .... G 260 450-6411
    Fort Wayne *(G-4733)*

Watcon Inc .... F 574 287-3397
    South Bend *(G-12988)*

Water Energizers Inc .... F 812 288-6900
    Jeffersonville *(G-8440)*

Water Tec LLC .... G 219 554-1790
    Hammond *(G-5957)*

Western Wyne Rgonal Sewage Dst 765 478-3788
    Cambridge City *(G-1263)*

3592 Carburetors, Pistons, Rings & Valves

Consolidated Pipe & Valve 574 262-3758
    Elkhart *(G-2769)*

Dover Corporation .... C 502 587-6783
    Jeffersonville *(G-8352)*

Federal-Mogul Powertrain LLC ....B 574 271-5954
South Bend (G-12776)

Parker-Hannifin Corporation ....E 260 587-9102
Ashley (G-289)

Precision Rings Incorporated ....E 317 247-4786
Indianapolis (G-7736)

Stfrancis Mdwest Hart Vlve Ctr ....G 877 788-2583
Indianapolis (G-8006)

Tecumseh Products Company ....B 812 883-3575
Salem (G-12307)

Tri State Valve Instrument Co ....G 812 434-0141
Evansville (G-3772)

Valve Serve LLC ....G 260 421-1927
Fort Wayne (G-4723)

▲ Victor Reinz Valve Seals LLC ....D 260 897-2827
Avilla (G-420)

3593 Fluid Power Cylinders & Actuators

Actuant Corporation ....E 574 254-1428
Mishawaka (G-9990)

Advantage Fluid Systems LLC ....G 800 317-1570
Indianapolis (G-6338)

Elevator Equipment Corporation ....D 765 966-7761
Richmond (G-11981)

▲ Five Star Hydraulics Inc ....E 219 762-1619
Portage (G-11763)

Hook Industrial Sales Inc ....F 317 545-8100
Indianapolis (G-7119)

International Automation Inc ....E 260 747-6151
Fort Wayne (G-4379)

▲ K M Specialty Pumps Inc ....F 812 925-3000
Chandler (G-1550)

▲ Logansport Machine Co Inc ....E 574 735-0225
Logansport (G-9350)

Micro-Precision Operations ....E 260 589-2136
Berne (G-620)

▼ Micromatic LLC ....D 260 589-2136
Berne (G-621)

PHD Inc ....G 260 747-6151
Fort Wayne (G-4527)

▼ R P S Hydraulics Sales & Svc ....E 219 845-5526
Hammond (G-5931)

▲ SMC Corporation of America ....B 317 899-3182
Noblesville (G-11184)

3594 Fluid Power Pumps & Motors

American Gorwood Corporation ....E 765 948-3401
Fairmount (G-3829)

Camco Manufacturing Inc ....F 574 264-1491
Elkhart (G-2747)

Crown Elec Svcs & Automtn Inc ....D 972 929-4700
Portage (G-11758)

D A Hochstetler & Sons LLP ....F 574 642-1144
Topeka (G-13416)

Deutsch LLC ....G 219 464-1557
Valparaiso (G-13528)

Elevator Equipment Corporation ....D 765 966-7761
Richmond (G-11981)

Freudenberg-Nok General Partnr ....B 260 894-7183
Ligonier (G-9285)

Gravel Conveyors Inc ....F 317 873-8686
Zionsville (G-14435)

Hy-Matic Mfg Inc ....E 260 347-3651
Kendallville (G-8479)

Hydro-Gear Inc ....E 317 821-0477
Indianapolis (G-7152)

Jomar Machining & Fabg Inc ....E 574 825-9837
Middlebury (G-9897)

Met-Pro Technologies LLC ....E 317 293-2930
Indianapolis (G-7485)

▲ Murray Equipment Inc ....D 260 484-0382
Fort Wayne (G-4406)

Nidec Motor Corporation ....D 812 385-2564
Princeton (G-11880)

Parker-Hannifin Corporation ....F 219 736-0400
Merrillville (G-9744)

Parker-Hannifin Corporation ....E 812 547-4710
Tell City (G-13171)

Parker-Hannifin Corporation ....G 502 810-5823
Jeffersonville (G-8412)

Parker-Hannifin Corporation ....C 574 528-9400
Syracuse (G-13139)

▼ R P S Hydraulics Sales & Svc ....E 219 845-5526
Hammond (G-5931)

Steel Parts Corporation ....B 765 675-2191
Tipton (G-13406)

◆ Terra Drive Systems Inc ....C 219 279-2801
Brookston (G-1108)

Terry Liquidation III Inc ....E 219 362-3557
La Porte (G-8829)

3596 Scales & Balances, Exc Laboratory

A H Emery Company ....E 812 466-5265
Terre Haute (G-13184)

Cullman Casting Corporation ....G 256 735-0900
North Vernon (G-11251)

▲ Indiana Scale Company Inc ....F 812 232-0893
Terre Haute (G-13255)

Indianapolis Scale Company ....G 317 856-6606
Lafayette (G-8923)

Powell Systems Inc ....E 765 884-0980
Fowler (G-4805)

Raco Industries LLC ....G 812 232-3676
Terre Haute (G-13314)

▲ Richards Scale Company ....G 812 246-3354
Sellersburg (G-12412)

Sinden Racing Service Inc ....F 317 243-7171
Indianapolis (G-7949)

▲ Technical Weighing Svcs Inc ....E 219 924-3366
Griffith (G-5793)

Valley Scale Company LLC ....F 812 282-5269
Clarksville (G-1699)

Winslow Scale Company ....D 812 466-5265
Terre Haute (G-13370)

3599 Machinery & Eqpt, Indl & Commercial, NEC

3d Machine Inc ....E 219 297-3674
Goodland (G-5156)

3rd Dimension LLC ....G 317 941-7958
Indianapolis (G-6290)

A & A Manufacturing Co Inc ....G 219 462-0822
Valparaiso (G-13479)

A & M Tool Inc ....G 812 934-6533
Batesville (G-488)

A & R Machine Shop LLP ....E 574 825-5686
Middlebury (G-9866)

A P Machine & Tool Inc ....F 812 232-4939
Terre Haute (G-13185)

▼ A-1 Production Inc ....E 260 347-0960
Kendallville (G-8450)

Absolute Custom Machine LLC ....G 812 724-2284
Owensville (G-11426)

Absolute Machining Inc ....G 260 747-4568
Fort Wayne (G-4034)

▲ Accraline Inc ....E 574 546-3484
Bremen (G-981)

Acme Industrial Inc ....E 260 422-6518
Columbia City (G-1759)

▲ Acro Engineering Inc ....E 812 663-6236
Greensburg (G-5588)

▲ Action Machine Inc ....F 574 287-9650
South Bend (G-12694)

Adept Tool and Engineering ....G 317 896-9250
Carmel (G-1302)

Advance Machine Works Corp ....E 260 483-1183
Fort Wayne (G-4042)

Advance Repair & Machining ....G 765 474-8000
Lafayette (G-8846)

▲ Advanced Machine & Tool Corp ....C 260 489-3572
Fort Wayne (G-4044)

Advanced Metal Etching Inc ....E 260 894-4189
Ligonier (G-9275)

Advantage Components Corp ....G 317 784-0299
Indianapolis (G-6337)

Aegis Sales & Engineering Inc ....F 260 483-4160
Fort Wayne (G-4048)

Aero Machine LLC ....E 219 548-0490
Valparaiso (G-13485)

▲ Aeromet Industries Inc ....D 219 924-7442
Griffith (G-5761)

▲ Ahaus Tool & Engineering Inc ....D 765 962-3573
Richmond (G-11952)

Aj Machine Inc ....G 260 248-4900
Columbia City (G-1762)

Ald Indy Inc ....G 317 826-3833
Fishers (G-3867)

All Points Tool & Mfg ....G 574 935-3944
Plymouth (G-11663)

▲ Alliance Tool & Equipment Inc ....F 260 432-2909
Fort Wayne (G-4060)

Allied Specialty Precision Inc ....D 574 255-4718
Mishawaka (G-9994)

American Fabricated Carbide Co ....E 317 773-5520
Noblesville (G-11059)

American Industrial McHy Inc ....F 219 755-4090
Merrillville (G-9697)

American Precision Svcs Inc ....E 219 977-4451
Gary (G-5027)

▲ AMG Engineering Machining Inc ....E 317 329-4000
Indianapolis (G-6396)

AMS Productions Machining Inc ....E 317 838-9273
Plainfield (G-11592)

◆ Amt Precision Parts Inc ....E 260 490-0223
Fort Wayne (G-4076)

Angola Wire Products Inc ....E 260 665-3061
Angola (G-193)

Apex Sales & Repair Llc ....E 812 248-9001
Sellersburg (G-12388)

Apollo Precision Machining Inc ....E 574 271-1197
South Bend (G-12708)

Applied Metals & Mch Works Inc ....E 260 424-4834
Fort Wayne (G-4083)

Aqua Nova ....G 812 941-8995
Floyds Knobs (G-4006)

Atlas Die LLC ....D 574 295-0277
Elkhart (G-2700)

Atlas Machine and Supply Inc ....F 812 423-7762
Evansville (G-3367)

Austin & Austin Inc ....F 574 586-2320
Goshen (G-5173)

Auto Center Inc ....G 317 545-3360
Indianapolis (G-6442)

Auto Specialty of Lafayette ....G 765 446-2311
Lafayette (G-8857)

Auto Truck Group LLC ....E 260 356-1610
Huntington (G-6188)

Avf Machining ....G 260 760-1531
Butler (G-1222)

B & C Machining Inc ....E 219 924-5411
Rensselaer (G-11915)

B & F Machine Products ....G 574 255-7447
Mishawaka (G-10002)

▲ B & J Specialty Inc ....D 260 761-5011
Wawaka (G-14029)

B S T Enterprises Inc ....G 260 493-4313
New Haven (G-10930)

▲ B&J Rocket America Inc ....E 574 825-5802
Middlebury (G-9874)

Banco Industries Inc ....F 260 347-9524
Kendallville (G-8460)

▼ Banks Machine & Engrg Inc ....D 317 642-4980
Shelbyville (G-12519)

Bbs Enterprises Inc ....E 574 255-3173
Mishawaka (G-10006)

Bcd & Associates ....G 317 873-5394
Zionsville (G-14421)

Beatty International Inc ....E 219 931-3000
Hammond (G-5846)

Beatty Machine & Mfg Co ....D 219 931-3000
Hammond (G-5847)

Bedford Machine & Tool Inc ....E 812 275-1948
Bedford (G-533)

Bel-Mar Products Corporation ....G 317 769-3262
Whitestown (G-14249)

Bemcor Inc ....F 219 937-1600
Hammond (G-5850)

Bishop Repair ....G 812 523-3246
Crothersville (G-2216)

Blackpoint Engineering LLC ....G 574 642-3152
Ligonier (G-9277)

Bolinger Machine Co ....F 317 241-2989
Indianapolis (G-6494)

Boreco Industries Inc ....G 574 255-4149
Mishawaka (G-10012)

▲ Boyer Machine & Tool Co Inc ....E 812 379-9581
Columbus (G-1861)

Brewer Machine & Mfg Inc ....E 317 398-3505
Shelbyville (G-12525)

Bristol Tool and Die Inc ....F 574 848-5354
Bristol (G-1050)

Browell Enterprises Inc ....F 765 447-2292
Lafayette (G-8865)

Bryan Machine Service Inc ....G 260 356-5530
Huntington (G-6195)

Bryant Industries Inc ....F 812 944-6010
New Albany (G-10755)

Bryant Machining & Welding LLC ....G 260 997-6059
Bryant (G-1199)

Buckles Tool and Engineering ....G 574 642-3471
Goshen (G-5181)

Burkholder Machine ....G 574 862-2004
Goshen (G-5182)

Busche Enterprise Division Inc ....D 260 636-7030
Albion (G-19)

Busche Performance Group Inc ....E 260 636-1069
Albion (G-20)

Busche Performance Group Inc ....D 260 349-0070
Kendallville (G-8462)

▲ Busche Performance Group Inc ....A 260 636-7030
Albion (G-21)

Butler Tool & Design Inc ....F 219 297-4531
Goodland *(G-5158)*
Buxton Engineering Inc.........................G....... 812 897-3609
Boonville *(G-910)*
C & P Machine Service Inc ....E 260 484-7723
Fort Wayne *(G-4131)*
C and S Machine Inc..............................G....... 812 687-7203
Plainville *(G-11654)*
C M Engineering Inc ....F 812 648-2038
Dugger *(G-2479)*
C M Grinding Inc ....F 574 234-6812
South Bend *(G-12731)*
▲ C&R Racing Incorporated ....D....... 317 293-4100
Indianapolis *(G-6530)*
Cad & Machining Services Inc..............F 317 535-1067
Whiteland *(G-14234)*
Calavera Tool Works LLC......................G....... 765 481-6775
Zionsville *(G-14424)*
CAM Co Inc..G....... 574 967-4496
Flora *(G-3992)*
Camtool Inc ....F 765 286-9725
Muncie *(G-10445)*
Cardemon Inc...F 765 857-1000
Ridgeville *(G-12080)*
Carmel Engineering Inc.........................F 765 279-8955
Kirklin *(G-8547)*
Cass County Machine Inc ....F 574 722-5714
Logansport *(G-9331)*
Cast Metals Technology.........................F 765 284-3888
Selma *(G-12422)*
Cauble Precision Machine Inc ....G....... 812 537-4884
Greendale *(G-5484)*
Centerline Manufacturing......................G....... 260 348-7400
Churubusco *(G-1651)*
Central States Fabricating ....F 574 288-5607
South Bend *(G-12733)*
Central Tool Co Inc ....G....... 317 485-5344
Fortville *(G-4769)*
Certa Craft Inc ....G....... 317 535-0226
Whiteland *(G-14236)*
Chalk Precision Machining LLC ....G....... 765 452-9202
Kokomo *(G-8606)*
Charleston Metal Products Inc ....E 260 837-8211
Waterloo *(G-14011)*
Charleston Metal Products Inc ....F 260 281-9972
Corunna *(G-2083)*
Chassix ....G....... 574 825-9457
Bristol *(G-1051)*
Checkered Past Racing Pdts LLC ....G....... 317 852-6978
Brownsburg *(G-1142)*
Chesterfield Tool & Engrg Inc...............E 765 378-5101
Daleville *(G-2338)*
Christie Machine Works Co Inc ....G....... 317 638-8840
Indianapolis *(G-6603)*
Cimtech Inc..E 812 948-1472
New Albany *(G-10760)*
CL Tech Inc..G....... 812 526-0995
Edinburgh *(G-2600)*
Clifty Engineering and Tool Co.............C....... 812 273-3272
Madison *(G-9452)*
Cnc Concepts Inc...................................G....... 574 269-2301
Warsaw *(G-13858)*
Cnc Industries Inc..................................D....... 260 490-5700
Fort Wayne *(G-4165)*
Cnc Machine Inc.....................................G....... 317 835-4575
Shelbyville *(G-12527)*
Complete Metal Fabrication Inc.............E 812 284-4470
Jeffersonville *(G-8342)*
Component Machine Inc ....G....... 317 635-8929
Indianapolis *(G-6642)*
Conrad Machine Co Inc..........................G....... 574 259-1190
Mishawaka *(G-10022)*
Continental Machining Products...........G....... 219 474-5061
Kentland *(G-8518)*
▲ Contract Indus Tooling Inc...............D....... 765 966-1134
Richmond *(G-11973)*
Cope Brothers Machine Shop................G....... 219 663-5561
Leroy *(G-9247)*
Corydon Machine & Tool Co Inc ....E 812 738-3107
Corydon *(G-2095)*
Country Components Inc ....G....... 812 345-9594
Edinburgh *(G-2602)*
County Line Companies LLC..................G....... 866 959-7866
Parker City *(G-11462)*
Crane Hill Machine Inc...........................E 812 358-3534
Seymour *(G-12439)*
Creative Craftsmen Inc..........................E 812 423-2844
Evansville *(G-3437)*
Creative McHining Concepts Inc ....G....... 317 896-9250
Westfield *(G-14148)*
Creative Tool and Machining ....F 812 378-3562
Columbus *(G-1884)*
Crossrads Rhbilitation Ctr Inc...............C....... 317 897-7320
Indianapolis *(G-6697)*
Crystal Machining Inc.............................G....... 317 727-8984
Greenwood *(G-5679)*
Cullip Industries Inc...............................F 574 293-8251
Elkhart *(G-2782)*
Culver Tool & Engineering Inc...............D....... 574 935-9611
Plymouth *(G-11678)*
Cunningham Pattern & Engrg Inc ....F 812 379-9571
Columbus *(G-1902)*
Custom Engineering Inc.........................G....... 812 424-3879
Evansville *(G-3450)*
Custom Engrg & Fabrication Inc............E 260 745-9299
Fort Wayne *(G-4195)*
Custom Honing Inc.................................G....... 574 233-2846
South Bend *(G-12747)*
Custom Keepsakes Machine EMB ....G....... 317 894-5506
Indianapolis *(G-6715)*
◆ Custom Machining Services Inc ....E 219 462-6128
Valparaiso *(G-13525)*
Customized Machining Inc.....................G....... 765 490-7894
Lafayette *(G-8886)*
D & E Machine Inc..................................G....... 765 653-8919
Greencastle *(G-5457)*
D & M Precision Machining Inc.............G....... 219 393-5132
Kingsbury *(G-8535)*
D E Key Machine Shop ....G....... 765 664-1720
Marion *(G-9519)*
D&D Automation Inc ....G....... 812 299-1045
Terre Haute *(G-13221)*
Da-Mar Industries Inc ....F 260 347-1662
Kendallville *(G-8471)*
Daily Grind Corporation ....F 574 875-8389
Elkhart *(G-2786)*
DAKA Manufacturing Inc.......................G....... 574 295-8036
Goshen *(G-5197)*
▲ Dakota Engineering Inc....................E 317 546-8460
Yorktown *(G-14403)*
Davis Tool & Machine Inc.......................F 317 896-9278
Westfield *(G-14157)*
Dawson Machine Shop Inc.....................F 812 649-4777
Rockport *(G-12167)*
De Witt Tool & Die Inc............................G....... 765 998-7320
Upland *(G-13469)*
▲ Decatur Mold Tool and Engrg ....C....... 812 346-5188
North Vernon *(G-11253)*
Dede Tool & Machine Inc.......................G....... 812 232-7365
Terre Haute *(G-13224)*
Degood Dmensional Concepts Inc.........F 574 834-5437
North Webster *(G-11291)*
Dekalb Tool and Engrg LLC....................F 260 357-1500
Garrett *(G-5001)*
Delbert M Dawson & Son Inc ....G....... 765 284-9711
Muncie *(G-10458)*
Demotte Manufacturing Inc...................G....... 219 987-6196
Demotte *(G-2435)*
Dennis Manufacturing Inc.....................G....... 812 755-4891
Campbellsburg *(G-1276)*
Denver Stone..E 317 244-5889
Indianapolis *(G-6734)*
Dependable Rubber Industrial...............G....... 765 447-5654
Lafayette *(G-8887)*
Dial-X Acquisition Company Inc............E 260 636-7588
Albion *(G-26)*
Die-Rite Machine and Tool Corp............G....... 574 522-2366
Elkhart *(G-2797)*
Disinger Machine Shop ....G....... 219 567-2357
Francesville *(G-4810)*
Donaldson Company Inc........................G....... 317 838-5568
Plainfield *(G-11606)*
Dons Automotive and Machine ....G....... 812 547-6292
Tell City *(G-13159)*
Duel & Tool & Gage Inc ....G....... 317 244-0129
Indianapolis *(G-6770)*
E & R Machine Company Inc ....G....... 317 293-1550
Indianapolis *(G-6781)*
E L S Inc..G....... 812 985-2272
Evansville *(G-3470)*
Eagle Cnc Machining Inc........................F 765 289-2816
Muncie *(G-10466)*
Eagle Creek Machining Company ....G....... 219 365-3621
Saint John *(G-12263)*
Eason Manufacturing Inc ....G....... 312 310-9430
Griffith *(G-5772)*
Eastside Machine Shop...........................G....... 317 549-2216
Indianapolis *(G-6793)*
Echelbarger Machining Co LLC.............F 765 252-1965
Kokomo *(G-8619)*
Ecm Photo Tooling Inc ....E 574 264-4433
Elkhart *(G-2813)*
Edge Technologies Inc ....G....... 317 408-0116
Indianapolis *(G-6805)*
Eds Machine & Tool ....G....... 812 295-7264
Loogootee *(G-9382)*
Eemsco Inc..E 812 426-2224
Evansville *(G-3472)*
Egenolf Contg & Rigging II Inc ....D....... 317 787-5301
Indianapolis *(G-6812)*
Egenolf Machine Inc ....D....... 317 787-5301
Indianapolis *(G-6814)*
Electro-Tech Inc ....G....... 219 937-0826
Hammond *(G-5877)*
Elite Machine and Tool Inc ....G....... 219 345-3424
Demotte *(G-2437)*
Elkhart Grinding Services Inc................G....... 574 293-2707
Elkhart *(G-2824)*
Ellis Machine Shop LLC ....G....... 812 779-7477
Hazleton *(G-6009)*
Elmco Engineering Inc ....E 317 788-4114
Indianapolis *(G-6844)*
Embree Machine Inc................................G....... 812 275-5729
Springville *(G-13063)*
Emprotech Steel Services LLC...............D....... 219 326-6900
La Porte *(G-8756)*
Endeavor Machined Products Inc ....G....... 574 232-1940
South Bend *(G-12763)*
Engel Manufacturing Co Inc ....G....... 574 232-3800
South Bend *(G-12764)*
Engineered Industrial Products..............G....... 317 684-4280
Indianapolis *(G-6868)*
Esco Enterprises Indiana Inc.................F 317 241-0318
Indianapolis *(G-6876)*
Euclid Machine & Tool Inc......................E 219 397-1374
East Chicago *(G-2528)*
Evart Engineering Co Inc ....F 765 354-2232
Middletown *(G-9935)*
Exact-Tech Machining Inc ....F 574 970-0197
Elkhart *(G-2839)*
Exacto Machine & Tool Inc.....................G....... 317 872-3136
Indianapolis *(G-6888)*
Excel Machine ....G....... 317 467-0299
Greenfield *(G-5531)*
Excel Machine Technologies Inc ....F 219 548-0708
Valparaiso *(G-13538)*
▲ Excel Manufacturing Inc....................D....... 812 523-6764
Seymour *(G-12448)*
Excel Tool Inc...D....... 812 522-6880
Seymour *(G-12449)*
Executive MGT Svcs Ind Inc ....G....... 317 594-6000
Indianapolis *(G-6892)*
Extreme Precision Products LLC ....G....... 812 839-0101
Madison *(G-9461)*
F S G Inc ....G....... 574 291-5998
South Bend *(G-12771)*
Fab2order Inc ....E 317 975-1056
Brownsburg *(G-1149)*
Farmers Machine Shop Inc ....G....... 812 425-1238
Evansville *(G-3500)*
Faztek LLC...F 260 482-7544
Fort Wayne *(G-4260)*
Feddema Industries Inc............................F 260 665-6463
Angola *(G-213)*
Ferdinand Machine Shop ....G....... 812 367-2590
Ferdinand *(G-3849)*
Filca LLC..G....... 812 637-3559
Lawrenceburg *(G-9141)*
Filtration Tech Systems LLC...................E 812 944-9368
New Albany *(G-10776)*
Fisher Tool & Design Inc ....F 812 867-8350
Evansville *(G-3506)*
Fitech Inc ....E 513 398-1414
Michigan City *(G-9794)*
Flamespray Machine Service...................G....... 260 726-6236
Portland *(G-11823)*
▲ Flare Inc ....G....... 260 490-1101
Fort Wayne *(G-4265)*
Fleming Machine Works Inc....................G....... 812 967-4086
Pekin *(G-11472)*
Flenar Manufacturing LLC ....G....... 574 893-4070
Rochester *(G-12124)*
Flexaust Company Inc..............................G....... 574 371-3248
Warsaw *(G-13875)*
Flexible Concepts Inc...............................D....... 574 296-0941
Elkhart *(G-2854)*
Force Cnc LLC ....G....... 812 273-0218
Madison *(G-9462)*
Fortville Feeders Inc ....E 317 485-5095
Fortville *(G-4775)*

SIC

Fourman Enterprises Inc.................F...... 812 546-5734
Hope (G-6113)

Frank W Martinez........................G...... 574 232-6081
South Bend (G-12782)

Franks Industries.........................G...... 765 647-2080
Brookville (G-1114)

Franks Machine Shop Tool & Die......G...... 574 288-6899
South Bend (G-12783)

Fred Anderson............................G...... 765 985-2099
Peru (G-11527)

Freed Machining & Tool Inc............G...... 765 538-3019
Westpoint (G-14205)

Friskney Gear & Machine Corp.........G...... 260 281-2200
Corunna (G-2084)

Fullenkamp Machine & Mfg Inc........F...... 260 726-8345
Portland (G-11824)

▲ Fulton Industries Inc.................E...... 574 968-3222
South Bend (G-12784)

G & N Warehouse & Packaging.........G...... 574 234-3717
South Bend (G-12785)

G and P Enterprises Ind Inc............G...... 812 723-3837
Paoli (G-11451)

Garrity Tool Company LLC..............D...... 317 541-1400
Indianapolis (G-6986)

Gary Bridge and Iron Co Inc............G...... 219 884-3792
Gary (G-5049)

General Machine Brokers Inc...........G...... 260 691-3800
Columbia City (G-1788)

General Products Corporation...........G...... 260 668-1440
Angola (G-217)

Generation Four Machine &.............G...... 219 297-3003
Goodland (G-5159)

Gentec Inc................................G...... 260 436-7333
Fort Wayne (G-4298)

▼ Genuine Machine Design Inc........G...... 219 866-8060
Rensselaer (G-11926)

Gillum Machine & Tool Inc..............F...... 765 893-4426
West Lebanon (G-14120)

Global Air Inc.............................F...... 317 634-5300
Indianapolis (G-7008)

Global Air Inc.............................G...... 317 251-1251
Indianapolis (G-7009)

GMI Corporation..........................G...... 317 736-5116
Franklin (G-4890)

Goad Crankshaft Service Inc...........G...... 812 477-1127
Evansville (G-3521)

Greenwood Models Inc..................G...... 317 859-2988
Greenwood (G-5700)

Greenwood Tool & Die Co Inc..........G...... 219 924-9663
Griffith (G-5775)

Greg Miner................................G...... 765 647-1012
Brookville (G-1115)

Greys Automotive Inc...................G...... 317 632-3562
Indianapolis (G-7048)

Grimm Mold & Die Co Inc...............F...... 219 778-4211
Rolling Prairie (G-12186)

Grind City Customs.......................G...... 317 981-5462
Indianapolis (G-7049)

Grindco Inc................................E...... 219 763-6130
Chesterton (G-1610)

Grinding Experts..........................G...... 219 838-7773
Highland (G-6047)

Griner Engineering Inc...................D...... 812 332-2220
Bloomington (G-734)

Guide Engineering LLC...................E...... 260 483-1153
Fort Wayne (G-4310)

◆ Gvs Technologies LLC.................F...... 574 293-0974
Elkhart (G-2901)

H & E Machined Specialties............F...... 260 424-2527
Fort Wayne (G-4311)

H & H Design & Tool Inc.................G...... 765 886-6199
Economy (G-2591)

H Proto Development Inc.................G...... 574 267-6372
Warsaw (G-13887)

H&E Cutter Grinding Inc.................E...... 765 825-0541
Connersville (G-2049)

Ham Enterprise LLC.......................G...... 317 831-2902
Martinsville (G-9610)

Hamilton Industrial Inc..................G...... 260 488-3662
Hamilton (G-5823)

Hardigg Industries Inc...................C...... 812 342-0139
Columbus (G-1937)

Harman Machine & Engineering.........G...... 574 266-5015
Elkhart (G-2907)

Haylex Manufacturing LLC...............E...... 765 288-1818
Muncie (G-10483)

Hdh Manufacturing Inc...................G...... 317 918-4088
Indianapolis (G-7082)

Hdh Manufacturing Inc...................G...... 317 918-4088
Indianapolis (G-7083)

Headco Industries Inc....................G...... 219 924-7758
Highland (G-6049)

Headco Industries Inc....................G...... 574 288-4471
South Bend (G-12795)

Herald Machine Works Inc...............F...... 219 949-0580
Gary (G-5063)

HI Point Machine and Tool Inc..........F...... 574 831-5361
New Paris (G-10982)

HI Tech Systems Inc......................G...... 317 704-1077
Indianapolis (G-7103)

HI-Tech Turning...........................G...... 260 997-6668
Bryant (G-1200)

Highland Machine Tool Inc...............E...... 812 923-8884
Floyds Knobs (G-4013)

◆ Highway Machine Co Inc..............E...... 812 385-3639
Princeton (G-11875)

Hilltop Machine Shop LLC................G...... 260 768-9196
Shipshewana (G-12617)

Hilltop Mch Sp Haubstadt LLC..........G...... 812 768-5717
Haubstadt (G-6002)

Hitarth LLC................................G...... 812 372-1744
Columbus (G-1939)

Hochbaum Machine Services Inc........E...... 219 996-6830
Hebron (G-6014)

Holbrook Manufacturing Inc.............G...... 317 736-9387
Franklin (G-4896)

Honing Stl Hsptlity Cncpts Inc..........G...... 317 332-5170
Indianapolis (G-7118)

Hoosier Industrial Supply................G...... 574 535-0712
Goshen (G-5239)

Hoosier Tool & Grinding Inc.............G...... 812 597-0213
Morgantown (G-10353)

Hope Machine.............................G...... 502 550-9532
Evansville (G-3542)

Hose Technology Inc.....................E...... 765 762-5501
Williamsport (G-14291)

▲ Hoverstream LLC.......................G...... 317 489-0075
Indianapolis (G-7139)

Howard Hopkins Inc......................F...... 765 827-5666
Connersville (G-2051)

Hudelson Sharpening & Mch Sp.........G...... 812 865-3951
Orleans (G-11362)

Hull Precision Machining Inc.............G...... 260 238-4372
Spencerville (G-13048)

Humphreys Welding Service.............G...... 317 881-9024
Indianapolis (G-7145)

Huntingburg Machine Works Inc........F...... 812 683-3531
Huntingburg (G-6169)

Huth Tool.................................G...... 260 749-9411
Fort Wayne (G-4350)

Hyco Machine & Mold Inc................G...... 574 522-5847
Elkhart (G-2925)

Illiana Grinding Machining Inc...........G...... 219 884-5828
Merrillville (G-9722)

Imco Industrial Machine Corp...........E...... 219 663-6100
Crown Point (G-2261)

Indiana Micro Met Etching Inc..........F...... 574 293-3342
Elkhart (G-2931)

Indiana Model Company Inc.............D...... 317 787-6358
Indianapolis (G-7184)

▲ Indiana Research Institute............E...... 812 378-4221
Columbus (G-1947)

Indiana Southern TI & Engrg Co.........G...... 812 967-2714
Borden (G-931)

Indiana Technology and Manufac.......G...... 574 936-2112
Plymouth (G-11692)

Industrial Control Service...............F...... 260 356-4698
Huntington (G-6216)

Industrial Engineering Inc................D...... 260 478-1514
Fort Wayne (G-4367)

Industrial Hydraulics Inc.................E...... 317 247-4421
Indianapolis (G-7208)

Industrial Machine........................G...... 812 547-5656
Tell City (G-13164)

Industrial Metal Products Inc............F...... 260 447-7900
Fort Wayne (G-4368)

▲ Industrial Metal-Fab Inc..............E...... 574 288-8368
South Bend (G-12812)

▲ Industrial Mint Wldg Machining.......E...... 219 393-5531
Kingsbury (G-8539)

Industrial Pattern Works Inc.............F...... 219 362-4547
La Porte (G-8771)

Industrial Rep Inc.........................G...... 260 316-4973
Fremont (G-4962)

Industrial Tool & Mfg Co.................G...... 219 932-8670
Hammond (G-5899)

Indy Custom Machine Inc................G...... 317 271-1544
Indianapolis (G-7215)

Injection Plastic & Mfg Co...............F...... 574 784-2070
Lapaz (G-9117)

Innovative 3d Mfg LLC...................G...... 317 560-5080
Franklin (G-4901)

▲ Innovative Tooling Solutions.........G...... 260 487-9970
Fort Wayne (G-4373)

Instrumental Machine & Dev Inc........D...... 574 267-7713
Warsaw (G-13893)

Intri-Cut Tool Company LLC.............F...... 260 672-9602
Roanoke (G-12104)

Iris Rubber Company Inc.................F...... 317 984-3561
Cicero (G-1662)

◆ J & A Machine Inc......................G...... 260 637-6215
Garrett (G-5012)

J & H Tool Inc.............................G...... 765 724-9691
Alexandria (G-45)

▲ J & J Welding Inc.......................E...... 812 838-4391
Mount Vernon (G-10396)

J & L Tool & Machine Inc................F...... 317 398-6281
Shelbyville (G-12540)

J & P Machine Inc.........................F...... 260 357-5157
Garrett (G-5013)

J & R Tool Inc.............................G...... 812 295-2557
Loogootee (G-9386)

▲ J & T Marine Specialists Inc..........G...... 317 890-9444
Indianapolis (G-7280)

▲ J B Tool Die & Engineering Co........G...... 260 483-9586
Fort Wayne (G-4386)

J Henrys Machine Shop LLC.............G...... 317 917-1052
Indianapolis (G-7286)

J L Harris Machine Co Inc...............G...... 574 834-2866
Leesburg (G-9237)

J M S Machine Inc........................G...... 260 244-0077
Columbia City (G-1799)

J P Corporation...........................G...... 317 783-1000
Beech Grove (G-598)

J R P Machine Products LLP.............G...... 260 622-4746
Ossian (G-11402)

J V C Machining..........................G...... 219 462-0363
Valparaiso (G-13562)

Jatex Inc..................................F...... 574 773-5928
Nappanee (G-10687)

Jbd Machining............................G...... 765 671-9050
Marion (G-9538)

Jenco Engineering Inc....................G...... 574 267-4608
Warsaw (G-13895)

▲ Jennerjahn Machine Inc...............E...... 765 998-2733
Matthews (G-9652)

Jimco Engineering Co.....................G...... 317 923-2290
Indianapolis (G-7305)

Jj Machine................................G...... 765 723-1511
New Ross (G-11005)

Joint & Clutch Service Inc...............G...... 317 264-5038
Indianapolis (G-7310)

Jomar Machining & Fabg Inc............E...... 574 825-9837
Middlebury (G-9897)

Jones Machine & Tool Inc...............E...... 812 364-4588
Fredericksburg (G-4945)

Jws Machine Inc..........................E...... 812 917-5571
Terre Haute (G-13263)

K & L Machining Inc......................G...... 812 526-4840
Edinburgh (G-2614)

K C Machine Inc..........................G...... 574 293-1822
Elkhart (G-2954)

K&T Performance Engrg LLC.............G...... 765 437-0185
Peru (G-11535)

K-Motion Racing Engines................G...... 765 742-8494
Lafayette (G-8935)

Kamplain Machine Co Inc................G...... 317 388-9111
Indianapolis (G-7331)

Kbc Machine Inc..........................G...... 317 638-7865
Indianapolis (G-7336)

Keller Machine & Welding Inc...........E...... 219 464-4915
Valparaiso (G-13566)

Kelly Metal Products Inc.................G...... 812 232-1221
Terre Haute (G-13265)

Ken Anliker...............................G...... 219 984-5676
Chalmers (G-1547)

▲ Kens Tool & Design....................F...... 812 268-6653
Sullivan (G-13085)

Kentuckiana Machine & Tool Inc........G...... 502 593-3975
Georgetown (G-5146)

Kerns Speed Shop........................G...... 812 275-4289
Bedford (G-556)

Keystone Machine Services Inc.........G...... 219 397-6792
East Chicago (G-2544)

Kiesler Machine Inc......................G...... 812 364-6610
Palmyra (G-11436)

King Investments Inc.....................F...... 812 752-6000
Scottsburg (G-12371)

King Machining Inc.......................G...... 317 271-3132
Indianapolis (G-7352)

Kings Custom Machine .... G 812 477-5262
  Evansville *(G-3591)*

Kirby Risk Corporation .... D 765 742-2254
  Lafayette *(G-8943)*

▲ Kirby Risk Corporation .... D 765 448-4567
  Lafayette *(G-8940)*

Kirk Enterprises .... G 260 665-3670
  Angola *(G-225)*

Kitterman Machine Co Inc 317 773-2283
  Noblesville *(G-11139)*

Klueg Tool & Machine Inc .... G 812 867-5702
  Evansville *(G-3595)*

▲ Kobelco Cmpsr Mfg Ind Inc .... D 574 295-3145
  Elkhart *(G-2973)*

Kocsis Brothers Machine Co .... E 219 397-8400
  East Chicago *(G-2545)*

KOI Enterprises Inc .... G 812 537-2335
  Lawrenceburg *(G-9146)*

Kokomo Metal Fabricators Inc 765 459-8173
  Kokomo *(G-8653)*

Konal Automated Systems Inc .... D 616 659-4774
  Elkhart *(G-2974)*

Kortzendorf Machine & Tool .... F 317 783-5449
  Indianapolis *(G-7367)*

L & D Industries Inc 260 925-4714
  Auburn *(G-340)*

L & L Engineering Co Inc 317 786-6886
  Beech Grove *(G-601)*

L & P Manufacturing Company .... G 812 405-2093
  Jonesville *(G-8449)*

L & R Machine Company Inc 317 787-7251
  Beech Grove *(G-602)*

La Porte Prcsion Mch Works LLC .... G 219 326-7000
  La Porte *(G-8782)*

Lafayette Quality Products Inc .... F 765 446-0890
  Lafayette *(G-8950)*

Lakeland Technology Inc .... E 574 267-1503
  Warsaw *(G-13900)*

Lamb Machine & Tool Co .... G 317 780-9106
  Indianapolis *(G-7376)*

Landis Equipment & Tool Rental .... G 812 847-2582
  Linton *(G-9309)*

Lansing Metallizing & Grinding .... G 219 931-1785
  Hammond *(G-5906)*

Larrys Machine 574 596-4994
  Goshen *(G-5263)*

Le Hue Machine & Tool Co Inc .... G 574 255-8404
  Mishawaka *(G-10069)*

Lear Machining & Waterjet Inc .... G 812 418-8111
  Columbus *(G-1957)*

Lee Machine Inc .... G 765 932-3100
  Rushville *(G-12228)*

Leis Machine Shop Inc .... G 574 278-6000
  Buffalo *(G-1204)*

Lengacher Machine Inc .... F 260 657-3114
  Grabill *(G-5378)*

Lennon Industries Inc .... G 219 996-6838
  Hebron *(G-6018)*

Leonard Eaton Tooling Inc .... G 574 295-5041
  Elkhart *(G-2994)*

Liberty Tool and Engineering .... G 765 354-9550
  Middletown *(G-9937)*

Lievore Custom Machine Inc .... G 574 848-0150
  Bristol *(G-1067)*

Lightbeam Technology .... G 219 397-1684
  East Chicago *(G-2548)*

Linden Machine Shop LLC .... G 765 339-7244
  Linden *(G-9304)*

◆ Lively Machine Company Inc .... G 812 425-5060
  Evansville *(G-3604)*

Lloyds Machine Co .... G 812 422-7064
  Evansville *(G-3605)*

Loading Dock Maintenance LLC .... G 260 424-3635
  Fort Wayne *(G-4439)*

Loughmiller Mch Tl Design Inc .... E 812 295-3903
  Loogootee *(G-9390)*

Luxemburg Machine LLC .... G 260 347-4192
  Kendallville *(G-8491)*

Lycro Products Co Inc .... E 574 862-4981
  Wakarusa *(G-13784)*

Lynn Tool Company Inc .... G 765 874-2471
  Lynn *(G-9430)*

M & S Screw Machine Products .... G 765 853-5022
  Modoc *(G-10174)*

M C Welding & Machining Co .... G 219 393-5718
  Kingsbury *(G-8540)*

M G Products Inc .... E 574 293-0752
  Elkhart *(G-3009)*

M T M Machining Inc .... F 219 872-8677
  Michigan City *(G-9813)*

M-Tech Machine Products .... G 812 637-3500
  West Harrison *(G-14040)*

Machine Rebuilders & Service .... F 260 482-8168
  Fort Wayne *(G-4448)*

Machine Tool Service Inc .... F 812 232-1912
  Terre Haute *(G-13277)*

Magna Machine & Tool Co Inc .... E 765 766-5388
  New Castle *(G-10910)*

Maitland Engineering Inc .... E 574 287-0155
  South Bend *(G-12850)*

▲ Major Tool and Machine Inc .... B 317 636-6433
  Indianapolis *(G-7446)*

Manchester Tool & Die Inc .... D 260 982-8524
  North Manchester *(G-11234)*

Manufactured Products .... G 765 552-2871
  Elwood *(G-3306)*

Maple City Machine Inc .... F 574 533-6742
  Goshen *(G-5278)*

Margaret Machine and Tool Co .... G 219 924-0859
  Griffith *(G-5783)*

Maschino Industries Inc .... G 812 346-3083
  North Vernon *(G-11270)*

Master Metal Machining Inc .... D 574 299-0222
  South Bend *(G-12853)*

▲ Masterbilt Incorporated .... F 574 287-6567
  South Bend *(G-12854)*

Matts Repair Inc .... F 219 696-6765
  Lowell *(G-9416)*

McD Machine Incorporated .... G 812 339-1240
  Bloomington *(G-770)*

Mcl/Screwdriver Systems Inc .... F 317 776-1970
  Noblesville *(G-11147)*

Mechanical Engineering Control .... E 574 294-7580
  Elkhart *(G-3025)*

Med Grind Inc .... G 574 965-4040
  Delphi *(G-2424)*

Melching Machine Inc .... E 260 622-4315
  Ossian *(G-11404)*

Mercer Machine Company Inc .... F 317 241-9903
  Indianapolis *(G-7479)*

Merit Tool & Manufacturing Inc .... F 765 396-9566
  Eaton *(G-2586)*

Mesco Manufacturing LLC .... D 812 663-3870
  Greensburg *(G-5622)*

Metal Fabricated Products Co .... G 812 372-7430
  Columbus *(G-1972)*

Metalcraft Precision Machining .... F 574 293-6700
  Elkhart *(G-3029)*

▲ Metaltec Inc .... G 219 362-9811
  La Porte *(G-8792)*

Metcalf Engineering Inc .... G 765 342-6792
  Martinsville *(G-9625)*

Michfab Machinery .... G 260 244-6117
  Columbia City *(G-1809)*

Micro Machine Works Inc .... G 574 293-1354
  Elkhart *(G-3034)*

▼ Micromatic LLC .... D 260 589-2136
  Berne *(G-621)*

Mid-States Tool and Mch Inc .... E 260 728-9797
  Decatur *(G-2394)*

Mid-West Metal Products Co Inc .... F 765 741-3140
  Muncie *(G-10522)*

Midcounty Machining Inc .... G 219 992-9380
  Lake Village *(G-9083)*

Midstate Manufacturing Corp .... F 317 738-0094
  Franklin *(G-4908)*

Midwest Accurate Grinding Svc .... F 219 696-4060
  Lowell *(G-9417)*

Midwest Bale Ties Inc .... E 765 364-0113
  Crawfordsville *(G-2173)*

Midwest Machining & Fabg .... F 219 924-0206
  Griffith *(G-5785)*

Miller Machine & Welding .... G 812 882-7566
  Vincennes *(G-13693)*

Miller Machine Shop LLC .... G 574 773-2900
  Nappanee *(G-10694)*

Miller Welding & Mechanic Svc .... G 812 923-3359
  Pekin *(G-11476)*

Mining Machine Parts Inc .... G 812 897-1256
  Boonville *(G-918)*

Minnich Mfg Inc .... G 260 489-5357
  Fort Wayne *(G-4476)*

Mitchum-Schaefer Inc .... D 317 546-4081
  Indianapolis *(G-7528)*

▲ Models LLC .... E 765 676-6700
  Lebanon *(G-9207)*

Modern Machine & Grinding Inc .... E 219 322-1201
  Dyer *(G-2503)*

Modern Machine & Tool Inc .... G 765 934-3110
  Van Buren *(G-13641)*

Monroe Manufacturing Tech Inc .... G 317 782-1005
  Indianapolis *(G-7536)*

Monticello Machine Co Inc .... G 574 583-9537
  Monticello *(G-10270)*

Moore Machine & Gear Inc .... G 812 963-3074
  Evansville *(G-3637)*

Moore Precision Machining LLC .... G 765 265-2386
  Connersville *(G-2065)*

Moran Engineering LLC .... G 574 266-6799
  Elkhart *(G-3050)*

Morris Holding Company LLC .... C 812 446-6141
  Brazil *(G-970)*

Morris Machine & Tool .... G 219 866-3018
  Rensselaer *(G-11932)*

Morris Machine Co Inc .... D 317 788-0371
  Indianapolis *(G-7543)*

Morris Mfg & Sls Corp .... C 812 446-6141
  Brazil *(G-971)*

Morris Precision Inc .... E 574 656-3089
  Noblesville *(G-11155)*

Morris Precision Inc .... F 574 656-8707
  Noblesville *(G-11156)*

Motsinger Auto Supply Inc .... G 317 782-8484
  Indianapolis *(G-7549)*

Mpp Inc .... E 260 422-5426
  Fort Wayne *(G-4482)*

Mudhole Machine Shop LLC .... G 765 533-4228
  Middletown *(G-9939)*

Multiple Machining Inc .... E 812 432-5946
  Dillsboro *(G-2470)*

Muncie Metal Products .... G 765 288-3421
  Muncie *(G-10529)*

Nathan Millis Tools LLC .... G 219 996-3305
  Hebron *(G-6019)*

Nector Machine & Fabricating .... G 219 322-6878
  Schererville *(G-12338)*

New Age Equipment Inc .... G 765 659-1524
  Frankfort *(G-4843)*

Nixon Tool Co Inc .... G 765 966-6608
  Richmond *(G-12024)*

Nmc Inc .... E 812 648-2636
  Dugger *(G-2482)*

Northeast Machine & Tool Co .... G 317 823-6594
  Indianapolis *(G-7592)*

▲ Northern Indiana Manufacturing .... E 574 342-2105
  Bourbon *(G-946)*

Northside Machine & Tool Inc .... F 765 654-4538
  Frankfort *(G-4845)*

Northside Machining Inc .... G 812 683-3500
  Huntingburg *(G-6176)*

Numerical Concepts Inc .... D 812 466-5261
  Terre Haute *(G-13293)*

Numerix Inc .... G 260 248-2942
  Columbia City *(G-1813)*

Oakley Industries LLC .... G 812 246-2600
  Sellersburg *(G-12410)*

Odon Machine & Manufacturing .... G 812 636-7781
  Odon *(G-11338)*

Odyssey Machine Inc .... G 812 951-1160
  Georgetown *(G-5151)*

OHM Enterprise LLC .... G 812 879-5455
  Gosport *(G-5354)*

Okaya USA .... G 317 362-0696
  Indianapolis *(G-7614)*

Oliver Machine & Tl Corp .... F 765 349-2271
  Martinsville *(G-9630)*

Oliver Machine and Tool Corp .... F 765 349-2271
  Mooresville *(G-10329)*

On Point Machining Inc .... G 219 393-5132
  Kingsbury *(G-8544)*

On Site Machining Corporation .... G 219 923-2292
  Munster *(G-10619)*

Opi Inc .... G 260 636-2352
  Albion *(G-31)*

Ortho Grind LLC .... G 260 493-1230
  Fort Wayne *(G-4512)*

Ossenbeck Mach Co .... G 937 564-6092
  Lawrenceburg *(G-9150)*

Ottinger Machine Co .... G 317 654-1700
  Indianapolis *(G-7637)*

Ottosons Industries Inc .... G 219 365-8330
  Cedar Lake *(G-1532)*

P & A Machine Inc .... G 317 634-3673
  Indianapolis *(G-7641)*

P & H Engineering Inc .... G 765 676-6323
  Jamestown *(G-8232)*

P & J Tool Co Inc .... G 317 546-4858
  Indianapolis *(G-7642)*

P M Fabricating Incorporated .... G 219 362-9926
  La Porte *(G-8802)*

P O C Industries Inc ....G..... 765 645-5015 Mays (G-9663)	R & B Mold and Die Inc ....G..... 219 324-4176 La Porte (G-8809)	▲ Russell Metal Products ....F ..... 317 841-9003 Fishers (G-3966)
P T I Machining Inc ....G..... 765 564-9966 Delphi (G-2425)	R & D Machine Shop Inc ....G..... 574 946-6109 Winamac (G-14318)	S & J Precision Inc.....................E ..... 812 944-9368 New Albany (G-10860)
Pamela S Taulman ....F ..... 812 378-5008 Columbus (G-1990)	R & R Tool Manufacturing Inc ......E ..... 219 362-1681 La Porte (G-8810)	S & S Machine & Tool Inc ....G..... 260 897-3823 Avilla (G-418)
Parametric Machining Inc ....F ..... 260 338-1564 Huntertown (G-6143)	R & S Welding & Fabricating ....G..... 574 946-6816 Winamac (G-14319)	S Edwards Incorporated.................G..... 317 831-0261 Mooresville (G-10338)
Parker-Hannifin Corporation.........E ..... 260 587-9102 Ashley (G-289)	R & Y Professional Tools LLC ....G..... 765 354-9076 Middletown (G-9940)	S&C Machine LLC ....G..... 812 768-6731 Haubstadt (G-6005)
Parsons Custom Machining Inc ......G..... 812 877-2700 Centerpoint (G-1539)	R A McCoy Inc ....G..... 260 636-2341 Albion (G-33)	San Mar ....G..... 574 286-6884 South Bend (G-12926)
Pauls Custom Machine................G..... 574 674-9633 Elkhart (G-3092)	R B Machine Company ....G..... 765 364-6716 Crawfordsville (G-2190)	Sardinia Machine ....G..... 812 591-2091 Westport (G-14211)
Paynter Machine Works Inc ....G..... 812 883-2808 Salem (G-12303)	R E Ferguson & Associates Inc ......G..... 317 839-9311 Plainfield (G-11639)	Schaefer Technologies Inc..............D..... 317 241-9444 Indianapolis (G-7902)
Peerless Pattern & Machine Co ....G..... 765 477-7719 Lafayette (G-8979)	Rapid Prototyping & Engrg ....G..... 812 526-9207 Edinburgh (G-2624)	Schlatters Inc ....G..... 219 567-9158 Francesville (G-4815)
▼ Perfecto Tool & Engineering Co ......E ..... 765 644-2821 Anderson (G-150)	Rauch Inc ....C..... 812 945-4063 New Albany (G-10854)	Scutt Tool & Die ....G..... 317 858-8725 Brownsburg (G-1170)
Performance Machining Inc ....G..... 812 432-9180 Dillsboro (G-2471)	Rayco Mch & Engrg Group Inc ....E ..... 317 291-7848 Indianapolis (G-7819)	Selco Engineering Inc ....E ..... 317 297-1888 Shelbyville (G-12566)
Pgi Mfg LLC............................D..... 574 968-3222 South Bend (G-12893)	Rayco Steel Process Inc ....F ..... 574 267-7676 Warsaw (G-13932)	Select Tool & Eng Inc ....G..... 574 295-6197 Elkhart (G-3160)
Piercy Machine Co Inc ....G..... 317 398-9296 Shelbyville (G-12556)	Reber Machine & Tool Co Inc ....G..... 765 288-0297 Muncie (G-10554)	Seymour Precision Machining..........G..... 812 524-1813 Seymour (G-12486)
Pinnacle Tool Inc ....G..... 812 336-5000 Bloomington (G-799)	Reeder & Kline Machine Co Inc ....E ..... 317 846-6591 Sheridan (G-12596)	Shaw Machining Services I ....G..... 765 663-2732 Rushville (G-12232)
Plakes Tooling Inc ....G..... 765 963-2745 Tipton (G-13401)	Rehco Products Inc ....F ..... 317 984-3319 Arcadia (G-269)	Sheridan Manufacturing Co Inc ....E ..... 317 758-6000 Sheridan (G-12598)
Pleasant Industries Inc ....G..... 260 638-4699 Yoder (G-14399)	Reliable Tool & Machine Co ....E ..... 260 347-4000 Kendallville (G-8507)	Shirley Machine & Engrg Inc ....E ..... 765 349-9040 Martinsville (G-9638)
Ploog Engineering Co Inc ....G..... 219 663-2854 Crown Point (G-2284)	Reliable Tool & Machine Co ....E ..... 260 347-4000 Kendallville (G-8508)	Shorts Machine Shop ....G..... 765 622-6259 Anderson (G-165)
Plymouth Foundry Inc ....E ..... 574 936-2106 Plymouth (G-11713)	Reliable Tool & Machine Co ....D..... 260 343-7150 Kendallville (G-8506)	Shull Machine Service Inc ....G..... 260 925-4198 Butler (G-1240)
Point Machine Products Inc ....G..... 574 289-2429 South Bend (G-12900)	Reliance Machine Company Inc ....D..... 765 284-0151 Muncie (G-10558)	Sibley Machine & Foundry Corp.........E ..... 574 232-2910 South Bend (G-12933)
Powder Metal Technicians Inc ....G..... 317 353-2812 Indianapolis (G-7711)	Reliance Machine Company Inc ....F ..... 765 857-1000 Ridgeville (G-12082)	Simko Machining Inc ....G..... 219 864-9535 Dyer (G-2509)
Prairies Edge Machining Inc ....G..... 765 986-2222 Williamsport (G-14295)	Reliant Engineering Inc ....E ..... 317 322-9084 Indianapolis (G-7832)	Single Source Inc ....F ..... 574 656-3400 North Liberty (G-11222)
Precision Agronomy ....G..... 219 552-0032 Lowell (G-9420)	Remington Machine Inc ....G..... 765 724-3389 Alexandria (G-50)	Slick Engineering Industries............G..... 765 354-2822 Middletown (G-9941)
▲ Precision Electric Inc................E ..... 574 256-1000 Mishawaka (G-10106)	Rencor Inc ....G..... 765 395-7949 Converse (G-2082)	Smith Small Engine Service.............G..... 812 232-1318 Terre Haute (G-13329)
Precision Enterprises LLC ....G..... 812 873-6391 Paris Crossing (G-11460)	Research Machining Services ....G..... 765 494-3710 West Lafayette (G-14101)	Snavelys Machine & Mfg Co Inc ....C..... 765 473-8395 Peru (G-11547)
Precision Fiber Solutions LLC..........G..... 317 421-9642 Franklin (G-4922)	Reuer Machine & Tool Inc ....G..... 219 362-2894 La Porte (G-8981)	Sordelet Tool & Die Inc..................G..... 260 483-7258 Fort Wayne (G-4636)
▼ Precision Laser Services Inc ....E ..... 260 744-4375 Fort Wayne (G-4551)	Reynolds & Co Inc ....E ..... 812 232-5313 Terre Haute (G-13319)	Specialty Cnc Incorporated ....G..... 812 825-7982 Bloomington (G-830)
Precision Mold & Tool Inc ....F ..... 765 284-4415 Muncie (G-10547)	Reynolds North ....G..... 812 235-5313 Terre Haute (G-13320)	Specialty Machine Stamping ....G..... 574 658-3350 Warsaw (G-13942)
Precision Racg Components LLC ....F ..... 317 248-4764 Indianapolis (G-7735)	Rf Manufacturing Inc ....G..... 317 773-8610 Noblesville (G-11176)	Spencer Machine and TI Co Inc.........E ..... 812 282-6300 Jeffersonville (G-8426)
Precision Tool & Die Inc ....G..... 765 664-4786 Marion (G-9556)	Rhyne Engines Inc......................G..... 219 845-1218 Gary (G-5092)	Spreuer & Son Inc......................F ..... 260 463-3513 Lagrange (G-9067)
Prodigy Group Inc ....E ..... 317 834-5480 Mooresville (G-10335)	Richters Machine & Tool ....G..... 260 495-5327 Fremont (G-4973)	Square 1 Dsign Manufacture Inc ....F ..... 866 647-7771 Shelbyville (G-12570)
Prodigy Mold & Tool Inc ....E ..... 812 753-3029 Haubstadt (G-6004)	Rix Laser Processing ....G..... 812 537-9230 Lawrenceburg (G-9155)	SSd Control Technology Inc ....E ..... 574 289-5942 South Bend (G-12950)
Progress Group Inc ....D..... 219 322-3700 Schererville (G-12342)	Rk Machine Inc ....F ..... 812 466-0550 Terre Haute (G-13321)	Stag Tool ....G..... 812 876-3281 Gosport (G-5355)
Promotor Engines & Components ......G..... 574 533-9898 Goshen (G-5313)	Rmt Inc ....F ..... 260 637-4649 Huntertown (G-6146)	Stamets Tool & Engineering ....G..... 260 925-1382 Auburn (G-358)
Provident Tool & Die Inc...............G..... 574 862-1233 Wakarusa (G-13791)	Roberts Precision Machining ....G..... 812 926-3233 Aurora (G-386)	Stamina Metal Products Inc ....G..... 574 534-7410 Goshen (G-5327)
PSc Machining and Engrg Inc ....F ..... 219 764-4270 Portage (G-11789)	Robertson Machine Co Inc ....G..... 317 881-9405 Greenwood (G-5741)	Stamping Specialty Co Inc..............G..... 812 829-0760 Spencer (G-13038)
Pumphreys Performance Engines ....G..... 812 358-4704 Medora (G-9682)	Rodex Machining ....G..... 260 768-4844 Shipshewana (G-12648)	Standish Steel Inc......................F ..... 812 834-5255 Bedford (G-580)
Qig LLC.................................E ..... 260 244-3591 Columbia City (G-1821)	Rohder Machine & Tool Inc ....F ..... 219 663-3697 Crown Point (G-2297)	Stanley Allen ....G..... 812 752-2720 Scottsburg (G-12383)
Qig LLC ....E ..... 260 244-3591 Columbia City (G-1822)	Ron Osborne Machining Inc ....G..... 812 637-1045 Lawrenceburg (G-9156)	▲ Star Engineering & Mch Co Inc ....E ..... 260 824-4825 Bluffton (G-894)
Quake Manufacturing Inc ....F ..... 260 432-8023 Fort Wayne (G-4570)	Rose Engineering Co Inc ....G..... 317 788-4446 Indianapolis (G-7862)	Star Tool & Die Inc ....F ..... 574 264-3815 Elkhart (G-3189)
Quality Machine & Tool Inc ....G..... 574 534-5664 Goshen (G-5314)	Ross Machining ....G..... 765 998-2400 Upland (G-13473)	Stephens Machine Inc ....D..... 765 459-4017 Kokomo (G-8702)
▲ Quality Machine & Tool Works.........D..... 812 379-2660 Columbus (G-2003)	Rotam Tool Corporation ....F ..... 260 982-8318 North Manchester (G-11242)	Stephens Machine Inc ....E ..... 765 459-9770 Kokomo (G-8703)
Quality Mch Repr & Engrg Inc ....G..... 317 375-1366 Indianapolis (G-7798)	Royalty Investments LLC ....E ..... 812 358-3534 Seymour (G-12481)	Sterling Machine Co Inc ....G..... 219 374-9360 Cedar Lake (G-1534)
Quality Tool & Machine Co ....G..... 219 464-2411 Valparaiso (G-13604)	RPM Machinery LLC ....F ..... 574 271-0800 South Bend (G-12923)	Steve Mitchell ....G..... 574 831-4848 New Paris (G-10996)
Quicks Machine & Tool Inc ....G..... 812 952-2135 Corydon (G-2109)	Rs Precision Machining ....G..... 219 362-4560 La Porte (G-8814)	▲ Steve Schmidt Racing Engines ....F ..... 317 898-1831 Indianapolis (G-8004)
Quicksilver Metals Inc ....G..... 765 482-1782 Lebanon (G-9219)	Rush Jaw Company The Inc ....G..... 317 729-5095 Shelbyville (G-12564)	Steves Machining & Rework............G..... 317 500-4627 Franklin (G-4934)

Stoney Creek Wash Machine Shop ....G...... 574 642-1155
   Millersburg *(G-9974)*
Stream Tek LLC.............................G...... 260 441-9300
   Fort Wayne *(G-4656)*
Stulls Mch & Fabrication Inc ....G...... 765 942-2717
   Ladoga *(G-8843)*
Stumlers Machine Inc ....G...... 812 944-2467
   New Albany *(G-10868)*
Summit Mfg & Machining ....F...... 574 546-4571
   Bremen *(G-1026)*
Sun Engineering Inc ....E...... 219 962-1191
   Lake Station *(G-9078)*
Sunman Engineering Inc ....G...... 812 623-4072
   Sunman *(G-13119)*
Superb Tooling Inc ....F...... 812 367-2102
   Ferdinand *(G-3863)*
Superior Machine & Tool Co ....F...... 260 493-4517
   Fort Wayne *(G-4667)*
Superior Machine Inc ....G...... 574 654-8243
   New Carlisle *(G-10887)*
Superior Piece Parts Inc ....F...... 574 277-4236
   Mishawaka *(G-10138)*
Superior Tool & Die Company ....G...... 574 293-2591
   Elkhart *(G-3201)*
Surface Enhancement ....G...... 574 269-1366
   Warsaw *(G-13945)*
Swansons Service Center ....G...... 574 858-9406
   Atwood *(G-310)*
Syltech Experimental ....G...... 765 489-1777
   Hagerstown *(G-5813)*
System Science Institute ....G...... 260 436-6096
   Fort Wayne *(G-4670)*
T & M Precision Inc ....G...... 513 253-2274
   Versailles *(G-13658)*
T & M Precision Inc ....G...... 812 689-5769
   Versailles *(G-13659)*
T & S Engineering LLC ....G...... 812 969-3860
   New Palestine *(G-10973)*
T F & T Inc...G...... 765 874-1628
   Lynn *(G-9432)*
T L Tate Manufacturing Inc ....G...... 765 452-8283
   Kokomo *(G-8706)*
T M E Inc ....G...... 219 769-6627
   Merrillville *(G-9756)*
T Shorter Manufacturing Inc ....G...... 574 264-4131
   Elkhart *(G-3203)*
T W Machine & Grinding ....G...... 260 799-4236
   Columbia City *(G-1839)*
T-N-T Performance Mch Sp LLC ....G...... 574 457-5056
   Syracuse *(G-13148)*
Tasco Industries Inc ....G...... 219 922-6100
   Highland *(G-6056)*
Task Force Tips Inc............................F...... 219 462-6161
   Valparaiso *(G-13627)*
Taurus Tech & Engrg LLC ....E...... 765 282-2090
   Muncie *(G-10568)*
Tempest Tool & Machine Inc ....F...... 812 346-6464
   North Vernon *(G-11283)*
Teresa L Powell CPA...........................G...... 765 962-1862
   Richmond *(G-12061)*
Terrel Automotive Machine Inc ....G...... 812 883-3859
   Salem *(G-12308)*
Test Rite Systems & Mfg Co LLC ....G...... 317 736-9192
   Franklin *(G-4937)*
▲ Tgm Manufacturing Inc ....F...... 260 758-3055
   Uniondale *(G-13466)*
Thinking Machine LLC.........................G...... 812 539-2968
   Lawrenceburg *(G-9158)*
Thomas Cubit Inc ....G...... 219 933-0566
   Hammond *(G-5949)*
▲ Thomas/Euclid Industries Inc ....D...... 317 783-7171
   Indianapolis *(G-8066)*
Three Daughters Corp ....E...... 260 925-2128
   Auburn *(G-361)*
Titan Metal Worx LLC ....E...... 260 422-4433
   Fort Wayne *(G-4688)*
Titus Inc ....F...... 574 936-3345
   Plymouth *(G-11728)*
▲ Tmak Inc ....E...... 219 874-7661
   Michigan City *(G-9853)*
Tool Room Service...............................G...... 765 287-0062
   Muncie *(G-10574)*
Top Notch Tool & Engineering.............G...... 812 663-2184
   Greensburg *(G-5637)*
Total Tote Inc ....F...... 260 982-8318
   North Manchester *(G-11246)*
Touchdown Machining Inc ....G...... 812 378-0300
   Columbus *(G-2023)*
Tr Manufacturing LLC ....G...... 260 357-4679
   Garrett *(G-5024)*

Trace Engineering Inc.........................G...... 765 354-4351
   Middletown *(G-9942)*
Trade Line Fabricating Inc ....E...... 812 637-1444
   Lawrenceburg *(G-9159)*
▼ Tree City Tool & Engrg Co Inc..........D...... 812 663-4196
   Greensburg *(G-5639)*
Tri Aerospace LLC ....E...... 812 872-2400
   Terre Haute *(G-13358)*
Tri Don LLC ....G...... 765 966-7300
   Richmond *(G-12069)*
Tri-State Machine Co Inc ....F...... 812 479-3159
   Evansville *(G-3774)*
Tri-State Machining Inc.......................G...... 260 422-2508
   Fort Wayne *(G-4701)*
Triangle Engineering Corp ....D...... 317 243-8549
   Indianapolis *(G-8097)*
Triangle Machine Inc...........................G...... 574 246-0165
   South Bend *(G-12979)*
Trison Industries Inc..........................G...... 812 945-7775
   Floyds Knobs *(G-4022)*
Troyer Brothers ....E...... 260 589-2244
   Decatur *(G-2410)*
Trp International LLC ....F...... 574 389-9941
   Elkhart *(G-3224)*
Trufab Stainless ....G...... 812 287-8278
   Bloomington *(G-844)*
Tsf Tool LLC ....G...... 765 537-9008
   Gosport *(G-5356)*
TT Machining & Fabricating LLC ....G...... 219 878-0399
   Michigan City *(G-9856)*
U S Valves Inc.....................................G...... 812 476-6662
   Evansville *(G-3782)*
Ultrexx Inc..C...... 260 897-2680
   Warsaw *(G-13955)*
▼ Union Tool Corp ....E...... 574 267-3211
   Warsaw *(G-13956)*
United Machine Corporation ....E...... 219 548-8050
   Valparaiso *(G-13633)*
United Tool Company Inc ....F...... 260 563-3143
   Wabash *(G-13760)*
Universal Metalcraft Inc ....E...... 260 547-4457
   Decatur *(G-2411)*
Universal Precision Instrs Inc ....G...... 574 264-3997
   Elkhart *(G-3238)*
US Automation LLC ....G...... 260 338-1100
   Huntertown *(G-6148)*
Uway Extrusion LLC ....F...... 765 592-6089
   Marshall *(G-9593)*
Valad McHning Cntrless Grnding ....G...... 574 291-5541
   South Bend *(G-12982)*
Value Tool & Engineering Inc..............D...... 574 246-1913
   South Bend *(G-12984)*
Van Com Inc ....E...... 574 255-9689
   Mishawaka *(G-10145)*
Versatile Automation Tech ....G...... 574 266-0780
   Elkhart *(G-3243)*
Versatile Fabrication LLC ....G...... 574 293-8504
   Elkhart *(G-3244)*
Vigo Machine Shop Inc ....E...... 812 235-8393
   Terre Haute *(G-13362)*
Vincennes Welding Co Inc ....F...... 812 882-9682
   Vincennes *(G-13712)*
Vision Machine Works Inc ....F...... 574 259-6500
   Mishawaka *(G-10148)*
Voege Precision Mch Pdts LLC ....G...... 317 867-4699
   Westfield *(G-14199)*
Voges Machine ....G...... 812 299-1546
   Terre Haute *(G-13363)*
Vorzeigen Machining Inc ....E...... 765 827-1500
   Connersville *(G-2077)*
W T Boone Enterprises Inc ....G...... 317 738-0275
   Franklin *(G-4939)*
Wagler Machining LLC ....G...... 812 866-2904
   Lexington *(G-9256)*
Waka Mfg Inc ....G...... 574 258-0019
   Mishawaka *(G-10149)*
▲ Walerko Tool and Engrg Corp..........E...... 574 295-2233
   Elkhart *(G-3252)*
Walkerton Tool & Die Inc ....G...... 574 586-3162
   Walkerton *(G-13813)*
Waterfield Automotive Mch Sp ....G...... 765 288-6262
   Muncie *(G-10580)*
Wauseon MCHne&mfg-Kndlvlle Div .....E...... 260 347-5095
   Kendallville *(G-8513)*
Wayne Machine Manufacturers ....G...... 765 962-0459
   Richmond *(G-12074)*
Wg S Global Services ....G...... 810 239-4947
   Tell City *(G-13176)*
Whiffen Machine and Press Repr ....G...... 812 876-1257
   Gosport *(G-5357)*

White Machine Inc...............................G...... 574 267-5895
   Warsaw *(G-13964)*
William F Shirley ....G...... 812 426-2599
   Evansville *(G-3813)*
Williams Tool & Machine Corp ....F...... 765 676-5859
   Jamestown *(G-8233)*
Wilson Machine Shop Inc ....G...... 812 392-2774
   Elizabethtown *(G-2652)*
Wilson Tool & Engineering Inc ....G...... 812 334-1110
   Bloomington *(G-857)*
Winn Machine Inc ....G...... 219 324-2978
   La Porte *(G-8833)*
Wirco Inc ....C...... 260 897-3768
   Avilla *(G-422)*
Wirecut Technologies Inc ....G...... 317 885-9915
   Indianapolis *(G-8205)*
Wolfe and Swickard Mch Co Inc ....D...... 317 241-2589
   Indianapolis *(G-8210)*
Workrite Machine & Tool Inc ....E...... 260 489-4778
   Fort Wayne *(G-4761)*
XYZ Machining Inc ....G...... 574 269-5541
   Warsaw *(G-13970)*
Yoder & Sons ....G...... 574 642-1196
   Middlebury *(G-9928)*
Young Machine Co Inc ....F...... 812 944-5807
   New Albany *(G-10877)*
Zook Machine Inc.................................G...... 765 563-6585
   Battle Ground *(G-525)*

36 ELECTRONIC AND OTHER ELECTRICAL EQUIPMENT AND COMPONENTS, EXCEPT COMPUTER

3612 Power, Distribution & Specialty Transformers

Ajax Tocco Magnethermic Corp ....G...... 317 352-9880
   Indianapolis *(G-6357)*
Ball Systems Inc ....E...... 317 804-2330
   Westfield *(G-14138)*
▲ Coil Tran Corp ....D...... 219 942-8511
   Hobart *(G-6076)*
▲ Custom Magnetics Inc ....E...... 773 463-6500
   North Manchester *(G-11227)*
Gasco LLC ....G...... 317 565-5000
   Noblesville *(G-11109)*
General Transmission Pdts LLC............F...... 574 284-2917
   South Bend *(G-12789)*
Hoffmaster Electric Inc.......................G...... 219 616-1313
   Schererville *(G-12323)*
Kay Industries Inc ....F...... 574 236-6220
   Plymouth *(G-11698)*
Powers Energy America Inc ....G...... 812 473-5500
   Evansville *(G-3680)*
R & R Regulators Inc ....F...... 574 522-5846
   Elkhart *(G-3134)*
R B Annis Instruments Inc ....G...... 765 848-1621
   Greencastle *(G-5476)*
Schneider Electric Usa Inc ....E...... 260 356-2060
   Huntington *(G-6247)*
Whiting Clean Energy Inc ....E...... 219 473-0653
   Whiting *(G-14277)*
▲ Xfmrs Inc ....A...... 317 834-1066
   Camby *(G-1272)*

3613 Switchgear & Switchboard Apparatus

◆ Advance MCS Electronics Inc ....F...... 574 642-3501
   Goshen *(G-5166)*
Advanced Control Panels Inc ....F...... 219 763-4000
   Portage *(G-11748)*
Blinkless Power Equipment LLC............G...... 317 844-7328
   Indianapolis *(G-6484)*
Bonner & Associates ....G...... 317 571-1911
   Carmel *(G-1321)*
Breakers Unlimited Inc ....G...... 317 474-9431
   Noblesville *(G-11072)*
Burt Products Inc.................................G...... 812 386-6890
   Princeton *(G-11867)*
Caddo Connections Inc ....E...... 219 874-8119
   La Porte *(G-8744)*
Circuit Breaker Sales Co Inc ....G...... 219 575-5420
   Crown Point *(G-2234)*
▼ Control Consultants of America ....G...... 219 989-3311
   Hammond *(G-5865)*
Controlled Automation Inc ....F...... 317 770-3870
   Noblesville *(G-11084)*

S I C

CTS Corporation ....G...... 574 293-7511
Berne *(G-611)*

▲ Custom Magnetics Inc ....E...... 773 463-6500
North Manchester *(G-11227)*

Direct Control Systems Inc ....G...... 765 282-7474
Muncie *(G-10460)*

Fabricated Specialties Inc ....G...... 219 996-4787
Hebron *(G-6012)*

▼ Fabtration LLC ....F...... 812 989-6730
Georgetown *(G-5144)*

Hoffmaster Electric Inc ....C...... 219 616-1313
Schererville *(G-12323)*

▲ Hubbell Incorporated Delaware ....B...... 574 234-7151
South Bend *(G-12806)*

Integrated Tech Resources ....G...... 317 757-5432
Indianapolis *(G-7249)*

Integratorcom Inc ....D...... 317 776-3500
Noblesville *(G-11130)*

Integrity Marketing Team Inc ....G...... 317 517-0012
Plainfield *(G-11617)*

J & J Industrial Services Inc ....G...... 219 362-4973
La Porte *(G-8772)*

▲ Janco Engineered Products LLC ....C...... 574 255-3169
Mishawaka *(G-10060)*

Landis Gyr Utilities Svcs Inc ....E...... 765 742-1001
Lafayette *(G-8953)*

Leman Engrg & Consulting Inc ....G...... 574 870-7732
Brookston *(G-1106)*

Mechanical Engineering Control ....F...... 574 294-7580
Elkhart *(G-3025)*

Pinder Instruments Company Inc ....E...... 219 924-7070
Munster *(G-10624)*

Proteus Solutions LLC ....G...... 317 222-1138
Indianapolis *(G-7783)*

Quality Industrial Supplies ....F...... 219 324-2654
La Porte *(G-8808)*

Richard J Bagan Inc ....E...... 260 244-5115
Columbia City *(G-1826)*

Schneder Elc Bldngs Amrcas Inc ....G...... 317 894-6374
Greenfield *(G-5571)*

Schneider Electric ....G...... 574 293-0877
Elkhart *(G-3158)*

Semcor Inc ....F...... 219 362-0222
La Porte *(G-8817)*

Siemens Industry Inc ....D...... 219 763-7927
Portage *(G-11794)*

▲ Sigma Switches Plus Inc ....E...... 574 294-5776
Elkhart *(G-3170)*

Standard Fusee Corporation ....E...... 765 472-4375
Peru *(G-11548)*

Sullivan Engineered Services ....G...... 812 294-1724
Henryville *(G-6033)*

Teaco Inc ....E...... 219 874-6234
Michigan City *(G-9852)*

▲ Touchplate Technologies Inc ....F...... 260 424-4323
Fort Wayne *(G-4696)*

Western Consolidated Tech Inc ....D...... 260 495-9866
Fremont *(G-4982)*

3621 Motors & Generators

American Mitsuba Corporation ....C...... 989 779-4962
Monroeville *(G-10191)*

An-Mar Wiring Systems Inc ....F...... 574 255-5523
Mishawaka *(G-9996)*

B & H Electric and Supply Inc ....E...... 812 522-5607
Seymour *(G-12431)*

Blinkless Power Equipment LLC ....G...... 317 844-7328
Indianapolis *(G-6484)*

▲ Bluffton Motor Works LLC ....C...... 800 579-8527
Bluffton *(G-867)*

◆ Borgwarner Pds Anderson LLC ....B...... 765 778-6499
Noblesville *(G-11068)*

Borgwarner Pds Anderson LLC ....C...... 765 778-6499
Anderson *(G-76)*

Burt Products Inc ....G...... 812 386-6890
Princeton *(G-11867)*

▲ Coil Tran Corp ....D...... 219 942-8511
Hobart *(G-6076)*

Contour Hardening Inc ....G...... 317 876-1530
Indianapolis *(G-6659)*

▲ Contour Hardening Inc ....E...... 888 867-2184
Indianapolis *(G-6660)*

Cummins Inc ....A...... 812 522-9366
Seymour *(G-12442)*

Cummins Inc ....B...... 812 377-5000
Columbus *(G-1891)*

Cummins Inc ....G...... 812 377-8601
Columbus *(G-1894)*

Cummins Inc ....E...... 812 377-2932
Columbus *(G-1895)*

Cummins Inc ....G...... 317 244-7251
Indianapolis *(G-6709)*

Cummins Inc ....G...... 317 610-2493
Indianapolis *(G-6710)*

Cummins Power Generation Inc ....E...... 574 262-4611
Elkhart *(G-2783)*

▲ Custom Magnetics Inc ....E...... 773 463-6500
North Manchester *(G-11227)*

D & E Auto Electric Inc ....F...... 219 763-3892
Portage *(G-11759)*

Double Eagle Industries Inc ....E...... 260 768-4121
Shipshewana *(G-12612)*

Electric Motors and Spc ....C...... 260 357-4141
Garrett *(G-5003)*

Electro Corporation ....F...... 219 393-5571
Kingsbury *(G-8536)*

Elevator Equipment Corporation ....D...... 765 966-7761
Richmond *(G-11981)*

Engenaire ....G...... 574 264-0391
Elkhart *(G-2834)*

Fowler Ridge II Wind Farm LLC ....E...... 713 354-2100
Fowler *(G-4799)*

◆ Franklin Electric Co Inc ....B...... 260 824-2900
Fort Wayne *(G-4285)*

Franklin Electric Intl ....G...... 260 824-2900
Fort Wayne *(G-4286)*

G & M Rebuilders Inc ....G...... 812 858-9233
Newburgh *(G-11029)*

General Electric Company ....B...... 260 439-2000
Fort Wayne *(G-4297)*

Go Electric Inc ....F...... 765 400-1347
Anderson *(G-111)*

▲ Hansen Corporation ....E...... 812 385-3000
Princeton *(G-11874)*

Hendershot Service Center Inc ....F...... 765 653-2600
Greencastle *(G-5464)*

Hillside Motor Sales LLC ....G...... 219 322-7700
Schererville *(G-12322)*

I Power Energy Systems LLC ....E...... 765 621-9980
Anderson *(G-120)*

Ies Subsidiary Holdings Inc ....F...... 330 830-3500
South Bend *(G-12807)*

Illinois Tool Works Inc ....E...... 317 298-5000
Indianapolis *(G-7160)*

Infrastructure and Energy ....F...... 765 828-2580
Indianapolis *(G-7228)*

Ipfw Student Housing ....G...... 260 481-4180
Fort Wayne *(G-4382)*

Ipower Technologies Inc ....E...... 317 574-0103
Anderson *(G-121)*

Jeannie and Rachel Heidenreich ....G...... 260 244-4583
Columbia City *(G-1801)*

▲ JMS Electronics Corporation ....E...... 574 522-0246
Elkhart *(G-2949)*

Jones Engineering Inc ....G...... 812 254-6456
Washington *(G-13989)*

Kay Industries Inc ....F...... 574 236-6220
Plymouth *(G-11698)*

Kay Industries Inc ....F...... 574 236-6220
Plymouth *(G-11699)*

Kendrion (mishawaka) LLC ....E...... 574 257-2422
Mishawaka *(G-10063)*

Leclanche SA ....G...... 765 610-0050
Anderson *(G-133)*

Liberty Green Renewables LLP ....B...... 812 951-3143
Georgetown *(G-5148)*

Lynx Motion Technology Corp ....E...... 812 923-7474
Greenville *(G-5650)*

Matrix Nac ....F...... 219 931-6600
Hammond *(G-5914)*

Mighty-Quip Industries ....G...... 260 615-1899
Fort Wayne *(G-4475)*

MO Trailer Corporation ....F...... 574 533-0824
Goshen *(G-5295)*

MRC Technology Inc ....F...... 574 232-9057
South Bend *(G-12867)*

OH Hunt Lines Inc ....G...... 260 856-2126
Cromwell *(G-2210)*

Pete D Limkemann ....G...... 260 403-4297
Fort Wayne *(G-4526)*

Qp Inc ....F...... 574 295-6884
Elkhart *(G-3125)*

Red Barn Industries Inc ....F...... 765 379-3197
Mulberry *(G-10419)*

Regal Beloit America Inc ....C...... 574 583-9171
Monticello *(G-10282)*

Regal Beloit America Inc ....G...... 260 416-5400
Fort Wayne *(G-4586)*

Remy Electric Motors LLC ....E...... 765 778-6466
Pendleton *(G-11503)*

Remy Power Products LLC ....A...... 765 778-6499
Pendleton *(G-11504)*

Scottorsville Sales and Svc ....G...... 765 250-5245
Lafayette *(G-8998)*

Semcor Inc ....F...... 219 362-0222
La Porte *(G-8817)*

Shooting Stars Synchro Inc ....G...... 317 710-1462
Noblesville *(G-11182)*

Siemens Industry Inc ....D...... 219 763-7927
Portage *(G-11794)*

▲ Southern Electric Coil LLC ....E...... 219 931-5500
Hammond *(G-5944)*

Sterling Electric Inc ....G...... 317 872-0471
Indianapolis *(G-8002)*

▲ Sterling Electric Inc ....G...... 317 872-0471
Indianapolis *(G-8001)*

▲ Summit/Ems Corporation ....E...... 574 722-1317
Logansport *(G-9366)*

▲ Vanair Manufacturing Inc ....C...... 219 879-5100
Michigan City *(G-9857)*

W W Williams Company LLC ....F...... 260 827-0553
Bluffton *(G-896)*

Warner Electric LLC ....C...... 260 244-6183
Columbia City *(G-1846)*

3624 Carbon & Graphite Prdts

Aerodine Composites LLC ....F...... 317 271-1207
Indianapolis *(G-6347)*

Aerodine Engineering Group LLC ....G...... 317 271-1207
Indianapolis *(G-6348)*

Applied Composites Engrg Inc ....E...... 317 243-4225
Indianapolis *(G-6411)*

Composite Specialties ....G...... 317 852-1408
Brownsburg *(G-1144)*

Demotte Manufacturing Inc ....G...... 219 987-6196
Demotte *(G-2435)*

Hickman Williams & Company ....B...... 812 522-6293
Seymour *(G-12454)*

Hickman Williams & Company ....F...... 708 656-8818
La Porte *(G-12807)*

Indy Prfmce Composites Inc ....G...... 317 858-7793
Brownsburg *(G-1154)*

3625 Relays & Indl Controls

ABB Flexible Automation Inc ....E...... 317 876-9090
Indianapolis *(G-6307)*

▲ Advanced Control Tech Inc ....G...... 317 806-2750
Indianapolis *(G-6332)*

Advantage Electronics Inc ....F...... 317 888-1946
Greenwood *(G-5659)*

AEL/Span LLC ....E...... 317 203-4602
Plainfield *(G-11591)*

▲ American Elctrnic Cmpnents Inc .....E...... 574 295-6330
Elkhart *(G-2682)*

Amt Parts International Corp ....E...... 260 490-0223
Fort Wayne *(G-4075)*

Aptiv Services Us LLC ....F...... 765 451-5011
Kokomo *(G-8591)*

Automation & Control Svcs Inc ....F...... 219 558-2060
Schererville *(G-12315)*

Axis Controls Inc ....G...... 260 414-4028
Fort Wayne *(G-4099)*

▼ B & M Electrical Co Inc ....F...... 765 448-4532
Lafayette *(G-8859)*

Benshaw Inc ....G...... 412 487-8235
Noblesville *(G-11067)*

◆ Borgwarner Pds Anderson LLC ....B...... 765 778-6499
Noblesville *(G-11068)*

Borgwarner Pds Anderson LLC ....C...... 765 778-6499
Anderson *(G-76)*

Brenda Sue Ware Eaton LLC ....G...... 317 462-2058
Greenfield *(G-5509)*

◆ Carson Manufacturing Co Inc ....F...... 317 257-3191
Indianapolis *(G-6560)*

▼ Control Consultants of America ....G...... 219 989-3311
Hammond *(G-5865)*

Control Solutions ....G...... 765 313-1984
West Lafayette *(G-14060)*

D & E Auto Electric Inc ....F...... 219 763-3892
Portage *(G-11759)*

Damping Technologies Inc ....E...... 574 258-7916
Mishawaka *(G-10031)*

Damping Technologies Inc ....E...... 574 258-7916
Mishawaka *(G-10032)*

Dayton-Phoenix Group Inc ....D...... 765 742-4410
West Lafayette *(G-14063)*

Direct Control Systems Inc ....G...... 765 282-7474
Muncie *(G-10460)*

Doron Distribution Inc ....G...... 317 594-9259
Indianapolis *(G-6759)*

Duesenburg Inc....G.... 260 496-9650
Fort Wayne (G-4223)
E C T Franklin Control Systems....G.... 765 939-2531
Richmond (G-11979)
Eaton & Hancock Associates....G.... 317 291-6513
Indianapolis (G-6795)
Eaton Corporation....C.... 574 283-5004
South Bend (G-12755)
Eaton Emts....G.... 765 587-4910
Muncie (G-10467)
Eaton Hydraulics LLC....G.... 260 248-5800
Columbia City (G-1782)
Eaton Partners LLC....G.... 765 458-7896
Liberty (G-9260)
Electro Corporation....F.... 219 393-5571
Kingsbury (G-8536)
Electromechanical RES Labs....E.... 812 948-8484
New Albany (G-10771)
Enginring Cncpts Unlimited Inc....G.... 317 826-1558
Fishers (G-3905)
Enoise Control Inc....G.... 317 774-1900
Westfield (G-14162)
Environmental Technology Inc....E.... 574 233-1202
South Bend (G-12765)
Flosource Inc....E.... 765 342-1360
Martinsville (G-9605)
Frakes Engineering Inc....E.... 317 577-3000
Indianapolis (G-6956)
Franklin Electric Co Inc....D.... 765 677-6900
Gas City (G-5124)
▲ Functional Devices Inc....G.... 765 883-5538
Sharpsville (G-12505)
G W Enterprises....G.... 260 868-2555
Butler (G-1228)
General Automation Company....F.... 317 849-7483
Indianapolis (G-6992)
GM Components Holdings LLC....G.... 765 451-9049
Kokomo (G-8629)
Harris Corporation....C.... 260 451-6000
Fort Wayne (G-4322)
Hitachi Automotive Systems....B.... 859 734-9451
Ligonier (G-9287)
▲ Horner Apg LLC....D.... 317 916-4274
Indianapolis (G-7127)
Horner Industrial Services Inc....G.... 317 916-4274
Indianapolis (G-7128)
Horner Industrial Services Inc....G.... 812 466-5281
Terre Haute (G-13249)
Horner Industrial Services Inc....G.... 260 434-1189
Fort Wayne (G-4348)
▼ Industrial Conductor Products....G.... 219 662-9477
Crown Point (G-2262)
Innovative Battery Power Inc....G.... 260 267-6582
Fort Wayne (G-4372)
ITT LLC....G.... 260 451-6000
Fort Wayne (G-4385)
▲ JMS Electronics Corporation....E.... 574 522-0246
Elkhart (G-2949)
Kcma & Services LLC....G.... 260 645-0885
Waterloo (G-14016)
▲ Kreuter Manufacturing Co Inc....G.... 574 831-4626
New Paris (G-10989)
L H Controls Inc....F.... 260 432-9020
Fort Wayne (G-4420)
Micro-Precision Operations....E.... 260 589-2136
Berne (G-620)
MRC Technology Inc....F.... 574 232-9057
South Bend (G-12867)
Neo Magnequench Dist LLC....G.... 765 778-7809
Pendleton (G-11496)
Nidec Motor Corporation....D.... 812 385-2564
Princeton (G-11880)
Nidec Motor Corporation....A.... 317 328-4079
Indianapolis (G-7587)
Power Components of Midwest....C.... 574 256-6990
Mishawaka (G-10105)
Pyromation Inc....C.... 260 484-2580
Fort Wayne (G-4566)
Remy Power Products LLC....A.... 765 778-6499
Pendleton (G-11504)
Riverside Mfg LLC....B.... 260 637-4470
Fort Wayne (G-4595)
Rockwell Automation Inc....E.... 219 924-3002
Munster (G-10626)
Ron Eaton....G.... 219 464-1607
Valparaiso (G-13610)
Rs2 Technologies LLC....F.... 877 682-3532
Munster (G-10628)
SBS Cybermetrix Inc....G.... 812 378-7960
Columbus (G-2011)
SGS Cybermetrix Inc....G.... 800 713-1203
Columbus (G-2013)
Siemens Industry Inc....D.... 219 763-7927
Portage (G-11794)
▲ Sigma Switches Plus Inc....E.... 574 294-5776
Elkhart (G-3170)
▲ SMC Corporation of America....B.... 317 899-3182
Noblesville (G-11184)
Tamara Eaton....G.... 219 872-9151
Michigan City (G-9851)
Teaco Inc....F.... 219 874-6234
Michigan City (G-9852)
Terry Eaton....G.... 812 687-7579
Plainville (G-11655)
▲ Touch Plate Technologies Inc....F.... 260 426-1565
Fort Wayne (G-4695)
▲ Touchplate Technologies Inc....F.... 260 424-4323
Fort Wayne (G-4696)
Touchtronics Inc....F.... 574 294-2570
Elkhart (G-3221)
West Side Automation....F.... 812 768-6878
Haubstadt (G-6008)
Western Consolidated Tech Inc....D.... 260 495-9866
Fremont (G-4982)
Wolfe and Swickard Mch Co Inc....D.... 317 241-2589
Indianapolis (G-8210)

3629 Electrical Indl Apparatus, NEC

▲ Amerawhip Inc....G.... 317 639-5248
Indianapolis (G-6383)
Delta Microinverter LLC....G.... 317 274-5935
Zionsville (G-14430)
▲ Empro Manufacturing Co Inc....E.... 317 823-3000
Indianapolis (G-6859)
▲ Energy Access Inc....F.... 317 329-1676
Indianapolis (G-6864)
Flat Electronics LLC....G.... 765 414-6635
Lafayette (G-8899)
Globalvue International LLC....G.... 866 974-1968
Indianapolis (G-7014)
Go Electric Inc....F.... 765 400-1347
Anderson (G-111)
Gregory Thomas Inc....G.... 219 324-3801
La Porte (G-8758)
▲ Kirby Risk Corporation....D.... 765 448-4567
Lafayette (G-8940)
Motion & Control Entps LLC....F.... 219 844-4224
Hammond (G-5918)
MRC Technology Inc....F.... 574 232-9057
South Bend (G-12867)
R B Annis Instruments Inc....G.... 765 848-1621
Greencastle (G-5476)
▲ Southwater Sourcing LLC....G.... 219 809-7106
Michigan City (G-9845)
▲ Xantrex Technology USA Inc....F.... 574 522-9628
Elkhart (G-3270)

3631 Household Cooking Eqpt

Betos Bar Inc....G.... 219 397-8247
East Chicago (G-2523)
Challenge Tool & Mfg Inc....D.... 260 749-9558
New Haven (G-10934)
Dynamic Packg Solutions Inc....C.... 574 848-1410
Bristol (G-1057)
Elixir Industries....E.... 574 294-5685
Elkhart (G-2816)
◆ Onward Manufacturing Company....D.... 260 358-4111
Huntington (G-6233)
Sterling Manufacturing LLC....G.... 260 451-9760
Fort Wayne (G-4648)
Thermodyne Food Service Pdts....E.... 260 428-2535
Fort Wayne (G-4682)

3632 Household Refrigerators & Freezers

Freezing Systems and Svc Inc....F.... 219 879-6236
Michigan City (G-9796)
▼ JC Refrigeration LLC....G.... 260 768-4067
Shipshewana (G-12622)
Whirlpool Corporation....C.... 812 426-4000
Evansville (G-3811)

3633 Household Laundry Eqpt

▲ Accra-Pac Inc....D.... 574 295-0000
Elkhart (G-2665)
Accra-Pac Inc....D.... 905 660-0444
Elkhart (G-2666)
Grassco Inc....G.... 260 749-5437
Fort Wayne (G-4304)
Souder Power Washing LLC....G.... 812 894-2544
Terre Haute (G-13336)
Whirlpool Corporation....A.... 317 837-5300
Plainfield (G-11651)

3634 Electric Household Appliances

Air Energy Systems Inc....G.... 317 290-8500
Indianapolis (G-6353)
▲ Battle Creek Equipment Co....E.... 260 495-3472
Fremont (G-4952)
Dometic Corporation....E.... 574 389-3759
Goshen (G-5202)
◆ Fanimation Inc....E.... 317 733-4113
Zionsville (G-14431)
Fulton Co R E M C....G.... 574 223-3156
Rochester (G-12125)
Hoosier Roaster Llc....G.... 574 257-1415
Mishawaka (G-10051)
▲ Hyndman Industrial Pdts Inc....E.... 260 483-6042
Fort Wayne (G-4354)
Naptown Vapors LLC....G.... 765 315-0554
Martinsville (G-9629)
▲ Royal Spa Corporation....D.... 317 781-0828
Indianapolis (G-7867)
Scott Fetzer Company....D.... 260 488-3531
Hamilton (G-5828)
Ultra-Heat Inc....F.... 574 522-6594
Elkhart (G-3232)

3635 Household Vacuum Cleaners

Arden Companies LLC....D.... 260 747-1657
Fort Wayne (G-4089)
Steamin Demon Inc....G.... 812 288-6754
Clarksville (G-1697)

3639 Household Appliances, NEC

Ebert Machine Company Inc....E.... 765 473-3728
Peru (G-11526)
◆ Sailrite Enterprises Inc....F.... 260 244-4647
Columbia City (G-1833)
Solfire Contract Mfg Inc....F.... 260 755-2115
Fort Wayne (G-4634)

3641 Electric Lamps

6605 E State LLC....G.... 260 433-7007
Fort Wayne (G-4033)
Acuity Brands Lighting Inc....B.... 765 362-1837
Crawfordsville (G-2132)
◆ American Ultraviolet Company....D.... 765 483-9514
Lebanon (G-9168)
Energy Saver Lights Inc....F.... 202 544-7868
Indianapolis (G-6866)
GE Lexington Lamp Plant....G.... 859 277-1161
Fort Wayne (G-4294)
General Electric Company....D.... 812 933-0700
Batesville (G-501)
Lomont Holdings Co Inc....E.... 800 545-9023
Angola (G-228)
▲ Pent Plastics Inc....C.... 260 897-3775
Kendallville (G-8502)
Tap-A-Lite Inc....E.... 219 932-8067
Hammond (G-5948)
Valeo North America Inc....A.... 248 619-8300
Seymour (G-12498)
▲ Vista Manufacturing Inc....E.... 574 264-0711
Elkhart (G-3247)

3643 Current-Carrying Wiring Devices

▲ Advanced Control Tech Inc....G.... 317 806-2750
Indianapolis (G-6332)
▲ Aearo Technologies LLC....A.... 317 692-6666
Indianapolis (G-6341)
◆ Almega/Tru-Flex Inc....E.... 574 546-2113
Bremen (G-982)
An-Mar Wiring Systems Inc....F.... 574 255-5523
Mishawaka (G-9996)
Bb Wiring LLC....G.... 765 376-0190
Crawfordsville (G-2135)
Bender Products Inc....E.... 574 255-5350
Mishawaka (G-10009)
Bowmar LLC....E.... 260 747-3121
Fort Wayne (G-4116)
Cloud Defensive LLC....G.... 812 760-5017
Newburgh (G-11025)
▲ Cme LLC....B.... 260 623-3700
Monroeville (G-10192)
Coleman Cable LLC....C.... 574 546-5115
Bremen (G-990)

S I C

Employee Codes: A=Over 500 employees, B=251-500
C=101-250, D=51-100, E=20-50, F=10-19, G=2-9
2018 Harris Indiana
Industrial Directory
659

▲ Connecta Corporation ....F 317 923-9282
Indianapolis (G-6651)

Contact Fabricators Ind Inc ....G 765 779-4125
Shirley (G-12661)

▲ E M F Corp ....E 260 665-9541
Angola (G-208)

E M F Corp ....E 260 488-2479
Hamilton (G-5821)

▲ Elkhart Supply Corp ....E 574 264-4156
Elkhart (G-2831)

Energypoint LLC ....G 317 275-7979
Carmel (G-1371)

Freudenberg-Nok General Partnr ....C 765 763-7246
Morristown (G-10369)

▲ Functional Devices Inc ....G 765 883-5538
Sharpsville (G-12505)

Group Dekko Inc ....F 260 637-3964
Laotto (G-9109)

▲ Group Dekko Inc ....D 260 357-3621
Garrett (G-5009)

Hitachi Cable America Inc ....B 812 945-9011
New Albany (G-10795)

▼ Independent Protection Co Inc ....C 574 533-4116
Goshen (G-5242)

Independent Protection Co Inc ....E 574 533-4116
Goshen (G-5243)

Independent Protection Co Inc ....D 574 831-5680
New Paris (G-10985)

Kendrion (mishawaka) LLC ....E 574 257-2422
Mishawaka (G-10063)

Kirby Risk Corporation ....B 765 447-1402
Lafayette (G-8942)

Lime City Manufacturing Co ....E 260 356-6826
Huntington (G-6224)

Llama Corporation ....G 888 701-7432
Decatur (G-2391)

Nidec Motor Corporation ....A 317 328-4079
Indianapolis (G-7587)

Odyssian Technology LLC ....G 574 257-7555
South Bend (G-12882)

Outman Industries Inc ....G 260 467-1576
Fort Wayne (G-4514)

Pent Assemblies ....D 260 347-5828
Kendallville (G-8501)

REA Magnet Wire Company Inc ....B 765 477-8000
Lafayette (G-8989)

Rees Inc ....F 260 495-9811
Fremont (G-4972)

Tap-A-Lite Inc ....E 219 932-8067
Hammond (G-5948)

Thomas & Betts Corp ....G 901 252-8000
Westfield (G-14194)

▲ Touchplate Technologies Inc ....F 260 424-4323
Fort Wayne (G-4696)

Ucom Inc ....F 260 829-1294
Orland (G-11358)

Western Consolidated Tech Inc ....D 260 495-9866
Fremont (G-4982)

3644 Noncurrent-Carrying Wiring Devices

Appleton Grp LLC ....D 219 326-5936
La Porte (G-8734)

Bo-Witt Products Inc ....E 812 526-5561
Edinburgh (G-2597)

E Squared Motorsports LLC ....G 317 626-2937
Avon (G-439)

Fastlane Raceway ....G 812 430-8818
Evansville (G-3501)

Gund Company Inc ....E 219 374-9944
Cedar Lake (G-1529)

Hoffmaster Electric Inc ....G 219 616-1313
Schererville (G-12323)

▲ Hubbell Incorporated Delaware ....B 574 234-7151
South Bend (G-12806)

Juncos Racing ....G 317 640-2348
Indianapolis (G-7321)

Lucas Oil Raceway ....F 317 291-4090
Indianapolis (G-7423)

Miller Raceway ....G 219 939-9688
Gary (G-5076)

Napier & Napier ....G 765 580-9116
Liberty (G-9266)

Raceway Commons ....G 303 503-4333
Indianapolis (G-7812)

Raceway Distributing Inc ....G 574 850-8191
Mishawaka (G-10115)

Raceway Hand Car Wash LLC ....G 260 242-9866
Kendallville (G-8505)

Regal Beloit America Inc ....C 574 583-9171
Monticello (G-10282)

▲ Touch Plate Technologies Inc ....F 260 426-1565
Fort Wayne (G-4695)

Winona Building Products LLC ....F 574 822-0100
Etna Green (G-3323)

3645 Residential Lighting Fixtures

▲ A Homestead Shoppe Inc ....E 574 784-2307
Lapaz (G-9116)

Fashion Flooring and Ltg Inc ....G 219 531-5667
Valparaiso (G-13540)

Lasalle Bristol Corporation ....E 574 295-4400
Bristol (G-1065)

◆ Lasalle Bristol Corporation ....C 574 295-4400
Elkhart (G-2985)

Metalite Corporation ....D 812 944-6600
New Albany (G-10828)

Professional Lighting Services ....F 317 844-4261
Carmel (G-1456)

Ward Industries Inc ....F 574 825-2548
Middlebury (G-9923)

3646 Commercial, Indl & Institutional Lighting Fixtures

Acuity Brands Inc ....F 765 362-1837
Crawfordsville (G-2131)

Acuity Brands Lighting Inc ....B 765 362-1837
Crawfordsville (G-2132)

Acuity Brands Lighting Inc ....F 317 849-1233
Fishers (G-3866)

Amerlight LLC ....G 812 602-3452
Evansville (G-3355)

B&D Lights LLC ....G 765 452-2761
Kokomo (G-8596)

▼ Craft Metal Products Inc ....G 317 545-3252
Indianapolis (G-6684)

Digital Cmmnties Intiative Inc ....G 317 580-0111
Carmel (G-1360)

Dream Lighting Inc ....G 574 206-4888
Elkhart (G-2800)

Eco Lighting Solutions LLC ....F 866 897-1234
Indianapolis (G-6800)

Green Illuminating Systems Inc ....G 317 869-7430
Noblesville (G-11113)

Lomont Holdings Co Inc ....E 800 545-9023
Angola (G-228)

Metalite Corporation ....D 812 944-6600
New Albany (G-10828)

Premiere Building Mtls Inc ....G 574 293-5800
Elkhart (G-3114)

Professional Grade Svcs LLC ....G 317 688-8898
Indianapolis (G-7772)

Semcor Inc ....F 219 362-0222
La Porte (G-8817)

Source Products Inc ....G 260 424-0864
Columbia City (G-1835)

Specified Lighting Fixs of Ind ....F 317 577-8100
Indianapolis (G-7970)

Specified Ltg Systems Ind Inc ....F 317 577-8100
Indianapolis (G-7971)

Ward Industries Inc ....F 574 825-2548
Middlebury (G-9923)

3647 Vehicular Lighting Eqpt

BTR Engineering ....G 812 360-9415
Bloomington (G-691)

Business Adventures Inc ....G 574 674-9996
Osceola (G-11371)

Dajac Inc ....G 317 608-0500
Westfield (G-14155)

◆ Grote Industries Inc ....A 812 273-2121
Madison (G-9463)

Grote Industries LLC ....A 812 265-8273
Madison (G-9464)

Hokey Spokes ....G 219 938-7360
Gary (G-5065)

J J Lites ....G 765 966-3252
Richmond (G-12004)

Jtn Services Inc ....G 765 653-7158
Greencastle (G-5465)

Lund International Holding Co ....E 765 742-7200
Lafayette (G-8963)

New Vision Manufacturing Inc ....G 812 522-5585
Seymour (G-12471)

North American Lighting Inc ....A 812 983-2663
Elberfeld (G-2637)

Patrick Industries Inc ....D 574 522-0871
Elkhart (G-3085)

▲ Tcb Enterprises LLC ....F 574 522-3971
Elkhart (G-3207)

Techshot Lighting LLC ....G 812 923-9591
Floyds Knobs (G-4020)

3648 Lighting Eqpt, NEC

Advanced Kinematics Inc ....G 574 533-8178
Goshen (G-5167)

Always Sun Tanning Center ....G 812 238-2786
Terre Haute (G-13192)

Ao Inc ....G 317 280-3000
Avon (G-427)

Around Campus LLC ....G 574 360-6571
South Bend (G-12711)

B and D Lighting ....G 317 414-8056
Indianapolis (G-6449)

Badger Daylighting Corp ....G 219 762-9177
Portage (G-11750)

Charm-Lite Inc ....G 765 644-6876
Anderson (G-84)

Circle City Lighting Inc ....G 317 439-0824
Noblesville (G-11081)

Cloud Defensive LLC ....G 812 760-5017
Newburgh (G-11025)

Comcast Spotlight ....G 317 502-5098
Indianapolis (G-6636)

Comcast Spotlight Muncie ....G 765 216-1728
Muncie (G-10446)

Dekker Lighting ....G 219 227-8520
Schererville (G-12320)

▲ General Manufacturing Inc ....E 260 824-3627
Bluffton (G-875)

Gmp Holdings LLC ....G 317 353-6580
Indianapolis (G-7016)

▲ Ikio Led Lighting LLC ....F 765 414-0835
Indianapolis (G-7157)

In The Spotlight LLC ....G 260 519-1805
North Manchester (G-11231)

J&L Lighting Solutions LLC ....G 317 413-8768
Indianapolis (G-7291)

Lake Effect Lighting LLC ....G 812 783-9482
Bloomington (G-761)

Lawncreations LLC ....G 574 536-1546
Millersburg (G-9971)

Logical Lighting and Controls ....G 317 244-8234
Indianapolis (G-7415)

Lumen Cache Inc ....G 317 222-1314
Indianapolis (G-7426)

Mag Instrument Inc ....G 574 262-1521
Elkhart (G-3015)

Metalite Corporation ....D 812 944-6600
New Albany (G-10828)

Mid-America Sound Corporation ....F 317 947-9880
Greenfield (G-5552)

Mobile Stadium Lighting LLC ....G 219 325-0000
La Porte (G-8796)

Natural Lighting LLC ....G 574 907-9457
Nappanee (G-10697)

Nu Led Lighting ....G 317 989-7352
Greenwood (G-5729)

Orka Technologies LLC ....G 812 378-9842
Columbus (G-1986)

Searchlight Social LLC ....G 317 983-3802
Kokomo (G-8692)

Spectrum Brands Inc ....B 317 773-6627
Noblesville (G-11187)

Spotlight LLC ....G 219 616-4421
Culver (G-2326)

Spotlight On Drama ....G 765 643-7170
Anderson (G-169)

▲ Touch Plate Technologies Inc ....F 260 426-1565
Fort Wayne (G-4695)

▲ Touchplate Technologies Inc ....F 260 424-4323
Fort Wayne (G-4696)

Triad Warsh Plant Scale House ....G 812 385-0909
Petersburg (G-11571)

Uberlux Inc ....G 317 580-0111
Carmel (G-1501)

Vista Worldwide LLC ....G 574 264-0711
Elkhart (G-3248)

Ward Industries Inc ....F 574 825-2548
Middlebury (G-9923)

3651 Household Audio & Video Eqpt

▲ A E Techron Inc ....F 574 295-9495
Elkhart (G-2657)

American Mobile Sound Ind LLC ....G 765 288-1500
Muncie (G-10430)

Boyer Enterprises Inc ....G 812 963-9180
Evansville (G-3394)

Continntal Broadcast Group LLC ....E 317 924-1071
Indianapolis (G-6657)

Csd Group Inc ....E 260 918-3500
New Haven *(G-10937)*

Dage-MTI Michigan City Inc ....G 219 872-5514
Michigan City *(G-9780)*

Damping Technologies Inc ....E 574 258-7916
Mishawaka *(G-10031)*

Digital Evolution ....G 317 839-7963
Plainfield *(G-11604)*

◆ Draper Inc.......................................B 765 987-7999
Spiceland *(G-13054)*

Ebey Sales & Service ....G 260 636-3286
Albion *(G-27)*

GM Components Holdings LLC ....G 765 451-9049
Kokomo *(G-8629)*

▲ Harman Embedded Audio LLC ....E 317 849-8175
Indianapolis *(G-7077)*

Harman Professional Inc ....G 574 294-8000
Elkhart *(G-2908)*

Haven Technologies Inc ....G 317 490-7197
Carmel *(G-1399)*

Image Vault LLC ....G 812 948-8400
New Albany *(G-10802)*

◆ Itech Holdings LLC ....E 317 567-5160
Indianapolis *(G-7276)*

Jon E Gee Enterprises Inc ....G 317 291-4522
Carmel *(G-1420)*

JP Technology Inc ....G 219 947-2525
Crown Point *(G-2270)*

Kas Satellite & Cable Inc ....G 260 833-3941
Angola *(G-224)*

Kauffman Enterprises Inc ....G 260 434-1590
Fort Wayne *(G-4404)*

Kelley Global Brands LLC ....G 833 554-8326
Noblesville *(G-11136)*

◆ Klipsch Group Inc ....C 317 860-8100
Indianapolis *(G-7360)*

Loys Sales Inc ....G 765 552-7250
Elwood *(G-3304)*

Mark Murray ....G 812 372-8390
Columbus *(G-1969)*

Michana Used Music and Media ....G 574 247-1188
Mishawaka *(G-10079)*

Mobile Communications Tech ....G 812 423-7322
Evansville *(G-3631)*

◆ MTS Products Corp ....E 574 295-3142
Elkhart *(G-3054)*

MTS Products Corp ....F 574 295-3142
Elkhart *(G-3055)*

Oscar Telecom Inc ....G 317 359-7000
Indianapolis *(G-7634)*

R B Annis Instruments Inc ....G 765 848-1621
Greencastle *(G-5476)*

Recon Group LLP ....G 855 874-8741
Greenfield *(G-5566)*

Rhodes Amplification LLC ....G 765 775-5100
West Lafayette *(G-14103)*

Rider Productions ....G 260 471-0099
Fort Wayne *(G-4593)*

▲ Skytech II Inc ....G 260 459-1703
Fort Wayne *(G-4629)*

▲ Skytech-Systems Inc ....F 260 459-1703
Fort Wayne *(G-4630)*

▲ Sony Dadc US Inc ....A 812 462-8100
Terre Haute *(G-13334)*

▲ Sports Select Usa Inc ....G 317 631-4011
Indianapolis *(G-7978)*

Tech Solutions and Sales Inc ....G 317 536-5846
Indianapolis *(G-8047)*

Technology Cons Group LLC ....G 219 525-4064
Merrillville *(G-9757)*

▲ U-Nitt LLC ....G 812 251-9980
Carmel *(G-1499)*

Uncle Alberts Amplifier Inc ....G 317 845-3037
Indianapolis *(G-8126)*

Vidicom Corporation ....F 219 923-7475
Hammond *(G-5956)*

3652 Phonograph Records & Magnetic Tape

Asahi TEC America Corporation ....G 765 962-8399
Richmond *(G-11956)*

Boeke Road Baptist Church Inc ....G 812 479-5342
Evansville *(G-3389)*

Cliff A Ostermeyer.............................G 615 361-7902
Indianapolis *(G-6621)*

◆ Rhi US Ltd ....G 219 237-2420
Hammond *(G-5934)*

▲ Sony Dadc US Inc ....A 812 462-8100
Terre Haute *(G-13334)*

◆ Voice of God Recordings Inc...........D 812 246-2137
Jeffersonville *(G-8439)*

▲ World Media Group Inc ....C 317 549-8484
Indianapolis *(G-8216)*

3661 Telephone & Telegraph Apparatus

Acd Suppliers LLC ....G 317 527-9715
Indianapolis *(G-6315)*

American Cmnty Bnk Ind Modem 2....G 219 627-3381
Saint John *(G-12259)*

Byte Blue Technology Solutions ....G 574 903-5637
Elkhart *(G-2741)*

C&D Technologies Inc ....G 765 762-2461
Attica *(G-298)*

Coriant Operations Inc ....D 219 785-1737
La Porte *(G-8745)*

GE Power Electronics Inc ....G 317 259-9264
Indianapolis *(G-6988)*

Great Deals Magazine ....F 765 649-3302
Anderson *(G-112)*

International Resources Inc ....G 317 813-5300
Indianapolis *(G-7261)*

Lyra LLC ....G 260 452-4058
Fort Wayne *(G-4445)*

Siemens AG ....G 574 522-6807
Elkhart *(G-3169)*

Smart Choice Mobile Inc ....F 574 830-5727
Elkhart *(G-3177)*

Sprint Spectrum LP ....G 765 983-6991
Richmond *(G-12053)*

◆ Telamon International Corp ....E 317 818-6888
Carmel *(G-1490)*

▲ Telamon Technologies Corp ....A 317 818-6888
Carmel *(G-1491)*

Telecom LLC ....G 317 805-1090
Indianapolis *(G-6282)*

3663 Radio & T V Communications, Systs & Eqpt, Broadcast/Studio

AAA Satellite Link ....G 765 642-7000
Anderson *(G-58)*

Abk Tracking Inc ....G 812 473-9554
Evansville *(G-3333)*

Acoustical Audio Designs LLC............F 812 282-7522
Jeffersonville *(G-8318)*

At T ....G 765 649-5900
Anderson *(G-70)*

B JS Electronics................................G 812 482-3484
Jasper *(G-8237)*

Broadcast Connection Inc ....G 765 847-2519
Williamsburg *(G-14283)*

Commtineo LLC ....F 219 476-3667
Wanatah *(G-13822)*

Corporate Systems Engrg LLC............D 317 322-7984
Indianapolis *(G-6671)*

Destiny Solutions Inc ....G 502 384-0031
Georgetown *(G-5142)*

Digital Solutions ....G 812 257-0333
Washington *(G-13980)*

Directv Inc ....G 260 471-3474
Fort Wayne *(G-4211)*

Dish Express ....G 812 962-3982
Evansville *(G-3458)*

Echostar Corporation ....E 574 271-0595
South Bend *(G-12757)*

Ejl Tech ....G 812 374-8808
Columbus *(G-1918)*

Furrion LLC ....F 574 327-6571
Elkhart *(G-2871)*

GH Products Inc.................................G 619 208-4823
West Lafayette *(G-14068)*

Grand Master LLC ....G 574 288-8273
South Bend *(G-12790)*

Gwin Enterprises ....G 317 881-6401
Indianapolis *(G-7061)*

Harman Professional Inc ....G 574 294-8000
Elkhart *(G-2908)*

Haven Technologies Inc ....G 317 490-7197
Carmel *(G-1399)*

I E M C ....G 219 464-2890
Valparaiso *(G-13558)*

Llama Corporation ....G 888 701-7432
Decatur *(G-2391)*

Managed Cmmunications Svcs LLC ....F 260 480-7885
Huntertown *(G-6142)*

Microwave Devices Inc.......................G 317 736-8833
Franklin *(G-4907)*

Motorola Solutions Inc ....G 317 716-8064
Indianapolis *(G-7548)*

Nello Capital Inc ....G 574 288-3632
South Bend *(G-12869)*

Orbital Installation Tech LLC ....G 317 774-3668
Noblesville *(G-11162)*

Raytheon Company ....E 317 306-4872
Indianapolis *(G-7821)*

Raytheon Company ....D 310 647-9438
Fort Wayne *(G-4577)*

▲ Ritron Inc ....D 317 846-1201
Carmel *(G-1468)*

▲ Satellite Oasis ....G 317 375-1097
Indianapolis *(G-7897)*

Shf Microwave Parts Co ....G 219 785-2602
La Porte *(G-8820)*

Spaceport Explrtion Centre Inc ....G 765 606-1512
New Whiteland *(G-11014)*

Telectro-Mek Inc ....G 260 747-0586
Fort Wayne *(G-4677)*

W Ay-FM Media Group Inc..................G 812 945-1043
New Albany *(G-10872)*

World Rdo Mssnary Fllwship Inc..........E 574 970-4252
Elkhart *(G-3268)*

3669 Communications Eqpt, NEC

A Plus Datacomm ....G 219 472-1644
Portage *(G-11747)*

Acterna LLC ....G 317 788-9351
Indianapolis *(G-6320)*

American Eagle Security Inc................G 219 980-1177
Merrillville *(G-9696)*

American Fire Company ....G 219 840-0630
Valparaiso *(G-13491)*

◆ Carson Manufacturing Co Inc ....F 317 257-3191
Indianapolis *(G-6560)*

Discount Detector Sales Inc ....G 765 866-0320
Crawfordsville *(G-2149)*

Dux Signal Kits LLC ....G 260 623-3017
Monroeville *(G-10194)*

General Dynamics Mission ....C 260 434-9500
Fort Wayne *(G-4296)*

Grunau Company Inc..........................G 317 872-7360
Indianapolis *(G-7054)*

Harris Corporation ....D 260 451-6180
Fort Wayne *(G-4321)*

Harris Corporation ....G 260 451-5597
Fort Wayne *(G-4323)*

Highway Safety Services Inc ....G 765 474-1000
Lafayette *(G-8915)*

Integratorcom Inc...............................G 317 849-2250
Indianapolis *(G-7250)*

J A Larr & Co ....G 317 627-3192
Indianapolis *(G-7282)*

Johnson Controls ....G 812 423-9000
Evansville *(G-3576)*

Johnson Controls ....G 260 692-6666
Monroe *(G-10183)*

Johnson Controls ....E 812 423-9000
Evansville *(G-3577)*

Logical Concepts ....D 317 885-6330
Greenwood *(G-5721)*

Lyra LLC ....G 260 452-4058
Fort Wayne *(G-4445)*

Messagenet Systems Inc ....G 317 566-1677
Carmel *(G-1438)*

Mgi Traffic Control Pdts Inc ....G 317 835-9212
Fairland *(G-3825)*

Mikes Metal Dectors ....G 812 366-3558
Georgetown *(G-5150)*

Molex LLC ....E 317 834-5600
Mooresville *(G-10323)*

National Exhaust Cleaning Inc ....F 317 831-4750
Mooresville *(G-10327)*

New Concept Metal Detector ....G 765 447-2681
Lafayette *(G-8976)*

Port Services LLC ....G 317 840-7606
Indianapolis *(G-7707)*

Pumpalarmcom LLC ....G 888 454-5051
Indianapolis *(G-7789)*

SC Supply Company LLC....................G 574 287-0252
South Bend *(G-12928)*

Sentinel Alarm Inc.............................G 219 874-6051
Trail Creek *(G-13442)*

▲ St Louis Group LLC ....E 317 975-3121
Indianapolis *(G-7981)*

Tct Technologies LLC ....G 317 833-6730
Fishers *(G-3974)*

3671 Radio & T V Receiving Electron Tubes

Applied Biomedical Techno ....G 219 465-2079
Valparaiso *(G-13495)*

HB Connect Inc ....D 260 422-1212
Fort Wayne *(G-4324)*

S
I
C

Iotron Industries USA Inc ....E 260 212-1722
　Columbia City *(G-1798)*

J&L Uebelhor Enterprises LLC ....G 812 367-1591
　Ferdinand *(G-3854)*

Vapourflow LLC ....G 812 284-5204
　Jeffersonville *(G-8438)*

3672 Printed Circuit Boards

Active Sensors Incorporated ....G 317 713-2973
　Indianapolis *(G-6322)*

Bluering Stencils ....E 260 203-5461
　Fort Wayne *(G-4114)*

▲ Cal-Comp USA (indiana) Inc ....B 956 342-5061
　Logansport *(G-9326)*

Carrier Corporation ....A 260 358-0888
　Huntington *(G-6196)*

David Kechel ....G 260 627-2749
　Leo *(G-9242)*

Divsys International LLC ....E 317 405-9427
　Indianapolis *(G-6752)*

Hamby ....G 765 664-4045
　Marion *(G-9528)*

Illinois Tool Works Inc ....C 260 347-8040
　Kendallville *(G-8480)*

Jtd Enterprises Inc ....G 574 533-9438
　Goshen *(G-5249)*

Kimball Elec Indianapolis ....D 812 634-4000
　Indianapolis *(G-7349)*

Kimball Electronics Inc ....B 812 634-4200
　Jasper *(G-8272)*

▲ Kimball Electronics Tampa Inc ....A 812 634-4000
　Jasper *(G-8275)*

Madison Electronics Inc ....E 812 689-4204
　Versailles *(G-13655)*

Pinder Instruments Company Inc ....E 219 924-7070
　Munster *(G-10624)*

Teaco Inc ....F 219 874-6234
　Michigan City *(G-9852)*

Tritech Manufacturing Inc ....E 260 747-9154
　Fort Wayne *(G-4705)*

3674 Semiconductors

▲ Advanced Control Tech Inc ....G 317 806-2750
　Indianapolis *(G-6332)*

Allegro Microsystems LLC ....G 765 854-2263
　Carmel *(G-1309)*

◆ American Ultraviolet Company ....D 765 483-9514
　Lebanon *(G-9168)*

Amerlight LLC ....G 812 602-3452
　Evansville *(G-3355)*

▲ Autosem Inc ....F 574 288-8866
　South Bend *(G-12718)*

Benson Solar Enterprises LLC ....G 855 533-7467
　Huntington *(G-6193)*

Bowmar LLC ....E 260 747-3121
　Fort Wayne *(G-4116)*

E-Certa Incorporated ....E 812 323-7824
　Bloomington *(G-717)*

Environmental Technology Inc ....E 574 233-1202
　South Bend *(G-12765)*

Fairchild Semiconductor Corp ....G 317 616-3641
　Carmel *(G-1377)*

Federal-Mogul LLC ....G 574 271-0274
　South Bend *(G-12775)*

Heraeus Electro-Nite Co LLC ....C 765 473-8275
　Peru *(G-11529)*

Indiana Intgrated Circuits LLC ....G 724 244-4560
　Granger *(G-5414)*

Infineon Tech Americas Corp ....G 765 454-2144
　Kokomo *(G-8646)*

Intel Corporation ....G 317 336-5464
　Mccordsville *(G-9671)*

Jdsu Acterna Holdings LLC ....G 317 788-9351
　Indianapolis *(G-7300)*

Leidos Inc ....C 812 863-3100
　Crane *(G-2128)*

Mark Lamaster ....G 765 534-4185
　Noblesville *(G-11146)*

Maxim Integrated Products Inc ....G 252 227-7202
　Westfield *(G-14175)*

Microchip Technology Inc ....G 317 773-8323
　Noblesville *(G-11150)*

Microscreen LLC ....E 574 232-4358
　South Bend *(G-12862)*

Millennia Technologies Inc ....G 574 830-5161
　Goshen *(G-5292)*

Nxp Usa Inc ....E 765 455-5100
　Kokomo *(G-8677)*

Paul Nelson ....G 765 352-0698
　Martinsville *(G-9632)*

▲ Payne-Sparkman Manufacturing ......F 812 944-4893
　New Albany *(G-10840)*

Perfection Products Inc ....E 765 482-7786
　Lebanon *(G-9215)*

Power Components of Midwest ....C 574 256-6990
　Mishawaka *(G-10105)*

Pursuit Defense Technology LLC ....G 630 687-3826
　Indianapolis *(G-7791)*

Pyromation Inc ....C 260 484-2580
　Fort Wayne *(G-4566)*

◆ Qualitex Inc ....F 260 244-7839
　Fort Wayne *(G-4571)*

Rapid Sensors Inc ....G 260 562-3614
　Howe *(G-6131)*

Raytheon Company ....E 317 306-4872
　Indianapolis *(G-7821)*

Semicndctor Cmponents Inds LLC ....G 765 868-5015
　Kokomo *(G-8694)*

Texas Instruments Incorporated ....F 317 574-2611
　Carmel *(G-1493)*

Viavi Solutions Inc ....B 317 788-9351
　Indianapolis *(G-8161)*

3675 Electronic Capacitors

A C Mallory Capacitors LLC ....D 317 612-1000
　Indianapolis *(G-6293)*

Eternal Energy LLC ....G 260 410-3056
　Fort Wayne *(G-4249)*

Greatbatch Ltd ....D 260 755-7484
　Warsaw *(G-13886)*

Integer Holdings Corporation ....G 260 373-1664
　Fort Wayne *(G-4377)*

Kirby Risk Corporation ....F 317 398-9713
　Shelbyville *(G-12543)*

Regal-Beloit Corporation ....D 260 416-5400
　Fort Wayne *(G-4587)*

3676 Electronic Resistors

Dayton-Phoenix Group Inc ....D 765 742-4410
　West Lafayette *(G-14063)*

▲ Khorporate Holdings Inc ....C 260 357-3365
　Laotto *(G-9110)*

Vishay Americas Inc ....G 765 778-4878
　Pendleton *(G-11510)*

3677 Electronic Coils & Transformers

Andon Specialties Inc ....G 317 983-1700
　Indianapolis *(G-6400)*

Andover Coils LLC ....D 765 447-1157
　Fishers *(G-3871)*

Arctic Clear Products Inc ....G 574 533-7671
　Goshen *(G-5172)*

Chemtrex LLC ....G 317 508-4223
　Noblesville *(G-11080)*

◆ Coil Tran Corp ....D 219 942-8511
　Hobart *(G-6076)*

Custom Magnetics Inc ....E 773 463-6500
　North Manchester *(G-11228)*

▲ Custom Magnetics Inc ....E 773 463-6500
　North Manchester *(G-11227)*

G G B Inc ....G 219 733-2897
　Westville *(G-14216)*

Hermetic Coil Co Inc ....E 812 735-2400
　Bicknell *(G-631)*

Kendrion (mishawaka) LLC ....E 574 257-2422
　Mishawaka *(G-10063)*

◆ Marshall Electric Corporation ....F 574 223-4367
　Rochester *(G-12136)*

▲ Midwest Coil LLC ....F 765 807-5429
　Lafayette *(G-8969)*

Performance Mstr Coil Proc Inc ....E 765 364-1300
　Crawfordsville *(G-2185)*

Qp Inc ....G 574 295-6884
　Elkhart *(G-3125)*

R B Annis Instruments Inc ....G 765 848-1621
　Greencastle *(G-5476)*

▲ REO-Usa Inc ....F 317 899-1395
　Indianapolis *(G-7834)*

Separation Technologies Inc ....G 219 548-5814
　Valparaiso *(G-13614)*

Sonicu LLC ....G 317 468-2345
　Greenfield *(G-5576)*

▲ Southern Electric Coil LLC ....G 219 931-5500
　Hammond *(G-5944)*

◆ Tetrasolv Inc ....F 765 643-3941
　Anderson *(G-176)*

Tri Star Filtration Inc ....G 317 337-0940
　Indianapolis *(G-8095)*

Vista Worldwide LLC ....G 574 264-0711
　Elkhart *(G-3248)*

Warner Electric LLC ....C 260 244-6183
　Columbia City *(G-1846)*

▲ Warsaw Coil Co Inc ....D 574 267-6041
　Warsaw *(G-13959)*

▲ Xfmrs Inc ....A 317 834-1066
　Camby *(G-1272)*

3678 Electronic Connectors

Accu-Mold LLC ....E 269 323-0388
　Mishawaka *(G-9989)*

Advanced Metal Etching Inc ....E 260 894-4189
　Ligonier *(G-9275)*

Alexander Machine ....G 812 879-4982
　Gosport *(G-5349)*

Assembly Masters Inc ....G 574 293-9026
　Mishawaka *(G-9999)*

CTS Corporation ....E 574 293-7511
　Elkhart *(G-2780)*

Edinburgh Connector Company ....D 812 526-8801
　Edinburgh *(G-2611)*

Kirby Risk Corporation ....B 765 447-1402
　Lafayette *(G-8942)*

Major League Electronics LLC ....E 812 670-4174
　Jeffersonville *(G-8394)*

Molex LLC ....G 317 770-4900
　Noblesville *(G-11154)*

Molex LLC ....E 317 834-5600
　Mooresville *(G-10323)*

PMG Incorporated ....G 574 291-3805
　South Bend *(G-12899)*

Smith Ruth C Rn Prof Electrlg ....G 812 423-4760
　Evansville *(G-3737)*

▲ Zh Brothers International Inc ....G 313 718-6732
　Mishawaka *(G-10153)*

3679 Electronic Components, NEC

A-1vet LLC ....G 317 498-1804
　Indianapolis *(G-6304)*

Acterna LLC ....E 317 788-9351
　Indianapolis *(G-6320)*

◆ Almega/Tru-Flex Inc ....E 574 546-2113
　Bremen *(G-982)*

Assembly Masters Inc ....F 574 293-9026
　Elkhart *(G-2698)*

▲ Autosem Inc ....F 574 288-8866
　South Bend *(G-12718)*

Avnet ....G 260 359-9513
　Huntington *(G-6189)*

B Q Products Inc ....E 317 786-5500
　Indianapolis *(G-6450)*

Broadwave Technologies Inc ....G 317 346-6101
　Franklin *(G-4873)*

C & G Wiring Inc ....F 574 333-3433
　Elkhart *(G-2742)*

Caddo Connections Inc ....E 219 874-8119
　La Porte *(G-8744)*

◆ Carson Manufacturing Co Inc ....F 317 257-3191
　Indianapolis *(G-6560)*

Cool-Shirts Inc ....G 317 826-1674
　Indianapolis *(G-6663)*

CTS Elctrnic Cmponents Cal Inc ....G 574 523-3800
　Elkhart *(G-2781)*

Dwyer Instruments Inc ....E 219 393-5250
　La Porte *(G-8752)*

◆ EJ Brooks Company ....D 800 348-4777
　Angola *(G-209)*

Electric-Tec LLC ....E 260 665-1252
　Angola *(G-211)*

Electro Transfer Systems Inc ....D 574 234-0600
　Mishawaka *(G-10040)*

Electronic Services LLC ....E 765 457-3894
　Kokomo *(G-8620)*

◆ Ets International Llc ....D 574 234-0700
　Mishawaka *(G-10043)*

Freedom Wire Inc ....F 260 856-3059
　Cromwell *(G-2208)*

Gartech Enterprises Inc ....G 812 794-4796
　Austin *(G-397)*

George Marshall ....G 317 839-6563
　Plainfield *(G-11612)*

Gimme Charge LLC ....G 317 759-4067
　Indianapolis *(G-7006)*

▲ Green Cubes Technology Corp ....E 502 416-1060
　Kokomo *(G-8633)*

Haven Technologies Inc ....G 317 490-7197
　Carmel *(G-1399)*

HB Connect Inc ....D 260 422-1212
　Fort Wayne *(G-4324)*

Heather Sound Amplification ....G 574 255-6100
　Mishawaka *(G-10049)*

Hermac Incorporated..................E...... 260 925-0312
Auburn (G-335)

▲ Hi-Pro Inc..................F...... 260 665-5038
Angola (G-218)

Hymns2go LLC..................G...... 317 577-0730
Fishers (G-3926)

Indiana Integrated Circuits In..................574 217-4612
South Bend (G-12810)

▼ Infinias LLC..................G...... 317 348-1249
Indianapolis (G-7226)

▼ Intelliray Inc..................G...... 260 547-4399
Decatur (G-2386)

Investwell Electronics Inc..................G...... 765 457-1911
Kokomo (G-8648)

Jag Wire LLC..................F...... 260 463-8537
Lagrange (G-9048)

K J S Associates..................G...... 317 842-7500
Indianapolis (G-7328)

K Ra International LLC..................574 258-7151
South Bend (G-12827)

Kadel Engineering Corporation..................E...... 317 745-2798
Danville (G-2350)

Kauffman Engineering Inc..................D...... 574 732-2154
Bremen (G-1007)

▲ Kauffman Engineering Inc..................D...... 765 483-4919
Lebanon (G-9195)

Kauffman Engineering Inc..................D...... 765 482-5640
Lebanon (G-9196)

Kauffman Engineering Inc..................D...... 574 722-3800
Logansport (G-9344)

Kendrion (mishawaka) LLC..................E...... 574 257-2422
Mishawaka (G-10063)

▲ Key Electronics Inc..................C...... 812 206-2500
Jeffersonville (G-8389)

Kimball Electronics Mfg Inc..................A...... 812 482-1600
Jasper (G-8274)

▲ Kimball Electronics Tampa Inc..................A...... 812 634-4000
Jasper (G-8275)

▲ Kirby Risk Corporation..................D...... 765 448-4567
Lafayette (G-8940)

▲ Kra International LLC..................574 259-3550
Mishawaka (G-10065)

Leidos Inc..................C...... 812 863-3100
Crane (G-2128)

Madison Electronics Inc..................F...... 812 689-4204
Versailles (G-13655)

▲ Mallory Sonalert Products Inc..................E...... 317 612-1000
Indianapolis (G-7448)

▲ Marian Worldwide Inc..................D...... 317 638-6525
Indianapolis (G-7454)

Mark Russell..................G...... 812 386-8069
Princeton (G-11877)

Microform Inc..................G...... 574 522-9851
Elkhart (G-3035)

Microwave Devices Inc..................G...... 317 736-8833
Franklin (G-4907)

Mier Products Inc..................E...... 765 457-0223
Kokomo (G-8666)

Mssl Wiring System Inc..................E...... 260 726-6501
Portland (G-11837)

▲ Mursix Corporation..................C...... 765 282-2221
Yorktown (G-14408)

Music Store..................G...... 812 949-3004
Clarksville (G-1689)

Northwind Electronics LLC..................F...... 317 288-0787
Indianapolis (G-7596)

▲ Orion Global Sourcing Inc..................G...... 812 332-3338
Bloomington (G-792)

Patrick Industries Inc..................D...... 574 293-2990
Elkhart (G-3089)

Pent Assemblies..................D...... 260 347-5828
Kendallville (G-8501)

Pinder Instruments Company Inc..................E...... 219 924-7070
Munster (G-10624)

Poly Electronics LLC..................D...... 574 522-0246
Elkhart (G-3101)

Polyphase Microwave Inc..................G...... 812 323-8708
Bloomington (G-800)

▲ Power Systems Innovations Inc..................G...... 812 480-4380
Newburgh (G-11043)

Precision Wire Assemblies Inc..................D...... 765 489-6302
Hagerstown (G-5812)

Precision Wire Inc..................G...... 574 834-7545
North Webster (G-11300)

Priority Electronics LLC..................G...... 260 749-0143
New Haven (G-10954)

Qualitronics Inc..................D...... 765 966-2039
Richmond (G-12039)

▲ Quality Plastics and Engrg Inc..................E...... 574 262-2621
Elkhart (G-3128)

▲ Regency Technologies Inc..................G...... 317 543-9740
Indianapolis (G-7827)

Rogers Electro-Matics Inc..................F...... 574 457-2305
Syracuse (G-13143)

Schumaker Technical Assembly..................G...... 765 742-7176
Lafayette (G-8997)

Signaling Solution Inc..................812 533-1345
Shelburn (G-12510)

▲ Skytech II Inc..................G...... 260 459-1703
Fort Wayne (G-4629)

▲ Skytech-Systems Inc..................G...... 260 459-1703
Fort Wayne (G-4630)

Stuart Manufacturing Inc..................F...... 260 403-2003
Fort Wayne (G-4658)

Tap-A-Lite Inc..................E...... 219 932-8067
Hammond (G-5948)

Technology Dynamics..................G...... 317 524-6338
Indianapolis (G-8050)

Techshot Inc..................E...... 812 923-9591
Greenville (G-5655)

Tempest Technical Sales Inc..................F...... 317 844-9236
Carmel (G-1492)

Top Shelf Acoustics LLC..................G...... 317 512-4569
Indianapolis (G-8081)

Tri TEC Systems Inc..................E...... 260 724-8874
Decatur (G-2409)

Vista Worldwide LLC..................G...... 574 264-0711
Elkhart (G-3248)

Walton Industrial Park Inc..................F...... 574 626-2929
Walton (G-13818)

Wattre Inc..................G...... 260 657-3701
Woodburn (G-14391)

Wilco Corporation..................F...... 317 228-9320
Indianapolis (G-8196)

ZF North America Inc..................B...... 765 429-1984
Lafayette (G-9028)

3691 Storage Batteries

Advanced Btry Charger Svc LLC..................G...... 260 563-3909
Wabash (G-13719)

B T Bttery Charger Systems Inc..................574 533-6030
Goshen (G-5176)

Batteries Plus..................317 219-0007
Noblesville (G-11064)

◆ Bulldog Battery Corporation..................C...... 260 563-0551
Wabash (G-13722)

C&D Technologies Inc..................765 762-2461
Attica (G-298)

Crown Battery Manufacturing Co..................G...... 260 423-3358
Fort Wayne (G-4188)

Ener1 Inc..................E...... 317 703-1800
Indianapolis (G-6862)

▲ Enerdel Inc..................C...... 317 703-1800
Indianapolis (G-6863)

Enersys..................D...... 574 266-0658
Elkhart (G-2833)

Exide Technologies..................317 876-7475
Indianapolis (G-6894)

Exide Technologies..................C...... 765 747-9980
Muncie (G-10470)

Greatbatch Ltd..................260 755-7484
Warsaw (G-13886)

Integer Holdings Corporation..................G...... 260 373-1664
Fort Wayne (G-4377)

Johnson Controls Inc..................D...... 260 489-6104
Fort Wayne (G-4397)

Johnson Controls Inc..................D...... 317 917-5043
Pittsboro (G-11583)

Knk Battery LLC..................G...... 765 426-2016
Otterbein (G-11420)

Span Inc..................F...... 317 347-2646
Lebanon (G-9226)

Tri-State Power Supply LLC..................G...... 812 537-2500
Lawrenceburg (G-9160)

Worldwide Battery Company LLC..................G...... 812 475-1326
Evansville (G-3816)

3692 Primary Batteries: Dry & Wet

C&D Technologies Inc..................C...... 765 762-2461
Attica (G-298)

Greatbatch Ltd..................F...... 260 755-7484
Warsaw (G-13886)

Integer Holdings Corporation..................G...... 260 373-1664
Fort Wayne (G-4377)

3694 Electrical Eqpt For Internal Combustion Engines

◆ Almega/Tru-Flex Inc..................E...... 574 546-2113
Bremen (G-982)

▲ Aristo LLC..................E...... 219 962-1032
Hobart (G-6069)

▼ B & M Electrical Co Inc..................F...... 765 448-4532
Lafayette (G-8859)

Ballantrae Inc..................B...... 800 372-3555
Pendleton (G-11483)

Borgwarner Pds (indiana) Inc..................A...... 800 372-3555
Pendleton (G-11485)

◆ Borgwarner Pds Anderson LLC..................B...... 765 778-6499
Noblesville (G-11068)

Borgwarner Pds Anderson LLC..................C...... 765 778-6499
Anderson (G-76)

Caddo Connections Inc..................G...... 219 874-8119
La Porte (G-8744)

▲ Cpx Inc..................D...... 219 474-5280
Kentland (G-8519)

Cummins Inc..................B...... 812 377-5000
Columbus (G-1891)

Cummins Inc..................F...... 812 377-8601
Columbus (G-1894)

Cummins Inc..................E...... 812 377-2932
Columbus (G-1895)

Cummins Inc..................G...... 317 244-7251
Indianapolis (G-6709)

Cummins Inc..................G...... 317 610-2493
Indianapolis (G-6710)

D & E Auto Electric Inc..................F...... 219 763-3892
Portage (G-11759)

Delco Electronics..................G...... 765 451-9325
Kokomo (G-8613)

Design Engineering..................G...... 219 926-2170
Chesterton (G-1602)

▲ E M F Corp..................E...... 260 665-9541
Angola (G-208)

E M F Corp..................E...... 260 488-2479
Hamilton (G-5821)

East Penn Manufacturing Co..................G...... 317 236-6288
Indianapolis (G-6791)

Federal-Mogul LLC..................G...... 574 271-0274
South Bend (G-12775)

GM Components Holdings LLC..................G...... 765 451-5011
Kokomo (G-8630)

Group Dekko Inc..................D...... 260 635-2134
Wolflake (G-14379)

Hitachi Automotive Systems..................B...... 859 734-9451
Ligonier (G-9287)

Indiana Research Institute..................F...... 812 378-5363
Columbus (G-1948)

Kirby Risk Corporation..................B...... 765 447-1402
Lafayette (G-8942)

La Fontaine Generator Exchange..................G...... 765 981-4561
La Fontaine (G-8723)

Motherson Sumi Systems Limited..................A...... 260 726-6501
Portland (G-11836)

Noel-Smyser Engineering Corp..................F...... 317 293-2215
Indianapolis (G-7590)

◆ Old Remco Holdings LLC..................C...... 765 778-6499
Pendleton (G-11498)

Patrick Industries Inc..................D...... 260 665-6112
Angola (G-235)

Porter Systems Inc..................G...... 317 867-0234
Westfield (G-14178)

Qualtronics LLC..................E...... 812 375-8880
Columbus (G-2004)

R & R Regulators LLC..................G...... 574 522-5846
Elkhart (G-3133)

R & R Regulators Inc..................G...... 574 522-5846
Elkhart (G-3134)

Reman Holdings LLC..................G...... 800 372-5131
Pendleton (G-11502)

Remy Electric Motors LLC..................E...... 765 778-6466
Pendleton (G-11503)

Remy Logistics LLC..................G...... 765 683-3700
Anderson (G-160)

Remy Power Products LLC..................A...... 765 778-6499
Pendleton (G-11504)

Standard Motor Products Inc..................C...... 574 259-6253
Mishawaka (G-10135)

◆ Technuity Inc..................G...... 800 887-2557
Indianapolis (G-8051)

United Starter Alternator LLC..................G...... 219 696-9095
Lowell (G-9424)

3695 Recording Media

Optical Media Mfg Inc..................E...... 317 822-1850
Indianapolis (G-7630)

R B Annis Instruments Inc..................765 848-1621
Greencastle (G-5476)

RPI Consultants LLC..................F...... 317 803-7431
Indianapolis (G-7868)

S I C

Sony Corporation of America ....G....... 812 462-8726
Terre Haute (G-13332)
Sony Dadc US Inc ....E....... 812 462-8116
Terre Haute (G-13333)
▲ Sony Dadc US Inc ....A....... 812 462-8100
Terre Haute (G-13334)
Sony Dadc US Inc ....B....... 812 462-8784
Terre Haute (G-13335)
Tclogic LLC ....G....... 317 464-5152
Indianapolis (G-8042)
Tech Enterprises Incorporated ....G....... 317 251-3816
Indianapolis (G-8045)

3699 Electrical Machinery, Eqpt & Splys, NEC

Academy Energy Group LLC ....G....... 312 931-7443
Newburgh (G-11017)
Adaptek Systems Inc ....E....... 260 637-8660
Fort Wayne (G-4041)
Advantage Cartridge Co Inc ....F....... 260 747-9941
Fort Wayne (G-4046)
Alliance Electric ....G....... 812 590-3500
Sellersburg (G-12387)
Allied Mfg Partners Inc ....G....... 260 428-2670
Fort Wayne (G-4062)
American Door Controls Inc ....G....... 812 988-4853
Morgantown (G-10349)
Applied Technology Group Inc ....F....... 260 482-2844
Fort Wayne (G-4084)
Automated Laser Corporation ....E....... 260 637-4140
Fort Wayne (G-4097)
Automation Consultants Inc ....G....... 502 552-4995
Floyds Knobs (G-4007)
Automtion Ctrl Panl Sltons Inc ....F....... 219 961-8308
Munster (G-10597)
B & H Electric and Supply Inc ....G....... 812 333-7303
Bloomington (G-669)
B Y M Electronics Inc ....G....... 574 674-5096
Granger (G-5393)
Babsco Supply Inc ....G....... 574 267-8999
Warsaw (G-13841)
Becker Elec ....G....... 812 362-9000
Rockport (G-12166)
Best Equipment Co Inc ....E....... 317 823-3050
Indianapolis (G-6469)
Broadwave Technologies Inc ....F....... 317 888-8316
Greenwood (G-5671)
Carmichael Electric LLC ....G....... 574 722-4028
Logansport (G-9327)
Chappys Rent To Own LLC ....G....... 765 622-9500
Anderson (G-83)
Chase Electric ....G....... 765 388-2183
New Castle (G-10896)
Cnc Laser Inc ....G....... 260 562-3953
Shipshewana (G-12608)
▲ Connecticut Electric Inc ....F....... 800 730-2557
Anderson (G-89)
Conzer Security Inc ....G....... 317 580-9460
Carmel (G-1342)
Copper Smith Electric ....G....... 260 849-4299
Berne (G-610)
Data Technologies Inc ....G....... 317 580-9161
Carmel (G-1352)
Digiop Inc ....E....... 800 968-3606
Indianapolis (G-6742)
Directed Photonics Inc ....F....... 317 877-3142
Noblesville (G-11093)
Don Moline Electric ....G....... 317 987-7606
Avon (G-438)
▲ E M F Corp ....G....... 260 665-9541
Angola (G-208)
Eaton Electric Holdings LLC ....G....... 317 578-7724
Fishers (G-3900)
Economy Electric Htg & Coolg ....G....... 219 923-4441
Highland (G-6044)
Electric Motor Sales & Service ....G....... 812 574-3233
Madison (G-9460)
Electric Plus ....G....... 812 336-4992
Bloomington (G-719)
▲ Energy Access Inc ....F....... 317 329-1676
Indianapolis (G-6864)
▲ Esaote North America Inc ....D....... 317 813-6000
Fishers (G-3907)
Expert Electric ....G....... 765 664-6642
Marion (G-9523)
Fairway Laser Systems Inc ....G....... 219 462-6892
Valparaiso (G-13539)
Flager Electric ....G....... 574 295-8007
Elkhart (G-2851)
Flight Integrity LLC ....G....... 812 455-6642
Newburgh (G-11028)

Fortes Bros Electric ....G....... 219 472-0111
Merrillville (G-9716)
G & T Distribution ....G....... 765 759-8611
Yorktown (G-14404)
Gabbard and Son Electric ....G....... 812 747-7621
Lawrenceburg (G-9142)
Global Sonics LLC ....G....... 765 522-5548
Roachdale (G-12093)
Group Dekko Inc ....C....... 260 357-5988
Garrett (G-5010)
Group Dekko Inc ....D....... 260 635-2134
Wolflake (G-14379)
Hitachi Automotive Systems ....B....... 859 734-9451
Ligonier (G-9423)
▲ Hubbell Incorporated Delaware ....B....... 574 234-7151
South Bend (G-12806)
Image Vault LLC ....G....... 812 948-8400
New Albany (G-10802)
Indiana Instruments Inc ....G....... 317 875-8032
Indianapolis (G-7180)
▼ Industrial Trning Unlmted Corp ....G....... 812 961-8801
Dugger (G-2480)
Indy Control Corp ....G....... 317 787-4639
Beech Grove (G-597)
▲ Innotek Inc ....C....... 800 826-5527
Auburn (G-337)
Instellus Inc ....G....... 734 415-3013
Griffith (G-5780)
Jason Incorporated ....C....... 847 215-1948
Richmond (G-12007)
Kelley Electric ....G....... 765 778-8203
Anderson (G-127)
Koester Metals Inc ....E....... 260 495-1818
Fremont (G-4964)
Lancon Electric Inc ....G....... 260 897-3285
Laotto (G-9113)
Lovetts Electronics ....G....... 812 446-1093
Brazil (G-967)
▲ Lumen Cache Incorporated ....G....... 317 739-4218
McCordsville (G-9673)
Lynn Bros Electric Inc ....G....... 219 762-6386
Portage (G-11774)
Magnetic Instrumentation Inc ....G....... 317 842-9000
Indianapolis (G-7438)
Magnetic Instrumentation LLC ....E....... 317 842-7500
Indianapolis (G-7439)
▲ Marian Inc ....A....... 317 638-6525
Indianapolis (G-7453)
Martin Electric Inc ....G....... 765 288-3254
Eaton (G-2585)
Master Electric Service LLC ....G....... 812 246-3707
Sellersburg (G-12407)
Meade Electric Co ....C....... 219 787-8317
Chesterton (G-1620)
Moffitt Consulting Services ....G....... 317 773-5570
Noblesville (G-11153)
Murphy Electric ....G....... 574 224-9473
Rochester (G-12141)
Nmm Electric ....G....... 219 864-9688
Dyer (G-2504)
Northwest Electric Connection ....G....... 219 465-5205
Carmel (G-1444)
Nrk Inc ....E....... 812 232-1800
Terre Haute (G-13292)
◆ Ogden Welding Systems Inc ....E....... 219 322-5252
Schererville (G-12341)
Ohio Valley Electric ....G....... 812 532-5288
Lawrenceburg (G-9149)
▲ PBM Industries Inc ....E....... 812 346-2648
North Vernon (G-11277)
Phil & Son Inc ....F....... 219 663-5757
Crown Point (G-2283)
Pioneer Electric ....G....... 765 762-2000
Williamsport (G-14294)
▲ Projected Sound Inc ....E....... 317 839-4111
Plainfield (G-11637)
Qp Inc ....F....... 574 295-6884
Elkhart (G-3125)
Quality Hydraulic & Mch Svc ....G....... 317 892-2596
Danville (G-2355)
Quick Panic Release LLC ....G....... 812 841-5733
Terre Haute (G-13313)
R C Electric ....E....... 317 600-3001
Indianapolis (G-7808)
Reese Forge Oma Ironwork ....G....... 219 775-1039
Lake Village (G-9086)
Ryco Electric ....G....... 219 319-0934
Schererville (G-12344)
Samtec Inc ....G....... 812 517-6081
Scottsburg (G-12379)

Seib Machine & Tool Co Inc ....G....... 812 453-6174
Evansville (G-3721)
Sentinel Alarm Systems Inc ....F....... 317 842-6482
Indianapolis (G-7912)
Silent Witness Enterprises ....G....... 219 365-6660
Saint John (G-12270)
Stage Ninja LLC ....G....... 317 829-1507
Indianapolis (G-7985)
Sumitomo Electric Carbide Inc ....G....... 317 859-1601
Greenwood (G-5751)
Sun Power Technologies LLC ....G....... 317 399-8113
Westfield (G-14192)
Superior Electric Nwi LLC ....G....... 219 696-0717
Lowell (G-9423)
T & H Sweeper Co ....G....... 765 641-9800
Anderson (G-172)
T Shorter Manufacturing Inc ....G....... 574 264-4131
Elkhart (G-3203)
Tap-A-Lite Inc ....E....... 219 932-8067
Hammond (G-5948)
Targamite LLC ....G....... 260 489-0046
Fort Wayne (G-4674)
Terick Sales ....G....... 574 626-3173
Walton (G-13817)
Thermo Cube Incorporated ....G....... 574 936-5096
Plymouth (G-11727)
Top In Sound Inc ....G....... 765 649-8111
Anderson (G-177)
▲ Touchplate Technologies Inc ....F....... 260 424-4323
Fort Wayne (G-4696)
Troyer Brothers Inc ....E....... 260 565-2244
Bluffton (G-895)
USA Vision Systems Inc ....G....... 949 583-1519
Fishers (G-3983)
V The Electric Brew ....G....... 574 296-7785
Elkhart (G-3239)
Vincent Aliano Elc Htg & Coolg ....G....... 812 332-3332
Bloomington (G-852)
William D Darr ....G....... 574 518-0453
Syracuse (G-13154)
X-Treme Lazer Tag ....G....... 812 238-8412
Terre Haute (G-13372)
Xfmrs Holdings Inc ....G....... 317 834-1066
Camby (G-1271)
Xwind LLC ....G....... 317 350-2080
Brownsburg (G-1177)

37 TRANSPORTATION EQUIPMENT

3711 Motor Vehicles & Car Bodies

1st Attack Engineering Inc ....G....... 260 837-2435
Waterloo (G-14009)
ABRA Auto Body & Glass LP ....E....... 317 839-8940
Plainfield (G-11590)
ADM Mobility Solutions Inc ....G....... 317 481-8707
Indianapolis (G-6327)
AM General Holdings LLC ....F....... 574 237-6222
South Bend (G-12699)
AM General LLC ....A....... 574 258-7523
Mishawaka (G-9995)
AM General LLC ....A....... 574 257-4268
South Bend (G-12701)
AM General LLC ....B....... 574 258-6699
South Bend (G-12702)
AM General LLC ....D....... 574 235-7326
South Bend (G-12700)
Android Industries LLC ....D....... 260 672-0112
Roanoke (G-12098)
Aptiv Services Us LLC ....F....... 765 451-5011
Kokomo (G-8591)
▲ B & B Industries Inc ....E....... 574 262-8551
Elkhart (G-2710)
Badlands Pick Up Van ACC Salv ....G....... 574 633-2156
Wyatt (G-14396)
Besi Manufacturing Inc ....F....... 812 427-4114
Vevay (G-13660)
C-Line Engineering Inc ....G....... 812 246-4822
Sellersburg (G-12390)
Capital City Transit LLC ....G....... 317 813-5800
Indianapolis (G-6547)
Checkered Racing & Chrome LLC ....F....... 812 275-2875
Spencer (G-13019)
Coachmen Recrtl Vehicles Co ....G....... 574 825-5821
Middlebury (G-9876)
Concept Cars Inc ....G....... 260 668-7553
Angola (G-204)
Daimler Trucks North Amer LLC ....G....... 317 769-8500
Whitestown (G-14252)
Damon Corporation ....F....... 574 264-2900
Elkhart (G-2789)

Damon Motor Coach E 574 536-3781
Elkhart (G-2790)
Discount Power Equipment G 765 642-0040
Anderson (G-96)
Elringklinger Mfg Ind Inc G 734 788-1776
Fort Wayne (G-4236)
Fishers Fire Station 92 G 317 595-3292
Fishers (G-3912)
▲ Flexform Technologies LLC E 574 295-3777
Elkhart (G-2853)
Ford Motor Company D 317 837-2302
Plainfield (G-11610)
Forest River Inc G 574 262-5466
Elkhart (G-2863)
Fred Sibley Sr G 574 264-2237
Elkhart (G-2869)
Freightliner Cstm Chassis Corp G 260 517-9678
Wakarusa (G-13777)
General Motors LLC G 419 576-9472
Bloomington (G-730)
General Motors LLC A 260 672-1224
Roanoke (G-12102)
General Motors LLC B 765 668-2000
Marion (G-9525)
Global Trnsp Organization LLC G 574 226-6372
Elkhart (G-2887)
▼ Goshen Coach Inc C 574 970-6300
Elkhart (G-2891)
Hardins Speed Service Co G 219 962-8080
Hobart (G-6079)
◆ Honda Manufacturing Ind LLC A 812 222-6000
Greensburg (G-5612)
Hoosier Hot Rods Classics Inc G 812 768-5221
Haubstadt (G-6003)
Howerton Racecar Works Inc F 317 241-0868
Indianapolis (G-7140)
▼ Independent Protection Co Inc C 574 533-4116
Goshen (G-5242)
Independent Protection Co Inc E 574 533-4116
Goshen (G-5243)
Independent Protection Co Inc D 574 831-5680
New Paris (G-10985)
Jbh Manufacturing LLC G 574 612-1379
Goshen (G-5247)
Jbm Race Cars LLC G 812 305-3666
Evansville (G-3572)
K & D Custom Coach Inc E 574 537-1716
Goshen (G-5250)
KFC Composite Engineering Inc G 219 369-9093
La Porte (G-8781)
LCI Industries D 574 535-1125
Elkhart (G-2989)
Lcm Realty LLC G 574 535-1125
Elkhart (G-2990)
Lippert Cmponents Intl Sls Inc G 574 312-7480
Elkhart (G-2998)
Lippert Components Inc D 574 537-8900
Goshen (G-5267)
Lippert Components Inc C 800 551-9149
Elkhart (G-2999)
Lippert Components Inc D 574 535-1125
Goshen (G-5268)
Lippert Components Inc F 574 312-6654
South Bend (G-12840)
Lippert Components Inc D 574 294-6852
Elkhart (G-3000)
Lippert Components Inc D 574 535-1125
South Bend (G-12841)
Lippert Components Inc E 574 535-1125
Goshen (G-5271)
Lippert Components Inc D 574 849-0869
Goshen (G-5273)
Lippert Components Inc C 574 971-4320
Goshen (G-5275)
Lippert Components Inc D 574 312-7445
Middlebury (G-9904)
Lippert Components Inc E 574 535-1125
Goshen (G-5272)
Lippert Components Mfg Inc A 574 535-1125
Elkhart (G-3002)
M-TEC Corporation C 574 294-1060
Elkhart (G-3011)
Mastersbilt Chassis Inc F 812 793-3666
Crothersville (G-2218)
Mc Ginley Fire Apparatus G 765 482-3152
Lebanon (G-9204)
▼ Medix Specialty Vehicles LLC C 574 266-0911
Elkhart (G-3028)
Medtec Ambulance Corporation C 574 534-2631
Goshen (G-5284)
Medtec Ambulance Corporation G 574 533-2924
Goshen (G-5285)
Midway Specialty Vehicles LLC E 574 264-2530
Elkhart (G-3038)
Mirrus Corporation Inc E 812 689-1411
Versailles (G-13656)
Nemesis Race Cars G 812 361-9743
Bloomington (G-778)
Nix Bus Sales Inc E 812 464-2576
Poseyville (G-11858)
NRC Modifications Inc F 574 825-3646
Middlebury (G-9912)
Olson Race Cars G 765 529-6933
New Castle (G-10914)
Race Cars USA LLC G 317 508-3500
Carmel (G-1462)
Race Engineering G 219 661-8904
Crown Point (G-2291)
Rayburn Automotive Inc G 317 535-8232
Whiteland (G-14244)
▲ Rebel Devil Customs G 303 921-7131
Noblesville (G-11173)
Renewed Performance Company F 765 675-7586
Tipton (G-13404)
Richard Sheets G 574 536-8247
Bristol (G-1080)
Ring-Co LLC G 317 641-7050
Trafalgar (G-13437)
Royale Phoenix Inc G 574 206-1216
Elkhart (G-3150)
◆ Schumacher Racing Corporation E 317 858-0356
Brownsburg (G-1169)
Sparkling Clean Inc G 812 422-4871
Evansville (G-3741)
Spitzers Racing Enterprises F 317 894-9533
Greenfield (G-5577)
Team Green Inc D 317 872-2700
Indianapolis (G-8043)
Think North America Inc E 313 565-6781
Elkhart (G-3213)
Thor Industries Inc C 574 970-7460
Elkhart (G-3214)
Tony Stewart Racing Entps LLC G 317 858-8620
Brownsburg (G-1175)
Toyota G 317 755-4791
Nineveh (G-11058)
Toyota Boshoku America Inc E 812 385-2040
Princeton (G-11885)
◆ Toyota Motor Mfg Ind Inc C 812 387-2266
Princeton (G-11887)
Travel Home Solutions G 260 592-7628
Pleasant Mills (G-11658)
Turtle Top Mini Motor Homes G 574 831-4340
Goshen (G-5343)
U B Machine Inc E 260 493-3381
New Haven (G-10962)
U S O of Indiana Inc G 317 704-2400
Indianapolis (G-8123)
◆ Utilimaster Holdings Inc A 800 237-7806
Bristol (G-1093)
Valparaiso Fire Fighters D 219 462-5291
Valparaiso (G-13634)
Vehicle Service Group LLC E 812 273-1622
Madison (G-9499)
Vehicle Service Group LLC G 800 445-9262
Madison (G-9500)
◆ Vehicle Service Group LLC B 800 640-5438
Madison (G-9501)
Vuteq Usa Inc G 812 385-2584
Princeton (G-11889)
Wave Express G 574 642-0630
Goshen (G-5345)
Wb Automotive Holdings Inc F 734 604-8962
Fort Wayne (G-4748)
Wgs Global Services LC C 812 548-4446
Tell City (G-13177)

3713 Truck & Bus Bodies

ABRA Auto Body & Glass LP E 317 839-8940
Plainfield (G-11590)
Accuride Corporation C 812 962-5000
Evansville (G-3336)
Accuride Emi LLC G 940 565-8505
Evansville (G-3337)
American Reliance Inds Co E 260 768-4704
Shipshewana (G-12603)
Arboc Specialty Vehicles LLC D 574 825-1720
Middlebury (G-9871)
Armor Parent Corp F 812 962-5000
Evansville (G-3366)
▲ Autocar LLC C 765 489-5499
Hagerstown (G-5803)
B & G Truck Conversions Inc F 574 892-6666
Argos (G-272)
Basiloid Products Corp E 812 692-5511
Elnora (G-3286)
Bay Bridge Manufacturing Inc E 574 848-7477
Bristol (G-1048)
Bentz Transport Products Inc F 260 622-9100
Zionsville (G-14422)
▲ Braun Motor Works Inc G 574 205-0102
Winamac (G-14303)
Brindle Products Inc E 260 627-2156
Grabill (G-5358)
Chads LLC G 812 323-7377
Ellettsville (G-3273)
Cowan Systems LLC G 317 241-4158
Indianapolis (G-6681)
Dana Driveshaft Products LLC B 260 432-2903
Marion (G-9520)
Delivery Concepts Inc E 574 522-3981
Elkhart (G-2793)
Delphi Body Works F 765 564-2212
Delphi (G-2417)
Double Eagle Industries Inc E 260 768-4121
Shipshewana (G-12612)
Eagle Craft Inc E 574 936-3196
Plymouth (G-11682)
Eaton Corporation C 260 925-3800
Auburn (G-328)
Eaton Corporation F 317 704-2520
Indianapolis (G-6796)
Ford Motor Company D 317 837-2302
Plainfield (G-11610)
Gea Inc G 812 944-1401
New Albany (G-10786)
General Motors LLC A 260 672-1224
Roanoke (G-12102)
Gerald S Zins G 812 623-4980
Milan (G-9944)
Grahams Wrecker Service Inc G 317 736-4355
Franklin (G-4892)
Gravel Conveyors Inc F 317 873-8686
Zionsville (G-14435)
◆ H & H Sales Company Inc F 260 637-3177
Huntertown (G-6139)
Hausers Reclamation & REM G 812 663-6378
Burney (G-1212)
Hendrickson International Corp C 260 349-6400
Kendallville (G-8478)
Hendrickson International Corp C 765 483-5350
Lebanon (G-9187)
Herberts Truck & Van G 812 663-6970
Greensburg (G-5608)
Independent Protection Co Inc E 574 533-4116
Goshen (G-5243)
Independent Protection Co Inc D 574 831-5680
New Paris (G-10985)
Indiana Custom Trucks LLC E 260 463-3244
Lagrange (G-9046)
Indiana Phoenix Inc D 260 897-4397
Avilla (G-406)
International Brake Inds Inc E 419 905-7468
South Bend (G-12817)
▲ Kiel NA LLC F 574 293-3600
Elkhart (G-2965)
Kneppers Inc F 260 636-2180
Albion (G-29)
▲ Kruz Inc E 574 772-6673
Knox (G-8571)
Leer Midwest F 574 522-5337
Elkhart (G-2992)
Lund International Holding Co E 765 742-7200
Lafayette (G-8963)
M H EBY Inc F 574 753-4000
Logansport (G-9353)
Manasek Acquisition Co LLC E 765 551-1600
Elwood (G-3305)
Mantra Enterprise LLC G 201 428-8709
Fishers (G-3944)
Marmon Highway Tech LLC E 317 787-0718
Indianapolis (G-7457)
▼ Mavron Inc F 574 267-3044
Warsaw (G-13904)
McNeilus Truck and Mfg Inc G 260 489-3031
Fort Wayne (G-4462)
Monroe Custom Utility Bodies D 317 894-8684
Greenfield (G-5558)
Mooresville Welding Inc G 317 831-2265
Mooresville (G-10324)

S I C

Morgan Olson LLC	G	269 659-0243		
Angola (G-231)				
NRC Modifications Inc	F	574 825-3646		
Middlebury (G-9912)				
Original Tractor Cab Co Inc	E	765 663-2214		
Arlington (G-282)				
Quality Tank Trucks & Eqp Inc	G	317 635-0000		
Indianapolis (G-7801)				
R & B Associates Inc	G	812 471-1550		
Evansville (G-3693)				
▲ Ramco Engineering Inc	E	574 266-1455		
Elkhart (G-3136)				
▲ Rowe Truck Equipment Inc	D	765 583-4461		
Otterbein (G-11421)				
Roys Disposal	G	812 721-3443		
Oakland City (G-11314)				
S CJ Incorporated	F	317 822-3477		
Indianapolis (G-7879)				
Sharp Wraps LLC	G	317 989-8447		
Zionsville (G-14462)				
▼ Sjc Industries Corp	G	574 264-7511		
Elkhart (G-3174)				
Spartan Motors Usa Inc	E	574 848-2000		
Bristol (G-1088)				
▼ Starcraft Corporation	E	574 534-7827		
Goshen (G-5329)				
◆ Supreme Corporation	A	574 642-4888		
Goshen (G-5332)				
Supreme Corporation	B	574 642-4888		
Goshen (G-5333)				
Supreme Corporation	B	260 894-9191		
Ligonier (G-9298)				
Supreme Corporation	C	574 642-4888		
Goshen (G-5334)				
◆ Supreme Industries Inc	D	574 642-3070		
Goshen (G-5336)				
◆ Utilimaster Holdings Inc	A	800 237-7806		
Bristol (G-1093)				
▲ Vanair Manufacturing Inc	C	219 879-5100		
Michigan City (G-9857)				
▲ Vanguard National Trailer Corp	B	219 253-2000		
Monon (G-10179)				
Wannemuehler Distribution Inc	F	812 422-3251		
Evansville (G-3809)				
Wiers Fleet Partners Inc	F	574 936-4076		
Plymouth (G-11737)				
Wimmer Lime Service Inc	G	765 948-4001		
Fairmount (G-3835)				

3714 Motor Vehicle Parts & Access

3d Engineering Inc	G	317 729-5430
Edinburgh (G-2593)		
▲ A-Fab LLC	D	812 897-0900
Boonville (G-904)		
Acadia	G	260 894-7125
Ligonier (G-9274)		
Accuride Corporation	C	812 962-5000
Evansville (G-3336)		
Accuride Emi LLC	G	940 565-8505
Evansville (G-3337)		
▲ Action Machine Inc	F	574 287-9650
South Bend (G-12694)		
Advance Prtective Coatings Inc	G	317 228-0123
Indianapolis (G-6330)		
Advanced Racg Suspensions Inc	F	317 896-3306
Indianapolis (G-6335)		
▲ Advics Manufacturing Ind LLC	B	812 298-1617
Terre Haute (G-13188)		
▲ Aero Industries Inc	D	317 808-1923
Indianapolis (G-6346)		
▲ Air Ride Technologies Inc	E	812 482-2932
Jasper (G-8235)		
▲ Aisin Drivetrain Inc	C	812 793-2427
Crothersville (G-2214)		
▲ Aisin USA Mfg Inc	B	812 523-1969
Seymour (G-12428)		
◆ All American Group Inc	E	574 262-0123
Elkhart (G-2674)		
◆ Allied Enterprises Inc	E	765 288-8849
Muncie (G-10428)		
Allied Tube & Conduit Corp	C	812 265-9255
Madison (G-9443)		
Allison Transm Holdings Inc	D	317 242-5000
Indianapolis (G-6371)		
Allison Transmission Inc	A	317 280-6206
Indianapolis (G-6372)		
◆ Allison Transmission Inc	D	317 242-5000
Indianapolis (G-6373)		
Allison Transmission Inc	F	317 242-5000
Indianapolis (G-6374)		

Allison Transmission Inc	D	317 242-2080
Indianapolis (G-6375)		
Allison Transmission Inc	D	317 821-5104
Indianapolis (G-6376)		
▲ Allomatic Products Company	C	800 686-4729
Sullivan (G-13078)		
AM General Holdings LLC	F	574 237-6222
South Bend (G-12699)		
AM General LLC	B	574 258-6699
South Bend (G-12702)		
AM General LLC	D	574 235-7326
South Bend (G-12700)		
American Gorwood Corporation	E	765 948-3401
Fairmount (G-3829)		
American Mitsuba Corporation	C	989 779-4962
Monroeville (G-10191)		
Americana Development Inc	C	574 295-3535
Elkhart (G-2688)		
Amsafe Partners Inc	E	574 266-8330
Elkhart (G-2690)		
Aptiv Services Us LLC	C	765 451-5011
Kokomo (G-8591)		
Aptiv Services Us LLC	G	765 451-5011
Kokomo (G-8592)		
Aptiv Services Us LLC	C	765 451-0732
Kokomo (G-8593)		
Aptiv Services Us LLC	C	765 451-5011
Kokomo (G-8594)		
▲ Aristo LLC	E	219 962-1032
Hobart (G-6069)		
Armor Parent Corp	F	812 962-5000
Evansville (G-3366)		
▲ Arvin Sango Inc	A	812 265-2888
Madison (G-9444)		
▲ Attc Manufacturing Inc	B	812 547-5060
Tell City (G-13156)		
Atwood Mobile Products LLC	D	574 266-4848
Elkhart (G-2702)		
Atwood Mobile Products LLC	D	574 264-2131
Elkhart (G-2703)		
▲ Atwood Mobile Products LLC	D	574 264-2131
Elkhart (G-2704)		
Atwood Mobile Products LLC	C	574 522-7891
Elkhart (G-2705)		
Atwood Mobile Products LLC	D	574 264-2131
Elkhart (G-2706)		
▲ Auburn Gear LLC	C	260 925-3200
Auburn (G-313)		
Auburn Manufacturing Inc	F	260 925-8651
Auburn (G-315)		
▼ Auto Bumper Exchange Inc	F	260 493-4408
Fort Wayne (G-4096)		
Autoform Tool & Mfg LLC	C	260 624-2014
Angola (G-195)		
Automated Products Intl LLC	F	260 463-2515
Lagrange (G-9032)		
Autoneum North America Inc	G	248 848-0100
Jeffersonville (G-8327)		
Avg North America Inc	F	765 748-3162
Gas City (G-5120)		
Avionic Structures of Indiana	G	765 671-7865
Marion (G-9511)		
▲ Avis Industrial Corporation	E	765 998-8100
Upland (G-13468)		
Axle Inc	G	574 264-9434
Elkhart (G-2709)		
▲ B & B Manufacturing Inc	D	219 324-0247
La Porte (G-8737)		
Ballantrae Inc	B	800 372-3555
Pendleton (G-11483)		
Barry Seat Cover & Auto Glass	F	574 288-4603
South Bend (G-12721)		
Bender Products Inc	E	574 255-5350
Mishawaka (G-10009)		
Bendix Coml Vhcl Systems LLC	B	260 356-9720
Huntington (G-6191)		
Benteler Automotive Corp	C	574 534-1499
Goshen (G-5178)		
Bentz Transport Products Inc	F	260 622-9100
Zionsville (G-14422)		
▲ Bludot Inc	G	574 277-2306
South Bend (G-12723)		
Borgwarner Inc	G	765 609-3801
Anderson (G-75)		
Borgwarner Pds (indiana) Inc	A	800 372-3555
Pendleton (G-11485)		
◆ Borgwarner Pds Anderson LLC	B	765 778-6499
Noblesville (G-11068)		
Borgwarner Pds Anderson LLC	C	765 778-6641
Pendleton (G-11486)		

Borgwarner Pds Anderson LLC	C	765 778-6499
Anderson (G-76)		
Bornemann Products Inc	C	574 546-2881
Warsaw (G-13851)		
▲ BRC Rubber & Plastics Inc	C	260 693-2171
Fort Wayne (G-4118)		
BRC Rubber & Plastics Inc	C	260 894-4121
Ligonier (G-9278)		
BRC Rubber & Plastics Inc	D	260 203-5300
Fort Wayne (G-4119)		
Brindle Products Inc	E	260 627-2156
Grabill (G-5358)		
Bwi Indiana Inc	E	937 260-2460
Greenfield (G-5510)		
C-Line Engineering Inc	G	812 246-4822
Sellersburg (G-12390)		
▲ Caltherm Corporation	E	812 372-0281
Columbus (G-1864)		
Caltherm Corporation	F	812 372-0281
Columbus (G-1865)		
Camaco Portage Mfg LLC	E	248 657-0246
Portage (G-11754)		
Cardinal Services Inc Indiana	E	574 267-3823
Warsaw (G-13855)		
Cardinal Services Inc Indiana	D	574 267-3823
Warsaw (G-13853)		
◆ Carlisle Industrial Brake & Fr	B	812 336-3811
Bloomington (G-696)		
▲ Carter Fuel Systems LLC	B	574 722-6141
Logansport (G-9328)		
Carter Fuel Systems LLC	B	574 735-0235
Logansport (G-9329)		
▲ Caterpillar Remn Powrtrn Indna	B	317 738-2117
Franklin (G-4875)		
CD & R Components Inc	E	812 852-4864
Batesville (G-496)		
Cedar Creek Studios Inc	G	260 627-7320
Leo (G-9241)		
Champion Racing Engines	G	317 335-2491
McCordsville (G-9665)		
Chemtrusion Inc	D	812 280-2910
Jeffersonville (G-8336)		
Colbin Tool Company Inc	E	574 457-3183
Syracuse (G-13130)		
Comhar LLC	F	812 399-2123
New Albany (G-10764)		
Component Machine Inc	G	317 635-8929
Indianapolis (G-6642)		
▲ Compositech Inc	E	800 231-6755
Indianapolis (G-6643)		
▲ Continental Manufacturing LLC	E	765 778-9999
Anderson (G-90)		
Continental Strl Plas Inc	E	260 627-0890
Grabill (G-5361)		
Conversion Components Inc	G	574 264-4181
Elkhart (G-2772)		
Cooper-Standard Automotive Inc	B	260 637-5824
Auburn (G-323)		
Coupled Products LLC	B	260 248-3200
Columbia City (G-1776)		
Coupled Products LLC	B	812 849-5304
Mitchell (G-10161)		
▼ Coupled Products LLC	B	260 248-3200
Columbia City (G-1777)		
Covidien LP	C	317 837-8199
Plainfield (G-11602)		
CTA Acoustics Inc	C	260 829-1030
Orland (G-11350)		
Cummins Emission Solutions Inc	E	608 987-3206
Columbus (G-1889)		
Cummins Inc	G	765 430-0093
Columbus (G-1898)		
Cummins Inc	B	812 377-5000
Columbus (G-1891)		
Cummins Inc	F	812 377-8601
Columbus (G-1894)		
Cummins Inc	E	812 377-2932
Columbus (G-1895)		
Cummins Inc	G	317 244-7251
Indianapolis (G-6709)		
Cummins Inc	G	317 610-2493
Indianapolis (G-6710)		
Cummins Midwest Regional Dist	D	901 302-8143
Whitestown (G-14251)		
▲ Custom Wood Products Inc	D	574 522-3300
Elkhart (G-2784)		
Cvg Sprague Devices LLC	G	614 289-5360
Michigan City (G-9778)		
▲ D & D Brake Sales Inc	D	317 485-5177
Fortville (G-4772)		

D & E Auto Electric Inc .... F 219 763-3892
Portage *(G-11759)*
D&D Motors .... G 765 358-3856
Gaston *(G-5131)*
Dallara LLC .... F 317 388-5400
Speedway *(G-13012)*
Dana Driveshaft Products LLC .... B 260 432-2903
Marion *(G-9520)*
Dana Light Axle Products LLC .... E 260 636-4300
Albion *(G-24)*
▲ Dana Light Axle Products LLC .... D 260 483-7174
Fort Wayne *(G-4199)*
Decker Sales Inc .... G 812 330-1580
Bloomington *(G-711)*
Delco Electronics .... G 765 455-9713
Kokomo *(G-8612)*
Delphi E & S Morgan Street Ops .... G 765 451-2571
Kokomo *(G-8614)*
Delphi Powertrain Systems LLC .... F 765 236-0025
Kokomo *(G-8615)*
Delphi Powertrain Systems LLC .... G 765 451-0732
Kokomo *(G-8616)*
Dexter Axle Company .... C 574 294-6651
Elkhart *(G-2794)*
Dexter Axle Company .... C 260 636-2195
Albion *(G-25)*
Dexter Axle Company .... D 260 495-5100
Fremont *(G-4958)*
◆ Dexter Axle Company .... D 574 295-7888
Elkhart *(G-2795)*
Dexter Axle Company .... D 574 294-6651
Elkhart *(G-2796)*
Diesel Punk Core .... G 812 631-0606
Bloomington *(G-712)*
Discount Power Equipment .... G 765 642-0040
Anderson *(G-96)*
▲ Diversified Mch Bristol LLC .... A 248 728-8642
Bristol *(G-1055)*
Dometic Corporation .... B 260 463-7657
Lagrange *(G-9037)*
Donaldson Company Inc .... B 765 659-4766
Frankfort *(G-4828)*
Donaldson Company Inc .... G 317 838-5568
Plainfield *(G-11606)*
Double T Manufacturing Corp .... F 574 262-1340
Elkhart *(G-2799)*
Dura Automotive Systems of Ind .... G 574 262-2655
Elkhart *(G-2803)*
Dwyer Enterprises .... G 317 573-9628
Carmel *(G-1364)*
Eaton Corporation .... C 260 925-3800
Auburn *(G-328)*
Eaton Corporation .... F 317 704-2520
Indianapolis *(G-6796)*
Elizabeth M Graham .... G 812 343-1267
Bargersville *(G-481)*
▲ Elsa LLC .... B 765 552-5200
Elwood *(G-3296)*
▲ Elsa Corporation .... B 765 552-5200
Elwood *(G-3297)*
Engineered Machined Pdts Inc .... D 317 462-8894
Greenfield *(G-5527)*
Engineered Machined Pdts Inc .... C 317 462-8894
Greenfield *(G-5528)*
▲ Enkei America Inc .... A 812 373-7000
Columbus *(G-1920)*
Enovapremier LLC .... D 812 385-0576
Princeton *(G-11870)*
Exhaust Productions Inc .... D 219 942-0069
Merrillville *(G-9714)*
Ezs Custom Woodworking .... G 574 831-3078
Nappanee *(G-10668)*
Fairfield Manufacturing Co Inc .... E 765 772-4547
Lafayette *(G-8895)*
▲ Fairfield Manufacturing Co Inc .... A 765 772-4000
Lafayette *(G-8896)*
Faurecia Emissions Contl Tech .... B 812 341-2620
Columbus *(G-1923)*
Faurecia Emissions Contl Tech .... D 248 758-8160
Fort Wayne *(G-4259)*
Faurecia Emissions Control .... A 812 348-4305
Columbus *(G-1924)*
Faurecia Emissions Control .... G 937 823-5393
Columbus *(G-1925)*
◆ Faurecia Emissions Control .... B 812 341-2000
Columbus *(G-1926)*
Faurecia Emissions Control .... B 812 341-2000
Columbus *(G-1927)*
Faurecia Emissions Control TEC .... G 812 341-2000
Columbus *(G-1928)*

Faurecia Exhaust Systems LLC .... C 812 341-2079
Columbus *(G-1929)*
FCA US LLC .... A 765 454-1705
Kokomo *(G-8622)*
FCA US LLC .... A 765 854-4234
Kokomo *(G-8623)*
FCA US LLC .... A 765 454-1005
Kokomo *(G-8625)*
FCA US LLC .... A 765 454-0018
Kokomo *(G-8624)*
▲ FCC (adams) LLC .... B 260 589-8555
Berne *(G-614)*
▲ FCC (indiana) Inc .... A 260 726-8023
Portland *(G-11819)*
FCC (north America) Inc .... E 260 726-8023
Portland *(G-11820)*
FCC Adams .... F 260 589-8555
Portland *(G-11821)*
Federal-Mogul LLC .... A 765 659-7207
Frankfort *(G-4830)*
Federal-Mogul LLC .... B 317 875-7259
Indianapolis *(G-6907)*
Fenwick Motor Sports .... G 765 522-1354
Bainbridge *(G-476)*
Firestone Industrial Pdts Inc .... G 317 575-7000
Indianapolis *(G-6924)*
Flex-N-Gate Corporation .... A 765 294-3050
Veedersburg *(G-13643)*
Flex-N-Gate Corporation .... C 260 665-8288
Angola *(G-214)*
Flora Racing .... G 574 233-0642
South Bend *(G-12781)*
Ford Motor Company .... D 317 837-2302
Plainfield *(G-11610)*
Fort Wayne Clutch Inc .... F 260 484-8505
Fort Wayne *(G-4271)*
Four Woods Laminating Inc .... E 260 593-2246
Topeka *(G-13419)*
Frank Wiss Racg Components Inc .... E 317 248-4764
Indianapolis *(G-6957)*
Freudenberg-Nok General Partnr .... B 260 894-7183
Ligonier *(G-9285)*
Freudenberg-Nok General Partnr .... E 734 354-5504
Shelbyville *(G-12535)*
Freudenberg-Nok General Partnr .... C 317 421-3400
Shelbyville *(G-12534)*
Freudenberg-Nok General Partnr .... C 765 763-7246
Morristown *(G-10369)*
FTC Products Corp .... G 219 567-2441
Francesville *(G-4813)*
▲ G E C O M Corp .... A 812 663-2270
Greensburg *(G-5601)*
Gartech Enterprises Inc .... E 812 794-4796
Austin *(G-397)*
▲ General Products Angola Corp .... C 260 665-8441
Angola *(G-216)*
GKN Sinter Metals LLC .... C 812 883-3381
Salem *(G-12288)*
▲ Global Forming LLC .... E 317 290-1000
Indianapolis *(G-7011)*
Global Glass Inc .... C 574 294-7681
Elkhart *(G-2885)*
GM Components Holdings LLC .... B 765 451-8440
Kokomo *(G-8628)*
GM Components Holdings LLC .... G 765 451-9049
Kokomo *(G-8629)*
Graber Manufacturing .... G 812 636-7725
Odon *(G-11327)*
Grede LLC .... C 765 521-8000
New Castle *(G-10903)*
Greg Moser Engineering Inc .... E 260 726-6689
Portland *(G-11827)*
Griner Engineering .... G 765 296-2955
Mulberry *(G-10417)*
▼ Gulf Stream Coach Inc .... C 574 773-7761
Nappanee *(G-10677)*
Hanwha Machinery America Corp .... B 574 546-2261
Bremen *(G-1001)*
Hapco Rebuilders Inc .... G 812 232-2550
Terre Haute *(G-13245)*
Hart Plastics Inc .... E 574 264-7060
Elkhart *(G-2909)*
Heads First .... G 219 785-4100
Westville *(G-14217)*
▲ Heartland Automotive Inc .... A 765 653-4263
Greencastle *(G-5462)*
Heartland Automotive LLC .... G 765 653-4263
Greencastle *(G-5463)*
Heavy Duty Manufacturing Inc .... F 260 432-2480
Fort Wayne *(G-4328)*

Hendrickson International Corp .... G 260 868-2131
Butler *(G-1230)*
Hendrickson International Corp .... C 260 349-6400
Kendallville *(G-8478)*
Hendrickson International Corp .... C 765 483-5350
Lebanon *(G-9187)*
▲ Hisada America Inc .... D 812 526-0756
Edinburgh *(G-2613)*
Hitachi Automotive Systems .... B 859 734-9451
Ligonier *(G-9287)*
▲ Hitachi Cble Auto Pdts USA Inc .... C 812 945-9011
New Albany *(G-10796)*
▲ Hitachi Powdered Mtls USA Inc .... C 812 663-5058
Greensburg *(G-5610)*
Hoosier Industrial Supply Inc .... F 574 533-8565
Goshen *(G-5240)*
Horizon Global Americas Inc .... C 517 767-4142
South Bend *(G-12804)*
Horner Industrial Services Inc .... F 317 634-7165
Indianapolis *(G-7129)*
I Hsg Inc .... G 765 778-6499
Anderson *(G-119)*
Icon Metal Forming LLC .... B 812 738-5900
Corydon *(G-2102)*
Illinois Tool Works Inc .... E 317 390-5940
Indianapolis *(G-7159)*
Illinois Tool Works Inc .... C 260 347-8040
Kendallville *(G-8480)*
▲ Indiana Automotive Fas Inc .... B 317 467-0100
Greenfield *(G-5538)*
Indiana Custom Trucks LLC .... E 260 463-3244
Lagrange *(G-9046)*
Indiana Heat Transfer Corp .... C 574 936-3171
Plymouth *(G-11690)*
▲ Indiana Marujun LLC .... E 765 584-7639
Winchester *(G-14332)*
▲ Indiana Mills & Manufacturing .... B 317 896-9531
Westfield *(G-14169)*
▲ Indiana Precision Forge LLC .... D 317 421-0102
Shelbyville *(G-12538)*
Indiana Research Institute .... F 812 378-5363
Columbus *(G-1948)*
Industrial Axle Company LLC .... D 574 294-6651
Elkhart *(G-2933)*
Industrial Axle Company LLC .... D 574 295-6077
Elkhart *(G-2934)*
Industrial Steering Pdts Inc .... E 260 488-1880
Hamilton *(G-5824)*
▼ Indy Cylinder Head .... E 317 862-3724
Indianapolis *(G-7216)*
▲ Integrated Energy Technologies .... E 812 421-7810
Evansville *(G-3563)*
International Brake Inds Inc .... E 419 905-7468
South Bend *(G-12817)*
Interstate Power Systems Inc .... E 952 854-2044
Gary *(G-5070)*
Jason Incorporated .... G 248 455-7919
Richmond *(G-12005)*
◆ Jasper Engine Exchange Inc .... A 812 482-1041
Jasper *(G-8261)*
Jasper Engine Exchange Inc .... D 812 482-1041
Leavenworth *(G-9164)*
Jasper Willow Springs Mo LLC .... G 800 827-7455
Jasper *(G-8266)*
JD Norman Industries Inc .... D 765 288-8098
Muncie *(G-10499)*
JD Norman Industries Inc .... E 765 584-6069
Winchester *(G-14334)*
Joe Wade Customs .... G 765 548-0333
Rosedale *(G-12204)*
Jrz Industries Inc .... G 574 834-4543
North Webster *(G-11295)*
K Min .... G 574 296-3500
Elkhart *(G-2955)*
Kampco Steel Products Inc .... E 574 294-5466
Elkhart *(G-2956)*
Kautex Inc .... B 260 897-3250
Avilla *(G-410)*
Kautex Inc .... B 937 238-8096
Avilla *(G-409)*
▲ Keihin Aircon North America .... C 765 213-4915
Muncie *(G-10502)*
▲ Keihin Ipt Mfg LLC .... A 317 462-3015
Greenfield *(G-5547)*
▲ Keihin North America Inc .... A 765 298-6030
Anderson *(G-126)*
Killer Camaros Custom Camaro .... G 260 255-2425
New Haven *(G-10946)*
Kinro Manufacturing Inc .... C 574 533-8337
Goshen *(G-5257)*

Kirby Risk Corporation ....B...... 765 447-1402	Mor/Ryde Inc ....C...... 574 293-1581	R Concepts Industries Inc ....D...... 574 295-6641
Lafayette *(G-8942)*	Elkhart *(G-3046)*	Elkhart *(G-3135)*
Kp Holdings LLC ....B...... 317 867-0234	Mor/Ryde International Inc ....C...... 574 293-1581	▲ Ramco Engineering Inc ....E...... 574 266-1455
Westfield *(G-14173)*	Elkhart *(G-3049)*	Elkhart *(G-3136)*
KYB Americas Corporation ....F...... 317 881-7772	Morris Holding Company LLC ....C...... 812 446-6141	Rance Aluminum Fabrication ....E...... 574 266-9028
Greenwood *(G-5714)*	Brazil *(G-970)*	Elkhart *(G-3137)*
▲ KYB Americas Corporation ....B...... 317 736-7774	Morris Mfg & Sls Corp ....C...... 812 446-6141	Raybestos Powertrain ....G...... 812 268-1370
Franklin *(G-4903)*	Brazil *(G-971)*	Sullivan *(G-13092)*
KYB Americas Corporation ....E...... 630 620-5555	Mosey Manufacturing Co Inc ....D...... 765 768-7462	Raybestos Powertrain LLC ....E...... 812 268-1211
Greenwood *(G-5715)*	Dunkirk *(G-2486)*	Sullivan *(G-13093)*
L & W Engineering Inc ....G...... 574 825-5351	Mosey Manufacturing Co Inc ....C...... 765 983-8870	Rayburn Automotive Inc ....G...... 317 535-8232
Middlebury *(G-9900)*	Richmond *(G-12020)*	Whiteland *(G-14244)*
Lakepark Industries Ind Inc ....D...... 260 768-7411	Mosey Manufacturing Co Inc ....D...... 765 983-8889	Rayco Mch & Engrg Group Inc ....E...... 317 291-7848
Shipshewana *(G-12628)*	Richmond *(G-12022)*	Indianapolis *(G-7819)*
Lances Driveshaft & Components ....G...... 219 762-2531	Motherson Sumi Systems Limited ....A...... 260 726-6501	Reliable Tool & Machine Co ....D...... 260 343-7150
Portage *(G-11772)*	Portland *(G-11836)*	Kendallville *(G-8506)*
Lau Industries Inc ....G...... 574 223-3181	Motorama Auto Ctr Inc ....G...... 317 831-0036	Reman Holdings LLC ....G...... 800 372-5131
Rochester *(G-12132)*	Mooresville *(G-10325)*	Pendleton *(G-11502)*
LCI Industries ....D...... 574 535-1125	▲ Mpt Muncie LLC ....E...... 765 587-1300	▲ Riverside Mfg Inc ....C...... 260 637-4470
Elkhart *(G-2989)*	Muncie *(G-10526)*	Fort Wayne *(G-4594)*
Lear Corporation ....D...... 317 481-0530	◆ Muncie Power Products Inc ....C...... 765 284-7721	Road Equipment ....G...... 219 887-6400
Indianapolis *(G-7391)*	Muncie *(G-10533)*	Gary *(G-5094)*
Lear Corporation ....G...... 260 244-1700	Muncie Power Products Inc ....G...... 765 896-9816	Robert Bosch LLC ....D...... 574 654-4000
Columbia City *(G-1808)*	Muncie *(G-10534)*	New Carlisle *(G-10886)*
Lear Corporation ....G...... 219 764-5101	◆ Mvo Usa Inc ....F...... 317 585-5785	Robert Bosch LLC ....C...... 260 636-1005
Portage *(G-11773)*	Indianapolis *(G-7562)*	Albion *(G-34)*
Lear Corporation ....G...... 765 653-2511	▲ Nagakura Engrg Works Co Inc ....C...... 812 375-1382	Rochester Manufacturing LLC ....G...... 574 224-2044
Greencastle *(G-5466)*	Columbus *(G-1978)*	Rochester *(G-12147)*
Lear Corporation ....E...... 574 935-3818	NERP LLC ....G...... 574 303-6377	Rocore Thermal Systems LLC ....G...... 317 227-2929
Plymouth *(G-11702)*	South Bend *(G-12872)*	Indianapolis *(G-7854)*
Lear Corporation ....B...... 219 852-0014	Niagara Lasalle Corporation ....E...... 800 262-2558	Roppel Industries Inc ....G...... 812 425-0267
Hammond *(G-5907)*	Hammond *(G-5921)*	Evansville *(G-3709)*
▲ Lingenfelter Prfmce Engrg Inc ....E...... 260 724-2552	Nishikawa Cooper LLC ....G...... 574 546-5938	▲ Ryobi Die Casting (usa) Inc ....A...... 317 398-3398
Decatur *(G-2390)*	Bremen *(G-1012)*	Shelbyville *(G-12565)*
Lippert Components Inc ....G...... 574 971-4100	Norco Industries Inc ....C...... 574 262-3400	S & H Metal Products Inc ....E...... 260 593-2565
Goshen *(G-5274)*	Elkhart *(G-3065)*	Topeka *(G-13428)*
Lippert Components Inc ....C...... 800 551-9149	Northern Trans & Differential ....G...... 219 764-4009	Safe Fleet Mirrors ....F...... 574 266-3700
Elkhart *(G-2999)*	Portage *(G-11785)*	Elkhart *(G-3153)*
Lippert Components Inc ....D...... 574 535-1125	Northwind Electronics LLC ....F...... 317 288-0787	▼ Saldana Racing Tanks Inc ....F...... 317 852-4193
Goshen *(G-5268)*	Indianapolis *(G-7596)*	Indianapolis *(G-7888)*
Lippert Components Inc ....D...... 574 294-6852	NSK Corporation ....C...... 765 458-5000	Smart Technologies LLC ....G...... 317 738-4338
Elkhart *(G-3000)*	Liberty *(G-9267)*	Franklin *(G-4933)*
Lippert Components Inc ....E...... 574 535-1125	NSK Precision America Inc ....C...... 317 738-5000	▲ SMI Manufacturing Inc ....G...... 812 428-2794
Goshen *(G-5272)*	Franklin *(G-4916)*	Newburgh *(G-11051)*
Lippert Components Inc ....D...... 574 849-0869	▲ NTN Driveshaft Inc ....A...... 812 342-7000	SMR Management Inc ....G...... 765 252-0257
Goshen *(G-5273)*	Columbus *(G-1982)*	Lafayette *(G-8999)*
Lippert Components Inc ....G...... 574 971-4320	◆ Old Remco Holdings LLC ....C...... 765 778-6499	Sonoco Prtective Solutions Inc ....D...... 260 726-9333
Goshen *(G-5275)*	Pendleton *(G-11498)*	Portland *(G-11847)*
Lippert Components Inc ....D...... 574 312-7445	Omnimax International Inc ....E...... 574 294-8576	▲ South Bend Clutch Inc ....E...... 574 256-5064
Middlebury *(G-9904)*	Elkhart *(G-3070)*	Mishawaka *(G-10131)*
Lippert Components Mfg Inc ....C...... 574 935-5122	Onspot of North America Inc ....E...... 812 346-1719	Spheros North America Inc ....F...... 574 264-2190
Plymouth *(G-11703)*	North Vernon *(G-11275)*	Elkhart *(G-3185)*
Madison Manufacturing Inc ....E...... 574 633-4433	Parker-Hannifin Corporation ....C...... 260 894-7125	Spitzers Racing Enterprises ....F...... 317 894-9533
Bremen *(G-1009)*	Ligonier *(G-9292)*	Greenfield *(G-5577)*
Magna Powertrain America Inc ....C...... 765 587-1300	Patterson Driveshaft Inc ....G...... 317 481-0495	Splendor Boats LLC ....F...... 260 352-2835
Muncie *(G-10515)*	Indianapolis *(G-7663)*	Silver Lake *(G-12681)*
Magna Powertrain America Inc ....C...... 765 587-1300	Perfection Wheel LLC ....F...... 260 358-9239	Standard Glass and Star Glass ....G...... 574 546-5912
Muncie *(G-10516)*	Huntington *(G-6237)*	Bremen *(G-1025)*
Mahomed Sales & Whsng LLC ....D...... 317 472-5800	Performance Rod & Custom Inc ....G...... 812 897-5805	◆ Stant USA Corp ....C...... 765 825-3121
Indianapolis *(G-7441)*	Boonville *(G-921)*	Connersville *(G-2072)*
Make It Mobile LLC ....E...... 260 562-1045	Performance Technology Inc ....G...... 574 862-2116	Stant USA Corp ....B...... 765 825-3121
Howe *(G-6128)*	Wakarusa *(G-13789)*	Connersville *(G-2073)*
Makuta Technics Inc ....F...... 317 642-0001	Peterson Sanko Corp ....G...... 765 966-9656	Starcraft Corporation ....G...... 574 534-7705
Shelbyville *(G-12550)*	Richmond *(G-12028)*	Goshen *(G-5328)*
▲ Mancor Indiana Inc ....E...... 765 779-4800	▲ Phillips Company Inc ....D...... 812 378-3797	▼ Starcraft Corporation ....E...... 574 534-7827
Anderson *(G-134)*	Columbus *(G-1994)*	Goshen *(G-5329)*
Mann+hummel Filtration Technol ....G...... 260 497-5560	▲ Pierce Company Inc ....E...... 765 998-8100	◆ State Wide Aluminum Inc ....D...... 574 262-2594
Fort Wayne *(G-4451)*	Upland *(G-13472)*	Elkhart *(G-3191)*
Martinrea Industries Inc ....C...... 812 346-5750	▲ Pk USA Inc ....B...... 317 395-5500	Steel Parts Manufacturing Inc ....E...... 765 675-2191
North Vernon *(G-11269)*	Shelbyville *(G-12558)*	Tipton *(G-13407)*
Mascot Truck Parts Usa LLC ....D...... 317 839-9525	▲ PMG Indiana LLC ....C...... 812 379-4606	Steel Tank & Fabricating Corp ....E...... 260 248-8971
Plainfield *(G-11623)*	Columbus *(G-1996)*	Columbia City *(G-1838)*
Mastersbilt Chassis Inc ....F...... 812 793-3666	Power Investments Inc ....C...... 317 738-2117	Stephen G Morrow Inc ....G...... 812 876-7837
Crothersville *(G-2218)*	Franklin *(G-4921)*	Spencer *(G-13040)*
Meritor Inc ....G...... 317 279-2180	Power Plant Service Inc ....E...... 260 432-6716	Sterling Industries Inc ....E...... 812 376-6560
Plainfield *(G-11627)*	Fort Wayne *(G-4542)*	Columbus *(G-2016)*
▲ Metaldyne Bsm LLC ....D...... 260 495-4315	Power Train Corp Fort Wayne ....F...... 317 241-9393	Stored Energy Solutions Inc ....G...... 574 457-2199
Fremont *(G-4968)*	Indianapolis *(G-7712)*	Anderson *(G-171)*
▲ Metaldyne M&A Bluffton LLC ....D...... 260 824-2360	Precision Racg Components LLC ....F...... 317 248-4764	Summit Coaches ....G...... 260 489-3556
Bluffton *(G-882)*	Indianapolis *(G-7735)*	Fort Wayne *(G-4662)*
▲ Miasa Automotive LLC ....E...... 765 751-9967	Price Motor Sport Engineering ....G...... 812 546-4220	Taylor Made Group Holdings Inc ....C...... 260 347-1368
Yorktown *(G-14407)*	Hope *(G-6118)*	Kendallville *(G-8512)*
Midwest Auto Repair Inc ....E...... 219 322-0364	Pridgeon & Clay Inc ....C...... 317 738-4885	Teal Automotive Inc ....E...... 765 768-7726
Schererville *(G-12334)*	Franklin *(G-4923)*	Dunkirk *(G-2489)*
Miller Mfg Corp ....E...... 574 773-4136	Pulliam Enterprises Inc ....E...... 574 259-1520	Team Oneway ....G...... 574 387-5417
Nappanee *(G-10695)*	Mishawaka *(G-10112)*	Granger *(G-5443)*
▲ Mobile Climate Control Corp ....D...... 574 534-1516	Pullman Company ....B...... 260 667-2200	▲ Techna-Fit Inc ....G...... 317 350-2153
Goshen *(G-5296)*	Angola *(G-241)*	Brownsburg *(G-1174)*
Mobile Dynamometer LLC ....G...... 765 271-5080	Quality Converters Inc ....E...... 260 829-6541	Tenneco Automotive Oper Co Inc ......C...... 260 894-9214
Kokomo *(G-8668)*	Orland *(G-11356)*	Ligonier *(G-9299)*

Tenneco Automotive Oper Co Inc ....D...... 574 296-9400
  Elkhart *(G-3211)*
Thermal Ceramics Inc.........................E...... 574 296-3500
  Elkhart *(G-3212)*
◆ TI Automotive Ligonier Corp ....B...... 260 894-3163
  Ligonier *(G-9300)*
TI Group Auto Systems LLC ....B...... 260 622-7900
  Ossian *(G-11414)*
TI Group Auto Systems LLC ....C...... 260 587-6100
  Ashley *(G-291)*
◆ Tire Rack Inc ....B...... 888 541-1777
  South Bend *(G-12972)*
TNT Truck Accessories LLC ....G...... 812 305-0714
  Haubstadt *(G-6006)*
◆ TOA (usa) LLC ....B...... 317 834-0522
  Mooresville *(G-10343)*
Townsend Transmissions LLC ....G...... 765 342-0042
  Martinsville *(G-9643)*
▲ Transportation Tech Inds ....F...... 812 962-5000
  Evansville *(G-3769)*
▲ Transwheel Corporation ....C...... 260 358-8660
  Huntington *(G-6256)*
Tri Aerospace LLC ....E...... 812 872-2400
  Terre Haute *(G-13358)*
▲ Tri State Cylinder Head ....E...... 812 421-0095
  Evansville *(G-3770)*
▲ Trin Inc ....E...... 260 587-9282
  Ashley *(G-292)*
▲ Tru-Flex LLC ....C...... 765 893-4403
  West Lebanon *(G-14122)*
Truckpro LLC ....F...... 765 482-6525
  Lebanon *(G-9230)*
TRW Automotive US LLC ....A...... 765 423-5377
  Lafayette *(G-9012)*
▲ TRW Commercial Steering ....A...... 765 423-5377
  Lafayette *(G-9013)*
▲ Tsuda USA Corporation ....F...... 317 468-9177
  Greenfield *(G-5582)*
Twb of Indiana ....G...... 812 342-6000
  Columbus *(G-2026)*
U B Machine Inc ....E...... 260 493-3381
  New Haven *(G-10962)*
Ugn Inc..C...... 219 464-7813
  Valparaiso *(G-13631)*
Ultimate Sports Inc ....G...... 765 423-2984
  West Lafayette *(G-14114)*
Ultra-Heat Inc ....F...... 574 522-6594
  Elkhart *(G-3232)*
United Components LLC ....F...... 812 867-4156
  Evansville *(G-3786)*
▲ Universal Bearings LLC ....C...... 574 546-2261
  Bremen *(G-1030)*
Valeo North America Inc ....A...... 812 663-8541
  Greensburg *(G-5640)*
Valeo North America Inc ....B...... 812 663-8541
  Greensburg *(G-5641)*
Valley Distributing Inc ....E...... 574 266-4455
  Elkhart *(G-3241)*
Vee Engineering Inc.........................D...... 260 424-6635
  Fort Wayne *(G-4725)*
Vessell Trim Co ....F...... 812 424-2963
  Evansville *(G-3797)*
Variiloc Distributors Inc ....G...... 317 273-0089
  Indianapolis *(G-8160)*
Vibration Eliminator Co Inc ....E...... 765 932-2858
  Rushville *(G-12237)*
Viking Inc ....E...... 260 244-6141
  Columbia City *(G-1845)*
Voegele Auto Supply LLC ....G...... 765 647-3541
  Brookville *(G-1130)*
Wabash National Corporation ....B...... 765 771-5300
  Lafayette *(G-9018)*
Wagler Competition Pdts LLC ....G...... 812 486-9360
  Odon *(G-11344)*
Warner Electric LLC.........................C...... 260 244-6183
  Columbia City *(G-1846)*
Webb Wheel Products Inc ....C...... 812 548-0477
  Tell City *(G-13175)*
Wellspring Components LLC..............G...... 260 768-7336
  Shipshewana *(G-12657)*
▲ Western Reman Industrial Inc .....G...... 765 472-2002
  Peru *(G-11557)*
Wheel Group Holdings LLC ....G...... 317 780-1661
  Indianapolis *(G-8189)*
▲ Wheels 4 Tots Inc ....G...... 219 987-6812
  Demotte *(G-2452)*
Woodys Hot Rodz LLc.......................G...... 812 637-1933
  Lawrenceburg *(G-9162)*
Xtrac Inc..F...... 317 472-2451
  Indianapolis *(G-8222)*

Zemco Mfg Inc..................................E...... 260 428-2650
  Fort Wayne *(G-4765)*

3715 Truck Trailers

▲ Agri - Traders & Repair LLC ....G...... 260 238-4225
  Spencerville *(G-13042)*
Agritraders Mfg Inc ....G...... 260 238-4225
  Spencerville *(G-13043)*
Aluminum Cargo Trailers Inc ....F...... 260 463-0185
  Lagrange *(G-9030)*
Alvin J Nix......................................G...... 812 347-2510
  Ramsey *(G-11892)*
Angels Wings Expedited ....F...... 574 339-3038
  South Bend *(G-12707)*
Atc Trailers Holdings Inc ....C...... 574 773-2440
  Nappanee *(G-10651)*
Brindle Products Inc ....E...... 260 627-2156
  Grabill *(G-5358)*
BSB Trans Inc..................................G...... 317 919-8778
  Greenwood *(G-5672)*
Bull Manufacturing LLC ....G...... 812 530-1064
  Brownstown *(G-1182)*
Bullseye Technologies Inc ....G...... 574 753-0102
  Elkhart *(G-2737)*
C & J Services & Supplies Inc ....G...... 317 569-7222
  Fort Wayne *(G-4130)*
Delphi Body Works ....F...... 765 564-2212
  Delphi *(G-2417)*
Diamonds Componets Inc..................E...... 574 358-0452
  Middlebury *(G-9881)*
Durcholz Excavating & Cnstr Co ....G...... 812 634-1764
  Huntingburg *(G-6161)*
Eaton Corporation ....D...... 574 288-4446
  South Bend *(G-12756)*
Fontaine Trailer Company ....G...... 574 772-6673
  Knox *(G-8566)*
Forest River Inc ....C...... 574 848-1335
  Bristol *(G-1060)*
Great Dane LLC ....A...... 812 443-4711
  Brazil *(G-962)*
◆ H & H Sales Company Inc ....F...... 260 637-3177
  Huntertown *(G-6139)*
H John Enterprise Inc ....E...... 574 293-6008
  Elkhart *(G-2903)*
Heartcare LLC ....G...... 260 432-7000
  Fort Wayne *(G-4327)*
Hendrickson International Corp ....C...... 765 483-5350
  Lebanon *(G-9187)*
Impact Trailers ....G...... 574 322-4369
  Elkhart *(G-2929)*
▼ Intech Trailers Inc ....D...... 574 773-9536
  Nappanee *(G-10685)*
▲ Kruz Inc ....E...... 574 772-6673
  Knox *(G-8571)*
Kuckuck Transport LLC ....G...... 260 609-0316
  South Whitley *(G-13001)*
Lakota Corp ....E...... 574 848-1636
  Bristol *(G-1064)*
Lantzs Coachworks Inc ....G...... 317 487-1111
  Indianapolis *(G-7380)*
LCI Industries ....D...... 574 535-1125
  Elkhart *(G-2989)*
Millers Superior Entps Inc ....F...... 877 475-5665
  Middlebury *(G-9909)*
Pace American Enterprises Inc ....E...... 800 247-5767
  Middlebury *(G-9914)*
▲ Quality Steel & Alum Pdts Inc......E...... 574 295-8715
  Elkhart *(G-3130)*
Rail Protection Plus LLC ....G...... 812 399-1084
  New Albany *(G-10853)*
Schwartzs Trailer Sales Inc..............G...... 317 773-2608
  Noblesville *(G-11181)*
Sternberg Inc ....E...... 812 867-0077
  Evansville *(G-3751)*
Strick Corporation ....B...... 260 692-6121
  Monroe *(G-10185)*
Strick Trailers LLC ....C...... 260 692-6121
  Monroe *(G-10186)*
Superior Mfg Inc..............................F...... 812 983-9900
  Elberfeld *(G-2639)*
Tail Wind Transport..........................F...... 574 343-2157
  Elkhart *(G-3204)*
Talbert Manufacturing Inc ....C...... 219 866-7141
  Rensselaer *(G-11942)*
Team Spirit Trlrs Elkhart Inc ....E...... 574 266-2966
  Elkhart *(G-3209)*
TEC Transport LLC ....G...... 765 534-3253
  Noblesville *(G-11193)*
▼ Travel Lite Inc ....E...... 574 831-3000
  New Paris *(G-10999)*

Truck Life LLC..................................F...... 219 655-0018
  Gary *(G-5110)*
United Trailers Inc ....G...... 574 848-7088
  Bristol *(G-1091)*
▼ Universal Trlr Crgo Group Inc........B...... 574 264-9661
  Bristol *(G-1092)*
▲ Vanguard National Trailer Corp .....A...... 219 253-2000
  Monon *(G-10179)*
Wabash National LP ....D...... 765 771-5300
  Lafayette *(G-9017)*
Wabash National Corporation ....C...... 765 659-3856
  Frankfort *(G-4859)*
Wabash National Corporation ....B...... 765 771-5300
  Lafayette *(G-9018)*
Wabash National Mfg LP ....D...... 765 771-5310
  Lafayette *(G-9019)*
▼ Wellco Holdings Inc ....B...... 574 264-9661
  Elkhart *(G-3257)*
Whitewater Valley Rvs Inc ....G...... 765 458-5171
  Liberty *(G-9272)*
Zieman Manufacturing Company ....G...... 574 522-5202
  Goshen *(G-5347)*

3716 Motor Homes

Aip/Fw Funding Inc ....G...... 212 627-2360
  Decatur *(G-2364)*
◆ All American Group Inc ....E...... 574 262-0123
  Elkhart *(G-2674)*
All American Group Inc ....G...... 574 262-9889
  Elkhart *(G-2675)*
All American Group Inc ....D...... 574 825-1720
  Middlebury *(G-9869)*
Bison Horse Trailers LLC ....G...... 574 658-4161
  Milford *(G-9950)*
Chariot Vans Inc ....E...... 574 264-7577
  Elkhart *(G-2755)*
Coach Line Motors.............................G...... 765 825-7893
  Connersville *(G-2043)*
◆ Damon Corporation ....F...... 574 262-2624
  Elkhart *(G-2787)*
Damon Corporation ....B...... 574 262-2624
  Elkhart *(G-2788)*
Damon Corporation ....F...... 574 264-2900
  Elkhart *(G-2789)*
▲ Ds Corp ....C...... 260 593-3850
  Topeka *(G-13417)*
Fiber-Tron Corp ....E...... 574 294-8545
  Elkhart *(G-2848)*
Fleetwood Motor Homes ....G...... 260 627-6800
  Spencerville *(G-13046)*
Forest River Inc ....C...... 574 262-3474
  Elkhart *(G-2862)*
Forest River Inc ....C...... 574 296-7700
  Elkhart *(G-2866)*
Gulf Stream Coach Inc ....A...... 574 773-7761
  Nappanee *(G-10676)*
▼ Gulf Stream Coach Inc ....C...... 574 773-7761
  Nappanee *(G-10677)*
Independent Protection Co Inc...........D...... 574 831-5680
  New Paris *(G-10985)*
▼ Jayco Inc ....A...... 574 825-5861
  Middlebury *(G-9896)*
Newmar Corporation ....A...... 574 773-7791
  Nappanee *(G-10699)*
▲ Phoenix Usa Inc ....E...... 574 266-2020
  Elkhart *(G-3095)*
Rev Recreation Group Inc ....E...... 260 728-9564
  Decatur *(G-2401)*
▲ Rev Recreation Group Inc.............C...... 260 728-2121
  Decatur *(G-2402)*
Rev Recreation Group Inc ....C...... 260 724-4217
  Decatur *(G-2403)*
Southside Mini Storage ....G...... 574 293-3270
  Elkhart *(G-3181)*
Sportsmobile Inc ....F...... 260 356-5435
  Huntington *(G-6251)*
▼ Starcraft Corporation ....E...... 574 534-7827
  Goshen *(G-5329)*
Thor Motor Coach ....G...... 574 266-1111
  Elkhart *(G-3215)*
▼ Thor Motor Coach Inc ....B...... 574 266-1111
  Elkhart *(G-3216)*
◆ Van Explorer Company Inc ....E...... 574 267-7666
  Warsaw *(G-13957)*
Zoomers Rv of Indiana LLC ....G...... 260 414-1978
  Wabash *(G-13769)*

3721 Aircraft

Aerial Drone Exposures Inc ....G...... 404 641-5563
  Indianapolis *(G-6343)*

Aerospace Waterjet Svcs LLC ....G 502 836-1112
   Marysville (G-9649)
Bae Systems Inc ....G 812 863-0514
   Odon (G-11319)
Bae Systems Controls Inc ....A 260 434-5195
   Fort Wayne (G-4100)
Bell Aerospace LLC ....G 904 505-4055
   Plainfield (G-11596)
Drone Works LLC ....G 812 917-4691
   Terre Haute (G-13225)
Drone1260wrx LLC ....G 773 957-3625
   Merrillville (G-9711)
Droneye Imaging LLC ....G 317 878-4065
   Trafalgar (G-13435)
Golden Age Aeroplane Work LLC ....G 812 358-5778
   Brownstown (G-1188)
Golden-Helvey Holdings Inc ....F 574 266-4500
   Elkhart (G-2889)
Hoosier Industrial Supply ....G 574 535-0712
   Goshen (G-5239)
Hull Aircraft Support LLC ....G 219 324-6247
   La Porte (G-8769)
I-Fly Drones LLC ....G 812 524-3863
   Seymour (G-12457)
Infinity Drones LLC ....G 812 457-7140
   Poseyville (G-11857)
Klx Aerospace Inc ....G 260 747-0671
   Fort Wayne (G-4413)
Live Bold Aerospace LLC ....G 260 438-5710
   Fort Wayne (G-4438)
Lockheed Martin Corporation ....B 317 821-4000
   Indianapolis (G-7414)
Raytheon Company ....E 317 306-4872
   Indianapolis (G-7821)
Robert J Robinson Aircraft ....G 317 787-7809
   Greenwood (G-5740)
Rollison Airplane Company Inc ....G 812 384-4972
   Bloomfield (G-645)
Sargent Aerospace Inc ....G 305 593-6038
   Franklin (G-4928)
Technology MGT Group Inc ....F 765 606-1512
   Anderson (G-173)
Thunderbird Aviation LLC ....G 847 303-3100
   Indianapolis (G-8073)
Tip To Tail Aerospace LLC ....G 765 437-6556
   Peru (G-11552)
UTC Aerospace Systems ....G 812 704-5200
   Jeffersonville (G-8437)
Utilities Aviation Specialists ....G 219 662-8175
   Crown Point (G-2317)

3724 Aircraft Engines & Engine Parts

Airtomic Repair Station ....G 317 738-0148
   Franklin (G-4865)
Avborne Accessory Group Inc ....E 317 738-0148
   Franklin (G-4869)
Bel-Mar Products Corporation ....G 317 769-3262
   Whitestown (G-14249)
Georgia Sstnment Solutions Inc ....G 575 621-2372
   Cicero (G-1661)
Global Air Inc ....G 317 251-1251
   Indianapolis (G-7010)
Honeywell International Inc ....B 765 284-3300
   Muncie (G-10490)
Honeywell International Inc ....D 317 580-6165
   Indianapolis (G-7116)
Honeywell International Inc ....A 574 935-0200
   Plymouth (G-11688)
Honeywell International Inc ....A 574 231-3000
   South Bend (G-12800)
Honeywell International Inc ....G 317 359-9505
   Indianapolis (G-7117)
Honeywell International Inc ....G 574 231-3000
   South Bend (G-12801)
Hsm ....G 317 573-8700
   Indianapolis (G-7142)
Innovtive Srcing Solutions Inc ....G 317 752-2952
   Fishers (G-3932)
Instellus Inc ....G 734 415-3013
   Griffith (G-5780)
▲ Integrated Energy Technologies......E 812 421-7810
   Evansville (G-3563)
Integrity EDM LLC ....F 317 333-7630
   Tipton (G-13392)
Midwest Arcft Mch & TI Co Inc ....E 317 839-1515
   Plainfield (G-11628)
▲ Ngh Retail LLC ....G 219 476-0772
   Valparaiso (G-13588)
Robert Perez ....G 317 291-7311
   Indianapolis (G-7849)

Rolls-Royce Corporation...................A 317 230-2000
   Plainfield (G-11641)
Rolls-Royce Corporation...................G 317 437-9326
   Indianapolis (G-7857)
Rolls-Royce Corporation...................G 317 230-8515
   West Lafayette (G-14104)
▲ Rolls-Royce Corporation...............A 317 230-2000
   Indianapolis (G-7858)
Rolls-Royce Corporation...................D 812 421-7810
   Evansville (G-3708)
Simpson Alloy Services Inc ....G 812 969-2766
   Elizabeth (G-2646)
Smiths Arospc Components Haute......G 812 235-5210
   Terre Haute (G-13330)
Teamair Mro Ltd ....G 812 584-3733
   Moores Hill (G-10299)
Thermal Structures Inc ....D 951 736-9911
   Plainfield (G-11646)
Tri Aerospace LLC ....E 812 872-2400
   Terre Haute (G-13358)
Turbines Inc ....E 812 877-2587
   Terre Haute (G-13359)
Twigg Corporation ....D 765 342-7126
   Martinsville (G-9644)
▲ Walerko Tool and Engrg Corp........E 574 295-2233
   Elkhart (G-3252)
Wbh Inc ....F 317 839-1515
   Plainfield (G-11650)
Wbh Inc ....F 317 269-1510
   Indianapolis (G-8180)

3728 Aircraft Parts & Eqpt, NEC

Allison Transmission Inc ....A 317 280-6206
   Indianapolis (G-6372)
Attco Machine Products Inc ....E 574 234-1063
   South Bend (G-12714)
B-D Industries Inc ....F 574 295-1420
   Elkhart (G-2712)
Bertrand Products Inc ....E 574 234-4181
   South Bend (G-12722)
Burris Engineering Inc ....F 317 862-1046
   Indianapolis (G-6522)
C F Roark Wldg Engrg Co Inc ....C 317 852-3163
   Brownsburg (G-1141)
Cook Aircraft Leasing Inc ....G 812 339-2044
   Bloomington (G-702)
First Gear Inc ....F 260 490-3238
   Fort Wayne (G-4263)
Golden-Helvey Holdings Inc ....D 574 266-4500
   Elkhart (G-2890)
Goodrich Corporation ....D 812 704-5200
   Jeffersonville (G-8370)
HB Connect Inc ....D 260 422-1212
   Fort Wayne (G-4324)
Honeywell International Inc ....G 574 231-2000
   South Bend (G-12799)
Iasa Group LLC ....G 260 484-1322
   Fort Wayne (G-4355)
Indiana Aircraft Hardware Co ....G 317 485-6500
   Fortville (G-4780)
Integrated De Icing Servi ....G 317 517-1643
   Indianapolis (G-7247)
Integrity Defense Services Inc..........F 812 675-4913
   Springville (G-13064)
Kem Krest Defense LLC ....F 574 389-2650
   Elkhart (G-2960)
Krisma Diversified ....G 317 413-4788
   Carmel (G-1425)
L&E Engineering LLC ....D 317 884-0017
   Greenwood (G-5716)
Liberty Advance Machine Inc ....G 812 372-1010
   Columbus (G-1961)
Lift Works Inc ....G 812 797-0479
   Greenwood (G-5720)
Mack Tool & Engineering Inc ....E 574 233-8424
   South Bend (G-12847)
▲ Midwest Aerospace Ltd ....F 219 365-7250
   Saint John (G-12265)
Mike Magiera Inc ....G 574 654-3044
   New Carlisle (G-10884)
MSP Aviation Inc ....E 812 333-6100
   Bloomington (G-777)
◆ Mvo Usa Inc ....F 317 585-5785
   Indianapolis (G-7562)
Odyssian Technology LLC ....G 574 257-7555
   South Bend (G-12882)
Precision Piece Parts Inc ....D 574 255-3185
   Mishawaka (G-10107)
Pynco Inc ....E 812 275-0900
   Bedford (G-567)

Q Air Inc ....G 219 476-7048
   Valparaiso (G-13603)
Rayco Mch & Engrg Group Inc ....E 317 291-7848
   Indianapolis (G-7819)
Regent Aerospace Corporation ....G 317 837-4000
   Plainfield (G-11640)
Rolls-Royce Corporation...................D 812 421-7810
   Evansville (G-3708)
Safran Nclles Svcs Amricas LLC........F 317 789-8188
   Indianapolis (G-7885)
Smart Manufacturing Inc ....G 765 482-7481
   Lebanon (G-9225)
Taft Aviation Property LLC ....G 317 769-4487
   Zionsville (G-14467)
Tri Aerospace LLC ....E 812 872-2400
   Terre Haute (G-13358)
Triumph Thermal Systems Inc ....G 419 273-1192
   Shelbyville (G-12580)
▲ Tube Processing Corp....................B 317 787-1321
   Indianapolis (G-8107)
Tube Processing Corp........................C 317 264-7760
   Indianapolis (G-8109)
U S S Inc ....G 260 693-1172
   Churubusco (G-1660)
Val Rollers Inc ....G 317 542-1968
   Indianapolis (G-8144)
Value Production Inc ....E 574 246-1913
   South Bend (G-12983)
Wbh Inc ....F 317 839-1515
   Plainfield (G-11650)
Wolf Technical Engineering LLC ....G 800 783-9653
   Indianapolis (G-8209)

3731 Shipbuilding & Repairing

Acl Professional Services Inc ....B 812 288-0100
   Jeffersonville (G-8317)
American Barge Line Company ....G 812 288-0100
   Jeffersonville (G-8323)
American Coml Barge Line LLC ....C 812 288-0100
   Jeffersonville (G-8324)
American Commercial Lines Inc ....C 812 288-0100
   Jeffersonville (G-8325)
Cargo Skiff Corporation ....G 812 873-6349
   Butlerville (G-1247)
Commercial Barge Line Company ......F 812 288-0100
   Jeffersonville (G-8341)
▲ Corn Island Shipyard Inc ....G 812 362-8808
   Grandview (G-5386)
General Dynamics Corporation ....G 260 637-4773
   Fort Wayne (G-4295)
Harvest Petroleum Inc ....G 219 924-8236
   Hammond (G-5890)
Innovations By ....G 260 413-1869
   Fort Wayne (G-4371)
Integrity Defense Services Inc..........F 812 675-4913
   Springville (G-13064)
Lake Lite Inc ....G 260 918-2758
   Laotto (G-9112)
Macks Welding ....F 812 265-6255
   Madison (G-9478)
Marine Builders Inc ....D 812 283-7932
   Jeffersonville (G-8396)
Nsa Crane ....G 812 854-4723
   Crane (G-2130)
Nswc Crane Division ....G 812 854-2865
   Bloomington (G-781)
Rolls-Royce Corporation....................G 317 230-8515
   West Lafayette (G-14104)
▲ Rolls-Royce Corporation...............A 317 230-2000
   Indianapolis (G-7858)
Smith Estill Marine Service ....G 812 282-7944
   Jeffersonville (G-8424)
▼ Smoker Craft Inc ....B 574 831-2103
   New Paris (G-10994)
Tpg Mt Vernon Marine LLC ....C 317 631-0234
   Indianapolis (G-8087)
Waterways Equipment Exchange........G 812 925-8104
   Chandler (G-1555)

3732 Boat Building & Repairing

Angola Canvas Co Inc ....F 260 665-9913
   Angola (G-191)
Atlas Dock Systems Inc ....G 317 714-3850
   New Castle (G-10892)
Boat Holdings LLC ....G 574 264-6336
   Elkhart (G-2728)
Brunswick Corporation ....C 260 459-8200
   Fort Wayne (G-4125)
Buckhorn Inc ....D 260 824-0997
   Bluffton (G-870)

Chief Powerboats Inc ....G....... 219 775-7024
Crown Point *(G-2233)*
Culvers Port Side Marina ....F....... 574 223-5090
Rochester *(G-12120)*
Destination Yachts Inc ....F....... 812 254-8800
Washington *(G-13979)*
Fiberglass Pdts & Boat Repr ....G....... 260 627-3209
Grabill *(G-5364)*
Fiberglass Pdts Boat Repairing ....G....... 260 337-5636
Saint Joe *(G-12255)*
Groh Inc ....G....... 260 463-2410
Lagrange *(G-9043)*
Harmon Boats Inc ....G....... 765 963-5358
Sharpsville *(G-12506)*
Highwater Marine LLC ....D....... 574 457-2082
Syracuse *(G-13134)*
▼ Highwater Marine LLC ....D....... 574 522-8381
Elkhart *(G-2916)*
Hoosier Marine ....G....... 812 879-5549
Quincy *(G-11890)*
Indianapolis Marine Co................F....... 317 545-4646
Indianapolis *(G-7202)*
J C Mfg Inc ....E....... 574 834-2881
North Webster *(G-11294)*
Kentuckiana Yacht Services LLC ....G....... 812 282-2660
Jeffersonville *(G-8387)*
Macks Welding ....F....... 812 265-6255
Madison *(G-9478)*
Mikes Boat Works LLC ....G....... 317 410-4981
Greenfield *(G-5553)*
N3 LLC ....G....... 317 845-9253
Indianapolis *(G-7568)*
▲ Neoteric Incorporated ....F....... 812 234-1120
Terre Haute *(G-13289)*
▼ Pontoon Boat LLC ....C....... 574 264-6336
Elkhart *(G-3102)*
Rollerboat Inc ....G....... 512 931-3936
Sellersburg *(G-12413)*
Rolls-Royce Corporation..............G....... 317 230-8515
West Lafayette *(G-14104)*
▲ Rolls-Royce Corporation...........A....... 317 230-2000
Indianapolis *(G-7858)*
Sherms Marine ....G....... 260 563-8051
Wabash *(G-13755)*
▼ Smoker Craft Inc ....B....... 574 831-2103
New Paris *(G-10994)*
Splendor Boats LLC ....F....... 260 352-2835
Silver Lake *(G-12681)*
▼ Starcraft Marine LLC ....B....... 574 831-2103
New Paris *(G-10995)*
▼ Sylvan Marine Inc ....B....... 574 831-2950
New Paris *(G-10997)*
Taylor Made Group Holdings Inc.........C....... 260 347-1368
Kendallville *(G-8512)*
Thomas Toll ....G....... 317 569-2628
Carmel *(G-1496)*
▼ Veada Industries Inc ....A....... 574 831-4775
New Paris *(G-11000)*
Wawasee Aluminum Works Inc ....E....... 574 457-2082
Syracuse *(G-13152)*
West Lakes Marine Inc ....F....... 260 854-2525
Rome City *(G-12201)*
Yacht Brite Proffesional Care ....G....... 219 874-1181
Michigan City *(G-9862)*
Yandt Boat Works ....G....... 219 851-8311
La Porte *(G-8834)*

3743 Railroad Eqpt

Adams & Westlake Ltd ....E....... 574 264-1141
Elkhart *(G-2668)*
Amsted Rail Company Inc.............D....... 219 931-1900
Hammond *(G-5843)*
Cai Rail ....G....... 317 669-2555
Carmel *(G-1325)*
General Signals Inc ....F....... 812 474-4256
Evansville *(G-3518)*
Hadady Corporation ....C....... 219 322-7417
Dyer *(G-2500)*
J P Industries Inc ....G....... 574 293-8763
Elkhart *(G-2942)*
▲ Kiel NA LLC ....F....... 574 293-3600
Elkhart *(G-2965)*
Locomotive S Professional.............G....... 219 398-9123
East Chicago *(G-2549)*
Mark Hedge..............................G....... 812 288-8037
Jeffersonville *(G-8397)*
Powerrail Holdings Inc ....F....... 765 827-4660
Connersville *(G-2068)*
Rolls-Royce Corporation..............G....... 317 230-8515
West Lafayette *(G-14104)*

▲ Rolls-Royce Corporation...........A....... 317 230-2000
Indianapolis *(G-7858)*
Stella Jones ....G....... 812 232-2316
Terre Haute *(G-13344)*
Tangent Rail Products Inc ....E....... 412 325-0202
Terre Haute *(G-13348)*
▲ Tcb Enterprises LLC ....F....... 574 522-3971
Elkhart *(G-3207)*
▲ Tcb Industries Inc ....F....... 574 522-3971
Elkhart *(G-3208)*
Transco Railway Products Inc ....D....... 574 753-6227
Logansport *(G-9370)*
▲ Western Reman Industrial LLC.......D....... 765 472-2002
Peru *(G-11558)*
Western-Cullen-Hayes Inc ....E....... 765 962-0526
Richmond *(G-12075)*

3751 Motorcycles, Bicycles & Parts

B B Cycles LLC ....G....... 812 723-4265
Paoli *(G-11443)*
Bike-N-Trikes ....G....... 317 835-4544
Boggstown *(G-899)*
Cheetah Trikes Inc ....G....... 812 256-9199
Charlestown *(G-1560)*
Choppers Kickstand LLC ....C....... 260 739-6966
Fort Wayne *(G-4148)*
▲ Compositech Inc ....E....... 800 231-6755
Indianapolis *(G-6643)*
David Tortora ....G....... 317 506-6902
Carmel *(G-1353)*
▲ Dngco LLC ....E....... 800 643-7332
Fort Wayne *(G-4216)*
Evansville Super Bike Shop.............F....... 812 477-1740
Evansville *(G-3491)*
Evill Cycles ....G....... 812 401-2045
Evansville *(G-3495)*
Gravis Ebikes Inc ....G....... 317 690-0616
Indianapolis *(G-7038)*
Horsepower Indy LLC ....G....... 317 757-8668
Indianapolis *(G-7131)*
Jrotten Chopper ....G....... 765 517-1779
Jonesboro *(G-8446)*
Ksm Enterprises ....G....... 317 773-7440
Fishers *(G-3937)*
Outdoor Performance ....G....... 765 732-3335
Liberty *(G-9268)*
R Falcone Powersports Inc ....G....... 317 803-2432
Indianapolis *(G-7809)*
Reality Motor Sports Inc...............G....... 765 662-3000
Marion *(G-9559)*
Red Hawk Choppers Inc...............G....... 765 307-2269
Crawfordsville *(G-2193)*
Renegade Trike Corp ....G....... 812 941-9900
Clarksville *(G-1693)*
Sram LLC ....G....... 317 481-1120
Indianapolis *(G-7979)*
Ss Custom Choppers LLC ....G....... 260 415-3793
Fort Wayne *(G-4643)*
Thugs Inc Choppers ....G....... 317 454-3762
Indianapolis *(G-8072)*
Time Out Trailers Inc ....G....... 574 294-7671
Elkhart *(G-3217)*
▲ Zh Brothers International Inc.........G....... 313 718-6732
Mishawaka *(G-10153)*

3761 Guided Missiles & Space Vehicles

Cypress Springs Enterprises................G....... 812 743-8888
Wheatland *(G-14231)*
Raytheon Company ....D....... 310 647-9438
Fort Wayne *(G-4577)*

3764 Guided Missile/Space Vehicle Propulsion Units & parts

Adranos Energetics LLC ....G....... 208 539-2439
West Lafayette *(G-14046)*
In Space LLC ....G....... 765 775-2107
West Lafayette *(G-14076)*
N Rolls-Royce Amercn Tech Inc ....C....... 317 230-4347
Indianapolis *(G-7567)*

3769 Guided Missile/Space Vehicle Parts & Eqpt, NEC

Attco Machine Products Inc................E....... 574 234-1063
South Bend *(G-12714)*
C F Roark Wldg Engrg Co Inc ....C....... 317 852-3163
Brownsburg *(G-1141)*
Cypress Springs Enterprises................G....... 812 743-8888
Wheatland *(G-14231)*

▲ Major Tool and Machine Inc ....B....... 317 636-6433
Indianapolis *(G-7446)*
Thermal Ceramics Inc..................E....... 574 296-3500
Elkhart *(G-3212)*

3792 Travel Trailers & Campers

All American Group Inc ....B....... 574 825-8555
Middlebury *(G-9868)*
◆ All American Group Inc ....E....... 574 262-0123
Elkhart *(G-2674)*
Bison Coach LLC ....E....... 574 658-4161
Milford *(G-9949)*
Cruiser Rv LLC ....D....... 260 562-3500
Howe *(G-6120)*
◆ Damon Corporation ....F....... 574 262-2624
Elkhart *(G-2787)*
▲ Dmi Holding Corp ....C....... 574 534-1224
Goshen *(G-5200)*
Dna Enterprises Inc ....C....... 574 534-0034
Goshen *(G-5201)*
▲ Ds Corp ....C....... 260 593-3850
Topeka *(G-13417)*
Eagle Craft Inc ....E....... 574 936-3196
Plymouth *(G-11682)*
▼ Evergreen Recrtl Vehicles LLC.......F....... 574 825-4298
Middlebury *(G-9886)*
Forest River Inc ....C....... 574 264-5179
Elkhart *(G-2861)*
Forest River Inc ....C....... 574 264-2513
Goshen *(G-5218)*
Forest River Inc ....F....... 574 389-4636
Middlebury *(G-9887)*
Forest River Inc ....C....... 574 642-3112
Goshen *(G-5219)*
Forest River Inc ....C....... 574 262-2212
Elkhart *(G-2864)*
Forest River Inc ....C....... 574 296-7700
Elkhart *(G-2866)*
Forest River Inc ....C....... 574 533-5934
Goshen *(G-5217)*
Forest River Inc ....C....... 574 262-3474
Elkhart *(G-2862)*
Forest River Inc ....C....... 574 848-1335
Bristol *(G-1060)*
Forest River Cherokee Inc ....G....... 260 593-2566
Topeka *(G-13418)*
Forest River Custom Extrusions ....E....... 574 975-0206
Goshen *(G-5220)*
Forest River Vibe ....G....... 574 296-2084
Elkhart *(G-2867)*
▼ Gulf Stream Coach Inc ....C....... 574 773-7761
Nappanee *(G-10677)*
Highland Ridge Rv Inc ....B....... 260 768-7771
Shipshewana *(G-12616)*
Homette Corporation ....G....... 574 294-6521
Elkhart *(G-2919)*
▼ Hy-Line Enterprises Intl Inc ....D....... 574 294-1112
Elkhart *(G-2924)*
Independent Protection Co Inc.........D....... 574 831-5680
New Paris *(G-10985)*
Indiana Interstate Entps LLC ....G....... 260 463-8100
Lagrange *(G-9047)*
Jason Industries Inc ....D....... 574 294-7595
Elkhart *(G-2945)*
▼ Jayco Inc ....A....... 574 825-5861
Middlebury *(G-9896)*
Keystone Rv Company.................C....... 574 535-2100
Goshen *(G-5254)*
Keystone Rv Company.................D....... 574 534-9430
Goshen *(G-5255)*
Keystone Rv Company.................C....... 574 535-2100
Goshen *(G-5256)*
Kropf Industries Inc ....E....... 574 533-2171
Goshen *(G-5258)*
◆ Kzrv LP ....B....... 260 768-4016
Shipshewana *(G-12624)*
L S R Conversions LLC ....F....... 574 206-9610
Elkhart *(G-2979)*
Layton Homes Corporation................G....... 574 294-6521
Elkhart *(G-2987)*
Layton Homes Corporation................D....... 574 294-6521
Elkhart *(G-2988)*
LGS Pace International Inc ....G....... 574 848-5665
Middlebury *(G-9903)*
Lippert Components Inc................C....... 574 971-4320
Goshen *(G-5275)*
Livin Lite Corp ....E....... 574 862-2228
Shipshewana *(G-12631)*
New Image Travel LLC ....E....... 812 426-1423
Evansville *(G-3643)*

S
I
C

Newmar Corporation ....A 574 773-7791
Nappanee *(G-10699)*

Rance Aluminum Fabrication ....E 574 266-9028
Elkhart *(G-3137)*

Ranch Fiberglass Inc ....D 574 294-7550
Elkhart *(G-3138)*

▼ Recreation By Design LLC ....D 574 294-2117
Elkhart *(G-3140)*

Skyline Champion Corporation ....B 574 294-6521
Elkhart *(G-3175)*

Skyline Homes Inc ....C 574 294-6521
Elkhart *(G-3176)*

Spectrum Rv LLC ....G 574 970-5554
Elkhart *(G-3184)*

▼ Starcraft Corporation ....E 574 534-7827
Goshen *(G-5329)*

♦ Starcraft Rv Inc ....B 800 945-4787
Middlebury *(G-9921)*

◆ Supreme Corporation ....A 574 642-4888
Goshen *(G-5332)*

Supreme Corporation ....B 260 894-9191
Ligonier *(G-9298)*

Switzerland Hills Inc ....E 812 594-2810
Patriot *(G-11469)*

▼ Thor Motor Coach Inc ....A 574 266-1111
Elkhart *(G-3216)*

Thorntons Welding ....G 812 332-8564
Bloomington *(G-841)*

TI Industries Inc ....E 419 666-8144
Elkhart *(G-3219)*

Truck Accessories Group Inc ....C 574 522-5337
Elkhart *(G-3226)*

Two Rivers Camping Club I ....G 812 838-3687
Mount Vernon *(G-10411)*

Wabash National LP ....D 765 771-5300
Lafayette *(G-9017)*

▼ Winnebago of Indiana LLC ....C 574 825-5250
Middlebury *(G-9926)*

Wolfpack Chassis LLC ....E 260 349-1887
Kendallville *(G-8514)*

◆ World Class North America LLC ......F 260 668-5511
Angola *(G-259)*

Yurts of America Inc ....G 317 377-9878
Indianapolis *(G-8225)*

3795 Tanks & Tank Components

AM General LLC ....A 574 258-7523
Mishawaka *(G-9995)*

Ceramix 101 ....G 219 531-6536
Valparaiso *(G-13521)*

Nix Sanitary Service ....G 812 475-9774
Boonville *(G-919)*

3799 Transportation Eqpt, NEC

Asw LLC ....G 260 432-1596
Columbia City *(G-1764)*

Bailey Chassis Company LLC ....G 615 822-7041
Haubstadt *(G-5997)*

BBC Distribution LLC ....G 574 266-3601
Elkhart *(G-2718)*

Bridgeview Manufacturing LLC ....E 574 970-0116
Elkhart *(G-2734)*

CC Manufacturing Inc ....F 574 293-1696
Elkhart *(G-2752)*

Chubbs Steel Sales Inc ....G 574 295-3166
Elkhart *(G-2757)*

Collins Trailers Inc ....G 574 294-2561
Elkhart *(G-2762)*

Competitive Designs Inc ....G 574 223-9406
Rochester *(G-12118)*

Creative Manufacturing Rv LLC ....F 574 333-3302
Elkhart *(G-2776)*

D Rv Luxury Suites LLC ....G 260 562-1075
Howe *(G-6121)*

▲ Dngco LLC ....E 800 643-7332
Fort Wayne *(G-4216)*

◆ Dorel Juvenile Group Inc ....C 800 457-5276
Columbus *(G-1912)*

▲ Drv Llc ....E 260 562-1075
Howe *(G-6122)*

Dutch Park Homes Inc ....E 574 642-0150
Goshen *(G-5206)*

E T & T Powder Coat ....G 574 293-2725
Elkhart *(G-2809)*

E Z Loader Boat Trailers Inc ....G 574 266-0092
Elkhart *(G-2810)*

Fiber-Tron Corp ....E 574 294-8545
Elkhart *(G-2848)*

Flj Transport LLC ....G 574 642-0200
Goshen *(G-5215)*

▼ Forest River Inc ....E 574 389-4600
Elkhart *(G-2865)*

Frontier Carriage ....G 574 965-4444
Delphi *(G-2421)*

Gardiner Rentals Bill ....G 765 447-5111
Lafayette *(G-8904)*

Goods On Target Sporting Inc ....G 812 623-2300
Sunman *(G-13111)*

Graber Manufacturing ....G 812 636-7725
Odon *(G-11327)*

Grand Design Rv LLC ....A 574 825-8000
Middlebury *(G-9890)*

Hadley Products Corporation ....F 574 266-3700
Elkhart *(G-2905)*

Hardins Speed Service Co ....G 219 962-8080
Hobart *(G-6079)*

Heritage Convertion LLC ....G 574 773-0750
Nappanee *(G-10679)*

Highland Ridge Rv Inc ....B 260 768-7771
Shipshewana *(G-12616)*

Hoosier Buggy Shop ....G 260 593-2192
Topeka *(G-13422)*

Hostetler Carriage ....G 260 463-9920
Lagrange *(G-9045)*

Iea Management Services Inc ....G 765 832-8526
Clinton *(G-1716)*

Iea Renewable Energy Inc ....G 765 832-8526
Clinton *(G-1717)*

IKON Group ....G 574 326-3661
Elkhart *(G-2928)*

Innovative Equipment Inc ....G 765 572-2367
Westpoint *(G-14206)*

J Q Tex Inc ....E 574 259-0329
Mishawaka *(G-10056)*

Landgrebe Manufacturing Inc ....G 219 462-9587
Valparaiso *(G-13570)*

Landjet International ....F 574 970-7805
Elkhart *(G-2984)*

Little Trailer Co Inc ....F 877 545-4897
Elkhart *(G-3005)*

Logistick Inc ....G 800 758-5840
South Bend *(G-12844)*

Martins Buggy Shop ....G 574 831-3699
Nappanee *(G-10692)*

Mighty Transport LLC ....G 812 401-7433
Chandler *(G-1552)*

Miller Carriage Co ....G 260 768-4553
Shipshewana *(G-12633)*

MO Trailer Corporation ....F 574 533-0824
Goshen *(G-5295)*

Mudd-Ox Inc ....F 260 768-7221
Shipshewana *(G-12638)*

Nomanco Trailers ....G 765 833-6711
Roann *(G-12097)*

Olympic Fiberglass Industries ....D 574 223-3101
Rochester *(G-12142)*

P R F ....G 219 477-8660
Portage *(G-11787)*

Parallax Group Inc ....G 800 443-4859
Anderson *(G-149)*

Perkinsville Power Sports ....G 765 734-1314
Anderson *(G-151)*

Professional Comp Naskart Inc ....G 765 552-9745
Elwood *(G-3309)*

Rapsure Inc ....G 574 773-2995
Nappanee *(G-10704)*

Recreational Customs Inc ....G 574 642-0632
Goshen *(G-5317)*

Ridge Trailers ....G 260 244-5443
Columbia City *(G-1828)*

Saladin Trailer Sales Inc ....F 812 692-5288
Elnora *(G-3291)*

Schwartzs Wheel & Clip C ....G 574 546-1302
Bremen *(G-1023)*

Showhaulers Trucks Inc ....E 574 825-6764
Middlebury *(G-9918)*

Sierra Motor Corp ....D 574 848-1300
Bristol *(G-1086)*

Slicers ....G 812 255-0655
Vincennes *(G-13706)*

Southern Indiana Linings & Coa ....G 812 206-7250
Charlestown *(G-1580)*

Spreuer & Son Inc ....F 260 463-3513
Lagrange *(G-9067)*

Structural Composites Ind Inc ....D 260 894-4083
Ligonier *(G-9296)*

◆ Supreme Industries Inc ....D 574 642-3070
Goshen *(G-5336)*

Sx4 ....G 812 907-2502
Palmyra *(G-11441)*

▼ T I B Inc ....E 574 892-5151
Argos *(G-278)*

Thor Industries Inc ....C 574 970-7460
Elkhart *(G-3214)*

Thorntons Mtrcycle Sls - Mdson ....G 812 574-6347
Madison *(G-9498)*

Three K Racing Enterprises ....G 765 482-4273
Lebanon *(G-9228)*

TRC Mfg Inc ....E 574 262-9299
South Bend *(G-12978)*

Trimas Corporation ....G 260 925-3700
Auburn *(G-364)*

Use What Youve Got Ministry ....G 317 924-4124
Indianapolis *(G-8140)*

Vintage Trailers Ltd ....G 574 522-2261
Elkhart *(G-3246)*

Wellspring Components LLC ....G 260 768-7336
Shipshewana *(G-12657)*

Zieman Manufacturing Company ....G 574 522-5202
Goshen *(G-5347)*

38 MEASURING, ANALYZING AND CONTROLLING INSTRUMENTS; PHOTOGRAPHIC, MEDICAL AN

3812 Search, Detection, Navigation & Guidance Systs & Instrs

Aptiv Services Us LLC ....F 765 451-5011
Kokomo *(G-8591)*

Ascension Space Technology LLP ....G 765 623-5164
Anderson *(G-69)*

Attco Machine Products Inc ....E 574 234-1063
South Bend *(G-12714)*

Bae Systems Inc ....G 812 863-0514
Odon *(G-11319)*

Bae Systems Controls Inc ....A 260 434-5195
Fort Wayne *(G-4100)*

Cyclone Adg LLC ....G 520 403-2927
New Albany *(G-10767)*

Cypress Springs Enterprises ....G 812 743-8888
Wheatland *(G-14231)*

Dcx-Chol Enterprises Inc ....D 260 407-1107
Fort Wayne *(G-4202)*

Federal-Mogul LLC ....G 574 271-0274
South Bend *(G-12775)*

First Gear Inc ....F 260 490-3238
Fort Wayne *(G-4263)*

Flir Detection Inc ....F 765 775-1701
West Lafayette *(G-14067)*

GM Components Holdings LLC ....G 765 451-9049
Kokomo *(G-8629)*

Harris Corporation ....B 260 451-5597
Fort Wayne *(G-4323)*

Harris Corporation ....G 812 202-5171
Crane *(G-2126)*

Harris Corporation ....C 812 202-5171
Crane *(G-2127)*

Harrison Manufacturing Inc ....G 812 466-1111
Avon *(G-445)*

Hobson Tool and Machine Co ....F 317 736-4203
Franklin *(G-4895)*

Hoosier Industrial Supply ....G 574 535-0712
Goshen *(G-5239)*

Pyromation Inc ....C 260 484-2580
Fort Wayne *(G-4566)*

Radar Assoc Corp ....G 219 838-8030
Munster *(G-10625)*

Raytheon Company ....E 317 306-4872
Indianapolis *(G-7821)*

Raytheon Company ....A 260 429-6000
Fort Wayne *(G-4576)*

Raytheon Company ....D 310 647-9438
Fort Wayne *(G-4577)*

Raytheon Company ....A 310 647-9438
Fort Wayne *(G-4578)*

Raytheon Company ....G 317 306-8471
Indianapolis *(G-7822)*

Reeds RFI Inc ....G 812 659-2872
Switz City *(G-13126)*

Silicis Technologies Inc ....E 317 896-5044
Westfield *(G-14189)*

Triumph Controls LLC ....F 317 421-8760
Shelbyville *(G-12578)*

U S S Inc ....G 260 693-1172
Churubusco *(G-1660)*

◆ Undersea Sensor Systems Inc ....C 260 244-3500
Columbia City *(G-1844)*

Value Production Inc ....E 574 246-1913
South Bend (G-12983)
Xtreme ADS Limited ....E 765 644-7323
Anderson (G-184)

3821 Laboratory Apparatus & Furniture

Beckman Coulter Inc ....D 317 471-8029
Indianapolis (G-6460)
◆ Chryso Inc ....E 812 256-4220
Charlestown (G-1561)
Cook Group Incorporated ....F 812 339-2235
Bloomington (G-704)
Current Technologies Inc ....F 765 364-0490
Crawfordsville (G-2147)
▲ Envigo Rms Inc ....C 317 806-6080
Indianapolis (G-6871)
Envigo Rms Inc ....G 317 806-6080
Greenfield (G-5530)
Fast Track Technologies LLC ....F 317 229-6080
Carmel (G-1378)
Helmer Inc ....C 317 773-9073
Noblesville (G-11120)
I2r ....G 812 235-6167
Terre Haute (G-13253)
Integrated Instrument Services ....F 317 248-1958
Indianapolis (G-7248)
Leco Corporation ....G 574 288-9017
South Bend (G-12838)
Merss Corporation ....G 317 632-7299
Indianapolis (G-7484)
N-Ovations Inc ....G 219 464-0441
Valparaiso (G-13583)
Parker-Hannifin Corporation ....F 608 824-0500
Tell City (G-13172)
◆ Poly-Wood LLC ....D 574 457-3284
Syracuse (G-13140)
Soil Dynamics Instruments Inc ....G 765 497-0511
West Lafayette (G-14108)
Templeton Coal Company Inc ....D 812 232-7037
Terre Haute (G-13351)
Wabash Instrument Corp ....F 260 563-8406
Wabash (G-13762)

3822 Automatic Temperature Controls

Abbott Controls Inc ....G 317 697-7102
Indianapolis (G-6308)
▲ Advanced Control Tech Inc ....G 317 806-2750
Indianapolis (G-6332)
Advantage Engineering Inc ....D 317 887-0729
Greenwood (G-5660)
Automated Logic Corporation ....E 765 286-1993
Muncie (G-10436)
Building Temp Solutions LLC ....F 260 449-9201
Fort Wayne (G-4126)
Caliente LLC ....E 260 426-3800
Fort Wayne (G-4137)
▲ Caltherm Corporation ....C 812 372-0281
Columbus (G-1864)
Caltherm Corporation ....F 812 372-0281
Columbus (G-1865)
Creative Control Systems ....G 260 432-9020
Fort Wayne (G-4184)
Digi International Inc ....G 877 272-3111
Mishawaka (G-10036)
Dimplex North America Limited ....G 317 890-0809
Indianapolis (G-6743)
Elliott-Williams Company Inc ....D 317 453-2295
Indianapolis (G-6843)
Executive Image Bldg Svcs Inc ....F 317 865-1366
Greenwood (G-5694)
Gillespie Mrrell Gen Contg LLC ....G 765 618-4084
Marion (G-9526)
Green Air LLC ....G 317 335-1706
Fishers (G-3987)
Hmmcopl LLC ....E 219 757-3575
Merrillville (G-9719)
Invensys Processs Systems Inc ....A 317 372-2839
Indianapolis (G-7264)
Jackson Systems LLC ....E 317 788-6800
Indianapolis (G-7295)
Johnson Controls Inc ....F 812 868-1374
Evansville (G-3578)
Johnson Controls Inc ....D 317 917-5043
Pittsboro (G-11583)
Johnson Sales Corp ....G 219 322-9558
Schererville (G-12326)
Nidec Motor Corporation ....A 317 328-4079
Indianapolis (G-7587)
OMI Industries Inc ....G 812 438-9218
Rising Sun (G-12090)
Open Control Systems LLC ....G 317 429-0627
Indianapolis (G-7626)
Pinder Instruments Company Inc ....E 219 924-7070
Munster (G-10624)
Pyromation Inc ....C 260 484-2580
Fort Wayne (G-4566)
Redi/Controls Inc ....G 317 494-6600
Franklin (G-4926)
Rees Inc ....F 260 495-9811
Fremont (G-4972)
Siemens Industry Inc ....D 317 381-0734
Indianapolis (G-7937)
Smart Temps LLC ....G 574 217-8847
Mishawaka (G-10127)
▲ SMC Corporation of America ....B 317 899-3182
Noblesville (G-11184)
Spensa Technologies Inc ....E 765 588-3592
West Lafayette (G-14110)
Suburban Manufacturing Company ....F 574 294-5681
Elkhart (G-3196)
Temperature Control Svcs LLC ....G 765 325-2439
Fishers (G-3975)
Temptek Inc ....G 317 887-6352
Greenwood (G-5752)
Thatcher Engineering Corp ....D 219 949-2084
Gary (G-5105)
▲ United Technologies Electr ....A 260 359-3514
Huntington (G-6260)

3823 Indl Instruments For Meas, Display & Control

Advanced Boiler Ctrl Svcs Inc ....F 708 429-7066
Crown Point (G-2223)
Agri-Tronix Corp ....F 317 738-4474
Franklin (G-4862)
Amatrol Inc ....C 812 288-8285
Jeffersonville (G-8322)
Ameriflo Inc ....E 317 844-2019
Indianapolis (G-6394)
AMG LLC ....E 317 329-4004
Indianapolis (G-6397)
Analyticalab Inc ....G 219 473-9777
Whiting (G-14267)
C & K Manufacturing Inc ....F 574 264-4063
Elkhart (G-2743)
Capital Tech Solutions LLC ....G 812 303-4357
Evansville (G-3409)
Cognex Corporation ....G 317 867-5079
Westfield (G-14144)
Complete Controls Inc ....G 260 489-0852
Fort Wayne (G-4170)
Cosworth Electronics LLC ....G 317 808-3800
Indianapolis (G-6674)
Covidien LP ....C 317 837-8199
Plainfield (G-11602)
Crown Elec Svcs & Automtn Inc ....D 972 929-4700
Portage (G-11758)
Damping Technologies Inc ....E 574 258-7916
Mishawaka (G-10031)
Dwyer Instruments Inc ....D 574 862-2590
Wakarusa (G-13775)
Dwyer Instruments Inc ....C 219 279-2031
Wolcott (G-14363)
Dwyer Instruments Inc ....G 219 879-8868
South Bend (G-12754)
Dwyer Instruments Inc ....D 260 723-5138
South Whitley (G-12997)
Dwyer Instruments Inc ....C 219 879-8000
Michigan City (G-9785)
Dwyer Instruments Inc ....F 219 879-8000
Michigan City (G-9786)
Emerson Electric Co ....G 219 465-2411
Valparaiso (G-13537)
Emerson Electric Co ....G 317 322-2055
Indianapolis (G-6853)
▲ Endress + Hauser Inc ....C 317 535-7138
Greenwood (G-5686)
Endress + Hauser Inc ....C 317 535-7138
Greenwood (G-5687)
▲ Endress + Huser Flowtec AG Inc ....C 317 535-7138
Greenwood (G-5688)
Endress+hauser (usa) Automatio ....D 317 535-2121
Greenwood (G-5689)
◆ Endress+hauser Wetzer USA Inc ....E 317 535-1362
Greenwood (G-5690)
Engineered Refr Shapes Svcs LLC ....G 765 778-8040
Pendleton (G-11488)
Envirnmntal Ctrl Solutions LLC ....G 317 358-5985
Indianapolis (G-6872)
Environmental Technology Inc ....E 574 233-1202
South Bend (G-12765)
Fire Aparatus Service Inc ....G 219 985-0788
Gary (G-5047)
Frew Process Group LLC ....G 317 565-5000
Noblesville (G-11107)
▲ Functional Devices Inc ....G 765 883-5538
Sharpsville (G-12505)
Gainescraft Inc ....G 765 932-3590
Rushville (G-12222)
Harman Professional Inc ....B 574 294-8000
Elkhart (G-2908)
Harris Corporation ....C 812 202-5171
Crane (G-2127)
Harris Corporation ....B 260 451-5597
Fort Wayne (G-4323)
Heraeus Electro-Nite Co LLC ....C 765 473-8275
Peru (G-11529)
▲ Hsm Eagle Ltd ....G 812 491-9666
Evansville (G-3545)
▲ Hurco Companies Inc ....C 317 293-5309
Indianapolis (G-7146)
Hurco Companies Inc ....G 317 347-6208
Indianapolis (G-7147)
Indiana Thermal Solutions LLC ....F 317 570-5400
Indianapolis (G-7195)
Integratorcom Inc ....D 317 776-3500
Noblesville (G-11130)
J & J Industrial Services Inc ....G 219 362-4973
La Porte (G-8772)
Leco Corporation ....G 574 288-9017
South Bend (G-12838)
Maxim Pipette Service Inc ....G 877 536-2946
Plainfield (G-11625)
▲ Milltronics Usa Inc ....E 317 293-5309
Indianapolis (G-7523)
Monitoring Solutions Inc ....E 317 856-9400
Indianapolis (G-7535)
Mtcr Site Services LLC ....G 812 598-6516
Newburgh (G-11039)
Norman Tool Inc ....G 812 867-3496
Evansville (G-3646)
Ovideon LLC ....G 812 577-3274
Lawrenceburg (G-9151)
Pyromation Inc ....C 260 484-2580
Fort Wayne (G-4566)
Quality Industrial Supplies ....F 219 324-2654
La Porte (G-8808)
Ray Kammer ....G 219 938-1708
Gary (G-5088)
Siemens Industry Inc ....D 219 763-7927
Portage (G-11794)
Superior Oprting Solutions Inc ....G 765 993-4094
Richmond (G-12056)
Syscon International Inc ....C 574 232-3900
South Bend (G-12964)
Technidyne Corporation ....E 812 948-2884
New Albany (G-10870)
▲ Texmo Prcision Castings US Inc ....D 574 269-1368
Warsaw (G-13951)
Thermco Instrument Corporation ....F 219 362-6258
La Porte (G-8831)
Thermphyscal Prpts RES Lab Inc ....G 765 463-1581
West Lafayette (G-14113)
▲ Zs Systems LLC ....G 765 586-2738
West Lafayette (G-14118)

3824 Fluid Meters & Counters

Bernard Hasten ....G 317 824-4544
Indianapolis (G-6467)
Custom Controls & Engineering ....G 812 663-0755
Greensburg (G-5596)
Dwyer Instruments Inc ....D 260 723-5138
South Whitley (G-12997)
Kendrion (mishawaka) LLC ....E 574 257-2422
Mishawaka (G-10063)
Madden Manufacturing Inc ....F 574 295-4292
Elkhart (G-3013)
▲ Mechanical Parts & Svcs Inc ....G 219 670-1986
Valparaiso (G-13580)
Memcor Inc ....F 260 356-4300
Huntington (G-6228)
Micro Motion Inc ....G 317 334-1893
Indianapolis (G-7498)
Midwest Meter Inc ....G 574 967-0175
Flora (G-3999)
Parker Exploration & Productio ....G 812 673-4017
Wadesville (G-13774)
▲ Phoenix America Inc ....E 260 432-9664
Fort Wayne (G-4529)

Prosperus LLC ....G.... 317 786-8990
Indianapolis *(G-7782)*
Scalar Design Engrg & Dist LLC ....G.... 765 429-5545
Lafayette *(G-8995)*
▲ **Steiner Enterprises Inc** ....F.... 765 429-6409
Lafayette *(G-9004)*

3825 Instrs For Measuring & Testing Electricity

Acterna LLC ....E.... 317 788-9351
Indianapolis *(G-6320)*
Advance Stores Company Inc ....G.... 317 253-5034
Indianapolis *(G-6331)*
Advantage Electronics Inc ....F.... 317 888-1946
Greenwood *(G-5659)*
App Engineering Incorporated ....F.... 317 755-3422
Indianapolis *(G-6407)*
Ball Systems Inc ....E.... 317 804-2330
Westfield *(G-14138)*
Chance Indiana Standards Lab ....F.... 317 787-6578
Indianapolis *(G-6593)*
Contact Products Inc ....E.... 219 838-1911
Munster *(G-10602)*
Doyle Manufacturing Inc ....G.... 574 848-5624
Bristol *(G-1056)*
Dwyer Instruments Inc ....D.... 260 723-5138
South Whitley *(G-12997)*
Emnet LLC ....G.... 574 360-1093
Granger *(G-5405)*
▲ **Empro Manufacturing Co Inc** ....E.... 317 823-3000
Indianapolis *(G-6859)*
Hgl Dynamics Inc ....G.... 317 782-3500
Indianapolis *(G-7100)*
▲ **Indiana Research Institute** ....E.... 812 378-4221
Columbus *(G-1947)*
Indiana Research Institute ....F.... 812 378-5363
Columbus *(G-1948)*
Innovative Rfid Inc ....G.... 260 433-5835
Huntertown *(G-6141)*
Jfw Industries Incorporated ....C.... 317 887-1340
Indianapolis *(G-7304)*
K J S Associates ....G.... 317 842-7500
Indianapolis *(G-7328)*
Kirby Risk Corporation ....B.... 765 447-1402
Lafayette *(G-8942)*
Landis+gyr Inc ....E.... 765 742-1001
Lafayette *(G-8954)*
Leco Corporation ....G.... 574 288-9017
South Bend *(G-12838)*
Magnetic Instrumentation Inc ....E.... 317 842-9000
Indianapolis *(G-7438)*
Matson Counsulting Engineers ....G.... 260 478-8813
Fort Wayne *(G-4457)*
Metrology Services LLC ....G.... 260 969-8424
Fort Wayne *(G-4468)*
Nano Universe LLC ....G.... 765 457-5860
Kokomo *(G-8675)*
Noel-Smyser Engineering Corp ....F.... 317 293-2215
Indianapolis *(G-7590)*
Pdma Inc ....G.... 317 844-7750
Indianapolis *(G-6275)*
Promethius Consulting LLC ....F.... 317 733-2388
Indianapolis *(G-7777)*
R K C Instrument ....F.... 574 273-6099
South Bend *(G-12911)*
◆ **Radian Research Inc** ....D.... 765 449-5500
Lafayette *(G-8988)*
Rail Scale Inc ....G.... 317 339-6486
Wilkinson *(G-14280)*
Renk Systems Corporation ....F.... 317 455-1367
Camby *(G-1268)*
SBS Cybermetrix Inc ....G.... 812 378-7960
Columbus *(G-2011)*
SGS Cybermetrix Inc ....G.... 800 713-1203
Columbus *(G-2013)*
Spectrum Industry ....G.... 812 231-8355
Terre Haute *(G-13340)*
System Solutions Inc ....G.... 317 877-7572
Cicero *(G-1668)*
Teaco Inc ....F.... 219 874-6234
Michigan City *(G-9852)*
▲ **Technical Weighing Svcs Inc** ....E.... 219 924-3366
Griffith *(G-5793)*

3826 Analytical Instruments

Anasazi Instruments Inc ....F.... 317 861-7657
New Palestine *(G-10967)*
Animated Dynamics Inc ....G.... 765 418-5359
West Lafayette *(G-14050)*
Astbury Water Technology Inc ....E.... 260 668-8900
Angola *(G-194)*
Beckman Coulter Inc ....D.... 317 471-8029
Indianapolis *(G-6460)*
Beckman Coulter Inc ....D.... 317 808-4200
Indianapolis *(G-6461)*
Beckman Coulter Inc ....G.... 317 808-4200
Indianapolis *(G-6462)*
Environmental Test Systems ....F.... 574 262-2060
Elkhart *(G-2835)*
Griffin Analytical Tech LLC ....E.... 765 775-1701
West Lafayette *(G-14072)*
Hach Company ....G.... 574 262-2060
Elkhart *(G-2904)*
Inchromatics LLC ....G.... 317 872-7401
Indianapolis *(G-7169)*
Infrared Lab Systems LLC ....F.... 317 896-1565
Westfield *(G-14170)*
Ipheion Development Corp ....G.... 240 281-1619
Indianapolis *(G-7265)*
Labtest Equipment Company ....D.... 219 462-3300
Valparaiso *(G-13568)*
Lazar Scientific Incorporated ....G.... 574 271-7020
Granger *(G-5418)*
Leco Corporation ....G.... 574 288-9017
South Bend *(G-12838)*
Lk Technologies Inc ....G.... 812 332-4449
Bloomington *(G-766)*
Lloyd Jr Frank P and Assoc ....G.... 317 388-9225
Indianapolis *(G-7410)*
Prosolia Inc ....G.... 317 275-5794
Indianapolis *(G-7781)*
◆ **R F Express Corp** ....G.... 219 510-5193
Valparaiso *(G-13606)*
Roche Diagnostics Corporation ....G.... 317 521-2000
Indianapolis *(G-7852)*
Sentech Corporation ....G.... 317 596-1988
Indianapolis *(G-7911)*
Smartgait LLC ....G.... 765 404-0726
West Lafayette *(G-14107)*
Templeton Coal Company Inc ....D.... 812 232-7037
Terre Haute *(G-13351)*
▲ **Trilithic Inc** ....C.... 317 895-3600
Indianapolis *(G-8099)*
Webber Manufacturing Company ....E.... 317 357-8681
Indianapolis *(G-8181)*

3827 Optical Instruments

Better Visions PC ....G.... 260 627-2669
Leo *(G-9239)*
Better Visions PC ....G.... 260 244-7542
Columbia City *(G-1766)*
Conmoto Enterprises Inc ....G.... 219 787-1622
Indianapolis *(G-6650)*
Control Development Inc ....F.... 574 288-7338
South Bend *(G-12742)*
◆ **Dave Jones Machinists LLC** ....G.... 574 256-5500
Mishawaka *(G-10034)*
G K Optical Company Inc ....E.... 317 881-2585
Indianapolis *(G-6975)*
Motion Engineering Company Inc ....G.... 317 804-7990
Westfield *(G-14177)*
Murrell Optical LLC ....G.... 317 280-0114
Indianapolis *(G-7561)*
S & S Optical Co Inc ....F.... 260 749-9614
New Haven *(G-10955)*
Sightwaveoptics ....G.... 317 513-8322
Zionsville *(G-14463)*
Thomas Optical LLC ....G.... 502 548-2163
Charlestown *(G-1584)*
Union Optical Eyecare Ctr Inc ....G.... 812 279-3466
Bedford *(G-587)*
Vision Aid Systems Inc ....G.... 317 888-0323
Greenwood *(G-5758)*

3829 Measuring & Controlling Devices, NEC

Accu-Chek Qulty Solutions LLC ....E.... 812 704-5491
Corydon *(G-2087)*
Adaptek Systems Inc ....E.... 260 637-8660
Fort Wayne *(G-4041)*
Advanced Designs Corp ....F.... 812 333-1922
Bloomington *(G-657)*
◆ **Ati Inc** ....G.... 812 431-5409
Mount Vernon *(G-10384)*
Automatic Tool Control ....E.... 317 328-8492
Indianapolis *(G-6445)*
Center For Diagnostic Imaging ....F.... 812 234-0555
Terre Haute *(G-13206)*
Chapman Environmental Controls ....G.... 574 674-8706
Osceola *(G-11374)*
Chesterfield Tool & Engrg Inc ....E.... 765 378-5101
Daleville *(G-2338)*
Containment Tech Group Inc ....G.... 317 862-5945
Indianapolis *(G-6654)*
Damping Technologies Inc ....E.... 574 258-7916
Mishawaka *(G-10031)*
Dose Shield Corporation ....G.... 317 576-0183
Markleville *(G-9587)*
Dyno One Inc ....E.... 812 526-0500
Edinburgh *(G-2609)*
Fleming Assoc Calibration Inc ....G.... 317 631-4605
Indianapolis *(G-6933)*
Hoosier Industrial Supply Inc ....F.... 574 533-8565
Goshen *(G-5240)*
Ias Corp ....G.... 209 836-8610
Peru *(G-11531)*
Indiana Veco Manufacturing ....E.... 765 932-2858
Rushville *(G-12223)*
Intech Automation Systems Corp ....G.... 209 836-8610
Peru *(G-11532)*
Integrtive Plygraph Trning LLC ....G.... 812 595-2884
Scottsburg *(G-12367)*
▲ **Lafayette Instrument Co Inc** ....E.... 765 423-1505
Lafayette *(G-8948)*
Linde Gas North America LLC ....G.... 888 345-0894
Terre Haute *(G-13275)*
Lomont Holdings Co Inc ....E.... 800 545-9023
Angola *(G-228)*
M RI Solutions ....E.... 317 218-3006
Indianapolis *(G-7433)*
▲ **Magwerks Corporation** ....F.... 317 241-8011
Danville *(G-2352)*
Matrix Technologies Inc ....G.... 765 284-3335
Muncie *(G-10518)*
Mattox & Moore Inc ....G.... 317 632-7534
Indianapolis *(G-7468)*
Micro-Precision Operations ....E.... 260 589-2136
Berne *(G-620)*
Moyer Process & Controls Co ....G.... 260 495-2405
Fremont *(G-4969)*
▲ **Nrp Jones LLC** ....D.... 219 362-4508
La Porte *(G-8800)*
Nuclear Measurements Corp ....G.... 317 546-2415
Indianapolis *(G-7604)*
P C Communication Inc ....G.... 219 838-2546
Highland *(G-6053)*
Piezotech LLC ....E.... 317 876-4670
Indianapolis *(G-7690)*
Power Place Products Inc ....G....
Boswell *(G-941)*
Pyromation Inc ....C.... 260 484-2580
Fort Wayne *(G-4566)*
RNS Imaging Inc ....G.... 812 523-2435
Seymour *(G-12480)*
Robco Engineered Rubber Pdts ....F.... 260 248-2888
Columbia City *(G-1829)*
Sensortec Inc ....E.... 260 497-8811
Fort Wayne *(G-4616)*
Sonam Technologies LLC ....G.... 844 887-6626
Crown Point *(G-2307)*
Stout Plastic Weld ....F.... 219 926-7622
Chesterton *(G-1634)*
Technical Controls Solutions ....G.... 260 416-0329
Churubusco *(G-1659)*
Therametric Technologies Inc ....F.... 317 565-8065
Noblesville *(G-11194)*
Vibromatic Company Inc ....E.... 317 773-3885
Noblesville *(G-11199)*
Wbh Inc ....F.... 317 269-1510
Indianapolis *(G-8180)*

3841 Surgical & Medical Instrs & Apparatus

3M Company ....B.... 317 692-6666
Indianapolis *(G-6288)*
3M Company ....B.... 574 948-8103
Plymouth *(G-11659)*
Accu-Mold LLC ....E.... 269 323-0388
Mishawaka *(G-9989)*
Admiral Medical Center Inc ....G.... 317 924-3757
Indianapolis *(G-6328)*
Advanced Mbility Solutions LLC ....G.... 812 438-2338
Rising Sun *(G-12085)*
Advanced Vscular Therapies Inc ....G.... 765 423-1720
Lafayette *(G-8847)*
▼ **Advantis Medical Inc** ....C.... 317 859-2300
Greenwood *(G-5661)*
After Action Med Dntl Sup LLC ....G.... 317 831-2699
Indianapolis *(G-6351)*
Airgas Usa LLC ....F.... 317 248-8072
Indianapolis *(G-6355)*

Alli Medical LLC .... G 317 625-4535
Westfield *(G-14134)*

Alpha Manufacturing and Design .... E 574 267-2171
Warsaw *(G-13837)*

AMD Group LLC .... F 317 202-9530
Indianapolis *(G-6382)*

American Veteran Group LLC .... G 317 600-4749
Westfield *(G-14136)*

Ameriflo2 Inc .... F 317 844-2019
Indianapolis *(G-6395)*

▼ Arcamed LLC .... E 317 375-7733
Indianapolis *(G-6413)*

Ascensia Diabetes Care US Inc .... E 201 875-8066
Mishawaka *(G-9998)*

Ash Access Technology Inc .... G 765 742-4813
Lafayette *(G-8854)*

Baxter Healthcare Corp .... G 847 948-2000
Hammond *(G-5845)*

Baxter Healthcare Corporation .... B 812 355-7167
Bloomington *(G-675)*

Baxter Healthcare Corporation .... E 317 291-0620
Indianapolis *(G-6459)*

Baxter Healthcare Corporation .... D 812 333-0887
Bloomington *(G-676)*

Bayer Healthcare LLC .... E 574 262-6136
Elkhart *(G-2716)*

Bbs Enterprises Inc .... E 574 255-3173
Mishawaka *(G-10006)*

Bcd & Associates .... G 317 873-5394
Zionsville *(G-14421)*

Bd Medical Development Inc .... G 219 310-8551
Crown Point *(G-2227)*

Becton Dickinson and Company .... B 317 561-2900
Plainfield *(G-11595)*

Bioanalytical Systems Inc .... C 765 463-4527
West Lafayette *(G-14053)*

◆ Biomet Inc .... A 574 267-6639
Warsaw *(G-13845)*

Biomet Europe Ltd .... G 574 267-2038
Warsaw *(G-13847)*

Biomet Inc .... G 574 372-6999
Warsaw *(G-13848)*

Biomet Sports Medicine LLC .... D 574 267-6639
Warsaw *(G-13850)*

Boston Scientific Corporation .... A 812 829-4877
Spencer *(G-13018)*

C & K Enterprises Inc .... E 260 624-3123
Angola *(G-201)*

Carecycle LLC .... G 317 372-7444
Indianapolis *(G-6554)*

▲ Catheter Research Inc .... C 317 872-0074
Indianapolis *(G-6568)*

Century Pharmaceuticals Inc .... F 317 849-4210
Indianapolis *(G-6586)*

▲ Circle M Spring Inc .... E 574 267-2883
Warsaw *(G-13857)*

Circle Medical Products Inc .... G 317 271-2626
Indianapolis *(G-6611)*

Community Diagnostic Center .... G 219 836-4599
Munster *(G-10601)*

Compassionate Procedures LLC .... G 317 259-4656
Indianapolis *(G-6641)*

Cook Biodevice LLC .... F 800 265-0945
Bloomington *(G-703)*

Cook Group Incorporated .... F 812 339-2235
Bloomington *(G-704)*

Cook Group Incorporated .... G 812 331-1025
Ellettsville *(G-3276)*

▲ Cook Incorporated .... A 812 339-2235
Bloomington *(G-705)*

Cook Incorporated .... C 812 339-2235
Ellettsville *(G-3277)*

Cook Incorporated .... A 812 829-4891
Spencer *(G-13020)*

Cook Incorporated .... C 812 876-7790
Bloomington *(G-706)*

Cook Medical LLC .... G 812 339-2235
Bloomington *(G-707)*

Corbett Phrmceuticals Dvcs LLC .... E 765 513-0674
Indianapolis *(G-6666)*

Cork Medical LLC .... G 317 361-4651
Indianapolis *(G-6667)*

Covidien LP .... C 317 837-8199
Plainfield *(G-11602)*

Cspine Inc .... G 574 936-7893
South Bend *(G-12743)*

Depuy Mitek LLC .... G 574 267-8143
Warsaw *(G-13863)*

▲ Depuy Synthes Inc .... B 574 267-8143
Warsaw *(G-13865)*

Ed Boilini .... G 317 921-0155
Indianapolis *(G-6802)*

Eli Lilly International Corp .... F 317 276-2000
Indianapolis *(G-6836)*

▲ Engineered Medical Systems .... D 317 246-5500
Indianapolis *(G-6869)*

▲ Esaote North America Inc .... D 317 813-6000
Fishers *(G-3907)*

First Gear Inc .... F 260 490-3238
Fort Wayne *(G-4263)*

Flw Plastics Inc .... E 812 546-0050
Hope *(G-6112)*

Fort Wyne Rdlgy Assn Fundation .... F 260 266-8120
Fort Wayne *(G-4283)*

Freudenberg Medical Mis Inc .... C 812 280-2400
Jeffersonville *(G-8364)*

Greatbatch Ltd .... G 260 755-7300
Fort Wayne *(G-4307)*

Greenwald Surgical Co Inc .... E 219 962-1604
Lake Station *(G-9075)*

Group Dekko Inc .... E 260 599-3405
Kendallville *(G-8477)*

Guidant Intercontinental Corp .... E 317 218-7012
Carmel *(G-1391)*

Hansa Medical Products Inc .... G 317 815-0708
Carmel *(G-1394)*

Helmer Inc .... C 317 773-9073
Noblesville *(G-11120)*

Hemocleanse Inc .... F 765 742-4813
Lafayette *(G-8913)*

Holgin Technologies LLC .... F 317 774-5181
Noblesville *(G-11121)*

Immunores-Therapeutics LLC .... G 860 514-0526
Indianapolis *(G-7166)*

Innovtive Surgical Designs Inc .... F 484 584-4230
Bloomington *(G-749)*

Inscope Medical Solutions Inc .... G 502 882-0183
Jeffersonville *(G-8381)*

Integrated Biomedical Tech .... F 574 264-0025
Elkhart *(G-2937)*

▲ Jemarkel Health-Tech LLC .... F 219 548-5881
Valparaiso *(G-13563)*

▲ Kilgore Manufacturing Co Inc .... D 260 248-2002
Columbia City *(G-1804)*

◆ King Systems Corporation .... B 317 776-6823
Noblesville *(G-11137)*

Kumplete Airway Solutions Inc .... G 219 680-0836
Crown Point *(G-2274)*

Lca-Vision Inc .... G 317 818-3980
Indianapolis *(G-7387)*

Lebanon Corp .... G 765 482-7273
Lebanon *(G-9199)*

LH Medical Corporation .... D 260 387-5194
Fort Wayne *(G-4432)*

Life Dme LLC .... G 219 795-1296
Merrillville *(G-9727)*

Magitek LLC .... G 260 488-2226
Hamilton *(G-5825)*

Mattox & Moore Inc .... G 317 632-7534
Indianapolis *(G-7468)*

Mectra Labs Inc .... E 812 384-3521
Bloomfield *(G-641)*

Med Devices LLC .... G 317 508-1699
Indianapolis *(G-7474)*

Med-Cut Inc .... D 574 269-1982
Warsaw *(G-13907)*

▲ Med2950 LLC .... F 317 545-5383
Indianapolis *(G-7475)*

Micropulse Inc .... C 260 625-3304
Columbia City *(G-1810)*

Miftek Corporation .... G 765 491-3848
West Lafayette *(G-14085)*

Nanovis LLC .... G 260 625-1502
Columbia City *(G-1811)*

Nemco Medical Ltd .... D 260 484-1500
Fort Wayne *(G-4494)*

Nextremity Solutions Inc .... G 732 383-7901
Warsaw *(G-13914)*

Nexxt Spine LLC .... F 317 436-7801
Noblesville *(G-11159)*

Nginstruments Inc .... D 574 268-2112
Warsaw *(G-13915)*

Omnitech Systems Inc .... E 219 531-5532
Valparaiso *(G-13595)*

On Guard .... G 317 753-5312
Indianapolis *(G-7621)*

Opsys Ltd .... G 765 236-6331
Bloomington *(G-790)*

Paragon Medical Inc .... G 574 594-2140
Pierceton *(G-11575)*

▲ Paragon Medical Inc .... B 574 594-2140
Pierceton *(G-11576)*

▲ Point Medical Corporation .... A 219 663-1775
Crown Point *(G-2285)*

Point Medical Corporation .... C 219 663-1775
Crown Point *(G-2286)*

▲ Polymer Technology Systems Inc .... D 317 870-5610
Indianapolis *(G-7706)*

Poyser Kelshaw Group LLC .... G 317 571-8493
Carmel *(G-1453)*

Predictive Wear LLC .... F 765 464-4891
West Lafayette *(G-14096)*

Promex Technologies LLC .... E 317 736-0128
Indianapolis *(G-7778)*

Prp Technologies LLC .... G 260 433-3769
Fort Wayne *(G-4564)*

Qig LLC .... G 260 244-3591
Columbia City *(G-1821)*

R 2 Diagnostics Inc .... G 574 288-4377
South Bend *(G-12910)*

Reed Immunodiagnostics LLC .... G 317 446-3582
Indianapolis *(G-7826)*

Restoration Med Polymers LLC .... G 260 625-1573
Columbia City *(G-1825)*

Rmi Holdings LLC .... E 317 214-7076
Warsaw *(G-13936)*

▲ Roche Diabetes Care Inc .... D 317 521-2000
Indianapolis *(G-7850)*

Roche Health Solutions Inc .... C 317 570-5100
Indianapolis *(G-7853)*

Rx Help Centers LLC .... G 866 478-9593
Indianapolis *(G-7876)*

Smiths Medical Asd Inc .... G 219 365-2376
Saint John *(G-12272)*

Smiths Medical Asd Inc .... E 219 554-2196
Gary *(G-5098)*

Sophysa USA Inc .... G 219 663-7711
Crown Point *(G-2308)*

▲ Sundance Enterprises Inc .... E 317 856-9780
Indianapolis *(G-8019)*

Symmetry Medical Inc .... C 574 267-8700
Warsaw *(G-13947)*

▲ Symmetry Medical Inc .... G 574 268-2252
Warsaw *(G-13948)*

Symmetry New Bedford RE LLC .... G 574 268-2252
Warsaw *(G-13950)*

T H S International Inc .... G 317 759-2869
Indianapolis *(G-8033)*

Thompson .... G 219 942-8133
Hobart *(G-6098)*

Tricounty Surgical and Assoc .... G 260 726-2890
Portland *(G-11853)*

Truarch Inc .... G 812 402-9511
Evansville *(G-3777)*

Universal Precision Instrs Inc .... G 574 264-3997
Elkhart *(G-3238)*

Vance Products Incorporated .... B 812 829-4891
Spencer *(G-13041)*

Vasmo Inc .... F 317 549-3722
Indianapolis *(G-8149)*

Vertical Power Co .... G 574 276-8094
Osceola *(G-11387)*

Vicair America LLC .... G 317 281-0809
Westfield *(G-14198)*

3842 Orthopedic, Prosthetic & Surgical Appliances/Splys

1st Choice Safety LLC .... G 260 797-5338
Fort Wayne *(G-4032)*

3M Company .... B 317 692-6666
Indianapolis *(G-6288)*

▲ Accra-Pac Inc .... D 574 295-0000
Elkhart *(G-2665)*

Accra-Pac Inc .... D 905 660-0444
Elkhart *(G-2666)*

Action Brace and Prosthetics .... F 317 347-4222
Indianapolis *(G-6321)*

Active Ankle Systems Inc .... F 812 258-0663
Jeffersonville *(G-8320)*

Advanced Limb Wound Care .... G 812 232-0957
Terre Haute *(G-13187)*

Advanced Orthopro Inc .... E 317 924-4444
Indianapolis *(G-6334)*

▲ Aearo Technologies LLC .... A 317 692-6666
Indianapolis *(G-6341)*

Affordable Sounds Inc .... G 260 493-7742
New Haven *(G-10926)*

Airgas Usa LLC .... F 317 248-8072
Indianapolis *(G-6355)*

Alli Medical LLC ....G.... 317 625-4535
Westfield *(G-14134)*
American Limb & Orthopedic Co ....G.... 574 522-3643
Elkhart *(G-2684)*
American Veteran Group LLC ....G.... 317 600-4749
Westfield *(G-14136)*
Assistive Technology Inc ....G.... 574 522-7201
Elkhart *(G-2699)*
Audio Diagnostics Inc ....G.... 765 477-7016
Lafayette *(G-8855)*
Automated Weapon Security Inc ....G.... 860 559-7176
Indianapolis *(G-6443)*
▲ Battle Creek Equipment Co ....E.... 260 495-3472
Fremont *(G-4952)*
Beltone Hearing Care ....G.... 812 274-4116
Madison *(G-9446)*
◆ Biomet Inc ....A.... 574 267-6639
Warsaw *(G-13845)*
Biomet Biologics LLC ....E.... 574 267-2038
Warsaw *(G-13846)*
Biomet Europe Ltd ....G.... 574 267-2038
Warsaw *(G-13847)*
Biomet Orthopedics LLC ....A.... 574 267-6639
Warsaw *(G-13849)*
Bionic Prosth & Orthos Grp LLC ....G.... 765 838-8222
Lafayette *(G-8861)*
Bionic Prosthetics and Ortho ....G.... 219 791-9200
Merrillville *(G-9701)*
Bionic Prosthetics and Ortho ....G.... 219 221-6119
Michigan City *(G-9769)*
Biopoly LLC ....E.... 260 999-6135
Fort Wayne *(G-4109)*
Bleys Prosthetics & Orthotics ....G.... 812 704-3894
Seymour *(G-12434)*
Braun Corporation ....B.... 574 946-7413
Winamac *(G-14302)*
Brewer Machine & Mfg Inc ....E.... 317 398-3505
Shelbyville *(G-12525)*
▲ Bryton Corporation ....F.... 317 334-8700
Indianapolis *(G-6516)*
Calumet Orthpd Prosthetics Co ....G.... 219 942-2148
Hobart *(G-6072)*
Central Brace & Limb Co Inc ....F.... 317 925-4296
Indianapolis *(G-6578)*
Central Brace & Limb Co Inc ....G.... 812 334-2524
Bloomington *(G-698)*
Central Brace & Limb Co Inc ....G.... 812 232-2145
Terre Haute *(G-13207)*
Central Brace & Limb Co Inc ....G.... 765 457-4868
Kokomo *(G-8605)*
Central Brace & Limb Co Inc ....G.... 317 872-1596
Indianapolis *(G-6579)*
▲ Circle City Medical Inc ....E.... 317 228-1144
Carmel *(G-1338)*
Cook Medical LLC ....G.... 812 339-2235
Bloomington *(G-707)*
Cooks Fabrication Inc ....G.... 317 782-1722
Indianapolis *(G-6661)*
Cortex Safety Technologies LLC ....G.... 317 414-5607
Carmel *(G-1344)*
Crossroads Orthotics & Cnsltn ....G.... 765 359-0041
Crawfordsville *(G-2145)*
Current Technologies Inc ....F.... 765 364-0490
Crawfordsville *(G-2147)*
Custom Outfitted Protection ....G.... 317 373-2092
Indianapolis *(G-6716)*
D J Investments Inc ....G.... 260 726-7346
Portland *(G-11814)*
D J Investments Inc ....G.... 765 348-3558
Hartford City *(G-5979)*
Del Palma Orthopedics Llc ....G.... 260 625-3169
Columbia City *(G-1778)*
Depuy Products Inc ....E.... 574 267-8143
Warsaw *(G-13864)*
Depuy Synthes Sales Inc ....F.... 574 267-8143
Warsaw *(G-13866)*
Djo LLC ....G.... 317 406-2000
Plainfield *(G-11605)*
▲ Ehob Inc ....C.... 317 972-4600
Indianapolis *(G-6815)*
Equippe Advanced Mobility ....G.... 317 807-6789
Greenwood *(G-5692)*
Fort Wayne Metals Res Pdts ....E.... 260 747-4154
Fort Wayne *(G-4273)*
Glove Corporation ....D.... 501 362-2437
Alexandria *(G-43)*
Golden-Helvey Holdings Inc ....D.... 574 266-4500
Elkhart *(G-2890)*
Hanger Prosthetics & ....G.... 812 479-1121
Evansville *(G-3531)*
Hanger Prsthetcs & Ortho Inc ....G.... 317 818-1459
Indianapolis *(G-6267)*
Hanger Prsthetcs & Ortho Inc ....F.... 219 844-2021
Hammond *(G-5889)*
Hanger Prsthetcs & Ortho Inc ....G.... 317 923-2351
Indianapolis *(G-7069)*
Hanger Prsthetcs & Ortho Inc ....G.... 765 966-5069
Richmond *(G-11995)*
Hanger Prsthetcs & Ortho Inc ....F.... 260 456-5998
Fort Wayne *(G-4318)*
Hanger Prsthetcs & Ortho Inc ....G.... 812 235-6451
Terre Haute *(G-13244)*
▲ Health Equipment Manufacturers ....E.... 260 495-3472
Fremont *(G-4961)*
Howmedica Osteonics Corp ....G.... 317 587-2008
Carmel *(G-1407)*
Infinity Products Inc ....G.... 317 272-3435
Avon *(G-448)*
Integrity Hearing ....G.... 317 882-9151
Noblesville *(G-11131)*
Invacare Corporation ....F.... 317 838-5500
Plainfield *(G-11619)*
Jatex Inc ....F.... 574 773-5928
Nappanee *(G-10687)*
Johnsons Orthotics Prosthetics ....G.... 317 272-9993
Avon *(G-450)*
▲ Kaldewei USA Inc ....G.... 866 822-2527
Fishers *(G-3936)*
Kenney Orthopedics Carmel LLC ....G.... 317 993-3664
Carmel *(G-1421)*
Kenney Orthopedics Seymour LLC ....G.... 812 271-1627
Seymour *(G-12462)*
Kenney Orthpdics Indnpolis LLC ....G.... 317 300-0814
Greenwood *(G-5713)*
Lafayette Dental Laboratory ....E.... 765 447-9341
Lafayette *(G-8947)*
Loving Care Ptnt/Wheelchair Tr ....G.... 219 427-1137
Merrillville *(G-9728)*
M & A Orthotics Inc ....G.... 317 281-5253
Fishers *(G-3941)*
Magnolia ....G.... 317 831-3221
Jasper *(G-8289)*
Maitland Engineering Inc ....E.... 574 287-0155
South Bend *(G-12850)*
Mathes Home Care ....G.... 812 944-2211
New Albany *(G-10823)*
Maxcare Orthtics Prsthtics LLC ....G.... 574 267-5852
Warsaw *(G-13905)*
Medical Device Bus Svcs Inc ....G.... 317 596-3320
Indianapolis *(G-7476)*
▲ Medical Device Bus Svcs Inc ....A.... 574 267-8143
Warsaw *(G-13908)*
Medtrnic Sofamor Danek USA Inc ....G.... 574 267-6826
Warsaw *(G-13909)*
Midwest Orthotic Services LLC ....E.... 219 736-9960
Merrillville *(G-9733)*
Midwest Orthotic Services LLC ....G.... 574 233-3352
Fort Wayne *(G-4472)*
Midwest Orthotic Services LLC ....D.... 574 233-3352
South Bend *(G-12863)*
Midwest Orthotic Services LLC ....G.... 317 334-1114
Indianapolis *(G-7509)*
Mobile Limb & Brace Inc ....G.... 765 463-4100
West Lafayette *(G-14087)*
Mobility Vehicles Indiana LLC ....G.... 317 471-7169
Knightstown *(G-8558)*
Ms Wheelchair Indiana Inc ....G.... 317 408-0947
Indianapolis *(G-7554)*
National Dentex LLC ....D.... 317 849-5143
Indianapolis *(G-7570)*
Nemcomed Fw LLC ....C.... 260 480-5226
Fort Wayne *(G-4495)*
Nemcomed Instrs & Implants ....G.... 800 255-4576
Fort Wayne *(G-4496)*
Neull Incorporated ....G.... 574 267-5575
Warsaw *(G-13912)*
Northern Brace Co Inc ....G.... 574 233-4221
South Bend *(G-12878)*
Northern Prosthetics Inc ....G.... 574 233-2459
South Bend *(G-12880)*
Oasis Lifestyle LLC ....E.... 574 948-0004
Plymouth *(G-11708)*
Orthopediatrics Corp ....D.... 574 268-6379
Warsaw *(G-13918)*
Orthopediatrics US Dist ....D.... 574 268-6379
Warsaw *(G-13919)*
Orthotic & Prosthetic Designs ....G.... 317 882-9002
Indianapolis *(G-7633)*
Orthotic & Prosthetic Lab ....F.... 812 479-6298
Evansville *(G-3657)*
Orthotic Prosthetic Specialist ....G.... 219 836-8668
Munster *(G-10620)*
OSI Specialties Inc ....E.... 317 293-4858
Indianapolis *(G-7635)*
Paragon Medical Inc ....G.... 317 570-5830
Indianapolis *(G-7654)*
Patriot Safety Products LLC ....G.... 317 945-7023
Fountaintown *(G-4792)*
Peyton Technical Services LLC ....F.... 812 738-2016
Corydon *(G-2107)*
▲ Point Medical Corporation ....A.... 219 663-1775
Crown Point *(G-2285)*
Positrax Inc ....D.... 317 293-4858
Indianapolis *(G-7708)*
Precision Medical Tech Inc ....E.... 574 267-6385
Warsaw *(G-13928)*
Precision Piece Parts Inc ....D.... 574 255-3185
Mishawaka *(G-10107)*
Prevail Prsthtics Orthtics Inc ....G.... 317 577-2273
Indianapolis *(G-7745)*
Prevail Prsthtics Orthtics Inc ....G.... 765 668-0890
Fort Wayne *(G-4558)*
Prevail Prsthtics Orthtics Inc ....E.... 260 483-5219
Fort Wayne *(G-4559)*
Prevail Prsthtics Orthtics Inc ....G.... 260 969-0605
Fort Wayne *(G-4560)*
Rayco Steel Process Inc ....F.... 574 267-7676
Warsaw *(G-13932)*
Rising Improvements LLC ....G.... 608 295-8301
South Bend *(G-12917)*
Rmi Holdings LLC ....E.... 317 214-7076
Warsaw *(G-13936)*
Safety Wear Fort Wayne ....E.... 260 456-3535
Fort Wayne *(G-4602)*
Sensorycritterscom ....G.... 260 373-0900
Fort Wayne *(G-4617)*
Soley Orthotics LLC ....G.... 317 373-7395
Indianapolis *(G-7962)*
Somer Inc ....E.... 317 873-1111
Zionsville *(G-14464)*
Spry-Clear Ear Inc ....G.... 219 934-9747
Griffith *(G-5790)*
Srt Prosthetics Orthotics LLC ....G.... 815 679-6900
Butler *(G-1241)*
Srt Prosthetics Orthotics LLC ....G.... 847 855-0030
Butler *(G-1242)*
Standard Fusee Corporation ....E.... 765 472-4375
Peru *(G-11548)*
Steel Grip Inc ....D.... 765 793-3652
Covington *(G-2120)*
Steel Grip Inc ....D.... 765 397-3344
Kingman *(G-8533)*
Surestep LLC ....E.... 574 233-3352
South Bend *(G-12962)*
▲ Symmetry Medical Inc ....G.... 574 268-2252
Warsaw *(G-13948)*
Tornier Inc ....G.... 574 268-0861
Warsaw *(G-13953)*
Transmed Associates Inc ....G.... 317 293-9993
Avon *(G-471)*
▲ Triple Inc ....G.... 574 267-1450
Warsaw *(G-13954)*
TW Enterprises LLC ....G.... 513 520-8453
Brookville *(G-1128)*
Ultra Athlete LLC ....G.... 317 520-9898
Carmel *(G-1502)*
▲ United Ortho ....F.... 260 422-5827
Fort Wayne *(G-4717)*
▲ United Surgical Inc ....G.... 260 422-5827
Fort Wayne *(G-4718)*
USA Medical Suppliers Ltd ....G.... 608 782-1855
Indianapolis *(G-8139)*
Walker Information Inc ....F.... 317 843-3939
Indianapolis *(G-8176)*
Warsaw Orthopedic Inc ....C.... 901 396-3133
Warsaw *(G-13963)*
Wheelchair Help LLC ....G.... 574 295-2220
Elkhart *(G-3259)*
Wheelchair of Indiana ....G.... 317 627-6560
Indianapolis *(G-8190)*
Wiley Young & Associates ....G.... 574 269-7006
Warsaw *(G-13967)*
Wilson Hearing Aid Center ....G.... 765 747-4131
Muncie *(G-10585)*
◆ Zimmer Inc ....B.... 330 343-8801
Warsaw *(G-13971)*
Zimmer Inc ....G.... 574 268-3100
Warsaw *(G-13972)*
Zimmer Inc ....G.... 574 371-1557
Warsaw *(G-13973)*

Zimmer Inc ....G...... 574 267-6131
Warsaw (G-13974)

Zimmer Biomet Holdings Inc ....B...... 574 267-6131
Warsaw (G-13975)

Zimmer Production Inc ....G...... 574 267-6131
Warsaw (G-13976)

Zimmer Us Inc ....D...... 574 267-6131
Warsaw (G-13977)

Zollman Plastic Surgery PC ....G...... 317 328-1100
Indianapolis (G-8227)

3843 Dental Eqpt & Splys

ABC Dental of Goshen ....G...... 574 534-8777
Goshen (G-5164)

Adec ....G...... 503 538-7478
Carmel (G-1301)

American Medical & Dntl Eqp LL ....G...... 219 628-2928
Valparaiso (G-13492)

Cooks Fabrication Inc ....G...... 317 782-1722
Indianapolis (G-6661)

Den-Craft Dental Laboratory ....G...... 219 663-7776
Crown Point (G-2245)

Dental Professional Labs ....E...... 219 769-6225
Merrillville (G-9710)

Exclusively Orthodontics Lab ....G...... 317 887-1076
Greenwood (G-5693)

Fidelity Dental Handpiece Svc ....G...... 317 254-0277
Indianapolis (G-6919)

G & H Wire Company Inc ....D...... 317 346-6655
Franklin (G-4888)

Gordon B Crawford DMD ....G...... 812 288-8560
Jeffersonville (G-8371)

Growing Smiles Inc ....G...... 317 787-6404
Indianapolis (G-7052)

Hayes Enterprises LLC ....G...... 260 636-3262
Albion (G-28)

Heraeus ....G...... 574 299-1862
South Bend (G-12796)

▲ Heraeus Kulzer LLC (mitsui) ....D...... 574 299-5466
South Bend (G-12797)

Heraus Kulzer Inc ....F...... 574 291-0661
South Bend (G-12798)

J F Jelenko Co ....G...... 914 273-8600
South Bend (G-12820)

Kathy Zuccarelli ....G...... 219 865-4095
Schererville (G-12328)

Knitting Mill Specialties ....G...... 219 942-8031
Hobart (G-6085)

Lafayette Dental Laboratory ....E...... 765 447-9341
Lafayette (G-8947)

Lehi Prosthetics Dental Lab ....G...... 765 288-4613
Muncie (G-10511)

Michael J Meyer D M D P C ....G...... 812 275-7112
Bedford (G-563)

National Dentex LLC ....D...... 317 849-5143
Indianapolis (G-7570)

▲ Orthodontic Design and Prod ....E...... 760 734-3995
Franklin (G-4917)

▲ Panoramic Rental Corp ....E...... 800 654-2027
Fort Wayne (G-4519)

Pearl Custom Plastic Molding ....G...... 765 763-6961
Gwynneville (G-5800)

Plaster Shak ....G...... 317 881-6518
Greenwood (G-5733)

Protero Corporation ....E...... 219 393-5591
Kingsford Heights (G-8546)

Ronald L Miller ....G...... 765 662-3881
Marion (G-9560)

Somer Inc ....E...... 317 873-1111
Zionsville (G-14464)

Terrafina Inc ....E...... 317 346-6655
Franklin (G-4936)

William Wesley Professional ....F...... 317 635-1000
Indianapolis (G-8200)

3844 X-ray Apparatus & Tubes

CXR Company Inc ....F...... 574 269-6020
Warsaw (G-13862)

3845 Electromedical & Electrotherapeutic Apparatus

Aeds & Safety Services LLC ....G...... 502 641-3118
Jeffersonville (G-8321)

B & J Specialty Inc ....F...... 260 636-2067
Kendallville (G-8458)

◆ Biomet Inc ....A...... 574 267-6639
Warsaw (G-13845)

Biomet Europe Ltd ....G...... 574 267-2038
Warsaw (G-13847)

Bionode LLC ....G...... 317 292-7686
Indianapolis (G-6476)

C Laser Inc ....G...... 317 641-5185
Kokomo (G-8603)

Cascade Metrix LLC ....G...... 317 572-7094
Fishers (G-3886)

Cook Group Incorporated ....F...... 812 339-2235
Bloomington (G-704)

Covidien LP ....C...... 317 837-8199
Plainfield (G-11602)

E3 Diagnostics Inc ....G...... 317 334-2000
Indianapolis (G-6784)

▲ Esaote North America Inc ....D...... 317 813-6000
Fishers (G-3907)

Faztech LLC ....G...... 812 327-0926
Bloomington (G-723)

Focus Surgery Inc ....F...... 317 541-1580
Indianapolis (G-6944)

Global Isotopes LLC ....G...... 317 578-1251
Noblesville (G-11111)

Greenwald Surgical Co Inc ....E...... 219 962-1604
Lake Station (G-9075)

Guidant Intercontinental Corp ....E...... 317 218-7012
Carmel (G-1391)

Indiana Laser Spine Center ....G...... 317 577-1800
Indianapolis (G-7181)

Innovtive Nurological Dvcs LLC ....G...... 317 674-2999
Carmel (G-1416)

Medishield ....G...... 502 939-9903
New Albany (G-10824)

Medtronic ....G...... 317 837-8664
Plainfield (G-11626)

Morel Company Llc ....F...... 812 932-6100
Batesville (G-511)

Mr-Link LLC ....G...... 765 476-3185
West Lafayette (G-14088)

Nanosonics Inc ....E...... 844 876-7466
Indianapolis (G-7569)

Orthoconcepts Inc ....G...... 317 727-0100
Indianapolis (G-7632)

Pda Solutions LLC ....G...... 219 629-4658
Munster (G-10622)

Philips Ultrasound Inc ....F...... 317 591-5242
Indianapolis (G-7684)

Plastic Assembly Tech Inc ....G...... 317 841-1202
Indianapolis (G-7700)

▲ Point Care Ultrasound LP ....G...... 317 459-8113
Indianapolis (G-7704)

Predictive Wear LLC ....F...... 765 464-4891
West Lafayette (G-14096)

Radiation Physics Consulting ....G...... 317 251-0193
Indianapolis (G-7814)

Sonacare Medical LLC ....E...... 888 874-4384
Indianapolis (G-7963)

Telamon Entp Ventures LLC ....G...... 317 818-6888
Carmel (G-1489)

3851 Ophthalmic Goods

2020 Lab Inc ....G...... 219 756-8703
Merrillville (G-9690)

▲ Aearo Technologies LLC ....A...... 317 692-6666
Indianapolis (G-6341)

American Contact Lens Service ....G...... 317 347-2900
Indianapolis (G-6387)

Armada Optical Services Inc ....F...... 812 476-6623
Evansville (G-3365)

City Optical Co Inc ....G...... 317 788-4243
Indianapolis (G-6616)

City Optical Co Inc ....D...... 317 924-1300
Indianapolis (G-6615)

Columbus Optical Service Inc ....G...... 812 372-2678
Columbus (G-1878)

Diversified Ophthalmics Inc ....F...... 317 780-1677
Indianapolis (G-6750)

Essilor Laboratories Amer Inc ....D...... 317 637-2391
Indianapolis (G-6878)

▲ Fatheadz Inc ....F...... 800 561-6640
Indianapolis (G-6906)

Frecker Optical Inc ....F...... 260 747-9653
Fort Wayne (G-4287)

G K Optical Company Inc ....E...... 317 881-2585
Indianapolis (G-6975)

Harmon Hrmon Uysugi Optmtrists ....F...... 812 723-4752
Paoli (G-11452)

Hetzler Ocular Prosthetics ....G...... 317 598-6298
Fishers (G-3925)

Jackson Vision Quest ....G...... 219 882-9397
Gary (G-5071)

Jasper Optical Lab ....G...... 812 634-9020
Jasper (G-8262)

Kokomo Optical Company Inc ....G...... 765 459-5137
Kokomo (G-8655)

Lenstech Optical Lab Inc ....E...... 317 882-1249
Greenwood (G-5718)

Luxottica Retail N Amer Inc ....E...... 219 736-0141
Merrillville (G-9729)

Luxottica Retail N Amer Inc ....E...... 317 293-9999
Indianapolis (G-7428)

◆ Samco Group Inc ....G...... 219 872-4413
Michigan City (G-9838)

Shimp Optical Corp ....G...... 317 636-4448
Indianapolis (G-7933)

Singer Optical Company Inc ....F...... 812 423-1179
Evansville (G-3732)

▲ Solar Bat Enterprises Inc ....G...... 812 986-3551
Brazil (G-978)

Spectacles of Carmel Inc ....G...... 317 848-9081
Carmel (G-1485)

Spectacles of Carmel Inc ....G...... 317 475-9011
Indianapolis (G-7972)

Tri State Optical ....E...... 765 289-4475
Muncie (G-10575)

Usv Optical Inc ....G...... 260 482-5033
Fort Wayne (G-4721)

Vision Associates ....G...... 765 288-1575
Muncie (G-10577)

3861 Photographic Eqpt & Splys

Able Printing & Bus Svcs LLC ....G...... 574 834-7006
North Webster (G-11288)

Aerial Imaging Resources LLC ....G...... 317 550-5970
Indianapolis (G-6344)

Camerabee LLC ....G...... 317 546-2999
Indianapolis (G-6544)

◆ Draper Inc ....B...... 765 987-7999
Spiceland (G-13054)

Gs Sales Inc ....G...... 317 595-6750
Westfield (G-14168)

Heartland Film Inc ....G...... 317 464-9405
Indianapolis (G-7085)

Image Inks Company ....G...... 317 432-5041
Indianapolis (G-7161)

Laser Systems ....G...... 219 465-1155
Valparaiso (G-13573)

Lasertone Inc ....F...... 812 473-5945
Evansville (G-3598)

Mid-America Environmental LLC ....F...... 812 475-1644
Evansville (G-3626)

Milestone AV Technologies LLC ....B...... 574 267-8101
Warsaw (G-13911)

Printing Technologies Inc ....E...... 800 428-3786
Indianapolis (G-7758)

Success Entrmt Group Intl Inc ....G...... 260 490-9990
Ossian (G-11409)

Success Holding Group Corp USA ....G...... 260 490-9990
Ossian (G-11410)

Xerox Corporation ....G...... 317 471-4220
Zionsville (G-14472)

3873 Watch & Clock Devices & Parts

▲ Hansen Corporation ....B...... 812 385-3000
Princeton (G-11874)

Montgomery Manufacturing Co ....G...... 812 724-2505
Owensville (G-11429)

Smokers Iron Works ....G...... 574 674-6683
Elkhart (G-3179)

Yoders Custom Service ....G...... 574 831-4717
New Paris (G-11002)

39 MISCELLANEOUS MANUFACTURING INDUSTRIES

3911 Jewelry: Precious Metal

Aaland Gem Company Inc ....G...... 219 769-4492
Merrillville (G-9691)

Alan W Long ....G...... 812 265-6717
Madison (G-9442)

Amore Forte LLC ....G...... 702 763-2550
Hammond (G-5842)

Argentum Jewelry Inc ....G...... 812 336-3100
Bloomington (G-665)

Ashleys Jewelry By Design Ltd ....G...... 219 926-9039
Chesterton (G-1596)

Brinker Mfg Jewelers Inc ....F...... 812 476-0651
Evansville (G-3402)

Collegiate Pride Inc ....G...... 260 726-7818
Portland (G-11812)

Crystal Source ....G...... 812 988-7009
Nashville (G-10721)

David Gonzales ....G.... 765 284-6960
Muncie (G-10454)
Design Msa Inc ....G.... 317 817-9000
Carmel (G-1355)
Downey Creations LLC ....D.... 317 248-9888
Indianapolis (G-6764)
Dyer Charles B and Ratliff Co ....G.... 317 634-3381
Indianapolis (G-6772)
Ed Stump Assembly Inc ....G.... 574 291-0058
South Bend (G-12758)
Edward E Petri Company ....G.... 317 636-5007
Indianapolis (G-6809)
Flawless Beauty LLC ....G.... 317 914-7952
Indianapolis (G-6932)
G Thrapp Jewelers Inc ....E.... 317 255-5555
Indianapolis (G-6977)
Ginas Creative Jewelry Inc ....G.... 317 272-0032
Avon (G-442)
Gold N Gems ....G.... 317 895-6002
Indianapolis (G-7018)
Golden Lion Inc ....G.... 765 446-9557
Lafayette (G-8909)
Goldstone Jewelry Inc ....G.... 765 742-1975
West Lafayette (G-14070)
Herff Jones LLC ....D.... 620 365-5181
Indianapolis (G-7090)
Herff Jones LLC ....G.... 800 837-4235
Indianapolis (G-7091)
◆ Herff Jones LLC ....C.... 800 419-5462
Indianapolis (G-7092)
Herff Jones Co Indiana - Inc ....G.... 317 297-3740
Indianapolis (G-7093)
Interntnal Damnd Gold Exch Ltd ....F.... 317 872-6666
Indianapolis (G-7262)
J C Sipe Inc ....G.... 317 848-0215
Indianapolis (G-7283)
J Lewis Small Co Inc ....D.... 765 552-5011
Elwood (G-3301)
Janette Walker ....G.... 219 937-9160
Hammond (G-5902)
Jewelers Boutique Inc ....G.... 317 788-7679
Indianapolis (G-7303)
Jostens Inc ....G.... 317 326-2782
Greenfield (G-5545)
Jostens Inc ....G.... 317 843-1958
Indianapolis (G-6270)
Peter Franklin Jewelers Inc ....G.... 260 749-4315
New Haven (G-10952)
Rogers Enterprises Inc ....G.... 317 851-5500
Greenwood (G-5742)
Ronaldo Designer Jewelry Inc ....D.... 812 972-7220
New Albany (G-10859)
Smokes - Berne ....G.... 260 849-4038
Berne (G-624)
Stall & Kessler Inc ....G.... 765 742-1259
Lafayette (G-9002)
Surplus Store and Exchange ....F.... 765 447-0200
Lafayette (G-9006)
Terri Logan Studios ....G.... 765 966-7876
Richmond (G-12062)
Verona LLC ....G.... 317 248-9888
Indianapolis (G-8151)
Welmer Jewelers Inc ....G.... 812 522-4082
Seymour (G-12499)

3914 Silverware, Plated & Stainless Steel Ware

▲ A-1 Awards Inc ....F.... 317 546-9000
Indianapolis (G-6301)
▲ Bruce Fox Inc ....C.... 812 945-3511
New Albany (G-10754)
Simply Silver ....G.... 260 824-4667
Bluffton (G-892)

3915 Jewelers Findings & Lapidary Work

Aaland Gem Company Inc ....G.... 219 769-4492
Merrillville (G-9691)
Alex and Ani LLC ....G.... 317 575-8449
Indianapolis (G-6361)
Chownings Jewelers ....G.... 765 294-4476
Veedersburg (G-13642)
▲ Diamond Tools Technology Inc ....F.... 847 537-8686
Indianapolis (G-6741)
RC Enterprises ....G.... 812 279-2755
Bedford (G-570)
▲ Woodburn Diamond Die Co Inc ....D.... 260 632-4217
Woodburn (G-14392)

3931 Musical Instruments

▲ Conn-Selmer Inc ....D.... 574 522-1675
Elkhart (G-2765)
Conn-Selmer Inc ....E.... 574 522-1675
Elkhart (G-2766)
Conn-Selmer Inc ....B.... 574 295-6730
Elkhart (G-2767)
Conn-Selmer Inc ....A.... 574 295-0079
Elkhart (G-2768)
Eddie S Guitars ....G.... 219 689-7007
Dyer (G-2497)
Flavoreeds ....G.... 260 373-2233
Fort Wayne (G-4266)
▲ Fox Products Corporation ....C.... 260 723-4888
South Whitley (G-12999)
▲ Gemeinhardt Musical Instr LLC ....E.... 574 295-5280
Elkhart (G-2876)
Goulding & Wood Inc ....F.... 317 637-5222
Indianapolis (G-7031)
▲ Humes & Berg Mfg Co Inc ....G.... 219 391-5880
East Chicago (G-2534)
▲ J J Babbitt Co ....G.... 574 315-1639
Elkhart (G-2941)
Jubilee Harps Inc ....G.... 812 426-2547
Evansville (G-3580)
Lucas Custom Instruments ....G.... 812 342-3093
Columbus (G-1965)
Main Music ....G.... 812 295-2020
Loogootee (G-9391)
Mountain Made Music Inc ....G.... 812 988-8869
Nashville (G-10731)
Normal City Music Co ....G.... 765 289-2041
Muncie (G-10539)
Piano Shop Llc ....G.... 812 951-2462
Georgetown (G-5152)
▲ Rees Harps Inc ....F.... 812 438-3032
Rising Sun (G-12091)
Self Care LLC ....G.... 317 295-8279
Indianapolis (G-7909)
Stanbinger Flutes Inc ....G.... 317 784-3012
Indianapolis (G-7986)
Steinway Piano Company Inc ....D.... 574 522-1675
Elkhart (G-3192)
Stone Custom Drum LLC ....G.... 260 403-7519
Fort Wayne (G-4651)
T Shorter Manufacturing Inc ....G.... 574 264-4131
Elkhart (G-3203)
Uniflex Relay Systems LLC ....G.... 765 232-4675
Union City (G-13462)
▲ Walter Piano Company Inc ....F.... 574 266-0615
Elkhart (G-3254)
Woodwind & Brasswind Inc ....F.... 574 251-3547
Indianapolis (G-8214)

3942 Dolls & Stuffed Toys

Kls Santas ....G.... 765 474-6951
Lafayette (G-8944)
Red Wagon ....G.... 260 768-3090
Shipshewana (G-12646)
Turner Dolls Inc ....G.... 812 834-5065
Heltonville (G-6029)
Virginias Very Own LLC ....G.... 812 834-5065
Heltonville (G-6030)

3944 Games, Toys & Children's Vehicles

4 Kids Books ....F.... 317 733-8710
Zionsville (G-14414)
B & B Specialties Inc ....G.... 574 277-0499
Granger (G-5391)
Chelseas Model Horses ....G.... 765 366-1082
Ladoga (G-8839)
▲ Chessex Manufacturing Co LLC ....F.... 260 471-9511
Fort Wayne (G-4146)
Christopher Engle ....G.... 812 876-3540
Ellettsville (G-3274)
Claywood Creation ....G.... 260 244-7719
Columbia City (G-1774)
▲ Continuum Games Incorporated ....G.... 877 405-2662
Indianapolis (G-6658)
Cosco Inc ....A.... 812 372-0141
Columbus (G-1883)
Country Cabin LLC ....G.... 812 232-4635
Terre Haute (G-13218)
Country Woodcrafts Inc ....G.... 260 244-7578
Columbia City (G-1775)
Dorel Juvenile Group Inc ....F.... 812 314-6629
Columbus (G-1910)
▲ Dorel USA Inc ....D.... 812 372-0141
Columbus (G-1914)
Eureka Science Corp ....G.... 317 821-0805
Camby (G-1266)
EVS Ltd ....F.... 574 233-5707
South Bend (G-12767)
Family Leisurecom Inc ....G.... 317 823-4448
Indianapolis (G-6903)
Flambeau Inc ....C.... 812 372-4899
Columbus (G-1931)
▲ Fundex Games Ltd ....D.... 317 248-1080
Indianapolis (G-6969)
Gameoto LLC ....G.... 317 883-9322
Indianapolis (G-6981)
Geist Bike and Hobby Company ....G.... 317 855-1346
Indianapolis (G-6990)
Gener8 LLC ....G.... 317 253-8737
Indianapolis (G-6991)
▲ Gigglicious LLC ....G.... 317 272-4064
Avon (G-441)
▲ Greenlight LLC ....F.... 317 287-0600
Indianapolis (G-7044)
Harris Bmo Bank National Assn ....G.... 219 939-0164
Gary (G-5059)
▲ Honey and ME ....G.... 317 668-3924
Franklin (G-4897)
Jigsaw Creations ....G.... 260 691-2196
Columbia City (G-1802)
K&D Crafts ....G.... 812 667-2575
Dillsboro (G-2469)
Kan Jam LLC ....G.... 317 804-9129
Westfield (G-14172)
Kite & Key LLC ....G.... 317 654-7703
Indianapolis (G-7355)
Lafayette Puzzle Factory LLC ....G.... 800 883-6408
Lafayette (G-8949)
Lightuptoyscom LLC ....E.... 812 246-1916
Sellersburg (G-12403)
Lpf Limited ....G.... 765 447-0939
Lafayette (G-8961)
Ludo Fact USA LLC ....D.... 765 588-9137
Lafayette (G-8962)
Marquette Council 3631 Kn ....G.... 219 864-3255
Griffith (G-5784)
Merritt Manufacturing Inc ....G.... 317 409-0148
Indianapolis (G-7483)
▲ Midwest Products Co Inc ....D.... 219 942-1134
Hobart (G-6092)
Milam Toys Inc ....G.... 765 362-2826
Crawfordsville (G-2174)
Old Lumber Yard Clay Factory ....F.... 260 627-3567
Grabill (G-5382)
▲ Peter Stone Company ....E.... 260 768-9150
Shipshewana (G-12643)
Planet Mind LLC ....G.... 765 452-2341
Kokomo (G-8681)
PNC Bank National Association ....G.... 812 948-4490
New Albany (G-10845)
Purrfectplay ....G.... 219 926-7604
Chesterton (G-1629)
RC Fun Parks LLC ....G.... 574 217-7715
Granger (G-5430)
Red Wagon ....G.... 260 768-3090
Shipshewana (G-12646)
Rix Products Inc ....G.... 812 426-1749
Evansville (G-3706)
▲ Round 2 LLC ....F.... 574 243-3000
South Bend (G-12918)
Scitt Inc ....G.... 574 208-6649
Mishawaka (G-10122)
Shepherds Loft ....G.... 812 486-2304
Montgomery (G-10241)
Snuggy Baby LLC ....G.... 260 418-6795
Fort Wayne (G-4632)
T & G Games Inc ....G.... 574 297-5455
Monticello (G-10284)
◆ Tedco Inc ....F.... 765 489-4527
Hagerstown (G-5814)
Timberline Scenery LLC ....G.... 260 244-5588
Columbia City (G-1842)
Wagon Train Ventures LLC ....G.... 260 625-5301
Fort Wayne (G-4732)
▲ Warren Industries Inc ....D.... 765 447-2151
Lafayette (G-9020)

3949 Sporting & Athletic Goods, NEC

Active Trading International ....G.... 260 637-1990
Fort Wayne (G-4040)
▲ AJS Belts ....G.... 219 628-0074
Valparaiso (G-13488)
American Playground Corp ....G.... 765 642-0288
Anderson (G-62)

American Playground Corp ....G....... 765 642-0288
Anderson *(G-63)*

American Whitetail Inc ....F....... 812 937-7185
Ferdinand *(G-3845)*

AP Acquisition LLC ....F....... 765 642-0288
Anderson *(G-67)*

Aquatic Renovation Systems Inc ....E....... 317 251-0207
Indianapolis *(G-6412)*

B & M Products ....G....... 574 238-7468
Goshen *(G-5174)*

Bad Boys Bllard Prductions LLC ....G....... 702 738-4950
Indianapolis *(G-6454)*

▲ Battle Creek Equipment Co ....E....... 260 495-3472
Fremont *(G-4952)*

Boomerang Ventures LLC ....G....... 317 852-7786
Danville *(G-2344)*

Braniff Game Birds ....G....... 574 784-3919
Lakeville *(G-9093)*

Brickyard Crossing ....G....... 317 492-6573
Indianapolis *(G-6506)*

C L Holdings LLC ....G....... 317 736-4414
Franklin *(G-4874)*

Cheercussion LLC ....F....... 317 762-4009
Carmel *(G-1336)*

▲ Chester Pool Systems Inc ....E....... 812 949-7333
New Albany *(G-10758)*

Chester Pool Systems Inc ....E....... 812 949-7333
New Albany *(G-10759)*

▲ Chicago Case Company ....G....... 317 636-3351
Indianapolis *(G-6600)*

Cloud Defensive LLC ....G....... 812 760-5017
Newburgh *(G-11025)*

▲ Compositech Inc ....E....... 800 231-6755
Indianapolis *(G-6643)*

Cover Care LLC ....G....... 513 297-4094
Westfield *(G-14146)*

Crossbow Group Inc ....G....... 317 603-0406
Westfield *(G-14150)*

David W Miller Miller Longbow ....G....... 765 482-3234
Lebanon *(G-9179)*

Deer Track Archery ....G....... 765 643-6847
Anderson *(G-92)*

Delilah Club Covers ....G....... 812 401-0012
Evansville *(G-3456)*

Delta Excell Incorporated ....E....... 765 642-0288
Anderson *(G-93)*

Destro Machines LLC ....G....... 412 999-1619
Lafayette *(G-8889)*

◆ Diamond Billiard Products Inc ....E....... 812 288-7665
Jeffersonville *(G-8351)*

Dick Baumgartners Basket ....E....... 765 220-1767
Richmond *(G-11977)*

▼ Divers Supply Company Inc ....D....... 317 923-4523
Indianapolis *(G-6745)*

Dmp LLC ....G....... 812 699-0086
Worthington *(G-14394)*

Duclas Fitness LLC ....G....... 812 217-8544
Evansville *(G-3466)*

▲ Dunn-Rite Products Inc ....E....... 765 552-9433
Elwood *(G-3295)*

Easton Technical Products Inc ....E....... 574 583-5131
Monticello *(G-10261)*

EMB Fishing LLC ....G....... 317 244-8741
Indianapolis *(G-6847)*

Empire Lacrosse & Sports Inc ....G....... 317 574-4529
Indianapolis *(G-6263)*

Escalade Incorporated ....D....... 812 467-4449
Evansville *(G-3481)*

Fairway Custom Golf ....G....... 317 842-0017
Fishers *(G-3910)*

Fallen Timber Bats LLC ....G....... 260 387-5841
Fort Wayne *(G-4254)*

Federal Cartridge Company ....G....... 765 966-7745
Richmond *(G-11986)*

Fields Outdoor Adventures LLP ....G....... 765 932-3964
Rushville *(G-12221)*

Fisherman S Lurecraft Shop Inc ....G....... 260 829-1274
Lagrange *(G-9042)*

Fishing Abilities Inc ....G....... 574 273-0842
South Bend *(G-12780)*

Flambeau Inc ....C....... 812 372-4899
Columbus *(G-1931)*

Flo Realty LLC ....G....... 317 636-6481
Indianapolis *(G-6938)*

Foot Locker Retail Inc ....G....... 317 578-1892
Indianapolis *(G-6947)*

Fort Wayne Pools ....C....... 260 459-4100
Fort Wayne *(G-4279)*

G & S Johnson Outdoors LLC ....G....... 574 267-3891
Warsaw *(G-13880)*

G L D Inc ....G....... 317 924-7981
Indianapolis *(G-6976)*

▲ Gameface Inc ....G....... 317 363-8855
Zionsville *(G-14433)*

◆ Gared Holdings LLC ....C....... 317 774-9840
Noblesville *(G-11108)*

Global Ozone Innovations LLC ....G....... 574 294-5797
Elkhart *(G-2886)*

▲ Global USA Inc ....G....... 317 219-5647
Noblesville *(G-11112)*

Graphic Fx Inc ....F....... 812 234-0000
Terre Haute *(G-13243)*

Harvard Sports Inc ....G....... 812 467-4449
Evansville *(G-3535)*

Hellbent Inc ....G....... 765 631-4934
Indianapolis *(G-7088)*

Hinton Keith & Hinton Tammy ....G....... 260 749-4867
New Haven *(G-10943)*

Home Run LLC ....G....... 219 531-1006
Valparaiso *(G-13556)*

Hook & Arrow ....G....... 260 739-6661
Fort Wayne *(G-4340)*

Hooker Deer Drag Co LLC ....G....... 812 623-2706
Sunman *(G-13112)*

Hubs Chub Inc ....F....... 317 758-5494
Sheridan *(G-12590)*

Hudson Aquatic Systems LLC ....F....... 260 665-1635
Angola *(G-220)*

▲ Impact Safety Inc ....G....... 317 852-3067
Indianapolis *(G-7167)*

▲ Imperial Marble Incorporated ....F....... 812 752-5384
Scottsburg *(G-12364)*

◆ Indian Industries Inc ....D....... 812 467-1200
Evansville *(G-3550)*

Indiana Baton Twirling Assoc ....G....... 317 769-6826
Lebanon *(G-9191)*

Indiana Section of Pga of Amer ....G....... 317 738-9696
Franklin *(G-4899)*

▲ Jay Orner Sons Billiard Co Inc ....G....... 317 243-0046
Indianapolis *(G-7299)*

Jns Sports ....G....... 317 852-8314
Brownsburg *(G-1158)*

Keesling Custom Pools & Patios ....G....... 317 823-3526
Indianapolis *(G-7339)*

▲ Kidstuff Playsystems Inc ....E....... 219 938-3331
Gary *(G-5072)*

L&N Supply LLC ....G....... 219 397-9500
East Chicago *(G-2546)*

Lake House ....G....... 574 265-6945
Winona Lake *(G-14350)*

Leisure Pool & Spa ....G....... 812 537-0071
Lawrenceburg *(G-9147)*

Lester Recreation Designs LLC ....G....... 317 888-2071
Greenwood *(G-5719)*

Life Less Ordinary LLC ....G....... 317 727-4277
Indianapolis *(G-7403)*

Master Corporation ....F....... 260 471-0001
Fort Wayne *(G-4455)*

Meditation Company ....G....... 574 217-3157
South Bend *(G-12859)*

Mid America Powered Vehicles ....G....... 812 925-7745
Chandler *(G-1551)*

▼ Midwest Gym Supply Inc ....F....... 812 265-4099
Madison *(G-9486)*

Mulry Manufacturing LLC ....G....... 317 253-2756
Indianapolis *(G-7557)*

Native Crossbows LLC ....G....... 765 641-2224
Anderson *(G-142)*

▲ Official Sports Intl Inc ....F....... 574 269-1404
Warsaw *(G-13917)*

Pathfinder School LLC ....F....... 317 791-8777
Indianapolis *(G-7660)*

Patriot Range Technologies ....G....... 708 354-3150
East Chicago *(G-2556)*

Peranis Hockey World ....G....... 317 288-5183
Indianapolis *(G-7673)*

Pieniadze Inc ....G....... 888 226-6241
Zionsville *(G-14456)*

Playfair Shuffleboard Company ....F....... 260 747-7288
Fort Wayne *(G-4534)*

Power Place Products Inc ....G....... 765 583-2333
West Lafayette *(G-14095)*

Powering Athletics ....G....... 260 672-1700
Fort Wayne *(G-4544)*

Proline Bowstrings ....G....... 513 259-3738
Liberty *(G-9270)*

Proteq Custom Gear LLC ....G....... 812 201-6002
Brazil *(G-975)*

Prt South LLC ....G....... 708 354-3786
East Chicago *(G-2566)*

R & R Bowling Inc ....G....... 574 252-4123
Mishawaka *(G-10114)*

Rbg Inc ....G....... 812 866-3983
Lexington *(G-9255)*

Reagent Chemical & RES Inc ....F....... 574 772-7424
Knox *(G-8578)*

Recreation Insites LLC ....G....... 317 578-0588
Fishers *(G-3961)*

Robert J Matt ....G....... 317 831-2400
Mooresville *(G-10337)*

Rome Cy Area Youth Ctr Basbal ....G....... 260 854-4599
Rome City *(G-12200)*

Royal Pin Leisure Ctr ....G....... 317 247-4426
Indianapolis *(G-7866)*

▲ Royal Spa Corporation ....D....... 317 781-0828
Indianapolis *(G-7867)*

Running Company LLC ....G....... 317 887-0606
Greenwood *(G-5745)*

S & W Swing Sets ....G....... 260 414-6200
New Haven *(G-10956)*

S P R Athletics LLC ....G....... 419 308-2732
Winchester *(G-14340)*

Sb Finishing ....G....... 317 598-0965
Indianapolis *(G-7899)*

Screwy Lewy Lures Inc ....G....... 812 786-7369
Corydon *(G-2112)*

Sea Quest Lures Inc ....G....... 219 762-4362
Portage *(G-11792)*

Send A Scent Arrow Co Inc ....G....... 317 297-5232
Indianapolis *(G-7910)*

Sevier Manufacturing ....G....... 317 892-2784
Brownsburg *(G-1171)*

Sg Helmets ....G....... 317 286-3616
Brownsburg *(G-1172)*

Sharps Baton Mfg Corp ....G....... 574 214-9389
Elkhart *(G-3164)*

Side Kick Lure Retriever ....G....... 812 329-9068
Bedford *(G-577)*

Sinden Racing Service Inc ....F....... 317 243-7171
Indianapolis *(G-7949)*

Sparkle Pools Inc ....F....... 812 232-1292
Terre Haute *(G-13337)*

Speedhook Specialists Inc ....G....... 877 773-4665
Schererville *(G-12347)*

Sports Licensed Division ....F....... 508 758-6101
Indianapolis *(G-7976)*

Standard Fusee Corporation ....E....... 765 472-4375
Peru *(G-11548)*

▲ Tarver Wolff LLC ....G....... 765 265-7416
Brookville *(G-1127)*

Team & Club Sporting Goods ....G....... 219 762-5477
Portage *(G-11797)*

Team Supreme Bait Company ....G....... 812 366-3200
Georgetown *(G-5154)*

Thundrbird Traditional Archery ....G....... 812 699-1099
Culver *(G-2327)*

Tippmann Sports LLC ....F....... 260 749-6022
Fort Wayne *(G-4687)*

Totschlager Game Calls LLC ....G....... 574 354-1620
Bourbon *(G-950)*

Touchdown Fishing Lures LLC ....G....... 812 873-8355
Paris Crossing *(G-11461)*

Triunity LLC ....G....... 317 703-1147
Noblesville *(G-11196)*

Uebelhors Golf ....G....... 317 881-4109
Indianapolis *(G-8124)*

Unique Outdoor Products LLC ....G....... 260 486-4955
Fort Wayne *(G-4714)*

Unique Products ....G....... 812 376-8887
Columbus *(G-2027)*

Urban-Ert Slings LLC ....G....... 317 223-6509
Clayton *(G-1709)*

Websters Sporting Goods Inc ....F....... 317 255-4855
Indianapolis *(G-8182)*

▲ Westfield Outdoor Inc ....C....... 317 334-0364
Indianapolis *(G-8186)*

White Flyer Targets ....G....... 574 772-3271
Knox *(G-8588)*

White River Outfitters LLC ....G....... 812 787-0921
Shoals *(G-12673)*

Wildman Enterprise ....G....... 317 985-0924
Greenfield *(G-5584)*

3952 Lead Pencils, Crayons & Artist's Mtrls

Chep (usa) Inc ....E....... 317 780-0700
Indianapolis *(G-6598)*

▲ Harcourt Industries Inc ....E....... 765 629-2625
Milroy *(G-9980)*

Playn2win LLC ....G....... 317 345-4653
Indianapolis *(G-7702)*

S
I
C

V M Integrated ....G....... 877 296-0621
Indianapolis (G-8143)
▲ Wolfe Engineered Plastics LLC ......G....... 812 623-8403
Sunman (G-13122)

3953 Marking Devices

A & M Rubber Stamps Inc ....G....... 219 836-0892
Munster (G-10591)
Arben Corp ....F....... 812 477-7763
Evansville (G-3360)
Bulldog Award Co Inc ....G....... 317 773-3379
Noblesville (G-11073)
Ehrgotts Signs & Stamps Inc ....G....... 317 353-2222
Indianapolis (G-6816)
Heartfelt Creations Inc ....G....... 574 773-3088
Goshen (G-5236)
Impressions That Count Inc ....G....... 317 423-0581
Indianapolis (G-7168)
Indiana Stamp Co Inc ....E....... 260 424-8973
Fort Wayne (G-4366)
Indianapolis Rubber Stamp Co ....F....... 317 263-9540
Indianapolis (G-7204)
J V C Rubber Stamp Company ....G....... 574 293-0113
Elkhart (G-2943)
Plastimatic Arts Corp ....E....... 574 254-9000
Mishawaka (G-10104)
Riverside Printing Co ....G....... 812 275-1950
Bedford (G-574)
▲ S & T Fulfillment LLC ....F....... 812 466-4900
Terre Haute (G-13323)
Seal Corp USA ....G....... 812 430-8441
Evansville (G-3719)
Sign A Rama ....G....... 812 477-7763
Evansville (G-3727)
Stamp Works ....G....... 765 962-5201
Richmond (G-12054)
Stampcrafter ....G....... 574 892-5206
Argos (G-277)
Toomuchfun Rubberstamps Inc ....G....... 260 557-4808
Fort Wayne (G-4693)
◆ Tyden Group Holdings Corp ....F....... 740 420-6777
Angola (G-253)

3955 Carbon Paper & Inked Ribbons

Cartridge Specialist Inc ....G....... 317 257-4465
Indianapolis (G-6562)
Lasertech Inc ....G....... 812 277-1321
Bedford (G-559)
Stenno Carbon Co ....F....... 317 890-8710
Indianapolis (G-8000)

3961 Costume Jewelry & Novelties

▲ Annie Oakley Enterprises Inc ....F....... 260 894-7100
Ligonier (G-9276)
◆ Dicksons Inc ....C....... 812 522-1308
Seymour (G-12445)
Ntr Metals LLC ....G....... 317 522-2891
Indianapolis (G-7603)
Rhinestone Supply LLC ....G....... 260 484-2711
Fort Wayne (G-4591)
Sisson & Son Mfg Jewelers ....G....... 574 967-4331
Flora (G-4003)
Swarovski North America Ltd ....G....... 317 841-0037
Indianapolis (G-8025)
Templeton Coal Company Inc ....G....... 812 232-7037
Terre Haute (G-13350)

3965 Fasteners, Buttons, Needles & Pins

Archimedes Inc ....G....... 260 347-3903
Kendallville (G-8455)
B&H Industries Corporation ....G....... 765 794-4428
Darlington (G-2360)
▲ Bollhoff Inc ....E....... 260 347-3903
Kendallville (G-8461)
Enterkin Manufacturing Co Inc ....E....... 317 462-4477
Greenfield (G-5529)
Freudenberg-Nok General Partnr ....F....... 765 763-7246
Morristown (G-10369)
Frickers Inc ....E....... 765 965-6655
Richmond (G-11988)
Nicholson Group LLC ....G....... 219 926-3528
Chesterton (G-1624)
▲ Rightway Fasteners Inc ....C....... 812 342-2700
Columbus (G-2009)
Scotts Fasteners & Supply LLC ....G....... 317 372-8743
Danville (G-2357)
Smart Machine Inc ....G....... 219 922-0706
Hammond (G-5942)

3991 Brooms & Brushes

▲ American Way Marketing Inc ....F....... 574 295-7466
Elkhart (G-2687)
City of Fort Wayne ....D....... 260 427-1235
Fort Wayne (G-4152)
▲ Crown Industries Inc ....E....... 219 791-9930
Crown Point (G-2239)
Jason Incorporated ....D....... 800 787-7325
Richmond (G-12006)
Midwest Finishing Systems Inc ....E....... 574 257-0099
Mishawaka (G-10087)
Power Brushes of Indiana Inc ....G....... 812 336-7395
Bloomington (G-801)
Reit-Price Mfg Co Incorporated ....G....... 765 964-3252
Union City (G-13460)
◆ Royal Brush Manufacturing Inc ....G....... 219 660-4170
Munster (G-10627)

3993 Signs & Advertising Displays

1global Ds LLC ....F....... 765 413-2211
Westfield (G-14131)
20 Minute Signs Plus ....G....... 765 413-1046
Lafayette (G-8844)
A Harris Verl Inc ....G....... 317 736-4680
Indianapolis (G-6296)
A Plus Sign Area Ltg Spcalists ....G....... 765 966-4857
Richmond (G-11951)
A S P Parrott Signs ....G....... 812 325-9102
Bloomington (G-653)
A Sign Above ....G....... 317 392-2144
Laurel (G-9127)
A Sign Odyssey LLC ....G....... 219 962-1247
Lake Station (G-9074)
A Sign-By-Design Inc ....E....... 317 876-7900
Zionsville (G-14415)
A To Z Sign Shop ....G....... 219 462-7489
Valparaiso (G-13481)
Aardvark Vinyl Signs ....G....... 260 833-0800
Angola (G-188)
Aarvee Associates LLC ....G....... 312 222-5665
Indianapolis (G-6305)
Absograph Sign Co ....G....... 630 940-4093
Valparaiso (G-13483)
Accent Signs & Graphics ....G....... 866 769-7446
French Lick (G-4983)
Ace Sign Company Inc ....G....... 812 232-4206
Terre Haute (G-13186)
Ace Sign Systems Inc ....G....... 765 288-1000
Muncie (G-10423)
ACS Sign Solution ....F....... 317 925-2835
Indianapolis (G-6318)
ACS Sign Solution ....G....... 317 201-4838
Indianapolis (G-6319)
ADM Custom Creations LLC ....G....... 765 499-0584
Hartford City (G-5977)
Advanced Sign & Graphics Inc ....F....... 765 284-8360
Muncie (G-10424)
Advanced Sign & Lighting Svc ....G....... 812 430-2817
Evansville (G-3344)
Advantage Signs & Graphics Inc ....G....... 219 853-1427
Hammond (G-5835)
Aerial Sign Co ....G....... 317 258-9696
Indianapolis (G-6345)
Affordable Sign & Neon Inc ....G....... 219 853-1855
Hammond (G-5836)
Affordable Signs ....G....... 260 349-1710
Kendallville (G-8451)
All American Tent & Awning Inc ....F....... 812 232-4220
Terre Haute (G-13190)
Alveys Sign Co Inc ....E....... 812 867-2567
Evansville (G-3350)
AMS Embroidery & Signs LLC ....G....... 513 313-1613
Brookville (G-1111)
Anderson Enterprises LLC ....G....... 317 569-1099
Carmel (G-1311)
Anderson Sign Pro ....G....... 765 642-0281
Anderson (G-66)
Any Reason Signs ....G....... 260 450-6756
Fort Wayne (G-4079)
AP Sign Group LLC ....E....... 317 257-1869
Indianapolis (G-6406)
Apex Electric & Sign Inc ....G....... 317 326-1325
Greenfield (G-5501)
Apex Electric & Sign Inc ....G....... 317 326-1325
Morristown (G-10365)
Aplus Signs ....G....... 765 966-4857
Richmond (G-11955)
Arben Corp ....F....... 812 477-7763
Evansville (G-3360)

Arizona Sport Shirts Inc ....E....... 317 481-2160
Indianapolis (G-6419)
Art Works Sign Co Inc ....G....... 574 360-9290
Mishawaka (G-9997)
ASAP Sign & Lighting Maint ....G....... 219 464-8865
Valparaiso (G-13499)
▲ Asempac Inc ....E....... 812 945-6303
New Albany (G-10747)
Athletic Avenue & More Inc ....G....... 812 547-7655
Tell City (G-13155)
Athletic Edge Inc ....F....... 260 489-6613
Fort Wayne (G-4095)
Auto & Sign Specialties Inc ....G....... 260 824-1987
Bluffton (G-866)
Auto Art & Signs ....G....... 765 448-6800
Lafayette (G-8856)
Awards Unlimited Inc ....G....... 765 447-9413
Lafayette (G-8858)
B & B Signs ....G....... 812 282-5366
Floyds Knobs (G-4008)
B B & H Signs Incorporated ....G....... 812 235-1340
Terre Haute (G-13196)
Bandit Signs ....G....... 574 370-7067
Elkhart (G-2713)
Baugh Enterprises Inc ....G....... 812 334-8189
Bloomington (G-674)
Bc Awards Inc ....G....... 317 852-3240
Brownsburg (G-1136)
Beacon Sign Company LLC ....G....... 317 272-2388
Avon (G-433)
Begley Sign Painting Inc ....G....... 317 835-2027
Fairland (G-3820)
Big Guy Signs LLC ....G....... 317 780-6000
Indianapolis (G-6473)
Bill Banner Signs ....G....... 765 209-2642
Falmouth (G-3836)
Billman Monument & Sign Co ....G....... 574 753-2394
Logansport (G-9325)
Biltz Signs ....G....... 574 594-2703
Warsaw (G-13844)
Bloomington Design Inc ....G....... 812 332-2033
Bloomington (G-687)
Blumling Design and Graphics ....G....... 765 477-7446
Lafayette (G-8863)
Bo-Mar Industries Inc ....E....... 317 899-1240
Indianapolis (G-6491)
Bob Prescott ....G....... 219 736-7804
Merrillville (G-9703)
Boezeman Enterprises Inc ....G....... 219 345-2732
Demotte (G-2432)
Booth Signs Inc ....G....... 812 376-7446
Columbus (G-1860)
Brand Wave LLC ....G....... 661 414-2115
Noblesville (G-11070)
Brick Street Embroidery ....G....... 574 453-3729
Leesburg (G-9233)
Broadway Auto Glass LLC ....F....... 219 884-5277
Merrillville (G-9704)
Brownsburg Signs & Graphics ....G....... 317 858-1907
Brownsburg (G-1138)
Built By Bill ....G....... 317 745-2666
Danville (G-2345)
Bulldog Award Co Inc ....G....... 317 773-3379
Noblesville (G-11073)
Burkhart Advertising Inc ....F....... 574 234-4444
South Bend (G-12728)
Burkhart Advertising Inc ....G....... 574 522-4421
Elkhart (G-2738)
Burkhart Advertising Inc ....G....... 574 233-2101
South Bend (G-12727)
Burkhart Advertising Inc ....E....... 260 482-9566
Fort Wayne (G-4127)
Business & Industrial Pdts Co ....G....... 812 376-6149
Columbus (G-1863)
Business Art & Design Inc ....G....... 317 782-9108
Beech Grove (G-593)
Buttons Galore Inc ....F....... 800 626-8168
Brownsburg (G-1139)
Buy Bulk Displays LLC ....G....... 574 222-4378
Osceola (G-11372)
C & H Signs Inc ....G....... 765 642-7777
Anderson (G-79)
Capital Custom Signs ....G....... 765 689-7170
Peru (G-11519)
Cardinal Manufacturing Co Inc ....F....... 317 283-4175
Indianapolis (G-6553)
Castleton Village Center Inc ....F....... 260 484-2600
Fort Wayne (G-4140)
▲ Castleton Village Center Inc ....F....... 260 471-5959
Fort Wayne (G-4141)

Castleton Village Center Inc	G	317 577-1995	
Indianapolis (G-6565)			
Ces Company Llc	G	317 290-0491	
Indianapolis (G-6590)			
Chads Signs Installations Inc	E	317 867-2737	
Noblesville (G-11079)			
Christys Design & Sign Co	G	317 882-5444	
Greenwood (G-5675)			
CJ Developers Inc	G	219 942-5051	
Hobart (G-6075)			
Classic City Signs Inc	G	260 927-8438	
Auburn (G-321)			
▲ Classic Trophy Co	F	260 483-1161	
Fort Wayne (G-4161)			
Clear Channel Outdoor Inc	E	317 686-2350	
Indianapolis (G-6619)			
Clermont Neon Sign Company	G	317 638-4123	
Brownsburg (G-1143)			
Clients Choice Ltd	G	812 853-2911	
Boonville (G-912)			
Clover Signs Co	F	812 442-7446	
Brazil (G-958)			
Cockerhams Signs & Graphics	G	812 358-3737	
Brownstown (G-1183)			
Columbus Signs	G	812 376-7877	
Columbus (G-1881)			
Commercial Signs	G	260 745-2678	
Fort Wayne (G-4168)			
Connections Sign Language Inte	G	812 491-6036	
Evansville (G-3428)			
Corsair Graphics	G	219 938-8317	
Gary (G-5040)			
Courtney Signs & Graphics Inc	G	317 841-3297	
Indianapolis (G-6679)			
Creative Inc	G	765 447-3500	
Lafayette (G-8882)			
Crichlow Industries Inc	G	317 925-5178	
Indianapolis (G-6692)			
Cumulus Intrmdate Holdings Inc	G	765 452-5704	
Kokomo (G-8609)			
Custom Sign & Engineeri	G	812 401-1550	
Newburgh (G-11026)			
Custom Signs Unlimited Co	G	260 483-4444	
Fort Wayne (G-4196)			
D D McKay and Associates	G	317 546-7446	
Indianapolis (G-6721)			
Delaplane & Son Neon & Sign	G	574 859-3431	
Camden (G-1273)			
Designs 4 U Inc	G	765 793-3026	
Covington (G-2118)			
Dezings By Cindy Ziese	G	219 819-8786	
Rensselaer (G-11921)			
Dg Graphics LLC	G	765 349-9500	
Martinsville (G-9601)			
Diskey Architectural Signage	F	260 424-0233	
Fort Wayne (G-4212)			
Doell Designs	G	260 486-4504	
Fort Wayne (G-4217)			
Don Anderson	G	574 278-7243	
Monticello (G-10259)			
Dxd Signs	G	219 588-4403	
Highland (G-6043)			
Earl R Hamilton	G	317 838-9386	
Plainfield (G-11607)			
▲ Economy Signs Inc	G	219 932-1233	
Hammond (G-5875)			
Ej Schmidt Inc	G	317 290-0491	
Avon (G-440)			
Everywhere Signs LLC	G	812 323-1471	
Bloomington (G-721)			
Express Sign & Neon Llc	G	812 882-0104	
Vincennes (G-13679)			
Fast Signs	G	574 254-0545	
South Bend (G-12772)			
Fastsigns	G	260 373-0911	
Fort Wayne (G-4258)			
Federal Heath Sign Company LLC	G	317 581-7790	
Carmel (G-1380)			
Fine Guys Inc	G	812 547-8630	
Tell City (G-13161)			
Fine Signs and Graphics	G	812 944-7446	
New Albany (G-10777)			
First Place Trophies	G	812 385-3279	
Princeton (G-11872)			
Flag & Banner Company Inc	F	317 299-4880	
Indianapolis (G-6931)			
Four Points Development Corp	F	317 357-3275	
Indianapolis (G-6951)			
French Lick Auto Signs	G	812 936-7777	
French Lick (G-4985)			
Future Signs Sales & Service	G	765 749-5180	
Winchester (G-14330)			
Future Wave Graphics Inc	G	574 389-8803	
Elkhart (G-2873)			
Gast Sign Co	G	219 759-4336	
Valparaiso (G-13547)			
Gc Solutions Inc	G	317 334-1149	
Indianapolis (G-6987)			
Geckos	G	765 762-0822	
Attica (G-301)			
Get Noticed Portable Signs	G	765 649-6645	
Anderson (G-110)			
Gindor Inc	G	574 642-4004	
Goshen (G-5225)			
Good Signs	G	317 738-4663	
Franklin (G-4891)			
▲ Grandview Aluminum Products	E	812 649-2569	
Grandview (G-5387)			
Granite Tee Signs LLC	G	317 670-4967	
Fort Branch (G-4027)			
Graphex International	G	219 696-4849	
Lowell (G-9406)			
Graphic Visions	G	812 331-7446	
Bloomington (G-733)			
Graphically Speaking	G	219 921-1572	
Chesterton (G-1609)			
Graphics Systems Inc	G	260 485-9667	
Fort Wayne (G-4302)			
Graycraft Signs Plus Inc	G	574 269-3780	
Warsaw (G-13885)			
Graycraft Signs Plus Inc	G	260 432-3760	
Fort Wayne (G-4305)			
Grayson Graphics	G	574 264-6466	
Elkhart (G-2895)			
Green Sign Co Inc	F	812 663-2550	
Greensburg (G-5603)			
Greenfield Signs Inc	G	317 469-3095	
Greenfield (G-5535)			
Greenwood Light & Sign Service	G	317 840-5729	
Boggstown (G-900)			
H L Signworks	G	812 325-5750	
Ellettsville (G-3279)			
◆ Hall Signs Inc	D	812 332-9355	
Bloomington (G-737)			
Hanks Neon & Plastic Service	G	812 423-7447	
Evansville (G-3532)			
Heres Your Sign Diy Workshop &	G	574 238-6369	
New Paris (G-10981)			
Hernandez Signs LLC	G	317 500-1303	
Indianapolis (G-7096)			
Hi-Rise Sign & Lighting LLC	G	812 825-4448	
Bloomington (G-740)			
Holloway Vinyl Signs Grap	G	765 717-1581	
Yorktown (G-14405)			
Hot Rod Car Care LLC	G	317 660-2077	
Indianapolis (G-7134)			
Hubbard Services Inc	G	317 881-2828	
Greenwood (G-5704)			
Hutchison Sign Co Inc	E	317 894-8787	
Indianapolis (G-7148)			
Hydrojet Signs	G	765 584-2125	
Winchester (G-14331)			
I F S Corp	G	317 898-6118	
Indianapolis (G-7153)			
▲ Icon International Inc	D	260 482-8700	
Fort Wayne (G-4356)			
Ideal Sign Corp	G	219 406-2092	
Valparaiso (G-13559)			
Image Group Inc	E	574 457-3111	
Syracuse (G-13135)			
Image One LLC	E	317 576-2700	
Fishers (G-3927)			
Imperial Trophy & Awards Co	G	260 432-8161	
Fort Wayne (G-4361)			
Indiana Dimensional Pdts LLC	D	574 834-7681	
North Webster (G-11293)			
Indiana Logo Sign Group	G	800 950-1093	
Indianapolis (G-7182)			
▲ Indiana Metal Craft Inc	D	812 336-2362	
Bloomington (G-747)			
Indiana Sign & Barricade Inc	E	317 377-8000	
Indianapolis (G-7191)			
Indiana Stamp Co Inc	E	260 424-8973	
Fort Wayne (G-4366)			
Indianapolis Signworks Inc	E	317 872-8722	
Indianapolis (G-7205)			
Indys Sign Source Inc	G	317 372-2260	
Indianapolis (G-7225)			
Insign Inc	G	317 251-0131	
Indianapolis (G-7241)			
Insignia Sign Shop LLC	G	317 356-4639	
Indianapolis (G-7242)			
Integrity Sign Solutions Inc	G	502 233-8755	
New Albany (G-10807)			
Isf Inc	E	317 251-1219	
Indianapolis (G-7274)			
J W P Vinyl Designs	G	812 873-8744	
Dupont (G-2491)			
J W Signs Inc	G	260 747-5168	
Fort Wayne (G-4388)			
Jabra Signs & Graphics	G	765 584-7100	
Winchester (G-14333)			
James Wafford	G	317 773-7200	
Noblesville (G-11135)			
Jef Enterprises Inc	F	812 425-0628	
Evansville (G-3573)			
Johnson Bros S Whitley Sign Co	F	260 723-5161	
South Whitley (G-13000)			
Johnson Engraving & Trophies	G	260 982-7868	
North Manchester (G-11232)			
Jrowe Signs	G	260 668-7100	
Angola (G-223)			
Jsn Advertising Inc	G	317 888-7591	
Indianapolis (G-7319)			
Karbach Holdings Corporation	F	219 924-2454	
Hobart (G-6083)			
Kay Company Inc	E	765 659-3388	
Frankfort (G-4840)			
Kellmark Corporation	E	574 264-9695	
Elkhart (G-2958)			
Kerham Inc	E	260 483-5444	
Fort Wayne (G-4409)			
Kinder Group Inc	C	765 457-5966	
Kokomo (G-8651)			
Konrady Graphics Inc	G	219 662-0436	
Crown Point (G-2273)			
L D Barger Wholesale Neon Inc	G	765 643-4506	
Anderson (G-131)			
▲ L R Green Co Inc	D	317 781-4200	
Indianapolis (G-7370)			
Landmark Signs Inc	D	219 762-9577	
Chesterton (G-1617)			
Legendary Designs Inc	G	260 768-9170	
Shipshewana (G-12630)			
Lesh Advertising Inc	G	574 859-2141	
Camden (G-1275)			
Lillich Sign Co Inc	F	260 463-3930	
Lagrange (G-9058)			
Link Electrical Service	G	812 288-8184	
Jeffersonville (G-8391)			
Lotus Design Group	G	812 206-7281	
Charlestown (G-1570)			
M F Y Designs Inc	G	260 563-6662	
Wabash (G-13734)			
Magic Light Neon Sign Company	G	765 361-5887	
Crawfordsville (G-2170)			
▼ Margison Graphics LLC	G	765 529-8250	
New Castle (G-10911)			
Markle Music	G	812 847-2103	
Linton (G-9310)			
Marshall Signs	G	260 350-1492	
Auburn (G-342)			
Martin Signs & Crane Services	G	317 908-9708	
Indianapolis (G-7460)			
Masco Corporation of Indiana	D	317 848-1812	
Indianapolis (G-7463)			
McCaffery Sign Designs	G	574 232-9991	
South Bend (G-12857)			
Mid America Sign Corporation	F	260 744-2200	
Fort Wayne (G-4471)			
Midwest Graphix LLC	G	812 649-2522	
Rockport (G-12169)			
Midwest Sign Company Inc	G	317 931-9535	
Seymour (G-12470)			
Military Neon Signs	G	574 258-9804	
Mishawaka (G-10088)			
Mjs Businesses LLC	G	317 845-1932	
Indianapolis (G-7530)			
MO Signs LLC	G	574 780-4075	
Plymouth (G-11707)			
Morgan Commercial Lettering	G	260 482-6430	
Fort Wayne (G-4481)			
Mullin Sign Studio	G	219 926-8937	
Chesterton (G-1623)			
Neon Accents	G	812 537-0102	
Lawrenceburg (G-9148)			
Neon Cactus	G	765 743-6081	
Lafayette (G-8975)			
New Hope Services Inc	E	812 288-8248	
Jeffersonville (G-8403)			

New Hope Services Inc ....E 812 752-4892
Scottsburg (G-12377)

Next Day Signs ....G 574 259-7446
Mishawaka (G-10095)

◆ Next Products LLC ....F 317 392-4701
Shelbyville (G-12554)

No-Sail Splash Guard Co Inc ....G 765 522-2100
Roachdale (G-12094)

North American Signs Inc ....D 574 234-5252
South Bend (G-12877)

North Star Signs Inc ....G 219 365-5935
Crown Point (G-2279)

Northwest Indus Specialist ....F 219 397-7446
East Chicago (G-2555)

▲ Olive Branch Etc Inc ....G 765 449-1884
Lafayette (G-8977)

Ovation Communications Inc ....G 812 401-9100
Evansville (G-3659)

Over Hill & Dale Sign Studio ....G 812 867-1664
Evansville (G-3660)

Paint The Town Graphics Inc ....E 260 422-9152
Fort Wayne (G-4518)

Pathfinder Communications Corp............E 574 295-2500
Elkhart (G-3077)

Pathfinder Communications Corp............G 574 266-5115
Elkhart (G-3078)

Perfect Sign LLC ....G 812 518-6459
Newburgh (G-11041)

Phantom Neon LLC ....G 765 362-2221
Crawfordsville (G-2186)

Phoenix Sign Works Inc ....G 317 432-4027
Indianapolis (G-7687)

Pioneer Signs Inc ....F 219 884-7587
Merrillville (G-9746)

Pjw Inc ....G 574 295-1203
Elkhart (G-3098)

Plainfield Sign Graphic Design ....G 317 839-9499
Plainfield (G-11636)

Plastimatic Arts Corp ....G 574 254-9000
Mishawaka (G-10104)

Precise Printing Plus Signs ....G 317 545-5117
Indianapolis (G-7729)

Premier Sign Group Inc ....G 317 613-4411
Indianapolis (G-7741)

Premiere Signs Co Inc ....F 574 533-8585
Goshen (G-5312)

Prentice Products Holdings LLC............E 260 747-3195
Fort Wayne (G-4556)

Printec Solutions Inc ....G 317 289-6510
Indianapolis (G-7751)

Professional Permits ....G 574 257-2954
Mishawaka (G-10111)

Progressive Design Apparel Inc............E 317 293-5888
Indianapolis (G-7775)

Pts Signs & Wraps ....G 317 653-1807
Indianapolis (G-7788)

Pyramid Sign & Design Inc ....G 765 447-4174
Lafayette (G-8986)

R&S Sign Design ....G 765 520-5594
New Castle (G-10916)

Radical Graphics & Sign Sp LLC............G 574 870-8873
Monticello (G-10281)

Raeco/Promo-Sports LLC ....E 574 537-9387
Goshen (G-5315)

Recognition Plus ....G 812 232-2372
Terre Haute (G-13316)

▲ Reddington Design Inc ....G 574 272-0790
South Bend (G-12914)

Redneck Monshiners Signs T-Shi ....G 812 844-0694
Salem (G-12304)

Reed Sign Service Inc ....G 765 459-4033
Kokomo (G-8688)

Region Signs Inc ....F 219 473-1616
Whiting (G-14275)

Reinforcements Design ....G 219 866-8626
Rensselaer (G-11935)

Richardson Entps Blmington LLC ....G 812 287-8179
Bloomington (G-811)

Rlr Associates Inc ....G 317 632-1300
Indianapolis (G-7848)

Ron Glasscock ....G 812 986-2342
Poland (G-11743)

Rookies Unlimited Inc ....G 765 536-2726
Summitville (G-13104)

Sabco Sign Co Inc ....G 317 882-3380
Greenwood (G-5746)

Safety Vehicle Emblem Inc ....F 317 885-7565
Indianapolis (G-7884)

Sampco Inc ....C 413 442-4043
South Bend (G-12925)

Seaton Springs Inc ....G 812 282-2440
Clarksville (G-1696)

Sexton Melinda ....G 812 522-4059
Seymour (G-12484)

Sig Media LLC ....G 317 858-7624
Indianapolis (G-7938)

Sign ....G 260 422-7446
Fort Wayne (G-4623)

Sign A Rama ....G 812 477-7763
Evansville (G-3727)

Sign A Rama ....G 812 537-5516
Lawrenceburg (G-9157)

Sign Age Inc ....G 765 778-5254
Pendleton (G-11505)

Sign Arama ....G 812 657-7449
Columbus (G-2014)

Sign Craft Industries Inc ....E 317 842-8664
Indianapolis (G-7940)

Sign Crafters Inc ....E 812 424-9011
Evansville (G-3728)

Sign Creations LLC ....G 574 855-1246
South Bend (G-12935)

Sign Deals Delivered ....G 574 276-7404
South Bend (G-12936)

Sign Factory ....G 574 255-7446
Mishawaka (G-10123)

Sign For It LLC ....G 317 834-4636
Mooresville (G-10340)

Sign Graphics ....G 574 834-7100
North Webster (G-11301)

Sign Graphics Evansville Inc ....G 812 476-9151
Evansville (G-3729)

Sign Group Inc ....G 317 228-8049
Indianapolis (G-7942)

Sign Group Inc ....F 317 875-6969
Indianapolis (G-7941)

Sign Guys Inc ....G 317 875-7446
Indianapolis (G-7943)

Sign Here Ltd ....G 317 487-8001
Indianapolis (G-7944)

Sign Masters ....G 765 525-7446
Saint Paul (G-12280)

Sign Pro of Fort Wayne Inc ....G 260 497-8484
Fort Wayne (G-4624)

Sign Pros ....G 765 289-2177
Muncie (G-10562)

Sign Pros Inc ....G 765 642-1175
Anderson (G-166)

Sign Pros of Marion ....G 765 677-1234
Marion (G-9562)

Sign Ser Homes ....G 317 214-8005
Noblesville (G-11183)

Sign Services ....G 317 546-1111
Indianapolis (G-7945)

Sign Shoppe ....G 260 483-1922
Fort Wayne (G-4625)

Sign Solutions Inc ....F 317 881-1818
Greenwood (G-5749)

Sign Source One I Group Inc ....G 219 736-5865
Hobart (G-6095)

Sign Write Signs LLC ....G 219 477-3840
Valparaiso (G-13618)

Sign-A-Rama ....G 317 477-2400
Greenfield (G-5573)

Signcenter Inc ....G 812 232-4994
Terre Haute (G-13326)

Signdoc Identity LLC ....G 317 247-9670
Indianapolis (G-7946)

Signplex LLC ....G 765 795-7446
Cloverdale (G-1737)

Signs By Design ....G 812 853-7784
Newburgh (G-11049)

Signs By Sulane Inc ....G 765 565-6773
Carthage (G-1516)

Signs In Time By Greg Inc ....G 260 749-7446
Fort Wayne (G-4626)

Signs Magic LLC ....G 812 473-5155
Evansville (G-3730)

Signs More ....G 317 392-9184
Shelbyville (G-12569)

Signs of Life LLC ....G 317 575-1049
Carmel (G-1480)

Signs of Seasons ....G 219 866-4507
Rensselaer (G-11938)

Signs of Times ....G 574 296-7464
Elkhart (G-3172)

Signs of Times Llc ....G 812 981-3000
New Albany (G-10862)

Signs On Time Inc ....F 219 661-4488
Crown Point (G-2304)

Signs Unlimited ....G 574 255-0500
Mishawaka (G-10124)

Signs Unlimited ....G 260 484-5769
Fort Wayne (G-4627)

Signs Xp Inc ....G 765 453-4812
Kokomo (G-8696)

Signtech Sign Services Inc ....G 574 537-8080
Goshen (G-5323)

Signworks ....G 219 462-5353
Valparaiso (G-13619)

Sjg Enterprises Inc ....G 574 269-4806
Warsaw (G-13940)

Skyline Signs Inc ....G 765 564-4422
Delphi (G-2427)

Smith Signs Inc ....G 574 255-6446
Mishawaka (G-10128)

Snykin Inc ....G 317 818-0618
Indianapolis (G-7956)

Sojane Technologies Inc ....G 317 915-1059
Indianapolis (G-7958)

Spark Marketing LLC ....G 219 301-0071
Schererville (G-12346)

Speckin Sign Service Inc ....G 317 539-5133
Greencastle (G-5478)

Spp Inc ....F 812 882-6203
Vincennes (G-13707)

Square 1 Designs & Signs ....G 219 552-0079
Shelby (G-12516)

Stackman Signs/Graphics Inc ....E 317 784-6120
Indianapolis (G-7984)

Stans Sign Design ....G 317 251-3838
Indianapolis (G-7994)

Steindler Signs ....G 219 733-2551
Wanatah (G-13825)

Stello Products Inc ....F 812 829-2246
Spencer (G-13039)

Stingel Enterprises Inc ....F 812 883-0054
Salem (G-12306)

◆ Stoffel Seals Corporation ....E 845 353-3800
Angola (G-248)

Stritto Sign Art Company ....G 317 356-2126
Indianapolis (G-8012)

Supreme Signs ....G 219 384-0198
Valparaiso (G-13625)

T G R Inc ....F 765 452-8225
Kokomo (G-8705)

T&S Signs ....G 317 996-3027
Martinsville (G-9639)

Tc4llc ....G 317 709-5429
Fishers (G-3973)

Team Hillman LLC ....F 260 426-2626
Fort Wayne (G-4676)

The Baldus Company Inc ....G 260 424-2366
Fort Wayne (G-4680)

Thousand One Inc ....G 765 962-3636
Richmond (G-12066)

Tko Enterprises Inc ....D 317 271-1398
Plainfield (G-11647)

Todays Signs and Graphics ....G 765 288-4771
Muncie (G-10571)

Tomlin Enterprises Inc ....G 866 994-9200
Fort Wayne (G-4690)

▲ Tower Advertising Products Inc ....D 260 593-2103
Topeka (G-13431)

Town & Country Industries Inc ....E 219 712-0893
Crown Point (G-2316)

Traffic Sign Company Inc ....G 317 845-9305
Indianapolis (G-8089)

Travis Britton ....G 317 762-6018
Indianapolis (G-8092)

Trulinesigns LLC ....G 219 644-7231
Dyer (G-2511)

Unique Signs ....G 812 384-4967
Bloomfield (G-646)

Universal Sign Group Inc ....G 317 697-1165
Plainfield (G-11649)

US Signcrafters Inc ....F 574 674-5055
Osceola (G-11385)

Van Der Weele Jon D ....G 574 892-5005
Argos (G-280)

Vart Grafix ....G 317 513-5522
Indianapolis (G-8148)

Vince Rogers Signs Inc ....G 574 264-0542
Elkhart (G-3245)

Vital Signs ....G 219 548-1605
Valparaiso (G-13635)

Vital Signs Marketing LLC ....G 765 453-5088
Kokomo (G-8713)

▲ Vkf Renzel Usa Corp ....F 219 661-6300
Crown Point (G-2318)

Wagner Signs Inc ....E 317 788-0202
Indianapolis (G-8175)
Ward Industries Inc ....F 574 825-2548
Middlebury (G-9923)
Weber Sign Service Inc ....G 219 872-5060
Trail Creek (G-13444)
Wendell Conger ....G 812 282-2564
Jeffersonville (G-8441)
Westlund Concepts ....F 317 819-0611
Lapel (G-9120)
Whiteco Industries Inc ....A 219 769-6601
Merrillville (G-9761)
Whitehead Signs Inc ....F 317 632-1800
Indianapolis (G-8193)
Wildside Signs ....G 812 358-3849
Vallonia (G-13478)
Williams Signs Inc ....G 765 448-6725
Lafayette (G-9025)
Winters Assoc Prmtnal Pdts Inc ....F 812 330-7000
Bloomington (G-858)
World Graffix LLC ....G 574 936-1927
Plymouth (G-11740)
XI Graphics Inc ....F 317 738-3434
Franklin (G-4942)
Ya-Nvr-No...G 260 833-8883
Orland (G-11360)
Young & Kenady Incorporated ....G 317 852-6300
Brownsburg (G-1178)

3995 Burial Caskets

Aurora Casket Company LLC ....G 812 926-1110
Aurora (G-371)
Aurora Casket Company LLC ....D 812 926-1111
Aurora (G-372)
Aurora Casket Company LLC ....B 800 457-1111
Aurora (G-370)
◆ Batesville Casket Company Inc ....A 812 934-7500
Batesville (G-491)
Batesville Casket Company Inc ....C 812 934-8102
Batesville (G-492)
Batesville Services Inc ....G 812 934-7000
Batesville (G-493)
Cressy Memorial Group Inc ....G 574 258-1800
Mishawaka (G-10025)
Elder Group Inc ....D 765 966-7676
Richmond (G-11980)
Goliath Casket Inc ....G 765 874-2380
Lynn (G-9427)
Hillenbrand Inc ....B 812 934-7500
Batesville (G-504)
◆ JM Hutton & Co Inc ....D 765 962-3591
Richmond (G-12008)
JM Hutton & Co Inc ....E 765 962-3506
Richmond (G-12009)
Majestic Caskets & Urns Inc ....G 812 523-3630
Seymour (G-12469)
Milso Industries Inc ....D 765 966-8012
Richmond (G-12018)
◆ Pontone Industries LLC ....C 765 966-8012
Richmond (G-12030)
Romark Industries Inc ....E 765 966-6211
Richmond (G-12047)
Specialty Enterprises Inc ....F 765 935-4556
Richmond (G-12052)
◆ Tiedemann-Bevs Industries LLC ....E 765 962-4914
Richmond (G-12067)
Vandor Corporation ....E 765 683-9760
Richmond (G-12072)
York Group Inc ....D 765 966-1576
Richmond (G-12078)

3996 Linoleum & Hard Surface Floor Coverings, NEC

▲ Eagle Flooring Brokers Inc ....G 260 422-6100
Fort Wayne (G-4231)
Quick Walk Systems Inc ....G 317 255-2247
Indianapolis (G-7804)
Sorbashock LLC ....G 574 520-9784
Fort Wayne (G-4635)

3999 Manufacturing Industries, NEC

ABS Mfg Rep Inc ....G 317 407-0406
Carmel (G-1299)
Accra Pac Holding Co LLC ....G 765 326-0005
Fort Wayne (G-4035)
Adaptive Mobility Inc ....F 317 347-6400
Indianapolis (G-6323)
Adec Industries ....G 574 522-7729
Elkhart (G-2669)

Advance Green Mfg Co Inc ....G 574 457-2695
Goshen (G-5165)
Advanced Manufacturing In ....G 260 273-9669
Geneva (G-5133)
▲ Agile Mfg Inc ....G 417 845-6065
Milford (G-9948)
Aidan Industries Incorporated ....G 812 239-2803
Terre Haute (G-13189)
Air Way Mfg ....G 269 749-2161
Hamilton (G-5819)
All Rvs Manufacturing Inc ....G 574 538-1559
Shipshewana (G-12602)
Allergyfree Inc ....G 765 349-0006
Martinsville (G-9595)
AM Manufacturing Company Ind ....F 800 342-6744
Munster (G-10594)
America Corn Cutter ....G 219 733-0885
Wanatah (G-13819)
American Chemical Service ....G 219 613-4114
Crown Point (G-2225)
▲ American Oak Preserving Co Inc ....E 574 896-2171
North Judson (G-11206)
Amusement Games Inc ....G 812 937-7084
Chrisney (G-1641)
Anchor Industries ....G 812 664-0772
Owensville (G-11427)
Anchor Industries Inc ....D 812 867-2421
Evansville (G-3357)
Anglers Manufacturing ....G 812 988-8040
Nashville (G-10713)
◆ ARC Industries ....G 812 471-1633
Evansville (G-3361)
ARC of Greater Boone Cnty Inc ....F 765 482-0051
Lebanon (G-9169)
Armor Contract Mfg Inc ....F 574 327-2962
Elkhart (G-2695)
ASAP Identification SEC Inc ....F 317 488-1030
Indianapolis (G-6424)
Ashe Industries ....G 219 852-6040
Hammond (G-5844)
Aspire Industries ....F 812 542-1561
New Albany (G-10748)
Aunt Netts Country Candles LLC ....G 765 557-2770
Elwood (G-3294)
Aus Embroidery Inc ....G 317 899-1225
Indianapolis (G-6440)
Austins Metal Mafia Inc ....G 812 619-6115
Cannelton (G-1286)
AVO Candle Company LLC ....G 812 822-2302
Bloomington (G-668)
Awards America ....E 219 462-7903
Valparaiso (G-13501)
B Honey & Candles ....G 574 642-1145
Shipshewana (G-12605)
◆ B&R Manufacturing Inc ....G 574 293-5669
Elkhart (G-2711)
B2 Manufacturing LLC ....G 765 993-4519
Fountain City (G-4784)
Bantam Industries Inc ....G 714 561-6122
Indianapolis (G-6456)
Bawel Industries LP ....G 812 634-8004
Jasper (G-8238)
Bbs Celebration Center ....G 765 730-6575
Yorktown (G-14402)
Becks Bird Feeders ....G 765 874-1496
Markleville (G-9586)
Benchmark Consumer Industries ....G 317 576-0931
Fishers (G-3878)
BF Goodrich Tire Manufacturing ....G 260 493-8100
Woodburn (G-14380)
Bittersweet Candle Company LLC ....F 317 782-3170
Indianapolis (G-6478)
Bkb Manufacturing Inc ....G 260 982-8524
North Manchester (G-11225)
▼ Braun Corporation ....B 574 946-6153
Winamac (G-14301)
Brothers Industries ....G 812 560-6224
Greensburg (G-5592)
Brunk Corp ....E 574 533-1109
Goshen (G-5180)
Burkhart Manufacturing Inc ....G 260 316-0715
Angola (G-200)
▲ Buztronics Inc ....D 317 876-3413
Brownsburg (G-1140)
Byers Scientific Mfg ....G 812 269-6218
Bloomington (G-693)
Byrd Industries ....G 812 867-5859
Evansville (G-3406)
C & B Industries LLC ....G 260 490-3000
Fort Wayne (G-4128)

C & C Industries ....G 260 804-6518
Fort Wayne (G-4129)
C & F Industries ....G 765 580-0378
Liberty (G-9257)
C & J K Industries Inc ....G 219 746-5760
Munster (G-10600)
C & P Distributing LLC ....E 574 256-1138
Mishawaka (G-10016)
C&B Industries LLC ....G 260 493-3288
Fort Wayne (G-4132)
CA Steel Country Candles ....G 812 290-8516
Aurora (G-374)
Cali Nail ....G 574 674-4126
Osceola (G-11373)
Caliente ....G 260 471-0700
Fort Wayne (G-4136)
▲ Candles By Dar Inc ....F 260 482-2099
Fort Wayne (G-4139)
Carousel Industries ....G 317 674-8111
Fishers (G-3885)
Carter Enterprises Inc ....G 317 984-1497
Arcadia (G-262)
Carters Manufacturing & Weld ....G 630 464-1520
Knox (G-8563)
CCM Industries Inc ....G 765 545-0597
Winchester (G-14326)
Cde Industries LLC ....G 317 573-6790
Indianapolis (G-6571)
Celestial Candle ....G 812 886-4819
Vincennes (G-13672)
Chapdells Tree & Plant Design ....G 317 845-9980
Fishers (G-3888)
Christian Candle Company ....G 317 427-8070
Indianapolis (G-6602)
Christys Candles Inc ....G 812 273-3072
Madison (G-9450)
Churchill Cigars ....G 812 273-2249
Madison (G-9451)
Cigarettes Plus ....G 574 267-3166
Warsaw (G-13856)
Clover Industries LLC ....G 574 892-5760
Argos (G-273)
Cobar Industries Inc ....G 317 691-7124
Indianapolis (G-6627)
Cobo Industries ....G 812 341-4318
Indianapolis (G-6628)
Coffman & Fairbanks Industries ....G 765 458-7896
Liberty (G-9259)
Commercial Technical Svcs Inc ....G 260 436-9898
Fort Wayne (G-4169)
Containmed Inc ....E 317 487-8800
Speedway (G-13011)
Cosmoprof ....G 317 897-0124
Indianapolis (G-6672)
Cottage Industries DBA ....G 765 617-8360
Alexandria (G-38)
Cottage Industries Inc ....G 260 482-1100
Fort Wayne (G-4181)
Country Barn Candles LLC ....G 812 299-2929
Terre Haute (G-13217)
Covidien LP ....E 317 837-8199
Plainfield (G-11602)
Crichlow Industries Inc ....G 317 925-5178
Indianapolis (G-6692)
Csn Industries Inc ....G 317 697-6549
Bargersville (G-479)
CT Industries LLC ....G 574 675-9422
Granger (G-5398)
Custom Fitz LLC ....G 219 405-0896
Porter (G-11803)
Custom Mfg & Fabrication LLC ....G 260 908-1088
Auburn (G-326)
D & F Industries Inc ....G 219 865-2926
Schererville (G-12319)
D A Merriman Inc ....G 260 636-3464
Albion (G-23)
D&A Industries Inc ....G 260 357-1830
Garrett (G-5000)
Damage Industries II LLC ....G 574 256-7006
Mishawaka (G-10029)
Darlage Investments LLC ....F 812 522-5929
Seymour (G-12443)
Davis Industries Inc ....G 317 871-0103
Indianapolis (G-6728)
Decatur Plastic Products Inc ....D 812 352-6050
North Vernon (G-11254)
▲ Derby Industries LLC ....G 765 778-6104
Anderson (G-94)
Dj Wreath Creations LLC ....G 317 723-3268
Indianapolis (G-6754)

DMC Distribution LLC............G....... 219 926-6401
Porter (G-11805)
Dmp Industries LLC............G....... 260 413-6701
Warsaw (G-13867)
Door Tech Industries Inc............G....... 219 322-3465
Dyer (G-2494)
Dragon Industries Incorporated............G....... 574 772-3508
Knox (G-8565)
Drummond Industries............F....... 260 348-5550
Fort Wayne (G-4221)
Dubois Equipment Company LLC............E....... 812 482-3644
Jasper (G-8248)
Dubois Manufacturing Inc............G....... 574 674-6988
Elkhart (G-2801)
Dynatect Manufacturing Inc............G....... 219 465-1898
Valparaiso (G-13531)
E-Beam Services Inc............G....... 765 447-6755
Lafayette (G-8893)
Earthy Industries LLC............G....... 260 483-7588
Fort Wayne (G-4232)
East Industries LLC............G....... 812 273-4358
Madison (G-9459)
Eastons Lettering Service............G....... 219 942-5101
Hobart (G-6078)
Echo Manufacturing LLC............G....... 574 333-3669
Elkhart (G-2812)
▲ Edsal Inc............G....... 219 427-1294
Gary (G-5043)
Eligius Industries LLC............G....... 574 267-5313
Warsaw (G-13869)
Elite Industries LLC............G....... 317 407-6869
Indianapolis (G-6838)
Elliott Manufacturing and Fabr............G....... 812 865-0516
Paoli (G-11449)
Ellwocks Auto Parts Restorat............G....... 812 962-4942
Newburgh (G-11027)
Energy Saver Lights Inc............F....... 202 544-7868
Indianapolis (G-6866)
English Industries LLC............G....... 812 218-9882
Jeffersonville (G-8355)
Enhanced Mfg Solutions LLC............G....... 812 932-1101
Batesville (G-499)
Excel Industries Inc............G....... 574 264-2131
Elkhart (G-2840)
Fabcore Industries LLC............G....... 260 438-3431
Fort Wayne (G-4252)
Farm Finds Candle Co LLC............G....... 260 437-5403
Fort Wayne (G-4255)
Fast Manufacturing LLC............G....... 219 778-8123
Rolling Prairie (G-12185)
Fia-Indiana............G....... 812 895-4700
Vincennes (G-13681)
Fillmanns Industries LLC............G....... 765 744-4772
Daleville (G-2339)
Filmtec Fabrications LLC............G....... 419 435-7504
Fort Wayne (G-4262)
Fire Star Industries LLC............G....... 317 432-3212
Greenwood (G-5695)
Floralcraft Distributors............G....... 574 262-2639
Elkhart (G-2859)
Foamiture............G....... 574 831-4775
New Paris (G-10980)
Forterra Concrete Inds Inc............G....... 812 426-5353
Evansville (G-3512)
Foy Industries............G....... 317 727-3905
Indianapolis (G-6954)
Frankinstein Industries Inc............G....... 217 918-4548
Indianapolis (G-6958)
Fruition Industries LLC............G....... 260 854-2325
Rome City (G-12199)
Fuel Fabrication LLC............G....... 219 390-7022
Crown Point (G-2255)
Fur Real Taxidermy LLC............G....... 812 667-6365
Cross Plains (G-2212)
G F M S Industries............G....... 219 464-1445
Valparaiso (G-13545)
Gdp Industries LLC............G....... 260 414-4003
Fort Wayne (G-4293)
Gem Industries Inc............G....... 574 773-4513
Nappanee (G-10673)
Geny Industries LLC............G....... 574 536-0297
Bremen (G-999)
Gnome Industries Inc............G....... 219 764-3337
Valparaiso (G-13549)
Goat Industries LLC............G....... 770 940-0433
Indianapolis (G-7017)
Gold Standard Truss LLC............G....... 219 987-7781
Demotte (G-2438)
Goodlife Industries Inc............G....... 317 339-6341
Indianapolis (G-7024)
Goodwill Industries............G....... 317 546-7251
Indianapolis (G-7027)
▲ Goodwill Industries............E....... 317 524-4293
Indianapolis (G-7028)
Goose Bumps LLC............G....... 765 491-2142
West Lafayette (G-14071)
Grand Products Inc............C....... 317 870-3122
Indianapolis (G-7034)
Graysville Mfg Inc............G....... 812 382-4616
Sullivan (G-13083)
Great Lakes Waterjet Inc............G....... 574 651-2158
Granger (G-5411)
Green Dog............G....... 260 483-1267
Fort Wayne (G-4308)
Green Mountain Industries LLC............G....... 812 585-1531
Centerpoint (G-1538)
Green Way Candle Company LLC............G....... 574 536-3802
Goshen (G-5230)
◆ H A Industries............G....... 219 931-6304
Hammond (G-5883)
Hager Industries Inc............G....... 317 219-6622
Noblesville (G-11117)
Hair Necessities............G....... 812 288-5887
Clarksville (G-1685)
Hangout At Flames LLC............G....... 765 483-2009
Lebanon (G-9186)
Havoc Motor Company LLC............G....... 973 407-9933
Elkhart (G-2910)
Haynes Honey LLC............G....... 260 563-6397
Wabash (G-13728)
Hensley Composites LLC............G....... 574 202-3840
Elkhart (G-2913)
Hentz Mfg LLC............G....... 260 469-0800
Fort Wayne (G-4331)
Hestad Industries Inc............G....... 574 271-7609
Granger (G-5412)
Hicks Mfg............G....... 317 219-9891
Carmel (G-1404)
High Velocity Manufacturing............G....... 260 413-8429
Fort Wayne (G-4333)
Highpoint Mfg LLC............G....... 812 273-8987
Madison (G-9466)
HK Manufacturing Inc............G....... 260 925-1680
Auburn (G-336)
Holiday House Inc............E....... 574 773-9536
Nappanee (G-10683)
Homestead Industries Inc............G....... 574 273-5274
Granger (G-5413)
Houghton Mifflin Harcourt Co............G....... 317 359-5585
Indianapolis (G-7137)
Hurst Enterprise............G....... 812 853-0901
Newburgh (G-11031)
Ilpea Industries Inc............F....... 812 752-2526
Evansville (G-3546)
Imagine Industries LLC............G....... 260 494-6530
Fort Wayne (G-4360)
Indiana Manufacturing Inst............G....... 765 494-4935
West Lafayette (G-14077)
Indiana Materials Proc LLC............F....... 260 244-6026
Columbia City (G-1795)
Industrial Utilities Inc............G....... 812 346-4489
North Vernon (G-11265)
Industries LLC............G....... 765 759-5577
Yorktown (G-14406)
◆ Ingredion Incorporated............E....... 317 635-4455
Indianapolis (G-7230)
Integritech Mfg Inc............G....... 574 656-3046
North Liberty (G-11217)
Irish Industries............G....... 773 213-2422
McCordsville (G-9672)
Iron Men Industries Inc............G....... 574 596-2251
Russiaville (G-12242)
Jacobs Country Candles LLC............G....... 765 557-0260
Elwood (G-3302)
Jacobs Mfg LLC............G....... 765 490-6111
Lafayette (G-8928)
▲ Jadco Ltd............F....... 219 661-2065
Crown Point (G-2265)
Jani Industries Inc............G....... 317 985-3916
Avon (G-449)
JG and JG Industries LLC............G....... 765 742-0260
Lafayette (G-8932)
Jlp Manufacturing LLC............G....... 765 647-2991
Brookville (G-1120)
Joy Ml Industries Inc............G....... 317 876-3917
Indianapolis (G-7314)
Jrds Industries............G....... 260 729-5037
Portland (G-11832)
Junoll Industries............G....... 574 586-2719
Walkerton (G-13804)
K&P Industries LLC............G....... 317 881-9245
Greenwood (G-5711)
K-M Machine & Mfg............G....... 765 886-5717
Economy (G-2592)
Karma Industries Inc............G....... 765 742-9200
Lafayette (G-8937)
Keck Fine Art............G....... 219 306-9474
Coal City (G-1741)
Keihin Ipt Mfg............G....... 317 578-5260
Indianapolis (G-7340)
Kemco Manufacturing LLC............G....... 574 546-2025
Bremen (G-1008)
KS Kreations............G....... 574 514-7366
Georgetown (G-5147)
▼ Kt Industries LLC............G....... 260 432-0027
Fort Wayne (G-4417)
Lafferty & Lafferty LLC............G....... 574 935-4852
Plymouth (G-11700)
Lamarvis Industries LLC............G....... 317 797-0483
Terre Haute (G-13269)
Lambright Country Chimes L L C............G....... 260 768-9138
Shipshewana (G-12629)
Lamco Finishers Inc............E....... 317 471-1010
Indianapolis (G-7379)
Lawrence Industries............G....... 260 432-9693
Columbia City (G-1807)
Lee Mfg LLC............G....... 260 403-2775
Fort Wayne (G-4429)
Leland Manufacturing............G....... 812 367-2068
Ferdinand (G-3857)
Lennon Industries............G....... 219 996-6024
Hebron (G-6017)
Lhp Software LLC............D....... 812 373-0870
Columbus (G-1960)
Licensed Eliquid Manufacturing............G....... 260 687-9213
Fort Wayne (G-4433)
Light Mine Candle Company LLC............G....... 317 353-7786
Indianapolis (G-7405)
Lighthouse Creat Candles Gifts............G....... 765 342-2920
Martinsville (G-9620)
Lil Girls Glam LLC............G....... 317 507-3443
Indianapolis (G-7406)
Lippert Extrusions............G....... 574 312-6467
Elkhart (G-3003)
▼ Litko Aerosystems Inc............G....... 219 462-9295
Valparaiso (G-13577)
Little Mfg LLC............G....... 812 453-8137
Boonville (G-916)
Lloyds of Indiana Inc............G....... 317 251-5430
Indianapolis (G-7411)
Lozano Wldg & Fabrication LLC............G....... 812 858-1379
Newburgh (G-11037)
▲ LSI Wallcovering Inc............D....... 502 458-1502
New Albany (G-10820)
Lsm Manufacturing LLC............G....... 260 409-4030
Grabill (G-5379)
Lucas Oil Products Inc............G....... 317 569-0039
Carmel (G-1428)
Luckmann Industries............G....... 317 464-0323
Indianapolis (G-7424)
M & J Shelton Enterprises Inc............G....... 260 745-1616
Fort Wayne (G-4446)
M & S Curtis LLC............G....... 317 946-8440
Indianapolis (G-7431)
M M Converting Inc............G....... 260 563-7411
Wabash (G-13735)
M2 Industries LLC............G....... 812 246-0651
Jeffersonville (G-8392)
Madison River Industries LLC............G....... 317 472-6375
Noblesville (G-11144)
Magic Candle Inc............G....... 317 357-1101
Indianapolis (G-7437)
Mainline Manufacturing Company............G....... 219 237-0770
Griffith (G-5782)
Mamon Global Industries Inc............G....... 317 721-1657
Fort Wayne (G-4450)
Martin Industries............G....... 502 553-6599
New Albany (G-10822)
▼ Master Spas Inc............C....... 260 436-9100
Fort Wayne (G-4456)
Maxwell Engineering Inc............G....... 260 745-4991
Fort Wayne (G-4458)
MBC Cereal Fines Inc............G....... 812 299-2191
Terre Haute (G-13281)
Medical Structures Mfg Corp............G....... 574 612-0353
Elkhart (G-3027)
Memories By Design Inc............G....... 317 254-1708
Indianapolis (G-7478)
Mercs Miniatures LLC............G....... 765 661-6724
Westfield (G-14176)

Merritt Manufacturing Inc ....G 317 422-1167
Bargersville (G-485)

Meteor Manufacturing LLC ....G 317 587-1414
Carmel (G-1439)

Michiana Lift Equipment Inc ....G 574 257-1665
Mishawaka (G-10082)

Mid America Prototyping Inc ....G 765 643-3200
Anderson (G-135)

Miles Systems Manufacturing ....G 574 988-0067
New Carlisle (G-10885)

Mitek Usa Inc ....D 219 924-3835
Griffith (G-5786)

Mk Mfg LLC ....G 260 768-4678
Shipshewana (G-12637)

Mobile Dental Van Mfg ....G 812 626-3010
Evansville (G-3632)

Modern Biology Incorporated ....E 765 523-3338
Lafayette (G-8972)

Moosein Industries LLC ....G 219 406-7306
Portage (G-11780)

Navspar Industries LLC ....G 812 344-1476
Columbus (G-1979)

Nemcomed Instrs & Implants ....G 800 255-4576
Fort Wayne (G-4496)

Nick-Em Builders LLC ....G 574 516-1060
Logansport (G-9360)

NM Industries LLC ....G 812 985-3608
Evansville (G-3645)

▲ Norco Industries ....G 800 347-2232
Elkhart (G-3064)

Nova Manufacturing ....G 512 750-5165
Avon (G-458)

NPS Xofigo Mfg Plant 5889 ....G 317 981-4129
Indianapolis (G-7602)

▲ Nuwave Manufacturing ....G 317 987-8229
Indianapolis (G-7606)

Omega Co ....G 317 831-4471
Mooresville (G-10330)

Osterfeld Industries ....G 219 926-4646
Chesterton (G-1626)

Outdoor Industries ....G 574 551-5936
Warsaw (G-13921)

Ovr There Industries Inc ....G 317 946-8365
Indianapolis (G-7639)

P & M Fabrication ....G 812 232-7640
Terre Haute (G-13295)

Panglass Industries Inc ....G 574 217-8505
Mishawaka (G-10099)

Papayan Industries ....G 765 387-7274
West Lafayette (G-14092)

Pbs Mfg LLC ....G 317 515-2875
Indianapolis (G-7665)

Pdk Industries Inc ....G 765 721-3085
Greencastle (G-5471)

Peerless Manufacturing ....G 260 897-3070
Laotto (G-9114)

Peerless Manufacturing LLC ....G 260 760-0880
Avilla (G-417)

Peerless Mfg Co ....G 260 357-3271
Garrett (G-5019)

Pgw Industries Inc ....G 317 322-3599
Indianapolis (G-7682)

Phantom Industries LLC ....G 812 276-5956
Jeffersonville (G-8414)

Pinnacle Manufacturing Group ....G 317 691-2460
Indianapolis (G-7694)

Pioneer Signs Inc ....F 219 884-7587
Merrillville (G-9746)

Planet Pets ....G 812 539-7316
Lawrenceburg (G-9152)

Plaquemaker Plus Inc ....G 317 594-5556
Fishers (G-3952)

Plastimatic Arts Corp ....E 574 254-9000
Mishawaka (G-10104)

Platinum Industries LLC ....G 765 744-8323
Fishers (G-3953)

Pollution Control Industries ....E 219 391-7020
East Chicago (G-2561)

Portable Left Foot Accelerator ....G 260 637-4447
Fort Wayne (G-4540)

Preciball USA ....G 812 257-5555
Washington (G-14000)

Predator Percussion LLC ....G 317 919-7659
New Whiteland (G-11013)

Prime Time Manufacturing ....G 574 862-3001
Wakarusa (G-13790)

Pro Series Products LLC ....G 812 793-3506
Crothersville (G-2219)

Procoat Products Inc ....G 812 352-6083
North Vernon (G-11279)

◆ Prowler Industries LLC ....F 877 477-6953
Greensburg (G-5630)

Prysm Inc ....G 317 324-1222
Carmel (G-1459)

Pure Image Laser and Spa LLC ....G 317 306-6603
Indianapolis (G-7790)

R M Mfg Housing Svc ....G 574 288-5207
South Bend (G-12912)

R N A Industries Corp ....G 765 288-4413
Redkey (G-11899)

Rappid Mfg Inc ....G 317 440-8084
Indianapolis (G-7816)

Raw Design and Fabrication LLC ....G 708 466-5835
Saint John (G-12269)

▲ Rbc Manufacturing Corp ....C 260 416-5400
Fort Wayne (G-4579)

RE Industries Inc ....G 219 987-1764
Demotte (G-2446)

Realize Inc ....F 317 915-0295
Noblesville (G-11172)

Redab Industries ....G 219 484-8382
Crown Point (G-2293)

Redman Industries LLC ....G 317 768-3004
Zionsville (G-14459)

Redstar Contract Manufacturing ....G 260 327-3145
Larwill (G-9126)

Reilly Industries Inc ....G 317 247-8141
Indianapolis (G-7829)

Resourcemfg ....G 574 206-1522
Elkhart (G-3144)

Ridge Iron LLC ....G 646 450-0092
Plymouth (G-11722)

Ring Industries Inc ....G 219 204-1577
Lake Village (G-9087)

Ronlewhorn Industries LLC ....G 765 661-9343
Indianapolis (G-7860)

Rose Industries LLC ....G 260 348-2610
Fort Wayne (G-4596)

Rosmarino Candles LLC ....G 970 218-2835
Bloomington (G-818)

Rowan Industries LLC ....G 574 302-1203
South Bend (G-12919)

Rustic Glow Candle Co LLC ....G 317 696-4264
Indianapolis (G-7875)

S & J Creative Design LLC ....G 765 251-0110
Wabash (G-13754)

Scaggs Moto Designs ....G 765 426-2526
West Lafayette (G-14106)

Schmigbob LLC ....G 219 781-7991
Crown Point (G-2300)

▲ Schwartz Manufacturing Inc ....G 260 589-3865
Berne (G-622)

Searle Exhibit Tech Inc ....F 317 787-3012
Indianapolis (G-7907)

Sebasty Manufacturing Inc ....G 574 505-1511
Laketon (G-9091)

Sentinel Services Inc ....F 574 360-5279
Granger (G-5432)

Shark-Co Mfg LLC ....G 317 670-6397
Lebanon (G-9223)

Sherrcom Industries LLC ....G 574 266-7389
Elkhart (G-3165)

Shields Mech & Fabrication LLC ....G 219 863-3972
Demotte (G-2447)

Sittin Pretty LLC ....G 219 947-4121
Crown Point (G-2306)

SLM Industries LLC ....G 317 537-1090
Indianapolis (G-7952)

SM Industries LLC ....G 219 613-5295
Saint John (G-12271)

Smart Pergola ....G 317 987-7750
Carmel (G-1482)

Smoke Smoke Smoke ....G 219 942-3331
Hobart (G-6096)

Smokestack Industries LLC ....G 812 267-8646
Elizabeth (G-2648)

So Industries LLC ....G 765 606-7596
Pendleton (G-11506)

Sonner Industries LLC ....G 574 370-9387
Middlebury (G-9919)

Specialty Manufacturing ....G 317 587-4999
Carmel (G-1484)

Star Manufacturing LLC ....G 574 329-6042
Elkhart (G-3188)

Startracks Custom Lifts ....G 574 596-5331
Elkhart (G-3190)

State Beauty Supply ....G 260 755-6361
Fort Wayne (G-4645)

Strategic Mfg & Sup Inc ....G 574 643-1050
South Bend (G-12957)

▲ T & S Equipment Company ....C 260 665-9521
Angola (G-249)

T S Manufacturing ....G 574 831-6647
New Paris (G-10998)

Tango Romeo Industries LLC ....G 765 623-1317
Pendleton (G-11507)

Taunyas Creative Cuts ....G 812 574-7722
Madison (G-9497)

Taurus Tech & Engrg LLC ....E 765 282-2090
Muncie (G-10568)

Taylor Made Candles ....G 812 663-6634
Greensburg (G-5636)

Tbin LLC ....G 812 491-9100
Princeton (G-11883)

▲ Techcom Inc ....G 317 865-2530
Indianapolis (G-8048)

Techcom Inc ....F 812 372-0960
Columbus (G-2020)

Terrapin Mfg ....G 717 339-6007
Fort Wayne (G-4679)

Thanatos Manufacturing LLC ....G 260 251-8498
Portland (G-11850)

The Eminence Hair Collectn LLC ....G 317 222-5085
Indianapolis (G-8057)

Thermtron Mfg Inc ....G 260 622-6000
Ossian (G-11413)

Thomas Strickler ....G 574 457-2473
Syracuse (G-13149)

Thomson Industries Inc ....G 574 529-2496
Syracuse (G-13150)

Thoroughbred Industries Inc ....G 260 486-8343
Fort Wayne (G-4683)

Thyssenkrupp Elevator Corp ....E 317 595-1125
Indianapolis (G-8074)

Timberlight Mfg Co ....G 317 694-1317
Martinsville (G-9642)

Titus Mfg LLC ....G 574 286-1928
Plymouth (G-11729)

Tomlinson Manufacturing ....G 800 881-9769
Indianapolis (G-8080)

Tomlinson Manufacturing ....G 317 209-9375
Avon (G-470)

Topgard LLC ....G 317 525-0700
Indianapolis (G-8082)

Topps Industries ....G 574 892-5016
Argos (G-279)

Trans Industries Incorporated ....G 219 977-9190
Gary (G-5108)

Transformation Industries LLC ....G 574 457-9320
South Bend (G-12977)

Tri-State Shtmtl & Mfg LLC ....G 260 402-8831
Fort Wayne (G-4703)

Trinity Displays Inc ....G 219 201-8733
Michigan City (G-9854)

True Precision Tech Inc ....G 765 252-9766
Kokomo (G-8710)

Trv Industries ....G 765 413-2301
Lafayette (G-9011)

Turnkey Instrument Solutions ....G 317 946-6354
Indianapolis (G-8114)

Twisod Wick Candle Company ....G 317 490-4789
Martinsville (G-9645)

Twisted Wick Candle Co ....G 812 988-6123
Nashville (G-10735)

Ultimate Mfg ....G 765 517-1160
Marion (G-9569)

Unplug Soy Candles LLC ....G 317 650-5776
Fortville (G-4783)

Vandelay Industries ....G 317 657-6205
Indianapolis (G-8147)

◆ Vestil Manufacturing Corp ....B 260 665-7586
Angola (G-258)

Vickie Hildreth ....G 812 350-3575
Columbus (G-2029)

Victory Mfg ....G 317 731-5063
Indianapolis (G-8162)

Village Candlemaker Inc ....G 812 988-7201
Nashville (G-10737)

Wabcoindustries LLC ....G 317 361-3653
Indianapolis (G-8174)

Walls Lawn & Garden Inc ....G 317 535-9059
Whiteland (G-14247)

Warm Glow Candle Company ....E 765 855-5483
Centerville (G-1544)

Wayne Manufacturing LLC ....G 260 432-2233
Fort Wayne (G-4741)

Whetstone Industries ....G 260 724-2461
Decatur (G-2412)

Whistle Stop ....G 219 253-4100
Monon (G-10180)

White Cap LLC ....G...... 812 425-6221
Evansville *(G-3812)*

Wiley Industries Inc ....G...... 317 574-1477
Carmel *(G-1510)*

Williams Bros Health Care Inc ....E...... 812 257-2505
Washington *(G-14007)*

Williams Bros Health Care Pha ....C...... 812 254-2497
Washington *(G-14008)*

Williams Bros Health Care Pha ....E...... 812 335-0000
Bloomington *(G-856)*

Wimmer Mfg Inc ....F...... 765 465-9846
New Castle *(G-10922)*

Windsong K-9 Coach Inc ....G...... 574 971-6358
Elkhart *(G-3260)*

XYZ Model Works ....G...... 260 413-1873
Decatur *(G-2413)*

Yankee Candle Company Inc ....G...... 812 526-5195
Edinburgh *(G-2632)*

Yankee Candle Company Inc ....G...... 812 234-1717
Terre Haute *(G-13373)*

Yellow Cup LLC ....G...... 260 403-3489
Fort Wayne *(G-4763)*

Yes Feed & Supply LLC ....G...... 765 361-9821
Crawfordsville *(G-2206)*

York Tank and Mfg LLC ....F...... 765 401-0667
Kingman *(G-8534)*

Young & Kenady Incorporated ....G...... 317 852-6300
Brownsburg *(G-1178)*

73 BUSINESS SERVICES

7372 Prepackaged Software

250ok LLC ....G...... 855 250-6529
Indianapolis *(G-6285)*

A Dine Tech Inc ....G...... 219 464-4764
Valparaiso *(G-13480)*

Accent Software Inc ....G...... 317 846-6025
Carmel *(G-1300)*

Adaptasoft Inc ....F...... 219 567-2547
Francesville *(G-4808)*

Aging Parent Software ....G...... 317 848-9548
Carmel *(G-1305)*

Akori Software ....G...... 574 595-5413
Rochester *(G-12115)*

Anabaptist Mennonite Biblical ....D...... 574 295-3726
Elkhart *(G-2691)*

App Press LLC ....G...... 317 661-4759
Indianapolis *(G-6408)*

Application Software ....G...... 317 814-8010
Greenfield *(G-5503)*

Application Software ....G...... 317 843-9775
Carmel *(G-1314)*

Application Software Inc ....G...... 317 823-3525
Indianapolis *(G-6410)*

Aptera Software Inc ....G...... 260 969-1410
Fort Wayne *(G-4087)*

Ark Software LLC ....G...... 317 835-7912
Fountaintown *(G-4788)*

Artemis Intl Solutions Corp ....G...... 708 665-3155
Valparaiso *(G-13498)*

Articode Inc ....G...... 317 569-8357
Carmel *(G-1315)*

Aspen Solutions Group Inc ....G...... 317 839-9274
Avon *(G-429)*

Aunalytics Inc ....G...... 574 307-9230
South Bend *(G-12716)*

Awave Software LLC ....G...... 219 285-1852
Munster *(G-10598)*

Black Ember LLC ....G...... 317 840-5523
Indianapolis *(G-6482)*

Blackboxit Inc ....G...... 260 489-8014
Fort Wayne *(G-4112)*

Blue Burro Inc ....G...... 904 825-9900
Bloomington *(G-689)*

Blue Pillar Inc ....E...... 317 723-6601
Indianapolis *(G-6488)*

Blue Sun Ventures Ltd ....G...... 317 426-0001
Indianapolis *(G-6490)*

Bluefin Software LLC ....G...... 574 643-1091
South Bend *(G-12724)*

Bolstra LLC ....G...... 317 660-9131
Carmel *(G-1320)*

Boomstick Interactive LLC ....G...... 812 528-4875
Indianapolis *(G-6496)*

Brangene LLC ....G...... 317 203-9172
Plainfield *(G-11597)*

Bronze Bow Software Inc ....G...... 260 672-9516
Roanoke *(G-12100)*

C&S Solutions ....G...... 812 895-0048
Vincennes *(G-13671)*

Cad/CAM Technologies Inc ....G...... 765 778-2020
Pendleton *(G-11487)*

Captivated LLC ....G...... 317 554-7400
Carmel *(G-1328)*

Casper Inc ....G...... 660 221-5906
Indianapolis *(G-6564)*

Catalyst Inc ....G...... 317 227-3499
Indianapolis *(G-6566)*

Cheddar Stacks Inc ....G...... 317 566-0425
Indianapolis *(G-6595)*

Clear Software LLC ....G...... 317 732-8831
Zionsville *(G-14427)*

Clinical Architecture LLC ....E...... 317 580-8400
Carmel *(G-1341)*

Compumark Industries Inc ....G...... 219 365-0508
Saint John *(G-12261)*

Computrain Learning Center Inc ....F...... 812 235-7419
Terre Haute *(G-13216)*

Cooperative Ventures Ind Corp ....G...... 317 259-7063
Carmel *(G-1343)*

Cornerstone Communications LLC ....F...... 317 802-0107
Indianapolis *(G-6669)*

Corvano LLC ....G...... 317 403-0471
Fishers *(G-3894)*

Createit Hlthcare Slutions Inc ....G...... 765 993-0988
Richmond *(G-11974)*

Crowdpixie LLC ....G...... 317 578-3137
Fishers *(G-3895)*

Crusaderbit Software LLC ....G...... 317 773-2317
Noblesville *(G-11088)*

Cummins Digital Ventures Inc ....E...... 812 377-5000
Columbus *(G-1887)*

Curvo Labs Inc ....G...... 619 316-1202
Evansville *(G-3448)*

D X Systems ....G...... 812 332-4699
Bloomington *(G-710)*

Dallara Research Center LLC ....G...... 317 388-5416
Speedway *(G-13013)*

Dallara USA Holding Inc ....G...... 317 388-5400
Speedway *(G-13014)*

Data-Vision Inc ....F...... 574 243-8625
Mishawaka *(G-10033)*

Dedicated Software ....G...... 260 341-4166
Yoder *(G-14397)*

Depth Plus Design LLC ....G...... 317 370-0532
Westfield *(G-14158)*

Determine Inc ....E...... 317 594-8600
Carmel *(G-1356)*

Determine Inc ....C...... 650 532-1500
Carmel *(G-1357)*

Determine Sourcing Inc ....G...... 408 570-9700
Carmel *(G-1358)*

Diverse Tech Services Inc ....F...... 317 432-6444
Indianapolis *(G-6748)*

Do Technologies LLC ....G...... 812 272-2306
Bloomington *(G-714)*

Dotstaff LLC ....E...... 317 806-6100
Indianapolis *(G-6760)*

Eat Here Indy LLC ....G...... 317 502-4419
Indianapolis *(G-6794)*

Edtechzone LLC ....G...... 317 902-7594
Cloverdale *(G-1725)*

Emarsys North America Inc ....E...... 844 693-6277
Indianapolis *(G-6846)*

Emplify LLC ....E...... 800 580-5344
Fishers *(G-3904)*

Enghouse Networks (us) Inc ....D...... 317 262-4666
Indianapolis *(G-6867)*

Envisio Design LLC ....G...... 574 274-4394
Mishawaka *(G-10042)*

Envista LLC ....D...... 317 208-9100
Carmel *(G-1372)*

Envista Concepts LLC ....E...... 317 208-9100
Carmel *(G-1373)*

Envista Entp Solutions LLC ....E...... 317 208-9100
Carmel *(G-1374)*

Envista Freight Managment LLC ....F...... 317 208-9100
Carmel *(G-1375)*

Eon Performance LLC ....G...... 847 997-8619
Indianapolis *(G-6874)*

Everything Underground Inc ....G...... 317 491-8148
Indianapolis *(G-6883)*

Exacttarget Inc ....G...... 317 423-3928
Indianapolis *(G-6890)*

Express Study LLC ....G...... 812 272-2247
Bloomington *(G-722)*

Finvantage LLC ....F...... 317 500-4949
Carmel *(G-1381)*

Fiserv Mrtg Servicing Systems ....C...... 574 282-3300
South Bend *(G-12779)*

Flynn Media LLC ....G...... 317 536-2972
Indianapolis *(G-6942)*

Frank R Komar CPA ....G...... 812 477-9110
Evansville *(G-3513)*

Freehold Games LLC ....G...... 574 656-9031
Walkerton *(G-13802)*

Gale Force Software Corp ....F...... 317 570-4900
Fishers *(G-3915)*

Genesys Telecom Labs Inc ....G...... 317 715-8545
Indianapolis *(G-7000)*

Genesys Telecom Labs Inc ....A...... 317 872-3000
Indianapolis *(G-7001)*

Getsaydo LLC ....G...... 317 800-8319
Indianapolis *(G-7003)*

Glidepath Com LLC ....G...... 317 288-4459
Fishers *(G-3917)*

Glio Software Inc ....G...... 314 856-5855
Carmel *(G-1385)*

Greenwell Software LLC ....G...... 812 295-4665
Loogootee *(G-9384)*

Guide Technologies LLC ....G...... 317 844-3162
Indianapolis *(G-7058)*

Healthcare Data Inc ....F...... 812 342-9947
Morgantown *(G-10352)*

Helios LLC ....E...... 317 554-9911
Indianapolis *(G-7087)*

Help Help LLC ....G...... 317 910-6631
Avon *(G-446)*

Holli Helms ....G...... 574 253-8923
Warsaw *(G-13890)*

Hot Shot Multimedia Entps LLC ....G...... 317 537-7527
South Bend *(G-12805)*

▲ Hurco Companies Inc ....G...... 317 293-5309
Indianapolis *(G-7146)*

Hyperbole Software Unltd ....G...... 812 839-6635
Madison *(G-9471)*

Identity Logix LLC ....G...... 219 379-5560
Munster *(G-10608)*

Ike Newton LLC ....G...... 317 902-1772
Greenwood *(G-5705)*

Ilab LLC ....D...... 317 218-3258
Indianapolis *(G-7158)*

Imminent Software Inc ....G...... 317 340-4562
Carmel *(G-1410)*

Indigo Bioautomation Inc ....E...... 317 493-2400
Carmel *(G-1412)*

Industrial Software LLC ....G...... 317 862-0650
Indianapolis *(G-7211)*

Indy Mobile Apps LLC ....G...... 508 685-5240
Greenwood *(G-5707)*

Infinite Ai Inc ....G...... 317 965-4850
Carmel *(G-1415)*

Infront Software LLC ....G...... 317 501-1871
Fishers *(G-3988)*

Innovtive Nurological Dvcs LLC ....G...... 317 674-2999
Carmel *(G-1416)*

Insertec Inc ....D...... 800 556-1911
Indianapolis *(G-7240)*

Intelligent Software Inc ....G...... 219 923-6166
Munster *(G-10610)*

Intempo Software Inc ....G...... 800 950-2221
Indianapolis *(G-7251)*

Intuitive Software LLC ....G...... 574 268-8239
Warsaw *(G-13894)*

Ip Software Inc ....G...... 317 569-1313
Indianapolis *(G-6269)*

Jem Software Development LLC ....G...... 812 339-2970
Bloomington *(G-753)*

Jim Couch ....G...... 574 533-5107
Goshen *(G-5248)*

JKL Software ....G...... 765 778-3032
Pendleton *(G-11491)*

Jpe Consulting LLP ....G...... 574 675-9552
Osceola *(G-11379)*

Kaplan Inc ....D...... 317 872-7220
Indianapolis *(G-7333)*

Keystone Consulting Services ....G...... 260 693-0250
Churubusco *(G-1654)*

Kgn Software ....G...... 812 618-4723
Evansville *(G-3588)*

Knowledge Diffusion Games LLC ....G...... 812 361-4424
Bloomington *(G-759)*

Lactor LLC ....G...... 765 496-6838
West Lafayette *(G-14080)*

Laney Software Co ....G...... 260 312-0759
South Bend *(G-12835)*

Leadtrack Software ....G...... 317 823-0748
Indianapolis *(G-7389)*

Leaf Hut Software LLC ....G...... 317 770-3632
Fishers *(G-3938)*

Lessonly Inc ....D...... 317 469-9194
Indianapolis (G-7399)

Lh Software Concepts LLC ....G...... 317 222-1779
Indianapolis (G-7401)

Lhp Software LLC ....C...... 812 373-0870
Columbus (G-1959)

Lincs Software Corp ....G...... 812 204-3619
Evansville (G-3603)

Long Tail Corporation ....G...... 260 918-0489
Fort Wayne (G-4441)

Lord Fms Games ....G...... 317 710-2253
Indianapolis (G-7419)

Lots of Software LLC ....G...... 317 578-8120
Fishers (G-3940)

Luxly LLC ....G...... 617 415-8031
Carmel (G-1429)

M2m Holdings Inc ....A...... 317 249-1700
Indianapolis (G-7434)

Maddenco Inc ....F...... 812 474-6245
Evansville (G-3609)

Mag Software Inc ....G...... 317 755-4080
Zionsville (G-14446)

Marshall & Poe LLC ....E...... 574 266-5244
Elkhart (G-3019)

Mellon Tax Service ....G...... 219 947-1660
Hobart (G-6091)

Mental Rehabilitation ....G...... 765 414-5590
Lafayette (G-8966)

Mesh Systems LLC ....E...... 317 661-4800
Carmel (G-1437)

Metakite Software LLC ....G...... 317 441-7385
Fishers (G-3946)

Micro Businessware Inc ....G...... 502 424-6613
Jeffersonville (G-8400)

Microsoft Corporation ....F...... 317 705-6900
Indianapolis (G-7501)

Middletowne Software LLC ....G...... 765 760-5007
Muncie (G-10524)

Mike Burroughs Sftwr Dev LLC ....G...... 317 927-7195
Indianapolis (G-7514)

Mike Jones Software ....G...... 317 845-7479
Indianapolis (G-7515)

Millstone Specialties Inc ....G...... 765 653-7382
Greencastle (G-5468)

▲ Milltronics Usa Inc ....E...... 317 293-5309
Indianapolis (G-7523)

Mobile Enerlytics LLC ....G...... 765 464-6909
West Lafayette (G-14086)

Nechanna One Productions Corp ....G...... 317 400-8908
Indianapolis (G-7582)

No Pass LLC ....G...... 516 713-6885
Kokomo (G-8676)

Nolan Brubaker Software LLC ....G...... 574 238-0676
Goshen (G-5300)

Novacove LLC ....G...... 219 775-2966
Indianapolis (G-7600)

Octiv Inc ....D...... 317 550-0148
Indianapolis (G-7609)

Old Gary Inc ....G...... 941 755-0976
Merrillville (G-9742)

Oprato Software LLC ....G...... 317 573-0168
Carmel (G-1446)

Osc Holdings LLC ....G...... 765 751-7000
Muncie (G-10540)

Oxinas Partners LLC ....G...... 812 725-8649
Jeffersonville (G-8411)

Paradigm Software Corp ....G...... 317 770-7862
Cicero (G-1664)

Pathology Computer Systems ....G...... 812 265-3264
Madison (G-9490)

Patriot Software Solutions Inc ....G...... 317 573-5431
Indianapolis (G-7661)

Pineapple Software Inc ....G...... 812 987-8277
Borden (G-937)

Policystat LLC ....D...... 317 644-1296
Carmel (G-1452)

Propellerheads ....G...... 317 219-0408
Muncie (G-10549)

Quality Council of Indiana ....G...... 812 533-4215
West Terre Haute (G-14128)

Quality Data Products Inc ....G...... 317 595-0700
Fishers (G-3959)

RAD Cube LLC ....F...... 317 456-7560
Indianapolis (G-7813)

Rebound Project LLP ....G...... 765 621-5604
Anderson (G-158)

Recon Group LLP ....G...... 855 874-8741
Greenfield (G-5566)

Regional Data Services Inc ....F...... 219 661-3200
Crown Point (G-2295)

Registration System LLC ....G...... 317 548-4090
Fishers (G-3963)

Relational Gravity Inc ....G...... 317 855-7685
Indianapolis (G-7831)

Relational Intelligence LLC ....G...... 317 669-8900
Westfield (G-14183)

Renaissnce Electronic Svcs LLC ....E...... 317 786-2235
Indianapolis (G-7833)

Rics Software Inc ....E...... 317 455-5338
Indianapolis (G-7843)

Rightrez ....G...... 812 219-1893
Bloomington (G-812)

Rob Nolley Inc ....G...... 317 825-5211
Shelbyville (G-12563)

Rough Notes Company Inc ....E...... 800 428-4384
Carmel (G-1470)

Rox Software Inc ....G...... 765 430-7616
Brookston (G-1107)

Rs2 Technologies LLC ....F...... 877 682-3532
Munster (G-10628)

Rt Software ....G...... 317 578-8518
Fishers (G-3965)

S & S Programming Inc ....G...... 765 423-4472
Lafayette (G-8994)

Sahasra Technologies Corp ....E...... 317 845-5326
Indianapolis (G-7887)

Sanborn Software Systems LLC ....G...... 317 283-7735
Indianapolis (G-7891)

Satellite Software ....G...... 574 842-3370
Plymouth (G-11724)

School Doctor Notes LLC ....G...... 317 660-1552
Carmel (G-1476)

Seasoned Software LLC ....G...... 260 431-5666
Fort Wayne (G-4613)

Sedona Inc ....G...... 219 764-9675
Portage (G-11793)

Sharpen Technologies Inc ....D...... 855 249-3357
Indianapolis (G-7923)

Sigma Micro Corp ....G...... 317 631-6580
Indianapolis (G-7939)

Sim 2 K Inc ....F...... 317 251-7920
Indianapolis (G-7947)

Simeoc LLC ....G...... 240 210-5685
South Bend (G-12937)

Simma Software Inc ....G...... 812 418-0526
Terre Haute (G-13327)

Sleepy Owl Software LLC ....G...... 765 299-2862
Bloomington (G-825)

Snappy Minds Llc ....G...... 812 661-8506
Jasper (G-8310)

Software Informatics Group LLC ....G...... 317 326-2598
Greenfield (G-5575)

Software Pub LLC ....G...... 260 486-7839
Fort Wayne (G-4633)

Software Sales Incorporated ....G...... 317 258-7442
Whitestown (G-14262)

Software Sneak ....G...... 219 510-5894
Valparaiso (G-13622)

Speak Modalities LLC ....G...... 765 742-4252
West Lafayette (G-14109)

Sports Software Inc ....G...... 812 738-2735
Corydon (G-2113)

Spotlight Cybersecurity LLC ....G...... 805 886-4456
Lafayette (G-9001)

Spring Ventures Infovation LLC ....G...... 317 847-1117
Greenwood (G-5750)

SS&c Technologies Inc ....G...... 812 266-2000
Evansville (G-12240)

Standard For Success LLC ....F...... 844 737-3825
Cloverdale (G-1739)

Steady Demand LLC ....G...... 765 404-1763
Lafayette (G-9003)

Structural LLC ....G...... 317 713-7500
Indianapolis (G-8013)

Sugar Coded Software LLC ....G...... 858 652-0797
Westfield (G-14191)

Sunyata Software LLC ....G...... 310 923-1821
Indianapolis (G-8020)

Swifttrip LLC ....G...... 812 206-5200
Jeffersonville (G-8432)

Symantec Corporation ....G...... 317 575-4010
Indianapolis (G-8029)

Synergy Software Group Inc ....G...... 765 229-4003
Union City (G-13461)

Tab Software ....G...... 260 490-7132
Fort Wayne (G-4673)

Tag Software ....G...... 219 866-3100
Rensselaer (G-11941)

Tech Innovation LLC ....G...... 317 506-8343
Indianapolis (G-8046)

Technalysis Inc ....E...... 317 291-1985
Indianapolis (G-8049)

Tgx Medical Systems LLC ....F...... 317 575-0300
Carmel (G-1494)

Thickstat Inc ....G...... 201 294-1896
Indianapolis (G-8061)

Three Dog Software Inc ....G...... 317 823-7080
Indianapolis (G-8071)

Tk Software Inc ....G...... 317 569-8887
Carmel (G-1498)

Trackahead LLC ....G...... 800 780-3519
Fishers (G-3979)

Trh Software Inc ....G...... 812 264-2428
Terre Haute (G-13357)

Trill Machine LLC ....G...... 219 730-0744
Kentland (G-8524)

Trivaeo LLC ....G...... 765 387-4451
Montezuma (G-10212)

Two El Exito ....G...... 574 830-5104
Goshen (G-5344)

Uber Dragon Studios Inc ....G...... 317 520-2837
Carmel (G-1500)

User Wise Software Ltd ....G...... 317 894-1385
Indianapolis (G-8141)

Vizai LLC ....G...... 630 677-6583
Indianapolis (G-8167)

Voidteam Studios ....G...... 765 414-9777
Lafayette (G-9016)

Web Software LLC ....F...... 765 452-3936
Kokomo (G-8716)

Wolfe Diversified Inds LLC ....G...... 765 683-9374
Pendleton (G-11511)

Wolfgang Software ....G...... 317 443-5147
Fishers (G-3985)

Yoder Software Inc ....G...... 574 302-6232
South Bend (G-12993)

76 MISCELLANEOUS REPAIR SERVICES

7692 Welding Repair

ABF Welding & Pipe LLC ....G...... 765 977-7349
Cambridge City (G-1252)

Absolute Welding Inc ....G...... 812 923-8001
Borden (G-926)

Accurate Tool & Engineering ....G...... 812 963-6677
Evansville (G-3335)

Ace Welding and Machine Inc ....G...... 812 379-9625
Columbus (G-1849)

▲ Acro Engineering Inc ....E...... 812 663-6236
Greensburg (G-5588)

Allied Boiler & Welding Co ....G...... 317 272-4820
Avon (G-426)

American Machine Fabrication ....G...... 812 944-4136
New Albany (G-10744)

Amos D Graber & Sons ....F...... 260 749-0526
New Haven (G-10929)

Annette Balfour ....G...... 765 286-1910
Muncie (G-10431)

Applied Metals & Mch Works Inc ....E...... 260 424-4834
Fort Wayne (G-4083)

Atp Welding Inc ....G...... 765 483-9273
Lebanon (G-9170)

Auto Truck Group LLC ....F...... 260 356-1610
Huntington (G-6188)

B&M Millwright Inc ....G...... 765 883-8177
Russiaville (G-12240)

Barks Welding Supplies ....G...... 812 732-4366
Corydon (G-2089)

Bel-Mar Products Corporation ....G...... 317 769-3262
Whitestown (G-14249)

Best Equipment & Welding Co ....E...... 317 271-8652
Indianapolis (G-6468)

Bobs Welding Repair ....G...... 765 744-4192
Farmland (G-3840)

Brand Sheet Metal Works Inc ....G...... 765 284-5594
Muncie (G-10443)

Brazing Preforms LLC ....G...... 317 705-6455
Noblesville (G-11071)

Buchanan Iron Works Inc ....G...... 219 785-4480
Westville (G-14214)

C & S Sandblasting & Wldg LLC ....G...... 317 867-6341
Westfield (G-14140)

C M Welding Inc ....G...... 765 258-4024
Frankfort (G-4820)

C-Way Tool and Die Inc ....G...... 812 256-6341
Charlestown (G-1559)

Campbells Welding & Machine ....G...... 574 643-6705
Royal Center (G-12212)

Carmel Welding and Supply ....F 317 846-3493
  Carmel *(G-1333)*

Carmichael Welding Inc ....G...... 812 825-5156
  Bloomfield *(G-636)*

Central Welding Inc ....G...... 317 784-7730
  Indianapolis *(G-6585)*

Century Tool & Engineering ....G...... 317 685-0942
  Indianapolis *(G-6587)*

Certified Welding Co Inc ....G...... 765 522-3238
  Bainbridge *(G-475)*

Chappos Inc ....G...... 219 942-8101
  Hobart *(G-6074)*

Chesterfield Tool & Engrg Inc.........E 765 378-5101
  Daleville *(G-2338)*

Chief Metal Works Inc ....G...... 765 932-2134
  Rushville *(G-12217)*

Circle R Industries Inc ....G...... 765 379-2768
  Rossville *(G-12210)*

City Welding & Fabrication ....G...... 765 569-5403
  Rockville *(G-12175)*

Cline Brothers Welding ....G...... 812 738-3537
  Corydon *(G-2093)*

Collins Tool & Die Inc ....G...... 812 273-4765
  Madison *(G-9453)*

Conley Welding Specialties Inc ....G...... 260 343-9051
  Kendallville *(G-8466)*

Country Welding LLC ....G...... 260 352-2938
  Silver Lake *(G-12675)*

Craig Welding and Mfg Inc ....E 574 353-7912
  Mentone *(G-9687)*

Custom Gage & Tool Co Inc............G...... 317 547-8257
  Indianapolis *(G-6713)*

◆ Custom Machining Services Inc ......E 219 462-6128
  Valparaiso *(G-13525)*

Da-Mar Industries Inc ....F 260 347-1662
  Kendallville *(G-8471)*

Davids Inc ....F 812 376-6870
  Columbus *(G-1905)*

Davis Tool & Machine Inc ....F 317 896-9278
  Westfield *(G-14157)*

Davron Fabricating ....G...... 765 339-7303
  New Richmond *(G-11004)*

Denver Stone ....E 317 244-5889
  Indianapolis *(G-6734)*

Diverse Fabrication Services ....G...... 317 781-8800
  Indianapolis *(G-6746)*

Dougs Welding Shop ....G...... 765 689-8396
  Bunker Hill *(G-1205)*

E & H Industrial Services LLC ....F 317 569-8819
  Carmel *(G-1365)*

E & S Metal Inc ....F 260 563-7714
  Wabash *(G-13726)*

East Side Welding Inc ....G...... 317 823-4065
  Indianapolis *(G-6792)*

Ebwa Industries Inc ....F 317 637-5860
  Indianapolis *(G-6797)*

Eckstein Welding & Fabrication ......G...... 812 934-2059
  Batesville *(G-498)*

Edco Welding and Hydraulic Inc ......F 317 783-2323
  Indianapolis *(G-6804)*

Egenolf Machine Inc ....D...... 317 787-5301
  Indianapolis *(G-6814)*

Englert & Meyer Corporation ....G...... 812 683-3540
  Huntingburg *(G-6163)*

Ernies Welding Shop ....G...... 812 326-2600
  Saint Anthony *(G-12245)*

▲ Ernstberger Enterprises Inc ....D...... 812 282-0488
  Jeffersonville *(G-8358)*

F T Moore and Sons Inc ....G...... 812 466-3762
  Terre Haute *(G-13333)*

Fabcreation ....G...... 812 246-6222
  Sellersburg *(G-12394)*

Fancil Robert Welding Svc LLC ....G...... 574 267-8627
  Warsaw *(G-13874)*

Faulkner Fabricating Inc ....F 574 342-0022
  Bourbon *(G-942)*

Fayette Welding Service Inc ....G...... 317 852-2929
  Brownsburg *(G-1150)*

▲ Flare Inc ....G...... 260 490-1101
  Fort Wayne *(G-4265)*

Four Star Welding ....G...... 574 825-3856
  Middlebury *(G-9888)*

Fullenkamp Machine & Mfg Inc ....F 260 726-8345
  Portland *(G-11824)*

G & N Warehouse & Packaging ....G...... 574 234-3717
  South Bend *(G-12785)*

Gary Earl ....G...... 812 279-6780
  Bedford *(G-544)*

General Sheet Metal Works Inc ....E 574 288-0611
  South Bend *(G-12788)*

Gerke Welding Inc...........................G...... 260 724-7701
  Decatur *(G-2380)*

Gibson Brothers Welding Inc ....F 765 948-5775
  Fairmount *(G-3832)*

Gillum Machine & Tool Inc ....F 765 893-4426
  West Lebanon *(G-14120)*

Gravelton Machine Shop Inc ....G...... 574 773-3413
  Nappanee *(G-10674)*

Greenwood Models Inc.....................G...... 317 859-2988
  Greenwood *(G-5700)*

H & H Design & Tool Inc ....G...... 765 886-6199
  Economy *(G-2591)*

H W Hasty Welding Inc ....G...... 765 482-8925
  Lebanon *(G-9184)*

Halcomb Welding LLC ....G...... 765 345-7156
  Spiceland *(G-13055)*

Harvs Welding Inc ....G...... 219 345-5959
  Wheatfield *(G-14224)*

Helfin Sheet Metal Inc ....G...... 260 563-2417
  Wabash *(G-13729)*

Hepton Welding LLC ....G...... 800 570-4238
  Nappanee *(G-10678)*

Herman Tool & Machine Inc ....F 574 594-5544
  Pierceton *(G-11572)*

Highland Machine Tool Inc ....E 812 923-8884
  Floyds Knobs *(G-4013)*

Hill Top Welding LLC ....G...... 765 585-2549
  Attica *(G-304)*

Hite Welding & Chassis ....G...... 765 741-0046
  Muncie *(G-10489)*

Hively Welding Co Inc ....G...... 219 843-5111
  Medaryville *(G-9679)*

Hochstetler Welding ....G...... 574 773-0600
  Nappanee *(G-10682)*

Hochstetler Welding ....G...... 260 463-2793
  Lagrange *(G-9044)*

Hoosier Machine & Welding Inc ....F 317 638-6286
  Indianapolis *(G-7122)*

Hoosier Spline Broach Corp ....E 765 452-8273
  Kokomo *(G-8639)*

Hoosier Welding ....G...... 765 521-4539
  New Castle *(G-10905)*

Hs Machine Welding ....G...... 812 752-2825
  Scottsburg *(G-12361)*

Hubbard Welding ....G...... 317 539-2758
  Clayton *(G-1707)*

Huehls Seal Coating & Lawn Car ....G...... 317 782-4069
  Indianapolis *(G-7143)*

Humphreys Welding Service ....G...... 317 881-9024
  Indianapolis *(G-7145)*

Huntington Sheet Metal Inc..............D...... 260 356-9011
  Huntington *(G-6213)*

▲ Imperial Stamping Corporation ....D...... 574 294-3780
  Elkhart *(G-2930)*

▼ Indiana Industrial Svcs LLC ....C...... 317 769-6099
  Whitestown *(G-14255)*

Innovative Metalworks LLC................G...... 260 839-0295
  Sidney *(G-12674)*

Instate Welding Service Inc ....G...... 260 483-0461
  Fort Wayne *(G-4375)*

J & J Repair ....G...... 574 831-3075
  Goshen *(G-5246)*

J & J Welding ....G...... 219 872-7282
  Michigan City *(G-9804)*

▲ J & J Welding ....E 812 838-4391
  Mount Vernon *(G-10396)*

J A Smit Inc ....G...... 812 424-8141
  Evansville *(G-3568)*

Jar Welding & Machine Inc ....G...... 812 752-6253
  Scottsburg *(G-12369)*

Jarrod Zachary Weld ....G...... 765 230-6424
  Crawfordsville *(G-2164)*

Jerry Lambert ....G...... 765 378-7599
  Daleville *(G-2340)*

Joe Woodrow ....G...... 765 866-0436
  New Market *(G-10963)*

Johns Welding and Fabrication ....G...... 574 936-1702
  Plymouth *(G-11697)*

Johnsons Welding Service ....G...... 317 835-2438
  Boggstown *(G-901)*

Jomar Machining & Fabg Inc ....E 574 825-9837
  Middlebury *(G-9897)*

K & B Trailer Sales Mfg ....G...... 574 946-4382
  Monterey *(G-10207)*

K Fab Inc ....G...... 812 663-6299
  Greensburg *(G-5618)*

K-K Tool and Design Inc ....E 260 758-2940
  Markle *(G-9578)*

Kammerer Inc ....G...... 260 349-9098
  Kendallville *(G-8484)*

Kammerer Inc ....G...... 260 347-0389
  Kendallville *(G-8485)*

Knepps Custom Welding ....G...... 765 525-5130
  Saint Paul *(G-12278)*

Knip Welding ....G...... 219 987-5123
  Demotte *(G-2442)*

Kocsis Brothers Machine Co ....E 219 397-8400
  East Chicago *(G-2545)*

Kortzendorf Machine & Tool ....F 317 783-5449
  Indianapolis *(G-7367)*

L & C Welding LLC ....G...... 260 593-3410
  Shipshewana *(G-12625)*

L & L Engineering Co Inc ....G...... 317 786-6886
  Beech Grove *(G-601)*

L & R Machine Company Inc ....G...... 317 787-7251
  Beech Grove *(G-602)*

Lane Shady Welding ....G...... 574 825-5553
  Middlebury *(G-9901)*

Lauck Manufacturing Co Inc ....F 317 787-6269
  Indianapolis *(G-7385)*

Lawson Welding Shop ....G...... 812 448-8984
  Harmony *(G-5975)*

Ldn Welding Corp ....G...... 219 996-5643
  Hebron *(G-6016)*

Leons Fabrication Inc ....F 219 365-5272
  Schererville *(G-12330)*

Lievore Custom Machine Inc ....G...... 574 848-0150
  Bristol *(G-1067)*

Linden Machine Shop LLC ....G...... 765 339-7244
  Linden *(G-9304)*

Lloyds Machine Co ....G...... 812 422-7064
  Evansville *(G-3605)*

Loading Dock Maintenance LLC ....G...... 260 424-3635
  Fort Wayne *(G-4439)*

Lockwood Welding Inc ....G...... 260 925-2086
  Waterloo *(G-14017)*

Loughmiller Mch TI Design Inc ....E 812 295-3903
  Loogootee *(G-9390)*

M T M Machining Inc ....F 219 872-8677
  Michigan City *(G-9813)*

▲ Major Tool and Machine Inc ....B...... 317 636-6433
  Indianapolis *(G-7446)*

Manier Welding & Fabrications ....G...... 765 675-6078
  Tipton *(G-13397)*

▼ Manufacturing Technology Inc ....C...... 574 230-0258
  South Bend *(G-12851)*

Martin Welding Shop ....G...... 574 862-2578
  Wakarusa *(G-13785)*

Matts Repair Inc ....F 219 696-6765
  Lowell *(G-9416)*

Mc Bride & Son Welding & Engrg ....G...... 260 724-3534
  Decatur *(G-2393)*

McGinn Tool & Engineering Co ....F 317 736-5512
  Franklin *(G-4905)*

Melching Machine Inc ....E 260 622-4315
  Ossian *(G-11404)*

Mervin M Burkholder ....G...... 574 862-4144
  Wakarusa *(G-13786)*

Metcalf Engineering Inc....................G...... 765 342-6792
  Martinsville *(G-9625)*

Midwest Machining & Fabg ....F 219 924-0206
  Griffith *(G-5785)*

Miller Machine & Welding ....G...... 812 882-7566
  Vincennes *(G-13693)*

Miller Welding & Mechanic Svc ....G...... 812 923-3359
  Pekin *(G-11476)*

Misner Welding & Construction ....G...... 812 648-2980
  Dugger *(G-2481)*

Mitchum-Schaefer Inc......................D...... 317 546-4081
  Indianapolis *(G-7528)*

▲ Moores Welding Service Inc ....G...... 260 627-2177
  Leo *(G-9244)*

Mooresville Welding Inc ....G...... 317 831-2265
  Mooresville *(G-10324)*

Morris Machine & Tool......................G...... 219 866-3018
  Rensselaer *(G-11932)*

Motsinger Auto Supply Inc ....G...... 317 782-8484
  Indianapolis *(G-7549)*

N K Welding Products Inc ....G...... 260 424-1901
  Fort Wayne *(G-4488)*

Nector Machine & Fabricating ....G...... 219 322-6878
  Schererville *(G-12338)*

Newlins Welding & Tank Maint ....G...... 765 245-2741
  Montezuma *(G-10210)*

Nichols Mfg Co Inc ....F 219 696-8577
  Lowell *(G-9418)*

Noble County Welding Inc ....F 260 897-4082
  Avilla *(G-416)*

Northeast Machine & Tool Co ....G...... 317 823-6594
  Indianapolis *(G-7592)*

Northside Machining Inc	G	812 683-3500	
Huntingburg (G-6176)			
O & R Precision Grinding Inc	E	260 368-9394	
Geneva (G-5137)			
OBrien Jack & Pat Enterprises	G	765 653-5070	
Greencastle (G-5470)			
OHM Automotive LLC	G	812 879-5455	
Bloomington (G-785)			
On Site Welding & Maintenance	G	812 755-4184	
Campbellsburg (G-1280)			
Onyett Welding & Machine Inc	G	812 582-2999	
Petersburg (G-11565)			
Overton & Sons Tl & Die Co Inc	E	317 831-4542	
Mooresville (G-10331)			
Owens Machine & Welding	G	574 583-9566	
Monticello (G-10277)			
P & H Engineering Inc	G	765 676-6323	
Jamestown (G-8232)			
Pannell & Son Welding Inc	G	765 948-3606	
Summitville (G-13100)			
Peerless Pattern & Machine Co	G	765 477-7719	
Lafayette (G-8979)			
Pgg Enterprises LLC	G	317 462-2871	
Greenfield (G-5563)			
Pierceton Welding & Fabg	G	260 352-0106	
Silver Lake (G-12678)			
Precision Pulse LLP	G	765 472-6002	
Peru (G-11540)			
Precision Tubes Inc	G	317 783-2339	
Indianapolis (G-7738)			
Precision Welding Corporation	G	260 637-5514	
Huntertown (G-6144)			
Pro-Weld LLC	G	219 922-8861	
Griffith (G-5787)			
Pruett Manufacturing Co Inc	F	812 234-9497	
Terre Haute (G-13312)			
PSc Machining and Engrg Inc	F	219 764-4270	
Portage (G-11789)			
Pyramid Equipment	F	219 778-2591	
Rolling Prairie (G-12193)			
Pyramid Equipment	G	219 778-4253	
Rolling Prairie (G-12194)			
Quality Die Set Corp	E	574 967-4411	
Logansport (G-9361)			
Quints Welding	G	574 936-9138	
Plymouth (G-11718)			
R & A Goodman Enterprises	G	765 296-3446	
Lafayette (G-8987)			
R & M Welding & Fabricating Sp	G	812 295-9130	
Loogootee (G-9392)			
R & R Tool Manufacturing Inc	E	219 362-1681	
La Porte (G-8810)			
R & S Welding & Fabricating	G	574 946-6816	
Winamac (G-14319)			
Rabers Buggy Shop LLC	G	812 486-3789	
Montgomery (G-10239)			
Ready Machine Tool & Die Corp	E	765 825-3108	
Connersville (G-2070)			
Red Forge Inc	G	812 934-9641	
Batesville (G-516)			
Rescom Management Systems Inc	E	812 254-5641	
Washington (G-14002)			
Richard Myers Mllwrght	G	765 883-8177	
Russiaville (G-12243)			
Robert L Wehr	G	812 482-2673	
Jasper (G-8302)			
Rods Welding Shop	G	812 859-4250	
Coal City (G-1744)			
Roembke Mfg & Design Inc	E	260 622-4030	
Ossian (G-11407)			
◆ Rogers Engineering and Mfg Co	E	765 478-5444	
Cambridge City (G-1261)			
Rons General Repair	G	765 732-3805	
West College Corner (G-14037)			
Rota Skipper Corporation	F	708 331-0660	
Crown Point (G-2298)			
S & S Service	G	812 952-2306	
Lanesville (G-9103)			
S-Tech Inc	G	812 793-3506	
Crothersville (G-2221)			
Saliwanchik & Sons Welding & F	G	219 362-9009	
La Porte (G-8815)			
Schenk Sons Wldg & Tree Svc In	G	812 985-3954	
Mount Vernon (G-10408)			
Schmucker Welding	G	574 773-0456	
Bremen (G-1021)			
Schuler Precision Tool LLC	G	260 982-2704	
North Manchester (G-11243)			
Seib Machine & Tool Co Inc	G	812 453-6174	
Evansville (G-3721)			

Seiler Excavating Inc	G	260 925-0507	
Auburn (G-355)			
Shoemaker Welding Co	G	574 656-4412	
North Liberty (G-11221)			
Six Mile Welding	G	260 768-3126	
Lagrange (G-9065)			
Slabaugh Welding LLC	G	574 773-5410	
Milford (G-9965)			
Smith Welding & Repair Service	G	260 563-0710	
Wabash (G-13756)			
Southwest Welding	G	574 862-4453	
Goshen (G-5325)			
Specialty Welding & Machine	G	812 969-2139	
Elizabeth (G-2649)			
Stahl Welding Inc	G	765 457-3386	
Kokomo (G-8699)			
▲ Star Engineering & Mch Co Inc	E	260 824-4825	
Bluffton (G-894)			
Starkey Welding Inc	G	765 932-2005	
Rushville (G-12235)			
Steel Works Welding Inc	F	812 268-0334	
Sullivan (G-13095)			
Stolle Tool Inc	F	765 935-5185	
Richmond (G-12055)			
Stout Plastic Weld	F	219 926-7622	
Chesterton (G-1634)			
Summerlot Engineered Pdts Inc	F	812 466-7266	
Rosedale (G-12206)			
Sun Engineering Inc	E	219 962-1191	
Lake Station (G-9078)			
Swags Welding Services LLC	G	260 417-7510	
Churubusco (G-1657)			
T & E Welding Inc	F	812 324-0140	
Petersburg (G-11570)			
T K Sales & Service	G	219 962-8982	
Gary (G-5104)			
TAS Welding & Gran Services LL	G	765 210-4274	
Wabash (G-13757)			
Technical Weighing Svcs Inc	G	219 924-3433	
Griffith (G-5792)			
Terrys Welding Inc	G	765 742-4191	
Lafayette (G-9009)			
Terrys Welding Inc	G	765 564-3331	
Delphi (G-2428)			
Thomas Cubit Inc	G	219 933-0566	
Hammond (G-5949)			
Thorntons Welding	G	812 332-8564	
Bloomington (G-841)			
Thrasher Welding and Mch Sp	G	260 475-5550	
Angola (G-250)			
Titus Inc	F	574 936-3345	
Plymouth (G-11728)			
Toolcraft LLC	E	260 749-0454	
Fort Wayne (G-4692)			
Total Concepts Design Inc	D	812 752-6534	
Scottsburg (G-12384)			
Trade Line Fabricating Inc	E	812 637-1444	
Lawrenceburg (G-9159)			
Tri-Esco Inc	G	765 446-7937	
Colburn (G-1755)			
Tri-State Machine Co Inc	F	812 479-3159	
Evansville (G-3774)			
▲ Tube Processing Corp	B	317 787-1321	
Indianapolis (G-8107)			
Tube Processing Corp	C	317 264-7760	
Indianapolis (G-8109)			
Tyco Welding	G	812 988-8770	
Nashville (G-10736)			
United Tool Company Inc	F	260 563-3143	
Wabash (G-13760)			
Vincennes Welding Co Inc	F	812 882-9682	
Vincennes (G-13712)			
Vision Machine Works Inc	F	574 259-6500	
Mishawaka (G-10148)			
Wagner Welding Incorporated	G	812 985-9929	
Evansville (G-3808)			
Walts Welding & Fabricating	G	812 637-5338	
West Harrison (G-14044)			
Weld Done	G	260 597-7237	
Ossian (G-11415)			
Weldors Inc	G	765 289-9074	
Muncie (G-10582)			
Whitley Welding & Fabg & Repr	G	260 723-5111	
South Whitley (G-13010)			
William F Shirley	G	812 426-2599	
Evansville (G-3813)			
Wilson Machine Shop Inc	G	812 392-2774	
Elizabethtown (G-2652)			
Wrib Manufacturing Inc	G	765 294-2841	
Veedersburg (G-13648)			

Yoders & Sons Repair Shop	G	260 593-2727	
Topeka (G-13433)			
Zimmer Welding Co	G	317 632-5212	
Indianapolis (G-8226)			
Zionsville Towing Inc	G	317 873-4550	
Zionsville (G-14474)			

7694 Armature Rewinding Shops

Altek Inc	G	812 385-2561	
Princeton (G-11863)			
American Encoder Repair Servic	D	219 872-2822	
Michigan City (G-9765)			
B & D Electric Inc	F	812 254-2122	
Washington (G-13978)			
Bassett Electric Motor Repair	G	260 925-0868	
Auburn (G-317)			
Best Electric Motor Service	G	765 583-2408	
Otterbein (G-11417)			
Buffington Electric Motors	G	574 935-5453	
Plymouth (G-11673)			
C & L Electric Motor Repr Inc	G	574 533-2643	
Goshen (G-5184)			
Columbus Industrial Electric	F	812 372-8414	
Columbus (G-1877)			
Eemsco Inc	E	812 426-2224	
Evansville (G-3472)			
Electric Motor Services Inc	E	219 931-2850	
Hammond (G-5876)			
Electric Power Service	G	260 493-4913	
Fort Wayne (G-4234)			
Electrical Motor Products Inc		877 455-1599	
Fort Wayne (G-4235)			
Electrik Connection Inc	G	219 362-4581	
La Porte (G-8754)			
Electro Corporation	F	219 393-5571	
Kingsbury (G-8536)			
Enyart Electric Motor Service	G	574 288-4731	
South Bend (G-12766)			
Flanders Electric Mtr Svc Inc	E	812 867-4014	
Evansville (G-3509)			
Flanders Electric Mtr Svc Inc	E	812 421-4300	
Evansville (G-3510)			
Gary Electric Motor Service Co	F	219 884-6555	
Valparaiso (G-13546)			
Gottman Electric Co Inc	G	812 838-0037	
Mount Vernon (G-10393)			
Harrison Electric Inc	F	219 879-0444	
Michigan City (G-9801)			
Hess Electric Motor Service	G	812 926-0346	
Aurora (G-378)			
Hoosier Industrial Electric	F	812 346-2232	
North Vernon (G-11262)			
▲ Horner Apg LLC	D	317 916-4274	
Indianapolis (G-7127)			
Horner Industrial Services Inc	D	317 639-4261	
Indianapolis (G-7130)			
Horner Industrial Services Inc	G	317 916-4274	
Indianapolis (G-7128)			
Horner Industrial Services Inc	G	812 466-5281	
Terre Haute (G-13249)			
Horner Industrial Services Inc	G	260 434-1189	
Fort Wayne (G-4348)			
les Subsidiary Holdings Inc	F	330 830-3500	
South Bend (G-12807)			
les Subsidiary Holdings Inc	D	219 937-0100	
Hammond (G-5897)			
Indian Creek Outdoor Power LLC	G	812 597-3055	
Morgantown (G-10354)			
Industrial Motor & Tool LLC	G	574 534-8282	
Goshen (G-5244)			
Jasper Electric Motor Inc	G	812 482-1660	
Jasper (G-8258)			
Jasper Electric Motor Inc	F	812 482-1660	
Jasper (G-8259)			
Kesters Electric Motor Service	G	574 269-2889	
Warsaw (G-13896)			
Kiemle-Hankins Company	F	219 213-2643	
Crown Point (G-2271)			
▲ Kirby Risk Corporation	D	765 448-4567	
Lafayette (G-8940)			
Kirby Risk Corporation	G	765 643-3384	
Anderson (G-130)			
Kirby Risk Corporation	E	765 423-4205	
Lafayette (G-8941)			
Kirby Risk Corporation	F	765 254-5460	
Muncie (G-10505)			
Kirby Risk Corporation	F	765 664-5185	
Marion (G-9540)			
Kochs Electric Inc	F	317 639-5624	
Indianapolis (G-7364)			

S
I
C

Kw Maintenance Services LLC ....E 574 232-2051
South Bend *(G-12833)*

Machine Rebuilders & Service ....F 260 482-8168
Fort Wayne *(G-4448)*

Magnetech Industrial Svc ....G 219 937-0100
Hammond *(G-5911)*

McBroom Electric Co Inc ....D 317 926-3451
Indianapolis *(G-7471)*

Mills Electric Co Inc ....G 219 931-3114
Hammond *(G-5916)*

Morgan Automotive ....G 765 378-0593
Chesterfield *(G-1588)*

Morrows Mt Vernon Elc Mtr Svc ....G 812 838-5641
Mount Vernon *(G-10402)*

Morse Lake Automotive ....G 317 984-4514
Cicero *(G-1663)*

Motor Electric Inc ....G 574 294-7123
Elkhart *(G-3051)*

Motorcraft Inc ....G 765 282-4272
Muncie *(G-10525)*

North Vernon Electric Inc ....F 812 392-2985
North Vernon *(G-11271)*

P H C Industries Inc ....G 260 423-9461
Fort Wayne *(G-4516)*

Peter Austin Co ....G 765 288-6397
Muncie *(G-10545)*

Phase Three Electric Inc ....G 812 945-9922
New Albany *(G-10842)*

▲ **Phazpak Inc** ....G 260 692-6416
Monroe *(G-10184)*

▲ **Precision Electric Inc** ....E 574 256-1000
Mishawaka *(G-10106)*

Pres-Del Electric Inc ....G 219 884-3146
Gary *(G-5086)*

Qp Inc ....F 574 295-6884
Elkhart *(G-3125)*

Quality Repair Services Inc ....F 317 881-0205
Greenwood *(G-5738)*

Robinson Industries Inc ....E 317 867-3214
Westfield *(G-14185)*

Robinson Industries Inc ....E 317 867-3214
Westfield *(G-14186)*

Ronald Holloway ....G 574 223-6825
Rochester *(G-12151)*

Three Star Electric Inc ....G 574 272-3136
South Bend *(G-12969)*

Tipton Engrg Elc Mtr Svcs Inc ....G 765 963-3380
Sharpsville *(G-12507)*

Truman Ritchie ....G 219 956-2211
Rensselaer *(G-11943)*

Wabash Valley Motor & Mch Inc ....G 812 466-7400
Terre Haute *(G-13366)*

Wagner Electric Fort Wayne Inc ....G 260 484-5532
Fort Wayne *(G-4730)*

Wills Electric Service Inc ....G 812 883-5653
Pekin *(G-11480)*

Wright Repairs Inc ....F 765 674-3300
Gas City *(G-5128)*

ALPHABETIC SECTION

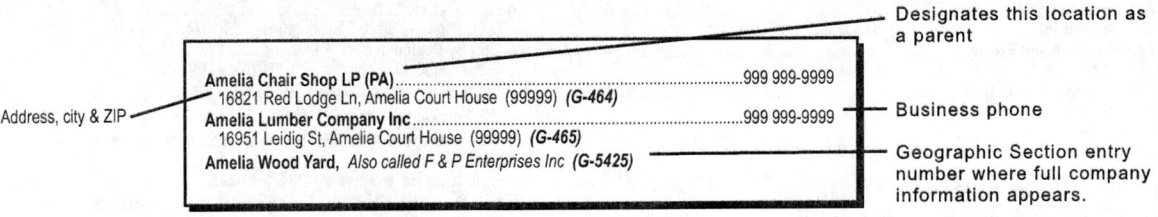
(ebs Composites) Engineered Bo....................574 266-3471
  3506 Henke St Elkhart (46514) *(G-2653)*

.dwg Tooling Technologies, Columbus *Also called dwg Design Services Corp* *(G-1915)*

03 Corp..812 597-0276
  6797 Morningstar Dr Morgantown (46160) *(G-10346)*

1 Up, Kokomo *Also called Web Software LLC* *(G-8716)*

100, Fort Wayne *Also called Deister Concentrator LLC* *(G-4204)*

101 Tool & Die LLC..................................260 203-2981
  6716 Metro Park Dr E Fort Wayne (46818) *(G-4031)*

103 Collection LLC..................................800 896-2945
  7402 Nature View Dr Schererville (46375) *(G-12312)*

124 Publishing LLC..................................574 784-0046
  124 S Michigan St Lakeville (46536) *(G-9092)*

1632 Inc..219 398-4155
  4202 Baring Ave East Chicago (46312) *(G-2514)*

1global Ds LLC......................................765 413-2211
  1225 Emerald Viking Ct Westfield (46074) *(G-14131)*

1st Attack Engineering Inc..........................260 837-2435
  2730 County Road 47 Waterloo (46793) *(G-14009)*

1st Choice Machining & Tooling, Madison *Also called Extreme Precision Products LLC* *(G-9461)*

1st Choice Safety LLC...............................260 797-5338
  4642 Pleasant Valley Dr Fort Wayne (46825) *(G-4032)*

1st Place Trophy Shop, Elkhart *Also called First Place Trophy Inc* *(G-2850)*

1st Source Products Inc.............................812 288-7466
  2822 Sable Mill Ln Jeffersonville (47130) *(G-8315)*

2 Bears LLC...317 375-1634
  4725 Brookville Rd Indianapolis (46201) *(G-6284)*

20 Minute Signs Plus................................765 413-1046
  3032 E 800 S Lafayette (47909) *(G-8844)*

200 Express...260 833-2125
  2040 N 200 W Angola (46703) *(G-186)*

2020 Lab Inc..219 756-8703
  2294 W 81st Ave Merrillville (46410) *(G-9690)*

243 Quarry..765 653-4100
  8090 S State Road 243 Cloverdale (46120) *(G-1723)*

250ok LLC...855 250-6529
  9247 N Meridian St # 301 Indianapolis (46260) *(G-6285)*

2fresh Prints LLC...................................317 947-7164
  10329 Galena Ct Indianapolis (46239) *(G-6286)*

2sweet Printing Service LLC.........................317 476-4402
  3320 Falcon Dr Indianapolis (46222) *(G-6287)*

3-K Racing, Lebanon *Also called Three K Racing Enterprises* *(G-9228)*

3-T Corp..812 424-7878
  2206 N Grand Ave Evansville (47711) *(G-3326)*

323ink LLC..812 282-3620
  2818 Sable Mill Ln Jeffersonville (47130) *(G-8316)*

37 Pipe & Supply LLC................................812 275-5676
  8987 Hc 37 Bedford (47421) *(G-526)*

39 Degrees North LLC................................855 447-3939
  908 N Walnut St Bloomington (47404) *(G-650)*

3b Tech Computers, South Bend *Also called 3btech Inc* *(G-12688)*

3btech Inc..574 233-0508
  3431 Wm Richards Dr B South Bend (46628) *(G-12688)*

3c Coman Ltd..317 650-5156
  800 W Ohio St Fortville (46040) *(G-4766)*

3d Engineering Inc..................................317 729-5430
  9064 S 600 W Edinburgh (46124) *(G-2593)*

3d Machine Inc......................................219 297-3674
  215 S Newton St Goodland (47948) *(G-5156)*

3d Parts Mfg LLC....................................317 860-6941
  3248 Dr Mar L King Jr Blv Martin Anderson (46013) *(G-56)*

3d Printing & Prototyping LLC.......................317 319-8515
  823 Cypress S Greenwood (46143) *(G-5657)*

3d Stone Inc..812 824-5805
  6700 S Victor Pike Bloomington (47403) *(G-651)*

3d Stone Purchaser Inc..............................812 824-5805
  6700 S Victor Pike Bloomington (47403) *(G-652)*

3M Company..765 348-3200
  304 S 075 E Hartford City (47348) *(G-5976)*

3M Company..317 692-6666
  5457 W 79th St Indianapolis (46268) *(G-6288)*

3M Company..574 948-8103
  2925 Gary Dr Plymouth (46563) *(G-11659)*

3M Indianapolis.....................................317 692-3000
  7911 Zionsville Rd Indianapolis (46268) *(G-6289)*

3rd Dimension Indus 3d Prtg, Indianapolis *Also called 3rd Dimension LLC* *(G-6290)*

3rd Dimension LLC...................................317 941-7958
  7168 Zionsville Rd Indianapolis (46268) *(G-6290)*

3w Enterprises LLC..................................847 366-6555
  2727 Industrial Pkwy Elkhart (46516) *(G-2654)*

4 Kids Books..317 733-8710
  4450 Weston Pointe Dr # 120 Zionsville (46077) *(G-14414)*

411 Newspaper.......................................219 922-8846
  1130 Camellia Dr Munster (46321) *(G-10590)*

4board LLC..317 997-3354
  802 N Meridian St Indianapolis (46204) *(G-6291)*

4d Manufacturing, North Judson *Also called Evelyn Dollahan* *(G-11211)*

5 Diamond X...574 601-8056
  10891 N Ravinia Blvd Monticello (47960) *(G-10250)*

500 Line, Syracuse *Also called Tranter Graphics Inc* *(G-13151)*

502 Mold Polishing LLC..............................502 436-0239
  1007 Wagon Trl Greenville (47124) *(G-5646)*

55 Monument Cir Level Off LLC.......................317 423-9472
  55 E Market St Indianapolis (46204) *(G-6292)*

5m Poultry LLC......................................812 890-5558
  10977 S County Road 500 E Carlisle (47838) *(G-1294)*

6605 E State LLC....................................260 433-7007
  2311 Forest Glade Fort Wayne (46845) *(G-4033)*

80/20 Inc...260 248-8030
  1701 S 400 E Columbia City (46725) *(G-1757)*

99 Nufab Rebar LLC..................................260 572-1315
  1610 S Grandstaff Dr Auburn (46706) *(G-311)*

A & A Custom Automation Inc (PA)....................812 464-3650
  2125 Bergdolt Rd Evansville (47711) *(G-3327)*

A & A Logging.......................................502 553-4132
  7006 Henryville Otisco Rd Henryville (47126) *(G-6031)*

A & A Machine Service Inc...........................317 745-7367
  4830 E Main St Avon (46123) *(G-423)*

A & A Manufacturing Co Inc..........................219 462-0822
  386 E State Road 2 Valparaiso (46383) *(G-13479)*

A & A Sheet Metal Products (PA).....................219 326-1288
  5122 N State Road 39 La Porte (46350) *(G-8725)*

A & B Fabricating & Maint Inc.......................574 353-1012
  516 N Morgan St Mentone (46539) *(G-9684)*

A & D Building, Evansville *Also called Red Spot Paint & Varnish Co* *(G-3698)*

A & D Constructors Inc (PA).........................812 428-3708
  1449 Kimber Ln Ste 103b Evansville (47715) *(G-3328)*

A & E Screen Printing...............................574 875-4488
  24266 County Road 45 Elkhart (46516) *(G-2655)*

A & H Enterprises LLC...............................317 398-3070
  60 E Washington St Shelbyville (46176) *(G-12517)*

A & I Products, Huntington *Also called ATI Products Inc* *(G-6187)*

A & L Spcialty Foods H C Trnsp, Indianapolis *Also called Park 100 Foods Inc* *(G-7656)*

A & M Innovations LLC...............................317 306-6118
  37 Erins Ct Whiteland (46184) *(G-14233)*

A & M Rubber Stamps Inc.............................219 836-0892
  424 Hickory Ln Munster (46321) *(G-10591)*

A & M Systems Inc...................................574 522-5000
  4121 Eastland Dr Elkhart (46516) *(G-2656)*

A & M Tool Inc......................................812 934-6533
  23102 Vote Rd Batesville (47006) *(G-488)*

A & M Woodworking...................................574 642-4555
  5545 S 1125 W Millersburg (46543) *(G-9968)*

A & R Machine Shop LLP..............................574 825-5686
  14719 County Road 20 Middlebury (46540) *(G-9866)*

A & S Logging Inc 574 896-3136
2340 E 800 S North Judson (46366) *(G-11205)*

A & T Concrete Supply Inc 812 753-4252
81 E State Road 168 Fort Branch (47648) *(G-4025)*

A & T Construction and Excvtg 219 314-2439
10212 W 128th Ave Cedar Lake (46303) *(G-1524)*

A & T Metal Fabricators LLC 219 949-5066
7000 W 21st Ave Gary (46406) *(G-5025)*

A & W Firearms 765 716-6856
8400 W County Road 400 S Yorktown (47396) *(G-14400)*

A B C Embroidery Inc 260 636-7311
3008 S 50 W Albion (46701) *(G-14)*

A B I Dept, North Judson *Also called Chester Inc (G-11209)*

A C C, Fort Wayne *Also called Applied Coating Converting LLC (G-4082)*

A C Mallory Capacitors LLC (PA) 317 612-1000
4411 S High School Rd Indianapolis (46241) *(G-6293)*

A Create Space Inc 317 254-2600
2750 E 55th St Ste D Indianapolis (46220) *(G-6294)*

A D I Screen Printing 765 457-8580
4758 E 00 Ns Kokomo (46901) *(G-8589)*

A Dine Tech Inc 219 464-4764
1609 Woodbine Dr Valparaiso (46383) *(G-13480)*

A E Techron Inc 574 295-9495
2507 Warren St Elkhart (46516) *(G-2657)*

A F Wolke Co Inc 812 738-4141
723 Quarry Rd Nw Corydon (47112) *(G-2086)*

A G A Gas Inc 317 783-2331
5825 Elmwood Ave Indianapolis (46203) *(G-6295)*

A H Emery Company 812 466-5265
4530 N 25th St Terre Haute (47805) *(G-13184)*

A Harris Verl Inc 317 736-4680
1331 N Capitol Ave Indianapolis (46202) *(G-6296)*

A Homestead Shoppe Inc (PA) 574 784-2307
330 E Vandalia St Lapaz (46537) *(G-9116)*

A Is For Apple Learning Center 219 629-3514
1510 173rd St Hammond (46324) *(G-5833)*

A J Coil Inc 574 353-7174
20015 Apple Rd Tippecanoe (46570) *(G-13380)*

A JS Furniture LLC 574 642-1273
5355 W 400 S Topeka (46571) *(G-13410)*

A L Brewster Plywood Inc 765 378-1040
232 Anderson Rd Chesterfield (46017) *(G-1586)*

A L E Enterprises 317 856-2981
4623 S High School Rd Indianapolis (46241) *(G-6297)*

A L S Inc 765 497-4750
3730 Westlake Ct West Lafayette (47906) *(G-14045)*

A Lit'le Bit of Heaven Farm, Arcadia *Also called Debra Schneider (G-263)*

A M A, Muncie *Also called Academy of Mdel Aronautics Inc (G-10422)*

A M A C O, Indianapolis *Also called American Art Clay Co Inc (G-6385)*

A M I, Bedford *Also called Aggregate Mfg Intl LLC (G-528)*

A M Manufacturing Co Inc 219 472-7272
9200 Calumet Ave Ste Nw07 Munster (46321) *(G-10592)*

A M T, Fort Wayne *Also called Advanced Machine & Tool Corp (G-4044)*

A Mayes Ing Inc 317 925-5777
3335 N Keystone Ave Indianapolis (46218) *(G-6298)*

A New Company Inc 574 293-9088
4811 Eastland Dr Elkhart (46516) *(G-2658)*

A New Covenant Woodwork LLC 812 737-2929
4305 Hooptown Rd Se Laconia (47135) *(G-8835)*

A P M, Scottsburg *Also called American Plastic Molding Corp (G-12355)*

A P Machine & Tool Inc 812 232-4939
1301 Elm St Terre Haute (47807) *(G-13185)*

A Pallet Company 317 687-9020
1305 Bedford St Indianapolis (46221) *(G-6299)*

A Plus Datacomm 219 472-1644
3282 Roswell Dr Portage (46368) *(G-11747)*

A Plus Images I N C 317 405-8955
5700 W Minn St Ste A5 Indianapolis (46241) *(G-6300)*

A Plus Sign Area Ltg Spcalists 765 966-4857
920 Progress Dr Richmond (47374) *(G-11951)*

A Pro-Build Company, Mooresville *Also called Carter Lee Building Component (G-10305)*

A Raymond Tinnerman, Logansport *Also called A Raymond Tinnerman Auto Inc (G-9319)*

A Raymond Tinnerman Auto Inc 574 722-5168
800 W County Road 250 S Logansport (46947) *(G-9319)*

A Rental Center, Linton *Also called Landis Equipment & Tool Rental (G-9309)*

A S C Industries Inc 574 264-1987
3604 County Road 6 E Elkhart (46514) *(G-2659)*

A S I, Bloomington *Also called Author Solutions LLC (G-667)*

A S I, Madison *Also called Arvin Sango Inc (G-9444)*

A S M Inc 260 724-8220
125 W Grant St Decatur (46733) *(G-2363)*

A S P Parrott Signs 812 325-9102
1820 S Walnut St Bloomington (47401) *(G-653)*

A Schulman Inc 574 935-5131
1301 Flora St Plymouth (46563) *(G-11660)*

A Schulman Inc 812 253-5238
2301 St Jseph Indus Pk Dr Evansville (47720) *(G-3329)*

A Sign Above 317 392-2144
25033 Us Highway 52 Laurel (47024) *(G-9127)*

A Sign Odyssey LLC 219 962-1247
727 Central Ave Lake Station (46405) *(G-9074)*

A Sign-By-Design Inc 317 876-7900
4725 W 106th St Zionsville (46077) *(G-14415)*

A T C, Indianapolis *Also called Automatic Tool Control (G-6445)*

A T G, Fort Wayne *Also called Applied Technology Group Inc (G-4084)*

A T L, Indianapolis *Also called Philips Ultrasound Inc (G-7684)*

A Time To Stitch Inc 812 422-5968
6916 Hogue Rd Evansville (47712) *(G-3330)*

A To Z Sheet Metal, Indianapolis *Also called Bright Sheet Metal Company Inc (G-6508)*

A To Z Sign Shop 219 462-7489
55 Us Highway 30 Bldg B Valparaiso (46383) *(G-13481)*

A W Manufacturing, Angola *Also called Angola Wire Products Inc (G-193)*

A W T, Indianapolis *Also called Astbury Water Technology Inc (G-6431)*

A&A Screen Printing 765 473-8783
311 W 8th St Peru (46970) *(G-11514)*

A&J Woodworking LLC 574 642-4551
12263 County Road 36 Goshen (46528) *(G-5162)*

A&M Commercial Cleaning LLC 765 720-3737
1138 Avenue D St Greencastle (46135) *(G-5453)*

A&M Tool & Die, Summitville *Also called Robert Atkins (G-13103)*

A-1 Awards Inc 317 546-9000
2500 N Ritter Ave Indianapolis (46218) *(G-6301)*

A-1 Door Specialties Inc 260 749-1635
212 Ullery St Ste 3 South Bend (46637) *(G-12689)*

A-1 Graphics Inc 765 289-1851
2500 W 7th St Muncie (47302) *(G-10420)*

A-1 Letter & Print Shop, Indianapolis *Also called A-1 Letter Shop Inc (G-6302)*

A-1 Letter Shop Inc 317 632-7212
417 E Ohio St Indianapolis (46204) *(G-6302)*

A-1 Machine, Terre Haute *Also called Rk Machine Inc (G-13321)*

A-1 Pallet Co Inc Clarksville 812 288-6339
1507 Progress Way Clarksville (47129) *(G-1671)*

A-1 Pallet Co Inc Clarksville (PA) 812 288-6339
940 Cottonwood Dr Clarksville (47129) *(G-1672)*

A-1 Production Inc 260 347-0960
5809 E Leighty Rd Kendallville (46755) *(G-8450)*

A-1 Shade Co 317 247-6447
5550 Marnette St Indianapolis (46241) *(G-6303)*

A-1 Welding & Repair 812 853-9701
5077 New York Dr Newburgh (47630) *(G-11016)*

A-1 Wire Tech Inc 815 226-0477
2900 Higgins Blvd Elkhart (46514) *(G-2660)*

A-1vet LLC 317 498-1804
4411 Dunn St Indianapolis (46226) *(G-6304)*

A-Fab LLC 812 897-0900
977 Hyrock Blvd Boonville (47601) *(G-904)*

A. Schulman, Evansville *Also called Matrixx Group Incorporated (G-3617)*

A/C Fabricating Corp 574 534-1415
1821 Century Dr Goshen (46528) *(G-5163)*

A1 Iron & Aluminum Co, South Bend *Also called Ironcraft Co Inc (G-12819)*

A1 Machine, Laotto *Also called Fulk Inc (G-9107)*

A1 Pallet Liquidators 765 356-4020
2700 Indiana Ave Anderson (46012) *(G-57)*

A1 Pallets Inc 812 425-0381
1801 W Maryland St Evansville (47712) *(G-3331)*

AAA Cabinet Guy LLC 574 299-9371
60822 Greenridge Ct South Bend (46614) *(G-12690)*

AAA Galvanizing - Joliet Inc 260 488-4477
7825 S Homestead Dr Hamilton (46742) *(G-5818)*

AAA Galvanizing - Joliet Inc 765 289-3427
2415 S Walnut St Muncie (47302) *(G-10421)*

AAA Galvanizing - Joliet Inc 574 935-4500
2631 Jim Neu Dr Plymouth (46563) *(G-11661)*

AAA Mudjackers 317 574-1990
5873 W 300 N Sharpsville (46068) *(G-12503)*

AAA Sales and Engineering, Angola *Also called AAA-Gpc Holdings LLC (G-187)*

AAA Satellite Link 765 642-7000
1529 W 2nd St Anderson (46016) *(G-58)*

AAA State of Play.com, Indianapolis *Also called Nvb Playgrounds Inc (G-7607)*

AAA Tool and Die Company Inc (PA) 574 246-1222
25101 Cleveland Rd South Bend (46628) *(G-12691)*

AAA-Gpc Holdings LLC (PA) 260 668-1468
1411 Wohlert St Angola (46703) *(G-187)*

Aacoa Inc (HQ) 574 262-4685
2551 County Road 10 W Elkhart (46514) *(G-2661)*

AAF International, Lebanon *Also called American Air Filter Co Inc (G-9167)*

Aaland Gem Company Inc 219 769-4492
8102 Georgia St Merrillville (46410) *(G-9691)*

Aam-Equipco Inc (PA) 574 272-8886
12838 Loop Ct Granger (46530) *(G-5388)*

Aardvark Furniture, Lafayette *Also called Wasu Inc (G-9022)*

Aardvark Graphics 574 267-4799
4121 Deer Run N Warsaw (46582) *(G-13834)*

Aardvark Vinyl Signs 260 833-0800
1875 W 275 N Angola (46703) *(G-188)*

(G-0000) Company's Geographic Section entry number

Aaron Asphalt Maintenance Seal 574 528-6370
  9031 E Circle Dr S Syracuse (46567) *(G-13128)*

Aaron Company Incorporated 219 838-0852
  4835 W 45th Ave Gary (46408) *(G-5026)*

Aarvee Associates LLC 312 222-5665
  9541 Valparaiso Ct Indianapolis (46268) *(G-6305)*

Abari Properties Development 317 721-9230
  5137 Red Yarrow Way Indianapolis (46254) *(G-6306)*

ABB Flexible Automation Inc 317 876-9090
  8401 Northwest Blvd Indianapolis (46278) *(G-6307)*

ABB Robotics, Indianapolis Also called ABB Flexible Automation Inc *(G-6307)*

Abbott Controls Inc 317 697-7102
  3535 Kessler Blvd N Dr Indianapolis (46222) *(G-6308)*

Abbott Laboratories 317 356-5478
  7155 Wadsworth Way Indianapolis (46219) *(G-6309)*

Abbott's Candy Shop, Hagerstown Also called Abbotts Candy and Gifts Inc *(G-5801)*

Abbotts Candy and Gifts Inc (PA) 765 489-4442
  48 E Walnut St Hagerstown (47346) *(G-5801)*

Abbp LLC 812 402-5966
  5320 Stringtown Rd Evansville (47711) *(G-3332)*

ABC Dental of Goshen 574 534-8777
  622 W Lincoln Ave Goshen (46526) *(G-5164)*

ABC Embroidery, Albion Also called A B C Embroidery Inc *(G-14)*

ABC Industries Inc (PA) 800 426-0921
  301 Kings Hwy Winona Lake (46590) *(G-14349)*

Abell Engineering & Mfg 317 687-1174
  2229 E New York St Indianapolis (46201) *(G-6310)*

Abell Tool Co Inc 317 887-0021
  446 Park 800 Dr Greenwood (46143) *(G-5658)*

Abercrombie Textiles I LLC 574 825-9800
  300 Wayne St Middlebury (46540) *(G-9867)*

Aberdeen Woods Apartments, Jeffersonville Also called New Hope Services Inc *(G-8403)*

ABF Welding & Pipe LLC 765 977-7349
  308 N 3rd St Cambridge City (47327) *(G-1252)*

ABI, Terre Haute Also called Advics Manufacturing Ind LLC *(G-13188)*

ABI Attachments Inc 877 788-7253
  520 S Byrkit St Mishawaka (46544) *(G-9988)*

ABI Plastics LLC 574 294-1700
  2510 Middlebury St Elkhart (46516) *(G-2662)*

Abigails Baking Company LLC 219 299-1785
  557 Chestnut St Valparaiso (46385) *(G-13482)*

Abk Tracking Inc 812 473-9554
  1201 N Weinbach Ave Evansville (47711) *(G-3333)*

Able Printing & Bus Svcs LLC 574 834-7006
  740 S Main St North Webster (46555) *(G-11288)*

Able Woodcrafters LLC 317 915-1225
  8180 River Bay Dr E Indianapolis (46240) *(G-6311)*

ABRA Auto Body & Glass LP 317 839-8940
  2170 E Main St Plainfield (46168) *(G-11590)*

ABRA Autobody & Glass, Plainfield Also called ABRA Auto Body & Glass LP *(G-11590)*

Abracadabra Graphics 812 336-1971
  5144 E State Road 45 Bloomington (47408) *(G-654)*

Abrasive Processing & Tech LLC (PA) 317 485-5157
  712 E Ohio St Fortville (46040) *(G-4767)*

Abrasive Products LLC 317 423-3957
  701 W Henry St Indianapolis (46225) *(G-6312)*

Abro Industries Inc (PA) 574 232-8289
  3580 Blackthorn Ct South Bend (46628) *(G-12692)*

ABS Mfg Rep Inc 317 407-0406
  1950 E Greyhound Pass # 18 Carmel (46033) *(G-1299)*

Absograph Sign Co 630 940-4093
  125 Windridge Rd Valparaiso (46385) *(G-13483)*

Absolute Custom Machine LLC 812 724-2284
  5954 S 1075 W Owensville (47665) *(G-11426)*

Absolute Machining Inc 260 747-4568
  3834 Vanguard Dr Fort Wayne (46809) *(G-4034)*

Absolute Printing Equipment, Indianapolis Also called Perfecta USA *(G-7677)*

Absolute Stone Polsg Repr LLC 317 709-9539
  3801 Crest Point Dr Westfield (46062) *(G-14132)*

Absolute Welding Inc (PA) 812 923-8001
  130 East St Borden (47106) *(G-926)*

Abtrex Industries Inc 574 234-7773
  59640 Market St South Bend (46614) *(G-12693)*

Abz Corp 317 758-2699
  4310 W State Road 38 Sheridan (46069) *(G-12587)*

AC Printing Inc 708 418-9100
  2647 Highway Ave Highland (46322) *(G-6034)*

Academy Energy Group LLC (PA) 312 931-7443
  106 State St Ste C Newburgh (47630) *(G-11017)*

Academy Inc 574 293-7113
  21291 Buckingham Rd Elkhart (46516) *(G-2663)*

Academy of Mdel Aronautics Inc 765 287-1256
  5161 E Memorial Dr Muncie (47302) *(G-10422)*

Acadia 260 894-7125
  1201 Gerber St Ligonier (46767) *(G-9274)*

Accel International 260 897-9990
  302 Progress Way Avilla (46710) *(G-400)*

Accelerated Curing Inc 260 726-3202
  304 E 100 N Portland (47371) *(G-11807)*

Accent Bicycles, Carmel Also called David Tortora *(G-1353)*

Accent Coatings LLC 317 712-0017
  9915 Glenburr Ct Fishers (46038) *(G-3865)*

Accent Complex Inc 574 522-2368
  1201 Richmond St Elkhart (46516) *(G-2664)*

Accent Fishing Product, Indianapolis Also called EMB Fishing LLC *(G-6847)*

Accent Limestone & Carving Inc 812 876-7040
  5900 N Maple Grove Rd Bloomington (47404) *(G-655)*

Accent Printing, Elkhart Also called Accent Complex Inc *(G-2664)*

Accent Signs & Graphics 866 769-7446
  11471 W County Road 75 N French Lick (47432) *(G-4983)*

Accent Software Inc 317 846-6025
  12409 Old Meridian St Carmel (46032) *(G-1300)*

Accent Wire Products 765 628-3587
  324 Shamrock Ave Greentown (46936) *(G-5643)*

Access Solutions 812 490-6026
  8322 Lancaster Dr Newburgh (47630) *(G-11018)*

Accessories By Sherwood, Elkhart Also called Floralcraft Distributors *(G-2858)*

Acclaim Graphics Inc 812 424-5035
  908 N Garvin St Evansville (47711) *(G-3334)*

Accordion Medical, Indianapolis Also called T H S International Inc *(G-8033)*

Accra Pac Holding Co LLC 765 326-0005
  6435 W Jefferson Blvd # 151 Fort Wayne (46804) *(G-4035)*

Accra-Pac Inc 574 295-0000
  1919 Superior St Elkhart (46516) *(G-2665)*

Accra-Pac Inc (PA) 905 660-0444
  2730 Middlebury St Elkhart (46516) *(G-2666)*

Accraline Inc 574 546-3484
  1420 W Bike St Bremen (46506) *(G-981)*

ACCRALINE INC-METAL SURGEONS, Bremen Also called Accraline Inc *(G-981)*

Accu-Chek Qulty Solutions LLC 812 704-5491
  1015 Old Forest Rd Nw Corydon (47112) *(G-2087)*

Accu-Label Inc 260 482-5223
  2021 Research Dr Fort Wayne (46808) *(G-4036)*

Accu-Mold LLC (HQ) 269 323-0388
  1702 E 7th St Mishawaka (46544) *(G-9989)*

Accu-Tech Automation Inc 317 352-1490
  1752 Lutherwood Dr Indianapolis (46219) *(G-6313)*

Accu-Tool Inc 260 248-4529
  831 E Short St Columbia City (46725) *(G-1758)*

Accuburn Williamsport Inc 765 762-1100
  304 W Washington St Williamsport (47993) *(G-14286)*

Accucast Inc 317 849-5521
  9705 Decatur Dr Indianapolis (46256) *(G-6314)*

Accucast Industries 219 929-1137
  1631 Pioneer Trl Chesterton (46304) *(G-1590)*

Accucraft Imaging Inc 219 933-3007
  5920 Hohman Ave Hammond (46320) *(G-5834)*

Accugear Inc 260 497-6600
  6710 Innovation Blvd Fort Wayne (46818) *(G-4037)*

Accuprint of Kentuckiana Inc 812 944-8603
  4101 Reas Ln New Albany (47150) *(G-10740)*

Accurate Castings Inc 219 393-3122
  3232 3rd Rd La Porte (46350) *(G-8726)*

Accurate Publishing Co 219 836-1397
  8445 Manor Ave Apt 301 Munster (46321) *(G-10593)*

Accurate Tool & Engineering 812 963-6677
  8501 Neu Rd Evansville (47720) *(G-3335)*

Accuride Corporation (HQ) 812 962-5000
  7140 Office Cir Evansville (47715) *(G-3336)*

Accuride Emi LLC 940 565-8505
  7140 Office Cir Evansville (47715) *(G-3337)*

Accutech Mold & Machine Inc 260 471-6102
  2817 Goshen Rd Fort Wayne (46808) *(G-4038)*

Accutemp Products Inc (PA) 260 493-0415
  8415 Clinton Park Dr Fort Wayne (46825) *(G-4039)*

Acd Suppliers LLC 317 527-9715
  5426 Wood Hollow Dr Indianapolis (46239) *(G-6315)*

Ace Extrusion LLC 812 463-5230
  1800 W Maryland St Evansville (47712) *(G-3338)*

Ace Extrusion LLC (PA) 812 868-8640
  14020 Highway 57 Evansville (47725) *(G-3339)*

Ace Extrusion LLC 812 463-5230
  1800 W Maryland St Evansville (47712) *(G-3340)*

Ace Extrusion LLC 812 436-4840
  701 N 9th Ave Evansville (47712) *(G-3341)*

Ace Metal Sales, Marysville Also called Solomon M Eicher *(G-9651)*

Ace Mobility Inc 317 241-2444
  9850 E 30th St Indianapolis (46229) *(G-6316)*

Ace Screen Printing LLC 317 861-7477
  4220 S 650 W New Palestine (46163) *(G-10965)*

Ace Sign & Awning, Terre Haute Also called All American Tent & Awning Inc *(G-13190)*

Ace Sign Company Inc 812 232-4206
  1140 3rd Ave Terre Haute (47807) *(G-13186)*

Ace Sign Systems Inc 765 288-1000
  3621 W Royerton Rd Muncie (47304) *(G-10423)*

Ace Tool & Engineering Co, Mooresville Also called S Edwards Incorporated *(G-10338)*

Ace Welding and Machine Inc 812 379-9625
  2461 N Indianapolis Rd Columbus (47201) *(G-1849)*

Acell Inc 765 464-8198
3589 Sgmre Pkwy N 220 Lafayette (47904) *(G-8845)*

Aceys Trophies & Awards 574 267-1426
301 S Scott St Warsaw (46580) *(G-13835)*

Achaemenian Shahpur 812 331-1317
314 W 2nd St Bloomington (47403) *(G-656)*

Achievers Institute LLC 812 278-8785
1440 Church Camp Rd Bedford (47421) *(G-527)*

Aci Construction Company Inc 317 549-1833
5108 Topp Dr Indianapolis (46218) *(G-6317)*

Acl, Jeffersonville *Also called American Commercial Lines Inc* *(G-8325)*

Acl Professional Services Inc 812 288-0100
1701 Utica Pike Jeffersonville (47130) *(G-8317)*

Acme Cabinets Corp 219 924-1800
1331 E Main St Griffith (46319) *(G-5760)*

Acme Coatings Inc 317 272-6202
240 Production Dr Avon (46123) *(G-424)*

Acme Industrial Inc 260 422-6518
2380 E Cardinal Dr Columbia City (46725) *(G-1759)*

Acme Masking Company Inc 317 272-6202
240 Production Dr Avon (46123) *(G-425)*

Acme Sports Inc 812 522-4008
800 E Tipton St Seymour (47274) *(G-12426)*

Acorn Ridge Highlands, Warsaw *Also called Hand Industries Inc* *(G-13888)*

Acorn Woodworks 317 867-4377
16116 Ditch Rd Westfield (46074) *(G-14133)*

Acoustical Audio Designs LLC 812 282-7522
2008 Coopers Ln Jeffersonville (47130) *(G-8318)*

Acro Engineering Inc 812 663-6236
1120 W Washington St Greensburg (47240) *(G-5588)*

ACS Sign Solution (PA) 317 925-2835
1110 E 22nd St Indianapolis (46202) *(G-6318)*

ACS Sign Solution 317 201-4838
115 E 21st St Indianapolis (46202) *(G-6319)*

ACS Sign Systems, Indianapolis *Also called ACS Sign Solution* *(G-6319)*

Act, Lagrange *Also called Aluminum Cargo Trailers Inc* *(G-9030)*

Act, Indianapolis *Also called Advanced Control Tech Inc* *(G-6332)*

Act Research, Columbus *Also called Americas Coml Trnsp RES Co LLC* *(G-1854)*

Act Systems International LLC 812 437-4609
1513 N Cullen Ave Evansville (47715) *(G-3342)*

Actega North America Inc 800 426-4657
650 W 67th Pl Schererville (46375) *(G-12313)*

Acterna LLC 317 788-9351
5808 Churchman Byp Indianapolis (46203) *(G-6320)*

Action Brace and Prosthetics 317 347-4222
5942 W 71st St Indianapolis (46278) *(G-6321)*

Action Cooling Towers Inc 219 285-2660
2649 S 500 W Morocco (47963) *(G-10359)*

Action Embroidery Inc 850 626-1796
4400 Charlestown Pike Jeffersonville (47130) *(G-8319)*

Action Filtration Inc (PA) 812 546-6262
221 Raymond St Hope (47246) *(G-6110)*

Action Machine Inc 574 287-9650
1847 Prairie Ave South Bend (46613) *(G-12694)*

Action Plus Shopper & Shoppers, Demotte *Also called Kankakee Valley Post News* *(G-2441)*

Active Ankle Systems Inc 812 258-0663
233 Quartermaster Ct Jeffersonville (47130) *(G-8320)*

Active Sensors Incorporated 317 713-2973
8520 Allison Pointe Blvd # 220 Indianapolis (46250) *(G-6322)*

Active Trading International 260 637-1990
6015 2 Highway Dr Ste G Fort Wayne (46818) *(G-4040)*

Actuant Corporation 574 254-1428
1217 E 7th St Mishawaka (46544) *(G-9990)*

Acuity Brands Inc 765 362-1837
1304 E Elmore St Crawfordsville (47933) *(G-2131)*

Acuity Brands Lighting Inc 765 362-1837
1615 E Elmore St Crawfordsville (47933) *(G-2132)*

Acuity Brands Lighting Inc 317 849-1233
12001 Exit 5 Pkwy Fishers (46037) *(G-3866)*

Acura Pharmaceutical Tech 574 842-3305
16235 State Road 17 Culver (46511) *(G-2324)*

Acutech LLC 574 262-8228
53905 County Road 9 Ste C Elkhart (46514) *(G-2667)*

Ad Craft Printers Incorporated 219 942-9799
3201 E 83rd Pl Merrillville (46410) *(G-9692)*

Ad Plex-Rhodes Inc 812 256-3396
100 Quality Ct Charlestown (47111) *(G-1556)*

Ad Vision Graphics Inc 812 476-4932
1820 N Hoosier Ave Evansville (47715) *(G-3343)*

Ad-Sign & Display Division, Indianapolis *Also called Phil Irwin Advertising Inc* *(G-7683)*

Ad-Vance Magnetics Inc 574 223-3158
625 Monroe St Rochester (46975) *(G-12113)*

Adams & Westlake Ltd 574 264-1141
940 N Michigan St Elkhart (46514) *(G-2668)*

Adams Smith (PA) 219 661-2812
10431 Floyd St Crown Point (46307) *(G-2222)*

Adaptasoft Inc 219 567-2547
106 E Montgomery St Francesville (47946) *(G-4808)*

Adaptek Systems Inc 260 637-8660
14224 Plank St Fort Wayne (46818) *(G-4041)*

Adaptive Mobility Inc 317 347-6400
7040 Guion Rd Indianapolis (46268) *(G-6323)*

Adavantage Direct, Fort Wayne *Also called Advantage Direct365 Corp* *(G-4047)*

Adcomm Bindery, Roachdale *Also called No-Sail Splash Guard Co Inc* *(G-12094)*

Addenda Corporation (HQ) 317 290-5007
5929 Lakeside Blvd Indianapolis (46278) *(G-6324)*

Adec 503 538-7478
13085 Hmlton Crssing Blvd Carmel (46032) *(G-1301)*

Adec Inc 574 848-7451
19670 State Road 120 Bristol (46507) *(G-1040)*

Adec Industries 574 522-7729
2700 Industrial Pkwy Elkhart (46516) *(G-2669)*

Adept Tool and Engineering 317 896-9250
11307 Green St Carmel (46033) *(G-1302)*

Adhesive Products Inc 317 899-0565
9635 Park Davis Dr Indianapolis (46235) *(G-6325)*

Adhesive Solutions Company LLC (PA) 260 691-0304
4201 N 450 E Columbia City (46725) *(G-1760)*

Adidas Group 317 895-7000
8677 Logo Athletic Ct Indianapolis (46219) *(G-6326)*

Adidas North America Inc 219 878-5822
601 Wabash St Ste 1205 Michigan City (46360) *(G-9764)*

Adidas Outlet Store Mich Cy, Michigan City *Also called Adidas North America Inc* *(G-9764)*

Adkev Inc 574 583-4420
1207 N 6th St Monticello (47960) *(G-10251)*

Adkins Sawmill Inc 812 849-4036
2929 Fleenor Rd Mitchell (47446) *(G-10154)*

Adlake, Elkhart *Also called Adams & Westlake Ltd* *(G-2668)*

ADM, Goodland *Also called Archer-Daniels-Midland Company* *(G-5157)*

ADM, Beech Grove *Also called Archer-Daniels-Midland Company* *(G-592)*

ADM, Nappanee *Also called Archer-Daniels-Midland Company* *(G-10646)*

ADM, Nappanee *Also called Archer-Daniels-Midland Company* *(G-10647)*

ADM, Bluffton *Also called Archer-Daniels-Midland Company* *(G-864)*

ADM, Indianapolis *Also called Archer-Daniels-Midland Company* *(G-6415)*

ADM, Rensselaer *Also called Archer-Daniels-Midland Company* *(G-11913)*

ADM, Decatur *Also called Archer-Daniels-Midland Company* *(G-2369)*

ADM, Evansville *Also called Archer-Daniels-Midland Company* *(G-3363)*

ADM, Huntertown *Also called Asphalt Drum Mixers Inc* *(G-6134)*

ADM, Attica *Also called Archer-Daniels-Midland Company* *(G-296)*

ADM, Rensselaer *Also called Archer-Daniels-Midland Company* *(G-11914)*

ADM, State Line *Also called Archer-Daniels-Midland Company* *(G-13071)*

ADM, Frankfort *Also called Archer-Daniels-Midland Company* *(G-4818)*

ADM, Crawfordsville *Also called Archer-Daniels-Midland Company* *(G-2134)*

ADM, Goshen *Also called Archer-Daniels-Midland Company* *(G-5171)*

ADM Custom Creations LLC 765 499-0584
6 Belfast Ct Hartford City (47348) *(G-5977)*

ADM Milling Co 812 838-4445
614 W 2nd St Mount Vernon (47620) *(G-10380)*

ADM Milling Co 317 783-3321
854 Bethel Ave Beech Grove (46107) *(G-591)*

ADM Mobility Solutions Inc 317 481-8707
8360 W Washington St Indianapolis (46231) *(G-6327)*

Admar Mold & Engineering Inc 574 848-7085
21426 Meadowview Ln Bristol (46507) *(G-1041)*

Admiral Medical Center Inc 317 924-3757
5435 Emerson Way Ste 210 Indianapolis (46226) *(G-6328)*

Admiral Petroleum Company 574 272-2051
52394 Ind St Rte 933 South Bend (46637) *(G-12695)*

Adranos Energetics LLC 208 539-2439
137 Prophet Dr West Lafayette (47906) *(G-14046)*

Adranos Rdx LLC 208 539-2439
137 Prophet Dr West Lafayette (47906) *(G-14047)*

Adrian Orchards Inc 317 784-0550
500 W Epler Ave Indianapolis (46217) *(G-6329)*

Advance Aero Inc 317 513-6071
135 E Harrison St Mooresville (46158) *(G-10300)*

Advance Auto Parts, Indianapolis *Also called Advance Stores Company Inc* *(G-6331)*

Advance Energy LLC 312 665-0022
3580 N Hobart Rd C Hobart (46342) *(G-6068)*

Advance Fabricators Inc 812 944-6941
980 Progress Blvd New Albany (47150) *(G-10741)*

Advance Green Mfg Co Inc 574 457-2695
2482 E Kercher Rd Goshen (46526) *(G-5165)*

Advance Leader, Kendallville *Also called Kpc Media Group Inc* *(G-8488)*

Advance Machine Works Corp 260 483-1183
2620 Independence Dr Fort Wayne (46808) *(G-4042)*

Advance MCS Electronics Inc (PA) 574 642-3501
67928 Us Highway 33 Goshen (46526) *(G-5166)*

Advance Prtective Coatings Inc 317 228-0123
8448 Moller Rd Indianapolis (46268) *(G-6330)*

Advance Repair & Machining 765 474-8000
3311 Imperial Pkwy Ste B Lafayette (47909) *(G-8846)*

Advance Stores Company Inc 317 253-5034
5125 N Keystone Ave Indianapolis (46205) *(G-6331)*

Advanced Assembly LLC......................260 244-1700
2101 S 600 E Columbia City (46725) *(G-1761)*

Advanced Bearing Materials LLC................812 663-3401
1515 W Main St Greensburg (47240) *(G-5589)*

Advanced Boiler Ctrl Svcs Inc (PA)............708 429-7066
7515 Cline Ave Crown Point (46307) *(G-2223)*

Advanced Btry Charger Svc LLC................260 563-3909
650 Valley Brook Ln Wabash (46992) *(G-13719)*

Advanced Cabinet Systems, Marion Also called J G Bowers Inc *(G-9536)*

Advanced Cabinet Systems Inc................765 677-8000
1629 S Joaquin Dr Marion (46953) *(G-9506)*

Advanced Control Panels Inc..................219 763-4000
1845 Willowcreek Rd Portage (46368) *(G-11748)*

Advanced Control Tech Inc....................317 806-2750
6805 Hillsdale Ct Indianapolis (46250) *(G-6332)*

Advanced Cutting Systems Inc.................260 423-3394
4030 Piper Dr Fort Wayne (46809) *(G-4043)*

Advanced Designs Corp (PA)..................812 333-1922
1169 W 2nd St Bloomington (47403) *(G-657)*

Advanced Drainage Systems..................317 917-7960
420 S Belmont Ave Indianapolis (46222) *(G-6333)*

Advanced Drainage Systems Inc...............812 443-2080
2340 E Us Highway 40 Brazil (47834) *(G-953)*

Advanced Engineering Inc.....................260 356-8077
5299 N Mishler Rd Huntington (46750) *(G-6184)*

Advanced Finishing Corporation...............317 335-2210
7724 Depot St Bldg A McCordsville (46055) *(G-9664)*

Advanced Inspection Solutions, Indianapolis Also called Conmoto Enterprises Inc *(G-6650)*

Advanced Kinematics Inc......................574 533-8178
15593 County Road 28 Goshen (46528) *(G-5167)*

Advanced Limb Wound Care...................812 232-0957
303 S 14th St Terre Haute (47807) *(G-13187)*

Advanced Machine & Tool Corp (PA)...........260 489-3572
3706 Transportation Dr Fort Wayne (46818) *(G-4044)*

Advanced Magnesium Alloys Corp..............765 643-5873
1820 E 32nd St Anderson (46013) *(G-59)*

Advanced Manufacturing In....................260 273-9669
500 W Line St Geneva (46740) *(G-5133)*

Advanced Mbility Solutions LLC................812 438-2338
4669 Cass Union Rd Rising Sun (47040) *(G-12085)*

Advanced Metal Etching Inc...................260 894-4189
801 Gerber St Ligonier (46767) *(G-9275)*

Advanced Metal Fabricators Inc................574 259-1263
1204 E 6th St Mishawaka (46544) *(G-9991)*

Advanced Mold & Engineering.................812 342-9000
7980 S International Dr Columbus (47201) *(G-1850)*

Advanced Mtlwrking Prctces LLC...............317 337-0441
4511 W 99th St Carmel (46032) *(G-1303)*

Advanced Ntrding Solutions LLC...............812 932-1010
1688 Lammers Pike Batesville (47006) *(G-489)*

Advanced Orthopro Inc (PA)...................317 924-4444
1820 N Illinois St Indianapolis (46202) *(G-6334)*

Advanced Print Solutions LLC..................513 405-3452
10108 State Road 101 Brookville (47012) *(G-1110)*

Advanced Products Tech Inc...................765 827-1166
5430 Western Ave Connersville (47331) *(G-2038)*

Advanced Protective Tech LLC.................877 548-9323
1101 Cumberland Xing # 180 Valparaiso (46383) *(G-13484)*

Advanced Prtctive Slutions LLC................765 720-9574
639 Gettysburg Coatesville (46121) *(G-1746)*

Advanced Racg Suspensions Inc...............317 896-3306
1698 Midwest Blvd Indianapolis (46214) *(G-6335)*

Advanced Radiant Systems, Fortville Also called Hale Industries Inc *(G-4778)*

Advanced Services LLC........................317 780-6909
5426 Elmwood Ave Indianapolis (46203) *(G-6336)*

Advanced Sign & Graphics Inc.................765 284-8360
3939 E Mcgalliard Rd Muncie (47303) *(G-10424)*

Advanced Sign & Lighting Svc.................812 430-2817
13350 N Green River Rd Evansville (47725) *(G-3344)*

Advanced Systems Intgrtion LLC...............260 447-5555
4534 Allen Martin Dr Fort Wayne (46806) *(G-4045)*

Advanced Vscular Therapies Inc...............765 423-1720
1125 N 13th St Lafayette (47904) *(G-8847)*

Advantage Cartridge Co Inc...................260 747-9941
3236 Illinois Rd Fort Wayne (46802) *(G-4046)*

Advantage Components Corp...................317 784-0299
2233 S West St Indianapolis (46225) *(G-6337)*

Advantage Direct365 Corp (PA)................260 490-1961
4111 Engleton Dr Fort Wayne (46804) *(G-4047)*

Advantage Electronics Inc.....................317 888-1946
525 E Stop 18 Rd Greenwood (46143) *(G-5659)*

Advantage Embroidery Inc.....................765 471-0188
1059 E 400 S Bringhurst (46913) *(G-1037)*

Advantage Engineering Inc (PA)...............317 887-0729
525 E Stop 18 Rd Greenwood (46143) *(G-5660)*

Advantage Fluid Systems LLC.................800 317-1570
8170 Zionsville Rd Indianapolis (46268) *(G-6338)*

Advantage Manufacturing......................317 237-4289
1802 W 10th St Indianapolis (46222) *(G-6339)*

Advantage Signs & Graphics Inc...............219 853-1427
6223 Hohman Ave Ste 3 Hammond (46324) *(G-5835)*

Advantage Thermal Service, Kendallville Also called MD Moxie LLC *(G-8494)*

Advantex Inc.................................812 339-6479
5981 E State Road 45 Bloomington (47408) *(G-658)*

Advantis Medical Inc.........................317 859-2300
2121 Southtech Dr Ste 600 Greenwood (46143) *(G-5661)*

Advent Precision Inc..........................317 908-6937
1740 Industry Dr Ste F Indianapolis (46219) *(G-6340)*

Adventureglass, North Webster Also called B Thystrup US Corporation *(G-11289)*

Advertiser, Hebron Also called Russ Print Shop *(G-6022)*

Advertiser Inc................................260 824-4770
2917 E State Road 124 C Bluffton (46714) *(G-862)*

Advertising Communications Gro...............317 843-2523
11690 Technology Dr Carmel (46032) *(G-1304)*

Advics Manufacturing Ind LLC.................812 298-1617
10550 James Adams St Terre Haute (47802) *(G-13188)*

Ae Sport, Fort Wayne Also called Amanda Elizabeth LLC *(G-4066)*

Ae Techron, Elkhart Also called A E Techron Inc *(G-2657)*

Aearo Company, Indianapolis Also called Aearo Technologies LLC *(G-6341)*

Aearo Technologies LLC (HQ).................317 692-6666
5457 W 79th St Indianapolis (46268) *(G-6341)*

Aearo Technologies LLC.......................317 692-6666
7911 Zionsville Rd Indianapolis (46268) *(G-6342)*

AEC America, Columbus Also called Indiana Research Institute *(G-1948)*

Aeds & Safety Services LLC...................502 641-3118
12 Abby Chase Jeffersonville (47130) *(G-8321)*

Aef Emblem, Carmel Also called Favor It Promotions Inc *(G-1379)*

Aegis Sales & Engineering Inc.................260 483-4160
5411 Industrial Rd Fort Wayne (46825) *(G-4048)*

AEL/Span LLC...............................317 203-4602
6032 Gateway Dr Plainfield (46168) *(G-11591)*

Aerchem LLC................................812 334-9996
3935 W Roll Ave Bloomington (47403) *(G-659)*

Aerial Drone Exposures Inc....................404 641-5563
2869 N Moreland Ave Indianapolis (46222) *(G-6343)*

Aerial Imaging Resources LLC.................317 550-5970
712 N New Jersey St Indianapolis (46202) *(G-6344)*

Aerial Sign Co...............................317 258-9696
1205 Cannonero Ct Indianapolis (46217) *(G-6345)*

Aero Industries Inc (PA)......................317 808-1923
4243 W Bradbury Ave Indianapolis (46241) *(G-6346)*

Aero Machine LLC...........................219 548-0490
1251 Transport Dr Ste A Valparaiso (46383) *(G-13485)*

Aero Metals Inc (PA).........................219 326-1976
1201 E Lincolnway La Porte (46350) *(G-8727)*

Aero-Flo Industries Inc.......................219 393-3555
3999 E Hupp Rd Bldg R34 La Porte (46350) *(G-8728)*

Aerodine Composites LLC.....................317 271-1207
8201 Indy Ln Indianapolis (46214) *(G-6347)*

Aerodine Engineering Group LLC..............317 271-1207
8201 Indy Ln Indianapolis (46214) *(G-6348)*

Aerofab, Indianapolis Also called Tube Processing Corp *(G-8107)*

Aeromet Industries Inc........................219 924-7442
739 S Arbogast St Griffith (46319) *(G-5761)*

Aeromotive Mfg Inc..........................765 552-0668
8421 N 750 W Elwood (46036) *(G-3293)*

Aeropro Holdings LLC........................317 849-9555
7035 E 86th St Indianapolis (46250) *(G-6349)*

Aerosmith Fastening Systems, Indianapolis Also called Hkn International LLC *(G-7110)*

Aerospace Products Company, Indianapolis Also called Wbh Inc *(G-8180)*

Aerospace Waterjet Svcs LLC.................502 836-1112
21608 New Market Rd Marysville (47141) *(G-9649)*

Aet Films, Rosedale Also called Taghleef Industries Inc *(G-12208)*

AF Ohab Company Inc........................317 225-4740
2346 S Lynhurst Dr # 302 Indianapolis (46241) *(G-6350)*

Afc Industries Inc............................574 264-1987
3604 County Road 6 E Elkhart (46514) *(G-2670)*

Afco Performance Group LLC (PA).............812 897-0900
977 Hyrock Blvd Boonville (47601) *(G-905)*

Afco Racing Products, Boonville Also called Afco Performance Group LLC *(G-905)*

Afequip.com, Indianapolis Also called AF Ohab Company Inc *(G-6350)*

Affinis Group LLC (PA).......................317 831-3830
1050 Indianapolis Rd Mooresville (46158) *(G-10301)*

Affordable Computer Repair, Yoder Also called Dedicated Software *(G-14397)*

Affordable Footwear & T-Shrt.................260 702-5134
4755 Blum Dr Fort Wayne (46835) *(G-4049)*

Affordable Furniture..........................317 881-7726
816 Us Highway 31 N Greenwood (46142) *(G-5662)*

Affordable Luxury Homes Inc..................260 758-2141
49 S 500 E Markle (46770) *(G-9575)*

Affordable Screen Printing EMB................574 278-7885
8262 N Kiger Dr Monticello (47960) *(G-10252)*

Affordable Sign & Neon Inc....................219 853-1855
534 Conkey St Ste 1 Hammond (46324) *(G-5836)*

Affordable Signs..............................260 349-1710
700 S Orchard St Kendallville (46755) *(G-8451)*

Affordable Sounds Inc 260 493-7742
10848 Rose Ave Ste 3 New Haven (46774) ***(G-10926)***
Afs Fluid Controls, Indianapolis *Also called Advantage Fluid Systems LLC* ***(G-6338)***
Aftco Manufacturing, Yorktown *Also called Aul In The Family Tool and Die* ***(G-14401)***
After Action Med Dntl Sup LLC 317 831-2699
4444 Decatur Blvd Ste 100 Indianapolis (46241) ***(G-6351)***
After Hours Embroidery 812 926-9355
406 2nd St Aurora (47001) ***(G-368)***
Afterimage Gis (PA) 765 744-1346
808 E Cooper Rd Muncie (47303) ***(G-10425)***
Aftermath Cidery and Winery 219 299-8463
454 Greenwich St Valparaiso (46383) ***(G-13486)***
AG Apparel and Screen Prtg LLC 260 483-3817
5515 Planeview Dr Fort Wayne (46825) ***(G-4050)***
AG Plus Inc (PA) 260 723-5141
401 N Main St South Whitley (46787) ***(G-12996)***
AG Plus Inc 260 623-6121
306 W South St Monroeville (46773) ***(G-10190)***
AG Printing Specialists LLC 866 445-6824
2880 Us Highway 231 S # 200 Lafayette (47909) ***(G-8848)***
AG Processing A Cooperative 574 773-4138
302 S Main St Nappanee (46550) ***(G-10644)***
AG Processing A Cooperative 574 831-2292
24120 County Road 142 1 Goshen (46526) ***(G-5168)***
AG Technologies Inc 574 224-8324
1268 E 100 S Rochester (46975) ***(G-12114)***
Agbest Cooperative Inc 765 358-3388
430 S Sycamore St Gaston (47342) ***(G-5129)***
Agdia Inc 574 264-2014
52642 County Road 1 Elkhart (46514) ***(G-2671)***
Aggreate Systems (PA) 260 854-4711
102 Industry Bnd Rome City (46784) ***(G-12197)***
Aggreate Systems 260 854-4711
106 Industry Bnd Rome City (46784) ***(G-12198)***
Aggregate Industries - Mwr Inc 260 665-2052
1310 W Maumee St Angola (46703) ***(G-189)***
Aggregate Mfg Intl LLC 812 278-9670
309 Oolitic Rd Bedford (47421) ***(G-528)***
Aggregate Service, Plymouth *Also called Stone Quary* ***(G-11725)***
Aggrock Quarries Inc 812 246-2582
5421 County Road 403 Charlestown (47111) ***(G-1557)***
Agi International Inc 317 536-2415
2525 N Shadeland Ave D5 Indianapolis (46219) ***(G-6352)***
Agile Mfg Inc 417 845-6065
720 Industrial Park Rd Milford (46542) ***(G-9948)***
Aging Parent Software 317 848-9548
872 Joann Ct Carmel (46032) ***(G-1305)***
Agrati - Park Forest LLC 219 531-2202
4001 Redbow Dr Valparaiso (46383) ***(G-13487)***
Agri - Traders & Repair LLC 260 238-4225
16702 Campbell Rd Spencerville (46788) ***(G-13042)***
Agri Processing Services LLC 765 860-5108
13789 Smokey Ridge Dr Carmel (46033) ***(G-1306)***
Agri-Tronix Corp 317 738-4474
2001 N Morton St Franklin (46131) ***(G-4862)***
Agricor Inc 765 662-0606
1626 S Joaquin Dr Marion (46953) ***(G-9507)***
Agritraders Mfg Inc 260 238-4225
16702 Campbell Rd Spencerville (46788) ***(G-13043)***
Ah Printing Service 219 933-7686
7421 Van Buren Ave Hammond (46324) ***(G-5837)***
Ahaus Tool & Engineering Inc 765 962-3573
200 Industrial Pkwy Richmond (47374) ***(G-11952)***
Ahf Industries Inc 812 936-9988
8647 W State Road 56 French Lick (47432) ***(G-4984)***
Aidan Industries Incorporated 812 239-2803
8539 E Sunset Ave Terre Haute (47805) ***(G-13189)***
Aids To Navigation/Buoys, Noblesville *Also called R R Forrest Company Inc* ***(G-11169)***
Ail, Evansville *Also called Lasertone Inc* ***(G-3598)***
Aim Media Indiana Oper LLC 317 462-5528
22 W New Rd Greenfield (46140) ***(G-5497)***
Aim Media Indiana Oper LLC 317 736-7101
30 S Water St Ste A Franklin (46131) ***(G-4863)***
Aim Media Indiana Oper LLC (PA) 812 372-7811
2980 N National Rd A Columbus (47201) ***(G-1851)***
Aim Media Indiana Oper LLC 812 372-7811
2980 N National Rd Ste A Columbus (47201) ***(G-1852)***
Aim Media Indiana Oper LLC 812 522-4871
100 Saint Louis Ave Seymour (47274) ***(G-12427)***
Aim Media Indiana Oper LLC 812 988-2221
147 E Main St Nashville (47448) ***(G-10712)***
Aim Media Indiana Oper LLC 812 358-2111
116 E Cross St Brownstown (47220) ***(G-1179)***
Aim Media Indiana Oper LLC 765 778-2324
126 W State St Pendleton (46064) ***(G-11482)***
Aim Media Indiana Oper LLC 317 462-5528
22 W New Rd Greenfield (46140) ***(G-5498)***
Aim Media Indiana Oper LLC 812 736-7101
30 S Water St Ste A Franklin (46131) ***(G-4864)***
Aim Media Indiana Oper LLC 317 462-5528
22 W New Rd Greenfield (46140) ***(G-5499)***
Aims, Carmel *Also called American Intl Mfg Slutions LLP* ***(G-1310)***
Aip/Fw Funding Inc (PA) 212 627-2360
1031 E Us Highway 224 Decatur (46733) ***(G-2364)***
Air & Energy, Mishawaka *Also called River Valley Sheet Metal Inc* ***(G-10118)***
Air Energy Systems Inc (PA) 317 290-8500
4790 W 73rd St Indianapolis (46268) ***(G-6353)***
Air Equipment & Engrg Inc 765 349-9259
60 Industrial Dr Martinsville (46151) ***(G-9594)***
Air Feet LLC 317 441-1817
191 Us Highway 31 S Ste C Greenwood (46142) ***(G-5663)***
Air Filters Sales & Service, Jeffersonville *Also called Purolator Pdts A Filtration Co* ***(G-8418)***
Air Fixtures Inc 260 982-2169
1108 N Sycamore St North Manchester (46962) ***(G-11224)***
Air Liquide Tom Utley 812 838-0599
721 W 6th St Mount Vernon (47620) ***(G-10381)***
Air Products and Chemicals Inc 260 868-9145
4590 County Road 59 Butler (46721) ***(G-1221)***
Air Products and Chemicals Inc 219 787-9551
246 Bailey Station Rd Chesterton (46304) ***(G-1591)***
Air Ride Technologies Inc 812 482-2932
350 S Saint Charles St Jasper (47546) ***(G-8235)***
Air Support Medical, Hope *Also called Flw Plastics Inc* ***(G-6112)***
Air Systems Compents LP 765 483-5841
843 Indianapolis Ave Lebanon (46052) ***(G-9166)***
Air Tech Comfort Systems 219 663-9778
9021 W 141st Ave Cedar Lake (46303) ***(G-1525)***
Air Technology Inc 574 231-0579
5706 S Bridgeton Ln South Bend (46614) ***(G-12696)***
Air Vac Sewer Systems, Rochester *Also called Aqseptence Group Inc* ***(G-12116)***
Air Way Mfg 269 749-2161
7540 S Homestead Dr Hamilton (46742) ***(G-5819)***
Air-Tech Industrial Design 317 797-1804
580 W Main St Monrovia (46157) ***(G-10201)***
Airgas Inc 317 632-7106
1441 Bates St Indianapolis (46201) ***(G-6354)***
Airgas Inc 812 376-9155
415 Park 800 Dr Ste A Greenwood (46143) ***(G-5664)***
Airgas Puritan Medical, Indianapolis *Also called Airgas Usa LLC* ***(G-6355)***
Airgas Usa LLC 812 362-7593
6500 N Us Highway 231 Rockport (47635) ***(G-12163)***
Airgas Usa LLC 812 838-8808
1101 Hwy 69 S Mount Vernon (47620) ***(G-10382)***
Airgas Usa LLC 317 248-8072
5701 Fortune Cir S Ste M Indianapolis (46241) ***(G-6355)***
Airgas Usa LLC 260 749-9576
4935 New Haven Ave Fort Wayne (46803) ***(G-4051)***
Airgas Usa LLC 317 783-2331
5825 Elmwood Ave Indianapolis (46203) ***(G-6356)***
Airgas Usa LLC 812 474-0440
2300 N Burkhardt Rd Evansville (47715) ***(G-3345)***
Airgas Usa LLC 812 537-4101
601 Front St Moores Hill (47032) ***(G-10296)***
Airgas Usa LLC 317 892-5221
8000 N County Road 225 E Pittsboro (46167) ***(G-11582)***
Airjet Inc 574 264-0123
2101 Kinro Ct Elkhart (46514) ***(G-2672)***
Airlift Services International, Alexandria *Also called Energy Inc* ***(G-41)***
Airodapt LLC 559 331-0156
809 E Stewart Dr Rensselaer (47978) ***(G-11911)***
Airomat, Fort Wayne *Also called Life Management Inc* ***(G-4435)***
Airtomic Repair Station 317 738-0148
215 Industrial Dr Franklin (46131) ***(G-4865)***
Ais Gauging, Terre Haute *Also called Industrial Maint Engrg Inc* ***(G-13256)***
Aisin Chemical Indiana LLC 812 793-2888
1004 Industrial Way Crothersville (47229) ***(G-2213)***
Aisin Drivetrain Inc 812 793-2427
1001 Industrial Way Crothersville (47229) ***(G-2214)***
Aisin USA Mfg Inc (HQ) 812 523-1969
1700 E 4th Street Rd Seymour (47274) ***(G-12428)***
Aj Express Broker Service 812 866-1380
73 N Rogers Rd Madison (47250) ***(G-9441)***
Aj Machine Inc 260 248-4900
507 S Line St Columbia City (46725) ***(G-1762)***
Ajax Tocco Magnethermic Corp 317 352-9880
2525 N Shadeland Ave A6 Indianapolis (46219) ***(G-6357)***
Ajax Tool Inc 260 747-7482
2828 Commercial Rd Fort Wayne (46809) ***(G-4052)***
Ajem Welding 812 595-3541
261 E State Road 256 Austin (47102) ***(G-394)***
Ajll LLC 812 477-3611
450 Plaza Dr Evansville (47715) ***(G-3346)***
AJS Belts 219 628-0074
215 Sauk Trl Valparaiso (46385) ***(G-13488)***
AJS Gyros To Go 812 951-1715
441 Rocky Meadow Rd Ne New Salisbury (47161) ***(G-11007)***
AK Industries Inc 574 936-6022
2055 Pidco Dr Plymouth (46563) ***(G-11662)***

AK Steel Corporation 812 362-7317
6500 N Us Highway 231 Rockport (47635) ***(G-12164)***
AK Supply Inc 317 895-0410
10501 E Washington St Indianapolis (46229) ***(G-6358)***
AK Tool and Die 574 286-9010
13990 Early Rd Mishawaka (46545) ***(G-9992)***
AK Tube LLC 317 736-8888
1001 Hurricane St Franklin (46131) ***(G-4866)***
AK Tube LLC 812 341-3200
150 W 450 S Columbus (47201) ***(G-1853)***
Akina Inc 765 464-0501
3495 Kent Ave Ste M200 West Lafayette (47906) ***(G-14048)***
Akka Plastics Inc 812 849-9256
1100 Teke Burton Dr Mitchell (47446) ***(G-10155)***
Akori Software 574 595-5413
1510 Cardinal Cir Rochester (46975) ***(G-12115)***
Akron Concrete Products Inc (PA) 574 893-4841
321 N Maple St Akron (46910) ***(G-1)***
Akron Foundry Inc 574 893-4548
502 E Main St Akron (46910) ***(G-2)***
Akzo Nobel Coatings Inc 574 372-2000
1102 Leiter Dr Warsaw (46580) ***(G-13836)***
Al Fe Corporate Group, Fort Wayne *Also called Al-Fe Heat Treating Inc* ***(G-4054)***
Al Fe Heat Treating-Ohio Inc (PA) 260 747-9422
6920 Pointe Inverness Way # 140 Fort Wayne (46804) ***(G-4053)***
Al Perry Enterprises Inc (PA) 812 867-7727
9203 Petersburg Rd Evansville (47725) ***(G-3347)***
Al's, La Porte *Also called Lakeshore Foods Corp* ***(G-8785)***
Al-Ex Inc 574 206-0100
3170 Windsor Ct Elkhart (46514) ***(G-2673)***
Al-Fe Heat Treating Inc (PA) 260 747-9422
6920 Pointe Inverness Way # 140 Fort Wayne (46804) ***(G-4054)***
Al-Fe Heat Treating Inc 888 747-2533
6920 Pointe Inverness Way Fort Wayne (46804) ***(G-4055)***
Al-Fe Heat Treating Inc 260 563-8321
200 Wedcor Ave Wabash (46992) ***(G-13720)***
Al-Fe Systems Inc 260 483-4411
2349 E Cardinal Dr Columbia City (46725) ***(G-1763)***
Al-Ko Kober, Elkhart *Also called Dexter Axle Company* ***(G-2796)***
Al-Marco Products, Fort Wayne *Also called Martin Spouting Inc* ***(G-4453)***
Alacheri Publishing LLC 317 755-6670
8335 Catamaran Dr Indianapolis (46236) ***(G-6359)***
Alan Daily 574 595-6253
7300 S 600 E Star City (46985) ***(G-13069)***
Alan W Long 812 265-6717
120 E Main St Madison (47250) ***(G-9442)***
Albanese Candy Retail, Merrillville *Also called Albanese Conf Group Inc* ***(G-9694)***
Albanese Conf Group Inc (PA) 219 942-1877
5441 E Lincoln Hwy Merrillville (46410) ***(G-9693)***
Albanese Conf Group Inc 219 738-2333
1910 W Us 30 Merrillville (46410) ***(G-9694)***
Albany Metal Treating Inc 765 789-6470
400 S Gray St Albany (47320) ***(G-10)***
Alberding Woodworking Inc 260 728-9526
7050 N 200 W Decatur (46733) ***(G-2365)***
Albert Ransom Logging Inc 812 567-2012
7300 Lauderdale Rd Dale (47523) ***(G-2330)***
Albertson Seed Sales 765 267-0680
3868 W County Road 1200 S Russellville (46175) ***(G-12238)***
Albertson's Sports Shop, Warsaw *Also called G & S Johnson Outdoors LLC* ***(G-13880)***
Albion New ERA, Albion *Also called All Printing and Publications* ***(G-15)***
Alcatraz Brewing Co., Indianapolis *Also called Tavistock Restaurants LLC* ***(G-8040)***
Alcoa, Newburgh *Also called Arconic Inc* ***(G-11021)***
Alcoa, Indianapolis *Also called Arconic Inc* ***(G-6416)***
Alcoa Csi, Crawfordsville *Also called Closure Systems Intl Inc* ***(G-2139)***
Alcoa Inc 765 447-1707
160 N 36th St Lafayette (47905) ***(G-8849)***
Alcoa Warrick LLC 812 853-6111
4400 W State Route 66 Newburgh (47630) ***(G-11019)***
Alconex Specialty Products (PA) 260 744-3446
4204 W Ferguson Rd Fort Wayne (46809) ***(G-4056)***
Alconex Specialty Products 260 744-3446
4201 Piper Dr Fort Wayne (46809) ***(G-4057)***
Ald Indy Inc 317 826-3833
12993 Parkside Dr Fishers (46038) ***(G-3867)***
Aldridge Cabinets 812 873-6723
10304 W 500 N Deputy (47230) ***(G-2458)***
Alebro LLC 317 876-9212
7690 Zionsville Rd Indianapolis (46268) ***(G-6360)***
Aleo Inc 317 324-8583
10396 Lakeland Dr Fishers (46037) ***(G-3868)***
Aleph Bet Document Centre 260 749-2288
13539 Old 24 E New Haven (46774) ***(G-10927)***
Alex and Ani LLC 317 575-8449
8702 Keystone Xing Indianapolis (46240) ***(G-6361)***
Alex Mid West, La Porte *Also called Alexandria Mw LLC* ***(G-8729)***
Alexander Machine 812 879-4982
7847 Jones Rd Gosport (47433) ***(G-5349)***
Alexander Screw Products Inc 317 898-5313
8750 Pendleton Pike Indianapolis (46226) ***(G-6362)***
Alexandria Extrsion Midamerica, Indianapolis *Also called Alexandria Extrusion Company* ***(G-6363)***
Alexandria Extrusion Company 317 545-1221
4925 Aluminum Dr Indianapolis (46218) ***(G-6363)***
Alexandria Mw LLC 219 324-9541
4747 W State Road 2 Ste B La Porte (46350) ***(G-8729)***
Alexandria Times-Tribune, Alexandria *Also called Elwood Publishing Co Inc* ***(G-40)***
Alexin LLC 260 353-3100
1390 S Adams St Bluffton (46714) ***(G-863)***
Algaewheel Inc 317 582-1400
201 N Illinois St # 1200 Indianapolis (46204) ***(G-6364)***
Algalco LLC 317 361-2787
6532 Castle Knoll Ct Indianapolis (46250) ***(G-6365)***
Alh Building Systems, Markle *Also called Affordable Luxury Homes Inc* ***(G-9575)***
Alig LLC 812 362-7593
6500 N Us Highway 231 Rockport (47635) ***(G-12165)***
All 4u Printing LLC 317 845-2955
6710 W 425 S Morgantown (46160) ***(G-10347)***
All About Organizing 513 238-8157
253 Charles A Liddle Dr # 1 Lawrenceburg (47025) ***(G-9130)***
All American Awards Inc 765 296-4333
11624 S Glick St Mulberry (46058) ***(G-10416)***
All American Components, Hoagland *Also called Bk International LLC* ***(G-6063)***
All American Group Inc (HQ) 574 262-0123
2831 Dexter Dr Elkhart (46514) ***(G-2674)***
All American Group Inc 574 262-9889
1251 N Nappanee St Elkhart (46514) ***(G-2675)***
All American Group Inc 574 262-0123
2831 Dexter Dr Elkhart (46514) ***(G-2676)***
All American Group Inc 574 825-8555
14489 Us Highway 20 Middlebury (46540) ***(G-9868)***
All American Group Inc 574 825-1720
51165 Greenfield Pkwy Middlebury (46540) ***(G-9869)***
All American Homes LLC (HQ) 574 266-3044
2831 Dexter Dr Elkhart (46514) ***(G-2677)***
All American Homes Indiana LLC 260 724-9171
1418 S 13th St Decatur (46733) ***(G-2366)***
All American Homes LLC 260 724-7391
309 S 13th St Decatur (46733) ***(G-2367)***
All American Screen Prtg LLC 765 914-7600
16914 Massey Rd Hagerstown (47346) ***(G-5802)***
All American Tent & Awning Inc 812 232-4220
1140 3rd Ave Terre Haute (47807) ***(G-13190)***
All American Vending, Indianapolis *Also called Window Man Inc* ***(G-8203)***
All Amrcan Shtter Cmpnents LLC 260 639-0112
14525 Bruick Ln Hoagland (46745) ***(G-6062)***
All Borders Expediting LLC 260 459-1434
1105 River Oak Run Fort Wayne (46804) ***(G-4058)***
All City Metal Craft Inc 317 782-9340
121 W Sumner Ave Indianapolis (46217) ***(G-6366)***
All Metal Polishing 219 980-3011
2777 E 83rd Pl Merrillville (46410) ***(G-9695)***
All N One 219 226-9263
905 Hub Ct Crown Point (46307) ***(G-2224)***
All Occasions Gift Shop LLC 513 314-5693
19062 S Main St Metamora (47030) ***(G-9762)***
All Points Tool & Mfg 574 935-3944
2743 Pioneer Dr Plymouth (46563) ***(G-11663)***
All Printing and Publications 260 636-2727
407 S Orange St Albion (46701) ***(G-15)***
All Pro Shearing Inc 317 691-1005
1905 Lawton Ave Indianapolis (46203) ***(G-6367)***
All Rvs Manufacturing Inc 574 538-1559
1055 N 625 W Shipshewana (46565) ***(G-12602)***
All Star Turf Management LLC 317 861-1234
7441 W Creekside Ct New Palestine (46163) ***(G-10966)***
All State Manufacturing Co Inc 812 466-2276
4024 2nd Pkwy Terre Haute (47804) ***(G-13191)***
All Steel Carports Inc 765 284-0694
2200 N Granville Ave Muncie (47303) ***(G-10426)***
All Steel Crprts Buildings LLC 765 284-0694
2200 N Granville Ave Muncie (47303) ***(G-10427)***
All-Flex Inc 812 949-8898
6451 S Park Dr Georgetown (47122) ***(G-5140)***
All-Phase Construction Co LLC 317 345-7057
10182 Orange Blossom Trl Fishers (46038) ***(G-3869)***
All-Pro Pump & Repair Inc 317 738-4203
7907 W 500 S Morgantown (46160) ***(G-10348)***
All-Rite Ready Mix Inc 812 926-0920
10513 Morgan Branch Rd Aurora (47001) ***(G-369)***
All-Weather Products Inc 812 867-6403
8346 Baumgart Rd Evansville (47725) ***(G-3348)***
Allegheny Ludlum LLC 765 529-9570
516 W State Road 38 New Castle (47362) ***(G-10890)***
Allegheny Ludlum Corp 412 394-2800
250 E Lafayette St Portland (47371) ***(G-11808)***
Allegheny Petroleum Pdts Co 812 897-0760
422 W Degonia Rd Boonville (47601) ***(G-906)***

ALPHABETIC

Allegiance Tool & Die Inc.....574 277-1819
12888 Industrial Park Dr Granger (46530) ***(G-5389)***
Allegion Public Ltd Company.....317 810-3700
11819 N Pennsylvania St Carmel (46032) ***(G-1307)***
Allegion S&S Holding Co Inc (HQ).....317 810-3700
11819 N Pennsylvania St Carmel (46032) ***(G-1308)***
Allegra Print & Imaging, Warsaw *Also called Hugh K Eagan* ***(G-13891)***
Allegra Print & Imaging, Elkhart *Also called Nea LLC* ***(G-3059)***
Allegra Print & Imaging, New Salisbury *Also called Cunningham Printing Inc* ***(G-11008)***
Allegra Print & Imaging, Indianapolis *Also called Wise Printing Inc* ***(G-8206)***
Allegro Microsystems LLC.....765 854-2263
11711 N Penn St Ste 240 Carmel (46032) ***(G-1309)***
Allen C Terhune & Associates (PA).....765 948-4164
122 S Main St Fairmount (46928) ***(G-3828)***
Allen Fabricators Inc.....260 458-0008
10106 Smith Rd Fort Wayne (46809) ***(G-4059)***
Allen Industries Inc (PA).....317 595-0730
6874 Hawthorn Park Dr Indianapolis (46220) ***(G-6368)***
Allen Machine & Tool, Scottsburg *Also called Stanley Allen* ***(G-12383)***
Allen-Davis Enterprises Inc.....574 303-2173
920 Brook Run Dr Apt 3b Mishawaka (46544) ***(G-9993)***
Allergyfree Inc.....765 349-0006
3755 Adams Dr Martinsville (46151) ***(G-9595)***
Alli Medical LLC.....317 625-4535
36 E Rowan Run Westfield (46074) ***(G-14134)***
Alliance Coating LLC.....574 772-3372
204 E Danker St Knox (46534) ***(G-8562)***
Alliance Electric.....812 590-3500
1002 Industrial Blvd Sellersburg (47172) ***(G-12387)***
Alliance Machine, Boonville *Also called Sons of Thunder* ***(G-922)***
Alliance Sheets LLC.....574 622-6020
1725 Commerce Ctr Dr Bristol (46507) ***(G-1042)***
Alliance Tool & Equipment Inc.....260 432-2909
3919 Engle Rd Fort Wayne (46804) ***(G-4060)***
Alliance Winding Equipment (PA).....260 478-2200
3939 Vanguard Dr Fort Wayne (46809) ***(G-4061)***
Allied Boiler & Welding Co.....317 272-4820
1974 N County Road 600 E Avon (46123) ***(G-426)***
Allied Enterprises Inc.....765 288-8849
3228 W Kilgore Ave Muncie (47304) ***(G-10428)***
Allied Mfg Partners Inc.....260 428-2670
4410 New Haven Ave Fort Wayne (46803) ***(G-4062)***
Allied OSI Labs, Indianapolis *Also called Positrax Inc* ***(G-7708)***
Allied Specialty Precision Inc.....574 255-4718
815 E Lowell Ave Mishawaka (46545) ***(G-9994)***
Allied Steel Rule Dies Inc.....317 634-9835
5811 W Minnesota St Indianapolis (46241) ***(G-6369)***
Allied Tube & Conduit Corp.....812 265-9255
4004 N Us 421 Madison (47250) ***(G-9443)***
Allied Tube & Conduit Corp.....765 459-8811
101 E Broadway St Kokomo (46901) ***(G-8590)***
Allin Plastics Engraving.....219 972-2223
2845 Garfield Ave Hammond (46322) ***(G-5838)***
Allison Parts Distribution, Indianapolis *Also called Allison Transmission Inc* ***(G-6376)***
Allison Payment Systems LLC (PA).....317 808-2400
2200 Production Dr Indianapolis (46241) ***(G-6370)***
Allison Transm Holdings Inc (PA).....317 242-5000
1 Allison Way Indianapolis (46222) ***(G-6371)***
Allison Transmission Inc.....317 280-6206
6040 W 62nd St Indianapolis (46278) ***(G-6372)***
Allison Transmission Inc (HQ).....317 242-5000
1 Allison Way Indianapolis (46222) ***(G-6373)***
Allison Transmission Inc.....317 242-5000
901 Grande Ave Indianapolis (46222) ***(G-6374)***
Allison Transmission Inc.....317 242-2080
2840 Fortune Cir Dr W A Indianapolis (46241) ***(G-6375)***
Allison Transmission Inc.....317 821-5104
5902 Decatur Blvd Indianapolis (46241) ***(G-6376)***
Allison Transmission Division, Indianapolis *Also called Allison Transmission Inc* ***(G-6374)***
Allomatic Products Company (HQ).....800 686-4729
609 E Chaney St Sullivan (47882) ***(G-13078)***
Alloy Custom Products LLC.....765 564-4684
9701 Old State Road 25 N Lafayette (47905) ***(G-8850)***
Allsports.....812 883-3561
210 N Main St Salem (47167) ***(G-12281)***
Allstate Mfg, Terre Haute *Also called All State Manufacturing Co Inc* ***(G-13191)***
Allterrain Paving & Cnstr LLC.....502 265-4731
2235 Corydon Pike New Albany (47150) ***(G-10742)***
Almega Wire Products, Bremen *Also called Almega/Tru-Flex Inc* ***(G-982)***
Almega/Tru-Flex Inc.....574 546-2113
3917 State Road 106 Bremen (46506) ***(G-982)***
Almet Inc.....260 493-1556
300 Hartzell Rd New Haven (46774) ***(G-10928)***
Almighty Business Cards LLC.....260 615-4663
9912 White Hill Ct Fort Wayne (46804) ***(G-4063)***
Almiras Bakery.....219 844-4334
2635 169th St Hammond (46323) ***(G-5839)***
Almix, Fort Wayne *Also called Asphalt Equipment Company Inc* ***(G-4093)***
Almost Famous Printing.....219 793-6388
1309 119th St Whiting (46394) ***(G-14266)***
Alocit USA.....317 631-9111
1128 S West St Indianapolis (46225) ***(G-6377)***
Alpaca Holler LLC.....513 544-6866
25327 Jacobs Rd Guilford (47022) ***(G-5796)***
Alpha Baking Co Inc.....574 234-0188
1910 Lincoln Way W South Bend (46628) ***(G-12697)***
Alpha Baking Co Inc.....219 324-7440
360 N Fail Rd La Porte (46350) ***(G-8730)***
Alpha Laser and Imaging, Evansville *Also called Mid-America Environmental LLC* ***(G-3626)***
Alpha Manufacturing and Design.....574 267-2171
2070 N Cessna Rd Warsaw (46582) ***(G-13837)***
Alpha Prime Computers.....260 347-4800
113 S Main St Kendallville (46755) ***(G-8452)***
Alpha Systems LLC.....574 295-5206
5120 Beck Dr Elkhart (46516) ***(G-2678)***
Alpha Water Conditioning.....765 281-8820
4021 N Broadway Ave Rear Muncie (47303) ***(G-10429)***
Alpha-Pure Corporation.....877 645-7676
251 N Roeske Ave Trail Creek (46360) ***(G-13440)***
AlphaGraphics, Carmel *Also called Kile Enterprises Inc* ***(G-1423)***
AlphaGraphics, South Bend *Also called Summit LLC* ***(G-12961)***
AlphaGraphics, Evansville *Also called Thomas E Slade Inc* ***(G-3760)***
AlphaGraphics, Elkhart *Also called Printed By Erik Inc* ***(G-3116)***
Alpine Enterprises.....574 773-5475
12844 N 700 W Nappanee (46550) ***(G-10645)***
Alro Group, Indianapolis *Also called Alro Steel Corporation* ***(G-6378)***
Alro Steel Corporation.....317 781-3800
5620 Churchman Ave Indianapolis (46203) ***(G-6378)***
Alro Steel Corporation.....260 749-1829
4929 New Haven Ave Fort Wayne (46803) ***(G-4064)***
Als Enviromental.....219 299-8127
2400 Cumberland Dr Valparaiso (46383) ***(G-13489)***
Als Woodcraft Inc.....812 967-4458
435 E Main St Borden (47106) ***(G-927)***
Alsip Pallet Company Inc.....219 322-3288
1154 Thiel Dr Schererville (46375) ***(G-12314)***
Altair Nanotechnologies Inc.....317 333-7617
3019 Enterprise Dr Anderson (46013) ***(G-60)***
Altapure LLC.....574 485-2145
1400 E Angela Blvd # 102 South Bend (46617) ***(G-12698)***
Altec Engineering Inc (PA).....574 293-1965
2401 W Mishawaka Rd Elkhart (46517) ***(G-2679)***
Altec Industries Inc.....317 872-3460
5201 W 84th St Indianapolis (46268) ***(G-6379)***
Altek Inc.....812 385-2561
1603 E Broadway St Princeton (47670) ***(G-11863)***
Altek Mfg. Co., Clarksville *Also called Precision Automation Co Inc* ***(G-1691)***
Alternative Container, Indianapolis *Also called Jenson Industries Inc* ***(G-7301)***
Alternative Fuel Solutions LLC.....260 224-1965
8380 N 200 W Huntington (46750) ***(G-6185)***
Alterra Plastics LLC.....812 271-1890
2213 Killion Ave Seymour (47274) ***(G-12429)***
Altivity Packaging, Portage *Also called Graphic Packaging Intl LLC* ***(G-11768)***
Altstadt Business Forms Inc (PA).....812 425-3393
1550 Baker Ave Evansville (47710) ***(G-3349)***
Altstadt Office City, Evansville *Also called Altstadt Business Forms Inc* ***(G-3349)***
Alum-Elec Structures Inc.....260 347-9362
250 W Grove St Kendallville (46755) ***(G-8453)***
Aluminum Cargo Trailers Inc.....260 463-0185
2840 N State Road 9 Lagrange (46761) ***(G-9030)***
Aluminum Conversion Inc.....260 856-2180
204 Parkway Cromwell (46732) ***(G-2207)***
Aluminum Extrusions.....574 206-0100
3170 Windsor Ct Elkhart (46514) ***(G-2680)***
Aluminum Foundries Inc.....765 584-6501
1036 N Old Highway 27 Winchester (47394) ***(G-14324)***
Aluminum Wldg & Mch Works Inc.....219 787-8066
225 W Dunes Hwy Chesterton (46304) ***(G-1592)***
Alveys Sign Co Inc.....812 867-2567
13100 Highway 57 Evansville (47725) ***(G-3350)***
Alvin J Nix.....812 347-2510
2820 Fairdale Rd Nw Ramsey (47166) ***(G-11892)***
Always Sun Tanning Center (PA).....812 238-2786
1420 N 25th St Terre Haute (47803) ***(G-13192)***
Alymat Publishing LLC.....812 933-9940
13198 N County Road 400 E Batesville (47006) ***(G-490)***
AM General Commercial, South Bend *Also called AM General LLC* ***(G-12700)***
AM General Holdings LLC (HQ).....574 237-6222
105 N Niles Ave South Bend (46617) ***(G-12699)***
AM General LLC.....574 235-7326
105 N Niles Ave South Bend (46617) ***(G-12700)***
AM General LLC.....574 258-7523
13200 Mckinley Hwy Mishawaka (46545) ***(G-9995)***
AM General LLC.....574 257-4268
105 N Niles Ave South Bend (46617) ***(G-12701)***
AM General LLC.....574 258-6699
711 W Chippewa Ave South Bend (46614) ***(G-12702)***

AM Manufacturing Company Ind 800 342-6744
9200 Calumet Ave Munster (46321) *(G-10594)*

AM Publishing Inc 317 806-0001
11650 Lantern Rd Ste 103 Fishers (46038) *(G-3870)*

AM Stabilizers Corporation 219 844-3980
705 Silhavy Rd Valparaiso (46383) *(G-13490)*

Am-Safe Commercial Products, Elkhart *Also called Amsafe Partners Inc* *(G-2690)*

AMA Usa Inc 317 329-6590
7998 Georgetown Rd # 400 Indianapolis (46268) *(G-6380)*

Amacor, Anderson *Also called Advanced Magnesium Alloys Corp* *(G-59)*

Amalgamated Incorporated 260 489-2549
6211 Discount Dr Fort Wayne (46818) *(G-4065)*

Amanda Elizabeth LLC 602 317-9633
3711 Vanguard Dr Ste C Fort Wayne (46809) *(G-4066)*

Amatrol Inc (PA) 812 288-8285
2400 Centennial Blvd Jeffersonville (47130) *(G-8322)*

Ambandash 260 415-1709
3826 Walden Run Fort Wayne (46815) *(G-4067)*

Ambassador Steel Corporation 317 834-3434
149 Sycamore Ln Mooresville (46158) *(G-10302)*

Ambre Blends 317 257-0202
7825 E 89th St Indianapolis (46256) *(G-6381)*

Ambu, Noblesville *Also called King Systems Corporation* *(G-11137)*

AMC Acquisition Corporation 215 572-0738
4840 Beck Dr Elkhart (46516) *(G-2681)*

Amcor Phrm Packg USA Inc 812 591-2332
1108 N State Road 3 Westport (47283) *(G-14208)*

Amcor Rigid Plastics Usa LLC 317 736-4313
3201 Bearing Dr Franklin (46131) *(G-4867)*

AMD Group LLC 317 202-9530
8925 N Meridian St # 250 Indianapolis (46260) *(G-6382)*

AMD Lasers, Indianapolis *Also called AMD Group LLC* *(G-6382)*

Amerawhip Inc 317 639-5248
1735 W 18th St Indianapolis (46202) *(G-6383)*

Amercan, Fort Wayne *Also called Scotia Corporation* *(G-4610)*

Ameri Kan 574 533-7032
1919 E Center St Warsaw (46580) *(G-13838)*

Ameri-Can Engineering, Argos *Also called T I B Inc* *(G-278)*

Ameri-Kan, Fort Wayne *Also called Rugged Steel Works LLC* *(G-4598)*

Ameri-Kart Corp 225 642-7874
17196 State Road 120 Bristol (46507) *(G-1043)*

Ameri-Kart Corp (HQ) 574 848-7462
17196 State Road 120 Bristol (46507) *(G-1044)*

Ameri-Tek Manufacturing Inc 574 753-8058
3332 Billiard Dr Logansport (46947) *(G-9320)*

Ameribridge LLC 317 826-2000
5425 Poindexter Dr Indianapolis (46235) *(G-6384)*

America Corn Cutter 219 733-0885
9203 Twin Acres Dr Wanatah (46390) *(G-13819)*

American Agri Curtains Div, Delphi *Also called Mar-Co Packaging Inc* *(G-2423)*

American Air Filter Co Inc 888 223-2003
210 N Enterprise Blvd Lebanon (46052) *(G-9167)*

American Art Clay Co Inc (PA) 317 243-0066
6060 Guion Rd Indianapolis (46254) *(G-6385)*

American Axle, Bluffton *Also called Metaldyne M&A Bluffton LLC* *(G-882)*

American Barge Line Company (HQ) 812 288-0100
1701 E Market St Jeffersonville (47130) *(G-8323)*

American Beverage Marketers, New Albany *Also called Clark Foods Inc* *(G-10761)*

American Beverage Marketers 812 944-3585
810 Progress Blvd New Albany (47150) *(G-10743)*

American Bottling Company 574 291-9000
4610 S Burnett Dr South Bend (46614) *(G-12703)*

American Bottling Company 260 484-4177
2711 Independence Dr Fort Wayne (46808) *(G-4068)*

American Bottling Company 765 987-7800
6083 State Rd Spiceland (47385) *(G-13053)*

American Chemical Service 219 613-4114
12227 S Williams Ct Crown Point (46307) *(G-2225)*

American Chiropractor Mag Inc 260 471-4090
5005 Riviera Ct Fort Wayne (46825) *(G-4069)*

American Chiropractor, The, Fort Wayne *Also called American Chiropractor Mag Inc (G-4069)*

American Classifieds 317 782-8111
359 E Thompson Rd Indianapolis (46227) *(G-6386)*

American Cmnty Bnk Ind Modem 2 .... 219 627-3381
7880 Wicker Ave Saint John (46373) *(G-12259)*

American Colloid Company 812 547-3567
11645 State Road 545 Troy (47588) *(G-13445)*

American Coml Barge Line LLC (HQ) 812 288-0100
1701 E Market St Jeffersonville (47130) *(G-8324)*

American Commercial Lines Inc (HQ) 812 288-0100
1701 E Market St Jeffersonville (47130) *(G-8325)*

American Communications Netwrk, Hagerstown *Also called Brian Bex Report Inc* *(G-5804)*

American Contact Lens Service 317 347-2900
5617 W 74th St Indianapolis (46278) *(G-6387)*

American Containers Inc (PA) 574 936-4068
2526 Western Ave Plymouth (46563) *(G-11664)*

American Door Controls Inc 812 988-4853
51 W State Road 45 Morgantown (46160) *(G-10349)*

American Eagle Security Inc 219 980-1177
6111 Harrison St Ste 126 Merrillville (46410) *(G-9696)*

American Elctrnc Cmpnents Inc 574 295-6330
1101 Lafayette St Elkhart (46516) *(G-2682)*

American Elkhart LLC 574 293-0333
2304 Charlotte Ave Elkhart (46517) *(G-2683)*

American Encoder Repair Servic 219 872-2822
7115 W Lynwood Dr Michigan City (46360) *(G-9765)*

American Express Travel 812 523-0106
709 A Ave E Seymour (47274) *(G-12430)*

American Fabricated Carbide Co 317 773-5520
1335 Pleasant St Noblesville (46060) *(G-11059)*

American Fabricating 812 897-0900
1302 N Rockport Rd Boonville (47601) *(G-907)*

American Fabricators Inc 219 844-4744
5832 Cline Ave Hammond (46323) *(G-5840)*

American Feeding Systems Inc 317 773-5517
15425 Endeavor Dr Noblesville (46060) *(G-11060)*

American Fibertech Corporation (PA) 219 261-3586
4 N New York St Remington (47977) *(G-11904)*

American Fibertech Corporation 219 261-3586
11349 Us Highway 52 S Clarks Hill (47930) *(G-1670)*

American Fire Company 219 840-0630
2603 Oakwood Dr Valparaiso (46383) *(G-13491)*

American Flame Inc 260 459-1703
9230 Conservation Way Fort Wayne (46809) *(G-4070)*

American Gardenworks Inc 765 869-4033
205 W Mauzy St Boswell (47921) *(G-939)*

American Gorwood Corporation 765 948-3401
619 E Jefferson St Fairmount (46928) *(G-3829)*

American Graphics Group 260 589-3117
269 S Jefferson St Berne (46711) *(G-606)*

American Green Technology Inc (HQ) 269 340-9975
52129 Ind St Rte 933 South Bend (46637) *(G-12704)*

American Heritage Shutters 317 598-6908
9450 Timberline Dr Indianapolis (46256) *(G-6388)*

American Home Fragrance, South Bend *Also called Lebermuth Company Inc* *(G-12837)*

American Hydraulic Hoses, Newburgh *Also called Cindon Inc* *(G-11024)*

American Hydro Systems Inc 866 357-5063
7201 Engle Rd Fort Wayne (46804) *(G-4071)*

American Hydroformers Inc 260 428-2660
2320 Meyer Rd Fort Wayne (46803) *(G-4072)*

American Industrial Corp 317 859-9900
1400 American Way Greenwood (46143) *(G-5665)*

American Industrial McHy Inc 219 755-4090
4015 W 83rd Pl Merrillville (46410) *(G-9697)*

American Integrated Mfg Co 317 445-2056
629 E Columbine Ln Westfield (46074) *(G-14135)*

American Intl Mfg Slutions LLP 317 443-5778
378 Abbedale Ct Carmel (46032) *(G-1310)*

American Keeper Corporation 765 521-2080
3300 S Commerce Dr New Castle (47362) *(G-10891)*

American Label Products Inc 317 873-9850
4949 W 106th St Zionsville (46077) *(G-14416)*

American Lawn Mower 800 633-1501
7444 Shadeland Stn Way Indianapolis (46256) *(G-6389)*

American Lawn Mower Co., Indianapolis *Also called Great States Corporation* *(G-7040)*

American Leak Detection, Fishers *Also called Ald Indy Inc* *(G-3867)*

American Licorice Company (PA) 510 487-5500
1900 Whirlpool Dr S La Porte (46350) *(G-8731)*

American Licorice Company 219 362-5790
1900 Whirlpool Dr S La Porte (46350) *(G-8732)*

American Limb & Orthopedic Co 574 522-3643
58382 State Road 19 # 122 Elkhart (46517) *(G-2684)*

American Machine Fabrication 812 944-4136
1223 E 8th St New Albany (47150) *(G-10744)*

American Meat Packing Div, La Porte *Also called Kane-Miller Corp* *(G-8775)*

American Medical & Dntl Eqp LL 219 628-2928
3201 Parker Dr Valparaiso (46383) *(G-13492)*

American Melt Blown Filtration 219 866-3500
1030 E Elm St Rensselaer (47978) *(G-11912)*

American Metal Coatings Inc 765 608-2100
6501 Production Dr Anderson (46013) *(G-61)*

American Millwork, Elkhart *Also called AMC Acquisition Corporation* *(G-2681)*

American Mitsuba Corporation 989 779-4962
21600 Monroeville Rd Monroeville (46773) *(G-10191)*

American Mobile Power, Fairmount *Also called American Gorwood Corporation* *(G-3829)*

American Mobile Sound Ind LLC 765 288-1500
2418 W 7th St Muncie (47302) *(G-10430)*

American Mtsuba Corp Ind Plant, Monroeville *Also called American Mitsuba Corporation* *(G-10191)*

American Natural Resources LLC 219 922-6444
120 N Broad St Griffith (46319) *(G-5762)*

American Natural Resources Str, Griffith *Also called American Natural Resources LLC* *(G-5762)*

American Oak Preserving Co Inc (PA) 574 896-2171
601 Mulberry St North Judson (46366) *(G-11206)*

American Orthpdics Prosthetics 765 447-0111
720 Farabee Ct Lafayette (47905) **(G-8851)**

American Pallet & Recycl Inc (PA) 219 322-4391
1203 Sheffield Ave Dyer (46311) **(G-2492)**

American Pellet Supply LLC 812 398-2225
10228 S Old 41 Carlisle (47838) **(G-1295)**

American Performance Engrg, Peru Also called K&T Performance Engrg LLC **(G-11535)**

American Petroleum 269 223-4135
11044 County Road 2 Middlebury (46540) **(G-9870)**

American Plastic Molding Corp 812 752-2292
965 S Elm St Scottsburg (47170) **(G-12355)**

American Playground, Anderson Also called Delta Excell Incorporated **(G-93)**

American Playground, Anderson Also called AP Acquisition LLC **(G-67)**

American Playground Corp 765 642-0288
505 E 31st St Ste X Anderson (46016) **(G-62)**

American Playground Corp 765 642-0288
2320 Jefferson St Anderson (46016) **(G-63)**

American Precision Svcs Inc 219 977-4451
7110 W 21st Ave Gary (46406) **(G-5027)**

American Printing 219 836-5600
8208 Calumet Ave Munster (46321) **(G-10595)**

American Printing Company (PA) 574 533-5399
2331 Eisenhower Dr N Goshen (46526) **(G-5169)**

American Printing Indiana LLC 765 825-7600
1047 Broadway St Anderson (46012) **(G-64)**

American Reliance Inds Co 260 768-4704
860 N Tuscany Dr Shipshewana (46565) **(G-12603)**

American Renolit Corporation (HQ) 219 324-6886
1207 E Lincolnway La Porte (46350) **(G-8733)**

American Reprographics Co LLC 574 287-2944
1303 Northside Blvd South Bend (46615) **(G-12705)**

American Reusable Energy LLC 317 965-2604
801 N Madison Ave Greenwood (46142) **(G-5666)**

American Roller Company LLC 574 586-3101
201 Industrial Park Dr Walkerton (46574) **(G-13801)**

American Sandblasting 574 233-1384
57375 Allen St South Bend (46619) **(G-12706)**

American School Health Assn 703 506-7675
501 N Morton St Ste 110 Bloomington (47404) **(G-660)**

American Scrap Processing Inc 219 398-1444
3601 Canal St East Chicago (46312) **(G-2515)**

American Senior Homecare 317 849-4968
4519 E 82nd St Ofc Indianapolis (46250) **(G-6390)**

American Speedy Printing, Indianapolis Also called Srnitson Cmmnications Group LLC **(G-7953)**

American Speedy Printing, Valparaiso Also called D-J Printing Specialists Inc **(G-13527)**

American Sportworks, Columbia City Also called Asw LLC **(G-1764)**

American Stair Corporation Inc 815 886-9600
3510 Calumet Ave Hammond (46320) **(G-5841)**

American Stationery Co 765 473-4438
300 N Park Ave Peru (46970) **(G-11515)**

American Steel Rule Die Inc 574 262-3437
3401 Reedy Dr Elkhart (46514) **(G-2685)**

American Stonecast Pdts Inc 574 206-0097
4315 Wyland Dr Elkhart (46516) **(G-2686)**

American Sunspace, Elkhart Also called Wallar Additions Inc **(G-3253)**

American Tool Service Inc (PA) 260 493-6351
7007 Trafalgar Dr Fort Wayne (46803) **(G-4073)**

American Tool Service Inc 317 782-3551
3955 Industrial Blvd Frnt Indianapolis (46254) **(G-6391)**

American Tourister 812 526-0344
11891 N Executive Dr Edinburgh (46124) **(G-2594)**

American Truck Company LLC 260 969-4510
7727 Freedom Way Fort Wayne (46818) **(G-4074)**

American Trucker, New Palestine Also called Informa Business Media Inc **(G-10971)**

American Ultraviolet Co., Inc., Lebanon Also called American Ultraviolet Company **(G-9168)**

American Ultraviolet Company (PA) 765 483-9514
212 S Mount Zion Rd Lebanon (46052) **(G-9168)**

American Veteran Group LLC 317 600-4749
17020 Emerald Green Cir Westfield (46074) **(G-14136)**

American Water Works Co Inc 765 362-3940
809 Banjo Dr Crawfordsville (47933) **(G-2133)**

American Way Marketing LLC 574 295-7466
400 Pine Creek Ct Elkhart (46516) **(G-2687)**

American Wedge Company Inc 812 883-1086
215 Tarr Ave Salem (47167) **(G-12282)**

American Whitetail Inc 812 937-7185
8478 E State Road 62 Ferdinand (47532) **(G-3845)**

American Wholesalers Inc (PA) 812 464-8781
3509 American Way Evansville (47711) **(G-3351)**

American Window and Glass Co (PA) 812 464-9400
2715 Lynch Rd Evansville (47711) **(G-3352)**

American Wire Rope & Sling of 877 634-2545
5760 Dividend Rd Indianapolis (46241) **(G-6392)**

American Woodmark Corporation 765 677-1690
5300 Eastside Parkway Dr Gas City (46933) **(G-5118)**

Americana Development Inc 574 295-3535
400 Collins Rd Elkhart (46516) **(G-2688)**

Americas Best Millwrk Supplrs 574 780-0066
10605 Nutmeg Rd Plymouth (46563) **(G-11665)**

Americas Cabinet Co of Ind 317 788-9533
7367 E Us Highway 40 Greenfield (46140) **(G-5500)**

Americas Coml Trnsp RES Co LLC 812 379-2085
4440 Middle Rd Columbus (47203) **(G-1854)**

Americhef USA, Kendallville Also called Kitchen-Quip Inc **(G-8487)**

Amerifab Inc 317 231-0100
3501 E 9th St Indianapolis (46201) **(G-6393)**

Ameriflo Inc 317 844-2019
1936 S Lynhurst Dr Ste P Indianapolis (46241) **(G-6394)**

Ameriflo2 Inc 317 844-2019
1936 S Lynhurst Dr Ste P Indianapolis (46241) **(G-6395)**

Ameriforce Media LLC 812 961-9478
400 W 7th St Ste 233 Bloomington (47404) **(G-661)**

Amerimax Fabricated Products 574 389-8960
206 Kesco Dr Bristol (46507) **(G-1045)**

Ameriqual Foods, Evansville Also called Ameriqual Group LLC **(G-3354)**

Ameriqual Group LLC (HQ) 812 867-1300
18200 Highway 41 N Evansville (47725) **(G-3353)**

Ameriqual Group LLC 812 867-1444
18200 Highway 41 N Evansville (47725) **(G-3354)**

Ameriqual Packaging, Evansville Also called Ameriqual Group LLC **(G-3353)**

Ameristamp Sign-A-Rama, Evansville Also called Arben Corp **(G-3360)**

Ameristeel, Muncie Also called Tishler Industries Inc **(G-10569)**

Amerlight LLC (PA) 812 602-3452
2800 Lynch Rd Ste B Evansville (47711) **(G-3355)**

AMG Engineering Machining Inc 317 329-4000
4030 Guion Ln Indianapolis (46268) **(G-6396)**

AMG LLC 317 329-4004
4030 Guion Ln Indianapolis (46268) **(G-6397)**

AMG Resources Corporation 219 949-8150
459 Cline Ave Gary (46406) **(G-5028)**

AMI Industries Inc 989 786-3755
1501 Wohlert St Angola (46703) **(G-190)**

Amish Country Popcorn Inc 260 589-8513
5433 S 150 E Berne (46711) **(G-607)**

Amish Hills Woodworking and MA 574 875-3558
64723 County Road 15 Goshen (46526) **(G-5170)**

Amish Robs Tattoos LLC 219 863-9727
106 S Main St Morocco (47963) **(G-10360)**

Amish Woodworking LLC 574 941-4439
8870 State Road 17 Plymouth (46563) **(G-11666)**

Amkus Rescue Systems, Valparaiso Also called Innovative Rescue Systems Inc **(G-13560)**

Amore Forte LLC 702 763-2550
7556 Monroe Ave Hammond (46324) **(G-5842)**

Amore Forte By Moni, Hammond Also called Amore Forte LLC **(G-5842)**

Amos D Graber & Sons 260 749-0526
5229 Bruick Rd New Haven (46774) **(G-10929)**

Amos-Hill Associates Inc 812 526-2671
112 Shelby Ave Edinburgh (46124) **(G-2595)**

AMP Americas LLC 312 300-6700
5431 E 600 N Fair Oaks (47943) **(G-3817)**

AMP CNG, Fair Oaks Also called AMP Americas LLC **(G-3817)**

Ampacet Corporation 812 466-5231
3701 N Fruitridge Ave Terre Haute (47804) **(G-13193)**

Ampacet Corporation 812 466-9828
3801 N Fruitridge Ave Terre Haute (47804) **(G-13194)**

Ampacet Research & Development, Terre Haute Also called Ampacet Corporation **(G-13194)**

Amri Ssci LLC 765 463-0112
3065 Kent Ave West Lafayette (47906) **(G-14049)**

Amrosia Metal Fabrication Inc 812 425-5707
1701 N Kentucky Ave Evansville (47711) **(G-3356)**

AMS Embroidery & Signs LLC 513 313-1613
110 S Main St Unit A Brookville (47012) **(G-1111)**

AMS of Indiana Inc (PA) 574 293-5526
3933 E Jackson Blvd Elkhart (46516) **(G-2689)**

AMS Pro Sound and Lightingame, Muncie Also called American Mobile Sound Ind LLC **(G-10430)**

AMS Productions Machining Inc 317 838-9273
800 Andico Rd Plainfield (46168) **(G-11592)**

Amsafe Partners Inc 574 266-8330
3802 Gallatin Way Elkhart (46514) **(G-2690)**

Amsted Rail Company Inc 219 931-1900
4831 Hohman Ave Hammond (46327) **(G-5843)**

Amt Parts International, Fort Wayne Also called Amt Precision Parts Inc **(G-4076)**

Amt Parts International Corp 260 490-0223
3606 Transportation Dr Fort Wayne (46818) **(G-4075)**

Amt Precision Parts, Fort Wayne Also called Amt Parts International Corp **(G-4075)**

Amt Precision Parts Inc 260 490-0223
3606 Transportation Dr Fort Wayne (46818) **(G-4076)**

Amtek Wholesale Signs, Salem Also called Stingel Enterprises Inc **(G-12306)**

Amusement Games Inc 812 937-7084
23b W Market St Chrisney (47611) **(G-1641)**

An-Mar Wiring Systems Inc 574 255-5523
711 E Grove St Mishawaka (46545) **(G-9996)**

Anabaptist Mennonite Biblical 574 295-3726
3003 Benham Ave Elkhart (46517) **(G-2691)**

Analyticalab Inc (PA) 219 473-9777
  1404 119th St Ste A Whiting (46394) *(G-14267)*

Anasazi Instruments Inc 317 861-7657
  23 S Westside Dr A New Palestine (46163) *(G-10967)*

Anatolia Group Ltd Partnership 203 343-7808
  640 E Michigan St Indianapolis (46202) *(G-6398)*

Anchor Enterprises 812 282-7220
  10 Arctic Spgs Jeffersonville (47130) *(G-8326)*

Anchor Glass Container Corp 765 584-6101
  603 E North St Winchester (47394) *(G-14325)*

Anchor Glass Container Corp 812 537-1655
  200 Belleview Dr Greendale (47025) *(G-5482)*

Anchor Industries 812 664-0772
  9248 W 280 S Owensville (47665) *(G-11427)*

Anchor Industries Inc 812 867-2421
  7701 Highway 41 N Evansville (47725) *(G-3357)*

Ancient Cellars 503 437-4827
  360 W 63rd St Indianapolis (46260) *(G-6399)*

Ancient Faith Ministries 219 728-6786
  1550 Birdie Way Chesterton (46304) *(G-1593)*

Anco Products, Elkhart *Also called Anderson Products Incorporated* *(G-2692)*

Andersen Corporation 260 694-6861
  219 W State Road 218 Poneto (46781) *(G-11744)*

Anderson Enterprises LLC 317 569-1099
  1496 Heathrow Ct Carmel (46033) *(G-1311)*

Anderson Machine Tool, Peru *Also called Fred Anderson* *(G-11527)*

Anderson Memorial Park 765 643-3211
  6805 Dr Martin Luther Anderson (46013) *(G-65)*

Anderson Parking Authority, Anderson *Also called City of Anderson* *(G-86)*

Anderson Products 765 794-4242
  700 E Rd Darlington (47940) *(G-2359)*

Anderson Products Incorporated 574 293-5574
  2500 17th St Elkhart (46517) *(G-2692)*

Anderson Sign Pro 765 642-0281
  633 Jackson St Anderson (46016) *(G-66)*

Anderson Silver Plating Co 574 294-6447
  541 Industrial Pkwy Elkhart (46516) *(G-2693)*

Anderson Winery and Vineyard 219 464-4936
  430 E Us Highway 6 Valparaiso (46383) *(G-13493)*

Andersons Agriculture Group LP 574 626-2522
  8086 E 900 Galveston (46932) *(G-4993)*

Andersons Agriculture Group LP 765 564-6135
  3902 N Anderson Dr Delphi (46923) *(G-2414)*

Andersons Agriculture Group LP 574 753-4974
  2345 S 400 E Logansport (46947) *(G-9321)*

Andersons Clymers Ethanol LLC 574 722-2627
  3389 W County Road 300 S Logansport (46947) *(G-9322)*

Andersons Fertilizer Service 765 538-3285
  527 W 1150 S Romney (47981) *(G-12202)*

Andis Logging Inc 812 723-2357
  76 W County Road 550 S Paoli (47454) *(G-11442)*

Andon Specialties Inc 317 983-1700
  5736 W 79th St Indianapolis (46278) *(G-6400)*

Andover Coils LLC 765 447-1157
  13865 Black Canyon Ct Fishers (46038) *(G-3871)*

Andresen Graphic Processors 317 291-7071
  10843 E County Road 950 N Brownsburg (46112) *(G-1133)*

Android Industries LLC 260 672-0112
  13004 Fogwell Pkwy Roanoke (46783) *(G-12098)*

Android Industries Fort Wayne, Roanoke *Also called Android Industries LLC* *(G-12098)*

Andys Global Inc 317 595-8825
  8445 Castlewood Dr Ste C Indianapolis (46250) *(G-6401)*

Anewco, Elkhart *Also called A New Company Inc* *(G-2658)*

Angel Falls Water Company 812 939-9107
  6621 S Old State Road 59 Clay City (47841) *(G-1701)*

Angelinas Cigars 574 935-5544
  1906 N Oak Dr Plymouth (46563) *(G-11667)*

Angels Wings Expedited 574 339-3038
  1246 Echo Dr South Bend (46614) *(G-12707)*

Angies Printing LLC 765 966-6237
  1751 Sheridan St Richmond (47374) *(G-11953)*

Angleboard, Elkhart *Also called Signode Industrial Group LLC* *(G-3171)*

Anglers Manufacturing 812 988-8040
  217 Salt Creek Rd Nashville (47448) *(G-10713)*

Angola Canvas Co Inc 260 665-9913
  2301 N Wayne St Angola (46703) *(G-191)*

Angola Wire Products Inc (PA) 260 665-9447
  803 Wohlert St Angola (46703) *(G-192)*

Angola Wire Products Inc 260 665-3061
  1300 Wohlert St Angola (46703) *(G-193)*

Anh Refractories Co., Gary *Also called Harbisonwalker Intl Inc* *(G-5057)*

Animal Finders Guide, Terre Haute *Also called Patrick & Sharon Hoctor* *(G-13297)*

Animalsink 317 496-8467
  7489 Windridge Way Brownsburg (46112) *(G-1134)*

Animated Dynamics Inc 765 418-5359
  1281 Win Hentschel Blvd West Lafayette (47906) *(G-14050)*

Anippe 317 979-1110
  11486 Enclave Blvd Fishers (46038) *(G-3872)*

Anliker Machine, Chalmers *Also called Ken Anliker* *(G-1547)*

Anna Daisys LLC 812 346-7623
  309 N State St North Vernon (47265) *(G-11247)*

Annabella Publications LLC 219 663-4244
  1385 Tanglewood Ct Crown Point (46307) *(G-2226)*

Annette Balfour 765 286-1910
  2201 E Memorial Dr Rear Muncie (47302) *(G-10431)*

Annie Oakley Enterprises Inc 260 894-7100
  300 Johnson St Ligonier (46767) *(G-9276)*

Annual Reports Inc 317 736-8838
  1250 Park Ave Franklin (46131) *(G-4868)*

Annual Reports Services, Franklin *Also called Annual Reports Inc* *(G-4868)*

Anodizing Technologies Inc 317 253-5725
  5868 N New Jersey St Indianapolis (46220) *(G-6402)*

Anokhi International Inc 260 750-0418
  10404 Antelope Ct Fort Wayne (46804) *(G-4077)*

ANR Pipeline Company 260 463-3342
  2255 W Us Highway 20 Lagrange (46761) *(G-9031)*

Anthony D Etienne Logging 812 843-5872
  15502 N State Road 66 Magnet (47520) *(G-9502)*

Anthony Wayne Rehabilitation C (PA) 260 744-6145
  8515 Bluffton Rd Fort Wayne (46809) *(G-4078)*

Anthony Wayne Rehabilitation C 317 972-1000
  2762 Rand Rd Indianapolis (46241) *(G-6403)*

Anton Alexander, Fort Wayne *Also called European Concepts LLC* *(G-4250)*

Antreasian Design Inc 317 546-3234
  3124 Ridgeview Dr Indianapolis (46226) *(G-6404)*

Any Reason Signs 260 450-6756
  9809 Johnson Rd Fort Wayne (46818) *(G-4079)*

Anyprint LLC 317 402-5979
  6546 Yorkshire Cir Zionsville (46077) *(G-14417)*

Ao Inc 317 280-3000
  9227 E Us Highway 36 Avon (46123) *(G-427)*

Aoc LLC 219 465-4384
  2552 Industrial Dr Valparaiso (46383) *(G-13494)*

Aom Bookshop 317 493-8095
  5239 Rockville Rd Ste B Indianapolis (46224) *(G-6405)*

AP Acquisition LLC 765 642-0288
  505 E 31st St Ste X Anderson (46016) *(G-67)*

AP Sign Group LLC 317 257-1869
  1160 W 16th St Indianapolis (46202) *(G-6406)*

Apartment Assn of Fort Wayne 260 482-2916
  3106 Lake Ave Ste A Fort Wayne (46805) *(G-4080)*

Aperion Care 219 874-5211
  1101 E Coolspring Ave Michigan City (46360) *(G-9766)*

Apex AG Solutions LLC 937 564-5421
  5532 Arba Pike Richmond (47374) *(G-11954)*

Apex Electric & Sign Inc 317 326-1325
  4328 E State Road 234 Greenfield (46140) *(G-5501)*

Apex Electric & Sign Inc (PA) 317 326-1325
  500 N Range Line Rd Morristown (46161) *(G-10365)*

Apex Metrology Solutions, Fort Wayne *Also called Metrology Services LLC* *(G-4468)*

Apex Sales & Repair Llc 812 248-9001
  7703 Locust Dr Sellersburg (47172) *(G-12388)*

Apex Tool and Manufacturing 812 425-8121
  2306 N New York Ave Evansville (47711) *(G-3358)*

Apexx Engineering, Montgomery *Also called Apexx Enterprises LLC* *(G-10213)*

Apexx Enterprises LLC 812 486-2443
  973 S 800 E Montgomery (47558) *(G-10213)*

API, Lagrange *Also called Automated Products Intl LLC* *(G-9032)*

API Americas Inc 812 689-6502
  604 Railroad Ave Osgood (47037) *(G-11388)*

API International Inc 317 894-1100
  6219 W Stoner Dr Greenfield (46140) *(G-5502)*

Aplus Signs 765 966-4857
  920 Progress Dr Richmond (47374) *(G-11955)*

APM&co Inc 317 409-5639
  616 W Us Highway 40 Lewisville (47352) *(G-9248)*

Apollo Design Technology Inc 260 497-9191
  4130 Fourier Dr Fort Wayne (46818) *(G-4081)*

Apollo North America Inc 317 573-0777
  301 E Carmel Dr Ste D500 Carmel (46032) *(G-1312)*

Apollo Outdoor Cstm Design Inc 317 718-2502
  7124 E County Road 150 S B Avon (46123) *(G-428)*

Apollo Precision Machining Inc 574 271-1197
  4085 Ralph Jones Dr South Bend (46628) *(G-12708)*

Apollo Prtg & Graphics Ctr Inc 574 287-3707
  731 S Michigan St South Bend (46601) *(G-12709)*

Apotex Corp 317 839-6550
  2516 Airwest Blvd Plainfield (46168) *(G-11593)*

Apothecarys Ointment LLC 574 930-6662
  2630 Prairie Ave South Bend (46614) *(G-12710)*

App Engineering Incorporated 317 755-3422
  5234 Elmwood Ave Indianapolis (46203) *(G-6407)*

App Factor 219 229-1039
  308 Carmody Dr Chesterton (46304) *(G-1594)*

App Press LLC 317 661-4759
  435 Virginia Ave Unit 607 Indianapolis (46203) *(G-6408)*

Appalachian Log HMS Fultn Elc 260 356-5431
  1268 Waterworks Rd Huntington (46750) *(G-6186)*

A L P H A B E T I C

Appalachian Log Structures...............................812 744-5711
  10994 Chesterville Rd Moores Hill (47032) *(G-10297)*

Apparel Design Group.....................................812 339-3355
  671 S Landmark Ave Ste A Bloomington (47403) *(G-662)*

Apparel Promotions Inc...................................574 294-7165
  21269 Buckingham Rd Elkhart (46516) *(G-2694)*

Appel-Olson LLC...219 926-6679
  942 N 651 E Westville (46391) *(G-14213)*

Apple American Group.....................................317 889-1167
  1251 Us Highway 31 N Greenwood (46142) *(G-5667)*

Apple American Language Inst............................812 867-7239
  9200 Moffett Ln Evansville (47725) *(G-3359)*

Apple Blossom Floral......................................765 649-2480
  1845 N Scatterfield Rd Anderson (46012) *(G-68)*

Apple Cyber LLC...812 822-1341
  3307 S Acadia Ct Bloomington (47401) *(G-663)*

Apple Designs, Ligonier *Also called Edna Troyer (G-9281)*

Apple Group Inc..765 675-4777
  122 N East St Tipton (46072) *(G-13387)*

Apple III LLC..317 691-2869
  3928 Kitty Hawk Ct Carmel (46033) *(G-1313)*

Apple Inc...812 342-4225
  2448 Woodland Farms Ct Columbus (47201) *(G-1855)*

Apple Ly Ever After Inc..................................219 838-9397
  3542 Highway Ave Highland (46322) *(G-6035)*

Apple Press Inc..317 253-7752
  6327 Ferguson St Indianapolis (46220) *(G-6409)*

Apple Terrace LLC.......................................260 347-9400
  515 Professional Way Kendallville (46755) *(G-8454)*

Applegate Livestock Eqp Inc (HQ)......................765 964-3715
  902 S State Road 32 Union City (47390) *(G-13452)*

Appleton Grp LLC..219 326-5936
  2362 N Us Highway 35 La Porte (46350) *(G-8734)*

Application Software.....................................317 814-8010
  117 Wood St Greenfield (46140) *(G-5503)*

Application Software.....................................317 843-9775
  13857 Kickapoo Trl Carmel (46033) *(G-1314)*

Application Software Inc..................................317 823-3525
  9801 Fall Creek Rd 101 Indianapolis (46256) *(G-6410)*

Applied Biomedical Techno................................219 465-2079
  4205 Victoria Dr Valparaiso (46383) *(G-13495)*

Applied Coating Converting LLC..........................260 436-4455
  3736 N Wells St Fort Wayne (46808) *(G-4082)*

Applied Composites Engrg Inc............................317 243-4225
  705 S Girls School Rd Indianapolis (46231) *(G-6411)*

Applied Laboratories Inc..................................812 372-2607
  3240 N Indianapolis Rd Columbus (47201) *(G-1856)*

Applied Material Solutions LLC...........................317 769-3829
  3610 Mossy Rock Dr Zionsville (46077) *(G-14418)*

Applied Metals & Mch Works Inc..........................260 424-4834
  1036 Saint Marys Ave Fort Wayne (46808) *(G-4083)*

Applied Technology Group Inc............................260 482-2844
  2230 W Coliseum Blvd Fort Wayne (46808) *(G-4084)*

Applied Thermal Tech Inc.................................574 269-7116
  2169 N 100 E Warsaw (46582) *(G-13839)*

Apr Plastic Fabricating Inc...............................206 482-8523
  Lima Rd Fort Wayne (46805) *(G-4085)*

Apr Plastic Fabricating Inc...............................260 482-8523
  2312 Cass St Fort Wayne (46808) *(G-4086)*

Apsco of Indiana, Fort Wayne *Also called Shank Brothers Inc (G-4618)*

Aptera Software Inc......................................260 969-1410
  201 W Main St Fort Wayne (46802) *(G-4087)*

Aptimise Composites LLC.................................260 484-3139
  8301 Clinton Park Dr Fort Wayne (46825) *(G-4088)*

Aptiv Services Us LLC....................................765 451-5011
  1 Corporate Dr Kokomo (46902) *(G-8591)*

Aptiv Services Us LLC....................................765 451-5011
  1 Corporate Dr Kokomo (46902) *(G-8592)*

Aptiv Services Us LLC....................................765 451-0732
  2151 E Lincoln Rd Kokomo (46902) *(G-8593)*

Aptiv Services Us LLC....................................765 451-5011
  2705 S Goyer Rd Kokomo (46902) *(G-8594)*

Aqseptence Group Inc....................................574 223-3980
  4217 N Old Us Highway 31 Rochester (46975) *(G-12116)*

Aqua Blast Corp...260 728-4433
  1025 W Commerce Dr Decatur (46733) *(G-2368)*

Aqua Nova...812 941-8995
  5914 W Luther Rd Floyds Knobs (47119) *(G-4006)*

Aqua Spa..219 548-4772
  2505 Laporte Ave Ste 119 Valparaiso (46383) *(G-13496)*

Aqua Systems, Avon *Also called New Aqua LLC (G-456)*

Aqua Utility Services LLC................................812 284-9243
  1829 E Spring St New Albany (47150) *(G-10745)*

Aquathin Air & Water Purifictn, Evansville *Also called Kendle Custom Inc (G-3583)*

Aquatic Renovation Systems Inc..........................317 251-0207
  2825 55th Pl Ste G Indianapolis (46220) *(G-6412)*

Aquatic Weed Control, Goshen *Also called Schuyler Corp (G-5321)*

Aquestive Therapeutics..................................219 762-4143
  6465 Ameriplex Dr Portage (46368) *(G-11749)*

AR Tee Enterprises Inc...................................574 848-5543
  19874 County Road 6 Bristol (46507) *(G-1046)*

Arben Corp..812 477-7763
  1300 N Royal Ave Evansville (47715) *(G-3360)*

Arboc Specialty Vehicles LLC............................574 825-1720
  51165 Greenfield Pkwy Middlebury (46540) *(G-9871)*

Arbor Industries Inc......................................574 825-2375
  117 14th Ave Middlebury (46540) *(G-9872)*

Arboramerica Inc...765 572-1212
  7852 W 200 S Westpoint (47992) *(G-14204)*

Arbuckle Industries Inc...................................317 835-7489
  4990 N 550 W Fairland (46126) *(G-3819)*

Arby's, Warsaw *Also called Tili LLC (G-13952)*

ARC Industries..812 471-1633
  615 W Virginia St Evansville (47710) *(G-3361)*

ARC of Greater Boone Cnty Inc..........................765 482-0051
  912 W Main St Lebanon (46052) *(G-9169)*

ARC Rehab Services, Lebanon *Also called ARC of Greater Boone Cnty Inc (G-9169)*

Arcamed LLC..317 375-7733
  5101 Decatur Blvd Ste A Indianapolis (46241) *(G-6413)*

Arcelormittal Burns Harbor LLC..........................219 787-2120
  250 W Us Highway 12 Burns Harbor (46304) *(G-1214)*

Arcelormittal Holdings LLC (HQ)..........................219 399-1200
  3210 Watling St East Chicago (46312) *(G-2516)*

Arcelormittal Indiana Harbor W, East Chicago *Also called Arcelormittal Indiana Hbr LLC (G-2517)*

Arcelormittal Indiana Hbr LLC............................219 399-1200
  3210 Watling St East Chicago (46312) *(G-2517)*

Arcelormittal Kote Inc (HQ)..............................574 654-1000
  30755 Edison Rd New Carlisle (46552) *(G-10878)*

Arcelormittal Minorca Mine Inc (HQ).....................219 399-1200
  3210 Watling St East Chicago (46312) *(G-2518)*

Arcelormittal USA LLC...................................219 787-2120
  250 W Us Highway 12 Chesterton (46304) *(G-1595)*

Arcelormittal USA LLC...................................312 899-3400
  3210 Watling St East Chicago (46312) *(G-2519)*

Arcelormittal USA LLC...................................219 399-6500
  3001 E Columbus Dr East Chicago (46312) *(G-2520)*

Arch Amarlite, Indianapolis *Also called Trulite GL Alum Solutions LLC (G-8104)*

Arch Wood Protection Inc.................................219 464-3949
  2852 Raystone Dr Valparaiso (46383) *(G-13497)*

Archaeasolutions Inc.....................................770 487-5303
  911 E Franklin St Evansville (47711) *(G-3362)*

Archer Products Inc......................................317 899-0700
  8756 E 33rd St Indianapolis (46226) *(G-6414)*

Archer-Daniels-Midland Company.........................219 297-4582
  4463 E Us Highway 24 Goodland (47948) *(G-5157)*

Archer-Daniels-Midland Company.........................317 783-3321
  854 Bethel Ave Beech Grove (46107) *(G-592)*

Archer-Daniels-Midland Company.........................574 773-4138
  252 S Jackson St Nappanee (46550) *(G-10646)*

Archer-Daniels-Midland Company.........................574 773-4131
  301 S Jackson St Nappanee (46550) *(G-10647)*

Archer-Daniels-Midland Company.........................260 824-0079
  1800 W Western Ave Bluffton (46714) *(G-864)*

Archer-Daniels-Midland Company.........................317 784-2200
  1901 S Sherman Dr Indianapolis (46203) *(G-6415)*

Archer-Daniels-Midland Company.........................219 866-2810
  1201 W State Road 114 Rensselaer (47978) *(G-11913)*

Archer-Daniels-Midland Company.........................260 728-8000
  7453 N Piqua Rd Decatur (46733) *(G-2369)*

Archer-Daniels-Midland Company.........................812 424-3581
  2350 Broadway Ave Evansville (47712) *(G-3363)*

Archer-Daniels-Midland Company.........................765 762-6763
  105 E Harrison St Attica (47918) *(G-296)*

Archer-Daniels-Midland Company.........................219 866-3939
  9179 W State Road 14 Rensselaer (47978) *(G-11914)*

Archer-Daniels-Midland Company.........................765 793-2512
  7979 S 1100 W State Line (47982) *(G-13071)*

Archer-Daniels-Midland Company.........................765 523-3286
  2906 S County Road 930 W Frankfort (46041) *(G-4818)*

Archer-Daniels-Midland Company.........................765 362-2965
  3696 E Elm St Crawfordsville (47933) *(G-2134)*

Archer-Daniels-Midland Company.........................812 268-4334
  323 N Holloway St Sullivan (47882) *(G-13079)*

Archer-Daniels-Midland Company.........................574 831-2292
  24120 County Road 142 Goshen (46526) *(G-5171)*

Archibald Brothers Intl Inc...............................812 941-8267
  209 Quality Ave Ste 1 New Albany (47150) *(G-10746)*

Archibald Frozen Desserts, New Albany *Also called Archibald Brothers Intl Inc (G-10746)*

Archimedes Inc..260 347-3903
  2705 Marion Dr Kendallville (46755) *(G-8455)*

Architectural Accents Inc.................................219 922-9333
  1547 Ridge Rd Munster (46321) *(G-10596)*

Architectural Metal Roofg Sup............................812 423-5257
  1400 N Cullen Ave Evansville (47715) *(G-3364)*

Architectural Plywood, New Albany *Also called Dimension Plywood Inc (G-10768)*

Architectural Stone Sales Inc.............................812 279-2421
  1728 30th St Bedford (47421) *(G-529)*

Arco Electric Products, Shelbyville *Also called Kirby Risk Corporation* **(G-12543)**
Arconic Forgings & Extrusions, Lafayette *Also called Arconic Inc* **(G-8852)**
Arconic Inc...765 771-3600
3131 Main St Lafayette (47905) **(G-8852)**
Arconic Inc...812 853-6111
State Highway 66 Newburgh (47630) **(G-11020)**
Arconic Inc...412 553-4545
2792 Laura Lynn Ln Newburgh (47630) **(G-11021)**
Arconic Inc...812 842-3300
4700 Darlington Rd Newburgh (47630) **(G-11022)**
Arconic Inc...317 241-9393
2334 Production Dr Indianapolis (46241) **(G-6416)**
Arctic Clear Products Inc...574 533-7671
1808 Barclay Dr Goshen (46528) **(G-5172)**
Arctic Ice Express Inc...812 333-0423
2423 W Industrial Park Dr Bloomington (47404) **(G-664)**
Arctrans LLC...317 231-1620
1414 S West St Ste B Indianapolis (46225) **(G-6417)**
Ardagh Glass Inc...765 651-1260
123 E Mckinley St Marion (46952) **(G-9508)**
Ardagh Glass Inc...765 768-7891
524 E Center St Dunkirk (47336) **(G-2483)**
Ardagh Glass Inc...765 662-1172
123 E Mckinley St Marion (46952) **(G-9509)**
Ardagh Glass Inc (HQ)...317 558-1002
10194 Crosspoint Blvd Indianapolis (46256) **(G-6418)**
Ardagh Is Services, Marion *Also called Ardagh Glass Inc* **(G-9509)**
Arden Companies LLC...260 747-1657
3510 Piper Dr Fort Wayne (46809) **(G-4089)**
Arden/Benhar Mills, Fort Wayne *Also called Arden Companies LLC* **(G-4089)**
Area 340, Lafayette *Also called Rieth-Riley Cnstr Co Inc* **(G-8993)**
Areva Pharmaceuticals Inc...855 853-4760
7112 Areva Dr Ne Georgetown (47122) **(G-5141)**
Argentum Jewelry Inc...812 336-3100
205 N College Ave Ste 100 Bloomington (47404) **(G-665)**
Aristo LLC...219 962-1032
4410 W 37th Ave Frnt Hobart (46342) **(G-6069)**
Aristo Catalyst Technology, Hobart *Also called Aristo LLC* **(G-6069)**
Aristocrat Inc...812 634-0460
1 Masterbrand Cabinets Dr Jasper (47546) **(G-8236)**
Aristoline Cabinet Inc...260 482-9719
5803 Industrial Rd Fort Wayne (46825) **(G-4090)**
Arizona Sport Shirts Inc...317 481-2160
100 Gasoline Aly Ste Az Indianapolis (46222) **(G-6419)**
Ark Model and Stampings Inc...317 549-3394
2401 N Ritter Ave Indianapolis (46218) **(G-6420)**
Ark Software LLC...317 835-7912
8930 N Timberlane Dr Fountaintown (46130) **(G-4788)**
Armada Optical Services Inc...812 476-6623
701 N Weinbach Ave # 410 Evansville (47711) **(G-3365)**
Armco...219 981-8864
6071 Broadway Merrillville (46410) **(G-9698)**
Armor Clad Inc...812 883-8734
6170 E State Road 56 Salem (47167) **(G-12283)**
Armor Contract Mfg Inc...574 327-2962
300 Comet Ave Elkhart (46514) **(G-2695)**
Armor Parent Corp (PA)...812 962-5000
7140 Office Cir Evansville (47715) **(G-3366)**
Armstrong Drilling Inc...765 455-2445
1490 S Michigan St Burlington (46915) **(G-1209)**
Around Campus LLC...574 360-6571
319 Lamonte Ter South Bend (46616) **(G-12711)**
Arrow Container LLC...317 882-6444
5343 Commerce Square Dr Indianapolis (46237) **(G-6421)**
Arrow Mining Inc (HQ)...270 683-4186
1216 E County Road 900 S Oakland City (47660) **(G-11306)**
Arrow Mining Inc...812 328-2117
1216 E County Road 900 S Oakland City (47660) **(G-11307)**
Arrow Mining Inc...812 328-6154
1216 E County Road 900 S Oakland City (47660) **(G-11308)**
Arrow Powder Coating LLC...317 822-8002
1030 E New York St Indianapolis (46202) **(G-6422)**
Arrow Vault Co Inc...765 742-1704
1312 Underwood St Lafayette (47904) **(G-8853)**
Arrowhead Composites, Muncie *Also called Arrowhead Plastic Engineering* **(G-10432)**
Arrowhead Plastic Engineering (PA)...765 286-0533
2909 S Hoyt Ave Muncie (47302) **(G-10432)**
Arrowhead Plastic Engineering...765 396-9113
1155 N Hartford St Eaton (47338) **(G-2581)**
Arrowhead Plastic Products, Eaton *Also called Arrowhead Plastic Engineering* **(G-2581)**
ARS Nebraska LLC...765 832-5210
515 E 4th St Clinton (47842) **(G-1713)**
Arson Press...812 345-3527
2415 E 4th St Bloomington (47408) **(G-666)**
Art Gallery, The, La Porte *Also called Hjj Inc* **(G-8765)**
Art Ovation...317 769-4301
7615 S State Road 267 Brownsburg (46112) **(G-1135)**
Art Works Sign Co Inc...574 360-9290
55581 Currant Rd Mishawaka (46545) **(G-9997)**

Artek Inc...260 484-4222
3311 Enterprise Rd Fort Wayne (46808) **(G-4091)**
Artemis International Inc...260 436-6899
3711 Vanguard Dr Ste A Fort Wayne (46809) **(G-4092)**
Artemis Intl Solutions Corp...708 665-3155
2600 Roosevelt Rd Valparaiso (46383) **(G-13498)**
Articode Inc...317 569-8357
12524 Gladecrest Dr Carmel (46033) **(G-1315)**
Artisan Interiors Inc (PA)...574 825-9494
526 S Main St Middlebury (46540) **(G-9873)**
Artisan Sheet Metal Corp...812 422-7393
1101 Rexing Rd Wadesville (47638) **(G-13770)**
Artisan Tool & Die Inc...765 288-6653
3805 W State Road 28 Muncie (47303) **(G-10433)**
Artisanz Fabrication Mch LLC...317 708-0228
2198 Reeves Rd Plainfield (46168) **(G-11594)**
Artistic Carton Company...260 925-6060
1201 S Grandstaff Dr Auburn (46706) **(G-312)**
Artistic Expressions Pubg...317 502-6213
111 E South C St Gas City (46933) **(G-5119)**
Artistic Stone Company Inc...812 256-2890
13909 Highway 62 Charlestown (47111) **(G-1558)**
Artsy Canvas...855 206-9045
9900 Westpoint Dr Ste 138 Indianapolis (46256) **(G-6423)**
Artys Logging...812 969-3124
7800 E Highway 11 Se Elizabeth (47117) **(G-2641)**
Arvin Sango Inc (HQ)...812 265-2888
2905 Wilson Ave Madison (47250) **(G-9444)**
Arvin's Creative Woodworking, Loogootee *Also called William R Arvin* **(G-9398)**
Asahi TEC America Corporation...765 962-8399
1757 Sheridan St Richmond (47374) **(G-11956)**
ASAP Identification SEC Inc...317 488-1030
212 W 10th St Ste F100 Indianapolis (46202) **(G-6424)**
ASAP Sign & Lighting Maint...219 464-8865
276 W State Road 130 Valparaiso (46385) **(G-13499)**
Asbestos Abatement & Mold...317 783-0350
816 E Elbert St Indianapolis (46227) **(G-6425)**
Asbury Hall, Evansville *Also called Sycamore Enterprises Inc* **(G-3756)**
ASC, Lebanon *Also called Air Systems Compents LP* **(G-9166)**
Asc Inc...765 472-5331
N Miami Industrial Park Peru (46970) **(G-11516)**
Ascensia Diabetes Care US Inc...201 875-8066
430 S Beiger St Mishawaka (46544) **(G-9998)**
Ascension Space Technology LLP...765 623-5164
7315 Colonial Ct Anderson (46013) **(G-69)**
Ascot Enterprises Inc (PA)...877 773-7751
503 S Main St Nappanee (46550) **(G-10648)**
Ascot Enterprises Inc...260 593-3733
129 Roy St Topeka (46571) **(G-13411)**
Ascot Enterprises Inc...574 773-7751
1901 Cheyenne St Nappanee (46550) **(G-10649)**
Ascot Enterprises Inc...574 773-3104
1901 Cheyenne St Nappanee (46550) **(G-10650)**
Ascot Plant 10, Nappanee *Also called Ascot Enterprises Inc* **(G-10649)**
Asempac Inc...812 945-6303
5300 Foundation Blvd New Albany (47150) **(G-10747)**
Asf Keystones, Hammond *Also called Amsted Rail Company Inc* **(G-5843)**
ASG Unlimited, Indianapolis *Also called Midwest Empire LLC* **(G-7504)**
Ash Access Technology Inc...765 742-4813
3601 Sagamore Pkwy N B Lafayette (47904) **(G-8854)**
Ash-Lin Inc...317 861-1540
386 E Brookville Rd Fountaintown (46130) **(G-4789)**
Asha, Bloomington *Also called American School Health Assn* **(G-660)**
Ashe Industries...219 852-6040
17 Highland St Hammond (46320) **(G-5844)**
Ashley Aluminum Foundry Inc...812 793-2654
125 S Armstrong St Crothersville (47229) **(G-2215)**
Ashley F Ward Inc...574 294-1502
56883 Elk Ct Elkhart (46516) **(G-2696)**
Ashley F Ward Inc...219 879-4177
2031 Tryon Rd Michigan City (46360) **(G-9767)**
Ashley Industrial Molding Inc (PA)...260 587-9155
310 S Wabash St Ashley (46705) **(G-283)**
Ashley Industrial Molding Inc...260 349-1982
100 S Progress Dr W Kendallville (46755) **(G-8456)**
Ashley Machine, Greensburg *Also called Mssh Inc* **(G-5624)**
Ashley Ward, Elkhart *Also called Ashley F Ward Inc* **(G-2696)**
Ashley Worldwide Inc (PA)...574 259-2481
13388 State Road 23 Granger (46530) **(G-5390)**
Ashleys Jewelry By Design Ltd...219 926-9039
221 Broadway Chesterton (46304) **(G-1596)**
Asl Technologies LLC...219 733-2777
10525 W Us Highway 30 3d Wanatah (46390) **(G-13820)**
Aspen Solutions Group Inc...317 839-9274
2076 Aspen Dr Avon (46123) **(G-429)**
Asphalt Cutbacks Inc...219 398-4230
3000 Gary Rd East Chicago (46312) **(G-2521)**
Asphalt Drum Mixers Inc...260 637-5729
1 Adm Pkwy Huntertown (46748) **(G-6134)**

A L P H A B E T I C

Asphalt Engineers Inc 574 289-5557
59755 Market St South Bend (46614) *(G-12712)*
Asphalt Equipment Company Inc (PA) 260 672-3004
13333 Us Highway 24 W Fort Wayne (46814) *(G-4093)*
Asphalt Materials Inc 574 267-5076
2820 Durbin St Warsaw (46580) *(G-13840)*
Asphalt Materials Inc (PA) 317 872-6010
5400 W 86th St Indianapolis (46268) *(G-6426)*
Asphalt Materials Inc 317 243-8304
7901 W Morris St Indianapolis (46231) *(G-6427)*
Asphalt Materials Inc 317 875-4670
5400 W 86th St Indianapolis (46268) *(G-6428)*
Asphalt Materials Inc 317 872-5580
4902 W 86th St Indianapolis (46268) *(G-6429)*
Asphalt Refining Co, Indianapolis *Also called Asphalt Materials Inc (G-6429)*
Aspire Industries 812 542-1561
5329 Foundation Blvd New Albany (47150) *(G-10748)*
Assa Abloy Door Group LLC 800 826-2617
2300 Johnson St Elkhart (46514) *(G-2697)*
Assembly Biosciences Inc (PA) 317 210-9311
11711 N Meridian St # 310 Carmel (46032) *(G-1316)*
Assembly Masters Inc 574 293-9026
56624 Elk Park Dr Elkhart (46516) *(G-2698)*
Assembly Masters Inc 574 293-9026
55807 Currant Rd Mishawaka (46545) *(G-9999)*
Assistive Technology Inc 574 522-7201
21279 Protecta Dr Elkhart (46516) *(G-2699)*
Assmann Corporation America (PA) 260 357-3181
300 N Taylor Rd Garrett (46738) *(G-4995)*
Associated Label Inc 812 877-3682
8402 E Davis Ave Terre Haute (47805) *(G-13195)*
Associated Materials LLC 260 451-9072
502 Incentive Dr Fort Wayne (46825) *(G-4094)*
Associated Mfg & Packg, Crawfordsville *Also called Yes Feed & Supply LLC (G-2206)*
Assurance Locking Systems LLC 317 786-8724
5673 Misty Ridge Cir Indianapolis (46237) *(G-6430)*
Astar Inc 574 234-2137
645 Wilber St South Bend (46628) *(G-12713)*
Astbury Water Technology Inc 260 668-8900
601 W 400 N Angola (46703) *(G-194)*
Astbury Water Technology Inc (PA) 317 328-7153
5940 W Raymond St Indianapolis (46241) *(G-6431)*
Astec Corp 317 872-7550
7750 Zionsville Rd # 650 Indianapolis (46268) *(G-6432)*
Asterion LLC 317 875-0051
5425 W 84th St Indianapolis (46268) *(G-6433)*
Astrazeneca Pharmaceuticals LP 812 429-5000
4601 Highway 62 E Mount Vernon (47620) *(G-10383)*
Astro Cutting Tools 765 478-3662
600 E Church St Cambridge City (47327) *(G-1253)*
Asw LLC 260 432-1596
2499 S 600 E Ste 102 Columbia City (46725) *(G-1764)*
AT Ferrell Company Inc (PA) 260 824-3400
1440 S Adams St Bluffton (46714) *(G-865)*
At T 765 649-5900
4711 S Scatterfield Rd Anderson (46013) *(G-70)*
At The Barn Winery 513 310-8810
1726 Einsel Rd Lawrenceburg (47025) *(G-9131)*
AT&T Corp 317 347-2163
7144 Lakeview Pkwy W Dr Indianapolis (46268) *(G-6434)*
AT&T Publishing, Indianapolis *Also called AT&T Corp (G-6434)*
Atc Plastics LLC (PA) 317 469-7552
8425 Woodfield Crossing B Indianapolis (46240) *(G-6435)*
Atc Trailers Holdings Inc 574 773-2440
306 S Nappanee St Nappanee (46550) *(G-10651)*
Atco-Gary Metal Tech LLC 219 885-3232
1931 E Main St Griffith (46319) *(G-5763)*
Athena Arts & Graphics Inc 317 876-8916
3500 Depauw Blvd Ste 1000 Indianapolis (46268) *(G-6436)*
Athentic Inc 219 362-8508
702 Ohio St La Porte (46350) *(G-8735)*
Athletes Management & Service 317 925-8200
3750 Guion Rd Ste 315 Indianapolis (46222) *(G-6437)*
Athletic Avenue & More Inc 812 547-7655
802 31st St Tell City (47586) *(G-13155)*
Athletic Edge Inc 260 489-6613
1133 Old Bridge Pl Fort Wayne (46825) *(G-4095)*
Athlinks, Evansville *Also called Chronotrack Systems Corp (G-3417)*
ATI 317 238-3073
6635 E 30th St Indianapolis (46219) *(G-6438)*
Ati Inc (PA) 812 431-5409
103 Brown St Mount Vernon (47620) *(G-10384)*
ATI Allegheny Ludlum, New Castle *Also called Allegheny Ludlum LLC (G-10890)*
ATI Casting Service, La Porte *Also called Tdy Industries LLC (G-8827)*
ATI Casting Service LLC (HQ) 219 362-1000
300 Philadelphia St La Porte (46350) *(G-8736)*
ATI Products Inc 260 358-9254
855 N Broadway St Huntington (46750) *(G-6187)*
Atkins Nutritionals Inc 317 622-4154
3023 N Dist Way Unit 200 Greenfield (46140) *(G-5504)*
Atkisson Enterprises Inc 765 675-7593
632 Mill St Tipton (46072) *(G-13388)*
Atlas Chem-Milling, Elkhart *Also called Atlas Die LLC (G-2700)*
Atlas Die LLC 574 295-0277
1627 W Lusher Ave Elkhart (46517) *(G-2700)*
Atlas Die Inc 574 295-0050
2000 Middlebury St Elkhart (46516) *(G-2701)*
Atlas Dock Systems Inc 317 714-3850
5363 W State Road 38 New Castle (47362) *(G-10892)*
Atlas Energy Indiana LLC 812 268-4900
32 S Court St Ste F Sullivan (47882) *(G-13080)*
Atlas Foundry Company Inc 765 662-2525
601 N Henderson Ave Marion (46952) *(G-9510)*
Atlas Machine and Supply Inc 812 423-7762
5001 Hitch Peters Rd Evansville (47711) *(G-3367)*
Atlas Specialty Products, Elkhart *Also called H John Enterprise Inc (G-2903)*
Atm, Angola *Also called Autoform Tool & Mfg LLC (G-195)*
Atmosphere Annealing LLC 812 346-1275
1300 Indtl Dr North Vernon (47265) *(G-11248)*
Atmosphere Dynamics Corp 317 392-6262
1107 Saint Joseph St Shelbyville (46176) *(G-12518)*
Atp Steel & Welding Supplies, Lebanon *Also called Atp Welding Inc (G-9170)*
Atp Welding Inc 765 483-9273
930 Hendricks Dr Lebanon (46052) *(G-9170)*
Attc Manufacturing Inc 812 547-5060
10455 State Road 37 Tell City (47586) *(G-13156)*
Attco Machine Products Inc 574 234-1063
2411 Foundation Dr South Bend (46628) *(G-12714)*
Attica Ready Mixed Concrete (PA) 765 762-2424
104 W Sycamore St Attica (47918) *(G-297)*
Atwood Concrete Construction, Waldron *Also called Larry Atwood (G-13800)*
Atwood Mobile Products, Elkhart *Also called Dura Automotive Systems of Ind (G-2803)*
Atwood Mobile Products LLC 574 266-4848
1120 N Main St Elkhart (46514) *(G-2702)*
Atwood Mobile Products LLC 574 264-2131
2040 Toledo Rd Elkhart (46516) *(G-2703)*
Atwood Mobile Products LLC (HQ) 574 264-2131
1120 N Main St Elkhart (46514) *(G-2704)*
Atwood Mobile Products LLC 574 522-7891
3308 Charlotte Ave Elkhart (46517) *(G-2705)*
Atwood Mobile Products LLC 574 264-2131
2701 Ada Dr Elkhart (46514) *(G-2706)*
Atwood Solutions, Elkhart *Also called Atwood Mobile Products LLC (G-2704)*
Aubry Lane LLC 317 644-6372
5333 W 86th St Indianapolis (46268) *(G-6439)*
Auburn Gear LLC (PA) 260 925-3200
400 E Auburn Dr Auburn (46706) *(G-313)*
Auburn Hardwood Molding 260 925-5959
1109 W Auburn Dr Auburn (46706) *(G-314)*
Auburn Manufacturing Inc 260 925-8651
1929 Wayne St Auburn (46706) *(G-315)*
Aucilla Incorporated 574 234-9036
3333 N Kenmore St South Bend (46628) *(G-12715)*
Audio Diagnostics Inc 765 477-7016
2320 Concord Rd Ste A Lafayette (47909) *(G-8855)*
Audio Source, Columbus *Also called Mark Murray (G-1969)*
Audiodiagnostics, Lafayette *Also called Audio Diagnostics Inc (G-8855)*
Augustin Prtg & Design Svcs (PA) 765 966-7130
211 Nw 7th St Richmond (47374) *(G-11957)*
Aul Brothers Tool & Die Inc 765 759-5124
9609 W Jackson St Muncie (47304) *(G-10434)*
Aul In The Family Tool and Die 765 759-5161
9801 W Jackson St Yorktown (47396) *(G-14401)*
Aunalytics Inc 574 307-9230
460 Stull St Ste 100 South Bend (46601) *(G-12716)*
Aunt Beth's Cookies, Mishawaka *Also called Aunt Beths Products Inc (G-10000)*
Aunt Beths Products Inc 574 259-6244
1828 Clover Rd Mishawaka (46545) *(G-10000)*
Aunt Millie's Bakeries, Fort Wayne *Also called Perfection Bakeries Inc (G-4524)*
Aunt Millie's Bakeries, Warsaw *Also called Perfection Bakeries Inc (G-13926)*
Aunt Millies 765 966-6691
415 N 12th St Richmond (47374) *(G-11958)*
Aunt Millies Bakeries, Fort Wayne *Also called Perfection Bakeries Inc (G-4525)*
Aunt Netts Country Candles LLC 765 557-2770
7374 W State Rd Elwood (46036) *(G-3294)*
Auntie Annes 765 288-8077
3501 N Grnville Ave Ste 3 Muncie (47303) *(G-10435)*
Auntie Annes 574 271-8740
6501 Grape Rd Ste 670a Mishawaka (46545) *(G-10001)*
Aurora Casket Company LLC (HQ) 800 457-1111
10944 Marsh Rd Aurora (47001) *(G-370)*
Aurora Casket Company LLC 812 926-1110
50 Factory Aurora (47001) *(G-371)*
Aurora Casket Company LLC 812 926-1111
202 Conwell St Aurora (47001) *(G-372)*
Aurora Services Inc 260 463-4901
7155 N 675 W Shipshewana (46565) *(G-12604)*

Aus Embroidery Inc...317 899-1225
  8745 Rawles Ave Ste C Indianapolis (46219) *(G-6440)*

Auspro Manufacturing Co Inc..................................574 264-3705
  5320 Beck Dr Elkhart (46516) *(G-2707)*

Austin & Austin Inc (PA)...574 586-2320
  59632 Timberwood Ln Goshen (46528) *(G-5173)*

Austin Powder Company...812 536-2885
  8146 S Old St Rd Rt 64 Hw Stendal (47585) *(G-13073)*

Austin Powder Company...812 342-1237
  13468 W Old Nashville Rd Columbus (47201) *(G-1857)*

Austin Tri-Hawk Automotive Inc..............................812 794-0062
  2001 W Just Indus Pkwy Austin (47102) *(G-395)*

Austin-Westran LLC (PA)..815 234-2811
  2876 Wooded Glen Ct Indianapolis (46268) *(G-6441)*

Austins Metal Mafia Inc..812 619-6115
  8175 Boyd Rd Cannelton (47520) *(G-1286)*

Author Solutions LLC (PA).......................................812 339-6000
  1663 S Liberty Dr Bloomington (47403) *(G-667)*

Auto & Sign Specialties Inc.....................................260 824-1987
  3124 E State Road 124 Bluffton (46714) *(G-866)*

Auto Art & Signs...765 448-6800
  420 Sagamore Pkwy N Lafayette (47904) *(G-8856)*

Auto Bumper Exchange Inc......................................260 493-4408
  2321 Bremer Rd Fort Wayne (46803) *(G-4096)*

Auto Center Inc...317 545-3360
  5461 Massachusetts Ave Indianapolis (46218) *(G-6442)*

Auto Extras Inc...574 855-2370
  1400 S Main St South Bend (46613) *(G-12717)*

Auto Specialty of Lafayette......................................765 446-2311
  313 Teal Rd Lafayette (47905) *(G-8857)*

Auto Truck Group LLC...260 356-1610
  1640 Riverfork Dr Huntington (46750) *(G-6188)*

Auto Wood Restoration...219 797-3775
  24 S Pennsylvania St Hanna (46340) *(G-5958)*

Autocar LLC..765 489-5499
  551 S Washington St Hagerstown (47346) *(G-5803)*

Autoform Tool & Mfg LLC...260 624-2014
  1501 Wohlert St Angola (46703) *(G-195)*

Automated Fuels, Terre Haute *Also called Spence/Banks Inc (G-13341)*

Automated Laser Corporation...................................260 637-4140
  14224 Plank St Fort Wayne (46818) *(G-4097)*

Automated Logic - Indiana, Muncie *Also called Automated Logic Corporation (G-10436)*

Automated Logic Corporation...................................765 286-1993
  117 N High St Muncie (47305) *(G-10436)*

Automated Products Intl LLC....................................260 463-2515
  2840 N State Road 9 Lagrange (46761) *(G-9032)*

Automated Routing Inc...812 357-2429
  16920 N State Road 545 Saint Meinrad (47577) *(G-12274)*

Automated Systems Technology, Mitchell *Also called C&M Conveyor Inc (G-10157)*

Automated Weapon Security Inc...............................860 559-7176
  9324 E 10th St Indianapolis (46229) *(G-6443)*

Automatic Fastner Tools...317 784-4111
  3250 Payne Dr Indianapolis (46227) *(G-6444)*

Automatic Pool Covers Inc.......................................317 579-2000
  17397 Oak Ridge Rd Westfield (46074) *(G-14137)*

Automatic Tool Control..317 328-8492
  4037 Guion Ln Indianapolis (46268) *(G-6445)*

Automation & Control Svcs Inc................................219 558-2060
  2440 Ontario St Schererville (46375) *(G-12315)*

Automation Consultants Inc......................................502 552-4995
  4003 Kendall Ct Floyds Knobs (47119) *(G-4007)*

Automobile Dealers Assn of Ind (PA).......................317 635-1441
  150 W Market St Ste 812 Indianapolis (46204) *(G-6446)*

Automotive Vibration Division, Ligonier *Also called Freudenberg-Nok General Partnr (G-9285)*

Automtic Pool Cver Prfssionals, Westfield *Also called Cover Care LLC (G-14146)*

Automtion Ctrl Panl Sltons Inc..................................219 961-8308
  514 Jenna Dr Munster (46321) *(G-10597)*

Autoneum North America Inc....................................248 848-0100
  100 River Ridge Pkwy Jeffersonville (47130) *(G-8327)*

Autosem Inc..574 288-8866
  1701 S Main St South Bend (46613) *(G-12718)*

Autotwirler, Clayton *Also called Wurk Metal Products Inc (G-1710)*

Autumn Interiors..317 894-1494
  11717 E Washington St Indianapolis (46229) *(G-6447)*

Auxilius Heavy Industries LLC.................................765 885-5099
  301 S Adeway Fowler (47944) *(G-4794)*

Avalign Cutting Tools Division, Warsaw *Also called Nginstruments Inc (G-13915)*

Avalon Drinkware, Indianapolis *Also called Avalon Enterprises Inc (G-6448)*

Avalon Enterprises Inc...317 894-8666
  12010 E Washington St Indianapolis (46229) *(G-6448)*

Avarrotes Luliana..574 232-6803
  1601 S Walnut St South Bend (46613) *(G-12719)*

Avborne Accessory Group Inc..................................317 738-0148
  215 Industrial Dr Franklin (46131) *(G-4869)*

Ave Maria Press Inc..574 287-2831
  1865 Moreau Dr Notre Dame (46556) *(G-11303)*

Aventine Renewable Energy......................................812 838-9598
  7201 Port Rd Mount Vernon (47620) *(G-10385)*

Aventine Renewable Fuels, Mount Vernon *Also called Aventine Renewable Energy (G-10385)*

Avenue Industries Inc...574 674-6971
  1453 3rd St Osceola (46561) *(G-11370)*

Avery Dennison Corporation.....................................765 221-9277
  5710 Douglas Way Anderson (46013) *(G-71)*

Avery Dennison Corporation.....................................260 481-4500
  3011 Independence Dr Fort Wayne (46808) *(G-4098)*

Avery Dennison Corporation.....................................219 696-7777
  270 Westmeadow Pl Lowell (46356) *(G-9399)*

Avery Dennison Corporation.....................................317 462-1988
  870 Anderson Blvd Greenfield (46140) *(G-5505)*

Avery Dennison Fasson, Greenfield *Also called Avery Dennison Corporation (G-5505)*

Avf Machining...260 760-1531
  5850 County Road 24 Butler (46721) *(G-1222)*

Avg North America Inc...765 748-3162
  5133 Eastside Parkway Dr Gas City (46933) *(G-5120)*

Aviation Fuel Group LLC..219 462-6081
  159 Brockton Pl Valparaiso (46385) *(G-13500)*

Avionic Structures of Indiana...................................765 671-7865
  4589 N Wabash Rd Marion (46952) *(G-9511)*

Avionics Mounts Inc...812 988-2949
  4510 State Road 46 E Nashville (47448) *(G-10714)*

Avis Industrial Corporation (PA)..............................765 998-8100
  1909 S Main St Upland (46989) *(G-13468)*

Avnet...260 359-9513
  3650 W 200 N Huntington (46750) *(G-6189)*

AVO Candle Company LLC.......................................812 822-2302
  2406 S Bryan St Bloomington (47403) *(G-668)*

Avon Carbon Capture RES Assoc.............................317 753-8829
  7468 Glensford Dr Avon (46123) *(G-430)*

Avon Mobile Wash...317 517-1890
  5518 Muirfield Way Avon (46123) *(G-431)*

Avon Sports Apparel Corp..317 887-2673
  3115 Meridian Parke Dr D Greenwood (46142) *(G-5668)*

Awards America...219 462-7903
  397 E Us Highway 30 Valparaiso (46383) *(G-13501)*

Awards Unlimited Inc...765 447-9413
  3031 Union St Lafayette (47904) *(G-8858)*

Awave Software LLC...219 285-1852
  1317 Macarthur Blvd Munster (46321) *(G-10598)*

Awning Innovations, Fishers *Also called Image One LLC (G-3927)*

Awningtec Usa Incorporated.....................................812 734-0423
  3265 Highway 62 Nw Corydon (47112) *(G-2088)*

Awol Metal Contorsion LLC......................................260 909-0411
  439 Prospect Ave Kendallville (46755) *(G-8457)*

Axis Controls Inc..260 414-4028
  6100 Lower Huntington Rd Fort Wayne (46809) *(G-4099)*

Axis Machine and Tool, Sellersburg *Also called Oakley Industries LLC (G-12410)*

Axis Mold Inc..574 292-8904
  53450 Tamarack Rd New Carlisle (46552) *(G-10879)*

Axis Unlimited LLC...574 370-8923
  24615 County Road 45 # 2 Elkhart (46516) *(G-2708)*

Axle Inc...574 264-9434
  53664 County Road 9 Elkhart (46514) *(G-2709)*

Axtrom Industries..812 859-4873
  170 Mt Calvery Rd Freedom (47431) *(G-4946)*

Axtrom Industries/Pallat Div, Freedom *Also called Axtrom Industries (G-4946)*

Aynes Custom Upholstery, Freedom *Also called Aynes Upholstery LLC (G-4947)*

Aynes Upholstery LLC..812 829-1321
  3220 Dunn Rd Freedom (47431) *(G-4947)*

Azimuth Custom Extrusions LLC.............................812 423-6180
  1618 Lynch Rd Evansville (47711) *(G-3368)*

Azland Inc...765 429-6200
  345 Burnetts Rd Ste 300 West Lafayette (47906) *(G-14051)*

Aztec Printing Inc (PA)...812 422-1462
  9800 Highway 66 Wadesville (47638) *(G-13771)*

Azz Galvanizing - Muncie, Muncie *Also called AAA Galvanizing - Joliet Inc (G-10421)*

Azz Galvanizing Hamilton, Hamilton *Also called AAA Galvanizing - Joliet Inc (G-5818)*

Azz Galvanizing Plymouth, Plymouth *Also called AAA Galvanizing - Joliet Inc (G-11661)*

B & A Cnstr & Design Inc..812 683-4600
  772 W 3rd St Huntingburg (47542) *(G-6150)*

B & B Engineering Inc..765 566-3460
  7102 E 300 S Bringhurst (46913) *(G-1038)*

B & B Industries Inc...574 262-8551
  1121 D I Dr Elkhart (46514) *(G-2710)*

B & B Manufacturing Inc..219 324-0247
  712 N Fail Rd La Porte (46350) *(G-8737)*

B & B Pallet..
  1301 N 9th St Clinton (47842) *(G-1714)*

B & B Sawmill Inc...812 834-5072
  7142 Leatherwood Rd Bedford (47421) *(G-530)*

B & B Signs..812 282-5366
  5060 Buck Creek Rd Floyds Knobs (47119) *(G-4008)*

B & B Specialties Inc...574 277-0499
  14234 Cleveland Rd Granger (46530) *(G-5391)*

B & B Washer Assemblies, Liberty *Also called Larry G Byrd (G-9263)*

B & C Machining Inc...219 924-5411
  320 E Merritt St Rensselaer (47978) *(G-11915)*

A
L
P
H
A
B
E
T
I
C

B & D Electric Inc 812 254-2122
  413 W Van Trees St Washington (47501) *(G-13978)*

B & D Manufacturing Inc 765 452-2761
  2100 E Carter St Kokomo (46901) *(G-8595)*

B & F Machine Products 574 255-7447
  606 S Byrkit St Mishawaka (46544) *(G-10002)*

B & G Sales 765 473-7668
  421 Harrison Ave Peru (46970) *(G-11517)*

B & G Truck Conversions Inc 574 892-6666
  10478 16th Rd Argos (46501) *(G-272)*

B & G Woodworking, Attica Also called Gloria J Burnworth *(G-302)*

B & H Electric and Supply Inc 812 333-7303
  4719 W Vernal Pike Bloomington (47404) *(G-669)*

B & H Electric and Supply Inc (PA) 812 522-5607
  740 C Ave E Seymour (47274) *(G-12431)*

B & J Specialty Inc (PA) 260 761-5011
  7919 N 100 E Wawaka (46794) *(G-14029)*

B & J Specialty Inc 260 636-2067
  4268 E Us Highway 6 Kendallville (46755) *(G-8458)*

B & L Custom Cabinets Inc 765 379-2471
  7427 N County Road 300 W Rossville (46065) *(G-12209)*

B & L Sheet Metal & Roofing 812 332-4309
  1301 N Monroe St Bloomington (47404) *(G-670)*

B & M Electrical Co Inc 765 448-4532
  710 Navco Dr Lafayette (47905) *(G-8859)*

B & M Products 574 238-7468
  18702 Monticello Dr Goshen (46528) *(G-5174)*

B & M Steel & Welding Inc 765 964-5868
  1251 S Jackson Pike Union City (47390) *(G-13453)*

B & S Products Corp 574 537-0770
  1917 Eisenhower Dr N Goshen (46526) *(G-5175)*

B & W Specialized Drilling 219 746-9463
  9002 Indianapolis Blvd B Highland (46322) *(G-6036)*

B and D Lighting 317 414-8056
  5635 Hickory Rd Indianapolis (46239) *(G-6449)*

B and R Engraving Inc 317 894-3599
  5825 W 300 N Greenfield (46140) *(G-5506)*

B B & H Signs Incorporated 812 235-1340
  2212 S 3rd St Terre Haute (47802) *(G-13196)*

B B & H Tool of Columbus Inc 812 372-3707
  2775 Roadway Dr Columbus (47201) *(G-1858)*

B B Cycles LLC 812 723-4265
  2547 N State Road 37 Paoli (47454) *(G-11443)*

B B Mining Inc (PA) 812 845-2717
  11700 Water Tank Rd Cynthiana (47612) *(G-2329)*

B C C Products Inc 317 494-6420
  2140 Earlywood Dr Franklin (46131) *(G-4870)*

B C I, Shelbyville Also called Installed Building Pdts LLC *(G-12539)*

B C Welding Inc 574 272-9008
  12801 Industrial Park Dr Granger (46530) *(G-5392)*

B D Custom Manufacturing Inc 574 848-0925
  1100 Bloomingdale Dr Bristol (46507) *(G-1047)*

B E A L I Inc 219 322-5158
  2401 Capri Dr Schererville (46375) *(G-12316)*

B G Hoadley Quarries Inc (PA) 812 332-1447
  3211 W Arlington Rd Bloomington (47404) *(G-671)*

B G Hoadley Quarries Inc 812 332-1447
  2200 W Tapp Rd Bloomington (47403) *(G-672)*

B Happy Peanut Butter LLC 317 733-3831
  340 Raintree Dr Zionsville (46077) *(G-14419)*

B Honey & Candles 574 642-1145
  2260 N 1000 W Shipshewana (46565) *(G-12605)*

B I P C O, Columbus Also called Business & Industrial Pdts Co *(G-1863)*

B JS Electronics 812 482-3484
  265 S Clay St Jasper (47546) *(G-8237)*

B K & M Inc 219 924-0184
  210 S Lindberg St Griffith (46319) *(G-5764)*

B L, Bloomington Also called B & L Sheet Metal & Roofing *(G-670)*

B M C Marketing Corp 260 693-2193
  300 E Pleasant St Churubusco (46723) *(G-1642)*

B M P Logging LLC 812 272-2149
  11202 Swamp Lake Rd Williams (47470) *(G-14281)*

B N Oil LLC 859 816-2244
  622 Arch St Lawrenceburg (47025) *(G-9132)*

B P Security 219 473-3700
  2815 Indianapolis Blvd Whiting (46394) *(G-14268)*

B Plus Enterprises Inc 219 733-9404
  122 S Illinois St Wanatah (46390) *(G-13821)*

B Q Products Inc 317 786-5500
  6233 Brookville Rd Indianapolis (46219) *(G-6450)*

B S T Enterprises Inc 260 493-4313
  1900 Summit St New Haven (46774) *(G-10930)*

B T Bttery Charger Systems Inc 574 533-6030
  17189 County Road 22 Goshen (46528) *(G-5176)*

B Thystrup US Corporation 574 834-2554
  201 E Epworth Forest Rd North Webster (46555) *(G-11289)*

B Trucking & Backhoe Inc 765 437-5960
  3491 E 700 N Windfall (46076) *(G-14346)*

B Walter & Company Inc 260 563-2181
  655 Factory St Wabash (46992) *(G-13721)*

B Y M Electronics Inc 574 674-5096
  10288 Anderson Rd Granger (46530) *(G-5393)*

B&B Goodiez 765 338-6833
  911 1/2 Western Ave Connersville (47331) *(G-2039)*

B&B Manufacturing, La Porte Also called B & B Manufacturing Inc *(G-8737)*

B&B Molders LLC 574 259-7838
  58471 Fir Rd Mishawaka (46544) *(G-10003)*

B&D Lights LLC 765 452-2761
  2100 E Carter St Kokomo (46901) *(G-8596)*

B&F Plastics Inc 765 962-6125
  540 N 8th St Richmond (47374) *(G-11959)*

B&G Curtis Dyna-Fog, Westfield Also called Curtis Dyna-Fog Ltd *(G-14151)*

B&H Industries Corporation 765 794-4428
  6425 E South St Darlington (47940) *(G-2360)*

B&J International 260 854-2215
  4268 E Us Highway 6 Kendallville (46755) *(G-8459)*

B&J Rocket America Inc 574 825-5802
  325 N Main St Middlebury (46540) *(G-9874)*

B&M Instruments, Warsaw Also called Lakeland Technology Inc *(G-13900)*

B&M Millwright Inc 765 883-8177
  2719 S 1280 W Russiaville (46979) *(G-12240)*

B&M Steel Fabrication, Union City Also called B & M Steel & Welding Inc *(G-13453)*

B&R Manufacturing Inc 574 293-5669
  2503 Marina Dr Elkhart (46514) *(G-2711)*

B&W Packaging Mfg LLC 812 280-9578
  4140 Capitol Dr New Albany (47150) *(G-10749)*

B-D Industries Inc 574 295-1420
  1715 Fieldhouse Ave Elkhart (46517) *(G-2712)*

B-Hive Printing 812 897-3905
  804 W Main St Boonville (47601) *(G-908)*

B.N.W. Industries, Tippecanoe Also called Lee E Norris Cnstr & Grn Co *(G-13383)*

B/C Precision Tool Inc 812 577-0642
  1000b Schenley Pl Greendale (47025) *(G-5483)*

B2 Manufacturing LLC 765 993-4519
  606 Century Dr Fountain City (47341) *(G-4784)*

B6 Manufacturing LLC 317 549-4290
  4701 Massachusetts Ave Indianapolis (46218) *(G-6451)*

Ba Romines Sheet Metal Inc 260 657-5500
  11827 Hood St Harlan (46743) *(G-5966)*

Babb Lumber Company Inc 812 886-0551
  700 Fulton Glass Rd Vincennes (47591) *(G-13668)*

Babbs Super-Value, Spencer Also called Babbs Supermarket Inc *(G-13017)*

Babbs Supermarket Inc 812 829-2231
  459 W Morgan St Spencer (47460) *(G-13017)*

Babcock Paving Inc 219 987-5450
  6049 Work St Demotte (46310) *(G-2431)*

Babsco Electric, Warsaw Also called Babsco Supply Inc *(G-13841)*

Babsco Supply Inc 574 267-8999
  2361 N Shelby Dr Warsaw (46580) *(G-13841)*

Bacchus Winery Golf Vinyrd LLC 574 732-4663
  14 Golfview Dr Logansport (46947) *(G-9323)*

Bach Tech Inc 219 531-7424
  67 S 500 W Valparaiso (46385) *(G-13502)*

Backdoor Baking Company LLC 317 927-7275
  301 Buckingham Dr Indianapolis (46208) *(G-6452)*

Backyard Company 317 727-0298
  5621 Woodland Trace Blvd Indianapolis (46237) *(G-6453)*

Bad Apple Macs LLC 812 274-0469
  605 W Main St Madison (47250) *(G-9445)*

Bad Boys Bllard Prductions LLC 702 738-4950
  9037 Matterhorn Rd Indianapolis (46234) *(G-6454)*

Bada Boom Fireworks LLC 219 472-6700
  4601 Cleveland St Gary (46408) *(G-5029)*

Badger Daylighting Corp 219 762-9177
  5597 Old Porter Rd Ste D Portage (46368) *(G-11750)*

Badlands Accessories Salvage, Wyatt Also called Badlands Pick Up Van ACC Salv *(G-14396)*

Badlands Pick Up Van ACC Salv 574 633-2156
  66521 State Rd 331 Wyatt (46595) *(G-14396)*

Bae Systems Inc 812 863-0514
  209 E Walnut St Odon (47562) *(G-11319)*

Bae Systems Controls Inc 260 434-5195
  4250 Airport Expy Fort Wayne (46809) *(G-4100)*

Bags By Brenda 765 779-4287
  3674 E 575 S Markleville (46056) *(G-9585)*

Bahr Bros Mfg Inc 765 664-6235
  2545 S Lincoln Blvd Marion (46953) *(G-9512)*

Bahr Brothers Manufacturing, Marion Also called Bahr Bros Mfg Inc *(G-9512)*

Bailey Chassis Company LLC 615 822-7041
  78 W 1100 S Haubstadt (47639) *(G-5997)*

Bailey Tools & Supply Inc 502 635-6348
  5716 E Morgan Ave Ste 9 Evansville (47715) *(G-3369)*

Bains Packing and Rfrgn 260 244-5209
  3922 W Old Trail Rd Columbia City (46725) *(G-1765)*

Bains' Packing & Refrigeration, Columbia City Also called Bains Packing and Rfrgn *(G-1765)*

Baird Home Corporation 812 883-1141
  1401 W Mulberry St Salem (47167) *(G-12284)*

Baird Homes of Distinction, Salem Also called Baird Home Corporation (G-12284)

Baird Ice Cream Co 812 283-3345
110 N Randolph Ave Clarksville (47129) (G-1673)

Baird Sawmill, Rockville Also called Michael O Baird (G-12177)

Baker Metalworks 260 572-9353
5843 County Road 59 Saint Joe (46785) (G-12252)

Baker Petrolite LLC 219 473-5329
2831 Indian Airforce Blvd Whiting (46394) (G-14269)

Bakesmart, Indianapolis Also called Blue Sun Ventures Ltd (G-6490)

Baldwin Logging Inc 812 834-1040
11763 State Road 58 E Norman (47264) (G-11202)

Balemaster Division, Crown Point Also called East Chicago Machine Tool Sls (G-2248)

Balfour Company, Indianapolis Also called Edward ONeil Associates (G-6810)

Ball Corporation 574 583-9418
1104 N 6th St Monticello (47960) (G-10253)

Ball Inc 317 736-8236
1900 Commerce Pkwy Franklin (46131) (G-4871)

Ball Metal Beverage Cont Corp 574 583-9418
501 N 6th St Monticello (47960) (G-10254)

Ball Metal Beverage Cont Div, Monticello Also called Ball Metal Beverage Cont
Corp (G-10254)

Ball State Daily News, Muncie Also called Ball State University (G-10437)

Ball State University 765 285-8218
276 Park Journalism Bldg Muncie (47306) (G-10437)

Ball Systems Inc 317 804-2330
16469 Southpark Dr Westfield (46074) (G-14138)

Ballantrae Inc 800 372-3555
600 Corporation Dr Pendleton (46064) (G-11483)

Baller Signs, Bluffton Also called Auto & Sign Specialties Inc (G-866)

Bamar Plastics Inc 574 234-4066
1702 Robinson St South Bend (46613) (G-12720)

Ban Transit, Howe Also called Nelson J Hochstetler (G-6130)

Banco Industries Inc 260 347-9524
11542 N State Road 3 Kendallville (46755) (G-8460)

Bandit Signs 574 370-7067
23970 Byrd Ave Elkhart (46516) (G-2713)

Bane Logging, Brownstown Also called William S Bane (G-1193)

Bane-Clene Corp (PA) 317 546-5448
3940 N Keystone Ave Indianapolis (46205) (G-6455)

Bane-Welker Equipment LLC 812 234-2627
300 W Margaret Dr Terre Haute (47802) (G-13197)

Banes Machine Shop, Lafayette Also called Homer Banes (G-8917)

Bangs Laboratories Inc 317 570-7020
9025 Technology Dr Fishers (46038) (G-3873)

Banks Machine & Engrg Inc 317 642-4980
1677 W 400 N Shelbyville (46176) (G-12519)

Banner Cablevision, The, Brownstown Also called Jackson County Banner (G-1189)

Banner Graphic, Greencastle Also called Truth Publishing Company Inc (G-5480)

Bantam Industries Inc 714 561-6122
2346 S Lynhurst Dr # 601 Indianapolis (46241) (G-6456)

Bar Keepers Friend, Indianapolis Also called Servaas Laboratories Inc (G-7915)

Bar Steel Service Center, Indianapolis Also called Mitchel & Scott Machine Co (G-7526)

Barber & Ross of Indiana, Knox Also called Scp Building Products LLC (G-8581)

Barber Manufacturing Co Inc (PA) 765 643-6905
1824 Brown St Anderson (46016) (G-72)

Barbs Homemade Noodles 812 486-3762
787 S 700 E Montgomery (47558) (G-10214)

Bare Metal Inc 812 948-1313
4160 Capitol Dr New Albany (47150) (G-10750)

Bargain Finder, The, Hammond Also called Service Publication Inc (G-5938)

Barger Engineering Inc 812 476-3077
2116 Lincoln Ave Evansville (47714) (G-3370)

Barger Packaging Inc 888 525-2845
2901 Oakland Ave Elkhart (46517) (G-2714)

Barger Packaging Corporation (HQ) 574 389-1860
2901 Oakland Ave Elkhart (46517) (G-2715)

Baril Coatings 260 665-8431
401 Growth Pkwy Angola (46703) (G-196)

Baril Coatings Usa LLC 260 665-8431
401 Growth Pkwy Angola (46703) (G-197)

Barkman Custom Woodworking 574 773-9212
30235 Us Highway 6 Nappanee (46550) (G-10652)

Barks Lumber Co Inc 812 732-4680
1800 Heth Wash Rd Sw Central (47110) (G-1545)

Barks Welding Supplies 812 732-4366
6125 Highway 135 Sw Corydon (47112) (G-2089)

Barley Island Brewing Co 317 770-5280
639 Conner St Noblesville (46060) (G-11061)

Barnes Executive Trnsp, Carmel Also called Luxly LLC (G-1429)

Barnett Industrial Inc 219 814-7500
3012 Grand Trunk Rd Valparaiso (46383) (G-13503)

Barnhizer Machining and Wldg, Liberty Also called James E Barnhizer (G-9261)

Baron Embroidery Corp 260 484-8700
103 S Main St Auburn (46706) (G-316)

Barr None Music Publishers/Lea 502 413-5443
1833 Valley Vista Dr Borden (47106) (G-928)

Barrett Manufacturing Inc 812 753-5808
901 E John St Fort Branch (47648) (G-4026)

Barrett Paving Materials Inc 765 935-3060
5834 Inke Rd Richmond (47374) (G-11960)

Barrington Packaging Systems I 847 382-8066
19 W South St Shelbyville (46176) (G-12520)

Barry A Wilcox 260 495-3677
207 S Wayne St Fremont (46737) (G-4951)

Barry Company Inc 812 333-1850
2037 S Yost Ave Bloomington (47403) (G-673)

Barry Company Inc 317 578-2486
13317 Britton Park Rd Fishers (46038) (G-3874)

Barry Seat Cover & Auto Glass 574 288-4603
1924 S Michigan St South Bend (46613) (G-12721)

Barry Stuckwisch 812 525-1052
1330 N State Road 11 Seymour (47274) (G-12432)

Barry Stuckwisch Mowing, Seymour Also called Barry Stuckwisch (G-12432)

Barsteel Corporation 219 650-7100
1000 E 80th Pl Ste 425n Merrillville (46410) (G-9699)

Bartel Printing Company Inc 574 267-7421
310 Cedar St Warsaw (46580) (G-13842)

Bartow Warehouse, Goshen Also called Brunk Corp (G-5180)

Baseline Tool Co Inc 260 761-4932
8458 N Baseline Rd Wawaka (46794) (G-14030)

Basi, West Lafayette Also called Bioanalytical Systems Inc (G-14053)

Basiloid Products Corp 812 692-5511
312 N East St Elnora (47529) (G-3286)

Bassett Electric Motor Repair 260 925-0868
215 E 11th St Auburn (46706) (G-317)

Bastell Perimeter Systems, Frankfort Also called Bell Machine Company Inc (G-4819)

Bastian Automation Engrg LLC 317 467-2583
2155 Fields Blvd Greenfield (46140) (G-5507)

Bastian Solutions, Greenfield Also called Bastian Automation Engrg LLC (G-5507)

Bastian Solutions, Indianapolis Also called Halo LLC (G-6266)

Bastine Pottery Inc 317 776-0210
16509 Cyntheanne Rd Noblesville (46060) (G-11062)

Batch Small Press LLC 317 410-8923
240 Newhart St Indianapolis (46217) (G-6457)

Bates Technologies LLC 317 841-2400
14560 Bergen Blvd Noblesville (46060) (G-11063)

Batesville Casket Company Inc (HQ) 812 934-7500
1 Batesville Blvd Batesville (47006) (G-491)

Batesville Casket Company Inc 812 934-8102
100 Eastern Ave Batesville (47006) (G-492)

Batesville Herald Tribune, Batesville Also called Community Holdings Indiana Inc (G-497)

Batesville Management Services, Batesville Also called Batesville Casket Company
Inc (G-491)

Batesville Products Inc (PA) 513 381-2057
434 Margaret St Lawrenceburg (47025) (G-9133)

Batesville Products Inc 812 926-4230
10367 Randall Ave Aurora (47001) (G-373)

Batesville Services Inc (HQ) 812 934-7000
1 Batesville Blvd Batesville (47006) (G-493)

Batesville Tool & Die Inc (HQ) 812 934-5616
177 Six Pine Ranch Rd Batesville (47006) (G-494)

Bath & Body Works LLC 219 531-2146
2410 Laporte Ave Ste 140 Valparaiso (46383) (G-13504)

Bath & Body Works LLC 317 468-0834
1519 N State St Greenfield (46140) (G-5508)

Bath & Body Works LLC 317 209-1517
10343 E Us Highway 36 Avon (46123) (G-432)

Bath Gallery Showroom 219 531-2150
709 Morthland Dr Valparaiso (46383) (G-13505)

Batteries Plus 317 219-0007
2640 Conner St Noblesville (46060) (G-11064)

Battery Xpress 765 759-2288
12549 Marina View Dr Indianapolis (46256) (G-6458)

Battisti Customs, Elkhart Also called Forest River Inc (G-2863)

Battle Creek Equipment Co (PA) 260 495-3472
702 S Reed Rd Fremont (46737) (G-4952)

Battle Creek Health Eqp Co, Fremont Also called Battle Creek Equipment Co (G-4952)

Baugh Enterprises Inc 812 334-8189
125 S Westplex Ave Bloomington (47404) (G-674)

Baum Cabinetry LLC 219 575-6309
4 Spectacle Dr Valparaiso (46383) (G-13506)

Bauman Harnish Rubber Co, Garrett Also called Griffith Rbr Mills of Garrett (G-5007)

Bawel Industries LP 812 634-8004
2667 S Meridian Rd Jasper (47546) (G-8238)

Baxter Biosciences, Bloomington Also called Baxter Phrm Solutions (G-677)

Baxter Design & Advertising 219 464-9237
656 Franklin St Valparaiso (46383) (G-13507)

Baxter Healthcare Corp. 847 948-2000
7048 Hohman Ave Hammond (46324) (G-5845)

Baxter Healthcare Corporation 812 355-7167
927 S Curry Pike Bloomington (47403) (G-675)

Baxter Healthcare Corporation 317 291-0620
6812 Corporate Dr Indianapolis (46278) (G-6459)

A
L
P
H
A
B
E
T
I
C

Baxter Healthcare Corporation 812 333-0887
2000 N Curry Pike Bloomington (47404) *(G-676)*

Baxter Heathcare Plasma Center 260 451-8119
7921 Coldwater Rd Fort Wayne (46825) *(G-4101)*

Baxter Lumber LLC 812 873-6868
12876 W Deputy Pike Rd Deputy (47230) *(G-2459)*

Baxter Phrm Solutions 812 355-5289
1801 N Curry Pike Bloomington (47404) *(G-677)*

Baxter Phrm Solutions LLC 812 333-0887
927 S Curry Pike Bloomington (47403) *(G-678)*

Baxter Printing Inc 219 923-1999
3837 Ridge Rd Highland (46322) *(G-6037)*

Bay Bridge Manufacturing Inc 574 848-7477
1301 Commerce Dr Bristol (46507) *(G-1048)*

Bay Valley Foods LLC 574 936-4061
1430 Western Ave Plymouth (46563) *(G-11668)*

Bayer Healthcare LLC 574 252-4734
3930 Edison Lakes Pkwy Mishawaka (46545) *(G-10004)*

Bayer Healthcare LLC 574 262-6136
3400 Middlebury St Elkhart (46516) *(G-2716)*

Bayer Healthcare LLC 574 252-4735
4100 Edison Lakes Pkwy Mishawaka (46545) *(G-10005)*

Bayer Healthcare LLC 574 255-3327
1025 N Michigan St Elkhart (46514) *(G-2717)*

Bayview Estates 574 457-4136
400 S Harkless Dr Syracuse (46567) *(G-13129)*

Bb Wiring LLC 765 376-0190
1413 W Us Highway 136 Crawfordsville (47933) *(G-2135)*

BBC Distribution LLC 574 266-3601
53320 Columbia Dr Elkhart (46514) *(G-2718)*

Bbs Celebration Center 765 730-6575
1019 S Yorkchester Dr Yorktown (47396) *(G-14402)*

Bbs Enterprises Inc 574 255-3173
55980 Russell Indus Pkwy Mishawaka (46545) *(G-10006)*

Bc Awards Inc 317 852-3240
480 E Nrthfeld Dr Ste 100 Brownsburg (46112) *(G-1136)*

Bc Publications Inc 765 334-8277
5812 W 850 N Carthage (46115) *(G-1512)*

Bcbg Max Azria Group LLC 319 753-0437
311 S Broadway Fort Wayne (46805) *(G-4102)*

Bcbg Max Azria Group LLC 515 964-7355
1132 S Elmhurst Fishers (46037) *(G-3875)*

Bcbg Max Azria Group LLC 515 993-4753
382 W Church St Evansville (47715) *(G-3371)*

Bcbg Max Azria Group LLC 574 289-3937
815 Trail Rd Albion (46701) *(G-16)*

Bcbg Max Azria Group LLC 620 694-4256
215 S 9th St Petersburg (47567) *(G-11561)*

Bcbg Max Azria Group LLC 620 442-1111
1712 North Bch Monticello (47960) *(G-10255)*

Bcbg Max Azria Group LLC 641 872-1842
1501 M St Fort Wayne (46804) *(G-4103)*

Bcbg Max Azria Group LLC 712 243-1965
41720 Winchester Rd Fort Wayne (46825) *(G-4104)*

Bcbg Max Azria Group LLC 712 277-3937
380 Huku Lii Pl Merrillville (46410) *(G-9700)*

Bcbg Max Azria Group LLC 913 631-0090
2325 Aberdeen Blvd Zionsville (46077) *(G-14420)*

Bcd & Associates 317 873-5394
10830 Bennett Pkwy Ste G Zionsville (46077) *(G-14421)*

BCI Defense LLC 574 546-2411
545 N Bowen Ave Bremen (46506) *(G-983)*

BCT, Indianapolis *Also called Templeton Myers Inc (G-8053)*

Bcw Diversified Inc 765 644-2033
514 E 31st St Anderson (46016) *(G-73)*

Bcw Supplies, Anderson *Also called Bcw Diversified Inc (G-73)*

Bd Medical Development Inc 219 310-8551
1140 Millennium Dr Crown Point (46307) *(G-2227)*

Beach Mold & Tool Inc 502 649-9915
4600 New Middle Rd Jeffersonville (47130) *(G-8328)*

Beacher Business Printers, Michigan City *Also called Montgomery & Associates Inc (G-9821)*

Beachfront Furniture 574 875-0817
60874 Ridgepoint Ct Elkhart (46517) *(G-2719)*

Beachwood Lumber Co Inc 574 858-9325
7878 W Old Road 30 Warsaw (46580) *(G-13843)*

Beachwood Manufacturing, Warsaw *Also called Beachwood Lumber Co Inc (G-13843)*

Beachy Machine Shop LLC 765 452-9051
3884 E 400 N Kokomo (46901) *(G-8597)*

Beacon House 219 756-2131
7203 Starling Dr Schererville (46375) *(G-12317)*

Beacon Industries Inc (PA) 812 526-0100
912 S Walnut St Edinburgh (46124) *(G-2596)*

Beacon Publishing Co Inc 812 637-0660
24486 Stateline Rd Ste F Lawrenceburg (47025) *(G-9134)*

Beacon Sign Company LLC 317 272-2388
9305 E Us Highway 36 Avon (46123) *(G-433)*

Beak It Bronze, Indianapolis *Also called Leon R Dixon (G-7397)*

Beal Systems Inc 260 693-0772
10772 E State Road 205 Laotto (46763) *(G-9104)*

Bear Creek Farms, Bryant *Also called Richards Restaurant Inc (G-1201)*

Bear Wallow Distillery, Columbus *Also called Old Copper Still Distlg Co LLC (G-1985)*

Bear Wallow Distillery 812 657-4923
4484 Old State Road 46 Nashville (47448) *(G-10715)*

Bearcat Corp 574 533-0448
2431 E Kercher Rd Goshen (46526) *(G-5177)*

Bearing Headquarters Co, Highland *Also called Headco Industries Inc (G-6049)*

Bearing Headquarters Co, South Bend *Also called Headco Industries Inc (G-12795)*

Bearing Service Company PA 773 734-5132
1951 N Griffith Blvd Griffith (46319) *(G-5765)*

Bears Den EMB & More LLC 260 724-4070
530 E 900 N Decatur (46733) *(G-2370)*

Beast Custom Athletic Printing 765 610-6802
418 W Fifth St Fairmount (46928) *(G-3830)*

Beatty International Inc (PA) 219 931-3000
940 150th St Hammond (46327) *(G-5846)*

Beatty Machine & Mfg Co 219 931-3000
940 150th St Hammond (46327) *(G-5847)*

Beauti Pleat Draperies Inc 317 887-1728
201 Moccosin Ct Greenwood (46142) *(G-5669)*

Beautiful Brides By TEC, Bloomington *Also called TEC Photography (G-836)*

Beaver Gravel Corporation 317 773-0679
16101 River Rd Noblesville (46062) *(G-11065)*

Beaver Materials, Noblesville *Also called Beaver Gravel Corporation (G-11065)*

Beaver Mouldings LLC 260 463-4822
3565 S 300 W Lagrange (46761) *(G-9033)*

Beaver Products Inc 317 773-0679
16101 River Rd Noblesville (46062) *(G-11066)*

Beaver Readi-Mix, Noblesville *Also called Ma-Ri-Al Corp (G-11143)*

Becker Elec 812 362-9000
6500 N Us Highway 231 Rockport (47635) *(G-12166)*

Beckett Bronze Company Inc (PA) 765 282-2261
401 W 23rd St Muncie (47302) *(G-10438)*

Beckett Bronze Company Inc 765 282-2261
106 E 20th St Muncie (47302) *(G-10439)*

Beckler Power Equipment 260 356-1188
1255 S Jefferson St Huntington (46750) *(G-6190)*

Beckman Coulter Inc 317 471-8029
5355 W 76th St Indianapolis (46268) *(G-6460)*

Beckman Coulter Inc 317 808-4200
5350 Lakeview Pkwy Indianapolis (46268) *(G-6461)*

Beckman Coulter Inc 317 808-4200
7451 Winton Dr Indianapolis (46268) *(G-6462)*

Becks 765 566-3900
709 Michigan Rd Burlington (46915) *(G-1210)*

Becks Bird Feeders 765 874-1496
8909 S State Road 109 Markleville (46056) *(G-9586)*

Beckys Die Cutting Inc 260 467-1714
701 Sherman Blvd Fort Wayne (46808) *(G-4105)*

Becton Dickinson and Company 317 561-2900
2350 Reeves Rd Plainfield (46168) *(G-11595)*

Bedder Way Company Inc 317 783-5105
3450 Developers Rd Indianapolis (46227) *(G-6463)*

Bedford Crane LLC 812 275-4411
957 J St Bedford (47421) *(G-531)*

Bedford Cut Stone Co, Bedford *Also called Architectural Stone Sales Inc (G-529)*

Bedford Limestone Suppliers 812 279-9120
1319 Breckenridge Rd Bedford (47421) *(G-532)*

Bedford Machine & Tool Inc 812 275-1948
2103 John Williams Blvd Bedford (47421) *(G-533)*

Bedford Stonecrafters Inc 812 275-2646
3160 Mitchell Rd Bedford (47421) *(G-534)*

Bee Window Incorporated 317 283-8522
115 Shadowlawn Dr Fishers (46038) *(G-3876)*

Beebe Cabinet Co Inc 574 293-3580
22695 State Road 120 Elkhart (46516) *(G-2720)*

Beechler Well Drlg & Pump Svc 317 849-2535
10211 E 116th St Fishers (46037) *(G-3877)*

Beechys Molding Plus 260 768-7030
1365 N 500 W Shipshewana (46565) *(G-12606)*

Beemak Plastics Inc 317 841-4398
7035 E 86th St Indianapolis (46250) *(G-6464)*

Beeman Jorgensen Inc 317 841-7677
7510 Allisonville Rd Indianapolis (46250) *(G-6465)*

Beemsterboer Slag Corp (PA) 219 931-7462
3411 Sheffield Ave Hammond (46327) *(G-5848)*

Beemsterboer Slag Corp 219 931-7462
3411 Sheffield Ave Hammond (46327) *(G-5849)*

Beemsterboer Slag Corp 219 392-1930
3210 Watling St East Chicago (46312) *(G-2522)*

Beer and Slabaugh Inc 574 773-3413
23965 Us Highway 6 Nappanee (46550) *(G-10653)*

Beer Baron LLC 317 735-2706
5764 Wheeler Rd Indianapolis (46216) *(G-6466)*

Begley Sign Painting Inc 317 835-2027
220 N Murnan Ln Fairland (46126) *(G-3820)*

Behning Inc 260 672-2663
287 N Main St Roanoke (46783) *(G-12099)*

Bel-Mar Products Corporation 317 769-3262
5 E Pierce St Whitestown (46075) *(G-14249)*

Belcher Gravel, Monrovia *Also called Bob Belcher (G-10202)*

Belden 1993 LLC 606 348-8433
2200 Us Highway 27 S Richmond (47374) *(G-11961)*

Belden Cdt, Richmond *Also called Belden Inc (G-11962)*

Belden Cdt, Richmond *Also called Belden Wire & Cable Co LLC (G-11963)*

Belden Inc 765 962-7561
350 Nw N St Richmond (47374) *(G-11962)*

Belden Inc 317 818-6300
401 Pennsylvania Pkwy Indianapolis (46280) *(G-6262)*

Belden Wire & Cable Co LLC 606 348-8433
2200 Us Highway 27 S Richmond (47374) *(G-11963)*

Belgian Horse Winery LLC 765 779-3002
7122 W County Road 625 N Middletown (47356) *(G-9933)*

Bell Aerospace LLC 904 505-4055
4510 Redcliff South Ln Plainfield (46168) *(G-11596)*

Bell Aquaculture LLC (PA) 765 369-3100
9885 W State Road 67 Redkey (47373) *(G-11896)*

Bell Duffens Optical, Indianapolis *Also called Essilor Laboratories Amer Inc (G-6878)*

Bell Graphics and Design LLC 765 827-5441
3207 Iowa Ave Connersville (47331) *(G-2040)*

Bell Machine Company Inc 765 654-5225
1400 Magnolia Ave Frankfort (46041) *(G-4819)*

Bell Pyrotechnics Incorporated 812 859-3888
3201 Mitten Rd Bowling Green (47833) *(G-952)*

Belmont Sand, Indianapolis *Also called Marietta Martin Materials Inc (G-7455)*

Beltone Hearing Care 812 274-4116
219 Clifty Dr Ste D Madison (47250) *(G-9446)*

Bemcor Inc 219 937-1600
940 150th St Hammond (46327) *(G-5850)*

Bemis Company Inc 812 466-2213
1350 N Fruitridge Ave Terre Haute (47804) *(G-13198)*

Bemr LLC 812 385-8509
106 N 1st Ave Princeton (47670) *(G-11864)*

Bench & Field Pet Foods LLC 800 525-4802
1025 W 11th St Mishawaka (46544) *(G-10007)*

Benchmark Consumer Industries 317 576-0931
7538 Timber Springs Dr N Fishers (46038) *(G-3878)*

Benchmark Fabricated Steel, Terre Haute *Also called Benchmark Inc (G-13199)*

Benchmark Fabricated Steel, Terre Haute *Also called Benchmark Inc (G-13200)*

Benchmark Inc (PA) 812 238-0659
4149 4th Pkwy Terre Haute (47804) *(G-13199)*

Benchmark Inc 812 238-2691
4149 4th Pkwy Terre Haute (47804) *(G-13200)*

Bender Mold & Machine Inc 574 255-5176
55951 Russell Indus Pkwy Mishawaka (46545) *(G-10008)*

Bender Plastics, Mishawaka *Also called Bender Products Inc (G-10009)*

Bender Products Inc 574 255-5350
55951 Russell Indus Pkwy Mishawaka (46545) *(G-10009)*

Bender Wholesale Distributors 574 264-4409
2911 Moose Trl Elkhart (46514) *(G-2721)*

Bendix Coml Vhcl Systems LLC 260 356-9720
1850 Riverfork Dr Huntington (46750) *(G-6191)*

Bendix Mc II 260 356-9720
1230 Sabine St Huntington (46750) *(G-6192)*

Benham Sawmill LLC 812 723-2644
150 W County Road 250 N Paoli (47454) *(G-11444)*

Benitos Printing 812 282-4855
214 E Maple St Jeffersonville (47130) *(G-8329)*

Bennett Printing 812 966-2917
1245 S County Road 925 W Medora (47260) *(G-9680)*

Bennett Tool & Die Inc 317 422-5140
910 Cherokee Ave Bargersville (46106) *(G-478)*

Bennington, Elkhart *Also called Pontoon Boat LLC (G-3102)*

Bennington Pontoon Boats, Elkhart *Also called Boat Holdings LLC (G-2728)*

Bens Quarry LLC 812 824-3730
303 E Ingram Rd Springville (47462) *(G-13060)*

Benshaw Inc 412 487-8235
235 Westchester Blvd Noblesville (46062) *(G-11067)*

Benson Solar Enterprises LLC 855 533-7467
1140 E Franklin St Huntington (46750) *(G-6193)*

Benteler Automotive Corp 574 534-1499
910 Eisenhower Dr S Goshen (46526) *(G-5178)*

Benthall Bros Inc (PA) 800 488-5995
15 Read St Evansville (47710) *(G-3372)*

Benton Review Newspaper 765 884-1902
204 N Adams Ave Fowler (47944) *(G-4795)*

Bentz Transport Products Inc 260 622-9100
3943 Weston Pointe Dr Zionsville (46077) *(G-14422)*

Berendsen Inc 812 423-6468
460 E Sycamore St Evansville (47713) *(G-3373)*

Berkey Machine Corporation 260 761-4002
7037a N Triplett St Wawaka (46794) *(G-14031)*

Bernard Hasten 317 824-4544
4525 Saguaro Trl Indianapolis (46268) *(G-6467)*

Berne Apparel Company (PA) 260 622-1500
2501 E 850 N Ossian (46777) *(G-11397)*

Berne Locker Storage 260 589-2806
524 W Franklin St Berne (46711) *(G-608)*

Berne Tri Weekly News Inc 260 589-2101
153 S Jefferson St Berne (46711) *(G-609)*

Berry Film Products Co Inc 812 306-2690
101 Oakley St Evansville (47710) *(G-3374)*

Berry Global Inc 812 334-7090
4100 W Profile Pkwy Bloomington (47404) *(G-679)*

Berry Global Inc 812 424-2904
4100 W Profile Pkwy Bloomington (47404) *(G-680)*

Berry Global Inc 812 558-3510
10485 E 1250 N Odon (47562) *(G-11320)*

Berry Global Inc 812 386-1525
889 W Gach Rd Princeton (47670) *(G-11865)*

Berry Global Inc 765 966-1414
630 Commerance Rd Richmond (47374) *(G-11964)*

Berry Global Inc 812 867-6671
3245 Kansas Rd Evansville (47725) *(G-3375)*

Berry Global Inc 765 962-4253
630 Commerce Rd Richmond (47374) *(G-11965)*

Berry Global Inc (HQ) 812 424-2904
101 Oakley St Evansville (47710) *(G-3376)*

Berry Global Group Inc (PA) 812 424-2904
101 Oakley St Evansville (47710) *(G-3377)*

Berry Plastics, Evansville *Also called Berry Global Inc (G-3376)*

Berry Plastics Group Inc 812 424-2904
101 Oakley St Evansville (47710) *(G-3378)*

Berry Plastics Ik LLC 641 648-5047
101 Oakley St Evansville (47710) *(G-3379)*

Berry Plastics Opco Inc 812 402-2903
9845 Hedden Rd Evansville (47725) *(G-3380)*

Berry Plastics Opco Inc (HQ) 812 424-2904
101 Oakley St Evansville (47710) *(G-3381)*

Bertrand Products Inc 574 234-4181
2323 Foundation Dr South Bend (46628) *(G-12722)*

Beryl Martin, Griffith *Also called Ccmp Inc (G-5769)*

Bes Racing Engines Inc 812 576-2371
27545 State Route 1 Guilford (47022) *(G-5797)*

Besi Manufacturing Inc 812 427-4114
503 Vineyard St Vevay (47043) *(G-13660)*

Besse Veneers Inc 906 428-3113
718 E Park St Trafalgar (46181) *(G-13434)*

Best Access Solutions, Indianapolis *Also called Dormakaba USA Inc (G-6758)*

Best Access Systems, Indianapolis *Also called Stanley Security Solutions Inc (G-7991)*

Best Access Systems, Indianapolis *Also called Stanley Security Solutions Inc (G-7992)*

Best Access Systems, Indianapolis *Also called Stanley Security Solutions Inc (G-7993)*

Best Beers LLC 812 332-1234
1100 S Strong Dr Bloomington (47403) *(G-681)*

Best Chairs Incorporated (PA) 812 367-1761
1 Best Dr Ferdinand (47532) *(G-3846)*

Best Chairs Incorporated 812 367-1761
1700 W Willowcreek Rd Paoli (47454) *(G-11445)*

Best Chairs Incorporated 812 367-1761
Highway 66 E Cannelton (47520) *(G-1287)*

Best Electric Motor Service 765 583-2408
11430 E Us Hwy 52 Otterbein (47970) *(G-11417)*

Best Equipment & Welding Co 317 271-8652
1960 Midwest Blvd Indianapolis (46214) *(G-6468)*

Best Equipment Co Inc (PA) 317 823-3050
5550 Poindexter Dr Indianapolis (46235) *(G-6469)*

Best Formed Plastics LLC 574 293-6128
21209 Protecta Dr Elkhart (46516) *(G-2722)*

Best Friends Inc 765 985-3872
252 W Harrison St Denver (46926) *(G-2453)*

Best Machine Co Inc 765 827-0250
1830 Virginia Ave Connersville (47331) *(G-2041)*

Best Metal Finishing Inc 812 689-9950
1050 Railroad Ave Osgood (47037) *(G-11389)*

Best Tires & Wheels 317 306-3379
320 N Morton St Franklin (46131) *(G-4872)*

Best Vineyards 812 969-9463
8373 Morgans Ln Se Elizabeth (47117) *(G-2642)*

Best Weld Inc 765 641-7720
1315 W 18th St Anderson (46016) *(G-74)*

Bestway Foam, Indianapolis *Also called Foamcraft Inc (G-6943)*

Beta Steel Corp 219 787-0001
6500 S Boundary Rd Portage (46368) *(G-11751)*

Bethlehem Packg Die Cutng Inc 812 282-8740
802 E 8th St New Albany (47150) *(G-10751)*

Betos Bar Inc 219 397-8247
1301 E Chicago Ave East Chicago (46312) *(G-2523)*

Better Built Barns Inc 812 477-2001
4415 E Morgan Ave Evansville (47715) *(G-3382)*

Better Built Products, Lowell *Also called V N C Inc (G-9425)*

Better Metal Systems LLC 888 958-5945
9445 Indianapolis Blvd J Highland (46322) *(G-6038)*

Better Metal Systems LLC 219 290-2539
7604 Oakdale Ave Hammond (46324) *(G-5851)*

Better Visions PC 260 627-2669
 10529 Hosler Rd A Leo (46765) *(G-9239)*
Better Visions PC 260 244-7542
 513 N Line St Columbia City (46725) *(G-1766)*
Better Way Partners LLC 574 831-3340
 70891 County Road 23 New Paris (46553) *(G-10975)*
Better Way Products, New Paris Also called Better Way Partners LLC *(G-10975)*
Bettner Wire Coating Dyes Inc 812 372-2732
 1230 Jackson St Columbus (47201) *(G-1859)*
Beulah Inc 219 309-5635
 808 N 360 W Valparaiso (46385) *(G-13508)*
Beutler Meat Processing Co 765 742-7285
 802 Wabash Ave Lafayette (47905) *(G-8860)*
Bev Can Printers Llc 219 617-6181
 1705 State St Bldg B La Porte (46350) *(G-8738)*
Bev Rexam Can Americas Inc 773 399-3000
 4750 Swisher Rd West Lafayette (47906) *(G-14052)*
Beveled Glass & Ltg Designs, Indianapolis Also called Larry Robertson Associates *(G-7381)*
Beverly G Inc 812 401-1819
 1818 Vann Ave Evansville (47714) *(G-3383)*
Beverly Industrial Service 812 667-5047
 4233 S Farmers Retreat Rd Dillsboro (47018) *(G-2463)*
Beverly Tent & Awning Co 219 931-3723
 7126 Calumet Ave Hammond (46324) *(G-5852)*
Beverlys Incense 219 558-2461
 9214 Maple Ct Saint John (46373) *(G-12260)*
Bex Screen Printing Inc 317 791-0375
 5602 Elmwood Ave Ste 214 Indianapolis (46203) *(G-6470)*
Beyond Monumental 317 454-8519
 202 E Market St Indianapolis (46204) *(G-6471)*
BF Goodrich, Woodburn Also called Michelin North America Inc *(G-14386)*
BF Goodrich Tire Manufacturing 260 493-8100
 18906 Old 24 Woodburn (46797) *(G-14380)*
BF Shaffer Co 812 949-8356
 2712 Clearstream Ct New Albany (47150) *(G-10752)*
Bhar Incorporated 260 749-5168
 6509 Moeller Rd Fort Wayne (46806) *(G-4106)*
Bhar Printing Inc 317 899-1020
 8745 Rawles Ave Indianapolis (46219) *(G-6472)*
Bhj Usa Inc 574 722-3933
 81 E Industrial Blvd Logansport (46947) *(G-9324)*
Bibles For Blind & Visually 812 466-3134
 3228 E Rose Hill Ave Terre Haute (47805) *(G-13201)*
Biblical Enterprises LLC 812 391-0071
 3428 S Burks Ct Bloomington (47401) *(G-682)*
Bidwhist Industries 219 879-2508
 5276 N Verma Dr La Porte (46350) *(G-8739)*
Biela Printing 219 874-8094
 1004 Kentucky St Michigan City (46360) *(G-9768)*
Big Als Athletics 765 836-5203
 303 S Walnut Mount Summit (47361) *(G-10378)*
Big B Distributors Inc 812 425-5235
 2727 N Kentucky Ave Evansville (47711) *(G-3384)*
Big Brick House Bakery LLP 260 563-1071
 4322 Marvin Dr Fort Wayne (46806) *(G-4107)*
Big Chops Famous Bbq, Lamar Also called Hilltop Processing Inc *(G-9100)*
Big Creek LLC 812 876-0835
 8248 Main St Stinesville (47464) *(G-13075)*
Big Dog Adhesives LLC 574 299-6768
 615 S 4th St Elkhart (46516) *(G-2723)*
Big E Publications Inc 317 485-4097
 505 N School St Fortville (46040) *(G-4768)*
Big Guy Signs LLC 317 780-6000
 5575 Elmwood Ave Ste C Indianapolis (46203) *(G-6473)*
Big Inch Fabricators Cnstr Inc 765 245-9353
 6127 W Us Highway 36 Montezuma (47862) *(G-10209)*
Big Picture Data Imaging LLC 812 235-0202
 608 N 13th St Terre Haute (47807) *(G-13202)*
Big Red, Indianapolis Also called Brama Inc *(G-6502)*
Big Red Liquors Inc 812 339-9552
 435 S Walnut St Bloomington (47401) *(G-683)*
Bigasspizzacutter.com, Indianapolis Also called Tgf Enterprises LLC *(G-8056)*
Biggerstaff & Son Excavating 317 784-6034
 5002 E Thompson Rd Indianapolis (46237) *(G-6474)*
Bike-N-Trikes 317 835-4544
 6597 W 300 N Boggstown (46110) *(G-899)*
Bill Baldwins Screenprinting 317 881-2712
 129 Totten Dr Greenwood (46143) *(G-5670)*
Bill Banner Signs 765 209-2642
 10697 N 600 E Falmouth (46127) *(G-3836)*
Bill Graber Logging 812 486-2709
 6722 E 400 N Montgomery (47558) *(G-10215)*
Bill Walters Concrete Inc 574 259-0056
 1134 E 12th St Mishawaka (46544) *(G-10010)*
Billman Monument & Sign Co 574 753-2394
 1137 Pleasant Hl Logansport (46947) *(G-9325)*
Bills Industries LLC 765 629-0227
 7794 S 175 W Milroy (46156) *(G-9977)*
Bills Pallets, Cloverdale Also called Billy D Snider *(G-1724)*

Bills Printing 765 962-7674
 1310 Nw 5th St Richmond (47374) *(G-11966)*
Billy D Snider 765 795-6426
 294 Bubble Loo Rd Cloverdale (46120) *(G-1724)*
Biltz Signs 574 594-2703
 5843 E Mckenna Rd Warsaw (46582) *(G-13844)*
Bimbo Baker US, Evansville Also called Bimbo Bakeries Usa Inc *(G-3385)*
Bimbo Bakeries Usa Inc 812 678-3471
 4878 E 450n Dubois (47527) *(G-2475)*
Bimbo Bakeries Usa Inc 219 844-0465
 3420 179th St Hammond (46323) *(G-5853)*
Bimbo Bakeries Usa Inc 317 273-0444
 8121 W 10th St Indianapolis (46214) *(G-6475)*
Bimbo Bakeries Usa Inc 812 479-6934
 6717 Toney Ln Evansville (47715) *(G-3385)*
Bio-Response Solutions Inc 317 386-3500
 200 Colin Ct Danville (46122) *(G-2343)*
Bioanalytical Systems Inc (PA) 765 463-4527
 2701 Kent Ave West Lafayette (47906) *(G-14053)*
Biodyne-Midwest LLC 888 970-0955
 10617 Majic Port Ln Fort Wayne (46819) *(G-4108)*
Biokorf LLC 765 727-0782
 1008 Ravinia Rd West Lafayette (47906) *(G-14054)*
Biolife Plasma Services LP 574 264-7204
 2715 Emerson Dr Elkhart (46514) *(G-2724)*
Biologics Modular LLC 317 456-9191
 1533 E Northfield Dr # 1000 Brownsburg (46112) *(G-1137)*
Biomet Inc (HQ) 574 267-6639
 345 E Main St Warsaw (46580) *(G-13845)*
Biomet Biologics LLC 574 267-2038
 56 E Bell Dr Warsaw (46582) *(G-13846)*
Biomet Europe Ltd 574 267-2038
 56 E Bell Dr Warsaw (46582) *(G-13847)*
Biomet Inc 574 372-6999
 737 N Detroit St Warsaw (46580) *(G-13848)*
Biomet Orthopedics LLC 574 267-6639
 56 E Bell Dr Warsaw (46582) *(G-13849)*
Biomet Sports Medicine LLC 574 267-6639
 56 E Bell Dr Warsaw (46582) *(G-13850)*
Bionic Prosth & Orthos Grp LLC 765 838-8222
 5 Executive Dr Ste D-2 Lafayette (47905) *(G-8861)*
Bionic Prosthetics & Orthotics, Merrillville Also called Bionic Prosthetics and Ortho *(G-9701)*
Bionic Prosthetics and Ortho (PA) 219 791-9200
 8695 Connecticut St Ste E Merrillville (46410) *(G-9701)*
Bionic Prosthetics and Ortho 219 221-6119
 1200 S Woodland Ave Ste A Michigan City (46360) *(G-9769)*
Bionode LLC 317 292-7686
 7987 Clearwater Pkwy Indianapolis (46240) *(G-6476)*
Biopoly LLC 260 999-6135
 7136 Gettysburg Pike Fort Wayne (46804) *(G-4109)*
Biosafe Engineering LLC 317 858-8099
 5750 W 80th St Indianapolis (46278) *(G-6477)*
Bioscience Vaccines Inc 765 464-5890
 1425 Innovation Pl West Lafayette (47906) *(G-14055)*
Biosolid Compost, Fort Wayne Also called City of Fort Wayne *(G-4151)*
Biotta Juices, Fishers Also called Caj Food Products Inc *(G-3884)*
Birch Wood 260 432-0011
 8151 Glencarin Blvd Fort Wayne (46804) *(G-4110)*
Bird Publishing Company 219 462-6330
 1600 Edgewater Beach Rd Valparaiso (46383) *(G-13509)*
Birdeye Inc 812 886-0598
 483 N Mount Zion Rd Vincennes (47591) *(G-13669)*
Birds Nest Inc 574 247-0201
 421 E University Dr Granger (46530) *(G-5394)*
Birkat Adonai LLC 219 221-9810
 4605 N Highway 11 Se Elizabeth (47117) *(G-2643)*
Bishop Repair 812 523-3246
 4514 S County Road 700 E Crothersville (47229) *(G-2216)*
Bison Coach LLC 574 658-4161
 1002 N Old State Road 15 Milford (46542) *(G-9949)*
Bison Horse Trailers LLC 574 658-4161
 804 S Higbee St Milford (46542) *(G-9950)*
Bittersweet Candle Company LLC 317 782-3170
 5230 Park Emerson Dr Indianapolis (46203) *(G-6478)*
Bittersweet LLC 574 642-1184
 2250 W 550 S Wolcottville (46795) *(G-14368)*
Bittersweet Publishing 317 640-3943
 9936 Boysenberry Dr Fishers (46038) *(G-3879)*
Bittinger Writings Inc 317 846-9136
 3011 Whispering Trl Carmel (46033) *(G-1317)*
Bituminous Materials & Sup LP 317 228-8203
 5400 W 86th St Indianapolis (46268) *(G-6479)*
Bixlers Logging, Lexington Also called Keith Bixler *(G-9252)*
Bizcard 317 436-8649
 9745 Fall Creek Rd Indianapolis (46256) *(G-6480)*
Bizik Masonry Corporation 219 659-1348
 2435 Indianapolis Blvd Whiting (46394) *(G-14270)*
Bk International LLC 260 639-0112
 14525 Bruick Ln Hoagland (46745) *(G-6063)*

(G-0000) Company's Geographic Section entry number

Bkb Manufacturing Inc..................................260 982-8524
607 S Wabash Rd North Manchester (46962) **(G-11225)**

Bkb Petroleum Inc.......................................574 389-8159
22700 Old Us 20 Elkhart (46516) **(G-2725)**

Black & Decker (us) Inc................................317 241-1200
5999 Crawfordsville Rd Indianapolis (46224) **(G-6481)**

Black Bear Recrtl Vehicles, Middlebury Also called Grand Design Rv LLC **(G-9890)**

Black Beauty Air Qulty 1 Mine, Wheatland Also called Peabody Midwest Mining LLC **(G-14232)**

Black Beauty Farmersburg, Pimento Also called Peabody Midwest Mining LLC **(G-11580)**

Black Beauty Mining, Oakland City Also called Peabody Midwest Mining LLC **(G-11313)**

Black Beauty Mining Div, Lynnville Also called Peabody Midwest Mining LLC **(G-9436)**

Black Books Publishing Inc.............................260 225-7479
653 Candlelite Ct Fort Wayne (46807) **(G-4111)**

Black Dog Vineyard Inc.................................812 877-1933
7622 N Meneely St Terre Haute (47805) **(G-13203)**

Black Ember LLC.......................................317 840-5523
1332 Cliff Ridge Ct Indianapolis (46217) **(G-6482)**

Black Equipment Company South........................812 477-6481
1187 Burch Dr Evansville (47725) **(G-3386)**

Black Jewell Popcorn, Columbus Also called LLC Black Jewell **(G-1963)**

Black Panther Mining LLC..............................812 745-2920
12661 N Agri Care Rd Oaktown (47561) **(G-11317)**

Black Plate Catering...................................317 634-8030
2025 E 46th St Indianapolis (46205) **(G-6483)**

Black Swan Vapors LLC.................................317 645-5210
118 W State St Pendleton (46064) **(G-11484)**

Black Tie Manufacturing Inc............................574 971-6034
2749 Jami St Elkhart (46514) **(G-2726)**

Blackboxit Inc...260 489-8014
111 E Ludwig Rd Ste 109 Fort Wayne (46825) **(G-4112)**

Blackerby & Associates.................................812 216-2370
444 Persimmon Dr Seymour (47274) **(G-12433)**

Blackfoot Powder Coating..............................812 531-9315
5729 N State Road 59 Brazil (47834) **(G-954)**

Blackhawk Millwright & Rigging.........................765 662-7922
1316 Ann St Kokomo (46901) **(G-8598)**

Blackpoint Engineering LLC............................574 642-3152
601 Sroufe St Ste 200 Ligonier (46767) **(G-9277)**

Blackwell Limestone, Norman Also called Justin Blackwell **(G-11203)**

Blackwood Solutions Inc...............................812 824-6728
205 N College Ave Ste 410 Bloomington (47404) **(G-684)**

Blanket Buddy, Crown Point Also called Blanket Hog **(G-2228)**

Blanket Hog...219 308-9532
10850 Bell St Crown Point (46307) **(G-2228)**

Blasdel Enterprises Inc.................................812 663-3213
495 W Mckee St Greensburg (47240) **(G-5590)**

Blasted Works...574 583-3211
214 N Main St Monticello (47960) **(G-10256)**

Blessing Enterprises Inc...............................219 736-9800
1420 E 91st Dr Merrillville (46410) **(G-9702)**

Blessing Tool & Die Inc................................574 875-1982
24366 County Road 45 Elkhart (46516) **(G-2727)**

Blessinger Brothers, Huntingburg Also called Englert & Meyer Corporation **(G-6163)**

Bleu Rooster Designs..................................317 845-0889
7444 River Highlands Dr Fishers (46038) **(G-3880)**

Bleys Prosthetics & Orthotics..........................812 704-3894
50 Hancock St Seymour (47274) **(G-12434)**

Blinkless Power Equipment LLC.........................317 844-7328
8802 Bash St Ste F Indianapolis (46256) **(G-6484)**

Blitz Manufacturing Co Ind.............................812 284-2548
263 America Pl Jeffersonville (47130) **(G-8330)**

Blocksom & Co (PA)...................................219 878-4455
450 Saint John Rd Ste 710 Michigan City (46360) **(G-9770)**

Blocksom & Co..219 878-4458
420 E 5th St Michigan City (46360) **(G-9771)**

Blondies Cookies Inc (PA).............................765 628-3978
303 N Meridian St Greentown (46936) **(G-5644)**

Blondies Cookies Inc...................................765 288-3872
3501 N Grnvlle Ave Ste 99 Muncie (47303) **(G-10440)**

Bloom Magazine.......................................812 323-8959
414 W 6th St Bloomington (47404) **(G-685)**

Bloom Pharmaceutical.................................260 615-2633
2831 Union Chapel Rd Fort Wayne (46845) **(G-4113)**

Bloomfield Mfg Co Inc.................................812 384-4441
46 W Spring St Bloomfield (47424) **(G-635)**

Bloomington Asphalt & Cnstr, Bloomington Also called Rogers Group Inc **(G-817)**

Bloomington Brewing Co, Bloomington Also called Lennies Inc **(G-765)**

Bloomington Concret Surfaces.........................812 345-0011
615 W Allen St Bloomington (47403) **(G-686)**

Bloomington Crushed Stone, Bloomington Also called Rogers Group Inc **(G-813)**

Bloomington Design Inc................................812 332-2033
6767 E State Road 46 Bloomington (47401) **(G-687)**

Bloomington Discount Prtg Inc.........................812 332-9789
1017 S Lincoln St Bloomington (47401) **(G-688)**

Bludot Inc..574 277-2306
4335 Meghan Beeler Ct South Bend (46628) **(G-12723)**

Blue Burro Inc..904 825-9900
8325 W Hinds Rd Bloomington (47403) **(G-689)**

Blue Collar...260 359-8030
23 E Washington St Huntington (46750) **(G-6194)**

Blue Creek Trail Map Co...............................765 455-9867
3506 Hawthorne Ln Kokomo (46902) **(G-8599)**

Blue Flame, Madison Also called Crestwood Equity Partners LP **(G-9455)**

Blue Grass Chemical Spc LLC (PA).....................812 948-1115
895 Industrial Blvd New Albany (47150) **(G-10753)**

Blue Guardian Publishing Co...........................317 506-0763
5252 Brianna Ln Indianapolis (46235) **(G-6485)**

Blue Marble Cocktails Inc..............................888 400-3090
6008 Corporate Way Indianapolis (46278) **(G-6486)**

Blue Octopus Printing Company.........................317 247-1997
2431 Directors Row Indianapolis (46241) **(G-6487)**

Blue Pillar Inc..317 723-6601
9025 River Rd Ste 150 Indianapolis (46240) **(G-6488)**

Blue Print Specialties Inc..............................765 742-6976
1500 Union St Lafayette (47904) **(G-8862)**

Blue Ribbon Products Inc..............................317 972-7970
8188 Allison Ave Indianapolis (46268) **(G-6489)**

Blue River Farm Supply Inc............................812 364-6675
14485 Greene St Ne Palmyra (47164) **(G-11435)**

Blue River Printing Inc.................................317 392-3676
55 E Washington St Shelbyville (46176) **(G-12521)**

Blue River Roasters LLC...............................317 392-9668
2138 Cherokee Dr Shelbyville (46176) **(G-12522)**

Blue River Services Inc................................812 738-2437
101 N Mulberry St Corydon (47112) **(G-2090)**

Blue River Stamping Inc...............................317 395-5600
600 Northridge Dr Shelbyville (46176) **(G-12523)**

Blue River Timber LLC.................................812 291-0411
2997 Gethsemane Church Rd Evansville (47712) **(G-3387)**

Blue Sun Ventures Ltd.................................317 426-0001
525 S Meridian St Indianapolis (46225) **(G-6490)**

Bluefin Software LLC..................................574 643-1091
105 E Jefferson Blvd # 800 South Bend (46601) **(G-12724)**

Bluering Stencils......................................260 203-5461
2248 Research Dr Fort Wayne (46808) **(G-4114)**

Bluffton Motor Works LLC (HQ).........................800 579-8527
410 E Spring St Bluffton (46714) **(G-867)**

Bluffton Rubber.......................................260 824-4501
810 Lancaster St Bluffton (46714) **(G-868)**

Blume Metal Sales LLC................................765 490-0600
695 W State Road 18 Brookston (47923) **(G-1101)**

Blumenau Alpacas.....................................219 713-6171
19950 Austin St Lowell (46356) **(G-9400)**

Blumling Design and Graphics..........................765 477-7446
3228 Olympia Dr Ste C Lafayette (47909) **(G-8863)**

Blush & Bobby Pins....................................317 789-5166
600 E Carmel Dr Ste 249 Carmel (46032) **(G-1318)**

Blush Salon Boutique..................................317 523-1635
11631 Maple St Fishers (46038) **(G-3881)**

Blythes Sport Shop Inc (PA)............................219 924-4403
138 N Broad St Griffith (46319) **(G-5766)**

Blythes Sport Shop Inc.................................219 476-0026
2810 Calumet Ave Valparaiso (46383) **(G-13510)**

Bm Creations Inc......................................219 922-8935
1313 E Main St Griffith (46319) **(G-5767)**

Bmi Refractory Services Inc............................219 885-2209
201 Mississippi St Gary (46402) **(G-5030)**

Bmo Harris Bank, Gary Also called Harris Bmo Bank National Assn **(G-5059)**

Bmr Group, Kimmell Also called Boyd Machine & Repair Co Inc **(G-8529)**

Bo-Mar Industries Inc..................................317 899-1240
3838 S Arlington Ave Indianapolis (46203) **(G-6491)**

Bo-Witt Products Inc..................................812 526-5561
500 N Walnut St Edinburgh (46124) **(G-2597)**

Boarder Magic By J & A.................................317 545-4401
902 W Banta Rd Indianapolis (46217) **(G-6492)**

Boardworks Inc.......................................219 464-8111
1203 Formula Dr Valparaiso (46383) **(G-13511)**

Boat Holdings LLC....................................574 264-6336
2805 Decio Dr Elkhart (46514) **(G-2728)**

Bob Belcher..317 996-3712
6624 W State Road 42 Monrovia (46157) **(G-10202)**

Bob Evans Farms Inc..................................317 846-3261
931 N Rangeline Rd Ste B Carmel (46032) **(G-1319)**

Bob Low Discount Tobacco.............................765 868-9713
221 W Morgan St Kokomo (46901) **(G-8600)**

Bob Prescott..219 736-7804
101 W 78th Pl Merrillville (46410) **(G-9703)**

Bobby Little Creations.................................219 313-5102
610 W Joliet St Crown Point (46307) **(G-2229)**

Bobs Quick Copy Shop.................................765 457-9160
1128 Emery St Kokomo (46902) **(G-8601)**

Bobs Welding Repair..................................765 744-4192
6447 W 250 S Farmland (47340) **(G-3840)**

Bock Industries Inc....................................574 295-8070
29851 County Road 20 Elkhart (46517) **(G-2729)**

A
L
P
H
A
B
E
T
I
C

Body Panels Co 812 962-6262
1101 N Governor St Evansville (47711) *(G-3388)*

Bodycote Thermal Proc Inc 812 662-0500
1930 N Montgomery Rd Greensburg (47240) *(G-5591)*

Bodycote Thermal Proc Inc 260 423-1691
3715 E Washington Blvd Fort Wayne (46803) *(G-4115)*

Bodycote Thermal Proc Inc 574 295-2491
908 County Road 1 N Elkhart (46514) *(G-2730)*

Bodycote Thermal Proc Inc 317 924-4321
500 W 21st St Indianapolis (46202) *(G-6493)*

Boe Knows Mold 260 760-7136
488 Courtney Dr New Haven (46774) *(G-10931)*

Boeke Road Baptist Church Inc 812 479-5342
2601 S Boeke Rd Evansville (47714) *(G-3389)*

Boezeman Enterprises Inc 219 345-2732
9941 N 1200 W Demotte (46310) *(G-2432)*

Boezeman Signs Graphic Design, Demotte *Also called Boezeman Enterprises Inc (G-2432)*

Bofrebo Industries Inc 219 322-1550
1145 Birch Dr Schererville (46375) *(G-12318)*

Boilers & More Inc 317 873-2007
8639 W 96th St Zionsville (46077) *(G-14423)*

Bolinger Machine Co 317 241-2989
23 N Alton Ave Indianapolis (46222) *(G-6494)*

Bollhoff Inc (HQ) 260 347-3903
2705 Marion Dr Kendallville (46755) *(G-8461)*

Bollock Interprises Inc 765 448-6000
900 Farabee Ct Lafayette (47905) *(G-8864)*

Bolstra LLC 317 660-9131
12400 N Meridian St # 120 Carmel (46032) *(G-1320)*

Bolttech Mannings Inc 219 310-8389
1170 Arrowhead Ct Crown Point (46307) *(G-2230)*

Bomarko Inc (PA) 574 936-9901
1955 N Oak Dr Plymouth (46563) *(G-11669)*

Bon L Manufacturing Company 815 351-6802
508 Wilson St Kentland (47951) *(G-8517)*

Bonar Inc 260 636-7430
307 Woods Dr Albion (46701) *(G-17)*

Bonar Well Drilling, Albion *Also called Bonar Inc (G-17)*

Bondline Adhesives Inc 812 423-4651
500 N Woods Ave Evansville (47712) *(G-3390)*

Bonner & Associates 317 571-1911
12310 Windsor Dr Carmel (46033) *(G-1321)*

Bonnie Doon Ice Cream Corp 574 255-9841
2704 Lincolnway W Mishawaka (46544) *(G-10011)*

Bonnier Corporation 317 231-5862
838 N Delaware St Indianapolis (46204) *(G-6495)*

Bontrager & Sons Projects, Goshen *Also called Daniel Bontrager (G-5198)*

Boomerang Bay LLC 812 236-2027
530 Farrington St Terre Haute (47807) *(G-13204)*

Boomerang Ventures LLC 317 852-7786
3367 N County Road 575 E Danville (46122) *(G-2344)*

Boomers 765 741-4031
2627 S Walnut St Muncie (47302) *(G-10441)*

Boomstick Interactive LLC 812 528-4875
6346 Stockwell Dr Indianapolis (46237) *(G-6496)*

Boondocks Logging LLC 812 247-3363
12471 Sanders Ln Shoals (47581) *(G-12664)*

Booth Signs Inc 812 376-7446
1307 12th St Columbus (47201) *(G-1860)*

Bootz Industries, Evansville *Also called Bootz Manufacturing Co LLC (G-3391)*

Bootz Industries, Evansville *Also called Bootz Manufacturing Co LLC (G-3392)*

Bootz Manufacturing Co LLC (PA) 812 423-5401
1400 Park St Evansville (47710) *(G-3391)*

Bootz Manufacturing Co LLC 812 423-5019
1600 N 1st Ave Evansville (47710) *(G-3392)*

Bootz Manufacturing Company 812 425-4646
2301 W Maryland St Evansville (47712) *(G-3393)*

Bootz Plumbing, Evansville *Also called Bootz Manufacturing Company (G-3393)*

Bordners Truck Repair & Algnmt, Cutler *Also called CD & Ws Bordner Entps Inc (G-2328)*

Boreco Industries Inc 574 255-4149
54530 Clover Rd Mishawaka (46545) *(G-10012)*

Borgwarner Inc 765 609-3801
6628 Production Dr Anderson (46013) *(G-75)*

Borgwarner Pds (indiana) Inc (HQ) 800 372-3555
600 Corporation Dr Pendleton (46064) *(G-11485)*

Borgwarner Pds Anderson LLC (HQ) 765 778-6499
13975 Borgwarner Dr Noblesville (46060) *(G-11068)*

Borgwarner Pds Anderson LLC 765 778-6641
600 Corporation Dr Pendleton (46064) *(G-11486)*

Borgwarner Pds Anderson LLC 765 778-6499
6628 Production Dr Anderson (46013) *(G-76)*

Borkholder Building Supply, Nappanee *Also called Borkholder Corporation (G-10654)*

Borkholder Corporation (PA) 574 773-4083
786 Us Highway 6 Nappanee (46550) *(G-10654)*

Borkholder Lavon 574 773-3714
492 Us Highway 6 Nappanee (46550) *(G-10655)*

Borkholder Wood Products 574 546-2613
2060 5th Rd Bremen (46506) *(G-984)*

Bornemann Products Inc 574 546-2881
2562 Walton Blvd Warsaw (46582) *(G-13851)*

Bosch Auto Proving Ground, New Carlisle *Also called Robert Bosch LLC (G-10886)*

Bosch Automotive, Albion *Also called Robert Bosch LLC (G-34)*

Bosphorus Breakfast Hookah Bar 317 624-1700
937 S East St Indianapolis (46225) *(G-6497)*

Boss Industries LLC 219 324-7776
1761 Genesis Dr La Porte (46350) *(G-8740)*

Boston Scientific Corporation 812 829-4877
780 Brookside Dr Spencer (47460) *(G-13018)*

Boston Tool Company Inc 765 935-6282
800 S 9th St Richmond (47374) *(G-11967)*

Botanic Choice, Hobart *Also called Indiana Botanic Gardens Inc (G-6081)*

Bottcher America Corporation 765 675-4449
717 Industrial Dr Tipton (46072) *(G-13389)*

Bottle Neck Solutions, North Judson *Also called Cold Craft Brewing LLC (G-11210)*

Bottom Line Management Inc 812 944-7388
1410 Johnson Ln Clarksville (47129) *(G-1674)*

Bottom Line Rv, Middlebury *Also called Jayco Inc (G-9896)*

Bounthanhs Egg Rolls 574 546-4276
1415 Us Highway 6 Nappanee (46550) *(G-10656)*

Bourbon Kitchen and Bath, Bourbon *Also called McKinney & Sell Inc (G-945)*

Bowell Ty & Michelle, Greendale *Also called Ty Bowells Farrier Service (G-5496)*

Bowen Printing Inc 574 936-3924
200 S Michigan St Plymouth (46563) *(G-11670)*

Bowman Art Glass Studio 765 281-4527
3929 W Kilgore Ave Muncie (47304) *(G-10442)*

Bowman Brothers Inc 317 253-6043
1831 E 64th St Indianapolis (46220) *(G-6498)*

Bowmans Tin Shop Inc 574 936-3234
113 E Laporte St Plymouth (46563) *(G-11671)*

Bowmar LLC 260 747-3121
8000 Bluffton Rd Fort Wayne (46809) *(G-4116)*

Boy-Conn Printers Inc 219 462-2665
803 Glendale Blvd Valparaiso (46383) *(G-13512)*

Boyd Corporation 574 389-1878
53208 Columbia Dr Elkhart (46514) *(G-2731)*

Boyd Machine & Repair Co Inc 260 635-2195
3794 W 50 S Kimmell (46760) *(G-8529)*

Boyer Enterprises Inc 812 963-9180
12311 Edgewater Dr Evansville (47720) *(G-3394)*

Boyer Machine & Tool Co Inc 812 379-9581
1080 S Gladstone Ave Columbus (47201) *(G-1861)*

BP Alternative Energy NA Inc 765 884-1000
91 S 100 E Fowler (47944) *(G-4796)*

BP Parallel LLC 812 424-2904
101 Oakley St Evansville (47710) *(G-3395)*

BP Wind Energy North Amer Inc 765 884-1000
91 S 100 E Fowler (47944) *(G-4797)*

Bpc Manufacturing Operation 574 936-9894
1755 N Oak Dr Plymouth (46563) *(G-11672)*

Bprex Closure Systems LLC 812 424-2904
101 Oakley St Evansville (47710) *(G-3396)*

Bprex Closures LLC (HQ) 812 424-2904
101 Oakley St Evansville (47710) *(G-3397)*

Bprex Closures LLC 812 424-2904
3245 Kansas Rd Evansville (47725) *(G-3398)*

Bprex Closures LLC 812 867-6671
3245 Kansas Rd Evansville (47725) *(G-3399)*

Bprex Closures LLC 812 386-1525
889 W Gach Rd Princeton (47670) *(G-11866)*

Brackett Heating & AC 812 476-1138
5233 Old Boonville Hwy Evansville (47715) *(G-3400)*

Braden Sutphin Ink Co 317 352-8781
1340 Sadlier Circle E Dr Indianapolis (46239) *(G-6499)*

Bradford Press 574 876-3601
302 W 3rd St Mishawaka (46544) *(G-10013)*

Bradley Environmental, Ladoga *Also called Bradley Innovation Group LLC (G-8838)*

Bradley Innovation Group LLC 765 942-7127
7442 S 750 E Ladoga (47954) *(G-8838)*

Brainstorm Print LLC 317 466-1600
2603 55th Pl Indianapolis (46220) *(G-6500)*

Bralin Laser Services Inc 260 357-6511
2233 County Road 72 Auburn (46706) *(G-318)*

Brallan Press LLC 317 525-4335
2102 E 161st St Westfield (46074) *(G-14139)*

Brallan Press LLC 765 337-7909
5835 N Tacoma Ave Indianapolis (46220) *(G-6501)*

Brama Inc 317 786-7770
5855 Kopetsky St Ste I Indianapolis (46217) *(G-6502)*

Brand Prtg & Photo-Litho Co (PA) 317 921-4095
8745 Rawles Ave Ste D Indianapolis (46219) *(G-6503)*

Brand Quick Printing, Indianapolis *Also called Brand Prtg & Photo-Litho Co (G-6503)*

Brand Restaurant Equipment, Muncie *Also called Brand Sheet Metal Works Inc (G-10443)*

Brand Sheet Metal Works Inc 765 284-5594
907 S Burlington Dr Muncie (47302) *(G-10443)*

Brand Wave Inc 661 414-2115
240 Yorkshire Cir Noblesville (46060) *(G-11069)*

(G-0000) Company's Geographic Section entry number

Brand Wave LLC 661 414-2115
240 Yorkshire Cir Noblesville (46060) *(G-11070)*

Branded By Jdh, Warsaw *Also called Aardvark Graphics (G-13834)*

Brandywine Vinyrd & Winery LLC 317 403-5669
8437 W 1200 N New Palestine (46163) *(G-10968)*

Brangene LLC 317 203-9172
815 Walton Dr Plainfield (46168) *(G-11597)*

Braniff Game Birds 574 784-3919
67510 Mulberry Rd Lakeville (46536) *(G-9093)*

Branik Inc 260 467-1808
3626 Illinois Rd Fort Wayne (46804) *(G-4117)*

Brashear 219 778-2422
8804 N 200 E La Porte (46350) *(G-8741)*

Brasilia Press Inc 574 262-9700
2911 Moose Trl Elkhart (46514) *(G-2732)*

Brass Products Division, Albion *Also called Parker-Hannifin Corporation (G-32)*

Brass Ring 317 635-7464
1245 Shelby St Indianapolis (46203) *(G-6504)*

Bratco Inc 812 536-4071
502 N 2nd St Holland (47541) *(G-6104)*

Braun Corporation (HQ) 574 946-6153
631 W 11th St Winamac (46996) *(G-14301)*

Braun Corporation 574 946-7413
627 W 11th St Winamac (46996) *(G-14302)*

Braun Lift, Winamac *Also called Braun Corporation (G-14301)*

Braun Motor Works Inc (PA) 574 205-0102
144 S 100 W Winamac (46996) *(G-14303)*

Braun Witte Pattern Works Inc 260 463-8210
4705 S 050 E Wolcottville (46795) *(G-14369)*

Bravo Trailers LLC 574 848-7500
19319 C R 8 Bristol (46507) *(G-1049)*

Bray Logging 812 863-7947
6399 E State Road 58 Owensburg (47453) *(G-11423)*

Brazeway Inc 317 392-2533
1109 Lincoln St Shelbyville (46176) *(G-12524)*

Brazing Preforms LLC 317 705-6455
15402 Stony Creek Way Noblesville (46060) *(G-11071)*

BRC Rubber & Plastics Inc 260 827-0871
810 Lancaster St Bluffton (46714) *(G-869)*

BRC Rubber & Plastics Inc 260 693-2171
589 S Main St Churubusco (46723) *(G-1643)*

BRC Rubber & Plastics Inc (PA) 260 693-2171
1029a W State Blvd Fort Wayne (46808) *(G-4118)*

BRC Rubber & Plastics Inc 260 894-4121
1497 Gerber St Ligonier (46767) *(G-9278)*

BRC Rubber & Plastics Inc 260 203-5300
1029 W State Blvd Fort Wayne (46808) *(G-4119)*

BRC Rubber & Plastics Inc 260 693-2171
1133 Gilkey Ave Hartford City (47348) *(G-5978)*

BRC Rubber & Plastics Inc 765 728-8510
623 W Monroe St Montpelier (47359) *(G-10289)*

BRC Rubber Group, Churubusco *Also called BRC Rubber & Plastics Inc (G-1643)*

BRC Rubber Group, Fort Wayne *Also called BRC Rubber & Plastics Inc (G-4118)*

Bread Box Bake Shop, Shipshewana *Also called Shipshewana Bread Box Corp (G-12649)*

Breakers Unlimited Inc 317 474-9431
15241 Stony Creek Way Noblesville (46060) *(G-11072)*

Breast Diagnostic Center, Fort Wayne *Also called Fort Wyne Rdlgy Assn Fundation (G-4283)*

Breckenridge Recrtl Pk Trlrs, Elkhart *Also called Damon Corporation (G-2787)*

Bredensteiner & Assoc Inc 317 921-2226
1920 Dr Martin Luther Kin Indianapolis (46202) *(G-6505)*

Breiner Company Inc 317 272-2521
259 Production Dr Avon (46123) *(G-434)*

Breitburn Operating LP 812 738-3338
3761 Corydon Ramsey Rd Nw Corydon (47112) *(G-2091)*

Bremen Castings Inc 574 546-2411
500 N Baltimore St Bremen (46506) *(G-985)*

Bremen Composites LLC 574 546-3791
425 Industrial Dr Bremen (46506) *(G-986)*

Bremen Corporation (HQ) 574 546-4238
405 Industrial Dr Bremen (46506) *(G-987)*

Bremen Wire Products, Bremen *Also called Kauffman Engineering Inc (G-1007)*

Bremtown Fine Cstm Cbnetry Inc 574 546-2781
1456 State Road 331 Bremen (46506) *(G-988)*

Brenco Exotic Woods, Hammond *Also called Brenco LLC (G-5854)*

Brenco LLC (PA) 219 844-9570
2300 Michigan St Hammond (46320) *(G-5854)*

Brenda Sue Ware Eaton LLC 317 462-2058
840 E Ridge Dr Greenfield (46140) *(G-5509)*

Brenmeer LLC 260 267-0249
5716 Wald Rd Fort Wayne (46818) *(G-4120)*

Brent Croxton Inc 317 846-7591
12755 Kiawah Dr Carmel (46033) *(G-1322)*

Brethren In Christ Media Minis (PA) 574 773-3164
69954 County Road 11 Nappanee (46550) *(G-10657)*

Brewer Machine & Mfg Inc 317 398-3505
1501 Miller Ave Shelbyville (46176) *(G-12525)*

Brewhouse Supplies LLC 219 286-7285
1555 W Lincolnway Ste 102 Valparaiso (46385) *(G-13513)*

Brewster Cabinets Paneling Ctr, Chesterfield *Also called A L Brewster Plywood Inc (G-1586)*

Breyden Products Inc 260 244-2995
4532 E Park 30 Dr Columbia City (46725) *(G-1767)*

Brian Bex Report Inc 765 489-5566
100 N Woodpecker Rd Hagerstown (47346) *(G-5804)*

Brian J Spilman 765 663-2860
2443 N 700 W Ste 100 Arlington (46104) *(G-281)*

Brian T Klem 812 342-4080
4270 W Jnathan Moore Pike Columbus (47201) *(G-1862)*

Brianza USA Corp 574 855-9520
3503 Cooper Dr Elkhart (46514) *(G-2733)*

Brick 812 522-8636
309 Walnut St Jonesville (47247) *(G-8447)*

Brick Road Brewery Corp 219 362-7623
308 Perry St La Porte (46350) *(G-8742)*

Brick Street Embroidery 574 453-3729
205 E Prairie St Leesburg (46538) *(G-9233)*

Brickyard Crossing 317 492-6573
2572 Moller Rd Indianapolis (46224) *(G-6506)*

Brics 317 257-5757
901 E 64th St Indianapolis (46220) *(G-6507)*

Bridgeview Manufacturing LLC 574 970-0116
5321 Beck Dr Elkhart (46516) *(G-2734)*

Bridgewell Resources LLC 812 285-1811
1274 Dutch Ln Jeffersonville (47130) *(G-8331)*

Bridon American Oakland, Oakland City *Also called Bridon-American Corporation (G-11309)*

Bridon-American Corporation 812 749-3115
11698 E 200 S Oakland City (47660) *(G-11309)*

Briggs Exploration Prod Co LLC 812 249-0564
4424 Vogel Rd Ste 404 Evansville (47715) *(G-3401)*

Bright Beacon, Lawrenceburg *Also called Beacon Publishing Co Inc (G-9134)*

Bright Corp 765 642-3114
3040 E 38th St Anderson (46013) *(G-77)*

Bright Ideas LLC 574 295-5533
2322 Primrose Ave Elkhart (46516) *(G-2735)*

Bright Sheet Metal Company Inc (PA) 317 291-7600
4212 W 71st St Ste A Indianapolis (46268) *(G-6508)*

Brighter Dayz Publishing LLC 317 793-1364
7210 Mars Dr Indianapolis (46241) *(G-6509)*

Brighton Collectibles LLC 317 580-0912
8702 Keystone Xing 142a Indianapolis (46240) *(G-6510)*

Brim Concrete Inc 765 564-4975
2485 W Gravel Pit Rd Delphi (46923) *(G-2415)*

Brindle Products Inc (PA) 260 627-2156
13633 David Dr Grabill (46741) *(G-5358)*

Brinker Mfg Jewelers Inc 812 476-0651
111 S Green Rver Rd Ste C Evansville (47715) *(G-3402)*

Brinkman Press Inc 317 722-0305
6945 Hawthorn Park Dr Indianapolis (46220) *(G-6511)*

Brinly-Hardy Company (PA) 812 218-7200
3230 Industrial Pkwy Jeffersonville (47130) *(G-8332)*

Briovarx 812 256-8600
1050 Patrol Rd Jeffersonville (47130) *(G-8333)*

Bristol Div, Bristol *Also called Skyline Corporation (G-1087)*

Bristol Myers 812 428-1927
2400 W Lloyd Expy Evansville (47712) *(G-3403)*

Bristol Pallet 574 862-1862
64466 State Road 19 Goshen (46526) *(G-5179)*

Bristol Tool and Die Inc 574 848-5354
710 Commerce Dr Bristol (46507) *(G-1050)*

Bristol-Myers Squibb Company 260 432-2764
7527 Aboite Center Rd Fort Wayne (46804) *(G-4121)*

Bristol-Myers Squibb Company 812 307-2000
6400 William Keck Byp Mount Vernon (47620) *(G-10386)*

Bristow Milling Co LLC 812 843-5176
4721 Water St Bristow (47515) *(G-1094)*

Briter Products Inc 574 386-8167
1901 N Bendix Dr South Bend (46628) *(G-12725)*

Britton Vault Co Douglas 765 893-4071
3486 W 400 S Williamsport (47993) *(G-14287)*

Broadcast Connection Inc 765 847-2519
2164 W New Garden Rd Williamsburg (47393) *(G-14283)*

Broadwave Technologies Inc 317 888-8316
500 Polk St Ste 25 Greenwood (46143) *(G-5671)*

Broadwave Technologies Inc 317 346-6101
2900 N Graham Rd Ste B Franklin (46131) *(G-4873)*

Broadway Auto Glass LLC 219 884-5277
6491 Broadway Merrillville (46410) *(G-9704)*

Broadway Press 765 644-8813
2112 Broadway St Anderson (46012) *(G-78)*

Broccoli Press LLC 317 815-4687
12624 Largo Dr Fishers (46037) *(G-3882)*

Brocks Incorporated 765 721-3068
6541 N Us Highway 231 Bainbridge (46105) *(G-473)*

Brockwood Farm 812 837-9607
7867 Axsom Branch Rd Nashville (47448) *(G-10716)*

Brogan Pharmaceuticals LLC 219 644-3693
9800 Connecticut Dr Crown Point (46307) *(G-2231)*

Broken Mold Customs Inc 219 863-1008
1207 Daisy St Se Demotte (46310) *(G-2433)*

A
L
P
H
A
B
E
T
I
C

Bronze Bow Software Inc 260 672-9516
7717 Aboite Rd Roanoke (46783) ***(G-12100)***
Brook Locker Plant 219 275-2611
243 W Main St Brook (47922) ***(G-1098)***
Brookes Candy Co 765 665-3646
247 Maple St Clinton (47842) ***(G-1715)***
Brookfield Sand & Gravel Inc (PA) 317 835-2235
8587 N 850 W Fairland (46126) ***(G-3821)***
Brooks Construction Co Inc 260 478-1990
6525 Ardmore Ave Fort Wayne (46809) ***(G-4122)***
Brooks Langeloh 219 691-3577
465 E Morsches Rd Columbia City (46725) ***(G-1768)***
Brookville Democrat, Brookville *Also called Whitewater Publications Inc* ***(G-1131)***
Brookville Tool Co, Brookville *Also called Greg Miner* ***(G-1115)***
Brookwood Cabinet Company Inc 260 749-5012
5912 Old Maumee Rd Fort Wayne (46803) ***(G-4123)***
Brothers Industries 812 560-6224
803 E Washington St Greensburg (47240) ***(G-5592)***
Brouillette Heating & Cooling 765 884-0176
403 W 5th St Fowler (47944) ***(G-4798)***
Browell Enterprises Inc 765 447-2292
711 N 31st St Lafayette (47904) ***(G-8865)***
Brown & Brown Fuel 219 984-5173
5774 S State Road 43 Chalmers (47929) ***(G-1546)***
Brown Advanced Mfg LLC 574 209-2003
545 N Bowen Ave Bremen (46506) ***(G-989)***
Brown County Democrat Inc 812 988-2221
147 E Main St Nashville (47448) ***(G-10717)***
Brown County Wine Company (PA) 812 988-6144
4520 State Road 46 E Nashville (47448) ***(G-10718)***
Brown Ridge Studio 812 335-0643
625 N Lwer Brdie Glyan Rd Bloomington (47408) ***(G-690)***
Browning, William Logging, Brookville *Also called William Browning* ***(G-1132)***
Browns Dairy Inc (PA) 219 464-4141
57 Monroe St Valparaiso (46383) ***(G-13514)***
Browns Simply Printings 317 490-7493
126 S Jefferson St Mooresville (46158) ***(G-10303)***
Brownsburg Custom Cabinets 317 271-1887
1747 Country Club Rd Indianapolis (46234) ***(G-6512)***
Brownsburg Signs & Graphics 317 858-1907
1016 E Main St Brownsburg (46112) ***(G-1138)***
Brownston Quality Tl & Design, Brownstown *Also called Brownstown Qlty Tl Automtn LLC* ***(G-1180)***
Brownstown Qlty Tl Automtn LLC 812 358-9059
1412 E State Road 250 Brownstown (47220) ***(G-1180)***
Brownstown Qulty Tl Design Inc 812 358-4593
1408 E State Road 250 Brownstown (47220) ***(G-1181)***
Brq Quickprint Inc 219 464-1070
1310 Lincolnway Valparaiso (46383) ***(G-13515)***
Bruce Fox Inc (PA) 812 945-3511
1909 Mcdonald Ln New Albany (47150) ***(G-10754)***
Bruce Payne 260 492-2259
5078 Stellhorn Rd Fort Wayne (46815) ***(G-4124)***
Bruco Industries, Fort Wayne *Also called Quikcut Incorporated* ***(G-4574)***
Brulin Holding Company Inc (PA) 317 923-3211
2920 Aj Brown Ave Indianapolis (46205) ***(G-6513)***
Brulin Holding Company Inc 317 923-3211
2920 Dr Andrew J Brown Indianapolis (46205) ***(G-6514)***
Brumate LLC 317 474-7352
640 E Michigan St C135 Indianapolis (46202) ***(G-6515)***
Brunk Corp (PA) 574 533-1109
803 Logan St Goshen (46528) ***(G-5180)***
Brunos Breads LLC 219 883-5126
2700 W 5th Ave Gary (46404) ***(G-5031)***
Brunsman Graphic Design, Connersville *Also called Bell Graphics and Design LLC* ***(G-2040)***
Brunswick Corporation 260 459-8200
1111 N Hadley Rd Fort Wayne (46804) ***(G-4125)***
Brush Strokes Inc 800 272-2307
19320 Haviland Dr South Bend (46637) ***(G-12726)***
Bryan Boilers, Peru *Also called Bryan Steam LLC* ***(G-11518)***
Bryan Machine Service Inc 260 356-5530
345 Commerce Dr Huntington (46750) ***(G-6195)***
Bryan Steam LLC 765 473-6651
783 Chili Ave Peru (46970) ***(G-11518)***
Bryant Ice Co Inc 765 459-4543
824 S Armstrong St Kokomo (46901) ***(G-8602)***
Bryant Industries Inc 812 944-6010
201b E 18th St New Albany (47150) ***(G-10755)***
Bryant Machining & Welding LLC 260 997-6059
1015 E State Road 67 Bryant (47326) ***(G-1199)***
Bryant Printing 765 521-3379
2601 Broad St New Castle (47362) ***(G-10893)***
Bryant Products Inc 812 522-5929
816 F Ave E Seymour (47274) ***(G-12435)***
Bryson C Toothaker 219 462-9179
45 Tayside St Valparaiso (46385) ***(G-13516)***
Bryton Corporation 317 334-8700
4011 Championship Dr Indianapolis (46268) ***(G-6516)***
BSB Trans Inc 317 919-8778
711 Legacy Blvd Greenwood (46143) ***(G-5672)***
Bsbw Cultured Marble Inc 812 246-5619
860 S Penn Ave Sellersburg (47172) ***(G-12389)***
BSC Vntres Acquisition Sub LLC 260 665-7521
100 Woodhull Dr Angola (46703) ***(G-198)***
Bst Corp 812 925-7911
1066 Hunter Blvd Boonville (47601) ***(G-909)***
BT Management Inc 219 794-9546
8605 Indiana Pl Merrillville (46410) ***(G-9705)***
BT&f LLC 574 272-6128
12441 Beckley St Ste 8 Granger (46530) ***(G-5395)***
Btd Manufacturing Inc (PA) 812 934-5616
177 Six Pine Ranch Rd Batesville (47006) ***(G-495)***
BTR Engineering 812 360-9415
2255 W Bolin Ln Bloomington (47403) ***(G-691)***
Buchan Logging Inc 260 728-2136
3333 E 600 N Decatur (46733) ***(G-2371)***
Buchan Logging Inc 260 749-4697
2802 Ryan Rd New Haven (46774) ***(G-10932)***
Buchan Saw Mill, New Haven *Also called Buchan Logging Inc* ***(G-10932)***
Buchanan Iron Works Inc 219 785-4480
103 Greenway St Westville (46391) ***(G-14214)***
Buchanan Publishing 317 546-4524
7835 E 56th St Apt B Indianapolis (46226) ***(G-6517)***
Buck & Company Inc 574 292-0874
12000 Buttercup Cir Granger (46530) ***(G-5396)***
Buck Creek Winery, Indianapolis *Also called Durm Vineyard Inc* ***(G-6771)***
Buckaroos Inc (PA) 317 899-9100
9855 Crosspoint Blvd # 142 Indianapolis (46256) ***(G-6518)***
Buckeye Corrugated Inc 330 576-0590
4001 S High School Rd B Indianapolis (46241) ***(G-6519)***
Buckhorn Inc 260 824-0997
785 Decker Dr Bluffton (46714) ***(G-870)***
Buckingham Pallets Inc 317 846-8601
12325 Camberly Ln Carmel (46033) ***(G-1323)***
Buckles Tool and Engineering 574 642-3471
68860 County Road 33 Goshen (46526) ***(G-5181)***
Buckner Inc (PA) 317 570-0533
9922 E 79th St Indianapolis (46256) ***(G-6520)***
Budco Tool and Die 574 522-4004
56935 Elk Ct Elkhart (46516) ***(G-2736)***
Buddy Eugene Publishing LLC 574 223-6048
2031 S 650 E Akron (46910) ***(G-3)***
Budget Blinds, Fishers *Also called Childress Corporation* ***(G-3889)***
Budget Blinds, Muncie *Also called J P Whitt Inc* ***(G-10498)***
Budget Inks LLC 877 636-4657
45 S Public Sq Angola (46703) ***(G-199)***
Budget Instant Print, Jeffersonville *Also called Budget Printing Centers Inc* ***(G-8334)***
Budget Printing Centers Inc (PA) 812 282-8832
902 E 10th St Jeffersonville (47130) ***(G-8334)***
Budget Sales Inc 260 657-5185
17606 Notestine Rd Woodburn (46797) ***(G-14381)***
Buehler Foods Inc 812 467-7255
4635 N 1st Ave Evansville (47710) ***(G-3404)***
Buehler's Buy Low 4182, Evansville *Also called Buehler Foods Inc* ***(G-3404)***
Buffington Custom Kitchens, Seymour *Also called Phoenix Custom Kitchens Inc* ***(G-12475)***
Buffington Electric Motors 574 935-5453
2520 Lake Ave Plymouth (46563) ***(G-11673)***
Buffington Farm Service, Plymouth *Also called Buffington Electric Motors* ***(G-11673)***
Buhrt Engineering & Cnstr 574 267-3720
27 E 250 N Warsaw (46582) ***(G-13852)***
Builders Iron Works Inc 574 254-1553
1016 E 12th St Mishawaka (46544) ***(G-10014)***
Building Temp Solutions LLC 260 449-9201
3811 Fourier Dr Fort Wayne (46818) ***(G-4126)***
Built By Bill 317 745-2666
360 E Columbia St Danville (46122) ***(G-2345)***
Buis Enterprises Inc 317 839-7394
6987 S County Road 750 E Plainfield (46168) ***(G-11598)***
Bulk Truck & Transport Service 812 866-2155
659 W Lagrange Rd Hanover (47243) ***(G-5959)***
Bull Hn Info Systems Inc 317 686-5500
1099 N Meridian St # 200 Indianapolis (46204) ***(G-6521)***
Bull Manufacturing LLC 812 530-1064
1943 E Us Highway 50 Brownstown (47220) ***(G-1182)***
Bull Moose Tube, Elkhart *Also called Bock Industries Inc* ***(G-2729)***
Bulldog Award Co Inc 317 773-3379
777 Conner St Noblesville (46060) ***(G-11073)***
Bulldog Battery Corporation (PA) 260 563-0551
98 E Canal St Wabash (46992) ***(G-13722)***
Bullseye Leveling, Elkhart *Also called Bullseye Technologies Inc* ***(G-2737)***
Bullseye Technologies Inc 574 753-0102
2925 Stephen Pl Elkhart (46514) ***(G-2737)***
Bumblebee Quick Print Inc 765 962-0368
211 Nw 7th St Richmond (47374) ***(G-11968)***
Bundy Bros & Sons Inc 812 966-2551
3 David St Medora (47260) ***(G-9681)***

Bunge North America Inc................................260 724-2101
1200 N 2nd St Decatur (46733) *(G-2372)*

Bunge North America Inc................................812 875-3113
7383 N 100 W Worthington (47471) *(G-14393)*

Bunge North America Foundation.......................219 261-2124
413 N Cressy Ave Remington (47977) *(G-11905)*

Bunge North America Foundation.......................765 763-7500
700 N Range Line Rd Morristown (46161) *(G-10366)*

Burco Molding Inc....................................317 773-5699
15015 Herriman Blvd Noblesville (46060) *(G-11074)*

Burgermeister, Herman MD, Portland *Also called Tricounty Surgical and Assoc (G-11853)*

Burgess Auction Resale, Albion *Also called Burgess Enterprises LLC (G-18)*

Burgess Enterprises LLC..............................260 615-5194
441 S 400 E Albion (46701) *(G-18)*

Burke Heating Systems Company, Fort Wayne *Also called Pac Corporation (G-4517)*

Burkert-Walton Inc...................................812 425-7157
1561 Allens Ln Evansville (47710) *(G-3405)*

Burkes Garden Wood Pdts LLC..........................765 344-1724
4774 S 1000 E Brazil (47834) *(G-955)*

Burkhart Advertising Inc (PA)........................574 233-2101
1335 Mishawaka Ave South Bend (46615) *(G-12727)*

Burkhart Advertising Inc.............................260 482-9566
4511 Executive Blvd Fort Wayne (46808) *(G-4127)*

Burkhart Advertising Inc.............................574 234-4444
1247 Mishawaka Ave South Bend (46615) *(G-12728)*

Burkhart Advertising Inc.............................574 522-4421
1600 W Beardsley Ave # 110 Elkhart (46514) *(G-2738)*

Burkhart Manufacturing Inc...........................260 316-0715
6534 N 450 W Angola (46703) *(G-200)*

Burkholder Machine...................................574 862-2004
25354 County Road 40 Goshen (46526) *(G-5182)*

Burks Door & Sash Inc................................317 844-2484
599 3rd Ave Sw Carmel (46032) *(G-1324)*

Burns Buldings, Macy *Also called Burns Construction Inc (G-9440)*

Burns Cabinets and Disp Inc..........................260 897-2219
140 Green Dr Avilla (46710) *(G-401)*

Burns Construction Inc...............................574 382-2315
6676 S Old Us Highway 31 Macy (46951) *(G-9440)*

Burnside Enterprises.................................765 664-4032
4796 N 300 E Marion (46952) *(G-9513)*

Burris Engineering Inc...............................317 862-1046
5430 S Franklin Rd Indianapolis (46239) *(G-6522)*

Burston Marketing Inc...............................574 262-4005
2802 Frederic Dr Elkhart (46514) *(G-2739)*

Burt Products Inc....................................812 386-6890
315 S West St Princeton (47670) *(G-11867)*

Burton Lumber Co Inc.................................812 866-4438
13980 W Polk Rd Lexington (47138) *(G-9249)*

Busakshamban, Fort Wayne *Also called Trellborg Sling Sltions US Inc (G-4700)*

Busche Alum Tchnlgies Franklin, Franklin *Also called Shipston Aluminum Tech Ind Inc (G-4932)*

Busche Aluminum Technologies, Franklin *Also called Shipston Alum Tech Intl Inc (G-4930)*

Busche Enterprise Division Inc.......................260 636-7030
1612 Progress Dr Albion (46701) *(G-19)*

Busche Performance Group Inc.........................260 636-7030
100 Progress Way W Avilla (46710) *(G-402)*

Busche Performance Group Inc.........................260 636-1069
600 S 7th St Albion (46701) *(G-20)*

Busche Performance Group Inc.........................260 349-0070
811 Commerce Dr Kendallville (46755) *(G-8462)*

Busche Performance Group Inc (HQ)....................260 636-7030
1563 E State Road 8 Albion (46701) *(G-21)*

Buschman Tank Cars Inc...............................219 984-5444
601 E 2nd St Reynolds (47980) *(G-11944)*

Bush Trophy Case & Embroidery, Anderson *Also called Wanda Harrington (G-182)*

Business & Industrial Pdts Co........................812 376-6149
3552 Mockingbird Dr Columbus (47203) *(G-1863)*

Business Adventures Inc..............................574 674-9996
1327 3rd St Osceola (46561) *(G-11371)*

Business Art & Design Inc............................317 782-9108
402 Main St Beech Grove (46107) *(G-593)*

Business Health......................................219 762-7105
5715 Independence Ave Portage (46368) *(G-11752)*

Business People Magazine, Fort Wayne *Also called Michiana Business Publications (G-4470)*

Business To Business, Mishawaka *Also called Michiana Executive Journal (G-10080)*

Busters Cement Products Inc (PA).....................765 529-0287
3450 S Spiceland Rd New Castle (47362) *(G-10894)*

Butcher Block..219 696-9111
17918 Grant Pl Lowell (46356) *(G-9401)*

Butler Mill Service Company..........................260 625-4930
2734 S 800 E Columbia City (46725) *(G-1769)*

Butler Mill Service Company..........................260 868-5123
4506 County Road 59 Butler (46721) *(G-1223)*

Butler Tool & Design Inc.............................219 297-4531
641 S Newton St Goodland (47948) *(G-5158)*

Butler Vineyards.....................................219 929-1400
401 Broadway Chesterton (46304) *(G-1597)*

Butler Vineyards (PA)................................812 332-6660
6202 E Robinson Rd Bloomington (47408) *(G-692)*

Butler Winery, Bloomington *Also called Butler Vineyards (G-692)*

Butler-Macdonald Inc.................................317 872-5115
5955 W 80th St Indianapolis (46278) *(G-6523)*

Butterfield Foods LLC...............................317 776-4775
635 Westfield Rd Noblesville (46060) *(G-11075)*

Butterworth Industries Inc...........................765 677-6725
5050 Eastside Parkway Dr Gas City (46933) *(G-5121)*

Buttons Galore Inc..................................800 626-8168
110 E College Ave Brownsburg (46112) *(G-1139)*

Buxton Engineering Inc...............................812 897-3609
1322 S Rockport Rd Boonville (47601) *(G-910)*

Buy Bulk Displays LLC................................574 222-4378
1610 3rd St Osceola (46561) *(G-11372)*

Buztronics Inc.......................................317 876-3413
464 Suthpoint Cir Ste 100 Brownsburg (46112) *(G-1140)*

Buzzi Unicem, Indianapolis *Also called Lone Star Industries Inc (G-6271)*

Buzzi Unicem USA Inc.................................317 780-9860
1112 W Thompson Rd Indianapolis (46217) *(G-6524)*

Bw Manufacturing, Kokomo *Also called Mier Products Inc (G-8666)*

Bway Corporation.....................................317 297-4638
6061 Guion Rd Indianapolis (46254) *(G-6525)*

Bway Corporation.....................................219 462-8915
4002 Montdale Park Dr Valparaiso (46383) *(G-13517)*

Bwi Group, Greenfield *Also called Bwi Indiana Inc (G-5510)*

Bwi Indiana Inc......................................937 260-2460
989 Opportunity Pkwy Greenfield (46140) *(G-5510)*

Bwt Custom Woodworking LLC...........................812 634-1800
1325 Franklin St Jasper (47546) *(G-8239)*

Bwt LLC..574 232-3338
802 Fellows St South Bend (46601) *(G-12729)*

Bwxt Nclear Oprtions Group Inc.......................812 838-1200
1400 Old Highway 69 S Mount Vernon (47620) *(G-10387)*

By The Sword Inc....................................877 433-9368
304 E Sunset Dr Huntingburg (47542) *(G-6151)*

By-Pass Paint Shop Inc (PA)..........................574 264-5334
1132 N Nappanee St Elkhart (46514) *(G-2740)*

Bybee Stone Company Inc..............................812 876-2215
6293 N Matthews Dr Ellettsville (47429) *(G-3272)*

Byers Scientific Mfg.................................812 269-6218
2332 W Industrial Park Dr Bloomington (47404) *(G-693)*

Byler Family Wood Working............................574 825-3339
60845 State Road 13 Goshen (46528) *(G-5183)*

Byler Sawmill..812 577-5761
9435 State Road 250 Bennington (47011) *(G-605)*

Byrd Industries......................................812 867-5859
8811 Whispering Tree Ln Evansville (47711) *(G-3406)*

Byte Blue Technology Solutions.......................574 903-5637
28571 County Road 16 Elkhart (46516) *(G-2741)*

Byway Brewing Company LLC............................312 543-7639
1939 Rosewood Ct Munster (46321) *(G-10599)*

C & A Tool Engineering Inc (HQ)......................260 693-2167
4100 N Us 33 Churubusco (46723) *(G-1644)*

C & A Tool Engineering Inc...........................260 693-2167
101 N Main St Churubusco (46723) *(G-1645)*

C & A Tool Engineering Inc...........................260 693-2167
100 Cole St Churubusco (46723) *(G-1646)*

C & A Tool Engineering Inc...........................260 693-2167
411 S Mulberry St Churubusco (46723) *(G-1647)*

C & A Tool Engineering Inc...........................260 693-2167
119 S Mulberry St Churubusco (46723) *(G-1648)*

C & A Tool Engineering Inc...........................260 693-2167
1015 W 15th St Auburn (46706) *(G-319)*

C & A Tool Engineering Inc...........................260 693-2167
118 N Main St Churubusco (46723) *(G-1649)*

C & A Tool Engineering Inc...........................260 693-2167
105 S Main St Churubusco (46723) *(G-1650)*

C & B Industries LLC................................260 490-3000
9009 Coldwater Rd Fort Wayne (46825) *(G-4128)*

C & C Industries.....................................260 804-6518
10214 Chestnut Plaza Dr Fort Wayne (46814) *(G-4129)*

C & C Iron Inc.......................................219 769-2511
6409 Hendricks St Merrillville (46410) *(G-9706)*

C & C Mailbox Products...............................765 358-4880
18100 N County Road 925 W Gaston (47342) *(G-5130)*

C & C Pallets and Lumber LLC.........................765 524-3214
1611 S County Road 275 W New Castle (47362) *(G-10895)*

C & E Exteriors Inc..................................317 984-5463
517 E S St Arcadia (46030) *(G-261)*

C & F Industries.....................................765 580-0378
5282 W Booth Rd Liberty (47353) *(G-9257)*

C & G Labeling.......................................317 396-2953
4057 Vincennes Rd Indianapolis (46268) *(G-6526)*

C & G Salsa Company LLC.............................317 569-9099
5282 E 156th St Noblesville (46062) *(G-11076)*

C & G Tool Inc.......................................812 524-7061
706 W Chestnut St Jonesville (47247) *(G-8448)*

C & G Wiring Inc.....................................574 333-3433
1824 Leer Dr Elkhart (46514) *(G-2742)*

C & H Signs Inc......................................765 642-7777
805 Morton St Anderson (46016) *(G-79)*

A
L
P
H
A
B
E
T
I
C

C & H Stone Co Inc...812 336-2560
  4000 S Rockport Rd Bloomington (47403) *(G-694)*

C & J Corporation..574 255-6793
  1530 Ken Mcintee Ct Mishawaka (46544) *(G-10015)*

C & J K Industries Inc...219 746-5760
  230 Timrick Dr Munster (46321) *(G-10600)*

C & J Plating & Grinding LLC...............................765 288-8728
  411 E 3rd St Muncie (47302) *(G-10444)*

C & J Security Solutions, Fort Wayne *Also called C & J Services & Supplies Inc (G-4130)*

C & J Services & Supplies Inc...............................317 569-7222
  5201 Investment Dr Fort Wayne (46808) *(G-4130)*

C & K Enterprises Inc..260 624-3123
  240 Growth Pkwy Angola (46703) *(G-201)*

C & K Manufacturing Inc.......................................574 264-4063
  25943 Forrest Hl Elkhart (46514) *(G-2743)*

C & K Tool, Angola *Also called C & K Enterprises Inc (G-201)*

C & K United Shtmtl & Mech..................................812 423-5090
  2805 Lincoln Ave Rear Evansville (47714) *(G-3407)*

C & L Electric Motor Repr Inc...............................574 533-2643
  1402 N Chicago Ave Goshen (46528) *(G-5184)*

C & L Lumber Inc..812 536-2171
  8836 W State Road 64 Huntingburg (47542) *(G-6152)*

C & L Sheet Metal LLC..812 449-9126
  2263 E Tennessee St Evansville (47711) *(G-3408)*

C & P Distributing LLC...574 256-1138
  2500 Miracle Ln Ste D Mishawaka (46545) *(G-10016)*

C & P Engineering & Mfg..765 825-4293
  1605 Kentucky Ave Connersville (47331) *(G-2042)*

C & P Machine Service Inc.....................................260 484-7723
  445 Council Dr Fort Wayne (46825) *(G-4131)*

C & R, Indianapolis *Also called C&R Racing Incorporated (G-6530)*

C & R Plating Corp...586 755-4900
  302 Factory St Columbia City (46725) *(G-1770)*

C & R Woodworks...317 422-9603
  8880 Huggin Hollow Rd Martinsville (46151) *(G-9596)*

C & S Family Inc..812 886-5500
  2205 S Old Decker Rd Vincennes (47591) *(G-13670)*

C & S Sandblasting & Wldg LLC.............................317 867-6341
  17623 Washington St Westfield (46074) *(G-14140)*

C & T Engineering Inc..812 522-5854
  322 Thompson Rd Seymour (47274) *(G-12436)*

C & W Inkd...317 352-1000
  6300 Brookville Rd Bldg B Indianapolis (46219) *(G-6527)*

C A Derr & Company...812 897-2920
  601 S 3rd St Boonville (47601) *(G-911)*

C A E, Marion *Also called Computer Age Engineering Inc (G-9518)*

C and S Machine Inc...812 687-7203
  19 Main St Plainville (47568) *(G-11654)*

C B Printing...765 569-0900
  792 N Us Highway 41 Rockville (47872) *(G-12174)*

C C Cook and Son Lbr Co Inc................................765 672-4235
  6236 W Us Highway 40 Reelsville (46171) *(G-11900)*

C D & R Components, Batesville *Also called CD & R Components Inc (G-496)*

C D I, Leesburg *Also called Composite Designs Inc (G-9235)*

C D I, Fort Wayne *Also called Complete Drives Inc (G-4171)*

C D Ventures Inc..765 482-9179
  820 Hendricks Dr Lebanon (46052) *(G-9171)*

C E Kersting & Sons...574 896-2766
  6800 S 300 W North Judson (46366) *(G-11207)*

C E M Printing & Specialities.................................269 684-6898
  50750 Marie Ct South Bend (46637) *(G-12730)*

C E R Metal Marking Corp.....................................219 924-9710
  2224 Industrial Dr Ste C Highland (46322) *(G-6039)*

C E W Enterprises, North Vernon *Also called Manar Inc (G-11268)*

C F Roark Wldg Engrg Co Inc................................317 852-3163
  136 N Green St Brownsburg (46112) *(G-1141)*

C F Slattery Steel Fabrication...............................812 948-9167
  2101 Logan St New Albany (47150) *(G-10756)*

C Fabco/L Inc...219 785-4181
  9811 W State Road 2 Ste 1 La Porte (46350) *(G-8743)*

C H Ellis LLC..317 636-3351
  2432 Se Ave Indianapolis (46201) *(G-6528)*

C J P Corporation..219 924-1685
  9445 Indianapolis Blvd A Highland (46322) *(G-6040)*

C L Holdings LLC..317 736-4414
  1441 Amy Ln Franklin (46131) *(G-4874)*

C Laser Inc..317 641-5185
  613 W Lincoln Rd Ste A Kokomo (46902) *(G-8603)*

C Lee Cook, Jeffersonville *Also called Dover Corporation (G-8352)*

C M Engineering Inc...812 648-2038
  8112 E Main St Dugger (47848) *(G-2479)*

C M Grinding Inc..574 234-6812
  55643 Fairview Ave South Bend (46628) *(G-12731)*

C M I Automotive of Indiana, Elkhart *Also called C M I Enterprises Inc (G-2744)*

C M I Enterprises Inc...305 685-9651
  2904 Leer Ct Elkhart (46514) *(G-2744)*

C M Welding Inc...765 258-4024
  4496 N County Road 0 Ew Frankfort (46041) *(G-4820)*

C Milligan Investments LLC...................................219 241-5811
  1208 Pine Creek Rd Valparaiso (46383) *(G-13518)*

C Modesitt Oil Production LLC...............................812 249-0678
  10807 S 625 W Rosedale (47874) *(G-12203)*

C R Graphics...317 881-6192
  485 E Pearl St Greenwood (46143) *(G-5673)*

C S I, Indianapolis *Also called Closure Systems Intl Inc (G-6624)*

C T C Corporation..812 849-2500
  3030 Poplar St Mitchell (47446) *(G-10156)*

C&A Woodworking Inc..574 875-1273
  24183 County Road 45 Elkhart (46516) *(G-2745)*

C&B Industries LLC..260 493-3288
  8515 Schwartz Rd Fort Wayne (46835) *(G-4132)*

C&C Deer Processing..812 836-2323
  5515 Advantage Rd Tell City (47586) *(G-13157)*

C&C Polo Enterprises Inc......................................317 577-8266
  9801 Fall Creek Rd Indianapolis (46256) *(G-6529)*

C&D Technologies Inc...765 762-2461
  200 W Main St Attica (47918) *(G-298)*

C&F Fabricating LLC..765 362-5922
  1831 E Elmore St Crawfordsville (47933) *(G-2136)*

C&H Plastic Letters & Signs, Anderson *Also called C & H Signs Inc (G-79)*

C&M Conveyor Inc...812 849-5647
  4598 State Road 37 Mitchell (47446) *(G-10157)*

C&M Fine Pack, Fort Wayne *Also called D&W Fine Pack LLC (G-4198)*

C&M Woodworking LLC..260 403-4555
  10225 Donald Ave Leo (46765) *(G-9240)*

C&P Machine, Fort Wayne *Also called C & P Machine Service Inc (G-4131)*

C&R Racing Incorporated (HQ)..............................317 293-4100
  6950 Guion Rd Indianapolis (46268) *(G-6530)*

C&S Machinery Inc..812 937-2160
  5440 E 2150 N Dale (47523) *(G-2331)*

C&S Solutions..812 895-0048
  2064 N Old Highway 41 Vincennes (47591) *(G-13671)*

C-Cat Inc..317 568-2899
  1726 W 15th St Indianapolis (46202) *(G-6531)*

C-L Building & Leasing Inc.....................................574 293-8959
  28468 County Road 26 Elkhart (46517) *(G-2746)*

C-Level, Avon *Also called Infinity Products Inc (G-448)*

C-Line Engineering Inc..812 246-4822
  1001 Somerset Ct Sellersburg (47172) *(G-12390)*

C-Way Tool and Die Inc...812 256-6341
  103 Industrial Way Charlestown (47111) *(G-1559)*

C. H. Ellis, Indianapolis *Also called C H Ellis LLC (G-6528)*

C.J. Boots Casket Company, Richmond *Also called Vandor Corporation (G-12072)*

C.P.i, Bloomington *Also called Circle - Prosco Inc (G-700)*

C5 Printing & Graphic Design, Connersville *Also called Codybro LLC (G-2044)*

CA Steel Country Candles......................................812 290-8516
  138 W Conwell St Apt 1 Aurora (47001) *(G-374)*

Cabco, Hammond *Also called Calumet Abrasives Co Inc (G-5855)*

Cabinet & Countertop Solutio................................219 775-3540
  127 Marr Ct Crown Point (46307) *(G-2232)*

Cabinet Cottage LLC...317 369-0051
  1111 Westfield Rd Noblesville (46062) *(G-11077)*

Cabinet Crafters Corp...765 724-7074
  120 S Sheridan St Alexandria (46001) *(G-37)*

Cabinetmaker Inc...812 723-3461
  1714 E Owl Hollow Rd Paoli (47454) *(G-11446)*

Cabinetmaker, The, Paoli *Also called Cabinetmaker Inc (G-11446)*

Cabinetry Green LLC...317 842-1550
  13818 Promise Rd Fishers (46038) *(G-3883)*

Cabinetry Ideas Inc..317 722-1300
  6113 Allisonville Rd Indianapolis (46220) *(G-6532)*

Cabinets & Counters Inc.......................................812 858-3300
  7000 Savannah Dr Newburgh (47630) *(G-11023)*

Cabinets & Furniture, Grabill *Also called Graber Cabinetry LLC (G-5366)*

Cabinets By Gentry...765 378-7900
  3516 Andover Rd Anderson (46013) *(G-80)*

Cabinets By Rick Inc..812 945-2220
  1630 Grant Line Rd New Albany (47150) *(G-10757)*

Cablecraft Motion Controls LLC (PA).......................260 749-5105
  2110 Summit St New Haven (46774) *(G-10933)*

Cac Wall Panels LP...260 437-4003
  14329 Rupert Rd Harlan (46743) *(G-5967)*

Cad & Machining Services Inc................................317 535-1067
  521 Williamson St Whiteland (46184) *(G-14234)*

Cad/CAM Technologies Inc.....................................765 778-2020
  178 S Heritage Way Pendleton (46064) *(G-11487)*

Caddo Connections Inc...219 874-8119
  2833 N Goldring Rd La Porte (46350) *(G-8744)*

Cadillac Coffee Company.......................................260 489-6281
  7221 Innovation Blvd Fort Wayne (46818) *(G-4133)*

Cai Rail...317 669-2555
  597 Industrial Dr Carmel (46032) *(G-1325)*

Caine Publishing LLC..312 215-5253
  2721 Floral Trl Long Beach (46360) *(G-9376)*

Caj Food Products Inc...888 524-6882
  11650 Olio Rd Ste 1000 Fishers (46037) *(G-3884)*

Cake Bake Shop Inc 317 257-2253
   6515 Carrollton Ave Indianapolis (46220) *(G-6533)*

Cal Pipe Manufacturing Inc 219 844-6800
   6451 Northwind Pkwy Hobart (46342) *(G-6070)*

Cal-Comp USA (indiana) Inc 956 342-5061
   1 Technology Way Logansport (46947) *(G-9326)*

Calavera Tool Works LLC 765 481-6775
   9823 Buttondown Ln Zionsville (46077) *(G-14424)*

Calcar Quarries Incorporated 812 723-2109
   731 Ne Main St Paoli (47454) *(G-11447)*

Calcean LLC 812 672-4995
   2213 Killion Ave Seymour (47274) *(G-12437)*

Caldwell Gravel Sales Tm, Morristown *Also called Cgs Services Inc (G-10367)*

Calf-Teria, Spencerville *Also called Rhinehart Development Corp (G-13050)*

Calhoun St Soup Salad Spirits 260 456-7005
   112 E Masterson Ave Fort Wayne (46803) *(G-4134)*

Cali Nail 574 674-4126
   941 Lincolnway W Osceola (46561) *(G-11373)*

Cali Nail Salon, Osceola *Also called Cali Nail (G-11373)*

Calico Precision Molding LLC 260 484-4500
   1211 Progress Rd Fort Wayne (46808) *(G-4135)*

Caliente 260 471-0700
   1123 E State Blvd Fort Wayne (46805) *(G-4136)*

Caliente LLC 260 426-3800
   315 E Wallace St Fort Wayne (46803) *(G-4137)*

California Pellet Mill Company, Crawfordsville *Also called CPM Acquisition Corp (G-2142)*

California Pellet Mill Company 765 362-2600
   1114 E Wabash Ave Crawfordsville (47933) *(G-2137)*

Call Leader, Elwood *Also called Elwood Publishing Co Inc (G-3298)*

Callisons Inc 574 896-5074
   7675 S 100 W North Judson (46366) *(G-11208)*

Calpipe Industries LLC 219 844-6800
   6451 Northwind Pkwy Hobart (46342) *(G-6071)*

Caltherm Corporation (HQ) 812 372-0281
   910 S Gladstone Ave Columbus (47201) *(G-1864)*

Caltherm Corporation 812 372-0281
   835 S Marr Rd Columbus (47201) *(G-1865)*

Calumet Wilbert Vault Co Inc 219 980-1173
   1920 W 41st Ave Gary (46408) *(G-5032)*

Calumet Abrasives Co Inc 219 844-2695
   3039 169th Pl Hammond (46323) *(G-5855)*

Calumet Breweries Inc 219 845-2242
   6535 Osborne Ave Hammond (46320) *(G-5856)*

Calumet Finance Corp 317 328-5660
   2780 Waterfront Pkwy Indianapolis (46214) *(G-6534)*

Calumet Gp LLC 317 328-5660
   2780 Wtrfrnt Pkwy Dr St Indianapolis (46214) *(G-6535)*

Calumet International Inc 317 328-5660
   2780 Waterfront Indianapolis (46214) *(G-6536)*

Calumet Karns City Ref LLC (HQ) 317 328-5660
   2780 Waterfront Indianapolis (46214) *(G-6537)*

Calumet Missouri LLC (HQ) 318 795-3800
   2780 Waterfront Pkwy E Dr Indianapolis (46214) *(G-6538)*

Calumet Operating LLC (HQ) 317 328-5660
   2780 Waterfront Pkwy Indianapolis (46214) *(G-6539)*

Calumet Orthpd Prosthetics Co 219 942-2148
   7554 Grand Blvd Hobart (46342) *(G-6072)*

Calumet Pallet Company Inc 219 932-4550
   4333 Ohio St Michigan City (46360) *(G-9772)*

Calumet Penreco, LLC, Indianapolis *Also called Calumet Karns City Ref LLC (G-6537)*

Calumet Press, The, Hammond *Also called Ckmt Associates Inc (G-5863)*

Calumet Refining LLC (HQ) 317 328-5660
   2780 Waterfront Pkwy Indianapolis (46214) *(G-6540)*

Calumet Shreveport Llc 317 328-5660
   2780 Waterfront Pkwy E Dr Indianapolis (46214) *(G-6541)*

Calumet Spcialty Pdts Partners, Indianapolis *Also called Calumet Refining LLC (G-6540)*

Calumet Spclty Pdts Prtners LP (PA) 317 328-5660
   2780 Waterfront Pkwy Indianapolis (46214) *(G-6542)*

Calumet Superior LLC 317 328-5660
   2780 Waterfront Pkwy 20 Indianapolis (46214) *(G-6543)*

Calumet Surface Hardening, Hammond *Also called D & D Industries Inc (G-5868)*

Calumite Company LLC 219 787-8667
   1605 Adler Cir Ste I Portage (46368) *(G-11753)*

CAM Co Inc 574 967-4496
   1776 N 200 E Flora (46929) *(G-3992)*

CAM Metal Fabrication LLC 260 982-6280
   911 W Main St North Manchester (46962) *(G-11226)*

Camaco Portage Mfg LLC 248 657-0246
   6515 Ameriplex Dr Ste B Portage (46368) *(G-11754)*

Camcar LLC 574 223-3131
   4366 N Old Us Highway 31 Rochester (46975) *(G-12117)*

Camco Manufacturing Inc 574 264-1491
   2912 Leer Ct Elkhart (46514) *(G-2747)*

Camera Art, Indianapolis *Also called Herff Jones LLC (G-7092)*

Camerabee LLC 317 546-2999
   7507 Crews Dr Indianapolis (46226) *(G-6544)*

Camilles Studio 219 365-5902
   11650 Wicker Ave Cedar Lake (46303) *(G-1526)*

Camo Diva, Fort Wayne *Also called Sugar Tree Incorporated (G-4660)*

Camoplast Crocker, Howe *Also called Exo-S US LLC (G-6125)*

Campbell Cobert Woodcraft 812 883-5399
   621 E Rudder Rd Salem (47167) *(G-12285)*

Campbell Logging 812 972-6280
   9100 W State Road 64 Birdseye (47513) *(G-634)*

Campbell Pet Company 812 692-5208
   120 N Odon St Elnora (47529) *(G-3287)*

Campbell Printing Co Inc 219 866-5913
   125 N Van Rensselaer St Rensselaer (47978) *(G-11916)*

Campbell Road Sawmill 260 238-4252
   17127 Campbell Rd Spencerville (46788) *(G-13044)*

Campbell Ventilation Inc 317 636-7211
   1544 Kennington St Indianapolis (46225) *(G-6545)*

Campbells Welding & Machine 574 643-6705
   202 E Day St Royal Center (46978) *(G-12212)*

Camtool Inc 765 286-9725
   3690 S Hoyt Ave Muncie (47302) *(G-10445)*

Can-Clay Corp 812 547-3461
   402 Washington St Cannelton (47520) *(G-1288)*

Cana Inc (PA) 574 266-6566
   2712 Old Us 20 W Elkhart (46514) *(G-2748)*

Cana Cabinetry, Elkhart *Also called Cana Inc (G-2748)*

Canature USA Inc (PA) 877 771-6789
   9760 Mayflower Carmel (46032) *(G-1326)*

Canature Watergroup Usa Inc (HQ) 877 771-6789
   9760 Mayflower Carmel (46032) *(G-1327)*

Candies Inc 260 747-7514
   4211 Earth Dr Fort Wayne (46809) *(G-4138)*

Candles By Dar Inc 260 482-2099
   3710 N Clinton St Fort Wayne (46805) *(G-4139)*

Candy Cents Vending Inc 317 378-9197
   7515 Somerset Bay Apt B Indianapolis (46240) *(G-6546)*

Candy Dish Inc 317 269-6262
   61 W Main St Nashville (47448) *(G-10719)*

Canines Choice Inc 765 662-2633
   1019 E 26th St Marion (46953) *(G-9514)*

Cannelburg Processing Plant 812 486-3223
   204 S Main St Cannelburg (47519) *(G-1283)*

Cannon Fabrication Company 765 629-2277
   7957 S State Road 3 Milroy (46156) *(G-9978)*

Cannon Timber LLC 219 754-1088
   418 E Oneida St La Crosse (46348) *(G-8719)*

CANTERBURY R V, Goshen *Also called Dna Enterprises Inc (G-5201)*

Canvas Shop LLC 260 768-7755
   850 Taylor Dr Shipshewana (46565) *(G-12607)*

Capco LLC 812 375-1700
   1349 Arcadia Dr Columbus (47201) *(G-1866)*

Cape Sandy Quarry, Leavenworth *Also called Mulzer Crushed Stone Inc (G-9165)*

Capital Adhesives & Packg Corp 317 834-5415
   1260 S Old State Road 67 Mooresville (46158) *(G-10304)*

Capital City Transit LLC 317 813-5800
   3421 W Washington St Indianapolis (46222) *(G-6547)*

Capital Custom Signs 765 689-7170
   1251 N Lancer St Peru (46970) *(G-11519)*

Capital Industries, Shelbyville *Also called Banks Machine & Engrg Inc (G-12519)*

Capital Machine Company Inc (PA) 317 638-6661
   2801 Roosevelt Ave Indianapolis (46218) *(G-6548)*

Capital Machines International, Indianapolis *Also called Capital Machine Company Inc (G-6548)*

Capital Tech Solutions LLC 812 303-4357
   1112 S Villa Dr Evansville (47714) *(G-3409)*

Capitol City Container Corp 317 875-0290
   8240 Zionsville Rd Indianapolis (46268) *(G-6549)*

Capitol City Glass Inc 317 635-2556
   1424 S East St Indianapolis (46225) *(G-6550)*

Capitol Source Network 260 248-9747
   366 E 600 N Columbia City (46725) *(G-1771)*

Caplas Neptune LLC 812 424-2904
   101 Oakley St Evansville (47710) *(G-3410)*

Capricorn Foods LLC (PA) 219 670-1872
   8880 Louisiana St Merrillville (46410) *(G-9707)*

Capriole Inc 812 923-9408
   10329 New Cut Rd Greenville (47124) *(G-5647)*

Capstone Commerce Company, Indianapolis *Also called Egenolf Enterprise Inc (G-6813)*

Captivated LLC 317 554-7400
   5483 Kenwood Pl Carmel (46033) *(G-1328)*

Captive Holdings LLC 812 424-2904
   101 Oakley St Evansville (47710) *(G-3411)*

Captive Plastics Inc (HQ) 812 424-2904
   101 Oakley St Evansville (47710) *(G-3412)*

Car-TEC, Ridgeville *Also called Cardemon Inc (G-12080)*

Carb-Rite, Schneider *Also called E J Bognar Inc (G-12354)*

Carbide Cutting Tools-Drake, Jasper *Also called Drake Corporation (G-8246)*

Carbon's Golden Malted, South Bend *Also called New Carbon Company LLC (G-12873)*

Carcapsule USA Inc 219 945-9493
   4590 W 61st Ave Hobart (46342) *(G-6073)*

Card Calendar Publishing LLC 812 234-5999
   2500 Prairieton Rd Terre Haute (47802) *(G-13205)*

A
L
P
H
A
B
E
T
I
C

Cardemon Inc..765 857-1000
  108 W 2nd St Ridgeville (47380) *(G-12080)*

Cardina L G, Fremont *Also called Cardinal Glass Industries Inc (G-4953)*

Cardinal Container Corp.......................................317 898-2715
  750 S Post Rd Indianapolis (46239) *(G-6551)*

Cardinal Ethanol LLC..765 964-3137
  1554 N County Rd 600 E Union City (47390) *(G-13454)*

Cardinal Glass Industries Inc.................................260 495-4105
  301 E Mcswain Dr Fremont (46737) *(G-4953)*

Cardinal Health 414 LLC.......................................317 981-4100
  4343 W 62nd St Indianapolis (46268) *(G-6552)*

Cardinal Manufacturing Co Inc................................317 283-4175
  1095 E 52nd St Indianapolis (46205) *(G-6553)*

Cardinal Metal Finishing LLC (PA)............................866 585-8024
  1500 E Murden St Kokomo (46901) *(G-8604)*

Cardinal Publishers Group, Indianapolis *Also called Tom Doherty Company Inc (G-8079)*

Cardinal Publishers Group.....................................317 846-8190
  14 Lakeview Ct Carmel (46033) *(G-1329)*

Cardinal Services Inc Indiana (PA)...........................574 267-3823
  504 N Bay Dr Warsaw (46580) *(G-13853)*

Cardinal Services Inc Indiana................................574 371-1305
  1770 E Smith St Warsaw (46580) *(G-13854)*

Cardinal Services Inc Indiana................................574 267-3823
  504 N Bay Dr Warsaw (46580) *(G-13855)*

Cardinal Spirits LLC..812 202-6789
  922 S Morton St Bloomington (47403) *(G-695)*

Carecycle LLC...317 372-7444
  8302 E 33rd St Indianapolis (46226) *(G-6554)*

Carenotes, Saint Meinrad *Also called St Meinrad Archabbey (G-12275)*

Carestone Inc...219 853-0600
  1646 Summer St Hammond (46320) *(G-5857)*

Cargill Incorporated..765 423-4302
  1502 Wabash Ave Lafayette (47905) *(G-8866)*

Cargill Incorporated..574 353-7621
  104 N Etna St Mentone (46539) *(G-9685)*

Cargill Incorporated..574 353-7623
  104 N Etna St Mentone (46539) *(G-9686)*

Cargill Incorporated..217 253-3389
  1281 Win Hentschel Blvd West Lafayette (47906) *(G-14056)*

Cargill Incorporated..402 533-4227
  1100 Indianapolis Blvd Hammond (46320) *(G-5858)*

Cargill Dry Corn Ingrdents Inc...............................317 632-1481
  1730 W Michigan St Indianapolis (46222) *(G-6555)*

Cargo Express, Middlebury *Also called Millers Superior Entps Inc (G-9909)*

Cargo Skiff Corporation.......................................812 873-6349
  1280 N County Road 500 E Butlerville (47223) *(G-1247)*

Cargo Systems Inc...574 264-1600
  2603 Glenview Dr Elkhart (46514) *(G-2749)*

Carico Enterprises LLC..765 384-4451
  3426 W Delphi Pike Marion (46952) *(G-9515)*

Carico Systems, Marion *Also called Carico Enterprises LLC (G-9515)*

Carl Dyers Original Moccasins................................812 667-5442
  5961 E State Rd 62 Friendship (47021) *(G-4991)*

Carl Hugness Publishing.......................................812 273-2472
  318 Mulberry St Madison (47250) *(G-9447)*

Carlex Glass America LLC......................................260 925-5656
  1900 Center St Auburn (46706) *(G-320)*

Carlex Glass America LLC......................................260 894-7750
  860 W Us Highway 6 Ligonier (46767) *(G-9279)*

Carlex Glass Company, Lafayette *Also called Carlex Indiana Assembly (G-8867)*

Carlex Glass Ind Inc-Auburn, Auburn *Also called Carlex Glass America LLC (G-320)*

Carlex Indiana Assembly (HQ).................................765 471-9399
  3701 David Howarth Dr Lafayette (47909) *(G-8867)*

Carlisle Industrial Brake & Fr...............................812 336-3811
  1031 E Hillside Dr Bloomington (47401) *(G-696)*

Carlisle Veneers Inc..812 398-2225
  10228 S Old 41 Carlisle (47838) *(G-1296)*

Carlson Motorsports...765 339-4407
  215 N High St Linden (47955) *(G-9303)*

Carlson Racing, Linden *Also called Carlson Motorsports (G-9303)*

Carlson Report, Indianapolis *Also called Raven Communications Inc (G-7818)*

Carlton Ventures Inc..317 637-2590
  1815 N Meridian St # 100 Indianapolis (46202) *(G-6556)*

Carlton West Oil Company LLC.................................812 375-9689
  3237 Nugent Blvd Columbus (47203) *(G-1867)*

Carman Industries Inc (PA)...................................812 288-4710
  1005 W Riverside Dr Jeffersonville (47130) *(G-8335)*

Carmel Countertops Inc..317 843-0331
  904 3rd Ave Sw Carmel (46032) *(G-1330)*

Carmel Engineering Inc..765 279-8955
  413 E Madison St Kirklin (46050) *(G-8547)*

Carmel Process Solutions Inc.................................317 705-0217
  484 E Carmel Dr Ste 213 Carmel (46032) *(G-1331)*

Carmel Sand & Gravel, Indianapolis *Also called Martin Marietta Materials Inc (G-6272)*

Carmel Trophies Plus..317 844-3770
  411 N Rangeline Rd Carmel (46032) *(G-1332)*

Carmel Trophies Plus, Carmel *Also called Carmel Trophies Plus (G-1332)*

Carmel Welding and Supply....................................317 846-3493
  550 S Rangeline Rd Carmel (46032) *(G-1333)*

Carmeuse Lime Inc...219 949-1450
  1 N Carmeuse Ln Gary (46406) *(G-5033)*

Carmeuse Lime Inc...773 221-9400
  1 N Carmeuse Ln Gary (46406) *(G-5034)*

Carmeuse Lime & Stone, Gary *Also called Carmeuse Lime Inc (G-5033)*

Carmeuse Lime & Stone, Gary *Also called Carmeuse Lime Inc (G-5034)*

Carmeuse Lime & Stone..219 787-9190
  165 Steel Dr Portage (46368) *(G-11755)*

Carmichael Electric LLC.......................................574 722-4028
  4334 Logansport Rd Logansport (46947) *(G-9327)*

Carmichael Welding Inc..812 825-5156
  9136 E State Road 54 Bloomfield (47424) *(G-636)*

Carother's Printing Company, South Bend *Also called Kill-N-Em Inc (G-12828)*

Carousel Industries...317 674-8111
  10419 Corning Way Fishers (46038) *(G-3885)*

Carousel Winery, Bedford *Also called Red Gate Farms Inc (G-573)*

Carousel Winery...812 849-1005
  6058 Lawrenceport Rd Mitchell (47446) *(G-10158)*

Carpenter Co..574 522-2800
  195 County Road 15 Elkhart (46516) *(G-2750)*

Carpenter Co..812 367-2211
  130 Scenic Industrial Dr Ferdinand (47532) *(G-3847)*

Carpenter Co Inc..317 297-2900
  5751 W 56th St Indianapolis (46254) *(G-6557)*

Carpenter Realtors, Indianapolis *Also called Carpenter Co Inc (G-6557)*

Carr Logging..812 863-7585
  9322 E State Road 58 Owensburg (47453) *(G-11424)*

Carr Metal Products Inc.......................................317 542-0691
  3735 N Arlington Ave Indianapolis (46218) *(G-6558)*

Carrara Industries Inc..765 643-3430
  1619 W 5th St Anderson (46016) *(G-81)*

Carrera Manufacturing Inc....................................260 726-9800
  1000 N Morton St Portland (47371) *(G-11809)*

Carriage House Woodworking...................................317 406-3042
  1601 E Main St Ste 12 Plainfield (46168) *(G-11599)*

Carrier Corporation...317 243-0851
  7310 W Morris St Indianapolis (46231) *(G-6559)*

Carrier Corporation...260 358-0888
  3650 W 200 N Huntington (46750) *(G-6196)*

Carris Reels Inc..269 545-3400
  31977 Us Highway 20 New Carlisle (46552) *(G-10880)*

Carroll County Comet, Flora *Also called Carroll Papers Inc (G-3993)*

Carroll County Comet, Delphi *Also called Carroll Papers Inc (G-2416)*

Carroll Distrg & Cnstr Sup Inc...............................317 984-2400
  20935 Cicero Rd Noblesville (46060) *(G-11078)*

Carroll Papers Inc (PA).......................................574 967-4135
  14 E Main St Flora (46929) *(G-3993)*

Carroll Papers Inc..765 564-2222
  114 E Franklin St Delphi (46923) *(G-2416)*

Carson Manufacturing Co Inc..................................317 257-3191
  5451 N Rural St Indianapolis (46220) *(G-6560)*

Cartec Company, Ridgeville *Also called Reliance Machine Company Inc (G-12082)*

Carter Cabinet Co Inc...317 985-5782
  5839 S 600 W New Palestine (46163) *(G-10969)*

Carter Enterprises Inc..317 984-1497
  119 W Main St Arcadia (46030) *(G-262)*

Carter Fuel Systems LLC (HQ).................................574 722-6141
  101 E Industrial Blvd Logansport (46947) *(G-9328)*

Carter Fuel Systems LLC.......................................574 735-0235
  91 E Industrial Blvd Logansport (46947) *(G-9329)*

Carter Lee Building Component................................317 834-5380
  9028 N Old State Road 67 Mooresville (46158) *(G-10305)*

Carter Manufacturing Company.................................765 563-3666
  896 E Carter Ct Brookston (47923) *(G-1102)*

Carter Septic Tank Inc..574 583-5796
  1720 N Buckeye St Monticello (47960) *(G-10257)*

Carter-Lee Building Components...............................317 639-5431
  1717 W Washington St Indianapolis (46222) *(G-6561)*

Carters Concrete Block Inc (PA)..............................574 722-2644
  5110 W Us Highway 24 Logansport (46947) *(G-9330)*

Carters Manufacturing & Weld.................................630 464-1520
  3270 S County Road 210 Knox (46534) *(G-8563)*

Cartesian Corp..765 742-0293
  230 Walnut St Lafayette (47905) *(G-8868)*

Carton Craft, New Albany *Also called Graphic Packaging Intl Inc (G-10789)*

Cartridge Specialist Inc......................................317 257-4465
  2440 E 57th St Indianapolis (46220) *(G-6562)*

Carver Non-Woven Tech LLC....................................260 627-0033
  706 E Depot St Fremont (46737) *(G-4954)*

Carvers Logging LLP...812 732-4932
  1801 Overlook Dr Sw Mauckport (47142) *(G-9653)*

Cascade Metrix LLC..317 572-7094
  11650 Olio Rd Ste 1000 Fishers (46037) *(G-3886)*

Case and Quart Inc..260 368-7808
  220 E Shore Dr Geneva (46740) *(G-5134)*

Case Indy Products Inc..317 677-0200
  1810 S Lynhurst Dr Ste L Indianapolis (46241) *(G-6563)*

Case New Holland LLC..765 482-5446
  420 S Enterprise Blvd Lebanon (46052) *(G-9172)*

(G-0000) Company's Geographic Section entry number

Case Show Homes LLC 317 669-6202
12965 Old Meridian St Carmel (46032) *(G-1334)*
Case Weinkauff 219 733-9484
671 E 100 S Valparaiso (46383) *(G-13519)*
Cash & Carry Lumber Co Inc 765 378-7575
14113 W Main St Daleville (47334) *(G-2337)*
Cash Concrete Products Inc (PA) 765 653-4007
1541 S County Road 450 E Greencastle (46135) *(G-5454)*
Cash Concrete Products Inc 765 653-4887
State Road 240 Greencastle (46135) *(G-5455)*
Cash Logging 812 843-5335
20198 N State Road 66 Mount Pleasant (47520) *(G-10377)*
Casino Printing For Less 765 742-0000
1400 Canal Rd Lafayette (47904) *(G-8869)*
Casper Inc 660 221-5906
4310 Stout Field North Dr Indianapolis (46241) *(G-6564)*
Cass County Byproducts, Logansport *Also called Bhj Usa Inc (G-9324)*
Cass County Machine Inc 574 722-5714
2915 Green Hills Dr Logansport (46947) *(G-9331)*
Cassini - D & D Mfg Inc 765 449-7992
800 S Earl Ave Lafayette (47904) *(G-8870)*
Cast Metals Technology 765 284-3888
11200 E State Road 32 Selma (47383) *(G-12422)*
Cast Products LP (HQ) 574 294-2684
3601 Charlotte Ave Elkhart (46517) *(G-2751)*
Cast Products LP 574 255-9619
1711 Clover Rd Mishawaka (46545) *(G-10017)*
Casters In Motion, Evansville *Also called Act Systems International LLC (G-3342)*
Casters In Motion USA Ltd LLC 812 437-4627
1513 N Cullen Ave Evansville (47715) *(G-3413)*
Casting Service, La Porte *Also called Kennametal Inc (G-8780)*
Castleton Village Center Inc 260 484-2600
6321 Huguenard Rd Ste A Fort Wayne (46818) *(G-4140)*
Castleton Village Center Inc (PA) 260 471-5959
6321 Huguenard Rd Ste A Fort Wayne (46818) *(G-4141)*
Castleton Village Center Inc 317 577-1995
450 E 96th St Indianapolis (46240) *(G-6565)*
Catalent Indiana LLC 812 355-6746
1300 S Patterson Dr Bloomington (47403) *(G-697)*
Catalyst Inc (PA) 317 227-3499
5420 W Sthern Ave Ste 104 Indianapolis (46241) *(G-6566)*
Catalyst Services Inc 219 972-7803
1940 N Lafayette Ct Griffith (46319) *(G-5768)*
Catalyst USA, Indianapolis *Also called Catalyst Inc (G-6566)*
Catchrs LLC 310 902-9723
365 E 75th St Indianapolis (46240) *(G-6567)*
Caterpillar Authorized Dealer, Fort Wayne *Also called Macallister Machinery Co Inc (G-4447)*
Caterpillar Authorized Dealer, Richmond *Also called Macallister Machinery Co Inc (G-12012)*
Caterpillar Inc 765 448-5000
3701 South St Lafayette (47905) *(G-8871)*
Caterpillar Inc 630 743-4094
6719 W 350 N Greenfield (46140) *(G-5511)*
Caterpillar Remn Powrtrn Indna (HQ) 317 738-2117
751 International Dr Franklin (46131) *(G-4875)*
Cathay Industries (usa) Inc (HQ) 219 531-5359
4901 Evans Ave Valparaiso (46383) *(G-13520)*
Cathay Pigments, Valparaiso *Also called Cathay Industries (usa) Inc (G-13520)*
Catheter Research Inc (PA) 317 872-0074
6102 Victory Way Indianapolis (46278) *(G-6568)*
Catholic Church School Market, Tell City *Also called Charles E Watts (G-13158)*
Catholic Moment 765 742-2050
610 Lingle Ave Lafayette (47901) *(G-8872)*
Catholic Press of Evansville 812 424-5536
4200 N Kentucky Ave Evansville (47711) *(G-3414)*
Cauble Precision Machine Inc 812 537-4884
1224 Foxwood Ct Greendale (47025) *(G-5484)*
Cause Printing Company 260 224-3515
5448 W 400 S Huntington (46750) *(G-6197)*
Cause Printing Company 765 573-3330
1102 W Ontario St Marion (46953) *(G-9516)*
Cave & Co. Printing, Westfield *Also called Damalak Printing Inc (G-14156)*
Cave & Company Printing 317 896-5337
104 W Main St Westfield (46074) *(G-14141)*
Cave Company Printing Inc 812 863-4333
5282 S Black Ankle Rd Bloomfield (47424) *(G-637)*
Cave Quarries Inc 812 936-7743
1156 N County Road 425 W Paoli (47454) *(G-11448)*
Cbfc LLC 317 352-0444
7698 Zionsville Rd Indianapolis (46268) *(G-6569)*
CC Manufacturing Inc 574 293-1696
54424 Susquehanna Ct Elkhart (46516) *(G-2752)*
CCI Big Boy Products, Warsaw *Also called Cardinal Services Inc Indiana (G-13855)*
CCI Contract Manufacturing, Warsaw *Also called Cardinal Services Inc Indiana (G-13854)*
CCM Industries Inc 765 545-0597
610 N 100 E Winchester (47394) *(G-14326)*
Ccmp Inc 219 922-8935
1313 E Main St Griffith (46319) *(G-5769)*
Ccoa of Indiana, Hammond *Also called Control Consultants of America (G-5865)*
Ccts Technology Group Inc 305 209-5743
8403 N Illinois St Indianapolis (46260) *(G-6570)*
CD & R Components Inc 812 852-4864
3247 W State Road 229 Batesville (47006) *(G-496)*
CD & Ws Bordner Entps Inc 765 268-2120
6559 S State Road 75 Cutler (46920) *(G-2328)*
CD Grafix LLC 812 945-4443
632 Providence Way Ste 3 Clarksville (47129) *(G-1675)*
Cdb Screen Printing Inc 765 472-4404
185 Madison Ave Peru (46970) *(G-11520)*
Cde Industries LLC 317 573-6790
4470 N Delaware St Indianapolis (46205) *(G-6571)*
Cdg Operation LLC 812 682-3770
6555 Griffin Rd New Harmony (47631) *(G-10924)*
Ce Systems Inc 812 372-8234
1045 S Gladstone Ave Columbus (47201) *(G-1868)*
Cecils Printing & Office Sups 812 683-4416
319 E 4th St Huntingburg (47542) *(G-6153)*
Ceco Metal Doors and Frames 317 787-3455
4010 S Meridian St Indianapolis (46217) *(G-6572)*
Cedar Creek Sawmill LLC 260 627-3985
15010 Page Rd Grabill (46741) *(G-5359)*
Cedar Creek Studios Inc 260 627-7320
7030 Hosler Rd Leo (46765) *(G-9241)*
Cedar Creek Winery 812 988-1111
36 E Franklin St Nashville (47448) *(G-10720)*
Cedar Creek Winery 765 342-9000
3820 Leonard Rd Martinsville (46151) *(G-9597)*
Cedar Shack 219 682-5531
11300 W 131st Pl Cedar Lake (46303) *(G-1527)*
Cedar Woodworking 812 486-2765
7932 E 625 N Montgomery (47558) *(G-10216)*
Ceg & Supply LLC 317 435-6398
1858 Haven Trl Martinsville (46151) *(G-9598)*
Cei, Columbus *Also called Columbus Engineering Inc (G-1876)*
Celebrate Season 609 261-5200
957 N Meridian St Sunman (47041) *(G-13109)*
Celebration Creations Inc 800 762-8286
5860 Michigan Rd Indianapolis (46228) *(G-6573)*
Celebration Halloween, Indianapolis *Also called Celebration Creations Inc (G-6573)*
Celebration Ice LLC 812 634-9801
4525 W Church Ave Jasper (47546) *(G-8240)*
Celebration Station, Merrillville *Also called Whiteco Industries Inc (G-9761)*
Celestial Candle 812 886-4819
138 E 17th St Vincennes (47591) *(G-13672)*
Celestial Designs LLC 317 733-3110
80 N First St Zionsville (46077) *(G-14425)*
Cellar Masters LLC 317 817-9473
8310 Allison Pointe Blvd Indianapolis (46250) *(G-6574)*
Cellofoam North America Inc 317 535-9008
150 Crossroads Dr Whiteland (46184) *(G-14235)*
Cellofoam North America Inc 317 535-0826
2615 Endress Pl Greenwood (46143) *(G-5674)*
Cemex 317 351-9912
1051 S Emerson Ave Indianapolis (46203) *(G-6575)*
Cemex Materials LLC 317 891-7500
6662 W 350 N Greenfield (46140) *(G-5512)*
Cemex Materials LLC 317 891-3015
1501 S Holt Rd Indianapolis (46241) *(G-6576)*
Cemex Materials LLC 317 891-3015
6662 W 350 N Greenfield (46140) *(G-5513)*
Cemex Materials LLC 317 769-5801
4360 Whitelick Dr Whitestown (46075) *(G-14250)*
Centennial Bindery LLC 812 472-4655
1330 Woerner Ave Clarksville (47129) *(G-1676)*
Center Concrete Inc 800 453-4224
4225 County Road 79 Butler (46721) *(G-1224)*
Center For Diagnostic Imaging 812 234-0555
4313 S 7th St Terre Haute (47802) *(G-13206)*
Center Line Mold & Tool Inc 812 526-0970
703 S Eisenhower Dr Edinburgh (46124) *(G-2598)*
Center Line Wood Works Inc 317 770-9486
14027 Brightwater Dr Fishers (46038) *(G-3887)*
Centerline Manufacturing 260 348-7400
18628 Wappes Rd Churubusco (46723) *(G-1651)*
Centerline Studio 317 423-3220
1011 E Beecher St Indianapolis (46203) *(G-6577)*
Centerline Woodworking 260 768-4116
695 S 600 W Lagrange (46761) *(G-9034)*
Central Brace & Limb Co Inc (PA) 317 925-4296
1901 N Capitol Ave Indianapolis (46202) *(G-6578)*
Central Brace & Limb Co Inc 812 334-2524
641 S Walker St Ste D Bloomington (47403) *(G-698)*
Central Brace & Limb Co Inc 812 232-2145
500 E Springhill Dr Ste G Terre Haute (47802) *(G-13207)*
Central Brace & Limb Co Inc 765 457-4868
802 S Berkley Rd Ste B Kokomo (46901) *(G-8605)*
Central Brace & Limb Co Inc 317 872-1596
1901 N Capitol Ave Indianapolis (46202) *(G-6579)*

ALPHABETIC

Central Coca-Cola Btlg Co Inc 765 423-5668
830 N 6th St Lafayette (47904) *(G-8873)*

Central Coca-Cola Btlg Co Inc 812 482-7475
641 Wernsing Rd Jasper (47546) *(G-8241)*

Central Coca-Cola Btlg Co Inc 765 642-9951
3200 E 38th St Anderson (46013) *(G-82)*

Central Coca-Cola Btlg Co Inc 812 232-9543
924 Lafayette Ave Terre Haute (47804) *(G-13208)*

Central Coca-Cola Btlg Co Inc 800 241-2653
1701 S Liberty Dr Bloomington (47403) *(G-699)*

Central Coca-Cola Btlg Co Inc 260 726-7126
1617 N Meridian St Portland (47371) *(G-11810)*

Central Coca-Cola Btlg Co Inc 800 241-2653
405 N Harrison St Shelbyville (46176) *(G-12526)*

Central Coca-Cola Btlg Co Inc 317 398-0129
5000 W 25th St Indianapolis (46224) *(G-6580)*

Central Coca-Cola Btlg Co Inc 574 291-1511
1400 W Ireland Rd South Bend (46614) *(G-12732)*

Central Coca-Cola Btlg Co Inc 260 478-2978
5010 Airport Expy Fort Wayne (46809) *(G-4142)*

Central Coca-Cola Btlg Co Inc 317 243-3771
3830 Hanna Cir Indianapolis (46241) *(G-6581)*

Central Concrete Supply LLC 812 481-2331
801 E 230s Jasper (47546) *(G-8242)*

Central Illinois Steel Company 219 882-1026
50 N Bridge St Gary (46404) *(G-5035)*

Central Ind Muldings Mllwk Inc 317 568-1639
2721 N Emerson Ave Indianapolis (46218) *(G-6582)*

Central Ind Oil Co 317 253-1131
5656 N Pennsylvania St Indianapolis (46220) *(G-6583)*

Central Indiana Ethanol LLC 765 384-4001
2955 W Delphi Pike Marion (46952) *(G-9517)*

Central Indiana Woodworkers 317 407-9228
1702 Misty Lake Dr Indianapolis (46260) *(G-6584)*

Central Overhead Door 219 696-1566
2080 W 172nd Ln Lowell (46356) *(G-9402)*

Central Packaging Inc 260 436-7225
7707 Vicksburg Pike Fort Wayne (46804) *(G-4143)*

Central Rubber & Plastics Inc 574 534-6411
17416 County Road 34 Goshen (46528) *(G-5185)*

Central States Fabricating 574 288-5607
3015 N Kenmore St South Bend (46628) *(G-12733)*

Central States Mfg Inc 219 879-4770
2051 Tryon Rd Michigan City (46360) *(G-9773)*

Central Tool Co Inc 317 485-5344
461 E Michigan St Fortville (46040) *(G-4769)*

Central Welding Inc 317 784-7730
6040 Gray Rd Indianapolis (46237) *(G-6585)*

Centre Township 765 482-1729
525 Ransdell Rd Lebanon (46052) *(G-9173)*

Centrifuge Chicago Corporation 219 852-5200
1721 Summer St Hammond (46320) *(G-5859)*

Centrifuge Support & Sups LLC 317 830-6141
8446 Abbey Dell Dr Camby (46113) *(G-1264)*

Centrum Force Fabrication 574 295-5367
204 W Clinton St Goshen (46526) *(G-5186)*

Centura Solid Surfacing Inc 317 867-5555
3525 W State Road 32 Westfield (46074) *(G-14142)*

Centurion Industries Inc (PA) 260 357-6665
1107 N Taylor Rd Garrett (46738) *(G-4996)*

Century Concrete Inc 765 739-6210
3725 W Us Highway 36 Bainbridge (46105) *(G-474)*

Century Foam Inc (PA) 574 293-5547
2600 S Nappanee St Elkhart (46517) *(G-2753)*

Century Grave & Vault Service 812 967-2110
2807 S Franklin School Rd Pekin (47165) *(G-11470)*

Century Marble Co Inc 317 867-5555
3525 W State Road 32 Westfield (46074) *(G-14143)*

Century Memorial, Bainbridge *Also called Century Concrete Inc (G-474)*

Century Pharmaceuticals Inc 317 849-4210
10377 Hague Rd Indianapolis (46256) *(G-6586)*

Century Steel Fabricating Inc 317 834-1295
4421 E County Line Rd Camby (46113) *(G-1265)*

Century Tool & Engineering 317 685-0942
1330 Deloss St Indianapolis (46203) *(G-6587)*

Century Tube, Madison *Also called Allied Tube & Conduit Corp (G-9443)*

Century Tube LLC 812 265-9255
4004 N Us 421 Madison (47250) *(G-9448)*

Cenveo Inc 317 791-5250
6302 Churchman Byp Indianapolis (46203) *(G-6588)*

Ceramica Inc 317 546-0087
6695 E 34th St Indianapolis (46226) *(G-6589)*

Ceramix 101 .... 219 531-6536
908 Roosevelt Rd Ste C Valparaiso (46383) *(G-13521)*

Ceran Inc 812 882-2680
2000 Chestnut St Vincennes (47591) *(G-13673)*

Ceres Solutions LLP 765 477-6542
3354 Us Highway 52 S Lafayette (47905) *(G-8874)*

Ceres Solutions Coop Inc 765 473-3922
6519 S State Road 19 Peru (46970) *(G-11521)*

Cerro Wire LLC 812 793-2929
1002 Industrial Way Crothersville (47229) *(G-2217)*

Certa Craft Inc 317 535-0226
140 Crossroads Dr Whiteland (46184) *(G-14236)*

Certainteed Corporation 812 645-0400
1001 W Industrial Dr Terre Haute (47802) *(G-13209)*

Certified Welding Co Inc 765 522-3238
5355 E County Road 500 N Bainbridge (46105) *(G-475)*

Cervella, Carmel *Also called Innovtive Nurological Dvcs LLC (G-1416)*

Ces Company Llc 317 290-0491
1331 N Capitol Ave Indianapolis (46202) *(G-6590)*

CF Gunworks LLC 317 538-1122
1157 S County Road 1000 E Frankfort (46041) *(G-4821)*

Cgenetech Inc 317 295-1925
7202 E 87th St Ste 100 Indianapolis (46256) *(G-6591)*

Cgm, Whitestown *Also called Precast Solutions Inc (G-14259)*

Cgs Services Inc 765 763-6258
2920 E Us Highway 52 Morristown (46161) *(G-10367)*

CH Ellis Co Inc (PA) 317 636-3351
2432 Southeastern Ave Indianapolis (46201) *(G-6592)*

Chad Simons 219 405-1620
803 Shannon Dr Chesterton (46304) *(G-1598)*

Chad's Towing and Recovery, Ellettsville *Also called Chads LLC (G-3273)*

Chads LLC 812 323-7377
6679 W Mcneely St Ellettsville (47429) *(G-3273)*

Chads Signs Installations Inc (PA) 317 867-2737
555 Park 32 West Dr Noblesville (46062) *(G-11079)*

Chalk Precision Machining LLC 765 452-9202
3095 N Washington St Kokomo (46901) *(G-8606)*

Challenge Plastic Products Inc 812 526-0582
110 W Industrial Dr Edinburgh (46124) *(G-2599)*

Challenge Tool & Mfg Inc 260 749-9558
11725 Lincoln Hwy E New Haven (46774) *(G-10934)*

Challenger Design, Nappanee *Also called Challenger Door Llc (G-10659)*

Challenger Door Llc (PA) 574 773-0470
1205 E Lincoln St Nappanee (46550) *(G-10658)*

Challenger Door Llc 574 773-8200
24785 Us Highway 6 Nappanee (46550) *(G-10659)*

Chameleon Lifestyles LLC 317 468-3246
1678 E Grey Feather Trl Greenfield (46140) *(G-5514)*

Champ Converters, Evansville *Also called Champ Torque Converters Inc (G-3415)*

Champ Torque Converters Inc 812 424-2602
1914 N Denby Ave Evansville (47711) *(G-3415)*

Champagne Lipstick 317 691-6045
135 Parkview Rd Carmel (46032) *(G-1335)*

Champion Home Builders Inc 260 593-2962
308 Sheridian Dr Topeka (46571) *(G-13412)*

Champion Manufacturing Inc 574 295-6893
2601 Industrial Pkwy Elkhart (46516) *(G-2754)*

Champion of Evansville LLC (PA) 812 424-2456
6827 Interchange Rd S Evansville (47715) *(G-3416)*

Champion Opco LLC 260 271-4076
2226 Research Dr Fort Wayne (46808) *(G-4144)*

Champion Racing Engines 317 335-2491
5002 W State Road 234 McCordsville (46055) *(G-9665)*

Champion Target 765 966-7745
232 Industrial Pkwy Richmond (47374) *(G-11969)*

Champion Window Mfr and Sups, Fort Wayne *Also called Champion Opco LLC (G-4144)*

Champion Wood Products Inc 812 282-9460
840 S Penn Ave Ste A Sellersburg (47172) *(G-12391)*

Chance Abrasives 219 871-0977
217 Twilight Dr Michigan City (46360) *(G-9774)*

Chance Indiana Standards Lab 317 787-6578
2919 Shelby St Indianapolis (46203) *(G-6593)*

Chao Center, The, West Lafayette *Also called Purdue Gmp Center LLC (G-14098)*

Chapdells Tree & Plant Design 317 845-9980
11480 E 111th St Fishers (46037) *(G-3888)*

Chapman Environmental Controls 574 674-8706
10463 Pleasant Valley Ct Osceola (46561) *(G-11374)*

Chapmans Cider Company LLC 260 444-1194
300 Industrial Dr Angola (46703) *(G-202)*

Chappos Inc 219 942-8101
101 N Wabash St Hobart (46342) *(G-6074)*

Chappys Rent To Own LLC 765 622-9500
615 S Scatterfield Rd # 1 Anderson (46012) *(G-83)*

Chariot Vans Inc 574 264-7577
2998 Paul Dr Elkhart (46514) *(G-2755)*

Charles Bane 765 855-5100
2009 Willow Grove Rd Centerville (47330) *(G-1541)*

Charles Coons 765 362-6509
2401 Indianapolis Rd Crawfordsville (47933) *(G-2138)*

Charles E Watts 812 547-8516
42 Zurich Way Tell City (47586) *(G-13158)*

Charles Kolb Logging 765 458-7766
7096 S Snowden Rd Liberty (47353) *(G-9258)*

Charles Kolb Sons Logging 765 647-4309
1135 John St Brookville (47012) *(G-1112)*

Charles W Knies Sawmill, Huntingburg *Also called Knies Sawmill Inc (G-6173)*

Charleston, Bremen *Also called Patrick Industries Inc (G-1014)*

Charleston Metal Products Inc (PA) 260 837-8211
350 Grant St Waterloo (46793) *(G-14010)*

Charleston Metal Products Inc 260 837-8211
350 Grant St Waterloo (46793) *(G-14011)*

Charleston Metal Products Inc 260 281-9972
1746 Us Highway 6 Corunna (46730) *(G-2083)*

Charm-Lite Inc 765 644-6876
2448 E 39th St Anderson (46013) *(G-84)*

Charmaran Corporation 260 347-3347
1451 Stonebraker Dr Kendallville (46755) *(G-8463)*

Chase Electric 765 388-2183
1467 S County Road 250 E New Castle (47362) *(G-10896)*

Chase Manufacturing LLC 574 546-4776
506 S Oakland Ave Nappanee (46550) *(G-10660)*

Chase N Corydon 812 738-3032
1881 Old Highway 135 Nw Corydon (47112) *(G-2092)*

Chase Plastic Services Inc 574 239-4090
5245 Dylan Dr South Bend (46628) *(G-12734)*

Chase Southport Emerson 317 266-7470
7120 Emblem Dr Indianapolis (46237) *(G-6594)*

Chassix 574 825-9457
51650 County Road 133 Bristol (46507) *(G-1051)*

Chateau Thomas Winery Inc (PA) 317 837-9463
6291 Cambridge Way Plainfield (46168) *(G-11600)*

Chattin Walter R Cotton 812 254-5031
2554 Union St Columbus (47201) *(G-1869)*

Checkered Past Racing Pdts LLC 317 852-6978
481 Southpoint Cir Ste 8 Brownsburg (46112) *(G-1142)*

Checkered Racing & Chrome LLC 812 275-2875
2221 N St Rd Spencer (47460) *(G-13019)*

Cheddar Stacks Inc 317 566-0425
5875 Castle Crk Indianapolis (46250) *(G-6595)*

Cheercussion Inc 317 762-4009
1091 3rd Ave Sw Carmel (46032) *(G-1336)*

Cheetah Building Products 812 466-1234
4600 N 13th St Terre Haute (47805) *(G-13210)*

Cheetah Trikes Inc 812 256-9199
7631 High Jackson Rd Charlestown (47111) *(G-1560)*

Chegar Manufacturing Co Inc 765 945-7444
951 N Independence St Windfall (46076) *(G-14347)*

Cheli Fuel 317 377-1480
2551 N Emerson Ave Indianapolis (46218) *(G-6596)*

Chelseas Model Horses 765 366-1082
7889 S Ladoga Rd Ladoga (47954) *(G-8839)*

Chem Tech Inc 574 848-1001
501 Bloomingdale Dr Bristol (46507) *(G-1052)*

Chem-Aqua 317 899-3660
8401 E 33rd St Indianapolis (46226) *(G-6597)*

Chem-Elec, North Webster *Also called Chematics Inc (G-11290)*

Chematics Inc 574 834-2406
4519 N Sr13 North Webster (46555) *(G-11290)*

Chemcoaters LLC 219 977-1929
700 Chase St Gary (46404) *(G-5036)*

Chemical Control Systems Inc (PA) 219 465-5103
403 Industrial Dr Griffith (46319) *(G-5770)*

Chemicals Solvents & Lubr 260 484-2000
8005 N Clinton St Fort Wayne (46825) *(G-4145)*

Chemigen Inc 317 902-6630
6584 Regents Park Dr Zionsville (46077) *(G-14426)*

Chemstation, Carmel *Also called Paradigm Industries Inc (G-1448)*

Chemtrex LLC 317 508-4223
6315 Edenshall Ln Noblesville (46062) *(G-11080)*

Chemtrusion Inc 812 280-2910
1403 Port Rd Jeffersonville (47130) *(G-8336)*

Chemtrusion-Indiana, Jeffersonville *Also called Chemtrusion Inc (G-8336)*

Chemtura Corporation 765 497-6782
5268 Grapevine Dr West Lafayette (47906) *(G-14057)*

Chep (usa) Inc 317 780-0700
606 W Troy Ave Indianapolis (46225) *(G-6598)*

Cherry Hill Shopping Park, Connersville *Also called Coach Line Motors (G-2043)*

Cherry Hill Vineyard LLC 317 846-5170
10236 Ditch Rd Carmel (46032) *(G-1337)*

Cherrytree Farms LLC 317 758-4495
4310 W State Road 38 Sheridan (46069) *(G-12588)*

Chessex Manufacturing Co LLC 260 471-9511
3415 Centennial Dr Fort Wayne (46808) *(G-4146)*

Chester Inc 574 896-5600
6020 S 500 W North Judson (46366) *(G-11209)*

Chester Pool Systems Inc 812 949-7333
5311 Foundation Blvd New Albany (47150) *(G-10758)*

Chester Pool Systems Inc 812 949-7333
5311 Foundation Blvd New Albany (47150) *(G-10759)*

Chesterfield Tool & Engrg Inc 765 378-5101
13710 W Commerce Rd Daleville (47334) *(G-2338)*

Chesterton Tribune Inc 219 926-1131
193 S Calumet Rd Chesterton (46304) *(G-1599)*

Cheyenne Enterprises LLC 317 253-7795
6949 Antelope Dr Indianapolis (46278) *(G-6599)*

Chicago Automated Labeling 219 531-0646
44 N 450 E Valparaiso (46383) *(G-13522)*

Chicago Case Company (PA) 317 636-3351
2432 Southeastern Ave Indianapolis (46201) *(G-6600)*

Chicago Color Graphics 312 856-1433
7258 Forest Ave Hammond (46324) *(G-5860)*

Chicago Faucet Company, Michigan City *Also called Geberit Manufacturing Inc (G-9797)*

Chicago Flame Hardening Co 773 768-3608
5200 Railroad Ave Ste 1 East Chicago (46312) *(G-2524)*

Chicago Specialty Steel Corp 219 922-8888
505 Industrial Dr Griffith (46319) *(G-5771)*

Chicago Steel Ltd Partnership 219 949-1111
700 Chase St Gary (46404) *(G-5037)*

Chicken Scratch LLC 260 486-9800
8003 Young Rd Fort Wayne (46835) *(G-4147)*

Chief Automotive Technologies, Madison *Also called Vehicle Service Group LLC (G-9500)*

Chief Automotive Technologies, Madison *Also called Vehicle Service Group LLC (G-9501)*

Chief Industries Inc 219 866-4121
1225 E Maple St Rensselaer (47978) *(G-11917)*

Chief Metal Works Inc 765 932-2134
1705 W Us Highway 52 Rushville (46173) *(G-12217)*

Chief Powerboats Inc 219 775-7024
280 Wood St Crown Point (46307) *(G-2233)*

Chikol Equities, Granger *Also called Sentinel Services Inc (G-5432)*

Childrens Better Health Inst, Indianapolis *Also called Saturday Evening Post Soc Inc (G-7898)*

Childress Corporation 317 774-8571
10403 Parmer Cir Fishers (46038) *(G-3889)*

Chinet Company 219 989-7040
6629 Indianapolis Blvd Hammond (46320) *(G-5861)*

Chisholm Lumber & Sup Co Inc 317 547-3535
3419 Roosevelt Ave Indianapolis (46218) *(G-6601)*

Choco-Pan, Indianapolis *Also called Confectionery Products Mfg Inc (G-6649)*

Chocolate Moose, The, Bloomington *Also called Penguin Enterprises LLC (G-797)*

Choppers Kickstand LLC 260 739-6966
3032 Maumee Ave Fort Wayne (46803) *(G-4148)*

Chore-Time Plty Prod Systems, Milford *Also called Ctb Inc (G-9951)*

Chore-Time Plty Prod Systems, Milford *Also called Ctb Inc (G-9952)*

Chowning Jewelers, Veedersburg *Also called Chownings Jewelers (G-13642)*

Chownings Jewelers 765 294-4476
115 E 2nd St Veedersburg (47987) *(G-13642)*

Chris Schwartz 260 615-9574
13631 Spencerville Rd Grabill (46741) *(G-5360)*

Christian Candle Company 317 427-8070
1509 Mary Dr Indianapolis (46241) *(G-6602)*

Christian Sound & Song Inc 574 294-2893
56718 Coppergate Dr Elkhart (46516) *(G-2756)*

Christie Machine Works Co Inc 317 638-8840
425 W Mccarty St Indianapolis (46225) *(G-6603)*

Christman Logging 502 525-2649
7641 N Bacon Ridge Rd Madison (47250) *(G-9449)*

Christopher Engle 812 876-3540
7251 W State Road 46 Ellettsville (47429) *(G-3274)*

Christopher Miller 812 442-0949
1892 E Us Highway 40 Brazil (47834) *(G-956)*

Christy's Candles & Gifts, Madison *Also called Christys Candles Inc (G-9450)*

Christys Candles Inc 812 273-3072
2631 Michigan Rd Madison (47250) *(G-9450)*

Christys Design & Sign Co 317 882-5444
500 Polk St Ste 17 Greenwood (46143) *(G-5675)*

Chromasource Inc 260 420-3000
2433 S Cr 600 E E Columbia City (46725) *(G-1772)*

Chromcraft Revington Inc (HQ) 662 562-8203
1330 Win Hentschel Blvd West Lafayette (47906) *(G-14058)*

Chrome Deposit Corporation (PA) 219 763-1571
6640 Melton Rd Portage (46368) *(G-11756)*

Chronicle-Tribune, Marion *Also called Paxton Media Group LLC (G-9550)*

Chronotrack Systems Corp (PA) 314 406-7243
6001 Old Boonville Hwy Evansville (47715) *(G-3417)*

Chrysler Foundry, Kokomo *Also called FCA US LLC (G-8624)*

Chrysler Transmission, Kokomo *Also called FCA US LLC (G-8622)*

Chryso Inc 812 256-4220
10600 Highway 62 Unit 7 Charlestown (47111) *(G-1561)*

Chubbs Steel Sales Inc 574 295-3166
57832 County Road 3 Elkhart (46517) *(G-2757)*

Chuck Bivens Services Inc 260 747-6195
10216 Airport Dr Fort Wayne (46809) *(G-4149)*

Chucks Cleaners 260 488-3362
3820 E Bellefontaine Rd Hamilton (46742) *(G-5820)*

Chucks Stace-Allen Inc 317 632-2401
2246 W Minnesota St # 50 Indianapolis (46221) *(G-6604)*

Church Untd Brethren In Chrst, Huntington *Also called United Brethren In Christ (G-6258)*

Churchill Cigars 812 273-2249
605 W 2nd St Madison (47250) *(G-9451)*

Chyall Pharmaceutical 765 237-3391
1281 Win Hentschel Blvd West Lafayette (47906) *(G-14059)*

Ciderleaf Tea Company Inc 812 375-1937
4525 Progress Dr Columbus (47201) *(G-1870)*

Cie, Marion *Also called Central Indiana Ethanol LLC (G-9517)*

Cigarette Discount Outlet, Michigan City *Also called Fast Lane Foods Inc* ***(G-9792)***
Cigarettes Plus 574 267-3166
843 N Lake St Warsaw (46580) ***(G-13856)***
Cimbar Performance Mineral, Mount Vernon *Also called United Minerals and Prpts Inc* ***(G-10412)***
Cimtech Inc 812 948-1472
325 Park East Blvd New Albany (47150) ***(G-10760)***
Cin-Nan Treasures 574 533-6593
808 Lynwood Dr Goshen (46526) ***(G-5187)***
Cinda B USA LLC 260 469-0803
1530 Progress Rd Fort Wayne (46808) ***(G-4150)***
Cindon Inc 812 853-5450
8400 Golden Dr Newburgh (47630) ***(G-11024)***
Cindys Crossstitch & Patterns 317 410-0764
2265 Reformers Ave Indianapolis (46203) ***(G-6605)***
Cindys In Stitches 317 841-1408
9836 N By Northeast Blvd Fishers (46037) ***(G-3890)***
Cinematic Captioning Systems 317 862-3418
8111 Bel Moore Blvd Indianapolis (46259) ***(G-6606)***
Circle - Prosco Inc 812 339-3653
401 N Gates Dr Bloomington (47404) ***(G-700)***
Circle City Heat Treating Inc 317 638-2252
2243 Massachusetts Ave Indianapolis (46218) ***(G-6607)***
Circle City Kombucha, Indianapolis *Also called Circle City Sonorans LLC* ***(G-6609)***
Circle City Lighting Inc 317 439-0824
21570 Anchor Bay Dr Noblesville (46062) ***(G-11081)***
Circle City Medical Inc 317 228-1144
10850 Ruby Ct Carmel (46032) ***(G-1338)***
Circle City Rebar LLC 317 917-8566
4002 Industrial Blvd Indianapolis (46254) ***(G-6608)***
Circle City Services Ltd 317 770-6287
176 Logan St Noblesville (46060) ***(G-11082)***
Circle City Sonorans LLC 317 401-9787
1121 N Arlington Ave Indianapolis (46219) ***(G-6609)***
Circle City Woodworking 765 637-6687
5574 Alcott Ln Indianapolis (46221) ***(G-6610)***
Circle M Spring Inc 574 267-2883
930 Executive Dr Warsaw (46580) ***(G-13857)***
Circle Medical Products Inc 317 271-2626
8202 Indy Ln Indianapolis (46214) ***(G-6611)***
Circle Printing LLC 812 663-7367
130 W Main St Greensburg (47240) ***(G-5593)***
Circle R Industries Inc 765 379-2768
5262 W 750 S Rossville (46065) ***(G-12210)***
Circle Y Farms, Springville *Also called Robert L Young* ***(G-13067)***
Circuit Breaker Sales Co Inc 219 575-5420
11181 Virginia St Crown Point (46307) ***(G-2234)***
Cisco Systems Inc 317 816-5200
11711 N Meridian St # 250 Carmel (46032) ***(G-1339)***
CIT, Richmond *Also called Contract Indus Tooling Inc* ***(G-11973)***
Citadel Architectural Pdts Inc 317 894-9400
3131 N Franklin Rd Ste A Indianapolis (46226) ***(G-6612)***
Citgo, Huntingburg *Also called Hucks Food Fuel* ***(G-6168)***
Citizens By-Products Coal Co (HQ) 317 927-4738
2020 N Meridian St Indianapolis (46202) ***(G-6613)***
Citizens Energy Group 317 261-8794
366 Kentucky Ave Indianapolis (46225) ***(G-6614)***
City of Anderson 765 648-6560
2801 Gene Gustin Way Anderson (46011) ***(G-85)***
City of Anderson 765 648-6715
1035 Main St Anderson (46016) ***(G-86)***
City of Columbia City 260 248-5118
925 E Van Buren St Columbia City (46725) ***(G-1773)***
City of Fort Wayne 260 749-8040
5510 Lake Ave Fort Wayne (46815) ***(G-4151)***
City of Fort Wayne 260 427-1235
1701 Lafayette St Fort Wayne (46803) ***(G-4152)***
City Optical Co Inc (PA) 317 924-1300
2839 Lafayette Rd Indianapolis (46222) ***(G-6615)***
City Optical Co Inc 317 788-4243
3636 S East St Indianapolis (46227) ***(G-6616)***
City Vision Center, Columbia City *Also called Better Visions PC* ***(G-1766)***
City Vision Center, Leo *Also called Better Visions PC* ***(G-9239)***
City Welding & Fabrication 765 569-5403
255 N Dormeyer Ave Rockville (47872) ***(G-12175)***
Cives Corporation 219 279-4000
337 N 700 W Wolcott (47995) ***(G-14362)***
Cives Steel Company, Wolcott *Also called Cives Corporation* ***(G-14362)***
CJ Automotive Indiana LLC (PA) 260 868-2147
100 Comm St Butler (46721) ***(G-1225)***
CJ Developers Inc 219 942-5051
150 N Illinois St Hobart (46342) ***(G-6075)***
CJ Logging LLC 812 360-0163
2336 S Cnservation Clb Rd Morgantown (46160) ***(G-10350)***
CJ Printing 219 924-1685
9445 Indianapolis Blvd A Hammond (46322) ***(G-5862)***
CJS Mens Wear 260 436-4788
6410 W Jefferson Blvd Fort Wayne (46804) ***(G-4153)***
Cjs Stop N Go 317 877-0681
5855 E 211th St Ste 34 Noblesville (46062) ***(G-11083)***
CK Products LLC 260 484-2517
6230 Innovation Blvd Fort Wayne (46818) ***(G-4154)***
Ckc Tool Inc 219 285-6415
508 S Polk St Morocco (47963) ***(G-10361)***
Ckc Tool Inc 219 285-6415
511 S Lincoln St Morocco (47963) ***(G-10362)***
Ckmt Associates Inc 219 924-2820
6405 Olcott St Hammond (46320) ***(G-5863)***
CL Tech Inc 812 526-0995
216 N Main St Edinburgh (46124) ***(G-2600)***
Clabber Girl, Terre Haute *Also called Hulman & Company* ***(G-13250)***
Clabber Girl Corporation 812 232-9446
900 Wabash Ave Terre Haute (47807) ***(G-13211)***
Claeys Candy Inc 574 287-1818
525 S Taylor St South Bend (46601) ***(G-12735)***
Clancys of Portage 219 764-4995
2542 Portage Mall Portage (46368) ***(G-11757)***
Clarcor Air Filtration Pdts (HQ) 502 969-2304
100 River Ridge Cir Jeffersonville (47130) ***(G-8337)***
Clark Dairy Equipment, Greenwood *Also called Robertson Machine Co Inc* ***(G-5741)***
Clark Foods Inc (PA) 812 949-3075
810 Progress Blvd New Albany (47150) ***(G-10761)***
Clark Millworks 260 665-1270
1587 S Old Us Highway 27 Angola (46703) ***(G-203)***
Clark's Snacks, New Albany *Also called Jones Popcorn Inc* ***(G-10810)***
Clarke American Checks Inc 812 283-9598
240 America Pl Jeffersonville (47130) ***(G-8338)***
Clarke American Checks Inc 812 283-9598
239 America Pl Jeffersonville (47130) ***(G-8339)***
Clarke American Checks Inc 812 283-9598
239 America Pl Jeffersonville (47130) ***(G-8340)***
Clarks Cnc LLC 812 508-1773
1718 S Jackson Pike Springville (47462) ***(G-13061)***
Classee Vinyl Windows LLC 574 825-7863
59323 County Road 35 Middlebury (46540) ***(G-9875)***
Classic Baluster, Brazil *Also called Burkes Garden Wood Pdts LLC* ***(G-955)***
Classic Baluster LLC 765 344-1619
4774 S 1000 E Brazil (47834) ***(G-957)***
Classic Buildings Inc 812 944-5821
2709 Blackiston Mill Rd Clarksville (47129) ***(G-1677)***
Classic Cabinetry 317 823-1853
10665 E 59th St Indianapolis (46236) ***(G-6617)***
Classic Chemical Corp 812 934-3289
7750 Zionsville Rd # 700 Indianapolis (46268) ***(G-6618)***
Classic City Signs Inc 260 927-8438
551 N Grandstaff Dr Auburn (46706) ***(G-321)***
Classic Die Services Inc 260 748-6907
6926 Trafalgar Dr Ste D Fort Wayne (46803) ***(G-4155)***
Classic Engraving 765 523-3355
7522 S 775 E Stockwell (47983) ***(G-13076)***
Classic Graphics, Fort Wayne *Also called Classic Media LLC* ***(G-4157)***
Classic Graphics Inc 260 482-3487
3219 E State Blvd Ste 2 Fort Wayne (46805) ***(G-4156)***
Classic Industries Inc 812 421-4006
2308 Commercial Ct Evansville (47720) ***(G-3418)***
Classic Kitchen & Granite 317 575-8883
9 E City Center Dr Carmel (46032) ***(G-1340)***
Classic Media LLC 260 482-3487
3219 E State Blvd Fort Wayne (46805) ***(G-4157)***
Classic Products Corp 260 748-6907
6926 Trafalgar Dr Ste D Fort Wayne (46803) ***(G-4158)***
Classic Products Corp (PA) 260 484-2695
4617 Industrial Rd Fort Wayne (46825) ***(G-4159)***
Classic Rock Face Block Inc 260 704-3113
520 Southview Ave Fort Wayne (46806) ***(G-4160)***
Classic Trophy Co 260 483-1161
210 Marciel Dr Fort Wayne (46825) ***(G-4161)***
Classic Truss WD Cmponents Inc 812 944-5821
2709 Blackiston Mill Rd Clarksville (47129) ***(G-1678)***
Classico Seating, Carmel *Also called Hanco Inc* ***(G-1393)***
Classique Hair Style 317 738-2104
50 S Water St Franklin (46131) ***(G-4876)***
Clay Critters, West Lafayette *Also called R Drew & Co Inc* ***(G-14100)***
Clay Factory, The, Grabill *Also called Old Lumber Yard Clay Factory* ***(G-5382)***
Clayhill Wind & Solar LLC 765 437-2395
3660 W 500 S Sharpsville (46068) ***(G-12504)***
Claymore Tools Inc 574 255-6483
1619 N Home St Mishawaka (46545) ***(G-10018)***
Clayton Dant Corporation 317 842-2420
120 Shadowlawn Dr Fishers (46038) ***(G-3891)***
Clayton Homes Inc 260 553-5500
1850 State Road 8 Garrett (46738) ***(G-4997)***
Clayton Homes Inc 812 423-4052
19410 Us 41 N Evansville (47725) ***(G-3419)***
Claywood Creation 260 244-7719
111 S Briarwood Ln Columbia City (46725) ***(G-1774)***

CLC Embroidery LLC 219 395-9600
   332 Wake Robin Dr Chesterton (46304) *(G-1600)*

Clean Air of Evansville, Evansville *Also called 3-T Corp (G-3326)*

CLEAN EXHAUST, Indianapolis *Also called Ccts Technology Group Inc (G-6570)*

Clean-Seal Inc 574 299-1888
   20900 Ireland Rd South Bend (46614) *(G-12736)*

Clear Channel Outdoor Inc 317 686-2350
   511 Madison Ave Indianapolis (46225) *(G-6619)*

Clear Decision Filtration Inc 219 567-2008
   4571 S 1450 W Francesville (47946) *(G-4809)*

Clear Ear Hearing Aid Center, Griffith *Also called Spry-Clear Ear Inc (G-5790)*

Clear Edge Filtration Inc 219 306-7339
   202 S Indiana Ave Crown Point (46307) *(G-2235)*

Clear Software LLC 317 732-8831
   10 S Main St Zionsville (46077) *(G-14427)*

Clear View Cstm Windows Doors 812 877-1000
   9630 E Us Highway 40 Terre Haute (47803) *(G-13212)*

Cleer Vision Tempered GL LLC 574 262-0449
   3401 County Road 6 E Elkhart (46514) *(G-2758)*

Cleer Vision Windows Inc 574 262-0449
   3401 County Road 6 E Elkhart (46514) *(G-2759)*

Cleer Vision Windows Inc 574 262-0449
   3401 County Road 6 E Elkhart (46514) *(G-2760)*

Clermont Neon Sign Company 317 638-4123
   491 Johnson Ln Ste B Brownsburg (46112) *(G-1143)*

Clients Choice Ltd 812 853-2911
   2144 Wildwood Dr Boonville (47601) *(G-912)*

Clif Bar & Company 510 596-6451
   7575 Georgetown Rd Indianapolis (46268) *(G-6620)*

Cliff A Ostermeyer 615 361-7902
   9375 College Dr Apt A Indianapolis (46240) *(G-6621)*

Clifty Engineering and Tool Co 812 273-3272
   2949 Clifty Dr Madison (47250) *(G-9452)*

Climate Systems Division, New Haven *Also called Parker-Hannifin Corporation (G-10951)*

Cline Brothers Welding 812 738-3537
   3490 Highway 62 Ne Corydon (47112) *(G-2093)*

Clinical Architecture LLC 317 580-8400
   11611 N Meridian St # 450 Carmel (46032) *(G-1341)*

Clinical Drug Information LLC (HQ) 317 735-5300
   8425 Woodfield Indianapolis (46240) *(G-6622)*

Clinton Custom Wood Turning 574 535-0543
   62172 County Road 33 Goshen (46528) *(G-5188)*

Clinton Harness Shop 574 533-9797
   13705 State Road 4 Goshen (46528) *(G-5189)*

Clm Pallet Recycling Inc (PA) 317 485-4080
   3103 W 1000 N Fortville (46040) *(G-4770)*

Clondalkin Pharma & Healthcare 317 328-7355
   6454 Saguaro Ct Indianapolis (46268) *(G-6623)*

Clondalkin Pharma & Healthcare 812 464-2461
   1100 E Louisiana St Evansville (47711) *(G-3420)*

Closure Systems Intl Inc (HQ) 317 390-5000
   7820 Innovation Blvd # 100 Indianapolis (46278) *(G-6624)*

Closure Systems Intl Inc 765 364-6300
   1604 E Elmore St Crawfordsville (47933) *(G-2139)*

Closure Systems Intl Inc 317 390-5000
   318 Glenn St Crawfordsville (47933) *(G-2140)*

Closure Systems Intl Inc 765 364-6300
   1205 E Elmore St Crawfordsville (47933) *(G-2141)*

Cloud Defensive LLC (PA) 812 760-5017
   717 Adams St Newburgh (47630) *(G-11025)*

Cloudburst Lawn Sprinkler Syst 260 492-8400
   1707 Brandywine Trl Fort Wayne (46845) *(G-4162)*

Clover Industrial Services LLC 317 879-5001
   1555 S Franklin Rd Ste D Indianapolis (46239) *(G-6625)*

Clover Industries LLC 574 892-5760
   20240 Michigan Rd Argos (46501) *(G-273)*

Clover Printing LLC 260 657-3003
   16840 State Road 37 Harlan (46743) *(G-5968)*

Clover Sheet Metal Company 574 293-5912
   28298 Clay St Elkhart (46517) *(G-2761)*

Clover Signs Co 812 442-7446
   932 W National Ave Brazil (47834) *(G-958)*

Cloverleaf Farms Dairy 219 938-5140
   6401 Melton Rd Gary (46403) *(G-5038)*

Clovis LLC 812 944-4791
   3333 Buffalo Trl Floyds Knobs (47119) *(G-4009)*

Clown Room, The, Lexington *Also called Rbg Inc (G-9255)*

Clp Towne Inc 574 233-3183
   24805 Us Highway 20 South Bend (46628) *(G-12737)*

Club Cyberia, Indianapolis *Also called Cyberia Ltd (G-6719)*

Clunette Elevator Co Inc 574 858-2281
   4316 W 600 N Leesburg (46538) *(G-9234)*

Clute Enterprises Inc 260 413-0810
   18706 Coldwater Rd Huntertown (46748) *(G-6135)*

CM Reed LLC (PA) 517 546-4100
   18463 Running Deer Ln Greendale (47025) *(G-5485)*

CM Tech 765 584-6501
   1036 N Old Highway 27 Winchester (47394) *(G-14327)*

CMa Steel & Fabrication Inc 260 207-9000
   3333 Independence Dr Fort Wayne (46808) *(G-4163)*

CMA Supply, Fort Wayne *Also called CMa Supply Co Fort Wayne Inc (G-4164)*

CMa Supply Co Fort Wayne Inc 260 471-9000
   3333 Independence Dr Fort Wayne (46808) *(G-4164)*

Cme LLC 260 623-3700
   21600 Monroeville Rd Monroeville (46773) *(G-10192)*

Cmg Inc 317 890-1999
   455 Rawles Ct Indianapolis (46229) *(G-6626)*

CMI Pgi Holdings LLC (HQ) 812 377-5000
   500 Jackson St Columbus (47201) *(G-1871)*

Cmj & Associates Corporation 765 962-1947
   160 Fort Wayne Ave Richmond (47374) *(G-11970)*

CMS, Whiteland *Also called Cad & Machining Services Inc (G-14234)*

CMS Technologies Inc 219 395-8272
   147 N Jackson Blvd Ste 1x Chesterton (46304) *(G-1601)*

Cnc Concepts Inc 574 269-2301
   3019 S County Farm Rd Warsaw (46580) *(G-13858)*

Cnc Industries Inc 260 490-5700
   3810 Fourier Dr Fort Wayne (46818) *(G-4165)*

Cnc Laser Inc 260 562-3953
   3408 N 915 W Shipshewana (46565) *(G-12608)*

Cnc Machine Inc 317 835-4575
   1380 N 450 W Shelbyville (46176) *(G-12527)*

Cnh Industrial America LLC 765 482-5409
   400 S Enterprise Blvd Lebanon (46052) *(G-9174)*

Cnhi LLC 574 936-3101
   214 N Michigan St Plymouth (46563) *(G-11674)*

Cnhi LLC 812 944-6481
   318 Pearl St Ste 100 New Albany (47150) *(G-10762)*

Cns Custom Woodworks Inc 812 350-2431
   1053 Hummingbird Ln Columbus (47203) *(G-1872)*

Co Experts, Kokomo *Also called G E Kerr Companies Inc (G-8627)*

Co-Alliance LLP 765 659-2596
   411b Eb Kellyb Rd Frankfort (46041) *(G-4822)*

Co-Alliance LLP 765 249-2233
   805 East St Michigantown (46057) *(G-9864)*

Co-Alliance LLP 765 659-3420
   6454 W Rte 28 Frankfort (46041) *(G-4823)*

Co-Alliance Ltd Lblty Partnr (PA) 317 745-4491
   5250 E Us Hwy 3 Avon (46123) *(G-435)*

Co-Op Trading, Fort Wayne *Also called Friends of Third World Inc (G-4288)*

Co-Tronics Inc 574 722-3850
   2935 W 100 N Peru (46970) *(G-11522)*

Coach Line Motors 765 825-7893
   2516 Western Ave Connersville (47331) *(G-2043)*

Coaches Connection Inc 260 356-0400
   200 E Park Dr Huntington (46750) *(G-6198)*

Coachmen Recreational Vehicle, Elkhart *Also called All American Group Inc (G-2675)*

Coachmen Recrtl Vehicles Co 574 825-5821
   423 N Main St Middlebury (46540) *(G-9876)*

Coast To Coast, Huntington *Also called Transwheel Corporation (G-6256)*

Cobar Industries Inc 317 691-7124
   8302 Christiana Ln Indianapolis (46256) *(G-6627)*

Coblentz Cabinet 812 687-7525
   8876 E 800 N Montgomery (47558) *(G-10217)*

Cobo Industries 812 341-4318
   6831 Ridge Vale Pl Apt 2b Indianapolis (46237) *(G-6628)*

Coca Cola Btlg Co Kokomo Ind (PA) 765 457-4421
   2305 Davis Rd Kokomo (46901) *(G-8607)*

Coca Cola Btlg Co Kokomo Ind 574 936-3220
   1701 Pidco Dr Plymouth (46563) *(G-11675)*

Coca-Cola, Kokomo *Also called Coca Cola Btlg Co Kokomo Ind (G-8607)*

Coca-Cola Bottling Co Cnsld 812 228-3200
   3223 Interstate Dr Evansville (47715) *(G-3421)*

Coca-Cola Bottling Co Inc 812 376-3381
   1334 Washington St Columbus (47201) *(G-1873)*

Coca-Cola Bottling Co Portland 260 726-7126
   1617 N Meridian St Portland (47371) *(G-11811)*

Cockerhams Signs & Graphics 812 358-3737
   1130 S County Road 150 W Brownstown (47220) *(G-1183)*

Codeweld Inc 317 784-4140
   905 E Edgewood Ave Indianapolis (46227) *(G-6629)*

Codybro LLC 765 827-5441
   3207 Iowa Ave Connersville (47331) *(G-2044)*

Coeus Technology Inc 765 203-2304
   2701 Entp Dr Ste 230 Anderson (46013) *(G-87)*

Coffee Lomont & Moyer Inc 260 422-7825
   1205 W Main St Fort Wayne (46808) *(G-4166)*

Coffeys Custom Upholstery 812 948-8611
   610 Silver St New Albany (47150) *(G-10763)*

Coffman & Fairbanks Industries 765 458-7896
   5282 W Booth Rd Liberty (47353) *(G-9259)*

Coffman Logging 812 732-4857
   2190 Lckford Bridge Rd Sw Corydon (47112) *(G-2094)*

Cognex Corporation 317 867-5079
   804 Allen Ct Westfield (46074) *(G-14144)*

Coil Tran Corp (PA) 219 942-8511
   160 S Illinois St Hobart (46342) *(G-6076)*

Cola Voce Music Inc 317 466-0624
   4600 Sunset Ave Indianapolis (46208) *(G-6630)*

A
L
P
H
A
B
E
T
I
C

Colbin Tool Company Inc 574 457-3183
1021 N Indiana Ave Syracuse (46567) ***(G-13130)***
Colby L Stanger 574 536-5835
15504 County Road 42 Goshen (46528) ***(G-5190)***
Cold Craft Brewing LLC 314 712-0883
424 Lane St North Judson (46366) ***(G-11210)***
Cold Heading Co 260 495-7003
900 S Cassell St Fremont (46737) ***(G-4955)***
Cold Heading Co 260 587-3231
103 W State Road 4 Hudson (46747) ***(G-6132)***
Cold Heading Co 260 495-4222
401 E Sidel St Fremont (46737) ***(G-4956)***
Coleman Cable LLC 574 546-5115
1115 W North St Bremen (46506) ***(G-990)***
Coleman Cable LLC 765 449-7227
3400 Union St Lafayette (47905) ***(G-8875)***
Coleman Sawmill Supply 812 865-4001
260 S 6th St Orleans (47452) ***(G-11361)***
Collective Press Inc 812 325-1385
401 W 6th St Ste J Bloomington (47404) ***(G-701)***
College Network Inc (PA) 800 395-3276
3815 River Crossing Pkwy # 260 Indianapolis (46240) ***(G-6631)***
Collegiate Pride Inc 260 726-7818
807 N Meridian St Portland (47371) ***(G-11812)***
Collier Pubg & Consulting 317 513-8176
5351 E Thompson Rd # 227 Indianapolis (46237) ***(G-6632)***
Collier's Glass Block Windows, South Bend *Also called Colliers Glassblock Inc* ***(G-12738)***
Colliers Glassblock Inc 574 288-8682
824 Park Ave South Bend (46616) ***(G-12738)***
Collins Caviar Company 269 231-5100
113 York St Michigan City (46360) ***(G-9775)***
Collins Tool & Die Inc 812 273-4765
2902 Wilson Ave Madison (47250) ***(G-9453)***
Collins Trailers Inc 574 294-2561
1053 Middleton Run Rd Elkhart (46516) ***(G-2762)***
Colluci Construction-Log Homes 812 843-5607
10591 Oriental Rd English (47118) ***(G-3312)***
Colonial Baking Co Inc 812 232-4466
660 N 1st St Terre Haute (47807) ***(G-13213)***
Colony Bay Cond Owners 260 436-4764
2118 Bayside Ct Apt A Fort Wayne (46804) ***(G-4167)***
Color Glo 812 926-2639
5083 Country Hills Dr Aurora (47001) ***(G-375)***
Color Master Inc (PA) 260 868-2320
810 S Broadway St Butler (46721) ***(G-1226)***
Color-Box LLC 765 983-7618
1056 Industries Rd Richmond (47374) ***(G-11971)***
Color-Box LLC (HQ) 765 966-7588
623 S G St Richmond (47374) ***(G-11972)***
Colorcon Inc 317 545-6211
3702 E 21st St Indianapolis (46218) ***(G-6633)***
Colorcon Inc 317 545-6211
6585 E 30th St Indianapolis (46219) ***(G-6634)***
Colorcon Inc 317 545-6211
6585 E 30th St Indianapolis (46219) ***(G-6635)***
Colorimetric, Elkhart *Also called Cast Products LP* ***(G-2751)***
Colorimetric Inc 574 255-9619
1711 Clover Rd Mishawaka (46545) ***(G-10019)***
Colormax Digital Imaging Inc (PA) 812 477-3805
626 Court St Evansville (47708) ***(G-3422)***
Colormax Imaging, Evansville *Also called Colormax Digital Imaging Inc* ***(G-3422)***
Colorworks, Indianapolis *Also called Gammons Metal & Mfg Co Inc* ***(G-6982)***
Columbia City Mill Service, Columbia City *Also called Butler Mill Service Company* ***(G-1769)***
Columbia City Ready Mix, Columbia City *Also called Speedway Redi Mix Inc* ***(G-1836)***
Columbian Home Products LLC 812 238-5041
1600 Beech St Terre Haute (47804) ***(G-13214)***
Columbus Canvas LLC 812 376-9414
8395 W State Road 46 Columbus (47201) ***(G-1874)***
Columbus Cstm Cbinets Furn LLC 812 379-9411
4475 Middle Rd Columbus (47203) ***(G-1875)***
Columbus Embroidery 812 273-0860
617 Green Rd Madison (47250) ***(G-9454)***
Columbus Engineering Inc 812 342-1231
6600 S 50 W Columbus (47201) ***(G-1876)***
Columbus Industrial Electric 812 372-8414
1625 N Indianapolis Rd Columbus (47201) ***(G-1877)***
Columbus Optical Service Inc 812 372-2678
2475 Cottage Ave Columbus (47201) ***(G-1878)***
Columbus Paint Supply 812 375-1118
3800 W C Folger Dr 150 Columbus (47201) ***(G-1879)***
Columbus Pallet Corporation 812 372-7272
1520 14th St Columbus (47201) ***(G-1880)***
Columbus Signs 812 376-7877
4540 E State St Columbus (47201) ***(G-1881)***
Columbus Vault Co 812 372-3210
3100 S Us Highway 31 Columbus (47201) ***(G-1882)***
Columbus Wholesale Optical, Columbus *Also called Columbus Optical Service Inc* ***(G-1878)***
Colwell Inc (HQ) 260 347-1981
2605 Marion Dr Kendallville (46755) ***(G-8464)***
Colwell Inc 260 347-1981
231 S Progress Dr E Kendallville (46755) ***(G-8465)***
Com-Tech Plastics Inc (PA) 812 421-3600
15000 Highway 41 N Evansville (47725) ***(G-3423)***
Com-Tech Plastics Inc 812 423-8270
9 N Kentucky Ave Evansville (47711) ***(G-3424)***
Combined Technologies Inc 574 251-4968
3620 W Mcgill St South Bend (46628) ***(G-12739)***
Combustion and Systems Inc 859 814-8847
116 N Walnut St Rising Sun (47040) ***(G-12086)***
Comcast, Muncie *Also called Ken-Bar Tool & Engineering Inc* ***(G-10503)***
Comcast Spotlight 317 502-5098
8415 Allison Pointe Blvd # 500 Indianapolis (46250) ***(G-6636)***
Comcast Spotlight Muncie 765 216-1728
420 W Washington St Muncie (47305) ***(G-10446)***
Comfort Quarters Conversions 574 262-3701
3507 Cooper Dr Elkhart (46514) ***(G-2763)***
Comfycaps By Cindy 269 683-6881
1825 Rainbow Bend Blvd Elkhart (46514) ***(G-2764)***
Comhar LLC 812 399-2123
3660 Security Pkwy New Albany (47150) ***(G-10764)***
Commercial Barge Line Company (HQ) 812 288-0100
1701 E Market St Jeffersonville (47130) ***(G-8341)***
Commercial Coatings Assoc LLC 812 483-5130
800 E Oregon St Evansville (47711) ***(G-3425)***
Commercial Electric Co Inc 260 726-9357
600 E Votaw St Portland (47371) ***(G-11813)***
Commercial Finishing Corp 317 267-0377
7199 English Ave Indianapolis (46219) ***(G-6637)***
Commercial Group Lifting Pdts 219 944-7200
1601 Cline Ave Gary (46406) ***(G-5039)***
Commercial Laundry Equipment 317 856-1234
5560 W Ralston Rd Indianapolis (46221) ***(G-6638)***
Commercial Pallet Recycl Inc (PA) 260 829-1021
5235 N State Road 327 Orland (46776) ***(G-11347)***
Commercial Print Shop Inc 260 724-3722
210 S 2nd St Decatur (46733) ***(G-2373)***
Commercial Printing of Lagro 260 782-2421
400 Clinton St Lagro (46941) ***(G-9072)***
Commercial Printing Service, Connersville *Also called Tatman Inc* ***(G-2075)***
Commercial Review, The, Portland *Also called Graphic Printing Co Inc* ***(G-11825)***
Commercial School of Lettering, Fort Wayne *Also called Commercial Signs* ***(G-4168)***
Commercial Signs 260 745-2678
513 E Hawthorne St Fort Wayne (46806) ***(G-4168)***
Commercial Star Inc 765 386-2800
4170 S State Road 75 Coatesville (46121) ***(G-1747)***
Commercial Structures Corp (PA) 574 773-7931
655 N Tomahawk Trl Nappanee (46550) ***(G-10661)***
Commercial Structures Corp 574 773-7931
65213 County Road 31 Goshen (46528) ***(G-5191)***
Commercial Technical Svcs Inc 260 436-9898
2809 Carrington Dr Fort Wayne (46804) ***(G-4169)***
Commodore Corporation 574 534-3067
1902 Century Dr Goshen (46528) ***(G-5192)***
Commodore Home Systems, Goshen *Also called Commodore Corporation* ***(G-5192)***
Common Sense Producing LLC 317 622-1682
1041 N Village Greene Dr Greenfield (46140) ***(G-5515)***
Commtineo LLC 219 476-3667
10525 W Us Highway 30 4c Wanatah (46390) ***(G-13822)***
Community Diagnostic Center 219 836-4599
10020 Don S Powers Dr Munster (46321) ***(G-10601)***
Community Healtcare System, Munster *Also called Community Diagnostic Center* ***(G-10601)***
Community Holdings Indiana Inc 765 622-1212
1133 Jackson St Anderson (46016) ***(G-88)***
Community Holdings Indiana Inc 574 722-5000
517 E Broadway Logansport (46947) ***(G-9332)***
Community Holdings Indiana Inc 317 272-5800
8109 Kingston St Ste 500 Avon (46123) ***(G-436)***
Community Holdings Indiana Inc 812 934-4343
475 N Huntersville Rd Batesville (47006) ***(G-497)***
Community Holdings Indiana Inc 765 932-2222
315 N Main St Rushville (46173) ***(G-12218)***
Community Holdings Indiana Inc 765 482-4650
117 E Washington St Lebanon (46052) ***(G-9175)***
Community Holdings Indiana Inc 765 459-3121
300 N Union St Kokomo (46901) ***(G-8608)***
Community Holdings Indiana Inc 317 873-6397
117 E Washington St Lebanon (46052) ***(G-9176)***
Community Holdings Indiana Inc 812 663-3111
135 S Franklin St Greensburg (47240) ***(G-5594)***
Community Media Group, Kentland *Also called Newton County Enterprises Inc* ***(G-8522)***
Community Papers Inc 317 241-7363
608 S Vine St Indianapolis (46241) ***(G-6639)***
Community Shopper, Fortville *Also called Big E Publications Inc* ***(G-4768)***
Community Vault Inc 574 255-3033
1120 N Merrifield Ave Mishawaka (46545) ***(G-10020)***
Companion Diagnostics Inc 860 227-9028
8206 Rockville Rd # 282 Indianapolis (46214) ***(G-6640)***

Company Pride Shirts LLC 812 526-5700
  8136 W 1200 S Edinburgh (46124) (G-2601)
Compassionate Procedures LLC 317 259-4656
  8140 Morningside Dr Indianapolis (46240) (G-6641)
Competition TI Engrg line Inc 812 524-1991
  2600 Montgomery Dr Seymour (47274) (G-12438)
Competitive Designs Inc 574 223-9406
  4477 Deere Trail Ct Rochester (46975) (G-12118)
Competitive Pallet Service, Jeffersonville Also called Ernest A Cooper (G-8357)
Complete Controls Inc 260 489-0852
  3923 Option Pass Fort Wayne (46818) (G-4170)
Complete Drives Inc (PA) 260 489-6033
  6419 Discount Dr Fort Wayne (46818) (G-4171)
Complete Finish Inc 260 587-3588
  200 S Parker Dr Ashley (46705) (G-284)
Complete Lumber Inc (PA) 812 473-6400
  5625 Old Boonville Hwy Evansville (47715) (G-3426)
Complete Metal Fabrication Inc 812 284-4470
  200 Salem Rd Jeffersonville (47130) (G-8342)
Complete Printer Inc 574 936-9505
  1920 Jim Neu Dr Plymouth (46563) (G-11676)
Complete Printing Service, Decatur Also called Commercial Print Shop Inc (G-2373)
Complete Property Care LLC 765 288-0890
  806 W Jackson St Muncie (47305) (G-10447)
Complete Prtg Solutions Inc 812 285-9200
  2199 Hamburg Pike Jeffersonville (47130) (G-8343)
Component Machine Inc 317 635-8929
  1631 Gent Ave Indianapolis (46202) (G-6642)
Composite Designs Inc 574 453-2902
  306 School St Leesburg (46538) (G-9235)
Composite Specialties 317 852-1408
  464 Johnson Ln Ste D Brownsburg (46112) (G-1144)
Compositech Inc 800 231-6755
  5315 Walt Pl Indianapolis (46254) (G-6643)
Composites Syndicate LLC 260 484-3139
  8301 Clinton Park Dr Fort Wayne (46825) (G-4172)
Composition LLC 317 979-7214
  14048 Woodlark Dr Fishers (46038) (G-3892)
Compost Bins Pro 317 873-0555
  10000 Fox Trce Zionsville (46077) (G-14428)
Compucomics 812 876-1480
  6079 N Holly Dr Ellettsville (47429) (G-3275)
Compumark Industries Inc 219 365-0508
  9853 Northcote Ave Saint John (46373) (G-12261)
Computer Age Engineering Inc 765 674-8551
  867 E 38th St Marion (46953) (G-9518)
Computer Solutions Systems Co 812 235-9008
  19 S 6th St Ste 900 Terre Haute (47807) (G-13215)
Computer Technology 812 283-5094
  1101 Watt St Jeffersonville (47130) (G-8344)
Computrain Learning Center Inc 812 235-7419
  530 Farrington St Terre Haute (47807) (G-13216)
Comtineo, Wanatah Also called Commtineo LLC (G-13822)
Conagra Brands Inc 317 329-3700
  4300 W 62nd St Indianapolis (46268) (G-6644)
Conagra Brands Inc 402 240-5000
  7579 Georgetown Rd Indianapolis (46268) (G-6645)
Conagra Brands Inc 765 563-3182
  162 E 900 S Brookston (47923) (G-1103)
Conagra Brands Inc 317 329-3700
  4300 W 62nd St Indianapolis (46268) (G-6646)
Conagra Brands Inc 740 387-2722
  750 E Drexel Pkwy Rensselaer (47978) (G-11918)
Conagra Brands Inc 219 866-3020
  750 E Drexel Pkwy Rensselaer (47978) (G-11919)
Conagra Dairy Foods Company 317 329-3700
  4300 W 62nd St Indianapolis (46268) (G-6647)
Concannons Pastry Shop 765 288-8551
  620 N Walnut St Muncie (47305) (G-10448)
Concept Cabinet Shop (PA) 317 272-7430
  7599 E Us Highway 36 Avon (46123) (G-437)
Concept Cars Inc 260 668-7553
  1280 N 290 W Angola (46703) (G-204)
Concept Prints Inc 317 290-1222
  6707 Guion Rd Indianapolis (46268) (G-6648)
Concept Tool & Engineering 812 352-0055
  508 5th St North Vernon (47265) (G-11249)
Concepts In Stone & Tile Inc 574 267-4712
  118 N Buffalo St Warsaw (46580) (G-13859)
Concord Realstate Corp 765 423-5555
  308 Erie St Lafayette (47904) (G-8876)
Concord Window Manufacturing, Lafayette Also called Concord Realstate Corp (G-8876)
Concrete & Asphalt Recycl Inc (HQ) 574 237-1928
  2010 Went Ave Mishawaka (46545) (G-10021)
Concrete Lady Inc (PA) 812 256-2765
  4910 Highway 3 Otisco (47163) (G-11416)
Concrete Pumping Michiana LLC 574 936-2140
  16200 Lincoln Hwy Plymouth (46563) (G-11677)
Concrete Supply LLC (PA) 812 474-6715
  4300 Vogel Rd Evansville (47715) (G-3427)

Coneqtec Corp 812 446-4055
  128 Ne 1st St Carbon (47837) (G-1292)
Confectionery Products Mfg Inc 317 269-7363
  1725 S Franklin Rd Ste A Indianapolis (46239) (G-6649)
Conforma Clad Inc 812 948-2118
  501 Park East Blvd New Albany (47150) (G-10765)
Conger Signs, Jeffersonville Also called Wendell Conger (G-8441)
Conley Welding Specialties Inc 260 343-9051
  605 S Orchard St Kendallville (46755) (G-8466)
Conmoto Enterprises Inc 219 787-1622
  6226 Graham Rd Indianapolis (46220) (G-6650)
Conn-Selmer Inc (HQ) 574 522-1675
  600 Industrial Pkwy Elkhart (46516) (G-2765)
Conn-Selmer Inc 574 522-1675
  2415 Industrial Pkwy Elkhart (46516) (G-2766)
Conn-Selmer Inc 574 295-6730
  500 Industrial Pkwy Elkhart (46516) (G-2767)
Conn-Selmer Inc 574 295-0079
  1000 Industrial Pkwy Elkhart (46516) (G-2768)
Connecta Corporation 317 923-9282
  3363 Boulevard Pl Indianapolis (46208) (G-6651)
Connecticut Electric Inc (PA) 800 730-2557
  1819 W 38th St Anderson (46013) (G-89)
Connection LLC 260 593-3999
  211 W Lake St Topeka (46571) (G-13413)
Connections Sign Language Inte 812 491-6036
  417 N Weinbach Ave # 107 Evansville (47711) (G-3428)
Connectronics, Edinburgh Also called Edinburgh Connector Company (G-2611)
Conner Saw Mill, Walton Also called Conner Sawmill Inc (G-13815)
Conner Sawmill Inc 574 626-3227
  300 North St Walton (46994) (G-13815)
Connies Satin Stitch 219 942-1887
  829 E 3rd St Hobart (46342) (G-6077)
Conopco Inc 219 659-3200
  1200 Calumet Ave Hammond (46320) (G-5864)
Conover Custom Fabrication Inc 317 784-1904
  2625 S Pennsylvania St Indianapolis (46225) (G-6652)
Conrad Machine Co Inc 574 259-1190
  926 E Mckinley Ave Mishawaka (46545) (G-10022)
Consolidated Nutrition Lc 574 773-4131
  301 S Jackson St Nappanee (46550) (G-10662)
Consolidated Pipe & Valve 574 262-3758
  53903 Juanita Dr Elkhart (46514) (G-2769)
Consolidated Printing Svcs Inc 765 468-6033
  201 E Henry St Farmland (47340) (G-3841)
Consolidated Recycling Co Inc (PA) 812 547-7951
  11210 Solomon Rd Troy (47588) (G-13446)
Constellation Mold Inc 812 424-5338
  4825 Hitch Peters Rd Evansville (47711) (G-3429)
Contact Concealment, La Porte Also called Shadowhouse Jiu-Jitsu Inc (G-8819)
Contact Fabricators Ind Inc 765 779-4125
  4449 N County Road 950 W Shirley (47384) (G-12661)
Contact Products Inc 219 838-1911
  8736 Schreiber Dr Munster (46321) (G-10602)
Container Life Cycle MGT LLC 317 357-9853
  3619 Terrace Ave Indianapolis (46203) (G-6653)
Container Service Corp 574 232-7474
  2811 Viridian Dr South Bend (46628) (G-12740)
Containmed Inc (PA) 317 487-8800
  1404 Main St Speedway (46224) (G-13011)
Containment Tech Group Inc (PA) 317 862-5945
  5460 Victory Dr Ste 300 Indianapolis (46203) (G-6654)
Contech Engnered Solutions LLC 317 407-4914
  10130 Bahamas Cir Fishers (46037) (G-3893)
Contech Engnered Solutions LLC 317 842-7766
  7164 Graham Rd Ste 120 Indianapolis (46250) (G-6655)
Contech Engnered Solutions LLC 812 849-3933
  Metric Industrial Park Mitchell (47446) (G-10159)
Contech Engnered Solutions LLC 812 849-3933
  200 John R Williams Ave Mitchell (47446) (G-10160)
Contego International Inc (PA) 574 223-5989
  1013 Arthur St Rochester (46975) (G-12119)
Continental Carbonic Pdts Inc 317 784-3311
  4140 Cashard Ave Indianapolis (46203) (G-6656)
Continental Carbonic Pdts Inc 574 273-2800
  4075 Ralph Jones Dr South Bend (46628) (G-12741)
Continental Diamond Tool Corp 260 493-1294
  1221 Hartzell St New Haven (46774) (G-10935)
Continental Enterprises Inc 260 447-7000
  6723 Hanna St Fort Wayne (46816) (G-4173)
Continental Express 574 294-5684
  2904 Half Hammond Ave Elkhart (46516) (G-2770)
Continental Industries Inc (PA) 574 262-4511
  100 W Windsor Ave Elkhart (46514) (G-2771)
Continental Machining Products 219 474-5061
  306 S 3rd St Kentland (47951) (G-8518)
Continental Manufacturing LLC 765 778-9999
  1524 Jackson St Anderson (46016) (G-90)
Continental Register Co, Elkhart Also called Continental Industries Inc (G-2771)

A
L
P
H
A
B
E
T
I
C

Continental Strl Plas Inc 260 355-4011
  1890 Riverfork Dr Huntington (46750) *(G-6199)*
Continental Strl Plas Inc 260 627-0890
  13811 Roth Rd Grabill (46741) *(G-5361)*
Continntal Broadcast Group LLC 317 924-1071
  1800 N Meridian St # 605 Indianapolis (46202) *(G-6657)*
Continntal Crpntry Cmpnnts LLC 219 369-4839
  9702 W Us Highway 30 Wanatah (46390) *(G-13823)*
Continuum Games Incorporated 877 405-2662
  221 S Franklin Rd Indianapolis (46219) *(G-6658)*
Contour Hardening Inc 317 876-1530
  8227 Northwest Blvd # 130 Indianapolis (46278) *(G-6659)*
Contour Hardening Inc (PA) 888 867-2184
  8401 Northwest Blvd Indianapolis (46278) *(G-6660)*
Contract Indus Tooling Inc (PA) 765 966-1134
  2351 Production Ct Richmond (47374) *(G-11973)*
Control Consultants of America (PA) 219 989-3311
  3800 179th St Hammond (46323) *(G-5865)*
Control Development Inc 574 288-7338
  2633 Foundation Dr South Bend (46628) *(G-12742)*
Control Solutions, Greenfield *Also called Schneder Elc Bldngs Amrcas Inc (G-5571)*
Control Solutions 765 313-1984
  221 Timbercrest Rd West Lafayette (47906) *(G-14060)*
Controlled Automation Inc 317 770-3870
  15421 Stony Creek Way A Noblesville (46060) *(G-11084)*
Conversion Components Inc 574 264-4181
  2605 Decio Dr Elkhart (46514) *(G-2772)*
Conversions By Bearcat, Goshen *Also called Bearcat Corp (G-5177)*
Convertastep LLC 260 969-8645
  4654 E Markle Rd Markle (46770) *(G-9576)*
Converto Mfg Co Inc 765 478-3205
  220 S Green St Cambridge City (47327) *(G-1254)*
Conzer Security Inc 317 580-9460
  231 1st Ave Sw Carmel (46032) *(G-1342)*
Cook Aircraft Leasing Inc 812 339-2044
  750 N Daniels Way Bloomington (47404) *(G-702)*
Cook Biodevice LLC 800 265-0945
  500 W Simpson Chapel Rd Bloomington (47404) *(G-703)*
Cook Compression Inc 502 515-6900
  2540 Centennial Blvd Jeffersonville (47130) *(G-8345)*
Cook Endoscopy, Bloomington *Also called Cook Incorporated (G-705)*
Cook Group Incorporated (PA) 812 339-2235
  750 N Daniels Way Bloomington (47404) *(G-704)*
Cook Group Incorporated 812 331-1025
  6300 N Matthews Dr Ellettsville (47429) *(G-3276)*
Cook Incorporated (HQ) 812 339-2235
  750 N Daniels Way Bloomington (47404) *(G-705)*
Cook Incorporated 812 339-2235
  6600 W Mcneely St Ellettsville (47429) *(G-3277)*
Cook Incorporated 812 829-4891
  1100 W Morgan St Spencer (47460) *(G-13020)*
Cook Incorporated 812 876-7790
  750 N Daniels Way Bloomington (47404) *(G-706)*
Cook Medical, Ellettsville *Also called Cook Group Incorporated (G-3276)*
Cook Medical LLC 812 339-2235
  400 N Daniels Way Bloomington (47404) *(G-707)*
Cook Pharmica LLC, Bloomington *Also called Catalent Indiana LLC (G-697)*
Cook Polymer Technology, Bloomington *Also called Sabin Corporation (G-820)*
Cook Urological, Spencer *Also called Cook Incorporated (G-13020)*
Cook Urological, Spencer *Also called Vance Products Incorporated (G-13041)*
Cooks Fabrication Inc 317 782-1722
  6011 E Hanna Ave Ste H Indianapolis (46203) *(G-6661)*
Cool Cayenne LLC 765 282-0977
  1701 W Jackson St Muncie (47303) *(G-10449)*
Cool Planet Awning Co, Indianapolis *Also called Cool Planet LLC (G-6662)*
Cool Planet LLC 317 927-9000
  340 S Mitthoeffer Rd Indianapolis (46229) *(G-6662)*
Cool-Shirts Inc 317 826-1674
  7654 Geist Estates Cir Indianapolis (46236) *(G-6663)*
Coomer & Sons Sawmill & Pallet 765 659-2846
  184 Roy Scott Pkwy Frankfort (46041) *(G-4824)*
Cooper-Standard Automotive Inc 260 925-0700
  725 W 15th St Auburn (46706) *(G-322)*
Cooper-Standard Automotive Inc 260 637-5824
  725 W 11th St Auburn (46706) *(G-323)*
Cooper-Standard Automotive Inc 260 925-0700
  207 S West St Auburn (46706) *(G-324)*
Cooper-Standard Automotive Inc 260 593-2156
  324 Morrow St Topeka (46571) *(G-13414)*
Cooper-Standard Automotive Inc 574 546-5938
  501 High Rd Bremen (46506) *(G-991)*
Cooperative Ventures Ind Corp 317 259-7063
  11550 N Meridian St # 180 Carmel (46032) *(G-1343)*
Cope Brothers Machine Shop 219 663-5561
  5301 E State Rd 231 Leroy (46355) *(G-9247)*
Copia Vineyards and Winery LLC 805 835-6094
  435 Virginia Ave Unit 707 Indianapolis (46203) *(G-6664)*
Copper Box, The, Jasper *Also called Helming Bros Inc (G-8254)*

Copper Brass Sale 574 295-3100
  3500 Charlotte Ave Elkhart (46517) *(G-2773)*
Copper Kettle Fudge LLC 260 417-1036
  4714 Union Chapel Rd Fort Wayne (46845) *(G-4174)*
Copper Smith Electric 260 849-4299
  992 W 700 S Berne (46711) *(G-610)*
Coppes Nappanee Co, Nappanee *Also called Coppes-Nappanee Company Inc (G-10663)*
Coppes-Nappanee Company Inc 574 773-0007
  401 E Market St Ste Xx Nappanee (46550) *(G-10663)*
Copy Quick, Fort Wayne *Also called Classic Graphics Inc (G-4156)*
Copy Solutions Inc 260 436-2679
  5928 W Jefferson Blvd Fort Wayne (46804) *(G-4175)*
Copy-Print Shop Inc 765 447-6868
  627 S Earl Ave Ste A Lafayette (47904) *(G-8877)*
Copyfire Typesetting Inc 317 894-0408
  1513 Touchstone Dr Indianapolis (46239) *(G-6665)*
Copymat Service Inc 765 743-5995
  135 S Chauncey Ave Lafayette (47906) *(G-8878)*
Cor-A-Vent Inc (PA) 574 255-1910
  2529 Lincolnway W Mishawaka (46544) *(G-10023)*
Cor-A-Vent Inc. 574 258-6161
  945 E 6th St Mishawaka (46544) *(G-10024)*
Coram USA LLC 260 451-8200
  6911 Innov Blvd Summi Par Summit Park Ii Fort Wayne (46818) *(G-4176)*
Corbett Phrmceuticals Dvcs LLC 765 513-0674
  7101 Red Lake Ct Indianapolis (46217) *(G-6666)*
Corbetts Custom Cabinetry LLC 812 670-6211
  6104 Carr Cir Jeffersonville (47130) *(G-8346)*
Corby Publishing LP 574 229-1107
  11961 Tyler Rd Lakeville (46536) *(G-9094)*
Core Biologic LLC 888 390-8838
  3201 Stellhorn Rd Fort Wayne (46815) *(G-4177)*
Core Laboratories LP 260 312-0455
  1726 Saint Joe River Dr Fort Wayne (46805) *(G-4178)*
Core Minerals Operating Co Inc 812 759-6950
  25 Nw Riverside Dr # 300 Evansville (47708) *(G-3430)*
Core Resources LLC 812 829-2240
  150 S Montgomery St Spencer (47460) *(G-13021)*
Core Wood Components LLC 574 370-4457
  612 Kollar St Elkhart (46514) *(G-2774)*
Core-Tech Inc 260 748-4477
  6000 Maumee Rd Fort Wayne (46803) *(G-4179)*
Corebiologic LLC 260 437-0353
  4415 Winding Brook Rd Fort Wayne (46814) *(G-4180)*
Coriant Operations Inc 219 785-1737
  3393 S Coulter Creek Dr La Porte (46350) *(G-8745)*
Cork Medical LLC 317 361-4651
  8000 Castleway Dr Indianapolis (46250) *(G-6667)*
Corn Island Shipyard Inc 812 362-8808
  9447 Indiana 66 Grandview (47615) *(G-5386)*
Cornelius Manufacturing Inc 812 636-4319
  5344 E 1250 N Elnora (47529) *(G-3288)*
Cornelius Printed Products Inc 317 923-1340
  1002 E 25th St Indianapolis (46205) *(G-6668)*
Corner Cabinet 317 859-6336
  405 E Main St Greenwood (46143) *(G-5676)*
Cornerstone Business Prtg LLC 574 642-4060
  510 Skyview Dr Middlebury (46540) *(G-9877)*
Cornerstone Cabinetry LLC 574 250-2690
  15510 Cleveland Rd Granger (46530) *(G-5397)*
Cornerstone Communications Inc 317 802-0107
  8910 Purdue Rd Ste 750 Indianapolis (46268) *(G-6669)*
Cornerstone Expediting LLC 317 893-2891
  7730 Gordon Way Indianapolis (46237) *(G-6670)*
Cornerstone Flooring & Lining, Brownsburg *Also called Cornerstone Industries Corp (G-1145)*
Cornerstone Industries Corp (PA) 317 852-6522
  8781 Motorsports Way Brownsburg (46112) *(G-1145)*
Cornerstone Mill Work 260 357-0754
  106 N Randolph St Garrett (46738) *(G-4998)*
Cornerstone Moulding Inc 574 546-4249
  1586 3rd Rd Bremen (46506) *(G-992)*
Cornerstone Woods Alpaca LLC 574 546-4179
  988 Elm Rd Bremen (46506) *(G-993)*
Coronado Stone Inc 812 284-2845
  4306 Charlestown Pike Jeffersonville (47130) *(G-8347)*
Corporate Office, Brazil *Also called Indiana Oxide Corporation (G-965)*
Corporate Packaging Solutions, Westfield *Also called Cps Inc (G-14147)*
Corporate Printing, Zionsville *Also called Mid West Digital Express Inc (G-14449)*
Corporate Shirts Direct Inc 317 474-6033
  2141 Holiday Ln Franklin (46131) *(G-4877)*
Corporate Systems Engrg LLC 317 322-7984
  1215 Brookville Way Indianapolis (46239) *(G-6671)*
Corporation Bonnier, Indianapolis *Also called Bonnier Corporation (G-6495)*
Corr-Wood Manufacturing Inc 812 867-0700
  10501 Hedden Rd Evansville (47725) *(G-3431)*
Correct Construction, Portage *Also called GI Properties Inc (G-11765)*
Corrosion Technologies Inc 317 894-0627
  6268 W Stoner Dr Ste C Greenfield (46140) *(G-5516)*

(G-0000) Company's Geographic Section entry number

Corrquest Automation Inc 812 596-0049
2060 Highway 335 Ne Crandall (47114) *(G-2124)*

Corrugated Packaging Systems 317 848-0000
17435 Tiller St Westfield (46074) *(G-14145)*

Corsair Graphics 219 938-8317
1038 E 11th Ct Gary (46403) *(G-5040)*

Cortex Safety Technologies LLC 317 414-5607
421 S Rangeline Rd Carmel (46032) *(G-1344)*

Corvano LLC 317 403-0471
11309 Guy St Fishers (46038) *(G-3894)*

Corydon Machine & Tool Co Inc 812 738-3107
615 Quarry Rd Nw Corydon (47112) *(G-2095)*

Corydon Stone & Asphalt Inc 812 738-2216
1100 Quarry Rd Nw Corydon (47112) *(G-2096)*

Corydon Stone and Asphalt, Corydon *Also called Goh A&C Inc* *(G-2099)*

Cosco Home & Office Pdts Div, Columbus *Also called Dorel Juvenile Group Inc* *(G-1912)*

Cosco Inc 812 372-0141
2525 State St Columbus (47201) *(G-1883)*

Cosmoprof 317 897-0124
9455 E Washington St Indianapolis (46229) *(G-6672)*

Cosmos Superior Foods LLC 317 975-2747
1020 3rd Ave Sw Bldg A Carmel (46032) *(G-1345)*

Cosner Ice Company Inc 812 279-8930
2404 U St Bedford (47421) *(G-535)*

Costume Delights, Ellettsville *Also called Higgins Dyan* *(G-3281)*

Costumes By Margie By Cher, Indianapolis *Also called Knotts and Frye Inc* *(G-7362)*

Cosworth LLC (HQ) 844 278-6941
5355 W 86th St Indianapolis (46268) *(G-6673)*

Cosworth Electronics LLC 317 808-3800
5355 W 86th St Indianapolis (46268) *(G-6674)*

Cottage Industries DBA 765 617-8360
7633 N 200 E Alexandria (46001) *(G-38)*

Cottage Industries Inc 260 482-1100
5325 Merchandise Dr Fort Wayne (46825) *(G-4181)*

Cottom Automated Bus Soluti 317 853-6531
13295 Illinois St Ste 313 Carmel (46032) *(G-1346)*

Cottonwood Corp (PA) 260 820-0415
1412 Evergreen Ct Ossian (46777) *(G-11398)*

Cottonwood Corp 260 565-3185
Rr 1 Craigville (46731) *(G-2121)*

Cottonwood Farm, Ossian *Also called Cottonwood Corp* *(G-11398)*

Couden Woodworks Inc 317 370-0835
23808 Couden Rd Noblesville (46060) *(G-11085)*

Cougar Bag Inc 317 831-9720
3310 Hancel Cir Mooresville (46158) *(G-10306)*

Counter Design Co Inc 812 477-1243
2381 N Cullen Ave Evansville (47715) *(G-3432)*

Counterfitters Inc 219 531-0848
359 Franklin St Ste C Valparaiso (46383) *(G-13523)*

Countertop Connections Inc 317 822-9858
3042 Hudson St Franklin (46131) *(G-4878)*

Countertops & More 317 346-0111
500 International Dr Franklin (46131) *(G-4879)*

Country Barn Candles LLC 812 299-2929
9835 Sable Ridge Ln Terre Haute (47802) *(G-13217)*

Country Cabin LLC 812 232-4635
5125 S Us Highway 41 Terre Haute (47802) *(G-13218)*

Country Cabinets 260 694-6777
3900 W State Road 218 Poneto (46781) *(G-11745)*

Country Charm 765 572-2588
2721 E Flint Rd Attica (47918) *(G-299)*

Country Club Computer 317 271-4000
8247 Indy Ct Indianapolis (46214) *(G-6675)*

Country Compact 574 831-6682
69594 County Road 117 New Paris (46553) *(G-10976)*

Country Components Inc 812 345-9594
8990 S Edinburgh Rd Edinburgh (46124) *(G-2602)*

Country Corner Woodworks LLC 574 825-6782
52133 State Road 13 Middlebury (46540) *(G-9878)*

Country Craftsman Wdwkg LLC 574 773-4911
8563 W 1100 N Nappanee (46550) *(G-10664)*

Country Estate Mobile Home Pk, Frankfort *Also called Paddack Brothers Inc* *(G-4849)*

Country Estates 812 925-6443
6222 Edwards Rd Boonville (47601) *(G-913)*

Country Hritg Wnery Vinyrd Inc 260 637-2980
185 County Road 68 Laotto (46763) *(G-9105)*

Country Maid, La Crosse *Also called Labraid Inc* *(G-8721)*

Country Mill Cabinet Co Inc 260 693-9289
7590 E 400 S Laotto (46763) *(G-9106)*

Country Moon Winery LLC 317 773-7942
16222 Prairie Baptist Rd Noblesville (46060) *(G-11086)*

Country Pines Inc 812 247-3315
11013 Country Pines Rd Shoals (47581) *(G-12665)*

Country Pines Printing, Shoals *Also called Country Pines Inc* *(G-12665)*

Country Sewing 260 347-9733
8929 E 1125 N Kendallville (46755) *(G-8467)*

Country Stitches Embroidery 219 324-7625
606 E 400 N La Porte (46350) *(G-8746)*

Country Stone 260 837-7134
2280 County Road 27 Waterloo (46793) *(G-14012)*

Country Stones and The Gravel, Waterloo *Also called Wilhelm Gravel Co Inc* *(G-14027)*

Country View Cabinets LLC 574 825-3150
11770 County Road 32 Goshen (46528) *(G-5193)*

Country View Furn Mfg & Uphl 812 636-5024
8659 N 1000 E Odon (47562) *(G-11321)*

Country Welding LLC 260 352-2938
11706 S 600 W Silver Lake (46982) *(G-12675)*

Country Woodcrafts Inc 260 244-7578
2283 E State Road 205 Columbia City (46725) *(G-1775)*

Country Woodshop LLC 574 642-3681
62870 County Road 43 Goshen (46528) *(G-5194)*

Country Woodworking LLC 812 636-6004
7650 E 1000 N Odon (47562) *(G-11322)*

Countrymark Coop Holdg Corp (PA) 800 808-3170
225 S East St Ste 144 Indianapolis (46202) *(G-6676)*

Countrymark Coop Holdg Corp 812 759-6962
7116 Eagle Crest Blvd Evansville (47715) *(G-3433)*

Countrymark Cooperative, Mount Vernon *Also called Countrymark Ref Logistics LLC* *(G-10388)*

Countrymark Ref Logistics LLC 812 838-4341
1200 Refinery Rd Mount Vernon (47620) *(G-10388)*

Countrymark Ref Logistics LLC 800 808-3170
225 S East St Ste 144 Indianapolis (46202) *(G-6677)*

Countryside Cabinetry LLC 765 597-2391
2881 E Lucas Rd Marshall (47859) *(G-9590)*

Countryside Printing 812 486-2454
7243 E 300 N Montgomery (47558) *(G-10218)*

Countryside Sawmill 812 486-2991
8753 E 450 N Montgomery (47558) *(G-10219)*

Countryside Tool 260 357-3839
1723 South Rd Garrett (46738) *(G-4999)*

County Line Cabinetry LLC 574 642-1202
705 N 1200 W Middlebury (46540) *(G-9879)*

County Line Companies LLC 866 959-7866
3535 N Cross 800 E Parker City (47368) *(G-11462)*

County Line Woodworking 574 935-7107
11594 N 1100 W Bremen (46506) *(G-994)*

County Materials, Seymour *Also called Lees Ready-Mix & Trucking* *(G-12466)*

County Materials Corp 317 262-4920
2050 S Harding St Indianapolis (46221) *(G-6678)*

County Materials Corp 317 323-6000
119 N Main St Maxwell (46154) *(G-9660)*

County of Lagrange 260 499-6353
300 E Factory St Lagrange (46761) *(G-9035)*

County of Steuben 260 833-2401
100 Lane 101 Crooked Lk Angola (46703) *(G-205)*

County West Sports 317 839-4076
1702 E Main St Plainfield (46168) *(G-11601)*

Countyline Marathon, Columbia City *Also called Iam Petroleum Inc* *(G-1793)*

Coupled Products LLC 260 248-3200
2651 S 600 E Columbia City (46725) *(G-1776)*

Coupled Products LLC 812 849-5304
1201 Orchard St Mitchell (47446) *(G-10161)*

Coupled Products LLC (PA) 260 248-3200
2651 S 600 E Columbia City (46725) *(G-1777)*

Courier Communications LLC 260 347-3044
2500 Marion Dr Kendallville (46755) *(G-8468)*

Courier Kendallville Inc (HQ) 260 347-3044
2500 Marion Dr Kendallville (46755) *(G-8469)*

Courier Printing, Kendallville *Also called Courier Communications LLC* *(G-8468)*

Courier Printing Co Allen Cnty 260 627-2728
13720 Main St Grabill (46741) *(G-5362)*

Courier-Times Inc 765 529-1111
201 S 14th St New Castle (47362) *(G-10897)*

Courtney Signs & Graphics Inc 317 841-3297
7535 E 71st St Indianapolis (46256) *(G-6679)*

Courtney Signs & Lighting, Indianapolis *Also called Courtney Signs & Graphics Inc* *(G-6679)*

Covalence Coated Products, Evansville *Also called Covalnce Spcialty Coatings LLC* *(G-3435)*

Covalnce Spcalty Adhesives LLC (HQ) 812 424-2904
101 Oakley St Evansville (47710) *(G-3434)*

Covalnce Spcialty Coatings LLC (HQ) 812 424-2904
101 Oakley St Evansville (47710) *(G-3435)*

Cover Care LLC 513 297-4094
17397 Oak Ridge Rd # 100 Westfield (46074) *(G-14146)*

Coverite-Custom Covers 574 278-7152
8593 N State Road 39 Monticello (47960) *(G-10258)*

Covers of Indiana Inc 317 244-0291
2906 Kentucky Ave Indianapolis (46221) *(G-6680)*

Covidien LP 317 837-8199
2824 Airwest Blvd Plainfield (46168) *(G-11602)*

Covington Products Inc 765 282-6626
112 W Fuson Rd Muncie (47302) *(G-10450)*

Cowan Systems LLC 317 241-4158
6238 W Minnesota St Indianapolis (46241) *(G-6681)*

Cowco Inc 812 346-8993
3780 S State Highway 7 North Vernon (47265) *(G-11250)*

Cowpokes Inc 765 642-3911
  1812 E 53rd St Anderson (46013) *(G-91)*

Cowpokes Western Outfitters, Anderson Also called Cowpokes Inc *(G-91)*

Cox John 765 463-6396
  140 Tamiami Ct West Lafayette (47906) *(G-14061)*

Coy & Associates 317 787-5089
  2305 E Banta Rd Indianapolis (46227) *(G-6682)*

Coy Oil Inc (PA) 812 838-3146
  7451 Sauerkraut Ln N Mount Vernon (47620) *(G-10389)*

Coy Oil Inc 618 966-2126
  7451 Sauerkraut Ln N Mount Vernon (47620) *(G-10390)*

Cozy Cat Inc 765 463-1254
  2101 Indian Trail Dr Lafayette (47906) *(G-8879)*

Cp Inc 765 825-4111
  27100 Hall Rd Connersville (47331) *(G-2045)*

CP Group Inc 765 551-7768
  867 Shawnee Ave Lafayette (47905) *(G-8880)*

CPC 812 358-5010
  811 Bloomington Rd Brownstown (47220) *(G-1184)*

Cpg - Ohio LLC 260 829-6721
  9880 W Maple St Orland (46776) *(G-11348)*

CPI AIRCRAFT INTERIORS, New Albany Also called Custom Plywood Inc *(G-10766)*

CPI Card Group - Indiana Inc 260 424-4920
  613 High St Fort Wayne (46808) *(G-4182)*

CPM Acquisition Corp 765 362-2600
  1114 E Wabash Ave Crawfordsville (47933) *(G-2142)*

CPM Conveyor LLC 765 918-5190
  5119 S Davis Bridge Rd Crawfordsville (47933) *(G-2143)*

Cpp Filter Corporation 765 446-8416
  730 Farabee Ct Lafayette (47905) *(G-8881)*

Cps Inc 317 804-2300
  17435 Tiller Ct Westfield (46074) *(G-14147)*

Cpx Inc (PA) 219 474-5280
  410 E Kent St Kentland (47951) *(G-8519)*

Cr Publications 219 931-6700
  640 Conkey St Hammond (46324) *(G-5866)*

CRA-Wal Inc 317 856-3701
  4001 S High School Rd Indianapolis (46241) *(G-6683)*

Craddock Finishing Corporation 812 425-2691
  1400 W Illinois St Evansville (47710) *(G-3436)*

Craddock Furniture, Evansville Also called Craddock Finishing Corporation *(G-3436)*

Craft Laboratories Inc 260 432-9467
  1901 Lakeview Dr Fort Wayne (46808) *(G-4183)*

Craft Metal Products Inc 317 545-3252
  2751 N Emerson Ave Indianapolis (46218) *(G-6684)*

Craftech Building Systems Inc 574 773-4167
  2676 E Market St Nappanee (46550) *(G-10665)*

Craftmark Bakery LLC 317 548-3929
  5202 Exploration Dr Indianapolis (46241) *(G-6685)*

Craftsman Lithograph, Roanoke Also called Behning Inc *(G-12099)*

Craftsnmoregalore LLC 574 303-2231
  710 W Melbourne Ave Logansport (46947) *(G-9333)*

Craig Hydraulic Enterprises 812 432-5108
  9790 Front St Dillsboro (47018) *(G-2464)*

Craig Welding and Mfg Inc 574 353-7912
  5158 N 825 E Mentone (46539) *(G-9687)*

Craigs Printing Co 812 358-5010
  811 Bloomington Rd Brownstown (47220) *(G-1185)*

Crane Composites 574 295-9391
  21067 Protecta Dr Elkhart (46516) *(G-2775)*

Crane Composites Inc 815 467-8600
  2424 E Kercher Rd Goshen (46526) *(G-5195)*

Crane Hill Machine Inc 812 358-3534
  2476 E Us Highway 50 Seymour (47274) *(G-12439)*

Crane Pro Services, Crown Point Also called Konecranes Inc *(G-2272)*

Crane Pro Services, Indianapolis Also called Konecranes Inc *(G-7366)*

Cranehill Mch & Fabrication, Seymour Also called Royalty Investments LLC *(G-12481)*

Cranewerks Inc 765 663-2909
  511 N Range Line Rd Morristown (46161) *(G-10368)*

Crankshaft Brewing Co 317 939-0138
  1630 E Northfield Dr Brownsburg (46112) *(G-1146)*

Crash Beds LLC 317 601-4436
  545 Christy Dr Ste 2101 Greenwood (46143) *(G-5677)*

Crates & Pallets, Fountaintown Also called Ash-Lin Inc *(G-4789)*

Crawal Division, Indianapolis Also called CRA-Wal Inc *(G-6683)*

Crawford County Concrete 812 739-2707
  7172 S Tower Rd Leavenworth (47137) *(G-9163)*

Crawford Industries LLC (PA) 800 428-0840
  1414 Crawford Dr Crawfordsville (47933) *(G-2144)*

Createc Corporation 317 566-0022
  6835 Guion Rd Ste A Indianapolis (46268) *(G-6686)*

Createit Hlthcare Slutions Inc 765 993-0988
  814 E Main St Ste 3 Richmond (47374) *(G-11974)*

Creations In Glass 219 326-7941
  725 Pine Lake Ave La Porte (46350) *(G-8747)*

Creative Cabinet Designs 812 637-3300
  414 White Ridge Rd Lawrenceburg (47025) *(G-9135)*

Creative Coatings, Fort Wayne Also called Creative Powder Coatings LLC *(G-4186)*

Creative Computer Services 317 729-5779
  4223 S Shelby 750 W Franklin (46131) *(G-4880)*

Creative Concept Ventures Inc 812 282-9442
  590 Missouri Ave Jeffersonville (47130) *(G-8348)*

Creative Construction Pubg 765 743-9704
  2720 S River Rd West Lafayette (47906) *(G-14062)*

Creative Control Systems 260 432-9020
  4115 Clubview Dr Fort Wayne (46804) *(G-4184)*

Creative Craftsmen Inc 812 423-2844
  5010 N Spring St Evansville (47711) *(G-3437)*

Creative Designs, Plainfield Also called R E Ferguson & Associates Inc *(G-11639)*

Creative Embroidery Designs 812 479-8280
  2545 Mjm Industrial Dr Evansville (47715) *(G-3438)*

Creative Finishing 812 591-8111
  6417 S County Road 220 Sw Greensburg (47240) *(G-5595)*

Creative Foam Corporation 574 546-4238
  405 Industrial Dr Bremen (46506) *(G-995)*

Creative Impressions Inc 317 244-9842
  6908 Carlsen Ave Indianapolis (46214) *(G-6687)*

Creative Inc 765 447-3500
  150 N 36th St Lafayette (47905) *(G-8882)*

Creative Industries Inc 317 248-1102
  1024 Western Dr Indianapolis (46241) *(G-6688)*

Creative Ldscp & Compost Co 317 776-2909
  18377 Deshane Ave Noblesville (46060) *(G-11087)*

Creative Ldscpg & Compost Co, Noblesville Also called Creative Ldscp & Compost Co *(G-11087)*

Creative Liquid Coatings Inc 260 349-1862
  2620 Marion Dr Kendallville (46755) *(G-8470)*

Creative Liquid Coatings Inc (PA) 260 349-1862
  2701 S Coliseum Blvd # 1284 Fort Wayne (46803) *(G-4185)*

Creative Logic Equipment Corp 317 271-1100
  5482 Ashurst St Indianapolis (46220) *(G-6689)*

Creative Manufacturing Rv LLC 574 333-3302
  330 E Windsor Ave Elkhart (46514) *(G-2776)*

Creative McHining Concepts Inc 317 896-9250
  17018 Westfield Park Rd Westfield (46074) *(G-14148)*

Creative Powder Coatings LLC 260 489-3580
  7505 Freedom Way Fort Wayne (46818) *(G-4186)*

Creative Publishing Concep 317 844-3549
  11614 Fairgreen Dr Carmel (46032) *(G-1347)*

Creative Solutions 219 778-4919
  3606 E Us Highway 20 Rolling Prairie (46371) *(G-12184)*

Creative Tool and Machining 812 378-3562
  4010 Middle Rd Columbus (47203) *(G-1884)*

Creative Tool Inc 260 338-1222
  2403 W Shoaff Rd Huntertown (46748) *(G-6136)*

Creative Woodworks LLC 260 450-1742
  9771 Maysville Rd Fort Wayne (46815) *(G-4187)*

Creed & Dyer Precast Inc 574 784-3361
  68186 Us Highway 31 Lakeville (46536) *(G-9095)*

Creek Chassis Inc 317 247-4480
  312 Gasoline Aly Indianapolis (46222) *(G-6690)*

Creek Motor Sports, Indianapolis Also called Creek Chassis Inc *(G-6690)*

Crenshaw Paving Inc 765 249-2342
  7304 E County Road 100 N Michigantown (46057) *(G-9865)*

Crescendo Inc 812 829-4759
  56 E Jefferson St Spencer (47460) *(G-13022)*

Crescent Oil Company Inc 317 634-1415
  1751 W Raymond St Indianapolis (46221) *(G-6691)*

Crescent Plastics Inc (PA) 812 428-9305
  955 E Diamond Ave Evansville (47711) *(G-3439)*

Crescent Plastics Inc 812 428-9300
  955 E Diamond Ave Evansville (47711) *(G-3440)*

Crescent-Cresline-Wabash Plast 812 428-9300
  600 N Cross Pointe Blvd Evansville (47715) *(G-3441)*

Cresline Plastic Pipe Co Inc (PA) 812 428-9300
  600 N Cross Pointe Blvd Evansville (47715) *(G-3442)*

Cresline-Northwest LLC (PA) 812 428-9300
  600 N Cross Pointe Blvd Evansville (47715) *(G-3443)*

Cresline-West Inc (PA) 812 428-9300
  955 E Diamond Ave Evansville (47711) *(G-3444)*

Cressy Memorial Group Inc 574 258-1800
  3925 Glaser Ct Mishawaka (46545) *(G-10025)*

Crestview Woodworking LLC 260 768-4707
  6510 W 450 N Shipshewana (46565) *(G-12609)*

Crestwood Equity Partners LP 812 265-3313
  3625 Clifty Dr Madison (47250) *(G-9455)*

Cretaceous Cures 317 379-7744
  15541 Wildflower Ln Westfield (46074) *(G-14149)*

Crichlow Industries Inc 317 925-5178
  6848 Hawthorn Park Dr Indianapolis (46220) *(G-6692)*

Crider Holcomb Partnership LLC 812 279-2200
  2611 16th St Bedford (47421) *(G-536)*

Crisman Sand Co Inc 219 762-2619
  251 Indiana Ave Valparaiso (46383) *(G-13524)*

Criterion Catalyst Technologys, Michigan City Also called Criterion Catalysts & Tech LP *(G-9776)*

Criterion Catalysts & Tech LP 219 874-6211
  1800 E Us Highway 12 Michigan City (46360) *(G-9776)*

Criterion Press Inc 317 236-1570
1400 N Meridian St Indianapolis (46202) *(G-6693)*
Critser Companies Inc 219 663-0052
120 Main St Crown Point (46307) *(G-2236)*
Crone Lumber Co Inc 765 342-1160
501 N Park Ave Martinsville (46151) *(G-9599)*
Crookedstick Sawmill LLC 317 714-8930
4546 S State Road 75 Coatesville (46121) *(G-1748)*
Crosbie Foundry Co Inc 574 262-1502
1600 Mishawaka St Elkhart (46514) *(G-2777)*
Cross Country Hardwoods LLC 812 571-4226
10071 Bill Peelman Rd Vevay (47043) *(G-13661)*
Cross Modular Set Inc 765 836-1511
4429 N Prairie Rd New Castle (47362) *(G-10898)*
Cross Printwear Inc 317 293-1776
3466 N Raceway Rd Indianapolis (46234) *(G-6694)*
Cross Rv Sales, Lagrange *Also called Indiana Interstate Entps LLC* *(G-9047)*
Crossbow Group Inc 317 603-0406
16356 Trace Blvd N Westfield (46074) *(G-14150)*
Crossing Creations 812 587-0212
6562 E 800 N Columbus (47203) *(G-1885)*
Crosspoint Polymer Tech LLC 812 426-1350
2301 St Jseph Indus Pk Dr Evansville (47720) *(G-3445)*
Crosspoint Power and Rfrgn LLC (PA) 317 240-1967
4301 W Morris St Indianapolis (46241) *(G-6695)*
Crosspoint Solutions, Indianapolis *Also called Cummins Crosspoint LLC* *(G-6707)*
Crosspower LLC 812 591-2009
1268 E County Road 1000 S Westport (47283) *(G-14209)*
Crossrads Cntrtops Cbnetry LLC 317 908-9254
604 S Audubon Rd Indianapolis (46219) *(G-6696)*
Crossrads Rhbilitation Ctr Inc 317 897-7320
8302 E 33rd St Indianapolis (46226) *(G-6697)*
Crossroads Door & Hardware Inc 812 234-9751
1301 Eagle St Terre Haute (47807) *(G-13219)*
Crossroads Galvanizing LLC 765 421-6741
4877 E Old 350 S Lafayette (47905) *(G-8883)*
Crossroads Imprints Inc 765 482-2931
107 W Main St Lebanon (46052) *(G-9177)*
Crossroads Lighting, Indianapolis *Also called Gmp Holdings LLC* *(G-7016)*
Crossroads Orthotics & Cnsltn 765 359-0041
821 S Washington St Crawfordsville (47933) *(G-2145)*
Crossroads Services Inc 219 972-3631
9200 Calumet Ave Ste 6 Munster (46321) *(G-10603)*
Crossroads Sourcing Group Ltd 847 940-4123
737 Edison Way Carmel (46032) *(G-1348)*
Crosswind Pharmaceuticals LLC 317 436-8522
9402 Uptown Dr Ste 1200 Indianapolis (46256) *(G-6698)*
Crowd Factor, Lafayette *Also called Goldden Corporation* *(G-8908)*
Crowdpixie LLC 317 578-3137
7594 Timber Springs Dr N Fishers (46038) *(G-3895)*
Crown Battery Manufacturing Co 260 423-3358
3000 E Washington Blvd Fort Wayne (46803) *(G-4188)*
Crown Bioscience Indiana Inc 317 872-6001
7918 Zionsville Rd Indianapolis (46268) *(G-6699)*
Crown Brick & Supply Inc (PA) 219 663-7880
820 Thomas St Crown Point (46307) *(G-2237)*
Crown Cab & Counter Top Inc 219 663-2725
500 Sheridan St Crown Point (46307) *(G-2238)*
Crown Coatings LLC 317 482-2766
770 E Broadway St Fortville (46040) *(G-4771)*
Crown Cork & Seal Usa Inc 765 362-3200
400 N Walnut St Crawfordsville (47933) *(G-2146)*
Crown E.S.A., Portage *Also called Crown Elec Svcs & Automtn Inc* *(G-11758)*
Crown Elec Svcs & Automtn Inc (HQ) 972 929-4700
5960 Southport Rd Portage (46368) *(G-11758)*
Crown Equipment Corporation 812 477-5511
2540 Diego Dr Evansville (47715) *(G-3446)*
Crown Equipment Corporation 574 293-1264
1125 Herman St Elkhart (46516) *(G-2778)*
Crown Equipment Corporation 765 520-2422
1817 I Ave New Castle (47362) *(G-10899)*
Crown Equipment Corporation 260 484-0055
9110 Avionics Dr Fort Wayne (46809) *(G-4189)*
Crown Equipment Corporation 765 653-4240
2600 State Rd 240 E Greencastle (46135) *(G-5456)*
Crown Equipment Corporation 317 875-7233
2495 E Perry Rd Plainfield (46168) *(G-11603)*
Crown Group Co 260 432-6900
4301 Engle Rd Fort Wayne (46804) *(G-4190)*
Crown Industries Inc 219 791-9930
10769 Broadway Crown Point (46307) *(G-2239)*
Crown Lift Trucks, Evansville *Also called Crown Equipment Corporation* *(G-3446)*
Crown Lift Trucks, Elkhart *Also called Crown Equipment Corporation* *(G-2778)*
Crown Lift Trucks, New Castle *Also called Crown Equipment Corporation* *(G-10899)*
Crown Lift Trucks, Greencastle *Also called Crown Equipment Corporation* *(G-5456)*
Crown Lift Trucks, Plainfield *Also called Crown Equipment Corporation* *(G-11603)*
Crown Lift Trucks-Ft Wayne, Fort Wayne *Also called Crown Equipment Corporation* *(G-4189)*
Crown Mtal Fbricators Erectors 219 661-8277
1031 E Summit St Crown Point (46307) *(G-2240)*
Crown Point Shopping News 219 663-4212
112 W Clark St Crown Point (46307) *(G-2241)*
Crown Products & Services Inc (PA) 317 564-4799
12821 E New M Ste 100 Carmel (46032) *(G-1349)*
Crown Supply Co Inc 812 522-6987
1191 King Ave Seymour (47274) *(G-12440)*
Crown Technology Inc 317 845-0045
7513 E 96th St Indianapolis (46256) *(G-6700)*
Crown Training & Development 219 947-0845
2642 E 84th Pl Merrillville (46410) *(G-9708)*
Croy Machine & Fabrication 260 565-3682
2744 Se Mulberry St Bluffton (46714) *(G-871)*
Cruiser Rv LLC 260 562-3500
160 W 750 N Howe (46746) *(G-6120)*
Crusaderbit Software LLC 317 773-2317
18493 Oakmont Dr Noblesville (46062) *(G-11088)*
Crusher Parts Direct LLC 812 822-1463
3905 W Farmer Ave Bloomington (47403) *(G-708)*
Crust N More Inc 317 890-7878
6815 E 34th St Indianapolis (46226) *(G-6701)*
Cryogenic Support Systems Inc 765 764-4961
1903 W State Road 63 Williamsport (47993) *(G-14288)*
Cryovac Inc 317 876-4100
7950 Allison Ave Indianapolis (46268) *(G-6702)*
Cryovac Division, Indianapolis *Also called Cryovac Inc* *(G-6702)*
Crystal Clear Inc 317 753-5393
2257 Willow Lake Dr Greenwood (46143) *(G-5678)*
Crystal Colors, South Bend *Also called Sugarpaste* *(G-12960)*
Crystal Graphics Inc 317 535-9202
530 Main St Whiteland (46184) *(G-14237)*
Crystal Healing Elements 312 623-1764
14018 Parley Ln Fishers (46038) *(G-3896)*
Crystal Industries Inc 574 264-6166
28870 Phillips St Elkhart (46514) *(G-2779)*
Crystal Lake LLC (PA) 574 267-3101
4217 W Old Road 30 Warsaw (46580) *(G-13860)*
Crystal Lake LLC 574 858-2514
6500 W Crystal Lake Rd Warsaw (46580) *(G-13861)*
Crystal Machining Inc 317 727-8984
1144 Tampico Rd Greenwood (46143) *(G-5679)*
Crystal Source (PA) 812 988-7009
150 S Old School Way Nashville (47448) *(G-10721)*
Crystal Valley Farms LLC (PA) 260 829-6550
9622 W 350 N Orland (46776) *(G-11349)*
Cs Kern Inc 765 289-8600
3401 S Hamilton Ave Muncie (47302) *(G-10451)*
Cs Technology, Terre Haute *Also called Computer Solutions Systems Co* *(G-13215)*
Csc-Indiana LLC 708 625-3255
2190 Summit St New Haven (46774) *(G-10936)*
Csd Group Inc 260 918-3500
3003 Ryan Rd New Haven (46774) *(G-10937)*
Csi, Crawfordsville *Also called Closure Systems Intl Inc* *(G-2141)*
CSI ELECTRONICS, Kokomo *Also called Electronic Services LLC* *(G-8620)*
Csi Print Supply, Indianapolis *Also called Cartridge Specialist Inc* *(G-6562)*
Csi Signs, Noblesville *Also called Chads Signs Installations Inc* *(G-11079)*
Csl Plasma Inc 260 454-5083
108 E Pettit Ave Fort Wayne (46806) *(G-4191)*
Csl Plasma Inc 317 688-5852
2750 E 46th St Indianapolis (46205) *(G-6703)*
Csl Plasma Inc 317 352-9157
5550 E Washington St Indianapolis (46219) *(G-6704)*
Csn Industries Inc 317 697-6549
571 Industrial Dr Bargersville (46106) *(G-479)*
Cspine Inc 574 936-7893
3501 Miller Dr South Bend (46634) *(G-12743)*
CT Industries LLC 574 675-9422
51622 Steeple Chase Dr Granger (46530) *(G-5398)*
CT Phoenix of Indiana Inc 812 838-2414
1600 W 4th St Mount Vernon (47620) *(G-10391)*
CTA Acoustics Inc 260 829-1030
9670 W Maple St Orland (46776) *(G-11350)*
Ctb Inc 574 658-4191
410 N Higbee St Milford (46542) *(G-9951)*
Ctb Inc (HQ) 574 658-4191
611 N Higbee St Milford (46542) *(G-9952)*
Ctb Inc 765 654-8517
1750 W State Road 28 Frankfort (46041) *(G-4825)*
Ctb Inc 574 658-9323
611 N Kigby St Milford (46542) *(G-9953)*
Ctb Inc 574 658-4191
410 N Higbee St Milford (46542) *(G-9954)*
CTB MN Investment Co Inc 765 654-8517
1750 W State Road 28 Frankfort (46041) *(G-4826)*
CTB MN Investment Co Inc (HQ) 574 658-4191
611 N Higbee St Milford (46542) *(G-9955)*
Cte Solutions, Plymouth *Also called Culver Tool & Engineering Inc* *(G-11678)*
Ctm, New Haven *Also called Challenge Tool & Mfg Inc* *(G-10934)*
Ctp Corporation 317 787-5747
2615 Endress Pl Greenwood (46143) *(G-5680)*

CTS Corporation....574 293-7511
1142 W Beardsley Ave Elkhart (46514) ***(G-2780)***
CTS Corporation....574 293-7511
406 E Parr Rd Berne (46711) ***(G-611)***
CTS Elctrnic Cmponents Cal Inc....574 523-3800
905 N West Blvd Elkhart (46514) ***(G-2781)***
Ctsi, Fort Wayne *Also called Commercial Technical Svcs Inc* ***(G-4169)***
Culligan, Muncie *Also called Driessen Water Inc* ***(G-10463)***
Cullip Industries Inc....574 293-8251
300 Comet Ave Elkhart (46514) ***(G-2782)***
Cullip Tool & Die, Elkhart *Also called Cullip Industries Inc* ***(G-2782)***
Cullman Casting Corporation....256 735-0900
3750 N County Road 75 W North Vernon (47265) ***(G-11251)***
Culpeper Wood Preservers, Shelbyville *Also called Jefferson Homebuilders Inc* ***(G-12541)***
Cultor Food Science....812 299-6700
100 Pfizer Dr Terre Haute (47802) ***(G-13220)***
Culture Media LLC....317 966-0847
5884 Lost Oaks Dr Carmel (46033) ***(G-1350)***
Culver Duck Farms Inc....574 825-9537
12215 County Road 10 Middlebury (46540) ***(G-9880)***
Culver Tool & Engineering Inc....574 935-9611
1901 Walter Glaub Dr Plymouth (46563) ***(G-11678)***
Culvers Port Side Marina....574 223-5090
1409 Wentzel St Rochester (46975) ***(G-12120)***
Cummins....812 524-6381
845 A Ave E Seymour (47274) ***(G-12441)***
Cummins - Allison Corp....317 872-6244
5696 W 74th St Indianapolis (46278) ***(G-6705)***
Cummins Americas Inc (HQ)....812 377-5000
500 Jackson St Columbus (47201) ***(G-1886)***
Cummins Crosspoint LLC (HQ)....317 243-7979
2601 Fortune Cir E 300c Indianapolis (46241) ***(G-6706)***
Cummins Crosspoint LLC....812 867-4400
7901 Highway 41 N Evansville (47725) ***(G-3447)***
Cummins Crosspoint LLC....317 244-7251
3621 W Morris St Indianapolis (46241) ***(G-6707)***
Cummins Crosspoint LLC....574 252-2154
3025 N Home St Mishawaka (46545) ***(G-10026)***
Cummins Crosspoint LLC....317 484-2146
4557 W Bradbury Ave Ste 3 Indianapolis (46241) ***(G-6708)***
Cummins Crosspoint LLC....260 482-3691
3415 W Coliseum Blvd Fort Wayne (46808) ***(G-4192)***
Cummins Digital Ventures Inc....812 377-5000
500 Jackson St Columbus (47201) ***(G-1887)***
Cummins Dist Holdco Inc (HQ)....812 377-5000
500 Jackson St Columbus (47201) ***(G-1888)***
Cummins Emission Solutions Inc (HQ)....608 987-3206
500 Jackson St Columbus (47201) ***(G-1889)***
Cummins Engine, Columbus *Also called Cummins Americas Inc* ***(G-1886)***
Cummins Engine Holding Co Inc....812 377-5000
500 Jackson St Columbus (47201) ***(G-1890)***
Cummins Engine Service....260 657-1436
20329 Notestine Rd Woodburn (46797) ***(G-14382)***
Cummins Inc (PA)....812 377-5000
500 Jackson St Columbus (47201) ***(G-1891)***
Cummins Inc....812 377-0150
2879 Prairie Stream Way Columbus (47203) ***(G-1892)***
Cummins Inc....812 377-6072
1460 N National Rd Columbus (47201) ***(G-1893)***
Cummins Inc....812 377-8601
2851 State St Columbus (47201) ***(G-1894)***
Cummins Inc....812 377-2932
910 S Marr Rd Columbus (47201) ***(G-1895)***
Cummins Inc....812 524-6455
1825 W 450 S Columbus (47201) ***(G-1896)***
Cummins Inc....812 374-4774
3540 W 450 S Columbus (47201) ***(G-1897)***
Cummins Inc....317 244-7251
3621 W Morris St Indianapolis (46241) ***(G-6709)***
Cummins Inc....765 430-0093
525 Jackson St Columbus (47201) ***(G-1898)***
Cummins Inc....317 610-2493
301 E Market St Indianapolis (46204) ***(G-6710)***
Cummins Inc....812 522-9366
800 E 3rd St Seymour (47274) ***(G-12442)***
Cummins Inc....812 377-7000
1900 Mckinley Ave Columbus (47201) ***(G-1899)***
Cummins Midwest Regional Dist (PA)....901 302-8143
4820 S Indianapolis Rd Whitestown (46075) ***(G-14251)***
Cummins Onan, Elkhart *Also called Cummins Power Generation Inc* ***(G-2783)***
Cummins Power Generation Inc....812 377-5000
301 Jackson St Columbus (47201) ***(G-1900)***
Cummins Power Generation Inc....574 262-4611
5125 Beck Dr Ste A Elkhart (46516) ***(G-2783)***
Cummins Repair Inc....260 632-4800
11110 Scipio Rd Harlan (46743) ***(G-5969)***
Cummins Sales and Service, Indianapolis *Also called Cummins Inc* ***(G-6710)***
Cummins Technical Center, Columbus *Also called Cummins Inc* ***(G-1899)***
Cummins-Allison, Indianapolis *Also called Cummins - Allison Corp* ***(G-6705)***
Cummins-Scania Xpi Mfg LLC (PA)....812 377-5000
1460 N National Rd Columbus (47201) ***(G-1901)***
Cumulus Intrmdate Holdings Inc....765 452-5704
4834 N Parkway Kokomo (46901) ***(G-8609)***
Cunningham Optical One, Muncie *Also called Tri State Optical Inc* ***(G-10575)***
Cunningham Pattern & Engrg Inc....812 379-9571
4399 N Us Highway 31 Columbus (47201) ***(G-1902)***
Cunningham Printing Inc....812 347-2438
175 W Whiskey Run Rd Ne New Salisbury (47161) ***(G-11008)***
Cunningham Quality Painting....317 925-8852
2060 Yandes St Indianapolis (46202) ***(G-6711)***
Cupprint LLC....574 323-5250
635 S Lafayette Blvd South Bend (46601) ***(G-12744)***
Current Publishing LLC....317 489-4444
30 S Rangeline Rd Carmel (46032) ***(G-1351)***
Current Technologies Inc....765 364-0490
Frontage Rd Crawfordsville (47933) ***(G-2147)***
Curtis Dyna-Fog Ltd....317 896-2561
525 Park St Westfield (46074) ***(G-14151)***
Curtis Products Inc (PA)....574 289-4891
401 N Bendix Dr South Bend (46628) ***(G-12745)***
Curtis Products Inc....574 289-4891
722 Carroll St South Bend (46601) ***(G-12746)***
Curvo Labs Inc (PA)....619 316-1202
58 Adams Ave Evansville (47713) ***(G-3448)***
Custom Art Screen Printing....260 456-3909
2800 Wayne Trce Fort Wayne (46803) ***(G-4193)***
Custom Blacksmith Shop....765 292-2745
29579 N State Road 19 Atlanta (46031) ***(G-293)***
Custom Blacksmithing, Atlanta *Also called Custom Blacksmith Shop* ***(G-293)***
Custom Blind Co....812 867-9280
21 W Sunrise Dr Evansville (47710) ***(G-3449)***
Custom Bottling & Packg Inc....877 401-7195
101 S Parker Dr Ashley (46705) ***(G-285)***
Custom Building Products Inc....765 656-0234
3800 W State Road 28 Frankfort (46041) ***(G-4827)***
Custom Built Barns Inc (PA)....765 457-9037
2312 N Plate St Kokomo (46901) ***(G-8610)***
Custom Built Cabinets and....812 427-9733
8587 Elmo Rayles Rd Vevay (47043) ***(G-13662)***
Custom Built Storage Sheds, Kokomo *Also called Custom Built Barns Inc* ***(G-8610)***
Custom Cabinet & Millwork....219 696-9827
17804 Holtz Rd Lowell (46356) ***(G-9403)***
Custom Cabinets & Furn LLC....812 486-2503
4578 N 875 E Montgomery (47558) ***(G-10220)***
Custom Candy Wrappers Company....574 247-0756
52092 Larkspur Cir Granger (46530) ***(G-5399)***
Custom Carton Inc....260 563-7411
3758 W Old 24 Wabash (46992) ***(G-13723)***
Custom Case Place LLC....260 715-1413
6435 W Jefferson Blvd Fort Wayne (46804) ***(G-4194)***
Custom Cast Stone Inc....317 896-1700
734 E 169th St Westfield (46074) ***(G-14152)***
Custom Coating Inc....260 925-0623
1937 Jacob St Auburn (46706) ***(G-325)***
Custom Coatings....317 392-7908
2446 N Michigan Rd Shelbyville (46176) ***(G-12528)***
Custom Compressor Svcs Corp....219 879-4966
104 Woodland Ct Ste A Michigan City (46360) ***(G-9777)***
Custom Controls & Engineering....812 663-0755
346 E North St Greensburg (47240) ***(G-5596)***
Custom Counters Inc....812 546-0052
2740 N State Road 9 Columbus (47203) ***(G-1903)***
Custom Covers Inc....765 481-7800
4548 W 50 S Lebanon (46052) ***(G-9178)***
Custom Crimp, Valparaiso *Also called Custom Machining Services Inc* ***(G-13525)***
Custom Cut Canvas LLC....260 221-3000
401 W Union St Ligonier (46767) ***(G-9280)***
Custom Design Laminates Inc....574 674-9174
10055 Mckinley Hwy Osceola (46561) ***(G-11375)***
Custom Die Casting Inc....765 935-3979
1134 Nw T St Richmond (47374) ***(G-11975)***
Custom Door Manufacturing....812 636-3667
8076 N 1100 E Loogootee (47553) ***(G-9380)***
Custom Draperies of Indiana....219 924-2500
7205 Calumet Ave Hammond (46324) ***(G-5867)***
Custom Drapery Service Inc....317 587-1518
1540 E 86th St Indianapolis (46240) ***(G-6712)***
Custom Durable Products, Elkhart *Also called Assistive Technology Inc* ***(G-2699)***
Custom Engineering Inc....812 424-3879
1900 Lynch Rd Evansville (47711) ***(G-3450)***
Custom Engrg & Fabrication Inc....260 745-9299
2211 Freeman St Fort Wayne (46802) ***(G-4195)***
Custom Expressions, Fort Wayne *Also called Athletic Edge Inc* ***(G-4095)***
Custom Fitz LLC....219 405-0896
10 Wagner Rd Porter (46304) ***(G-11803)***
Custom Forms Inc (PA)....765 463-6162
1400 Canal Rd Ste B Lafayette (47904) ***(G-8884)***
Custom Formulating & Blending, Bristol *Also called F B C Inc* ***(G-1059)***

Custom Gage & Tool Co Inc 317 547-8257
7305 E 30th St Indianapolis (46219) *(G-6713)*
Custom Golf By Uebelhor, Indianapolis *Also called Uebelhors Golf (G-8124)*
Custom Hardwood Cabinetry 260 623-3147
12504 Fackler Rd Monroeville (46773) *(G-10193)*
Custom Honing Inc 574 233-2846
24840 Us Highway 20 South Bend (46628) *(G-12747)*
Custom Imprint, Merrillville *Also called BT Management Inc (G-9705)*
Custom Imprint Corporation 800 378-3397
8605 Indiana Pl Merrillville (46410) *(G-9709)*
Custom Interior Dynamics LLC 317 632-0477
3314 Prospect St Indianapolis (46203) *(G-6714)*
Custom Keepsakes Machine EMB 317 894-5506
915 Tanninger Dr Indianapolis (46239) *(G-6715)*
Custom Kiln Works 812 535-3561
4400 W Concannon Ave West Terre Haute (47885) *(G-14123)*
Custom Machine Mfr LLC 574 251-0292
4111 Technology Dr South Bend (46628) *(G-12748)*
Custom Machine Shop, Lafayette *Also called Browell Enterprises Inc (G-8865)*
Custom Machining Inc (PA) 317 392-2328
1204 Hale Rd Shelbyville (46176) *(G-12529)*
Custom Machining Services Inc 219 462-6128
326 N 400 E Valparaiso (46383) *(G-13525)*
Custom Magnetics Inc (PA) 773 463-6500
801 W Main St North Manchester (46962) *(G-11227)*
Custom Magnetics Inc 773 463-6500
801 W Main St North Manchester (46962) *(G-11228)*
Custom Manufacturing Solutions, Bloomington *Also called OHM Automotive LLC (G-785)*
Custom Manufacturing Solutions, Gosport *Also called OHM Enterprise LLC (G-5354)*
Custom Marble Unlimited 574 594-2948
10379 S Roosevelt St Silver Lake (46982) *(G-12676)*
Custom Metal Fabrication LLC 574 257-8851
603 W 9th St Mishawaka (46544) *(G-10027)*
Custom Metal Industries, Greenfield *Also called Edwards Steel Inc (G-5522)*
Custom Mfg & Fabrication LLC 260 908-1088
5536 County Road 31 Auburn (46706) *(G-326)*
Custom Millwork & Display LLC 574 289-9772
1607 S Main St South Bend (46613) *(G-12749)*
Custom Millwork & Display Inc 574 289-4000
2102 W Washington St # 1 South Bend (46628) *(G-12750)*
Custom Moulding 812 636-7110
9061 E 875 N Odon (47562) *(G-11323)*
Custom Mtal Fnshng-Indiana LLC 765 489-4089
9705 State Road 38 Hagerstown (47346) *(G-5805)*
Custom Outfitted Protection 317 373-2092
9309 Memorial Park Dr 1b Indianapolis (46216) *(G-6716)*
Custom Packaging Inc 317 876-9559
7248 Haverhill Ct Indianapolis (46250) *(G-6717)*
Custom Plastics LLC 574 259-2340
1950 E Mckinley Ave Mishawaka (46545) *(G-10028)*
Custom Plywood Inc 812 944-7300
301 Quality Ave New Albany (47150) *(G-10766)*
Custom Polish & Chrome 260 665-7448
114 Lange Ln Angola (46703) *(G-206)*
Custom Polishing, Lynnville *Also called Doug Wilcox (G-9434)*
Custom Poly Packaging, Fort Wayne *Also called D and M Enterprises LLC (G-4197)*
Custom Precision Components, Ossian *Also called Roembke Mfg & Design Inc (G-11407)*
Custom Printing Co, Brownstown *Also called CPC (G-1184)*
Custom Qlting Pllow Cshion Svc 219 464-7316
102 Harmel Dr Valparaiso (46383) *(G-13526)*
Custom Secure Handles LLC 812 764-4948
6283 W County Road 600 S Greensburg (47240) *(G-5597)*
Custom Sewing Service 812 428-7015
2644 N Heidelbach Ave Evansville (47711) *(G-3451)*
Custom Sign & Engineeri 812 401-1550
5344 Vann Rd Newburgh (47630) *(G-11026)*
Custom Signs, Lawrenceburg *Also called Neon Accents (G-9148)*
Custom Signs Unlimited Co 260 483-4444
1410 Goshen Ave Fort Wayne (46808) *(G-4196)*
Custom Sound Designs, New Haven *Also called Csd Group Inc (G-10937)*
Custom Steel Technologies LLC 812 546-2299
701 South St Hope (47246) *(G-6111)*
Custom Tables & Cabinets 812 486-3831
5127 E 300 N Montgomery (47558) *(G-10221)*
Custom Tees 765 449-4893
1516 Sherwood Dr Lafayette (47909) *(G-8885)*
Custom TS & Trophies 219 926-4174
30 E Burwell Dr Porter (46304) *(G-11804)*
Custom Tube Co, Fort Wayne *Also called Jae Enterprises Inc (G-4391)*
Custom Tube Co, Fort Wayne *Also called Jae Enterprises Inc (G-4392)*
Custom Urethanes Inc 219 924-1644
10010 Express Dr Highland (46322) *(G-6041)*
Custom Wood Finishing 574 642-1213
10561 County Road 44 Millersburg (46543) *(G-9969)*
Custom Wood Floor, Evansville *Also called Custom Woodworking (G-3452)*
Custom Wood Products Inc 574 522-3300
1901 W Hively Ave Elkhart (46517) *(G-2784)*
Custom Woodworking 812 339-6601
732 S Village Dr Bloomington (47403) *(G-709)*
Custom Woodworking 812 422-6786
3314 Kratzville Rd Evansville (47710) *(G-3452)*
Custom Woodworks Inc 317 867-2929
17440 Westfield Park Rd Westfield (46074) *(G-14153)*
Custom-Flex, West Lebanon *Also called Tru-Flex LLC (G-14122)*
Customer 1st LLC (PA) 812 967-6727
8899 E Daily Rd Lot 51 Pekin (47165) *(G-11471)*
Customer 1st Safes & Services, Pekin *Also called Customer 1st LLC (G-11471)*
Customized Machining Inc 765 490-7894
5596 Keeneland Way Lafayette (47905) *(G-8886)*
Cut-Pro Indexable Tooling LLC 260 668-2400
212 Growth Pkwy Angola (46703) *(G-207)*
Cutting Edge Craftsmen LLC 317 757-6975
1125 Brookside Ave C20 Indianapolis (46202) *(G-6718)*
Cutting Edge Wire EDM Inc 765 284-3820
1800 W Mt Pleasant Blvd Muncie (47302) *(G-10452)*
Cvg Sprague Devices LLC 614 289-5360
527 W Us Highway 20 Michigan City (46360) *(G-9778)*
CVI Sheet Metal Contractors, Indianapolis *Also called Campbell Ventilation Inc (G-6545)*
CXR Company Inc 574 269-6020
2599 N Fox Farm Rd Warsaw (46580) *(G-13862)*
Cyberia Ltd 317 721-2582
6800 E 30th St Indianapolis (46219) *(G-6719)*
Cyclone Adg LLC 520 403-2927
166 Mills Ln New Albany (47150) *(G-10767)*
Cyclone Manufacturing Co Inc 260 774-3311
151 N Washington St Urbana (46990) *(G-13476)*
Cyclone Shop Inc 812 683-2887
2403 S 600w Huntingburg (47542) *(G-6154)*
Cylicron LLC 812 283-4600
5171 Maritime Jeffersonville (47130) *(G-8349)*
Cylinder Div, Goodland *Also called Parker-Hannifin Corporation (G-5160)*
Cypress Springs Enterprises 812 743-8888
11536 E Lucky Point Rd Wheatland (47597) *(G-14231)*
D & D Auto Detailing Sups, New Haven *Also called Dennis Adams Inc (G-10938)*
D & D Brake Sales Inc 317 485-5177
State Rd 234 & Cnty Rd 20 St State Ro Fortville (46040) *(G-4772)*
D & D Industries Inc 219 844-5600
6805 Mccook Ave Hammond (46323) *(G-5868)*
D & D Manufacturing Inc (PA) 812 432-3294
7415 E County Road 50 S Dillsboro (47018) *(G-2465)*
D & D Mouldings & Millwork 317 770-5500
15509 Stony Creek Way Noblesville (46060) *(G-11089)*
D & E Auto Electric Inc 219 763-3892
5665 Old Porter Rd Portage (46368) *(G-11759)*
D & E Machine Inc 765 653-8919
944 W County Road 350 N Greencastle (46135) *(G-5457)*
D & E Printing Company Inc 317 852-9048
2 E Main St Brownsburg (46112) *(G-1147)*
D & E Workshop 260 593-0195
9680 W 700 S Topeka (46571) *(G-13415)*
D & F Industries Inc 219 865-2926
315 Nottingham Ln Schererville (46375) *(G-12319)*
D & J Custom Embroidery 219 874-9061
707 E 11th St Michigan City (46360) *(G-9779)*
D & J Tool Co Inc 260 636-2682
300 S 7th St Albion (46701) *(G-22)*
D & M Precision Machining Inc 219 393-5132
1 Kingsbury Indstrl Park Kingsbury (46345) *(G-8535)*
D & M Printing Inc 812 847-4837
13 N Main St Linton (47441) *(G-9306)*
D & M Systems Inc 812 327-2384
6516 S Thomas Ct Owensburg (47453) *(G-11425)*
D & M Tool Corporation (HQ) 812 279-8882
699 Washboard Rd Springville (47462) *(G-13062)*
D & S Industries Inc 574 848-7144
207 W St Joseph St Bristol (46507) *(G-1053)*
D & S Machine Inc 317 826-2900
10640 Deme Dr Ste R Indianapolis (46236) *(G-6720)*
D & V Precision Sheetmetal 317 462-2601
205 S 400 W Greenfield (46140) *(G-5517)*
D & W Inc 574 264-9674
941 Oak St Elkhart (46514) *(G-2785)*
D 1 Mold & Tool LLC 765 378-0693
8201 N State Road 9 Alexandria (46001) *(G-39)*
D A Hochstetler & Sons LLP 574 642-1144
4165 S 500 W Topeka (46571) *(G-13416)*
D A Merriman Inc 260 636-3464
2259 E State Road 8 Albion (46701) *(G-23)*
D and E Surplus LLC 260 351-3200
4205 S 900 E Wolcottville (46795) *(G-14370)*
D and M Enterprises LLC 260 483-4008
3216 Congressional Pkwy Fort Wayne (46808) *(G-4197)*
D and R Custom Logging, Warsaw *Also called Graber Ronald D Yoder & (G-13883)*
D and S Pallet 765 866-7263
3174 S 600 W Crawfordsville (47933) *(G-2148)*
D C C, Elkhart *Also called Quality Plastics and Engrg Inc (G-3128)*

ALPHABETIC

D D McKay and Associates 317 546-7446
  4068 Pendleton Way Indianapolis (46226) *(G-6721)*

D E Key Machine Shop 765 664-1720
  1442 E 450 N Marion (46952) *(G-9519)*

D H Gravel Company 765 893-4914
  7794 S State Road 263 Williamsport (47993) *(G-14289)*

D J Investments Inc 260 726-7346
  111 W North St Ste C Portland (47371) *(G-11814)*

D J Investments Inc 765 348-3558
  1608 N Cherry St Hartford City (47348) *(G-5979)*

D K Enterprises LLC 260 356-9011
  1675 Riverfork Dr Huntington (46750) *(G-6200)*

D K Tools & Engineering 812 325-4532
  6250 Spearsville Rd Morgantown (46160) *(G-10351)*

D L Miller Woodworking 260 562-9329
  5345 N 400 W Shipshewana (46565) *(G-12610)*

D M Sales & Engineering Inc 317 783-5493
  1325 Sunday Dr Indianapolis (46217) *(G-6722)*

D R Pattern Inc 260 868-5585
  1835 County Road 61 Butler (46721) *(G-1227)*

D Rv Luxury Suites LLC 260 562-1075
  1000 Interchange Dr Howe (46746) *(G-6121)*

D S E Inc 812 376-0310
  2651 Cessna Dr Columbus (47203) *(G-1904)*

D S M, Evansville Also called DSM Engineering Plastics Inc *(G-3465)*

D Terrell & Company, Washington Also called Douglas P Terrell *(G-13981)*

D Timber Inc 219 374-8085
  14405 Clark St Crown Point (46307) *(G-2242)*

D W Stewart 260 463-2607
  104 E Wayne St Lagrange (46761) *(G-9036)*

D X Systems 812 332-4699
  317 W 17th St Bloomington (47404) *(G-710)*

D&A Industries Inc 260 357-1830
  5079 County Road 19 Garrett (46738) *(G-5000)*

D&A Transportation, South Bend Also called Pro-Tote System Inc *(G-12905)*

D&D Automation Inc 812 299-1045
  1207 E Dallas Dr Terre Haute (47802) *(G-13221)*

D&D Manufacturing, Union Mills Also called Hot Stamping & Printing *(G-13463)*

D&D Motors 765 358-3856
  10240 N Langdon Rd Gaston (47342) *(G-5131)*

D&G Publishing Inc 317 531-8678
  17336 Tilbury Way Westfield (46074) *(G-14154)*

D&G Timber Inc 812 486-3356
  21198 Us Highway 231 Odon (47562) *(G-11324)*

D&J Custom Embroidery, Michigan City Also called D & J Custom Embroidery *(G-9779)*

D&W Fine Pack LLC 260 432-3027
  7707 Vicksburg Pike Fort Wayne (46804) *(G-4198)*

D-J Printing Specialists Inc 219 465-1164
  2600 Roosevelt Rd 200-4 Valparaiso (46383) *(G-13527)*

DA Inc (HQ) 812 503-2302
  1800 Patrol Rd Charlestown (47111) *(G-1562)*

Da-Lite, Warsaw Also called Milestone AV Technologies LLC *(G-13911)*

Da-Mar Industries Inc (PA) 260 347-1662
  201 W Ohio St Kendallville (46755) *(G-8471)*

Dads Root Beer Company LLC 812 482-5352
  950 S Saint Charles St Jasper (47546) *(G-8243)*

Daechang Seat Co   Ltd USA 317 755-3663
  8150 Woodland Dr Indianapolis (46278) *(G-6723)*

Daed Toolworks 317 861-7419
  3255 W Birdsong Ct Greenfield (46140) *(G-5518)*

Dage-MTI Michigan City Inc 219 872-5514
  701 N Roeske Ave Michigan City (46360) *(G-9780)*

Daily Grind Corporation 574 875-8389
  58711 Runway Rd Elkhart (46516) *(G-2786)*

Daily Peru Tribune Pubg Co 765 473-6641
  26 W 3rd St Peru (46970) *(G-11523)*

Daimler Trucks North Amer LLC 317 769-8500
  4140 Anson Blvd Whitestown (46075) *(G-14252)*

Dairy Farmers America Inc 574 533-3141
  1110 S 9th St Goshen (46526) *(G-5196)*

Dairychem Laboratories Inc 317 849-8400
  9120 Technology Ln Fishers (46038) *(G-3897)*

Dajac Inc 317 608-0500
  17406 Tiller Ct Ste 600 Westfield (46074) *(G-14155)*

DAKA Manufacturing Inc 574 295-8036
  24578 Copper Ridge Dr Goshen (46526) *(G-5197)*

Dakota Engineering Inc 317 546-8460
  2401 N Executive Park Dr Yorktown (47396) *(G-14403)*

Dallara LLC 317 388-5400
  1201 Main St Speedway (46224) *(G-13012)*

Dallara Indycar Factory, Speedway Also called Dallara LLC *(G-13012)*

Dallara Research Center LLC 317 388-5416
  1201 Main St Ste B Speedway (46224) *(G-13013)*

Dallara USA Holding Inc (PA) 317 388-5400
  1201 Main St Ste B Speedway (46224) *(G-13014)*

Dallas Group of America Inc 812 283-6675
  1402 Fabricon Blvd Jeffersonville (47130) *(G-8350)*

Dallas Towing Service, Evansville Also called Sparkling Clean Inc *(G-3741)*

Daltech Enterprises Inc 260 527-4590
  810 S Broad St Fremont (46737) *(G-4957)*

Daltech Force, Fremont Also called Daltech Enterprises Inc *(G-4957)*

Damage Industries II LLC 574 256-7006
  55685 Currant Rd Mishawaka (46545) *(G-10029)*

Damalak Printing Inc 317 896-5337
  104 W Main St Westfield (46074) *(G-14156)*

Daman Products Company Inc 574 259-7841
  1811 N Home St Mishawaka (46545) *(G-10030)*

Damon Corporation (HQ) 574 262-2624
  2958 Gateway Dr Elkhart (46514) *(G-2787)*

Damon Corporation 574 262-2624
  2824 Jami St Elkhart (46514) *(G-2788)*

Damon Corporation 574 264-2900
  2958 Paul Dr Elkhart (46514) *(G-2789)*

Damon Motor Coach 574 536-3781
  604 Middleton Run Rd Elkhart (46516) *(G-2790)*

Damping Technologies Inc 574 258-7916
  12970 Mckinley Hwy Ste 1 Mishawaka (46545) *(G-10031)*

Damping Technologies Inc (PA) 574 258-7916
  55656 Currant Rd Mishawaka (46545) *(G-10032)*

Dan Goode Cabinet 317 541-9878
  3839 Englewood Dr Indianapolis (46226) *(G-6724)*

Dana Driveshaft Products LLC 260 432-2903
  400 S Miller Ave Marion (46953) *(G-9520)*

Dana Light Axle Products LLC 260 636-4300
  401 E Park Dr Albion (46701) *(G-24)*

Dana Light Axle Products LLC (HQ) 260 483-7174
  2100 W State Blvd Fort Wayne (46808) *(G-4199)*

Dana Sealing Products, Avilla Also called Victor Reinz Valve Seals LLC *(G-420)*

Dance Sophisticates 317 634-7728
  1605 Prospect St Indianapolis (46203) *(G-6725)*

Dance World Bazaar Corporation 812 663-7679
  1553 N Commerce East Dr Greensburg (47240) *(G-5598)*

Danco Anodizing, Warsaw Also called Riepen LLC *(G-13935)*

Daniel Bontrager 574 825-5656
  14872 County Road 126 Goshen (46528) *(G-5198)*

Daniel Griffin 765 492-3257
  2019 E 50 N Cayuga (47928) *(G-1518)*

Daniel Korb Laundry Company (PA) 812 425-6121
  4905 Bellemeade Ave Evansville (47715) *(G-3453)*

Daniel Skaggs & Company 765 342-0071
  610 W Dickson St Martinsville (46151) *(G-9600)*

Daniels Vineyard LLC 317 894-6860
  6311 W Stoner Dr Greenfield (46140) *(G-5519)*

Danisco USA, Terre Haute Also called E I Du Pont De Nemours & Co *(G-13228)*

Danisco USA Inc 812 299-6700
  11 W Litesse Dr Terre Haute (47802) *(G-13222)*

Danish Woodworking, Carmel Also called Carmel Countertops Inc *(G-1330)*

Danny Webb Plumbing 574 936-2746
  18391 6th Rd Plymouth (46563) *(G-11679)*

Dannys Fireworks 219 324-5757
  2415 Monroe St La Porte (46350) *(G-8748)*

Danubius Machine Inc 219 662-7787
  11205 Delaware Pkwy Crown Point (46307) *(G-2243)*

Danwood Industries 219 369-1484
  7606 S Young Rd La Porte (46350) *(G-8749)*

Danzer Services Inc (PA) 812 526-2601
  206 S Holland St Edinburgh (46124) *(G-2603)*

Danzer Veneer Americas Inc 812 526-6789
  206 S Holland St Edinburgh (46124) *(G-2604)*

Daramic LLC 812 738-8274
  3430 Cline Rd Nw Corydon (47112) *(G-2097)*

Daredevil Brewing Co 317 512-2202
  1151 Main St Indianapolis (46224) *(G-6726)*

Dargie Racing Engines, Richmond Also called Michael Dargie *(G-12017)*

Dark Star Inc 765 759-4764
  1309 S Nebo Rd 400w Muncie (47304) *(G-10453)*

Dark Star Printing & Advg, Muncie Also called Dark Star Inc *(G-10453)*

Darlage Investments LLC 812 522-5929
  860 F Ave E Seymour (47274) *(G-12443)*

Darling Ingredients Inc 317 784-4486
  700 W Southern Ave Indianapolis (46225) *(G-6727)*

Darlington Cookie Company (PA) 800 754-2202
  8001 E 196th St Noblesville (46062) *(G-11090)*

Darlington Farms, Noblesville Also called Darlington Cookie Company *(G-11090)*

Darlite Designs, Fort Wayne Also called Candles By Dar Inc *(G-4139)*

Darrins Coffee Company 317 732-5037
  9122 Crawfordsville Rd Clermont (46234) *(G-1711)*

Das Big Dawg Brewhaus LLC 765 965-9463
  3407 National Rd W Richmond (47374) *(G-11976)*

Data Label Inc (PA) 812 232-0408
  1000 Spruce St Terre Haute (47807) *(G-13223)*

Data Print Initiatives LLC 260 489-2665
  1710 Dividend Rd Fort Wayne (46808) *(G-4200)*

Data Technologies Inc 317 580-9161
  231 1st Ave Sw Carmel (46032) *(G-1352)*

Data-Vision Inc 574 243-8625
  4215 Edison Lakes Pkwy # 140 Mishawaka (46545) *(G-10033)*

(G-0000) Company's Geographic Section entry number

Datagraphic Printing, Chesterton *Also called Four Part Inc (G-1607)*

Daubert Vci Inc 574 772-9310
1805 Pacific Ave Knox (46534) *(G-8564)*

Daugherty Cabinets 574 272-9205
51719 Gumwood Rd Granger (46530) *(G-5400)*

Dave Jones Machinists LLC 574 256-5500
1212 N Merrifield Ave Mishawaka (46545) *(G-10034)*

Dave OMara Paving Inc (PA) 812 346-1214
1100 E O And M Ave North Vernon (47265) *(G-11252)*

Dave Turner 765 674-3360
109 E South D St Gas City (46933) *(G-5122)*

Davern Machine Shop 765 505-1051
1248 E 500 S Dana (47847) *(G-2342)*

David Alan Chocolatier, Lebanon *Also called Lebanon Corp (G-9199)*

David Company, Fishers *Also called David Indus Process PDT Co (G-3898)*

David Gonzales 765 284-6960
701 E Mcgalliard Rd Muncie (47303) *(G-10454)*

David Indus Process PDT Co 317 577-0351
10142 Brooks School Rd # 102 Fishers (46037) *(G-3898)*

David Kechel 260 627-2749
12921 Leo Rd Leo (46765) *(G-9242)*

David M Pszonka 219 988-2235
93 S 695 W Hebron (46341) *(G-6011)*

David R Webb Company Inc (HQ) 812 526-2601
206 S Holland St Edinburgh (46124) *(G-2605)*

David Tortora 317 506-6902
11700 Oak Tree Way Carmel (46032) *(G-1353)*

David W Miller Miller Longbow 765 482-3234
1304 S East St Apt C Lebanon (46052) *(G-9179)*

Davids Inc 812 376-6870
905 S Gladstone Ave Columbus (47201) *(G-1905)*

Davies-Imperial Coatings Inc 219 933-0877
1275 State St Hammond (46320) *(G-5869)*

Daviess County Metal Sales 812 486-4299
9929 E Us Highway 50 Cannelburg (47519) *(G-1284)*

Davis Crushed Stone & Lime, Depauw *Also called John S Davis Inc (G-2457)*

Davis Hezakih Corp 260 768-7300
255 E Main St Shipshewana (46565) *(G-12611)*

Davis Hotel, Shipshewana *Also called Davis Hezakih Corp (G-12611)*

Davis Industries Inc 317 871-0103
4090 Westover Dr Indianapolis (46268) *(G-6728)*

Davis Machine & Tool Inc 812 526-2674
920 S Walnut St Edinburgh (46124) *(G-2606)*

Davis Tool & Machine Inc 317 896-9278
19224 Eagletown Rd Westfield (46074) *(G-14157)*

Davis Tool and Gage Company 317 852-5400
5125 E County Road 450 N Brownsburg (46112) *(G-1148)*

Davis Vachon Artworks 260 489-9160
227 W Wallen Rd Fort Wayne (46825) *(G-4201)*

Davis Water Conditioning, Rensselaer *Also called Davis Water Services Inc (G-11920)*

Davis Water Services Inc 219 394-2270
4898 S 1000 W Rensselaer (47978) *(G-11920)*

Davron Fabricating 765 339-7303
3873 W 750 N New Richmond (47967) *(G-11004)*

Dawn Food Products Inc 800 333-3296
9601 Georgia St Crown Point (46307) *(G-2244)*

Dawn Food Products Frozen Div, Crown Point *Also called Dawn Food Products Inc (G-2244)*

Dawson Machine Shop Inc 812 649-4777
614 N State Road 161 Rockport (47635) *(G-12167)*

Dawson Sheet Metal, Muncie *Also called Delbert M Dawson & Son Inc (G-10458)*

Daylight Engineering Inc (PA) 812 983-2518
11022 Elberfeld Rd Elberfeld (47613) *(G-2633)*

Dayton Progress Corporation 260 726-6861
1314 N Meridian St Portland (47371) *(G-11815)*

Dayton-Phoenix Group Inc (HQ) 765 742-4410
4750 Swisher Rd West Lafayette (47906) *(G-14063)*

Db Polishing 574 518-2443
6445 W 1350 N Nappanee (46550) *(G-10666)*

Dbfederal, Indianapolis *Also called Dbisp LLC (G-6729)*

Dbisp LLC 317 222-1671
5847 W 74th St Indianapolis (46278) *(G-6729)*

DC Coaters Inc 765 675-6006
550 Industrial Dr Tipton (46072) *(G-13390)*

DC Construction Services Inc 317 577-0276
9465 Counselors Row # 200 Indianapolis (46240) *(G-6730)*

Dc's Mobile Electronics, Evansville *Also called Dcs Car Audio (G-3454)*

DCI, Carmel *Also called Digital Cmmnties Intiative Inc (G-1360)*

Dcs Car Audio 812 437-8488
1732 W Franklin St A Evansville (47712) *(G-3454)*

Dcx-Chol Enterprises Inc 260 407-1107
1615 E Wallace St Fort Wayne (46803) *(G-4202)*

Dd Stoops Laser Engraving 765 868-4999
315 W Markland Ave Kokomo (46901) *(G-8611)*

De Harts Pallet & Lbr Mfg Co, Austin *Also called Dehart Pallet & Lumber Co (G-396)*

De Masqu Productions Ltd 812 556-0061
601 Main St Jasper (47546) *(G-8244)*

De Vols Ornamental Iron 765 482-1171
4540 E State Road 32 Lebanon (46052) *(G-9180)*

De Witt Tool & Die Inc 765 998-7320
10040 E 500 S Upland (46989) *(G-13469)*

Dean Boslers 812 476-8787
3820 E Morgan Ave Evansville (47715) *(G-3455)*

Dean Co Inc 317 891-2518
6153 W 400 N Greenfield (46140) *(G-5520)*

Dean Food of Decatur, Decatur *Also called Suiza Dairy Group LLC (G-2407)*

Dean Foods Co 214 303-3400
1430 Western Ave Plymouth (46563) *(G-11680)*

Dean Foods Company 574 223-2141
1700 N Old Us 31 Rochester (46975) *(G-12121)*

Dearborn Coatings LLC 513 600-9580
25768 Mount Pleasant Rd Lawrenceburg (47025) *(G-9136)*

Dearborn Crane and Engrg Co (PA) 574 259-2444
1133 E 5th St Mishawaka (46544) *(G-10035)*

Dearborn Overhead Crane, Mishawaka *Also called Dearborn Crane and Engrg Co (G-10035)*

Death Studios 219 362-4321
431 Pine Lake Ave La Porte (46350) *(G-8750)*

Deatons Waterfront Svcs LLC 317 336-7180
215 S Madison St Fortville (46040) *(G-4773)*

Debbies Handmade Soap 765 747-5090
1140 E County Road 500 S Muncie (47302) *(G-10455)*

Debra Schneider 317 420-9360
25610 Salem Church Rd Arcadia (46030) *(G-263)*

Debrand Inc (PA) 260 969-8333
10105 Auburn Park Dr Fort Wayne (46825) *(G-4203)*

Debrand Fine Chocolates, Fort Wayne *Also called Debrand Inc (G-4203)*

Dec-O-Art Inc 574 294-6451
3914 Lexington Park Dr Elkhart (46514) *(G-2791)*

Decatur Daily Democrat, Decatur *Also called Decatur Publishing Co Inc (G-2374)*

Decatur Mold Tool and Engrg 812 346-5188
3330 N State Rd 7 North Vernon (47265) *(G-11253)*

Decatur Plastic Products Inc 812 352-6050
655 Montrow Pkwy North Vernon (47265) *(G-11254)*

Decatur Plastic Products Inc (PA) 812 346-5159
3250 N State Highway 7 North Vernon (47265) *(G-11255)*

Decatur Publishing Co Inc 260 724-2121
141 S 2nd St Decatur (46733) *(G-2374)*

Decatur Wire Die, Hoagland *Also called Dwd Industries LLC (G-6064)*

Decker Sales Inc 812 330-1580
5100 E Four Boys Trl Bloomington (47408) *(G-711)*

Deco Corporation 812 342-4767
6510 S 50 W Columbus (47201) *(G-1906)*

Deco Products, Columbus *Also called Deco Corporation (G-1906)*

Decor Ironworks Inc 219 865-1222
1483 Joliet St Dyer (46311) *(G-2493)*

Decora Cabinets, Jasper *Also called Masterbrand Cabinets Inc (G-8292)*

Dede Tool & Machine Inc 812 232-7365
799 W Springhill Dr Terre Haute (47802) *(G-13224)*

Dedicated Software 260 341-4166
6018 Hamilton Rd Yoder (46798) *(G-14397)*

Dedrick Tool & Die Inc 260 824-3334
2929 E State Road 124 Bluffton (46714) *(G-872)*

Deem & Loureiro Inc 770 652-9871
8111 Bayberry Ct Indianapolis (46250) *(G-6731)*

Deep Pockets Foods LLC 317 815-4898
13283 Aquamarine Dr Carmel (46033) *(G-1354)*

Deep Three Inc 260 705-2283
17607 Rupert Rd Spencerville (46788) *(G-13045)*

Deer Country Equipment LLC 812 522-1922
1250 W 2nd St Seymour (47274) *(G-12444)*

Deer Ridgewood Craft LLC 812 535-3744
5330 Yuma Rd West Terre Haute (47885) *(G-14124)*

Deer Run Sawmill LLC 812 732-4608
8242 Vly Cy Mckport Rd Sw Mauckport (47142) *(G-9654)*

Deer Track Archery 765 643-6847
648 W 500 S Anderson (46013) *(G-92)*

Deerwood Group 219 866-5521
792 E State Road 16 Monon (47959) *(G-10175)*

Defelice Engineering Inc 317 834-2832
7451 N Ridgeway Ln Mooresville (46158) *(G-10307)*

Deflecto LLC (HQ) 317 849-9555
7035 E 86th St Indianapolis (46250) *(G-6732)*

Defrukuscn LLC 219 718-2128
2158 45th St 520 Highland (46322) *(G-6042)*

Degler Mktg & Mailing Svcs 317 873-5550
8930 Cooper Rd Zionsville (46077) *(G-14429)*

Degood Dmensional Concepts Inc 574 834-5437
7815 N State Road 13 North Webster (46555) *(G-11291)*

Dehart Pallet & Lumber Co 812 794-2974
2737 E State Road 256 Austin (47102) *(G-396)*

Dehco Inc (HQ) 574 294-2684
3601 Charlotte Ave Elkhart (46517) *(G-2792)*

Deister Concentrator LLC 260 747-2700
9205 Avionics Dr Fort Wayne (46809) *(G-4204)*

Deister Machine Company Inc (PA) 260 426-7495
1933 E Wayne St Fort Wayne (46803) *(G-4205)*

Deister Machine Company Inc 260 426-7495
901 Glasgow Ave Fort Wayne (46803) *(G-4206)*

Deister Machine Company Inc 260 422-0354
1604 E Berry St Fort Wayne (46803) *(G-4207)*

Deka Battery, Indianapolis *Also called East Penn Manufacturing Co* *(G-6791)*

Dekalb Metal Finishing Inc 260 925-1820
625 W 15th St Auburn (46706) *(G-327)*

Dekalb Tool and Engrg LLC 260 357-1500
700 E Quincy St Garrett (46738) *(G-5001)*

Dekker Lighting 219 227-8520
2142 Us Highway 41 Schererville (46375) *(G-12320)*

Dekker Vacuum Technologies Inc 219 861-0661
935 S Woodland Ave Michigan City (46360) *(G-9781)*

Dekko Acquisition Parent Inc (PA) 260 347-0700
6928 N 400 E Kendallville (46755) *(G-8472)*

Dekko Techinal Center, Laotto *Also called Group Dekko Inc* *(G-9109)*

Del Palma Orthopedics Llc 260 625-3169
5865 E State Road 14 Columbia City (46725) *(G-1778)*

Delaplane & Son Neon & Sign 574 859-3431
7768 E 550 N Camden (46917) *(G-1273)*

Delaplane Son Neon & Sign Svc, Camden *Also called Delaplane & Son Neon & Sign* *(G-1273)*

Delaware County Home Bldrs Inc 765 289-6328
2411 N Dr Martin Luther Muncie (47303) *(G-10456)*

Delaware County Mobile Homes, Muncie *Also called Delaware County Home Bldrs Inc* *(G-10456)*

Delaware Dynamics LLC 765 284-3335
700 S Mulberry St Muncie (47302) *(G-10457)*

Delaware Machinery, Muncie *Also called Matrix Technologies Inc* *(G-10518)*

Delbert Kemp 812 486-3325
3590 N 700 E Montgomery (47558) *(G-10222)*

Delbert M Dawson & Son Inc 765 284-9711
1405 W Kilgore Ave Muncie (47305) *(G-10458)*

Delco Electronics 765 455-9713
3700 Orleans Dr Kokomo (46902) *(G-8612)*

Delco Electronics 765 451-9325
4221 Coventry Dr Kokomo (46902) *(G-8613)*

Delco Remy America, Pendleton *Also called Ballantrae Inc* *(G-11483)*

Delilah Club Covers 812 401-0012
4812 Tippecanoe Dr Evansville (47715) *(G-3456)*

Delivery Concepts Inc (PA) 574 522-3981
29301 County Road 20 Elkhart (46517) *(G-2793)*

Delmar Knepp Logging 812 486-2565
10293 E 600 N Loogootee (47553) *(G-9381)*

Delp Printing & Mailing Inc 317 872-9744
7750 Zionsville Rd # 200 Indianapolis (46268) *(G-6733)*

Delphi, Kokomo *Also called Aptiv Services Us LLC* *(G-8592)*

Delphi, Kokomo *Also called Aptiv Services Us LLC* *(G-8593)*

Delphi, Kokomo *Also called Aptiv Services Us LLC* *(G-8594)*

Delphi Body Works 765 564-2212
313 S Washington St Delphi (46923) *(G-2417)*

Delphi E & S Morgan Street Ops 765 451-2571
1501 E 200 N Kokomo (46901) *(G-8614)*

Delphi Pdts & Svc Solutions, Plainfield *Also called AEL/Span LLC* *(G-11591)*

Delphi Powertrain Systems LLC 765 236-0025
1501 E 200 N Kokomo (46901) *(G-8615)*

Delphi Powertrain Systems LLC 765 451-0732
2151 E Lincoln Rd Kokomo (46902) *(G-8616)*

Delphi Products Co Inc 800 382-7903
2065 W Us Highway 421 Delphi (46923) *(G-2418)*

Delphi Products Company, Delphi *Also called Dpc Inc* *(G-2419)*

Delphos Herald of Indiana (PA) 812 537-0063
126 W High St Lawrenceburg (47025) *(G-9137)*

Delphos Herald of Indiana Inc (HQ) 812 537-0063
126 W High St Lawrenceburg (47025) *(G-9138)*

Delphos Herald of Indiana Inc 812 438-2011
235 Main St Rising Sun (47040) *(G-12087)*

Delta Excell Incorporated 765 642-0288
505 E 31st St Ste X Anderson (46016) *(G-93)*

Delta Faucet Company 812 663-4433
1425 W Main St Greensburg (47240) *(G-5599)*

Delta Microinverter LLC 317 274-5935
6779 Woodcliff Cir Zionsville (46077) *(G-14430)*

Delta Tool Manufacturing Inc 574 223-4863
1090 W 325 S Rochester (46975) *(G-12122)*

Deluxe Homes 219 256-1701
1888 S Rolling Meadows Dr Westville (46391) *(G-14215)*

Deluxe Soap Company LLC 260 422-5614
6031 State Road 1 Saint Joe (46785) *(G-12253)*

Demotte Decorative Stone Inc 219 987-5461
6611 W State Road 10 Demotte (46310) *(G-2434)*

Demotte Manufacturing Inc 219 987-6196
5844 W State Road 10 Demotte (46310) *(G-2435)*

Demotte Yard, Demotte *Also called Legacy Vulcan LLC* *(G-2443)*

Den-Craft Dental Laboratory 219 663-7776
1776 E North St Crown Point (46307) *(G-2245)*

Dennis Adams Inc 260 493-4829
5108 N Webster Rd New Haven (46774) *(G-10938)*

Dennis Etiennes Logging Inc 812 843-4518
14370 Ureka Rd Cannelton (47520) *(G-1289)*

Dennis K Marvell 812 779-5107
3700 W 250 N Patoka (47666) *(G-11465)*

Dennis Manufacturing Inc 812 755-4891
250 Hwy 56 Campbellsburg (47108) *(G-1276)*

Dennis Polk & Associates Inc 574 831-3555
4916 N Sr 15 New Paris (46553) *(G-10977)*

Dennisign, Fort Wayne *Also called Tomlin Enterprises Inc* *(G-4690)*

Dental Enterprises, Kingsford Heights *Also called Protero Corporation* *(G-8546)*

Dental Professional Labs 219 769-6225
8040 Cleveland Pl Merrillville (46410) *(G-9710)*

Dentisse Inc 260 444-3046
6415 Mutual Dr Fort Wayne (46825) *(G-4208)*

Denver Stone 317 244-5889
3148 S Holt Rd Indianapolis (46221) *(G-6734)*

Denver Stone Machine Co, Indianapolis *Also called Denver Stone* *(G-6734)*

Dependable Metal Treating Inc 260 347-5744
902 Dowling St Kendallville (46755) *(G-8473)*

Dependable Rubber Industrial 765 447-5654
201 Farabee Dr S Ste C Lafayette (47905) *(G-8887)*

Depth Plus Design LLC 317 370-0532
505 Birch St Westfield (46074) *(G-14158)*

Depuy Mitek LLC 574 267-8143
700 Orthopaedic Dr Warsaw (46582) *(G-13863)*

Depuy Products Inc (HQ) 574 267-8143
700 Orthopaedic Dr Warsaw (46582) *(G-13864)*

Depuy Synthes Inc (HQ) 574 267-8143
700 Orthopaedic Dr Warsaw (46582) *(G-13865)*

Depuy Synthes Sales Inc 574 267-8143
700 Orthopaedic Dr Warsaw (46582) *(G-13866)*

Derby Inc 574 233-4500
24350 State Road 23 South Bend (46614) *(G-12751)*

Derby Industries, South Bend *Also called Derby Inc* *(G-12751)*

Derby Industries LLC 765 778-6104
4301 W 73rd St Anderson (46011) *(G-94)*

Dereeltech LLC 812 293-4786
9571 Barker Dr Bldg 3 Nabb (47147) *(G-10639)*

Descon, Brownsburg *Also called Young & Kenady Incorporated* *(G-1178)*

Deshazo LLC 317 867-7677
1022 Kendall Ct Ste 2 Westfield (46074) *(G-14159)*

Design & Mfg Solutions LLC 765 478-9393
15421 W Hunnicut Rd Cambridge City (47327) *(G-1255)*

Design Engineering 219 926-2170
600 River Dr Chesterton (46304) *(G-1602)*

Design Engineering Company, Chesterton *Also called Design Engineering* *(G-1602)*

Design Media Connections LLC 317 819-2022
9365 Counselors Row # 104 Indianapolis (46240) *(G-6735)*

Design Msa Inc 317 817-9000
200 S Rangeline Rd # 217 Carmel (46032) *(G-1355)*

Design Time, Goshen *Also called Zieman Manufacturing Company* *(G-5347)*

Design Works Inc 317 815-8619
6240 E 116th St Fishers (46038) *(G-3899)*

Designs 4 U Inc 765 793-3026
1350 W 100 N Covington (47932) *(G-2118)*

Desirable Scents 317 504-4976
3843 Daisy Dr Lafayette (47905) *(G-8888)*

Destin Products Division, Elkhart *Also called Sigma Switches Plus Inc* *(G-3170)*

Destination Yachts Inc 812 254-8800
2610 S 140 W Washington (47501) *(G-13979)*

Destiny Solutions Inc 502 384-0031
8265 State Road 64 Georgetown (47122) *(G-5142)*

Destro Machines LLC 412 999-1619
1905 Mulligan Way Apt D Lafayette (47909) *(G-8889)*

Determine Inc 317 594-8600
12800 N Meridian St # 425 Carmel (46032) *(G-1356)*

Determine Inc (PA) 650 532-1500
615 W Carmel Dr Ste 100 Carmel (46032) *(G-1357)*

Determine Sourcing Inc 408 570-9700
615 W Carmel Dr Ste 100 Carmel (46032) *(G-1358)*

Detweilers Cabinet Shop 765 629-2698
6053 W State Road 244 Milroy (46156) *(G-9979)*

Deufol Sunman Inc (HQ) 812 623-1140
924 S Meridian St Sunman (47041) *(G-13110)*

Deutsch Kase Haus Inc, Middlebury *Also called Middlebury Cheese Company LLC* *(G-9906)*

Deutsch LLC 219 464-1557
1753 Crestview Dr Valparaiso (46383) *(G-13528)*

Deuxfreres LLC 317 241-7600
1351 S Girls School Rd Indianapolis (46231) *(G-6736)*

Developmental Natural Res 317 543-4886
8750 Sugar Pine Pt Indianapolis (46256) *(G-6737)*

Devening Block Inc (PA) 812 372-4458
895 Jonesville Rd Columbus (47201) *(G-1907)*

Dewalt Service Center 017, Indianapolis *Also called Black & Decker (us) Inc* *(G-6481)*

Dewig Bros Meats 812 768-6208
100 W Maple St Haubstadt (47639) *(G-5998)*

Dewig Bros Packing Co Inc 812 768-6208
100 E Maple St Haubstadt (47639) *(G-5999)*

Dewig Deer Processing, Owensville *Also called Kenny Dewig Meats Sausage Inc* *(G-11428)*

Dewilde Glass Inc 765 742-0229
712 Ste 1 Wide Water Dr Lafayette (47904) *(G-8890)*

Dexstar Wheel, Elkhart *Also called Americana Development Inc (G-2688)*

Dexter Axle Company 574 295-7888
902 S Division St Bristol (46507) *(G-1054)*

Dexter Axle Company 574 294-6651
21611 Protecta Dr Elkhart (46516) *(G-2794)*

Dexter Axle Company 260 636-2195
500 S 7th St Albion (46701) *(G-25)*

Dexter Axle Company 260 495-5100
301 W Pearl St Fremont (46737) *(G-4958)*

Dexter Axle Company (HQ) 574 295-7888
2900 Industrial Pkwy Elkhart (46516) *(G-2795)*

Dexter Axle Company 574 294-6651
21608 Protecta Dr Elkhart (46516) *(G-2796)*

Dexter Axle Division, Albion *Also called Dexter Axle Company (G-25)*

Dexterous Mold and Tool Inc 812 422-8046
2535 Locust Creek Dr Evansville (47720) *(G-3457)*

Dezigns By Cindy Ziese 219 819-8786
5270 W 300 N Rensselaer (47978) *(G-11921)*

Df Global Mfg, Indianapolis *Also called Mary Jonas (G-7462)*

Dg Graphics LLC 765 349-9500
1809 E Morgan St Martinsville (46151) *(G-9601)*

Dgp Intelsius LLC 317 452-4006
7696 Zionsville Rd Indianapolis (46268) *(G-6738)*

DH Machine Inc 574 773-9211
352 N Tomahawk Trl Nappanee (46550) *(G-10667)*

Di Cologne Group 260 616-0158
14214 Brafferton Pkwy Fort Wayne (46814) *(G-4209)*

Diabco Life Sciences LLC 317 697-9988
484 E Carmel Dr Carmel (46032) *(G-1359)*

Dial-X Acquisition Company Inc 260 636-7588
3903 S State Road 9 Albion (46701) *(G-26)*

Dial-X Automated Equipment, Albion *Also called Dial-X Acquisition Company Inc (G-26)*

Diamond Billiard Products Inc 812 288-7665
4700 New Middle Rd Jeffersonville (47130) *(G-8351)*

Diamond Chain Company Inc (HQ) 800 872-4246
402 Kentucky Ave Indianapolis (46225) *(G-6739)*

Diamond Construction Svcs LLC 513 314-3609
6534 Hartford Pike Aurora (47001) *(G-376)*

Diamond Foods LLC 209 467-6000
4943 N 900 E Van Buren (46991) *(G-13639)*

Diamond Hoosier 317 773-1411
518 Sunset Dr Noblesville (46060) *(G-11091)*

Diamond III Inc 812 882-6269
4298 E Bristol Dr Vincennes (47591) *(G-13674)*

Diamond Manufacturing Company 219 874-2374
600 Royal Rd Michigan City (46360) *(G-9782)*

Diamond Mfg Co Midwest, Michigan City *Also called Diamond Manufacturing Company (G-9782)*

Diamond Mining Lead 317 340-7760
929 Evening Dr Ste A Indianapolis (46201) *(G-6740)*

Diamond Plastics Corporation 765 287-9234
4100 Niles Rd Muncie (47302) *(G-10459)*

Diamond Stone Technologies Inc 812 276-6043
2237 Industrial Dr Bedford (47421) *(G-537)*

Diamond Tools Technology Inc 847 537-8686
9339 Castlegate Dr Indianapolis (46256) *(G-6741)*

Diamonds Componets Inc 574 358-0452
420 N Main St Ste 6 Middlebury (46540) *(G-9881)*

Diane Dixon 812 836-4179
8172 Triplett Rd Rome (47574) *(G-12196)*

Dick Baumgartners Basket 765 220-1767
707 Beeson Rd Richmond (47374) *(G-11977)*

Dickey Consumer Products Inc 317 773-8330
15268 Stony Creek Way # 100 Noblesville (46060) *(G-11092)*

Dicksons Inc 812 522-1308
709 B Ave E Seymour (47274) *(G-12445)*

Dicksons Inspirational Gifts, Seymour *Also called Dicksons Inc (G-12445)*

Die Protection Tech LLC 812 837-9507
6040 Crooked Creek Rd Nashville (47448) *(G-10722)*

Die-Mensional Metal Stamping 812 265-3946
2950 Wilson Ave Madison (47250) *(G-9456)*

Die-Rite Machine and Tool Corp 574 522-2366
129 Rush Ct Elkhart (46516) *(G-2797)*

Dieco of Indiana Inc 765 825-4151
5130 Western Ave Connersville (47331) *(G-2046)*

Diedrich Drill Inc 219 326-7788
5 Fisher St La Porte (46350) *(G-8751)*

Diesel Punk Core 812 631-0606
3520 S Mcdougal St Bloomington (47403) *(G-712)*

Diesel Rx Products, Shelbyville *Also called Wap Inc (G-12584)*

Dietech Corporation 260 724-8946
1001 W Commerce Dr Decatur (46733) *(G-2375)*

Dietrich Industries Inc 219 931-3741
1435 165th St Hammond (46320) *(G-5870)*

Digger Specialties Inc (PA) 574 546-5999
3446 Us Highway 6 Bremen (46506) *(G-996)*

Digi International Inc 877 272-3111
435 Park Place Cir # 100 Mishawaka (46545) *(G-10036)*

Digiop Inc 800 968-3606
9340 Priority Way West Dr Indianapolis (46240) *(G-6742)*

Digistitch 574 538-3960
16123 County Road 40 Goshen (46528) *(G-5199)*

Digital Carvings LLC 812 269-6123
927 E Meadowlands Dr Ellettsville (47429) *(G-3278)*

Digital Cmmnties Intiative Inc 317 580-0111
12579 Pembrooke Cir Carmel (46032) *(G-1360)*

Digital Color Graphics, Indianapolis *Also called Diversfied Cmmunications Group (G-6749)*

Digital Evolution 317 839-7963
2028 Stafford Rd Ste D Plainfield (46168) *(G-11604)*

Digital Helium LLC 219 365-4038
9301 W 94th Pl Saint John (46373) *(G-12262)*

Digital Printing Incorporated 812 265-2205
2906 Clifty Dr Madison (47250) *(G-9457)*

Digital Reprographics Inc 260 483-8066
3311 Congressional Pkwy Fort Wayne (46808) *(G-4210)*

Digital Solutions 812 257-0333
402 S State Road 57 Washington (47501) *(G-13980)*

Dilden Bros Inc 765 742-1717
1426 Canal Rd Lafayette (47904) *(G-8891)*

Dilden Bros Well & Drilling, Lafayette *Also called Dilden Bros Inc (G-8891)*

Dillman Farm Incorporated 812 825-5525
4955 W State Road 45 Bloomington (47403) *(G-713)*

Dillon Pattern Works Inc 765 642-3549
1010 W 21st St Anderson (46016) *(G-95)*

Dimension Plywood Inc 812 944-6491
415 Industrial Blvd New Albany (47150) *(G-10768)*

Dimensional Imprinting Inc 260 417-0202
13579 Whitaker Dr Milton (47357) *(G-9987)*

Dimensions Furniture Inc 317 218-0025
341 Gradle Dr Carmel (46032) *(G-1361)*

Dimensions In Tooling Inc 574 273-1505
12635 Sandy Dr Granger (46530) *(G-5401)*

Dimplex North America Limited 317 890-0809
221 S Franklin Rd Ste 300 Indianapolis (46219) *(G-6743)*

Direct Cnnect Prtg Dgital Svcs, Indianapolis *Also called Rhr Corporation (G-7837)*

Direct Control Systems Inc 765 282-7474
4200 W County Road 750 N Muncie (47303) *(G-10460)*

Direct Conveyors LLC 317 346-7777
551 Earlywood Dr Franklin (46131) *(G-4881)*

Directed Photonics Inc 317 877-3142
7178 Oakbay Dr Noblesville (46062) *(G-11093)*

Directional Business Intellige 317 770-0805
149 Stony Creek Overlook Noblesville (46060) *(G-11094)*

Directional Drilling Co LLC 812 208-3392
112 W Main St Farmersburg (47850) *(G-3837)*

Directv Inc 260 471-3474
10020 Lima Rd Ste A Fort Wayne (46818) *(G-4211)*

Dirty Squeegee Screen Prtg LLC 574 358-0003
57319 County Road 35 Middlebury (46540) *(G-9882)*

Discount Detector Sales Inc 765 866-0320
7488 S 600 W Crawfordsville (47933) *(G-2149)*

Discount Labels LLC 812 945-2617
4115 Profit Ct New Albany (47150) *(G-10769)*

Discount Power Equipment 765 642-0040
2650 E State Road 236 Anderson (46017) *(G-96)*

Dish Express 812 962-3982
1101 N Fulton Ave Evansville (47710) *(G-3458)*

Disinger Machine Shop 219 567-2357
4045 S 1450 W Francesville (47946) *(G-4810)*

Diskey Architectural Signage 260 424-0233
450 E Brackenridge St Fort Wayne (46802) *(G-4212)*

Diskit Sales Division, Lafayette *Also called Perry Foam Products Inc (G-8980)*

Dispensit 317 776-8740
17555 Willow View Rd Noblesville (46062) *(G-11095)*

Display Craft 260 726-4535
803 W Water St Portland (47371) *(G-11816)*

Displaysource, Fort Wayne *Also called Icon International Inc (G-4356)*

Dist Council 91 .... 812 962-9191
409 Millner Industrial Dr Evansville (47710) *(G-3459)*

Distance Learning Systems Ind 888 955-3276
107 N State Road 135 # 302 Greenwood (46142) *(G-5681)*

Distinct Images Inc 317 613-4413
6830 Hawthorn Park Dr Indianapolis (46220) *(G-6744)*

Distinctive Creations, Nashville *Also called Pit Bull Leather Company Inc (G-10733)*

Distinctive Elements 260 704-2464
10208 Kilkea Pl Fort Wayne (46835) *(G-4213)*

Distrbteurs De Monnaie Std Inc, Indianapolis *Also called Standard Change-Makers Inc (G-7987)*

Ditech Inc 812 526-0850
1151 S Walnut St Edinburgh (46124) *(G-2607)*

Ditto Sales Inc (PA) 812 482-3043
2332 Cathy Ln Jasper (47546) *(G-8245)*

Ditto Sales Inc 812 424-4098
1817 W Virginia St Evansville (47712) *(G-3460)*

A
L
P
H
A
B
E
T
I
C

Divers Supply Company Inc...317 923-4523
50 W 33rd St Indianapolis (46208) ***(G-6745)***
Diverse Fabrication Services...317 781-8800
5508 Elmwood Ave Ste 317 Indianapolis (46203) ***(G-6746)***
Diverse Managed Services, Indianapolis *Also called Diverse Tech Services Inc* ***(G-6748)***
Diverse Sales Solutions LLC...317 514-2403
4947 Oakbrook Ct Indianapolis (46254) ***(G-6747)***
Diverse Tech Services Inc...317 432-6444
7176 Waldemar Dr Indianapolis (46268) ***(G-6748)***
Diverse Woodworking LLC...812 366-3000
505 Maplewood Blvd Georgetown (47122) ***(G-5143)***
Diversfied Cmmunications Group...317 755-3191
2629 Rand Rd Indianapolis (46241) ***(G-6749)***
Diversified Coating & Fabg Inc...260 563-2858
3406 W 50 N Wabash (46992) ***(G-13724)***
Diversified Mch Bristol LLC...248 728-8642
51650 County Road 133 Bristol (46507) ***(G-1055)***
Diversified Ophthalmics Inc...317 780-1677
4555 Independence Sq Indianapolis (46203) ***(G-6750)***
Diversified Pattern & Engrg Co...260 897-3771
100 Progress Way Avilla (46710) ***(G-403)***
Diversified Products Div, Elkhart *Also called Elixir Industries* ***(G-2816)***
Diversified Qulty Svcs Ind LLC...765 644-7712
1315 W 18th St Anderson (46016) ***(G-97)***
Diversified Tools & Machine...260 489-0272
2701 W Wallen Rd Fort Wayne (46818) ***(G-4214)***
Diversified Wear Products, Gary *Also called Refax Inc* ***(G-5090)***
Diversity Press LLC...317 241-4234
4026 W 10th St Indianapolis (46222) ***(G-6751)***
Diversity-Vuteq LLC...812 761-0210
825 E 350 S Princeton (47670) ***(G-11868)***
Divine Grace Homecare...219 290-5911
4224 Connecticut St Gary (46409) ***(G-5041)***
Division 60, Indianapolis *Also called Gardner Glass Products Inc* ***(G-6984)***
Division of Clones Plus, Madison *Also called Pathology Computer Systems* ***(G-9490)***
Divsys International LLC...317 405-9427
8110 Zionsville Rd Indianapolis (46268) ***(G-6752)***
Dixie Chopper, Coatesville *Also called Magic Circle Corporation* ***(G-1751)***
Dixie Metal Spinning Corp...317 541-1330
4730 Industrial Pkwy Indianapolis (46226) ***(G-6753)***
Dj Wreath Creations LLC...317 723-3268
6829 Meadowgreen Dr Indianapolis (46236) ***(G-6754)***
Djo LLC...317 406-2000
790 Columbia Rd Plainfield (46168) ***(G-11605)***
Dkm Embroidery Inc...260 471-4070
3203 Caprice Ct Fort Wayne (46808) ***(G-4215)***
DL Schwartz Co LLC...260 692-1464
2188 S Us Highway 27 Berne (46711) ***(G-612)***
Dla Document Services...812 854-1465
300 Highway 361 Bldg 18 Crane (47522) ***(G-2125)***
DMC Distribution LLC...219 926-6401
172 S 19th St Porter (46304) ***(G-11805)***
DMD Pharmaceuticals, Noblesville *Also called Dickey Consumer Products Inc* ***(G-11092)***
Dmg Mori Usa Inc...317 913-0978
6848 Hillsdale Ct Indianapolis (46250) ***(G-6755)***
Dmi, Bristol *Also called Diversified Mch Bristol LLC* ***(G-1055)***
Dmi Distribution Inc...765 287-0035
401 S Lincoln St Muncie (47302) ***(G-10461)***
Dmi Furniture Inc...812 683-2123
703 N Chestnut St Huntingburg (47542) ***(G-6155)***
Dmi Furniture Inc...812 683-4035
213 W 1st St Huntingburg (47542) ***(G-6156)***
Dmi Holding Corp (HQ)...574 534-1224
2164 Caragana Ct Goshen (46526) ***(G-5200)***
Dmp Industries LLC...260 413-6701
1411 E Springhill Rd Warsaw (46580) ***(G-13867)***
Dmp LLC...812 699-0086
2868 W 325 N Worthington (47471) ***(G-14394)***
Dmray Sawmill Inc...812 723-1109
6001 E Us Highway 150 Hardinsburg (47125) ***(G-5964)***
Dna Enterprises Inc...574 534-0034
2470 E Kercher Rd Goshen (46526) ***(G-5201)***
Dngco LLC (PA)...800 643-7332
7625 Disalle Blvd Fort Wayne (46825) ***(G-4216)***
Dnm Converters & Cores...502 599-5225
107 E Lynnwood Dr Clarksville (47129) ***(G-1679)***
Do It Best, Attica *Also called Neumayr Lumber Co Inc* ***(G-308)***
Do It Best, Merrillville *Also called Leeps Supply Co Inc* ***(G-9726)***
Do Technologies LLC...812 272-2306
730 N Walnut St Apt 202 Bloomington (47404) ***(G-714)***
Dobbins Interior Woodworks...812 221-0058
5916 E County Road 300 S Dillsboro (47018) ***(G-2466)***
Dockside...574 400-0848
1835 Lincoln Way E South Bend (46613) ***(G-12752)***
Docutech Document Service...219 690-3038
1601 Northview Dr Lowell (46356) ***(G-9404)***
Dodd Saw Mills Inc...812 268-4811
85 E County Road 450 N Sullivan (47882) ***(G-13081)***
Dodd Wood Products Inc...812 268-0798
85 E County Road 450 N Sullivan (47882) ***(G-13082)***
Dodge Heating and Coolg Contrs, Angola *Also called Knox Inc* ***(G-226)***
DOE Run Tooling Inc...812 265-3057
8550 E Doe Run Rd Madison (47250) ***(G-9458)***
Doell Designs...260 486-4504
5211 Stellhorn Rd Fort Wayne (46815) ***(G-4217)***
Doerr Printing Co...317 568-0135
4222 E 18th St Indianapolis (46218) ***(G-6756)***
Dog Ear Publishing...317 228-3656
4011 Vincennes Rd Indianapolis (46268) ***(G-6757)***
Dole...812 576-2186
6575 Stonegate Dr Guilford (47022) ***(G-5798)***
Domar Machine & Tool Inc...574 295-8791
56740 Elk Park Dr Elkhart (46516) ***(G-2798)***
Dometic Corporation...574 389-3759
2482 Century Dr Goshen (46528) ***(G-5202)***
Dometic Corporation...260 463-7657
509 S Poplar St Lagrange (46761) ***(G-9037)***
Dominion Building Products, Elkhart *Also called Assa Abloy Door Group LLC* ***(G-2697)***
Don Anderson...574 278-7243
10739 N 650 E Monticello (47960) ***(G-10259)***
Don Case...765 748-1325
3200 E County Road 350 N Muncie (47303) ***(G-10462)***
Don Detzer LLC...812 362-7599
12859 N County Road 125 W Tennyson (47637) ***(G-13179)***
Don Hartman Oil Co Inc...765 643-5026
4193 Alexandria Pike Anderson (46012) ***(G-98)***
Don Jones Oil Company, Vincennes *Also called Pioneer Oil Company Inc* ***(G-13697)***
Don Michiel Prints LLC...812 550-7767
5217 Normandy Pl Evansville (47715) ***(G-3461)***
Don Moline Electric...317 987-7606
6957 E County Road 100 S Avon (46123) ***(G-438)***
Don R Fruchey Inc...260 493-3626
2121 Wayne Haven St Fort Wayne (46803) ***(G-4218)***
Don R Kill Publishing Inc...574 271-9381
50742 Old Lantern Trl Granger (46530) ***(G-5402)***
Donald H & Susan K Minch...260 726-9486
2825 W 400 N Portland (47371) ***(G-11817)***
Donald L Gard...219 663-7945
11629 Burr St Crown Point (46307) ***(G-2246)***
Donaldson Company Inc...765 659-4766
3260 W State Road 28 Frankfort (46041) ***(G-4828)***
Donaldson Company Inc...952 887-3131
303 N 6th St Monticello (47960) ***(G-10260)***
Donaldson Company Inc...317 838-5568
1251 S Perry Rd Plainfield (46168) ***(G-11606)***
Donaldson Company Inc...812 637-9200
1802 Boardwalk Dr Lawrenceburg (47025) ***(G-9139)***
Donaldson Country Home, Lebanon *Also called Donaldsons Chocolates Inc* ***(G-9181)***
Donaldsons Chocolates Inc...765 482-3334
600 S State Road 39 Lebanon (46052) ***(G-9181)***
Donnie Michaels Kicks...765 457-4083
3780 S Reed Rd Kokomo (46902) ***(G-8617)***
Dons Automotive and Machine...812 547-6292
1047 6th St Tell City (47586) ***(G-13159)***
Donut Bank Bakery, Evansville *Also called Donut Bank Inc* ***(G-3462)***
Donut Bank Inc (PA)...812 426-0011
1031 E Diamond Ave Evansville (47711) ***(G-3462)***
Donuts N Coffee Inc...812 376-2796
2222 State St Columbus (47201) ***(G-1908)***
Door Service Supply...317 496-0391
4075 Primrose Path Greenwood (46142) ***(G-5682)***
Door Tech Industries Inc...219 322-3465
2733 Quinn Pl Dyer (46311) ***(G-2494)***
Doors & Drawers Inc...574 533-3509
2302 Dierdorff Rd Goshen (46526) ***(G-5203)***
Dorel Home Furnishings Inc...812 372-0141
2525 State St Columbus (47201) ***(G-1909)***
Dorel Juvenile Group, Columbus *Also called Dorel USA Inc* ***(G-1914)***
Dorel Juvenile Group Inc...812 314-6629
500 S Gladstone Ave Columbus (47201) ***(G-1910)***
Dorel Juvenile Group Inc...812 372-0141
505 S Cherry St Columbus (47201) ***(G-1911)***
Dorel Juvenile Group Inc (HQ)...800 457-5276
2525 State St Columbus (47201) ***(G-1912)***
Dorel Juvenile Group Inc...812 372-0141
2525 State St Columbus (47201) ***(G-1913)***
Dorel USA Inc (HQ)...812 372-0141
2525 State St Columbus (47201) ***(G-1914)***
Doris Drapery Boutique...765 472-5850
68 N Broadway Peru (46970) ***(G-11524)***
Dorma...317 468-6742
215 W New Rd Greenfield (46140) ***(G-5521)***
Dormakaba USA Inc...317 806-4605
6161 E 75th St Indianapolis (46250) ***(G-6758)***
Doron Distribution Inc...317 594-9259
10625 Deme Dr Ste C Indianapolis (46236) ***(G-6759)***
Dose Shield Corporation...317 576-0183
530 Oakmont Ln Markleville (46056) ***(G-9587)***

DOT America Inc..260 244-5700
335 Towerview Dr Columbia City (46725) *(G-1779)*

Dotstaff LLC..317 806-6100
5875 Castle Creek Pkwy N Indianapolis (46250) *(G-6760)*

Dotted Lime Resale LLC.................................317 908-3905
4232 Zachary Ln Westfield (46062) *(G-14160)*

Doty, Leroy E. Builder, Crown Point *Also called Leroy E Doty Cabinet Shop* *(G-2275)*

Double E Distributing Co Inc (PA).....................812 334-2220
2214 E Rock Creek Dr Bloomington (47401) *(G-715)*

Double E Dstrbtng Co, Bloomington *Also called Double E Distributing Co Inc* *(G-715)*

Double E Enterprise Inc...................................812 689-0671
205 Western Ave Osgood (47037) *(G-11390)*

Double Eagle Industries Inc..............................260 768-4121
775 N 740 W Shipshewana (46565) *(G-12612)*

Double Envelope Corp.....................................260 434-0500
10804 Lake Shasta Ct Fort Wayne (46804) *(G-4219)*

Double H Manufacturing Corp............................765 664-9090
2548 W 26th St Marion (46953) *(G-9521)*

Double H Plastics, Marion *Also called Double H Manufacturing Corp* *(G-9521)*

Double L Woodworking L L C..............................260 768-3155
12478 County Road 34 Goshen (46528) *(G-5204)*

Double T Manufacturing Corp............................574 262-1340
27139 County Road 6 Elkhart (46514) *(G-2799)*

Doug Wilcox...812 476-1957
1188 W State Route 68 Lynnville (47619) *(G-9434)*

Douglas Dye and Associates.............................317 844-1709
501 Industrial Dr Carmel (46032) *(G-1362)*

Douglas Industries LLC...................................260 327-3692
2277 N Binkley Rd Larwill (46764) *(G-9121)*

Douglas K Gresham.......................................812 445-3174
1540 N County Road 900 W Seymour (47274) *(G-12446)*

Douglas P Terrell..812 254-1976
1289 S State Road 57 Washington (47501) *(G-13981)*

Dougs Welding Shop......................................765 689-8396
10541 S Strawtown Pike Bunker Hill (46914) *(G-1205)*

Dove Printing Services...................................317 843-8222
8425 Wdfld Xing Blvd Indianapolis (46240) *(G-6761)*

Dover Chemical Corporation.............................219 852-0042
3000 Sheffield Ave Hammond (46327) *(G-5871)*

Dover Corporation (PA)..................................502 587-6783
2540 Centennial Blvd Jeffersonville (47130) *(G-8352)*

Dovetail Woodworks......................................812 448-8832
8390 N County Road 500 W Brazil (47834) *(G-959)*

Dovey Corporation..765 649-2576
3220 W 25th St Anderson (46011) *(G-99)*

Dow Agroscience..765 743-0015
1281 Win Hentschel Blvd West Lafayette (47906) *(G-14064)*

Dow Agrosciences LLC...................................317 252-5602
5110 E 69th St Indianapolis (46220) *(G-6762)*

Dow Agrosciences LLC (HQ).............................317 337-3000
9330 Zionsville Rd Indianapolis (46268) *(G-6763)*

Dow Silicones Corporation...............................260 347-5813
111 S Progress Dr E Kendallville (46755) *(G-8474)*

Dow Theory Forecasts Inc................................219 931-6480
7412 Calumet Ave Ste 1 Hammond (46324) *(G-5872)*

Down-Lite International Inc...............................513 229-3696
8984 W State Road 236 Middletown (47356) *(G-9934)*

Downey Creations Inc....................................317 248-9888
1811 Executive Dr Ste R Indianapolis (46241) *(G-6764)*

Doyle Logging Etienne, Magnet *Also called Anthony D Etienne Logging* *(G-9502)*

Doyle Manufacturing Inc.................................574 848-5624
16630 County Road 10 Bristol (46507) *(G-1056)*

Dpa Investments Inc.....................................219 873-0914
1750 E Us Highway 12 Michigan City (46360) *(G-9783)*

Dpc Inc...765 564-3752
2065 W Us Highway 421 Delphi (46923) *(G-2419)*

DPG, West Lafayette *Also called Dayton-Phoenix Group Inc* *(G-14063)*

Dpi, Madison *Also called Digital Printing Incorporated* *(G-9457)*

Dpp, North Vernon *Also called Decatur Plastic Products Inc* *(G-11255)*

Dps Printing...260 503-9681
950 Liberty Dr Columbia City (46725) *(G-1780)*

Dr Pepper Bottling Co.....................................765 647-3576
261 Webers Ln Brookville (47012) *(G-1113)*

Dr Pepper Bottling Company.............................812 332-1200
214 W 17th St Bloomington (47404) *(G-716)*

Dr Pepper Snapple Group I..............................260 484-4177
2711 Independence Dr Fort Wayne (46808) *(G-4220)*

Dr Restorations Inc.......................................317 646-7150
4252 N Raceway Rd Clermont (46234) *(G-1712)*

Dr Tavel Premium Optical, Indianapolis *Also called City Optical Co Inc* *(G-6616)*

Dr Tavel's One Hour Optical, Indianapolis *Also called City Optical Co Inc* *(G-6615)*

Dragon ESP Ltd...574 893-1569
8857 E State Road 14 Akron (46910) *(G-4)*

Dragon Industries Incorporated.........................574 772-3508
2120 E State Road 10 Knox (46534) *(G-8565)*

Drake Corporation..636 464-5070
9930 E 56th St Indianapolis (46236) *(G-6765)*

Drake Corporation..812 683-2101
1180 Wernsing Rd Jasper (47546) *(G-8246)*

Draper Inc (PA)...765 987-7999
411 S Pearl St Spiceland (47385) *(G-13054)*

Dream Kraft LLC..317 545-2988
4037 N Drexel Ave Indianapolis (46226) *(G-6766)*

Dream Lighting Inc..574 206-4888
2111 Industrial Pkwy Elkhart (46516) *(G-2800)*

Dream Mill, Elwood *Also called Aunt Netts Country Candles LLC* *(G-3294)*

Dreamwork Stones LLC..................................317 709-2202
4161 Kattman Ct Carmel (46074) *(G-1363)*

Drews Deer Processing...................................812 279-6246
8122 Us Highway 50 W Mitchell (47446) *(G-10162)*

Driessen Water Inc.......................................765 529-4905
1509 N Wheeling Ave Muncie (47303) *(G-10463)*

Drilling & Trenching Sup Inc.............................317 825-0919
860 Elston Dr Shelbyville (46176) *(G-12530)*

Drilling World, Shelbyville *Also called Drilling & Trenching Sup Inc* *(G-12530)*

Drinkgp LLC...317 410-4748
5707 Brockton Dr Apt 115 Indianapolis (46220) *(G-6767)*

Drive Process Services Inc...............................765 741-9717
6017 W Hellis Dr Muncie (47304) *(G-10464)*

Drone Works LLC...812 917-4691
933 S 5th St Apt 3 Terre Haute (47807) *(G-13225)*

Drone1260wrx LLC.......................................773 957-3625
6841 E 85th Ct Merrillville (46410) *(G-9711)*

Droneye Imaging LLC.....................................317 878-4065
5127 S 200 W Trafalgar (46181) *(G-13435)*

Drp Mold Inc...765 349-3355
70 James Baldwin Dr Martinsville (46151) *(G-9602)*

Drs Graphix Group Inc....................................317 569-1855
3855 E 96th St Ste L Indianapolis (46240) *(G-6768)*

Drug Plastics and Glass Co Inc..........................765 385-0035
5 Bottle Dr Oxford (47971) *(G-11431)*

Drug Plastics Closures Inc...............................812 526-0555
2875 W 800 N Edinburgh (46124) *(G-2608)*

Drummond Industries.....................................260 348-5550
2826 White Oak Ave Fort Wayne (46805) *(G-4221)*

Drv Llc...260 562-1075
160 W 750 N Howe (46746) *(G-6122)*

Dry Inc...503 977-9204
7201 Engle Rd Fort Wayne (46804) *(G-4222)*

Dry Cleaners Secret, Fort Wayne *Also called Dry Inc* *(G-4222)*

Ds Corp..260 593-3850
1115 W Lake St Topeka (46571) *(G-13417)*

Ds Products Inc...260 563-9030
202 Wedcor Ave Wabash (46992) *(G-13725)*

Ds Smith Rapak, Indianapolis *Also called Grrk Holdings Inc* *(G-7053)*

Ds Wood Products Inc....................................574 642-3855
14322 County Road 40 Goshen (46528) *(G-5205)*

DS Woods Custom Cabinets.............................260 692-6565
2231 N Us Highway 27 Decatur (46733) *(G-2376)*

DSM Coating Resins Inc..................................765 659-4721
3110 W State Road 28 Frankfort (46041) *(G-4829)*

DSM Engineering Plastics Inc............................812 435-7500
2267 W Mill Rd Evansville (47720) *(G-3463)*

DSM Engineering Plastics Inc............................812 435-7638
2267 W Mill Rd Evansville (47720) *(G-3464)*

DSM Engineering Plastics Inc (HQ)......................248 530-5500
2267 W Mill Rd Evansville (47720) *(G-3465)*

DTE, Clinton *Also called ARS Nebraska LLC* *(G-1713)*

Du Bois Equipment Company, Jasper *Also called Dubois Machine Co Inc* *(G-8249)*

Dual Machine & Tool Co Inc..............................812 256-2202
310 Randolph St Charlestown (47111) *(G-1563)*

Dual Machine Corporation................................317 921-9850
1951 Bloyd Ave Indianapolis (46218) *(G-6769)*

Dualtech Inc...317 738-9043
450 Blue Chip Ct Franklin (46131) *(G-4882)*

Dubois Cnty Block & Brick Inc...........................812 482-6293
2208 Newton St Jasper (47546) *(G-8247)*

Dubois Co Block & Brick, Jasper *Also called Dubois Cnty Block & Brick Inc* *(G-8247)*

Dubois County Free Press LLC...........................812 639-9651
4288 W 630s Huntingburg (47542) *(G-6157)*

Dubois Equipment Company LLC.........................812 482-3644
620 3rd Ave Jasper (47546) *(G-8248)*

Dubois Machine Co Inc...................................812 482-3644
620 3rd Ave Jasper (47546) *(G-8249)*

Dubois Manufacturing Inc................................574 674-6988
30561 Old Us 20 Elkhart (46514) *(G-2801)*

Dubois Wood Products, Huntingburg *Also called Dubois Wood Realty Inc* *(G-6160)*

Dubois Wood Products Inc (PA)..........................812 683-3613
707 E 6th St Huntingburg (47542) *(G-6158)*

Dubois Wood Products Inc...............................812 683-5105
610 E 5th St Huntingburg (47542) *(G-6159)*

Dubois Wood Realty Inc..................................812 683-3613
707 E 6th St Huntingburg (47542) *(G-6160)*

Duboisspencer Counties Pubg (PA).....................812 367-2041
113 W 6th St Ferdinand (47532) *(G-3848)*

Dubose Strapping Inc....................................765 361-0000
4414 E 400 S Crawfordsville (47933) *(G-2150)*

A
L
P
H
A
B
E
T
I
C

Duclas Fitness LLC 812 217-8544
　114 Williamsburg Dr Evansville (47715) *(G-3466)*

Duel & Tool & Gage Inc 317 244-0129
　1553 S Concord St Indianapolis (46241) *(G-6770)*

Duesenburg Inc 260 496-9650
　3330 Congressional Pkwy Fort Wayne (46808) *(G-4223)*

Dugherty Inc 260 375-2010
　609 E 1st St Warren (46792) *(G-13828)*

Dugout 765 642-8528
　2203 Broadway St Anderson (46012) *(G-100)*

Dulceria Garza Inc 219 397-1062
　4120 Deal St East Chicago (46312) *(G-2525)*

Duley Press Inc 574 259-5203
　2906 N Home St Mishawaka (46545) *(G-10037)*

Dumor Water Specialists Inc 574 522-9500
　4405 Wyland Dr Elkhart (46516) *(G-2802)*

Dump & Go, Elkhart *Also called Quality Steel & Alum Pdts Inc (G-3130)*

Duncan Logging Inc 812 564-2488
　13628 S Watts St Coalmont (47845) *(G-1745)*

Duncan Service Company 765 452-6799
　701 S Main St Kokomo (46901) *(G-8618)*

Duncan Supply Co Inc 765 446-0105
　510 Morland Dr Lafayette (47905) *(G-8892)*

Duncan Systems, Elkhart *Also called Lippert Components Inc (G-3000)*

Dune Ridge Winery LLC 219 548-4605
　1903 Cheyenne Cir Valparaiso (46383) *(G-13529)*

Duneland Alpacas Ltd 219 877-4417
　1394 N County Line Rd Michigan City (46360) *(G-9784)*

Duneland Specialties Inc 219 464-1616
　2005 Calumet Ave Valparaiso (46383) *(G-13530)*

Dungan Aerial Services Inc 765 827-1355
　4290 N County Road 450 W Connersville (47331) *(G-2047)*

Dunham Rubber & Belting Corp (PA) 317 888-3002
　682 Commerce Parkway W Dr Greenwood (46143) *(G-5683)*

Dunham Rubber & Belting Corp 800 876-5340
　4004 Lower Huntington Rd Fort Wayne (46809) *(G-4224)*

Dunham Rubber Belting Corp 317 604-5313
　245 Northridge Dr Shelbyville (46176) *(G-12531)*

Dunn-Rite Products Inc (PA) 765 552-9433
　2200 S J St Elwood (46036) *(G-3295)*

Dupont 219 261-2124
　600 Harrington St Remington (47977) *(G-11906)*

Dupont 9 Building Company LLC 260 432-4913
　2518 E Dupont Rd Fort Wayne (46825) *(G-4225)*

Dupont and Tonkel Partners LLC 260 444-2264
　10501 Day Lily Dr Fort Wayne (46825) *(G-4226)*

Dupont Commons LLC 260 637-3215
　10316 Valley Hills Ln Fort Wayne (46825) *(G-4227)*

Dupont Nutrition & Health, Terre Haute *Also called E I Du Pont De Nemours & Co (G-13226)*

Dupont Orthodontics 260 490-3554
　2121 E Dupont Rd Fort Wayne (46825) *(G-4228)*

Dura Automotive Systems of Ind 574 262-2655
　2700 Jeanwood Dr Elkhart (46514) *(G-2803)*

Dura Bull, Alexandria *Also called Glove Corporation (G-43)*

Dura Products Inc 855 502-3872
　504 Demoss Ave Arcadia (46030) *(G-264)*

Dura-Vent Corp 574 936-2432
　1435 N Michigan St Ste 3 Plymouth (46563) *(G-11681)*

Durakool, Elkhart *Also called American Elctrnic Cmpnents Inc (G-2682)*

Duramark Technologies Inc 317 867-5700
　16450 Southpark Dr Westfield (46074) *(G-14161)*

Duramold Castings Inc 574 251-1111
　1901 N Bendix Dr South Bend (46628) *(G-12753)*

Durcholz Excavating & Cnstr Co 812 634-1764
　4308 S State Road 162 Huntingburg (47542) *(G-6161)*

Durcholz Excvtg & Cnstr Co In, Huntingburg *Also called Durcholz Excavating & Cnstr Co (G-6161)*

Durm Vineyard Inc 317 862-9463
　11747 Indian Creek Rd S Indianapolis (46259) *(G-6771)*

Duro Inc 574 293-6860
　24478 County Road 45 Elkhart (46516) *(G-2804)*

Duro Recycling Inc 574 522-2572
　24478 County Road 45 Elkhart (46516) *(G-2805)*

Dutch Country Woodworking Inc 260 499-4847
　200 Industrial Pkwy Lagrange (46761) *(G-9038)*

Dutch Kettle LLC 574 546-4033
　6375 Fir Rd Bremen (46506) *(G-997)*

Dutch Made Inc 260 657-3331
　16836 State Road 37 Harlan (46743) *(G-5970)*

Dutch Made Inc (PA) 260 657-3311
　10415 Roth Rd Grabill (46741) *(G-5363)*

Dutch Park Homes Inc 574 642-0150
　2249 Lincolnway E Goshen (46526) *(G-5206)*

Dutchcraft Corporation 260 463-8366
　50 S 375 W Lagrange (46761) *(G-9039)*

Dutchtown Homes 812 354-2197
　1011 N State Road 257 Otwell (47564) *(G-11422)*

Dux Signal Kits LLC 260 623-3017
　23132 Monroeville Rd Monroeville (46773) *(G-10194)*

Dvs Refractories, Gary *Also called Shanxi-Indiana LLC (G-5097)*

Dvs Refractories LLC 219 886-2004
　1040 N Union St Gary (46403) *(G-5042)*

Dwd Industries LLC (HQ) 260 728-9272
　1921 Patterson St Decatur (46733) *(G-2377)*

Dwd Industries LLC 260 639-3254
　11117 English St Hoagland (46745) *(G-6064)*

Dwd Miller Inc 812 853-8497
　10399 Telephone Rd Chandler (47610) *(G-1548)*

dwg Design Services Corp 812 372-0864
　1220 Washington St Columbus (47201) *(G-1915)*

Dwight Smith Logging 812 834-5546
　815 Roberts Ln Heltonville (47436) *(G-6026)*

Dwyer Enterprises 317 573-9628
　12075 Waterford Ln Carmel (46033) *(G-1364)*

Dwyer Instruments Inc 574 862-2590
　55 Ward St Wakarusa (46573) *(G-13775)*

Dwyer Instruments Inc 219 279-2031
　204 E Sherry Ln Wolcott (47995) *(G-14363)*

Dwyer Instruments Inc 219 879-8868
　6850 Enterprise Dr South Bend (46628) *(G-12754)*

Dwyer Instruments Inc 260 723-5138
　367 W 1st St South Whitley (46787) *(G-12997)*

Dwyer Instruments Inc 219 879-8000
　102 Hwy 212 Michigan City (46360) *(G-9785)*

Dwyer Instruments Inc 219 393-5250
　3999 E Hupp Rd Bldg R64 La Porte (46350) *(G-8752)*

Dwyer Instruments Inc 219 879-8000
　102 Indiana Highway 212 Michigan City (46360) *(G-9786)*

Dwyer-Wilbert Inc 765 962-3605
　1014 National Rd W Richmond (47374) *(G-11978)*

Dwyer-Wilbert Monument, Richmond *Also called Dwyer-Wilbert Inc (G-11978)*

Dx 4 LLC 260 410-3749
　3000 Engle Rd Fort Wayne (46809) *(G-4229)*

Dxd Signs 219 588-4403
　9231 Spring St Highland (46322) *(G-6043)*

Dye Woodworks, Carmel *Also called Douglas Dye and Associates (G-1362)*

Dyer Charles B and Ratliff Co 317 634-3381
　238 S Meridian St Fl 3 Indianapolis (46225) *(G-6772)*

Dyer Signwerks Inc 219 322-7722
　1000 Richard Rd Dyer (46311) *(G-2495)*

Dyer Vault Company Inc 219 865-2521
　1750 Sheffield Ave Dyer (46311) *(G-2496)*

Dyna Technology Inc 219 663-2920
　11025 Delaware Pkwy Crown Point (46307) *(G-2247)*

Dyna-Fab Corporation 765 893-4423
　3893 S State Road 263 West Lebanon (47991) *(G-14119)*

Dynaloy LLC 317 788-5694
　6445 Olivia Ln Indianapolis (46226) *(G-6773)*

Dynamark Graphics Group Inc 317 569-1855
　3855 E 96th St Ste L Indianapolis (46240) *(G-6774)*

Dynamark Graphics Group Inc (PA) 317 328-2555
　7210 Zionsville Rd Indianapolis (46268) *(G-6775)*

Dynamark Graphics Group Inc 317 328-2565
　7210 Zionsville Rd Indianapolis (46268) *(G-6776)*

Dynamark Graphics Group Inc 317 634-2963
　7210 Zionsville Rd Indianapolis (46268) *(G-6777)*

Dynamic Aerospace and Defense, Elkhart *Also called Dynamic Metals LLC (G-2807)*

Dynamic Composites LLC 260 625-8686
　2670 S 700 E Columbia City (46725) *(G-1781)*

Dynamic Designs Scottys 219 809-7268
　3409 Franklin St Michigan City (46360) *(G-9787)*

Dynamic Dies Inc 317 247-4706
　2321 Executive Dr Indianapolis (46241) *(G-6778)*

Dynamic Holdings LLC (HQ) 260 969-3500
　7575 W Jefferson Blvd Fort Wayne (46804) *(G-4230)*

Dynamic Industrial Group LLC 574 295-5525
　54347 Highland Blvd Elkhart (46514) *(G-2806)*

Dynamic Landscape & Design Co, Indianapolis *Also called Dynamic Landscapes LLC (G-6779)*

Dynamic Landscapes LLC 317 409-3487
　1022 Halifax Ln Indianapolis (46231) *(G-6779)*

Dynamic Metals LLC 574 262-2497
　54347 Highland Blvd Elkhart (46514) *(G-2807)*

Dynamic Packg Solutions Inc 574 848-1410
　406 Kesco Dr Bristol (46507) *(G-1057)*

Dynatect Manufacturing Inc 219 465-1898
　386 E State Road 2 Valparaiso (46383) *(G-13531)*

Dyno Nobel Inc 219 253-2525
　905 Burbank Rd Indianapolis (46219) *(G-6780)*

Dyno Nobel Inc 260 731-4431
　7860 W 400 N Pennville (47369) *(G-11513)*

Dyno Nobel Inc 859 278-4770
　4 Nw 2nd St Evansville (47708) *(G-3467)*

Dyno One Inc 812 526-0500
　14671 N 250 W Edinburgh (46124) *(G-2609)*

E & B Paving Inc (HQ) 765 643-5358
　286 W 300 N Anderson (46012) *(G-101)*

E & B Paving Inc 765 674-5848
　3888 S Garthwaite Rd Marion (46953) *(G-9522)*

E & B Paving Inc.....765 289-7131
4308 E County Road 350 N Muncie (47303) *(G-10465)*
E & B Paving Inc.....260 356-0828
875 N Broadway St Huntington (46750) *(G-6201)*
E & B Paving Inc.....765 472-3626
Cemetary Rd Peru (46970) *(G-11525)*
E & B Paving Inc.....317 781-1030
17042 Middletown Ave Noblesville (46060) *(G-11096)*
E & B Paving Inc.....317 773-4132
17042 Middletown Ave Noblesville (46060) *(G-11097)*
E & B Paving Inc.....317 773-8216
15215 River Rd Noblesville (46062) *(G-11098)*
E & H Bridge & Grating Inc.....812 277-8343
1 Lavender Ln Bedford (47421) *(G-538)*
E & H Industrial Services LLC.....317 569-8819
5515 Salem Dr S Carmel (46033) *(G-1365)*
E & H Tubing Inc.....812 358-3894
848 W Sweet St Brownstown (47220) *(G-1186)*
E & H Tubing Inc (HQ).....812 358-3894
848 W Sweet St Brownstown (47220) *(G-1187)*
E & L Construction Inc.....765 525-7081
1375 N 800 E Manilla (46150) *(G-9503)*
E & R Fabricating Inc.....812 275-0388
8854 State Road 37 Bedford (47421) *(G-539)*
E & R Machine Company Inc.....317 293-1550
8910 Crawfordsville Rd Indianapolis (46234) *(G-6781)*
E & R Manufacturing Company.....765 279-8826
504 N Illinois St Kirklin (46050) *(G-8548)*
E & S Metal Inc.....260 563-7714
3673 W Old 24 Wabash (46992) *(G-13726)*
E & S Wood Creations LLC.....260 768-3033
2030 N 450 W Lagrange (46761) *(G-9040)*
E C Schleyer Pump Co Inc.....765 643-3334
501 Sycamore St Anderson (46016) *(G-102)*
E C T Franklin Control Systems.....765 939-2531
1831 W Main St Richmond (47374) *(G-11979)*
E F M Corporation.....812 372-4421
1480 14th St Columbus (47201) *(G-1916)*
E Fab Incorporated.....317 786-9593
513 National Ave Ste A Indianapolis (46227) *(G-6782)*
E H Baare Corporation (PA).....765 778-7895
3620 W 73rd St Anderson (46011) *(G-103)*
E I Du Pont De Nemours & Co.....812 299-6700
11 W Litesse Dr Terre Haute (47802) *(G-13226)*
E I Du Pont De Nemours & Co.....812 299-6700
11 W Litesse Dr Terre Haute (47802) *(G-13227)*
E I Du Pont De Nemours & Co.....812 299-6700
33 W Litesse Dr Terre Haute (47802) *(G-13228)*
E Industries Inc.....574 522-7550
4526 Chester Dr Elkhart (46516) *(G-2808)*
E J Bognar Inc.....412 344-9900
23810 Highland St Schneider (46376) *(G-12354)*
E James Dant (PA).....812 476-2271
1620 Harmony Way Evansville (47720) *(G-3468)*
E James Dant.....812 476-2271
2520 E Morgan Ave Apt D Evansville (47711) *(G-3469)*
E L M, Indianapolis *Also called Ewing Light Metals Co Inc (G-6886)*
E L S Inc.....812 985-2272
10435 Upper Mt Vernon Rd Evansville (47712) *(G-3470)*
E M Cummings Veneers Inc.....812 944-2269
601 E 4th St New Albany (47150) *(G-10770)*
E M F Corp (PA).....260 665-9541
505 Pokagon Trl Angola (46703) *(G-208)*
E M F Corp.....260 488-2479
7335 S Enterprise Dr Hamilton (46742) *(G-5821)*
E M P, Greenfield *Also called Engineered Machined Pdts Inc (G-5527)*
E M S, Indianapolis *Also called Engineered Medical Systems (G-6869)*
E M Woodworking.....812 486-2696
6000 N 450 E Montgomery (47558) *(G-10223)*
E P I, Kingsbury *Also called Environmental Products Inc (G-8537)*
E P I, Merrillville *Also called Exhaust Productions Inc (G-9714)*
E P I, Indianapolis *Also called Epi Printers Inc (G-6875)*
E S A I, South Bend *Also called Ed Stump Assembly Inc (G-12758)*
E S C O, Elkhart *Also called Elkhart Supply Corp (G-2831)*
E S I, Garrett *Also called Enzyme Solutions Inc (G-5004)*
E Squared Motorsports LLC.....317 626-2937
1511 N County Road 600 E Avon (46123) *(G-439)*
E T & T Powder Coat.....574 293-2725
58391 Ventura Dr Elkhart (46517) *(G-2809)*
E T and T Enterprises, Elkhart *Also called E T & T Powder Coat (G-2809)*
E T S, Mishawaka *Also called Electro Transfer Systems Inc (G-10040)*
E Z Choice.....219 852-4281
5529 Calumet Ave Hammond (46320) *(G-5873)*
E Z Loader Boat Trailers Inc.....574 266-0092
125 W Belvedere Rd Elkhart (46514) *(G-2810)*
E Z'S Custom Woodworking, Nappanee *Also called Ezs Custom Woodworking (G-10668)*
E&P Technologies LLC.....317 828-8482
14254 Trailwind Ct Carmel (46032) *(G-1366)*
E&S Wallcovering.....812 256-6668
9018 Stonemour Way Charlestown (47111) *(G-1564)*
E-Beam Services Inc.....765 447-6755
3400 Union St Lafayette (47905) *(G-8893)*
E-Certa Incorporated.....812 323-7824
3930 S Walnut St Bloomington (47401) *(G-717)*
E-Collar Technologies Inc.....260 357-0051
2120 Forrest Park Dr Garrett (46738) *(G-5002)*
E-Pak Machinery Inc.....219 393-5541
1535 S State Road 39 La Porte (46350) *(G-8753)*
E-Tank Ltd.....317 296-0510
999 W Troy Ave Indianapolis (46225) *(G-6783)*
E-Z Sweep & Rake LLC.....574 533-2083
2556a Southside Park Dr Goshen (46526) *(G-5207)*
E3 Diagnostics Inc.....317 334-2000
8770 Commerce Park Pl D Indianapolis (46268) *(G-6784)*
E3 Gordon Stowe, Indianapolis *Also called E3 Diagnostics Inc (G-6784)*
EAB INDUSTRIES, Evansville *Also called Evansville Assn For The Blind (G-3482)*
Eagle Bearing, Evansville *Also called Hsm Eagle Ltd (G-3545)*
Eagle Cnc Machining Inc.....765 289-2816
801 W Riggin Rd Muncie (47303) *(G-10466)*
Eagle Consulting Inc.....317 590-0485
7968 Zionsville Rd Indianapolis (46268) *(G-6785)*
Eagle Craft Inc.....574 936-3196
904 Markley Dr Plymouth (46563) *(G-11682)*
Eagle Creek Machining Company.....219 365-3621
9680 Industrial Dr Saint John (46373) *(G-12263)*
Eagle Flooring Brokers Inc.....260 422-6100
220 Fernhill Ave Fort Wayne (46805) *(G-4231)*
Eagle Industries Inc.....812 282-1393
131 E Court Ave Ste 200 Jeffersonville (47130) *(G-8353)*
Eagle Magnetic Company Inc.....317 297-1030
7417 Crawfordsville Rd Indianapolis (46214) *(G-6786)*
Eagle Nest Workshop.....812 876-3215
3230 Pheasant Ln Spencer (47460) *(G-13023)*
Eagle Packaging Inc.....260 281-2333
2301 W Wilden Ave Goshen (46528) *(G-5208)*
Eagle Pet Products Inc.....574 259-7834
1025 W 11th St Mishawaka (46544) *(G-10038)*
Eagle Precision Machining Inc.....260 637-4649
2420 Shoaff R Huntertown (46748) *(G-6137)*
EAGLE PRINT, Lawrenceburg *Also called Delphos Herald of Indiana Inc (G-9138)*
Eagle Ready-Mix Inc.....574 642-4455
65723 Us Highway 33 Goshen (46526) *(G-5209)*
Eagle River Coal LLC.....618 252-0490
250 N Cross Pointe Blvd Evansville (47715) *(G-3471)*
Eagle Sign & Design, New Albany *Also called Richardson Imaging Svcs Inc (G-10855)*
Eagle Tile, Fort Wayne *Also called Eagle Flooring Brokers Inc (G-4231)*
Earl Chupp.....574 372-8400
9151 W 750 N Etna Green (46524) *(G-3320)*
Earl R Hamilton.....317 838-9386
312 Wayside Dr Plainfield (46168) *(G-11607)*
Earl's Indy, Indianapolis *Also called Esco Enterprises Indiana Inc (G-6876)*
Earth Drops Handcrafted Soaps.....812 336-2491
3065 N Prow Rd Bloomington (47404) *(G-718)*
Earth First Kentuckiana Inc.....812 248-0712
5511 County Road 403 Charlestown (47111) *(G-1565)*
Earth First Kentuckiana Inc (PA).....812 923-1227
9251 Highway 150 Greenville (47124) *(G-5648)*
Earth Mama Compost.....317 759-4589
10830 Lafayette Rd Indianapolis (46278) *(G-6787)*
Earthchain Magnetic Pro.....317 803-8034
9930 E 56th St Indianapolis (46236) *(G-6788)*
Earthway Products Inc.....574 848-7491
1009 Maple St Bristol (46507) *(G-1058)*
Earthwise Plastics Inc.....765 673-0308
100 Earthwise Way Gas City (46933) *(G-5123)*
Earthwise Woodworks LLC.....317 887-0142
1119 Falkirk Ct Greenwood (46143) *(G-5684)*
Earthy Industries LLC.....260 483-7588
2609 East Dr Fort Wayne (46805) *(G-4232)*
Eash Design, Elkhart *Also called Eash LLC (G-2811)*
Eash LLC.....574 295-4450
107 Rush Ct Elkhart (46516) *(G-2811)*
Easley Enterprises Inc.....317 636-4516
205 N College Ave Indianapolis (46202) *(G-6789)*
Easley Winery, Indianapolis *Also called Easley Enterprises Inc (G-6789)*
Eason Manufacturing Inc.....312 310-9430
601 Industrial Dr Ste B Griffith (46319) *(G-5772)*
East 40 Sports Apparel Inc.....812 877-3695
215 Deming Ln Terre Haute (47803) *(G-13229)*
East Chicago Machine Tool Sls.....219 663-4525
980 Crown Ct Crown Point (46307) *(G-2248)*
East Fork Studio & Press Inc.....765 458-6103
104 Ne First St Brownsville (47325) *(G-1195)*
East Heat Wood Pellets LLC.....317 638-4840
217 S Belmont Ave Ste E Indianapolis (46222) *(G-6790)*
East Industries LLC.....812 273-4358
831 W Main St Madison (47250) *(G-9459)*

A L P H A B E T I C

East Penn Manufacturing Co 317 236-6288
918 S Senate Ave Indianapolis (46225) ***(G-6791)***
East Side Jersey Dairy Inc 812 536-2207
300 W Main St Holland (47541) ***(G-6105)***
East Side Jersey Dairy Inc 765 649-1261
722 Broadway St Anderson (46012) ***(G-104)***
East Side Welding Inc 317 823-4065
10148 Pendleton Pike Indianapolis (46236) ***(G-6792)***
Eastern Banner Supply Corp 812 448-2222
932 W National Ave Brazil (47834) ***(G-960)***
Eastern Red Cedar Products LLC (PA) 812 365-2495
9611 S County Road 425 E Marengo (47140) ***(G-9504)***
Easterwood, Warsaw *Also called Indiana Vac-Form* ***(G-13892)***
Easton Technical Products Inc 574 583-5131
2709 S Freeman Rd Monticello (47960) ***(G-10261)***
Eastons Lettering Service 219 942-5101
514 E 3rd St Hobart (46342) ***(G-6078)***
Eastside Machine Shop 317 549-2216
4500 Dunn St Indianapolis (46226) ***(G-6793)***
Easywater, Fishers *Also called Freije Treatment Systems Inc* ***(G-3913)***
Eat Dessert First Inc 812 438-9600
10023 State Road 156 Patriot (47038) ***(G-11467)***
Eat Here Indy LLC (PA) 317 502-4419
5255 Winthrop Ave Ste 110 Indianapolis (46220) ***(G-6794)***
Eaton & Hancock Associates 317 291-6513
2066 Oldfields Cir Indianapolis (46228) ***(G-6795)***
Eaton Corporation 260 925-3800
201 Brandon St Auburn (46706) ***(G-328)***
Eaton Corporation 574 283-5004
2930 Foundation Dr South Bend (46628) ***(G-12755)***
Eaton Corporation 317 704-2520
7365 Winton Dr Indianapolis (46268) ***(G-6796)***
Eaton Corporation 574 288-4446
2930 Foundation Dr South Bend (46628) ***(G-12756)***
Eaton Electric Holdings LLC 317 578-7724
7599 Timber Springs Dr S Fishers (46038) ***(G-3900)***
Eaton Emts 765 587-4910
703 W 13th St Muncie (47302) ***(G-10467)***
Eaton Hydraulics LLC 260 248-5800
1380 S Williams Dr Columbia City (46725) ***(G-1782)***
Eaton Partners LLC 765 458-7896
5282 W Booth Rd Liberty (47353) ***(G-9260)***
Eaton Septic Tank Company 765 396-3275
14601 N State Road 3n Eaton (47338) ***(G-2582)***
Ebc LLC 812 234-4111
1075 Crawford St Terre Haute (47807) ***(G-13230)***
Ebenezer Sportswear, Gas City *Also called Dave Turner* ***(G-5122)***
Ebert Machine Company Inc 765 473-3728
2177 S State Road 19 Peru (46970) ***(G-11526)***
Ebey Sales & Service 260 636-3286
1037 E Baseline Rd Albion (46701) ***(G-27)***
Ebs Logging LLC 812 346-9248
3600 E County Road 600 N North Vernon (47265) ***(G-11256)***
Ebsc, Elkhart *Also called (ebs Composites) Engineered Bo* ***(G-2653)***
Ebwa Industries Inc 317 637-5860
1556 Deloss St Indianapolis (46201) ***(G-6797)***
Eca Enterprises Inc 812 526-6734
906 S Walnut St Edinburgh (46124) ***(G-2610)***
Echelbarger Machining Co LLC 765 252-1965
2614 Precision Dr Kokomo (46902) ***(G-8619)***
Echelbrger Precision Machining, Kokomo *Also called Echelbarger Machining Co LLC* ***(G-8619)***
Echo Engrg & Prod Sups Inc (PA) 317 876-8848
5406 W 78th St Indianapolis (46268) ***(G-6798)***
Echo Manufacturing LLC 574 333-3669
21888 Beck Dr Elkhart (46516) ***(G-2812)***
Echo Publications 219 696-3756
15863 Stevenson Pl Lowell (46356) ***(G-9405)***
Echo Supply, Indianapolis *Also called Echo Engrg & Prod Sups Inc* ***(G-6798)***
Echo, The, Bluffton *Also called News Banner Publications Inc* ***(G-883)***
Echostar Corporation 574 271-0595
3725 Cleveland Road Ext South Bend (46628) ***(G-12757)***
Eckco Inc 574 257-0299
12962 Jefferson Blvd Mishawaka (46545) ***(G-10039)***
Eckhart & Company Inc 317 347-2665
4011 W 54th St Indianapolis (46254) ***(G-6799)***
Eckhart Woodworking Inc 260 692-6218
424 S Van Buren St Monroe (46772) ***(G-10181)***
Eckstein Welding & Fabrication 812 934-2059
11385 N Delaware Rd Batesville (47006) ***(G-498)***
Eclipse Imports, Indianapolis *Also called Futon Factory Inc* ***(G-6971)***
Ecm Photo Tooling Inc 574 264-4433
26082 Heatherfield Dr Elkhart (46514) ***(G-2813)***
Eco Golf, Knox *Also called Hoosier Custom Plastics LLC* ***(G-8567)***
Eco Lighting Solutions LLC 866 897-1234
8730 Corporation Dr Indianapolis (46256) ***(G-6800)***
Eco Partners Inc 317 450-3346
515 Twin Oaks Dr Carmel (46032) ***(G-1367)***

Eco Services Operations Corp 219 932-7651
2000 Michigan St Hammond (46320) ***(G-5874)***
Eco Water of Southern Indiana 812 734-1407
7685 Highway 135 Ne New Salisbury (47161) ***(G-11009)***
Eco-Bat America LLC 317 247-1303
7870 W Morris St Indianapolis (46231) ***(G-6801)***
Ecojacks LLC 574 306-0414
503 E Broad St South Whitley (46787) ***(G-12998)***
Ecolab Inc 317 816-0983
160 W Carmel Dr Ste 255 Carmel (46032) ***(G-1368)***
Ecolab Inc 260 375-4710
2847 E 600 S Warren (46792) ***(G-13829)***
Ecolab Inc 260 359-3280
970 E Tipton St Huntington (46750) ***(G-6202)***
Ecom Publishing Inc 574 862-2179
114 S Elkhart St Wakarusa (46573) ***(G-13776)***
Economy Electric Htg & Coolg 219 923-4441
9031 Grace St Highland (46322) ***(G-6044)***
Economy Offset Printers Inc 574 534-6270
2516 Industrial Park Dr A Goshen (46526) ***(G-5210)***
Economy Signs Inc 219 932-1233
546 Conkey St Hammond (46324) ***(G-5875)***
Ecovantage LLC 260 337-0338
6878 County Road 62 Saint Joe (46785) ***(G-12254)***
Ecowater, New Salisbury *Also called Eco Water of Southern Indiana* ***(G-11009)***
ECR Fuel, Ladoga *Also called Emerald Cast Rnewable Fuel LLC* ***(G-8840)***
Ect, Richmond *Also called E C T Franklin Control Systems* ***(G-11979)***
Ecu, Fishers *Also called Enginring Cncpts Unlimited Inc* ***(G-3905)***
Ed and Daves Wood Chips LLC 574 699-1263
419 Sycamore Ct Galveston (46932) ***(G-4994)***
Ed Boilini 317 921-0155
24 E 40th St Indianapolis (46205) ***(G-6802)***
Ed Lloyd Co 812 342-2505
13240 S 100 W Columbus (47201) ***(G-1917)***
Ed Nickels 219 887-6128
5793 Taney Pl Merrillville (46410) ***(G-9712)***
Ed Sons Inc (PA) 317 897-8821
8335 Pendleton Pike Indianapolis (46226) ***(G-6803)***
Ed Stump Assembly Inc 574 291-0058
60856 Us 31 S South Bend (46614) ***(G-12758)***
Edco Welding and Hydraulic Inc 317 783-2323
861 W Troy Ave Indianapolis (46225) ***(G-6804)***
Edcoat Limited Partnership 574 654-9105
30350 Edison Rd New Carlisle (46552) ***(G-10881)***
Eddie S Guitars 219 689-7007
2111 Northwinds Dr Dyer (46311) ***(G-2497)***
Eden Foods Inc 765 396-3344
201 E Babb Rd Eaton (47338) ***(G-2583)***
Edge Manufacturing Inc 260 827-0482
1274 S Adams St Bluffton (46714) ***(G-873)***
Edge Technologies Inc 317 408-0116
4455 W 62nd St Indianapolis (46268) ***(G-6805)***
Edgewood Building Supply, Carmel *Also called Edgewood Corporation Indiana* ***(G-1369)***
Edgewood Corporation Indiana 317 786-9208
430 W Carmel Dr Carmel (46032) ***(G-1369)***
Edgewood Metal Fab LLC 574 546-5947
1265 B Rd Bremen (46506) ***(G-998)***
Edibleindy, Indianapolis *Also called Rubenstein LLC* ***(G-7871)***
Edinburgh Connector Company 812 526-8801
908 S Walnut St Edinburgh (46124) ***(G-2611)***
Editions Ltd Gallery Fine Arts 317 466-9940
838 E 65th St Indianapolis (46220) ***(G-6806)***
EDM Specialties Inc 317 856-4700
7746 Milhouse Rd Indianapolis (46241) ***(G-6807)***
Edna B LLC 574 271-4300
51265 Golfview Ct Granger (46530) ***(G-5403)***
Edna Troyer 260 894-4405
6316 W 825 N Ligonier (46767) ***(G-9281)***
EDS, Jeffersonville *Also called Energy Delivery Solutions LLC* ***(G-8354)***
EDS, Indianapolis *Also called Endowment Development Services* ***(G-6861)***
Eds Machine & Tool 812 295-7264
1250 Mount Pleasant Rd Loogootee (47553) ***(G-9382)***
Eds Trading Post Inc 317 933-4867
8012 S Nineveh Rd Nineveh (46164) ***(G-11057)***
Eds Wood Craft 812 768-6617
300 E Gibson St Haubstadt (47639) ***(G-6000)***
Edsal Inc 219 427-1294
700 Chase St Ste 400 Gary (46404) ***(G-5043)***
Edtechzone LLC 317 902-7594
10741 S County Road 850 E Cloverdale (46120) ***(G-1725)***
Education Connection Pubg LLC 317 876-3355
4923 W 78th St Indianapolis (46268) ***(G-6808)***
Edw C Levy Co 765 364-9251
New Core Rd Crawfordsville (47933) ***(G-2151)***
Edward E Petri Company 317 636-5007
20 N Meridian St Ste 206 Indianapolis (46204) ***(G-6809)***
Edward ONeil Associates 317 244-5400
1810 S Raceway Rd Indianapolis (46231) ***(G-6810)***

Edwards Steel Inc ... 317 462-9451
2042 E Main St Greenfield (46140) **(G-5522)**
Edys Grd Ice Cream, Fort Wayne *Also called Nestle Dreyers Ice Cream Co* **(G-4497)**
Eemsco Inc ... 812 426-2224
600 W Eichel Ave Evansville (47710) **(G-3472)**
Efficient Plastics Solutions ... 574 965-4690
9745 N 850 W Delphi (46923) **(G-2420)**
Efil Pharmaceuticals Corp ... 765 491-7247
3706 Litchfield Pl West Lafayette (47906) **(G-14065)**
Efp LLC (HQ) ... 574 295-4690
223 Middleton Run Rd Elkhart (46516) **(G-2814)**
Efurnituremax LLC ... 317 697-9504
8070 Castleton Rd 117 Indianapolis (46250) **(G-6811)**
Egenolf Contg & Rigging II Inc ... 317 787-5301
350 Wisconsin St Indianapolis (46225) **(G-6812)**
Egenolf Enterprise Inc ... 317 501-5069
2855 N Evanklin Rd Ste Indianapolis (46226) **(G-6813)**
Egenolf Machine Inc ... 317 787-5301
2916 Bluff Rd Ste A Indianapolis (46225) **(G-6814)**
Egg Innovations LLC (PA) ... 574 267-7545
4799 W 100 N Warsaw (46580) **(G-13868)**
Ehob Inc ... 317 972-4600
250 N Belmont Ave Indianapolis (46222) **(G-6815)**
Ehrgotts Signs & Stamps Inc ... 317 353-2222
7173 W Us Highway 40 Indianapolis (46229) **(G-6816)**
Eichstedt Manufacturing Inc ... 574 288-8881
23020 Ireland Rd South Bend (46614) **(G-12759)**
Eis Fibercoating Inc ... 574 722-5192
616 E Main St Logansport (46947) **(G-9334)**
Eiseles Honey LLC ... 317 896-5830
8146 Zionsville Rd Indianapolis (46268) **(G-6817)**
EJ Brooks Company (HQ) ... 800 348-4777
409 Hoosier Dr Angola (46703) **(G-209)**
EJ Brooks Company (HQ) ... 260 624-4800
409 Hoosier Dr Angola (46703) **(G-210)**
Ej Schmidt Inc ... 317 290-0491
8100 E Us Highway 36 # 1 Avon (46123) **(G-440)**
Ej Usa Inc ... 765 744-1184
201 N Illinois St # 1900 Indianapolis (46204) **(G-6818)**
Ejl Tech ... 812 374-8808
461 S Mapleton St Ste B Columbus (47201) **(G-1918)**
Ekmi, Fort Wayne *Also called Elringklinger Mfg Ind Inc* **(G-4236)**
El Mexicano Inc ... 260 456-6843
2301 Fairfield Ave # 102 Fort Wayne (46807) **(G-4233)**
El Mexicano Newspaper, Fort Wayne *Also called El Mexicano Inc* **(G-4233)**
El Popular Inc ... 219 397-3728
910 E Chicago Ave East Chicago (46312) **(G-2526)**
El Popular Sausage Factory LLC ... 219 476-7040
555 Eastport Centre Dr Valparaiso (46383) **(G-13532)**
El Puente LLC ... 574 533-9082
1906 W Clinton St Goshen (46526) **(G-5211)**
El Shaddai Inc ... 260 359-9080
517 N Jefferson St Huntington (46750) **(G-6203)**
Elan Corp PLC ... 317 442-1502
11237 Wedgefield Ct Fishers (46037) **(G-3901)**
Elanco Animal Division, Plainfield *Also called Eli Lilly and Company* **(G-11608)**
Elanco Animal Health, Fishers *Also called Eli Lilly and Company* **(G-3903)**
Elanco Animal Health, Indianapolis *Also called Eli Lilly and Company* **(G-6824)**
Elanco Animal Health, Indianapolis *Also called Eli Lilly and Company* **(G-6830)**
Elanco Animal Health, Greenfield *Also called Eli Lilly and Company* **(G-5524)**
Elanco Animal Health, Indianapolis *Also called Eli Lilly and Company* **(G-6832)**
Elanco Animal Health, Indianapolis *Also called Eli Lilly and Company* **(G-6833)**
Elanco Animal Health, Indianapolis *Also called Eli Lilly and Company* **(G-6834)**
Elanco Animal Health, Indianapolis *Also called Eli Lilly and Company* **(G-6835)**
Elanco US Inc (HQ) ... 877 352-6261
2500 Innovation Way N Greenfield (46140) **(G-5523)**
Elder Group Inc ... 765 966-7676
4251 W Industries Rd Richmond (47374) **(G-11980)**
Electonic Systems Division, Fort Wayne *Also called Harris Corporation* **(G-4321)**
Electri-Tec Inc., Angola *Also called Electric-Tec LLC* **(G-211)**
Electric Coating Tech LLC ... 219 378-1930
4407 Railroad Ave East Chicago (46312) **(G-2527)**
Electric Metal Fab Inc ... 812 988-9353
4889 Helmsburg Rd Nashville (47448) **(G-10723)**
Electric Motor Company, Rensselaer *Also called Truman Ritchie* **(G-11943)**
Electric Motor Sales & Service ... 812 574-3233
1540 W Jpg Niblo Rd Madison (47250) **(G-9460)**
Electric Motor Services Inc (PA) ... 219 931-2850
6350 Indianapolis Blvd Hammond (46320) **(G-5876)**
Electric Motors and Spc ... 260 357-4141
701 W King St Garrett (46738) **(G-5003)**
Electric Plus ... 812 336-4992
1030 W 17th St Bloomington (47404) **(G-719)**
Electric Power Service ... 260 493-4913
5423 State Road 930 Fort Wayne (46803) **(G-4234)**
Electric-Tec LLC ... 260 665-1252
509 Growth Pkwy Angola (46703) **(G-211)**
Electrical Motor Products Inc ... 877 455-1599
15009 Dunton Rd Fort Wayne (46845) **(G-4235)**
Electrik Connection Inc ... 219 362-4581
106 Washington St La Porte (46350) **(G-8754)**
Electro Corporation ... 219 393-5571
1st Rd Kingsbury Indus Pa Kingsbury (46345) **(G-8536)**
Electro Painters Inc ... 317 875-8816
14712 Alsong Ct Carmel (46032) **(G-1370)**
Electro Seal Corporation ... 219 926-8606
914 Broadway Chesterton (46304) **(G-1603)**
Electro Transfer Systems Inc (PA) ... 574 234-0600
1810 Clover Rd Mishawaka (46545) **(G-10040)**
Electro-Coat Technologies ... 574 266-7356
2501 Jeanwood Dr Elkhart (46514) **(G-2815)**
Electro-Spec Inc ... 317 738-9199
1800 Commerce Pkwy Franklin (46131) **(G-4883)**
Electro-Tech Inc ... 219 937-0826
5334 Sohl Ave Hammond (46320) **(G-5877)**
Electromechanical RES Labs ... 812 948-8484
2560 Charlestown Rd New Albany (47150) **(G-10771)**
Electron Beam Welding, Indianapolis *Also called Ebwa Industries Inc* **(G-6797)**
Electronic Services LLC ... 765 457-3894
1942 S Elizabeth St Kokomo (46902) **(G-8620)**
Elegan Customwear, Valparaiso *Also called Elegan Sportswear Inc* **(G-13534)**
Elegan Graphics ... 219 462-9921
5905 Murvihill Rd Valparaiso (46383) **(G-13533)**
Elegan Sportswear Inc ... 219 464-8416
212 Lincolnway Valparaiso (46383) **(G-13534)**
Elegant Needleworks Inc ... 765 284-9427
7500 N Janna Dr Muncie (47303) **(G-10468)**
Elektrisola Incorporated ... 317 375-8192
2400 N Shadeland Ave B Indianapolis (46219) **(G-6819)**
Element Armament LLC ... 317 442-7924
5120 N 400 W Bargersville (46106) **(G-480)**
Element Elite Tumbling ... 502 751-5654
4601 Commerce Pass Sellersburg (47172) **(G-12392)**
Element Homes ... 219 310-2505
11061 Broadway Crown Point (46307) **(G-2249)**
Element of Fun Travel ... 317 435-9185
10327 Forest Hills Dr Demotte (46310) **(G-2436)**
Element Pro Services LLC ... 574 271-5259
50961 Partridge Woods Dr Granger (46530) **(G-5404)**
Elemental Inc ... 812 684-8036
512 S Park Dr Huntingburg (47542) **(G-6162)**
Elemental S A Protection ... 765 717-7325
509 N Forest Ave Muncie (47304) **(G-10469)**
Elements ... 812 881-9400
4 N 2nd St Vincennes (47591) **(G-13675)**
Elements Elearning LLC ... 317 986-2113
4543 Melbourne Rd Indianapolis (46228) **(G-6820)**
Elengas Customwear ... 317 577-1677
12463 Norman Pl Fishers (46037) **(G-3902)**
Elephant Enterprises ... 248 366-5383
7618 Tapper Ave Hammond (46324) **(G-5878)**
Elevator Equipment Corporation ... 765 966-7761
2230 Nw 12th St Richmond (47374) **(G-11981)**
Elevator One LLC ... 317 634-8001
120 E Market St Indianapolis (46204) **(G-6821)**
Eleys Woodworking ... 765 584-3531
3602 W 200 N Winchester (47394) **(G-14328)**
Elf Machinery LLC ... 219 393-5541
1535 S State Road 39 La Porte (46350) **(G-8755)**
Elgin Fastener Group LLC ... 812 689-8917
1415 S Benham Rd Versailles (47042) **(G-13653)**
Eli Lilly ... 812 242-5900
1445 S 1st St Terre Haute (47802) **(G-13231)**
Eli Lilly and Co ... 317 433-1244
10871 Monarch Springs Ct Noblesville (46060) **(G-11099)**
Eli Lilly and Company (PA) ... 317 276-2000
Lilly Corporate Ctr Indianapolis (46285) **(G-6822)**
Eli Lilly and Company ... 317 276-2000
1400 W Raymond St Indianapolis (46221) **(G-6823)**
Eli Lilly and Company ... 317 748-1622
12023 Quarry Ct Fishers (46037) **(G-3903)**
Eli Lilly and Company ... 317 276-2000
2401 Directors Row Indianapolis (46241) **(G-6824)**
Eli Lilly and Company ... 317 277-1079
1223 W Morris St Dock 312 Indianapolis (46221) **(G-6825)**
Eli Lilly and Company ... 317 276-7907
355 E Merrill St Indianapolis (46225) **(G-6826)**
Eli Lilly and Company ... 317 276-2000
450 S Meridian St Indianapolis (46225) **(G-6827)**
Eli Lilly and Company ... 317 651-7790
1223 S Harding St Indianapolis (46221) **(G-6828)**
Eli Lilly and Company ... 317 276-2000
Lilly Corporate Center Indianapolis (46285) **(G-6829)**
Eli Lilly and Company ... 317 277-0147
30 S Meridian St Fl 5 Indianapolis (46204) **(G-6830)**
Eli Lilly and Company ... 317 276-2000
2500 Innovation Way N Greenfield (46140) **(G-5524)**

Eli Lilly and Company 317 433-3624
　2222 Stanley Rd Plainfield (46168) (G-11608)
Eli Lilly and Company 317 276-7907
　1280 S Dakota St Indianapolis (46225) (G-6831)
Eli Lilly and Company 317 276-5925
　1402 S Dakota St Indianapolis (46225) (G-6832)
Eli Lilly and Company 317 276-2000
　1555 S Harding St Indianapolis (46221) (G-6833)
Eli Lilly and Company 317 276-2118
　639 S Delaware St Indianapolis (46225) (G-6834)
Eli Lilly and Company 317 276-2000
　2301 Executive Dr Indianapolis (46241) (G-6835)
Eli Lilly International Corp (HQ) 317 276-2000
　893 S Delaware St Indianapolis (46225) (G-6836)
Elie Cleaning Services LLC 317 983-3388
　10475 Crosspoint Blvd # 250 Indianapolis (46256) (G-6837)
Eligius Industries LLC 574 267-5313
　728 Dogwood Ln Warsaw (46582) (G-13869)
Elite Crete Systems Inc (PA) 219 465-7671
　1151 Transport Dr Valparaiso (46383) (G-13535)
Elite Industries LLC 317 407-6869
　6331 Muirfield Way Indianapolis (46237) (G-6838)
Elite Machine and Tool Inc 219 345-3424
　10192 N 600 E Demotte (46310) (G-2437)
Elite Printing Inc 317 781-9701
　4239 Madison Ave Indianapolis (46227) (G-6839)
Elite Printing Inc (PA) 317 257-2744
　2138 E 52nd St Indianapolis (46205) (G-6840)
Elite Protective Coatings 317 476-1712
　3632 Woodland Streams Dr Greenwood (46143) (G-5685)
Elixir Industries 574 294-5685
　640 Collins Rd Elkhart (46516) (G-2816)
Elixir Industries 574 294-5685
　640 Collins Rd Elkhart (46516) (G-2817)
Elixir Industries 574 294-5685
　2040 Industrial Pkwy Elkhart (46516) (G-2818)
Elizabeth M Graham 812 343-1267
　379 W Old South St Bargersville (46106) (G-481)
Elk Trailers, Elkhart Also called CC Manufacturing Inc (G-2752)
Elkcases Inc 574 295-7700
　23143 Heaton Vis Elkhart (46514) (G-2819)
Elkhart Bedding Co Inc 574 293-6200
　2124 Sterling Ave Elkhart (46516) (G-2820)
Elkhart Binding Inc 574 522-5455
　51784 State Road 19 Elkhart (46514) (G-2821)
Elkhart Brass Manufacturing Co 800 346-0250
　1302 W Beardsley Ave Elkhart (46514) (G-2822)
Elkhart Cases Inc 574 295-7700
　23143 Heaton Vis Elkhart (46514) (G-2823)
Elkhart County Gravel Inc (PA) 574 831-2815
　19242 Us Highway 6 New Paris (46553) (G-10978)
Elkhart County Gravel Inc 574 831-2815
　2042 W 300 N Warsaw (46582) (G-13870)
Elkhart County Gravel Inc 574 825-7913
　56570 County Road 35 Middlebury (46540) (G-9883)
Elkhart Grinding Services Inc 574 293-2707
　121 Rush Ct Elkhart (46516) (G-2824)
Elkhart Hinge Co Inc 574 293-2841
　1839 W Lusher Ave Elkhart (46517) (G-2825)
Elkhart Metal Polishing Inc 574 206-0666
　1926 Leininger Ave Elkhart (46517) (G-2826)
Elkhart Plastics Inc 574 389-9911
　1400 Leininger Ave Elkhart (46517) (G-2827)
Elkhart Plastics Inc (PA) 574 232-8066
　3300 N Kenmore St South Bend (46628) (G-12760)
Elkhart Plastics Inc 574 370-1079
　316 Lake Shore Dr Michigan City (46360) (G-9788)
Elkhart Plastics Inc 574 232-8066
　3300 N Kenmore St South Bend (46628) (G-12761)
Elkhart Plastics Inc 574 825-9797
　51703 Packard Dr Middlebury (46540) (G-9884)
Elkhart Plating Corp 574 294-1800
　1913 14th St Elkhart (46516) (G-2828)
Elkhart Products Corporation (HQ) 574 264-3181
　1255 Oak St Elkhart (46514) (G-2829)
Elkhart Products Corporation 260 368-7246
　700 Rainbow Rd Geneva (46740) (G-5135)
Elkhart Steel Service Inc (PA) 574 262-2552
　23321 C R 106 Elkhart (46514) (G-2830)
Elkhart Supply Corp 574 264-4156
　1126 Kent St Elkhart (46514) (G-2831)
Elkhart Tool and Die Inc 574 295-8500
　2400 15th St Elkhart (46517) (G-2832)
Elkhart Yard, Elkhart Also called Legacy Vulcan LLC (G-2993)
Elko Inc 812 473-8400
　940 N Boeke Rd Evansville (47711) (G-3473)
Elko Plastic Fabricators Div, Evansville Also called Elko Inc (G-3473)
Ell Enterprises Inc 317 783-7838
　2950 E Hanna Ave Indianapolis (46227) (G-6841)

Elliott Co of Indianapolis 317 291-1213
　9200 Zionsville Rd Indianapolis (46268) (G-6842)
Elliott Company, Indianapolis Also called Elliott Co of Indianapolis (G-6842)
Elliott Manufacturing and Fabr 812 865-0516
　2302 W Coffee Dr N Paoli (47454) (G-11449)
Elliott Stone Co Inc (PA) 812 275-5556
　7056 State Road 158 Bedford (47421) (G-540)
Elliott-Williams Company Inc 317 453-2295
　3500 E 20th St Indianapolis (46218) (G-6843)
Ellis Machine Shop LLC 812 779-7477
　1318 E 870 N Hazleton (47640) (G-6009)
Ellwocks Auto Parts Restorat 812 962-4942
　5820 Lisa Ln Newburgh (47630) (G-11027)
Elm Packaging, Decatur Also called Tp/Elm Acquisition Sbusid Inc (G-2408)
Elmco Engineering Inc (PA) 317 788-4114
　6107 Churchman Road Byp Bypass Indianapolis (46203) (G-6844)
Elmos 574 371-2050
　1900 Plaza Dr Warsaw (46580) (G-13871)
Elpers Truck Equipment LLC 812 423-5787
　8136 Baumgart Rd Evansville (47725) (G-3474)
Elringklinger Mfg Ind Inc 734 788-1776
　2677 Persistence Dr Fort Wayne (46808) (G-4236)
Elsa LLC 765 552-5200
　1240 S State Road 37 Elwood (46036) (G-3296)
Elsa Corporation (HQ) 765 552-5200
　1240 S State Road 37 Elwood (46036) (G-3297)
Elsie Manufacturing Co Inc 260 837-8841
　600 W Maple St Waterloo (46793) (G-14013)
Elt Tooling, Elkhart Also called Tube Form Solutions LLC (G-3228)
Elucence Products, Indianapolis Also called Kenra Professional LLC (G-7343)
Elvin L Nuest Sales and Servic 219 863-5216
　420 S Bill St Francesville (47946) (G-4811)
Elwood Fuel and Cigs LLC 317 244-5744
　1050 S High School Rd Indianapolis (46241) (G-6845)
Elwood Operations, Dunkirk Also called Mosey Manufacturing Co Inc (G-2487)
Elwood Publishing Co Inc (HQ) 765 552-3355
　317 S Anderson St Elwood (46036) (G-3298)
Elwood Publishing Co Inc 765 724-4469
　1 Harrison Sq Alexandria (46001) (G-40)
Elysian Company LLC 574 267-2259
　110 E Center St Warsaw (46580) (G-13872)
Em Black Oxide 574 233-4933
　3702 W Sample St Ste 4052 South Bend (46619) (G-12762)
Em Printing & Embroidery LLC 812 373-0082
　2221 Pear Tree Ct Columbus (47201) (G-1919)
EM&s, Garrett Also called Electric Motors and Spc (G-5003)
Emarsys North America Inc 844 693-6277
　10 W Market St Ste 1350 Indianapolis (46204) (G-6846)
EMB Fishing LLC 317 244-8741
　8133 Winterset Cir Indianapolis (46214) (G-6847)
Embree Machine Inc 812 275-5729
　1435 Greer Ln Springville (47462) (G-13063)
Embroidery Designs, Monticello Also called Unique Graphic Designs Inc (G-10287)
Embroidery Express, Terre Haute Also called Mary Duncan (G-13279)
Embroidery N Things Inc 317 859-8963
　3520 W Whiteland Rd Bargersville (46106) (G-482)
Embroidery Nation 574 967-3928
　209 Manor Dr Flora (46929) (G-3994)
Embroidery Plus Inc 317 243-3445
　5514 W Washington St Indianapolis (46241) (G-6848)
Embroidery Solutions U S 812 923-9152
　8301 Pekin Rd Ste 1 Greenville (47124) (G-5649)
Embroidme, Avon Also called Tma Enterprises Inc (G-469)
Embroidme 219 465-1400
　2254 Morthland Dr Valparaiso (46385) (G-13536)
EMC Corporation 317 706-8600
　8888 Keystone Xing # 700 Indianapolis (46240) (G-6849)
EMC Precision Machining II LLC 317 758-4451
　701 S Main St Sheridan (46069) (G-12589)
EMC Projects 317 420-8005
　1409 N New Jersey St Indianapolis (46202) (G-6850)
EMC Stamping, La Porte Also called Dwyer Instruments Inc (G-8752)
Emc2 ....317 435-8021
　3539 N Colorado Ave Indianapolis (46218) (G-6851)
Emco Gears Inc 317 243-3836
　703 S Girls School Rd Indianapolis (46231) (G-6852)
Emcon Technologies, Columbus Also called Faurecia Emissions Control (G-1926)
Emerald Cast Renewable Fuel LLC 765 942-5019
　329 W College St Ladoga (47954) (G-8840)
Emergency Radio Service LLC (PA) 317 821-0422
　9144 N 900 W Ligonier (46767) (G-9282)
Emerson Climate Tech Inc 765 932-2956
　616 Conrad Harcourt Way Rushville (46173) (G-12219)
Emerson Climate Tech Inc 937 498-3671
　6579 W 350 N Ste A Greenfield (46140) (G-5525)
Emerson Climate Tech Inc 765 932-1902
　500 Conrad Harcourt Way Rushville (46173) (G-12220)
Emerson Climate Tech Inc 317 968-4250
　6579 W 350 N Ste A Greenfield (46140) (G-5526)

(G-0000) Company's Geographic Section entry number

Emerson Electric Co 219 465-2411
2300 Evans Ave Valparaiso (46383) *(G-13537)*

Emerson Electric Co 317 322-2055
8320 Brookville Rd Ste E Indianapolis (46239) *(G-6853)*

Emerson Industrial Automation 574 583-9171
705 N 6th St Monticello (47960) *(G-10262)*

Emery Winslow Scale Co., Terre Haute *Also called A H Emery Company (G-13184)*

Emhart Teknologies LLC 765 728-2433
7345 N 400 E Montpelier (47359) *(G-10290)*

Emi LLC 812 437-9100
5701 Old Boonville Hwy Evansville (47715) *(G-3475)*

EMI Quality Plating, Evansville *Also called Emi LLC (G-3475)*

EMI Quality Plating, Evansville *Also called Evantek Manufacturing Inds LLC (G-3493)*

Emmis Communications Corp (PA) 317 266-0100
40 Monument Cir Ste 700 Indianapolis (46204) *(G-6854)*

Emmis Operating Company (HQ) 317 266-0100
40 Monument Cir Ste 700 Indianapolis (46204) *(G-6855)*

Emmis Publishing LP (HQ) 317 266-0100
40 Monument Cir Ste 100 Indianapolis (46204) *(G-6856)*

Emmis Publishing Corporation (HQ) 317 266-0100
40 Monument Cir Ste 700 Indianapolis (46204) *(G-6857)*

Emnet LLC 574 360-1093
12441 Beckley St Ste 6 Granger (46530) *(G-5405)*

Emp, Greenfield *Also called Engineered Machined Pdts Inc (G-5528)*

Emp, Fishers *Also called Enterprise Marking Pdts Inc (G-3906)*

Emp of Evansville 812 962-1309
4 Chestnut St Evansville (47713) *(G-3476)*

Emphymab Biotech LLC 317 274-5935
351 W 10th St Indianapolis (46202) *(G-6858)*

Empire Lacrosse & Sports Inc 317 574-4529
9700 Lake Shore Dr E B Indianapolis (46280) *(G-6263)*

Emplify LLC 800 580-5344
11787 Lantern Rd Ste 201 Fishers (46038) *(G-3904)*

Empro Manufacturing Co Inc 317 823-3000
10920 E 59th St Indianapolis (46236) *(G-6859)*

Emprotech Steel Services LLC 219 326-6900
3234 N State Road 39 La Porte (46350) *(G-8756)*

Emquip Corporation 317 849-3977
6909 E 32nd St Indianapolis (46226) *(G-6860)*

EMT Industries Inc 574 533-1273
12065 Covered Wagon Ct Granger (46530) *(G-5406)*

Enbi Global Inc (PA) 317 395-7324
1703 Mccall Dr Shelbyville (46176) *(G-12532)*

Enbi Indiana Inc (PA) 317 398-3267
1703 Mccall Dr Shelbyville (46176) *(G-12533)*

Encom Inc 812 421-7700
4825 N Spring St Evansville (47711) *(G-3477)*

Encom Polymers, Evansville *Also called Encom Inc (G-3477)*

Endeavor Machined Products Inc 574 232-1940
1705 N Bendix Dr South Bend (46628) *(G-12763)*

Endocyte Inc 765 463-7175
3000 Kent Ave Ste A1-100 West Lafayette (47906) *(G-14066)*

Endowment Development Services 317 542-9829
921 E 86th St Ste 100 Indianapolis (46240) *(G-6861)*

Endress + Hauser Inc (HQ) 317 535-7138
2350 Endress Pl Greenwood (46143) *(G-5686)*

Endress + Hauser Inc 317 535-7138
2413 Endress Pl Greenwood (46143) *(G-5687)*

Endress + Huser Flowtec AG Inc 317 535-7138
2330 Endress Pl Greenwood (46143) *(G-5688)*

Endress+hauser (usa) Automatio 317 535-2121
2340 Endress Pl Greenwood (46143) *(G-5689)*

Endress+hauser Wetzer USA Inc 317 535-1362
2413 Endress Pl Greenwood (46143) *(G-5690)*

Endresshauser, Greenwood *Also called Endress + Huser Flowtec AG Inc (G-5688)*

Endurance Metals LLC 765 960-5834
1300 Rose City Blvd Richmond (47374) *(G-11982)*

Enduring Graphics, Valparaiso *Also called National Equipment Inc (G-13586)*

Endustra Filter Manufacturers, Schererville *Also called Bofrebo Industries Inc (G-12318)*

Ener1 Inc (HQ) 317 703-1800
8740 Hague Rd Bldg 7 Indianapolis (46256) *(G-6862)*

Enerdel Inc (PA) 317 703-1800
8740 Hague Rd Bldg 7 Indianapolis (46256) *(G-6863)*

Energy Access Inc 317 329-1676
5344 W 79th St Indianapolis (46268) *(G-6864)*

Energy Delivery Solutions LLC 502 271-8753
3315 Industrial Pkwy Jeffersonville (47130) *(G-8354)*

Energy Drilling LLC 618 943-5314
1290 N State Road 67 Vincennes (47591) *(G-13676)*

Energy Inc 765 948-3504
8201 N State Road 9 Alexandria (46001) *(G-41)*

Energy Quest Inc 317 827-9212
8553 Bash St Ste 107 Indianapolis (46250) *(G-6865)*

Energy Saver Lights Inc 202 544-7868
2530 Brandywine Ct Indianapolis (46241) *(G-6866)*

Energy Two Inc 812 497-3113
184 E County Road 800 N Seymour (47274) *(G-12447)*

Energypoint LLC 317 275-7979
12400 N Meridian St # 180 Carmel (46032) *(G-1371)*

Enersys 574 266-0658
1353 Wade Dr Elkhart (46514) *(G-2833)*

Engel Manufacturing Co Inc 574 232-3800
411 W Indiana Ave South Bend (46613) *(G-12764)*

Engenaire 574 264-0391
30068 Westlake Dr Elkhart (46514) *(G-2834)*

Enghouse Networks (us) Inc (HQ) 317 262-4666
333 N Alabama St Ste 240 Indianapolis (46204) *(G-6867)*

Engineered Bar Products Div, Pittsboro *Also called Steel Dynamics Inc (G-11588)*

Engineered Conveyors Inc (PA) 765 459-4545
1055 Home Ave Kokomo (46902) *(G-8621)*

Engineered Industrial Products 317 684-4280
5652 W 74th St Indianapolis (46278) *(G-6868)*

Engineered Machined Pdts Inc 317 462-8894
125 N Blue Rd Greenfield (46140) *(G-5527)*

Engineered Machined Pdts Inc 317 462-8894
317462 8894 Greenfield (46140) *(G-5528)*

Engineered Medical Systems 317 246-5500
2055 Executive Dr Indianapolis (46241) *(G-6869)*

Engineered Products Inc 219 662-2080
1203 E Summit St Crown Point (46307) *(G-2250)*

Engineered Rubber & Plastics 574 254-1405
646 Rivers Edge Ct Mishawaka (46544) *(G-10041)*

Engineered Seals Division, Syracuse *Also called Parker-Hannifin Corporation (G-13139)*

Engineered Steel Concepts Inc 219 924-9056
9241 Spring St Highland (46322) *(G-6045)*

Engineering Services, Columbia City *Also called Webco Inc (G-1847)*

Enginered Refr Shapes Svcs LLC (PA) 765 778-8040
3370 W 1000 S Pendleton (46064) *(G-11488)*

Enginring Cncpts Unlimited Inc 317 826-1558
8950 Technology Dr Fishers (46038) *(G-3905)*

Englehardt Custom Woodworking 812 425-9282
4125 Kedzie Ave Evansville (47712) *(G-3478)*

Engler Machine & Tool Inc 812 386-6254
1106 W 150 S Princeton (47670) *(G-11869)*

Englert & Meyer Corporation 812 683-3540
6720 S 585w Huntingburg (47542) *(G-6163)*

English Industries LLC 812 218-9882
2781 Jefferson Centre Way Jeffersonville (47130) *(G-8355)*

English Resources Inc 812 423-6716
816 Nw 2nd St Evansville (47708) *(G-3479)*

Engrave Inc 812 537-8693
140 Industrial Dr Lawrenceburg (47025) *(G-9140)*

Engraving and Stamp Center Inc 812 336-0606
218 N Madison St Bloomington (47404) *(G-720)*

Enhanced Mfg Solutions LLC 812 932-1101
23 Hillcrest Estates Dr Batesville (47006) *(G-499)*

Enhancement Power Products 317 359-3461
398 N Mitchner Ave Indianapolis (46219) *(G-6870)*

Enjoy Life Natural Brands LLC 773 632-2163
301 Salem Rd Jeffersonville (47130) *(G-8356)*

Enkei America Inc (PA) 812 373-7000
2900 Inwood Dr Columbus (47201) *(G-1920)*

Enkei America Moldings Inc 812 373-7000
2680 Norcross Dr Columbus (47201) *(G-1921)*

Enmac LLC 812 298-8711
13200 S Us Highway 41 Terre Haute (47802) *(G-13232)*

Enoise Control Inc 317 774-1900
129 Penn St Westfield (46074) *(G-14162)*

Enovapremier LLC 812 385-0576
858 E 350 S Princeton (47670) *(G-11870)*

Enpak LLC 574 268-7273
939 E Pound Dr N Warsaw (46582) *(G-13873)*

Enterkin Manufacturing Co Inc 317 462-4477
165 W New Rd Greenfield (46140) *(G-5529)*

Enterprise Marking Pdts Inc 317 867-7600
12840 Ford Dr Fishers (46038) *(G-3906)*

Enterprise Marking Products 317 867-7600
17450 Tiller Ct Westfield (46074) *(G-14163)*

Enterprise MGT Solutions LLC (PA) 219 545-8544
1900 W 62nd Ave Merrillville (46410) *(G-9713)*

Entertainment Express 219 763-3610
3460 Anthony Dr Portage (46368) *(G-11760)*

Entree Vous Greenwood 317 881-0800
1642 Olive Br Parke Ln Greenwood (46143) *(G-5691)*

Envelope Service Inc 260 432-6277
7101 Lincoln Pkwy Fort Wayne (46804) *(G-4237)*

Envigo Rms Inc (HQ) 317 806-6080
8520 Allison Pointe Blvd # 400 Indianapolis (46250) *(G-6871)*

Envigo Rms Inc 317 806-6080
6825 W 400 N Ste 170 Greenfield (46140) *(G-5530)*

Envirmmntal Ctrl Solutions LLC 317 358-5985
5115 N Richardt Ave Indianapolis (46226) *(G-6872)*

Enviro Filters, Gary *Also called Enviro Filtration Inc (G-5044)*

Enviro Filtration Inc (PA) 815 469-2871
4719 Roosevelt St Gary (46408) *(G-5044)*

Enviro Finishing of Indiana 765 966-8183
511 Industrial Pkwy Richmond (47374) *(G-11983)*

Enviro Ink 260 748-0636
6926 Quemetco Ct Ste A Fort Wayne (46803) *(G-4238)*

Enviromental Services Pdts Mfg, Akron *Also called Dragon ESP Ltd (G-4)*

Environment Tech of Fort Wayne, South Bend *Also called Environmental Technology Inc (G-12765)*

Environmental Management & Dev 765 874-1539
  105 W Sherman St Lynn (47355) *(G-9426)*

Environmental Products Inc 219 393-3446
  Fourth Road Kingsbury Kingsbury (46345) *(G-8537)*

Environmental Technology Inc 574 233-1202
  1850 N Sheridan St South Bend (46628) *(G-12765)*

Environmental Test Systems 574 262-2060
  3504 Henke St Elkhart (46514) *(G-2835)*

Enviropeel USA, Indianapolis *Also called Precision Cams Inc (G-7731)*

Enviropeel USA 317 631-9100
  1128 S West St Indianapolis (46225) *(G-6873)*

Enviroplas Inc 812 868-0808
  15220 Foundation Ave Evansville (47725) *(G-3480)*

Envirotech Extrusion Inc 765 966-8068
  4810 Woodside Dr Richmond (47374) *(G-11984)*

Envisio Design LLC 574 274-4394
  2406 Schumacher Dr Mishawaka (46545) *(G-10042)*

Envisioit, Mishawaka *Also called Envisio Design LLC (G-10042)*

Envision Epoxy 317 448-3400
  16517 Anderson Way Noblesville (46062) *(G-11100)*

Envision Graphics Inc 260 925-2266
  506 Brandon St Auburn (46706) *(G-329)*

Envista LLC (PA) 317 208-9100
  11555 N Meridian St # 300 Carmel (46032) *(G-1372)*

Envista Concepts LLC 317 208-9100
  11711 N Meridian St # 415 Carmel (46032) *(G-1373)*

Envista Entp Solutions LLC 317 208-9100
  11711 N Meridian St # 415 Carmel (46032) *(G-1374)*

Envista Freight Managment LLC 317 208-9100
  11711 N Meridian St # 415 Carmel (46032) *(G-1375)*

Enyart Electric Motor Service 574 288-4731
  1313 Prairie Ave South Bend (46613) *(G-12766)*

Enzyme Solutions Inc (PA) 260 553-9100
  2105 Forrest Park Dr Garrett (46738) *(G-5004)*

Enzyme Solutions Inc 800 523-1323
  10219 River Rapids Run Fort Wayne (46845) *(G-4239)*

Eon Performance LLC 847 997-8619
  1526 Woodson Dr Apt 209 Indianapolis (46227) *(G-6874)*

EP Graphics Inc (HQ) 877 589-2145
  169 S Jefferson St Berne (46711) *(G-613)*

Epac, Chesterton *Also called Harford Industries Inc (G-1612)*

Epco Products Inc 260 747-8888
  3736 Vanguard Dr Fort Wayne (46809) *(G-4240)*

Epi Printers Inc 317 579-4870
  7502 E 86th St Indianapolis (46256) *(G-6875)*

Epw LLC 574 293-5090
  1500 W Hively Ave Ste A Elkhart (46517) *(G-2836)*

Equipment Technologies, Mooresville *Also called Et Works LLC (G-10309)*

Equipment Technologies Inc (PA) 800 861-2142
  2201 Hancel Pkwy Mooresville (46158) *(G-10308)*

Equippe Advanced Mobility 317 807-6789
  3209 W Smi Val Rd Ste 146 Greenwood (46142) *(G-5692)*

Equippe Mobility Resources, Greenwood *Also called Equippe Advanced Mobility (G-5692)*

Erapsco 260 248-3524
  4868 E Park 30 Dr Columbia City (46725) *(G-1783)*

Erbeco, Fort Wayne *Also called Bloom Pharmaceutical (G-4113)*

ERC Mining Indiana Corp 812 665-9780
  15127 W 700 N Jasonville (47438) *(G-8234)*

Erie Haven Concrete, Fort Wayne *Also called Erie-Haven Inc (G-4241)*

Erie Haven Inc 260 665-2052
  1310 W Maumee St Angola (46703) *(G-212)*

Erie-Haven Inc (PA) 260 478-1674
  3909 Limestone Dr Fort Wayne (46809) *(G-4241)*

Erie-Haven Inc 260 353-1133
  235 S Adams St Bluffton (46714) *(G-874)*

Erie-Haven Inc 260 478-1674
  1204 S Union St Auburn (46706) *(G-330)*

Erl, New Albany *Also called Electromechanical RES Labs (G-10771)*

Erl Properties Inc 812 948-8484
  2560 Charlestown Rd New Albany (47150) *(G-10772)*

Erler Industries Inc (PA) 812 346-4421
  418 Stockwell St North Vernon (47265) *(G-11257)*

Ernest A Cooper 812 284-0436
  1502 Production Rd Jeffersonville (47130) *(G-8357)*

Ernest Enterprises Inc 765 584-5700
  1041 N Old Highway 27 Winchester (47394) *(G-14329)*

Ernest Heighway 765 847-2865
  9347 N State Road 227 Fountain City (47341) *(G-4785)*

Ernies Welding Shop 812 326-2600
  3854 E 450 S Saint Anthony (47575) *(G-12245)*

Ernst Concrete 260 726-8282
  1125 W Water St Portland (47371) *(G-11818)*

Ernst Concrete Enterprises 812 284-5205
  4710 Utica Sellersburg Rd Sellersburg (47172) *(G-12393)*

Ernstberger Enterprises Inc 812 282-0488
  211 Eastern Blvd Jeffersonville (47130) *(G-8358)*

Erny Sheet Metal Inc 812 482-1044
  1020 2nd Ave Jasper (47546) *(G-8250)*

Ers Holding Company Inc (PA) 260 894-4145
  9144 N 900 W Ligonier (46767) *(G-9283)*

Ers Tower LLC 260 894-4145
  9144 N 900 W Ligonier (46767) *(G-9284)*

Erss, Pendleton *Also called Engineered Refr Shapes Svcs LLC (G-11488)*

Ertel Cellars Winery Inc 812 933-1500
  3794 E County Road 1100 N Batesville (47006) *(G-500)*

Ertl Enterprises Inc 765 622-9900
  2316 Jefferson St Anderson (46016) *(G-105)*

Ertl Fabricating Inc 765 393-1376
  2316 Jefferson St Anderson (46016) *(G-106)*

Ervins Millwork Shop LLC 260 768-3222
  8645 W 100 S Shipshewana (46565) *(G-12613)*

Es Deicing 260 422-2020
  3500 Meyer Rd Fort Wayne (46806) *(G-4242)*

Esaote North America Inc 317 813-6000
  11907 Exit 5 Pkwy Fishers (46037) *(G-3907)*

Esarey Hardwood Creations LLC 419 610-6486
  534 Hoffman Dr New Albany (47150) *(G-10773)*

Esc Promotions, Pendleton *Also called Wolfe Diversified Inds LLC (G-11511)*

Escalade Incorporated (PA) 812 467-4449
  817 Maxwell Ave Evansville (47711) *(G-3481)*

Escalade Sports, Evansville *Also called Indian Industries Inc (G-3550)*

Esco Enterprises Indiana Inc 317 241-0318
  302 Gasoline Aly Indianapolis (46222) *(G-6876)*

Esco Industries Inc 574 522-4500
  1701 Conant St Elkhart (46516) *(G-2837)*

Esco Technologies Inc 317 346-0393
  690 S State St Franklin (46131) *(G-4884)*

Esm Group Inc 219 393-5502
  5th Rd Bldg 4 Kingsbury (46345) *(G-8538)*

Espich Printing Inc 260 244-0132
  107 Hoosier Dr Columbia City (46725) *(G-1784)*

Essenhaus Inc 574 825-6790
  240 W Us Highway 20 Middlebury (46540) *(G-9885)*

Essenhaus Foods, Middlebury *Also called Essenhaus Inc (G-9885)*

Essential Sealing Products Inc 219 787-8711
  307 Melton Rd Ste B Chesterton (46304) *(G-1604)*

Essentra, Indianapolis *Also called Clondalkin Pharma & Healthcare (G-6623)*

Essentra Packaging US Inc 317 328-7355
  6454 Saguaro Ct Indianapolis (46268) *(G-6877)*

Essex Group Inc (HQ) 260 461-4000
  1601 Wall St Fort Wayne (46802) *(G-4243)*

Essex Group Inc 260 461-4000
  1601 Wall St Fort Wayne (46802) *(G-4244)*

Essex Group Inc 260 461-4183
  1700 Taylor St Fort Wayne (46802) *(G-4245)*

Essex Group Inc 260 461-4994
  3405 Meyer Rd Ste 170 Fort Wayne (46803) *(G-4246)*

Essex Group Inc 260 248-5500
  2580 S 600 E Columbia City (46725) *(G-1785)*

Essex Group Inc 260 248-5500
  2601 S 600 E Columbia City (46725) *(G-1786)*

Essex Group Inc 704 598-0222
  601 Wall St Fort Wayne (46802) *(G-4247)*

Essex Group Inc 260 424-1708
  3405 Meyer Rd Ste 170 Fort Wayne (46803) *(G-4248)*

Essex Group Inc 317 738-4365
  3200 Essex Dr Franklin (46131) *(G-4885)*

Essex Wire & Cable Division, Fort Wayne *Also called Essex Group Inc (G-4248)*

Essilor Laboratories Amer Inc 317 637-2391
  1718 Lafayette Rd Indianapolis (46222) *(G-6878)*

Essroc Corp 317 351-9910
  1051 S Emerson Ave Indianapolis (46203) *(G-6879)*

Estes Design and Manufacturing 317 899-2203
  470 S Mitthoeffer Rd Indianapolis (46229) *(G-6880)*

Estes Designs 317 899-5556
  7510 E 39th St Indianapolis (46226) *(G-6881)*

Estes Waste Solutions LLC 812 283-6400
  5005 Hamburg Pike Jeffersonville (47130) *(G-8359)*

Esteves Group USA, Decatur *Also called Esteves-Dwd LLC (G-2378)*

Esteves-Dwd LLC 260 728-9272
  1921 Patterson St Decatur (46733) *(G-2378)*

Et Printing 317 219-7966
  746 Westfield Rd Noblesville (46062) *(G-11101)*

Et Sprayers, Mooresville *Also called Equipment Technologies Inc (G-10308)*

Et Works LLC (PA) 317 834-4500
  2201 Hancel Pkwy Mooresville (46158) *(G-10309)*

Eta Engineering, Avilla *Also called Eta Fabrication Inc (G-404)*

Eta Fabrication Inc 260 897-3711
  10605 E Baseline Rd Avilla (46710) *(G-404)*

Etching Industries Corporation 317 591-3500
  3233 N Post Rd Indianapolis (46226) *(G-6882)*

Eternal Energy LLC 260 410-3056
  1530 Progress Rd Fort Wayne (46808) *(G-4249)*

Ets International Llc 574 234-0700
  1810 Clover Rd Mishawaka (46545) *(G-10043)*

Ettensohn & Company LLC 812 547-5491
9018 State Road 237 Tell City (47586) (G-13160)

Euclid Machine & Tool Inc (PA) 219 397-1374
4450 Euclid Ave East Chicago (46312) (G-2528)

EUCLID MACHINE CO, Indianapolis Also called Thomas/Euclid Industries Inc (G-8066)

Eureka Science Corp 317 821-0805
7631 Reynolds Rd Camby (46113) (G-1266)

Euronique Inc 812 983-3337
7633 Saint Johns Rd Elberfeld (47613) (G-2634)

European Concepts LLC 888 797-9005
5607 Newland Pl Fort Wayne (46835) (G-4250)

Evangel Press, Nappanee Also called Brethren In Christ Media Minis (G-10657)

Evans Adhesive Corporation 812 859-4245
7140 State Highway 246 Spencer (47460) (G-13024)

Evans Limestone Co 812 279-9744
1201 Limestone Dr Bedford (47421) (G-541)

Evans Metal Products Co Inc 574 264-2166
2400 Johnson St Elkhart (46514) (G-2838)

Evansville Assn For The Blind 812 422-1181
500 N 2nd Ave Evansville (47710) (G-3482)

Evansville Bindery Inc 812 423-2222
221 E Columbia St Evansville (47711) (G-3483)

Evansville Block Co Inc 812 422-2864
1700 W Franklin St Ste 14 Evansville (47712) (G-3484)

Evansville Courier Co (HQ) 812 464-7500
300 E Walnut St Evansville (47713) (G-3485)

Evansville Lithograph Co Inc 812 477-0506
3112 E Walnut St Evansville (47714) (G-3486)

Evansville Living, Evansville Also called Tucker Publishing Group Inc (G-3778)

Evansville Metal Products Inc (PA) 812 423-5632
119 Ladonna Blvd Evansville (47711) (G-3487)

Evansville Metal Products Inc 812 421-6589
2086 N 6th Ave Evansville (47710) (G-3488)

Evansville Pallets 812 550-0199
2203 N Kentucky Ave Evansville (47711) (G-3489)

Evansville Print Specialist 812 423-5831
2217 W Franklin St Evansville (47712) (G-3490)

Evansville Super Bike Shop 812 477-1740
1980 N Burkhardt Rd Evansville (47715) (G-3491)

Evansville Tool & Die Inc 812 422-7101
4900 N Saint Joseph Ave Evansville (47720) (G-3492)

Evantek Manufacturing Inds LLC 812 437-9100
5701 Old Boonville Hwy Evansville (47715) (G-3493)

Evart Engineering Co Inc 765 354-2232
1340 State St Middletown (47356) (G-9935)

Evelyn Dollahan 574 896-2971
520 E 625 S North Judson (46366) (G-11211)

Event Print, Hartford City Also called Printers Express Inc (G-5988)

Everett Charles Technologies, Munster Also called Contact Products Inc (G-10602)

Evergreen Drilling LLC 812 961-7701
21 Se 3rd St Ste 1 Evansville (47708) (G-3494)

Evergreen Recrtl Vehicles LLC (PA) 574 825-4298
10758 County Road 2 Middlebury (46540) (G-9886)

Evergreen Rv, Middlebury Also called Evergreen Recrtl Vehicles LLC (G-9886)

Everything Underground Inc 317 491-8148
6945 Westlake Rd Indianapolis (46214) (G-6883)

Everywhere Signs LLC 812 323-1471
2630 N Walnut St Bloomington (47404) (G-721)

Evia Custom Cabinets LLC 317 987-5504
14221 Avian Way Carmel (46033) (G-1376)

Evill Cycles 812 401-2045
606 Bell Ave Evansville (47712) (G-3495)

Evonik Corporation 765 477-4300
1650 Lilly Rd Lafayette (47909) (G-8894)

Evoqua Water Technologies LLC 317 280-4255
6111 Guion Rd Indianapolis (46254) (G-6884)

Evoqua Water Technologies LLC 317 280-4251
6125 Guion Rd Indianapolis (46254) (G-6885)

EVS Ltd 574 233-5707
3702 W Sample St South Bend (46619) (G-12767)

Ewing Light Metals Co Inc 317 926-4591
3451 Terrace Ave Indianapolis (46203) (G-6886)

Ewing Printing Company Inc 812 882-2415
516 Vigo St Vincennes (47591) (G-13677)

Ewireless LLC 317 536-0400
4625 N Capitol Ave Indianapolis (46208) (G-6887)

Exact Sheet Metal & Skylights 219 670-3520
763 Seminole Ct Crown Point (46307) (G-2251)

Exact-Tech Machining Inc 574 970-0197
1140 County Road 6 W Elkhart (46514) (G-2839)

Exactifab 812 420-2723
10309 N Industrial Pk Dr Brazil (47834) (G-961)

Exacto Machine & Tool Inc 317 872-3136
3402 W 79th St Indianapolis (46268) (G-6888)

Exactseal Inc 317 559-2220
7601 E 88th Pl Ste 3b Indianapolis (46256) (G-6889)

Exacttarget Inc (HQ) 317 423-3928
20 N Meridian St Ste 200 Indianapolis (46204) (G-6890)

Excel Business Printing Inc 317 259-1075
6302 Rucker Rd Ste A Indianapolis (46220) (G-6891)

Excel Co-Op Inc 219 984-5950
319 N Us Highway 421 Reynolds (47980) (G-11945)

Excel Co-Op Inc 574 967-4166
64 W 100 N Flora (46929) (G-3995)

Excel Coop Inc 574 967-3943
11179 S Us Highway 231 Brookston (47923) (G-1104)

Excel Industries Inc 574 264-2131
3308 Charlotte Ave Elkhart (46517) (G-2840)

Excel Machine 317 467-0299
3103 W Us Highway 40 Greenfield (46140) (G-5531)

Excel Machine Technologies Inc 219 548-0708
405 Elm St Valparaiso (46383) (G-13538)

Excel Manufacturing Inc 812 523-6764
1705 E 4th Street Rd Seymour (47274) (G-12448)

Excel Rubber, Granger Also called EMT Industries Inc (G-5406)

Excel Tool Inc 812 522-6880
2020 1st Ave Seymour (47274) (G-12449)

Excell, Lagrange Also called E & S Wood Creations LLC (G-9040)

Excell Color Graphics Inc 260 482-2720
2623 Camino Ct Fort Wayne (46808) (G-4251)

Excell Usa Inc 812 895-1687
1065 E Beckes Ln Vincennes (47591) (G-13678)

Excellon Technologies, Fort Wayne Also called HB Connect Inc (G-4324)

Excenart, West Lafayette Also called Proaxis Inc (G-14097)

Exchange Publishing Corp 574 831-2138
19401 Industrial Dr New Paris (46553) (G-10979)

Excista Corporation 734 224-3652
14213 Calming Waters Fishers (46038) (G-3908)

Exclusive Reality Inc, Clermont Also called Dr Restorations Inc (G-1712)

Exclusively Orthodontics Lab 317 887-1076
4475 Country Ln Greenwood (46142) (G-5693)

Executive Image Bldg Svcs Inc 317 865-1366
500 Polk St Ste 11 Greenwood (46143) (G-5694)

Executive MGT Svcs Ind Inc 317 594-6000
1605 Prospect St Indianapolis (46203) (G-6892)

Exelead Inc 317 347-2800
6925 Guion Rd Indianapolis (46268) (G-6893)

Exelis Inc., Electronic, Crane Also called Harris Corporation (G-2126)

Exemplary Foam Inc (PA) 574 295-8888
1235 W Hively Ave Elkhart (46517) (G-2841)

Exeon Processors LLC (PA) 765 674-2266
232 W Pearl St Jonesboro (46938) (G-8444)

Exhaust Productions Inc (PA) 219 942-0069
2777 E 83rd Pl Merrillville (46410) (G-9714)

Exhibit A Plastics LLC 765 386-6702
4170 S State Road 75 Coatesville (46121) (G-1749)

Exide Technologies 317 876-7475
5945 W 84th St Ste B Indianapolis (46278) (G-6894)

Exide Technologies 765 747-9980
2601 W Mt Pleasant Blvd Muncie (47302) (G-10470)

Exo-S US LLC 260 562-4131
6505 N State Road 9 Howe (46746) (G-6123)

Exo-S US LLC 260 562-4100
6505 N State Road 9 Howe (46746) (G-6124)

Exo-S US LLC (HQ) 260 562-4100
6505 N State Road 9 Howe (46746) (G-6125)

Exotic Metal Treating Inc 317 784-8565
6234 E Hanna Ave Indianapolis (46203) (G-6895)

Expanded Metals Co Ind LLC 574 287-6471
1400 Riverside Dr South Bend (46616) (G-12768)

Expedition Log Homes 219 663-5555
11091 Marion Pl Crown Point (46307) (G-2252)

Expert Electric 765 664-6642
2916 E Bocock Rd Marion (46952) (G-9523)

Expert Woodworks 219 345-2705
9126 N 200 E Lake Village (46349) (G-9082)

Exploding Brain Press 219 393-0796
607 Franklin St Michigan City (46360) (G-9789)

Explorer Sport Trucks, Warsaw Also called Van Explorer Company Inc (G-13957)

Expo Designers Co Inc 317 784-5610
720 S Belmont Ave Indianapolis (46221) (G-6896)

Expodesign, Indianapolis Also called Expo Designers Co Inc (G-6896)

Express Bindings 317 269-8114
212 W 10th St Ste F130 Indianapolis (46202) (G-6897)

Express Impressions Prtg LLC 765 966-2679
1334 Fairacres Rd Richmond (47374) (G-11985)

Express Machine 812 719-5979
6115 Sugar Maple Rd Cannelton (47520) (G-1290)

Express Mart, West Terre Haute Also called Mid-West Oil Company Inc (G-14127)

Express Motor Vehicle ADM LLC 812 909-0116
1111 S Green River Rd # 100 Evansville (47715) (G-3496)

Express Motors 812 437-9495
1059 E Riverside Dr Evansville (47714) (G-3497)

Express Press, South Bend Also called Systems & Services of Michiana (G-12965)

Express Press 4, South Bend Also called Express Press Indiana Inc (G-12770)

Express Press Indiana Inc (PA) 574 277-3355
325 N Dixie Way South Bend (46637) (G-12769)

Express Press Indiana Inc 219 874-2223
3505 W Mcgill St South Bend (46628) (G-12770)

Express Print, Frankfort *Also called Smith Business Supply Inc* ***(G-4853)***
Express Printing & Copying........219 762-3508
2554 Portage Mall Portage (46368) ***(G-11761)***
Express Sign & Neon Llc........812 882-0104
119 S 15th St Vincennes (47591) ***(G-13679)***
Express Study LLC........812 272-2247
2420 E Rock Creek Dr Bloomington (47401) ***(G-722)***
Exton Inc........574 533-0447
2134 Dierdorff Rd 27 Goshen (46526) ***(G-5212)***
Extra, The, Shelbyville *Also called Shelbyville Newspapers Inc* ***(G-12568)***
Extract Talent, Indianapolis *Also called Strategic Talent LLC* ***(G-8011)***
Extranet Talent........317 362-0140
3502 Woodview Trce Indianapolis (46268) ***(G-6898)***
Extreme Metal Fab Inc........812 988-9353
4889 Helmsburg Rd Nashville (47448) ***(G-10724)***
Extreme Precision Products LLC........812 839-0101
11388 N West Fork Rd Madison (47250) ***(G-9461)***
Extreme Quality Prints........812 987-7617
1938 E Oak St New Albany (47150) ***(G-10774)***
Extreme Trailer Service LLC........812 406-1984
117 Industrial Way Charlestown (47111) ***(G-1566)***
Extrusion Division, Evansville *Also called Ace Extrusion LLC* ***(G-3340)***
EZ Cut Tool LLC........260 748-0732
110 Rose Ave New Haven (46774) ***(G-10939)***
EZ Loader Northcentral, Elkhart *Also called E Z Loader Boat Trailers Inc* ***(G-2810)***
Ezs Custom Woodworking........574 831-3078
24314 County Road 46 Nappanee (46550) ***(G-10668)***
F & F Contracting........574 867-4471
7315 E 300 N Grovertown (46531) ***(G-5795)***
F & F Machine Specialties, Mishawaka *Also called Bbs Enterprises Inc* ***(G-10006)***
F & F Screw Machine Products........574 293-0362
4302 Wyland Dr Elkhart (46516) ***(G-2842)***
F & N Woodworking LLC........260 463-8938
2105 W 450 S Lagrange (46761) ***(G-9041)***
F & R Draperies........812 284-4682
827 Eastern Blvd Ste R6 Clarksville (47129) ***(G-1680)***
F A I, Princeton *Also called Federal Assembly Inc* ***(G-11871)***
F B C Inc (PA)........574 848-5288
1123 Commerce Dr Bristol (46507) ***(G-1059)***
F D Deskins Company Inc........317 284-4014
12554 Spire View Dr Fishers (46037) ***(G-3909)***
F D Ramsey & Co Inc........219 362-2452
708 Ridgeway St La Porte (46350) ***(G-8757)***
F E Harding Paving Co Inc........317 846-7401
5145 E 96th St Indianapolis (46240) ***(G-6899)***
F R Sheet Metal Co Inc........219 949-2290
7428 W 15th Ave Gary (46406) ***(G-5045)***
F Robert Gardner Co Inc........317 634-2333
1621 E New York St Indianapolis (46201) ***(G-6900)***
F S G Inc........574 291-5998
222 E Walter St South Bend (46614) ***(G-12771)***
F T Moore and Sons Inc........812 466-3762
3648 E Broadlands Ave Terre Haute (47805) ***(G-13233)***
F W A Decks & Fencing........219 865-3275
2401 Hickory Dr Dyer (46311) ***(G-2498)***
F.E.D., Indianapolis *Also called Fiberglass Engrg & Design Inc* ***(G-6918)***
Fab Con, Bedford *Also called Sigma Steel Inc* ***(G-578)***
Fab Solutions LLC........765 744-2671
10135 W 800 S Redkey (47373) ***(G-11897)***
Fab-Tech Industries........765 478-4191
14271 W Us Highway 40 Cambridge City (47327) ***(G-1256)***
Fab2order Inc........317 975-1056
1145 E Northfield Dr Brownsburg (46112) ***(G-1149)***
Fabco Publishing, Indianapolis *Also called Flag & Banner Company Inc* ***(G-6931)***
Fabcomp, Yorktown *Also called Dakota Engineering Inc* ***(G-14403)***
Fabcore Industries LLC........260 438-3431
928 Pencross Dr Fort Wayne (46845) ***(G-4252)***
Fabcreation........812 246-6222
7412 Highway 31 E Sellersburg (47172) ***(G-12394)***
Fabri-Tech Inc........317 849-7755
8236 N 600 W McCordsville (46055) ***(G-9666)***
Fabric Services, Bristol *Also called Mpr Corporation* ***(G-1073)***
Fabricated Metals Corp........219 734-6896
2180 N State Road 149 Chesterton (46304) ***(G-1605)***
Fabricated Metals Corp........219 871-0230
4991a W Us Highway 20 Michigan City (46360) ***(G-9790)***
Fabricated Specialties Inc........219 996-4787
511 N Main St Hebron (46341) ***(G-6012)***
Fabricated Steel Corporation........317 899-0012
9809 Park Davis Dr Indianapolis (46235) ***(G-6901)***
Fabshop........317 549-1681
8732 W County Road 1075 S Reelsville (46171) ***(G-11901)***
Fabstar Inc........765 230-0261
200 E Maple St Cayuga (47928) ***(G-1519)***
Fabtration LLC........812 989-6730
526 Maplewood Blvd Georgetown (47122) ***(G-5144)***
Fabtron Corporation........260 925-9553
1820 Sprott St Auburn (46706) ***(G-331)***
Facet Engineering........317 745-5070
1 Hickory Ct Danville (46122) ***(G-2346)***
Faerber's Bee Window, Fishers *Also called Bee Window Incorporated* ***(G-3876)***
Fairchild Semiconductor Corp........317 616-3641
11805 N Pennsylvania St Carmel (46032) ***(G-1377)***
Fairfield Gas Way........260 744-2186
4230 Fairfield Ave Fort Wayne (46807) ***(G-4253)***
Fairfield Manufacturing Co Inc........765 772-4547
2309 Concord Rd Lafayette (47909) ***(G-8895)***
Fairfield Manufacturing Co Inc (HQ)........765 772-4000
2400 Sagamore Pkwy S Lafayette (47905) ***(G-8896)***
Fairmont Homes LLC (HQ)........574 773-7941
502 S Oakland Ave Nappanee (46550) ***(G-10669)***
Fairmont Homes LLC........574 773-2041
1961 E Market St Nappanee (46550) ***(G-10670)***
Fairmount News........765 948-4164
122 S Main St Fairmount (46928) ***(G-3831)***
Fairview Fittings & Mfg........574 206-8884
23845 County Road 6 Elkhart (46514) ***(G-2843)***
Fairview Woodworking........260 768-3255
8655 W 100 S Shipshewana (46565) ***(G-12614)***
Fairway Custom Golf........317 842-0017
12500 Brooks School Rd Fishers (46037) ***(G-3910)***
Fairway Laser Systems Inc........219 462-6892
950 Transport Dr Valparaiso (46383) ***(G-13539)***
Fairylan LLC........219 866-3077
7175 N 700 W Rensselaer (47978) ***(G-11922)***
Faith Music Missions, Evansville *Also called Boeke Road Baptist Church Inc* ***(G-3389)***
Faith Walkers........219 873-1900
7358 W Johnson Rd Michigan City (46360) ***(G-9791)***
Faith Walkers Screen Printing, Michigan City *Also called Faith Walkers* ***(G-9791)***
Falcon Manufacturing LLC........317 884-3600
6200 S International Dr Columbus (47201) ***(G-1922)***
Falcon Metal Fabrication Inc........317 255-9365
2210 W 60th St Indianapolis (46228) ***(G-6902)***
Fall Creek Corporation........765 482-1861
917 E Walnut St Lebanon (46052) ***(G-9182)***
Fall Creek Enterprises, Lebanon *Also called Fall Creek Corporation* ***(G-9182)***
Fallen Timber Bats LLC........260 387-5841
1136 Tina Marie Ct Fort Wayne (46825) ***(G-4254)***
Falls Cities Printing Inc........812 949-9051
323 Vincennes St New Albany (47150) ***(G-10775)***
Family Design, Gary *Also called Aaron Company Incorporated* ***(G-5026)***
Family Leisurecom Inc........317 823-4448
11811 Pendleton Pike Indianapolis (46236) ***(G-6903)***
Family Vineyard........812 322-1720
3944 N Delaware St Indianapolis (46205) ***(G-6904)***
Fan-Tastic Vent........800 521-0298
1120 N Main St Elkhart (46514) ***(G-2844)***
Fanattic-Bedz, Noblesville *Also called Rwb & Associates LLC* ***(G-11178)***
Fancil Robert Welding Svc LLC........574 267-8627
721 S Buffalo St Warsaw (46580) ***(G-13874)***
Fancil Welding Service, Warsaw *Also called Fancil Robert Welding Svc LLC* ***(G-13874)***
Fanimation Inc........317 733-4113
10983 Bennett Pkwy Zionsville (46077) ***(G-14431)***
Fanstand Prints........317 579-9413
7050 E 116th St Ste 200 Fishers (46038) ***(G-3911)***
Farbest Farms Inc........812 481-1034
4689 S 400w Huntingburg (47542) ***(G-6164)***
Farbest Foods........812 886-2125
3672 S Keller Rd Vincennes (47591) ***(G-13680)***
Farbest Foods Inc........812 683-4200
4689 S 400w Huntingburg (47542) ***(G-6165)***
Farbest Foods Intl Inc........812 683-4200
4689 S 400w Huntingburg (47542) ***(G-6166)***
Faries-Mcmeekan Inc........574 293-3526
28858 County Road 20 Elkhart (46517) ***(G-2845)***
Faris Mailing Inc........317 246-3315
701 N Holt Rd Ste 3 Indianapolis (46222) ***(G-6905)***
Farm Boy Meats of Evansville........812 425-5231
2761 N Kentucky Ave Evansville (47711) ***(G-3498)***
Farm Fab........574 862-4775
65511 County Road 9 Goshen (46526) ***(G-5213)***
Farm Finds Candle Co LLC........260 437-5403
831 Woodland Xing Fort Wayne (46825) ***(G-4255)***
Farm Innovators Inc........574 936-5096
2255 Walter Glaub Dr Plymouth (46563) ***(G-11683)***
Farmer Bros Co........812 424-3309
1905 N Kentucky Ave Evansville (47711) ***(G-3499)***
Farmer Tank Incorporated........574 264-4625
25575 Woodlawn Ave Elkhart (46514) ***(G-2846)***
Farmers Brothers Coffee, Evansville *Also called Farmer Bros Co* ***(G-3499)***
Farmers Exchange, New Paris *Also called Exchange Publishing Corp* ***(G-10979)***
Farmers Machine Shop Inc........812 425-1238
1511 E Virginia St Evansville (47711) ***(G-3500)***
Farmland Lumber, South Whitley *Also called Steve Reiff Inc* ***(G-13005)***
Farmweek, Knightstown *Also called Mayhill Publications Inc* ***(G-8556)***
Fas Plastic Enterprises Inc........812 265-2928
3408 W State Road 56 Hanover (47243) ***(G-5960)***

Fas-N-Fast, Chesterton Also called Nicholson Group LLC **(G-1624)**

Fashion City 260 744-6753
1108 E Pontiac St Ste 2 Fort Wayne (46803) **(G-4256)**

Fashion Flooring and Ltg Inc 219 531-5667
2510 Beech St Valparaiso (46383) **(G-13540)**

Fasi Coatings LLC 219 985-0788
3905 W Ridge Rd Gary (46408) **(G-5046)**

Fasi Codings, Gary Also called Fire Aparatus Service Inc **(G-5047)**

Faske Wood Moulding Inc 812 923-5601
10215 Saint Johns Rd Borden (47106) **(G-929)**

Fasson Roll North America Div, Fort Wayne Also called Avery Dennison
Corporation **(G-4098)**

Fast Holster LLC 317 727-5243
10376 Harrow Pl Indianapolis (46280) **(G-6264)**

Fast Land Food, Kokomo Also called H & H Partnership Inc **(G-8634)**

Fast Lane Foods Inc 219 879-3300
4211 Franklin St Michigan City (46360) **(G-9792)**

Fast Manufacturing LLC 219 778-8123
3956 E 800 N Rolling Prairie (46371) **(G-12185)**

Fast Print Incorporated 260 484-5487
3050 E State Blvd Fort Wayne (46805) **(G-4257)**

Fast Signs 574 254-0545
2411 Mishawaka Ave South Bend (46615) **(G-12772)**

Fast Track Technologies LLC 317 229-6080
484 E Carmel Dr Carmel (46032) **(G-1378)**

Fastener Equipment Corporation 708 957-5100
1150 Loudermilk Ln Valparaiso (46383) **(G-13541)**

Fastlane Raceway 812 430-8818
10040 Brook Meadow Dr Evansville (47711) **(G-3501)**

Fastsigns, Bloomington Also called Richardson Entps Blmington LLC **(G-811)**

Fastsigns, South Bend Also called Fast Signs **(G-12772)**

Fastsigns, Indianapolis Also called Snykin Inc **(G-7956)**

Fastsigns, Greenwood Also called Hubbard Services Inc **(G-5704)**

Fastsigns, Indianapolis Also called I F S Corp **(G-7153)**

Fastsigns, Elkhart Also called Pathfinder Communications Corp **(G-3078)**

Fastsigns, Indianapolis Also called Gc Solutions Inc **(G-6987)**

Fastsigns 260 373-0911
3014 N Clinton St Fort Wayne (46805) **(G-4258)**

Fasttimes Fabrication Cus 574 858-9222
115 S Walnut St Etna Green (46524) **(G-3321)**

Fat Quarter Annies Qui 317 918-1481
2975 W Crosscreek Dr Monrovia (46157) **(G-10203)**

Fatheadz Eyewear, Indianapolis Also called Fatheadz Inc **(G-6906)**

Fatheadz Inc 800 561-6640
1125 W 16th St Indianapolis (46202) **(G-6906)**

Faulkenberg Printing Co Inc 317 638-1359
1670 Amy Ln Franklin (46131) **(G-4886)**

Faulkens Floorcover 574 300-4260
2045 N Meade St South Bend (46628) **(G-12773)**

Faulkner Fabricating Inc 574 342-0022
4050 Lincoln Hwy Bourbon (46504) **(G-942)**

Faulkners Bindery 765 292-2285
1596 E 400 S Atlanta (46031) **(G-294)**

Faurecia Clean Mobility, Columbus Also called Faurecia Emissions Control TEC **(G-1928)**

Faurecia Emissions Contl Tech 812 341-2620
950 W 450 S 4 Columbus (47201) **(G-1923)**

Faurecia Emissions Contl Tech 248 758-8160
4510 Airport Expy Fort Wayne (46809) **(G-4259)**

Faurecia Emissions Control 812 348-4305
601 S Gladstone Ave Columbus (47201) **(G-1924)**

Faurecia Emissions Control 937 823-5393
960 W 450 S Columbus (47201) **(G-1925)**

Faurecia Emissions Control (HQ) 812 341-2000
950 W 450 S Columbus (47201) **(G-1926)**

Faurecia Emissions Control 812 341-2000
950 W 450 S Bldg 2 Columbus (47201) **(G-1927)**

Faurecia Emissions Control TEC, Columbus Also called Faurecia Exhaust Systems
LLC **(G-1929)**

Faurecia Emissions Control TEC 812 341-2000
950 W 450 S Columbus (47201) **(G-1928)**

Faurecia Exhaust Systems LLC 812 341-2079
950 W 450 S Columbus (47201) **(G-1929)**

Favor It Promotions Inc 317 733-1112
4250 W 99th St Carmel (46032) **(G-1379)**

Favre Gunshop, Terre Haute Also called Favres Gun Shop **(G-13234)**

Favres Gun Shop 812 235-0198
520 N 42nd St Terre Haute (47803) **(G-13234)**

Fayette Tool and Engineering 765 825-7518
5432 Western Ave Connersville (47331) **(G-2048)**

Fayette Welding Service Inc 317 852-2929
7555 S State Road 267 Brownsburg (46112) **(G-1150)**

Faztech LLC 812 327-0926
7069 S Leisure Ln Bloomington (47401) **(G-723)**

Faztek LLC 260 482-7544
6935 Lincoln Pkwy Fort Wayne (46804) **(G-4260)**

Fbapower, Richmond Also called Pretty Brilliant LLC **(G-12031)**

Fbf Originals Inc 765 349-7474
1201 S Ohio St Martinsville (46151) **(G-9603)**

FBN Corporation 765 728-2438
890 W Huntington St Montpelier (47359) **(G-10291)**

Fbsa LLC 574 542-2001
7346 W 400 N Rochester (46975) **(G-12123)**

FCA US LLC 765 454-1705
2401 S Reed Rd Kokomo (46902) **(G-8622)**

FCA US LLC 765 854-4234
3660 State Rd 931 Kokomo (46901) **(G-8623)**

FCA US LLC 765 454-0018
1947 S Elizabeth St Kokomo (46902) **(G-8624)**

FCA US LLC 765 454-1005
1001 E Boulevard Kokomo (46902) **(G-8625)**

FCC (adams) LLC 260 589-8555
936 E Parr Rd Berne (46711) **(G-614)**

FCC (indiana) Inc 260 726-8023
555 Industrial Park Dr Portland (47371) **(G-11819)**

FCC (north America) Inc (HQ) 260 726-8023
555 Industrial Dr Portland (47371) **(G-11820)**

FCC Adams 260 589-8555
555 Industrial Dr Portland (47371) **(G-11821)**

FCC North America, Berne Also called FCC (adams) LLC **(G-614)**

Fdc Graphics Films Inc 574 273-4400
3820 Wlliam Richardson Dr South Bend (46628) **(G-12774)**

FDS Northwood LLC 765 289-2481
2727 S County Road 762 E Selma (47383) **(G-12423)**

Feddema Industries Inc 260 665-6463
1305 Wohlert St Angola (46703) **(G-213)**

Federal Assembly Inc 812 386-7062
115 S Hall St Princeton (47670) **(G-11871)**

Federal Cartridge Company 765 966-7745
232 Industrial Pkwy Richmond (47374) **(G-11986)**

Federal Heath Sign Company LLC 317 581-7790
160 W Carmel Dr Ste 236 Carmel (46032) **(G-1380)**

Federal Mogul, South Bend Also called Federal-Mogul Powertrain LLC **(G-12776)**

Federal Sign, Carmel Also called Federal Heath Sign Company LLC **(G-1380)**

Federal-Mogul LLC 765 659-7207
2845 W State Road 28 Frankfort (46041) **(G-4830)**

Federal-Mogul LLC 574 271-0274
5435 Dylan Dr Ste 200 South Bend (46628) **(G-12775)**

Federal-Mogul LLC 260 497-5563
9602 Coldwater Rd Fort Wayne (46825) **(G-4261)**

Federal-Mogul LLC 317 875-7259
8325 N Norfolk St Indianapolis (46268) **(G-6907)**

Federal-Mogul Powertrain LLC 574 271-5954
3605 W Cleveland Road Ext South Bend (46628) **(G-12776)**

Federated Auto Parts, Lawrenceburg Also called KOI Enterprises Inc **(G-9146)**

Federated Media, Elkhart Also called Pathfinder Communications Corp **(G-3077)**

Federated Publications Inc 765 962-1575
1175 N A St Richmond (47374) **(G-11987)**

Federated Publicators, Richmond Also called Federated Publications Inc **(G-11987)**

Fedex Office & Print Svcs Inc 317 631-6862
120 Monument Cir Ste 107 Indianapolis (46204) **(G-6908)**

Fedex Office & Print Svcs Inc 317 974-0378
10 S West St Indianapolis (46204) **(G-6909)**

Fedex Office & Print Svcs Inc 317 917-1529
241 W Washington St Indianapolis (46204) **(G-6910)**

Fedex Office & Print Svcs Inc 317 849-9683
6091 E 82nd St Indianapolis (46250) **(G-6911)**

Fedex Office & Print Svcs Inc 574 271-0398
2202 S Bend Ave Ste C South Bend (46635) **(G-12777)**

Fedex Office & Print Svcs Inc 219 462-6270
2505 Laporte Ave Ste 115 Valparaiso (46383) **(G-13542)**

Fedex Office & Print Svcs Inc 317 337-2679
3269 W 86th St Ste A Indianapolis (46268) **(G-6912)**

Fedex Office & Print Svcs Inc 317 295-1063
5030 W Pike Plaza Rd Indianapolis (46254) **(G-6913)**

Fedex Office & Print Svcs Inc 317 839-3896
2245 E Main St Ste 190 Plainfield (46168) **(G-11609)**

Fedex Office & Print Svcs Inc 765 449-4950
3520 South St Lafayette (47905) **(G-8897)**

Fedex Office & Print Svcs Inc 317 251-2406
1050 Broad Ripple Ave Indianapolis (46220) **(G-6914)**

Fedex Office & Print Svcs Inc 317 885-6480
8231 Us 31 S Indianapolis (46227) **(G-6915)**

Feeding Concepts Inc 317 773-2040
15235 Herriman Blvd Noblesville (46060) **(G-11102)**

Fehrenbacher Cabinets Inc 812 963-3377
8944 Big Cynthiana Rd Evansville (47720) **(G-3502)**

Fehring F N & Son Printers 219 933-0439
7336 Calumet Ave Hammond (46324) **(G-5879)**

Fehring Printers, Hammond Also called Fehring F N & Son Printers **(G-5879)**

Fellwocks Automotive 812 867-3658
10004 Darmstadt Rd Evansville (47710) **(G-3503)**

Femyer Drapery Shop 765 282-3398
4409 W Burton Dr Muncie (47304) **(G-10471)**

Fender 4 Star Meat Processing, Spencer Also called Fender 4 Star Meats
Processing **(G-13025)**

Fender 4 Star Meats Processing 812 829-3240
  1494 Rocky Hill Rd Spencer (47460) *(G-13025)*

Fenders Inc 574 293-3717
  5304 Beck Dr Elkhart (46516) *(G-2847)*

Fenwick Motor Sports 765 522-1354
  112 S Washington St Bainbridge (46105) *(G-476)*

Fenwick Pharma LLC 765 296-7443
  8812 Fenwick Ct Lafayette (47905) *(G-8898)*

Feralloy Corporation 219 787-9698
  6755 Waterway Dr Portage (46368) *(G-11762)*

Ferdinand Machine Shop 812 367-2590
  825 Main St Ferdinand (47532) *(G-3849)*

Ferdinand Processing Inc 812 367-2073
  1182 E 5th St Ferdinand (47532) *(G-3850)*

Ferguson 317 254-5965
  1057 E 54th St Ste A Indianapolis (46220) *(G-6916)*

Ferguson Equipment Inc 574 234-4303
  25170 Edison Rd South Bend (46628) *(G-12778)*

Ferguson Waterworks 219 440-5254
  450 Kennedy Ave Schererville (46375) *(G-12321)*

Fergys Cabinets 765 529-0116
  2506 Grand Ave New Castle (47362) *(G-10900)*

Ferree Logging LLC 812 786-1676
  2150 Leonard Rd Nw Corydon (47112) *(G-2098)*

Ferrellgas LP 574 936-2725
  11867 Lincoln Hwy Plymouth (46563) *(G-11684)*

Ferret, Elkhart *Also called Smco Inc (G-3178)*

Ferrill-Fisher Incorporated 812 935-9000
  8768 N Wayport Rd Bloomington (47404) *(G-724)*

Ferry Street Woodworks 812 427-9663
  319 Ferry St Vevay (47043) *(G-13663)*

Fertilizer Plant, Reynolds *Also called Excel Co-Op Inc (G-11945)*

Ffesar Inc 812 378-4220
  6564 W Black Tail Way McCordsville (46055) *(G-9667)*

Fia-Indiana 812 895-4700
  3320 S Keller Rd Vincennes (47591) *(G-13681)*

Fiber Bond Corporation 219 879-4541
  110 Menke Rd Trail Creek (46360) *(G-13441)*

Fiber Technologies LLC 812 569-4641
  2517 E Caray Ct Bloomington (47401) *(G-725)*

Fiber-Tron Corp 574 294-8545
  29877 Old Us 33 Elkhart (46516) *(G-2848)*

Fiberbond, Trail Creek *Also called Fiber Bond Corporation (G-13441)*

Fiberglas & Plastic Fabg 317 549-1779
  2832 N Webster Ave Indianapolis (46219) *(G-6917)*

Fiberglass Engrg & Design Inc 317 293-0002
  7421 Crawfordsville Rd Indianapolis (46214) *(G-6918)*

Fiberglass Pdts & Boat Repr 260 627-3209
  12401 Bay Heights Blvd Grabill (46741) *(G-5364)*

Fiberglass Pdts Boat Repairing 260 337-5636
  311 Spencer St Saint Joe (46785) *(G-12255)*

Fibertech Inc 812 983-2642
  11744 Blue Bell Rd Elberfeld (47613) *(G-2635)*

Fibrosan USA 574 612-4736
  2926 Paul Dr Elkhart (46514) *(G-2849)*

Fickle Peach Inc 765 282-5211
  117 E Charles St Muncie (47305) *(G-10472)*

Fideli Publishing 888 343-3542
  119 W Morgan St Martinsville (46151) *(G-9604)*

Fidelity Dental Handpiece Svc 317 254-0277
  4330 Black Oak Dr Indianapolis (46228) *(G-6919)*

Fiedeke Vinyl Coverings Inc 574 534-3408
  811 Eisenhower Dr N Goshen (46526) *(G-5214)*

Fiekert Homestead Wine, Rising Sun *Also called Kenneth Fiekert (G-12089)*

Field Construction 574 664-2010
  5222 E County Road 650 N Twelve Mile (46988) *(G-13450)*

Field Rubber Products Inc 317 773-3787
  3211 Conner St Noblesville (46060) *(G-11103)*

Fielders Choice Direct, Oxford *Also called Landec Ag Inc (G-11433)*

Fields Outdoor Adventures LLP 765 932-3964
  126 S Perkins St Rushville (46173) *(G-12221)*

Figure Eight Brewing LLC 219 477-2000
  150 Washington St Valparaiso (46383) *(G-13543)*

Filca LLC 812 637-3559
  22806 Stateline Rd Lawrenceburg (47025) *(G-9141)*

Fill-Rite Division, Fort Wayne *Also called Tuthill Corporation (G-4709)*

Fillmanns Industries LLC 765 744-4772
  3921 S Highbanks Rd Daleville (47334) *(G-2339)*

Filmtec Fabrications LLC 419 435-7504
  9609 Ardmore Ave Fort Wayne (46809) *(G-4262)*

Filson Earthwork Company 317 774-3180
  21785 Riverwood Ave Noblesville (46062) *(G-11104)*

Filters Plus 812 430-0347
  6227 Calloway Dr Evansville (47715) *(G-3504)*

Filtration Parts Incorporated 704 661-8135
  513 N Melville St Rensselaer (47978) *(G-11923)*

Filtration Plus Inc 219 879-0663
  4208 N 900 W Michigan City (46360) *(G-9793)*

Filtration Tech Systems LLC 812 944-9368
  4345 Security Pkwy New Albany (47150) *(G-10776)*

Financial Times-Prentice Hall, Indianapolis *Also called Pearson Education Inc (G-7668)*

Findley Foster Corp 812 524-7279
  14 S County Road 1250 E Seymour (47274) *(G-12450)*

Fine Guys Inc 812 547-8630
  1001 Main St Tell City (47586) *(G-13161)*

Fine Print, Bloomington *Also called Wraco Enterprises Inc (G-859)*

Fine Signs and Graphics 812 944-7446
  802 E 8th St New Albany (47150) *(G-10777)*

Fineline Digital Group Inc 317 872-4490
  8081 Zionsville Rd Indianapolis (46268) *(G-6920)*

Fineline Graphics Incorporated 317 872-4490
  8081 Zionsville Rd Indianapolis (46268) *(G-6921)*

Fineline Printing Group, Indianapolis *Also called Fineline Graphics Incorporated (G-6921)*

Fingerhut Bakery Inc (PA) 574 896-5937
  119 Lane St North Judson (46366) *(G-11212)*

Finish Alternatives 317 440-2899
  705 Northfield Ct Indianapolis (46227) *(G-6922)*

Finish Design Woodworking Inc 812 284-9240
  2819 Sable Mill Ln Jeffersonville (47130) *(G-8360)*

Finite Filtation Company 219 789-8084
  120 Las Olas Ct Crown Point (46307) *(G-2253)*

Finley Creek Vineyards Inc 317 769-5483
  795 S Us 421 Zionsville (46077) *(G-14432)*

Finvantage LLC 317 500-4949
  275 Medical Dr Unit 633 Carmel (46082) *(G-1381)*

Finvantage Solutions, Carmel *Also called Finvantage LLC (G-1381)*

Finzer Roller Inc 812 829-1455
  650 W Market St Spencer (47460) *(G-13026)*

Finzer Roller Indiana, Spencer *Also called Finzer Roller Inc (G-13026)*

Fire Aparatus Service Inc 219 985-0788
  3905 W Ridge Rd Gary (46408) *(G-5047)*

Fire King International LLC (HQ) 812 948-8400
  101 Security Pkwy New Albany (47150) *(G-10778)*

Fire King International LLC 812 948-2795
  900 Park Pl New Albany (47150) *(G-10779)*

Fire King Security Group, New Albany *Also called Fki Security Group LLC (G-10781)*

Fire King Security Pdts LLC 812 948-8400
  111 Security Pkwy New Albany (47150) *(G-10780)*

Fire Star Industries LLC 317 432-3212
  4644 Brentridge Pkwy Greenwood (46143) *(G-5695)*

Firehouse Printing LLC 812 547-3109
  711 Humboldt St Tell City (47586) *(G-13162)*

Firesmoke Org 317 690-2542
  323 N Delaware St Indianapolis (46204) *(G-6923)*

Firestone Industrial Pdts Inc (HQ) 317 575-7000
  250 W 96th St Fl 2 Indianapolis (46260) *(G-6924)*

First Choice Forestry & Log 574 271-9425
  51101 Old Cottage Dr Granger (46530) *(G-5407)*

First Class Printing 317 808-2222
  6800 E 30th St Indianapolis (46219) *(G-6925)*

First Databank Inc 317 571-7200
  500 E 96th St Ste 500 # 500 Indianapolis (46240) *(G-6926)*

First Flash Line, Fort Wayne *Also called Moose Lake Products Co (G-4480)*

First Gear Engineering & Tech, Fort Wayne *Also called First Gear Inc (G-4263)*

First Gear Inc 260 490-3238
  7606 Freedom Way Fort Wayne (46818) *(G-4263)*

First Image 219 791-9900
  1447 E 86th Pl Merrillville (46410) *(G-9715)*

First Metals & Plastics Inc 812 379-4400
  3805 Jonesville Rd Columbus (47201) *(G-1930)*

First Place Trophies 812 385-3279
  1595 E State Road 64 Princeton (47670) *(G-11872)*

First Place Trophy Inc 574 293-6147
  24888 County Road 20 Elkhart (46517) *(G-2850)*

First Quality Printing Inc 317 506-8633
  8745 Rawles Ave Ste D Indianapolis (46219) *(G-6927)*

First Quality Printing Center 317 546-5531
  5498 Emerson Way Indianapolis (46226) *(G-6928)*

Fischer Woodcraft Inc 317 627-6035
  1024 Timber Grove Pl Beech Grove (46107) *(G-594)*

Fischer Woodworking Inc 812 985-9488
  3190 Ford Rd N Mount Vernon (47620) *(G-10392)*

Fiserv Inc 317 576-6700
  2307 Directors Row Indianapolis (46241) *(G-6929)*

Fiserv Mrtg Servicing Systems (HQ) 574 282-3300
  3575 Moreau Ct 2 South Bend (46628) *(G-12779)*

Fish Boys, The, Indianapolis *Also called Algaewheel Inc (G-6364)*

Fish Factory 219 929-9375
  676 Mississinewa Rd Chesterton (46304) *(G-1606)*

Fisher & Company Incorporated 586 746-2000
  2301 Saint George Rd Evansville (47711) *(G-3505)*

Fisher Clinical Services Inc 317 277-0337
  1220 W Morris St Indianapolis (46221) *(G-6930)*

Fisher Packing Company 260 726-7355
  300 W Walnut St Portland (47371) *(G-11822)*

Fisher Specialties Inc 260 385-8251
  11515 Roberts Rd Harlan (46743) *(G-5971)*

Fisher Tool & Design Inc 812 867-8350
  8231 Burch Park Dr Evansville (47725) *(G-3506)*

Fisherman S Lurecraft Shop Inc 260 829-1274
  513 W Central Ave Lagrange (46761) *(G-9042)*

Fishers Fire Station 92 .... 317 595-3292
  11595 Brooks School Rd Fishers (46037) *(G-3912)*

Fishers Sun Herald, Fishers *Also called Topics Newspapers Inc (G-3978)*

Fishing Abilities Inc 574 273-0842
  22770 Adams Rd South Bend (46628) *(G-12780)*

Fitch Inc 260 637-0835
  3708 Mccomb Rd Huntertown (46748) *(G-6138)*

Fitech Divison, Michigan City *Also called Ashley F Ward Inc (G-9767)*

Fitech Inc 513 398-1414
  2031 Tryon Rd Michigan City (46360) *(G-9794)*

Five Star Fabulous LLC 260 579-3401
  6931 Lincoln Pkwy Fort Wayne (46804) *(G-4264)*

Five Star Hydraulics Inc 219 762-1619
  1210 Crisman Rd Portage (46368) *(G-11763)*

Five Star Sheets LLC 574 654-8058
  54370 Smilax Rd New Carlisle (46552) *(G-10882)*

Five Starr Inc 812 367-1554
  453 W 9th St Ferdinand (47532) *(G-3851)*

Fives N Amercn Combustn Inc 219 662-9600
  730 N Main St Crown Point (46307) *(G-2254)*

Fix & Sons Manufacturing Inc 765 724-4041
  219 E Washington St Alexandria (46001) *(G-42)*

Fki Security Group LLC (PA) 812 948-8400
  101 Security Pkwy New Albany (47150) *(G-10781)*

FL Smidth 812 402-9210
  1315 N Cullen Ave Ste 102 Evansville (47715) *(G-3507)*

Flag & Banner Company Inc 317 299-4880
  5450 Lafayette Rd Ste 5 Indianapolis (46254) *(G-6931)*

Flager Electric 574 295-8007
  224 S Main St Elkhart (46516) *(G-2851)*

Flags International LLC 574 674-5125
  10845 Mckinley Hwy Osceola (46561) *(G-11376)*

Flair Molded Plastics Inc 812 425-6155
  2521 Lynch Rd Evansville (47711) *(G-3508)*

Flambeau Inc 812 372-4899
  4325 Middle Rd Columbus (47203) *(G-1931)*

Flamespray Machine Service 260 726-6236
  237 E Votaw St Portland (47371) *(G-11823)*

Flanders Electric Mtr Svc Inc 812 867-4014
  500 E Buena Vista Rd Evansville (47711) *(G-3509)*

Flanders Electric Mtr Svc Inc 812 421-4300
  1050 E Maryland St Evansville (47711) *(G-3510)*

Flare Inc 260 490-1101
  6210 Discount Dr Fort Wayne (46818) *(G-4265)*

Flat Electronics LLC 765 414-6635
  4315 Commerce Dr 440-101 Lafayette (47905) *(G-8899)*

Flat Rock 219 852-5262
  6732 Calumet Ave Hammond (46324) *(G-5880)*

Flat Rock Furniture Inc (PA) 317 398-1501
  1424 Miller Ave Waldron (46182) *(G-13798)*

Flat Roll Div - Jeffersonville, Jeffersonville *Also called Steel Dynamics Inc (G-8428)*

Flavor Burst Co LLP 317 745-2952
  499 Commerce Dr Danville (46122) *(G-2347)*

Flavoreeds 260 373-2233
  3535 N Anthony Blvd Fort Wayne (46805) *(G-4266)*

Flawless Beauty LLC 317 914-7952
  4951 Tuscany Ln Indianapolis (46254) *(G-6932)*

Fleenor Sawmill Inc 812 752-3594
  571 N State Road 39 Scottsburg (47170) *(G-12356)*

Fleetwood Homes, Decatur *Also called Rev Recreation Group Inc (G-2401)*

Fleetwood Homes, Decatur *Also called Rev Recreation Group Inc (G-2402)*

Fleetwood Homes, Decatur *Also called Rev Recreation Group Inc (G-2403)*

Fleetwood Motor Homes 260 627-6800
  17728 Lochner Rd Spencerville (46788) *(G-13046)*

Fleming Air Flow, Indianapolis *Also called Fleming Assoc Calibration Inc (G-6933)*

Fleming Assoc Calibration Inc 317 631-4605
  1060 N Capitol Ave E100 Indianapolis (46204) *(G-6933)*

Fleming Machine Works Inc 812 967-4086
  9934 S Fleming Rd Pekin (47165) *(G-11472)*

Flenar Manufacturing LLC 574 893-4070
  2906 Ft Wayne Rd Rochester (46975) *(G-12124)*

Fletcher Heating & Cooling 812 865-2984
  2049 W County Road 500 N Paoli (47454) *(G-11450)*

Fletchs Apple Lane 317 489-2697
  5441 Senour Rd Indianapolis (46239) *(G-6934)*

Flex-N-Gate Corporation 765 294-3050
  1200 E 8th St Veedersburg (47987) *(G-13643)*

Flex-N-Gate Corporation 260 665-8288
  3000 Woodhull Dr Angola (46703) *(G-214)*

Flex-Tech Inc 317 546-0183
  5108 Massachusetts Ave Indianapolis (46218) *(G-6935)*

Flexaust Company Inc 574 371-3248
  1605 W Center St Warsaw (46580) *(G-13875)*

Flexaust Inc (HQ) 574 267-7909
  1510 Armstrong Rd Warsaw (46580) *(G-13876)*

Flexco Products Inc 574 294-2502
  2415 Bryant St Elkhart (46516) *(G-2852)*

Flexcon, Richmond *Also called Shell Packaging Corporation (G-12048)*

Flexform Technologies LLC 574 295-3777
  4955 Beck Dr Elkhart (46516) *(G-2853)*

Flexible Concepts Inc 574 296-0941
  1620 Middlebury St Elkhart (46516) *(G-2854)*

Flexible Marketing Group 574 296-0941
  1620 Middlebury St Elkhart (46516) *(G-2855)*

Flexible Materials Inc (PA) 812 280-7000
  3101 Hamburg Pike Ste B Jeffersonville (47130) *(G-8361)*

Flexible Materials Inc 812 280-9578
  3101 Hamburg Pike Ste A Jeffersonville (47130) *(G-8362)*

Flexible Materials Inc 812 948-7786
  3595 Lafayette Pkwy Floyds Knobs (47119) *(G-4010)*

Flexible Technologies Inc 574 936-2432
  1435 N Michigan St Ste 3 Plymouth (46563) *(G-11685)*

Flexseals Manufacturing LLC 574 293-0333
  2304 Charlotte Ave Elkhart (46517) *(G-2856)*

Flextech Corporation 574 271-9797
  53585 Lakefield Dr Elkhart (46514) *(G-2857)*

Flickinger Industries Inc 260 432-4527
  1801 Carlton Ave Fort Wayne (46802) *(G-4267)*

Flight Dept, South Bend *Also called Leco Corporation (G-12838)*

Flight Integrity LLC 812 455-6642
  2111 Eaglewood Dr Newburgh (47630) *(G-11028)*

Flinn Farms Bedford Seed Inc 812 279-4136
  917 17th St Bedford (47421) *(G-542)*

Flint & Walling Inc 260 347-1781
  95 N Oak St Kendallville (46755) *(G-8475)*

Flint Group Print Media N Amer, Indianapolis *Also called Flint Group US LLC (G-6936)*

Flint Group US LLC 317 471-8435
  4910 W 78th St Indianapolis (46268) *(G-6936)*

Flint Group US LLC 317 870-4422
  4910 W 78th St Indianapolis (46268) *(G-6937)*

Flint Group US LLC 574 269-4603
  3025 E Old Road 30 Warsaw (46582) *(G-13877)*

Flint Ink North America Div, Indianapolis *Also called Flint Group US LLC (G-6937)*

Flint Ink North America Div, Warsaw *Also called Flint Group US LLC (G-13877)*

Flir Detection Inc 765 775-1701
  3000 Kent Ave West Lafayette (47906) *(G-14067)*

Flir Systems, West Lafayette *Also called Flir Detection Inc (G-14067)*

Flj Transport LLC 574 642-0200
  1025 Lantern Ln Goshen (46526) *(G-5215)*

Flo Realty LLC 317 636-6481
  1 Indiana Sq Indianapolis (46204) *(G-6938)*

Flodders Sawmill 765 628-0280
  10861 E 100 N Greentown (46936) *(G-5645)*

Flomatic International, Sellersburg *Also called Manitowoc Beverage Eqp Inc (G-12405)*

Floortech 317 887-6825
  1280 W Southport Rd Indianapolis (46217) *(G-6939)*

Flora Racing 574 233-0642
  3319 W Sample St South Bend (46619) *(G-12781)*

Flora Wastewater Treatment 574 967-3005
  507 N Division St Flora (46929) *(G-3996)*

Floralcraft Distributors (PA) 574 262-2639
  1805 Leer Dr Elkhart (46514) *(G-2858)*

Floralcraft Distributors 574 262-2639
  52876 Park Six Dr Elkhart (46514) *(G-2859)*

Flosource Inc 765 342-1360
  489 Gardner Ave Martinsville (46151) *(G-9605)*

Flow Center Products Inc 765 364-9460
  2065 S Nucor Rd Crawfordsville (47933) *(G-2152)*

Flowserve Corporation 219 763-1000
  6675 Daniel Burnham Dr F Portage (46368) *(G-11764)*

Floyd County Brewing Company L 502 724-3202
  129 W Main St New Albany (47150) *(G-10782)*

Flp Woodworks 260 424-3904
  1510 Boone St Fort Wayne (46808) *(G-4268)*

Fluid Handling Technology Inc 317 216-9629
  7692 Zionsville Rd Indianapolis (46268) *(G-6940)*

Fluid Power Division, Hammond *Also called Niagara Lasalle Corporation (G-5921)*

Flutes Inc (PA) 317 870-6010
  8252 Zionsville Rd Indianapolis (46268) *(G-6941)*

Flw Plastics Inc 812 546-0050
  199 Raymond St Hope (47246) *(G-6112)*

Flying Turtle Publishing LLC 219 221-8488
  7216 Birch Ave Hammond (46324) *(G-5881)*

Flying W Trophy Div, Indianapolis *Also called Professional Bowling Ball Svc (G-7770)*

Flynn Interactive, Indianapolis *Also called Flynn Media LLC (G-6942)*

Flynn Media LLC 317 536-2972
  9334 Champton Dr Indianapolis (46256) *(G-6942)*

Flynn Sons Sand & Gravel 812 636-4400
  11971 N Us Highway 231 Odon (47562) *(G-11325)*

Flyover Enterprises Inc 317 417-1747
  1068 Chipmunk Ln Pendleton (46064) *(G-11489)*

Foam Fabricators Inc 812 948-1696
  950 Progress Blvd New Albany (47150) *(G-10783)*

Foam Rubber LLC 765 521-2000
  2000 Troy Ave New Castle (47362) *(G-10901)*

Foam Rubber Products, New Castle *Also called Foam Rubber LLC (G-10901)*

Foamcraft Inc (PA) 317 545-3626
  9230 Harrison Park Ct Indianapolis (46216) *(G-6943)*

Foamcraft Inc 574 293-8569
  900 Industrial Pkwy Elkhart (46516) *(G-2860)*

Foamcraft Inc 574 534-4343
  2506 Industrial Park Dr Goshen (46526) *(G-5216)*

Foamcraft Inc 812 849-3350
  100 N Industrial Pkwy Mitchell (47446) *(G-10163)*

Foamex, Fort Wayne *Also called Fxi Inc (G-4291)*

Foamex, Auburn *Also called Fxi Inc (G-333)*

Foamiture 574 831-4775
  19240 Tarman Rd New Paris (46553) *(G-10980)*

Focal Point Cabinetry, Osceola *Also called Custom Design Laminates Inc (G-11375)*

Focus Mold & Machine Inc 812 422-9627
  1145 Indy Ct Evansville (47725) *(G-3511)*

Focus Surgery Inc 317 541-1580
  4000 Pendleton Way Indianapolis (46226) *(G-6944)*

Foertsch Construction Co Inc (PA) 812 529-8211
  12724 N State Road 245 Lamar (47550) *(G-9099)*

Fogwell Technologies 260 410-1898
  10525 W Yoder Rd Roanoke (46783) *(G-12101)*

Foil Die International Inc 260 359-9011
  1054 W 900 N Huntington (46750) *(G-6204)*

Foil Form Inc 260 359-9011
  1054 W 900 N Huntington (46750) *(G-6205)*

Foil Laminating Inc 574 935-3645
  1000 Pidco Dr Plymouth (46563) *(G-11686)*

Foley Pattern Company Inc 260 925-4113
  500 W 11th St Auburn (46706) *(G-332)*

Fontaine Trailer Company 574 772-6673
  1201 W Culver Rd Knox (46534) *(G-8566)*

Fontaine Truck Equipment Co, Indianapolis *Also called Marmon Highway Tech LLC (G-7457)*

Fontana Fasteners Inc (HQ) 765 654-0477
  3595 W State Road 28 Frankfort (46041) *(G-4831)*

Food & Fuel Upland 765 998-0840
  280 N Main St Upland (46989) *(G-13470)*

Food Specialties Inc 317 271-0862
  1727 Expo Ln Indianapolis (46214) *(G-6945)*

Foods Peer 317 735-4283
  1825 Stout Field Ter Indianapolis (46241) *(G-6946)*

Foot Locker Retail Inc 317 578-1892
  6020 E 82nd St Ste 632 Indianapolis (46250) *(G-6947)*

Foppers Gourmet Pet Treat Bky, Logansport *Also called Nick-Em Builders LLC (G-9360)*

For Bare Feet Inc 765 349-7474
  1201 S Ohio St Martinsville (46151) *(G-9606)*

Force Cnc LLC 812 273-0218
  940 Lanier Dr Madison (47250) *(G-9462)*

Ford Motor Company 317 837-2302
  2675 Reeves Rd Ste 101 Plainfield (46168) *(G-11610)*

Ford Sawmills Inc 812 324-2134
  2019 E Old Terre Haute Rd Vincennes (47591) *(G-13682)*

Forecast Sales Inc 317 829-0147
  2719 Tobey Dr Indianapolis (46219) *(G-6948)*

Foremost Fabricators, Goshen *Also called Patrick Industries Inc (G-5308)*

Foremost Farms USA Cooperative 317 842-7755
  7202 E 87th St Ste 112 Indianapolis (46256) *(G-6949)*

Foremost Flexible Fabricating 812 663-4756
  824 N Michigan Ave Greensburg (47240) *(G-5600)*

Foremost Flexible Products, Greensburg *Also called Foremost Flexible Fabricating (G-5600)*

Forest Commodities Inc (PA) 765 349-3291
  1789 S Old State Road 67 Martinsville (46151) *(G-9607)*

Forest Products Group Inc 765 659-1807
  901 Blinn Ave Frankfort (46041) *(G-4832)*

Forest Products Group Ind Div, Frankfort *Also called Forest Products Group Inc (G-4832)*

Forest Products Mfg Co (PA) 812 482-5625
  51 E 30th St Jasper (47546) *(G-8251)*

Forest River Inc 574 264-5179
  2901 County Road 7 N Elkhart (46514) *(G-2861)*

Forest River Inc 574 533-5934
  3010 College Ave Goshen (46528) *(G-5217)*

Forest River Inc 574 264-2513
  2780 County Road 36 Goshen (46527) *(G-5218)*

Forest River Inc 574 262-3474
  2745 Northland Dr Elkhart (46514) *(G-2862)*

Forest River Inc 574 262-5466
  3601 County Road 6 E Elkhart (46514) *(G-2863)*

Forest River Inc 574 848-1335
  1280 Commerce Dr Bristol (46507) *(G-1060)*

Forest River Inc 574 389-4636
  51773 County Road 39 Middlebury (46540) *(G-9887)*

Forest River Inc 574 642-3112
  2367 Century Dr Goshen (46528) *(G-5219)*

Forest River Inc 574 262-2212
  914 County Road 1 N Elkhart (46514) *(G-2864)*

Forest River Inc (HQ) 574 389-4600
  900 County Road 1 N Elkhart (46514) *(G-2865)*

Forest River Inc 574 296-7700
  3603 S Nappanee St Elkhart (46517) *(G-2866)*

Forest River Cherokee Inc 260 593-2566
  402 Lehman Ave Topeka (46571) *(G-13418)*

Forest River Custom Extrusions 574 975-0206
  712 Eisenhower Dr S Goshen (46526) *(G-5220)*

Forest River Vibe 574 296-2084
  411 County Road 15 Elkhart (46516) *(G-2867)*

Forget ME Not Printing Ltd 317 508-7401
  7858 Bosinney Cir Indianapolis (46256) *(G-6950)*

Form Wood Industries Inc 812 284-3676
  1601 Production Rd Jeffersonville (47130) *(G-8363)*

Form/TEC Plastics Incorporated 765 342-2300
  1000 Industrial Dr Martinsville (46151) *(G-9608)*

Formal Affairs Tuxedo Shop 574 875-6654
  23797 Us Highway 33 Elkhart (46517) *(G-2868)*

Formflex, Bloomingdale *Also called Futurex Industries Inc (G-647)*

Forsyth Brothers Concrete Pdts (PA) 812 466-4080
  4500 N Fruitridge St Terre Haute (47805) *(G-13235)*

Fort Meyers, Fort Wayne *Also called United Oil Corp (G-4716)*

Fort Wayne Awning Co Inc 260 478-1636
  7105 Ardmore Ave Fort Wayne (46809) *(G-4269)*

Fort Wayne Box & Pallet LLC 260 409-4067
  7739 Hessen Cassel Rd Fort Wayne (46816) *(G-4270)*

Fort Wayne Business Weekly, Fort Wayne *Also called Kpc Media Group Inc (G-4415)*

Fort Wayne Clutch & Driveline, Fort Wayne *Also called Fort Wayne Clutch Inc (G-4271)*

Fort Wayne Clutch Inc (PA) 260 484-8505
  2424 Goshen Rd Fort Wayne (46808) *(G-4271)*

Fort Wayne Fabrication 260 459-8848
  3303 Freeman St Fort Wayne (46802) *(G-4272)*

Fort Wayne Metals Res Pdts 260 747-4154
  9307 Avionics Dr Fort Wayne (46809) *(G-4273)*

Fort Wayne Metals Res Pdts (PA) 260 747-4154
  9609 Ardmore Ave Fort Wayne (46809) *(G-4274)*

Fort Wayne Metals RES Pdts 260 747-4154
  3401 Mcarthur Dr Fort Wayne (46809) *(G-4275)*

Fort Wayne Mold & Engrg Inc 260 747-9168
  4501 Earth Dr Fort Wayne (46809) *(G-4276)*

Fort Wayne Newspapers Inc 260 461-8444
  600 W Main St Fort Wayne (46802) *(G-4277)*

Fort Wayne Plastics Inc 260 432-2520
  510 Sumpter St Fort Wayne (46804) *(G-4278)*

Fort Wayne Pools 260 459-4100
  6930 Gettysburg Pike Fort Wayne (46804) *(G-4279)*

Fort Wayne Printing Co Inc 260 471-7744
  909 Production Rd Fort Wayne (46808) *(G-4280)*

Fort Wayne Wire Die Inc (PA) 260 747-1681
  2424 American Way Fort Wayne (46809) *(G-4281)*

Fort Wayne Wire Die Inc 260 747-1681
  2424 American Way Fort Wayne (46809) *(G-4282)*

Fort Wyne Rdlgy Assn Fundation 260 266-8120
  3707 New Vision Dr Fort Wayne (46845) *(G-4283)*

Forterra Concrete Inds Inc 812 426-5353
  1213 Stanley Ave Evansville (47711) *(G-3512)*

Fortes Bros Electric 219 472-0111
  3931 W 77th Pl Merrillville (46410) *(G-9716)*

Fortville Automotive Sup Inc 317 485-5114
  305 W Broadway St Fortville (46040) *(G-4774)*

Fortville Feeders Inc (PA) 317 485-5095
  750 E Broadway St Fortville (46040) *(G-4775)*

Fosbel Inc 219 883-4479
  1 N Broadway Gary (46402) *(G-5048)*

Fostek 540 587-5870
  201 S Main St Mishawaka (46544) *(G-10044)*

Foundry Services Inc 317 955-8112
  10482 Winghaven Dr Noblesville (46060) *(G-11105)*

Fountain Acres Foods 765 847-1897
  1140 W Whitewater Rd Fountain City (47341) *(G-4786)*

Fountain County Neighbor 765 762-2411
  113 S Perry St Attica (47918) *(G-300)*

Fountain Food and Fueling 765 847-5257
  402 Us Highway 27 N Fountain City (47341) *(G-4787)*

Fountaintown Forge Inc 317 861-5403
  5513 S 100 E Fountaintown (46130) *(G-4790)*

Four Part Inc 219 926-7777
  132 S Calumet Rd Chesterton (46304) *(G-1607)*

Four Points Development Corp 317 357-3275
  6368 Harrison Ridge Blvd Indianapolis (46236) *(G-6951)*

Four Season Oil Inc 317 215-1214
  1237 American Ave Plainfield (46168) *(G-11611)*

Four Season Sports Inc 812 279-0384
  2828 Washington Ave Bedford (47421) *(G-543)*

Four Star Fabricators Inc 812 354-9995
  810 S Industrial Park Dr Petersburg (47567) *(G-11562)*

Four Star Field Services 812 354-9995
  804 S Industrial Park Dr # 10 Petersburg (47567) *(G-11563)*

Four Star Printing 765 620-9728
  1001 E Sigler St Frankton (46044) *(G-4943)*

Four Star Screen Printing LLC 765 533-3006
  1379 N Cadiz Pike New Castle (47362) *(G-10902)*

Four Star Welding 574 825-3856
  11400 W 300n Middlebury (46540) *(G-9888)*

(G-0000) Company's Geographic Section entry number

Four Woods Laminating Inc (PA) 260 593-2246
  7550 W 500 S Topeka (46571) *(G-13419)*

Fourman Enterprises Inc 812 546-5734
  701 South St Hope (47246) *(G-6113)*

Fourth Freedom Forum Inc 574 534-3402
  212 S Main St Ste 1 Goshen (46526) *(G-5221)*

Fourth Shift Inc 317 567-3072
  2145 Ransdell St Indianapolis (46225) *(G-6952)*

Fowler Ridge II Wind Farm LLC 713 354-2100
  91 S 100 E Fowler (47944) *(G-4799)*

Fowler Ridge IV Wind Farm LLC 765 884-1029
  2870 W State Road 18 Fowler (47944) *(G-4800)*

Fox Products Corporation 260 723-4888
  6110 S State Road 5 South Whitley (46787) *(G-12999)*

Fox Smoothies LLC 812 333-3051
  4000 E Stonegate Dr Bloomington (47401) *(G-726)*

Fox Studios Inc 317 253-0135
  6027 Gladden Dr Indianapolis (46220) *(G-6953)*

Foy Industries 317 727-3905
  6953 Dean Rd Indianapolis (46220) *(G-6954)*

Fpc Feed & Manufacturing 765 468-7768
  10727 W State Road 32 Parker City (47368) *(G-11463)*

Fr Chinook LLC 317 356-1666
  7441 Chinook Cir Indianapolis (46219) *(G-6955)*

Frakes Electric Company, Westfield *Also called Robinson Industries Inc (G-14185)*

Frakes Engineering Inc 317 577-3000
  7950 Castleway Dr Ste 160 Indianapolis (46250) *(G-6956)*

Frakes Industrial Sales & Svc, Westfield *Also called Robinson Industries Inc (G-14186)*

Frame Shop, The, Indianapolis *Also called Franklin Barry Gallery (G-6959)*

Francesville Vulcan Materials 219 567-9155
  14530 W 700 S Francesville (47946) *(G-4812)*

Francisco Mining, Francisco *Also called Peabody Midwest Mining LLC (G-4817)*

Franco Corporation 765 675-6691
  600 Industrial Dr Tipton (46072) *(G-13391)*

Frank H Monroe Htg & Coolg Inc 812 945-2566
  595 Industrial Blvd New Albany (47150) *(G-10784)*

Frank Miller Lumber Co Inc (PA) 800 345-2643
  1690 Frank Miller Rd Union City (47390) *(G-13455)*

Frank Miller Lumber Co Inc 812 883-8077
  7016 E Old 56 Salem (47167) *(G-12286)*

Frank R Komar CPA 812 477-9110
  1431 S Green River Rd Evansville (47715) *(G-3513)*

Frank W Martinez 574 232-6081
  54555 Pine Rd South Bend (46628) *(G-12782)*

Frank Wiss Racg Components Inc 317 248-4764
  140 Gasoline Aly Indianapolis (46222) *(G-6957)*

Franke Plating Works Inc 260 422-8477
  2109 E Washington Blvd Fort Wayne (46803) *(G-4284)*

Frankfort Newspaper 859 254-2385
  251 E Clinton St Frankfort (46041) *(G-4833)*

Frankinstein Industries Inc 217 918-4548
  6800 E 30th St Indianapolis (46219) *(G-6958)*

Franklin Barry Gallery 317 822-8455
  617 Massachusetts Ave Indianapolis (46204) *(G-6959)*

Franklin Electric Co Inc (PA) 260 824-2900
  9255 Coverdale Rd Fort Wayne (46809) *(G-4285)*

Franklin Electric Co Inc 765 677-6900
  100 Schaffer Dr Gas City (46933) *(G-5124)*

Franklin Electric Intl (HQ) 260 824-2900
  9255 Coverdale Rd Fort Wayne (46809) *(G-4286)*

Franklin Publishing Inc 800 634-1993
  5373 Ashby Ct Greenwood (46143) *(G-5696)*

Franklin Stamping Inds Inc 765 282-5138
  105 W Fuson Rd Muncie (47302) *(G-10473)*

Franklin Township Civic League 317 862-1774
  8822 Southeastern Ave Indianapolis (46239) *(G-6960)*

FRANKLIN TOWNSHIP INFORMER, Indianapolis *Also called Franklin Township Civic League (G-6960)*

Franklins Mercantile 812 876-0426
  7115 Kimberly Ln Spencer (47460) *(G-13027)*

Franks Industries 765 647-2080
  9021 State Road 101 Brookville (47012) *(G-1114)*

Franks Machine Shop Tool & Die 574 288-6899
  24133 State Road 2 South Bend (46619) *(G-12783)*

Franks Wood Shop 317 738-2039
  3170 Compass Dr Franklin (46131) *(G-4887)*

Franks Woodworking 765 378-0424
  3314 E 500 N Anderson (46012) *(G-107)*

Frascio International LLC 317 663-0030
  1011 3rd Ave Sw Carmel (46032) *(G-1382)*

Frazier Products 317 781-9781
  3445 S Harding St Indianapolis (46217) *(G-6961)*

Frech U S A Inc 219 874-2812
  6000 Ohio St Michigan City (46360) *(G-9795)*

Frecker Optical Inc 260 747-9653
  7115 Old Trail Rd Fort Wayne (46809) *(G-4287)*

Freckles Graphics Inc 765 448-4692
  3835 Fortune Dr Lafayette (47905) *(G-8900)*

Fred Anderson 765 985-2099
  4757 N 400 E Peru (46970) *(G-11527)*

Fred D McCrary 812 354-6520
  4295 W County Road 350 N Petersburg (47567) *(G-11564)*

Fred Jay Stewart 765 284-1386
  4001 E Centennial Ave Muncie (47303) *(G-10474)*

Fred S Carver Inc (HQ) 260 563-7577
  1569 Morris St Wabash (46992) *(G-13727)*

Fred Sibley Enterprises, Elkhart *Also called Fred Sibley Sr (G-2869)*

Fred Sibley Sr 574 264-2237
  25551 Homewood Ave Elkhart (46514) *(G-2869)*

Fred Smith Store Fixtures Inc 812 347-2363
  6405 Highway 337 Nw Depauw (47115) *(G-2456)*

Fred Weber Inc 317 262-4920
  2050 S Harding St Indianapolis (46221) *(G-6962)*

Frederick Tool Corp 574 295-6700
  24615 County Road 45 # 4 Elkhart (46516) *(G-2870)*

Freds Driveways Inc 317 770-6094
  1101 Westfield Rd Noblesville (46062) *(G-11106)*

Freduenberg-Nok Sealing Tech, Shelbyville *Also called Freudenberg-Nok General Partnr (G-12535)*

Freed Machining & Tool Inc 765 538-3019
  6033 W 800 S Westpoint (47992) *(G-14205)*

Freedman Mobility Seating, Rochester *Also called Fbsa LLC (G-12123)*

Freedom Corrugated LLC 317 290-1140
  5505 W 74th St Indianapolis (46268) *(G-6963)*

Freedom Lumber Company, Monroeville *Also called Monroeville Box Pallet & Wood (G-10197)*

Freedom Valley Cabinets 812 875-2509
  7483 Old Glory Ln Freedom (47431) *(G-4948)*

Freedom Wire Inc 260 856-3059
  458 Olive St Cromwell (46732) *(G-2208)*

Freehold Games LLC 574 656-9031
  69080 Sycamore Rd Walkerton (46574) *(G-13802)*

Freezing Systems and Svc Inc 219 879-6236
  107 Freyer Rd Michigan City (46360) *(G-9796)*

Freight Trnsp RES Assoc Inc 888 988-1699
  1720 N Kinser Pike # 210 Bloomington (47404) *(G-727)*

Freightliner Cstm Chassis Corp 260 517-9678
  66540 State Road 19 Wakarusa (46573) *(G-13777)*

Freije Treatment Systems Inc 888 766-7258
  9715 Kincaid Dr Ste 1100 Fishers (46037) *(G-3913)*

Freije Treatment Systems Inc 317 508-3848
  7435 E 86th St Indianapolis (46256) *(G-6964)*

Fremont Coatings Div 260 495-4445
  302 E Mcswain Dr Fremont (46737) *(G-4959)*

Fremont Plastics, Fremont *Also called Thermform Engineered Qulty LLC (G-4977)*

French International Coatings 574 505-0774
  15205 E 200 S Akron (46910) *(G-5)*

French Lick Auto Signs (PA) 812 936-7777
  9451 W State Road 56 French Lick (47432) *(G-4985)*

French Tips 812 923-9055
  102 Lafollette Sta S Floyds Knobs (47119) *(G-4011)*

Fresh Air Screens, Indianapolis *Also called Kitty Mac Inc (G-7356)*

Fresh Start Inc 812 254-3398
  113 N Industrial Park Rd Washington (47501) *(G-13982)*

Fretina Corp 812 547-6471
  2001 Main St Tell City (47586) *(G-13163)*

Freudenberg Medical Mis Inc (HQ) 812 280-2400
  2301 Centennial Blvd Jeffersonville (47130) *(G-8364)*

Freudenberg-Nok General Partnr 317 421-3400
  1700 Miller Ave Shelbyville (46176) *(G-12534)*

Freudenberg-Nok General Partnr 765 763-7246
  487 W Main St Morristown (46161) *(G-10369)*

Freudenberg-Nok General Partnr 734 354-5504
  877 Miller Ave Ste B Shelbyville (46176) *(G-12535)*

Freudenberg-Nok General Partnr 260 894-7183
  1497 Gerber St Ligonier (46767) *(G-9285)*

Freudenberg-Nok General Partnr 765 763-7246
  487 W Main St Morristown (46161) *(G-10370)*

Frew Process Group LLC 317 565-5000
  15305 Stony Creek Way Noblesville (46060) *(G-11107)*

Frick Services Inc (PA) 260 761-3311
  3154 Depot St Wawaka (46794) *(G-14032)*

Frickers Inc 765 965-6655
  3237 Chester Blvd Richmond (47374) *(G-11988)*

Friends of Third World Inc (PA) 260 422-6821
  611 W Wayne St Fort Wayne (46802) *(G-4288)*

Friendship Homes Division, Nappanee *Also called Fairmont Homes LLC (G-10669)*

Friskney Gear & Machine Corp 260 281-2200
  106 N Bridge St Corunna (46730) *(G-2084)*

Friskney Gear Division, Corunna *Also called Friskney Gear & Machine Corp (G-2084)*

Frito-Lay North America Inc 765 659-1831
  323 S County Road 300 W Frankfort (46041) *(G-4834)*

Frito-Lay North America Inc 765 471-1833
  3435 S 460 E Lafayette (47905) *(G-8901)*

Frito-Lay North America Inc 812 877-2425
  6541 State Road 42 Terre Haute (47803) *(G-13236)*

Frito-Lay North America Inc 765 659-4517
  2611 W County Road 0 Ns Frankfort (46041) *(G-4835)*

A
L
P
H
A
B
E
T
I
C

Froggy Print LLC 317 965-7954
1219 E Thornton Dr Bloomington (47401) ***(G-728)***
Front End Digital Inc 317 652-6134
11899 Stepping Stone Dr Fishers (46037) ***(G-3914)***
Front Line Manufacturing, Warsaw *Also called Frontline Mfg Inc* ***(G-13878)***
Frontier Additive Mfg LLC 765 413-5568
2418 W Co Rd 400 S Crawfordsville (47933) ***(G-2153)***
Frontier Carriage 574 965-4444
7872 W 1000 N Delphi (46923) ***(G-2421)***
Frontier Engineering 317 823-6885
12469 E 65th St Indianapolis (46236) ***(G-6965)***
Frontline Mfg Inc 574 269-6751
2466 W 200 N Warsaw (46580) ***(G-13878)***
Frontline Mfg Inc (PA) 574 453-2902
2446 N 200 W Warsaw (46580) ***(G-13879)***
Frozen Garden LLC 219 286-3578
315 E 316 N Ste C Valparaiso (46383) ***(G-13544)***
Frugal Times 317 326-4165
2309 W 100 N Greenfield (46140) ***(G-5532)***
Fruit Hills Winery Orchrd LLC 574 848-9463
55535 State Road 15 Bristol (46507) ***(G-1061)***
Fruition Industries LLC 260 854-2325
105 Warmer Dr Rome City (46784) ***(G-12199)***
Ft Wayne Reader 260 420-8580
1301 Lafayette St Ste 202 Fort Wayne (46802) ***(G-4289)***
FTC Products Corp 219 567-2441
Hwy 421 N One Half Mile Francesville (47946) ***(G-4813)***
Ftic, Jamestown *Also called Fukai Toyotetsu Indiana Corp* ***(G-8230)***
Ftr Trnsportation Intelligence 888 988-1699
1720 N Kinser Pike Bloomington (47404) ***(G-729)***
Fuel Bladder Distributors Inc 317 852-9156
3800 N State Road 267 B Brownsburg (46112) ***(G-1151)***
Fuel Fabrication LLC 219 390-7022
14727 Reeder Ct Crown Point (46307) ***(G-2255)***
Fuel Prfmce Enhancement LLC 317 979-2316
10640 Deme Dr Ste H Indianapolis (46236) ***(G-6966)***
Fuel Recovery Service Inc 317 372-3029
125 W South St Unit 2690 Indianapolis (46206) ***(G-6967)***
Fuentes Distributing 219 808-2147
6811 New Hampshire Ave Hammond (46323) ***(G-5882)***
Fuhrman Precision Services 260 728-9600
10484 N 200 W Decatur (46733) ***(G-2379)***
Fukai Toyotetsu Indiana Corp 765 676-4800
1100 N Lebanon St Jamestown (46147) ***(G-8230)***
Fulk Inc 260 338-1012
40 County Road 70 Laotto (46763) ***(G-9107)***
Full Circle Printing & Mktg, Avon *Also called Jt Printing LLC* ***(G-451)***
Full Color Direct LLC 317 538-4500
3808 Churchman Woods Blvd Indianapolis (46203) ***(G-6968)***
Full Court Press, Indianapolis *Also called Hardingpoorman Inc* ***(G-7074)***
Full Court Press Printing, Indianapolis *Also called Hardingpoorman Group Inc* ***(G-7075)***
Full Metal Solutions LLC 812 725-9660
295a America Pl Jeffersonville (47130) ***(G-8365)***
Full Press LLC 260 433-7731
5714 Evard Rd Fort Wayne (46835) ***(G-4290)***
Fullenkamp Machine & Mfg Inc 260 726-8345
1507 N Meridian St Portland (47371) ***(G-11824)***
Fuller Architectural Hardwoods, Daleville *Also called Cash & Carry Lumber Co Inc* ***(G-2337)***
Fullifillment Center, Peru *Also called Asc Inc* ***(G-11516)***
Fulton Co R E M C 574 223-3156
1448 W S R 14 Rochester (46975) ***(G-12125)***
Fulton Industries, South Bend *Also called Pgi Mfg LLC* ***(G-12893)***
Fulton Industries Inc (PA) 574 968-3222
100 E Wayne St Ste 320 South Bend (46601) ***(G-12784)***
Functional Devices Inc 765 883-5538
101 Commerce Dr Sharpsville (46068) ***(G-12505)***
Fundex Games Ltd 317 248-1080
1901 W 16th St Indianapolis (46202) ***(G-6969)***
Fur Real Taxidermy LLC 812 667-6365
4339 E County Road 900 S Cross Plains (47017) ***(G-2212)***
Furnace Design Technology LLC 317 896-5506
16903 Spring Mill Rd Westfield (46074) ***(G-14164)***
Furniture Sales & Marketing 317 849-1508
7219 Knollvalley Ln Indianapolis (46256) ***(G-6970)***
Furrion LLC 574 327-6571
52567 Independence Ct Elkhart (46514) ***(G-2871)***
Fusion Designs, Goshen *Also called Country Woodshop LLC* ***(G-5194)***
Fusion Wood Products LLC 574 389-0307
1600 W Mishawaka Rd Elkhart (46517) ***(G-2872)***
Futaba Indiana America Corp 812 895-4700
3320 S Keller Rd Vincennes (47591) ***(G-13683)***
Futon Factory Inc (PA) 317 549-8639
5920 E 34th St Indianapolis (46218) ***(G-6971)***
Future Mold Inc 812 941-8661
100 Galvin Way New Albany (47150) ***(G-10785)***
Future Signs Sales & Service 765 749-5180
709 S Main St Winchester (47394) ***(G-14330)***
Future Tool & Engineering Co 812 376-8699
3400 Scott Dr Columbus (47201) ***(G-1932)***
Future Wave Graphics Inc 574 389-8803
54257 County Road 7 Apt 4 Elkhart (46514) ***(G-2873)***
Futuretek 317 631-0098
535 N Livingston Ave Indianapolis (46222) ***(G-6972)***
Futurex Industries Inc 812 299-5708
10000 S Carlisle St Terre Haute (47802) ***(G-13237)***
Futurex Industries Inc 765 597-2221
101 Guionrd Rd Marshall (47859) ***(G-9591)***
Futurex Industries Inc (PA) 765 498-3900
80 E Smith St Bloomingdale (47832) ***(G-647)***
Futurex Industries Inc 765 498-8900
1 N Main St Bloomingdale (47832) ***(G-648)***
Fuzion Products LLC 317 536-0745
6312 Southeastern Ave Indianapolis (46203) ***(G-6973)***
Fwp, Fort Wayne *Also called Fort Wayne Plastics Inc* ***(G-4278)***
Fxi Inc 260 747-7485
3005 Commercial Rd Fort Wayne (46809) ***(G-4291)***
Fxi Inc 260 925-1073
2211 Wayne St Auburn (46706) ***(G-333)***
Fyt Fuels LLC 520 304-6451
1722 W 400 N Rensselaer (47978) ***(G-11924)***
G & B Directional Boring LLC 574 538-8132
2620 N 850 W Shipshewana (46565) ***(G-12615)***
G & G Metal Spinners Inc 317 923-3225
1717 Cornell Ave Indianapolis (46202) ***(G-6974)***
G & G Millwright Service LLC 260 571-4908
11052 S 600 E La Fontaine (46940) ***(G-8722)***
G & H Wire Company Inc 317 346-6655
2165 Earlywood Dr Franklin (46131) ***(G-4888)***
G & J 765 457-9889
1252 N Main St Kokomo (46901) ***(G-8626)***
G & M Rebuilders Inc 812 858-9233
7140 Savannah Dr Newburgh (47630) ***(G-11029)***
G & N Fabrications LLC 317 698-9539
1315 Sumac Ct Carmel (46033) ***(G-1383)***
G & N Warehouse & Packaging 574 234-3717
209 College St South Bend (46628) ***(G-12785)***
G & P Machinery, Indianapolis *Also called Grinding and Polsg McHy Corp* ***(G-7050)***
G & R Woodworking LLC 812 687-7701
7747 N 775 E Montgomery (47558) ***(G-10224)***
G & S Johnson Outdoors LLC 574 267-3891
3400 E Us Highway 30 Warsaw (46580) ***(G-13880)***
G & S Rural Woodworking 765 348-7781
1102 S 200 E Hartford City (47348) ***(G-5980)***
G & S Super Abrasives Inc 260 665-5562
1601 Wohlert St Angola (46703) ***(G-215)***
G & T Distribution 765 759-8611
9108 W Sutherland Ave Yorktown (47396) ***(G-14404)***
G & T Industries Inc 812 634-2252
290 E 30th St Jasper (47546) ***(G-8252)***
G & T Industries of Indiana 812 634-2252
2741 Cathy Ln Jasper (47546) ***(G-8253)***
G & W Herbs 574 646-2134
10517 W 1100 N Nappanee (46550) ***(G-10671)***
G and G Peppers LLC 765 358-4519
12245 N County Road 450 W Gaston (47342) ***(G-5132)***
G and P Enterprises Ind Inc 812 723-3837
782 N Greenbriar Dr Paoli (47454) ***(G-11451)***
G C G Industries Inc 260 482-7454
4636 Newaygo Rd Fort Wayne (46808) ***(G-4292)***
G C I, Nappanee *Also called Grrreat Creations* ***(G-10675)***
G D C, Goshen *Also called Gdc Inc* ***(G-5222)***
G E C O M Corp (HQ) 812 663-2270
1025 E Barachel Ln Greensburg (47240) ***(G-5601)***
G E Kerr Companies Inc 417 426-5504
2600 W Jefferson St Kokomo (46901) ***(G-8627)***
G F M S Industries 219 464-1445
166 Wessex Ct Valparaiso (46385) ***(G-13545)***
G G B Inc 219 733-2897
7512 S 800 W Westville (46391) ***(G-14216)***
G K Optical Company Inc (HQ) 317 881-2585
2902 N Mitthoeffer Pl Indianapolis (46229) ***(G-6975)***
G L D Inc (PA) 317 924-7981
6427 N Ewing St Indianapolis (46220) ***(G-6976)***
G M D, Rensselaer *Also called Genuine Machine Design Inc* ***(G-11926)***
G M S I Inc 574 457-4646
6521 E Cornelius Rd Syracuse (46567) ***(G-13131)***
G T A Drum Inc 574 288-3459
1410 Napier St South Bend (46601) ***(G-12786)***
G Thrapp Jewelers Inc 317 255-5555
5609 N Illinois St Indianapolis (46208) ***(G-6977)***
G W Enterprises 260 868-2555
7063 County Road 24 Butler (46721) ***(G-1228)***
G&H Orthodontics, Franklin *Also called G & H Wire Company Inc* ***(G-4888)***
G&L Machine 260 488-2100
5920 County Road 4 Hamilton (46742) ***(G-5822)***
G4 Tool and Technology Inc 574 970-0844
1827 Fieldhouse Ave Elkhart (46517) ***(G-2874)***
Gabbard and Son Electric 812 747-7621
252 Charles A Liddle Dr # 7 Lawrenceburg (47025) ***(G-9142)***

Gabriel Intl Group LLC (PA) 812 537-5400
136 Industrial Dr Lawrenceburg (47025) *(G-9143)*

Gabriel Products Inc 502 291-5388
2303 Cypress Pt Jeffersonville (47130) *(G-8366)*

Gac Chemical Corporation 317 917-0319
1598 S Senate Ave Indianapolis (46225) *(G-6978)*

Gad-A-Bout Screenprinting Inc 765 855-5681
403 E School St Centerville (47330) *(G-1542)*

GAF Materials, Mount Vernon *Also called Standard Industries Inc (G-10409)*

GAF Materials, Michigan City *Also called Standard Industries Inc (G-9847)*

Gagan Petroleum Inc 765 254-1330
5302 N Wheeling Ave Muncie (47304) *(G-10475)*

Gainescraft Inc 765 932-3590
203 N Hannah St Rushville (46173) *(G-12222)*

Galaxy Arts 219 836-6033
8748 Madison Ave Munster (46321) *(G-10604)*

Galaxy Arts and Sciences, Munster *Also called Galaxy Arts (G-10604)*

Galaxy Container LLC 574 936-6300
1001 Pidco Dr Plymouth (46563) *(G-11687)*

Galbe Magazine LLC 248 742-5231
10540 Combs Ave Indianapolis (46280) *(G-6265)*

Galbreath LLC (HQ) 219 946-6631
480 E 150 S Winamac (46996) *(G-14304)*

Galbreath LLC 574 946-6631
480 E 150 S Winamac (46996) *(G-14305)*

Gale Enameling Co Inc 317 839-7474
10095 Old National Rd Indianapolis (46231) *(G-6979)*

Gale Force Software Corp 317 570-4900
11800 Exit 5 Pkwy Ste 102 Fishers (46037) *(G-3915)*

Galfab LLC (PA) 574 946-7767
612 W 11th St Winamac (46996) *(G-14306)*

Gallagher Drilling Inc (PA) 812 477-6746
115 Se 3rd St Fl 2 Evansville (47708) *(G-3514)*

Gallery of Kitchens, Vincennes *Also called Warren Homes Inc (G-13716)*

Galloway Fabricating 574 453-3802
3776 E 750 N Leesburg (46538) *(G-9236)*

Galvanized Division, Bristol *Also called Quality Galvanized Pdts Inc (G-1076)*

Game Face Brands, Zionsville *Also called Pieniadze Inc (G-14456)*

Game Face Graphix LLC 317 340-0973
8903 Squire Boone Ct Camby (46113) *(G-1267)*

Game Plan Graphics LLC 812 663-3238
123 N Broadway St Greensburg (47240) *(G-5602)*

Game Vault 317 209-7795
3734 Pursley Ln Indianapolis (46235) *(G-6980)*

Gameface Inc 317 363-8855
1555 W Oak St Ste 100 Zionsville (46077) *(G-14433)*

Gameoto LLC 317 883-9322
3400 Bloomsbury Ln Indianapolis (46228) *(G-6981)*

Gammons Metal & Mfg Co Inc 317 546-7091
2900 N Richardt Ave Indianapolis (46219) *(G-6982)*

Ganal Corporation 260 749-2161
915 Lincoln Hwy E New Haven (46774) *(G-10940)*

Gannett Co Inc 765 423-5512
823 Park East Blvd Ste C Lafayette (47905) *(G-8902)*

Gannett Co Inc 765 962-1575
1175 North Dr Richmond (47374) *(G-11989)*

Gannett Co Inc 765 423-5511
1501 Veterans Mem Pkwy E Lafayette (47905) *(G-8903)*

Gannon Mtal Fbrcators Erectors 219 398-0299
418 E Chicago Ave East Chicago (46312) *(G-2529)*

Gapco Inc 317 787-6440
1817 Inisheer Ct Indianapolis (46217) *(G-6983)*

Gaps, Elkhart *Also called Graphic Arts & Publ Svcs (G-2894)*

Gardiner Rentals Bill 765 447-5111
510 Veterans Mem Pkwy E Lafayette (47905) *(G-8904)*

Gardner Glass Products Inc 317 464-0881
1705 Lafayette Rd Indianapolis (46222) *(G-6984)*

Gared Holdings LLC 317 774-9840
9200 E 146th St Ste A Noblesville (46060) *(G-11108)*

Gared Sports, Noblesville *Also called Gared Holdings LLC (G-11108)*

Garphik Mechanix, Fort Wayne *Also called Wayne Press Incorporated (G-4743)*

GARPHYTTAN WIRE, South Bend *Also called Suzuki Garphyttan Corp (G-12963)*

Garr Custom Pallets Inc 812 352-8887
750 S Stonehenge North Vernon (47265) *(G-11258)*

Garrett Printing, Garrett *Also called Scott Culbertson (G-5022)*

Garrett Printing & Graphics 812 422-6005
1405 N 1st Ave Evansville (47710) *(G-3515)*

Garrett Products 260 357-5988
1605 Dekko Dr Garrett (46738) *(G-5005)*

Garrity Stone Inc 317 546-0893
3137 N Ritter Ave Indianapolis (46218) *(G-6985)*

Garrity Tool Company LLC 317 541-1400
3555 Developers Rd Ste A Indianapolis (46227) *(G-6986)*

Gartech Enterprises Inc 812 794-4796
3037 W State Road 256 Austin (47102) *(G-397)*

Gartland Foundry Company Inc 812 232-0226
330 Grant St Terre Haute (47802) *(G-13238)*

Garver Manufacturing Inc 765 964-5828
224 N Columbia St Union City (47390) *(G-13456)*

Gary Bridge and Iron Co Inc 219 884-3792
3700 Roosevelt St Gary (46408) *(G-5049)*

Gary Devoss 765 369-2492
409 S Spencer St Redkey (47373) *(G-11898)*

Gary Earl 812 279-6780
411 County Complex Rd Bedford (47421) *(G-544)*

Gary Electric Motor Service Co 219 884-6555
393 E Us Highway 30 Valparaiso (46383) *(G-13546)*

Gary Machinery LLC 219 980-5700
1931 E Main St Griffith (46319) *(G-5773)*

Gary Metal Mfg LLC 219 885-3232
2700 E 5th Ave Gary (46402) *(G-5050)*

Gary Muslim Center 219 885-3018
1473 W 15th Ave Gary (46407) *(G-5051)*

Gary Printing Inc 219 886-1767
1950 W 11th Ave Gary (46404) *(G-5052)*

Gary Ratcliff 765 538-3170
9950 Us Highway 231 S Lafayette (47909) *(G-8905)*

Gary Sign Co, Merrillville *Also called Pioneer Signs Inc (G-9746)*

Gary Vehicle Maintenance-Fuel 219 881-0219
1000 Madison St Gary (46402) *(G-5053)*

Gary W Martin 812 926-0935
9588 Old State Road 350 Aurora (47001) *(G-377)*

Gary's Welding and Machining, Bedford *Also called Gary Earl (G-544)*

Garyrae Inc 574 255-7141
800 Cleveland St Mishawaka (46544) *(G-10045)*

Gas City B & K Inc 765 674-9651
928 E Main St Gas City (46933) *(G-5125)*

Gasco LLC 317 565-5000
15305 Stony Creek Way Noblesville (46060) *(G-11109)*

Gaska Tape Inc 574 294-5431
1810 W Lusher Ave Elkhart (46517) *(G-2875)*

Gast Sign Co 219 759-4336
499 W Us Highway 30 Valparaiso (46385) *(G-13547)*

Gateway Galvinizing Inc 812 284-5241
1117 Brown Forman Rd Jeffersonville (47130) *(G-8367)*

Gator Buckets, Ladoga *Also called New Market Plastics Inc (G-8841)*

Gator Cases Inc 260 627-8070
2499 S 600 E Columbia City (46725) *(G-1787)*

Gaunt Family LLC 812 473-3167
7001 Red Wing Dr Evansville (47715) *(G-3516)*

Gbi Air Systems Inc 574 272-0600
50867 Post Rd Granger (46530) *(G-5408)*

GC Fuller Mfg Co Inc 812 539-2831
1 Shurlite Dr Lawrenceburg (47025) *(G-9144)*

Gc Solutions Inc 317 334-1149
3702 W 86th St Ste B Indianapolis (46268) *(G-6987)*

Gd Cox Inc 317 398-0035
105 S Harrison St Shelbyville (46176) *(G-12536)*

Gdc Inc (PA) 574 533-3128
815 Logan St Goshen (46528) *(G-5222)*

Gdp Industries LLC 260 414-4003
7431 Regina Dr Fort Wayne (46815) *(G-4293)*

GE Lexington Lamp Plant 859 277-1161
433 Council Dr Fort Wayne (46825) *(G-4294)*

GE Power Electronics Inc 317 259-9264
3148 E 48th St Indianapolis (46205) *(G-6988)*

Gea Inc 812 944-1401
615 State St New Albany (47150) *(G-10786)*

Gear Up Awards, Terre Haute *Also called Larry H Poole (G-13272)*

Geberit Manufacturing Inc 219 879-4466
1100 Boone Dr Michigan City (46360) *(G-9797)*

Gebhart's Woodworking & Lumber, Cayuga *Also called John Gebhart Woodworkings (G-1521)*

Geckos 765 762-0822
111 S Perry St Attica (47918) *(G-301)*

Gehl Industries Inc 574 773-7663
9547 W 1050 N Nappanee (46550) *(G-10672)*

Geiger & Peters Inc 317 322-7740
761 S Sherman Dr Indianapolis (46203) *(G-6989)*

Geist Bike and Hobby Company 317 855-1346
8150 Oaklandon Rd Ste 103 Indianapolis (46236) *(G-6990)*

Gem Industries Inc 574 773-4513
1400 Northwood Dr Nappanee (46550) *(G-10673)*

Gem-Rose Corp 317 773-6400
597 Christian Ave Noblesville (46060) *(G-11110)*

Gemeinhardt Company, LLC, Elkhart *Also called Gemeinhardt Musical Instr LLC (G-2876)*

Gemeinhardt Musical Instr LLC 574 295-5280
3302 S Nappanee St Elkhart (46517) *(G-2876)*

Gemini Oil LLC 260 571-8388
1323 W 600 S Warren (46792) *(G-13830)*

Gemstone, Elkhart *Also called Newlett Inc (G-3061)*

Gen Enterprises 574 498-6777
3500 18b Rd Tippecanoe (46570) *(G-13381)*

Genchem International LLC 317 574-4970
484 E Carmel Dr Ste 142 Carmel (46032) *(G-1384)*

Gener8 LLC 317 253-8737
1901 W 16th St Indianapolis (46202) *(G-6991)*

General Alum & Chemical, Indianapolis *Also called Gac Chemical Corporation (G-6978)*

General Aluminum Mfg Company 260 356-3900
1345 Henry St Huntington (46750) *(G-6206)*
General Aluminum Mfg Company 260 495-2600
303 E Swager St Fremont (46737) *(G-4960)*
General Automation Company 317 849-7483
9325 Uptown Dr Ste 700 Indianapolis (46256) *(G-6992)*
General Cable Industries Inc 317 271-8447
7950 Rockville Rd Indianapolis (46214) *(G-6993)*
General Cable Industries Inc 765 664-2321
440 E 8th St Marion (46953) *(G-9524)*
General Cable Industries Inc 317 271-8447
7920 Rockville Rd Indianapolis (46214) *(G-6994)*
General Cage LLC 765 552-5039
1106 Meridian St Ste 325 Anderson (46016) *(G-108)*
General Crafts Corp 574 533-1936
602 E Madison St Goshen (46526) *(G-5223)*
General Devices Co Inc 317 897-7000
1410 S Post Rd Ste 100 Indianapolis (46239) *(G-6995)*
General Dynamics Corporation 260 637-4773
1124 Falcon Creek Pkwy Fort Wayne (46845) *(G-4295)*
General Dynamics Mission 260 434-9500
1700 Magnavox Way Ste 200 Fort Wayne (46804) *(G-4296)*
General Electric Betz, East Chicago *Also called Suez Wts Usa Inc* *(G-2569)*
General Electric Company 260 439-2000
433 Council Dr Fort Wayne (46825) *(G-4297)*
General Electric Company 812 933-0700
1736 Lammers Pike Batesville (47006) *(G-501)*
General Fabr 260 593-3858
7360 S State Road 5 Topeka (46571) *(G-13420)*
General Fabrication, Topeka *Also called General Fabr (G-13420)*
General Fabricators Inc 317 787-9354
5230 S Harding St Indianapolis (46217) *(G-6996)*
General Furniture & Bedg Pdts 317 849-2670
7249 Fulham Dr Indianapolis (46250) *(G-6997)*
General Machine & Saw Co Ind, South Bend *Also called General Mch & Saw Co of Ind (G-12787)*
General Machine Brokers Inc 260 691-3800
1295 E 600 N Columbia City (46725) *(G-1788)*
General Manufacturing Inc 260 824-3627
1336 W Wiley Ave Bluffton (46714) *(G-875)*
General Material Handling Co 317 888-5735
1302 Kings Cove Ct Indianapolis (46260) *(G-6998)*
General Mch & Saw Co of Ind 574 232-6077
3636 Gagnon St South Bend (46628) *(G-12787)*
General Mills Inc 317 509-3709
12222 Bedrock Ct Fishers (46037) *(G-3916)*
General Motors LLC 419 576-9472
3112 E Kensington Park Dr Bloomington (47401) *(G-730)*
General Motors LLC 260 672-1224
12200 Lafayette Center Rd Roanoke (46783) *(G-12102)*
General Motors LLC 765 668-2000
2400 W 2nd St Marion (46952) *(G-9525)*
General Motors LLC 812 379-7360
105 Gm Dr Bedford (47421) *(G-545)*
General Mrgans Scrnprint Shppe, Corydon *Also called Blue River Services Inc (G-2090)*
General Products Angola Corp 260 665-8441
1411 Wohlert St Angola (46703) *(G-216)*
General Products Corporation 260 668-1440
1411 Wohlert St Angola (46703) *(G-217)*
General Rbr Plas of Evansville (PA) 812 464-5153
1902 N Kentucky Ave Evansville (47711) *(G-3517)*
General Sheet Metal Works Inc (PA) 574 288-0611
25101 Cleveland Rd South Bend (46628) *(G-12788)*
General Signals Inc 812 474-4256
5611 E Morgan Ave Evansville (47715) *(G-3518)*
General Stamping & Metalworks, South Bend *Also called General Sheet Metal Works Inc (G-12788)*
General Steel 317 251-9583
5335 N Tacoma Ave Ste 16 Indianapolis (46220) *(G-6999)*
General Transmission Pdts LLC 574 284-2917
105 N Niles Ave South Bend (46617) *(G-12789)*
Generation Four Machine & 219 297-3003
319 N Newton St Goodland (47948) *(G-5159)*
Generations Collision Services, Franklin *Also called Grahams Wrecker Service Inc (G-4892)*
Genesco Inc 812 234-9722
3401 S Us Highway 41 A13b Terre Haute (47802) *(G-13239)*
Genesis Molding Inc 574 256-9271
55901 Currant Rd Mishawaka (46545) *(G-10046)*
Genesis Plastics and Engrg LLC 812 752-6742
640 N Wilson Rd Scottsburg (47170) *(G-12357)*
Genesis Plastics Solutions LLC 812 283-4435
2200 Centennial Blvd Jeffersonville (47130) *(G-8368)*
Genesis Plastics Welding Inc 317 485-7887
720 E Broadway St Fortville (46040) *(G-4776)*
Genesis Products Inc 574 262-4054
2924 County Road 6 E Elkhart (46514) *(G-2877)*
Genesis Products Inc 574 266-8293
3130 Tuscany Dr Elkhart (46514) *(G-2878)*

Genesis Products LLC (PA) 877 266-8292
2608 Almac Ct Elkhart (46514) *(G-2879)*
Genesis Products, Plant 2, Elkhart *Also called Genesis Products Inc (G-2878)*
Genesys Telecom Labs Inc 317 715-8545
5501 W 79th St Indianapolis (46268) *(G-7000)*
Genesys Telecom Labs Inc 317 872-3000
7601 Interactive Way Indianapolis (46278) *(G-7001)*
Geneva Manufacturing Inc 260 368-7555
110 5th St Geneva (46740) *(G-5136)*
Genoa Healthcare LLC 219 427-1837
1100 W 6th Ave Gary (46402) *(G-5054)*
Genova Products Inc 219 866-5136
1100 E Elm St Rensselaer (47978) *(G-11925)*
Genpak LLC 812 752-3111
845 S Elm St Scottsburg (47170) *(G-12358)*
Gensic Creative Metals, Fort Wayne *Also called Coffee Lomont & Moyer Inc (G-4166)*
Gentec Inc 260 436-7333
3632 Illinois Rd Fort Wayne (46804) *(G-4298)*
Genteq, Fort Wayne *Also called Regal-Beloit Corporation (G-4587)*
Genteq, Fort Wayne *Also called Regal Beloit America Inc (G-4586)*
Gentrys Cabinet Inc 765 643-6611
415 Main St Anderson (46016) *(G-109)*
Genuine Machine Design Inc 219 866-8060
509 E Drexel Pkwy Rensselaer (47978) *(G-11926)*
Geny Industries LLC 574 536-0297
621 E Plymouth St Bremen (46506) *(G-999)*
Geo Pfaus Sons Company Inc 800 732-8645
800 Wall St Jeffersonville (47130) *(G-8369)*
Geo Specialty Chemicals Inc (PA) 765 448-9412
401 S Earl Ave Ste 3 Lafayette (47904) *(G-8906)*
Geo-Flo Products Corporation 812 275-8513
905 Williams Park Dr Bedford (47421) *(G-546)*
Georg Utz Inc 812 526-2240
14000 N 250 W Edinburgh (46124) *(G-2612)*
George Koch Sons LLC (HQ) 812 465-9600
10 S 11th Ave Evansville (47712) *(G-3519)*
George Koch Sons MGT Inc 812 422-3257
10 S 11th Ave Evansville (47712) *(G-3520)*
George Marshall 317 839-6563
648 S East St Plainfield (46168) *(G-11612)*
George P Stewart Printing Co 317 924-5143
2901 N Tacoma Ave Indianapolis (46218) *(G-7002)*
George Voyles Logging, Salem *Also called George Voyles Sawmill Inc (G-12287)*
George Voyles Sawmill Inc 812 472-3968
4887 W Apple Ln Salem (47167) *(G-12287)*
Georges Custom Wood Working 812 944-3344
1603 Beechwood Ave New Albany (47150) *(G-10787)*
Georgetown Donuts 260 493-6719
6328 E State Blvd Fort Wayne (46815) *(G-4299)*
Georgetown Truss Company Inc 812 951-2647
9627 State Road 64 Georgetown (47122) *(G-5145)*
Georgia Sstnment Solutions Inc 575 621-2372
1024 Gallium Dr Cicero (46034) *(G-1661)*
Georgia-Pacific, Richmond *Also called Color-Box LLC (G-11972)*
Georgia-Pacific LLC 219 776-0069
604 Na Sandifer Rd Wheatfield (46392) *(G-14222)*
Georgia-Pacific LLC 219 956-3100
484 E 1400 N Wheatfield (46392) *(G-14223)*
Ger, Valparaiso *Also called Global Energy Resources LLC (G-13548)*
Gerald S Zins 812 623-4980
12988 E State Road 48 Milan (47031) *(G-9944)*
Gerard 219 924-6388
9311 Southmoor Ave Highland (46322) *(G-6046)*
Gerardot Performance Products 260 623-3048
108 W Barnhart St Monroeville (46773) *(G-10195)*
Gerber Manufacturing, Granger *Also called Ashley Worldwide Inc (G-5390)*
Gerdau Ameristeel US Inc 765 286-5454
1810 S Macedonia Ave Muncie (47302) *(G-10476)*
Gerdau Macsteel Inc 260 356-9520
25 Commercial Rd Huntington (46750) *(G-6207)*
Gerdau Macsteel Atmosphere Ann 812 346-1275
1300 Industrial Dr North Vernon (47265) *(G-11259)*
Gerke Welding & Fabrication, Decatur *Also called Gerke Welding Inc (G-2380)*
Gerke Welding Inc 260 724-7701
10815 N 000 Rd Decatur (46733) *(G-2380)*
Gesco Group LLC (PA) 260 747-5088
4422 Earth Dr Fort Wayne (46809) *(G-4300)*
Gessner Woodworking 812 389-2594
106 N 1000 E Celestine (47521) *(G-1535)*
Get Noticed Portable Signs 765 649-6645
1842 Lowell Ave Anderson (46011) *(G-110)*
Get Printing Inc 574 533-6827
432 Blackport Dr Goshen (46528) *(G-5224)*
Get Published Inc 812 334-5279
1663 S Liberty Dr Ste 200 Bloomington (47403) *(G-731)*
Getsaydo LLC 317 800-8319
5255 Winthrop Ave Indianapolis (46220) *(G-7003)*
Gettelfinger Holdings LLC 812 923-9065
5773 Scottsville Rd Floyds Knobs (47119) *(G-4012)*

(G-0000) Company's Geographic Section entry number

GH Products Inc 619 208-4823
   3917 Sunnycroft Pl West Lafayette (47906) *(G-14068)*

Ghk Truss LLC 812 282-6600
   521 N Clark Blvd Clarksville (47129) *(G-1681)*

Ghost Forge L T D (PA) 765 362-8654
   1009 S Elm St Crawfordsville (47933) *(G-2154)*

Ghost Frge Rubenesque Fashions, Crawfordsville *Also called Ghost Forge L T D (G-2154)*

Ghost Trail Winery LLC 317 387-0052
   5528 W 62nd St Indianapolis (46268) *(G-7004)*

GI Properties Inc (PA) 219 763-1177
   6610 Melton Rd Portage (46368) *(G-11765)*

GI Tape & Label 574 269-2836
   701 N Union St Warsaw (46580) *(G-13881)*

Gibbs Susie Framing & Art 765 428-2434
   514 Main St Lafayette (47901) *(G-8907)*

Gibson Brothers Welding Inc 765 948-5775
   1520 W 900 S Fairmount (46928) *(G-3832)*

Gibson County Coal LLC 812 385-1816
   2579 W Gibson Coal Rd Princeton (47670) *(G-11873)*

Gibson County Sand & Grav Inc 812 851-5800
   2997 W State Road 68 Haubstadt (47639) *(G-6001)*

Gifts That Last, Madison *Also called Alan W Long (G-9442)*

Gigglicious LLC 317 272-4064
   1782 Rudgate Dr Avon (46123) *(G-441)*

Giggling Wenches Handcrafts 765 482-9776
   2123 Hannah Ct Lebanon (46052) *(G-9183)*

Gilberts Machine, Uniondale *Also called Tgm Manufacturing Inc (G-13466)*

Giles Agency Incorporated 317 842-5546
   7002 Graham Rd Ste 219 Indianapolis (46220) *(G-7005)*

Giles Chemical Corporation 812 537-4852
   200 Brown St Greendale (47025) *(G-5486)*

Giles Manufacturing, Greendale *Also called Giles Chemical Corporation (G-5486)*

Giles Manufacturing Company 812 537-4852
   200 Brown St Greendale (47025) *(G-5487)*

Gill Carbide Saw & TI Svc LLC 317 698-6787
   8471 Waverly Rd Martinsville (46151) *(G-9609)*

Gillespie Mrrell Gen Contg LLC 765 618-4084
   1240 S Adams St Marion (46953) *(G-9526)*

Gillis Company 574 273-9086
   51093 Bittersweet Rd Granger (46530) *(G-5409)*

Gillum Machine & Tool Inc 765 893-4426
   3365 W State Road 28 West Lebanon (47991) *(G-14120)*

Gilpin Inc 260 724-9155
   1819 Patterson St Decatur (46733) *(G-2381)*

Gilpin Custom Woodworking 260 413-6618
   10611 Coopers Hawk Trce Roanoke (46783) *(G-12103)*

Gimme Charge LLC 317 759-4067
   2245 Kessler Blvd E Dr Indianapolis (46220) *(G-7006)*

Ginas Creative Jewelry Inc 317 272-0032
   8100 E Us Highway 36 # 7 Avon (46123) *(G-442)*

Ginas Essentials 812 406-3276
   7705 Carrol Rd Nabb (47147) *(G-10640)*

Gindor Inc 574 642-4004
   66101 Us Highway 33 Goshen (46526) *(G-5225)*

Ginger Oliviae Publishing LLC 765 762-3132
   303 S 2nd St Williamsport (47993) *(G-14290)*

Gingerbread House Publications 260 622-4868
   11216 N 500 E Ossian (46777) *(G-11399)*

Giraffe X Graphics Inc 317 546-4944
   5746 Wheeler Rd Indianapolis (46216) *(G-7007)*

Girtz Engineering, Monticello *Also called Girtz Industries Inc (G-10263)*

Girtz Industries Inc 844 464-4789
   5262 N East Shafer Dr Monticello (47960) *(G-10263)*

Giveaway, The, Scottsburg *Also called Green Banner Publications Inc (G-12359)*

Gjs Home and Office Furniture 765 472-2478
   21 E Main St Peru (46970) *(G-11528)*

GKN Aerospace Muncie Inc 765 747-7147
   3901 S Delaware Dr Muncie (47302) *(G-10477)*

GKN Sinter Metals LLC 812 883-3381
   198 S Imperial Dr Salem (47167) *(G-12288)*

Glacier Bottling Company LLC 574 293-0357
   23155 Old Us 20 Elkhart (46516) *(G-2880)*

Glander 317 889-1039
   1678 Ashwood Dr Greenwood (46143) *(G-5697)*

Glas-Col LLC 812 235-6167
   711 Hulman St Terre Haute (47802) *(G-13240)*

Glas-Col Div, Terre Haute *Also called Templeton Coal Company Inc (G-13350)*

Glasmont, Indianapolis *Also called Oldcastle Buildingenvelope Inc (G-7617)*

Glasrite Div, Indianapolis *Also called PSC Industries Inc (G-7785)*

Glass Surgeons 219 374-2500
   12604 Havenwood Pass Cedar Lake (46303) *(G-1528)*

Glaze Mfg Co 574 612-1401
   53612 Tara Ln Elkhart (46514) *(G-2881)*

Glaze Tool and Engineering Inc 260 493-4557
   1610 Summit St New Haven (46774) *(G-10941)*

Glcc Laurel LLC 765 497-6100
   1 Geddes Way West Lafayette (47906) *(G-14069)*

Gldn Rule Truss & Metal Sales 812 866-1800
   4886 S 850 W Lexington (47138) *(G-9250)*

Gleason Corporation 574 533-1141
   612 E Reynolds St Goshen (46526) *(G-5226)*

Gleason Industrial Pdts Inc 574 533-1141
   612 E Reynolds St Goshen (46526) *(G-5227)*

Glenwood M Brown Co LLC 260 710-4428
   209 County Road 56 Laotto (46763) *(G-9108)*

Glidden Professional Paint Ctr, Lafayette *Also called PPG Architectural Finishes Inc (G-8981)*

Glidden Professional Paint Ctr, Indianapolis *Also called PPG Architectural Finishes Inc (G-7713)*

Glidden Racing Engines 317 535-5225
   5026 N Graham Rd Whiteland (46184) *(G-14238)*

Glidepath Com LLC 317 288-4459
   12175 Visionary Way Fishers (46038) *(G-3917)*

Glio Software Inc 314 856-5855
   14262 Overbrook Dr Carmel (46074) *(G-1385)*

Global 317 494-6174
   600 Ironwood Dr Ste N Franklin (46131) *(G-4889)*

Global Air Inc (PA) 317 634-5300
   913 Bates St Indianapolis (46202) *(G-7008)*

Global Air Inc 317 251-1251
   6450 Rucker Rd Indianapolis (46220) *(G-7009)*

Global Air Inc 317 251-1251
   6450 Rucker Rd Indianapolis (46220) *(G-7010)*

Global Building Products LLC 574 296-6868
   1121 Herman St Elkhart (46516) *(G-2882)*

Global Composites Inc 574 522-9956
   58190 County Road 3 Elkhart (46517) *(G-2883)*

Global Composites Inc 574 522-0475
   56807 Elk Park Dr Elkhart (46516) *(G-2884)*

Global Cutting Solutions 812 683-5808
   613 E 7th St Huntingburg (47542) *(G-6167)*

Global Energy Resources LLC 219 712-2556
   5206 Garden Gtwy Valparaiso (46383) *(G-13548)*

Global Forming LLC 317 290-1000
   913 Bates St Indianapolis (46202) *(G-7011)*

Global Glass Inc 574 294-7681
   28967 Old Us 33 Elkhart (46516) *(G-2885)*

Global Isotopes LLC (PA) 317 578-1251
   14395 Bergen Blvd Noblesville (46060) *(G-11111)*

Global Mold Solutions Inc 574 259-6262
   1702 E 7th St Mishawaka (46544) *(G-10047)*

Global Moulding, Elkhart *Also called Global Composites Inc (G-2883)*

Global Odor Ctrl Tech Mid Amer, Dillsboro *Also called Craig Hydraulic Enterprises (G-2464)*

Global Ozone Innovations LLC 574 294-5797
   425 Pine Creek Ct Elkhart (46516) *(G-2886)*

Global Packaging LLC 317 896-2089
   16707 Southpark Dr Westfield (46074) *(G-14165)*

Global Plastics Inc 317 299-2345
   6739 Guion Rd Indianapolis (46268) *(G-7012)*

Global Precision Parts, Wabash *Also called Ds Products Inc (G-13725)*

Global Sonics LLC 765 522-5548
   5 Big Walnut Acres Roachdale (46172) *(G-12093)*

Global Stone Portage LLC 219 787-9190
   6600 Us Highway 12 Portage (46368) *(G-11766)*

Global Trnsp Organization LLC 574 226-6372
   3402 Reedy Dr Elkhart (46514) *(G-2887)*

Global USA Inc 317 219-5647
   23044 State Road 37 N Noblesville (46060) *(G-11112)*

Global Water Technologies Inc 317 452-4488
   351 W 10th St Ste 537 Indianapolis (46202) *(G-7013)*

Globaltech Manufacturing L 317 571-1910
   14465 Welford Way Carmel (46032) *(G-1386)*

Globalvue International LLC 866 974-1968
   6402 Corporate Dr Indianapolis (46278) *(G-7014)*

Globe Asphalt Paving Co Inc 317 568-4344
   6445 E 30th St Indianapolis (46219) *(G-7015)*

Globe Mechanical Inc 812 949-2001
   20 W 7th St New Albany (47150) *(G-10788)*

Gloria J Burnworth 765 366-3950
   2875 N 70 W Attica (47918) *(G-302)*

Glove Corporation 501 362-2437
   301 N Harrison St Ste X Alexandria (46001) *(G-43)*

Glowire, Laotto *Also called Beal Systems Inc (G-9104)*

GLS Machining & Design LLC 765 754-8248
   12516 N 300 W Alexandria (46001) *(G-44)*

Glue + Paper Workshop LLC 773 275-8935
   410 E St Clair Ave Beverly Shores (46301) *(G-630)*

Glueboss Adhesive Company LLC 855 458-2677
   435 Harrison St Elkhart (46516) *(G-2888)*

Glynn Johnson, Indianapolis *Also called Von Duprin LLC (G-8168)*

GM Components Holdings LLC 765 451-8440
   2100 E Lincoln Rd Kokomo (46902) *(G-8628)*

GM Components Holdings LLC 765 451-9049
   2033 E Blvd Plant 9 9 Plant Kokomo (46904) *(G-8629)*

GM Components Holdings LLC 765 451-5011
   2150 E Lincoln Rd Kokomo (46902) *(G-8630)*

GMI, Eaton *Also called Graphic Menus Inc (G-2584)*

GMI Corporation 317 736-5116
  700 International Dr Franklin (46131) *(G-4890)*

Gmp Holdings LLC 317 353-6580
  2525 N Shadeland Ave Indianapolis (46219) *(G-7016)*

Gnome Industries Inc 219 764-3337
  808 N 360 W Rear Valparaiso (46385) *(G-13549)*

Go Electric Inc 765 400-1347
  1920 Purdue Pkwy Ste 400 Anderson (46016) *(G-111)*

Go Print LLC 765 778-1111
  1260 W 700 S Pendleton (46064) *(G-11490)*

Goad Crankshaft Service Inc 812 477-1127
  3514 E Morgan Ave Evansville (47715) *(G-3521)*

Goat Industries LLC 770 940-0433
  17 S Pennsylvania St Indianapolis (46204) *(G-7017)*

Goatee Shirt Printing 219 916-2443
  1039 N 200 W Valparaiso (46385) *(G-13550)*

Godfrey Marine, Elkhart *Also called Highwater Marine LLC (G-2916)*

Goetz Printing 812 243-2086
  415 Barton Ave Terre Haute (47803) *(G-13241)*

Goetz Printing & Copy Center, Terre Haute *Also called Goetz Printing (G-13241)*

Goh A&C Inc 812 738-2217
  1100 Quarry Rd Nw Corydon (47112) *(G-2099)*

Goh Con Inc (PA) 812 282-1349
  1630 Broadway St Clarksville (47129) *(G-1682)*

Gohmann Asphalt & Construction, Clarksville *Also called Goh Con Inc (G-1682)*

Gohn Bros Manufacturing Co 574 825-2400
  105 S Main St Middlebury (46540) *(G-9889)*

Gold Medal Awards, Bunker Hill *Also called Timothy White (G-1207)*

Gold N Gems 317 895-6002
  10202 E Washington St # 1325 Indianapolis (46229) *(G-7018)*

Gold Standard Truss LLC 219 987-7781
  817 15th St Se Demotte (46310) *(G-2438)*

Goldden Corporation (PA) 765 423-4366
  3601 Sagamore Pkwy N E Lafayette (47904) *(G-8908)*

Golden Age Aeroplane Work LLC 812 358-5778
  2375 E State Road 250 Brownstown (47220) *(G-1188)*

Golden Beam Metals LLC 317 806-2750
  6805 Hillsdale Ct Indianapolis (46250) *(G-7019)*

Golden Frame Inc 812 232-0048
  509 E Voorhees St Terre Haute (47802) *(G-13242)*

Golden Lion Inc 765 446-9557
  3416 State Road 38 E Lafayette (47905) *(G-8909)*

Golden Lion Jewelers, Lafayette *Also called Golden Lion Inc (G-8909)*

Golden Pride Hair Company LLC 812 777-9604
  1226 N Illinois St S205 Indianapolis (46202) *(G-7020)*

Golden Threads 765 557-7801
  516 N Anderson St Ste C Elwood (46036) *(G-3299)*

Golden Trngle Lbrcant Svcs LLC 317 875-9465
  5009 W 81st St Indianapolis (46268) *(G-7021)*

Golden Valley Microwave Foods, Rensselaer *Also called Conagra Brands Inc (G-11918)*

Golden-Helvey Holdings Inc 574 266-4500
  1020 County Road 6 W Elkhart (46514) *(G-2889)*

Golden-Helvey Holdings Inc 574 266-4500
  1020 County Road 6 W Elkhart (46514) *(G-2890)*

Goldleaf Promotional Products 317 202-2754
  6630 Ferguson St Indianapolis (46220) *(G-7022)*

Goldman Machine Services 812 359-5440
  5233 W County Road 600 N Richland (47634) *(G-11950)*

Goldshield Fiber Glass Inc 260 728-2476
  2004 Patterson St Decatur (46733) *(G-2382)*

Goldstone Jewelry Inc 765 742-1975
  3617 Montclair St West Lafayette (47906) *(G-14070)*

Goliath Casket Inc 765 874-2380
  8261 S 350 E Lynn (47355) *(G-9427)*

Gonzalez International Inc 317 558-3700
  3629 Oak Hollow Ct Carmel (46033) *(G-1387)*

Gonzalez Pallets 317 644-1242
  105 S Denny St Indianapolis (46201) *(G-7023)*

Good Earth Compost LLC 812 824-7928
  650 E Empire Mill Rd Bloomington (47401) *(G-732)*

Good Impressions Printing, Zionsville *Also called Zogman Enterprises Inc (G-14475)*

Good Impressions Printing Inc 317 873-6809
  170 W Hawthorne St Zionsville (46077) *(G-14434)*

Good Signs 317 738-4663
  368 S Main St Ste 1 Franklin (46131) *(G-4891)*

Goodlife Industries Inc 317 339-6341
  3925 E 26th St Indianapolis (46218) *(G-7024)*

Goodman & Wolfe, Terre Haute *Also called Mervis Industries Inc (G-13284)*

Goodprint LLC 201 926-0133
  611 N Park Ave Apt 106 Indianapolis (46204) *(G-7025)*

Goodrich Corporation 812 704-5200
  510 Patrol Rd Jeffersonville (47130) *(G-8370)*

Goods Candies 765 785-6776
  State Rd 234 Kennard (47351) *(G-8516)*

Goods On Target Sporting Inc 812 623-2300
  8663 E Hoff Rd Sunman (47041) *(G-13111)*

Goodtime Manufacturing LLC 317 876-3661
  5136 W 81st St Indianapolis (46268) *(G-7026)*

Goodtime Technology Dev, Indianapolis *Also called Goodtime Manufacturing LLC (G-7026)*

Goodwill Inds of Centl Ind 317 587-0281
  1122 Keystone Way Carmel (46032) *(G-1388)*

Goodwill Industries 317 546-7251
  9704 Beaumont Rd Indianapolis (46216) *(G-7027)*

Goodwill Industries 317 524-4293
  1635 W Michigan St Indianapolis (46222) *(G-7028)*

Goodyear Tire & Rubber Company 219 762-0651
  6791 Melton Rd Portage (46368) *(G-11767)*

Goon Jonn 574 306-2927
  107 E Market St Warsaw (46580) *(G-13882)*

Goose Bumps LLC 765 491-2142
  187 Turnberry Ct West Lafayette (47906) *(G-14071)*

Goose Graphics L L C 260 563-4516
  4943 Coventry Pkwy Fort Wayne (46804) *(G-4301)*

Gordon B Crawford DMD 812 288-8560
  1804 E Park Pl Jeffersonville (47130) *(G-8371)*

Gordon Lumber Company 219 924-0500
  806 W Avenue H Griffith (46319) *(G-5774)*

Gorilla Plastic Rbr Group LLC 317 635-9616
  3401 Newton Ave Indianapolis (46201) *(G-7029)*

Goshen Case Company, Elkhart *Also called MTS Products Corp (G-3055)*

Goshen Coach Inc 574 970-6300
  1826 Leer Dr Elkhart (46514) *(G-2891)*

Gospel Echoes Team Association (PA) 574 533-0221
  1809 E Monroe St Ste C Goshen (46528) *(G-5228)*

Gosport Manufacturing Co Inc 812 879-4224
  11 Lousisa St Gosport (47433) *(G-5350)*

Gotokiosk LLC 800 206-0177
  109 E Andrews St Monroe (46772) *(G-10182)*

Gottman Electric Co Inc 812 838-0037
  3350 Old Highway 62 Mount Vernon (47620) *(G-10393)*

Goudy Brothers Boiler Co Inc 765 459-4416
  100 W Spraker St Kokomo (46901) *(G-8631)*

Gould Solenoid Valve Co 317 547-5289
  4707 Massachusetts Ave Indianapolis (46218) *(G-7030)*

Goulding & Wood Inc 317 637-5222
  823 Massachusetts Ave Indianapolis (46204) *(G-7031)*

Gourmet Express 219 921-9927
  1256 Morthland Dr Valparaiso (46385) *(G-13551)*

Goyal Products, Fort Wayne *Also called Alliance Winding Equipment (G-4061)*

Gr Huber Enterprises Inc 574 293-7113
  21291 Buckingham Rd Elkhart (46516) *(G-2892)*

Graber 812 636-7699
  6608 E 1000 N Odon (47562) *(G-11326)*

Graber Box & Pallet Fmly Lmt P 260 657-5657
  16301 Trammel Rd Grabill (46741) *(G-5365)*

Graber Cabinetry LLC 260 627-2243
  15210 Grabill Rd Grabill (46741) *(G-5366)*

Graber Furniture 812 295-4939
  6377 N 1200 E Loogootee (47553) *(G-9383)*

Graber Lumber LP 260 238-4124
  17528 Cuba Rd Spencerville (46788) *(G-13047)*

Graber Manufacturing 812 636-7725
  Ct Rd 1050 N Odon (47562) *(G-11327)*

Graber Manufacturing & Repair, Odon *Also called Graber Manufacturing (G-11327)*

Graber Manufacturing LLC 260 657-3400
  12836 Cuba Rd Grabill (46741) *(G-5367)*

Graber Ronald D Yoder & 574 268-9512
  1515 Fox Farm Rd Warsaw (46580) *(G-13883)*

Graber Steel & Fab LLC 812 636-8418
  8528 N 900 E Odon (47562) *(G-11328)*

Graber Therm-O-Loc Windows 812 486-3273
  9058 E 500 N Montgomery (47558) *(G-10225)*

Graber Woodworks Inc 812 486-2861
  5155 N 900 E Montgomery (47558) *(G-10226)*

Grabers Kountry Korner 812 636-4399
  8902 N 900 E Odon (47562) *(G-11329)*

Grabers Portable Band Mill 812 636-4158
  10722 N 1000 E Odon (47562) *(G-11330)*

Grabill Cabinet Company Inc 877 472-2782
  13844 Sawmill Dr Grabill (46741) *(G-5368)*

Grabill Country Meat 1 Inc 260 627-3691
  13211 West St Grabill (46741) *(G-5369)*

Grabill Home Food Service, Grabill *Also called Grabill Country Meat 1 Inc (G-5369)*

Grabill Truss Incorporated 260 627-0933
  14005 David Ln Grabill (46741) *(G-5370)*

Grabill Truss Manufacturing, Grabill *Also called Grabill Truss Incorporated (G-5370)*

Grabill Woodworking Specialty 260 627-5982
  13830 Grabill Rd Grabill (46741) *(G-5371)*

Grable Burial Vault Services 574 753-4514
  322 Highland St Logansport (46947) *(G-9335)*

Grace Amazing Graphics 812 737-2841
  250 W Highway 11 Se Laconia (47135) *(G-8836)*

Grace Digital Printing 317 903-6172
  7304 Atmore Dr Indianapolis (46217) *(G-7032)*

Grace Island Spcalty Foods Inc 260 357-3336
  5840 County Road 11 Garrett (46738) *(G-5006)*

Grace Manufacturing Inc 574 267-8000
  1500 W Center St Warsaw (46580) *(G-13884)*

(G-0000) Company's Geographic Section entry number

Grace W R & Co-Co 317 876-4100
  7950 Allison Ave Indianapolis (46268) **(G-7033)**

Gracies Paw Prints 317 910-9969
  10053 Parkshore Dr Fishers (46038) **(G-3918)**

Graessle-Mercer Co 812 522-5478
  100 N Pine St Seymour (47274) **(G-12451)**

Grafco Industries Ltd Partnr (HQ) 812 424-2904
  101 Oakley St Evansville (47710) **(G-3522)**

Grafcor Inc 765 966-7030
  601 Nw 5th St Richmond (47374) **(G-11990)**

Grafton Peek Incorporated 317 557-8377
  280 W Main St Greenwood (46142) **(G-5698)**

Graham Cheese Corporation 812 692-5237
  Hwy 57 N Elnora (47529) **(G-3289)**

Graham Packaging Company LP 812 868-8012
  5504 Foundation Dr Evansville (47725) **(G-3523)**

Grahams Wrecker Service Inc 317 736-4355
  159 W Monroe St Franklin (46131) **(G-4892)**

Grain Millers, Marion Also called Agricor Inc **(G-9507)**

Grain Processing Corporation 812 257-0480
  1443 S 300 W Washington (47501) **(G-13983)**

Grand Design Rv LLC 574 825-8000
  11333 County Road 2 Middlebury (46540) **(G-9890)**

Grand Junction Brewery 317 804-9583
  1189 E 181st St Westfield (46074) **(G-14166)**

Grand Master LLC 574 288-8273
  1619 Miami St South Bend (46613) **(G-12790)**

Grand Products Inc 317 870-3122
  1650 S Girls School Rd Indianapolis (46231) **(G-7034)**

Grandma Hams Farm LLC 317 253-0635
  5436 N Delaware St Indianapolis (46220) **(G-7035)**

Grandview Aluminum Products 812 649-2569
  110 W 4th St Grandview (47615) **(G-5387)**

Granger Gazette 574 277-2679
  50841 Stonebridge Dr Granger (46530) **(G-5410)**

Granite and Marble, Westfield Also called Absolute Stone Polsg Repr LLC **(G-14132)**

Granite Engineering & Tool Co (PA) 812 375-9077
  51 S Us Highway 31 Columbus (47201) **(G-1933)**

Granite Innovations Inc 219 690-1081
  18178 Clay St Hebron (46341) **(G-6013)**

Granite Marble & More Inc 765 939-4846
  425 Nw K St Richmond (47374) **(G-11991)**

Granite Tee Signs LLC 317 670-4967
  7884 S Andee Ln Fort Branch (47648) **(G-4027)**

Granitech 574 674-6988
  3954 Lexington Park Dr Elkhart (46514) **(G-2893)**

Grant County Ready Mix, Marion Also called Speedway Redi Mix Inc **(G-9563)**

Grant County Steel Inc 765 668-7547
  2201 S Branson St Marion (46953) **(G-9527)**

Graphex International 219 696-4849
  792 W 181st Ave Lowell (46356) **(G-9406)**

Graphic 22, Chesterton Also called Graphic22 Inc **(G-1608)**

Graphic Arts & Publ Svcs 574 294-1770
  2121 Roys Ave Elkhart (46517) **(G-2894)**

Graphic Enterprises, Brookville Also called Huelseman Printing Co **(G-1117)**

Graphic Expressions 219 663-2085
  6707 Broadway Merrillville (46410) **(G-9717)**

Graphic Expressions Inc 317 577-9622
  13025 New Britton Dr Fishers (46038) **(G-3919)**

Graphic Fx Inc 812 234-0000
  1130 Walnut St Terre Haute (47807) **(G-13243)**

Graphic Menus Inc 765 396-3003
  16555 N State Road 3n Eaton (47338) **(G-2584)**

Graphic Packaging Intl 765 289-7391
  301 S Butterfield Rd Muncie (47303) **(G-10478)**

Graphic Packaging Intl Inc 812 949-4393
  2549 Charlestown Rd Ste 1 New Albany (47150) **(G-10789)**

Graphic Packaging Intl Inc 812 948-1608
  1502 Beeler St New Albany (47150) **(G-10790)**

Graphic Packaging Intl LLC 260 347-7612
  301 S Progress Dr E Kendallville (46755) **(G-8476)**

Graphic Packaging Intl LLC 219 762-4855
  5900 Carlson Ave Portage (46368) **(G-11768)**

Graphic Printing Co Inc 765 768-6022
  209 S Main St Dunkirk (47336) **(G-2484)**

Graphic Printing Co Inc (PA) 260 726-8141
  309 W Main St Portland (47371) **(G-11825)**

Graphic Ventures Inc 812 288-6093
  648 N Clark Blvd Clarksville (47129) **(G-1683)**

Graphic Visions 812 331-7446
  1314 W Kirkwood Ave Bloomington (47404) **(G-733)**

Graphic Vsons Screen Prtg Sgns, Bloomington Also called Graphic Visions **(G-733)**

Graphic22 Inc 219 921-5409
  1505 S Calumet Rd Ste 2 Chesterton (46304) **(G-1608)**

Graphically Speaking 219 921-1572
  349 Sand Creek Dr Chesterton (46304) **(G-1609)**

Graphicorp 317 867-3099
  8587 Zionsville Rd 206 Indianapolis (46268) **(G-7036)**

Graphics 55, Alexandria Also called Robert Burkhart **(G-52)**

Graphics Lab Uv Printing Inc 765 457-5784
  1041 S Union St Kokomo (46902) **(G-8632)**

Graphics Output, Fort Wayne Also called Two B Enterprises Inc **(G-4711)**

Graphics Systems Inc 260 485-9667
  8421 Mayhew Rd Fort Wayne (46835) **(G-4302)**

Graphics Unlimited 765 288-6816
  500 S Celia Ave B Muncie (47303) **(G-10479)**

Graphie-Tees, South Bend Also called Mito-Craft Inc **(G-12864)**

Graphik Mechanix Inc 260 426-7001
  1116 N Wells St Fort Wayne (46808) **(G-4303)**

Graphix Unlimited Inc 574 546-3770
  3947 State Road 106 Bremen (46506) **(G-1000)**

Grassco Inc 260 749-5437
  6430 E State Blvd Fort Wayne (46815) **(G-4304)**

Grateful Heart Enterprises LLC 765 838-2266
  5082 Glacier Way Lafayette (47909) **(G-8910)**

Grateful Heart Gallery & Gifts, Lafayette Also called Grateful Heart Enterprises LLC **(G-8910)**

Gravel Conveyors Inc (PA) 317 873-8686
  5005 W 106th St Zionsville (46077) **(G-14435)**

Gravel Doctor Indianapolis LLC 317 399-4585
  7611 Dornock Dr Indianapolis (46237) **(G-7037)**

Gravelton Machine Shop Inc 574 773-3413
  23965 Us Highway 6 Nappanee (46550) **(G-10674)**

Gravis Ebikes Inc 317 690-0616
  7220 N Audubon Rd Indianapolis (46250) **(G-7038)**

Graybull Organic Wines Inc 317 797-2186
  7365 Lakeside Dr Indianapolis (46278) **(G-7039)**

Graycraft Signs Plus, Warsaw Also called Sjg Enterprises Inc **(G-13940)**

Graycraft Signs Plus Inc 574 269-3780
  3304 Lake City Hwy Warsaw (46580) **(G-13885)**

Graycraft Signs Plus Inc (PA) 260 432-3760
  2428 Getz Rd Fort Wayne (46804) **(G-4305)**

Grayson Graphics 574 264-6466
  3008 Mobile Dr Elkhart (46514) **(G-2895)**

Grayson Thermal Systems Corp 317 739-3290
  980 Hurricane Rd Franklin (46131) **(G-4893)**

Graysville Mfg Inc 812 382-4616
  4391 N County Road 875 W Sullivan (47882) **(G-13083)**

Grc Enterprises Inc 219 932-2220
  3477 Watling St East Chicago (46312) **(G-2530)**

Great American Desk Co Inc 574 293-3591
  1600 W Mishawaka Rd Elkhart (46517) **(G-2896)**

Great American Puzzle Factory, Indianapolis Also called Fundex Games Ltd **(G-6969)**

Great Dane LLC 812 443-4711
  2664 E Us Highway 40 Brazil (47834) **(G-962)**

Great Dane Trailers, Brazil Also called Great Dane LLC **(G-962)**

Great Deals Magazine 765 649-3302
  1232 Broadway St Ste 300 Anderson (46012) **(G-112)**

Great Lakes Forest Pdts Inc 574 389-9663
  21658 Buckingham Rd Elkhart (46516) **(G-2897)**

Great Lakes Forest Pdts Inc (PA) 574 389-9663
  21861 Protecta Dr Elkhart (46516) **(G-2898)**

Great Lakes Waterjet Inc 574 651-2158
  53100 Corydon Ct Granger (46530) **(G-5411)**

Great Panes Glass Co 260 426-0203
  1307 N Wells St Fort Wayne (46808) **(G-4306)**

Great States Corporation 317 392-3615
  7444 Shadeland Stn Way Indianapolis (46256) **(G-7040)**

Greatbatch Ltd 260 755-7300
  4545 Kroemer Rd Fort Wayne (46818) **(G-4307)**

Greatbatch Ltd 260 755-7484
  265 E Bell Dr Ste A Warsaw (46582) **(G-13886)**

Greatbatch Medical, Fort Wayne Also called Greatbatch Ltd **(G-4307)**

Greatbatch Medical, Fort Wayne Also called Integer Holdings Corporation **(G-4377)**

Greatbatch Medical, Warsaw Also called Greatbatch Ltd **(G-13886)**

Greatbatch Medical, Indianapolis Also called Integer Holdings Corporation **(G-7246)**

Greazy Pickle LLC 260 726-9200
  211 W Main St Portland (47371) **(G-11826)**

Grede LLC 765 521-8000
  2700 Plum St New Castle (47362) **(G-10903)**

Green Air LLC 317 335-1706
  13967 Hawkstone Dr Fishers (46040) **(G-3987)**

Green Apple Active LLC 910 585-1151
  17304 Tilbury Way Westfield (46074) **(G-14167)**

Green Apple Active LLC 317 698-1032
  10529 Titan Run Carmel (46032) **(G-1389)**

Green Apple Utilities Llc 440 278-0183
  1475 W Oak St Unit 5063 Zionsville (46077) **(G-14436)**

Green Banner Publications Inc (PA) 812 967-3176
  490 E State Road 60 Pekin (47165) **(G-11473)**

Green Banner Publications Inc 812 752-3171
  730 N Gardner St Scottsburg (47170) **(G-12359)**

Green Banner Publications Inc 812 752-3171
  183 E Mcclain Ave Scottsburg (47170) **(G-12360)**

Green Banner Publications Inc 812 883-5555
  105 E Walnut St Salem (47167) **(G-12289)**

Green Cow Power LLC 219 984-5915
  24130 County Road 40 Goshen (46526) **(G-5229)**

Green Cubes Technology Corp (PA) 502 416-1060
   4124 Cartwright Dr Kokomo (46902) *(G-8633)*

Green Dog 260 483-1267
   3421 N Anthony Blvd Fort Wayne (46805) *(G-4308)*

Green Fast Cure LLC 812 486-2510
   5461 E 300 N Montgomery (47558) *(G-10227)*

Green Forest Sawmill LLC 812 745-3335
   407 W Main St Oaktown (47561) *(G-11318)*

Green Illuminating Systems Inc 317 869-7430
   10330 Pleasant St Ste 600 Noblesville (46060) *(G-11113)*

Green Lake Tube LLC (PA) 219 397-0495
   4500 Euclid Ave East Chicago (46312) *(G-2531)*

Green Leaf Inc 812 877-1546
   9490 N Baldwin St Fontanet (47851) *(G-4024)*

Green Mountain Industries LLC 812 585-1531
   603 W State Road 46 Centerpoint (47840) *(G-1538)*

Green Pipe & Supply Inc 219 762-1077
   46 Sunset Trl Portage (46368) *(G-11769)*

Green Plains Bluffton LLC 260 846-0011
   1441 S Adams St Bluffton (46714) *(G-876)*

Green Plains Inc 812 985-7480
   8999 W Franklin Rd Mount Vernon (47620) *(G-10394)*

Green Plus Plastics LLC 317 672-2410
   3131 N Franklin Rd Ste L Indianapolis (46226) *(G-7041)*

Green Plus Plastics LLC 931 510-0525
   3131 N Franklin Rd Ste L Indianapolis (46226) *(G-7042)*

Green Sign Co Inc 812 663-2550
   1045 E Freeland Rd Greensburg (47240) *(G-5603)*

Green Steak Pulling Inc 812 254-6858
   1312 E 200 N Washington (47501) *(G-13984)*

Green Stream Company 574 293-1949
   29414 Phillips St Elkhart (46514) *(G-2899)*

Green Tek LLC 317 294-1614
   4925 Jennings Dr Carmel (46033) *(G-1390)*

Green Thumb of Indiana Inc 260 897-2319
   9999 E Baseline Rd Avilla (46710) *(G-405)*

Green Tree Plastics LLC 812 402-4127
   1107 E Virginia St Evansville (47711) *(G-3524)*

Green Way Candle Company LLC 574 536-3802
   63 Greenway Dr Goshen (46526) *(G-5230)*

Greencastle Offset Inc 765 653-4026
   20 S Jackson St Greencastle (46135) *(G-5458)*

Greencastle Offset Printing, Greencastle *Also called Greencastle Offset Inc (G-5458)*

Greencycle Inc 317 773-3350
   2695 Cicero Rd Noblesville (46060) *(G-11114)*

Greencycle of Indiana Inc 317 780-8175
   1103 W Troy Ave Indianapolis (46225) *(G-7043)*

Greencycle of Indiana Inc 317 769-5668
   4227 S Perry Worth Rd Whitestown (46075) *(G-14253)*

Greene County Pallet Inc 812 384-8362
   1338 N Harv-Wright Rd Bloomfield (47424) *(G-638)*

Greenfield Coffee Company 317 498-9568
   303 E Lincoln St Greenfield (46140) *(G-5533)*

Greenfield Feeders Inc 317 462-6363
   3599 W Us Highway 40 Greenfield (46140) *(G-5534)*

Greenfield Signs Inc 317 469-3095
   716 W Main St Greenfield (46140) *(G-5535)*

GREENLIGHT COLLECTIBLES, Indianapolis *Also called Greenlight LLC (G-7044)*

Greenlight LLC 317 287-0600
   5855 W 74th St Indianapolis (46278) *(G-7044)*

Greenline Screen Printing 317 572-1155
   6830 Hawthorn Park Dr Indianapolis (46220) *(G-7045)*

Greensburg Daily News, Greensburg *Also called Community Holdings Indiana Inc (G-5594)*

Greensburg Printing Co Inc 812 663-8265
   116 N Franklin St Greensburg (47240) *(G-5604)*

Greensgroomer Worldwide Inc (PA) 317 388-0695
   10992 E Us Highway 136 A Indianapolis (46234) *(G-7046)*

Greensignco.com, Greensburg *Also called Green Sign Co Inc (G-5603)*

Greenville Technology Inc 765 221-7576
   3511 W 73rd St Anderson (46011) *(G-113)*

Greenwald Surgical Co Inc 219 962-1604
   2688 Dekalb St Lake Station (46405) *(G-9075)*

Greenwell Software LLC 812 295-4665
   9750 N 1300 E Loogootee (47553) *(G-9384)*

Greenwood Draperie Corp 317 882-0130
   965 Apple Valley Rd Greenwood (46142) *(G-5699)*

Greenwood Draperies, Greenwood *Also called Greenwood Draperie Corp (G-5699)*

Greenwood Light & Sign Service 317 840-5729
   7955 W 400 N Boggstown (46110) *(G-900)*

Greenwood Models Inc 317 859-2988
   350 Commerce Parkway W Dr Greenwood (46143) *(G-5700)*

Greenwood Tool & Die Co Inc 219 924-9663
   231 S Lindberg St Griffith (46319) *(G-5775)*

Grefco Minerals Inc 765 362-6000
   2510 N Concord Rd Crawfordsville (47933) *(G-2155)*

Greg Miner 765 647-1012
   10068 Oxford Pike Brookville (47012) *(G-1115)*

Greg Moser Engineering Inc 260 726-6689
   102 Performance Dr Portland (47371) *(G-11827)*

Gregory & Appel 317 823-0131
   11738 Capistrano Dr Indianapolis (46236) *(G-7047)*

Gregory Thomas Inc (PA) 219 324-3801
   1823 N Circle View Ln La Porte (46350) *(G-8758)*

Gregs Tool & Machine 812 373-9329
   1537 Hutchins Ave Ste D Columbus (47201) *(G-1934)*

Greif Inc 219 746-3753
   17405 Holtz Rd Lowell (46356) *(G-9407)*

Greys Automotive Inc 317 632-3562
   1604 W Minnesota St Indianapolis (46221) *(G-7048)*

Grid Element Sled 219 462-2687
   460 Bond Ave Ste D Valparaiso (46385) *(G-13552)*

Grid Elements 219 615-9683
   20 Tower Rd Valparaiso (46385) *(G-13553)*

Griffen Plmbng-Heating-Cooling 574 295-2440
   2310 Toledo Rd Elkhart (46516) *(G-2900)*

Griffen Plumbing & Heating, Elkhart *Also called Griffen Plmbng-Heating-Cooling (G-2900)*

Griffin Analytical Tech LLC 765 775-1701
   3000 Kent Ave Ste E1 West Lafayette (47906) *(G-14072)*

Griffin Industries LLC 812 659-3399
   7358 S Griffin Rd Newberry (47449) *(G-11015)*

Griffin Industries LLC 812 379-9528
   345 Water St Columbus (47201) *(G-1935)*

Griffin Logging, Cayuga *Also called Daniel Griffin (G-1518)*

Griffin Logging LLC 765 592-5701
   4967 W Craig St Mecca (47860) *(G-9678)*

Griffin Trailers, Elkhart *Also called Chubbs Steel Sales Inc (G-2757)*

Griffith Machine & Fabricating 219 980-8855
   3750 W 47th Ave Gary (46408) *(G-5055)*

Griffith Rbr Mills of Garrett (HQ) 260 357-3125
   400 N Taylor Rd Garrett (46738) *(G-5007)*

Griffith Rbr Mills of Garrett 260 357-0876
   507 N Lee St Garrett (46738) *(G-5008)*

Grimm Mold & Die Co Inc 219 778-4211
   200 S Depot St Rolling Prairie (46371) *(G-12186)*

Grind City Customs 317 981-5462
   7145 E 46th St Indianapolis (46226) *(G-7049)*

Grindco Inc 219 763-6130
   288 W 1050 N Chesterton (46304) *(G-1610)*

Grinding and Polsg McHy Corp 317 898-0750
   2801 Tobey Dr Indianapolis (46219) *(G-7050)*

Grinding Experts 219 838-7773
   2736 Condit St Ste C Highland (46322) *(G-6047)*

Griner Engineering 765 296-2955
   515 W Jackson St Mulberry (46058) *(G-10417)*

Griner Engineering Inc 812 332-2220
   2500 N Curry Pike Bloomington (47404) *(G-734)*

Grinon Industries LLC 317 388-5100
   7649 Winton Dr Indianapolis (46268) *(G-7051)*

Grip-Tite, Granger *Also called BT&f LLC (G-5395)*

Gro-Tec Inc 765 853-1246
   10324 W Us Highway 36 Modoc (47358) *(G-10173)*

Groh Inc 260 463-2410
   406 W North St Lagrange (46761) *(G-9043)*

Groovemade LLC 574 834-1138
   713 S Main St North Webster (46555) *(G-11292)*

Gross & Sons Lumber and Veneer 574 457-5214
   8516 E 1250 N Syracuse (46567) *(G-13132)*

Gross Roofing Sheet Metals 765 965-0068
   1751 Sheridan St Richmond (47374) *(G-11992)*

Grote Industries Inc (PA) 812 273-2121
   2600 Lanier Dr Madison (47250) *(G-9463)*

Grote Industries LLC 812 265-8273
   2600 Lanier Dr Madison (47250) *(G-9464)*

Grotrian Tool & Die 260 894-3558
   300 Sroufe St Ligonier (46767) *(G-9286)*

Group Dekko Inc 260 635-2134
   1075 S Washington St Wolflake (46796) *(G-14379)*

Group Dekko Inc 260 599-3405
   6928 N 400 E Dock101 Kendallville (46755) *(G-8477)*

Group Dekko Inc (HQ) 260 357-3621
   2505 Dekko Dr Garrett (46738) *(G-5009)*

Group Dekko Inc 260 637-3964
   11913 E 450 S Laotto (46763) *(G-9109)*

Group Dekko Inc 260 357-5988
   1605 Dekko Dr Garrett (46738) *(G-5010)*

Group Dekko Holdings Inc (HQ) 260 347-0700
   2505 Dekko Dr Garrett (46738) *(G-5011)*

Grove Forest Products 812 432-3312
   16423 N State Route 156 Rising Sun (47040) *(G-12088)*

Growing Child 765 464-0920
   2336 Northwestern Ave West Lafayette (47906) *(G-14073)*

Growing Smiles Inc 317 787-6404
   7210 Madison Ave Ste O Indianapolis (46227) *(G-7052)*

Growlers 219 924-0245
   2816 Highway Ave Highland (46322) *(G-6048)*

Growth Principals LLC 812 320-1574
   1155 E Benson Ct Bloomington (47401) *(G-735)*

Grrk Holdings Inc 317 872-0172
   7430 New Augusta Rd Indianapolis (46268) *(G-7053)*

(G-0000) Company's Geographic Section entry number

Grrreat Creations..574 773-5331
597 Shawnee St Nappanee (46550) *(G-10675)*

Grunau Company Inc...317 872-7360
4341 W 96th St Indianapolis (46268) *(G-7054)*

Grundfos Pumps Mfg Corp..................................317 925-9661
2005 Dr Martin L King Jr Indianapolis (46202) *(G-7055)*

Gryphon Print Studio...574 514-1644
3702 W Sample St South Bend (46619) *(G-12791)*

Gs Sales Inc..317 595-6750
2802 Pyrenean Pl Westfield (46074) *(G-14168)*

Gsi Group Inc..317 787-3047
5900 Elmwood Ave Indianapolis (46203) *(G-7056)*

Gsp-2700 LLC...219 885-3232
2700 E 5th Ave Gary (46402) *(G-5056)*

Gt Computers LLC..502 550-7490
1006 State St New Albany (47150) *(G-10791)*

Gt Stamping Inc...574 533-4108
1025 S 10th St Goshen (46526) *(G-5231)*

Gta Containers Inc..574 288-3459
4201 Linden Ave South Bend (46619) *(G-12792)*

Gta Containers Inc (PA).....................................574 288-3459
4201 Linden Ave South Bend (46619) *(G-12793)*

Gta Enterprises Inc...260 478-7800
4422 Airport Expy Ste 220 Fort Wayne (46809) *(G-4309)*

Gti Static Solutions, La Porte *Also called Gregory Thomas Inc* *(G-8758)*

GTW Enterprises Inc..219 362-2278
183 W 800 N La Porte (46350) *(G-8759)*

Guardian Couplings LLC......................................219 874-5248
300 Indiana 212 Michigan City (46360) *(G-9798)*

Guardian Fire Systems Inc..................................317 752-2768
435 W Garden St Fortville (46040) *(G-4777)*

Guardian Ind Inc..219 874-5248
300 Indiana Highway 212 Michigan City (46360) *(G-9799)*

Guardian Industries, Michigan City *Also called Guardian Ind Inc* *(G-9799)*

Guardian Industries LLC.....................................812 422-6987
5401 Highway 41 N Evansville (47711) *(G-3525)*

Guardian Mold Prevent Corp................................708 878-5788
906 Jackson Pl Dyer (46311) *(G-2499)*

Guardian Tech Group Ind LLC...............................765 364-0863
1100 E Elmore St Crawfordsville (47933) *(G-2156)*

Guereca Woodworking..260 724-3994
310 Eastbrook Dr Decatur (46733) *(G-2383)*

Guidant Intercontinental Corp...............................317 218-7012
11711 N Meridian St # 850 Carmel (46032) *(G-1391)*

Guide Book Publishing..317 259-0599
5929 Haverford Ave Indianapolis (46220) *(G-7057)*

Guide Engineering LLC..260 483-1153
1515 Dividend Rd Fort Wayne (46808) *(G-4310)*

Guide Technologies LLC (PA)................................317 844-3162
250 E 96th St Ste 525 Indianapolis (46240) *(G-7058)*

Gul For Media Development...................................317 726-9544
15505 Wandering Way Noblesville (46060) *(G-11115)*

Gulf Stream Coach Inc..574 773-7761
2404 E Market St Nappanee (46550) *(G-10676)*

Gulf Stream Coach Inc (PA)..................................574 773-7761
503 S Oakland Ave Nappanee (46550) *(G-10677)*

Gulf Stream Coach Plant 59, Nappanee *Also called Gulf Stream Coach Inc* *(G-10676)*

Gulsad Inc...317 541-1940
4084 Pendleton Way Indianapolis (46226) *(G-7059)*

Gund Company Inc..219 374-9944
10501 W 133rd Ave Cedar Lake (46303) *(G-1529)*

Gustafson, Elkhart *Also called Patrick Industries Inc* *(G-3085)*

Gutierrez Mexican Bakery & Mkt............................574 534-9979
122 S Main St Goshen (46526) *(G-5232)*

Gutman, Anthony & Mary, Versailles *Also called T & M Precision Inc* *(G-13659)*

Gutter One Supply...317 872-1257
8026 Woodland Dr Indianapolis (46278) *(G-7060)*

Guy Cardboard...812 989-4809
2860 N Highway 11 Se Elizabeth (47117) *(G-2644)*

Guys Wood N Things...812 689-0433
340 N County Road 300 W Holton (47023) *(G-6107)*

Gvm Inc..765 689-5010
8497 S Us Highway 31 Bunker Hill (46914) *(G-1206)*

Gvs Filter Technology Inc....................................317 442-3925
4522 Winterspring Cres Zionsville (46077) *(G-14437)*

Gvs Technologies LLC..574 293-0974
5308 Beck Dr Elkhart (46516) *(G-2901)*

Gwaltney Drilling Inc..812 254-5085
101 Se 3rd St Washington (47501) *(G-13985)*

Gwin Enterprises..317 881-6401
7294 S Delaware St Indianapolis (46227) *(G-7061)*

Gypsum Express Ltd...812 247-2648
9720 Us Highway 50 Shoals (47581) *(G-12666)*

Gypsum Express Ltd...219 987-2181
1214 Forsythia St Se Demotte (46310) *(G-2439)*

Gypsy Moon Ragdolls Inc.....................................260 589-2852
423 Wabash St Berne (46711) *(G-615)*

Gyrewide Publications & Bad.................................765 721-7676
1925 Windemere Dr Greencastle (46135) *(G-5459)*

H & A Products Inc..574 226-0079
28761 Holiday Pl Elkhart (46517) *(G-2902)*

H & B Pork Inc...219 261-3053
6032 N 1200 E Wolcott (47995) *(G-14364)*

H & E Machined Specialties..................................260 424-2527
1321 E Wallace St Fort Wayne (46803) *(G-4311)*

H & H Commercial Heat Treating............................765 288-3618
2200 E 8th St Muncie (47302) *(G-10480)*

H & H Design & Tool Inc......................................765 886-6199
222 2nd St Economy (47339) *(G-2591)*

H & H Home Improvement Inc................................812 288-8700
1120 N Taggart Ave Clarksville (47129) *(G-1684)*

H & H Manufacturing Inc......................................812 664-3582
499 N 150 W Patoka (47666) *(G-11466)*

H & H Metal Products Inc.....................................812 256-0444
104 Industrial Way Charlestown (47111) *(G-1567)*

H & H Partnership Inc...765 513-4739
174 E North St Kokomo (46901) *(G-8634)*

H & H Sales Company Inc.....................................260 637-3177
16339 Lima Rd Huntertown (46748) *(G-6139)*

H & H Sheet Metal Inc..317 787-0883
875 Bethel Ave Beech Grove (46107) *(G-595)*

H & M Bay Inc...410 463-5430
3410 Meyer Rd Fort Wayne (46803) *(G-4312)*

H & M Pallet, Milroy *Also called Milroy Pallet Inc* *(G-9984)*

H & M Tool & Die Inc...812 663-8252
242 W Mckee St Greensburg (47240) *(G-5605)*

H & N Machine Division of, Waterloo *Also called Charleston Metal Products Inc* *(G-14011)*

H & P Tool Co Inc...765 962-4504
610 S G St Richmond (47374) *(G-11993)*

H & R Industrial LLC..765 868-8408
816 Millbrook Ln Kokomo (46901) *(G-8635)*

H & S Custom Countertops Inc..............................812 422-6314
5705 E Morgan Ave Evansville (47715) *(G-3526)*

H & W Molders Inc..812 423-9340
1031 W Tennessee St Evansville (47710) *(G-3527)*

H 20 Factory, Newburgh *Also called H20 Factory* *(G-11030)*

H A Industries..219 931-6304
4527 Columbia Ave Hammond (46327) *(G-5883)*

H A King Co Inc...260 482-6376
3210 Clairmont Ct Fort Wayne (46808) *(G-4313)*

H A P Industries Inc..765 948-3385
7220 S 200 W Jonesboro (46938) *(G-8445)*

H and H 3d Plastics Inc.......................................812 699-0379
12759 W 300 N Linton (47441) *(G-9307)*

H C J B World Radio, Elkhart *Also called World Rdo Mssnary Fllwship Inc* *(G-3268)*

H C Schumacher Machine Co Inc............................317 787-9361
3619 S Arlington Ave Indianapolis (46203) *(G-7062)*

H D I, Logansport *Also called Hopper Development Inc* *(G-9336)*

H D Williams Co...812 372-6476
1637 Franklin St Columbus (47201) *(G-1936)*

H E D, Indianapolis *Also called Heat Exchanger Design Inc* *(G-7086)*

H John Enterprise Inc...574 293-6008
21066 Protecta Dr Elkhart (46516) *(G-2903)*

H L Signworks...812 325-5750
616 Robin Dr Ellettsville (47429) *(G-3279)*

H M C, Princeton *Also called Highway Machine Co Inc* *(G-11875)*

H M C Screen Printing Inc....................................317 773-8532
954 Conner St Noblesville (46060) *(G-11116)*

H P Oil, Jeffersonville *Also called Hoosier Penn Oil Co Inc* *(G-8376)*

H P Products, Hartford City *Also called Harold Precision Products Inc* *(G-5981)*

H P Products Corporation.....................................812 331-8793
502 W 4th St Bloomington (47404) *(G-736)*

H P Schmitt Packing Co Inc..................................260 724-3146
976 Waynesboro Rd Decatur (46733) *(G-2384)*

H Proto Development Inc......................................574 267-6372
332 N 300 E Warsaw (46582) *(G-13887)*

H T D, Columbus *Also called Hoosier Tool & Die Co Inc* *(G-1942)*

H W Hasty Welding Inc..765 482-8925
125 W 300 N Lebanon (46052) *(G-9184)*

H W Molders...812 423-3552
1500 W Missouri St Evansville (47710) *(G-3528)*

H&E Cutter Grinding Inc.......................................765 825-0541
6251 Industrial Ave N Connersville (47331) *(G-2049)*

H-C Liquidating Corp..574 535-9300
1002 Eisenhower Dr N Goshen (46526) *(G-5233)*

H20 Factory..812 858-1948
7899 Bell Oaks Dr Newburgh (47630) *(G-11030)*

H3 Sportgear LLC (HQ).......................................317 595-7500
11988 Fishers Crossing Dr # 161 Fishers (46038) *(G-3920)*

Haas Cabinet Co Inc (PA)....................................812 246-4431
625 W Utica St Sellersburg (47172) *(G-12395)*

Hach Company...574 262-2060
3504 Henke St Elkhart (46514) *(G-2904)*

Hachette Book Group Inc.....................................765 483-9900
121 N Enterprise Blvd Lebanon (46052) *(G-9185)*

Hackett Publishing Company (PA)...........................317 635-9250
3333 Massachusetts Ave Indianapolis (46218) *(G-7063)*

A
L
P
H
A
B
E
T
I
C

Hackett Publishing Company................................317 635-9250
　832 Pierson St Indianapolis (46204) *(G-7064)*

Hackman Borthers Show Feed, Brownstown *Also called Mark Hackman* *(G-1190)*

Hackman Cabinet Co....................................812 522-4118
　1156 Darcis Dr Seymour (47274) *(G-12452)*

Hackney Home Furnishings Inc.................317 895-4300
　9420 E 33rd St Indianapolis (46235) *(G-7065)*

Hadady Corporation.................................219 322-7417
　1832 Lake St Dyer (46311) *(G-2500)*

Hadley Products Corporation....................574 266-3700
　319 Roske Dr Elkhart (46516) *(G-2905)*

Hagemier Products.................................812 526-0377
　6181 S 550 E Franklin (46131) *(G-4894)*

Hager Inc (PA).......................................260 483-7075
　6844 N Clinton St Fort Wayne (46825) *(G-4314)*

Hager Industries Inc................................317 219-6622
　230 Riverwood Dr Noblesville (46062) *(G-11117)*

Hagerstown Gravel & Cnstr........................765 489-4812
　14064 Olive Branch Rd Hagerstown (47346) *(G-5806)*

Hagerstown Plastics Inc..........................765 939-3849
　621 S J St Richmond (47374) *(G-11994)*

Hahn Enterprises Inc...............................574 862-4491
　911 E Waterford St Wakarusa (46573) *(G-13778)*

Haines Engineering.................................260 589-3388
　6262 S 550 E Berne (46711) *(G-616)*

Hair Associates LLC (PA).........................317 844-7207
　1115 Woodgate Dr Carmel (46033) *(G-1392)*

Hair Huggers LLC...................................317 776-9977
　10561 Creektree Ln Fishers (46038) *(G-3921)*

Hair Necessities....................................812 288-5887
　1124 Eastern Blvd Clarksville (47129) *(G-1685)*

Haire Machine Corporation........................219 947-4545
　3019 E 84th Pl Merrillville (46410) *(G-9718)*

Halcomb Welding LLC..............................765 345-7156
　8017 S Mill Rd Spiceland (47385) *(G-13055)*

Hale Industries Inc.................................317 577-0337
　315 N Madison St Fortville (46040) *(G-4778)*

Hall Signs Inc......................................812 332-9355
　4495 W Vernal Pike Bloomington (47404) *(G-737)*

Hallett Enterprises Inc............................317 495-7800
　3916 E Traction Rd Crawfordsville (47933) *(G-2157)*

Hallett Gutter Cover, Crawfordsville *Also called Hallett Enterprises Inc (G-2157)*

Halo LLC (PA).......................................317 575-9992
　10585 N Meridian St Fl 3 Indianapolis (46290) *(G-6266)*

Halo Metalworks Inc................................317 481-0100
　4000 W 10th St Indianapolis (46222) *(G-7066)*

Halox Division, Hammond *Also called Hammond Group Inc (G-5885)*

Halsen Brothers Sheet Metal....................574 583-3358
　300 Tioga Rd Monticello (47960) *(G-10264)*

Halstab, Hammond *Also called Hammond Group Inc (G-5884)*

Ham Enterprise LLC................................317 831-2902
　160 E Morgan St Martinsville (46151) *(G-9610)*

Ham Enterprises Machine Co.....................765 342-7966
　4590 Jordan Rd Martinsville (46151) *(G-9611)*

Hamby...765 664-4045
　2104 S Valley Ave Marion (46953) *(G-9528)*

Hamilton Bros Inc...................................317 241-2571
　1840 Midwest Blvd Indianapolis (46214) *(G-7067)*

Hamilton Canvas Inc...............................219 763-1686
　2305 Hamstrom Rd Ste F Portage (46368) *(G-11770)*

Hamilton Exhibits LLC (PA).......................317 898-9300
　9150 E 33rd St Indianapolis (46235) *(G-7068)*

Hamilton Industrial Inc............................260 488-3662
　6610 S State Road 1 Hamilton (46742) *(G-5823)*

Hamilton Iron Works Inc...........................574 533-3784
　208 W Lincoln Ave Goshen (46526) *(G-5234)*

Hamilton News Inc..................................260 488-3780
　9115 Sunflower Cv Fort Wayne (46819) *(G-4315)*

Hammer Industries Inc.............................812 422-6953
　1504 N 1st Ave Evansville (47710) *(G-3529)*

Hammer Time Forge................................812 448-2171
　8969 N 200 W 8969 W N200 Brazil (47834) *(G-963)*

Hammond Drapery, Hammond *Also called Custom Draperies of Indiana (G-5867)*

Hammond Group Inc (PA).........................219 931-9360
　1414 Field St Bldg B Hammond (46320) *(G-5884)*

Hammond Group Inc................................219 933-1560
　6530 Schneider St Hammond (46320) *(G-5885)*

Hammond Group Inc................................219 845-0031
　2323 165th St Hammond (46320) *(G-5886)*

Hammond Lead Products, Hammond *Also called Hammond Group Inc (G-5886)*

Hammond Lead Products Llc.....................219 931-9360
　1414 Field St Bldg B Hammond (46320) *(G-5887)*

Hammond Steel Components LLC...............630 816-1343
　3200 Sheffield Ave Hammond (46327) *(G-5888)*

Hammond Works, Hammond *Also called Dover Chemical Corporation (G-5871)*

Hampels Woodland Products......................574 293-2124
　61292 County Road 7 Elkhart (46517) *(G-2906)*

Hampton Equipment LLC..........................260 740-8704
　7127 Hessen Cassel Rd Fort Wayne (46816) *(G-4316)*

Hampton Ironworks Inc............................219 929-6448
　542 Dunewood Dr Chesterton (46304) *(G-1611)*

Hamster Press Klingel-Engle Pu, Ellettsville *Also called Christopher Engle (G-3274)*

Hanco Inc..800 968-6655
　1374 Clay Spring Dr Carmel (46032) *(G-1393)*

Hancor Inc...812 443-2080
　2340 E Us Highway 40 Brazil (47834) *(G-964)*

Hand Industries Inc.................................574 267-3525
　315 S Hand Ave Warsaw (46580) *(G-13888)*

Handle Bar, The, Kokomo *Also called G & J (G-8626)*

Handle With Care Packaging.....................812 250-1920
　2007 N Green River Rd Evansville (47715) *(G-3530)*

Handle With Kare LLC..............................260 420-1698
　1723 Alabama Ave Fort Wayne (46805) *(G-4317)*

Handson (HQ).......................................812 246-4481
　4700 Utica Sellersburg Rd Sellersburg (47172) *(G-12396)*

Hanger Clinic, Evansville *Also called Hanger Prosthetics & (G-3531)*

Hanger Clinic, Fort Wayne *Also called Hanger Prsthetcs & Ortho Inc (G-4318)*

Hanger Orthopedics, Indianapolis *Also called Hanger Prsthetcs & Ortho Inc (G-6267)*

Hanger Orthotics, Indianapolis *Also called Hanger Prsthetcs & Ortho Inc (G-7069)*

Hanger Prosthetics &..............................812 479-1121
　7145 E Virginia St # 4000 Evansville (47715) *(G-3531)*

Hanger Prsthetcs & Ortho Inc....................317 818-1459
　10435 N Pennsylvna St Indianapolis (46280) *(G-6267)*

Hanger Prsthetcs & Ortho Inc....................219 844-2021
　7324 Indianapolis Blvd Hammond (46324) *(G-5889)*

Hanger Prsthetcs & Ortho Inc....................317 923-2351
　1330 N Illinois St Indianapolis (46202) *(G-7069)*

Hanger Prsthetcs & Ortho Inc....................765 966-5069
　1200 Chester Blvd Richmond (47374) *(G-11995)*

Hanger Prsthetcs & Ortho Inc....................260 456-5998
　4666 W Jefferson Blvd Fort Wayne (46804) *(G-4318)*

Hanger Prsthetcs & Ortho Inc....................812 235-6451
　4142 S 7th St Terre Haute (47802) *(G-13244)*

Hangout At Flames LLC...........................765 483-2009
　3776 N State Road 39 Lebanon (46052) *(G-9186)*

Hanks Neon & Plastic Service....................812 423-7447
　910 Keck Ave Evansville (47711) *(G-3532)*

Hanlon Solutions Resource Inc..................317 776-4880
　3501 Conner St Ste X Noblesville (46060) *(G-11118)*

Hanover Machine & Tool Inc......................812 265-6265
　3408 W State Road 56 Hanover (47243) *(G-5961)*

Hansa Medical Products Inc......................317 815-0708
　2000 W 106th St Carmel (46032) *(G-1394)*

Hansen Corporation.................................812 385-3000
　901 S 1st St Princeton (47670) *(G-11874)*

Hansford Co...317 255-4756
　7420 N Park Ave Indianapolis (46240) *(G-7070)*

Hansford Prevent LLC.............................317 985-2346
　5658 Buck Pond Ct Indianapolis (46237) *(G-7071)*

Hanson Aggregates, Charlestown *Also called Aggrock Quarries Inc (G-1557)*

Hanson Aggregates East LLC....................812 883-2191
　1510 W Market St Salem (47167) *(G-12290)*

Hanson Aggregates East LLC....................260 490-9006
　1820 W Washington Ctr Fort Wayne (46818) *(G-4319)*

Hanson Aggregates Midwest LLC...............812 246-1942
　5417 State Rd 403 Sellersburg (47172) *(G-12397)*

Hanson Aggregates Midwest LLC...............419 399-4846
　22821 Dawkins Rd Woodburn (46797) *(G-14383)*

Hanson Aggregates Midwest LLC...............812 689-5017
　606 W County Road 300 S Versailles (47042) *(G-13654)*

Hanson Aggregates Midwest LLC...............260 747-3105
　6100 Ardmore Ave Fort Wayne (46809) *(G-4320)*

Hanson Aggregates Midwest LLC...............812 889-2120
　313 S State Road 203 Lexington (47138) *(G-9251)*

Hanson Aggregates Midwest LLC...............812 346-6100
　610 S County Road 250 E North Vernon (47265) *(G-11260)*

Hanson Aggregates Midwest LLC...............765 653-7205
　State Rd 243 Cty Rd 900 S State Road Cloverdale (46120) *(G-1726)*

Hanson Aggrgates Southeast Inc................317 788-4086
　4200 S Harding St Indianapolis (46217) *(G-7072)*

Hanson Agrigoods Midwest Inc..................317 635-9048
　8950 S State Road 243 Cloverdale (46120) *(G-1727)*

Hanson Pipe Precast...............................219 873-9509
　302 Elmwood Dr Michigan City (46360) *(G-9800)*

Hanwha Machinery America Corp................574 546-2261
　431 N Birkey St Bremen (46506) *(G-1001)*

Hapco Rebuilders Inc..............................812 232-2550
　129 N 2nd St Terre Haute (47807) *(G-13245)*

Happy Apple Educational Svcs...................765 338-9293
　502 Hill St Connersville (47331) *(G-2050)*

Happy Headgear LLC...............................574 892-5792
　128 Westview Ct Argos (46501) *(G-274)*

Happy Valley Sand & Gravel Inc..................317 839-6800
　4232 E Us Highway 40 Plainfield (46168) *(G-11613)*

Harbisonwalker Intl Inc............................219 881-4440
　76 N Bridge St Gary (46404) *(G-5057)*

Harbisonwalker Intl Inc............................219 883-3335
　76 N Bridge St Gary (46404) *(G-5058)*

2018 Harris Indiana
Industrial Directory

(G-0000) Company's Geographic Section entry number

Harcourt Industries Inc 765 629-2625
7765 S 175 W Milroy (46156) **(G-9980)**

Harcourt Outlines, Milroy Also called Harcourt Industries Inc **(G-9980)**

Hard Chrome Co, Evansville Also called Industrial Research Inc **(G-3557)**

Hard Surface Fabrications Inc 574 259-4843
810 S Beiger St Mishawaka (46544) **(G-10048)**

Hardesty Printing Co Inc (PA) 574 223-4553
1218 N State Road 25 Rochester (46975) **(G-12126)**

Hardesty Printing Co Inc 574 267-7591
411 W Market St Warsaw (46580) **(G-13889)**

Hardigg Battery Products, Columbus Also called Hardigg Industries Inc **(G-1937)**

Hardigg Industries Inc 812 342-0139
2405 Norcross Dr Columbus (47201) **(G-1937)**

Harding Materials Inc 317 846-7401
5145 E 96th St Indianapolis (46240) **(G-7073)**

Hardingpoorman Inc 317 876-3355
4923 W 78th St Indianapolis (46268) **(G-7074)**

Hardingpoorman Group Inc 317 876-3355
4923 W 78th St Indianapolis (46268) **(G-7075)**

Hardins Speed Service Co 219 962-8080
3649 Illinois St Hobart (46342) **(G-6079)**

Hardware Retailing, Indianapolis Also called National Retail Hardware Assn **(G-7576)**

Hardwood Door Mfg LLC 812 486-3313
5084 N 575 E Montgomery (47558) **(G-10228)**

Hardwood Flooring, Vevay Also called Cross Country Hardwoods LLC **(G-13661)**

Hardwoods By Bill LLC 219 465-5346
2450 Honelee Ct Valparaiso (46385) **(G-13554)**

Hare Canvas Products 260 758-8800
300 N Tracy St Markle (46770) **(G-9577)**

Harford Industries Inc 219 929-6455
1635 Starwood Dr Chesterton (46304) **(G-1612)**

Haring Contractors Inc 812 744-6870
11231 State Road 350 Moores Hill (47032) **(G-10298)**

Harl Plastics, Elkhart Also called Hart Plastics Inc **(G-2909)**

Harlan Bakeries LLC (PA) 317 272-3600
7597 E Us Highway 36 Avon (46123) **(G-443)**

Harlan Bakeries-Avon LLC 317 272-3600
7597 E Us Highway 36 Avon (46123) **(G-444)**

Harlan Cabinets Inc 260 657-5154
12707 Spencerville Rd Harlan (46743) **(G-5972)**

Harlan Development Company 317 352-1583
404 S Kitley Ave Indianapolis (46219) **(G-7076)**

Harland Clarke, Jeffersonville Also called Clarke American Checks Inc **(G-8338)**

Harman Embedded Audio LLC 317 849-8175
6602 E 75th St Ste 520 Indianapolis (46250) **(G-7077)**

Harman Machine & Engineering 574 266-5015
53905 County Road 9 Ste C Elkhart (46514) **(G-2907)**

Harman Professional Inc 574 294-8000
1718 W Mishawaka Rd Elkhart (46517) **(G-2908)**

Harmon Boats Inc 765 963-5358
596 W Meridian St Sharpsville (46068) **(G-12506)**

Harmon Coatings LLC 317 326-4298
4528 N 25 W Greenfield (46140) **(G-5536)**

Harmon Hrmon Uysugi Optmtrists (PA) 812 723-4752
488 W Hospital Rd Ste 1 Paoli (47454) **(G-11452)**

Harmony Marketing Group, Bourbon Also called Harmony Press Inc **(G-943)**

Harmony Press Inc (PA) 800 525-3742
115 N Main St Bourbon (46504) **(G-943)**

Harmony Winery 317 585-9463
7350 Village Square Ln # 200 Fishers (46038) **(G-3922)**

Harold Precision Products Inc 765 348-2710
1600 Gilkey Ave Hartford City (47348) **(G-5981)**

Harper Direct LLC 214 245-5026
5100 Schenley Pl Greendale (47025) **(G-5488)**

Harpercollins Publishers LLC 219 324-4880
2205 E Lincolnway La Porte (46350) **(G-8760)**

Harpercollins Return Center, La Porte Also called Harpercollins Publishers LLC **(G-8760)**

Harpring Steel Inc 812 256-6326
109 Industrial Way Charlestown (47111) **(G-1568)**

Harps On Main, Rising Sun Also called Rees Harps Inc **(G-12091)**

Harrell Family LLC 317 770-4550
15525 Stony Creek Way Noblesville (46060) **(G-11119)**

Harringtons Noodles Inc 574 546-3861
1451 Dogwood Rd Bremen (46506) **(G-1002)**

Harris Bmo Bank National Assn 219 939-0164
6001 Melton Rd Gary (46403) **(G-5059)**

Harris Burial Services 812 939-3605
1440 W County Road 800 S Clay City (47841) **(G-1702)**

Harris City Stone Co, Laurel Also called New Point Stone Co Inc **(G-9128)**

Harris City Stone Company, Greensburg Also called New Point Stone Co Inc **(G-5627)**

Harris Corporation 260 451-6180
1919 W Cook Rd Fort Wayne (46818) **(G-4321)**

Harris Corporation 260 451-6000
7310 Innovation Blvd Fort Wayne (46818) **(G-4322)**

Harris Corporation 260 451-5597
1919 W Cook Rd Fort Wayne (46818) **(G-4323)**

Harris Corporation 812 202-5171
27548 N 1400 E Crane (47522) **(G-2126)**

Harris Corporation 812 202-5171
27548 N 1400 E Crane (47522) **(G-2127)**

Harris Kayot, Fort Wayne Also called Brunswick Corporation **(G-4125)**

Harris Oil Co, Evansville Also called Michael R Harris **(G-3625)**

Harris Pre Cast Inc (PA) 219 362-2457
1877 W Severs Rd La Porte (46350) **(G-8761)**

Harris Rebar Nufab LLC (PA) 260 925-5440
1342 S Grandstaff Dr Auburn (46706) **(G-334)**

Harris Stone Service Inc 765 522-6241
5588 N County Road 50 E Bainbridge (46105) **(G-477)**

Harris Sugar Bush LLC (PA) 765 653-5108
999 E County Road 325 N Greencastle (46135) **(G-5460)**

Harrison Cnty Democrate 812 734-0560
229 E Chestnut St Corydon (47112) **(G-2100)**

Harrison Concrete 812 275-6682
1218 7th St Bedford (47421) **(G-547)**

Harrison Electric Inc 219 879-0444
10855 W 400 N Michigan City (46360) **(G-9801)**

Harrison Hauling Inc 574 862-3196
64341 County Road 11 Goshen (46526) **(G-5235)**

Harrison Macdonald & Sons 765 742-9012
302 Ferry St Ste 300 Lafayette (47901) **(G-8911)**

Harrison Manufacturing Inc 812 466-1111
9973 E Us Highway 36 Avon (46123) **(G-445)**

Harrison Sand and Gravel Co (PA) 812 663-2021
992 S County Road 800 E Greensburg (47240) **(G-5606)**

Harrison Steel Castings Co (PA) 765 762-2481
900 S Mound St Attica (47918) **(G-303)**

Harry & Izzys Northside LLC 317 915-8045
4050 E 82nd St Indianapolis (46250) **(G-7078)**

Harry B Higley & Sons Inc 219 558-8183
9550 Calumet St Dyer (46311) **(G-2501)**

Harsco Corporation 219 397-0200
5222 Indianapolis Blvd East Chicago (46312) **(G-2532)**

Harsco Corporation 219 944-6250
7100 W 9th Ave Gary (46406) **(G-5060)**

Hart Plastics Inc 574 264-7060
2907 Park Six Ct Elkhart (46514) **(G-2909)**

Hart Publishers Inc 260 672-8978
2955 E 630 N Huntington (46750) **(G-6208)**

Hartford Bakery Inc 812 425-4642
500 N Fulton Ave Evansville (47710) **(G-3533)**

Hartford City Division, Hartford City Also called BRC Rubber & Plastics Inc **(G-5978)**

Hartford City News Times 765 348-0110
100 N Jefferson St Hartford City (47348) **(G-5982)**

Hartford Heat Treatment 812 725-8272
37 W 5th St New Albany (47150) **(G-10792)**

Hartford TEC Glass Co Inc (PA) 765 348-1282
735 E Water St Hartford City (47348) **(G-5983)**

Hartland Distillations Inc 812 464-4446
2410 Lynch Rd Evansville (47711) **(G-3534)**

Hartland Products Inc 219 778-9034
5022 E Oaknoll Rd Rolling Prairie (46371) **(G-12187)**

Hartland Winery LLC 260 587-3316
2409 County Road 4 Ashley (46705) **(G-286)**

Hartley Interiors, Arcadia Also called Sylvia Kay Hartley **(G-270)**

Hartley J Company Inc 812 376-9708
101 N National Rd Columbus (47201) **(G-1938)**

Hartman Brothers Heat & AC 260 493-4402
535 Green St New Haven (46774) **(G-10942)**

Hartman Logging 765 653-3889
1158 W Us Highway 40 Greencastle (46135) **(G-5461)**

Harts Handmade Naturals LLC 317 407-9988
1354 Westridge Ct Greenwood (46142) **(G-5701)**

Hartson-Kennedy Cabinet Top Co (PA) 765 668-8144
522 W 22nd St Marion (46953) **(G-9529)**

Hartwell's Premium Products, Greenwood Also called Grafton Peek Incorporated **(G-5698)**

Hartzells Homemade Ice Cream 812 332-3502
107 N Dunn St Bloomington (47408) **(G-738)**

Harvard Business Publishing 317 815-8232
1033 3rd Ave Sw Ste 202 Carmel (46032) **(G-1395)**

Harvard Sports Inc 812 467-4449
817 Maxwell Ave Evansville (47711) **(G-3535)**

Harvest Cafe Coffee & Tea LLC 317 585-9162
2225 E 54th St Ste A Indianapolis (46220) **(G-7079)**

Harvest Fuels LLC 832 895-6621
12716 Norfolk Ln Carmel (46032) **(G-1396)**

Harvest Land Co-Op Inc 765 489-4141
4379 Jacksonburg Rd Hagerstown (47346) **(G-5807)**

Harvest Land Co-Op Inc 317 861-5080
1124 W Railroad St Fountaintown (46130) **(G-4791)**

Harvest Moon Winery LLC 317 258-4615
9407 N Captain Cir McCordsville (46055) **(G-9668)**

Harvest Petroleum Inc 219 924-8236
9518 Primrose Ln Hammond (46321) **(G-5890)**

Harvey Adhesives Inc 877 547-5558
10328 E Lakeshore Dr Carmel (46033) **(G-1397)**

Harvey Hinklemeyers 765 452-1942
1554 S Dixon Rd Kokomo (46902) **(G-8636)**

Harvs Welding Inc 219 345-5959
8700 N 400 W Wheatfield (46392) *(G-14224)*

Hasser Enterprises Inc 765 583-1444
8023 Us Highway 52 W West Lafayette (47906) *(G-14074)*

Hatch Prints 312 952-1908
901 N Saint Peter St South Bend (46617) *(G-12794)*

Hatfield Publications LLC 317 581-9804
1401 Olde Briar Ln Carmel (46032) *(G-1398)*

Hausers Reclamation & REM 812 663-6378
811 W Sheridan St Burney (47240) *(G-1212)*

Hautau Tube Cutoff Systems LLC 765 647-1600
11199 State Road 101 Brookville (47012) *(G-1116)*

Haven Manufacturing Ind Inc 260 622-4150
6935 N State Road 1 Ossian (46777) *(G-11400)*

Haven Technologies Inc 317 490-7197
12202 Hancock St Carmel (46032) *(G-1399)*

Havoc Motor Company LLC 973 407-9933
207 Parkview Ave E Elkhart (46514) *(G-2910)*

Hawaiian Smoothie LLC 317 598-1730
12395 Eddington Pl Fishers (46037) *(G-3923)*

Hawaiian Smoothie LLC 317 881-7290
1251 Us Highway 31 N Greenwood (46142) *(G-5702)*

Hawk Enterprises Elkhart Inc (PA) 574 264-6772
2902 Park Six Ct Elkhart (46514) *(G-2911)*

Hawk Precision Components Inc 812 755-4501
596 W Oak St Campbellsburg (47108) *(G-1277)*

Hawkins Inc 765 288-8930
4601 S Delaware Dr Muncie (47302) *(G-10481)*

Hawkins Darryal 765 282-6021
1001 E 18th St Muncie (47302) *(G-10482)*

Hawkins Industrial Resource Co, Muncie Also called Hawkins Darryal *(G-10482)*

Hawkins Machine & Tool Inc 812 522-5529
2166 N County Road 900 E Seymour (47274) *(G-12453)*

Hawkins Print Shop, La Porte Also called Riden Inc *(G-8812)*

Hawthorne Products Inc 765 768-6585
16828 N State Road 167n Dunkirk (47336) *(G-2485)*

Hawthorne Publishing 317 867-5183
15601 Oak Rd Carmel (46033) *(G-1400)*

Hayabusa LLC 317 594-1188
5025 E 82nd St Indianapolis (46250) *(G-7080)*

Hayes Enterprises LLC 260 636-3262
2174 N River Rd W Albion (46701) *(G-28)*

Haylex Manufacturing LLC 765 288-1818
4401 S Delaware Dr Muncie (47302) *(G-10483)*

Haynes Honey LLC 260 563-6397
1269 E 500 S Wabash (46992) *(G-13728)*

Haynes International Inc 765 457-3790
2000 W Defenbaugh St Kokomo (46902) *(G-8637)*

Haynes International Inc 219 326-8530
3238 N Hwy 39 La Porte (46352) *(G-8762)*

Haynes International Inc (PA) 765 456-6000
1020 W Park Ave Kokomo (46901) *(G-8638)*

Hayward & Sams LLP 260 351-4166
4250 E 1175 S Stroh (46789) *(G-13077)*

Hayward Tyler Inc 812 867-2848
12540 Kenai Dr Evansville (47725) *(G-3536)*

Haywood Printing Co Inc 765 742-4085
300 N 5th St Lafayette (47901) *(G-8912)*

HB, Lafayette Also called Holder Bedding Inc *(G-8916)*

HB Connect Inc 260 422-1212
1105 Sherman Blvd Fort Wayne (46808) *(G-4324)*

Hc Farms 765 289-9909
1010 E County Road 700 N Muncie (47303) *(G-10484)*

Hco Holding I Corporation 317 248-1344
4351 W Morris St Indianapolis (46241) *(G-7081)*

Hd Mechanical Inc 219 924-6050
507 Industrial Dr Griffith (46319) *(G-5776)*

Hd Supply Construction Supply 260 471-7619
4510 Industrial Rd Fort Wayne (46825) *(G-4325)*

Hdh Manufacturing Inc 317 918-4088
4008 W 10th St Indianapolis (46222) *(G-7082)*

Hdh Manufacturing Inc (PA) 317 918-4088
3534 Nolen Dr Indianapolis (46234) *(G-7083)*

Headco Industries Inc 219 924-7758
9922 Express Dr Highland (46322) *(G-6049)*

Headco Industries Inc 574 288-4471
1625 Commerce Dr South Bend (46628) *(G-12795)*

Headlands Ltd 260 426-9884
9125 E 480 S Wolcottville (46795) *(G-14371)*

Heads 1st, Westville Also called Heads First *(G-14217)*

Heads First 219 785-4100
7 Plain St Westville (46391) *(G-14217)*

Headsight Inc 574 546-5022
4845 3b Rd Bremen (46506) *(G-1003)*

Headstamp Fine Brass LLC 812 212-8326
1120 Delaware Rd Batesville (47006) *(G-502)*

Heagy Vineyards LLC 317 752-4484
10330 Holaday Dr Carmel (46032) *(G-1401)*

Healey Custom Cabinetry LLC 574 946-4000
802 N Us Highway 35 Winamac (46996) *(G-14307)*

Healing Elements LLC 260 355-7181
3102 Mallard Cove Ln Fort Wayne (46804) *(G-4326)*

Health Employment Law Update, Evansville Also called Rutkowski & Associates Inc *(G-3712)*

Health Equipment Manufacturers 260 495-3472
702 S Reed Rd Fremont (46737) *(G-4961)*

Health Probe, Morgantown Also called Healthcare Data Inc *(G-10352)*

Healthcare Data Inc 812 342-9947
5693 S Bear Wallow Rd # 100 Morgantown (46160) *(G-10352)*

Hearing Aid Outlet, Portland Also called D J Investments Inc *(G-11814)*

Hearing Aid Outlet, Hartford City Also called D J Investments Inc *(G-5979)*

Heartcare LLC 260 432-7000
7806 W Jefferson Blvd D Fort Wayne (46804) *(G-4327)*

Heartfelt Creations Inc 574 773-3088
2147 Eisenhower Dr N Goshen (46526) *(G-5236)*

Hearth Glow Inc 260 839-3205
2234 E 1450 N North Manchester (46962) *(G-11229)*

Hearthcraft, Clarksville Also called Bottom Line Management Inc *(G-1674)*

Hearthmark LLC 765 557-3000
1501 E 9th St Muncie (47302) *(G-10485)*

Hearthmark LLC (HQ) 765 557-3000
9999 E 121st St Fishers (46037) *(G-3924)*

Hearthside Food Solutions LLC 219 878-1522
502 W Us Highway 20 Michigan City (46360) *(G-9802)*

Hearthstone of Indiana 812 988-2127
3204 Helmsburg Rd Nashville (47448) *(G-10725)*

Heartland Adhesives Inc 219 310-8645
7519 Boardwalk Crown Point (46307) *(G-2256)*

Heartland Automotive Inc 765 653-4263
300 S Warren Dr Greencastle (46135) *(G-5462)*

Heartland Automotive Inc 765 653-4263
300 S Warren Dr Greencastle (46135) *(G-5463)*

Heartland Castings Inc 260 837-8311
675 E Union St Waterloo (46793) *(G-14014)*

Heartland Distillers LLC 317 598-9775
9402 Uptown Dr Ste 1000 Indianapolis (46256) *(G-7084)*

Heartland Filled Machine LLC 574 223-6931
5176 State Road 110 Rochester (46975) *(G-12127)*

Heartland Film Inc 317 464-9405
1043 Virginia Ave Ste 2 Indianapolis (46203) *(G-7085)*

Heartland Food Products Group, Indianapolis Also called Tc Heartland LLC *(G-8041)*

Heartland Food Products Group, Carmel Also called Tc Heartland LLC *(G-1487)*

Heartland Steel Processing LLC 812 299-4157
455 W Industrial Dr Terre Haute (47802) *(G-13246)*

Heartland Table Pads Inc 888 487-2377
401 N Main St Wolcottville (46795) *(G-14372)*

Hearts Rmned Lifestyle Cir LLC 800 807-0485
1052 N County Line Rd Gary (46403) *(G-5061)*

Heartwood Manufacturing Inc 812 933-0388
1646 Lammers Pike Batesville (47006) *(G-503)*

Heat Exchanger Design Inc 317 917-1566
901 E Beecher St Indianapolis (46203) *(G-7086)*

Heat Wagons Inc 219 464-8818
342 N 400 E Valparaiso (46383) *(G-13555)*

Heather Sound Amplification 574 255-6100
1717 E 6th St Mishawaka (46544) *(G-10049)*

Heaven Sent Gurmet Cookies Inc 219 980-1066
3745 Broadway Gary (46409) *(G-5062)*

Heavy Duty Manufacturing Inc 260 432-2480
4317 Clubview Dr Fort Wayne (46804) *(G-4328)*

Hebron Ventures Global, Fort Wayne Also called Hebron Ventures North America *(G-4329)*

Hebron Ventures North America 260 437-7733
344 Field St Fort Wayne (46805) *(G-4329)*

HECKAMAN HOMES, Nappanee Also called Craftech Building Systems Inc *(G-10665)*

Heckley Printing 260 434-1370
6134 Constitution Dr Fort Wayne (46804) *(G-4330)*

Heco, Chesterton Also called Grindco Inc *(G-1610)*

Hector Engineering Co 812 876-5274
123 E Dewey Dr Ellettsville (47429) *(G-3280)*

Heflin Hflin Oil Gas Producers 812 536-3464
9823 S County Road 800 E Stendal (47585) *(G-13074)*

Heidenreich Woodworking Inc 317 861-9331
4175 S Kelly Dr New Palestine (46163) *(G-10970)*

Heidipops Gourmet Popcorn LLC 317 863-0844
2498 Futura Pkwy Ste 165 Plainfield (46168) *(G-11614)*

Heidtman Steel Products Inc 419 691-4646
4400 County Road 59 Butler (46721) *(G-1229)*

Heitink Veneers Incorporated 812 336-6436
1141 N Snrise Gretings Ct Bloomington (47404) *(G-739)*

Helena Agri-Enterprises LLC 765 583-4458
502 W Oxford St Otterbein (47970) *(G-11418)*

Helena Agri-Enterprises LLC 765 869-5518
210 N 1st St Ambia (47917) *(G-55)*

Helena Agri-Enterprises LLC 260 565-3196
2300 N State Road 301 Craigville (46731) *(G-2122)*

Helena Agri-Enterprises LLC 812 654-3177
5262 E Us Highway 50 Dillsboro (47018) *(G-2467)*

Helena Agri-Enterprises LLC 574 268-4762
321 Thurman Poe Way Huntington (46750) *(G-6209)*

Helfin Sheet Metal Inc 260 563-2417
1965 S Wabash St Wabash (46992) *(G-13729)*

Helfrich Engineering Inc 812 985-3118
9401 Hogue Rd Evansville (47712) *(G-3537)*

Helgeson Steel Inc 574 293-5576
1130 Verdant St Ste 1 Elkhart (46516) *(G-2912)*

Helios LLC 317 554-9911
8001 Woodland Dr Indianapolis (46278) *(G-7087)*

Hellbent Inc 765 631-4934
833 N Denny St Indianapolis (46201) *(G-7088)*

Hellweg Holdings LLC 317 909-6764
12940 Rocky Pointe Rd McCordsville (46055) *(G-9669)*

Helmer Inc 317 773-9073
14400 Bergen Blvd Noblesville (46060) *(G-11120)*

Helmer Scientific, Noblesville Also called Helmer Inc *(G-11120)*

Helming Bros Inc (PA) 812 634-9797
1030 Fairview Ave Jasper (47546) *(G-8254)*

Helms Enterprise, Warsaw Also called Holli Helms *(G-13890)*

Helmsburg Sawmill Inc 812 988-6161
2230 State Road 45 Nashville (47448) *(G-10726)*

Helmuth Cabinet Shop, Etna Green Also called Millwood Custom Cabinets *(G-3322)*

Helmuth Quality Power System 574 457-2002
100 S Huntington St Syracuse (46567) *(G-13133)*

Help Help LLC 317 910-6631
1935 Acorn Ct Avon (46123) *(G-446)*

Helsel, Campbellsburg Also called Netshape Technologies LLC *(G-1278)*

Helvie & Sons Inc 765 674-1372
5418 S Lincoln Blvd Marion (46953) *(G-9530)*

Hemocleanse Inc (PA) 765 742-4813
3601 Sagamore Pkwy N B Lafayette (47904) *(G-8913)*

Hendershot Service Center Inc 765 653-2600
711 N Jackson St Greencastle (46135) *(G-5464)*

Hendricks County Flyer 317 272-5800
8109 Kingston St Ste 500 Avon (46123) *(G-447)*

Hendrickson International Corp 260 868-2131
201 W Cherry St Butler (46721) *(G-1230)*

Hendrickson International Corp 260 349-6400
101 S Progress Dr W Kendallville (46755) *(G-8478)*

Hendrickson International Corp 765 483-5350
180 N Mount Zion Rd Lebanon (46052) *(G-9187)*

Hendrickson Suspension, Butler Also called Hendrickson International Corp *(G-1230)*

Hendrickson Trlr Suspntn, Lebanon Also called Hendrickson International Corp *(G-9187)*

Henkel (HQ) 765 284-5050
3416 S Hoyt Ave Muncie (47302) *(G-10486)*

Hennessey Montage Prints 317 841-7562
6471 Brauer Ln Carmel (46033) *(G-1402)*

Henry Fligeltaub Co Div, Evansville Also called Joe W Morgan Inc *(G-3575)*

Henry Holsters LLC 812 369-2266
1604 State Ferry Rd Solsberry (47459) *(G-12684)*

Henry Pratt Company LLC 219 931-0405
403 Conkey St Hammond (46324) *(G-5891)*

Henschen Sand and Gravel 260 367-2636
4635 N 800 E Howe (46746) *(G-6126)*

Hensley Composites LLC 574 202-3840
1705 W Lexington Ave Elkhart (46514) *(G-2913)*

Hensley Custom Cabinetry 219 843-5331
3281 E 400 N Rensselaer (47978) *(G-11927)*

Hensley Fabricating & Eqp Co 574 498-6514
17624 State Road 331 Tippecanoe (46570) *(G-13382)*

Hensley Hydra-Haulers, Tippecanoe Also called Hensley Fabricating & Eqp Co *(G-13382)*

Hentz Mfg LLC 260 469-0800
1530 Progress Rd Fort Wayne (46808) *(G-4331)*

Hepton Welding LLC 800 570-4238
9352 W Hepton Rd Nappanee (46550) *(G-10678)*

Heraeus 574 299-1862
1822 Se Macgregor Rd South Bend (46614) *(G-12796)*

Heraeus Electro-Nite Co LLC 765 473-8275
1025 Industrial Pkwy Peru (46970) *(G-11529)*

Heraeus Kulzer LLC (mitsui) 574 299-5466
300 Heraeus Dr South Bend (46614) *(G-12797)*

Herald Bulletin, The, Anderson Also called Community Holdings Indiana Inc *(G-88)*

Herald Journal, The, Monticello Also called Home News Enterprises LLC *(G-10265)*

Herald Machine Works Inc (PA) 219 949-0580
7100 Industrial Hwy Gary (46406) *(G-5063)*

Herald Times, Bloomington Also called Hoosier Times Inc *(G-741)*

Heraus Kulzer Inc 574 291-0661
4315 S Lafayette Blvd South Bend (46614) *(G-12798)*

Herb Rahman & Sons Inc 812 367-2513
9426 E County Road 2100 N Ferdinand (47532) *(G-3852)*

Herbert S Sawmill 812 663-9347
3438 E County Road 700 S Greensburg (47240) *(G-5607)*

Herbert Vernon Sawmill, Greensburg Also called Herbert S Sawmill *(G-5607)*

Herberts Truck & Van 812 663-6970
1625 N Carver St Greensburg (47240) *(G-5608)*

Herco, Bicknell Also called Hermetic Coil Co Inc *(G-631)*

Heres Your Sign Diy Workshop & 574 238-6369
18808 County Road 46 New Paris (46553) *(G-10981)*

Herff Jones LLC 317 612-3400
4625 W 62nd St Indianapolis (46268) *(G-7089)*

Herff Jones LLC 620 365-5181
4601 W 62nd St Indianapolis (46268) *(G-7090)*

Herff Jones LLC 800 837-4235
4601 W 62nd St Indianapolis (46268) *(G-7091)*

Herff Jones LLC (HQ) 800 419-5462
4501 W 62nd St Indianapolis (46268) *(G-7092)*

Herff Jones Co Indiana - Inc 317 297-3740
4625 W 62nd St Indianapolis (46268) *(G-7093)*

Herff Jones Yearbooks 717 334-9123
4625 W 62nd St Indianapolis (46268) *(G-7094)*

Heritage Arms, Huntington Also called Heritage Tool and Die Inc *(G-6210)*

Heritage Asphalt LLC 317 872-6010
5400 W 86th St Indianapolis (46268) *(G-7095)*

Heritage Cabinets LLC 812 963-3435
11911 Winery Rd Wadesville (47638) *(G-13772)*

Heritage Convertion LLC 574 773-0750
2112 Beech Rd Nappanee (46550) *(G-10679)*

Heritage Financial Group Inc (PA) 574 522-8000
120 W Lexington Ave # 200 Elkhart (46516) *(G-2914)*

Heritage Fine Furn & Cabinetry 812 205-5437
818 E Franklin St Evansville (47711) *(G-3538)*

Heritage Group Safety, Indianapolis Also called Asphalt Materials Inc *(G-6428)*

Heritage Hardwoods KY Inc (PA) 812 288-5855
1507 Production Rd Jeffersonville (47130) *(G-8372)*

Heritage Log Homes, Moores Hill Also called Appalachian Log Structures *(G-10297)*

Heritage Log Homes 812 427-2591
10648 Stevens Rd Vevay (47043) *(G-13664)*

Heritage Products Inc 765 364-9002
2000 Smith Ave Crawfordsville (47933) *(G-2158)*

Heritage Tool and Die Inc 260 359-8121
679 W Markle Rd Huntington (46750) *(G-6210)*

Heritage Unlimited LLC (PA) 574 538-8021
11641 County Road 30 Goshen (46528) *(G-5237)*

Heritage Wire Die Inc 260 728-9300
10484 N 200 W Decatur (46733) *(G-2385)*

Hermac Incorporated 260 925-0312
540 North St Auburn (46706) *(G-335)*

Herman Tool & Machine Inc 574 594-5544
2 Arnolt Dr Pierceton (46562) *(G-11572)*

Hermans' Christmas Land, Pierceton Also called Herman Tool & Machine Inc *(G-11572)*

Hermetic Coil Co Inc 812 735-2400
12005 E Davis Ln Bicknell (47512) *(G-631)*

Hermetic Coil Co Inc 812 735-2401
12005 E Davis Ln Bicknell (47512) *(G-632)*

Hernandez Signs LLC 317 500-1303
2937 S Rybolt Ave Indianapolis (46241) *(G-7096)*

Heron Blue Publications LLC 317 696-0674
11157 Valeside Cres Carmel (46032) *(G-1403)*

Heron Printing Co Inc 317 865-0007
159 Walnut St Indianapolis (46227) *(G-7097)*

Herrero Printing Co, Wolcottville Also called Headlands Ltd *(G-14371)*

Hess Electric Motor Service 812 926-0346
242 Railroad Ave Ste 2 Aurora (47001) *(G-378)*

Hessit Works Inc 812 829-6246
4181 S Us Highway 231 Freedom (47431) *(G-4949)*

Hessville Cable & Sling Co 773 768-8181
1601 Cline Ave Gary (46406) *(G-5064)*

Hestad Industries Inc 574 271-7609
52265 Wood Haven Dr Granger (46530) *(G-5412)*

Heston Log Homes Inc 219 778-4074
10409 N 200 E La Porte (46350) *(G-8763)*

Hetty Incorporated (PA) 219 836-2517
8244 Calumet Ave Munster (46321) *(G-10605)*

Hetty Incorporated 219 933-0833
6937 Calumet Ave Hammond (46324) *(G-5892)*

Hetzler Ocular Prosthetics (PA) 317 598-6298
10173 Allisonville Rd # 200 Fishers (46038) *(G-3925)*

Hewitt Manufacturing Company 765 525-9829
5365 S 600 E Waldron (46182) *(G-13799)*

Hewlett-Packard Co 765 534-4468
9471 Tiger Ct Lapel (46051) *(G-9119)*

Heyerly Bakery, Ossian Also called Heyerlys Bakery Inc *(G-11401)*

Heyerlys Bakery Inc 260 622-4196
107 N Jefferson St Ossian (46777) *(G-11401)*

Heywood Williams Inc 574 295-8400
601 County Road 17 Elkhart (46516) *(G-2915)*

Hf Chlor-Alkali LLC (PA) 317 591-0000
9307 E 56th St Indianapolis (46216) *(G-7098)*

Hf Group LLC 260 982-2107
1010 N Sycamore St North Manchester (46962) *(G-11230)*

Hg Metal Fabrication 317 491-3381
1426 N Graham Ave Indianapolis (46219) *(G-7099)*

Hg Metals, Indianapolis Also called Hgmc Supply Inc *(G-7101)*

Hgc Custom Chrome 260 447-4731
17507 Wayne St Yoder (46798) *(G-14398)*

Hgl Dynamics Inc 317 782-3500
2461 Directors Row Ste J Indianapolis (46241) *(G-7100)*

A
L
P
H
A
B
E
T
I
C

Hgmc Supply Inc 317 351-9500
   5402 Massachusetts Ave Indianapolis (46218) *(G-7101)*

Hh Rellim Inc 812 662-9944
   3494 E Base Rd Greensburg (47240) *(G-5609)*

HI Def Machining LLC 812 493-9943
   3508 N State Road 7 Madison (47250) *(G-9465)*

HI Point Machine and Tool Inc 574 831-5361
   19519 Industrial Dr 2 New Paris (46553) *(G-10982)*

HI Tech Foam Products Inc 317 614-1515
   9900 Westpoint Dr Ste 116 Indianapolis (46256) *(G-7102)*

HI Tech Label Inc 765 659-1800
   357 E Washington St Frankfort (46041) *(G-4836)*

HI Tech Systems Inc (PA) 317 704-1077
   8575 Zionsville Rd Indianapolis (46268) *(G-7103)*

HI Tech Veneer, Jeffersonville Also called JDC Veneers Inc *(G-8384)*

HI Tech Veneer LLC 812 284-9775
   276 America Pl Jeffersonville (47130) *(G-8373)*

Hi-Perfrmnce Sperabrasives Inc 317 899-1050
   9133 Pendleton Pike Ste G Indianapolis (46236) *(G-7104)*

Hi-Pro Inc 260 665-5038
   1410 Wohlert St Ste C Angola (46703) *(G-218)*

Hi-Rise Sign & Lighting LLC 812 825-4448
   6524 W Ison Rd Bloomington (47403) *(G-740)*

Hi-Tech Concrete Inc 765 477-5550
   3691 S 500 E Lafayette (47905) *(G-8914)*

Hi-Tech Foam Products LLC (HQ) 270 684-8331
   550 Bell St Indianapolis (46202) *(G-7105)*

Hi-Tech Housing Inc 574 848-5593
   1103 Maple St Bristol (46507) *(G-1062)*

Hi-Tech Hydraulics, Rensselaer Also called B & C Machining Inc *(G-11915)*

HI-Tech Turning 260 997-6668
   303 N Hendricks St Bryant (47326) *(G-1200)*

Hi-Temp Refractories, Crawfordsville Also called Ht Enterprises Inc *(G-2160)*

Hiatt Enterprises (PA) 765 289-7756
   1716 N Wheeling Ave Ste 1 Muncie (47303) *(G-10487)*

Hiatt Enterprises Inc 765 289-2700
   506 N Mckinley Ave Muncie (47303) *(G-10488)*

Hiatt Printing, Muncie Also called Hiatt Enterprises Inc *(G-10487)*

Hiatt Printing, Muncie Also called Hiatt Enterprises Inc *(G-10488)*

Hibbing International Friction 765 529-7001
   2001 Troy Ave New Castle (47362) *(G-10904)*

Hickman Williams & Company 812 522-6293
   2083 Upper Heiskell Ct Seymour (47274) *(G-12454)*

Hickman Williams & Company 708 656-8818
   2321 W Progress Dr La Porte (46350) *(G-8764)*

Hickman Williams & Co, La Porte Also called Hickman Williams & Company *(G-8764)*

Hickory Furniture Designs Inc 765 642-0700
   415 E 38th St Anderson (46013) *(G-114)*

Hickory Valley Woodworking LLC 812 486-2857
   10432 E 625 N Loogootee (47553) *(G-9385)*

Hicks Farms 812 852-4055
   3871 W County Road 1050 N Osgood (47037) *(G-11391)*

Hicks Mfg 317 219-9891
   3333 Walnut Creek Dr N Carmel (46032) *(G-1404)*

Hidinghilda LLC 260 760-7093
   1510 Calvert Ct Fort Wayne (46845) *(G-4332)*

Hielo Services LLC 219 973-1952
   3011 Crabapple Ln Hobart (46342) *(G-6080)*

Higgins Dyan 812 876-0754
   5680 W Mcneely St Ellettsville (47429) *(G-3281)*

High End Concepts Inc 317 630-9901
   225 E 10th St Indianapolis (46202) *(G-7106)*

High Note Publishing 765 313-1699
   571 S 1400 E34 Swayzee (46986) *(G-13123)*

High Value Metal Inc 812 522-6468
   101 Blish St Seymour (47274) *(G-12455)*

High Velocity Manufacturing 260 413-8429
   4710 Arden Dr Fort Wayne (46804) *(G-4333)*

Highland Computer Forms Inc 260 665-6268
   1510 Wohlert St Angola (46703) *(G-219)*

Highland Machine Tool Inc 812 923-8884
   3461 E Luther Rd Floyds Knobs (47119) *(G-4013)*

Highland Park Services Inc 317 954-0456
   5345 Winthrop Ave Indianapolis (46220) *(G-7107)*

Highland Ridge Rv Inc 260 768-7771
   3195 N State Road 5 Shipshewana (46565) *(G-12616)*

Highmark Pack Systems, Fort Wayne Also called Highmark Technologies LLC *(G-4334)*

Highmark Technologies LLC 260 483-0012
   8343 Clinton Park Dr Fort Wayne (46825) *(G-4334)*

Highpoint Mfg LLC 812 273-8987
   3501 N Jefferson Lake Rd Madison (47250) *(G-9466)*

Hightech Signs, Fort Wayne Also called Castleton Village Center Inc *(G-4140)*

Hightech Signs, Fort Wayne Also called Castleton Village Center Inc *(G-4141)*

Hightech Signs, Indianapolis Also called Castleton Village Center Inc *(G-6565)*

Highwater Marine LLC 574 457-2082
   300 E Chicago St Syracuse (46567) *(G-13134)*

Highwater Marine LLC (PA) 574 522-8381
   4500 Middlebury St Elkhart (46516) *(G-2916)*

Highway Machine Co Inc 812 385-3639
   3010 S Old Us Highway 41 Princeton (47670) *(G-11875)*

Highway Press Inc 812 283-6462
   2199 Hamburg Pike Jeffersonville (47130) *(G-8374)*

Highway Safety Services Inc 765 474-1000
   3215 Imperial Pkwy Lafayette (47909) *(G-8915)*

Hilex Poly 812 346-1066
   1001 2nd St North Vernon (47265) *(G-11261)*

Hill & Griffith Company 317 241-9233
   3637 Farnsworth St Indianapolis (46241) *(G-7108)*

Hill Top Welding LLC 765 585-2549
   217 N State Road 55 Attica (47918) *(G-304)*

Hill's Pet Products, Richmond Also called Hills Pet Nutrition Inc *(G-11996)*

Hillcrest Mobile Homes Court, Crawfordsville Also called Charles Coons *(G-2138)*

Hillcrest Pallets 812 883-3636
   5445 W Kansas Church Rd Salem (47167) *(G-12291)*

Hillenbrand Inc (PA) 812 934-7500
   1 Batesville Blvd Batesville (47006) *(G-504)*

Hills Pet Nutrition Inc 765 966-4549
   2859 Salisbury Rd N Richmond (47374) *(G-11996)*

Hills Pet Nutrition Inc 765 935-7071
   2325 Union Pike Richmond (47374) *(G-11997)*

Hillshire Brands Company 260 456-4802
   1108 E Pontiac St Fort Wayne (46803) *(G-4335)*

Hillside Motor Sales LLC 219 322-7700
   1212 W Us Highway 30 Schererville (46375) *(G-12322)*

Hilltop Basic Resources Inc 812 594-2293
   14208 State Road 156 Patriot (47038) *(G-11468)*

Hilltop Leather 317 831-4855
   450 S Indiana St Mooresville (46158) *(G-10310)*

Hilltop Leather 317 508-3404
   1820 Observatory Rd Martinsville (46151) *(G-9612)*

Hilltop Machine Shop LLC 260 768-9196
   10515 W Us Highway 20 Shipshewana (46565) *(G-12617)*

Hilltop Mch Sp Haubstadt LLC 812 768-5717
   4958 E 1200 S Haubstadt (47639) *(G-6002)*

Hilltop Metal Fabricating LLC 574 773-4975
   71024 County Road 13 Nappanee (46550) *(G-10680)*

Hilltop Processing Inc 812 544-2174
   13371 N State Road 245 Lamar (47550) *(G-9100)*

Hilltop Specialties LLC 574 773-4975
   71024 County Road 13 Nappanee (46550) *(G-10681)*

Hilltop Wood Working 270 604-1962
   4406 W County Road 1050 S Madison (47250) *(G-9467)*

Hilltop Woodworking 812 689-3462
   4406 W County Road 1050 S Madison (47250) *(G-9468)*

Hiltys Woodwork 260 627-2905
   10615 Schwartz Rd Fort Wayne (46835) *(G-4336)*

Him Gentlemans Boutique 812 924-7441
   314 Pearl St New Albany (47150) *(G-10793)*

Hindi Petroleum Group II Inc 317 574-0619
   993 Deer Lake Dr Carmel (46032) *(G-1405)*

Hinen Printing Co 260 248-8984
   117 W Market St Columbia City (46725) *(G-1789)*

Hines Bindery Systems Service 317 839-6432
   212 E Main St Plainfield (46168) *(G-11615)*

Hingecraft Corporation 574 293-6543
   3601 Lexington Park Dr Elkhart (46514) *(G-2917)*

Hinsdale Farms Ltd 574 848-0344
   605 Kesco Dr Bristol (46507) *(G-1063)*

Hinshaw Tool & Die, Lynn Also called T F & T Inc *(G-9432)*

Hinton Keith & Hinton Tammy 260 749-4867
   442 Lincoln Hwy W New Haven (46774) *(G-10943)*

Hintz Equipment Inc 765 362-6115
   1091 N Terrace Rd Thorntown (46071) *(G-13375)*

Hipsher Tool & Die Inc 260 563-4143
   1593 S State Road 115 Wabash (46992) *(G-13730)*

Hirata Corporation of America (HQ) 317 856-8600
   5625 Decatur Blvd Indianapolis (46241) *(G-7109)*

His, Anderson Also called Don Hartman Oil Co Inc *(G-98)*

Hisada America Inc 812 526-0756
   1191 S Walnut St Ste 102 Edinburgh (46124) *(G-2613)*

Hitachi Automotive Systems 859 734-9451
   925 N Main St Ligonier (46767) *(G-9287)*

Hitachi Cable America Inc 812 945-9011
   5301 Foundation Blvd New Albany (47150) *(G-10794)*

Hitachi Cable America Inc 812 945-9011
   5300 Grant Line Rd New Albany (47150) *(G-10795)*

Hitachi Cble Auto Pdts USA Inc (HQ) 812 945-9011
   5300 Grant Line Rd New Albany (47150) *(G-10796)*

Hitachi Powdered Mtls USA Inc (PA) 812 663-5058
   1024 E Barachel Ln Greensburg (47240) *(G-5610)*

Hitarth LLC 812 372-1744
   1609 Cottage Ave Ste G Columbus (47201) *(G-1939)*

Hite Welding & Chassis 765 741-0046
   1715 E 18th St Muncie (47302) *(G-10489)*

Hites Hardwood Lumber Corp 574 278-7783
   309 S East St Buffalo (47925) *(G-1203)*

Hitzer Inc 260 589-8536
   269 E Main St Berne (46711) *(G-617)*

2018 Harris Indiana
Industrial Directory

(G-0000) Company's Geographic Section entry number

Hively Welding Co Inc...219 843-5111
  14695 W State Road 14 Medaryville (47957) *(G-9679)*

Hjj Inc...219 362-4421
  1533 Weller Ave La Porte (46350) *(G-8765)*

HK Manufacturing Inc..260 925-1680
  203 Hunters Rdg Auburn (46706) *(G-336)*

HK Petroleum Ltd...229 366-1313
  606 E Main St Madison (47250) *(G-9469)*

Hkn International LLC..317 243-5959
  5621 Dividend Rd Indianapolis (46241) *(G-7110)*

Hmh, Indianapolis *Also called Houghton Mifflin Harcourt Co* *(G-7137)*

Hmi Machinery, Topeka *Also called Honeyville Metal Inc* *(G-13421)*

Hmmcopl LLC...219 757-3575
  1000 E 80th Pl Ste 777s Merrillville (46410) *(G-9719)*

HMS Zoo Diets Inc...260 824-5157
  1222 Echo Ln Bluffton (46714) *(G-877)*

Hmt LLC...219 736-9901
  4100 W 82nd Ave Merrillville (46410) *(G-9720)*

Hobart Electronics Division, Hobart *Also called Coil Tran Corp* *(G-6076)*

Hobart Locker & Meat Pkg Co.................................219 942-5952
  8602 Randolph St Crown Point (46307) *(G-2257)*

Hobson Tool and Machine Co...................................317 736-4203
  3061 N Morton St Franklin (46131) *(G-4895)*

Hochbaum Machine Services Inc..............................219 996-6830
  11 Wood Ct Hebron (46341) *(G-6014)*

Hochstetler Welding..574 773-0600
  7262 W 1350 N Nappanee (46550) *(G-10682)*

Hochstetler Welding..260 463-2793
  2520 W 350 N Lagrange (46761) *(G-9044)*

Hoehn Hardwoods...812 968-3242
  2285 Fogel Rd Se Corydon (47112) *(G-2101)*

Hoehn Plastics Inc...812 874-3646
  11481 W 925 S Poseyville (47633) *(G-11856)*

Hoffman Quality Graphics.......................................574 223-5738
  2096 Sycamore Dr Rochester (46975) *(G-12128)*

Hoffman Sls & Specialty Co Inc................................317 846-6428
  3222 Birch Canyon Dr Carmel (46033) *(G-1406)*

Hoffmaster Electric Inc..219 616-1313
  1635 Hartley Dr Schererville (46375) *(G-12323)*

Hog Slat Incorporated..765 828-0828
  18506 S Rangeline Rd Universal (47884) *(G-13467)*

Hog Slat Incorporated..574 967-4145
  200 N Meridian Line Rd Camden (46917) *(G-1274)*

Hogan Stamping LLC..812 656-8222
  305 Maple St West Harrison (47060) *(G-14039)*

Hogen Industries Inc Indiana...................................317 591-5070
  4655 Massachusetts Ave Indianapolis (46218) *(G-7111)*

Hoist Liftruck Mfg LLC (HQ)....................................708 552-2722
  4407 Railroad Ave East Chicago (46312) *(G-2533)*

Hokey Spokes...219 938-7360
  739 N Montgomery St Gary (46403) *(G-5065)*

Holbrook Manufacturing Inc....................................317 736-9387
  291 Province St Franklin (46131) *(G-4896)*

Holder Bedding Inc..765 642-1256
  1923 W 8th St Anderson (46016) *(G-115)*

Holder Bedding Inc (PA)...765 447-7907
  230 Farabee Dr N Lafayette (47905) *(G-8916)*

Holgin Technologies LLC...317 774-5181
  15335 Endeavor Dr Ste 100 Noblesville (46060) *(G-11121)*

Holic LLC...765 444-8115
  710 Norfleet Dr W Middletown (47356) *(G-9936)*

Holiday House Inc...574 773-9536
  1852 W Market St Nappanee (46550) *(G-10683)*

Holland Colours Americas Inc..................................765 935-0329
  1501 Progress Dr Richmond (47374) *(G-11998)*

Holland House, Indianapolis *Also called Hackney Home Furnishings Inc* *(G-7065)*

Holland Metal Fab Inc..574 522-1434
  1550 W Lusher Ave Elkhart (46517) *(G-2918)*

Hollands Deer Processing LLC..................................765 472-5876
  1848 W Lovers Lane Rd Peru (46970) *(G-11530)*

Holli Helms...574 253-8923
  1 Ems B37 Ln Lot 46 Warsaw (46582) *(G-13890)*

Hollingsworth & Associates, Osceola *Also called R B Tool & Machinery Co* *(G-11383)*

HOLLINGSWORTH LUMBER, Russiaville *Also called Hollingsworth Sawmill Inc* *(G-12241)*

Hollingsworth Sawmill Inc.......................................765 883-5836
  6810 W 400 S Russiaville (46979) *(G-12241)*

Holloway Electric Motor Svc, Rochester *Also called Ronald Holloway* *(G-12151)*

Holloway House Inc...317 485-4272
  309 Business Park Dr Fortville (46040) *(G-4779)*

Holloway Vinyl Signs Grap.......................................765 717-1581
  4100 S Native Ct Yorktown (47396) *(G-14405)*

Holm Industries, Scottsburg *Also called Ilpea Industries Inc* *(G-12362)*

Holman Septic Tank Sls Redymix...............................812 689-1913
  4896 S Old Michigan Rd Holton (47023) *(G-6108)*

Holman's Septic Tank Sales, Holton *Also called Holman Septic Tank Sls Redymix* *(G-6108)*

Holmes & Company Inc...260 244-6149
  807 E Ellsworth St Columbia City (46725) *(G-1790)*

Holscher Products Inc..765 884-8021
  407 W Main St Fowler (47944) *(G-4801)*

Holsum of Fort Wayne Inc (HQ)................................260 456-2130
  136 Murray St Fort Wayne (46803) *(G-4337)*

Holsum of Fort Wayne Inc.......................................219 362-4561
  800 Boyd Blvd La Porte (46350) *(G-8766)*

Holzmeyer Die & Mold Mfg Corp...............................812 386-6015
  333 S 2nd Ave Princeton (47670) *(G-11876)*

Home & Lawn Services..260 633-9155
  7420 Nature Trail Dr Fort Wayne (46835) *(G-4338)*

Home - Little Creek Winery......................................812 319-3951
  4116 Koressel Rd Evansville (47720) *(G-3539)*

Home City Ice Company..317 638-0437
  55 S State Ave Indianapolis (46201) *(G-7112)*

Home City Ice Company..317 926-2451
  2000 Dr M Lther Kng Dr Martin Indianapolis (46202) *(G-7113)*

Home City Ice Company..765 762-6096
  200 S Market St Attica (47918) *(G-305)*

Home City Ice Company..219 661-8369
  668 N Madison St Crown Point (46307) *(G-2258)*

Home City Ice Company..317 926-2451
  3602 W Washington St Indianapolis (46241) *(G-7114)*

Home Design Products, Alexandria *Also called Resin Partners Inc* *(G-51)*

Home Design Products, Anderson *Also called Resin Partners Inc* *(G-161)*

Home Guard Industries Inc.......................................260 627-6060
  13101 Main St Grabill (46741) *(G-5372)*

Home News Enterprises LLC.....................................812 342-1056
  3330 W International Ct Columbus (47201) *(G-1940)*

Home News Enterprises LLC.....................................574 583-5121
  114 S Main St Monticello (47960) *(G-10265)*

Home Pdts Intl - N Amer Inc.....................................773 890-1010
  885 N Chestnut St Seymour (47274) *(G-12456)*

Home Phone Inc...812 280-3657
  414 Spring St Jeffersonville (47130) *(G-8375)*

Home Reserve LLC...260 969-6939
  3015 Cannongate Dr Fort Wayne (46808) *(G-4339)*

Home Reserve.com, Fort Wayne *Also called Home Reserve LLC* *(G-4339)*

Home Run LLC...219 531-1006
  312 N 325 E Ste B Valparaiso (46383) *(G-13556)*

Home Works, Lafayette *Also called James A Andrew Inc* *(G-8929)*

Home-Style Industries, Elkhart *Also called Lippert Components Inc* *(G-2999)*

Homecrest, Jasper *Also called Masterbrand Cabinets Inc* *(G-8291)*

Homecrest Cabinetry, Goshen *Also called H-C Liquidating Corp* *(G-5233)*

Homeowners Equity & Rlty Corp................................219 981-1700
  306 W Ridge Rd Gary (46408) *(G-5066)*

Homer Banes..765 449-8551
  520 S Earl Ave Lafayette (47904) *(G-8917)*

Homes & Lifestyles Magazine...................................574 674-6639
  11859 Lincolnway Osceola (46561) *(G-11377)*

Homeshield, Richmond *Also called Imperial Products LLC* *(G-12001)*

Homestead Industries Inc..574 273-5274
  53193 Chelle Ln Granger (46530) *(G-5413)*

Homestead Primitives Inc..812 782-3521
  704 W School St Francisco (47649) *(G-4816)*

Homestead Properties Inc..812 866-4415
  10214 W Deputy Pike Rd Deputy (47230) *(G-2460)*

Hometown Energy..812 663-3391
  1430 W Main St Greensburg (47240) *(G-5611)*

Homette Corporation (HQ).......................................574 294-6521
  2520 Bypass Rd Elkhart (46514) *(G-2919)*

Honda Manufacturing Ind LLC..................................812 222-6000
  2755 N Michigan Ave Greensburg (47240) *(G-5612)*

Honey and ME..317 668-3924
  2908 N Graham Rd A Franklin (46131) *(G-4897)*

Honey Creek Machine Inc..812 299-5255
  1537 W Harlan Dr Terre Haute (47802) *(G-13247)*

Honey Pastry, Bloomington *Also called Achaemenian Shahpur* *(G-656)*

Honeycomb Products Inc...317 787-9351
  405 W Raymond St Indianapolis (46225) *(G-7115)*

Honeyville Metal Inc..800 593-8377
  4200 S 900 W Topeka (46571) *(G-13421)*

Honeywell Authorized Dealer, New Albany *Also called Frank H Monroe Htg & Coolg Inc* *(G-10784)*

Honeywell Authorized Dealer, Indianapolis *Also called Abbott Controls Inc* *(G-6308)*

Honeywell Authorized Dealer, Monticello *Also called Halsen Brothers Sheet Metal* *(G-10264)*

Honeywell Authorized Dealer, Evansville *Also called Jack Frost LLC* *(G-3571)*

Honeywell Authorized Dealer, Middlebury *Also called Washburn Heating & AC* *(G-9924)*

Honeywell Authorized Dealer, Michigan City *Also called Paniccia Heating & Cooling* *(G-9827)*

Honeywell Friction Materials, Fortville *Also called D & D Brake Sales Inc* *(G-4772)*

Honeywell International Inc......................................765 284-3300
  201 E 18th St Muncie (47302) *(G-10490)*

Honeywell International Inc......................................317 580-6165
  9355 Delegates Row Indianapolis (46240) *(G-7116)*

Honeywell International Inc......................................574 935-0200
  504 E Garro St Plymouth (46563) *(G-11688)*

Honeywell International Inc......................................574 231-2000
  3520 Westmoor St South Bend (46628) *(G-12799)*

Honeywell International Inc 574 231-3000
3520 Westmoor St South Bend (46628) *(G-12800)*

Honeywell International Inc 317 359-9505
1775 N Sherman Dr Ste A Indianapolis (46218) *(G-7117)*

Honeywell International Inc 574 231-3000
3520 Westmoor St South Bend (46628) *(G-12801)*

Honing Stl Hsptlity Cncpts Inc 317 332-5170
5807 Tempest Dr Indianapolis (46237) *(G-7118)*

Hoogies Sports House Inc 574 533-9875
825 Logan St Goshen (46528) *(G-5238)*

Hook & Arrow 260 739-6661
7536 Winchester Rd Fort Wayne (46819) *(G-4340)*

Hook Development Inc 260 432-7771
2731 Brooklyn Ave Fort Wayne (46802) *(G-4341)*

Hook Industrial Sales Inc (PA) 260 432-9441
2731 Brooklyn Ave Fort Wayne (46802) *(G-4342)*

Hook Industrial Sales Inc 317 545-8100
2138 N Olney St Indianapolis (46218) *(G-7119)*

Hooker Corner Winery LLC 765 585-1225
444 W State Road 26 Pine Village (47975) *(G-11581)*

Hooker Deer Drag Co LLC 812 623-2706
27499 Lawrenceville Rd Sunman (47041) *(G-13112)*

Hoople Country Kitchens Inc 812 649-2351
714 N 5th St Rockport (47635) *(G-12168)*

Hoosier All-Stars Inc 317 408-0513
303 E Arch St Portland (47371) *(G-11828)*

Hoosier Badge & Trophies Inc 317 257-4441
6161 Hillside Ave Fl 1 Indianapolis (46220) *(G-7120)*

Hoosier Bat Company, Valparaiso *Also called Home Run LLC* **(G-13556)**

Hoosier Box and Skid Inc 574 256-2111
2401 Schumacher Dr Mishawaka (46545) *(G-10050)*

Hoosier Buggy Shop 260 593-2192
5245 S 600 W Topeka (46571) *(G-13422)*

Hoosier Container Inc 765 966-2541
1001 Indiana Ave Richmond (47374) *(G-11999)*

Hoosier Crane Service Company 574 523-2945
3500 Charlotte Ave Elkhart (46517) *(G-2920)*

Hoosier Crush Corp 765 292-6375
325 E Michael Dr Atlanta (46031) *(G-295)*

Hoosier Custom Plastics LLC 574 772-2120
201 Hamilton Dr Knox (46534) *(G-8567)*

Hoosier Custom Woodworking 574 642-3764
67348 County Road 33 Millersburg (46543) *(G-9970)*

Hoosier Daddy Woodworks 812 949-2801
1903 Depauw Ave New Albany (47150) *(G-10797)*

Hoosier Data Forms, Indianapolis *Also called Cornelius Printed Products Inc* **(G-6668)**

Hoosier Drilling Contrs Inc 812 689-1260
8364 S Us 421 Madison (47250) *(G-9470)*

Hoosier Engineering Co Inc 260 694-6887
7726 S Meridian Rd Poneto (46781) *(G-11746)*

Hoosier Ethanol Energy LLC 260 407-6161
110 W Berry St Ste 1200 Fort Wayne (46802) *(G-4343)*

Hoosier Feeder Company Inc 765 445-3333
100 W Morgan St Knightstown (46148) *(G-8550)*

Hoosier Fiberglass Industries 812 232-5027
2011 S 3rd St Terre Haute (47802) *(G-13248)*

Hoosier Fire Equipment Inc (PA) 219 462-1707
4009 Montdale Park Dr Valparaiso (46383) *(G-13557)*

Hoosier Gasket Corporation (PA) 317 545-2000
2400 Enterprise Park Pl Indianapolis (46218) *(G-7121)*

Hoosier Horse Review LLC 765 212-1320
7301 S County Road 400 W Muncie (47302) *(G-10491)*

Hoosier Hot Rods Classics Inc 812 768-5221
189 E State Road 68 Haubstadt (47639) *(G-6003)*

Hoosier Hrdwood Rclamation LLC 765 299-6507
1471 S 600 W Crawfordsville (47933) *(G-2159)*

Hoosier Industrial Electric 812 346-2232
Rodgers Park Dr North Vernon (47265) *(G-11262)*

Hoosier Industrial Supply 574 535-0712
2516 Industrial Park Dr Goshen (46526) *(G-5239)*

Hoosier Industrial Supply Inc 574 533-8565
1223 N Chicago Ave Goshen (46528) *(G-5240)*

Hoosier Interior Doors Inc 574 534-3072
523 E Lincoln Ave Goshen (46528) *(G-5241)*

Hoosier Jiffy Print, Marion *Also called L & L Press Inc* **(G-9541)**

Hoosier Jiffy Print 260 563-8715
675 Stitt St Wabash (46992) *(G-13731)*

Hoosier Machine & Welding Inc 317 638-6286
451 Arbor Ave Indianapolis (46221) *(G-7122)*

Hoosier Manufacturing LLC 260 493-9990
9312 Avionics Dr Fort Wayne (46809) *(G-4344)*

Hoosier Marine 812 879-5549
10151 N Us Highway 231 Quincy (47456) *(G-11890)*

Hoosier Metal Polish Inc 219 474-6011
304 N Fairground Rd Kentland (47951) *(G-8520)*

Hoosier Metal Products Inc 812 372-5151
1402 Union St Columbus (47201) *(G-1941)*

Hoosier Oxygen Company, Indianapolis *Also called Indiana Oxygen Company Inc* **(G-7188)**

Hoosier Pallet 765 629-2899
4126 W 900 S Milroy (46156) *(G-9981)*

Hoosier Penn Oil Co Inc 812 284-9433
2990 Industrial Pkwy Jeffersonville (47130) *(G-8376)*

Hoosier Powder Coating LLC 574 253-7737
9583 W 1350 N Nappanee (46550) *(G-10684)*

Hoosier Precast LLC 812 883-4665
200 Tarr Ave Salem (47167) *(G-12292)*

Hoosier Press Inc 765 649-3716
1027 Meridian St Anderson (46016) *(G-116)*

Hoosier Pride Plastics Inc 260 497-7080
6120 Highview Dr Fort Wayne (46818) *(G-4345)*

Hoosier Printing Co Inc 219 836-8877
8208 Calumet Ave Munster (46321) *(G-10606)*

Hoosier Racing Tire Corp 574 784-3409
65465 Sr 931 Lakeville (46536) *(G-9096)*

Hoosier Ready Mix LLC 812 254-7625
1115 S 300 W Washington (47501) *(G-13986)*

Hoosier Reproduction Services 765 664-3162
1417 W Kem Rd Marion (46952) *(G-9531)*

Hoosier Roaster Llc 574 257-1415
2212 Lincolnway W Mishawaka (46544) *(G-10051)*

Hoosier Roll Shop Services LLC 219 844-8077
7020 Cline Ave Hammond (46323) *(G-5893)*

Hoosier Shred 317 915-7473
9325 Uptown Dr Ste 1400 Indianapolis (46256) *(G-7123)*

Hoosier Shred Llc 317 989-9333
9525 Brigantine Ct Indianapolis (46256) *(G-7124)*

Hoosier Spline Broach Corp 765 452-8273
1401 Touby Pike Kokomo (46901) *(G-8639)*

Hoosier Spring Co Inc 574 291-7550
4604 S Burnett Dr South Bend (46614) *(G-12802)*

Hoosier Stamping LLC 812 993-2040
7988 Gardner Rd Chandler (47610) *(G-1549)*

Hoosier Stamping & Mfg Corp (PA) 812 426-2778
1865 W Franklin St Evansville (47712) *(G-3540)*

Hoosier Tank and Mfg Inc 574 232-8368
1710 N Sheridan St South Bend (46628) *(G-12803)*

Hoosier Times Inc (HQ) 812 331-4270
1900 S Walnut St Bloomington (47401) *(G-741)*

Hoosier Times Inc 765 342-3311
60 S Jefferson St Martinsville (46151) *(G-9613)*

Hoosier Times Inc 812 275-3372
2139 16th St Bedford (47421) *(G-548)*

Hoosier Times Inc 812 332-4401
301 Main St Beech Grove (46107) *(G-596)*

Hoosier Tire, Lakeville *Also called Hoosier Racing Tire Corp* **(G-9096)**

Hoosier Tool & Die Co Inc 812 376-8286
2860 N National Rd Ste B Columbus (47201) *(G-1942)*

Hoosier Tool & Grinding Inc 812 597-0213
1382 N Fruitdale Rd Morgantown (46160) *(G-10353)*

Hoosier Toolmaking & Engrg Inc 260 493-9990
6930 Derek Dr Fort Wayne (46803) *(G-4346)*

Hoosier Trim Products LLC 317 271-4007
1850 Expo Ln Indianapolis (46214) *(G-7125)*

Hoosier Truck & Trailer Srv 317 887-4887
4301 W Southport Rd Indianapolis (46217) *(G-7126)*

Hoosier Wallbeds Inc 812 926-0055
8787 State Road 48 Aurora (47001) *(G-379)*

Hoosier Wallbeds Incorporated 812 747-7154
23036 Stateline Rd Lawrenceburg (47025) *(G-9145)*

Hoosier Welding 765 521-4539
1726 S County Road 125 W New Castle (47362) *(G-10905)*

Hoosier Wheel, Evansville *Also called Hoosier Stamping & Mfg Corp* **(G-3540)**

Hoosier Wheel LLC 812 421-6900
700 Schrader Dr Evansville (47712) *(G-3541)*

Hoosier Wood Creations Inc 574 831-6330
19881 County Road 146 New Paris (46553) *(G-10983)*

Hoosier Wood Works 812 325-9823
118 E Ridgeview Dr Bloomington (47401) *(G-742)*

Hoosier Woodworking McHy LLC 812 944-3302
3306 Cobblers Ct New Albany (47150) *(G-10798)*

Hoostier Topics, Cloverdale *Also called Spencer Evening World* **(G-1738)**

Hooven - Dayton Corp 765 935-3999
165 Industrial Pkwy Richmond (47374) *(G-12000)*

Hoover Sheet Metal, Indianapolis *Also called Sanbar of Indiana Inc* **(G-7890)**

Hoover Well Drilling Inc 574 831-4901
20477 County Road 46 New Paris (46553) *(G-10984)*

Hope Hardwoods Inc 812 546-4427
1006 Seminary St Hope (47246) *(G-6114)*

Hope Machine 502 550-9532
3110 Bellemeade Ave Evansville (47714) *(G-3542)*

Hope Powder Coat Inc 812 546-5555
220 Raymond St Hope (47246) *(G-6115)*

Hope Star Journal, Hope *Also called Indiana News Media LLC* **(G-6116)**

Hopkins & Woods, Martinsville *Also called Metcalf Engineering Inc* **(G-9625)**

Hopkins Gravel Sand & Concrete 317 831-2704
540 State Road 267 Mooresville (46158) *(G-10311)*

Hopper Development Inc 574 753-6621
1332 18th St Logansport (46947) *(G-9336)*

Hopwood Cellars 317 873-4099
12 E Cedar St Zionsville (46077) *(G-14438)*

(G-0000) Company's Geographic Section entry number

Horizon Atomtn Fabrication LLC 765 896-9491
3620 S Hoyt Ave Muncie (47302) *(G-10492)*

Horizon Biotechnologies LLC 317 534-2540
1740 S Morgantown Rd Greenwood (46143) *(G-5703)*

Horizon Global Americas Inc 517 767-4142
3310 Wlliam Richardson Dr South Bend (46628) *(G-12804)*

Horizon Management Services (PA) 219 852-3200
7412 Calumet Ave Hammond (46324) *(G-5894)*

Horizon Publications Inc 260 244-5153
927 W Connexion Way Columbia City (46725) *(G-1791)*

Horizon Publishing Company LLC 219 852-3200
7412 Calumet Ave Ste 100 Hammond (46324) *(G-5895)*

Horizon Terra Incorporated (HQ) 812 280-0000
101 River Ridge Cir Jeffersonville (47130) *(G-8377)*

Horizon Vinyl Windows Inc 260 632-0207
7434 Brush College Rd Woodburn (46797) *(G-14384)*

Horn Pre-Cast Inc 812 372-4458
895 Jonesville Rd Columbus (47201) *(G-1943)*

Horneco Fabrication Inc 260 672-2064
13020 Redding Dr Fort Wayne (46814) *(G-4347)*

Horner Advanced Products Group, Indianapolis Also called Horner Apg LLC *(G-7127)*

Horner Apg LLC (PA) 317 916-4274
59 S State Ave Indianapolis (46201) *(G-7127)*

Horner Electric, Fort Wayne Also called Horner Industrial Services Inc *(G-4348)*

Horner Industrial Services Inc 317 916-4274
59 S State Ave Indianapolis (46201) *(G-7128)*

Horner Industrial Services Inc 812 466-5281
3601 Scherer Rd Terre Haute (47804) *(G-13249)*

Horner Industrial Services Inc 317 634-7165
2045 E Washington St Indianapolis (46201) *(G-7129)*

Horner Industrial Services Inc 260 434-1189
4421 Ardmore Ave Fort Wayne (46809) *(G-4348)*

Horner Industrial Services Inc 317 639-4261
1521 E Washington St Indianapolis (46201) *(G-7130)*

Horoho Printing Company Inc 765 452-8862
500 N Philips St Kokomo (46901) *(G-8640)*

Horse Circuit News Inc 800 537-3958
8098 E County Road 400 S New Castle (47362) *(G-10906)*

Horse N Around Animal & Tack 765 618-2032
7288 S 825 E Upland (46989) *(G-13471)*

Horsepower Indy LLC 317 757-8668
4 Gasoline Aly Ste D Indianapolis (46222) *(G-7131)*

Hose & Go 574 295-7800
2623 S Nappanee St Elkhart (46517) *(G-2921)*

Hose Assemblies, Mishawaka Also called Slb Corporation *(G-10125)*

Hose Technology Inc 765 762-5501
2520 E Us Hwy 41 Williamsport (47993) *(G-14291)*

Hosetract Industries Ltd 260 489-8828
6433 Discount Dr Fort Wayne (46818) *(G-4349)*

Hostetler Carriage 260 463-9920
3200 W 300 S Lagrange (46761) *(G-9045)*

Hot Cake 317 889-2253
6845 Bluff Rd Indianapolis (46217) *(G-7132)*

Hot Off Press 317 253-5987
5838 Bonnie Brae St Indianapolis (46228) *(G-7133)*

Hot Off Press 260 591-8331
832 Manchester Ave Wabash (46992) *(G-13732)*

Hot Rod Car Care LLC 317 660-2077
7242 E 86th St Indianapolis (46250) *(G-7134)*

Hot Shot Multimedia Entps LLC 317 537-7527
1610 Hilltop Dr South Bend (46614) *(G-12805)*

Hot Shot USA, South Bend Also called Hot Shot Multimedia Entps LLC *(G-12805)*

Hot Stamping & Printing 219 767-2429
6601 W 900 S Union Mills (46382) *(G-13463)*

Hot Stone LLC 812 949-4969
202 Pearl St New Albany (47150) *(G-10799)*

Hotel Tango Distillery, Indianapolis Also called Hotel Tango Whiskey Inc *(G-7135)*

Hotel Tango Whiskey Inc 317 653-1806
702 Virginia Ave Indianapolis (46203) *(G-7135)*

Hotel Vanities Intl LLC (PA) 317 787-2330
5514 Stockwell Ct Indianapolis (46237) *(G-7136)*

Hotmix Inc (PA) 812 926-1471
110 Forest Ave Aurora (47001) *(G-380)*

Hotmix Inc 812 663-2020
992 S County Road 800 E Greensburg (47240) *(G-5613)*

Houck Industries Inc 812 663-5675
814 E Randall St Greensburg (47240) *(G-5614)*

Houghton Mifflin Harcourt Co 317 359-5585
2700 N Richardt Ave Indianapolis (46219) *(G-7137)*

Houghton Mifflin Harcourt Pubg 317 359-5585
2700 N Richardt Ave Indianapolis (46219) *(G-7138)*

House of Bluez 812 401-2583
111 S Green Rver Rd Ste F Evansville (47715) *(G-3543)*

Housefield Marketing, Indianapolis Also called Omnisource Marketing Group Inc *(G-7620)*

Hovair Automotive, Franklin Also called Production Hdlg Systems Inc *(G-4924)*

Hoverstream LLC 317 489-0075
4801 Van Cleave St Indianapolis (46226) *(G-7139)*

How Pubs USA 219 933-9251
601 45th St Munster (46321) *(G-10607)*

Howard & Sons Cement Products 574 293-1906
2912 Oakland Ave Elkhart (46517) *(G-2922)*

Howard Hopkins Inc 765 827-5666
129 Fiant St Connersville (47331) *(G-2051)*

Howard Pblctions Vidette Times, Valparaiso Also called Lee Publications Inc *(G-13574)*

Howard Print Shop 765 453-6161
2111 W Alto Rd Kokomo (46902) *(G-8641)*

Howden Roots LLC (HQ) 765 827-9200
900 W Mount St Connersville (47331) *(G-2052)*

Howe House Ltd Editions Inc (PA) 765 742-6831
624 South St Lafayette (47901) *(G-8918)*

Howe Industries, Indianapolis Also called CH Ellis Co Inc *(G-6592)*

Howerton Racecar Works Inc 317 241-0868
360 Gasoline Aly Indianapolis (46222) *(G-7140)*

Howerton Racing Products, Indianapolis Also called Howerton Racecar Works Inc *(G-7140)*

Howmedica Osteonics Corp 317 587-2008
12348 Hancock St Carmel (46032) *(G-1407)*

Howmet Castings & Services Inc 219 326-7400
1110 E Lincolnway La Porte (46350) *(G-8767)*

HP Inc 317 566-6200
10201 N Illinois St # 240 Indianapolis (46290) *(G-6268)*

HP Inc 317 334-3400
7520 Georgetown Rd Indianapolis (46268) *(G-7141)*

HP Products A Ferguson Entp, Bloomington Also called H P Products Corporation *(G-736)*

Hpi Wire Assemblies, Angola Also called Hi-Pro Inc *(G-218)*

Hpp Mold & Tool, Fort Wayne Also called Hoosier Pride Plastics Inc *(G-4345)*

Hrezo Engineering, Greendale Also called Hrezo Industrial Eqp & Engrg *(G-5489)*

Hrezo Industrial Eqp & Engrg 812 537-4700
1025 Ridge Ave Greendale (47025) *(G-5489)*

Hrh Door Corp 812 479-5680
5425 Oak Grove Rd Ste J Evansville (47715) *(G-3544)*

Hrr Enterprises Inc 219 362-9050
1755 Genesis Dr La Porte (46350) *(G-8768)*

Hs Machine Welding 812 752-2825
733 W Bellevue Ave Scottsburg (47170) *(G-12361)*

Hs Processing, Butler Also called Heidtman Steel Products Inc *(G-1229)*

Hsm 317 573-8700
9525 Delegates Row Indianapolis (46240) *(G-7142)*

Hsm Eagle Ltd 812 491-9666
6149 Wedeking Ave Evansville (47715) *(G-3545)*

Ht Enterprises Inc 765 794-4174
5070 N Old State Road 55 Crawfordsville (47933) *(G-2160)*

HTI 574 722-2814
500 W Clinton St Ste 2 Logansport (46947) *(G-9337)*

Hu/Man Tech, Noblesville Also called Huver Manufacturing Tech LLC *(G-11122)*

Hub City Stl & Fabrication LLC 260 760-0370
4487 S Arba Pike Union City (47390) *(G-13457)*

Hub States Corporation 317 816-9955
112 W Carmel Dr Carmel (46032) *(G-1408)*

Hubbard & Cravens Coffee, Indianapolis Also called Suncoast Coffee Inc *(G-8018)*

Hubbard Feeds, Shipshewana Also called Ridley USA Inc *(G-12647)*

Hubbard Inc 317 535-1926
6774 N Us Highway 31 Whiteland (46184) *(G-14239)*

Hubbard Services Inc 317 881-2828
1280 Us Highway 31 N T Greenwood (46142) *(G-5704)*

Hubbard Welding 317 539-2758
10114 S County Road 100 W Clayton (46118) *(G-1707)*

Hubbell Incorporated Delaware (HQ) 574 234-7151
3902 W Sample St South Bend (46619) *(G-12806)*

Hubbell Raco Division, South Bend Also called Hubbell Incorporated Delaware *(G-12806)*

Huber Brothers Inc 317 392-1566
3955 N 100 W Shelbyville (46176) *(G-12537)*

Huber Industries, Aurora Also called Batesville Products Inc *(G-373)*

Huber Orchard Winery & Gift, Borden Also called Huber Orchards Inc *(G-930)*

Huber Orchards Inc 812 923-9463
19816 Huber Rd Borden (47106) *(G-930)*

Hubs Chub Inc 317 758-5494
2451 W 246th St Sheridan (46069) *(G-12590)*

Hubs-Chub, Sheridan Also called Hubs Chub Inc *(G-12590)*

Huckleberry Winery 317 850-4445
3057 Amber Way Bargersville (46106) *(G-483)*

Hucks Food Fuel 812 683-5566
601 N Main St Huntingburg (47542) *(G-6168)*

Hudec Construction Company 219 922-9811
148 N Ivanhoe Ct Griffith (46319) *(G-5777)*

Hudec Woodworking Company, Griffith Also called Hudec Construction Company *(G-5777)*

Hudelson Fabrication, Orleans Also called Lana Hudelson *(G-11363)*

Hudelson Sharpening & Mch Sp 812 865-3951
27 W Quarry Rd Orleans (47452) *(G-11362)*

Hudson Aquatic Systems LLC 260 665-1635
1100 Wohlert St Angola (46703) *(G-220)*

Hudson Concrete Products Inc 812 825-2917
10017 E New Ln Solsberry (47459) *(G-12685)*

Hudson Sales & Service, Solsberry Also called Hudson Concrete Products Inc *(G-12685)*

Huehls Seal Coating & Lawn Car 317 782-4069
312 E Epler Ave Indianapolis (46227) *(G-7143)*

Huelseman Printing Co 765 647-3947
9085 Bath Rd Brookville (47012) *(G-1117)*

Hugh K Eagan 574 269-5411
201 W Center St Warsaw (46580) *(G-13891)*

Hughes Paving Company Inc 812 678-2126
11907 Hwy 56 French Lick (47432) *(G-4986)*

Huhtamaki Inc 219 972-4264
6629 Indianapolis Blvd Hammond (46320) *(G-5896)*

Huhtamaki Inc 765 664-2330
1001 E 38th St Ste B Marion (46953) *(G-9532)*

Huhtamaki Foodservice, Hammond *Also called Huhtamaki Inc (G-5896)*

Hull Aircraft Support LLC 219 324-6247
602 Lakeside St La Porte (46350) *(G-8769)*

Hull Precision Machining Inc 260 238-4372
6974 State Road 1 Spencerville (46788) *(G-13048)*

Hulletts Backhoe Service, Peru *Also called Tracy K Hullett (G-11553)*

Hulman & Company (PA) 812 232-9446
900 Wabash Ave Terre Haute (47807) *(G-13250)*

Human Element Therapeutics 317 446-4062
4601 E Viola Dr Mooresville (46158) *(G-10312)*

Humes & Berg Mfg Co Inc 219 391-5880
4801 Railroad Ave East Chicago (46312) *(G-2534)*

Humphrey Printing Co 317 241-6049
2346 S Lynhurst Dr 407c Indianapolis (46241) *(G-7144)*

Humphrey Printing Company Inc 765 452-0093
1001 E Summit St Crown Point (46307) *(G-2259)*

Humphrey Tool Coinc 574 753-3853
120 Water St Logansport (46947) *(G-9338)*

Humphreys Welding Service 317 881-9024
810 Front Royal Dr Indianapolis (46227) *(G-7145)*

Huncilman Inc 812 945-3544
2072 Mcdonald Ave New Albany (47150) *(G-10800)*

Hunt and Sons Memorial LLC 317 745-0940
2655 E Main St Danville (46122) *(G-2348)*

Hunt Wesson Foods, Rensselaer *Also called Conagra Brands Inc (G-11919)*

Hunter Nutrition Inc 765 563-1003
200 Ns St Brookston (47923) *(G-1105)*

Hunter Sheep Nutrition, Brookston *Also called Hunter Nutrition Inc (G-1105)*

Hunters Ridge Winery LLC 812 967-9463
9945 E Garrison Hollow Rd Salem (47167) *(G-12293)*

Huntingburg Machine Works Inc 812 683-3531
309 N Main St Huntingburg (47542) *(G-6169)*

Huntingburg Vault Co, Huntingburg *Also called Tretter Boeglin (G-6182)*

Huntington Alloys Corporation 574 262-3451
2900 Higgins Blvd Elkhart (46514) *(G-2923)*

Huntington County Tab Inc 260 356-1107
1670 Etna Ave Huntington (46750) *(G-6211)*

Huntington Sheet Metal Inc 260 356-9011
2060 Old Us Highway 24 Huntington (46750) *(G-6212)*

Huntington Sheet Metal Inc (PA) 260 356-9011
1675 Riverfork Dr Huntington (46750) *(G-6213)*

Huntington Tool & Die Inc 260 356-5940
9 Commercial Rd Huntington (46750) *(G-6214)*

Hunts Maintenance Inc 219 785-2333
107 Greenway St Westville (46391) *(G-14218)*

Hurco Companies Inc (PA) 317 293-5309
1 Technology Way Indianapolis (46268) *(G-7146)*

Hurco Companies Inc. 317 347-6208
7220 Winton Dr Indianapolis (46268) *(G-7147)*

Hurco Usa, Inc., Indianapolis *Also called Milltronics Usa Inc (G-7523)*

Hurricane Compressor Company, Leo *Also called K Grimmer Industries Inc (G-9243)*

Hurricane Ditcher Company Inc 812 886-9663
2425 S Cathlinette Rd Vincennes (47591) *(G-13684)*

Hurst Jeff Custom Woodworking 812 367-1430
8134 S State Road 162 Ferdinand (47532) *(G-3853)*

Hurst Custom Cabinets Inc 812 683-3378
1003 S Cherry St Huntingburg (47542) *(G-6170)*

Hurst Enterprise 812 853-0901
7866 Owens Dr Newburgh (47630) *(G-11031)*

Hurst Manufacturing Division, Princeton *Also called Nidec Motor Corporation (G-11880)*

Husqvrna Cnsmr Otdr Prod NA 812 883-3575
1555 S Jackson St Salem (47167) *(G-12294)*

Hutchison Sign Co Inc 317 894-8787
215 S Munsie St Indianapolis (46229) *(G-7148)*

Huth Tool 260 749-9411
6930 Derek Dr Fort Wayne (46803) *(G-4350)*

Huth Tool & Machine Corp 260 749-9411
6930 Derek Dr Fort Wayne (46803) *(G-4351)*

Huthone LLC 260 248-2384
707 Burke St Columbia City (46725) *(G-1792)*

Huver Manufacturing Tech LLC 317 460-8605
10210 Carmine Dr Noblesville (46060) *(G-11122)*

Hux Oil Corp 812 894-2096
5451 Riley Rd Terre Haute (47802) *(G-13251)*

HWH Embroidery Inc 317 895-0201
5255 N Tacoma Ave Ste 2 Indianapolis (46220) *(G-7149)*

Hy-Flex Corporation 765 571-5125
8774 S State Road 109 Knightstown (46148) *(G-8551)*

Hy-Line Enterprises Intl Inc 574 294-1112
25369 Vernon Xing Elkhart (46514) *(G-2924)*

Hy-Line North America LLC 260 375-3041
1029 Mill Site Dr Warren (46792) *(G-13831)*

Hy-Matic Mfg Inc 260 347-3651
205 W Ohio St Kendallville (46755) *(G-8479)*

Hy-Pro Corporation 317 849-3535
6810 Layton Rd Anderson (46011) *(G-117)*

Hy-Pro Filtration, Anderson *Also called Hy-Pro Corporation (G-117)*

Hy-TEC Fiberglass Inc 260 489-6601
2201 Suppliers Ct Fort Wayne (46818) *(G-4352)*

Hy-Tech Machining Systems LLC 765 649-6852
2900 S Scatterfield Rd Anderson (46013) *(G-118)*

Hyco Machine & Mold Inc 574 522-5847
121 Rush Ct Elkhart (46516) *(G-2925)*

Hydratrend, Indianapolis *Also called Uridynamics Inc (G-8135)*

Hydraulic Press Brick Company 317 290-1140
6618 N Tidewater Rd Mooresville (46158) *(G-10313)*

Hydraulic Press Brick Company (HQ) 317 290-1140
3600 Woodview Trce # 300 Indianapolis (46268) *(G-7150)*

Hydrite Chemical Co. 812 232-5411
2400 Erie Canal Rd Terre Haute (47802) *(G-13252)*

Hydro Conduit of Texas LP 317 769-2261
4360 Whitelick Dr Whitestown (46075) *(G-14254)*

Hydro Extruder LLC 765 825-1141
5120 Western Ave Connersville (47331) *(G-2053)*

Hydro Extruder LLC 574 262-2667
3406 Reedy Dr Elkhart (46514) *(G-2926)*

Hydro Extrusion North Amer LLC 888 935-5757
400 S Main St North Liberty (46554) *(G-11215)*

Hydro Extrusion North Amer LLC 888 935-5757
400 S Main St North Liberty (46554) *(G-11216)*

Hydro Fire Protection Inc 317 780-6980
5851 S Harding St Indianapolis (46217) *(G-7151)*

Hydro Systems Mfg Inc 260 436-4476
3632 Illinois Rd Ofc Fort Wayne (46804) *(G-4353)*

Hydro-Exc Inc 219 922-9886
321 E Main St Griffith (46319) *(G-5778)*

Hydro-Gear Inc 317 821-0477
5101 Decatur Blvd Indianapolis (46241) *(G-7152)*

Hydrojet Signs 765 584-2125
707 N Co Rd 400 E Winchester (47394) *(G-14331)*

Hydrojet Signs and Fabricating, Winchester *Also called Hydrojet Signs (G-14331)*

Hymns To Go, Fishers *Also called Hymns2go LLC (G-3926)*

Hymns2go LLC 317 577-0730
10315 Stonebridge Ct Fishers (46037) *(G-3926)*

Hyndman Industrial Pdts Inc 260 483-6042
4031 Merchant Rd Ste A Fort Wayne (46818) *(G-4354)*

Hynes Kokomo LLC 330 799-3221
1817 W Defenbaugh St Kokomo (46902) *(G-8642)*

Hyperbole Creations, Madison *Also called Hyperbole Software Unltd (G-9471)*

Hyperbole Software Unltd 812 839-6635
9383 E Tate Ridge Rd Madison (47250) *(G-9471)*

Hytek Hose & Coupling Div, La Porte *Also called Terry Liquidation III Inc (G-8828)*

I A S, Peru *Also called Intech Automation Systems Corp (G-11532)*

I B P, Washington *Also called Tyson Fresh Meats Inc (G-14005)*

I C Mattresses & More LLC 765 635-7239
1525 W 1850 N Summitville (46070) *(G-13099)*

I C R, Indianapolis *Also called Innovative Chemical Resources (G-7235)*

I C S, Huntington *Also called Industrial Control Service (G-6216)*

I D I, Logansport *Also called Indiana Dimension Inc (G-9340)*

I E M C 219 464-2890
1150 Lincolnway Ste 1 Valparaiso (46385) *(G-13558)*

I E Products, Fort Wayne *Also called Ie Products Mad Dasher Inc (G-4357)*

I E Signs & Graphics LLC 574 936-4652
1221 W Garro St Plymouth (46563) *(G-11689)*

I F S Corp 317 898-6118
9433 E Washington St Indianapolis (46229) *(G-7153)*

I H C, Paoli *Also called Indiana Handle Company Inc (G-11453)*

I Hsg Inc 765 778-6499
2902 Enterprise Dr Anderson (46013) *(G-119)*

I Love Salad LLC 317 688-7512
4825 E 96th St Indianapolis (46240) *(G-7154)*

I M I, Greenfield *Also called Irving Materials Inc (G-5542)*

I M I, Washington *Also called Irving Materials Inc (G-13987)*

I M I, Springport *Also called Irving Materials Inc (G-13059)*

I M I, Bluffton *Also called Irving Materials Inc (G-880)*

I M I, Muncie *Also called Irving Materials Inc (G-10497)*

I M I, Connersville *Also called Irving Materials Inc (G-2056)*

I M I, Cambridge City *Also called Irving Materials Inc (G-1257)*

I M I, Anderson *Also called Irving Materials Inc (G-122)*

I M I, Noblesville *Also called Irving Materials Inc (G-11132)*

I M I, Noblesville *Also called Irving Materials Inc (G-11133)*

I M I, Huntingburg *Also called Irving Materials Inc (G-6172)*

I M I, Crawfordsville *Also called Irving Materials Inc (G-2163)*

I M I, Lafayette *Also called Irving Materials Inc (G-8926)*

I M I, West Lafayette *Also called Irving Materials Inc (G-14078)*
I M I, Fishers *Also called Irving Materials Inc (G-3989)*
I M I, Indianapolis *Also called Irving Materials Inc (G-7268)*
I M I, Elwood *Also called Irving Materials Inc (G-3300)*
I M I, Bedford *Also called Irving Materials Inc (G-554)*
I M I, Kokomo *Also called Irving Materials Inc (G-8649)*
I M I, Swayzee *Also called Irving Materials Inc (G-13125)*
I M I, Peru *Also called Irving Materials Inc (G-11533)*
I M I, Tipton *Also called Irving Materials Inc (G-13394)*
I M I, Marion *Also called Irving Materials Inc (G-9535)*
I M I, Bloomington *Also called Irving Materials Inc (G-751)*
I M I, Whiteland *Also called Irving Materials Inc (G-14241)*
I M I, Indianapolis *Also called Irving Materials Inc (G-7269)*
I M I, Indianapolis *Also called Irving Materials Inc (G-7270)*
I M I, Indianapolis *Also called Irving Materials Inc (G-7271)*
I M I, Logansport *Also called Irving Materials Inc (G-9342)*
I M I, Mooresville *Also called Irving Materials Inc (G-10315)*
I M I, Brookville *Also called Irving Materials Inc (G-1119)*
I M I, Huntington *Also called Irving Materials Inc (G-6219)*
I M L, Winchester *Also called Indiana Marujun LLC (G-14332)*

I N C O M Wholesale Supply 574 722-2442
2865 E Market St Logansport (46947) *(G-9339)*

I Noodles 765 447-2288
111 N Chauncey Ave West Lafayette (47906) *(G-14075)*

I P Callison & Sons, North Judson *Also called Callisons Inc (G-11208)*

I P F, Shelbyville *Also called Indiana Precision Forge LLC (G-12538)*

I Power, Anderson *Also called Ipower Technologies Inc (G-121)*

I Power Energy Systems LLC 765 621-9980
4640 Dr M L King Jr Blvd Martin Anderson (46013) *(G-120)*

I S M A Report, Indianapolis *Also called Indiana State Medical Assn (G-7192)*

I T D Inc 765 825-0151
6050 Industrial Ave N Connersville (47331) *(G-2054)*

I T Equipment, Plymouth *Also called Industrial Transmission Eqp (G-11694)*

I-69 Trailer Center, Markle *Also called Novae Corp (G-9581)*

I-Fly Drones LLC 812 524-3863
5269 E County Road 400 S Seymour (47274) *(G-12457)*

I/N Tek & I/N Kote, New Carlisle *Also called Arcelormittal Kote Inc (G-10878)*

I/N Tek LP 574 654-1000
30755 Edison Rd New Carlisle (46552) *(G-10883)*

I2r 812 235-6167
711 Hulman St Terre Haute (47802) *(G-13253)*

Iaire LLC (PA) 317 806-2750
6805 Hillsdale Ct Indianapolis (46250) *(G-7155)*

IAm Aw TI Die Makers LL 229 ....574 333-5955
2618 Lowell Ave Elkhart (46516) *(G-2927)*

Iam Petroleum Inc (PA) 260 625-9951
5126 W County Line Rd N Columbia City (46725) *(G-1793)*

Ias Corp 209 836-8610
206 N Grant St Peru (46970) *(G-11531)*

Iasa Group LLC (PA) 260 484-1322
1905 Production Rd Fort Wayne (46808) *(G-4355)*

Iasta, Carmel *Also called Determine Inc (G-1356)*

IBC Advanced Alloys, Franklin *Also called IBC US Holdings Inc (G-4898)*

IBC Advanced Alloys Copper, Franklin *Also called Nonferrous Products Inc (G-4914)*

IBC Coatings Technologies Ltd 317 418-3725
902 Hendricks Dr Lebanon (46052) *(G-9188)*

IBC Materials & Tech LLC 765 482-9802
902 Hendricks Dr Lebanon (46052) *(G-9189)*

IBC US Holdings Inc 317 738-2558
401 Arvin Rd Franklin (46131) *(G-4898)*

IBJ Book Publishing LLC 317 564-9924
11550 N Meridian St # 115 Carmel (46032) *(G-1409)*

IBJ Corporation 317 634-6200
41 E Washington St # 200 Indianapolis (46204) *(G-7156)*

Icbo, Indianapolis *Also called International Code Council Inc (G-7252)*

Ice Cream On Wheels Inc 800 884-9793
2011 N Griffith Blvd Griffith (46319) *(G-5779)*

Ice Cream Specialties Inc 765 474-2989
2600 Concord Rd Lafayette (47909) *(G-8919)*

Ice Logging LLC 312 860-0897
515 Linden Ln Chesterfield (46017) *(G-1587)*

Ice River Springs Kentland LLC 219 474-6300
306 E Bailie St Kentland (47951) *(G-8521)*

ICI Americas Inc 317 535-5626
43 N Us Highway 31 Whiteland (46184) *(G-14240)*

ICO Polymers North America Inc 219 392-3375
4404 Euclid Ave East Chicago (46312) *(G-2535)*

ICO Polymers North America Inc 219 392-3375
4404 Euclid Ave East Chicago (46312) *(G-2536)*

Icon International Inc (PA) 260 482-8700
8333 Clinton Park Dr Fort Wayne (46825) *(G-4356)*

Icon Metal Forming LLC 812 738-5900
2190 Landmark Ave Ne Corydon (47112) *(G-2102)*

Ict, Lagrange *Also called Indiana Custom Trucks LLC (G-9046)*

Ideal Archtectural Doors Plywd, New Albany *Also called Ideal Wood Products (G-10801)*

Ideal Coatings LLC 574 358-0182
11431 County Road 10 Middlebury (46540) *(G-9891)*

Ideal Inc 765 457-6222
1037 S Union St Kokomo (46902) *(G-8643)*

Ideal Janitor Supply, Kokomo *Also called Ideal Inc (G-8643)*

Ideal Pro Cnc Inc 260 693-1954
6231 N 650 E Churubusco (46723) *(G-1652)*

Ideal Sign Corp 219 406-2092
507 N 325 W Valparaiso (46385) *(G-13559)*

Ideal Wood Products 812 949-5181
890 Central Ct New Albany (47150) *(G-10801)*

Idemitsu Lubricants Amer Corp (HQ) 812 284-3300
701 Port Rd Jeffersonville (47130) *(G-8378)*

Idenitee 317 462-4606
3626 W Us Highway 40 Greenfield (46140) *(G-5537)*

Identity Logix LLC 219 379-5560
10048 Wellington Ter Munster (46321) *(G-10608)*

Identitylogix, Munster *Also called Identity Logix LLC (G-10608)*

IDI, Noblesville *Also called Industrial DIctrics Hldngs Inc (G-11128)*

IDI Composites International, Noblesville *Also called Industrial Dielectrics Inc (G-11127)*

IDI Fabrication Inc (PA) 317 776-6577
14444 Herriman Blvd Noblesville (46060) *(G-11123)*

Idp, North Webster *Also called Indiana Dimensional Pdts LLC (G-11293)*

Idra North America Inc 765 459-0085
1510 Ann St Kokomo (46901) *(G-8644)*

Idx - Louisville, Jeffersonville *Also called Horizon Terra Incorporated (G-8377)*

Idx Corporation 812 280-0000
101 River Ridge Cir Jeffersonville (47130) *(G-8379)*

Ie Products Mad Dasher Inc 260 747-0545
4410 Tielker Rd Fort Wayne (46809) *(G-4357)*

Iea Management Services Inc 765 832-8526
3900 White Ave Clinton (47842) *(G-1716)*

Iea Renewable Energy Inc 765 832-8526
3900 White Ave Clinton (47842) *(G-1717)*

Ierc, Elkhart *Also called CTS Elctrnic Cmponents Cal Inc (G-2781)*

Ies Subsidiary Holdings Inc 330 830-3500
1125 S Walnut St South Bend (46619) *(G-12807)*

Ies Subsidiary Holdings Inc 219 937-0100
1825 Summer St Hammond (46320) *(G-5897)*

Ifc Fence LLC 219 977-4000
3245 W 46th Ave Gary (46408) *(G-5067)*

Igh Steel Fabrication Inc 765 482-7534
1001 Ransdell Rd Lebanon (46052) *(G-9190)*

Iic, Granger *Also called Indiana Intgrated Circuits LLC (G-5414)*

Iis, Bloomington *Also called Inari Information Services (G-743)*

Ijs Custom Printing LLC 219 769-2050
2023 W 75th Pl Unit 33 Merrillville (46410) *(G-9721)*

Ike Newton LLC 317 902-1772
949 Fry Rd Greenwood (46142) *(G-5705)*

Ikelite Underwater Systems, Indianapolis *Also called Divers Supply Company Inc (G-6745)*

Ikio Led Lighting LLC 765 414-0835
8470 Allison Pointe Blvd # 128 Indianapolis (46250) *(G-7157)*

IKON Group 574 326-3661
330 E Windsor Ave Elkhart (46514) *(G-2928)*

Ilab LLC 317 218-3258
111 Monument Cir Ste 882 Indianapolis (46204) *(G-7158)*

Ilf Industries 260 749-1931
9702 Greenmoor Dr New Haven (46774) *(G-10944)*

Illiana Grinding Machining Inc 219 884-5828
5341 Broadway Merrillville (46410) *(G-9722)*

Illiana Remedial Action Inc 219 844-4862
6550 Osborne Ave Hammond (46320) *(G-5898)*

Illiana Steel Inc 219 397-3250
4407 Railroad Ave East Chicago (46312) *(G-2537)*

Illiana Storage & Processing, East Chicago *Also called Illiana Steel Inc (G-2537)*

Illinois Lubricants LLC 260 436-2444
1300 Arprt N Off Park Ste Fort Wayne (46825) *(G-4358)*

Illinois Precision, Bicknell *Also called Hermetic Coil Co Inc (G-632)*

Illinois Tool Works Inc 317 390-5940
7130 W Mccarty St Indianapolis (46241) *(G-7159)*

Illinois Tool Works Inc 317 298-5000
4141 W 54th St Indianapolis (46254) *(G-7160)*

Illinois Tool Works Inc 219 874-4217
1919 E Us Highway 12 Michigan City (46360) *(G-9803)*

Illinois Tool Works Inc 260 347-8040
2720 Marion Dr Kendallville (46755) *(G-8480)*

Illuminated Image, Angola *Also called Lomont Holdings Co Inc (G-228)*

Ilpea Industries Inc (HQ) 812 752-2526
745 S Gardner St Scottsburg (47170) *(G-12362)*

Ilpea Industries Inc 812 752-2526
745 S Gardner St Scottsburg (47170) *(G-12363)*

Ilpea Industries Inc 812 752-2526
2500 Lynch Rd Evansville (47711) *(G-3546)*

IM Impressed 219 838-7959
9540 Fran Lin Pkwy Munster (46321) *(G-10609)*

Im Indiana Holdings Inc 260 478-1674
6300 Ardmore Ave Fort Wayne (46809) *(G-4359)*

Image Builders/Rowland Prtg, Noblesville Also called Rowland Printing Co Inc **(G-11177)**

Image Concepts Inc 317 408-5558
6215 Buttonwood Dr Noblesville (46062) **(G-11124)**

Image Group Inc 574 457-3111
4598 E 1200 N Syracuse (46567) **(G-13135)**

Image House Inc 219 947-0800
1001 E Summit St Crown Point (46307) **(G-2260)**

Image Inks Company 317 432-5041
7363 Red Rock Rd Indianapolis (46236) **(G-7161)**

Image Manufacturing, Connersville Also called Howard Hopkins Inc **(G-2051)**

Image One LLC (PA) 317 576-2700
11899 Exit 5 Pkwy Fishers (46037) **(G-3927)**

Image Vault LLC 812 948-8400
101 Security Pkwy New Albany (47150) **(G-10802)**

Imagination Graphics 812 423-6503
2323 W Franklin St Evansville (47712) **(G-3547)**

Imagination Publications LLC 574 256-6666
203 N Main St Mishawaka (46544) **(G-10052)**

Imagine Industries LLC 260 494-6530
525 Victoria Station Way Fort Wayne (46814) **(G-4360)**

Imagineering Enterprises Inc 574 287-0642
3722 Foundation Ct South Bend (46628) **(G-12808)**

Imagineering Enterprises Inc (PA) 574 287-2941
1302 W Sample St South Bend (46619) **(G-12809)**

Imagineering Enterprises Inc 317 635-8565
2719 N Emerson Ave Ste A Indianapolis (46218) **(G-7162)**

Imagineering Finishing Tech, South Bend Also called Imagineering Enterprises Inc **(G-12808)**

Imagineering Finishing Tech, South Bend Also called Imagineering Enterprises Inc **(G-12809)**

Imaj Data Company, Indianapolis Also called RPI Consultants LLC **(G-7868)**

IMC, Indianapolis Also called Indiana Model Company Inc **(G-7184)**

Imco Industrial Machine Corp 219 663-6100
1201 S Main St Crown Point (46307) **(G-2261)**

IMD, Warsaw Also called Instrumental Machine & Dev Inc **(G-13893)**

Imerys Steelcasting Usa Inc 219 921-1012
620 E Us Highway 6 Westville (46391) **(G-14219)**

Imh Fabrication Inc (PA) 317 252-5566
1121 E 46th St Indianapolis (46205) **(G-7163)**

Imh Fabrication Inc 317 252-5566
2073 Dr Andrew J Brown Indianapolis (46202) **(G-7164)**

Imh Products, Indianapolis Also called Imh Fabrication Inc **(G-7163)**

IMI Bloomfield 812 384-0045
9 E Judson St Bloomfield (47424) **(G-639)**

IMI Irving Material, Greenwood Also called Irving Materials Inc **(G-5708)**

IMI South LLC 812 945-6605
1732 Lincoln Ave New Albany (47150) **(G-10803)**

IMI South LLC 812 273-1428
3650 N Hwy 7 Madison (47250) **(G-9472)**

IMI South LLC 812 738-4173
3060 Cline Rd Nw Corydon (47112) **(G-2103)**

IMI South LLC 812 284-9732
1221 Highway 31 E Clarksville (47129) **(G-1686)**

IMI Southwest Inc (HQ) 812 424-3554
1816 W Lloyd Expy Evansville (47712) **(G-3548)**

Imine Corporation 877 464-6388
8520 Allison Pointe Blvd Indianapolis (46250) **(G-7165)**

Immi, Westfield Also called Indiana Mills & Manufacturing **(G-14169)**

Imminent Software Inc 317 340-4562
6575 Brauer Ln Carmel (46033) **(G-1410)**

Immunores-Therapeutics LLC 860 514-0526
Noyes Pavillion 5th Fl E Indianapolis (46202) **(G-7166)**

Impact, Frankfort Also called Co-Alliance LLP **(G-4822)**

Impact Cnc LLC (PA) 260 244-5511
1380 S Williams Dr Columbia City (46725) **(G-1794)**

Impact Forge Group LLC (HQ) 812 342-4437
2805 Norcross Dr Columbus (47201) **(G-1944)**

Impact Forge Group LLC 812 342-5527
2705 Norcross Dr Columbus (47201) **(G-1945)**

Impact Forge Group LLC 219 261-2115
18325 S 580 W Remington (47977) **(G-11907)**

Impact Safety Inc 317 852-3067
7991 W 21st St Ste D1 Indianapolis (46214) **(G-7167)**

Impact Trailers 574 322-4369
4607 Wyland Dr Elkhart (46516) **(G-2929)**

Imperial Designs 765 985-2712
6599 N State Road 19 Denver (46926) **(G-2454)**

Imperial Fabrics, Nappanee Also called Ascot Enterprises Inc **(G-10648)**

Imperial Marble Incorporated 812 752-5384
325 W Lovers Ln Scottsburg (47170) **(G-12364)**

Imperial Petroleum Inc (PA) 812 867-1433
11600 German Pines Dr Evansville (47725) **(G-3549)**

Imperial Products LLC 765 966-0322
451 Industrial Pkwy Richmond (47374) **(G-12001)**

Imperial Stamping Company, Elkhart Also called Imperial Stamping Corporation **(G-2930)**

Imperial Stamping Corporation 574 294-3780
4801 Middlebury St Elkhart (46516) **(G-2930)**

Imperial Trophy & Awards Co 260 432-8161
2405 W Jefferson Blvd Fort Wayne (46802) **(G-4361)**

Impression Printing 765 342-6977
389 E Walnut St Martinsville (46151) **(G-9614)**

Impressions LLC 765 490-2575
3007 1/2 Kossuth St Lafayette (47904) **(G-8920)**

Impressions That Count Inc 317 423-0581
917 Greer St Indianapolis (46203) **(G-7168)**

Impressive Printing 812 913-1101
515 E Daisy Ln New Albany (47150) **(G-10804)**

Impressive Stamping & Mfg Co 260 824-2610
1690 E 250 N Bluffton (46714) **(G-878)**

Imprint It All 812 234-0024
1419 S 25th St Terre Haute (47803) **(G-13254)**

IMS, East Chicago Also called Tms International LLC **(G-2571)**

Imw, Kingsbury Also called Industrial Mint Wldg Machining **(G-8539)**

In Business For Life Inc 317 691-6169
12400 N Meridian St # 150 Carmel (46032) **(G-1411)**

In Ductile LLC 317 776-8000
1600 S 8th St Noblesville (46060) **(G-11125)**

In Line Industries, La Porte Also called Kenco Plastics Inc **(G-8779)**

In Space LLC 765 775-2107
3495 Kent Ave Ste G100 West Lafayette (47906) **(G-14076)**

In The Spotlight LLC 260 519-1805
3106 E 1450 N North Manchester (46962) **(G-11231)**

In, Technology Center, Indianapolis Also called General Cable Industries Inc **(G-6994)**

In-Fab Inc 812 279-8144
2030 John Williams Blvd Bedford (47421) **(G-549)**

In-Print 219 956-3001
886 E 900 N Wheatfield (46392) **(G-14225)**

Inari Information Services 812 331-2298
804 N College Ave Ste 101 Bloomington (47404) **(G-743)**

Incense Incense 317 544-9444
256 Canal West Cir Danville (46122) **(G-2349)**

Inchromatics LLC 317 872-7401
1545 Trace Ln Indianapolis (46260) **(G-7169)**

Indalex Inc 765 457-1117
1500 E Murden St Kokomo (46901) **(G-8645)**

Indco Inc 812 945-4383
4040 Earnings Way New Albany (47150) **(G-10805)**

Independent Cabinets 502 594-6026
12910 Highway 60 Memphis (47143) **(G-9683)**

Independent Concrete Pipe Co (PA) 419 841-3361
2050 S Harding St Indianapolis (46221) **(G-7170)**

Independent Concrete Pipe Co 800 875-4920
2050 S Harding St Indianapolis (46221) **(G-7171)**

Independent Concrete Pipe Co 317 262-4920
2050 S Harding St Indianapolis (46221) **(G-7172)**

Independent Concrete Pipe Co 317 262-4920
2050 S Harding St Indianapolis (46221) **(G-7173)**

Independent Concrete Pipe Co 317 262-4920
2050 S Harding St Indianapolis (46221) **(G-7174)**

Independent Concrete Pipe Co 317 326-2600
8 E Junction St Maxwell (46154) **(G-9661)**

Independent Limestone Co LLC 812 824-4951
6001 S Rockport Rd Bloomington (47403) **(G-744)**

Independent Protection Co Inc (PA) 574 533-4116
1607 S Main St Goshen (46526) **(G-5242)**

Independent Protection Co Inc 574 533-4116
1607 S Main St Goshen (46526) **(G-5243)**

Independent Protection Co Inc 574 831-5680
67895 Industrial Dr New Paris (46553) **(G-10985)**

Independent Rail Corporation 317 780-8480
6233 Brookville Rd Indianapolis (46219) **(G-7175)**

Independent Water Tech, Carmel Also called Canature Watergroup Usa Inc **(G-1327)**

Indian Creek Outdoor Power LLC 812 597-3055
320 E State Road 135 Morgantown (46160) **(G-10354)**

Indian Creek Quarries LLC 812 388-5622
12587 Mount Olive Rd Williams (47470) **(G-14282)**

Indian Industries Inc (HQ) 812 467-1200
817 Maxwell Ave Evansville (47711) **(G-3550)**

Indiana Aircraft Hardware Co 317 485-6500
221 S Main St Fortville (46040) **(G-4780)**

Indiana American Water Company, Crawfordsville Also called American Water Works Co Inc **(G-2133)**

Indiana Architectural Plywood (PA) 317 878-4822
750 E Park St Trafalgar (46181) **(G-13436)**

Indiana Artisan Inc 317 607-8715
203 Surrey Hl Noblesville (46062) **(G-11126)**

Indiana Automotive Fas Inc 317 467-0100
1300 Anderson Blvd Greenfield (46140) **(G-5538)**

Indiana Baking Co 260 483-5997
5109 Executive Blvd Fort Wayne (46808) **(G-4362)**

Indiana Barrier Wall LLC 260 747-5777
7107 Smith Rd Fort Wayne (46809) **(G-4363)**

Indiana Baton Twirling Assoc 317 769-6826
6920 S 280 E Lebanon (46052) **(G-9191)**

Indiana Bevel Inc 317 596-0001
8605 South St Fishers (46038) **(G-3928)**

Indiana Botanic Gardens Inc 219 947-4040
  3401 W 37th Ave Hobart (46342) *(G-6081)*
Indiana Bottle Company Inc (PA) 812 752-8700
  300 W Lovers Ln Scottsburg (47170) *(G-12365)*
Indiana Box Company (HQ) 260 356-9660
  1200 Riverfork Dr Huntington (46750) *(G-6215)*
Indiana Box Company 317 462-7743
  2200 Royal Dr Greenfield (46140) *(G-5539)*
Indiana Bridge-Midwest Stl Inc 765 288-1985
  1810 S Macedonia Ave Muncie (47302) *(G-10493)*
Indiana Business Magazine 317 692-1200
  1100 Waterway Blvd Indianapolis (46202) *(G-7176)*
Indiana Cardinal, Evansville Also called Martin Holding Company LLC *(G-3614)*
Indiana Carton Company Inc 574 546-3848
  1721 W Bike St Bremen (46506) *(G-1004)*
Indiana City Brewing LLC 317 643-1103
  24 Shelby St Indianapolis (46202) *(G-7177)*
Indiana Coatings Division, Fort Wayne Also called Crown Group Co *(G-4190)*
Indiana Concession Supply LLC 317 353-1667
  2402 N Shadeland Ave R Indianapolis (46219) *(G-7178)*
Indiana Custom Embroidery, Indianapolis Also called Profit Finders Incorporated *(G-7773)*
Indiana Custom Machining, Columbus Also called Pamela S Taulman *(G-1990)*
Indiana Custom Trucks LLC (PA) 260 463-3244
  2840 N State Road 9 2 Lagrange (46761) *(G-9046)*
Indiana Cut Stone Inc 812 275-0264
  616 Guthrie Rd Bedford (47421) *(G-550)*
Indiana Daily Student, Bloomington Also called Trustees Indiana University *(G-846)*
Indiana Dimension Inc 574 739-2319
  1621 W Market St Logansport (46947) *(G-9340)*
Indiana Dimensional Pdts LLC 574 834-7681
  7224 N State Road 13 North Webster (46555) *(G-11293)*
Indiana Division, Whiteland Also called Cellofoam North America Inc *(G-14235)*
Indiana Division, Indianapolis Also called Independent Concrete Pipe Co *(G-7174)*
Indiana Division, South Bend Also called Abtrex Industries Inc *(G-12693)*
Indiana Drilling Company Inc (PA) 812 477-1575
  1410 N Cullen Ave Evansville (47715) *(G-3551)*
Indiana Ductile, Noblesville Also called In Ductile LLC *(G-11125)*
Indiana Fabric Solutions Inc 812 279-0255
  1350 9th St Bedford (47421) *(G-551)*
Indiana Factory Outlet Marine 260 799-4764
  3450 S 1100 W-57 Larwill (46764) *(G-9122)*
Indiana Fan & Fabrication, Indianapolis Also called Horner Industrial Services Inc *(G-7129)*
Indiana Fiber Works 317 524-5711
  625 E 11th St Indianapolis (46202) *(G-7179)*
Indiana Fine Blanking, Knox Also called Mpi Products LLC *(G-8575)*
Indiana Fine Blanking 574 772-3850
  1200 Kloeckner Dr Knox (46534) *(G-8568)*
Indiana Flame Service 219 787-7129
  250 W Us Highway 12 Chesterton (46304) *(G-1613)*
Indiana Furniture Inds Inc 812 678-2396
  4897 E 45 N Dubois (47527) *(G-2476)*
Indiana Galvanizing LLC 574 822-9102
  51702 Lovejoy Dr Middlebury (46540) *(G-9892)*
Indiana Gratings Inc 765 342-7191
  210 W Douglas St Martinsville (46151) *(G-9615)*
Indiana Hand Piece Repair 260 436-0765
  9530 Old Grist Mill Pl Fort Wayne (46835) *(G-4364)*
Indiana Handle Company Inc 812 723-3159
  1514 W Main St Paoli (47454) *(G-11453)*
Indiana Harbor Coke Company LP 219 397-5769
  3210 Watling St East Chicago (46312) *(G-2538)*
Indiana Hardwood Specialists 812 829-4866
  4341 N Us Highway 231 Spencer (47460) *(G-13028)*
Indiana Heat Transfer Corp. 574 936-3171
  500 W Harrison St Plymouth (46563) *(G-11690)*
Indiana Imprint LLC 812 704-2773
  3006 Bishop Rd Jeffersonville (47130) *(G-8380)*
Indiana Industrial Svcs LLC (PA) 317 769-6099
  5294 Performance Way Whitestown (46075) *(G-14255)*
Indiana Instruments Inc 317 875-8032
  8032 Gordon Dr Indianapolis (46278) *(G-7180)*
Indiana Integrated Circuits In 574 217-4612
  1400 E Angela Blvd South Bend (46617) *(G-12810)*
Indiana Interstate Entps LLC 260 463-8100
  1695 E Us Highway 20 Lagrange (46761) *(G-9047)*
Indiana Intgrated Circuits LLC 724 244-4560
  14659 Horseshoe Bend Ct Granger (46530) *(G-5414)*
Indiana Knitwear Corporation (PA) 317 462-4413
  230 E Osage St Greenfield (46140) *(G-5540)*
Indiana KY III Interstate Qua 812 985-9966
  6508 Uebelhack Rd Mount Vernon (47620) *(G-10395)*
Indiana Laser Spine Center 317 577-1800
  8202 Clearvista Pkwy 9e Indianapolis (46256) *(G-7181)*
Indiana Letterpress LLC 574 967-0154
  315 S Sycamore St Flora (46929) *(G-3997)*
Indiana Limestone Company, Bloomington Also called Indiana Lmstone Acqisition LLC *(G-745)*

Indiana Lmstone Acqisition LLC 812 275-3341
  123 S College Ave Bloomington (47404) *(G-745)*
Indiana Logging Company Corp 765 523-2616
  8228 S 350 E Lafayette (47909) *(G-8921)*
Indiana Logo Sign Group 800 950-1093
  600 E 96th St Ste 460 Indianapolis (46240) *(G-7182)*
Indiana Lumber Inc. 812 837-9493
  8215 S State Road 446 Bloomington (47401) *(G-746)*
Indiana Manufacturing Inst 765 494-4935
  1105 Challenger Ave West Lafayette (47906) *(G-14077)*
Indiana Marine Products, Angola Also called Patrick Industries Inc *(G-235)*
Indiana Marujun LLC 765 584-7639
  200 Inks Dr Winchester (47394) *(G-14332)*
Indiana Materials Proc LLC 260 244-6026
  5750 E Rail Connect Dr Columbia City (46725) *(G-1795)*
Indiana Metal Craft Inc 812 336-2362
  4602 W Innovation Dr Bloomington (47404) *(G-747)*
Indiana Metal Stamping Co 574 936-2964
  500 W Harrison St Plymouth (46563) *(G-11691)*
Indiana Metal Treating Inc 317 636-2421
  512 S Harding St Indianapolis (46221) *(G-7183)*
Indiana Micro Met Etching Inc 574 293-3342
  4615 Wyland Dr Elkhart (46516) *(G-2931)*
Indiana Mills & Manufacturing (PA) 317 896-9531
  18881 Immi Way Westfield (46074) *(G-14169)*
Indiana Model Company Inc 317 787-6358
  6136 E Hanna Ave Indianapolis (46203) *(G-7184)*
Indiana Nanotech LLC 317 385-1578
  7750 Centerstone Dr Indianapolis (46259) *(G-7185)*
Indiana News Media LLC 812 546-4940
  645 Harrison St Hope (47246) *(G-6116)*
Indiana Newspapers LLC (HQ) 317 444-4000
  130 S Meridian St Indianapolis (46225) *(G-7186)*
Indiana Newspapers LLC 812 886-9955
  702 Main St Vincennes (47591) *(G-13685)*
Indiana Newspapers LLC 317 444-3800
  8278 Georgetown Rd Indianapolis (46268) *(G-7187)*
Indiana Newspapers LLC 765 213-5700
  345 S High St Muncie (47305) *(G-10494)*
Indiana Ordnance Works Inc (PA) 812 256-4478
  11020 E Fitzpatrick Ln Pekin (47165) *(G-11474)*
Indiana Oxide Corporation 812 446-2525
  10665 N State Road 59 Brazil (47834) *(G-965)*
Indiana Oxygen Company Inc (PA) 317 290-0003
  6099 Corporate Way Indianapolis (46278) *(G-7188)*
Indiana Oxygen Company Inc 765 662-8700
  2215 S Western Ave Marion (46953) *(G-9533)*
Indiana Packers Corporation (HQ) 765 564-3680
  Hwy 421 S & Cr 100 N Delphi (46923) *(G-2422)*
Indiana Pallet Co Inc 219 398-4223
  724 E Chicago Ave East Chicago (46312) *(G-2539)*
Indiana Petroleum Contractors (PA) 812 477-1575
  1410 N Cullen Ave Evansville (47715) *(G-3552)*
Indiana Phoenix Inc. 260 897-4397
  200 Dekko Dr Avilla (46710) *(G-406)*
Indiana Pickle Company LLC 317 698-7292
  8434 Silverado Dr Indianapolis (46237) *(G-7189)*
Indiana Plastics Inc 574 294-3253
  2221 Industrial Pkwy Elkhart (46516) *(G-2932)*
Indiana Precast Inc. 812 372-7771
  895 Jonesville Rd Columbus (47201) *(G-1946)*
Indiana Precision Forge LLC 317 421-0102
  302 Northbrook Dr Shelbyville (46176) *(G-12538)*
Indiana Precision Plastics Inc 765 762-2452
  701 State Road 28 E Williamsport (47993) *(G-14292)*
Indiana Precision Tooling Inc 812 667-5141
  4233 S Farmers Retreat Rd Dillsboro (47018) *(G-2468)*
Indiana Quarriers & Carvers 812 935-8383
  8383 N Stinesville Rd Gosport (47433) *(G-5351)*
Indiana Refractories Inc 260 426-3286
  1815 S Anthony Blvd Fort Wayne (46803) *(G-4365)*
Indiana Research Institute (PA) 812 378-4221
  4571 N Long Rd Columbus (47203) *(G-1947)*
Indiana Research Institute 812 378-5363
  1402 Hutchins Ave Columbus (47201) *(G-1948)*
Indiana Review, Bloomington Also called Trustees Indiana University *(G-847)*
Indiana Ribbon Inc (PA) 219 279-2112
  106 N 2nd St Wolcott (47995) *(G-14365)*
Indiana Ribbon Inc. 219 279-2112
  106 N 2nd St Wolcott (47995) *(G-14366)*
Indiana Rug Company 574 252-4653
  900 Cleveland St Mishawaka (46544) *(G-10053)*
Indiana Scale Company Inc 812 232-0893
  1607 Maple Ave Terre Haute (47804) *(G-13255)*
Indiana Seal 317 841-3547
  9329 Castlegate Dr Indianapolis (46256) *(G-7190)*
Indiana Section of Pga of Amer 317 738-9696
  2625 Hurricane Rd Franklin (46131) *(G-4899)*
Indiana Sign & Barricade Inc 317 377-8000
  5240 E 25th St Indianapolis (46218) *(G-7191)*

Indiana Skydiving Center.................................765 659-5557
  3009 W State Road 28 Frankfort (46041) *(G-4837)*

Indiana Southern Hardwoods.......................812 326-2053
  2739 S Saint Anthony Rd W Huntingburg (47542) *(G-6171)*

Indiana Southern Millwork Inc (PA)................812 346-6129
  819 Buckeye St North Vernon (47265) *(G-11263)*

Indiana Southern Mold Corp..........................812 346-2622
  2945 N State Highway 3 North Vernon (47265) *(G-11264)*

Indiana Southern TI & Engrg Co....................812 967-2714
  21718 Martinsburg Rd Borden (47106) *(G-931)*

Indiana Spray Foam.......................................219 696-6100
  17958 Grant Pl Unit A Lowell (46356) *(G-9408)*

Indiana Stamp Co Inc (PA)............................260 424-8973
  1319 Production Rd Fort Wayne (46808) *(G-4366)*

Indiana Standards Laboratory, Indianapolis *Also called Chance Indiana Standards Lab (G-6593)*

Indiana State Medical Assn...........................317 261-2060
  322 Canal Walk Ste Cl Indianapolis (46202) *(G-7192)*

Indiana Steel & Engrg Inc (PA)......................812 275-3363
  957 J St Bedford (47421) *(G-552)*

Indiana Steel and Tube, Brownstown *Also called E & H Tubing Inc (G-1187)*

Indiana Steel Fabricating Inc (PA)................317 247-4545
  4545 W Bradbury Ave Indianapolis (46241) *(G-7193)*

Indiana Steel Fabricating Inc........................765 742-1031
  925 S 1st St Lafayette (47905) *(G-8922)*

Indiana Steel Rule & Die, Indianapolis *Also called Indiana Steel Rule Die Inc (G-7194)*

Indiana Steel Rule Die Inc............................317 352-9859
  6331 English Ave Indianapolis (46219) *(G-7194)*

Indiana Stone Works.....................................812 279-0448
  11438 Us Highway 50 W Bedford (47421) *(G-553)*

Indiana Technology and Manufac..................574 936-2112
  6100 Michigan Rd Plymouth (46563) *(G-11692)*

Indiana Thermal Solutions LLC....................317 570-5400
  6872 Hillsdale Ct # 375 Indianapolis (46250) *(G-7195)*

Indiana Ticket Company, Muncie *Also called Muncie Novelty Company Inc (G-10532)*

Indiana Tool & Mfg Co Inc.............................574 936-5548
  6100 Michigan Rd Plymouth (46563) *(G-11693)*

Indiana Tool Inc...765 825-7117
  6260 Industrial Ave N Connersville (47331) *(G-2055)*

Indiana Town Planner LLC............................219 384-3555
  7654 Starling Dr Schererville (46375) *(G-12324)*

Indiana Truss Co LLC....................................812 522-5929
  860 F Ave E Seymour (47274) *(G-12458)*

Indiana Tube Corporation (HQ).....................812 467-7155
  2100 Lexington Rd Evansville (47720) *(G-3553)*

Indiana U Bolts Inc.......................................317 870-1940
  300 E Railroad St Waterloo (46793) *(G-14015)*

Indiana University Bloomington....................812 855-2816
  1215 E Atwater Ave Bloomington (47401) *(G-748)*

Indiana Vac-Form...574 269-1725
  2030 N Boeing Rd Warsaw (46582) *(G-13892)*

Indiana Veco Manufacturing.........................765 932-2858
  1104 N Fort Wayne Rd Rushville (46173) *(G-12223)*

Indiana Veneer, Montpelier *Also called FBN Corporation (G-10291)*

Indiana Veneers Corp (PA)............................317 926-2458
  1121 E 24th St Indianapolis (46205) *(G-7196)*

Indiana Whiskey Co.......................................574 339-1737
  1115 W Sample St South Bend (46619) *(G-12811)*

Indiana Wholesale Wine Lq Co......................317 667-0231
  1240 Brookville Way Ste 1 Indianapolis (46239) *(G-7197)*

Indiana Wire Assembly, Hamilton *Also called E M F Corp (G-5821)*

Indiana Wire Die Co, Huntington *Also called Royer Enterprises Inc (G-6245)*

Indiana Wire Products Inc............................812 663-7441
  915 N Ireland St Greensburg (47240) *(G-5615)*

Indiana Wood Products Inc..........................574 825-2129
  58228 County Road 43 Middlebury (46540) *(G-9893)*

Indianapolis - Pipe, Indianapolis *Also called Cemex Materials LLC (G-6576)*

Indianapolis Badge Name Plate, Indianapolis *Also called Crichlow Industries Inc (G-6692)*

Indianapolis Business Journal, Indianapolis *Also called IBJ Corporation (G-7156)*

Indianapolis Division, Indianapolis *Also called Southwark Metal Mfg Co (G-7965)*

Indianapolis Drum Service, Indianapolis *Also called Container Life Cycle MGT LLC (G-6653)*

Indianapolis Fabrications LLC......................317 600-3522
  1125 Brookside Ave G50 Indianapolis (46202) *(G-7198)*

Indianapolis Gatorade..................................317 821-6400
  5858 Decatur Blvd Indianapolis (46241) *(G-7199)*

Indianapolis Granite & MBL Inc....................317 259-4478
  5360 Winthrop Ave Indianapolis (46220) *(G-7200)*

Indianapolis I&I, Indianapolis *Also called Paragon Medical Inc (G-7654)*

Indianapolis Industrial Pdts.........................317 359-3078
  2320 Duke St Indianapolis (46205) *(G-7201)*

Indianapolis Marine Co.................................317 545-4646
  4979 Massachusetts Ave Indianapolis (46218) *(G-7202)*

Indianapolis Metal Spinning Co....................317 273-7440
  1924 Midwest Blvd Indianapolis (46214) *(G-7203)*

Indianapolis Recorder, Indianapolis *Also called George P Stewart Printing Co (G-7002)*

Indianapolis Rubber Stamp Co......................317 263-9540
  955 N Pennsylvania St Indianapolis (46204) *(G-7204)*

Indianapolis Scale Company........................317 856-6606
  3619 N 500 E Lafayette (47905) *(G-8923)*

Indianapolis Signworks Inc...........................317 872-8722
  5349 W 86th St Indianapolis (46268) *(G-7205)*

Indianapolis Star, Indianapolis *Also called Indiana Newspapers LLC (G-7187)*

Indianapolis Star, The, Indianapolis *Also called Indiana Newspapers LLC (G-7186)*

Indianapolis Thermal Proc, Indianapolis *Also called Honeycomb Products Inc (G-7115)*

Indianapolis Wdwkg Intl LLC........................317 841-7800
  9160 Ford Cir Fishers (46038) *(G-3929)*

Indianapolis Welding Co, Indianapolis *Also called Christie Machine Works Co Inc (G-6603)*

Indianapolis, In Plant, Indianapolis *Also called General Cable Industries Inc (G-6993)*

Indianian Wood Crafts, Walkerton *Also called Indianian Woodcrafts (G-13803)*

Indianian Woodcrafts...................................574 586-3741
  72099 Spruce Rd Walkerton (46574) *(G-13803)*

Indierail, Indianapolis *Also called Independent Rail Corporation (G-7175)*

Indigo Bioautomation Inc.............................317 493-2400
  385 W City Center Dr # 200 Carmel (46032) *(G-1412)*

Indigo Printing & Graphics...........................260 432-1320
  15732 Golden Eagle Cv Huntertown (46748) *(G-6140)*

Indilabel LLC...317 839-8814
  2198 Reeves Rd Ste 4c Plainfield (46168) *(G-11616)*

Individual Mausoleum Co, Aurora *Also called Superior Vault Co Inc (G-391)*

Induction Iron Incorporated.........................813 969-3300
  403 N 7th Ave Evansville (47710) *(G-3554)*

Indus LLC (PA)...502 553-1770
  3050 Autumn Hill Trl New Albany (47150) *(G-10806)*

Industrial Adhesives Indiana........................317 271-2100
  8202 Indy Ln Indianapolis (46214) *(G-7206)*

Industrial Anodizing Co Inc..........................317 637-4641
  1610 W Washington St Indianapolis (46222) *(G-7207)*

Industrial Axle Company LLC........................574 294-6651
  21611 Protecta Dr Elkhart (46516) *(G-2933)*

Industrial Axle Company LLC (HQ)................574 295-6077
  21608 Protecta Dr Elkhart (46516) *(G-2934)*

Industrial Combustion Engnrs, Gary *Also called Industrial Combustn Engineers (G-5068)*

Industrial Combustn Engineers.....................219 949-5066
  7000 W 21st Ave Gary (46406) *(G-5068)*

Industrial Conductor Products......................219 662-9477
  10172 Florida Ln Crown Point (46307) *(G-2262)*

Industrial Control Service.............................260 356-4698
  1321 W Park Dr Huntington (46750) *(G-6216)*

Industrial Contrs Shtmtl Div, Evansville *Also called Industrial Contrs Skanska Inc (G-3555)*

Industrial Contrs Skanska Inc......................812 423-7832
  1001 Mount Auburn Rd Evansville (47720) *(G-3555)*

Industrial Dielectrics Inc.............................317 773-1766
  407 S 7th St Noblesville (46060) *(G-11127)*

Industrial Division, Geneva *Also called Elkhart Products Corporation (G-5135)*

Industrial Dlctrics Hldngs Inc (PA)................317 773-1766
  407 S 7th St Noblesville (46060) *(G-11128)*

Industrial Elec Maint Co, Valparaiso *Also called I E M C (G-13558)*

Industrial Engineering Inc............................260 478-1514
  4430 Tielker Rd Fort Wayne (46809) *(G-4367)*

Industrial Engineering NC, Fort Wayne *Also called Industrial Engineering Inc (G-4367)*

Industrial Graphic Design.............................260 856-2110
  203 Industrial Dr Cromwell (46732) *(G-2209)*

Industrial Hydraulics Inc..............................317 247-4421
  1005 Western Dr Indianapolis (46241) *(G-7208)*

Industrial Lumber Products Inc....................219 324-7697
  251 N State Road 39 La Porte (46350) *(G-8770)*

Industrial Machine......................................812 547-5656
  1645 Main St Tell City (47586) *(G-13164)*

Industrial Machine & Tool, New Albany *Also called Bryant Industries Inc (G-10755)*

Industrial Maint Engrg Inc............................812 466-5478
  5350 N 13th St Terre Haute (47805) *(G-13256)*

Industrial Metal Products Inc.......................260 447-7900
  4519 Allen Martin Dr Fort Wayne (46806) *(G-4368)*

Industrial Metal-Fab Inc..............................574 288-8368
  2806 W Sample St South Bend (46619) *(G-12812)*

Industrial Mint Wldg Machining (PA)..............219 393-5531
  2nd & Hupp Rd Kingsbury (46345) *(G-8539)*

Industrial Motor & Tool LLC..........................574 534-8282
  60282 County Road 21 Goshen (46528) *(G-5244)*

Industrial Organic Inks Inc...........................219 878-0613
  1608 Fox Point Dr Chesterton (46304) *(G-1614)*

Industrial Pallet, Clarks Hill *Also called American Fibertech Corporation (G-1670)*

Industrial Pallet Corporation........................574 583-4800
  5091 S Stone Dr Monticello (47960) *(G-10266)*

Industrial Pattern Works Inc.........................219 362-4547
  119 Koomler Dr La Porte (46350) *(G-8771)*

Industrial Plastics Group LLC.......................812 831-4053
  911 E Virginia St Evansville (47711) *(G-3556)*

Industrial Plating Inc...................................765 447-5036
  120 N 36th St Lafayette (47905) *(G-8924)*

Industrial Rep Inc..260 316-4973
  1184 E State Road 120 Fremont (46737) *(G-4962)*

Industrial Research Inc................................812 401-2333
  510 Dresden St Evansville (47710) *(G-3557)*

Industrial Sales & Supply Inc 317 240-0560
5640 Professional Cir Indianapolis (46241) ***(G-7209)***
Industrial Services Co, Evansville *Also called Van Zandt Enterprises Inc* ***(G-3792)***
Industrial Services Group Inc 317 334-0921
6450 Guion Rd Indianapolis (46268) ***(G-7210)***
Industrial Sewing Machine Co 812 425-2255
2750 N Burkhardt Rd # 107 Evansville (47715) ***(G-3558)***
Industrial Software LLC 317 862-0650
7657 Stones River Ct Indianapolis (46259) ***(G-7211)***
Industrial Steel Cnstr Inc 219 885-5610
86 N Bridge St Gary (46404) ***(G-5069)***
Industrial Steel Co Division, Elkhart *Also called Flexco Products Inc* ***(G-2852)***
Industrial Steering Pdts Inc (PA) 260 488-1880
7790 S Homestead Dr Hamilton (46742) ***(G-5824)***
Industrial Tool & Die, Connersville *Also called I T D Inc* ***(G-2054)***
Industrial Tool & Die Corp 812 424-9971
2201 Lexington Rd Evansville (47720) ***(G-3559)***
Industrial Tool & Mfg Co 219 932-8670
4901 Calumet Ave Hammond (46327) ***(G-5899)***
Industrial Transmission Eqp 574 936-3028
2033 Western Ave Plymouth (46563) ***(G-11694)***
Industrial Trning Unlmted Corp (PA) 812 961-8801
8141 E State St Dugger (47848) ***(G-2480)***
Industrial Tube Components Inc 317 431-2188
6114 N County Road 50 W Lizton (46149) ***(G-9316)***
Industrial Utilities Inc 812 346-4489
3680 E County Road 450 S North Vernon (47265) ***(G-11265)***
Industrial Water MGT Inc 317 889-0836
140 S Park Blvd Greenwood (46143) ***(G-5706)***
Industrial Woodkraft Inc (PA) 812 897-4893
811 Hyrock Blvd Boonville (47601) ***(G-914)***
Industries LLC 765 759-5577
13501 W River Valley Rd Yorktown (47396) ***(G-14406)***
Indy Aerospace Inc 817 521-6508
2801 Fortune Cir E Ste J Indianapolis (46241) ***(G-7212)***
Indy Auto Graphics, Indianapolis *Also called Hot Rod Car Care LLC* ***(G-7134)***
Indy Color Printing LLC 317 371-8829
6220 Hardegan St Indianapolis (46227) ***(G-7213)***
Indy Composite Works Inc 317 280-9766
3945 Guion Ln Ste A Indianapolis (46268) ***(G-7214)***
Indy Control Corp 317 787-4639
308 Main St Beech Grove (46107) ***(G-597)***
Indy Custom Machine Inc 317 271-1544
8267 Indy Ct Indianapolis (46214) ***(G-7215)***
Indy Cylinder Head 317 862-3724
8621 Stheastern Ave Ste B Indianapolis (46239) ***(G-7216)***
Indy Glass Center Inc 317 591-5000
6366 E 32nd Ct Indianapolis (46226) ***(G-7217)***
Indy Hanger, Indianapolis *Also called Innovative Fabrication LLC* ***(G-7237)***
Indy Holsters LLC 317 370-7451
1705 Cold Spring Dr Brownsburg (46112) ***(G-1152)***
Indy Medical Supplies LLC 866 744-9013
650 S 800 E Zionsville (46077) ***(G-14439)***
Indy Metal Finishing Co 317 858-5353
451 Suthpoint Cir Ste 400 Brownsburg (46112) ***(G-1153)***
Indy Metro Woman Magazine 317 843-1344
8961 Crystal Lake Dr Indianapolis (46240) ***(G-7218)***
Indy Mobile Apps LLC 508 685-5240
264 Legacy Blvd Greenwood (46143) ***(G-5707)***
Indy Pallet Company Inc 317 843-0452
1017 Indianpipe Cir Carmel (46033) ***(G-1413)***
Indy Parts Inc 317 243-7171
2 Gasoline Aly A Indianapolis (46222) ***(G-7219)***
Indy Powder Coating Inc 317 244-2231
4300 W 10th St Indianapolis (46222) ***(G-7220)***
Indy Powder Coatings LLC 317 236-7177
10482 Winghaven Dr Noblesville (46060) ***(G-11129)***
Indy Prfmce Composites Inc 317 858-7793
1185 E Northfield Dr A Brownsburg (46112) ***(G-1154)***
Indy Rapid 3d LLC 812 243-4175
10117 Falcon Cove Cir Indianapolis (46236) ***(G-7221)***
Indy Sports Magazine, Indianapolis *Also called Indy Sports Preview Program* ***(G-7222)***
Indy Sports Preview Program 317 259-0570
1089 3rd Ave Sw Ste 207 Indianapolis (46205) ***(G-7222)***
Indy Stud Welding 317 416-3617
2654 Allen Ave Indianapolis (46203) ***(G-7223)***
Indy Tube Fabrication LLC 317 883-2000
398 Cincinnati St Franklin (46131) ***(G-4900)***
Indy Web Inc 317 356-3622
3151 Madison Ave A Indianapolis (46227) ***(G-7224)***
Indy Wiring Services LLC 317 371-7044
150 Gasoline Aly Brownsburg (46112) ***(G-1155)***
Indybake Products LLC 812 877-1588
9445 E Us Highway 40 Terre Haute (47803) ***(G-13257)***
Indycoast Partners LLC 317 454-1050
2258 Finchley Rd Carmel (46032) ***(G-1414)***
Indys Sign Source Inc 317 372-2260
5501 W 86th St Ste C Indianapolis (46268) ***(G-7225)***
Infineon Tech Americas Corp 765 454-2144
2529 Commerce Dr Ste H Kokomo (46902) ***(G-8646)***
Infinias LLC 317 348-1249
9340 Priority Way West Dr Indianapolis (46240) ***(G-7226)***
Infinite Ai Inc 317 965-4850
1950 E Greyhound Pass Carmel (46033) ***(G-1415)***
Infinity Drones LLC 812 457-7140
5700 High School Rd Poseyville (47633) ***(G-11857)***
Infinity Performance Inc 317 479-1017
7002 N Park Ave Indianapolis (46220) ***(G-7227)***
Infinity Printing Promoti 317 332-4811
14563 Sowers Dr Fishers (46038) ***(G-3930)***
Infinity Products Inc 317 272-3435
141 Casco Dr Avon (46123) ***(G-448)***
Info Publishing Impact LLC 317 912-3642
9869 Worthington Blvd Fishers (46038) ***(G-3931)***
Info-Lite, Indianapolis *Also called Sojane Technologies Inc* ***(G-7958)***
Infobind Systems Inc 260 248-4989
1116 N Wells St Fort Wayne (46808) ***(G-4369)***
Informa Business Media Inc 317 233-1310
4639 W Stonehaven Ln New Palestine (46163) ***(G-10971)***
Infrared Lab Systems LLC 317 896-1565
17408 Tiller Ct Ste 1900 Westfield (46074) ***(G-14170)***
Infrared Technologies LLC 317 326-2019
6531 E 200 N Greenfield (46140) ***(G-5541)***
Infrastructure and Energy (PA) 765 828-2580
2647 Waterfront Pkwy Indianapolis (46214) ***(G-7228)***
Infront Software LLC 317 501-1871
10785 Harbor Bay Ct Fishers (46040) ***(G-3988)***
Ingredion Incorporated 317 295-4122
5521 W 74th St Indianapolis (46268) ***(G-7229)***
Ingredion Incorporated 317 635-4455
1050 W Raymond St Indianapolis (46221) ***(G-7230)***
Ingredion Incorporated 317 635-4455
1515 Drover St Indianapolis (46221) ***(G-7231)***
Ingroup 317 817-9997
200 W Washington St M12 Indianapolis (46204) ***(G-7232)***
Inhabit Inc 317 636-1699
211 S Ritter Ave Ste B Indianapolis (46219) ***(G-7233)***
Injection Mold Inc 812 346-7002
134 E O And M Ave North Vernon (47265) ***(G-11266)***
Injection Plastic & Mfg Co 574 784-2070
12140 Us Hwy 6 E Lapaz (46537) ***(G-9117)***
Injection Plastics 574 784-2070
12798 2a Rd St 2 Lapaz (46537) ***(G-9118)***
Ink Angel Inc 574 534-4415
1827 Bashor Rd Goshen (46526) ***(G-5245)***
Ink Angel Rubber Stamp, Goshen *Also called Ink Angel Inc* ***(G-5245)***
Ink Spot 260 482-4492
215 W State Blvd Fort Wayne (46808) ***(G-4370)***
Ink Spot Printing, Cedar Lake *Also called Jk Graphics Inc* ***(G-1531)***
Ink Spot Tattoo 260 244-0025
302 S Main St Columbia City (46725) ***(G-1796)***
Ink Well, Indianapolis *Also called Carlton Ventures Inc* ***(G-6556)***
Ink Well Business Center 812 476-9147
1326 N Weinbach Ave Evansville (47711) ***(G-3560)***
Inkme LLC 574 520-1203
54732 Scrmento Meadows Dr Osceola (46561) ***(G-11378)***
Inland Paper Board & Packaging 317 879-9710
5461 W 79th St Indianapolis (46268) ***(G-7234)***
Inline Shirt Printing LLC 765 647-6356
5062 State Road 252 Brookville (47012) ***(G-1118)***
Inner City Sports TS 812 402-4143
3012 Covert Ave Evansville (47714) ***(G-3561)***
Innerprint Inc 317 509-6511
12940 Rocky Pointe Rd McCordsville (46055) ***(G-9670)***
Innocor Foam Tech - Acp Inc 574 294-7694
1900 W Lusher Ave Elkhart (46517) ***(G-2935)***
Innomark Communications, Richmond *Also called Grafcor Inc* ***(G-11990)***
Innotek Inc 800 826-5527
923 Cardinal Ct Auburn (46706) ***(G-337)***
Innotek Pet Products, Auburn *Also called Innotek Inc* ***(G-337)***
Innovations By 260 413-1869
2611 Lincroft Dr Fort Wayne (46845) ***(G-4371)***
Innovative 3d Mfg LLC 317 560-5080
600 International Dr Franklin (46131) ***(G-4901)***
Innovative Battery Power Inc 260 267-6582
10827 Middleford Pl Fort Wayne (46818) ***(G-4372)***
Innovative Casting Tech, Franklin *Also called Dualtech Inc* ***(G-4882)***
Innovative Chemical Resources 317 695-6001
6464 Rucker Rd Indianapolis (46220) ***(G-7235)***
Innovative Composites Ltd 574 857-2224
5408 State St Ste 25 Rochester (46975) ***(G-12129)***
Innovative Concepts Group 317 408-0292
8624 Quarterhorse Dr Indianapolis (46256) ***(G-7236)***
Innovative Consumer Packaging, Crawfordsville *Also called Crawford Industries LLC* ***(G-2144)***
Innovative Corp 317 804-5977
17401 Tiller Ct Ste H Westfield (46074) ***(G-14171)***
Innovative Energy Inc 219 696-3639
10653 W 181st Ave Lowell (46356) ***(G-9409)***

ALPHABETIC

Innovative Equipment Inc 765 572-2367
   9227 W 600 S Westpoint (47992) *(G-14206)*

Innovative Fabrication LLC 317 215-5988
   801 S Emerson Ave Indianapolis (46203) *(G-7237)*

Innovative Home Offices, Westfield *Also called Innovative Corp* *(G-14171)*

Innovative Metalworks LLC 260 839-0295
   106 S Main St Sidney (46562) *(G-12674)*

Innovative Mold & Machine Inc 317 634-1177
   2702 Brill Rd Indianapolis (46225) *(G-7238)*

Innovative Packaging Assoc Inc (PA) 260 356-6577
   1312 Flaxmill Rd Huntington (46750) *(G-6217)*

Innovative Rescue Systems Inc 219 548-1028
   4201 Montdale Dr Valparaiso (46383) *(G-13560)*

Innovative Rfid Inc 260 433-5835
   105 Twin Eagles Blvd W Huntertown (46748) *(G-6141)*

Innovative Tooling Solutions 260 487-9970
   6225 Commodity Ct Fort Wayne (46818) *(G-4373)*

Innovtive Hydrlic Slutions LLC 317 252-0120
   3015 S Harding St Indianapolis (46217) *(G-7239)*

Innovtive Nurological Dvcs LLC 317 674-2999
   13295 Illinois St Ste 312 Carmel (46032) *(G-1416)*

Innovtive Srcing Solutions Inc 317 752-2952
   12752 Broncos Dr Fishers (46037) *(G-3932)*

Innovtive Surgical Designs Inc 484 584-4230
   3903 S Walnut St Bloomington (47401) *(G-749)*

Inovateus Solar LLC 574 485-1400
   19890 State Line Rd South Bend (46637) *(G-12813)*

Inscope Medical Solutions Inc 502 882-0183
   2533 Centennial Blvd Jeffersonville (47130) *(G-8381)*

Insertec Inc (PA) 800 556-1911
   4011 W 54th St Indianapolis (46254) *(G-7240)*

Inside Systems 317 831-3772
   1053 E Jessup Way Mooresville (46158) *(G-10314)*

Insight Equity Holdings LLC 219 378-1930
   4407 Railroad Ave East Chicago (46312) *(G-2540)*

Insign Inc 317 251-0131
   5812 Linton Ln Indianapolis (46220) *(G-7241)*

Insignia Sign Shop LLC 317 356-4639
   7225 E Raymond St Indianapolis (46239) *(G-7242)*

Inson Tool & Machine Inc 812 752-3754
   833 S Gardner St Scottsburg (47170) *(G-12366)*

Inspired Fire Glass Studio & G 765 474-1981
   2124 State Road 25 W Lafayette (47909) *(G-8925)*

Installed Building Pdts LLC 317 398-3216
   886 W Mausoleum Rd Shelbyville (46176) *(G-12539)*

Instant Auto Finance Inc 260 483-9000
   2500 Spy Run Ave Fort Wayne (46805) *(G-4374)*

Instant Copy, Lafayette *Also called Twin Prints Inc* *(G-9014)*

Instant Memorabilia Inc 219 661-8942
   12880 Jefferson Dr Crown Point (46307) *(G-2263)*

Instant Rain Irrigation LLC 260 336-1237
   5420 W 450 N Shipshewana (46565) *(G-12618)*

Instant Refund Tax Service 317 536-1689
   10059 E Washington St Indianapolis (46229) *(G-7243)*

Instant Warehouse 765 342-3430
   1290 Morton Ave Martinsville (46151) *(G-9616)*

Instantwhip-Indianapolis Inc 317 899-1533
   9125 Burk Rd Indianapolis (46229) *(G-7244)*

Instate Welding Service Inc 260 483-0461
   4911 Industrial Rd Fort Wayne (46825) *(G-4375)*

Instellus Inc (PA) 734 415-3013
   425 N Broad St Ste 4 Griffith (46319) *(G-5780)*

Instellus Technology Solutions, Griffith *Also called Instellus Inc* *(G-5780)*

Institute of Mennonite Studies, Elkhart *Also called Anabaptist Mennonite Biblical* *(G-2691)*

Instru-Med, Warsaw *Also called Med-Cut Inc* *(G-13907)*

Instrumental Machine & Dev Inc 574 267-7713
   2098 N Pound Dr W Warsaw (46582) *(G-13893)*

Insty-Prints, Jeffersonville *Also called Creative Concept Ventures Inc* *(G-8348)*

Insty-Prints, Indianapolis *Also called Printing Partners East Inc* *(G-7756)*

Insty-Prints 317 788-1504
   930 E Hanna Ave Indianapolis (46227) *(G-7245)*

Insty-Prints of South Bend 574 289-6977
   129 S Lafayette Blvd South Bend (46601) *(G-12814)*

Insul-Coustic Corporation 260 420-1480
   2701 S Coliseum Blvd Fort Wayne (46803) *(G-4376)*

Insulation Fabricators Inc (HQ) 219 845-2008
   2501 165th St Ste 3 Hammond (46320) *(G-5900)*

Insulation Specialties of Amer 219 733-2502
   1095 Kabert Dr Wanatah (46390) *(G-13824)*

Insurance Publishing Plus, Carmel *Also called Rough Notes Company Inc* *(G-1471)*

Intat Precision Inc 765 932-5323
   2148 N State Road 3 Rushville (46173) *(G-12224)*

Intech Automation Systems Corp 209 836-8610
   206 N Grant St Peru (46970) *(G-11532)*

Intech Trailers Inc 574 773-9536
   1940 W Market St Nappanee (46550) *(G-10685)*

Integer Holdings Corporation 260 373-1664
   4545 Kroemer Rd Fort Wayne (46818) *(G-4377)*

Integer Holdings Corporation 317 454-8800
   3737 N Arlington Ave Indianapolis (46218) *(G-7246)*

Integra Certified Document 574 295-4611
   605 Mason St Elkhart (46516) *(G-2936)*

Integral Technologies Inc 812 550-1770
   2605 Eastside Park Rd # 1 Evansville (47715) *(G-3562)*

Integrated Biomedical Tech 574 264-0025
   2931 Moose Trl Elkhart (46514) *(G-2937)*

Integrated Custom Components, Fort Wayne *Also called Iasa Group LLC* *(G-4355)*

Integrated De Icing Servi 317 517-1643
   7899 S Service Rd Ste H Indianapolis (46241) *(G-7247)*

Integrated Energy Technologies 812 421-7810
   225 W Morgan Ave Ste A Evansville (47710) *(G-3563)*

Integrated Instrument Services 317 248-1958
   5601 Fortune Cir S Ste A Indianapolis (46241) *(G-7248)*

Integrated Mfg & Assembly LLC 260 244-1700
   2101 S 600 E Columbia City (46725) *(G-1797)*

Integrated Orthotic Lab Inc 317 852-4640
   1630 E Northfield Dr # 400 Brownsburg (46112) *(G-1156)*

Integrated Sealing Systems Div, Ligonier *Also called Parker-Hannifin Corporation* *(G-9292)*

Integrated Systems Management 765 565-6108
   7002 W 1000 N B Carthage (46115) *(G-1513)*

Integrated Tech Resources 317 757-5432
   2445 Directors Row Ste J Indianapolis (46241) *(G-7249)*

Integrative Flavors, Michigan City *Also called Williams West & Witts Pdts Co* *(G-9860)*

Integratorcom Inc 317 776-3500
   14670 Cumberland Rd Noblesville (46060) *(G-11130)*

Integratorcom Inc 317 849-2250
   6161 E 75th St Indianapolis (46250) *(G-7250)*

Integritech Mfg Inc 574 656-3046
   67911 State Road 23 North Liberty (46554) *(G-11217)*

Integrity Bio-Fuels LLC 765 763-6020
   780 E Industrial Dr Morristown (46161) *(G-10371)*

Integrity Custom Concepts LLC 574 252-2366
   244 S Olive St Ste S South Bend (46619) *(G-12815)*

Integrity Defense Services Inc 812 675-4913
   1463 S State Road 45 Springville (47462) *(G-13064)*

Integrity EDM LLC 317 333-7630
   641 Cleveland St Tipton (46072) *(G-13392)*

Integrity Hearing (PA) 317 882-9151
   5628 Merritt Cir Noblesville (46062) *(G-11131)*

Integrity Machine Systems 317 897-3338
   22 S Westside Dr New Palestine (46163) *(G-10972)*

Integrity Marketing Team Inc 317 517-0012
   4067 Cheltonham Ct Plainfield (46168) *(G-11617)*

Integrity Molding Inc 812 524-1243
   2710 Montgomery Dr Seymour (47274) *(G-12459)*

Integrity Pallet LLC 574 612-2119
   9385 W 750 N Shipshewana (46565) *(G-12619)*

Integrity Qntum Innvations LLC 765 537-9037
   6830 Hancock Ridge Rd Martinsville (46151) *(G-9617)*

Integrity Rttional Molding LLC 317 837-1101
   701 N Carr Rd Plainfield (46168) *(G-11618)*

Integrity Sign Solutions Inc 502 233-8755
   4302 Security Pkwy New Albany (47150) *(G-10807)*

Integrity Woodcrafting 260 562-2067
   4285 N 500 W Shipshewana (46565) *(G-12620)*

Integrtive Plygraph Trning LLC 812 595-2884
   1352 S Phillips Ln Scottsburg (47170) *(G-12367)*

Intek Manufacturing LLC 260 637-4100
   11118 Coldwater Rd # 200 Fort Wayne (46845) *(G-4378)*

Intel Corporation 317 336-5464
   6088 Crossfield Trl Mccordsville (46055) *(G-9671)*

Intelligent Software Inc 219 923-6166
   9609 Cypress Ave Munster (46321) *(G-10610)*

Intelliray Inc 260 547-4399
   10262 N 550 W Decatur (46733) *(G-2386)*

Intempo Software Inc 800 950-2221
   8777 Purdue Rd Ste 340 Indianapolis (46268) *(G-7251)*

Intense Incense 765 457-3602
   1211 N Morrison St Kokomo (46901) *(G-8647)*

Interactions Inc 574 722-6207
   1031 N 3rd St Logansport (46947) *(G-9341)*

Interactive Engineering Inc 574 272-5851
   15925 Fair Banks Ct Granger (46530) *(G-5415)*

Interactive Intelligence, Indianapolis *Also called Genesys Telecom Labs Inc* *(G-7000)*

Interactive Surface Tech LLC 812 246-0900
   1511 Avco Blvd Sellersburg (47172) *(G-12398)*

Interchurch Print Shop, Indianapolis *Also called Perfect Impressions Printing* *(G-7674)*

Interfaith Resources, Heltonville *Also called Special Ideas Incorporated* *(G-6028)*

Interglobal Way Network LLC 574 971-4490
   3002 Coast Ct Elkhart (46514) *(G-2938)*

Interior Design Surfaces Inc 317 829-3970
   5078 Huntington Dr Carmel (46033) *(G-1417)*

Interior Fixs & Millwk Co Inc 812 446-0933
   995 E Barnett St Knightsville (47857) *(G-8561)*

Intermetco Processing Inc 812 423-5914
   1901 W Louisiana St Evansville (47710) *(G-3564)*

Internal Honing Service, Paoli *Also called G and P Enterprises Ind Inc* *(G-11451)*

(G-0000) Company's Geographic Section entry number

International A I Inc 812 824-2473
7909 S Fairfax Rd Bloomington (47401) ***(G-750)***
International Automation Inc (PA) 260 747-6151
9009 Clubridge Dr Fort Wayne (46809) ***(G-4379)***
International Bakers Services 574 287-7111
1902 N Sheridan St South Bend (46628) ***(G-12816)***
International Brake Inds Inc 419 905-7468
4300 Quality Dr South Bend (46628) ***(G-12817)***
International Code Council Inc 317 879-1677
1223 S Richland St Indianapolis (46221) ***(G-7252)***
International Cryogenics Inc 317 297-4777
4040 Championship Dr Indianapolis (46268) ***(G-7253)***
International English Inc 260 868-2670
3597 County Road 75 Butler (46721) ***(G-1231)***
International Food Tech Inc 812 853-9432
8499 Spencer Dr Newburgh (47630) ***(G-11032)***
International Label Mfg LLC 812 235-5071
1925 S 13th St Terre Haute (47802) ***(G-13258)***
International Metals Proc Inc 317 895-4141
3131 N Franklin Rd Ste E Indianapolis (46226) ***(G-7254)***
International Paper Company 317 871-6999
4901 W 79th St Indianapolis (46268) ***(G-7255)***
International Paper Company 260 868-2151
2626 County Road 71 Butler (46721) ***(G-1232)***
International Paper Company 317 481-4000
7536 Miles Dr Indianapolis (46231) ***(G-7256)***
International Paper Company 765 364-5342
801 N Englewood Dr Crawfordsville (47933) ***(G-2161)***
International Paper Company 317 510-6410
4350 Sam Jones Expy Indianapolis (46241) ***(G-7257)***
International Paper Company 765 675-6732
815 Industrial Dr Tipton (46072) ***(G-13393)***
International Paper Company 317 715-9080
8501 Moller Rd Indianapolis (46268) ***(G-7258)***
International Paper Company 260 747-9111
3904 W Ferguson Rd Fort Wayne (46809) ***(G-4380)***
International Paper Company 800 643-7244
320 S 25th St Ste 2 Terre Haute (47803) ***(G-13259)***
International Paper Company 219 844-6509
2501 165th St Ste 3 Hammond (46320) ***(G-5901)***
International Paper Company 765 359-0107
1823 E Elmore St Crawfordsville (47933) ***(G-2162)***
International Paper Company 812 326-2125
3565 E 550 S St Rt 6 Saint Anthony (47575) ***(G-12246)***
International Paper Company 317 875-4101
8501 Moller Rd Indianapolis (46268) ***(G-7259)***
International Paper Company 765 492-3341
2585 E 200 N Cayuga (47928) ***(G-1520)***
International Paper Company 317 390-3300
2135 Stout Field East Dr Indianapolis (46241) ***(G-7260)***
International Resources Inc 317 813-5300
9325 Uptown Dr Ste 900 Indianapolis (46256) ***(G-7261)***
International Steel Company 812 425-3311
2138 N 6th Ave Evansville (47710) ***(G-3565)***
International Wire Group Inc 574 546-4680
833 Legner St Bremen (46506) ***(G-1005)***
International Wood Inc 812 883-5778
803 N Deer Run Rd Salem (47167) ***(G-12295)***
Interntional Pipe Cons Sls LLC 765 388-2222
900 New York Ave New Castle (47362) ***(G-10907)***
Interntnal Damnd Gold Exch Ltd 317 872-6666
6010 W 86th St Ste 114 Indianapolis (46278) ***(G-7262)***
Interntonal Revolving Door Div, Evansville *Also called International Steel Company* ***(G-3565)***
Interpak Inc 765 482-9179
820 Hendricks Dr Lebanon (46052) ***(G-9192)***
Interplastic Corporation 574 234-1105
1545 S Olive St South Bend (46619) ***(G-12818)***
Interplastic Corporation 574 259-1505
1460 E 12th St Mishawaka (46544) ***(G-10054)***
Interrachem LLC 812 858-3147
5722 Prospect Dr Newburgh (47630) ***(G-11033)***
Interstate Block Corporation 812 273-1742
3148 Clifty Dr Madison (47250) ***(G-9473)***
Interstate Forestry, Plymouth *Also called Intrst Forestry Inc* ***(G-11695)***
Interstate Gravel, Williamsport *Also called Rogers Group Inc* ***(G-14296)***
Interstate Metals LLC 765 893-4449
3454 W State Road 28 West Lebanon (47991) ***(G-14121)***
Interstate Power Systems Inc 952 854-2044
2601 E 15th Ave Gary (46402) ***(G-5070)***
Interstate Powersystems, Gary *Also called Interstate Power Systems Inc* ***(G-5070)***
Interstate Truss LLC 260 463-6124
4875 N 675 W Shipshewana (46565) ***(G-12621)***
Intervention Diagnostics Inc 317 432-6091
6925 Hawthorn Park Dr Indianapolis (46220) ***(G-7263)***
Intimus International NA, Wabash *Also called Olympia Business Systems Inc* ***(G-13744)***
Intratek Engineering, Fort Wayne *Also called Intratek Inc* ***(G-4381)***
Intratek Inc 260 484-3377
3209 Clearfield Ct Fort Wayne (46808) ***(G-4381)***
Intri-Cut Tool Company LLC 260 672-9602
5130 E 900 N Roanoke (46783) ***(G-12104)***
Intrst Forestry Inc 574 936-1284
10200 W County Line Rd Plymouth (46563) ***(G-11695)***
Intuitive Software LLC 574 268-8239
1015 Logan St Warsaw (46580) ***(G-13894)***
Invacare Corporation 317 838-5500
1100 Whitaker Rd Plainfield (46168) ***(G-11619)***
Invensys Processs Systems Inc 317 372-2839
101 W Ohio St Indianapolis (46204) ***(G-7264)***
Inventure Electronics, Goshen *Also called Jtd Enterprises Inc* ***(G-5249)***
Inventure Foods Inc 260 824-2800
705 W Dustman Rd Bluffton (46714) ***(G-879)***
Investwell Electronics Inc 765 457-1911
329 E Firmin St Kokomo (46902) ***(G-8648)***
INX International Ink Co 765 939-6625
1056 Industries Rd Richmond (47374) ***(G-12002)***
Ionic Cut Stone Inc 812 829-3416
1201 Kelley Farm Dr Spencer (47460) ***(G-13029)***
Iotron Industries USA Inc 260 212-1722
4394 E Park 30 Dr Columbia City (46725) ***(G-1798)***
Ip Moulding Inc 574 825-5845
219 W Us Highway 20 Middlebury (46540) ***(G-9894)***
Ip Software Inc 317 569-1313
10333 N Meridian St Indianapolis (46290) ***(G-6269)***
Ipfw Student Housing 260 481-4180
2101 E Coliseum Blvd # 100 Fort Wayne (46805) ***(G-4382)***
Ipg, Evansville *Also called Industrial Plastics Group LLC* ***(G-3556)***
Ipheion Custom Technologies, Indianapolis *Also called Ipheion Development Corp* ***(G-7265)***
Ipheion Development Corp 240 281-1619
3421 Breckenridge Dr Indianapolis (46228) ***(G-7265)***
Ipower Technologies Inc 317 574-0103
4640 Dr Mrtn Lthr Kng Jr Anderson (46013) ***(G-121)***
Ips, Evansville *Also called Smith & Butterfield Co Inc* ***(G-3736)***
Ips Indiana, Indianapolis *Also called Ips-Integrated Prj Svcs LLC* ***(G-7266)***
Ips-Integrated Prj Svcs LLC 317 247-1200
320 N Meridian St Ste 212 Indianapolis (46204) ***(G-7266)***
Ira Preservation Partners 317 722-0710
3271 E 79th St Apt C Indianapolis (46240) ***(G-7267)***
IRD Group Inc 812 425-3311
2138 N 6th Ave Evansville (47710) ***(G-3566)***
Ireco Metals Inc 574 936-2146
1433 Western Ave Plymouth (46563) ***(G-11696)***
Iris Rubber Company Inc 317 984-3561
10 E Jackson St Cicero (46034) ***(G-1662)***
Irish Cupcakes Inc 574 289-8669
58727 Baugo Cove Dr Elkhart (46517) ***(G-2939)***
Irish Industries 773 213-2422
13006 Rocky Pointe Rd McCordsville (46055) ***(G-9672)***
Iron Bull Mfg LLC 765 597-2480
5947 N 350 E Marshall (47859) ***(G-9592)***
Iron Men Industries Inc 574 596-2251
6086 W 250 S Russiaville (46979) ***(G-12242)***
Iron Out Inc 800 654-0791
7201 Engle Rd Fort Wayne (46804) ***(G-4383)***
Ironcraft Co Inc 574 272-0866
50655 Ind St Rte 933 South Bend (46637) ***(G-12819)***
Irongate V LLC 219 464-8704
214 Edgewood Dr Valparaiso (46385) ***(G-13561)***
Ironhorse Detailing Inc 812 939-3300
8445 S State Road 59 Clay City (47841) ***(G-1703)***
IRONMONGER SPRING DIVISION, Walton *Also called Walton Industrial Park Inc* ***(G-13818)***
Iroquois Bio-Energy Co LLC (HQ) 219 866-5990
751 W State Road 114 Rensselaer (47978) ***(G-11928)***
Irsco Marking Products, Indianapolis *Also called Indianapolis Rubber Stamp Co* ***(G-7204)***
Irvine Shade & Door Inc (PA) 574 522-1446
1000 Verdant St Elkhart (46516) ***(G-2940)***
Irvine Window Coverings, Elkhart *Also called Irvine Shade & Door Inc* ***(G-2940)***
Irving Materials Inc (PA) 317 326-3101
8032 N State Road 9 Greenfield (46140) ***(G-5542)***
Irving Materials Inc 812 424-3551
6000 Oak Grove Rd Evansville (47715) ***(G-3567)***
Irving Materials Inc 765 825-2581
1998 S State Road 121 Connersville (47331) ***(G-2056)***
Irving Materials Inc 765 644-8819
1601 N Scatterfield Rd Anderson (46012) ***(G-122)***
Irving Materials Inc 317 770-1745
17050 River Rd Noblesville (46062) ***(G-11132)***
Irving Materials Inc 317 773-3640
12798 State Road 38 E Noblesville (46060) ***(G-11133)***
Irving Materials Inc 317 335-2121
10959 Olio Rd Fishers (46040) ***(G-3989)***
Irving Materials Inc 317 784-5433
5560 S Belmont Ave Indianapolis (46217) ***(G-7268)***
Irving Materials Inc 765 654-5333
28 Lewis Smith Rd Frankfort (46041) ***(G-4838)***
Irving Materials Inc 765 482-5620
417 S West St Lebanon (46052) ***(G-9193)***
Irving Materials Inc 765 342-3369
1502 Rogers Rd Martinsville (46151) ***(G-9618)***

ALPHABETIC

Irving Materials Inc.....812 254-0820
611 W Main St Washington (47501) *(G-13987)*
Irving Materials Inc.....765 836-4007
4304 E County Road 350 N Muncie (47303) *(G-10495)*
Irving Materials Inc.....765 288-5566
4312 E County Road 350 N Muncie (47303) *(G-10496)*
Irving Materials Inc.....765 755-3447
1078 E Luray Rd Springport (47386) *(G-13059)*
Irving Materials Inc.....260 824-3428
2321 E 150 N Bluffton (46714) *(G-880)*
Irving Materials Inc.....765 288-0288
4304 E County Road 350 N Muncie (47303) *(G-10497)*
Irving Materials Inc.....574 653-2749
500 Erie Stone Rd Huntington (46750) *(G-6218)*
Irving Materials Inc.....765 478-4914
14413 W Us Highway 40 Cambridge City (47327) *(G-1257)*
Irving Materials Inc.....574 946-3754
1132 S Us Highway 35 Winamac (46996) *(G-14308)*
Irving Materials Inc.....812 883-4242
784 N Wilson Rd Scottsburg (47170) *(G-12368)*
Irving Materials Inc.....812 683-4444
615 W 12th St Huntingburg (47542) *(G-6172)*
Irving Materials Inc.....765 362-6904
3350 State Road 32 E Crawfordsville (47933) *(G-2163)*
Irving Materials Inc.....765 423-2533
2903 Old State Road 25 N Lafayette (47905) *(G-8926)*
Irving Materials Inc.....765 743-3806
301 Ahlers Dr West Lafayette (47906) *(G-14078)*
Irving Materials Inc.....219 261-2441
318 W South St Remington (47977) *(G-11908)*
Irving Materials Inc.....765 922-7991
6377 W 600 S Swayzee (46986) *(G-13124)*
Irving Materials Inc.....765 552-5041
2500 S D St Elwood (46036) *(G-3300)*
Irving Materials Inc.....765 728-5335
5067 E Cummins Rd Montpelier (47359) *(G-10292)*
Irving Materials Inc.....812 275-7450
1307 Bundy Ln Bedford (47421) *(G-554)*
Irving Materials Inc.....765 452-4044
1315 S Dixon Rd Kokomo (46902) *(G-8649)*
Irving Materials Inc.....765 922-7931
6455 W 600 S Swayzee (46986) *(G-13125)*
Irving Materials Inc.....317 888-0157
6695 W Fifth Valley Rd Greenwood (46142) *(G-5708)*
Irving Materials Inc.....765 778-4760
5002 S State Road 67 Anderson (46013) *(G-123)*
Irving Materials Inc.....765 472-5370
351 N 150 W Peru (46970) *(G-11533)*
Irving Materials Inc.....765 675-6327
929 E Jefferson St Tipton (46072) *(G-13394)*
Irving Materials Inc.....765 922-7285
3888 S Garthwaite Rd Marion (46953) *(G-9534)*
Irving Materials Inc.....765 674-2271
3892 S Garthwaite Rd Marion (46953) *(G-9535)*
Irving Materials Inc.....812 333-8530
1800 N Kinser Pike Bloomington (47404) *(G-751)*
Irving Materials Inc.....317 535-7566
600 Tracy Rd Whiteland (46184) *(G-14241)*
Irving Materials Inc.....317 872-0152
4700 W 96th St Indianapolis (46268) *(G-7269)*
Irving Materials Inc.....317 843-2944
5244 E 96th St Indianapolis (46240) *(G-7270)*
Irving Materials Inc.....317 783-3381
4200 S Harding St Ste X Indianapolis (46217) *(G-7271)*
Irving Materials Inc.....574 722-3420
2245 S County Road 150 E Logansport (46947) *(G-9342)*
Irving Materials Inc.....317 243-7391
4330 W Morris St Indianapolis (46241) *(G-7272)*
Irving Materials Inc.....317 831-0224
501 N Samuel Moore Pkwy Mooresville (46158) *(G-10315)*
Irving Materials Inc.....317 899-2187
3130 N Post Rd Indianapolis (46226) *(G-7273)*
Irving Materials Inc.....765 647-6533
1352 Fairfield Ave Brookville (47012) *(G-1119)*
Irving Materials Inc.....260 356-7214
500 Erie Stone Rd Huntington (46750) *(G-6219)*
Irwin Hodson Group Indiana LLC.....260 482-8052
2980 E Coliseum Blvd Fort Wayne (46805) *(G-4384)*
Isf Inc.....317 251-1219
6468 Rucker Rd Indianapolis (46220) *(G-7274)*
Isg Burns Harbor Services LLC.....219 787-2120
250 W Us Highway 12 Burns Harbor (46304) *(G-1215)*
ISI Inc.....317 631-7980
1212 E Michigan St Indianapolis (46202) *(G-7275)*
Isolatek International, Huntington *Also called United States Mineral Pdts Co (G-6259)*
It Factor Publications Inc.....219 228-8424
2158 45th St Ste 224 Highland (46322) *(G-6050)*
Italian House On Park, The, Westfield *Also called Wolfies Grill 5 LLC (G-14203)*
Italmac USA Inc.....574 243-0217
12743 Heather Park Dr # 104 Granger (46530) *(G-5416)*
Itamco Company, Plymouth *Also called Indiana Tool & Mfg Co Inc (G-11693)*
Itech Digital, Indianapolis *Also called Itech Holdings LLC (G-7276)*
Itech Holdings LLC.....317 567-5160
6330 E 75th St Ste 132 Indianapolis (46250) *(G-7276)*
Itera LLC.....574 538-3838
19260 County Road 46 # 3 New Paris (46553) *(G-10986)*
Itestout.com, Indianapolis *Also called College Network Inc (G-6631)*
Its, Westpoint *Also called Innovative Equipment Inc (G-14206)*
Its Personal Laser Engraving.....812 934-6657
3243 County Rd 1150 E Batesville (47006) *(G-505)*
Itsuwa Usa LLC.....812 375-0323
1349 Arcadia Dr Columbus (47201) *(G-1949)*
ITT Communications Systems, Fort Wayne *Also called ITT LLC (G-4385)*
ITT LLC.....260 451-6000
1919 W Cook Rd Fort Wayne (46818) *(G-4385)*
Itu Learnlab, Dugger *Also called Industrial Trning Unlmted Corp (G-2480)*
ITW Gema, Indianapolis *Also called Illinois Tool Works Inc (G-7160)*
ITW Gema.....317 298-5000
4141 W 54th St Indianapolis (46254) *(G-7277)*
ITW Tomco, Kendallville *Also called Illinois Tool Works Inc (G-8480)*
Iu East Business Office.....765 973-8218
2325 Chester Blvd Richmond (47374) *(G-12003)*
Iuniverse, Bloomington *Also called Get Published Inc (G-731)*
Iuniverse Inc.....812 330-2909
1663 S Liberty Dr Bloomington (47403) *(G-752)*
IVc Industrial Coatings Inc.....812 442-5080
2831 E Industrial Park Dr Brazil (47834) *(G-966)*
Ivy Hill Packaging Division, Indianapolis *Also called Multi Packaging Solutions Inc (G-7558)*
Ivy Woodworks LLC.....317 842-4085
8634 Burrell Ln Indianapolis (46256) *(G-7278)*
Izzy Better Together, Middlebury *Also called Izzy Plus (G-9895)*
Izzy Plus.....574 821-1200
11451 Harter Dr Middlebury (46540) *(G-9895)*
J & A Machine Inc.....260 637-6215
219 E Quincy St Garrett (46738) *(G-5012)*
J & B Pallet, Warsaw *Also called Meagan Inc (G-13906)*
J & C Printing Co, Scottsburg *Also called Journal and Chronicle Inc (G-12370)*
J & F Steel Corporation.....219 764-3500
310 Tech Dr Burns Harbor (46304) *(G-1216)*
J & H Tool Inc.....765 724-9691
109 S Clinton St Alexandria (46001) *(G-45)*
J & J Cabinets.....219 374-6816
13418 Wicker Ave Cedar Lake (46303) *(G-1530)*
J & J Engineering Inc.....317 462-2309
610 W Osage St Greenfield (46140) *(G-5543)*
J & J Industrial Services Inc.....219 362-4973
2204 E Lincolnway Bldg D La Porte (46350) *(G-8772)*
J & J Pallet Corp.....812 948-9382
2234 E Market St New Albany (47150) *(G-10808)*
J & J Pallet Corp (PA).....812 944-8670
2234 E Market St New Albany (47150) *(G-10809)*
J & J Pallet Corp.....812 288-4487
640 Miller Ave Clarksville (47129) *(G-1687)*
J & J Printing Co.....765 642-6642
2107 State St Anderson (46012) *(G-124)*
J & J Repair.....574 831-3075
22064 County Road 142 Goshen (46526) *(G-5246)*
J & J Stables.....812 279-2581
4081 S Leatherwood Rd Bedford (47421) *(G-555)*
J & J Welding.....219 872-7282
4100 W 700 N Michigan City (46360) *(G-9804)*
J & J Welding Inc.....812 838-4391
1114 W 4th St Mount Vernon (47620) *(G-10396)*
J & J Woodcrafters.....765 436-2466
2416 N State Road 75 Thorntown (46071) *(G-13376)*
J & K Associates.....317 255-3588
6302 Rucker Rd Ste C Indianapolis (46220) *(G-7279)*
J & L Cabinet Design Group, Greenwood *Also called Joseph Lee (G-5710)*
J & L Dimensional Services Inc.....219 325-3588
16 Industrial Pkwy La Porte (46350) *(G-8773)*
J & L Tool & Machine Inc.....317 398-6281
1441 Miller Ave Shelbyville (46176) *(G-12540)*
J & N Stone Inc.....574 862-4251
905 E Waterford St Wakarusa (46573) *(G-13779)*
J & N Stone Inc.....260 627-2404
13729 David Dr Grabill (46741) *(G-5373)*
J & P Custom Plating Inc.....260 726-9696
807 N Meridian St Portland (47371) *(G-11829)*
J & P Machine Inc.....260 357-5157
1213 S Franklin St Garrett (46738) *(G-5013)*
J & R Tool Inc.....812 295-2557
11919 E 250 N Loogootee (47553) *(G-9386)*
J & T Marine Specialists Inc.....317 890-9444
810 S Mitthoeffer Rd Indianapolis (46239) *(G-7280)*
J 2 Systems and Supply LLC.....317 602-3940
803 E 38th St Indianapolis (46205) *(G-7281)*
J A Larr & Co.....317 627-3192
4040 E 82nd St Ste C9 Indianapolis (46250) *(G-7282)*

776 2018 Harris Indiana Industrial Directory (G-0000) Company's Geographic Section entry number

J A Smit Inc 812 424-8141
1500 N Fulton Ave Evansville (47710) *(G-3568)*

J Aime Music Publishing LLC 574 772-2934
10040 E 50 S Knox (46534) *(G-8569)*

J and G Enterprises 219 778-4319
5556 E 300 N Rolling Prairie (46371) *(G-12188)*

J B Enterprises, Elkhart Also called Collins Trailers Inc *(G-2762)*

J B Tool Die & Engineering Co 260 483-9586
1509 Dividend Rd Fort Wayne (46808) *(G-4386)*

J C Mfg Inc (PA) 574 834-2881
7248 N State Road 13 North Webster (46555) *(G-11294)*

J C Penney Optical, Fort Wayne Also called Usv Optical Inc *(G-4721)*

J C Sipe Inc 317 848-0215
3000 E 96th St Indianapolis (46240) *(G-7283)*

J C Sipe Jewelers, Indianapolis Also called J C Sipe Inc *(G-7283)*

J Coffey Metal Masters Inc 317 780-1864
2514 Bethel Ave Indianapolis (46203) *(G-7284)*

J D Gould Company Inc 317 542-1876
4707 Massachusetts Ave Indianapolis (46218) *(G-7285)*

J D Petro and Associates Inc 317 736-6566
40 W Court St Ste B Franklin (46131) *(G-4902)*

J DS Big Boys Toys 219 365-7807
13361 W 83rd Pl Saint John (46373) *(G-12264)*

J Ennis Fabrics Inc (usa) 877 953-6647
853 Columbia Rd Ste 125 Plainfield (46168) *(G-11620)*

J F Jelenko Co 914 273-8600
300 Heraeus Dr South Bend (46614) *(G-12820)*

J G Bowers Inc 765 677-1000
1629 S Joaquin Dr Marion (46953) *(G-9536)*

J G Cabinet & Counter Inc 260 723-4275
2571 S State Road 5 Larwill (46764) *(G-9123)*

J Game Ventures LLC 812 241-7096
2675 Rothchild Pl Apt 207 Brownsburg (46112) *(G-1157)*

J H J Inc 574 256-6966
15314 Harrison Rd Mishawaka (46544) *(G-10055)*

J Henrys Machine Shop LLC 317 917-1052
1111 S East St Indianapolis (46225) *(G-7286)*

J J Babbitt Co 574 315-1639
2201 Industrial Pkwy Elkhart (46516) *(G-2941)*

J J Lites 765 966-3252
4469 Webster Rd Richmond (47374) *(G-12004)*

J Jesse Inc 574 862-4538
904 Nelsons Pkwy Wakarusa (46573) *(G-13780)*

J L Harris Machine Co Inc 574 834-2866
4953 N 700 E Leesburg (46538) *(G-9237)*

J L Mfg & Fab, Berne Also called JI Manfcturing Fabrication Inc *(G-618)*

J L Squared Inc 317 354-1513
1347 Sadlier Circle S Dr Indianapolis (46239) *(G-7287)*

J Lewis Small Co Inc 765 552-5011
9147 W 1000 N Elwood (46036) *(G-3301)*

J M Hutton & Company, Richmond Also called JM Hutton & Co Inc *(G-12008)*

J M McCormick 317 874-4444
8214 Allison Ave Indianapolis (46268) *(G-7288)*

J M S Machine Inc 260 244-0077
307 Diamond Ave Columbia City (46725) *(G-1799)*

J M Woodworking Co Inc 260 627-8362
10832 Witmer Rd Grabill (46741) *(G-5374)*

J Miller Cabinet Company, Columbia City Also called J Miller Cabinetry Inc *(G-1800)*

J Miller Cabinetry Inc 260 691-2032
5874 N 350 E Columbia City (46725) *(G-1800)*

J N P Custom Designs Inc 317 253-2198
550 W 65th St Indianapolis (46260) *(G-7289)*

J O Mory Sheet Metal Division, Avilla Also called JO Mory Inc *(G-407)*

J O Wolf Tool & Die Inc 260 672-2605
550 Condit St Huntington (46750) *(G-6220)*

J P Corporation 317 783-1000
227 Main St Beech Grove (46107) *(G-598)*

J P Industries Inc 574 293-8763
726 Middleton Run Rd Elkhart (46516) *(G-2942)*

J P Whitt Inc 765 759-0521
827 S Tillotson Ave Muncie (47304) *(G-10498)*

J Plus Products Inc 317 660-1003
4000 W 106th St Carmel (46032) *(G-1418)*

J Porter Mfg Co 812 853-9395
8900 Woodland Dr Newburgh (47630) *(G-11034)*

J Q Tex Inc 574 259-0329
1033 E 5th St Mishawaka (46544) *(G-10056)*

J R Graber & Sons Inc 260 657-5620
12916 Cuba Rd Grabill (46741) *(G-5375)*

J R Newby 765 664-3501
405 N Henderson Ave Marion (46952) *(G-9537)*

J R P Machine Products LLP 260 622-4746
420 Carol Ann Ln Ossian (46777) *(G-11402)*

J Robert Switzer 765 474-1307
1020 Beck Ln Lafayette (47909) *(G-8927)*

J T D Spiral Inc 260 497-1300
6212 Highview Dr Fort Wayne (46818) *(G-4387)*

J Tees 812 524-9292
9389 N County Road 100 E Seymour (47274) *(G-12460)*

J Trockman & Sons Inc 812 425-5271
1017 Bayse St Evansville (47714) *(G-3569)*

J V C Machining 219 462-0363
766 N 500 E Valparaiso (46383) *(G-13562)*

J V C Rubber Stamp Company 574 293-0113
816 W Beardsley Ave Elkhart (46514) *(G-2943)*

J V Crane & Engineering Inc 219 942-8566
425 S Shelby St Hobart (46342) *(G-6082)*

J W Hicks Inc (PA) 219 736-2212
8955 Louisiana St Merrillville (46410) *(G-9723)*

J W Jones Company LLC 765 537-2279
2468 S State Road 67 Paragon (46166) *(G-11458)*

J W Model & Engineering Inc 317 788-7471
5508 Elmwood Ave Ste 406 Indianapolis (46203) *(G-7290)*

J W P Vinyl Designs 812 873-8744
5210 E Private Road 415 S Dupont (47231) *(G-2491)*

J W Signs Inc 260 747-5168
2511 Alma Ave Fort Wayne (46809) *(G-4388)*

J W Woodworking Inc 574 831-3033
72057 County Road 17 New Paris (46553) *(G-10987)*

J Y Design & Print Inc 260 357-3759
1036 State Road 8 Garrett (46738) *(G-5014)*

J&J Manufacturing 574 646-2069
7663 W 800 N Nappanee (46550) *(G-10686)*

J&J Packaging, Sunman Also called Deufol Sunman Inc *(G-13110)*

J&J Sprts Screen Prtg Sprit Wr 812 909-2686
3012 Covert Ave Ste B Evansville (47714) *(G-3570)*

J&J Welding, Michigan City Also called J & J Welding *(G-9804)*

J&L Lighting Solutions LLC 317 413-8768
21 N Pennsylvania St Indianapolis (46204) *(G-7291)*

J&L Uebelhor Enterprises LLC 812 367-1591
1440 Virginia St Ferdinand (47532) *(G-3854)*

J-I-T Distributing Inc 574 251-0292
4111 Technology Dr South Bend (46628) *(G-12821)*

J2 S&S, Indianapolis Also called J 2 Systems and Supply LLC *(G-7281)*

J4 Printing LLC 260 417-5382
1008 Orlando Dr Fort Wayne (46825) *(G-4389)*

Jabra Signs & Graphics 765 584-7100
406 S Brown St Winchester (47394) *(G-14333)*

Jac Jmr Inc 219 663-6700
1849 E Summit St Crown Point (46307) *(G-2264)*

Jack Frost LLC 812 477-7244
1510 Yokel Rd Evansville (47711) *(G-3571)*

Jack House LLC 251 990-5960
106 W Wabash St Converse (46919) *(G-2079)*

Jack Howard 317 788-7643
1915 S State Ave Indianapolis (46203) *(G-7292)*

Jack Laurie Coml Floors Inc 317 569-2095
7998 Georgetown Rd # 1000 Indianapolis (46268) *(G-7293)*

Jack Mix 812 923-8679
3400 Lawrence Banet Rd Floyds Knobs (47119) *(G-4014)*

Jack O'Brien Welding Service, Greencastle Also called OBrien Jack & Pat
Enterprises *(G-5470)*

Jackson Brothers Lumber Co 812 847-7812
59 State Rd S Linton (47441) *(G-9308)*

Jackson County Banner 812 358-2111
116 E Cross St Brownstown (47220) *(G-1189)*

Jackson Group Inc 317 791-9000
5804 Churchman Byp Indianapolis (46203) *(G-7294)*

Jackson Hewitt Tax Service, Warsaw Also called Worth Tax and Financial Svc *(G-13969)*

Jackson Hewitt Tax Service 574 255-2200
922 S Beiger St Mishawaka (46544) *(G-10057)*

Jackson Systems LLC 317 788-6800
5418 Elmwood Ave Indianapolis (46203) *(G-7295)*

Jackson Vision Quest 219 882-9397
521 Broadway Gary (46402) *(G-5071)*

Jackson-Jennings LLC 812 522-4911
103 Community Dr Seymour (47274) *(G-12461)*

Jacobs & Brichford LLC 765 692-0056
2957 S State Road 1 Connersville (47331) *(G-2057)*

Jacobs Country Candles LLC 765 557-0260
1420 S K St Elwood (46036) *(G-3302)*

Jacobs Machine & Tool Co Inc 317 831-2917
315 E Washington St Mooresville (46158) *(G-10316)*

Jacobs Mfg LLC 765 490-6111
218 Trowbridge Dr Lafayette (47909) *(G-8928)*

Jacobs Mfg LLC 574 583-3883
806 N 1st St Monticello (47960) *(G-10267)*

Jacobsen Prof Lawn Care Inc 765 246-7737
6302 E County Road 100 N Coatesville (46121) *(G-1750)*

Jacyl Technology Inc (PA) 260 471-6067
6020 Huguenard Rd Fort Wayne (46818) *(G-4390)*

Jacyl Web Design, Fort Wayne Also called Jacyl Technology Inc *(G-4390)*

Jadco Ltd 219 661-2065
401 N Jackson St Crown Point (46307) *(G-2265)*

Jadcore LLC 812 234-2724
300 N Fruitridge Ave A Terre Haute (47803) *(G-13260)*

Jae Enterprises Inc 260 747-0568
8000 Baer Rd Fort Wayne (46809) *(G-4391)*

Jae Enterprises Inc (PA) 260 489-6249
7707 Freedom Way Fort Wayne (46818) *(G-4392)*

Jaeger-Ntek Sling Slutions Inc 219 324-1111
115 Koomler Dr La Porte (46350) *(G-8774)*

Jag Metal Solutions Inc 765 445-4459
234 W Warrick St Knightstown (46148) *(G-8552)*

Jag Metal Spinning Inc 812 533-5501
1022 Crawford St Sandford (47885) *(G-12310)*

Jag Wire LLC 260 463-8537
130 E 200 N Lagrange (46761) *(G-9048)*

Jah Coatings LLC 317 550-7169
6415 E 11th St Indianapolis (46219) *(G-7296)*

Jam Graphics Inc 317 896-5662
176 Logan St 314 Noblesville (46060) *(G-11134)*

Jam Printing Inc 765 649-9292
1200 Meridian St Anderson (46016) *(G-125)*

Jam-Ko Engineering Company 574 294-7684
21496 Buckingham Rd Elkhart (46516) *(G-2944)*

James A Andrew Inc 765 269-9807
665 Maple Point Dr Lafayette (47904) *(G-8929)*

James David Inc 260 744-0579
11323 Nightingale Cv Roanoke (46783) *(G-12105)*

James E Barnhizer 765 458-9344
2302 Omar Fields Dr Liberty (47353) *(G-9261)*

James Electronics Div, North Manchester *Also called Custom Magnetics Inc (G-11228)*

James Electronics Div., North Manchester *Also called Custom Magnetics Inc (G-11227)*

James F Reilly 3 Ent 574 277-8267
1969 E Mckinley Ave Mishawaka (46545) *(G-10058)*

James G Henager 812 795-2230
8837 S State Road 57 Elberfeld (47613) *(G-2636)*

James J Maginot Printing 219 836-5692
8720 Calumet Ave Munster (46321) *(G-10611)*

James Lake Vineyard Inc 260 495-9463
6208 N Van Guilder Rd Fremont (46737) *(G-4963)*

James Mobile Oil Change 219 455-5321
291 S Chase Dr Crown Point (46307) *(G-2266)*

James R McNutt 317 899-6955
3130 N Mitthoefer Rd Indianapolis (46235) *(G-7297)*

James W Hager 765 643-0188
5731 N 100 E Alexandria (46001) *(G-46)*

James Wafford 317 773-7200
1720 S 10th St Noblesville (46060) *(G-11135)*

Jamil Packaging Corporation (PA) 574 256-2600
1420 Industrial Dr Mishawaka (46544) *(G-10059)*

Jamplast Inc 812 838-8562
6450 Leonard Rd N Mount Vernon (47620) *(G-10397)*

Janco Engineered Products LLC 574 255-3169
1217 E 7th St Mishawaka (46544) *(G-10060)*

Janesville Acoustics, Richmond *Also called Jason Incorporated (G-12005)*

Janette Walker 219 937-9160
1050 Eaton St Hammond (46320) *(G-5902)*

Jani Industries Inc 317 985-3916
2256 N County Road 800 E Avon (46123) *(G-449)*

Janis Buhl 765 478-5448
26 W Church St Cambridge City (47327) *(G-1258)*

Jar Welding & Machine Inc 812 752-6253
1217 S Gardner St Scottsburg (47170) *(G-12369)*

Jarden Brands Consumables, Fishers *Also called Hearthmark LLC (G-3924)*

Jarden Home Brands, Muncie *Also called Hearthmark LLC (G-10485)*

Jarrod Zachary Weld 765 230-6424
3384 E State Road 32 Crawfordsville (47933) *(G-2164)*

Jason Incorporated 248 455-7919
3031 W Industries Rd Richmond (47374) *(G-12005)*

Jason Incorporated 800 787-7325
2350 Salisbury Rd N Richmond (47374) *(G-12006)*

Jason Incorporated 847 215-1948
2350 Salisbury Rd N Richmond (47374) *(G-12007)*

Jason Industries Inc 574 294-7595
1500 W Lusher Ave Elkhart (46517) *(G-2945)*

Jason Randall Designs 317 319-6747
361 W 300 S Kokomo (46902) *(G-8650)*

Jasper Chair Company Inc 812 482-5239
534 E 8th St Jasper (47546) *(G-8255)*

Jasper Desk Company Inc (PA) 812 482-4132
415 E 6th St Jasper (47546) *(G-8256)*

Jasper Desk Company Inc 812 482-6827
415 E 6th St Jasper (47546) *(G-8257)*

Jasper Electric Motor Inc (HQ) 812 482-1660
815 Wernsing Rd Jasper (47546) *(G-8258)*

Jasper Electric Motor Inc 812 482-1660
733 W Division Rd Jasper (47546) *(G-8259)*

Jasper EMB & Screen Prtg 812 482-4787
310 Main St Jasper (47546) *(G-8260)*

Jasper EMB & Screenprinting, Jasper *Also called Jasper EMB & Screen Prtg (G-8260)*

Jasper Engine Exchange Inc (PA) 812 482-1041
815 Wernsing Rd Jasper (47546) *(G-8261)*

Jasper Engine Exchange Inc 812 482-1041
6400 E Industrial Ln Leavenworth (47137) *(G-9164)*

Jasper Engines & Transmissions, Jasper *Also called Jasper Engine Exchange Inc (G-8261)*

Jasper Group, Jasper *Also called Jasper Seating Company Inc (G-8264)*

Jasper Group, Paoli *Also called Jasper Seating Company Inc (G-11454)*

Jasper Optical Lab 812 634-9020
231 S Us Highway 231 Jasper (47546) *(G-8262)*

Jasper Plastics Solutions, Syracuse *Also called Jp Incorporated - Indiana (G-13136)*

Jasper Rubber Products Inc (PA) 812 482-3242
1010 1st Ave W Jasper (47546) *(G-8263)*

Jasper Seating Company Inc (PA) 812 482-3204
225 Clay St Jasper (47546) *(G-8264)*

Jasper Seating Company Inc 812 936-9977
8084 W County Road 25 S French Lick (47432) *(G-4987)*

Jasper Seating Company Inc 812 326-2361
4582 S Cross St Saint Anthony (47575) *(G-12247)*

Jasper Seating Company Inc 812 723-1323
1352 W Hospital Rd Paoli (47454) *(G-11454)*

Jasper Veneer Inc 812 482-4245
810 W 14th St Jasper (47546) *(G-8265)*

Jasper Willow Springs Mo LLC 800 827-7455
815 Wernsing Rd Jasper (47546) *(G-8266)*

JAT Inc LLC 317 201-3684
1638 Lancashire Ct Apt E Indianapolis (46260) *(G-7298)*

Jatech Scientific Inc (PA) 765 345-2085
117 S Franklin St Knightstown (46148) *(G-8553)*

Jatex Inc 574 773-5928
551 Shawnee St Nappanee (46550) *(G-10687)*

Java Roaster 765 742-2037
130 N 3rd St Lafayette (47901) *(G-8930)*

Jay C Food 84 .... 812 886-9311
1400 Washington Ave Vincennes (47591) *(G-13686)*

Jay Costas Companies Inc 219 663-4364
1492 N Main St Crown Point (46307) *(G-2267)*

Jay Mobile Home Additions 260 726-9274
2443 N 200 W Portland (47371) *(G-11830)*

Jay Orner Sons Billiard Co Inc (PA) 317 243-0046
6333 Rockville Rd Indianapolis (46214) *(G-7299)*

Jay Retail Systems LLC 574 842-2313
402 W Cass St Culver (46511) *(G-2325)*

Jayco Inc (HQ) 574 825-5861
903 S Main St Middlebury (46540) *(G-9896)*

JB Graphics Inc 317 819-0008
1422 Keystone Way Carmel (46032) *(G-1419)*

Jbd Machining 765 671-9050
1702 W Jeffras Ave Marion (46952) *(G-9538)*

Jbh Manufacturing LLC 574 612-1379
57210 County Road 23 Goshen (46528) *(G-5247)*

Jbm Race Cars LLC 812 305-3666
7901 Newburgh Rd Evansville (47715) *(G-3572)*

Jbs Powder Coating LLC 812 952-1204
7320 Thomas Ave Ne Lanesville (47136) *(G-9101)*

Jbs United Inc 800 382-9909
4310 W State Road 38 Sheridan (46069) *(G-12591)*

Jbs United Inc 317 758-2609
322 S Main St Sheridan (46069) *(G-12592)*

Jbs United Animal Hlth II LLC 317 758-2616
322 S Main St Sheridan (46069) *(G-12593)*

Jbs United Trading Inc 317 758-4495
4310 W State Road 38 Sheridan (46069) *(G-12594)*

JC Distributers Inc 502 276-6311
505 Amelie Dr Ste 2 Jeffersonville (47130) *(G-8382)*

JC Metal Fabrication 574 340-1109
15393 Kelly Rd Mishawaka (46544) *(G-10061)*

JC Moag Corporation 812 284-8400
249 America Pl Jeffersonville (47130) *(G-8383)*

JC Printing 574 721-9000
301 Burlington Ave Logansport (46947) *(G-9343)*

JC Printing & Mailing 765 742-6829
3711 Piney Grove Dr Colburn (47905) *(G-1752)*

JC Refrigeration LLC 260 768-4067
6495 W 200 N Shipshewana (46565) *(G-12622)*

JC Treeations Inc 219 322-2911
842 Manistee Ave Schererville (46375) *(G-12325)*

Jci Jones Chemicals Inc 317 787-8382
600 Bethel Ave Beech Grove (46107) *(G-599)*

Jcr Automation Inc 260 749-6606
1426 Ryan Rd New Haven (46774) *(G-10945)*

Jcs Enterprises Inc. 812 284-4827
757 E Lewis & Clark Pkwy Clarksville (47129) *(G-1688)*

JD Materials 219 662-1418
11563 Baker St Crown Point (46307) *(G-2268)*

JD Metal Concepts Inc 812 342-9111
1522 Bridle Way Blvd Columbus (47201) *(G-1950)*

JD Norman Industries Inc 765 288-8098
3301 W Mt Pleasant Blvd Muncie (47302) *(G-10499)*

JD Norman Industries Inc 765 584-6069
1099 Rainbow Dr Winchester (47394) *(G-14334)*

JDC Veneers Inc 812 284-9775
276 America Pl Jeffersonville (47130) *(G-8384)*

Jds Pugh Cabinets Inc 317 835-2910
5720 N London Rd Fairland (46126) *(G-3822)*

2018 Harris Indiana
Industrial Directory

(G-0000) Company's Geographic Section entry number

Jdsu Acterna Holdings LLC....317 788-9351
5808 Churchman Byp Indianapolis (46203) *(G-7300)*
Jeannie and Rachel Heidenreich....260 244-4583
1240 N Airport Rd Columbia City (46725) *(G-1801)*
Jeannine Stassen....765 289-3756
1217 W University Ave Muncie (47303) *(G-10500)*
Jeans Extrusions Inc....812 883-2581
201 Jeans Dr Salem (47167) *(G-12296)*
Jec Steel Company (PA)....574 326-3829
1137 Verdant St Elkhart (46516) *(G-2946)*
Jeco Plastic Products LLC....317 839-4943
885 Andico Rd Plainfield (46168) *(G-11621)*
Jeda Equipment Services Inc....317 842-9377
13270 Summerwood Ln Fishers (46038) *(G-3933)*
Jef Enterprises Inc (PA)....812 425-0628
1200 W Columbia St Evansville (47710) *(G-3573)*
Jeff Halls Logging Inc....812 941-8020
2358 W Riley Rd Floyds Knobs (47119) *(G-4015)*
Jeff Hury Hardwood Floors Pntg....812 204-8650
629 S Norman Ave Evansville (47714) *(G-3574)*
Jeffboat LLC....812 288-0200
1701 E Market St Jeffersonville (47130) *(G-8385)*
Jefferson Homebuilders Inc....317 398-0874
701 W Mausoleum Rd Shelbyville (46176) *(G-12541)*
Jeffreys Good Soap LLC....219 926-3447
709 Plaza Dr Ste 151 Chesterton (46304) *(G-1615)*
Jeld-Wen Inc....260 894-7111
200 Gerber St Ligonier (46767) *(G-9288)*
Jem Printing Inc....812 376-9264
808 3rd St Ste C Columbus (47201) *(G-1951)*
Jem Software Development LLC....812 339-2970
2957 N Ramble Rd E Bloomington (47408) *(G-753)*
Jemarkel Health-Tech LLC....219 548-5881
2701 Beech St Ste R Valparaiso (46383) *(G-13563)*
Jemdd LLC....260 768-4156
5680 W 100 N Lagrange (46761) *(G-9049)*
Jenco Engineering Inc....574 267-4608
27 E 250 N Warsaw (46582) *(G-13895)*
Jennerjahn Machine Inc....765 998-2733
901 S Massachusetts Ave Matthews (46957) *(G-9652)*
Jennings County Pallets Inc....812 458-6288
5195 E Us Highway 50 Butlerville (47223) *(G-1248)*
Jennings County Pallets Inc (PA)....812 458-6288
5195 E Us Highway 50 Butlerville (47223) *(G-1249)*
Jenny Lynn Soap Company LLC....219 863-8243
402 S Mckinley Ave Rensselaer (47978) *(G-11929)*
Jennys Backery....260 447-9592
4151 Diplomat Plaza Ctr Fort Wayne (46806) *(G-4393)*
Jensen Cabinet Inc....260 456-2131
205 Murray St Fort Wayne (46803) *(G-4394)*
Jensen Publications Inc....317 514-8864
7333 Fox Hollow Rdg Zionsville (46077) *(G-14440)*
Jenson Industries Inc....317 871-0122
8219 Zionsville Rd Indianapolis (46268) *(G-7301)*
Jer-Maur Corporation....812 384-8290
119 E Main St Bloomfield (47424) *(G-640)*
Jerden Industries Inc....812 332-1762
1104 S Morton St Bloomington (47403) *(G-754)*
Jeremy Parker....765 284-5414
3501 N Grnvlle Ave Ste 95 Muncie (47303) *(G-10501)*
Jerico Metal Specialties Inc....812 339-3182
1111 W 17th St Ste 1 Bloomington (47404) *(G-755)*
Jerry L Fuelling....317 709-6978
8470 E 300 S Zionsville (46077) *(G-14441)*
Jerry Lambert....765 378-7599
10010 S County Road 900 W Daleville (47334) *(G-2340)*
Jerry Lewis Cnstr & Excvtg, Greencastle *Also called Lewis Jerry Cnstr & Excvtg* *(G-5467)*
Jessco, Wakarusa *Also called J Jesse Inc* *(G-13780)*
Jessen Manufacturing Co Inc....574 295-3836
1409 W Beardsley Ave Elkhart (46514) *(G-2947)*
Jessup Paper Box LLC....765 588-9137
4775 Dale Dr Lafayette (47905) *(G-8931)*
Jet City Specialties, Ligonier *Also called Blackpoint Engineering LLC* *(G-9277)*
Jet Engineering, Warsaw *Also called Symmetry Medical Mfg Inc* *(G-13949)*
Jet Technologies Inc....574 264-3613
53893 N Park Ave Elkhart (46514) *(G-2948)*
Jeter Winery Inc....317 862-9193
7302 Kita Dr Indianapolis (46259) *(G-7302)*
Jewelers Boutique Inc....317 788-7679
3320 Madison Ave Indianapolis (46227) *(G-7303)*
Jezroc Metalworks LLC....317 417-1132
205 S 1100 E Zionsville (46077) *(G-14442)*
Jfs Milling Inc....812 324-2022
5167 N State Road 67 Bruceville (47516) *(G-1197)*
Jfw Industries Incorporated....317 887-1340
5134 Commerce Square Dr Indianapolis (46237) *(G-7304)*
JG and JG Industries LLC....765 742-0260
1609 Hart St Lafayette (47904) *(G-8932)*
JG Grinestoppers, Warsaw *Also called Super Car Wash of Warsaw* *(G-13943)*
Jgr Enterprises LLC....586 264-3400
6525 Daniel Burnham Dr D Portage (46368) *(G-11771)*
Jiffy Lube, Fort Wayne *Also called Illinois Lubricants LLC* *(G-4358)*
Jiffy Lube....317 882-5823
320 S Emerson Ave Greenwood (46143) *(G-5709)*
Jigsaw Creations....260 691-2196
5867 N 350 E Columbia City (46725) *(G-1802)*
Jim Couch....574 533-5107
1206 Westbrooke Ct Goshen (46528) *(G-5248)*
Jim Graber Logging LLC....812 636-7000
10514 N 1000 E Odon (47562) *(G-11331)*
Jim Rhodes Logging....812 739-4221
2121 W State Road 62 English (47118) *(G-3313)*
Jimco Engineering Co....317 923-2290
3315 Sutherland Ave Indianapolis (46218) *(G-7305)*
Jinnings Equipment LLC....260 447-4343
4434 Allen Martin Dr Fort Wayne (46806) *(G-4395)*
Jj Machine....765 723-1511
8834 E 400 S New Ross (47968) *(G-11005)*
Jk Graphics Inc....219 374-5930
12546 Parrish Ave Cedar Lake (46303) *(G-1531)*
JKL Software....765 778-3032
210 E Water St Pendleton (46064) *(G-11491)*
Jknk Ventures Inc....812 246-0900
1511 Avco Blvd Sellersburg (47172) *(G-12399)*
Jkp Printing Inc....574 246-1650
1701 Linden Ave South Bend (46628) *(G-12822)*
Jkr Inc....260 665-1067
301 Growth Pkwy Angola (46703) *(G-221)*
Jl Manfcturing Fabrication Inc....260 589-3723
3633 E 800 S Berne (46711) *(G-618)*
Jl Vincent Enterprises, Peru *Also called Vickery Tape & Label Co Inc* *(G-11555)*
JL Walter & Associates Inc....317 524-3600
1211 Roosevelt Ave Indianapolis (46202) *(G-7306)*
Jlb Industrial LLC....765 561-1751
5066 S The Farm Rd Rushville (46173) *(G-12225)*
Jlm Pharmatech, Seymour *Also called Pd Sub LLC* *(G-12474)*
Jlp Manufacturing LLC....765 647-2991
6059 Graf Rd Brookville (47012) *(G-1120)*
JM Christian LLC....317 460-0984
882 N 350 E Chesterton (46304) *(G-1616)*
JM Fittings LLC....260 747-9200
9910 Airport Dr Fort Wayne (46809) *(G-4396)*
JM Hutton & Co Inc (PA)....765 962-3591
1501 S 8th St Richmond (47374) *(G-12008)*
JM Hutton & Co Inc....765 962-3506
1117 N E St Richmond (47374) *(G-12009)*
JM Hutton & Company, Richmond *Also called JM Hutton & Co Inc* *(G-12009)*
JM Machine....219 464-4477
354 W Division Rd Valparaiso (46385) *(G-13564)*
JMS Electronics Corporation....574 522-0246
4400 Wyland Dr Elkhart (46516) *(G-2949)*
JMS Engineered Plastics Inc....574 277-3228
52275 State Road 933 South Bend (46637) *(G-12823)*
JMS Mold & Engineering Co Inc....574 272-0198
50941 Ind St Rte 933 South Bend (46637) *(G-12824)*
Jmt, Mooresville *Also called Jacobs Machine & Tool Co Inc* *(G-10316)*
Jnp Custom Designs, Indianapolis *Also called J N P Custom Designs Inc* *(G-7289)*
Jns Sports....317 852-8314
6390 N County Road 550 E Brownsburg (46112) *(G-1158)*
JO Mory Inc....260 897-3541
201 Progress Way Avilla (46710) *(G-407)*
Joans T-Shirt Printing LLC....812 934-2616
16 E Boehringer St Batesville (47006) *(G-506)*
Job Scholar LLC....419 564-9574
4399 E 300 N Huntington (46750) *(G-6221)*
Job Shop Coating Inc....317 462-9714
18 E Pierson St Greenfield (46140) *(G-5544)*
Jobsite Mobile Offices, Rochester *Also called Jobsite Trailer Corporation* *(G-12130)*
Jobsite Trailer Corporation....574 224-4000
1393 N Lucas St Rochester (46975) *(G-12130)*
Joe Lorey Music, Jasper *Also called B JS Electronics* *(G-8237)*
Joe Tricker....630 759-0251
13114 Zinfandel Pl Fishers (46038) *(G-3934)*
Joe W Morgan Inc....812 423-5914
1901 W Louisiana St Evansville (47710) *(G-3575)*
Joe Wade Customs....765 548-0333
324 N Main St Rosedale (47874) *(G-12204)*
Joe Woodrow....765 866-0436
107 W Main St New Market (47965) *(G-10963)*
Jofco Inc (PA)....812 482-5154
225 Clay St Jasper (47546) *(G-8267)*
Jofco Inc....812 482-5154
305 E 12th Ave Jasper (47546) *(G-8268)*
Jofco, International, Jasper *Also called Jofco Inc* *(G-8267)*
John Davern, Dana *Also called Davern Machine Shop* *(G-2342)*
John Deere Authorized Dealer, Seymour *Also called Deer Country Equipment LLC* *(G-12444)*

A L P H A B E T I C

John Deere Landscapes, Merrillville *Also called Siteone Landscape Supply LLC* ***(G-9754)***
John G Wagler 812 709-1681
9639 N 1150 E Odon (47562) ***(G-11332)***
John Garrison Woodworking LLC 765 795-4681
2951 Combes Rd Quincy (47456) ***(G-11891)***
John Gebhart Woodworkings 765 492-3898
5352 N Fable St Cayuga (47928) ***(G-1521)***
John King 317 801-3080
6515 Olivia Ln Indianapolis (46226) ***(G-7307)***
John Ley Monument Sales Inc 260 347-7346
101 Progress Way Avilla (46710) ***(G-408)***
John M Wooley Lumber Company 317 831-2700
200 E South St Mooresville (46158) ***(G-10317)***
John Pater Design Fabrication 812 926-4845
5298 Hartford Pike Aurora (47001) ***(G-381)***
John Remmler Well Drilling 812 663-8178
3970 N County Rd 500 N Greensburg (47240) ***(G-5616)***
John S Davis Inc 812 347-2707
8605 Big John Rd Nw Depauw (47115) ***(G-2457)***
John Thrasher, Camby *Also called Wax Shield* ***(G-1270)***
John Wallace Builder Inc 765 447-3614
301 S 675 E Lafayette (47905) ***(G-8933)***
John Wiley and Sons Publishing, Indianapolis *Also called Wiley Publishing Inc* ***(G-8198)***
Johnco Corp 317 576-4417
8770 Commerce Park Pl F Indianapolis (46268) ***(G-7308)***
Johnny Bontrager 260 463-8912
1735 N 400 W Lagrange (46761) ***(G-9050)***
Johnny Graber Woodworking 260 466-4957
11522 Notestine Rd Grabill (46741) ***(G-5376)***
Johnny Lemas 260 833-8850
2314 N 200 W Angola (46703) ***(G-222)***
Johns Architectural Media 630 450-7539
10544 Mimosa St Dyer (46311) ***(G-2502)***
Johns Butcher Shop 574 773-4632
158 N Main St Nappanee (46550) ***(G-10688)***
Johns Fine Cabinetry 765 296-2388
594 N 850 E Colburn (47905) ***(G-1753)***
Johns Manville Corporation 765 973-5200
814 Richmond Ave Richmond (47374) ***(G-12010)***
Johns Manville Corporation 574 546-4666
1215 W Dewey St Bremen (46506) ***(G-1006)***
Johns Welding and Fabrication 574 936-1702
1203 N Michigan St Plymouth (46563) ***(G-11697)***
Johnson & Johnson 732 524-0400
10284 Seagrave Dr Fishers (46037) ***(G-3935)***
Johnson & Johnson 317 539-8300
2100 Innovation Blvd Mooresville (46158) ***(G-10318)***
Johnson Bros S Whitley Sign Co 260 723-5161
304 N Calhoun St South Whitley (46787) ***(G-13000)***
Johnson Brothers Sign Co ., South Whitley *Also called Johnson Bros S Whitley Sign Co* ***(G-13000)***
Johnson Contrls Authorized Dlr, Lafayette *Also called Duncan Supply Co Inc* ***(G-8892)***
Johnson Controls 812 423-9000
2225 N Burkhardt Rd Evansville (47715) ***(G-3576)***
Johnson Controls 260 692-6666
424 S Vanburen St Monroe (46772) ***(G-10183)***
Johnson Controls 812 423-9000
800 Canal St Evansville (47713) ***(G-3577)***
Johnson Controls 317 826-2130
11820 Pendleton Pike Indianapolis (46236) ***(G-7309)***
Johnson Controls Inc 260 489-6104
1300 Airport North Off Pa Fort Wayne (46825) ***(G-4397)***
Johnson Controls Inc 317 917-5043
314 Brixton Woods West Dr Pittsboro (46167) ***(G-11583)***
Johnson Controls Inc 260 347-0500
300 S Progress Dr E Kendallville (46755) ***(G-8481)***
Johnson Controls Inc 219 736-7105
2293 N Main St Crown Point (46307) ***(G-2269)***
Johnson Controls Inc 260 485-9999
6010 Brandy Chase Cv Fort Wayne (46815) ***(G-4398)***
Johnson Controls Inc 260 479-4400
8710 Indianapolis Rd Fort Wayne (46809) ***(G-4399)***
Johnson Controls Inc 812 868-1374
8401 N Kentucky Ave Ste H Evansville (47725) ***(G-3578)***
Johnson Eh Construction LLC 812 344-8450
8079 Grandview Rd Columbus (47201) ***(G-1952)***
Johnson Engraving & Trophies 260 982-7868
1302 Beckley St North Manchester (46962) ***(G-11232)***
Johnson Hardware, Elkhart *Also called L E Johnson Products Inc* ***(G-2977)***
Johnson Materials 812 373-9044
450 Franklin St Columbus (47201) ***(G-1953)***
Johnson Plastics & Sup Co Inc 812 424-5554
1414 Baker Ave Evansville (47710) ***(G-3579)***
Johnson Safe Company 317 876-7233
8750 E 200 S Zionsville (46077) ***(G-14443)***
Johnson Sales Corp 219 322-9558
1145 Birch Dr Schererville (46375) ***(G-12326)***
Johnsons Orthotics Prosthetics 317 272-9993
5055 E Us Highway 36 # 200 Avon (46123) ***(G-450)***
Johnsons Welding Service 317 835-2438
7908 W 525 N Boggstown (46110) ***(G-901)***
Joint & Clutch Service Inc 317 264-5038
2075 Kentucky Ave Indianapolis (46221) ***(G-7310)***
Jojos Pretzels 260 768-7759
205 N Harrison St Shipshewana (46565) ***(G-12623)***
Jolar Enterprises 574 875-8369
58052 Ox Bow Dr Elkhart (46516) ***(G-2950)***
Jolene D Pavey 765 473-6171
4641 S 50 W Peru (46970) ***(G-11534)***
Jolliff Diesel Service 812 692-5725
7325 E 1500 N Elnora (47529) ***(G-3290)***
Jolliff, Phillip, Elnora *Also called Jolliff Diesel Service* ***(G-3290)***
Jomar Machining & Fabg Inc 574 825-9837
13393 County Road 22 Middlebury (46540) ***(G-9897)***
Jon E Gee Enterprises Inc 317 291-4522
4000 W 106th St Carmel (46032) ***(G-1420)***
Jones & Sons Inc (PA) 812 254-4731
1262 S State Road 57 Washington (47501) ***(G-13988)***
Jones & Sons Inc 812 882-2957
784 S 6th Street Rd Vincennes (47591) ***(G-13687)***
Jones & Sons Inc 812 299-2287
3527 Erie Canal Rd Terre Haute (47802) ***(G-13261)***
Jones & Webb Associates Inc 317 236-9755
151 N Delaware St Ste 120 Indianapolis (46204) ***(G-7311)***
Jones Engineering Inc 812 254-6456
897 W 150 S Washington (47501) ***(G-13989)***
Jones Fabrication & Machining 812 466-2237
5600 N Us Highway 41 Terre Haute (47805) ***(G-13262)***
Jones Machine & Tool Inc 812 364-4588
14710 N Xrd Nw Fredericksburg (47120) ***(G-4945)***
Jones Popcorn Inc 812 941-8810
125 Quality Ave New Albany (47150) ***(G-10810)***
Jones Trucking Inc 765 537-2279
2468 S State Road 67 Paragon (46166) ***(G-11459)***
Jonesville Desk, North Vernon *Also called Indiana Southern Millwork Inc* ***(G-11263)***
Jordan Manufacturing Co Inc (PA) 800 328-6522
1200 S 6th St Monticello (47960) ***(G-10268)***
Josam Company (PA) 219 872-5531
525 W Us Highway 20 Michigan City (46360) ***(G-9805)***
Joseph & Jones LLC 317 691-0328
6170 Guilford Ave Indianapolis (46220) ***(G-7312)***
Joseph Fisher 765 435-7231
6492 E 850 N Waveland (47989) ***(G-14028)***
Joseph Lee 317 931-9446
438 S Emerson Ave 211 Greenwood (46143) ***(G-5710)***
Joseph M Schmidt 260 223-3498
7741 N 200 E Decatur (46733) ***(G-2387)***
Jossey-Bass Publishers 877 762-2974
10475 Crosspoint Blvd Indianapolis (46256) ***(G-7313)***
Jostens Inc 317 326-2782
5220 N Sugar Hills Dr Greenfield (46140) ***(G-5545)***
Jostens Inc 317 843-1958
9700 Lake Shore Dr E D Indianapolis (46280) ***(G-6270)***
Journal and Chronicle Inc 812 752-5060
39 E Wardell St Scottsburg (47170) ***(G-12370)***
Journal and Courier, Lafayette *Also called Gannett Co Inc* ***(G-8902)***
Journal Gazette Foundation 260 424-5257
600 W Main St Fort Wayne (46802) ***(G-4400)***
Journal of American History, Bloomington *Also called Indiana University Bloomington* ***(G-748)***
Journal Publishing Co Inc 812 876-2254
211 N Sale St Ellettsville (47429) ***(G-3282)***
Journeyman Tool & Mold Inc 574 237-1880
3601 Gagnon St South Bend (46628) ***(G-12825)***
Journeymann Precision Press 260 724-6934
10921 N State Road 101 Decatur (46733) ***(G-2388)***
Joy Ml Industries Inc 317 876-3917
8707 Arbor Lake Dr # 1523 Indianapolis (46268) ***(G-7314)***
Joy Sweet Cupcakes 219 276-3791
7230 Bell St Schererville (46375) ***(G-12327)***
Joyce Consulting LLC 317 577-8504
9132 Sargent Manor Ct Indianapolis (46256) ***(G-7315)***
Joyce/Dayton Corp 260 726-9361
1621 N Meridian St Portland (47371) ***(G-11831)***
Joyful Noise Recordings LLC 317 632-3220
1030 Orange St Indianapolis (46203) ***(G-7316)***
Jp Incorporated - Indiana 574 457-2062
501 W Railroad Ave Syracuse (46567) ***(G-13136)***
JP Custom Cabinetry Inc 219 956-3587
13467 Whippoorwill Ln Wheatfield (46392) ***(G-14226)***
JP Ownership Group Inc 317 791-1122
5804 Churchman Byp Indianapolis (46203) ***(G-7317)***
JP Signs, Dupont *Also called J W P Vinyl Designs* ***(G-2491)***
JP Technology Inc 219 947-2525
10769 Broadway Crown Point (46307) ***(G-2270)***
Jpc LLC 574 293-8030
2926 Paul Dr Elkhart (46514) ***(G-2951)***
Jpc Mat, Elkhart *Also called Jpc LLC* ***(G-2951)***

ALPHABETIC SECTION

Kaiser Press LLC

Jpe Consulting LLP.....574 675-9552
10451 Dunn Rd Osceola (46561) ***(G-11379)***
Jpg Machine & Tool LLC.....812 265-4512
1263 W Jpg Woodfill Rd # 212 Madison (47250) ***(G-9474)***
Jpt Enterprises Inc.....260 672-1605
6435 W Jefferson Blvd Fort Wayne (46804) ***(G-4401)***
Jr & Sons Woodworking, Lagrange *Also called Johnny Bontrager* ***(G-9050)***
JR Grber Sons Fmly Ltd Prtnr.....260 657-1071
15822 Trammel Rd Grabill (46741) ***(G-5377)***
Jrds Industries.....260 729-5037
1700 N Meridian St Portland (47371) ***(G-11832)***
Jrotten Chopper.....765 517-1779
6563 Wheeling Pike Jonesboro (46938) ***(G-8446)***
Jrowe Signs.....260 668-7100
311 S Superior St Angola (46703) ***(G-223)***
Jrp Machine Co.....317 955-1905
1607 Deloss St Ste B Indianapolis (46201) ***(G-7318)***
Jrs Custom Cabinets Co.....219 696-7205
16855 Mississippi St Lowell (46356) ***(G-9410)***
JRS Custom Fabrication.....765 676-4170
5998 S 500 W Jamestown (46147) ***(G-8231)***
Jrs Wood Shop.....765 498-2663
6950 W 1025 N Kingman (47952) ***(G-8532)***
Jrz Industries Inc.....574 834-4543
133 S East St North Webster (46555) ***(G-11295)***
Jsi, French Lick *Also called Jasper Seating Company Inc* ***(G-4987)***
Jsj Furniture Corporation.....256 768-2871
11451 Harter Dr Middlebury (46540) ***(G-9898)***
Jsj Furniture Corporation.....574 825-5871
11451 Harter Dr Middlebury (46540) ***(G-9899)***
Jsn Advertising Inc.....317 888-7591
8522 Madison Ave Indianapolis (46227) ***(G-7319)***
Jt Composites LLC.....317 297-9520
312 Gasoline Aly Ste C Indianapolis (46222) ***(G-7320)***
Jt Printing LLC.....317 271-7700
77 Park Place Blvd Avon (46123) ***(G-451)***
Jt-Fencing LLC.....765 323-8591
4027 Amethyst Dr Lafayette (47909) ***(G-8934)***
Jtd Enterprises Inc.....574 533-9438
609 N Harrison St Goshen (46528) ***(G-5249)***
Jtm Home & Building.....219 690-1445
16005 Chestnut St Lowell (46356) ***(G-9411)***
Jtn Services Inc.....765 653-7158
4421 S Us Highway 231 Greencastle (46135) ***(G-5465)***
Jubilee Harps Inc.....812 426-2547
2405 Diefenbach Rd Evansville (47720) ***(G-3580)***
Judson Harness & Saddlery.....765 569-0918
4889 E 350 N Rockville (47872) ***(G-12176)***
Jujuberry LLC.....765 673-0058
2020 S Western Ave Marion (46953) ***(G-9539)***
Juncos Racing.....317 640-2348
4401 Gilman St Indianapolis (46224) ***(G-7321)***
Junoll Industries.....574 586-2719
27045 Tyler Rd Walkerton (46574) ***(G-13804)***
Jupiter Aluminum Corporation.....219 932-3322
205 E Carey St Fairland (46126) ***(G-3823)***
Jupiter Aluminum Corporation (PA).....219 932-3322
1745 165th St Ste 6 Hammond (46320) ***(G-5903)***
Jupiter Coil Coating, Fairland *Also called Jupiter Aluminum Corporation* ***(G-3823)***
Jurgen Associates Inc.....317 786-3513
5180 Commerce Cir Indianapolis (46237) ***(G-7322)***
Jus Rite Engineering Inc.....574 522-9600
56977 Elk Ct Elkhart (46516) ***(G-2952)***
Just Desserts Inc.....317 872-2253
7768 Zionsville Rd # 300 Indianapolis (46268) ***(G-7323)***
Just For Granite.....317 842-8255
5277 Emco Dr Indianapolis (46220) ***(G-7324)***
Just Ink LLC.....800 948-7671
1657 Commerce Dr Ste 9b South Bend (46628) ***(G-12826)***
Just Monograms LLC.....812 827-3693
535 University Dr Jasper (47546) ***(G-8269)***
Just Signs Now Advertising, Indianapolis *Also called Jsn Advertising Inc* ***(G-7319)***
Just Standout LLC.....317 531-6956
951 E 86th St Ste 200e Indianapolis (46240) ***(G-7325)***
Justin Blackwell.....812 834-6350
7071 State Road 446 Norman (47264) ***(G-11203)***
Justin Mollo.....812 361-7694
7890 Spearsville Rd Morgantown (46160) ***(G-10355)***
Jws Machine Inc.....812 917-5571
501 S Airport St Terre Haute (47803) ***(G-13263)***
K & B Trailer Sales Mfg.....574 946-4382
93 E 800 N Monterey (46960) ***(G-10207)***
K & D Custom Coach Inc.....574 537-1716
2313 Eisenhower Dr N Goshen (46526) ***(G-5250)***
K & I Hard Chrome Inc.....812 948-1166
1900 E Main St New Albany (47150) ***(G-10811)***
K & I Sash & Door, Evansville *Also called Kentucky-Indiana Lumber Co Inc* ***(G-3584)***
K & K Fence Inc.....317 359-5425
6520 Brookville Rd Indianapolis (46219) ***(G-7326)***
K & K Inc.....574 266-8040
2617 Glenview Dr Elkhart (46514) ***(G-2953)***
K & K Industries Inc.....812 486-3281
8518 E 550 N Montgomery (47558) ***(G-10229)***
K & L Machining Inc.....812 526-4840
6973 S Us Highway 31 Edinburgh (46124) ***(G-2614)***
K & M Tool & Die Inc.....765 482-9464
406 S Patterson St Lebanon (46052) ***(G-9194)***
K & N Carpet, Fort Wayne *Also called Todd K Hockemeyer Inc* ***(G-4689)***
K & P Products, Mishawaka *Also called Vision Machine Works Inc* ***(G-10148)***
K & S Pallet Inc.....260 422-1264
1025 Osage St Fort Wayne (46808) ***(G-4402)***
K A Components, Otterbein *Also called Kerkhoff Associates Inc* ***(G-11419)***
K and S Farm and Machine Shop.....812 663-8567
4620 S County Road 550 E Greensburg (47240) ***(G-5617)***
K C Creations.....937 748-8181
11612 Breckenridge Ct Indianapolis (46236) ***(G-7327)***
K C Designs Printing, Bloomington *Also called Kc Designs* ***(G-757)***
K C Machine Inc.....574 293-1822
56850 Elk Park Dr Elkhart (46516) ***(G-2954)***
K Fab Inc.....812 663-6299
1940 N Montgomery Rd Greensburg (47240) ***(G-5618)***
K Grimmer Industries Inc (PA).....317 736-3800
17301 Juniper Ln Leo (46765) ***(G-9243)***
K Irpcheadstart Program.....219 345-2011
10448 N 450 E Demotte (46310) ***(G-2440)***
K J Pallets.....812 342-6476
10110 S 500 W Columbus (47201) ***(G-1954)***
K J S Associates.....317 842-7500
8431 Castlewood Dr Indianapolis (46250) ***(G-7328)***
K Lash & Son Inc.....260 347-3660
910 Harlash St Kendallville (46755) ***(G-8482)***
K M I, Fremont *Also called Koester Metals Inc* ***(G-4964)***
K M Specialty Pumps Inc.....812 925-3000
8055 Highway 62 W Chandler (47610) ***(G-1550)***
K Min.....574 296-3500
2730 Industrial Pkwy Elkhart (46516) ***(G-2955)***
K Mold and Engineering Inc.....574 272-5858
51383 Bittersweet Rd Granger (46530) ***(G-5417)***
K Ra International LLC.....574 258-7151
3300 W Sample St Ste 1206 South Bend (46619) ***(G-12827)***
K S Oil Corp.....812 453-3026
11625 Ramblewood Ct Evansville (47712) ***(G-3581)***
K Tech Specialty Coatings Inc.....260 587-3888
111 W Garfield St Ashley (46705) ***(G-287)***
K V S Inc.....260 925-0525
1105 W Auburn Dr Auburn (46706) ***(G-338)***
K W Deer Processing.....812 824-2492
1715 E Rayletown Rd Bloomington (47401) ***(G-756)***
K&D Crafts.....812 667-2575
13020 Southfork Rd Dillsboro (47018) ***(G-2469)***
K&M Indiana LLC.....812 256-3351
301 Pike St Charlestown (47111) ***(G-1569)***
K&P Industries LLC.....317 881-9245
1200 Tanglewood Dr Greenwood (46142) ***(G-5711)***
K&T Performance Engrg LLC.....765 437-0185
1975 N Lancer St Peru (46970) ***(G-11535)***
K-K Tool and Design Inc.....260 758-2940
50 Countryside Dr Markle (46770) ***(G-9578)***
K-M Machine & Mfg.....765 886-5717
12691 Indian Trail Rd Economy (47339) ***(G-2592)***
K-Motion Racing Engines.....765 742-8494
2381 N 24th St Lafayette (47904) ***(G-8935)***
K2m Printing.....812 623-3040
5250 E State Road 48 Sunman (47041) ***(G-13113)***
Kabert Fiberglass, Lynn *Also called Kabert Industries Inc* ***(G-9429)***
Kabert Industries Inc.....765 874-2335
514 W Church St Lynn (47355) ***(G-9428)***
Kabert Industries Inc.....765 874-1300
2681 E 800 S Lynn (47355) ***(G-9429)***
Kable Tool & Engineering.....260 726-9670
530 E 300 N Portland (47371) ***(G-11833)***
Kadar Wood Shop, Gary *Also called William A Kadar* ***(G-5116)***
Kadel Engineering Corporation.....317 745-2798
1627 E Main St Danville (46122) ***(G-2350)***
Kadet Products Inc.....765 552-7341
2403 S J St Elwood (46036) ***(G-3303)***
Kaeb Sales Inc.....574 862-2777
27481 County Road 40 Wakarusa (46573) ***(G-13781)***
Kahn's Fine Wines Marketplace, Indianapolis *Also called Cellar Masters LLC* ***(G-6574)***
Kaho Brothers Inc.....812 659-2901
460 E Broad St Lyons (47443) ***(G-9439)***
Kain Tool Inc.....260 829-6569
9775 W Maple St Orland (46776) ***(G-11351)***
Kairos Specialty Metals Corp.....765 836-5540
404 W Main St Mount Summit (47361) ***(G-10379)***
Kaiser Press LLC.....317 619-7092
2525 E 91st St Indianapolis (46240) ***(G-7329)***

ALPHABETIC

Kaiser Tool Company Inc 260 484-3620
  3620 Centennial Dr Fort Wayne (46808) (G-4403)

Kaldewei USA Inc 866 822-2527
  14074 Trade Center Dr # 217 Fishers (46038) (G-3936)

Kaleidoscope Inc 765 423-1951
  1214 North St Lafayette (47904) (G-8936)

Kalems Enterprises Inc 317 399-1645
  8455 Castlewood Dr Ste H Indianapolis (46250) (G-7330)

Kalenborn Abresist Corporation (HQ) 800 348-0717
  5541 N State Road 13 Urbana (46990) (G-13477)

Kaley Centerless Grinding, South Bend Also called Valad McHning Cntrless
Grnding (G-12982)

Kammerer Dynamics Inc 260 349-9098
  5780 E Concrete Dr Kendallville (46755) (G-8483)

Kammerer Inc 260 349-9098
  303 W Wayne St Kendallville (46755) (G-8484)

Kammerer Inc (PA) 260 347-0389
  2348 E Kammerer Rd Kendallville (46755) (G-8485)

Kampco Steel Products Inc 574 294-5466
  57533 County Road 3 Elkhart (46517) (G-2956)

Kamplain Machine Co Inc 317 388-9111
  6360 La Pas Trl Indianapolis (46268) (G-7331)

Kamps Inc 317 634-8360
  1905 S Belmont Ave Indianapolis (46221) (G-7332)

Kamrex Inc 317 204-3779
  7367 Business Center Dr Avon (46123) (G-452)

Kan Jam LLC 317 804-9129
  17401 Tiller Ct Ste A Westfield (46074) (G-14172)

Kane-Miller Corp 219 362-9050
  1755 Genesis Dr La Porte (46350) (G-8775)

Kaniewski & Odle Trckg & Repr, Williamsport Also called Cryogenic Support Systems
Inc (G-14288)

Kankakee Valley Post News 219 987-5111
  827 S Halleck St Demotte (46310) (G-2441)

Kankakee Valley Publishing Co 219 866-5111
  117 N Van Rensselaer St Rensselaer (47978) (G-11930)

Kankakee Valley Steel Inc 219 828-4011
  12632 N 400 E Wheatfield (46392) (G-14227)

Kanoff Enterprises 574 575-6787
  928 W Berry Ave Mishawaka (46545) (G-10062)

Kant Slam Door Check Company, Bloomfield Also called Bloomfield Mfg Co Inc (G-635)

Kaplan Inc 317 872-7220
  7835 Woodland Dr Ste 100 Indianapolis (46278) (G-7333)

Kaplan Enterprises Inc 219 933-7993
  4334 Calumet Ave Hammond (46320) (G-5904)

Karbach Holdings Corporation 219 924-2454
  1701 Northwind Pkwy Hobart (46342) (G-6083)

Karemar Productions 765 766-5117
  6789 E State Road 36 Mooreland (47360) (G-10295)

Karens Kountry Krafts 765 238-2873
  3916 Viking Trl New Castle (47362) (G-10908)

Karma Industries Inc 765 742-9200
  525 Wabash Ave Lafayette (47905) (G-8937)

Karran USA 410 975-0128
  1291 E Ramsey Rd Vincennes (47591) (G-13688)

Karton King, Bloomington Also called Big Red Liquors Inc (G-683)

Karyn K Cleveland 317 698-6787
  8471 Waverly Rd Martinsville (46151) (G-9619)

Kas Satellite & Cable Inc (PA) 260 833-3941
  60 Lane 165 Jimmerson Lk Angola (46703) (G-224)

Kasco Mfg Co Inc 317 398-7973
  170 W 600 N Shelbyville (46176) (G-12542)

Kasnak Designs, Brownsburg Also called Kasnak Restorations Inc (G-1159)

Kasnak Restorations Inc 317 852-9770
  5505 N County Road 1000 E Brownsburg (46112) (G-1159)

Kaspar Broadcasting Co Inc (PA) 765 659-3388
  1401 W Barner St 3 Frankfort (46041) (G-4839)

Kasting Printing Service 317 881-9411
  7146 S Meridian St Indianapolis (46217) (G-7334)

Kathy Zuccarelli 219 865-4095
  1314 Eagle Ridge Dr Schererville (46375) (G-12328)

Kathys Sewing Inc 260 623-6387
  10118 Grotrian Rd Monroeville (46773) (G-10196)

Kauffman Engineering Inc 574 732-2154
  510 E 2nd St Bremen (46506) (G-1007)

Kauffman Engineering Inc (PA) 765 483-4919
  701 Ransdell Rd Lebanon (46052) (G-9195)

Kauffman Engineering Inc 765 482-5640
  202 S Mount Zion Rd Lebanon (46052) (G-9196)

Kauffman Engineering Inc 574 722-3800
  830 State Road 25 S Logansport (46947) (G-9344)

Kauffman Enterprises Inc 260 434-1590
  7875 Shaker Ct Fort Wayne (46804) (G-4404)

Kautex Inc 937 238-8096
  210 Green Dr Avilla (46710) (G-409)

Kautex Inc 260 897-3250
  210 Green Dr Avilla (46710) (G-410)

Kawneer Company Inc 317 882-2314
  1040 Sierra Dr Ste 1500 Greenwood (46143) (G-5712)

Kay Company Inc 765 659-3388
  509 W Barner St Frankfort (46041) (G-4840)

Kay Industries Inc 574 236-6220
  7834 Queen Rd Plymouth (46563) (G-11698)

Kay Industries Inc (PA) 574 236-6220
  7834 Queen Rd Plymouth (46563) (G-11699)

Kayco, Frankfort Also called Kay Company Inc (G-4840)

Kays Graphics Inc 317 236-9755
  151 N Delaware St Ste 120 Indianapolis (46204) (G-7335)

Kbc Machine 317 446-6163
  408 Woodland East Dr Greenfield (46140) (G-5546)

Kbc Machine Inc 317 638-7865
  1740 Wales Ave Indianapolis (46218) (G-7336)

Kbi Inc 765 763-6114
  2618 E Us Highway 52 Morristown (46161) (G-10372)

Kbs Coatings, Valparaiso Also called Advanced Protective Tech LLC (G-13484)

Kbshimmer Bath and Body Inc 317 979-2307
  2820 S State Road 63 Terre Haute (47802) (G-13264)

Kc Designs 812 876-4020
  2801 W Bristol Dr Bloomington (47404) (G-757)

Kc Engineering Inc 317 352-9742
  5602 Elmwood Ave Ste 118 Indianapolis (46203) (G-7337)

KCARC Formerly: Knox, Vincennes Also called Knox County Association (G-13689)

Kci Crane Pro Services 812 479-0488
  2710 Eastside Park Rd C Evansville (47715) (G-3582)

Kcma & Services LLC 260 645-0885
  1954 County Road 43 Waterloo (46793) (G-14016)

Kds Industries LLC 574 333-2720
  21790 Beck Dr Elkhart (46516) (G-2957)

Keck Fine Art 219 306-9474
  13855 Bond Rd Coal City (47427) (G-1741)

Keco Engineered Coatings Inc (PA) 317 356-7279
  1030 S Kealing Ave Indianapolis (46203) (G-7338)

Keefer Graphic Imaging Inc 260 426-7500
  2433 S 600 E Columbia City (46725) (G-1803)

Keefer Printing Company Inc 260 424-4543
  3824 Transportation Dr Fort Wayne (46818) (G-4405)

Keen Screen 812 945-5336
  3314 Grant Line Rd New Albany (47150) (G-10812)

Keener Corporatio - South, Connersville Also called Keener Corporation (G-2060)

Keener Corporation (PA) 765 825-2100
  950 Conwell St Connersville (47331) (G-2058)

Keener Corporation 765 825-2100
  950 Conwell St Connersville (47331) (G-2059)

Keener Corporation 765 825-2711
  950 Conwell St Connersville (47331) (G-2060)

Keesling Custom Pools & Patios 317 823-3526
  10424 Rainbow Ln Indianapolis (46236) (G-7339)

Keihin Aircon North America 765 213-4915
  4400 N Superior Dr Muncie (47303) (G-10502)

Keihin Ipt Mfg 317 578-5260
  9900 Westpoint Dr Indianapolis (46256) (G-7340)

Keihin Ipt Mfg LLC 317 462-3015
  400 W New Rd Greenfield (46140) (G-5547)

Keihin North America Inc (HQ) 765 298-6030
  2701 Enterprise Dr # 100 Anderson (46013) (G-126)

Keil Chemical Corporation 219 931-2630
  3000 Sheffield Ave Hammond (46327) (G-5905)

Keith Bixler 812 866-1637
  352 S Getty Rd Lexington (47138) (G-9252)

Keith Ison 765 938-1460
  615 Conrad Harcourt Way Rushville (46173) (G-12226)

Keline Manufacturing, Elkhart Also called J P Industries Inc (G-2942)

Kelk Publishing LLC 812 268-6356
  249 W Washington St Sullivan (47882) (G-13084)

Kellco, Georgetown Also called Kentuckiana Machine & Tool Inc (G-5146)

Keller Logging LLC 219 309-0379
  210 W 375 S Valparaiso (46385) (G-13565)

Keller Machine & Welding Inc 219 464-4915
  5705 Murvihill Rd Valparaiso (46383) (G-13566)

Keller Tool 812 873-7344
  1085 N County Road 500 E Butlerville (47223) (G-1250)

Keller Tools, Butlerville Also called Keller Tool (G-1250)

Kellers Limestone Service 219 326-1688
  2074 N 50 W La Porte (46350) (G-8776)

Kelley Cadillac LLC 260 434-4646
  811 Avenue Of Autos Fort Wayne (46804) (G-4406)

Kelley Electric 765 778-8203
  2905 Enterprise Dr Anderson (46013) (G-127)

Kelley Global Brands LLC 833 554-8326
  984 Logan St Ste 301 Noblesville (46060) (G-11136)

Kelley Pagels Enterprises LLC 219 872-8552
  500 Huron Michigan City (46360) (G-9806)

Kellmark Corporation 574 264-9695
  2501 Ada Dr Elkhart (46514) (G-2958)

Kellogg Company 812 877-1588
  9445 Us Hwy 40 Seelyville (47878) (G-12386)

Kellogg's Snacks, Terre Haute Also called Indybake Products LLC (G-13257)

Kellum Imprints Inc 812 347-2546
   1675 Highway 64 Nw Ramsey (47166) (G-11893)

Kellum Imprints & Trophies, Ramsey Also called Kellum Imprints Inc (G-11893)

Kelly Box and Packaging Corp (PA) 260 432-4570
   2801 Covington Rd Fort Wayne (46802) (G-4407)

Kelly Metal Products Inc 812 232-1221
   1415 E Pugh St Terre Haute (47802) (G-13265)

Kelwood Designs LLC Cabinetry 574 862-2472
   25440 County Road 138 Goshen (46526) (G-5251)

Kem Krest Corporation 574 389-2650
   2040 Toledo Rd Elkhart (46516) (G-2959)

Kem Krest Defense LLC 574 389-2650
   3221 Magnum Dr Elkhart (46516) (G-2960)

Kemco International Inc 260 829-1263
   9915 W Maple St Orland (46776) (G-11352)

Kemco Manufacturing LLC 574 546-2025
   617 E Plymouth St Bremen (46506) (G-1008)

Kemira Water Solutions Inc 219 397-2646
   3761 Canal St East Chicago (46312) (G-2541)

Kemira Water Solutions Inc 219 397-2646
   3761 Canal St East Chicago (46312) (G-2542)

Kemiron Great Lakes LLC 219 397-2646
   3761 Canal St East Chicago (46312) (G-2543)

Kemtune Inc 260 745-0722
   2015 S Calhoun St Fort Wayne (46802) (G-4408)

Ken Anliker 219 984-5676
   2785 S 75 W Chalmers (47929) (G-1547)

Ken Co Hartland, Rolling Prairie Also called Hartland Products Inc (G-12187)

Ken Tex Crude Producers Inc 812 723-2108
   2401 Mondavi Blvd Lafayette (47909) (G-8938)

Ken-Bar Tool & Engineering Inc 765 284-4408
   3121 S Walnut St Muncie (47302) (G-10503)

Kenco Plastics Inc 219 324-6621
   809 Pine Lake Ave La Porte (46350) (G-8777)

Kenco Plastics Inc (PA) 219 362-7565
   2022 W 450 N La Porte (46350) (G-8778)

Kenco Plastics Inc 219 326-5501
   809 Pine Lake Ave La Porte (46350) (G-8779)

Kendall Enterprise, Indianapolis Also called Proshred Indianapolis Inc (G-7780)

Kendallville Iron & Metal Inc 260 347-1958
   243 E Lisbon Rd Kendallville (46755) (G-8486)

Kendallville Recycle Center, Kendallville Also called New-Indy Hartford City LLC (G-8499)

Kendalville Mall 260 897-2697
   109 N Baum St Avilla (46710) (G-411)

Kendle Custom Inc 812 985-5917
   11711 Boberg Rd Evansville (47712) (G-3583)

Kendrion (mishawaka) LLC 574 257-2422
   56733 Magnetic Dr Mishawaka (46545) (G-10063)

Kenley Corporation 765 825-7150
   950 Conwell St Connersville (47331) (G-2061)

Kenn Feld Group LLC (PA) 260 632-4242
   4724 N State Road 101 Woodburn (46797) (G-14385)

Kennametal Consora Clad, New Albany Also called Kennametal Inc (G-10813)

Kennametal Inc 812 948-2118
   501 Park East Blvd New Albany (47150) (G-10813)

Kennametal Inc 574 534-2585
   1201 Eisenhower Dr N Goshen (46526) (G-5252)

Kennametal Inc 219 362-1000
   300 Philadelphia St La Porte (46350) (G-8780)

Kennametal Inc 317 696-8798
   9217 Backwater Dr Indianapolis (46250) (G-7341)

Kennametal Stellite LP 574 534-9532
   1201 Eisenhower Dr N Goshen (46526) (G-5253)

Kennedy Enterprises Inc 765 724-2225
   2310 Broadway St Anderson (46012) (G-128)

Kennedy Metal Products Inc 219 322-9388
   1050 Kennedy Ave Schererville (46375) (G-12329)

Kennedy Tank & Mfg Co 317 787-1311
   833 E Sumner Ave Indianapolis (46227) (G-7342)

Kenneth Fiekert 812 551-5122
   412 S High St Rising Sun (47040) (G-12089)

Kenneth Fuhrman 812 482-4612
   6711 N 550w Jasper (47546) (G-8270)

Kenney Orthopedics Carmel (HQ) 317 993-3664
   755 W Carmel Dr Carmel (46032) (G-1421)

Kenney Orthopedics Seymour LLC (HQ) 812 271-1627
   629 E Tipton St Seymour (47274) (G-12462)

Kenney Orthpdics Indnpolis LLC (HQ) 317 300-0814
   33 E County Line Rd Ste E Greenwood (46143) (G-5713)

Kenny Dewig Meats Sausage Inc 812 724-2333
   9208 W State Road 165 Owensville (47665) (G-11428)

Kennyleeholmescom 574 612-2526
   25855 Kiser Ct Elkhart (46514) (G-2961)

Kenra Professional LLC (HQ) 317 356-6491
   7445 Company Dr Indianapolis (46237) (G-7343)

Kens Tool & Design 812 268-6653
   2437 N Section St Sullivan (47882) (G-13085)

Kent Brenneke 260 446-5383
   14038 Scipio Rd Harlan (46743) (G-5973)

Kent Machine Inc 765 778-7777
   8677 S State Road 9 Pendleton (46064) (G-11492)

Kent Nutrition Group Inc 574 722-5368
   2407 S County Road 400 E Logansport (46947) (G-9345)

Kentner Creek, Wabash Also called West Plains Distribution LLC (G-13767)

Kentuckiana Machine & Tool 502 301-9005
   4550 Lazy Creek Rd Ne Lanesville (47136) (G-9102)

Kentuckiana Machine & Tool Inc 502 593-3975
   518 Maplewood Blvd Georgetown (47122) (G-5146)

Kentuckiana Publishing 812 273-2259
   307 Jefferson St Madison (47250) (G-9475)

Kentuckiana Wire Rope & Supply 812 282-3667
   3335 Industrial Pkwy Jeffersonville (47130) (G-8386)

Kentuckiana Yacht Services LLC 812 282-2660
   700 E Market St Jeffersonville (47130) (G-8387)

Kentucky Concrete Indiana LLC 812 282-6671
   2220 Hamburg Pike Jeffersonville (47130) (G-8388)

Kentucky Korner, Clarksville Also called Jcs Enterprises Inc (G-1688)

Kentucky Wood Floors LLC 812 256-2164
   533 Louis Smith Rd Borden (47106) (G-932)

Kentucky-Indiana Lumber Co Inc 812 464-2428
   1700 N Kentucky Ave Evansville (47711) (G-3584)

Kep Chem Inc 574 739-0501
   616 Center Ave Logansport (46947) (G-9346)

Keppler Steel and Fabricating 765 289-1529
   1401 S Macedonia Ave Muncie (47302) (G-10504)

Kerham Inc 260 483-5444
   205 E Collins Rd Fort Wayne (46825) (G-4409)

Kerkhoff Associates Inc (PA) 765 583-4491
   21 W Oxford St Otterbein (47970) (G-11419)

Kern's Speed & Racing Products, Bedford Also called Kerns Speed Shop (G-556)

Kerns Speed Shop 812 275-4289
   203 Newton St Bedford (47421) (G-556)

Kerr Concrete Pipe Co 317 569-9949
   600 E Carmel Dr Ste 154 Carmel (46032) (G-1422)

Kerr Group LLC 812 424-2904
   315 Se 2nd St Evansville (47713) (G-3585)

Kerry Inc 812 464-9151
   1515 Park St Evansville (47710) (G-3586)

Kerry Inc 812 464-9151
   1615 N Fulton Ave Evansville (47710) (G-3587)

Kerst Pallet 765 585-3026
   945 N Milligan Hill Rd Attica (47918) (G-306)

Kessco Water LLC (PA) 765 362-3890
   2207b Indianapolis Rd Crawfordsville (47933) (G-2165)

Kessington LLC 574 266-4500
   1020 County Road 6 W Elkhart (46514) (G-2962)

Kessington Machine Products, Elkhart Also called Kessington LLC (G-2962)

Kester Logging Inc 765 672-8170
   5596 S County Road 625 W Reelsville (46171) (G-11902)

Kesters Electric Motor Service 574 269-2889
   1408 Armstrong Rd Warsaw (46580) (G-13896)

Ketch Publishing 812 327-0072
   4675 N Benton Dr Bloomington (47408) (G-758)

Keter North America LLC 765 298-6800
   6435 S Scatterfield Rd Anderson (46013) (G-129)

Kettle Processed Foods, Morristown Also called Park 100 Foods Inc (G-10375)

Keurig Dr Pepper Inc 812 522-3823
   1450 Schleter Rd Seymour (47274) (G-12463)

Keusch Glass Inc 812 482-2566
   403 E 23rd St Jasper (47546) (G-8271)

Kevin Coomer Pallet Co 765 324-2294
   8930 W County Road 650 S Colfax (46035) (G-1756)

Kevin Kolish Corp 574 946-3238
   436 N Monticello St Winamac (46996) (G-14309)

Kewanna Metal Specialties Inc (PA) 574 653-2554
   419 W Main St Kewanna (46939) (G-8525)

Kewanna Screen Printing Inc 574 653-2683
   109 Toner St Kewanna (46939) (G-8526)

Key Electronics Inc 812 206-2500
   2533 Centennial Blvd Jeffersonville (47130) (G-8389)

Key Fasteners Corp 260 589-2626
   525 Key Way Dr Berne (46711) (G-619)

Key Made Now 317 664-8582
   317 N Kenyon St Indianapolis (46219) (G-7344)

Key Millwork Inc 260 426-6501
   1830 Wayne Trce Fort Wayne (46803) (G-4410)

Key Sheet Metal Inc 317 546-7151
   1128 E Maryland St Indianapolis (46202) (G-7345)

Keys R US 317 616-0267
   3210 E Thompson Rd Indianapolis (46227) (G-7346)

Keystone Automotive Inds Inc 574 206-1421
   2304 Charlotte Ave Elkhart (46517) (G-2963)

Keystone Automotive Industries, Huntington Also called Transmetco Corporation (G-6255)

Keystone Concrete Inc (PA) 260 693-6437
   12628 Us Highway 33 N Churubusco (46723) (G-1653)

Keystone Consulting Services 260 693-0250
   114 Mill St Churubusco (46723) (G-1654)

Keystone Designs Inc 574 269-5531
   3606 E Us Highway 30 Warsaw (46580) (G-13897)

A
L
P
H
A
B
E
T
I
C

Keystone Engrg & Mfg Corp (PA) 317 271-6192
  9786 E County Road 200 N Avon (46123) *(G-453)*
Keystone Machine Services Inc 219 397-6792
  1520 E Chicago Ave East Chicago (46312) *(G-2544)*
Keystone Rv Company 574 535-2100
  2420 Hackberry Dr Goshen (46526) *(G-5254)*
Keystone Rv Company (HQ) 574 534-9430
  2642 Hackberry Dr Goshen (46526) *(G-5255)*
Keystone Rv Company 574 535-2100
  2425 Davis Dr Goshen (46526) *(G-5256)*
Keywest LLC 317 821-8419
  4811 S High School Rd Indianapolis (46221) *(G-7347)*
Keywest Metal 219 513-8429
  2034 N Griffith Blvd Griffith (46319) *(G-5781)*
Keywest Metal 219 654-4063
  6338 E 35th Ave Hobart (46342) *(G-6084)*
KFC Composite Engineering Inc 219 369-9093
  3451 S State Road 104 La Porte (46350) *(G-8781)*
Kgn Software LLC 812 618-4723
  5100 Vogel Rd Evansville (47715) *(G-3588)*
Kh, Crown Point *Also called Kiemle-Hankins Company (G-2271)*
Kh Woodworking 317 702-5094
  739 W North St Greenfield (46140) *(G-5548)*
Khamis Fine Jewelers Inc 317 841-8440
  9763 Fall Creek Rd Indianapolis (46256) *(G-7348)*
Khorporate Holdings Inc (PA) 260 357-3365
  6492 State Road 205 Laotto (46763) *(G-9110)*
Kibbechem Inc 574 266-1234
  1139 All Pro Dr Elkhart (46514) *(G-2964)*
Kick Out Jams LLC 765 763-0225
  6559 E 1200 N Morristown (46161) *(G-10373)*
Kids At Heart Publishing LLC 765 478-5773
  215 W Main St Cambridge City (47327) *(G-1259)*
Kids Place, Scottsburg *Also called New Hope Services Inc (G-12377)*
Kids World Productions Inc 317 674-6090
  11551 Willow Bend Dr Zionsville (46077) *(G-14444)*
Kidstuff Playsystems Inc 219 938-3331
  5400 Miller Ave Gary (46403) *(G-5072)*
Kiel Media LLC 219 544-2060
  16 E Main St La Crosse (46348) *(G-8720)*
Kiel NA LLC 574 293-3600
  2009 Middlebury St Elkhart (46516) *(G-2965)*
Kiel North America, Elkhart *Also called Kiel NA LLC (G-2965)*
Kiemle-Hankins Company 219 213-2643
  1011 E Summit St Crown Point (46307) *(G-2271)*
Kiesler Machine Inc 812 364-6610
  13700 S Mrtn Mathis Rd Ne Palmyra (47164) *(G-11436)*
Kihm Metal Technologies, Brazil *Also called Ms Manufacturing LLC (G-972)*
Kik Aerosol Socal LLC 626 363-6200
  1919 Superior St Elkhart (46516) *(G-2966)*
Kik Cusrtom Products, Elkhart *Also called Accra-Pac Inc (G-2666)*
Kik Custom Manufacuring, Elkhart *Also called Kik Custom Products Inc (G-2968)*
Kik Custom Pdts Los Angeles, Elkhart *Also called Kik Aerosol Socal LLC (G-2966)*
Kik Custom Products 574 294-8695
  1919 Superior St Elkhart (46516) *(G-2967)*
Kik Custom Products Inc 574 295-0000
  2730 Middlebury St Elkhart (46516) *(G-2968)*
Kik-Indiana, Elkhart *Also called Accra-Pac Inc (G-2665)*
Kile Enterprises Inc 317 844-6629
  1051 3rd Ave Sw Carmel (46032) *(G-1423)*
Kilgore Manufacturing Co Inc 260 248-2002
  445 S Line St Columbia City (46725) *(G-1804)*
Kilgore Mfg Plant No 1, Columbia City *Also called Kilgore Manufacturing Co Inc (G-1804)*
Kill-N-Em Inc 574 233-6655
  2118 Franklin St South Bend (46613) *(G-12828)*
Killer Camaros Custom Camaro 260 255-2425
  4762 Zelt Cv New Haven (46774) *(G-10946)*
Killer Car Customs, New Haven *Also called Killer Camaros Custom Camaro (G-10946)*
Kimalco Inc 812 463-3105
  213 W Division St Ste J Evansville (47710) *(G-3589)*
Kimalco Mattress, Evansville *Also called Kimalco Inc (G-3589)*
Kimball Elec Indianapolis 812 634-4000
  2950 N Catherwood Ave Indianapolis (46219) *(G-7349)*
Kimball Electronics Inc 317 357-3175
  2402 N Shadeland Ave Indianapolis (46219) *(G-7350)*
Kimball Electronics Inc 317 545-5383
  6205 E 30th St Indianapolis (46219) *(G-7351)*
Kimball Electronics Inc 812 634-4200
  1038 E 15th St Jasper (47546) *(G-8272)*
Kimball Electronics Group LLC (HQ) 812 634-4000
  1205 Kimball Blvd Jasper (47546) *(G-8273)*
Kimball Electronics Mfg Inc 812 482-1600
  1600 Royal St Jasper (47549) *(G-8274)*
Kimball Electronics Tampa Inc (HQ) 812 634-4000
  1205 Kimball Blvd Jasper (47546) *(G-8275)*
Kimball Furniture Group LLC 812 482-8517
  1037 E 15th St Jasper (47549) *(G-8276)*
Kimball Furniture Group LLC 812 634-3526
  340 E 11th Ave Jasper (47549) *(G-8277)*

Kimball Furniture Group LLC 812 482-8401
  1620 Cherry St Jasper (47549) *(G-8278)*
Kimball Furniture Group LLC 812 883-1850
  200 Kimball Blvd Salem (47167) *(G-12297)*
Kimball Furniture Group LLC (HQ) 812 482-1600
  1600 Royal St Jasper (47549) *(G-8279)*
Kimball Hospitality Inc 812 482-8090
  1180 E 16th St Jasper (47549) *(G-8280)*
Kimball Hospitality Inc (HQ) 812 482-8090
  1600 Royal St Jasper (47549) *(G-8281)*
Kimball International Inc (PA) 812 482-1600
  1600 Royal St Jasper (47549) *(G-8282)*
Kimball National Office F 812 634-3356
  340 E 11th Ave Jasper (47549) *(G-8283)*
Kimball Office, Jasper *Also called Kimball Furniture Group LLC (G-8276)*
Kimball Office, Jasper *Also called Kimball Furniture Group LLC (G-8278)*
Kimball Office, Salem *Also called Kimball Furniture Group LLC (G-12297)*
Kimball Office Inc 812 634-3220
  1155 W 12th Ave Jasper (47546) *(G-8284)*
Kimball Office Inc (HQ) 812 482-1600
  1600 Royal St Jasper (47549) *(G-8285)*
Kimber Creek Limited, Zionsville *Also called Mgtc Inc (G-14448)*
Kims Scrub Connection LLC 812 867-1237
  200 S Green River Rd Evansville (47715) *(G-3590)*
Kin Naturals LLC 219 213-9516
  2158 45th St Highland (46322) *(G-6051)*
Kinco, Seymour *Also called King Industrial Corporation (G-12464)*
Kinder Group Inc 765 457-5966
  1915 E North St Kokomo (46901) *(G-8651)*
Kinetico Water Systems, Crawfordsville *Also called Kessco Water LLC (G-2165)*
King Industrial Corporation 812 522-3261
  105 S Obrien St Seymour (47274) *(G-12464)*
King Investments Inc 812 752-6000
  505 E Mcclain Ave Scottsburg (47170) *(G-12371)*
King Machining Inc 317 271-3132
  1213 Indy Way Indianapolis (46214) *(G-7352)*
King of Tarpaulins The, Gosport *Also called Gosport Manufacturing Co Inc (G-5350)*
King Systems Corporation 317 776-6823
  15011 Herriman Blvd Noblesville (46060) *(G-11137)*
King Tut Inc 317 938-9907
  4720 Pebblepointe Pass Zionsville (46077) *(G-14445)*
King's Antenna Service, Angola *Also called Kas Satellite & Cable Inc (G-224)*
King's Copies, Indianapolis *Also called Rrc Corporation (G-7869)*
King-Tuesley Enterprises Inc (PA) 800 428-3266
  5616 Progress Rd Indianapolis (46241) *(G-7353)*
Kingery Group Inc 317 823-9585
  6574 Breckenridge Dr Indianapolis (46236) *(G-7354)*
Kings Custom Machine 812 477-5262
  2700 N Cullen Ave Evansville (47715) *(G-3591)*
Kings-Qlity Rstrtion Svcs LLC 812 944-4347
  1818 E Market St New Albany (47150) *(G-10814)*
Kingsbury Castings Div, La Porte *Also called Accurate Castings Inc (G-8726)*
Kingsford Products Inc (PA) 740 862-4450
  1819 Patterson St Decatur (46733) *(G-2389)*
Kinkos Inc 765 449-4950
  3520 South St Lafayette (47905) *(G-8939)*
Kinro Manufacturing Inc 574 535-1125
  3501 County Road 6 E Elkhart (46514) *(G-2969)*
Kinro Manufacturing Inc 574 535-1125
  3501 County Road 6 E Elkhart (46514) *(G-2970)*
Kinro Manufacturing Inc (HQ) 574 535-1125
  3501 County Road 6 E Elkhart (46514) *(G-2971)*
Kinro Manufacturing Inc 574 535-1125
  3501 County Road 6 E Elkhart (46514) *(G-2972)*
Kinro Manufacturing Inc 574 533-8337
  1206 Eisenhower Dr S Goshen (46526) *(G-5257)*
Kinser Timber Products Inc 812 876-4775
  8283 W Hedrick Rd Gosport (47433) *(G-5352)*
Kinser Trucking, Gosport *Also called Kinser Timber Products Inc (G-5352)*
Kinsers Hardwood 812 834-5568
  7805 Bartlettsville Rd Heltonville (47436) *(G-6027)*
Kirby Machine Company LLC 317 773-6700
  1709 Cherry St Noblesville (46060) *(G-11138)*
Kirby Risk Corporation (PA) 765 448-4567
  1815 Sagamore Pkwy N Lafayette (47904) *(G-8940)*
Kirby Risk Corporation 765 643-3384
  633 Broadway St Anderson (46012) *(G-130)*
Kirby Risk Corporation 765 664-5185
  1221 S Adams St Marion (46953) *(G-9540)*
Kirby Risk Corporation 765 423-4205
  714 S 1st St Lafayette (47905) *(G-8941)*
Kirby Risk Corporation 317 398-9713
  2325 E Michigan Rd Shelbyville (46176) *(G-12543)*
Kirby Risk Corporation 765 447-1402
  3574 Mccarty Ln Lafayette (47905) *(G-8942)*
Kirby Risk Corporation 765 254-5460
  1619 S Walnut St Muncie (47302) *(G-10505)*
Kirby Risk Corporation 765 742-2254
  1700 Schuyler Ave Lafayette (47904) *(G-8943)*

(G-0000) Company's Geographic Section entry number

Kirby Risk Electric Motor Repr, Lafayette *Also called Kirby Risk Corporation* ***(G-8941)***
Kirby Risk Electrical Supply, Lafayette *Also called Kirby Risk Corporation* ***(G-8940)***
Kirby Risk Electrical Supply, Anderson *Also called Kirby Risk Corporation* ***(G-130)***
Kirby Risk Precision Machining, Lafayette *Also called Kirby Risk Corporation* ***(G-8943)***
Kirby Risk Servicenter, Lafayette *Also called Kirby Risk Corporation* ***(G-8942)***
Kirby Tool and Die Inc...812 369-7779
2716 N Pierce Dr Solsberry (47459) ***(G-12686)***
Kirchoff Custom Sports...812 434-0355
311 Eissler Rd Evansville (47711) ***(G-3592)***
Kirk Enterprises...260 665-3670
333 Hoosier Dr Angola (46703) ***(G-225)***
Kirklin Waste Water Treatment...765 279-5251
800 N Main St Kirklin (46050) ***(G-8549)***
Kissel Printers Inc...812 424-5333
901 W Delaware St Evansville (47710) ***(G-3593)***
Kissy Face Lipstick LLC...260 797-5024
1542 Reed Rd Apt E Fort Wayne (46815) ***(G-4411)***
Kitchen & Baths By Untd HM Sup, Muncie *Also called United Home Supply Inc* ***(G-10576)***
Kitchen Craft Cabinetry, Jasper *Also called Masterbrand Cabinets Inc* ***(G-8290)***
Kitchen Jewels Inc (PA)...812 482-9663
1330 Franklin St Jasper (47546) ***(G-8286)***
Kitchen Kompact Inc...812 282-6681
911 E 11th St Jeffersonville (47130) ***(G-8390)***
Kitchen Konnection Inc...812 277-0393
227 Eastlake Dr Bedford (47421) ***(G-557)***
Kitchen Krafts...765 458-6858
302 E Union St Liberty (47353) ***(G-9262)***
Kitchen Queen LLC...812 662-8399
58 W County Rd 650 N Saint Paul (47272) ***(G-12277)***
Kitchen-Quip Inc...260 837-8311
338 S Oak St Kendallville (46755) ***(G-8487)***
Kitchen/Bath Design Center, Harlan *Also called Dutch Made Inc* ***(G-5970)***
Kite & Key LLC...317 654-7703
5825 Alpine Ave Indianapolis (46224) ***(G-7355)***
Kitterman Machine Co Inc...317 773-2283
87 S 8th St Noblesville (46060) ***(G-11139)***
Kitty Mac Inc...888 549-0783
4010 W 86th St Ste D Indianapolis (46268) ***(G-7356)***
Kleeman Cabinetry...812 926-0428
9814 Hueseman Rd Aurora (47001) ***(G-382)***
Kleen-Rite Supply Inc...812 422-7483
1101 E Diamond Ave Evansville (47711) ***(G-3594)***
Kleidoscope Quilting...812 932-3264
24 Saratoga Dr Batesville (47006) ***(G-507)***
Klem Hospitality, Saint Anthony *Also called Jasper Seating Company Inc* ***(G-12247)***
Klemm's Sausage Company, Indianapolis *Also called Klemms Meat Market* ***(G-7357)***
Klemms Meat Market...317 632-1963
1845 Shelby St Indianapolis (46203) ***(G-7357)***
Klene Pipe Structures Inc...812 663-6445
515 N Anderson St Greensburg (47240) ***(G-5619)***
Kleptz Aluminum Inc...812 238-2946
1135 Poplar St Terre Haute (47807) ***(G-13266)***
Kleptz Aluminum & Vinyl Pdts, Terre Haute *Also called Kleptz Aluminum Inc* ***(G-13266)***
Klh Audio, Noblesville *Also called Kelley Global Brands LLC* ***(G-11136)***
Klh Holding Corporation (HQ)...317 634-3976
2002 Lafayette Rd Indianapolis (46222) ***(G-7358)***
Klincher Locknut, Indianapolis *Also called Dual Machine Corporation* ***(G-6769)***
Kline Cabinet Makers LLC...317 326-3049
16 S Main St Maxwell (46154) ***(G-9662)***
Klinge Coatings, Indianapolis *Also called Klinge Enameling Company Inc* ***(G-7359)***
Klinge Enameling Company Inc...317 359-8291
5001 Prospect St Indianapolis (46203) ***(G-7359)***
Klipsch Group Inc (HQ)...317 860-8100
3502 Woodview Trce # 200 Indianapolis (46268) ***(G-7360)***
Klosterman Baking Co...317 359-5545
5867 Churchman Ave Indianapolis (46203) ***(G-7361)***
Klotz Special Formula Products...260 490-0489
7424 Freedom Way Fort Wayne (46818) ***(G-4412)***
Klotz Synthetic Lubricants, Fort Wayne *Also called Klotz Special Formula Products* ***(G-4412)***
Kls Santas...765 474-6951
4406 Chisholm Trl Lafayette (47909) ***(G-8944)***
Klueg Tool & Machine Inc...812 867-5702
14420 Darmstadt Rd Evansville (47725) ***(G-3595)***
Klx Aerospace Inc...260 747-0671
4250 Airport Expy Fort Wayne (46809) ***(G-4413)***
KMC Controls, New Paris *Also called Kreuter Manufacturing Co Inc* ***(G-10989)***
KMC Corporation...574 267-7033
602 Leiter Dr Warsaw (46580) ***(G-13898)***
KMC Enterprises Inc...765 584-1533
1094 N Old Highway 27 Winchester (47394) ***(G-14335)***
Kmi, Palmyra *Also called Kiesler Machine Inc* ***(G-11436)***
Kml Inc (PA)...260 897-3723
108 S Main St Laotto (46763) ***(G-9111)***
Kms, Hobart *Also called Knitting Mill Specialties* ***(G-6085)***
Kn Platech America Corporation...317 392-7707
1755 Mccall Dr Shelbyville (46176) ***(G-12544)***
Knapke & Sons Inc...260 639-0112
14525 Bruick Ln Hoagland (46745) ***(G-6065)***
Knapp Engraving, Montgomery *Also called Cedar Woodworking* ***(G-10216)***
Knauf Insulation Inc...317 421-3341
240 Elizabeth St Shelbyville (46176) ***(G-12545)***
Knauf Insulation Inc...317 398-4434
400 Walker St Shelbyville (46176) ***(G-12546)***
Knauf Insulation Inc (HQ)...317 398-4434
1 Knauf Dr Shelbyville (46176) ***(G-12547)***
Knepp Logging...812 486-3741
2946 N 900 E Loogootee (47553) ***(G-9387)***
Kneppers Inc (PA)...260 636-2180
2359 N 300 E Albion (46701) ***(G-29)***
Knepps Custom Welding...765 525-5130
7586 N County Road 450 W Saint Paul (47272) ***(G-12278)***
Knepps Logging Bandmilling...812 486-7721
5220 N 650 E Montgomery (47558) ***(G-10230)***
Knies Sawmill Inc...812 683-3402
2238 E 550s Huntingburg (47542) ***(G-6173)***
Knights Woodworking LLC...812 988-2106
3991 State Road 46 W Nashville (47448) ***(G-10727)***
Knightstown Banner LLC...765 345-2292
24 N Washington St Knightstown (46148) ***(G-8554)***
Knip Welding...219 987-5123
8446 W 1000 N Demotte (46310) ***(G-2442)***
Knitting Mill Specialties...219 942-8031
291 N County Line Rd Hobart (46342) ***(G-6085)***
Knk Battery LLC...765 426-2016
9117 E State Road 26 Otterbein (47970) ***(G-11420)***
Knothole Woodworks LLC...317 600-8151
3852 W State Road 38 Sheridan (46069) ***(G-12595)***
Knotts and Frye Inc...317 925-6406
3818 N Illinois St Indianapolis (46208) ***(G-7362)***
Knowledge Diffusion Games LLC...812 361-4424
1441 S Fnbrook Ln Ste 100 Bloomington (47401) ***(G-759)***
Knox City Sand & Gravel, Vincennes *Also called Rogers Group Inc* ***(G-13703)***
Knox County Association (PA)...812 886-4312
2525 N 6th St Vincennes (47591) ***(G-13689)***
Knox Enterprises Inc...317 714-3073
1 Technology Way Indianapolis (46268) ***(G-7363)***
Knox Fertilizer Company Inc...574 772-6275
2660 E 100 S Knox (46534) ***(G-8570)***
Knox Inc...260 665-6617
101 Fox Lake Rd Angola (46703) ***(G-226)***
Knox Tool & Die Inc...574 255-1256
2027 N Merrifield Ave Mishawaka (46545) ***(G-10064)***
Knoy Apparel...765 448-1031
1164 S Creasy Ln Lafayette (47905) ***(G-8945)***
Knu LLC...812 367-2068
1 Best Dr Ferdinand (47532) ***(G-3855)***
Knu Contract, Ferdinand *Also called Knu LLC* ***(G-3855)***
Kobaltec LLC...219 462-1483
1450 Clark Rd Valparaiso (46385) ***(G-13567)***
Kobelco Cmpsr Mfg Ind Inc...574 295-3145
3000 Hammond Ave Elkhart (46516) ***(G-2973)***
Koch Enterprises Inc (PA)...812 465-9800
14 S 11th Ave Evansville (47712) ***(G-3596)***
Koch Industries Inc...260 356-7191
502 E Hosler Rd Huntington (46750) ***(G-6222)***
Kochs Electric Inc...317 639-5624
202 E Palmer St Indianapolis (46225) ***(G-7364)***
Kocsis Brothers Machine Co...219 397-8400
4321 Railroad Ave East Chicago (46312) ***(G-2545)***
Koehler Welding Supply Inc...812 574-4103
2352 Michigan Rd Madison (47250) ***(G-9476)***
Koester Financial Services, Evansville *Also called Vigo Coaf Inc* ***(G-3800)***
Koester Metals Inc (PA)...260 495-1818
301 W Water St Fremont (46737) ***(G-4964)***
Koetter Sawmill, Borden *Also called Koetter Woodworking* ***(G-933)***
Koetter Woodworking...812 923-8875
533 Louis Smith Rd Borden (47106) ***(G-933)***
Koetter Woodworking Inc (PA)...812 923-8875
533 Louis Smith Rd Borden (47106) ***(G-934)***
KOI Enterprises Inc...812 537-2335
601 Saint Clair St Lawrenceburg (47025) ***(G-9146)***
Kokoku Wire Industries Corp...574 287-5610
406 Manitou Pl South Bend (46616) ***(G-12829)***
Kokomo Cabinetry...765 457-2385
1516 N Locke St Kokomo (46901) ***(G-8652)***
Kokomo Castings, Kokomo *Also called FCA US LLC* ***(G-8625)***
Kokomo Electronic Assembly, Kokomo *Also called GM Components Holdings LLC* ***(G-8628)***
Kokomo Masonry & Supply, Logansport *Also called Carters Concrete Block Inc* ***(G-9330)***
Kokomo Metal Fabricators Inc...765 459-8173
1931 E North St Kokomo (46901) ***(G-8653)***
Kokomo Opalescent Glass Co...765 457-8136
1310 S Market St Kokomo (46902) ***(G-8654)***
Kokomo Optical Company Inc...765 459-5137
501 E Lincoln Rd Kokomo (46902) ***(G-8655)***
Kokomo Power Electronics, Kokomo *Also called Delphi Powertrain Systems LLC* ***(G-8615)***

ALPHABETIC

Kokomo Press LLC 317 575-9903
　5019 Westwood Dr Carmel (46033) **(G-1424)**

Kokomo Spring Company Inc 765 459-5156
　320 Rainbow Dr Kokomo (46902) **(G-8656)**

Kokomo Tribune, Kokomo *Also called Community Holdings Indiana Inc* **(G-8608)**

Kokomo Truck Store 765 459-5118
　901 E Markland Ave Kokomo (46901) **(G-8657)**

Kolossos Inc 312 952-6991
　2715 Duffy Ln Long Beach (46360) **(G-9377)**

Komodo Pharmaceuticals Inc 317 485-0023
　8064 W 1000 S Fortville (46040) **(G-4781)**

Komun Scents 317 308-0714
　4635 Falcon Run Way Indianapolis (46254) **(G-7365)**

Konal Automated Systems Inc 616 659-4774
　1500 W Hively Ave Ste E Elkhart (46517) **(G-2974)**

Konecranes Inc 219 661-9602
　1255 Erie Ct Ste B Crown Point (46307) **(G-2272)**

Konecranes Inc 317 546-8122
　1345 Brookville Way Ste E Indianapolis (46239) **(G-7366)**

Konrady Graphics Inc 219 662-0436
　4070 Bush Hill Ct Crown Point (46307) **(G-2273)**

Koomler & Sons Inc 260 482-7641
　3820 Superior Ridge Dr Fort Wayne (46808) **(G-4414)**

Koontz-Wagner Maintenance Svcs, South Bend *Also called Kw Maintenance Services LLC* **(G-12833)**

Kopelov Cut Stone Inc 812 675-0099
　2321 39th St Bedford (47421) **(G-558)**

Kopy Kat, Jeffersonville *Also called The Office Sup of Southern Ind* **(G-8434)**

Kortzendorf Machine & Tool 317 783-5449
　1450 Sunday Dr Indianapolis (46217) **(G-7367)**

Kostyo Woodworking Inc 812 466-7350
　3399 Fort Harrison Rd Terre Haute (47804) **(G-13267)**

Kountry Kraft Wood Products 574 831-6736
　68604 County Road 15 New Paris (46553) **(G-10988)**

Kountry Wood Products LLC (PA) 574 773-5673
　352 Shawnee St Nappanee (46550) **(G-10689)**

Kousei USA Inc 812 373-7315
　2396 Norcross Dr Columbus (47201) **(G-1955)**

Kova Fertilizer Inc (PA) 812 663-5081
　1330 N Anderson St Greensburg (47240) **(G-5620)**

Kovenz Memorial Shop, La Porte *Also called Harris Pre Cast Inc* **(G-8761)**

Kozs Quality Printing Inc 219 696-6711
　17934 Grant Pl A Lowell (46356) **(G-9412)**

Kp Holdings LLC 317 867-0234
　2000 E 196th St Westfield (46074) **(G-14173)**

Kp Pharmaceutical Tech Inc 812 330-8121
　1212 W Rappel Ave Bloomington (47404) **(G-760)**

Kpc Media Group Inc (PA) 260 347-0400
　102 N Main St Kendallville (46755) **(G-8488)**

Kpc Media Group Inc 260 925-2611
　118 W 9th St Auburn (46706) **(G-339)**

Kpc Media Group Inc 678 645-0000
　45 S Public Sq Angola (46703) **(G-227)**

Kpc Media Group Inc 260 426-2640
　3306 Independence Dr Fort Wayne (46808) **(G-4415)**

Kq Servicing LLC 812 486-9244
　22383 Third Rd Loogootee (47553) **(G-9388)**

Kra International LLC (PA) 574 259-3550
　1810 Clover Rd Mishawaka (46545) **(G-10065)**

Krafft Gravel Inc (PA) 260 238-4653
　6031 County Road 68 Spencerville (46788) **(G-13049)**

Kraft Heinz Foods Company 260 347-1300
　151 W Ohio St Kendallville (46755) **(G-8489)**

Kraft N Kreations 812 243-1754
　4589 S Robinson Pl West Terre Haute (47885) **(G-14125)**

Kraigs Custom Woodworking 574 904-7501
　1810 E 12th St Mishawaka (46544) **(G-10066)**

Kramer Furn & Cab Makers Inc 812 526-2711
　12600 N Presidential Way Edinburgh (46124) **(G-2615)**

Krazy Klothes Ltd (PA) 317 687-8310
　1101 S Illinois St Indianapolis (46225) **(G-7368)**

Kreamo Bakers, South Bend *Also called Alpha Baking Co Inc* **(G-12697)**

Kreig De Vault 317 238-6234
　1 Indiana Sq Ste 2050 Indianapolis (46204) **(G-7369)**

Kremers Urban Phrmcuticals Inc (HQ) 812 523-5347
　1101 C Ave W Seymour (47274) **(G-12465)**

Kretler Tool & Engineering 260 897-2662
　104 Well St Avilla (46710) **(G-412)**

Kreuter Manufacturing Co Inc (PA) 574 831-4626
　19476 Industrial Dr New Paris (46553) **(G-10989)**

Krisma Diversified 317 413-4788
　12986 Abraham Run Carmel (46033) **(G-1425)**

Kristens Homemade Delight 765 566-2200
　703 Michigan Rd Burlington (46915) **(G-1211)**

Kroger Co 574 294-6092
　130 W Hively Ave Elkhart (46517) **(G-2975)**

Kroger Co 574 291-0740
　1217 E Ireland Rd South Bend (46614) **(G-12830)**

Kroger Limited Partnership II 765 364-5200
　800 N Englewood Dr Crawfordsville (47933) **(G-2166)**

Kromet America Inc 812 346-5117
　2700 Concord Rd Lafayette (47909) **(G-8946)**

Kronmiller Machine & Tool 260 436-1355
　2230 Lakeview Dr Fort Wayne (46808) **(G-4416)**

Kropf Industries Inc 574 533-2171
　58647 State Road 15 Goshen (46528) **(G-5258)**

Krs, Evansville *Also called Kleen-Rite Supply Inc* **(G-3594)**

Kruis Mold & Engineering Inc 574 293-4613
　2221 Industrial Pkwy Elkhart (46516) **(G-2976)**

Krukemeier Machine and Tool Co 317 784-7042
　4949 Subway St Beech Grove (46107) **(G-600)**

Krupp Gerlach Company 765 294-0045
　1291 E 8th St Veedersburg (47987) **(G-13644)**

Kruz Inc (PA) 574 772-6673
　1201 W Culver Rd Knox (46534) **(G-8571)**

Krystil Klear Filtration, Winamac *Also called S&F Manufacturing Inc* **(G-14321)**

KS Kreations 574 514-7366
　7700 Greenbrier Rd Ne Georgetown (47122) **(G-5147)**

Ksm Enterprises 317 773-7440
　12190 Halite Ln Fishers (46038) **(G-3937)**

Kt Cakes 812 442-6047
　13699 N Rock Run Ch Rd Rosedale (47874) **(G-12205)**

Kt Industries LLC 260 432-0027
　3925 Ardmore Ave Fort Wayne (46802) **(G-4417)**

KTI Cutting Tools Inc 260 749-1465
　7007 Trafalgar Dr Fort Wayne (46803) **(G-4418)**

Ktr Corporation 219 872-9100
　122 Anchor Rd Michigan City (46360) **(G-9807)**

Kubota Authorized Dealer, Terre Haute *Also called Bane-Welker Equipment LLC* **(G-13197)**

Kuckuck Transport LLC 260 609-0316
　2165 S 625 W South Whitley (46787) **(G-13001)**

Kuert Concrete Inc (PA) 574 232-9911
　3402 Lincoln Way W South Bend (46628) **(G-12831)**

Kuert Concrete Inc 574 293-0430
　18370 Us Highway 20 Goshen (46528) **(G-5259)**

Kuert Concrete Inc 574 223-2414
　1101 W 13th St Rochester (46975) **(G-12131)**

Kuert Concrete Inc 574 453-3993
　155 W 600 N Warsaw (46582) **(G-13899)**

Kuharic Enterprises 574 288-9410
　57890 Crumstown Hwy South Bend (46619) **(G-12832)**

Kuhn & Sons Inc 812 424-8268
　210 S Morton Ave Evansville (47713) **(G-3597)**

Kumplete Airway Solutions Inc 219 680-0836
　625 Fairfield Dr Crown Point (46307) **(G-2274)**

Kuntry Lumber and Farm Sup Ltd 260 463-3242
　2875 S 00ew Lagrange (46761) **(G-9051)**

Kuri TEC Manufacturing Inc 765 764-6000
　2600 E Us Hwy 41 Williamsport (47993) **(G-14293)**

Kustom Kilms LLC 317 512-5813
　2410 Chestnut St Columbus (47201) **(G-1956)**

Kustom Kilns 5 LLC 260 820-3636
　1400 E Polymer Dr Terre Haute (47802) **(G-13268)**

Kvk US Technologies Inc 765 529-1100
　1016 S 25th St New Castle (47362) **(G-10909)**

Kw Maintenance Services LLC 574 232-2051
　3801 Voorde Dr Ste B South Bend (46628) **(G-12833)**

Kwik Kopy Business Center 130, Evansville *Also called Ovation Communications Inc* **(G-3659)**

Kwik Kopy Printing, Crawfordsville *Also called North Enterprises Inc* **(G-2179)**

Kwik Lok Corporation Indiana 260 493-1220
　1222 Ryan Rd New Haven (46774) **(G-10947)**

KYB Americas Corporation 317 881-7772
　850 N Graham Rd Greenwood (46143) **(G-5714)**

KYB Americas Corporation (HQ) 317 736-7774
　2625 N Morton St Franklin (46131) **(G-4903)**

KYB Americas Corporation 630 620-5555
　850 N Graham Rd Ste C Greenwood (46143) **(G-5715)**

Kyle Machine & Tool Inc 317 736-4743
　5228 E 300 S Franklin (46131) **(G-4904)**

Kyles Incense LLC 219 682-4278
　5330 Delaware St Merrillville (46410) **(G-9724)**

Kylin Therapeutics Inc 765 412-6661
　3000 Kent Ave West Lafayette (47906) **(G-14079)**

Kys, Jeffersonville *Also called Kentuckiana Yacht Services LLC* **(G-8387)**

Kzrv LP 260 768-4016
　985 N 900 W Shipshewana (46565) **(G-12624)**

L & C Welding LLC 260 593-3410
　11705 W 300 S Shipshewana (46565) **(G-12625)**

L & D Industries Inc 260 925-4714
　201 Fulton St Auburn (46706) **(G-340)**

L & L Engineering Co Inc 317 786-6886
　4925 Subway St Beech Grove (46107) **(G-601)**

L & L Fittings Mfg, Fort Wayne *Also called JM Fittings LLC* **(G-4396)**

L & L Press Inc 765 664-3162
　1417 W Kem Rd Marion (46952) **(G-9541)**

L & L Woodworking LLC 574 535-4613
　13614 N 700 W Nappanee (46550) **(G-10690)**

(G-0000) Company's Geographic Section entry number

L & N Woodworking..260 768-7008
  2240 N 925 W Shipshewana (46565) *(G-12626)*

L & P Manufacturing Company...............................812 405-2093
  207 Rodgers Ln Jonesville (47247) *(G-8449)*

L & R Machine Company Inc...................................317 787-7251
  3136 S Emerson Ave Beech Grove (46107) *(G-602)*

L & S Lumber...765 886-1452
  7501 State Road 38 Greens Fork (47345) *(G-5587)*

L & W Engineering Inc..574 825-5351
  107 Industrial Pkwy E Middlebury (46540) *(G-9900)*

L A M B Woodworking...260 768-7992
  5510 W 200 N Shipshewana (46565) *(G-12627)*

L and D Custom Woodworking.................................812 486-2958
  3610 N 900 E Montgomery (47558) *(G-10231)*

L B Foster Company..260 244-2887
  2658 S 700 E Columbia City (46725) *(G-1805)*

L C Typesetting Company Inc..................................574 232-4700
  2611 S Main St South Bend (46614) *(G-12834)*

L D Barger Wholesale Neon Inc..............................765 643-4506
  749 E 500 S Anderson (46013) *(G-131)*

L E Johnson Products Inc Inc (PA)..........................574 293-5664
  2100 Sterling Ave Elkhart (46516) *(G-2977)*

L E Johnson Products Inc..574 293-5664
  1133 E Lusher Ave Elkhart (46516) *(G-2978)*

L H Carbide Corporation (HQ).................................260 432-5563
  4420 Clubview Dr Fort Wayne (46804) *(G-4419)*

L H Controls Inc...260 432-9020
  4208 Clubview Dr Fort Wayne (46804) *(G-4420)*

L H Stamping Corporation (HQ)...............................260 432-5563
  4420 Clubview Dr Fort Wayne (46804) *(G-4421)*

L J T, South Bend *Also called Lock Joint Tube LLC (G-12843)*

L L Welding..765 565-6006
  501 N East St Carthage (46115) *(G-1514)*

L M Products Inc..765 643-3802
  1325 Meridian St Anderson (46016) *(G-132)*

L M Woodworking..574 534-9177
  62270 County Road 33 Goshen (46528) *(G-5260)*

L R Green Co Inc..317 781-4200
  5650 Elmwood Ave Indianapolis (46203) *(G-7370)*

L R Nisley & Sons..574 642-1245
  62724 County Road 35 Goshen (46528) *(G-5261)*

L S Manufacturing, Elkhart *Also called Patrick Industries Inc (G-3088)*

L S R Conversions LLC...574 206-9610
  25771 Miner Rd Elkhart (46514) *(G-2979)*

L Thorn Company Inc (PA)......................................812 246-4461
  6000 Grant Line Rd New Albany (47150) *(G-10815)*

L W Woodworking LLC...260 463-8938
  4635 S 200 W Wolcottville (46795) *(G-14373)*

L&E Engineering Company, Greenwood *Also called L&E Engineering LLC (G-5716)*

L&E Engineering LLC..317 884-0017
  254 N Graham Rd Greenwood (46143) *(G-5716)*

L&N Supply LLC..219 397-9500
  4016 Deodar St East Chicago (46312) *(G-2546)*

L&S Sanitation Service...765 932-5410
  270 S 100 W Rushville (46173) *(G-12227)*

L5 Solutions LLC..317 436-1044
  7950 Castleway Dr Ste 160 Indianapolis (46250) *(G-7371)*

La Farga, New Haven *Also called Sdi Lafarga LLC (G-10958)*

La Fontaine Generator Exchange.............................765 981-4561
  202 Logan St La Fontaine (46940) *(G-8723)*

La Fontaine Gravel Inc..765 981-4849
  1244 E 1050 S La Fontaine (46940) *(G-8724)*

La Grange County, Lagrange *Also called County of Lagrange (G-9035)*

La Grange Publishing Co Inc...................................260 463-3243
  Hc 9 Box S Lagrange (46761) *(G-9052)*

La Michoacana...574 293-9799
  246 W Lusher Ave Elkhart (46517) *(G-2980)*

La Ola Latino Americana...317 822-0345
  2401 W Washington St Indianapolis (46222) *(G-7372)*

La Porte Prcsion Mch Works LLC.............................219 326-7000
  1756 Genesis Dr La Porte (46350) *(G-8782)*

La Porte Smokes and Beverages.............................219 575-7754
  609 E Lincolnway La Porte (46350) *(G-8783)*

La Porte Technologies LLC (PA)..............................219 362-1000
  300 Philadelphia St La Porte (46350) *(G-8784)*

La Voz De Ind Bilngual Newsppr, Indianapolis *Also called La Voz De Indiana Inc (G-7373)*

La Voz De Indiana Inc...317 423-0957
  2911 W Washington St Indianapolis (46222) *(G-7373)*

La Zee Tek..260 351-3274
  5610 S State Road 327 Hudson (46747) *(G-6133)*

Label Logic Inc..574 266-6007
  516 Pine Creek Ct Elkhart (46516) *(G-2981)*

Label Tech Inc...765 747-1234
  2601 S Walnut St Muncie (47302) *(G-10506)*

Labels Unlimited, New Albany *Also called Discount Labels LLC (G-10769)*

Labraid Inc..219 754-2501
  9404 W 2100 S La Crosse (46348) *(G-8721)*

Labtest Equipment Company...................................219 462-3300
  72 Timber Dr Valparaiso (46385) *(G-13568)*

Lacap Container Corp...317 835-4282
  521 One Half E Hndrcks St Shelbyville (46176) *(G-12548)*

Lacay Fabrication and Mfg Inc................................574 288-4678
  2801 Glenview Dr Elkhart (46514) *(G-2982)*

Laconia Laser Engraving..812 786-3641
  2825 Mosquito Creek Rd Se Laconia (47135) *(G-8837)*

Lacopa International Inc..317 410-1483
  5028 Hill Valley Dr Pittsboro (46167) *(G-11584)*

Lactor LLC...765 496-6838
  3221 Covington St West Lafayette (47906) *(G-14080)*

Lafarge North America Inc......................................219 378-1193
  3210 Watling St East Chicago (46312) *(G-2547)*

Lafayette Dental Laboratory...................................765 447-9341
  5628 Roseberry Rdg Lafayette (47905) *(G-8947)*

Lafayette Instrument Co Inc (PA)............................765 423-1505
  3700 Sagamore Pkwy N Lafayette (47904) *(G-8948)*

Lafayette Interior Fashions, West Lafayette *Also called Lafayette Venetian Blind Inc (G-14082)*

Lafayette Marketing Inc..765 474-5374
  3180 W 250 N West Lafayette (47906) *(G-14081)*

Lafayette Puzzle Factory LLC..................................800 883-6408
  4315 Commerce Dr Lafayette (47905) *(G-8949)*

Lafayette Quality Products Inc................................765 446-0890
  111 Farabee Dr S Lafayette (47905) *(G-8950)*

Lafayette Tent & Awning Co....................................765 742-4277
  125 S 5th St Lafayette (47901) *(G-8951)*

Lafayette Venetian Blind Inc (PA)...........................765 464-2500
  3000 Klondike Rd West Lafayette (47906) *(G-14082)*

Lafayette Wire Products Inc....................................765 474-7896
  2700 Concord Rd Lafayette (47909) *(G-8952)*

Laff or Die Productions...219 942-3790
  221 N Colorado St Hobart (46342) *(G-6086)*

Lafferty & Lafferty LLC...574 935-4852
  8923 8a Rd Plymouth (46563) *(G-11700)*

Lafree Enterprises...574 674-5906
  11645 Mckinley Hwy Osceola (46561) *(G-11380)*

Lagnaippe LLC...812 288-9291
  802 E 8th St New Albany (47150) *(G-10816)*

Lagrange Products Inc..260 495-3025
  607 S Wayne St Fremont (46737) *(G-4965)*

Lagrange Publishing Co Inc....................................260 463-2166
  50 W 100 S Lagrange (46761) *(G-9053)*

Lagwana Printing Inc..260 463-4901
  4425 W Us Highway 20 # 3 Lagrange (46761) *(G-9054)*

Laibe Corporation..317 231-2250
  1414 Bates St Indianapolis (46201) *(G-7374)*

Laidig Inc..574 256-0204
  14535 Dragoon Trl Mishawaka (46544) *(G-10067)*

Laird Plastics Inc...317 890-1808
  3439 N Shadeland Ave # 5 Indianapolis (46226) *(G-7375)*

Lake Air Balance..219 988-2449
  639 W 250 S Hebron (46341) *(G-6015)*

Lake Area Promotional Spc, Warsaw *Also called Goon Jonn (G-13882)*

Lake Cable of Indiana Inc.......................................847 238-3000
  2700 Evans Ave Valparaiso (46383) *(G-13569)*

Lake Copper Conductors LLC...................................847 238-3000
  4430 Eastland Dr Elkhart (46516) *(G-2983)*

Lake County Sand & Gravel LLC..............................219 988-4540
  2115 W Lincoln Hwy Merrillville (46410) *(G-9725)*

Lake Effect Lighting LLC...812 783-9482
  3635 E Cleve Butcher Rd Bloomington (47401) *(G-761)*

Lake George Material & Sup Co...............................219 942-1912
  450 S Ohio St Hobart (46342) *(G-6087)*

Lake House..574 265-6945
  720 E Canal St Winona Lake (46590) *(G-14350)*

Lake Lite Inc..260 918-2758
  105 W Simon St Laotto (46763) *(G-9112)*

Lake States Veneer Inc...260 244-4767
  732 S Columbia Pkwy Columbia City (46725) *(G-1806)*

Lake Tool & Die Inc..574 457-8274
  1009 W Brooklyn St Syracuse (46567) *(G-13137)*

Lakeland Technology Inc...574 267-1503
  542 E 200 N Warsaw (46582) *(G-13900)*

Lakemaster Inc..765 288-3718
  2407 S Walnut St Muncie (47302) *(G-10507)*

Lakepark Industries Ind Inc.....................................260 768-7411
  750 E Middlebury St Shipshewana (46565) *(G-12628)*

Laker Winery LLC...812 934-4633
  1001 Western Ave Batesville (47006) *(G-508)*

Lakeshore Foods Corp..219 362-8513
  702 E Lincolnway Ste 1 La Porte (46350) *(G-8785)*

Lakeshore Graphics, Crown Point *Also called Adams Smith (G-2222)*

Lakeside Woodworking..812 687-7901
  8024 N 775 E Odon (47562) *(G-11333)*

Lakestreet Enterprises LLC......................................260 768-7991
  75 N 700 W Lagrange (46761) *(G-9055)*

Laketon Refining Corporation..................................260 982-0703
  2784 W Lukens Lake Rd Laketon (46943) *(G-9090)*

Lakeview Engineered Pdts Inc.................................260 432-3479
  2500 W Jefferson Blvd Fort Wayne (46802) *(G-4422)*

Lakeview Woodworking....................................574 642-1335
  10190 County Road 34 Goshen (46528) *(G-5262)*

Lakota Corp...574 848-1636
  4 Stoutco Dr Bristol (46507) *(G-1064)*

Lakota Language Consortium.........................888 525-6828
  2620 N Walnut St Ste 1280 Bloomington (47404) *(G-762)*

Lal Acquisition Inc (PA)................................765 288-3691
  9501 S Center Rd Muncie (47302) *(G-10508)*

Lamarvis Industries LLC................................317 797-0483
  1429 S 13th 1/2 St Terre Haute (47802) *(G-13269)*

Lamaster Radiation Consulting, Noblesville Also called Mark Lamaster *(G-11146)*

Lamb Machine & Tool Co................................317 780-9106
  3510 E Raymond St Indianapolis (46203) *(G-7376)*

Lambel Corporation.......................................317 849-6828
  7902 E 88th St Indianapolis (46256) *(G-7377)*

Lambert Asphlting Slcating Inc.......................317 985-8061
  12649 White Rabbit Dr Indianapolis (46235) *(G-7378)*

Lambert Metal Finishing Inc...........................260 493-0529
  6912 Derek Dr Fort Wayne (46803) *(G-4423)*

Lambright Country Chimes L L C......................260 768-9138
  8340 Us High Way 20 Shipshewana (46565) *(G-12629)*

Lambright Woodworking LLC............................260 593-2721
  7785 W 300 S Topeka (46571) *(G-13423)*

Lambrights Inc...260 463-2178
  2450 W Us Highway 20 Lagrange (46761) *(G-9056)*

Lamco Finishers Inc......................................317 471-1010
  8260 Zionsville Rd Indianapolis (46268) *(G-7379)*

Lami-Crafts Inc..812 232-3012
  2806 S 7th St Terre Haute (47802) *(G-13270)*

Laminated Tops of Central Ind........................812 824-6299
  711 E Dillman Rd Bloomington (47401) *(G-763)*

Laminated Tops of Terre Haute........................812 235-2920
  700 N 5th St Terre Haute (47807) *(G-13271)*

Laminating Specialties Inc Ind........................765 385-0023
  5833 E Old Us Highway 52 Templeton (47986) *(G-13178)*

Laminique Inc..765 482-4222
  540 Ransdell Rd Lebanon (46052) *(G-9197)*

Lana Hudelson..812 865-3951
  27 W Quarry Rd Orleans (47452) *(G-11363)*

Lancaster Custom Cabinets Inc.......................812 949-4750
  5301 Grant Line Rd New Albany (47150) *(G-10817)*

Lances Driveshaft & Components.....................219 762-2531
  2076 Dombey Rd Portage (46368) *(G-11772)*

Lancon Electric Inc.......................................260 897-3285
  101 S Main St Laotto (46763) *(G-9113)*

Land Enterprises..317 774-9475
  7116 Summer Oak Dr Noblesville (46062) *(G-11140)*

Land OLakes Inc..765 962-9561
  505 N 4th St Richmond (47374) *(G-12011)*

Landec Ag Inc..765 385-1000
  201 N Michigan St Oxford (47971) *(G-11432)*

Landec Ag Inc (HQ)......................................765 385-1000
  201 N Michigan St Oxford (47971) *(G-11433)*

Landgrebe Manufacturing Inc.........................219 462-9587
  208 N 250 W Valparaiso (46385) *(G-13570)*

Landis Equipment & Tool Rental......................812 847-2582
  390 S Main St Linton (47441) *(G-9309)*

Landis Gyr Utilities Svcs Inc..........................765 742-1001
  2800 Duncan Rd Lafayette (47904) *(G-8953)*

Landis+gyr Inc..765 742-1001
  2800 Duncan Rd Lafayette (47904) *(G-8954)*

Landjet International.....................................574 970-7805
  21240 Protecta Dr Elkhart (46516) *(G-2984)*

Landmark Home & Land Co Inc (PA)................219 874-4065
  1902 Washington St Michigan City (46360) *(G-9808)*

Landmark Signs Inc......................................219 762-9577
  7424 Industrial Ave Chesterton (46304) *(G-1617)*

Landmark Signs Group, Chesterton Also called Landmark Signs Inc *(G-1617)*

Landmark Wood Products Inc.........................812 338-2641
  118 W Sawmill Rd English (47118) *(G-3314)*

Landrums Mch Tl Repr & Svcs........................574 256-0312
  1002 Saint Jerome St Mishawaka (46544) *(G-10068)*

Landsberg Indanapolis Div 1015, Indianapolis Also called Orora North America *(G-7631)*

Landscape Products, Frankfort Also called Ostler Enterprises Inc *(G-4847)*

Lane Byler Winery...260 920-4377
  5858 County Road 35 Auburn (46706) *(G-341)*

Lane Quick..812 896-1890
  1304 S Jackson St Salem (47167) *(G-12298)*

Lane Shady Welding......................................574 825-5553
  56322 County Road 35 Middlebury (46540) *(G-9901)*

Laney Software Co..260 312-0759
  17144 Moonlite Dr South Bend (46614) *(G-12835)*

Langenwlter Crpt Dyg Vlparaiso......................219 531-7601
  185 Wexford Rd Valparaiso (46385) *(G-13571)*

Langfords Delivery Service.............................317 996-3594
  10 Nw Union Church Rd Monrovia (46157) *(G-10204)*

Langley Fine Art Prints..................................219 872-0087
  2019 Somerset Rd Long Beach (46360) *(G-9378)*

Languell Printing Inc.....................................317 889-3545
  547 N Greenbriar Dr Greenwood (46142) *(G-5717)*

Lannett Company, Seymour Also called Kremers Urban Phrmcuticals Inc *(G-12465)*

Lansing Building Products Inc.........................765 448-4363
  1425 Industrial Dr Lafayette (47905) *(G-8955)*

Lansing Metalizing & Grinding, Hammond Also called Lansing Metallizing & Grinding *(G-5906)*

Lansing Metallizing & Grinding.......................219 931-1785
  4742 Calumet Ave Hammond (46327) *(G-5906)*

Lanthier Winery & Restaurant.........................812 273-2409
  123 Mill St Madison (47250) *(G-9477)*

Lantzs Coachworks Inc..................................317 487-1111
  505 S Tibbs Ave Lot 3251 Indianapolis (46241) *(G-7380)*

Laotto Brewing LLC......................................260 897-3152
  7530 E Swan Rd Avilla (46710) *(G-413)*

LAp Cstm EMB Grment Prtg LLC.....................260 782-0762
  2472 E State Road 524 Wabash (46992) *(G-13733)*

Lape Steel, Elkhart Also called Elkhart Steel Service Inc *(G-2830)*

Lapell Post, Pendleton Also called Pendleton Times *(G-11500)*

Lapis Services Inc..219 464-9131
  1101 Cumberland Xing Valparaiso (46383) *(G-13572)*

Laptop Publishing LLC...................................317 379-5716
  3531 Rolling Springs Dr Carmel (46033) *(G-1426)*

Largus Printing, Munster Also called Largus Speedy Print Corp *(G-10612)*

Largus Speedy Print Corp..............................219 922-8414
  732 45th Ave Munster (46321) *(G-10612)*

Larkin Woodworks.......................................765 795-5332
  709 S Lafayette St Cloverdale (46120) *(G-1728)*

Larry Atwood...765 525-6851
  6597 S 250 E Waldron (46182) *(G-13800)*

Larry Flowers Wholesale...............................765 747-5156
  2948 S Chippewa Ln Muncie (47302) *(G-10509)*

Larry G Byrd..765 458-7285
  2312 W County Road 250 S Liberty (47353) *(G-9263)*

Larry Graber Cabinets...................................812 486-2713
  9407 E 500 N Montgomery (47558) *(G-10232)*

Larry H Poole...812 466-9345
  7826 E Rose Hill Ave Terre Haute (47805) *(G-13272)*

Larry Robertson Associates...........................812 537-4090
  1056 Millwood Ct Indianapolis (46260) *(G-7381)*

Larrys Canvas Cleaning.................................260 463-2220
  403 E Central Ave Lagrange (46761) *(G-9057)*

Larrys Machine..574 596-4994
  18374 Dennis Ave Goshen (46528) *(G-5263)*

Larrys Tls Hydraulic Jack Svcs........................317 243-8666
  702 S Lynhurst Dr Indianapolis (46241) *(G-7382)*

Las Perlas Tapatias Inc.................................765 447-0601
  11 N Earl Ave Lafayette (47904) *(G-8956)*

Las Perlas Tapatias Mexican RE, Lafayette Also called Las Perlas Tapatias Inc *(G-8956)*

Lasalle Bristol, Elkhart Also called Lasalle Bristol Corporation *(G-2985)*

Lasalle Bristol Corporation.............................574 936-9894
  1755 N Oak Dr Plymouth (46563) *(G-11701)*

Lasalle Bristol Corporation.............................574 295-4400
  1203 N Division St Bristol (46507) *(G-1065)*

Lasalle Bristol Corporation (HQ)......................574 295-4400
  601 County Road 17 Elkhart (46516) *(G-2985)*

Lasalles Landing Vineyard LLC.......................574 277-2711
  51739 Lilac Rd South Bend (46628) *(G-12836)*

Laser Graphx Inc...574 834-4443
  7196 N State Road 13 North Webster (46555) *(G-11296)*

Laser Images, Fort Wayne Also called Kaiser Tool Company Inc *(G-4403)*

Laser Marking Technologies............................812 852-7999
  873 W County Road 600 N Osgood (47037) *(G-11392)*

Laser Plus..574 269-1246
  3950 N Blue Heron Dr Warsaw (46582) *(G-13901)*

Laser Systems...219 465-1155
  104 Billings St Ste A Valparaiso (46383) *(G-13573)*

Lasertech Inc..812 277-1321
  4684 Dixie Hwy Bedford (47421) *(G-559)*

Lasertone Inc...812 473-5945
  700 N Weinbach Ave # 101 Evansville (47711) *(G-3598)*

Laserwash...765 359-0582
  1529 S Washington St Crawfordsville (47933) *(G-2167)*

Lasher Lumber Inc.......................................812 836-2618
  15147 State Road 145 Tell City (47586) *(G-13165)*

Lasikplus Vision Center, Indianapolis Also called Lca-Vision Inc *(G-7387)*

Lassus Bros Oil Inc.......................................260 625-4003
  10225 Illinois Rd Fort Wayne (46814) *(G-4424)*

Last Round Coffee LLC..................................317 292-0500
  389 E Washington St Morgantown (46160) *(G-10356)*

Lastec, Indianapolis Also called Wood-Mizer Holdings Inc *(G-8212)*

Lastec, Lizton Also called Wood-Mizer Holdings Inc *(G-9318)*

Lastec LLC..317 892-4444
  7865 N County Road 100 E Lizton (46149) *(G-9317)*

Lasting Impressions, Noblesville Also called Bulldog Award Co Inc *(G-11073)*

Latch Gard Co Inc..574 862-2373
  1900 Fieldhouse Ave Elkhart (46517) *(G-2986)*

Latham Manufacturing Corp...........................260 459-4115
  6932 Gettysburg Pike Fort Wayne (46804) *(G-4425)*

Lather Up LLC 260 638-4978
  2040 W 900 N-90 Markle (46770) *(G-9579)*

Laticrete International Inc 317 298-8510
  4620 W 84th St Ste 200 Indianapolis (46268) *(G-7383)*

Laticrete International Inc 317 298-8510
  4620 W 84th St Ste 200 Indianapolis (46268) *(G-7384)*

Lattice Works, Evansville *Also called Plastic Extrusions Company (G-3674)*

Lau Industries Inc 574 223-3181
  510 N State Road 25 Rochester (46975) *(G-12132)*

Lauck Manufacturing Co Inc 317 787-6269
  735 Bacon St Indianapolis (46227) *(G-7385)*

Lauer Log Homes 260 486-7010
  6630 Reed Rd Fort Wayne (46835) *(G-4426)*

Laughery Gravel Co, Osgood *Also called Schmaltz Ready Mix Concrete (G-11394)*

Laughery Valley AG Co-Op Inc (PA) 812 689-4401
  336 N Buckeye St Osgood (47037) *(G-11393)*

Laundry Room, The, Columbus *Also called Brian T Klem (G-1862)*

Lava Lips 317 965-6629
  6821 Grosvenor Pl Indianapolis (46220) *(G-7386)*

Lavender Patch Fabr Quilts LLC 574 848-0011
  20615 Baltimore Oriole Dr Bristol (46507) *(G-1066)*

Law Valve of Texas, New Albany *Also called Erl Properties Inc (G-10772)*

Lawncreations LLC 574 536-1546
  10592 County Rd Millersburg (46543) *(G-9971)*

Lawrence Cnty Fabrication Corp 812 849-0124
  240 S Meridian Rd Mitchell (47446) *(G-10164)*

Lawrence Industries 260 432-9693
  2921 E 400 S Columbia City (46725) *(G-1807)*

Lawrence Industries Inc 260 432-9693
  10403 Arbor Trl Fort Wayne (46804) *(G-4427)*

Lawrence Shirks 574 223-5118
  4920 State Road 110 Rochester (46975) *(G-12133)*

Lawrenco Steel Inc 812 466-7115
  4000 E Evans Ave Terre Haute (47805) *(G-13273)*

Lawson Welding Shop 812 448-8984
  10516 N County 200e Harmony (47853) *(G-5975)*

Layton Elkhart, Elkhart *Also called Layton Homes Corporation (G-2988)*

Layton Homes Corporation (HQ) 574 294-6521
  2520 Bypass Rd Elkhart (46514) *(G-2987)*

Layton Homes Corporation 574 294-6521
  411 County Road 15 Elkhart (46516) *(G-2988)*

Lazar Scientific Incorporated 574 271-7020
  12692 Sandy Dr Ste 116 Granger (46530) *(G-5418)*

Lb Mold Inc 812 526-2030
  1031 S Main St Edinburgh (46124) *(G-2616)*

Lb Woodworking, Nappanee *Also called Borkholder Lavon (G-10655)*

Lca-Vision Inc 317 818-3980
  8930 Keystone Xing Indianapolis (46240) *(G-7387)*

Lcas Inc 541 219-0229
  233 Center St Hobart (46342) *(G-6088)*

Lcf Enterprises LLC 260 483-3248
  10316 Valley Hills Ln Fort Wayne (46825) *(G-4428)*

LCI Industries (PA) 574 535-1125
  3501 County Road 6 E Elkhart (46514) *(G-2989)*

Lcm Realty LLC 574 535-1125
  3501 County Road 6 E Elkhart (46514) *(G-2990)*

Lcm Realty IV LLC 574 312-6182
  2469 E Kercher Rd Goshen (46526) *(G-5264)*

LDI Ltd LLC (PA) 317 237-5400
  54 Monument Cir Ste 800 Indianapolis (46204) *(G-7388)*

Ldn Welding Corp 219 996-5643
  17907 Union St Hebron (46341) *(G-6016)*

Le Air Co Inc 812 988-1313
  1313 Timber Crest Rd Nashville (47448) *(G-10728)*

Le Hue Machine & Tool Co Inc 574 255-8404
  1915 N Cedar St Mishawaka (46545) *(G-10069)*

Le Kem of Indiana Inc 812 932-5536
  1863 Lammers Pike Batesville (47006) *(G-509)*

Le Park Mold & Tool, Elkhart *Also called Mike H Inc (G-3041)*

Leach & Sons WaterCare (PA) 317 248-8954
  671 E Main St Danville (46122) *(G-2351)*

Leach and Sons Water Systems, Danville *Also called Leach & Sons WaterCare (G-2351)*

Leader Publishing Co of Salem 812 883-4446
  117 E Walnut St 119 Salem (47167) *(G-12299)*

Leadtrack Software 317 823-0748
  11415 Sturgen Bay Ln Indianapolis (46236) *(G-7389)*

Leaf Hut Software LLC 317 770-3632
  8430 Weaver Woods Pl Fishers (46038) *(G-3938)*

Leap Frogz Screanprinting EMB 317 786-2441
  3307 Madison Ave Indianapolis (46227) *(G-7390)*

Lear Corporation 317 481-0530
  4409 W Morris St Indianapolis (46241) *(G-7391)*

Lear Corporation 260 244-1700
  2101 S 600 E Columbia City (46725) *(G-1808)*

Lear Corporation 219 764-5101
  6750 Daniel Burnham Dr A Portage (46368) *(G-11773)*

Lear Corporation 765 653-2511
  750 S Fillmore Rd Greencastle (46135) *(G-5466)*

Lear Corporation 574 935-3818
  2000 Walter Glaub Dr Plymouth (46563) *(G-11702)*

Lear Corporation 219 852-0014
  1401 165th St Hammond (46320) *(G-5907)*

Lear Lawn & Garden, Muncie *Also called Lear Manufacturing (G-10510)*

Lear Machining & Waterjet Inc 812 418-8111
  4056 N Long Rd Columbus (47203) *(G-1957)*

Lear Manufacturing 765 282-6273
  2204 N Wolfe St Muncie (47303) *(G-10510)*

Learman Electronic Tool Assoc 574 226-0420
  1513 S 6th St Elkhart (46516) *(G-2991)*

Leasenet Incorporated 317 575-4098
  8888 Keystone Xing # 1300 Indianapolis (46240) *(G-7392)*

Lebanon Berg Vault Co Inc 765 482-0302
  730 E Elm St Lebanon (46052) *(G-9198)*

Lebanon Corp (PA) 765 482-7273
  1700 N Lebanon St Lebanon (46052) *(G-9199)*

Lebanon Reporter 765 482-4650
  117 E Washington St Lebanon (46052) *(G-9200)*

Lebanon Reporter, The, Lebanon *Also called Community Holdings Indiana Inc (G-9175)*

Lebermuth Company Inc (PA) 574 259-7000
  4004 Technology Dr South Bend (46628) *(G-12837)*

Leclanche SA 765 610-0050
  2705 Enterprise Dr Anderson (46013) *(G-133)*

Leclere Manufacturing Inc 812 683-5627
  2905 Newton St Jasper (47546) *(G-8287)*

Leco Corporation 574 288-9017
  4100 Lathrop St South Bend (46628) *(G-12838)*

Ledgerwood & Sons Sawmill 812 939-8212
  246 Pleasant View Rd Coal City (47427) *(G-1742)*

Lee E Norris Cnstr & Grn Co (PA) 574 353-7855
  7930 N 700 E Tippecanoe (46570) *(G-13383)*

Lee Enterprises Inc Times 219 933-3200
  601 45th St Munster (46321) *(G-10613)*

Lee Machine Inc 765 932-3100
  505 E 11th St Rushville (46173) *(G-12228)*

Lee Mfg LLC 260 403-2775
  9529 Marquis Ln Fort Wayne (46835) *(G-4429)*

Lee Publications Inc 219 462-5151
  1111 Glendale Blvd Valparaiso (46383) *(G-13574)*

Lee Publications Inc 219 933-9251
  601 45th St Munster (46321) *(G-10614)*

Lee Supply Corp 812 333-4343
  1821 W 3rd St Bloomington (47404) *(G-764)*

Lee's Ready Mix, North Vernon *Also called Lees Ready-Mix & Trucking Inc (G-11267)*

Lee's Ready-Mix, Columbus *Also called Lees Ready-Mix & Trucking Inc (G-1958)*

Lee's Wood Products, Elkhart *Also called Duro Inc (G-2804)*

Leed Selling Tools Corp (PA) 812 867-4340
  9700 Highway 57 Evansville (47725) *(G-3599)*

Leed Selling Tools Corp 812 482-7888
  5312 W Ireland Center St Ireland (47545) *(G-8229)*

Leed Thermal Processing Inc 317 637-5102
  1718 N Luett Ave Indianapolis (46222) *(G-7393)*

Leepoxy Plastics Inc 260 747-7411
  3706 W Ferguson Rd Fort Wayne (46809) *(G-4430)*

Leeps Supply Co 219 696-9511
  7332 Mcconnell Ave Lowell (46356) *(G-9413)*

Leeps Supply Co Inc (PA) 219 756-5337
  8001 Tyler St Merrillville (46410) *(G-9726)*

Leer Midwest 574 522-5337
  58391 Ventura Dr Elkhart (46517) *(G-2992)*

Lees Ready-Mix & Trucking 812 522-7270
  1122 E 4th Street Rd Seymour (47274) *(G-12466)*

Lees Ready-Mix & Trucking Inc (PA) 812 346-9767
  1100 W Jfk Dr North Vernon (47265) *(G-11267)*

Lees Ready-Mix & Trucking Inc 812 372-1800
  1460 Blessing Rd Columbus (47201) *(G-1958)*

Legacy Resources Co LP (PA) 317 328-5660
  2780 Wtrfrnt Pw E Dr # 200 Indianapolis (46214) *(G-7394)*

Legacy Screen Printing Promoti 219 262-4000
  1086 N State Road 149 Chesterton (46304) *(G-1618)*

Legacy Screen Prtg Prmtons LLC 219 262-4000
  503 Gardena St Michigan City (46360) *(G-9809)*

Legacy Vulcan LLC 219 987-3040
  832 15th St Se Demotte (46310) *(G-2443)*

Legacy Vulcan LLC 219 465-3066
  4105 Montdale Park Dr Valparaiso (46383) *(G-13575)*

Legacy Vulcan LLC 574 293-1536
  2500 W Lusher Ave Elkhart (46517) *(G-2993)*

Legacy Vulcan LLC 219 462-5832
  651 Axe Ave Valparaiso (46383) *(G-13576)*

Legacy Vulcan LLC 219 567-9155
  14530 W 700 S Francesville (47946) *(G-4814)*

Legacy Vulcan LLC 219 253-6686
  6857 N Us Highway 421 Monon (47959) *(G-10176)*

Legacy Vulcan LLC 219 696-5467
  9331 W 205th Ave Lowell (46356) *(G-9414)*

Legacy Wood Creations LLC 574 773-4405
  24675 County Road 54 Nappanee (46550) *(G-10691)*

Legend Valley Products, Winamac *Also called Braun Motor Works Inc (G-14303)*

A
L
P
H
A
B
E
T
I
C

Legendary Designs Inc 260 768-9170
2685 N 850 W Shipshewana (46565) *(G-12630)*

Leggett & Platt Incorporated 219 866-7181
1132 N Cullen St Rensselaer (47978) *(G-11931)*

Leggett & Platt 0714, Kouts Also called Leggett & Platt Incorporated *(G-8717)*

Leggett & Platt Incorporated 260 347-2600
2225 Production Rd Kendallville (46755) *(G-8490)*

Leggett & Platt Incorporated 219 766-2261
State Road 8 Kouts (46347) *(G-8717)*

Leggett & Platt Incorporated 574 825-9561
402 N Main St Middlebury (46540) *(G-9902)*

Lehi Prosthetics Dental Lab 765 288-4613
1501 W Jackson St Muncie (47303) *(G-10511)*

Lehigh Cement Company LLC 812 849-2191
180 N Meridian Rd Mitchell (47446) *(G-10165)*

Lehigh Cement Company LLC 877 534-4442
3084 W County Road 225 S Logansport (46947) *(G-9347)*

Lehigh Cement Company LLC 812 246-5472
301 Highway 31 Sellersburg (47172) *(G-12400)*

Lehigh Hanson Ecc Inc 574 753-5121
3084 W County Road 225 S Logansport (46947) *(G-9348)*

Lehigh Hanson Ecc Inc 812 246-5472
Hwy 31 Sellersburg (47172) *(G-12401)*

Lehigh Hanson Ecc Inc 812 246-7700
301 Highway 31 Sellersburg (47172) *(G-12402)*

Lehman Manufacturing, Kentland Also called Hoosier Metal Polish Inc *(G-8520)*

Lehue Machine and Tool 574 329-5456
55981 Wynnewood Dr Osceola (46561) *(G-11381)*

Leibering Dimension Inc 812 367-2971
514 W 8th St Ferdinand (47532) *(G-3856)*

Leidos Inc 812 863-3100
14064 Westgate Ct Crane (47522) *(G-2128)*

Lein Corporation 765 674-6950
3301 S Hamaker St Marion (46953) *(G-9542)*

Leis Machine Shop Inc 574 278-6000
6033 E Hwy 16 Buffalo (47925) *(G-1204)*

Leistner Aquatic Services Inc 317 535-6099
6237 N 25 W Whiteland (46184) *(G-14242)*

Leisure Pool & Spa 812 537-0071
159 Florence Dr Lawrenceburg (47025) *(G-9147)*

Leland Manufacturing 812 367-2068
1 Best Dr Ferdinand (47532) *(G-3857)*

Leman Engrg & Consulting Inc 574 870-7732
520 E 1050 S Brookston (47923) *(G-1106)*

Lemler Pallet Inc 574 646-2707
9200 Apple Rd Bourbon (46504) *(G-944)*

Lenex Steel Company 317 818-1622
2325 S 6th St Terre Haute (47802) *(G-13274)*

Lengacher Machine Inc 260 657-3114
17305 Grabill Rd Grabill (46741) *(G-5378)*

Lengerich Meats Inc 260 638-4123
3095 W Van Horn St Zanesville (46799) *(G-14413)*

Lennies Inc 812 323-2112
1795 E 10th St Bloomington (47408) *(G-765)*

Lennon Industries 219 996-6024
1102 Norbeh Dr Hebron (46341) *(G-6017)*

Lennon Industries Inc 219 996-6838
3629 E 157th Ave Hebron (46341) *(G-6018)*

Lennox Ind Production Lxud 240 .... 317 253-0353
6542 E Westfield Blvd Indianapolis (46220) *(G-7395)*

Lennox Lir Lennox Inds Intl 317 334-1339
8148 Woodland Dr Indianapolis (46278) *(G-7396)*

Lens Tech, Greenwood Also called Lenstech Optical Lab Inc *(G-5718)*

Lenscrafters, Indianapolis Also called Luxottica Retail N Amer Inc *(G-7428)*

Lenscrafters, Merrillville Also called Luxottica Retail N Amer Inc *(G-9729)*

Lenstech Optical Lab Inc 317 882-1249
1064 Greenwood Sprng Blvd Greenwood (46143) *(G-5718)*

Leon R Dixon 317 545-1956
5206 Fawn Hill Ct Indianapolis (46226) *(G-7397)*

Leonard Eaton Tooling Inc 574 295-5041
435 Roske Dr Elkhart (46516) *(G-2994)*

Leons Fabrication Inc 219 365-5272
8850 Parrish Ave Schererville (46375) *(G-12330)*

Lep Special Fasteners, Frankfort Also called Fontana Fasteners Inc *(G-4831)*

Lepark Mold & Tool 574 262-0518
2504 Jeanwood Dr Elkhart (46514) *(G-2995)*

Leroy E Doty Cabinet Shop 219 663-1139
4514 W 105th Ave Crown Point (46307) *(G-2275)*

Leroy R Sollars 765 284-9417
305 1/2 Rd N Selma (47383) *(G-12424)*

Lesac Corporation (PA) 219 879-3215
700 W Michigan Blvd Michigan City (46360) *(G-9810)*

Lesco Inc 317 876-7968
8569 Zionsville Rd Indianapolis (46268) *(G-7398)*

Lesh Advertising Inc 574 859-2141
6938 E State Road 218 Camden (46917) *(G-1275)*

Leslie Webber Media & Pubg LLC 317 774-0598
6685 Braemar Ave N Noblesville (46062) *(G-11141)*

Leslie-Fisher Engineering Inc 765 457-7796
2832 E Boulevard Kokomo (46902) *(G-8658)*

Lessonly Inc 317 469-9194
407 Fulton St 302 Indianapolis (46202) *(G-7399)*

Lester Recreation Designs LLC 317 888-2071
751 Nonchalant Ct Greenwood (46142) *(G-5719)*

Letica Corporation 248 652-0557
701 E Depot St Fremont (46737) *(G-4966)*

Lewger Machine & Tool, Kendallville Also called Da-Mar Industries Inc *(G-8471)*

Lewis Bakeries, Vincennes Also called Lewis Brothers Bakeries Inc *(G-13690)*

Lewis Bakeries, La Porte Also called Holsum of Fort Wayne Inc *(G-8766)*

Lewis Brothers Bakeries Inc (PA) 812 425-4642
500 N Fulton Ave Evansville (47710) *(G-3600)*

Lewis Brothers Bakeries Inc 812 886-6533
2792 S Old Decker Rd Vincennes (47591) *(G-13690)*

Lewis Jerry Cnstr & Excvtg 765 653-2800
1249 N Jackson St Greencastle (46135) *(G-5467)*

Lex Tooling LLC 765 675-6301
604 Berryman Pike Tipton (46072) *(G-13395)*

Lexington Pharmaceuticals 317 870-0370
8496 Georgetown Rd Indianapolis (46268) *(G-7400)*

Lfab, Indianapolis Also called Indianapolis Fabrications LLC *(G-7198)*

LFD Bearings LLC 574 245-0375
4505 Wyland Dr Ste 1100 Elkhart (46516) *(G-2996)*

Lgin LLC 260 562-2233
6825 N 375 E Howe (46746) *(G-6127)*

LGS Pace International Inc 574 848-5665
11550 Harter Dr Middlebury (46540) *(G-9903)*

LGS Plumbing Inc 219 663-2177
1112 E Summit St Crown Point (46307) *(G-2276)*

LH Industries Corp (PA) 260 432-5563
4420 Clubview Dr Fort Wayne (46804) *(G-4431)*

LH Medical Corporation 260 387-5194
6932 Gettysburg Pike Fort Wayne (46804) *(G-4432)*

Lh Software Concepts LLC 317 222-1779
3601 W 69th St Indianapolis (46268) *(G-7401)*

Lhp Engineering Solutions, Columbus Also called Lhp Software LLC *(G-1959)*

Lhp Engineering Solutions, Columbus Also called Lhp Software LLC *(G-1960)*

Lhp Software LLC 812 373-0870
1888 Poshard Dr Columbus (47203) *(G-1959)*

Lhp Software LLC (PA) 812 373-0870
305 Franklin St Columbus (47201) *(G-1960)*

LI, Lafayette Also called Lafayette Instrument Co Inc *(G-8948)*

Liberation 219 736-7329
5308 Gull Dr Schererville (46375) *(G-12331)*

Liberty Advance Machine Inc 812 372-1010
3210 Scott Dr Columbus (47201) *(G-1961)*

Liberty Book & Bb Manufactures (PA) 317 633-1450
901 E Maryland St Indianapolis (46202) *(G-7402)*

Liberty Cut Stone Inc 812 935-5515
9921 N Liberty Hollow Rd Gosport (47433) *(G-5353)*

Liberty Green Renewables LLP 812 951-3143
5019 Georges Hill Rd Ne Georgetown (47122) *(G-5148)*

Liberty Herald 765 458-5114
10 N Market St Liberty (47353) *(G-9264)*

Liberty Homes Inc (PA) 574 533-0438
1101 Eisenhower Dr N Goshen (46526) *(G-5265)*

Liberty Industries LC 812 853-0595
3266 Tower Rd Newburgh (47630) *(G-11035)*

Liberty Signs, Monticello Also called Don Anderson *(G-10259)*

Liberty Tool and Engineering 765 354-9550
277 N 11th St Middletown (47356) *(G-9937)*

Libertyworks, Indianapolis Also called N Rolls-Royce Amercn Tech Inc *(G-7567)*

Libs Mike & Choclat Fctry LLC 812 424-8750
6201 Hogue Rd Evansville (47712) *(G-3601)*

Licensed Eliquid Manufacturing 260 687-9213
6746 E State Blvd Fort Wayne (46815) *(G-4433)*

Lid, Carmel Also called Long Item Development Corp *(G-1427)*

Lids, Terre Haute Also called Genesco Inc *(G-13239)*

Lids Corporation 260 471-4287
4201 Coldwater Rd Ste 506 Fort Wayne (46805) *(G-4434)*

Lids Kids, Fort Wayne Also called Lids Corporation *(G-4434)*

Lievore Custom Machine Inc 574 848-0150
55265 County Road 14 Bristol (46507) *(G-1067)*

Life Dme LLC 219 795-1296
8896 Louisiana St Merrillville (46410) *(G-9727)*

Life Less Ordinary LLC 317 727-4277
9032 Sargent Creek Dr Indianapolis (46256) *(G-7403)*

Life Management Inc (PA) 260 747-7408
2916 Engle Rd Fort Wayne (46809) *(G-4435)*

Life Path Business Sevices, Indianapolis Also called Life Path Numerology Center *(G-7404)*

Life Path Numerology Center 317 638-9752
108 S Elder Ave Indianapolis (46222) *(G-7404)*

Lifoam Industries LLC 410 889-1023
9999 E 121st St Fishers (46037) *(G-3939)*

Lift 812 394-5438
6535 W Market St Fairbanks (47849) *(G-3818)*

Lift Works Inc 812 797-0479
5253 Mount Pleasant S St Greenwood (46142) *(G-5720)*

Lift-A-Loft, Muncie Also called Lal Acquisition Inc *(G-10508)*

(G-0000) Company's Geographic Section entry number

Lift-A-Loft Manufacturing Inc 317 288-3691
9501 S Center Rd Muncie (47302) *(G-10512)*

Liftco Inc 574 266-5551
3301 Reedy Dr Elkhart (46514) *(G-2997)*

Light & Ink Corp 812 421-1400
1018 E Diamond Ave Evansville (47711) *(G-3602)*

Light Beam Technologies Inc 260 635-2195
3794 W 50 S Kimmell (46760) *(G-8530)*

Light House Homes Center (PA) 765 448-4502
3918 Harry Ave Lafayette (47905) *(G-8957)*

Light House Woodworking DBA 260 704-0589
5553 County Road 79a Saint Joe (46785) *(G-12256)*

Light Mine Candle Company LLC 317 353-7786
1701 Redbay Dr Indianapolis (46234) *(G-7405)*

Lightbeam Technology 219 397-1684
4809 Tod Ave East Chicago (46312) *(G-2548)*

Lighthouse Creat Candles Gifts 765 342-2920
1190 E Morgan St Martinsville (46151) *(G-9620)*

Lighthouse Industries Inc (PA) 219 879-1550
107 Eastwood Rd Ste D Michigan City (46360) *(G-9811)*

Lighthouse Publ Ministries 260 209-6948
9903 Canopy Ln Fort Wayne (46835) *(G-4436)*

Lightning Printing 765 362-5999
115 N Washington St Crawfordsville (47933) *(G-2168)*

Lightuptoyscom LLC (PA) 812 246-1916
8512 Commerce Park Dr Sellersburg (47172) *(G-12403)*

Ligonier Woodworking 260 894-9969
1068 E Perry Rd Ligonier (46767) *(G-9289)*

Lil Girl's Glam Spa Bus, Indianapolis *Also called Lil Girls Glam LLC (G-7406)*

Lil Girls Glam LLC 317 507-3443
2333 Rostock Ct Indianapolis (46229) *(G-7406)*

Lillich Sign Co Inc 260 463-3930
1333 Industrial Dr N Lagrange (46761) *(G-9058)*

Lillsun Manufacturing Co Inc 260 356-6514
1350 Harris St Huntington (46750) *(G-6223)*

Lime City Manufacturing Co 260 356-6826
1470 Etna Ave Huntington (46750) *(G-6224)*

Lime City Press LLC 260 344-3435
9712 N 300 W Huntington (46750) *(G-6225)*

Limelight Publishing 765 448-4461
1600 Main St Lafayette (47904) *(G-8958)*

Limmco Tool, New Albany *Also called Lukemeier Indus Mold & Mch Co (G-10821)*

Lincoln Industries Inc 812 897-0715
110 W Division St Boonville (47601) *(G-915)*

Lincoln Printing Corporation 260 424-5200
3310 Congressional Pkwy Fort Wayne (46808) *(G-4437)*

Lincs Software Corp 812 204-3619
1133 W Mill Rd Ste 210 Evansville (47710) *(G-3603)*

Lindal North America Inc 812 657-7142
6010 S International Dr Columbus (47201) *(G-1962)*

Lindas 812 265-0099
4630 W Lea Ln Hanover (47243) *(G-5962)*

Lindas Gone Buggie 219 299-0174
28 E 36th Pl Hobart (46342) *(G-6089)*

Linde Gas North America LLC 219 989-9304
3930 Michigan St Hammond (46323) *(G-5908)*

Linde Gas North America LLC 888 345-0894
834 S 10th St Terre Haute (47807) *(G-13275)*

Linde LLC 574 234-4887
3809 W Calvert St South Bend (46613) *(G-12839)*

Linde LLC 219 324-0498
7996 N State Road 39 La Porte (46350) *(G-8786)*

Linden Machine Shop LLC 765 339-7244
220 N Main St Linden (47955) *(G-9304)*

Linder Oil Co Inc 260 622-4680
820 Industrial Pkwy Ossian (46777) *(G-11403)*

Line-X of Indy, Indianapolis *Also called Advance Prtective Coatings Inc (G-6330)*

Linear Publishing Corp 317 722-8500
921 E 86th St Ste 108 Indianapolis (46240) *(G-7407)*

Liner Products LLC 812 723-0244
1468 W Hospital Rd Paoli (47454) *(G-11455)*

Lingenfelter Prfmce Engrg Inc 260 724-2552
1557 Winchester Rd Decatur (46733) *(G-2390)*

Lingenfelter Racing, Decatur *Also called Lingenfelter Prfmce Engrg Inc (G-2390)*

Linguistics Club, Bloomington *Also called Trustees Indiana University (G-848)*

Link Electrical Service 812 288-8184
1018 E 7th St Jeffersonville (47130) *(G-8391)*

Link Engineering LLC (PA) 765 457-1166
1719 N Main St Kokomo (46901) *(G-8659)*

Link Graphics, Evansville *Also called Light & Ink Corp (G-3602)*

Link Printing Services LLC 317 826-9852
12237 Old Stone Dr Indianapolis (46236) *(G-7408)*

Link Rental Company Inc 574 946-7373
103 E Pearl St Winamac (46996) *(G-14310)*

Linkel Company (PA) 812 934-5190
1081 Morris Rd Batesville (47006) *(G-510)*

Linkster's, Winamac *Also called Link Rental Company Inc (G-14310)*

Linton Daily Citizen, Linton *Also called Russ Publishing (G-9313)*

Lipper Components, Goshen *Also called Lippert Components Inc (G-5272)*

Lippert Cmponents Intl Sls Inc 574 312-7480
3501 County Road 6 E Elkhart (46514) *(G-2998)*

Lippert Components Inc 574 534-8177
2602 College Ave Goshen (46528) *(G-5266)*

Lippert Components Inc 574 537-8900
2703 College Ave Goshen (46528) *(G-5267)*

Lippert Components Inc (HQ) 800 551-9149
3501 County Road 6 E Elkhart (46514) *(G-2999)*

Lippert Components Inc 574 535-1125
2703 College Ave Goshen (46528) *(G-5268)*

Lippert Components Inc 574 537-8900
1701 Century Dr Goshen (46528) *(G-5269)*

Lippert Components Inc 574 312-6654
1280 S Olive St South Bend (46619) *(G-12840)*

Lippert Components Inc 574 294-6852
29391 Old Us 33 Elkhart (46516) *(G-3000)*

Lippert Components Inc 574 535-1125
1902 W Sample St South Bend (46619) *(G-12841)*

Lippert Components Inc 574 534-2163
1010 Eisenhower Dr S Goshen (46526) *(G-5270)*

Lippert Components Inc 574 295-8166
2503 Banks Ct Elkhart (46514) *(G-3001)*

Lippert Components Inc 574 535-1125
2703 College Ave Goshen (46528) *(G-5271)*

Lippert Components Inc 574 535-1125
2703 College Ave Goshen (46528) *(G-5272)*

Lippert Components Inc 574 849-0869
2703 College Ave Goshen (46528) *(G-5273)*

Lippert Components Inc 574 971-4100
2703 College Ave Goshen (46528) *(G-5274)*

Lippert Components Inc 574 971-4320
2703 College Ave Goshen (46528) *(G-5275)*

Lippert Components Inc 574 312-7445
51040 Greenfield Pkwy Middlebury (46540) *(G-9904)*

Lippert Components Mfg Inc (HQ) 574 535-1125
3501 County Road 6 E Elkhart (46514) *(G-3002)*

Lippert Components Mfg Inc 574 935-5122
1101 N Oak Dr Plymouth (46563) *(G-11703)*

Lippert Extrusions 574 312-6467
1722 W Mishawaka Rd Elkhart (46517) *(G-3003)*

Lippert Interior Solutions, Goshen *Also called Lippert Components Inc (G-5266)*

Lippert Interiors, Goshen *Also called Lippert Components Inc (G-5270)*

Liquid Packaging Solutions Inc 219 393-3600
3999 E Hupp Rd Bldg R43 La Porte (46350) *(G-8787)*

Liquid Technologies Elkhart 574 596-1883
208 N Elkhart St Wakarusa (46573) *(G-13782)*

Liquidspring LLC 765 474-7816
4899 E 400 S Lafayette (47905) *(G-8959)*

Literature Sales 219 873-3093
613 Franklin St Michigan City (46360) *(G-9812)*

Litho Press Inc 317 634-6468
1747 Massachusetts Ave Indianapolis (46201) *(G-7409)*

Lithogrphic Communications LLC 219 924-9779
9701 Indiana Pkwy Munster (46321) *(G-10615)*

Lithotone Inc (PA) 574 294-5521
1313 W Hively Ave Elkhart (46517) *(G-3004)*

Litko Aerosystems Inc 219 462-9295
316 E 316 N Ste 6 Valparaiso (46383) *(G-13577)*

Little Cricket Letterpress 317 762-2044
702 Chestnut Ave Winona Lake (46590) *(G-14351)*

Little Green Apple 219 836-5025
923 Ridge Rd Unit A Munster (46321) *(G-10616)*

Little Green Apple 317 272-1168
8100 E Us Highway 36 # 12 Avon (46123) *(G-454)*

Little Green Apple 812 853-8761
8449 Bell Oaks Dr Newburgh (47630) *(G-11036)*

Little Green Apple Hallmark 219 661-0420
10827 Broadway Crown Point (46307) *(G-2277)*

Little I Publications LLC 317 467-9297
120 Lake View Ct N Greenfield (46140) *(G-5549)*

Little Mfg LLC 812 453-8137
2122 N State Route 61 Boonville (47601) *(G-916)*

Little Trailer Co Inc 877 545-4897
29877 Old Us 33 Elkhart (46516) *(G-3005)*

Littler Diecast A Brahm Corp 765 789-4456
500 W Walnut St Albany (47320) *(G-11)*

Live Bold Aerospace LLC 260 438-5710
6914 Hiltonia Dr Fort Wayne (46819) *(G-4438)*

Live Engine Test Building, Anderson *Also called Borgwarner Pds Anderson LLC (G-76)*

Lively Machine Company Inc 812 425-5060
4404 Upper Mt Vernon Rd Evansville (47712) *(G-3604)*

Livin Lite Corp 574 862-2228
985 N 900 W Shipshewana (46565) *(G-12631)*

Livin' Lite Rv, Shipshewana *Also called Livin Lite Corp (G-12631)*

Livings Graphics Inc 574 264-4114
2111 Cassopolis St Elkhart (46514) *(G-3006)*

Ljt Texas LLC (HQ) 800 257-6859
515 W Ireland Rd South Bend (46614) *(G-12842)*

Lk Technologies Inc 812 332-4449
1590 S Liberty Dr Ste A Bloomington (47403) *(G-766)*

Llama Corporation 888 701-7432
   2937 E 900 N Decatur (46733) **(G-2391)**

LLC Black Jewell 800 948-2302
   417 Washington St Columbus (47201) **(G-1963)**

LLC Tipton Mills 716 825-4422
   835 S Mapleton St Columbus (47201) **(G-1964)**

Lloyd & Mona Sulivan 812 522-9191
   2169 N County Road 400 E Seymour (47274) **(G-12467)**

Lloyd Jr Frank P and Assoc 317 388-9225
   4461 Sylvan Rd Indianapolis (46228) **(G-7410)**

Lloyds Machine Co 812 422-7064
   2214 St Joseph Ind Pk Dr Evansville (47720) **(G-3605)**

Lloyds of Indiana Inc 317 251-5430
   2507 Roosevelt Ave Indianapolis (46218) **(G-7411)**

Lm Sugarbush LLC 812 967-4491
   29618 Green Rd Borden (47106) **(G-935)**

LMC Workholding, Logansport Also called Logansport Machine Co Inc **(G-9350)**

Lnl Logging, Martinsville Also called Poplar Log Homes Inc **(G-9633)**

Loaded Pharmaceuticals Inc 317 300-1996
   3417 Pinetop Dr Indianapolis (46227) **(G-7412)**

Loading Dock Maintenance LLC 260 424-3635
   5032 Moeller Rd Fort Wayne (46806) **(G-4439)**

Lock Joint Tube LLC (HQ) 574 299-5326
   515 W Ireland Rd South Bend (46614) **(G-12843)**

Lock Joint Tube Texas, South Bend Also called Ljt Texas LLC **(G-12842)**

Lockerbie Square Cab Co Inc 317 635-1134
   4350 W 10th St Indianapolis (46222) **(G-7413)**

Lockheed Martin Corporation 317 821-4000
   5101 Decatur Blvd Ste A Indianapolis (46241) **(G-7414)**

Lockwood Welding Inc 260 925-2086
   2450 County Road 32 Waterloo (46793) **(G-14017)**

Locoli Inc (PA) 219 365-3125
   1650 Us Highway 41 Ste E Schererville (46375) **(G-12332)**

Locomotive S Professional 219 398-9123
   4949 Huish Dr East Chicago (46312) **(G-2549)**

Lodos Theranostics LLC 765 427-2492
   132 Vigo Ct West Lafayette (47906) **(G-14083)**

Loeb-Lorman Metals Inc 574 892-5063
   402 West St Argos (46501) **(G-275)**

Loewenstein Furniture Inc 800 521-5381
   1204 E 6th St Huntingburg (47542) **(G-6174)**

Log Home Construction Indiana, Manilla Also called E & L Construction Inc **(G-9503)**

Log Lifestyles Inc 574 850-6158
   72300 Walkerton Trl Walkerton (46574) **(G-13805)**

Logan Stampings Inc 574 722-3101
   1100 E Main St Logansport (46947) **(G-9349)**

Logan Street Signs and Banners, Noblesville Also called James Wafford **(G-11135)**

Logansport Machine Co Inc 574 735-0225
   1200 W Linden Ave Logansport (46947) **(G-9350)**

Logansport Pharos Press 574 753-4169
   3175 Billiard Dr Logansport (46947) **(G-9351)**

Loggers Incorporated 812 939-2797
   7755 S County Rd 50 Clay City (47841) **(G-1704)**

Logging 812 216-3544
   10680 W Seymour Rd Seymour (47274) **(G-12468)**

Logical Concepts 317 885-6330
   494 S Emerson Ave Ste E1 Greenwood (46143) **(G-5721)**

Logical Lighting and Controls 317 244-8234
   5054 Crawfordsville Rd Indianapolis (46224) **(G-7415)**

Logistick Inc 800 758-5840
   19880 State Line Rd South Bend (46637) **(G-12844)**

Logo Apparel Plus, Floyds Knobs Also called Gettelfinger Holdings LLC **(G-4012)**

Logo Boys Inc 574 256-6844
   3102 N Home St Mishawaka (46545) **(G-10070)**

Logo Connxtion, Terre Haute Also called Vco Inc **(G-13361)**

Logo Designs Inc 812 293-4750
   7619 Bthlehem New Wash Rd New Washington (47162) **(G-11012)**

Logo Shop, The, Hagerstown Also called Pheonix Inc **(G-5811)**

Logo USA Corporation (PA) 317 867-8518
   320 Parkway Cir Westfield (46074) **(G-14174)**

Logo Zone Inc 574 753-7569
   731 Lakeview Dr Logansport (46947) **(G-9352)**

Logos, Tell City Also called Fine Guys Inc **(G-13161)**

Logos Express Inc 317 272-1200
   1225 Ransdell Ct Lebanon (46052) **(G-9201)**

Lomont Holdings Co Inc 800 545-9023
   1825 W Maumee St Angola (46703) **(G-228)**

Lone Star Industries Inc (HQ) 317 706-3314
   10401 N Meridian St # 400 Indianapolis (46290) **(G-6271)**

Lone Star Industries Inc 574 674-8873
   55284 Corwin Rd Elkhart (46514) **(G-3007)**

Lone Star Industries Inc 260 482-4559
   4805 Investment Dr Fort Wayne (46808) **(G-4440)**

Lone Star Industries Inc 317 780-9860
   1112 W Thompson Rd Indianapolis (46217) **(G-7416)**

Lone Star Tool & Die Weld 812 346-9681
   432 4th St Vernon (47282) **(G-13651)**

Long Item Development Corp 317 844-9491
   5753 Turnbull Ct Carmel (46033) **(G-1427)**

Long Leather Works LLC 812 336-5309
   203 W Gordon Pike Bloomington (47403) **(G-767)**

Long Tail Corporation (PA) 260 918-0489
   5738 Coventry Ln Fort Wayne (46804) **(G-4441)**

Long Tail Technology, Fort Wayne Also called Long Tail Corporation **(G-4441)**

Longbow Machining LLC 812 599-6728
   1666 S Rogers Rd Lexington (47138) **(G-9253)**

Longhorn Sand and Gravel LLC 574 656-3231
   30430 Osborne Rd North Liberty (46554) **(G-11218)**

Longhorn Sand and Gravel LLC 574 532-2788
   1434 Fallcreek Dr Mishawaka (46544) **(G-10071)**

Longs Landing of Bedford 812 278-8986
   2831 U St Bedford (47421) **(G-560)**

Lonn Manufacturing Inc 317 897-1440
   5450 W 84th St Indianapolis (46268) **(G-7417)**

Loogootee Tribune Inc 812 295-2500
   514 N John F Kennedy Ave Loogootee (47553) **(G-9389)**

Look Trailers, Middlebury Also called LGS Pace International Inc **(G-9903)**

Lord Corporation 317 259-4161
   5101 E 65th St Indianapolis (46220) **(G-7418)**

Lord Fms Games 317 710-2253
   7244 Rooses Way Indianapolis (46217) **(G-7419)**

Lorentson Manufacturing Co (PA) 765 452-4425
   1111 Rank Pkwy Kokomo (46901) **(G-8660)**

Lotec Inc 574 294-1506
   2000 Industrial Pkwy Elkhart (46516) **(G-3008)**

Lots of Software LLC 317 578-8120
   13534 Kelsey Ln Fishers (46038) **(G-3940)**

Lotus Design Group 812 206-7281
   113 Industrial Way Charlestown (47111) **(G-1570)**

Lou Mary Donuts Inc 765 474-9131
   1830 S 4th St Lafayette (47905) **(G-8960)**

Louanna Stilwell 812 631-0647
   6451 S County Road 1075 E Velpen (47590) **(G-13649)**

Loudon Printing Co Inc 574 967-3944
   507 W Columbia St Flora (46929) **(G-3998)**

Loughmiller Mch TI & Design, Loogootee Also called Loughmiller Mch TI Design
Inc **(G-9390)**

Loughmiller Mch TI Design Inc 812 295-3903
   12851 E 150 N Loogootee (47553) **(G-9390)**

Louis Dreyfus Co AG Inds LLC 574 566-2100
   7344 S State Road 15 Claypool (46510) **(G-1706)**

Louisiana-Pacific Corporation 574 825-5845
   219 W Us Highway 20 Middlebury (46540) **(G-9905)**

Louisville Veneer Corp 502 500-7176
   301 E Elm St New Albany (47150) **(G-10818)**

Loutsa Inc 317 273-0123
   7435 W 10th St Indianapolis (46214) **(G-7420)**

Love Controls, Michigan City Also called Dwyer Instruments Inc **(G-9786)**

Lovett Pallet Recycling LLC 317 638-4840
   217 S Belmont Ave Ste E Indianapolis (46222) **(G-7421)**

Lovetts Electronics 812 446-1093
   840 E Pinckley St Brazil (47834) **(G-967)**

Loving Care Ptnt/Wheelchair Tr 219 427-1137
   6115 Johnson St Merrillville (46410) **(G-9728)**

Low Vision Store, Greenwood Also called Vision Aid Systems Inc **(G-5758)**

Lowe Machine Tools LLC 248 705-7562
   7080 Willowleaf Ct Noblesville (46062) **(G-11142)**

Lowell Concrete Products Inc 219 696-3339
   9312 W 181st Ave Lowell (46356) **(G-9415)**

Lowell Quarry, Lowell Also called Legacy Vulcan LLC **(G-9414)**

Lowell Tribune, Lowell Also called Pilcher Publishing Co Inc **(G-9419)**

Lowery's Candies, Muncie Also called Lowerys Home Made Candies **(G-10513)**

Lowerys Home Made Candies 765 288-7300
   6255 W Kilgore Ave Muncie (47304) **(G-10513)**

Lowes Pellets and Grain Inc (PA) 812 663-7863
   2372 W State Road 46 Greensburg (47240) **(G-5621)**

Loy's Music Center, Elwood Also called Loys Sales Inc **(G-3304)**

Loyal Mfg Corp 317 359-3185
   1121 S Shortridge Rd Indianapolis (46239) **(G-7422)**

Loys Sales Inc 765 552-7250
   715 S 22nd St Elwood (46036) **(G-3304)**

Lozano Wldg & Fabrication LLC 812 858-1379
   8677 Hanover Dr Newburgh (47630) **(G-11037)**

Lozier Machinery Incorporated 812 945-2558
   695 Industrial Blvd New Albany (47150) **(G-10819)**

LP Middlebury, Middlebury Also called Louisiana-Pacific Corporation **(G-9905)**

Lpf Limited 765 447-0939
   4315 Commerce Dr Lafayette (47905) **(G-8961)**

LPI Paving & Excavating (PA) 260 726-9564
   1401 W Votaw St Portland (47371) **(G-11834)**

Lsc Communications Inc 812 234-1585
   200 Hulman St Terre Haute (47802) **(G-13276)**

Lsc Communications Us LLC 765 362-1300
   600 W State Road 32 Crawfordsville (47933) **(G-2169)**

Lsc Communications Us LLC 574 267-7101
   2801 W Old Road 30 Warsaw (46580) **(G-13902)**

Lsc Communications Us LLC 812 256-3396
   100 Quality Ct Charlestown (47111) **(G-1571)**

LSI, Granger *Also called Lazar Scientific Incorporated* (G-5418)
LSI Wallcovering Inc (PA) 502 458-1502
　2073 Mcdonald Ave New Albany (47150) (G-10820)
Lsm Manufacturing LLC 260 409-4030
　15303 Roth Rd Grabill (46741) (G-5379)
LTV Steel Co 219 391-2076
　3001 Dickey Rd East Chicago (46312) (G-2550)
Lube-Line Corporation (PA) 260 637-3779
　906 Carroll Rd Fort Wayne (46845) (G-4442)
Lucas Bus Forms & Swift Prtg 260 482-7644
　3020 Cngrnnal Pkwy Ste Ab Fort Wayne (46808) (G-4443)
Lucas Custom Instruments 812 342-3093
　13360 W Becks Grove Rd Columbus (47201) (G-1965)
Lucas Oil Pro Plling Prmotions 812 246-3350
　5511 County Road 403 Charlestown (47111) (G-1572)
Lucas Oil Products Inc 317 569-0039
　1143 W 116th St Carmel (46032) (G-1428)
Lucas Oil Raceway 317 291-4090
　10267 E Us Highway 136 Indianapolis (46234) (G-7423)
Lucas Oil Racing Inc 812 738-1147
　3199 Harrison Way Nw Corydon (47112) (G-2104)
Lucent Polymers Inc 812 492-7214
　1800 Lynch Rd Evansville (47711) (G-3606)
Luckmann Industries 317 464-0323
　3135 Jackson St Indianapolis (46222) (G-7424)
Lucky Straw Inc 219 397-9910
　405 E 151st St East Chicago (46312) (G-2551)
Ludo Fact USA LLC 765 588-9137
　4775 Dale Dr Lafayette (47905) (G-8962)
Ludwick Graphics Inc (PA) 574 233-2165
　1312 Honan Dr South Bend (46614) (G-12845)
Lue Manufacturing Inc 574 862-4249
　27667 County Road 40 Wakarusa (46573) (G-13783)
Lufkin Industries Inc 765 472-2935
　401 Blair Pike Peru (46970) (G-11536)
Lui Plus 812 309-9350
　7933 Valley Stream Dr Indianapolis (46237) (G-7425)
Luick Quality Gage & Tool, Muncie *Also called Haylex Manufacturing LLC* (G-10483)
Lukemeier Indus Mold & Mch Co 812 945-3375
　4300 Security Pkwy New Albany (47150) (G-10821)
Lumber WD Furn Mg Sell WD Flrg, South Whitley *Also called Ecojacks LLC* (G-12998)
Lumen Cache Incorporated 317 739-4218
　13402 Chrisfield Ln McCordsville (46055) (G-9673)
Lumen Cache Inc 317 222-1314
　11216 Fall Creek Rd Indianapolis (46256) (G-7426)
Luna Press Productions LLC 317 398-8895
　118 S Harrison St Shelbyville (46176) (G-12549)
Lund International Holding Co 765 742-7200
　3565 E 300 N Lafayette (47905) (G-8963)
Lush 317 842-5874
　4507 E 82nd St Indianapolis (46250) (G-7427)
Lute Supply 260 480-2441
　5406 Keystone Dr Fort Wayne (46825) (G-4444)
Luxemburg Machine LLC 260 347-4192
　5638 E Us Highway 6 Kendallville (46755) (G-8491)
Luxly LLC 617 415-8031
　14549 Brackney Ln Carmel (46032) (G-1429)
Luxottica Retail N Amer Inc 317 293-9999
　4020 Lafayette Rd Indianapolis (46254) (G-7428)
Luxottica Retail N Amer Inc 219 736-0141
　2212 Southlake Mall Merrillville (46410) (G-9729)
Lycro Products Co Inc 574 862-4981
　66557 State Road 19 Wakarusa (46573) (G-13784)
Lynch Fireworks Display Inc 812 537-1750
　56 Oakey Ave Greendale (47025) (G-5490)
Lynn Bros Electric Inc 219 762-6386
　5685 Old Porter Rd Portage (46368) (G-11774)
Lynn Tool Company Inc 765 874-2471
　107 Elm St Lynn (47355) (G-9430)
Lyntech Engineering Inc 574 224-2300
　6310 E State Road 14 Rochester (46975) (G-12134)
Lynx Motion Technology Corp 812 923-7474
　9540 Highway 150 Greenville (47124) (G-5650)
Lyra LLC 260 452-4058
　3711 Astoria Way Fort Wayne (46818) (G-4445)
Lyric and Line Tshirt Company, Fort Wayne *Also called Black Books Publishing Inc* (G-4111)
M & A Orthotics Inc 317 281-5253
　9065 Chadwell Ct Apt 208 Fishers (46037) (G-3941)
M & C LLC 812 482-7447
　3626 N Newton St Jasper (47546) (G-8288)
M & D Draperies 812 886-4608
　2022 Jackson Dr Vincennes (47591) (G-13691)
M & H Woodworking LLC 812 486-2570
　3591 N 775 E Montgomery (47558) (G-10233)
M & J Shelton Enterprises Inc 260 745-1616
　2131 Fairfield Ave Fort Wayne (46802) (G-4446)
M & K Services, South Bend *Also called Northern Indiana Ordnance Co* (G-12879)
M & M Printing, New Albany *Also called Mike Mugler* (G-10831)
M & M Svc Stn Eqp Spcalist Inc 317 347-8001
　2228 Yandes St Indianapolis (46205) (G-7429)

M & M Trim Inc 317 791-7009
　6525 Capitol Reef Ln Indianapolis (46237) (G-7430)
M & R Pattern Inc 219 778-4675
　6205 Fail Rd La Porte (46350) (G-8788)
M & S Curtis LLC 317 946-8440
　10015 Chester Dr Indianapolis (46240) (G-7431)
M & S Indus Met Fabricators, Huntington *Also called M & S Indus Met Fbricators Inc* (G-6226)
M & S Indus Met Fbricators Inc 260 356-0300
　5 Commercial Rd Huntington (46750) (G-6226)
M & S Screw Machine Products 765 853-5022
　S Main St Modoc (47358) (G-10174)
M & S Steel Corp 260 357-5184
　217 E Railroad St Garrett (46738) (G-5015)
M & W Concrete Pipe & Supply 812 426-2871
　1213 Stanley Ave Evansville (47711) (G-3607)
M A C Corporation 317 545-3341
　4717 Massachusetts Ave Indianapolis (46218) (G-7432)
M A Studio Inc 574 275-2200
　3153 S 900 W San Pierre (46374) (G-12309)
M and B Fabricating LLC 219 762-5032
　826 N 360 W Valparaiso (46385) (G-13578)
M and G Dirt and Gravel LLC 219 778-9341
　4203 N 600 E Rolling Prairie (46371) (G-12189)
M B S, Sellersburg *Also called Manitowoc Beverage Systems Inc* (G-12406)
M C F Business Product & Svcs, Evansville *Also called E James Dant* (G-3469)
M C L Window Coverings Inc (PA) 317 577-2670
　11815 Technology Ln Fishers (46038) (G-3942)
M C Welding & Machining Co 219 393-5718
　I Kingsbury Industrial Pa Kingsbury (46345) (G-8540)
M D Holdings LLC 317 831-7030
　451 E County Line Rd Mooresville (46158) (G-10319)
M E C, Westfield *Also called Motion Engineering Company Inc* (G-14177)
M F Y Designs Inc 260 563-6662
　1051 N State Road 15 Wabash (46992) (G-13734)
M G Products Inc 574 293-0752
　4707 Chester Dr Elkhart (46516) (G-3009)
M H EBY Inc 574 753-4000
　2909 W County Road 300 S Logansport (46947) (G-9353)
M I C Fremont, Fremont *Also called Metal Improvement Company LLC* (G-4967)
M L X Graphics, Terre Haute *Also called Phoenix Color Corp* (G-13303)
M M Converting Inc 260 563-7411
　3758 W Old 24 Wabash (46992) (G-13735)
M M Paltech Inc 219 932-5308
　518 Hoffman St Hammond (46327) (G-5909)
M M Printing Plus 574 658-9345
　634 E Beer Rd Milford (46542) (G-9956)
M Nelson & Associates Inc 317 228-1422
　4250 W 99th St 140 Carmel (46032) (G-1430)
M P L, Fairland *Also called Marstone Products Ltd* (G-3824)
M Pro LLC 765 459-4750
　4812 N Parkway Kokomo (46901) (G-8661)
M R S Printing Erectors Inc 317 888-1314
　4258 Redman Dr Greenwood (46142) (G-5722)
M RI Solutions 317 218-3006
　8805 N Meridian St Indianapolis (46260) (G-7433)
M Ross Masson, Indianapolis *Also called Masson M Ross Co Inc* (G-7464)
M S Aronstam Jewelers, Carmel *Also called Design Msa Inc* (G-1355)
M S Powder Coating 260 356-0300
　5 Commercial Rd Huntington (46750) (G-6227)
M S W, Indianapolis *Also called Mahomed Sales & Whsng LLC* (G-7441)
M T I, Lebanon *Also called Metal Technology of Indiana* (G-9205)
M T M Machining Inc 219 872-8677
　311 Indiana Highway 212 Michigan City (46360) (G-9813)
M U Holdings Inc 765 675-8054
　815 W Jefferson St Bldg 4 Tipton (46072) (G-13396)
M&M Machines 260 349-1922
　111 W Lisle St Kendallville (46755) (G-8492)
M&M Performance Inc 574 536-6103
　16077 Prairie Rose Ave Goshen (46528) (G-5276)
M-3 & Associates, Granger *Also called Wait Industries LLC* (G-5451)
M-3 and Associates Inc 574 294-3988
　28244 Clay St Elkhart (46517) (G-3010)
M-TEC Corporation 574 294-1060
　701 Collins Rd Elkhart (46516) (G-3011)
M-Tech Machine Products 812 637-3500
　27755 Daugherty Ln Ste A West Harrison (47060) (G-14040)
M.A.S. Products, Elkhart *Also called Mid America Screw Products* (G-3036)
M2 Industries LLC 812 246-0651
　2200 Utica Pike Jeffersonville (47130) (G-8392)
M2m Holdings Inc 317 249-1700
　450 E 96th St Ste 300 Indianapolis (46240) (G-7434)
M4 Sciences LLC 765 479-6215
　1800 Woodland Ave West Lafayette (47906) (G-14084)
MA Metal Co Inc 812 526-2666
　2860 N National Rd Columbus (47201) (G-1966)
Ma-Ri-Al Corp 317 773-0679
　16101 River Rd Noblesville (46062) (G-11143)

A
L
P
H
A
B
E
T
I
C

Maax Aker Plastics, Plymouth *Also called Maax Inc (G-11704)*
Maax Inc 574 936-3838
  1001 N Oak Dr Plymouth (46563) *(G-11704)*
Mac Designs 317 580-9390
  1009 3rd Ave Sw Carmel (46032) *(G-1431)*
Mac Industrial Services, Mount Vernon *Also called Michrochem LLC (G-10401)*
Mac Machine & Metal Works Inc 765 825-5873
  100 N Grand Ave Connersville (47331) *(G-2062)*
Macallister Machinery Co Inc 260 483-6469
  2500 W Coliseum Blvd Fort Wayne (46808) *(G-4447)*
Macallister Machinery Co Inc 765 966-0759
  4791 E Main St Richmond (47374) *(G-12012)*
Macdonald Classified Service, Lafayette *Also called Harrison Macdonald & Sons (G-8911)*
Mach 1 Paper and Poly Pdts Inc 574 522-4500
  1801 Minnie St Elkhart (46516) *(G-3012)*
Machine Keys Inc 765 228-4208
  309 N Timber Ridge Ct Muncie (47304) *(G-10514)*
Machine Rebuilders & Service 260 482-8168
  4801 Projects Dr Fort Wayne (46825) *(G-4448)*
Machine Tool Service Inc 812 232-1912
  117 Elm St Terre Haute (47807) *(G-13277)*
Machined Castings Spc LLC 574 223-5694
  290 Blacketor Dr Rochester (46975) *(G-12135)*
Machining Center Inc 317 787-1965
  5935 Kopetsky Dr Ste E Indianapolis (46217) *(G-7435)*
Machining Solutions 574 292-3227
  942 S 27th St South Bend (46615) *(G-12846)*
Mack Tool & Engineering Inc 574 233-8424
  2820 Viridian Dr South Bend (46628) *(G-12847)*
Macks Welding 812 265-6255
  2890 Wilson Ave Madison (47250) *(G-9478)*
Maco Press Inc 317 846-5754
  560 3rd Ave Sw Carmel (46032) *(G-1432)*
Maco Reprograhics LLC 812 464-8108
  600 Court St Evansville (47708) *(G-3608)*
Macor 574 255-2658
  1025 W 11th St Mishawaka (46544) *(G-10072)*
Macpactor Inc 502 643-7845
  414 Spring St Jeffersonville (47130) *(G-8393)*
Macs Express Inc 765 865-9700
  428 E Center Rd Kokomo (46902) *(G-8662)*
Mactac, Columbus *Also called Morgan Adhesives Company LLC (G-1976)*
Mad Hatters Unlimited 219 852-6011
  4846 Pine Ave Hammond (46327) *(G-5910)*
Madden Manufacturing Inc 574 295-4292
  1317 Princeton St Elkhart (46516) *(G-3013)*
Maddenco Inc 812 474-6245
  4847 E Virginia St Ste G Evansville (47715) *(G-3609)*
Maddock Construction Eqp LLC 812 349-3000
  239 W Grimes Ln Bloomington (47403) *(G-768)*
Made Rite Manufacturing Inc 812 967-2652
  3967 E Sullivan Ln Salem (47167) *(G-12300)*
Madelyn Harwood Inc 317 839-7890
  7454 Hawthorne Dr Plainfield (46168) *(G-11622)*
Madillion Plastics Inc 574 293-4434
  836 Summa Dr Elkhart (46516) *(G-3014)*
Madison Boat & Barge, Madison *Also called Macks Welding (G-9478)*
Madison Cabinets Inc 260 639-3915
  14727 Bruick Dr Hoagland (46745) *(G-6066)*
Madison County Cabinets Inc 765 778-4646
  9592 W 650 S Pendleton (46064) *(G-11493)*
Madison Courier 812 265-3641
  310 Courier Sq Madison (47250) *(G-9479)*
Madison Electronics Inc 812 689-4204
  475 S Tanglewood Rd Versailles (47042) *(G-13655)*
Madison Manufacturing Inc 574 633-4433
  66990 State Road 331 Bremen (46506) *(G-1009)*
Madison Plating Inc 812 273-2211
  2520 Lanier Dr Ste A Madison (47250) *(G-9480)*
Madison Precision Products Inc 812 273-4702
  94 E 400 N Madison (47250) *(G-9481)*
Madison River Industries LLC 317 472-6375
  16567 River Rd Noblesville (46062) *(G-11144)*
Madison Tool and Die Inc 812 273-2250
  3000 Michigan Rd Madison (47250) *(G-9482)*
Madison Truss Company 812 273-5482
  5426 N Olive Branch Rd Madison (47250) *(G-9483)*
Madison Vineyards Inc 812 273-6500
  1456 E 400 N Madison (47250) *(G-9484)*
Madison, The, Mishawaka *Also called J H J Inc (G-10055)*
Madsen Wire LLC 260 829-6561
  101 Madsen St Orland (46776) *(G-11353)*
Madsen Wire Products, Orland *Also called Noble Wire Products Inc (G-11354)*
Mae of America Inc 765 561-4539
  7960 Castleway Dr Ste 131 Indianapolis (46250) *(G-7436)*
Mafcote Wabash Paper Coating 260 563-4181
  301 Wedcor Ave Wabash (46992) *(G-13736)*
Mag Instrument Inc 574 262-1521
  25845 Meadow Oak Ln Elkhart (46514) *(G-3015)*

Mag Software Inc 317 755-4080
  49 Boone Vlg Ste 275 Zionsville (46077) *(G-14446)*
Magaws of Boston 765 935-6170
  5774 State Road 227 S Richmond (47374) *(G-12013)*
Magaws of Boston The, Richmond *Also called Magaws of Boston (G-12013)*
Magazine Fulfillment Corp 219 874-4245
  613 Franklin St Michigan City (46360) *(G-9814)*
Magic Candle Inc 317 357-1101
  203 S Audubon Rd Indianapolis (46219) *(G-7437)*
Magic Circle Corporation 765 246-7737
  6302 E County Road 100 N Coatesville (46121) *(G-1751)*
Magic Company 260 747-1502
  405 Lower Huntington Rd Fort Wayne (46819) *(G-4449)*
Magic Glass Lafayette, Lafayette *Also called Dewilde Glass Inc (G-8890)*
Magic Light Neon Sign Company 765 361-5887
  408 California St Crawfordsville (47933) *(G-2170)*
Magic Premium Snacks, Fort Wayne *Also called Magic Company (G-4449)*
Magitek LLC 260 488-2226
  5618 County Road 6 Hamilton (46742) *(G-5825)*
Magna Machine & Tool Co Inc 765 766-5388
  3722 N Messick Rd New Castle (47362) *(G-10910)*
Magna Powertrain America Inc 765 587-1300
  4701 S Cowan Rd Muncie (47302) *(G-10515)*
Magna Powertrain America Inc 765 587-1300
  1400 W Fuson Rd Muncie (47302) *(G-10516)*
Magneco/Metrel Inc 219 885-4190
  201 Mississippi St Gary (46402) *(G-5073)*
Magnequench Inc 765 778-7809
  237 S Pendleton Ave Ste C Pendleton (46064) *(G-11494)*
Magnetech Industrial Svc 219 937-0100
  1825 Summer St Hammond (46320) *(G-5911)*
Magnetic Concepts Corporation 317 580-4021
  611 3rd Ave Sw Carmel (46032) *(G-1433)*
Magnetic Instrumentation Inc (PA) 317 842-9000
  8431 Castlewood Dr Indianapolis (46250) *(G-7438)*
Magnetic Instrumentation LLC 317 842-7500
  8431 Castlewood Dr Indianapolis (46250) *(G-7439)*
Magnets R US Inc 574 633-0061
  63300 State Road 331 South Bend (46614) *(G-12848)*
Magnifiscents 317 549-3880
  5207 E 38th St Indianapolis (46218) *(G-7440)*
Magnolia 317 831-3221
  311 W 36th St Jasper (47546) *(G-8289)*
Magnolia Products LLC 812 306-8638
  314 Ridgeway Ave Evansville (47713) *(G-3610)*
Magnum Drilling Svcs Inc 812 985-3981
  10020 Carmel Ct Evansville (47712) *(G-3611)*
Magnum Industries, Goshen *Also called Magnum Venus Products Inc (G-5277)*
Magnum Venus Products Inc 727 573-2955
  320 N Main St Goshen (46528) *(G-5277)*
Magwerks Corporation 317 241-8011
  501 Commerce Dr Danville (46122) *(G-2352)*
Maher Cnstr Roofg & Siding, Terre Haute *Also called Maher Supply Inc (G-13278)*
Maher Supply Inc 812 234-7699
  910 N 10th St Terre Haute (47807) *(G-13278)*
Mahogany Scents 574 271-1364
  53154 Bracken Fern Dr South Bend (46637) *(G-12849)*
Mahomed Sales & Whsng LLC 317 472-5800
  8258 Zionsville Rd Indianapolis (46268) *(G-7441)*
Mahoney Foundries Inc (PA) 260 347-1768
  209 W Ohio St Kendallville (46755) *(G-8493)*
Mailboxes and Parcel Depot, Jasper *Also called M & C LLC (G-8288)*
Mailroom LLC 765 254-0000
  4801 N Wheeling Ave Muncie (47304) *(G-10517)*
Main Event Mdsg Group LLC 317 570-8900
  6880 Hillsdale Ct Indianapolis (46250) *(G-7442)*
Main Music 812 295-2020
  12958 E Us Highway 50 Loogootee (47553) *(G-9391)*
Main One Media, Indianapolis *Also called Main1media LLC (G-7443)*
Main Street Computers 574 772-7890
  4 S Main St Apt A Knox (46534) *(G-8572)*
Main Street Sports, Bloomfield *Also called Jer-Maur Corporation (G-640)*
Main1media LLC 317 841-7000
  8459 Castlewood Dr Ste D Indianapolis (46250) *(G-7443)*
Maingate Inc 317 243-2000
  7900 Rockville Rd Indianapolis (46214) *(G-7444)*
Mainline Conveyor Systems Inc 317 831-2795
  10970 N Holland Dr S Mooresville (46158) *(G-10320)*
Mainline Manufacturing Company 219 237-0770
  329 N Colfax St Griffith (46319) *(G-5782)*
Mains Enterprises Inc 765 425-0162
  9762 N Nashville Rd Wilkinson (46186) *(G-14279)*
Maitland Engineering Inc 574 287-0155
  2713 Foundation Dr South Bend (46628) *(G-12850)*
Majestic Block & Supply Inc 317 842-6602
  7711 Loma Ct Fishers (46038) *(G-3943)*
Majestic Block and Brick Inc 317 831-2455
  520 S Park Dr Mooresville (46158) *(G-10321)*

(G-0000) Company's Geographic Section entry number

Majestic Caskets & Urns Inc 812 523-3630
2019 2nd Ave Seymour (47274) *(G-12469)*

Majestic Drapieries 574 259-3080
400 S West St Mishawaka (46544) *(G-10073)*

Majestic Marble Imports Inc 317 237-4400
1100 E Maryland St Indianapolis (46202) *(G-7445)*

Majestic Tool Inc 812 426-0332
9333 W Boonvl New Harmony Evansville (47720) *(G-3612)*

Majesty Enterprises Inc 812 752-6446
2068 S Jimtown Ln Scottsburg (47170) *(G-12372)*

Majesty Express, Scottsburg *Also called Majesty Enterprises Inc (G-12372)*

Major League Electronics LLC 812 670-4174
2533 Cenennial Blvd Jeffersonville (47130) *(G-8394)*

Major Medical Sales, Indianapolis *Also called Writt Sales & Supply Co Inc (G-8220)*

Major Tool and Machine Inc 317 636-6433
1458 E 19th St Indianapolis (46218) *(G-7446)*

Make It Black Seal Coating 219 629-6230
824 Lake St Hobart (46342) *(G-6090)*

Make It Mobile LLC 260 562-1045
770 E State Road 120 Howe (46746) *(G-6128)*

Makuta Technics Inc 317 642-0001
2155 Intelliplex Dr Shelbyville (46176) *(G-12550)*

Malibu C, Indianapolis *Also called Malibu Wellness Inc (G-7447)*

Malibu Wellness Inc 317 624-7560
6050 E Hanna Ave Ste 1 Indianapolis (46203) *(G-7447)*

Mallory Sonalert Products Inc 317 612-1000
4411 S High School Rd Indianapolis (46241) *(G-7448)*

Mallow Run LLC 317 422-1556
6964 W Whiteland Rd Bargersville (46106) *(G-484)*

Malone Hardwoods, Boswell *Also called Power Place Products Inc (G-941)*

Maloney Group Inc 812 285-7400
6300 E Highway 62 Jeffersonville (47130) *(G-8395)*

Mammoth Hats Inc 812 849-2772
1773 Huron Williams Rd Mitchell (47446) *(G-10166)*

Mamon Global Industries Inc 317 721-1657
1009 Manck Dr Fort Wayne (46814) *(G-4450)*

Managed Cmmunications Svcs LLC 260 480-7885
18511 Lima Rd Huntertown (46748) *(G-6142)*

Manar Inc (PA) 812 526-2891
905 S Walnut St Edinburgh (46124) *(G-2617)*

Manar Inc 812 346-2858
1050 W Jfk Dr North Vernon (47265) *(G-11268)*

Manasek Acquisition Co LLC 765 551-1600
11700 N State Road 37 Elwood (46036) *(G-3305)*

Manchester Industries Inc VA 765 489-4521
63 Paul R Foulke Pkwy Hagerstown (47346) *(G-5808)*

Manchester Metals, North Manchester *Also called Mm Holdings I LLC (G-11236)*

Manchester North News Journal 260 982-6383
1306 State Road 114 W North Manchester (46962) *(G-11233)*

Manchester Tank & Equipment Co, Goshen *Also called McWane Inc (G-5283)*

Manchester Tank & Equipment Co 812 275-5931
905 X St Bedford (47421) *(G-561)*

Manchester Tank & Equipment Co 574 295-8200
3630 Manchester Dr Elkhart (46514) *(G-3016)*

Manchester Tool & Die Inc 260 982-8524
601 S Wabash Rd North Manchester (46962) *(G-11234)*

Manchester Tool and Die Plant 260 982-0702
405 Beckley St North Manchester (46962) *(G-11235)*

Mancor Indiana Inc 765 779-4800
7825 American Way Anderson (46013) *(G-134)*

Mandala Screen Printing Inc 574 946-6290
950 E 250 N Winamac (46996) *(G-14311)*

Manier Welding & Fabrications 765 675-6078
859 Market Rd Tipton (46072) *(G-13397)*

Manitex International Inc 574 772-5380
5420 E State Road 8 Knox (46534) *(G-8573)*

Manitex Sabre, Knox *Also called Manitex International Inc (G-8573)*

Manitex Sabre Inc 574 772-5380
5420 E State Road 8 Knox (46534) *(G-8574)*

Manitowoc 540 375-9300
2100 Future Dr Sellersburg (47172) *(G-12404)*

Manitowoc Beverage Eqp Inc (HQ) 812 246-7000
2100 Future Dr Sellersburg (47172) *(G-12405)*

Manitowoc Beverage Systems Inc 800 367-4233
2100 Future Dr Sellersburg (47172) *(G-12406)*

Manley Meats Inc 260 592-7313
302 S 400 E Decatur (46733) *(G-2392)*

Mann Distribution Inc 317 293-6785
7 Barbara Ct Indianapolis (46222) *(G-7449)*

Mann Road Sawmill Inc 765 342-2700
7060 New Harmony Rd Martinsville (46151) *(G-9621)*

Mann+hummel Filtration Technol 260 497-5560
9602 Coldwater Rd Ste 104 Fort Wayne (46825) *(G-4451)*

Mannon L Walters Inc 812 867-5946
500 N Congress Ave Ste D Evansville (47715) *(G-3613)*

Mansfield - King LLC 317 788-0750
6501 Julian Ave Indianapolis (46219) *(G-7450)*

Manta Rugs 765 869-5940
305 N Harrison St Boswell (47921) *(G-940)*

Mantech Manifold 260 479-2383
9105 Clubridge Dr Fort Wayne (46809) *(G-4452)*

Mantra Enterprise LLC 201 428-8709
12694 Balbo Pl Fishers (46037) *(G-3944)*

Manufactured Products 765 552-2871
2700 S K St Elwood (46036) *(G-3306)*

Manufacturing Facility, Evansville *Also called Bprex Closures LLC (G-3399)*

Manufacturing Technology Inc (PA) 574 230-0258
1702 W Washington St South Bend (46628) *(G-12851)*

Manufacturing Technology Inc 574 233-9490
402 N Sheridan St South Bend (46619) *(G-12852)*

Manuwal Sawmill Inc 574 936-8187
15771 14th Rd Plymouth (46563) *(G-11705)*

Map of Easton 574 293-0966
3733 Lexington Park Dr Elkhart (46514) *(G-3017)*

Maple Acres 260 636-2073
535 S 500 E Avilla (46710) *(G-414)*

Maple City Machine Inc 574 533-6742
1762 E Kercher Rd Goshen (46526) *(G-5278)*

Maple City Woodworking Corp 574 642-3342
2948 Hackberry Dr Goshen (46526) *(G-5279)*

Maple Leaf Inc (PA) 574 453-4455
101 E Church St Leesburg (46538) *(G-9238)*

Maple Leaf Farms, Leesburg *Also called Maple Leaf Inc (G-9238)*

Maple Leaf Farms Inc (HQ) 574 453-4500
9166 N 200 E Milford (46542) *(G-9957)*

Maple Leaf Farms Inc 574 658-4121
9179 N 200 E Milford (46542) *(G-9958)*

Maple Leaf Graphics Inc 317 410-0321
13540 Kensington Pl Carmel (46032) *(G-1434)*

Maple Leaf Woodworking 260 768-8166
3950 W 200 N Lagrange (46761) *(G-9059)*

Maple-Hunter Decals 812 894-9759
8075 St Rd 46 Riley (47871) *(G-12084)*

Maplehurst Bakeries, Brownsburg *Also called Weston Foods Us Inc (G-1176)*

Maplehurst Bakeries LLC 317 858-9000
1760 Industrial Dr Greenwood (46143) *(G-5723)*

Maplehurst Bakeries LLC (HQ) 317 858-9000
50 Maplehurst Dr Brownsburg (46112) *(G-1160)*

Mapleleaf Printing Co Inc 574 534-7790
301 W Lincoln Ave Goshen (46526) *(G-5280)*

Mappa Mundi Magazine 574 896-4952
307 Lane St North Judson (46366) *(G-11213)*

Mar Kel Inc 812 853-6133
4111 Merchant Dr Newburgh (47630) *(G-11038)*

Mar-Co Packaging Inc 765 564-3979
1124 Samuel Milroy Rd Delphi (46923) *(G-2423)*

Mar-Kel Quick Print, Newburgh *Also called Mar Kel Inc (G-11038)*

Marathon Oil, Fort Wayne *Also called Fairfield Gas Way (G-4253)*

Marburger Foods, Peru *Also called Mpi Holdings Inc (G-11538)*

Marc Woodworking Inc 317 635-9663
1719 English Ave Indianapolis (46201) *(G-7451)*

Marco Plastics Inc 812 333-0062
1616 S Huntington Dr Bloomington (47401) *(G-769)*

Marcotte Cabinets 574 520-1342
51286 Ironwood Rd Granger (46530) *(G-5419)*

Marcums Welding & Stl Proc Inc 765 763-7279
454 E Main St Morristown (46161) *(G-10374)*

Margaret Machine and Tool Co 219 924-0859
206 S Lindberg St Griffith (46319) *(G-5783)*

Margco International LLC 317 568-4274
6445 E 30th St Indianapolis (46219) *(G-7452)*

Margins Printing LLC 773 981-4251
4163 Georgia St Gary (46409) *(G-5074)*

Margison Graphics LLC 765 529-8250
1813 S Memorial Dr New Castle (47362) *(G-10911)*

Margison Sign Company, New Castle *Also called Margison Graphics LLC (G-10911)*

Mariah Foods Corp 812 378-3366
1333 Indiana Ave Columbus (47201) *(G-1967)*

Marian Inc 317 638-6525
1011 E Saint Clair St Indianapolis (46202) *(G-7453)*

Marian Worldwide Inc (PA) 317 638-6525
1011 E Saint Clair St Indianapolis (46202) *(G-7454)*

Marie S Embroidery 219 931-2561
7132 Madison Ave Hammond (46324) *(G-5912)*

Marietta Martin Materials Inc 765 459-3194
2400 W 50 S Kokomo (46902) *(G-8663)*

Marietta Martin Materials Inc 317 831-7391
8520 Old State Road 37 N Martinsville (46151) *(G-9622)*

Marietta Martin Materials Inc 317 789-4020
5620 S Belmont Ave Indianapolis (46217) *(G-7455)*

Marietta Martin Materials Inc 317 776-4460
15215 River Rd Noblesville (46062) *(G-11145)*

Marine Builders Inc 812 283-7932
208 Church St Jeffersonville (47130) *(G-8396)*

Marine Mooring Inc 574 594-5787
3404 N 600 E Warsaw (46582) *(G-13903)*

Marine Precast, Decatur *Also called Prestress Services Inc (G-2399)*

Marion Manufacturing, West Terre Haute *Also called Marion Tool & Die Inc (G-14126)*

A
L
P
H
A
B
E
T
I
C

Marion Metal Products Inc.....765 662-8333
401 N Henderson Ave Marion (46952) ***(G-9543)***
Marion Paper Box Company.....765 664-6435
600 E 18th St Marion (46953) ***(G-9544)***
Marion Steel Fabrication Inc.....765 664-1478
1819 S Branson St Marion (46953) ***(G-9545)***
Marion Tent & Awning Co.....765 664-7722
225 W Swayzee St Marion (46952) ***(G-9546)***
Marion Tool & Die Inc (PA).....812 533-9800
1126 W National Ave West Terre Haute (47885) ***(G-14126)***
Marion, In Plant, Marion *Also called General Cable Industries Inc* ***(G-9524)***
Marion-Kay Spices, Brownstown *Also called Reidco Inc* ***(G-1191)***
Marios Athletic Zone.....219 845-1800
6942 Indianapolis Blvd Hammond (46324) ***(G-5913)***
Mark & Jessies Firework Shack.....812 372-3855
3515 Hollowell St Columbus (47201) ***(G-1968)***
Mark Concrete Products Inc.....317 398-8616
1126 Miller Ave Shelbyville (46176) ***(G-12551)***
Mark Fore Sales, Fort Wayne *Also called Kerham Inc* ***(G-4409)***
Mark Hackman.....812 522-8257
3640 S County Road 400 E Brownstown (47220) ***(G-1190)***
Mark Hedge.....812 288-8037
1501 Cameron Dr Jeffersonville (47130) ***(G-8397)***
Mark Heister Design Inc.....312 527-0422
1600 Indiana Ave La Porte (46350) ***(G-8789)***
Mark Lamaster.....765 534-4185
16271 E 191st St Noblesville (46060) ***(G-11146)***
Mark Middleton.....812 967-2853
5691 S Olive Branch Rd Pekin (47165) ***(G-11475)***
Mark Morin Logging.....812 327-4917
757 N Walnut St West Baden Springs (47469) ***(G-14034)***
Mark Murray.....812 372-8390
3475 Commerce Dr Columbus (47201) ***(G-1969)***
Mark Parmenter.....812 829-6583
358 S East St Spencer (47460) ***(G-13030)***
Mark Russell.....812 386-8069
610 E Christian St Princeton (47670) ***(G-11877)***
Mark Tool & Die Inc.....765 533-4932
50 W Main St Markleville (46056) ***(G-9588)***
Mark-Line Industries LLC (PA).....574 825-5851
51687 County Road 133 Bristol (46507) ***(G-1068)***
Market Place Publications.....219 769-7733
7091 Broadway Ste D Merrillville (46410) ***(G-9730)***
Marketing Services Group Inc.....317 381-2268
2601 S Holt Rd Indianapolis (46241) ***(G-7456)***
Markle Classic Signs, Linton *Also called Markle Music* ***(G-9310)***
Markle Music.....812 847-2103
44 S Main St Linton (47441) ***(G-9310)***
Markle Water Treatment Plant.....260 758-3482
460 Parkview Dr Markle (46770) ***(G-9580)***
Markley Enterprise Inc.....574 295-4195
800 Lillian Ave Elkhart (46516) ***(G-3018)***
Marksmen Tool & Die Inc.....765 584-3600
230 N Jackson St Winchester (47394) ***(G-14336)***
Marley-Wylain Company (HQ).....630 560-3703
500 Blaine St Michigan City (46360) ***(G-9815)***
Marley-Wylain Company.....219 879-6561
500 Blaine St Michigan City (46360) ***(G-9816)***
Marmon Highway Tech LLC.....317 787-0718
2770 Bluff Rd Indianapolis (46225) ***(G-7457)***
Marner Door Manufacturing LLC.....812 486-3128
4254 N 525 E Montgomery (47558) ***(G-10234)***
Maron Products Incorporated.....574 259-1971
1301 Industrial Dr Mishawaka (46544) ***(G-10074)***
Marque, Elkhart *Also called Sjc Industries Corp* ***(G-3174)***
Marquette Council 3631 Kn.....219 864-3255
1400 S Broad St Griffith (46319) ***(G-5784)***
Marquise Enterprises Ltd.....317 578-3400
7330 E 86th St Ste 100 Indianapolis (46256) ***(G-7458)***
Marshall & Poe Bus Cons & CP, Elkhart *Also called Marshall & Poe LLC* ***(G-3019)***
Marshall & Poe LLC (PA).....574 266-5244
818 Erwin St Elkhart (46514) ***(G-3019)***
Marshall Companies Indiana.....317 769-2666
6850 S 280 E Lebanon (46052) ***(G-9202)***
Marshall Crane, Lebanon *Also called Marshall Companies Indiana* ***(G-9202)***
Marshall Electric Corporation (PA).....574 223-4367
425 N State Road 25 Rochester (46975) ***(G-12136)***
Marshall Gas Controls, Elkhart *Also called S H Leggitt Company* ***(G-3152)***
Marshall Signs.....260 350-1492
1270 Rohm Dr Auburn (46706) ***(G-342)***
Marson International LLC.....574 295-4222
1001 Sako Ct Elkhart (46516) ***(G-3020)***
Marstone Products Ltd.....800 466-7465
203 N Edgerton St Fairland (46126) ***(G-3824)***
Marteck Inc.....317 824-0240
7998 Georgetown Rd # 600 Indianapolis (46268) ***(G-7459)***
Martin Brown Publishers LLC.....765 459-8258
1138 S Webster St Kokomo (46902) ***(G-8664)***
Martin Ekwlor Phrmcuticals Inc.....765 962-4410
2800 Southeast Pkwy Richmond (47374) ***(G-12014)***
Martin Electric Inc.....765 288-3254
5501 E Eaton Albany Pike Eaton (47338) ***(G-2585)***
Martin Grgory Cnvyor Engrg LLC.....812 923-9814
1549 Pirtle Dr Georgetown (47122) ***(G-5149)***
Martin Holding Company LLC.....812 401-9988
605 W Eichel Ave Evansville (47710) ***(G-3614)***
Martin Industries.....502 553-6599
4235 Earnings Way New Albany (47150) ***(G-10822)***
Martin Marietta Aggregates, Kokomo *Also called Marietta Martin Materials Inc* ***(G-8663)***
Martin Marietta Aggregates, Martinsville *Also called Marietta Martin Materials Inc* ***(G-9622)***
Martin Marietta Materials Inc.....317 846-8540
11010 Hazel Dell Pkwy Indianapolis (46280) ***(G-6272)***
Martin Mretta Magnesia Spc LLC.....765 795-3536
2010 E County Road 800 S Cloverdale (46120) ***(G-1729)***
Martin Signs & Crane Services.....317 908-9708
7204 E 46th St Indianapolis (46226) ***(G-7460)***
Martin Spouting Inc.....260 485-5703
10165 Saint Joe Rd Fort Wayne (46835) ***(G-4453)***
Martin Truss Manufacturing.....574 862-4457
62332 County Road 1 Elkhart (46517) ***(G-3021)***
Martin Welding Shop.....574 862-2578
27585 County Road 40 Wakarusa (46573) ***(G-13785)***
Martin Yale Industries LLC.....260 563-0641
251 Wedcor Ave Wabash (46992) ***(G-13737)***
Martinrea Industries Inc.....812 346-5750
505 Industrial Dr North Vernon (47265) ***(G-11269)***
Martins Buggy Shop.....574 831-3699
24070 County Road 46 Nappanee (46550) ***(G-10692)***
Martins Wood Works.....574 862-4080
66227 County Road 9 Goshen (46526) ***(G-5281)***
Martinson Cabinet Shop.....219 926-1566
1245 W Us Highway 20 Chesterton (46304) ***(G-1619)***
Martinson Custom Kitchens, Chesterton *Also called Martinson Cabinet Shop* ***(G-1619)***
Martinsville Asphalt & Cnstr, Martinsville *Also called Rogers Group Inc* ***(G-9634)***
Martinsville Milling Co Inc.....317 253-2581
8391 N Illinois St Indianapolis (46260) ***(G-7461)***
Martinsville Vault Company.....765 342-4576
5910 Hacker Creek Rd Martinsville (46151) ***(G-9623)***
Marv Kahlig & Sons Inc.....260 335-2212
3229 S 500 E Portland (47371) ***(G-11835)***
Marvelous Woodworking LLC.....317 679-5890
5475 S 175 W Lebanon (46052) ***(G-9203)***
Marwood Inc.....812 288-8344
2901 Hamburg Pike Jeffersonville (47130) ***(G-8398)***
Mary Duncan.....812 238-3637
601 W Honey Creek Dr Terre Haute (47802) ***(G-13279)***
Mary Jonas.....317 500-0600
2104 Dr Andrw J Brwn Ave Indianapolis (46202) ***(G-7462)***
Mary Lou Donuts, Lafayette *Also called Lou Mary Donuts Inc* ***(G-8960)***
Maschino Industries Inc.....812 346-3083
1405 S County Road 750 W North Vernon (47265) ***(G-11270)***
Maschino Woodworks.....812 230-7428
739 N Forest Dr Terre Haute (47803) ***(G-13280)***
Masco Corporation of Indiana (HQ).....317 848-1812
55 E 111th St Indianapolis (46280) ***(G-6273)***
Masco Corporation of Indiana.....317 848-1812
300 S Carroll Rd Indianapolis (46229) ***(G-7463)***
Mascot Truck Parts Usa LLC.....317 839-9525
849 Whitaker Rd Ste D Plainfield (46168) ***(G-11623)***
Maso Inc.....260 432-3568
2200 Lafontain St Fort Wayne (46802) ***(G-4454)***
Masolite, Fort Wayne *Also called Maso Inc* ***(G-4454)***
Mason Corporation.....219 865-8040
1049 Us Highway 41 Schererville (46375) ***(G-12333)***
Mason Total Property Care.....260 385-3573
3706 Norland Ln New Haven (46774) ***(G-10948)***
Masson M Ross Co Inc.....317 632-8021
567 N Highland Ave Indianapolis (46202) ***(G-7464)***
Mast Woodworking.....812 636-7938
9922 E 1000 N Odon (47562) ***(G-11334)***
Master Brand Cabinets, Goshen *Also called Masterbrand Cabinets Inc* ***(G-5282)***
Master Built Racing Accessory, Crothersville *Also called Mastersbilt Chassis Inc* ***(G-2218)***
Master Corporation.....260 471-0001
6206 Discount Dr Fort Wayne (46818) ***(G-4455)***
Master Electric Service LLC.....812 246-3707
1233 Bringham Dr Ste A Sellersburg (47172) ***(G-12407)***
Master Manufacturing Company.....812 425-1561
4703 Ohara Dr Evansville (47711) ***(G-3615)***
Master Metal Engineering, South Bend *Also called Master Metal Machining Inc* ***(G-12853)***
Master Metal Machining Inc.....574 299-0222
4520 S Burnett Dr South Bend (46614) ***(G-12853)***
Master Piece Krafts LLC.....260 768-4330
4875 N 675 W Shipshewana (46565) ***(G-12632)***
Master Roll Mfg's, Kingsbury *Also called Mayfield-Glenn Group Inc* ***(G-8541)***
Master Spas Inc.....260 436-9100
6927 Lincoln Pkwy Fort Wayne (46804) ***(G-4456)***
Master Sports, Fort Wayne *Also called Master Corporation* ***(G-4455)***

796 2018 Harris Indiana Industrial Directory (G-0000) Company's Geographic Section entry number

Masterbilt Incorporated....574 287-6567
325 S Walnut St South Bend (46601) ***(G-12854)***
Masterbrand Cabinets Inc....812 482-2527
1 Masterbrand Cabinets Dr Jasper (47546) ***(G-8290)***
Masterbrand Cabinets Inc....765 966-3940
1340 Rose City Blvd Richmond (47374) ***(G-12015)***
Masterbrand Cabinets Inc (HQ)....812 482-2527
1 Masterbrand Cabinets Dr Jasper (47546) ***(G-8291)***
Masterbrand Cabinets Inc....574 535-9300
1002 Eisenhower Dr N Goshen (46526) ***(G-5282)***
Masterbrand Cabinets Inc....812 482-2527
6385 E State Road 164 Celestine (47521) ***(G-1536)***
Masterbrand Cabinets Inc....812 482-2513
1491 S Meridian Rd Jasper (47546) ***(G-8292)***
Masterbrand Cabinets Inc....812 367-1104
614 W 3rd St Ferdinand (47532) ***(G-3858)***
Masterbrand Cabinets Inc....812 482-2527
1009 N Geiger St Huntingburg (47542) ***(G-6175)***
Masterbrand Cabinets Inc....256 362-5530
1 Masterbrand Cabinets Dr Jasper (47546) ***(G-8293)***
Mastercraft Inc (PA)....260 463-8702
711 S Poplar St Lagrange (46761) ***(G-9060)***
Masterguard, Veedersburg *Also called Flex-N-Gate Corporation* ***(G-13643)***
Mastersbilt Chassis Inc....812 793-3666
6520 S Us Highway 31 Crothersville (47229) ***(G-2218)***
Matam Corp....317 264-9908
1434 N New Jersey St Indianapolis (46202) ***(G-7465)***
Matchless Machine & Tool Co....765 342-4550
55 James Baldwin Dr Martinsville (46151) ***(G-9624)***
Material Sciences, East Chicago *Also called Electric Coating Tech LLC* ***(G-2527)***
Materials Processing Inc....317 803-3010
3500 Depauw Blvd Indianapolis (46268) ***(G-7466)***
Mathes Home Care....812 944-2211
1621 Charlestown Rd New Albany (47150) ***(G-10823)***
Matheson Tri-Gas Inc....812 838-5518
1101 Holler Rd Mount Vernon (47620) ***(G-10398)***
Matheson Tri-Gas Inc....812 257-0470
1285 S 300 W Washington (47501) ***(G-13990)***
Matheson Tri-Gas Inc....317 892-5221
8000 N County Road 225 E Pittsboro (46167) ***(G-11585)***
Matjack Division Indianapolis, Indianapolis *Also called Indianapolis Industrial Pdts* ***(G-7201)***
Matrix Imaging, Indianapolis *Also called Matrix Photo Laboratories Inc* ***(G-7467)***
Matrix Label Systems Inc....317 839-1973
4692 S County Road 600 E Plainfield (46168) ***(G-11624)***
Matrix Manufacturing Inc....260 854-4659
4935 S 300 E Wolcottville (46795) ***(G-14374)***
Matrix Nac....219 931-6600
4508 Columbia Ave Hammond (46327) ***(G-5914)***
Matrix North American Cnstr, Hammond *Also called Matrix Nac* ***(G-5914)***
Matrix Photo Laboratories Inc....317 635-4756
118 W North St Indianapolis (46204) ***(G-7467)***
Matrix Technologies Inc....765 284-3335
700 S Mulberry St Muncie (47302) ***(G-10518)***
Matrix Tool Inc....574 259-3093
1210 S Merrifield Ave Mishawaka (46544) ***(G-10075)***
Matrixx Group Incorporated....812 421-3600
820 E Columbia St Evansville (47711) ***(G-3616)***
Matrixx Group Incorporated....812 421-3600
15000b Highway 41 N Evansville (47725) ***(G-3617)***
Matrixx Group Incorporated....812 423-5218
5001 Ohara Dr Evansville (47711) ***(G-3618)***
Matrixx-Qtr Inc....812 429-0901
15000 Highway 41 N Evansville (47725) ***(G-3619)***
Matson Counsulting Engineers....260 478-8813
3131 Engle Rd Fort Wayne (46809) ***(G-4457)***
Matthew Warren Inc....574 722-8200
500 E Ottawa St Logansport (46947) ***(G-9354)***
Matthew Warren Spring, Logansport *Also called Matthew Warren Inc* ***(G-9354)***
Matthews Aurora Fnrl Solutions, Aurora *Also called Aurora Casket Company LLC* ***(G-370)***
Mattox & Moore Inc....317 632-7534
1503 E Riverside Dr Indianapolis (46202) ***(G-7468)***
Matts Repair Inc....219 696-6765
9412 W 181st Ave Lowell (46356) ***(G-9416)***
Mauckport Sand & Gravel....812 732-8800
3200 W Highway 11 Sw Mauckport (47142) ***(G-9655)***
Maul Technology, Winchester *Also called Vhc Ltd* ***(G-14343)***
Maul Technology Co....765 584-2101
300 W Martin St Winchester (47394) ***(G-14337)***
Maumee Machine & Tool, Harlan *Also called Kent Brenneke* ***(G-5973)***
Maureen Sharp....765 379-3644
153 N Gaddis St Rossville (46065) ***(G-12211)***
Maurer Constructors Inc....812 236-5950
10109 N Harmony Border St Brazil (47834) ***(G-968)***
Maurer Environmental Drilling....574 272-7524
51711 Emmons Rd South Bend (46637) ***(G-12855)***
Maurice Lukens Jr....765 345-2971
38 W Grant St Knightstown (46148) ***(G-8555)***
Maury Boyd & Associates Inc....317 849-6110
9241 Castlegate Dr Indianapolis (46256) ***(G-7469)***
Mautz Paint Factory....574 289-2497
1201 S Main St South Bend (46601) ***(G-12856)***
Maverick Molding, Mishawaka *Also called Paul Tirotta* ***(G-10102)***
Maverick Packaging Inc....574 264-2891
3505 Reedy Dr Elkhart (46514) ***(G-3022)***
Mavron Inc....574 267-3044
152 S Zimmer Rd Warsaw (46580) ***(G-13904)***
Max Powder Coating Inc....812 752-4200
1250 S Main St Bldg A Scottsburg (47170) ***(G-12373)***
Maxcare Bionics, Avon *Also called Transmed Associates Inc* ***(G-471)***
Maxcare Orthtics Prsthtics LLC....574 267-5852
3159 E Center Street Ext Warsaw (46582) ***(G-13905)***
Maxim Automation Inc....317 418-9561
13528 Water Crest Dr Fishers (46038) ***(G-3945)***
Maxim Integrated Products Inc....252 227-7202
16848 Southpark Dr Westfield (46074) ***(G-14175)***
Maxim Pipette Service Inc....877 536-2946
4310 Saratoga Pkwy # 100 Plainfield (46168) ***(G-11625)***
Maximum Screen Printing....502 802-4652
3310 E 10th St Jeffersonville (47130) ***(G-8399)***
Maximum Spndle Utilization Inc....812 526-8250
1141 S Walnut St Edinburgh (46124) ***(G-2618)***
Maxwell Engineering Inc....260 745-4991
616 E Wallace St Fort Wayne (46803) ***(G-4458)***
Maxwell Milling Indiana Inc....765 489-3506
4359 N State Road 1 Hagerstown (47346) ***(G-5809)***
May and Co Inc....317 236-6500
3210 Greensview Dr Greenwood (46143) ***(G-5724)***
Mayco International LLC....765 348-5780
1701 W Mcdonald St Hartford City (47348) ***(G-5984)***
Mayco Intl Hartford Cy, Hartford City *Also called Mayco International LLC* ***(G-5984)***
Mayfield-Glenn Group Inc....219 393-7117
3999 Hupp Rd Bldg R23 Kingsbury (46345) ***(G-8541)***
Mayhew Oil & Gas Development, Mount Vernon *Also called Mayhew Oil & Gas LLC* ***(G-10399)***
Mayhew Oil & Gas LLC....812 985-9966
6508 Uebelhack Rd Mount Vernon (47620) ***(G-10399)***
Mayhill Publications Inc (PA)....765 345-5133
27 N Jefferson St Knightstown (46148) ***(G-8556)***
Mays+red Spot Coatings LLC....317 558-2024
5611 E 71st St Indianapolis (46220) ***(G-7470)***
MBC Cereal Fines Inc....812 299-2191
9748 S Carlisle St Terre Haute (47802) ***(G-13281)***
Mbsi Holdings LLC....574 295-1214
58120 County Road 3 Elkhart (46517) ***(G-3023)***
Mc Bride & Son Welding & Engrg....260 724-3534
409 Bellmont Rd Decatur (46733) ***(G-2393)***
Mc Custom Cabinets Inc....502 641-1528
2157 W Salem Rd Underwood (47177) ***(G-13451)***
Mc Ginley Fire Apparatus....765 482-3152
901 W Washington St Lebanon (46052) ***(G-9204)***
Mc Kay Printing Services, Michigan City *Also called Kelley Pagels Enterprises LLC* ***(G-9806)***
Mc Metalcraft Inc....574 259-8101
1210 Willow St Mishawaka (46545) ***(G-10076)***
Mc Metalcraft Inc....574 259-8101
1210 Willow St Mishawaka (46545) ***(G-10077)***
MCB Accessories, Greenfield *Also called Monroe Custom Utility Bodies* ***(G-5558)***
McBeth Designs Inc....317 848-7313
820 W Main St Carmel (46032) ***(G-1435)***
McBride & Son Welding & Engrg, Decatur *Also called Mc Bride & Son Welding & Engrg* ***(G-2393)***
McBroom Electric Co Inc....317 926-3451
800 W 16th St Indianapolis (46202) ***(G-7471)***
McBroom Industrial Services, Indianapolis *Also called McBroom Electric Co Inc* ***(G-7471)***
McC, Goshen *Also called Mobile Climate Control Corp* ***(G-5296)***
MCC, Pendleton *Also called Madison County Cabinets Inc* ***(G-11493)***
McCaffery Sign Designs....574 232-9991
1310 S Main St Ste 2 South Bend (46601) ***(G-12857)***
McCammon Engineering Corp....812 356-4455
1863 W County Road 500 S Sullivan (47882) ***(G-13086)***
McClamroch AG LLC....765 362-4495
115 W 580 N Crawfordsville (47933) ***(G-2171)***
McCombs and Son Company....765 825-4581
201 W 6th St Connersville (47331) ***(G-2063)***
McCormick & Company Inc....574 234-8101
3425 Lathrop St South Bend (46628) ***(G-12858)***
McCormick Printing Impressions....765 675-9556
618 Oak St Tipton (46072) ***(G-13398)***
McCoy Bolt Works Inc....260 482-4476
2811 Congressional Pkwy Fort Wayne (46808) ***(G-4459)***
McCrary, Fred D Oil Co, Petersburg *Also called Fred D McCrary* ***(G-11564)***
McCreary Concrete Products Inc (PA)....765 932-3058
810 N Fort Wayne Rd Rushville (46173) ***(G-12229)***
McCreary Concrete Products Inc....317 844-5157
875 Industrial Dr Tipton (46072) ***(G-13399)***
McCrory Publishing....260 485-1812
2530 Deerwood Dr Fort Wayne (46825) ***(G-4460)***

ALPHABETIC

McD Machine Incorporated.................................812 339-1240
  2345 W Industrial Park Dr Bloomington (47404) *(G-770)*

McDowell Enterprises Inc.................................574 293-1042
  2010 Superior St Elkhart (46516) *(G-3024)*

McF Business Products & Svcs, Evansville *Also called E James Dant (G-3468)*

McGill Manufacturing Co Inc..............................219 465-2200
  2300 Evans Ave Valparaiso (46383) *(G-13579)*

McGill Manufacturing Company, Valparaiso *Also called Regal Beloit America Inc (G-13607)*

McGinn Tool & Engineering Co.............................317 736-5512
  1001 Yandes St Franklin (46131) *(G-4905)*

McGinty Conveyors Inc....................................317 240-4315
  5002 W Washington St Indianapolis (46241) *(G-7472)*

McGrews Well Drilling Inc................................574 857-3875
  7413 S 125 W Rochester (46975) *(G-12137)*

McHenry Manufacturing Inc................................260 824-8146
  1325 W Wiley Ave Bluffton (46714) *(G-881)*

McI/Screwdriver Systems Inc..............................317 776-1970
  14800 Herriman Blvd Noblesville (46060) *(G-11147)*

McIntire Concrete..765 759-7111
  4701 W County Road 1000 N Muncie (47303) *(G-10519)*

McKinney & Sell Inc......................................877 665-3300
  117 E Center St Bourbon (46504) *(G-945)*

McKinney Corporation.....................................765 448-4800
  4710 Fastline Dr Lafayette (47905) *(G-8964)*

McKinneys Embroidery & Sup Co............................317 984-9039
  201 E Broadway Ave Arcadia (46030) *(G-265)*

McLaughlin Services LLC (PA).............................260 897-4328
  333 Progress Way Avilla (46710) *(G-415)*

McLean's Screen Printing, Greensburg *Also called Dance World Bazaar Corporation (G-5598)*

McMillan Express...260 447-7648
  3505 Wayne Trce Fort Wayne (46806) *(G-4461)*

McNeil Coatings Consultants..............................317 885-1557
  1132 Kay Dr Greenwood (46142) *(G-5725)*

McNeilus Truck and Mfg Inc...............................260 489-3031
  7520 Freedom Way Fort Wayne (46818) *(G-4462)*

McPhersons (us) Inc......................................812 623-2225
  957 N Meridian St Sunman (47041) *(G-13114)*

McWane Inc...574 534-9328
  62626 Stephanie St Goshen (46526) *(G-5283)*

MD Laird Inc...317 842-6338
  8255 Craig St Ste 110 Indianapolis (46250) *(G-7473)*

MD Moxie LLC...260 347-1203
  5966 E Concrete Dr Kendallville (46755) *(G-8494)*

Md/Lf Incorporated.......................................765 575-8130
  187 S Denny Dr New Castle (47362) *(G-10912)*

Mdl Mold Die Components Inc..............................812 373-0021
  4572 N Long Rd Columbus (47203) *(G-1970)*

Mdl Woodworking LLC......................................260 242-1824
  1011 W Packard Ave Fort Wayne (46807) *(G-4463)*

Mead Johnson & Company LLC (HQ)..........................812 429-5000
  2400 W Lloyd Expy Evansville (47712) *(G-3620)*

Mead Johnson & Company LLC...............................812 429-5000
  62 W State Rd Mount Vernon (47620) *(G-10400)*

Mead Johnson Nutrition, Evansville *Also called Mead Johnson & Company LLC (G-3620)*

Mead Johnson Nutritionals, Mount Vernon *Also called Mead Johnson & Company LLC (G-10400)*

Meade Electric Co..219 787-8317
  246 Bailey Station Rd Chesterton (46304) *(G-1620)*

Meadors & Assoc Inc......................................317 736-6944
  203 Earlywood Dr Franklin (46131) *(G-4906)*

Meagan Inc...574 267-8626
  711 S Buffalo St Warsaw (46580) *(G-13906)*

Mears Machine Corp.......................................317 745-0656
  2983 S County Road 300 E Danville (46122) *(G-2353)*

Measure Press Inc..812 473-0361
  526 S Lincoln Park Dr Evansville (47714) *(G-3621)*

Meca, Elkhart *Also called Mechanical Engineering Control (G-3025)*

Mechanical Engineering Control...........................574 294-7580
  57236 Nagy Dr Elkhart (46517) *(G-3025)*

Mechanical Parts & Svcs Inc..............................219 670-1986
  304 Burlington Beach Rd Valparaiso (46383) *(G-13580)*

Mechanovent Corporation..................................219 326-1767
  171 Factory St La Porte (46350) *(G-8790)*

Meck Die Inc...574 262-5441
  29029 Phillips St Elkhart (46514) *(G-3026)*

Mectra Labs Inc..812 384-3521
  600 S Us Hwy 231 Blmfield Bloomfield (47424) *(G-641)*

Med Devices LLC..317 508-1699
  6335 Old Orchard Rd Indianapolis (46226) *(G-7474)*

Med Grind Inc..574 965-4040
  7848 N Us Highway 421 Delphi (46923) *(G-2424)*

Med-Cut Inc..574 269-1982
  727 N Detroit St Warsaw (46580) *(G-13907)*

Med-Rep Inc..317 574-0497
  236 John St Carmel (46032) *(G-1436)*

Med2950 LLC..317 545-5383
  2950 N Catherwood Ave Indianapolis (46219) *(G-7475)*

Medcast, Warsaw *Also called Texmo Prcision Castings US Inc (G-13951)*

Medegen Holdings LLC.....................................219 473-1674
  648 114th St Whiting (46394) *(G-14271)*

Medical Device Bus Svcs Inc..............................317 596-3320
  8904 Bash St Ste A Indianapolis (46256) *(G-7476)*

Medical Device Bus Svcs Inc (HQ).........................574 267-8143
  700 Orthopaedic Dr Warsaw (46582) *(G-13908)*

Medical Structures Mfg Corp..............................574 612-0353
  1803 Minnie St Elkhart (46516) *(G-3027)*

Medical Systems Division, Merrillville *Also called Parker-Hannifin Corporation (G-9744)*

Medishield..502 939-9903
  1598 Rector Ln New Albany (47150) *(G-10824)*

Meditation Company.......................................574 217-3157
  830 Oak Ridge Dr South Bend (46617) *(G-12859)*

Medix Specialty Vehicles LLC.............................574 266-0911
  3008 Mobile Dr Elkhart (46514) *(G-3028)*

Medreco Inc..765 458-7444
  757 S State Road 101 Liberty (47353) *(G-9265)*

Medtec Ambulance Corporation (HQ)........................574 534-2631
  2429 Lincolnway E Goshen (46526) *(G-5284)*

Medtec Ambulance Corporation.............................574 533-2924
  2429 Lincolnway E Goshen (46526) *(G-5285)*

Medtric LLC..765 586-8228
  3000 Kent Ave Ste D1-104 Lafayette (47906) *(G-8965)*

Medtrnic Sofamor Danek USA Inc...........................574 267-6826
  2500 Silveus Xing Warsaw (46582) *(G-13909)*

Medtronic..317 837-8664
  2824 Airwest Blvd Plainfield (46168) *(G-11626)*

Medventure Technology, Jeffersonville *Also called Freudenberg Medical Mis Inc (G-8364)*

Meese Inc..812 273-1008
  1745 Cragmont St Madison (47250) *(G-9485)*

Meese Orbitron Dunne Co, Madison *Also called Meese Inc (G-9485)*

Mega Brands America, Lafayette *Also called Warren Industries Inc (G-9020)*

Megacon Games, Westfield *Also called Mercs Miniatures LLC (G-14176)*

Megan Inc..574 267-8626
  711 S Buffalo St Warsaw (46580) *(G-13910)*

Meggitt Control Systems, Troy *Also called Troy Meggitt Inc (G-13448)*

Meggitt Sensing Systems, Indianapolis *Also called Piezotech LLC (G-7690)*

Mehringer Metal Design LLC...............................812 634-6100
  919 E 14th St Ste 102 Jasper (47546) *(G-8294)*

Meier Winery & Vinyard LLC...............................812 382-4220
  4251 N State Road 63 Sullivan (47882) *(G-13087)*

Meilink Safe Company.....................................812 941-0024
  101 Security Pkwy New Albany (47150) *(G-10825)*

Meister Cook LLC...260 399-6692
  3217 Stellhorn Rd Ste A Fort Wayne (46815) *(G-4464)*

Mel Rhon Inc...574 546-4559
  124 E Plymouth St Bremen (46506) *(G-1010)*

Melching Machine Inc.....................................260 622-4315
  1630 Baker Dr Ossian (46777) *(G-11404)*

Melissa King...219 989-1497
  3542 170th Pl Hammond (46323) *(G-5915)*

Mellon Tax Service.......................................219 947-1660
  101 Center St Hobart (46342) *(G-6091)*

Melrose Group LLC..317 437-6784
  6833 Fair Ridge Dr Indianapolis (46221) *(G-7477)*

Melrose Pyrotechnics (PA)................................219 393-5522
  Kingsbury Industrial Park Kingsbury (46345) *(G-8542)*

Memcor Inc...260 356-4300
  1320 Flaxmill Rd Huntington (46750) *(G-6228)*

Memcor-Truohm, Huntington *Also called Memcor Inc (G-6228)*

Memering Farms...812 254-8170
  3867 N State Road 57 Washington (47501) *(G-13991)*

Memorial Arts Studio, San Pierre *Also called M A Studio Inc (G-12309)*

Memories By Design Inc...................................317 254-1708
  5615 Central Ave Indianapolis (46220) *(G-7478)*

Menard Inc...812 466-1234
  4600 N 13th St Terre Haute (47805) *(G-13282)*

Menard Inc...260 441-0406
  7702 Southtown Xing Fort Wayne (46816) *(G-4465)*

Mendoza Mexican Mix......................................219 791-9034
  7425 Madison St Merrillville (46410) *(G-9731)*

Mendozas Inc...219 791-9034
  7425 Madison St Merrillville (46410) *(G-9732)*

Mennonite Inc Inc..574 535-6050
  1700 S Main St Goshen (46526) *(G-5286)*

Mental Rehabilitation....................................765 414-5590
  1322 Fairfax Dr Lafayette (47909) *(G-8966)*

Mepco, Evansville *Also called Moore Engineering & Prod Co (G-3636)*

Mercantile 1, Nashville *Also called Mercantile Store (G-10729)*

Mercantile Store (PA)....................................812 988-6939
  44 N Van Buren St Nashville (47448) *(G-10729)*

Mercer Machine Company Inc...............................317 241-9903
  1421 S Holt Rd Indianapolis (46241) *(G-7479)*

Merchants Metals Inc.....................................317 783-7678
  6701 Bluff Rd Indianapolis (46217) *(G-7480)*

Merchants Metals LLC.....................................574 831-4060
  71347 County Road 23 New Paris (46553) *(G-10990)*

Merck Sharp & Dohme Corp.................................317 286-3038
  8440 Woodfld Xing 490 Indianapolis (46240) *(G-7481)*

(G-0000) Company's Geographic Section entry number

Mercs Miniatures LLC 765 661-6724
   46 W Clear Lake Ln Westfield (46074) *(G-14176)*

Merediths Inc 765 966-5084
   800 S 7th St Richmond (47374) *(G-12016)*

Meridian Brick LLC 812 894-2454
   5601 E Price Dr Terre Haute (47802) *(G-13283)*

Meridian Closet, Indianapolis *Also called Bedder Way Company Inc* *(G-6463)*

Meridian Metalform Inc 812 422-1524
   1025 W Tennessee St Evansville (47710) *(G-3622)*

Merin Interiors Indianapolis 317 251-6603
   1145 Woodmere Dr Indianapolis (46260) *(G-7482)*

Merit Tool & Manufacturing Inc 765 396-9566
   120 N Hartford St Eaton (47338) *(G-2586)*

Meritor Inc 317 279-2180
   849 Whitaker Rd Plainfield (46168) *(G-11627)*

Meriwether Tool & Engineering 260 744-6955
   10108 Smith Rd Fort Wayne (46809) *(G-4466)*

Merkley & Sons Inc 812 482-7020
   3994 W 180n Jasper (47546) *(G-8295)*

Merkley Packing Co, Jasper *Also called Merkley & Sons Inc* *(G-8295)*

Merrill Corporation 574 255-2988
   606 N Main St Mishawaka (46545) *(G-10078)*

Merrill Manufacturing Inc 812 752-6688
   1052 S Bond St Scottsburg (47170) *(G-12374)*

Merrill Pharmacy, Mishawaka *Also called Merrill Corporation* *(G-10078)*

Merrillville Awning & Tent, Merrillville *Also called Blessing Enterprises Inc* *(G-9702)*

Merriman Kiln & Mill Service, Bedford *Also called Merriman Steel and Equipment* *(G-562)*

Merriman Steel and Equipment 812 849-2784
   10430 Tunnelton Rd Bedford (47421) *(G-562)*

Merritt Manufacturing Inc 317 409-0148
   1350 W Southport Rd Ste C Indianapolis (46217) *(G-7483)*

Merritt Manufacturing Inc 317 422-1167
   2146 N 400 W Bargersville (46106) *(G-485)*

Merritt Sand and Gravel Inc (PA) 260 665-2513
   2007 County Road 39 Waterloo (46793) *(G-14018)*

Merss Corporation 317 632-7299
   1017 W 23rd St Indianapolis (46208) *(G-7484)*

Mervin Knepps Molding 812 486-2971
   6349 N 900 E Montgomery (47558) *(G-10235)*

Mervin M Burkholder 574 862-4144
   26253 County Road 42 Wakarusa (46573) *(G-13786)*

Mervis & Sons, Kokomo *Also called Mervis Industries Inc* *(G-8665)*

Mervis Industries Inc 812 232-1251
   830 S 13th St Terre Haute (47807) *(G-13284)*

Mervis Industries Inc 765 454-5800
   990 E Carter St Kokomo (46901) *(G-8665)*

Mesco Manufacturing LLC 812 663-3870
   900 E Randall St Greensburg (47240) *(G-5622)*

Mesh Systems LLC (PA) 317 661-4800
   12400 N Meridian St # 175 Carmel (46032) *(G-1437)*

Meshberger Stone Inc 812 579-5241
   3415 S 650 E Columbus (47203) *(G-1971)*

Meshberger Stone Inc 765 525-6442
   15 E State Road 252 Flat Rock (47234) *(G-3991)*

Message The, Evansville *Also called Catholic Press of Evansville* *(G-3414)*

Messagenet Systems Inc 317 566-1677
   101 E Carmel Dr Ste 105 Carmel (46032) *(G-1438)*

Messenger LLC 260 925-1700
   318 E 7th St Auburn (46706) *(G-343)*

Messenger, The, Attica *Also called Fountain County Neighbor* *(G-300)*

Mestek Inc 317 831-5314
   101 Linel Dr Mooresville (46158) *(G-10322)*

Met Pak Specialties Inc 260 420-2217
   2701 S Coliseum Blvd # 1172 Fort Wayne (46803) *(G-4467)*

Met-Pro Technologies LLC 317 293-2930
   6040 Guion Rd Indianapolis (46254) *(G-7485)*

Metakite Software LLC 317 441-7385
   8430 Weaver Woods Pl Fishers (46038) *(G-3946)*

Metal Art Inc 765 354-4571
   7730 N Raider Rd Middletown (47356) *(G-9938)*

Metal Building Components Mbci, Shelbyville *Also called Nci Group Inc* *(G-12553)*

Metal Dynamics Ltd 812 949-7998
   30 E 10th St New Albany (47150) *(G-10826)*

Metal Etching Tech Associates, Fort Wayne *Also called Bluering Stencils* *(G-4114)*

Metal Fab Engineering Inc 574 278-7150
   9341 S State Road 39 Winamac (46996) *(G-14312)*

Metal Fabricated Products Co 812 372-7430
   925 S Marr Rd Columbus (47201) *(G-1972)*

Metal Finishing Co Inc 317 546-9004
   3901 E 26th St Indianapolis (46218) *(G-7486)*

Metal Forming Industries, Russellville *Also called St Clair Group Inc* *(G-12239)*

Metal Improvement Company LLC 260 495-4445
   302 E Mcswain Dr Fremont (46737) *(G-4967)*

Metal Improvement Company LLC 317 875-6030
   5945 W 84th St Ste D Indianapolis (46278) *(G-7487)*

Metal Masters Inc 812 421-9162
   4600 Broadway Ave Evansville (47712) *(G-3623)*

Metal Plate Polishing, Fort Wayne *Also called Mpp Inc* *(G-4482)*

Metal Resources Inc 219 886-2710
   201 Mississippi St Slip 9 Gary (46402) *(G-5075)*

Metal Sales Manufacturing Corp 812 246-1866
   7800 Highway 60 Sellersburg (47172) *(G-12408)*

Metal Sales Manufacturing Corp 812 941-0041
   999 Park Pl New Albany (47150) *(G-10827)*

Metal Services LLC 219 787-1514
   250 W Us Highway 12 Burns Harbor (46304) *(G-1217)*

Metal Solutions Inc 317 781-6734
   5756 Churchman Ave Indianapolis (46203) *(G-7488)*

Metal Source LLC 260 563-8833
   1733 S Wabash St Wabash (46992) *(G-13738)*

Metal Spinners Inc (PA) 260 665-2158
   914 Wohlert St Angola (46703) *(G-229)*

Metal Spinners Inc. 260 665-7741
   800 Growth Pkwy Angola (46703) *(G-230)*

Metal Technologies, Auburn *Also called West Allis Gray Iron* *(G-367)*

Metal Technologies Inc 812 384-9800
   Sr 54 E Rr 1 Bloomfield (47424) *(G-642)*

Metal Technologies Inc (PA) 812 384-9800
   909 E State Road 54 Bloomfield (47424) *(G-643)*

Metal Technologies Auburn LLC 260 925-4717
   1401 S Grandstaff Dr Auburn (46706) *(G-344)*

Metal Technologies Inc Alabama (PA) 260 925-4717
   1401 S Grandstaff Dr Auburn (46706) *(G-345)*

Metal Technologies Indiana Inc (PA) 260 925-4717
   1401 S Grandstaff Dr Auburn (46706) *(G-346)*

Metal Technology of Indiana 765 482-1100
   810 Hendricks Dr Lebanon (46052) *(G-9205)*

Metalcraft Inc 260 761-3001
   3330 W Us Highway 6 Wawaka (46794) *(G-14033)*

Metalcraft Precision Machining 574 293-6700
   56854 Elk Ct Elkhart (46516) *(G-3029)*

Metaldyne Bsm LLC 260 495-4315
   307 S Tillotson St Fremont (46737) *(G-4968)*

Metaldyne Fremont, Fremont *Also called Metaldyne Bsm LLC* *(G-4968)*

Metaldyne M&A Bluffton LLC 260 824-2360
   131 W Harvest Rd Bluffton (46714) *(G-882)*

Metalite Corporation 812 944-6600
   1815 Troy St New Albany (47150) *(G-10828)*

Metalized Coatings LLC 219 851-0683
   1540 Genesis Dr La Porte (46350) *(G-8791)*

Metallic Seals Inc 317 780-0773
   2735 Brill Rd Indianapolis (46225) *(G-7489)*

Metalloid Corporation 260 356-3200
   500 Jackson St Huntington (46750) *(G-6229)*

Metallurgical Processing, Fort Wayne *Also called Bodycote Thermal Proc Inc* *(G-4115)*

Metals and Additives LLC (PA) 317 290-5007
   5929 Lakeside Blvd Indianapolis (46278) *(G-7490)*

Metals and Additives Corp Inc 812 446-2525
   10665 N State Road 59 Brazil (47834) *(G-969)*

Metals Division, Elkhart *Also called Elixir Industries* *(G-2817)*

Metalstamp Inc 574 232-5997
   24545 State Road 23 South Bend (46614) *(G-12860)*

Metaltec Inc 219 362-9811
   11 Pine Lake Ave Ste C La Porte (46350) *(G-8792)*

Metalworking Lubricants Co 317 269-2444
   1509 S Senate Ave Indianapolis (46225) *(G-7491)*

Metcalf Engineering Inc 765 342-6792
   290 E Morgan St Martinsville (46151) *(G-9625)*

Meteor Manufacturing LLC 317 587-1414
   3814 Rolling Springs Dr Carmel (46033) *(G-1439)*

Metfab Inc 317 322-0385
   1329 Sadlier Circle W Dr Indianapolis (46239) *(G-7492)*

Metro Area Printing, Indianapolis *Also called Kalems Enterprises Inc* *(G-7330)*

Metro Plastics Tech Inc 317 776-0860
   17145 Metro Park Ct Noblesville (46060) *(G-11148)*

Metrology Services LLC 260 969-8424
   3020 Cngrnonal Pkwy Ste G Fort Wayne (46808) *(G-4468)*

Metropolitan Printing Svcs LLC 812 332-7279
   720 S Morton St Bloomington (47403) *(G-771)*

Metropolitan Printing, Rrd, Bloomington *Also called Metropolitan Printing Svcs LLC* *(G-771)*

Mettle Creek, Cambridge City *Also called Western Wayne News* *(G-1262)*

Metzger Dairy Inc 260 564-5445
   4837 W 100 S Kimmell (46760) *(G-8531)*

Meuth Construction Supply Inc 812 424-8554
   2201 Bergdolt Rd Evansville (47711) *(G-3624)*

Mexicano Newsletter 260 704-0682
   2301 Fairfield Ave # 102 Fort Wayne (46807) *(G-4469)*

Meyer Custom Woodworking Inc 812 695-2021
   2657 E State Road 56 Dubois (47527) *(G-2477)*

Meyer Engineering Inc 812 663-6535
   1420 W Main St Greensburg (47240) *(G-5623)*

Meyer Foods Inc 317 773-6594
   18247 Pennington Rd Noblesville (46060) *(G-11149)*

Meyer Ice Cream LLC 812 941-8267
   209 Quality Ave Ste 3 New Albany (47150) *(G-10829)*

Meyer Industries Inc 317 769-3497
   6851 S Indianapolis Rd Whitestown (46075) *(G-14256)*

A
L
P
H
A
B
E
T
I
C

Meyer Mill Oak Woodcrafters 317 462-1413
1539 E 300 N Greenfield (46140) *(G-5550)*

Meyer Mill Weddings, Greenfield *Also called Meyer Mill Oak Woodcrafters (G-5550)*

Meyer Plastics Inc (PA) 317 259-4131
5167 E 65th St Indianapolis (46220) *(G-7493)*

Meyer Plastics Inc 765 447-2195
100 Creasy Ct Lafayette (47905) *(G-8967)*

Mf Printing LLC 317 462-6895
133 Mcclellan Rd Greenfield (46140) *(G-5551)*

Mgi Traffic Control Pdts Inc 317 835-9212
102 W Washington St Fairland (46126) *(G-3825)*

Mgpi Processing Inc 812 532-4100
7 Ridge Ave Greendale (47025) *(G-5491)*

Mgtc Inc 317 786-1693
5757 Kopetsky Dr Ste D Indianapolis (46217) *(G-7494)*

Mgtc Inc (HQ) 317 780-0609
11541 Trail Ridge Pl Zionsville (46077) *(G-14447)*

Mgtc Inc 317 873-8697
11541 Trail Ridge Pl Zionsville (46077) *(G-14448)*

Mhia, Franklin *Also called Mitsubishi Heavy Industries (G-4910)*

MI Tierra 812 376-0668
1461 Central Ave Columbus (47201) *(G-1973)*

Mi-Tech Tungsten Metals LLC 317 549-4290
4701 Massachusetts Ave Indianapolis (46218) *(G-7495)*

Miasa Automotive LLC 765 751-9967
2101 S West St Yorktown (47396) *(G-14407)*

Mica Shop Inc 574 533-1102
2122 Lincolnway E Goshen (46526) *(G-5287)*

Michael and Sons Incorporated (PA) 812 876-4736
2606 E Calvertville Rd Bloomfield (47424) *(G-644)*

Michael Dargie 765 935-2241
1700 Nw 11th St Richmond (47374) *(G-12017)*

Michael Deom Professional 812 836-2206
9394 Abner Rd Tell City (47586) *(G-13166)*

Michael J Meyer D M D P C 812 275-7112
1504 Dental Dr Bedford (47421) *(G-563)*

MICHAEL JONES, South Bend *Also called Ultra Montane Associates Inc (G-12980)*

Michael L Baker 812 967-2160
8779 E New Phladelphia Rd Salem (47167) *(G-12301)*

Michael O Baird 765 569-6721
4484 N Guion Rd Rockville (47872) *(G-12177)*

Michael R Harris 812 425-9411
20 Nw 1st St Rear 208 Evansville (47708) *(G-3625)*

Michael Skaggs 812 732-8809
Rr 1 Mauckport (47142) *(G-9656)*

Michana Used Music and Media 574 247-1188
4609 Grape Rd Ofc Mishawaka (46545) *(G-10079)*

Michele L Gravel 317 889-0521
8607 Depot Dr Indianapolis (46217) *(G-7496)*

Michelin North America Inc 260 493-8100
18906 Old 24 Woodburn (46797) *(G-14386)*

Michfab Machinery 260 244-6117
201 Towerview Dr Columbia City (46725) *(G-1809)*

Michiana Business Publications 260 497-0433
7729 Westfield Dr Fort Wayne (46825) *(G-4470)*

Michiana Cabinet & Refacing LL 574 277-0801
50520 Park Ln E Granger (46530) *(G-5420)*

Michiana Carwash Systems LLC 574 320-2331
15228 County Road 22 Goshen (46528) *(G-5288)*

Michiana Column & Truss LLC 574 862-2828
611 E Waterford St Wakarusa (46573) *(G-13787)*

Michiana Column & Truss LLC 574 862-2828
611 E Waterford St Wakarusa (46573) *(G-13788)*

Michiana Compressor, Elkhart *Also called Michiana Forklift Inc (G-3031)*

Michiana Directional Drilling, Bristol *Also called Niblock Excavating Inc (G-1074)*

Michiana Elkhart Inc 574 206-0620
51505 State Road 19 Elkhart (46514) *(G-3030)*

Michiana Executive Journal 574 256-6666
203 N Main St Mishawaka (46544) *(G-10080)*

Michiana Forklift Inc 574 326-3702
2921 Moose Trl Elkhart (46514) *(G-3031)*

Michiana Global Mold Inc 574 259-6262
1702 E 7th St Mishawaka (46544) *(G-10081)*

Michiana Impreglon Center, Michigan City *Also called Secorp Inc (G-9842)*

Michiana Laminated Products 260 562-2871
7130 N 050 E Howe (46746) *(G-6129)*

Michiana Lift Equipment Inc 574 257-1665
709 S Byrkit St Mishawaka (46544) *(G-10082)*

Michiana Metal Fabricatio 574 256-9010
1310 E 6th St Mishawaka (46544) *(G-10083)*

Michiana Metal Fabrication 574 256-9010
1227 W Beardsley Ave Elkhart (46514) *(G-3032)*

Michiana Metal Finishing Inc 574 206-0666
2805 Frederic Dr Elkhart (46514) *(G-3033)*

Michiana Pallet Recycle Inc 574 232-8566
55022 Pear Rd South Bend (46628) *(G-12861)*

Michiana Plastics Inc 574 259-6262
1702 E 7th St Mishawaka (46544) *(G-10084)*

Michigan City Baking, Michigan City *Also called Hearthside Food Solutions LLC (G-9802)*

Michigan City News Dispatch, Michigan City *Also called News Dispatch (G-9823)*

Michigan City Paper Box Co 219 872-8383
1206 Pine St Michigan City (46360) *(G-9817)*

Michrochem LLC 812 838-1832
901 E 3rd St Mount Vernon (47620) *(G-10401)*

Micro Businessware Inc 502 424-6613
1008 E 10th St Jeffersonville (47130) *(G-8400)*

Micro Machine Works Inc 574 293-1354
835 Lillian Ave Elkhart (46516) *(G-3034)*

Micro Metl Corporation (PA) 800 662-4822
3035 N Shadeland Ave # 300 Indianapolis (46226) *(G-7497)*

Micro Motion Inc 317 334-1893
8525 Northwest Blvd Indianapolis (46278) *(G-7498)*

Micro Tool & Machine Co Inc 574 272-9141
51836 Purdue Ct Granger (46530) *(G-5421)*

Micro-Precision Operations 260 589-2136
525 Berne St Berne (46711) *(G-620)*

Microchip Technology Inc 317 773-8323
9779 E 146th St Ste 130 Noblesville (46060) *(G-11150)*

Microform Inc 574 522-9851
21053 Protecta Dr Ste A Elkhart (46516) *(G-3035)*

Micrology Laboratories Llc 574 533-3351
1303 Eisenhower Dr S Goshen (46526) *(G-5289)*

Micromatic LLC (PA) 260 589-2136
525 Berne St Berne (46711) *(G-621)*

Micrometl Indianapolis 317 524-5400
3035 N Shadeland Ave Indianapolis (46226) *(G-7499)*

Micronutrients Division, Indianapolis *Also called Micronutrients USA LLC (G-7500)*

Micronutrients USA LLC 317 486-5880
1550 Research Way Indianapolis (46231) *(G-7500)*

Micropulse Inc (PA) 260 625-3304
5865 E State Road 14 Columbia City (46725) *(G-1810)*

Microscreen LLC 574 232-4358
1106 High St South Bend (46601) *(G-12862)*

Microsoft Corporation 317 705-6900
8702 Keystone Xing Ste 66 Indianapolis (46240) *(G-7501)*

Microwave Devices Inc 317 736-8833
240 N Forsythe St Franklin (46131) *(G-4907)*

Microwave Plant, Garrett *Also called Griffith Rbr Mills of Garrett (G-5008)*

Microworks Inc 219 661-8620
2200 W 97th Pl Crown Point (46307) *(G-2278)*

Mid America Coop Education 317 726-6910
6302 Rucker Rd Indianapolis (46220) *(G-7502)*

Mid America Powered Vehicles 812 925-7745
1699 S Stevenson Stn Rd Chandler (47610) *(G-1551)*

Mid America Print Council 765 463-3971
2217 Miami Trl Lafayette (47906) *(G-8968)*

Mid America Prototyping Inc 765 643-3200
428 E 21st St Anderson (46016) *(G-135)*

Mid America Screw Products 574 294-6905
21559 Protecta Dr Elkhart (46516) *(G-3036)*

Mid America Sign Corporation (PA) 260 744-2200
1319 Production Rd Fort Wayne (46808) *(G-4471)*

Mid American Sound, Greenfield *Also called Mid-America Sound Corporation (G-5552)*

Mid Central Land & Exploration 812 476-9393
5825 Dawnwood Dr Carmel (46033) *(G-1440)*

Mid State Water Treatment 765 884-1220
1009 E 5th St Fowler (47944) *(G-4802)*

Mid Valley Supply Co, Indianapolis *Also called M & M Svc Stn Eqp Spcalist Inc (G-7429)*

Mid West Digital Express Inc 317 733-1214
10815 Deandra Dr Zionsville (46077) *(G-14449)*

Mid-America Environmental LLC 812 475-1644
5815 Metro Center Dr Evansville (47715) *(G-3626)*

Mid-America Golf Car, Chandler *Also called Mid America Powered Vehicles (G-1551)*

Mid-America Sound Corporation 317 947-9880
6643 W 400 N Greenfield (46140) *(G-5552)*

Mid-City Plating Company Inc 765 289-2374
921 E Charles St Muncie (47305) *(G-10520)*

Mid-Continent Coal and Coke Co 219 787-8171
1150 E Boundary Rd Portage (46368) *(G-11775)*

Mid-County Machining, Lake Village *Also called Midcounty Machining Inc (G-9083)*

Mid-State Automation Inc 765 795-5500
12389 Camp Otto Rd Cloverdale (46120) *(G-1730)*

Mid-States Tool and Mch Inc 260 728-9797
2220 Patterson St Decatur (46733) *(G-2394)*

Mid-Town Petro Acquisition LLC 219 728-4110
950 Wabash Ave Chesterton (46304) *(G-1621)*

Mid-West Homes For Pets, Muncie *Also called Mid-West Metal Products Co Inc (G-10521)*

Mid-West Metal Products Co Inc (PA) 888 741-1044
3142 S Cowan Rd Muncie (47302) *(G-10521)*

Mid-West Metal Products Co Inc 765 741-3140
3500 S Hoyt Ave Muncie (47302) *(G-10522)*

Mid-West Metal Products Co Inc 765 741-3137
2100 W Mt Pleasant Blvd Muncie (47302) *(G-10523)*

Mid-West Oil Company Inc 812 533-1227
15 E National Ave West Terre Haute (47885) *(G-14127)*

Mid-West Spring Mfg Co 574 353-1409
105 N Etna St Mentone (46539) *(G-9688)*

Midcountry Media Inc......................................765 345-5133
27 N Jefferson St Knightstown (46148) *(G-8557)*

Midcounty Machining Inc...................................219 992-9380
9313 N 300 W Lake Village (46349) *(G-9083)*

Middlebury Cheese Company LLC (HQ)..............574 825-9511
11275 W 250 N Middlebury (46540) *(G-9906)*

Middlebury Hardwood Pdts Inc (HQ).................574 825-9524
101 Joan Dr Middlebury (46540) *(G-9907)*

Middletown Enterprises Inc...............................765 348-3100
105 N Wabash Ave Hartford City (47348) *(G-5985)*

Middletowne Software LLC.................................765 760-5007
2006 S Daly Ave Muncie (47302) *(G-10524)*

Mide Products LLC..574 333-5906
22420 Forsythia Dr Goshen (46528) *(G-5290)*

Midland Plastics Co Division.............................317 352-7785
3001 E 30th St Indianapolis (46218) *(G-7503)*

Midland Powder LLC...812 402-4070
4 Nw 2nd St Evansville (47708) *(G-3627)*

Midnite Grafix...812 386-9430
3437 S 125 E Princeton (47670) *(G-11878)*

Midstate Manufacturing Corp...........................317 738-0094
3250 N Graham Rd Franklin (46131) *(G-4908)*

Midstates Tool & Die and Engrg........................574 264-3521
3407 Cooper Dr Elkhart (46514) *(G-3037)*

Midway Specialty Vehicles LLC.........................574 264-2530
2940 Dexter Dr Elkhart (46514) *(G-3038)*

Midwest Accurate Grinding Svc.........................219 696-4060
17211 Morse St Lowell (46356) *(G-9417)*

Midwest Aerospace Ltd...................................219 365-7250
9465 Joliet St Saint John (46373) *(G-12265)*

Midwest AG Fly Services Inc.............................812 275-5579
120 S Teddy Bird Ln Bedford (47421) *(G-564)*

Midwest Aircraft, Plainfield *Also called Wbh Inc (G-11650)*

Midwest Arcft Mch & TI Co Inc..........................317 839-1515
204 N Mill St Plainfield (46168) *(G-11628)*

Midwest Auto Repair Inc.................................219 322-0364
1901 Lincolnwood Rd Schererville (46375) *(G-12334)*

Midwest Bale Ties Inc.....................................765 364-0113
1200 E Wabash Ave Crawfordsville (47933) *(G-2172)*

Midwest Bale Ties Inc.....................................765 364-0113
1200 E Wabash Ave Crawfordsville (47933) *(G-2173)*

Midwest Bc...219 369-4839
755 S 500 W La Porte (46350) *(G-8793)*

Midwest Bio-Products Inc................................765 793-3426
618 Liberty St Covington (47932) *(G-2119)*

Midwest Blind & Shade Co...............................574 271-0770
4115 Grape Rd Mishawaka (46545) *(G-10085)*

Midwest Cabinet Solutions Inc.........................765 664-3938
1001 E 24th St Marion (46953) *(G-9547)*

Midwest Calcium Carbonates LLC......................217 222-1800
7925 S State Road 243 Cloverdale (46120) *(G-1731)*

Midwest Caviar LLC..812 338-3610
439 E State Road 64 English (47118) *(G-3315)*

Midwest Cnstr Components..............................765 654-8719
1729 W State Road 28 Frankfort (46041) *(G-4841)*

Midwest Coil LLC...765 807-5429
2304 Brothers Dr Ste A Lafayette (47909) *(G-8969)*

Midwest Color Printing LLC.............................812 822-2947
2458 S Walnut St Bloomington (47401) *(G-772)*

Midwest Custom Finishing Inc.........................219 874-0099
800 Royal Rd Michigan City (46360) *(G-9818)*

Midwest Custom Finishing Inc (PA)...................574 258-0099
1906 Clover Rd Mishawaka (46545) *(G-10086)*

Midwest Custom Woodworking.........................574 349-1645
409 E Lafayette St Lagrange (46761) *(G-9061)*

Midwest Division, Francesville *Also called Legacy Vulcan LLC (G-4814)*

Midwest Division - Bluffton, Bluffton *Also called W W Williams Company LLC (G-896)*

Midwest Empire LLC.......................................317 786-7446
3747 S Meridian St Indianapolis (46217) *(G-7504)*

Midwest Energy Partners LLC..........................317 600-3235
201 S Capitol Ave Ste 510 Indianapolis (46225) *(G-7505)*

Midwest Exterminators, Bedford *Also called Midwest AG Fly Services Inc (G-564)*

Midwest Fabrication LLC.................................574 276-5041
16100 Branchwood Ln Granger (46530) *(G-5422)*

Midwest Fast Structures LLC...........................812 886-3060
2341 S Old Decker Rd Vincennes (47591) *(G-13692)*

Midwest Film Factory, Auburn *Also called Scher Maihem Publishing Ltd (G-352)*

Midwest Finishing Systems Inc........................574 257-0099
1906 Clover Rd Mishawaka (46545) *(G-10087)*

Midwest Gasket Corporation...........................765 629-2221
100 S Railroad St Milroy (46156) *(G-9982)*

Midwest Graphics Inc.....................................317 780-4600
5550 Elmwood Ct Indianapolis (46203) *(G-7506)*

Midwest Graphix LLC......................................812 649-2522
1540 S County Road 100 W D Rockport (47635) *(G-12169)*

Midwest Gym Supply Inc (PA)..........................812 265-4099
775 Scott Ct Madison (47250) *(G-9486)*

Midwest Indus Met Fbrction Inc.......................260 356-5262
281 Thurman Poe Way Huntington (46750) *(G-6230)*

Midwest Industrial Metal.................................260 358-0373
2080 Old Us Highway 24 Huntington (46750) *(G-6231)*

Midwest Industrial Tanks, Elkhart *Also called Axis Unlimited LLC (G-2708)*

Midwest Leather & Vinyl.................................574 266-1700
1434 Johnson St Elkhart (46514) *(G-3039)*

Midwest Logging & Veneer..............................765 342-2774
50 Rose St Martinsville (46151) *(G-9626)*

Midwest Machining & Fabg..............................219 924-0206
711 W Main St Griffith (46319) *(G-5785)*

Midwest Manufacturing, Terre Haute *Also called Menard Inc (G-13282)*

Midwest Metal Products Inc............................219 879-8595
111 Mariner Dr Michigan City (46360) *(G-9819)*

Midwest Meter Inc...574 967-0175
200 Commercial Dr Flora (46929) *(G-3999)*

Midwest Mfg Resources Inc............................317 821-9872
3902 Hanna Cir Ste J Indianapolis (46241) *(G-7507)*

Midwest Mold Remediation.............................502 386-6559
912 Webster Blvd Jeffersonville (47130) *(G-8401)*

Midwest Nonwovens Indiana LLC......................317 241-8956
4555 W Bradbury Ave Ste 4 Indianapolis (46241) *(G-7508)*

Midwest Orthotic and Tech Ctr, South Bend *Also called Midwest Orthotic Services LLC (G-12863)*

Midwest Orthotic and Tech Ctr, Indianapolis *Also called Midwest Orthotic Services LLC (G-7509)*

Midwest Orthotic Services LLC.........................219 736-9960
114 E 90th Dr Merrillville (46410) *(G-9733)*

Midwest Orthotic Services LLC.........................574 233-3352
417 Fernhill Ave Fort Wayne (46805) *(G-4472)*

Midwest Orthotic Services LLC (PA)...................574 233-3352
17530 Dugdale Dr South Bend (46635) *(G-12863)*

Midwest Orthotic Services LLC.........................317 334-1114
3445 W 96th St Indianapolis (46268) *(G-7509)*

Midwest Parenting Publications, Indianapolis *Also called Linear Publishing Corp (G-7407)*

Midwest Pipecoating Inc.................................219 322-4564
925 Kennedy Ave Schererville (46375) *(G-12335)*

Midwest Plastics Company Inc.........................574 674-0161
401 Lincolnway W Osceola (46561) *(G-11382)*

Midwest Poultry Services LP (PA)......................574 353-7232
9951 W State Road 25 Mentone (46539) *(G-9689)*

Midwest Pre-Finishing Inc..............................260 728-9487
8826 N 000 Rd Decatur (46733) *(G-2395)*

Midwest Precision Machining...........................260 459-6866
3626 Illinois Rd Fort Wayne (46804) *(G-4473)*

Midwest Printing...812 238-1641
1925 S 13th St Terre Haute (47802) *(G-13285)*

Midwest Products Co Inc (PA)..........................219 942-1134
400 S Indiana St Hobart (46342) *(G-6092)*

Midwest Pullet Farm, Mentone *Also called Midwest Poultry Services LP (G-9689)*

Midwest Remediation.....................................317 826-0940
5858 Thunderbird Rd Indianapolis (46236) *(G-7510)*

Midwest Roll Forming & Mfg Inc.......................574 594-2100
1 Arnolt Dr Pierceton (46562) *(G-11573)*

Midwest Rotational Molding LLC.......................574 294-6891
22165 Sunset Ln Elkhart (46516) *(G-3040)*

Midwest Rubber Products Inc..........................317 237-4037
2457 E Washington St Indianapolis (46201) *(G-7511)*

Midwest Rubber Sales Inc...............................765 468-7105
2135 N 900 W Farmland (47340) *(G-3842)*

Midwest Sheet Metal Inc.................................574 223-3332
2467 E 200 N Rochester (46975) *(G-12138)*

Midwest Sign Company Inc..............................317 931-9535
819 N Obrien St Seymour (47274) *(G-12470)*

Midwest Spring & Stamping, Mentone *Also called Mid-West Spring Mfg Co (G-9688)*

Midwest Steekl Acqusition, East Chicago *Also called Midwest Steel & Tube LLC (G-2552)*

Midwest Steel & Tube LLC...............................219 398-2200
4500 Euclid Ave East Chicago (46312) *(G-2552)*

Midwest Stl Rule Cutng Die Inc........................317 780-4600
5570 Elmwood Ct Indianapolis (46203) *(G-7512)*

Midwest Surface Prep LLC..............................317 726-1336
5835 White Oak Ct Indianapolis (46220) *(G-7513)*

Midwest Tile & Concrete Pdts, Woodburn *Also called Midwest Tile and Concrete Pdts (G-14388)*

Midwest Tile and Concrete Pdts (PA).................260 749-5173
4309 Webster Rd Woodburn (46797) *(G-14387)*

Midwest Tile and Concrete Pdts.......................260 749-5173
4309 Webster Rd Woodburn (46797) *(G-14388)*

Midwest Tire & Auto Repair, Schererville *Also called Midwest Auto Repair Inc (G-12334)*

Midwest Tool & Die Corp.................................260 483-4282
1126 Sunset Lake Cv Fort Wayne (46845) *(G-4474)*

Midwest Tube Mills Inc (PA).............................812 265-1553
2855 Michigan Rd Madison (47250) *(G-9487)*

Midwest Veneer Products Co...........................765 728-2950
6104 N Main Street Rd Montpelier (47359) *(G-10293)*

Midwest Water Controls, Gary *Also called Ray Kammer (G-5088)*

Midwest Wheelcoaters LLC.............................219 874-0099
800 Royal Rd Michigan City (46360) *(G-9820)*

Midwest-Tek Inc...812 981-3551
4345 Security Pkwy New Albany (47150) *(G-10830)*

Midwestern Pallet Service Inc....260 563-1526
3632 W Old 24 Wabash (46992) ***(G-13739)***
Mier Products Inc....765 457-0223
1500 Ann St Kokomo (46901) ***(G-8666)***
Miftek Corporation....765 491-3848
1231 Cumberland Ave West Lafayette (47906) ***(G-14085)***
Mighty Transport LLC....812 401-7433
246 Green Valley Dr Chandler (47610) ***(G-1552)***
Mighty-Quip Industries....260 615-1899
921 E Dupont Rd 894 Fort Wayne (46825) ***(G-4475)***
Mignone Communications, Berne *Also called EP Graphics Inc* ***(G-613)***
Mik Mocha Prints LLC....812 376-8891
4637 Clairmont Dr Columbus (47203) ***(G-1974)***
Mike Burroughs Sftwr Dev LLC....317 927-7195
4001 N Meridian St Indianapolis (46208) ***(G-7514)***
Mike Gross....574 529-2201
68080 County Road 23 New Paris (46553) ***(G-10991)***
Mike H Inc....574 262-0518
2508 Jeanwood Dr Elkhart (46514) ***(G-3041)***
Mike Jones Software....317 845-7479
8903 Powderhorn Ln Indianapolis (46256) ***(G-7515)***
Mike Magiera Inc....574 654-3044
8011 N 850 E New Carlisle (46552) ***(G-10884)***
Mike Mugler....812 945-4266
3712 Dove Cir New Albany (47150) ***(G-10831)***
Mike-Sells West Virginia Inc....317 241-7422
5767 Dividend Rd Indianapolis (46241) ***(G-7516)***
Mikes Boat Works LLC....317 410-4981
610 Pratt St Greenfield (46140) ***(G-5553)***
Mikes Creative Woodworks LLC....502 649-3665
2405 Arrowhead Dr Charlestown (47111) ***(G-1573)***
Mikes Metal Dectors....812 366-3558
9350 Indian Bluff Rd Ne Georgetown (47122) ***(G-5150)***
Miko-Hone Machine Co Inc....574 642-4701
2424 Supreme Ct Goshen (46528) ***(G-5291)***
Mikro Furniture....812 877-9550
7975 E Chandler Ave Terre Haute (47803) ***(G-13286)***
Milagro Packaging, Princeton *Also called Southland Container Corp* ***(G-11882)***
Milam Toys Inc....765 362-2826
5072 N Us Highway 231 Crawfordsville (47933) ***(G-2174)***
Milan Food Bank....812 654-3682
201 Josephine St Milan (47031) ***(G-9945)***
Milani Custom Homes LLC....219 455-5804
5222 Connecticut St Merrillville (46410) ***(G-9734)***
Miles Farm Service, Boonville *Also called Miles Farm Supply LLC* ***(G-917)***
Miles Farm Supply LLC....812 359-4463
7187 State Hwy 66 E Boonville (47601) ***(G-917)***
Miles Printing Corporation....317 870-6115
4923 W 78th St Indianapolis (46268) ***(G-7517)***
Miles Systems Manufacturing....574 988-0067
7385 N Walker Rd New Carlisle (46552) ***(G-10885)***
Milestone AV Technologies LLC....574 267-8101
3100 N Detroit St Warsaw (46582) ***(G-13911)***
Milestone Cabinetry....219 947-0600
2916 E 83rd Pl Merrillville (46410) ***(G-9735)***
Milestone Contractors LP....765 772-7500
3301 S 460 E Lafayette (47905) ***(G-8970)***
Milestone Contractors LP....812 579-5248
3410 S 650 E Columbus (47203) ***(G-1975)***
Military Facilities....812 854-1762
300 Highway 361 Crane (47522) ***(G-2129)***
Military Neon Signs....574 258-9804
3304 Wild Cherry Rdg W Mishawaka (46544) ***(G-10088)***
Mill Creek Custom Deluxe Box....765 934-3901
3815 N 900 E Van Buren (46991) ***(G-13640)***
Mill End Drapery Inc....317 257-4800
4720 N Keystone Ave Indianapolis (46205) ***(G-7518)***
Mill Steel Co....765 622-4545
444 E 29th St Anderson (46016) ***(G-136)***
Millburn Peat Company Inc....219 362-7025
1733 E Division Rd La Porte (46350) ***(G-8794)***
Millcraft Paper Company....317 240-3500
2735 Fortune Cir W Ste A Indianapolis (46241) ***(G-7519)***
Millenium Sheet Metal Inc....574 935-9101
6730 W County Line Rd Plymouth (46563) ***(G-11706)***
Millennia Technologies Inc....574 830-5161
21948 Shirley Dr Goshen (46526) ***(G-5292)***
Millennial Fireworks....812 732-5126
10645 Highway 135 Sw Mauckport (47142) ***(G-9657)***
Millennium Supply Inc....765 764-7000
1111 E Main St Attica (47918) ***(G-307)***
Millennium Tool Inc....812 273-1566
619 Thomas Hill Rd Madison (47250) ***(G-9488)***
Miller Block Co, Evansville *Also called Evansville Block Co Inc* ***(G-3484)***
Miller Brothers Builders Inc....574 533-8602
1819 E Monroe St Goshen (46528) ***(G-5293)***
Miller Cabinetry & Furn LLC....260 657-5052
16016 Trammel Rd Grabill (46741) ***(G-5380)***
Miller Canvas Shop....574 658-3563
13279 N 400 W Milford (46542) ***(G-9959)***
Miller Carriage Co....260 768-4553
3035 N 850 W Shipshewana (46565) ***(G-12633)***
Miller Chemical Tech & MGT, Franklin *Also called Miller Chemical Tech & MGT Inc* ***(G-4909)***
Miller Chemical Tech & MGT Inc....317 560-5437
980 Hurricane Rd Ste B Franklin (46131) ***(G-4909)***
Miller Custom Forest Products....765 478-3057
4715 W County Road 800 N Connersville (47331) ***(G-2064)***
Miller Door & Trim Inc....574 533-8141
1702 E Monroe St Goshen (46528) ***(G-5294)***
Miller Hardwoods LLC....574 773-9371
8760 W 1350 N Nappanee (46550) ***(G-10693)***
Miller Industrial Fluids, Indianapolis *Also called Petrochoice Holdings Inc* ***(G-7680)***
Miller Machine & Welding....812 882-7566
2610 S Old Decker Rd Vincennes (47591) ***(G-13693)***
Miller Machine Shop LLC....574 773-2900
2028 Beech Rd Nappanee (46550) ***(G-10694)***
Miller Machine Works, Frankfort *Also called New Age Equipment Inc* ***(G-4843)***
Miller Maid Cabinets Inc....317 786-0418
6815 S Emerson Ave Ste D Indianapolis (46237) ***(G-7520)***
Miller Meat Poultry, Orland *Also called Crystal Valley Farms LLC* ***(G-11349)***
Miller Mfg Corp....574 773-4136
901 E Lincoln St Nappanee (46550) ***(G-10695)***
Miller Milling Inc....260 768-9171
700 E North Village Dr Shipshewana (46565) ***(G-12634)***
Miller Plating & Metal Finishi....812 424-3837
3200 N 6th Ave Evansville (47710) ***(G-3628)***
Miller Poultry, Orland *Also called Pine Manor Inc* ***(G-11355)***
Miller Raceway....219 939-9688
4900 Melton Rd Gary (46403) ***(G-5076)***
Miller Rainbow Printing Inc....812 275-3355
813 16th St Bedford (47421) ***(G-565)***
Miller Steel Fabricators....260 768-7321
3235 N 675 W Shipshewana (46565) ***(G-12635)***
Miller Veneers Inc....317 638-2326
3724 E 13th St Indianapolis (46201) ***(G-7521)***
Miller Waste Mills Inc....507 454-6900
8111 Zionsville Rd Indianapolis (46268) ***(G-7522)***
Miller Welding & Mechanic Svc....812 923-3359
9556 Voyles Rd Pekin (47165) ***(G-11476)***
Millercarlson, Carmel *Also called Cortex Safety Technologies LLC* ***(G-1344)***
Millers Custom Cabinets....260 768-7830
8170 W State Road 120 Shipshewana (46565) ***(G-12636)***
Millers Custom Care Candes....574 658-4976
12711 N 400 W Milford (46542) ***(G-9960)***
Millers Locker Plant....765 234-2381
1979 N Summer Dr Crawfordsville (47933) ***(G-2175)***
Millers Mill....574 825-2010
55514 County Road 8 Middlebury (46540) ***(G-9908)***
Millers Quick Production....812 278-8374
6581 State Road 54 W Springville (47462) ***(G-13065)***
Millers Saw Mill....812 883-5246
76 E Miller Sawmill Rd Salem (47167) ***(G-12302)***
Millers Superior Entps Inc (PA)....877 475-5665
11550 Harter Dr Middlebury (46540) ***(G-9909)***
Millers Windmill Service....574 825-2877
14386 County Road 14 Middlebury (46540) ***(G-9910)***
Millers Woodnthings Inc....574 825-2996
11894 County Road 14 Middlebury (46540) ***(G-9911)***
Milliner Printing Company Inc....260 563-5717
425 S Wabash St Wabash (46992) ***(G-13740)***
Millmade Inc....812 424-7778
9 N Kentucky Ave Evansville (47711) ***(G-3629)***
Millmark Enterprises Inc....574 389-9904
1935 Markle Ave Elkhart (46517) ***(G-3042)***
Mills Custom Powder Coating....812 766-0308
1444 E County Road 475 S Winslow (47598) ***(G-14357)***
Mills Electric Co Inc....219 931-3114
4828 Calumet Ave Hammond (46327) ***(G-5916)***
Millstone Specialties Inc....765 653-7382
1001 Sherwood Dr Greencastle (46135) ***(G-5468)***
Milltronics Usa Inc (HQ)....317 293-5309
1 Technology Way Indianapolis (46268) ***(G-7523)***
Millwood Box & Pallet....765 628-7330
4665 E 600 N Kokomo (46901) ***(G-8667)***
Millwood Custom Cabinets....574 646-3009
7427 N 800 W Etna Green (46524) ***(G-3322)***
Millwork Specialties Co Inc....219 362-2960
1405 Lake St La Porte (46350) ***(G-8795)***
Milroy Canning Company....765 629-2221
100 S Railroad St Milroy (46156) ***(G-9983)***
Milroy Pallet Inc....765 629-2919
3018 W 1050 S Milroy (46156) ***(G-9984)***
Milso Industries Inc....765 966-8012
401 Industrial Pkwy Richmond (47374) ***(G-12018)***
Miltec Circuits, Leo *Also called David Kechel* ***(G-9242)***
Milwaukee Hand Truck, Goshen *Also called Gleason Industrial Pdts Inc* ***(G-5227)***
Minds Eye Graphics Inc....260 724-2050
1019 W Commerce Dr Decatur (46733) ***(G-2396)***

Mine Equipment Mill Supply Co 812 402-4070
   4 Nw 2nd St 2 Evansville (47708) *(G-3630)*
Mining Machine Parts Inc 812 897-1256
   420 S 3rd St Boonville (47601) *(G-918)*
Mining Media Inc 317 802-7116
   6043 Primrose Ave Indianapolis (46220) *(G-7524)*
Minnich Mfg Inc 260 489-5357
   2421 W Wallen Rd Fort Wayne (46818) *(G-4476)*
Minnick Concrete Products Inc 260 432-5031
   222 N Thomas Rd Fort Wayne (46808) *(G-4477)*
Minnick Services, Fort Wayne *Also called Minnick Concrete Products Inc (G-4477)*
Minor Products Company Inc 812 448-3611
   Staunton Rd N Staunton (47881) *(G-13072)*
Minteq International Inc 219 397-5978
   3001 Dickey Rd East Chicago (46312) *(G-2553)*
Minteq International Inc 219 886-9555
   1 N Broadway Gary (46402) *(G-5077)*
Minteq Shapes and Services Inc 219 762-4863
   1789 Schiller St Portage (46368) *(G-11776)*
Minute Print It Inc 765 482-9019
   312 W South St Lebanon (46052) *(G-9206)*
Minuteman Press, Indianapolis *Also called Printing Concepts Inc (G-7754)*
Minuteman Press, Indianapolis *Also called Print Sharp Enterprises Inc (G-7750)*
Minuteman Press, Schererville *Also called Quality Printing of NW Ind (G-12343)*
Minuteman Press 317 209-1677
   6377 Rockville Rd Indianapolis (46214) *(G-7525)*
Minuteman Press 317 316-0566
   746 Westfield Rd Noblesville (46062) *(G-11151)*
Mirrus Corporation Inc 812 689-1411
   225 N Us Highway 421 Versailles (47042) *(G-13656)*
Mirteq Holdings Inc 260 490-3706
   2201 Suppliers Ct Fort Wayne (46818) *(G-4478)*
Mirwec Film Incorporated 812 331-7194
   601 S Liberty Dr Bloomington (47403) *(G-773)*
Mishawaka LLC 574 259-1981
   609 E Jefferson Blvd Mishawaka (46545) *(G-10089)*
Mishawaka Brewing Company 574 256-9993
   408 W Cleveland Rd Granger (46530) *(G-5423)*
Mishawaka Devision, Mishawaka *Also called Ncp Coatings Inc (G-10094)*
Mishawaka Door LLC 574 259-2822
   58743 Executive Dr Mishawaka (46544) *(G-10090)*
Mishawaka Food Pantry Inc 574 220-6213
   315 Lincolnway W Mishawaka (46544) *(G-10091)*
Mishawaka Frozen Custard 574 255-8000
   3921 N Main St Mishawaka (46545) *(G-10092)*
Mishawaka Sheet Metal, Elkhart *Also called Patrick Industries Inc (G-3087)*
Mishawaka Whse & Distrg LLC 574 259-6011
   2017 Elder Rd Mishawaka (46545) *(G-10093)*
Misner Welding & Construction 812 648-2980
   6922 E County Road 425 S Dugger (47848) *(G-2481)*
Miss Print, Munster *Also called Hetty Incorporated (G-10605)*
Miss Print, Hammond *Also called Hetty Incorporated (G-5892)*
MISSION 1 COMMUNICATIONS, Ligonier *Also called Ers Tower LLC (G-9284)*
Mission Announcement Co 626 332-4084
   100 N Park Ave Peru (46970) *(G-11537)*
Mission Woodworking Inc 574 848-5697
   502 Kesco Dr Bristol (46507) *(G-1069)*
Mississippi Lime Company 800 437-5463
   570 E Boundary Rd Portage (46368) *(G-11777)*
Mitchel & Scott Machine Co, Indianapolis *Also called Mitchel Group Incorporated (G-7527)*
Mitchel & Scott Machine Co 317 639-5331
   1841 Ludlow Ave Indianapolis (46201) *(G-7526)*
Mitchel Group Incorporated (PA) 317 639-5331
   1841 Ludlow Ave Indianapolis (46201) *(G-7527)*
Mitchell Crushed Stone, Mitchell *Also called Rogers Group Inc (G-10170)*
Mitchell Fabrics Inc 309 674-8631
   3532 Coleman Ct Ste B Lafayette (47905) *(G-8971)*
Mitchell Industries Inc 812 849-4931
   1407 W Main St Mitchell (47446) *(G-10167)*
Mitchell Plastics, Charlestown *Also called K&M Indiana LLC (G-1569)*
Mitchell Smith Auto Service, Anderson *Also called Mitchell Smith Racing (G-137)*
Mitchell Smith Racing 765 640-0237
   4570 W State Road 32 Anderson (46011) *(G-137)*
Mitchell Veneers Inc 812 941-9663
   4250 Earnings Way New Albany (47150) *(G-10832)*
Mitchell-Fleming Printing Inc 317 462-5467
   420 W Osage St Greenfield (46140) *(G-5554)*
Mitchum-Schaefer Inc 317 546-4081
   4901 W Raymond St Indianapolis (46241) *(G-7528)*
Mitek Usa Inc 219 924-3835
   905 W Glen Park Ave Griffith (46319) *(G-5786)*
Miter Craft Inc 317 462-3621
   708 Lake Dr Greenfield (46140) *(G-5555)*
Mito-Craft Inc 574 287-4555
   505 S Logan St South Bend (46615) *(G-12864)*
Mitsubishi Climate Control, Franklin *Also called Mitsubishi Heavy Industries (G-4911)*
Mitsubishi Heavy Industries 714 960-3785
   1200 N Mitsubishi Pkwy Franklin (46131) *(G-4910)*

Mitsubishi Heavy Industries (HQ) 317 346-5000
   1200 N Mitsubishi Pkwy Franklin (46131) *(G-4911)*
Mitsubsh Trbchrgr & Engn AM In 317 346-5291
   1200 N Mitsubishi Pkwy A Franklin (46131) *(G-4912)*
Mittal Steel -Ihw- 3 Sp, East Chicago *Also called Arcelormittal Minorca Mine Inc (G-2518)*
Mittal Steel USA 219 787-2113
   71 Detroit Rd Chesterton (46304) *(G-1622)*
Mj Finishing 574 646-2080
   5311 E County Line Rd Bremen (46506) *(G-1011)*
MJB Wood Group Inc 574 295-5228
   1600 Fieldhouse Ave Ste A Elkhart (46517) *(G-3043)*
Mjp & Company LLC 317 631-7263
   1728 E New York St Indianapolis (46201) *(G-7529)*
Mjs Businesses LLC 317 845-1932
   5381 E 82nd St Indianapolis (46250) *(G-7530)*
Mjs Concrete 260 341-5640
   19427 Notestine Rd Woodburn (46797) *(G-14389)*
Mk Interiors, Indianapolis *Also called American Heritage Shutters (G-6388)*
Mk Mfg LLC 260 768-4678
   8895 W 250 N Shipshewana (46565) *(G-12637)*
Mm Holdings I LLC 260 982-2191
   205 Wabash Rd North Manchester (46962) *(G-11236)*
Mm Window Fashions 317 585-4933
   7485 Vineyard Dr Fishers (46038) *(G-3947)*
MM&m Electrical Supply, Cedar Lake *Also called Gund Company Inc (G-1529)*
MO Signs LLC 574 780-4075
   1842 W Jefferson St Plymouth (46563) *(G-11707)*
MO Trailer Corporation 574 533-0824
   2211 W Wilden Ave Goshen (46528) *(G-5295)*
Mo-Wood Products Inc (HQ) 812 482-5625
   51 E 30th St Jasper (47546) *(G-8296)*
Mo3d Printing LLC 317 345-0061
   19257 Pathway Pointe Noblesville (46062) *(G-11152)*
Moan Racing Products LLC 317 644-3100
   4812 S 50 W Greenfield (46140) *(G-5556)*
Mobel Incorporated (PA) 812 367-1214
   2130 Industrial Park Rd Ferdinand (47532) *(G-3859)*
Mobilcraft Wood Products, Elkhart *Also called Patrick Industries Inc (G-3082)*
Mobile Climate Control Corp (HQ) 574 534-1516
   17103 State Road 4 Goshen (46528) *(G-5296)*
Mobile Communications Tech 812 423-7322
   945 N Peerless Rd Evansville (47712) *(G-3631)*
Mobile Dental Van Mfg 812 626-3010
   800 Cedar Hill Dr Evansville (47710) *(G-3632)*
Mobile Distillery, Indianapolis *Also called Joseph & Jones LLC (G-7312)*
Mobile Drill Intl, Indianapolis *Also called Mobile Drill Operating Co LLC (G-7531)*
Mobile Drill Operating Co LLC 317 260-8108
   3807 Madison Ave Indianapolis (46227) *(G-7531)*
Mobile Dynamometer LLC 765 271-5080
   1309 E Markland Ave Kokomo (46901) *(G-8668)*
Mobile Enerlytics LLC 765 464-6909
   1281 Win Hentschel Blvd West Lafayette (47906) *(G-14086)*
Mobile Limb & Brace Inc 765 463-4100
   2041 Klondike Rd West Lafayette (47906) *(G-14087)*
Mobile Mini Inc 260 749-6611
   5314 Maumee Rd Fort Wayne (46803) *(G-4479)*
Mobile Mini Inc 317 782-1513
   2104 W Epler Ave Indianapolis (46217) *(G-7532)*
Mobile Stadium Lighting LLC 219 325-0000
   707 N Fail Rd La Porte (46350) *(G-8796)*
Mobility Vehicles Indiana LLC 317 471-7169
   11389 N Goose Rd Knightstown (46148) *(G-8558)*
Mobius Learning, Carmel *Also called Cooperative Ventures Ind Corp (G-1343)*
Models LLC (PA) 765 676-6700
   2275 S 500 W Lebanon (46052) *(G-9207)*
Modern Biology Incorporated 765 523-3338
   2211 South St Lafayette (47904) *(G-8972)*
Modern Die Systems Inc 765 552-3145
   1104 N J St Elwood (46036) *(G-3307)*
Modern Door Corporation 574 586-3117
   1300 Virginia St Walkerton (46574) *(G-13806)*
Modern Drop Forge Company 708 388-1806
   8757 Colorado St Merrillville (46410) *(G-9736)*
Modern Drop Forge Company LLC (PA) 708 489-4208
   8757 Colorado St Merrillville (46410) *(G-9737)*
Modern Forge Companies LLC 708 388-1806
   8757 Colorado St Merrillville (46410) *(G-9738)*
Modern Forge Indiana LLC 219 945-5945
   8757 Colorado St Merrillville (46410) *(G-9739)*
Modern Graphics, Peru *Also called Reprocomm Inc (G-11544)*
Modern Machine & Grinding Inc 219 322-1201
   2001 Clark Rd Dyer (46311) *(G-2503)*
Modern Machine & Tool Inc 765 934-3110
   106 W Main St Van Buren (46991) *(G-13641)*
Modern Materials Inc 574 223-4509
   435 N State Road 25 Rochester (46975) *(G-12139)*
Modern Muscle Car Factory Inc 574 329-6390
   30446 County Road 12 Elkhart (46514) *(G-3044)*

A
L
P
H
A
B
E
T
I
C

Modern Powder Coating LLC 765 342-7039
  801 S Ohio St Martinsville (46151) *(G-9627)*
Modern Printing Co 260 347-1679
  117 E Williams St Kendallville (46755) *(G-8495)*
Modern Welding & Boiler Works 812 232-5039
  3500 Plum St Terre Haute (47803) *(G-13287)*
Modernfold Inc (HQ) 800 869-9685
  215 W New Rd Greenfield (46140) *(G-5557)*
Modrak Products Company Inc 219 838-0308
  3700 Clark Rd Gary (46408) *(G-5078)*
Modular Builders Inc 574 223-4934
  2756 Ft Wayne Rd Rochester (46975) *(G-12140)*
Modular Green Systems LLC 260 547-4121
  5889 N 700 W-1 Craigville (46731) *(G-2123)*
Moeller Printing Co Inc 317 353-2224
  4401 E New York St Indianapolis (46201) *(G-7533)*
Mofab Inc (PA) 765 649-1288
  1415 Fairview St Anderson (46016) *(G-138)*
Mofab Inc 765 649-1288
  619 W 14th St Anderson (46016) *(G-139)*
Moffitt Consulting Services 317 773-5570
  15365 Cherry Tree Rd Noblesville (46062) *(G-11153)*
Mohawk Laboratories 317 899-3660
  8401 E 33rd St Indianapolis (46226) *(G-7534)*
Molargik Woodworking Inc 260 357-6625
  1116 S Hamsher St Garrett (46738) *(G-5016)*
Mold Busters LLC 812 989-0008
  136 Lee Dr Floyds Knobs (47119) *(G-4016)*
Mold Removal Team of Hammond 219 554-9719
  6938 Grand Ave Hammond (46323) *(G-5917)*
Mold Service Inc 260 868-2920
  2911 County Road 59 Butler (46721) *(G-1233)*
Mold Stoppers of Indiana 812 325-1609
  1135 N Logan Rd Bloomington (47404) *(G-774)*
Molded Acstcal Pdts Easton Inc 610 253-7135
  3733 Lexington Park Dr Elkhart (46514) *(G-3045)*
Molded Acstcal Pdts Easton Inc 574 968-3124
  13065 Anderson Rd Granger (46530) *(G-5424)*
Molded Foam LLC 574 848-1500
  1203 S Division St Bristol (46507) *(G-1070)*
Molded Foam Products, Bristol *Also called Molded Foam LLC (G-1070)*
Molding Products Division, South Bend *Also called Interplastic Corporation (G-12818)*
Molex LLC 317 770-4900
  10 S 9th St Noblesville (46060) *(G-11154)*
Molex LLC 317 834-5600
  1500 Hancel Pkwy Mooresville (46158) *(G-10323)*
Momaki Publishing LLC 847 454-4641
  1701 W 55th Ave Merrillville (46410) *(G-9740)*
Momentive Performance Mtls, Garrett *Also called Momentive Performance Mtls Inc (G-5017)*
Momentive Performance Mtls Inc 260 357-2000
  420 N Taylor Rd Garrett (46738) *(G-5017)*
Mominee Studios Inc 812 473-1691
  5001 Lincoln Ave Evansville (47715) *(G-3633)*
Moms Homemade Pies Co LLC 765 453-4417
  3700 S Lafountain St Kokomo (46902) *(G-8669)*
Monark Marine, New Paris *Also called Starcraft Marine LLC (G-10995)*
Monitoring Solutions Inc 317 856-9400
  4440 S High School Rd C Indianapolis (46241) *(G-7535)*
Monogram Comfort Foods LLC 574 848-0344
  605 Kesco Dr Bristol (46507) *(G-1071)*
Monogram Frozen Foods LLC 574 848-0344
  605 Kesco Dr Bristol (46507) *(G-1072)*
Monon Meat Packing Company 219 253-6363
  402 N Railroad St Monon (47959) *(G-10177)*
Monosol LLC (HQ) 219 762-3165
  707 E 80th Pl Ste 301 Merrillville (46410) *(G-9741)*
Monosol LLC 219 763-7589
  1500 Louis Sullivan Dr Portage (46368) *(G-11778)*
Monosol LLC 219 324-9459
  1609 Genesis Dr La Porte (46350) *(G-8797)*
Monosol LLC 219 762-3165
  1701 County Line Rd Portage (46368) *(G-11779)*
Monroe Custom Utility Bodies 317 894-8684
  3312 N 600 W Greenfield (46140) *(G-5558)*
Monroe Manufacturing Tech Inc 317 782-1005
  5508 Elmwood Ave Ste 422 Indianapolis (46203) *(G-7536)*
Monroe Wood Works 317 979-0964
  10203 Heather Hills Rd Indianapolis (46229) *(G-7537)*
Monroeville Box Pallet & Wood 260 623-3128
  20009 Monroeville Rd Monroeville (46773) *(G-10197)*
Monsanto 260 341-3227
  1290 S 1000 W Farmland (47340) *(G-3843)*
Monsanto Company 574 870-0397
  371 N Diener Rd Reynolds (47980) *(G-11946)*
Monsanto Company 219 733-2938
  10201 S 700 W Union Mills (46382) *(G-13464)*
Monsanto Company 574 583-0028
  306 N Main St Monticello (47960) *(G-10269)*
Monsanto Company 317 945-7121
  908 N Independence St Windfall (46076) *(G-14348)*

Monsanto Cotton 229 759-0035
  738 Rusher Ln Evansville (47725) *(G-3634)*
Monster House Press 440 364-4548
  1608 S Buffstone Ct Bloomington (47401) *(G-775)*
Montech USA, Columbia City *Also called Richard J Bagan Inc (G-1826)*
Montezuma Jewelry, Muncie *Also called David Gonzales (G-10454)*
Montgomery & Associates Inc 219 879-0088
  911 Franklin St Michigan City (46360) *(G-9821)*
Montgomery Manufacturing Co 812 724-2505
  202 S Main St Owensville (47665) *(G-11429)*
Montgomery Tent & Awning Co 317 357-9759
  5054 E 10th St Indianapolis (46201) *(G-7538)*
Monticello Machine Co Inc 574 583-9537
  7779 E 175 N Monticello (47960) *(G-10270)*
Monticello Vault Burial Co 574 583-3206
  2304 N 750 E Monticello (47960) *(G-10271)*
Montro Company 812 268-4390
  240 E Depot St Sullivan (47882) *(G-13088)*
Monument Chemical LLC (PA) 317 223-2630
  6510 Telecom Dr Ste 425 Indianapolis (46278) *(G-7539)*
Monument Construction Inc 317 472-0271
  430 Msschstts Ave Ste 104 Indianapolis (46204) *(G-7540)*
Monument Lighthouse Chart 317 657-0160
  8503 Summertree Ln Indianapolis (46256) *(G-7541)*
Monumental Stone Works Inc 765 866-0658
  105 S 3rd St New Market (47965) *(G-10964)*
Moody Meats 317 272-4533
  235 N Avon Ave Avon (46123) *(G-455)*
Moon Fabricating Corp 765 459-4194
  700 W Morgan St Kokomo (46901) *(G-8670)*
Mooney Copy Service Inc 812 423-6626
  40 E Sycamore St Evansville (47713) *(G-3635)*
Moonlight Mold & Machine Inc 765 868-9860
  924 Millbrook Ln Kokomo (46901) *(G-8671)*
Moonshine Leather Company Inc 812 988-1326
  38 S Van Buren St Nashville (47448) *(G-10730)*
Moore Engineering & Prod Co (PA) 812 479-1051
  2104 Lincoln Ave Evansville (47714) *(G-3636)*
Moore Machine & Gear Inc 812 963-3074
  10920 N Saint Joseph Ave Evansville (47720) *(G-3637)*
Moore Metal Works & A/C L L C 812 422-9473
  3712 Upper Mt Vernon Rd Evansville (47712) *(G-3638)*
Moore Precision Machining LLC (PA) 765 265-2386
  1400 Madison St Connersville (47331) *(G-2065)*
Moores Country Wood Crafting 317 984-3326
  507 Demoss Ave Arcadia (46030) *(G-266)*
Moores Inc 574 533-6089
  316 W Douglas St Goshen (46526) *(G-5297)*
Moores Pie Shop Inc 765 457-2428
  115 W Elm St Kokomo (46901) *(G-8672)*
Moores Welding Service Inc 260 627-2177
  13131 Leo Rd Leo (46765) *(G-9244)*
Mooresville Welding Inc 317 831-2265
  220 E Washington St Mooresville (46158) *(G-10324)*
Moorfeed Acquisition LLC 317 545-7171
  1445 Brookville Way Ste R Indianapolis (46239) *(G-7542)*
Moorfeed Corporation 317 545-7171
  4162 N Ems Blvd Greenfield (46140) *(G-5559)*
Moorfeed Parts Automation, Indianapolis *Also called Moorfeed Acquisition LLC (G-7542)*
Moormann Bros Mfg Co, Rushville *Also called Gainescraft Inc (G-12222)*
Moose Lake Products Co. 260 432-2768
  6528 Constitution Dr Fort Wayne (46804) *(G-4480)*
Moose Lodge 219 362-2446
  925 Boyd Blvd La Porte (46350) *(G-8798)*
Moose Lodge No 492, La Porte *Also called Moose Lodge (G-8798)*
Moosein Industries LLC 219 406-7306
  1256 Camelot Mnr Portage (46368) *(G-11780)*
Mopar Detail Connection, Newburgh *Also called Ellwocks Auto Parts Restorat (G-11027)*
Mor-Ryde Service Center, Elkhart *Also called Mor/Ryde Inc (G-3046)*
Mor/Ryde Inc 574 293-1581
  1966 Sterling Ave Elkhart (46516) *(G-3046)*
Mor/Ryde International Inc 574 293-1581
  1536 Grant St Elkhart (46514) *(G-3047)*
Mor/Ryde International Inc 574 293-1581
  23208 Cooper Dr Elkhart (46514) *(G-3048)*
Mor/Ryde International Inc (PA) 574 293-1581
  1966 Moyer Ave Elkhart (46516) *(G-3049)*
Moran Engineering LLC 574 266-6799
  28973 Buttercup Ln Elkhart (46514) *(G-3050)*
More Wallace, Indianapolis *Also called R R Donnelley Inc (G-7810)*
Morel Company Llc 812 932-6100
  100 Progress Dr Batesville (47006) *(G-511)*
Moreton Printing Co 812 926-1692
  511 2nd St Aurora (47001) *(G-383)*
Morgan Adhesives Company LLC 812 342-2004
  2576 Norcross Dr Columbus (47201) *(G-1976)*
Morgan Automotive 765 378-0593
  4443 State Road 32 E Chesterfield (46017) *(G-1588)*

Morgan Commercial Lettering 260 482-6430
434 Merkler St Fort Wayne (46825) *(G-4481)*

Morgan County Sand & Gravel Co, Martinsville *Also called Rogers Group Inc (G-9635)*

Morgan Excavating 812 385-6036
5268 S 875 E Oakland City (47660) *(G-11310)*

Morgan Foods Inc 812 794-1170
90 W Morgan St Austin (47102) *(G-398)*

Morgan Francis, Arlington *Also called Original Tractor Cab Co Inc (G-282)*

Morgan Francis Flagpoles & ACC, Indianapolis *Also called Superior Metal Tech LLC (G-8022)*

Morgan Olson LLC 269 659-0243
300 Growth Pkwy Angola (46703) *(G-231)*

Morgan Thermal Ceramics, Elkhart *Also called Thermal Ceramics Inc (G-3212)*

Morin Corp 219 465-8334
302 Elmhurst Ave Valparaiso (46385) *(G-13581)*

Morning Song Wild Bird Feed, Reynolds *Also called Scotts Miracle-Gro Company (G-11948)*

Morris Holding Company LLC (PA) 812 446-6141
1015 E Mechanic St Brazil (47834) *(G-970)*

Morris Machine & Tool 219 866-3018
828 N Scott St Rensselaer (47978) *(G-11932)*

Morris Machine Co Inc 317 788-0371
6480 S Belmont Ave Indianapolis (46217) *(G-7543)*

Morris Mfg & Sls Corp 812 446-6141
1015 E Mechanic St Brazil (47834) *(G-971)*

Morris Mold and Machine Co 317 923-6653
912 E 21st St Indianapolis (46202) *(G-7544)*

Morris Precision Inc 574 656-3089
102 Lilac Ct Noblesville (46062) *(G-11155)*

Morris Precision Inc 574 656-8707
102 Lilac Ct Noblesville (46062) *(G-11156)*

Morris Printing Company Inc 317 639-5553
1502 N College Ave Indianapolis (46202) *(G-7545)*

Morrows Electric Motor Service, Mount Vernon *Also called Morrows Mt Vernon Elc Mtr Svc (G-10402)*

Morrows Mt Vernon Elc Mtr Svc 812 838-5641
214 W 2nd St Mount Vernon (47620) *(G-10402)*

Morse Lake Automotive 317 984-4514
8300 E 216th St Cicero (46034) *(G-1663)*

Morse Metal Fab Inc 574 674-6237
51111 Bittersweet Rd Granger (46530) *(G-5425)*

Mortar Net Usa Ltd 800 664-6638
326 Melton Rd Burns Harbor (46304) *(G-1218)*

Mortgageserv, South Bend *Also called Fiserv Mrtg Servicing Systems (G-12779)*

Morton Buildings Inc 765 932-3979
1224 S State Road 3 Rushville (46173) *(G-12230)*

Morton Buildings Inc 260 563-2118
1873 S State Rte 115 Wabash (46992) *(G-13741)*

Moseley Laboratories Inc 317 866-8460
6108 W Stoner Dr Greenfield (46140) *(G-5560)*

Moser Engineering, Portland *Also called Greg Moser Engineering Inc (G-11827)*

Mosey Manufacturing Co Inc (PA) 765 983-8800
262 Fort Wayne Ave Richmond (47374) *(G-12019)*

Mosey Manufacturing Co Inc 765 768-7462
11340 W 450 S Dunkirk (47336) *(G-2486)*

Mosey Manufacturing Co Inc 765 552-3504
11340 W 450 S Dunkirk (47336) *(G-2487)*

Mosey Manufacturing Co Inc 765 983-8870
1700 N F St Richmond (47374) *(G-12020)*

Mosey Manufacturing Co Inc 765 983-8870
534 N 17th St Richmond (47374) *(G-12021)*

Mosey Manufacturing Co Inc 765 983-8889
1700 N F St Richmond (47374) *(G-12022)*

Mosey Manufacturing Plant 7, Richmond *Also called Mosey Manufacturing Co Inc (G-12022)*

Mosey Plant II, Richmond *Also called Mosey Manufacturing Co Inc (G-12020)*

Mosier Log Homes, Corydon *Also called Mosier Pallet & Lumber Co (G-2105)*

Mosier Pallet & Lumber Co 812 366-4817
3600 Tee Rd Ne Corydon (47112) *(G-2105)*

Mosiers Tarps 260 563-3332
4021 S State Road 15 Wabash (46992) *(G-13742)*

Moss Glass, Indianapolis *Also called Moss L Glass Co Inc (G-7546)*

Moss L Glass Co Inc 765 642-4946
5265 E 82nd St Indianapolis (46250) *(G-7546)*

Mossberg & Company Inc (PA) 574 289-9253
301 E Sample St South Bend (46601) *(G-12865)*

Mossberg & Company Inc 574 236-1094
4100 Technology Dr South Bend (46628) *(G-12866)*

Mossberg Industries, Laotto *Also called Khorporate Holdings Inc (G-9110)*

Mossberg Industries Inc (HQ) 260 357-5141
204 N 2nd St Garrett (46738) *(G-5018)*

Mossman Metal Works 765 676-6055
3595 W 200 S Lebanon (46052) *(G-9208)*

Motherson Sumi Systems Limited 260 726-6501
700 Industrial Dr Portland (47371) *(G-11836)*

Mothersoy Inc 812 424-5357
424 S Kentucky Ave Evansville (47714) *(G-3639)*

Motion & Control Entps LLC 219 844-4224
7917 New Jersey Ave Hammond (46323) *(G-5918)*

Motion Engineering Company Inc 317 804-7990
17338 Wstfeld Pk Rd Ste 4 Westfield (46074) *(G-14177)*

Motionwear LLC 317 780-4182
1315 Sunday Dr Indianapolis (46217) *(G-7547)*

Motor Electric Inc 574 294-7123
4700 Eastland Dr Elkhart (46516) *(G-3051)*

Motorama Auto Ctr Inc (PA) 317 831-0036
10509 N Old State Road 67 Mooresville (46158) *(G-10325)*

Motorama Kart Parts, Mooresville *Also called Motorama Auto Ctr Inc (G-10325)*

Motorcraft Inc 765 282-4272
1219 S Walnut St Muncie (47302) *(G-10525)*

Motorola Inc 765 455-5100
2723 Albright Rd Kokomo (46902) *(G-8673)*

Motorola Solutions Inc 317 716-8064
2461 Directors Row Ste C Indianapolis (46241) *(G-7548)*

Motsinger Auto Supply Inc 317 782-8484
345 W Hanna Ave Indianapolis (46217) *(G-7549)*

Mould-Rite Inc 812 967-3200
5885 E Old Pekin Rd Pekin (47165) *(G-11477)*

Mountain Made Music Inc 812 988-8869
3315 Hoover Rd Nashville (47448) *(G-10731)*

Mountjoy Wooding 317 897-6792
1221 Schleicher Ave Indianapolis (46229) *(G-7550)*

Mountville Mats 574 753-8858
5270 E Country Club Rd Logansport (46947) *(G-9355)*

Mouron & Company Inc 317 243-7955
1025 Western Dr Indianapolis (46241) *(G-7551)*

Movie Poster Print 812 679-7301
4114 Washington St Columbus (47203) *(G-1977)*

Moyer Process & Controls Co 260 495-2405
105 N Wayne St Fremont (46737) *(G-4969)*

Moyers Inc 574 264-3119
3502 Reedy Dr Elkhart (46514) *(G-3052)*

Mp Steel Indiana LLC (PA) 260 347-1203
5966 E Concrete Dr Kendallville (46755) *(G-8496)*

Mpi Holdings Inc 765 473-3086
3311 S State Road 19 Peru (46970) *(G-11538)*

Mpi Products LLC 574 772-3850
1200 Kloeckner Dr Knox (46534) *(G-8575)*

Mpp, Noblesville *Also called Netshape Technologies LLC (G-11158)*

Mpp Inc 260 422-5426
2413 Meyer Rd Fort Wayne (46803) *(G-4482)*

Mpr Corporation 574 848-5100
103 Hinsdale Farm Rd Bristol (46507) *(G-1073)*

MPS, Wabash *Also called Midwestern Pallet Service Inc (G-13739)*

MPS Indianapolis Inc 317 241-2020
2020 Production Dr Indianapolis (46241) *(G-7552)*

MPS Printing Inc 812 273-4446
339 Clifty Dr Madison (47250) *(G-9489)*

Mpsi, Valparaiso *Also called Mechanical Parts & Svcs Inc (G-13580)*

Mpt Muncie LLC 765 587-1300
4701 S Cowan Rd Muncie (47302) *(G-10526)*

Mpt Muncie East, Muncie *Also called Magna Powertrain America Inc (G-10516)*

Mr B'S Sporting Goods, Kendallville *Also called Mr BS Sports & Design (G-8497)*

Mr BS Sports & Design 260 347-4830
117 S Main St Kendallville (46755) *(G-8497)*

Mr Copy Inc 812 334-2679
501 E 10th St Bloomington (47408) *(G-776)*

Mr Copyrite 219 462-1108
308 Lincolnway Valparaiso (46383) *(G-13582)*

Mr Fuel 317 531-0891
140 Holwager Dr Spiceland (47385) *(G-13056)*

Mr Heat Inc 219 345-5629
11735 N State Road 55 Demotte (46310) *(G-2444)*

Mr Mhammads Sweet-Bean Snacks 317 519-0728
4212 Village Bend Ln Indianapolis (46254) *(G-7553)*

Mr Pin Shi Peter Lee 574 264-9754
23329 Century Dr Elkhart (46514) *(G-3053)*

Mr Tintz 219 844-5500
6806 Indianapolis Blvd D Hammond (46324) *(G-5919)*

Mr Trophy, Argos *Also called Van Der Weele Jon D (G-280)*

Mr-Link LLC 765 476-3185
3024 Benton St West Lafayette (47906) *(G-14088)*

MRC Technology Inc 574 232-9057
1901 S Lafayette Blvd South Bend (46613) *(G-12867)*

Mrs International, Fort Wayne *Also called Machine Rebuilders & Service (G-4448)*

Mrs T'S Bakery, Bremen *Also called Mel Rhon Inc (G-1010)*

Ms & J Quality Screw Mch Pdts 812 623-3002
8925 E County Road 1000 N Sunman (47041) *(G-13115)*

Ms Manufacturing LLC 812 442-7468
301 N Murphy Ave Brazil (47834) *(G-972)*

Ms Wheelchair Indiana Inc. 317 408-0947
9106 Tansel Ct Indianapolis (46234) *(G-7554)*

MSC Property Management Div, La Porte *Also called Millwork Specialties Co Inc (G-8795)*

Msca LLC 574 583-6220
303 N 6th St Monticello (47960) *(G-10272)*

MSI, Anderson *Also called Muhlen Sohn Industries LP (G-140)*

Msk Mold Inc 812 985-5457
2591 Juanita Ave Wadesville (47638) *(G-13773)*

A
L
P
H
A
B
E
T
I
C

MSP Aviation Inc 812 333-6100
  239 W Grimes Ln Bloomington (47403) *(G-777)*

Mssh Inc 812 663-2180
  901 N Carver St Greensburg (47240) *(G-5624)*

Mssl Wiring System Inc 260 726-6501
  700 Industrial Dr Portland (47371) *(G-11837)*

Mt Olive Manufacturing Inc. 317 834-8525
  3304 Hancel Cir Mooresville (46158) *(G-10326)*

MT Publishing Company Inc 812 468-8022
  209 Nw 8th St Evansville (47708) *(G-3640)*

Mt Vernon Coal Transfer Co 812 838-5531
  3300 Bluff Rd Mount Vernon (47620) *(G-10403)*

Mt. Vernon Barge Service, Indianapolis *Also called Tpg Mt Vernon Marine LLC (G-8087)*

Mt. Vernon Democrat, Mount Vernon *Also called News Publishing Company LLC (G-10404)*

MTA Technology LLC 765 447-2221
  2624 Salem St Lafayette (47904) *(G-8973)*

Mtcr Site Services LLC 812 598-6516
  6033 Vann Rd Newburgh (47630) *(G-11039)*

Mtd, Fort Wayne *Also called Midwest Tool & Die Corp (G-4474)*

Mtd Products Inc 317 986-2042
  5353 W 79th St Indianapolis (46268) *(G-7555)*

Mtr Machining Concept Inc 260 587-3381
  2878 W 800 S Ashley (46705) *(G-288)*

MTS Products Corp (PA) 574 295-3142
  28672 Holiday Pl Elkhart (46517) *(G-3054)*

MTS Products Corp 574 295-3142
  28672 Holiday Pl Elkhart (46517) *(G-3055)*

Mud Creek Publishing Inc 317 577-9659
  8335 Allison Pointe Trl # 200 Indianapolis (46250) *(G-7556)*

Mudd-Ox Inc 260 768-7221
  8525 W 750 N Shipshewana (46565) *(G-12638)*

Mudhole Machine Shop LLC 765 533-4228
  5121 N County Road 200 W Middletown (47356) *(G-9939)*

Muehlhausen Spring Company 574 626-2351
  602 Michele Ln Walton (46994) *(G-13816)*

Muehlhausen Spring Company 574 859-2481
  488 N 705 E Flora (46929) *(G-4000)*

Muhlen Sohn Industries LP 765 640-9674
  4640 Martin Lut Anderson (46013) *(G-140)*

Mulhern Belting Inc 219 879-2385
  910 Indiana Highway 212 Michigan City (46360) *(G-9822)*

Mullet Custom Interiors LLC 574 773-9442
  106 3b Rd Nappanee (46550) *(G-10696)*

Mulligans Sports Pub 765 868-8230
  1134 Home Ave Kokomo (46902) *(G-8674)*

Mullin Sign Studio 219 926-8937
  48 E 1050 N Chesterton (46304) *(G-1623)*

Mullinix Packages Inc (HQ) 260 747-3149
  3511 Engle Rd Fort Wayne (46809) *(G-4483)*

Mulry Manufacturing LLC 317 253-2756
  4261 Kessler Lane East Dr Indianapolis (46220) *(G-7557)*

Multi Packaging Solutions Inc 317 241-2020
  2020 Production Dr Indianapolis (46241) *(G-7558)*

Multi Packaging Solutions Ind, Indianapolis *Also called MPS Indianapolis Inc (G-7552)*

Multi-Color Corporation 812 752-0586
  2281 S Us Highway 31 Scottsburg (47170) *(G-12375)*

Multi-Color Corporation 812 752-3187
  2281 S Us Highway 31 Scottsburg (47170) *(G-12376)*

Multimactic New Haven LLC 260 868-1067
  201 Re Jones Rd Butler (46721) *(G-1234)*

Multimatic Indiana Inc 260 868-1000
  201 Re Jones Rd Butler (46721) *(G-1235)*

Multimatic New Haven LLC (PA) 260 868-1067
  2808 Adams Center Rd Fort Wayne (46803) *(G-4484)*

Multiple Machining Inc 812 432-5946
  10150 Lenover St Dillsboro (47018) *(G-2470)*

Multiple Resource Solution 317 862-2584
  6925 S Carroll Rd Indianapolis (46259) *(G-7559)*

Multiplex Company Inc (HQ) 812 246-7000
  2100 Future Dr Sellersburg (47172) *(G-12409)*

Multiseal Inc 812 428-3422
  4320 Hitch Peters Rd Evansville (47711) *(G-3641)*

Multitech Swiss Machining LLC 260 894-4180
  711 Gerber St Ligonier (46767) *(G-9290)*

Mulzer Crush Stone, Rockport *Also called Mulzer Crushed Stone Inc (G-12170)*

Mulzer Crushed Stone Inc 812 365-2145
  Old Hwy 64e English (47118) *(G-3316)*

Mulzer Crushed Stone Inc (HQ) 812 547-7921
  534 Mozart St Tell City (47586) *(G-13167)*

Mulzer Crushed Stone Inc 812 723-4137
  3880 W Us Highway 150 Paoli (47454) *(G-11456)*

Mulzer Crushed Stone Inc 812 547-7921
  3300 Green River Dr Evansville (47715) *(G-3642)*

Mulzer Crushed Stone Inc 812 937-2442
  4590 E Aw Mulzer Dr Dale (47523) *(G-2332)*

Mulzer Crushed Stone Inc 812 649-5055
  411 Washington St Rockport (47635) *(G-12170)*

Mulzer Crushed Stone Inc 812 739-4777
  19925 S Alton Fredonia Rd Leavenworth (47137) *(G-9165)*

Mulzer Crushed Stone Inc 812 547-3467
  3rd Lafayette St Tell City (47586) *(G-13168)*

Mulzer Crushed Stone Inc 812 256-3346
  15602 Charlstwn Bethlehem Charlestown (47111) *(G-1574)*

Mulzer Security, Charlestown *Also called Mulzer Crushed Stone Inc (G-1574)*

Muncie Cabinet Discounters 765 216-7367
  4205 N Wheeling Ave Muncie (47304) *(G-10527)*

Muncie Casting Corp 765 288-2611
  1406 E 18th St Muncie (47302) *(G-10528)*

Muncie Metal Products 765 288-3421
  820 E Willard St Muncie (47302) *(G-10529)*

Muncie Metal Spinning Inc 765 288-1937
  1100 E 20th St Muncie (47302) *(G-10530)*

Muncie Mold & Engineering LLC 765 282-0522
  704 S Burlington Dr Muncie (47302) *(G-10531)*

Muncie Novelty Company Inc 765 288-8301
  9610 N State Road 67 Muncie (47303) *(G-10532)*

Muncie Power Products Inc (HQ) 765 284-7721
  201 E Jackson St Ste 500 Muncie (47305) *(G-10533)*

Muncie Power Products Inc 765 896-9816
  1210 E Seymour St Muncie (47302) *(G-10534)*

Muncie Precision Hard Chrome 765 288-2489
  1001 E 18th St Muncie (47302) *(G-10535)*

Muncie Sand & Gravel Inc 765 282-6422
  4210 E Mcgalliard Rd Muncie (47303) *(G-10536)*

Munster Steel Co Inc 219 924-5198
  1501 Huehn St Hammond (46327) *(G-5920)*

Muroplex Therapeutics Inc 317 502-0545
  5701 Carrollton Ave Indianapolis (46220) *(G-7560)*

Murpac of Fort Wayne LLC 260 424-2299
  3405 Meyer Rd Ste 135 Fort Wayne (46803) *(G-4485)*

Murphy Electric 574 224-9473
  4606 W 100 N Rochester (46975) *(G-12141)*

Murray Equipment Inc 260 484-0382
  2515 Charleston Pl Fort Wayne (46808) *(G-4486)*

Murrays Tin Cup 260 349-1002
  2004 W North St Kendallville (46755) *(G-8498)*

Murrell Optical LLC 317 280-0114
  4150 Lafayette Rd Ste C Indianapolis (46254) *(G-7561)*

Mursix Corporation 765 282-2221
  2401 N Executive Park Dr Yorktown (47396) *(G-14408)*

Music Store 812 949-3004
  307 W Lewis & Clark Pkwy Clarksville (47129) *(G-1689)*

Music Town Distributors, Indianapolis *Also called Cliff A Ostermeyer (G-6621)*

Muzfeed Inc 815 252-7676
  6304 Tanbark Trl Fort Wayne (46835) *(G-4487)*

Mvo Usa Inc 317 585-5785
  8802 Bash St Ste A Indianapolis (46256) *(G-7562)*

Mvp Dumpsters Inc 317 502-3155
  8093 S 600 W Pendleton (46064) *(G-11495)*

Mwf LLC 812 936-5303
  8228 W State Road 56 West Baden Springs (47469) *(G-14035)*

My Choice Recycling Inc 219 313-1388
  1952 Us Hwy 41 Schrrville Schererville (46375) *(G-12336)*

My County Publishing LLC 765 630-8221
  15 1/2 S Indiana St Greencastle (46135) *(G-5469)*

My Daily Wedding Deals LLC 812 603-6149
  4822 Crystal River Ct Indianapolis (46240) *(G-7563)*

My Pneumatic Tools and Service 317 364-3324
  7032 E Shelby 1100 S Greensburg (47240) *(G-5625)*

My-Te Products Inc 317 897-9880
  9880 E 30th St Indianapolis (46229) *(G-7564)*

Mycogen Corporation (HQ) 317 337-3000
  9330 Zionsville Rd Indianapolis (46268) *(G-7565)*

Mycogen Crop Protection Inc 317 337-3000
  9330 Zionsville Rd Indianapolis (46268) *(G-7566)*

Myers Cabinet Company 765 342-7781
  409 E Pike St Martinsville (46151) *(G-9628)*

Myers Designs Inc 317 955-2450
  6061 Logansport Rd # 140 Logansport (46947) *(G-9356)*

Myers Enterprises Inc 812 636-7350
  102 W Main St Odon (47562) *(G-11335)*

Myers Frozen Food Provisioners 765 525-6304
  405 W Dorsey St Saint Paul (47272) *(G-12279)*

Myers Spring Co Inc 574 753-5105
  720 Water St Logansport (46947) *(G-9357)*

Myers Wood Products 765 597-2147
  1287 E 1200 N Bloomingdale (47832) *(G-649)*

Mystique Winery and Vinyrd LLC 812 922-5612
  13000 Gore Rd Lynnville (47619) *(G-9435)*

Mytex Polymers US Corp 812 280-2900
  1403 Port Rd Jeffersonville (47130) *(G-8402)*

N & K Cabinet Inc 765 552-6997
  2510 S F St Elwood (46036) *(G-3308)*

N & R Woodworking Llc 812 787-0644
  10546 N 700 E Odon (47562) *(G-11336)*

N E W Interstate Concrete Inc 812 234-5983
  2223 E Margaret Dr Terre Haute (47802) *(G-13288)*

N K Welding Products Inc 260 424-1901
  302 W Superior St Fort Wayne (46802) *(G-4488)*

(G-0000) Company's Geographic Section entry number

N R S, Fort Wayne *Also called National Rcreation Systems Inc (G-4491)*

N Rolls-Royce Amercn Tech Inc.................................317 230-4347
2059 S Tibbs Ave Indianapolis (46241) *(G-7567)*

N-Complete Inc...765 649-2244
804 Lincoln St Anderson (46016) *(G-141)*

N-Ovations Inc..219 464-0441
506 Franklin St Valparaiso (46383) *(G-13583)*

N.E.W. Indiana Co.,, Columbus *Also called Nagakura Engrg Works Co Inc (G-1978)*

N3 LLC..317 845-9253
7001 Hawthorn Park Dr A Indianapolis (46220) *(G-7568)*

N3 Boatworks, Indianapolis *Also called N3 LLC (G-7568)*

Naas Heating and Cooling, Princeton *Also called Naas Inc (G-11879)*

Naas Inc..812 385-3578
200 Tennessee St Princeton (47670) *(G-11879)*

Nachi America Inc (HQ)..317 535-5527
715 Pushville Rd Greenwood (46143) *(G-5726)*

Nachi Technology Inc...317 535-5000
713 Pushville Rd Greenwood (46143) *(G-5727)*

Nachi Tool America Inc...317 535-0320
717 Pushville Rd Greenwood (46143) *(G-5728)*

Nachurs Alpine Solutions Corp................................812 738-1333
3185 Cline Rd Nw Corydon (47112) *(G-2106)*

Nagakura Engrg Works Co Inc.................................812 375-1382
630 S Mapleton St Columbus (47201) *(G-1978)*

Nagys Winery LLC..219 331-0588
109 Shorewood Dr Valparaiso (46385) *(G-13584)*

Nai Print Solutions..317 392-1207
168 W Hendricks St Shelbyville (46176) *(G-12552)*

Nail Pro...219 322-9220
246 W Us Highway 30 Schererville (46375) *(G-12337)*

Nalc LLC...502 548-9590
8090 S State Road 243 Cloverdale (46120) *(G-1732)*

Nalco Co, East Chicago *Also called Phoenix Services LLC (G-2557)*

Nalleys Woodworking...812 923-1299
4747 Saint Johns Rd Greenville (47124) *(G-5651)*

Namacle LLC..574 320-1436
1235 W Hively Ave Elkhart (46517) *(G-3056)*

Nampac, Indianapolis *Also called North America Packaging Corp (G-7591)*

Nano Universe LLC...765 457-5860
514 Rudgate Ln Kokomo (46901) *(G-8675)*

Nanochem Technologies LLC...................................574 970-2436
1203 Kent St Elkhart (46514) *(G-3057)*

Nanolayer Technologies LLC...................................260 414-4458
3523 Knoll Rd Fort Wayne (46809) *(G-4489)*

Nanolayer Technology, Fort Wayne *Also called Nanolayer Technologies LLC (G-4489)*

Nanosonics Inc...844 876-7466
7205 E 87th St Indianapolis (46256) *(G-7569)*

Nanovis LLC (PA)...260 625-1502
5865 E State Road 14 Columbia City (46725) *(G-1811)*

Nanshn Amrc Adv Alum Tech LLC.............................765 838-8645
3600 Us Highway 52 S Lafayette (47905) *(G-8974)*

Nap Asset Holdings Ltd (PA)..................................812 482-2000
1180 Wernsing Rd Jasper (47546) *(G-8297)*

Nap Gladu, Jasper *Also called Nap Asset Holdings Ltd (G-8297)*

NAPA Autoparts Fortville, Fortville *Also called Fortville Automotive Sup Inc (G-4774)*

Napier & Napier..765 580-9116
2369 S Us Highway 27 Liberty (47353) *(G-9266)*

Napolean Quarry, Batesville *Also called New Point Stone Co Inc (G-512)*

Napoleon Hardwood Lbr Co Inc................................812 852-4090
1522 S Mill Creek Rd Greensburg (47240) *(G-5626)*

Napoleon Lumber Co..812 852-4545
Us Hwy 421 S Napoleon (47034) *(G-10641)*

Naptown Etching..317 733-8776
7313 Mayflower Park Dr Zionsville (46077) *(G-14450)*

Naptown Vapors LLC (PA)......................................765 315-0554
339 Morton Ave Ste B Martinsville (46151) *(G-9629)*

Narrow Gate Publishing LLC...................................219 464-8579
113 Shorewood Dr Valparaiso (46385) *(G-13585)*

Nasco Industries Inc...812 254-7393
3 Ne 21st St Washington (47501) *(G-13992)*

Nasg Indiana LLC...765 381-4310
3401 W 8th St Muncie (47302) *(G-10537)*

Nash Sheet Metal Co...812 397-5306
4295 E County Road 800 N Shelburn (47879) *(G-12508)*

Natcon, South Bend *Also called National Consolidated Corp (G-12868)*

Nathan Millis Tools LLC..219 996-3305
115 Poplar Ct Hebron (46341) *(G-6019)*

National Athletic Sportswear..................................260 436-2248
3911 Option Pass Fort Wayne (46818) *(G-4490)*

National Cigar Corporation (PA)...............................765 659-3326
407 N Main St Frankfort (46041) *(G-4842)*

National Consolidated Corp....................................574 289-7885
25855 State Road 2 South Bend (46619) *(G-12868)*

National Dentex LLC..317 849-5143
6402 Castleplace Dr Indianapolis (46250) *(G-7570)*

National Equipment Inc..219 462-1205
358 Harrison Blvd Valparaiso (46383) *(G-13586)*

National Exhaust Cleaning Inc................................317 831-4750
634 E State Road 42 Mooresville (46158) *(G-10327)*

National Federation of (PA)...................................317 972-6900
690 W Washington St Indianapolis (46204) *(G-7571)*

National Group, The, Lafayette *Also called Copy-Print Shop Inc (G-8877)*

National Gypsum Co, Shoals *Also called New Ngc Inc (G-12667)*

National Gypsum Company, Rensselaer *Also called New Ngc Inc (G-11933)*

National Gypsum Company, Clinton *Also called New Ngc Inc (G-1718)*

National Handicapped Workshop...............................765 287-8331
5900 W Kilgore Ave Muncie (47304) *(G-10538)*

National Ice Corp..317 887-9446
5333 Commerce Square Dr F Indianapolis (46237) *(G-7572)*

National Lib Bindery Co of Ind.................................317 636-5606
55 S State Ave Ste 100 Indianapolis (46201) *(G-7573)*

National Material LP...219 397-5088
4506 Cline Ave East Chicago (46312) *(G-2554)*

National Notification Ctr LLC..................................317 613-6060
20 N Meridian St Ste 300 Indianapolis (46204) *(G-7574)*

National Office Furniture Inc (HQ)............................812 482-1600
1610 Royal St Jasper (47549) *(G-8298)*

National Oilwell Varco Inc.....................................317 897-3099
9870 E 30th St Indianapolis (46229) *(G-7575)*

National Printfast, Indianapolis *Also called Kingery Group Inc (G-7354)*

National Printing Converters, Brazil *Also called NP Converters Inc (G-973)*

National Products Inc..574 457-4565
201 E Medusa St Syracuse (46567) *(G-13138)*

National Products LLC...219 393-5536
1st Rd Kingsbury Indus Pa Kingsbury (46345) *(G-8543)*

National Rcreation Systems Inc................................260 482-6023
1300-D Airport N Off Park Fort Wayne (46825) *(G-4491)*

National Retail Hardware Assn.................................317 290-0338
136 N Delaware St Ste 200 Indianapolis (46204) *(G-7576)*

National Screen Printing Co, Indianapolis *Also called High End Concepts Inc (G-7106)*

National Stock Dog Registry, Butler *Also called International English Inc (G-1231)*

National Tube Form, Fort Wayne *Also called Whipp In Holdings LLC (G-4752)*

National Tube Form, Fort Wayne *Also called Nelson Global Products Inc (G-4493)*

Nationwide Publishing Company...............................260 312-3924
12110 Glen Lake Dr Fort Wayne (46814) *(G-4492)*

Native Crossbows LLC...765 641-2224
2310 Broadway St Anderson (46012) *(G-142)*

Natural Answers..219 922-3663
2300 Ramblewood Dr Ste C Highland (46322) *(G-6052)*

Natural Coating Systems.......................................765 642-2464
3220 W 25th St Anderson (46011) *(G-143)*

Natural Lighting LLC...574 907-9457
29618 County Road 146 Nappanee (46550) *(G-10697)*

Naturegenic Inc (PA)...765 807-5525
1281 Win Hentschel Blvd West Lafayette (47906) *(G-14089)*

Natures Alpine Solutions, Corydon *Also called Nachurs Alpine Solutions Corp (G-2106)*

Natures Woodshop LLC..317 691-1462
7438 Cotherstone Ct Indianapolis (46256) *(G-7577)*

Naval Surface Wrfre Cntr Cran, Crane *Also called Military Facilities (G-2129)*

Navistar Cmponent Holdings LLC (HQ)........................317 352-4500
5565 Brookville Rd Indianapolis (46219) *(G-7578)*

Navspar Industries LLC..812 344-1476
1671 Wrenwood Dr Columbus (47201) *(G-1979)*

NC Coatings LLC...574 213-4754
30338 County Road 56 Nappanee (46550) *(G-10698)*

NCH Corporation...317 899-3660
8401 E 33rd St Indianapolis (46226) *(G-7579)*

Nci Group Inc..317 392-3536
1780 Mccall Dr Shelbyville (46176) *(G-12553)*

Ncp Coatings Inc..574 255-9678
1413 Clover Rd Mishawaka (46545) *(G-10094)*

Ncs Pearson Inc...317 297-0259
2629 Waterfront Pkwy E Dr Indianapolis (46214) *(G-7580)*

ND Prints..
3924 W Washington St Indianapolis (46241) *(G-7581)*

Nda Energized Coatings.......................................260 499-0307
855 E Mishawaka Rd Elkhart (46517) *(G-3058)*

Ndiana Warm Floors Inc.......................................260 668-8836
935 N 275 W Ste B Angola (46703) *(G-232)*

Nea LLC..574 295-0024
131 W Marion St Elkhart (46516) *(G-3059)*

Nebo Ridge Bicycles, Carmel *Also called Nebo Ridge Enterprises LLC (G-1441)*

Nebo Ridge Enterprises LLC...................................317 471-1089
4335 W 106th St Ste 900 Carmel (46032) *(G-1441)*

Nechanna One Productions Corp..............................317 400-8908
11252 Redskin Ln Apt G Indianapolis (46235) *(G-7582)*

Nector Machine & Fabricating..................................219 322-6878
595 Kennedy Ave Schererville (46375) *(G-12338)*

Neeta Sweet Cupcakes n Minis................................574 286-7032
52101 Goldenrod Ln Granger (46530) *(G-5426)*

Nello Capital Inc (PA)..574 288-3632
105 E Jefferson Blvd South Bend (46601) *(G-12869)*

Nello Corporation, South Bend *Also called Nello Inc (G-12870)*

Nello Inc (HQ)...574 288-3632
1201 S Sheridan St South Bend (46619) *(G-12870)*

Nelson Acquisition LLC..574 753-6377
130 E Industrial Blvd Logansport (46947) *(G-9358)*

Nelson Global Products Inc................................608 719-1752
  3405 Engle Rd Fort Wayne (46809) *(G-4493)*

Nelson J Hochstetler.......................................260 499-0315
  1935 W 450 N Howe (46746) *(G-6130)*

Nelson Tube Company, Logansport Also called Nelson Acquisition LLC *(G-9358)*

Nemco Medical Ltd..260 484-1500
  8727 Clinton Park Dr Fort Wayne (46825) *(G-4494)*

Nemcomed Fw LLC..260 480-5226
  8551 N Clinton St Fort Wayne (46825) *(G-4495)*

Nemcomed Instrs & Implants...............................800 255-4576
  8727 Clinton Park Dr Fort Wayne (46825) *(G-4496)*

Nemesis Race Cars...812 361-9743
  6155 S Ison Rd Bloomington (47403) *(G-778)*

Neo Industries Inc (HQ)....................................574 217-4078
  1400 E Angela Blvd South Bend (46617) *(G-12871)*

Neo Industries LLC..219 762-6075
  1775 Willowcreek Rd Portage (46368) *(G-11781)*

Neo Industries (indiana) Inc.............................219 762-6075
  1775 Willowcreek Rd Portage (46368) *(G-11782)*

Neo Magnequench Dist LLC................................765 778-7809
  237 S Pendleton Ave Pendleton (46064) *(G-11496)*

Neodyne Technologies, Indianapolis Also called Robert Perez *(G-7849)*

Neon Accents..812 537-0102
  101 W Eads Pkwy Lawrenceburg (47025) *(G-9148)*

Neon Bay...574 583-6366
  5014 E Indiana Beach Rd Monticello (47960) *(G-10273)*

Neon Cactus...765 743-6081
  360 Brown St Lafayette (47901) *(G-8975)*

Neon Glassworks LLC..765 497-1135
  3330 Crawford St West Lafayette (47906) *(G-14090)*

Neon Safety Group LLC.....................................317 774-5144
  6896 Carters Grove Dr Noblesville (46062) *(G-11157)*

Neosphere Energy Inc.......................................219 781-7893
  1802 Robinhood Blvd Ste 4 Schererville (46375) *(G-12339)*

Neoteric Hovercraft, Terre Haute Also called Neoteric Incorporated *(G-13289)*

Neoteric Incorporated......................................812 234-1120
  1649 Tippecanoe St Terre Haute (47807) *(G-13289)*

Neptune Flotation LLC.......................................317 588-3600
  101 W 103rd St Indianapolis (46290) *(G-6274)*

NERP LLC...574 303-6377
  58016 Crumstown Hwy South Bend (46619) *(G-12872)*

Nerx Biosciences Inc...317 251-7408
  351 W 10th St Ste 510 Indianapolis (46202) *(G-7583)*

Nestle Dreyers Ice Cream Co.............................260 483-3102
  3426 N Wells St Fort Wayne (46808) *(G-4497)*

Nestle Usa Inc..765 778-6000
  4301 W 73rd St Anderson (46011) *(G-144)*

Nestor Sales LLC...574 295-5535
  205 County Road 17 Elkhart (46516) *(G-3060)*

Netshape Technologies LLC (HQ).........................812 248-9273
  14670 Cumberland Rd Noblesville (46060) *(G-11158)*

Netshape Technologies LLC................................812 755-4501
  596 W Oak St Campbellsburg (47108) *(G-1278)*

Neubau Contracting..970 406-8084
  1701 E Circle Dr Bloomington (47401) *(G-779)*

Neuhaus Industrial Machining I............................260 710-2845
  1830 Wayne Trce Fort Wayne (46803) *(G-4498)*

Neull Incorporated..574 267-5575
  4002 N State Road 15 Warsaw (46582) *(G-13912)*

Neumayr Lumber Co Inc.....................................765 764-4148
  401 S Union St Attica (47918) *(G-308)*

New Age Equipment Inc.....................................765 659-1524
  3309 Washington Ave Frankfort (46041) *(G-4843)*

New Albany Tribune, New Albany Also called Cnhi LLC *(G-10762)*

New Aqua LLC (PA)...317 272-3000
  7785 E Us Highway 36 Avon (46123) *(G-456)*

New Business Corporation..................................219 886-2700
  444 Rutledge St Gary (46404) *(G-5079)*

New Carbon Company LLC (PA)...........................574 247-2270
  4101 Wliam Richardson Dr South Bend (46628) *(G-12873)*

New Castle Courier Times, New Castle Also called Courier-Times Inc *(G-10897)*

New Castle Foundry, New Castle Also called Grede LLC *(G-10903)*

New Castle Modular Inc.....................................765 521-0788
  6990 W Washington St Indianapolis (46241) *(G-7584)*

New Castle Saw Mill..765 529-6635
  2910 Outer Dr New Castle (47362) *(G-10913)*

New Concept Metal Detector..............................765 447-2681
  511 N Earl Ave Lafayette (47904) *(G-8976)*

New Dalton Foundry LLC (PA)..............................574 267-8111
  1900 E Jefferson St Warsaw (46580) *(G-13913)*

New Die Concepts Inc..260 420-9504
  302 E Wallace St Fort Wayne (46803) *(G-4499)*

New Elements LLC..219 465-1389
  212 Morthland Dr Valparaiso (46383) *(G-13587)*

New England Sheets LLC....................................978 487-2500
  3600 Wdview Trce Ste 300 Indianapolis (46268) *(G-7585)*

New Haven Bakery, New Haven Also called Ganal Corporation *(G-10940)*

New Haven Trophies & Shirts..............................260 749-0269
  710 Broadway St New Haven (46774) *(G-10949)*

New Holland Richmond Inc..................................765 962-7724
  3100 W Industries Rd Richmond (47374) *(G-12023)*

New Hope Services Inc (PA)................................812 288-8248
  725 Wall St Jeffersonville (47130) *(G-8403)*

New Hope Services Inc......................................812 752-4892
  1642 W Mcclain Ave Ste 1 Scottsburg (47170) *(G-12377)*

New Horizons Baking Company............................260 495-7055
  700 W Water St Fremont (46737) *(G-4970)*

New Image Prtg & Design Inc..............................260 969-0410
  3233 Lafayette St Fort Wayne (46806) *(G-4500)*

New Image Travel LLC.......................................812 426-1423
  2336 Glenview Dr Evansville (47720) *(G-3643)*

New Market Plastics Inc (PA)..............................317 758-5494
  10099 S Us Highway 231 Ladoga (47954) *(G-8841)*

New Market Welding, New Market Also called Joe Woodrow *(G-10963)*

New Mlennium Bldg Systems LLC (HQ)...................260 969-3500
  7575 W Jefferson Blvd Fort Wayne (46804) *(G-4501)*

New Mlennium Bldg Systems LLC.........................260 868-6000
  6115 County Road 42 Butler (46721) *(G-1236)*

New Nello Operating Co LLC...............................574 288-3632
  1201 S Sheridan St South Bend (46619) *(G-12874)*

New Ngc Inc..812 247-2424
  9720 Us Highway 50 Shoals (47581) *(G-12667)*

New Ngc Inc..219 866-7570
  1325 E Maple St Rensselaer (47978) *(G-11933)*

New Ngc Inc..765 828-0898
  75 Ivy Ln Clinton (47842) *(G-1718)*

New Paradigms Industrial Art..............................219 762-4046
  6520 Lakewood Ave Portage (46368) *(G-11783)*

New Philosopher Prss..406 992-5791
  5156 N Brummetts Creek Rd Bloomington (47408) *(G-780)*

New Point Products Inc......................................812 663-6311
  8563 E State Rte 46 New Point (47263) *(G-11003)*

New Point Products Martguild, New Point Also called New Point Products Inc *(G-11003)*

New Point Stone Co Inc (PA)...............................812 663-2021
  992 S County Road 800 E Greensburg (47240) *(G-5627)*

New Point Stone Co Inc.....................................812 663-2422
  3671 S County Road 220 Sw Greensburg (47240) *(G-5628)*

New Point Stone Co Inc.....................................812 852-4225
  8792 N County Road 300 W Batesville (47006) *(G-512)*

New Point Stone Co Inc.....................................765 698-2227
  24031 Derbyshire Rd Laurel (47024) *(G-9128)*

New Process Graphics LLC..................................260 489-1700
  310 W Cook Rd Fort Wayne (46825) *(G-4502)*

New Process Steel LP..260 868-1445
  4258 County Road 61 Butler (46721) *(G-1237)*

New Readers Press...317 514-6515
  6414 Woodhaven Ct Avon (46123) *(G-457)*

New Style of Crossroads LLC..............................260 593-3800
  9585 W 700 S Topeka (46571) *(G-13424)*

New Vision Manufacturing Inc.............................812 522-5585
  835 E 10th St Seymour (47274) *(G-12471)*

New Wolcott Enterprise......................................219 279-2167
  125 W Market St Wolcott (47995) *(G-14367)*

New York Blower Company..................................217 347-3233
  171 Factory St La Porte (46350) *(G-8799)*

New-Indy Containerboard, Hartford City Also called New-Indy Hartford City LLC *(G-5986)*

New-Indy Hartford City LLC (HQ)..........................765 348-5440
  501 S Spring St Hartford City (47348) *(G-5986)*

New-Indy Hartford City LLC.................................260 347-4739
  606 Uhl Dr Kendallville (46755) *(G-8499)*

Newbury Farm & Logging LLC.............................574 825-9969
  3650 N 1150 W Shipshewana (46565) *(G-12639)*

Newco Metals Inc...765 644-6649
  1515 E 22nd St Anderson (46016) *(G-145)*

Newco Metals Inc (PA).......................................317 485-7721
  7268 S State Road 13 Pendleton (46064) *(G-11497)*

Newco Metals Processing, Bedford Also called Recycling Services Indiana Inc *(G-572)*

Newcomb Printing Services Inc...........................219 874-3201
  605 E 9th St Michigan City (46360) *(G-9763)*

Newjac Inc..765 483-2190
  415 S Grant St Lebanon (46052) *(G-9209)*

Newlett Inc..574 294-8899
  435 Harrison St Elkhart (46516) *(G-3061)*

Newlins Welding & Tank Maint............................765 245-2741
  5360 W Us Highway 36 Montezuma (47862) *(G-10210)*

Newman Logging Inc...260 351-3550
  6340 E 700 S Wolcottville (46795) *(G-14375)*

Newmar Corporation (PA)...................................574 773-7791
  355 Delaware St Nappanee (46550) *(G-10699)*

Newport Pallet Inc..217 497-8220
  1888 S State Rd 63 Newport (47966) *(G-11056)*

Newport Pallet Inc..765 505-9463
  1110 W Industrial Dr Hillsdale (47854) *(G-6061)*

News & Tribune, New Albany Also called Southern Indiana Bus Source *(G-10863)*

News 4 U Magazine, Evansville Also called Emp of Evansville *(G-3476)*

News and Sun, Dunkirk Also called Graphic Printing Co Inc *(G-2484)*

News and Tribune..812 206-2168
  221 Spring St Jeffersonville (47130) *(G-8404)*

News Banner Publications Inc 260 824-0224
  125 N Johnson St Bluffton (46714) *(G-883)*

News Dispatch (HQ) 219 874-7211
  422 Franklin St Ste B Michigan City (46360) *(G-9823)*

News Examiner Circulation Dept 765 825-2914
  406 N Central Ave Connersville (47331) *(G-2066)*

News Publishing Company LLC (HQ) 812 547-3424
  537 Main St Tell City (47586) *(G-13169)*

News Publishing Company LLC (HQ) 502 633-4334
  542 7th St Tell City (47586) *(G-13170)*

News Publishing Company LLC 812 649-4440
  541 Main St Rockport (47635) *(G-12171)*

News Publishing Company LLC 812 838-4811
  132 E 2nd St Mount Vernon (47620) *(G-10404)*

News Publishing Company Inc (HQ) 260 461-8444
  600 W Main St Fort Wayne (46802) *(G-4503)*

News Reminder 574 583-5121
  114 S Main St Monticello (47960) *(G-10274)*

News-Gazette 765 584-4501
  224 W Franklin St Winchester (47394) *(G-14338)*

News-Sentinel, Fort Wayne *Also called Fort Wayne Newspapers Inc (G-4277)*

News-Sun, The, Fairmount *Also called Allen C Terhune & Associates (G-3828)*

News-Times, Hartford City *Also called Hartford City News Times (G-5982)*

Newsletter Express Ltd 317 876-8916
  3500 Depauw Blvd Ste 1000 Indianapolis (46268) *(G-7586)*

Newsom Industries Inc 812 372-2844
  1919 15th St Columbus (47201) *(G-1980)*

Newspaper Holding Inc 812 231-4200
  222 S 7th St Terre Haute (47807) *(G-13290)*

Newspaper Holding Inc 812 254-0480
  102 E Van Trees St Washington (47501) *(G-13993)*

Newspaper Solutions, Avon *Also called Ao Inc (G-427)*

Newton Business Forms 812 256-5399
  104 Bates Dr Charlestown (47111) *(G-1575)*

Newton County Enterprises Inc 219 474-5532
  305 E Graham St Kentland (47951) *(G-8522)*

Newton County Stone Co, Kentland *Also called Rogers Group Inc (G-8523)*

Nexgen Mold & Tool Inc 812 945-3375
  4300 Security Pkwy New Albany (47150) *(G-10833)*

Next Day Signs, Indianapolis *Also called Sign Guys Inc (G-7943)*

Next Day Signs, Indianapolis *Also called D D McKay and Associates (G-6721)*

Next Day Signs 574 259-7446
  13565 Us 20 Mishawaka (46545) *(G-10095)*

Next Day Signs & Images, Mishawaka *Also called Next Day Signs (G-10095)*

Next Products LLC 317 392-4701
  2201 E Michigan Rd Shelbyville (46176) *(G-12554)*

Nextremity Solutions Inc 732 383-7901
  210 N Buffalo St Warsaw (46580) *(G-13914)*

Nexus Valve Inc 317 257-6050
  9982 E 121st St Fishers (46037) *(G-3948)*

Nexxt Spine LLC 317 436-7801
  14425 Bergen Blvd Ste B Noblesville (46060) *(G-11159)*

Nf Friction Composites Inc 414 365-1550
  1441 Holland St Logansport (46947) *(G-9359)*

Ngh Retail LLC 219 476-0772
  315 E 316 N Ste A Valparaiso (46383) *(G-13588)*

Ngh Retail LLC 219 476-0772
  301 W 550 N Valparaiso (46385) *(G-13589)*

Nginstruments Inc 574 268-2112
  4643 N State Road 15 Warsaw (46582) *(G-13915)*

Nhk Seating of America Inc (HQ) 765 659-4781
  2298 W State Road 28 Frankfort (46041) *(G-4844)*

Niagara Bottling LLC 909 758-5313
  1250 Whitaker Rd Plainfield (46168) *(G-11629)*

Niagara Lasalle Corporation 800 262-2558
  1412 150th St Hammond (46327) *(G-5921)*

Niagara Lasalle Corporation (HQ) 219 853-6000
  1412 150th St Hammond (46327) *(G-5922)*

Nibco Inc (PA) 574 295-3000
  1516 Middlebury St Elkhart (46516) *(G-3062)*

Nibco Inc 812 256-8500
  105 Quality Ct Charlestown (47111) *(G-1576)*

Nibco Inc 574 296-1240
  701 Eisenhower Dr N Goshen (46526) *(G-5298)*

Nibco Inc 812 256-8500
  204 Pike St Charlestown (47111) *(G-1577)*

Niblock Excavating Inc (PA) 574 848-4437
  906 Maple St Bristol (46507) *(G-1074)*

Niblock Excavating Inc 260 248-2100
  1080 Spartan Dr Ste C Columbia City (46725) *(G-1812)*

Nice-Pak Products Inc 845 365-1700
  1 Nice Pak Rd Mooresville (46158) *(G-10328)*

Nice-Pak Products Inc 317 839-0373
  381 Airtech Pkwy Plainfield (46168) *(G-11630)*

Nicholas Precision Works LLC 260 306-3426
  1101 Taylor St North Manchester (46962) *(G-11237)*

Nicholls Printing 574 233-1388
  1219 Mishawaka Ave South Bend (46615) *(G-12875)*

Nichols Mfg Co Inc 219 696-8577
  1006 W 203rd Ave Lowell (46356) *(G-9418)*

Nichols Operating LLC 812 753-3600
  8157 S 100 W Fort Branch (47648) *(G-4028)*

Nicholson & Sons Printing Inc 812 283-1200
  209 Eastern Blvd Jeffersonville (47130) *(G-8405)*

Nicholson Group LLC 219 926-3528
  450 E 1400 N Chesterton (46304) *(G-1624)*

Nicholson Printing, Jeffersonville *Also called Nicholson & Sons Printing Inc (G-8405)*

Nick-Em Builders LLC 574 516-1060
  1005 W Broadway Logansport (46947) *(G-9360)*

Nickel Enterprises, Elkhart *Also called Patrick Industries Inc (G-3083)*

Nickell Moulding Company Inc 574 295-5223
  3015 Mobile Dr Elkhart (46514) *(G-3063)*

Nickolick Development 812 422-8526
  4209 Highway 41 N Ste 26 Evansville (47711) *(G-3644)*

Nickolick, Joe J, Evansville *Also called Nickolick Development (G-3644)*

Nickprint Inc (PA) 317 489-3033
  484 E Carmel Dr Carmel (46032) *(G-1442)*

Nicks Automotive Inc 765 964-6843
  2741 N 700 E Union City (47390) *(G-13458)*

Nicorr LLC 574 353-1700
  1260 20th Rd Tippecanoe (46570) *(G-13384)*

Nidec Motor Corporation 812 385-2564
  1551 E Broadway St Princeton (47670) *(G-11880)*

Nidec Motor Corporation 317 328-4079
  2831 Waterfront Pkwy E Dr Indianapolis (46214) *(G-7587)*

Nielsen Company 812 889-3493
  1602 S 1066 W Lexington (47138) *(G-9254)*

Nielsen Enterprises Inc 574 277-3748
  51950 Chicory Ln Granger (46530) *(G-5427)*

Nik-O-Lok Company, Indianapolis *Also called Standard Change-Makers Inc (G-7988)*

Nike Inc 219 879-1320
  917 Lighthouse Pl Michigan City (46360) *(G-9824)*

Nippon Steel & Sumikin 219 228-0110
  400 Northbrook Dr Shelbyville (46176) *(G-12555)*

Nipro Phrmpckging Amricas Corp 812 591-2332
  1108 N State Road 3 Westport (47283) *(G-14210)*

Nisco, Topeka *Also called Nishikawa Cooper LLC (G-13425)*

Nishikawa Cooper LLC 260 593-2156
  2785 Persistence Dr Fort Wayne (46808) *(G-4504)*

Nishikawa Cooper LLC (HQ) 260 593-2156
  324 Morrow St Topeka (46571) *(G-13425)*

Nishikawa Cooper LLC 574 546-5938
  501 High Rd Bremen (46506) *(G-1012)*

Nishikawa of America Inc (HQ) 260 593-2156
  324 Morrow St Topeka (46571) *(G-13426)*

Nisley, L R & Sons, Goshen *Also called L R Nisley & Sons (G-5261)*

Nisource Inc 877 647-5990
  2755 Raystone Dr Valparaiso (46383) *(G-13590)*

Nistem, Zionsville *Also called Nitto Inc (G-14451)*

Nitrex Inc 317 346-7700
  350 Blue Chip Ct Franklin (46131) *(G-4913)*

Nitto Inc 317 879-2840
  10505 Bennett Pkwy 300 Zionsville (46077) *(G-14451)*

Nix Bus Sales Inc 812 464-2576
  Hwy 165 N Poseyville (47633) *(G-11858)*

Nix Equipment LLC 812 874-2231
  160 W Main St Poseyville (47633) *(G-11859)*

Nix Sanitary Service 812 475-9774
  703 S 2nd St Boonville (47601) *(G-919)*

Nixon Tool Co Inc 765 966-6608
  301 N 3rd St Richmond (47374) *(G-12024)*

NJ Logging LLC 812 597-0782
  1825 W Three Story Hl Rd Morgantown (46160) *(G-10357)*

Nlmk Indiana LLC 219 787-8200
  6500 S Boundary Rd Portage (46368) *(G-11784)*

NM Industries LLC 812 985-3608
  300 Kirchoff Blvd Evansville (47712) *(G-3645)*

Nmc Inc 812 648-2636
  8068 E Main St Dugger (47848) *(G-2482)*

Nmm Electric 219 864-9688
  1900 Hart St Dyer (46311) *(G-2504)*

No Pass LLC 516 713-6885
  2512 Lauren Ln Kokomo (46901) *(G-8676)*

No Sag 260 347-2600
  2225 Production Rd Kendallville (46755) *(G-8500)*

No-Load Fund Investor Inc 317 571-1471
  10534 Coppergate Carmel (46032) *(G-1443)*

No-Sail Splash Guard Co Inc 765 522-2100
  10254 N Us Highway 231 Roachdale (46172) *(G-12094)*

Noah Worcester Derm Society 317 257-5907
  8365 Keystone Xing Indianapolis (46240) *(G-7588)*

Nobbe Concrete Products Inc 765 647-4017
  11177 Us Highway 52 Brookville (47012) *(G-1121)*

Noble Composites Inc 574 533-1462
  2424 E Kercher Rd Goshen (46526) *(G-5299)*

Noble County Welding Inc 260 897-4082
  635 S Van Scoyoc St Avilla (46710) *(G-416)*

(PA)=Parent Co (HQ)=Headquarters (DH)=Div Headquarters

Noble Industrial Fabrications, Avilla *Also called Noble County Welding Inc* **(G-416)**

Noble Industries Inc 317 773-1926
17575 Presley Dr Noblesville (46060) **(G-11160)**

Noble Wire Products Inc 317 773-1926
101 Madsen St Orland (46776) **(G-11354)**

Noblesville Daily Times, The, Noblesville *Also called Schurz Communications Inc* **(G-11180)**

Noblesville Pack & Ship 317 776-6306
199 N 9th St Noblesville (46060) **(G-11161)**

Noblesville Sand & Gravel, Noblesville *Also called Marietta Martin Materials Inc* **(G-11145)**

Noblitt Fabricating, Columbus *Also called Noblitt International Corp* **(G-1981)**

Noblitt International Corp 812 372-9969
4735 N Indianapolis Rd Columbus (47203) **(G-1981)**

Nochar Inc 317 613-3046
8650 Commerce Park Pl K Indianapolis (46268) **(G-7589)**

Noel Studio Inc 317 297-1117
75 N Main St Zionsville (46077) **(G-14452)**

Noel-Smyser Engineering Corp 317 293-2215
4005 Industrial Blvd Indianapolis (46254) **(G-7590)**

Noir Magazine, Highland *Also called It Factor Publications Inc* **(G-6050)**

Nolan Brubaker Software LLC 574 238-0676
434 S Silverwood Ln A Goshen (46526) **(G-5300)**

Nolan Co, Jeffersonville *Also called Eagle Industries Inc* **(G-8353)**

Nomanco Trailers 765 833-6711
State Road 400 N Roann (46974) **(G-12097)**

Nonferrous Products Inc 317 738-2558
401 Arvin Rd Franklin (46131) **(G-4914)**

Noodle Alley 574 258-1889
2370 Miracle Ln Mishawaka (46545) **(G-10096)**

Noodle Shop Co - Colorado Inc 219 548-0921
71 Silhavy Rd Ste 101 Valparaiso (46383) **(G-13591)**

Nor-Cote International Inc 800 488-9180
506 Lafayette Ave Crawfordsville (47933) **(G-2176)**

Nor-Cote International Inc (HQ) 765 230-7252
605 Lafayette Ave Crawfordsville (47933) **(G-2177)**

Nor-Cote International Inc 765 362-9180
605 Lafayette Ave Crawfordsville (47933) **(G-2178)**

Norco Industries 800 347-2232
2800 Northland Dr Elkhart (46514) **(G-3064)**

Norco Industries Inc 574 262-3400
2600 Jeanwood Dr Elkhart (46514) **(G-3065)**

Norlightspresscom 812 675-8054
762 State Road 458 Bedford (47421) **(G-566)**

Normal City Music Co 765 289-2041
2112 W Berwyn Rd Muncie (47304) **(G-10539)**

Norman Stein & Associates 260 749-5468
9520 Paulding Rd New Haven (46774) **(G-10950)**

Norman Tool Inc 812 867-3496
15415 Old State Rd Albion (47725) **(G-3646)**

Norres North America Inc 855 667-7370
2520 Foundation Dr South Bend (46628) **(G-12876)**

Norris Thermal Tech Inc 574 353-7855
7930 N 700 E Tippecanoe (46570) **(G-13385)**

Norstam Veneers Inc 812 732-4391
2990 Overlook Dr Sw Mauckport (47142) **(G-9658)**

North America Packaging Corp 317 291-2396
6061 Guion Rd Indianapolis (46254) **(G-7591)**

North America Packaging Corp 219 462-8915
4002 Montdale Park Dr Valparaiso (46383) **(G-13592)**

North American Composites, Mishawaka *Also called Interplastic Corporation* **(G-10054)**

North American Extrusn & Assem 260 636-3336
200 E Park Dr Albion (46701) **(G-30)**

North American Latex Corp 812 268-6608
49 Industrial Park Dr Sullivan (47882) **(G-13089)**

North American Lighting Inc 812 983-2663
11833 Industrial Park Dr Elberfeld (47613) **(G-2637)**

North American Manufacturing 765 948-3337
619 E Jefferson St Fairmount (46928) **(G-3833)**

North American Signs Inc (PA) 574 234-5252
3601 Lathrop St South Bend (46628) **(G-12877)**

North American Stamping Group, Muncie *Also called Nasg Indiana LLC* **(G-10537)**

North Central Ind Shavings LLC 765 395-3875
307 E Dunn St Converse (46919) **(G-2080)**

North Central Pallets Inc 574 892-6142
13990 State Road 10 Argos (46501) **(G-276)**

North Coast Organics LLC 260 246-0289
629 E Wash Blvd Fort Wyne Fort Wayne (46802) **(G-4505)**

North Enterprises Inc 765 362-4410
123 E Main St Crawfordsville (47933) **(G-2179)**

North Manchester Ethanol LLC 260 774-3532
868 E 800 N North Manchester (46962) **(G-11238)**

North Star Distributing, Lafayette *Also called Ice Cream Specialties Inc* **(G-8919)**

North Star Signs Inc 219 365-5935
9117 Fairbanks St Crown Point (46307) **(G-2279)**

North Star Stone Inc 219 464-7272
312 N 325 E Valparaiso (46383) **(G-13593)**

North Street Companies LLC 317 457-4520
216 W North St Greenfield (46140) **(G-5561)**

North Vernon Division, North Vernon *Also called Martinrea Industries Inc* **(G-11269)**

North Vernon Electric Inc 812 392-2985
1511 E Buckeye St North Vernon (47265) **(G-11271)**

North Vernon Plain Dlr & Sun 812 346-3973
528 E O And M Ave North Vernon (47265) **(G-11272)**

North Vernon Sun, North Vernon *Also called North Vernon Plain Dlr & Sun* **(G-11272)**

North Webster Construction Inc 574 834-4448
7240 N State Road 13 North Webster (46555) **(G-11297)**

North Woods Village 574 247-1866
1409 E Day Rd Mishawaka (46545) **(G-10097)**

Northbend Pattern Works Inc 812 637-3000
28080 Ziegler Blvd West Harrison (47060) **(G-14041)**

Northeast Machine & Tool Co 317 823-6594
10655 E 59th St Indianapolis (46236) **(G-7592)**

Northern Box Company Inc 574 264-2161
1328 Mishawaka St Elkhart (46514) **(G-3066)**

Northern Brace Co Inc (PA) 574 233-4221
610 N Michigan St Ste 104 South Bend (46601) **(G-12878)**

Northern Brace Nthrn Prsthtics, South Bend *Also called Northern Brace Co Inc* **(G-12878)**

Northern Division, Indianapolis *Also called Altec Industries Inc* **(G-6379)**

Northern Gases and Sups Inc (PA) 574 594-2551
1426 S State Road 13 Pierceton (46562) **(G-11574)**

Northern Ind Indus Catings LLC 574 893-4621
619 E Main St Akron (46910) **(G-6)**

Northern Indiana Manufacturing (PA) 574 342-2105
202 S Ecker Ave Bourbon (46504) **(G-946)**

Northern Indiana Mfg, Chesterton *Also called Electro Seal Corporation* **(G-1603)**

Northern Indiana Oil LLC 765 749-3791
212 W 10th St Ste D365 Indianapolis (46202) **(G-7593)**

Northern Indiana Ordnance Co 574 289-5938
60161 Mayflower Rd South Bend (46614) **(G-12879)**

Northern Indiana Packg Co Inc (HQ) 260 356-9660
1200 Riverfork Dr Huntington (46750) **(G-6232)**

Northern Indiana Truss 574 858-0505
2208 N 500 W Warsaw (46580) **(G-13916)**

Northern Prosthetics Inc 574 233-2459
610 N Michigan St Ste 104 South Bend (46601) **(G-12880)**

Northern Tool and Die 260 495-7314
501 E Depot St Fremont (46737) **(G-4971)**

Northern Trans & Differential 219 764-4009
6641 Melton Rd Portage (46368) **(G-11785)**

Northern Wood Products Inc 574 586-3068
3573 Thorn Rd Walkerton (46574) **(G-13807)**

Northfield Block Company 800 424-0190
901 E Troy Ave Indianapolis (46203) **(G-7594)**

Northside Machine, Dugger *Also called Nmc Inc* **(G-2482)**

Northside Machine & Tool Inc 765 654-4538
1604 N County Road 0 Ew Frankfort (46041) **(G-4845)**

Northside Machining Inc 812 683-3500
407 W 12th St Huntingburg (47542) **(G-6176)**

Northside Pattern Works Inc 317 290-0501
4370 Saguaro Trl Indianapolis (46268) **(G-7595)**

Northtech Machine LLC 812 967-7400
102 Walnut St Borden (47106) **(G-936)**

Northwest Alum Fabricators Inc 219 844-4354
6103 Kennedy Ave Hammond (46323) **(G-5923)**

Northwest Electric Connection 219 465-5205
5894 Hollow Oak Trl Carmel (46033) **(G-1444)**

Northwest Farm Fertilizers 219 785-2331
4725 S Us Highway 421 Westville (46391) **(G-14220)**

Northwest Indus Specialist 219 397-7446
4333 Indianapolis Blvd East Chicago (46312) **(G-2555)**

Northwest Interiors Inc 574 294-2326
405 Pine Creek Ct Elkhart (46516) **(G-3067)**

Northwest News & Printing 260 637-9003
3306 Independence Dr Fort Wayne (46808) **(G-4506)**

Northwind Electronics LLC 317 288-0787
8875 Bash St Indianapolis (46256) **(G-7596)**

Northwind Pharmaceuticals LLC 800 722-0772
212 W 10th St Ste A310 Indianapolis (46202) **(G-7597)**

Norton Packaging Inc 574 867-6002
5190 N Industrial Pkwy Hamlet (46532) **(G-5831)**

Notables 765 649-1648
1325 Meridian St Anderson (46016) **(G-146)**

Notre Dame Press, Notre Dame *Also called University Notre Dame Du Lac* **(G-11305)**

Nouvex, New Albany *Also called Poly Group LLC* **(G-10846)**

Nov Oak Woodworking 812 422-1973
913 Washington Ave Evansville (47713) **(G-3647)**

Nova Flex Group 317 334-1444
7812 Moller Rd Indianapolis (46268) **(G-7598)**

Nova Graphics Inc 317 577-6682
7805 E 89th St Indianapolis (46256) **(G-7599)**

Nova Manufacturing 512 750-5165
1153 S Avon Ave Avon (46123) **(G-458)**

Nova Packaging Group Inc 765 651-2600
2409 W 2nd St Marion (46952) **(G-9548)**

Nova Pak, Marion *Also called Nova Packaging Group Inc* **(G-9548)**

Nova Polymers Incorporated 812 476-0339
2650 Eastside Park Rd Evansville (47715) **(G-3648)**

Novacove LLC 219 775-2966
4162 Viva Ln Indianapolis (46239) *(G-7600)*

Novae Corp 260 982-7075
11870 N 650 E North Manchester (46962) *(G-11239)*

Novae Corp (PA) 260 758-9800
1 Novae Pkwy Markle (46770) *(G-9581)*

Novaprints, Indianapolis *Also called Nova Graphics Inc (G-7599)*

Novartis Animal Health US Inc 317 276-2348
2500 Innovation Way N Greenfield (46140) *(G-5562)*

Novartis Corporation 317 852-3839
30 Lakeshore Pl Brownsburg (46112) *(G-1161)*

Novelis Corporation 812 462-2287
5901 N 13th St Terre Haute (47805) *(G-13291)*

Novels By Nellotie 812 583-1196
393 Sonny Dorsett Rd Mitchell (47446) *(G-10168)*

Novipax LLC 201 791-7600
7950 Allison Ave Indianapolis (46268) *(G-7601)*

Novolex Inc 812 346-1066
1001 2nd St North Vernon (47265) *(G-11273)*

NP Converters Inc 812 448-2555
18 S Murphy Ave Brazil (47834) *(G-973)*

Npp Packaging Graphics 317 522-2010
610 White Oak Ct Zionsville (46077) *(G-14453)*

NPS Xofigo Mfg Plant 5889 .... 317 981-4129
4343 N 62nd St Indianapolis (46268) *(G-7602)*

NRC Modifications Inc 574 825-3646
51045 Greenfield Pkwy Middlebury (46540) *(G-9912)*

Nrk Inc 812 232-1800
1126 S 13th St Terre Haute (47802) *(G-13292)*

Nrp Jones LLC (PA) 219 362-4508
302 Philadelphia St La Porte (46350) *(G-8800)*

Nsa Crane 812 854-4723
300 Highway 361 Crane (47522) *(G-2130)*

Nsignia Screenprinting, Fort Wayne *Also called Brenmeer LLC (G-4120)*

NSK Corporation 317 837-8879
1581 Perry Rd Ste A Plainfield (46168) *(G-11631)*

NSK Corporation 765 458-5000
1112 E Kitchel Rd Liberty (47353) *(G-9267)*

NSK Corporation, Liberty Plant, Liberty *Also called NSK Corporation (G-9267)*

NSK Corporation, Plainfield Wh, Plainfield *Also called NSK Corporation (G-11631)*

NSK Precision America Hq, Franklin *Also called NSK Precision America Inc (G-4915)*

NSK Precision America Inc (HQ) 317 738-5000
3450 Bearing Dr Franklin (46131) *(G-4915)*

NSK Precision America Inc. 317 738-5000
3450 Bearing Dr Franklin (46131) *(G-4916)*

Nst Campbellsburg Inc 812 755-4501
596 W Oak St Campbellsburg (47108) *(G-1279)*

Nswc Crane Division 812 854-2865
3217 S Rogers St Bloomington (47403) *(G-781)*

Ntk Precision Axle Corporation 765 656-1000
741 S County Road 200 W Frankfort (46041) *(G-4846)*

NTN Driveshaft Inc 812 342-7000
8251 S International Dr Columbus (47201) *(G-1982)*

Ntr Metals LLC 317 522-2891
4014 W 10th St Indianapolis (46222) *(G-7603)*

Nu Led Lighting 317 989-7352
1147 Old Vines Ct Greenwood (46143) *(G-5729)*

Nu-TEC Industries Inc 219 844-1233
1319 Saint Andrews Dr Schererville (46375) *(G-12340)*

Nuaxon Bioscience Inc 812 762-4400
899 S College Mall Rd # 161 Bloomington (47401) *(G-782)*

Nuclear Measurements Corp 317 546-2415
2460 N Arlington Ave Indianapolis (46218) *(G-7604)*

Nucor Building Systems, Waterloo *Also called Nucor Corporation (G-14020)*

Nucor Cold Finish 219 937-1442
12451 Shelby Pl Crown Point (46307) *(G-2280)*

Nucor Corporation 260 337-1800
6610 County Rd 60 Saint Joe (46785) *(G-12257)*

Nucor Corporation 260 837-7891
305 Industrial Pkwy Waterloo (46793) *(G-14019)*

Nucor Corporation 765 364-1323
4537 S Nucor Rd Crawfordsville (47933) *(G-2180)*

Nucor Corporation 260 837-7891
305 Industrial Pkwy Waterloo (46793) *(G-14020)*

Nucor Steel Corp 765 364-1323
4537 S Nucor Rd Crawfordsville (47933) *(G-2181)*

Nugent Sand Company 812 372-7508
5205 W State Road 46 Columbus (47201) *(G-1983)*

Numark Industries Company Ltd 317 718-2502
7124 E County Road 150 S Avon (46123) *(G-459)*

Numerical Concepts Inc 812 466-5261
4040 1st Pkwy Terre Haute (47804) *(G-13293)*

Numerix Inc 260 248-2942
406 Diamond Ave Ste B Columbia City (46725) *(G-1813)*

Nunn Milling Company Inc 812 425-3303
4700 New Harmony Rd Evansville (47720) *(G-3649)*

Nussmeier Engraving Co 812 425-1339
933 Main St Evansville (47708) *(G-3650)*

Nutritional Research Assoc (PA) 260 723-4931
407 E Broad St South Whitley (46787) *(G-13002)*

Nuvo Inc (PA) 317 254-2400
3951 N Meridian St # 200 Indianapolis (46208) *(G-7605)*

Nuvo Newsweekly, Indianapolis *Also called Nuvo Inc (G-7605)*

Nuwave Manufacturing 317 987-8229
68 N Gale St Ste G Indianapolis (46201) *(G-7606)*

Nvb Playgrounds Inc 317 826-2777
10725 Hidden Oak Way Indianapolis (46236) *(G-7607)*

Nvic, North Vernon *Also called Vernon North Industry Corp (G-11285)*

Nvsd LLC 502 561-0007
2235 Corydon Pike New Albany (47150) *(G-10834)*

Nwi Print & Mail LLC 219 916-1358
1050 Flagstone Dr Dyer (46311) *(G-2505)*

Nwitimescom 219 933-3200
601 45th St Munster (46321) *(G-10617)*

Nxp Usa Inc 765 455-5100
2733 Albright Rd Kokomo (46902) *(G-8677)*

Nyloncraft Inc (HQ) 574 256-1521
616 W Mckinley Ave Mishawaka (46545) *(G-10098)*

O & P Lab, Evansville *Also called Orthotic & Prosthetic Lab (G-3657)*

O & R Precision Grinding Inc 260 368-9394
5315 W 900 S Geneva (46740) *(G-5137)*

O D P, Franklin *Also called Orthodontic Design and Prod (G-4917)*

O'Sullivans Italian Pub, Fort Wayne *Also called T F S Inc (G-4672)*

O-M Distributors Inc 219 853-1900
724 Hoffman St Hammond (46327) *(G-5924)*

O3 Solutions, Huntertown *Also called Clute Enterprises Inc (G-6135)*

Oak Hill Winery LLC 765 395-3632
111 E Marion St Converse (46919) *(G-2081)*

Oak Lief 765 642-9010
3211 Jay Dr Anderson (46012) *(G-147)*

Oak Security Group LLC 317 585-9830
8904 Bash St Ste K Indianapolis (46256) *(G-7608)*

Oak Tree Experimental Farm, Washington *Also called Perdue Farms Inc (G-13999)*

Oak View Tooling Inc 260 244-7677
724 E Swihart St Columbia City (46725) *(G-1814)*

Oak-Rite Mfg Corp 317 839-2301
701 N Carr Rd Plainfield (46168) *(G-11632)*

Oaken Barrel Brewing Co Inc 317 887-2287
50 Airport Pkwy Ste L Greenwood (46143) *(G-5730)*

Oakenbarrel.com, Greenwood *Also called Oaken Barrel Brewing Co Inc (G-5730)*

Oakley Industries LLC 812 246-2600
1229 Bringham Dr Ste B Sellersburg (47172) *(G-12410)*

Oasis Bath, Plymouth *Also called Oasis Lifestyle LLC (G-11708)*

Oasis Lifestyle LLC 574 948-0004
1400 Pidco Dr Plymouth (46563) *(G-11708)*

OBrien Jack & Pat Enterprises 765 653-5070
1208 W County Road 125 S Greencastle (46135) *(G-5470)*

OBryan Barrel Company Inc 812 479-6741
5501 Old Boonville Hwy Evansville (47715) *(G-3651)*

Observer, The, Notre Dame *Also called University Notre Dame Du Lac (G-11304)*

Oce Copiers 812 479-0000
5625 E Virginia St Evansville (47715) *(G-3652)*

Oce Corporate Printing Div 260 436-7395
6915 Innovation Blvd Fort Wayne (46818) *(G-4507)*

Octapharma Plasma Inc 574 234-9568
2102 S Michigan St South Bend (46613) *(G-12881)*

Octiv Inc 317 550-0148
54 Monument Cir Ste 200 Indianapolis (46204) *(G-7609)*

Odb Inc 260 673-0062
7203 Wintergreen Dr Fort Wayne (46814) *(G-4508)*

Odin Corporation of Delaware 317 849-3770
6736 E 82nd St Indianapolis (46250) *(G-7610)*

Odon Feed and Grain Inc 812 636-7392
500 S East St Odon (47562) *(G-11337)*

Odon Journal, Odon *Also called Myers Enterprises Inc (G-11335)*

Odon Machine & Manufacturing 812 636-7781
409 W Elnora St Odon (47562) *(G-11338)*

Odon Vault Co. 812 636-7386
2909 E Kylie Ct Bloomington (47401) *(G-783)*

Odyssey Machine Inc 812 951-1160
9627 State Road 64 Georgetown (47122) *(G-5151)*

Odyssian Technology LLC 574 257-7555
511 E Colfax Ave South Bend (46617) *(G-12882)*

Oeding Corporation 812 367-1271
443 W 16th St Ferdinand (47532) *(G-3860)*

OEM Solution Center, Indianapolis *Also called Cummins Crosspoint LLC (G-6708)*

Oerlikon Balzers Coating USA 765 935-7424
1580 Progress Dr Richmond (47374) *(G-12025)*

Oerlikon Fairfield, Lafayette *Also called Fairfield Manufacturing Co Inc (G-8895)*

Oerlikon Fairfield, Lafayette *Also called Fairfield Manufacturing Co Inc (G-8896)*

Oesterling Chimney Sweep Inc 812 372-3512
2360 N National Rd Columbus (47201) *(G-1984)*

Office Furniture Warehouse Inc 317 872-6477
7121 Royal Oakland Ct Indianapolis (46236) *(G-7611)*

Office Hub, Shelbyville *Also called A & H Enterprises LLC (G-12517)*

Official Sports Intl Inc 574 269-1404
4120 Corridor Dr Warsaw (46582) *(G-13917)*

Offset House Inc 317 849-5155
  9374 Castlegate Dr Indianapolis (46256) (G-7612)

OFFSET HOUSE PRINTING, Indianapolis Also called Offset House Inc (G-7612)

Offset One Inc 260 456-8828
  1609 S Calhoun St Fort Wayne (46802) (G-4509)

Ofs Brands Holdings Inc 800 521-5381
  1204 E 6th St Huntingburg (47542) (G-6177)

Ogden Welding Systems Inc 219 322-5252
  372 Division St Schererville (46375) (G-12341)

OH Hunt Lines Inc 260 856-2126
  591 N Jefferson St Cromwell (46732) (G-2210)

OH Pharmaceutical Co Ltd 219 644-3239
  9800 Connecticut Dr Crown Point (46307) (G-2281)

OHara Sports Inc 219 836-5554
  9450 Calumet Ave Munster (46321) (G-10618)

Ohio County News, The, Rising Sun Also called Delphos Herald of Indiana Inc (G-12087)

Ohio River Metal Services Inc 812 282-4770
  5150 Loop Rd Jeffersonville (47130) (G-8406)

Ohio River Trading Co 765 653-4100
  8090 S State Road 243 Cloverdale (46120) (G-1733)

Ohio River Veneer LLC 812 824-7928
  650 E Empire Mill Rd Bloomington (47401) (G-784)

Ohio Table Pad of Indiana 260 463-2139
  1400 N Detroit St Lagrange (46761) (G-9062)

Ohio Transmission Corporation 812 466-2734
  1502 Lafayette Ave Terre Haute (47804) (G-13294)

Ohio Valley Caviar 812 338-4367
  1927 E Shelton Rd English (47118) (G-3317)

Ohio Valley Creative Enrgy Inc 502 468-9787
  626 Albany St New Albany (47150) (G-10835)

Ohio Valley Door Corp 812 945-5285
  2143 Willow St New Albany (47150) (G-10836)

Ohio Valley Electric 812 532-5288
  800 Aep Dr Lawrenceburg (47025) (G-9149)

Ohio Valley Fuel Injection 812 987-5857
  5905 Stacy Rd Charlestown (47111) (G-1578)

Ohio Valley Ready Mix, Jeffersonville Also called Kentucky Concrete Indiana LLC (G-8388)

Ohio Valley Ready Mix Inc 812 282-6671
  2220 Hamburg Pike Jeffersonville (47130) (G-8407)

OHM Automotive LLC 812 879-5455
  3748 S Claybridge Dr Bloomington (47401) (G-785)

OHM Enterprise LLC 812 879-5455
  2534 State Highway 67 Gosport (47433) (G-5354)

Oil and Go, Crown Point Also called Jay Costas Companies Inc (G-2267)

Oil Palace Limited 317 679-9187
  4525 Lafayette Rd Ste L Indianapolis (46254) (G-7613)

Oil Technology Inc 219 322-2724
  1203 Sheffield Ave Dyer (46311) (G-2506)

Oilfield Research Inc 812 424-2907
  1204 N 1st Ave Evansville (47710) (G-3653)

Okaya USA 317 362-0696
  8227 Northwest Blvd Indianapolis (46278) (G-7614)

Old Barn Creations LLC 219 324-2553
  2634 N Vermeer Ln La Porte (46350) (G-8801)

Old Bob's, Avon Also called Woodland Manufacturing & Sup (G-472)

Old Capital Printing LLC 812 946-9444
  3314 Grant Line Rd Ste 3 New Albany (47150) (G-10837)

Old Castle Precast, Carmel Also called Kerr Concrete Pipe Co (G-1422)

Old Copper Still Distlg Co LLC 812 342-0765
  885 Baywood Ct Columbus (47201) (G-1985)

Old Dutch Sand Co Inc 219 938-7020
  4600 E 15th Ave Gary (46403) (G-5080)

Old Fashion Woods, Warsaw Also called H Proto Development Inc (G-13887)

Old Fort Distillery Inc 260 705-5128
  12311 Saint Joe Rd Grabill (46741) (G-5381)

Old Gary Inc 941 755-0976
  1433 E 83rd Ave Merrillville (46410) (G-9742)

Old Guy Woodcrafters LLC 574 527-9044
  1312 Freedom Pkwy Winona Lake (46590) (G-14352)

Old Hoosier Meats 574 825-2940
  101 Wayne St Middlebury (46540) (G-9913)

Old Jim Customs LLC 812 431-1460
  4001 Vogel Rd Evansville (47715) (G-3654)

Old Lumber Yard Clay Factory 260 627-3567
  13716 3rd St Grabill (46741) (G-5382)

Old Paths Tract Society Inc 812 247-2560
  11298 Old Paths Ln Shoals (47581) (G-12668)

Old Ras Inc 260 563-7461
  4525 W Old 24 Wabash (46992) (G-13743)

Old Remco Holdings LLC (HQ) 765 778-6499
  600 Corporation Dr Pendleton (46064) (G-11498)

Old World Fudge & Cds Dogs LLC 260 610-2249
  206 Raleigh Ct Columbia City (46725) (G-1815)

Oldcastle Apg Midwest Inc (HQ) 317 786-0971
  901 E Troy Ave Indianapolis (46203) (G-7615)

Oldcastle Buildingenvelope Inc 317 876-1155
  8441 Bearing Dr Indianapolis (46268) (G-7616)

Oldcastle Buildingenvelope Inc 317 876-1155
  8441 Bearing Dr Indianapolis (46268) (G-7617)

Oldenburg Pallet Inc 812 933-0568
  19349 Tony Rd Batesville (47006) (G-513)

Oleta Publishing Co Inc 765 730-7195
  3009 S Sugar Maple St Yorktown (47396) (G-14409)

Olive Branch Etc Inc 765 449-1884
  181 Sagamore Pkwy S Lafayette (47905) (G-8977)

Olive Leaf LLC 812 323-3073
  879 S College Mall Rd Bloomington (47401) (G-786)

Olive Mill 317 574-9200
  10 S Rangeline Rd Carmel (46032) (G-1445)

OLIVE MILL THE, Carmel Also called Olive Mill (G-1445)

Oliver Machine & TI Corp 765 349-2271
  110 Industrial Dr Martinsville (46151) (G-9630)

Oliver Machine and Tool Corp 765 349-2271
  110 Industrial Dr Mooresville (46158) (G-10329)

Oliver Wine Company Inc (PA) 812 822-0466
  200 E Winery Rd Bloomington (47404) (G-787)

Oliver Winery, Bloomington Also called Oliver Wine Company Inc (G-787)

Olon Industries Inc (us) 812 256-6400
  600 Patrol Rd Jeffersonville (47130) (G-8408)

Olon Industries Inc (us) 812 254-0427
  2510 E National Hwy Washington (47501) (G-13994)

Olon Industries Inc (us) 812 254-6718
  2510 E National Hwy Washington (47501) (G-13995)

Olson Race Cars 765 529-6933
  129 N 26th St New Castle (47362) (G-10914)

Olympia Business Systems Inc 800 225-5644
  251 Wedcor Ave Wabash (46992) (G-13744)

Olympia Candy Kitchen 574 533-5040
  136 N Main St Goshen (46526) (G-5301)

Olympic Fiberglass Industries 574 223-3101
  1235 E 4th St Rochester (46975) (G-12142)

Olympus Manufacturing Systems 219 465-1520
  4703 N Calumet Ave Valparaiso (46383) (G-13594)

Omco, Pierceton Also called Midwest Roll Forming & Mfg Inc (G-11573)

Omega, Bristol Also called Reschcor Inc (G-1079)

Omega Co 317 831-4471
  12494 N Woodlawn Dr Mooresville (46158) (G-10330)

Omega Enterprises Inc 765 584-1990
  732 W Washington St Winchester (47394) (G-14339)

Omega National Products LLC 574 295-5353
  1010 Rowe St Elkhart (46516) (G-3068)

Omega One Connect Inc 317 626-3445
  3825 E 78th St Indianapolis (46240) (G-7618)

Omg Cupcakes & Sweets LLC 317 281-7926
  9797 Hidden Hills Ln Indianapolis (46234) (G-7619)

OMI Industries Inc 812 438-9218
  1300 Barbour Way Rising Sun (47040) (G-12090)

Omicron Biochemicals Inc 574 287-6910
  115 S Hill St South Bend (46617) (G-12883)

Omni Auto Parts, Fort Wayne Also called Omnisource LLC (G-4510)

Omni Looseleaf Inc 219 253-8020
  4087 E Monon Rd Monticello (47960) (G-10275)

Omni Oxide, Indianapolis Also called Metals and Additives LLC (G-7490)

Omni Plastics LLC 812 422-0888
  2300 Lynch Rd Evansville (47711) (G-3655)

Omni Technologies Inc (PA) 812 537-4102
  779 Rudolph Way Greendale (47025) (G-5492)

Omni-Tron Tooling & Engrg (PA) 574 262-2083
  1649 Brookwood Dr Elkhart (46514) (G-3069)

Omnimax International Inc 574 294-8576
  160 County Road 15 Elkhart (46516) (G-3070)

Omnimax International Inc 574 848-7432
  2341 E Market St Nappanee (46550) (G-10700)

Omnimax International Inc 574 773-7981
  2341 E Market St Nappanee (46550) (G-10701)

Omnisource LLC (HQ) 260 422-5541
  7575 W Jefferson Blvd Fort Wayne (46804) (G-4510)

Omnisource Holdings LLC (HQ) 260 969-3500
  7575 W Jefferson Blvd Fort Wayne (46804) (G-4511)

Omnisource Marketing Group Inc 317 575-3300
  8925 N Meridian St # 150 Indianapolis (46260) (G-7620)

Omnitech Systems Inc 219 531-5532
  450 Campbell St Ste 2 Valparaiso (46385) (G-13595)

Omr North America Inc 317 956-9509
  4755 Gilman St Speedway (46224) (G-13015)

On Guard 317 753-5312
  10329 Vandergriff Rd Indianapolis (46239) (G-7621)

On Point Machining Inc 219 393-5132
  7111 Union Center Rd Kingsbury (46345) (G-8544)

On Semiconductor, Kokomo Also called Semicndctor Cmponents Inds LLC (G-8694)

On Site Machining Corporation 219 923-2292
  1148 Park Dr Munster (46321) (G-10619)

On Site Welding & Maintenance 812 755-4184
  7632 E County Road 240 N Campbellsburg (47108) (G-1280)

On Spot of North America, North Vernon Also called Onspot of North America Inc (G-11275)

On The Go Portble Wtr Sftnr LL 260 482-9614
  3905 W Roll Ave Bloomington (47403) (G-788)

One Eight Seven Incorporated 219 886-2060
1050 Michigan St Gary (46402) **(G-5081)**
One Source Labs, New Albany *Also called Workflow Solutions LLC* **(G-10875)**
One Stop Travel Shop Inc 812 339-9496
317 E Dodds St Bloomington (47401) **(G-789)**
ONeal Wood Products Inc 765 342-2709
1120 Lenvoil Rd Martinsville (46151) **(G-9631)**
Onfield Apparel Group LLC 317 895-7249
8677 Logo Athletic Ct Indianapolis (46219) **(G-7622)**
Onion Enterprises Inc 317 762-6007
5705 W 73rd St Indianapolis (46278) **(G-7623)**
Online Packaging Incorporated 219 872-0925
124 Tri Quad Dr Michigan City (46360) **(G-9825)**
Only Alpha, Fort Wayne *Also called Trivector Manufacturing Inc* **(G-4706)**
Onsite Construction Services 312 723-8060
416 Jefferson Ave Chesterton (46304) **(G-1625)**
Onspot of North America Inc (HQ) 203 377-0777
1075 Rodgers Park Dr North Vernon (47265) **(G-11274)**
Onspot of North America Inc 812 346-1719
1075 Rodgers Park Dr North Vernon (47265) **(G-11275)**
Onu Acre LLC 765 565-1355
9350 W 800 N Carthage (46115) **(G-1515)**
Onward Manufacturing Company (HQ) 260 358-4111
1000 E Market St Huntington (46750) **(G-6233)**
Onyett Fabricators, Petersburg *Also called Smgf LLC* **(G-11568)**
Onyett Welding & Machine Inc 812 582-2999
409 N 8th St Petersburg (47567) **(G-11565)**
Onyett, A.B. & Sons, Petersburg *Also called Onyett Welding & Machine Inc* **(G-11565)**
Ooshirts Inc 317 246-9083
7800 Records St Ste C Indianapolis (46226) **(G-7624)**
Ooten Pattern Works 317 244-7348
1101 N Eleanor St Indianapolis (46214) **(G-7625)**
Open Canvas LLC 317 908-6524
103 N University St West Lafayette (47906) **(G-14091)**
Open Control Systems LLC 317 429-0627
905 N Capitol Ave Ste 200 Indianapolis (46204) **(G-7626)**
Open Gate Design & Decor, Anderson *Also called Open Gate LLC* **(G-148)**
Open Gate LLC 765 734-1314
2834 N 900 W Anderson (46011) **(G-148)**
Open Range Rv, Shipshewana *Also called Highland Ridge Rv Inc* **(G-12616)**
Opflex Environmental Tech, Indianapolis *Also called Opflex Technologies LLC* **(G-7629)**
Opflex Solutions Inc 800 568-7036
733 S West St Indianapolis (46225) **(G-7627)**
Opflex Technologies LLC 317 731-6123
2525 N Shadeland Ave Indianapolis (46219) **(G-7628)**
Opflex Technologies LLC (HQ) 518 568-7036
733 S West St Indianapolis (46225) **(G-7629)**
Opi Inc 260 636-2352
71 E 400 S Ste A Albion (46701) **(G-31)**
Opportunities 574 518-0606
6122 N 675 E North Webster (46555) **(G-11298)**
Oprato Software LLC 317 573-0168
14155 Wicksworth Way Carmel (46032) **(G-1446)**
Opsys Ltd 765 236-6331
2600 S Henderson St # 204 Bloomington (47401) **(G-790)**
Optical Media Mfg Inc 317 822-1850
310 N Alabama St Ste 320 Indianapolis (46204) **(G-7630)**
Optimum System Products Inc 812 289-1905
20304 New Market Rd Marysville (47141) **(G-9650)**
Oracle America Inc 317 581-0078
701 Congressional Blvd Carmel (46032) **(G-1447)**
Orange Cnty Wldg & Fabrication 812 653-5754
6063 N County Road 200 E Orleans (47452) **(G-11364)**
Orange County Concrete Inc 812 865-2425
409 E Jefferson St Orleans (47452) **(G-11365)**
Orange County Processing 812 865-2028
5028 N State Road 37 Orleans (47452) **(G-11366)**
Orbital Installation Tech LLC 317 774-3668
9750 E 150 St Ste 1200 Noblesville (46060) **(G-11162)**
Orchard Lane Cabinets 574 825-7568
14425 County Road 126 Goshen (46528) **(G-5302)**
Orchid Systems, Carmel *Also called Messagenet Systems Inc* **(G-1438)**
Org Chem Group LLC (PA) 812 464-4446
2406 Lynch Rd Evansville (47711) **(G-3656)**
Organi Gro, New Castle *Also called Md/Lf Incorporated* **(G-10912)**
Organic Bread of Heaven, Gary *Also called Brunos Breads LLC* **(G-5031)**
Organized Living Inc 812 334-8839
1500 S Strong Dr Bloomington (47403) **(G-791)**
Orica USA Inc 812 256-7800
2000 Coopers Ln Ste A1 Jeffersonville (47130) **(G-8409)**
Original Tractor Cab Co Inc 765 663-2214
6849 W Front St Arlington (46104) **(G-282)**
Orion Global Sourcing Inc 812 332-3338
1516 S Walnut St Bloomington (47401) **(G-792)**
Orion Lighting, Elkhart *Also called Premiere Building Mtls Inc* **(G-3114)**
Orion Safety Products, Peru *Also called Standard Fusee Corporation* **(G-11548)**
Orka Technologies LLC 812 378-9842
2182 W 500 N Columbus (47201) **(G-1986)**

Ornamental Division, Anderson *Also called Mofab Inc* **(G-139)**
Ornamental Iron Works 219 988-4929
5300 Massachusetts St Merrillville (46410) **(G-9743)**
Orora North America 317 879-4628
4635 W 84th St Ste 500 Indianapolis (46268) **(G-7631)**
Orpro Prosthetics & Orthotics, Richmond *Also called Hanger Prsthetcs & Ortho Inc* **(G-11995)**
Orr Paving Inc 317 839-4110
3442 S State Road 267 Plainfield (46168) **(G-11633)**
Ortho Grind LLC 260 493-1230
7007 Trafalgar Dr Fort Wayne (46803) **(G-4512)**
Orthoconcepts Inc 317 727-0100
10947 Echo Grove Cir Indianapolis (46236) **(G-7632)**
Orthodontic Design and Prod (PA) 760 734-3995
2165 Earlywood Dr Franklin (46131) **(G-4917)**
Orthopediatrics Corp 574 268-6379
2850 Frontier Dr Warsaw (46582) **(G-13918)**
Orthopediatrics US Dist 574 268-6379
2850 Frontier Dr Warsaw (46582) **(G-13919)**
Orthopedic Precision Instrs, Albion *Also called Opi Inc* **(G-31)**
Orthotic & Prosthetic Designs 317 882-9002
5120 Commerce Cir Ste 104 Indianapolis (46237) **(G-7633)**
Orthotic & Prosthetic Lab 812 479-6298
125 N Weinbach Ave # 330 Evansville (47711) **(G-3657)**
Orthotic Prosthetic Specialist 219 836-8668
625 Ridge Rd Ste D Munster (46321) **(G-10620)**
Ortman Meat Processing Inc 574 946-7113
2035 S State Road 119 Winamac (46996) **(G-14313)**
Orville Redenbacher Popcorn, Brookston *Also called Conagra Brands Inc* **(G-1103)**
Osborn Intl 765 965-3722
1400 Industries Rd Richmond (47374) **(G-12026)**
Osborn Manufacturing Corp 574 267-6156
960 N Lake St Warsaw (46580) **(G-13920)**
Osc Holdings LLC 765 751-7000
1150 W Kilgore Ave Muncie (47305) **(G-10540)**
Oscar Telecom Inc 317 359-7000
802 N Grant Ave Indianapolis (46201) **(G-7634)**
Osgood Journal, Versailles *Also called Ripley Publishing Co Inc* **(G-13657)**
OSI Specialties Inc 317 293-4858
6299 Guion Rd Indianapolis (46268) **(G-7635)**
Osr Inc 812 342-7642
7715 S International Dr Columbus (47201) **(G-1987)**
Ossenbeck Mach Co 937 564-6092
4755 Eileens Way Lawrenceburg (47025) **(G-9150)**
Ossian Plant, Ossian *Also called Ti Group Auto Systems LLC* **(G-11414)**
Ossian Printing, Kendallville *Also called Modern Printing Co* **(G-8495)**
Osterfeld Industries 219 926-4646
1050 Broadway Stsuite8 Chesterton (46304) **(G-1626)**
Osterholt Construction Inc 260 672-3493
6486 N Mayne Rd Roanoke (46783) **(G-12106)**
Osterholt Truss, Roanoke *Also called Osterholt Construction Inc* **(G-12106)**
Ostler Enterprises Inc 765 656-1275
1624 W Armstrong Rd Frankfort (46041) **(G-4847)**
Oswalt Menu Company Inc 317 257-8039
1433 Alimingo Dr Indianapolis (46260) **(G-7636)**
Otech, Rolling Prairie *Also called OTech Corporation* **(G-12190)**
OTech Corporation 219 778-8001
4744 E Oaknoll Rd Rolling Prairie (46371) **(G-12190)**
Otis Elevator Company 812 331-5605
320 W 8th St Ste 201 Bloomington (47404) **(G-793)**
Otis Elevator Company 812 471-9770
6050 Wedeking Ave Ste 10b Evansville (47715) **(G-3658)**
Otp Industrial Solutions, Terre Haute *Also called Ohio Transmission Corporation* **(G-13294)**
Ottenweller Co Inc (PA) 260 484-3166
3011 Congressional Pkwy Fort Wayne (46808) **(G-4513)**
Ottinger Machine Co 317 654-1700
2900 N Richardt Ave Indianapolis (46219) **(G-7637)**
Ottinger Machine Shop, Indianapolis *Also called Ottinger Machine Co* **(G-7637)**
Ottosons Industries Inc 219 365-8330
12742 Wicker Ave Ste B Cedar Lake (46303) **(G-1532)**
Our Country Home Entps Inc (PA) 260 657-5605
12120 Water St Harlan (46743) **(G-5974)**
Our Daily Brew, Fort Wayne *Also called Odb Inc* **(G-4508)**
Our Little Books LLC 812 987-2475
306 Brighton Ave Jeffersonville (47130) **(G-8410)**
Out of Sight Screen Co Inc 317 430-1705
3910 Cranbrook Dr Indianapolis (46240) **(G-7638)**
Outdoor Action Wear Spc, Brazil *Also called Solar Bat Enterprises Inc* **(G-978)**
Outdoor Industries 574 551-5936
221 S Hand Ave Warsaw (46580) **(G-13921)**
Outdoor Performance 765 732-3335
2920 S Us Highway 27 Liberty (47353) **(G-9268)**
Outdoor Roomscapes Inc 574 965-2009
11965 W 800 N Monticello (47960) **(G-10276)**
Outfitter 765 289-6456
1800 N Wheeling Ave Muncie (47303) **(G-10541)**
Outman Industries Inc 260 467-1576
1830 Wayne Trce Fort Wayne (46803) **(G-4514)**

Outsource Technologies Inc 574 233-1303
   1832 N Kenmore St South Bend (46628) *(G-12884)*

Outtadaway LLC 219 866-8885
   503 W Washington St Rensselaer (47978) *(G-11934)*

Ovation Communications Inc 812 401-9100
   1326 N Weinbach Ave Evansville (47711) *(G-3659)*

Over Hill & Dale Sign Studio 812 867-1664
   1100 Indy Ct Evansville (47725) *(G-3660)*

Overgaards Artcraft Printers 574 234-8464
   2213 S Michigan St South Bend (46613) *(G-12885)*

Overton & Sons Tl & Die Co Inc 317 736-7700
   2155 Mcclain Dr Franklin (46131) *(G-4918)*

Overton & Sons Tl & Die Co Inc (PA) 317 831-4542
   1250 S Old State Road 67 Mooresville (46158) *(G-10331)*

Overton & Sons Tl & Die Co Inc 317 831-4542
   1250 S Old State Road 67 Mooresville (46158) *(G-10332)*

Overton Carbide Tool & Engrg, Franklin *Also called Overton & Sons Tl & Die Co Inc (G-4918)*

Overton Industries, Mooresville *Also called Overton & Sons Tl & Die Co Inc (G-10331)*

Overton Mold Inc 317 831-9595
   1248 S Old State Road 67 Mooresville (46158) *(G-10333)*

Ovideon LLC 812 577-3274
   135 Short St Side Lawrenceburg (47025) *(G-9151)*

Ovr There Industries Inc 317 946-8365
   5825 Bonnie Brae St Indianapolis (46228) *(G-7639)*

Owen County Pallet 812 859-4617
   9628 Stahl Rd Worthington (47471) *(G-14395)*

Owen Leader Inc 812 829-3936
   114 E Franklin St Spencer (47460) *(G-13031)*

Owen Valley Winery LLC 812 828-0883
   491 Timber Ridge Rd Spencer (47460) *(G-13032)*

Owen Woodworking 317 331-6936
   3012 S State Road 39 Danville (46122) *(G-2354)*

Owens Corning Sales LLC 765 647-4131
   128 W 8th St Brookville (47012) *(G-1122)*

Owens Corning Sales LLC 765 647-2857
   6102 Holland Rd Brookville (47012) *(G-1123)*

Owens Corning Sales LLC 260 563-2111
   3711 Mill St Wabash (46992) *(G-13745)*

Owens Corning Sales LLC 219 465-4324
   2552 Industrial Dr Valparaiso (46383) *(G-13596)*

Owens Corning Sales LLC 260 665-7318
   1211 Wohlert St Angola (46703) *(G-233)*

Owens Corning Sales Therm, Wabash *Also called Owens Corning Sales LLC (G-13745)*

Owens Fuel Center 260 358-1211
   2718 Guilford St Huntington (46750) *(G-6234)*

Owens Machine & Welding 574 583-9566
   1110 N 6th St Monticello (47960) *(G-10277)*

Owens Machinery Inc 812 968-3285
   1502 W Palmyra Lake Rd Palmyra (47164) *(G-11437)*

Owings Patterns Inc 812 944-5577
   3011 Progress Way Sellersburg (47172) *(G-12411)*

Oxbo International Corporation 260 768-3217
   10605 W 750 N Shipshewana (46565) *(G-12640)*

Oxbow Carbon & Minerals 219 473-0359
   2815 Indianapolis Blvd Whiting (46394) *(G-14272)*

Oxford Cabinet Company LLC 765 223-2101
   141 S Us Highway 27 Liberty (47353) *(G-9269)*

Oxford House Incorporated 765 884-3265
   606 W State Road 18 Fowler (47944) *(G-4803)*

Oxford Industries Inc 317 569-0866
   8701 Keystone Xing 14b Indianapolis (46240) *(G-7640)*

Oxinas Partners LLC 812 725-8649
   702 N Shore Dr Ste 101 Jeffersonville (47130) *(G-8411)*

Oxygen Education, Jeffersonville *Also called Amatrol Inc (G-8322)*

Oza Compound Products 260 483-0406
   1221 Production Rd Fort Wayne (46808) *(G-4515)*

Ozinga Bros Inc 219 956-3418
   11607 N State Road 49 Wheatfield (46392) *(G-14228)*

Ozinga Bros Inc 574 546-2550
   524 N Bowen Ave Bremen (46506) *(G-1013)*

Ozinga Bros Inc 574 642-4455
   65723 Us Highway 33 Goshen (46526) *(G-5303)*

Ozinga Bros Inc 574 971-8239
   1700 Egbert Ave Goshen (46528) *(G-5304)*

Ozinga Bros Inc 219 949-9800
   1575 Adler Cir Ste B Portage (46368) *(G-11786)*

Ozinga Bros Inc 219 662-0925
   1211 E Summit St Crown Point (46307) *(G-2282)*

Ozinga Indiana Rdymx Con Inc 219 949-9800
   400 Blaine St Gary (46406) *(G-5082)*

Ozinga Ready Mix, Wheatfield *Also called Ozinga Bros Inc (G-14228)*

Ozinga Ready Mix, Portage *Also called Ozinga Bros Inc (G-11786)*

P & A Machine Inc 317 634-3673
   3025 English Ave Indianapolis (46201) *(G-7641)*

P & E Products 765 969-2644
   637 W 17th St Connersville (47331) *(G-2067)*

P & H Engineering Inc 765 676-6323
   6745 Middle Jamestown Rd Jamestown (46147) *(G-8232)*

P & H Iron & Supply Inc 219 853-0240
   1435 Summer St Hammond (46320) *(G-5925)*

P & H LLC 765 654-5291
   309 Harvard Ter Frankfort (46041) *(G-4848)*

P & J Industries Inc 260 894-7143
   1494 Gerber St Ligonier (46767) *(G-9291)*

P & J Sectional Housing 260 982-7231
   14385 N 200 E North Manchester (46962) *(G-11240)*

P & J Tool Co Inc 317 546-4858
   3525 Massachusetts Ave Indianapolis (46218) *(G-7642)*

P & M Fabrication 812 232-7640
   2820 S Center St Terre Haute (47802) *(G-13295)*

P & R Farms LLC 812 326-2010
   5195 E State Road 64 Saint Anthony (47575) *(G-12248)*

P C Communication Inc 219 838-2546
   2301 Ridgewood St Highland (46322) *(G-6053)*

P D Q, Columbia City *Also called PDQ Workholding LLC (G-1817)*

P F Apple LLC 317 773-8683
   19541 Heather Ln Noblesville (46060) *(G-11163)*

P H C Industries Inc 260 423-9461
   3115 Pittsburg St Fort Wayne (46803) *(G-4516)*

P H Drew Incorporated 317 297-5152
   2450 N Raceway Rd Indianapolis (46234) *(G-7643)*

P J J T Distributors Inc 812 254-2218
   501 N Meridian St Washington (47501) *(G-13996)*

P J Marketing Services Inc 574 259-8843
   20950 Ireland Rd South Bend (46614) *(G-12886)*

P Js Custom Embroidering LLC 219 787-9161
   252 Haglund Rd Chesterton (46304) *(G-1627)*

P M Fabricating Incorporated 219 362-9926
   2008 Ohio St La Porte (46350) *(G-8802)*

P M I LLC 812 374-3856
   12595 N Executive Dr Edinburgh (46124) *(G-2619)*

P M P Design, Fishers *Also called Plaquemaker Plus Inc (G-3952)*

P O C Industries Inc 765 645-5015
   8944 N Crossway Mays (46155) *(G-9663)*

P R F 219 477-8660
   6737 Central Ave Ste D Portage (46368) *(G-11787)*

P S C Fabricating, Evansville *Also called PSC Industries Inc (G-3688)*

P T I Machining Inc 765 564-9966
   5395 W 200 N Delphi (46923) *(G-2425)*

P&M Beverage Imports, Plainfield *Also called Pepito Miller Bev Imports LLC (G-11635)*

P-Americas LLC 219 836-1800
   9300 Calumet Ave Munster (46321) *(G-10621)*

P-Americas LLC 812 794-4455
   1402 W State Road 256 Austin (47102) *(G-399)*

P-Americas LLC 812 522-3421
   1811 1st Ave Seymour (47274) *(G-12472)*

P-Americas LLC 317 876-6800
   5411 W 78th St Indianapolis (46268) *(G-7644)*

P-Americas LLC 765 647-3576
   261 Webers Ln Brookville (47012) *(G-1124)*

P-Americas LLC 812 332-1200
   214 W 17th St Bloomington (47404) *(G-794)*

P-Americas LLC 765 289-0270
   2901 N Walnut St Muncie (47303) *(G-10542)*

P413 Corporation 317 769-0679
   7163 Whitestown Pkwy Zionsville (46077) *(G-14454)*

Pac Banner Works, Mishawaka *Also called Plastimatic Arts Corp (G-10104)*

Pac Corporation 260 637-8792
   211 Soaring Eagle Ct Fort Wayne (46845) *(G-4517)*

Pace American Enterprises Inc (HQ) 800 247-5767
   11550 Harter Dr Middlebury (46540) *(G-9914)*

Pace Tool and Engineering Inc 812 373-9885
   2675 Grissom St Columbus (47203) *(G-1988)*

Pacemaker Buildings, North Webster *Also called North Webster Construction Inc (G-11297)*

Pack Printing 317 437-9779
   1916 Haynes Ave Indianapolis (46240) *(G-7645)*

Packaging Corporation America 812 882-7631
   408 E Saint Clair St Vincennes (47591) *(G-13694)*

Packaging Corporation America 812 376-9301
   3460 Commerce Dr Columbus (47201) *(G-1989)*

Packaging Corporation America 812 526-5919
   12599 N Presidential Way Edinburgh (46124) *(G-2620)*

Packaging Corporation America 765 674-9781
   520 S 1st St Gas City (46933) *(G-5126)*

Packaging Corporation America 317 247-0193
   7752 W Morris St Indianapolis (46231) *(G-7646)*

Packaging Corporation America 812 522-3100
   2200 D Ave E Seymour (47274) *(G-12473)*

Packaging Corporation America 812 482-4598
   240 S Truman Rd Jasper (47546) *(G-8299)*

Packaging Group Corp (PA) 219 879-2500
   2125 E Us Highway 12 C Michigan City (46360) *(G-9826)*

Packaging Lgstics Slutions LLC 502 807-8346
   3001 E Lobo Rdg New Albany (47150) *(G-10838)*

Packaging Logic Inc 219 326-1350
   239 Factory St La Porte (46350) *(G-8803)*

Packerware, Evansville *Also called Berry Film Products Co Inc (G-3374)*

Packetvac LLC 317 414-6137
　7018 W 71st St Indianapolis (46278) (G-7647)
Pacmoore Products Inc 317 831-2666
　100 Pacmoore Pkwy Mooresville (46158) (G-10334)
Pactiv Corporation 574 936-7065
　1411 Pidco Dr Plymouth (46563) (G-11709)
Paddack Brothers Inc 765 659-4777
　4410 W Old State Road 28 Frankfort (46041) (G-4849)
Paden Engineering Co Inc 812 546-4447
　100 Raymond St Hope (47246) (G-6117)
Padgett Inc 812 945-2391
　901 E 4th St New Albany (47150) (G-10839)
Pag Holdings Inc 814 446-2525
　10665 N State Road 59 Brazil (47834) (G-974)
Pag Holdings Inc (HQ) 317 290-5006
　5929 Lakeside Blvd Indianapolis (46278) (G-7648)
Pages Editorial Services Inc 765 674-4212
　113 E Old Kokomo Rd Marion (46953) (G-9549)
Paige Marschall 574 277-1631
　12622 Alexander Dr Granger (46530) (G-5428)
Paige's Custom Lettering, Granger Also called Paige Marschall (G-5428)
Paint The Town Graphics Inc 260 422-9152
　1828 W Main St Fort Wayne (46808) (G-4518)
Paklab, Orland Also called Universal Packg Systems Inc (G-11359)
Palacio Tropical 574 289-0742
　2012 W Western Ave South Bend (46619) (G-12887)
Palibrio 812 671-9757
　1663 S Liberty Dr Bloomington (47403) (G-795)
Palladium Item, The, Richmond Also called Gannett Co Inc (G-11989)
Pallet Builder Inc 765 948-3345
　1520 W 900 S Fairmount (46928) (G-3834)
Pallet One of Indiana Inc 260 768-4021
　5345 W 200 N Shipshewana (46565) (G-12641)
Pallet Recyclers LLC 812 402-0095
　4200 Upper Mt Vernon Rd Evansville (47712) (G-3661)
Palletone Indiana Trnsp LLC 260 768-4021
　5345 W 200 N Shipshewana (46565) (G-12642)
Pallets Viveros LLC 765 307-0112
　1815 W 575 N Crawfordsville (47933) (G-2182)
Palmetto Planters LLC 765 396-4446
　1153 N Hartford St Eaton (47338) (G-2587)
Palmor Products Inc (PA) 800 872-2822
　1990 John Bart Rd Lebanon (46052) (G-9210)
Pam Franz, Greenwood Also called Exclusively Orthodontics Lab (G-5693)
Pamela S Taulman 812 378-5008
　982 S Marr Rd Columbus (47201) (G-1990)
Panacea Paints & Coatings Inc 260 728-4222
　1013 W Commerce Dr Decatur (46733) (G-2397)
Panda Prints 574 322-1050
　19647 County Road 8 Bristol (46507) (G-1075)
Pandora Printing 574 551-9624
　1831 Rosemont Ave Warsaw (46580) (G-13922)
Panel Solutions Inc (PA) 574 389-8494
　5015 Verdant St Elkhart (46516) (G-3071)
Panel Solutions Inc 574 295-0222
　5015 Berdant Dr Elkhart (46516) (G-3072)
Panel Solutions/Tape Tech, Elkhart Also called Panel Solutions Inc (G-3071)
Pangloss Industries Inc 574 217-8505
　2215 Waters Edge Ct Mishawaka (46545) (G-10099)
Panhandle Eastrn Pipe Line LP 317 873-2410
　9371 Zionsville Rd Indianapolis (46268) (G-7649)
Paniccia Heating & Cooling 219 872-2198
　5076 N Bleck Rd Michigan City (46360) (G-9827)
Pannell & Son Welding Inc 765 948-3606
　207 N Summit St Summitville (46070) (G-13100)
Panolam Industries Inc 574 264-0702
　25603 Borg Rd Elkhart (46514) (G-3073)
Panoramic Rental Corp 800 654-2027
　4321 Goshen Rd Fort Wayne (46818) (G-4519)
Panther Graphics LLC 317 223-3845
　5740 Decatur Blvd Indianapolis (46241) (G-7650)
Papa Murphy's, Lafayette Also called Rico Aroma LLC (G-8992)
Papayan Industries 765 387-7274
　906 Rose St West Lafayette (47906) (G-14092)
Paper of Montgomery County 765 361-8888
　201 E Jefferson St # 200 Crawfordsville (47933) (G-2183)
Paper of Wabash County Inc 260 563-8326
　606 N State Road 13 Wabash (46992) (G-13746)
Paper Products, Muncie Also called Larry Flowers Wholesale (G-10509)
Paper Street Press 765 894-0027
　1841 King Eider Dr West Lafayette (47906) (G-14093)
Paper Tigers Inc 317 573-9040
　8702 Keystone Xing Indianapolis (46240) (G-7651)
Papers Inc 574 534-2591
　134 S Main St Goshen (46526) (G-5305)
Papers Inc 574 269-2932
　114 W Market St Warsaw (46580) (G-13923)
Paperworks Industries Inc 260 563-3102
　455 Factory St Wabash (46992) (G-13747)

Paperworks Industries Inc 260 569-3352
　455 Factory St Wabash (46992) (G-13748)
Papyrus, Indianapolis Also called Paper Tigers Inc (G-7651)
Par Digital Imaging 317 787-3330
　3330 Madison Ave Indianapolis (46227) (G-7652)
Par-Kan Company LLC 260 352-2141
　2915 W 900 S Silver Lake (46982) (G-12677)
Paradigm Industries Inc 317 574-8590
　12236 Hancock St Carmel (46032) (G-1448)
Paradigm Software Corp 317 770-7862
　1020 Seaport Dr Cicero (46034) (G-1664)
Paradise Ink Inc 812 402-4465
　619 N Burkhardt Rd Ste G Evansville (47715) (G-3662)
Paradise Machine & Tool Corp 317 247-4606
　6820 W Minnesota St Indianapolis (46241) (G-7653)
Paragon Manufacturing Inc 260 665-1492
　700 Wohlert St Angola (46703) (G-234)
Paragon Medical Inc 317 570-5830
　7350 E 86th St Indianapolis (46256) (G-7654)
Paragon Medical Inc 574 594-2140
　22 Pequignot Dr Pierceton (46562) (G-11575)
Paragon Medical Inc (PA) 574 594-2140
　8 Matchett Dr Pierceton (46562) (G-11576)
Paragon Printing Center Inc 574 533-5835
　117 S Main St Goshen (46526) (G-5306)
Paragon Tube Corporation 260 424-1266
　1605 Winter St Fort Wayne (46803) (G-4520)
Parallax Group Inc 800 443-4859
　600 Broadway St Anderson (46012) (G-149)
Paralogics LLC 765 587-4618
　301 S Batterfill Rd Muncie (47303) (G-10543)
Parametric Machining Inc 260 338-1564
　16335 Lima Rd Ste 3 Huntertown (46748) (G-6143)
Paramount Plastics Inc 574 264-2143
　2810 Jeanwood Dr Elkhart (46514) (G-3074)
Paramount Printing Ltd Inc 219 980-0445
　2400 W 47th Ave Gary (46408) (G-5083)
Paramount Tube Division, Indianapolis Also called Precision Products Group Inc (G-6276)
Paramount Tube Division, Fort Wayne Also called Precision Products Group Inc (G-4552)
Paratex Products, Michigan City Also called Blocksom & Co (G-9771)
Parco Incorporated 260 451-0810
　9100 Front St Fort Wayne (46818) (G-4521)
Parent Co. Glassteel, Goshen Also called Stability America Inc (G-5326)
Pariah 317 250-0612
　5702 Crittenden Ave Indianapolis (46220) (G-7655)
Paringa Resources Limited (PA) 314 422-4150
　6724 E Morgan Ave Ste B Evansville (47715) (G-3663)
Park 100 Business Printing, Indianapolis Also called Graphicorp (G-7036)
Park 100 Foods Inc 317 549-4545
　6908 E 30th St Indianapolis (46219) (G-7656)
Park 100 Foods Inc (PA) 765 675-3480
　326 E Adams St Tipton (46072) (G-13400)
Park 100 Foods Inc 765 763-6064
　205 Central Pkwy Morristown (46161) (G-10375)
Park County Aggregates LLC 765 245-2344
　5081 N State Road 59 Rockville (47872) (G-12178)
Park Developement, Anderson Also called Anderson Memorial Park (G-65)
Park Ohio, Huntington Also called General Aluminum Mfg Company (G-6206)
Parke County Sentinel, Rockville Also called Torch Newspapers Inc (G-12182)
Parker Exploration & Productio 812 673-4017
　2940 Donner Rd Wadesville (47638) (G-13774)
Parker-Hannifin Corporation 219 736-0400
　1201 E 86th Pl Ste H Merrillville (46410) (G-9744)
Parker-Hannifin Corporation 812 547-4710
　2002 Main St Tell City (47586) (G-13171)
Parker-Hannifin Corporation 260 894-7125
　1201 Gerber St Ligonier (46767) (G-9292)
Parker-Hannifin Corporation 574 533-1111
　1525 S 10th St Goshen (46526) (G-5307)
Parker-Hannifin Corporation 608 824-0500
　2002 Main St Tell City (47586) (G-13172)
Parker-Hannifin Corporation 574 528-9400
　501 S Sycamore St Syracuse (46567) (G-13139)
Parker-Hannifin Corporation 502 810-5823
　100 River Ridge Cir Jeffersonville (47130) (G-8412)
Parker-Hannifin Corporation 260 587-9102
　201 S Parker Dr Ashley (46705) (G-289)
Parker-Hannifin Corporation 260 636-2104
　903 N Orange St Albion (46701) (G-32)
Parker-Hannifin Corporation 219 297-3182
　715 S Iroquois St Goodland (47948) (G-5160)
Parker-Hannifin Corporation 260 748-6000
　10801 Rose Ave New Haven (46774) (G-10951)
Parkers Custom Ironworks LLC 812 897-3007
　1100 Mount Gilead Rd Boonville (47601) (G-920)
Parking Bumper Company, Universal Also called Hog Slat Incorporated (G-13467)
Parlor City Trophy & Apparel 260 824-0216
　224 W Market St Bluffton (46714) (G-884)

A
L
P
H
A
B
E
T
I
C

Parr Corp...574 264-9614
3200 County Road 6 E Elkhart (46514) ***(G-3075)***
Parr Technologies LLC...574 264-9614
3200 County Road 6 E Elkhart (46514) ***(G-3076)***
Parretts Meat Proc & Catrg...574 967-3711
603 Railroad St Flora (46929) ***(G-4001)***
Parretts Mt Proc Hog Roasting, Flora *Also called Parretts Meat Proc & Catrg* ***(G-4001)***
Parrish of Indiana Inc...317 859-0934
1020 Beal Ct Indianapolis (46217) ***(G-7657)***
Parsing Laser Designs LLC...317 677-4316
365 Austin Dr Avon (46123) ***(G-460)***
Parsley Seal Coating Stripping, Ellettsville *Also called Parsleys Seal Coating Inc* ***(G-3283)***
Parsleys Seal Coating Inc...812 876-5450
305 Ridge Springs Ln Ellettsville (47429) ***(G-3283)***
Parson Adhesives Inc...812 401-7277
2545 Eastside Park Rd Evansville (47715) ***(G-3664)***
Parsons Custom Machining Inc...812 877-2700
3029 N County Road 100 E Centerpoint (47840) ***(G-1539)***
Partners Marketing, Indianapolis *Also called Printing Partners Inc* ***(G-7755)***
Parts Cleaning Tech LLC...317 241-9379
2263 Distributors Dr Indianapolis (46241) ***(G-7658)***
Party Cask...812 234-3008
1652 S 25th St Terre Haute (47803) ***(G-13296)***
Party Cask Southeast, Terre Haute *Also called Party Cask* ***(G-13296)***
Past & Present Soap & Snd LLC...812 852-4328
10674 N County Road 350 W Batesville (47006) ***(G-514)***
Pasteleria Gresil LLC...317 299-8801
5348 W 38th St Indianapolis (46254) ***(G-7659)***
Patco Distribution, East Chicago *Also called Universal Services Inc* ***(G-2577)***
Pate & Lyle, Lafayette *Also called Tate Lyle Ingrdnts Amricas LLC* ***(G-9008)***
Pates Slaughtering & Proc...812 866-4710
Off Hwy 62 Hanover (47243) ***(G-5963)***
Pathfinder Amramp LLC...260 356-0500
2824 Theater Ave Huntington (46750) ***(G-6235)***
Pathfinder Cmnty Connection, Huntington *Also called Pathfinder Services Inc* ***(G-6236)***
Pathfinder Communications Corp (PA)...574 295-2500
421 S 2nd St Ste 100 Elkhart (46516) ***(G-3077)***
Pathfinder Communications Corp...574 266-5115
1846 Cassopolis St Elkhart (46514) ***(G-3078)***
Pathfinder School LLC...317 791-8777
6050 Churchman Byp Indianapolis (46203) ***(G-7660)***
Pathfinder Services Inc (PA)...260 356-0500
2824 Theater Ave Huntington (46750) ***(G-6236)***
Pathology Computer Systems...812 265-3264
131 E Main St Madison (47250) ***(G-9490)***
Patora Fine Jewelers, Indianapolis *Also called Interntnal Damnd Gold Exch Ltd* ***(G-7262)***
Patricia J Nickels Inc...502 489-4358
8324 Cypress Dr Charlestown (47111) ***(G-1579)***
Patrick & Sharon Hoctor...812 898-2678
13469 S Trueblood Pl Terre Haute (47802) ***(G-13297)***
Patrick Aluminum Inc...574 262-1907
2708 Frederic Dr Elkhart (46514) ***(G-3079)***
Patrick Custom Carbon...815 721-5150
475 Northpoint Ct Ste 400 Brownsburg (46112) ***(G-1162)***
Patrick Industries Inc (PA)...574 294-7511
107 W Franklin St Elkhart (46516) ***(G-3080)***
Patrick Industries Inc...574 522-7710
1808 W Hively Ave Elkhart (46517) ***(G-3081)***
Patrick Industries Inc...574 255-9692
5020 Lincolnway E Mishawaka (46544) ***(G-10100)***
Patrick Industries Inc...574 293-1521
1930 W Lusher Ave Elkhart (46517) ***(G-3082)***
Patrick Industries Inc...574 294-5758
3905 Lexington Park Dr Elkhart (46514) ***(G-3083)***
Patrick Industries Inc...574 293-1521
1926 W Lusher Ave Elkhart (46517) ***(G-3084)***
Patrick Industries Inc...574 522-0871
57766 County Road 3 Elkhart (46517) ***(G-3085)***
Patrick Industries Inc...574 522-6100
107 Rush Ct Elkhart (46516) ***(G-3086)***
Patrick Industries Inc...574 294-5959
28505 C R 20 W Elkhart (46517) ***(G-3087)***
Patrick Industries Inc...574 294-8828
56741 Elk Park Dr Elkhart (46516) ***(G-3088)***
Patrick Industries Inc...574 534-5300
3352 Maple City Dr Goshen (46526) ***(G-5308)***
Patrick Industries Inc...574 293-2990
2520 Industrial Pkwy Elkhart (46516) ***(G-3089)***
Patrick Industries Inc...574 295-9660
4906 Hoffman St Ste B Elkhart (46516) ***(G-3090)***
Patrick Industries Inc...260 665-6112
409 Growth Pkwy Angola (46703) ***(G-235)***
Patrick Industries Inc...574 546-5222
1849 Dogwood Rd Bremen (46506) ***(G-1014)***
Patrick Industries Inc...574 294-1975
2300 W Mishawaka Rd Elkhart (46517) ***(G-3091)***
Patrick Industries Inc...574 255-9692
5020 Lincolnway E Mishawaka (46544) ***(G-10101)***
Patriot Arms...812 859-4293
13379 State Highway 246 Coal City (47427) ***(G-1743)***
Patriot Label Inc...812 877-1611
9192 E Us Highway 40 Terre Haute (47803) ***(G-13298)***
Patriot Packaging LLC...812 346-0700
1002 Rodgers Park Dr North Vernon (47265) ***(G-11276)***
Patriot Plant, Patriot *Also called Hilltop Basic Resources Inc* ***(G-11468)***
Patriot Porcelain LLC...574 583-5128
114 Constitution Plz Monticello (47960) ***(G-10278)***
Patriot Products LLC...317 736-8007
3022 Hudson St Franklin (46131) ***(G-4919)***
Patriot Range Technologies, East Chicago *Also called Prt South LLC* ***(G-2566)***
Patriot Range Technologies...708 354-3150
4400 Homerlee Ave Ste 1 East Chicago (46312) ***(G-2556)***
Patriot Safety Products LLC...317 945-7023
11299 N 650 W Fountaintown (46130) ***(G-4792)***
Patriot Software Solutions Inc...317 573-5431
1311 W 96th St Ste 220 Indianapolis (46260) ***(G-7661)***
Patriotic Fireworks Inc...317 381-0529
1314 S High School Rd Indianapolis (46241) ***(G-7662)***
Pats Cleaning Service Rob...574 272-3067
18840 Darden Rd South Bend (46637) ***(G-12888)***
Pats Custom Printing and EMB...765 456-1532
1003 N Buckeye St Kokomo (46901) ***(G-8678)***
Patterson Driveshaft Inc...317 481-0495
8360 W Washington St Indianapolis (46231) ***(G-7663)***
Patty Processing Inc...574 936-9901
1955 N Oak Dr Plymouth (46563) ***(G-11710)***
Paul E Potts...812 354-3241
8689 W Private Road 375 N Hazleton (47640) ***(G-6010)***
Paul H Rohe Co Inc...812 926-1471
110 Forest Ave Aurora (47001) ***(G-384)***
Paul Knepp Saw Mill, Montgomery *Also called Paul Knepp Sawmill Inc* ***(G-10236)***
Paul Knepp Sawmill Inc...812 486-3773
3589 N 900 E Montgomery (47558) ***(G-10236)***
Paul Marshall and Son Log...260 724-2852
4895 E 600 N Decatur (46733) ***(G-2398)***
Paul Nelson...765 352-0698
4009 E Rembrandt Dr Martinsville (46151) ***(G-9632)***
Paul Tirotta...574 255-4101
1701 E 6th St Mishawaka (46544) ***(G-10102)***
Pauls Custom Machine...574 674-9633
30924 County Road 8 Elkhart (46514) ***(G-3092)***
Pauls Seating Inc...574 522-0630
56912 Elk Ct Elkhart (46516) ***(G-3093)***
Pauls Welding...574 646-2015
7930 W 1000 N Nappanee (46550) ***(G-10702)***
Paulus Plastic Company Inc...574 834-7663
304 E George St North Webster (46555) ***(G-11299)***
Paust Inc (PA)...765 962-1507
14 N 10th St Richmond (47374) ***(G-12027)***
Paust Printers, Richmond *Also called Paust Inc* ***(G-12027)***
Pavement Coatings Inc...812 424-3400
2120 N Grand Ave Evansville (47711) ***(G-3665)***
Paver Rescue Inc...317 259-4880
7802 E 88th St Indianapolis (46256) ***(G-7664)***
Paws Depot, Elnora *Also called Campbell Pet Company* ***(G-3287)***
Paxton Media Group, Frankfort *Also called Times* ***(G-4856)***
Paxton Media Group LLC...765 664-5111
610 S Adams St Marion (46953) ***(G-9550)***
Paxxal Inc...317 296-7724
14425 Bergen Blvd Ste A Noblesville (46060) ***(G-11164)***
Payne George A Petroleum Engr...812 853-3813
5844 Sharon Rd Newburgh (47630) ***(G-11040)***
Payne's Die Cutting, Fort Wayne *Also called Bruce Payne* ***(G-4124)***
Payne-Sparkman Manufacturing...812 944-4893
2571 Roanoke Ave New Albany (47150) ***(G-10840)***
Paynes Fine Cabrinetry...765 589-9176
7705 E 300 N Lafayette (47905) ***(G-8978)***
Paynter Machine Works Inc...812 883-2808
1302 E Hackberry St Salem (47167) ***(G-12303)***
Paytons Barbecue...765 294-2716
119 E Washington St Veedersburg (47987) ***(G-13645)***
Pb Metal Works...765 489-1311
50 Paul R Foulke Pkwy Hagerstown (47346) ***(G-5810)***
PBM Industries Inc...812 346-2648
1150 J F K Dr North Vernon (47265) ***(G-11277)***
Pbs Company, Wabash *Also called Poly Plastics Ltd* ***(G-13750)***
Pbs Mfg LLC...317 515-2875
5693 Federalist Ct Indianapolis (46254) ***(G-7665)***
PC Imprints...812 622-0855
158b Lockwood St Poseyville (47633) ***(G-11860)***
PC Max Inc...812 337-0630
2534 E 3rd St Bloomington (47401) ***(G-796)***
PCA, Columbus *Also called Packaging Corporation America* ***(G-1989)***
PCA, Edinburgh *Also called Packaging Corporation America* ***(G-2620)***
PCA, Jasper *Also called Packaging Corporation America* ***(G-8299)***
PCA Publishing Inc...317 658-2055
8845 Jackson St Indianapolis (46231) ***(G-7666)***

PCA Suthern Ind Corrugated LLC......................812 376-9301
  3460 Commerce Dr Columbus (47201) *(G-1991)*
PCA/Gas City 323, Gas City Also called Packaging Corporation America *(G-5126)*
Pd Sub LLC...812 524-0534
  2223 Killion Ave Seymour (47274) *(G-12474)*
Pda Solutions LLC..219 629-4658
  8840 Calumet Ave Ste 103 Munster (46321) *(G-10622)*
Pdb II Inc...219 865-1888
  2661 Tower Ct Dyer (46311) *(G-2507)*
Pdi, Columbus Also called Power Drives Inc *(G-1997)*
Pdi, Columbus Also called Phillips Company Inc *(G-1994)*
Pdk Industries Inc...765 721-3085
  6145 S County Road 375 W Greencastle (46135) *(G-5471)*
Pdma Inc..317 844-7750
  10201 N Illinois St # 420 Indianapolis (46290) *(G-6275)*
PDQ Tooling LLC...260 244-2984
  1100-1 S Williams Dr Columbia City (46725) *(G-1816)*
PDQ Workholding LLC....................................260 244-2919
  1100 S Williams Dr 1 Columbia City (46725) *(G-1817)*
Peabody Bear Run Mining LLC.........................812 659-7126
  7100 Eagle Crest Blvd Evansville (47715) *(G-3666)*
Peabody Energy Corporation...........................314 342-3400
  6280 S 1025 E Oakland City (47660) *(G-11311)*
Peabody Energy Corporation...........................812 795-4026
  6280 S And 1025 E Oakland City (47660) *(G-11312)*
Peabody Midwest Mining LLC..........................812 743-2910
  Se 610 E And Se 700 S S 7 Wheatland (47597) *(G-14232)*
Peabody Midwest Mining LLC.........................812 743-9292
  Air Quality 1 Vincennes (47591) *(G-13695)*
Peabody Midwest Mining LLC.........................812 644-7323
  3066 S 900 E Montgomery Cannelburg (47519) *(G-1285)*
Peabody Midwest Mining LLC.........................812 495-6070
  5526 E French Dr Pimento (47866) *(G-11580)*
Peabody Midwest Mining LLC (HQ)...................812 434-8500
  566 Dickeyville Rd Lynnville (47619) *(G-9436)*
Peabody Midwest Mining LLC...........................812 795-0040
  6280 S 1025 E Oakland City (47660) *(G-11313)*
Peabody Midwest Mining LLC...........................812 254-7714
  1281 S 300 W Washington (47501) *(G-13997)*
Peabody Midwest Mining LLC...........................812 782-3209
  County Rd 850 E Francisco (47649) *(G-4817)*
Peabody Wild Boar Mining LLC.......................812 434-8500
  566 Dickeyville Rd Lynnville (47619) *(G-9437)*
Peace Love Cupcakes....................................812 239-1591
  3833 N 25th St Terre Haute (47805) *(G-13299)*
Peace Valley Cabinets Inc...............................812 238-5134
  1111 E Royse Dr Terre Haute (47802) *(G-13300)*
Peace Valley Cabinets Inc...............................812 486-3831
  5127 E 300 N Montgomery (47558) *(G-10237)*
Peace Water Winery......................................317 810-1330
  37 W Main St Carmel (46032) *(G-1449)*
Peafield Products Inc.....................................317 839-8473
  4692 S County Road 600 E Plainfield (46168) *(G-11634)*
Peanut Butter and Jelly.................................317 205-9211
  5501 E 71st St Ste 4 Indianapolis (46220) *(G-7667)*
Pearl Custom Plastic Molding..........................765 763-6961
  7072 E Mulberry St Gwynneville (46144) *(G-5800)*
Pearl Launderers & Cleaners, Evansville Also called Daniel Korb Laundry
Company *(G-3453)*
Pearl of Wisdom, Crawfordsville Also called Milam Toys Inc *(G-2174)*
Pearson Education Inc...................................765 483-6500
  199 Pearson Pkwy Lebanon (46052) *(G-9211)*
Pearson Education Inc...................................765 483-6738
  150 Pearson Pkwy Lebanon (46052) *(G-9212)*
Pearson Education Inc...................................317 428-3049
  800 E 96th St Ste 300 Indianapolis (46240) *(G-7668)*
Pearson Education Inc...................................317 715-2150
  5550 W 74th St Indianapolis (46268) *(G-7669)*
Pearson Printing Company..............................765 664-8769
  3239 S Washington St Marion (46953) *(G-9551)*
Peepers Reading Glasses, Michigan City Also called Samco Group Inc *(G-9838)*
Peer Foods, Columbus Also called Mariah Foods Corp *(G-1967)*
Peerless Gear, Salem Also called Husqvrna Cnsmr Otdr Prod NA *(G-12294)*
Peerless Machine & Tool Corp.........................765 662-2586
  1804 W 2nd St Marion (46952) *(G-9552)*
Peerless Machinery Inc...................................574 210-5990
  4406 Technology Dr South Bend (46628) *(G-12889)*
Peerless Manufacturing, Garrett Also called Peerless Mfg Co *(G-5019)*
Peerless Manufacturing..................................260 897-3070
  103 W Simon St Laotto (46763) *(G-9114)*
Peerless Manufacturing LLC............................260 760-0880
  2084 N 800 E Avilla (46710) *(G-417)*
Peerless Mfg Co...260 357-3271
  800 E King St Garrett (46738) *(G-5019)*
Peerless of Georgetown, Fort Wayne Also called Grassco Inc *(G-4304)*
Peerless Pattern & Machine Co........................765 477-7719
  3521 Coleman Ct Lafayette (47905) *(G-8979)*
Peerless Printing & Off Sups, Marion Also called Peerless Printing Corp *(G-9553)*

Peerless Printing Corp...................................765 664-8341
  513 S Washington St Marion (46953) *(G-9553)*
Peerless Pump Company, Indianapolis Also called Sterling Fluid Systems USA LLC *(G-8003)*
Peggy Williams...765 724-3862
  3049 E 1100 N Alexandria (46001) *(G-47)*
Pelican Bay Solutions LLC..............................574 268-4456
  126 E Deerwood Ct Warsaw (46582) *(G-13924)*
Pems, Monroe Also called Phazpak Inc *(G-10184)*
Pendleton Door Company................................765 778-4164
  8680 S 750 W Pendleton (46064) *(G-11499)*
Pendleton Times...765 778-2324
  6837 S State Road 67 Pendleton (46064) *(G-11500)*
Pendleton Woolen Mills Inc.............................219 879-0326
  401 Lighthouse Pl Michigan City (46360) *(G-9828)*
Pendry Coatings LLC.....................................574 268-2956
  1119 Seymour Midwest Dr Warsaw (46580) *(G-13925)*
Pengad/Indy, Muncie Also called Pengad/West Inc *(G-10544)*
Pengad/West Inc..765 286-3000
  1106 E Seymour St Ste A Muncie (47302) *(G-10544)*
Penguin Enterprises LLC................................812 333-0475
  401 S Walnut St Bloomington (47401) *(G-797)*
Penguin Random House LLC............................800 672-7836
  199 Pearson Pkwy Lebanon (46052) *(G-9213)*
Penguin Random House LLC............................765 362-5125
  1021 N State Road 47 Crawfordsville (47933) *(G-2184)*
Penlines Publishing LLC................................219 884-2632
  212 W 49th Ave Gary (46408) *(G-5084)*
Penn Tool, Indianapolis Also called Precision Tubes Inc *(G-7738)*
Pennville Custom Cabinetry, Portland Also called Commercial Electric Co Inc *(G-11813)*
Pent Assemblies...260 347-5828
  6928 N 400 E Kendallville (46755) *(G-8501)*
Pent Plastics Inc (PA)..................................260 897-3775
  6928 N 400 E Kendallville (46755) *(G-8502)*
Pentera Group Inc...317 543-2055
  921 E 86th St Ste 100 Indianapolis (46240) *(G-7670)*
Pentzer Printing Inc.......................................812 372-2896
  4505 Kelly St Columbus (47203) *(G-1992)*
Penway Inc...812 526-2645
  900 S Walnut St Edinburgh (46124) *(G-2621)*
Penz Products Inc..574 255-4736
  1320 S Merrifield Ave Mishawaka (46544) *(G-10103)*
People's Exchange, The, Lagrange Also called Lagwana Printing Inc *(G-9054)*
Pepcon Concrete Inc......................................765 964-6572
  1567 Frank Miller Rd Union City (47390) *(G-13459)*
Pepito Miller Bev Imports LLC.........................317 416-3215
  4188 Scioto Dr Plainfield (46168) *(G-11635)*
Pepka Spring Company Inc.............................765 459-3114
  810 S Waugh St Kokomo (46901) *(G-8679)*
Pepsi Beverage Company...............................574 271-0633
  5435 Dylan Dr South Bend (46628) *(G-12890)*
Pepsi Beverages Company..............................219 836-1800
  9300 Calumet Ave Munster (46321) *(G-10623)*
Pepsi Bottling Ventures LLC...........................765 659-7313
  2611 W County Road 0 Ns Frankfort (46041) *(G-4850)*
Pepsi-Cola, Logansport Also called Interactions Inc *(G-9341)*
Pepsi-Cola, Frankfort Also called Pepsi Bottling Ventures LLC *(G-4850)*
Pepsi-Cola...812 634-1844
  2811 Market St Jasper (47546) *(G-8300)*
Pepsi-Cola Metro Btlg Co Inc...........................812 332-1200
  214 W 17th St Bloomington (47404) *(G-798)*
Pepsico, Munster Also called P-Americas LLC *(G-10621)*
Pepsico, Austin Also called P-Americas LLC *(G-399)*
Pepsico, Seymour Also called P-Americas LLC *(G-12472)*
Pepsico, Munster Also called Pepsi Beverages Company *(G-10623)*
Pepsico, Jasper Also called Pepsi-Cola *(G-8300)*
Pepsico, Indianapolis Also called P-Americas LLC *(G-7644)*
Pepsico, Brookville Also called P-Americas LLC *(G-1124)*
Pepsico, Bloomington Also called P-Americas LLC *(G-794)*
Pepsico, Muncie Also called P-Americas LLC *(G-10542)*
Pepsico...317 334-0153
  5010 W 81st St Indianapolis (46268) *(G-7671)*
Pepsico...317 821-6400
  5858 Decatur Blvd Indianapolis (46241) *(G-7672)*
Pepsico Inc..260 579-3461
  3939 N Wells St Fort Wayne (46808) *(G-4522)*
Peranis Hockey World....................................317 288-5183
  7325 E 96th St Ste F Indianapolis (46250) *(G-7673)*
Perch Tree Inc..630 450-4591
  11377 Hawkshead Ln # 200 Fishers (46037) *(G-3949)*
Perdue Farms Inc...812 254-8500
  65 S 200 W Washington (47501) *(G-13998)*
Perdue Farms Inc...812 886-0593
  500 Perdue Rd Vincennes (47591) *(G-13696)*
Perdue Farms Inc...765 436-7990
  4586 N Us Highway 52 Thorntown (46071) *(G-13377)*
Perdue Farms Inc...757 787-5210
  100 W 400 N Washington (47501) *(G-13999)*

(PA)=Parent Co (HQ)=Headquarters (DH)=Div Headquarters

Perdue Farms Inc 765 325-2997
5490 N 500 E Lebanon (46052) *(G-9214)*

Perdue Printed Products Inc 260 456-7575
1902 S Harrison St Fort Wayne (46802) *(G-4523)*

Perfect Impressions Printing 317 923-1756
3901 N Meridian St Ste 15 Indianapolis (46208) *(G-7674)*

Perfect Manufacturing LLC 317 924-5284
450 W 16th Pl Indianapolis (46202) *(G-7675)*

Perfect Pallets Inc (PA) 888 553-5559
450 W 16th Pl Indianapolis (46202) *(G-7676)*

Perfect Pig Inc 219 984-5355
332 W 100 N Reynolds (47980) *(G-11947)*

Perfect Plastic Printing Corp 317 888-9447
3967 Woodmore Dr Greenwood (46142) *(G-5731)*

Perfect Seating LLC 317 733-1284
10730 Bennett Pkwy A Zionsville (46077) *(G-14455)*

Perfect Sign LLC 812 518-6459
1944 Lakes Edge Dr Newburgh (47630) *(G-11041)*

Perfecta USA 317 862-7371
5505 S Franklin Rd Indianapolis (46239) *(G-7677)*

Perfection Bakeries Inc (PA) 260 424-8245
350 Pearl St Fort Wayne (46802) *(G-4524)*

Perfection Bakeries Inc 260 483-5481
4001 Kraft Pkwy Fort Wayne (46808) *(G-4525)*

Perfection Bakeries Inc 574 269-9706
2557 E Us Highway 30 Warsaw (46580) *(G-13926)*

Perfection Kitchen & Bath Ctr, Selma *Also called Perfection Kitchen & Bath Ctr (G-12425)*

Perfection Kitchen & Bath Ctr 765 289-7594
10210 E Katie Ln Selma (47383) *(G-12425)*

Perfection Mold & Tool Inc 574 292-0824
1116 Mishawaka Ave South Bend (46615) *(G-12891)*

Perfection Products Inc 765 482-7786
1320 Indianapolis Ave Lebanon (46052) *(G-9215)*

Perfection Wheel LLC 260 358-9239
255 N Briant St Huntington (46750) *(G-6237)*

Perfecto Tool & Engineering Co 765 644-2821
1124 W 53rd St Anderson (46013) *(G-150)*

Performance Coatings Spc LLC 574 606-8153
7030 W 665 S Topeka (46571) *(G-13427)*

Performance Machining Inc 812 432-9180
13350 Us Highway 50 Dillsboro (47018) *(G-2471)*

Performance Minerals Corp (PA) 219 365-8356
10220 Wicker Ave Ste 3s Saint John (46373) *(G-12266)*

Performance Mstr Coil Proc Inc 765 364-1300
3752 E 350 S Crawfordsville (47933) *(G-2185)*

Performance Powder Coating 765 438-5224
1124 S Union St Kokomo (46902) *(G-8680)*

Performance Rod & Custom Inc 812 897-5805
913 W Main St Boonville (47601) *(G-921)*

Performance Technology Inc 574 862-2116
65251 State Road 19 Wakarusa (46573) *(G-13789)*

Performance Tool Inc 260 726-6572
103 Performance Dr Portland (47371) *(G-11838)*

Perfumery 812 777-0657
621 Park East Blvd New Albany (47150) *(G-10841)*

Peri Formwork Systems Inc 317 390-0062
5550 S East St Ste E Indianapolis (46227) *(G-7678)*

Perimeter Solutions LP 219 933-1560
1326 Summer St Hammond (46320) *(G-5926)*

Perkinsville Power Sports 765 734-1314
2834 N 900 W Anderson (46011) *(G-151)*

Perm Industries Inc 219 365-5000
9660 Industrial Dr Saint John (46373) *(G-12267)*

Perm Machine & Tool Co, Saint John *Also called Perm Industries Inc (G-12267)*

Perma Lubrication 317 241-0797
2346 S Lynhurst Dr Ste J Indianapolis (46241) *(G-7679)*

Perma Lubrication 219 531-9155
2503 Chicago St Ste A Valparaiso (46383) *(G-13597)*

Perma-Green Supreme Inc 219 548-3801
5609 Murvihill Rd Valparaiso (46383) *(G-13598)*

Permalatt Products Inc 574 546-6311
3462 Us Highway 6 Bremen (46506) *(G-1015)*

Permawick Company Inc 812 376-0703
3110 Permawick Dr Columbus (47201) *(G-1993)*

Permo Wick, Columbus *Also called Caltherm Corporation (G-1865)*

Perry County News, Tell City *Also called News Publishing Company LLC (G-13169)*

Perry Equipment, Crawfordsville *Also called McClamroch AG LLC (G-2171)*

Perry Foam Products Inc (PA) 765 474-3404
2335 S 30th St Lafayette (47909) *(G-8980)*

Perry Material Sales, Terre Haute *Also called Prairie Group (G-13307)*

Perry Products Inc 260 668-7860
959 Growth Pkwy Angola (46703) *(G-236)*

Perry's Specialties, Churubusco *Also called Perrys Country Store (G-1655)*

Perrys Country Store 260 693-0084
3530 N Us Highway 33 Churubusco (46723) *(G-1655)*

Peru Hardwood Products Inc 765 473-4844
2678 N Mexico Rd Peru (46970) *(G-11539)*

Peru Tribune, Peru *Also called Daily Peru Tribune Pubg Co (G-11523)*

Pete D Limkemann 260 403-4297
724 S Doyle Rd Fort Wayne (46803) *(G-4526)*

Pete's Peaches, Washington *Also called Southern Indiana Chemical (G-14003)*

Peter Austin Co 765 288-6397
900 W 1st St Muncie (47305) *(G-10545)*

Peter Franklin Jewelers Inc (PA) 260 749-4315
507 Broadway St New Haven (46774) *(G-10952)*

Peter Stone Company 260 768-9150
805 E North Village Dr Shipshewana (46565) *(G-12643)*

Peters & Marske, Michigan City *Also called M T M Machining Inc (G-9813)*

Peters Enterprises 260 493-6435
217 State Road 930 W New Haven (46774) *(G-10953)*

Peters Equipment, New Haven *Also called Peters Enterprises (G-10953)*

Peterson Sanko Corp 765 966-9656
505 Industrial Pkwy Richmond (47374) *(G-12028)*

Petoskey Plastics Inc 765 348-9808
1100 W Grant St Hartford City (47348) *(G-5987)*

Petrochoice Holdings Inc 317 634-7300
1751 W Raymond St Indianapolis (46221) *(G-7680)*

Petrogas International Corp 260 484-0859
2444 Woodland Trl Auburn (46706) *(G-347)*

Petroleum Solutions Inc 574 546-2133
809 Douglas Rd Bremen (46506) *(G-1016)*

Pettigrew 260 868-2032
7725 County Road 32 Butler (46721) *(G-1238)*

Pettit Printing Inc 260 563-2346
789 S Carroll St Wabash (46992) *(G-13749)*

Peyton Technical Services LLC 812 738-2016
1548 Highway 62 Nw Corydon (47112) *(G-2107)*

Pfeiffer Winery & Vineyard 812 952-2650
940 Saint Peters Ch Rd Ne Corydon (47112) *(G-2108)*

Pfizer Inc 574 232-9927
6879 Entp Dr Ste 500 South Bend (46628) *(G-12892)*

Pfizer Inc 212 733-2323
411 E Dallas Dr Terre Haute (47802) *(G-13301)*

Pfortune Art & Design, Indianapolis *Also called Pfortune Art & Design Inc (G-7681)*

Pfortune Art & Design Inc 317 872-4123
9549 Valparaiso Ct Indianapolis (46268) *(G-7681)*

Pfrank Quarter Horses 765 220-0257
3921 Park Elwood Rd Richmond (47374) *(G-12029)*

Pgc Landscaping & Mulch, Evansville *Also called Pgc Mulch LLC (G-3667)*

Pgc Mulch LLC 812 455-0700
1501 N 7th Ave Evansville (47710) *(G-3667)*

Pgg Enterprises LLC 317 462-2871
6331 E Us Highway 40 Greenfield (46140) *(G-5563)*

Pgi Mfg LLC (PA) 574 968-3222
100 E Wayne St Ste 320 South Bend (46601) *(G-12893)*

Pgp Corp 812 285-7700
701 Loop Rd Jeffersonville (47130) *(G-8413)*

Pgp International Inc 812 867-5129
5404 Foundation Blvd Evansville (47725) *(G-3668)*

Pgs LLC (PA) 812 988-4030
120 E Main St Nashville (47448) *(G-10732)*

Pgw Industries Inc 317 322-3599
1445 Brookville Way Ste S Indianapolis (46239) *(G-7682)*

Ph Inc 877 467-4763
2400 Walter Glaub Dr Plymouth (46563) *(G-11711)*

Phantom Industries LLC 812 276-5956
734 Spring St Jeffersonville (47130) *(G-8414)*

Phantom Neon LLC 765 362-2221
100 E North St Crawfordsville (47933) *(G-2186)*

Phantom Signs, Crawfordsville *Also called Phantom Neon LLC (G-2186)*

Pharma Form Finders LLC 317 362-1191
11164 Muirfield Trce Fishers (46037) *(G-3950)*

Pharos Tribune, Logansport *Also called Community Holdings Indiana Inc (G-9332)*

Phase Three Electric Inc 812 945-9922
2115 E Market St New Albany (47150) *(G-10842)*

Phaze One LLC 812 634-9545
4533 Baden Strasse Jasper (47546) *(G-8301)*

Phazpak Inc 260 692-6416
259 N Van Buren St Monroe (46772) *(G-10184)*

PHD Inc 260 747-6151
9030 Clubridge Dr Fort Wayne (46809) *(G-4527)*

PHD Inc 260 356-0120
4763 N Us Highway 24 E Huntington (46750) *(G-6238)*

Phend and Brown Inc (PA) 574 658-4166
367 E 1250 N Milford (46542) *(G-9961)*

Phenix Tube Corp 260 424-3734
2701 S Coliseum Blvd # 1148 Fort Wayne (46803) *(G-4528)*

Pheonix Inc 765 489-3030
98 W Main St Hagerstown (47346) *(G-5811)*

Phil & Son Inc 219 663-5757
871 N Madison St Crown Point (46307) *(G-2283)*

Phil Etienne Timber, Saint Croix *Also called Phil Etiennes Timber Harvest (G-12251)*

Phil Etiennes Timber Harvest 812 843-5132
25993 Saint Croix Rd Saint Croix (47576) *(G-12251)*

Phil Irwin Advertising Inc 317 547-5117
5995 E 30th St Indianapolis (46218) *(G-7683)*

Philip Konrad & Sons Inc...574 772-3966
  1315 E State Road 10 Knox (46534) *(G-8576)*

Philip Pins...219 769-1059
  3701 W 79th Pl Merrillville (46410) *(G-9745)*

Philip Reinisch Company Llc...812 326-2626
  5170 S 3rd St Saint Anthony (47575) *(G-12249)*

Philips Ultrasound Inc...317 591-5242
  7518 E 39th St Indianapolis (46226) *(G-7684)*

Phillips Company Inc...812 378-3797
  6330 E 100 S Columbus (47201) *(G-1994)*

Phillips Diversified Services...260 248-2975
  309 N Washington St Columbia City (46725) *(G-1818)*

Phillips Pattern & Casting Inc (PA)................................765 288-2319
  801 W Riggin Rd Muncie (47303) *(G-10546)*

Phoenix America Inc...260 432-9664
  4717 Clubview Dr Fort Wayne (46804) *(G-4529)*

Phoenix Assembly LLC (HQ).......................................317 884-3600
  164 S Park Blvd Greenwood (46143) *(G-5732)*

Phoenix Assembly Indiana LLC....................................317 884-3600
  6200 S International Dr Columbus (47201) *(G-1995)*

Phoenix Brands LLC (PA)...203 975-0319
  2601 Fortune Cir E 102b Indianapolis (46241) *(G-7685)*

Phoenix Brands LLC...317 231-8044
  2601 Fortune Cir E 102b Indianapolis (46241) *(G-7686)*

Phoenix Closures LLC..765 658-1800
  2000 S Jackson St Greencastle (46135) *(G-5472)*

Phoenix Color Corp...812 234-1585
  200 Hulman St Terre Haute (47802) *(G-13302)*

Phoenix Color Corp...812 238-1551
  200 Hulman St Terre Haute (47802) *(G-13303)*

Phoenix Custom Kitchens Inc......................................812 523-1890
  6600 N Us Highway 31 Seymour (47274) *(G-12475)*

Phoenix Drum Dryer Inc...574 251-9040
  1531 Kemble Ave South Bend (46613) *(G-12894)*

Phoenix Engineering & Mfg Inc...................................574 251-9040
  1531 Kemble Ave South Bend (46613) *(G-12895)*

Phoenix Fbrcators Erectors LLC (PA).............................317 271-7002
  182 S County Road 900 E Avon (46123) *(G-461)*

Phoenix Mixers, Avilla *Also called Indiana Phoenix Inc (G-406)*

Phoenix Pallet Inc...574 262-0458
  2901 Dexter Dr Elkhart (46514) *(G-3094)*

Phoenix Safe International LLC.....................................765 483-0954
  382 N Mount Zion Rd Lebanon (46052) *(G-9216)*

Phoenix Services LLC...219 397-0650
  3001 Dickey Rd East Chicago (46312) *(G-2557)*

Phoenix Services LLC...219 399-7808
  3236 Watling St East Chicago (46312) *(G-2558)*

Phoenix Sign Works Inc...317 432-4027
  5345 Lexington Ave Indianapolis (46219) *(G-7687)*

Phoenix Specialities Ltd...219 345-5812
  2798 W 800 N Lake Village (46349) *(G-9084)*

Phoenix Specialties Ltd...219 345-5812
  2279 E State Road 10 Lake Village (46349) *(G-9085)*

Phoenix Usa Inc...574 266-2020
  2601 Marina Dr Elkhart (46514) *(G-3095)*

Photo Screen Service Inc..317 636-7712
  1505 Southeastern Ave Indianapolis (46201) *(G-7688)*

Photo Specialties...812 944-5111
  232 Maevi Dr New Albany (47150) *(G-10843)*

Phytex, Sheridan *Also called United Animal Health Inc (G-12600)*

Phytoption LLC...765 490-7738
  3495 Kent Ave Ste P100 West Lafayette (47906) *(G-14094)*

Pia Automation US Inc...812 474-3126
  5825 Old Boonville Hwy Evansville (47715) *(G-3669)*

Piano Shop Llc...812 951-2462
  9161 In 64 Georgetown (47122) *(G-5152)*

Pickle Bites...219 902-6315
  7451 Olcott Ave Hammond (46323) *(G-5927)*

Pickle Prints LLC...317 344-2495
  12639 Teaberry Ln Carmel (46032) *(G-1450)*

Pickled Pedaler...317 877-0624
  499 Banbury Rd Noblesville (46062) *(G-11165)*

Pickslays Woodworking...530 388-8697
  1313 Wooster Rd Winona Lake (46590) *(G-14353)*

Picture Perfect Printing...765 482-4241
  1301 Ashley Dr Lebanon (46052) *(G-9217)*

Piece Vallet Cabinets, Montgomery *Also called Custom Tables & Cabinets (G-10221)*

Piedmont Heat Treating, Fort Wayne *Also called Al-Fe Heat Treating Inc (G-4055)*

Piedmont Plastics Inc...317 947-4500
  7768 Zionsville Rd Indianapolis (46268) *(G-7689)*

Pieniadze Inc...888 226-6241
  1555 W Oak St Ste 100 Zionsville (46077) *(G-14456)*

Pier-Mac Plastics Inc...260 726-9844
  1000 N Morton St Portland (47371) *(G-11839)*

Pierce Company Inc (HQ)...765 998-8100
  35 N 8th St Upland (46989) *(G-13472)*

Pierce Oil Co Inc...812 268-6356
  115 W Jackson St Sullivan (47882) *(G-13090)*

Pierce Tracy...765 748-2361
  4663 State Road 32 E Anderson (46017) *(G-152)*

Pierceton Case & Tray, Pierceton *Also called Paragon Medical Inc (G-11576)*

Pierceton I&I, Pierceton *Also called Paragon Medical Inc (G-11575)*

Pierceton Rubber Products Inc....................................574 594-3002
  3076 S 900 E Pierceton (46562) *(G-11577)*

Pierceton Welding & Fabg..260 352-0106
  9730 S State Road 15 Silver Lake (46982) *(G-12678)*

Piercy Machine Co Inc...317 398-9296
  945 W 300 S Shelbyville (46176) *(G-12556)*

Piezotech LLC (HQ)...317 876-4670
  8431 Georgetown Rd # 300 Indianapolis (46268) *(G-7690)*

Pigeon Switch Pottery...812 567-4124
  1896 Pigeon Switch Tennyson (47637) *(G-13180)*

Pike County Publishing Corp (PA)................................812 354-8500
  820 E Poplar St Petersburg (47567) *(G-11566)*

Pike Lumber Company Inc..574 893-4511
  440 W County Rd1450 N Carbon (47837) *(G-1293)*

Pike Publishing...812 354-4701
  407 E Walnut St Petersburg (47567) *(G-11567)*

Pilcher Publishing Co Inc..219 696-7711
  318 E Commercial Ave Lowell (46356) *(G-9419)*

Pilkington North America Inc......................................317 346-0621
  1001 Hurricane St Franklin (46131) *(G-4920)*

Pilkington North America Inc......................................317 392-7000
  300 Northridge Dr Shelbyville (46176) *(G-12557)*

Pillar Innovations LLC...812 474-9080
  9844 Hedden Rd Evansville (47725) *(G-3670)*

Pillow Pals Inc...812 853-8241
  6566 Sharon Rd Newburgh (47630) *(G-11042)*

Pillsbury Company LLC...812 944-8411
  707 Pillsbury Ln New Albany (47150) *(G-10844)*

Pilot News, Plymouth *Also called Cnhi LLC (G-11674)*

Pimmler Holdings Inc (PA)..574 583-8090
  3137 S Freeman Rd Monticello (47960) *(G-10279)*

Pin Point Av LLC...317 750-3120
  8226 Kentallen Ct Indianapolis (46236) *(G-7691)*

Pin-Up Curls LLC...260 241-5871
  1835 Marietta Dr Fort Wayne (46804) *(G-4530)*

Pinch of Sugar...812 476-7650
  519 N Green River Rd Evansville (47715) *(G-3671)*

Pinder Industries, Munster *Also called Pinder Instruments Company Inc (G-10624)*

Pinder Instruments Company Inc..................................219 924-7070
  9751 Indiana Pkwy Ste A Munster (46321) *(G-10624)*

Pinder Polyurethane & Plas Inc...................................219 397-8248
  481 E 151st St East Chicago (46312) *(G-2559)*

Pine Manor Inc (HQ)...800 532-4186
  9622 W 350 N Orland (46776) *(G-11355)*

Pineapple Software Inc...812 987-8277
  707 Lake Shore Dr Borden (47106) *(G-937)*

Ping Custom Drapery Workroom...................................317 984-3251
  11313 E 234th St Cicero (46034) *(G-1665)*

Ping's Custom Drapery, Cicero *Also called Ping Custom Drapery Workroom (G-1665)*

Pingleton Sawmill Inc...765 653-2878
  525 S County Road 550 W Greencastle (46135) *(G-5473)*

Pink Lipstick and Company...317 992-6818
  5744 Brendon Way West Dr Indianapolis (46226) *(G-7692)*

Pinnacle Equipment Company Inc................................317 259-1180
  1616 Milburn St Indianapolis (46202) *(G-7693)*

Pinnacle Manufacturing Group.....................................317 691-2460
  5622 Liberty Creek Dr E Indianapolis (46254) *(G-7694)*

Pinnacle Oil Holdings LLC..317 875-9465
  8175 Allison Ave Indianapolis (46268) *(G-7695)*

Pinnacle Oil Holdings LLC (PA).....................................317 875-9465
  5009 W 81st St Indianapolis (46268) *(G-7696)*

Pinnacle Oil Trading LLC...317 875-9465
  8175 Allison Ave Indianapolis (46268) *(G-7697)*

Pinnacle Seating Inc..574 522-2636
  1011 Herman St Elkhart (46516) *(G-3096)*

Pinnacle Tool Inc...812 336-5000
  1830 S Walnut St Bloomington (47401) *(G-799)*

Pinnacle Woodworking LLC...765 345-2301
  9708 S County Road 650 W Knightstown (46148) *(G-8559)*

Pinpoint Printer...812 577-0630
  541 Green Blvd Aurora (47001) *(G-385)*

Pintegra/Whosser Data Forms, Indianapolis *Also called Printegra Corp (G-7752)*

Pinup Curls Salon...260 267-9659
  6222 Covington Rd Fort Wayne (46804) *(G-4531)*

Pioneer Cane & Handle Co..812 859-4415
  3016 E River Rd Clay City (47841) *(G-1705)*

Pioneer Electric...765 762-2000
  107 Fall St Williamsport (47993) *(G-14294)*

Pioneer Metal Finishing LLC......................................574 287-7239
  2424 Foundation Dr South Bend (46628) *(G-12896)*

Pioneer Oil Company Inc..812 494-2800
  400 Main St Vincennes (47591) *(G-13697)*

Pioneer Oilfield Services LLC.....................................812 882-0999
  1290 N State Road 67 Vincennes (47591) *(G-13698)*

Pioneer Plastics Corporation.....................................574 264-0702
  25603 Borg Rd Elkhart (46514) *(G-3097)*

Pioneer Signs Inc...219 884-7587
  3289 E 83rd Pl Merrillville (46410) *(G-9746)*

A
L
P
H
A
B
E
T
I
C

PIP Printing, Columbus *Also called Jem Printing Inc* *(G-1951)*

PIP Printing, Indianapolis *Also called Dynamark Graphics Group Inc* *(G-6774)*

PIP Printing, Indianapolis *Also called Ed Sons Inc* *(G-6803)*

PIP Printing, Indianapolis *Also called Drs Graphix Group Inc* *(G-6768)*

PIP Printing, Indianapolis *Also called Dynamark Graphics Group Inc* *(G-6775)*

PIP Printing, Indianapolis *Also called Dynamark Graphics Group Inc* *(G-6776)*

PIP Printing, New Albany *Also called Lagnaippe LLC* *(G-10816)*

PIP Printing, Indianapolis *Also called Dynamark Graphics Group Inc* *(G-6777)*

PIP Printing 317 843-5755
11711 N Penn St Ste 107 Carmel (46032) *(G-1451)*

PIP Printing & Marketting Svcs, Anderson *Also called Jam Printing Inc* *(G-125)*

Pipe Creek Jr 765 922-7991
6377 W 600 S Sims (46986) *(G-12683)*

Pipeconx, Evansville *Also called Ace Extrusion LLC* *(G-3341)*

Pipeconx 800 443-9081
701 N 9th Ave Evansville (47712) *(G-3672)*

Piro Shoes LLC 888 849-0916
8327 Weaver Woods Pl Fishers (46038) *(G-3951)*

Pirod Inc (HQ) 574 936-7221
1545 Pidco Dr Plymouth (46563) *(G-11712)*

Pit Bull Leather Company Inc 812 988-6007
20 N Van Buren St Nashville (47448) *(G-10733)*

Pitney Bowes Inc 317 769-8300
5490 Industrial Ct Whitestown (46075) *(G-14257)*

Pitney Bowes Inc 260 436-7395
5071 W 74th St Indianapolis (46268) *(G-7698)*

Pitney Bowes Inc 317 769-8300
5490 Industrial Ct Whitestown (46075) *(G-14258)*

Pittman Mine Service LLC 812 847-2340
2878 N State Road 59 Linton (47441) *(G-9311)*

Pittsburgh Glass Works LLC 812 867-6601
424 E Inglefield Rd Evansville (47725) *(G-3673)*

Pittsfield of Indiana, Hamilton *Also called Pittsfield Products Inc* *(G-5826)*

Pittsfield Products Inc 260 488-2124
7365 S Enterprise Dr Hamilton (46742) *(G-5826)*

Pizo Operating Company LLC 317 243-0811
7901 W Morris St Indianapolis (46231) *(G-7699)*

PJmort Woodworking 574 542-9680
8835 S 1000 E Monterey (46960) *(G-10208)*

Pjw Inc 574 295-1203
56199 Parkway Ave Elkhart (46516) *(G-3098)*

Pk USA Inc (HQ) 317 395-5500
600 Northridge Dr Shelbyville (46176) *(G-12558)*

Plainfield Sign Graphic Design 317 839-9499
8285 E County Road 300 S Plainfield (46168) *(G-11636)*

Plakes Tooling Inc 765 963-2745
881 S 725 W Tipton (46072) *(G-13401)*

Planet Mind Learning Store, Kokomo *Also called Planet Mind LLC* *(G-8681)*

Planet Mind LLC 765 452-2341
108 N Main St Kokomo (46901) *(G-8681)*

Planet Pets 812 539-7316
1099 W Eads Pkwy Lawrenceburg (47025) *(G-9152)*

Planks Printing Service Inc 574 533-1739
505 S 9th St Goshen (46526) *(G-5309)*

Plant Engineering Services Inc (PA) 260 281-2917
744 County Road 8 Corunna (46730) *(G-2085)*

Plaquemaker Plus Inc 317 594-5556
10080 E 121st St Ste 118 Fishers (46037) *(G-3952)*

Plas-Tech Molding & Design Inc 260 761-3006
7037b N Triplett St Brimfield (46794) *(G-1036)*

Plasfinco LLC 812 346-3900
1060 Jfk Dr North Vernon (47265) *(G-11278)*

Plaster Shak 317 881-6518
1797 Old State Road 37 Greenwood (46143) *(G-5733)*

Plastic Assembly Tech Inc 317 841-1202
8445 Castlewood Dr Ste B Indianapolis (46250) *(G-7700)*

Plastic Cardz 260 440-1964
1925 Wayside Dr Fort Wayne (46818) *(G-4532)*

Plastic Cardz LLC 260 431-6380
12721 Us Highway 24 W Fort Wayne (46814) *(G-4533)*

Plastic Components Inc 574 264-7514
1210 County Road 6 W Elkhart (46514) *(G-3099)*

Plastic Composites Co, Fort Wayne *Also called Aptimise Composites LLC* *(G-4088)*

Plastic Composites Co., Fort Wayne *Also called Composites Syndicate LLC* *(G-4172)*

Plastic Extrusions Company 812 479-3232
6500 Newburgh Rd Evansville (47715) *(G-3674)*

Plastic Line Manufacturing 219 769-8022
9070 Louisiana St Merrillville (46410) *(G-9747)*

Plastic Molding Mfg Inc 574 234-9036
5102 Dylan Dr South Bend (46628) *(G-12897)*

Plastic Moldings Company Llc 317 392-4139
1451 Miller Ave Shelbyville (46176) *(G-12559)*

Plastic Package LLC 916 921-3399
1900 Whirlpool Dr Ste 300 La Porte (46350) *(G-8804)*

Plastic Processors Inc 260 488-3999
7450 S Homestead Dr Hamilton (46742) *(G-5827)*

Plastic Solutions, Inc., South Bend *Also called PSI Molded Plastics Ind Inc* *(G-12907)*

Plasticraft-Complete Acrylics 765 610-9502
4441 S Scatterfield Rd Anderson (46013) *(G-153)*

Plastics Fabg & Distrg LLC 574 233-7527
219 E Tutt St South Bend (46601) *(G-12898)*

Plastics Research and Dev Inc 812 279-8885
747 Washboard Rd Springville (47462) *(G-13066)*

Plastimatic Arts Corp 574 254-9000
3622 N Home St Mishawaka (46545) *(G-10104)*

Plateplus Inc 219 392-3400
4303 Kennedy Ave East Chicago (46312) *(G-2560)*

Plating Products Inc 775 241-0416
1020 S Main St Kokomo (46902) *(G-8682)*

Platinum Display Group 317 731-5026
5855 Kopetsky Dr Indianapolis (46217) *(G-7701)*

Platinum Industries LLC 765 744-8323
11625 Suncatcher Dr Fishers (46037) *(G-3953)*

Play 2 Win Screenprinting LLC 765 426-0679
8975 E 200 S Oxford (47971) *(G-11434)*

Playfair Shuffleboard Company 260 747-7288
7021 Bluffton Rd Fort Wayne (46809) *(G-4534)*

Playn2win LLC 317 345-4653
7948 Preservation Dr Indianapolis (46278) *(G-7702)*

Pleasant Industries Inc 260 638-4699
6045 Hamilton Rd Yoder (46798) *(G-14399)*

Pletchers Poultry Processing 574 831-2329
66786 County Road 17 Goshen (46526) *(G-5310)*

Plexiclass Awards Disc Tropies, Elkhart *Also called Smokers Iron Works* *(G-3179)*

Pliant Corp International, Evansville *Also called Pliant International LLC* *(G-3676)*

Pliant Corp International (PA) 812 424-2904
101 Oakley St Evansville (47710) *(G-3675)*

Pliant International LLC 812 424-2904
101 Oakley St Evansville (47710) *(G-3676)*

Pliant Packaging Canada LLC 812 424-2904
101 Oakley St Evansville (47710) *(G-3677)*

PLM Holdings Inc 812 232-0624
3956 S State Road 63 Terre Haute (47802) *(G-13304)*

Ploog Engineering Co Inc 219 663-2854
814 N Indiana Ave Crown Point (46307) *(G-2284)*

Pls, New Albany *Also called Packaging Lgstics Slutions LLC* *(G-10838)*

Plumrose USA Inc 574 295-8190
24402 County Road 45 Elkhart (46516) *(G-3100)*

Pluto, French Lick *Also called Ahf Industries Inc* *(G-4984)*

Plymouth Foundry Inc 574 936-2106
523 W Harrison St Plymouth (46563) *(G-11713)*

Plymouth Oil and Gas Inc 574 875-4808
57592 Hearthstone Ct Goshen (46528) *(G-5311)*

Plymouth Pdts Acquisition Inc 574 936-4757
1800 Jim Neu Dr Ste 7 Plymouth (46563) *(G-11714)*

Plymouth Ready Mart Inc 574 936-5251
422 N Michigan St Plymouth (46563) *(G-11715)*

Plymouth Tube Co CARbn&ally, Winamac *Also called Plymouth Tube Company* *(G-14316)*

Plymouth Tube Company 574 946-6191
572 W State Road 14 Winamac (46996) *(G-14314)*

Plymouth Tube Company 574 653-2575
718 E Main St Kewanna (46939) *(G-8527)*

Plymouth Tube Company 574 946-3125
572 W State Road 14 Winamac (46996) *(G-14315)*

Plymouth Tube Company 574 946-6657
572 W State Road 14 Winamac (46996) *(G-14316)*

PMC, Shelbyville *Also called Plastic Moldings Company Llc* *(G-12559)*

PMC, Saint John *Also called Performance Minerals Corp* *(G-12266)*

PMG, Indianapolis *Also called Pinnacle Manufacturing Group* *(G-7694)*

PMG Incorporated 574 291-3805
5534 Colonial Ln South Bend (46614) *(G-12899)*

PMG Indiana LLC (HQ) 812 379-4606
1751 Arcadia Dr Columbus (47201) *(G-1996)*

Pmp Enterprise, Centerville *Also called Charles Bane* *(G-1541)*

Pmw Holdings LLC 317 339-4685
2255 Colfax Ln Indianapolis (46260) *(G-7703)*

PNC Bank National Association 812 948-4490
5170 Charlestown Rd Ste 1 New Albany (47150) *(G-10845)*

Png Speed and Custom Ctr LLC 317 858-1919
454 Johnson Ln Ste A Brownsburg (46112) *(G-1163)*

Poco A Poco LLC 317 443-5753
7611 Hursh Rd Leo (46765) *(G-9245)*

Poet Biorefining - Portland 260 726-7154
1542 S 200 W Portland (47371) *(G-11840)*

Poet Brfining - Cloverdale LLC 765 795-3235
2265 E County Road 800 S Cloverdale (46120) *(G-1734)*

Poet Brfining- Portland 18200, Portland *Also called Premier Ethanol LLC* *(G-11841)*

Poet Brfining- Portland 18200, Portland *Also called Premier Ethanol LLC* *(G-11842)*

Poet Brfnng- Alexandria 21200, Alexandria *Also called Ultimate Ethanol LLC* *(G-54)*

Poet Brfnng- N Mnchster 24000, North Manchester *Also called North Manchester Ethanol LLC* *(G-11238)*

Point Care Ultrasound LP 317 459-8113
5904 E Southport Rd Indianapolis (46237) *(G-7704)*

Point Machine Products Inc 574 289-2429
621 S Scott St South Bend (46601) *(G-12900)*

Point Medical Corporation (PA).................................219 663-1775
  891 E Summit St Crown Point (46307) *(G-2285)*

Point Medical Corporation...219 663-1775
  891 E Summit St Crown Point (46307) *(G-2286)*

Poiry Partners LLC (PA)..260 424-1030
  2535 Wayne Trce Fort Wayne (46803) *(G-4535)*

Polar Ice, Indianapolis *Also called Home City Ice Company (G-7114)*

Polar King International Inc..260 428-2530
  4424 New Haven Ave Fort Wayne (46803) *(G-4536)*

Polar Kraft Boats, Syracuse *Also called Wawasee Aluminum Works Inc (G-13152)*

Polar Seal Inc..260 356-2369
  4461 W 500 N Huntington (46750) *(G-6239)*

Policystat LLC...317 644-1296
  550 Congressional Blvd # 100 Carmel (46032) *(G-1452)*

Polk, Dennis Equipment, New Paris *Also called Dennis Polk & Associates Inc (G-10977)*

Pollution Control Industries......................................219 391-7020
  4343 Kennedy Ave East Chicago (46312) *(G-2561)*

Poly Electronics LLC...574 522-0246
  4400 Wyland Dr Elkhart (46516) *(G-3101)*

Poly Group LLC...812 590-4750
  3000 Tech Ave Ste 2221 New Albany (47150) *(G-10846)*

Poly HI Solidur Inc...260 479-4100
  2710 American Way Fort Wayne (46809) *(G-4537)*

Poly Plastics Ltd..260 569-9088
  98 E Canal St Wabash (46992) *(G-13750)*

Poly Pro Tools, Zionsville *Also called Remco Products Corporation (G-14460)*

Poly-Seal LLC...812 306-2573
  101 Oakley St Evansville (47710) *(G-3678)*

Poly-Tainer Inc..317 883-2072
  999 Gerdt Ct Ste C Greenwood (46143) *(G-5734)*

Poly-Wood LLC..574 457-3284
  1001 W Brooklyn St Syracuse (46567) *(G-13140)*

Polycon Industries Inc..219 738-1000
  8919 Colorado St Merrillville (46410) *(G-9748)*

Polydyn3, Elkhart *Also called Patrick Industries Inc (G-3086)*

Polyfreeze LLC..812 547-7951
  11210 Solomon Rd Troy (47588) *(G-13447)*

Polyfusion LLC...260 624-7659
  395 Lane 101 Angola (46703) *(G-237)*

Polyfusion LLC...260 624-7659
  959 Growth Pkwy Ste D Angola (46703) *(G-238)*

Polygon...317 240-1130
  2346 S Lynhurst Dr F201e Indianapolis (46241) *(G-7705)*

Polygon Company (PA)...574 586-3145
  103 Industrial Park Dr Walkerton (46574) *(G-13808)*

Polygon Company..574 586-3145
  Tenesse St Walkerton (46574) *(G-13809)*

Polyjohn Enterprises Corp (PA).................................219 659-1152
  2500 Gaspar Ave Whiting (46394) *(G-14273)*

Polymer Additives Group, Indianapolis *Also called Pag Holdings Inc (G-7648)*

Polymer Equipment Co Inc..765 855-3448
  1219 E Main St Centerville (47330) *(G-1543)*

Polymer Science Inc (PA)...574 583-3751
  2577 S Freeman Rd Monticello (47960) *(G-10280)*

Polymer Technology Systems Inc (HQ).......................317 870-5610
  7736 Zionsville Rd Indianapolis (46268) *(G-7706)*

Polymicrospheres Division, Indianapolis *Also called Vasmo Inc (G-8149)*

Polymod Technologies Inc...260 436-1322
  4146 Engleton Dr Fort Wayne (46804) *(G-4538)*

Polyone Corporation...574 267-1100
  3454 N Detroit St Warsaw (46582) *(G-13927)*

Polyone Corporation...812 466-5116
  3915 1st Pkwy Terre Haute (47804) *(G-13305)*

Polyphase Microwave Inc...812 323-8708
  1983 S Liberty Dr Bloomington (47403) *(G-800)*

Polyram Compounds LLC..703 439-7945
  15000 Foundation Ave Evansville (47725) *(G-3679)*

Polytec Packaging Solution, Fort Wayne *Also called Calico Precision Molding LLC (G-4135)*

Pond Champs, Fort Wayne *Also called Sanco Industries Inc (G-4603)*

Pontone Industries LLC..765 966-8012
  401 Industrial Pkwy Richmond (47374) *(G-12030)*

Pontoon Boat LLC..574 264-6336
  2805 Decio Dr Elkhart (46514) *(G-3102)*

Pool Enterprises, Nashville *Also called Helmsburg Sawmill Inc (G-10726)*

Poolguard, North Vernon *Also called PBM Industries Inc (G-11277)*

Poore Brothers - Bluffton LLC...................................260 824-2800
  705 W Dustman Rd Bluffton (46714) *(G-885)*

Pop Tique Popcorn...260 459-3767
  4206 W Jefferson Blvd C3 Fort Wayne (46804) *(G-4539)*

Poplar Log Homes Inc..765 342-9910
  2635 Little Hurricane Rd Martinsville (46151) *(G-9633)*

Poppy Co...317 442-2491
  10915 N State Road 267 Brownsburg (46112) *(G-1164)*

Porchlight Group Inc..317 804-1166
  7 Launch Way Ste 610 Fishers (46038) *(G-3954)*

Port Services LLC..317 840-7606
  6127 Gunyon Way Indianapolis (46237) *(G-7707)*

Portable Left Foot Accelerator..................................260 637-4447
  429 E Dupont Rd Ste 203 Fort Wayne (46825) *(G-4540)*

Portage Custom Wear LLC..219 841-9070
  2536 Portage Mall Portage (46368) *(G-11788)*

Portals of Light Inc..765 981-2651
  1186 E 700 N Marion (46952) *(G-9554)*

Porter Case Inc...574 289-2616
  3718 W Western Ave South Bend (46619) *(G-12901)*

Porter County Fabricators...219 663-4665
  13405 Montgomery St Crown Point (46307) *(G-2287)*

Porter County Ir & Met Recycle.................................219 996-7630
  552 S 600 W Ste 1 Hebron (46341) *(G-6020)*

Porter Engineered Systems, Westfield *Also called Porter Systems Inc (G-14178)*

Porter Engineered Systems, Westfield *Also called Porter Systems Inc (G-14179)*

Porter Systems Inc..317 867-0234
  2000 E 196th St Westfield (46074) *(G-14178)*

Porter Systems Inc..317 867-0234
  2000 E 196th St Westfield (46074) *(G-14179)*

Portland Division, Portland *Also called Joyce/Dayton Corp (G-11831)*

Portland Plastics, South Bend *Also called Elkhart Plastics Inc (G-12760)*

Poseidon Barge Ltd...260 422-8767
  3101 New Haven Ave Fort Wayne (46803) *(G-4541)*

Posey County News...812 682-3950
  801 North St New Harmony (47631) *(G-10925)*

Positrax Inc..317 293-4858
  6299 Guion Rd Indianapolis (46268) *(G-7708)*

Positron Corporation (PA)...574 295-8777
  4614 Wyland Dr Elkhart (46516) *(G-3103)*

Post and Mail, Columbia City *Also called Horizon Publications Inc (G-1791)*

Poster Display Co, Indianapolis *Also called L R Green Co Inc (G-7370)*

Posters 2 Prints LLC..317 769-3784
  9389 Timberwolf Ln Zionsville (46077) *(G-14457)*

Posters 2 Prints LLC..800 598-5837
  9900 Westpoint Dr Ste 138 Indianapolis (46256) *(G-7709)*

Posters2prints LLC..317 414-8972
  10428 Starboard Way Indianapolis (46256) *(G-7710)*

Postle Aluminum Co, Elkhart *Also called Postle Operating LLC (G-3105)*

Postle Aluminum Company LLC (HQ)..........................574 389-0800
  511 Pine Creek Ct Elkhart (46516) *(G-3104)*

Postle Operating LLC (HQ)..574 389-0800
  511 Pine Creek Ct Elkhart (46516) *(G-3105)*

Postmasters, Indianapolis *Also called Anthony Wayne Rehabilitation C (G-6403)*

Powder Coating/Holscher Pwdr, Fowler *Also called Holscher Products Inc (G-4801)*

Powder Metal Technicians Inc...................................317 353-2812
  8462 Brookville Rd Indianapolis (46239) *(G-7711)*

Powder Processing & Tech LLC.................................219 462-4141
  5103 Evans Ave Valparaiso (46383) *(G-13599)*

Powdercoil Technologies LLC....................................708 634-2343
  9800 Connecticut Dr Crown Point (46307) *(G-2288)*

Powdertech Corp...219 462-4141
  5103 Evans Ave Valparaiso (46383) *(G-13600)*

Powell Systems Inc...765 884-0613
  604 E 9th St Fowler (47944) *(G-4804)*

Powell Systems Inc...765 884-0980
  83 S Meridian Rd Fowler (47944) *(G-4805)*

Power Brushes of Indiana Inc...................................812 336-7395
  2506 S Milton Dr Bloomington (47403) *(G-801)*

Power Components of Midwest..................................574 256-6990
  56641 Twin Branch Dr Mishawaka (46545) *(G-10105)*

Power Drives Inc...812 344-4351
  6077 Acorn Dr Columbus (47201) *(G-1997)*

Power Gear, Mishawaka *Also called Actuant Corporation (G-9990)*

Power House Brewing Co..812 343-1302
  12377 W 50 S Columbus (47201) *(G-1998)*

Power Investments Inc (HQ)......................................317 738-2117
  400 N Forsythe St Franklin (46131) *(G-4921)*

Power Place Products Inc...765 583-2333
  4840 Us Highway 231 N West Lafayette (47906) *(G-14095)*

Power Place Products Inc..
  317 N Old Us Highway 41 Boswell (47921) *(G-941)*

Power Plant Service Inc...260 432-6716
  2500 W Jefferson Blvd Fort Wayne (46802) *(G-4542)*

Power Systems Innovations Inc..................................812 480-4380
  3247 Commerce Dr Newburgh (47630) *(G-11043)*

Power Train, Lebanon *Also called Truckpro LLC (G-9230)*

Power Train Corp Fort Wayne (PA)............................317 241-9393
  2334 Production Dr Indianapolis (46241) *(G-7712)*

Power Wall Systems LLC..317 348-1260
  11253 Tall Trees Dr Fishers (46038) *(G-3955)*

Powerclean Inc (PA)..260 483-1375
  3404 Metro Dr N Ste B Fort Wayne (46818) *(G-4543)*

Powerclean Industrial Services, Fort Wayne *Also called Powerclean Inc (G-4543)*

Powerhouse Engines LLC..765 576-1418
  10771 S 100 E Lynn (47355) *(G-9431)*

Powering Athletics...260 672-1700
  3711 Vanguard Dr Ste F Fort Wayne (46809) *(G-4544)*

Powerrail Holdings Inc...765 827-4660
  1321 N Illinois Ave Connersville (47331) *(G-2068)*

Powerrail Mfg, Connersville *Also called Powerrail Holdings Inc (G-2068)*

Powers Energy America Inc 812 473-5500
1100 Erie Ave Evansville (47715) *(G-3680)*

Powers Welding Shop, Evansville *Also called J A Smit Inc* *(G-3568)*

Poynter Sheet Metal Inc 317 893-1193
775 Commerce Parkway W Dr Greenwood (46143) *(G-5735)*

Poyser Kelshaw Group LLC 317 571-8493
4936 Regency Pl Carmel (46033) *(G-1453)*

PPG 4313, New Albany *Also called PPG Industries Inc* *(G-10847)*

PPG 4315, Jeffersonville *Also called PPG Industries Inc* *(G-8415)*

PPG 4361, Indianapolis *Also called PPG Industries Inc* *(G-7715)*

PPG 4363, Indianapolis *Also called PPG Industries Inc* *(G-7718)*

PPG 4364, Indianapolis *Also called PPG Industries Inc* *(G-7717)*

PPG 4365, Indianapolis *Also called PPG Industries Inc* *(G-7716)*

PPG 4366, Avon *Also called PPG Industries Inc* *(G-462)*

PPG 4367, Indianapolis *Also called PPG Industries Inc* *(G-7714)*

PPG 4369, Carmel *Also called PPG Industries Inc* *(G-1454)*

PPG 4371, Westfield *Also called PPG Industries Inc* *(G-14180)*

PPG 4378, Terre Haute *Also called PPG Industries Inc* *(G-13306)*

PPG 4379, Vincennes *Also called PPG Industries Inc* *(G-13699)*

PPG 4380, Evansville *Also called PPG Industries Inc* *(G-3682)*

PPG 4382, Evansville *Also called PPG Industries Inc* *(G-3683)*

PPG 4383, Fort Wayne *Also called PPG Industries Inc* *(G-4545)*

PPG 5547, Indianapolis *Also called PPG Industries Inc* *(G-7719)*

PPG 9259, Fishers *Also called PPG Industries Inc* *(G-3956)*

PPG Aerospace, Indianapolis *Also called PRC - Desoto International Inc* *(G-7728)*

PPG Architectural Finishes Inc 765 447-9334
15 N Earl Ave Lafayette (47904) *(G-8981)*

PPG Architectural Finishes Inc 317 787-9393
7025 Madison Ave Indianapolis (46227) *(G-7713)*

PPG Industries 812 867-6601
424 E Inglefield Rd Evansville (47725) *(G-3681)*

PPG Industries Inc 317 745-0427
5201 E Us Highway 36 # 209 Avon (46123) *(G-462)*

PPG Industries Inc 317 849-2340
5977 E 82nd St Indianapolis (46250) *(G-7714)*

PPG Industries Inc 317 267-0511
952 N Delaware St Indianapolis (46202) *(G-7715)*

PPG Industries Inc 812 424-4774
306 N 7th Ave Evansville (47710) *(G-3682)*

PPG Industries Inc 812 473-0339
2211 N Burkhardt Rd Ste D Evansville (47715) *(G-3683)*

PPG Industries Inc 317 897-3836
10009 E Washington St Indianapolis (46229) *(G-7716)*

PPG Industries Inc 317 577-2344
7275 E 116th St Fishers (46038) *(G-3956)*

PPG Industries Inc 260 373-2373
2510 Independence Dr Fort Wayne (46808) *(G-4545)*

PPG Industries Inc 317 598-9448
10564 E 96th St Ste 6 Fishers (46037) *(G-3957)*

PPG Industries Inc 812 285-0546
3310 E Highway 62 Ste 6 Jeffersonville (47130) *(G-8415)*

PPG Industries Inc 317 787-9393
7025 Madison Ave Indianapolis (46227) *(G-7717)*

PPG Industries Inc 317 870-0345
10111 N Michigan Rd Carmel (46032) *(G-1454)*

PPG Industries Inc 812 944-4164
3314 Grant Line Rd Ste 1 New Albany (47150) *(G-10847)*

PPG Industries Inc 317 251-9494
2311 E 53rd St Indianapolis (46220) *(G-7718)*

PPG Industries Inc 317 546-5714
6951 E 30th St Ste E Indianapolis (46219) *(G-7719)*

PPG Industries Inc 812 232-0672
1700 Wabash Ave Terre Haute (47807) *(G-13306)*

PPG Industries Inc 812 882-0440
417 Main St Vincennes (47591) *(G-13699)*

PPG Industries Inc 317 867-5934
3132 E State Road 32 Westfield (46074) *(G-14180)*

Ppi Acquisition LLC 765 674-8627
1424 W 35th St Marion (46953) *(G-9555)*

PQ Corporation 812 288-7186
1101 Quartz Rd Clarksville (47129) *(G-1690)*

Pragmatics Inc 574 295-7908
29477 County Road 16 Elkhart (46516) *(G-3106)*

Prairie Creek Book Store, Montgomery *Also called Prairie Creek Prtg & Bk Str* *(G-10238)*

Prairie Creek Prtg & Bk Str 812 636-7243
9309 E 800 N Montgomery (47558) *(G-10238)*

Prairie Farms Dairy Inc 765 649-1261
722 Broadway St Anderson (46012) *(G-154)*

Prairie Gold Rush 812 342-3608
17390 S State Road 58 Seymour (47274) *(G-12476)*

Prairie Group 812 877-9886
5222 E Margaret Dr Terre Haute (47803) *(G-13307)*

Prairie Mills Products LLC 574 223-3177
401 E 4th St Rochester (46975) *(G-12143)*

Prairie Scents LLC 765 361-6908
1817 N State Road 47 Crawfordsville (47933) *(G-2187)*

Prairie Sun Vineyard LLC 219 741-5918
3131 N 700 E Rolling Prairie (46371) *(G-12191)*

Prairies Edge Machining Inc 765 986-2222
4920 W Division Rd Williamsport (47993) *(G-14295)*

Praise Gathering Music Group 765 640-4428
9 W 10th St Anderson (46016) *(G-155)*

Praiseworthy Press LLC 765 536-2077
151 W Indiana St Summitville (46070) *(G-13101)*

Pratt (jet Corr) Inc 219 548-9191
3155 S State Road 49 Valparaiso (46383) *(G-13601)*

Pratt Industries USA, Valparaiso *Also called Pratt (jet Corr) Inc* *(G-13601)*

Pratt Paper (in) LLC 219 477-1040
3050 Anthony Pratt Dr Valparaiso (46383) *(G-13602)*

Pratt Visual Solutions Company 800 428-7728
3035 N Shadeland Ave Indianapolis (46226) *(G-7720)*

Praxair Inc 219 398-3777
166 Indiana 130 Whiting (46394) *(G-14274)*

Praxair Inc 765 456-1128
2100 E Lincoln Rd Kokomo (46902) *(G-8683)*

Praxair Inc 219 949-8407
Clark & Dean Mitchell Rds Gary (46406) *(G-5085)*

Praxair Inc 317 240-2500
1500 Polco St Indianapolis (46222) *(G-7721)*

Praxair Inc 219 398-3700
4400 Kennedy Ave East Chicago (46312) *(G-2562)*

Praxair Inc 219 326-7808
3076 N State Road 39 La Porte (46350) *(G-8805)*

Praxair Inc 219 397-6940
2551 Dickie Rd East Chicago (46312) *(G-2563)*

Praxair Inc 765 447-8171
2655 Teal Rd Ste E Lafayette (47905) *(G-8982)*

Praxair Inc 812 537-2898
601 Front St Lawrenceburg (47025) *(G-9153)*

Praxair Distribution Inc 317 481-4550
1400 Polco St Indianapolis (46222) *(G-7722)*

Praxair Distribution Inc 260 423-4468
1725 Edsall Ave Fort Wayne (46803) *(G-4546)*

Praxair Distribution Inc 317 481-4550
1400 Polco St Indianapolis (46222) *(G-7723)*

Praxair Surface Tech Inc 317 240-2500
1555 Main St Indianapolis (46224) *(G-7724)*

Praxair Surface Tech Inc (HQ) 317 240-2500
1500 Polco St Indianapolis (46222) *(G-7725)*

Praxair Surface Tech Inc 317 240-2544
1245 Main St Indianapolis (46224) *(G-7726)*

Praxair Surface Tech Inc 317 240-2192
1555 Main St Indianapolis (46224) *(G-7727)*

PRC, Indianapolis *Also called Precision Racg Components LLC* *(G-7735)*

PRC - Desoto International Inc 317 290-1600
6022 Corporate Way Indianapolis (46278) *(G-7728)*

Prd, Springville *Also called Plastics Research and Dev Inc* *(G-13066)*

Pre-Owned Auto Center, Indianapolis *Also called Auto Center Inc* *(G-6442)*

Precast Solutions Inc 317 545-6557
6145 S Indianapolis Rd Whitestown (46075) *(G-14259)*

Precast Specialties Inc 260 623-6131
111 Utility Dr Monroeville (46773) *(G-10198)*

Preciball USA 812 257-5555
219 E Main St Ste 4x Washington (47501) *(G-14000)*

Precise Manufacturing, Fort Wayne *Also called Whitcraft Enterprises Inc* *(G-4753)*

Precise Mold and Plate, Columbus *Also called Precise Tooling Solutions Inc* *(G-1999)*

Precise Printing Plus Signs 317 545-5117
4501 N Edmondson Ave Indianapolis (46226) *(G-7729)*

Precise Title Inc 219 987-2286
8917 24th St Sw Demotte (46310) *(G-2445)*

Precise Tooling Solutions Inc 812 378-0247
3150 Scott Dr Columbus (47201) *(G-1999)*

Precisely Write Inc 317 585-7701
9801 Fall Creek Rd 202 Indianapolis (46256) *(G-7730)*

Precision Abrasive Machinery 765 378-3315
14200 W Commerce Rd Daleville (47334) *(G-2341)*

Precision Agronomy 219 552-0032
23305 Whitcomb St Lowell (46356) *(G-9420)*

Precision Automation Co Inc 812 283-7963
2120 Addmore Ln Clarksville (47129) *(G-1691)*

Precision Battery Fabricat 260 563-5138
375 Wedcor Ave Wabash (46992) *(G-13751)*

Precision Battery Fabrication, Wabash *Also called Bulldog Battery Corporation* *(G-13722)*

Precision Buffing and Polsg 574 262-3430
54194 Adams St Elkhart (46514) *(G-3107)*

Precision Building, Elkhart *Also called Precision Buffing and Polsg* *(G-3107)*

Precision Cams Inc (PA) 317 631-9100
3510 E Raymond St Indianapolis (46203) *(G-7731)*

Precision Cams Inc 317 780-0117
3510 E Raymond St Indianapolis (46203) *(G-7732)*

Precision Chemical LLC 317 570-1538
9723 Kincaid Dr Fishers (46037) *(G-3958)*

Precision Colors LLC 260 969-6402
2617 Meyer Rd Fort Wayne (46803) *(G-4547)*

(G-0000) Company's Geographic Section entry number

Precision Cryogenic Systems 317 273-2800
7804 Rockville Rd Indianapolis (46214) *(G-7733)*
Precision Die Technologies 260 482-5001
4716 Speedway Dr Fort Wayne (46825) *(G-4548)*
Precision Electric Inc 574 256-1000
1508 W 6th St Mishawaka (46544) *(G-10106)*
Precision Electronics, Mishawaka *Also called Precision Electric Inc (G-10106)*
Precision Enterprises LLC 812 873-6391
9775 S County Road 550 W Paris Crossing (47270) *(G-11460)*
Precision Fabrication Inc 260 422-4448
710 Hanover St Fort Wayne (46803) *(G-4549)*
Precision Fiber Solutions LLC 317 421-9642
590 Lake Shore Rd Franklin (46131) *(G-4922)*
Precision Gage LLC 260 925-4717
1401 S Grandstaff Dr Auburn (46706) *(G-348)*
Precision Heat Treating Corp 260 749-5125
2711 Adams Center Rd Fort Wayne (46803) *(G-4550)*
Precision Industries Corp 574 522-2626
601 Wagner Ave Elkhart (46516) *(G-3108)*
Precision Label Incorporated 812 877-3811
8890 E Davis Ave Terre Haute (47805) *(G-13308)*
Precision Laser Services Inc 260 744-4375
14730 Lima Rd Fort Wayne (46818) *(G-4551)*
Precision Medical Tech Inc 574 267-6385
2059 N Pound Dr W Warsaw (46582) *(G-13928)*
Precision Mill Work & Plastics, South Bend *Also called Precision Millwork & Plas Inc (G-12902)*
Precision Millwork & Plas Inc 574 243-8720
3311 Wlliam Richardson Dr South Bend (46628) *(G-12902)*
Precision Mold & Tool Inc 765 284-4415
2401 S Monroe St Muncie (47302) *(G-10547)*
Precision Multi Media 765 359-0466
604 Mill St Crawfordsville (47933) *(G-2188)*
Precision Piece Parts Inc 574 255-3185
712 S Logan St Mishawaka (46544) *(G-10107)*
Precision Plastics Indiana Inc 260 244-6114
900 W Connexion Way Columbia City (46725) *(G-1819)*
Precision Polishing & Buffing 317 352-0165
1038 S Kealing Ave Indianapolis (46203) *(G-7734)*
Precision Print LLC 765 789-8799
10910 E County Road 500 N Albany (47320) *(G-12)*
Precision Products Group Inc (PA) 330 698-4711
10201 N Illinois St # 390 Indianapolis (46290) *(G-6276)*
Precision Products Group Inc 260 484-4111
1430 Progress Rd Fort Wayne (46808) *(G-4552)*
Precision Products Group Inc 301 474-3100
10201 N Illinois St # 390 Indianapolis (46290) *(G-6277)*
Precision Pulse LLP 765 472-6002
4995 E 550 S Peru (46970) *(G-11540)*
Precision Racg Components LLC 317 248-4764
140 Gasoline Aly Indianapolis (46222) *(G-7735)*
Precision Rings Incorporated 317 247-4786
5611 Progress Rd Indianapolis (46241) *(G-7736)*
Precision Rubber Plate Co Inc 317 783-3226
5620 Elmwood Ave Indianapolis (46203) *(G-7737)*
Precision Stamping Inc 574 522-8987
720 Collins Rd Elkhart (46516) *(G-3109)*
Precision Stitch Indiana Inc 765 473-6734
404 W Canal St Peru (46970) *(G-11541)*
Precision Stone Works 812 683-1102
1984 W 950s Huntingburg (47542) *(G-6178)*
Precision Surveillance Corp 219 397-4295
3468 Watling St East Chicago (46312) *(G-2564)*
Precision Tool, New Paris *Also called Steve Mitchell (G-10996)*
Precision Tool & Die Inc 765 664-4786
1735 W Factory Ave Marion (46952) *(G-9556)*
Precision Tubes Inc 317 783-2339
5730 Kopetsky Dr Ste C Indianapolis (46217) *(G-7738)*
Precision Utilities Group Inc 260 485-8300
5916 E State Blvd Fort Wayne (46815) *(G-4553)*
Precision Welding Corporation 260 637-5514
16403 Lima Rd Huntertown (46748) *(G-6144)*
Precision Wire Assemblies Inc 765 489-6302
551 E Main St Hagerstown (47346) *(G-5812)*
Precision Wire Inc 574 834-7545
7493 E 800 N North Webster (46555) *(G-11300)*
Precision Wire Service, North Webster *Also called Precision Wire Inc (G-11300)*
Precision Wire Technologies, Fort Wayne *Also called Pwt Group LLC (G-4565)*
Precision Wood Products, Mishawaka *Also called Garyrae Inc (G-10045)*
Precision Woodcrafters, Decatur *Also called A S M Inc (G-2363)*
Precisionair LLC 219 380-9267
1828 N Summit Dr La Porte (46350) *(G-8806)*
Precisn Fbrctn of Shlbyvle Inc 765 544-2204
7340 E State Road 44 Shelbyville (46176) *(G-12560)*
Precoat Metals Corp (HQ) 317 462-7761
1950 E Main St Greenfield (46140) *(G-5564)*
Precoat Metals Corp 219 393-3561
858 E Hupp Rd La Porte (46350) *(G-8807)*
Precoat Metals Corp 317 462-7761
1950 E Main St Greenfield (46140) *(G-5565)*
Predator Percussion LLC 317 919-7659
1174 Dark Star Ct New Whiteland (46184) *(G-11013)*
Predictive Wear LLC 765 464-4891
1401 Shining Armor Ln West Lafayette (47906) *(G-14096)*
Preferred Enterprises Inc 765 457-0637
2215 Carr Dr Kokomo (46902) *(G-8684)*
Preferred Metal Services Inc 219 988-2386
1146 Sunnyslope Dr Crown Point (46307) *(G-2289)*
Preferred Popcorn LLC 308 850-6631
3055 W Bradford Rd Ne Palmyra (47164) *(G-11438)*
Preferred Print 317 371-8829
6220 Hardegan St Indianapolis (46227) *(G-7739)*
Preferred Seating Company LLC 317 782-3323
633 Yosemite Dr Indianapolis (46217) *(G-7740)*
Preferred Tank & Tower Inc (PA) 270 826-7950
5444 E Indiana St Pmb 374 Evansville (47715) *(G-3684)*
Pregis LLC 574 936-7065
1411 Pidco Dr Plymouth (46563) *(G-11716)*
Preh Ima Atomtn Evansville Inc, Evansville *Also called Pia Automation US Inc (G-3669)*
Premier AG Co-Op Inc (PA) 812 522-4911
811 W 2nd St Seymour (47274) *(G-12477)*
Premier Claim Services, Indianapolis *Also called Renaissnce Electronic Svcs LLC (G-7833)*
Premier Components LLC 219 776-9372
346 S 725 W Hebron (46341) *(G-6021)*
Premier Compounding, Terre Haute *Also called Jadcore LLC (G-13260)*
Premier Concepts Inc 574 269-7570
2371 N Rainbow Dr Warsaw (46582) *(G-13929)*
Premier Consulting Inc (PA) 260 496-9300
1712 Dividend Rd Fort Wayne (46808) *(G-4554)*
Premier Cstm Coatings LLC Ind 317 557-7841
4676 Rainmaker Row Greenwood (46143) *(G-5736)*
Premier Ethanol LLC 260 726-2681
1542 S 200 W Portland (47371) *(G-11841)*
Premier Ethanol LLC 260 726-7154
1542 S 200 W Portland (47371) *(G-11842)*
Premier Fiberglass Co Inc 574 264-5457
55080 Phillips St Elkhart (46514) *(G-3110)*
Premier Homes, Clarksville *Also called Classic Buildings Inc (G-1677)*
Premier Hydraulic Augers Inc 260 456-8518
2707 Lofty Dr Fort Wayne (46808) *(G-4555)*
Premier Kitchen & Bath Inc 574 294-6805
24615 County Road 45 # 1 Elkhart (46516) *(G-3111)*
Premier Label Company Inc 765 289-5000
1205 E Washington St Muncie (47305) *(G-10548)*
Premier Lumber Company 219 801-6018
6717 Atcheson Dr Chesterton (46304) *(G-1628)*
Premier Mold 574 293-2846
1671 W Franklin St Elkhart (46516) *(G-3112)*
Premier Powder Coating, Huntington *Also called Pulley-Kellam Co Inc (G-6240)*
Premier Print & Svcs Group Inc 574 273-2525
6910 N Main St Unit 11 Granger (46530) *(G-5429)*
Premier Printing 765 459-8339
1708 W Taylor St Kokomo (46901) *(G-8685)*
Premier Prints 812 987-1129
3018 Seminole Dr Jeffersonville (47130) *(G-8416)*
Premier Sign Group Inc 317 613-4411
740 E 52nd St Ste 7 Indianapolis (46205) *(G-7741)*
Premier Strctres Acqsition Inc 574 522-4011
4200 Middlebury St Elkhart (46516) *(G-3113)*
Premier Truss & Lumber Company 574 498-6022
18140 State Road 331 Tippecanoe (46570) *(G-13386)*
Premier Wire Die, Fort Wayne *Also called Premier Consulting Inc (G-4554)*
Premiere Advertising 317 722-2400
2704 E 62nd St Ste B Indianapolis (46220) *(G-7742)*
Premiere Building Mtls Inc 574 293-5800
631 Collins Rd Elkhart (46516) *(G-3114)*
Premiere Services, Goshen *Also called Premiere Signs Co Inc (G-5312)*
Premiere Signs Co Inc 574 533-8585
400 N Main St Goshen (46528) *(G-5312)*
Premiere Structures, Elkhart *Also called Premier Strctres Acqsition Inc (G-3113)*
Premium Srfc Fbrication of Ind 317 867-1013
17401 Tiller Ct Ste D Westfield (46074) *(G-14181)*
Prentice Products Holdings LLC 260 747-3195
4236 W Ferguson Rd Fort Wayne (46809) *(G-4556)*
Pres-Del Electric Inc 219 884-3146
4172 Broadway Gary (46408) *(G-5086)*
Preserving Past 574 835-0833
3764 E Jackson Blvd Elkhart (46516) *(G-3115)*
Press 96, Indianapolis *Also called Priority Press Inc (G-6278)*
Press Control Systems 317 887-1369
1864 S Crooked Ln Greenwood (46143) *(G-5737)*
Press Dispatch, Petersburg *Also called Pike County Publishing Corp (G-11566)*
Press-Seal Gasket Corporation 260 436-0521
2424 W State Blvd Fort Wayne (46808) *(G-4557)*
Presstime Graphics Inc 812 234-3815
1016 Poplar St Terre Haute (47807) *(G-13309)*

ALPHABETIC

Pressure Systems Inc 317 755-3050
　16 Gazebo Dr Indianapolis (46227) *(G-7743)*
Prestige Printing Inc 812 372-2500
　1307 12th St Columbus (47201) *(G-2000)*
Preston Farms LLC 812 364-6123
　3055 W Bradford Rd Ne Palmyra (47164) *(G-11439)*
Preston Leaderbrand 812 828-0883
　491 Timber Ridge Rd Spencer (47460) *(G-13033)*
Prestress Services Inc 260 724-7117
　7855 Nw Winchester Rd Decatur (46733) *(G-2399)*
Pretty Brilliant LLC 765 277-2308
　822 E Main St Richmond (47374) *(G-12031)*
Pretty In Prints LLC 317 252-3672
　4022 Carrollton Ave Indianapolis (46205) *(G-7744)*
Pretty Incrdbl Communications, Jeffersonville *Also called Printing Inc Louisville
KY (G-8417)*
Pretzels Inc 574 941-2201
　2910 Commerce St Plymouth (46563) *(G-11717)*
Pretzels Inc (PA) 260 824-4838
　123 W Harvest Rd Bluffton (46714) *(G-886)*
Prevail Design Systems LLC 260 245-1245
　5130 Willow Bluff Trl Huntertown (46748) *(G-6145)*
Prevail Prsthtics Orthtics Inc 317 577-2273
　6330 E 75th St Ste 126 Indianapolis (46250) *(G-7745)*
Prevail Prsthtics Orthtics Inc 765 668-0890
　7735 W Jefferson Blvd C Fort Wayne (46804) *(G-4558)*
Prevail Prsthtics Orthtics Inc (PA) 260 483-5219
　7735 W Jefferson Blvd Fort Wayne (46804) *(G-4559)*
Prevail Prsthtics Orthtics Inc 260 969-0605
　3906 New Vision Dr Fort Wayne (46845) *(G-4560)*
Prevention Response Technology, Rushville *Also called Prt Inc (G-12231)*
PRI-Pak Inc 812 260-2291
　2000 Schenley Pl Greendale (47025) *(G-5493)*
Price Motor Sport Engineering 812 546-4220
　205 Main St Hope (47246) *(G-6118)*
Pridgeon & Clay Inc 317 738-4885
　150 Arvin Rd Franklin (46131) *(G-4923)*
Prime Conveyor Inc 219 736-1994
　8903 Louisiana St Merrillville (46410) *(G-9749)*
Prime Source LLC 812 867-8921
　4609 E Boonv New Harmo Rd Evansville (47725) *(G-3685)*
Prime Tech Inc 317 715-1162
　3131 N Franklin Rd Ste B Indianapolis (46226) *(G-7746)*
Prime Time Manufacturing 574 862-3001
　66149 State Road 19 Wakarusa (46573) *(G-13790)*
Primed & Ready LLC 317 694-2028
　5036 E 65th St Indianapolis (46220) *(G-7747)*
Primet Fluid Power, Hammond *Also called Motion & Control Entps LLC (G-5918)*
Primex Color Compounding 800 222-5116
　1235 N F St Richmond (47374) *(G-12032)*
Primex Design Fabrication Corp 765 935-2990
　400 Industrial Pkwy Richmond (47374) *(G-12033)*
Primex Plastics Corporation (HQ) 765 966-7774
　1235 N F St Richmond (47374) *(G-12034)*
Prince Manufacturing Corp 260 357-4484
　320 N Taylor Rd Garrett (46738) *(G-5020)*
Princeton Daily Clarion, Princeton *Also called Princeton Publishing Inc (G-11881)*
Princeton Publishing Inc 812 385-2525
　100 N Gibson St Princeton (47670) *(G-11881)*
Prinit Press, Richmond *Also called Augustin Prtg & Design Svcs (G-11957)*
Prinova Solutions 219 879-7356
　1700 E Us Highway 12 Michigan City (46360) *(G-9829)*
Print and Save LLP 317 567-1459
　4420 W Washington St Indianapolis (46241) *(G-7748)*
Print Center Inc 219 874-9683
　2902 Ridge Rd Long Beach (46360) *(G-9379)*
Print Ideas 317 299-8766
　2233 Country Club Rd Indianapolis (46234) *(G-7749)*
Print It Wear It Inc 317 946-1456
　679 Brentwood Dr Shelbyville (46176) *(G-12561)*
Print Management Solutions 574 234-7269
　1833 Hass Dr South Bend (46635) *(G-12903)*
Print My Merch LLC 574 323-5541
　3702 W Sample St Ste 1103 South Bend (46619) *(G-12904)*
Print My Merch LLC 765 269-6772
　14208 Dragoon Trl Mishawaka (46544) *(G-10108)*
Print Place Inc 260 768-7878
　8100 W Us Highway 20 B Shipshewana (46565) *(G-12644)*
Print Sharp Enterprises Inc 317 899-2754
　4371 Sellers St Indianapolis (46226) *(G-7750)*
Print Source Corporation 260 589-2842
　213 E Perry St Bluffton (46714) *(G-887)*
Print Tech, Evansville *Also called Acclaim Graphics Inc (G-3334)*
Print Works of Lafayette Inc 765 446-9735
　3217 Olympia Dr Lafayette (47909) *(G-8983)*
Print2promo Group Inc 219 778-4649
　7592 E 400 N Rolling Prairie (46371) *(G-12192)*
Printcraft Press Inc 765 457-2141
　524 S Union St Kokomo (46901) *(G-8686)*

Printcrafters Inc 812 838-4106
　304 W 4th St Mount Vernon (47620) *(G-10405)*
Printec Solutions Inc 317 289-6510
　8130 Wysong Dr Indianapolis (46219) *(G-7751)*
Printed By Erik Inc 574 295-1203
　660 County Road 15 Elkhart (46516) *(G-3116)*
Printegra Corp 317 328-0022
　1002 E 25th St Indianapolis (46205) *(G-7752)*
Printer Plus 812 945-5955
　410 Pearl St New Albany (47150) *(G-10848)*
Printer Zink Inc 765 644-3959
　1047 Broadway St Anderson (46012) *(G-156)*
Printers Express Inc 765 348-0069
　112 N Jefferson St Hartford City (47348) *(G-5988)*
Printers Group 317 835-7720
　4485 W 600 N Fairland (46126) *(G-3826)*
Printers Plus, Elkhart *Also called Livings Graphics Inc (G-3006)*
Printing All Stars 812 288-9291
　802 E 8th St New Albany (47150) *(G-10849)*
Printing Center Inc 317 545-8518
　3503 N Shadeland Ave Indianapolis (46226) *(G-7753)*
Printing Company LLC 812 367-2668
　8765 S Club Rd Ferdinand (47532) *(G-3861)*
Printing Complex, The, Indianapolis *Also called Printing Center Inc (G-7753)*
Printing Concepts Inc 317 899-2754
　4371 Sellers St Indianapolis (46226) *(G-7754)*
Printing Creations Inc 765 759-9679
　2410 S Vine St Yorktown (47396) *(G-14410)*
Printing Emporium Inc 574 256-0059
　235 E Mckinley Ave Ste 2 Mishawaka (46545) *(G-10109)*
Printing In Time Inc 502 807-3545
　8213 Lotticks Cornr Rd Se Elizabeth (47117) *(G-2645)*
Printing Inc Louisville KY 502 368-6555
　1600 Dutch Ln Ste A Jeffersonville (47130) *(G-8417)*
Printing Partners Inc (PA) 317 635-2282
　929 W 16th St Indianapolis (46202) *(G-7755)*
Printing Partners East Inc 317 356-2522
　929 W 16th St Indianapolis (46202) *(G-7756)*
Printing Phantom 765 719-2097
　3101 W County Road 100 S Greencastle (46135) *(G-5474)*
Printing Place Inc-Photos Plus 260 665-8444
　1500 N Wayne St Ste B Angola (46703) *(G-239)*
Printing Plus Inc 317 574-1313
　505 E 116th St Carmel (46032) *(G-1455)*
Printing Press, The, Fort Wayne *Also called Lucas Bus Forms & Swift Prtg (G-4443)*
Printing Services Inc 317 300-0363
　5333 Commerce Square Dr Indianapolis (46237) *(G-7757)*
Printing Solutions 812 923-0756
　6220 Sarles Creek Rd Floyds Knobs (47119) *(G-4017)*
Printing Technologies Inc 800 428-3786
　6266 Morenci Trl Indianapolis (46268) *(G-7758)*
Printmaster LLC 260 459-1900
　4120 Engleton Dr Fort Wayne (46804) *(G-4561)*
Printpack Inc 812 663-5091
　930 E Barachel Ln Ste 200 Greensburg (47240) *(G-5629)*
Printpack Inc 812 334-5500
　2121 N Angelina Ln Bloomington (47404) *(G-802)*
Printwerk Graphics & Design 219 322-7722
　1000 Richard Rd Dyer (46311) *(G-2508)*
Printworks Inc 317 535-1250
　655 Tracy Rd Whiteland (46184) *(G-14243)*
Priority Business Forms, Indianapolis *Also called Priority Press Inc (G-7759)*
Priority Communications, Indianapolis *Also called Telecom LLC (G-6282)*
Priority Electronics LLC 260 749-0143
　10104 Paulding Rd New Haven (46774) *(G-10954)*
Priority Plastics Inc (PA) 260 726-7000
　500 Industrial Dr Portland (47371) *(G-11843)*
Priority Press Inc (PA) 317 241-4234
　4026 W 10th St Indianapolis (46222) *(G-7759)*
Priority Press Inc 317 240-0103
　4026 W 10th St Indianapolis (46222) *(G-7760)*
Priority Press Inc 317 848-9695
　9609 N College Ave Indianapolis (46280) *(G-6278)*
Priority Printing LLC 317 241-4234
　4026 W 10th St Indianapolis (46222) *(G-7761)*
Prized Possession 317 842-1498
　6606 Avalon Forest Dr Indianapolis (46250) *(G-7762)*
Prn Graphics LLC 317 426-3545
　3822 N Illinois St Indianapolis (46208) *(G-7763)*
Prn Incorporated 317 624-4401
　9449 Priority Way West Dr Indianapolis (46240) *(G-7764)*
Pro Clean LLC 574 867-1000
　607 E Plymouth St Hamlet (46532) *(G-5832)*
Pro Epuipment Service 317 322-7858
　451 S Kenmore Rd Indianapolis (46219) *(G-7765)*
Pro Fab, Mishawaka *Also called C & J Corporation (G-10015)*
Pro Foods America Inc 317 826-8526
　11971 Promontory Ct Indianapolis (46236) *(G-7766)*
Pro Industies, Franklin *Also called C L Holdings LLC (G-4874)*

Pro Laminators, Sellersburg *Also called Jknk Ventures Inc* ***(G-12399)***
Pro Pallet LLC 219 292-3389
1584 Blaine St Gary (46406) ***(G-5087)***
Pro Prints 812 932-3800
394 Northside Dr Batesville (47006) ***(G-515)***
Pro Prints Gear, Marion *Also called Ppi Acquisition LLC* ***(G-9555)***
Pro Series Products LLC 812 793-3506
208 N Armstrong St Crothersville (47229) ***(G-2219)***
Pro Tech Automation Inc 317 201-3875
8236 N Hall Rd Monrovia (46157) ***(G-10205)***
Pro Tech Metal Finishing 260 894-4011
214 Heckner Dr Ligonier (46767) ***(G-9293)***
Pro Tool & Engineering Inc 574 256-5911
3723 N Home St Mishawaka (46545) ***(G-10110)***
Pro Traument Scale, Franklin *Also called Agri-Tronix Corp* ***(G-4862)***
Pro-Blast Equip, Fort Wayne *Also called Professional Metal Refinishing* ***(G-4562)***
Pro-Form Plastics Inc 812 522-4433
11624 E State Road 250 Crothersville (47229) ***(G-2220)***
Pro-Kote Indy 317 872-0001
8813 Robbins Rd Indianapolis (46268) ***(G-7767)***
Pro-Mark Bldg Solutions LLC 812 798-1178
575 N 1000 W Linton (47441) ***(G-9312)***
Pro-Motor Engines, Goshen *Also called Promotor Engines & Components* ***(G-5313)***
Pro-Prep, Indianapolis *Also called Websters Sporting Goods Inc* ***(G-8182)***
Pro-Tech Tool & Engineering 765 258-3613
890 E County Road 600 N Frankfort (46041) ***(G-4851)***
Pro-Tex All Co, Evansville *Also called Kuhn & Sons Inc* ***(G-3597)***
Pro-Tote System Inc 574 287-6006
1705 S Olive St South Bend (46613) ***(G-12905)***
Pro-Weld LLC 219 922-8861
4710 Oaklane Dr Griffith (46319) ***(G-5787)***
Proair LLC (HQ) 574 264-5494
2900 County Road 6 W Elkhart (46514) ***(G-3117)***
Proair LLC 574 264-5494
2900 County Road 6 W Elkhart (46514) ***(G-3118)***
Proaxis Inc 765 742-4200
345 Burnetts Rd West Lafayette (47906) ***(G-14097)***
Process Systems & Services (PA) 812 427-2331
13395 Innovation Dr Florence (47020) ***(G-4004)***
Proco, Fort Wayne *Also called Protective Coatings Inc* ***(G-4563)***
Procoat Inc 317 263-5071
920 E New York St Indianapolis (46202) ***(G-7768)***
Procoat Products Inc 812 352-6083
604 W Montrow Indus Pkwy North Vernon (47265) ***(G-11279)***
Procyon Pharmaceuticals Inc 765 778-9710
206 Jh Walker Dr Pendleton (46064) ***(G-11501)***
Prodigy Group Inc 317 834-5480
310 Indianapolis Rd Ste E Mooresville (46158) ***(G-10335)***
Prodigy Mold & Tool Inc 812 753-3029
88 E 1100 S Haubstadt (47639) ***(G-6004)***
Product Engineering Company, Columbus *Also called E F M Corporation* ***(G-1916)***
Production Dynamics, Valparaiso *Also called Task Force Tips Inc* ***(G-13627)***
Production Hdlg Systems Inc 317 738-0485
211 Province St Franklin (46131) ***(G-4924)***
Production Machining Company 812 466-2885
4850 N 13th St Terre Haute (47805) ***(G-13310)***
Production Plastic Molding 317 872-4669
3402 W 79th St Indianapolis (46268) ***(G-7769)***
Production Plating, Indianapolis *Also called Progressive Plating Company* ***(G-7776)***
Production Systems Assoc, Huntingburg *Also called Masterbrand Cabinets Inc* ***(G-6175)***
Productivity Fabricators Inc 765 966-2896
2332 Flatley Rd Richmond (47374) ***(G-12035)***
Productivity Resources Inc 317 245-4040
325 Pickwick Ct Noblesville (46062) ***(G-11166)***
Proedge Inc 219 552-9550
23326 Shelby Rd Shelby (46377) ***(G-12515)***
Profab Custom Metal Works Inc 812 865-3999
7040 N State Road 337 Orleans (47452) ***(G-11367)***
Professional Bowling Ball Svc 317 786-4329
2630 Madison Ave Indianapolis (46225) ***(G-7770)***
Professional Comp Naskart Inc 765 552-9745
1224 S H St Elwood (46036) ***(G-3309)***
Professional Diabetes Center, Indianapolis *Also called Admiral Medical Center Inc* ***(G-6328)***
Professional Fabricators Inc 260 665-2555
1103 Redding Ln Angola (46703) ***(G-240)***
Professional Gifting Inc 317 257-3466
6366 Guilford Ave 300 Indianapolis (46220) ***(G-7771)***
Professional Grade Svcs LLC 317 688-8898
10428 Windward Dr Indianapolis (46234) ***(G-7772)***
Professional Lighting Services 317 844-4261
1091 3rd Ave Sw Carmel (46032) ***(G-1456)***
Professional Metal Refinishing 260 436-2828
2415 W State Blvd Fort Wayne (46808) ***(G-4562)***
Professional Permits 574 257-2954
2319 Lincolnway E Mishawaka (46544) ***(G-10111)***
Professional Print & Copy, Bluffton *Also called Professional Print Brokers* ***(G-888)***
Professional Print Brokers 260 824-2328
2020 N Main St Ste B Bluffton (46714) ***(G-888)***
Profit Finders Incorporated 317 251-7792
6438 Rucker Rd Indianapolis (46220) ***(G-7773)***
Proform, Fort Wayne *Also called Dx 4 LLC* ***(G-4229)***
Proforma Corporate Solutions, Granger *Also called Nielsen Enterprises Inc* ***(G-5427)***
Proforma Premier Printing 317 842-9181
10252 Eastwind Ct Indianapolis (46256) ***(G-7774)***
Proforma Print Promo Group 574 931-2941
3702 W Sample St South Bend (46619) ***(G-12906)***
Proforma Viking, Fort Wayne *Also called Viking Business Products Inc* ***(G-4727)***
Progress Examiner 812 865-3242
233 S 2nd St Orleans (47452) ***(G-11368)***
Progress Group Inc 219 322-3700
918 Kennedy Ave Schererville (46375) ***(G-12342)***
Progress Rail Services Corp 765 472-2002
588 W 7th St Peru (46970) ***(G-11542)***
Progress Rail Services Corp 219 397-5326
175 W Chicago Ave East Chicago (46312) ***(G-2565)***
Progress Tool & Die Shop, Tipton *Also called Atkisson Enterprises Inc* ***(G-13388)***
Progressive Design Apparel Inc 317 293-5888
7260 Georgetown Rd Indianapolis (46268) ***(G-7775)***
Progressive Plastics Inc 765 552-2004
2200 S J St Elwood (46036) ***(G-3310)***
Progressive Plating Company 317 923-2413
2064 Columbia Ave Indianapolis (46202) ***(G-7776)***
Progressive Printing Co Inc 765 653-3814
115 N Jackson St Ste 1 Greencastle (46135) ***(G-5475)***
Progressive Tool & Machine 812 346-1837
241 Coovert St Columbus (47201) ***(G-2001)***
Progressive Woodcraft LLC 574 546-9010
2550 Birch Rd Bremen (46506) ***(G-1017)***
Projected Sound Inc 317 839-4111
469 Avon Ave Plainfield (46168) ***(G-11637)***
Prokuma Incorporated 812 461-1681
110 N Main St Evansville (47711) ***(G-3686)***
Prolam Products Inc 812 867-1662
10245 Hedden Rd Evansville (47725) ***(G-3687)***
Proline Bowstrings 513 259-3738
1957 S Hubble Rd Liberty (47353) ***(G-9270)***
Prolon Inc 574 522-8900
1040 Sako Ct Elkhart (46516) ***(G-3119)***
Promethius Consulting LLC 317 733-2388
9519 Valparaiso Ct Indianapolis (46268) ***(G-7777)***
Promex Technologies LLC 317 736-0128
7510 E 82nd St Indianapolis (46256) ***(G-7778)***
Promotion Extras, Lebanon *Also called Hangout At Flames LLC* ***(G-9186)***
Promotional Products, Brownsburg *Also called Bc Awards Inc* ***(G-1136)***
Promotor Engines & Components 574 533-9898
1814 Lincolnway E Goshen (46526) ***(G-5313)***
Propellerheads 317 219-0408
4319 W Clara Ln Muncie (47304) ***(G-10549)***
Proportion-Air Inc (PA) 317 335-2602
8250 N 600 W McCordsville (46055) ***(G-9674)***
Prosco Inc 317 353-2920
3818 Prospect St Indianapolis (46203) ***(G-7779)***
Proseries Products, Scottsburg *Also called King Investments Inc* ***(G-12371)***
Proshred Indianapolis Inc 317 578-3650
3140 N Shadeland Ave Indianapolis (46226) ***(G-7780)***
Prosolia Inc 317 275-5794
6500 Tech Ctr Dr Ste 200 Indianapolis (46278) ***(G-7781)***
Prosperus LLC 317 786-8990
5644 S Meridian St Ste E Indianapolis (46217) ***(G-7782)***
Protect Perry, Indianapolis *Also called Innovtive Hydrlic Slutions LLC* ***(G-7239)***
Protective Coatings, Winamac *Also called Kevin Kolish Corp* ***(G-14309)***
Protective Coatings Inc 260 424-2900
1602 Birchwood Ave Fort Wayne (46803) ***(G-4563)***
Proteq Custom Gear LLC 812 201-6002
3057 W County Road 1200 N Brazil (47834) ***(G-975)***
Protero Corporation 219 393-5591
605 Grayton Rd Kingsford Heights (46346) ***(G-8546)***
Proteus Solutions LLC 317 222-1138
2367 Black Gold Dr Indianapolis (46234) ***(G-7783)***
Proton Mold Tool Inc 812 923-7263
6126 Saint Marys Rd Floyds Knobs (47119) ***(G-4018)***
Prototech Enterprises Inc 317 250-9644
1788 Spruce Dr Carmel (46033) ***(G-1457)***
Prototype Baker Engineering 574 266-7223
53050 Elkhart East Blvd Elkhart (46514) ***(G-3120)***
Prototype Systems Inc 317 634-3040
481 Gradle Dr Carmel (46032) ***(G-1458)***
Provident Tool & Die Inc 574 862-1233
66100 State Road 19 Wakarusa (46573) ***(G-13791)***
Provision Publishing LLC 765 282-3928
3141 E Shockley Rd Muncie (47302) ***(G-10550)***
Prowler Industries LLC 877 477-6953
1220 N Liberty Cir E Greensburg (47240) ***(G-5630)***
Prox Company Inc 812 232-4324
1179 E Garden Dr S Terre Haute (47802) ***(G-13311)***
Prp Technologies LLC 260 433-3769
3201 Stellhorn Rd Fort Wayne (46815) ***(G-4564)***

ALPHABETIC

Prp Wine International...317 288-0005
8310 Allison Pointe Blvd # 205 Indianapolis (46250) *(G-7784)*
Prt Inc...765 938-3333
700 W 5th St Rushville (46173) *(G-12231)*
Prt South LLC...708 354-3786
4400 Homerlee Ave Ste 1 East Chicago (46312) *(G-2566)*
Pruett Manufacturing Co Inc...812 234-9497
3953 Trey Cir Terre Haute (47803) *(G-13312)*
Pryor Safe & Lock, Indianapolis *Also called S C Pryor Inc (G-7878)*
Prysm Inc...317 324-1222
11711 N College Ave # 140 Carmel (46032) *(G-1459)*
PSC, East Chicago *Also called Precision Surveillance Corp (G-2564)*
PSC Industries Inc...812 425-9071
900 E Virginia St Evansville (47711) *(G-3688)*
PSC Industries Inc...317 547-5439
6790 E 32nd St Indianapolis (46226) *(G-7785)*
PSc Machining and Engrg Inc...219 764-4270
6672 Melton Rd Portage (46368) *(G-11789)*
Psd and More LLC (PA)...317 770-4577
15260 Herriman Blvd Noblesville (46060) *(G-11167)*
Psd Concepts, Noblesville *Also called Psd and More LLC (G-11167)*
PSI, Monticello *Also called Polymer Science Inc (G-10280)*
PSI Group Inc...317 297-3211
5071 W 74th St Indianapolis (46268) *(G-7786)*
PSI Molded Plastics Ind Inc...574 288-2100
3615 Voorde Dr South Bend (46628) *(G-12907)*
PSI Repair Services Inc...812 485-5575
5825 Old Boonville Hwy Evansville (47715) *(G-3689)*
Pt Services Inc...574 970-0512
2701 Industrial Pkwy # 125 Elkhart (46516) *(G-3121)*
Pt Tool Machine...219 275-3633
5183 E 894 S Brook (47922) *(G-1099)*
Ptc Alliance Corporation...765 259-3334
1480 Nw 11th St Richmond (47374) *(G-12036)*
Ptc Tubular Products LLC (HQ)...765 259-3334
1480 Nw 11th St Richmond (47374) *(G-12037)*
Ptf Cabinets & Tops LLC...317 786-4367
1310 W Troy Ave Ste A Indianapolis (46225) *(G-7787)*
PTG Inc...317 892-4625
5838 E County Road 800 N Brownsburg (46112) *(G-1165)*
PTG Silicones Inc...812 948-8719
827 Progress Blvd New Albany (47150) *(G-10850)*
Pts Diagnostics, Indianapolis *Also called Polymer Technology Systems Inc (G-7706)*
Pts Signs & Wraps...317 653-1807
1720 Orchid Ct Indianapolis (46219) *(G-7788)*
Pubco Inc...219 874-4245
613 Franklin St Michigan City (46360) *(G-9830)*
Publishers Consulting Corp...219 874-4245
613 Franklin St Michigan City (46360) *(G-9831)*
Publishers Sovereign Grace...765 296-5538
307 S Glick St Mulberry (46058) *(G-10418)*
Puck Supply & Machine LLC...574 293-3333
56644 Elk Park Dr Elkhart (46516) *(G-3122)*
Puff Hut, Fort Wayne *Also called United Media Group Inc (G-4715)*
Pugh's Cabinets, Fairland *Also called Jds Pugh Cabinets Inc (G-3822)*
Pulaski County Press Inc...574 946-6628
114 W Main St Winamac (46996) *(G-14317)*
Pull Rite, Mishawaka *Also called Pulliam Enterprises Inc (G-10112)*
Pulley-Kellam Co Inc (PA)...260 356-6326
245 Erie St Huntington (46750) *(G-6240)*
Pulliam Enterprises Inc...574 259-1520
13790 Jefferson Blvd Mishawaka (46545) *(G-10112)*
Pullman Company...260 667-2200
503 Weatherhead St Angola (46703) *(G-241)*
Pulse Energy...812 268-6700
3137 N Old 41 Sullivan (47882) *(G-13091)*
Pump Meter Solutions...317 984-7867
6660 E 266th St Ste 100 Arcadia (46030) *(G-267)*
Pumpalarmcom LLC...888 454-5051
203 W Morris St Indianapolis (46225) *(G-7789)*
Pumphreys Performance Engines...812 358-4704
1820 S State Road 235 Medora (47260) *(G-9682)*
Pumpkin Patch Market Inc...574 825-3312
10532 Us Highway 20 Middlebury (46540) *(G-9915)*
Pumpkinvine Quilting Inc...574 825-1151
500 Spring Valley Dr # 3 Middlebury (46540) *(G-9916)*
Punjab Empire Inc...765 987-8786
5809 S State Road 3 Spiceland (47385) *(G-13057)*
Pur-SE, Greendale *Also called CM Reed LLC (G-5485)*
Purdue Exponent, The, West Lafayette *Also called Purdue Student Pubg Foundation (G-14099)*
Purdue Gmp Center LLC...765 464-8414
3070 Kent Ave West Lafayette (47906) *(G-14098)*
Purdue Student Pubg Foundation...765 743-1111
460 Northwestern Ave West Lafayette (47906) *(G-14099)*
Purdy Concrete Inc (PA)...765 477-7687
3633 Old Us Highway 231 S Lafayette (47909) *(G-8984)*
Purdy Materials Inc...765 474-8993
3633 Old Us Highway 231 S Lafayette (47909) *(G-8985)*
Pure Edible Oils, Indianapolis *Also called Northern Indiana Oil LLC (G-7593)*
Pure Flow Airdog, Shelbyville *Also called W A P LLC (G-12583)*
Pure Image Laser and Spa LLC...317 306-6603
5222 S East St Ste B1 Indianapolis (46227) *(G-7790)*
Purina Animal Nutrition LLC...765 962-8547
1759 Sheridan St Richmond (47374) *(G-12038)*
Purina Animal Nutrition LLC...765 659-4791
2472 W State Road 28 Frankfort (46041) *(G-4852)*
Purina Animal Nutrition LLC...812 424-5501
2124 Lynch Rd Evansville (47711) *(G-3690)*
Purina Animal Nutrition LLC...574 658-4137
346 W 1350 N Milford (46542) *(G-9962)*
Purina Mills LLC...812 424-5501
2124 Lynch Rd Evansville (47711) *(G-3691)*
Purina Mills LLC...574 658-4137
346 W 1350 N Milford (46542) *(G-9963)*
Puritan Water Conditioning...765 362-6340
216 Lafayette Ave Crawfordsville (47933) *(G-2189)*
Purolator Pdts A Filtration Co (HQ)...866 925-2247
100 River Ridge Cir Jeffersonville (47130) *(G-8418)*
Purple Door Press...219 690-1046
8833 W 156th Ct Lowell (46356) *(G-9421)*
Purrfectplay...219 926-7604
790 Graham Dr Chesterton (46304) *(G-1629)*
Pursuit Defense Technology LLC...630 687-3826
1405 Barth Ave Indianapolis (46203) *(G-7791)*
Pussob Apparel & Printing LLC...574 229-5795
1643 Columbian Ave Elkhart (46514) *(G-3123)*
Putnam Plastics Inc (PA)...765 795-6102
30 W Stardust Rd Cloverdale (46120) *(G-1735)*
PVA Unlimited, Warsaw *Also called Seymour Midwest LLC (G-13939)*
PVA Unlimited Inc...574 269-2782
2234 E Hendricks St Warsaw (46580) *(G-13930)*
Pwt Group LLC...260 490-6477
6320 Highview Dr Fort Wayne (46818) *(G-4565)*
Pynco Inc...812 275-0900
2605 35th St Bedford (47421) *(G-567)*
Pyramid Equipment (PA)...219 778-2591
211 S Prairie St Rolling Prairie (46371) *(G-12193)*
Pyramid Equipment...219 778-4253
8 S Depot St Rolling Prairie (46371) *(G-12194)*
Pyramid Metallizing Inc...219 879-9967
3155 W Dunes Hwy Michigan City (46360) *(G-9832)*
Pyramid Paper Products Inc...812 372-0288
725 S Mapleton St Columbus (47201) *(G-2002)*
Pyramid Plastic Group Inc...260 327-3145
1560 N State Road 5 Larwill (46764) *(G-9124)*
Pyramid Sign & Design Inc...765 447-4174
515 Farabee Dr S Lafayette (47905) *(G-8986)*
Pyrimont Operating Solutions, Fishers *Also called Front End Digital Inc (G-3914)*
Pyro Industrial Services Inc...219 787-5700
6610 Shepherd Ave Portage (46368) *(G-11790)*
Pyro Shield Inc...219 661-8600
1171 Erie Court Crown Pt Crown Point Crown Point (46307) *(G-2290)*
Pyromation Inc...260 484-2580
5211 Industrial Rd Fort Wayne (46825) *(G-4566)*
Pyrotechnic Productions Inc...812 448-8196
2749 E County Road 1200 N Brazil (47834) *(G-976)*
Pyrotek Incorporated...260 248-4141
4447 E Park 30 Dr Columbia City (46725) *(G-1820)*
Q Air Inc...219 476-7048
4008 Murvihill Rd Valparaiso (46383) *(G-13603)*
Q C I, Orland *Also called Quality Converters Inc (G-11356)*
Q Graphics Inc (PA)...765 564-2314
108 E Main St Delphi (46923) *(G-2426)*
Q Graphics Inc...574 967-3733
103 W Walnut St Flora (46929) *(G-4002)*
Q S I Inc...574 282-1200
3024 Mishawaka Ave South Bend (46615) *(G-12908)*
Q-Edge Corporation...317 203-6800
1581 Perry Rd Ste B Plainfield (46168) *(G-11638)*
Qbc Catering...812 364-4293
2124 E County Line Rd S Palmyra (47164) *(G-11440)*
Qci, West Terre Haute *Also called Quality Council of Indiana (G-14128)*
Qfs Holdings LLC...317 634-2543
2457 E Washington St B Indianapolis (46201) *(G-7792)*
Qig LLC...260 244-3591
225 Towerview Dr Columbia City (46725) *(G-1821)*
Qig LLC...260 244-3591
225 Towerview Dr Columbia City (46725) *(G-1822)*
Qmp Inc...574 262-1575
2925 Stephen Pl Elkhart (46514) *(G-3124)*
Qp Inc...574 295-6884
530 E Lexington Ave # 155 Elkhart (46516) *(G-3125)*
Qrs Inc...812 948-1323
1001 Floyd St New Albany (47150) *(G-10851)*
Qsens Equipment Solutions LLC...317 443-6167
7602 Dartmouth Rd Indianapolis (46260) *(G-7793)*
Qsi Printers and Mailers, South Bend *Also called Q S I Inc (G-12908)*

Qsp Printing Inc 317 773-0864
5920 E 161st St Noblesville (46062) (G-11168)

Qtg Pepsi Co Larry Davi 317 830-4020
9101 Orly Rd Indianapolis (46241) (G-7794)

Quad 4 Plastics Inc 574 293-8660
1840 Borneman Ave Elkhart (46517) (G-3126)

Quad Plus LLC 219 844-9214
3535 165th St Hammond (46323) (G-5928)

Quad/Graphics Inc 260 748-5300
6502 Nelson Rd Fort Wayne (46803) (G-4567)

Quadrant Engrg Plastic Pdts, Fort Wayne Also called Quadrant Epp Usa Inc (G-4569)

Quadrant Epp Usa Inc 260 479-4700
4115 Polymer Pl Fort Wayne (46809) (G-4568)

Quadrant Epp Usa Inc 260 479-4100
2710 American Way Fort Wayne (46809) (G-4569)

Quake Manufacturing Inc 260 432-8023
3923 Engle Rd Fort Wayne (46804) (G-4570)

Quaker Chemical Corp 765 668-2441
2400 W 2nd St Marion (46952) (G-9557)

Quaker Oats Company 317 821-6442
5858 Decatur Blvd Indianapolis (46241) (G-7795)

Qualidie Corp 317 632-6845
515 N Luett Ave Indianapolis (46222) (G-7796)

Qualitex Inc 260 244-7839
4185 E Park 30 Dr 30th Fort Wayne (46814) (G-4571)

Qualitronics Inc (PA) 765 966-2039
1200 Nw O St Richmond (47374) (G-12039)

Quality Coatings Inc 812 925-3314
1700 N State St Chandler (47610) (G-1553)

Quality Connections of Indiana 812 279-5852
618 H St Bedford (47421) (G-568)

Quality Converters Inc 260 829-6541
9675 W Maple St Orland (46776) (G-11356)

Quality Council of Indiana 812 533-4215
602 W Paris Ave West Terre Haute (47885) (G-14128)

Quality Data Products Inc 317 595-0700
10142 Brooks School Rd # 210 Fishers (46037) (G-3959)

Quality Die Set Corp 574 967-4411
600 Water St Logansport (46947) (G-9361)

Quality Drapery Corporation 765 481-2370
1334 W Main St Lebanon (46052) (G-9218)

Quality Engineered Products 574 294-6943
56802 Elk Ct Elkhart (46516) (G-3127)

Quality Fabricated Solutions, Indianapolis Also called Qfs Holdings LLC (G-7792)

Quality Fabrication Ind Inc 765 529-9776
3174 S Commerce Dr New Castle (47362) (G-10915)

Quality Fence Ltd 260 768-4986
6450 W 275 N Shipshewana (46565) (G-12645)

Quality Foam Designs, Nappanee Also called Teach Enterprises Inc (G-10708)

Quality Galvanized Pdts Inc 574 848-5151
19473 County Road 8 Bristol (46507) (G-1076)

Quality Graphics Corp 219 845-7084
7801 Northcote Ave Hammond (46324) (G-5929)

Quality Hardwood Products Inc 260 982-2043
2234 E 1450 N North Manchester (46962) (G-11241)

Quality Hardwood Sales, Knightstown Also called Maurice Lukens Jr (G-8555)

Quality Hardwood Sales, Nappanee Also called Ufp Nappanee LLC (G-10709)

Quality Hydraulic & Mch Svc 317 892-2596
4905 E County Road 450 N Danville (46122) (G-2355)

Quality Imagination Corp 317 753-0042
4405 Massachusetts Ave Indianapolis (46218) (G-7797)

Quality Imprssons Print Design, Crown Point Also called Jac Jmr Inc (G-2264)

Quality Industrial Service, Michigan City Also called Tmak Inc (G-9853)

Quality Industrial Services, La Porte Also called Quality Industrial Supplies (G-8808)

Quality Industrial Supplies 219 324-2654
517 Brighton St La Porte (46350) (G-8808)

Quality Inspection and Gage, Columbia City Also called Qig LLC (G-1822)

Quality Machine & Tool Inc 574 534-5664
924 E Lincoln Ave Goshen (46528) (G-5314)

Quality Machine & Tool Works 812 379-2660
1201 Michigan Ave Columbus (47201) (G-2003)

Quality Mch Repr & Engrg Inc 317 375-1366
4032 S East St Indianapolis (46227) (G-7798)

Quality Metal Products, Elkhart Also called Qmp Inc (G-3124)

Quality Mold & Engineering 812 346-6577
230 N State Highways 3/7 Vernon (47282) (G-13652)

Quality Molded Products Inc 574 272-3733
19850 State Line Rd South Bend (46637) (G-12909)

Quality Pallet 765 348-4840
1506 W Park Ave Hartford City (47348) (G-5989)

Quality Pallet 765 212-2215
1000 E Seymour St Muncie (47302) (G-10551)

Quality Pallets Inc 812 873-6818
8740 W County Road 700 S Commiskey (47227) (G-2036)

Quality Pdts Northwestern Ind, Valparaiso Also called Steelco Industrial Lubricants (G-13624)

Quality Plastics and Engrg Inc 574 262-2621
2507 Decio Dr Elkhart (46514) (G-3128)

Quality Pnt Prstned Fnshes Inc 574 294-6944
28827 Us Highway 33 Elkhart (46516) (G-3129)

Quality Printing, Anderson Also called Printer Zink Inc (G-156)

Quality Printing of NW Ind 219 322-6677
2315 Us Highway 41 Schererville (46375) (G-12343)

Quality Repair Services Inc 317 881-0205
411 Knight Dr Greenwood (46142) (G-5738)

Quality Steel & Alum Pdts Inc 574 295-8715
28620 County Road 20 Elkhart (46517) (G-3130)

Quality Steel & Aluminium 574 294-7221
56741 Elk Park Dr Elkhart (46516) (G-3131)

Quality Steel Treating Co Inc 317 357-8691
3860 Prospect St Indianapolis (46203) (G-7799)

Quality Surfaces 812 876-5838
2087 Franklin Rd Spencer (47460) (G-13034)

Quality Systems LLC 317 326-4660
5603 W Raymond St Ste N Indianapolis (46241) (G-7800)

Quality Tank Trucks & Eqp Inc 317 635-0000
3301 Moore Ave Indianapolis (46201) (G-7801)

Quality Tool & Machine Co 219 464-2411
393 S State Road 49 Valparaiso (46383) (G-13604)

Quality Tool Co Inc 260 484-0187
1431 Production Rd Fort Wayne (46808) (G-4572)

Quality Tool Design Inc 765 377-4055
1645 E County Road 175 N Connersville (47331) (G-2069)

Quality Typesetting 317 787-4466
5501 S East St Indianapolis (46227) (G-7802)

Quality Vault Company 812 336-8127
1908 W Allen St Bloomington (47403) (G-803)

Qualtech Tool & Engrg Inc 260 726-6572
103 Performance Dr Portland (47371) (G-11844)

Qualtronics LLC 812 375-8880
4775 Progress Dr Columbus (47201) (G-2004)

Quanex Corp Lasalle Steel Div 219 853-6202
1412 150th St Hammond (46327) (G-5930)

Quanex Heat Treat 260 356-9520
25 Commercial Rd Huntington (46750) (G-6241)

Quanex Homeshield LLC 765 966-0322
451 Industrial Pkwy Richmond (47374) (G-12040)

Quantum 7 Group LLC 812 824-9378
3523 E Harbor Dr Bloomington (47401) (G-804)

Quantum Covers LLC 219 307-0893
1313 Peachtree Dr Valparaiso (46383) (G-13605)

Quantum Creative LLC 812 381-2586
6320 E Bender Rd Bloomington (47401) (G-805)

Quantum Tech USA 360 400-0905
3271 N Obrien Pl Bloomington (47404) (G-806)

Quantumgraphix LLC 317 819-0009
10302 N College Ave Indianapolis (46280) (G-6279)

Quantumtech LLC 786 512-0827
5042 Brandywine Dr # 322 Indianapolis (46241) (G-7803)

Quarterly Group 812 526-5600
5020 Somerset Ln Columbus (47201) (G-2005)

Queen Ann Custom Drapies 317 802-6130
4000 W 106th St Ste 125 Carmel (46032) (G-1460)

Queen Ann Draperies, Carmel Also called Queen Ann Custom Drapies (G-1460)

Queen City Candy LLC 812 537-5203
601 Rudolph Way Greendale (47025) (G-5494)

Quemetco, Indianapolis Also called Eco-Bat America LLC (G-6801)

Quick Click Marketing Inc 765 857-2167
9270 N Us Highway 27 Ridgeville (47380) (G-12081)

Quick Copy & Design, Indianapolis Also called Kays Graphics Inc (G-7335)

Quick Panic Release LLC 812 841-5733
2216 Dutch Ln Terre Haute (47802) (G-13313)

Quick Print, Valparaiso Also called Brq Quickprint Inc (G-13515)

Quick Sign & Shirt, Hobart Also called CJ Developers Inc (G-6075)

Quick Tanks Inc (PA) 260 347-3850
522 Krueger St Kendallville (46755) (G-8503)

Quick Tanks Inc 260 347-3850
522 Krueger St Kendallville (46755) (G-8504)

Quick Turn Anodizing LLC 877 716-1150
6973 S Us Highway 31 Edinburgh (46124) (G-2622)

Quick Walk Systems Inc 317 255-2247
5315 N Pennsylvania St Indianapolis (46220) (G-7804)

Quick Well Service Inc 812 426-1924
4209 Highway 41 N Evansville (47711) (G-3692)

Quickblades 260 359-2072
1640 Riverfork Dr Ste A Huntington (46750) (G-6242)

Quicks Machine & Tool Inc 812 952-2135
5523 Corydon Ridge Rd Ne Corydon (47112) (G-2109)

Quicksign, Indianapolis Also called Sign Craft Industries Inc (G-7940)

Quicksilver Metals Inc 765 482-1782
2805 N State Road 39 Lebanon (46052) (G-9219)

Quikcut Incorporated 260 447-8090
4630 Allen Martin Dr Fort Wayne (46806) (G-4573)

Quikcut Incorporated (PA) 260 447-3880
4630 Allen Martin Dr Fort Wayne (46806) (G-4574)

Quikrete Companies Inc 317 251-2281
3100 E 56th St Indianapolis (46220) (G-7805)

A
L
P
H
A
B
E
T
I
C

Quikset Bollard Company............................502 648-6734
  2234 E Market St New Albany (47150) *(G-10852)*

Quilt Designs At Old Bag Fctry, Elkhart *Also called Quilt Designs Inc* **(G-3132)**

Quilt Designs Inc..574 534-2502
  23669 Wilshire Blvd E Elkhart (46516) *(G-3132)*

Quilt Expressions..317 913-1916
  12514 Reynolds Dr Ste B Fishers (46038) *(G-3960)*

Quilters Garden...812 539-4939
  9 E Center St Lawrenceburg (47025) *(G-9154)*

Quints Welding..574 936-9138
  8888 King Rd Plymouth (46563) *(G-11718)*

R & A Goodman Enterprises.........................765 296-3446
  1109 S 1025 E Lafayette (47905) *(G-8987)*

R & B Associates Inc.....................................812 471-1550
  5920 Oak Grove Rd Evansville (47715) *(G-3693)*

R & B Fine Printing Inc.................................219 365-9490
  9720 Industrial Dr Saint John (46373) *(G-12268)*

R & B Mold and Die Inc.................................219 324-4176
  1560 Lake St La Porte (46350) *(G-8809)*

R & D Concrete Products of Ind....................260 837-6511
  2397 County Road 27 Waterloo (46793) *(G-14021)*

R & D Machine Shop Inc................................574 946-6109
  935 N Us Highway 35 Winamac (46996) *(G-14318)*

R & D Mold & Engineering Inc......................574 257-1070
  1710 Clover Rd Mishawaka (46545) *(G-10113)*

R & E Pallet Inc...219 873-9671
  1843 E Us Highway 12 Michigan City (46360) *(G-9833)*

R & K Incinerator Inc....................................260 565-3214
  6125 W 100 S Decatur (46733) *(G-2400)*

R & L Die Co Inc..765 759-6880
  4801 S County Road 700 W Yorktown (47396) *(G-14411)*

R & M Enterprises...765 795-6395
  2908 N Routiers Ave Indianapolis (46219) *(G-7806)*

R & M Tool Engineering Inc..........................812 352-0240
  2895 N State Highway 7 North Vernon (47265) *(G-11280)*

R & M Welding & Fabricating Sp (PA)...........812 295-9130
  1192 State Road 550 Loogootee (47553) *(G-9392)*

R & R Bowling Inc..574 252-4123
  1504 Chestnut St Mishawaka (46545) *(G-10114)*

R & R Custom Woodworking Inc....................574 773-5436
  30480 County Road 52 Nappanee (46550) *(G-10703)*

R & R Engineering Co Inc.............................765 536-2331
  801 S Main St Summitville (46070) *(G-13102)*

R & R Manufacturing.....................................260 244-5621
  1150 W 150 N Columbia City (46725) *(G-1823)*

R & R Plastics Inc...219 393-5505
  4th Rd Kingsbury Indus Pa Kingsbury (46345) *(G-8545)*

R & R Regulators Inc.....................................574 522-5846
  24545 County Road 45 Elkhart (46516) *(G-3133)*

R & R Regulators Inc.....................................574 522-5846
  1801 Minnie St Elkhart (46516) *(G-3134)*

R & R Technologies LLC (PA)........................812 526-2655
  7560 E County Line Rd Edinburgh (46124) *(G-2623)*

R & R Tool Manufacturing Inc......................219 362-1681
  1540 Lake St La Porte (46350) *(G-8810)*

R & S Plating Inc...317 925-2396
  2302 Bloyd Ave Indianapolis (46218) *(G-7807)*

R & S Welding & Fabricating........................574 946-6816
  961 W 25 S Winamac (46996) *(G-14319)*

R & Y Professional Tools LLC........................765 354-9076
  102 S 15th St Middletown (47356) *(G-9940)*

R 2 Diagnostics Inc......................................574 288-4377
  1801 Commerce Dr South Bend (46628) *(G-12910)*

R A McCoy Inc...260 636-2341
  1512 Progress Dr Albion (46701) *(G-33)*

R B Annis Instruments Inc............................765 848-1621
  117 W Franklin St Greencastle (46135) *(G-5476)*

R B Machine Company....................................765 364-6716
  2907 S 550 E Crawfordsville (47933) *(G-2190)*

R B Tool & Machinery Co...............................574 679-0082
  10120 Glenwood Ave Osceola (46561) *(G-11383)*

R Booe & Son Hardwoods Inc.......................812 835-2663
  481 N Meridian Rd Centerpoint (47840) *(G-1540)*

R C Electric...317 600-3001
  3659 W 10th St Indianapolis (46222) *(G-7808)*

R C Laser Inc...812 923-1918
  540 E State Road 60 Pekin (47165) *(G-11478)*

R Concepts Industries Inc...........................574 295-6641
  555 County Road 15 Elkhart (46516) *(G-3135)*

R D Laney Family Honey Company.................574 656-8701
  25725 New Rd North Liberty (46554) *(G-11219)*

R D-N-P Drilling Inc......................................219 956-3481
  3759 W 900 N Wheatfield (46392) *(G-14229)*

R Drew & Co Inc..765 420-7232
  4866 N 9th Street Rd West Lafayette (47906) *(G-14100)*

R E Casebeer & Sons Inc..............................812 829-3284
  661 W Market St Spencer (47460) *(G-13035)*

R E Ferguson & Associates Inc.....................317 839-9311
  7851 Quail Rdg S Plainfield (46168) *(G-11639)*

R F Express Corp...219 510-5193
  2601 Vale Park Rd Valparaiso (46383) *(G-13606)*

R Falcone Powersports Inc...........................317 803-2432
  2416 W 16th St Indianapolis (46222) *(G-7809)*

R J Hanlon Company Inc (PA).......................317 867-2900
  17408 Tiller Ct Ste 600 Westfield (46074) *(G-14182)*

R K C Instrument...574 273-6099
  4245 Meghan Beeler Ct South Bend (46628) *(G-12911)*

R M I, Warsaw *Also called Rmi Holdings LLC* **(G-13936)**

R M Mfg Housing Svc.....................................574 288-5207
  1001 S Mayflower Rd L South Bend (46619) *(G-12912)*

R N A Industries Corp...................................765 288-4413
  251 E Sheridan St Redkey (47373) *(G-11899)*

R P S Hydraulics Sales & Svc........................219 845-5526
  3550 179th St Ste 7 Hammond (46323) *(G-5931)*

R P Wakefield Company Inc...........................260 837-8841
  600 W Maple St Waterloo (46793) *(G-14022)*

R R Donnelley & Sons Company.....................260 624-2350
  611 W Mill St Angola (46703) *(G-242)*

R R Donnelley & Sons Company.....................574 267-7101
  2801 W Old Road 30 Warsaw (46580) *(G-13931)*

R R Donnelley & Sons Company.....................812 523-1800
  709 A Ave E Seymour (47274) *(G-12478)*

R R Donnelley Inc...317 631-2203
  201 S Capitol Ave Ste 201 # 201 Indianapolis (46225) *(G-7810)*

R R Forrest Company Inc..............................317 502-3286
  58 Chesterfield Dr Noblesville (46060) *(G-11169)*

R R M, Rochester *Also called Rochester Rttional Molding Inc* **(G-12149)**

R S C, East Chicago *Also called Refractory Service Corporation* **(G-2567)**

R S E Tool and Die Inc..................................574 848-7966
  State Rd 15 N Bristol (46507) *(G-1077)*

R T P Company, Indianapolis *Also called Miller Waste Mills Inc* **(G-7522)**

R V Window Manufacture, Plymouth *Also called Lippert Components Mfg Inc* **(G-11703)**

R W Machine Incorporated.............................317 769-6798
  3463 S 500 E Whitestown (46075) *(G-14260)*

R&D Investment Holdings Inc........................260 749-1301
  6900 Nelson Rd Fort Wayne (46803) *(G-4575)*

R&R Signs, Plainfield *Also called Earl R Hamilton* **(G-11607)**

R&S Sign Design..765 520-5594
  3963 S State Road 103 New Castle (47362) *(G-10916)*

R2 Pharma LLC...317 810-6205
  11550 N Meridian St # 290 Carmel (46032) *(G-1461)*

R3 Composites Corp (PA)..............................260 627-0033
  14123 Roth Rd Grabill (46741) *(G-5383)*

Rabb & Howe Cabinet Top Co........................317 926-6442
  2571 Winthrop Ave Indianapolis (46205) *(G-7811)*

Rabbit Lane LLC..317 733-8380
  1765 Continental Dr Zionsville (46077) *(G-14458)*

Rabboni Book Publishing Co LLC...................765 254-9969
  1100 N Saybrook Ln Muncie (47304) *(G-10552)*

Rabers Buggy Shop LLC.................................812 486-3789
  7209 E 300 N Montgomery (47558) *(G-10239)*

Rabers Whl Works & Buggy Works...................812 486-2786
  7226 E 300 N Montgomery (47558) *(G-10240)*

Race Cars USA LLC..317 508-3500
  1530 Woodlake Ct Carmel (46032) *(G-1462)*

Race Engineering...219 661-8904
  725 E Goldsborough St # 4 Crown Point (46307) *(G-2291)*

Raceway Commons...303 503-4333
  55 S Raceway Rd Indianapolis (46231) *(G-7812)*

Raceway Distributing Inc...............................574 850-8191
  2803 N Main St Mishawaka (46545) *(G-10115)*

Raceway Hand Car Wash LLC.........................260 242-9866
  606 Fairview Blvd Kendallville (46755) *(G-8505)*

Racing Fuel Ignite...765 733-0833
  2950 W Delphi Pike Marion (46952) *(G-9558)*

Raco Industries LLC.......................................812 232-3676
  1607 Maple Ave Terre Haute (47804) *(G-13314)*

RAD Cube LLC...317 456-7560
  9449 Priority Way West Dr Indianapolis (46240) *(G-7813)*

Radar Assoc Corp..219 838-8030
  1117 Melbrook Dr Munster (46321) *(G-10625)*

Radecki Galleries Inc....................................574 287-0266
  721 E Jefferson Blvd South Bend (46617) *(G-12913)*

Radel Wood Products Inc..............................765 472-2940
  1630 W Logansport Rd Peru (46970) *(G-11543)*

Radian Research Inc......................................765 449-5500
  3852 Fortune Dr Lafayette (47905) *(G-8988)*

Radiation Physics Consulting.........................317 251-0193
  7022 Warwick Rd Indianapolis (46220) *(G-7814)*

Radiator Specialty Company...........................574 546-5606
  860 870 Legner Dr Bremen (46506) *(G-1018)*

Radical Graphics & Sign Sp LLC.....................574 870-8873
  4805 E Honeycreek Ct Monticello (47960) *(G-10281)*

Radio Station Wrbi, Batesville *Also called The Findlay Publishing Co* **(G-519)**

Raeco/Promo-Sports LLC.................................574 537-9387
  2249 Lincolnway E Goshen (46526) *(G-5315)*

Rail Protection Plus LLC................................812 399-1084
  3913 Horne Ave New Albany (47150) *(G-10853)*

Rail Scale Inc...317 339-6486
  5303 N 800 E Wilkinson (46186) *(G-14280)*

(G-0000) Company's Geographic Section entry number

Railworks Wood Products Inc.................................812 789-5331
　3818 S County Road 50 E Winslow (47598) *(G-14358)*
Rain Song Farms LLC...317 640-4534
　19539 Pilgrim Rd Noblesville (46060) *(G-11170)*
Rain Song Winery, Noblesville *Also called Rain Song Farms LLC (G-11170)*
Rainbow Design Inc...260 593-2856
　1100 W Us Highway 20 Lagrange (46761) *(G-9063)*
Rainbow Printing Inc..812 275-3372
　2139 16th St Bedford (47421) *(G-569)*
Rainbows Stained Glass.....................................812 265-0030
　1782 E Telegraph Hill Rd Madison (47250) *(G-9491)*
Raine Inc..765 622-7687
　6401 S Madison Ave Anderson (46013) *(G-157)*
Rajo Guns Corp..812 422-6945
　2106 W Franklin St Evansville (47712) *(G-3694)*
Ralph Ransom Logging, Newburgh *Also called Ralph Ransom Veneers (G-11044)*
Ralph Ransom Veneers......................................812 858-9956
　6599 Heathervale Ct Newburgh (47630) *(G-11044)*
Ralston Yard, Valparaiso *Also called Legacy Vulcan LLC (G-13576)*
Ram Apparel, Alexandria *Also called Ram Graphics Inc (G-48)*
Ram Graphics Inc..765 724-7783
　1509 S Longwood Dr Alexandria (46001) *(G-48)*
Ram North America Inc.......................................317 984-1971
　25415 State Road 19 Arcadia (46030) *(G-268)*
Ram Services Rfrgn & Mech.................................317 679-8541
　5170 Atherton North Dr Indianapolis (46219) *(G-7815)*
Ramar Industries Inc..765 288-7319
　6200 N Wheeling Ave Muncie (47304) *(G-10553)*
Ramco Builder and Supply LLC............................574 223-7802
　4572 N Old Us Highway 31 Rochester (46975) *(G-12144)*
Ramco Engineering Inc.......................................574 266-1455
　2805 Frederic Dr Elkhart (46514) *(G-3136)*
Ramco of Indiana, Angola *Also called Jkr Inc (G-221)*
Ramco Supply, Rochester *Also called Ramco Builder and Supply LLC (G-12144)*
Ramer Chair Co...574 862-4179
　25445 County Road 38 Goshen (46526) *(G-5316)*
Ramer Chair Shop, Goshen *Also called Ramer Chair Co (G-5316)*
Ramsey Popcorn Co Inc......................................812 347-2441
　5645 Clover Valley Rd Nw Ramsey (47166) *(G-11894)*
Ramsey's Sheet Metal, La Porte *Also called F D Ramsey & Co Inc (G-8757)*
Rance Aluminum Fabrication................................574 266-9028
　3012 Mobile Dr Elkhart (46514) *(G-3137)*
Ranch Fiberglass Inc..574 294-7550
　28564 Holiday Pl Elkhart (46517) *(G-3138)*
Randall Corp...812 425-7122
　1105 E Virginia St Evansville (47711) *(G-3695)*
Randall Lowe & Sons Sawmill..............................812 936-2254
　6543 W County Road 875 S French Lick (47432) *(G-4988)*
Randall Rents of Indiana Inc................................219 763-1155
　6480 Us Highway 20 Portage (46368) *(G-11791)*
Randolph Carpet-Tile Cleaning.............................317 401-2300
　59 W Armitage Dr Cicero (46034) *(G-1666)*
Random House Inc...410 386-7717
　1019 N State Road 47 Crawfordsville (47933) *(G-2191)*
Randy Gehlhausen...812 327-4454
　2808 E Daniel St Bloomington (47401) *(G-807)*
Randy Harvey Pro Shop, Mishawaka *Also called R & R Bowling Inc (G-10114)*
Rankin Pump and Supply Co Inc...........................812 238-2535
　130 N 11th St Terre Haute (47807) *(G-13315)*
Rapar Inc...812 254-9886
　705 W National Hwy Washington (47501) *(G-14001)*
Rapid Prototyping & Engrg...................................812 526-9207
　3340 W Presidential Way Edinburgh (46124) *(G-2624)*
Rapid Ribbons, Goshen *Also called Planks Printing Service Inc (G-5309)*
Rapid Rule Co Inc..574 784-2273
　69159 Pine Rd North Liberty (46554) *(G-11220)*
Rapid Sensors Inc...260 562-3614
　6060 N 160 W Howe (46746) *(G-6131)*
Rappid Mfg Inc..317 440-8084
　8219 Indy Ct Indianapolis (46214) *(G-7816)*
Rapsure Inc..574 773-2995
　305 S Main St Nappanee (46550) *(G-10704)*
Rapt Pen LLC..317 547-8113
　3614 N Grant Ave Indianapolis (46218) *(G-7817)*
Rasche Bro Logging...812 357-7782
　12242 E Monte Casino Rd Ferdinand (47532) *(G-3862)*
Rasure Prints..812 454-6222
　3960 Wood Castle Rd Evansville (47711) *(G-3696)*
Ratcliff Enterprises, Lafayette *Also called Gary Ratcliff (G-8905)*
Ratech Industries, Lowell *Also called Innovative Energy Inc (G-9409)*
Rathburn Tool and Mfg, Auburn *Also called Three Daughters Corp (G-361)*
Rau Creations..317 774-8789
　14617 Strauss Dr Apt 2412 Carmel (46032) *(G-1463)*
Rauch Inc (PA)..812 945-4063
　845 Park Pl New Albany (47150) *(G-10854)*
Raven Communications Inc.................................317 576-9889
　6939 Lantern Rd Indianapolis (46256) *(G-7818)*

Raver Ready Mix Concrete LLC............................812 662-7900
　7935 E State Road 46 Greensburg (47240) *(G-5631)*
Raw Design and Fabrication LLC..........................708 466-5835
　8821 Mallard Ln Saint John (46373) *(G-12269)*
Ray Brothers Noble Canning Co...........................765 552-9432
　1361 S 500 E Tipton (46072) *(G-13402)*
Ray Kammer...219 938-1708
　6805 Forest Ave Gary (46403) *(G-5088)*
Ray's Wood Products, Martinsville *Also called Terry L Ray (G-9641)*
Raybestos Powertrain.......................................812 268-1370
　110 Industrial Park Dr Sullivan (47882) *(G-13092)*
Raybestos Powertrain LLC..................................812 268-1211
　312 S St Clair St Sullivan (47882) *(G-13093)*
Rayburn Automotive Inc.....................................317 535-8232
　4725 N Graham Rd Whiteland (46184) *(G-14244)*
Rayco Marketing..574 293-8416
　29675 Old Us 20 Elkhart (46514) *(G-3139)*
Rayco Mch & Engrg Group Inc.............................317 291-7848
　970 Western Dr Indianapolis (46241) *(G-7819)*
Rayco Steel Process Inc.....................................574 267-7676
　207 S Lincoln St Warsaw (46580) *(G-13932)*
Raymond Little Print Shop...................................317 246-9083
　7800 Records St Ste C Indianapolis (46226) *(G-7820)*
Raymond Truex...574 858-2260
　5383 W 400 N Warsaw (46582) *(G-13933)*
Raytheon Company..317 306-4872
　6125 E 21st St Indianapolis (46219) *(G-7821)*
Raytheon Company..317 306-8471
　6125 E 21st St Indianapolis (46219) *(G-7822)*
Raytheon Company..260 429-6000
　1010 Production Rd Fort Wayne (46808) *(G-4576)*
Raytheon Company..310 647-9438
　1010 Production Rd Fort Wayne (46808) *(G-4577)*
Raytheon Company..310 647-9438
　1010 Production Rd Fort Wayne (46808) *(G-4578)*
RB Apparel, Bloomington *Also called RB Concepts (G-808)*
RB Concepts..317 735-2172
　8451 S Marcy Ct Bloomington (47401) *(G-808)*
Rbc Manufacturing Corp.....................................260 416-5400
　1946 W Cook Rd Fort Wayne (46818) *(G-4579)*
Rbc Prcision Pdts - Bremen Inc...........................574 546-4455
　225 Industrial Dr Bremen (46506) *(G-1019)*
Rbc Prcsion Pdts - Plymth Inc (HQ).....................574 935-3027
　2928 Gary Dr Plymouth (46563) *(G-11719)*
Rbg Inc..812 866-3983
　9186 W Henry Rd Lexington (47138) *(G-9255)*
Rbk Development Inc..574 267-5879
　1058 W 400 N Warsaw (46582) *(G-13934)*
RBM Manufacturing Inc......................................765 364-6933
　566 S 200 E Crawfordsville (47933) *(G-2192)*
Rbs Tees Co...812 522-8675
　1102 Gaiser Dr Seymour (47274) *(G-12479)*
RC Canada Dry Bottling Company, Seymour *Also called Keurig Dr Pepper Inc (G-12463)*
RC Cola, Evansville *Also called Royal Crown Bottling Corp (G-3710)*
RC Enterprise LLC...317 225-6747
　1389 W 86th St Ste 143 Indianapolis (46260) *(G-7823)*
RC Enterprises..812 279-2755
　2611 16th St 301 Bedford (47421) *(G-570)*
RC Fun Parks LLC...574 217-7715
　12990 Adams Rd Granger (46530) *(G-5430)*
RCO-Reed Corporation..317 736-8014
　1050 Eastview Dr Franklin (46131) *(G-4925)*
Rcr Metal Fab LLC...219 923-9104
　713 N Oakwood St Griffith (46319) *(G-5788)*
Rcs Contractor Supplies Inc................................317 773-6279
　5000 Conner St Noblesville (46060) *(G-11171)*
Rd Rubber Products Inc......................................260 357-3571
　1600 South Rd Garrett (46738) *(G-5021)*
RD Smith Manufacturing Inc................................260 829-6709
　5990 N State Road 327 Orland (46776) *(G-11357)*
RE Industries Inc...219 987-1764
　1328 15th St Se Ste 4 Demotte (46310) *(G-2446)*
RE Winset Music, Kendallville *Also called Sacred Selections (G-8509)*
REA Magnet Wire Company Inc............................765 477-8000
　2800 Concord Rd Lafayette (47909) *(G-8989)*
REA Magnet Wire Company Inc............................260 421-5400
　4300 New Haven Ave Fort Wayne (46803) *(G-4580)*
REA Magnet Wire NH, Fort Wayne *Also called REA Magnet Wire Company Inc (G-4580)*
Reactor Services Intl Inc.....................................219 924-0507
　238 S Linburg Griffith (46319) *(G-5789)*
Reading Bakery Systems Ta.................................317 337-0000
　7517 Winton Dr Indianapolis (46268) *(G-7824)*
Ready Machine Tool & Die Corp...........................765 825-3108
　1321 N Illinois Ave Connersville (47331) *(G-2070)*
Ready Pac Foods Inc..574 935-9800
　2050 N Oak Dr Plymouth (46563) *(G-11720)*
Reagent Chemical & RES Inc...............................574 772-3271
　317 Kloeckner Dr Knox (46534) *(G-8577)*
Reagent Chemical & RES Inc...............................574 772-7424
　1705 Pacific Ave Knox (46534) *(G-8578)*

A L P H A B E T I C

Real Alloy Recycling LLC 262 637-9858
4525 W Old 24 Wabash (46992) **(G-13752)**
Real Alloy Recycling LLC 260 563-2409
305 Dimension Ave Wabash (46992) **(G-13753)**
Real Estate Sign Services, Indianapolis *Also called Insign Inc* **(G-7241)**
Real Image Llc 765 675-7325
501 N Main St Tipton (46072) **(G-13403)**
Real Log Homes, Attica *Also called Country Charm* **(G-299)**
Real Power, Indianapolis *Also called Contour Hardening Inc* **(G-6659)**
Real Wood Works 812 277-1462
2802 N Poor Farm Rd Bedford (47421) **(G-571)**
Reality Motor Sports Inc 765 662-3000
1322 N Baldwin Ave Marion (46952) **(G-9559)**
Realize Inc 317 915-0295
15515 Endeavor Dr Noblesville (46060) **(G-11172)**
Rebar Corp of Indiana 260 471-2002
5601 Industrial Rd Fort Wayne (46825) **(G-4581)**
Rebel Devil Customs 303 921-7131
14164 E 239th St Noblesville (46060) **(G-11173)**
Reber Machine & Tool Co Inc 765 288-0297
1112 S Liberty St Muncie (47302) **(G-10554)**
Rebound Project LLP 765 621-5604
1125 N Madison Ave Anderson (46011) **(G-158)**
Reckon Plating Inc 260 744-4339
5300 Hanna St Fort Wayne (46806) **(G-4582)**
Recognition Plus 812 232-2372
25 S 6th St Terre Haute (47807) **(G-13316)**
Recon Group LLP 855 874-8741
6719 W 350 N Greenfield (46140) **(G-5566)**
Reconserve of Indiana 310 458-1574
1150 E Harlan Dr Terre Haute (47802) **(G-13317)**
Record / Play Tek Inc 574 848-5233
110 E Vistula St Bristol (46507) **(G-1078)**
Recovery Technologies LLC 260 745-3902
2001 E Pontiac St Bldg 8 Fort Wayne (46803) **(G-4583)**
Recreation By Design LLC 574 294-2117
57420 County Road 3 Elkhart (46517) **(G-3140)**
Recreation Insites LLC 317 578-0588
12237 Westmorland Dr Fishers (46037) **(G-3961)**
Recreation Nation, Elkhart *Also called Dehco Inc* **(G-2792)**
Recreational Customs Inc 574 642-0632
67928 Us Highway 33 Goshen (46526) **(G-5317)**
Recycle Design Inc 765 374-0316
804 Hazlett St Anderson (46016) **(G-159)**
Recycled New, Elkhart *Also called Duro Recycling Inc* **(G-2805)**
Recycledgranite.com, Schererville *Also called My Choice Recycling Inc* **(G-12336)**
Recycling Center Inc 765 966-8295
630 S M St Richmond (47374) **(G-12041)**
Recycling Services Indiana Inc 812 279-8114
4635 Peerless Rd Bedford (47421) **(G-572)**
Recycling Works Inc 574 293-3751
605 Mason St Elkhart (46516) **(G-3141)**
Red Barn Industries Inc 765 379-3197
5665 W County Road 700 N Mulberry (46058) **(G-10419)**
Red Bull Armory LLC 757 287-7738
440 Peaceful Valley Rd Mitchell (47446) **(G-10169)**
Red Bull North America Inc 216 401-3950
7533 Chapel Hill Ct Newburgh (47630) **(G-11045)**
Red Case LLC 317 250-5538
1005 Churchman Ave Beech Grove (46107) **(G-603)**
Red Cedar Center, Fort Wayne *Also called Anthony Wayne Rehabilitation C* **(G-4078)**
Red Cloud Adhesives Inc 219 331-3239
9800 Connecticut Dr Crown Point (46307) **(G-2292)**
Red Forge Inc 812 934-9641
4552 State Road 46 E Batesville (47006) **(G-516)**
Red Gate Farms Inc 812 277-9750
8987 State Road 37 Bedford (47421) **(G-573)**
Red Gold 765 254-1705
3500 S Cowan Rd Muncie (47302) **(G-10555)**
Red Gold Inc 260 726-8140
957 W 200 S Portland (47371) **(G-11845)**
Red Gold Inc 260 368-9017
705 Williams St Geneva (46740) **(G-5138)**
Red Gold LP 765 754-8750
2595 W State Road 28 Alexandria (46001) **(G-49)**
Red Hawk Choppers Inc 765 307-2269
212 N Washington St Crawfordsville (47933) **(G-2193)**
Red Lark Press Inc 260 224-7974
230 George St Huntington (46750) **(G-6243)**
Red Line Graphics Incorporated (PA) 317 591-9400
6430 S Belmont Ave Indianapolis (46217) **(G-7825)**
Red Rover Wholesale, Fort Wayne *Also called Big Brick House Bakery LLP* **(G-4107)**
Red Spot Paint & Varnish Co (HQ) 812 428-9100
1107 E Louisiana St Evansville (47711) **(G-3697)**
Red Spot Paint & Varnish Co 812 428-9100
1111 E Louisiana St Evansville (47711) **(G-3698)**
Red Spot Paint & Varnish Co 812 428-9100
1016 E Columbia St Evansville (47711) **(G-3699)**
Red Star Contract Mfg Inc 260 327-3145
1560 N State Road 5 Larwill (46764) **(G-9125)**
Red Tortilla Inc 260 403-2681
921 E Dupont Rd Ste 913 Fort Wayne (46825) **(G-4584)**
Red Wagon 260 768-3090
255 N Harrison St Ste 206 Shipshewana (46565) **(G-12646)**
Red Wing Shoe Company Inc 317 219-6777
17017 Mercantile Blvd Noblesville (46060) **(G-11174)**
Redab Industries 219 484-8382
10425 Maine Dr Crown Point (46307) **(G-2293)**
Reddi-Pac Inc 574 266-6933
1301 N Nappanee St Elkhart (46514) **(G-3142)**
Reddington Design Inc 574 272-0790
4221 Ralph Jones Ct South Bend (46628) **(G-12914)**
Redi/Controls Inc 317 494-6600
161 R J Pkwy Franklin (46131) **(G-4926)**
Redlin Custom Woodworking LLC 317 578-1852
8507 Barstow Dr Fishers (46038) **(G-3962)**
Redman Industries LLC 317 768-3004
6696 E Stonegate Dr Zionsville (46077) **(G-14459)**
Redneck Monshiners Signs T-Shi 812 844-0694
2810 W Terry Ave Salem (47167) **(G-12304)**
Redspot Paint and Varnish Co 812 428-9100
1107 E La St Evansville (47711) **(G-3700)**
Redstar Contract Manufacturing 260 327-3145
1560 N State Road 5 Larwill (46764) **(G-9126)**
Reed Contracting Company 765 452-2638
113 W Jefferson St Kokomo (46901) **(G-8687)**
Reed Immunodiagnostics LLC 317 446-3582
351 W 10th St Indianapolis (46202) **(G-7826)**
Reed Manufacturing Services, Franklin *Also called RCO-Reed Corporation* **(G-4925)**
Reed Minerals 219 944-6250
7100 W 9th Ave Gary (46406) **(G-5089)**
Reed Raymond Trust 317 831-7246
133 Justin Dr Mooresville (46158) **(G-10336)**
Reed Sign Service Inc 765 459-4033
113 W Jefferson St Kokomo (46901) **(G-8688)**
Reeder & Kline Machine Co Inc 317 846-6591
501 W 261st St Sheridan (46069) **(G-12596)**
Reeders Cleaners 812 945-4833
1205 Eastern Blvd Clarksville (47129) **(G-1692)**
Reeds Plastic Tops Inc 765 282-1471
2150 E Memorial Dr Muncie (47302) **(G-10556)**
Reeds RFI Inc 812 659-2872
248 N 475 W Switz City (47465) **(G-13126)**
Reelcraft Industries Inc 855 634-9109
2842 E Business 30 Columbia City (46725) **(G-1824)**
Rees Inc 260 495-9811
405 S Reed Rd Fremont (46737) **(G-4972)**
Rees Harps Inc 812 438-3032
222 Main St Rising Sun (47040) **(G-12091)**
Reese Forge Orna Ironwork 219 775-1039
6873 W 700 N Lake Village (46349) **(G-9086)**
Reeves Feed & Grain LLC 812 453-3313
96 N Walnut St Poseyville (47633) **(G-11861)**
Reeves Manufacturing Inc 765 935-3875
1214 Sheridan St Richmond (47374) **(G-12042)**
Refax Inc 219 977-0414
3240 W 5th Ave Gary (46406) **(G-5090)**
Refax Wear Products Inc 219 977-0414
3240 W 5th Ave Gary (46406) **(G-5091)**
Reflectix Inc 765 533-4332
1 School St Markleville (46056) **(G-9589)**
Refractory Service Corporation (PA) 219 397-7108
4900 Cline Ave East Chicago (46312) **(G-2567)**
Refractory Service Corporation 219 853-0885
4902 Calumet Ave Hammond (46327) **(G-5932)**
Refractory Specialists LLC 260 969-1099
3525 Metro Dr N Fort Wayne (46818) **(G-4585)**
Refreshment Services Inc 812 466-0602
3875 4th Pkwy Terre Haute (47804) **(G-13318)**
Refrigeration Package Corp 812 867-0900
11425 N Green River Rd Evansville (47725) **(G-3701)**
Refrigeration Sys of Evans, Evansville *Also called Evansville Metal Products Inc* **(G-3487)**
Regal Inc 765 747-1155
305 N Gray St Muncie (47303) **(G-10557)**
Regal Beloit America Inc 574 583-9171
705 N 6th St Monticello (47960) **(G-10282)**
Regal Beloit America Inc 219 465-2200
2300 Evans Ave Valparaiso (46383) **(G-13607)**
Regal Beloit America Inc 260 416-5400
1946 W Cook Rd Fort Wayne (46818) **(G-4586)**
Regal Beloit America Inc 219 465-2200
2300 Evans Ave Valparaiso (46383) **(G-13608)**
Regal Marketing, Muncie *Also called Regal Inc* **(G-10557)**
Regal Mills Odon 812 295-2299
2805 N 1200 E Loogootee (47553) **(G-9393)**
Regal Mold & Die, Elkhart *Also called Ruco Inc* **(G-3151)**
Regal Printing Inc 317 844-1723
485 Gradle Dr Carmel (46032) **(G-1464)**

Regal Publications LLC 260 693-0698
  120 W Washington St Churubusco (46723) (G-1656)

Regal-Beloit Corporation 260 416-5400
  1946 W Cook Rd Fort Wayne (46818) (G-4587)

Regency Pad Corp 731 587-9596
  2625 Kotter Ave Evansville (47715) (G-3702)

Regency Technologies Inc 317 543-9740
  3880 Pendleton Way # 900 Indianapolis (46226) (G-7827)

Regent Aerospace Corporation 317 837-4000
  2501 E Perry Rd Plainfield (46168) (G-11640)

Regin Manufacturing, Indianapolis Also called AMG LLC (G-6397)

Region Communications Inc 219 662-8888
  7590 E 109th Ave Crown Point (46307) (G-2294)

Region Signs Inc 219 473-1616
  1345 119th St Whiting (46394) (G-14275)

Regional Data Services Inc 219 661-3200
  1260 Arrowhead Ct Crown Point (46307) (G-2295)

Register Publications, Lawrenceburg Also called Delphos Herald of Indiana (G-9137)

Registration System LLC 317 548-4090
  7 Launch Way Fishers (46038) (G-3963)

Regulations Update Svcs LLC 812 334-4020
  1819 N Hartstrait Rd Bloomington (47404) (G-809)

Rehco Products Inc 317 984-3319
  700 S East St Arcadia (46030) (G-269)

Reiberg Ceramics 317 283-8441
  5723 N Meridian St Indianapolis (46208) (G-7828)

Reidco Inc 812 358-3000
  1351 W Us Highway 50 Brownstown (47220) (G-1191)

Reilly Industries Inc 317 247-8141
  1500 S Tibbs Ave Indianapolis (46241) (G-7829)

Reinforcements Design 219 866-8626
  3195 1/2 W Clark St Rensselaer (47978) (G-11935)

Reising Son Originals 812 437-1831
  5120 Middle Mt Vernon Rd Evansville (47712) (G-3703)

Reiss Orna & Structurall Pdts 317 925-2371
  3739 N Illinois St Indianapolis (46208) (G-7830)

Reit-Price Mfg Co Incorporated 765 964-3252
  522 W Chestnut St Union City (47390) (G-13460)

Relational Gravity Inc 317 855-7685
  12623 Tealwood Dr Indianapolis (46236) (G-7831)

Relational Intelligence LLC 317 669-8900
  14948 Annabel Ct Westfield (46074) (G-14183)

Relevo Inc 317 644-0099
  5883 William Conner Way Carmel (46033) (G-1465)

Relevo Labs LLC 317 900-6949
  5883 William Conner Way Carmel (46033) (G-1466)

Reliable Metalcraft, Mishawaka Also called Mc Metalcraft Inc (G-10077)

Reliable Metalcraft Corp, Mishawaka Also called Mc Metalcraft Inc (G-10076)

Reliable Polishing Co 765 744-7824
  12517 W State Road 32 Parker City (47368) (G-11464)

Reliable Prod Machining & Wldg, Kendallville Also called Reliable Tool & Machine
Co (G-8506)

Reliable Sealants LLC 765 672-4455
  3382 W County Road 875 S Reelsville (46171) (G-11903)

Reliable Tool & Machine Co (PA) 260 343-7150
  301 W Ohio St Kendallville (46755) (G-8506)

Reliable Tool & Machine Co 260 347-4000
  902 S Main St Kendallville (46755) (G-8507)

Reliable Tool & Machine Co 260 347-4000
  800 Weston Ave Kendallville (46755) (G-8508)

Reliance Machine Company Inc (PA) 765 284-0151
  4605 S Walnut St Muncie (47302) (G-10558)

Reliance Machine Company Inc 765 857-1000
  108 W 2nd St Ridgeville (47380) (G-12082)

Reliant Engineering Inc 317 322-9084
  1329 Sadlier Circle W Dr Indianapolis (46239) (G-7832)

REM Industries Inc 574 862-2127
  902 Nelsons Pkwy Wakarusa (46573) (G-13792)

Reman Holdings LLC (HQ) 800 372-5131
  600 Corporation Dr Pendleton (46064) (G-11502)

Remco Products Corporation 317 876-9856
  4735 W 106th St Zionsville (46077) (G-14460)

Remedium Services Group LLC 317 660-6868
  11711 N College Ave Carmel (46032) (G-1467)

Remington Machine Inc 765 724-3389
  6 Twin Oaks St Alexandria (46001) (G-50)

Remmler Drilling & Pump Svc, Greensburg Also called John Remmler Well Drilling (G-5616)

Remy Electric Motors LLC 765 778-6466
  600 Corporation Dr Pendleton (46064) (G-11503)

Remy Logistics LLC (HQ) 765 683-3700
  2902 Enterprise Dr Anderson (46013) (G-160)

Remy Power Products LLC 765 778-6499
  600 Corporation Dr Pendleton (46064) (G-11504)

Renaissnce Electronic Svcs LLC 317 786-2235
  1502 W Edgewood Ave Ste A Indianapolis (46217) (G-7833)

Rencor Inc 765 395-7949
  12833 S 1000 E Converse (46919) (G-2082)

Renegade Trike Corp 812 941-9900
  1309 Providence Way Clarksville (47129) (G-1693)

Renewed Performance Company 765 675-7586
  1095 Development Dr Tipton (46072) (G-13404)

Renk Systems Corporation 317 455-1367
  8880 Union Mills Dr Camby (46113) (G-1268)

Renosys, Indianapolis Also called Aquatic Renovation Systems Inc (G-6412)

Rensew Inc 574 257-0665
  706 E Broadway St Mishawaka (46545) (G-10116)

Rensselaer Eagle Vault Corp 219 866-5123
  250 N Mckinley Ave Rensselaer (47978) (G-11936)

Rensselaer Print Co 219 866-5000
  116 N Cullen St Rensselaer (47978) (G-11937)

Rensselaer Products, Rensselaer Also called Genova Products Inc (G-11925)

Rensselaer Republican, Rensselaer Also called Kankakee Valley Publishing Co (G-11930)

Rensselaer Septic Tanks, Rensselaer Also called Rensselaer Eagle Vault Corp (G-11936)

Rentown Cabinets 574 546-2569
  2735 Birch Rd Bremen (46506) (G-1020)

REO-Usa Inc 317 899-1395
  8450 E 47th St Indianapolis (46226) (G-7834)

Repaco, Evansville Also called Refrigeration Package Corp (G-3701)

Replas of Texas Inc 812 421-3600
  15000 Highway 41 N Evansville (47725) (G-3704)

Reprocomm Inc (PA) 765 472-5700
  179 N Miami St Peru (46970) (G-11544)

Reprocomm Inc 765 423-2578
  511 Ferry St Lafayette (47901) (G-8990)

Republic Etching Carving 812 366-8111
  5925 Highway 135 Ne New Salisbury (47161) (G-11010)

Republic Inc 812 342-8028
  333 2nd St Columbus (47201) (G-2006)

Republican 317 745-2777
  6 E Main St Danville (46122) (G-2356)

Republican Newspaper, Danville Also called Republican (G-2356)

Reschcor Inc (PA) 574 295-2413
  2123 Blakesley Pkwy Bristol (46507) (G-1079)

Reschcor Inc 574 295-2413
  2711 Industrial Pkwy Elkhart (46516) (G-3143)

Resco Products Inc 219 844-7830
  5501 Kennedy Ave Hammond (46323) (G-5933)

Rescom Management Systems Inc 812 254-5641
  3625 W 450 S Washington (47501) (G-14002)

Research, Indianapolis Also called Indiana Nanotech LLC (G-7185)

Research Machining Services 765 494-3710
  694 S Russell St West Lafayette (47907) (G-14101)

Residual Pays Daily 260 267-1617
  2313 Florida Dr Apt C15 Fort Wayne (46805) (G-4588)

Residue Regency Pad, Evansville Also called Residue West Inc (G-3705)

Residue West Inc 731 587-9596
  2625 Kotter Ave Evansville (47715) (G-3705)

Resin Partners Inc 765 724-7761
  602 S Fairview St Alexandria (46001) (G-51)

Resin Partners Inc (HQ) 765 298-6800
  6435 S Scatterfield Rd Anderson (46013) (G-161)

Resistance Wire, Fort Wayne Also called Hyndman Industrial Pdts Inc (G-4354)

Resource Ventures LLC 260 432-9177
  6714 Pointe Inverness Way # 200 Fort Wayne (46804) (G-4589)

Resource Ventures II LLC 260 969-3500
  7575 W Jefferson Blvd Fort Wayne (46804) (G-4590)

Resourcemfg 574 206-1522
  3243 Northview Dr Elkhart (46514) (G-3144)

Restoration Med Polymers LLC 260 625-1573
  5865 E State Road 14 Columbia City (46725) (G-1825)

Restorco Inc 812 882-3987
  1202 Barnett St Vincennes (47591) (G-13700)

Resumes Today, Indianapolis Also called Athena Arts & Graphics Inc (G-6436)

Rethceif Enterprises LLC 260 622-7200
  420 Industrial Pkwy Ossian (46777) (G-11405)

Rethceif Packaging, Ossian Also called Rethceif Enterprises LLC (G-11405)

Rettig Enterprises Inc 765 567-2441
  1950 E 800 N West Lafayette (47906) (G-14102)

Reuer Machine & Tool Inc 219 362-2894
  1733 E State Road 2 La Porte (46350) (G-8811)

Rev Group, Decatur Also called Goldshield Fiber Glass Inc (G-2382)

Rev Recreation Group Inc 260 728-9564
  1031 E Us Highway 224 Decatur (46733) (G-2401)

Rev Recreation Group Inc (HQ) 260 728-2121
  1031 E Us Highway 224 Decatur (46733) (G-2402)

Rev Recreation Group Inc 260 724-4217
  1803 Winchester St Decatur (46733) (G-2403)

Revere Industries 317 638-1521
  111 Monument Cir Ste 3200 Indianapolis (46204) (G-7835)

Revere Industries LLC (PA) 317 580-2420
  16855 Suthpark Dr Ste 100 Westfield (46074) (G-14184)

Revere Plastics Systems LLC 812 670-2240
  5171 Maritime Jeffersonville (47130) (G-8419)

Reversible Rollers, Chesterfield Also called Smiths Enterprises Inc (G-1589)

Revolver LLC 317 418-1824
  13904 Town Center Blvd # 800 Noblesville (46060) (G-11175)

Reward Inc 574 936-7196
  11040 4a Rd Plymouth (46563) *(G-11721)*

Rewind 812 361-0411
  118 E 6th St Bloomington (47408) *(G-810)*

Rewright Printing 219 513-8133
  9222 Indianapolis Blvd D Highland (46322) *(G-6054)*

Rex Alton & Companies Inc 812 882-8519
  2341 S Old Decker Rd Vincennes (47591) *(G-13701)*

Rex Alton Trucking, Vincennes *Also called Rex Alton & Companies Inc (G-13701)*

Rex Byers Htg & Coolg Systems 765 459-8858
  4108 Cartwright Dr Kokomo (46902) *(G-8689)*

Rexam, Princeton *Also called Bprex Closures LLC (G-11866)*

Rexford Rand Corp (PA) 219 872-5561
  2123 E Us Highway 12 Michigan City (46360) *(G-9834)*

Rexnord Industries LLC 865 220-7700
  1304 Turfway Dr Avon (46123) *(G-463)*

Rexnord Industries LLC 317 273-5500
  1304 Turfway Dr Avon (46123) *(G-464)*

Reynolds & Co Inc 812 232-5313
  1916 S 25th St Terre Haute (47802) *(G-13319)*

Reynolds North 812 235-5313
  1025 N Fruitridge Ave Terre Haute (47804) *(G-13320)*

Reynoldsrussell Entps LLC 317 431-5886
  2324 Jefferson St Anderson (46016) *(G-162)*

Rf Manufacturing Inc 317 773-8610
  1780 S 10th St Noblesville (46060) *(G-11176)*

RFI, Columbus *Also called Rightway Fasteners Inc (G-2009)*

Rga, Fort Wayne *Also called Rubber & Gasket Co Amer Inc (G-4597)*

Rheem Sales Company Inc 479 648-4900
  1240 Brookville Way Indianapolis (46239) *(G-7836)*

Rhi US Ltd 219 237-2420
  2929 Carlson Dr Ste 201 Hammond (46323) *(G-5934)*

Rhinehart Development Corp 260 238-4442
  5345 County Road 68 Spencerville (46788) *(G-13050)*

Rhinehart Finishing LLC 260 238-4442
  5345 County Road 68 Spencerville (46788) *(G-13051)*

Rhinestone Supply LLC 260 484-2711
  921 E Dupont Rd Ste 233 Fort Wayne (46825) *(G-4591)*

Rhodes Amplification LLC 765 775-5100
  4209 State Road 43 N West Lafayette (47906) *(G-14103)*

Rhon Inc 574 297-5217
  802 N 1st St Monticello (47960) *(G-10283)*

Rhr Corporation 317 788-1504
  930 E Hanna Ave Indianapolis (46227) *(G-7837)*

Rhyne & Associates Inc 317 786-4459
  3560 Madison Ave Indianapolis (46227) *(G-7838)*

Rhyne Competition Engines, Gary *Also called Rhyne Engines Inc (G-5092)*

Rhyne Engines Inc 219 845-1218
  5733 W 25th Ave Gary (46406) *(G-5092)*

Rhyne, R E & Company, Indianapolis *Also called Rhyne & Associates Inc (G-7838)*

Ricca Chemical Company LLC 812 932-1161
  1490 Lammers Pike Batesville (47006) *(G-517)*

Rice Flooring 574 830-5147
  58794 Chase Trl Elkhart (46516) *(G-3145)*

Rich Glas Products, Jonesboro *Also called H A P Industries Inc (G-8445)*

Rich Manufacturing Inc 765 436-2744
  1990 John Bart Rd Lebanon (46052) *(G-9220)*

Richard E Leonard LLC 812 882-7343
  2101 Mckinley Ave Vincennes (47591) *(G-13702)*

Richard Greg Etienne Logging 812 843-5132
  11133 Trumpet Rd Derby (47525) *(G-2462)*

Richard J Bagan Inc 260 244-5115
  1280 S Williams Dr Columbia City (46725) *(G-1826)*

Richard Myers Mllwrght 765 883-8177
  2719 S 1280 W Russiaville (46979) *(G-12243)*

Richard Sheets 574 536-8247
  15569 State Road 120 Bristol (46507) *(G-1080)*

Richard Squier Pallets Inc 260 281-2434
  2522 Us Highway 6 Waterloo (46793) *(G-14023)*

Richard Young 812 546-5208
  10477 E 600 N Columbus (47203) *(G-2007)*

Richards Bakery 260 424-4012
  1130 N Wells St Fort Wayne (46808) *(G-4592)*

Richards Printery 812 406-0295
  9357 Arthur Coffman Rd Greenville (47124) *(G-5652)*

Richards Restaurant Inc 260 997-6823
  8341 N 400 E Bryant (47326) *(G-1201)*

Richards Scale Company 812 246-3354
  820 S Penn Ave Sellersburg (47172) *(G-12412)*

Richardson Entps Blmington LLC 812 287-8179
  2454 S Walnut St Bloomington (47401) *(G-811)*

Richardson Imaging Svcs Inc 888 561-0007
  4239 Earnings Way New Albany (47150) *(G-10855)*

Richardson Molding LLC (PA) 812 342-0139
  2405 Norcross Dr Columbus (47201) *(G-2008)*

Richardson Molding LLC 317 787-9463
  5601 S Meridian St Ste B Indianapolis (46217) *(G-7839)*

Richeson Cabinet, Indianapolis *Also called Richeson Contracting Inc (G-7840)*

Richeson Contracting Inc 317 889-5995
  5325 Commerce Square Dr Indianapolis (46237) *(G-7840)*

Richeys Mold and Tool Inc 812 752-1059
  101 E Owen St Scottsburg (47170) *(G-12378)*

Richmond Baking Co 765 962-8535
  520 N 6th St Richmond (47374) *(G-12043)*

Richmond Baking Georgia Inc 765 962-8535
  520 N 6th St Richmond (47374) *(G-12044)*

Richmond Casting Company 765 935-4090
  1775 Rich Rd Richmond (47374) *(G-12045)*

Richmond Pattern 765 935-7342
  301 N 3rd St Richmond (47374) *(G-12046)*

Richmonds Feed Service Inc 574 862-2984
  704 E Waterford St Wakarusa (46573) *(G-13793)*

Richters Machine & Tool 260 495-5327
  4395 E 300 N Fremont (46737) *(G-4973)*

Rick Black Associates LLC 765 838-3498
  3233 E 200 N Lafayette (47905) *(G-8991)*

Rick Singleton 574 259-5555
  203 N Main St Mishawaka (46544) *(G-10117)*

Rick's Tool Company, Columbia City *Also called Rickie Allan Pease (G-1827)*

Ricker Oil Company Inc 317 780-1777
  4002 S East St Indianapolis (46227) *(G-7841)*

Ricker Oil Company Inc 317 920-0850
  3750 E Fall Creek Parkway Indianapolis (46205) *(G-7842)*

Rickie Allan Pease 260 244-7579
  406 Diamond Ave Columbia City (46725) *(G-1827)*

Rickles Pickles 260 495-9024
  103 W Toledo St Fremont (46737) *(G-4974)*

Ricks Custom Sheet Metal LLC 812 825-3959
  13089 E Newton Dr Solsberry (47459) *(G-12687)*

Rico Aroma LLC 765 471-1700
  2324 Teal Rd Lafayette (47905) *(G-8992)*

Rics Software Inc 317 455-5338
  129 E Market St Ste 1100 Indianapolis (46204) *(G-7843)*

Riddell Technologies LLC 219 213-9602
  1351 W 95th Ct Crown Point (46307) *(G-2296)*

Riddle Ridge Woodworks 812 596-4503
  1731 E Denton Rd English (47118) *(G-3318)*

Riden Inc 219 362-5511
  315 Lincolnway La Porte (46350) *(G-8812)*

Rider Productions 260 471-0099
  4934 Hillegas Rd Fort Wayne (46818) *(G-4593)*

Ridg-U-Rak Inc 574 273-8036
  51738 Foxdale Ln Granger (46530) *(G-5431)*

Ridge Iron Inc 646 450-0092
  1911 Western Ave Plymouth (46563) *(G-11722)*

Ridge Trailers 260 244-5443
  3330 E Lincolnway Columbia City (46725) *(G-1828)*

Ridley USA Inc 260 768-4103
  135 Main St Shipshewana (46565) *(G-12647)*

Riebel Roque Inc 317 849-3680
  6027 Castlebar Cir Indianapolis (46220) *(G-7844)*

Riebel Roque Publishing Co, Indianapolis *Also called Riebel Roque Inc (G-7844)*

Riegseckers Woodworks Inc 574 642-3504
  15600 County Road 38 Goshen (46528) *(G-5318)*

Rieke Corporation (HQ) 260 925-3700
  500 W 7th St Auburn (46706) *(G-349)*

Rieke Packaging Systems, Auburn *Also called Rieke Corporation (G-349)*

Riepen LLC 574 269-5900
  2450 Deelyn Dr Warsaw (46580) *(G-13935)*

Rieth-Riley Cnstr Co Inc 765 447-2324
  3425 Ofarrell Rd Ste 1 Lafayette (47905) *(G-8993)*

Rieth-Riley Cnstr Co Inc 574 288-8321
  25200 State Road 23 South Bend (46614) *(G-12915)*

Rieth-Riley Cnstr Co Inc 574 875-5183
  7500 W 5th Ave Gary (46406) *(G-5093)*

Rigdon Incorporated 765 393-2283
  209 S 500 W Anderson (46011) *(G-163)*

Right Angle Stl & Fabrication 574 862-2432
  29508 County Road 38 Wakarusa (46573) *(G-13794)*

Rightrez 812 219-1893
  3010 E David Dr Bloomington (47401) *(G-812)*

Rightway Fasteners Inc 812 342-2700
  7945 S International Dr Columbus (47201) *(G-2009)*

Rihm Foods, Cambridge City *Also called Rihm Inc (G-1260)*

Rihm Inc (PA) 765 478-3426
  8360 E County Road 950 S Cambridge City (47327) *(G-1260)*

Riley Equipment, Vincennes *Also called C & S Family Inc (G-13670)*

Rim Molding and Engrg Inc 574 294-1932
  1500 W Hively Ave Ste B Elkhart (46517) *(G-3146)*

Ring Industries Inc 219 204-1577
  3572 W State Road 10 # 13 Lake Village (46349) *(G-9087)*

Ring-Co LLC 317 641-7050
  8402 S 250 W Trafalgar (46181) *(G-13437)*

Rink Printing Company Inc 574 232-7935
  814 S Main St South Bend (46601) *(G-12916)*

Rink Riverside Printing, South Bend *Also called Rink Printing Company Inc (G-12916)*

Rinker Materials, Greenfield *Also called Cemex Materials LLC (G-5512)*

Rinker Materials 317 241-8237
   1501 S Holt Rd Indianapolis (46241) *(G-7845)*

Rinker Materials Corp 317 353-2118
   1030 S Kitley Ave Indianapolis (46203) *(G-7846)*

Ripley Publishing Co Inc 812 689-6364
   115 S Washington St Versailles (47042) *(G-13657)*

Risco Products Inc 317 392-6150
   1344 N Michigan Rd Shelbyville (46176) *(G-12562)*

Rise Inc 260 665-9408
   1600 Wohlert St Angola (46703) *(G-243)*

Rising Improvements LLC 608 295-8301
   17526 Douglas Rd Lot 9 South Bend (46635) *(G-12917)*

Risley's Art Gallery, Evansville *Also called Randall Corp (G-3695)*

Ristance, Mishawaka *Also called Standard Motor Products Inc (G-10135)*

Rite Way Industries Inc 812 206-8665
   4201 Reas Ln New Albany (47150) *(G-10856)*

Rite-Way Steel Inc 574 262-3465
   25687 Woodlawn Ave Elkhart (46514) *(G-3147)*

Ritron Inc 317 846-1201
   505 W Carmel Dr Carmel (46032) *(G-1468)*

Rittenhouse Square 260 824-4200
   312 S Main St Bluffton (46714) *(G-889)*

Ritter's Frozen Custard, Mishawaka *Also called Mishawaka Frozen Custard (G-10092)*

Ritters Frozen Custard Inc 317 859-1038
   3219 W County Line Rd Greenwood (46142) *(G-5739)*

Rivars Inc (PA) 765 789-6119
   9900 Westpoint Dr Ste 132 Indianapolis (46256) *(G-7847)*

River City Winery 317 868-8223
   25 N Main St Franklin (46131) *(G-4927)*

River City Winery LLC 812 945-9463
   321 Pearl St New Albany (47150) *(G-10857)*

River Valley Plastics Inc 574 262-5221
   1090 D I Dr Elkhart (46514) *(G-3148)*

River Valley Sheet Metal Inc 574 259-2538
   58785 Executive Dr Mishawaka (46544) *(G-10118)*

Rivera Screenprinting 812 663-0816
   1010 E State Road 46 Burney (47240) *(G-1213)*

Riverside Mfg Inc (PA) 260 637-4470
   14510 Lima Rd Fort Wayne (46818) *(G-4594)*

Riverside Mfg LLC (HQ) 260 637-4470
   14510 Lima Rd Fort Wayne (46818) *(G-4595)*

Riverside Printing Co 812 275-1950
   1407 I St Bedford (47421) *(G-574)*

Riverside Recycle, New Albany *Also called Qrs Inc (G-10851)*

Riverside Tool Corp (HQ) 574 522-6798
   3504 Henke St Elkhart (46514) *(G-3149)*

Rix Laser Processing 812 537-9230
   252 Charles A Liddle Dr Lawrenceburg (47025) *(G-9155)*

Rix Products Inc 812 426-1749
   3747 Hogue Rd Evansville (47712) *(G-3706)*

Rj Fuel Services Inc 812 350-2897
   6815 W State Road 252 Edinburgh (46124) *(G-2625)*

Rk Machine Inc 812 466-0550
   3170 N 25th St Terre Haute (47804) *(G-13321)*

Rko Enterprises LLC 812 273-8813
   2850 Clifty Dr Madison (47250) *(G-9492)*

Rlr Associates Inc 317 632-1300
   1302 N Illinois St Indianapolis (46202) *(G-7848)*

Rmg Cabinet 219 712-6129
   6809 Columbia Ave Hammond (46324) *(G-5935)*

Rmi Holdings LLC 317 214-7076
   4130 Corridor Dr Warsaw (46582) *(G-13936)*

Rmt Inc 260 637-4649
   2420 W Shoaff Rd Huntertown (46748) *(G-6146)*

Rng Performance LLC 260 602-5613
   24315 S County Line Rd E Monroeville (46773) *(G-10199)*

Rnk Intl C/O, Greenwood *Also called Wessels Company (G-5759)*

RNS Imaging Inc 812 523-2435
   574 Lasher Dr Seymour (47274) *(G-12480)*

Ro Vic Wood Products Inc 812 283-9199
   254 America Pl C Jeffersonville (47130) *(G-8420)*

Road Apple Psychotherapy 574 230-3449
   740 S 1100 E Knox (46534) *(G-8579)*

Road Equipment 219 887-6400
   3450 Grant St Gary (46408) *(G-5094)*

Road Runner Expediting, Greenwood *Also called Franklin Publishing Inc (G-5696)*

Road Solutions, Indianapolis *Also called King-Tuesley Enterprises Inc (G-7353)*

Roadhog Inc 317 858-7050
   464 Southpoint Cir Brownsburg (46112) *(G-1166)*

Roadworks Manufacturing, Lafayette *Also called Lund International Holding Co (G-8963)*

Roann Publishers 574 831-2795
   22425 County Road 42 Goshen (46526) *(G-5319)*

Roanoke Woodworking Inc 260 672-8462
   7477 E State Road 114-92 Roanoke (46783) *(G-12107)*

Rob Nolley Inc 317 825-5211
   1110 Fallway Ct Shelbyville (46176) *(G-12563)*

Robco Engineered Rubber Pdts 260 248-2888
   707 E Short St Columbia City (46725) *(G-1829)*

Robert Atkins (PA) 765 536-4164
   303 E North Main St Summitville (46070) *(G-13103)*

Robert Bosch LLC 574 654-4000
   32104 State Road 2 New Carlisle (46552) *(G-10886)*

Robert Bosch LLC 260 636-1005
   1613 Progress Dr Albion (46701) *(G-34)*

Robert Burkhart 219 448-0365
   434 W State Road 28 Alexandria (46001) *(G-52)*

Robert D Meadows 812 797-8294
   3568 Peerless Rd Bedford (47421) *(G-575)*

Robert Dietrick Co Inc 260 244-4668
   777 E Short St Columbia City (46725) *(G-1830)*

Robert J Matt 317 831-2400
   246 E Washington St Mooresville (46158) *(G-10337)*

Robert J Robinson Aircraft 317 787-7809
   904 N Matthews Rd Greenwood (46143) *(G-5740)*

Robert L Wehr 812 482-2673
   1527 W 100s Jasper (47546) *(G-8302)*

Robert L Young 812 863-4475
   4436 S Young Dr Springville (47462) *(G-13067)*

Robert Perez 317 291-7311
   3945 Guion Ln Ste A Indianapolis (46268) *(G-7849)*

Robert W Sheffer 219 464-2095
   4411 Evans Ave Valparaiso (46383) *(G-13609)*

Robert Weed Plywood Corp 574 848-7631
   705 Maple St Bristol (46507) *(G-1081)*

Roberts Precision Machining 812 926-3233
   8007 Us Highway 50 Aurora (47001) *(G-386)*

Roberts Precission Machining, Aurora *Also called Roberts Precision Machining (G-386)*

Robertson Crushed Stone Inc 812 633-4881
   6300 Hwy 64 Nw Milltown (47145) *(G-9976)*

Robertson Machine Co Inc 317 881-9405
   430 E Main St Greenwood (46143) *(G-5741)*

Robinson Engineering & Oil Co (PA) 812 477-1575
   1410 N Cullen Ave Evansville (47715) *(G-3707)*

Robinson Industries Inc 317 867-3214
   17111 Westfield Park Rd Westfield (46074) *(G-14185)*

Robinson Industries Inc 317 867-3214
   17111 Westfield Park Rd Westfield (46074) *(G-14186)*

Robinson International Inc 812 637-0678
   2147 Seeley Rd West Harrison (47060) *(G-14042)*

Robinson Lumber Company Inc 812 944-8020
   1750 Ormond Rd New Albany (47150) *(G-10858)*

Roche Applied Sciences, Indianapolis *Also called Roche Diagnostics Corporation (G-7852)*

Roche Diabetes Care Inc 317 521-2000
   9115 Hague Rd Indianapolis (46256) *(G-7850)*

Roche Diagnostics Corporation (HQ) 800 428-5076
   9115 Hague Rd Indianapolis (46256) *(G-7851)*

Roche Diagnostics Corporation 317 521-2000
   7988 Centerpoint Dr Indianapolis (46256) *(G-7852)*

Roche Health Solutions Inc 317 570-5100
   9115 Hague Rd Indianapolis (46256) *(G-7853)*

Rochester Cement Products 574 223-3917
   2184 Sweetgum Rd Rochester (46975) *(G-12145)*

Rochester Concrete Plant, Rochester *Also called Kuert Concrete Inc (G-12131)*

Rochester Heat Treating Co 574 224-4328
   8039 E Cherokee Rd Syracuse (46567) *(G-13141)*

Rochester Homes Inc (PA) 574 223-4321
   1345 N Lucas St Rochester (46975) *(G-12146)*

Rochester Manufacturing LLC 574 224-2044
   2903 Ft Wayne Rd Rochester (46975) *(G-12147)*

Rochester Metal Products Corp (PA) 574 223-3164
   616 Indiana Ave Rochester (46975) *(G-12148)*

Rochester Metal Products Corp 765 288-6624
   2100 N Granville Ave Muncie (47303) *(G-10559)*

Rochester Rttional Molding Inc 574 223-8844
   1952 E Lucas St Rochester (46975) *(G-12149)*

Rochester Sentinel, The, Rochester *Also called Sentinel Corp (G-12153)*

Rock Creek Stone LLC 260 694-6880
   781 N 500 W Bluffton (46714) *(G-890)*

Rock Equipment, Paragon *Also called J W Jones Company LLC (G-11458)*

Rock Garden Engraving 765 647-3357
   268 Main St Brookville (47012) *(G-1125)*

Rock Hard Stones Custom 219 613-0112
   2023 W 75th Pl Merrillville (46410) *(G-9750)*

Rock Hollow Golf Club, Peru *Also called Stone Quary (G-11549)*

Rock N' Roll Alley, Lafayette *Also called Custom Tees (G-8885)*

Rock Run Industries LLC 574 361-0848
   11665 W 600 S Millersburg (46543) *(G-9972)*

Rock-Tenn Paperboard Products, Columbus *Also called Westrock Rkt Company (G-2033)*

Rockport Roll Shop LLc 812 362-6419
   6500 N Us Highway 231 Rockport (47635) *(G-12172)*

Rockport Works, Rockport *Also called AK Steel Corporation (G-12164)*

Rocktenn-Knox, Knox *Also called Westrock Cp LLC (G-8587)*

Rockville Woodworks 765 569-6483
   2282 N Marshall Rd Rockville (47872) *(G-12179)*

Rockwell Automation Inc 219 924-3002
   225 45th St Munster (46321) *(G-10626)*

A
L
P
H
A
B
E
T
I
C

Rockwell Diversified Woodworks 317 758-4797
  26715 Dunbar Rd Sheridan (46069) *(G-12597)*

Rocore Thermal Systems LLC (PA) 317 227-2929
  2401 Directors Row Ste R Indianapolis (46241) *(G-7854)*

Rod Welding and Auto, Coal City *Also called Rods Welding Shop* *(G-1744)*

Rodeghero Enterprise 574 935-0568
  10605 Nutmeg Rd Plymouth (46563) *(G-11723)*

Rodeswood LLC 574 457-4496
  14852 County Road 50 Syracuse (46567) *(G-13142)*

Rodex Machining 260 768-4844
  7400 W 650 N Shipshewana (46565) *(G-12648)*

Rodgers Enterprises LLC 765 396-3143
  17920 N State Road 3n Eaton (47338) *(G-2588)*

Rodman's Auto Wood Restoration, Hanna *Also called Auto Wood Restoration* *(G-5958)*

Rodney Sloan Logging 812 934-5321
  1324 E Salem Rd Batesville (47006) *(G-518)*

Rods Welding Shop 812 859-4250
  2135 Beech Church Rd Coal City (47427) *(G-1744)*

Roeder Industries 812 654-3322
  406 W Carr St Milan (47031) *(G-9946)*

Roembke Mfg & Design Inc (PA) 260 622-4135
  1580 Baker Dr Ossian (46777) *(G-11406)*

Roembke Mfg & Design Inc 260 622-4030
  1580 Baker Dr Ossian (46777) *(G-11407)*

Rogers & Hollands Jewelers, Greenwood *Also called Rogers Enterprises Inc* *(G-5742)*

Rogers Cabinetry 574 664-9931
  2527 N County Road 925 E Logansport (46947) *(G-9362)*

Rogers Electro-Matics Inc 574 457-2305
  405 W Chicago St Syracuse (46567) *(G-13143)*

Rogers Engineering and Mfg Co 765 478-5444
  112 S Center St Cambridge City (47327) *(G-1261)*

Rogers Enterprises Inc 317 851-5500
  1251 Us Highway 31 N Greenwood (46142) *(G-5742)*

Rogers Group Inc 812 333-8560
  1100 N Oard Rd Bloomington (47404) *(G-813)*

Rogers Group Inc 765 342-9655
  1500 Rogers Rd Martinsville (46151) *(G-9634)*

Rogers Group Inc 765 342-6898
  1500 Rogers Rd Martinsville (46151) *(G-9635)*

Rogers Group Inc 812 824-8565
  7885 S Victor Pike Bloomington (47403) *(G-814)*

Rogers Group Inc 219 474-5125
  235 E Us Highway 24 Kentland (47951) *(G-8523)*

Rogers Group Inc 812 332-6341
  2944 E Covenanter Dr Bloomington (47401) *(G-815)*

Rogers Group Inc 812 849-3530
  3020 State Road 60 W Mitchell (47446) *(G-10170)*

Rogers Group Inc 812 882-3640
  1200 S 6th Street Rd Vincennes (47591) *(G-13703)*

Rogers Group Inc 812 333-6324
  550 S Adams St Bloomington (47403) *(G-816)*

Rogers Group Inc 765 893-4463
  3255 W 650 S Williamsport (47993) *(G-14296)*

Rogers Group Inc 812 333-8550
  1110 N Oard Rd Bloomington (47404) *(G-817)*

Rogers Group Inc 765 762-2660
  429 W Washington St Williamsport (47993) *(G-14297)*

Rogers Group Inc 812 275-7860
  938 Sieboldt Quarry Rd Springville (47462) *(G-13068)*

Rogers Marketing & Printing 317 838-7203
  7588 E County Road 100 S Avon (46123) *(G-465)*

Roh Custom Cabinetry LLC 260 802-1158
  6784 W Stat Rd 114 Lot 21 Silver Lake (46982) *(G-12679)*

Rohder Machine & Tool Inc 219 663-3697
  1023 E Summit St Crown Point (46307) *(G-2297)*

Rohe, Paul H, Aurora *Also called Valley Asphalt Corporation* *(G-392)*

Roi Marketing Company 317 644-0797
  5868 W 71st St 101 Indianapolis (46278) *(G-7855)*

Rol Publications 812 366-4154
  3600 Amy Ln Ne Greenville (47124) *(G-5653)*

Roland International Co LLC 319 400-1106
  1016 3rd Ave Sw Ste 207 Carmel (46032) *(G-1469)*

Rolands Processing 574 831-4301
  68417 County Road 15 New Paris (46553) *(G-10992)*

Roll Coater Inc 317 652-1102
  9908 Blue Ridge Way Indianapolis (46234) *(G-7856)*

Roll Forming Corporation 812 284-0650
  1205 N Access Dr Jeffersonville (47130) *(G-8421)*

Rollerboat 512 931-3936
  2810 Coopers Ln Sellersburg (47172) *(G-12413)*

Rollin Mini Barns LLC 812 687-7581
  6950 E 800 N Odon (47562) *(G-11339)*

Rollison Airplane Company Inc 812 384-4972
  County Road 300 S Bloomfield (47424) *(G-645)*

Rolls-Royce Corporation 317 230-2000
  758 Columbia Rd Ste 199 Plainfield (46168) *(G-11641)*

Rolls-Royce Corporation 317 437-9326
  2840 Fortune Cir W Indianapolis (46241) *(G-7857)*

Rolls-Royce Corporation 317 230-8515
  1801 Newman Rd West Lafayette (47906) *(G-14104)*

Rolls-Royce Corporation (HQ) 317 230-2000
  450 S Meridian St Indianapolis (46225) *(G-7858)*

Rolls-Royce Corporation 812 421-7810
  225 W Morgan Ave Ste A Evansville (47710) *(G-3708)*

Rolls-Royce Liftfan Factory, Plainfield *Also called Rolls-Royce Corporation* *(G-11641)*

Rolls-Royce PLC 317 306-2441
  4151 Arnold Ave Martinsville (46151) *(G-9636)*

Rollway Bearing, Valparaiso *Also called Regal Beloit America Inc* *(G-13608)*

Roman Marblene Company Inc 812 738-1367
  1560 Quarry Rd Nw Corydon (47112) *(G-2110)*

Romanart Inc 219 736-9150
  7302 Taft St Merrillville (46410) *(G-9751)*

Romark Industries Inc 765 966-6211
  1751 S 8th St Richmond (47374) *(G-12047)*

Romculinary LLC 630 235-3338
  1933 N Talbott St Indianapolis (46202) *(G-7859)*

Rome Cy Area Youth Ctr Basbal 260 854-4599
  705 Kelly Street Ext Rome City (46784) *(G-12200)*

Romotech, New Paris *Also called Rotational Molding Tech Inc* *(G-10993)*

Ron Eaton 219 464-1607
  333 E 600 N Valparaiso (46383) *(G-13610)*

Ron Glasscock 812 986-2342
  3282 N County Road 700 E Poland (47868) *(G-11743)*

Ron Osborne Machining Inc 812 637-1045
  25660 Mount Pleasant Rd Lawrenceburg (47025) *(G-9156)*

Ronald Chileen Furniture 574 542-4505
  9369 Ohio St Rochester (46975) *(G-12150)*

Ronald Holloway 574 223-6825
  426 Main St Rochester (46975) *(G-12151)*

Ronald L Miller 765 662-3881
  1102 N Wabash Ave Marion (46952) *(G-9560)*

Ronald Lee Allen 812 644-7649
  8271 S 1125 E Loogootee (47553) *(G-9394)*

Ronald Wright Logging LLC 812 338-2665
  61 S Pleasant Hill Rd English (47118) *(G-3319)*

Ronaldo Designer Jewelry Inc (PA) 812 972-7220
  115 E Spring St Ste 102 New Albany (47150) *(G-10859)*

Ronlewhorn Industries LLC 765 661-9343
  4226 Sunset Ave Indianapolis (46208) *(G-7860)*

Ronnie Elmore Jr 765 719-1681
  1193 E State Road 42 Cloverdale (46120) *(G-1736)*

Rons General Repair 765 732-3805
  403 Ramsey St West College Corner (47003) *(G-14037)*

Rons Halloween, Indianapolis *Also called Patriotic Fireworks Inc* *(G-7662)*

Roof Masters Plus 765 572-1321
  7800 W 650 S Westpoint (47992) *(G-14207)*

Roofing & Insulation Sup Inc 317 547-4373
  6555 E 30th St Ste D2 Indianapolis (46219) *(G-7861)*

Rookies Unlimited Inc 765 536-2726
  103 South Mnr Summitville (46070) *(G-13104)*

Roost 317 842-3735
  7371 E 116th St Fishers (46038) *(G-3964)*

Roppel Industries Inc 812 425-0267
  920 Keck Ave Evansville (47711) *(G-3709)*

Rose Acre Farms Inc 219 253-6681
  5408 W State Road 16 Monon (47959) *(G-10178)*

Rose Brother Graphics, Columbus *Also called Crossing Creations* *(G-1885)*

Rose Engineering Co Inc 317 788-4446
  1105 Martin St Indianapolis (46227) *(G-7862)*

Rose Industries LLC 260 348-2610
  6030 Almond Bluff Pass Fort Wayne (46804) *(G-4596)*

Rose-Wall Mfg Inc 317 894-4497
  5827 W Us Highway 40 Greenfield (46140) *(G-5567)*

Rosedale Filters LLC 219 879-4700
  700 W Michigan Blvd Michigan City (46360) *(G-9835)*

Roses Square Dance Acc 812 865-2821
  448 E Liberty Rd Orleans (47452) *(G-11369)*

Roskovenski Sand & Gravel Inc 765 832-6748
  3200 E 1850 S Clinton (47842) *(G-1719)*

Rosmarino Candles LLC 970 218-2835
  310 S High St Bloomington (47401) *(G-818)*

Ross Engineering & Machine 574 586-7791
  70100 Stephens St Walkerton (46574) *(G-13810)*

Ross Machining 765 998-2400
  8855 E 500 S Upland (46989) *(G-13473)*

Ross-Gage Inc (PA) 317 283-2323
  8502 Brookville Rd Indianapolis (46239) *(G-7863)*

Rosskovenski Concrete & Rdymx 765 832-6103
  12927 S State Road 63 Clinton (47842) *(G-1720)*

Rossroads Rv, Topeka *Also called Ds Corp* *(G-13417)*

Rosswyvern Press LLC 859 421-0864
  2224 Birch Dr Clarksville (47129) *(G-1694)*

Rota Skipper Corporation 708 331-0660
  130 E 168th St Crown Point (46307) *(G-2298)*

Rotam Tool Corporation (PA) 260 982-8318
  11606 N State Road 15 North Manchester (46962) *(G-11242)*

Rotam Tooling, North Manchester *Also called Total Tote Inc* *(G-11246)*

Rotation Dynamics Corporation 219 325-8808
  1164 E 150 N La Porte (46350) *(G-8813)*

Rotational Molding Tech Inc....574 831-6450
67742 County Road 23 # 1 New Paris (46553) ***(G-10993)***
Roudebush Company Incorporated....574 595-7115
583 S State Rd 119 Star City (46985) ***(G-13070)***
Rough Notes Company Inc....800 428-4384
11690 Technology Dr Carmel (46032) ***(G-1470)***
Rough Notes Company Inc (PA)....317 582-1600
11690 Technology Dr Carmel (46032) ***(G-1471)***
Round 2 LLC....574 243-3000
4073 Meghan Beeler Ct South Bend (46628) ***(G-12918)***
Round Town Brewery LLC....317 657-6397
950 S White River Pkwy W Indianapolis (46204) ***(G-7864)***
Round Two Begins Corporation....574 825-9800
300 Wayne St Middlebury (46540) ***(G-9917)***
Round World Products Inc....317 257-7352
75 Executive Dr Ste B Carmel (46032) ***(G-1472)***
Roundabout Entertainment Guide, Madison *Also called Kentuckiana Publishing* ***(G-9475)***
Row Printing....317 796-3289
7177 Golden Oak Brownsburg (46112) ***(G-1167)***
Row Printing Inc....317 441-4301
4406 Quail Creek Trce N Pittsboro (46167) ***(G-11586)***
Rowan Industries LLC....574 302-1203
52555 Kenilworth Rd South Bend (46637) ***(G-12919)***
Rowe Conveyor LLC (PA)....317 602-1024
1729 Us Highway 31 S Fj Greenwood (46143) ***(G-5743)***
Rowe Truck Equipment Inc (PA)....765 583-4461
102 W 1st St Otterbein (47970) ***(G-11421)***
Rowland Printing Co Inc....317 773-1829
199 N 9th St Noblesville (46060) ***(G-11177)***
Rox Software Inc....765 430-7616
1192 E Dollar Ct Brookston (47923) ***(G-1107)***
Roy Umbarger and Sons Inc....317 422-5195
111 N Baldwin St Bargersville (46106) ***(G-486)***
Royal & Langnickel Brush Mfg, Munster *Also called Royal Brush Manufacturing Inc* ***(G-10627)***
Royal Acres Equestrian Center....219 874-7519
9375 W 300 N Michigan City (46360) ***(G-9836)***
Royal Adhesives & Sealants LLC (HQ)....574 246-5000
2001 W Washington St South Bend (46628) ***(G-12920)***
Royal Adhesives & Sealants LLC....574 246-5000
2001 W Washington St South Bend (46628) ***(G-12921)***
Royal ARC Welding Company....260 587-3711
640 County Road 27 Ashley (46705) ***(G-290)***
Royal Box Group LLC....317 462-7743
2200 Royal Dr Greenfield (46140) ***(G-5568)***
Royal Box Group LLC....765 728-2416
1200 Riverfork Dr Huntington (46750) ***(G-6244)***
Royal Brush Manufacturing Inc....219 660-4170
515 45th St Munster (46321) ***(G-10627)***
Royal Center Locker Plant Inc....574 643-3275
104 S Chicago St Royal Center (46978) ***(G-12213)***
Royal Center Record....574 643-3165
120 Michael Ln Royal Center (46978) ***(G-12214)***
Royal Crown Bottling Corp (HQ)....812 424-7978
1100 Independence Ave Evansville (47714) ***(G-3710)***
Royal Elastomers, South Bend *Also called Royal Adhesives & Sealants LLC* ***(G-12920)***
Royal Feeds, Evansville *Also called Royal Inc* ***(G-3711)***
Royal Food Products Inc....317 782-2660
7001 Hawthorn Park Dr A Indianapolis (46220) ***(G-7865)***
Royal Holdings Inc....574 246-5000
2001 W Washington St South Bend (46628) ***(G-12922)***
Royal Imprints Inc....800 894-3151
711 Gerber St Ligonier (46767) ***(G-9294)***
Royal Inc....812 424-4925
1210 N Fulton Ave Evansville (47710) ***(G-3711)***
Royal Outdoor Products Inc....574 658-9442
401 E Syracuse St Milford (46542) ***(G-9964)***
Royal Pin Leisure Centers Inc....317 881-8686
1010 Us Highway 31 S Greenwood (46143) ***(G-5744)***
Royal Pin Leisure Ctr....317 247-4426
6441 W Washington St Indianapolis (46241) ***(G-7866)***
Royal Rubber Company, South Bend *Also called Rubber Shop Inc* ***(G-12924)***
Royal Spa Corporation (PA)....317 781-0828
2041 W Epler Ave Indianapolis (46217) ***(G-7867)***
Royal Spa Manufacturing, Indianapolis *Also called Royal Spa Corporation* ***(G-7867)***
Royal Stamping Inc....260 925-3312
530 North St Auburn (46706) ***(G-350)***
Royal Tool & Molding Inc....574 643-6800
412 S Chicago St Royal Center (46978) ***(G-12215)***
Royale Phoenix Inc....574 206-1216
53972 N Park Ave Elkhart (46514) ***(G-3150)***
Royalty, Seymour *Also called Crane Hill Machine Inc* ***(G-12439)***
Royalty Investments LLC....812 358-3534
2476 E Us Highway 50 Seymour (47274) ***(G-12481)***
Royalty Publishing Company, Bedford *Also called Achievers Institute LLC* ***(G-527)***
Royer Corporation....800 457-8997
805 East St Madison (47250) ***(G-9493)***
Royer Enterprises Inc....260 359-0689
6780 N 362 W Huntington (46750) ***(G-6245)***
Roys Disposal....812 721-3443
924 E County Road 1150 S Oakland City (47660) ***(G-11314)***
Royster Clark Closed....812 397-2617
2745 W State Road 48 Shelburn (47879) ***(G-12509)***
RPC Machinery Inc....765 458-5655
424 N Industrial Park Rd Liberty (47353) ***(G-9271)***
Rpf Inc....317 727-6386
6643 W Boggstown Rd Boggstown (46110) ***(G-902)***
Rph On Call LLC....317 622-4800
1115 N 300 W Greenfield (46140) ***(G-5569)***
RPI Consultants LLC....317 803-7431
5666 Winthrop Ave Indianapolis (46220) ***(G-7868)***
RPM Machinery LLC....574 271-0800
3953 Ralph Jones Dr South Bend (46628) ***(G-12923)***
RPM Tool, Princeton *Also called Bemr LLC* ***(G-11864)***
RPS Hydraulic Sales & Service, Hammond *Also called R P S Hydraulics Sales & Svc* ***(G-5931)***
RPS Printing Services, Plainfield *Also called Buis Enterprises Inc* ***(G-11598)***
Rpt, Bristol *Also called Record / Play Tek Inc* ***(G-1078)***
RR Donnelley & Sons Company....765 362-1300
1009 Sloan St Crawfordsville (47933) ***(G-2194)***
Rrc Corporation....317 687-8325
1002 E Garfield Dr Indianapolis (46203) ***(G-7869)***
Rs Pallet Inc....574 596-8777
19816 County Road 6 Bristol (46507) ***(G-1082)***
Rs Precision Machining....219 362-4560
7909 N Wilhelm Rd La Porte (46350) ***(G-8814)***
Rs Used Oil Services Inc....866 778-7336
4501 W 99th St Ste 1000 Carmel (46032) ***(G-1473)***
Rs2 Technologies LLC....877 682-3532
400 Fisher St Ste G Munster (46321) ***(G-10628)***
RSI, Griffith *Also called Reactor Services Intl Inc* ***(G-5789)***
Rst Custom Woodworking LL....317 602-2490
1015 E 42nd St Indianapolis (46205) ***(G-7870)***
Rt Software....317 578-8518
13534 Kelsey Ln Fishers (46038) ***(G-3965)***
RTC....260 503-9770
1901 N Airport Rd Columbia City (46725) ***(G-1831)***
RTC Threaders, Columbia City *Also called RTC* ***(G-1831)***
Rubber & Gasket Co Amer Inc....260 432-9070
3328 Congressional Pkwy Fort Wayne (46808) ***(G-4597)***
Rubber Shop Inc....574 291-6440
500 W Chippewa Ave South Bend (46614) ***(G-12924)***
Ruben Martinez....574 735-0803
1936 E Private Road 340 N Logansport (46947) ***(G-9363)***
Rubenstein LLC....317 946-2752
7982 Fishback Rd Indianapolis (46278) ***(G-7871)***
Rubicon Foods LLC....317 826-8793
7320 E 86th St Ste 400 Indianapolis (46256) ***(G-7872)***
Ruby Enterprises Inc....765 649-2060
1150 W 29th St Anderson (46016) ***(G-164)***
Ruco Inc....574 262-4110
1817 Leer Dr Elkhart (46514) ***(G-3151)***
Rudys Food & Fuel LLC....812 547-2530
9780 W State Road 66 Tell City (47586) ***(G-13173)***
Rugged Steel Works LLC....260 444-4241
4325 Meyer Rd Fort Wayne (46806) ***(G-4598)***
Running Around Screen Printing....260 248-1216
227 W Van Buren St Columbia City (46725) ***(G-1832)***
Running Company LLC....317 887-0606
1251 Us Highway 31 N # 112 Greenwood (46142) ***(G-5745)***
Rural Land Inc....812 843-4518
14370 Ureka Rd Cannelton (47520) ***(G-1291)***
Rusach International Inc....317 638-0298
100 Raymond St Hope (47246) ***(G-6119)***
Rush County Stone Co Inc....765 629-2211
5814 W State Road 244 Milroy (46156) ***(G-9985)***
Rush County Wood Products....765 629-0603
2437 W 900 S Milroy (46156) ***(G-9986)***
Rush Hour Station....812 323-7874
421 E 3rd St Bloomington (47401) ***(G-819)***
Rush Jaw Company The Inc....317 729-5095
6870 W 100 S Shelbyville (46176) ***(G-12564)***
Rushville Republican, Rushville *Also called Community Holdings Indiana Inc* ***(G-12218)***
Russ Print Shop....219 996-3142
131 N Main St Hebron (46341) ***(G-6022)***
Russ Publishing....812 847-4487
79 S Main St Linton (47441) ***(G-9313)***
Russel Warfield Inc....317 243-7650
1132 Rosner Dr Indianapolis (46224) ***(G-7873)***
Russell Distributing, Westfield *Also called Furnace Design Technology LLC* ***(G-14164)***
Russell Metal Products....317 841-9003
9238 Alton Ct Fishers (46037) ***(G-3966)***
Russell's Septic Tank Service, Mount Vernon *Also called Russells Excvtg & Septic Tanks* ***(G-10406)***
Russells Excvtg & Septic Tanks....812 838-2471
6800 Leonard Rd S Mount Vernon (47620) ***(G-10406)***
Russells Tube Forming Inc....317 241-4072
220 Gasoline Aly Indianapolis (46222) ***(G-7874)***

ALPHABETIC

Rust Publishing In LLC....765 653-5151
100 N Jackson St Greencastle (46135) ***(G-5477)***
Rustic Acres Woodworks....765 886-5699
4600 W New Garden Rd Williamsburg (47393) ***(G-14284)***
Rustic Glow Candle Co LLC....317 696-4264
7605 Indian Lake Rd Indianapolis (46236) ***(G-7875)***
Rustic N Chic LLC....219 987-4957
1917 W 1100 N Wheatfield (46392) ***(G-14230)***
Rutkowski & Associates Inc....812 476-4520
206 Charmwood Ct Evansville (47715) ***(G-3712)***
Ruwaldt Packing Co Inc....219 942-2911
6510 E Ridge Rd Hobart (46342) ***(G-6093)***
Rvp, Elkhart *Also called River Valley Plastics Inc* ***(G-3148)***
Rwb & Associates LLC....317 219-6572
16217 Stony Ridge Dr Noblesville (46060) ***(G-11178)***
Rwh Woodworking....317 714-5179
240 W Osage St Greenfield (46140) ***(G-5570)***
Rwp West LLC....208 549-2410
705 Maple St Bristol (46507) ***(G-1083)***
Rx Help Centers LLC....866 478-9593
3905 Vincennes Rd Ste 200 Indianapolis (46268) ***(G-7876)***
Rx Honing Machine Corp....574 259-1606
1301 E 5th St Mishawaka (46544) ***(G-10119)***
Ryan Fuelling....260 403-6450
6928 Nighthawk Dr Fort Wayne (46835) ***(G-4599)***
Ryan Oil Co LLC....812 422-4168
123 Nw 4th St Ste 2 Evansville (47708) ***(G-3713)***
Ryco Electric....219 319-0934
710 65th St Schererville (46375) ***(G-12344)***
Ryerson Tull Inc (HQ)....219 764-3500
310 Tech Dr Burns Harbor (46304) ***(G-1219)***
Ryobi Die Casting (usa) Inc (HQ)....317 398-3398
800 W Mausoleum Rd Shelbyville (46176) ***(G-12565)***
Ryobi Press Parts....800 901-3304
241 N Rangeline Rd Carmel (46032) ***(G-1474)***
S & G Excavating Inc (PA)....812 234-4848
545 E Margaret Dr Terre Haute (47802) ***(G-13322)***
S & H Cabinets....574 773-7465
70932 County Road 3 Nappanee (46550) ***(G-10705)***
S & H Metal Products Inc....260 593-2565
122 Redman Dr Topeka (46571) ***(G-13428)***
S & J Creative Design LLC....765 251-0110
6037 E 450 S Wabash (46992) ***(G-13754)***
S & J Manufacturing LLC....812 662-6640
712 S Christy Rd Greensburg (47240) ***(G-5632)***
S & J Precision Inc....812 944-9368
4345 Security Pkwy New Albany (47150) ***(G-10860)***
S & M Precast Inc....812 294-3703
16700 Sima Gray Rd Henryville (47126) ***(G-6032)***
S & R Concessions LLC....260 570-3247
813 E 9th St Auburn (46706) ***(G-351)***
S & R Welding Inc....317 710-0360
113 Pennsylvania Ct Indianapolis (46225) ***(G-7877)***
S & S Industry & Manufacturing....219 963-0213
3311 Liverpool Rd Lake Station (46405) ***(G-9076)***
S & S Machine & Tool Inc....260 897-3823
731 W Albion St Avilla (46710) ***(G-418)***
S & S Machine Co, Evansville *Also called William F Shirley* ***(G-3813)***
S & S Optical Co Inc....260 749-9614
416 Ann St New Haven (46774) ***(G-10955)***
S & S Precast Inc....574 946-4123
840 W 25 S Winamac (46996) ***(G-14320)***
S & S Programming Inc....765 423-4472
3601 Sagamore Pkwy N F Lafayette (47904) ***(G-8994)***
S & S Service....812 952-2306
7608 Main St Ne Lanesville (47136) ***(G-9103)***
S & T Fulfillment LLC....812 466-4900
351 S Airport St Terre Haute (47803) ***(G-13323)***
S & W Electric, La Porte *Also called Electrik Connection Inc* ***(G-8754)***
S & W Swing Sets....260 414-6200
17007 Doty Rd New Haven (46774) ***(G-10956)***
S C Pryor Inc....317 352-1281
5424 Brookville Rd Indianapolis (46219) ***(G-7878)***
S CJ Incorporated....317 822-3477
2021 W Raymond St Indianapolis (46221) ***(G-7879)***
S E P, Rosedale *Also called Summerlot Engineered Pdts Inc* ***(G-12206)***
S Edwards Incorporated....317 831-0261
292 W Harrison St Mooresville (46158) ***(G-10338)***
S G I, Indianapolis *Also called Sign Group Inc* ***(G-7941)***
S G I, Indianapolis *Also called Service Graphics Inc* ***(G-7917)***
S H Leggitt Company....574 264-0230
831 E Windsor Ave Unit 9 Elkhart (46514) ***(G-3152)***
S Huck Food and Fuel....812 886-4323
2816 N 6th St Vincennes (47591) ***(G-13704)***
S L Thomas Family Winery Inc....812 273-3755
208 E 2nd St Madison (47250) ***(G-9494)***
S P R Athletics LLC....419 308-2732
4662 N 100 E Winchester (47394) ***(G-14340)***
S P X Corp....574 594-9681
5 Arnolt Dr Pierceton (46562) ***(G-11578)***
S Phillippe Lawn & Landscape....765 724-2020
2806 E 1100 N Alexandria (46001) ***(G-53)***
S S M Inc....317 357-4552
4000 Southeastern Ave Indianapolis (46203) ***(G-7880)***
S T Laminating, Elkhart *Also called Double T Manufacturing Corp* ***(G-2799)***
S T Praxair Technology Inc....317 240-2500
1500 Polco St Indianapolis (46222) ***(G-7881)***
S U S, Logansport *Also called SUs Cast Products Inc* ***(G-9367)***
S W Industries Inc....317 788-4221
2024 Bluff Rd Indianapolis (46225) ***(G-7882)***
S&C Machine LLC....812 768-6731
1197 W 1000 S Haubstadt (47639) ***(G-6005)***
S&F Manufacturing Inc....574 278-7865
9449 S 550 W Winamac (46996) ***(G-14321)***
S&S Machinery Repair LLC....812 521-2368
12807 W Us Highway 50 Norman (47264) ***(G-11204)***
S-B Capable Concepts LLC....812 420-2565
11542 N Murphy Rd Brazil (47834) ***(G-977)***
S-Tech Inc....812 793-3506
208 N Armstrong St Crothersville (47229) ***(G-2221)***
S.B.I., Brownsburg *Also called Fuel Bladder Distributors Inc* ***(G-1151)***
S.E.S., Henryville *Also called Sullivan Engineered Services* ***(G-6033)***
Sabco Sign Co Inc....317 882-3380
1620 W Smith Valley Rd C Greenwood (46142) ***(G-5746)***
Sabert Corporation....260 747-3149
3511 Engle Rd Fort Wayne (46809) ***(G-4600)***
Sabic Innovative Plas US LLC....812 372-0197
945 S Marr Rd Columbus (47201) ***(G-2010)***
Sabic Innovative Plastics Mt V....812 838-4385
1 Lexan Ln Mount Vernon (47620) ***(G-10407)***
Sabin Corporation....812 323-4500
3800 W Constitution Ave Bloomington (47403) ***(G-820)***
Sac Acquisition LLC....317 575-1795
8702 Keystone Xing # 165 Indianapolis (46240) ***(G-7883)***
Saco Industries Inc....219 690-9900
17151 Morse St Lowell (46356) ***(G-9422)***
Sacoma International Llc....812 526-5600
955 S Walnut St Edinburgh (46124) ***(G-2626)***
Sacred Selections....260 347-3758
112 N Shore Dr Kendallville (46755) ***(G-8509)***
Safe Fleet Mirrors....574 266-3700
319 Roske Dr Elkhart (46516) ***(G-3153)***
Safelite Autoglass, Fort Wayne *Also called Safelite Glass Corp* ***(G-4601)***
Safelite Glass Corp....260 423-2477
3927 New Haven Ave Fort Wayne (46803) ***(G-4601)***
Safety First, Columbus *Also called Dorel Juvenile Group Inc* ***(G-1913)***
Safety Vehicle Emblem Inc....317 885-7565
5235 Commerce Cir Indianapolis (46237) ***(G-7884)***
Safety Wear Fort Wayne....260 456-3535
1121 E Wallace St Fort Wayne (46803) ***(G-4602)***
Safety-Kleen Systems Inc....219 397-1131
601 Riley Rd East Chicago (46312) ***(G-2568)***
Safran Nclles Svcs Amricas LLC....317 789-8188
725 S Girls School Rd Indianapolis (46231) ***(G-7885)***
Saftlite, Bluffton *Also called General Manufacturing Inc* ***(G-875)***
Sagamore Ready Mix....317 573-5410
5001 E 106th St Indianapolis (46280) ***(G-6280)***
Sagamore Ready-Mix LLC....317 783-3768
4550 S Harding St Indianapolis (46217) ***(G-7886)***
Sagamore Ready-Mix LLC (PA)....317 570-6201
9170 E 131st St Fishers (46038) ***(G-3967)***
Sager Metal Strip Company LLC....219 874-3609
100 Boone Dr Michigan City (46360) ***(G-9837)***
Sahasra Technologies Corp (PA)....317 845-5326
9449 Priority Way West Dr Indianapolis (46240) ***(G-7887)***
Sailrite Enterprises Inc....260 244-4647
2390 E 100 S Columbia City (46725) ***(G-1833)***
Saint Adrian Meats Sausage LLC....317 403-3305
6115 E State Road 47 Lebanon (46052) ***(G-9221)***
Saint Clair Boat Works, Carmel *Also called Thomas Toll* ***(G-1496)***
Saint-Gobain Abrasives Inc....317 837-0700
1001 Perry Rd Plainfield (46168) ***(G-11642)***
Saladin Trailer Sales Inc....812 692-5288
637 E Highway 57 Elnora (47529) ***(G-3291)***
Salamonie Mills Inc....260 375-2200
525 N Wayne St Warren (46792) ***(G-13832)***
Saldana Racing Products, Indianapolis *Also called Saldana Racing Tanks Inc* ***(G-7888)***
Saldana Racing Tanks Inc....317 852-4193
3754 N Raceway Rd Indianapolis (46234) ***(G-7888)***
Salem Leader, The, Salem *Also called Leader Publishing Co of Salem* ***(G-12299)***
Salesman Sawmill Inc....812 382-9154
3396 N County Road 550 W Sullivan (47882) ***(G-13094)***
Saliwanchik & Sons Welding & F....219 362-9009
3707 N Us Highway 35 La Porte (46350) ***(G-8815)***
Salt Creek Harvest LLC....708 927-5569
314 W 700 N Valparaiso (46385) ***(G-13611)***
Salt Creek Winery, Freetown *Also called Twin Willows LLC* ***(G-4950)***
Salt Creek Woodworks....219 730-7553
2755 Heavilin Rd Valparaiso (46385) ***(G-13612)***

Sam Mouron Equipment Co Inc 317 776-1799
15535 Stony Creek Way Noblesville (46060) *(G-11179)*
Sam's Windmill Service, Middlebury *Also called Millers Windmill Service (G-9910)*
Samaron Corp 574 970-7070
3310 Magnum Dr Elkhart (46516) *(G-3154)*
Samco Group Inc (PA) 219 872-4413
9935 E Us Highway 12 Michigan City (46360) *(G-9838)*
Samco Inc 812 279-8131
1000 U St Bedford (47421) *(G-576)*
Samco Inc 812 926-4282
19992 N Manchester Rd Sunman (47041) *(G-13116)*
Sampan Screen Print New Image 812 282-8499
202 Ash St Jeffersonville (47130) *(G-8422)*
Sampco Inc 413 442-4043
915 W Ireland Rd South Bend (46614) *(G-12925)*
Sampco of Indiana, South Bend *Also called Sampco Inc (G-12925)*
Sampler Inc (PA) 765 663-2233
7138 W 235 S Homer (46146) *(G-6109)*
Sampson Fiberglass Inc 574 255-4356
2424 N Home St Mishawaka (46545) *(G-10120)*
Sams Technical Publishing LLC 317 396-9850
9850 E 30th St Indianapolis (46229) *(G-7889)*
Samswoodworking 574 772-6482
4725 S 750 E Knox (46534) *(G-8580)*
Samtec Inc 812 517-6081
861 S Lake Rd S Scottsburg (47170) *(G-12379)*
San Jo Steel Inc 317 888-6227
610 W Main St Ste A Greenwood (46142) *(G-5747)*
San Mar 574 286-6884
54555 Pine Rd South Bend (46628) *(G-12926)*
Sanbar of Indiana Inc 317 375-6220
1721 S Franklin Rd # 100 Indianapolis (46239) *(G-7890)*
Sanborn Software Systems LLC 317 283-7735
402 E 43rd St Indianapolis (46205) *(G-7891)*
Sanco Industries Inc 260 467-1791
1819 S Calhoun St Fort Wayne (46802) *(G-4603)*
Sanco Industries Inc (PA) 260 426-6281
1819 S Calhoun St Fort Wayne (46802) *(G-4604)*
Sand Designs Inc 574 293-5791
2609 E Jackson Blvd Elkhart (46516) *(G-3155)*
Sand Dune Publishing Compa 219 938-7118
8719 Indian Boundary Gary (46403) *(G-5095)*
Sander Processing 812 481-0044
6614 E State Road 164 Celestine (47521) *(G-1537)*
Sanders Pre-Cast Concrete 317 769-5503
6051 S Indianapolis Rd Whitestown (46075) *(G-14261)*
Sanders Saw Mill Inc 812 738-4793
2999 N Gethsemane Rd Nw Corydon (47112) *(G-2111)*
Sandin Mfg Inc 219 872-2253
250 Indiana Highway 212 Michigan City (46360) *(G-9839)*
Sandman Products LLC 574 264-7700
2604 Glenview Dr Elkhart (46514) *(G-3156)*
Sandpaper America, Indianapolis *Also called Mjp & Company LLC (G-7529)*
Sandpaper America Inc 317 631-7263
1728 E New York St Indianapolis (46201) *(G-7892)*
Sandpaper Studio LLC 317 435-7479
6403 N 300 E Whiteland (46184) *(G-14245)*
Sandra Rice Noodle 317 823-8323
10625 Pendleton Pike A11 Indianapolis (46236) *(G-7893)*
Sandusky Abrasive Wheel Co 219 879-6601
532 W 4th St Michigan City (46360) *(G-9840)*
Sandusky-Chicago Abrasive Whl, Michigan City *Also called Sandusky Abrasive Wheel Co (G-9840)*
Sandy Little Coal Co Inc 812 529-8216
12568 N State Road 245 Evanston (47531) *(G-3325)*
Saniserv, Mooresville *Also called M D Holdings LLC (G-10319)*
Saniserv 317 831-7030
451 E County Line Rd Mooresville (46158) *(G-10339)*
Sanitation Equipment, Elkhart *Also called Global Ozone Innovations LLC (G-2886)*
Sanko Gosei Tech USA Inc 260 749-5168
6509 Moeller Rd Fort Wayne (46806) *(G-4605)*
Sanlo Inc 219 879-0241
400 Hwy 212 Michigan City (46360) *(G-9841)*
Sanmar Tool & Manufacturing 574 232-6081
54555 Pine Rd South Bend (46628) *(G-12927)*
Sanofi US Services Inc 317 228-5750
5225 W 81st St Indianapolis (46268) *(G-7894)*
Sansher Corporation 260 484-2000
8005 N Clinton St Fort Wayne (46825) *(G-4606)*
Santarossa Mosaic Tile Co Inc (PA) 317 632-9494
2707 Roosevelt Ave Indianapolis (46218) *(G-7895)*
Sapp Inc 317 512-8353
600 S Kyle St Edinburgh (46124) *(G-2627)*
Sapp USA, Edinburgh *Also called Sapp Inc (G-2627)*
Sapper's Farm Market, Hobart *Also called Sappers Market and Greenhouses (G-6094)*
Sappers Market and Greenhouses 219 942-4995
1155 S Lake Park Ave Hobart (46342) *(G-6094)*
Saran Industries LLC (PA) 317 897-2170
1500 E Murden St Kokomo (46901) *(G-8690)*
Saran Industries LLC 317 897-2170
1425 S Curry Pike Bloomington (47403) *(G-821)*
Sardinia Machine 812 591-2091
12337 S State Road 3 Westport (47283) *(G-14211)*
Sarge's Shooting Bags, Pendleton *Also called Tango Romeo Industries LLC (G-11507)*
Sargent Aerospace Inc 305 593-6038
7500 Nw 26th St Franklin (46131) *(G-4928)*
Sargent Controls & Aerospace, Franklin *Also called Airtomic Repair Station (G-4865)*
Satco Inc 317 856-0301
4221 S High School Rd Indianapolis (46241) *(G-7896)*
Satek Winery, Fremont *Also called James Lake Vineyard Inc (G-4963)*
Satellite Industries, Bristol *Also called Satellite Shelters (G-1084)*
Satellite Oasis 317 375-1097
8464 Brookville Rd Indianapolis (46239) *(G-7897)*
Satellite Shelters 574 350-2150
1686 Commerce Dr Bristol (46507) *(G-1084)*
Satellite Software 574 842-3370
15231 12th Rd Plymouth (46563) *(G-11724)*
Sater Enterprises 812 477-1529
5401 Vogel Rd Ste 430 Evansville (47715) *(G-3714)*
Saturday Evening Post Soc Inc 317 634-1100
1100 Waterway Blvd Indianapolis (46202) *(G-7898)*
Saturn Wheel Company Inc 260 375-4720
507 E 9th St Warren (46792) *(G-13833)*
Sauder Woodworking Co 800 537-1530
13737 Main St Grabill (46741) *(G-5384)*
Sav-or Pack, Avon *Also called Rogers Marketing & Printing (G-465)*
Saver Systems, Richmond *Also called Merediths Inc (G-12016)*
Savor Flavor LLC 812 667-1030
13721 Prosperity Ridge Rd Dillsboro (47018) *(G-2472)*
Savran Technologies LLC 765 409-2050
2533 Yeoman Ln West Lafayette (47906) *(G-14105)*
Say Help, Avon *Also called Help Help LLC (G-446)*
Saybolt LP 812 282-7242
905 Eastern Blvd Ste C Clarksville (47129) *(G-1695)*
Sb Finishing 317 598-0965
6844 Hawthorn Park Dr Indianapolis (46220) *(G-7899)*
Sbd Reprographics, South Bend *Also called American Reprographics Co LLC (G-12705)*
SBS Cybermetrix Inc 812 378-7960
635 S Mapleton St Columbus (47201) *(G-2011)*
SC Supply Company LLC 574 287-0252
1908 Portage Ave South Bend (46616) *(G-12928)*
Scaggs Lrgent Scrnprinting LLC 765 362-5477
201 E Main St Crawfordsville (47933) *(G-2195)*
Scaggs Moto Designs 765 426-2526
4909 Leicester Way West Lafayette (47906) *(G-14106)*
Scalable Press 510 396-5226
7800 Records St Indianapolis (46226) *(G-7900)*
Scalar Design Engrg & Dist LLC 765 429-5545
836 Shawnee Ave Lafayette (47905) *(G-8995)*
Scale Computing Inc (PA) 317 856-9959
525 S Meridian St Indianapolis (46225) *(G-7901)*
Scandinavian Sleep Products, Greenwood *Also called May and Co Inc (G-5724)*
Scepter Inc 812 735-2500
6467 N Scepter Rd Bicknell (47512) *(G-633)*
Scepter Steel Inc 317 996-2103
380 Maple St Monrovia (46157) *(G-10206)*
Scg Acquisition Company LLC 574 294-1506
2000 Industrial Pkwy Elkhart (46516) *(G-3157)*
Schachtpfister Inc 260 356-9775
232 E Washington St Ste 3 Huntington (46750) *(G-6246)*
Schaefer Technologies, Indianapolis *Also called Mitchum-Schaefer Inc (G-7528)*
Schaefer Technologies Inc 317 241-9444
4901 W Raymond St Indianapolis (46241) *(G-7902)*
Schaefers Indiana Turf Corp 260 489-3391
5202 W Washington Ctr Rd Fort Wayne (46818) *(G-4607)*
Schafer Gear Works-South Bend, South Bend *Also called Schafer Industries Inc (G-12929)*
Schafer Industries Inc (PA) 574 234-4116
4701 Nimtz Pkwy South Bend (46628) *(G-12929)*
Schafer Powder Coating Inc 317 228-9987
4518 W 99th St Carmel (46032) *(G-1475)*
Schaffsteins Truck Clean LLC 812 464-2424
601 N 9th Ave Evansville (47712) *(G-3715)*
Schatzi Press 317 335-2335
10004 Springstone Rd McCordsville (46055) *(G-9675)*
Scheffer International Inc 219 736-6200
1155 Arrowhead Ct Crown Point (46307) *(G-2299)*
Scheidler Machine Incorporated 812 662-6555
3551 N Old Us Highway 421 Greensburg (47240) *(G-5633)*
Schenk Sons Wldg & Tree Svc In 812 985-3954
11018 Altheide Rd Mount Vernon (47620) *(G-10408)*
Schenkel's All-Star Dairy, Huntington *Also called Suiza Dairy Group LLC (G-6254)*
Scher Maihem Publishing Ltd 260 897-2697
650 North St Auburn (46706) *(G-352)*
Scherer Industrial Group, Indianapolis *Also called Horner Industrial Services Inc (G-7130)*
Schererville Branch, Saint John *Also called American Cmnty Bnk Ind Modem 2 (G-12259)*
Scheumann Cabinet Co 260 747-3509
8809 Winchester Rd Fort Wayne (46819) *(G-4608)*

ALPHABETIC

Schick Sand & Gravel, Muncie *Also called Muncie Sand & Gravel Inc* (G-10536)

Schimpff Confectionery 812 283-8367
347 Spring St Jeffersonville (47130) (G-8423)

Schindler Electric Inc 317 858-8215
25 S Green St Brownsburg (46112) (G-1168)

Schindler Woodwork 513 314-5943
6006 English Hill Rd Cedar Grove (47016) (G-1522)

Schlabach Hardwoods 574 642-1157
11186 County Road 34 Goshen (46528) (G-5320)

Schlabach Window & Glass LLC 765 628-2024
5337 E 250 N Kokomo (46901) (G-8691)

Schlatters Inc 219 567-9158
16179 W 500 S Francesville (47946) (G-4815)

Schmalbach-Lubeca, Franklin *Also called Amcor Rigid Plastics Usa LLC* (G-4867)

Schmaltz Ready Mix Concrete (PA) 812 689-5140
705 Tanglewood Rd Osgood (47037) (G-11394)

Schmidt Cabinet Co Inc 812 347-1031
1355 Highway 64 Ne New Salisbury (47161) (G-11011)

Schmidt Contracting Inc 812 482-3923
1111 Maurice St Jasper (47546) (G-8303)

Schmidt Marken Designs 219 785-4238
3403 S Wozniak Rd La Porte (46350) (G-8816)

Schmigbob LLC 219 781-7991
5366 E 111th Ave Crown Point (46307) (G-2300)

Schmucker Welding 574 773-0456
3208 Beech Rd Bremen (46506) (G-1021)

Schmucker Woodworking LLC 260 413-9784
13131 Ehle Rd New Haven (46774) (G-10957)

Schmuckers Wood Shop 260 485-1434
9966 Eby Rd Fort Wayne (46835) (G-4609)

Schneder Elc Bldngs Amrcas Inc 317 894-6374
6191 W 400 N Ste 100 Greenfield (46140) (G-5571)

Schneder Elc Slar Invrters USA, Elkhart *Also called Xantrex Technology USA Inc* (G-3270)

Schneider Electric 574 293-0877
4714 Hoffman St Elkhart (46516) (G-3158)

Schneider Electric Usa Inc 260 356-2060
6 Commercial Rd Huntington (46750) (G-6247)

Schneiders Wood Shop Inc 812 522-4621
5910 N Us Highway 31 Seymour (47274) (G-12482)

Schnuck Markets Inc 812 853-9505
8301 Bell Oaks Dr Newburgh (47630) (G-11046)

Schnucks, Newburgh *Also called Schnuck Markets Inc* (G-11046)

Scholars Inn Bakehouse 812 331-6029
125 N College Ave Bloomington (47404) (G-822)

School Doctor Notes LLC 317 660-1552
11555 N Meridian St # 100 Carmel (46032) (G-1476)

Schott Gemtron Corporation 812 882-2680
2000 Chestnut St Vincennes (47591) (G-13705)

Schouten Metal Craft Inc 317 546-2639
2211 E 44th St Indianapolis (46205) (G-7903)

Schrock Aggregate Company Inc (HQ) 574 862-4167
111 Industrial Dr Wakarusa (46573) (G-13795)

Schrock Cabinet 812 482-2527
5231 Oak Grove Rd Jasper (47547) (G-8304)

Schrock Excavating Inc (PA) 574 862-4167
111 Industrial Dr Wakarusa (46573) (G-13796)

Schug Awards LLC 765 447-0002
229 S 30th St Lafayette (47909) (G-8996)

Schuler Precision Tool LLC 260 982-2704
6177 W State Road 114 North Manchester (46962) (G-11243)

Schuler Products Co 812 852-4419
8968 N Us 421 Napoleon (47034) (G-10642)

Schulman 812 253-5238
1700 Lynch Rd Evansville (47711) (G-3716)

Schumacher Racing Corporation 317 858-0356
1681 E Northfield Dr A Brownsburg (46112) (G-1169)

Schumaker Technical Assembly 765 742-7176
681 N 36th St Lafayette (47905) (G-8997)

Schurz Communications Inc (HQ) 574 247-7237
1301 E Douglas Rd Ste 200 Mishawaka (46545) (G-10121)

Schurz Communications Inc 574 235-6496
225 W Colfax Ave South Bend (46626) (G-12930)

Schurz Communications Inc 317 773-9960
802 Mulberry St Noblesville (46060) (G-11180)

Schuster Glass Studio 812 988-7377
3847 Mount Liberty Rd Nashville (47448) (G-10734)

Schuster Sheet Metal Inc 574 293-4802
418 Roske Dr Elkhart (46516) (G-3159)

Schuster's Building Products, Indianapolis *Also called Oldcastle Apg Midwest Inc* (G-7615)

Schutte Lithography Inc 812 469-3500
2716 Kotter Ave Evansville (47715) (G-3717)

Schutz Brothers Inc 260 982-8581
1604 East St North Manchester (46962) (G-11244)

Schuyler Corp 574 533-2597
2105 Carmen Ct Goshen (46526) (G-5321)

Schwans Home Service Inc 317 882-6624
1763 Industrial Dr Greenwood (46143) (G-5748)

Schwartz Elmer D Mfg Co, Berne *Also called Schwartz Manufacturing Inc* (G-622)

Schwartz Manufacturing Inc 260 589-3865
1261 W 200 S Berne (46711) (G-622)

Schwartz Wheel Co 574 546-0101
2750 3b Rd Bremen (46506) (G-1022)

Schwartz Woodworking 260 593-3193
4810 S 950 W Millersburg (46543) (G-9973)

Schwartz Woodworking LLC 260 854-9457
7240 S 075 W B Wolcottville (46795) (G-14376)

Schwartz's Custom Woodworking, Grabill *Also called Chris Schwartz* (G-5360)

Schwartz's Wheel Repair, Bremen *Also called Schwartzs Wheel & Clip C* (G-1023)

Schwartzs Trailer Sales Inc 317 773-2608
117 Cicero Rd Noblesville (46060) (G-11181)

Schwartzs Wheel & Clip C 574 546-1302
4199 Cedar Rd Bremen (46506) (G-1023)

Schwartzville Pallet 260 244-4144
4861 W 300 S Columbia City (46725) (G-1834)

Schwarz Partners LP (PA) 317 290-1140
3600 Woodview Trce # 300 Indianapolis (46268) (G-7904)

Schwarz Pharma 812 523-3457
1101 C Ave W Seymour (47274) (G-12483)

SCI, Ligonier *Also called Structural Composites Ind Inc* (G-9296)

Science Fiction Public, East Chicago *Also called 1632 Inc* (G-2514)

Science For Today and Tomorrow, Mishawaka *Also called Scitt Inc* (G-10122)

Scitt Inc 574 208-6649
1840 E 12th St Mishawaka (46544) (G-10122)

Scot Industries Inc 608 778-2251
1729 W Auburn Dr Auburn (46706) (G-353)

Scotia Corporation 260 479-8800
7707 Freedom Way Fort Wayne (46818) (G-4610)

Scott Art Castings, Carmel *Also called Poyser Kelshaw Group LLC* (G-1453)

Scott Billman 317 293-9921
5411 Maplewood Dr Indianapolis (46224) (G-7905)

Scott County Jurnl & Chronicle, Scottsburg *Also called Green Banner Publications Inc* (G-12360)

Scott Culbertson 260 357-6430
1202 S Hamsher St Garrett (46738) (G-5022)

Scott Fetzer Company 260 488-3531
7715 S Homestead Dr Hamilton (46742) (G-5828)

Scott Pet Products Inc (PA) 765 569-4636
1543 N Us Highway 41 Rockville (47872) (G-12180)

Scott Printing LLC 812 306-7477
8823 Old State Rd Evansville (47711) (G-3718)

Scott Steel Services Inc 219 663-4740
1203 E Summit St Crown Point (46307) (G-2301)

Scottorsville Sales and Svc 765 250-5245
602 S Earl Ave Lafayette (47904) (G-8998)

Scotts Company LLC 317 596-7830
13053 Parkside Dr Fishers (46038) (G-3968)

Scotts Company LLC 219 663-3830
825 S Main St Crown Point (46307) (G-2302)

Scotts Fasteners & Supply LLC 317 372-8743
1945 W County Road 300 S Danville (46122) (G-2357)

Scotts Grant County Asp Inc 765 664-2754
2686 S 300 W Marion (46953) (G-9561)

Scotts Miracle-Gro Company 219 984-6110
10 E 100 S Reynolds (47980) (G-11948)

Scp Building Products LLC 574 772-2955
1001 W Culver Rd Knox (46534) (G-8581)

Scp Holdings Inc 260 925-2588
1700 S Indiana Ave Auburn (46706) (G-354)

Scp Limited, Auburn *Also called Specilzed Cmpnent Prts Ltd LLC* (G-357)

Scrapbook Nook 812 967-3306
205 W State Road 60 Pekin (47165) (G-11479)

Scrapwood Sawmill 574 223-2725
3488 S Wabash Rd Rochester (46975) (G-12152)

Screen Art Advertising Co Inc 260 483-6514
457 Ley Rd Ste B Fort Wayne (46825) (G-4611)

Screen Print Express Inc 765 521-2727
1107 Fleming St New Castle (47362) (G-10917)

Screen Printing, New Castle *Also called Screen Print Express Inc* (G-10917)

Screen Printing, Granger *Also called Sir Graphics Inc* (G-5436)

Screen Printing Plus, Vincennes *Also called Spp Inc* (G-13707)

Screen Printing Super Store 317 804-9904
17408 Tiller Ct Ste 100 Westfield (46074) (G-14187)

Screen Tech Designs, Columbus *Also called D S E Inc* (G-1904)

Screenprint Special Tees LLC 317 396-0349
4353 W 96th St Ste 200 Indianapolis (46268) (G-7906)

Screw Conveyor Corporation (PA) 219 931-1450
700 Hoffman St Hammond (46327) (G-5936)

Screw Conveyor Pacific Corp (PA) 219 931-1450
700 Hoffman St Hammond (46327) (G-5937)

Screw Machine Products, La Porte *Also called Nrp Jones LLC* (G-8800)

Screwy Lewy Lures Inc 812 786-7369
1820 Owans Ln Ne Corydon (47112) (G-2112)

Scribe Publications Inc 219 791-9254
2050 W 86th Ave Merrillville (46410) (G-9752)

Scurvy Palace Publishing LLC 317 809-4591
6149 New Harmony Rd Martinsville (46151) (G-9637)

Scutt Tool & Die 317 858-8725
3245 N State Road 267 Brownsburg (46112) (G-1170)

SD, Kokomo *Also called Stephens Machine Inc (G-8702)*
SDI, Fort Wayne *Also called Steel Dynamics Inc (G-4646)*
Sdi Lafarga LLC 260 748-6565
1640 Ryan Rd New Haven (46774) *(G-10958)*
SDP Manufacturing Inc 765 768-5000
400 Industrial Dr Dunkirk (47336) *(G-2488)*
Se-Cur-All Cabinets, La Porte *Also called A & A Sheet Metal Products (G-8725)*
Sea Quest Lures Inc 219 762-4362
2141 Whippoorwill St Portage (46368) *(G-11792)*
Seal Corp USA 812 430-8441
1175 E Diamond Ave Evansville (47711) *(G-3719)*
Seal Products LLC 260 436-5628
10515 Majic Port Ln Fort Wayne (46819) *(G-4612)*
Seal Tran Div, Richmond *Also called Transcendia Inc (G-12068)*
Sealcorpusa Inc 866 868-0791
1175 E Diamond Ave Evansville (47711) *(G-3720)*
Sealwrap Systems LLC 317 462-3310
325 E Main St Greenfield (46140) *(G-5572)*
Sealy Components, Rensselaer *Also called Leggett & Platt Incorporated (G-11931)*
Searchlight Social LLC 317 983-3802
1694 S 200 E Kokomo (46902) *(G-8692)*
Searle Exhibit Tech Inc 317 787-3012
3500 E 20th St Ste 3 Indianapolis (46218) *(G-7907)*
Seasoned Software Inc 260 431-5666
13030 Callison Ct Fort Wayne (46845) *(G-4613)*
Seat Tech, Goshen *Also called Seating Technology Inc (G-5322)*
Seating Technology Inc 574 971-4100
2703 College Ave Goshen (46528) *(G-5322)*
Seaton Springs Inc 812 282-2440
632 Eastern Blvd B Clarksville (47129) *(G-1696)*
Seavac USA LLC 260 747-7123
9304 Yeager Ln Fort Wayne (46809) *(G-4614)*
Sebasty Manufacturing Inc 574 505-1511
10321 N Troyer Rd Laketon (46943) *(G-9091)*
Sechler's Fine Pickles, Saint Joe *Also called Sechlers Pickles Inc (G-12258)*
Sechlers Pickles Inc (PA) 260 337-5461
5686 State Rd 1 Saint Joe (46785) *(G-12258)*
Secorp Inc 219 874-5010
205 Woodcreek Dr 1 Michigan City (46360) *(G-9842)*
Security Automation Systems, Noblesville *Also called Integratorcom Inc (G-11130)*
Security Paks Intl LLC 317 536-2662
11405 N Penn St Ste 106 Carmel (46032) *(G-1477)*
Sedona Inc 219 764-9675
3195 Willowcreek Rd Portage (46368) *(G-11793)*
Seed & Satchel LLC 317 892-2557
4298 E County Road 1000 N Pittsboro (46167) *(G-11587)*
Segura Publishing Company 574 631-3143
1045 W Washington St South Bend (46601) *(G-12931)*
Seib Machine & Tool Co Inc 812 453-6174
14314 Bender Rd Evansville (47720) *(G-3721)*
Seibs Welding, Evansville *Also called Seib Machine & Tool Co Inc (G-3721)*
Seiler & Sons 812 858-9598
5922 Seiler Rd Newburgh (47630) *(G-11047)*
Seiler Excavating Inc 260 925-0507
6310 County Road 31 Auburn (46706) *(G-355)*
Seismic Vision LLC 219 548-8704
967 Misty Glen Dr Valparaiso (46385) *(G-13613)*
Selby Publishing & Printing 765 453-5417
3405 Zartman Rd Kokomo (46902) *(G-8693)*
Selco Engineering Inc 317 297-1888
1677 W 400 N Shelbyville (46176) *(G-12566)*
Seleco Inc 317 872-4148
8427 Zionsville Rd Indianapolis (46268) *(G-7908)*
Select Embroidery/Top It Off 812 337-8049
1713 N College Ave Ste 3 Bloomington (47404) *(G-823)*
Select Gourmet Popcorn 812 212-2202
9632 N County Road 800 E Sunman (47041) *(G-13117)*
Select Tool & Eng Inc 574 295-6197
21537 Protecta Dr Elkhart (46516) *(G-3160)*
Self Care LLC 317 295-8279
4816 Bridgefield Dr Indianapolis (46254) *(G-7909)*
Self Reliance Outfitters, Indianapolis *Also called Pathfinder School LLC (G-7660)*
Selking International Inc 574 522-2001
836 Verdant St Elkhart (46516) *(G-3161)*
Selking International Inc (HQ) 260 482-3000
2807 Goshen Rd Fort Wayne (46808) *(G-4615)*
Sellersburg Metals & Wldg Co 812 248-0811
1000 Service Dr Sellersburg (47172) *(G-12414)*
Selmer Paris, Elkhart *Also called Conn-Selmer Inc (G-2765)*
Selvins Marble & Gran Sp LLC 317 370-4237
10806 Deandra Dr Zionsville (46077) *(G-14461)*
Semcor Inc 219 362-0222
1500 Genesis Dr La Porte (46350) *(G-8817)*
Semcor Manufacturing, La Porte *Also called Semcor Inc (G-8817)*
Semicndctor Cmponents Inds LLC 765 868-5015
2529 Commerce Dr Ste B Kokomo (46902) *(G-8694)*
Seminole Stone Inc 812 634-7115
1503 S Meridian Rd Jasper (47546) *(G-8305)*

Semmaterials LP 574 267-5076
2820 Durbin St Warsaw (46580) *(G-13937)*
Semstream LP 765 482-8105
550 W 125 S Lebanon (46052) *(G-9222)*
Send A Scent Arrow Co Inc 317 297-5232
4257 Wedgewood Ct Indianapolis (46254) *(G-7910)*
Senior Pathways Magazine LLC 812 697-1750
115 Rossmoore Dr New Albany (47150) *(G-10861)*
Sensortec Inc 260 497-8811
7620 Disalle Blvd Fort Wayne (46825) *(G-4616)*
Sensorycritterscom 260 373-0900
4715 Lima Rd Fort Wayne (46808) *(G-4617)*
Sentech Corporation 317 596-1988
8358 Masters Rd Indianapolis (46250) *(G-7911)*
Sentinel Alarm Inc 219 874-6051
2815 E Michigan Blvd Trail Creek (46360) *(G-13442)*
Sentinel Alarm Systems Inc. 317 842-6482
7520 E 88th Pl Indianapolis (46256) *(G-7912)*
Sentinel Cardio Scan Division, Carmel *Also called Med-Rep Inc (G-1436)*
Sentinel Corp 574 223-2111
118 E 8th St Rochester (46975) *(G-12153)*
Sentinel Services Inc. 574 360-5279
51618 Autumn Ridge Dr Granger (46530) *(G-5432)*
Separation By Design Inc 812 424-1239
1601 Buchanan St Evansville (47720) *(G-3722)*
Separation Technologies Inc 219 548-5814
463 E Us Highway 30 # 4 Valparaiso (46383) *(G-13614)*
Sepro Corporation (PA) 317 580-8282
11550 N Meridian St # 600 Carmel (46032) *(G-1478)*
Sera Tech Biologicals 765 288-2699
1318 S Madison St Muncie (47302) *(G-10560)*
Serenade Foods, Milford *Also called Maple Leaf Farms Inc (G-9957)*
Serenade Foods, Milford *Also called Maple Leaf Farms Inc (G-9958)*
Serie Hardwoods Inc 765 275-2321
2521 E Bethel Rd Attica (47918) *(G-309)*
Sermatech Intl Canada Corp 317 240-2500
1500 Polco St Indianapolis (46222) *(G-7913)*
Sermatech-Aeroforge, Muncie *Also called GKN Aerospace Muncie Inc (G-10477)*
Sermershiems Fiberglass Inc 812 424-4701
3817 N Saint Joseph Ave Evansville (47720) *(G-3723)*
Servaas Inc (PA) 317 633-2020
1100 Waterway Blvd Indianapolis (46202) *(G-7914)*
Servaas Laboratories Inc 317 636-7760
5240 Walt Pl Indianapolis (46254) *(G-7915)*
Servants Inc (PA) 812 634-2201
3145 Lottes Dr Jasper (47546) *(G-8306)*
Servants Inc 812 634-2201
3145 Lottes Dr Jasper (47546) *(G-8307)*
Server Partners LLC 317 917-2000
101 E Michigan St Indianapolis (46204) *(G-7916)*
Service Graphics Inc 317 471-8246
8350 Allison Ave Indianapolis (46268) *(G-7917)*
Service Printers Inc 574 266-6710
28574 Phillips St Elkhart (46514) *(G-3162)*
Service Publication Inc 219 845-4445
7147 Kennedy Ave Hammond (46323) *(G-5938)*
Service Steel Framing Inc 260 868-5853
206 Depot St Butler (46721) *(G-1239)*
Servsteel Inc 219 736-6030
8880 Mississippi St Gary (46410) *(G-5096)*
SESCO, Fort Wayne *Also called Systems Engineering and Sls Co (G-4671)*
Set Enterprises of Mi Inc 812 346-1700
1 Steel Way North Vernon (47265) *(G-11281)*
Setco LLC (HQ) 812 424-2904
101 Oakley St Evansville (47710) *(G-3724)*
Setser Fabricating LLC 812 546-2169
15601 E 225 N Columbus (47203) *(G-2012)*
Sevenoks Inc 800 523-8715
3539 Monroe St La Porte (46350) *(G-8818)*
Sevier Manufacturing 317 892-2784
103 Oak Hill Dr Brownsburg (46112) *(G-1171)*
Sew Creative Threads LLC 574 266-7397
189 County Road 6 W Elkhart (46514) *(G-3163)*
Sew Unique Inc 317 257-0503
9054 Sweet Bay Ct Indianapolis (46260) *(G-7918)*
Sewing Connection L L C 317 745-1501
786 Cheltenham Way Avon (46123) *(G-466)*
Sexton, Bloomington *Also called Quality Vault Company (G-803)*
Sexton Melinda 812 522-4059
622 W 2nd St Seymour (47274) *(G-12484)*
Sexton & Associates, Seymour *Also called Sexton Melinda (G-12484)*
Sexton Plywood & Veneer Co 812 454-0488
227 Rosemarie Ct Evansville (47715) *(G-3725)*
Sexton Vault Company, Bloomington *Also called Wilbert Sexton Corporation (G-854)*
Seymour Division, Seymour *Also called Packaging Corporation America (G-12473)*
Seymour Manufacturing Co Inc (HQ) 812 522-2900
500 N Broadway St Seymour (47274) *(G-12485)*
Seymour Midwest LLC (PA) 574 267-7875
2666 S Country Club Rd Warsaw (46580) *(G-13938)*

Seymour Midwest LLC 574 269-2782
  2234 E Hendricks St Warsaw (46580) (G-13939)

Seymour Precision Machining 812 524-1813
  1733 1st Ave Seymour (47274) (G-12486)

Seymour Trbune A Cal Ltd Prtnr 812 522-4871
  100 Saint Louis Ave Seymour (47274) (G-12487)

Seymour Tubing Inc (HQ) 812 523-0842
  1515 E 4th Street Rd Seymour (47274) (G-12488)

Sg Helmets 317 286-3616
  8599 Motorsports Way Brownsburg (46112) (G-1172)

Sg Solutions LLC 812 535-6000
  444 W Sandford Ave West Terre Haute (47885) (G-14129)

Sg Trading Post, Fort Wayne Also called Dkm Embroidery Inc (G-4215)

SGS Cybermetrix Inc (HQ) 800 713-1203
  2860 N National Rd A Columbus (47201) (G-2013)

Sha-Do Corp 574 848-9296
  1501 Bloomingdale Dr Bristol (46507) (G-1085)

Shackelford Graphics 317 783-3582
  5640 S Meridian St Ste C Indianapolis (46217) (G-7919)

Shade By Design Inc 317 602-3513
  10501 E Washington St Indianapolis (46229) (G-7920)

Shade Express, Elkhart Also called Continental Express (G-2770)

Shade Techniques LLC 765 396-9903
  4191 E Gregory Rd Eaton (47338) (G-2589)

Shadow Cruiser, Howe Also called Cruiser Rv LLC (G-6120)

Shadow Custom Graphics 317 481-9710
  4703 W Vermont St Indianapolis (46222) (G-7921)

Shadow Graphix Inc 317 481-9710
  4703 W Vermont St Indianapolis (46222) (G-7922)

Shadowhouse Jiu-Jitsu Inc 219 873-4556
  3707 N Promenade Cir La Porte (46350) (G-8819)

Shady Creek Vineyard 219 874-9463
  2030 Tryon Rd Michigan City (46360) (G-9843)

Shady Frog Winery LLC 317 366-3370
  3059 Woodhaven Way Bargersville (46106) (G-487)

Shakour Industries Inc 574 289-0100
  4550 S Burnett Dr South Bend (46614) (G-12932)

Shalee Oils LLC 765 329-4057
  400 Bob Barry Dr Hartford City (47348) (G-5990)

Shamrock Cabinets Inc 812 482-7969
  5785 W 150n Jasper (47546) (G-8308)

Shamrock Engineering Inc 812 867-0009
  1020 W Morton St Oakland City (47660) (G-11315)

Shank Brothers Inc (PA) 260 744-4802
  3710 Piper Dr Fort Wayne (46809) (G-4618)

Shannon Door, Carmel Also called Burks Door & Sash Inc (G-1324)

Shanxi-Indiana LLC 219 885-2209
  201 Mississippi St Gary (46402) (G-5097)

Shape Man, Mishawaka Also called South Bend Screen Process Inc (G-10133)

Shar Systems Inc 260 432-5312
  3210 Freeman St Fort Wayne (46802) (G-4619)

Sharbade, Indianapolis Also called Mulry Manufacturing LLC (G-7557)

Shark-Co Mfg LLC 317 670-6397
  1231 Indianapolis Ave Lebanon (46052) (G-9223)

Sharon Sperry 219 736-0121
  1106 W 73rd Ave Merrillville (46410) (G-9753)

Sharon's Tolebooth, Merrillville Also called Sharon Sperry (G-9753)

Sharp Printing Services Inc 317 842-5159
  8645 E 116th St Fishers (46038) (G-3969)

Sharp Shirt Printing LLC 260 413-9346
  2831 Union Chapel Rd Fort Wayne (46845) (G-4620)

Sharp Wraps LLC 317 989-8447
  1664 Williams Way Zionsville (46077) (G-14462)

Sharp's Creations, Elkhart Also called Sharps Baton Mfg Corp (G-3164)

Sharp's Woodshop, Shelbyville Also called Vernon Sharp (G-12582)

Sharpen Technologies Inc 855 249-3357
  211 N Penn St Ste 400 Indianapolis (46204) (G-7923)

Sharps Baton Mfg Corp 574 214-9389
  57330 Orchard Ridge Dr Elkhart (46516) (G-3164)

Sharyls Hair With Flare 765 885-5121
  104 N Madison Ave Fowler (47944) (G-4806)

Shaughnessy-Kniep-Hawe-paper 317 837-7041
  865 Perry Rd Plainfield (46168) (G-11643)

Shaw Machining Services I 765 663-2732
  1866 N 450 W Rushville (46173) (G-12232)

Shaw Polymers LLC (PA) 219 779-9450
  530 N Indiana Ave Crown Point (46307) (G-2303)

She Lettered 317 844-4555
  555 Pine Dr Indianapolis (46260) (G-7924)

Shear Line Golf, Noblesville Also called Triunity LLC (G-11196)

Shearer Business Products, Kokomo Also called Shearer Printing Service Inc (G-8695)

Shearer Printing Service Inc 765 457-3274
  107 W Markland Ave Kokomo (46901) (G-8695)

Sheet Metal Models Inc 317 783-1303
  2702 National Ave Indianapolis (46227) (G-7925)

Sheet Metal Models/Machine TI, Indianapolis Also called Sheet Metal Models Inc (G-7925)

Sheet Metal Services Inc 219 924-1206
  9944 Express Dr Highland (46322) (G-6055)

Sheet Mtl Wkrs Local No 20 .... 317 541-0050
  2828 E 45th St Ste A Indianapolis (46205) (G-7926)

Sheets LLC 317 290-1140
  3600 Woodview Trce # 300 Indianapolis (46268) (G-7927)

Shelby Engineering Co Inc 317 784-1135
  2233 S West St Indianapolis (46225) (G-7928)

Shelby Gravel Inc (PA) 317 398-4485
  157 E Rampart St Shelbyville (46176) (G-12567)

Shelby Gravel Inc 812 526-2731
  7520 E 650 S Edinburgh (46124) (G-2628)

Shelby Gravel Inc 317 804-8100
  17701 Spring Mill Rd Westfield (46074) (G-14188)

Shelby Gravel Inc 317 738-3445
  451 Arvin Rd Franklin (46131) (G-4929)

Shelby Gravel Inc 317 784-6678
  2701 S Emerson Ave Indianapolis (46203) (G-7929)

Shelby Gravel Inc 765 932-3292
  982 S Flatrock River Rd Rushville (46173) (G-12233)

Shelby Gravel Inc 317 216-7556
  10770 E County Road 300 N Indianapolis (46234) (G-7930)

Shelby Materials, Shelbyville Also called Shelby Gravel Inc (G-12567)

Shelby Materials, Indianapolis Also called Shelby Gravel Inc (G-7930)

Shelby Products Corporation 317 398-4870
  27687 Ste Rte 1 West Harrison (47060) (G-14043)

Shelby Upholstering Interiors, Indianapolis Also called Shelby Westside Upholstering (G-7931)

Shelby Westside Upholstering 317 631-8911
  3136 W 16th St Indianapolis (46222) (G-7931)

Shelbyville Newspapers Inc 317 398-6631
  123 E Washington St Shelbyville (46176) (G-12568)

Shelbyville Plant, Shelbyville Also called Pilkington North America Inc (G-12557)

Shelf Tag Supply Corporation 317 580-4030
  611 3rd Ave Sw Carmel (46032) (G-1479)

Shell 765 282-4635
  2001 W Mcgalliard Rd Muncie (47304) (G-10561)

Shell Packaging Corporation 765 965-6861
  400 Industrial Pkwy Richmond (47374) (G-12048)

Shell Pipe Line Corporation 765 962-1329
  1221 S 9th St Richmond (47374) (G-12049)

Shells Inc 574 342-2673
  502 Old Us Highway 30 E Bourbon (46504) (G-947)

Shelters Specialty & Supply, Angola Also called Ndiana Warm Floors Inc (G-232)

Shelton Powder Coating LLC 574 323-8369
  51345 Bittersweet Rd Granger (46530) (G-5433)

Shenango LLC 812 235-2058
  1200 College Ave Terre Haute (47802) (G-13324)

Shepherd Distributing 317 991-3877
  2154 S Lynhurst Dr Indianapolis (46241) (G-7932)

Shepherds Loft 812 486-2304
  8008 E 625 N Montgomery (47558) (G-10241)

Sheridan Manufacturing Co Inc 317 758-6000
  508 S Main St Sheridan (46069) (G-12598)

Sherman Enterprises 260 636-6225
  4426 S 100 W Albion (46701) (G-35)

Sherms Marine 260 563-8051
  8662 S 400 W Wabash (46992) (G-13755)

Sherrcom Industries LLC 574 266-7389
  51005 Twilight Dr Elkhart (46514) (G-3165)

Sherry Print Solutions Inc 708 255-5457
  66 E 602 N Valparaiso (46383) (G-13615)

Sherwood, Elkhart Also called Floralcraft Distributors (G-2859)

Sherwood Industries Inc 574 262-2639
  1805 Leer Dr Elkhart (46514) (G-3166)

Sherwood Plastics, Bristol Also called Ameri-Kart Corp (G-1043)

Sherwood-Templeton Coal Co Inc 812 232-7037
  701 Wabash Ave Ste 501 Terre Haute (47807) (G-13325)

Shetlers Famous Staineless 260 368-9069
  10113 S 450 E Geneva (46740) (G-5139)

Shf Microwave Parts Co 219 785-2602
  7102 W 500 S La Porte (46350) (G-8820)

Shield Restraint Systems Inc (HQ) 574 266-8330
  3802 Gallatin Way Elkhart (46514) (G-3167)

Shields Designs, Martinsville Also called Form/TEC Plastics Incorporated (G-9608)

Shields Mech & Fabrication LLC 219 863-3972
  11474 Chateau Ln Demotte (46310) (G-2447)

Shilling Sales Inc 260 426-2626
  414 E Wayne St Fort Wayne (46802) (G-4621)

Shiloh Custom Woodworks 812 636-0100
  9394 E 1000 N Odon (47562) (G-11340)

Shiloh Industries Inc 260 925-4711
  1200 Power Dr Auburn (46706) (G-356)

Shiloh Industries Inc 574 594-9681
  5 Arnolt Dr Pierceton (46562) (G-11579)

Shimp Optical Corp 317 636-4448
  932 S Meridian St Ste 101 Indianapolis (46225) (G-7933)

Shinabargar Custom Stairs 219 462-1735
  176 Goodview Dr Valparaiso (46385) (G-13616)

Ship It Now Store, The, Indianapolis Also called Gulsad Inc (G-7059)

Shipping Plus, Boonville Also called B-Hive Printing (G-908)

Shipshewana Bread Box Corp 260 768-4629
140 One Half N Morton St Shipshewana (46565) *(G-12649)*

Shipston Alum Tech Intl Inc (HQ) 317 738-0282
1450 Commerce Pkwy Franklin (46131) *(G-4930)*

Shipston Alum Tech Intl LLC (HQ) 317 738-0282
1450 Commerce Pkwy Franklin (46131) *(G-4931)*

Shipston Aluminum Tech Ind Inc 317 738-0282
1450 Commerce Pkwy Franklin (46131) *(G-4932)*

Shirks Wood Products, Rochester *Also called Lawrence Shirks (G-12133)*

Shirley Adams Publications, Avon *Also called Sewing Connection L L C (G-466)*

Shirley Engraving Co Inc 317 634-4084
4026 W 10th St Indianapolis (46222) *(G-7934)*

Shirley Foods Inc 765 738-6511
505 Walnut St Shirley (47384) *(G-12662)*

Shirley Machine & Engrg Inc (PA) 765 349-9040
200 Robert Curry Dr Martinsville (46151) *(G-9638)*

Shirt Shack 812 550-0158
12593 Apache Pass Evansville (47720) *(G-3726)*

Shirtails 812 858-8605
4944 State Route 261 Newburgh (47630) *(G-11048)*

Shirts N Things S N T Graphics 317 271-3515
1115 Country Club Rd Indianapolis (46234) *(G-7935)*

Shivom Jay Steels Intl LLC 574 271-7222
14260 Meridian Xing Granger (46530) *(G-5434)*

Shoals News 812 247-2828
311 High St Shoals (47581) *(G-12669)*

Shoemaker Inc 260 625-4321
12120 Yellow River Rd Fort Wayne (46818) *(G-4622)*

Shoemaker Welding Co 574 656-4412
65508 State Road 23 North Liberty (46554) *(G-11221)*

Shooting Stars Synchro Inc 317 710-1462
21480 Candlewick Rd Noblesville (46062) *(G-11182)*

Shopping Guide News Inc 574 223-5417
617 Main St Rochester (46975) *(G-12154)*

Shoremet LLC 219 390-3336
3601 Enterprise Ave Valparaiso (46383) *(G-13617)*

Shorts Machine Shop 765 622-6259
509 E 29th St Anderson (46016) *(G-165)*

Shotmizer Unit Dose Packaging, Kokomo *Also called Link Engineering LLC (G-8659)*

Shouse Sawmill 812 743-2017
4679 S State Road 241 Monroe City (47557) *(G-10188)*

Showhaulers Trucks Inc 574 825-6764
114 Industrial Pkwy E Middlebury (46540) *(G-9918)*

Shreve Manufacturing, Elkhart *Also called Elkhart Brass Manufacturing Co (G-2822)*

Shrock Manufacturing Inc 574 264-4126
2746 Jami St Elkhart (46514) *(G-3168)*

Shull Machine Service Inc 260 925-4198
3877 County Road 49 Butler (46721) *(G-1240)*

Shupan & Sons, Indianapolis *Also called Trinity Metals LLC (G-8102)*

Shur Ply, Lagrange *Also called Dutch Country Woodworking Inc (G-9038)*

Shuttleworth LLC (HQ) 260 356-8500
10 Commercial Rd Huntington (46750) *(G-6248)*

Shuttleworth North America, Huntington *Also called Shuttleworth LLC (G-6248)*

Si Plastics, Jeffersonville *Also called Southern Indiana Plastics Inc (G-8425)*

Sibley Machine & Foundry Corp 574 232-2910
206 E Tutt St South Bend (46601) *(G-12933)*

Side Kick Lure Retriever 812 329-9068
109 Steeple Ridge Ln Bedford (47421) *(G-577)*

Sideline Graphix 765 520-9042
319 Parkview Dr New Castle (47362) *(G-10918)*

Sidney & Janice Bond 812 366-8160
4400 Sunrise Ct Sellersburg (47172) *(G-12415)*

Sieboldt Quarry, Springville *Also called Rogers Group Inc (G-13068)*

Siemens AG 574 522-6807
2720 E Jackson Blvd Elkhart (46516) *(G-3169)*

Siemens Energy Inc 317 677-1340
201 S Capitol Ave A Indianapolis (46225) *(G-7936)*

Siemens Industrial Services, Portage *Also called Siemens Industry Inc (G-11794)*

Siemens Industry Inc 317 381-0734
7800 Col H Weir Cook Mem Indianapolis (46241) *(G-7937)*

Siemens Industry Inc 219 763-7927
6625 Daniel Burnham Dr Portage (46368) *(G-11794)*

Sierra Interiors, Bristol *Also called Sierra Motor Corp (G-1086)*

Sierra Machine 574 232-5694
26378 Lakeview Dr South Bend (46619) *(G-12934)*

Sierra Motor Corp 574 848-1300
19224 County Road 8 Bristol (46507) *(G-1086)*

Sig Media LLC (PA) 317 858-7624
5423 Landrum Dr Indianapolis (46234) *(G-7938)*

Sightwaveoptics 317 513-8322
4139 Creekside Pass Zionsville (46077) *(G-14463)*

Sigma Micro Corp 317 631-6580
714 N Senate Ave Indianapolis (46202) *(G-7939)*

Sigma Steel Inc (PA) 812 275-4489
1218 5th St Bedford (47421) *(G-578)*

Sigma Switches Plus Inc 574 294-5776
4703 Wyland Dr Elkhart (46516) *(G-3170)*

Sign 260 422-7446
2932 E Dupont Rd Fort Wayne (46825) *(G-4623)*

Sign A Rama 812 477-7763
1300 N Royal Ave Evansville (47715) *(G-3727)*

Sign A Rama 812 537-5516
1210 W Eads Pkwy Lawrenceburg (47025) *(G-9157)*

Sign Age Inc 765 778-5254
8521 S State Road 9 Pendleton (46064) *(G-11505)*

Sign Arama 812 657-7449
3192 Washington St Columbus (47201) *(G-2014)*

Sign Art Etc, Lafayette *Also called Olive Branch Etc Inc (G-8977)*

Sign Craft Industries Inc 317 842-8664
8816 Corporation Dr Indianapolis (46256) *(G-7940)*

Sign Crafters Inc (PA) 812 424-9011
1508 Stringtown Rd Evansville (47711) *(G-3728)*

Sign Creations LLC 574 855-1246
55234 Holmes Rd South Bend (46628) *(G-12935)*

Sign Deals Delivered 574 276-7404
19355 Sundale Dr South Bend (46614) *(G-12936)*

Sign Experts, Lafayette *Also called Creative Inc (G-8882)*

Sign Express, Terre Haute *Also called B B & H Signs Incorporated (G-13196)*

Sign Fab, Indianapolis *Also called Isf Inc (G-7274)*

Sign Factory, Indianapolis *Also called Mjs Businesses LLC (G-7530)*

Sign Factory 574 255-7446
55811 Elder Rd Mishawaka (46545) *(G-10123)*

Sign For It LLC 317 834-4636
68 W Main St Mooresville (46158) *(G-10340)*

Sign Graphics 574 834-7100
7196 N State Road 13 North Webster (46555) *(G-11301)*

Sign Graphics Evansville Inc 812 476-9151
6020 Feltman Dr Evansville (47711) *(G-3729)*

Sign Group Inc (PA) 317 875-6969
5370 W 84th St Indianapolis (46268) *(G-7941)*

Sign Group Inc 317 228-8049
5370 W 84th St Indianapolis (46268) *(G-7942)*

Sign Guys Inc 317 875-7446
5442 W 86th St Indianapolis (46268) *(G-7943)*

Sign Here Ltd 317 487-8001
4444 Decatur Blvd # 1200 Indianapolis (46241) *(G-7944)*

Sign Masters 765 525-7446
207 S Taylor St Saint Paul (47272) *(G-12280)*

Sign Pro, Kokomo *Also called Cumulus Intrmdate Holdings Inc (G-8609)*

Sign Pro of Fort Wayne Inc 260 497-8484
7710 Lima Rd Fort Wayne (46818) *(G-4624)*

Sign Pros 765 289-2177
3509 W County Road 400 N Muncie (47304) *(G-10562)*

Sign Pros Inc 765 642-1175
633 Jackson St Anderson (46016) *(G-166)*

Sign Pros of Marion 765 677-1234
4260 S 400 W Marion (46953) *(G-9562)*

Sign Ser Homes 317 214-8005
50 N 9th St Noblesville (46060) *(G-11183)*

Sign Services 317 546-1111
1305 W 29th St Indianapolis (46208) *(G-7945)*

Sign Shoppe 260 483-1922
4619 Lima Rd Fort Wayne (46808) *(G-4625)*

Sign Solutions Inc 317 881-1818
505 Commerce Parkway W Dr Greenwood (46143) *(G-5749)*

Sign Source One I Group Inc 219 736-5865
3429 Michigan St Hobart (46342) *(G-6095)*

Sign Write Signs LLC 219 477-3840
1451 Joliet Rd Valparaiso (46385) *(G-13618)*

Sign's By Tomorrow, Merrillville *Also called Bob Prescott (G-9703)*

Sign-A-Rama, Evansville *Also called Sign A Rama (G-3727)*

Sign-A-Rama, Indianapolis *Also called Ces Company Llc (G-6590)*

Sign-A-Rama, Indianapolis *Also called A Harris Verl Inc (G-6296)*

Sign-A-Rama, Lawrenceburg *Also called Sign A Rama (G-9157)*

Sign-A-Rama, Avon *Also called Ej Schmidt Inc (G-440)*

Sign-A-Rama 317 477-2400
842 S State St Greenfield (46140) *(G-5573)*

Signaling Solution Inc 812 533-1345
6274 N County Road 25 E Shelburn (47879) *(G-12510)*

Signature Formulations LLC 317 878-4086
3 Trafalgar Sq Trafalgar (46181) *(G-13438)*

Signature Industries Inc 260 350-3688
1775 E Us Highway 20 # 4 Lagrange (46761) *(G-9064)*

Signature Metals Inc 317 335-2207
6315 Pin Oak Dr McCordsville (46055) *(G-9676)*

Signature Products, Fort Wayne *Also called R&D Investment Holdings Inc (G-4575)*

Signcenter Inc 812 232-4994
333 N Fruitridge Ave Terre Haute (47803) *(G-13326)*

Signdoc Identity LLC 317 247-9670
3150 Rand Rd Indianapolis (46241) *(G-7946)*

Signet Cabinetry Inc 812 248-0612
1400 Service Dr Sellersburg (47172) *(G-12416)*

Signet Millwork Inc 812 248-0612
1400 Service Dr Sellersburg (47172) *(G-12417)*

Signgrafx & Engraving, Richmond *Also called Thousand One Inc (G-12066)*

Signode Industrial Group LLC 574 266-6933
1301 N Nappanee St Elkhart (46514) *(G-3171)*

(PA)=Parent Co (HQ)=Headquarters (DH)=Div Headquarters

Signplex LLC 765 795-7446
   4 W Market St Cloverdale (46120) *(G-1737)*

Signs By Design 812 853-7784
   4133 Merchant Dr Ste 5 Newburgh (47630) *(G-11049)*

Signs By Sulane Inc 765 565-6773
   5920 W 850 N Carthage (46115) *(G-1516)*

Signs By Tmrrow Indanapolis NW, Indianapolis *Also called Aarvee Associates LLC (G-6305)*

Signs In Time By Greg Inc 260 749-7446
   4306 Lake Ave Fort Wayne (46815) *(G-4626)*

Signs Magic LLC 812 473-5155
   716 N Weinbach Ave Evansville (47711) *(G-3730)*

Signs More 317 392-9184
   628 Highpointe Blvd Shelbyville (46176) *(G-12569)*

Signs Now, Evansville *Also called Signs Magic LLC (G-3730)*

Signs Now, Indianapolis *Also called Four Points Development Corp (G-6951)*

Signs Now, Clarksville *Also called Seaton Springs Inc (G-1696)*

Signs of Life LLC 317 575-1049
   10940 Timber Ln Carmel (46032) *(G-1480)*

Signs of Seasons 219 866-4507
   2675 W Clark St Rensselaer (47978) *(G-11938)*

Signs of Times, Poland *Also called Ron Glasscock (G-11743)*

Signs of Times 574 296-7464
   2201 S Nappanee St Elkhart (46517) *(G-3172)*

Signs of Times Llc 812 981-3000
   714 Mount Tabor Rd New Albany (47150) *(G-10862)*

Signs On Time Inc 219 661-4488
   10740 Broadway Crown Point (46307) *(G-2304)*

Signs Unlimited 574 255-0500
   4121 Lincolnway E Mishawaka (46544) *(G-10124)*

Signs Unlimited 260 484-5769
   1412 Goshen Ave Fort Wayne (46808) *(G-4627)*

Signs Xp Inc 765 453-4812
   1609 Cherry Hill Ln Kokomo (46902) *(G-8696)*

Signtech Sign Services Inc 574 537-8080
   1508 Bashor Rd Goshen (46528) *(G-5323)*

Signworks 219 462-5353
   2003 Calumet Ave Valparaiso (46383) *(G-13619)*

Sila Seal, Indianapolis *Also called Meyer Plastics Inc (G-7493)*

Silberline Mfg Co Inc 260 728-2111
   2010 Guy Brown Dr Decatur (46733) *(G-2404)*

Silberline of Indiana, Decatur *Also called Silberline Mfg Co Inc (G-2404)*

Silcotec Inc 219 324-4411
   707 Boyd Blvd La Porte (46350) *(G-8821)*

Silent Witness Enterprises 219 365-6660
   9804 W Oakridge Dr Saint John (46373) *(G-12270)*

Silgan Containers Mfg Corp 219 362-7002
   300 N Fail Rd La Porte (46350) *(G-8822)*

Silgan Containers Mfg Corp 219 845-1500
   2501 165th St Ste 2 Hammond (46320) *(G-5939)*

Silgan Containers Mfg Corp 219 362-7002
   300 N Fail Rd La Porte (46350) *(G-8823)*

Silgan Plastics Corporation 812 522-0900
   3779 N County Road 850 E Seymour (47274) *(G-12489)*

Silgan Plastics LLC 260 894-3118
   910 Gerber St Ligonier (46767) *(G-9295)*

Silgan Plastics LLC 812 522-0900
   3779 N County Road 850 E Seymour (47274) *(G-12490)*

Silgan Plastics Llc 812 522-0900
   S O Brien St Seymour (47274) *(G-12491)*

Silgan White Cap Corporation 812 425-6222
   2201 W Maryland St Evansville (47712) *(G-3731)*

Silgan White Cap Corporation 765 983-9200
   1701 Williamsburg Pike Richmond (47374) *(G-12050)*

Silicis Technologies Inc 317 896-5044
   17225 Westfield Park Rd Westfield (46074) *(G-14189)*

Silk Mountain Creation 317 815-1660
   620 S Rangeline Rd Ste P Carmel (46032) *(G-1481)*

Silva Military Solutions, Fort Wayne *Also called Innovations By (G-4371)*

Silver Petroleum Corp 260 824-2220
   409 N Main St Bluffton (46714) *(G-891)*

Sim 2 K Inc 317 251-7920
   6330 E 75th St Ste 336 Indianapolis (46250) *(G-7947)*

Simeoc LLC 240 210-5685
   18125 Chipstead Dr South Bend (46637) *(G-12937)*

Simko Industrial Fabricators 219 933-9100
   4545 Ash Ave Hammond (46327) *(G-5940)*

Simko Machining Inc 219 864-9535
   51 Chateau Dr Dyer (46311) *(G-2509)*

Simko Sons Indus Refractories 219 933-9100
   4545 Ash Ave Hammond (46327) *(G-5941)*

Simma Software Inc 812 418-0526
   5940 S Ernest St Terre Haute (47802) *(G-13327)*

Simmons Winery & Farm Market 812 546-0091
   8111 E 450 N Columbus (47203) *(G-2015)*

Simon and Sons 812 852-3636
   5802 N Us Highway 421 Osgood (47037) *(G-11395)*

Simple Cremations Burials LLC 765 592-6226
   459 N 9th St Clinton (47842) *(G-1721)*

Simple Quarters LLC 812 216-8602
   2340 Quarter Path Rd Cicero (46034) *(G-1667)*

Simple To Elegant 812 234-8700
   1601 S 3rd St Terre Haute (47802) *(G-13328)*

Simplified Imaging LLC 219 663-5122
   1126 Arrowhead Ct Crown Point (46307) *(G-2305)*

Simply Silver 260 824-4667
   1165 Fawncrest Ct Bluffton (46714) *(G-892)*

Simply Socks Yarn Company 260 416-2397
   1408 Clara Ave Fort Wayne (46805) *(G-4628)*

Simpson Alloy Services Inc 812 969-2766
   7017 Highway 111 Se Elizabeth (47117) *(G-2646)*

Sims Cabinet Co Inc (PA) 317 634-1747
   431 N Holmes Ave Indianapolis (46222) *(G-7948)*

Sims-Lohman Inc 317 467-0710
   725 E Main St Greenfield (46140) *(G-5574)*

Sincerely Different LLC 574 292-1727
   51860 Sharon Ct Granger (46530) *(G-5435)*

Sinclair Glass, Hartford City *Also called Middletown Enterprises Inc (G-5985)*

Sinden Racing Service Inc 317 243-7171
   1201 Main St Indianapolis (46224) *(G-7949)*

Sinflex Paper Co Inc 765 789-6688
   301 S Butterfield Rd Muncie (47303) *(G-10563)*

Singer Optical Company Inc 812 423-1179
   1401 N Royal Ave Evansville (47715) *(G-3732)*

Single Source Inc 574 656-3400
   791 Industrial Pkwy North Liberty (46554) *(G-11222)*

Singles Ministry, The, Tippecanoe *Also called Gen Enterprises (G-13381)*

Sinks N More, Whiting *Also called Polyjohn Enterprises Corp (G-14273)*

Sir Graphics Inc 574 272-9330
   12599 Industrial Park Dr Granger (46530) *(G-5436)*

Sirmax North America Inc 765 639-0300
   2915 Dr Martin Luther Kin Anderson (46016) *(G-167)*

Sisco Box, Evansville *Also called Sisco Corporation (G-3733)*

Sisco Corporation 812 422-2090
   1231 E Michigan St Evansville (47711) *(G-3733)*

Sisson & Son Mfg Jewelers 574 967-4331
   7 W Main St Flora (46929) *(G-4003)*

Sisson Steel Inc 812 354-8701
   739 S State Road 61 Winslow (47598) *(G-14359)*

Sissys Ceramics 951 550-7728
   30803 County Road 20 Elkhart (46517) *(G-3173)*

Siswd Processing (PA) 812 574-4080
   6556 N Shun Pike Rd 534 Madison (47250) *(G-9495)*

Sit Can Happen LLC 812 346-4188
   130 N County Road 400 W North Vernon (47265) *(G-11282)*

Site Enhancement Services, South Bend *Also called North American Signs Inc (G-12877)*

Siteone Landscape Supply LLC 219 769-2351
   4068 W 82nd Ct Merrillville (46410) *(G-9754)*

Sitesuccess Inc 219 808-4076
   521 Saint Andrews Dr Schererville (46375) *(G-12345)*

Sittin Pretty LLC 219 947-4121
   9470 Randolph St Crown Point (46307) *(G-2306)*

Six Mile Welding 260 768-3126
   40 S 600 W Lagrange (46761) *(G-9065)*

Six Sigma Mold Inc 219 285-6539
   511 S Lincoln St Morocco (47963) *(G-10363)*

Sjc Industries Corp 574 264-7511
   1110 D I Dr Elkhart (46514) *(G-3174)*

Sjg Enterprises Inc 574 269-4806
   3304 Lake City Hwy Warsaw (46580) *(G-13940)*

SJS Components LLC 260 578-0192
   6778 S State Road 13 Warsaw (46580) *(G-13941)*

Sk Beer, Indianapolis *Also called Sun King Brewing Company LLC (G-8017)*

Skid Row Wood Products Inc 812 828-0349
   2270 Wood Dr Spencer (47460) *(G-13036)*

Skinny and Company LLC 888 865-4278
   5762 W 74th St Ste 117 Indianapolis (46278) *(G-7950)*

Skirt & Satchel 812 727-0292
   101 W Kirkwood Ave # 107 Bloomington (47404) *(G-824)*

Skjodt Ink, Carmel *Also called Maple Leaf Graphics Inc (G-1434)*

Skjodt-Brrett Cntract Pckg LLC 765 482-6856
   401 S Enterprise Blvd Lebanon (46052) *(G-9224)*

Sky Fire Group LLC 812 623-8980
   21868 Lake Tambo Rd Sunman (47041) *(G-13118)*

Sky King Unlimited Inc 574 271-9170
   50571 Indiana Sr 533 South Bend (46637) *(G-12938)*

Sky Thunder LLC 812 397-0102
   6521 N Us Highway 41 Shelburn (47879) *(G-12511)*

Skydive Indianapolis, Frankfort *Also called Indiana Skydiving Center (G-4837)*

Skyline Champion Corporation (PA) 574 294-6521
   2520 Bypass Rd Elkhart (46514) *(G-3175)*

Skyline Corporation 574 848-7621
   State Route 15 Bristol (46507) *(G-1087)*

Skyline Homes Inc (HQ) 574 294-6521
   2520 Bypass Rd Elkhart (46514) *(G-3176)*

Skyline Mainsfield, Elkhart *Also called Homette Corporation (G-2919)*

Skyline Signs & Awnings, Delphi *Also called Skyline Signs Inc (G-2427)*

Skyline Signs Inc 765 564-4422
1989 W Mill St Delphi (46923) (G-2427)

Skytech II Inc 260 459-1703
9230 Conservation Way Fort Wayne (46809) (G-4629)

Skytech-Systems Inc 260 459-1703
9230 Conservation Way Fort Wayne (46809) (G-4630)

Skyward Publishing LLC 317 791-2212
2709 Westbrook Ave Indianapolis (46241) (G-7951)

Slabach Logging LLC 260 768-4644
7615 W 200 N Shipshewana (46565) (G-12650)

Slabaugh Metal Fab 574 546-2882
2320 4c Rd Bremen (46506) (G-1024)

Slabaugh Metal Fab LLC 574 342-0554
1855 12th Rd Bourbon (46504) (G-948)

Slabaugh Welding LLC 574 773-5410
3942 W 1350 N Milford (46542) (G-9965)

Slabaughs Meat Processing 574 773-0381
72700 County Road 101 Nappanee (46550) (G-10706)

Slate Mechanical Inc 765 452-9611
4602 W 100 N Kokomo (46901) (G-8697)

Slater Publishing Co, Westville Also called WAr - LLC- Westville Prtg (G-14221)

Slaters Concrete Products 260 347-0164
322 E Wayne St Kendallville (46755) (G-8510)

Slatile Roofing and Shtmtl Co 574 233-7485
1703 S Ironwood Dr Ste A South Bend (46613) (G-12939)

Slavica Publishers, Bloomington Also called Trustees Indiana University (G-845)

Slb Corporation 574 255-9774
1906 E Mckinley Ave Mishawaka (46545) (G-10125)

Sledgehammer Printing 812 629-2160
4956 State Route 261 Newburgh (47630) (G-11050)

Sleepmadecom LLC 662 350-0999
2625 Kotter Ave Evansville (47715) (G-3734)

Sleepy Hollow Leather Inc 219 926-1071
108 Lincoln St Chesterton (46304) (G-1630)

Sleepy Hollow Lock and Key, Chesterton Also called Sleepy Hollow Leather Inc (G-1630)

Sleepy Owl Software LLC 765 299-2862
3030 E Amy Ln Bloomington (47408) (G-825)

Slicers 812 255-0655
2715 Washington Ave Vincennes (47591) (G-13706)

Slick Engineering Industries 765 354-2822
8768 W State Road 236 Middletown (47356) (G-9941)

Slip Harris Company LLC 812 923-5674
5971 Buttontown Rd Greenville (47124) (G-5654)

Slipcover Xpress Inc 260 482-7177
10607 Leo Rd Fort Wayne (46825) (G-4631)

SLM Industries LLC 317 537-1090
8606 Allsnvlle Rd Ste 134 Indianapolis (46250) (G-7952)

Sloan, Rodney Logging, Batesville Also called Rodney Sloan Logging (G-518)

Slon Inc (PA) 765 884-1792
206 N Harrison Ave Fowler (47944) (G-4807)

SM Industries LLC 219 613-5295
13701 Limerick Dr Saint John (46373) (G-12271)

Small Parts Inc (HQ) 574 753-6323
600 Humphrey St Logansport (46947) (G-9364)

Small Parts Inc 574 739-6236
112 E Mildred St Logansport (46947) (G-9365)

Small Town Printers LLC 812 596-1536
6265 Sand Hill Rd Se Elizabeth (47117) (G-2647)

Smallwood Consulting LLC 812 406-8040
7018 Plum Creek Dr Sellersburg (47172) (G-12418)

Smart Choice Mobile Inc 574 830-5727
4542 Elkhart Rd Elkhart (46517) (G-3177)

Smart Machine Inc 219 922-0706
9941 Express Dr Hammond (46322) (G-5942)

Smart Manufacturing Inc 765 482-7481
515 N State Road 75 Lebanon (46052) (G-9225)

Smart Pergola 317 987-7750
12958 Brighton Ave Carmel (46032) (G-1482)

Smart Products, Muncie Also called Sp Holdings Inc (G-10564)

Smart Systems 800 348-0823
303 S Byrkit St Mishawaka (46544) (G-10126)

Smart Technologies LLC 317 738-4338
317 E Creekside Ct W Franklin (46131) (G-4933)

Smart Temps, Mishawaka Also called Digi International Inc (G-10036)

Smart Temps LLC 574 217-8847
435 Park Place Cir # 100 Mishawaka (46545) (G-10127)

Smartgait LLC 765 404-0726
3000 Kent Ave Ste C2-108 West Lafayette (47906) (G-14107)

SMC Corporation of America (HQ) 317 899-3182
10100 Smc Blvd Noblesville (46060) (G-11184)

Smco Inc 574 295-1482
2505 Laura Ct Elkhart (46517) (G-3178)

Smelly Gourmet, The, Metamora Also called All Occasions Gift Shop LLC (G-9762)

Smgf LLC 812 354-8899
3377 N State Road 57 Petersburg (47567) (G-11568)

SMI Manufacturing Inc 812 428-2794
7457 W State Route 66 Newburgh (47630) (G-11051)

SMI Marketing, Newburgh Also called SMI Manufacturing Inc (G-11051)

Smith & Associates, Cloverdale Also called Trio Milling Inc (G-1740)

Smith & Butterfield Co Inc (HQ) 812 422-3261
2800 Lynch Rd Ste D Evansville (47711) (G-3735)

Smith & Butterfield Co Inc 812 422-3261
2800 Lynch Rd Ste 2 Evansville (47711) (G-3736)

Smith Brothers Berne Inc (PA) 260 589-2131
356 Monroe St Berne (46711) (G-623)

Smith Business Supply Inc 765 654-4442
358 N Columbia St Frankfort (46041) (G-4853)

Smith Consulting Inc 765 728-5980
850 W Huntington St Montpelier (47359) (G-10294)

Smith Dairy Wayne Division, Richmond Also called Smithfoods Richmond Inc (G-12051)

Smith Estill Marine Service 812 282-7944
4210 E Hwy 62 Jeffersonville (47130) (G-8424)

Smith Excavating 812 636-0054
10122 E1400 N Odon (47562) (G-11341)

Smith Graphics & Design, Mishawaka Also called Smith Signs Inc (G-10128)

Smith Machine and Tool 574 223-2318
3392 Wabash Ave Rochester (46975) (G-12155)

Smith Metal Finishing, Fort Wayne Also called Lambert Metal Finishing Inc (G-4423)

Smith Printing, Linton Also called D & M Printing Inc (G-9306)

Smith Ready Mix Inc (PA) 219 462-3191
251 Lincolnway Valparaiso (46383) (G-13620)

Smith Ready Mix Inc 219 374-5581
9018 W 133rd Ave Cedar Lake (46303) (G-1533)

Smith Ready Mix Inc 219 874-6219
3608 E Michigan Blvd Michigan City (46360) (G-9844)

Smith Ready Mix Inc 219 374-5581
251 Lincolnway Valparaiso (46383) (G-13621)

Smith Ruth C Rn Prof Electrlg 812 423-4760
715 N 1st Ave Ste 20 Evansville (47710) (G-3737)

Smith Signs Inc 574 255-6446
317 Capital Ave Mishawaka (46544) (G-10128)

Smith Small Engine Service 812 232-1318
1515 N 25th St Terre Haute (47803) (G-13329)

Smith Welding & Repair Service 260 563-0710
1605 S Baumbauer Rd Wabash (46992) (G-13756)

Smith's Small Engines, Terre Haute Also called Smith Small Engine Service (G-13329)

Smithfield Direct LLC 812 867-6644
8426 Baumgart Rd Evansville (47725) (G-3738)

Smithfield Direct LLC 765 473-3086
3311 S State Road 19 Peru (46970) (G-11545)

Smithfield Foods 765 473-3086
3311 S State Road 19 Peru (46970) (G-11546)

Smithfoods Richmond Inc 330 683-8710
1590 Nw 11th St Richmond (47374) (G-12051)

Smithland Butchering Co Inc 317 729-5398
11420 S Us Highway 31 Elizabethtown (47232) (G-2651)

Smiths Arospc Components Haute 812 235-5210
333 S 3rd St Terre Haute (47807) (G-13330)

Smiths Enterprises Inc 765 378-6267
1124 Dilts St Chesterfield (46017) (G-1589)

Smiths Medical Asd Inc 219 365-2376
12010 W 90th Ave Saint John (46373) (G-12272)

Smiths Medical Asd Inc 219 554-2196
5700 W 23rd Ave Gary (46406) (G-5098)

Smiths TAC Shack 765 345-5590
117 E Main St Knightstown (46148) (G-8560)

Smitson Cmmnications Group LLC 317 876-8916
3500 Depauw Blvd Ste 1000 Indianapolis (46268) (G-7953)

Smitty's Indianapolis Marine, Indianapolis Also called Indianapolis Marine Co (G-7202)

Smock Material Handling Co 317 890-3200
3420 Park Davis Cir Indianapolis (46235) (G-7954)

Smoke Smoke Smoke 219 942-3331
1165 W 37th Ave Hobart (46342) (G-6096)

Smoker Craft, New Paris Also called Sylvan Marine Inc (G-10997)

Smoker Craft Inc (PA) 574 831-2103
68143 Clunette St New Paris (46553) (G-10994)

Smoker Friendly 812 556-0244
2913 Newton St Jasper (47546) (G-8309)

Smokers Host 307 .... 765 938-1877
1510 N Main St Rushville (46173) (G-12234)

Smokers Iron Works 574 674-6683
30907 County Road 16 Elkhart (46516) (G-3179)

Smokes - Berne 260 849-4038
428 Wind Ridge Trl Berne (46711) (G-624)

Smokestack Industries LLC 812 267-8646
11090 Majestic Blvd Se Elizabeth (47117) (G-2648)

SMR Management Inc 765 252-0257
2139 Klondike Rd Lafayette (47906) (G-8999)

SMS, South Bend Also called Strategic Mfg & Sup Inc (G-12957)

SMS Group Inc 219 880-0256
201 Mssissippi St Ste 12a Gary (46402) (G-5099)

SMS Technical Services, Gary Also called SMS Group Inc (G-5099)

Smurfit Stone Container, Wabash Also called Paperworks Industries Inc (G-13747)

Snapple Beverage Corp 812 424-7978
1100 Independence Ave Evansville (47714) (G-3739)

Snappy Minds Llc 812 661-8506
1330 Cobblestone Rd Jasper (47546) (G-8310)

Snark Publishing LLC.....574 256-1027
340 Park Ave Mishawaka (46545) ***(G-10129)***
Snavely Machine, Peru *Also called Snavelys Machine & Mfg Co Inc* ***(G-11547)***
Snavelys Machine & Mfg Co Inc.....765 473-8395
1070 Industrial Pkwy Peru (46970) ***(G-11547)***
Snax In Pax Inc.....260 593-3066
204 Hawpatch Dr Topeka (46571) ***(G-13429)***
Snodgrass Sheet Metal.....317 783-3181
1930 S State Ave Indianapolis (46203) ***(G-7955)***
Snooks Land Holding Inc.....812 876-4540
7800 N Mt Tabor Rd Ellettsville (47429) ***(G-3284)***
Snow Management Group.....574 252-5253
14009 Jefferson Blvd Mishawaka (46545) ***(G-10130)***
Snt Graphics, Indianapolis *Also called Shirts N Things S N T Graphics* ***(G-7935)***
Snuggy Baby LLC.....260 418-6795
835 W Berry St Fort Wayne (46802) ***(G-4632)***
Snyder & Co Inc.....765 447-3452
406 S Earl Ave Lafayette (47904) ***(G-9000)***
Snykin Inc.....317 818-0618
3915 E 96th St Indianapolis (46240) ***(G-7956)***
So Industries LLC.....765 606-7596
4197 W 950 S Pendleton (46064) ***(G-11506)***
Soap Guy, The, La Porte *Also called Tall Cotton Marketing LLC* ***(G-8825)***
Soapequipment.com, Hagerstown *Also called Willow Way LLC* ***(G-5817)***
Soapy Soap Company.....812 575-0005
2786 E Bressingham Way Bloomington (47401) ***(G-826)***
Society For Ethnmusicology Inc.....812 855-6672
800 E 3rd St Bloomington (47405) ***(G-827)***
Socks For The Homeless Inc.....317 568-3942
3518 N Gladstone Ave Indianapolis (46218) ***(G-7957)***
Sofamor/Danek Group Mfg Div, Warsaw *Also called Warsaw Orthopedic Inc* ***(G-13963)***
Soft Stop, Anderson *Also called Ruby Enterprises Inc* ***(G-164)***
Software House, Goshen *Also called Jim Couch* ***(G-5248)***
Software Informatics Group LLC.....317 326-2598
869 N 300 W Greenfield (46140) ***(G-5575)***
Software Pub LLC.....260 486-7839
4104 Wyndemere Pass Fort Wayne (46835) ***(G-4633)***
Software Sales Incorporated.....317 258-7442
3370 S 450 E Whitestown (46075) ***(G-14262)***
Software Sneak.....219 510-5894
259 Indiana Ave Valparaiso (46383) ***(G-13622)***
Soil Dynamics Instruments Inc.....765 497-0511
3309 Elkhart St West Lafayette (47906) ***(G-14108)***
Soil-Max Inc.....888 764-5629
1201 S 1st St Terre Haute (47802) ***(G-13331)***
Sojane Technologies Inc.....317 915-1059
7526 E 82nd St Ste 110 Indianapolis (46256) ***(G-7958)***
Solae, Remington *Also called Bunge North America Foundation* ***(G-11905)***
Solae, Remington *Also called Dupont* ***(G-11906)***
Solae.....260 724-2101
1200 N 2nd St Decatur (46733) ***(G-2405)***
Solae LLC.....800 325-7108
413 N Cressy Ave Remington (47977) ***(G-11909)***
Solae LLC.....219 261-2124
413 N Cressy Ave Remington (47977) ***(G-11910)***
Solar America Solutions LLC.....317 688-8581
9263 Castlegate Dr Indianapolis (46256) ***(G-7959)***
Solar Bat Enterprises Inc.....812 986-3551
3628 E County Road 600 N Brazil (47834) ***(G-978)***
Solar Goes Green, Huntington *Also called Benson Solar Enterprises LLC* ***(G-6193)***
Solar Sources Inc (PA).....317 788-0084
6755 Gray Rd Indianapolis (46237) ***(G-7960)***
Solar Sources Inc.....812 354-8776
625 N 9th St Petersburg (47567) ***(G-11569)***
Solar Sources Underground LLC (PA).....317 788-0084
6755 Gray Rd Indianapolis (46237) ***(G-7961)***
Solas Ray Lighting, Anderson *Also called Continental Manufacturing LLC* ***(G-90)***
Solema USA Inc.....765 361-0806
315 Glenn St Crawfordsville (47933) ***(G-2196)***
Soley Orthotics LLC.....317 373-7395
5787 W 74th St Indianapolis (46278) ***(G-7962)***
Solfire Contract Mfg Inc.....260 755-2115
4939 Decatur Rd Fort Wayne (46806) ***(G-4634)***
Solid Rock Gbc.....260 723-4806
213 Reed St South Whitley (46787) ***(G-13003)***
Solid Surface Craftsmen Inc.....317 535-2333
100 Crossroads Dr Ste D Whiteland (46184) ***(G-14246)***
Soliven Brough, Fort Wayne *Also called Safety Wear Fort Wayne* ***(G-4602)***
Solomon M Eicher.....812 289-1252
7809 Henderson Rd Marysville (47141) ***(G-9651)***
Solotat Industries LLC.....574 320-1436
1233 W Hively Ave Elkhart (46517) ***(G-3180)***
Soltek, Evansville *Also called Boyer Enterprises Inc* ***(G-3394)***
Solution Tree Inc (PA).....812 336-7700
555 N Morton St Bloomington (47404) ***(G-828)***
Solutions For Print LLC.....812 584-2701
9530 N 100 W Fountaintown (46130) ***(G-4793)***
Somer Dental Laboratories, Zionsville *Also called Somer Inc* ***(G-14464)***
Somer Inc.....317 873-1111
11707 N Michigan Rd Zionsville (46077) ***(G-14464)***
Somersaults LLC.....317 747-7496
10285 Normandy Ct Fishers (46040) ***(G-3990)***
Somersaults Life Archives, Fishers *Also called Somersaults LLC* ***(G-3990)***
Sommer Awning Group, Indianapolis *Also called AP Sign Group LLC* ***(G-6406)***
Sommer Letter Company LLC.....260 414-6686
3916 N County Line Rd E Huntertown (46748) ***(G-6147)***
Sommers Graphics Group, South Bend *Also called Sommers Graphics Inc* ***(G-12940)***
Sommers Graphics Inc.....574 282-2000
60750 Greenridge Ct South Bend (46614) ***(G-12940)***
Sonacare Medical LLC.....888 874-4384
4000 Pendleton Way Indianapolis (46226) ***(G-7963)***
Sonam Technologies LLC.....844 887-6626
9800 Connecticut Dr Crown Point (46307) ***(G-2307)***
Sonicu LLC.....317 468-2345
19 W Main St Greenfield (46140) ***(G-5576)***
Sonner Industries LLC.....574 370-9387
58639 County Road 35 Middlebury (46540) ***(G-9919)***
Sonny Scaffolds Inc (PA).....317 831-3900
319 Harlan Dr Mooresville (46158) ***(G-10341)***
Sonobuoytechsystems, Columbia City *Also called Erapsco* ***(G-1783)***
Sonoco Products Company.....812 526-5511
6502 S Us Highway 31 Edinburgh (46124) ***(G-2629)***
Sonoco Products Company.....574 893-4521
1535 S State Road 19 Th Akron (46910) ***(G-7)***
Sonoco Prtective Solutions Inc.....260 726-9333
1619 N Meridian St Portland (47371) ***(G-11846)***
Sonoco Prtective Solutions Inc.....260 726-9333
1619 N Meridian St Portland (47371) ***(G-11847)***
Sons of Thunder.....812 897-4908
1233 Mount Gilead Rd Boonville (47601) ***(G-922)***
Sony Corporation of America.....812 462-8726
1800 N Fruitridge Ave Terre Haute (47804) ***(G-13332)***
Sony Dadc US Inc.....812 462-8116
3181 N Fruitridge Ave Terre Haute (47804) ***(G-13333)***
Sony Dadc US Inc (HQ).....812 462-8100
1800 N Fruitridge Ave Terre Haute (47804) ***(G-13334)***
Sony Dadc US Inc.....812 462-8784
1600 N Fruitridge Ave Terre Haute (47804) ***(G-13335)***
Sophysa USA Inc.....219 663-7711
503 E Summit St Ste 5 Crown Point (46307) ***(G-2308)***
Sorbashock LLC.....574 520-9784
204 Barouche Pl Fort Wayne (46845) ***(G-4635)***
Sordelet Tool & Die Inc.....260 483-7258
1925 Lakeview Dr Fort Wayne (46808) ***(G-4636)***
Sorensen Custom Cabinets.....765 292-2225
21 E 400 S Tipton (46072) ***(G-13405)***
Sorg Millwork.....260 639-3223
10744 Us Highway 27 S Fort Wayne (46816) ***(G-4637)***
Souder Power Washing LLC.....812 894-2544
7425 E Troy Ct Terre Haute (47802) ***(G-13336)***
Soulful Scents LLC.....317 319-8001
19388 Golden Meadow Way Noblesville (46060) ***(G-11185)***
Sound & Graphics.....219 963-7293
2580 Central Ave A Lake Station (46405) ***(G-9077)***
Source Hospitality Mfg Group, Washington *Also called Troy Stuart* ***(G-14004)***
Source Products Inc.....260 424-0864
9875 S Washington Rd Columbia City (46725) ***(G-1835)***
South Bend Brew Werks LLC.....801 209-2987
216 S Michigan St South Bend (46601) ***(G-12941)***
South Bend Chocolate Co Inc (PA).....574 233-2577
3300 W Sample St Ste 110 South Bend (46619) ***(G-12942)***
South Bend Clutch Inc.....574 256-5064
709 W Jefferson Blvd Mishawaka (46545) ***(G-10131)***
South Bend Ethanol LLC.....574 703-3360
3201 W Calvert St South Bend (46613) ***(G-12943)***
South Bend Form Tool Co Inc.....574 289-2441
408 W Indiana Ave South Bend (46613) ***(G-12944)***
South Bend Metal Products Co, South Bend *Also called Shakour Industries Inc* ***(G-12932)***
South Bend Modern Molding Inc.....574 255-0711
605 Laurel St Mishawaka (46544) ***(G-10132)***
South Bend Screen Process Inc (PA).....574 254-9000
3622 N Home St Mishawaka (46545) ***(G-10133)***
South Bend Smoke Time Inc.....574 318-4837
1841 S Bend Ave South Bend (46637) ***(G-12945)***
South Bend Tribune.....574 971-5651
114 S Main St Goshen (46526) ***(G-5324)***
South Bend Tribune Corp (HQ).....574 235-6161
225 W Colfax Ave South Bend (46626) ***(G-12946)***
South Bend Woodworks LLC.....574 232-8875
707 S Scott St South Bend (46601) ***(G-12947)***
South Gibson Star-Times Inc.....812 753-3553
203 S Mccreary St Fort Branch (47648) ***(G-4029)***
South Shore Slag LLC (PA).....219 881-6544
3411 Sheffield Ave Hammond (46327) ***(G-5943)***
South Whtly Trbne Prctn News.....260 723-4771
113 S State St South Whitley (46787) ***(G-13004)***

Southcorp Packaging North Amer, Valparaiso *Also called North America Packaging Corp* ***(G-13592)***
Southeast Ind Solid Waste Proc, Madison *Also called Siswd Processing* ***(G-9495)***
Southeastern Aluminum Pdts Inc.....904 781-8200
9770 Mayflower Park Dr # 200 Carmel (46032) ***(G-1483)***
Southern Bowl, Greenwood *Also called Royal Pin Leisure Centers Inc* ***(G-5744)***
Southern Electric Coil LLC.....219 931-5500
5025 Columbia Ave Hammond (46327) ***(G-5944)***
Southern Fuel LLC.....219 689-3552
1250 N Mckinley Ave Rensselaer (47978) ***(G-11939)***
Southern Ind Archtectural Pdts, Evansville *Also called Wagner Welding Incorporated* ***(G-3808)***
Southern Indiana Bus Source.....812 206-6397
318 Pearl St Ste 100 New Albany (47150) ***(G-10863)***
Southern Indiana Chemical (PA).....812 687-7118
358 E 900 N Washington (47501) ***(G-14003)***
Southern Indiana Collar Co.....812 486-3714
1692 N 725 E Montgomery (47558) ***(G-10242)***
Southern Indiana Collar Mfg Co, Montgomery *Also called Southern Indiana Collar Co* ***(G-10242)***
Southern Indiana Linings & Coa.....812 206-7250
113 Industrial Way Charlestown (47111) ***(G-1580)***
Southern Indiana Plastics Inc (PA).....812 280-7474
1606 Dutch Ln Jeffersonville (47130) ***(G-8425)***
Southern Indiana Sawmill LLC.....502 664-5723
3325 N Highland Rd Salem (47167) ***(G-12305)***
Southern Indiana Supply Inc.....812 482-2267
1059 Wernsing Rd Jasper (47546) ***(G-8311)***
Southern Indiana Treating, Huntingburg *Also called Steinkamp Warehouses Inc* ***(G-6179)***
Southern Indiana Vinyl Window, Odon *Also called Vernon Greyber* ***(G-11343)***
Southern Mold and Tool Inc.....812 752-3333
915 S Elm St Scottsburg (47170) ***(G-12380)***
Southfield Corporation.....812 824-1355
7100 S Old State Road 37 Bloomington (47403) ***(G-829)***
Southfield Corporation.....317 773-5340
15215 N River Ave Noblesville (46060) ***(G-11186)***
Southlake Lift Truck.....219 962-4695
3601 Arizona St Gary (46405) ***(G-5100)***
Southlake Machine Corp.....219 285-6150
112 N Polk St Morocco (47963) ***(G-10364)***
Southland Container Corp.....812 385-0774
Rr 1 Box 174 Princeton (47670) ***(G-11882)***
Southland Metals Inc.....574 252-4441
4042 Southampton Dr Mishawaka (46544) ***(G-10134)***
Southside Mini Storage.....574 293-3270
2031 W Mishawaka Rd Elkhart (46517) ***(G-3181)***
Southside Plating Works Inc.....219 293-5508
2010 Superior St Elkhart (46516) ***(G-3182)***
Southside Publishing, Indianapolis *Also called Southsider* ***(G-7964)***
Southside Solidification Svcs, Carmel *Also called Remedium Services Group LLC* ***(G-1467)***
Southside Times, Beech Grove *Also called Hoosier Times Inc* ***(G-596)***
Southside Times The, Indianapolis *Also called Times Leader Publications LLC* ***(G-8076)***
Southsider.....317 781-0023
6025 Madison Ave Ste B Indianapolis (46227) ***(G-7964)***
Southwark Metal Mfg Co.....317 823-5300
10401 E 59th St Indianapolis (46236) ***(G-7965)***
Southwater Sourcing LLC.....219 809-7106
200 Tomahawk Dr Michigan City (46360) ***(G-9845)***
Southwest Grafix and AP Inc.....812 425-5104
2229 W Franklin St Evansville (47712) ***(G-3740)***
Southwest Welding.....574 862-4453
25389 State Road 119 Goshen (46526) ***(G-5325)***
Southwire, Bremen *Also called Coleman Cable LLC* ***(G-990)***
Sp Holdings Inc.....765 284-9545
3401 N Commerce Dr Muncie (47303) ***(G-10564)***
Sp3.....260 547-4150
3531 W Us Highway 224 Decatur (46733) ***(G-2406)***
Space Kraft.....317 871-6999
4901 W 79th St Indianapolis (46268) ***(G-7966)***
Spaceguard Inc.....812 523-3044
711 S Commerce Dr Seymour (47274) ***(G-12492)***
Spaceguard Products, Seymour *Also called Spaceguard Inc* ***(G-12492)***
Spaceport Explrtion Centre Inc.....765 606-1512
144 Tracy Ridge Blvd New Whiteland (46184) ***(G-11014)***
Span Inc.....317 347-2646
724 Esplanade St Lebanon (46052) ***(G-9226)***
Spankys Paintball.....812 752-7375
2799 E State Road 356 Scottsburg (47170) ***(G-12381)***
Spark Marketing LLC.....219 301-0071
1112 Us Highway 41 # 102 Schererville (46375) ***(G-12346)***
Sparkle Pools Inc.....812 232-1292
2225 N 25th St Terre Haute (47804) ***(G-13337)***
Sparkling Clean Inc.....812 422-4871
1018 Bayse St Evansville (47714) ***(G-3741)***
Sparkman Mfg Inc.....812 873-6052
9197 N Jake Gayle Rd Commiskey (47227) ***(G-2037)***
Sparks Belting Company Inc.....800 451-4537
3420 179th St 3b Hammond (46323) ***(G-5945)***
Spartan Motors Usa Inc.....574 848-2000
603 Earthway Blvd Bristol (46507) ***(G-1088)***
Spartech LLC.....765 281-5100
1401 E Memorial Dr Muncie (47302) ***(G-10565)***
Spartech Plastics, Warsaw *Also called Polyone Corporation* ***(G-13927)***
Spaulding Products and Mfg Co, West Lafayette *Also called Cox John* ***(G-14061)***
Spawn Mate Inc.....812 948-2174
2049 Indiana Ave New Albany (47150) ***(G-10864)***
Speak Modalities LLC.....765 742-4252
6137 Naschette Pkwy West Lafayette (47906) ***(G-14109)***
Special Cutting Tools, Angola *Also called Feddema Industries Inc* ***(G-213)***
Special Fabrication Services.....812 384-5384
418 E Highway 57 Elnora (47529) ***(G-3292)***
Special Ideas Incorporated.....812 834-5691
511 Diamond Rd Heltonville (47436) ***(G-6028)***
Special K Alpacas.....260 638-4515
10562 N Meridian Rd Ossian (46777) ***(G-11408)***
Special Metals Corporation.....574 262-3451
2900 Higgins Blvd Elkhart (46514) ***(G-3183)***
Special Product Services Inc.....260 632-1302
22416 Front St Woodburn (46797) ***(G-14390)***
Speciality Manufacturing, Charlestown *Also called Specialty Manufacturing of Ind* ***(G-1581)***
Specialized Printed Products, Fort Wayne *Also called Hager Inc* ***(G-4314)***
Specialized Services Inc.....317 485-8561
514 S Main St Fortville (46040) ***(G-4782)***
Specialties Co LLC.....260 432-3973
201 S Thomas Rd Fort Wayne (46808) ***(G-4638)***
Specialty Adhesive Film Co (PA).....812 926-0156
10510 Randall Ave Aurora (47001) ***(G-387)***
Specialty Cnc Incorporated.....812 825-7982
4900 W State Road 45 Bloomington (47403) ***(G-830)***
Specialty Coating Systems Inc (HQ).....317 451-8549
7645 Woodland Dr Indianapolis (46278) ***(G-7967)***
Specialty Coatings LLC.....812 431-3375
702 Fairway Dr Apt A Evansville (47710) ***(G-3742)***
Specialty Engrg Tl & Die LLC.....260 356-2678
875 E State St Huntington (46750) ***(G-6249)***
Specialty Enterprises Inc.....765 935-4556
2931 Us Highway 35 N Richmond (47374) ***(G-12052)***
Specialty Food Group LLC.....219 531-2142
463 E Us Highway 30 Valparaiso (46383) ***(G-13623)***
Specialty Indus Coatings Corp.....574 784-3711
555 N Michigan Rd Lakeville (46536) ***(G-9097)***
Specialty Machine Stamping.....574 658-3350
3890 N 300 W Warsaw (46582) ***(G-13942)***
Specialty Machines, Warsaw *Also called Specialty Machine Stamping* ***(G-13942)***
Specialty Manufacturing.....317 587-4999
11595 N Meridian St # 705 Carmel (46032) ***(G-1484)***
Specialty Manufacturing of Ind.....812 256-4633
15412 Highway 62 Ste 2 Charlestown (47111) ***(G-1581)***
Specialty Process Eqp Ctrl Inc.....812 473-8528
333 Plaza East Blvd Ste G Evansville (47715) ***(G-3743)***
Specialty Products & Polymers.....269 684-5931
50869 Hawthorne Meadow Dr South Bend (46628) ***(G-12948)***
Specialty Rim Supply Inc (PA).....812 234-3002
500 S 9th St Terre Haute (47807) ***(G-13338)***
Specialty Shoppe.....574 772-7873
1307 S Heaton St Knox (46534) ***(G-8582)***
Specialty Stainless (PA).....317 337-9800
4337 W 96th St Ste 500 Indianapolis (46268) ***(G-7968)***
Specialty Steel Works Inc (PA).....877 289-2277
1412 150th St Hammond (46327) ***(G-5946)***
Specialty Tool & Die Company.....765 452-9209
1614 Rank Parkway Ct Kokomo (46901) ***(G-8698)***
Specialty Tool LLC.....260 493-6351
6011 E Hanna Ave Ste D Indianapolis (46203) ***(G-7969)***
Specialty Tooling Inc.....812 464-8521
2391 Lexington Rd Evansville (47720) ***(G-3744)***
Specialty Welding & Machine.....812 969-2139
9280 Lotticks Comr Rd Se Elizabeth (47117) ***(G-2649)***
Specified Lighting Fixs of Ind (PA).....317 577-8100
8904 Bash St Ste B Indianapolis (46256) ***(G-7970)***
Specified Ltg Systems Ind Inc.....317 577-8100
8904 Bash St Ste B Indianapolis (46256) ***(G-7971)***
Specilzed Cmpnent Prts Ltd LLC.....260 925-2588
1700 S Indiana Ave Auburn (46706) ***(G-357)***
Speckin Sign Service Inc.....317 539-5133
845 Indianapolis Rd Greencastle (46135) ***(G-5478)***
Spectacles of Carmel Inc.....317 848-9081
30 1st St Sw Carmel (46032) ***(G-1485)***
Spectacles of Carmel Inc.....317 475-9011
7945 Lieber Rd Indianapolis (46260) ***(G-7972)***
Spectacular Soirees.....812 841-4311
2270 Ohio Blvd Terre Haute (47803) ***(G-13339)***
Spectra Metal Sales Inc.....317 822-8291
1711 W New York St Indianapolis (46222) ***(G-7973)***
Spectrum.....812 923-7830
2530 Edwrdsvlle Galena Rd Georgetown (47122) ***(G-5153)***
Spectrum.....812 941-6899
1608 Vance Ave New Albany (47150) ***(G-10865)***

ALPHABETIC

Spectrum Brands Inc 317 773-6627
20975 Creek Rd Noblesville (46060) ***(G-11187)***
Spectrum Finishing LLC 260 463-7300
1340 Industrial Dr N Lagrange (46761) ***(G-9066)***
Spectrum Industry 812 231-8355
500 8th Ave Terre Haute (47804) ***(G-13340)***
Spectrum Marketing 765 643-5566
1629 Pearl St Anderson (46016) ***(G-168)***
Spectrum Press Inc 812 335-1945
1300 N Loesch Rd Bloomington (47404) ***(G-831)***
Spectrum Print & Marketing 317 908-7471
7546 Corsican Cir Avon (46123) ***(G-467)***
Spectrum Rv LLC 574 970-5554
2801 Dexter Dr Elkhart (46514) ***(G-3184)***
Spectrum Services Inc 574 272-7605
12911 Industrial Park Dr # 7 Granger (46530) ***(G-5437)***
Speechlesstees LLC 260 417-9394
810 Lemonwood Ct Fort Wayne (46825) ***(G-4639)***
Speedgrip Chuck, Elkhart *Also called Lotec Inc* ***(G-3008)***
Speedgrip Chuck Company, Elkhart *Also called Scg Acquisition Company LLC* ***(G-3157)***
Speedhook Specialists Inc 877 773-4665
2321 Deerpath Dr W Schererville (46375) ***(G-12347)***
Speedread Technologies, Indianapolis *Also called Bernard Hasten* ***(G-6467)***
Speedway Cnstr Pdts Corp 260 203-9806
4817 Industrial Rd Fort Wayne (46825) ***(G-4640)***
Speedway LLC 765 827-0321
300 N Central Ave Connersville (47331) ***(G-2071)***
Speedway LLC 317 867-3699
17645 Little Chicago Rd Noblesville (46062) ***(G-11188)***
Speedway LLC 317 838-5479
3066 E Main St Plainfield (46168) ***(G-11644)***
Speedway LLC 219 929-1054
502 Gateway Blvd N Chesterton (46304) ***(G-1631)***
Speedway LLC 317 770-0225
3150 Conner St Noblesville (46060) ***(G-11189)***
Speedway LLC 317 783-6361
5960 S East St Indianapolis (46227) ***(G-7974)***
Speedway Redi Mix Inc 260 496-8877
4820 Industrial Rd Fort Wayne (46825) ***(G-4641)***
Speedway Redi Mix Inc 765 671-1020
1620 W Factory Ave Marion (46952) ***(G-9563)***
Speedway Redi Mix Inc 260 244-7205
400 S Whitley St Columbia City (46725) ***(G-1836)***
Speedway Redi Mix Inc 260 356-5600
1217 W Park Dr Huntington (46750) ***(G-6250)***
Speedway Redi Mix Inc 260 665-5999
260 E 300 N Angola (46703) ***(G-244)***
Speedway Sand & Gravel Inc 574 893-7355
2896 S 1600 E Silver Lake (46982) ***(G-12680)***
Speedway Superamerica 3303, Noblesville *Also called Speedway LLC* ***(G-11188)***
Speedway Superamerica 3304, Noblesville *Also called Speedway LLC* ***(G-11189)***
Speedway Superamerica 3338, Plainfield *Also called Speedway LLC* ***(G-11644)***
Speedway Superamerica 5522, Chesterton *Also called Speedway LLC* ***(G-1631)***
Speedway Superamerica 7102, Indianapolis *Also called Speedway LLC* ***(G-7974)***
Speedway Superamerica 7556, Connersville *Also called Speedway LLC* ***(G-2071)***
Speer Ron Sawmill & Lumber Co 812 834-5515
5667 Leesville Rd Bedford (47421) ***(G-579)***
Spence/Banks Inc (PA) 812 234-3538
700 N 1st St Terre Haute (47807) ***(G-13341)***
Spencer Cnty Journal-Democrat, Rockport *Also called News Publishing Company LLC* ***(G-12171)***
Spencer County Leader, Ferdinand *Also called Duboisspencer Counties Pubg* ***(G-3848)***
Spencer Evening World (PA) 812 829-2255
114 E Franklin St Spencer (47460) ***(G-13037)***
Spencer Evening World 765 795-4438
1 N Main St Cloverdale (46120) ***(G-1738)***
Spencer Industries Inc (PA) 812 937-4561
902 Buffaloville Rd Dale (47523) ***(G-2333)***
Spencer Logging 812 595-0987
5297 N State Road 39 Scottsburg (47170) ***(G-12382)***
Spencer Machine and Tl Co Inc 812 282-6300
6205 Gheens Mill Rd Jeffersonville (47130) ***(G-8426)***
Spencer Printing Inc 765 288-6111
4404 S Madison St Muncie (47302) ***(G-10566)***
Spensa Technologies Inc 765 588-3592
1281 Win Hentschel Blvd West Lafayette (47906) ***(G-14110)***
Spensatech, West Lafayette *Also called Spensa Technologies Inc* ***(G-14110)***
Sperry & Rice LLC (PA) 765 647-4141
9146 Us Highway 52 Brookville (47012) ***(G-1126)***
Spheros North America Inc (PA) 574 264-2190
22150 Challenger Dr Elkhart (46514) ***(G-3185)***
SPI Binding Co Inc 765 794-4992
610 W South St Darlington (47940) ***(G-2361)***
SPI Industries, South Bend *Also called Quality Molded Products Inc* ***(G-12909)***
Spiceland Wood Products Inc 765 987-8156
609 S Pearl St Spiceland (47385) ***(G-13058)***
Spin Zone, Granger *Also called Sportcrafters Inc* ***(G-5438)***
Spin-Cast Plastics Inc 574 232-8066
3300 N Kenmore St South Bend (46628) ***(G-12949)***
Spindle-Tech Inc 812 926-1114
14434 Goose Run Rd Aurora (47001) ***(G-388)***
Spiral-Fab Inc 812 427-3006
10034 E State Road 156 Vevay (47043) ***(G-13665)***
Spiritbuilding Publishing 765 623-2238
15591 N State Road 9 Summitville (46070) ***(G-13105)***
SPIRITUAL BOOK ASSOCIATES, Notre Dame *Also called Ave Maria Press Inc* ***(G-11303)***
Spitzer Enterprises, Greenfield *Also called Dean Co Inc* ***(G-5520)***
Spitzers Racing Enterprises 317 894-9533
6135 W 400 N Greenfield (46140) ***(G-5577)***
Splendor Boats LLC 260 352-2835
9526 S State Road 15 Silver Lake (46982) ***(G-12681)***
Sport Form Inc 260 589-2200
151 W Main St Berne (46711) ***(G-625)***
Sportcrafters Inc (PA) 574 243-4994
51345 Bittersweet Rd Granger (46530) ***(G-5438)***
Sports Chronicle LLC 317 353-9365
1934 Alvee Cir Indianapolis (46239) ***(G-7975)***
Sports Hotline 765 664-8732
1950 W Westholme Dr Marion (46952) ***(G-9564)***
Sports Licensed Division 508 758-6101
8677 Logo Athletic Ct Indianapolis (46219) ***(G-7976)***
Sports Licensed Division 317 895-7000
8677 Logo Athletic Ct Indianapolis (46219) ***(G-7977)***
Sports Locker Room, Shelbyville *Also called Gd Cox Inc* ***(G-12536)***
Sports Screen Impact 812 926-9355
718 Green Blvd Aurora (47001) ***(G-389)***
Sports Select Usa Inc 317 631-4011
1920 N Shadeland Ave Indianapolis (46219) ***(G-7978)***
Sports Software Inc 812 738-2735
1290 Spencer Ave Corydon (47112) ***(G-2113)***
Sports Unlimited Printed AP 574 772-4239
6 S Cleveland St Knox (46534) ***(G-8583)***
Sportscenter Inc 260 436-6198
5511 Coventry Ln Fort Wayne (46804) ***(G-4642)***
Sportsmania Sales Inc 317 873-5501
260 S First St Ste 4 Zionsville (46077) ***(G-14465)***
Sportsmobile Inc 260 356-5435
250 Court St Huntington (46750) ***(G-6251)***
Spotlight Cybersecurity LLC 805 886-4456
250 Main St Ste 590 Lafayette (47901) ***(G-9001)***
Spotlight LLC 219 616-4421
1300 Academy Rd Culver (46511) ***(G-2326)***
Spotlight On Drama 765 643-7170
3551 W 8th Street Rd Anderson (46011) ***(G-169)***
Spotlight Strategies, Franklin *Also called Xl Graphics Inc* ***(G-4942)***
Spp Inc 812 882-6203
1001 Main St Vincennes (47591) ***(G-13707)***
Spray Sand & Gravel Inc (PA) 812 523-8081
1635 Murray Hill Dr Seymour (47274) ***(G-12493)***
Spray Sand & Gravel Inc 812 522-5417
6492 E State Road 258 Seymour (47274) ***(G-12494)***
Spreuer & Son Inc 260 463-3513
115 E Spring St Lagrange (46761) ***(G-9067)***
Sprigati LLC 219 484-9455
8250 Baring Ave Munster (46321) ***(G-10629)***
Spring Ventures Infovation LLC 317 847-1117
1846 Saratoga Dr Greenwood (46143) ***(G-5750)***
Springhill Wholesale Inc 812 299-2181
1430 E Springhill Dr Terre Haute (47802) ***(G-13342)***
Springs Valley Herald, French Lick *Also called Springs Valley Publishing Co* ***(G-4989)***
Springs Valley Publishing Co 812 936-9630
7303 W County Road 175 S French Lick (47432) ***(G-4989)***
Sprint Spectrum LP 765 983-6991
3721 E Main St Richmond (47374) ***(G-12053)***
Sprunger Engineering, Elkhart *Also called Elkcases Inc* ***(G-2819)***
Sprunger Engineering, Elkhart *Also called Elkhart Cases Inc* ***(G-2823)***
Spry-Clear Ear Inc 219 934-9747
827 W Glen Park Ave Griffith (46319) ***(G-5790)***
Spunlite, Muncie *Also called Muncie Metal Spinning Inc* ***(G-10530)***
Spurlino Mtls Indianapolis LLC 765 339-4055
11528 N Us Highway 231 Linden (47955) ***(G-9305)***
SPX Corporation 812 849-5647
4598 State Road 37 Mitchell (47446) ***(G-10171)***
SPX Corporation 219 879-6561
500 Blaine St Michigan City (46360) ***(G-9846)***
SPX Corporation 704 752-4400
300 Growth Pkwy Angola (46703) ***(G-245)***
Square 1 Designs & Signs 219 552-0079
23316 Shelby Rd Shelby (46377) ***(G-12516)***
Square 1 Dsign Manufacture Inc 866 647-7771
1 Clark Rd Shelbyville (46176) ***(G-12570)***
Square Donuts Inc 812 232-6463
935 Wabash Ave Terre Haute (47807) ***(G-13343)***
Squeeze Play, Muncie *Also called Jeremy Parker* ***(G-10501)***
Sr Petroleum Inc 574 383-5879
15482 Bryanton Ct Granger (46530) ***(G-5439)***

Sram LLC 317 481-1120
  5315 Walt Pl Indianapolis (46254) *(G-7979)*
Srg Global Evansville, Evansville *Also called Srg Global Trim Inc* *(G-3745)*
Srg Global Trim Inc (HQ) 812 473-6200
  601 N Congress Ave Evansville (47715) *(G-3745)*
SRK Filters LLC 765 647-9962
  5010 Beesley Rd Cedar Grove (47016) *(G-1523)*
Srt Prosthetics Orthotics LLC 815 679-6900
  408 E Washington St Butler (46721) *(G-1241)*
Srt Prosthetics Orthotics LLC 847 855-0030
  408 E Washington St Butler (46721) *(G-1242)*
Ss Custom Choppers LLC 260 415-3793
  804 W Wildwood Ave Fort Wayne (46807) *(G-4643)*
SS&c Technologies Inc 812 266-2000
  110 N Fulton Ave Evansville (47710) *(G-3746)*
SSd Control Technology Inc 574 289-5942
  1801 S Main St South Bend (46613) *(G-12950)*
Ssi, Fort Wayne *Also called System Science Institute* *(G-4670)*
SSP Technologies Inc 888 548-4668
  709 Plaza Dr Ste 2 Chesterton (46304) *(G-1632)*
Sssi Inc 219 762-8901
  1865 Willowcreek Rd Portage (46368) *(G-11795)*
Sssi Inc 219 880-0818
  1 N Broadway Gary (46402) *(G-5101)*
Ssw International Inc 219 763-1199
  1111 State Road 149 Burns Harbor (46304) *(G-1220)*
St Augustines Press Inc (PA) 574 291-3500
  17917 Killington Way South Bend (46614) *(G-12951)*
St Clair Group Inc 765 435-3091
  7903 W County Road 1325 N Russellville (46175) *(G-12239)*
St Clair Press 317 612-9100
  1203 E Saint Clair St Indianapolis (46202) *(G-7980)*
St Henry Tile Co Inc 260 589-2880
  155 E Buckeye St Berne (46711) *(G-626)*
St John Sports, Schererville *Also called Locoli Inc* *(G-12332)*
St Louis Group LLC 317 975-3121
  8888 Keystone Xing # 650 Indianapolis (46240) *(G-7981)*
St Meinrad Archabbey (PA) 812 357-6611
  200 Hill Dr Saint Meinrad (47577) *(G-12275)*
St Meinrad Archabbey 812 357-6611
  State Rte 545 Saint Meinrad (47577) *(G-12276)*
St Regis Culvert Inc 317 353-8065
  1101 S Kitley Ave Indianapolis (46203) *(G-7982)*
St Reigs Crystal, Indianapolis *Also called Etching Industries Corporation* *(G-6882)*
ST&I, Mishawaka *Also called Substrate Treatments Lubr Inc* *(G-10137)*
Staab Sheet Metal Inc 317 241-2553
  2720 S Tibbs Ave Ste 1x Indianapolis (46241) *(G-7983)*
Stability America Inc 574 642-3029
  2928 Elder Dr Goshen (46526) *(G-5326)*
Stackman Signs/Graphics Inc 317 784-6120
  5520 S Harding St Indianapolis (46217) *(G-7984)*
Stadry Enclosure Co 812 284-2244
  213 Riverwood Dr Jeffersonville (47130) *(G-8427)*
Stafco, Columbia City *Also called Steel Tank & Fabricating Corp* *(G-1838)*
Stafford Construction Inc 574 287-9696
  111 Cherry St South Bend (46601) *(G-12952)*
Stafford Gravel Inc 260 868-2503
  4225 County Road 79 Butler (46721) *(G-1243)*
Stag Tool 812 876-3281
  3755 W Burma Rd Gosport (47433) *(G-5355)*
Stage Door Graphics 317 398-9011
  207 S Harrison St Shelbyville (46176) *(G-12571)*
Stage Ninja LLC 317 829-1507
  1060 N Capitol Ave E350 Indianapolis (46204) *(G-7985)*
Stahl Equipment Inc 812 925-3341
  718 W Lincoln Ave Chandler (47610) *(G-1554)*
Stahl Welding Inc 765 457-3386
  2610 S Goyer Rd Kokomo (46902) *(G-8699)*
Stainless Steel Kitchens 574 272-2530
  12911 Industrial Park Dr # 3 Granger (46530) *(G-5440)*
Stalcop LLC (PA) 765 436-7926
  1217 W Main St Thorntown (46071) *(G-13378)*
Stalcop Cold US, Thorntown *Also called Stalcop LLC* *(G-13378)*
Stall & Kessler Inc 765 742-1259
  333 Columbia St Lafayette (47901) *(G-9002)*
Stall Kessler's Diamond Center, Lafayette *Also called Stall & Kessler Inc* *(G-9002)*
Stallion Sportswear Inc (PA) 765 584-5097
  117 S Main St Winchester (47394) *(G-14341)*
Stalter Glass Inc 574 825-2225
  400 N Main St Middlebury (46540) *(G-9920)*
Stamets Tool & Engineering 260 925-1382
  510 North St Auburn (46706) *(G-358)*
Stamina Metal Products Inc 574 534-7410
  901 E Madison St Goshen (46528) *(G-5327)*
Stamp N Scrap Ink Corp 219 440-7239
  1043 Sheffield Ave Dyer (46311) *(G-2510)*
Stamp Works 765 962-5201
  121 S 5th St Richmond (47374) *(G-12054)*

Stampcrafter 574 892-5206
  324 Weidner Ave Argos (46501) *(G-277)*
Stamping Plant, Batesville *Also called Batesville Casket Company Inc* *(G-492)*
Stamping Specialty Co Inc 812 829-0760
  State Roads 46 & 43 Spencer (47460) *(G-13038)*
Stamprint Inc 574 233-3900
  2609 S Main St South Bend (46614) *(G-12953)*
Stan Clamme (PA) 765 348-0008
  725 E Water St Hartford City (47348) *(G-5991)*
Stanbinger Flutes Inc 317 784-3012
  5920 S East St Indianapolis (46227) *(G-7986)*
Stanbio Laboratory LP 830 249-0772
  1814 Leer Dr Elkhart (46514) *(G-3186)*
Standard & News, Lagrange *Also called Lagrange Publishing Co Inc* *(G-9053)*
Standard Change-Makers Inc (PA) 317 899-6955
  3130 N Mitthoefer Rd Indianapolis (46235) *(G-7987)*
Standard Change-Makers Inc 317 899-6955
  3130 N Mitthoefer Rd Indianapolis (46235) *(G-7988)*
Standard Coal Lab, Washington *Also called Peabody Midwest Mining LLC* *(G-13997)*
Standard Die Supply of Indiana (PA) 317 236-6200
  927 S Pennsylvania St Indianapolis (46225) *(G-7989)*
Standard Fertilizer Company 812 663-8391
  2006 S County Road 60 Sw Greensburg (47240) *(G-5634)*
Standard For Success LLC 844 737-3825
  10741 S County Road 850 E Cloverdale (46120) *(G-1739)*
Standard Fusee Corporation 765 472-4375
  3157 N 500 W Peru (46970) *(G-11548)*
Standard Glass and Star Glass 574 546-5912
  404 N Bowen Ave Bremen (46506) *(G-1025)*
Standard Industries Inc 812 838-4861
  901 Givens Rd Mount Vernon (47620) *(G-10409)*
Standard Industries Inc 219 872-1111
  505 N Roeske Ave Michigan City (46360) *(G-9847)*
Standard Label Co 574 522-3548
  4200 Wyland Dr Elkhart (46516) *(G-3187)*
Standard Locknut LLC 317 399-2230
  1045 E 169th St Westfield (46074) *(G-14190)*
Standard Motor Products Inc 574 259-6253
  1718 N Home St Mishawaka (46545) *(G-10135)*
Standard Pattern Company Inc 260 456-4870
  2136 Lafayette St Fort Wayne (46803) *(G-4644)*
Standard Plastic Corp 260 824-0214
  850 Decker Dr Bluffton (46714) *(G-893)*
Standish Steel Inc 812 834-5255
  280 Standish Steel Dr Bedford (47421) *(G-580)*
Standout Creations LLC 765 203-9110
  1078 E 500 S Anderson (46013) *(G-170)*
Standout Socks 317 531-6950
  3704 Ontario Cir Indianapolis (46268) *(G-7990)*
Stands Photography 812 723-3922
  792 S Ridgecrest Ln Paoli (47454) *(G-11457)*
Stanger Excavating, Goshen *Also called Colby L Stanger* *(G-5190)*
Stanley Allen 812 752-2720
  1176 Allen St Scottsburg (47170) *(G-12383)*
Stanley Fastening Systems LP 317 398-0761
  501 W New Rd Greenfield (46140) *(G-5578)*
Stanley Oliver Products LLC 260 499-3506
  3545 E 100 N Lagrange (46761) *(G-9068)*
Stanley Security Solutions Inc 317 598-0421
  6161 E 75th St Indianapolis (46250) *(G-7991)*
Stanley Security Solutions Inc 678 533-3846
  6161 E 75th St Indianapolis (46250) *(G-7992)*
Stanley Security Solutions Inc 317 849-2250
  6161 E 75th St Indianapolis (46250) *(G-7993)*
Stanley-Bostitch, Greenfield *Also called Stanley Fastening Systems LP* *(G-5578)*
Stans Sign Design 317 251-3838
  6373 Rucker Rd Indianapolis (46220) *(G-7994)*
Stant USA Corp (HQ) 765 825-3121
  1620 Columbia Ave Connersville (47331) *(G-2072)*
Stant USA Corp 765 825-3121
  1620 Columbia Ave Connersville (47331) *(G-2073)*
Stanton & Associates Inc 574 247-5522
  6910 N Main St Unit 15 Granger (46530) *(G-5441)*
Stapert Tool & Machine Co Inc 317 787-2387
  2958 Carson Ave Indianapolis (46203) *(G-7995)*
Staples Pipe & Muffler (PA) 812 522-3569
  1365 S County Road 650 E Butlerville (47223) *(G-1251)*
Star, Crown Point *Also called Crown Point Shopping News* *(G-2241)*
Star Automation Inc 812 475-9947
  5625 Vogel Rd Ste B Evansville (47715) *(G-3747)*
Star Case Manufacturing Co LLC 219 922-4440
  648 Superior Ave Munster (46321) *(G-10630)*
Star Engineering & Mch Co Inc 260 824-4825
  1717 Lancaster St Bluffton (46714) *(G-894)*
Star Manufacturing LLC 574 329-6042
  53509 Lakefield Dr Elkhart (46514) *(G-3188)*
Star Metal Products 317 631-5902
  2075 S Belmont Ave Indianapolis (46221) *(G-7996)*
Star Nail 765 453-0743
  1500 E Markland Ave Kokomo (46901) *(G-8700)*

(PA)=Parent Co (HQ)=Headquarters (DH)=Div Headquarters

Star Nova US LLC (PA) 269 830-5802
3702 W Sample St South Bend (46619) ***(G-12954)***

Star Packaging Company Inc 317 357-3707
4001 Prospect St Indianapolis (46203) ***(G-7997)***

Star Quality Awards Inc 812 273-1740
322 Crestwood Dr Madison (47250) ***(G-9496)***

Star Technology Inc 260 837-7833
200 Executive Dr Waterloo (46793) ***(G-14024)***

Star Tool & Die Inc 574 264-3815
53088 Faith Ave Elkhart (46514) ***(G-3189)***

Star Water Systems, Kendallville *Also called Flint & Walling Inc* ***(G-8475)***

Star Weld, Rushville *Also called Starkey Welding Inc* ***(G-12235)***

Star-Seal of Tennessee, Evansville *Also called Pavement Coatings Inc* ***(G-3665)***

Starburst Sales, North Judson *Also called American Oak Preserving Co Inc* ***(G-11206)***

Starcraft Accessories, Goshen *Also called Starcraft Corporation* ***(G-5328)***

Starcraft Bus, Goshen *Also called Forest River Inc* ***(G-5219)***

Starcraft Corporation 574 534-7705
2006 Century Dr Goshen (46528) ***(G-5328)***

Starcraft Corporation (HQ) 574 534-7827
1123 S Indiana Ave Goshen (46526) ***(G-5329)***

Starcraft Marine LLC 574 831-2103
68143 Clunette St New Paris (46553) ***(G-10995)***

Starcraft Rv Inc 800 945-4787
903 S Main St Middlebury (46540) ***(G-9921)***

Starglas of Bremen, Bremen *Also called Standard Glass and Star Glass* ***(G-1025)***

Stark Truss Company Inc 219 866-2772
1317 N Owen St Rensselaer (47978) ***(G-11940)***

Starke County Recycling Inc 574 772-2594
3055 S Us Highway 35 Knox (46534) ***(G-8584)***

Starken Printing Co Inc 317 839-6852
131 N Mill St Plainfield (46168) ***(G-11645)***

Starkey Welding Inc 765 932-2005
709 W 1st St Rushville (46173) ***(G-12235)***

Starlight Printing 812 486-3905
3792 N 525 E Montgomery (47558) ***(G-10243)***

Starquest Products, Elkhart *Also called Kinro Manufacturing Inc* ***(G-2971)***

Starquest Products LLC 574 537-0486
2006 Century Dr Goshen (46528) ***(G-5330)***

Startracks Custom Lifts 574 596-5331
1227 W Beardsley Ave Elkhart (46514) ***(G-3190)***

State Beauty Supply 260 755-6361
3123 E State Blvd Fort Wayne (46805) ***(G-4645)***

State Gear Company Inc 317 634-3521
3510 E Raymond St Indianapolis (46203) ***(G-7998)***

State Line Woodworking 260 768-4577
6520 N 675 W Shipshewana (46565) ***(G-12651)***

State Plating, Indianapolis *Also called Wrr Inc* ***(G-8221)***

State Wide Aluminum Inc (HQ) 574 262-2594
3518 County Road 6 E Elkhart (46514) ***(G-3191)***

State Wide Window, Elkhart *Also called State Wide Aluminum Inc* ***(G-3191)***

Stateline Woodturnings LLC 260 768-4507
7005 W 650 N Shipshewana (46565) ***(G-12652)***

States Engineering, Fort Wayne *Also called Chuck Bivens Services Inc* ***(G-4149)***

Station 21 American Drill 219 661-0021
201 N Main St Crown Point (46307) ***(G-2309)***

Statzer C Mark, Wabash *Also called Tru-Cut Machine & Tool Inc* ***(G-13759)***

Ste Inc 260 358-9254
855 N Broadway St Huntington (46750) ***(G-6252)***

Steady Demand LLC 765 404-1763
3200 South St Ste 6 Lafayette (47904) ***(G-9003)***

Stealth Furniture, Spencerville *Also called Deep Three Inc* ***(G-13045)***

Steam Specialties Inc 317 849-5601
11100 Allisonville Rd Fishers (46038) ***(G-3970)***

Steamin Demon Inc 812 288-6754
1041 S Clark Blvd Clarksville (47129) ***(G-1697)***

Stedman Machine Company 812 926-0038
129 Franklin St Aurora (47001) ***(G-390)***

Steel Avenue Inc 517 238-2220
3848 Cottage Ave Mishawaka (46544) ***(G-10136)***

Steel Dynamics Inc 260 248-2600
2601 County Rd 700 E Columbia City (46725) ***(G-1837)***

Steel Dynamics Inc 260 868-8000
4500 County Road 59 Butler (46721) ***(G-1244)***

Steel Dynamics Inc 812 218-1490
5134 Loop Rd Jeffersonville (47130) ***(G-8428)***

Steel Dynamics Inc 317 892-7000
8000 N County Road 225 E Pittsboro (46167) ***(G-11588)***

Steel Dynamics Inc (PA) 260 969-3500
7575 W Jefferson Blvd Fort Wayne (46804) ***(G-4646)***

Steel Grip Inc 765 793-3652
1200 Pearl St Covington (47932) ***(G-2120)***

Steel Grip Inc 765 397-3344
42233 S Kingman Rd Kingman (47952) ***(G-8533)***

Steel Grip Safety Apparel, Kingman *Also called Steel Grip Inc* ***(G-8533)***

Steel Manufacturing, East Chicago *Also called Green Lake Tube LLC* ***(G-2531)***

Steel Parts Corporation 765 675-2191
801 Berryman Pike Tipton (46072) ***(G-13406)***

Steel Parts Manufacturing Inc (HQ) 765 675-2191
801 Berryman Pike Tipton (46072) ***(G-13407)***

Steel Services Inc 317 783-5255
1110 W Thompson Rd Indianapolis (46217) ***(G-7999)***

Steel Storage Inc 574 282-2618
1408 Elwood Ave Ste A South Bend (46628) ***(G-12955)***

Steel Structural Products LLC (HQ) 812 670-4195
1195 Port Rd Jeffersonville (47130) ***(G-8429)***

Steel Tank & Fabricating Corp 260 248-8971
365 S James St Columbia City (46725) ***(G-1838)***

Steel Technologies LLC 502 245-2110
5830 Southport Rd Portage (46368) ***(G-11796)***

Steel Technologies LLC 812 663-9704
1811 N Montgomery Rd Greensburg (47240) ***(G-5635)***

Steel Technologies LLC 765 362-3110
3560 S Nucor Rd Crawfordsville (47933) ***(G-2197)***

Steel Warehouse of Ohio LLC 574 236-5100
2722 Tucker Dr South Bend (46619) ***(G-12956)***

Steel Works Welding Inc 812 268-0334
2768 S County Road 100 W Sullivan (47882) ***(G-13095)***

Steelco Industrial Lubricants 219 462-0333
358 Ruge St Valparaiso (46385) ***(G-13624)***

Steelmaster Machine & Tl Corp 574 825-7670
106 Industrial Pkwy E Middlebury (46540) ***(G-9922)***

Steeltech Partners LLC 812 849-0124
240 S Meridian Rd Mitchell (47446) ***(G-10172)***

Steffy Wood Products Inc 260 665-8016
701 W Mill St Angola (46703) ***(G-246)***

Steindler Signs 219 733-2551
105 Koselke St Wanatah (46390) ***(G-13825)***

Steiner Enterprises Inc 765 429-6409
3532 Coleman Ct Ste B Lafayette (47905) ***(G-9004)***

Steinkamp Warehouses Inc 812 683-3860
1000 N Main St Huntingburg (47542) ***(G-6179)***

Steinway Piano Company Inc (HQ) 574 522-1675
600 Industrial Pkwy Elkhart (46516) ***(G-3192)***

Stella Jones 812 232-2316
2901 Ohio Blvd Terre Haute (47803) ***(G-13344)***

Stella-Jones Corporation 812 789-5331
3818 S County Road 50 E Winslow (47598) ***(G-14360)***

Stello Products Inc 812 829-2246
840 W Hillside Ave Spencer (47460) ***(G-13039)***

Stemwood Corp 812 945-6646
2710 Grant Line Rd New Albany (47150) ***(G-10866)***

Stemwood Manufacturing LLC 812 945-6646
2710 Grant Line Rd New Albany (47150) ***(G-10867)***

Stenidy Industries Inc 317 873-5343
10305 Cottonwood Ct Zionsville (46077) ***(G-14466)***

Stenno Carbon Co 317 890-8710
1410 S Post Rd Ste 100 Indianapolis (46239) ***(G-8000)***

Stensland Engines Inc 260 623-6859
4933 Morgan Rd Monroeville (46773) ***(G-10200)***

Stephen G Morrow Inc 812 876-7837
2632 Schooling Rd Spencer (47460) ***(G-13040)***

Stephen Libs Candy Co Inc 812 473-0048
6225 Vogel Rd Evansville (47715) ***(G-3748)***

Stephen Libs Finer Chocolate, Evansville *Also called Stephen Libs Candy Co Inc* ***(G-3748)***

Stephens Fabrication Inc 765 459-9770
1817 W Defenbaugh St Kokomo (46902) ***(G-8701)***

Stephens Machine Inc (PA) 765 459-4017
1600 Dodge St Kokomo (46902) ***(G-8702)***

Stephens Machine Inc 765 459-9770
1801 S Berkley Rd Kokomo (46902) ***(G-8703)***

Stephens Woodworking 812 487-2818
5928 Bonnell Rd Guilford (47022) ***(G-5799)***

Stephenson Block Inc 574 264-6660
2211 Grant St Elkhart (46514) ***(G-3193)***

Steritech-Usa Inc 260 745-7272
314 E Wallace St Fort Wayne (46803) ***(G-4647)***

Sterling Berry Corporation 812 424-2904
101 Oakley St Evansville (47710) ***(G-3749)***

Sterling Boiler and Mech LLC (PA) 812 479-5447
1420 Kimber Ln Evansville (47715) ***(G-3750)***

Sterling Electric Inc (PA) 317 872-0471
7997 Allison Ave Indianapolis (46268) ***(G-8001)***

Sterling Electric Inc 317 872-0471
7973 Allison Ave Indianapolis (46268) ***(G-8002)***

Sterling Fluid Systems USA LLC (HQ) 317 925-9661
2005 Dr Mrtn Lthr Kng Jr Indianapolis (46202) ***(G-8003)***

Sterling Formulations LLC 317 490-0823
1402 S Nor St Shelbyville (46176) ***(G-12572)***

Sterling Industries Inc 812 376-6560
4015 N Long Rd Columbus (47203) ***(G-2016)***

Sterling Machine Co Inc 219 374-9360
10501 W 133rd Ave Lot 6 Cedar Lake (46303) ***(G-1534)***

Sterling Manufacturing LLC 260 451-9760
144 E Collins Rd Fort Wayne (46825) ***(G-4648)***

Sterling Sales and Engineering 765 376-0454
324 S Sterling Ave Veedersburg (47987) ***(G-13646)***

Sternberg Inc 812 867-0077
8950 N Kentucky Ave Evansville (47725) ***(G-3751)***

848 2018 Harris Indiana Industrial Directory (G-0000) Company's Geographic Section entry number

Sternberg International Isuzu, Evansville *Also called Sternberg Inc* ***(G-3751)***
Sterno Delivery, La Porte *Also called Sevenoks Inc* ***(G-8818)***
Steuben County Parks, Angola *Also called County of Steuben* ***(G-205)***
Steuben Fabg & Engrg Inc....260 665-3001
2797 Woodhull Dr Angola (46703) ***(G-247)***
Steve Mitchell....574 831-4848
69420 County Road 27 New Paris (46553) ***(G-10996)***
Steve Reiff Inc (PA)....260 723-4360
5650 W 800 S South Whitley (46787) ***(G-13005)***
Steve Schmidt Racing Engines....317 898-1831
8560 E 30th St Indianapolis (46219) ***(G-8004)***
Steve's Automotive Center, Spencer *Also called Stephen G Morrow Inc* ***(G-13040)***
Steven A Williams....812 664-3405
2922 Teakwood Landing Dr Sellersburg (47172) ***(G-12419)***
Steven Block....765 749-5394
7805 N Tanglewood Ln Muncie (47304) ***(G-10567)***
Stevens Ironworks Inc....219 987-6332
6852 Mercedes Ln Demotte (46310) ***(G-2448)***
Steves Cabinets & More....765 296-9419
934 S 750 E Colburn (47905) ***(G-1754)***
Steves Machining & Rework....317 500-4627
1299 Paris Dr Franklin (46131) ***(G-4934)***
Steves Pallets....260 856-2047
3868 N 1025 W Cromwell (46732) ***(G-2211)***
Steves Pallets Inc....574 457-3620
12661 N Pleasant Grove Rd Syracuse (46567) ***(G-13144)***
Stewart Graphics Inc (PA)....812 283-0455
1419 Fabricon Blvd Jeffersonville (47130) ***(G-8430)***
Stewart Trucking, Muncie *Also called Fred Jay Stewart* ***(G-10474)***
Stewart Warner South Wind....812 547-7071
2445 Directors Row Ste G Indianapolis (46241) ***(G-8005)***
Stfrancis Mdwest Hart Vlve Ctr....877 788-2583
5330 E Stop 11 Rd Indianapolis (46237) ***(G-8006)***
Stickle Steam Specialties Co....317 636-6563
2215 Valley Ave Indianapolis (46218) ***(G-8007)***
Stien Designs & Graphics Inc....260 347-9136
106 S Main St Kendallville (46755) ***(G-8511)***
Stiffler Handy Product, Indianapolis *Also called Alexander Screw Products Inc* ***(G-6362)***
Stillions Saw Mill....812 824-6542
7208 S Rockport Rd Bloomington (47403) ***(G-832)***
Stillions Sawmill, Bloomington *Also called Stillions Saw Mill* ***(G-832)***
Stines Printing....260 356-5994
549 Warren St Huntington (46750) ***(G-6253)***
Stingel Enterprises Inc....812 883-0054
1002 Webb St Salem (47167) ***(G-12306)***
Stitch N Frame....260 478-1301
4220 Bluffton Rd Fort Wayne (46809) ***(G-4649)***
Stitch N Time, Seymour *Also called Lloyd & Mona Sulivan* ***(G-12467)***
Stlogics, Indianapolis *Also called Sahasra Technologies Corp* ***(G-7887)***
Sto-Away Power Crane Inc....219 942-9797
9306 Grand Blvd Crown Point (46307) ***(G-2310)***
Stock 420, Fort Wayne *Also called Stock Building Supply LLC* ***(G-4650)***
Stock Building Supply LLC....260 490-0616
2219 Contractors Way Fort Wayne (46818) ***(G-4650)***
Stoffel Seals Corporation (HQ)....845 353-3800
409 Hoosier Dr Angola (46703) ***(G-248)***
Stogdill Sports....812 524-7081
1244 Hickory Hill Rd Seymour (47274) ***(G-12495)***
Stolle Tool Inc....765 935-5185
4693 Webster Rd Richmond (47374) ***(G-12055)***
Stolls Woodworking LLC....812 486-5117
8779 N 1025 E Odon (47562) ***(G-11342)***
Stolz Structural Inc....812 983-4720
7735 Saint Johns Rd Elberfeld (47613) ***(G-2638)***
Stone Artisans Ltd....317 362-0107
7952 Zionsville Rd Indianapolis (46268) ***(G-8008)***
Stone Center of Indiana LLC (PA)....317 849-9100
5272 E 65th St Indianapolis (46220) ***(G-8009)***
Stone City Ironworks Inc....812 279-3023
1771 Us Highway 50 E Bedford (47421) ***(G-581)***
Stone City Products Inc....812 275-3373
1206 7th St Bedford (47421) ***(G-582)***
Stone Coal Services LLC....812 455-8215
2200 E Boonvle Nw Harmony Evansville (47725) ***(G-3752)***
Stone Custom Drum LLC....260 403-7519
2701 S Coliseum Blvd Fort Wayne (46803) ***(G-4651)***
Stone Industrial Division, Indianapolis *Also called Precision Products Group Inc* ***(G-6277)***
Stone Industrial Inc....301 474-3100
1430 Progress Rd Fort Wayne (46808) ***(G-4652)***
Stone Quary....574 936-2975
10988 11th Rd Plymouth (46563) ***(G-11725)***
Stone Quary (PA)....765 473-5578
350 N 150 W Peru (46970) ***(G-11549)***
Stone Sand & Concrete Sales, Tell City *Also called Mulzer Crushed Stone Inc* ***(G-13168)***
Stone Street Quarries Inc....260 639-6511
5536 Hoagland Rd Hoagland (46745) ***(G-6067)***
Stonehenge Concrete & Gravel....260 726-8282
1125 W Water St Portland (47371) ***(G-11848)***
Stoneware 3....812 696-2679
830a S Charles St Farmersburg (47850) ***(G-3838)***
Stoney Acres Woodworking LLC....260 768-4367
2685 S 1000 W Shipshewana (46565) ***(G-12653)***
Stoney Creek Wash Machine Shop....574 642-1155
66365 E County Line Rd Millersburg (46543) ***(G-9974)***
Stoney Creek Winery....574 642-4454
10315 County Road 146 Millersburg (46543) ***(G-9975)***
Stoneybrook Wood Products, West Harrison *Also called Shelby Products Corporation* ***(G-14043)***
Stop & Shred....260 483-6200
5325 Industrial Rd Ste B Fort Wayne (46825) ***(G-4653)***
Storageworks Inc....317 577-3511
12000 Exit 5 Pkwy Fishers (46037) ***(G-3971)***
Stored Energy Solutions Inc....574 457-2199
3619 W 73rd St Anderson (46011) ***(G-171)***
Stork News Northwest Indiana....219 405-0499
1541 Duffer Dr Chesterton (46304) ***(G-1633)***
Stork News Northwest Indiana....219 808-5221
2880 Tulip Ln Hobart (46342) ***(G-6097)***
Storm Graphics Inc....812 402-5202
4707 Bayard Park Dr Evansville (47714) ***(G-3753)***
Storm Trailers, Elkhart *Also called H & A Products Inc* ***(G-2902)***
Stotlar Hill LLC....260 497-0808
4723 E Washington Blvd Fort Wayne (46803) ***(G-4654)***
Stout Plastic Weld....219 926-7622
425 S 15th St Chesterton (46304) ***(G-1634)***
Strahman Holdings Inc (HQ)....317 818-5030
10201 N Illinois St # 200 Indianapolis (46290) ***(G-6281)***
Stranco Inc....219 874-5221
1306 W Us Highway 20 Michigan City (46360) ***(G-9848)***
Strand Diagnostics LLC....317 455-2100
5770 Decatur Blvd Ste A Indianapolis (46241) ***(G-8010)***
Strataflo Products Inc....260 482-4366
2010 Lakeview Dr Fort Wayne (46808) ***(G-4655)***
Strategic Mfg & Sup Inc....574 643-1050
59661 Moonbeam Ct South Bend (46614) ***(G-12957)***
Strategic Talent LLC....317 489-4000
3502 Woodview Trce Indianapolis (46268) ***(G-8011)***
Stratikore....574 807-0028
1714 E Lincolnway La Porte (46350) ***(G-8824)***
Strauss Bakeries Inc (PA)....574 293-9027
228 W High St Elkhart (46516) ***(G-3194)***
Strauss Veal Feeds Inc (PA)....260 982-8611
600 Strauss Provimi Rd North Manchester (46962) ***(G-11245)***
Strawtown Pottery & Antiques....317 984-5080
12738 Strawtown Ave Noblesville (46060) ***(G-11190)***
Stream Tek LLC....260 441-9300
4520 Ellenwood Dr Fort Wayne (46806) ***(G-4656)***
Streamside Woodshop LLC....260 768-7887
2275 N 925 W Shipshewana (46565) ***(G-12654)***
Street Department, Fort Wayne *Also called City of Fort Wayne* ***(G-4152)***
Streetscape Products Limited, Greensburg *Also called Hh Rellim Inc* ***(G-5609)***
Strescore Inc....574 233-1117
24445 State Road 23 South Bend (46614) ***(G-12958)***
Strick Corporation....260 692-6121
301 N Polk St Monroe (46772) ***(G-10185)***
Strick Trailers LLC....260 692-6121
301 N Polk St Monroe (46772) ***(G-10186)***
Stritto Sign Art Company....317 356-2126
1401 N Sherman Dr Indianapolis (46201) ***(G-8012)***
Stroh Fixit Shop, Stroh *Also called Hayward & Sams LLP* ***(G-13077)***
Strohbeck Cabinet Install....812 923-5013
4339 Country View Dr Floyds Knobs (47119) ***(G-4019)***
Structural LLC....317 713-7500
54 Monument Cir Indianapolis (46204) ***(G-8013)***
Structural Composites Ind Inc....260 894-4083
1118 Gerber St Ligonier (46767) ***(G-9296)***
Structural Iron & Fab Inc....260 758-2273
480 W Scott St Markle (46770) ***(G-9582)***
Structural Source....260 489-0035
1510 Holliston Trl Fort Wayne (46825) ***(G-4657)***
Stuart Integrated Systems, Fort Wayne *Also called Stuart Manufacturing Inc* ***(G-4658)***
Stuart Manufacturing Inc....260 403-2003
1830 Wayne Trce Unit 407 Fort Wayne (46803) ***(G-4658)***
Studio A Advertising, Mishawaka *Also called Rick Singleton* ***(G-10117)***
Studio Indiana....812 332-5073
430 N Sewell Rd Bloomington (47408) ***(G-833)***
Studio Printers....574 772-0900
1202 S Heaton St Knox (46534) ***(G-8585)***
Stueben, Fort Wayne *Also called Hamilton News Inc* ***(G-4315)***
Stulls Machining Center Inc....765 942-2717
209 E College St Ladoga (47954) ***(G-8842)***
Stulls Mch & Fabrication Inc....765 942-2717
213 E Locust St Ladoga (47954) ***(G-8843)***
Stumlers Machine Inc....812 944-2467
222 E 4th St New Albany (47150) ***(G-10868)***
Stump Home Specialties Mfg Inc....574 291-0050
2220 S Main St South Bend (46613) ***(G-12959)***

ALPHABETIC

Stump Printing Co Inc 260 723-5171
  101 Carroll Rd South Whitley (46787) *(G-13006)*

Stump's, South Whitley *Also called Stump Printing Co Inc (G-13006)*

Sturm Heat Treating Inc 317 357-2368
  1110 S Drexel Ave Indianapolis (46203) *(G-8014)*

Stutz Products Corp 765 348-2510
  606 S Walnut St Hartford City (47348) *(G-5992)*

Styled Rite Company Inc 219 931-9844
  1500 Polk St Gary (46407) *(G-5102)*

Styled-Rite, Gary *Also called Trim-A-Seal of Indiana Inc (G-5109)*

Styrene Solutions LLC 574 876-4610
  115 E Windsor Ave Elkhart (46514) *(G-3195)*

Substrate Treatments Lubr Inc 574 258-0904
  1309 S Byrkit Ave Mishawaka (46544) *(G-10137)*

Suburban Manufacturing Company 574 294-5681
  1136 Verdant St Elkhart (46516) *(G-3196)*

Success Entrmt Group Intl Inc 260 490-9990
  215 N Jefferson St Ossian (46777) *(G-11409)*

Success Holding Group Corp USA 260 490-9990
  215 N Jefferson St Ossian (46777) *(G-11410)*

Success Holding Group Intl Inc 260 450-1982
  215 N Jefferson St Ossian (46777) *(G-11411)*

Sues Custom Shirts 812 535-4429
  4932 N Orchard Pl Sandford (47885) *(G-12311)*

Suez Wts Usa Inc 219 397-0554
  3210 Watling St East Chicago (46312) *(G-2569)*

Sugar Abd Bruno, Indianapolis *Also called Progressive Design Apparel Inc (G-7775)*

Sugar Coded Software LLC 858 652-0797
  16743 Ashley Blvd Apt C Westfield (46074) *(G-14191)*

Sugar Creek Candies Inc 765 681-1607
  1688 W Hoosier Blvd Peru (46970) *(G-11550)*

Sugar Creek Fabricators Inc 765 361-0891
  503 W 300 N Crawfordsville (47933) *(G-2198)*

Sugar Creek Gravel & Stone 765 362-1646
  1400 Ladoga Rd Crawfordsville (47933) *(G-2199)*

Sugar Spice Cupcake Event Plg 260 610-5103
  443 Pasadena Dr Fort Wayne (46807) *(G-4659)*

Sugar Tree Incorporated 260 417-3362
  9185 Lima Rd Fort Wayne (46818) *(G-4660)*

Sugarcube Systems Inc 765 543-6709
  2746 Margesson Xing Lafayette (47909) *(G-9005)*

Sugarpaste 574 276-8703
  2211 S Michigan St South Bend (46613) *(G-12960)*

Suggs Custom Design Solutions 574 549-2174
  336 W Garfield Ave Elkhart (46516) *(G-3197)*

Suiza Dairy Group LLC 260 355-2273
  1019 Flaxmill Rd Huntington (46750) *(G-6254)*

Suiza Dairy Group LLC 260 724-2136
  400 Chamber Dr Decatur (46733) *(G-2407)*

Suke Inc 219 689-0321
  2903 Acorn Ct Crown Point (46307) *(G-2311)*

Sullair LLC (HQ) 219 879-5451
  3700 E Michigan Blvd Michigan City (46360) *(G-9849)*

Sullivan Daily Times, Sullivan *Also called Pierce Oil Co Inc (G-13090)*

Sullivan Engineered Services 812 294-1724
  316 Mount Zion Rd Henryville (47126) *(G-6033)*

Sullivan Group Inc 574 773-2108
  302 Dal Mar Way Nappanee (46550) *(G-10707)*

Sullivan IMI 812 268-3306
  939 S Section St Sullivan (47882) *(G-13096)*

Sullivan-Palatek Inc 219 874-2497
  1201 W Us Highway 20 Michigan City (46360) *(G-9850)*

Sumco LLC 317 241-7600
  1351 S Girls School Rd Indianapolis (46231) *(G-8015)*

Sumitomo Electric Carbide Inc 317 859-1601
  595 S Emerson Ave Greenwood (46143) *(G-5751)*

Summerlot Engineered Pdts Inc 812 466-7266
  11655 N Us Highway 41 Rosedale (47874) *(G-12206)*

Summit LLC 574 287-7468
  201 N Main St South Bend (46601) *(G-12961)*

Summit Brands, Fort Wayne *Also called Iron Out Inc (G-4383)*

Summit Brands 260 483-2519
  3404 Conestoga Dr Fort Wayne (46808) *(G-4661)*

Summit Coaches 260 489-3556
  6215 Commodity Ct Fort Wayne (46818) *(G-4662)*

Summit Foundry Systems Inc 260 749-7740
  2100 Wayne Haven St Fort Wayne (46803) *(G-4663)*

Summit Industrial Technologies 260 494-3461
  1400 Arprt N Off Park Ste Fort Wayne (46825) *(G-4664)*

Summit Manufacturing Corp 317 823-2848
  10586 E 59th St Indianapolis (46236) *(G-8016)*

Summit Manufacturing Corp 260 428-2600
  2320 Meyer Rd Fort Wayne (46803) *(G-4665)*

Summit Mfg & Machining 574 546-4571
  723 High Rd Bremen (46506) *(G-1026)*

Summit Seating Inc 574 264-9636
  2601 Northland Dr Elkhart (46514) *(G-3198)*

Summit/Ems Corporation 574 722-1317
  1509 Woodlawn Ave Logansport (46947) *(G-9366)*

Sun Chemical Corporation 765 659-6000
  2642 W State Road 28 Frankfort (46041) *(G-4854)*

Sun Chemical Corporation 812 235-8031
  1350 N Fruitridge Ave Terre Haute (47804) *(G-13345)*

Sun Control Center LLC 260 490-9902
  6032 Highview Dr Ste E Fort Wayne (46818) *(G-4666)*

Sun Energy Group LLC 812 683-1178
  2740 W 1100s Huntingburg (47542) *(G-6180)*

Sun Engineering Inc 219 962-1191
  950 Marquette Rd Lake Station (46405) *(G-9078)*

Sun King Brewing Company LLC 317 602-3702
  135 N College Ave Indianapolis (46202) *(G-8017)*

Sun Polymers International Inc 317 834-6410
  100 Sun Polymers Dr Mooresville (46158) *(G-10342)*

Sun Power Technologies LLC 317 399-8113
  17406 Tiller Ct Ste 900 Westfield (46074) *(G-14192)*

Sun Rise Metal Shop 260 463-4026
  3070 W 350 S Topeka (46571) *(G-13430)*

Suncoast Coffee Inc (PA) 317 251-3198
  1114 E 52nd St Indianapolis (46205) *(G-8018)*

Sundae's, Indianapolis *Also called Buckner Inc (G-6520)*

Sundance Enterprises Inc 317 856-9780
  3902 Hanna Cir Ste E Indianapolis (46241) *(G-8019)*

Sundance Solutions, Indianapolis *Also called Sundance Enterprises Inc (G-8019)*

Sunequinox, Harlan *Also called Our Country Home Entps Inc (G-5974)*

Sunman Engineering Inc 812 623-4072
  131 W Washington St Sunman (47041) *(G-13119)*

Sunnybrook Rv, Middlebury *Also called Winnebago of Indiana LLC (G-9926)*

Sunpress South, Morgantown *Also called All 4u Printing LLC (G-10347)*

Sunright America Inc 812 342-3430
  6205 S International Dr Columbus (47201) *(G-2017)*

Sunrise Coal LLC (PA) 812 299-2800
  1183 E Canvasback Dr Terre Haute (47802) *(G-13346)*

Sunrise Coal LLC 812 398-2200
  1466 E State Road 58 Carlisle (47838) *(G-1297)*

Sunrise Energy LLC 812 886-9990
  1290 N State Road 67 Vincennes (47591) *(G-13708)*

Sunyata Software LLC 310 923-1821
  8415 Autumn Leaf Ct Apt E Indianapolis (46268) *(G-8020)*

Super Blend Inc 260 463-7486
  105 S 500 E Lagrange (46761) *(G-9069)*

Super Car Wash of Warsaw 574 269-6922
  2223 E Center St Warsaw (46580) *(G-13943)*

Super Hicksgas Fuel 219 345-2656
  5768 E State Road 10 Demotte (46310) *(G-2449)*

Super Seal Inc 765 639-4993
  548 E 1800 N Summitville (46070) *(G-13106)*

Superb Horticulture LLC 800 567-8264
  2811 Us Highway 31 Plymouth (46563) *(G-11726)*

Superb Tooling Inc 812 367-2102
  250 Scenic Industrial Dr Ferdinand (47532) *(G-3863)*

Superioir Essex, Franklin *Also called Essex Group Inc (G-4885)*

Superior AG Resources Coop Inc 812 724-4455
  504 S 2nd St Owensville (47665) *(G-11430)*

Superior Aluminum Alloys LLC 260 749-7599
  14214 Edgerton Rd New Haven (46774) *(G-10959)*

Superior Canopy Corporation 260 488-4065
  2435 E Bellefontaine Rd Hamilton (46742) *(G-5829)*

Superior Coatings Inc 574 546-0591
  1730 W Dewey St Bremen (46506) *(G-1027)*

Superior Distribution 618 242-5560
  2570 N Shadeland Ave Indianapolis (46219) *(G-8021)*

Superior Electric Nwi LLC 219 696-0717
  8900 W 156th Ave Lowell (46356) *(G-9423)*

Superior Equipment & Mfg 260 925-0152
  717 Lakeshore Dr Auburn (46706) *(G-359)*

Superior Essex, Fort Wayne *Also called Essex Group Inc (G-4243)*

Superior Essex, Fort Wayne *Also called Essex Group Inc (G-4245)*

Superior Fabrication Inc 812 649-2630
  1654 S County Road 200 W Rockport (47635) *(G-12173)*

Superior Fiberglass & Resins, Elkhart *Also called Superior Oil Company Inc (G-3199)*

Superior Hardwoods, Montezuma *Also called Timberland Resources Inc (G-10211)*

Superior Ice Co Inc 812 847-4312
  492 A St Nw Linton (47441) *(G-9314)*

Superior Laminating Inc 574 361-7266
  60894 County Road 19 Goshen (46528) *(G-5331)*

Superior Layout 812 371-1709
  1417 Chestnut St Columbus (47201) *(G-2018)*

Superior Machine & Tool Co 260 493-4517
  6911 Trafalgar Dr Fort Wayne (46803) *(G-4667)*

Superior Machine Inc 574 654-8243
  33721 Early Rd New Carlisle (46552) *(G-10887)*

Superior Manufacturing Div Mag 260 456-3596
  2015 S Calhoun St Fort Wayne (46802) *(G-4668)*

Superior Mattress Inc 812 422-5761
  213 W Division St Ste C Evansville (47710) *(G-3754)*

Superior Metal Tech LLC 317 897-9850
  9850 E 30th St Indianapolis (46229) *(G-8022)*

Superior Mfg Inc 812 983-9900
11333 Elberfeld Rd Elberfeld (47613) *(G-2639)*

Superior Oil Company Inc 574 264-0161
1030 All Pro Dr Elkhart (46514) *(G-3199)*

Superior Oprting Solutions Inc 765 993-4094
4307 National Rd W Richmond (47374) *(G-12056)*

Superior Piece Parts Inc 574 277-4236
54015 Fir Rd Mishawaka (46545) *(G-10138)*

Superior Precision Inc 260 229-3871
602 Hathaway Dr South Whitley (46787) *(G-13007)*

Superior Print Inc 812 246-6311
840 S Indiana Ave Sellersburg (47172) *(G-12420)*

Superior Sample Co Inc 260 894-3136
520 Gerber St Ligonier (46767) *(G-9297)*

Superior Satellite, Plainfield Also called Digital Evolution *(G-11604)*

Superior Seating Inc 574 389-9011
21468 C St Elkhart (46516) *(G-3200)*

Superior Tool & Die Company (PA) 574 293-2591
2325 S Nappanee St Elkhart (46517) *(G-3201)*

Superior Truss & Components 574 457-8925
72298 State Road 13 Syracuse (46567) *(G-13145)*

Superior Truss & Panel Inc 708 339-1200
7592 Melton Rd Gary (46403) *(G-5103)*

Superior Vault Co Inc (PA) 812 256-5545
500 Pike St Charlestown (47111) *(G-1582)*

Superior Vault Co Inc 812 539-1830
714 Green Blvd Aurora (47001) *(G-391)*

Superior Veneer & Plywood LLC 812 941-8850
1819 Dewey St New Albany (47150) *(G-10869)*

Superior Wood Products, Warsaw Also called Rbk Development Inc *(G-13934)*

Superior Woodcrafts LLC 260 357-3743
1111 S Franklin St Garrett (46738) *(G-5023)*

Supersweet Farm Service, Nappanee Also called AG Processing A Cooperative *(G-10644)*

Supersweet Farm Service, Goshen Also called AG Processing A Cooperative *(G-5168)*

Supper Wash 574 269-2233
2233 E Center St Warsaw (46580) *(G-13944)*

Suppress TEC LLC 812 453-5813
7599 Saint Johns Rd Elberfeld (47613) *(G-2640)*

Supreme Corporation (HQ) 574 642-4888
2581 Kercher Rd Goshen (46528) *(G-5332)*

Supreme Corporation 574 642-4888
2581 Kercher Rd Goshen (46528) *(G-5333)*

Supreme Corporation 260 894-9191
1491 Gerber St Ligonier (46767) *(G-9298)*

Supreme Corporation 574 642-4888
2581 Kercher Rd Goshen (46528) *(G-5334)*

Supreme Corporation Georgia 574 228-4130
2581 Kercher Rd Goshen (46528) *(G-5335)*

Supreme Industries Inc (HQ) 574 642-3070
2581 Kercher Rd Goshen (46528) *(G-5336)*

Supreme Signs 219 384-0198
265 Springhill Dr Valparaiso (46385) *(G-13625)*

Supremex Midwest Inc (PA) 317 253-4321
5331 N Tacoma Ave Indianapolis (46220) *(G-8023)*

Supremex Midwest Inc 317 253-4321
5331 N Tacoma Ave Indianapolis (46220) *(G-8024)*

Sur-Loc Inc 260 495-4065
501 E Swager St Fremont (46737) *(G-4975)*

Sure-Flo Seamless Gutters Inc 260 622-4372
9192 N 750 E Ossian (46777) *(G-11412)*

Surestep LLC 574 233-3352
17530 Dugdale Dr South Bend (46635) *(G-12962)*

Surface Enhancement 574 269-1366
125 W 250 N Warsaw (46582) *(G-13945)*

Surplus Store and Exchange 765 447-0200
1650 Main St Lafayette (47904) *(G-9006)*

SUs Cast Products Inc 574 753-4111
1825 W Market St Logansport (46947) *(G-9367)*

Sushiya-US 260 444-4263
14328 Brafferton Pkwy Fort Wayne (46814) *(G-4669)*

Susies Sandbar 574 269-5355
1360 W Center St Warsaw (46580) *(G-13946)*

Sutter Home Winery 317 848-3003
1503 Cool Creek Dr Carmel (46033) *(G-1486)*

Suzuki Garphyttan Corp 574 232-8800
4404 Nimtz Pkwy South Bend (46628) *(G-12963)*

Swager Communications Inc 260 495-2515
501 E Swager St Fremont (46737) *(G-4976)*

Swags Welding Services LLC 260 417-7510
6650 E Mcguire Rd Churubusco (46723) *(G-1657)*

Swan Real Estate Mgmt Inc 765 664-1478
815 N Western Ave Marion (46952) *(G-9565)*

Swanel Beverage, Hammond Also called Swanel Inc *(G-5947)*

Swanel Inc 219 932-7676
6044 Erie Ave Hammond (46320) *(G-5947)*

Swansons Service Center 574 858-9406
U S 30 County Road 650 W Atwood (46502) *(G-310)*

Swarovski North America Ltd 317 841-0037
6020 E 82nd St Ste 430 Indianapolis (46250) *(G-8025)*

Swartzentruber Sawmill 812 486-3350
5912 N 900 E Montgomery (47558) *(G-10244)*

Swartzndrber Hrdwood Creat LLC 574 534-2502
17229 County Road 18 Goshen (46528) *(G-5337)*

Sweet Art Gallery, Indianapolis Also called Sweet Art Inc *(G-8026)*

Sweet Art Inc 317 787-3647
8320 Brookville Rd Ste P Indianapolis (46239) *(G-8026)*

Sweet LLC 812 455-0886
4523 Erinwood Ct Evansville (47725) *(G-3755)*

Sweet N Sassy Cupcakes 317 652-6132
8440 Coppel Ln Indianapolis (46259) *(G-8027)*

Sweet Properties LLC 812 283-8367
347 Spring St Jeffersonville (47130) *(G-8431)*

Sweet Things Candy & Gifts, Indianapolis Also called Sweet Things Inc *(G-8028)*

Sweet Things Inc (PA) 317 872-8720
2288 W 86th St Indianapolis (46260) *(G-8028)*

Swi 812 342-2409
3475 W International Ct Columbus (47201) *(G-2019)*

Swift Fuels LLC 765 464-8336
1435 Win Hentschel Blvd # 205 West Lafayette (47906) *(G-14111)*

Swifttrip LLC 812 206-5200
702 N Shore Dr Jeffersonville (47130) *(G-8432)*

Swings N Things 260 336-8811
4755 W Us Highway 20 Lagrange (46761) *(G-9070)*

Swiss Alps Printing & Off Sups, Vevay Also called Swiss Alps Printing Inc *(G-13666)*

Swiss Alps Printing Inc 812 427-3844
108 W Pike St Vevay (47043) *(G-13666)*

Swiss Caps, Patriot Also called Switzerland Hills Inc *(G-11469)*

Swiss Labs Machine & Engrg Inc 317 346-6190
2854 N Graham Rd Franklin (46131) *(G-4935)*

Swiss Metal Spinning Co 260 692-1401
2301 W 200 S Monroe (46772) *(G-10187)*

Swiss Perfection LLC 574 457-4457
100 S Huntington St Syracuse (46567) *(G-13146)*

Swiss Woodworking & Sales 260 849-9669
371 W 500 S Berne (46711) *(G-627)*

Swissland Milk Company Inc 260 589-2761
818 Welty St Berne (46711) *(G-628)*

Switzer Buildings, Bremen Also called Bremen Composites LLC *(G-986)*

Switzerland Hills Inc 812 594-2810
19091 Us Highway 250 Patriot (47038) *(G-11469)*

Sx4 .... 812 967-2502
3363 E Wetzel Rd Palmyra (47164) *(G-11441)*

Sycamore Coal Inc 812 491-4000
1183 E Canvasback Dr Terre Haute (47802) *(G-13347)*

Sycamore Enterprises Inc 812 491-0901
6534 Toney Ln Evansville (47715) *(G-3756)*

Sycamore Printing Center, Avon Also called Sycamore Services Inc *(G-468)*

Sycamore Services Inc 317 745-5456
77 Park Place Blvd Avon (46123) *(G-468)*

Sycamore Winery LLC 812 243-0565
3980 N Gosnell Pl West Terre Haute (47885) *(G-14130)*

Syltech Experimental 765 489-1777
13931 Clyde Oler Rd Hagerstown (47346) *(G-5813)*

Sylvan Marine Inc (PA) 574 831-2950
68143 Clunette St New Paris (46553) *(G-10997)*

Sylvia Kay Hartley (PA) 317 984-3424
103 E Main St Arcadia (46030) *(G-270)*

Symantec Corporation 317 575-4010
8888 Keystone Xing # 1300 Indianapolis (46240) *(G-8029)*

Symmetry Medical, Warsaw Also called Ultrexx Inc *(G-13955)*

Symmetry Medical Inc 574 267-8700
486 W 350 N Warsaw (46582) *(G-13947)*

Symmetry Medical Inc (HQ) 574 268-2252
3724 N State Road 15 Warsaw (46582) *(G-13948)*

Symmetry Medical Mfg Inc 574 371-2284
3724 N State Road 15 Warsaw (46582) *(G-13949)*

Symmetry New Bedford RE LLC 574 268-2252
3724 N State Road 15 Warsaw (46582) *(G-13950)*

Syndicate Sales Inc (PA) 765 457-7277
2025 N Wabash Ave Kokomo (46901) *(G-8704)*

Synergy Feeds LLC 260 723-5141
401 N Main St South Whitley (46787) *(G-13008)*

Synergy Software Group Inc 765 229-4003
814 W Oak St Union City (47390) *(G-13461)*

Synermed International Inc 317 896-1565
17408 Tiller Ct Ste 1900 Westfield (46074) *(G-14193)*

Syntag Rfld 317 685-5292
602 N Park Ave Indianapolis (46204) *(G-8030)*

Synthes USA, Warsaw Also called Depuy Synthes Inc *(G-13865)*

Syracuse Glass Inc 574 457-5516
1107 S Huntington St D Syracuse (46567) *(G-13147)*

Syscon International Inc 574 232-3900
1108 High St South Bend (46601) *(G-12964)*

Syscon-Plantstar, South Bend Also called Syscon International Inc *(G-12964)*

Sysgenomics LLC 574 302-5396
51210 Lexingham Dr Granger (46530) *(G-5442)*

Systec Conveyors, Indianapolis Also called Systec Corporation *(G-8031)*

A
L
P
H
A
B
E
T
I
C

Systec Corporation 317 890-9230
   3245 N Mitthoefer Rd Indianapolis (46235) *(G-8031)*

System Science Institute 260 436-6096
   4710 Arden Dr Fl 1 Fort Wayne (46804) *(G-4670)*

System Solutions Inc 317 877-7572
   4 Forest Bay Ln Cicero (46034) *(G-1668)*

Systems & Services of Michiana (PA) 574 273-1111
   3505 W Mcgill St South Bend (46628) *(G-12965)*

Systems & Services of Michiana 574 277-3355
   325 N Dixie Way Ste 300 South Bend (46637) *(G-12966)*

Systems and Services, South Bend *Also called Systems & Services of Michiana (G-12966)*

Systems Contracting Corp 765 361-2991
   4537 S Nucor Rd Crawfordsville (47933) *(G-2200)*

Systems Engineering and Sls Co 260 422-1671
   3805 E Pontiac St Fort Wayne (46803) *(G-4671)*

Syzygy Media Inc 317 509-8987
   12940 Rocky Pointe Rd McCordsville (46055) *(G-9677)*

T & D Printing, New Haven *Also called T N D Printing (G-10960)*

T & D Property Specialist, Winamac *Also called Thomas P Kasten (G-14322)*

T & E Welding Inc 812 324-0140
   10 W Locust St Petersburg (47567) *(G-11570)*

T & G Games Inc 574 297-5455
   4900 N Boxman Pl Monticello (47960) *(G-10284)*

T & H Sweeper Co 765 641-9800
   4134 S Scatterfield Rd Anderson (46013) *(G-172)*

T & J Plating Inc 765 664-9669
   2439 W 11th St Marion (46953) *(G-9566)*

T & L Sharpening Inc 574 583-3868
   2663 S Freeman Rd Monticello (47960) *(G-10285)*

T & L Tool & Die II Co Inc 574 722-6246
   911 Calla St Logansport (46947) *(G-9368)*

T & M Equipment Company Inc (PA) 219 942-2299
   2880 E 83rd Pl Merrillville (46410) *(G-9755)*

T & M Equipment Company Inc 317 293-9255
   6501 Guion Rd Indianapolis (46268) *(G-8032)*

T & M Precision Inc 513 253-2274
   1861 S Us Highway 421 Versailles (47042) *(G-13658)*

T & M Precision Inc (PA) 812 689-5769
   1861 S Us Highway 421 Versailles (47042) *(G-13659)*

T & M Rubber Inc 574 533-3173
   1102 S 10th St Goshen (46526) *(G-5338)*

T & S Engineering LLC 812 969-3860
   34 N Depot St Ste B New Palestine (46163) *(G-10973)*

T & S Equipment Company 260 665-9521
   2999 N Wayne St Angola (46703) *(G-249)*

T & T Tool & Stamping Inc 765 789-4670
   1090 W Walnut St Albany (47320) *(G-13)*

T A T Apparrel and Promotions, Indianapolis *Also called Thoughts Are Things (G-8069)*

T and T Hydraulics Inc 765 548-2355
   7443 S 625 W Rosedale (47874) *(G-12207)*

T B K Tarp Sales & Service, Gary *Also called T K Sales & Service (G-5104)*

T F & T Inc 765 874-1628
   603 Linden St Lynn (47355) *(G-9432)*

T F S Inc 260 422-5896
   1808 W Main St Fort Wayne (46808) *(G-4672)*

T G R Inc 765 452-8225
   1257 E Morgan St Kokomo (46901) *(G-8705)*

T G R Signs, Kokomo *Also called T G R Inc (G-8705)*

T H S International Inc 317 759-2869
   3510 E 96th St Ste 27 Indianapolis (46240) *(G-8033)*

T I B Inc 574 892-5151
   775 N Michigan St Argos (46501) *(G-278)*

T J B Inc 219 293-8030
   2926 Paul Dr Elkhart (46514) *(G-3202)*

T J Snuggles Inc 574 546-4404
   1851 Dogwood Rd Bremen (46506) *(G-1028)*

T K Sales & Service 219 962-8982
   669 S Grand Blvd Gary (46403) *(G-5104)*

T L E LLC 317 257-1424
   17039 Mercantile Blvd Noblesville (46060) *(G-11191)*

T L Tate Manufacturing Inc 765 452-8283
   1500 N Webster St Kokomo (46901) *(G-8706)*

T M E Inc 219 769-6627
   9100 Lane St Bldg C-2 Merrillville (46410) *(G-9756)*

T M G, Anderson *Also called Technology MGT Group Inc (G-173)*

T N D Printing 260 493-4949
   514 Broadway St Ste 100 New Haven (46774) *(G-10960)*

T n Z Technology LLC 812 438-1205
   5770 Woods Ridge Rd Dillsboro (47018) *(G-2473)*

T Productions Inc 574 257-8610
   504 S Byrkit St Mishawaka (46544) *(G-10139)*

T R Bulger Inc 219 879-8525
   3123 E Michigan Blvd Trail Creek (46360) *(G-13443)*

T S F Co Inc 812 985-2630
   2930 Saint Philip Rd S Evansville (47712) *(G-3757)*

T S Manufacturing 574 831-6647
   68563 County Road 17 New Paris (46553) *(G-10998)*

T Shorter Manufacturing Inc 574 264-4131
   2931 Dexter Dr Elkhart (46514) *(G-3203)*

T W Machine & Grinding 260 799-4236
   7150 N 350 W Columbia City (46725) *(G-1839)*

T&S Signs 317 996-3027
   6205 Beech Grove Rd Martinsville (46151) *(G-9639)*

T&T Coatings Inc 317 408-3752
   8544 E Hadley Rd Camby (46113) *(G-1269)*

T-Flyerz Printing and Prom LLC 260 729-7392
   6073 N Us Highway 27 Bryant (47326) *(G-1202)*

T-N-T Performance Mch Sp LLC 574 457-5056
   210 E Maple Grove St Syracuse (46567) *(G-13148)*

T. E. Scott, Rockville *Also called Scott Pet Products Inc (G-12180)*

T.K.O. Graphix, Plainfield *Also called Tko Enterprises Inc (G-11647)*

T1design, Indianapolis *Also called Travis Britton (G-8092)*

Tab Software 260 490-7132
   8118 Victoria Woods Pl Fort Wayne (46825) *(G-4673)*

Tab Technologies 765 482-7561
   437 W 150 S Lebanon (46052) *(G-9227)*

Tabco Business Forms Inc 812 882-2836
   638 Broadway St Vincennes (47591) *(G-13709)*

Table Logix, Evansville *Also called Prolam Products Inc (G-3687)*

Tacair Publications 260 429-7975
   15922 Wappes Rd Churubusco (46723) *(G-1658)*

Tackle Service Center, Mooresville *Also called Robert J Matt (G-10337)*

Taft Aviation Property LLC 317 769-4487
   11329 E State Road 32 Zionsville (46077) *(G-14467)*

Tag Software 219 866-3100
   4093 N Us Highway 231 Rensselaer (47978) *(G-11941)*

Taggarts Custom Sndblst LLC 765 825-4584
   1740 Georgia Ave Connersville (47331) *(G-2074)*

Taghleef Industries Inc 302 326-5500
   3600 E Head Ave Rosedale (47874) *(G-12208)*

Tail Wind Logistics, Elkhart *Also called Tail Wind Transport (G-3204)*

Tail Wind Transport 574 343-2157
   2991 Paul Dr Elkhart (46514) *(G-3204)*

Tailgaters Inc 812 827-3600
   802 S Main St Huntingburg (47542) *(G-6181)*

Talbert Manufacturing Inc (PA) 219 866-7141
   1628 W State Road 114 Rensselaer (47978) *(G-11942)*

Tale Chaser Publishing Inc 765 962-4309
   54 S 14th St Richmond (47374) *(G-12057)*

Tall Cotton Marketing LLC 312 320-5862
   3522 S State Road 104 La Porte (46350) *(G-8825)*

Talon Products LLC 574 218-0100
   1690 Commerce Dr Bristol (46507) *(G-1089)*

Talon Terra LLC 219 393-1400
   399 E Hupp Rd La Porte (46350) *(G-8826)*

Tamara Eaton 219 872-9151
   1213 E Coolspring Ave Michigan City (46360) *(G-9851)*

Tamarack Petroleum Company Inc 812 567-4023
   2611 E Kelly Rd Tennyson (47637) *(G-13181)*

Tamco Manufacturing Co 574 294-1909
   2717 Oakland Ave Elkhart (46517) *(G-3205)*

Tamwall Demountable Partitions, Indianapolis *Also called Tamwall Inc (G-8034)*

Tamwall Inc 317 546-5055
   4362 Sellers St Indianapolis (46226) *(G-8034)*

Tangent Rail Products Inc 812 789-5331
   3818 S County Road 50 E Winslow (47598) *(G-14361)*

Tangent Rail Products Inc 412 325-0202
   2901 Ohio Blvd Ste 252 Terre Haute (47803) *(G-13348)*

Tanglewood Press, Indianapolis *Also called Tanglewood Publishing Inc (G-8035)*

Tanglewood Publishing Inc 812 877-9488
   1060 N Capitol Ave E395 Indianapolis (46204) *(G-8035)*

Tango Romeo Industries LLC 765 623-1317
   5567 S Cladwell Dr Pendleton (46064) *(G-11507)*

Tanimura & Antle, Plymouth *Also called Ready Pac Foods Inc (G-11720)*

Tank Construction & Service Co 317 509-6294
   6145 S Indianapolis Rd Whitestown (46075) *(G-14263)*

Tap-A-Lite Inc 219 932-8067
   820 165th St Hammond (46324) *(G-5948)*

Targamite LLC 260 489-0046
   6917 Innovation Blvd Fort Wayne (46818) *(G-4674)*

Target Printing Inc 260 744-6038
   3233 Lafayette St Fort Wayne (46806) *(G-4675)*

Tarpenning-Lafollette Co Inc 317 780-1500
   404 W Gimber St Indianapolis (46225) *(G-8036)*

Tartan Properties LLC 317 714-7337
   3419 Roosevelt Ave Indianapolis (46218) *(G-8037)*

Tarter Woodworking Inc 765 349-4193
   440 Rolling Woods Dr Martinsville (46151) *(G-9640)*

Tarver Wolff LLC 765 265-7416
   1149 Brookhaven Rd Brookville (47012) *(G-1127)*

TAS Welding & Gran Services LL 765 210-4274
   5459 W Old 24 Wabash (46992) *(G-13757)*

Tasco Industries Inc 219 922-6100
   10018 Express Dr Highland (46322) *(G-6056)*

Tascon Corp 317 547-6127
   2213 Duke St Indianapolis (46205) *(G-8038)*

Task Force Tips Inc (PA) 219 462-6161
   3701 Innovation Way Valparaiso (46383) *(G-13626)*

Task Force Tips Inc 219 462-6161
3701 Innovation Way Valparaiso (46383) ***(G-13627)***
Tasty Rich, Indianapolis *Also called Food Specialties Inc* ***(G-6945)***
Tasus Corporation (HQ) 812 333-6500
300 N Daniels Way Bloomington (47404) ***(G-834)***
Tate Lyle Ingrdnts Amricas LLC 765 474-5474
3300 Us Highway 52 S Lafayette (47905) ***(G-9007)***
Tate Lyle Ingrdnts Amricas LLC 765 448-7123
2245 Sagamore Pkwy N Lafayette (47904) ***(G-9008)***
Tate Soaps & Surfactants Inc 765 868-4488
1500 N Webster St Kokomo (46901) ***(G-8707)***
Tatman Inc 765 825-2164
815 N Central Ave Connersville (47331) ***(G-2075)***
Taught It LLC 317 469-4120
8440 Wdfld Xing Blvd Indianapolis (46240) ***(G-8039)***
Taunyas Creative Cuts 812 574-7722
220 Clifty Dr Madison (47250) ***(G-9497)***
Taurus Tech & Engrg LLC 765 282-2090
5101 W County Road 400 S Muncie (47302) ***(G-10568)***
Taurus Tool & Engineering, Muncie *Also called Taurus Tech & Engrg LLC* ***(G-10568)***
Tavistock Restaurants LLC 317 488-1230
49 W Maryland St Ste 104 Indianapolis (46204) ***(G-8040)***
Taylor Chain, East Chicago *Also called Grc Enterprises Inc* ***(G-2530)***
Taylor Communications Inc 317 392-3235
1750 Miller Ave Shelbyville (46176) ***(G-12573)***
Taylor Made Awards, Greencastle *Also called Taylor Made Enterprises* ***(G-5479)***
Taylor Made Candles 812 663-6634
7864 W County Road 80 N Greensburg (47240) ***(G-5636)***
Taylor Made Enterprises 765 653-8481
1292 N Jackson St Greencastle (46135) ***(G-5479)***
Taylor Made Group Holdings Inc 260 347-1368
1101 Stonebraker Dr Kendallville (46755) ***(G-8512)***
Taylor Made Systems Indiana, Kendallville *Also called Taylor Made Group Holdings Inc* ***(G-8512)***
Tb Plastic Extrusions Michiana 574 266-7409
54432 Adams St Elkhart (46514) ***(G-3206)***
Tbin LLC 812 491-9100
1698 S 100 W Princeton (47670) ***(G-11883)***
Tbk America Inc 765 962-0147
3700 W Industries Rd Richmond (47374) ***(G-12058)***
TC Burton Enterprises LLC 317 446-8776
11764 Marigold Cir Fishers (46038) ***(G-3972)***
Tc Graphics, Evansville *Also called Schaffsteins Truck Clean LLC* ***(G-3715)***
Tc Heartland LLC 317 876-7121
4635 W 84th St Ste 300 Indianapolis (46268) ***(G-8041)***
Tc Heartland LLC (PA) 317 566-9750
14300 Clay Terrace Blvd # 249 Carmel (46032) ***(G-1487)***
Tc Pallets & Peddler Sweet LLC 812 283-1090
1414 E 10th St Jeffersonville (47130) ***(G-8433)***
Tc Printing 812 865-5127
8381 W State Road 56 French Lick (47432) ***(G-4990)***
Tc Printing & More LLC 812 936-3069
8304 W Us Highway 150 West Baden Springs (47469) ***(G-14036)***
Tc4llc 317 709-5429
9217 Muir Ln Fishers (46037) ***(G-3973)***
Tcb Enterprises LLC 574 522-3971
4600 Wyland Dr Elkhart (46516) ***(G-3207)***
Tcb Industries Inc 574 522-3971
4519 Wyland Dr Elkhart (46516) ***(G-3208)***
Tclogic LLC 317 464-5152
429 N Penn St Ste 300 Indianapolis (46204) ***(G-8042)***
TCS Cabinets 765 208-5350
557 E 1450 N Summitville (46070) ***(G-13107)***
Tct Technologies LLC 317 833-6730
10735 Sky Prairie St Fishers (46038) ***(G-3974)***
Td Consulting LLC 260 925-3089
812 Allison Blvd Auburn (46706) ***(G-360)***
Td Innovations 530 477-9780
515 S Woodscrest Dr # 202 Bloomington (47401) ***(G-835)***
Tdc Logging LLC 574 289-4243
24890 Edison Rd South Bend (46628) ***(G-12967)***
Tdf of Indiana Inc 812 597-4009
7209 E Mahalasville Rd Morgantown (46160) ***(G-10358)***
Tdk Graphics Inc 219 663-7799
1180 N Main St Crown Point (46307) ***(G-2312)***
TDS, Brookston *Also called Terra Drive Systems Inc* ***(G-1108)***
Tdy Industries LLC 260 726-8121
250 E Lafayette St Portland (47371) ***(G-11849)***
Tdy Industries LLC 219 362-1000
300 Philadelphia St La Porte (46350) ***(G-8827)***
Tea Unwrapped LLC 317 558-8550
15486 Herriman Blvd Noblesville (46060) ***(G-11192)***
Teach Enterprises Inc 574 773-3108
72377 Airline Dr Nappanee (46550) ***(G-10708)***
Teaco Inc 219 874-6234
2117 Ohio St Michigan City (46360) ***(G-9852)***
Teal Automotive Inc 765 768-7726
450 Industrial Dr Dunkirk (47336) ***(G-2489)***
Team & Club Sporting Goods 219 762-5477
6218 Old Porter Rd Portage (46368) ***(G-11797)***
Team Gear Printing LLC 765 935-4748
3451 Dorothy Ln Richmond (47374) ***(G-12059)***
Team Gear Printing LLC 765 977-2995
4714 National Rd E Richmond (47374) ***(G-12060)***
Team Green Inc 317 872-2700
7615 Zionsville Rd Indianapolis (46268) ***(G-8043)***
Team Hillman LLC 260 426-2626
414 E Wayne St Fort Wayne (46802) ***(G-4676)***
Team Image LLC (PA) 317 468-0802
121 S Pennsylvania St Greenfield (46140) ***(G-5579)***
Team Image LLC 317 477-7468
212 E Main St Greenfield (46140) ***(G-5580)***
Team Oneway 574 387-5417
12911 Industrial Park Dr Granger (46530) ***(G-5443)***
Team Pride Athletic AP Corp 574 224-8326
2196 Sweetgum Rd Rochester (46975) ***(G-12156)***
Team Spirit 219 924-6272
10429 Columbia Ave Munster (46321) ***(G-10631)***
Team Spirit Trlrs Elkhart Inc 574 266-2966
25954 Pierina Dr Elkhart (46514) ***(G-3209)***
Team Supreme Bait Company 812 366-3200
7565 Pleasant Vly Rd Ne Georgetown (47122) ***(G-5154)***
Teamair Mro Ltd 812 584-3733
12978 Josephs Field Ln Moores Hill (47032) ***(G-10299)***
TEC Hoist LLC 708 598-2300
1349 E Main St Griffith (46319) ***(G-5791)***
TEC Inc 765 827-3868
3594 S County Road 350 E Connersville (47331) ***(G-2076)***
TEC Photography 812 332-9847
1011 W Gourley Pike Bloomington (47404) ***(G-836)***
TEC Transport LLC 765 534-3253
20218 Cyntheanne Rd Noblesville (46060) ***(G-11193)***
TEC-Air LLC 219 301-7084
9200 Calumet Ave Ste Nw1 Munster (46321) ***(G-10632)***
TEC-Tool Inc 812 526-3158
220 N Main St Indianapolis (46214) ***(G-8044)***
Tech Castings LLC 765 535-4100
1102 South St Shirley (47384) ***(G-12663)***
Tech Enterprises Incorporated 317 251-3816
5868 Haverford Ave Indianapolis (46220) ***(G-8045)***
Tech Group North America Inc 765 650-2300
2810 W State Road 28 Frankfort (46041) ***(G-4855)***
Tech Innovation LLC 317 506-8343
8517 Oakmont Ln Indianapolis (46260) ***(G-8046)***
Tech Solutions and Sales Inc 317 536-5846
6898 Hawthorn Park Dr Indianapolis (46220) ***(G-8047)***
TECH WEIGH MANUFACTURING, Griffith *Also called Technical Weighing Svcs Inc* ***(G-5793)***
Techcom Inc (PA) 317 865-2530
7515 Company Dr Ste A Indianapolis (46237) ***(G-8048)***
Techcom Inc 812 372-0960
4630 Progress Dr Columbus (47201) ***(G-2020)***
Techknowledgey Inc (PA) 574 971-4267
1840 W Lincoln Ave Goshen (46526) ***(G-5339)***
Techna Fit of Indiana 317 350-2153
493 Southpoint Cir B Brownsburg (46112) ***(G-1173)***
Techna-Fit Inc 317 350-2153
493 Southpoint Cir B Brownsburg (46112) ***(G-1174)***
Technalysis Inc 317 291-1985
7172 Waldemar Dr Indianapolis (46268) ***(G-8049)***
Technical Controls Solutions 260 416-0329
2640 N 825 E Churubusco (46723) ***(G-1659)***
Technical Water Treatment Inc 574 277-1949
51431 Autumn Ridge Dr Granger (46530) ***(G-5444)***
Technical Weighing Svcs Inc 219 924-3433
1000 Reder Rd Griffith (46319) ***(G-5792)***
Technical Weighing Svcs Inc (PA) 219 924-3366
1004 Reder Rd Griffith (46319) ***(G-5793)***
Technicote Inc 812 466-9844
3200 N 25th St Terre Haute (47804) ***(G-13349)***
Technidyne Corporation (PA) 812 948-2884
100 Quality Ave New Albany (47150) ***(G-10870)***
Technifab Products Inc (PA) 812 442-0520
10339 N Industrial Pk Dr Brazil (47834) ***(G-979)***
Techniplas, Mishawaka *Also called Nyloncraft Inc* ***(G-10098)***
Technology Cons Group LLC 219 525-4064
1421 E 91st Dr Merrillville (46410) ***(G-9757)***
Technology Dynamics 317 524-6338
9105 E 56th St Ste 2150 Indianapolis (46216) ***(G-8050)***
Technology MGT Group Inc 765 606-1512
16 Edgewood Dr Anderson (46011) ***(G-173)***
Technuity Inc 800 887-2557
6040 W 79th St Indianapolis (46278) ***(G-8051)***
Techseal Division, Goshen *Also called Parker-Hannifin Corporation* ***(G-5307)***
Techshot Inc 812 923-9591
7200 Highway 150 Greenville (47124) ***(G-5655)***
Techshot Lighting LLC 812 923-9591
5605 Featheringill Rd # 102 Floyds Knobs (47119) ***(G-4020)***

ALPHABETIC

Tecnoplast Usa LLC 317 769-4929
  3619 W 73rd St Ste 1 Anderson (46011) *(G-174)*

Tecumseh Peerless Gear Mch Div, Salem *Also called Tecumseh Products
Company (G-12307)*

Tecumseh Products Company 812 883-3575
  1555 S Jackson St Salem (47167) *(G-12307)*

Tedco Inc (PA) 765 489-4527
  498 S Washington St Hagerstown (47346) *(G-5814)*

Tedco Inc 765 489-5807
  303 W Main St Hagerstown (47346) *(G-5815)*

Tedco Toys, Hagerstown *Also called Tedco Inc (G-5814)*

Tedrows Wood Products Inc 812 247-2260
  7910 Coal Hollow Rd Shoals (47581) *(G-12670)*

Teeki Hut Custom Tees Inc 317 205-3589
  807 Broad Ripple Ave Indianapolis (46220) *(G-8052)*

Tejas Tubular Products Inc 574 249-0623
  31140 Edison Rd New Carlisle (46552) *(G-10888)*

Tek Print LLC 812 336-2525
  812 14th St Bedford (47421) *(G-583)*

Teklad Diets, Indianapolis *Also called Envigo Rms Inc (G-6871)*

Tekmodo Structures LLC 574 970-5800
  1701 Conant St Elkhart (46516) *(G-3210)*

Teknor Apex Co 812 246-3357
  6637 Westwood Dr Charlestown (47111) *(G-1583)*

Telamon Corporation (PA) 317 818-6888
  1000 E 116th St Carmel (46032) *(G-1488)*

Telamon Entp Ventures LLC 317 818-6888
  1000 E 116th St Carmel (46032) *(G-1489)*

Telamon International, Carmel *Also called Telamon Technologies Corp (G-1491)*

Telamon International Corp (PA) 317 818-6888
  1000 E 116th St Carmel (46032) *(G-1490)*

Telamon Technologies Corp 317 818-6888
  1000 E 116th St Carmel (46032) *(G-1491)*

Telecom LLC 317 805-1090
  10401 N Meridian St # 401 Indianapolis (46290) *(G-6282)*

Telecommunications Pdts Div, Fort Wayne *Also called Essex Group Inc (G-4244)*

Telectro-Mek Inc 260 747-0586
  2700 Nuttman Ave Fort Wayne (46802) *(G-4677)*

Tell City Concrete Supply, Tell City *Also called Mulzer Crushed Stone Inc (G-13167)*

Tell City Concrete Supply, Evansville *Also called Mulzer Crushed Stone Inc (G-3642)*

Tellabs, La Porte *Also called Coriant Operations Inc (G-8745)*

Temperature Control Svcs LLC 765 325-2439
  13920 Wendessa Dr Fishers (46038) *(G-3975)*

Tempest Technical Sales Inc (PA) 317 844-9236
  13295 Illinois St Ste 329 Carmel (46032) *(G-1492)*

Tempest Tool & Machine Inc 812 346-6464
  7235 W Us Highway 50 North Vernon (47265) *(G-11283)*

Temple Inland 765 362-1074
  801 N Englewood Dr Crawfordsville (47933) *(G-2201)*

Temple-Inland Inc 765 675-6732
  815 Industrial Dr Tipton (46072) *(G-13408)*

Templeton Coal Company Inc (PA) 812 232-7037
  701 Wabash Ave Ste 501 Terre Haute (47807) *(G-13350)*

Templeton Coal Company Inc 812 232-7037
  711 Hulman St Terre Haute (47802) *(G-13351)*

Templeton Myers Inc 317 898-6688
  351 S Post Rd Indianapolis (46219) *(G-8053)*

Temptek Inc 317 887-6352
  525 E Stop 18 Rd Greenwood (46143) *(G-5752)*

Ten Cate Enbi Inc (indiana) 317 398-3267
  1703 Mccall Dr Shelbyville (46176) *(G-12574)*

Ten Point Trim Corp 317 875-5424
  4750 Nw Plaza West Dr Zionsville (46077) *(G-14468)*

Tendre Press LLC 812 606-9563
  134 N Overhill Dr Bloomington (47408) *(G-837)*

Tenneco, Angola *Also called Pullman Company (G-241)*

Tenneco Automotive Oper Co Inc 260 894-9214
  1490 Gerber St Ligonier (46767) *(G-9299)*

Tenneco Automotive Oper Co Inc 574 296-9400
  4825 Hoffman St Elkhart (46516) *(G-3211)*

Tennplasco, Edinburgh *Also called Manar Inc (G-2617)*

Teragraphics Ink LLC 765 430-2863
  204 E Pine Ave West Lafayette (47906) *(G-14112)*

Teresa L Powell CPA 765 962-1862
  321 Sw 1st St Richmond (47374) *(G-12061)*

Terex Corporation 574 342-0086
  4470 Lincoln Hwy Bourbon (46504) *(G-949)*

Terex Corporation 260 497-0728
  7727 Freedom Way Fort Wayne (46818) *(G-4678)*

Terick Sales 574 626-3173
  3519 E County Road 800 S Walton (46994) *(G-13817)*

Terick Sales & Service, Walton *Also called Terick Sales (G-13817)*

Ternet Metal Finishing Inc 260 897-3903
  150 Green Dr Avilla (46710) *(G-419)*

Terra Drive Systems Inc 219 279-2801
  9098 W 800 S Brookston (47923) *(G-1108)*

Terra Transit, Goshen *Also called Independent Protection Co Inc (G-5243)*

Terrafina Inc 317 346-6655
  2165 Earlywood Dr Franklin (46131) *(G-4936)*

Terrance Smith Distributing 765 644-3396
  2215 N Madison Ave Anderson (46011) *(G-175)*

Terrapin Mfg 717 339-6007
  4109 Evard Rd Fort Wayne (46835) *(G-4679)*

Terre Haute Coca-Cola Btlg Co 812 232-9543
  924 Lafayette Ave Terre Haute (47804) *(G-13352)*

Terre Haute Wilbert Burial Vlt 812 235-0339
  509 E Preston St Terre Haute (47802) *(G-13353)*

Terrecorp Inc 317 951-8325
  2121 Hillside Ave Indianapolis (46218) *(G-8054)*

Terrel Automotive Machine Inc 812 883-3859
  707 S Main St Salem (47167) *(G-12308)*

Terri Logan Studios 765 966-7876
  2101 Reeveston Rd Richmond (47374) *(G-12062)*

Terronics Development Corp 765 552-0808
  7565 W 900 N Elwood (46036) *(G-3311)*

Terry Eaton 812 687-7579
  2761 E 900 N Plainville (47568) *(G-11655)*

Terry L Ray 765 342-3180
  340 S Sycamore St Martinsville (46151) *(G-9641)*

Terry Liquidation III Inc (PA) 219 362-9908
  210 Philadelphia St La Porte (46350) *(G-8828)*

Terry Liquidation III Inc 219 362-3557
  28 Industrial Pkwy La Porte (46350) *(G-8829)*

Terrys Sewer Service 219 756-5238
  8235 Lincoln St Merrillville (46410) *(G-9758)*

Terrys Welding Inc 765 742-4191
  707 Widewater Dr Lafayette (47904) *(G-9009)*

Terrys Welding Inc 765 564-3331
  9176 W 132 N Delphi (46923) *(G-2428)*

Terz Design and Imprinting LLC 765 965-9762
  2305 Vi Post Rd Richmond (47374) *(G-12063)*

Tesco, Syracuse *Also called Thomas Strickler (G-13149)*

Tesla Wireless Company LLC 219 363-7922
  10525 W Us Highway 30 4c Wanatah (46390) *(G-13826)*

Test Gauge & Backflow Supply, Indianapolis *Also called Prosperus LLC (G-7782)*

Test Rite Systems & Mfg Co LLC 317 736-9192
  1650 N 800 E Franklin (46131) *(G-4937)*

Testimony Publications 812 602-3031
  901 Jobes Ln Evansville (47712) *(G-3758)*

Testworth Laboratories Inc 260 244-5137
  401 S Main St Columbia City (46725) *(G-1840)*

Tetrafab Corporation 812 258-0000
  3429 Knobs Valley Dr Floyds Knobs (47119) *(G-4021)*

Tetrasolv Filtration, Anderson *Also called Tetrasolv Inc (G-176)*

Tetrasolv Inc 765 643-3941
  1424 Abraham Dr Anderson (46013) *(G-176)*

Texacon Cut Stone LLC 812 824-3211
  4790 Fluck Mill Rd Bloomington (47403) *(G-838)*

Texas Instruments Incorporated 317 574-2611
  12900 N Meridian St # 175 Carmel (46032) *(G-1493)*

Texas Monthly, Indianapolis *Also called Emmis Publishing LP (G-6856)*

Texmo Prcision Castings US Inc 574 269-1368
  596 E 200 N Warsaw (46582) *(G-13951)*

Tf Fulfillment, Indianapolis *Also called Tfi Inc (G-8055)*

TFC Canopy, Garrett *Also called Centurion Industries Inc (G-4996)*

Tfco Incorporated (PA) 219 324-4166
  2606 N State Road 39 La Porte (46350) *(G-8830)*

Tfi Inc 317 290-1333
  6355 Morenci Trl Indianapolis (46268) *(G-8055)*

Tfx Plating Company LLC 765 289-2436
  2401 N Executive Park Dr Yorktown (47396) *(G-14412)*

Tgc Auto Care Products Inc 765 962-7725
  421 S 33rd St Richmond (47374) *(G-12064)*

Tgf Enterprises LLC 440 840-9704
  11075 Woods Bay Ln Indianapolis (46236) *(G-8056)*

Tgm Manufacturing Inc 260 758-3055
  5980 N 400 W Uniondale (46791) *(G-13466)*

Tgx Medical Systems LLC 317 575-0300
  12220 N Meridian St # 175 Carmel (46032) *(G-1494)*

Thadco, Bloomington *Also called Winters Assoc Prmtnal Pdts Inc (G-858)*

Thanatos Manufacturing LLC 260 251-8498
  4263 W 200 S Portland (47371) *(G-11850)*

Thatcher Engineering Corp 219 949-2084
  7100 Industrial Hwy Gary (46406) *(G-5105)*

The Baldus Company Inc 260 424-2366
  440 E Brackenridge St Fort Wayne (46802) *(G-4680)*

The Criterion Newspaper, Indianapolis *Also called Criterion Press Inc (G-6693)*

The Eminence Hair Collectn LLC 317 222-5085
  5401 S East St Ste 107 Indianapolis (46227) *(G-8057)*

THE FALCON MINT, Portland *Also called Collegiate Pride Inc (G-11812)*

The Findlay Publishing Co 812 222-8000
  133 S Main St Batesville (47006) *(G-519)*

The Goshen News, Goshen *Also called Triple Crown Media LLC (G-5342)*

The Office Sup of Southern Ind (PA) 812 283-5523
  417 Spring St Jeffersonville (47130) *(G-8434)*

(G-0000) Company's Geographic Section entry number

The Pro Shear Corporation Corp 260 408-1010
  3405 Meyer Rd Ste 100 Fort Wayne (46803) *(G-4681)*

The Tap 812 486-9795
  101 N College Ave Bloomington (47404) *(G-839)*

The Truth, Elkhart *Also called Truth Publishing Company Inc* *(G-3227)*

Therametric Technologies Inc 317 565-8065
  9880 Douglas Floyd Pkwy Noblesville (46060) *(G-11194)*

Theraptic Elmnts By Lori Myers 765 480-2525
  3901 High St Logansport (46947) *(G-9369)*

Therm-O-Lite LLC 574 234-4004
  3502 W Sample St South Bend (46619) *(G-12968)*

Therma-Tru Corp 260 868-5811
  601 Re Jones Rd Butler (46721) *(G-1245)*

Therma-Tru Corp 260 868-5811
  601 Re Jones Rd Dock13 Butler (46721) *(G-1246)*

Thermafiber Inc (HQ) 260 563-2111
  3711 Mill St Wabash (46992) *(G-13758)*

Thermal Ceramics Inc 574 296-3500
  2730 Industrial Pkwy Elkhart (46516) *(G-3212)*

Thermal Product Solutions 708 758-6530
  1470 Mackinaw Pl Schererville (46375) *(G-12348)*

Thermal Structures Inc 951 736-9911
  2800 Airwest Blvd Plainfield (46168) *(G-11646)*

Thermal Tech & Temp Inc 219 808-1258
  772 N Madison St Crown Point (46307) *(G-2313)*

Thermco Instrument Corporation 219 362-6258
  1201 W Us Highway 20 La Porte (46350) *(G-8831)*

Thermform Engineered Qulty LLC 260 495-9842
  500 W Water St Fremont (46737) *(G-4977)*

Thermo Cube Incorporated 574 936-5096
  2255 Walter Glaub Dr Plymouth (46563) *(G-11727)*

Thermo Products LLC (HQ) 574 896-2133
  5235 W State Road 10 # 5 North Judson (46366) *(G-11214)*

Thermo Transfer Inc 317 398-3503
  1601 Miller Ave Shelbyville (46176) *(G-12575)*

Thermo-Cycler Industries Inc (PA) 219 767-2990
  111 E Hamilton St Union Mills (46382) *(G-13465)*

Thermodynamic Process Ctrl LLC 317 780-5743
  5730 Kopetsky Dr Ste B Indianapolis (46217) *(G-8058)*

Thermodyne Food Service Pdts 260 428-2535
  4418 New Haven Ave Fort Wayne (46803) *(G-4682)*

Thermography Indianapolis LLC 317 370-5111
  4000 N Meridian St Apt 10 Indianapolis (46208) *(G-8059)*

Thermolite Windows System, South Bend *Also called Therm-O-Lite LLC* *(G-12968)*

Thermoseal Co Ed Munoz Inc 812 428-3343
  800 E Oregon St Evansville (47711) *(G-3759)*

Thermoset Plastics Division, Indianapolis *Also called Lord Corporation* *(G-7418)*

Thermovision Thermography 317 306-6622
  3815 River Crosng Pkwy Ste 100 Indianapolis (46240) *(G-8060)*

Thermphyscal Prpts RES Lab Inc 765 463-1581
  3080 Kent Ave West Lafayette (47906) *(G-14113)*

Thermtron Mfg Inc 260 622-6000
  1625 Baker Dr Ossian (46777) *(G-11413)*

Thermwood Corporation 812 937-4476
  904 Buffaloville Rd Dale (47523) *(G-2334)*

Thickstat Inc 201 294-1896
  5251 S East St Ste 331 Indianapolis (46227) *(G-8061)*

Thieme and Wagner Brewing Co 765 477-0667
  1619 Stonevalley Ct Lafayette (47909) *(G-9010)*

Think North America Inc 313 565-6781
  3221 Magnum Dr Elkhart (46516) *(G-3213)*

Thinking Machine LLC 812 539-2968
  798 Greentree Rd Lawrenceburg (47025) *(G-9158)*

Thinkshortcut Publishing LLC 765 935-1127
  2695 Inke Rd Richmond (47374) *(G-12065)*

This & That Products 812 299-2688
  3784 Hotel St Terre Haute (47802) *(G-13354)*

This That EMB Screen Prtg LLC 317 541-8548
  3724 N Dequincy St Indianapolis (46218) *(G-8062)*

Thm Publishing Indianapolis, Carmel *Also called Thm Publishing Sacramento LLC* *(G-1495)*

Thm Publishing Sacramento LLC 317 810-1340
  301 E Carmel Dr Ste Ce800 Carmel (46032) *(G-1495)*

Thomas & Betts Corp 901 252-8000
  16577 Brookhollow Dr Westfield (46062) *(G-14194)*

Thomas & Skinner Inc (PA) 317 923-2501
  1120 E 23rd St Indianapolis (46205) *(G-8063)*

Thomas & Skinner Inc 812 689-4811
  525 Western Ave Osgood (47037) *(G-11396)*

Thomas Chateau Winery 812 339-9463
  118 N Walnut St Bloomington (47404) *(G-840)*

Thomas Cubit Inc 219 933-0566
  110 Brunswick St Hammond (46327) *(G-5949)*

Thomas E Slade Inc 812 471-7100
  6220 Vogel Rd Evansville (47715) *(G-3760)*

Thomas Green LLC 317 337-0000
  7517 Winton Dr Indianapolis (46268) *(G-8064)*

Thomas L Wehr 317 835-7824
  8192 W 700 N Fairland (46126) *(G-3827)*

Thomas Medical, Indianapolis *Also called Catheter Research Inc* *(G-6568)*

Thomas Monuments Inc 317 244-6525
  7009 W Washington St Indianapolis (46241) *(G-8065)*

Thomas Optical LLC 502 548-2163
  954 Market St Charlestown (47111) *(G-1584)*

Thomas P Kasten 574 806-4663
  4620 N Us Highway 35 Winamac (46996) *(G-14322)*

Thomas Strickler 574 457-2473
  6749 E Cornelius Rd Syracuse (46567) *(G-13149)*

Thomas Toll 317 569-2628
  1929 W 136th St Carmel (46032) *(G-1496)*

Thomas/Euclid Industries Inc 317 783-7171
  2575 Bethel Ave Indianapolis (46203) *(G-8066)*

Thomasville Furniture Inds Inc 336 476-2175
  442 165th St Hammond (46324) *(G-5950)*

Thomco Inc 317 359-3539
  1414 Sadlier Circle W Dr Indianapolis (46239) *(G-8067)*

Thompson 219 942-8133
  421 Driftwood Dr Hobart (46342) *(G-6098)*

Thompson Printing Service Inc 317 783-7448
  447 E Elbert St Indianapolis (46227) *(G-8068)*

Thomson Industries Inc 574 529-2496
  1209 Shore Ln Syracuse (46567) *(G-13150)*

Thomson Reuters Corporation 317 570-9387
  8670 Harrison Pkwy Fishers (46038) *(G-3976)*

Thor Industries Inc (PA) 574 970-7460
  601 E Beardsley Ave Elkhart (46514) *(G-3214)*

Thor Motor Coach 574 266-1111
  4221 Pine Creek Rd Elkhart (46516) *(G-3215)*

Thor Motor Coach Inc 574 266-1111
  520 County Road 15 Elkhart (46516) *(G-3216)*

Thorgren Tool & Molding Co 219 462-1801
  1100 Evans Ave Valparaiso (46383) *(G-13628)*

Thormax Enterprises LLC 812 530-7744
  6976 Lydia Ln Seymour (47274) *(G-12496)*

Thornes Homes Inc 812 275-4656
  3211 State Road 37 S Bedford (47421) *(G-584)*

Thornton's Welding Serv, Bloomington *Also called Thorntons Welding* *(G-841)*

Thorntons Mtrcycle Sls - Mdson 812 574-6347
  217 Clifty Dr Madison (47250) *(G-9498)*

Thorntons Welding 812 332-8564
  4439 W Arlington Rd Bloomington (47404) *(G-841)*

Thoroughbred Industries Inc 260 486-8343
  6902 Brackenwood Ct Fort Wayne (46835) *(G-4683)*

Thoughts Are Things 317 585-8053
  8035 Clearwater Dr Indianapolis (46256) *(G-8069)*

Thousand One Inc 765 962-3636
  1001 S E St Richmond (47374) *(G-12066)*

Thrasher Welding and Mch Sp 260 475-5550
  2085 S 600 W Angola (46703) *(G-250)*

Thread Creations Inc 765 521-3886
  2004 S Memorial Dr New Castle (47362) *(G-10919)*

Thread Letter Emblem, Noblesville *Also called T L E LLC* *(G-11191)*

Threads Embroidery, North Webster *Also called Groovemade LLC* *(G-11292)*

Three Cups LLC 317 633-8082
  310 W Michigan St Ste A Indianapolis (46202) *(G-8070)*

Three Daughters Corp 260 925-2128
  5005 County Road 29 Auburn (46706) *(G-361)*

Three Dog Software Inc 317 823-7080
  5258 Hickory Lake Dr Indianapolis (46235) *(G-8071)*

Three Floyds Brewing Co 219 922-4425
  9750 Indiana Pkwy Munster (46321) *(G-10633)*

Three K Racing Enterprises 765 482-4273
  2685 S 25 W Lebanon (46052) *(G-9228)*

Three Little Monkeys 765 778-9370
  129 S Pendleton Ave # 3 Pendleton (46064) *(G-11508)*

Three Points Alpaca Farm LLC 812 363-3876
  944 Locust Ave Batesville (47006) *(G-520)*

Three Rivers Comprsd AR Sstms 260 248-8908
  1075 S 50 E Columbia City (46725) *(G-1841)*

Three Rivers Distilling Co LLC 260 745-9355
  220 E Wallace St Fort Wayne (46803) *(G-4684)*

Three Star Electric Inc 574 272-3136
  52620 Helmen Ave South Bend (46637) *(G-12969)*

Thrift Products Heating Spc, Peru *Also called Ebert Machine Company Inc* *(G-11526)*

Thrifty Nickel Want ADS, Indianapolis *Also called American Classifieds* *(G-6386)*

Thrify Nickel Wnt ADS Evansvil 812 428-8484
  999 N Congress Ave Evansville (47715) *(G-3761)*

Throttle Jockey, Kokomo *Also called Graphics Lab Uv Printing Inc* *(G-8632)*

Thrush Co Inc 765 472-3351
  340 W 8th St Peru (46970) *(G-11551)*

Thrust Industries Inc 812 437-3643
  10334 Hedden Rd Evansville (47725) *(G-3762)*

Thugs Inc Choppers 317 454-3762
  735 N Lynhurst Dr Indianapolis (46224) *(G-8072)*

Thunder Rolls Express 812 667-5111
  13449 State Road 129 Canaan (47224) *(G-1281)*

Thunderbird Aviation LLC 847 303-3100
  8623 E Washington St Indianapolis (46219) *(G-8073)*

Thundrbird Traditional Archery 812 699-1099
  306 N Ohio St Culver (46511) *(G-2327)*

A
L
P
H
A
B
E
T
I
C

Thyme In Kitchen LLC 812 624-0344
2308 W Franklin St Ste A Evansville (47712) *(G-3763)*

Thyssenkrupp Crankshaft Co LLC 765 294-0045
1291 E 8th St Veedersburg (47987) *(G-13647)*

Thyssenkrupp Elevator Corp 317 595-1125
8665 Bash St Indianapolis (46256) *(G-8074)*

TI Automotive Ligonier Corp 260 894-3163
925 N Main St Ligonier (46767) *(G-9300)*

TI Group Auto Systems LLC 260 587-6100
507 H L Thompson Jr Dr Ashley (46705) *(G-291)*

TI Group Auto Systems LLC 260 622-7900
1200 Baker Dr Ossian (46777) *(G-11414)*

Tic Toc Trophy Shop Inc 574 893-4234
930 E Rochester St Akron (46910) *(G-8)*

Tiedemann-Bevs Industries LLC 765 962-4914
4225 W Industries Rd Richmond (47374) *(G-12067)*

Tiedmann and Sons, Richmond *Also called Tiedemann-Bevs Industries LLC* *(G-12067)*

Tiem, Columbus *Also called Toyota Industrial Eqp Mfg Inc* *(G-2024)*

Tier 1 Medical LLC 317 316-7871
11404 Regency Ln Carmel (46033) *(G-1497)*

Tiffany Marble of Indianapolis 317 894-9141
6301 W 400 N Greenfield (46140) *(G-5581)*

Tili LLC 574 267-6995
1980 N Detroit St Warsaw (46580) *(G-13952)*

Timber & Logging, Mauckport *Also called Michael Skaggs* *(G-9656)*

Timber Creek Design Co Inc 317 297-5336
7230 Guion Rd Indianapolis (46268) *(G-8075)*

Timber Line Crating LP 260 238-3075
17501 Campbell Rd Spencerville (46788) *(G-13052)*

Timber Ox Inc 317 758-5942
2133 E 226th St Cicero (46034) *(G-1669)*

Timber Ox Green, Cicero *Also called Timber Ox Inc* *(G-1669)*

Timberland Resources Inc 765 245-2634
6429 W 100 N Montezuma (47862) *(G-10211)*

Timberlight Mfg Co 317 694-1317
1155 S Shore Dr Martinsville (46151) *(G-9642)*

Timberline Industries, Brazil *Also called Christopher Miller* *(G-956)*

Timberline Scenery LLC 260 244-5588
700 Hill Dr Columbia City (46725) *(G-1842)*

Timberline Woodworking Inc 219 766-2733
304 E Mentor St Kouts (46347) *(G-8718)*

Time Out Trailers Inc 574 294-7671
4636 Chester Dr Elkhart (46516) *(G-3217)*

Times 765 296-3622
211 N Jackson St Frankfort (46041) *(G-4856)*

Times Leader Publications LLC 317 300-8782
7670 Us 31 S Indianapolis (46227) *(G-8076)*

Times Mail, Bedford *Also called Miller Rainbow Printing Inc* *(G-565)*

Times, The, Munster *Also called Lee Enterprises Inc Times* *(G-10613)*

Timken Company 574 288-7188
3502 W Sample St South Bend (46619) *(G-12970)*

Timken Company 574 287-1566
3010 Mishawaka Ave South Bend (46615) *(G-12971)*

Timken Furnaces Agency, South Bend *Also called Timken Company* *(G-12971)*

Timothy J Troyer 574 546-1115
1657 3rd Rd Bremen (46506) *(G-1029)*

Timothy Reed Carry ME Mus Pubg 812 322-7187
610 S Washington St Apt D Bloomington (47401) *(G-842)*

Timothy White 765 689-8270
191 S Elm St Bunker Hill (46914) *(G-1207)*

Tinas Ceramics & Things 812 917-4190
1001 N 3rd St Terre Haute (47807) *(G-13355)*

Tinchers Creative Woodworks 765 344-0062
11206 E Ferndale Rd Rockville (47872) *(G-12181)*

Tint Unlimited 812 402-6102
204 N 9th Ave Ste C Evansville (47712) *(G-3764)*

Tints & Prints By Tierney LLC 317 769-5895
4211 Honeysuckle Ln Zionsville (46077) *(G-14469)*

Tiny Timbers, Deputy *Also called Homestead Properties Inc* *(G-2460)*

Tip To Tail Aerospace LLC 765 437-6556
1697 W Hoosier Blvd 11 Peru (46970) *(G-11552)*

Tippecanoe Laboratories, Lafayette *Also called Evonik Corporation* *(G-8894)*

Tippecanoe Press Inc 317 392-1207
230 N Knightstown Rd Shelbyville (46176) *(G-12576)*

Tippmann Ordnance, Fort Wayne *Also called Allied Mfg Partners Inc* *(G-4062)*

Tippmann Products LLC 260 438-7946
3905 Goeglein Rd Fort Wayne (46815) *(G-4685)*

Tippmann Sports LLC (HQ) 800 533-4831
2955 Adams Center Rd Fort Wayne (46803) *(G-4686)*

Tippmann Sports LLC 260 749-6022
2955 Adams Center Rd Fort Wayne (46803) *(G-4687)*

Tipsy Glass LLC 260 251-0021
704 W Race St Portland (47371) *(G-11851)*

Tipton Engrg Elc Mtr Svcs Inc 765 963-3380
159 W Vine St Sharpsville (46068) *(G-12507)*

Tipton Mills Foods LLC 812 372-0900
835 S Mapleton St Columbus (47201) *(G-2021)*

Tire Rack Inc (PA) 888 541-1777
7101 Vorden Pkwy South Bend (46628) *(G-12972)*

Tire Rack, The, South Bend *Also called Tire Rack Inc* *(G-12972)*

Tisa, Princeton *Also called Toyota Boshoku Indiana LLC* *(G-11886)*

Tishler Industries Inc (PA) 765 286-5454
1810 S Macedonia Ave Muncie (47302) *(G-10569)*

Titan Manufacturing Co 219 662-7238
13128 Iowa St Crown Point (46307) *(G-2314)*

Titan Metal Spinning Inc 260 665-1067
301 Growth Pkwy Angola (46703) *(G-251)*

Titan Metal Worx LLC 260 422-4433
5225 New Haven Ave Fort Wayne (46803) *(G-4688)*

Titanium Eagles Nutrition 219 781-6018
4700 Central Ave Lake Station (46405) *(G-9079)*

Titanium LLC 765 236-6906
847 N 300 E Kokomo (46901) *(G-8708)*

Titanium Rails Nutrition LLC 219 940-3704
1709 E 37th Ave Hobart (46342) *(G-6099)*

Tite-Lok, Fort Wayne *Also called Universal Consolidated Methods* *(G-4719)*

Title Ten Manufacturing LLC 765 388-2482
401 W Willard St Muncie (47302) *(G-10570)*

Titus Inc 574 936-3345
9887 6b Rd Plymouth (46563) *(G-11728)*

Titus Mfg LLC 574 286-1928
7991 Lilac Rd Plymouth (46563) *(G-11729)*

Tj Maintenance LLC 219 776-8427
8591 N 300 W Lake Village (46349) *(G-9088)*

Tj Performance LLC 765 580-0481
4331 N Jobe Rd Brownsville (47325) *(G-1196)*

Tjs Roaster 812 985-9615
11835 Old Highway 66 Evansville (47712) *(G-3765)*

Tk Finishing 574 233-1617
3702 W Sample St Ste 4045 South Bend (46619) *(G-12973)*

Tk Sales and Marketing LLC 812 430-5103
2301 Mount Auburn Rd Evansville (47720) *(G-3766)*

Tk Software Inc (PA) 317 569-8887
11495 N Penn St Ste 220 Carmel (46032) *(G-1498)*

Tko Enterprises Inc 317 271-1398
2751 Stafford Rd Plainfield (46168) *(G-11647)*

Tl Enterprises LLC 574 262-4706
2901 E Bristol St Ste D Elkhart (46514) *(G-3218)*

Tl Industries Inc 419 666-8144
21746 Buckingham Rd Elkhart (46516) *(G-3219)*

Tls By Design 765 683-1971
10737 Sand Key Cir Indianapolis (46256) *(G-8077)*

Tma Enterprises Inc 317 272-0694
7900 E Us Highway 36 C Avon (46123) *(G-469)*

Tmak Inc 219 874-7661
200 Winski Dr Michigan City (46360) *(G-9853)*

Tmf Center Inc 765 762-3800
105 Slauter Ln Williamsport (47993) *(G-14298)*

Tmf Center Inc (PA) 765 762-1000
300 W Washington St Williamsport (47993) *(G-14299)*

Tmgg LLC 812 687-7444
714 5th St Plainville (47568) *(G-11656)*

TMI Contractors, Mount Vernon *Also called Tron Mechanical Incorporated* *(G-10410)*

Tmr Group, Whitestown *Also called Tank Construction & Service Co* *(G-14263)*

Tms International LLC 219 881-0266
1 N Broadway Gary (46402) *(G-5106)*

Tms International LLC 219 762-2176
1575 Adler Cir Ste E Portage (46368) *(G-11798)*

Tms International LLC 219 864-0044
833 W Lincoln Hwy 310w Schererville (46375) *(G-12349)*

Tms International LLC 219 885-7491
1 N Broadway Stop 380 Gary (46402) *(G-5107)*

Tms International LLC 219 881-0155
3001 Dickey Rd East Chicago (46312) *(G-2570)*

Tms International LLC 219 397-6550
3001 Dickey Rd Ste 392 East Chicago (46312) *(G-2571)*

Tnemec Company Inc 317 884-1806
458 Park 800 Dr Greenwood (46143) *(G-5753)*

TNT Construction 260 726-2643
114 Jack Imel Ave Portland (47371) *(G-11852)*

TNT Truck Accessories LLC 812 305-0714
152 W 1275 S Haubstadt (47639) *(G-6006)*

To a Tee Inc 317 757-8842
7125 Girls School Ave Indianapolis (46241) *(G-8078)*

TOA (usa) LLC 317 834-0522
2000 Pleiades Dr Mooresville (46158) *(G-10343)*

TOA Winchester LLC 765 584-7639
200 Inks Dr Winchester (47394) *(G-14342)*

Tobacco Zone Inc 317 268-6808
4306 Stillwater Way Plainfield (46168) *(G-11648)*

Toco Inc 317 627-8854
4307 Blackwood Ct Greenwood (46143) *(G-5754)*

Todays Signs and Graphics 765 288-4771
1804 N Wheeling Ave Ste 1 Muncie (47303) *(G-10571)*

Todd Couch Regional Office 312 863-2520
10804 Knightsbridge Ln Fishers (46037) *(G-3977)*

Todd K Hockemeyer Inc 260 639-3591
12108 Us Highway 27 S Fort Wayne (46816) *(G-4689)*

Todd L Wise..260 799-4828
5440 W 450 S Albion (46701) **(G-36)**

Tokai Rika of Indiana, Ashley Also called Trin Inc **(G-292)**

Tom Cooks, Evansville Also called Industrial Sewing Machine Co **(G-3558)**

Tom Doherty Company Inc.....................317 352-8200
2402 N Shadeland Ave A Indianapolis (46219) **(G-8079)**

Tom Spencer Concrete Products.............812 659-2318
Road 600 W St Rd Switz City (47465) **(G-13127)**

Tomken Plastic Tech Inc.......................765 284-2472
4601 N Superior Dr Muncie (47303) **(G-10572)**

Tomlin Enterprises Inc.........................866 994-9200
6926 Quemetco Ct Fort Wayne (46803) **(G-4690)**

Tomlinson Manufacturing......................800 881-9769
1125 Brookside Ave Ste C1 Indianapolis (46202) **(G-8080)**

Tomlinson Manufacturing......................317 209-9375
9165 E Us Highway 36 Avon (46123) **(G-470)**

Toms Donuts of Auburn LLC..................260 927-1224
202 S Dewey St Auburn (46706) **(G-362)**

Toms Interior Windows LLC...................574 233-0799
3702 W Sample St Ste 1133 South Bend (46619) **(G-12974)**

Tonne Winery.....................................765 896-9821
101 W Royerton Rd Muncie (47303) **(G-10573)**

Tony Stewart Racing Entps LLC..............317 858-8620
438 Southpoint Cir Brownsburg (46112) **(G-1175)**

Tonya Gerhardt..................................260 434-1370
6134 Constitution Dr Fort Wayne (46804) **(G-4691)**

Tool Dynamics LLC..............................812 379-4243
835 S Marr Rd Columbus (47201) **(G-2022)**

Tool Room Service..............................765 287-0062
1403 S Liberty St Muncie (47302) **(G-10574)**

Toolcraft LLC...................................260 749-0454
2620 Adams Center Rd Fort Wayne (46803) **(G-4692)**

Toolmasters Inc.................................574 256-1881
1203 E 6th St Mishawaka (46544) **(G-10140)**

Toomuchfun Rubberstamps Inc...............260 557-4808
11738 Winchester Rd Fort Wayne (46819) **(G-4693)**

Top Design Cnc Inc............................219 662-2915
41 N 400 E Valparaiso (46383) **(G-13629)**

Top Fuel Crossfit...............................219 281-7001
1674 E North St Crown Point (46307) **(G-2315)**

Top In Sound Inc................................765 649-8111
3273 N State Road 9 Anderson (46012) **(G-177)**

Top Lock Corporation..........................317 831-2000
319 Harlan Dr Mooresville (46158) **(G-10344)**

Top Notch Tool & Engineering................812 663-2184
930 E Main St Greensburg (47240) **(G-5637)**

Top Shelf Acoustics LLC.......................317 512-4569
8175 Ehlerbrook Rd Indianapolis (46237) **(G-8081)**

Topgard LLC......................................317 525-0700
1125 Brookside Ave Indianapolis (46202) **(G-8082)**

Topics Newspapers Inc........................888 357-7827
13095 Publishers Dr Fishers (46038) **(G-3978)**

Topp Industries Incorporated................574 223-3681
420 N State Road 25 Rochester (46975) **(G-12157)**

Topps Industries................................574 892-5016
820 Dewey St Argos (46501) **(G-279)**

Topspeed...260 665-8889
319 Pokagon Trl Angola (46703) **(G-252)**

Topstitch Inc...................................574 293-6633
921 Summa Dr Elkhart (46516) **(G-3220)**

Toray Resin Company..........................317 398-7833
821 W Mausoleum Rd Shelbyville (46176) **(G-12577)**

Torch Newspapers Inc.........................765 569-2033
125 W High St Rockville (47872) **(G-12182)**

Tordilleria Del Valle............................765 654-9590
905 Walnut Ave Frankfort (46041) **(G-4857)**

Tornier Inc.......................................574 268-0861
100 Capital Dr Ste 201 Warsaw (46582) **(G-13953)**

Torsion Plastics LLC..........................330 552-2184
5400 Foundation Blvd Evansville (47725) **(G-3767)**

Torti Products Inc.............................219 730-2071
2735 Glenwood St Highland (46322) **(G-6057)**

Tortillas Nuevo Leon, Hammond Also called O-M Distributors Inc **(G-5924)**

Tosmo America Inc............................812 953-1481
819 Buckeye St North Vernon (47265) **(G-11284)**

Total Cleaning Solutions LLC.................260 471-7761
4620 Lima Rd Fort Wayne (46808) **(G-4694)**

Total Concepts Design Inc....................812 752-6534
1054 S Taylor Mill Rd Scottsburg (47170) **(G-12384)**

Total Control Systems, Fort Wayne Also called Murray Equipment Inc **(G-4486)**

Total Electronics, Logansport Also called Cal-Comp USA (indiana) Inc **(G-9326)**

Total Tote Inc...................................260 982-8318
11606 N State Road 15 North Manchester (46962) **(G-11246)**

Totschlager Game Calls LLC.................574 354-1620
4820 8a Rd Bourbon (46504) **(G-950)**

Touch Plate, Fort Wayne Also called Touchplate Technologies Inc **(G-4696)**

Touch Plate Lighting Controls, Fort Wayne Also called Touch Plate Technologies Inc **(G-4695)**

Touch Plate Technologies Inc................260 426-1565
1830 Wayne Trce Ste 9 Fort Wayne (46803) **(G-4695)**

Touchdown Fishing Lures LLC................812 873-8355
5975 W State Highway 250 Paris Crossing (47270) **(G-11461)**

Touchdown Machining Inc.....................812 378-0300
432 S Mapleton St Columbus (47201) **(G-2023)**

Touchplate Technologies Inc.................260 424-4323
1830 Wayne Trce Ste 9 Fort Wayne (46803) **(G-4696)**

Touchtronics Inc................................574 294-2570
57315 Nagy Dr Ste A Elkhart (46517) **(G-3221)**

Touchwood Trans Inc..........................317 941-0009
7142 Chesterton Ln Indianapolis (46237) **(G-8083)**

Tower Advertising Products Inc (PA).........260 593-2103
1015 W Lake St Topeka (46571) **(G-13431)**

Tower Automotive Operations...............260 925-5113
801 W 15th St Auburn (46706) **(G-363)**

Tower Innovations, Newburgh Also called Liberty Industries LC **(G-11035)**

Tower Ribbons, Topeka Also called Tower Advertising Products Inc **(G-13431)**

Tower Structural Laminating, Ligonier Also called Supreme Corporation **(G-9298)**

Town & Country Industries Inc...............219 712-0893
1001 E Summit St Crown Point (46307) **(G-2316)**

Town & Country Press Inc.....................574 936-9505
1920 Jim Neu Dr Plymouth (46563) **(G-11730)**

Town & Country Printing, Crown Point Also called Town & Country Industries Inc **(G-2316)**

Town Country Printing.........................765 452-0093
315 N Main St Kokomo (46901) **(G-8709)**

Towne Air Freight, South Bend Also called Clp Towne Inc **(G-12737)**

Towne Post Network Inc.......................317 288-7101
11216 Fall Creek Rd 125 Indianapolis (46256) **(G-8084)**

Townepost LLC..................................317 288-7101
12135 Southcreek Ct Indianapolis (46236) **(G-8085)**

Townsend Sales Inc............................317 736-4047
4141 S 25 W Trafalgar (46181) **(G-13439)**

Townsend Transmissions LLC................765 342-0042
1051 S Old State Road 67 Martinsville (46151) **(G-9643)**

Toyo Seiko North America Inc................574 288-2000
3507 N Olive Rd Ste E South Bend (46628) **(G-12975)**

Toyoshima Indiana Inc.........................317 638-3511
735 Saint Paul St Indianapolis (46203) **(G-8086)**

Toyoshima Special Steel USA, Indianapolis Also called Toyoshima Indiana Inc **(G-8086)**

Toyota...317 755-4791
8192 Sweetwater Dr Nineveh (46164) **(G-11058)**

Toyota Boshoku America Inc..................812 385-2040
1698 S 100 W Princeton (47670) **(G-11884)**

Toyota Boshoku America Inc..................812 385-2040
1698 S 100 W Princeton (47670) **(G-11885)**

Toyota Boshoku Indiana, Princeton Also called Tbin LLC **(G-11883)**

Toyota Boshoku Indiana LLC.................812 491-9100
1698 S 100 W Princeton (47670) **(G-11886)**

Toyota Industrial Eqp Mfg Inc (HQ)..........812 342-0060
5555 Inwood Dr Columbus (47201) **(G-2024)**

Toyota Industries N Amer Inc (HQ)..........812 341-3810
3030 Barker Dr Columbus (47201) **(G-2025)**

Toyota Motor Mfg Ind Inc (HQ)..............812 387-2266
4000 S Tulip Tree Dr Princeton (47670) **(G-11887)**

Tp/Elm Acquisition Sbusid Inc (HQ).........260 728-2161
2110 Patterson St Decatur (46733) **(G-2408)**

Tpg Mt Vernon Marine LLC..................317 631-0234
1341 N Capitol Ave Indianapolis (46202) **(G-8087)**

Tpr, Indianapolis Also called Beeman Jorgensen Inc **(G-6465)**

Tprl, West Lafayette Also called Thermphyscal Prpts RES Lab Inc **(G-14113)**

Tr Manufacturing LLC.........................260 357-4679
1106 S Cowen St Garrett (46738) **(G-5024)**

Trace Engineering Inc..........................765 354-4351
400 Locust St Middletown (47356) **(G-9942)**

Trackahead LLC.................................800 780-3519
12175 Visionary Way Fishers (46038) **(G-3979)**

Tracy K Hullett..................................765 472-3349
268 W 3rd St Peru (46970) **(G-11553)**

Trade Line Fabricating Inc.....................812 637-1444
22422 Stateline Rd Lawrenceburg (47025) **(G-9159)**

Tradebe Environmental Svcs LLC (HQ)......800 388-7242
1433 E 83rd Ave Ste 200 Merrillville (46410) **(G-9759)**

Tradebe GP (HQ)...............................800 388-7242
4343 Kennedy Ave East Chicago (46312) **(G-2572)**

Tradebe Industrial Svcs LLC (HQ)...........800 388-7242
1433 E 83rd Ave Ste 200 East Chicago (46312) **(G-2573)**

Trademark Screen Printing....................317 885-3258
173 E Broadway St Greenwood (46143) **(G-5755)**

Traders Point Winery..........................317 879-9463
5520 W 84th St Indianapolis (46268) **(G-8088)**

Trading Post.....................................574 935-5460
523 E Jefferson St Plymouth (46563) **(G-11731)**

Traffic Sign Company Inc......................317 845-9305
9402 Uptown Dr Ste 1500 Indianapolis (46256) **(G-8089)**

Traffic Signal Company, Indianapolis Also called Doron Distribution Inc **(G-6759)**

Trafford Holdings Ltd..........................888 232-4444
1663 S Liberty Dr Bloomington (47403) **(G-843)**

Trafford Publishing, Bloomington Also called Trafford Holdings Ltd **(G-843)**

Trailer Life Publishing, Elkhart *Also called TI Enterprises LLC (G-3218)*

Trailmaster, Mishawaka *Also called J Q Tex Inc (G-10056)*

Train Co, La Porte *Also called Kenco Plastics Inc (G-8777)*

Trane US Inc...812 421-8725
1024 E Sycamore St Evansville (47714) *(G-3768)*

Trane US Inc...317 255-8777
5355 N Post Rd Indianapolis (46216) *(G-8090)*

Trane US Inc...574 282-4880
3725 Cleveland Rd Ste 300 South Bend (46628) *(G-12976)*

Trane US Inc...260 489-0884
6602 Innovation Blvd Fort Wayne (46818) *(G-4697)*

Trane US Inc...765 932-7200
1300 N Benjamin St Rushville (46173) *(G-12236)*

Trans Industries Incorporated...............219 977-9190
6325 W 5th Ave Gary (46406) *(G-5108)*

Trans-Flo, Fort Wayne *Also called Im Indiana Holdings Inc (G-4359)*

Transcendia Inc.....................................765 935-1520
300 Industrial Pkwy Richmond (47374) *(G-12068)*

Transco Railway Products Inc...............574 753-6227
1331 18th St Logansport (46947) *(G-9370)*

Transformation Industries LLC..............574 457-9320
615 Cushing St South Bend (46616) *(G-12977)*

Transformations By Wieland Inc............800 440-9337
310 Racquet Dr Fort Wayne (46825) *(G-4698)*

Transhield Inc (PA)...............................574 742-4333
2932 Thorne Dr Elkhart (46514) *(G-3222)*

Transmed Associates Inc (PA)...............317 293-9993
8131 Kingston St Ste 700 Avon (46123) *(G-471)*

Transmetco Corporation........................260 355-0089
1750 Riverfork Dr Huntington (46750) *(G-6255)*

Transportation Tech Inds (HQ)..............812 962-5000
7140 Office Cir Evansville (47715) *(G-3769)*

Transwheel Corporation (HQ)................260 358-8660
3000 Yeoman Way Huntington (46750) *(G-6256)*

Tranter Graphics Inc.............................574 834-2626
8094 N State Road 13 Syracuse (46567) *(G-13151)*

Travel Home Solutions...........................260 592-7628
2242 Mulberry St Pleasant Mills (46780) *(G-11658)*

Travel Lite Inc.......................................574 831-3000
71913 County Road 23 New Paris (46553) *(G-10999)*

Travel Star Products, Goshen *Also called Exton Inc (G-5212)*

Traveling Bookbinder Inc.......................317 441-4901
10712 Talisman Dr Noblesville (46060) *(G-11195)*

Traveling Satchel LLC...........................317 502-3241
1501 Oakwood Trl Indianapolis (46260) *(G-8091)*

Travis Britton..317 762-6018
315 N Franklin Rd Indianapolis (46219) *(G-8092)*

Travis C and Jan B Page.......................812 398-5507
9606 S County Road 18 Sw Carlisle (47838) *(G-1298)*

Travomatic Corp Indiana Div.................812 522-8177
2230 D Ave E Seymour (47274) *(G-12497)*

TRC Mfg Inc..574 262-9299
17460 Fleetwood Ln South Bend (46635) *(G-12978)*

Tre Paper Co Inc....................................765 649-2536
5395 S 50 W Anderson (46013) *(G-178)*

Tredegar Corporation.............................812 466-0266
3400 Fort Harrison Rd Terre Haute (47804) *(G-13356)*

Tree City Saw Mill.................................812 663-6363
2663 E County Road 500 S Greensburg (47240) *(G-5638)*

Tree City Sawmill, Greensburg *Also called Tree City Saw Mill (G-5638)*

Tree City Tool & Engrg Co Inc...............812 663-4196
1954 N Montgomery Rd Greensburg (47240) *(G-5639)*

Tree Pro, West Lafayette *Also called Lafayette Marketing Inc (G-14081)*

Treehugger Maple Syrup LLC................765 698-3728
15203 Ott Rd Laurel (47024) *(G-9129)*

Trellborg Sling Prfiles US Inc...............330 995-5125
1151 Bloomingdale Dr Bristol (46507) *(G-1090)*

Trellborg Sling Sltions US Inc..............260 748-5895
2531 Bremer Rd Fort Wayne (46803) *(G-4699)*

Trellborg Sling Sltions US Inc (HQ).......260 749-9631
2531 Bremer Rd Fort Wayne (46803) *(G-4700)*

Tremain Ceramic Tile & Flr Cvg............317 542-1491
8105 E 47th St Indianapolis (46226) *(G-8093)*

Trendway Corporation............................317 870-3269
5273 Lakeview Pkwy S Dr Indianapolis (46268) *(G-8094)*

Trenwa Inc..812 427-2217
13268 Innovation Dr Florence (47020) *(G-4005)*

Tretter Boeglin Inc................................812 683-4598
475 W 19th St Huntingburg (47542) *(G-6182)*

Trey Exploration Inc..............................812 858-3146
2699 Sr 261 Newburgh (47630) *(G-11052)*

Trh Software Inc....................................812 264-2428
1503 7th Ave Terre Haute (47807) *(G-13357)*

Tri Aerospace LLC................................812 872-2400
1055 S Hunt St Terre Haute (47803) *(G-13358)*

Tri Don LLC...765 966-7300
5679 Park Elwood Rd Richmond (47374) *(G-12069)*

Tri Star Embroidery, Fort Branch *Also called Barrett Manufacturing Inc (G-4026)*

Tri Star Filtration Inc............................317 337-0940
5319 W 86th St Indianapolis (46268) *(G-8095)*

Tri State Cylinder Head.........................812 421-0095
1712 Read St Evansville (47710) *(G-3770)*

Tri State Flasher Co, Evansville *Also called T S F Co Inc (G-3757)*

Tri State Hydraulic Indus Sup, Greendale *Also called Tri-State Hydraulics Indus Sup (G-5495)*

Tri State Mold.......................................859 240-7643
7255 State Route 56 W Rising Sun (47040) *(G-12092)*

Tri State Monument Company................812 386-7303
106 E Brumfield Ave Princeton (47670) *(G-11888)*

Tri State Optical Inc..............................765 289-4475
1608 W Mcgalliard Rd Muncie (47304) *(G-10575)*

Tri State Powder Coating LLC...............812 425-7010
800 Bayse St Evansville (47713) *(G-3771)*

Tri State Printing & Embroider..............812 316-0094
24 N 1st St Vincennes (47591) *(G-13710)*

Tri State Valve Instrument Co................812 434-0141
1200 N Willow Rd Ste 103 Evansville (47711) *(G-3772)*

Tri TEC Systems Inc.............................260 724-8874
125 W Grant St Decatur (46733) *(G-2409)*

Tri-Esco Inc..765 446-7937
101 N 36th St Colburn (47905) *(G-1755)*

Tri-S, Jeffersonville *Also called Steel Structural Products LLC (G-8429)*

Tri-Seals Division, Goshen *Also called Triangle Rubber Co LLC (G-5340)*

Tri-Star Glove, Plainville *Also called Tmgg LLC (G-11656)*

Tri-State Forest Products Inc.................317 328-1850
6740 Guion Rd Indianapolis (46268) *(G-8096)*

Tri-State Hardwood Company................260 351-3111
7050 S State Rd 3 South Milford (46786) *(G-12994)*

Tri-State Homes and Garages...............812 867-2411
7703 Baumgart Rd Evansville (47725) *(G-3773)*

Tri-State Hydraulics Indus Sup.............812 537-3485
752 Oberting Rd Greendale (47025) *(G-5495)*

Tri-State Industries Inc.........................219 933-1710
4923 Columbia Ave Hammond (46327) *(G-5951)*

Tri-State Machine Co Inc.......................812 479-3159
2410 N Burkhardt Rd Evansville (47715) *(G-3774)*

Tri-State Machining Inc.........................260 422-2508
2515 Mcdonald St Fort Wayne (46803) *(G-4701)*

Tri-State Mechanical Inc.......................260 471-0345
4530 Secretary Dr Fort Wayne (46808) *(G-4702)*

Tri-State Metals Inc..............................219 397-0470
220 W Chicago Ave East Chicago (46312) *(G-2574)*

Tri-State Power Supply LLC..................812 537-2500
48 Doughty Rd Lawrenceburg (47025) *(G-9160)*

Tri-State Printing & EMB LLC................812 743-2825
6250 S State Road 61 Monroe City (47557) *(G-10189)*

Tri-State Shtmtl & Mfg LLC...................260 402-8831
1738 Traders Xing Fort Wayne (46845) *(G-4703)*

Tri-State Trailer and Truck, Evansville *Also called R & B Associates Inc (G-3693)*

Tri-State Trophies, Evansville *Also called Jef Enterprises Inc (G-3573)*

Triad Mining Co of Indiana, Oakland City *Also called Arrow Mining Inc (G-11307)*

Triad Mining Inc...................................812 328-2117
1216 E County Road 900 S Oakland City (47660) *(G-11316)*

Triad Warsh Plant Scale House..............812 385-0909
4251 W County Road 125 S Petersburg (47567) *(G-11571)*

Triangle Asphalt Paving Corp................765 482-5701
501 Sam Ralston Rd Lebanon (46052) *(G-9229)*

Triangle Engineering Corp....................317 243-8549
2206 Production Dr Indianapolis (46241) *(G-8097)*

Triangle Machine Inc............................574 246-0165
3702 W Sample St Ste 1125 South Bend (46619) *(G-12979)*

Triangle Printing Inc.............................317 786-3488
6107 Homestead Dr Indianapolis (46227) *(G-8098)*

Triangle Publishing...............................765 677-2544
4201 S Washington St Marion (46953) *(G-9567)*

Triangle Rubber Co LLC (PA)................574 533-3118
1924 Elkhart Rd Goshen (46526) *(G-5340)*

Triangle Rubber Co LLC........................574 533-3118
1801 Eisenhower Dr N Goshen (46526) *(G-5341)*

Tribine Industries LLC..........................316 282-8011
6991 E 750 N Logansport (46947) *(G-9371)*

Tribune Showprint Inc...........................574 943-3281
107 S Oak St Earl Park (47942) *(G-2513)*

Tribune Star, Terre Haute *Also called Newspaper Holding Inc (G-13290)*

Tribune, The, Seymour *Also called Seymour Trbune A Cal Ltd Prtnr (G-12487)*

Tricounty Surgical and Assoc................260 726-2890
510b W Votaw St Ste B Portland (47371) *(G-11853)*

Trident Engraving Inc............................812 282-2098
3114 New Chapel Rd Jeffersonville (47130) *(G-8435)*

Trifab & Construction Inc (PA)..............219 845-1300
2433 167th St Hammond (46323) *(G-5952)*

Trilithic Inc (HQ)..................................317 895-3600
5808 Churchman Byp Indianapolis (46203) *(G-8099)*

Trill Machine LLC.................................219 730-0744
104 W Washington St Kentland (47951) *(G-8524)*

Trillium Cabinet Company Inc...............317 471-8870
4357 W 96th St Indianapolis (46268) *(G-8100)*

Trilogy Gallery, Nashville *Also called Pgs LLC (G-10732)*

Trim-A-Door...317 769-8746
4036 Perry Blvd Whitestown (46075) *(G-14264)*

Trim-A-Seal of Indiana Inc (PA)...............................219 883-2180
1500 Polk St Gary (46407) *(G-5109)*

Trim-Lok Inc..574 227-1143
1642 Gateway Ct Elkhart (46514) *(G-3223)*

Trimas Corporation..260 925-3700
500 W 7th St Auburn (46706) *(G-364)*

Trimax Machine LLC...812 887-9281
5852 N Rod And Gun Clb Bruceville (47516) *(G-1198)*

Trimble Combustion Systems Inc..............................812 623-4545
215 Nieman St Ste 2 Sunman (47041) *(G-13120)*

Trin Inc (HQ)..260 587-9282
803 H L Thompson Jr Dr Ashley (46705) *(G-292)*

Trinity Cmmnications Group Inc...............................260 484-1029
2524 Merivale St Fort Wayne (46805) *(G-4704)*

Trinity Cstm Built Pallets LLC..................................260 466-4625
12802 Irving Rd New Haven (46774) *(G-10961)*

Trinity Displays Inc...219 201-8733
50 Marine Dr Apt E8 Michigan City (46360) *(G-9854)*

Trinity Guardion..812 932-2600
4 S Park Ave Ste 204 Batesville (47006) *(G-521)*

Trinity Metals LLC..317 358-8265
2440 N Shadeland Ave Indianapolis (46219) *(G-8101)*

Trinity Metals LLC (HQ)...317 358-8265
6400 English Ave Indianapolis (46219) *(G-8102)*

Trinkets & Forget ME Nots, Carmel *Also called Anderson Enterprises LLC (G-1311)*

Trio Milling Inc..765 795-4088
4222 E County Road 1000 S Cloverdale (46120) *(G-1740)*

Triple Crown Media LLC...574 533-2151
114 S Main St Goshen (46526) *(G-5342)*

Triple H Tool Co..812 567-4600
7677 Folsomville Rd Tennyson (47637) *(G-13182)*

Triple Inc..574 267-1450
610 E Bell Dr Warsaw (46582) *(G-13954)*

Triple J Ironworks Inc..765 544-9152
211 S Main St Carthage (46115) *(G-1517)*

Triple S Logging, Decatur *Also called Joseph M Schmidt (G-2387)*

Triplet Tool and Die Co Inc......................................812 867-2494
8039 Burch Park Dr Evansville (47725) *(G-3775)*

Triplex Industries Inc..574 256-9253
55901 Currant Rd Mishawaka (46545) *(G-10141)*

Triplex Plating Inc...219 874-3209
1555 E Us Highway 12 Michigan City (46360) *(G-9855)*

Trison Industries Inc..812 945-7775
3203 Old Hill Rd Floyds Knobs (47119) *(G-4022)*

Tristate Plastic Tops..812 853-7827
4395 State Route 261 Newburgh (47630) *(G-11053)*

Tritech Manufacturing Inc..260 747-9154
2728 Commercial Rd Fort Wayne (46809) *(G-4705)*

Triton Brewing, Indianapolis *Also called Beer Baron LLC (G-6466)*

Triton Metal Products Inc...260 488-1800
7790 S Homestead Dr Hamilton (46742) *(G-5830)*

Triton Plant, Angola *Also called BSC Vntres Acquisition Sub LLC (G-198)*

Triumph Controls LLC..317 421-8760
1960 N Michigan Rd Shelbyville (46176) *(G-12578)*

Triumph Group Operations Inc.................................317 392-5000
850 Elston Dr Shelbyville (46176) *(G-12579)*

Triumph Thermal Systems Inc..................................419 273-1192
1960 N Michigan Rd Shelbyville (46176) *(G-12580)*

Triunity LLC..317 703-1147
15209 Herriman Blvd Noblesville (46060) *(G-11196)*

Trivaeo LLC...765 387-4451
4250 N River Rd Montezuma (47862) *(G-10212)*

Trivalence Technologies LLC....................................800 209-2517
3290 Claremont Ave Evansville (47712) *(G-3776)*

Trivector Manufacturing Inc.....................................260 637-0141
4404 Engle Ridge Dr Fort Wayne (46804) *(G-4706)*

Trivett Contracting Inc..317 539-5150
5981 Liberty Pkwy Clayton (46118) *(G-1708)*

Tron Mechanical Incorporated..................................812 838-4715
331 W 2nd St Mount Vernon (47620) *(G-10410)*

Trophies & Awards Inc...260 925-4672
1916 Wayne St Auburn (46706) *(G-365)*

Troves..260 672-0878
270 N Main St Roanoke (46783) *(G-12108)*

Troy Meggitt Inc (HQ)..812 547-7071
3 Industrial Dr Troy (47588) *(G-13448)*

Troy Stuart...812 887-0403
1 Fountain View Est # 2 Washington (47501) *(G-14004)*

Troyer Brothers...260 589-2244
6691 W State Road 124 Decatur (46733) *(G-2410)*

Troyer Brothers Inc...260 565-2244
6691 W State Rd 124 Bluffton (46714) *(G-895)*

Troyer Products, Elkhart *Also called Samaron Corp (G-3154)*

Trp International LLC..574 389-9941
21840 Protecta Dr Elkhart (46516) *(G-3224)*

Tru-Cut Inc...765 683-9920
3111 S Madison Ave Anderson (46016) *(G-179)*

Tru-Cut Machine & Tool Inc......................................260 569-1802
556 E Baumbauer Rd Lot 41 Wabash (46992) *(G-13759)*

Tru-Flex LLC (HQ)..765 893-4403
2391 S State Road 263 West Lebanon (47991) *(G-14122)*

Tru-Form Metal Products Inc....................................574 266-8020
1025 D I Dr Elkhart (46514) *(G-3225)*

Tru-Form Steel & Wire Inc (PA).................................765 348-5001
1204 Gilkey Ave Hartford City (47348) *(G-5993)*

Tru-Form Steel & Wire Inc..765 348-5001
1822 Joe Bonham Dr Hartford City (47348) *(G-5994)*

Truarch Inc...812 402-9511
3101 N Green River Rd Evansville (47715) *(G-3777)*

Truck Accessories Group Inc....................................574 522-5337
58288 Ventura Dr Elkhart (46517) *(G-3226)*

Truck Life LLC...219 655-0018
7900 Melton Rd Gary (46403) *(G-5110)*

Truck Stylin & Collision, Rochester *Also called Truck Stylin Unlimited (G-12158)*

Truck Stylin Unlimited...574 223-8800
2123 Southway 31 Rochester (46975) *(G-12158)*

Truckpro LLC...765 482-6525
450 N Enterprise Blvd Lebanon (46052) *(G-9230)*

Trudel Family Ltd Partnership...................................260 627-5626
14101 Leo Rd Leo (46765) *(G-9246)*

True Chem Inc...317 769-2701
283 Innisbrooke Ave Greenwood (46142) *(G-5756)*

True Flight Arrow Co, Monticello *Also called Easton Technical Products Inc (G-10261)*

True Precision Tech Inc..765 252-9766
1602 Ehavens St Kokomo (46901) *(G-8710)*

True Stories Publishing Co LLC.................................765 425-8224
48 N Whitcomb Ave Indianapolis (46224) *(G-8103)*

Trufab Stainless..812 287-8278
2126 W Industrial Park Dr Bloomington (47404) *(G-844)*

Trulinesigns Inc..219 644-7231
13105 81st Ave Dyer (46311) *(G-2511)*

Trulite GL Alum Solutions LLC..................................317 273-0646
7701 W New York St Indianapolis (46214) *(G-8104)*

Truman Ritchie..219 956-2211
262 E 550 N Rensselaer (47978) *(G-11943)*

Truss Manufacturing Company, Tipton *Also called Truss Partners LLC (G-13409)*

Truss Partners LLC..765 675-5700
840 S 550 W Tipton (46072) *(G-13409)*

Truss Systems Inc...812 897-3064
810 Hyrock Blvd Boonville (47601) *(G-923)*

Trusslink..219 362-3968
512 Washington St La Porte (46350) *(G-8832)*

Trustees Indiana University.......................................812 856-4186
2611 E 10th St Rm 160 Bloomington (47408) *(G-845)*

Trustees Indiana University.......................................812 855-0763
120 Ernie Pyle Hall Ind Bloomington (47405) *(G-846)*

Trustees Indiana University.......................................812 855-3439
465 Ballantine Hall 1020 1020 E Bloomington (47405) *(G-847)*

Trustees Indiana University.......................................812 855-4848
900 E 7th St Bloomington (47405) *(G-848)*

Truth Publishing Company Inc (PA)..........................574 294-1661
421 S 2nd St Ste 100 Elkhart (46516) *(G-3227)*

Truth Publishing Company Inc..................................765 653-5151
100 N Jackson St Greencastle (46135) *(G-5480)*

Trutle Run Winery, Corydon *Also called Pfeiffer Winery & Vineyard (G-2108)*

Trv Industries...765 413-2301
1213 Hartford St Apt 5 Lafayette (47904) *(G-9011)*

TRW Automotive Commercial Stee, Lafayette *Also called TRW Automotive US LLC (G-9012)*

TRW Automotive US LLC...765 423-5377
800 Heath St Lafayette (47904) *(G-9012)*

TRW Commercial Steering..765 423-5377
800 Heath St Lafayette (47904) *(G-9013)*

TS Tech Indiana LLC..765 465-4294
3800 Brooks Dr New Castle (47362) *(G-10920)*

Ts2 Tctical Spec-Solutions Inc.................................765 437-3650
11 Hillcrest Cir Bedford (47421) *(G-585)*

TSA America LLC..317 915-1950
6898 Hawthorn Park Dr Indianapolis (46220) *(G-8105)*

Tsb LLC..812 314-8331
12550 N Presidential Way Edinburgh (46124) *(G-2630)*

Tsf Tool LLC..765 537-9008
5044 S Salem Church Rd Gosport (47433) *(G-5356)*

Tssi, Shelburn *Also called Signaling Solution Inc (G-12510)*

Tsuda USA Corporation..317 468-9177
2934 Jannetides Blvd Greenfield (46140) *(G-5582)*

Tsune America LLC...812 378-9875
12550 N Presidential Way Edinburgh (46124) *(G-2631)*

TT Machining & Fabricating LLC................................219 878-0399
228 Indiana Highway 212 Michigan City (46360) *(G-9856)*

Tt2 LLC...260 438-4575
14516 Lima Rd Fort Wayne (46818) *(G-4707)*

Tube Fabrication Inds Inc...574 753-6377
130 E Industrial Blvd Logansport (46947) *(G-9372)*

Tube Form Solutions LLC (PA)..................................574 295-5041
435 Roske Dr Elkhart (46516) *(G-3228)*

Tube Form Solutions LLC...574 266-5230
4221 Pine Creek Rd Elkhart (46516) *(G-3229)*

Tube Processing Corp.....317 787-5747
604 E Legrande Ave Indianapolis (46203) ***(G-8106)***
Tube Processing Corp (PA).....317 787-1321
604 E Legrande Ave Indianapolis (46203) ***(G-8107)***
Tube Processing Corp.....317 782-9486
3750 Shelby St Indianapolis (46227) ***(G-8108)***
Tube Processing Corp.....317 264-7760
3555 Madison Ave Indianapolis (46227) ***(G-8109)***
Tube Processing Corp.....317 787-1321
604 E Legrande Ave Indianapolis (46203) ***(G-8110)***
Tubesock, Inc., Shelbyville *Also called Rob Nolley Inc* ***(G-12563)***
Tubular Engrg & Sls Co Inc.....765 536-2225
107 S Main St Summitville (46070) ***(G-13108)***
Tucker Publishing Group Inc.....812 426-2115
223 Nw 2nd St Ste 200 Evansville (47708) ***(G-3778)***
Tuff Shed.....317 481-8388
4250 W Morris St Indianapolis (46241) ***(G-8111)***
Tuff Stuff Sales and Svc Inc.....765 354-4151
8520 W State Road 236 Middletown (47356) ***(G-9943)***
Tuff Tool Inc.....262 612-8300
6003 Highgate Pl Fort Wayne (46815) ***(G-4708)***
Tulip Tree Creamery LLC.....317 331-5469
6330 Corporate Dr Ste D Indianapolis (46278) ***(G-8112)***
Tulox Plastics Corporation.....765 664-5155
1007 W Overlook Rd Marion (46952) ***(G-9568)***
Tungsten Company LLC.....317 788-6732
6124 Lazy Ln Indianapolis (46259) ***(G-8113)***
Tupy American Foundry Corp.....317 859-0066
200 N Emerson Ave Ste C Greenwood (46143) ***(G-5757)***
Turbines Inc.....812 877-2587
7303 Maynard Wheeler Ln Terre Haute (47803) ***(G-13359)***
Turkey Roost Publishing LLC.....402 972-6388
4500 S Calloway Dr Hardinsburg (47125) ***(G-5965)***
Turner Contracting Inc.....812 834-5954
1044 Old Us Highway 50 E Bedford (47421) ***(G-586)***
Turner Dolls Inc.....812 834-5065
3522 Pleasant Run Rd Heltonville (47436) ***(G-6029)***
Turner Paving Company.....765 962-4408
1458 Nw 5th St Richmond (47374) ***(G-12070)***
Turnkey Instrument Solutions.....317 946-6354
1132 Southeastern Ave Indianapolis (46202) ***(G-8114)***
Turnomat, Wakarusa *Also called Provident Tool & Die Inc* ***(G-13791)***
Turonis Forget ME Not Inn.....812 477-7500
4 N Weinbach Ave Evansville (47711) ***(G-3779)***
Turtle Top, Goshen *Also called Independent Protection Co Inc* ***(G-5242)***
Turtle Top, New Paris *Also called Independent Protection Co Inc* ***(G-10985)***
Turtle Top Mini Motor Homes.....574 831-4340
1607 S Main St Goshen (46526) ***(G-5343)***
Tusca 2.....812 876-2857
3815 N Collins Dr Bloomington (47404) ***(G-849)***
Tuthill Corporation.....260 747-7529
8825 Aviation Dr Fort Wayne (46809) ***(G-4709)***
Tuthill Corporation.....260 747-7529
8825 Aviation Dr Fort Wayne (46809) ***(G-4710)***
Tuthill Transfer Systems, Fort Wayne *Also called Tuthill Corporation* ***(G-4710)***
Tuttle A Dant Clayton Company, Fishers *Also called Clayton Dant Corporation* ***(G-3891)***
Tuttle Aluminum Intl Inc (PA).....317 842-2420
120 Shadowlawn Dr Fishers (46038) ***(G-3980)***
TW Enterprises LLC.....513 520-8453
9021 Meyer Rd Brookville (47012) ***(G-1128)***
TW Performance Coatings LLC.....317 331-8664
8110 Christian Ln Indianapolis (46217) ***(G-8115)***
Tway Company Incorporated.....317 636-2591
1609 Oliver Ave Indianapolis (46221) ***(G-8116)***
Tway Lifting Products, Indianapolis *Also called Tway Company Incorporated* ***(G-8116)***
Twb of Indiana.....812 342-6000
3030 Barker Dr Columbus (47201) ***(G-2026)***
Twice Daily LLC.....812 484-5417
640 S Bennighof Ave Evansville (47714) ***(G-3780)***
Twigg Corporation (HQ).....765 342-7126
659 E York St Martinsville (46151) ***(G-9644)***
Twin Air Products Inc.....574 295-1129
4602 Chester Dr Elkhart (46516) ***(G-3230)***
Twin City Journal Reporter.....765 674-0070
407 E Main St Gas City (46933) ***(G-5127)***
Twin Coatings & Finishes.....317 557-0633
10216 E 25th St Indianapolis (46229) ***(G-8117)***
Twin Lakes Canvas Inc.....574 583-2000
1103 N 6th St Monticello (47960) ***(G-10286)***
Twin Maple Tool Inc.....574 586-7500
324 Liberty St Walkerton (46574) ***(G-13811)***
Twin Prints Inc.....765 742-8656
701 Main St Lafayette (47901) ***(G-9014)***
Twin Sparrow Press.....917 331-5247
9833 Whitehall Gdn Munster (46321) ***(G-10634)***
Twin Spires Cabinetry LLC.....502 644-4183
316 E Court Ave Jeffersonville (47130) ***(G-8436)***
Twin Willows LLC.....812 497-0254
7603 W County Road 925 N Freetown (47235) ***(G-4950)***
Twincorp Inc.....812 934-9226
2135 N Huntersville Rd Batesville (47006) ***(G-522)***
Twinrocker Hand Made Paper Inc.....765 563-3119
100 E 3rd St Brookston (47923) ***(G-1109)***
Twisod Wick Candle Company.....317 490-4789
1115 Twin Br Martinsville (46151) ***(G-9645)***
Twisted Lime Bartending.....317 607-6836
6459 N Lynnfield Ct Indianapolis (46254) ***(G-8118)***
Twisted Mtal Fbrication Svcs I.....219 923-8045
1331 Azalea Dr Munster (46321) ***(G-10635)***
Twisted Wick Candle Co.....812 988-6123
102 S Van Buren St Nashville (47448) ***(G-10735)***
Two B Enterprises Inc.....260 245-0119
6909 Quemetco Ct Fort Wayne (46803) ***(G-4711)***
Two Ees Winery.....260 672-2000
6808 N Us Highway 24 E Huntington (46750) ***(G-6257)***
Two El Exito.....574 830-5104
117 Brookside Mnr Goshen (46526) ***(G-5344)***
Two Rivers Camping Club I.....812 838-3687
623 W 7th St Mount Vernon (47620) ***(G-10411)***
Two Sticks Inc.....219 926-7910
147 E Us Highway 20 Chesterton (46304) ***(G-1635)***
Twoson Tool Company, Yorktown *Also called Mursix Corporation* ***(G-14408)***
Ty Bowells Farrier Service.....812 537-3990
170 Us Highway 50 E Greendale (47025) ***(G-5496)***
Tyco Welding.....812 988-8770
6473 State Road 46 E Nashville (47448) ***(G-10736)***
Tyden Brooks, Angola *Also called EJ Brooks Company* ***(G-210)***
Tyden Group Holdings Corp (HQ).....740 420-6777
409 Hoosier Dr Angola (46703) ***(G-253)***
Tydenbrooks, Angola *Also called EJ Brooks Company* ***(G-209)***
Tyler Truss Systems Inc.....765 221-5050
7883 W Fall Creek Dr Pendleton (46064) ***(G-11509)***
Tyson Corporation (PA).....317 241-8396
2301 S Holt Rd Indianapolis (46241) ***(G-8119)***
Tyson Foods Inc.....812 347-2452
495 Highway 64 Nw Ramsey (47166) ***(G-11895)***
Tyson Foods Inc.....574 753-6121
2125 S County Road 125 W Logansport (46947) ***(G-9373)***
Tyson Foods Inc.....812 738-3219
545 Valley Rd Corydon (47112) ***(G-2114)***
Tyson Foods Inc.....260 726-3118
1355 W Tyson Rd Portland (47371) ***(G-11854)***
Tyson Fresh Meats Inc.....812 486-2800
Rr 3 Washington (47501) ***(G-14005)***
Tyson Fresh Meats Inc.....574 753-6134
Hwy 35 S Logansport (46947) ***(G-9374)***
U B Klem Furniture Co Inc.....812 326-2236
3861 E Schnellville Rd Saint Anthony (47575) ***(G-12250)***
U B Machine Inc.....260 493-3381
1615 Lincoln Hwy E New Haven (46774) ***(G-10962)***
U S Aggregates Inc.....765 966-8155
6340 State Road 121 Richmond (47374) ***(G-12071)***
U S Aggregates Inc (HQ).....317 872-6010
5400 W 86th St Indianapolis (46268) ***(G-8120)***
U S Aggregates Inc.....765 362-2500
3607 N Us Highway 231 Crawfordsville (47933) ***(G-2202)***
U S Aggregates Inc.....765 564-2580
2195 W Us Highway 421 Delphi (46923) ***(G-2429)***
U S Aggregates Inc.....765 564-2282
Us 421n Delphi (46923) ***(G-2430)***
U S Aggregates Inc.....765 436-7665
6990 N 875 W Thorntown (46071) ***(G-13379)***
U S Air Filtration Inc.....260 486-7399
3450 Stellhorn Rd Ste B Fort Wayne (46815) ***(G-4712)***
U S Filter.....317 280-4251
6125 Guion Rd Indianapolis (46254) ***(G-8121)***
U S Filter Distribution.....317 271-1463
1680 Expo Ln Indianapolis (46214) ***(G-8122)***
U S Granules Corporation.....574 936-2146
1433 Western Ave Plymouth (46563) ***(G-11732)***
U S O of Indiana Inc.....317 704-2400
3905 Vincennes Rd Ste 204 Indianapolis (46268) ***(G-8123)***
U S S Inc.....260 693-1172
9745 E State Road 205-57 Churubusco (46723) ***(G-1660)***
U S Sheet Metal and Roofing Co.....812 425-2428
1701 N 1st Ave Evansville (47710) ***(G-3781)***
U S Valves Inc.....812 476-6662
640 S Hebron Ave Evansville (47714) ***(G-3782)***
U-Bolts Engineering, Summitville *Also called R & R Engineering Co Inc* ***(G-13102)***
U-Haul, Chesterton *Also called Stout Plastic Weld* ***(G-1634)***
U-Nitt LLC.....812 251-9980
13640 Akers Dr Carmel (46074) ***(G-1499)***
U. S. Signcrafters, Osceola *Also called US Signcrafters Inc* ***(G-11385)***
U. S. Steel, Gary *Also called United States Steel Corp* ***(G-5111)***
U.S. Centrifuge, Indianapolis *Also called US Innovation Group Inc* ***(G-8137)***
U.S.I. Custom Blinds, Clarksville *Also called United Services Inc* ***(G-1698)***
Ubelhor Construction Inc.....812 357-2220
26018 State Road 145 Bristow (47515) ***(G-1095)***

Ubelhor Woodworking, Bristow *Also called Ubelhor Construction Inc* **(G-1095)**

Uber Dragon Studios Inc 317 520-2837
  1404 Spruce Dr Carmel (46033) **(G-1500)**

Uberlux Inc 317 580-0111
  12579 Pembrooke Cir Carmel (46032) **(G-1501)**

UC Ink LLC 765 220-5502
  6549 S Kirker Rd West College Corner (47003) **(G-14038)**

Ucom Inc 260 829-1294
  9725 W Maple St Orland (46776) **(G-11358)**

Uebelhors Golf 317 881-4109
  7611 S Meridian St Indianapolis (46217) **(G-8124)**

Ufp Granger LLC 574 277-7670
  50415 Herbert St Granger (46530) **(G-5445)**

Ufp Nappanee LLC 574 773-2505
  493 Shawnee St Nappanee (46550) **(G-10709)**

UFS Corporation 219 464-2027
  330 N 400 E Valparaiso (46383) **(G-13630)**

Ugn Inc 219 464-7813
  2252 Industrial Dr Valparaiso (46383) **(G-13631)**

Ugo Bars LLC 812 322-3499
  1019 W Howe St Bloomington (47403) **(G-850)**

Uhi Worldwide Inc., Elkhart *Also called Ultra-Heat Inc* **(G-3232)**

Uiw Supply, Columbus *Also called United Industrial & Wldg LLC* **(G-2028)**

Ulrich Chemical Inc 317 898-8632
  3111 N Post Rd Indianapolis (46226) **(G-8125)**

Ultimate Bowling Products, Franklin *Also called B C C Products Inc* **(G-4870)**

Ultimate Ethanol LLC 765 724-4384
  13179 N 100 E Alexandria (46001) **(G-54)**

Ultimate Mfg 765 517-1160
  4794 S Lincoln Blvd Marion (46953) **(G-9569)**

Ultimate Sports Inc 765 423-2984
  820 Hillcrest Rd West Lafayette (47906) **(G-14114)**

Ultra Athlete LLC 317 520-9898
  2800 N Mridian St Ste 125 Carmel (46032) **(G-1502)**

Ultra Elec Precsion Air & Land 260 327-4112
  4794 E Park 30 Dr Columbia City (46725) **(G-1843)**

Ultra Electronics, Columbia City *Also called Undersea Sensor Systems Inc* **(G-1844)**

Ultra Manufacturing, Goshen *Also called Austin & Austin Inc* **(G-5173)**

Ultra Manufacturing Inc 574 586-2320
  648 Stephens St Walkerton (46574) **(G-13812)**

Ultra Montane Associates Inc 574 289-9786
  206 Marquette Ave South Bend (46617) **(G-12980)**

Ultra Tech Racing Engines 574 674-6028
  11301 Idlewood Dr Osceola (46561) **(G-11384)**

Ultra-Fab Products Inc 574 294-7571
  57985 State Road 19 Elkhart (46517) **(G-3231)**

Ultra-Heat Inc 574 522-6594
  1314 Perkins Ave Elkhart (46516) **(G-3232)**

Ultra/Glas of Lakeville Inc 574 784-8958
  520 Industrial Dr Lakeville (46536) **(G-9098)**

Ultrexx Inc 260 897-2680
  3724 N State Road 15 Warsaw (46582) **(G-13955)**

Un Communications Group Inc 317 844-8622
  1429 Chase Ct Carmel (46032) **(G-1503)**

Un Printing & Mailing, Carmel *Also called Un Communications Group Inc* **(G-1503)**

Un Seen Press Co 317 867-5594
  17272 Futch Way Westfield (46074) **(G-14195)**

Un Seen Tesh, Westfield *Also called Un Seen Press Co* **(G-14195)**

Uncle Alberts Amplifier Inc 317 845-3037
  7709 Hague Rd Indianapolis (46256) **(G-8126)**

Under Staircase Brewing Co LLC 260 580-2586
  4927 S Camden Dr Fort Wayne (46825) **(G-4713)**

Undersea Sensor Systems Inc (HQ) 260 244-3500
  4868 E Park 30 Dr Columbia City (46725) **(G-1844)**

Uniflex Relay Systems LLC 765 232-4675
  526 W Division St Union City (47390) **(G-13462)**

Uniform Hood Lace Inc 317 896-9555
  18881 Immi Way Ste B Westfield (46074) **(G-14196)**

Unifrax I LLC 574 654-7100
  54401 Smilax Rd New Carlisle (46552) **(G-10889)**

Unilever Hpc USA, Hammond *Also called Unilever United States Inc* **(G-5953)**

Unilever United States Inc 219 659-3200
  1200 Calumet Ave Hammond (46320) **(G-5953)**

Unimin Corporation 812 683-2179
  1405 Industrial Park Dr Huntingburg (47542) **(G-6183)**

Union Electric Steel Corp 219 464-1031
  3702 Montdale Dr Valparaiso (46383) **(G-13632)**

Union Optical Eyecare Ctr Inc 812 279-3466
  3250 16th St Bedford (47421) **(G-587)**

Union Tool Corp 574 267-3211
  1144 N Detroit St Warsaw (46580) **(G-13956)**

Unique Global Solutions LLC 765 779-5030
  5729 S 200 E Anderson (46017) **(G-180)**

Unique Graphic Designs Inc 574 583-7119
  1279 N State Road 39 Monticello (47960) **(G-10287)**

Unique Outdoor Products LLC 260 486-4955
  4211 Chetham Dr Fort Wayne (46835) **(G-4714)**

Unique Products 812 376-8887
  3129 25th St Columbus (47203) **(G-2027)**

Unique Signs 812 384-4967
  1650 N Warren Rd Bloomfield (47424) **(G-646)**

Unique Specialty Services LLC 219 395-8898
  307 S 18th St Chesterton (46304) **(G-1636)**

Unique Tape Manufacturing LLC 219 617-4204
  117 Broadway Chesterton (46304) **(G-1637)**

Unique-Prescotech Inc 479 646-2973
  1900 N New York Ave Evansville (47711) **(G-3783)**

Uniseal Inc (HQ) 812 425-1361
  1014 Uhlhorn St Evansville (47710) **(G-3784)**

Uniseal Inc. 812 425-1361
  1000 Grove St Evansville (47710) **(G-3785)**

Unit Step, Indianapolis *Also called S S M Inc* **(G-7880)**

United Air Works Inc 317 576-0040
  9715 Decatur Dr Indianapolis (46256) **(G-8127)**

United Animal Health Inc (PA) 317 758-4495
  322 S Main St Sheridan (46069) **(G-12599)**

United Animal Health Inc 207 771-0965
  4310 W State Road 38 Sheridan (46069) **(G-12600)**

United Brethren In Christ 260 356-2312
  302 Lake St Huntington (46750) **(G-6258)**

United Cabinet Corporation Nit 812 482-2561
  1 Masterbrand Cabinets Dr Jasper (47546) **(G-8312)**

United Coatings Tech Inc 574 287-4774
  1011 S Main St South Bend (46601) **(G-12981)**

United Components LLC 812 867-4156
  14601 Highway 41 N Evansville (47725) **(G-3786)**

United Conveyor Corporation 574 256-0991
  13077 Mckinley Hwy Mishawaka (46545) **(G-10142)**

United Drugs, Bloomington *Also called Williams Bros Health Care Pha* **(G-856)**

United Feeds 317 627-5637
  1513 Brook Mill Ct Carmel (46032) **(G-1504)**

United Hero Apparel Printing 812 306-1998
  928 Beverly Ave Evansville (47710) **(G-3787)**

United Home Supply Inc 765 288-2737
  3600 N Everbrook Ln Ste C Muncie (47304) **(G-10576)**

United Industrial & Wldg LLC 812 526-4050
  8720 N Us Highway 31 Columbus (47201) **(G-2028)**

United Machine & Design Inc 812 442-7468
  301 N Murphy Ave Brazil (47834) **(G-980)**

United Machine Corporation 219 548-8050
  753 Axe Ave Valparaiso (46383) **(G-13633)**

United Mechanical Tech Inc 219 608-0717
  6808 Swan Ln Schererville (46375) **(G-12350)**

United Media Group Inc 260 436-7417
  2801 Freeman St Fort Wayne (46802) **(G-4715)**

United Methodist Pubg Hse 812 654-1325
  6358 E County Road 50 N Milan (47031) **(G-9947)**

United Minerals 812 842-0978
  3699 Darlington Rd Newburgh (47630) **(G-11054)**

United Minerals and Prpts Inc 812 838-5236
  2700 Bluff Rd Mount Vernon (47620) **(G-10412)**

United Oil Corp 260 489-3511
  Hwy 33 And Wash Ctr Rd Fort Wayne (46808) **(G-4716)**

United Ortho 260 422-5827
  2235 Pennsylvania St Fort Wayne (46803) **(G-4717)**

United Ortho Enterprises, Fort Wayne *Also called United Surgical Inc* **(G-4718)**

United Ortho Enterprises, Fort Wayne *Also called United Ortho* **(G-4717)**

United Parcel Service Inc 317 776-9494
  14350 Mundy Dr Ste 800 Noblesville (46060) **(G-11197)**

United Pet Foods Inc 574 674-5981
  30809 Corwin Rd Elkhart (46514) **(G-3233)**

United Pies of Elkhart Inc 574 294-3419
  1016 Middlebury St Elkhart (46516) **(G-3234)**

United Precision Gear Co Inc 317 784-4665
  4937 Camden St Indianapolis (46227) **(G-8128)**

United Ribtype Company, Fort Wayne *Also called Indiana Stamp Co Inc* **(G-4366)**

United Roll Forming Corp 574 294-2800
  58288 County Road 3 Elkhart (46517) **(G-3235)**

United Services Inc (PA) 812 989-3320
  118 W Lewis & Clark Pkwy Clarksville (47129) **(G-1698)**

United Shade LLC 574 262-0954
  2904 Airport Pkwy Elkhart (46514) **(G-3236)**

United Sign Advertising, Indianapolis *Also called Stackman Signs/Graphics Inc* **(G-7984)**

United Starter Alternator LLC 219 696-9095
  404 Mocking Bird Ln Lowell (46356) **(G-9424)**

United States Cold Storage Inc 765 482-2653
  415 S Mount Zion Rd Lebanon (46052) **(G-9231)**

United States Filter 812 471-0414
  6050 Wedeking Ave Evansville (47715) **(G-3788)**

United States Gypsum Company 812 247-2101
  12802 Deep Cut Lake Rd Shoals (47581) **(G-12671)**

United States Gypsum Company 812 388-6866
  8754 E State Road 450 Shoals (47581) **(G-12672)**

United States Gypsum Company 219 392-4600
  301 Riley Rd East Chicago (46312) **(G-2575)**

United States Mineral Pdts Co 260 356-2040
  701 N Broadway St Huntington (46750) **(G-6259)**

United States Steel Corp 219 888-2000
  1 N Broadway Gary (46402) **(G-5111)**

United States Steel Corp 219 762-3131
  6300 Us Highway 12 Portage (46368) (G-11799)
United States Steel Corp 219 391-2045
  101 E 129th St East Chicago (46312) (G-2576)
United Surgical Inc 260 422-5827
  2235 Pennsylvania St Fort Wayne (46803) (G-4718)
United Technologies Electr 260 359-3514
  3650 W 200 N Huntington (46750) (G-6260)
United Tool & Engineering Inc 574 259-1953
  337 Campbell St Mishawaka (46544) (G-10143)
United Tool Company Inc 260 563-3143
  838 Lafontaine Ave Wabash (46992) (G-13760)
United Trailers Inc 574 848-7088
  19985 County Road 8 Bristol (46507) (G-1091)
Universal Bearing, Bremen Also called Hanwha Machinery America Corp (G-1001)
Universal Bearings LLC (HQ) 574 546-2261
  431 N Birkey St Bremen (46506) (G-1030)
Universal Blower Pac Inc 317 773-7256
  440 Park 32 West Dr Noblesville (46062) (G-11198)
Universal Coatings LLC 574 520-3403
  1204 Pierina Dr Elkhart (46514) (G-3237)
Universal Consolidated Methods 260 637-2575
  3522 Astoria Way Fort Wayne (46818) (G-4719)
Universal Door Carrier Inc 317 241-3447
  1609 S Sigsbee St Indianapolis (46241) (G-8129)
Universal Export Partnr LLC 219 939-9529
  5528 Melton Rd Gary (46403) (G-5112)
Universal Forest Products, Granger Also called Ufp Granger LLC (G-5445)
Universal Forest Products Inc 574 277-7670
  50415 Herbert St Granger (46530) (G-5446)
Universal Forest Products Indi 574 273-6326
  51070 Bittersweet Rd Granger (46530) (G-5447)
Universal Metalcraft Inc 260 547-4457
  4215 W 750 N Decatur (46733) (G-2411)
Universal Operating Inc 812 477-1584
  1521 S Green River Rd Evansville (47715) (G-3789)
Universal Package LLC 812 937-3605
  4360 E 2150 N Dale (47523) (G-2335)
Universal Package Systems, Dale Also called Universal Package LLC (G-2335)
Universal Packg Systems Inc 260 829-6721
  9880 W Naples St Orland (46776) (G-11359)
Universal Precision Instrs Inc 574 264-3997
  2921 Lavanture Pl Elkhart (46514) (G-3238)
Universal Services Inc 219 397-4373
  475 E 151st St East Chicago (46312) (G-2577)
Universal Sign Group Inc 317 697-1165
  5083 Nicodemus Dr Plainfield (46168) (G-11649)
Universal Tool & Engrg Co 317 842-8999
  105 Rush Ct Fishers (46038) (G-3981)
Universal Transparent Bag Co 317 634-6425
  230 W Mccarty St Indianapolis (46225) (G-8130)
Universal Trlr Crgo Group Inc (HQ) 574 264-9661
  14054 C R 4 Bristol (46507) (G-1092)
University Notre Dame Du Lac 574 631-7471
  024 S Dinnina Hl Notre Dame (46556) (G-11304)
University Notre Dame Du Lac 574 631-6346
  310 Flanner Hall Fl 3 Notre Dame (46556) (G-11305)
University of Evansville 812 479-2963
  1800 Lincoln Ave Evansville (47722) (G-3790)
University of Evansville Press, Evansville Also called University of Evansville (G-3790)
Univertical Holdings Inc (HQ) 260 665-1500
  203 Weatherhead St Angola (46703) (G-254)
Univertical LLC (HQ) 260 665-1500
  203 Weatherhead St Angola (46703) (G-255)
Univertical LLC 260 665-1500
  203 Weatherhead St Angola (46703) (G-256)
Univertical Semicdtr Pdts Inc 260 665-1500
  203 Weatherhead St Angola (46703) (G-257)
Unknown, Garrett Also called Clayton Homes Inc (G-4997)
Unknown, Evansville Also called DSM Engineering Plastics Inc (G-3464)
Unlimited Ink Custom Screen 765 889-3212
  6239 W 250 S Russiaville (46979) (G-12244)
Unplug Soy Candles LLC 317 650-5776
  1360 E Broadway St Ste C Fortville (46040) (G-4783)
Upland Brewing Co., Bloomington Also called Upland Brewing Company Inc (G-851)
Upland Brewing Company 317 602-3931
  4842 N College Ave Indianapolis (46205) (G-8131)
Upland Brewing Company Inc 812 330-7421
  350 W 11th St Bloomington (47404) (G-851)
Upland Stop & Go LLC 765 998-0840
  7175 E 600 S Upland (46989) (G-13474)
Upland Village Laundry LLC 765 998-1260
  87 E Berry Ave Upland (46989) (G-13475)
Upper Level Networks 317 863-0955
  16545 Southpark Dr Westfield (46074) (G-14197)
Upper Level Sports LLC 317 681-3754
  2303 E Riverside Dr Indianapolis (46208) (G-8132)
Upright Iron Works Inc 219 922-1994
  1036 Reder Rd Griffith (46319) (G-5794)

UPS, Indianapolis Also called C&C Polo Enterprises Inc (G-6529)
UPS, Noblesville Also called United Parcel Service Inc (G-11197)
UPS Store 5219 .... 219 750-9597
  417 W 81st Ave Merrillville (46410) (G-9760)
UPS Store 6991, Zionsville Also called P413 Corporation (G-14454)
Upside Prints Corporation 812 319-4883
  727 N Cross Pointe Blvd C Evansville (47715) (G-3791)
Upside Prints Corporation 812 205-7374
  1011 15th St Bedford (47421) (G-588)
Urban Forest Products Llc 219 697-2900
  3126 E 500 S Brook (47922) (G-1100)
Urban Logging Company LLC 317 710-4070
  404 W 44th St Indianapolis (46208) (G-8133)
Urban Swirl (PA) 574 387-4035
  7130 Heritage Square Dr # 440 Granger (46530) (G-5448)
Urban-Ert Slings LLC 317 223-6509
  1510 E County Road 900 S Clayton (46118) (G-1709)
Ureas Music Group LLC 317 426-3103
  4340 N Illinois St Indianapolis (46208) (G-8134)
Uridynamics Inc 317 915-7896
  6786 Hawthorn Park Dr Indianapolis (46220) (G-8135)
Urschel Air Leasing LLC 219 464-4811
  1200 Cutting Edge Dr Chesterton (46304) (G-1638)
Urschel Laboratories Inc (PA) 219 464-4811
  1200 Cutting Edge Dr Chesterton (46304) (G-1639)
Urserys LLC 619 206-1761
  3439 Connecticut St Gary (46409) (G-5113)
US Automation LLC 260 338-1100
  7143 State Road 3 Huntertown (46748) (G-6148)
US Biopsy, Indianapolis Also called Promex Technologies LLC (G-7778)
US Centrifuge Systems LLC 317 299-2020
  1428 W Henry St Ste C Indianapolis (46221) (G-8136)
US Crane & Hoist Inc 219 963-1400
  721 E 25th Pl Lake Station (46405) (G-9080)
US Exploration Eqp Co Div, Indianapolis Also called Precision Cams Inc (G-7732)
US Foam, Fort Wayne Also called US Foam Corporation (G-4720)
US Foam Corporation 260 456-4998
  1829 E Creighton Ave Fort Wayne (46803) (G-4720)
US Innovation Group Inc 800 899-2040
  1428 W Henry St Ste C Indianapolis (46221) (G-8137)
US Metals 219 515-2756
  833 W Lincoln Hwy Schererville (46375) (G-12351)
US Metals Inc 219 398-1350
  425 W 151st St Ste 2 East Chicago (46312) (G-2578)
US Molders Inc 219 984-5058
  59 W 100 N Reynolds (47980) (G-11949)
US Oilfield Company LLC 888 584-7565
  8925 N Mrdian Ste Ste 120 Carmel (46032) (G-1505)
US Signcrafters Inc 574 674-5055
  216 Lincolnway E Osceola (46561) (G-11385)
US Solids Control, Carmel Also called US Oilfield Company LLC (G-1505)
US Water Systems Inc 317 209-0889
  1209 Country Club Rd Indianapolis (46234) (G-8138)
USA Flap, Aurora Also called Specialty Adhesive Film Co (G-387)
USA Medical Suppliers Ltd 608 782-1855
  9658 Oakhaven Ct Indianapolis (46256) (G-8139)
USA Today 212 715-2188
  13095 Publishers Dr Fishers (46038) (G-3982)
USA Travel Magazine 317 834-3683
  7213 Bethany Park Martinsville (46151) (G-9646)
USA Vision Systems Inc 949 583-1519
  12550 Promise Creek Ln Fishers (46038) (G-3983)
Use What Youve Got Ministry 317 924-4124
  3549 Boulevard Pl Indianapolis (46208) (G-8140)
Useful Home Products LLC 765 459-0095
  186 Champagne Ct Kokomo (46901) (G-8711)
Useful Products LLC 877 304-9036
  429 W Jasper St Goodland (47948) (G-5161)
Uselman Packing Co 765 832-2112
  75 E 4th St Clinton (47842) (G-1722)
User Wise Software Ltd 317 894-1385
  11720 E Washington St Indianapolis (46229) (G-8141)
USI, West Lafayette Also called Ultimate Sports Inc (G-14114)
Usv Optical Inc 260 482-5033
  4201 Coldwater Rd Ste 4 Fort Wayne (46805) (G-4721)
Usw Lu 6103-07 .... 219 762-4433
  1919 Willowcreek Rd Portage (46368) (G-11800)
UT Electronic Controls, Huntington Also called United Technologies Electr (G-6260)
UTC Aerospace Systems 812 704-5200
  510 Patrol Rd Jeffersonville (47130) (G-8437)
Utilimaster Holdings Inc 800 237-7806
  603 Earthway Blvd Bristol (46507) (G-1093)
Utilities Aviation Specialists 219 662-8175
  401 W Summit St Crown Point (46307) (G-2317)
Utility Access Solutions Inc 765 744-6528
  205 S Walnut St Ridgeville (47380) (G-12083)
Utility Systems, Indianapolis Also called Magnetic Instrumentation LLC (G-7439)
Utility Systems, Indianapolis Also called Magnetic Instrumentation Inc (G-7438)

(G-0000) Company's Geographic Section entry number

Utility Systems Specialists, Churubusco *Also called U S S Inc* ***(G-1660)***
Uway Extrusion LLC....765 592-6089
48 N Parke Ave Marshall (47859) ***(G-9593)***
V & H Fiberglass Repair....574 772-4920
680 N Us Highway 35 Knox (46534) ***(G-8586)***
V & P Printing....260 495-3741
3655 N 300 E Fremont (46737) ***(G-4978)***
V Global Holdings LLC....317 247-8141
6330 E 75th St Ste 144 Indianapolis (46250) ***(G-8142)***
V I P Tooling Inc....317 398-0753
739 E Franklin St Shelbyville (46176) ***(G-12581)***
V J Shimp Optical, Indianapolis *Also called Shimp Optical Corp* ***(G-7933)***
V M Integrated....877 296-0621
8501 Bash St Ste 1000 Indianapolis (46250) ***(G-8143)***
V N C Inc....219 696-5031
585 N Nichols St Lowell (46356) ***(G-9425)***
V The Electric Brew....574 296-7785
113 E Lexington Ave Elkhart (46516) ***(G-3239)***
Vahala Foam Inc....574 293-1287
903 Herman St Elkhart (46516) ***(G-3240)***
Val Rollers Inc....317 542-1968
2345 N Butler Ave Indianapolis (46218) ***(G-8144)***
Valad McHning Cntrless Grnding....574 291-5541
2825 S Main St South Bend (46614) ***(G-12982)***
Valbruna Slater Stainless Inc....260 434-2800
2400 Taylor St Fort Wayne (46802) ***(G-4722)***
Valeo Engine Cooling, Greensburg *Also called Valeo North America Inc* ***(G-5640)***
Valeo Engine Cooling, Greensburg *Also called Valeo North America Inc* ***(G-5641)***
Valeo North America Inc....248 619-8300
1231 A Ave N Seymour (47274) ***(G-12498)***
Valeo North America Inc....812 663-8541
1100 E Barachel Ln Greensburg (47240) ***(G-5640)***
Valeo North America Inc....812 663-8541
1100 E Barachel Ln Greensburg (47240) ***(G-5641)***
Valero Renewable Fuels Co LLC....812 833-3900
7201 Port Rd Mount Vernon (47620) ***(G-10413)***
Valesco Manufacturing Inc (PA)....765 522-2740
9875 N County Road 600 E Roachdale (46172) ***(G-12095)***
Valesco Manufacturing Inc....812 636-6001
7857 N 1100 E Loogootee (47553) ***(G-9395)***
Validated Custom Solutions LLC (PA)....317 259-7604
905 N Capitol Ave 200 Indianapolis (46204) ***(G-8145)***
Valley Asphalt Corporation....812 926-1471
110 4th St Aurora (47001) ***(G-392)***
Valley Distributing Inc....574 266-4455
2820 Lillian Ave Elkhart (46514) ***(G-3241)***
Valley Line Wood Products LLC....260 768-7807
2935 N 500 W Shipshewana (46565) ***(G-12655)***
Valley Manufacturing, Elkhart *Also called Valley Distributing Inc* ***(G-3241)***
Valley Press Tc....812 234-8030
629 S 9th St Terre Haute (47807) ***(G-13360)***
Valley Sanitation....574 893-7070
8526 Fort Wayne Rd Akron (46910) ***(G-9)***
Valley Scale Company LLC....812 282-5269
751 W Kenwood Ave Clarksville (47129) ***(G-1699)***
Valley Screen Process Co Inc....574 256-0901
58740 Executive Dr Mishawaka (46544) ***(G-10144)***
Valley Sharpening Inc....574 674-9077
102 Osceola Ave Osceola (46561) ***(G-11386)***
Valley Tile Corporation....812 268-3328
2437 N Section St Sullivan (47882) ***(G-13097)***
Valley Tool & Die Stampings....574 722-4566
6408 W Us Highway 24 Logansport (46947) ***(G-9375)***
Valmont Industries Inc....574 935-3058
1545 Pidco Dr Plymouth (46563) ***(G-11733)***
Valmont Industries Inc....574 295-6942
3403 Charlotte Ave Elkhart (46517) ***(G-3242)***
Valmont Site Pro 1, Plymouth *Also called Ph Inc* ***(G-11711)***
Valmont Structures, Plymouth *Also called Pirod Inc* ***(G-11712)***
Valparaiso Fire Fighters....219 462-5291
2065 Cumberland Dr Valparaiso (46383) ***(G-13634)***
Valpo Velvet Shoppe, Valparaiso *Also called Browns Dairy Inc* ***(G-13514)***
Value Production Inc....574 246-1913
2629 Foundation Dr South Bend (46628) ***(G-12983)***
Value Tool & Engineering Inc (PA)....574 246-1913
2629 Foundation Dr South Bend (46628) ***(G-12984)***
Valve Serve LLC....260 421-1927
2020 E Wa Blvd Ste 550 Fort Wayne (46803) ***(G-4723)***
Valvoline Express....765 473-4891
318 W Main St Peru (46970) ***(G-11554)***
Van Com Inc....574 255-9689
1030 N Merrifield Ave Mishawaka (46545) ***(G-10145)***
Van Der Weele Jon D....574 892-5005
200 W Walnut St Argos (46501) ***(G-280)***
Van Duyne Block and Gravel....574 223-6656
2602 S 500 E Rochester (46975) ***(G-12159)***
Van Explorer Company Inc (PA)....574 267-7666
2749 N Fox Farm Rd Warsaw (46580) ***(G-13957)***
Van Gard Vault Co Inc....219 980-6233
4401 W Ridge Rd Gary (46408) ***(G-5114)***
Van Gard Vault Co Inc....219 949-7723
5100 Industrial Hwy Gary (46406) ***(G-5115)***
Van Go Inc....574 862-2807
7187 N 1150 W Shipshewana (46565) ***(G-12656)***
Van Guard Vault, Gary *Also called Van Gard Vault Co Inc* ***(G-5115)***
Van Keppel Redi-Mix Inc....219 987-2811
200 5th Ave Ne Demotte (46310) ***(G-2450)***
Van Schouwen Farms....219 696-0877
19306 Clay St Hebron (46341) ***(G-6023)***
Van Westrum Corporation....317 926-3200
1750 E 37th St Indianapolis (46218) ***(G-8146)***
Van Zandt Enterprises Inc....812 423-3511
1701 N Kentucky Ave Evansville (47711) ***(G-3792)***
Van's Home Center, Auburn *Also called Vans TV & Appliance Inc* ***(G-366)***
Vanair Manufacturing Inc (PA)....219 879-5100
10896 W 300 N Michigan City (46360) ***(G-9857)***
Vance Products Incorporated....812 829-4891
1100 W Morgan St Spencer (47460) ***(G-13041)***
Vandelay Industries....317 657-6205
348 Palmyra Dr Indianapolis (46239) ***(G-8147)***
Vander Parts Co, Evansville *Also called Vandergriff & Associates Inc* ***(G-3793)***
Vandergriff & Associates Inc....812 422-6033
1930 Allens Ln Evansville (47720) ***(G-3793)***
Vandivier Tudor Monuments....317 736-5292
951 N Main St Franklin (46131) ***(G-4938)***
Vandor Corporation....765 683-9760
4251 W Industries Rd Richmond (47374) ***(G-12072)***
Vanguard National Trailer Corp (HQ)....219 253-2000
289 Water Tower Dr Monon (47959) ***(G-10179)***
Vans Cabinet Shop....574 658-9625
1704 E Mock Rd Milford (46542) ***(G-9966)***
Vans Industrial Inc....219 931-4881
231 Condit St Hammond (46320) ***(G-5954)***
Vans Iron Works (PA)....219 934-1935
1604 Mourning Dove Dr Munster (46321) ***(G-10636)***
Vans TV & Appliance Inc....260 927-8267
106 Peckhart Ct Auburn (46706) ***(G-366)***
Vapourflow LLC....812 284-5204
590 Missouri Ave Ste 105 Jeffersonville (47130) ***(G-8438)***
Varied Products Indiana Inc....219 763-2526
2180 N State Road 149 Chesterton (46304) ***(G-1640)***
Varsity Sports Inc....219 987-7200
603 N Halleck St Demotte (46310) ***(G-2451)***
Vart Grafix....317 513-5522
5102 Sandhurst Dr Indianapolis (46217) ***(G-8148)***
Vasmo Inc....317 549-3722
4101 E 30th St Ste 2 Indianapolis (46218) ***(G-8149)***
Vault....317 784-4000
700 Main St Beech Grove (46107) ***(G-604)***
Vault Plant, The, Whitestown *Also called Meyer Industries Inc* ***(G-14256)***
Vauterbuilt Inc....219 712-2384
16448 Clay St Hebron (46341) ***(G-6024)***
Vb Air Suspension North Amer, Elkhart *Also called Liftco Inc* ***(G-2997)***
Vco Inc....812 235-3540
1210 Wabash Ave Terre Haute (47807) ***(G-13361)***
Vdk Printing LLC....260 602-8212
3822 Live Oak Blvd Fort Wayne (46804) ***(G-4724)***
Vead Dodd Sawmill Inc....812 268-4486
165 E County Road 300 N Sullivan (47882) ***(G-13098)***
Veada Industries Inc....574 831-4775
19240 Tarman Rd New Paris (46553) ***(G-11000)***
Veco Indiana Manufacturing, Rushville *Also called Vibration Eliminator Co Inc* ***(G-12237)***
Vectren Corporation (PA)....812 491-4000
1 Vectren Sq Evansville (47708) ***(G-3794)***
Vectren Corporation....812 424-6411
20 Nw 4th St Evansville (47708) ***(G-3795)***
Vectren Fuels, Inc., Terre Haute *Also called Sycamore Coal Inc* ***(G-13347)***
Vee Engineering Inc (PA)....765 778-7895
3620 W 73rd St Anderson (46011) ***(G-181)***
Vee Engineering Inc....260 424-6635
3805 Reynolds St Fort Wayne (46803) ***(G-4725)***
Vehicle Service Group LLC....812 273-1622
2700 Lanier Dr Madison (47250) ***(G-9499)***
Vehicle Service Group LLC....800 445-9262
996 Industrial Dr Madison (47250) ***(G-9500)***
Vehicle Service Group LLC (HQ)....800 640-5438
2700 Lanier Dr Madison (47250) ***(G-9501)***
Veitsch-Radex America LLC....219 237-2420
9245 Calumet Ave Ste 100 Munster (46321) ***(G-10637)***
Velko Hinge Inc....219 924-6363
9325 Kennedy Ct Munster (46321) ***(G-10638)***
Veneer Curry Sales LLC....812 945-6623
1014 E 6th St New Albany (47150) ***(G-10871)***
Veneer Services LLC....317 346-0711
1457 Sunday Dr Indianapolis (46217) ***(G-8150)***
Vent Division, Elkhart *Also called Elixir Industries* ***(G-2818)***
Ventline, Bristol *Also called Dexter Axle Company* ***(G-1054)***

ALPHABETIC

Venture & Alliance Group, Carmel *Also called Telamon International Corp* *(G-1490)*

Venture Indus 765 348-5780
1701 W Mcdonald St Hartford City (47348) *(G-5995)*

Vera Bradley Inc 219 878-1093
505 Lighthouse Pl Michigan City (46360) *(G-9858)*

Vera Bradley Inc 260 482-4673
12420 Stonebridge Rd Roanoke (46783) *(G-12109)*

Vera Bradley Inc (PA) 877 708-8372
12420 Stonebridge Rd Roanoke (46783) *(G-12110)*

Vera Bradley International LLC (HQ) 260 482-4673
12420 Stonebridge Rd Roanoke (46783) *(G-12111)*

Verallia North America, Indianapolis *Also called Ardagh Glass Inc* *(G-6418)*

Verallia North America 765 768-7891
524 E Center St Dunkirk (47336) *(G-2490)*

Verizon Business, Noblesville *Also called Mcl/Screwdriver Systems Inc* *(G-11147)*

Vermette Machine Company Inc 219 931-5406
7 143rd St Hammond (46327) *(G-5955)*

Vermont Foundry Company, Kendallville *Also called Mahoney Foundries Inc* *(G-8493)*

Vernon A Stevens 812 626-0010
3901 Bergdolt Rd Evansville (47711) *(G-3796)*

Vernon Greyber 812 636-7880
9808 E 1100 N Odon (47562) *(G-11343)*

Vernon North Industry Corp (HQ) 812 346-8772
3750 N County Road 75 W North Vernon (47265) *(G-11285)*

Vernon Sharp 317 398-0631
2202 W Mckay Rd Shelbyville (46176) *(G-12582)*

Verns Woodworking 574 773-7930
491 4th Rd Bremen (46506) *(G-1031)*

Verona LLC 317 248-9888
2346 S Lynhurst Dr C101 Indianapolis (46241) *(G-8151)*

Versa Machinery, Elkhart *Also called Versatile Automation Tech* *(G-3243)*

Versatile Automation Tech 574 266-0780
4850 Green Ct Elkhart (46516) *(G-3243)*

Versatile Fabrication LLC 574 293-8504
4431 Pine Creek Rd Elkhart (46516) *(G-3244)*

Versatile Metal Works LLC 765 754-7470
204 S Washington St Frankton (46044) *(G-4944)*

Versatile Processing Group Inc (PA) 317 577-8930
9820 Westpoint Dr Ste 300 Indianapolis (46256) *(G-8152)*

Versteel, Jasper *Also called Ditto Sales Inc* *(G-8245)*

Vertellus, Indianapolis *Also called V Global Holdings LLC* *(G-8142)*

Vertellus Agriculture & Ntrtn, Indianapolis *Also called VSI Liquidating Inc* *(G-8171)*

Vertellus Holdings LLC (PA) 317 247-8141
201 N Illinois St # 1800 Indianapolis (46204) *(G-8153)*

Vertellus Intgrted Pyrdnes LLC 317 247-8141
201 N Illinois St # 1800 Indianapolis (46204) *(G-8154)*

Vertellus LLC (PA) 317 247-8141
201 N Illinois St # 1800 Indianapolis (46204) *(G-8155)*

Vertellus Sbh Holdings LLC 317 247-8141
201 N Illinois St # 1800 Indianapolis (46204) *(G-8156)*

Vertex Building Materials LLC 765 547-1883
9111 Whitewater Dr Brookville (47012) *(G-1129)*

Vertical Plus Mri America LLC 574 257-4674
3838 N Main St Ste 1a Mishawaka (46545) *(G-10146)*

Vertical Power Co 574 276-8094
10254 Jefferson Rd Osceola (46561) *(G-11387)*

Vertical Sale 260 438-4299
3838 Sherman Blvd Fort Wayne (46808) *(G-4726)*

Vertical Vision Inc 812 432-3763
2417 S County Road 750 E Dillsboro (47018) *(G-2474)*

Vesco, Richmond *Also called Martin Ekwlor Phrmcuticals Inc* *(G-12014)*

Vessell Trim Co 812 424-2963
955 E Riverside Dr Evansville (47713) *(G-3797)*

Vest Pallet Co 812 839-6247
8795 N Scotts Ridge Rd Canaan (47224) *(G-1282)*

Vesta Ingredients Inc 317 895-9000
5767 Thunderbird Rd Indianapolis (46236) *(G-8157)*

Vesta Pharmaceuticals Inc 317 895-9000
5767 Thunderbird Rd Indianapolis (46236) *(G-8158)*

Vestil Manufacturing Corp (PA) 260 665-7586
2999 N Wayne St Angola (46703) *(G-258)*

Vet Signs LLC 937 733-4727
2171 State Route 227 N Richmond (47374) *(G-12073)*

Vevay Newspapers Inc 812 427-2311
111 W Market St Vevay (47043) *(G-13667)*

Vf Outdoor LLC 317 843-9419
8702 Keystone Xing Indianapolis (46240) *(G-8159)*

Vgmc, Geneva *Also called Geneva Manufacturing Inc* *(G-5136)*

Vhc Ltd (HQ) 765 584-2101
300 W Martin St Winchester (47394) *(G-14343)*

Via Development Corp (PA) 888 225-5842
867 E 38th St Marion (46953) *(G-9570)*

Viannos Village Cretan Oil 219 513-6720
2011 Idlewild Ct Highland (46322) *(G-6058)*

Viariloc Distributors Inc 317 273-0089
1717 Expo Ln Indianapolis (46214) *(G-8160)*

Viavi Solutions Inc 317 788-9351
5808 Churchman Byp Indianapolis (46203) *(G-8161)*

Vibcon Corp 317 984-3543
6660 E 266th St Ste 200 Arcadia (46030) *(G-271)*

Vibracoustic North America L P 260 894-7199
1496 Gerber St Ligonier (46767) *(G-9301)*

Vibration Control Tech LLC 260 894-7199
1492 Gerber St Ligonier (46767) *(G-9302)*

Vibration Eliminator, Rushville *Also called Indiana Veco Manufacturing* *(G-12223)*

Vibration Eliminator Co Inc 765 932-2858
1104 N Fort Wayne Rd Rushville (46173) *(G-12237)*

Vibromatic Company Inc (PA) 317 773-3885
1301 S 6th St Noblesville (46060) *(G-11199)*

Vibronics Inc 812 853-2300
10744 W Highway 662 Newburgh (47630) *(G-11055)*

Vicair America LLC 317 281-0809
16461 Chalet Cir Westfield (46074) *(G-14198)*

Vice Bros Pattern Shop & Fndry 260 782-2585
1010 W State Road 524 Lagro (46941) *(G-9073)*

Vickers Graphics Inc 765 868-4646
329 S 00 Ew Kokomo (46902) *(G-8712)*

Vickery Drilling Co 812 473-4671
2526 N Burkhardt Rd Evansville (47715) *(G-3798)*

Vickery Tape & Label Co Inc 765 472-1974
20 W Canal St Peru (46970) *(G-11555)*

Vickie Hildreth 812 350-3575
2331 N Marr Rd Columbus (47203) *(G-2029)*

Vicksmetal Armco Associates (PA) 765 659-5555
150 S County Road 300 W Frankfort (46041) *(G-4858)*

Victor Reinz Valve Seals LLC 260 897-2827
301 Progress Way Avilla (46710) *(G-420)*

Victorian House Scones LLC 765 742-2709
1305 Richards St Lafayette (47904) *(G-9015)*

Victorias Vineyard 765 348-3070
426 S Willman Rd Hartford City (47348) *(G-5996)*

Victory Mfg 317 731-5063
933 N Lynhurst Dr Indianapolis (46224) *(G-8162)*

Vidal Plastics LLC 812 431-8075
616 N Norman Ave Evansville (47711) *(G-3799)*

Video Video, Fort Wayne *Also called Kauffman Enterprises Inc* *(G-4404)*

Vidicom Corporation 219 923-7475
124 Sibley St Hammond (46320) *(G-5956)*

Vidimos Inc 219 397-2728
3858 Indiana Harbor Dr East Chicago (46312) *(G-2579)*

Vierks Fine Jewelry, Lafayette *Also called Surplus Store and Exchange* *(G-9006)*

Vigo Coal Inc 812 759-8446
250 N Cross Pointe Blvd Evansville (47715) *(G-3800)*

Vigo Coal Company, Evansville *Also called Vigo Coal Operating Co Inc* *(G-3801)*

Vigo Coal Operating Co Inc (PA) 812 759-8446
250 N Cross Pointe Blvd Evansville (47715) *(G-3801)*

Vigo Machine Shop Inc 812 235-8393
3920 Locust St Terre Haute (47803) *(G-13362)*

Vigred Sports, Auburn *Also called Baron Embroidery Corp* *(G-316)*

Viking Business Products Inc 260 489-7787
7530 Disalle Blvd Fort Wayne (46825) *(G-4727)*

Viking Formed Products, Elkhart *Also called All American Group Inc* *(G-2674)*

Viking Inc 260 244-6141
2740 E Business 30 Columbia City (46725) *(G-1845)*

Viking Mine Corning Pit, Cannelburg *Also called Peabody Midwest Mining LLC* *(G-1285)*

Viking Paper Company 574 936-6300
1001 Pidco Dr Plymouth (46563) *(G-11734)*

Village Candlemaker Inc 812 988-7201
157 S Van Buren St Nashville (47448) *(G-10737)*

Village Custom Embroidery Inc 317 733-3110
80 N First St Zionsville (46077) *(G-14470)*

Village Workshop Inc 812 933-1527
3047 Washington St Oldenburg (47036) *(G-11346)*

Vin Elite Imports Inc 317 264-9250
55 S State Ave Ste 358 Indianapolis (46201) *(G-8163)*

Vince Rogers Signs Inc 574 264-0542
400 W Crawford St Elkhart (46514) *(G-3245)*

Vincennes Sun Commercial 812 886-9955
702 Main St Vincennes (47591) *(G-13711)*

Vincennes Sun-Commercial, Vincennes *Also called Indiana Newspapers LLC* *(G-13685)*

Vincennes Welding Co Inc 812 882-9682
923 N 13th St Vincennes (47591) *(G-13712)*

Vincent Aliano Elc Htg & Coolg 812 332-3332
5128 W Vernal Pike Bloomington (47404) *(G-852)*

Vindhurst Sheet Metal LLC 812 422-0143
2010 N Grand Ave Evansville (47711) *(G-3802)*

Vineyard Fishery Products LLC 317 902-0753
3032 Ruckle St Indianapolis (46205) *(G-8164)*

Vintage Chemical Enterprises 260 745-7272
314 E Wallace St Fort Wayne (46803) *(G-4728)*

Vintage Publishing LLC 812 719-7200
7643 Miranda Dr Evansville (47711) *(G-3803)*

Vintage Trailers Ltd 574 522-2261
4660 Pine Creek Rd Elkhart (46516) *(G-3246)*

Vinyl Creator 260 318-5133
11889 N Angling Rd-57 Wolcottville (46795) *(G-14377)*

Vinyl Therm of Indiana, Rushville *Also called Keith Ison* *(G-12226)*

Vires Backhoe and Dumptruc 812 595-1630
2571 E Doty Mill Rd Deputy (47230) *(G-2461)*
Virginias Very Own LLC 812 834-5065
3522 Pleasant Run Rd Heltonville (47436) *(G-6030)*
Virtuoso Distillers LLC 574 876-4450
4211 Grape Rd Mishawaka (46545) *(G-10147)*
Virtus Inc 812 932-0131
1896 Lammers Pike Batesville (47006) *(G-523)*
Vishay Americas Inc 765 778-4878
555 S Pendleton Ave Pendleton (46064) *(G-11510)*
Vision Aid Systems Inc 317 888-0323
916 E Main St Ste 114 Greenwood (46143) *(G-5758)*
Vision Associates 765 288-1575
1904 W Mcgalliard Rd Muncie (47304) *(G-10577)*
Vision IV Inc 812 423-0119
14110 Castle Brook Rd Evansville (47725) *(G-3804)*
Vision Machine Works Inc 574 259-6500
56540 Twin Branch Dr Mishawaka (46545) *(G-10148)*
Vision Quest, Merrillville *Also called 2020 Lab Inc* *(G-9690)*
Visions Printing LLC 317 960-2322
6015 E 34th St Ste A Indianapolis (46226) *(G-8165)*
Vista Grphic Cmmunications LLC 317 898-2000
7915 E 30th St Indianapolis (46219) *(G-8166)*
Vista Manufacturing Inc (PA) 574 264-0711
53345 Columbia Dr Elkhart (46514) *(G-3247)*
Vista Worldwide LLC 574 264-0711
53345 Columbia Dr Elkhart (46514) *(G-3248)*
Visual Values, New Castle *Also called R&S Sign Design* *(G-10916)*
Vita Nonwovens LLC 260 747-0990
9403 Avionics Dr Fort Wayne (46809) *(G-4729)*
Vita Vet Laboratories Inc 765 662-9398
1920 W Westholme Dr Marion (46952) *(G-9571)*
Vital Signs 219 548-1605
4411 Evans Ave Ste D Valparaiso (46383) *(G-13635)*
Vital Signs Marketing LLC 765 453-5088
2850 Bridgestone Cir Kokomo (46902) *(G-8713)*
Vitality Bowls 317 581-9496
110 W Main St Carmel (46032) *(G-1506)*
Vitamins Inc 219 879-7356
1700 E Us Highway 12 Michigan City (46360) *(G-9859)*
Vitamorph Labs LLC 219 237-0174
9445 Indianapolis Blvd # 1049 Highland (46322) *(G-6059)*
Vitracoat America Inc (PA) 574 262-2188
2807 Marina Dr Elkhart (46514) *(G-3249)*
Vivid Leds Inc 800 974-3570
1108 Dora Dr Sellersburg (47172) *(G-12421)*
Vivolac Cultures Corporation 317 866-9528
6108 W Stoner Dr Greenfield (46140) *(G-5583)*
Vixen Composites LLC 574 970-1224
2965 Lavanture Pl Elkhart (46514) *(G-3250)*
Vizai LLC 630 677-6583
7151 Jessman Road East Dr E Indianapolis (46256) *(G-8167)*
Vkf Renzel Usa Corp 219 661-6300
1311 Merrillville Rd Crown Point (46307) *(G-2318)*
Voege Precision Machine Pdts, Westfield *Also called Voege Precision Mch Pdts LLC* *(G-14199)*
Voege Precision Mch Pdts LLC 317 867-4699
17808 Commerce Dr Westfield (46074) *(G-14199)*
Voegele Auto Supply LLC 765 647-3541
12 Murphy St Brookville (47012) *(G-1130)*
Vogel Brothers Corporation 812 376-2775
860 Repp Dr Columbus (47201) *(G-2030)*
Voges Machine 812 299-1546
4876 W Kennett Dr Terre Haute (47802) *(G-13363)*
Voges Machine Shop, Terre Haute *Also called Voges Machine* *(G-13363)*
Voges Restoration and Wdwkg 812 299-1546
5696 W Cantrell Dr Terre Haute (47802) *(G-13364)*
Vogler Copperworks LLC 812 630-9010
308 S Vine St Haubstadt (47639) *(G-6007)*
Voice of God Recordings Inc 812 246-2137
5911 Charlestown Pike Jeffersonville (47130) *(G-8439)*
Voidteam Network, Lafayette *Also called Voidteam Studios* *(G-9016)*
Voidteam Studios 765 414-9777
2930 Greenbush St Lafayette (47904) *(G-9016)*
Voluforms, Jeffersonville *Also called Stewart Graphics Inc* *(G-8430)*
Vomela 574 522-6016
4505 Wyland Dr Ste 800 Elkhart (46516) *(G-3251)*
Von Duprin LLC (HQ) 317 429-2866
2720 Tobey Dr Indianapolis (46219) *(G-8168)*
Von Duprin LLC 317 899-2760
2720 Tobey Dr Indianapolis (46219) *(G-8169)*
Vorzeigen Machining Inc 765 827-1500
5650 Industrial Ave S Connersville (47331) *(G-2077)*
Voss Industries, Jeffersonville *Also called Pgp Corp* *(G-8413)*
Voter Registration 219 755-3795
2293 N Main St Crown Point (46307) *(G-2319)*
VSC, Clarksville *Also called Valley Scale Company LLC* *(G-1699)*
VSI Acquisition Corp 317 247-8141
201 N Illinois St Indianapolis (46204) *(G-8170)*
VSI Liquidating Inc (HQ) 317 247-8141
201 N Illinois St # 1800 Indianapolis (46204) *(G-8171)*
Vti Packaging Specialties 574 277-4119
12912 Industrial Park Dr Granger (46530) *(G-5449)*
Vtty, Indianapolis *Also called Victory Mfg* *(G-8162)*
Vulcraft Division, Saint Joe *Also called Nucor Corporation* *(G-12257)*
Vuteq Usa Inc 812 385-2584
819 E 350 S Princeton (47670) *(G-11889)*
Vw Co 812 397-0102
6521 N Us Highway 41 Shelburn (47879) *(G-12512)*
Vytec Inc 574 277-4295
12912 Industrial Park Dr Granger (46530) *(G-5450)*
W & J Sawmill Llc 812 486-2719
9533 E 600 N Montgomery (47558) *(G-10245)*
W & M Enterprises Inc 812 537-4656
370 Industrial Dr Lawrenceburg (47025) *(G-9161)*
W & M Manufacturing Inc 260 726-9800
1000 N Morton St Portland (47371) *(G-11855)*
W & M Woodworking 260 854-3126
3180 E 450 S Lagrange (46761) *(G-9071)*
W & S Woodworking 812 486-3673
6460 N 1100 E Loogootee (47553) *(G-9396)*
W & W Fabricating Inc 765 362-2182
2597 S Us Highway 231 Crawfordsville (47933) *(G-2203)*
W & W Gravel Co Incorporated (PA) 260 672-3591
8031 W County Line Rd S Roanoke (46783) *(G-12112)*
W & W Locker 260 344-3400
8896 W 600 N Andrews (46702) *(G-185)*
W & W Pallet Co LLC 812 486-3548
7799 E 300 N Montgomery (47558) *(G-10246)*
W A P LLC 317 421-3180
705 W Mausoleum Rd Shelbyville (46176) *(G-12583)*
W A P Company, Martinsville *Also called Wallace Construction Inc* *(G-9647)*
W Ay-FM Media Group Inc 812 945-1043
3211 Grant Line Rd Ste 1 New Albany (47150) *(G-10872)*
W B I, Liberty *Also called Winslow-Browning Inc* *(G-9273)*
W C Grant Company Incorporated 260 484-6688
9665 N 100 W-90 Markle (46770) *(G-9583)*
W F Meyers Company Inc 812 275-4485
1008 13th St Bedford (47421) *(G-589)*
W H I, Westfield *Also called Wholesale Hrdwood Intriors Inc* *(G-14202)*
W J Hagerty & Sons Ltd Inc 574 288-4991
3801 Linden Ave South Bend (46619) *(G-12985)*
W Kendall & Sons Inc (PA) 219 733-2412
10270 W Us Highway 30 Wanatah (46390) *(G-13827)*
W M G, Indianapolis *Also called World Media Group Inc* *(G-8216)*
W M Kelley Co Inc 812 945-3529
620 Durgee Rd New Albany (47150) *(G-10873)*
W Martin Gary 812 926-0935
8467 Lower Dillsboro Rd Aurora (47001) *(G-393)*
W R Grace & Co - Conn 219 398-2040
5215 Kennedy Ave East Chicago (46312) *(G-2580)*
W R Grace Davison Chemical Div, East Chicago *Also called W R Grace & Co - Conn* *(G-2580)*
W Robbins & Sons Inc 765 522-1736
207 N West St Roachdale (46172) *(G-12096)*
W S F Fire Store 812 421-3826
1279 Maxwell Ave Evansville (47711) *(G-3805)*
W T Boone Enterprises Inc 317 738-0275
159 Cincinnati St Franklin (46131) *(G-4939)*
W W G Inc 317 783-6413
5602 Elmwood Ave Ste 222 Indianapolis (46203) *(G-8172)*
W W Williams Company LLC 260 827-0553
610 W Washington St Bluffton (46714) *(G-896)*
W-M Lumber and Wood Pdts Inc 812 944-6711
1801 E Main St New Albany (47150) *(G-10874)*
W/S Packaging Group Inc 317 578-4454
8444 Castlewood Dr # 400 Indianapolis (46250) *(G-8173)*
Wabash Castings Inc 260 563-8371
3837 Mill St Wabash (46992) *(G-13761)*
Wabash Environmental Pdts LLC 765 464-3440
120 Burke Ct West Lafayette (47906) *(G-14115)*
Wabash Instrument Corp 260 563-8406
300 Olive St Wabash (46992) *(G-13762)*
Wabash Metal Products Inc (HQ) 260 563-1184
1569 Morris St Wabash (46992) *(G-13763)*
Wabash Mpi, Wabash *Also called Wabash Metal Products Inc* *(G-13763)*
Wabash National LP (HQ) 765 771-5300
1000 Sagamore Pkwy S Lafayette (47905) *(G-9017)*
Wabash National Corporation 765 659-3856
901 W Morrison St Frankfort (46041) *(G-4859)*
Wabash National Corporation (PA) 765 771-5300
1000 Sagamore Pkwy S Lafayette (47905) *(G-9018)*
Wabash National Mfg LP 765 771-5310
1000 Sagamore Pkwy S Lafayette (47905) *(G-9019)*
Wabash Plain Dealer 260 563-2131
123 W Canal St Wabash (46992) *(G-13764)*
Wabash Plastics Inc (PA) 812 428-9300
600 N Cross Pointe Blvd Evansville (47715) *(G-3806)*

Wabash Plastics Inc......812 867-2447
1300 Burch Dr Evansville (47725) *(G-3807)*
Wabash Printing Company......765 650-1701
3776 Campus Suites Blvd # 222 West Lafayette (47906) *(G-14116)*
Wabash Sand & Gravel, Williamsport *Also called Rogers Group Inc (G-14297)*
Wabash Snacks, Bluffton *Also called Poore Brothers - Bluffton LLC (G-885)*
Wabash Steel LLC......317 818-1622
2007 Oliphant Dr Vincennes (47591) *(G-13713)*
Wabash Valley Magazine......812 231-4294
721 Wabash Ave Ste 411 Terre Haute (47807) *(G-13365)*
Wabash Valley Manufacturing......260 352-2102
505 E Main St Silver Lake (46982) *(G-12682)*
Wabash Valley Motor & Mch Inc......812 466-7400
3909 N Fruitridge Ave Terre Haute (47805) *(G-13366)*
Wabash Valley Packaging Corp......812 299-7181
1303 E Industrial Dr Terre Haute (47802) *(G-13367)*
Wabash Valley Publishing LLC......812 494-2152
611 N 7th St Vincennes (47591) *(G-13714)*
Wabash Valley Tool & Engrg......260 563-7690
1253 S State Road 115 Wabash (46992) *(G-13765)*
Wabash Welding Services Inc (PA)......260 563-2363
150 Smith St Wabash (46992) *(G-13766)*
Wabcoindustries LLC......317 361-3653
5540 W Henry St Indianapolis (46241) *(G-8174)*
Waddell Printing Co, Lagrange *Also called La Grange Publishing Co Inc (G-9052)*
Wag-Way Tool Incorporated......812 886-0598
483 N Mount Zion Rd Vincennes (47591) *(G-13715)*
Waggway Tool, Vincennes *Also called Birdeye Inc (G-13669)*
Wagler Competition Pdts LLC......812 486-9360
9612 N 675 E Odon (47562) *(G-11344)*
Wagler Machining LLC......812 866-2904
11778 W State Road 256 Lexington (47138) *(G-9256)*
Wagler Mini Barn Products......812 687-7372
8972 N 550 E Plainville (47568) *(G-11657)*
Wagler Woodworking......812 486-6357
19866 Us Highway 231 Loogootee (47553) *(G-9397)*
Waglers Custom Cabinets......812 486-2878
8170 E 200 N Montgomery (47558) *(G-10247)*
Wagner Electric Fort Wayne Inc......260 484-5532
3610 N Clinton St Fort Wayne (46805) *(G-4730)*
Wagner Signs Inc......317 788-0202
2802 E Troy Ave Indianapolis (46203) *(G-8175)*
Wagner Truss Manufacturing......812 852-2206
9410 N Us 421 Napoleon (47034) *(G-10643)*
Wagner Welding Incorporated......812 985-9929
9201 Hogue Rd Evansville (47712) *(G-3808)*
Wagners Plasti Craft Co......260 627-3147
5705 Union Chapel Rd Fort Wayne (46845) *(G-4731)*
Wagon Train Ventures LLC......260 625-5301
6712 Felger Rd Fort Wayne (46818) *(G-4732)*
Wait Industries LLC......574 347-4320
11930 Pacific Dr Granger (46530) *(G-5451)*
Waka Mfg Inc......574 258-0019
945 E 5th St Mishawaka (46544) *(G-10149)*
Wakarusa Ag LLC......574 862-1163
711 E Waterford St Wakarusa (46573) *(G-13797)*
Wakarusa Tribune, Wakarusa *Also called Ecom Publishing Inc (G-13776)*
Wakelam John......812 752-5243
160 E State Road 356 Scottsburg (47170) *(G-12385)*
Wakelam Lumber Company, Scottsburg *Also called Wakelam John (G-12385)*
Walburn Kitchens, Muncie *Also called Walburn Service Inc (G-10578)*
Walburn Service Inc......765 289-3383
109 S Claypool Rd Muncie (47303) *(G-10578)*
Walerko Tool and Engrg Corp......574 295-2233
1935 W Lusher Ave Elkhart (46517) *(G-3252)*
Walker Information Inc......317 843-3939
8940 River Crossing Blvd Indianapolis (46240) *(G-8176)*
Walker Shores Development Co, Angola *Also called Univertical Semicdtr Pdts Inc (G-257)*
Walkerton Plant, Walkerton *Also called American Roller Company LLC (G-13801)*
Walkerton Tool & Die Inc......574 586-3162
106 Industrial Park Dr Walkerton (46574) *(G-13813)*
Wall Control Services Inc......260 450-6411
5742 Industrial Rd Fort Wayne (46825) *(G-4733)*
Wall's Enterprises, Whiteland *Also called Walls Lawn & Garden Inc (G-14247)*
Wallace Construction Inc......317 422-5356
9790 Old State Road 37 N Martinsville (46151) *(G-9647)*
Wallace Grain Co Inc......317 758-4434
604 S Main St Sheridan (46069) *(G-12601)*
Wallar Additions Inc (PA)......574 262-1989
30012 County Road 10 Elkhart (46514) *(G-3253)*
Wallets Belts & Stuff LLC......219 218-3576
2042 Schrage Ave Whiting (46394) *(G-14276)*
Walls Lawn & Garden Inc......317 535-9059
201 N Us Highway 31 Whiteland (46184) *(G-14247)*
Wallys Construction......812 254-4154
1279 S 3t Washington (47501) *(G-14006)*
Wallys Lockshop......765 748-2282
606 W 11th St Muncie (47302) *(G-10579)*
Walnut Acres Sawmill LLC......765 344-0027
6218 E 100 N Rockville (47872) *(G-12183)*
Walnut Lane Woodworking......574 633-2114
12530 Shively Rd Bremen (46506) *(G-1032)*
Walnut Street Hardwoods......574 287-1023
25490 Trunk Trl South Bend (46619) *(G-12986)*
Walsh & Kelly Inc......219 924-5900
24358 State Road 23 South Bend (46614) *(G-12987)*
Walter Piano Company Inc......574 266-0615
1705 County Road 6 E # 200 Elkhart (46514) *(G-3254)*
Walters Cabinet Shop......765 452-9634
471 E 1300 S Kokomo (46901) *(G-8714)*
Walters Development LLC......260 747-7531
6600 Ardmore Ave Fort Wayne (46809) *(G-4734)*
Walton Industrial Park Inc......574 626-2929
7585 S Us Hwy 35 Walton (46994) *(G-13818)*
Walton Logging......812 365-9635
991 S State Road 66 Marengo (47140) *(G-9505)*
Walts Welding & Fabricating......812 637-5338
5664 Bischoff Hill Rd West Harrison (47060) *(G-14044)*
Wamingo Publishing LLP......317 443-1326
5441 Hibben Ave Indianapolis (46219) *(G-8177)*
Wampum Hardware, Pennville *Also called Dyno Nobel Inc (G-11513)*
Wanafeed Corporation......317 862-4032
4410 Northeastern Ave Indianapolis (46239) *(G-8178)*
Wanamaker Feed & Seed Company, Indianapolis *Also called Wanafeed Corporation (G-8178)*
Wanda Harrington......765 642-1628
5215 S 100 W Anderson (46013) *(G-182)*
Waninger & Sons Timber Co, Fulda *Also called Waninger Knneth Sons Log Tmber (G-4992)*
Waninger Knneth Sons Log Tmber......812 357-5200
Hwy 545 Fulda (47536) *(G-4992)*
Wannemuehler Distribution Inc......812 422-3251
516 N 7th Ave Evansville (47710) *(G-3809)*
Wap Inc......877 421-3187
705 W Mausoleum Rd Shelbyville (46176) *(G-12584)*
WAr - LLC- Westville Prtg......219 785-2821
361 W Main St Westville (46391) *(G-14221)*
Ward Corporation (PA)......260 426-8700
642 Growth Ave Fort Wayne (46808) *(G-4735)*
Ward Corporation......260 489-2281
7603 Opportunity Dr Fort Wayne (46825) *(G-4736)*
Ward Forging Co Inc......812 923-7463
3311 E Luther Rd Floyds Knobs (47119) *(G-4023)*
Ward Heat Treating, Fort Wayne *Also called Ward Corporation (G-4736)*
Ward Industries Inc......574 825-2548
58582 State Road 13 Middlebury (46540) *(G-9923)*
Ward Production Machine, Fort Wayne *Also called Ward Corporation (G-4735)*
Warfytr, Brookville *Also called Tarver Wolff LLC (G-1127)*
Warm Glow Candle Company......765 855-5483
519 W Water St Centerville (47330) *(G-1544)*
Warner Bodies, Elwood *Also called Manasek Acquisition Co LLC (G-3305)*
Warner Electric LLC......260 244-6183
4578 E Park 30 Dr Columbia City (46725) *(G-1846)*
Warnke Associates Inc......574 586-3331
8401 N Tippecanoe Dr Walkerton (46574) *(G-13814)*
Warren Homes Inc......812 882-1059
2807 Adams Meyer Ln Vincennes (47591) *(G-13716)*
Warren Industries Inc (HQ)......765 447-2151
3200 South St Lafayette (47904) *(G-9020)*
Warren Power Attachments......317 892-4737
4614 E County Road 1000 N Pittsboro (46167) *(G-11589)*
Warren Printing Services LLC......812 738-6508
217 E Chestnut St Corydon (47112) *(G-2115)*
Warrick Publishing Co Inc (HQ)......812 897-2330
204 W Locust St Boonville (47601) *(G-924)*
Warrior Oil Service Inc......317 738-9777
809 Overstreet St Franklin (46131) *(G-4940)*
Warrior Rack, Muncie *Also called Title Ten Manufacturing LLC (G-10570)*
Warsaw Black Oxide Inc......574 491-2975
310 S Walnut St Burket (46508) *(G-1208)*
Warsaw Chemical Company Inc......574 267-3251
390 Argonne Rd Warsaw (46580) *(G-13958)*
Warsaw Coil Co Inc......574 267-6041
1809 W Winona Ave Warsaw (46580) *(G-13959)*
Warsaw Custom Cabinet......574 267-5794
904 Chestnut Ave Winona Lake (46590) *(G-14354)*
Warsaw Custom Cabinet (PA)......574 267-5794
1697 W 350 S Warsaw (46580) *(G-13960)*
Warsaw Cut Glass Company Inc......574 267-6581
505 S Detroit St Warsaw (46580) *(G-13961)*
Warsaw Electropolishing, Warsaw *Also called Surface Enhancement (G-13945)*
Warsaw Foundry Company Inc......574 267-8772
1212 N Detroit St Warsaw (46580) *(G-13962)*
Warsaw Mfg Div, Warsaw *Also called R R Donnelley & Sons Company (G-13931)*
Warsaw Orthopedic Inc......901 396-3133
2500 Silveus Xing Warsaw (46582) *(G-13963)*
Washburn Heating & AC......574 825-7697
54761 County Road 8 Middlebury (46540) *(G-9924)*

Washington 2 Mount Publi 812 332-1600
403 E 3rd St Bloomington (47401) ***(G-853)***
Washington County Addition, Salem *Also called Green Banner Publications Inc* ***(G-12289)***
Washington Times Herald, Washington *Also called Newspaper Holding Inc* ***(G-13993)***
Wasser Brewing Company LLC 765 653-3240
102 E Franklin St Greencastle (46135) ***(G-5481)***
Waste 1 ....765 477-9138
3304 Concord Rd Lafayette (47909) ***(G-9021)***
Wastequip Mfg 574 946-6631
461 E Rosser Rd Winamac (46996) ***(G-14323)***
Wasu Inc 765 448-4450
24 N Earl Ave Lafayette (47904) ***(G-9022)***
Watcon Inc (PA) 574 287-3397
2215 S Main St South Bend (46613) ***(G-12988)***
Water Energizers Inc 812 288-6900
3008 Middle Rd Ste A Jeffersonville (47130) ***(G-8440)***
Water Front Rabbitry, Odon *Also called Graber* ***(G-11326)***
Water Sciences 260 485-4655
327 Ley Rd Fort Wayne (46825) ***(G-4737)***
Water Tec LLC 219 554-1790
7020 Cline Ave Hammond (46323) ***(G-5957)***
Waterfield Automotive Mch Sp 765 288-6262
3600 S Meeker Ave Muncie (47302) ***(G-10580)***
Waterloo Press Inc 260 837-3781
415 W Railroad St Waterloo (46793) ***(G-14025)***
Waterstone Technology 317 644-0862
12429 Springbrooke Run Carmel (46033) ***(G-1507)***
Waterways Equipment Exchange (PA) 812 925-8104
1699 S Stevenson Stn Rd Chandler (47610) ***(G-1555)***
Wattre Inc 260 657-3701
9301 Roberts Rd Woodburn (46797) ***(G-14391)***
Waupaca Foundry Inc 812 547-0700
9856 State Hwy 66 Tell City (47586) ***(G-13174)***
Waupaca Pallet 812 547-1565
11225 Solomon Rd Troy (47588) ***(G-13449)***
Wauseon MCHne&mfg-Kndlvlle Div 260 347-5095
708 S Orchard St Kendallville (46755) ***(G-8513)***
Wave Express 574 642-0630
67952 Us Highway 33 Goshen (46526) ***(G-5345)***
Wawasee Aluminum Works Inc 574 457-2082
300 E Chicago St Syracuse (46567) ***(G-13152)***
Wax Connections Inc 219 778-2325
3628 E Us Highway 20 Rolling Prairie (46371) ***(G-12195)***
Wax Shield 317 831-1349
11818 N Bens Ct Camby (46113) ***(G-1270)***
Wayne Black Oxide Inc 260 484-0280
4505 Executive Blvd Fort Wayne (46808) ***(G-4738)***
Wayne Burial Vault Company 317 357-4656
602 S Emerson Ave Indianapolis (46203) ***(G-8179)***
Wayne Chemical Inc 260 432-1120
7114 Homestead Rd Fort Wayne (46814) ***(G-4739)***
Wayne Combustion Systems, Fort Wayne *Also called Wayne/Scott Fetzer Company* ***(G-4745)***
Wayne Concepts Mfg Inc 260 482-8615
5005 Speedway Dr Fort Wayne (46825) ***(G-4740)***
Wayne Machine Manufacturers 765 962-0459
1747 S 5th St Richmond (47374) ***(G-12074)***
Wayne Manufacturing Corp 260 637-5586
6505 State Road 205 Laotto (46763) ***(G-9115)***
Wayne Manufacturing LLC 260 432-2233
5642 Coventry Ln Fort Wayne (46804) ***(G-4741)***
Wayne Meats, Milan *Also called Milan Food Bank* ***(G-9945)***
Wayne Metal Protection Company 260 492-2529
2413 Meyer Rd Fort Wayne (46803) ***(G-4742)***
Wayne Metals LLC (PA) 260 758-3121
400 E Logan St Markle (46770) ***(G-9584)***
Wayne Newspapers, Cambridge City *Also called Janis Buhl* ***(G-1258)***
Wayne Press Incorporated 260 744-3022
1716 S Harrison St Fort Wayne (46802) ***(G-4743)***
Wayne Steel Supply Inc 260 489-6249
7707 Freedom Way Fort Wayne (46818) ***(G-4744)***
Wayne/Scott Fetzer Company 260 425-9200
801 Glasgow Ave Fort Wayne (46803) ***(G-4745)***
Waynedale Mill Inc 260 436-7100
6701 Ideal Ave Fort Wayne (46809) ***(G-4746)***
Waynedale News Inc 260 747-4535
2505 Lower Huntington Rd A Fort Wayne (46809) ***(G-4747)***
Wayseeker LLC 574 529-0199
9521 N Koher Rd E Syracuse (46567) ***(G-13153)***
Wb Automotive Holdings Inc 734 604-8962
3405 Meyer Rd Fort Wayne (46803) ***(G-4748)***
Wb Refractory Service Inc 317 450-7386
5342 Maplewood Dr Speedway (46224) ***(G-13016)***
Wbh Inc 317 839-1515
204 N Mill St Plainfield (46168) ***(G-11650)***
Wbh Inc (PA) 317 269-1510
123 N Pine St Indianapolis (46202) ***(G-8180)***
WC Redmon Co Inc 765 473-6683
200 Harrison Ave Peru (46970) ***(G-11556)***
Wcm Tool & Machine Inc 812 422-2315
810 E Division St Evansville (47711) ***(G-3810)***
Wdmi Inc 574 291-7100
715 W Ireland Rd South Bend (46614) ***(G-12989)***
Wdmi Inc 765 868-9646
1397 E Havens St Kokomo (46901) ***(G-8715)***
Wearly Monuments Inc (PA) 765 284-9796
4000 W Kilgore Ave Muncie (47304) ***(G-10581)***
Wearlypocock Monuments 574 223-2010
1229 Main St Rochester (46975) ***(G-12160)***
Weas Engineering Inc 317 867-4477
17297 Oak Ridge Rd Westfield (46074) ***(G-14200)***
Weatherall Company, Charlestown *Also called Weatherall Indiana Inc* ***(G-1585)***
Weatherall Indiana Inc 812 256-3378
106 Industrial Way Charlestown (47111) ***(G-1585)***
Weaver Air Products LLC 317 848-4420
1033 3rd Ave Sw Ste 212 Carmel (46032) ***(G-1508)***
Weaver Fine Cabinets Furniture 812 342-4833
14400 W Georgetown Rd Columbus (47201) ***(G-2031)***
Weaver Logging 260 589-9985
2896 West St Berne (46711) ***(G-629)***
Weaver Woodworking 260 565-3647
7795 E 300 S Bluffton (46714) ***(G-897)***
Web Converting, Fort Wayne *Also called Web Industries Dallas Inc* ***(G-4749)***
Web Converting of Fort Wayne, Fort Wayne *Also called Web Industries Fort Wayne Inc* ***(G-4750)***
Web Industries Dallas Inc 260 432-0027
3925 Ardmore Ave Fort Wayne (46802) ***(G-4749)***
Web Industries Fort Wayne Inc 260 432-0027
3925 Ardmore Ave Fort Wayne (46802) ***(G-4750)***
Web Software LLC 765 452-3936
2115 W Alto Rd Ste A Kokomo (46902) ***(G-8716)***
Webb Wheel Products Inc 812 548-0477
9840 W State Route 66 Tell City (47586) ***(G-13175)***
Webb, Danny Plumbing & Heating, Plymouth *Also called Danny Webb Plumbing* ***(G-11679)***
Webber Manufacturing Company 317 357-8681
8498 Brookville Rd Indianapolis (46239) ***(G-8181)***
Webco Inc 260 244-4233
303 Towerview Dr Columbia City (46725) ***(G-1847)***
Weber Sign Service Inc 219 872-5060
320 Trail St Trail Creek (46360) ***(G-13444)***
Weberdings Carving Shop Inc 812 934-3710
1230 State Road 46 E Batesville (47006) ***(G-524)***
Webster Custom Canvas Inc 574 834-4497
221 N Main St North Webster (46555) ***(G-11302)***
Webster West Inc 812 346-5666
1050 Rodgers Park Dr North Vernon (47265) ***(G-11286)***
Webster West Packaging, North Vernon *Also called Webster West Inc* ***(G-11286)***
Websters Sporting Goods Inc 317 255-4855
5060 E 62nd St Ste 114 Indianapolis (46220) ***(G-8182)***
Websters Tom Custom WD Turning, Indianapolis *Also called Prized Possession* ***(G-7762)***
Wedj-FM, Indianapolis *Also called Continntal Broadcast Group LLC* ***(G-6657)***
Wee Engineer Inc 765 449-4280
282 Delaware St Dayton (47941) ***(G-2362)***
Weekly Herald, The, Madison *Also called Madison Courier* ***(G-9479)***
Wegener Steel and Fabricating 219 462-3911
906 Evans Ave Valparaiso (46383) ***(G-13636)***
Wehr Engineering, Fairland *Also called Thomas L Wehr* ***(G-3827)***
Wehr Welding & Repair Shop, Jasper *Also called Robert L Wehr* ***(G-8302)***
Weil-Mclain, Michigan City *Also called Marley-Wylain Company* ***(G-9815)***
Weil-Mclain, Michigan City *Also called Marley-Wylain Company* ***(G-9816)***
Welch Packaging LLC (HQ) 574 295-2460
1020 Herman St Elkhart (46516) ***(G-3255)***
Welch Packaging Group Inc (PA) 574 295-2460
1020 Herman St Elkhart (46516) ***(G-3256)***
Welch Packaging Marion LLC 765 651-2600
2409 W 2nd St Marion (46952) ***(G-9572)***
Welcome Friends, Terre Haute *Also called Mikro Furniture* ***(G-13286)***
Weld & Fabrication Shop, Batesville *Also called Red Forge Inc* ***(G-516)***
Weld Done 260 597-7237
5945 E Us Highway 224 Ossian (46777) ***(G-11415)***
Weld-Done Shop, Ossian *Also called Weld Done* ***(G-11415)***
Welded Products Div, Mishawaka *Also called Van Com Inc* ***(G-10145)***
Weldors Inc 765 289-9074
2702 S Monroe St Muncie (47302) ***(G-10582)***
Weldy Enterprises, Wakarusa *Also called Hahn Enterprises Inc* ***(G-13778)***
Welformed, Elkhart *Also called Genesis Products Inc* ***(G-2877)***
Well Ink 765 743-3413
360 Brown St West Lafayette (47906) ***(G-14117)***
Wellco Holdings Inc (HQ) 574 264-9661
1503 Mcnaughton Ave Elkhart (46514) ***(G-3257)***
Wellpet LLC 574 259-7834
1025 W 11th St Mishawaka (46544) ***(G-10150)***
Wells Robe Sales & Rental 317 542-9062
5702 E 40th St Indianapolis (46226) ***(G-8183)***
Wells Unlimited Robes Service, Indianapolis *Also called Wells Robe Sales & Rental* ***(G-8183)***

ALPHABETIC

Wellspring Components LLC 260 768-7336
1085 N 850 W Shipshewana (46565) *(G-12657)*

Welmer Jewelers Inc 812 522-4082
106 S Chestnut St Seymour (47274) *(G-12499)*

Wendell Conger 812 282-2564
3730 Utica Sellersburg Rd Jeffersonville (47130) *(G-8441)*

Wendell Denton 317 736-8397
4257 S 200 E Franklin (46131) *(G-4941)*

Wenzel Acquisition Inc 260 495-9898
5610 N West St Fremont (46737) *(G-4979)*

Wenzel Metal Spinning Inc (PA) 260 495-9898
701 W Water St Fremont (46737) *(G-4980)*

Wenzel Metal Spinning Inc Ind 260 495-9898
701 W Water St Fremont (46737) *(G-4981)*

Werner Sawmill Inc 812 482-7565
3545 N 550w Jasper (47546) *(G-8313)*

Werrco Inc 812 358-8665
5994 W State Road 58 Brownstown (47220) *(G-1192)*

Werrco Tools & Machines, Brownstown Also called Werrco Inc *(G-1192)*

Wert Fixture & Display Inc 317 577-0905
6951 E 30th St Ste C Indianapolis (46219) *(G-8184)*

Wesley Publishing House, The, Fishers Also called Wesleyan Church Corporation *(G-3984)*

Wesleyan Church Corporation (PA) 317 774-7900
13300 Olio Rd Ste X Fishers (46037) *(G-3984)*

Wessels Company 317 888-9800
101 Tank St Greenwood (46143) *(G-5759)*

West Allis Gray Iron 260 925-4717
1401 S Grandstaff Dr Auburn (46706) *(G-367)*

West Executive Offices, Mishawaka Also called Patrick Industries Inc *(G-10100)*

West Fork Whiskey Co 812 583-9797
1660 Bellefontaine St Indianapolis (46202) *(G-8185)*

West Lakes Boat Mart, Rome City Also called West Lakes Marine Inc *(G-12201)*

West Lakes Marine Inc (PA) 260 854-2525
85 E Holiday Pt Rome City (46784) *(G-12201)*

West Plains Distribution LLC 260 563-9500
1600 S Olive St Wabash (46992) *(G-13767)*

West Plains Mining LLC 260 563-9500
6601 W Old 24 Wabash (46992) *(G-13768)*

West Point Woodworking LLC 260 768-4750
6565 W 200 N Shipshewana (46565) *(G-12658)*

West Side Automation 812 768-6878
78 W 1100 S Haubstadt (47639) *(G-6008)*

West Side Community News, Indianapolis Also called Community Papers Inc *(G-6639)*

Westech Building Products Inc 812 985-3628
7451 Highway 62 E Mount Vernon (47620) *(G-10414)*

Western Consolidated Tech Inc (HQ) 260 495-9866
700 W Swager St Fremont (46737) *(G-4982)*

Western Green LLC 812 963-3373
5401 St Wndl Cynthiana Rd Poseyville (47633) *(G-11862)*

Western Metal Fabricators, Fishers Also called Tuttle Aluminum Intl Inc *(G-3980)*

Western Products Indiana Inc 765 529-6230
387 W State Road 38 New Castle (47362) *(G-10921)*

Western Reman Industrial Inc (HQ) 765 472-2002
588 W 7th St Peru (46970) *(G-11557)*

Western Reman Industrial LLC 765 472-2002
588 W 7th St Peru (46970) *(G-11558)*

Western Wayne News 765 478-5448
26 W Church St Cambridge City (47327) *(G-1262)*

Western Wyne Rgonal Sewage Dst 765 478-3788
200 S Plum St Cambridge City (47327) *(G-1263)*

Western-Cullen-Hayes Inc 765 962-0526
120 N 3rd St Richmond (47374) *(G-12075)*

Westfield Donuts 317 896-5856
212 E Main St Westfield (46074) *(G-14201)*

Westfield Outdoor Inc 317 334-0364
8675 Purdue Rd Indianapolis (46268) *(G-8186)*

Westfield Steel Inc 812 466-3500
3345 Fort Harrison Rd Terre Haute (47804) *(G-13368)*

Westlund Concepts 317 819-0611
806 N Woodward St Lapel (46051) *(G-9120)*

Weston Foods Us Inc (HQ) 317 858-9000
50 Maplehurst Dr Brownsburg (46112) *(G-1176)*

Westrock Cp LLC 574 936-2118
1100 Pidco Dr Plymouth (46563) *(G-11735)*

Westrock Cp LLC 574 772-5545
6595 E State Road 10 Knox (46534) *(G-8587)*

Westrock Cp LLC 812 372-8873
3101 State St Columbus (47201) *(G-2032)*

Westrock Cp LLC 574 256-0318
1925 Stone Ct Mishawaka (46545) *(G-10151)*

Westrock CP LLC 219 762-4855
5900 Carlson Ave Portage (46368) *(G-11801)*

Westrock CP LLC 574 296-2817
1535 Fieldhouse Ave Elkhart (46517) *(G-3258)*

Westrock Mwv LLC 317 787-3361
6302 Churchman Byp Indianapolis (46203) *(G-8187)*

Westrock Rkt Company 574 936-2118
1810 Pidco Dr Plymouth (46563) *(G-11736)*

Westrock Rkt Company 765 396-3317
800 S Romy St Ste A Eaton (47338) *(G-2590)*

Westrock Rkt Company 812 372-8873
3101 State St Columbus (47201) *(G-2033)*

Westwood Paper Co 317 843-1212
4489 Camborne Dr Carmel (46033) *(G-1509)*

Wg S Global Services 810 239-4947
9856 W State Road 66 Tell City (47586) *(G-13176)*

Wge Equipment Solutions LLC 260 636-7218
306 Stable Dr Fort Wayne (46825) *(G-4751)*

Wgs Global Services LC 812 548-4446
840 5th St Tell City (47586) *(G-13177)*

Whallon Machinery Inc 574 643-9561
205 N Chicago St Royal Center (46978) *(G-12216)*

Whb International Inc 317 820-3001
101 W Ohio St Ste 810 Indianapolis (46204) *(G-8188)*

Wheel Group Holdings LLC 317 780-1661
5720 Kopetsky Dr Ste I Indianapolis (46217) *(G-8189)*

Wheel Horse Sales & Service 574 272-4242
51465 Ind St Rte 933 South Bend (46637) *(G-12990)*

Wheel One, Indianapolis Also called Wheel Group Holdings LLC *(G-8189)*

Wheelchair Help LLC 574 295-2220
515 East St Elkhart (46516) *(G-3259)*

Wheelchair of Indiana 317 627-6560
4717 Boulevard Pl Indianapolis (46208) *(G-8190)*

Wheels 4 Tots Inc 219 987-6812
10700 W 1300 N Demotte (46310) *(G-2452)*

Wheels In Sky 812 249-8233
1026 Monterey Ave Terre Haute (47803) *(G-13369)*

Whetstone Industries 260 724-2461
1121 Marshall St Decatur (46733) *(G-2412)*

Whiffen Machine and Press Repr 812 876-1257
9967 N Brown Ln Gosport (47433) *(G-5357)*

Whipp In Holdings LLC (PA) 260 478-2363
3405 Engle Rd Fort Wayne (46809) *(G-4752)*

Whirlpool Corporation 812 426-4000
5401 Highway 41 N Evansville (47711) *(G-3811)*

Whirlpool Corporation 317 837-5300
2801 Airwest Blvd Plainfield (46168) *(G-11651)*

Whiskey Business 317 823-5078
11915 Pendleton Pike D Indianapolis (46236) *(G-8191)*

Whisler Custom Leather Co 765 212-8932
1108 E Royerton Rd Muncie (47303) *(G-10583)*

Whistle Stop 219 253-4100
10012 N Us Highway 421 Monon (47959) *(G-10180)*

Whitaker Glass & Mirror LLC 765 482-1500
104 E Superior St Lebanon (46052) *(G-9232)*

Whitaker Skid and Crate, Corydon Also called Whitakerr Dalemon *(G-2116)*

Whitakerr Dalemon 812 738-2396
1240 Old N Bridge Rd Ne Corydon (47112) *(G-2116)*

Whitcomb Yard, Valparaiso Also called Legacy Vulcan LLC *(G-13575)*

Whitcraft Enterprises Inc 260 422-6518
4323 Merchant Rd Fort Wayne (46818) *(G-4753)*

White Aspen Woodworking LLC 765 471-4962
4241 Fletcher Dr Lafayette (47909) *(G-9023)*

White Cap 153, Fort Wayne Also called Hd Supply Construction Supply *(G-4325)*

White Cap LLC 812 425-6221
2201 W Maryland St Evansville (47712) *(G-3812)*

White County Egg Farms, Monon Also called Rose Acre Farms Inc *(G-10178)*

White Flyer Targets, Knox Also called Reagent Chemical & RES Inc *(G-8577)*

White Flyer Targets 574 772-3271
317 Kloeckner Dr Knox (46534) *(G-8588)*

White Machine Inc 574 267-5895
1903 White Industrial Dr Warsaw (46580) *(G-13964)*

White Oak Land & Timber LLC 812 482-5102
560 E 25th St Jasper (47546) *(G-8314)*

White River Gravel Company Inc 317 834-6818
10151 Hague Rd Indianapolis (46256) *(G-8192)*

White River Outfitters LLC 812 787-0921
314 Main St Shoals (47581) *(G-12673)*

White Rver Fndry/Creative Arts, Spencer Also called Mark Parmenter *(G-13030)*

White Water Truss Llc 765 489-6261
79 Paul R Foulke Pkwy Hagerstown (47346) *(G-5816)*

Whiteco Industries Inc (PA) 219 769-6601
1000 E 80th Pl Ste 700n Merrillville (46410) *(G-9761)*

Whitehead Signs Inc 317 632-1800
1801 Deloss St Indianapolis (46201) *(G-8193)*

Whites Woodworks 765 341-6678
1835 Pumpkinvine Hill Rd Martinsville (46151) *(G-9648)*

Whitesell Prcsion Cmpnents Inc 812 282-4014
100 Technology Way Jeffersonville (47130) *(G-8442)*

Whitestown - Precast, Whitestown Also called Hydro Conduit of Texas LP *(G-14254)*

Whitetail Heartbeat 260 336-1052
61755 State Road 13 Middlebury (46540) *(G-9925)*

Whitetower Collection LLC 847 826-0927
976 Wexford Dr Lafayette (47905) *(G-9024)*

Whitewater Publications Inc 765 647-4221
531 Main St Brookville (47012) *(G-1131)*

Whitewater Valley Rvs Inc 765 458-5171
853 S State Road 101 Liberty (47353) *(G-9272)*

Whiting Clean Energy Inc 219 473-0653
2155 Standard Ave Whiting (46394) *(G-14277)*

Whiting Metals LLC 219 659-6955
2230 Indianapolis Blvd Whiting (46394) *(G-14278)*

Whitley Evergreen Inc (HQ) 260 723-5131
201 W 1st St South Whitley (46787) *(G-13009)*

Whitley Feeds Div, South Whitley Also called Nutritional Research Assoc *(G-13002)*

Whitley Welding & Fabg & Repr 260 723-5111
7700 S State Road 5 South Whitley (46787) *(G-13010)*

Whitlocks Pressure Wash 765 825-5868
5649 Industrial Ave S Connersville (47331) *(G-2078)*

Whitman Publications Inc 574 268-2062
401 Kings Hwy Winona Lake (46590) *(G-14355)*

Whitney Tool Company Inc 812 275-4491
906 R St Bedford (47421) *(G-590)*

Wholeaf Aloe Distributors 219 322-7217
46 Oak Ct Schererville (46375) *(G-12352)*

Wholesale Drainage Supply Inc 812 397-5100
8300 N Us Highway 41 Shelburn (47879) *(G-12513)*

Wholesale Hrdwood Intriors Inc 317 867-3660
17715 Commerce Dr Ste 300 Westfield (46074) *(G-14202)*

Wholesale Stone Distribution, Richmond Also called Granite Marble & More Inc *(G-11991)*

Wholistic Gardens 260 573-1088
4840 County Road 4 Waterloo (46793) *(G-14026)*

Whyte Haus 260 484-5666
1629 Channel Pl Fort Wayne (46825) *(G-4754)*

Whyte Horse Winery LLC 574 583-2345
1510 S Airport Rd Monticello (47960) *(G-10288)*

Wible Lumber Inc 260 351-2441
7155 S State Rte 3 South Milford (46786) *(G-12995)*

Wichman Woodworking Inc 812 522-8450
8305 N County Road 300 E Seymour (47274) *(G-12500)*

Wick - Fab Inc 260 897-3303
307 E Fourth St Avilla (46710) *(G-421)*

Wick's Air Filter, Fort Wayne Also called Wicks Air Filter Service Inc *(G-4755)*

Wicker Gallery 219 942-0783
619 E 3rd St Hobart (46342) *(G-6100)*

Wickfab Steel Fabrication, Avilla Also called Wick - Fab Inc *(G-421)*

Wicks Air Filter Service Inc 260 426-1782
2607 Mcdonald St Fort Wayne (46803) *(G-4755)*

Wicks Pie 765 584-8401
217 Se Greenville Ave Winchester (47394) *(G-14344)*

Wicks Pies Inc 765 584-8401
217 Se Greenville Ave Winchester (47394) *(G-14345)*

Widows Walk 812 285-8850
415 E Riverside Dr Clarksville (47129) *(G-1700)*

Wiers Fleet Partners Inc (PA) 574 936-4076
2111 Jim Neu Dr Plymouth (46563) *(G-11737)*

Wiese Holding Company 317 241-8600
4549 W Bradbury Ave Indianapolis (46241) *(G-8194)*

Wiggins Press LLC 574 273-1769
15945 Preswick Ln Granger (46530) *(G-5452)*

Wilbert Burial Vault Co Inc 317 547-1387
2165 N Sherman Dr Indianapolis (46218) *(G-8195)*

Wilbert Burial Vault Co Inc 812 753-3601
301 S Us Highway 41 Fort Branch (47648) *(G-4030)*

Wilbert Sexton Corporation 812 882-3555
426 S 15th St Vincennes (47591) *(G-13717)*

Wilbert Sexton Corporation (PA) 812 336-6469
1908 W Allen St Bloomington (47403) *(G-854)*

Wilbert Sexton Corporation 812 334-0883
2332 W 3rd St Bloomington (47404) *(G-855)*

Wilbert Sexton Corporation 812 372-3210
3100 S Us Highway 31 Columbus (47201) *(G-2034)*

Wilco Corporation 317 228-9320
5352 W 79th St Indianapolis (46268) *(G-8196)*

Wild Birds Unlimited, Granger Also called Birds Nest Inc *(G-5394)*

Wild Boar Mine 812 922-1015
2277 Tecumseh Rd Lynnville (47619) *(G-9438)*

Wildcat Creek Winery, Lafayette Also called Rick Black Associates LLC *(G-8991)*

Wildman Business Group LLC 866 369-1552
800 S Buffalo St Warsaw (46580) *(G-13965)*

Wildman Corporate Apparel, Warsaw Also called Wildman Business Group LLC *(G-13965)*

Wildman Corporate Apparel Ltd 574 269-7266
800 S Buffalo St Ste 1 Warsaw (46580) *(G-13966)*

Wildman Enterprise 317 985-0924
516 Grove St Greenfield (46140) *(G-5584)*

Wildside Signs 812 358-3849
10207 N State Road 135 Vallonia (47281) *(G-13478)*

Wildwood Floral Co LLC 916 220-4900
6347 Forest View Dr Indianapolis (46260) *(G-8197)*

Wildwood Millwork LLC 574 535-9104
2408 Lincolnway E Goshen (46526) *(G-5346)*

Wiley Young & Associates 574 269-7006
121 W Market St Ste B Warsaw (46580) *(G-13967)*

Wiley Industries Inc 317 574-1477
1311 Woodgate Dr Carmel (46033) *(G-1510)*

Wiley Metal Fabricating Inc (PA) 765 671-7865
4589 N Wabash Rd Marion (46952) *(G-9573)*

Wiley Metal Fabricating Inc 765 674-9707
816 W 34th St Marion (46953) *(G-9574)*

Wiley Publishing Inc 317 842-2032
10475 Croinpoint Blvd 100 Indianapolis (46256) *(G-8198)*

Wilhelm AG Lime, Peru Also called Jolene D Pavey *(G-11534)*

Wilhelm Gravel, Waterloo Also called Country Stone *(G-14012)*

Wilhelm Gravel Co Inc 260 837-6511
2280 County Road 27 Waterloo (46793) *(G-14027)*

Wilhite Industries Inc 812 853-8771
5833 S Yankeetown Rd Boonville (47601) *(G-925)*

Wilhoite Monuments Inc 765 286-7423
4710 S Madison St Muncie (47302) *(G-10584)*

Wilkerson Logging Inc 812 988-4960
4263 Hoover Rd Nashville (47448) *(G-10738)*

Wilkerson Sawmill 812 988-7436
5400 Hoover Rd Nashville (47448) *(G-10739)*

Wilkes Printing Inc 812 847-0005
1089 1st St Se Linton (47441) *(G-9315)*

William A Kadar 219 884-7404
5015 Broadway Gary (46409) *(G-5116)*

William Browning 765 647-6397
7015 Jefferson St Brookville (47012) *(G-1132)*

William D Darr 574 518-0453
5416 E 950 N Syracuse (46567) *(G-13154)*

William F Bane Co, Indianapolis Also called Bane-Clene Corp *(G-6455)*

William F Shirley 812 426-2599
2721 W Mill Rd Evansville (47720) *(G-3813)*

William H Sadlier Inc 219 465-0453
4405 Blair Ln Valparaiso (46383) *(G-13637)*

William Leman Co (PA) 574 546-2371
114 N Center St Bremen (46506) *(G-1033)*

William R Arvin 812 486-5255
200 Brooks Ave Loogootee (47553) *(G-9398)*

William Roam LLC 317 356-2715
6501 Julian Ave Indianapolis (46219) *(G-8199)*

William S Bane 812 358-5790
1414 E Us Highway 50 Brownstown (47220) *(G-1193)*

William Wesley Professional 317 635-1000
5605 W 73rd St Indianapolis (46278) *(G-8200)*

Williams Backhoe Service, Sellersburg Also called Steven A Williams *(G-12419)*

Williams Bros Health Care Inc 812 257-2505
7 Williams Brothers Dr Washington (47501) *(G-14007)*

Williams Bros Health Care Pha 812 335-0000
574 S Landmark Ave Bloomington (47403) *(G-856)*

Williams Bros Health Care Pha (PA) 812 254-2497
10 Williams Brothers Dr Washington (47501) *(G-14008)*

Williams Bros Logging LLC 270 547-0266
2880 Overlook Dr Sw Mauckport (47142) *(G-9659)*

Williams Companies Inc 765 886-6149
6690 W Davis Meyers Rd Williamsburg (47393) *(G-14285)*

Williams Plastics LLC 317 398-1630
2201 E Michigan Rd Shelbyville (46176) *(G-12585)*

Williams Printing Inc 765 468-6033
201 E Henry St Farmland (47340) *(G-3844)*

Williams Signs Inc 765 448-6725
6407 Whippoorwill Ln Lafayette (47905) *(G-9025)*

Williams Tool & Machine Corp 765 676-5859
54 W Main St Jamestown (46147) *(G-8233)*

Williams West & Witts Pdts Co 219 879-8236
3501 W Dunes Hwy Michigan City (46360) *(G-9860)*

Williams Woods Pubg Svcs LLC 317 270-0976
3921 English Ave Indianapolis (46201) *(G-8201)*

Williamsburg Furniture Inc 574 387-5691
3300 W Sample St South Bend (46619) *(G-12991)*

Williamsburg Furniture Inc (PA) 800 582-8183
2096 Cheyenne St Nappanee (46550) *(G-10710)*

Williamsport Tire Mart LLC 765 762-6315
18 Front St Williamsport (47993) *(G-14300)*

Willie and Associates Inc 219 662-9046
11188 State St Crown Point (46307) *(G-2320)*

Willis Curtis Genie Jr 317 377-4711
4606 N Ritter Ave Indianapolis (46226) *(G-8202)*

Willow Way LLC 765 886-4640
12873 We Oler Rd Hagerstown (47346) *(G-5817)*

Willowgreen Inc 260 490-2222
10351 Dawsons Creek Blvd B Fort Wayne (46825) *(G-4756)*

Wills Electric Motor Serv, Pekin Also called Wills Electric Service Inc *(G-11480)*

Wills Electric Service Inc 812 883-5653
85 E Shorts Corner Rd Pekin (47165) *(G-11480)*

Wills-Stockton Acres LLC 765 366-7307
4757 N 360 E Crawfordsville (47933) *(G-2204)*

Wilmes Window Mfg Co Inc (PA) 812 275-7575
234 W 23rd St Ferdinand (47532) *(G-3864)*

Wilo AM & Wshw FM, Frankfort Also called Kaspar Broadcasting Co Inc *(G-4839)*

Wilson Autotech, Crawfordsville Also called Wilson Enterprises Inc *(G-2205)*

Wilson Burial Vault Inc 260 356-5722
446 W Markle Rd Huntington (46750) *(G-6261)*

Wilson Enterprises Inc (PA) 765 362-1089
2008 Indianapolis Rd Crawfordsville (47933) *(G-2205)*

A
L
P
H
A
B
E
T
I
C

Wilson Fertilizer & Grain Inc (PA) 574 223-3175
  1827 E Lucas St Rochester (46975) *(G-12161)*
Wilson Hearing Aid Center 765 747-4131
  3716 N Wheeling Ave Muncie (47304) *(G-10585)*
Wilson Machine Shop Inc 812 392-2774
  7780 W County Road 800 N Elizabethtown (47232) *(G-2652)*
Wilson Printing 317 745-5868
  527 N County Road 50 E Danville (46122) *(G-2358)*
Wilson Tool & Engineering Inc 812 334-1110
  2460 N Curry Pike Bloomington (47404) *(G-857)*
Wilsons Locker & Proc Plant 812 358-2632
  324 N Bolles St Brownstown (47220) *(G-1194)*
Wilsons Slaughtering & Proc, Brownstown Also called Wilsons Locker & Proc
Plant *(G-1194)*
Wimmer Burial Vaults, New Castle Also called Wimmer Vaults Inc *(G-10923)*
Wimmer Lime Service Inc 765 948-4001
  7497 S 150 E Fairmount (46928) *(G-3835)*
Wimmer Mfg Inc 765 465-9846
  201 W County Road 100 S New Castle (47362) *(G-10922)*
Wimmer Vaults Inc. 765 529-5702
  900 New York Ave New Castle (47362) *(G-10923)*
Winamac Coil Spring Inc 574 653-2186
  512 N Smith St Kewanna (46939) *(G-8528)*
Winamac Cold Draw, Winamac Also called Plymouth Tube Company *(G-14314)*
Winandy Greenhouse Company 765 935-2111
  2211 Peacock Rd Richmond (47374) *(G-12076)*
Winchester Steel 812 591-2071
  10622 S County Road 100 W Westport (47283) *(G-14212)*
Winco Printing & Gift Shop, Roanoke Also called James David Inc *(G-12105)*
Wind Deco, Zionsville Also called Fanimation Inc *(G-14431)*
Windmill Brewing 219 440-2189
  2121 Gettler St Dyer (46311) *(G-2512)*
Window Makeover, Noblesville Also called Harrell Family LLC *(G-11119)*
Window Man Inc 317 755-3207
  5575 Elmwood Ave Ste B Indianapolis (46203) *(G-8203)*
Windsong K-9 Coach Inc 574 971-6358
  52711 County Road 11 Elkhart (46514) *(G-3260)*
Windsor Steel Inc 574 294-1060
  2210 Middlebury St Elkhart (46516) *(G-3261)*
Windsor Wartcare 574 266-6555
  3100 Windsor Ct Elkhart (46514) *(G-3262)*
Windstream Technologies Inc 812 953-1481
  819 Buckeye St North Vernon (47265) *(G-11287)*
Windy Knoll Winery 812 726-1600
  845 N Atkinson Rd Vincennes (47591) *(G-13718)*
Wine & Canvas South Bend LLC 574 807-1562
  51213 County Road 11 Elkhart (46514) *(G-3263)*
Wine and Canvas Dev LLC (PA) 317 345-1567
  5151 E 82nd St Ste 700 Indianapolis (46250) *(G-8204)*
Wine and Canvas Dev LLC 317 914-2806
  1005 Hawthorne Dr Columbus (47203) *(G-2035)*
Wine N Vine 765 282-3300
  1524 E Mcgalliard Rd Muncie (47303) *(G-10586)*
Winfield American, The, Crown Point Also called Region Communications Inc *(G-2294)*
Winfield Solutions LLC 317 838-3733
  923 Whitaker Rd Ste G Plainfield (46168) *(G-11652)*
Wingards Sales LLC 260 768-7961
  3715 N State Road 5 Shipshewana (46565) *(G-12659)*
Wings N Things Fabrication 260 432-2992
  1829 Kroemer Rd Fort Wayne (46808) *(G-4757)*
Winn Machine Inc 219 324-2978
  720 Boyd Blvd La Porte (46350) *(G-8833)*
Winnebago of Indiana LLC 574 825-5250
  201 14th Ave Middlebury (46540) *(G-9926)*
Winner's Circle, Spencer Also called Crescendo Inc *(G-13022)*
Winning Edge of Rochester Inc 574 223-6090
  221 Rouch Place Dr Rochester (46975) *(G-12162)*
Winona Building Products LLC 574 822-0100
  9876 W Old Road 30 Etna Green (46524) *(G-3323)*
Winona Powder Coating Inc (PA) 574 267-8311
  9876 W Old Road 30 Etna Green (46524) *(G-3324)*
Winona Pvd Coatings LLC 574 269-3255
  1180 Polk Dr Warsaw (46582) *(G-13968)*
Winski Brothers Inc 765 654-5323
  751 W Washington St Frankfort (46041) *(G-4860)*
Winslow Scale Company 812 466-5265
  4530 N 25th St Terre Haute (47805) *(G-13370)*
Winslow-Browning Inc 765 458-5157
  215 Brownsville Ave Liberty (47353) *(G-9273)*
Winters Assoc Prmtnal Pdts Inc (PA) 812 330-7000
  1048 W 17th St Bloomington (47404) *(G-858)*
Winzerwald Winery LLC 812 357-7000
  26300 N Indian Lake Rd Bristow (47515) *(G-1096)*
Winzerwald Winery LLC 812 357-7000
  26300 N Indian Lake Rd Bristow (47515) *(G-1097)*
Wirco Inc (PA) 260 897-3768
  105 Progress Way Avilla (46710) *(G-422)*
Wire America Inc 260 969-1700
  1613 E Wallace St Fort Wayne (46803) *(G-4758)*

Wire Design, Elkhart Also called Patrick Industries Inc *(G-3089)*
Wire-Tek Inc 812 623-8300
  234 Industrial Dr Sunman (47041) *(G-13121)*
Wirecut Technologies Inc 317 885-9915
  5328 Commerce Square Dr Indianapolis (46237) *(G-8205)*
Wise Business Forms Inc 260 489-1561
  4301 Merchant Rd Fort Wayne (46818) *(G-4759)*
Wise Industries Inc (del) 219 947-5333
  1596 Lilac Ct Hobart (46342) *(G-6101)*
Wise Printing Inc 317 861-6220
  3721 S Fallow Trl New Palestine (46163) *(G-10974)*
Wise Printing Inc 317 351-9477
  1429 Sadlier Circle W Dr Indianapolis (46239) *(G-8206)*
Wiseguys Seating & Accessry Co 574 294-6030
  2701 Industrial Pkwy Elkhart (46516) *(G-3264)*
Wisemans Custom Cabinets Inc 812 678-3601
  4501 E State Road 56 Dubois (47527) *(G-2478)*
Wishful Thinking, Nashville Also called Crystal Source *(G-10721)*
Witham Machine 317 835-2076
  8429 W 525 N Boggstown (46110) *(G-903)*
Witt Galvanizing 574 935-4500
  2631 Jim Neu Dr Plymouth (46563) *(G-11738)*
Witt Industries Inc 765 289-3427
  2415 S Walnut St Muncie (47302) *(G-10587)*
Witt Industries Inc 574 935-4500
  2631 Jim Neu Dr Plymouth (46563) *(G-11739)*
Wittmer Distributors 812 636-7786
  11057 N 700 E Odon (47562) *(G-11345)*
Wittmer Woodworking LLC 812 486-3115
  4637 E 200 N Montgomery (47558) *(G-10248)*
Wittrock Enterprises LLC 812 222-0373
  8829 E State Road 46 Greensburg (47240) *(G-5642)*
Wittrock Healthcare, Greensburg Also called Wittrock Enterprises LLC *(G-5642)*
Wiw Inc 219 663-7900
  424 Wessex Rd Crown Point (46307) *(G-2321)*
Wnc of Dayton LLC 937 999-8868
  3969 E 82nd St Indianapolis (46240) *(G-8207)*
Wolf Corporation 260 749-9393
  3434 Adams Center Rd Fort Wayne (46803) *(G-4760)*
Wolf Printing LLC 317 577-1771
  7120 Graham Rd Indianapolis (46250) *(G-8208)*
Wolf Technical Engineering LLC 800 783-9653
  9855 Crnpint Blvd Ste 126 Indianapolis (46256) *(G-8209)*
Wolf's Bar-B-Q Restaurant, Evansville Also called Wolfs Bar B Q Inc *(G-3814)*
Wolfe and Swickard Mch Co Inc 317 241-2589
  1344 S Tibbs Ave Indianapolis (46241) *(G-8210)*
Wolfe Diversified Inds LLC (PA) 765 683-9374
  9408 W Constellation Dr Pendleton (46064) *(G-11511)*
Wolfe Engineered Plastics LLC 812 623-8403
  215 Nieman St Sunman (47041) *(G-13122)*
Wolfgang Software 317 443-5147
  10401 Cotton Blossom Dr Fishers (46038) *(G-3985)*
Wolfies Grill 5 LLC 317 804-5619
  219 Park St Westfield (46074) *(G-14203)*
Wolfpack Chassis LLC 260 349-1887
  800 Weston Ave Kendallville (46755) *(G-8514)*
Wolfs Bar B Q Inc 812 424-8891
  6600 N 1st Ave Evansville (47710) *(G-3814)*
Wolke Paint Manufacturer, Corydon Also called A F Wolke Co Inc *(G-2086)*
Wonder Nail LLC 317 462-8404
  1909 Melody Ln Greenfield (46140) *(G-5585)*
Wood Creations Inc 574 522-7765
  800 Industrial Pkwy Elkhart (46516) *(G-3265)*
WOOD KOVERS, Valparaiso Also called Heat Wagons Inc *(G-13555)*
Wood Lighter Cases LLC 812 969-3908
  7705 Pine Hill Dr Se Elizabeth (47117) *(G-2650)*
Wood Medic Inc 765 778-4544
  9494 S 300 W Pendleton (46064) *(G-11512)*
Wood Spc By Fehrenbacher 812 963-9414
  8920 Big Cynthiana Rd Evansville (47720) *(G-3815)*
Wood Specialists LLC 219 779-9026
  12120 Chase St Crown Point (46307) *(G-2322)*
Wood Technologies LLC 260 627-8858
  13804 Antwerp Rd Grabill (46741) *(G-5385)*
Wood Truss Systems Inc 765 751-9990
  5600 W Shoreline Ter Muncie (47304) *(G-10588)*
Wood-Mizer LLC 317 271-1542
  8180 W 10th St Indianapolis (46214) *(G-8211)*
Wood-Mizer Holdings Inc (PA) 317 271-1542
  8180 W 10th St Indianapolis (46214) *(G-8212)*
Wood-Mizer Holdings Inc. 317 892-4444
  7865 N County Rd Ste 100 Lizton (46149) *(G-9318)*
Woodburn Diamond Die Co Inc (PA) 260 632-4217
  23012 Tile Mill Rd Woodburn (46797) *(G-14392)*
Woodburn Graphics Inc 812 232-0323
  25 S 6th St Terre Haute (47807) *(G-13371)*
Woodcrafters LLC 765 469-5103
  8472 N 100 E Denver (46926) *(G-2455)*
Woodcrest Manufacturing Inc (PA) 765 472-4471
  150 E Washington Ave Peru (46970) *(G-11559)*

(G-0000) Company's Geographic Section entry number

Woodcrest Manufacturing Inc.....765 472-5361
217 E Canal St Peru (46970) *(G-11560)*
Wooden Concept Inc.....317 293-3137
7410 Dobson St Indianapolis (46268) *(G-8213)*
Woodenware USA, Etna Green *Also called Earl Chupp (G-3320)*
Woodfield Printing Inc.....317 848-2000
9700 Lake Shore Dr E Indianapolis (46280) *(G-6283)*
Woodgrain Construction Inc.....317 873-5608
3380 S 875 E Zionsville (46077) *(G-14471)*
Woodhollow LLC.....219 384-2802
9603 Spring St Rear Highland (46322) *(G-6060)*
Woodland Lbor Rltons Cnsulting.....219 879-6095
15 Bristol Dr Michigan City (46360) *(G-9861)*
Woodland Manufacturing & Sup.....317 271-2266
10896 E Us Highway 36 Avon (46123) *(G-472)*
Woodland Park Inc.....574 825-2104
111 Crystal Heights Blvd Middlebury (46540) *(G-9927)*
Woodland Restoration LLC.....219 509-3078
96 Hickory Ave Hebron (46341) *(G-6025)*
Woodland Ridge Woodworking.....812 821-8032
5182 W Woodland Rd Ellettsville (47429) *(G-3285)*
Woodpart International, Elkhart *Also called Woodparts International Corp (G-3266)*
Woodparts International Corp.....574 293-0566
729 Mason St Elkhart (46516) *(G-3266)*
Woods Enterprises.....574 232-7449
26795 State Road 2 South Bend (46619) *(G-12992)*
Woods of Amber.....765 763-6926
632 S Washington St Morristown (46161) *(G-10376)*
Woods Printing Company Inc.....812 536-2261
601 W Main St Holland (47541) *(G-6106)*
Woods Unlimited Inc.....574 656-3382
67850 Sycamore Rd North Liberty (46554) *(G-11223)*
Woodside Custom Canvas LLC.....260 593-2420
9305 W 650 S Topeka (46571) *(G-13432)*
Woodside Woodworks.....260 499-3220
4795 S 200 W Wolcottville (46795) *(G-14378)*
Woodsong Publishing.....812 528-0875
5989 Spring Meadow Ln Seymour (47274) *(G-12501)*
Woodwind & Brasswind Inc.....574 251-3547
6625 Network Way Ste 200 Indianapolis (46278) *(G-8214)*
Woodworking By Design, Hoagland *Also called Knapke & Sons Inc (G-6065)*
Woodworking By Rich.....317 535-5750
119 Ardmoor Dr Whiteland (46184) *(G-14248)*
Woodwright Door & Trim Inc.....574 522-1667
808 9th St Elkhart (46516) *(G-3267)*
Woodys Hot Rodz LLc.....812 637-1933
23950 Salt Fork Rd Lawrenceburg (47025) *(G-9162)*
Woodys Paint Spot Ltd.....574 255-0348
3860 W Shore Dr Bremen (46506) *(G-1034)*
Workers In Vineyard Inc.....317 245-7256
8650 Coralberry Ln Indianapolis (46239) *(G-8215)*
Workflow Solutions LLC.....502 627-0257
2125 E Spring St New Albany (47150) *(G-10875)*
Workrite Machine & Tool Inc.....260 489-4778
6319 Discount Dr Fort Wayne (46818) *(G-4761)*
Workroom Inc.....574 269-6624
204 13th St Winona Lake (46590) *(G-14356)*
World Class North America LLC.....260 668-5511
1460 Wohlert St Angola (46703) *(G-259)*
World Graffix LLC.....574 936-1927
14717 Lincoln Hwy Plymouth (46563) *(G-11740)*
World Media Group Inc.....317 549-8484
2301 Whispering Dr Indianapolis (46239) *(G-8216)*
World Missionary Press Inc.....574 831-2111
19168 County Road 146 New Paris (46553) *(G-11001)*
World Rdo Mssnary Fllwship Inc.....574 970-4252
2830 17th St Elkhart (46517) *(G-3268)*
Worldcell Extrusions, Elkhart *Also called Worldwide Foam Ltd (G-3269)*
Worldwide Battery Company LLC.....812 475-1326
6050 Wedeking Ave Ste 5 Evansville (47715) *(G-3816)*
Worldwide Door Cmpnnts Ind Inc.....219 992-9225
8218 N 279 W Lake Village (46349) *(G-9089)*
Worldwide Foam Ltd (PA).....574 968-8268
1806 Conant St Elkhart (46516) *(G-3269)*
Worley Lumber Company Inc.....812 967-3521
5803 E Hurst Rd Pekin (47165) *(G-11481)*
Worth Publications LLC.....219 808-4001
13398 Hayes Ct Crown Point (46307) *(G-2323)*
Worth Tax and Financial Svc.....574 267-4687
3201 E Center Street Ext Warsaw (46582) *(G-13969)*
Worthington Steel Company.....219 929-4000
100 Worthington Dr Porter (46304) *(G-11806)*
Worwag Coatings LLC (HQ).....765 447-2137
3420 Kossuth St Lafayette (47905) *(G-9026)*
Woundvision.....317 775-6054
212 W 10th St Ste F180 Indianapolis (46202) *(G-8217)*
Wraco Enterprises Inc.....812 339-3987
125 S Westplex Ave Bloomington (47404) *(G-859)*
Wraith Arms Resolutions LLC.....812 380-1208
9602 E 475s Velpen (47590) *(G-13650)*
Wri, Peru *Also called Western Reman Industrial Inc (G-11557)*
Wrib Manufacturing Inc.....765 294-2841
110 E Jackson St Veedersburg (47987) *(G-13648)*
Wright Brothers Implements LLC.....812 967-3029
17606 State Road 60 Borden (47106) *(G-938)*
Wright Coatings Corporation.....317 937-6768
8620 W 82nd St Indianapolis (46278) *(G-8218)*
Wright Implement I LLC.....812 522-1922
1250 W 2nd St Seymour (47274) *(G-12502)*
Wright Repairs Inc.....765 674-3300
5900 Eastside Parkway Dr Gas City (46933) *(G-5128)*
Wrights Timber Products.....812 383-7138
201 S Hymera Church St Shelburn (47879) *(G-12514)*
Wrights Woodworking.....765 723-1546
8862 E 500 S New Ross (47968) *(G-11006)*
Writeguard Business Systems.....317 849-7292
5102 E 65th St Indianapolis (46220) *(G-8219)*
Writers of Vision.....812 239-6347
4118 W County Road 975 N Farmersburg (47850) *(G-3839)*
Writt Sales & Supply Co Inc.....317 356-5478
7155 Wadsworth Way Indianapolis (46219) *(G-8220)*
Wrr Inc.....317 577-1149
8908 Gary Pl Indianapolis (46256) *(G-8221)*
Wsg Manufacturing LLC.....765 934-2101
4485 S Perry Worth Rd Whitestown (46075) *(G-14265)*
Wt Products Inc.....765 216-7998
3005 W Woodbridge Dr Muncie (47304) *(G-10589)*
Wth Publications Inc.....574 646-2007
8690 Apple Rd Bldg 1 Bourbon (46504) *(G-951)*
Wunder Co Inc.....219 962-8573
3200 E 37th Ave Lake Station (46405) *(G-9081)*
Wurk Metal Products Inc.....317 828-0170
2425 E County Road 800 S Clayton (46118) *(G-1710)*
Www.psychmxgrafix.com, Greenfield *Also called Moan Racing Products LLC (G-5556)*
Wynn Wire Die Services Inc.....260 471-1395
1919 Lakeview Dr Fort Wayne (46808) *(G-4762)*
Wyrco LLC.....317 691-2832
13603 E 131st St Fishers (46037) *(G-3986)*
X Press Storage LLC.....219 942-1227
401 S Shelby St Hobart (46342) *(G-6102)*
X Printwear Inc.....812 336-0700
2121 S Yost Ave Bloomington (47403) *(G-860)*
X-L Box Inc.....219 763-3736
1035 N State Road 149 Valparaiso (46385) *(G-13638)*
X-Press Printing, Portage *Also called Express Printing & Copying (G-11761)*
X-Treme Lazer Tag.....812 238-8412
844 W Johnson Dr Terre Haute (47802) *(G-13372)*
Xantrex Technology USA Inc (HQ).....574 522-9628
541 Roske Dr Ste A Elkhart (46516) *(G-3270)*
Xerox Corporation.....765 778-6249
2828 Enterprise Dr Anderson (46013) *(G-183)*
Xerox Corporation.....317 471-4220
4545 Northwestern Dr Zionsville (46077) *(G-14472)*
Xfmrs Holdings Inc (PA).....317 834-1066
7570 E Landersdale Rd Camby (46113) *(G-1271)*
Xfmrs Inc.....317 834-1066
7570 E Landersdale Rd Camby (46113) *(G-1272)*
Xl Graphics Inc.....317 738-3434
170 Commerce Dr Franklin (46131) *(G-4942)*
Xlibris Corporation.....812 671-9162
1663 S Liberty Dr Ste 200 Bloomington (47403) *(G-861)*
Xtrac Inc.....317 472-2451
6183 W 80th St Indianapolis (46278) *(G-8222)*
Xtreme ADS Limited.....765 644-7323
1735 W 53rd St Anderson (46013) *(G-184)*
Xtreme Alternative Def Systems, Anderson *Also called Xtreme ADS Limited (G-184)*
Xtreme Graphics.....812 989-6948
3301 Justinian Jeffersonville (47130) *(G-8443)*
Xwind LLC.....317 350-2080
1185 E Northfield Dr C Brownsburg (46112) *(G-1177)*
XYZ Machining Inc.....574 269-5541
5141 W 100 S Warsaw (46580) *(G-13970)*
XYZ Model Works.....260 413-1873
10334 N 500 W Decatur (46733) *(G-2413)*
Ya-Nvr-No.....260 833-8883
8405 N 650 W Orland (46776) *(G-11360)*
Yacht Brite Proffesional Care.....219 874-1181
101 Kenwood Pl Michigan City (46360) *(G-9862)*
Yager Pallet.....219 365-2766
9155 Calumet Ave Saint John (46373) *(G-12273)*
Yahweh Design and Printing.....765 874-1003
6567 E 700 S Lynn (47355) *(G-9433)*
Yamaguchi Mfg Usa Inc.....765 973-9130
1771 Sheridan St Richmond (47374) *(G-12077)*
Yamaha Marine Precision Propel.....317 545-9080
2427 N Ritter Ave Indianapolis (46218) *(G-8223)*
Yandt Boat Works.....219 851-8311
308 Grayson Rd La Porte (46350) *(G-8834)*
Yanfeng US Automotive.....260 347-0500
300 S Progress Dr E Kendallville (46755) *(G-8515)*

ALPHABETIC

Yankee Candle Company Inc 812 526-5195
  11740 Ne Executive Dr Edinburgh (46124) *(G-2632)*

Yankee Candle Company Inc 812 234-1717
  3401 S Us Highway 41 E14 Terre Haute (47802) *(G-13373)*

Yankee Steel Inc 812 232-5353
  431 N 14th St Terre Haute (47807) *(G-13374)*

Yannis Furs Inc 317 580-0914
  8805 Crestview Dr Indianapolis (46240) *(G-8224)*

Yardarm Marine Products Inc 317 831-4950
  2100 Hancel Pkwy Mooresville (46158) *(G-10345)*

Yb Normal Custom Wood Working 260 338-2003
  16335 Lima Rd Huntertown (46748) *(G-6149)*

Yellow Banks Clay Company Inc 812 567-4703
  12733 Yellowbanks Trl Dale (47523) *(G-2336)*

Yellow Banks Recreation Center, Dale *Also called Yellow Banks Clay Company Inc (G-2336)*

Yellow Creek Gravel Service, Goshen *Also called Harrison Hauling Inc (G-5235)*

Yellow Cup LLC 260 403-3489
  1025 Northwood Blvd Fort Wayne (46805) *(G-4763)*

Yellow Dog Anodizing 574 343-2247
  2730 Almac Ct Elkhart (46514) *(G-3271)*

Yellow Dog Extrusion Company, Elkhart *Also called Patrick Aluminum Inc (G-3079)*

Yellow Dog Woodworking LLC 502 817-9395
  4747 Saint Johns Rd Greenville (47124) *(G-5656)*

Yellow Door Publishing LLC 574 256-5797
  637 Misty Harbour Ct Mishawaka (46544) *(G-10152)*

Yellowstone Rv, Nappanee *Also called Gulf Stream Coach Inc (G-10677)*

Yes Feed & Supply LLC 765 361-9821
  2065 S Nucor Rd Crawfordsville (47933) *(G-2206)*

Ynot Metal Inc 517 617-6039
  301 Growth Pkwy Angola (46703) *(G-260)*

Yoder & Sons 574 642-1196
  13781 County Road 20 # 1 Middlebury (46540) *(G-9928)*

Yoder & Sons Pallets 260 625-2835
  4757 W 300 S Columbia City (46725) *(G-1848)*

Yoder Kitchen Corp (PA) 574 773-3197
  501 S Main St Nappanee (46550) *(G-10711)*

Yoder Software Inc 574 302-6232
  1121 N Notre Dame Ave South Bend (46617) *(G-12993)*

Yoder Woodworking 574 825-0402
  60157 County Road 35 Middlebury (46540) *(G-9929)*

Yoder Woodworking Inc 574 546-5100
  2534 State Road 331 Bremen (46506) *(G-1035)*

Yoder's Lockworks, New Paris *Also called Yoders Custom Service (G-11002)*

Yoder's Meat Shop, Shipshewana *Also called Yoders Meats Inc (G-12660)*

Yoders & Sons Repair Shop 260 593-2727
  6035 W 800 S Topeka (46571) *(G-13433)*

Yoders Cabinets 812 486-3826
  5207 N 775 E Montgomery (47558) *(G-10249)*

Yoders Custom Service 574 831-4717
  18638 County Road 46 New Paris (46553) *(G-11002)*

Yoders Meats Inc 260 768-4715
  435 S Van Buren St Shipshewana (46565) *(G-12660)*

Yoders Monuments Inc 260 768-7934
  409 Bristol Ave Middlebury (46540) *(G-9930)*

Yoders Quality Barns 260 565-4122
  7207 E State Road 124 Bluffton (46714) *(G-898)*

Yogurtz 317 853-6600
  12561 N Meridian St Carmel (46032) *(G-1511)*

Yoli Inc 812 945-8530
  1404 Bell Ln Ste 1 New Albany (47150) *(G-10876)*

Yongli America LLC 219 763-7920
  6625 Daniel Burnham Dr Portage (46368) *(G-11802)*

York Group Inc 765 966-1576
  620 S J St Richmond (47374) *(G-12078)*

York Group Inc 765 966-0077
  1620 Rich Rd Richmond (47374) *(G-12079)*

York Tank and Mfg LLC 765 401-0667
  4438 S Roberts St Kingman (47952) *(G-8534)*

York Technology, Richmond *Also called York Group Inc (G-12079)*

You Can Do It Printer, Columbus *Also called Prestige Printing Inc (G-2000)*

Young & Kenady Incorporated 317 852-6300
  463 Suthpoint Cir Ste 600 Brownsburg (46112) *(G-1178)*

Young Machine Co Inc 812 944-5807
  904 Industrial Blvd New Albany (47150) *(G-10877)*

Youniquely Yours 219 942-1489
  955 Duck Creek Ct Hobart (46342) *(G-6103)*

Your Face Our Place Print Shop 812 567-4510
  3877 State Road 161 N Tennyson (47637) *(G-13183)*

Your Window Washer LLC 317 701-1710
  15566 Outside Trl Noblesville (46060) *(G-11200)*

Yudu, Fort Wayne *Also called Tt2 LLC (G-4707)*

Yuma, Shelbyville *Also called Yushiro Manufacturing Amer Inc (G-12586)*

Yurts of America Inc 317 377-9878
  4375 Sellers St Indianapolis (46226) *(G-8225)*

Yushiro Manufacturing Amer Inc 317 398-9862
  783 W Mausoleum Rd Shelbyville (46176) *(G-12586)*

Z Hotel, Warsaw *Also called Zimmer Inc (G-13971)*

Z-Athletic, Inc., Noblesville *Also called Global USA Inc (G-11112)*

Zachary Confections Inc 765 659-4751
  2130 W State Road 28 Frankfort (46041) *(G-4861)*

Zehrhaus Inc 260 486-3198
  8516 Samantha Dr Fort Wayne (46835) *(G-4764)*

Zeller Elevator Co 812 985-5888
  8875 Meinschein Rd Mount Vernon (47620) *(G-10415)*

Zels 219 864-1011
  7889 W Lincoln Hwy Schererville (46375) *(G-12353)*

Zemco Mfg Inc 260 428-2650
  2320 Meyer Rd Fort Wayne (46803) *(G-4765)*

Zentis North America LLC 574 941-1100
  2050 N Oak Dr Plymouth (46563) *(G-11741)*

Zentis Sweet Ovtions Holdg LLC 574 941-1100
  2050 N Oak Dr Plymouth (46563) *(G-11742)*

Zeppelin Commander Press Inc 317 839-9025
  1026 Kirkwood Dr Plainfield (46168) *(G-11653)*

Zevacor Molecular, Noblesville *Also called Global Isotopes LLC (G-11111)*

ZF North America Inc 765 429-1678
  9th & Greenbush Lafayette (47904) *(G-9027)*

ZF North America Inc 765 429-1984
  4820 Dale Dr Lafayette (47905) *(G-9028)*

Zh Brothers International Inc 313 718-6732
  5625 Irish Way Apt 2 Mishawaka (46545) *(G-10153)*

Zieman Manufacturing Company 574 522-5202
  2475 E Kercher Rd Goshen (46526) *(G-5347)*

Zig-Zag Crnr Qilts Baskets LLC 317 326-3115
  7872 N Troy Rd Greenfield (46140) *(G-5586)*

Ziggity Systems Inc 574 825-5849
  101 Industrial Pkwy E Middlebury (46540) *(G-9931)*

Zimco Materials Inc 219 883-0870
  2555 E 15th Ave Gary (46402) *(G-5117)*

Zimmer Inc (HQ) 330 343-8801
  1800 W Center St Warsaw (46580) *(G-13971)*

Zimmer Inc 574 268-3100
  1800 W Center St Warsaw (46580) *(G-13972)*

Zimmer Inc 574 371-1557
  1113 W Lake St Warsaw (46580) *(G-13973)*

Zimmer Inc 574 267-6131
  1777 W Center St Warsaw (46580) *(G-13974)*

Zimmer Biomet, Warsaw *Also called Biomet Inc (G-13845)*

Zimmer Biomet, Warsaw *Also called Zimmer Us Inc (G-13977)*

Zimmer Biomet Holdings Inc (PA) 574 267-6131
  345 E Main St Warsaw (46580) *(G-13975)*

Zimmer Medwest, Warsaw *Also called Wiley Young & Associates (G-13967)*

Zimmer Metal Sales LLC 574 862-1800
  64470 State Road 19 Goshen (46526) *(G-5348)*

Zimmer Production Inc 574 267-6131
  345 E Main St Warsaw (46580) *(G-13976)*

Zimmer Us Inc 574 267-6131
  1800 W Center St Warsaw (46580) *(G-13977)*

Zimmer Welding Co 317 632-5212
  16 N Harding St Indianapolis (46222) *(G-8226)*

Zimmerman Art Glass Company 812 738-2206
  300 E Chestnut St Corydon (47112) *(G-2117)*

Zimmerman-Newcomer Gravel 574 658-4063
  1775 E 1150 N Milford (46542) *(G-9967)*

Zinn Cabinets Plus, Bringhurst *Also called Zinn Kitchens Inc (G-1039)*

Zinn Kitchens Inc 574 967-4179
  1211 S Center St Bringhurst (46913) *(G-1039)*

Zionsville Custom Cabinets 317 339-0380
  10830 Bennett Pkwy Ste E Zionsville (46077) *(G-14473)*

Zionsville Times Sentinel, Lebanon *Also called Community Holdings Indiana Inc (G-9176)*

Zionsville Towing Inc 317 873-4550
  4901 W 106th St Zionsville (46077) *(G-14474)*

Zip-A-Tee Shirt Inc 219 879-5556
  120 Glencove Dr Michigan City (46360) *(G-9863)*

Zipp Print, Mishawaka *Also called Printing Emporium Inc (G-10109)*

Zipp Speed Weaponry, Indianapolis *Also called Compositech Inc (G-6643)*

Zogman Enterprises Inc 317 873-6809
  170 W Hawthorne St Zionsville (46077) *(G-14475)*

Zojila LLC 765 404-3767
  2004 N 9th St Lafayette (47904) *(G-9029)*

Zollman Plastic Surgery PC 317 328-1100
  8227 Northwest Blvd # 290 Indianapolis (46278) *(G-8227)*

Zoo Zone, Evansville *Also called Ad Vision Graphics Inc (G-3343)*

Zoofari Gardens, Indianapolis *Also called Industrial Sales & Supply Inc (G-7209)*

Zook Machine Inc 765 563-6585
  100 W 1250 S Battle Ground (47920) *(G-525)*

Zoom Seating, Middlebury *Also called Jsj Furniture Corporation (G-9898)*

Zoom Seating 574 825-3368
  11451 Harter Dr Middlebury (46540) *(G-9932)*

Zoomers Rv of Indiana LLC 260 414-1978
  1090 Manchester Ave Wabash (46992) *(G-13769)*

Zps America LLC 317 452-4030
  4950 W 79th St Indianapolis (46268) *(G-8228)*

Zr Tactical Solutions LLC 317 721-9787
  15223 Herriman Blvd Ste 4 Noblesville (46060) *(G-11201)*

Zrts, Noblesville *Also called Zr Tactical Solutions LLC (G-11201)*

Zs Systems LLC...765 586-2738

3339 Cardigan Ct West Lafayette (47906) *(G-14118)*

Ztmt Inc..502 296-4032
1750 Hidden Place Dr Georgetown (47122) *(G-5155)*

Zvibleman, Barry, Indianapolis *Also called Onion Enterprises Inc (G-7623)*

PRODUCT INDEX

• Product categories are listed in alphabetical order.

A

ABRASIVES
ABRASIVES: sandpaper
ACCELERATION INDICATORS & SYSTEM COMPONENTS: Aerospace
ACCELERATORS, RUBBER PROCESSING: Cyclic or Acyclic
ACCOUNTING MACHINES & CASH REGISTERS
ACCOUNTING SVCS: Certified Public
ACIDS: Boric
ACRYLONITRILE BUTADIENE STYRENE RESINS
ACTUATORS: Indl, NEC
ADAPTERS: Well
ADDITIVE BASED PLASTIC MATERIALS: Plasticizers
ADHESIVES
ADHESIVES & SEALANTS
ADHESIVES & SEALANTS WHOLESALERS
ADHESIVES: Adhesives, paste
ADHESIVES: Epoxy
ADULT EDUCATION SCHOOLS, PUBLIC
ADVERTISING AGENCIES
ADVERTISING AGENCIES: Consultants
ADVERTISING DISPLAY PRDTS
ADVERTISING MATERIAL DISTRIBUTION
ADVERTISING REPRESENTATIVES: Electronic Media
ADVERTISING REPRESENTATIVES: Newspaper
ADVERTISING REPRESENTATIVES: Printed Media
ADVERTISING REPRESENTATIVES: Radio
ADVERTISING SPECIALTIES, WHOLESALE
ADVERTISING SVCS: Billboards
ADVERTISING SVCS: Bus Card
ADVERTISING SVCS: Direct Mail
ADVERTISING SVCS: Outdoor
ADVERTISING SVCS: Transit
AERIAL WORK PLATFORMS
AEROSOLS
AGENTS, BROKERS & BUREAUS: Personal Service
AGRICULTURAL DISINFECTANTS
AGRICULTURAL EQPT: BARN, SILO, POULTRY, DAIRY/LIVESTOCK MACH
AGRICULTURAL EQPT: Elevators, Farm
AGRICULTURAL EQPT: Fertilizng, Sprayng, Dustng/Irrigatn Mach
AGRICULTURAL EQPT: Fillers & Unloaders, Silo
AGRICULTURAL EQPT: Grounds Mowing Eqpt
AGRICULTURAL EQPT: Harvesters, Fruit, Vegetable, Tobacco
AGRICULTURAL EQPT: Planting Machines
AGRICULTURAL EQPT: Tractors, Farm
AGRICULTURAL EQPT: Trailers & Wagons, Farm
AGRICULTURAL EQPT: Turf & Grounds Eqpt
AGRICULTURAL EQPT: Weeding Machines
AGRICULTURAL MACHINERY & EQPT REPAIR
AGRICULTURAL MACHINERY & EQPT: Wholesalers
AIR CLEANING SYSTEMS
AIR CONDITIONERS, AUTOMOTIVE: Wholesalers
AIR CONDITIONERS: Motor Vehicle
AIR CONDITIONING & VENTILATION EQPT & SPLYS: Wholesales
AIR CONDITIONING EQPT, WHOLE HOUSE: Wholesalers
AIR CONDITIONING UNITS: Complete, Domestic Or Indl
AIR COOLERS: Metal Plate
AIR DUCT CLEANING SVCS
AIR MATTRESSES: Plastic
AIR POLLUTION CONTROL EQPT & SPLYS WHOLESALERS
AIR POLLUTION MEASURING SVCS
AIR PURIFICATION EQPT
AIR-CONDITIONING SPLY SVCS
AIRCRAFT & AEROSPACE FLIGHT INSTRUMENTS & GUIDANCE SYSTEMS
AIRCRAFT & HEAVY EQPT REPAIR SVCS
AIRCRAFT ASSEMBLY PLANTS
AIRCRAFT CLEANING & JANITORIAL SVCS
AIRCRAFT CONTROL SYSTEMS:
AIRCRAFT CONTROL SYSTEMS: Electronic Totalizing Counters
AIRCRAFT ENGINES & ENGINE PARTS: Exhaust Systems
AIRCRAFT ENGINES & ENGINE PARTS: Mount Parts

AIRCRAFT ENGINES & PARTS
AIRCRAFT EQPT & SPLYS WHOLESALERS
AIRCRAFT FLIGHT INSTRUMENT REPAIR SVCS
AIRCRAFT PARTS & AUX EQPT: Adapter Assy, Hydromatic Prop
AIRCRAFT PARTS & AUXILIARY EQPT: Assys, Subassemblies/Parts
AIRCRAFT PARTS & AUXILIARY EQPT: Body Assemblies & Parts
AIRCRAFT PARTS & AUXILIARY EQPT: Deicing Eqpt
AIRCRAFT PARTS & AUXILIARY EQPT: Gears, Power Transmission
AIRCRAFT PARTS & AUXILIARY EQPT: Military Eqpt & Armament
AIRCRAFT PARTS & AUXILIARY EQPT: Nacelles
AIRCRAFT PARTS & AUXILIARY EQPT: Refueling Eqpt, In Flight
AIRCRAFT PARTS & AUXILIARY EQPT: Research & Development, Mfr
AIRCRAFT PARTS & EQPT, NEC
AIRCRAFT SEATS
AIRCRAFT UPHOLSTERY REPAIR SVCS
AIRCRAFT: Airplanes, Fixed Or Rotary Wing
AIRCRAFT: Motorized
AIRCRAFT: Nonmotorized & Lighter-Than-air
ALARMS: Burglar
ALARMS: Fire
ALCOHOL, GRAIN: For Beverage Purposes
ALCOHOL, INDL: Grain
ALCOHOL: Ethyl & Ethanol
ALCOHOLISM COUNSELING, NONTREATMENT
ALKALIES & CHLORINE
ALTERNATORS & GENERATORS: Battery Charging
ALTERNATORS: Automotive
ALUMINUM
ALUMINUM PRDTS
ALUMINUM: Rolling & Drawing
AMMONIUM PHOSPHATE
AMMUNITION
AMMUNITION: Cartridges Case, 30 mm & Below
AMMUNITION: Cores, Bullet, 30 mm & Below
AMMUNITION: Missile Warheads
AMMUNITION: Small Arms
AMPLIFIERS
AMUSEMENT & RECREATION SVCS: Amusement Arcades
AMUSEMENT & RECREATION SVCS: Fishing Lakes & Piers, Op
AMUSEMENT & RECREATION SVCS: Instruction Schools, Camps
AMUSEMENT & RECREATION SVCS: Karate Instruction
AMUSEMENT & RECREATION SVCS: Night Club, Exc Alcoholic Bev
AMUSEMENT MACHINES: Coin Operated
AMUSEMENT PARK DEVICES & RIDES
ANALYZERS: Blood & Body Fluid
ANALYZERS: Network
ANALYZERS: Petroleum Prdts
ANALYZERS: Respiratory
ANESTHESIA EQPT
ANIMAL BASED MEDICINAL CHEMICAL PRDTS
ANIMAL FEED & SUPPLEMENTS: Livestock & Poultry
ANIMAL FEED: Wholesalers
ANIMAL FOOD & SUPPLEMENTS: Bird Food, Prepared
ANIMAL FOOD & SUPPLEMENTS: Bone Meal
ANIMAL FOOD & SUPPLEMENTS: Dog
ANIMAL FOOD & SUPPLEMENTS: Dog & Cat
ANIMAL FOOD & SUPPLEMENTS: Feed Concentrates
ANIMAL FOOD & SUPPLEMENTS: Feed Premixes
ANIMAL FOOD & SUPPLEMENTS: Feed Supplements
ANIMAL FOOD & SUPPLEMENTS: Kelp Meal & Pellets
ANIMAL FOOD & SUPPLEMENTS: Livestock
ANIMAL FOOD & SUPPLEMENTS: Poultry
ANIMAL FOOD & SUPPLEMENTS: Stock Feeds, Dry
ANNEALING: Metal
ANODIZING SVC
ANTENNAS: Radar Or Communications
ANTIFREEZE
ANTIQUE & CLASSIC AUTOMOBILE RESTORATION

ANTIQUE FURNITURE RESTORATION & REPAIR
ANTIQUE SHOPS
APPAREL DESIGNERS: Commercial
APPLIANCE PARTS: Porcelain Enameled
APPLIANCES, HOUSEHOLD OR COIN OPERATED: Laundry Dryers
APPLIANCES, HOUSEHOLD: Drycleaning Machines, Incl Coin-Op
APPLIANCES, HOUSEHOLD: Kitchen, Major, Exc Refrigs & Stoves
APPLIANCES, HOUSEHOLD: Sewing Machines & Attchmnts, Domestic
APPLIANCES, HOUSEHOLD: Shampooers, Carpet
APPLIANCES: Household, Refrigerators & Freezers
APPLIANCES: Major, Cooking
APPLIANCES: Small, Electric
APPLICATIONS SOFTWARE PROGRAMMING
AQUARIUM ACCESS, METAL
AQUARIUMS & ACCESS: Glass
ARCHITECTURAL PANELS OR PARTS: Porcelain Enameled
ARCHITECTURAL SVCS
ARCHITECTURAL SVCS: Engineering
ARMATURE REPAIRING & REWINDING SVC
ARMATURES: Automotive
ARMOR PLATES
ART & ORNAMENTAL WARE: Pottery
ART DEALERS & GALLERIES
ART DESIGN SVCS
ART GALLERIES
ART GOODS & SPLYS WHOLESALERS
ART GOODS, WHOLESALE
ART RESTORATION SVC
ART SPLY STORES
ARTIFICIAL FLOWER SHOPS
ARTISTS' MATERIALS, WHOLESALE
ARTISTS' MATERIALS: Boards, Drawing
ARTISTS' MATERIALS: Chalks, Carpenters', Blackboard, Etc
ARTISTS' MATERIALS: Mixtures, Gold Or Bronze
ARTISTS' MATERIALS: Palettes
ARTISTS' MATERIALS: Pencils & Leads
ARTWORK: Framed
ASBESTOS PRDTS: Table Pads & Padding
ASBESTOS REMOVAL EQPT
ASH TRAYS: Stamped Metal
ASPHALT & ASPHALT PRDTS
ASPHALT COATINGS & SEALERS
ASPHALT MINING & BITUMINOUS STONE QUARRYING SVCS
ASPHALT PLANTS INCLUDING GRAVEL MIX TYPE
ASSEMBLING SVC: Clocks
ASSEMBLING SVC: Plumbing Fixture Fittings, Plastic
ASSOCIATIONS: Business
ASSOCIATIONS: Real Estate Management
ASSOCIATIONS: Trade
ATOMIZERS
AUDIO & VIDEO EQPT, EXC COMMERCIAL
AUDIO COMPONENTS
AUDIO ELECTRONIC SYSTEMS
AUDIO-VISUAL PROGRAM PRODUCTION SVCS
AUDIOLOGICAL EQPT: Electronic
AUDIOLOGISTS' OFFICES
AUTHOR
AUTHORS' AGENTS & BROKERS
AUTO & HOME SUPPLY STORES: Auto & Truck Eqpt & Parts
AUTO & HOME SUPPLY STORES: Automotive Access
AUTO & HOME SUPPLY STORES: Automotive parts
AUTO & HOME SUPPLY STORES: Batteries, Automotive & Truck
AUTO & HOME SUPPLY STORES: Speed Shops, Incl Race Car Splys
AUTO & HOME SUPPLY STORES: Trailer Hitches, Automotive
AUTO & HOME SUPPLY STORES: Truck Eqpt & Parts
AUTOCLAVES: Laboratory
AUTOMATIC REGULATING CONTROL: Building Svcs Monitoring, Auto
AUTOMATIC REGULATING CONTROLS: AC & Refrigeration

INDEX

AUTOMATIC REGULATING CONTROLS: Appliance Regulators
AUTOMATIC REGULATING CONTROLS: Appliance, Exc Air-Cond/Refr
AUTOMATIC REGULATING CONTROLS: Electric Heat
AUTOMATIC REGULATING CONTROLS: Hardware, Environmental Reg
AUTOMATIC REGULATING CONTROLS: Pneumatic Relays, Air-Cond
AUTOMATIC REGULATING CONTROLS: Pressure, Air-Cond Sys
AUTOMATIC TELLER MACHINES
AUTOMATIC VENDING MACHINES: Mechanisms & Parts
AUTOMOBILES & OTHER MOTOR VEHICLES WHOLE-SALERS
AUTOMOBILES: Midget, Power Driven
AUTOMOBILES: Wholesalers
AUTOMOTIVE & TRUCK GENERAL REPAIR SVC
AUTOMOTIVE AIR CONDITIONING REPAIR SHOPS
AUTOMOTIVE BODY SHOP
AUTOMOTIVE BODY, PAINT & INTERIOR REPAIR & MAINTENANCE SVC
AUTOMOTIVE COLLISION SHOPS
AUTOMOTIVE CUSTOMIZING SVCS, NONFACTORY BASIS
AUTOMOTIVE GLASS REPLACEMENT SHOPS
AUTOMOTIVE LETTERING SVCS
AUTOMOTIVE PARTS, ACCESS & SPLYS
AUTOMOTIVE PARTS: Plastic
AUTOMOTIVE PRDTS: Rubber
AUTOMOTIVE REPAIR SHOPS: Alternators/Generator, Rebuild/Rpr
AUTOMOTIVE REPAIR SHOPS: Auto Front End Repair
AUTOMOTIVE REPAIR SHOPS: Brake Repair
AUTOMOTIVE REPAIR SHOPS: Diesel Engine Repair
AUTOMOTIVE REPAIR SHOPS: Electrical Svcs
AUTOMOTIVE REPAIR SHOPS: Engine Rebuilding
AUTOMOTIVE REPAIR SHOPS: Engine Repair
AUTOMOTIVE REPAIR SHOPS: Engine Repair, Exc Diesel
AUTOMOTIVE REPAIR SHOPS: Machine Shop
AUTOMOTIVE REPAIR SHOPS: Muffler Shop, Sale/Rpr/Installation
AUTOMOTIVE REPAIR SHOPS: Torque Converter Repair
AUTOMOTIVE REPAIR SHOPS: Trailer Repair
AUTOMOTIVE REPAIR SVC
AUTOMOTIVE SPLYS & PARTS, NEW, WHOL: Auto Servicing Eqpt
AUTOMOTIVE SPLYS & PARTS, NEW, WHOL: Testing Eqpt, Electric
AUTOMOTIVE SPLYS & PARTS, NEW, WHOLESALE: Brakes
AUTOMOTIVE SPLYS & PARTS, NEW, WHOLESALE: Bumpers
AUTOMOTIVE SPLYS & PARTS, NEW, WHOLESALE: Engines/Eng Parts
AUTOMOTIVE SPLYS & PARTS, NEW, WHOLESALE: Hardware
AUTOMOTIVE SPLYS & PARTS, NEW, WHOLESALE: Trailer Parts
AUTOMOTIVE SPLYS & PARTS, NEW, WHOLESALE: Trim
AUTOMOTIVE SPLYS & PARTS, NEW, WHOLESALE: Wheels
AUTOMOTIVE SPLYS & PARTS, USED, WHOLESALE
AUTOMOTIVE SPLYS & PARTS, WHOLESALE, NEC
AUTOMOTIVE SPLYS, USED, WHOLESALE & RETAIL
AUTOMOTIVE SVCS, EXC REPAIR & CARWASHES: Customizing
AUTOMOTIVE SVCS, EXC REPAIR & CARWASHES: Insp & Diagnostic
AUTOMOTIVE SVCS, EXC REPAIR & CARWASHES: Lubrication
AUTOMOTIVE SVCS, EXC REPAIR & CARWASHES: Maintenance
AUTOMOTIVE SVCS, EXC REPAIR: Carwash, Self-Service
AUTOMOTIVE SVCS, EXC REPAIR: Truck Wash
AUTOMOTIVE SVCS, EXC REPAIR: Washing & Polishing
AUTOMOTIVE SVCS, EXC RPR/CARWASHES: High Perf Auto Rpr/Svc
AUTOMOTIVE TOPS INSTALLATION OR REPAIR: Canvas Or Plastic
AUTOMOTIVE TOWING & WRECKING SVC
AUTOMOTIVE TOWING SVCS
AUTOMOTIVE TRANSMISSION REPAIR SVC
AUTOMOTIVE UPHOLSTERY SHOPS
AUTOMOTIVE WELDING SVCS
AUTOMOTIVE: Bodies

AUTOMOTIVE: Seat Frames, Metal
AUTOMOTIVE: Seating
AWNINGS & CANOPIES
AWNINGS & CANOPIES: Awnings, Fabric, From Purchased Matls
AWNINGS & CANOPIES: Fabric
AWNINGS: Fiberglass
AWNINGS: Metal
AXLES
AXLES: Rolled Or Forged, Made In Steel Mills

B

BACKHOES
BADGES: Identification & Insignia
BAGS: Canvas
BAGS: Garment Storage Exc Paper Or Plastic Film
BAGS: Paper
BAGS: Plastic
BAGS: Plastic & Pliofilm
BAGS: Plastic, Made From Purchased Materials
BAGS: Rubber Or Rubberized Fabric
BAGS: Textile
BAGS: Trash, Plastic Film, Made From Purchased Materials
BAIT, FISHING, WHOLESALE
BAKERIES, COMMERCIAL: On Premises Baking Only
BAKERIES: On Premises Baking & Consumption
BAKERY MACHINERY
BAKERY PRDTS: Biscuits, Baked, Baking Powder & Raised
BAKERY PRDTS: Bread, All Types, Fresh Or Frozen
BAKERY PRDTS: Buns, Bread Type, Fresh Or Frozen
BAKERY PRDTS: Cakes, Bakery, Exc Frozen
BAKERY PRDTS: Cones, Ice Cream
BAKERY PRDTS: Cookies
BAKERY PRDTS: Cookies & crackers
BAKERY PRDTS: Croissants, Exc Frozen
BAKERY PRDTS: Doughnuts, Exc Frozen
BAKERY PRDTS: Dry
BAKERY PRDTS: Frozen
BAKERY PRDTS: Pastries, Danish, Frozen
BAKERY PRDTS: Pastries, Exc Frozen
BAKERY PRDTS: Pies, Bakery, Frozen
BAKERY PRDTS: Pies, Exc Frozen
BAKERY PRDTS: Pretzels
BAKERY PRDTS: Wholesalers
BAKERY: Wholesale Or Wholesale & Retail Combined
BALL CLAY MINING
BALUNS
BANNERS: Fabric
BANQUET HALL FACILITIES
BAR JOISTS & CONCRETE REINFORCING BARS: Fabricated
BARBECUE EQPT
BARBER SHOPS
BARGES BUILDING & REPAIR
BARRELS: Shipping, Metal
BARS, COLD FINISHED: Steel, From Purchased Hot-Rolled
BARS, PLATES & SHEETS: Zinc & Zinc Alloy Bars, Plates, Etc
BARS: Cargo, Stabilizing, Metal
BARS: Concrete Reinforcing, Fabricated Steel
BASES, BEVERAGE
BATCHING PLANTS: Aggregate Concrete & Bulk Cement
BATH SHOPS
BATHMATS: Rubber
BATHROOM ACCESS & FITTINGS: Vitreous China & Earthenware
BATHROOM FIXTURES: Plastic
BATTERIES, EXC AUTOMOTIVE: Wholesalers
BATTERIES: Lead Acid, Storage
BATTERIES: Rechargeable
BATTERIES: Storage
BATTERIES: Wet
BATTERY CASES: Plastic Or Plastics Combination
BATTERY CHARGERS
BATTERY CHARGERS: Storage, Motor & Engine Generator Type
BATTERY CHARGING GENERATORS
BATTERY WELLS OR BOXES: Concrete
BAUXITE MINING
BEARINGS & PARTS Ball
BEARINGS: Ball & Roller
BEARINGS: Roller & Parts
BEAUTY & BARBER SHOP EQPT
BEAUTY SALONS
BEDDING & BEDSPRINGS STORES

BEDDING, BEDSPREAD, BLANKET/SHEET: Pillowcase, Purchd Mtrl
BEDDING, BEDSPREADS, BLANKETS & SHEETS
BEDS: Hospital
BEDS: Institutional
BEDSPREADS & BED SETS, FROM PURCHASED MATERIALS
BEDSPREADS, COTTON
BEEKEEPERS' SPLYS
BEER & ALE WHOLESALERS
BEER & ALE, WHOLESALE: Beer & Other Fermented Malt Liquors
BEER, WINE & LIQUOR STORES
BEER, WINE & LIQUOR STORES: Wine
BELTING: Rubber
BELTS & BELT PRDTS
BELTS: Conveyor, Made From Purchased Wire
BELTS: Indl
BELTS: Seat, Automotive & Aircraft
BENCHES: Seating
BENTONITE MINING
BERYLLIUM
BEVERAGES, ALCOHOLIC: Beer
BEVERAGES, ALCOHOLIC: Beer & Ale
BEVERAGES, ALCOHOLIC: Bourbon Whiskey
BEVERAGES, ALCOHOLIC: Brandy & Brandy Spirits
BEVERAGES, ALCOHOLIC: Cocktails
BEVERAGES, ALCOHOLIC: Cordials
BEVERAGES, ALCOHOLIC: Distilled Liquors
BEVERAGES, ALCOHOLIC: Vodka
BEVERAGES, ALCOHOLIC: Wine Coolers
BEVERAGES, ALCOHOLIC: Wines
BEVERAGES, NONALCOHOLIC: Bottled & canned soft drinks
BEVERAGES, NONALCOHOLIC: Carbonated
BEVERAGES, NONALCOHOLIC: Carbonated, Canned & Bottled, Etc
BEVERAGES, NONALCOHOLIC: Cider
BEVERAGES, NONALCOHOLIC: Flavoring extracts & syrups, nec
BEVERAGES, NONALCOHOLIC: Soft Drinks, Canned & Bottled, Etc
BEVERAGES, WINE & DISTILLED ALCOHOLIC, WHOLESALE: Liquor
BEVERAGES, WINE & DISTILLED ALCOHOLIC, WHOLESALE: Wine
BICYCLE ASSEMBLY SVCS
BICYCLE SHOPS
BICYCLES, PARTS & ACCESS
BILLIARD & POOL TABLES & SPLYS
BILLIARD EQPT & SPLYS WHOLESALERS
BILLIARD TABLE REPAIR SVCS
BINDING SVC: Books & Manuals
BINDING SVC: Trade
BINOCULARS
BINS: Prefabricated, Metal Plate
BIOLOGICAL PRDTS: Blood Derivatives
BIOLOGICAL PRDTS: Exc Diagnostic
BIOLOGICAL PRDTS: Extracts
BIOLOGICAL PRDTS: Tuberculins
BIOLOGICAL PRDTS: Veterinary
BLACKPLATE
BLACKSMITH SHOP
BLADES: Knife
BLANKBOOKS & LOOSELEAF BINDERS
BLANKBOOKS: Scrapbooks
BLAST FURNACE & RELATED PRDTS
BLASTING SVC: Sand, Metal Parts
BLINDS & SHADES: Vertical
BLINDS : Window
BLINDS, WOOD
BLOCKS & BRICKS: Concrete
BLOCKS: Landscape Or Retaining Wall, Concrete
BLOCKS: Paving
BLOCKS: Paving, Asphalt, Not From Refineries
BLOCKS: Paving, Concrete
BLOCKS: Standard, Concrete Or Cinder
BLOWERS & FANS
BLOWERS & FANS
BLUEPRINTING SVCS
BOAT & BARGE COMPONENTS: Metal, Prefabricated
BOAT BUILDING & REPAIR
BOAT BUILDING & REPAIRING: Fiberglass
BOAT BUILDING & REPAIRING: Houseboats
BOAT BUILDING & REPAIRING: Motorized

BOAT BUILDING & REPAIRING: Non-Motorized
BOAT BUILDING & REPAIRING: Pontoons, Exc Aircraft & In-flat
BOAT BUILDING & REPAIRING: Yachts
BOAT DEALERS
BOAT DEALERS: Marine Splys & Eqpt
BOAT DEALERS: Motor
BOAT LIFTS
BOAT REPAIR SVCS
BOAT YARD: Boat yards, storage & incidental repair
BOATS & OTHER MARINE EQPT: Plastic
BODIES: Truck & Bus
BODY PARTS: Automobile, Stamped Metal
BOILER & HEATING REPAIR SVCS
BOILER REPAIR SHOP
BOILERS: Low-Pressure Heating, Steam Or Hot Water
BOLTS: Metal
BOOK STORES
BOOK STORES: Religious
BOOKS, WHOLESALE
BORING MILL
BOTTLE CAPS & RESEALERS: Plastic
BOTTLED GAS DEALERS: Liquefied Petro, Dlvrd To Cus-tomers
BOTTLED GAS DEALERS: Propane
BOTTLED WATER DELIVERY
BOTTLES: Plastic
BOULDER: Crushed & Broken
BOUTIQUE STORES
BOWL COVERS: Plastic
BOWLING EQPT & SPLY STORES
BOWLING EQPT & SPLYS
BOXES & CRATES: Rectangular, Wood
BOXES & SHOOK: Nailed Wood
BOXES: Ammunition, Metal
BOXES: Ammunition, Wood
BOXES: Corrugated
BOXES: Mail Or Post Office, Collection/Storage, Sheet Metal
BOXES: Outlet, Electric Wiring Device
BOXES: Packing & Shipping, Metal
BOXES: Paperboard, Folding
BOXES: Paperboard, Set-Up
BOXES: Plastic
BOXES: Solid Fiber
BOXES: Wirebound, Wood
BOXES: Wooden
BRAKES & BRAKE PARTS
BRASS & BRONZE PRDTS: Die-casted
BRASS FOUNDRY, NEC
BRASSWORK: Ornamental, Structural
BRAZING SVCS
BRAZING: Metal
BREAKER POINT SETS: Internal Combustion Engines
BRICK, STONE & RELATED PRDTS WHOLESALERS
BRICKS & BLOCKS: Structural
BRICKS : Flooring, Clay
BRICKS: Concrete
BRIDGE COMPONENTS: Bridge sections, prefabricated, highway
BRISTLES: Dressed
BROADCASTING & COMMUNICATION EQPT: Transmit-Re-ceiver, Radio
BROADCASTING & COMMUNICATIONS EQPT: Studio Eqpt, Radio & TV
BROADCASTING & COMMUNICATIONS EQPT: Transmitting, Radio/TV
BROADCASTING STATIONS, RADIO: Educational
BROKERS & DEALERS: Stock
BROKERS: Loan
BROKERS: Printing
BRONZE FOUNDRY, NEC
BROOMS & BRUSHES
BROOMS & BRUSHES: Household Or Indl
BROOMS & BRUSHES: Paintbrushes
BROOMS & BRUSHES: Street Sweeping, Hand Or Machine
BRUSHES
BUFFING FOR THE TRADE
BUILDING & OFFICE CLEANING SVCS
BUILDING & STRUCTURAL WOOD MBRS: Timbers, Struct, Lam Lumber
BUILDING & STRUCTURAL WOOD MEMBERS
BUILDING & STRUCTURAL WOOD MEMBERS: Arches, Laminated Lumber
BUILDING CLEANING & MAINTENANCE SVCS
BUILDING COMPONENTS: Structural Steel

BUILDING MAINTENANCE SVCS, EXC REPAIRS
BUILDING PRDTS & MATERIALS DEALERS
BUILDING PRDTS: Concrete
BUILDING PRDTS: Stone
BUILDINGS & COMPONENTS: Prefabricated Metal
BUILDINGS: Mobile, For Commercial Use
BUILDINGS: Portable
BUILDINGS: Prefabricated, Wood
BUILDINGS: Prefabricated, Wood
BUMPERS: Motor Vehicle
BURIAL VAULTS, FIBERGLASS
BURIAL VAULTS: Concrete Or Precast Terrazzo
BURIAL VAULTS: Stone
BURLAP & BURLAP PRDTS
BURNERS: Gas, Indl
BURNERS: Oil, Domestic Or Indl
BURNING: Metal
BUSHINGS & BEARINGS
BUSHINGS & BEARINGS: Bronze, Exc Machined
BUSINESS ACTIVITIES: Non-Commercial Site
BUSINESS FORMS WHOLESALERS
BUSINESS FORMS: Printed, Continuous
BUSINESS FORMS: Printed, Manifold
BUSINESS MACHINE REPAIR, ELECTRIC
BUSINESS SUPPORT SVCS
BUSINESS TRAINING SVCS
BUTTONS
Barium

C

CABINETS & CASES: Sewing Machine, Wood
CABINETS & CASES: Show, Display & Storage, Exc Wood
CABINETS: Bathroom Vanities, Wood
CABINETS: Entertainment
CABINETS: Entertainment Units, Household, Wood
CABINETS: Factory
CABINETS: Kitchen, Metal
CABINETS: Kitchen, Wood
CABINETS: Office, Metal
CABINETS: Office, Wood
CABINETS: Radio, Plastic
CABINETS: Show, Display, Etc, Wood, Exc Refrigerated
CABINETS: Stereo, Wood
CABLE & OTHER PAY TELEVISION DISTRIBUTION
CABLE & PAY TELEVISION SVCS: Closed Circuit
CABLE TELEVISION
CABLE WIRING SETS: Battery, Internal Combustion Engines
CABLE: Fiber
CABLE: Fiber Optic
CABLE: Noninsulated
CABLE: Steel, Insulated Or Armored
CAFES
CAGES: Wire
CALENDARS, WHOLESALE
CALIBRATING SVCS, NEC
CAMERA & PHOTOGRAPHIC SPLYS STORES
CAMERAS & RELATED EQPT: Photographic
CAMPERS: Truck Mounted
CAMPERS: Truck, Slide-In
CAMSHAFTS
CAN LIDS & ENDS
CANDLE SHOPS
CANDLES
CANDLES: Wholesalers
CANDY & CONFECTIONS: Candy Bars, Including Chocolate Covered
CANDY & CONFECTIONS: Chocolate Candy, Exc Solid Chocolate
CANDY & CONFECTIONS: Fudge
CANDY & CONFECTIONS: Licorice
CANDY & CONFECTIONS: Popcorn Balls/Other Trtd Popcorn Prdts
CANDY, NUT & CONFECTIONERY STORES: Candy
CANDY: Hard
CANDY: Soft
CANNED SPECIALTIES
CANOPIES: Sheet Metal
CANS & CASES: Capacitor Or Condenser, Stamped Metal
CANS & TUBES: Ammunition, Board Laminated With Metal Foil
CANS: Composite Foil-Fiber, Made From Purchased Materials
CANS: Metal
CANVAS PRDTS
CANVAS PRDTS: Air Cushions & Mattresses

CANVAS PRDTS: Convertible Tops, Car/Boat, Fm Purchased Mtrl
CANVAS PRDTS: Shades, Made From Purchased Materials
CAPACITORS: Fixed Or Variable
CAPACITORS: NEC
CAPS: Plastic
CAR WASH EQPT
CAR WASH EQPT & SPLYS WHOLESALERS
CAR WASHES
CARBIDES
CARBON & GRAPHITE PRDTS, NEC
CARBON BLACK
CARBURETORS
CARDS: Color
CARDS: Greeting
CARDS: Identification
CARPET & UPHOLSTERY CLEANING SVCS
CARPET & UPHOLSTERY CLEANING SVCS: On Customer Premises
CARPET DYEING & FINISHING
CARPETS, RUGS & FLOOR COVERING
CARPORTS: Prefabricated Metal
CARRIAGES: Horse Drawn
CARS: Electric
CASEMENTS: Aluminum
CASES, WOOD
CASES: Carrying
CASES: Carrying, Clothing & Apparel
CASES: Plastic
CASES: Sample Cases
CASES: Shipping, Nailed Or Lock Corner, Wood
CASES: Shipping, Wood, Wirebound
CASINGS: Storage, Missile & Missile Components
CASKET LININGS
CASKETS & ACCESS
CASKETS WHOLESALERS
CAST STONE: Concrete
CASTERS
CASTINGS GRINDING: For The Trade
CASTINGS: Aerospace, Aluminum
CASTINGS: Aerospace, Nonferrous, Exc Aluminum
CASTINGS: Aluminum
CASTINGS: Brass, Bronze & Copper
CASTINGS: Brass, NEC, Exc Die
CASTINGS: Commercial Investment, Ferrous
CASTINGS: Die, Aluminum
CASTINGS: Die, Nonferrous
CASTINGS: Die, Zinc
CASTINGS: Ductile
CASTINGS: Gray Iron
CASTINGS: Machinery, Aluminum
CASTINGS: Precision
CASTINGS: Steel
CASTINGS: Titanium
CASTINGS: Zinc
CATALOG & MAIL-ORDER HOUSES
CATALOG SALES
CATALOG SHOWROOMS
CATALYSTS: Chemical
CATAPULTS
CATERERS
CATTLE WHOLESALERS
CAULKING COMPOUNDS
CEMENT & CONCRETE RELATED PRDTS & EQPT: Bitumi-nous
CEMENT ROCK: Crushed & Broken
CEMENT: Hydraulic
CEMENT: Portland
CEMETERIES
CERAMIC FIBER
CERAMIC FLOOR & WALL TILE WHOLESALERS
CHAIN: Tire, Made From Purchased Wire
CHAIN: Welded, Made From Purchased Wire
CHAIN: Wire
CHAINS: Forged
CHANGE MAKING MACHINES
CHASSIS: Automobile House Trailer
CHASSIS: Automobile Trailer
CHASSIS: Motor Vehicle
CHAUFFEUR SVCS
CHEMICAL & FERTILIZER MINING
CHEMICAL CLEANING SVCS
CHEMICAL ELEMENTS
CHEMICAL PROCESSING MACHINERY & EQPT
CHEMICAL SPLYS FOR FOUNDRIES

CHEMICALS & ALLIED PRDTS WHOLESALERS, NEC
CHEMICALS & ALLIED PRDTS, WHOL: Chemical, Organic, Synthetic
CHEMICALS & ALLIED PRDTS, WHOL: Food Additives/Preservatives
CHEMICALS & ALLIED PRDTS, WHOLESALE: Alkalines
CHEMICALS & ALLIED PRDTS, WHOLESALE: Aromatic
CHEMICALS & ALLIED PRDTS, WHOLESALE: Carbon Dioxide
CHEMICALS & ALLIED PRDTS, WHOLESALE: Chemical Additives
CHEMICALS & ALLIED PRDTS, WHOLESALE: Chemicals, Indl
CHEMICALS & ALLIED PRDTS, WHOLESALE: Chemicals, Indl & Heavy
CHEMICALS & ALLIED PRDTS, WHOLESALE: Dry Ice
CHEMICALS & ALLIED PRDTS, WHOLESALE: Essential Oils
CHEMICALS & ALLIED PRDTS, WHOLESALE: Indl Gases
CHEMICALS & ALLIED PRDTS, WHOLESALE: Oxygen
CHEMICALS & ALLIED PRDTS, WHOLESALE: Plastics Film
CHEMICALS & ALLIED PRDTS, WHOLESALE: Plastics Materials, NEC
CHEMICALS & ALLIED PRDTS, WHOLESALE: Plastics Prdts, NEC
CHEMICALS & ALLIED PRDTS, WHOLESALE: Polyurethane Prdts
CHEMICALS & ALLIED PRDTS, WHOLESALE: Resins
CHEMICALS & ALLIED PRDTS, WHOLESALE: Resins, Plastics
CHEMICALS & ALLIED PRDTS, WHOLESALE: Spec Clean/Sanitation
CHEMICALS & ALLIED PRDTS, WHOLESALE: Syn Resin, Rub/Plastic
CHEMICALS & ALLIED PRDTS, WHOLESALE: Waxes, Exc Petroleum
CHEMICALS & OTHER PRDTS DERIVED FROM COKING
CHEMICALS, AGRICULTURE: Wholesalers
CHEMICALS: Agricultural
CHEMICALS: Alkalies
CHEMICALS: Aluminum Compounds
CHEMICALS: Ammonium Salts & Compounds
CHEMICALS: Bromine, Elemental
CHEMICALS: Caustic Soda
CHEMICALS: Compounds Or Salts, Iron, Ferric Or Ferrous
CHEMICALS: Copper Compounds Or Salts, Inorganic
CHEMICALS: Fire Retardant
CHEMICALS: High Purity, Refined From Technical Grade
CHEMICALS: Hydrogen Sulfide
CHEMICALS: Inorganic, NEC
CHEMICALS: Lead Compounds/Salts, Inorganic, Not Pigments
CHEMICALS: Magnesium Compounds Or Salts, Inorganic
CHEMICALS: Medicinal
CHEMICALS: Medicinal, Organic, Uncompounded, Bulk
CHEMICALS: Metal Compounds Or Salts, Inorganic, NEC
CHEMICALS: NEC
CHEMICALS: Nonmetallic Compounds
CHEMICALS: Organic, NEC
CHEMICALS: Phenol
CHEMICALS: Reagent Grade, Refined From Technical Grade
CHEMICALS: Soda Ash
CHEMICALS: Sulfur, Incl Rcvrd/Refined, Fm Sour Natural Gas
CHEMICALS: Tin, Stannic/Stannous, Compounds/Salts, Inorganic
CHEMICALS: Water Treatment
CHICKEN SLAUGHTERING & PROCESSING
CHILD & YOUTH SVCS, NEC
CHILDREN'S WEAR STORES
CHINA & GLASS REPAIR SVCS
CHLORINE
CHOCOLATE, EXC CANDY FROM BEANS: Chips, Powder, Block, Syrup
CHOCOLATE, EXC CANDY FROM PURCH CHOC: Chips, Powder, Block
CHROMATOGRAPHY EQPT
CHUCKS
CHURCHES
CIGAR & CIGARETTE HOLDERS
CIGAR STORES
CIGARETTE & CIGAR PRDTS & ACCESS
CIGARETTE FILTERS
CIGARETTE STORES
CIRCUIT BOARDS, PRINTED: Television & Radio
CIRCUITS: Electronic
CLAMPS & COUPLINGS: Hose

CLAMPS: Metal
CLAY PRDTS: Architectural
CLAY: Ground Or Treated
CLEANING & DESCALING SVC: Metal Prdts
CLEANING & DYEING PLANTS, EXC RUGS
CLEANING COMPOUNDS: Rifle Bore
CLEANING EQPT: Commercial
CLEANING EQPT: Floor Washing & Polishing, Commercial
CLEANING EQPT: High Pressure
CLEANING OR POLISHING PREPARATIONS, NEC
CLEANING PRDTS: Degreasing Solvent
CLEANING PRDTS: Disinfectants, Household Or Indl Plant
CLEANING PRDTS: Drain Pipe Solvents Or Cleaners
CLEANING PRDTS: Drycleaning Preparations
CLEANING PRDTS: Dusting Cloths, Chemically Treated
CLEANING PRDTS: Laundry Preparations
CLEANING PRDTS: Metal Polish
CLEANING PRDTS: Polishing Preparations & Related Prdts
CLEANING PRDTS: Sanitation Preparations
CLEANING PRDTS: Sanitation Preps, Disinfectants/Deodorants
CLEANING PRDTS: Specialty
CLEANING SVCS: Industrial Or Commercial
CLOSURES: Closures, Stamped Metal
CLOSURES: Plastic
CLOTHING & ACCESS, WOMEN, CHILDREN & INFANT, WHOL: Handbags
CLOTHING & ACCESS, WOMEN, CHILDREN & INFANT, WHOL: Uniforms
CLOTHING & ACCESS, WOMENS, CHILDREN & INFANTS, WHOL: Hats
CLOTHING & ACCESS: Costumes, Lodge
CLOTHING & ACCESS: Costumes, Masquerade
CLOTHING & ACCESS: Costumes, Theatrical
CLOTHING & ACCESS: Handicapped
CLOTHING & ACCESS: Men's Miscellaneous Access
CLOTHING & APPAREL STORES: Custom
CLOTHING & FURNISHINGS, MEN'S & BOYS', WHOLESALE: Shirts
CLOTHING & FURNISHINGS, MEN'S & BOYS', WHOLESALE: Uniforms
CLOTHING & FURNISHINGS, MENS & BOYS, WHOL: Sportswear/Work
CLOTHING STORES, NEC
CLOTHING STORES: Designer Apparel
CLOTHING STORES: Formal Wear
CLOTHING STORES: Leather
CLOTHING STORES: Square Dance Apparel
CLOTHING STORES: T-Shirts, Printed, Custom
CLOTHING STORES: Uniforms & Work
CLOTHING: Access
CLOTHING: Access, Women's & Misses'
CLOTHING: Anklets & Socks
CLOTHING: Athletic & Sportswear, Men's & Boys'
CLOTHING: Athletic & Sportswear, Women's & Girls'
CLOTHING: Children's, Girls'
CLOTHING: Clergy Vestments
CLOTHING: Coats, Hunting & Vests, Men's
CLOTHING: Costumes
CLOTHING: Dresses
CLOTHING: Gowns & Dresses, Wedding
CLOTHING: Gowns, Formal
CLOTHING: Hats & Caps, NEC
CLOTHING: Hats & Headwear, Knit
CLOTHING: Leather
CLOTHING: Leather & Sheep-Lined
CLOTHING: Maternity
CLOTHING: Men's & boy's clothing, nec
CLOTHING: Outerwear, Lthr, Wool/Down-Filled, Men, Youth/Boy
CLOTHING: Outerwear, Women's & Misses' NEC
CLOTHING: Robes & Dressing Gowns
CLOTHING: Shirts
CLOTHING: Shirts, Dress, Men's & Boys'
CLOTHING: Sleeping Garments, Men's & Boys'
CLOTHING: Socks
CLOTHING: Sportswear, Women's
CLOTHING: Sweaters & Sweater Coats, Knit
CLOTHING: T-Shirts & Tops, Knit
CLOTHING: Tailored Suits & Formal Jackets
CLOTHING: Ties, Neck & Bow, Men's & Boys'
CLOTHING: Trousers & Slacks, Men's & Boys'
CLOTHING: Tuxedos, From Purchased Materials
CLOTHING: Uniforms & Vestments
CLOTHING: Uniforms, Men's & Boys'

CLOTHING: Uniforms, Military, Men/Youth, Purchased Materials
CLOTHING: Uniforms, Team Athletic
CLOTHING: Waterproof Outerwear
CLOTHING: Work Apparel, Exc Uniforms
CLOTHING: Work, Men's
COAL GASIFICATION
COAL MINING SERVICES
COAL MINING SVCS: Bituminous, Contract Basis
COAL MINING: Bituminous & Lignite Surface
COAL MINING: Bituminous Coal & Lignite-Surface Mining
COAL MINING: Bituminous Underground
COAL MINING: Bituminous, Strip
COAL MINING: Bituminous, Surface, NEC
COAL PREPARATION PLANT: Bituminous or Lignite
COAL, MINERALS & ORES, WHOLESALE: Coal
COATING COMPOUNDS: Tar
COATING OR WRAPPING SVC: Steel Pipe
COATING SVC
COATING SVC: Aluminum, Metal Prdts
COATING SVC: Hot Dip, Metals Or Formed Prdts
COATING SVC: Metals & Formed Prdts
COATING SVC: Metals, With Plastic Or Resins
COATING SVC: Rust Preventative
COATING SVC: Silicon
COATINGS: Air Curing
COATINGS: Epoxy
COATINGS: Polyurethane
COFFEE SVCS
COIL WINDING SVC
COILS & ROD: Extruded, Aluminum
COILS & TRANSFORMERS
COILS: Electric Motors Or Generators
COIN-OPERATED LAUNDRY
COIN-OPERATED MACHINES & MECHANISMS, WHOLESALE
COKE OVEN PRDTS: Beehive
COLLECTION AGENCIES
COLOGNES
COLOR PIGMENTS
COLORING & FINISHING SVC: Aluminum Or Formed Prdts
COLORS: Pigments, Inorganic
COLORS: Pigments, Organic
COMBINATION UTILITIES, NEC
COMBINED ELEMENTARY & SECONDARY SCHOOLS, PRIVATE
COMFORTERS & QUILTS, FROM MANMADE FIBER OR SILK
COMMERCIAL & INDL SHELVING WHOLESALERS
COMMERCIAL & OFFICE BUILDINGS RENOVATION & REPAIR
COMMERCIAL ART & GRAPHIC DESIGN SVCS
COMMERCIAL ART & ILLUSTRATION SVCS
COMMERCIAL EQPT WHOLESALERS, NEC
COMMERCIAL EQPT, WHOLESALE: Comm Cooking & Food Svc Eqpt
COMMERCIAL EQPT, WHOLESALE: Merchandising Machines
COMMERCIAL EQPT, WHOLESALE: Neon Signs
COMMERCIAL EQPT, WHOLESALE: Restaurant, NEC
COMMERCIAL EQPT, WHOLESALE: Scales, Exc Laboratory
COMMERCIAL EQPT, WHOLESALE: Store Fixtures & Display Eqpt
COMMERCIAL EQPT, WHOLESALE: Vending Machines, Coin-Operated
COMMERCIAL PRINTING & NEWSPAPER PUBLISHING COMBINED
COMMODITY CONTRACTS BROKERS, DEALERS
COMMON SAND MINING
COMMUNICATION HEADGEAR: Telephone
COMMUNICATIONS EQPT & SYSTEMS, NEC
COMMUNICATIONS EQPT WHOLESALERS
COMMUNICATIONS EQPT: Microwave
COMMUNICATIONS SVCS
COMMUNICATIONS SVCS, NEC
COMMUNICATIONS SVCS: Data
COMMUNICATIONS SVCS: Internet Connectivity Svcs
COMMUNICATIONS SVCS: Internet Host Svcs
COMMUNICATIONS SVCS: Online Svc Providers
COMMUNICATIONS SVCS: Proprietary Online Svcs Networks
COMMUNITY CENTER
COMPACT DISC PLAYERS
COMPACT LASER DISCS: Prerecorded
COMPOSITION STONE: Plastic

COMPOST
COMPRESSORS, AIR CONDITIONING: Wholesalers
COMPRESSORS: Air & Gas
COMPRESSORS: Air & Gas, Including Vacuum Pumps
COMPRESSORS: Refrigeration & Air Conditioning Eqpt
COMPRESSORS: Repairing
COMPRESSORS: Wholesalers
COMPUTER & COMPUTER SOFTWARE STORES
COMPUTER & COMPUTER SOFTWARE STORES: Peripheral Eqpt
COMPUTER & COMPUTER SOFTWARE STORES: Software & Access
COMPUTER & COMPUTER SOFTWARE STORES: Software, Bus/Non-Game
COMPUTER & DATA PROCESSING EQPT REPAIR & MAINTENANCE
COMPUTER & OFFICE MACHINE MAINTENANCE & REPAIR
COMPUTER & SFTWR STORE: Modem, Monitor, Terminal/Disk Drive
COMPUTER FACILITIES MANAGEMENT SVCS
COMPUTER FORMS
COMPUTER GRAPHICS SVCS
COMPUTER HARDWARE REQUIREMENTS ANALYSIS
COMPUTER INTERFACE EQPT: Indl Process
COMPUTER PAPER WHOLESALERS
COMPUTER PERIPHERAL EQPT REPAIR & MAINTENANCE
COMPUTER PERIPHERAL EQPT, NEC
COMPUTER PERIPHERAL EQPT, WHOLESALE
COMPUTER PERIPHERAL EQPT: Graphic Displays, Exc Terminals
COMPUTER PHOTOGRAPHY OR PORTRAIT SVC
COMPUTER PROGRAMMING SVCS
COMPUTER PROGRAMMING SVCS: Custom
COMPUTER RELATED MAINTENANCE SVCS
COMPUTER SOFTWARE DEVELOPMENT
COMPUTER SOFTWARE DEVELOPMENT & APPLICATIONS
COMPUTER SOFTWARE SYSTEMS ANALYSIS & DESIGN: Custom
COMPUTER STORAGE DEVICES, NEC
COMPUTER SYSTEMS ANALYSIS & DESIGN
COMPUTER TERMINALS
COMPUTER-AIDED ENGINEERING SYSTEMS SVCS
COMPUTER-AIDED MANUFACTURING SYSTEMS SVCS
COMPUTERS, NEC
COMPUTERS, NEC, WHOLESALE
COMPUTERS, PERIPHERALS & SOFTWARE, WHOLESALE: Mainframe
COMPUTERS, PERIPHERALS & SOFTWARE, WHOLESALE: Software
COMPUTERS: Mainframe
COMPUTERS: Mini
COMPUTERS: Personal
CONCERT MANAGEMENT SVCS
CONCRETE BUGGIES: Powered
CONCRETE BUILDING PRDTS WHOLESALERS
CONCRETE PRDTS
CONCRETE PRDTS, PRECAST, NEC
CONCRETE: Asphaltic, Not From Refineries
CONCRETE: Ready-Mixed
CONDENSERS: Heat Transfer Eqpt, Evaporative
CONDENSERS: Refrigeration
CONDUITS & FITTINGS: Electric
CONFECTIONERY PRDTS WHOLESALERS
CONFECTIONS & CANDY
CONFINEMENT SURVEILLANCE SYS MAINTENANCE & MONITORING SVCS
CONNECTORS & TERMINALS: Electrical Device Uses
CONNECTORS: Cord, Electric
CONNECTORS: Electrical
CONNECTORS: Electronic
CONSTRUCTION & MINING MACHINERY WHOLESALERS
CONSTRUCTION & ROAD MAINTENANCE EQPT: Drags, Road
CONSTRUCTION EQPT REPAIR SVCS
CONSTRUCTION EQPT: Airport
CONSTRUCTION EQPT: Attachments
CONSTRUCTION EQPT: Backhoes, Tractors, Cranes & Similar Eqpt
CONSTRUCTION EQPT: Buckets, Excavating, Clamshell, Etc
CONSTRUCTION EQPT: Bulldozers
CONSTRUCTION EQPT: Catch Basin Cleaners
CONSTRUCTION EQPT: Cranes

CONSTRUCTION EQPT: Entrenching Machines
CONSTRUCTION EQPT: Finishers & Spreaders
CONSTRUCTION EQPT: Hammer Mills, Port, Incl Rock/Ore Crush
CONSTRUCTION EQPT: Spreaders, Aggregates
CONSTRUCTION EQPT: Subgraders
CONSTRUCTION EQPT: Tractors
CONSTRUCTION EQPT: Wrecker Hoists, Automobile
CONSTRUCTION MATERIALS, WHOL: Concrete/Cinder Bldg Prdts
CONSTRUCTION MATERIALS, WHOLESALE: Aggregate
CONSTRUCTION MATERIALS, WHOLESALE: Air Ducts, Sheet Metal
CONSTRUCTION MATERIALS, WHOLESALE: Architectural Metalwork
CONSTRUCTION MATERIALS, WHOLESALE: Asphalt Felts & coating
CONSTRUCTION MATERIALS, WHOLESALE: Awnings
CONSTRUCTION MATERIALS, WHOLESALE: Block, Concrete & Cinder
CONSTRUCTION MATERIALS, WHOLESALE: Building, Exterior
CONSTRUCTION MATERIALS, WHOLESALE: Building, Interior
CONSTRUCTION MATERIALS, WHOLESALE: Concrete Mixtures
CONSTRUCTION MATERIALS, WHOLESALE: Door Frames
CONSTRUCTION MATERIALS, WHOLESALE: Drywall Materials
CONSTRUCTION MATERIALS, WHOLESALE: Fiberglass Building Mat
CONSTRUCTION MATERIALS, WHOLESALE: Glass
CONSTRUCTION MATERIALS, WHOLESALE: Gravel
CONSTRUCTION MATERIALS, WHOLESALE: Insulation, Mineral Wool
CONSTRUCTION MATERIALS, WHOLESALE: Lime Building Prdts
CONSTRUCTION MATERIALS, WHOLESALE: Lime, Exc Agricultural
CONSTRUCTION MATERIALS, WHOLESALE: Limestone
CONSTRUCTION MATERIALS, WHOLESALE: Millwork
CONSTRUCTION MATERIALS, WHOLESALE: Molding, All Materials
CONSTRUCTION MATERIALS, WHOLESALE: Pallets, Wood
CONSTRUCTION MATERIALS, WHOLESALE: Particleboard
CONSTRUCTION MATERIALS, WHOLESALE: Paving Materials
CONSTRUCTION MATERIALS, WHOLESALE: Plywood
CONSTRUCTION MATERIALS, WHOLESALE: Prefabricated Structures
CONSTRUCTION MATERIALS, WHOLESALE: Roofing & Siding Material
CONSTRUCTION MATERIALS, WHOLESALE: Sand
CONSTRUCTION MATERIALS, WHOLESALE: Septic Tanks
CONSTRUCTION MATERIALS, WHOLESALE: Sewer Pipe, Clay
CONSTRUCTION MATERIALS, WHOLESALE: Siding, Exc Wood
CONSTRUCTION MATERIALS, WHOLESALE: Stone, Crushed Or Broken
CONSTRUCTION MATERIALS, WHOLESALE: Tile & Clay Prdts
CONSTRUCTION MATERIALS, WHOLESALE: Trim, Sheet Metal
CONSTRUCTION MATERIALS, WHOLESALE: Veneer
CONSTRUCTION MATERIALS, WHOLESALE: Windows
CONSTRUCTION MATLS, WHOL: Composite Board Prdts, Woodboard
CONSTRUCTION MATLS, WHOL: Doors, Combination, Screen-Storm
CONSTRUCTION MATLS, WHOL: Lumber, Rough, Dressed/Finished
CONSTRUCTION SAND MINING
CONSTRUCTION: Agricultural Building
CONSTRUCTION: Athletic & Recreation Facilities
CONSTRUCTION: Bridge
CONSTRUCTION: Commercial & Institutional Building
CONSTRUCTION: Commercial & Office Building, New
CONSTRUCTION: Commercial & Office Buildings, Prefabricated
CONSTRUCTION: Dams, Waterways, Docks & Other Marine
CONSTRUCTION: Drainage System
CONSTRUCTION: Farm Building
CONSTRUCTION: Food Prdts Manufacturing or Packing Plant
CONSTRUCTION: Foundation & Retaining Wall

CONSTRUCTION: Grain Elevator
CONSTRUCTION: Heavy Highway & Street
CONSTRUCTION: Indl Building & Warehouse
CONSTRUCTION: Indl Buildings, New, NEC
CONSTRUCTION: Multi-Family Housing
CONSTRUCTION: Pharmaceutical Manufacturing Plant
CONSTRUCTION: Pipeline, NEC
CONSTRUCTION: Pond
CONSTRUCTION: Residential, Nec
CONSTRUCTION: Scaffolding
CONSTRUCTION: Sewer Line
CONSTRUCTION: Single-Family Housing
CONSTRUCTION: Single-family Housing, New
CONSTRUCTION: Steel Buildings
CONSTRUCTION: Street Surfacing & Paving
CONSTRUCTION: Swimming Pools
CONSTRUCTION: Transmitting Tower, Telecommunication
CONSTRUCTION: Utility Line
CONSTRUCTION: Waste Water & Sewage Treatment Plant
CONSULTING SVC: Actuarial
CONSULTING SVC: Business, NEC
CONSULTING SVC: Chemical
CONSULTING SVC: Computer
CONSULTING SVC: Data Processing
CONSULTING SVC: Educational
CONSULTING SVC: Engineering
CONSULTING SVC: Executive Placement & Search
CONSULTING SVC: Financial Management
CONSULTING SVC: Management
CONSULTING SVC: Marketing Management
CONSULTING SVC: Online Technology
CONSULTING SVC: Telecommunications
CONSULTING SVCS, BUSINESS: Energy Conservation
CONSULTING SVCS, BUSINESS: Environmental
CONSULTING SVCS, BUSINESS: Publishing
CONSULTING SVCS, BUSINESS: Safety Training Svcs
CONSULTING SVCS, BUSINESS: Sys Engnrg, Exc Computer/Prof
CONSULTING SVCS, BUSINESS: Systems Analysis & Engineering
CONSULTING SVCS, BUSINESS: Systems Analysis Or Design
CONSULTING SVCS, BUSINESS: Testing, Educational Or Personnel
CONSULTING SVCS: Oil
CONSULTING SVCS: Scientific
CONTACT LENSES
CONTACTS: Electrical
CONTAINERS, GLASS: Food
CONTAINERS, GLASS: Packers' Ware
CONTAINERS: Air Cargo, Metal
CONTAINERS: Cargo, Wood
CONTAINERS: Cargo, Wood & Metal Combination
CONTAINERS: Cargo, Wood & Wood With Metal
CONTAINERS: Corrugated
CONTAINERS: Food & Beverage
CONTAINERS: Food, Liquid Tight, Including Milk
CONTAINERS: Food, Metal
CONTAINERS: Glass
CONTAINERS: Metal
CONTAINERS: Plastic
CONTAINERS: Plywood & Veneer, Wood
CONTAINERS: Sanitary, Food
CONTAINERS: Shipping & Mailing, Fiber
CONTAINERS: Shipping, Bombs, Metal Plate
CONTAINERS: Shipping, Wood
CONTAINERS: Wood
CONTRACTORS: Appliance Installation
CONTRACTORS: Asphalt
CONTRACTORS: Awning Installation
CONTRACTORS: Banking Machine Installation & Svc
CONTRACTORS: Blasting, Exc Building Demolition
CONTRACTORS: Boiler Maintenance Contractor
CONTRACTORS: Building Eqpt & Machinery Installation
CONTRACTORS: Building Sign Installation & Mntnce
CONTRACTORS: Building Site Preparation
CONTRACTORS: Carpentry Work
CONTRACTORS: Carpentry, Cabinet & Finish Work
CONTRACTORS: Carpentry, Cabinet Building & Installation
CONTRACTORS: Carpet Laying
CONTRACTORS: Chimney Construction & Maintenance
CONTRACTORS: Closed Circuit Television Installation
CONTRACTORS: Closet Organizers, Installation & Design
CONTRACTORS: Coating, Caulking & Weather, Water & Fire
CONTRACTORS: Commercial & Office Building

INDEX

CONTRACTORS: Communications Svcs
CONTRACTORS: Computerized Controls Installation
CONTRACTORS: Concrete
CONTRACTORS: Construction Site Cleanup
CONTRACTORS: Construction Site Metal Structure Coating
CONTRACTORS: Countertop Installation
CONTRACTORS: Demolition, Building & Other Structures
CONTRACTORS: Demountable Partition Installation
CONTRACTORS: Directional Oil & Gas Well Drilling Svc
CONTRACTORS: Dock Eqpt Installation, Indl
CONTRACTORS: Drapery Track Installation
CONTRACTORS: Drywall
CONTRACTORS: Earthmoving
CONTRACTORS: Electrical
CONTRACTORS: Electronic Controls Installation
CONTRACTORS: Epoxy Application
CONTRACTORS: Excavating
CONTRACTORS: Excavating Slush Pits & Cellars Svcs
CONTRACTORS: Fence Construction
CONTRACTORS: Fiberglass Work
CONTRACTORS: Fire Detection & Burglar Alarm Systems
CONTRACTORS: Fire Sprinkler System Installation Svcs
CONTRACTORS: Floor Laying & Other Floor Work
CONTRACTORS: Flooring
CONTRACTORS: Food Svcs Eqpt Installation
CONTRACTORS: Foundation & Footing
CONTRACTORS: Gas Detection & Analysis Svcs
CONTRACTORS: Gas Field Svcs, NEC
CONTRACTORS: Gas Leak Detection
CONTRACTORS: General Electric
CONTRACTORS: Glass Tinting, Architectural & Automotive
CONTRACTORS: Glass, Glazing & Tinting
CONTRACTORS: Grave Excavation
CONTRACTORS: Gutters & Downspouts
CONTRACTORS: Heating & Air Conditioning
CONTRACTORS: Heating Systems Repair & Maintenance Svc
CONTRACTORS: Highway & Street Construction, General
CONTRACTORS: Highway & Street Paving
CONTRACTORS: Highway & Street Resurfacing
CONTRACTORS: Home & Office Intrs Finish, Furnish/Remodel
CONTRACTORS: Hydraulic Well Fracturing Svcs
CONTRACTORS: Indl Building Renovation, Remodeling & Repair
CONTRACTORS: Insulation Installation, Building
CONTRACTORS: Irrigation Land Leveling
CONTRACTORS: Kitchen Cabinet Installation
CONTRACTORS: Lighting Syst
CONTRACTORS: Machine Rigging & Moving
CONTRACTORS: Machinery Installation
CONTRACTORS: Masonry & Stonework
CONTRACTORS: Mechanical
CONTRACTORS: Millwrights
CONTRACTORS: Oil & Gas Aerial Geophysical Exploration Svcs
CONTRACTORS: Oil & Gas Building, Repairing & Dismantling Svc
CONTRACTORS: Oil & Gas Field Fire Fighting Svcs
CONTRACTORS: Oil & Gas Well Casing Cement Svcs
CONTRACTORS: Oil & Gas Well Drilling Svc
CONTRACTORS: Oil & Gas Well Spudding Svcs
CONTRACTORS: Oil & Gas Wells Pumping Svcs
CONTRACTORS: Oil & Gas Wells Svcs
CONTRACTORS: Oil Field Lease Tanks: Erectg, Clng/Rprg Svcs
CONTRACTORS: Oil Field Mud Drilling Svcs
CONTRACTORS: Oil/Gas Well Construction, Rpr/Dismantling Svcs
CONTRACTORS: On-Site Welding
CONTRACTORS: Paint & Wallpaper Stripping
CONTRACTORS: Painting & Wall Covering
CONTRACTORS: Painting, Commercial
CONTRACTORS: Painting, Commercial, Exterior
CONTRACTORS: Painting, Indl
CONTRACTORS: Parking Lot Maintenance
CONTRACTORS: Patio & Deck Construction & Repair
CONTRACTORS: Pavement Marking
CONTRACTORS: Petroleum Storage Tanks, Pumping & Draining
CONTRACTORS: Pile Driving
CONTRACTORS: Pipe Laying
CONTRACTORS: Plaster & Drywall Work
CONTRACTORS: Plumbing
CONTRACTORS: Power Generating Eqpt Installation

CONTRACTORS: Prefabricated Window & Door Installation
CONTRACTORS: Process Piping
CONTRACTORS: Refractory or Acid Brick Masonry
CONTRACTORS: Renovation, Aircraft Interiors
CONTRACTORS: Roof Repair
CONTRACTORS: Roofing
CONTRACTORS: Safe Or Vault Installation
CONTRACTORS: Sandblasting Svc, Building Exteriors
CONTRACTORS: Seismograph Survey Svcs
CONTRACTORS: Septic System
CONTRACTORS: Sheet Metal Work, NEC
CONTRACTORS: Sheet metal Work, Architectural
CONTRACTORS: Ship Boiler & Tank Cleaning & Repair
CONTRACTORS: Siding
CONTRACTORS: Single-family Home General Remodeling
CONTRACTORS: Steeplejacks
CONTRACTORS: Stone Masonry
CONTRACTORS: Storage Tank Erection, Metal
CONTRACTORS: Structural Iron Work, Structural
CONTRACTORS: Structural Steel Erection
CONTRACTORS: Svc Well Drilling Svcs
CONTRACTORS: Terrazzo Work
CONTRACTORS: Tile Installation, Ceramic
CONTRACTORS: Trenching
CONTRACTORS: Tuck Pointing & Restoration
CONTRACTORS: Underground Utilities
CONTRACTORS: Ventilation & Duct Work
CONTRACTORS: Vinyl Flooring Installation, Tile & Sheet
CONTRACTORS: Warm Air Heating & Air Conditioning
CONTRACTORS: Water Intake Well Drilling Svc
CONTRACTORS: Water Well Drilling
CONTRACTORS: Water Well Servicing
CONTRACTORS: Window Treatment Installation
CONTRACTORS: Windows & Doors
CONTRACTORS: Wood Floor Installation & Refinishing
CONTRACTORS: Wrecking & Demolition
CONTROL CIRCUIT DEVICES
CONTROL EQPT: Electric
CONTROL EQPT: Electric Buses & Locomotives
CONTROL EQPT: Noise
CONTROL PANELS: Electrical
CONTROLS & ACCESS: Indl, Electric
CONTROLS & ACCESS: Motor
CONTROLS: Automatic Temperature
CONTROLS: Electric Motor
CONTROLS: Environmental
CONTROLS: Marine & Navy, Auxiliary
CONTROLS: Relay & Ind
CONTROLS: Thermostats
CONTROLS: Truck, Indl Battery
CONTROLS: Water Heater
CONVENIENCE STORES
CONVERTERS: Data
CONVERTERS: Phase Or Rotary, Electrical
CONVERTERS: Torque, Exc Auto
CONVEYOR SYSTEMS
CONVEYOR SYSTEMS: Bulk Handling
CONVEYOR SYSTEMS: Pneumatic Tube
CONVEYOR SYSTEMS: Robotic
CONVEYORS & CONVEYING EQPT
COOKING & FOOD WARMING EQPT: Commercial
COOKING & FOODWARMING EQPT: Commercial
COOKING & FOODWARMING EQPT: Popcorn Machines, Commercial
COOKING WARE: Cooking Ware, Porcelain Enameled
COOKWARE, STONEWARE: Coarse Earthenware & Pottery
COOLING TOWERS: Metal
COOLING TOWERS: Wood
COOPERAGE STOCK PRODUCTS
COPPER PRDTS: Refined, Primary
COPPER: Rolling & Drawing
COPY MACHINES WHOLESALERS
COPYRIGHT BUYING & LICENSING
CORRUGATING MACHINES
COSMETIC PREPARATIONS
COSMETICS & TOILETRIES
COSTUME JEWELRY & NOVELTIES: Exc Semi & Precious
COSTUME JEWELRY & NOVELTIES: Ornament, Exc Precious Mtl/Gem
COSTUME JEWELRY & NOVELTIES: Rosaries & Sm Religious Items
COSTUMES & WIGS STORES
COUNTER & SINK TOPS
COUNTERS & COUNTING DEVICES
COUNTERS OR COUNTER DISPLAY CASES, EXC WOOD

COUNTERS OR COUNTER DISPLAY CASES, WOOD
COUNTERS: Mechanical
COUNTING DEVICES: Controls, Revolution & Timing
COUNTING DEVICES: Gauges, Press Temp Corrections Computing
COUNTING DEVICES: Production
COUNTING DEVICES: Tachometer, Centrifugal
COUNTRY CLUBS
COUPLINGS: Hose & Tube, Hydraulic Or Pneumatic
COUPLINGS: Shaft
COURIER OR MESSENGER SVCS
COURIER SVCS: Ground
COURIER SVCS: Package By Vehicle
COURIER SVCS: Parcel By Vehicle
COVERS: Automobile Seat
COVERS: Automotive, Exc Seat & Tire
COVERS: Canvas
COVERS: Slip Made Of Fabric, Plastic, Etc.
CRADLES: Drum
CRANE & AERIAL LIFT SVCS
CRANES: Indl Plant
CRANES: Indl Truck
CRANES: Overhead
CRANKSHAFTS & CAMSHAFTS: Machining
CRATES: Berry, Wood Wirebound
CREATIVE SVCS: Advertisers, Exc Writers
CREDIT INST, SHORT-TERM BUSINESS: Financing Dealers
CROWNS & CLOSURES
CRUDE PETROLEUM & NATURAL GAS PRODUCTION
CRUDE PETROLEUM & NATURAL GAS PRODUCTION
CRUDE PETROLEUM PRODUCTION
CRYOGENIC COOLING DEVICES: Infrared Detectors, Masers
CULTURE MEDIA
CULVERTS: Metal Plate
CULVERTS: Sheet Metal
CUPOLAS: Metal Plate
CUPS & PLATES: Foamed Plastics
CUPS: Plastic Exc Polystyrene Foam
CURBING: Granite Or Stone
CURTAIN & DRAPERY FIXTURES: Poles, Rods & Rollers
CURTAIN WALLS: Building, Steel
CURTAINS: Window, From Purchased Materials
CUSHIONS & PILLOWS
CUSHIONS & PILLOWS: Boat
CUT STONE & STONE PRODUCTS
CUTLERY
CUTTING EQPT: Glass Cutters
CYCLIC CRUDES & INTERMEDIATES
CYLINDER & ACTUATORS: Fluid Power
CYLINDERS: Pressure
CYLINDERS: Pump

D

DAIRY EQPT
DAIRY PRDTS STORE: Cheese
DAIRY PRDTS STORE: Ice Cream, Packaged
DAIRY PRDTS WHOLESALERS: Fresh
DAIRY PRDTS: Butter
DAIRY PRDTS: Cheese
DAIRY PRDTS: Dairy Based Desserts, Frozen
DAIRY PRDTS: Dietary Supplements, Dairy & Non-Dairy Based
DAIRY PRDTS: Dips & Spreads, Cheese Based
DAIRY PRDTS: Evaporated Milk
DAIRY PRDTS: Fermented & Cultured Milk Prdts
DAIRY PRDTS: Frozen Desserts & Novelties
DAIRY PRDTS: Ice Cream & Ice Milk
DAIRY PRDTS: Ice Cream, Bulk
DAIRY PRDTS: Ice Cream, Packaged, Molded, On Sticks, Etc.
DAIRY PRDTS: Milk & Cream, Cultured & Flavored
DAIRY PRDTS: Milk, Condensed & Evaporated
DAIRY PRDTS: Milk, Fluid
DAIRY PRDTS: Milk, Processed, Pasteurized, Homogenized/Btld
DAIRY PRDTS: Natural Cheese
DAIRY PRDTS: Powdered Baby Formula
DAIRY PRDTS: Processed Cheese
DAIRY PRDTS: Sour Cream
DAIRY PRDTS: Whipped Topping, Exc Frozen Or Dry Mix
DAIRY PRDTS: Yogurt, Exc Frozen
DATA PROCESSING & PREPARATION SVCS
DATA PROCESSING SVCS
DECALS, WHOLESALE

DECORATIVE WOOD & WOODWORK
DEFENSE SYSTEMS & EQPT
DEGREASING MACHINES
DEHYDRATION EQPT
DEICING OR DEFROSTING FLUID
DENTAL EQPT
DENTAL EQPT & SPLYS
DENTAL EQPT & SPLYS WHOLESALERS
DENTAL EQPT & SPLYS: Dental Hand Instruments, NEC
DENTAL EQPT & SPLYS: Dental Materials
DENTAL EQPT & SPLYS: Enamels
DENTAL EQPT & SPLYS: Hand Pieces & Parts
DENTAL EQPT & SPLYS: Orthodontic Appliances
DENTAL EQPT & SPLYS: Plaster
DENTAL EQPT & SPLYS: Teeth, Artificial, Exc In Dental Labs
DENTAL INSTRUMENT REPAIR SVCS
DENTISTS' OFFICES & CLINICS
DEODORANTS: Personal
DERMATOLOGICALS
DESIGN SVCS, NEC
DESIGN SVCS: Commercial & Indl
DESIGN SVCS: Computer Integrated Systems
DETECTORS: Water Leak
DETINNING: Cans & Scrap
DIAGNOSTIC SUBSTANCES
DIAGNOSTIC SUBSTANCES OR AGENTS: Blood Derivative
DIAGNOSTIC SUBSTANCES OR AGENTS: In Vitro
DIAGNOSTIC SUBSTANCES OR AGENTS: Microbiology &
  Virology
DIAMONDS, GEMS, WHOLESALE
DIAMONDS: Cutting & Polishing
DICE & DICE CUPS
DIE CUTTING SVC: Paper
DIE SETS: Presses, Metal Stamping
DIES & TOOLS: Special
DIES: Cutting, Exc Metal
DIES: Diamond, Metalworking
DIES: Extrusion
DIES: Paper Cutting
DIES: Plastic Forming
DIES: Steel Rule
DIES: Wire Drawing & Straightening
DIFFERENTIAL ASSEMBLIES & PARTS
DIODES: Light Emitting
DIRECT SELLING ESTABLISHMENTS, NEC
DIRECT SELLING ESTABLISHMENTS: Food Svc, Coffee-
  Cart
DISC JOCKEYS
DISCS & TAPE: Optical, Blank
DISPENSING EQPT & PARTS, BEVERAGE: Beer
DISPENSING EQPT & PARTS, BEVERAGE: Cold, Exc Coin-
  Operated
DISPENSING EQPT & PARTS, BEVERAGE: Coolers,
  Milk/Water, Elec
DISPENSING EQPT & PARTS, BEVERAGE: Fountain/Other
  Beverage
DISPLAY FIXTURES: Showcases, Wood, Exc Refrigerated
DISPLAY FIXTURES: Wood
DISPLAY ITEMS: Corrugated, Made From Purchased Materi-
  als
DISTILLATES: Hardwood
DISTILLERS DRIED GRAIN & SOLUBLES
DOCK EQPT & SPLYS, INDL
DOCK OPERATION SVCS, INCL BLDGS, FACILITIES,
  OPERS & MAINT
DOLLIES: Industrial
DOOR FRAMES: Wood
DOOR OPERATING SYSTEMS: Electric
DOORS & WINDOWS WHOLESALERS: All Materials
DOORS & WINDOWS: Storm, Metal
DOORS: Fiberglass
DOORS: Fire, Metal
DOORS: Folding, Plastic Or Plastic Coated Fabric
DOORS: Garage, Overhead, Metal
DOORS: Garage, Overhead, Wood
DOORS: Glass
DOORS: Safe & Vault, Metal
DOORS: Screen, Metal
DOORS: Wooden
DOWELS & DOWEL RODS
DOWNSPOUTS: Sheet Metal
DRAINAGE PRDTS: Concrete
DRAPERIES & CURTAINS
DRAPERIES & DRAPERY FABRICS, COTTON
DRAPERIES: Plastic & Textile, From Purchased Materials

DRAPERY & UPHOLSTERY STORES: Draperies
DRILL BITS
DRILLING MACHINERY & EQPT: Oil & Gas
DRILLING MACHINERY & EQPT: Water Well
DRINK MIXES, NONALCOHOLIC: Cocktail
DRINKING PLACES: Alcoholic Beverages
DRINKING PLACES: Bars & Lounges
DRINKING PLACES: Tavern
DRIVE SHAFTS
DRIVES: High Speed Indl, Exc Hydrostatic
DRIVES: Hydrostatic
DROP CLOTHS: Fabric
DRUG STORES
DRUG TESTING KITS: Blood & Urine
DRUGS & DRUG PROPRIETARIES, WHOLESALE
DRUGS & DRUG PROPRIETARIES, WHOLESALE: Pharma-
  ceuticals
DRUGS: Parasitic & Infective Disease Affecting
DRUMS: Knockout Or Reflux, Metal Plate
DRYCLEANING & LAUNDRY SVCS: Commercial & Family
DRYCLEANING PLANTS
DUCTING: Plastic
DUCTS: Sheet Metal
DUMPSTERS: Garbage
DURABLE GOODS WHOLESALERS, NEC
DUST OR FUME COLLECTING EQPT: Indl
DYES & PIGMENTS: Organic

E

EATING PLACES
EDITING SVCS
EDUCATIONAL SVCS
EDUCATIONAL SVCS, NONDEGREE GRANTING: Continu-
  ing Education
EGG WHOLESALERS
ELASTOMERS
ELECTRIC MOTOR REPAIR SVCS
ELECTRIC SERVICES
ELECTRIC TOOL REPAIR SVCS
ELECTRICAL APPARATUS & EQPT WHOLESALERS
ELECTRICAL CURRENT CARRYING WIRING DEVICES
ELECTRICAL DISCHARGE MACHINING, EDM
ELECTRICAL EQPT & SPLYS
ELECTRICAL EQPT FOR ENGINES
ELECTRICAL EQPT REPAIR & MAINTENANCE
ELECTRICAL EQPT REPAIR SVCS
ELECTRICAL EQPT REPAIR SVCS: High Voltage
ELECTRICAL EQPT: Automotive, NEC
ELECTRICAL EQPT: Household
ELECTRICAL GOODS, WHOLESALE: Batteries, Storage, Indl
ELECTRICAL GOODS, WHOLESALE: Burglar Alarm Systems
ELECTRICAL GOODS, WHOLESALE: Connectors
ELECTRICAL GOODS, WHOLESALE: Electrical Appliances,
  Major
ELECTRICAL GOODS, WHOLESALE: Electronic Parts
ELECTRICAL GOODS, WHOLESALE: Facsimile Or Fax Eqpt
ELECTRICAL GOODS, WHOLESALE: Fire Alarm Systems
ELECTRICAL GOODS, WHOLESALE: Garbage Disposals
ELECTRICAL GOODS, WHOLESALE: Generators
ELECTRICAL GOODS, WHOLESALE: Light Bulbs & Related
  Splys
ELECTRICAL GOODS, WHOLESALE: Lighting Fittings & Ac-
  cess
ELECTRICAL GOODS, WHOLESALE: Lighting Fixtures,
  Comm & Indl
ELECTRICAL GOODS, WHOLESALE: Mobile telephone Eqpt
ELECTRICAL GOODS, WHOLESALE: Motors
ELECTRICAL GOODS, WHOLESALE: Rectifiers
ELECTRICAL GOODS, WHOLESALE: Security Control Eqpt
  & Systems
ELECTRICAL GOODS, WHOLESALE: Signaling, Eqpt
ELECTRICAL GOODS, WHOLESALE: Switchgear
ELECTRICAL GOODS, WHOLESALE: Video Eqpt
ELECTRICAL GOODS, WHOLESALE: Wire & Cable
ELECTRICAL MEASURING INSTRUMENT REPAIR & CALI-
  BRATION SVCS
ELECTRICAL SPLYS
ELECTRICAL SUPPLIES: Porcelain
ELECTROLYZING SVC: Steel, Light Gauge
ELECTROMEDICAL EQPT
ELECTRONIC COMPONENTS
ELECTRONIC DEVICES: Solid State, NEC
ELECTRONIC EQPT REPAIR SVCS
ELECTRONIC LOADS & POWER SPLYS
ELECTRONIC PARTS & EQPT WHOLESALERS

ELECTRONIC TRAINING DEVICES
ELECTROPLATING & PLATING SVC
ELEMENTARY & SECONDARY SCHOOLS, SPECIAL EDU-
  CATION
ELEVATORS & EQPT
ELEVATORS WHOLESALERS
ELEVATORS: Automobile
ELEVATORS: Installation & Conversion
ELEVATORS: Stair, Motor Powered
EMBLEMS: Embroidered
EMBOSSING SVC: Paper
EMBROIDERING & ART NEEDLEWORK FOR THE TRADE
EMBROIDERING SVC
EMBROIDERY ADVERTISING SVCS
EMBROIDERY KITS
EMERGENCY ALARMS
EMPLOYMENT AGENCY SVCS
ENAMELING SVC: Metal Prdts, Including Porcelain
ENCLOSURES: Electronic
ENGINE PARTS & ACCESS: Internal Combustion
ENGINE REBUILDING: Diesel
ENGINEERING SVCS
ENGINEERING SVCS: Acoustical
ENGINEERING SVCS: Building Construction
ENGINEERING SVCS: Electrical Or Electronic
ENGINEERING SVCS: Energy conservation
ENGINEERING SVCS: Heating & Ventilation
ENGINEERING SVCS: Industrial
ENGINEERING SVCS: Machine Tool Design
ENGINEERING SVCS: Mechanical
ENGINEERING SVCS: Petroleum
ENGINEERING SVCS: Structural
ENGINES & ENGINE PARTS: Guided Missile, Research &
  Develpt
ENGINES: Diesel & Semi-Diesel Or Duel Fuel
ENGINES: Gasoline, NEC
ENGINES: Internal Combustion, NEC
ENGINES: Steam
ENGRAVING SVC, NEC
ENGRAVING SVC: Jewelry & Personal Goods
ENGRAVING SVCS
ENGRAVING: Steel line, For The Printing Trade
ENGRAVINGS: Plastic
ENTERTAINMENT SVCS
ENVELOPES
ENVELOPES WHOLESALERS
ENZYMES
EPOXY RESINS
EQUIPMENT: Pedestrian Traffic Control
EQUIPMENT: Rental & Leasing, NEC
ETCHING & ENGRAVING SVC
ETCHING SVC: Metal
ETHANOLAMINES
ETHYLENE-PROPYLENE RUBBERS: EPDM Polymers
EXCAVATING EQPT
EXERCISE SALON
EXHAUST SYSTEMS: Eqpt & Parts
EXPLOSIVES
EXPLOSIVES, EXC AMMO & FIREWORKS WHOLESALERS
EXPLOSIVES, FUSES & DETONATORS: Primary explosives
EXPLOSIVES: Black Powder
EXTERMINATING PRDTS: Household Or Indl Use
EXTRACTS, FLAVORING
EXTRACTS: Dying Or Tanning, Natural
EYEGLASSES
EYEGLASSES: Sunglasses
EYES: Artificial

F

FABRIC STORES
FABRICATED METAL PRODUCTS, NEC
FABRICS & CLOTH: Quilted
FABRICS & YARN: Plastic Coated
FABRICS: Acrylic, Broadwoven
FABRICS: Alpacas, Cotton
FABRICS: Alpacas, Mohair, Woven
FABRICS: Apparel & Outerwear, Broadwoven
FABRICS: Apparel & Outerwear, Cotton
FABRICS: Basket Weave, Cotton
FABRICS: Bonded-Fiber, Exc Felt
FABRICS: Broadwoven, Cotton
FABRICS: Broadwoven, Synthetic Manmade Fiber & Silk
FABRICS: Canvas
FABRICS: Canvas & Heavy Coarse, Cotton
FABRICS: Chemically Coated & Treated

FABRICS: Coated Or Treated
FABRICS: Denims
FABRICS: Drills, Cotton
FABRICS: Fiberglass, Broadwoven
FABRICS: Furniture Denim
FABRICS: Glass & Fiberglass, Broadwoven
FABRICS: Laminated
FABRICS: Metallized
FABRICS: Nonwoven
FABRICS: Print, Cotton
FABRICS: Resin Or Plastic Coated
FABRICS: Slip Cover, From Manmade Fiber Or Silk
FABRICS: Stockinettes, Knit
FABRICS: Trimmings
FABRICS: Upholstery, Cotton
FABRICS: Upholstery, Wool
FABRICS: Wool, Broadwoven
FACE PLATES
FACILITIES SUPPORT SVCS
FACILITY RENTAL & PARTY PLANNING SVCS
FAMILY CLOTHING STORES
FANS, BLOWING: Indl Or Commercial
FANS, VENTILATING: Indl Or Commercial
FANS: Ceiling
FARM & GARDEN MACHINERY WHOLESALERS
FARM MACHINERY REPAIR SVCS
FARM PRDTS, RAW MATERIALS, WHOLESALE: Feathers
FARM SPLY STORES
FARM SPLYS WHOLESALERS
FARM SPLYS, WHOLESALE: Equestrian Eqpt
FARM SPLYS, WHOLESALE: Feed
FARM SPLYS, WHOLESALE: Fertilizers & Agricultural Chemicals
FARM SPLYS, WHOLESALE: Garden Splys
FARM SPLYS, WHOLESALE: Insecticides
FARM SPLYS, WHOLESALE: Limestone, Agricultural
FARM SPLYS, WHOLESALE: Saddlery
FASTENERS: Brads, Alum, Brass/Other Nonferrous Metal/Wire
FASTENERS: Metal
FASTENERS: Metal
FASTENERS: Notions, NEC
FASTENERS: Wire, Made From Purchased Wire
FAUCETS & SPIGOTS: Metal & Plastic
FEATHERS & FEATHER PRODUCTS
FENCES & FENCING MATERIALS
FENCES OR POSTS: Ornamental Iron Or Steel
FENCING DEALERS
FENCING MATERIALS: Docks & Other Outdoor Prdts, Wood
FENCING MATERIALS: Plastic
FENCING MATERIALS: Wood
FENCING: Chain Link
FENDERS: Automobile, Stamped Or Pressed Metal
FERTILIZER MINERAL MINING
FERTILIZER, AGRICULTURAL: Wholesalers
FERTILIZERS: NEC
FERTILIZERS: Nitrogenous
FERTILIZERS: Phosphatic
FIBER & FIBER PRDTS: Organic, Noncellulose
FIBER & FIBER PRDTS: Protein
FIBER & FIBER PRDTS: Soybean
FIBER & FIBER PRDTS: Synthetic Cellulosic
FIBER & FIBER PRDTS: Vinyl
FIBERS: Carbon & Graphite
FILM & SHEET: Unsupported Plastic
FILM DEVELOPING SVCS
FILM PROCESSING & FINISHING LABORATORY
FILM: Motion Picture
FILTER ELEMENTS: Fluid & Hydraulic Line
FILTERING MEDIA: Pottery
FILTERS
FILTERS & SOFTENERS: Water, Household
FILTERS: Air
FILTERS: Air Intake, Internal Combustion Engine, Exc Auto
FILTERS: General Line, Indl
FILTRATION DEVICES: Electronic
FINANCIAL INVESTMENT ADVICE
FINANCIAL SVCS
FINDINGS & TRIMMINGS: Fabric
FINGERNAILS, ARTIFICIAL
FINGERPRINTING SVCS
FINISHING AGENTS
FINISHING SVCS
FIRE ALARM MAINTENANCE & MONITORING SVCS
FIRE ARMS, SMALL: Guns Or Gun Parts, 30 mm & Below

FIRE ARMS, SMALL: Pistols Or Pistol Parts, 30 mm & below
FIRE CONTROL EQPT REPAIR SVCS, MILITARY
FIRE CONTROL OR BOMBING EQPT: Electronic
FIRE DETECTION SYSTEMS
FIRE EXTINGUISHER SVC
FIRE EXTINGUISHERS, WHOLESALE
FIRE OR BURGLARY RESISTIVE PRDTS
FIRE PROTECTION EQPT
FIREARMS & AMMUNITION, EXC SPORTING, WHOLESALE
FIREARMS: Large, Greater Than 30mm
FIREARMS: Small, 30mm or Less
FIREPLACE EQPT & ACCESS
FIREWORKS
FIREWORKS DISPLAY SVCS
FIRST AID SPLYS, WHOLESALE
FISH & SEAFOOD PROCESSORS: Fresh Or Frozen
FISHING EQPT REPAIR SVCS
FISHING EQPT: Lures
FITTINGS & ASSEMBLIES: Hose & Tube, Hydraulic Or Pneumatic
FITTINGS: Pipe
FITTINGS: Pipe, Fabricated
FIXTURES & EQPT: Kitchen, Metal, Exc Cast Aluminum
FIXTURES: Cut Stone
FLAGPOLES
FLARES
FLAT GLASS: Sheet
FLAT GLASS: Tempered
FLAT GLASS: Window, Clear & Colored
FLOCKING METAL PRDTS
FLOOR COVERING STORES
FLOOR COVERING STORES: Carpets
FLOOR COVERINGS WHOLESALERS
FLOOR COVERINGS: Rubber
FLOOR COVERINGS: Textile Fiber
FLOOR COVERINGS: Tile, Support Plastic
FLOOR COVERINGS: Twisted Paper, Grass, Reed, Coir, Etc
FLOORING & SIDING: Metal
FLOORING: Baseboards, Wood
FLOORING: Hard Surface
FLOORING: Hardwood
FLOORING: Rubber
FLORIST: Flowers, Fresh
FLORISTS
FLORISTS' SPLYS, WHOLESALE
FLOWERS & NURSERY STOCK, WHOLESALE
FLOWERS, ARTIFICIAL, WHOLESALE
FLOWERS: Artificial & Preserved
FLUES & PIPES: Stove Or Furnace
FLUID METERS & COUNTING DEVICES
FLUID POWER PUMPS & MOTORS
FLUID POWER VALVES & HOSE FITTINGS
FM & AM RADIO TUNERS
FOAM CHARGE MIXTURES
FOAM RUBBER
FOAMS & RUBBER, WHOLESALE
FOIL & LEAF: Metal
FOIL: Laminated To Paper Or Other Materials
FOLIAGE: Artificial & Preserved
FOOD COLORINGS
FOOD PRDTS, CANNED OR FRESH PACK: Vegetable Juices
FOOD PRDTS, CANNED: Barbecue Sauce
FOOD PRDTS, CANNED: Beans & Bean Sprouts
FOOD PRDTS, CANNED: Broth, Chicken
FOOD PRDTS, CANNED: Chili Sauce, Tomato
FOOD PRDTS, CANNED: Fruit Butters
FOOD PRDTS, CANNED: Fruits
FOOD PRDTS, CANNED: Fruits
FOOD PRDTS, CANNED: Jams, Including Imitation
FOOD PRDTS, CANNED: Jams, Jellies & Preserves
FOOD PRDTS, CANNED: Mexican, NEC
FOOD PRDTS, CANNED: Soups, Exc Seafood
FOOD PRDTS, CANNED: Spaghetti & Other Pasta Sauce
FOOD PRDTS, CANNED: Tomatoes
FOOD PRDTS, CONFECTIONERY, WHOLESALE: Snack Foods
FOOD PRDTS, CONFECTIONERY, WHOLESALE: Syrups, Fountain
FOOD PRDTS, FISH & SEAFOOD: Caviar, Preserved
FOOD PRDTS, FISH & SEAFOOD: Prepared Cakes & Sticks
FOOD PRDTS, FISH & SEAFOOD: Seafood, Frozen, Prepared
FOOD PRDTS, FROZEN: Fruits, Juices & Vegetables
FOOD PRDTS, FROZEN: NEC

FOOD PRDTS, FROZEN: Pizza
FOOD PRDTS, FROZEN: Snack Items
FOOD PRDTS, FROZEN: Soups
FOOD PRDTS, FRUITS & VEGETABLES, FRESH, WHOLESALE: Vegetable
FOOD PRDTS, MEAT & MEAT PRDTS, WHOLESALE: Cured Or Smoked
FOOD PRDTS, MEAT & MEAT PRDTS, WHOLESALE: Fresh
FOOD PRDTS, WHOL: Canned Goods, Fruit, Veg, Seafood/Meats
FOOD PRDTS, WHOLESALE: Beverages, Exc Coffee & Tea
FOOD PRDTS, WHOLESALE: Chocolate
FOOD PRDTS, WHOLESALE: Coffee & Tea
FOOD PRDTS, WHOLESALE: Coffee, Green Or Roasted
FOOD PRDTS, WHOLESALE: Cooking Oils & Shortenings
FOOD PRDTS, WHOLESALE: Corn
FOOD PRDTS, WHOLESALE: Flour
FOOD PRDTS, WHOLESALE: Grain Elevators
FOOD PRDTS, WHOLESALE: Grains
FOOD PRDTS, WHOLESALE: Health
FOOD PRDTS, WHOLESALE: Honey
FOOD PRDTS, WHOLESALE: Organic & Diet
FOOD PRDTS, WHOLESALE: Specialty
FOOD PRDTS, WHOLESALE: Spices & Seasonings
FOOD PRDTS, WHOLESALE: Syrups, Exc Fountain Use
FOOD PRDTS, WHOLESALE: Water, Distilled
FOOD PRDTS: Animal & marine fats & oils
FOOD PRDTS: Baking Powder
FOOD PRDTS: Baking Powder, Soda, Yeast & Leavenings
FOOD PRDTS: Breakfast Bars
FOOD PRDTS: Cereals
FOOD PRDTS: Chicken, Processed, Fresh
FOOD PRDTS: Chili Pepper Or Powder
FOOD PRDTS: Coconut Oil
FOOD PRDTS: Coffee
FOOD PRDTS: Coffee Roasting, Exc Wholesale Grocers
FOOD PRDTS: Corn Chips & Other Corn-Based Snacks
FOOD PRDTS: Corn Flour
FOOD PRDTS: Corn Meal
FOOD PRDTS: Corn Oil, Crude
FOOD PRDTS: Corn Oil, Refined
FOOD PRDTS: Cottonseed Oil, Cake & Meal
FOOD PRDTS: Dessert Mixes & Fillings
FOOD PRDTS: Doughs & Batters
FOOD PRDTS: Dressings, Salad, Raw & Cooked Exc Dry Mixes
FOOD PRDTS: Duck Slaughtering & Processing
FOOD PRDTS: Ducks, Processed, NEC
FOOD PRDTS: Edible Oil Prdts, Exc Corn Oil
FOOD PRDTS: Edible fats & oils
FOOD PRDTS: Eggs, Processed
FOOD PRDTS: Eggs, Processed, Frozen
FOOD PRDTS: Flavored Ices, Frozen
FOOD PRDTS: Flour & Other Grain Mill Products
FOOD PRDTS: Flour Mixes & Doughs
FOOD PRDTS: Flours & Flour Mixes, From Purchased Flour
FOOD PRDTS: Fruit Juices
FOOD PRDTS: Fruits & Vegetables, Pickled
FOOD PRDTS: Fruits, Dehydrated Or Dried
FOOD PRDTS: Honey
FOOD PRDTS: Ice, Blocks
FOOD PRDTS: Ice, Cubes
FOOD PRDTS: Macaroni, Noodles, Spaghetti, Pasta, Etc
FOOD PRDTS: Meat Meal & Tankage, Inedible
FOOD PRDTS: Mixes, Pancake From Purchased Flour
FOOD PRDTS: Mixes, Pizza
FOOD PRDTS: Nuts & Seeds
FOOD PRDTS: Oils & Fats, Animal
FOOD PRDTS: Olive Oil
FOOD PRDTS: Onions, Pickled
FOOD PRDTS: Pasta, Rice/Potatoes, Uncooked, Pkgd
FOOD PRDTS: Pasta, Uncooked, Packaged With Other Ingredients
FOOD PRDTS: Peanut Butter
FOOD PRDTS: Pickles, Vinegar
FOOD PRDTS: Popcorn, Unpopped
FOOD PRDTS: Potato & Corn Chips & Similar Prdts
FOOD PRDTS: Potato Chips & Other Potato-Based Snacks
FOOD PRDTS: Preparations
FOOD PRDTS: Prepared Sauces, Exc Tomato Based
FOOD PRDTS: Prepared Seafood Sauces Exc Tomato & Dry
FOOD PRDTS: Rabbit, Processed, Frozen
FOOD PRDTS: Salads
FOOD PRDTS: Sandwiches
FOOD PRDTS: Seasonings & Spices

FOOD PRDTS: Soup Mixes, Dried
FOOD PRDTS: Soybean Protein Concentrates & Isolates
FOOD PRDTS: Starch, Corn
FOOD PRDTS: Starches
FOOD PRDTS: Sugar, Maple, Indl
FOOD PRDTS: Syrup, Maple
FOOD PRDTS: Syrup, Sorghum, For Sweetening
FOOD PRDTS: Tea
FOOD PRDTS: Tortillas
FOOD PRDTS: Turkey, Processed, NEC
FOOD PRDTS: Vegetable Oil Mills, NEC
FOOD PRDTS: Wheat Flour
FOOD PRDTS: Wheat gluten
FOOD PRODUCTS MACHINERY
FOOD STORES: Grocery, Chain
FOOD STORES: Grocery, Independent
FOOD STORES: Supermarkets, Chain
FOOD STORES: Supermarkets, Independent
FOOD WARMING EQPT: Commercial
FOOTWEAR, WHOLESALE: Boots
FORGINGS
FORGINGS: Anchors
FORGINGS: Armor Plate, Iron Or Steel
FORGINGS: Automotive & Internal Combustion Engine
FORGINGS: Bearing & Bearing Race, Nonferrous
FORGINGS: Construction Or Mining Eqpt, Ferrous
FORGINGS: Engine Or Turbine, Nonferrous
FORGINGS: Gear & Chain
FORGINGS: Iron & Steel
FORGINGS: Machinery, Nonferrous
FORGINGS: Metal , Ornamental, Ferrous
FORGINGS: Nonferrous
FORGINGS: Nuclear Power Plant, Ferrous
FORGINGS: Pump & Compressor, Ferrous
FORMS HANDLING EQPT
FORMS: Concrete, Sheet Metal
FOUNDRIES: Aluminum
FOUNDRIES: Brass, Bronze & Copper
FOUNDRIES: Gray & Ductile Iron
FOUNDRIES: Iron
FOUNDRIES: Nonferrous
FOUNDRIES: Steel
FOUNDRIES: Steel Investment
FOUNDRY MACHINERY & EQPT
FRACTIONATION PRDTS OF CRUDE PETROLEUM, HY-
   DROCARBONS, NEC
FRAMES & FRAMING WHOLESALE
FRAMES: Chair, Metal
FREIGHT TRANSPORTATION ARRANGEMENTS
FREON
FRICTION MATERIAL, MADE FROM POWDERED METAL
FUEL ADDITIVES
FUEL BRIQUETTES & WAXES
FUEL DEALERS: Coal
FUEL DEALERS: Wood
FUEL OIL DEALERS
FUELS: Diesel
FUELS: Ethanol
FUELS: Nuclear
FUELS: Oil
FUNERAL HOMES & SVCS
FUNGICIDES OR HERBICIDES
FUR APPAREL STORES
FUR STRIPPING
FUR: Coats & Other Apparel
FURNACE CASINGS: Sheet Metal
FURNACES & OVENS: Fuel-Fired
FURNACES & OVENS: Indl
FURNACES: Indl, Electric
FURNACES: Warm Air, Electric
FURNITURE & CABINET STORES: Cabinets, Custom Work
FURNITURE & CABINET STORES: Custom
FURNITURE & FIXTURES Factory
FURNITURE COMPONENTS: Porcelain Enameled
FURNITURE PARTS: Metal
FURNITURE REPAIR & MAINTENANCE SVCS
FURNITURE STOCK & PARTS: Carvings, Wood
FURNITURE STOCK & PARTS: Dimension Stock, Hardwood
FURNITURE STOCK & PARTS: Frames, Upholstered Furni-
   ture, Wood
FURNITURE STOCK & PARTS: Hardwood
FURNITURE STOCK & PARTS: Turnings, Wood
FURNITURE STORES
FURNITURE STORES: Custom Made, Exc Cabinets
FURNITURE STORES: Office

FURNITURE STORES: Outdoor & Garden
FURNITURE WHOLESALERS
FURNITURE, GARDEN: Concrete
FURNITURE, HOUSEHOLD: Wholesalers
FURNITURE, MATTRESSES: Wholesalers
FURNITURE, OFFICE: Wholesalers
FURNITURE, OUTDOOR & LAWN: Wholesalers
FURNITURE, WHOLESALE: Beds & Bedding
FURNITURE, WHOLESALE: Dining Room
FURNITURE, WHOLESALE: Filing Units
FURNITURE, WHOLESALE: Theater Seats
FURNITURE: Bar furniture
FURNITURE: Bedroom, Metal
FURNITURE: Bedroom, Wood
FURNITURE: Bookcases & Partitions, Office, Exc Wood
FURNITURE: Bookcases, Wood
FURNITURE: Box Springs, Assembled
FURNITURE: Chair & Couch Springs, Assembled
FURNITURE: Chairs, Folding
FURNITURE: Chairs, Household Upholstered
FURNITURE: Chairs, Household Wood
FURNITURE: Chairs, Household, Metal
FURNITURE: Chairs, Office Exc Wood
FURNITURE: Chairs, Office Wood
FURNITURE: Console Tables, Wood
FURNITURE: Cribs, Metal
FURNITURE: Cut Stone
FURNITURE: Desks & Tables, Office, Exc Wood
FURNITURE: Desks & Tables, Office, Wood
FURNITURE: Desks, Household, Wood
FURNITURE: Desks, Metal
FURNITURE: Desks, Wood
FURNITURE: Dining Room, Wood
FURNITURE: End Tables, Wood
FURNITURE: Fiberglass & Plastic
FURNITURE: Foundations & Platforms
FURNITURE: Garden, Exc Wood, Metal, Stone Or Concrete
FURNITURE: High Chairs, Children's, Wood
FURNITURE: Hospital
FURNITURE: Hotel
FURNITURE: Household, Metal
FURNITURE: Household, NEC
FURNITURE: Household, Upholstered On Metal Frames
FURNITURE: Household, Upholstered, Exc Wood Or Metal
FURNITURE: Household, Wood
FURNITURE: Hydraulic Barber & Beauty Shop Chairs
FURNITURE: Institutional, Exc Wood
FURNITURE: Juvenile, Wood
FURNITURE: Kitchen & Dining Room
FURNITURE: Kitchen & Dining Room, Metal
FURNITURE: Lawn & Garden, Except Wood & Metal
FURNITURE: Lawn & Garden, Metal
FURNITURE: Lawn, Wood
FURNITURE: Living Room, Upholstered On Wood Frames
FURNITURE: Mattresses & Foundations
FURNITURE: Mattresses, Box & Bedsprings
FURNITURE: Mattresses, Innerspring Or Box Spring
FURNITURE: NEC
FURNITURE: Novelty, Wood
FURNITURE: Nursery, Wood
FURNITURE: Office Panel Systems, Exc Wood
FURNITURE: Office, Exc Wood
FURNITURE: Office, Wood
FURNITURE: Outdoor, Wood
FURNITURE: Picnic Tables Or Benches, Park
FURNITURE: Recliners, Upholstered On Wood Frames
FURNITURE: Restaurant
FURNITURE: Rockers, Wood, Exc Upholstered
FURNITURE: School
FURNITURE: Screens, privacy, Wood
FURNITURE: Silverware Chests, Wood
FURNITURE: Sofa Beds Or Convertible Sofas)
FURNITURE: Storage Chests, Household, Wood
FURNITURE: Table Tops, Marble
FURNITURE: Tables & Table Tops, Wood
FURNITURE: Tables, Household, Metal
FURNITURE: Tables, Office, Wood
FURNITURE: Theater
FURNITURE: Unfinished, Wood
FURNITURE: Upholstered
FURNITURE: Vehicle
FURNITURE: Waterbed Frames, Wood
FURNITURE: Wicker & Rattan
FUSES & FUSE EQPT
Furs

G

GAMES & TOYS: Baby Carriages & Restraint Seats
GAMES & TOYS: Banks
GAMES & TOYS: Bingo Boards
GAMES & TOYS: Board Games, Children's & Adults'
GAMES & TOYS: Books, Picture & Cutout
GAMES & TOYS: Child Restraint Seats, Automotive
GAMES & TOYS: Craft & Hobby Kits & Sets
GAMES & TOYS: Darts & Dart Games
GAMES & TOYS: Dolls & Doll Clothing
GAMES & TOYS: Dolls, Exc Stuffed Toy Animals
GAMES & TOYS: Electronic
GAMES & TOYS: Hobby Horses
GAMES & TOYS: Kits, Science, Incl Microscopes/Chemistry
   Sets
GAMES & TOYS: Models, Airplane, Toy & Hobby
GAMES & TOYS: Models, Automobile & Truck, Toy & Hobby
GAMES & TOYS: Models, Railroad, Toy & Hobby
GAMES & TOYS: Puzzles
GAMES & TOYS: Strollers, Baby, Vehicle
GARBAGE CONTAINERS: Plastic
GAS & OIL FIELD EXPLORATION SVCS
GAS & OIL FIELD SVCS, NEC
GAS APPLIANCE REPAIR SVCS
GAS FIELD MACHINERY & EQPT
GAS PROCESSING SVC
GAS PRODUCTION & DISTRIBUTION: Coke Oven
GAS: Refinery
GASES & LIQUIDIED PETROLEUM GASES
GASES: Acetylene
GASES: Carbon Dioxide
GASES: Flourinated Hydrocarbon
GASES: Helium
GASES: Indl
GASES: Neon
GASES: Nitrogen
GASES: Oxygen
GASKET MATERIALS
GASKETS
GASKETS & SEALING DEVICES
GASOLINE FILLING STATIONS
GATES: Ornamental Metal
GAUGE BLOCKS
GAUGES
GEARS
GEARS: Power Transmission, Exc Auto
GENEALOGICAL INVESTIGATION SVCS
GENERAL MERCHANDISE STORES, NEC
GENERAL MERCHANDISE, NONDURABLE, WHOLESALE
GENERATING APPARATUS & PARTS: Electrical
GENERATION EQPT: Electronic
GENERATOR SETS: Motor
GENERATORS: Electric
GENERATORS: Vehicles, Gas-Electric Or Oil-Electric
GIFT SHOP
GIFT WRAP: Paper, Made From Purchased Materials
GIFT, NOVELTY & SOUVENIR STORES: Artcraft & carvings
GIFT, NOVELTY & SOUVENIR STORES: Gifts & Novelties
GIFT, NOVELTY & SOUVENIR STORES: Trading Cards,
   Sports
GIFTS & NOVELTIES: Wholesalers
GLASS FABRICATORS
GLASS PRDTS, FROM PURCHASED GLASS: Glassware
GLASS PRDTS, FROM PURCHASED GLASS: Mirrored
GLASS PRDTS, FROM PURCHASED GLASS: Mirrors,
   Framed
GLASS PRDTS, FROM PURCHASED GLASS: Windshields
GLASS PRDTS, FROM PURCHD GLASS: Strengthened Or
   Reinforced
GLASS PRDTS, PRESSED OR BLOWN: Blocks & Bricks
GLASS PRDTS, PRESSED OR BLOWN: Bulbs, Electric
   Lights
GLASS PRDTS, PRESSED OR BLOWN: Candlesticks
GLASS PRDTS, PRESSED OR BLOWN: Furnishings & Ac-
   cess
GLASS PRDTS, PRESSED OR BLOWN: Glass Fibers, Textile
GLASS PRDTS, PRESSED OR BLOWN: Glassware, Art Or
   Decorative
GLASS PRDTS, PRESSED OR BLOWN: Glassware, Novelty
GLASS PRDTS, PRESSED OR BLOWN: Reflector, Lighting
   Eqpt
GLASS PRDTS, PURCHASED GLASS: Glassware, Scien-
   tific/Tech

GLASS PRDTS, PURCHSD GLASS: Ornamental, Cut, Engraved/Décor
GLASS STORE: Leaded Or Stained
GLASS STORES
GLASS: Fiber
GLASS: Flat
GLASS: Insulating
GLASS: Leaded
GLASS: Pressed & Blown, NEC
GLASS: Stained
GLASS: Tempered
GLASSWARE STORES
GLASSWARE: Cut & Engraved
GLOBAL POSITIONING SYSTEMS & EQPT
GLOVES: Fabric
GLOVES: Leather
GLOVES: Woven Or Knit, From Purchased Materials
GLYCERIN
GO-CART DEALERS
GOLF CARTS: Wholesalers
GOLF CLUB & EQPT REPAIR SVCS
GOLF COURSES: Public
GOLF EQPT
GOLF GOODS & EQPT
GOVERNMENT, LEGISLATIVE BODIES: Local
GOVERNORS: Diesel Engine, Pump
GRADING SVCS
GRAIN & FIELD BEANS WHOLESALERS
GRANITE: Cut & Shaped
GRANITE: Dimension
GRAPHIC ARTS & RELATED DESIGN SVCS
GRAPHIC LAYOUT SVCS: Printed Circuitry
GRATINGS: Open Steel Flooring
GRATINGS: Tread, Fabricated Metal
GRAVEL & PEBBLE MINING
GRAVEL MINING
GREASES & INEDIBLE FATS, RENDERED
GREASES: Lubricating
GREENHOUSES: Prefabricated Metal
GRILLS & GRILLWORK: Woven Wire, Made From Purchased Wire
GRINDING SAND MINING
GRINDING SVC: Precision, Commercial Or Indl
GRINDING SVCS: Ophthalmic Lens, Exc Prescription
GRITS: Crushed & Broken
GROCERIES WHOLESALERS, NEC
GROCERIES, GENERAL LINE WHOLESALERS
GUARD PROTECTIVE SVCS
GUIDED MISSILES & SPACE VEHICLES
GUIDED MISSILES & SPACE VEHICLES: Research & Development
GUIDED MISSILES/SPACE VEHICLE PARTS/AUX EQPT: Research/Devel
GUM & WOOD CHEMICALS
GUN SVCS
GUTTERS
GUTTERS: Sheet Metal
GYPSUM BOARD
GYPSUM PRDTS

H

HAIR & HAIR BASED PRDTS
HAIR CARE PRDTS
HAIR CARE PRDTS: Tonics
HAIR DRESSING, FOR THE TRADE
HAIRDRESSERS
HAND TOOLS, NEC: Wholesalers
HANDBAGS
HANDBAGS: Men's
HANDBAGS: Women's
HANDLES: Wood
HANDYMAN SVCS
HANGERS: Garment, Wire
HARDBOARD & FIBERBOARD PRDTS
HARDWARE
HARDWARE & BUILDING PRDTS: Plastic
HARDWARE & EQPT: Stage, Exc Lighting
HARDWARE STORES
HARDWARE STORES: Builders'
HARDWARE STORES: Door Locks & Lock Sets
HARDWARE STORES: Pumps & Pumping Eqpt
HARDWARE STORES: Tools
HARDWARE WHOLESALERS
HARDWARE, WHOLESALE: Builders', NEC
HARDWARE, WHOLESALE: Chains

HARDWARE, WHOLESALE: Garden Tools, Hand
HARDWARE, WHOLESALE: Rivets
HARDWARE, WHOLESALE: Screws
HARDWARE, WHOLESALE: Security Devices, Locks
HARDWARE: Builders'
HARDWARE: Cabinet
HARDWARE: Casket
HARDWARE: Door Opening & Closing Devices, Exc Electrical
HARDWARE: Furniture
HARDWARE: Furniture, Builders' & Other Household
HARDWARE: Plastic
HARDWARE: Saddlery
HARNESS ASSEMBLIES: Cable & Wire
HARNESS WIRING SETS: Internal Combustion Engines
HARNESSES, HALTERS, SADDLERY & STRAPS
HEADPHONES: Radio
HEALTH AIDS: Exercise Eqpt
HEARING AIDS
HEARING TESTING SVCS
HEAT EXCHANGERS: After Or Inter Coolers Or Condensers, Etc
HEAT TREATING SALTS
HEAT TREATING: Metal
HEATER RADIANTS: Clay
HEATERS: Induction & Dielectric
HEATERS: Room & Wall, Including Radiators
HEATERS: Space, Exc Electric
HEATING & AIR CONDITIONING EQPT & SPLYS WHOLESALERS
HEATING & AIR CONDITIONING UNITS, COMBINATION
HEATING EQPT & SPLYS
HEATING EQPT: Complete
HEATING EQPT: Induction
HEATING SYSTEMS: Radiant, Indl Process
HEATING UNITS & DEVICES: Indl, Electric
HELICOPTERS
HELMETS: Athletic
HITCHES: Trailer
HOBBY GOODS, WHOLESALE
HOBBY, TOY & GAME STORES: Arts & Crafts & Splys
HOBBY, TOY & GAME STORES: Dolls & Access
HOBBY, TOY & GAME STORES: Toys & Games
HOISTING SLINGS
HOISTS
HOLDING COMPANIES: Investment, Exc Banks
HOLDING COMPANIES: Personal, Exc Banks
HOME ENTERTAINMENT EQPT: Electronic, NEC
HOME FURNISHINGS WHOLESALERS
HOME HEALTH CARE SVCS
HOME MOVIES DEVELOPING & PROCESSING
HOMEFURNISHING STORES: Metalware
HOMEFURNISHING STORES: Pottery
HOMEFURNISHING STORES: Venetian Blinds
HOMEFURNISHING STORES: Window Furnishings
HOMEFURNISHINGS & SPLYS, WHOLESALE: Decorative
HOMEFURNISHINGS, WHOLESALE: Blinds, Vertical
HOMEFURNISHINGS, WHOLESALE: Carpets
HOMEFURNISHINGS, WHOLESALE: Decorating Splys
HOMEFURNISHINGS, WHOLESALE: Draperies
HOMEFURNISHINGS, WHOLESALE: Pottery
HOMEFURNISHINGS, WHOLESALE: Wood Flooring
HOMES, MODULAR: Wooden
HOMES: Log Cabins
HONES
HONING & LAPPING MACHINES
HOOPS: Iron & Steel
HOPPERS: Sheet Metal
HORSE & PET ACCESSORIES: Textile
HORSE ACCESS: Harnesses & Riding Crops, Etc, Exc Leather
HORSE DRAWN VEHICLE REPAIR SVCS
HORSESHOEING SVCS
HORSESHOES
HOSE: Flexible Metal
HOSE: Plastic
HOSE: Pneumatic, Rubber Or Rubberized Fabric, NEC
HOSE: Rubber
HOSES & BELTING: Rubber & Plastic
HOT TUBS
HOTEL & MOTEL RESERVATION SVCS
HOTLINE
HOUSEHOLD APPLIANCE STORES
HOUSEHOLD APPLIANCE STORES: Air Cond Rm Units, Self-Contnd

HOUSEHOLD APPLIANCE STORES: Electric Household, Major
HOUSEHOLD ARTICLES, EXC KITCHEN: Pottery
HOUSEHOLD ARTICLES: Metal
HOUSEHOLD FURNISHINGS, NEC
HOUSEWARE STORES
HOUSEWARES, ELECTRIC: Appliances, Personal
HOUSEWARES, ELECTRIC: Cooking Appliances
HOUSEWARES, ELECTRIC: Heaters, Space
HOUSEWARES, ELECTRIC: Lighters, Cigarette
HOUSEWARES, ELECTRIC: Roasters
HOUSEWARES: Dishes, Plastic
HOUSEWARES: Kettles & Skillets, Cast Iron
HOUSING COMPONENTS: Prefabricated, Concrete
HOUSINGS: Motor
HUMIDIFIERS & DEHUMIDIFIERS
HYDRAULIC EQPT REPAIR SVC
Hard Rubber & Molded Rubber Prdts

I

ICE
ICE: Dry
IGNEOUS ROCK: Crushed & Broken
IGNITER GRAINS: Boron Potassium Nitrate
IGNITION SYSTEMS: Internal Combustion Engine
INCENSE
INCINERATORS
INDL & PERSONAL SVC PAPER WHOLESALERS
INDL & PERSONAL SVC PAPER, WHOL: Bags, Paper/Disp Plastic
INDL & PERSONAL SVC PAPER, WHOL: Boxes, Corrugtd/Solid Fiber
INDL & PERSONAL SVC PAPER, WHOL: Paper, Wrap/Coarse/Prdts
INDL & PERSONAL SVC PAPER, WHOLESALE: Boxes & Containers
INDL & PERSONAL SVC PAPER, WHOLESALE: Patterns, Paper
INDL & PERSONAL SVC PAPER, WHOLESALE: Sanitary Food
INDL & PERSONAL SVC PAPER, WHOLESALE: Shipping Splys
INDL EQPT CLEANING SVCS
INDL EQPT SVCS
INDL GASES WHOLESALERS
INDL MACHINERY & EQPT WHOLESALERS
INDL MACHINERY REPAIR & MAINTENANCE
INDL PATTERNS: Foundry Cores
INDL PATTERNS: Foundry Patternmaking
INDL PROCESS INSTRUMENTS: Absorp Analyzers, Infrared, X-Ray
INDL PROCESS INSTRUMENTS: Analyzers
INDL PROCESS INSTRUMENTS: Boiler Controls, Power & Marine
INDL PROCESS INSTRUMENTS: Data Loggers
INDL PROCESS INSTRUMENTS: Digital Display, Process Variables
INDL PROCESS INSTRUMENTS: Fluidic Devices, Circuit & Systems
INDL PROCESS INSTRUMENTS: Indl Flow & Measuring
INDL PROCESS INSTRUMENTS: On-Stream Gas Or Liquid Analysis
INDL PROCESS INSTRUMENTS: Temperature
INDL PROCESS INSTRUMENTS: Water Quality Monitoring/Cntrl Sys
INDL SPLYS WHOLESALERS
INDL SPLYS, WHOL: Fasteners, Incl Nuts, Bolts, Screws, Etc
INDL SPLYS, WHOLESALE: Abrasives
INDL SPLYS, WHOLESALE: Adhesives, Tape & Plasters
INDL SPLYS, WHOLESALE: Barrels, New Or Reconditioned
INDL SPLYS, WHOLESALE: Bearings
INDL SPLYS, WHOLESALE: Bins & Containers, Storage
INDL SPLYS, WHOLESALE: Fasteners & Fastening Eqpt
INDL SPLYS, WHOLESALE: Filters, Indl
INDL SPLYS, WHOLESALE: Fittings
INDL SPLYS, WHOLESALE: Gaskets
INDL SPLYS, WHOLESALE: Gaskets & Seals
INDL SPLYS, WHOLESALE: Gears
INDL SPLYS, WHOLESALE: Power Transmission, Eqpt & Apparatus
INDL SPLYS, WHOLESALE: Rope, Exc Wire
INDL SPLYS, WHOLESALE: Rubber Goods, Mechanical
INDL SPLYS, WHOLESALE: Seals
INDL SPLYS, WHOLESALE: Sewing Thread
INDL SPLYS, WHOLESALE: Signmaker Eqpt & Splys

INDL SPLYS, WHOLESALE: Tools
INDL SPLYS, WHOLESALE: Tools, NEC
INDL TOOL GRINDING SVCS
INDL TRUCK REPAIR SVCS
INDUCTORS
INDUSTRIAL & COMMERCIAL EQPT INSPECTION SVCS
INFORMATION RETRIEVAL SERVICES
INGOT, EXTRUSION: Extrusion ingot, aluminum: rolling mills
INGOTS: Steel
INK: Duplicating
INK: Letterpress Or Offset
INK: Printing
INSECTICIDES
INSECTICIDES & PESTICIDES
INSPECTION & TESTING SVCS
INSPECTION SVCS, TRANSPORTATION
INSTR, MEASURE & CONTROL: Gauge, Oil Pressure & Water Temp
INSTRUMENTS, LAB: Spectroscopic/Optical Properties Measuring
INSTRUMENTS, LABORATORY: Spectrometers
INSTRUMENTS, MEASURING & CNTRL: Radiation & Testing, Nuclear
INSTRUMENTS, MEASURING & CNTRL: Testing, Abrasion, Etc
INSTRUMENTS, MEASURING & CNTRLG: Thermometers/Temp Sensors
INSTRUMENTS, MEASURING & CONTROLLING: Breathalyzers
INSTRUMENTS, MEASURING & CONTROLLING: Ion Chambers
INSTRUMENTS, MEASURING & CONTROLLING: Leak Detection, Liquid
INSTRUMENTS, MEASURING & CONTROLLING: Polygraph
INSTRUMENTS, MEASURING & CONTROLLING: Weather Tracking
INSTRUMENTS, MEASURING/CNTRLNG: Med Diagnostic Sys, Nuclear
INSTRUMENTS, OPTICAL: Aiming Circles, Fire Control
INSTRUMENTS, OPTICAL: Glasses, Field Or Opera
INSTRUMENTS, OPTICAL: Magnifying, NEC
INSTRUMENTS, SURGICAL & MED: Needles & Syringes, Hypodermic
INSTRUMENTS, SURGICAL & MEDICAL: Blood & Bone Work
INSTRUMENTS, SURGICAL & MEDICAL: Blood Transfusion
INSTRUMENTS, SURGICAL & MEDICAL: Catheters
INSTRUMENTS, SURGICAL & MEDICAL: Inhalation Therapy
INSTRUMENTS, SURGICAL & MEDICAL: Lasers, Ophthalmic
INSTRUMENTS, SURGICAL & MEDICAL: Lasers, Surgical
INSTRUMENTS, SURGICAL & MEDICAL: Muscle Exercise, Ophthalmic
INSTRUMENTS: Analytical
INSTRUMENTS: Analyzers, Radio Apparatus, NEC
INSTRUMENTS: Analyzers, Spectrum
INSTRUMENTS: Differential Pressure, Indl
INSTRUMENTS: Electronic, Analog-Digital Converters
INSTRUMENTS: Eye Examination
INSTRUMENTS: Flow, Indl Process
INSTRUMENTS: Frequency Meters, Electrical, Mech & Electronic
INSTRUMENTS: Indl Process Control
INSTRUMENTS: Liquid Level, Indl Process
INSTRUMENTS: Measuring & Controlling
INSTRUMENTS: Measuring Electricity
INSTRUMENTS: Measuring, Electrical Energy
INSTRUMENTS: Medical & Surgical
INSTRUMENTS: Nautical
INSTRUMENTS: Power Measuring, Electrical
INSTRUMENTS: Pressure Measurement, Indl
INSTRUMENTS: Refractometers, Indl Process
INSTRUMENTS: Temperature Measurement, Indl
INSTRUMENTS: Test, Electrical, Engine
INSTRUMENTS: Test, Electronic & Electric Measurement
INSTRUMENTS: Test, Electronic & Electrical Circuits
INSTRUMENTS: Thermal Conductive, Indl
INSTRUMENTS: Vibration
INSULATION & CUSHIONING FOAM: Polystyrene
INSULATION & ROOFING MATERIALS: Wood, Reconstituted
INSULATION MATERIALS WHOLESALERS
INSULATION: Fiberglass
INSULATORS & INSULATION MATERIALS: Electrical
INSURANCE AGENTS, NEC
INTEGRATED CIRCUITS, SEMICONDUCTOR NETWORKS, ETC

INTERCOMMUNICATION EQPT REPAIR SVCS
INTERCOMMUNICATIONS SYSTEMS: Electric
INTERIOR DECORATING SVCS
INTERIOR DESIGN SVCS, NEC
INTRAVENOUS SOLUTIONS
INVERTERS: Nonrotating Electrical
INVESTORS, NEC
IRON & STEEL PRDTS: Hot-Rolled
IRON ORES

J

JANITORIAL EQPT & SPLYS WHOLESALERS
JEWELERS' FINDINGS/MTRLS: Gem Prep, Settings, Real/Imitation
JEWELRY & PRECIOUS STONES WHOLESALERS
JEWELRY APPAREL
JEWELRY FINDINGS & LAPIDARY WORK
JEWELRY FINDINGS WHOLESALERS
JEWELRY REPAIR SVCS
JEWELRY STORES
JEWELRY STORES: Precious Stones & Precious Metals
JEWELRY STORES: Watches
JEWELRY, PRECIOUS METAL: Cigar & Cigarette Access
JEWELRY, PRECIOUS METAL: Mountings & Trimmings
JEWELRY, PRECIOUS METAL: Rings, Finger
JEWELRY, PRECIOUS METAL: Settings & Mountings
JEWELRY, PRECIOUS METAL: Studs, Precious & Semi Metal/Stone
JEWELRY, WHOLESALE
JEWELRY: Decorative, Fashion & Costume
JEWELRY: Precious Metal
JIGS & FIXTURES
JOB PRINTING & NEWSPAPER PUBLISHING COMBINED
JOB TRAINING & VOCATIONAL REHABILITATION SVCS
JOB TRAINING SVCS
JOINTS & COUPLINGS
JOINTS: Expansion
JOISTS: Long-Span Series, Open Web Steel

K

KEYS: Machine
KILNS & FURNACES: Ceramic
KITCHEN & TABLE ARTICLES: Coarse Earthenware
KITCHEN CABINET STORES, EXC CUSTOM
KITCHEN CABINETS WHOLESALERS
KITCHEN UTENSILS: Food Handling & Processing Prdts, Wood
KITCHEN UTENSILS: Wooden
KITCHENWARE STORES
KNIVES: Agricultural Or indl

L

LABELS: Cotton, Printed
LABELS: Paper, Made From Purchased Materials
LABORATORIES, TESTING: Product Testing
LABORATORIES, TESTING: Product Testing, Safety/Performance
LABORATORIES: Biotechnology
LABORATORIES: Commercial Nonphysical Research
LABORATORIES: Dental
LABORATORIES: Dental & Medical X-Ray
LABORATORIES: Dental, Crown & Bridge Production
LABORATORIES: Electronic Research
LABORATORIES: Noncommercial Research
LABORATORIES: Physical Research, Commercial
LABORATORIES: Testing
LABORATORY APPARATUS & FURNITURE
LABORATORY APPARATUS, EXC HEATING & MEASURING
LABORATORY APPARATUS: Crushing & Grinding
LABORATORY APPARATUS: Physics, NEC
LABORATORY APPARATUS: Pipettes, Hemocytometer
LABORATORY CHEMICALS: Organic
LABORATORY EQPT: Chemical
LABORATORY EQPT: Clinical Instruments Exc Medical
LABORATORY EQPT: Sterilizers
LADDERS: Metal
LADDERS: Permanent Installation, Metal
LAMINATED PLASTICS: Plate, Sheet, Rod & Tubes
LAMINATING MATERIALS
LAMINATING SVCS
LAMP & LIGHT BULBS & TUBES
LAMP BULBS & TUBES, ELECTRIC: Light, Complete
LAMP BULBS & TUBES/PARTS, ELECTRIC: Generalized Applications

LAMPS: Incandescent, Filament
LAMPS: Ultraviolet
LAND SUBDIVIDERS & DEVELOPERS: Commercial
LAND SUBDIVISION & DEVELOPMENT
LANGUAGE SCHOOLS
LANTERNS
LAPIDARY WORK: Jewel Cut, Drill, Polish, Recut/Setting
LASER SYSTEMS & EQPT
LASERS: Welding, Drilling & Cutting Eqpt
LAUNDRY & GARMENT SVCS, NEC: Garment Alteration & Repair
LAUNDRY EQPT: Commercial
LAUNDRY EQPT: Household
LAUNDRY SVC: Treated Eqpt Sply, Mats, Rugs, Mops, Etc
LAWN & GARDEN EQPT
LAWN & GARDEN EQPT STORES
LAWN & GARDEN EQPT: Blowers & Vacuums
LAWN & GARDEN EQPT: Carts Or Wagons
LAWN & GARDEN EQPT: Grass Catchers, Lawn Mower
LAWN & GARDEN EQPT: Lawnmowers, Residential, Hand Or Power
LAWN & GARDEN EQPT: Tractors & Eqpt
LAWN MOWER REPAIR SHOP
LEAD
LEAD & ZINC
LEASING & RENTAL SVCS: Cranes & Aerial Lift Eqpt
LEASING & RENTAL: Construction & Mining Eqpt
LEASING & RENTAL: Medical Machinery & Eqpt
LEASING & RENTAL: Mobile Home Sites
LEASING & RENTAL: Modular Office Trailers
LEASING & RENTAL: Other Real Estate Property
LEASING & RENTAL: Trucks, Without Drivers
LEASING: Passenger Car
LEASING: Residential Buildings
LEATHER GOODS: Harnesses Or Harness Parts
LEATHER GOODS: Holsters
LEATHER GOODS: NEC
LEATHER GOODS: Personal
LEATHER GOODS: Saddles Or Parts
LEATHER GOODS: Straps
LEATHER GOODS: Wallets
LEATHER TANNING & FINISHING
LEATHER: Accessory Prdts
LEATHER: Bookbinders'
LEATHER: Bridal
LEATHER: Equestrian Prdts
LEGAL & TAX SVCS
LEGAL OFFICES & SVCS
LESSORS: Farm Land
LICENSE TAGS: Automobile, Stamped Metal
LIGHT SENSITIVE DEVICES: Solid State
LIGHTING EQPT: Bicycle Lamps
LIGHTING EQPT: Flashlights
LIGHTING EQPT: Locomotive & Railroad Car Lights
LIGHTING EQPT: Miners' Lamps
LIGHTING EQPT: Motor Vehicle
LIGHTING EQPT: Motor Vehicle, Flasher Lights
LIGHTING EQPT: Motor Vehicle, Headlights
LIGHTING EQPT: Motor Vehicle, NEC
LIGHTING EQPT: Reflectors, Metal, For Lighting Eqpt
LIGHTING EQPT: Searchlights
LIGHTING EQPT: Spotlights
LIGHTING FIXTURES WHOLESALERS
LIGHTING FIXTURES, NEC
LIGHTING FIXTURES: Decorative Area
LIGHTING FIXTURES: Fluorescent, Commercial
LIGHTING FIXTURES: Indl & Commercial
LIGHTING FIXTURES: Motor Vehicle
LIGHTING FIXTURES: Residential
LIGHTING FIXTURES: Residential, Electric
LIGHTING MAINTENANCE SVC
LIME
LIMESTONE: Crushed & Broken
LIMESTONE: Cut & Shaped
LIMESTONE: Dimension
LIMESTONE: Ground
LINEN SPLY SVC: Non-Clothing
LINEN SPLY SVC: Uniform
LINERS & COVERS: Fabric
LIPSTICK
LIQUEFIED PETROLEUM GAS DEALERS
LITHOGRAPHIC PLATES
LIVESTOCK WHOLESALERS, NEC
LOCK & KEY SVCS
LOCKERS

LOCKS
LOCKS & LOCK SETS, WHOLESALE
LOCKS: Coin-Operated
LOCKS: Safe & Vault, Metal
LOCKSMITHS
LOCOMOTIVES & PARTS
LOGGING
LOGGING CAMPS & CONTRACTORS
LOGGING: Fuel Wood Harvesting
LOGGING: Timber, Cut At Logging Camp
LOGGING: Veneer Logs
LOGGING: Wood Chips, Produced In The Field
LOOSELEAF BINDERS
LOOSELEAF BINDERS: Forms & Fillers, Ruled Or Printed Only
LOTIONS OR CREAMS: Face
LOTIONS: SHAVING
LUBRICANTS: Corrosion Preventive
LUBRICATING EQPT: Indl
LUBRICATING OIL & GREASE WHOLESALERS
LUBRICATING SYSTEMS: Centralized
LUBRICATION SYSTEMS & EQPT
LUGGAGE & BRIEFCASES
LUGGAGE & LEATHER GOODS STORES
LUGGAGE: Traveling Bags
LUMBER & BLDG MATLS DEALER, RET: Electric Constructn Matls
LUMBER & BLDG MATRLS DEALERS, RET: Bath Fixtures, Eqpt/Sply
LUMBER & BLDG MTRLS DEALERS, RET: Closets, Interiors/Access
LUMBER & BLDG MTRLS DEALERS, RET: Doors, Storm, Wood/Metal
LUMBER & BLDG MTRLS DEALERS, RET: Planing Mill Prdts/Lumber
LUMBER & BLDG MTRLS DEALERS, RET: Windows, Storm, Wood/Metal
LUMBER & BUILDING MATERIAL DEALERS, RETAIL: Roofing Material
LUMBER & BUILDING MATERIALS DEALER, RET: Door & Window Prdts
LUMBER & BUILDING MATERIALS DEALER, RET: Masonry Matls/Splys
LUMBER & BUILDING MATERIALS DEALERS, RET: Solar Heating Eqpt
LUMBER & BUILDING MATERIALS DEALERS, RETAIL: Brick
LUMBER & BUILDING MATERIALS DEALERS, RETAIL: Cement
LUMBER & BUILDING MATERIALS DEALERS, RETAIL: Countertops
LUMBER & BUILDING MATERIALS DEALERS, RETAIL: Lime & Plaster
LUMBER & BUILDING MATERIALS DEALERS, RETAIL: Modular Homes
LUMBER & BUILDING MATERIALS DEALERS, RETAIL: Sand & Gravel
LUMBER & BUILDING MATERIALS DEALERS, RETAIL: Siding
LUMBER & BUILDING MATERIALS RET DEALERS: Millwork & Lumber
LUMBER & BUILDING MATLS DEALERS, RET: Concrete/Cinder Block
LUMBER: Dimension, Hardwood
LUMBER: Fiberboard
LUMBER: Hardwood Dimension
LUMBER: Hardwood Dimension & Flooring Mills
LUMBER: Kiln Dried
LUMBER: Piles, Foundation & Marine Construction, Treated
LUMBER: Plywood, Hardwood
LUMBER: Plywood, Hardwood or Hardwood Faced
LUMBER: Plywood, Prefinished, Hardwood
LUMBER: Plywood, Softwood
LUMBER: Plywood, Softwood
LUMBER: Rails, Fence, Round Or Split
LUMBER: Resawn, Small Dimension
LUMBER: Treated
LUMBER: Veneer, Hardwood
LUMBER: Veneer, Softwood

M

MACHINE PARTS: Stamped Or Pressed Metal
MACHINE SHOPS
MACHINE TOOL ACCESS: Boring Attachments
MACHINE TOOL ACCESS: Cams
MACHINE TOOL ACCESS: Collars

MACHINE TOOL ACCESS: Cutting
MACHINE TOOL ACCESS: Diamond Cutting, For Turning, Etc
MACHINE TOOL ACCESS: End Mills
MACHINE TOOL ACCESS: Files
MACHINE TOOL ACCESS: Knives, Metalworking
MACHINE TOOL ACCESS: Machine Attachments & Access, Drilling
MACHINE TOOL ACCESS: Milling Machine Attachments
MACHINE TOOL ACCESS: Tools & Access
MACHINE TOOL ACCESS: Wheel Turning Eqpt, Diamond Point, Etc
MACHINE TOOL ATTACHMENTS & ACCESS
MACHINE TOOLS & ACCESS
MACHINE TOOLS, METAL CUTTING: Die Sinking
MACHINE TOOLS, METAL CUTTING: Drilling & Boring
MACHINE TOOLS, METAL CUTTING: Electron-Discharge
MACHINE TOOLS, METAL CUTTING: Exotic, Including Explosive
MACHINE TOOLS, METAL CUTTING: Facing, Flange
MACHINE TOOLS, METAL CUTTING: Grind, Polish, Buff, Lapp
MACHINE TOOLS, METAL CUTTING: Home Workshop
MACHINE TOOLS, METAL CUTTING: Plasma Process
MACHINE TOOLS, METAL CUTTING: Robot, Drilling, Cutting, Etc
MACHINE TOOLS, METAL CUTTING: Saws, Power
MACHINE TOOLS, METAL CUTTING: Tool Replacement & Rpr Parts
MACHINE TOOLS, METAL CUTTING: Vertical Turning & Boring
MACHINE TOOLS, METAL FORMING: Forging Machinery & Hammers
MACHINE TOOLS, METAL FORMING: Headers
MACHINE TOOLS, METAL FORMING: Magnetic Forming
MACHINE TOOLS, METAL FORMING: Mechanical, Pneumatic Or Hyd
MACHINE TOOLS, METAL FORMING: Nail Heading
MACHINE TOOLS, METAL FORMING: Presses, Hyd & Pneumatic
MACHINE TOOLS, METAL FORMING: Pressing
MACHINE TOOLS, METAL FORMING: Punching & Shearing
MACHINE TOOLS, METAL FORMING: Rebuilt
MACHINE TOOLS, METAL FORMING: Spinning, Metal
MACHINE TOOLS: Metal Cutting
MACHINE TOOLS: Metal Forming
MACHINERY & EQPT, AGRICULTURAL, WHOL: Grain Elev Eqpt/Splys
MACHINERY & EQPT, AGRICULTURAL, WHOLESALE: Garden, NEC
MACHINERY & EQPT, AGRICULTURAL, WHOLESALE: Landscaping Eqpt
MACHINERY & EQPT, AGRICULTURAL, WHOLESALE: Lawn & Garden
MACHINERY & EQPT, AGRICULTURAL, WHOLESALE: Livestock Eqpt
MACHINERY & EQPT, AGRICULTURAL, WHOLESALE: Poultry Eqpt
MACHINERY & EQPT, AGRICULTURAL, WHOLESALE: Tractors
MACHINERY & EQPT, INDL, WHOL: Environ Pollution Cntrl, Air
MACHINERY & EQPT, INDL, WHOLESALE: Chemical Process
MACHINERY & EQPT, INDL, WHOLESALE: Compaction
MACHINERY & EQPT, INDL, WHOLESALE: Conveyor Systems
MACHINERY & EQPT, INDL, WHOLESALE: Engines & Parts, Diesel
MACHINERY & EQPT, INDL, WHOLESALE: Engs/Transportation Eqpt
MACHINERY & EQPT, INDL, WHOLESALE: Heat Exchange
MACHINERY & EQPT, INDL, WHOLESALE: Hoists
MACHINERY & EQPT, INDL, WHOLESALE: Hydraulic Systems
MACHINERY & EQPT, INDL, WHOLESALE: Indl Machine Parts
MACHINERY & EQPT, INDL, WHOLESALE: Instruments & Cntrl Eqpt
MACHINERY & EQPT, INDL, WHOLESALE: Lift Trucks & Parts
MACHINERY & EQPT, INDL, WHOLESALE: Machine Tools & Access
MACHINERY & EQPT, INDL, WHOLESALE: Machine Tools & Metalwork

MACHINERY & EQPT, INDL, WHOLESALE: Plastic Prdts Machinery
MACHINERY & EQPT, INDL, WHOLESALE: Processing & Packaging
MACHINERY & EQPT, INDL, WHOLESALE: Safety Eqpt
MACHINERY & EQPT, INDL, WHOLESALE: Sawmill
MACHINERY & EQPT, INDL, WHOLESALE: Sewing
MACHINERY & EQPT, INDL, WHOLESALE: Tool & Die Makers
MACHINERY & EQPT, INDL, WHOLESALE: Trailers, Indl
MACHINERY & EQPT, INDL, WHOLESALE: Waste Compactors
MACHINERY & EQPT, INDL, WHOLESALE: Water Pumps
MACHINERY & EQPT, INDL, WHOLESALE: Woodworking
MACHINERY & EQPT, WHOLESALE: Construction, General
MACHINERY & EQPT, WHOLESALE: Contractors Materials
MACHINERY & EQPT: Farm
MACHINERY & EQPT: Gas Producers, Generators/Other Rltd Eqpt
MACHINERY & EQPT: Liquid Automation
MACHINERY & EQPT: Metal Finishing, Plating Etc
MACHINERY & EQPT: Metal Pickling
MACHINERY & EQPT: Petroleum Refinery
MACHINERY & EQPT: Vibratory Parts Handling Eqpt
MACHINERY BASES
MACHINERY, COMM LAUNDRY: Rug Cleaning, Drying Or Napping
MACHINERY, COMMERCIAL LAUNDRY & Drycleaning: Ironers
MACHINERY, COMMERCIAL LAUNDRY & Drycleaning: Pressing
MACHINERY, COMMERCIAL LAUNDRY: Dryers, Incl Coin-Operated
MACHINERY, COMMERCIAL LAUNDRY: Washing, Incl Coin-Operated
MACHINERY, ENGRAVING TRADES: Blocks, Wood
MACHINERY, EQPT & SUPPLIES: Parking Facility
MACHINERY, FOOD PRDTS: Cream Separators
MACHINERY, FOOD PRDTS: Cutting, Chopping, Grinding, Mixing
MACHINERY, FOOD PRDTS: Dairy & Milk
MACHINERY, FOOD PRDTS: Ovens, Bakery
MACHINERY, FOOD PRDTS: Slicers, Commercial
MACHINERY, MAILING: Canceling
MACHINERY, MAILING: Postage Meters
MACHINERY, METALWORKING: Assembly, Including Robotic
MACHINERY, METALWORKING: Coil Winding, For Springs
MACHINERY, METALWORKING: Cutting & Slitting
MACHINERY, OFFICE: Duplicating
MACHINERY, OFFICE: Shorthand
MACHINERY, PAPER INDUSTRY: Coating & Finishing
MACHINERY, PAPER INDUSTRY: Converting, Die Cutting & Stampng
MACHINERY, PAPER INDUSTRY: Cutting
MACHINERY, PRINTING TRADES: Copy Holders
MACHINERY, PRINTING TRADES: Plates
MACHINERY, SEWING: Sewing & Hat & Zipper Making
MACHINERY, TEXTILE: Embroidery
MACHINERY, TEXTILE: Silk Screens
MACHINERY, WOODWORKING: Bandsaws
MACHINERY, WOODWORKING: Cabinet Makers'
MACHINERY, WOODWORKING: Sanding, Exc Portable Floor Sanders
MACHINERY, WOODWORKING: Scarfing
MACHINERY, WOODWORKING: Veneer Mill
MACHINERY/EQPT, INDL, WHOL: Machinist Precision Measrng Tool
MACHINERY: Assembly, Exc Metalworking
MACHINERY: Automotive Maintenance
MACHINERY: Automotive Related
MACHINERY: Billing
MACHINERY: Bottling & Canning
MACHINERY: Bridge Or Gate, Hydraulic
MACHINERY: Centrifugal
MACHINERY: Construction
MACHINERY: Cryogenic, Industrial
MACHINERY: Custom
MACHINERY: Deburring
MACHINERY: Die Casting
MACHINERY: Electronic Component Making
MACHINERY: Electronic Teaching Aids
MACHINERY: Gas Separators
MACHINERY: Gear Cutting & Finishing
MACHINERY: General, Industrial, NEC
MACHINERY: Glassmaking

MACHINERY: Grinding
MACHINERY: Ice Cream
MACHINERY: Ice Making
MACHINERY: Industrial, NEC
MACHINERY: Jack Screws
MACHINERY: Kilns
MACHINERY: Kilns, Cement
MACHINERY: Labeling
MACHINERY: Metalworking
MACHINERY: Milling
MACHINERY: Mining
MACHINERY: Packaging
MACHINERY: Paint Making
MACHINERY: Paper Industry Miscellaneous
MACHINERY: Pharmaciutical
MACHINERY: Plastic Working
MACHINERY: Pottery Making
MACHINERY: Printing Presses
MACHINERY: Road Construction & Maintenance
MACHINERY: Robots, Molding & Forming Plastics
MACHINERY: Semiconductor Manufacturing
MACHINERY: Service Industry, NEC
MACHINERY: Specialty
MACHINERY: Stone Working
MACHINERY: Textile
MACHINERY: Thread Rolling
MACHINERY: Tire Shredding
MACHINERY: Wire Drawing
MACHINERY: Woodworking
MACHINES: Forming, Sheet Metal
MACHINISTS' TOOLS & MACHINES: Measuring, Metalworking Type
MACHINISTS' TOOLS: Measuring, Precision
MACHINISTS' TOOLS: Precision
MAGAZINES, WHOLESALE
MAGNETIC SHIELDS, METAL
MAGNETIC TAPE, AUDIO: Prerecorded
MAGNETS: Ceramic
MAGNETS: Permanent
MAIL-ORDER HOUSE, NEC
MAIL-ORDER HOUSES: Clothing, Exc Women's
MAIL-ORDER HOUSES: Computer Eqpt & Electronics
MAIL-ORDER HOUSES: Educational Splys & Eqpt
MAIL-ORDER HOUSES: Electronic Kits & Parts
MAIL-ORDER HOUSES: Fitness & Sporting Goods
MAIL-ORDER HOUSES: Furniture & Furnishings
MAIL-ORDER HOUSES: Gift Items
MAIL-ORDER HOUSES: Record & Tape, Music Or Video Club
MAILBOX RENTAL & RELATED SVCS
MAILING SVCS, NEC
MANAGEMENT CONSULTING SVCS: Administrative
MANAGEMENT CONSULTING SVCS: Automation & Robotics
MANAGEMENT CONSULTING SVCS: Banking & Finance
MANAGEMENT CONSULTING SVCS: Business
MANAGEMENT CONSULTING SVCS: Business Planning & Organizing
MANAGEMENT CONSULTING SVCS: Distribution Channels
MANAGEMENT CONSULTING SVCS: General
MANAGEMENT CONSULTING SVCS: Hospital & Health
MANAGEMENT CONSULTING SVCS: Industrial
MANAGEMENT CONSULTING SVCS: Industry Specialist
MANAGEMENT CONSULTING SVCS: Manufacturing
MANAGEMENT CONSULTING SVCS: Planning
MANAGEMENT CONSULTING SVCS: Quality Assurance
MANAGEMENT CONSULTING SVCS: Training & Development
MANAGEMENT SERVICES
MANAGEMENT SVCS: Business
MANAGEMENT SVCS: Construction
MANAGEMENT SVCS: Industrial
MANHOLES & COVERS: Metal
MANICURE PREPARATIONS
MANPOWER TRAINING
MANUFACTURED & MOBILE HOME DEALERS
MANUFACTURING INDUSTRIES, NEC
MAPMAKING SVCS
MARBLE BOARD
MARBLE, BUILDING: Cut & Shaped
MARINAS
MARINE CARGO HANDLING SVCS: Marine Terminal
MARINE HARDWARE
MARINE RELATED EQPT
MARINE SPLYS WHOLESALERS
MARINE SVC STATIONS
MARKETS: Meat & fish

MARKING DEVICES
MARKING DEVICES: Canceling Stamps, Hand, Rubber Or Metal
MARKING DEVICES: Embossing Seals & Hand Stamps
MARKING DEVICES: Embossing Seals, Corporate & Official
MARKING DEVICES: Figures, Metal
MARKING DEVICES: Postmark Stamps, Hand, Rubber Or Metal
MARKING DEVICES: Time Stamps, Hand, Rubber Or Metal
MASQUERADE OR THEATRICAL COSTUMES STORES
MASSAGE MACHINES, ELECTRIC: Barber & Beauty Shops
MATERIAL GRINDING & PULVERIZING SVCS NEC
MATERIALS HANDLING EQPT WHOLESALERS
MATS OR MATTING, NEC: Rubber
MATS, MATTING & PADS: Nonwoven
MATS: Table, Plastic & Textile
MATTRESS STORES
MEAT & FISH MARKETS: Freezer Provisioners, Meat
MEAT & MEAT PRDTS WHOLESALERS
MEAT CUTTING & PACKING
MEAT MARKETS
MEAT PRDTS: Bacon, Side & Sliced, From Purchased Meat
MEAT PRDTS: Canned
MEAT PRDTS: Cured, From Slaughtered Meat
MEAT PRDTS: Dried Beef, From Purchased Meat
MEAT PRDTS: Frozen
MEAT PRDTS: Lamb, From Slaughtered Meat
MEAT PRDTS: Meat By-Prdts, From Slaughtered Meat
MEAT PRDTS: Pigs Feet, Cooked & Pickled, From Purchased Meat
MEAT PRDTS: Pork, From Slaughtered Meat
MEAT PRDTS: Prepared Pork Prdts, From Purchased Meat
MEAT PRDTS: Roast Beef, From Purchased Meat
MEAT PRDTS: Sausages & Related Prdts, From Purchased Meat
MEAT PRDTS: Sausages, From Purchased Meat
MEAT PRDTS: Sausages, From Slaughtered Meat
MEAT PRDTS: Snack Sticks, Incl Jerky, From Purchased Meat
MEAT PROCESSED FROM PURCHASED CARCASSES
MEATS, PACKAGED FROZEN: Wholesalers
MEDIA: Magnetic & Optical Recording
MEDICAL & HOSPITAL EQPT WHOLESALERS
MEDICAL & SURGICAL SPLYS: Absorbent Cotton, Sterilized
MEDICAL & SURGICAL SPLYS: Bandages & Dressings
MEDICAL & SURGICAL SPLYS: Belts, Linemen's Safety
MEDICAL & SURGICAL SPLYS: Braces, Orthopedic
MEDICAL & SURGICAL SPLYS: Clothing, Fire Resistant & Protect
MEDICAL & SURGICAL SPLYS: Ear Plugs
MEDICAL & SURGICAL SPLYS: Foot Appliances, Orthopedic
MEDICAL & SURGICAL SPLYS: Ligatures
MEDICAL & SURGICAL SPLYS: Limbs, Artificial
MEDICAL & SURGICAL SPLYS: Orthopedic Appliances
MEDICAL & SURGICAL SPLYS: Personal Safety Eqpt
MEDICAL & SURGICAL SPLYS: Prosthetic Appliances
MEDICAL & SURGICAL SPLYS: Supports, Abdominal, Ankle, Etc
MEDICAL & SURGICAL SPLYS: Technical Aids, Handicapped
MEDICAL & SURGICAL SPLYS: Trusses, Orthopedic & Surgical
MEDICAL & SURGICAL SPLYS: Walkers
MEDICAL & SURGICAL SPLYS: Welders' Hoods
MEDICAL CENTERS
MEDICAL EQPT REPAIR SVCS, NON-ELECTRIC
MEDICAL EQPT: Defibrillators
MEDICAL EQPT: Diagnostic
MEDICAL EQPT: Electromedical Apparatus
MEDICAL EQPT: Electrotherapeutic Apparatus
MEDICAL EQPT: Heart-Lung Machines, Exc Iron Lungs
MEDICAL EQPT: Laser Systems
MEDICAL EQPT: Pacemakers
MEDICAL EQPT: Patient Monitoring
MEDICAL EQPT: Ultrasonic Scanning Devices
MEDICAL EQPT: Ultrasonic, Exc Cleaning
MEDICAL FIELD ASSOCIATION
MEDICAL RESCUE SQUAD
MEDICAL, DENTAL & HOSPITAL EQPT, WHOL: Hosptl Eqpt/Furniture
MEDICAL, DENTAL & HOSPITAL EQPT, WHOLESALE: Med Eqpt & Splys
MEDICAL, DENTAL & HOSPITAL EQPT, WHOLESALE: Orthopedic
MEDICAL, DENTAL & HOSPITAL EQPT, WHOLESALE: Safety

MEDICAL, DENTAL/HOSPITAL EQPT, WHOL: Veterinarian Eqpt/Sply
MEMBERSHIP ORGANIZATIONS, LABOR UNIONS & SIMILAR: Trade
MEMBERSHIP ORGANIZATIONS, NEC: Charitable
MEMBERSHIP ORGANIZATIONS, NEC: Personal Interest
MEMBERSHIP ORGANIZATIONS, PROFESSIONAL: Health Association
MEMBERSHIP ORGANIZATIONS, REL: Churches, Temples & Shrines
MEMBERSHIP ORGANIZATIONS, RELIGIOUS: Baptist Church
MEMBERSHIP ORGANIZATIONS, RELIGIOUS: Nonchurch
MEMBERSHIP ORGS, RELIGIOUS: Non-Denominational Church
MEMORIALS, MONUMENTS & MARKERS
MEN'S & BOYS' CLOTHING ACCESS STORES
MEN'S & BOYS' CLOTHING WHOLESALERS, NEC
MEN'S & BOYS' HATS STORES
MEN'S & BOYS' SPORTSWEAR CLOTHING STORES
MEN'S & BOYS' SPORTSWEAR WHOLESALERS
MERCHANDISING MACHINE OPERATORS: Vending
MESH, REINFORCING: Plastic
METAL & STEEL PRDTS: Abrasive
METAL COMPONENTS: Prefabricated
METAL CUTTING SVCS
METAL DETECTORS
METAL FABRICATORS: Architechtural
METAL FABRICATORS: Plate
METAL FABRICATORS: Sheet
METAL FINISHING SVCS
METAL MINING SVCS
METAL ORES, NEC
METAL RESHAPING & REPLATING SVCS
METAL SERVICE CENTERS & OFFICES
METAL SLITTING & SHEARING
METAL SPINNING FOR THE TRADE
METAL STAMPING, FOR THE TRADE
METAL STAMPINGS: Perforated
METAL TREATING COMPOUNDS
METALS SVC CENTERS & WHOL: Structural Shapes, Iron Or Steel
METALS SVC CENTERS & WHOLESALERS: Cable, Wire
METALS SVC CENTERS & WHOLESALERS: Concrete Reinforcing Bars
METALS SVC CENTERS & WHOLESALERS: Ferrous Metals
METALS SVC CENTERS & WHOLESALERS: Flat Prdts, Iron Or Steel
METALS SVC CENTERS & WHOLESALERS: Foundry Prdts
METALS SVC CENTERS & WHOLESALERS: Iron & Steel Prdt, Ferrous
METALS SVC CENTERS & WHOLESALERS: Misc Nonferrous Prdts
METALS SVC CENTERS & WHOLESALERS: Pipe & Tubing, Steel
METALS SVC CENTERS & WHOLESALERS: Plates, Metal
METALS SVC CENTERS & WHOLESALERS: Rails & Access
METALS SVC CENTERS & WHOLESALERS: Rope, Wire, Exc Insulated
METALS SVC CENTERS & WHOLESALERS: Sheets, Metal
METALS SVC CENTERS & WHOLESALERS: Stampings, Metal
METALS SVC CENTERS & WHOLESALERS: Steel
METALS SVC CENTERS & WHOLESALERS: Tubing, Metal
METALS SVC CNTRS & WHOL: Metal Wires, Ties, Cables/Screening
METALS SVC CTRS & WHOLESALERS: Aluminum Bars, Rods, Etc
METALS: Primary Nonferrous, NEC
METALWORK: Miscellaneous
METALWORK: Ornamental
METALWORKING MACHINERY WHOLESALERS
METEOROLOGIC TRACKING SYSTEMS
METERING DEVICES: Water Quality Monitoring & Control Systems
METERS: Liquid
METERS: Magnetic Flow, Indl Process
MGMT CONSULTING SVCS: Matls, Incl Purch, Handle & Invntry
MICA PRDTS: Built-Up Or Sheet
MICA: Built-Up
MICROCIRCUITS, INTEGRATED: Semiconductor
MICROPROCESSORS
MICROWAVE COMPONENTS
MILITARY INSIGNIA, TEXTILE

INDEX

MILL PRDTS: Structural & Rail
MILLINERY SUPPLIES: Veils & Veiling, Bridal, Funeral, Etc
MILLING: Cereal Flour, Exc Rice
MILLING: Chemical
MILLING: Feed, Wheat
MILLING: Grains, Exc Rice
MILLING: Wheat Germ
MILLS: Ferrous & Nonferrous
MILLWORK
MIMEOGRAPHING SVCS
MINE & QUARRY SVCS: Nonmetallic Minerals
MINE DEVELOPMENT, METAL
MINERAL ABRASIVES MINING SVCS
MINERAL PIGMENT MINING
MINERAL WOOL
MINERALS: Ground Or Otherwise Treated
MINERALS: Ground or Treated
MINIATURES
MINING MACHINERY & EQPT WHOLESALERS
MINING MACHINES & EQPT: Feeders, Ore & Aggregate
MINING MACHINES & EQPT: Rock Crushing, Stationary
MINING SVCS, NEC: Anthracite
MINING: Oil Shale
MINING: Tar Sand
MIRRORS: Motor Vehicle
MISCELLANEOUS FINANCIAL INVEST ACT: Mineral Leasing Dealers
MISCELLANEOUS FINANCIAL INVEST ACT: Oil/Gas Lease Brokers
MISSILE GUIDANCE SYSTEMS & EQPT
MITTENS: Leather
MITTENS: Rubber
MIXING EQPT
MIXTURES & BLOCKS: Asphalt Paving
MOBILE COMMUNICATIONS EQPT
MOBILE HOME REPAIR SVCS
MOBILE HOMES
MOBILE HOMES WHOLESALERS
MOBILE HOMES, EXC RECREATIONAL
MOBILE HOMES: Indl Or Commercial Use
MOBILE HOMES: Personal Or Private Use
MODELS
MODELS: General, Exc Toy
MODULES: Computer Logic
MOLDED RUBBER PRDTS
MOLDING COMPOUNDS
MOLDING SAND MINING
MOLDINGS & TRIM: Metal, Exc Automobile
MOLDINGS & TRIM: Wood
MOLDINGS OR TRIM: Automobile, Stamped Metal
MOLDINGS: Picture Frame
MOLDS: Indl
MOLDS: Plastic Working & Foundry
MONOFILAMENTS: Nontextile
MONUMENTS & GRAVE MARKERS, EXC TERRAZZO
MONUMENTS: Concrete
MONUMENTS: Cut Stone, Exc Finishing Or Lettering Only
MOPS: Floor & Dust
MOTEL: Franchised
MOTION PICTURE & VIDEO PRODUCTION SVCS
MOTION PICTURE PRODUCTION ALLIED SVCS
MOTOR & GENERATOR PARTS: Electric
MOTOR HOMES
MOTOR REBUILDING SVCS, EXC AUTOMOTIVE
MOTOR REPAIR SVCS
MOTOR SCOOTERS & PARTS
MOTOR VEHICLE ASSEMBLY, COMPLETE: Ambulances
MOTOR VEHICLE ASSEMBLY, COMPLETE: Autos, Incl Specialty
MOTOR VEHICLE ASSEMBLY, COMPLETE: Bus/Large Spclty Vehicles
MOTOR VEHICLE ASSEMBLY, COMPLETE: Buses, All Types
MOTOR VEHICLE ASSEMBLY, COMPLETE: Fire Department Vehicles
MOTOR VEHICLE ASSEMBLY, COMPLETE: Military Motor Vehicle
MOTOR VEHICLE ASSEMBLY, COMPLETE: Motor Homes, Self Containd
MOTOR VEHICLE ASSEMBLY, COMPLETE: Snow Plows
MOTOR VEHICLE ASSEMBLY, COMPLETE: Truck & Tractor Trucks
MOTOR VEHICLE ASSEMBLY, COMPLETE: Truck Tractors, Highway
MOTOR VEHICLE ASSEMBLY, COMPLETE: Trucks, Pickup

MOTOR VEHICLE ASSEMBLY, COMPLETE: Wreckers, Tow Truck
MOTOR VEHICLE DEALERS: Automobiles, New & Used
MOTOR VEHICLE DEALERS: Cars, Used Only
MOTOR VEHICLE PARTS & ACCESS: Air Conditioner Parts
MOTOR VEHICLE PARTS & ACCESS: Axel Housings & Shafts
MOTOR VEHICLE PARTS & ACCESS: Bearings
MOTOR VEHICLE PARTS & ACCESS: Body Components & Frames
MOTOR VEHICLE PARTS & ACCESS: Brakes, Air
MOTOR VEHICLE PARTS & ACCESS: Brakes, Vacuum
MOTOR VEHICLE PARTS & ACCESS: Cleaners, air
MOTOR VEHICLE PARTS & ACCESS: Clutches
MOTOR VEHICLE PARTS & ACCESS: Connecting Rods
MOTOR VEHICLE PARTS & ACCESS: Cylinder Heads
MOTOR VEHICLE PARTS & ACCESS: Electrical Eqpt
MOTOR VEHICLE PARTS & ACCESS: Engines & Parts
MOTOR VEHICLE PARTS & ACCESS: Engs & Trans, Factory, Rebuilt
MOTOR VEHICLE PARTS & ACCESS: Fuel Pumps
MOTOR VEHICLE PARTS & ACCESS: Fuel Systems & Parts
MOTOR VEHICLE PARTS & ACCESS: Gas Tanks
MOTOR VEHICLE PARTS & ACCESS: Gears
MOTOR VEHICLE PARTS & ACCESS: Heaters
MOTOR VEHICLE PARTS & ACCESS: Instrument Board Assemblies
MOTOR VEHICLE PARTS & ACCESS: Manifolds
MOTOR VEHICLE PARTS & ACCESS: Mufflers, Exhaust
MOTOR VEHICLE PARTS & ACCESS: Oil Pumps
MOTOR VEHICLE PARTS & ACCESS: Pickup Truck Bed Liners
MOTOR VEHICLE PARTS & ACCESS: Propane Conversion Eqpt
MOTOR VEHICLE PARTS & ACCESS: Thermostats
MOTOR VEHICLE PARTS & ACCESS: Trailer Hitches
MOTOR VEHICLE PARTS & ACCESS: Transmission Housings Or Parts
MOTOR VEHICLE PARTS & ACCESS: Transmissions
MOTOR VEHICLE PARTS & ACCESS: Universal Joints
MOTOR VEHICLE PARTS & ACCESS: Wheel rims
MOTOR VEHICLE PARTS & ACCESS: Wipers, Windshield
MOTOR VEHICLE PARTS & ACCESS: Wiring Harness Sets
MOTOR VEHICLE RACING & DRIVER SVCS
MOTOR VEHICLE SPLYS & PARTS WHOLESALERS: New
MOTOR VEHICLE SPLYS & PARTS WHOLESALERS: Used
MOTOR VEHICLE: Hardware
MOTOR VEHICLE: Radiators
MOTOR VEHICLE: Shock Absorbers
MOTOR VEHICLE: Steering Mechanisms
MOTOR VEHICLE: Wheels
MOTOR VEHICLES & CAR BODIES
MOTOR VEHICLES, WHOLESALE: Commercial
MOTOR VEHICLES, WHOLESALE: Fire Trucks
MOTOR VEHICLES, WHOLESALE: Truck tractors
MOTOR VEHICLES, WHOLESALE: Trucks, commercial
MOTORCYCLE & BICYCLE PARTS: Gears
MOTORCYCLE ACCESS
MOTORCYCLE DEALERS
MOTORCYCLE PARTS & ACCESS DEALERS
MOTORCYCLE REPAIR SHOPS
MOTORCYCLES & RELATED PARTS
MOTORCYCLES: Wholesalers
MOTORS: Electric
MOTORS: Generators
MOUNTING SVC: Swatches & Samples
MOWERS & ACCESSORIES
MULTILITHING SVCS
MUSEUMS & ART GALLERIES
MUSIC BROADCASTING SVCS
MUSIC DISTRIBUTION APPARATUS
MUSIC LICENSING TO RADIO STATIONS
MUSICAL INSTRUMENT LESSONS
MUSICAL INSTRUMENT PARTS & ACCESS, WHOLESALE
MUSICAL INSTRUMENT REPAIR
MUSICAL INSTRUMENTS & ACCESS: Carrying Cases
MUSICAL INSTRUMENTS & ACCESS: NEC
MUSICAL INSTRUMENTS & ACCESS: Pianos
MUSICAL INSTRUMENTS & ACCESS: Pipe Organs
MUSICAL INSTRUMENTS & ACCESS: Stands
MUSICAL INSTRUMENTS & PARTS: Percussion
MUSICAL INSTRUMENTS & PARTS: Woodwind
MUSICAL INSTRUMENTS & SPLYS STORES
MUSICAL INSTRUMENTS & SPLYS STORES: Pianos

MUSICAL INSTRUMENTS & SPLYS STORES: String instruments
MUSICAL INSTRUMENTS WHOLESALERS
MUSICAL INSTRUMENTS: Bassoons
MUSICAL INSTRUMENTS: Guitars & Parts, Electric & Acoustic
MUSICAL INSTRUMENTS: Harps & Parts
MUSICAL INSTRUMENTS: Mouthpieces
MUSICAL INSTRUMENTS: Piccolos & Parts
MUSICAL INSTRUMENTS: Reeds

N

NAIL SALONS
NAILS: Steel, Wire Or Cut
NAME PLATES: Engraved Or Etched
NATIONAL SECURITY FORCES
NATIONAL SECURITY, GOVERNMENT: Military Training Schools
NATURAL GAS COMPRESSING SVC, On-Site
NATURAL GAS DISTRIBUTION TO CONSUMERS
NATURAL GAS LIQUIDS PRODUCTION
NATURAL GAS LIQUIDS PRODUCTION
NATURAL GAS PRODUCTION
NATURAL LIQUEFIED PETROLEUM GAS PRODUCTION
NATURAL PROPANE PRODUCTION
NEWS DEALERS & NEWSSTANDS
NEWSPAPER COLUMN WRITING SVCS
NICKEL ALLOY
NONFERROUS: Rolling & Drawing, NEC
NONMETALLIC MINERALS & CONCENTRATE WHOLESALERS
NONMETALLIC MINERALS: Support Activities, Exc Fuels
NOTARIES PUBLIC
NOVELTIES
NOVELTIES & SPECIALTIES: Metal
NOVELTIES, PAPER, WHOLESALE
NOVELTIES: Paper, Made From Purchased Materials
NOVELTIES: Plastic
NOZZLES & SPRINKLERS Lawn Hose
NOZZLES: Fire Fighting
NURSERIES & LAWN & GARDEN SPLY STORE, RET: Lawn/Garden Splys
NURSERIES & LAWN & GARDEN SPLY STORES, RETAIL: Fertilizer
NURSERIES & LAWN & GARDEN SPLY STORES, RETAIL: Lawn Ornament
NURSERIES & LAWN/GARDEN SPLY STORE, RET: Lawnmowers/Tractors
NURSERIES/LAWN/GARDEN SPLY STORE, RET: Christmas Tree, Natrl
NURSERY & GARDEN CENTERS
NYLON FIBERS
NYLON RESINS

O

OFFICE EQPT WHOLESALERS
OFFICE EQPT, WHOLESALE: Photocopy Machines
OFFICE MACHINES, NEC
OFFICE SPLY & STATIONERY STORES
OFFICE SPLY & STATIONERY STORES: Office Forms & Splys
OFFICE SPLYS, NEC, WHOLESALE
OFFICES & CLINICS OF DOCTORS OF MEDICINE: Radiologist
OFFICES & CLINICS OF DOCTORS OF MEDICINE: Surgeon, Plastic
OFFICES & CLINICS OF HEALTH PRACTITIONERS: Nutritionist
OFFICES & CLINICS OF HEALTH PRACTITIONERS: Physical Therapy
OFFICES & CLINICS OF OPTOMETRISTS: Specialist, Optometrists
OIL & GAS FIELD EQPT: Drill Rigs
OIL & GAS FIELD MACHINERY
OIL FIELD MACHINERY & EQPT
OIL FIELD SVCS, NEC
OIL TREATING COMPOUNDS
OILS & GREASES: Blended & Compounded
OILS & GREASES: Lubricating
OILS: Core Or Binders
OILS: Cutting
OILS: Lubricating
OILS: Lubricating
OINTMENTS
ON-LINE DATABASE INFORMATION RETRIEVAL SVCS

OPEN PIT IRON MINING, NEC
OPERATOR: Nonresidential Buildings
OPHTHALMIC GOODS
OPHTHALMIC GOODS WHOLESALERS
OPHTHALMIC GOODS: Eyewear, Protective
OPHTHALMIC GOODS: Frames & Parts, Eyeglass & Spectacle
OPHTHALMIC GOODS: Frames, Lenses & Parts, Eyeglasses
OPHTHALMIC GOODS: Lenses, Ophthalmic
OPHTHALMIC GOODS: Spectacles
OPTICAL GOODS STORES
OPTICAL GOODS STORES: Contact Lenses, Prescription
OPTICAL GOODS STORES: Eyeglasses, Prescription
OPTICAL GOODS STORES: Opticians
OPTICAL INSTRUMENTS & APPARATUS
OPTICAL INSTRUMENTS & LENSES
OPTICAL ISOLATORS
OPTOMETRISTS' OFFICES
ORDNANCE
ORGAN TUNING & REPAIR SVCS
ORGANIZATIONS: Medical Research
ORGANIZATIONS: Religious
ORGANIZATIONS: Research Institute
ORGANIZERS, CLOSET & DRAWER Plastic
ORIENTED STRANDBOARD
ORNAMENTS: Lawn
OSCILLATORS
OUTBOARD MOTORS & PARTS
OVENS: Infrared
OVERSHOES: Plastic

P

PACKAGE DESIGN SVCS
PACKAGING & LABELING SVCS
PACKAGING MATERIALS, INDL: Wholesalers
PACKAGING MATERIALS, WHOLESALE
PACKAGING MATERIALS: Paper
PACKAGING MATERIALS: Paper, Coated Or Laminated
PACKAGING MATERIALS: Plastic Film, Coated Or Laminated
PACKAGING MATERIALS: Polystyrene Foam
PACKING & CRATING SVC
PACKING & CRATING SVCS: Containerized Goods For Shipping
PACKING MATERIALS: Mechanical
PACKING SVCS: Shipping
PACKING: Metallic
PACKING: Rubber
PADDING: Foamed Plastics
PADS: Mattress
PADS: Permanent Waving
PAILS: Plastic
PAINT STORE
PAINTING SVC: Metal Prdts
PAINTS & ADDITIVES
PAINTS & ALLIED PRODUCTS
PAINTS & VARNISHES: Plastics Based
PAINTS, VARNISHES & SPLYS WHOLESALERS
PAINTS, VARNISHES & SPLYS, WHOLESALE: Paints
PAINTS: Asphalt Or Bituminous
PAINTS: Oil Or Alkyd Vehicle Or Water Thinned
PAINTS: Waterproof
PALLET REPAIR SVCS
PALLET SPACERS: Fiber, Made From Purchased Materials
PALLETS
PALLETS & SKIDS: Wood
PALLETS: Corrugated
PALLETS: Plastic
PALLETS: Wooden
PANEL & DISTRIBUTION BOARDS & OTHER RELATED APPARATUS
PANEL & DISTRIBUTION BOARDS: Electric
PANELS & SECTIONS: Prefabricated, Concrete
PANELS, CORRUGATED: Plastic
PANELS: Building, Metal
PANELS: Building, Plastic, NEC
PANELS: Building, Wood
PANELS: Electric Metering
PANELS: Wood
PAPER & BOARD: Die-cut
PAPER CONVERTING
PAPER MANUFACTURERS: Exc Newsprint
PAPER PRDTS: Feminine Hygiene Prdts
PAPER PRDTS: Infant & Baby Prdts
PAPER PRDTS: Molded Pulp Prdts
PAPER PRDTS: Sanitary Tissue Paper

PAPER, WHOLESALE: Printing
PAPER: Adhesive
PAPER: Art
PAPER: Bristols
PAPER: Building, Insulating & Packaging
PAPER: Business Form
PAPER: Carbon
PAPER: Cardboard
PAPER: Catalog
PAPER: Coated & Laminated, NEC
PAPER: Coated, Exc Photographic, Carbon Or Abrasive
PAPER: Corrugated
PAPER: Milk Filter
PAPER: Specialty Or Chemically Treated
PAPER: Tissue
PAPER: Wallpaper
PAPER: Waxed, Made From Purchased Materials
PAPER: Wrapping & Packaging
PAPERBOARD
PAPERBOARD CONVERTING
PAPERBOARD PRDTS: Container Board
PAPERBOARD PRDTS: Folding Boxboard
PAPERBOARD PRDTS: Packaging Board
PAPERBOARD: Boxboard
PAPERBOARD: Chipboard
PARACHUTES
PARTITIONS & FIXTURES: Except Wood
PARTITIONS: Nonwood, Floor Attached
PARTITIONS: Solid Fiber, Made From Purchased Materials
PARTITIONS: Wood & Fixtures
PARTS: Metal
PATENT OWNERS & LESSORS
PATTERNS: Indl
PAVERS
PAVING MATERIALS: Coal Tar, Not From Refineries
PAVING MATERIALS: Prefabricated, Concrete
PAVING MIXTURES
PAWN SHOPS
PEAT MINING & PROCESSING SVCS
PENCILS & PENS WHOLESALERS
PERFUME: Perfumes, Natural Or Synthetic
PERFUMES
PERLITE: Processed
PERSONAL CREDIT INSTITUTIONS: Consumer Finance Companies
PERSONAL CREDIT INSTITUTIONS: Financing, Autos, Furniture
PERSONAL SVCS
PERSONAL SVCS, NEC
PET & PET SPLYS STORES
PET COLLARS, LEASHES, MUZZLES & HARNESSES: Leather
PET FOOD WHOLESALERS
PET SPLYS
PET SPLYS WHOLESALERS
PETROLEUM & PETROLEUM PRDTS, WHOLESALE Crude Oil
PETROLEUM & PETROLEUM PRDTS, WHOLESALE Engine Fuels & Oils
PETROLEUM & PETROLEUM PRDTS, WHOLESALE Fuel Oil
PETROLEUM & PETROLEUM PRDTS, WHOLESALE Petroleum Brokers
PETROLEUM & PETROLEUM PRDTS, WHOLESALE Petroleum Terminals
PETROLEUM & PETROLEUM PRDTS, WHOLESALE: Bulk Stations
PETROLEUM BULK STATIONS & TERMINALS
PETROLEUM PRDTS WHOLESALERS
PHARMACEUTICAL PREPARATIONS: Druggists' Preparations
PHARMACEUTICAL PREPARATIONS: Medicines, Capsule Or Ampule
PHARMACEUTICAL PREPARATIONS: Proprietary Drug PRDTS
PHARMACEUTICAL PREPARATIONS: Solutions
PHARMACEUTICAL PREPARATIONS: Tablets
PHARMACEUTICALS
PHARMACEUTICALS: Medicinal & Botanical Prdts
PHARMACIES & DRUG STORES
PHOTOCOPYING & DUPLICATING SVCS
PHOTOFINISHING LABORATORIES
PHOTOGRAPHIC & OPTICAL GOODS EQPT REPAIR SVCS
PHOTOGRAPHIC EQPT & SPLYS

PHOTOGRAPHIC EQPT & SPLYS, WHOLESALE: Motion Picture Camera
PHOTOGRAPHIC EQPT & SPLYS: Diazotype Or Whiteprint Reprod
PHOTOGRAPHIC EQPT & SPLYS: Film, Cloth & Paper, Sensitized
PHOTOGRAPHIC EQPT & SPLYS: Printing Eqpt
PHOTOGRAPHIC EQPT & SPLYS: Toners, Prprd, Not Chem Plnts
PHOTOGRAPHIC SVCS
PHOTOGRAPHY SVCS: Portrait Studios
PHOTOGRAPHY SVCS: Still Or Video
PHOTOTYPESETTING SVC
PHYSICAL EXAMINATION & TESTING SVCS
PHYSICIANS' OFFICES & CLINICS: Medical doctors
PIANO TUNING & REPAIR SVCS
PICTURE FRAMES: Wood
PICTURE FRAMING SVCS, CUSTOM
PICTURE TUBE REPROCESSING
PIECE GOODS & NOTIONS WHOLESALERS
PIECE GOODS, NOTIONS & DRY GOODS, WHOL: Jute Piece Goods
PIECE GOODS, NOTIONS & DRY GOODS, WHOL: Textiles, Woven
PIECE GOODS, NOTIONS & DRY GOODS, WHOL: Trimmings, Apparel
PIECE GOODS, NOTIONS & DRY GOODS, WHOLESALE: Fabrics
PIECE GOODS, NOTIONS & DRY GOODS, WHOLESALE: Fabrics, Knit
PIECE GOODS, NOTIONS & OTHER DRY GOODS, WHOL: Flags/Banners
PIECE GOODS, NOTIONS & OTHER DRY GOODS, WHOLESALE: Fabrics
PIECE GOODS, NOTIONS/DRY GOODS, WHOL: Drapery Mtrl, Woven
PIECE GOODS, NOTIONS/DRY GOODS, WHOL: Nylon Piece, Woven
PIGMENTS, INORGANIC: Chrome Green, Chrome Yellow, Zinc Yellw
PIGMENTS, INORGANIC: Metallic & Mineral, NEC
PILE DRIVING EQPT
PINS
PINS: Dowel
PIPE & FITTING: Fabrication
PIPE & TUBES: Copper & Copper Alloy
PIPE & TUBES: Seamless
PIPE CLEANERS
PIPE FITTINGS: Plastic
PIPE, CULVERT: Concrete
PIPE, SEWER: Concrete
PIPE: Concrete
PIPE: Plastic
PIPE: Sheet Metal
PIPE: Water, Cast Iron
PIPELINES: Natural Gas
PIPES & TUBES
PIPES & TUBES: Steel
PIPES & TUBES: Welded
PIPES OR FITTINGS: Sewer, Clay
PISTONS & PISTON RINGS
PLANING MILL, NEC
PLANING MILLS: Millwork
PLANTS: Artificial & Preserved
PLAQUES: Clay, Plaster/Papier-Mache, Factory Production
PLAQUES: Picture, Laminated
PLASMAS
PLASTERING ACCESS: Metal
PLASTIC COLORING & FINISHING
PLASTIC PRDTS
PLASTIC PRDTS REPAIR SVCS
PLASTIC WOOD
PLASTICS FILM & SHEET
PLASTICS FILM & SHEET: Polyethylene
PLASTICS FILM & SHEET: Polypropylene
PLASTICS FILM & SHEET: Polyvinyl
PLASTICS FILM & SHEET: Vinyl
PLASTICS FINISHED PRDTS: Laminated
PLASTICS MATERIAL & RESINS
PLASTICS MATERIALS, BASIC FORMS & SHAPES WHOLESALERS
PLASTICS PROCESSING
PLASTICS SHEET: Packing Materials
PLASTICS: Blow Molded
PLASTICS: Cast

INDEX

PLASTICS: Extruded
PLASTICS: Finished Injection Molded
PLASTICS: Injection Molded
PLASTICS: Molded
PLASTICS: Polystyrene Foam
PLASTICS: Thermoformed
PLATEMAKING SVC: Color Separations, For The Printing Trade
PLATEMAKING SVC: Embossing, For The Printing Trade
PLATES
PLATES: Aluminum
PLATES: Sheet & Strip, Exc Coated Prdts
PLATES: Steel
PLATES: Truss, Metal
PLATING & FINISHING SVC: Decorative, Formed Prdts
PLATING & POLISHING SVC
PLATING COMPOUNDS
PLATING SVC: Chromium, Metals Or Formed Prdts
PLATING SVC: Electro
PLATING SVC: Gold
PLATING SVC: NEC
PLAYGROUND EQPT
PLEATING & STITCHING SVC
PLUGS: Electric
PLUMBING & HEATING EQPT & SPLY, WHOL: Htg Eqpt/Panels, Solar
PLUMBING & HEATING EQPT & SPLY, WHOLESALE: Hydronic Htg Eqpt
PLUMBING & HEATING EQPT & SPLYS WHOLESALERS
PLUMBING & HEATING EQPT & SPLYS, WHOL: Pipe/Fitting, Plastic
PLUMBING & HEATING EQPT & SPLYS, WHOL: Plumbing Fitting/Sply
PLUMBING & HEATING EQPT & SPLYS, WHOL: Water Purif Eqpt
PLUMBING & HEATING EQPT & SPLYS, WHOLESALE: Convectors
PLUMBING & HEATING EQPT & SPLYS, WHOLESALE: Steam Fittings
PLUMBING & HEATING EQPT & SPLYS, WHOLESALE: Wood Burn Stove
PLUMBING & HEATING EQPT, WHOLESALE: Water Heaters/Purif
PLUMBING FIXTURES
PLUMBING FIXTURES: Plastic
PLUMBING FIXTURES: Vitreous
POINT OF SALE DEVICES
POLISHING SVC: Metals Or Formed Prdts
POLYETHYLENE RESINS
POLYSTYRENE RESINS
POLYVINYL CHLORIDE RESINS
PONTOONS: Rubber
POPCORN & SUPPLIES WHOLESALERS
POSTERS
POSTS: Lamp, Metal
POTTERY
POTTING SOILS
POULTRY & POULTRY PRDTS WHOLESALERS
POULTRY & SMALL GAME SLAUGHTERING & PROCESSING
POULTRY SLAUGHTERING & PROCESSING
POWDER: Aluminum Atomized
POWDER: Iron
POWDER: Metal
POWDER: Silver
POWER GENERATORS
POWER OUTLETS & SOCKETS
POWER SPLY CONVERTERS: Static, Electronic Applications
POWER SUPPLIES: Transformer, Electronic Type
POWER TOOL REPAIR SVCS
POWER TOOLS, HAND: Drill Attachments, Portable
POWER TOOLS, HAND: Drills & Drilling Tools
POWER TOOLS, HAND: Guns, Pneumatic, Chip Removal
POWER TRANSMISSION EQPT WHOLESALERS
POWER TRANSMISSION EQPT: Aircraft
POWER TRANSMISSION EQPT: Mechanical
POWER TRANSMISSION EQPT: Vehicle
POWERED GOLF CART DEALERS
PRECAST TERRAZZO OR CONCRETE PRDTS
PRECIOUS METALS
PRECIOUS STONE MINING SVCS, NEC
PRECISION INSTRUMENT REPAIR SVCS
PRERECORDED TAPE, CD & RECORD STORE: Record, Disc/Tape

PRERECORDED TAPE, COMPACT DISC & RECORD STORES: Records
PRESSED FIBER & MOLDED PULP PRDTS, EXC FOOD PRDTS
PRESSES
PRESTRESSED CONCRETE PRDTS
PRIMARY FINISHED OR SEMIFINISHED SHAPES
PRIMARY METAL PRODUCTS
PRINT CARTRIDGES: Laser & Other Computer Printers
PRINTED CIRCUIT BOARDS
PRINTERS & PLOTTERS
PRINTERS' SVCS: Folding, Collating, Etc
PRINTERS: Computer
PRINTERS: Magnetic Ink, Bar Code
PRINTING & BINDING: Books
PRINTING & BINDING: Pamphlets
PRINTING & EMBOSSING: Plastic Fabric Articles
PRINTING & ENGRAVING: Card, Exc Greeting
PRINTING & ENGRAVING: Invitation & Stationery
PRINTING & STAMPING: Fabric Articles
PRINTING & WRITING PAPER WHOLESALERS
PRINTING MACHINERY
PRINTING MACHINERY, EQPT & SPLYS: Wholesalers
PRINTING PLATES: Stereotyping
PRINTING TRADES MACHINERY & EQPT REPAIR SVCS
PRINTING, COMMERCIAL: Announcements, NEC
PRINTING, COMMERCIAL: Business Forms, NEC
PRINTING, COMMERCIAL: Cards, Visiting, Incl Business, NEC
PRINTING, COMMERCIAL: Decals, NEC
PRINTING, COMMERCIAL: Envelopes, NEC
PRINTING, COMMERCIAL: Imprinting
PRINTING, COMMERCIAL: Invitations, NEC
PRINTING, COMMERCIAL: Labels & Seals, NEC
PRINTING, COMMERCIAL: Letterpress & Screen
PRINTING, COMMERCIAL: Literature, Advertising, NEC
PRINTING, COMMERCIAL: Magazines, NEC
PRINTING, COMMERCIAL: Promotional
PRINTING, COMMERCIAL: Publications
PRINTING, COMMERCIAL: Screen
PRINTING, COMMERCIAL: Stationery, NEC
PRINTING, COMMERCIAL: Tickets, NEC
PRINTING, COMMERCIAL: Wrappers, NEC
PRINTING, LITHOGRAPHIC: Advertising Posters
PRINTING, LITHOGRAPHIC: Calendars
PRINTING, LITHOGRAPHIC: Calendars & Cards
PRINTING, LITHOGRAPHIC: Color
PRINTING, LITHOGRAPHIC: Decals
PRINTING, LITHOGRAPHIC: Forms & Cards, Business
PRINTING, LITHOGRAPHIC: Forms, Business
PRINTING, LITHOGRAPHIC: Maps
PRINTING, LITHOGRAPHIC: Menus
PRINTING, LITHOGRAPHIC: Offset & photolithographic printing
PRINTING, LITHOGRAPHIC: On Metal
PRINTING, LITHOGRAPHIC: Post Cards, Picture
PRINTING, LITHOGRAPHIC: Posters & Decals
PRINTING, LITHOGRAPHIC: Transfers, Decalcomania Or Dry
PRINTING: Books
PRINTING: Books
PRINTING: Broadwoven Fabrics. Cotton
PRINTING: Checkbooks
PRINTING: Commercial, NEC
PRINTING: Engraving & Plate
PRINTING: Flexographic
PRINTING: Gravure, Business Form & Card
PRINTING: Gravure, Forms, Business
PRINTING: Gravure, Imprinting
PRINTING: Gravure, Job
PRINTING: Gravure, Labels
PRINTING: Gravure, Rotogravure
PRINTING: Gravure, Stationery & Invitation
PRINTING: Intaglio
PRINTING: Laser
PRINTING: Letterpress
PRINTING: Lithographic
PRINTING: Manmade Fiber & Silk, Broadwoven Fabric
PRINTING: Offset
PRINTING: Screen, Broadwoven Fabrics, Cotton
PRINTING: Screen, Fabric
PRINTING: Screen, Manmade Fiber & Silk, Broadwoven Fabric
PRINTING: Thermography
PROFESSIONAL EQPT & SPLYS, WHOLESALE: Analytical Instruments

PROFESSIONAL EQPT & SPLYS, WHOLESALE: Engineers', NEC
PROFESSIONAL EQPT & SPLYS, WHOLESALE: Optical Goods
PROFESSIONAL INSTRUMENT REPAIR SVCS
PROFILE SHAPES: Unsupported Plastics
PROMOTION SVCS
PROPELLERS: Boat & Ship, Cast
PROPELLERS: Boat & Ship, Machined
PROTECTION EQPT: Lightning
PROTECTIVE FOOTWEAR: Rubber Or Plastic
PUBLIC ORDER & SAFETY OFFICES, GOVERNMENT: Level Of Govt
PUBLIC RELATIONS & PUBLICITY SVCS
PUBLIC RELATIONS SVCS
PUBLISHERS: Art Copy & Poster
PUBLISHERS: Book
PUBLISHERS: Books, No Printing
PUBLISHERS: Comic Books, No Printing
PUBLISHERS: Directories, NEC
PUBLISHERS: Globe Cover Maps
PUBLISHERS: Guides
PUBLISHERS: Magazines, No Printing
PUBLISHERS: Miscellaneous
PUBLISHERS: Music Book
PUBLISHERS: Music Book & Sheet Music
PUBLISHERS: Newsletter
PUBLISHERS: Newspaper
PUBLISHERS: Newspapers, No Printing
PUBLISHERS: Periodical, With Printing
PUBLISHERS: Periodicals, Magazines
PUBLISHERS: Periodicals, No Printing
PUBLISHERS: Posters
PUBLISHERS: Shopping News
PUBLISHERS: Technical Manuals
PUBLISHERS: Technical Manuals & Papers
PUBLISHERS: Telephone & Other Directory
PUBLISHERS: Textbooks, No Printing
PUBLISHERS: Trade journals, No Printing
PUBLISHING & BROADCASTING: Internet Only
PUBLISHING & PRINTING: Art Copy
PUBLISHING & PRINTING: Book Music
PUBLISHING & PRINTING: Books
PUBLISHING & PRINTING: Catalogs
PUBLISHING & PRINTING: Guides
PUBLISHING & PRINTING: Magazines: publishing & printing
PUBLISHING & PRINTING: Music, Book
PUBLISHING & PRINTING: Newsletters, Business Svc
PUBLISHING & PRINTING: Newspapers
PUBLISHING & PRINTING: Pamphlets
PUBLISHING & PRINTING: Periodical Statistical Reports
PUBLISHING & PRINTING: Posters
PUBLISHING & PRINTING: Shopping News
PUBLISHING & PRINTING: Trade Journals
PUBLISHING & PRINTING: Yearbooks
PULP MILLS
PULP MILLS: Chemical & Semichemical Processing
PULP MILLS: Mechanical & Recycling Processing
PUMPS
PUMPS & PARTS: Indl
PUMPS & PUMPING EQPT REPAIR SVCS
PUMPS & PUMPING EQPT WHOLESALERS
PUMPS: Domestic, Water Or Sump
PUMPS: Measuring & Dispensing
PUMPS: Oil, Measuring Or Dispensing
PUNCHES: Forming & Stamping
PURCHASING SVCS
PURIFICATION & DUST COLLECTION EQPT
PURIFIERS: Centrifugal

Q

QUICKLIME
QUILTING SVC
QUILTING SVC & SPLYS, FOR THE TRADE
QUILTING: Individuals

R

RACETRACKS
RACEWAYS
RACKS & SHELVING: Household, Wood
RACKS: Bicycle, Automotive
RACKS: Display
RACKS: Railroad Car, Vehicle Transportation, Steel
RACKS: Trash, Metal Rack
RADAR SYSTEMS & EQPT

RADIO & TELEVISION COMMUNICATIONS EQUIPMENT
RADIO BROADCASTING & COMMUNICATIONS EQPT
RADIO BROADCASTING STATIONS
RADIO COMMUNICATIONS: Airborne Eqpt
RADIO RECEIVER NETWORKS
RADIO, TELEVISION & CONSUMER ELECTRONICS
STORES: Antennas
RADIO, TELEVISION & CONSUMER ELECTRONICS
STORES: Eqpt, NEC
RADIO, TELEVISION & CONSUMER ELECTRONICS
STORES: TV Sets
RAIL & STRUCTURAL SHAPES: Aluminum rail & structural
shapes
RAILINGS: Prefabricated, Metal
RAILROAD CAR RENTING & LEASING SVCS
RAILROAD CAR REPAIR SVCS
RAILROAD CROSSINGS: Steel Or Iron
RAILROAD EQPT
RAILROAD EQPT & SPLYS WHOLESALERS
RAILROAD EQPT: Brakes, Air & Vacuum
RAILROAD EQPT: Cars & Eqpt, Train, Freight Or Passenger
RAILROAD EQPT: Locomotives & Parts, Electric Or Nonelectric
RAILROAD EQPT: Locomotives & Parts, Indl
RAILROAD EQPT: Tenders, Locomotive
RAILROAD EQPT: Trackless Trolley Buses
RAILROAD MAINTENANCE & REPAIR SVCS
RAILROAD TIES: Concrete
RAMPS: Prefabricated Metal
REAL ESTATE AGENCIES & BROKERS
REAL ESTATE AGENTS & MANAGERS
REAL ESTATE BROKERS: Manufactured Homes, On-Site
REAL ESTATE MANAGERS: Cemetery
REAL ESTATE OPERATORS, EXC DEVEL: Theater Bldg,
Owner & Op
REAL ESTATE OPERATORS, EXC DEVELOPERS: Commercial/Indl Bldg
REAL ESTATE OPS, EXC DEVELOPER: Residential Bldg, 4
Or Less
RECORDING HEADS: Speech & Musical Eqpt
RECORDS & TAPES: Prerecorded
RECOVERY SVC: Iron Ore, From Open Hearth Slag
RECREATIONAL & SPORTING CAMPS
RECREATIONAL CAMPS
RECREATIONAL DEALERS: Campers/Pickup Coaches Truck
Mounted
RECREATIONAL SPORTING EQPT REPAIR SVCS
RECREATIONAL VEHICLE DEALERS
RECREATIONAL VEHICLE PARTS & ACCESS STORES
RECREATIONAL VEHICLE: Wholesalers
RECYCLING: Paper
REELS: Cable, Metal
REELS: Fiber, Textile, Made From Purchased Materials
REELS: Wood
REFINERS & SMELTERS: Aluminum
REFINERS & SMELTERS: Antimony, Primary
REFINERS & SMELTERS: Nonferrous Metal
REFINING LUBRICATING OILS & GREASES, NEC
REFINING: Petroleum
REFLECTIVE ROAD MARKERS, WHOLESALE
REFRACTORIES: Brick
REFRACTORIES: Clay
REFRACTORIES: Foundry, Clay
REFRACTORIES: Glasshouse
REFRACTORIES: Nonclay
REFRACTORIES: Tile & Brick, Exc Plastic
REFRACTORY CASTABLES
REFRACTORY MATERIALS WHOLESALERS
REFRIGERATION & HEATING EQUIPMENT
REFRIGERATION EQPT & SPLYS WHOLESALERS
REFRIGERATION EQPT & SPLYS, WHOLESALE: Beverage
Coolers
REFRIGERATION EQPT & SPLYS, WHOLESALE: Commercial Eqpt
REFRIGERATION EQPT: Complete
REFRIGERATION SVC & REPAIR
REFRIGERATOR REPAIR SVCS
REFUSE SYSTEMS
REGISTERS: Air, Metal
REGULATORS: Generator Voltage
REGULATORS: Transmission & Distribution Voltage
REGULATORS: Voltage, Automotive
REHABILITATION CTR, RESIDENTIAL WITH HEALTH CARE
INCIDENTAL
REHABILITATION SVCS

RELAYS & SWITCHES: Indl, Electric
RELAYS: Electronic Usage
RELIGIOUS SPLYS WHOLESALERS
RELOCATION SVCS
REMOVERS & CLEANERS
REMOVERS: Paint
RENTAL CENTERS: Party & Banquet Eqpt & Splys
RENTAL SVCS: Business Machine & Electronic Eqpt
RENTAL SVCS: Costume
RENTAL SVCS: Golf Cart, Power
RENTAL SVCS: Lawn & Garden Eqpt
RENTAL SVCS: Oil Eqpt
RENTAL SVCS: Recreational Vehicle
RENTAL SVCS: Sporting Goods, NEC
RENTAL SVCS: Stores & Yards Eqpt
RENTAL SVCS: Tent & Tarpaulin
RENTAL: Passenger Car
RENTAL: Portable Toilet
RENTAL: Video Tape & Disc
RESEARCH, DEV & TESTING SVCS, COMM: Chem Lab,
Exc Testing
RESEARCH, DEVELOPMENT & TEST SVCS, COMM: Cmptr
Hardware Dev
RESEARCH, DEVELOPMENT & TESTING SVCS, COMM:
Agricultural
RESEARCH, DEVELOPMENT & TESTING SVCS, COMM:
Research Lab
RESEARCH, DEVELOPMENT & TESTING SVCS, COMMERCIAL: Economic
RESEARCH, DEVELOPMENT & TESTING SVCS, COMMERCIAL: Medical
RESEARCH, DEVELOPMENT & TESTING SVCS, COMMERCIAL: Physical
RESEARCH, DVLPMT & TESTING SVCS, COMM: Merger,
Acq & Reorg
RESEARCH, DVLPT & TEST SVCS, COMM: Mkt Analysis or
Research
RESEARCH, DVLPT & TESTING SVCS, COMM: Mkt, Bus &
Economic
RESIDENTIAL MENTAL HEALTH & SUBSTANCE ABUSE FACILITIES
RESIDENTIAL REMODELERS
RESIDUES
RESINS: Custom Compound Purchased
RESISTORS
RESISTORS & RESISTOR UNITS
RESPIRATORS
RESTAURANT EQPT: Food Wagons
RESTAURANT RESERVATION SVCS
RESTAURANTS: Fast Food
RESTAURANTS:Full Svc, American
RESTAURANTS:Full Svc, Barbecue
RESTAURANTS:Full Svc, Family, Chain
RESTAURANTS:Full Svc, Family, Independent
RESTAURANTS:Full Svc, Mexican
RESTAURANTS:Limited Svc, Chicken
RESTAURANTS:Limited Svc, Coffee Shop
RESTAURANTS:Limited Svc, Ice Cream Stands Or Dairy
Bars
RESTAURANTS:Limited Svc, Lunch Counter
RESTAURANTS:Limited Svc, Pizza
RESTAURANTS:Limited Svc, Pizzeria, Chain
RESUME WRITING SVCS
RETAIL BAKERY: Bread
RETAIL BAKERY: Cakes
RETAIL BAKERY: Cookies
RETAIL BAKERY: Doughnuts
RETAIL BAKERY: Pretzels
RETAIL LUMBER YARDS
RETAIL STORES, NEC
RETAIL STORES: Alarm Signal Systems
RETAIL STORES: Artificial Limbs
RETAIL STORES: Audio-Visual Eqpt & Splys
RETAIL STORES: Awnings
RETAIL STORES: Business Machines & Eqpt
RETAIL STORES: Canvas Prdts
RETAIL STORES: Christmas Lights & Decorations
RETAIL STORES: Cleaning Eqpt & Splys
RETAIL STORES: Cosmetics
RETAIL STORES: Decals
RETAIL STORES: Drafting Eqpt & Splys
RETAIL STORES: Electronic Parts & Eqpt
RETAIL STORES: Engines & Parts, Air-Cooled
RETAIL STORES: Fire Extinguishers
RETAIL STORES: Flags

RETAIL STORES: Hair Care Prdts
RETAIL STORES: Hearing Aids
RETAIL STORES: Ice
RETAIL STORES: Infant Furnishings & Eqpt
RETAIL STORES: Medical Apparatus & Splys
RETAIL STORES: Monuments, Finished To Custom Order
RETAIL STORES: Motors, Electric
RETAIL STORES: Orthopedic & Prosthesis Applications
RETAIL STORES: Perfumes & Colognes
RETAIL STORES: Pet Splys
RETAIL STORES: Plumbing & Heating Splys
RETAIL STORES: Rubber Stamps
RETAIL STORES: Spas & Hot Tubs
RETAIL STORES: Technical Aids For The Handicapped
RETAIL STORES: Telephone & Communication Eqpt
RETAIL STORES: Tents
RETAIL STORES: Vaults & Safes
RETAIL STORES: Water Purification Eqpt
RETAIL STORES: Welding Splys
RETAIL STORES: Wheelchair Lifts
REUPHOLSTERY & FURNITURE REPAIR
REUPHOLSTERY SVCS
REWINDING SVCS
RIBBONS, NEC
RINGS: Angle
ROBOTS: Assembly Line
RODS: Extruded, Aluminum
RODS: Plastic
ROLL COVERINGS: Rubber
ROLL FORMED SHAPES: Custom
ROLLING MACHINERY: Steel
ROLLING MILL EQPT: Galvanizing Lines
ROLLING MILL MACHINERY
ROLLING MILL ROLLS: Cast Steel
ROLLS & BLANKETS, PRINTERS': Rubber Or Rubberized
Fabric
ROLLS & ROLL COVERINGS: Rubber
ROOF DECKS
ROOFING GRANULES
ROOFING MATERIALS: Asphalt
ROOFING MATERIALS: Sheet Metal
ROOFING MEMBRANE: Rubber
ROPE
RUBBER
RUBBER PRDTS
RUBBER PRDTS REPAIR SVCS
RUBBER PRDTS: Automotive, Mechanical
RUBBER PRDTS: Mechanical
RUBBER PRDTS: Silicone
RUBBER PRDTS: Sponge
RUBBER STAMP, WHOLESALE
RUBBER STRUCTURES: Air-Supported
RULERS: Metal
RUST ARRESTING COMPOUNDS: Animal Or Vegetable Oil
Based
RUST PROOFING SVC: Hot Dipping, Metals & Formed Prdts
RUST REMOVERS

S

SADDLERY STORES
SAFE DEPOSIT BOXES
SAFES & VAULTS: Metal
SAFETY EQPT & SPLYS WHOLESALERS
SAFETY INSPECTION SVCS
SALES PROMOTION SVCS
SALT
SAMPLE BOOKS
SAND & GRAVEL
SAND MINING
SAND: Hygrade
SANDBLASTING EQPT
SANDBLASTING SVC: Building Exterior
SANITARY SVCS: Hazardous Waste, Collection & Disposal
SANITARY SVCS: Medical Waste Disposal
SANITARY SVCS: Nonhazardous Waste Disposal Sites
SANITARY SVCS: Refuse Collection & Disposal Svcs
SANITARY SVCS: Rubbish Collection & Disposal
SANITARY SVCS: Sanitary Landfill, Operation Of
SANITARY SVCS: Sewage Treatment Facility
SANITARY SVCS: Waste Materials, Recycling
SANITARY WARE: Metal
SANITATION CHEMICALS & CLEANING AGENTS
SASHES: Door Or Window, Metal
SATCHELS
SATELLITE COMMUNICATIONS EQPT

INDEX

SATELLITES: Communications
SAW BLADES
SAWDUST & SHAVINGS
SAWING & PLANING MILLS
SAWING & PLANING MILLS: Custom
SAWMILL MACHINES
SAWS & SAWING EQPT
SAWS: Hand, Metalworking Or Woodworking
SCAFFOLDS: Mobile Or Stationary, Metal
SCALE REPAIR SVCS
SCALES & BALANCES, EXC LABORATORY
SCALES: Indl
SCALES: Railroad Track
SCANNING DEVICES: Optical
SCHOOL BUS SVC
SCHOOLS: Vocational, NEC
SCIENTIFIC INSTRUMENTS WHOLESALERS
SCISSORS: Hand
SCRAP & WASTE MATERIALS, WHOLESALE: Ferrous Metal
SCRAP & WASTE MATERIALS, WHOLESALE: Metal
SCRAP & WASTE MATERIALS, WHOLESALE: Nonferrous Metals Scrap
SCRAP & WASTE MATERIALS, WHOLESALE: Paper
SCRAP STEEL CUTTING
SCREENS: Projection
SCREENS: Window, Metal
SCREW MACHINE PRDTS
SCREWS: Metal
SEALANTS
SEALING COMPOUNDS: Sealing, synthetic rubber or plastic
SEALS: Hermetic
SEALS: Oil, Rubber
SEARCH & DETECTION SYSTEMS, EXC RADAR
SEARCH & NAVIGATION SYSTEMS
SEAT BELTS: Automobile & Aircraft
SEATING: Bleacher, Portable
SEATING: Stadium
SECURITIES DEALING
SECURITY CONTROL EQPT & SYSTEMS
SECURITY DEVICES
SECURITY GUARD SVCS
SECURITY SYSTEMS SERVICES
SEEDS & BULBS WHOLESALERS
SELF-DEFENSE & ATHLETIC INSTRUCTION SVCS
SEMICONDUCTORS & RELATED DEVICES
SENSORS: Radiation
SENSORS: Temperature, Exc Indl Process
SENSORS: Ultraviolet, Solid State
SEPTIC TANKS: Concrete
SERVICES, NEC
SEWAGE & WATER TREATMENT EQPT
SEWER CLEANING & RODDING SVC
SEWER CLEANING EQPT: Power
SEWING CONTRACTORS
SEWING MACHINE REPAIR SHOP
SEWING MACHINES & PARTS: Indl
SEWING, NEEDLEWORK & PIECE GOODS STORES: Notions, Incl Trim
SEWING, NEEDLEWORK & PIECE GOODS STORES: Sewing & Needlework
SHADES: Lamp & Light, Residential
SHADES: Window
SHALE: Expanded
SHAPES & PILINGS, STRUCTURAL: Steel
SHAPES: Extruded, Aluminum, NEC
SHAVING PREPARATIONS
SHEET METAL SPECIALTIES, EXC STAMPED
SHEETING: Laminated Plastic
SHEETING: Window, Plastic
SHEETS & STRIPS: Aluminum
SHEETS: Solid Fiber, Made From Purchased Materials
SHELLAC
SHELTERED WORKSHOPS
SHELVING, MADE FROM PURCHASED WIRE
SHELVING: Office & Store, Exc Wood
SHIELDS OR ENCLOSURES: Radiator, Sheet Metal
SHIMS: Metal
SHIP BLDG & RPRG: Drilling & Production Platforms, Oil/Gas
SHIP BUILDING & REPAIRING: Cargo, Commercial
SHIP BUILDING & REPAIRING: Ferryboats
SHIP BUILDING & REPAIRING: Lighters, Marine
SHIP BUILDING & REPAIRING: Military
SHIP BUILDING & REPAIRING: Towboats
SHIPBUILDING & REPAIR
SHOE & BOOT ACCESS

SHOE MATERIALS: Counters
SHOE MATERIALS: Inner Parts
SHOE MATERIALS: Quarters
SHOE MATERIALS: Uppers
SHOE STORES
SHOE STORES: Athletic
SHOE STORES: Custom & Orthopedic
SHOES & BOOTS WHOLESALERS
SHOES: Athletic, Exc Rubber Or Plastic
SHOES: Canvas, Rubber Soled
SHOES: Infants' & Children's
SHOES: Men's
SHOES: Men's, Dress
SHOES: Moccasins
SHOES: Plastic Or Rubber
SHOPPING CENTERS & MALLS
SHOT PEENING SVC
SHOWCASES & DISPLAY FIXTURES: Office & Store
SHOWER STALLS: Metal
SHOWER STALLS: Plastic & Fiberglass
SHREDDERS: Indl & Commercial
SHUTTERS, DOOR & WINDOW: Metal
SHUTTERS, DOOR & WINDOW: Plastic
SIDING & STRUCTURAL MATERIALS: Wood
SIDING MATERIALS
SIDING: Sheet Metal
SIGN LETTERING & PAINTING SVCS
SIGN PAINTING & LETTERING SHOP
SIGNALING APPARATUS: Electric
SIGNALS: Traffic Control, Electric
SIGNS & ADVERTISING SPECIALTIES
SIGNS & ADVERTISING SPECIALTIES: Artwork, Advertising
SIGNS & ADVERTISING SPECIALTIES: Novelties
SIGNS & ADVERTISING SPECIALTIES: Scoreboards, Electric
SIGNS & ADVERTISING SPECIALTIES: Signs
SIGNS & ADVERTSG SPECIALTIES: Displays/Cutouts Window/Lobby
SIGNS, ELECTRICAL: Wholesalers
SIGNS, EXC ELECTRIC, WHOLESALE
SIGNS: Electrical
SIGNS: Neon
SILICONES
SILK SCREEN DESIGN SVCS
SILVERWARE
SIMULATORS: Flight
SINK TOPS, PLASTIC LAMINATED
SINKS: Vitreous China
SIRENS: Vehicle, Marine, Indl & Warning
SKIDS: Wood
SKILL TRAINING CENTER
SLAB & TILE: Precast Concrete, Floor
SLABS: Steel
SLAG: Crushed Or Ground
SLAUGHTERING & MEAT PACKING
SLIDES & EXHIBITS: Prepared
SMOKE DETECTORS
SNOW REMOVAL EQPT: Residential
SNOWMOBILES
SOAPS & DETERGENTS
SOAPS & DETERGENTS: Textile
SOCIAL SVCS, HANDICAPPED
SOCKETS & RECEPTACLES: Lamp, Electric Wiring Devices
SOFT DRINKS WHOLESALERS
SOFTWARE PUBLISHERS: Application
SOFTWARE PUBLISHERS: Business & Professional
SOFTWARE PUBLISHERS: Computer Utilities
SOFTWARE PUBLISHERS: Education
SOFTWARE PUBLISHERS: Home Entertainment
SOFTWARE PUBLISHERS: NEC
SOFTWARE PUBLISHERS: Publisher's
SOFTWARE TRAINING, COMPUTER
SOIL TESTING KITS
SOLAR CELLS
SOLAR HEATING EQPT
SOLID CONTAINING UNITS: Concrete
SOLVENTS
SOLVENTS: Organic
SONAR SYSTEMS & EQPT
SOUND EQPT: Electric
SOUVENIR SHOPS
SOYBEAN PRDTS
SPACE PROPULSION UNITS & PARTS
SPACE VEHICLE EQPT
SPEAKER SYSTEMS

SPECIAL PRODUCT SAWMILLS, NEC
SPECIALTY FOOD STORES: Vitamin
SPEED CHANGERS
SPICE & HERB STORES
SPONGES: Bleached & Dyed
SPOOLS: Fiber, Made From Purchased Materials
SPOOLS: Indl
SPORTING & ATHLETIC GOODS: Arrows, Archery
SPORTING & ATHLETIC GOODS: Bags, Golf
SPORTING & ATHLETIC GOODS: Bags, Rosin
SPORTING & ATHLETIC GOODS: Basketball Eqpt & Splys, NEC
SPORTING & ATHLETIC GOODS: Batons
SPORTING & ATHLETIC GOODS: Boomerangs
SPORTING & ATHLETIC GOODS: Bowling Balls
SPORTING & ATHLETIC GOODS: Bowling Pins
SPORTING & ATHLETIC GOODS: Bows, Archery
SPORTING & ATHLETIC GOODS: Buckets, Fish & Bait
SPORTING & ATHLETIC GOODS: Camping Eqpt & Splys
SPORTING & ATHLETIC GOODS: Crossbows
SPORTING & ATHLETIC GOODS: Decoys, Duck & Other Game Birds
SPORTING & ATHLETIC GOODS: Fish & Bait Baskets Or Creels
SPORTING & ATHLETIC GOODS: Fishing Eqpt
SPORTING & ATHLETIC GOODS: Fishing Tackle, General
SPORTING & ATHLETIC GOODS: Game Calls
SPORTING & ATHLETIC GOODS: Gymnasium Eqpt
SPORTING & ATHLETIC GOODS: Lacrosse Eqpt & Splys, NEC
SPORTING & ATHLETIC GOODS: Ping-Pong Tables
SPORTING & ATHLETIC GOODS: Pools, Swimming, Exc Plastic
SPORTING & ATHLETIC GOODS: Pools, Swimming, Plastic
SPORTING & ATHLETIC GOODS: Shafts, Golf Club
SPORTING & ATHLETIC GOODS: Shooting Eqpt & Splys, General
SPORTING & ATHLETIC GOODS: Shuffleboards & Shuffleboard Eqpt
SPORTING & ATHLETIC GOODS: Soccer Eqpt & Splys
SPORTING & ATHLETIC GOODS: Target Shooting Eqpt
SPORTING & ATHLETIC GOODS: Targets, Archery & Rifle Shooting
SPORTING & ATHLETIC GOODS: Team Sports Eqpt
SPORTING & ATHLETIC GOODS: Tennis Eqpt & Splys
SPORTING & ATHLETIC GOODS: Trap Racks, Clay Targets
SPORTING & ATHLETIC GOODS: Water Sports Eqpt
SPORTING & REC GOODS, WHOLESALE: Boats, Canoes, Etc/Eqpt
SPORTING & RECREATIONAL GOODS & SPLYS WHOLESALERS
SPORTING & RECREATIONAL GOODS, WHOLESALE: Athletic Goods
SPORTING & RECREATIONAL GOODS, WHOLESALE: Bicycle
SPORTING & RECREATIONAL GOODS, WHOLESALE: Bowling
SPORTING & RECREATIONAL GOODS, WHOLESALE: Fishing Tackle
SPORTING & RECREATIONAL GOODS, WHOLESALE: Golf
SPORTING & RECREATIONAL GOODS, WHOLESALE: Hunting
SPORTING & RECREATIONAL GOODS, WHOLESALE: Outboard Motors
SPORTING CAMPS
SPORTING GOODS
SPORTING GOODS STORES, NEC
SPORTING GOODS STORES: Archery Splys
SPORTING GOODS STORES: Bait & Tackle
SPORTING GOODS STORES: Camping & Backpacking Eqpt
SPORTING GOODS STORES: Firearms
SPORTING GOODS STORES: Fishing Eqpt
SPORTING GOODS STORES: Football Eqpt
SPORTING GOODS STORES: Playground Eqpt
SPORTING GOODS STORES: Soccer Splys
SPORTING GOODS STORES: Specialty Sport Splys, NEC
SPORTING GOODS STORES: Team sports Eqpt
SPORTING GOODS: Archery
SPORTING GOODS: Hammocks & Other Net Prdts
SPORTING GOODS: Skin Diving Eqpt
SPORTING GOODS: Surfboards
SPORTS APPAREL STORES
SPORTS CLUBS, MANAGERS & PROMOTERS
SPORTS PROMOTION SVCS
SPRAYING EQPT: Agricultural

SPRINGS: Coiled Flat
SPRINGS: Gun, Precision
SPRINGS: Mechanical, Precision
SPRINGS: Precision
SPRINGS: Sash Balances
SPRINGS: Steel
SPRINGS: Torsion Bar
SPRINGS: Upholstery, Unassembled
SPRINGS: Wire
SPRINKLING SYSTEMS: Fire Control
STACKING MACHINES: Automatic
STAGE LIGHTING SYSTEMS
STAINLESS STEEL
STAINS: Biological
STAINS: Wood
STAIRCASES & STAIRS, WOOD
STAMPING: Fabric Articles
STAMPINGS: Automotive
STAMPINGS: Metal
STANDS: Ground Servicing, Aircraft
STAPLES, MADE FROM PURCHASED WIRE
STARTERS & CONTROLLERS: Motor, Electric
STARTERS: Electric Motor
STARTERS: Motor
STATIC ELIMINATORS: Ind
STATIONARY & OFFICE SPLYS, WHOL: Computer/Photo-
  copying Splys
STATIONER'S SUNDRIES: Rubber
STATIONERY & OFFICE SPLYS WHOLESALERS
STATIONERY PRDTS
STATORS REWINDING SVCS
STEEL & ALLOYS: Tool & Die
STEEL FABRICATORS
STEEL MILLS
STEEL SHEET: Cold-Rolled
STEEL WOOL
STEEL, COLD-ROLLED: Sheet Or Strip, From Own Hot-
  Rolled
STEEL, COLD-ROLLED: Strip NEC, From Purchased Hot-
  Rolled
STEEL, COLD-ROLLED: Strip Or Wire
STEEL, HOT-ROLLED: Sheet Or Strip
STEEL: Cold-Rolled
STEEL: Galvanized
STENCILS & LETTERING MATERIALS: Die-Cut
STERILIZERS, BARBER & BEAUTY SHOP
STITCHING SVCS
STOCK: Vehicle, Hardwood
STONE: Cast Concrete
STONE: Crushed & Broken, NEC
STONE: Dimension, NEC
STONE: Quarrying & Processing, Own Stone Prdts
STONEWARE PRDTS: Pottery
STORE FIXTURES, EXC REFRIGERATED: Wholesalers
STORE FIXTURES: Exc Wood
STORE FIXTURES: Wood
STORES: Auto & Home Supply
STORES: Drapery & Upholstery
STOVES: Wood & Coal Burning
STRAIGHTENERS
STRAIN GAGES: Solid State
STRAPPING
STRAPS: Bindings, Textile
STRAPS: Cotton Webbing
STRAWS: Drinking, Made From Purchased Materials
STRUCTURAL SUPPORT & BUILDING MATERIAL: Concrete
STUCCO
STUDIOS: Artist
STUDIOS: Artists & Artists' Studios
STUDIOS: Sculptor's
STYRENE
SUBMARINE BUILDING & REPAIR
SUNDRIES & RELATED PRDTS: Medical & Laboratory, Rub-
  ber
SUPERMARKETS & OTHER GROCERY STORES
SURFACE ACTIVE AGENTS
SURGICAL & MEDICAL INSTRUMENTS WHOLESALERS
SURGICAL APPLIANCES & SPLYS
SURGICAL APPLIANCES & SPLYS
SURGICAL EQPT: See Also Instruments
SURGICAL IMPLANTS
SURVEYING SVCS: Photogrammetric Engineering
SUSPENSION SYSTEMS: Acoustical, Metal
SVC ESTABLISH EQPT, WHOLESALE: Carpet/Rug Clean
  Eqpt & Sply

SVC ESTABLISHMENT EQPT, WHOL: Concrete Burial Vaults
  & Boxes
SVC ESTABLISHMENT EQPT, WHOLESALE: Beauty Parlor
  Eqpt & Sply
SVC ESTABLISHMENT EQPT, WHOLESALE: Electrolysis
  Eqpt & Splys
SVC ESTABLISHMENT EQPT, WHOLESALE: Firefighting
  Eqpt
SWIMMING POOL EQPT: Filters & Water Conditioning Sys-
  tems
SWIMMING POOL SPLY STORES
SWIMMING POOLS, EQPT & SPLYS: Wholesalers
SWITCHBOARD APPARATUS, EXC INSTRUMENTS
SWITCHES
SWITCHES: Electric Power
SWITCHES: Electric Power, Exc Snap, Push Button, Etc
SWITCHES: Electronic
SWITCHES: Electronic Applications
SWITCHES: Thermostatic
SWITCHGEAR & SWITCHBOARD APPARATUS
SWITCHGEAR & SWITCHGEAR ACCESS, NEC
SYNCHROS
SYNTHETIC RESIN FINISHED PRDTS, NEC
SYSTEMS ENGINEERING: Computer Related
SYSTEMS INTEGRATION SVCS
SYSTEMS INTEGRATION SVCS: Office Computer Automa-
  tion
SYSTEMS SOFTWARE DEVELOPMENT SVCS

T

TABLE OR COUNTERTOPS, PLASTIC LAMINATED
TABLES: Lift, Hydraulic
TACKS: Nonferrous Metal Or Wire
TAGS & LABELS: Paper
TALLOW: Animal
TANK REPAIR SVCS
TANKS & OTHER TRACKED VEHICLE CMPNTS
TANKS: Cryogenic, Metal
TANKS: Fuel, Including Oil & Gas, Metal Plate
TANKS: Lined, Metal
TANKS: Plastic & Fiberglass
TANKS: Standard Or Custom Fabricated, Metal Plate
TANKS: Storage, Farm, Metal Plate
TANKS: Water, Metal Plate
TANNING SALONS
TAPE SLITTING SVCS
TAPE STORAGE UNITS: Computer
TAPE: Rubber
TAPES, ADHESIVE: Medical
TAPES: Coated Fiberglass, Pipe Sealing Or Insulating
TAPES: Fabric
TAPES: Insulating
TAPES: Plastic Coated
TAPES: Pressure Sensitive
TARPAULINS
TARPAULINS, WHOLESALE
TATTOO PARLORS
TAX RETURN PREPARATION SVCS
TAXIDERMISTS
TECHNICAL MANUAL PREPARATION SVCS
TECHNICAL WRITING SVCS
TELECOMMUNICATION SYSTEMS & EQPT
TELECOMMUNICATIONS CARRIERS & SVCS: Wired
TELECOMMUNICATIONS CARRIERS & SVCS: Wireless
TELEMARKETING BUREAUS
TELEPHONE ANSWERING MACHINES
TELEPHONE CENTRAL OFFICE EQPT: Dial Or Manual
TELEPHONE EQPT: Modems
TELEPHONE EQPT: NEC
TELEPHONE SVCS
TELEPHONE: Fiber Optic Systems
TELEPHONE: Sets, Exc Cellular Radio
TELEVISION BROADCASTING STATIONS
TELEVISION SETS
TEMPERING: Metal
TEMPLES, RELIGIOUS
TENTS: All Materials
TEST BORING SVC: Anthracite Mining
TESTERS: Battery
TESTERS: Environmental
TESTERS: Gas, Exc Indl Process
TESTERS: Hardness
TESTERS: Physical Property
TESTERS: Water, Exc Indl Process
TEXTILE & APPAREL SVCS

TEXTILE FABRICATORS
TEXTILE: Finishing, Cotton Broadwoven
TEXTILE: Goods, NEC
TEXTILES: Bagging, Jute
TEXTILES: Jute & Flax Prdts
TEXTILES: Padding & Wadding
TEXTILES: Wool Waste, Processes
THEATRICAL PRODUCTION SVCS
THEOLOGICAL SEMINARIES
THERMOCOUPLES
THERMOPLASTIC MATERIALS
THERMOSTAT REPAIR SVCS
THERMOSTATS: Refrigeration
THREAD WHOLESALERS
THREAD: Embroidery
THREAD: Needle & Handicraft
TIES, FORM: Metal
TILE: Brick & Structural, Clay
TILE: Clay, Drain & Structural
TILE: Rubber
TIMBER PRDTS WHOLESALERS
TIMERS: Indl, Clockwork Mechanism Only
TIN
TIRE & INNER TUBE MATERIALS & RELATED PRDTS
TIRE DEALERS
TIRE INFLATORS: Hand Or Compressor Operated
TIRE INNER-TUBES
TIRES & INNER TUBES
TIRES & TUBES WHOLESALERS
TIRES & TUBES, WHOLESALE: Automotive
TIRES: Auto
TIRES: Cushion Or Solid Rubber
TIRES: Motorcycle, Pneumatic
TITANIUM MILL PRDTS
TOBACCO & PRDTS, WHOLESALE: Smokeless
TOBACCO & PRDTS, WHOLESALE: Smoking
TOBACCO LEAF PROCESSING
TOBACCO STORES & STANDS
TOBACCO: Chewing
TOBACCO: Cigarettes
TOBACCO: Cigars
TOBACCO: Smoking
TOILETRIES, COSMETICS & PERFUME STORES
TOILETRIES, WHOLESALE: Toilet Soap
TOILETRIES, WHOLESALE: Toiletries
TOILETS, PORTABLE, WHOLESALE
TOILETS: Metal
TOILETS: Portable Chemical, Plastics
TOOL & DIE STEEL
TOOL REPAIR SVCS
TOOLS: Carpenters', Including Levels & Chisels, Exc Saws
TOOLS: Hand
TOOLS: Hand, Carpet Layers
TOOLS: Hand, Ironworkers'
TOOLS: Hand, Power
TOOLS: Hand, Stonecutters'
TOOTHPASTES, GELS & TOOTHPOWDERS
TOWELS: Indl
TOWERS, SECTIONS: Transmission, Radio & Television
TOWING BARS & SYSTEMS
TOYS
TOYS & HOBBY GOODS & SPLYS, WHOLESALE:
  Arts/Crafts Eqpt/Sply
TOYS & HOBBY GOODS & SPLYS, WHOLESALE: Board
  Games
TOYS & HOBBY GOODS & SPLYS, WHOLESALE: Model
  Kits
TOYS & HOBBY GOODS & SPLYS, WHOLESALE: Toys &
  Games
TOYS & HOBBY GOODS & SPLYS, WHOLESALE: Video
  Games
TOYS, HOBBY GOODS & SPLYS WHOLESALERS
TOYS: Dolls, Stuffed Animals & Parts
TOYS: Electronic
TOYS: Kites
TRADING STAMP PROMOTION & REDEMPTION
TRAFFIC CONTROL FLAGGING SVCS
TRAILER COACHES: Automobile
TRAILERS & CHASSIS: Camping
TRAILERS & PARTS: Boat
TRAILERS & PARTS: Horse
TRAILERS & PARTS: Truck & Semi's
TRAILERS & TRAILER EQPT
TRAILERS OR VANS: Horse Transportation, Fifth-Wheel Type
TRAILERS: Bodies

INDEX

TRAILERS: Camping, Tent-Type
TRAILERS: Demountable Cargo Containers
TRAILERS: House, Exc Permanent Dwellings
TRAILERS: Semitrailers, Truck Tractors
TRAILERS: Truck, Chassis
TRANSDUCERS: Electrical Properties
TRANSFORMERS: Distribution
TRANSFORMERS: Electronic
TRANSFORMERS: Furnace, Electric
TRANSFORMERS: Power Related
TRANSFORMERS: Specialty
TRANSLATION & INTERPRETATION SVCS
TRANSMISSIONS: Motor Vehicle
TRANSPORTATION EPQT & SPLYS, WHOL: Aircraft Engs/Eng Parts
TRANSPORTATION EPQT & SPLYS, WHOLESALE: Acft/Space Vehicle
TRANSPORTATION EPQT & SPLYS, WHOLESALE: Combat Vehicles
TRANSPORTATION EPQT & SPLYS, WHOLESALE: Pulleys
TRANSPORTATION EPQT & SPLYS, WHOLESALE: Tanks & Tank Compnts
TRANSPORTATION EPQT/SPLYS, WHOL: Marine Propulsn Mach/Eqpt
TRANSPORTATION EQPT & SPLYS WHOLESALERS, NEC
TRANSPORTATION EQUIPMENT, NEC
TRANSPORTATION SVCS, WATER: Canal Barge Operations
TRANSPORTATION: Bus Transit Systems
TRANSPORTATION: Water Freight, NEC
TRAP ROCK: Crushed & Broken
TRAPS: Stem
TRAVEL AGENCIES
TRAVEL TRAILER DEALERS
TRAVEL TRAILERS & CAMPERS
TRAVELER ACCOMMODATIONS, NEC
TROPHIES, NEC
TROPHIES, SILVER
TROPHIES, WHOLESALE
TROPHIES: Metal, Exc Silver
TROPHY & PLAQUE STORES
TRUCK & BUS BODIES: Ambulance
TRUCK & BUS BODIES: Automobile Wrecker Truck
TRUCK & BUS BODIES: Beverage Truck
TRUCK & BUS BODIES: Cement Mixer
TRUCK & BUS BODIES: Dump Truck
TRUCK & BUS BODIES: Garbage Or Refuse Truck
TRUCK & BUS BODIES: Motor Vehicle, Specialty
TRUCK & BUS BODIES: Tank Truck
TRUCK & BUS BODIES: Truck Beds
TRUCK & BUS BODIES: Truck Cabs, Motor Vehicles
TRUCK & BUS BODIES: Truck Tops
TRUCK & BUS BODIES: Truck, Motor Vehicle
TRUCK & BUS BODIES: Van Bodies
TRUCK BODIES: Body Parts
TRUCK BODY SHOP
TRUCK DRIVER SVCS
TRUCK GENERAL REPAIR SVC
TRUCK PAINTING & LETTERING SVCS
TRUCK PARTS & ACCESSORIES: Wholesalers
TRUCKING & HAULING SVCS: Contract Basis
TRUCKING & HAULING SVCS: Haulage & Cartage, Light, Local
TRUCKING & HAULING SVCS: Heavy Machinery, Local
TRUCKING & HAULING SVCS: Lumber & Log, Local
TRUCKING & HAULING SVCS: Steel, Local
TRUCKING, DUMP
TRUCKING: Except Local
TRUCKING: Local, With Storage
TRUCKING: Local, Without Storage
TRUCKS & TRACTORS: Industrial
TRUCKS: Forklift
TRUCKS: Indl
TRUSSES & FRAMING: Prefabricated Metal
TRUSSES: Wood, Floor
TRUSSES: Wood, Roof
TUB CONTAINERS: Plastic
TUBE & PIPE MILL EQPT
TUBE & TUBING FABRICATORS
TUBES: Extruded Or Drawn, Aluminum
TUBES: Finned, For Heat Transfer
TUBES: Gas Or Vapor
TUBES: Generator, Electron Beam, Beta Ray
TUBES: Light Sensing & Emitting
TUBES: Mailing
TUBES: Paper

TUBES: Steel & Iron
TUBES: Television
TUBES: Welded, Aluminum
TUBES: Wrought, Welded Or Lock Joint
TUBING, COLD-DRAWN: Mech Or Hypodermic Sizes, Stainless
TUBING: Flexible, Metallic
TUBING: Plastic
TUBING: Rubber
TUBING: Seamless
TUNGSTEN CARBIDE
TUNGSTEN MILL PRDTS
TURBINES & TURBINE GENERATOR SET UNITS, COMPLETE
TURBINES & TURBINE GENERATOR SET UNITS: Gas, Complete
TURBINES & TURBINE GENERATOR SETS
TURBINES & TURBINE GENERATOR SETS & PARTS
TURBINES: Steam
TURBO-GENERATORS
TYPESETTING SVC
TYPESETTING SVC: Computer
TYPESETTING SVC: Linotype Composition, For Printing Trade
TYPOGRAPHY

U

ULTRASONIC EQPT: Cleaning, Exc Med & Dental
UNIFORM SPLY SVCS: Indl
UNIFORM STORES
UNISEX HAIR SALONS
UNIVERSITY
UNSUPPORTED PLASTICS: Floor Or Wall Covering
UPHOLSTERERS' EQPT & SPLYS WHOLESALERS
UPHOLSTERY WORK SVCS
UREA
URNS: Cut Stone
USED CAR DEALERS
USED MERCHANDISE STORES
UTENSILS: Household, Cooking & Kitchen, Metal
UTILITY TRAILER DEALERS

V

VACUUM CLEANERS: Household
VACUUM CLEANERS: Indl Type
VACUUM PUMPS & EQPT: Laboratory
VACUUM SYSTEMS: Air Extraction, Indl
VALUE-ADDED RESELLERS: Computer Systems
VALVES
VALVES & PARTS: Gas, Indl
VALVES & PIPE FITTINGS
VALVES & REGULATORS: Pressure, Indl
VALVES Solenoid
VALVES: Aerosol, Metal
VALVES: Aircraft
VALVES: Aircraft, Control, Hydraulic & Pneumatic
VALVES: Control, Automatic
VALVES: Fluid Power, Control, Hydraulic & pneumatic
VALVES: Indl
VAN CONVERSIONS
VAN CONVERSIONS
VARIETY STORES
VAULTS & SAFES WHOLESALERS
VEGETABLE OILS: Medicinal Grade, Refined Or Concentrated
VEHICLES: All Terrain
VEHICLES: Recreational
VENDING MACHINE REPAIR SVCS
VENDING MACHINES & PARTS
VENETIAN BLINDS & SHADES
VETERINARY PHARMACEUTICAL PREPARATIONS
VETERINARY PRDTS: Instruments & Apparatus
VIALS: Glass
VIDEO & AUDIO EQPT, WHOLESALE
VIDEO CAMERA-AUDIO RECORDERS: Household Use
VIDEO EQPT
VIDEO TAPE PRODUCTION SVCS
VIDEO TRIGGERS EXC REMOTE CONTROL TV DEVICES
VIDEO TRIGGERS: Remote Control TV Devices
VINYL RESINS, NEC
VISUAL COMMUNICATIONS SYSTEMS
VITAMINS: Natural Or Synthetic, Uncompounded, Bulk
VOCATIONAL REHABILITATION AGENCY

W

WALL & CEILING SQUARES: Concrete
WALL COVERINGS WHOLESALERS
WALLBOARD: Decorated, Made From Purchased Materials
WALLBOARD: Gypsum
WALLPAPER STORE
WALLS: Curtain, Metal
WAREHOUSING & STORAGE FACILITIES, NEC
WAREHOUSING & STORAGE, REFRIGERATED: Cold Storage Or Refrig
WAREHOUSING & STORAGE, REFRIGERATED: Frozen Or Refrig Goods
WAREHOUSING & STORAGE: Bulk St & Termnls, Hire, Petro/Chem
WAREHOUSING & STORAGE: Farm Prdts
WAREHOUSING & STORAGE: General
WAREHOUSING & STORAGE: General
WAREHOUSING & STORAGE: Miniwarehouse
WAREHOUSING & STORAGE: Self Storage
WARM AIR HEAT & AC EQPT & SPLYS, WHOLESALE Fan, Heat & Vent
WARM AIR HEATING & AC EQPT & SPLYS, WHOLESALE Air Filters
WARM AIR HEATING/AC EQPT/SPLYS, WHOL Warm Air Htg Eqpt/Splys
WARRANTY INSURANCE: Automobile
WASHERS
WASHERS: Lock
WASHERS: Rubber
WASHING MACHINES: Household
WATCH REPAIR SVCS
WATER HEATERS
WATER PURIFICATION EQPT: Household
WATER PURIFICATION PRDTS: Chlorination Tablets & Kits
WATER SOFTENER SVCS
WATER TREATMENT EQPT: Indl
WATER: Mineral, Carbonated, Canned & Bottled, Etc
WATER: Pasteurized, Canned & Bottled, Etc
WATERPROOFING COMPOUNDS
WAX Sealing wax
WAXES: Mineral, Natural
WAXES: Petroleum, Not Produced In Petroleum Refineries
WEATHER STRIP: Sponge Rubber
WEB SEARCH PORTALS: Internet
WEIGHING MACHINERY & APPARATUS
WELDING & CUTTING APPARATUS & ACCESS, NEC
WELDING EQPT
WELDING EQPT & SPLYS WHOLESALERS
WELDING EQPT & SPLYS: Resistance, Electric
WELDING EQPT & SPLYS: Wire, Bare & Coated
WELDING EQPT REPAIR SVCS
WELDING EQPT: Electric
WELDING EQPT: Electrical
WELDING MACHINES & EQPT: Ultrasonic
WELDING REPAIR SVC
WELDING SPLYS, EXC GASES: Wholesalers
WELDMENTS
WELL LOGGING EQPT
WESTERN APPAREL STORES
WET CORN MILLING
WHEELCHAIR LIFTS
WHEELCHAIRS
WHEELS
WHEELS & GRINDSTONES, EXC ARTIFICIAL: Abrasive
WHEELS & PARTS
WHEELS: Abrasive
WHEELS: Buffing & Polishing
WHEELS: Disc, Wheelbarrow, Stroller, Etc, Stamped Metal
WHIRLPOOL BATHS: Hydrotherapy
WHISTLES
WICKING
WINCHES
WIND CHIMES
WINDINGS: Coil, Electronic
WINDMILLS: Electric Power Generation
WINDMILLS: Farm Type
WINDOW & DOOR FRAMES
WINDOW CLEANING SVCS
WINDOW FRAMES & SASHES: Plastic
WINDOW FRAMES, MOLDING & TRIM: Vinyl
WINDOWS, LOUVER: Metal
WINDOWS: Frames, Wood
WINDOWS: Storm, Wood
WINDOWS: Wood

WINE CELLARS, BONDED: Wine, Blended
WIRE
WIRE & CABLE: Nonferrous, Building
WIRE & WIRE PRDTS
WIRE FABRIC: Welded Steel
WIRE MATERIALS: Copper
WIRE MATERIALS: Steel
WIRE PRDTS: Ferrous Or Iron, Made In Wiredrawing Plants
WIRE PRDTS: Steel & Iron
WIRE ROPE CENTERS
WIRE: Communication
WIRE: Magnet
WIRE: Mesh
WIRE: Nonferrous
WIRE: Nonferrous, Appliance Fixture
WIRE: Steel, Insulated Or Armored
WOMEN'S & CHILDREN'S CLOTHING WHOLESALERS, NEC
WOMEN'S & GIRLS' SPORTSWEAR WHOLESALERS
WOMEN'S CLOTHING STORES

WOOD & WOOD BY-PRDTS, WHOLESALE
WOOD PRDTS
WOOD PRDTS: Applicators
WOOD PRDTS: Battery Separators
WOOD PRDTS: Brackets
WOOD PRDTS: Bungs
WOOD PRDTS: Hampers, Laundry
WOOD PRDTS: Letters
WOOD PRDTS: Mantels
WOOD PRDTS: Moldings, Unfinished & Prefinished
WOOD PRDTS: Mulch Or Sawdust
WOOD PRDTS: Mulch, Wood & Bark
WOOD PRDTS: Outdoor, Structural
WOOD PRDTS: Panel Work
WOOD PRDTS: Porch Work
WOOD PRDTS: Shoe & Boot Prdts
WOOD PRDTS: Signboards
WOOD PRDTS: Spokes
WOOD PRDTS: Trim
WOOD PRDTS: Trophy Bases

WOOD PRODUCTS: Reconstituted
WOOD TREATING: Creosoting
WOOD TREATING: Structural Lumber & Timber
WOOD TREATING: Vehicle Lumber
WOOD TREATING: Wood Prdts, Creosoted
WOODWORK & TRIM: Interior & Ornamental
WOODWORK: Carved & Turned
WOODWORK: Interior & Ornamental, NEC
WOVEN WIRE PRDTS, NEC
WREATHS: Artificial

X

X-RAY EQPT & TUBES
X-RAY EQPT REPAIR SVCS

Y

YARN MILLS: Texturizing, Throwing & Twisting
YARN WHOLESALERS
YARN: Animal Fiber, Spun

INDEX

PRODUCT SECTION

Product category —→ **BOXES:** *Folding*

Edgar & Son Paperboard ....G..... 999 999-9999
Yourtown *(G-11480)*
Ready Box Co ....E...... 999 999-9999
City —→ Anytown *(G-7097)*

Indicates approximate employment figure
A = Over 500 employees, B = 251-500
C = 101-250, D = 51-100, E = 20-50
F = 10-19, G = 2-9

Business phone

Geographic Section entry number where full
company information appears.

See footnotes for symbols and codes identification.

- Refer to the Industrial Product Index preceding this section to locate product headings.

ABRASIVES

3M Company ....B...... 765 348-3200
Hartford City *(G-5976)*
3M Company ....B...... 317 692-6666
Indianapolis *(G-6288)*
Abrasive Products LLC ....G..... 317 423-3957
Indianapolis *(G-6312)*
Advanced Cutting Systems Inc ....E..... 260 423-3394
Fort Wayne *(G-4043)*
Andersons Agriculture Group LP ....F..... 765 564-6135
Delphi *(G-2414)*
Chance Abrasives ....G..... 219 871-0977
Michigan City *(G-9774)*
Drake Corporation ....E...... 812 683-2101
Jasper *(G-8246)*
Harsco Corporation ....E...... 219 944-6250
Gary *(G-5060)*
Mjp & Company LLC ....G..... 317 631-7263
Indianapolis *(G-7529)*
Reed Minerals ....G..... 219 944-6250
Gary *(G-5089)*
Royer Enterprises Inc ....F...... 260 359-0689
Huntington *(G-6245)*
Woodburn Diamond Die Co Inc ......D...... 260 632-4217
Woodburn *(G-14392)*

ABRASIVES: sandpaper

Sandpaper America Inc ....G..... 317 631-7263
Indianapolis *(G-7892)*
Sandpaper Studio LLC ....G..... 317 435-7479
Whiteland *(G-14245)*

ACCELERATION INDICATORS & SYSTEM COMPONENTS: Aerospace

Federal-Mogul LLC ....G..... 574 271-0274
South Bend *(G-12775)*
First Gear Inc ....F...... 260 490-3238
Fort Wayne *(G-4263)*
Harrison Manufacturing Inc ....G..... 812 466-1111
Avon *(G-445)*
Hobson Tool and Machine Co ....F...... 317 736-4203
Franklin *(G-4895)*

ACCELERATORS, RUBBER PROCESSING: Cyclic or Acyclic

Coeus Technology Inc ....G..... 765 203-2304
Anderson *(G-87)*

ACCOUNTING MACHINES & CASH REGISTERS

Jay Retail Systems LLC ....G..... 574 842-2313
Culver *(G-2325)*

ACCOUNTING SVCS: Certified Public

Frank R Komar CPA ....G..... 812 477-9110
Evansville *(G-3513)*

ACIDS: Boric

Eco Services Operations Corp ....E...... 219 932-7651
Hammond *(G-5874)*

ACRYLONITRILE BUTADIENE STYRENE RESINS

DSM Engineering Plastics Inc ....F...... 812 435-7500
Evansville *(G-3463)*

DSM Engineering Plastics Inc ....C...... 248 530-5500
Evansville *(G-3465)*

ACTUATORS: Indl, NEC

Flosource Inc ....E...... 765 342-1360
Martinsville *(G-9605)*
Micro-Precision Operations ....E...... 260 589-2136
Berne *(G-620)*
SMC Corporation of America ....B...... 317 899-3182
Noblesville *(G-11184)*

ADAPTERS: Well

Paulus Plastic Company Inc ....G..... 574 834-7663
North Webster *(G-11299)*

ADDITIVE BASED PLASTIC MATERIALS: Plasticizers

Excista Corporation ....G..... 734 224-3652
Fishers *(G-3908)*
Injection Plastics ....G..... 574 784-2070
Lapaz *(G-9118)*

ADHESIVES

Alpha Systems LLC ....F...... 574 295-5206
Elkhart *(G-2678)*
Big Dog Adhesives LLC ....G..... 574 299-6768
Elkhart *(G-2723)*
Bondline Adhesives Inc ....F...... 812 423-4651
Evansville *(G-3390)*
Capital Adhesives & Packg Corp ....F...... 317 834-5415
Mooresville *(G-10304)*
Chem Tech Inc ....F...... 574 848-1001
Bristol *(G-1052)*
Evans Adhesive Corporation ....G..... 812 859-4245
Spencer *(G-13024)*
Glueboss Adhesive Company LLC ....G..... 855 458-2677
Elkhart *(G-2888)*
Harvey Adhesives Inc ....G..... 877 547-5558
Carmel *(G-1397)*
Heartland Adhesives Inc ....G..... 219 310-8645
Crown Point *(G-2256)*
Industrial Adhesives Indiana ......G..... 317 271-2100
Indianapolis *(G-7206)*
Lomont Holdings Co Inc ....E...... 800 545-9023
Angola *(G-228)*
Lord Corporation ....D...... 317 259-4161
Indianapolis *(G-7418)*
Parr Corp ....G..... 574 264-9614
Elkhart *(G-3075)*
Parr Technologies LLC ....F...... 574 264-9614
Elkhart *(G-3076)*
Parson Adhesives Inc ....E...... 812 401-7277
Evansville *(G-3664)*
Patrick Industries Inc ....C...... 574 294-7511
Elkhart *(G-3080)*
PPG Architectural Finishes Inc ....G..... 765 447-9334
Lafayette *(G-8981)*
PPG Architectural Finishes Inc ....G..... 317 787-9393
Indianapolis *(G-7713)*
Technicote Inc ....D...... 812 466-9844
Terre Haute *(G-13349)*
Testworth Laboratories Inc ....F...... 260 244-5137
Columbia City *(G-1840)*

ADHESIVES & SEALANTS

3M Company ....B...... 317 692-6666
Indianapolis *(G-6288)*
Adhesive Solutions Company LLC ....G..... 260 691-0304
Columbia City *(G-1760)*

Cast Products LP ....E...... 574 294-2684
Elkhart *(G-2751)*
Coleman Cable LLC ....C...... 765 449-7227
Lafayette *(G-8875)*
Covalnce Spcalty Adhesives LLC ....B...... 812 424-2904
Evansville *(G-3434)*
Custom Building Products Inc ....D...... 765 656-0234
Frankfort *(G-4827)*
Davies-Imperial Coatings Inc ....E...... 219 933-0877
Hammond *(G-5869)*
Dehco Inc ....D...... 574 294-2684
Elkhart *(G-2792)*
Flexible Materials Inc ....D...... 812 280-9578
Jeffersonville *(G-8362)*
Gdc Inc ....C...... 574 533-3128
Goshen *(G-5222)*
Hco Holding I Corporation ....E...... 317 248-1344
Indianapolis *(G-7081)*
Iron Out Inc ....E...... 800 654-0791
Fort Wayne *(G-4383)*
Laticrete International Inc ....G..... 317 298-8510
Indianapolis *(G-7384)*
Marian Worldwide Inc ....D...... 317 638-6525
Indianapolis *(G-7454)*
Morgan Adhesives Company LLC .....B...... 812 342-2004
Columbus *(G-1976)*
PSC Industries Inc ....E...... 317 547-5439
Indianapolis *(G-7785)*
Royal Adhesives & Sealants LLC ....D...... 574 246-5000
South Bend *(G-12920)*
Royal Holdings Inc ....C...... 574 246-5000
South Bend *(G-12922)*
Sealcorpusa Inc ....E...... 866 868-0791
Evansville *(G-3720)*
Transcendia Inc ....C...... 765 935-1520
Richmond *(G-12068)*
Warsaw Chemical Company Inc ......D...... 574 267-3251
Warsaw *(G-13958)*

ADHESIVES & SEALANTS WHOLESALERS

Adhesive Solutions Company LLC ....G..... 260 691-0304
Columbia City *(G-1760)*

ADHESIVES: Adhesives, paste

Red Cloud Adhesives Inc ....G..... 219 331-3239
Crown Point *(G-2292)*

ADHESIVES: Epoxy

Baril Coatings ....F...... 260 665-8431
Angola *(G-196)*
Royal Adhesives & Sealants LLC ....E...... 574 246-5000
South Bend *(G-12921)*

ADULT EDUCATION SCHOOLS, PUBLIC

Pathfinder School LLC ....F...... 317 791-8777
Indianapolis *(G-7660)*

ADVERTISING AGENCIES

Charles E Watts ....G..... 812 547-8516
Tell City *(G-13158)*
Clondalkin Pharma & Healthcare ....C...... 812 464-2461
Evansville *(G-3420)*
Degler Mktg & Mailing Svcs ....E...... 317 873-5550
Zionsville *(G-14429)*
Don R Kill Publishing Inc ....G..... 574 271-9381
Granger *(G-5402)*
Dow Theory Forecasts Inc ....E...... 219 931-6480
Hammond *(G-5872)*

PRODUCT

Goldleaf Promotional Products ....G...... 317 202-2754
Indianapolis **(G-7022)**

Harrison Macdonald & Sons ....F...... 765 742-9012
Lafayette **(G-8911)**

Oswalt Menu Company Inc ....G...... 317 257-8039
Indianapolis **(G-7636)**

Ovation Communications Inc ....G...... 812 401-9100
Evansville **(G-3659)**

Printing Creations Inc ....G...... 765 759-9679
Yorktown **(G-14410)**

Rick Singleton ....E...... 574 259-5555
Mishawaka **(G-10117)**

Rowland Printing Co Inc ....F...... 317 773-1829
Noblesville **(G-11177)**

Shilling Sales Inc ....E...... 260 426-2626
Fort Wayne **(G-4621)**

ADVERTISING AGENCIES: Consultants

Advertising Communications Gro........E...... 317 843-2523
Carmel **(G-1304)**

Baxter Design & Advertising ....G...... 219 464-9237
Valparaiso **(G-13507)**

Sexton Melinda...................................G...... 812 522-4059
Seymour **(G-12484)**

ADVERTISING DISPLAY PRDTS

Prysm Inc ....G...... 317 324-1222
Carmel **(G-1459)**

Trinity Displays Inc ....G...... 219 201-8733
Michigan City **(G-9854)**

ADVERTISING MATERIAL DISTRIBUTION

C & W Inkd ....F...... 317 352-1000
Indianapolis **(G-6527)**

Sampco Inc ....C...... 413 442-4043
South Bend **(G-12925)**

ADVERTISING REPRESENTATIVES: Electronic Media

Federal Heath Sign Company LLC........G...... 317 581-7790
Carmel **(G-1380)**

ADVERTISING REPRESENTATIVES: Newspaper

Aim Media Indiana Oper LLC ....E...... 317 736-7101
Franklin **(G-4863)**

Big E Publications Inc ....G...... 317 485-4097
Fortville **(G-4768)**

TI Enterprises LLC..............................F...... 574 262-4706
Elkhart **(G-3218)**

ADVERTISING REPRESENTATIVES: Printed Media

Indy Metro Woman Magazine.................G...... 317 843-1344
Indianapolis **(G-7218)**

ADVERTISING REPRESENTATIVES: Radio

W Ay-FM Media Group Inc....................G...... 812 945-1043
New Albany **(G-10872)**

ADVERTISING SPECIALTIES, WHOLESALE

Able Printing & Bus Svcs LLC...............G...... 574 834-7006
North Webster **(G-11288)**

Abracadabra Graphics ....G...... 812 336-1971
Bloomington **(G-654)**

Apparel Promotions Inc ....G...... 574 294-7165
Elkhart **(G-2694)**

Apple Group Inc ....E...... 765 675-4777
Tipton **(G-13387)**

Awards Unlimited Inc ....G...... 765 447-9413
Lafayette **(G-8858)**

Baugh Enterprises Inc.........................F...... 812 334-8189
Bloomington **(G-674)**

Bc Awards Inc ....G...... 317 852-3240
Brownsburg **(G-1136)**

Burston Marketing Inc ....F...... 574 262-4005
Elkhart **(G-2739)**

Celestial Designs LLC ....G...... 317 733-3110
Zionsville **(G-14425)**

Dark Star Inc ....F...... 765 759-4764
Muncie **(G-10453)**

Discount Labels LLC ....A...... 812 945-2617
New Albany **(G-10769)**

Duneland Specialties Inc......................G...... 219 464-1616
Valparaiso **(G-13530)**

Favor It Promotions Inc ....F...... 317 733-1112
Carmel **(G-1379)**

Flag & Banner Company Inc ....F...... 317 299-4880
Indianapolis **(G-6931)**

Integrity Sign Solutions Inc ....G...... 502 233-8755
New Albany **(G-10807)**

Jer-Maur Corporation ....G...... 812 384-8290
Bloomfield **(G-640)**

Omnisource Marketing Group Inc ....G...... 317 575-3300
Indianapolis **(G-7620)**

P J Marketing Services Inc ....G...... 574 259-8843
South Bend **(G-12886)**

Paust Inc ....F...... 765 962-1507
Richmond **(G-12027)**

Preferred Enterprises Inc ....G...... 765 457-0637
Kokomo **(G-8684)**

Premiere Advertising ....G...... 317 722-2400
Indianapolis **(G-7742)**

Printing Solutions ....G...... 812 923-0756
Floyds Knobs **(G-4017)**

Shilling Sales Inc ....E...... 260 426-2626
Fort Wayne **(G-4621)**

Star Quality Awards Inc ....G...... 812 273-1740
Madison **(G-9496)**

Winters Assoc Prmtnal Pdts Inc ....F...... 812 330-7000
Bloomington **(G-858)**

ADVERTISING SVCS: Billboards

Burkhart Advertising Inc ....F...... 574 233-2101
South Bend **(G-12727)**

Burkhart Advertising Inc ....E...... 260 482-9566
Fort Wayne **(G-4127)**

Clear Channel Outdoor Inc ....E...... 317 686-2350
Indianapolis **(G-6619)**

Whiteco Industries Inc.........................A...... 219 769-6601
Merrillville **(G-9761)**

ADVERTISING SVCS: Bus Card

Spark Marketing LLC ....G...... 219 301-0071
Schererville **(G-12346)**

ADVERTISING SVCS: Direct Mail

American Express Travel ....C...... 812 523-0106
Seymour **(G-12430)**

Crossrads Rhbilitation Ctr Inc ....C...... 317 897-7320
Indianapolis **(G-6697)**

Degler Mktg & Mailing Svcs ....E...... 317 873-5550
Zionsville **(G-14429)**

Ovation Communications Inc ....G...... 812 401-9100
Evansville **(G-3659)**

Presstime Graphics Inc ....E...... 812 234-3815
Terre Haute **(G-13309)**

Printwerk Graphics & Design ....G...... 219 322-7722
Dyer **(G-2508)**

Prototype Systems Inc ....E...... 317 634-3040
Carmel **(G-1458)**

Storm Graphics Inc ....G...... 812 402-5202
Evansville **(G-3753)**

Valley Press Tc ....F...... 812 234-8030
Terre Haute **(G-13360)**

ADVERTISING SVCS: Outdoor

Burkhart Advertising Inc ....G...... 574 522-4421
Elkhart **(G-2738)**

Burkhart Advertising Inc ....F...... 574 234-4444
South Bend **(G-12728)**

Sig Media LLC ....G...... 317 858-7624
Indianapolis **(G-7938)**

Weber Sign Service Inc ....G...... 219 872-5060
Trail Creek **(G-13444)**

ADVERTISING SVCS: Transit

Sig Media LLC ....G...... 317 858-7624
Indianapolis **(G-7938)**

United Media Group Inc ....G...... 260 436-7417
Fort Wayne **(G-4715)**

AERIAL WORK PLATFORMS

Altec Industries Inc.............................C...... 317 872-3460
Indianapolis **(G-6379)**

AEROSOLS

Kik Aerosol Socal LLC ....C...... 626 363-6200
Elkhart **(G-2966)**

AGENTS, BROKERS & BUREAUS: Personal Service

Distance Learning Systems Ind.............E...... 888 955-3276
Greenwood **(G-5681)**

Happy Headgear LLC ....G...... 574 892-5792
Argos **(G-274)**

AGRICULTURAL DISINFECTANTS

Koch Industries Inc.............................G...... 260 356-7191
Huntington **(G-6222)**

AGRICULTURAL EQPT: BARN, SILO, POULTRY, DAIRY/LIVESTOCK MACH

Applegate Livestock Eqp Inc.................D...... 765 964-3715
Union City **(G-13452)**

Cardinal Services Inc Indiana ....G...... 574 267-3823
Warsaw **(G-13853)**

Dpc Inc ....E...... 765 564-3752
Delphi **(G-2419)**

Rhinehart Development Corp ....E...... 260 238-4442
Spencerville **(G-13050)**

Swiss Perfection LLC ....F...... 574 457-4457
Syracuse **(G-13146)**

AGRICULTURAL EQPT: Elevators, Farm

Haines Engineering ....G...... 260 589-3388
Berne **(G-616)**

AGRICULTURAL EQPT: Fertilizng, Sprayng, Dustng/Irrigatn Mach

Gvm Inc...G...... 765 689-5010
Bunker Hill **(G-1206)**

AGRICULTURAL EQPT: Fillers & Unloaders, Silo

Laidig Inc ....E...... 574 256-0204
Mishawaka **(G-10067)**

AGRICULTURAL EQPT: Grounds Mowing Eqpt

Barry Stuckwisch.................................G...... 812 525-1052
Seymour **(G-12432)**

AGRICULTURAL EQPT: Harvesters, Fruit, Vegetable, Tobacco

Reed Raymond Trust.............................G...... 317 831-7246
Mooresville **(G-10336)**

Shelby Engineering Co Inc ....E...... 317 784-1135
Indianapolis **(G-7928)**

AGRICULTURAL EQPT: Planting Machines

Carter Manufacturing Company ....G...... 765 563-3666
Brookston **(G-1102)**

AGRICULTURAL EQPT: Tractors, Farm

Coram USA LLC ....F...... 260 451-8200
Fort Wayne **(G-4176)**

Wright Brothers Implements LLC...........G...... 812 967-3029
Borden **(G-938)**

AGRICULTURAL EQPT: Trailers & Wagons, Farm

Cornelius Manufacturing Inc ....D...... 812 636-4319
Elnora **(G-3288)**

Fpc Feed & Manufacturing.....................G...... 765 468-7768
Parker City **(G-11463)**

K & B Trailer Sales Mfg.........................G...... 574 946-4382
Monterey **(G-10207)**

Par-Kan Company LLC ....D...... 260 352-2141
Silver Lake **(G-12677)**

AGRICULTURAL EQPT: Turf & Grounds Eqpt

All Star Turf Management LLC................G...... 317 861-1234
New Palestine **(G-10966)**

Commercial Star Inc ....F...... 765 386-2800
Coatesville **(G-1747)**

AGRICULTURAL EQPT: Weeding Machines

Valesco Manufacturing Inc....................G...... 765 522-2740
Roachdale (G-12095)
Valesco Manufacturing Inc....................G...... 812 636-6001
Loogootee (G-9395)

AGRICULTURAL MACHINERY & EQPT REPAIR

Deer Country Equipment LLC..............E 812 522-1922
Seymour (G-12444)
K and S Farm and Machine Shop.........F 812 663-8567
Greensburg (G-5617)
S & S Service.......................................G...... 812 952-2306
Lanesville (G-9103)
Wright Implement I LLC.......................E 812 522-1922
Seymour (G-12502)

AGRICULTURAL MACHINERY & EQPT: Wholesalers

Chester Inc ....E 574 896-5600
North Judson (G-11209)
Deer Country Equipment LLC..............E 812 522-1922
Seymour (G-12444)
Delphi Products Co Inc ....F 800 382-7903
Delphi (G-2418)
Dennis Polk & Associates Inc..............G...... 574 831-3555
New Paris (G-10977)
Miles Farm Supply LLC ....F 812 359-4463
Boonville (G-917)
National Equipment Inc ....G...... 219 462-1205
Valparaiso (G-13586)
Schlabach Window & Glass LLC.........G...... 765 628-2024
Kokomo (G-8691)
Schlatters Inc ....G...... 219 567-9158
Francesville (G-4815)
Wright Implement I LLC.......................E 812 522-1922
Seymour (G-12502)

AIR CLEANING SYSTEMS

3-T Corp..G...... 812 424-7878
Evansville (G-3326)
Clarcor Air Filtration Pdts ....D...... 502 969-2304
Jeffersonville (G-8337)
Wabash Environmental Pdts LLC ....G...... 765 464-3440
West Lafayette (G-14115)

AIR CONDITIONERS, AUTOMOTIVE: Wholesalers

Proair LLC..D...... 574 264-5494
Elkhart (G-3117)

AIR CONDITIONERS: Motor Vehicle

Mitsubishi Heavy Industries ....C...... 317 346-5000
Franklin (G-4911)
Proair LLC..D...... 574 264-5494
Elkhart (G-3117)
Proair LLC..F 574 264-5494
Elkhart (G-3118)
Toyota Industries N Amer Inc ....B 812 341-3810
Columbus (G-2025)
Twin Air Products Inc ....G...... 574 295-1129
Elkhart (G-3230)

AIR CONDITIONING & VENTILATION EQPT & SPLYS: Wholesales

Aero-Flo Industries Inc.......................G...... 219 393-3555
La Porte (G-8728)

AIR CONDITIONING EQPT, WHOLE HOUSE: Wholesalers

Koch Enterprises Inc...........................G...... 812 465-9800
Evansville (G-3596)

AIR CONDITIONING UNITS: Complete, Domestic Or Indl

Dometic Corporation ....B 260 463-7657
Lagrange (G-9037)

AIR COOLERS: Metal Plate

Caliente LLC.......................................E 260 426-3800
Fort Wayne (G-4137)

AIR DUCT CLEANING SVCS

National Exhaust Cleaning Inc ....F 317 831-4750
Mooresville (G-10327)
Poynter Sheet Metal Inc ....B 317 893-1193
Greenwood (G-5735)

AIR MATTRESSES: Plastic

Brianza USA Corp ....G...... 574 855-9520
Elkhart (G-2733)
Vixen Composites LLC.........................F 574 970-1224
Elkhart (G-3250)

AIR POLLUTION CONTROL EQPT & SPLYS WHOLESALERS

3-T Corp..G...... 812 424-7878
Evansville (G-3326)

AIR POLLUTION MEASURING SVCS

Chapman Environmental Controls........G...... 574 674-8706
Osceola (G-11374)

AIR PURIFICATION EQPT

Air-Tech Industrial Design ....G...... 317 797-1804
Monrovia (G-10201)
American Green Technology Inc ....F 269 340-9975
South Bend (G-12704)
Iaire LLC...G...... 317 806-2750
Indianapolis (G-7155)

AIR-CONDITIONING SPLY SVCS

Gbi Air Systems Inc ....G...... 574 272-0600
Granger (G-5408)

AIRCRAFT & AEROSPACE FLIGHT INSTRUMENTS & GUIDANCE SYSTEMS

Aptiv Services Us LLC.........................F 765 451-5011
Kokomo (G-8591)
Ascension Space Technology LLP ....G...... 765 623-5164
Anderson (G-69)
Bae Systems Inc ....G...... 812 863-0514
Odon (G-11319)
Cyclone Adg LLC ....G...... 520 403-2927
New Albany (G-10767)
Dcx-Chol Enterprises Inc ....D...... 260 407-1107
Fort Wayne (G-4202)
GM Components Holdings LLC..............G...... 765 451-9049
Kokomo (G-8629)
Hoosier Industrial Supply ....G...... 574 535-0712
Goshen (G-5239)
Silicis Technologies Inc ....E 317 896-5044
Westfield (G-14189)

AIRCRAFT & HEAVY EQPT REPAIR SVCS

Newlins Welding & Tank Maint ....G...... 765 245-2741
Montezuma (G-10210)
Shelby Products Corporation ....G...... 317 398-4870
West Harrison (G-14043)

AIRCRAFT ASSEMBLY PLANTS

Aerospace Waterjet Svcs LLC ....G...... 502 836-1112
Marysville (G-9649)
Bae Systems Controls Inc....................A...... 260 434-5195
Fort Wayne (G-4100)
Bell Aerospace LLC ....G...... 904 505-4055
Plainfield (G-11596)
Golden-Helvey Holdings Inc ....F 574 266-4500
Elkhart (G-2889)
Hoosier Industrial Supply ....G...... 574 535-0712
Goshen (G-5239)
Klx Aerospace Inc...............................G...... 260 747-0671
Fort Wayne (G-4413)
Live Bold Aerospace LLC ....G...... 260 438-5710
Fort Wayne (G-4438)
Lockheed Martin Corporation...............B 317 821-4000
Indianapolis (G-7414)
Raytheon Company ....E 317 306-4872
Indianapolis (G-7821)
Robert J Robinson Aircraft ....G...... 317 787-7809
Greenwood (G-5740)
Rollison Airplane Company Inc.............G...... 812 384-4972
Bloomfield (G-645)
Sargent Aerospace Inc ....G...... 305 593-6038
Franklin (G-4928)

(continued)

Technology MGT Group Inc...................F 765 606-1512
Anderson (G-173)
Thunderbird Aviation LLC....................G...... 847 303-3100
Indianapolis (G-8073)
Tip To Tail Aerospace LLC ....G...... 765 437-6556
Peru (G-11552)
UTC Aerospace Systems ....G...... 812 704-5200
Jeffersonville (G-8437)

AIRCRAFT CLEANING & JANITORIAL SVCS

Turbines Inc.......................................E 812 877-2587
Terre Haute (G-13359)

AIRCRAFT CONTROL SYSTEMS:

Triumph Controls LLC..........................F 317 421-8760
Shelbyville (G-12578)

AIRCRAFT CONTROL SYSTEMS: Electronic Totalizing Counters

U S S Inc ....G...... 260 693-1172
Churubusco (G-1660)

AIRCRAFT ENGINES & ENGINE PARTS: Exhaust Systems

Integrated Energy Technologies ....E 812 421-7810
Evansville (G-3563)

AIRCRAFT ENGINES & ENGINE PARTS: Mount Parts

Georgia Sstnment Solutions Inc ....G...... 575 621-2372
Cicero (G-1661)

AIRCRAFT ENGINES & PARTS

Airtomic Repair Station........................G...... 317 738-0148
Franklin (G-4865)
Avborne Accessory Group Inc ....E 317 738-0148
Franklin (G-4869)
Bel-Mar Products Corporation..............G...... 317 769-3262
Whitestown (G-14249)
Global Air Inc......................................G...... 317 251-1251
Indianapolis (G-7010)
Honeywell International Inc ....B 765 284-3300
Muncie (G-10490)
Honeywell International Inc ....D...... 317 580-6165
Indianapolis (G-7116)
Honeywell International Inc ....A...... 574 935-0200
Plymouth (G-11688)
Honeywell International Inc ....A...... 574 231-3000
South Bend (G-12800)
Honeywell International Inc ....G...... 317 359-9505
Indianapolis (G-7117)
Honeywell International Inc ....A...... 574 231-3000
South Bend (G-12801)
Hsm ....G...... 317 573-8700
Indianapolis (G-7142)
Innovtive Srcing Solutions Inc ....G...... 317 752-2952
Fishers (G-3932)
Instellus Inc ....G...... 734 415-3013
Griffith (G-5780)
Integrity EDM LLC...............................F 317 333-7630
Tipton (G-13392)
Midwest Arcft Mch & TI Co Inc ....E 317 839-1515
Plainfield (G-11628)
Ngh Retail LLC....................................G...... 219 476-0772
Valparaiso (G-13588)
Robert Perez.......................................G...... 317 291-7311
Indianapolis (G-7849)
Rolls-Royce Corporation......................A...... 317 230-2000
Plainfield (G-11641)
Rolls-Royce Corporation......................G...... 317 437-9326
Indianapolis (G-7857)
Rolls-Royce Corporation......................G...... 317 230-8515
West Lafayette (G-14104)
Rolls-Royce Corporation......................A...... 317 230-2000
Indianapolis (G-7858)
Rolls-Royce Corporation......................D...... 812 421-7810
Evansville (G-3708)
Simpson Alloy Services Inc ....G...... 812 969-2766
Elizabeth (G-2646)
Smiths Arospc Components Haute.......G...... 812 235-5210
Terre Haute (G-13330)
Teamair Mro Ltd ....G...... 812 584-3733
Moores Hill (G-10299)
Thermal Structures Inc........................D...... 951 736-9911
Plainfield (G-11646)

PRODUCT

Tri Aerospace LLC ....E 812 872-2400
Terre Haute (G-13358)
Turbines Inc ....E 812 877-2587
Terre Haute (G-13359)
Twigg Corporation ....D 765 342-7126
Martinsville (G-9644)
Walerko Tool and Engrg Corp .....E 574 295-2233
Elkhart (G-3252)
Wbh Inc ....F 317 839-1515
Plainfield (G-11650)
Wbh Inc ....F 317 269-1510
Indianapolis (G-8180)

AIRCRAFT EQPT & SPLYS WHOLESALERS

Midwest Arcft Mch & TI Co Inc ....E 317 839-1515
Plainfield (G-11628)

AIRCRAFT FLIGHT INSTRUMENT REPAIR SVCS

Troy Meggitt Inc ....D 812 547-7071
Troy (G-13448)

AIRCRAFT PARTS & AUX EQPT: Adapter Assy, Hydromatic Prop

HB Connect Inc ....D 260 422-1212
Fort Wayne (G-4324)

AIRCRAFT PARTS & AUXILIARY EQPT: Assys, Subassemblies/Parts

Bertrand Products Inc ....E 574 234-4181
South Bend (G-12722)
Iasa Group LLC ....G 260 484-1322
Fort Wayne (G-4355)

AIRCRAFT PARTS & AUXILIARY EQPT: Body Assemblies & Parts

Liberty Advance Machine Inc ....G 812 372-1010
Columbus (G-1961)

AIRCRAFT PARTS & AUXILIARY EQPT: Deicing Eqpt

Smart Manufacturing Inc ....G 765 482-7481
Lebanon (G-9225)

AIRCRAFT PARTS & AUXILIARY EQPT: Gears, Power Transmission

First Gear Inc ....F 260 490-3238
Fort Wayne (G-4263)

AIRCRAFT PARTS & AUXILIARY EQPT: Military Eqpt & Armament

Integrity Defense Services Inc .....F 812 675-4913
Springville (G-13064)
Mvo Usa Inc ....F 317 585-5785
Indianapolis (G-7562)

AIRCRAFT PARTS & AUXILIARY EQPT: Nacelles

Safran Nclles Svcs Amricas LLC ....F 317 789-8188
Indianapolis (G-7885)

AIRCRAFT PARTS & AUXILIARY EQPT: Refueling Eqpt, In Flight

Taft Aviation Property LLC ....G 317 769-4487
Zionsville (G-14467)

AIRCRAFT PARTS & AUXILIARY EQPT: Research & Development, Mfr

U S S Inc ....G 260 693-1172
Churubusco (G-1660)
Wolf Technical Engineering LLC ....G 800 783-9653
Indianapolis (G-8209)

AIRCRAFT PARTS & EQPT, NEC

Attco Machine Products Inc ....E 574 234-1063
South Bend (G-12714)
B-D Industries Inc ....F 574 295-1420
Elkhart (G-2712)

Burris Engineering Inc ....F 317 862-1046
Indianapolis (G-6522)
C F Roark Wldg Engrg Co Inc ....C 317 852-3163
Brownsburg (G-1141)
Cook Aircraft Leasing Inc ....G 812 339-2044
Bloomington (G-702)
Golden-Helvey Holdings Inc ....D 574 266-4500
Elkhart (G-2890)
Goodrich Corporation ....D 812 704-5200
Jeffersonville (G-8370)
Honeywell International Inc ....G 574 231-2000
South Bend (G-12799)
Indiana Aircraft Hardware Co ....G 317 485-6500
Fortville (G-4780)
Integrated De Icing Servi ....G 317 517-1643
Indianapolis (G-7247)
Kem Krest Defense LLC ....F 574 389-2650
Elkhart (G-2960)
Krisma Diversified ....G 317 413-4788
Carmel (G-1425)
L&E Engineering LLC ....G 317 884-0017
Greenwood (G-5716)
Lift Works Inc ....G 812 797-0479
Greenwood (G-5720)
Mack Tool & Engineering Inc ....E 574 233-8424
South Bend (G-12847)
Midwest Aerospace Ltd ....F 219 365-7250
Saint John (G-12265)
Mike Magiera Inc ....G 574 654-3044
New Carlisle (G-10884)
MSP Aviation Inc ....E 812 333-6100
Bloomington (G-777)
Odyssian Technology LLC ....G 574 257-7555
South Bend (G-12882)
Precision Piece Parts Inc ....D 574 255-3185
Mishawaka (G-10107)
Pynco Inc ....E 812 275-0900
Bedford (G-567)
Q Air Inc ....G 219 476-7048
Valparaiso (G-13603)
Rayco Mch & Engrg Group Inc ....E 317 291-7848
Indianapolis (G-7819)
Regent Aerospace Corporation ......G 317 837-4000
Plainfield (G-11640)
Rolls-Royce Corporation ....D 812 421-7810
Evansville (G-3708)
Tri Aerospace LLC ....E 812 872-2400
Terre Haute (G-13358)
Triumph Thermal Systems Inc ....G 419 273-1192
Shelbyville (G-12580)
Tube Processing Corp ....B 317 787-1321
Indianapolis (G-8107)
Tube Processing Corp ....C 317 264-7760
Indianapolis (G-8109)
Val Rollers Inc ....G 317 542-1968
Indianapolis (G-8144)
Value Production Inc ....G 574 246-1913
South Bend (G-12983)
Wbh Inc ....F 317 839-1515
Plainfield (G-11650)

AIRCRAFT SEATS

Wolf Technical Engineering LLC ....G 800 783-9653
Indianapolis (G-8209)

AIRCRAFT UPHOLSTERY REPAIR SVCS

Indy Aerospace Inc ....G 817 521-6508
Indianapolis (G-7212)

AIRCRAFT: Airplanes, Fixed Or Rotary Wing

Golden Age Aeroplane Work LLC ....G 812 358-5778
Brownstown (G-1188)
Hull Aircraft Support LLC ....G 219 324-6247
La Porte (G-8769)

AIRCRAFT: Motorized

Aerial Drone Exposures Inc ....G 404 641-5563
Indianapolis (G-6343)
Drone Works LLC ....G 812 917-4691
Terre Haute (G-13225)
Drone1260wrx LLC ....G 773 957-3625
Merrillville (G-9711)
Droneye Imaging LLC ....G 317 878-4065
Trafalgar (G-13435)
I-Fly Drones LLC ....G 812 524-3863
Seymour (G-12457)
Infinity Drones LLC ....G 812 457-7140
Poseyville (G-11857)

AIRCRAFT: Nonmotorized & Lighter-Than-air

Bae Systems Inc ....G 812 863-0514
Odon (G-11319)

ALARMS: Burglar

Harris Corporation ....B 260 451-5597
Fort Wayne (G-4323)
Logical Concepts ....D 317 885-6330
Greenwood (G-5721)
Sentinel Alarm Inc ....G 219 874-6051
Trail Creek (G-13442)

ALARMS: Fire

American Fire Company ....G 219 840-0630
Valparaiso (G-13491)
National Exhaust Cleaning Inc ....F 317 831-4750
Mooresville (G-10327)

ALCOHOL, GRAIN: For Beverage Purposes

Grain Processing Corporation ....F 812 257-0480
Washington (G-13983)

ALCOHOL, INDL: Grain

Grain Processing Corporation ....F 812 257-0480
Washington (G-13983)
Old Copper Still Distlg Co LLC ....G 812 342-0765
Columbus (G-1985)

ALCOHOL: Ethyl & Ethanol

Andersons Clymers Ethanol LLC ....G 574 722-2627
Logansport (G-9322)
Cardinal Ethanol LLC ....D 765 964-3137
Union City (G-13454)
Green Plains Bluffton LLC ....D 260 846-0011
Bluffton (G-876)
Green Plains Inc ....E 812 985-7480
Mount Vernon (G-10394)
Hoosier Ethanol Energy LLC ....G 260 407-6161
Fort Wayne (G-4343)
North Manchester Ethanol LLC ....G 260 774-3532
North Manchester (G-11238)
Poet Brfining - Cloverdale LLC ....D 765 795-3235
Cloverdale (G-1734)
Premier Ethanol LLC ....G 260 726-2681
Portland (G-11841)
Premier Ethanol LLC ....G 260 726-7154
Portland (G-11842)
Ultimate Ethanol LLC ....G 765 724-4384
Alexandria (G-54)
Valero Renewable Fuels Co LLC ....E 812 833-3900
Mount Vernon (G-10413)

ALCOHOLISM COUNSELING, NONTREATMENT

Fresh Start Inc ....F 812 254-3398
Washington (G-13982)

ALKALIES & CHLORINE

Warsaw Chemical Company Inc ....D 574 267-3251
Warsaw (G-13958)

ALTERNATORS & GENERATORS: Battery Charging

Borgwarner Pds (indiana) Inc ....A 800 372-3555
Pendleton (G-11485)
Old Remco Holdings LLC ....C 765 778-6499
Pendleton (G-11498)
Reman Holdings LLC ....G 800 372-5131
Pendleton (G-11502)

ALTERNATORS: Automotive

B & M Electrical Co Inc ....F 765 448-4532
Lafayette (G-8859)
D & E Auto Electric Inc ....F 219 763-3892
Portage (G-11759)
Hitachi Automotive Systems ....B 859 734-9451
Ligonier (G-9287)
Remy Electric Motors LLC ....E 765 778-6466
Pendleton (G-11503)
Remy Power Products LLC ....A 765 778-6499
Pendleton (G-11504)

ALUMINUM

Arconic Inc ....B.... 812 853-6111
  Newburgh (G-11020)
Arconic Inc ....B.... 412 553-4545
  Newburgh (G-11021)
Closure Systems Intl Inc ....C.... 317 390-5000
  Indianapolis (G-6624)
Closure Systems Intl Inc ....C.... 317 390-5000
  Crawfordsville (G-2140)
Closure Systems Intl Inc ....B.... 765 364-6300
  Crawfordsville (G-2141)
G&L Machine ....G.... 260 488-2100
  Hamilton (G-5822)
Industrial Sales & Supply Inc ....F.... 317 240-0560
  Indianapolis (G-7209)
Kingsford Products Inc ....G.... 740 862-4450
  Decatur (G-2389)
Nanshn Amrc Adv Alum Tech LLC ....C.... 765 838-8645
  Lafayette (G-8974)
Old Ras Inc ....G.... 260 563-7461
  Wabash (G-13743)
Scepter Inc ....D.... 812 735-2500
  Bicknell (G-633)

ALUMINUM PRDTS

Alexin LLC ....D.... 260 353-3100
  Bluffton (G-863)
Aluminum Extrusions ....G.... 574 206-0100
  Elkhart (G-2680)
Bon L Manufacturing Company ....C.... 815 351-6802
  Kentland (G-8517)
Brazeway Inc ....D.... 317 392-2533
  Shelbyville (G-12524)
Dyna Technology Inc ....G.... 219 663-2920
  Crown Point (G-2247)
Hautau Tube Cutoff Systems LLC ....F.... 765 647-1600
  Brookville (G-1116)
Hydro Extruder LLC ....D.... 765 825-1141
  Connersville (G-2053)
Hydro Extruder LLC ....C.... 574 262-2667
  Elkhart (G-2926)
Hydro Extrusion North Amer LLC ....C.... 888 935-5757
  North Liberty (G-11215)
Indalex Inc ....G.... 765 457-1117
  Kokomo (G-8645)
Indiana Gratings Inc ....F.... 765 342-7191
  Martinsville (G-9615)
Kinro Manufacturing Inc ....C.... 574 533-8337
  Goshen (G-5257)
Lakemaster Inc ....E.... 765 288-3718
  Muncie (G-10507)
McKinney Corporation ....E.... 765 448-4800
  Lafayette (G-8964)
Napier & Napier ....G.... 765 580-9116
  Liberty (G-9266)
Omnimax International Inc ....E.... 574 294-8576
  Elkhart (G-3070)
Parco Incorporated ....F.... 260 451-0810
  Fort Wayne (G-4521)
Patrick Aluminum Inc ....G.... 574 262-1907
  Elkhart (G-3079)
Patrick Industries Inc ....C.... 574 255-9692
  Mishawaka (G-10101)
Plymouth Tube Company ....C.... 574 946-6191
  Winamac (G-14314)
Stalcop LLC ....D.... 765 436-7926
  Thorntown (G-13378)
Torsion Plastics LLC ....F.... 330 552-2184
  Evansville (G-3767)
Tredegar Corporation ....D.... 812 466-0266
  Terre Haute (G-13356)

ALUMINUM: Rolling & Drawing

Alcoa Warrick LLC ....G.... 812 853-6111
  Newburgh (G-11019)
Alconex Specialty Products ....E.... 260 744-3446
  Fort Wayne (G-4057)
REA Magnet Wire Company Inc ....B.... 765 477-8000
  Lafayette (G-8989)
Revere Industries ....G.... 317 638-1521
  Indianapolis (G-7835)
Rockport Roll Shop LLc ....E.... 812 362-6419
  Rockport (G-12172)
Spectra Metal Sales Inc ....G.... 317 822-8291
  Indianapolis (G-7973)

AMMONIUM PHOSPHATE

Andersons Agriculture Group LP ....E.... 574 626-2522
  Galveston (G-4993)

AMMUNITION

Military Facilities ....G.... 812 854-1762
  Crane (G-2129)

AMMUNITION: Cartridges Case, 30 mm & Below

Flexible Marketing Group ....G.... 574 296-0941
  Elkhart (G-2855)

AMMUNITION: Cores, Bullet, 30 mm & Below

Blythes Sport Shop Inc ....F.... 219 924-4403
  Griffith (G-5766)

AMMUNITION: Missile Warheads

Flexible Marketing Group ....G.... 574 296-0941
  Elkhart (G-2855)

AMMUNITION: Small Arms

A & W Firearms ....G.... 765 716-6856
  Yorktown (G-14400)
Northern Indiana Ordnance Co ....G.... 574 289-5938
  South Bend (G-12879)
Solotat Industries LLC ....G.... 574 320-1436
  Elkhart (G-3180)
Sons of Thunder ....G.... 812 897-4908
  Boonville (G-922)

AMPLIFIERS

American Mobile Sound Ind LLC ....G.... 765 288-1500
  Muncie (G-10430)
Harman Professional Inc ....B.... 574 294-8000
  Elkhart (G-2908)
Rhodes Amplification LLC ....G.... 765 775-5100
  West Lafayette (G-14103)
Uncle Alberts Amplifier Inc ....G.... 317 845-3037
  Indianapolis (G-8126)

AMUSEMENT & RECREATION SVCS: Amusement Arcades

Coach Line Motors ....G.... 765 825-7893
  Connersville (G-2043)

AMUSEMENT & RECREATION SVCS: Fishing Lakes & Piers, Op

Leistner Aquatic Services Inc ....G.... 317 535-6099
  Whiteland (G-14242)

AMUSEMENT & RECREATION SVCS: Instruction Schools, Camps

Meditation Company ....G.... 574 217-3157
  South Bend (G-12859)

AMUSEMENT & RECREATION SVCS: Karate Instruction

Donnie Michaels Kicks ....G.... 765 457-4083
  Kokomo (G-8617)

AMUSEMENT & RECREATION SVCS: Night Club, Exc Alcoholic Bev

Acd Suppliers LLC ....G.... 317 527-9715
  Indianapolis (G-6315)

AMUSEMENT MACHINES: Coin Operated

Advance Green Mfg Co Inc ....G.... 574 457-2695
  Goshen (G-5165)
C & P Distributing LLC ....E.... 574 256-1138
  Mishawaka (G-10016)
Grand Products Inc. ....C.... 317 870-3122
  Indianapolis (G-7034)

AMUSEMENT PARK DEVICES & RIDES

County Line Companies LLC ....G.... 866 959-7866
  Parker City (G-11462)
Fab2order Inc ....E.... 317 975-1056
  Brownsburg (G-1149)

Grinding Experts ....G.... 219 838-7773
  Highland (G-6047)
Ham Enterprise LLC ....G.... 317 831-2902
  Martinsville (G-9610)
Trp International LLC ....F.... 574 389-9941
  Elkhart (G-3224)

ANALYZERS: Blood & Body Fluid

Predictive Wear LLC ....F.... 765 464-4891
  West Lafayette (G-14096)

ANALYZERS: Network

Promethius Consulting LLC ....F.... 317 733-2388
  Indianapolis (G-7777)

ANALYZERS: Petroleum Prdts

Lazar Scientific Incorporated ....G.... 574 271-7020
  Granger (G-5418)

ANALYZERS: Respiratory

Faztech LLC ....G.... 812 327-0926
  Bloomington (G-723)

ANESTHESIA EQPT

Flw Plastics Inc ....E.... 812 546-0050
  Hope (G-6112)
Kumplete Airway Solutions Inc ....G.... 219 680-0836
  Crown Point (G-2274)

ANIMAL BASED MEDICINAL CHEMICAL PRDTS

Animalsink ....G.... 317 496-8467
  Brownsburg (G-1134)

ANIMAL FEED & SUPPLEMENTS: Livestock & Poultry

Archer-Daniels-Midland Company ....G.... 574 831-2292
  Goshen (G-5171)
Blue River Farm Supply Inc ....G.... 812 364-6675
  Palmyra (G-11435)
Bristow Milling Co LLC ....G.... 812 843-5176
  Bristow (G-1094)
Bundy Bros & Sons Inc ....F.... 812 966-2551
  Medora (G-9681)
Cargill Incorporated ....G.... 574 353-7621
  Mentone (G-9685)
Cargill Incorporated ....E.... 574 353-7623
  Mentone (G-9686)
Cargill Incorporated ....E.... 217 253-3389
  West Lafayette (G-14056)
Cargill Incorporated ....B.... 402 533-4227
  Hammond (G-5858)
Consolidated Nutrition Lc ....G.... 574 773-4131
  Nappanee (G-10662)
Egg Innovations LLC ....G.... 574 267-7545
  Warsaw (G-13868)
Envigo Rms Inc. ....C.... 317 806-6080
  Indianapolis (G-6871)
Envigo Rms Inc. ....G.... 317 806-6080
  Greenfield (G-5530)
Excel Coop Inc ....G.... 574 967-3943
  Brookston (G-1104)
Frick Services Inc ....E.... 260 761-3311
  Wawaka (G-14032)
Griffin Industries LLC ....E.... 812 659-3399
  Newberry (G-11015)
Griffin Industries LLC ....E.... 812 379-9528
  Columbus (G-1935)
Harvest Land Co-Op Inc ....F.... 765 489-4141
  Hagerstown (G-5807)
HMS Zoo Diets Inc ....G.... 260 824-5157
  Bluffton (G-877)
Hog Slat Incorporated ....G.... 574 967-4145
  Camden (G-1274)
Innovative Concepts Group ....G.... 317 408-0292
  Indianapolis (G-7236)
Jbs United Inc ....F.... 800 382-9909
  Sheridan (G-12591)
Jbs United Inc ....E.... 317 758-2609
  Sheridan (G-12592)
Jbs United Trading Inc ....G.... 317 758-4495
  Sheridan (G-12594)
Jfs Milling Inc ....E.... 812 324-2022
  Bruceville (G-1197)

PRODUCT

Lambrights Inc ....D...... 260 463-2178
Lagrange (G-9056)

Land OLakes Inc ....F...... 765 962-9561
Richmond (G-12011)

Laughery Valley AG Co-Op Inc ....G...... 812 689-4401
Osgood (G-11393)

Mark Hackman ....G...... 812 522-8257
Brownstown (G-1190)

Novartis Animal Health US Inc ....G...... 317 276-2348
Greenfield (G-5562)

Nutritional Research Assoc ....F...... 260 723-4931
South Whitley (G-13002)

Purina Animal Nutrition LLC ....E...... 765 659-4791
Frankfort (G-4852)

Purina Animal Nutrition LLC ....E...... 812 424-5501
Evansville (G-3690)

Purina Animal Nutrition LLC ....E...... 574 658-4137
Milford (G-9962)

Purina Mills LLC ....E...... 574 658-4137
Milford (G-9963)

Regal Mills Odon ....G...... 812 295-2299
Loogootee (G-9393)

Scotts Miracle-Gro Company ....D...... 219 984-6110
Reynolds (G-11948)

United Feeds ....G...... 317 627-5637
Carmel (G-1504)

Wallace Grain Co Inc ....F...... 317 758-4434
Sheridan (G-12601)

Wilson Fertilizer & Grain Inc ....G...... 574 223-3175
Rochester (G-12161)

ANIMAL FEED: Wholesalers

AG Processing A Cooperative ....E...... 574 773-4138
Nappanee (G-10644)

Flinn Farms Bedford Seed Inc ....G...... 812 279-4136
Bedford (G-542)

Lambrights Inc ....D...... 260 463-2178
Lagrange (G-9056)

Nutritional Research Assoc ....F...... 260 723-4931
South Whitley (G-13002)

Synergy Feeds LLC ....E...... 260 723-5141
South Whitley (G-13008)

Wilson Fertilizer & Grain Inc ....G...... 574 223-3175
Rochester (G-12161)

ANIMAL FOOD & SUPPLEMENTS: Bird Food, Prepared

Birds Nest Inc ....G...... 574 247-0201
Granger (G-5394)

Sappers Market and Greenhouses ....G...... 219 942-4995
Hobart (G-6094)

ANIMAL FOOD & SUPPLEMENTS: Bone Meal

Synergy Feeds LLC ....E...... 260 723-5141
South Whitley (G-13008)

ANIMAL FOOD & SUPPLEMENTS: Dog

Bench & Field Pet Foods LLC ....G...... 800 525-4802
Mishawaka (G-10007)

Canines Choice Inc ....G...... 765 662-2633
Marion (G-9514)

Nestle Usa Inc ....C...... 765 778-6000
Anderson (G-144)

Trio Milling Inc ....G...... 765 795-4088
Cloverdale (G-1740)

ANIMAL FOOD & SUPPLEMENTS: Dog & Cat

Bhj Usa Inc ....E...... 574 722-3933
Logansport (G-9324)

Eagle Pet Products Inc ....D...... 574 259-7834
Mishawaka (G-10038)

Hills Pet Nutrition Inc ....C...... 765 966-4549
Richmond (G-11996)

Hills Pet Nutrition Inc ....C...... 765 935-7071
Richmond (G-11997)

Macor ....G...... 574 255-2658
Mishawaka (G-10072)

Nutritional Research Assoc ....F...... 260 723-4931
South Whitley (G-13002)

United Pet Foods Inc ....F...... 574 674-5981
Elkhart (G-3233)

Wellpet LLC ....D...... 574 259-7834
Mishawaka (G-10150)

ANIMAL FOOD & SUPPLEMENTS: Feed Concentrates

Hunter Nutrition Inc ....G...... 765 563-1003
Brookston (G-1105)

Winfield Solutions LLC ....G...... 317 838-3733
Plainfield (G-11652)

ANIMAL FOOD & SUPPLEMENTS: Feed Premixes

Gro-Tec Inc ....F...... 765 853-1246
Modoc (G-10173)

ANIMAL FOOD & SUPPLEMENTS: Feed Supplements

Micronutrients USA LLC ....D...... 317 486-5880
Indianapolis (G-7500)

Super Blend Inc ....G...... 260 463-7486
Lagrange (G-9069)

ANIMAL FOOD & SUPPLEMENTS: Kelp Meal & Pellets

Matam Corp ....G...... 317 264-9908
Indianapolis (G-7465)

ANIMAL FOOD & SUPPLEMENTS: Livestock

Cargill Dry Corn Ingrdents Inc ....D...... 317 632-1481
Indianapolis (G-6555)

Flinn Farms Bedford Seed Inc ....G...... 812 279-4136
Bedford (G-542)

Kent Nutrition Group Inc ....E...... 574 722-5368
Logansport (G-9345)

Reconserve of Indiana ....G...... 310 458-1574
Terre Haute (G-13317)

Richmonds Feed Service Inc ....G...... 574 862-2984
Wakarusa (G-13793)

Ridley USA Inc ....E...... 260 768-4103
Shipshewana (G-12647)

Strauss Veal Feeds Inc ....E...... 260 982-8611
North Manchester (G-11245)

United Animal Health Inc ....D...... 317 758-4495
Sheridan (G-12599)

United Animal Health Inc ....F...... 207 771-0965
Sheridan (G-12600)

Wanafeed Corporation ....G...... 317 862-4032
Indianapolis (G-8178)

ANIMAL FOOD & SUPPLEMENTS: Poultry

Pine Manor Inc ....B...... 800 532-4186
Orland (G-11355)

ANIMAL FOOD & SUPPLEMENTS: Stock Feeds, Dry

Odon Feed and Grain Inc ....G...... 812 636-7392
Odon (G-11337)

Purina Animal Nutrition LLC ....E...... 765 962-8547
Richmond (G-12038)

Purina Mills LLC ....F...... 812 424-5501
Evansville (G-3691)

ANNEALING: Metal

Atmosphere Annealing LLC ....E...... 812 346-1275
North Vernon (G-11248)

ANODIZING SVC

Aacoa Inc ....C...... 574 262-4685
Elkhart (G-2661)

B-D Industries Inc ....F...... 574 295-1420
Elkhart (G-2712)

Brunswick Corporation ....C...... 260 459-8200
Fort Wayne (G-4125)

Industrial Anodizing Co Inc ....E...... 317 637-4641
Indianapolis (G-7207)

Indy Metal Finishing Co ....G...... 317 858-5353
Brownsburg (G-1153)

Poiry Partners LLC ....E...... 260 424-1030
Fort Wayne (G-4535)

Quick Turn Anodizing LLC ....G...... 877 716-1150
Edinburgh (G-2622)

Riepen LLC ....D...... 574 269-5900
Warsaw (G-13935)

Superior Metal Tech LLC ....D...... 317 897-9850
Indianapolis (G-8022)

Yellow Dog Anodizing ....G...... 574 343-2247
Elkhart (G-3271)

ANTENNAS: Radar Or Communications

Reeds RFI Inc ....G...... 812 659-2872
Switz City (G-13126)

ANTIFREEZE

Camco Manufacturing Inc ....F...... 574 264-1491
Elkhart (G-2747)

Universal Services Inc ....G...... 219 397-4373
East Chicago (G-2577)

ANTIQUE & CLASSIC AUTOMOBILE RESTORATION

Hoosier Hot Rods Classics Inc ....G...... 812 768-5221
Haubstadt (G-6003)

ANTIQUE FURNITURE RESTORATION & REPAIR

Columbus Cstm Cbinets Furn LLC ....G...... 812 379-9411
Columbus (G-1875)

Deer Ridgewood Craft LLC ....G...... 812 535-3744
West Terre Haute (G-14124)

Kasnak Restorations Inc ....G...... 317 852-9770
Brownsburg (G-1159)

ANTIQUE SHOPS

Cowpokes Inc ....E...... 765 642-3911
Anderson (G-91)

Northern Indiana Ordnance Co ....G...... 574 289-5938
South Bend (G-12879)

Radecki Galleries Inc ....G...... 574 287-0266
South Bend (G-12913)

Strawtown Pottery & Antiques ....G...... 317 984-5080
Noblesville (G-11190)

APPAREL DESIGNERS: Commercial

Troves ....G...... 260 672-0878
Roanoke (G-12108)

APPLIANCE PARTS: Porcelain Enameled

Long Item Development Corp ....G...... 317 844-9491
Carmel (G-1427)

APPLIANCES, HOUSEHOLD OR COIN OPERATED: Laundry Dryers

Whirlpool Corporation ....A...... 317 837-5300
Plainfield (G-11651)

APPLIANCES, HOUSEHOLD: Drycleaning Machines, Incl Coin-Op

Grassco Inc ....G...... 260 749-5437
Fort Wayne (G-4304)

APPLIANCES, HOUSEHOLD: Kitchen, Major, Exc Refrigs & Stoves

Solfire Contract Mfg Inc ....F...... 260 755-2115
Fort Wayne (G-4634)

APPLIANCES, HOUSEHOLD: Sewing Machines & Attchmnts, Domestic

Sailrite Enterprises Inc ....F...... 260 244-4647
Columbia City (G-1833)

APPLIANCES, HOUSEHOLD: Shampooers, Carpet

Steamin Demon Inc ....G...... 812 288-6754
Clarksville (G-1697)

APPLIANCES: Household, Refrigerators & Freezers

Freezing Systems and Svc Inc ....F...... 219 879-6236
Michigan City (G-9796)

JC Refrigeration LLC ....G...... 260 768-4067
Shipshewana (G-12622)

Whirlpool Corporation ....C...... 812 426-4000
Evansville (G-3811)

APPLIANCES: Major, Cooking

Challenge Tool & Mfg Inc ....D 260 749-9558
New Haven *(G-10934)*
Dynamic Packg Solutions Inc ....C 574 848-1410
Bristol *(G-1057)*
Elixir Industries ....E 574 294-5685
Elkhart *(G-2816)*
Sterling Manufacturing LLC ....G 260 451-9760
Fort Wayne *(G-4648)*
Thermodyne Food Service Pdts ....E 260 428-2535
Fort Wayne *(G-4682)*

APPLIANCES: Small, Electric

Battle Creek Equipment Co ....E 260 495-3472
Fremont *(G-4952)*
Fulton Co R E M C ....G 574 223-3156
Rochester *(G-12125)*
Royal Spa Corporation ....D 317 781-0828
Indianapolis *(G-7867)*

APPLICATIONS SOFTWARE PROGRAMMING

Wall Control Services Inc ....G 260 450-6411
Fort Wayne *(G-4733)*

AQUARIUM ACCESS, METAL

Spectrum Brands Inc ....E 317 773-6627
Noblesville *(G-11187)*

AQUARIUMS & ACCESS: Glass

Spectrum Brands Inc ....E 317 773-6627
Noblesville *(G-11187)*

ARCHITECTURAL PANELS OR PARTS: Porcelain Enameled

Form Wood Industries Inc ....E 812 284-3676
Jeffersonville *(G-8363)*

ARCHITECTURAL SVCS

Meyer Custom Woodworking Inc ....G 812 695-2021
Dubois *(G-2477)*

ARCHITECTURAL SVCS: Engineering

Deem & Loureiro Inc ....G 770 652-9871
Indianapolis *(G-6731)*

ARMATURE REPAIRING & REWINDING SVC

Best Electric Motor Service ....G 765 583-2408
Otterbein *(G-11417)*
Flanders Electric Mtr Svc Inc ....E 812 421-4300
Evansville *(G-3510)*
les Subsidiary Holdings Inc ....F 330 830-3500
South Bend *(G-12807)*
Machine Rebuilders & Service ....F 260 482-8168
Fort Wayne *(G-4448)*
Morrows Mt Vernon Elc Mtr Svc ....G 812 838-5641
Mount Vernon *(G-10402)*
Morse Lake Automotive ....G 317 984-4514
Cicero *(G-1663)*
Robinson Industries Inc ....E 317 867-3214
Westfield *(G-14186)*

ARMATURES: Automotive

Aristo LLC ....E 219 962-1032
Hobart *(G-6069)*

ARMOR PLATES

By The Sword Inc ....F 877 433-9368
Huntingburg *(G-6151)*

ART & ORNAMENTAL WARE: Pottery

Donald H & Susan K Minch ....G 260 726-9486
Portland *(G-11817)*
Grateful Heart Enterprises LLC ....G 765 838-2266
Lafayette *(G-8910)*
Strawtown Pottery & Antiques ....G 317 984-5080
Noblesville *(G-11190)*

ART DEALERS & GALLERIES

Gibbs Susie Framing & Art ....G 765 428-2434
Lafayette *(G-8907)*
Hjj Inc ....G 219 362-4421
La Porte *(G-8765)*

Noel Studio Inc ....F 317 297-1117
Zionsville *(G-14452)*
Pfortune Art & Design Inc ....G 317 872-4123
Indianapolis *(G-7681)*
Randall Corp ....G 812 425-7122
Evansville *(G-3695)*

ART DESIGN SVCS

Annual Reports Inc ....E 317 736-8838
Franklin *(G-4868)*
World Media Group Inc ....C 317 549-8484
Indianapolis *(G-8216)*

ART GALLERIES

Editions Ltd Gallery Fine Arts ....G 317 466-9940
Indianapolis *(G-6806)*

ART GOODS & SPLYS WHOLESALERS

Bottom Line Management Inc ....F 812 944-7388
Clarksville *(G-1674)*

ART GOODS, WHOLESALE

Noel Studio Inc ....F 317 297-1117
Zionsville *(G-14452)*

ART RESTORATION SVC

Radecki Galleries Inc ....G 574 287-0266
South Bend *(G-12913)*

ART SPLY STORES

Stitch N Frame ....G 260 478-1301
Fort Wayne *(G-4649)*
Twinrocker Hand Made Paper Inc ....G 765 563-3119
Brookston *(G-1109)*

ARTIFICIAL FLOWER SHOPS

Youniquely Yours ....G 219 942-1489
Hobart *(G-6103)*

ARTISTS' MATERIALS, WHOLESALE

Double E Distributing Co Inc ....G 812 334-2220
Bloomington *(G-715)*
Yellow Banks Clay Company Inc ....F 812 567-4703
Dale *(G-2336)*

ARTISTS' MATERIALS: Boards, Drawing

Wolfe Engineered Plastics LLC ....G 812 623-8403
Sunman *(G-13122)*

ARTISTS' MATERIALS: Chalks, Carpenters', Blackboard, Etc

V M Integrated ....G 877 296-0621
Indianapolis *(G-8143)*

ARTISTS' MATERIALS: Mixtures, Gold Or Bronze

Playn2win LLC ....G 317 345-4653
Indianapolis *(G-7702)*

ARTISTS' MATERIALS: Palettes

Chep (usa) Inc ....E 317 780-0700
Indianapolis *(G-6598)*

ARTISTS' MATERIALS: Pencils & Leads

Harcourt Industries Inc ....E 765 629-2625
Milroy *(G-9980)*

ARTWORK: Framed

Keck Fine Art ....G 219 306-9474
Coal City *(G-1741)*

ASBESTOS PRDTS: Table Pads & Padding

Heartland Table Pads LLC ....G 888 487-2377
Wolcottville *(G-14372)*

ASBESTOS REMOVAL EQPT

Wall Control Services Inc ....G 260 450-6411
Fort Wayne *(G-4733)*

ASH TRAYS: Stamped Metal

Versatile Fabrication LLC ....G 574 293-8504
Elkhart *(G-3244)*

ASPHALT & ASPHALT PRDTS

Asphalt Materials Inc ....F 574 267-5076
Warsaw *(G-13840)*
Asphalt Materials Inc ....B 317 872-6010
Indianapolis *(G-6426)*
Asphalt Materials Inc ....G 317 875-4670
Indianapolis *(G-6428)*
Asphalt Materials Inc ....E 317 872-5580
Indianapolis *(G-6429)*
Babcock Paving Inc ....G 219 987-5450
Demotte *(G-2431)*
Calcar Quarries Incorporated ....F 812 723-2109
Paoli *(G-11447)*
Corydon Stone & Asphalt Inc ....E 812 738-2216
Corydon *(G-2096)*
E & B Paving Inc ....E 765 643-5358
Anderson *(G-101)*
E & B Paving Inc ....D 317 773-4132
Noblesville *(G-11097)*
Goh Con Inc ....E 812 282-1349
Clarksville *(G-1682)*
Hotmix Inc ....G 812 926-1471
Aurora *(G-380)*
Hotmix Inc ....G 812 663-2020
Greensburg *(G-5613)*
Niblock Excavating Inc ....D 574 848-4437
Bristol *(G-1074)*
Paul H Rohe Co Inc ....F 812 926-1471
Aurora *(G-384)*
Rogers Group Inc ....E 812 882-3640
Vincennes *(G-13703)*
Triangle Asphalt Paving Corp ....E 765 482-5701
Lebanon *(G-9229)*
Walsh & Kelly Inc ....D 219 924-5900
South Bend *(G-12987)*

ASPHALT COATINGS & SEALERS

Bituminous Materials & Sup LP ....G 317 228-8203
Indianapolis *(G-6479)*
Central States Mfg Inc ....D 219 879-4770
Michigan City *(G-9773)*
Dave OMara Paving Inc ....G 812 346-1214
North Vernon *(G-11252)*
Fosbel Inc ....G 219 883-4479
Gary *(G-5048)*
K Tech Specialty Coatings Inc ....F 260 587-3888
Ashley *(G-287)*
Metal Sales Manufacturing Corp ....E 812 941-0041
New Albany *(G-10827)*
Sampco Inc ....C 413 442-4043
South Bend *(G-12925)*
Schmidt Contracting Inc ....F 812 482-3923
Jasper *(G-8303)*
Standard Industries Inc ....C 219 872-1111
Michigan City *(G-9847)*
Thermoseal Co Ed Munoz Inc ....G 812 428-3343
Evansville *(G-3759)*
Triangle Asphalt Paving Corp ....E 765 482-5701
Lebanon *(G-9229)*

ASPHALT MINING & BITUMINOUS STONE QUARRYING SVCS

Goh A&C Inc ....E 812 738-2217
Corydon *(G-2099)*
Hanson Agrigoods Midwest Inc ....F 317 635-9048
Cloverdale *(G-1727)*

ASPHALT PLANTS INCLUDING GRAVEL MIX TYPE

Brooks Construction Co Inc ....E 260 478-1990
Fort Wayne *(G-4122)*
Critser Companies Inc ....G 219 663-0052
Crown Point *(G-2236)*
Harding Materials Inc ....G 317 846-7401
Indianapolis *(G-7073)*

ASSEMBLING SVC: Clocks

Smokers Iron Works ....G 574 674-6683
Elkhart *(G-3179)*

PRODUCT

ASSEMBLING SVC: Plumbing Fixture Fittings, Plastic

Buckaroos Inc ....F 317 899-9100
Indianapolis *(G-6518)*

Eca Enterprises Inc ....E 812 526-6734
Edinburgh *(G-2610)*

LGS Plumbing Inc ....E 219 663-2177
Crown Point *(G-2276)*

ASSOCIATIONS: Business

National Retail Hardware Assn ....E 317 290-0338
Indianapolis *(G-7576)*

News Banner Publications Inc ....E 260 824-0224
Bluffton *(G-883)*

Speedway Redi Mix Inc ....G 765 671-1020
Marion *(G-9563)*

Super Blend Inc ....G 260 463-7486
Lagrange *(G-9069)*

ASSOCIATIONS: Real Estate Management

Heritage Financial Group Inc ....D 574 522-8000
Elkhart *(G-2914)*

Millwork Specialties Co Inc ....G 219 362-2960
La Porte *(G-8795)*

ASSOCIATIONS: Trade

Automobile Dealers Assn of Ind ....G 317 635-1441
Indianapolis *(G-6446)*

ATOMIZERS

All Rvs Manufacturing Inc ....G 574 538-1559
Shipshewana *(G-12602)*

ARC of Greater Boone Cnty Inc ....F 765 482-0051
Lebanon *(G-9169)*

Aspire Industries ....F 812 542-1561
New Albany *(G-10748)*

BF Goodrich Tire Manufacturing ....G 260 493-8100
Woodburn *(G-14380)*

Derby Industries LLC ....G 765 778-6104
Anderson *(G-94)*

Lucas Oil Products Inc ....G 317 569-0039
Carmel *(G-1428)*

Nemcomed Instrs & Implants ....G 800 255-4576
Fort Wayne *(G-4496)*

True Precision Tech Inc ....G 765 252-9766
Kokomo *(G-8710)*

AUDIO & VIDEO EQPT, EXC COMMERCIAL

Damping Technologies Inc ....E 574 258-7916
Mishawaka *(G-10031)*

Draper Inc ....B 765 987-7999
Spiceland *(G-13054)*

Ebey Sales & Service ....G 260 636-3286
Albion *(G-27)*

Image Vault LLC ....G 812 948-8400
New Albany *(G-10802)*

Klipsch Group Inc ....C 317 860-8100
Indianapolis *(G-7360)*

Loys Sales Inc ....G 765 552-7250
Elwood *(G-3304)*

Michana Used Music and Media ....G 574 247-1188
Mishawaka *(G-10079)*

R B Annis Instruments Inc ....G 765 848-1621
Greencastle *(G-5476)*

Recon Group LLP ....G 855 874-8741
Greenfield *(G-5566)*

Sony Dadc US Inc ....A 812 462-8100
Terre Haute *(G-13334)*

Sports Select Usa Inc ....G 317 631-4011
Indianapolis *(G-7978)*

Technology Cons Group LLC ....G 219 525-4064
Merrillville *(G-9757)*

AUDIO COMPONENTS

A E Techron Inc ....F 574 295-9495
Elkhart *(G-2657)*

AUDIO ELECTRONIC SYSTEMS

Boyer Enterprises Inc ....G 812 963-9180
Evansville *(G-3394)*

Csd Group Inc ....E 260 918-3500
New Haven *(G-10937)*

GM Components Holdings LLC ....G 765 451-9049
Kokomo *(G-8629)*

Harman Embedded Audio LLC ....E 317 849-8175
Indianapolis *(G-7077)*

Jon E Gee Enterprises Inc ....G 317 291-4522
Carmel *(G-1420)*

Rider Productions ....G 260 471-0099
Fort Wayne *(G-4593)*

Tech Solutions and Sales Inc ....G 317 536-5846
Indianapolis *(G-8047)*

AUDIO-VISUAL PROGRAM PRODUCTION SVCS

Creative Impressions Inc ....F 317 244-9842
Indianapolis *(G-6687)*

Technology Cons Group LLC ....G 219 525-4064
Merrillville *(G-9757)*

Top In Sound Inc ....G 765 649-8111
Anderson *(G-177)*

AUDIOLOGICAL EQPT: Electronic

E3 Diagnostics Inc ....G 317 334-2000
Indianapolis *(G-6784)*

AUDIOLOGISTS' OFFICES

Audio Diagnostics Inc ....G 765 477-7016
Lafayette *(G-8855)*

AUTHOR

1632 Inc ....G 219 398-4155
East Chicago *(G-2514)*

AUTHORS' AGENTS & BROKERS

Georg Utz Inc ....E 812 526-2240
Edinburgh *(G-2612)*

AUTO & HOME SUPPLY STORES: Auto & Truck Eqpt & Parts

3d Engineering Inc ....G 317 729-5430
Edinburgh *(G-2593)*

Advance Stores Company Inc ....G 317 253-5034
Indianapolis *(G-6331)*

Engler Machine & Tool Inc ....F 812 386-6254
Princeton *(G-11869)*

Morse Lake Automotive ....G 317 984-4514
Cicero *(G-1663)*

AUTO & HOME SUPPLY STORES: Automotive Access

Broadway Auto Glass LLC ....F 219 884-5277
Merrillville *(G-9704)*

AUTO & HOME SUPPLY STORES: Automotive parts

Bailey Chassis Company LLC ....G 615 822-7041
Haubstadt *(G-5997)*

Component Machine Inc ....G 317 635-8929
Indianapolis *(G-6642)*

Greys Automotive Inc ....G 317 632-3562
Indianapolis *(G-7048)*

Hardins Speed Service Co ....G 219 962-8080
Hobart *(G-6079)*

KOI Enterprises Inc ....G 812 537-2335
Lawrenceburg *(G-9146)*

Lingenfelter Prfmce Engrg Inc ....E 260 724-2552
Decatur *(G-2390)*

Mastersbilt Chassis Inc ....F 812 793-3666
Crothersville *(G-2218)*

Promotor Engines & Components ....G 574 533-9898
Goshen *(G-5313)*

Whb International Inc ....G 317 820-3001
Indianapolis *(G-8188)*

AUTO & HOME SUPPLY STORES: Batteries, Automotive & Truck

Batteries Plus ....G 317 219-0007
Noblesville *(G-11064)*

Tri-State Power Supply LLC ....G 812 537-2500
Lawrenceburg *(G-9160)*

AUTO & HOME SUPPLY STORES: Speed Shops, Incl Race Car Splys

Competitive Designs Inc ....G 574 223-9406
Rochester *(G-12118)*

K-Motion Racing Engines ....G 765 742-8494
Lafayette *(G-8935)*

Olson Race Cars ....G 765 529-6933
New Castle *(G-10914)*

Price Motor Sport Engineering ....G 812 546-4220
Hope *(G-6118)*

Ultra Tech Racing Engines ....G 574 674-6028
Osceola *(G-11384)*

AUTO & HOME SUPPLY STORES: Trailer Hitches, Automotive

Pyramid Equipment ....F 219 778-2591
Rolling Prairie *(G-12193)*

AUTO & HOME SUPPLY STORES: Truck Eqpt & Parts

Nicks Automotive Inc ....F 765 964-6843
Union City *(G-13458)*

RPM Machinery LLC ....F 574 271-0800
South Bend *(G-12923)*

Truck Stylin Unlimited ....G 574 223-8800
Rochester *(G-12158)*

AUTOCLAVES: Laboratory

Helmer Inc ....C 317 773-9073
Noblesville *(G-11120)*

AUTOMATIC REGULATING CONTROL: Building Svcs Monitoring, Auto

Executive Image Bldg Svcs Inc ....F 317 865-1366
Greenwood *(G-5694)*

Johnson Controls Inc ....F 812 868-1374
Evansville *(G-3578)*

Johnson Controls Inc ....D 317 917-5043
Pittsboro *(G-11583)*

AUTOMATIC REGULATING CONTROLS: AC & Refrigeration

Elliott-Williams Company Inc ....D 317 453-2295
Indianapolis *(G-6843)*

Gillespie Mrrell Gen Contg LLC ....G 765 618-4084
Marion *(G-9526)*

Siemens Industry Inc ....D 317 381-0734
Indianapolis *(G-7937)*

AUTOMATIC REGULATING CONTROLS: Appliance Regulators

Creative Control Systems ....G 260 432-9020
Fort Wayne *(G-4184)*

AUTOMATIC REGULATING CONTROLS: Appliance, Exc Air-Cond/Refr

Johnson Sales Corp ....G 219 322-9558
Schererville *(G-12326)*

AUTOMATIC REGULATING CONTROLS: Electric Heat

Dimplex North America Limited ....G 317 890-0809
Indianapolis *(G-6743)*

Jackson Systems LLC ....E 317 788-6800
Indianapolis *(G-7295)*

AUTOMATIC REGULATING CONTROLS: Hardware, Environmental Reg

Spensa Technologies Inc ....E 765 588-3592
West Lafayette *(G-14110)*

AUTOMATIC REGULATING CONTROLS: Pneumatic Relays, Air-Cond

SMC Corporation of America ....B 317 899-3182
Noblesville *(G-11184)*

AUTOMATIC REGULATING CONTROLS: Pressure, Air-Cond Sys

Caliente LLC ....E 260 426-3800
Fort Wayne *(G-4137)*

AUTOMATIC TELLER MACHINES

Chase N Corydon................F...... 812 738-3032
Corydon (G-2092)
Chase Southport Emerson................G...... 317 266-7470
Indianapolis (G-6594)
Elmos................G...... 574 371-2050
Warsaw (G-13871)
Fairfield Gas Way................G...... 260 744-2186
Fort Wayne (G-4253)

AUTOMATIC VENDING MACHINES:
Mechanisms & Parts

Window Man Inc................G...... 317 755-3207
Indianapolis (G-8203)

AUTOMOBILES & OTHER MOTOR VEHICLES WHOLESALERS

Fenwick Motor Sports................G...... 765 522-1354
Bainbridge (G-476)
Wabash National Corporation................B...... 765 771-5300
Lafayette (G-9018)

AUTOMOBILES: Midget, Power Driven

Three K Racing Enterprises................G...... 765 482-4273
Lebanon (G-9228)

AUTOMOBILES: Wholesalers

Benteler Automotive Corp................C...... 574 534-1499
Goshen (G-5178)

AUTOMOTIVE & TRUCK GENERAL REPAIR SVC

Auto Center Inc................G...... 317 545-3360
Indianapolis (G-6442)
Auto Specialty of Lafayette................G...... 765 446-2311
Lafayette (G-8857)
Awol Metal Contorsion LLC................G...... 260 909-0411
Kendallville (G-8457)
Barry Seat Cover & Auto Glass................F...... 574 288-4603
South Bend (G-12721)
Dons Automotive and Machine................G...... 812 547-6292
Tell City (G-13159)
Hendershot Service Center Inc................F...... 765 653-2600
Greencastle (G-5464)
Independent Protection Co Inc................E...... 574 533-4116
Goshen (G-5243)
Jasper Engine Exchange Inc................A...... 812 482-1041
Jasper (G-8261)
Kerns Speed Shop................G...... 812 275-4289
Bedford (G-556)
Macallister Machinery Co Inc................D...... 260 483-6469
Fort Wayne (G-4447)
Marmon Highway Tech LLC................E...... 317 787-0718
Indianapolis (G-7457)
Midwest Auto Repair Inc................E...... 219 322-0364
Schererville (G-12334)
Mitchell Smith Racing................G...... 765 640-0237
Anderson (G-137)
OHM Automotive LLC................G...... 812 879-5455
Bloomington (G-785)
Selking International Inc................G...... 574 522-2001
Elkhart (G-3161)
Selking International Inc................E...... 260 482-3000
Fort Wayne (G-4615)

AUTOMOTIVE AIR CONDITIONING REPAIR SHOPS

Mitsubishi Heavy Industries................E...... 714 960-3785
Franklin (G-4910)

AUTOMOTIVE BODY SHOP

ABRA Auto Body & Glass LP................E...... 317 839-8940
Plainfield (G-11590)
Hgc Custom Chrome................G...... 260 447-4731
Yoder (G-14398)
Nicks Automotive Inc................F...... 765 964-6843
Union City (G-13458)
Vessell Trim Co................F...... 812 424-2963
Evansville (G-3797)

AUTOMOTIVE BODY, PAINT & INTERIOR REPAIR & MAINTENANCE SVC

Indiana Custom Trucks LLC................E...... 260 463-3244
Lagrange (G-9046)
Marmon Highway Tech LLC................E...... 317 787-0718
Indianapolis (G-7457)
Northern Ind Indus Catings LLC................G...... 574 893-4621
Akron (G-6)

AUTOMOTIVE COLLISION SHOPS

Keystone Automotive Inds Inc................G...... 574 206-1421
Elkhart (G-2963)

AUTOMOTIVE CUSTOMIZING SVCS, NONFACTORY BASIS

Bearcat Corp................E...... 574 533-0448
Goshen (G-5177)

AUTOMOTIVE GLASS REPLACEMENT SHOPS

Barry Seat Cover & Auto Glass................F...... 574 288-4603
South Bend (G-12721)
Broadway Auto Glass LLC................F...... 219 884-5277
Merrillville (G-9704)
Dewilde Glass Inc................G...... 765 742-0229
Lafayette (G-8890)

AUTOMOTIVE LETTERING SVCS

Hot Rod Car Care LLC................G...... 317 660-2077
Indianapolis (G-7134)
Pyramid Sign & Design Inc................G...... 765 447-4174
Lafayette (G-8986)

AUTOMOTIVE PARTS, ACCESS & SPLYS

A-Fab LLC................D...... 812 897-0900
Boonville (G-904)
Acadia................G...... 260 894-7125
Ligonier (G-9274)
Accuride Emi LLC................G...... 940 565-8505
Evansville (G-3337)
Action Machine Inc................F...... 574 287-9650
South Bend (G-12694)
Aero Industries Inc................D...... 317 808-1923
Indianapolis (G-6346)
Air Ride Technologies Inc................E...... 812 482-2932
Jasper (G-8235)
All American Group Inc................E...... 574 262-0123
Elkhart (G-2674)
Allied Tube & Conduit Corp................C...... 812 265-9255
Madison (G-9443)
Allison Transm Holdings Inc................D...... 317 242-5000
Indianapolis (G-6371)
Allison Transmission Inc................A...... 317 280-6206
Indianapolis (G-6372)
Allison Transmission Inc................F...... 317 242-5000
Indianapolis (G-6374)
Allison Transmission Inc................C...... 317 821-5104
Indianapolis (G-6376)
AM General Holdings LLC................F...... 574 237-6222
South Bend (G-12699)
AM General LLC................B...... 574 258-6699
South Bend (G-12702)
American Mitsuba Corporation................C...... 989 779-4962
Monroeville (G-10191)
Amsafe Partners Inc................E...... 574 266-8330
Elkhart (G-2690)
Aptiv Services Us LLC................G...... 765 451-5011
Kokomo (G-8592)
Aptiv Services Us LLC................C...... 765 451-0732
Kokomo (G-8593)
Aptiv Services Us LLC................C...... 765 451-5011
Kokomo (G-8594)
Aristo LLC................E...... 219 962-1032
Hobart (G-6069)
Attc Manufacturing Inc................B...... 812 547-5060
Tell City (G-13156)
Atwood Mobile Products LLC................D...... 574 266-4848
Elkhart (G-2702)
Atwood Mobile Products LLC................D...... 574 264-2131
Elkhart (G-2703)
Atwood Mobile Products LLC................D...... 574 264-2131
Elkhart (G-2704)
Atwood Mobile Products LLC................C...... 574 522-7891
Elkhart (G-2705)
Atwood Mobile Products LLC................D...... 574 264-2131
Elkhart (G-2706)

Auburn Manufacturing Inc................F...... 260 925-8651
Auburn (G-315)
Auto Bumper Exchange Inc................F...... 260 493-4408
Fort Wayne (G-4096)
Autoform Tool & Mfg LLC................C...... 260 624-2014
Angola (G-195)
Autoneum North America Inc................G...... 248 848-0100
Jeffersonville (G-8327)
Avg North America Inc................F...... 765 748-3162
Gas City (G-5120)
Avionic Structures of Indiana................G...... 765 671-7865
Marion (G-9511)
Axle Inc................G...... 574 264-9434
Elkhart (G-2709)
B & B Manufacturing Inc................D...... 219 324-0247
La Porte (G-8737)
Barry Seat Cover & Auto Glass................F...... 574 288-4603
South Bend (G-12721)
Bender Products Inc................E...... 574 255-5350
Mishawaka (G-10009)
Bendix Coml Vhcl Systems LLC................B...... 260 356-9720
Huntington (G-6191)
Benteler Automotive Corp................C...... 574 534-1499
Goshen (G-5178)
Bentz Transport Products Inc................F...... 260 622-9100
Zionsville (G-14422)
Borgwarner Inc................G...... 765 609-3801
Anderson (G-75)
Borgwarner Pds Anderson LLC................B...... 765 778-6499
Noblesville (G-11068)
Borgwarner Pds Anderson LLC................C...... 765 778-6641
Pendleton (G-11486)
Bornemann Products Inc................G...... 574 546-2881
Warsaw (G-13851)
BRC Rubber & Plastics Inc................C...... 260 693-2171
Fort Wayne (G-4118)
BRC Rubber & Plastics Inc................C...... 260 894-4121
Ligonier (G-9278)
BRC Rubber & Plastics Inc................D...... 260 203-5300
Fort Wayne (G-4119)
Brindle Products Inc................E...... 260 627-2156
Grabill (G-5358)
C-Line Engineering Inc................E...... 812 246-4822
Sellersburg (G-12390)
Cardinal Services Inc Indiana................D...... 574 267-3823
Warsaw (G-13853)
Carter Fuel Systems LLC................B...... 574 735-0235
Logansport (G-9329)
CD & R Components Inc................E...... 812 852-4864
Batesville (G-496)
Cedar Creek Studios Inc................G...... 260 627-7320
Leo (G-9241)
Chemtrusion Inc................D...... 812 280-2910
Jeffersonville (G-8336)
Colbin Tool Company Inc................E...... 574 457-3183
Syracuse (G-13130)
Component Machine Inc................G...... 317 635-8929
Indianapolis (G-6642)
Compositech Inc................E...... 800 231-6755
Indianapolis (G-6643)
Continental Manufacturing LLC................E...... 765 778-9999
Anderson (G-90)
Continental Strl Plas Inc................E...... 260 627-0890
Grabill (G-5361)
Conversion Components Inc................G...... 574 264-4181
Elkhart (G-2772)
Cooper-Standard Automotive Inc................B...... 260 637-5824
Auburn (G-323)
Coupled Products LLC................B...... 260 248-3200
Columbia City (G-1776)
Coupled Products LLC................B...... 812 849-5304
Mitchell (G-10161)
Coupled Products LLC................B...... 260 248-3200
Columbia City (G-1777)
Covidien LP................C...... 317 837-8199
Plainfield (G-11602)
Cummins Inc................G...... 765 430-0093
Columbus (G-1898)
Cummins Inc................B...... 812 377-5000
Columbus (G-1891)
Cummins Inc................F...... 812 377-8601
Columbus (G-1894)
Cummins Inc................E...... 812 377-2932
Columbus (G-1895)
Cummins Inc................G...... 317 244-7251
Indianapolis (G-6709)
Cummins Inc................G...... 317 610-2493
Indianapolis (G-6710)
Cummins Midwest Regional Dist................D...... 901 302-8143
Whitestown (G-14251)

Employee Codes: A=Over 500 employees, B=251-500
C=101-250, D=51-100, E=20-50, F=10-19, G=2-9

2018 Harris Indiana
Industrial Directory

905

PRODUCT

Custom Wood Products Inc.................D....... 574 522-3300
Elkhart *(G-2784)*
Cvg Sprague Devices LLC....................G....... 614 289-5360
Michigan City *(G-9778)*
Dallara LLC..F....... 317 388-5400
Speedway *(G-13012)*
Dana Light Axle Products LLC............E....... 260 636-4300
Albion *(G-24)*
Dana Light Axle Products LLC............D....... 260 483-7174
Fort Wayne *(G-4199)*
Delco Electronics..................................G....... 765 455-9713
Kokomo *(G-8612)*
Delphi E & S Morgan Street Ops..........G....... 765 451-2571
Kokomo *(G-8614)*
Delphi Powertrain Systems LLC..........F....... 765 236-0025
Kokomo *(G-8615)*
Delphi Powertrain Systems LLC...........G....... 765 451-0732
Kokomo *(G-8616)*
Diesel Punk Core..................................G....... 812 631-0606
Bloomington *(G-712)*
Diversified Mch Bristol LLC..................A....... 248 728-8642
Bristol *(G-1055)*
Dometic Corporation.............................B....... 260 463-7657
Lagrange *(G-9037)*
Donaldson Company Inc.......................G....... 317 838-5568
Plainfield *(G-11606)*
Double T Manufacturing Corp..............F....... 574 262-1340
Elkhart *(G-2799)*
Dura Automotive Systems of Ind..........G....... 574 262-2655
Elkhart *(G-2803)*
Eaton Corporation................................F....... 317 704-2520
Indianapolis *(G-6796)*
Elizabeth M Graham..............................G....... 812 343-1267
Bargersville *(G-481)*
Engineered Machined Pdts Inc.............C....... 317 462-8894
Greenfield *(G-5528)*
Enovapremier LLC.................................D....... 812 385-0576
Princeton *(G-11870)*
Ezs Custom Woodworking.....................G....... 574 831-3078
Nappanee *(G-10668)*
Faurecia Emissions Control.................A....... 812 348-4305
Columbus *(G-1924)*
Faurecia Emissions Control.................B....... 812 341-2000
Columbus *(G-1927)*
FCA US LLC...A....... 765 454-1005
Kokomo *(G-8625)*
FCA US LLC...A....... 765 454-0018
Kokomo *(G-8624)*
FCC Adams...F....... 260 589-8555
Portland *(G-11821)*
Federal-Mogul LLC................................A....... 765 659-7207
Frankfort *(G-4830)*
Federal-Mogul LLC................................B....... 317 875-7259
Indianapolis *(G-6907)*
Fenwick Motor Sports...........................G....... 765 522-1354
Bainbridge *(G-476)*
Firestone Industrial Pdts Inc.................G....... 317 575-7000
Indianapolis *(G-6924)*
Flex-N-Gate Corporation......................A....... 765 294-3050
Veedersburg *(G-13643)*
Flex-N-Gate Corporation.......................C....... 260 665-8288
Angola *(G-214)*
Ford Motor Company.............................D....... 317 837-2302
Plainfield *(G-11610)*
Fort Wayne Clutch Inc...........................F....... 260 484-8505
Fort Wayne *(G-4271)*
Four Woods Laminating Inc...................E....... 260 593-2246
Topeka *(G-13419)*
Frank Wiss Racg Components Inc........E....... 317 248-4764
Indianapolis *(G-6957)*
Freudenberg-Nok General Partnr..........E....... 734 354-5504
Shelbyville *(G-12535)*
Freudenberg-Nok General Partnr..........C....... 317 421-3400
Shelbyville *(G-12534)*
Freudenberg-Nok General Partnr..........C....... 765 763-7246
Morristown *(G-10369)*
GKN Sinter Metals LLC.........................C....... 812 883-3381
Salem *(G-12288)*
Global Forming LLC...............................E....... 317 290-1000
Indianapolis *(G-7011)*
GM Components Holdings LLC............B....... 765 451-8440
Kokomo *(G-8628)*
Grede LLC..C....... 765 521-8000
New Castle *(G-10903)*
Greg Moser Engineering Inc..................E....... 260 726-6689
Portland *(G-11827)*
Gulf Stream Coach Inc...........................C....... 574 773-7761
Nappanee *(G-10677)*
Hart Plastics Inc.....................................E....... 574 264-7060
Elkhart *(G-2909)*
Heartland Automotive Inc......................A....... 765 653-4263
Greencastle *(G-5462)*
Heartland Automotive LLC....................G....... 765 653-4263
Greencastle *(G-5463)*
Hendrickson International Corp............G....... 260 868-2131
Butler *(G-1230)*
Hendrickson International Corp............C....... 260 349-6400
Kendallville *(G-8478)*
Hendrickson International Corp............C....... 765 483-5350
Lebanon *(G-9187)*
Hisada America Inc...............................D....... 812 526-0756
Edinburgh *(G-2613)*
Hitachi Automotive Systems.................B....... 859 734-9451
Ligonier *(G-9287)*
Hitachi Cble Auto Pdts USA Inc............C....... 812 945-9011
New Albany *(G-10796)*
Hitachi Powdered Mtls USA Inc............C....... 812 663-5058
Greensburg *(G-5610)*
Hoosier Industrial Supply Inc................F....... 574 533-8565
Goshen *(G-5240)*
Horner Industrial Services Inc..............F....... 317 634-7165
Indianapolis *(G-7129)*
I Hsg Inc...G....... 765 778-6499
Anderson *(G-119)*
Icon Metal Forming LLC.........................B....... 812 738-5900
Corydon *(G-2102)*
Illinois Tool Works Inc............................E....... 317 390-5940
Indianapolis *(G-7159)*
Illinois Tool Works Inc............................C....... 260 347-8040
Kendallville *(G-8480)*
Indiana Automotive Fas Inc...................B....... 317 467-0100
Greenfield *(G-5538)*
Indiana Custom Trucks LLC..................E....... 260 463-3244
Lagrange *(G-9046)*
Indiana Marujun LLC..............................E....... 765 584-7639
Winchester *(G-14332)*
Indiana Mills & Manufacturing...............B....... 317 896-9531
Westfield *(G-14169)*
Interstate Power Systems Inc................E....... 952 854-2044
Gary *(G-5070)*
Jason Incorporated................................G....... 248 455-7919
Richmond *(G-12005)*
Jasper Willow Springs Mo LLC..............G....... 800 827-7455
Jasper *(G-8266)*
Jrz Industries Inc...................................G....... 574 834-4543
North Webster *(G-11295)*
K Min..G....... 574 296-3500
Elkhart *(G-2955)*
Kampco Steel Products Inc....................E....... 574 294-5466
Elkhart *(G-2956)*
Kautex Inc...B....... 937 238-8096
Avilla *(G-409)*
Kinro Manufacturing Inc.........................C....... 574 533-8337
Goshen *(G-5257)*
Kirby Risk Corporation............................B....... 765 447-1402
Lafayette *(G-8942)*
Kp Holdings LLC......................................B....... 317 867-0234
Westfield *(G-14173)*
KYB Americas Corporation....................F....... 317 881-7772
Greenwood *(G-5714)*
Lakepark Industries Ind Inc....................D....... 260 768-7411
Shipshewana *(G-12628)*
Lau Industries Inc....................................D....... 574 223-3181
Rochester *(G-12132)*
LCI Industries...D....... 574 535-1125
Elkhart *(G-2989)*
Lear Corporation.......................................G....... 260 244-1700
Columbia City *(G-1808)*
Lear Corporation.......................................G....... 219 764-5101
Portage *(G-11773)*
Lear Corporation.......................................G....... 765 653-2511
Greencastle *(G-5466)*
Lear Corporation.......................................E....... 574 935-3818
Plymouth *(G-11702)*
Lear Corporation.......................................B....... 219 852-0014
Hammond *(G-5907)*
Lingenfelter Prfmce Engrg Inc...............E....... 260 724-2552
Decatur *(G-2390)*
Lippert Components Inc..........................G....... 574 971-4100
Goshen *(G-5274)*
Lippert Components Inc..........................C....... 800 551-9149
Elkhart *(G-2999)*
Lippert Components Inc..........................D....... 574 535-1125
Goshen *(G-5268)*
Lippert Components Inc..........................D....... 574 294-6852
Elkhart *(G-3000)*
Lippert Components Inc..........................E....... 574 535-1125
Goshen *(G-5272)*
Lippert Components Inc..........................D....... 574 849-0869
Goshen *(G-5273)*
Lippert Components Inc..........................C....... 574 971-4320
Goshen *(G-5275)*
Lippert Components Inc..........................D....... 574 312-7445
Middlebury *(G-9904)*
Lippert Components Mfg Inc..................C....... 574 935-5122
Plymouth *(G-11703)*
Magna Powertrain America Inc..............C....... 765 587-1300
Muncie *(G-10515)*
Magna Powertrain America Inc..............E....... 765 587-1300
Muncie *(G-10516)*
Mahomed Sales & Whsng LLC...............D....... 317 472-5800
Indianapolis *(G-7441)*
Make It Mobile LLC..................................E....... 260 562-1045
Howe *(G-6128)*
Makuta Technics Inc.................................F....... 317 642-0001
Shelbyville *(G-12550)*
Mancor Indiana Inc...................................E....... 765 779-4800
Anderson *(G-134)*
Mann+hummel Filtration Technol...........G....... 260 497-5560
Fort Wayne *(G-4451)*
Martinrea Industries Inc..........................C....... 812 346-5750
North Vernon *(G-11269)*
Mascot Truck Parts Usa LLC..................D....... 317 839-9525
Plainfield *(G-11623)*
Mastersbilt Chassis Inc...........................F....... 812 793-3666
Crothersville *(G-2218)*
Meritor Inc...G....... 317 279-2180
Plainfield *(G-11627)*
Metaldyne Bsm LLC..................................D....... 260 495-4315
Fremont *(G-4968)*
Metaldyne M&A Bluffton LLC..................D....... 260 824-2360
Bluffton *(G-882)*
Midwest Auto Repair Inc...........................E....... 219 322-0364
Schererville *(G-12334)*
Mobile Dynamometer LLC.........................G....... 765 271-5080
Kokomo *(G-8668)*
Mosey Manufacturing Co Inc...................D....... 765 768-7462
Dunkirk *(G-2486)*
Mosey Manufacturing Co Inc...................D....... 765 983-8889
Richmond *(G-12022)*
Motorama Auto Ctr Inc..............................G....... 317 831-0036
Mooresville *(G-10325)*
Muncie Power Products Inc.....................C....... 765 284-7721
Muncie *(G-10533)*
Muncie Power Products Inc.....................G....... 765 896-9816
Muncie *(G-10534)*
Mvo Usa Inc...F....... 317 585-5785
Indianapolis *(G-7562)*
Niagara Lasalle Corporation...................E....... 800 262-2558
Hammond *(G-5921)*
Nishikawa Cooper LLC.............................A....... 574 546-5938
Bremen *(G-1012)*
Norco Industries Inc..................................C....... 574 262-3400
Elkhart *(G-3065)*
NSK Corporation..C....... 765 458-5000
Liberty *(G-9267)*
NSK Precision America Inc......................C....... 317 738-5000
Franklin *(G-4916)*
NTN Driveshaft Inc....................................A....... 812 342-7000
Columbus *(G-1982)*
Omnimax International Inc.......................E....... 574 294-8576
Elkhart *(G-3070)*
Onspot of North America Inc...................E....... 812 346-1719
North Vernon *(G-11275)*
Perfection Wheel LLC...............................F....... 260 358-9239
Huntington *(G-6237)*
Peterson Sanko Corp.................................G....... 765 966-9656
Richmond *(G-12028)*
Phillips Company Inc.................................D....... 812 378-3797
Columbus *(G-1994)*
Pierce Company Inc...................................E....... 765 998-8100
Upland *(G-13472)*
Power Plant Service Inc............................E....... 260 432-6716
Fort Wayne *(G-4542)*
Power Train Corp Fort Wayne...................F....... 317 241-9393
Indianapolis *(G-7712)*
Price Motor Sport Engineering.................G....... 812 546-4220
Hope *(G-6118)*
Pridgeon & Clay Inc...................................C....... 317 738-4885
Franklin *(G-4923)*
Quality Converters Inc...............................E....... 260 829-6541
Orland *(G-11356)*
Ramco Engineering Inc..............................E....... 574 266-1455
Elkhart *(G-3136)*
Raybestos Powertrain................................G....... 812 268-1370
Sullivan *(G-13092)*
Rayco Mch & Engrg Group Inc.................E....... 317 291-7848
Indianapolis *(G-7819)*
Riverside Mfg Inc.......................................C....... 260 637-4470
Fort Wayne *(G-4594)*

906

2018 Harris Indiana
Industrial Directory

(G-0000) Company's Geographic Section entry number

Road Equipment ....G....... 219 887-6400
  Gary (G-5094)
Robert Bosch LLC ....D....... 574 654-4000
  New Carlisle (G-10886)
Rochester Manufacturing LLC...........G....... 574 224-2044
  Rochester (G-12147)
Rocore Thermal Systems LLC ....E....... 317 227-2929
  Indianapolis (G-7854)
Safe Fleet Mirrors............................F....... 574 266-3700
  Elkhart (G-3153)
SMR Management Inc ....G....... 765 252-0257
  Lafayette (G-8999)
Sonoco Prtective Solutions Inc ....D....... 260 726-9333
  Portland (G-11847)
Spheros North America Inc ....F....... 574 264-2190
  Elkhart (G-3185)
Spitzers Racing Enterprises ....F....... 317 894-9533
  Greenfield (G-5577)
Splendor Boats LLC ....F....... 260 352-2835
  Silver Lake (G-12681)
Standard Glass and Star Glass ....G....... 574 546-5912
  Bremen (G-1025)
Stant USA Corp ....C....... 765 825-3121
  Connersville (G-2072)
Stant USA Corp ....B....... 765 825-3121
  Connersville (G-2073)
Starcraft Corporation........................G....... 574 534-7705
  Goshen (G-5328)
Starcraft Corporation........................E....... 574 534-7827
  Goshen (G-5329)
Steel Tank & Fabricating Corp............E....... 260 248-8971
  Columbia City (G-1838)
Summit Coaches ....G....... 260 489-3556
  Fort Wayne (G-4662)
Team Oneway ....G....... 574 387-5417
  Granger (G-5443)
Thermal Ceramics Inc.......................E....... 574 296-3500
  Elkhart (G-3212)
TI Automotive Ligonier Corp ....B....... 260 894-3163
  Ligonier (G-9300)
TI Group Auto Systems LLC ....B....... 260 622-7900
  Ossian (G-11414)
TI Group Auto Systems LLC ....C....... 260 587-6100
  Ashley (G-291)
TNT Truck Accessories LLC ....G....... 812 305-0714
  Haubstadt (G-6006)
Tri Aerospace LLC ....E....... 812 872-2400
  Terre Haute (G-13358)
Tru-Flex LLC....................................C....... 765 893-4403
  West Lebanon (G-14122)
Truckpro LLC...................................F....... 765 482-6525
  Lebanon (G-9230)
TRW Automotive US LLC ....A....... 765 423-5377
  Lafayette (G-9012)
TRW Commercial Steering ....A....... 765 423-5377
  Lafayette (G-9013)
Twb of Indiana ....G....... 812 342-6000
  Columbus (G-2026)
U B Machine Inc ....E....... 260 493-3381
  New Haven (G-10962)
Ugn Inc...C....... 219 464-7813
  Valparaiso (G-13631)
Ultimate Sports Inc ....G....... 765 423-2984
  West Lafayette (G-14114)
United Components LLC.....................F....... 812 867-4156
  Evansville (G-3786)
Valeo North America Inc ....A....... 812 663-8541
  Greensburg (G-5640)
Valeo North America Inc ....B....... 812 663-8541
  Greensburg (G-5641)
Vee Engineering Inc.........................D....... 260 424-6635
  Fort Wayne (G-4725)
Vessell Trim Co ....F....... 812 424-2963
  Evansville (G-3797)
V$iariloc Distributors Inc ....G....... 317 273-0089
  Indianapolis (G-8160)
Voegele Auto Supply LLC ....G....... 765 647-3541
  Brookville (G-1130)
Wabash National Corporation ....B....... 765 771-5300
  Lafayette (G-9018)
Wagler Competition Pdts LLC ....G....... 812 486-9360
  Odon (G-11344)
Warner Electric LLC..........................C....... 260 244-6183
  Columbia City (G-1846)
Webb Wheel Products Inc..................C....... 812 548-0477
  Tell City (G-13175)
Wellspring Components LLC ....G....... 260 768-7336
  Shipshewana (G-12657)
Xtrac Inc ....F....... 317 472-2451
  Indianapolis (G-8222)

Zemco Mfg Inc..................................E....... 260 428-2650
  Fort Wayne (G-4765)

AUTOMOTIVE PARTS: Plastic

Ace Mobility Inc................................F....... 317 241-2444
  Indianapolis (G-6316)
Bremen Composites LLC ....D....... 574 546-3791
  Bremen (G-986)
Diversity-Vuteq LLC ....C....... 812 761-0210
  Princeton (G-11868)
Enovapremier LLC ....D....... 812 385-0576
  Princeton (G-11870)
Futaba Indiana America Corp ....B....... 812 895-4700
  Vincennes (G-13683)
Indy Parts Inc ....G....... 317 243-7171
  Indianapolis (G-7219)
JMS Engineered Plastics Inc ....D....... 574 277-3228
  South Bend (G-12823)
K&M Indiana LLC ....C....... 812 256-3351
  Charlestown (G-1569)
M&M Performance Inc ....G....... 574 536-6103
  Goshen (G-5276)
Mgtc Inc ....G....... 317 873-8697
  Zionsville (G-14448)
Odyssey Machine Inc ....G....... 812 951-1160
  Georgetown (G-5151)

AUTOMOTIVE PRDTS: Rubber

Aeropro Holdings LLC ....G....... 317 849-9555
  Indianapolis (G-6349)
Central Rubber & Plastics Inc..............E....... 574 534-6411
  Goshen (G-5185)
Exactseal Inc ....G....... 317 559-2220
  Indianapolis (G-6889)
Goodtime Manufacturing LLC ....G....... 317 876-3661
  Indianapolis (G-7026)
Klh Holding Corporation ....E....... 317 634-3976
  Indianapolis (G-7358)
No-Sail Splash Guard Co Inc ....G....... 765 522-2100
  Roachdale (G-12094)
Servaas Inc ....G....... 317 633-2020
  Indianapolis (G-7914)
South Bend Modern Molding Inc..........D....... 574 255-0711
  Mishawaka (G-10132)

AUTOMOTIVE REPAIR SHOPS: Alternators/Generator, Rebuild/Rpr

Jeannie and Rachel Heidenreich..........G....... 260 244-4583
  Columbia City (G-1801)

AUTOMOTIVE REPAIR SHOPS: Auto Front End Repair

Fort Wayne Clutch Inc ....F....... 260 484-8505
  Fort Wayne (G-4271)

AUTOMOTIVE REPAIR SHOPS: Brake Repair

Auto Specialty of Lafayette.................G....... 765 446-2311
  Lafayette (G-8857)

AUTOMOTIVE REPAIR SHOPS: Diesel Engine Repair

Bryant Products Inc...........................F....... 812 522-5929
  Seymour (G-12435)
Cummins Crosspoint LLC ....E....... 317 243-7979
  Indianapolis (G-6706)
Jolliff Diesel Service ....G....... 812 692-5725
  Elnora (G-3290)
Power Investments Inc ....F....... 317 738-2117
  Franklin (G-4921)

AUTOMOTIVE REPAIR SHOPS: Electrical Svcs

G & M Rebuilders Inc.........................G....... 812 858-9233
  Newburgh (G-11029)
Martin Electric Inc ....G....... 765 288-3254
  Eaton (G-2585)
Regal-Beloit Corporation ....D....... 260 416-5400
  Fort Wayne (G-4587)

AUTOMOTIVE REPAIR SHOPS: Engine Rebuilding

C & P Machine Service Inc ....E....... 260 484-7723
  Fort Wayne (G-4131)

Chappos Inc ....G....... 219 942-8101
  Hobart (G-6074)
Performance Technology Inc................G....... 574 862-2116
  Wakarusa (G-13789)
Three K Racing Enterprises.................G....... 765 482-4273
  Lebanon (G-9228)

AUTOMOTIVE REPAIR SHOPS: Engine Repair

Cummins Crosspoint LLC ....G....... 317 484-2146
  Indianapolis (G-6708)
Indian Creek Outdoor Power LLC ....G....... 812 597-3055
  Morgantown (G-10354)
Morgan Automotive ....G....... 765 378-0593
  Chesterfield (G-1588)
Pyramid Equipment ....F....... 219 778-2591
  Rolling Prairie (G-12193)

AUTOMOTIVE REPAIR SHOPS: Engine Repair, Exc Diesel

Ccts Technology Group Inc ....G....... 305 209-5743
  Indianapolis (G-6570)

AUTOMOTIVE REPAIR SHOPS: Machine Shop

Champion Racing Engines ....G....... 317 335-2491
  McCordsville (G-9665)
Frank Wiss Racg Components Inc.........E....... 317 248-4764
  Indianapolis (G-6957)
Greg Moser Engineering Inc ....E....... 260 726-6689
  Portland (G-11827)
H & E Machined Specialties ....F....... 260 424-2527
  Fort Wayne (G-4311)
Reynoldsrussell Entps LLC ....G....... 317 431-5886
  Anderson (G-162)
Waterfield Automotive Mch Sp ....G....... 765 288-6262
  Muncie (G-10580)

AUTOMOTIVE REPAIR SHOPS: Muffler Shop, Sale/Rpr/Installation

Auto Specialty of Lafayette.................G....... 765 446-2311
  Lafayette (G-8857)

AUTOMOTIVE REPAIR SHOPS: Torque Converter Repair

Champ Torque Converters Inc..............G....... 812 424-2602
  Evansville (G-3415)

AUTOMOTIVE REPAIR SHOPS: Trailer Repair

Rugged Steel Works LLC ....F....... 260 444-4241
  Fort Wayne (G-4598)

AUTOMOTIVE REPAIR SVC

B & M Electrical Co Inc......................F....... 765 448-4532
  Lafayette (G-8859)
Best Weld Inc ....F....... 765 641-7720
  Anderson (G-74)
Lances Driveshaft & Components ....G....... 219 762-2531
  Portage (G-11772)
Mc Ginley Fire Apparatus....................G....... 765 482-3152
  Lebanon (G-9204)
Midwest Auto Repair Inc ....E....... 219 322-0364
  Schererville (G-12334)
Morgan Automotive ....G....... 765 378-0593
  Chesterfield (G-1588)

AUTOMOTIVE SPLYS & PARTS, NEW, WHOL: Auto Servicing Eqpt

C & P Machine Service Inc ....E....... 260 484-7723
  Fort Wayne (G-4131)
MRC Technology Inc...........................F....... 574 232-9057
  South Bend (G-12867)

AUTOMOTIVE SPLYS & PARTS, NEW, WHOL: Testing Eqpt, Electric

Remy Logistics LLC ....G....... 765 683-3700
  Anderson (G-160)

AUTOMOTIVE SPLYS & PARTS, NEW, WHOLESALE: Brakes

Hibbing International Friction ....F 765 529-7001
New Castle (G-10904)

Smart Technologies LLC ....G 317 738-4338
Franklin (G-4933)

AUTOMOTIVE SPLYS & PARTS, NEW, WHOLESALE: Bumpers

Auto Bumper Exchange Inc ....F 260 493-4408
Fort Wayne (G-4096)

AUTOMOTIVE SPLYS & PARTS, NEW, WHOLESALE: Engines/Eng Parts

3d Engineering Inc ....G 317 729-5430
Edinburgh (G-2593)

Mirrus Corporation Inc ....E 812 689-1411
Versailles (G-13656)

AUTOMOTIVE SPLYS & PARTS, NEW, WHOLESALE: Hardware

Conversion Components Inc ....G 574 264-4181
Elkhart (G-2772)

Wb Automotive Holdings Inc ....F 734 604-8962
Fort Wayne (G-4748)

AUTOMOTIVE SPLYS & PARTS, NEW, WHOLESALE: Trailer Parts

Chubbs Steel Sales Inc ....E 574 295-3166
Elkhart (G-2757)

Jayco Inc ....A 574 825-5861
Middlebury (G-9896)

Ridge Trailers ....G 260 244-5443
Columbia City (G-1828)

AUTOMOTIVE SPLYS & PARTS, NEW, WHOLESALE: Trim

Toyota Boshoku America Inc ....E 812 385-2040
Princeton (G-11885)

AUTOMOTIVE SPLYS & PARTS, NEW, WHOLESALE: Wheels

Marmon Highway Tech LLC ....E 317 787-0718
Indianapolis (G-7457)

AUTOMOTIVE SPLYS & PARTS, USED, WHOLESALE

Auto Bumper Exchange Inc ....F 260 493-4408
Fort Wayne (G-4096)

AUTOMOTIVE SPLYS & PARTS, WHOLESALE, NEC

Action Machine Inc ....F 574 287-9650
South Bend (G-12694)

Afco Performance Group LLC ....G 812 897-0900
Boonville (G-905)

Allied Enterprises Inc ....E 765 288-8849
Muncie (G-10428)

Borgwarner Pds Anderson LLC ....B 765 778-6499
Noblesville (G-11068)

Boyer Machine & Tool Co Inc ....E 812 379-9581
Columbus (G-1861)

Jason Industries Inc ....D 574 294-7595
Elkhart (G-2945)

KOI Enterprises Inc ....G 812 537-2335
Lawrenceburg (G-9146)

Meritor Inc ....G 317 279-2180
Plainfield (G-11627)

Motsinger Auto Supply Inc ....G 317 782-8484
Indianapolis (G-7549)

Promotor Engines & Components ....G 574 533-9898
Goshen (G-5313)

Staples Pipe & Muffler ....G 812 522-3569
Butlerville (G-1251)

AUTOMOTIVE SPLYS, USED, WHOLESALE & RETAIL

Acd Suppliers LLC ....G 317 527-9715
Indianapolis (G-6315)

Aom Bookshop ....G 317 493-8095
Indianapolis (G-6405)

Cortex Safety Technologies LLC ....G 317 414-5607
Carmel (G-1344)

AUTOMOTIVE SVCS, EXC REPAIR & CARWASHES: Customizing

K & D Custom Coach Inc ....E 574 537-1716
Goshen (G-5250)

AUTOMOTIVE SVCS, EXC REPAIR & CARWASHES: Insp & Diagnostic

Auto Specialty of Lafayette ....G 765 446-2311
Lafayette (G-8857)

Qualitex Inc ....F 260 244-7839
Fort Wayne (G-4571)

AUTOMOTIVE SVCS, EXC REPAIR & CARWASHES: Lubrication

Jiffy Lube ....F 317 882-5823
Greenwood (G-5709)

Morse Lake Automotive ....G 317 984-4514
Cicero (G-1663)

AUTOMOTIVE SVCS, EXC REPAIR & CARWASHES: Maintenance

Esco Enterprises Indiana Inc ....F 317 241-0318
Indianapolis (G-6876)

Wilson Enterprises Inc ....G 765 362-1089
Crawfordsville (G-2205)

AUTOMOTIVE SVCS, EXC REPAIR: Carwash, Self-Service

Paulus Plastic Company Inc ....G 574 834-7663
North Webster (G-11299)

Whitlocks Pressure Wash ....F 765 825-5868
Connersville (G-2078)

AUTOMOTIVE SVCS, EXC REPAIR: Truck Wash

Schaffsteins Truck Clean LLC ....F 812 464-2424
Evansville (G-3715)

AUTOMOTIVE SVCS, EXC REPAIR: Washing & Polishing

Elie Cleaning Services LLC ....F 317 983-3388
Indianapolis (G-6837)

AUTOMOTIVE SVCS, EXC RPR/CARWASHES: High Perf Auto Rpr/Svc

Competitive Designs Inc ....G 574 223-9406
Rochester (G-12118)

Illinois Lubricants LLC ....G 260 436-2444
Fort Wayne (G-4358)

Lingenfelter Prfmce Engrg Inc ....E 260 724-2552
Decatur (G-2390)

Mitchell Smith Racing ....G 765 640-0237
Anderson (G-137)

Rhyne Engines Inc ....G 219 845-1218
Gary (G-5092)

AUTOMOTIVE TOPS INSTALLATION OR REPAIR: Canvas Or Plastic

Mosiers Tarps ....G 260 563-3332
Wabash (G-13742)

AUTOMOTIVE TOWING & WRECKING SVC

Chads LLC ....G 812 323-7377
Ellettsville (G-3273)

Hendershot Service Center Inc ....F 765 653-2600
Greencastle (G-5464)

AUTOMOTIVE TOWING SVCS

Grahams Wrecker Service Inc ....G 317 736-4355
Franklin (G-4892)

Sparkling Clean Inc ....G 812 422-4871
Evansville (G-3741)

Zionsville Towing Inc ....G 317 873-4550
Zionsville (G-14474)

AUTOMOTIVE TRANSMISSION REPAIR SVC

Metaldyne M&A Bluffton LLC ....D 260 824-2360
Bluffton (G-882)

Northern Trans & Differential ....G 219 764-4009
Portage (G-11785)

Tecumseh Products Company ....B 812 883-3575
Salem (G-12307)

Truckpro LLC ....F 765 482-6525
Lebanon (G-9230)

AUTOMOTIVE UPHOLSTERY SHOPS

Barry Seat Cover & Auto Glass ....F 574 288-4603
South Bend (G-12721)

AUTOMOTIVE WELDING SVCS

Chappos Inc ....G 219 942-8101
Hobart (G-6074)

Ernies Welding Shop ....G 812 326-2600
Saint Anthony (G-12245)

Harvs Welding Inc ....G 219 345-5959
Wheatfield (G-14224)

Mooresville Welding Inc ....G 317 831-2265
Mooresville (G-10324)

Pgg Enterprises LLC ....G 317 462-2871
Greenfield (G-5563)

T K Sales & Service ....G 219 962-8982
Gary (G-5104)

AUTOMOTIVE: Bodies

ABRA Auto Body & Glass LP ....E 317 839-8940
Plainfield (G-11590)

ADM Mobility Solutions Inc ....G 317 481-8707
Indianapolis (G-6327)

KFC Composite Engineering Inc ....G 219 369-9093
La Porte (G-8781)

AUTOMOTIVE: Seat Frames, Metal

Kiel NA LLC ....F 574 293-3600
Elkhart (G-2965)

AUTOMOTIVE: Seating

Advanced Assembly LLC ....F 260 244-1700
Columbia City (G-1761)

Fisher & Company Incorporated ....C 586 746-2000
Evansville (G-3505)

Johnson Controls Inc ....D 317 917-5043
Pittsboro (G-11583)

Johnson Controls Inc ....D 260 347-0500
Kendallville (G-8481)

Johnson Controls Inc ....D 219 736-7105
Crown Point (G-2269)

Johnson Controls Inc ....G 260 485-9999
Fort Wayne (G-4398)

Johnson Controls Inc ....C 260 479-4400
Fort Wayne (G-4399)

Johnson Controls Inc ....F 812 868-1374
Evansville (G-3578)

Nhk Seating of America Inc ....E 765 659-4781
Frankfort (G-4844)

Pauls Seating Inc ....G 574 522-0630
Elkhart (G-3093)

Superior Seating Inc ....E 574 389-9011
Elkhart (G-3200)

Toyota Boshoku America Inc ....F 812 385-2040
Princeton (G-11884)

Toyota Boshoku Indiana LLC ....A 812 491-9100
Princeton (G-11886)

TS Tech Indiana LLC ....G 765 465-4294
New Castle (G-10920)

AWNINGS & CANOPIES

All American Tent & Awning Inc ....F 812 232-4220
Terre Haute (G-13190)

Awningtec Usa Incorporated ....E 812 734-0423
Corydon (G-2088)

Signdoc Identity LLC ....G 317 247-9670
Indianapolis (G-7946)

AWNINGS & CANOPIES: Awnings, Fabric, From Purchased Matls

Beverly Tent & Awning Co ....G 219 931-3723
Hammond (G-5852)

Blessing Enterprises Inc ....F 219 736-9800
Merrillville (G-9702)

Canvas Shop LLC ....G...... 260 768-7755
  Shipshewana (G-12607)
Cool Planet LLC ....G...... 317 927-9000
  Indianapolis (G-6662)
Lafayette Tent & Awning Co ....E...... 765 742-4277
  Lafayette (G-8951)
Larrys Canvas Cleaning ....G...... 260 463-2220
  Lagrange (G-9057)
Lomont Holdings Co Inc ....E...... 800 545-9023
  Angola (G-228)
Marion Tent & Awning Co ....G...... 765 664-7722
  Marion (G-9546)
T J Snuggles Inc ....E...... 574 546-4404
  Bremen (G-1028)
Twin Lakes Canvas Inc ....G...... 574 583-2000
  Monticello (G-10286)
Webster Custom Canvas Inc ....G...... 574 834-4497
  North Webster (G-11302)

AWNINGS & CANOPIES: Fabric

Shade By Design Inc ....G...... 317 602-3513
  Indianapolis (G-7920)
Woodside Custom Canvas LLC ....G...... 260 593-2420
  Topeka (G-13432)

AWNINGS: Fiberglass

American Window and Glass Inc ....C...... 812 464-9400
  Evansville (G-3352)

AWNINGS: Metal

Champion of Evansville LLC ....F...... 812 424-2456
  Evansville (G-3416)
Champion Opco LLC ....E...... 260 271-4076
  Fort Wayne (G-4144)
H & H Home Improvement Inc ....G...... 812 288-8700
  Clarksville (G-1684)
Key Sheet Metal Inc ....G...... 317 546-7151
  Indianapolis (G-7345)
Marion Tent & Awning Co ....G...... 765 664-7722
  Marion (G-9546)
Styled Rite Company Inc ....G...... 219 931-9844
  Gary (G-5102)

AXLES

Dexter Axle Company ....C...... 260 636-2195
  Albion (G-25)
Dexter Axle Company ....D...... 574 295-7888
  Elkhart (G-2795)
Dexter Axle Company ....D...... 574 294-6651
  Elkhart (G-2796)
Graber Manufacturing ....G...... 812 636-7725
  Odon (G-11327)
Industrial Axle Company LLC ....D...... 574 294-6651
  Elkhart (G-2933)
Industrial Axle Company LLC ....D...... 574 295-6077
  Elkhart (G-2934)

AXLES: Rolled Or Forged, Made In Steel Mills

Ntk Precision Axle Corporation ....B...... 765 656-1000
  Frankfort (G-4846)

BACKHOES

B Trucking & Backhoe Inc ....G...... 765 437-5960
  Windfall (G-14346)
Ramar Industries Inc ....G...... 765 288-7319
  Muncie (G-10553)
Steven A Williams ....G...... 812 664-3405
  Sellersburg (G-12419)
Tracy K Hullett ....G...... 765 472-3349
  Peru (G-11553)
Vires Backhoe and Dumptruc ....G...... 812 595-1630
  Deputy (G-2461)

BADGES: Identification & Insignia

ASAP Identification SEC Inc ....G...... 317 488-1030
  Indianapolis (G-6424)

BAGS: Canvas

Meese Inc ....D...... 812 273-1008
  Madison (G-9485)

BAGS: Garment Storage Exc Paper Or Plastic Film

Bags By Brenda ....G...... 765 779-4287
  Markleville (G-9585)

BAGS: Paper

Lesac Corporation ....E...... 219 879-3215
  Michigan City (G-9810)
Westrock Cp LLC ....G...... 574 936-2118
  Plymouth (G-11735)

BAGS: Plastic

Essentra Packaging US Inc ....F...... 317 328-7355
  Indianapolis (G-6877)
Gen Enterprises ....G...... 574 498-6777
  Tippecanoe (G-13381)
Jadcore LLC ....C...... 812 234-2724
  Terre Haute (G-13260)
Printpack Inc ....B...... 812 663-5091
  Greensburg (G-5629)
Witham Machine ....G...... 317 835-2076
  Boggstown (G-903)

BAGS: Plastic & Pliofilm

Cougar Bag Inc ....E...... 317 831-9720
  Mooresville (G-10306)
Grrk Holdings Inc ....E...... 317 872-0172
  Indianapolis (G-7053)
Novipax LLC ....D...... 201 791-7600
  Indianapolis (G-7601)

BAGS: Plastic, Made From Purchased Materials

All-Flex Inc ....G...... 812 949-8898
  Georgetown (G-5140)
Cpg - Ohio LLC ....F...... 260 829-6721
  Orland (G-11348)
D and M Enterprises LLC ....F...... 260 483-4008
  Fort Wayne (G-4197)
Eagle Industries Inc ....F...... 812 282-1393
  Jeffersonville (G-8353)
Hilex Poly ....F...... 812 346-1066
  North Vernon (G-11261)
Novolex Inc ....C...... 812 346-1066
  North Vernon (G-11273)
Putnam Plastics Inc ....E...... 765 795-6102
  Cloverdale (G-1735)
Universal Transparent Bag Co ....G...... 317 634-6425
  Indianapolis (G-8130)

BAGS: Rubber Or Rubberized Fabric

Boyd Corporation ....F...... 574 389-1878
  Elkhart (G-2731)

BAGS: Textile

Raine Inc ....F...... 765 622-7687
  Anderson (G-157)
Ts2 Tctical Spec-Solutions Inc ....G...... 765 437-3650
  Bedford (G-585)

BAGS: Trash, Plastic Film, Made From Purchased Materials

Adec Inc ....C...... 574 848-7451
  Bristol (G-1040)
Berry Global Group Inc ....F...... 812 424-2904
  Evansville (G-3377)

BAIT, FISHING, WHOLESALE

Fisherman S Lurecraft Shop Inc ....G...... 260 829-1274
  Lagrange (G-9042)

BAKERIES, COMMERCIAL: On Premises Baking Only

Abigails Baking Company LLC ....G...... 219 299-1785
  Valparaiso (G-13482)
Almiras Bakery ....E...... 219 844-4334
  Hammond (G-5839)
B&B Goodiez ....G...... 765 338-6833
  Connersville (G-2039)
Babbs Supermarket Inc ....D...... 812 829-2231
  Spencer (G-13017)

Backdoor Baking Company LLC ....G...... 317 927-7275
  Indianapolis (G-6452)
Brunos Breads LLC ....F...... 219 883-5126
  Gary (G-5031)
Buehler Foods Inc ....C...... 812 467-7255
  Evansville (G-3404)
Colonial Baking Co Inc ....C...... 812 232-4466
  Terre Haute (G-13213)
Concannons Pastry Shop ....F...... 765 288-8551
  Muncie (G-10448)
Confectionery Products Mfg Inc ....G...... 317 269-7363
  Indianapolis (G-6649)
Eat Dessert First Inc ....G...... 812 438-9600
  Patriot (G-11467)
Enjoy Life Natural Brands LLC ....F...... 773 632-2163
  Jeffersonville (G-8356)
Fingerhut Bakery Inc ....F...... 574 896-5937
  North Judson (G-11212)
Ganal Corporation ....G...... 260 749-2161
  New Haven (G-10940)
Gutierrez Mexican Bakery & Mkt ....G...... 574 534-9979
  Goshen (G-5232)
Harlan Bakeries LLC ....G...... 317 272-3600
  Avon (G-443)
Harlan Bakeries-Avon LLC ....B...... 317 272-3600
  Avon (G-444)
Hearthside Food Solutions LLC ....G...... 219 878-1522
  Michigan City (G-9802)
Heyerlys Bakery Inc ....F...... 260 622-4196
  Ossian (G-11401)
Holsum of Fort Wayne Inc ....C...... 219 362-4561
  La Porte (G-8766)
Indiana Baking Co ....F...... 260 483-5997
  Fort Wayne (G-4362)
Irish Cupcakes Inc ....G...... 574 289-8669
  Elkhart (G-2939)
Klosterman Baking Co ....E...... 317 359-5545
  Indianapolis (G-7361)
Kroger Co ....D...... 574 294-6092
  Elkhart (G-2975)
Kroger Co ....C...... 574 291-0740
  South Bend (G-12830)
Lakeshore Foods Corp ....C...... 219 362-8513
  La Porte (G-8785)
Lewis Brothers Bakeries Inc ....C...... 812 886-6533
  Vincennes (G-13690)
Neeta Sweet Cupcakes n Minis ....G...... 574 286-7032
  Granger (G-5426)
Omg Cupcakes & Sweets LLC ....G...... 317 281-7926
  Indianapolis (G-7619)
Peace Love Cupcakes ....G...... 812 239-1591
  Terre Haute (G-13299)
Schnuck Markets Inc ....C...... 812 853-9505
  Newburgh (G-11046)
Shipshewana Bread Box Corp ....E...... 260 768-4629
  Shipshewana (G-12649)
Strauss Bakeries Inc ....D...... 574 293-9027
  Elkhart (G-3194)
Sugar Spice Cupcake Event Plg ....G...... 260 610-5103
  Fort Wayne (G-4659)
Sweet N Sassy Cupcakes ....G...... 317 652-6132
  Indianapolis (G-8027)
Tyson Foods Inc ....B...... 260 726-3118
  Portland (G-11854)

BAKERIES: On Premises Baking & Consumption

Brunos Breads LLC ....F...... 219 883-5126
  Gary (G-5031)
Craftmark Bakery LLC ....F...... 317 548-3929
  Indianapolis (G-6685)
Donut Bank Inc ....E...... 812 426-0011
  Evansville (G-3462)
Grabers Kountry Korner ....E...... 812 636-4399
  Odon (G-11329)
Heyerlys Bakery Inc ....F...... 260 622-4196
  Ossian (G-11401)
Richards Bakery ....F...... 260 424-4012
  Fort Wayne (G-4592)
Scholars Inn Bakehouse ....D...... 812 331-6029
  Bloomington (G-822)
Strauss Bakeries Inc ....D...... 574 293-9027
  Elkhart (G-3194)

BAKERY MACHINERY

A M Manufacturing Co Inc ....E...... 219 472-7272
  Munster (G-10592)
Reading Bakery Systems Ta ....F...... 317 337-0000
  Indianapolis (G-7824)

PRODUCT

BAKERY PRDTS: Biscuits, Baked, Baking Powder & Raised

Jennys Backery.................................G....... 260 447-9592
Fort Wayne (G-4393)

BAKERY PRDTS: Bread, All Types, Fresh Or Frozen

Hartford Bakery Inc..........................B....... 812 425-4642
Evansville (G-3533)

Holsum of Fort Wayne Inc ....C....... 260 456-2130
Fort Wayne (G-4337)

Lewis Brothers Bakeries Inc ....C....... 812 425-4642
Evansville (G-3600)

Perfection Bakeries Inc ....C....... 260 424-8245
Fort Wayne (G-4524)

Weston Foods Us Inc ....A....... 317 858-9000
Brownsburg (G-1176)

BAKERY PRDTS: Buns, Bread Type, Fresh Or Frozen

Kbi Inc...D....... 765 763-6114
Morristown (G-10372)

BAKERY PRDTS: Cakes, Bakery, Exc Frozen

Achaemenian Shahpur......................G....... 812 331-1317
Bloomington (G-656)

Jay C Food 84...................................G....... 812 886-9311
Vincennes (G-13686)

Moms Homemade Pies Co LLC ....G....... 765 453-4417
Kokomo (G-8669)

Pasteleria Gresil LLC ....G....... 317 299-8801
Indianapolis (G-7659)

Ricker Oil Company Inc.....................D....... 317 920-0850
Indianapolis (G-7842)

Sweet LLC...G....... 812 455-0886
Evansville (G-3755)

BAKERY PRDTS: Cones, Ice Cream

Hartzells Homemade Ice Cream ....F....... 812 332-3502
Bloomington (G-738)

BAKERY PRDTS: Cookies

Aunt Beths Products Inc ....G....... 574 259-6244
Mishawaka (G-10000)

Blondies Cookies Inc.........................F....... 765 628-3978
Greentown (G-5644)

Blondies Cookies Inc.........................G....... 765 288-3872
Muncie (G-10440)

Darlington Cookie Company...............D....... 800 754-2202
Noblesville (G-11090)

Hearthside Food Solutions LLC ....B....... 219 878-1522
Michigan City (G-9802)

Richmond Baking Co..........................C....... 765 962-8535
Richmond (G-12043)

BAKERY PRDTS: Cookies & crackers

Almiras Bakery.................................E....... 219 844-4334
Hammond (G-5839)

Buehler Foods Inc..............................C....... 812 467-7255
Evansville (G-3404)

Clif Bar & Company ....G....... 510 596-6451
Indianapolis (G-6620)

Fingerhut Bakery Inc ....F....... 574 896-5937
North Judson (G-11212)

Grace Island Spcalty Foods Inc...........G....... 260 357-3336
Garrett (G-5006)

Heaven Sent Gurmet Cookies Inc ......G....... 219 980-1066
Gary (G-5062)

Heyerlys Bakery Inc..........................F....... 260 622-4196
Ossian (G-11401)

Indybake Products LLC.......................D....... 812 877-1588
Terre Haute (G-13257)

Richmond Baking Georgia Inc.............G....... 765 962-8535
Richmond (G-12044)

Schnuck Markets Inc ....C....... 812 853-9505
Newburgh (G-11046)

Shipshewana Bread Box Corp.............E....... 260 768-4629
Shipshewana (G-12649)

Strauss Bakeries Inc..........................D....... 574 293-9027
Elkhart (G-3194)

Weston Foods Us Inc ....A....... 317 858-9000
Brownsburg (G-1176)

BAKERY PRDTS: Croissants, Exc Frozen

Dawn Food Products Inc.....................C....... 800 333-3296
Crown Point (G-2244)

BAKERY PRDTS: Doughnuts, Exc Frozen

Donut Bank Inc..................................E....... 812 426-0011
Evansville (G-3462)

Georgetown Donuts ....G....... 260 493-6719
Fort Wayne (G-4299)

Square Donuts Inc.............................G....... 812 232-6463
Terre Haute (G-13343)

Westfield Donuts...............................G....... 317 896-5856
Westfield (G-14201)

BAKERY PRDTS: Dry

Las Perlas Tapatias Inc ....G....... 765 447-0601
Lafayette (G-8956)

Victorian House Scones LLC..............G....... 765 742-2709
Lafayette (G-9015)

BAKERY PRDTS: Frozen

Alpha Baking Co Inc ....C....... 219 324-7440
La Porte (G-8730)

Lewis Brothers Bakeries Inc ....C....... 812 886-6533
Vincennes (G-13690)

Printer Zink Inc.................................D....... 765 644-3959
Anderson (G-156)

Wicks Pies Inc..................................E....... 765 584-8401
Winchester (G-14345)

BAKERY PRDTS: Pastries, Danish, Frozen

Labraid Inc.......................................G....... 219 754-2501
La Crosse (G-8721)

BAKERY PRDTS: Pastries, Exc Frozen

Sweet Art Inc....................................G....... 317 787-3647
Indianapolis (G-8026)

BAKERY PRDTS: Pies, Bakery, Frozen

Moores Pie Shop Inc..........................G....... 765 457-2428
Kokomo (G-8672)

United Pies of Elkhart Inc..................G....... 574 294-3419
Elkhart (G-3234)

BAKERY PRDTS: Pies, Exc Frozen

Joy Sweet Cupcakes ....G....... 219 276-3791
Schererville (G-12327)

Moores Pie Shop Inc..........................G....... 765 457-2428
Kokomo (G-8672)

United Pies of Elkhart Inc..................G....... 574 294-3419
Elkhart (G-3234)

BAKERY PRDTS: Pretzels

Auntie Annes....................................F....... 765 288-8077
Muncie (G-10435)

Auntie Annes....................................G....... 574 271-8740
Mishawaka (G-10001)

Jojos Pretzels...................................F....... 260 768-7759
Shipshewana (G-12623)

Mike-Sells West Virginia Inc ....F....... 317 241-7422
Indianapolis (G-7516)

Pretzels Inc......................................C....... 260 824-4838
Bluffton (G-886)

BAKERY PRDTS: Wholesalers

Harlan Bakeries LLC..........................G....... 317 272-3600
Avon (G-443)

Harlan Bakeries-Avon LLC ....B....... 317 272-3600
Avon (G-444)

Lewis Brothers Bakeries Inc ....C....... 812 886-6533
Vincennes (G-13690)

BAKERY: Wholesale Or Wholesale & Retail Combined

Alpha Baking Co Inc ....F....... 574 234-0188
South Bend (G-12697)

Aunt Millies.......................................G....... 765 966-6691
Richmond (G-11958)

Bimbo Bakeries Usa Inc ....E....... 219 844-0465
Hammond (G-5853)

Bimbo Bakeries Usa Inc ....E....... 317 273-0444
Indianapolis (G-6475)

Bimbo Bakeries Usa Inc ....E....... 812 479-6934
Evansville (G-3385)

Fountain Acres Foods ....F....... 765 847-1897
Fountain City (G-4786)

Just Desserts Inc...............................F....... 317 872-2253
Indianapolis (G-7323)

Kristens Homemade Delight ....G....... 765 566-2200
Burlington (G-1211)

Kt Cakes..G....... 812 442-6047
Rosedale (G-12205)

Lou Mary Donuts Inc ....F....... 765 474-9131
Lafayette (G-8960)

Maplehurst Bakeries LLC ....C....... 317 858-9000
Greenwood (G-5723)

Mel Rhon Inc.....................................G....... 574 546-4559
Bremen (G-1010)

New Horizons Baking Company..........D....... 260 495-7055
Fremont (G-4970)

Perfection Bakeries Inc ....D....... 260 483-5481
Fort Wayne (G-4525)

Perfection Bakeries Inc ....G....... 574 269-9706
Warsaw (G-13926)

Pinch of Sugar...................................G....... 812 476-7650
Evansville (G-3671)

Richards Bakery................................F....... 260 424-4012
Fort Wayne (G-4592)

Scholars Inn Bakehouse.....................D....... 812 331-6029
Bloomington (G-822)

Torti Products Inc ....G....... 219 730-2071
Highland (G-6057)

BALL CLAY MINING

Unimin Corporation ....G....... 812 683-2179
Huntingburg (G-6183)

BALUNS

Marshall Electric Corporation.............F....... 574 223-4367
Rochester (G-12136)

BANNERS: Fabric

Eastern Banner Supply Corp...............G....... 812 448-2222
Brazil (G-960)

Expo Designers Co Inc ....E....... 317 784-5610
Indianapolis (G-6896)

BANQUET HALL FACILITIES

Grafton Peek Incorporated.................E....... 317 557-8377
Greenwood (G-5698)

BAR JOISTS & CONCRETE REINFORCING BARS: Fabricated

Rebar Corp of Indiana ....G....... 260 471-2002
Fort Wayne (G-4581)

BARBECUE EQPT

Betos Bar Inc....................................G....... 219 397-8247
East Chicago (G-2523)

Onward Manufacturing Company ....D....... 260 358-4111
Huntington (G-6233)

BARBER SHOPS

Cozy Cat Inc......................................G....... 765 463-1254
Lafayette (G-8879)

BARGES BUILDING & REPAIR

American Barge Line Company...........G....... 812 288-0100
Jeffersonville (G-8323)

American Coml Barge Line LLC ....C....... 812 288-0100
Jeffersonville (G-8324)

American Commercial Lines Inc ....C....... 812 288-0100
Jeffersonville (G-8325)

Commercial Barge Line Company ....F....... 812 288-0100
Jeffersonville (G-8341)

Corn Island Shipyard Inc...................G....... 812 362-8808
Grandview (G-5386)

Macks Welding ....F....... 812 265-6255
Madison (G-9478)

Smith Estill Marine Service ....G....... 812 282-7944
Jeffersonville (G-8424)

BARRELS: Shipping, Metal

North America Packaging Corp............C....... 317 291-2396
Indianapolis (G-7591)

OBryan Barrel Company Inc...............E....... 812 479-6741
Evansville (G-3651)

(G-0000) Company's Geographic Section entry number

BARS, COLD FINISHED: Steel, From Purchased Hot-Rolled

Niagara Lasalle Corporation ....E 800 262-2558
  Hammond (G-5921)
Niagara Lasalle Corporation ....C 219 853-6000
  Hammond (G-5922)
Steel Technologies LLC ....D 812 663-9704
  Greensburg (G-5635)
Ward Forging Co Inc.............................G 812 923-7463
  Floyds Knobs (G-4023)

BARS, PLATES & SHEETS: Zinc & Zinc Alloy Bars, Plates, Etc

Metal Source LLC ....E 260 563-8833
  Wabash (G-13738)

BARS: Cargo, Stabilizing, Metal

Liftco Inc...E 574 266-5551
  Elkhart (G-2997)

BARS: Concrete Reinforcing, Fabricated Steel

Circle City Rebar LLC ....F 317 917-8566
  Indianapolis (G-6608)
CMa Steel & Fabrication Inc...................G 260 207-9000
  Fort Wayne (G-4163)
Custom Secure Handles LLC...................G 812 764-4948
  Greensburg (G-5597)
Fabtration LLC ....F 812 989-6730
  Georgetown (G-5144)
H & R Industrial LLC..............................D 765 868-8408
  Kokomo (G-8635)
High Value Metal Inc..............................G 812 522-6468
  Seymour (G-12455)
Ironhorse Detailing Inc ....G 812 939-3300
  Clay City (G-1703)
J & F Steel Corporation ....G 219 764-3500
  Burns Harbor (G-1216)
Millmark Enterprises Inc ....F 574 389-9904
  Elkhart (G-3042)
Mor/Ryde International Inc.....................D 574 293-1581
  Elkhart (G-3048)
Mor/Ryde International Inc.....................E 574 293-1581
  Elkhart (G-3049)
Sherman Enterprises ....G 260 636-6225
  Albion (G-35)
Stolz Structural Inc ....G 812 983-4720
  Elberfeld (G-2638)
Trivett Contracting Inc ....E 317 539-5150
  Clayton (G-1708)
US Metals Inc.......................................G 219 398-1350
  East Chicago (G-2578)
Wayne Steel Supply Inc.........................E 260 489-6249
  Fort Wayne (G-4744)

BASES, BEVERAGE

North Street Companies LLC.................G 317 457-4520
  Greenfield (G-5561)

BATCHING PLANTS: Aggregate Concrete & Bulk Cement

Lehigh Hanson Ecc Inc ....C 812 246-7700
  Sellersburg (G-12402)

BATH SHOPS

Oasis Lifestyle LLC...............................E 574 948-0004
  Plymouth (G-11708)

BATHMATS: Rubber

Innocor Foam Tech - Acp Inc.................F 574 294-7694
  Elkhart (G-2935)

BATHROOM ACCESS & FITTINGS: Vitreous China & Earthenware

A Create Space Inc ....G 317 254-2600
  Indianapolis (G-6294)

BATHROOM FIXTURES: Plastic

Hotel Vanities Intl LLC...........................F 317 787-2330
  Indianapolis (G-7136)

BATTERIES, EXC AUTOMOTIVE: Wholesalers

Batteries Plus ....G 317 219-0007
  Noblesville (G-11064)
Worldwide Battery Company LLC ....G 812 475-1326
  Evansville (G-3816)

BATTERIES: Lead Acid, Storage

Enersys ....D 574 266-0658
  Elkhart (G-2833)
Exide Technologies ....D 317 876-7475
  Indianapolis (G-6894)
Exide Technologies ....C 765 747-9980
  Muncie (G-10470)
Johnson Controls Inc ....D 260 489-6104
  Fort Wayne (G-4397)
Johnson Controls Inc ....D 317 917-5043
  Pittsboro (G-11583)

BATTERIES: Rechargeable

Span Inc ....F 317 347-2646
  Lebanon (G-9226)

BATTERIES: Storage

Advanced Btry Charger Svc LLC ....G 260 563-3909
  Wabash (G-13719)
B T Bttery Charger Systems Inc ....G 574 533-6030
  Goshen (G-5176)
Batteries Plus ....G 317 219-0007
  Noblesville (G-11064)
Bulldog Battery Corporation ....C 260 563-0551
  Wabash (G-13722)
C&D Technologies Inc ....C 765 762-2461
  Attica (G-298)
Crown Battery Manufacturing Co..........G 260 423-3358
  Fort Wayne (G-4188)
Ener1 Inc ....E 317 703-1800
  Indianapolis (G-6862)
Enerdel Inc...C 317 703-1800
  Indianapolis (G-6863)
Greatbatch Ltd ....F 260 755-7484
  Warsaw (G-13886)
Integer Holdings Corporation ....G 260 373-1664
  Fort Wayne (G-4377)
Knk Battery LLC....................................G 765 426-2016
  Otterbein (G-11420)
Tri-State Power Supply LLC ....G 812 537-2500
  Lawrenceburg (G-9160)
Worldwide Battery Company LLC ....G 812 475-1326
  Evansville (G-3816)

BATTERIES: Wet

C&D Technologies Inc ....C 765 762-2461
  Attica (G-298)
Greatbatch Ltd ....F 260 755-7484
  Warsaw (G-13886)
Integer Holdings Corporation ....G 260 373-1664
  Fort Wayne (G-4377)

BATTERY CASES: Plastic Or Plastics Combination

Captive Holdings LLC...........................G 812 424-2904
  Evansville (G-3411)

BATTERY CHARGERS

Energy Access Inc ....F 317 329-1676
  Indianapolis (G-6864)
Flat Electronics LLC ....G 765 414-6635
  Lafayette (G-8899)
Go Electric Inc......................................F 765 400-1347
  Anderson (G-111)
MRC Technology Inc.............................F 574 232-9057
  South Bend (G-12867)

BATTERY CHARGERS: Storage, Motor & Engine Generator Type

Leclanche SA ....G 765 610-0050
  Anderson (G-133)

BATTERY CHARGING GENERATORS

Technuity Inc ....G 800 887-2557
  Indianapolis (G-8051)

BATTERY WELLS OR BOXES: Concrete

Bill Walters Concrete Inc.......................F 574 259-0056
  Mishawaka (G-10010)

BAUXITE MINING

Arconic Inc ....B 412 553-4545
  Newburgh (G-11021)

BEARINGS & PARTS Ball

NSK Corporation ....C 765 458-5000
  Liberty (G-9267)

BEARINGS: Ball & Roller

Emerson Industrial Automation.............G 574 583-9171
  Monticello (G-10262)
McGill Manufacturing Co Inc ....A 219 465-2200
  Valparaiso (G-13579)
Nachi Technology Inc............................C 317 535-5000
  Greenwood (G-5727)
NSK Corporation ....E 317 837-8879
  Plainfield (G-11631)
NSK Precision America Inc ....C 317 738-5000
  Franklin (G-4915)
NSK Precision America Inc ....C 317 738-5000
  Franklin (G-4916)
Rbc Prcsion Pdts - Plymouth Inc...........D 574 935-3027
  Plymouth (G-11719)
Regal Beloit America Inc ....C 219 465-2200
  Valparaiso (G-13607)
Regal Beloit America Inc ....C 219 465-2200
  Valparaiso (G-13608)
Timken Company ....B 574 288-7188
  South Bend (G-12970)
Timken Company ....C 574 287-1566
  South Bend (G-12971)

BEARINGS: Roller & Parts

Bearing Service Company PA................G 773 734-5132
  Griffith (G-5765)
Standard Locknut LLC ....C 317 399-2230
  Westfield (G-14190)

BEAUTY & BARBER SHOP EQPT

AM Manufacturing Company Ind..........F 800 342-6744
  Munster (G-10594)
Amusement Games Inc ....G 812 937-7084
  Chrisney (G-1641)
Anchor Industries Inc............................D 812 867-2421
  Evansville (G-3357)
Containmed Inc.....................................E 317 487-8800
  Speedway (G-13011)
Dubois Equipment Company LLC.........E 812 482-3644
  Jasper (G-8248)
Dynatect Manufacturing Inc..................G 219 465-1898
  Valparaiso (G-13531)
East Industries LLC ....G 812 273-4358
  Madison (G-9459)
Foamiture...G 574 831-4775
  New Paris (G-10980)
H A Industries ....G 219 931-6304
  Hammond (G-5883)
Ilpea Industries Inc ....F 812 752-2526
  Evansville (G-3546)
Indiana Manufacturing Inst ....G 765 494-4935
  West Lafayette (G-14077)
Indiana Materials Proc LLC...................F 260 244-6026
  Columbia City (G-1795)
Mitek Usa Inc ....D 219 924-3835
  Griffith (G-5786)
Nuwave Manufacturing ....G 317 987-8229
  Indianapolis (G-7606)
Peerless Mfg Co ....G 260 357-3271
  Garrett (G-5019)
State Beauty Supply ....G 260 755-6361
  Fort Wayne (G-4645)
Taunyas Creative Cuts ....G 812 574-7722
  Madison (G-9497)
Tbin LLC ....G 812 491-9100
  Princeton (G-11883)
Yankee Candle Company Inc.................G 812 526-5195
  Edinburgh (G-2632)
Yankee Candle Company Inc.................G 812 234-1717
  Terre Haute (G-13373)

P
R
O
D
U
C
T

BEAUTY SALONS

Kenra Professional LLC ....F 317 356-6491
Indianapolis (G-7343)

BEDDING & BEDSPRINGS STORES

Futon Factory Inc ....F 317 549-8639
Indianapolis (G-6971)

BEDDING, BEDSPREAD, BLANKET/SHEET: Pillowcase, Purchd Mtrl

Pillow Pals Inc ....G 812 853-8241
Newburgh (G-11042)

BEDDING, BEDSPREADS, BLANKETS & SHEETS

Blanket Hog ....G 219 308-9532
Crown Point (G-2228)

BEDS: Hospital

Kci Crane Pro Services ....G 812 479-0488
Evansville (G-3582)
Medreco Inc ....G 765 458-7444
Liberty (G-9265)

BEDS: Institutional

Champion Manufacturing Inc ....D 574 295-6893
Elkhart (G-2754)

BEDSPREADS & BED SETS, FROM PURCHASED MATERIALS

Artisan Interiors Inc ....E 574 825-9494
Middlebury (G-9873)
Ascot Enterprises Inc ....E 877 773-7751
Nappanee (G-10648)

BEDSPREADS, COTTON

Down-Lite International Inc ....G 513 229-3696
Middletown (G-9934)

BEEKEEPERS' SPLYS

Haynes Honey LLC ....G 260 563-6397
Wabash (G-13728)

BEER & ALE WHOLESALERS

Barley Island Brewing Co ....F 317 770-5280
Noblesville (G-11061)
Calumet Breweries Inc ....E 219 845-2242
Hammond (G-5856)
Indiana City Brewing LLC ....F 317 643-1103
Indianapolis (G-7177)
Mishawaka Brewing Company ....E 574 256-9993
Granger (G-5423)
Tavistock Restaurants LLC ....D 317 488-1230
Indianapolis (G-8040)

BEER & ALE, WHOLESALE: Beer & Other Fermented Malt Liquors

Sun King Brewing Company LLC ....G 317 602-3702
Indianapolis (G-8017)
Terrance Smith Distributing ....D 765 644-3396
Anderson (G-175)

BEER, WINE & LIQUOR STORES

Big Red Liquors Inc ....G 812 339-9552
Bloomington (G-663)
Crankshaft Brewing Co ....G 317 939-0138
Brownsburg (G-1146)
Four Points Development Corp ....F 317 357-3275
Indianapolis (G-6951)
Party Cask ....G 812 234-3008
Terre Haute (G-13296)
Rihm Inc ....G 765 478-3426
Cambridge City (G-1260)
Thomas Chateau Winery ....G 812 339-9463
Bloomington (G-840)

BEER, WINE & LIQUOR STORES: Wine

Brown County Wine Company ....G 812 988-6144
Nashville (G-10718)
Cedar Creek Winery ....G 812 988-1111
Nashville (G-10720)

James Lake Vineyard Inc ....G 260 495-9463
Fremont (G-4963)
Oliver Wine Company Inc ....D 812 822-0466
Bloomington (G-787)
Prp Wine International ....G 317 288-0005
Indianapolis (G-7784)
Red Gate Farms Inc ....G 812 277-9750
Bedford (G-573)
Wine N Vine ....G 765 282-3300
Muncie (G-10586)

BELTING: Rubber

Dunham Rubber Belting Corp ....G 317 604-5313
Shelbyville (G-12531)

BELTS & BELT PRDTS

Rubber & Gasket Co Amer Inc ....G 260 432-9070
Fort Wayne (G-4597)

BELTS: Conveyor, Made From Purchased Wire

Pro Tech Automation Inc ....G 317 201-3875
Monrovia (G-10205)
Yongli America LLC ....G 219 763-7920
Portage (G-11802)

BELTS: Indl

Muhlen Sohn Industries LP ....F 765 640-9674
Anderson (G-140)

BELTS: Seat, Automotive & Aircraft

Gerardot Performance Products ....G 260 623-3048
Monroeville (G-10195)
Jack House LLC ....G 251 990-5960
Converse (G-2079)
Shield Restraint Systems Inc ....C 574 266-8330
Elkhart (G-3167)
Wolf Technical Engineering LLC ....G 800 783-9653
Indianapolis (G-8209)

BENCHES: Seating

Recycle Design Inc ....G 765 374-0316
Anderson (G-159)

BENTONITE MINING

American Colloid Company ....G 812 547-3567
Troy (G-13445)

BERYLLIUM

Goldman Machine Services ....G 812 359-5440
Richland (G-11950)

BEVERAGES, ALCOHOLIC: Beer

Barley Island Brewing Co ....F 317 770-5280
Noblesville (G-11061)
Beer Baron LLC ....G 317 735-2706
Indianapolis (G-6466)
Best Beers LLC ....G 812 332-1234
Bloomington (G-681)
Brick Road Brewery Corp ....G 219 362-7623
La Porte (G-8742)
Calumet Breweries Inc ....E 219 845-2242
Hammond (G-5856)
Das Big Dawg Brewhaus LLC ....G 765 965-9463
Richmond (G-11976)
Figure Eight Brewing LLC ....E 219 477-2000
Valparaiso (G-13543)
Indiana City Brewing LLC ....F 317 643-1103
Indianapolis (G-7177)
Lennies Inc ....D 812 323-2112
Bloomington (G-765)
Mishawaka Brewing Company ....E 574 256-9993
Granger (G-5423)
Round Town Brewery LLC ....G 317 657-6397
Indianapolis (G-7864)
Sun King Brewing Company LLC ....G 317 602-3702
Indianapolis (G-8017)
Tavistock Restaurants LLC ....D 317 488-1230
Indianapolis (G-8040)
The Tap ....F 812 486-9795
Bloomington (G-839)
Three Floyds Brewing LLC ....G 219 922-4425
Munster (G-10633)
Upland Brewing Company ....G 317 602-3931
Indianapolis (G-8131)

Upland Brewing Company Inc ....E 812 330-7421
Bloomington (G-851)
Wasser Brewing Company LLC ....G 765 653-3240
Greencastle (G-5481)

BEVERAGES, ALCOHOLIC: Beer & Ale

Byway Brewing Company LLC ....G 312 543-7639
Munster (G-10599)
Chapmans Cider Company LLC ....G 260 444-1194
Angola (G-202)
Crankshaft Brewing Co ....G 317 939-0138
Brownsburg (G-1146)
Daredevil Brewing Co ....G 317 512-2202
Indianapolis (G-6726)
Dockside ....G 574 400-0848
South Bend (G-12752)
Drinkgp LLC ....G 317 410-4748
Indianapolis (G-6767)
Floyd County Brewing Company L .....G 502 724-3202
New Albany (G-10782)
Grand Junction Brewery ....G 317 804-9583
Westfield (G-14166)
Irongate V LLC ....G 219 464-8704
Valparaiso (G-13561)
Laotto Brewing LLC ....G 260 897-3152
Avilla (G-413)
Oaken Barrel Brewing Co Inc ....E 317 887-2287
Greenwood (G-5730)
Pepito Miller Bev Imports LLC ....G 317 416-3215
Plainfield (G-11635)
Power House Brewing Co ....G 812 343-1302
Columbus (G-1998)
South Bend Brew Werks LLC ....G 801 209-2987
South Bend (G-12941)
Terrance Smith Distributing ....G 765 644-3396
Anderson (G-175)
Thieme and Wagner Brewing Co ......G 765 477-0667
Lafayette (G-9010)
Turonis Forget ME Not Inn ....E 812 477-7500
Evansville (G-3779)
Under Staircase Brewing Co LLC ......G 260 580-2586
Fort Wayne (G-4713)
Windmill Brewing ....G 219 440-2189
Dyer (G-2512)

BEVERAGES, ALCOHOLIC: Bourbon Whiskey

West Fork Whiskey Co ....G 812 583-9797
Indianapolis (G-8185)

BEVERAGES, ALCOHOLIC: Brandy & Brandy Spirits

Hotel Tango Whiskey Inc ....E 317 653-1806
Indianapolis (G-7135)

BEVERAGES, ALCOHOLIC: Cocktails

Blue Marble Cocktails Inc ....E 888 400-3090
Indianapolis (G-6486)

BEVERAGES, ALCOHOLIC: Cordials

PRI-Pak Inc ....C 812 260-2291
Greendale (G-5493)

BEVERAGES, ALCOHOLIC: Distilled Liquors

Bear Wallow Distillery ....G 812 657-4923
Nashville (G-10715)
Cardinal Spirits LLC ....E 812 202-6789
Bloomington (G-695)
Easley Enterprises Inc ....E 317 636-4516
Indianapolis (G-6789)
Heartland Distillers LLC ....G 317 598-9775
Indianapolis (G-7084)
Indiana Whiskey Co ....G 574 339-1737
South Bend (G-12811)
Mgpi Processing Inc ....F 812 532-4100
Greendale (G-5491)
Old Fort Distillery Inc ....G 260 705-5128
Grabill (G-5381)
Royal Inc ....F 812 424-4925
Evansville (G-3711)
Three Rivers Distilling Co LLC ....G 260 745-9355
Fort Wayne (G-4684)
Virtuoso Distillers LLC ....G 574 876-4450
Mishawaka (G-10147)

BEVERAGES, ALCOHOLIC: Vodka

Joseph & Jones LLC ....G....... 317 691-0328
Indianapolis *(G-7312)*

BEVERAGES, ALCOHOLIC: Wine Coolers

Brumate LLC ....G....... 317 474-7352
Indianapolis *(G-6515)*
Pepito Miller Bev Imports LLC ....G....... 317 416-3215
Plainfield *(G-11635)*
PRI-Pak Inc ....C....... 812 260-2291
Greendale *(G-5493)*

BEVERAGES, ALCOHOLIC: Wines

Ajll LLC ....G....... 812 477-3611
Evansville *(G-3346)*
Ancient Cellars ....G....... 503 437-4827
Indianapolis *(G-6399)*
At The Barn Winery ....G....... 513 310-8810
Lawrenceburg *(G-9131)*
Bacchus Winery Golf Vinyrd LLC ....G....... 574 732-4663
Logansport *(G-9323)*
Belgian Horse Winery LLC ....G....... 765 779-3002
Middletown *(G-9933)*
Best Vineyards ....G....... 812 969-9463
Elizabeth *(G-2642)*
Brandywine Vinyrd & Winery LLC ....G....... 317 403-5669
New Palestine *(G-10968)*
Brewhouse Supplies LLC ....G....... 219 286-7285
Valparaiso *(G-13513)*
Brown County Wine Company ....G....... 812 988-6144
Nashville *(G-10718)*
Butler Vineyards ....G....... 219 929-1400
Chesterton *(G-1597)*
Butler Vineyards ....G....... 812 332-6660
Bloomington *(G-692)*
Carousel Winery ....G....... 812 849-1005
Mitchell *(G-10158)*
Cedar Creek Winery ....G....... 765 342-9000
Martinsville *(G-9597)*
Cedar Creek Winery ....G 812 988-1111
Nashville *(G-10720)*
Cellar Masters LLC ....E....... 317 817-9473
Indianapolis *(G-6574)*
Chateau Thomas Winery Inc ....E....... 317 837-9463
Plainfield *(G-11600)*
Copia Vineyards and Winery LLC ....G....... 805 835-6094
Indianapolis *(G-6664)*
Country Hrtg Wnery Vinyrd Inc ....F 260 637-2980
Laotto *(G-9105)*
Country Moon Winery LLC ....G....... 317 773-7942
Noblesville *(G-11086)*
Dune Ridge Winery LLC ....G....... 219 548-4605
Valparaiso *(G-13529)*
Ertel Cellars Winery Inc ....E....... 812 933-1500
Batesville *(G-500)*
Family Vineyard ....G....... 812 322-1720
Indianapolis *(G-6904)*
Finley Creek Vineyards LLC ....G....... 317 769-5483
Zionsville *(G-14432)*
Fruit Hills Winery Orchrd LLC ....G....... 574 848-9463
Bristol *(G-1061)*
Ghost Trail Winery LLC ....G....... 317 387-0052
Indianapolis *(G-7004)*
Graybull Organic Wines Inc ....G....... 317 797-2186
Indianapolis *(G-7039)*
Harmony Winery ....G....... 317 585-9463
Fishers *(G-3922)*
Harvest Moon Winery LLC ....G....... 317 258-4615
McCordsville *(G-9668)*
Home - Little Creek Winery ....G....... 812 319-3951
Evansville *(G-3539)*
Hooker Corner Winery LLC ....G....... 765 585-1225
Pine Village *(G-11581)*
Hopwood Cellars ....G....... 317 873-4099
Zionsville *(G-14438)*
Huckleberry Winery ....G....... 317 850-4445
Bargersville *(G-483)*
Indiana Artisan Inc ....G....... 317 607-8715
Noblesville *(G-11126)*
Indiana Wholesale Wine Lq Co ....G....... 317 667-0231
Indianapolis *(G-7197)*
James Lake Vineyard Inc ....G....... 260 495-9463
Fremont *(G-4963)*
Laker Winery LLC ....G....... 812 934-4633
Batesville *(G-508)*
Lane Byler Winery ....G....... 260 920-4377
Auburn *(G-341)*
Lanthier Winery & Restaurant ....F 812 273-2409
Madison *(G-9477)*

Madison Vineyards Inc ....G....... 812 273-6500
Madison *(G-9484)*
Mallow Run LLC ....G....... 317 422-1556
Bargersville *(G-484)*
Mystique Winery and Vinyrd LLC ....G....... 812 922-5612
Lynnville *(G-9435)*
Nagys Winery LLC ....G....... 219 331-0588
Valparaiso *(G-13584)*
Oak Hill Winery LLC ....G....... 765 395-3632
Converse *(G-2081)*
Oliver Wine Company Inc ....D....... 812 822-0466
Bloomington *(G-787)*
Owen Valley Winery LLC ....G....... 812 828-0883
Spencer *(G-13032)*
Peace Water Winery ....G....... 317 810-1330
Carmel *(G-1449)*
Pfeiffer Winery & Vineyard ....G....... 812 952-2650
Corydon *(G-2108)*
Prairie Sun Vineyard LLC ....G....... 219 741-5918
Rolling Prairie *(G-12191)*
Preston Leaderbrand ....F....... 812 828-0883
Spencer *(G-13033)*
Prp Wine International ....G....... 317 288-0005
Indianapolis *(G-7784)*
Red Gate Farms Inc ....G....... 812 277-9750
Bedford *(G-573)*
Rick Black Associates LLC ....G....... 765 838-3498
Lafayette *(G-8991)*
River City Winery ....G....... 317 868-8223
Franklin *(G-4927)*
River City Winery LLC ....G....... 812 945-9463
New Albany *(G-10857)*
S L Thomas Family Winery Inc ....G....... 812 273-3755
Madison *(G-9494)*
Shady Creek Vineyard ....G....... 219 874-9463
Michigan City *(G-9843)*
Shady Frog Winery LLC ....G....... 317 366-3370
Bargersville *(G-487)*
Simmons Winery & Farm Market ....G....... 812 546-0091
Columbus *(G-2015)*
Stoney Creek Winery ....G....... 574 642-4454
Millersburg *(G-9975)*
Sutter Home Winery ....G....... 317 848-3003
Carmel *(G-1486)*
Thomas Chateau Winery ....G....... 812 339-9463
Bloomington *(G-840)*
Tonne Winery ....G....... 765 896-9821
Muncie *(G-10573)*
Traders Point Winery ....G....... 317 879-9463
Indianapolis *(G-8088)*
Twin Willows LLC ....G....... 812 497-0254
Freetown *(G-4950)*
Two Ees Winery ....G....... 260 672-2000
Huntington *(G-6257)*
Vineyard Fishery Products LLC ....G....... 317 902-0753
Indianapolis *(G-8164)*
Whyte Horse Winery LLC ....G....... 574 583-2345
Monticello *(G-10288)*
Windy Knoll Winery ....G....... 812 726-1600
Vincennes *(G-13718)*
Winzerwald Winery LLC ....G....... 317 357-7000
Bristow *(G-1096)*
Wolfies Grill 5 LLC ....G....... 317 804-5619
Westfield *(G-14203)*

BEVERAGES, NONALCOHOLIC: Bottled & canned soft drinks

American Beverage Marketers ....G....... 812 944-3585
New Albany *(G-10743)*
American Bottling Company ....E....... 260 484-4177
Fort Wayne *(G-4068)*
American Bottling Company ....E....... 574 291-9000
South Bend *(G-12703)*
Central Coca-Cola Btlg Co Inc ....D....... 765 642-9951
Anderson *(G-82)*
Central Coca-Cola Btlg Co Inc ....D....... 812 232-9543
Terre Haute *(G-13208)*
Central Coca-Cola Btlg Co Inc ....E....... 574 291-1511
South Bend *(G-12732)*
Central Coca-Cola Btlg Co Inc ....C....... 260 478-2978
Fort Wayne *(G-4142)*
Clark Foods Inc ....D....... 812 949-3075
New Albany *(G-10761)*
Coca Cola Btlg Co Kokomo Ind ....D....... 765 457-4421
Kokomo *(G-8607)*
Coca Cola Btlg Co Kokomo Ind ....E....... 574 936-3220
Plymouth *(G-11675)*
Coca-Cola Bottling Co Cnsld ....D....... 812 228-3200
Evansville *(G-3421)*

Coca-Cola Bottling Co Inc ....E....... 812 376-3381
Columbus *(G-1873)*
Coca-Cola Bottling Co Portland ....D....... 260 726-7126
Portland *(G-11811)*
Indianapolis Gatorade ....G....... 317 821-6400
Indianapolis *(G-7199)*
JC Distributers Inc ....G....... 502 276-6311
Jeffersonville *(G-8382)*
P-Americas LLC ....C....... 317 876-6800
Indianapolis *(G-7644)*
Party Cask ....G....... 812 234-3008
Terre Haute *(G-13296)*
Pepsi Beverage Company ....G....... 574 271-0633
South Bend *(G-12890)*
Quaker Oats Company ....E....... 317 821-6442
Indianapolis *(G-7795)*
Red Bull North America Inc ....G....... 216 401-3950
Newburgh *(G-11045)*
Shepherd Distributing ....G....... 317 991-3877
Indianapolis *(G-7932)*
Snapple Beverage Corp ....G....... 812 424-7978
Evansville *(G-3739)*
Success Holding Group Intl Inc ....G....... 260 450-1982
Ossian *(G-11411)*
Terre Haute Coca-Cola Btlg Co ....D....... 812 232-9543
Terre Haute *(G-13352)*

BEVERAGES, NONALCOHOLIC: Carbonated

Battery Xpress ....G....... 765 759-2288
Indianapolis *(G-6458)*
Capitol Source Network ....G....... 260 248-9747
Columbia City *(G-1771)*
Central Coca-Cola Btlg Co Inc ....E....... 317 243-3771
Indianapolis *(G-6581)*
Dads Root Beer Company LLC ....G....... 812 482-5352
Jasper *(G-8243)*
P-Americas LLC ....C....... 219 836-1800
Munster *(G-10621)*
P-Americas LLC ....C....... 812 794-4455
Austin *(G-399)*
P-Americas LLC ....E....... 765 647-3576
Brookville *(G-1124)*
P-Americas LLC ....C....... 812 332-1200
Bloomington *(G-794)*
Pepsi Beverages Company ....G....... 219 836-1800
Munster *(G-10623)*
Pepsi-Cola ....G....... 812 634-1844
Jasper *(G-8300)*
Pepsico ....F....... 317 334-0153
Indianapolis *(G-7671)*
Pepsico ....G....... 317 821-6400
Indianapolis *(G-7672)*
Pepsico Inc ....F....... 260 579-3461
Fort Wayne *(G-4522)*

BEVERAGES, NONALCOHOLIC: Carbonated, Canned & Bottled, Etc

Ahf Industries Inc ....C....... 812 936-9988
French Lick *(G-4984)*
Circle City Sonorans LLC ....G....... 317 401-9787
Indianapolis *(G-6609)*
Manitowoc ....F....... 540 375-9300
Sellersburg *(G-12404)*
P-Americas LLC ....E....... 765 289-0270
Muncie *(G-10542)*
Refreshment Services Inc ....E....... 812 466-0602
Terre Haute *(G-13318)*
Vin Elite Imports Inc ....G....... 317 264-9250
Indianapolis *(G-8163)*

BEVERAGES, NONALCOHOLIC: Cider

Adrian Orchards Inc ....G....... 317 784-0550
Indianapolis *(G-6329)*
Millers Mill ....G....... 574 825-2010
Middlebury *(G-9908)*

BEVERAGES, NONALCOHOLIC: Flavoring extracts & syrups, nec

C A Derr & Company ....G....... 812 897-2920
Boonville *(G-911)*
Central Coca-Cola Btlg Co Inc ....E....... 317 243-3771
Indianapolis *(G-6581)*
Cultor Food Science ....G....... 812 299-6700
Terre Haute *(G-13220)*
International Bakers Services ....E....... 574 287-7111
South Bend *(G-12816)*

PRODUCT

Moseley Laboratories Inc..................E....... 317 866-8460
  Greenfield (G-5560)
Savor Flavor LLC..............................G....... 812 667-1030
  Dillsboro (G-2472)
Tate Lyle Ingrdnts Amricas LLC...........B....... 765 474-5474
  Lafayette (G-9007)
Vitamins Inc.....................................E....... 219 879-7356
  Michigan City (G-9859)

BEVERAGES, NONALCOHOLIC: Soft Drinks, Canned & Bottled, Etc

American Bottling Company................E....... 765 987-7800
  Spiceland (G-13053)
Central Coca-Cola Btlg Co Inc.............E....... 765 423-5668
  Lafayette (G-8873)
Central Coca-Cola Btlg Co Inc.............E....... 317 398-0129
  Indianapolis (G-6580)
Central Coca-Cola Btlg Co Inc.............G....... 812 482-7475
  Jasper (G-8241)
Central Coca-Cola Btlg Co Inc.............G....... 800 241-2653
  Bloomington (G-699)
Central Coca-Cola Btlg Co Inc.............G....... 260 726-7126
  Portland (G-11810)
Central Coca-Cola Btlg Co Inc.............G....... 800 241-2653
  Shelbyville (G-12526)
Dr Pepper Bottling Co........................G....... 765 647-3576
  Brookville (G-1113)
Dr Pepper Bottling Company...............G....... 812 332-1200
  Bloomington (G-716)
Dr Pepper Snapple Group I..................G....... 260 484-4177
  Fort Wayne (G-4220)
Interactions Inc................................D....... 574 722-6207
  Logansport (G-9341)
Keurig Dr Pepper Inc..........................D....... 812 522-3823
  Seymour (G-12463)
P-Americas LLC.................................E....... 812 522-3421
  Seymour (G-12472)
Pepsi Bottling Ventures LLC...............D....... 765 659-7313
  Frankfort (G-4850)
Pepsi-Cola Metro Btlg Co Inc..............E....... 812 332-1200
  Bloomington (G-798)
PRI-Pak Inc.....................................C....... 812 260-2291
  Greendale (G-5493)
Qtg Pepsi Co Larry Davi.....................G....... 317 830-4020
  Indianapolis (G-7794)
Royal Crown Bottling Corp.................C....... 812 424-7978
  Evansville (G-3710)
Swanel Inc......................................D....... 219 932-7676
  Hammond (G-5947)

BEVERAGES, WINE & DISTILLED ALCOHOLIC, WHOLESALE: Liquor

Clancys of Portage............................F....... 219 764-4995
  Portage (G-11757)

BEVERAGES, WINE & DISTILLED ALCOHOLIC, WHOLESALE: Wine

Durm Vineyard Inc............................G....... 317 862-9463
  Indianapolis (G-6771)
Indiana Wholesale Wine Lq Co.............G....... 317 667-0231
  Indianapolis (G-7197)
Prp Wine International.........................G....... 317 288-0005
  Indianapolis (G-7784)
Vin Elite Imports Inc..........................G....... 317 264-9250
  Indianapolis (G-8163)

BICYCLE ASSEMBLY SVCS

Walton Industrial Park Inc...................F....... 574 626-2929
  Walton (G-13818)

BICYCLE SHOPS

Sportcrafters Inc...............................G....... 574 243-4994
  Granger (G-5438)

BICYCLES, PARTS & ACCESS

David Tortora...................................G....... 317 506-6902
  Carmel (G-1353)
Evansville Super Bike Shop..................F....... 812 477-1740
  Evansville (G-3491)
Zh Brothers International Inc................G....... 313 718-6732
  Mishawaka (G-10153)

BILLIARD & POOL TABLES & SPLYS

Bad Boys Bllard Prductions LLC...........G....... 702 738-4950
  Indianapolis (G-6454)

Diamond Billiard Products Inc..............E....... 812 288-7665
  Jeffersonville (G-8351)
Jay Orner Sons Billiard Co Inc.............G....... 317 243-0046
  Indianapolis (G-7299)
Unique Products................................G....... 812 376-8887
  Columbus (G-2027)

BILLIARD EQPT & SPLYS WHOLESALERS

Diamond Billiard Products Inc..............E....... 812 288-7665
  Jeffersonville (G-8351)
Jay Orner Sons Billiard Co Inc.............G....... 317 243-0046
  Indianapolis (G-7299)
Playfair Shuffleboard Company.............F....... 260 747-7288
  Fort Wayne (G-4534)

BILLIARD TABLE REPAIR SVCS

Jay Orner Sons Billiard Co Inc.............G....... 317 243-0046
  Indianapolis (G-7299)

BINDING SVC: Books & Manuals

A-1 Awards Inc.................................F....... 317 546-9000
  Indianapolis (G-6301)
Acclaim Graphics Inc.........................G....... 812 424-5035
  Evansville (G-3334)
Athena Arts & Graphics Inc.................G....... 317 876-8916
  Indianapolis (G-6436)
Baxter Printing Inc............................G....... 219 923-1999
  Highland (G-6037)
Brand Prtg & Photo-Litho Co................G....... 317 921-4095
  Indianapolis (G-6503)
C J P Corporation.............................G....... 219 924-1685
  Highland (G-6040)
Cecils Printing & Office Sups...............G....... 812 683-4416
  Huntingburg (G-6153)
Ckmt Associates Inc..........................E....... 219 924-2820
  Hammond (G-5863)
Clarke American Checks Inc.................E....... 812 283-9598
  Jeffersonville (G-8339)
Classic Graphics Inc..........................F....... 260 482-3487
  Fort Wayne (G-4156)
Consolidated Printing Svcs Inc.............F....... 765 468-6033
  Farmland (G-3841)
Courier Printing Co Allen Cnty..............G....... 260 627-2728
  Grabill (G-5362)
Creative Concept Ventures Inc.............G....... 812 282-9442
  Jeffersonville (G-8348)
Crossrads Rhbilitation Ctr Inc..............C....... 317 897-7320
  Indianapolis (G-6697)
Digital Printing Incorporated................F....... 812 265-2205
  Madison (G-9457)
Doerr Printing Co..............................G....... 317 568-0135
  Indianapolis (G-6756)
Dynamark Graphics Group Inc..............G....... 317 634-2963
  Indianapolis (G-6777)
Dynamark Graphics Group Inc..............E....... 317 328-2555
  Indianapolis (G-6775)
Ed Sons Inc.....................................F....... 317 897-8821
  Indianapolis (G-6803)
Elkhart Binding Inc............................G....... 574 522-5455
  Elkhart (G-2821)
Epi Printers Inc.................................D....... 317 579-4870
  Indianapolis (G-6875)
Evansville Bindery Inc........................G....... 812 423-2222
  Evansville (G-3483)
Ewing Printing Company Inc.................F....... 812 882-2415
  Vincennes (G-13677)
Express Bindings...............................G....... 317 269-8114
  Indianapolis (G-6897)
Express Press Indiana Inc....................E....... 574 277-3355
  South Bend (G-12769)
Faulkenberg Printing Co Inc.................F....... 317 638-1359
  Franklin (G-4886)
Fedex Office & Print Svcs Inc...............E....... 317 631-6862
  Indianapolis (G-6908)
Fedex Office & Print Svcs Inc...............E....... 317 849-9683
  Indianapolis (G-6911)
Fedex Office & Print Svcs Inc...............E....... 574 271-0398
  South Bend (G-12777)
Fedex Office & Print Svcs Inc...............E....... 317 337-2679
  Indianapolis (G-6912)
Fedex Office & Print Svcs Inc...............G....... 317 295-1063
  Indianapolis (G-6913)
Fedex Office & Print Svcs Inc...............F....... 317 251-2406
  Indianapolis (G-6914)
Fedex Office & Print Svcs Inc...............E....... 317 885-6480
  Indianapolis (G-6915)
Fedex Office & Print Svcs Inc...............F....... 765 449-4950
  Lafayette (G-8897)

Goetz Printing.................................F....... 812 243-2086
  Terre Haute (G-13241)
Graessle-Mercer Co...........................E....... 812 522-5478
  Seymour (G-12451)
Granger Gazette...............................G....... 574 277-2679
  Granger (G-5410)
Green Banner Publications Inc..............E....... 812 967-3176
  Pekin (G-11473)
Greencastle Offset Inc.......................G....... 765 653-4026
  Greencastle (G-5458)
Greensburg Printing Co Inc.................G....... 812 663-8265
  Greensburg (G-5604)
Hager Inc.......................................G....... 260 483-7075
  Fort Wayne (G-4314)
Hardesty Printing Co Inc.....................F....... 574 223-4553
  Rochester (G-12126)
Hardesty Printing Co Inc.....................G....... 574 267-7591
  Warsaw (G-13889)
Hetty Incorporated............................E....... 219 836-2517
  Munster (G-10605)
Hetty Incorporated............................G....... 219 933-0833
  Hammond (G-5892)
Hf Group LLC...................................B....... 260 982-2107
  North Manchester (G-11230)
Hiatt Enterprises Inc..........................G....... 765 289-2700
  Muncie (G-10488)
Hiatt Enterprises Inc..........................E....... 765 289-7756
  Muncie (G-10487)
Hinen Printing Co..............................G....... 260 248-8984
  Columbia City (G-1789)
Howard Print Shop.............................G....... 765 453-6161
  Kokomo (G-8641)
Image Group Inc...............................E....... 574 457-3111
  Syracuse (G-13135)
Infobind Systems Inc..........................G....... 260 248-4989
  Fort Wayne (G-4369)
Insty-Prints of South Bend..................G....... 574 289-6977
  South Bend (G-12814)
Journal and Chronicle Inc....................G....... 812 752-5060
  Scottsburg (G-12370)
Kays Graphics Inc.............................G....... 317 236-9755
  Indianapolis (G-7335)
L & L Press Inc.................................F....... 765 664-3162
  Marion (G-9541)
La Grange Publishing Co Inc................F....... 260 463-3243
  Lagrange (G-9052)
Lamco Finishers Inc...........................E....... 317 471-1010
  Indianapolis (G-7379)
Laminating Specialties Inc Ind.............G....... 765 385-0023
  Templeton (G-13178)
Largus Speedy Print Corp...................E....... 219 922-8414
  Munster (G-10612)
Lincoln Printing Corporation................E....... 260 424-5200
  Fort Wayne (G-4437)
Ludwick Graphics Inc.........................F....... 574 233-2165
  South Bend (G-12845)
Mar Kel Inc.....................................G....... 812 853-6133
  Newburgh (G-11038)
Masco Corporation of Indiana..............D....... 317 848-1812
  Indianapolis (G-7463)
Maureen Sharp.................................G....... 765 379-3644
  Rossville (G-12211)
Maury Boyd & Associates Inc...............F....... 317 849-6110
  Indianapolis (G-7469)
Millcraft Paper Company.....................E....... 317 240-3500
  Indianapolis (G-7519)
Miller Rainbow Printing Inc..................E....... 812 275-3355
  Bedford (G-565)
Montgomery & Associates Inc...............F....... 219 879-0088
  Michigan City (G-9821)
North Vernon Plain Dlr & Sun...............E....... 812 346-3973
  North Vernon (G-11272)
Offset House Inc...............................F....... 317 849-5155
  Indianapolis (G-7612)
Offset One Inc..................................F....... 260 456-8828
  Fort Wayne (G-4509)
Overgaards Artcraft Printers................G....... 574 234-8464
  South Bend (G-12885)
PIP Printing.....................................G....... 317 843-5755
  Carmel (G-1451)
Plastimatic Arts Corp.........................G....... 574 254-9000
  Mishawaka (G-10104)
Presstime Graphics Inc.......................E....... 812 234-3815
  Terre Haute (G-13309)
Printer Zink Inc.................................D....... 765 644-3959
  Anderson (G-156)
Printing Place Inc-Photos Plus..............F....... 260 665-8444
  Angola (G-239)
Progressive Printing Co Inc..................G....... 765 653-3814
  Greencastle (G-5475)

Quality Printing of NW Ind ....G..... 219 322-6677
Schererville *(G-12343)*
Reprocomm Inc ....F..... 765 423-2578
Lafayette *(G-8990)*
Reprocomm Inc ....E..... 765 472-5700
Peru *(G-11544)*
Rhr Corporation ....G..... 317 788-1504
Indianapolis *(G-7837)*
Riden Inc ....G..... 219 362-5511
La Porte *(G-8812)*
Rink Printing Company Inc ....E..... 574 232-7935
South Bend *(G-12916)*
Rise Inc ....E..... 260 665-9408
Angola *(G-243)*
Rowland Printing Co Inc ....F..... 317 773-1829
Noblesville *(G-11177)*
RR Donnelley & Sons Company ....A..... 765 362-1300
Crawfordsville *(G-2194)*
Schutte Lithography Inc ....E..... 812 469-3500
Evansville *(G-3717)*
Service Graphics Inc ....D..... 317 471-8246
Indianapolis *(G-7917)*
Service Printers Inc ....E..... 574 266-6710
Elkhart *(G-3162)*
Spectrum Press Inc ....E..... 812 335-1945
Bloomington *(G-831)*
SPI Binding Co Inc ....E..... 765 794-4992
Darlington *(G-2361)*
Stamprint Inc ....G..... 574 233-3900
South Bend *(G-12953)*
Stines Printing ....G..... 260 356-5994
Huntington *(G-6253)*
Tabco Business Forms Inc ....G..... 812 882-2836
Vincennes *(G-13709)*
Tatman Inc ....E..... 765 825-2164
Connersville *(G-2075)*
Thomas E Slade Inc ....F..... 812 471-7100
Evansville *(G-3760)*
Tippecanoe Press Inc ....F..... 317 392-1207
Shelbyville *(G-12576)*
Voice of God Recordings Inc ....D..... 812 246-2137
Jeffersonville *(G-8439)*
W Robbins & Sons Inc ....G..... 765 522-1736
Roachdale *(G-12096)*
WAr - LLC- Westville Prtg ....G..... 219 785-2821
Westville *(G-14221)*
Whitewater Publications Inc ....E..... 765 647-4221
Brookville *(G-1131)*
Woodburn Graphics Inc ....E..... 812 232-0323
Terre Haute *(G-13371)*

BINDING SVC: Trade

Blasted Works ....G..... 574 583-3211
Monticello *(G-10256)*

BINOCULARS

Sightwaveoptics ....G..... 317 513-8322
Zionsville *(G-14463)*

BINS: Prefabricated, Metal Plate

Ctb Inc ....A..... 574 658-4191
Milford *(G-9952)*
Ctb Inc ....G..... 574 658-9323
Milford *(G-9953)*
Ctb Inc ....G..... 574 658-4191
Milford *(G-9954)*

BIOLOGICAL PRDTS: Blood Derivatives

Csl Plasma Inc ....D..... 317 352-9157
Indianapolis *(G-6704)*

BIOLOGICAL PRDTS: Exc Diagnostic

Apotex Corp ....E..... 317 839-6550
Plainfield *(G-11593)*
Biosafe Engineering LLC ....E..... 317 858-8099
Indianapolis *(G-6477)*
Bioscience Vaccines Inc ....G..... 765 464-5890
West Lafayette *(G-14055)*
Corebiologic LLC ....G..... 260 437-0353
Fort Wayne *(G-4180)*
Energy Two Inc ....G..... 812 497-3113
Seymour *(G-12447)*
Harlan Development Company ....G..... 317 352-1583
Indianapolis *(G-7076)*
Nerx Biosciences Inc ....F..... 317 251-7408
Indianapolis *(G-7583)*
Sera Tech Biologicals ....G..... 765 288-2699
Muncie *(G-10560)*

Vasmo Inc ....F..... 317 549-3722
Indianapolis *(G-8149)*

BIOLOGICAL PRDTS: Extracts

Extranet Talent ....G..... 317 362-0140
Indianapolis *(G-6898)*

BIOLOGICAL PRDTS: Tuberculins

Ctp Corporation ....D..... 317 787-5747
Greenwood *(G-5680)*

BIOLOGICAL PRDTS: Veterinary

Envigo Rms Inc ....C..... 317 806-6080
Indianapolis *(G-6871)*
Envigo Rms Inc ....G..... 317 806-6080
Greenfield *(G-5530)*
Indy Medical Supplies LLC ....G..... 866 744-9013
Zionsville *(G-14439)*

BLACKPLATE

Black Plate Catering ....G..... 317 634-8030
Indianapolis *(G-6483)*

BLACKSMITH SHOP

Amos D Graber & Sons ....F..... 260 749-0526
New Haven *(G-10929)*
Fabcreation ....G..... 812 246-6222
Sellersburg *(G-12394)*

BLADES: Knife

Pettigrew ....G..... 260 868-2032
Butler *(G-1238)*

BLANKBOOKS & LOOSELEAF BINDERS

Clarke American Checks Inc ....C..... 812 283-9598
Jeffersonville *(G-8339)*
Eckhart & Company Inc ....E..... 317 347-2665
Indianapolis *(G-6799)*
Futurex Industries Inc ....E..... 765 498-8900
Bloomingdale *(G-648)*
Harcourt Industries Inc ....E..... 765 629-2625
Milroy *(G-9980)*
Lamco Finishers Inc ....E..... 317 471-1010
Indianapolis *(G-7379)*
Leed Selling Tools Corp ....C..... 812 482-7888
Ireland *(G-8229)*
Nussmeier Engraving Co ....E..... 812 425-1339
Evansville *(G-3650)*
Printegra Corp ....D..... 317 328-0022
Indianapolis *(G-7752)*
Raine Inc ....F..... 765 622-7687
Anderson *(G-157)*
SPI Binding Co Inc ....E..... 765 794-4992
Darlington *(G-2361)*

BLANKBOOKS: Scrapbooks

Scrapbook Nook ....G..... 812 967-3306
Pekin *(G-11479)*

BLAST FURNACE & RELATED PRDTS

Worthington Steel Company ....C..... 219 929-4000
Porter *(G-11806)*

BLASTING SVC: Sand, Metal Parts

Abrasive Processing & Tech LLC ....F..... 317 485-5157
Fortville *(G-4767)*
Chief Metal Works Inc ....G..... 765 932-2134
Rushville *(G-12217)*
Complete Finish Inc ....E..... 260 587-3588
Ashley *(G-284)*
Klinge Enameling Company Inc ....E..... 317 359-8291
Indianapolis *(G-7359)*
Midwest Surface Prep LLC ....G..... 317 726-1336
Indianapolis *(G-7513)*
New Paradigms Industrial Art ....G..... 219 762-4046
Portage *(G-11783)*
P & H LLC ....G..... 765 654-5291
Frankfort *(G-4848)*
Performance Powder Coating ....G..... 765 438-5224
Kokomo *(G-8680)*
Schaffsteins Truck Clean LLC ....F..... 812 464-2424
Evansville *(G-3715)*
Steve Reiff Inc ....D..... 260 723-4360
South Whitley *(G-13005)*

W Kendall & Sons Inc ....G..... 219 733-2412
Wanatah *(G-13827)*

BLINDS & SHADES: Vertical

Mitchell Fabrics Inc ....E..... 309 674-8631
Lafayette *(G-8971)*
Oxford House Incorporated ....D..... 765 884-3265
Fowler *(G-4803)*
Vertical Plus Mri America LLC ....G..... 574 257-4674
Mishawaka *(G-10146)*
Vertical Sale ....G..... 260 438-4299
Fort Wayne *(G-4726)*
Vertical Vision Inc ....G..... 812 432-3763
Dillsboro *(G-2474)*

BLINDS : Window

Horizon Vinyl Windows Inc ....G..... 260 632-0207
Woodburn *(G-14384)*
Irvine Shade & Door Inc ....D..... 574 522-1446
Elkhart *(G-2940)*
Lafayette Venetian Blind Inc ....A..... 765 464-2500
West Lafayette *(G-14082)*
Merin Interiors Indianapolis ....G..... 317 251-6603
Indianapolis *(G-7482)*
Midwest Blind & Shade Co ....G..... 574 271-0770
Mishawaka *(G-10085)*
United Services Inc ....G..... 812 989-3320
Clarksville *(G-1698)*

BLINDS, WOOD

J P Whitt Inc ....G..... 765 759-0521
Muncie *(G-10498)*

BLOCKS & BRICKS: Concrete

Camilles Studio ....G..... 219 365-5902
Cedar Lake *(G-1526)*
Crown Brick & Supply Inc ....E..... 219 663-7880
Crown Point *(G-2237)*
Devening Block Inc ....E..... 812 372-4458
Columbus *(G-1907)*
Dubois Cnty Block & Brick Inc ....F..... 812 482-6293
Jasper *(G-8247)*
Irving Materials Inc ....D..... 317 326-3101
Greenfield *(G-5542)*
Majestic Block & Supply Inc ....G..... 317 842-6602
Fishers *(G-3943)*
R & D Concrete Products of Ind ....F..... 260 837-6511
Waterloo *(G-14021)*
Slon Inc ....F..... 765 884-1792
Fowler *(G-4807)*
Southfield Corporation ....E..... 812 824-1355
Bloomington *(G-829)*
W Martin Gary ....G..... 812 926-0935
Aurora *(G-393)*

BLOCKS: Landscape Or Retaining Wall, Concrete

Engineered Products Inc ....G..... 219 662-2080
Crown Point *(G-2250)*
Menard Inc ....A..... 812 466-1234
Terre Haute *(G-13282)*

BLOCKS: Paving

Orr Paving Inc ....G..... 317 839-4110
Plainfield *(G-11633)*

BLOCKS: Paving, Asphalt, Not From Refineries

Globe Asphalt Paving Co Inc ....E..... 317 568-4344
Indianapolis *(G-7015)*
Irving Materials Inc ....D..... 317 326-3101
Greenfield *(G-5542)*

BLOCKS: Paving, Concrete

Hessit Works Inc ....G..... 812 829-6246
Freedom *(G-4949)*
Stotlar Hill LLC ....G..... 260 497-0808
Fort Wayne *(G-4654)*

BLOCKS: Standard, Concrete Or Cinder

Cash Concrete Products Inc ....F..... 765 653-4007
Greencastle *(G-5454)*
Jones & Sons Inc ....E..... 812 254-4731
Washington *(G-13988)*

Employee Codes: A=Over 500 employees, B=251-500
C=101-250, D=51-100, E=20-50, F=10-19, G=2-9

2018 Harris Indiana
Industrial Directory

915

PRODUCT

Lafarge North America Inc ....G....... 219 378-1193
East Chicago (G-2547)

Northfield Block Company ....G....... 800 424-0190
Indianapolis (G-7594)

Shelby Gravel Inc ....F....... 317 738-3445
Franklin (G-4929)

Slaters Concrete Products ....G....... 260 347-0164
Kendallville (G-8510)

St Henry Tile Co Inc ....E....... 260 589-2880
Berne (G-626)

Van Duyne Block and Gravel ....G....... 574 223-6656
Rochester (G-12159)

BLOWERS & FANS

Abtrex Industries Inc ....E....... 574 234-7773
South Bend (G-12693)

Blocksom & Co ....E....... 219 878-4458
Michigan City (G-9771)

Buck & Company Inc ....G....... 574 292-0874
Granger (G-5396)

Cor-A-Vent Inc ....E....... 574 258-6161
Mishawaka (G-10024)

CTB MN Investment Co Inc ....E....... 574 658-4191
Milford (G-9955)

Dexter Axle Company ....C....... 574 295-7888
Bristol (G-1054)

Donaldson Company Inc ....G....... 812 637-9200
Lawrenceburg (G-9139)

Donaldson Company Inc ....B....... 765 659-4766
Frankfort (G-4828)

Donaldson Company Inc ....G....... 952 887-3131
Monticello (G-10260)

Donaldson Company Inc ....G....... 317 838-5568
Plainfield (G-11606)

E & S Metal Inc ....F....... 260 563-7714
Wabash (G-13726)

Eta Fabrication Inc ....F....... 260 897-3711
Avilla (G-404)

F D Ramsey & Co Inc ....G....... 219 362-2452
La Porte (G-8757)

Fan-Tastic Vent ....G....... 800 521-0298
Elkhart (G-2844)

Gbi Air Systems Inc ....G....... 574 272-0600
Granger (G-5408)

Kabert Industries Inc ....D....... 765 874-2335
Lynn (G-9428)

Pro Clean LLC ....G....... 574 867-1000
Hamlet (G-5832)

Spectrum Brands Inc ....E....... 317 773-6627
Noblesville (G-11187)

Terronics Development Corp ....G....... 765 552-0808
Elwood (G-3311)

Wicks Air Filter Service Inc ....G....... 260 426-1782
Fort Wayne (G-4755)

BLOWERS & FANS

Aero-Flo Industries Inc ....G....... 219 393-3555
La Porte (G-8728)

Howden Roots LLC ....G....... 765 827-9200
Connersville (G-2052)

Mechanovent Corporation ....G....... 219 326-1767
La Porte (G-8790)

BLUEPRINTING SVCS

Blue Print Specialties Inc ....G....... 765 742-6976
Lafayette (G-8862)

Copy Solutions Inc ....G....... 260 436-2679
Fort Wayne (G-4175)

J & L Dimensional Services Inc ......E....... 219 325-3588
La Porte (G-8773)

Maco Reprograhics LLC ....G....... 812 464-8108
Evansville (G-3608)

BOAT & BARGE COMPONENTS: Metal, Prefabricated

Marion Metal Products Inc ....E....... 765 662-8333
Marion (G-9543)

BOAT BUILDING & REPAIR

Angola Canvas Co Inc ....F....... 260 665-9913
Angola (G-191)

Atlas Dock Systems Inc ....G....... 317 714-3850
New Castle (G-10892)

Boat Holdings LLC ....G....... 574 264-6336
Elkhart (G-2728)

Buckhorn Inc ....D....... 260 824-0997
Bluffton (G-870)

Chief Powerboats Inc ....G....... 219 775-7024
Crown Point (G-2233)

Culvers Port Side Marina ....F....... 574 223-5090
Rochester (G-12120)

Fiberglass Pdts & Boat Repr ....G....... 260 627-3209
Grabill (G-5364)

Fiberglass Pdts Boat Repairing ......G....... 260 337-5636
Saint Joe (G-12255)

Highwater Marine LLC ....D....... 574 457-2082
Syracuse (G-13134)

Hoosier Marine ....G....... 812 879-5549
Quincy (G-11890)

Indianapolis Marine Co ....F....... 317 545-4646
Indianapolis (G-7202)

Mikes Boat Works LLC ....G....... 317 410-4981
Greenfield (G-5553)

N3 LLC ....G....... 317 845-9253
Indianapolis (G-7568)

Neoteric Incorporated ....F....... 812 234-1120
Terre Haute (G-13289)

Pontoon Boat LLC ....C....... 574 264-6336
Elkhart (G-3102)

Sylvan Marine Inc ....B....... 574 831-2950
New Paris (G-10997)

Taylor Made Group Holdings Inc .....C....... 260 347-1368
Kendallville (G-8512)

Veada Industries Inc ....A....... 574 831-4775
New Paris (G-11000)

West Lakes Marine Inc ....F....... 260 854-2525
Rome City (G-12201)

Yandt Boat Works ....G....... 219 851-8311
La Porte (G-8834)

BOAT BUILDING & REPAIRING: Fiberglass

Harmon Boats Inc ....G....... 765 963-5358
Sharpsville (G-12506)

Highwater Marine LLC ....D....... 574 522-8381
Elkhart (G-2916)

Macks Welding ....F....... 812 265-6255
Madison (G-9478)

Splendor Boats LLC ....F....... 260 352-2835
Silver Lake (G-12681)

BOAT BUILDING & REPAIRING: Houseboats

Destination Yachts Inc ....F....... 812 254-8800
Washington (G-13979)

BOAT BUILDING & REPAIRING: Motorized

Smoker Craft Inc ....B....... 574 831-2103
New Paris (G-10994)

Thomas Toll ....G....... 317 569-2628
Carmel (G-1496)

Wawasee Aluminum Works Inc ....E....... 574 457-2082
Syracuse (G-13152)

BOAT BUILDING & REPAIRING: Non-Motorized

Groh Inc ....G....... 260 463-2410
Lagrange (G-9043)

Rollerboat Inc ....G....... 512 931-3936
Sellersburg (G-12413)

Sherms Marine ....G....... 260 563-8051
Wabash (G-13755)

BOAT BUILDING & REPAIRING: Pontoons, Exc Aircraft & Inflat

Brunswick Corporation ....C....... 260 459-8200
Fort Wayne (G-4125)

J C Mfg Inc ....E....... 574 834-2881
North Webster (G-11294)

Starcraft Marine LLC ....B....... 574 831-2103
New Paris (G-10995)

BOAT BUILDING & REPAIRING: Yachts

Kentuckiana Yacht Services LLC ....G....... 812 282-2660
Jeffersonville (G-8387)

Rolls-Royce Corporation ....G....... 317 230-8515
West Lafayette (G-14104)

Rolls-Royce Corporation ....A....... 317 230-2000
Indianapolis (G-7858)

Yacht Brite Proffesional Care ....G....... 219 874-1181
Michigan City (G-9862)

BOAT DEALERS

Smoker Craft Inc ....B....... 574 831-2103
New Paris (G-10994)

Splendor Boats LLC ....F....... 260 352-2835
Silver Lake (G-12681)

Webster Custom Canvas Inc ....G....... 574 834-4497
North Webster (G-11302)

BOAT DEALERS: Marine Splys & Eqpt

Lake Lite Inc ....G....... 260 918-2758
Laotto (G-9112)

BOAT DEALERS: Motor

Culvers Port Side Marina ....F....... 574 223-5090
Rochester (G-12120)

Sherms Marine ....G....... 260 563-8051
Wabash (G-13755)

West Lakes Marine Inc ....F....... 260 854-2525
Rome City (G-12201)

BOAT LIFTS

Deatons Waterfront Svcs LLC ....F....... 317 336-7180
Fortville (G-4773)

Yardarm Marine Products Inc ....E....... 317 831-4950
Mooresville (G-10345)

BOAT REPAIR SVCS

Harmon Boats Inc ....G....... 765 963-5358
Sharpsville (G-12506)

BOAT YARD: Boat yards, storage & incidental repair

Fiberglass Pdts Boat Repairing ....G....... 260 337-5636
Saint Joe (G-12255)

Harmon Boats Inc ....G....... 765 963-5358
Sharpsville (G-12506)

Leco Corporation ....G....... 574 288-9017
South Bend (G-12838)

BOATS & OTHER MARINE EQPT: Plastic

Poppy Co ....G....... 317 442-2491
Brownsburg (G-1164)

BODIES: Truck & Bus

ABRA Auto Body & Glass LP ....E....... 317 839-8940
Plainfield (G-11590)

Accuride Emi LLC ....G....... 940 565-8505
Evansville (G-3337)

Arboc Specialty Vehicles LLC ....D....... 574 825-1720
Middlebury (G-9871)

Basiloid Products Corp ....C....... 812 692-5511
Elnora (G-3286)

Braun Motor Works Inc ....G....... 574 205-0102
Winamac (G-14303)

Dana Driveshaft Products LLC ....B....... 260 432-2903
Marion (G-9520)

Eagle Craft Inc ....E....... 574 936-3196
Plymouth (G-11682)

Eaton Corporation ....C....... 260 925-3800
Auburn (G-328)

Eaton Corporation ....F....... 317 704-2520
Indianapolis (G-6796)

Ford Motor Company ....D....... 317 837-2302
Plainfield (G-11610)

General Motors LLC ....A....... 260 672-1224
Roanoke (G-12102)

Gravel Conveyors Inc ....F....... 317 873-8686
Zionsville (G-14435)

Hendrickson International Corp ....C....... 260 349-6400
Kendallville (G-8478)

Hendrickson International Corp ....C....... 765 483-5350
Lebanon (G-9187)

Independent Protection Co Inc ....D....... 574 831-5680
New Paris (G-10985)

International Brake Inds Inc ....E....... 419 905-7468
South Bend (G-12817)

Kiel NA LLC ....F....... 574 293-3600
Elkhart (G-2965)

Lund International Holding Co ....E....... 765 742-7200
Lafayette (G-8963)

Marmon Highway Tech LLC ....E....... 317 787-0718
Indianapolis (G-7457)

Original Tractor Cab Co Inc ....E....... 765 663-2214
Arlington (G-282)

Quality Tank Trucks & Eqp Inc ....G...... 317 635-0000
Indianapolis *(G-7801)*
Ramco Engineering Inc ....E...... 574 266-1455
Elkhart *(G-3136)*
Spartan Motors Usa Inc ....E...... 574 848-2000
Bristol *(G-1088)*
Starcraft Corporation ....E...... 574 534-7827
Goshen *(G-5329)*
Supreme Corporation ....A...... 574 642-4888
Goshen *(G-5334)*
Supreme Industries Inc ....D...... 574 642-3070
Goshen *(G-5336)*
Utilimaster Holdings Inc ....A...... 800 237-7806
Bristol *(G-1093)*
Vanair Manufacturing Inc ....C...... 219 879-5100
Michigan City *(G-9857)*

BODY PARTS: Automobile, Stamped Metal

Afco Performance Group LLC ....G...... 812 897-0900
Boonville *(G-905)*
Auto Extras Inc ....G...... 574 855-2370
South Bend *(G-12717)*
Fukai Toyotetsu Indiana Corp................F...... 765 676-4800
Jamestown *(G-8230)*
Futaba Indiana America Corp ....B...... 812 895-4700
Vincennes *(G-13683)*
Heritage Products Inc ....C...... 765 364-9002
Crawfordsville *(G-2158)*
Kousei USA Inc ....G...... 812 373-7315
Columbus *(G-1955)*
Lift ....G...... 812 394-5438
Fairbanks *(G-3818)*
Metal Fab Engineering Inc ....F...... 574 278-7150
Winamac *(G-14312)*
Multimactic New Haven LLC ....D...... 260 868-1067
Butler *(G-1234)*
Multimatic Indiana Inc ....C...... 260 868-1000
Butler *(G-1235)*
Multimatic New Haven LLC ....G...... 260 868-1067
Fort Wayne *(G-4484)*
Omr North America Inc ....F...... 317 956-9509
Speedway *(G-13015)*
Patrick Custom Carbon ....G...... 815 721-5150
Brownsburg *(G-1162)*
Pk USA Inc ....B...... 317 395-5500
Shelbyville *(G-12558)*
Specialty Rim Supply Inc ....G...... 812 234-3002
Terre Haute *(G-13338)*
Techna Fit of Indiana ....G...... 317 350-2153
Brownsburg *(G-1173)*

BOILER & HEATING REPAIR SVCS

Complete Controls Inc ....G...... 260 489-0852
Fort Wayne *(G-4170)*

BOILER REPAIR SHOP

Power Plant Service Inc ....E...... 260 432-6716
Fort Wayne *(G-4542)*

BOILERS: Low-Pressure Heating, Steam Or Hot Water

Bryan Steam LLC ....D...... 765 473-6651
Peru *(G-11518)*
Marley-Wylain Company ....C...... 630 560-3703
Michigan City *(G-9815)*
Marley-Wylain Company ....G...... 219 879-6561
Michigan City *(G-9816)*

BOLTS: Metal

Agrati - Park Forest LLC ....E...... 219 531-2202
Valparaiso *(G-13487)*
B K & M Inc ....G...... 219 924-0184
Griffith *(G-5764)*
Cold Heading Co ....D...... 260 495-7003
Fremont *(G-4955)*
Cold Heading Co ....E...... 260 587-3231
Hudson *(G-6132)*
Cold Heading Co ....D...... 260 495-4222
Fremont *(G-4956)*
Elgin Fastener Group LLC ....G...... 812 689-8917
Versailles *(G-13653)*
Fontana Fasteners Inc ....C...... 765 654-0477
Frankfort *(G-4831)*
Key Fasteners Corp ....D...... 260 589-2626
Berne *(G-619)*
McCoy Bolt Works Inc ....D...... 260 482-4476
Fort Wayne *(G-4459)*

R & R Engineering Co Inc ....E...... 765 536-2331
Summitville *(G-13102)*
Rohder Machine & Tool Inc ....F...... 219 663-3697
Crown Point *(G-2297)*
Steve Mitchell ....G...... 574 831-4848
New Paris *(G-10996)*

BOOK STORES

Embroidme ....G...... 219 465-1400
Valparaiso *(G-13536)*
Prairie Creek Prtg & Bk Str ....G...... 812 636-7243
Montgomery *(G-10238)*
Un Communications Group Inc ....E...... 317 844-8622
Carmel *(G-1503)*
United Brethren In Christ ....F...... 260 356-2312
Huntington *(G-6258)*

BOOK STORES: Religious

Bibles For Blind & Visually ....G...... 812 466-3134
Terre Haute *(G-13201)*

BOOKS, WHOLESALE

Tom Doherty Company Inc ....G...... 317 352-8200
Indianapolis *(G-8079)*

BORING MILL

Hy-Tech Machining Systems LLC ....F...... 765 649-6852
Anderson *(G-118)*

BOTTLE CAPS & RESEALERS: Plastic

Berry Global Inc ....G...... 812 334-7090
Bloomington *(G-679)*
Berry Global Inc ....G...... 812 386-1525
Princeton *(G-11865)*
Berry Global Inc ....G...... 765 966-1414
Richmond *(G-11964)*
Berry Global Inc ....E...... 812 867-6671
Evansville *(G-3375)*
Berry Global Inc ....B...... 765 962-4253
Richmond *(G-11965)*
Berry Plastics Opco Inc ....G...... 812 402-2903
Evansville *(G-3380)*
Berry Plastics Opco Inc ....E...... 812 424-2904
Evansville *(G-3381)*
BP Parallel LLC ....G...... 812 424-2904
Evansville *(G-3395)*
Bprex Closure Systems LLC ....G...... 812 424-2904
Evansville *(G-3396)*
Bprex Closures LLC ....D...... 812 424-2904
Evansville *(G-3397)*
Bprex Closures LLC ....B...... 812 867-6671
Evansville *(G-3399)*
Caplas Neptune LLC ....G...... 812 424-2904
Evansville *(G-3410)*
Closure Systems Intl Inc ....B...... 765 364-6300
Crawfordsville *(G-2141)*
Pliant International LLC ....G...... 812 424-2904
Evansville *(G-3676)*
Pliant Packaging Canada LLC ....G...... 812 424-2904
Evansville *(G-3677)*

BOTTLED GAS DEALERS: Liquefied Petro, Dlvrd To Customers

Ferrellgas LP ....G...... 574 936-2725
Plymouth *(G-11684)*

BOTTLED GAS DEALERS: Propane

Crestwood Equity Partners LP ....G...... 812 265-3313
Madison *(G-9455)*
Oeding Corporation ....G...... 812 367-1271
Ferdinand *(G-3860)*

BOTTLED WATER DELIVERY

American Water Works Co Inc ....G...... 765 362-3940
Crawfordsville *(G-2133)*

BOTTLES: Plastic

Ahf Industries Inc ....C...... 812 936-9988
French Lick *(G-4984)*
Berry Global Group Inc ....F...... 812 424-2904
Evansville *(G-3377)*
Drug Plastics and Glass Co Inc ....D...... 765 385-0035
Oxford *(G-11431)*
Indiana Bottle Company Inc ....E...... 812 752-8700
Scottsburg *(G-12365)*

North America Packaging Corp ....C...... 317 291-2396
Indianapolis *(G-7591)*
Poly-Tainer Inc ....C...... 317 883-2072
Greenwood *(G-5734)*
Polycon Industries Inc ....C...... 219 738-1000
Merrillville *(G-9748)*
Setco LLC ....B...... 812 424-2904
Evansville *(G-3724)*
Silgan Plastics LLC ....D...... 260 894-3118
Ligonier *(G-9295)*
Silgan Plastics LLC ....C...... 812 522-0900
Seymour *(G-12490)*
Silgan Plastics LLC ....F...... 812 522-0900
Seymour *(G-12491)*
Specialty Manufacturing of Ind ....E...... 812 256-4633
Charlestown *(G-1581)*
Travomatic Corp Indiana Div ....G...... 812 522-8177
Seymour *(G-12492)*

BOULDER: Crushed & Broken

Bens Quarry LLC ....G...... 812 824-3730
Springville *(G-13060)*
Hanson Aggrgates Southeast Inc ....D...... 317 788-4086
Indianapolis *(G-7072)*

BOUTIQUE STORES

Formal Affairs Tuxedo Shop ....G...... 574 875-6654
Elkhart *(G-2868)*
House of Bluez ....G...... 812 401-2583
Evansville *(G-3543)*

BOWL COVERS: Plastic

Bprex Closures LLC ....D...... 812 386-1525
Princeton *(G-11866)*

BOWLING EQPT & SPLY STORES

Hoogies Sports House Inc ....G...... 574 533-9875
Goshen *(G-5238)*
Kerham Inc ....E...... 260 483-5444
Fort Wayne *(G-4409)*

BOWLING EQPT & SPLYS

R & R Bowling Inc ....G...... 574 252-4123
Mishawaka *(G-10114)*

BOXES & CRATES: Rectangular, Wood

Knights Woodworking LLC ....G...... 812 988-2106
Nashville *(G-10727)*

BOXES & SHOOK: Nailed Wood

A S M Inc ....G...... 260 724-8220
Decatur *(G-2363)*
American Fibertech Corporation ....E...... 219 261-3586
Clarks Hill *(G-1670)*
Bryant Products Inc ....F...... 812 522-5929
Seymour *(G-12435)*
C & C Mailbox Products ....G...... 765 358-4880
Gaston *(G-5130)*
C E Kersting & Sons ....G...... 574 896-2766
North Judson *(G-11207)*
Findley Foster Corp ....G...... 812 524-7279
Seymour *(G-12450)*
Hoosier Box and Skid Inc ....G...... 574 256-2111
Mishawaka *(G-10050)*
Indiana Wood Products Inc ....D...... 574 825-2129
Middlebury *(G-9893)*
Industrial Woodkraft Inc ....E...... 812 897-4893
Boonville *(G-914)*
Leclere Manufacturing Inc ....G...... 812 683-5627
Jasper *(G-8287)*

BOXES: Ammunition, Metal

Bway Corporation ....D...... 219 462-8915
Valparaiso *(G-13517)*

BOXES: Ammunition, Wood

Douglas Industries LLC ....G...... 260 327-3692
Larwill *(G-9121)*

BOXES: Corrugated

American Containers Inc ....D...... 574 936-4068
Plymouth *(G-11664)*
Capitol City Container Corp ....E...... 317 875-0290
Indianapolis *(G-6549)*

Cardinal Container Corp ....E 317 898-2715
Indianapolis (G-6551)
Color-Box LLC ....D 765 966-7588
Richmond (G-11972)
Container Service Corp ....D 574 232-7474
South Bend (G-12740)
CRA-Wal Inc ....D 317 856-3701
Indianapolis (G-6683)
Custom Packaging Inc ....F 317 876-9559
Indianapolis (G-6717)
Five Star Sheets LLC ....D 574 654-8058
New Carlisle (G-10882)
Galaxy Container LLC ....G 574 936-6300
Plymouth (G-11687)
Hoosier Container Inc ....E 765 966-2541
Richmond (G-11999)
Indiana Box Company ....E 317 462-7743
Greenfield (G-5539)
International Paper Company .....C 260 868-2151
Butler (G-1232)
International Paper Company .....D 765 364-5342
Crawfordsville (G-2161)
International Paper Company .....D 812 326-2125
Saint Anthony (G-12246)
International Paper Company .....E 317 875-4101
Indianapolis (G-7259)
International Paper Company .....G 765 492-3341
Cayuga (G-1520)
International Paper Company .....D 317 390-3300
Indianapolis (G-7260)
International Paper Company .....C 317 510-6410
Indianapolis (G-7257)
International Paper Company .....E 800 643-7244
Terre Haute (G-13259)
Jamil Packaging Corporation .....E 574 256-2600
Mishawaka (G-10059)
Kelly Box and Packaging Corp ....D 260 432-4570
Fort Wayne (G-4407)
Lacap Container Corp ....E 317 835-4282
Shelbyville (G-12548)
Marion Paper Box Company ......F 765 664-6435
Marion (G-9544)
Met Pak Specialties Inc ....F 260 420-2217
Fort Wayne (G-4467)
Northern Box Company Inc ......E 574 264-2161
Elkhart (G-3066)
Northern Indiana Packg Co Inc ....F 260 356-9660
Huntington (G-6232)
Nova Packaging Group Inc ......E 765 651-2600
Marion (G-9548)
Orora North America ....E 317 879-4628
Indianapolis (G-7631)
Packaging Corporation America ....C 812 882-7631
Vincennes (G-13694)
Packaging Corporation America ....B 812 376-9301
Columbus (G-1989)
Packaging Corporation America ....D 812 526-5919
Edinburgh (G-2620)
Packaging Corporation America ....D 765 674-9781
Gas City (G-5126)
Packaging Corporation America ....G 317 247-0193
Indianapolis (G-7646)
Packaging Corporation America ....E 812 522-3100
Seymour (G-12473)
Packaging Corporation America ....E 812 482-4598
Jasper (G-8299)
Packaging Lgstics Slutions LLC ....E 502 807-8346
New Albany (G-10838)
Packaging Logic Inc ....E 219 326-1350
La Porte (G-8803)
PCA Suthern Ind Corrugated LLC ....G 812 376-9301
Columbus (G-1991)
Pratt (jet Corr) Inc ....B 219 548-9191
Valparaiso (G-13601)
Pyramid Paper Products Inc .....E 812 372-0288
Columbus (G-2002)
Royal Box Group LLC ....D 765 728-2416
Huntington (G-6244)
Servants Inc ....D 812 634-2201
Jasper (G-8306)
Servants Inc ....D 812 634-2201
Jasper (G-8307)
Sisco Corporation ....D 812 422-2090
Evansville (G-3733)
Southland Container Corp ....F 812 385-0774
Princeton (G-11882)
Wabash Valley Packaging Corp ....F 812 299-7181
Terre Haute (G-13367)
Webster West Inc ....E 812 346-5666
North Vernon (G-11286)

Welch Packaging LLC ....D 574 295-2460
Elkhart (G-3255)
Welch Packaging Marion LLC .....D 765 651-2600
Marion (G-9572)
Westrock Cp LLC ....E 574 772-5545
Knox (G-8587)
Westrock Cp LLC ....C 812 372-8873
Columbus (G-2032)
Westrock Cp LLC ....C 574 256-0318
Mishawaka (G-10151)

BOXES: Mail Or Post Office, Collection/Storage, Sheet Metal

C & C Mailbox Products ....G 765 358-4880
Gaston (G-5130)
Mailroom LLC ....G 765 254-0000
Muncie (G-10517)
PSI Group Inc ....G 317 297-3211
Indianapolis (G-7786)
R & R Manufacturing ....G 260 244-5621
Columbia City (G-1823)

BOXES: Outlet, Electric Wiring Device

Hubbell Incorporated Delaware ....B 574 234-7151
South Bend (G-12806)

BOXES: Packing & Shipping, Metal

Ball Corporation ....F 574 583-9418
Monticello (G-10253)
Flexible Marketing Group ....G 574 296-0941
Elkhart (G-2855)

BOXES: Paperboard, Folding

Artistic Carton Company ....E 260 925-6060
Auburn (G-312)
Barger Packaging Corporation .....D 574 389-1860
Elkhart (G-2715)
Combined Technologies Inc ......E 574 251-4968
South Bend (G-12739)
Custom Carton Inc ....F 260 563-7411
Wabash (G-13723)
Glaze Mfg Co ....F 574 612-1401
Elkhart (G-2881)
Indiana Carton Company Inc .....D 574 546-3848
Bremen (G-1004)
Tre Paper Co Inc ....E 765 649-2536
Anderson (G-178)
Westrock Cp LLC ....G 574 936-2118
Plymouth (G-11735)

BOXES: Paperboard, Set-Up

American Containers Inc ....D 574 936-4068
Plymouth (G-11664)
Artistic Carton Company ....E 260 925-6060
Auburn (G-312)
Barger Packaging Corporation .....D 574 389-1860
Elkhart (G-2715)
Dgp Intelsius LLC ....D 317 452-4006
Indianapolis (G-6738)
Jessup Paper Box LLC ....E 765 588-9137
Lafayette (G-8931)
Pathfinder Services Inc ....E 260 356-0500
Huntington (G-6236)
Reddi-Pac Inc ....E 574 266-6933
Elkhart (G-3142)

BOXES: Plastic

Resin Partners Inc ....E 765 298-6800
Anderson (G-161)

BOXES: Solid Fiber

Graphic Packaging Intl Inc ....D 812 949-4393
New Albany (G-10789)
Smith Consulting Inc ....E 765 728-5980
Montpelier (G-10294)

BOXES: Wirebound, Wood

J R Graber & Sons Inc ....F 260 657-5620
Grabill (G-5375)
Minor Products Company Inc .....G 812 448-3611
Staunton (G-13072)
Zehrhaus Inc ....G 260 486-3198
Fort Wayne (G-4764)

BOXES: Wooden

Ash-Lin Inc ....F 317 861-1540
Fountaintown (G-4789)
F & F Contracting ....G 574 867-4471
Grovertown (G-5795)
JR Grber Sons Fmly Ltd Prtnr .....G 260 657-1071
Grabill (G-5377)
Whitakerr Dalemon ....G 812 738-2396
Corydon (G-2116)

BRAKES & BRAKE PARTS

Bludot Inc ....G 574 277-2306
South Bend (G-12723)
Bwi Indiana Inc ....E 937 260-2460
Greenfield (G-5510)
Carlisle Industrial Brake & Fr .....B 812 336-3811
Bloomington (G-696)
D & D Brake Sales Inc ....D 317 485-5177
Fortville (G-4772)
Horizon Global Americas Inc .....C 517 767-4142
South Bend (G-12804)
Indiana Precision Forge LLC .....D 317 421-0102
Shelbyville (G-12538)
International Brake Inds Inc ....E 419 905-7468
South Bend (G-12817)
NERP LLC ....G 574 303-6377
South Bend (G-12872)
Techna-Fit Inc ....G 317 350-2153
Brownsburg (G-1174)

BRASS & BRONZE PRDTS: Die-casted

Aero Metals Inc ....B 219 326-1976
La Porte (G-8727)

BRASS FOUNDRY, NEC

Ashley Aluminum Foundry Inc .....G 812 793-2654
Crothersville (G-2215)
Sterling Sales and Engineering ....G 765 376-0454
Veedersburg (G-13646)

BRASSWORK: Ornamental, Structural

Le Air Co Inc ....G 812 988-1313
Nashville (G-10728)

BRAZING SVCS

Applied Metals & Mch Works Inc ....E 260 424-4834
Fort Wayne (G-4083)
Brazing Preforms LLC ....G 317 705-6455
Noblesville (G-11071)
Tube Processing Corp ....B 317 787-1321
Indianapolis (G-8107)
Tube Processing Corp ....C 317 264-7760
Indianapolis (G-8109)

BRAZING: Metal

D & D Industries Inc ....G 219 844-5600
Hammond (G-5868)
Electro Seal Corporation ....G 219 926-8606
Chesterton (G-1603)

BREAKER POINT SETS: Internal Combustion Engines

La Fontaine Generator Exchange ....G 765 981-4561
La Fontaine (G-8723)

BRICK, STONE & RELATED PRDTS WHOLESALERS

Camilles Studio ....G 219 365-5902
Cedar Lake (G-1526)
Crown Brick & Supply Inc ....E 219 663-7880
Crown Point (G-2237)
Devening Block Inc ....E 812 372-4458
Columbus (G-1907)
Dubois Cnty Block & Brick Inc .....F 812 482-6293
Jasper (G-8247)
Independent Concrete Pipe Co .....E 317 262-4920
Indianapolis (G-7172)
Millburn Peat Company Inc ....E 219 362-7025
La Porte (G-8794)
Mulzer Crushed Stone Inc ....E 812 256-3346
Charlestown (G-1574)
Ozinga Indiana Rdymx Con Inc .....F 219 949-9800
Gary (G-5082)

Park County Aggregates LLC ....G...... 765 245-2344
Rockville (G-12178)
Stone Center of Indiana LLC..............E...... 317 849-9100
Indianapolis (G-8009)

BRICKS & BLOCKS: Structural

Ceramica Inc...............................F....... 317 546-0087
Indianapolis (G-6589)

BRICKS : Flooring, Clay

Santarossa Mosaic Tile Co Inc ....C... 317 632-9494
Indianapolis (G-7895)

BRICKS: Concrete

Majestic Block and Brick Inc ....E...... 317 831-2455
Mooresville (G-10321)

BRIDGE COMPONENTS: Bridge sections, prefabricated, highway

Bedford Crane LLC ....E...... 812 275-4411
Bedford (G-531)
Indiana Steel & Engrg Inc.................E...... 812 275-3363
Bedford (G-552)
Wabash Steel LLC..........................G...... 317 818-1622
Vincennes (G-13713)

BRISTLES: Dressed

Preciball USA ....G...... 812 257-5555
Washington (G-14000)

BROADCASTING & COMMUNICATION EQPT: Transmit-Receiver, Radio

Ritron Inc ....D...... 317 846-1201
Carmel (G-1468)
World Rdo Mssnary Fllwship Inc............E... 574 970-4252
Elkhart (G-3268)

BROADCASTING & COMMUNICATIONS EQPT: Studio Eqpt, Radio & TV

Grand Master LLC..........................G... 574 288-8273
South Bend (G-12790)

BROADCASTING & COMMUNICATIONS EQPT: Transmitting, Radio/TV

Harman Professional Inc ....B...... 574 294-8000
Elkhart (G-2908)

BROADCASTING STATIONS, RADIO: Educational

DMC Distribution LLC......................G...... 219 926-6401
Porter (G-11805)

BROKERS & DEALERS: Stock

Cook Group Incorporated ....F...... 812 339-2235
Bloomington (G-704)

BROKERS: Loan

Wallar Additions Inc......................E...... 574 262-1989
Elkhart (G-3253)

BROKERS: Printing

C E M Printing & Specialities ....G...... 269 684-6898
South Bend (G-12730)
Chicago Color Graphics ....G...... 312 856-1433
Hammond (G-5860)
Dynamark Graphics Group Inc ....E...... 317 328-2555
Indianapolis (G-6775)
Hager Inc.................................G...... 260 483-7075
Fort Wayne (G-4314)
Hiatt Enterprises Inc ....E...... 765 289-7756
Muncie (G-10487)
Maury Boyd & Associates Inc...............F...... 317 849-6110
Indianapolis (G-7469)

BRONZE FOUNDRY, NEC

Leon R Dixon..............................G...... 317 545-1956
Indianapolis (G-7397)
Mark Parmenter............................G...... 812 829-6583
Spencer (G-13030)

Wilhoite Monuments Inc....................G...... 765 286-7423
Muncie (G-10584)

BROOMS & BRUSHES

Midwest Finishing Systems Inc.............E... 574 257-0099
Mishawaka (G-10087)
Reit-Price Mfg Co Incorporated ....G... 765 964-3252
Union City (G-13460)

BROOMS & BRUSHES: Household Or Indl

Jason Incorporated........................D...... 800 787-7325
Richmond (G-12006)
Power Brushes of Indiana Inc..............G... 812 336-7395
Bloomington (G-801)

BROOMS & BRUSHES: Paintbrushes

Crown Industries Inc ....E... 219 791-9930
Crown Point (G-2239)

BROOMS & BRUSHES: Street Sweeping, Hand Or Machine

City of Fort Wayne ....D...... 260 427-1235
Fort Wayne (G-4152)

BRUSHES

American Way Marketing Inc ....F... 574 295-7466
Elkhart (G-2687)
Royal Brush Manufacturing Inc.............E... 219 660-4170
Munster (G-10627)

BUFFING FOR THE TRADE

Precision Polishing & Buffing ....G...... 317 352-0165
Indianapolis (G-7734)

BUILDING & OFFICE CLEANING SVCS

Allen Industries Inc.....................G...... 317 595-0730
Indianapolis (G-6368)

BUILDING & STRUCTURAL WOOD MBRS: Timbers, Struct, Lam Lumber

Brenco LLC................................G...... 219 844-9570
Hammond (G-5854)
Shelby Products Corporation ....G...... 317 398-4870
West Harrison (G-14043)

BUILDING & STRUCTURAL WOOD MEMBERS

Continntal Crpntry Cmpnnts LLC...........E...... 219 369-4839
Wanatah (G-13823)
Custom Millwork & Display LLC.............G... 574 289-9772
South Bend (G-12749)
Ghk Truss LLC ....E...... 812 282-6600
Clarksville (G-1681)
Indiana Truss Co LLC ....G...... 812 522-5929
Seymour (G-12458)
Interstate Truss LLC ....G...... 260 463-6124
Shipshewana (G-12621)
James G Henager...........................G...... 812 795-2230
Elberfeld (G-2636)
Kentucky-Indiana Lumber Co Inc...........E...... 812 464-2428
Evansville (G-3584)
Madison Truss Company ....G...... 812 273-5482
Madison (G-9483)
Northern Indiana Truss....................G... 574 858-0505
Warsaw (G-13916)
Osterholt Construction Inc ....G...... 260 672-3493
Roanoke (G-12106)
Superior Truss & Components ....G... 574 457-8925
Syracuse (G-13145)
Trusslink ....G...... 219 362-3968
La Porte (G-8832)
Tyler Truss Systems Inc ....F...... 765 221-5050
Pendleton (G-11509)
Ufp Granger LLC ....E... 574 277-7670
Granger (G-5445)

BUILDING & STRUCTURAL WOOD MEMBERS: Arches, Laminated Lumber

Composite Designs Inc ....G... 574 453-2902
Leesburg (G-9235)

BUILDING CLEANING & MAINTENANCE SVCS

A & H Enterprises LLC ....G...... 317 398-3070
Shelbyville (G-12517)
Complete Property Care LLC ....G...... 765 288-0890
Muncie (G-10447)
Onsite Construction Services..............E...... 312 723-8060
Chesterton (G-1625)
Professional Grade Svcs LLC ....G...... 317 688-8898
Indianapolis (G-7772)

BUILDING COMPONENTS: Structural Steel

Aggreate Systems..........................G...... 260 854-4711
Rome City (G-12198)
Almet Inc.................................D...... 260 493-1556
New Haven (G-10928)
Alum-Elec Structures Inc ....G...... 260 347-9362
Kendallville (G-8453)
Benchmark Inc.............................G...... 812 238-0659
Terre Haute (G-13199)
C & C Iron Inc ....E...... 219 769-2511
Merrillville (G-9706)
Cives Corporation ....C...... 219 279-4000
Wolcott (G-14362)
Custom Steel Technologies LLC ....G...... 812 546-2299
Hope (G-6111)
Evans Metal Products Co Inc...............F...... 574 264-2166
Elkhart (G-2838)
Four Star Fabricators Inc ....D...... 812 354-9995
Petersburg (G-11562)
Gary Bridge and Iron Co Inc ....G...... 219 884-3792
Gary (G-5049)
Geiger & Peters Inc ....D...... 317 322-7740
Indianapolis (G-6989)
Harpring Steel Inc ....E...... 812 256-6326
Charlestown (G-1568)
Helgeson Steel Inc ....F...... 574 293-5576
Elkhart (G-2912)
M & S Steel Corp ....E...... 260 357-5184
Garrett (G-5015)
Marion Steel Fabrication Inc ....E...... 765 664-1478
Marion (G-9545)
Munster Steel Co Inc ....G...... 219 924-5198
Hammond (G-5920)
P H Drew Incorporated ....E...... 317 297-5152
Indianapolis (G-7643)
Preferred Tank & Tower Inc................G...... 270 826-7950
Evansville (G-3684)
Productivity Fabricators Inc ....G...... 765 966-2896
Richmond (G-12035)
Rex Alton & Companies Inc ....E...... 812 882-8519
Vincennes (G-13701)
Service Steel Framing Inc ....F...... 260 868-5853
Butler (G-1239)
Sigma Steel Inc ....E...... 812 275-4489
Bedford (G-578)
Sisson Steel Inc ....F...... 812 354-8701
Winslow (G-14359)
Stahl Equipment Inc ....E...... 812 925-3341
Chandler (G-1554)

BUILDING MAINTENANCE SVCS, EXC REPAIRS

D J Investments Inc ....G...... 260 726-7346
Portland (G-11814)
Padgett Inc...............................C...... 812 945-2391
New Albany (G-10839)

BUILDING PRDTS & MATERIALS DEALERS

A L Brewster Plywood Inc ....G...... 765 378-1040
Chesterfield (G-1586)
Complete Lumber Inc ....F...... 812 473-6400
Evansville (G-3426)
Earth First Kentuckiana Inc ....G...... 812 248-0712
Charlestown (G-1565)
Gutter One Supply ....G...... 317 872-1257
Indianapolis (G-7060)
K Lash & Son Inc ....G...... 260 347-3660
Kendallville (G-8482)
Kuntry Lumber and Farm Sup Ltd.........E...... 260 463-3242
Lagrange (G-9051)
Maher Supply Inc ....E...... 812 234-7699
Terre Haute (G-13278)
Richardson Molding LLC ....G...... 317 787-9463
Indianapolis (G-7839)
Steinkamp Warehouses Inc ....E...... 812 683-3860
Huntingburg (G-6179)

Tartan Properties LLC ....G...... 317 714-7337
Indianapolis *(G-8037)*
Tremain Ceramic Tile & Flr Cvg ....E...... 317 542-1491
Indianapolis *(G-8093)*
Woodland Manufacturing & Sup ....F...... 317 271-2266
Avon *(G-472)*

BUILDING PRDTS: Concrete

B & G Sales ....G...... 765 473-7668
Peru *(G-11517)*
Flyover Enterprises Inc ....G...... 317 417-1747
Pendleton *(G-11489)*
Homeowners Equity & Rlty Corp.........G...... 219 981-1700
Gary *(G-5066)*
Omnimax International Inc ....E...... 574 848-7432
Nappanee *(G-10700)*
Quikrete Companies Inc ....E...... 317 251-2281
Indianapolis *(G-7805)*
Southern Indiana Supply Inc ....G...... 812 482-2267
Jasper *(G-8311)*

BUILDING PRDTS: Stone

Artistic Stone Company Inc ....G...... 812 256-2890
Charlestown *(G-1558)*
Superior Canopy Corporation ....E...... 260 488-4065
Hamilton *(G-5829)*

BUILDINGS & COMPONENTS: Prefabricated Metal

All American Homes LLC ....G...... 260 724-7391
Decatur *(G-2367)*
Asphalt Equipment Company Inc.........G...... 260 672-3004
Fort Wayne *(G-4093)*
Benchmark Inc ....F...... 812 238-2691
Terre Haute *(G-13200)*
Biologics Modular LLC ....G...... 317 456-9191
Brownsburg *(G-1137)*
Burns Construction Inc ....E...... 574 382-2315
Macy *(G-9440)*
Classic Buildings Inc...................E...... 812 944-5821
Clarksville *(G-1677)*
CTB MN Investment Co Inc ....E...... 574 658-4191
Milford *(G-9955)*
Falcon Metal Fabrication Inc............F...... 317 255-9365
Indianapolis *(G-6902)*
Jobsite Trailer Corporation ....E...... 574 224-4000
Rochester *(G-12130)*
Lacopa International Inc..................G...... 317 410-1483
Pittsboro *(G-11584)*
Laidig Inc ....E...... 574 256-0204
Mishawaka *(G-10067)*
Lakemaster Inc ....E...... 765 288-3718
Muncie *(G-10507)*
Maurer Constructors Inc ....G...... 812 236-5950
Brazil *(G-968)*
Miller Brothers Builders Inc ....E...... 574 533-8602
Goshen *(G-5293)*
Mobile Mini Inc ....G...... 260 749-6611
Fort Wayne *(G-4479)*
Morton Buildings Inc ....F...... 260 563-2118
Wabash *(G-13741)*
Sigma Steel Inc ....E...... 812 275-4489
Bedford *(G-578)*
Wagler Mini Barn Products ....G...... 812 687-7372
Plainville *(G-11657)*
Woodland Manufacturing & Sup ....F...... 317 271-2266
Avon *(G-472)*
Yoders Quality Barns.......................G...... 260 565-4122
Bluffton *(G-898)*

BUILDINGS: Mobile, For Commercial Use

Commercial Structures Corp ....E...... 574 773-7931
Nappanee *(G-10661)*
Commercial Structures Corp ....G...... 574 773-7931
Goshen *(G-5191)*
Jobsite Trailer Corporation ....E...... 574 224-4000
Rochester *(G-12130)*
Mark-Line Industries LLC ....C...... 574 825-5851
Bristol *(G-1068)*
Whitley Evergreen Inc ....D...... 260 723-5131
South Whitley *(G-13009)*

BUILDINGS: Portable

(ebs Composites) Engineered Bo ....F...... 574 266-3471
Elkhart *(G-2653)*
All Steel Carports Inc ....G...... 765 284-0694
Muncie *(G-10426)*

Chief Industries Inc..........................C...... 219 866-4121
Rensselaer *(G-11917)*
Five Starr Inc ....G...... 812 367-1554
Ferdinand *(G-3851)*
Mobile Mini Inc ....F...... 317 782-1513
Indianapolis *(G-7532)*
Mor/Ryde International Inc ....D...... 574 293-1581
Elkhart *(G-3047)*
Morton Buildings Inc ....F...... 765 932-3979
Rushville *(G-12230)*
Rollin Mini Barns LLC ....G...... 812 687-7581
Odon *(G-11339)*

BUILDINGS: Prefabricated, Wood

(ebs Composites) Engineered Bo ....F...... 574 266-3471
Elkhart *(G-2653)*
Affordable Luxury Homes Inc................D...... 260 758-2141
Markle *(G-9575)*
Burns Construction Inc ....E...... 574 382-2315
Macy *(G-9440)*
Classic Buildings Inc...................E...... 812 944-5821
Clarksville *(G-1677)*
Continntal Crpntry Cmpnnts LLC.........E...... 219 369-4839
Wanatah *(G-13823)*
Landmark Home & Land Co Inc.........G...... 219 874-4065
Michigan City *(G-9808)*
Light House Homes Center ....F...... 765 448-4502
Lafayette *(G-8957)*
Mbsi Holdings LLC ....G...... 574 295-1214
Elkhart *(G-3023)*
Midwest Fast Structures LLC ....G...... 812 886-3060
Vincennes *(G-13692)*
Miller Brothers Builders Inc ....E...... 574 533-8602
Goshen *(G-5293)*
Modular Builders Inc ....E...... 574 223-4934
Rochester *(G-12140)*
Morton Buildings Inc ....G...... 260 563-2118
Wabash *(G-13741)*
Mosier Pallet & Lumber Co ....G...... 812 366-4817
Corydon *(G-2105)*
Neubau Contracting ....G...... 970 406-8084
Bloomington *(G-779)*
TNT Construction ....G...... 260 726-2643
Portland *(G-11852)*
Tuff Shed ....G...... 317 481-8388
Indianapolis *(G-8111)*

BUILDINGS: Prefabricated, Wood

Custom Built Barns Inc ....G...... 765 457-9037
Kokomo *(G-8610)*
Jobsite Trailer Corporation ....E...... 574 224-4000
Rochester *(G-12130)*
Skyline Champion Corporation ....B...... 574 294-6521
Elkhart *(G-3175)*
Tri-State Homes and Garages.............G...... 812 867-2411
Evansville *(G-3773)*
Woodland Manufacturing & Sup ....F...... 317 271-2266
Avon *(G-472)*

BUMPERS: Motor Vehicle

R Concepts Industries Inc..................D...... 574 295-6641
Elkhart *(G-3135)*

BURIAL VAULTS, FIBERGLASS

Cressy Memorial Group Inc ....G...... 574 258-1800
Mishawaka *(G-10025)*

BURIAL VAULTS: Concrete Or Precast Terrazzo

Akron Concrete Products Inc ....F...... 574 893-4841
Akron *(G-1)*
Anderson Memorial Park.......................F...... 765 643-3211
Anderson *(G-65)*
Arrow Vault Co Inc ....G...... 765 742-1704
Lafayette *(G-8853)*
Britton Vault Co Douglas.....................G...... 765 893-4071
Williamsport *(G-14287)*
Calumet Wilbert Vault Co Inc ....F...... 219 980-1173
Gary *(G-5032)*
Century Concrete Inc.........................G...... 765 739-6210
Bainbridge *(G-474)*
Century Grave & Vault Service ....G...... 812 967-2110
Pekin *(G-11470)*
Columbus Vault Co ....G...... 812 372-3210
Columbus *(G-1882)*
Community Vault Inc ....G...... 574 255-3033
Mishawaka *(G-10020)*

Forsyth Brothers Concrete Pdts ....G...... 812 466-4080
Terre Haute *(G-13235)*
Game Vault ....G...... 317 209-7795
Indianapolis *(G-6980)*
Grable Burial Vault Services ....G...... 574 753-4514
Logansport *(G-9335)*
Harris Burial Services ....G...... 812 939-3605
Clay City *(G-1702)*
Harris Pre Cast Inc ....G...... 219 362-2457
La Porte *(G-8761)*
Howard & Sons Cement Products.........G...... 574 293-1906
Elkhart *(G-2922)*
Kreig De Vault ....G...... 317 238-6234
Indianapolis *(G-7369)*
Lebanon Berg Vault Co Inc ....G...... 765 482-0302
Lebanon *(G-9198)*
Mark Concrete Products Inc ....G...... 317 398-8616
Shelbyville *(G-12551)*
Meyer Industries Inc ....G...... 317 769-3497
Whitestown *(G-14256)*
Minnick Concrete Products Inc ....E...... 260 432-5031
Fort Wayne *(G-4477)*
Monticello Vault Burial Co ....G...... 574 583-3206
Monticello *(G-10271)*
Odon Vault Co ....G...... 812 636-7386
Bloomington *(G-783)*
Quality Vault Company ....F...... 812 336-8127
Bloomington *(G-803)*
Rosskovenski Concrete & Rdymx.........G...... 765 832-6103
Clinton *(G-1720)*
Superior Vault Co Inc ....F...... 812 256-5545
Charlestown *(G-1582)*
Superior Vault Co Inc.........................G...... 812 539-1830
Aurora *(G-391)*
Terre Haute Wilbert Burial Vlt ....F...... 812 235-0339
Terre Haute *(G-13353)*
Tretter Boeglin Inc ....G...... 812 683-4598
Huntingburg *(G-6182)*
Van Gard Vault Co Inc ....G...... 219 980-6233
Gary *(G-5114)*
Van Gard Vault Co Inc.........................E...... 219 949-7723
Gary *(G-5115)*
Vault ....G...... 317 784-4000
Beech Grove *(G-604)*
Wayne Burial Vault Company ....G...... 317 357-4656
Indianapolis *(G-8179)*
Wilbert Burial Vault Co Inc ....F...... 317 547-1387
Indianapolis *(G-8195)*
Wilbert Burial Vault Co Inc ....E...... 812 753-3601
Fort Branch *(G-4030)*
Wilbert Sexton Corporation ....G...... 812 336-6469
Bloomington *(G-854)*
Wilbert Sexton Corporation ....G...... 812 372-3210
Columbus *(G-2034)*
Wilson Burial Vault Inc ....G...... 260 356-5722
Huntington *(G-6261)*
Wimmer Vaults Inc ....G...... 765 529-5702
New Castle *(G-10923)*

BURIAL VAULTS: Stone

Dwyer-Wilbert Inc ....G...... 765 962-3605
Richmond *(G-11978)*
Simple Cremations Burials LLC ....G...... 765 592-6226
Clinton *(G-1721)*
Wilbert Sexton Corporation ....G...... 812 334-0883
Bloomington *(G-855)*

BURLAP & BURLAP PRDTS

3w Enterprises LLC ....G...... 847 366-6555
Elkhart *(G-2654)*

BURNERS: Gas, Indl

Trimble Combustion Systems Inc ....G...... 812 623-4545
Sunman *(G-13120)*

BURNERS: Oil, Domestic Or Indl

Wayne/Scott Fetzer Company ....E...... 260 425-9200
Fort Wayne *(G-4745)*

BURNING: Metal

Chicago Flame Hardening Co...............E...... 773 768-3608
East Chicago *(G-2524)*
Estes Designs ....G...... 317 899-5556
Indianapolis *(G-6881)*

2018 Harris Indiana
Industrial Directory

(G-0000) Company's Geographic Section entry number

BUSHINGS & BEARINGS

Complete Drives Inc ....F 260 489-6033
Fort Wayne (G-4171)
LFD Bearings LLC....................G 574 245-0375
Elkhart (G-2996)

BUSHINGS & BEARINGS: Bronze, Exc Machined

Beckett Bronze Company Inc ....E 765 282-2261
Muncie (G-10439)

BUSINESS ACTIVITIES: Non-Commercial Site

103 Collection LLC ....G 800 896-2945
Schererville (G-12312)
1632 Inc ....G 219 398-4155
East Chicago (G-2514)
1global Ds LLC....................F 765 413-2211
Westfield (G-14131)
A & W Firearms ....G 765 716-6856
Yorktown (G-14400)
A-1vet LLC ....G 317 498-1804
Indianapolis (G-6304)
Aeds & Safety Services LLC ....G 502 641-3118
Jeffersonville (G-8321)
Airodapt LLC ....G 559 331-0156
Rensselaer (G-11911)
Amore Forte LLC....................G 702 763-2550
Hammond (G-5842)
Anokhi International Inc ....G 260 750-0418
Fort Wayne (G-4077)
Apr Plastic Fabricating Inc ....E 206 482-8523
Fort Wayne (G-4085)
Ascension Space Technology LLP ......G 765 623-5164
Anderson (G-69)
Best Friends Inc ....G 765 985-3872
Denver (G-2453)
Big Brick House Bakery LLP ....G 260 563-1071
Fort Wayne (G-4107)
Boomstick Interactive LLC..........G 812 528-4875
Indianapolis (G-6496)
Brangene LLC ....G 317 203-9172
Plainfield (G-11597)
Brian J Spilman ....G 765 663-2860
Arlington (G-281)
Byler Sawmill....................G 812 577-5761
Bennington (G-605)
Captivated LLC....................G 317 554-7400
Carmel (G-1328)
Corby Publishing LP ....G 574 229-1107
Lakeville (G-9094)
Crowdpixie LLC....................G 317 578-3137
Fishers (G-3895)
Custom Secure Handles LLC..........G 812 764-4948
Greensburg (G-5597)
Dajac Inc ....G 317 608-0500
Westfield (G-14155)
David M Pszonka....................G 219 988-2235
Hebron (G-6011)
David Tortora ....G 317 506-6902
Carmel (G-1353)
Deep Three Inc ....G 260 705-2283
Spencerville (G-13045)
Digistitch....................G 574 538-3960
Goshen (G-5199)
Digital Cmmnties Intiative Inc ....G 317 580-0111
Carmel (G-1360)
Diverse Sales Solutions LLC ....G 317 514-2403
Indianapolis (G-6747)
Divine Grace Homecare..........G 219 290-5911
Gary (G-5041)
Drinkgp LLC ....G 317 410-4748
Indianapolis (G-6767)
Dux Signal Kits LLC....................G 260 623-3017
Monroeville (G-10194)
Dynamic Landscapes LLC ....E 317 409-3487
Indianapolis (G-6779)
E&P Technologies LLC....................G 317 828-8482
Carmel (G-1366)
Efurnituremax LLC ....G 317 697-9504
Indianapolis (G-6811)
EMB Fishing LLC ....G 317 244-8741
Indianapolis (G-6847)
Eon Performance LLC..........G 847 997-8619
Indianapolis (G-6874)
European Concepts LLC..........G 888 797-9005
Fort Wayne (G-4250)

Express Study LLC....................G 812 272-2247
Bloomington (G-722)
Freehold Games LLC....................G 574 656-9031
Walkerton (G-13802)
Galbe Magazine LLC....................G 248 742-5231
Indianapolis (G-6265)
Gerald S Zins....................G 812 623-4980
Milan (G-9944)
Giles Agency Incorporated ....G 317 842-5546
Indianapolis (G-7005)
Gimme Charge LLC....................G 317 759-4067
Indianapolis (G-7006)
Gonzalez International Inc ....G 317 558-3700
Carmel (G-1387)
Graber ....G 812 636-7699
Odon (G-11326)
Graber Box & Pallet Fmly Lmt P ......E 260 657-5657
Grabill (G-5365)
Graber Lumber LP ....E 260 238-4124
Spencerville (G-13047)
Greene County Pallet Inc ....F 812 384-8362
Bloomfield (G-638)
Hdh Manufacturing Inc ....G 317 918-4088
Indianapolis (G-7083)
Hearts Rmned Lifestyle Cir LLC ......G 800 807-0485
Gary (G-5061)
Hellweg Holdings LLC ....G 317 909-6764
McCordsville (G-9669)
Help Help LLC....................G 317 910-6631
Avon (G-446)
Hoosier Woodworking McHy LLC ....G 812 944-3302
New Albany (G-10798)
Ike Newton LLC....................G 317 902-1772
Greenwood (G-5705)
Innovations By ....G 260 413-1869
Fort Wayne (G-4371)
Interntional Pipe Cons Sls LLC ......F 765 388-2222
New Castle (G-10907)
Job Scholar LLC ....G 419 564-9574
Huntington (G-6221)
Johnny Graber Woodworking..........G 260 466-4957
Grabill (G-5376)
Kelwood Designs LLC Cabinetry ......G 574 862-2472
Goshen (G-5251)
Lh Software Concepts LLC..........G 317 222-1779
Indianapolis (G-7401)
Ligonier Woodworking ....G 260 894-9969
Ligonier (G-9289)
Lord Fms Games ....G 317 710-2253
Indianapolis (G-7419)
Lyra LLC ....G 260 452-4058
Fort Wayne (G-4445)
Magaws of Boston....................G 765 935-6170
Richmond (G-12013)
Mammoth Hats Inc ....F 812 849-2772
Mitchell (G-10166)
Mantra Enterprise LLC ....G 201 428-8709
Fishers (G-3944)
Mercs Miniatures LLC....................G 765 661-6724
Westfield (G-14176)
Modular Green Systems LLC ....G 260 547-4121
Craigville (G-2123)
Mr Mhammads Sweet-Bean Snacks ......G 317 519-0728
Indianapolis (G-7553)
MTA Technology LLC....................F 765 447-2221
Lafayette (G-8973)
Muzfeed Inc ....G 815 252-7676
Fort Wayne (G-4487)
Nelson J Hochstetler....................G 260 499-0315
Howe (G-6130)
North Coast Organics LLC ....G 260 246-0289
Fort Wayne (G-4505)
Omega One Connect Inc ....G 317 626-3445
Indianapolis (G-7618)
Owen County Pallet ....G 812 859-4617
Worthington (G-14395)
Packetvac LLC ....G 317 414-6137
Indianapolis (G-7647)
Phaze One LLC....................G 812 634-9545
Jasper (G-8301)
Pillow Pals Inc....................G 812 853-8241
Newburgh (G-11042)
Plant Engineering Services Inc ......G 260 281-2917
Corunna (G-2085)
Priority Electronics LLC ....G 260 749-0143
New Haven (G-10954)
Qualtronics LLC....................E 812 375-8880
Columbus (G-2004)
Rapar Inc....................G 812 254-9886
Washington (G-14001)

RC Enterprise LLC....................G 317 225-6747
Indianapolis (G-7823)
Rf Manufacturing Inc ....G 317 773-8610
Noblesville (G-11176)
Rob Nolley Inc ....G 317 825-5211
Shelbyville (G-12563)
Ronald Lee Allen ....G 812 644-7649
Loogootee (G-9394)
RTC ....G 260 503-9770
Columbia City (G-1831)
Ruben Martinez ....G 574 735-0803
Logansport (G-9363)
Rubenstein LLC ....G 317 946-2752
Indianapolis (G-7871)
S & R Concessions LLC ....F 260 570-3247
Auburn (G-351)
Setser Fabricating LLC ....G 812 546-2169
Columbus (G-2012)
Snappy Minds Llc ....G 812 661-8506
Jasper (G-8310)
Snuggy Baby LLC ....G 260 418-6795
Fort Wayne (G-4632)
Standard For Success LLC ....F 844 737-3825
Cloverdale (G-1739)
Sugarcube Systems Inc ....G 765 543-6709
Lafayette (G-9005)
Tc4llc ....G 317 709-5429
Fishers (G-3973)
Tgf Enterprises LLC....................G 440 840-9704
Indianapolis (G-8056)
Three Points Alpaca Farm LLC ......G 812 363-3876
Batesville (G-520)
Trill Machine LLC ....G 219 730-0744
Kentland (G-8524)
Trinity Displays Inc ....G 219 201-8733
Michigan City (G-9854)
Trivaeo LLC ....G 765 387-4451
Montezuma (G-10212)
True Chem Inc ....G 317 769-2701
Greenwood (G-5756)
Tt2 LLC....................G 260 438-4575
Fort Wayne (G-4707)
TW Enterprises LLC ....G 513 520-8453
Brookville (G-1128)
Uberlux Inc ....G 317 580-0111
Carmel (G-1501)
Unique Global Solutions LLC ....G 765 779-5030
Anderson (G-180)
Vizai LLC ....G 630 677-6583
Indianapolis (G-8167)
Voidteam Studios ....G 765 414-9777
Lafayette (G-9016)
Wall Control Services Inc ....G 260 450-6411
Fort Wayne (G-4733)
Wittmer Distributors ....G 812 636-7786
Odon (G-11345)

BUSINESS FORMS WHOLESALERS

Allison Payment Systems LLC ....C 317 808-2400
Indianapolis (G-6370)
Altstadt Business Forms Inc ....F 812 425-3393
Evansville (G-3349)
Brand Prtg & Photo-Litho Co..........G 317 921-4095
Indianapolis (G-6503)
Custom Forms Inc ....G 765 463-6162
Lafayette (G-8884)
Excel Business Printing Inc ....G 317 259-1075
Indianapolis (G-6891)
Lucas Bus Forms & Swift Prtg ....G 260 482-7644
Fort Wayne (G-4443)
Moreton Printing Co ....G 812 926-1692
Aurora (G-383)
Perdue Printed Products Inc..........G 260 456-7575
Fort Wayne (G-4523)
Stewart Graphics Inc ....E 812 283-0455
Jeffersonville (G-8430)

BUSINESS FORMS: Printed, Continuous

Highland Computer Forms Inc ....E 260 665-6268
Angola (G-219)
Writeguard Business Systems ....G 317 849-7292
Indianapolis (G-8219)

BUSINESS FORMS: Printed, Manifold

Altstadt Business Forms Inc ....F 812 425-3393
Evansville (G-3349)
Anchor Enterprises....................G 812 282-7220
Jeffersonville (G-8326)

P
R
O
D
U
C
T

Cornelius Printed Products Inc ....E 317 923-1340
Indianapolis *(G-6668)*

E James Dant ....G 812 476-2271
Evansville *(G-3469)*

Falls Cities Printing Inc ....F 812 949-9051
New Albany *(G-10775)*

International Label Mfg LLC ....F 812 235-5071
Terre Haute *(G-13258)*

Label Tech Inc ....E 765 747-1234
Muncie *(G-10506)*

Lincoln Printing Corporation ....E 260 424-5200
Fort Wayne *(G-4437)*

NP Converters Inc ....E 812 448-2555
Brazil *(G-973)*

Pengad/West Inc ....E 765 286-3000
Muncie *(G-10544)*

R R Donnelley & Sons Company ....B 260 624-2350
Angola *(G-242)*

Stewart Graphics Inc ....E 812 283-0455
Jeffersonville *(G-8430)*

Taylor Communications Inc ....D 317 392-3235
Shelbyville *(G-12573)*

Tippecanoe Press Inc ....F 317 392-1207
Shelbyville *(G-12576)*

Wise Business Forms Inc ....C 260 489-1561
Fort Wayne *(G-4759)*

Woodburn Graphics Inc ....E 812 232-0323
Terre Haute *(G-13371)*

BUSINESS MACHINE REPAIR, ELECTRIC

Cummins - Allison Corp ....G 317 872-6244
Indianapolis *(G-6705)*

Lasertone Inc ....F 812 473-5945
Evansville *(G-3598)*

Mid-America Environmental LLC ....F 812 475-1644
Evansville *(G-3626)*

Shearer Printing Service Inc ....E 765 457-3274
Kokomo *(G-8695)*

BUSINESS SUPPORT SVCS

Land Enterprises ....G 317 774-9475
Noblesville *(G-11140)*

Sues Custom Shirts ....G 812 535-4429
Sandford *(G-12311)*

BUSINESS TRAINING SVCS

Kaplan Inc ....D 317 872-7220
Indianapolis *(G-7333)*

Nechanna One Productions Corp ....G 317 400-8908
Indianapolis *(G-7582)*

BUTTONS

Frickers Inc ....E 765 965-6655
Richmond *(G-11988)*

Barium

Ascensia Diabetes Care US Inc ....E 201 875-8066
Mishawaka *(G-9998)*

CABINETS & CASES: Sewing Machine, Wood

Sew Creative Threads LLC ....G 574 266-7397
Elkhart *(G-3163)*

CABINETS & CASES: Show, Display & Storage, Exc Wood

Cabinets & Counters Inc ....E 812 858-3300
Newburgh *(G-11023)*

Carr Metal Products Inc ....C 317 542-0691
Indianapolis *(G-6558)*

Crown Cab & Counter Top Inc ....F 219 663-2725
Crown Point *(G-2238)*

Metal Dynamics Ltd ....E 812 949-7998
New Albany *(G-10826)*

CABINETS: Bathroom Vanities, Wood

Cassini - D & D Mfg Inc ....G 765 449-7992
Lafayette *(G-8870)*

Double T Manufacturing Corp ....F 574 262-1340
Elkhart *(G-2799)*

CABINETS: Entertainment

Eds Wood Craft ....E 812 768-6617
Haubstadt *(G-6000)*

Fehrenbacher Cabinets Inc ....E 812 963-3377
Evansville *(G-3502)*

Heather Sound Amplification ....G 574 255-6100
Mishawaka *(G-10049)*

Innovative Corp ....E 317 804-5977
Westfield *(G-14171)*

Madison Cabinets Inc ....G 260 639-3915
Hoagland *(G-6066)*

Shamrock Cabinets Inc ....E 812 482-7969
Jasper *(G-8308)*

Walters Cabinet Shop ....G 765 452-9634
Kokomo *(G-8714)*

William A Kadar ....G 219 884-7404
Gary *(G-5116)*

CABINETS: Entertainment Units, Household, Wood

Graber Cabinetry LLC ....E 260 627-2243
Grabill *(G-5366)*

J & J Woodcrafters ....G 765 436-2466
Thorntown *(G-13376)*

Larry Graber Cabinets ....G 812 486-2713
Montgomery *(G-10232)*

Rbk Development Inc ....E 574 267-5879
Warsaw *(G-13934)*

Timberline Woodworking Inc ....G 219 766-2733
Kouts *(G-8718)*

CABINETS: Factory

Challenger Door Llc ....E 574 773-8200
Nappanee *(G-10659)*

Concept Cabinet Shop ....G 317 272-7430
Avon *(G-437)*

Country Corner Woodworks LLC ....G 574 825-6782
Middlebury *(G-9878)*

Country Mill Cabinet Co Inc ....F 260 693-9289
Laotto *(G-9106)*

Creative Cabinet Designs ....G 812 637-3300
Lawrenceburg *(G-9135)*

Creative Woodworks LLC ....G 260 450-1742
Fort Wayne *(G-4187)*

Deerwood Group ....G 219 866-5521
Monon *(G-10175)*

Joseph Lee ....G 317 931-9446
Greenwood *(G-5710)*

Lancaster Custom Cabinets Inc ....G 812 949-4750
New Albany *(G-10817)*

Rabb & Howe Cabinet Top Co ....F 317 926-6442
Indianapolis *(G-7811)*

Richeson Contracting Inc ....E 317 889-5995
Indianapolis *(G-7840)*

Signet Millwork LLC ....E 812 248-0612
Sellersburg *(G-12417)*

Top Design Cnc Inc ....G 219 662-2915
Valparaiso *(G-13629)*

United Cabinet Corporation Nit ....G 812 482-2561
Jasper *(G-8312)*

United Home Supply Inc ....G 765 288-2737
Muncie *(G-10576)*

Willie and Associates Inc ....G 219 662-9046
Crown Point *(G-2320)*

CABINETS: Kitchen, Metal

Stainless Steel Kitchens ....G 574 272-2530
Granger *(G-5440)*

Warren Homes Inc ....G 812 882-1059
Vincennes *(G-13716)*

CABINETS: Kitchen, Wood

AAA Cabinet Guy LLC ....G 574 299-9371
South Bend *(G-12690)*

Academy Inc ....G 574 293-7113
Elkhart *(G-2663)*

Acme Cabinets Corp ....G 219 924-1800
Griffith *(G-5760)*

Advanced Cabinet Systems Inc ....D 765 677-8000
Marion *(G-9506)*

Aldridge Cabinets ....G 812 873-6723
Deputy *(G-2458)*

All About Organizing ....G 513 238-8157
Lawrenceburg *(G-9130)*

American Woodmark Corporation ....B 765 677-1690
Gas City *(G-5118)*

Americas Cabinet Co of Ind ....G 317 788-9533
Greenfield *(G-5500)*

Architectural Accents Inc ....F 219 922-9333
Munster *(G-10596)*

Aristoline Cabinet Inc ....E 260 482-9719
Fort Wayne *(G-4090)*

B & L Custom Cabinets Inc ....G 765 379-2471
Rossville *(G-12209)*

Baum Cabinetry LLC ....G 219 575-6309
Valparaiso *(G-13506)*

Beebe Cabinet Co Inc ....F 574 293-3580
Elkhart *(G-2720)*

Bremtown Fine Cstm Cbnetry Inc ....D 574 546-2781
Bremen *(G-988)*

Brookwood Cabinet Company Inc ....F 260 749-5012
Fort Wayne *(G-4123)*

Burns Cabinets and Disp Inc ....G 260 897-2219
Avilla *(G-401)*

C & R Woodworks ....G 317 422-9603
Martinsville *(G-9596)*

Cabinet & Countertop Solutio ....G 219 775-3540
Crown Point *(G-2232)*

Cabinet Cottage LLC ....G 317 369-0051
Noblesville *(G-11077)*

Cabinet Crafters Corp ....G 765 724-7074
Alexandria *(G-37)*

Cabinetmaker Inc ....G 812 723-3461
Paoli *(G-11446)*

Cabinetry Green LLC ....G 317 842-1550
Fishers *(G-3883)*

Cabinetry Ideas Inc ....G 317 722-1300
Indianapolis *(G-6532)*

Cabinets By Gentry ....G 765 378-7900
Anderson *(G-80)*

Cabinets By Rick Inc ....G 812 945-2220
New Albany *(G-10757)*

Carriage House Woodworking ....G 317 406-3042
Plainfield *(G-11599)*

Carter Cabinet Co Inc ....G 317 985-5782
New Palestine *(G-10969)*

Cedar Woodworking ....G 812 486-2765
Montgomery *(G-10216)*

Coblentz Cabinet..................................G 812 687-7525
Montgomery *(G-10217)*

Columbus Cstm Cbinets Furn LLC ......G 812 379-9411
Columbus *(G-1875)*

Commercial Electric Co Inc ....E 260 726-9357
Portland *(G-11813)*

Coppes-Nappanee Company Inc ....F 574 773-0007
Nappanee *(G-10663)*

Corbetts Custom Cabinetry LLC ....G 812 670-6211
Jeffersonville *(G-8346)*

Corner Cabinet ....G 317 859-6336
Greenwood *(G-5676)*

Cornerstone Cabinetry LLC ....G 574 250-2690
Granger *(G-5397)*

Counterfitters Inc ....G 219 531-0848
Valparaiso *(G-13523)*

Countertop Connections Inc ....G 317 822-9858
Franklin *(G-4878)*

Countertops & More ....G 317 346-0111
Franklin *(G-4879)*

Country Cabinets ....G 260 694-6777
Poneto *(G-11745)*

Country View Cabinets LLC ....G 574 825-3150
Goshen *(G-5193)*

Countryside Cabinetry LLC ....G 765 597-2391
Marshall *(G-9590)*

County Line Cabinetry LLC ....G 574 642-1202
Middlebury *(G-9879)*

Crossrads Cntrtops Cbnetry LLC ....G 317 908-9254
Indianapolis *(G-6696)*

Crown Cab & Counter Top Inc ....F 219 663-2725
Crown Point *(G-2238)*

Crown Supply Co Inc ....F 812 522-6987
Seymour *(G-12440)*

Custom Built Cabinets and ....G 812 427-9733
Vevay *(G-13662)*

Custom Cabinet & Millwork ....G 219 696-9827
Lowell *(G-9403)*

Custom Cabinets & Furn LLC ....F 812 486-2503
Montgomery *(G-10220)*

Custom Design Laminates Inc ....F 574 674-9174
Osceola *(G-11375)*

Custom Tables & Cabinets ....G 812 486-3831
Montgomery *(G-10221)*

Dan Goode Cabinet ....G 317 541-9878
Indianapolis *(G-6724)*

Daugherty Cabinets ....G 574 272-9205
Granger *(G-5400)*

Doors & Drawers Inc ....F 574 533-3509
Goshen *(G-5203)*

Douglas Dye and Associates ....G 317 844-1709
Carmel *(G-1362)*

DS Woods Custom Cabinets ....G 260 692-6565
Decatur *(G-2376)*

Dutch Made Inc ....C 260 657-3311
  Grabill (G-5363)
Dutch Made Inc ....G 260 657-3331
  Harlan (G-5970)
E & S Wood Creations LLC ....F 260 768-3033
  Lagrange (G-9040)
Eds Wood Craft ....G 812 768-6617
  Haubstadt (G-6000)
Elko Inc ....E 812 473-8400
  Evansville (G-3473)
Evia Custom Cabinets LLC ....G 317 987-5504
  Carmel (G-1376)
Fehrenbacher Cabinets Inc ....E 812 963-3377
  Evansville (G-3502)
Fergys Cabinets ....G 765 529-0116
  New Castle (G-10900)
Finish Alternatives ....G 317 440-2899
  Indianapolis (G-6922)
Fusion Wood Products LLC ....G 574 389-0307
  Elkhart (G-2872)
Gentrys Cabinet Inc ....G 765 643-6611
  Anderson (G-109)
Graber Cabinetry LLC ....E 260 627-2243
  Grabill (G-5366)
Graber Furniture ....G 812 295-4939
  Loogootee (G-9383)
Graber Woodworks Inc ....G 812 486-2861
  Montgomery (G-10226)
Grabill Cabinet Company Inc ....C 877 472-2782
  Grabill (G-5368)
Grabill Woodworking Specialty ....G 260 627-5982
  Grabill (G-5371)
Granitech ....E 574 674-6988
  Elkhart (G-2893)
H-C Liquidating Corp ....A 574 535-9300
  Goshen (G-5233)
Haas Cabinet Co Inc ....C 812 246-4431
  Sellersburg (G-12395)
Hackman Cabinet Co ....G 812 522-4118
  Seymour (G-12452)
Hardwood Door Mfg LLC ....G 812 486-3313
  Montgomery (G-10228)
Harlan Cabinets Inc ....D 260 657-5154
  Harlan (G-5972)
Healey Custom Cabinetry LLC ....G 574 946-4000
  Winamac (G-14307)
Herb Rahman & Sons Inc ....G 812 367-2513
  Ferdinand (G-3852)
Heritage Cabinets LLC ....G 812 963-3435
  Wadesville (G-13772)
Heritage Fine Furn & Cabinetry ....G 812 205-5437
  Evansville (G-3538)
Houck Industries Inc ....E 812 663-5675
  Greensburg (G-5614)
Hurst Custom Cabinets Inc ....G 812 683-3378
  Huntingburg (G-6170)
Independent Cabinets ....G 502 594-6026
  Memphis (G-9683)
Innovative Corp ....E 317 804-5977
  Westfield (G-14171)
Interior Fixs & Mllwk Co Inc ....G 812 446-0933
  Knightsville (G-8561)
J & J Cabinets ....G 219 374-6816
  Cedar Lake (G-1530)
J and G Enterprises ....G 219 778-4319
  Rolling Prairie (G-12188)
J G Cabinet & Counter Inc ....G 260 723-4275
  Larwill (G-9123)
J Miller Cabinetry Inc ....G 260 691-2032
  Columbia City (G-1800)
James G Henager ....G 812 795-2230
  Elberfeld (G-2636)
Jds Pugh Cabinets Inc ....F 317 835-2910
  Fairland (G-3822)
John Pater Design Fabrication ....F 812 926-4845
  Aurora (G-381)
Johnny Bontrager ....G 260 463-8912
  Lagrange (G-9050)
Johnny Graber Woodworking ....G 260 466-4957
  Grabill (G-5376)
Johns Fine Cabinetry ....G 765 296-2388
  Colburn (G-1753)
JP Custom Cabinetry Inc ....G 219 956-3587
  Wheatfield (G-14226)
Jrs Custom Cabinets Co ....E 219 696-7205
  Lowell (G-9410)
Kelwood Designs LLC Cabinetry ....G 574 862-2472
  Goshen (G-5251)
Kitchen Jewels Inc ....E 812 482-9663
  Jasper (G-8286)

Kitchen Kompact Inc ....C 812 282-6681
  Jeffersonville (G-8390)
Kitchen Konnection Inc ....G 812 277-0393
  Bedford (G-557)
Kline Cabinet Makers LLC ....F 317 326-3049
  Maxwell (G-9662)
Kokomo Cabinetry ....G 765 457-2385
  Kokomo (G-8652)
Kountry Wood Products LLC ....C 574 773-5673
  Nappanee (G-10689)
Kramer Furn & Cab Makers Inc ....F 812 526-2711
  Edinburgh (G-2615)
Lambright Woodworking LLC ....E 260 593-2721
  Topeka (G-13423)
Lami-Crafts Inc ....G 812 232-3012
  Terre Haute (G-13270)
Laminique Inc ....E 765 482-4222
  Lebanon (G-9197)
Leroy E Doty Cabinet Shop ....G 219 663-1139
  Crown Point (G-2275)
Lockerbie Square Cab Co Inc ....G 317 635-1134
  Indianapolis (G-7413)
Madison Cabinets Inc ....G 260 639-3915
  Hoagland (G-6066)
Madison County Cabinets Inc ....F 765 778-4646
  Pendleton (G-11493)
Marcotte Cabinets ....G 574 520-1342
  Granger (G-5419)
Martinson Cabinet Shop ....G 219 926-1566
  Chesterton (G-1619)
Masterbrand Cabinets Inc ....G 812 482-2527
  Jasper (G-8290)
Masterbrand Cabinets Inc ....B 765 966-3940
  Richmond (G-12015)
Masterbrand Cabinets Inc ....B 812 482-2527
  Jasper (G-8291)
Masterbrand Cabinets Inc ....G 574 535-9300
  Goshen (G-5282)
Masterbrand Cabinets Inc ....D 812 482-2527
  Celestine (G-1536)
Masterbrand Cabinets Inc ....C 812 482-2513
  Jasper (G-8292)
Masterbrand Cabinets Inc ....A 812 367-1104
  Ferdinand (G-3858)
Masterbrand Cabinets Inc ....C 812 482-2527
  Huntingburg (G-6175)
Masterbrand Cabinets Inc ....B 256 362-5530
  Jasper (G-8293)
Mc Custom Cabinets Inc ....G 502 641-1528
  Underwood (G-13451)
McKinney & Sell Inc ....G 877 665-3300
  Bourbon (G-945)
Meyer Custom Woodworking Inc ....G 812 695-2021
  Dubois (G-2477)
Michiana Cabinet & Refacing LL ....G 574 277-0801
  Granger (G-5420)
Milestone Cabinetry ....G 219 947-0600
  Merrillville (G-9735)
Miller Cabinetry & Furn LLC ....G 260 657-5052
  Grabill (G-5380)
Miller Maid Cabinets Inc ....F 317 786-0418
  Indianapolis (G-7520)
Millers Custom Cabinets ....G 260 768-7830
  Shipshewana (G-12636)
Mouron & Company Inc ....F 317 243-7955
  Indianapolis (G-7551)
Muncie Cabinet Discounters ....G 765 216-7367
  Muncie (G-10527)
Myers Cabinet Company ....G 765 342-7781
  Martinsville (G-9628)
N & K Cabinet Inc ....G 765 552-6997
  Elwood (G-3308)
Orchard Lane Cabinets ....G 574 825-7568
  Goshen (G-5302)
Oxford Cabinet Company LLC ....G 765 223-2101
  Liberty (G-9269)
Patrick Industries Inc ....E 574 293-1521
  Elkhart (G-3084)
Paynes Fine Cabinetry ....G 765 589-9176
  Lafayette (G-8978)
Peace Valley Cabinets Inc ....G 812 238-5134
  Terre Haute (G-13300)
Peace Valley Cabinets Inc ....G 812 486-3831
  Montgomery (G-10237)
Philip Konrad & Sons Inc ....F 574 772-3966
  Knox (G-8576)
Phoenix Custom Kitchens Inc ....G 812 523-1890
  Seymour (G-12475)
Plastic Line Manufacturing ....E 219 769-8022
  Merrillville (G-9747)

Pumpkin Patch Market Inc ....G 574 825-3312
  Middlebury (G-9915)
R & R Custom Woodworking Inc ....E 574 773-5436
  Nappanee (G-10703)
Rabb & Howe Cabinet Top Co ....F 317 926-6442
  Indianapolis (G-7811)
Radel Wood Products Inc ....F 765 472-2940
  Peru (G-11543)
Rainbow Design Inc ....E 260 593-2856
  Lagrange (G-9063)
Rbk Development Inc ....E 574 267-5879
  Warsaw (G-13934)
Rmg Cabinet ....G 219 712-6129
  Hammond (G-5935)
Rogers Cabinetry ....G 574 664-9931
  Logansport (G-9362)
Roh Custom Cabinetry LLC ....E 260 802-1158
  Silver Lake (G-12679)
Ronald Chileen Furniture ....G 574 542-4505
  Rochester (G-12150)
Rush County Wood Products ....G 765 629-0603
  Milroy (G-9986)
S & H Cabinets ....G 574 773-7465
  Nappanee (G-10705)
Saco Industries Inc ....B 219 690-9900
  Lowell (G-9422)
Schmidt Cabinet Co Inc ....E 812 347-1031
  New Salisbury (G-11011)
Schrock Cabinet ....G 812 482-2527
  Jasper (G-8304)
Shamrock Cabinets Inc ....G 812 482-7969
  Jasper (G-8308)
Signet Cabinetry Inc ....G 812 248-0612
  Sellersburg (G-12416)
Sims Cabinet Co Inc ....E 317 634-1747
  Indianapolis (G-7948)
Sorensen Custom Cabinets ....G 765 292-2225
  Tipton (G-13405)
Spiceland Wood Products Inc ....F 765 987-8156
  Spiceland (G-13058)
Steves Cabinets & More ....G 765 296-9419
  Colburn (G-1754)
Strohbeck Cabinet Install ....G 812 923-5013
  Floyds Knobs (G-4019)
Superior Laminating Inc ....F 574 361-7266
  Goshen (G-5331)
TCS Cabinets ....G 765 208-5350
  Summitville (G-13107)
Trillium Cabinet Company Inc ....G 317 471-8870
  Indianapolis (G-8100)
Twin Spires Cabinetry LLC ....G 502 644-4183
  Jeffersonville (G-8436)
Vans Cabinet Shop ....G 574 658-9625
  Milford (G-9966)
Village Workshop Inc ....G 812 933-1527
  Oldenburg (G-11346)
Waglers Custom Cabinets ....G 812 486-2878
  Montgomery (G-10247)
Walburn Service Inc ....G 765 289-3383
  Muncie (G-10578)
Walters Cabinet Shop ....G 765 452-9634
  Kokomo (G-8714)
Warsaw Custom Cabinet ....G 574 267-5794
  Winona Lake (G-14354)
Warsaw Custom Cabinet ....G 574 267-5794
  Warsaw (G-13960)
William A Kadar ....G 219 884-7404
  Gary (G-5116)
William R Arvin ....G 812 486-5255
  Loogootee (G-9398)
Wisemans Custom Cabinets Inc ....G 812 678-3601
  Dubois (G-2478)
Yoder Kitchen Corp ....E 574 773-3197
  Nappanee (G-10711)
Yoders Cabinets ....G 812 486-3826
  Montgomery (G-10249)
Zinn Kitchens Inc ....E 574 967-4179
  Bringhurst (G-1039)
Zionsville Custom Cabinets ....G 317 339-0380
  Zionsville (G-14473)

CABINETS: Office, Metal

All State Manufacturing Co Inc ....F 812 466-2276
  Terre Haute (G-13191)
Deerwood Group ....G 219 866-5521
  Monon (G-10175)

CABINETS: Office, Wood

A L E Enterprises ....G 317 856-2981
  Indianapolis (G-6297)

PRODUCT

Custom Hardwood Cabinetry ....G...... 260 623-3147
Monroeville (G-10193)

Delbert Kemp ....E...... 812 486-3325
Montgomery (G-10222)

Eds Wood Craft ....G...... 812 768-6617
Haubstadt (G-6000)

Gehl Industries Inc ....F...... 574 773-7663
Nappanee (G-10672)

Hensley Custom Cabinetry ....G...... 219 843-5331
Rensselaer (G-11927)

Laminated Tops of Terre Haute ....G...... 812 235-2920
Terre Haute (G-13271)

Leroy E Doty Cabinet Shop ....G...... 219 663-1139
Crown Point (G-2275)

Rabb & Howe Cabinet Top Co ....F...... 317 926-6442
Indianapolis (G-7811)

Steffy Wood Products Inc ....E...... 260 665-8016
Angola (G-246)

CABINETS: Radio, Plastic

Midwest Cabinet Solutions Inc ....F...... 765 664-3938
Marion (G-9547)

CABINETS: Show, Display, Etc, Wood, Exc Refrigerated

Beebe Cabinet Co Inc ....F...... 574 293-3580
Elkhart (G-2720)

Coppes-Nappanee Company Inc ....F...... 574 773-0007
Nappanee (G-10663)

Deem & Loureiro Inc ....G...... 770 652-9871
Indianapolis (G-6731)

Freedom Valley Cabinets ....G...... 812 875-2509
Freedom (G-4948)

Graber Cabinetry LLC ....E...... 260 627-2243
Grabill (G-5366)

Jensen Cabinet Inc ....E...... 260 456-2131
Fort Wayne (G-4394)

Middlebury Hardwood Pdts Inc ....C...... 574 825-9524
Middlebury (G-9907)

Timberline Woodworking Inc ....G...... 219 766-2733
Kouts (G-8718)

Wagners Plasti Craft Co ....G...... 260 627-3147
Fort Wayne (G-4731)

Wert Fixture & Display Inc ....G...... 317 577-0905
Indianapolis (G-8184)

Woods Unlimited Inc ....G...... 574 656-3382
North Liberty (G-11223)

Zehrhaus Inc ....G...... 260 486-3198
Fort Wayne (G-4764)

CABINETS: Stereo, Wood

Kimball International Inc ....B...... 812 482-1600
Jasper (G-8282)

CABLE & OTHER PAY TELEVISION DISTRIBUTION

Vectren Corporation ....E...... 812 424-6411
Evansville (G-3795)

Vision Aid Systems Inc ....G...... 317 888-0323
Greenwood (G-5758)

CABLE & PAY TELEVISION SVCS: Closed Circuit

American Eagle Security Inc ....G...... 219 980-1177
Merrillville (G-9696)

CABLE TELEVISION

Essex Group Inc ....C...... 260 424-1708
Fort Wayne (G-4248)

Times ....E...... 765 296-3622
Frankfort (G-4856)

CABLE WIRING SETS: Battery, Internal Combustion Engines

East Penn Manufacturing Co ....G...... 317 236-6288
Indianapolis (G-6791)

CABLE: Fiber

Apollo North America Inc ....G...... 317 573-0777
Carmel (G-1312)

C-Cat Inc ....F...... 317 568-2899
Indianapolis (G-6531)

CABLE: Fiber Optic

Precision Utilities Group Inc ....C...... 260 485-8300
Fort Wayne (G-4553)

CABLE: Noninsulated

Khorporate Holdings Inc ....C...... 260 357-3365
Laotto (G-9110)

CABLE: Steel, Insulated Or Armored

Sanlo Inc ....D...... 219 879-0241
Michigan City (G-9841)

Tway Company Incorporated ....E...... 317 636-2591
Indianapolis (G-8116)

CAFES

Harvest Cafe Coffee & Tea LLC ....G...... 317 585-9162
Indianapolis (G-7079)

South Bend Chocolate Co Inc ....F...... 574 233-2577
South Bend (G-12942)

CAGES: Wire

Fix & Sons Manufacturing Inc ....F...... 765 724-4041
Alexandria (G-42)

General Cage LLC ....E...... 765 552-5039
Anderson (G-108)

Mid-West Metal Products Co Inc ....D...... 765 741-3137
Muncie (G-10523)

Rabers Buggy Shop LLC ....G...... 812 486-3789
Montgomery (G-10239)

CALENDARS, WHOLESALE

Kellmark Corporation ....E...... 574 264-9695
Elkhart (G-2958)

Tfi Inc ....F...... 317 290-1333
Indianapolis (G-8055)

CALIBRATING SVCS, NEC

Qig LLC ....E...... 260 244-3591
Columbia City (G-1821)

Qig LLC ....E...... 260 244-3591
Columbia City (G-1822)

CAMERA & PHOTOGRAPHIC SPLYS STORES

Roi Marketing Company ....G...... 317 644-0797
Indianapolis (G-7855)

CAMERAS & RELATED EQPT: Photographic

Camerabee LLC ....G...... 317 546-2999
Indianapolis (G-6544)

CAMPERS: Truck Mounted

Indiana Interstate Entps LLC ....G...... 260 463-8100
Lagrange (G-9047)

CAMPERS: Truck, Slide-In

Cruiser Rv LLC ....D...... 260 562-3500
Howe (G-6120)

CAMSHAFTS

Hapco Rebuilders Inc ....G...... 812 232-2550
Terre Haute (G-13245)

CAN LIDS & ENDS

Ball Metal Beverage Cont Corp ....C...... 574 583-9418
Monticello (G-10254)

CANDLE SHOPS

Past & Present Soap & Snd LLC ....G...... 812 852-4328
Batesville (G-514)

Taylor Made Candles ....G...... 812 663-6634
Greensburg (G-5636)

Village Candlemaker Inc ....G...... 812 988-7201
Nashville (G-10737)

Yankee Candle Company Inc ....G...... 812 526-5195
Edinburgh (G-2632)

Yankee Candle Company Inc ....G...... 812 234-1717
Terre Haute (G-13373)

CANDLES

AVO Candle Company LLC ....G...... 812 822-2302
Bloomington (G-668)

B Honey & Candles ....G...... 574 642-1145
Shipshewana (G-12605)

Bittersweet Candle Company LLC ....F...... 317 782-3170
Indianapolis (G-6478)

CA Steel Country Candles ....G...... 812 290-8516
Aurora (G-374)

Celestial Candle ....G...... 812 886-4819
Vincennes (G-13672)

Christian Candle Company ....G...... 317 427-8070
Indianapolis (G-6602)

Christys Candles Inc ....G...... 812 273-3072
Madison (G-9450)

Country Barn Candles LLC ....G...... 812 299-2929
Terre Haute (G-13217)

Farm Finds Candle Co LLC ....G...... 260 437-5403
Fort Wayne (G-4255)

Green Way Candle Company LLC ....G...... 574 536-3802
Goshen (G-5230)

Homestead Industries Inc ....G...... 574 273-5274
Granger (G-5413)

Jacobs Country Candles LLC ....G...... 765 557-0260
Elwood (G-3302)

KS Kreations ....G...... 574 514-7366
Georgetown (G-5147)

Light Mine Candle Company LLC ....G...... 317 353-7786
Indianapolis (G-7405)

Lighthouse Creat Candles Gifts ....G...... 765 342-2920
Martinsville (G-9620)

Magic Candle Inc ....G...... 317 357-1101
Indianapolis (G-7437)

Rosmarino Candles LLC ....G...... 970 218-2835
Bloomington (G-818)

Rustic Glow Candle Co LLC ....G...... 317 696-4264
Indianapolis (G-7875)

Schwartz Manufacturing Inc ....G...... 260 589-3865
Berne (G-622)

Taylor Made Candles ....G...... 812 663-6634
Greensburg (G-5636)

Timberlight Mfg Co ....G...... 317 694-1317
Martinsville (G-9642)

Twisod Wick Candle Company ....G...... 317 490-4789
Martinsville (G-9645)

Twisted Wick Candle Co ....G...... 812 988-6123
Nashville (G-10735)

Unplug Soy Candles LLC ....G...... 317 650-5776
Fortville (G-4783)

Village Candlemaker Inc ....G...... 812 988-7201
Nashville (G-10737)

Warm Glow Candle Company ....E...... 765 855-5483
Centerville (G-1544)

CANDLES: Wholesalers

Yankee Candle Company Inc ....G...... 812 526-5195
Edinburgh (G-2632)

Yankee Candle Company Inc ....G...... 812 234-1717
Terre Haute (G-13373)

CANDY & CONFECTIONS: Candy Bars, Including Chocolate Covered

Donaldsons Chocolates Inc ....F...... 765 482-3334
Lebanon (G-9181)

Whiskey Business ....G...... 317 823-5078
Indianapolis (G-8191)

CANDY & CONFECTIONS: Chocolate Candy, Exc Solid Chocolate

Debrand Inc ....D...... 260 969-8333
Fort Wayne (G-4203)

Libs Mike & Choclat Fctry LLC ....G...... 812 424-8750
Evansville (G-3601)

CANDY & CONFECTIONS: Fudge

Copper Kettle Fudge LLC ....G...... 260 417-1036
Fort Wayne (G-4174)

Old World Fudge & Cds Dogs LLC ....G...... 260 610-2249
Columbia City (G-1815)

CANDY & CONFECTIONS: Licorice

American Licorice Company ....E...... 510 487-5500
La Porte (G-8731)

American Licorice Company ....C...... 219 362-5790
La Porte (G-8732)

CANDY & CONFECTIONS: Popcorn Balls/Other Trtd Popcorn Prdts

Heidipops Gourmet Popcorn LLC ....G....... 317 863-0844
  Plainfield (G-11614)
Wsg Manufacturing LLC ....G....... 765 934-2101
  Whitestown (G-14265)

CANDY, NUT & CONFECTIONERY STORES: Candy

Abbotts Candy and Gifts Inc ....E....... 765 489-4442
  Hagerstown (G-5801)
Lowerys Home Made Candies ....E....... 765 288-7300
  Muncie (G-10513)
Olympia Candy Kitchen ....F....... 574 533-5040
  Goshen (G-5301)
Schimpff Confectionery ....F....... 812 283-8367
  Jeffersonville (G-8423)
South Bend Chocolate Co Inc ....F....... 574 233-2577
  South Bend (G-12942)
Stephen Libs Candy Co Inc ....F....... 812 473-0048
  Evansville (G-3748)
Sweet Things Inc ....F....... 317 872-8720
  Indianapolis (G-8028)

CANDY: Hard

David M Pszonka ....G....... 219 988-2235
  Hebron (G-6011)

CANDY: Soft

Queen City Candy LLC ....G....... 812 537-5203
  Greendale (G-5494)

CANNED SPECIALTIES

Frito-Lay North America Inc ....B....... 765 659-1831
  Frankfort (G-4834)
Mead Johnson & Company LLC ....B....... 812 429-5000
  Evansville (G-3620)
Vitamins Inc ....E....... 219 879-7356
  Michigan City (G-9859)

CANOPIES: Sheet Metal

Centurion Industries Inc ....D....... 260 357-6665
  Garrett (G-4996)
Scotia Corporation ....E....... 260 479-8800
  Fort Wayne (G-4610)
Superior Canopy Corporation ....E....... 260 488-4065
  Hamilton (G-5829)

CANS & CASES: Capacitor Or Condenser, Stamped Metal

Kirby Risk Corporation ....F....... 317 398-9713
  Shelbyville (G-12543)
Productivity Resources Inc ....G....... 317 245-4040
  Noblesville (G-11166)

CANS & TUBES: Ammunition, Board Laminated With Metal Foil

Tube Fabrication Inds Inc ....E....... 574 753-6377
  Logansport (G-9372)

CANS: Composite Foil-Fiber, Made From Purchased Materials

Jt Composites LLC ....G....... 317 297-9520
  Indianapolis (G-7320)

CANS: Metal

Ameri Kan ....G....... 574 533-7032
  Warsaw (G-13838)
Ball Inc ....F....... 317 736-8236
  Franklin (G-4871)
Bev Rexam Can Americas Inc ....G....... 773 399-3000
  West Lafayette (G-14052)
Bway Corporation ....D....... 219 462-8915
  Valparaiso (G-13517)
Crown Cork & Seal Usa Inc ....D....... 765 362-3200
  Crawfordsville (G-2146)
Norton Packaging Inc ....E....... 574 867-6002
  Hamlet (G-5831)
Powell Systems Inc ....G....... 765 884-0613
  Fowler (G-4804)
R & M Welding & Fabricating Sp ....G....... 812 295-9130
  Loogootee (G-9392)

Silgan Containers Mfg Corp ....D....... 219 845-1500
  Hammond (G-5939)
Silgan Containers Mfg Corp ....D....... 219 362-7002
  La Porte (G-8823)
Silgan White Cap Corporation ....C....... 812 425-6222
  Evansville (G-3731)
Silgan White Cap Corporation ....C....... 765 983-9200
  Richmond (G-12050)

CANVAS PRDTS

Coverite-Custom Covers ....G....... 574 278-7152
  Monticello (G-10258)
Dometic Corporation ....B....... 260 463-7657
  Lagrange (G-9037)
Fort Wayne Awning Co Inc ....G....... 260 478-1636
  Fort Wayne (G-4269)
Hare Canvas Products ....G....... 260 758-8800
  Markle (G-9577)
Marine Mooring Inc ....E....... 574 594-5787
  Warsaw (G-13903)
Meese Inc ....D....... 812 273-1008
  Madison (G-9485)
Miller Canvas Shop ....G....... 574 658-3563
  Milford (G-9959)
Veada Industries Inc ....A....... 574 831-4775
  New Paris (G-11000)
Vessell Trim Co ....F....... 812 424-2963
  Evansville (G-3797)

CANVAS PRDTS: Air Cushions & Mattresses

Cork Medical LLC ....G....... 317 361-4651
  Indianapolis (G-6667)

CANVAS PRDTS: Convertible Tops, Car/Boat, Fm Purchased Mtrl

Angola Canvas Co Inc ....F....... 260 665-9913
  Angola (G-191)

CANVAS PRDTS: Shades, Made From Purchased Materials

AK Supply Inc ....F....... 317 895-0410
  Indianapolis (G-6358)

CAPACITORS: Fixed Or Variable

Kirby Risk Corporation ....D....... 765 448-4567
  Lafayette (G-8940)

CAPACITORS: NEC

A C Mallory Capacitors LLC ....D....... 317 612-1000
  Indianapolis (G-6293)
Eternal Energy LLC ....G....... 260 410-3056
  Fort Wayne (G-4249)
Greatbatch Ltd ....F....... 260 755-7484
  Warsaw (G-13886)
Integer Holdings Corporation ....G....... 260 373-1664
  Fort Wayne (G-4377)
Kirby Risk Corporation ....F....... 317 398-9713
  Shelbyville (G-12543)
Regal-Beloit Corporation ....D....... 260 416-5400
  Fort Wayne (G-4587)

CAPS: Plastic

Drug Plastics Closures Inc ....D....... 812 526-0555
  Edinburgh (G-2608)

CAR WASH EQPT

Hose & Go ....G....... 574 295-7800
  Elkhart (G-2921)
Kelley Cadillac LLC ....G....... 260 434-4646
  Fort Wayne (G-4406)
Laserwash ....G....... 765 359-0582
  Crawfordsville (G-2167)
Michiana Carwash Systems LLC ....G....... 574 320-2331
  Goshen (G-5288)
Super Car Wash of Warsaw ....F....... 574 269-6922
  Warsaw (G-13943)
Supper Wash ....G....... 574 269-2233
  Warsaw (G-13944)

CAR WASH EQPT & SPLYS WHOLESALERS

Whitlocks Pressure Wash ....F....... 765 825-5868
  Connersville (G-2078)

CAR WASHES

Super Car Wash of Warsaw ....F....... 574 269-6922
  Warsaw (G-13943)

CARBIDES

Gill Carbide Saw & Tl Svc LLC ....G....... 317 698-6787
  Martinsville (G-9609)
Karyn K Cleveland ....G....... 317 698-6787
  Martinsville (G-9619)

CARBON & GRAPHITE PRDTS, NEC

Aerodine Composites LLC ....F....... 317 271-1207
  Indianapolis (G-6347)
Aerodine Engineering Group LLC ....G....... 317 271-1207
  Indianapolis (G-6348)
Demotte Manufacturing Inc ....G....... 219 987-6196
  Demotte (G-2435)
Hickman Williams & Company ....G....... 812 522-6293
  Seymour (G-12454)
Hickman Williams & Company ....F....... 708 656-8818
  La Porte (G-8764)
Indy Prfmce Composites Inc ....G....... 317 858-7793
  Brownsburg (G-1154)

CARBON BLACK

Dean Co Inc ....G....... 317 891-2518
  Greenfield (G-5520)

CARBURETORS

Tecumseh Products Company ....B....... 812 883-3575
  Salem (G-12307)

CARDS: Color

Colwell Inc ....C....... 260 347-1981
  Kendallville (G-8464)
Colwell Inc ....C....... 260 347-1981
  Kendallville (G-8465)

CARDS: Greeting

Behning Inc ....G....... 260 672-2663
  Roanoke (G-12099)
Celebrate Season ....F....... 609 261-5200
  Sunman (G-13109)
Kellmark Corporation ....E....... 574 264-9695
  Elkhart (G-2958)
McPhersons (us) Inc ....C....... 812 623-2225
  Sunman (G-13114)
Nussmeier Engraving Co ....E....... 812 425-1339
  Evansville (G-3650)

CARDS: Identification

CPI Card Group - Indiana Inc ....C....... 260 424-4920
  Fort Wayne (G-4182)
Roi Marketing Company ....G....... 317 644-0797
  Indianapolis (G-7855)
Stoffel Seals Corporation ....E....... 845 353-3800
  Angola (G-248)

CARPET & UPHOLSTERY CLEANING SVCS

Kings-Qlity Rstrtion Svcs LLC ....F....... 812 944-4347
  New Albany (G-10814)

CARPET & UPHOLSTERY CLEANING SVCS: On Customer Premises

Bane-Clene Corp ....E....... 317 546-5448
  Indianapolis (G-6455)

CARPET DYEING & FINISHING

Langenwlter Crpt Dyg Vlparaiso ....G....... 219 531-7601
  Valparaiso (G-13571)

CARPETS, RUGS & FLOOR COVERING

Advanced Services LLC ....F....... 317 780-6909
  Indianapolis (G-6336)
Anna Daisys LLC ....G....... 812 346-7623
  North Vernon (G-11247)
Envirotech Extrusion Inc ....E....... 765 966-8068
  Richmond (G-11984)
Indiana Rug Company ....G....... 574 252-4653
  Mishawaka (G-10053)
Jpc LLC ....F....... 574 293-8030
  Elkhart (G-2951)

Employee Codes: A=Over 500 employees, B=251-500
C=101-250, D=51-100, E=20-50, F=10-19, G=2-9

2018 Harris Indiana
Industrial Directory

PRODUCT

925

Manta Rugs.................................G....... 765 869-5940
  Boswell (G-940)
Todd K Hockemeyer Inc ....G....... 260 639-3591
  Fort Wayne (G-4689)

CARPORTS: Prefabricated Metal

All Steel Crprts Buildings LLC..............G....... 765 284-0694
  Muncie (G-10427)

CARRIAGES: Horse Drawn

Frontier Carriage..........................G....... 574 965-4444
  Delphi (G-2421)
Graber Manufacturing ....G....... 812 636-7725
  Odon (G-11327)
Hoosier Buggy Shop ....G....... 260 593-2192
  Topeka (G-13422)
Hostetler Carriage ....G....... 260 463-9920
  Lagrange (G-9045)
Iea Renewable Energy Inc ....G....... 765 832-8526
  Clinton (G-1717)
Martins Buggy Shop ....G....... 574 831-3699
  Nappanee (G-10692)
Schwartzs Wheel & Clip C ....G....... 574 546-1302
  Bremen (G-1023)
Wellspring Components LLC................G....... 260 768-7336
  Shipshewana (G-12657)

CARS: Electric

M-TEC Corporation ....C....... 574 294-1060
  Elkhart (G-3011)

CASEMENTS: Aluminum

Meridian Metalform Inc ....G....... 812 422-1524
  Evansville (G-3622)

CASES, WOOD

Meyer Custom Woodworking Inc ....G....... 812 695-2021
  Dubois (G-2477)

CASES: Carrying

CH Ellis Co Inc ....E....... 317 636-3351
  Indianapolis (G-6592)
Derby Inc...................................D....... 574 233-4500
  South Bend (G-12751)
MTS Products Corp ....E....... 574 295-3142
  Elkhart (G-3054)

CASES: Carrying, Clothing & Apparel

Oxford Industries Inc ....G....... 317 569-0866
  Indianapolis (G-7640)
Porter Case Inc............................G....... 574 289-2616
  South Bend (G-12901)
Tetrafab Corporation ....E....... 812 258-0000
  Floyds Knobs (G-4021)

CASES: Plastic

Integer Holdings Corporation ....C....... 317 454-8800
  Indianapolis (G-7246)
Shadowhouse Jiu-Jitsu Inc..................G....... 219 873-4556
  La Porte (G-8819)

CASES: Sample Cases

Indiana Dimensional Pdts LLC ....D....... 574 834-7681
  North Webster (G-11293)
Markley Enterprise Inc.....................D....... 574 295-4195
  Elkhart (G-3018)

CASES: Shipping, Nailed Or Lock Corner, Wood

Monroeville Box Pallet & Wood ....E....... 260 623-3128
  Monroeville (G-10197)

CASES: Shipping, Wood, Wirebound

Case Indy Products Inc ....G....... 317 677-0200
  Indianapolis (G-6563)

CASINGS: Storage, Missile & Missile Components

C F Roark Wldg Engrg Co Inc..............C....... 317 852-3163
  Brownsburg (G-1141)

CASKET LININGS

Elder Group Inc............................D....... 765 966-7676
  Richmond (G-11980)
Tiedemann-Bevs Industries LLC...........E....... 765 962-4914
  Richmond (G-12067)

CASKETS & ACCESS

Aurora Casket Company LLC ....G....... 812 926-1110
  Aurora (G-371)
Aurora Casket Company LLC ....D....... 812 926-1111
  Aurora (G-372)
Aurora Casket Company LLC ....B....... 800 457-1111
  Aurora (G-370)
Batesville Casket Company Inc.............A....... 812 934-7500
  Batesville (G-491)
Batesville Casket Company Inc.............C....... 812 934-8102
  Batesville (G-492)
Batesville Services Inc.....................C....... 812 934-7000
  Batesville (G-493)
Goliath Casket Inc..........................G....... 765 874-2380
  Lynn (G-9427)
Hillenbrand Inc............................C....... 812 934-7500
  Batesville (G-504)
JM Hutton & Co Inc ....D....... 765 962-3591
  Richmond (G-12008)
JM Hutton & Co Inc ....E....... 765 962-3506
  Richmond (G-12009)
Majestic Caskets & Urns Inc ....G....... 812 523-3630
  Seymour (G-12469)
Milso Industries Inc ....D....... 765 966-8012
  Richmond (G-12018)
Pontone Industries LLC ....C....... 765 966-8012
  Richmond (G-12030)
Romark Industries Inc ....E....... 765 966-6211
  Richmond (G-12047)
Specialty Enterprises Inc ....F....... 765 935-4556
  Richmond (G-12052)
Vandor Corporation ....E....... 765 683-9760
  Richmond (G-12072)
York Group Inc ....D....... 765 966-1576
  Richmond (G-12078)

CASKETS WHOLESALERS

Christopher Miller ....G....... 812 442-0949
  Brazil (G-956)
Milso Industries Inc ....D....... 765 966-8012
  Richmond (G-12018)
Vandor Corporation ....E....... 765 683-9760
  Richmond (G-12072)

CAST STONE: Concrete

Custom Cast Stone Inc.....................D....... 317 896-1700
  Westfield (G-14152)
Monumental Stone Works Inc..............E....... 765 866-0658
  New Market (G-10964)

CASTERS

Casters In Motion USA Ltd LLC............G....... 812 437-4627
  Evansville (G-3413)

CASTINGS GRINDING: For The Trade

C M Grinding Inc ....F....... 574 234-6812
  South Bend (G-12731)
Daily Grind Corporation ....F....... 574 875-8389
  Elkhart (G-2786)
Elkhart Grinding Services Inc...............G....... 574 293-2707
  Elkhart (G-2824)
Grind City Customs ....G....... 317 981-5462
  Indianapolis (G-7049)
Honing Stl Hsptlity Cncpts Inc ....G....... 317 332-5170
  Indianapolis (G-7118)
Med Grind Inc.............................G....... 574 965-4040
  Delphi (G-2424)
Ortho Grind LLC..........................G....... 260 493-1230
  Fort Wayne (G-4512)
T W Machine & Grinding ....G....... 260 799-4236
  Columbia City (G-1839)

CASTINGS: Aerospace, Aluminum

Flextech Corporation ....G....... 574 271-9797
  Elkhart (G-2857)
Kessington LLC ....D....... 574 266-4500
  Elkhart (G-2962)

CASTINGS: Aerospace, Nonferrous, Exc Aluminum

Tech Castings LLC ....E....... 765 535-4100
  Shirley (G-12663)

CASTINGS: Aluminum

Aluminum Foundries Inc...................C....... 765 584-6501
  Winchester (G-14324)
Dillon Pattern Works Inc ....F....... 765 642-3549
  Anderson (G-95)
Ewing Light Metals Co Inc ....F....... 317 926-4591
  Indianapolis (G-6886)
Foley Pattern Company Inc ....E....... 260 925-4113
  Auburn (G-332)
General Aluminum Mfg Company ....D....... 260 356-3900
  Huntington (G-6206)
Mahoney Foundries Inc ....D....... 260 347-1768
  Kendallville (G-8493)
Montro Company ....G....... 812 268-4390
  Sullivan (G-13088)
Muncie Casting Corp ....E....... 765 288-2611
  Muncie (G-10528)
Ph Inc.....................................B....... 877 467-4763
  Plymouth (G-11711)
Phillips Pattern & Casting Inc ....F....... 765 288-2319
  Muncie (G-10546)
Pirod Inc...................................F....... 574 936-7221
  Plymouth (G-11712)
Shipston Alum Tech Intl Inc ....G....... 317 738-0282
  Franklin (G-4930)
Shipston Alum Tech Intl LLC ....C....... 317 738-0282
  Franklin (G-4931)
Vice Bros Pattern Shop & Fndry ....G....... 260 782-2585
  Lagro (G-9073)
Wingards Sales LLC ....G....... 260 768-7961
  Shipshewana (G-12659)

CASTINGS: Brass, Bronze & Copper

Cunningham Pattern & Engrg Inc ....F....... 812 379-9571
  Columbus (G-1902)
Foundry Services Inc.......................C....... 317 955-8112
  Noblesville (G-11105)
Poyser Kelshaw Group LLC ....G....... 317 571-8493
  Carmel (G-1453)

CASTINGS: Brass, NEC, Exc Die

Ewing Light Metals Co Inc ....F....... 317 926-4591
  Indianapolis (G-6886)
Mahoney Foundries Inc ....D....... 260 347-1768
  Kendallville (G-8493)
Phillips Pattern & Casting Inc ....F....... 765 288-2319
  Muncie (G-10546)

CASTINGS: Commercial Investment, Ferrous

Aero Metals Inc ....B....... 219 326-1976
  La Porte (G-8727)
J & T Marine Specialists Inc................G....... 317 890-9444
  Indianapolis (G-7280)
Texmo Prcision Castings US Inc ....D....... 574 269-1368
  Warsaw (G-13951)

CASTINGS: Die, Aluminum

Aluminum Foundries Inc...................C....... 765 584-6501
  Winchester (G-14324)
Batesville Products Inc ....D....... 513 381-2057
  Lawrenceburg (G-9133)
Custom Die Casting Inc....................F....... 765 935-3979
  Richmond (G-11975)
Enkei America Moldings Inc ....G....... 812 373-7000
  Columbus (G-1921)
FCA US LLC ....A....... 765 454-1005
  Kokomo (G-8625)
General Aluminum Mfg Company ....C....... 260 495-2600
  Fremont (G-4960)
General Motors LLC........................A....... 812 379-7360
  Bedford (G-545)
George Koch Sons MGT Inc ....G....... 812 422-3257
  Evansville (G-3520)
Grandview Aluminum Products ....E....... 812 649-2569
  Grandview (G-5387)
Hill & Griffith Company ....E....... 317 241-9233
  Indianapolis (G-7108)
Kitchen-Quip Inc ....E....... 260 837-8311
  Kendallville (G-8487)
Koch Enterprises Inc ....G....... 812 465-9800
  Evansville (G-3596)

(G-0000) Company's Geographic Section entry number

Littler Diecast A Brahm Corp ....D 765 789-4456
  Albany *(G-11)*
Madison Precision Products Inc ....B 812 273-4702
  Madison *(G-9481)*
Noblitt International Corp ....E 812 372-9969
  Columbus *(G-1981)*
Revere Industries LLC.........................G 317 580-2420
  Westfield *(G-14184)*
Ryobi Die Casting (usa) Inc ....A 317 398-3398
  Shelbyville *(G-12565)*
Shiloh Industries Inc...........................E 260 925-4711
  Auburn *(G-356)*
SUs Cast Products Inc ....D 574 753-4111
  Logansport *(G-9367)*
Whb International Inc ....G 317 820-3001
  Indianapolis *(G-8188)*

CASTINGS: Die, Nonferrous

Brooks Langeloh ....G 219 691-3577
  Columbia City *(G-1768)*
Hill & Griffith Company ....E 317 241-9233
  Indianapolis *(G-7108)*
Indiana Gratings Inc ....F 765 342-7191
  Martinsville *(G-9615)*
S P X Corp ....G 574 594-9681
  Pierceton *(G-11578)*

CASTINGS: Die, Zinc

Custom Die Casting Inc ....F 765 935-3979
  Richmond *(G-11975)*

CASTINGS: Ductile

Accurate Castings Inc ....D 219 393-3122
  La Porte *(G-8726)*
In Ductile LLC......................................E 317 776-8000
  Noblesville *(G-11125)*
Intat Precision Inc ....B 765 932-5323
  Rushville *(G-12224)*
Transportation Tech Inds ....F 812 962-5000
  Evansville *(G-3769)*

CASTINGS: Gray Iron

Accucast Inc ....G 317 849-5521
  Indianapolis *(G-6314)*
Akron Foundry Inc ....D 574 893-4548
  Akron *(G-2)*
Bahr Bros Mfg Inc ....E 765 664-6235
  Marion *(G-9512)*
Bremen Castings Inc ....C 574 546-2411
  Bremen *(G-985)*
Gartland Foundry Company Inc ....C 812 232-0226
  Terre Haute *(G-13238)*
Metal Technologies Inc Alabama..........D 260 925-4717
  Auburn *(G-345)*
Mm Holdings I LLC ....C 260 982-2191
  North Manchester *(G-11236)*
Navistar Cmponent Holdings LLC........B 317 352-4500
  Indianapolis *(G-7578)*
New Dalton Foundry LLC ....G 574 267-8111
  Warsaw *(G-13913)*
Plymouth Foundry Inc ....E 574 936-2106
  Plymouth *(G-11713)*
Richmond Casting Company ....E 765 935-4090
  Richmond *(G-12045)*
Rochester Metal Products Corp ....B 574 223-3164
  Rochester *(G-12148)*
Warsaw Foundry Company Inc ....D 574 267-8772
  Warsaw *(G-13962)*
Waupaca Foundry Inc...........................A 812 547-0700
  Tell City *(G-13174)*

CASTINGS: Machinery, Aluminum

AAA-Gpc Holdings LLC........................D 260 668-1468
  Angola *(G-187)*
Busche Performance Group Inc ....C 260 636-7030
  Avilla *(G-402)*
Machined Castings Spc LLC.................F 574 223-5694
  Rochester *(G-12135)*

CASTINGS: Precision

Duramold Castings Inc ....E 574 251-1111
  South Bend *(G-12753)*

CASTINGS: Steel

Harrison Steel Castings Co...................A 765 762-2481
  Attica *(G-303)*

Shenango LLC.......................................F 812 235-2058
  Terre Haute *(G-13324)*

CASTINGS: Titanium

Symmetry Medical Mfg Inc ....D 574 371-2284
  Warsaw *(G-13949)*

CASTINGS: Zinc

Heartland Castings Inc ....E 260 837-8311
  Waterloo *(G-14014)*
Tdy Industries LLC ....C 219 362-1000
  La Porte *(G-8827)*

CATALOG & MAIL-ORDER HOUSES

Johnny Lemas ....G 260 833-8850
  Angola *(G-222)*
Sacred Selections ....G 260 347-3758
  Kendallville *(G-8509)*
Sailrite Enterprises Inc ....F 260 244-4647
  Columbia City *(G-1833)*

CATALOG SALES

Stump Printing Co Inc ....C 260 723-5171
  South Whitley *(G-13006)*

CATALOG SHOWROOMS

Dutch Made Inc ....G 260 657-3331
  Harlan *(G-5970)*

CATALYSTS: Chemical

Atmosphere Dynamics Corp.................G 317 392-6262
  Shelbyville *(G-12518)*
Catalyst Services Inc ....E 219 972-7803
  Griffith *(G-5768)*
Criterion Catalysts & Tech LP...............C 219 874-6211
  Michigan City *(G-9776)*
Reactor Services Intl Inc ....E 219 924-0507
  Griffith *(G-5789)*

CATAPULTS

Egenolf Contg & Rigging II Inc ....D 317 787-5301
  Indianapolis *(G-6812)*

CATERERS

Grafton Peek Incorporated...................E 317 557-8377
  Greenwood *(G-5698)*
Heaven Sent Gurmet Cookies Inc ....G 219 980-1066
  Gary *(G-5062)*
Milan Food Bank ....G 812 654-3682
  Milan *(G-9945)*
Parretts Meat Proc & Catrg ....F 574 967-3711
  Flora *(G-4001)*

CATTLE WHOLESALERS

P & R Farms LLC..................................G 812 326-2010
  Saint Anthony *(G-12248)*

CAULKING COMPOUNDS

Cast Products LP ....D 574 255-9619
  Mishawaka *(G-10017)*
Colorimetric Inc....................................E 574 255-9619
  Mishawaka *(G-10019)*
Reliable Sealants LLC ....G 765 672-4455
  Reelsville *(G-11903)*
Weatherall Indiana Inc..........................F 812 256-3378
  Charlestown *(G-1585)*

CEMENT & CONCRETE RELATED PRDTS & EQPT: Bituminous

Nobbe Concrete Products Inc ....G 765 647-4017
  Brookville *(G-1121)*

CEMENT ROCK: Crushed & Broken

Rock Creek Stone LLC ....G 260 694-6880
  Bluffton *(G-890)*

CEMENT: Hydraulic

Busters Cement Products Inc................F 765 529-0287
  New Castle *(G-10894)*
Essroc Corp..G 317 351-9910
  Indianapolis *(G-6879)*

Irving Materials Inc ....F 765 922-7285
  Marion *(G-9534)*
Lafarge North America Inc ....G 219 378-1193
  East Chicago *(G-2547)*
Lehigh Cement Company LLC...............C 812 849-2191
  Mitchell *(G-10165)*
Lehigh Hanson Ecc Inc ....B 812 246-5472
  Sellersburg *(G-12401)*
Light House Homes Center....................F 765 448-4502
  Lafayette *(G-8957)*

CEMENT: Portland

Buzzi Unicem USA Inc..........................E 317 780-9860
  Indianapolis *(G-6524)*
Lehigh Cement Company LLC...............G 877 534-4442
  Logansport *(G-9347)*
Lehigh Cement Company LLC...............C 812 246-5472
  Sellersburg *(G-12400)*
Lehigh Hanson Ecc Inc ....C 574 753-5121
  Logansport *(G-9348)*
Lone Star Industries Inc ....D 317 706-3314
  Indianapolis *(G-6271)*
Lone Star Industries Inc ....G 574 674-8873
  Elkhart *(G-3007)*
Lone Star Industries Inc ....G 260 482-4559
  Fort Wayne *(G-4440)*
Lone Star Industries Inc ....G 317 780-9860
  Indianapolis *(G-7416)*

CEMETERIES

Anderson Memorial Park.......................F 765 643-3211
  Anderson *(G-65)*

CERAMIC FIBER

Insulation Specialties of Amer...............E 219 733-2502
  Wanatah *(G-13824)*
Thermal Ceramics Inc...........................E 574 296-3500
  Elkhart *(G-3212)*
Unifrax I LLC...C 574 654-7100
  New Carlisle *(G-10889)*

CERAMIC FLOOR & WALL TILE WHOLESALERS

Laticrete International Inc ....G 317 298-8510
  Indianapolis *(G-7383)*

CHAIN: Tire, Made From Purchased Wire

Onspot of North America Inc ....G 203 377-0777
  North Vernon *(G-11274)*
Onspot of North America Inc ....E 812 346-1719
  North Vernon *(G-11275)*

CHAIN: Welded, Made From Purchased Wire

Grc Enterprises Inc...............................E 219 932-2220
  East Chicago *(G-2530)*

CHAIN: Wire

Kentuckiana Wire Rope & Supply ....F 812 282-3667
  Jeffersonville *(G-8386)*

CHAINS: Forged

Diamond Chain Company Inc................C 800 872-4246
  Indianapolis *(G-6739)*

CHANGE MAKING MACHINES

James R McNutt....................................G 317 899-6955
  Indianapolis *(G-7297)*
Standard Change-Makers Inc ....C 317 899-6955
  Indianapolis *(G-7987)*
Standard Change-Makers Inc ....F 317 899-6955
  Indianapolis *(G-7988)*

CHASSIS: Automobile House Trailer

World Class North America LLC............F 260 668-5511
  Angola *(G-259)*

CHASSIS: Automobile Trailer

Bailey Chassis Company LLC ....G 615 822-7041
  Haubstadt *(G-5997)*

CHASSIS: Motor Vehicle

Aptiv Services Us LLC..........................F 765 451-5011
  Kokomo *(G-8591)*

P R O D U C T

C-Line Engineering Inc..................G...... 812 246-4822
  Sellersburg (G-12390)
Checkered Racing & Chrome LLC ....F 812 275-2875
  Spencer (G-13019)
LCI Industries.................................D...... 574 535-1125
  Elkhart (G-2989)
Lcm Realty LLC.............................G...... 574 535-1125
  Elkhart (G-2990)
Lippert Cmponents Intl Sls Inc............G...574 312-7480
  Elkhart (G-2998)
Lippert Components Inc...................G...... 574 537-8900
  Goshen (G-5267)
Lippert Components Inc...................C...... 800 551-9149
  Elkhart (G-2999)
Lippert Components Inc...................D...... 574 535-1125
  Goshen (G-5268)
Lippert Components Inc...................F...... 574 312-6654
  South Bend (G-12840)
Lippert Components Inc...................D...... 574 294-6852
  Elkhart (G-3000)
Lippert Components Inc...................D...... 574 535-1125
  South Bend (G-12841)
Lippert Components Inc...................E...... 574 535-1125
  Goshen (G-5271)
Lippert Components Inc...................G...... 574 849-0869
  Goshen (G-5273)
Lippert Components Inc...................C...... 574 971-4320
  Goshen (G-5275)
Lippert Components Inc...................D...... 574 312-7445
  Middlebury (G-9904)
Lippert Components Inc...................E...... 574 535-1125
  Goshen (G-5272)
Lippert Components Mfg Inc............A...... 574 535-1125
  Elkhart (G-3002)
U B Machine Inc............................E...... 260 493-3381
  New Haven (G-10962)
Vehicle Service Group LLC............E...... 812 273-1622
  Madison (G-9499)
Vehicle Service Group LLC............G...... 800 445-9262
  Madison (G-9500)
Vehicle Service Group LLC............B...... 800 640-5438
  Madison (G-9501)
Wb Automotive Holdings Inc............F...... 734 604-8962
  Fort Wayne (G-4748)

CHAUFFEUR SVCS

Luxly LLC......................................G...... 617 415-8031
  Carmel (G-1429)

CHEMICAL & FERTILIZER MINING

Royster Clark Closed.....................G...... 812 397-2617
  Shelburn (G-12509)

CHEMICAL CLEANING SVCS

Paradigm Industries Inc..................G...... 317 574-8590
  Carmel (G-1448)

CHEMICAL ELEMENTS

Crystal Healing Elements................G...... 312 623-1764
  Fishers (G-3896)
Distinctive Elements.......................G...... 260 704-2464
  Fort Wayne (G-4213)
Element Armament LLC...................G...... 317 442-7924
  Bargersville (G-480)
Element Elite Tumbling....................G...... 502 751-5654
  Sellersburg (G-12392)
Element Homes..............................G...... 219 310-2505
  Crown Point (G-2249)
Element of Fun Travel.....................G...... 317 435-9185
  Demotte (G-2436)
Element Pro Services LLC...............G...... 574 271-5259
  Granger (G-5404)
Elemental Inc.................................G...... 812 684-8036
  Huntingburg (G-6162)
Elemental S A Protection.................G...... 765 717-7325
  Muncie (G-10469)
Elements......................................G...... 812 881-9400
  Vincennes (G-13675)
Grid Element Sled..........................G...... 219 462-2687
  Valparaiso (G-13552)
Grid Elements................................G...... 219 615-9683
  Valparaiso (G-13553)
Healing Elements LLC.....................G...... 260 355-7181
  Fort Wayne (G-4326)
Human Element Therapeutics ....G...... 317 446-4062
  Mooresville (G-10312)
New Elements LLC..........................G...... 219 465-1389
  Valparaiso (G-13587)

Theraptic Elmnts By Lori Myers..........G...... 765 480-2525
  Logansport (G-9369)

CHEMICAL PROCESSING MACHINERY & EQPT

Curtis Dyna-Fog Ltd......................D...... 317 896-2561
  Westfield (G-14151)
Perma-Green Supreme Inc...............E...... 219 548-3801
  Valparaiso (G-13598)
Shar Systems Inc...........................E...... 260 432-5312
  Fort Wayne (G-4619)
Wayne Chemical Inc........................E...... 260 432-1120
  Fort Wayne (G-4739)

CHEMICAL SPLYS FOR FOUNDRIES

I N C O M Wholesale Supply............G...... 574 722-2442
  Logansport (G-9339)

CHEMICALS & ALLIED PRDTS WHOLESALERS, NEC

Adhesive Products Inc....................G...... 317 899-0565
  Indianapolis (G-6325)
Airgas Usa LLC.............................E...... 812 474-0440
  Evansville (G-3345)
Bane-Clene Corp............................E...... 317 546-5448
  Indianapolis (G-6455)
Bangs Laboratories Inc...................F...... 317 570-7020
  Fishers (G-3873)
Cast Products LP............................E...... 574 294-2684
  Elkhart (G-2751)
Craft Laboratories Inc.....................F...... 260 432-9467
  Fort Wayne (G-4183)
Hydrite Chemical Co.......................E...... 812 232-5411
  Terre Haute (G-13252)
Pendry Coatings LLC......................G...... 574 268-2956
  Warsaw (G-13925)

CHEMICALS & ALLIED PRDTS, WHOL: Chemical, Organic, Synthetic

Defrukuscn LLC.............................G...... 219 718-2128
  Highland (G-6042)
Green Tek LLC...............................G...... 317 294-1614
  Carmel (G-1390)

CHEMICALS & ALLIED PRDTS, WHOL: Food Additives/Preservatives

Kolossos Inc.................................G...... 312 952-6991
  Long Beach (G-9377)

CHEMICALS & ALLIED PRDTS, WHOLESALE: Alkalines

Bio-Response Solutions Inc..............F...... 317 386-3500
  Danville (G-2343)

CHEMICALS & ALLIED PRDTS, WHOLESALE: Aromatic

OMI Industries Inc..........................G...... 812 438-9218
  Rising Sun (G-12090)

CHEMICALS & ALLIED PRDTS, WHOLESALE: Carbon Dioxide

Swanel Inc....................................D...... 219 932-7676
  Hammond (G-5947)

CHEMICALS & ALLIED PRDTS, WHOLESALE: Chemical Additives

Paradigm Industries Inc..................G...... 317 574-8590
  Carmel (G-1448)

CHEMICALS & ALLIED PRDTS, WHOLESALE: Chemicals, Indl

J 2 Systems and Supply LLC...........G...... 317 602-3940
  Indianapolis (G-7281)
Kml Inc..E...... 260 897-3723
  Laotto (G-9111)
Nochar Inc....................................G...... 317 613-3046
  Indianapolis (G-7589)
Prosco Inc....................................G...... 317 353-2920
  Indianapolis (G-7779)

Vertellus Intgrted Pyrdnes LLC.........C...... 317 247-8141
  Indianapolis (G-8154)
Warsaw Chemical Company Inc..........D...... 574 267-3251
  Warsaw (G-13958)

CHEMICALS & ALLIED PRDTS, WHOLESALE: Chemicals, Indl & Heavy

Ulrich Chemical Inc........................D...... 317 898-8632
  Indianapolis (G-8125)

CHEMICALS & ALLIED PRDTS, WHOLESALE: Dry Ice

Continental Carbonic Pdts Inc..........G...... 574 273-2800
  South Bend (G-12741)

CHEMICALS & ALLIED PRDTS, WHOLESALE: Essential Oils

Lebermuth Company Inc...................D...... 574 259-7000
  South Bend (G-12837)

CHEMICALS & ALLIED PRDTS, WHOLESALE: Indl Gases

Linde LLC.....................................G...... 574 234-4887
  South Bend (G-12839)

CHEMICALS & ALLIED PRDTS, WHOLESALE: Oxygen

Williams Bros Health Care Inc...........E...... 812 257-2505
  Washington (G-14007)
Williams Bros Health Care Pha..........E...... 812 335-0000
  Bloomington (G-856)
Williams Bros Health Care Pha..........C...... 812 254-2497
  Washington (G-14008)

CHEMICALS & ALLIED PRDTS, WHOLESALE: Plastics Film

American Renolit Corporation............C...... 219 324-6886
  La Porte (G-8733)
Laird Plastics Inc...........................G...... 317 890-1808
  Indianapolis (G-7375)

CHEMICALS & ALLIED PRDTS, WHOLESALE: Plastics Materials, NEC

Celestial Designs LLC.....................G...... 317 733-3110
  Zionsville (G-14425)

CHEMICALS & ALLIED PRDTS, WHOLESALE: Plastics Prdts, NEC

Ameri-Kart Corp.............................C...... 574 848-7462
  Bristol (G-1044)
Nibco Inc......................................C...... 574 296-1240
  Goshen (G-5298)

CHEMICALS & ALLIED PRDTS, WHOLESALE: Polyurethane Prdts

Pinder Polyurethane & Plas Inc.........G...... 219 397-8248
  East Chicago (G-2559)

CHEMICALS & ALLIED PRDTS, WHOLESALE: Resins

Pmw Holdings LLC.........................G...... 317 339-4685
  Indianapolis (G-7703)

CHEMICALS & ALLIED PRDTS, WHOLESALE: Resins, Plastics

General Rbr Plas of Evansville...........E...... 812 464-5153
  Evansville (G-3517)

CHEMICALS & ALLIED PRDTS, WHOLESALE: Spec Clean/Sanitation

Dynaloy LLC..................................F...... 317 788-5694
  Indianapolis (G-6773)
Koehler Welding Supply Inc..............F...... 812 574-4103
  Madison (G-9476)
Online Packaging Incorporated..........E...... 219 872-0925
  Michigan City (G-9825)
Tgc Auto Care Products Inc..............G...... 765 962-7725
  Richmond (G-12064)

CHEMICALS & ALLIED PRDTS, WHOLESALE: Syn Resin, Rub/Plastic

Ampacet Corporation ....C 812 466-5231
Terre Haute **(G-13193)**

CHEMICALS & ALLIED PRDTS, WHOLESALE: Waxes, Exc Petroleum

Kuhn & Sons Inc ....E 812 424-8268
Evansville **(G-3597)**

CHEMICALS & OTHER PRDTS DERIVED FROM COKING

Citizens Energy Group ....D 317 261-8794
Indianapolis **(G-6614)**
Hawkins Inc ....E 765 288-8930
Muncie **(G-10481)**

CHEMICALS, AGRICULTURE: Wholesalers

Helena Agri-Enterprises LLC ....G 765 583-4458
Otterbein **(G-11418)**
Helena Agri-Enterprises LLC ....F 812 654-3177
Dillsboro **(G-2467)**
Helena Agri-Enterprises LLC ....E 574 268-4762
Huntington **(G-6209)**
Miles Farm Supply LLC ....F 812 359-4463
Boonville **(G-917)**
Vertellus Intgrted Pyrdnes LLC ....C 317 247-8141
Indianapolis **(G-8154)**
Winfield Solutions LLC ....G 317 838-3733
Plainfield **(G-11652)**

CHEMICALS: Agricultural

AG Technologies Inc ....G 574 224-8324
Rochester **(G-12114)**
Dow Agroscience ....G 765 743-0015
West Lafayette **(G-14064)**
Dow Agrosciences LLC ....G 317 252-5602
Indianapolis **(G-6762)**
Dow Agrosciences LLC ....A 317 337-3000
Indianapolis **(G-6763)**
Dupont 9 Building Company LLC ....G 260 432-4913
Fort Wayne **(G-4225)**
Dupont and Tonkel Partners LLC ....G 260 444-2264
Fort Wayne **(G-4226)**
Dupont Commons LLC ....G 260 637-3215
Fort Wayne **(G-4227)**
Dupont Orthodontics ....G 260 490-3554
Fort Wayne **(G-4228)**
E I Du Pont De Nemours & Co ....G 812 299-6700
Terre Haute **(G-13227)**
Eli Lilly International Corp ....F 317 276-2000
Indianapolis **(G-6836)**
Harvest Land Co-Op Inc ....F 765 489-4141
Hagerstown **(G-5807)**
Helena Agri-Enterprises LLC ....G 260 565-3196
Craigville **(G-2122)**
Helena Agri-Enterprises LLC ....E 574 268-4762
Huntington **(G-6209)**
Kep Chem Inc ....G 574 739-0501
Logansport **(G-9346)**
King-Tuesley Enterprises Inc ....E 800 428-3266
Indianapolis **(G-7353)**
Landec Ag Inc ....F 765 385-1000
Oxford **(G-11432)**
Landec Ag Inc ....F 765 385-1000
Oxford **(G-11433)**
Monsanto ....G 260 341-3227
Farmland **(G-3843)**
Monsanto Company ....D 574 870-0397
Reynolds **(G-11946)**
Monsanto Company ....C 219 733-2938
Union Mills **(G-13464)**
Monsanto Company ....G 574 583-0028
Monticello **(G-10269)**
Monsanto Company ....E 317 945-7121
Windfall **(G-14348)**
Monsanto Cotton ....G 229 759-0035
Evansville **(G-3634)**
Mycogen Corporation ....F 317 337-3000
Indianapolis **(G-7565)**
Mycogen Crop Protection Inc ....E 317 337-3000
Indianapolis **(G-7566)**
Roy Umbarger and Sons Inc ....F 317 422-5195
Bargersville **(G-486)**
Southern Indiana Chemical ....G 812 687-7118
Washington **(G-14003)**

Superior AG Resources Coop Inc ....G 812 724-4455
Owensville **(G-11430)**

CHEMICALS: Alkalies

Kik Custom Products Inc ....E 574 295-0000
Elkhart **(G-2968)**

CHEMICALS: Aluminum Compounds

Gac Chemical Corporation ....G 317 917-0319
Indianapolis **(G-6978)**
Industrial Maint Engrg Inc ....G 812 466-5478
Terre Haute **(G-13256)**

CHEMICALS: Ammonium Salts & Compounds

V Global Holdings LLC ....A 317 247-8141
Indianapolis **(G-8142)**

CHEMICALS: Bromine, Elemental

Glcc Laurel LLC ....C 765 497-6100
West Lafayette **(G-14069)**

CHEMICALS: Caustic Soda

Hf Chlor-Alkali LLC ....E 317 591-0000
Indianapolis **(G-7098)**

CHEMICALS: Compounds Or Salts, Iron, Ferric Or Ferrous

Crown Technology Inc ....E 317 845-0045
Indianapolis **(G-6700)**

CHEMICALS: Copper Compounds Or Salts, Inorganic

St Clair Group Inc ....D 765 435-3091
Russellville **(G-12239)**

CHEMICALS: Fire Retardant

Prt Inc ....G 765 938-3333
Rushville **(G-12231)**

CHEMICALS: High Purity, Refined From Technical Grade

Helena Agri-Enterprises LLC ....G 765 583-4458
Otterbein **(G-11418)**
Kml Inc ....E 260 897-3723
Laotto **(G-9111)**

CHEMICALS: Hydrogen Sulfide

Alig LLC ....G 812 362-7593
Rockport **(G-12165)**

CHEMICALS: Inorganic, NEC

Airgas Usa LLC ....G 812 362-7593
Rockport **(G-12163)**
Akzo Nobel Coatings Inc ....F 574 372-2000
Warsaw **(G-13836)**
Allen Industries Inc ....G 317 595-0730
Indianapolis **(G-6368)**
Amalgamated Incorporated ....G 260 489-2549
Fort Wayne **(G-4065)**
Arch Wood Protection Inc ....F 219 464-3949
Valparaiso **(G-13497)**
Astec Corp ....G 317 872-7550
Indianapolis **(G-6432)**
Craft Laboratories Inc ....F 260 432-9467
Fort Wayne **(G-4183)**
Davies-Imperial Coatings Inc ....E 219 933-0877
Hammond **(G-5869)**
Dover Chemical Corporation ....E 219 852-0042
Hammond **(G-5871)**
Dpa Investments Inc ....G 219 873-0914
Michigan City **(G-9783)**
E I Du Pont De Nemours & Co ....D 812 299-6700
Terre Haute **(G-13228)**
E J Bognar Inc ....F 412 344-9900
Schneider **(G-12354)**
Elements Elearning LLC ....G 317 986-2113
Indianapolis **(G-6820)**
Geo Specialty Chemicals Inc ....G 765 448-9412
Lafayette **(G-8906)**
Giles Manufacturing Company ....G 812 537-4852
Greendale **(G-5487)**

Helena Agri-Enterprises LLC ....G 765 869-5518
Ambia **(G-55)**
Helena Agri-Enterprises LLC ....F 812 654-3177
Dillsboro **(G-2467)**
Hydrite Chemical Co ....E 812 232-5411
Terre Haute **(G-13252)**
Industrial Water MGT Inc ....G 317 889-0836
Greenwood **(G-5706)**
J 2 Systems and Supply LLC ....G 317 602-3940
Indianapolis **(G-7281)**
Jci Jones Chemicals Inc ....F 317 787-8382
Beech Grove **(G-599)**
Kem Krest Corporation ....F 574 389-2650
Elkhart **(G-2959)**
Metalworking Lubricants Co ....E 317 269-2444
Indianapolis **(G-7491)**
Nanolayer Technologies LLC ....F 260 414-4458
Fort Wayne **(G-4489)**
Nochar Inc ....G 317 613-3046
Indianapolis **(G-7589)**
PQ Corporation ....E 812 288-7186
Clarksville **(G-1690)**
Prosco Inc ....G 317 353-2920
Indianapolis **(G-7779)**
Reagent Chemical & RES Inc ....D 574 772-3271
Knox **(G-8577)**
Shoremet LLC ....F 219 390-3336
Valparaiso **(G-13617)**
Substrate Treatments Lubr Inc ....G 574 258-0904
Mishawaka **(G-10137)**
W R Grace & Co - Conn ....E 219 398-2040
East Chicago **(G-2580)**
Waterstone Technology ....E 317 644-0862
Carmel **(G-1507)**
Wayne Chemical Inc ....E 260 432-1120
Fort Wayne **(G-4739)**

CHEMICALS: Lead Compounds/Salts, Inorganic, Not Pigments

Hammond Group Inc ....E 219 931-9360
Hammond **(G-5884)**
Indiana Oxide Corporation ....F 812 446-2525
Brazil **(G-965)**
Metals and Additives LLC ....F 317 290-5007
Indianapolis **(G-7490)**
Metals and Additives Corp Inc ....E 812 446-2525
Brazil **(G-969)**
Perimeter Solutions LP ....C 219 933-1560
Hammond **(G-5926)**

CHEMICALS: Magnesium Compounds Or Salts, Inorganic

Dallas Group of America Inc ....D 812 283-6675
Jeffersonville **(G-8350)**
Giles Chemical Corporation ....G 812 537-4852
Greendale **(G-5486)**

CHEMICALS: Medicinal

Cgenetech Inc ....G 317 295-1925
Indianapolis **(G-6591)**
Efil Pharmaceuticals Corp ....G 765 491-7247
West Lafayette **(G-14065)**
Vertellus Intgrted Pyrdnes LLC ....C 317 247-8141
Indianapolis **(G-8154)**

CHEMICALS: Medicinal, Organic, Uncompounded, Bulk

VSI Acquisition Corp ....C 317 247-8141
Indianapolis **(G-8170)**

CHEMICALS: Metal Compounds Or Salts, Inorganic, NEC

Dmp LLC ....G 812 699-0086
Worthington **(G-14394)**
Remedium Services Group LLC ....F 317 660-6868
Carmel **(G-1467)**

CHEMICALS: NEC

Addenda Corporation ....G 317 290-5007
Indianapolis **(G-6324)**
Agri Processing Services LLC ....G 765 860-5108
Carmel **(G-1306)**
American Colloid Company ....G 812 547-3567
Troy **(G-13445)**

PRODUCT

Arch Wood Protection Inc ....F 219 464-3949
Valparaiso (G-13497)

Asterion LLC ....E 317 875-0051
Indianapolis (G-6433)

Baker Petrolite LLC ....G 219 473-5329
Whiting (G-14269)

Bangs Laboratories Inc ....F 317 570-7020
Fishers (G-3873)

Biodyne-Midwest LLC ....F 888 970-0955
Fort Wayne (G-4108)

Boomers ....G 765 741-4031
Muncie (G-10441)

Custom Building Products Inc ....D 765 656-0234
Frankfort (G-4827)

Eco Services Operations Corp ....E 219 932-7651
Hammond (G-5874)

Esm Group Inc ....F 219 393-5502
Kingsbury (G-8538)

Harsco Corporation ....E 219 397-0200
East Chicago (G-2532)

Hydrite Chemical Co ....E 812 232-5411
Terre Haute (G-13252)

Innovative Chemical Resources ....G 317 695-6001
Indianapolis (G-7235)

Interrachem LLC ....G 812 858-3147
Newburgh (G-11033)

Kemco International Inc ....F 260 829-1263
Orland (G-11352)

Kemira Water Solutions Inc ....G 219 397-2646
East Chicago (G-2541)

Kenra Professional LLC ....F 317 356-6491
Indianapolis (G-7343)

Klinge Enameling Company Inc ....E 317 359-8291
Indianapolis (G-7359)

Le Kem of Indiana Inc ....G 812 932-5536
Batesville (G-509)

Lehigh Hanson Ecc Inc ....C 574 753-5121
Logansport (G-9348)

Metals and Additives Corp Inc ....E 812 446-2525
Brazil (G-969)

Metalworking Lubricants Co ....G 317 269-2444
Indianapolis (G-7491)

Miller Chemical Tech & MGT Inc ....G 317 560-5437
Franklin (G-4909)

Nochar Inc ....G 317 613-3046
Indianapolis (G-7589)

Polyfusion LLC ....G 260 624-7659
Angola (G-238)

Prosco Inc ....G 317 353-2920
Indianapolis (G-7779)

Quaker Chemical Corp ....G 765 668-2441
Marion (G-9557)

Ricca Chemical Company LLC ....F 812 932-1161
Batesville (G-517)

Robinson International Inc ....E 812 637-0678
West Harrison (G-14042)

Sanco Industries Inc ....G 260 467-1791
Fort Wayne (G-4603)

Sanco Industries Inc ....E 260 426-6281
Fort Wayne (G-4604)

Sterling Formulations LLC ....G 317 490-0823
Shelbyville (G-12572)

Total Cleaning Solutions LLC ....G 260 471-7761
Fort Wayne (G-4694)

United States Mineral Pdts Co ....D 260 356-2040
Huntington (G-6259)

Univertical LLC ....D 260 665-1500
Angola (G-255)

Yushiro Manufacturing Amer Inc ....E 317 398-9862
Shelbyville (G-12586)

CHEMICALS: Nonmetallic Compounds

Esm Group Inc ....F 219 393-5502
Kingsbury (G-8538)

CHEMICALS: Organic, NEC

Blue Grass Chemical Spc LLC ....E 812 948-1115
New Albany (G-10753)

Chemtura Corporation ....C 765 497-6782
West Lafayette (G-14057)

Classic Chemical Corp ....G 812 934-3289
Indianapolis (G-6618)

Dover Chemical Corporation ....E 219 852-0042
Hammond (G-5871)

Energy Quest Inc ....G 317 827-9212
Indianapolis (G-6865)

Enzyme Solutions Inc ....F 260 553-9100
Garrett (G-5004)

Evonik Corporation ....A 765 477-4300
Lafayette (G-8894)

Fyt Fuels LLC ....G 520 304-6451
Rensselaer (G-11924)

Gdc Inc ....C 574 533-3128
Goshen (G-5222)

Global Energy Resources LLC ....G 219 712-2556
Valparaiso (G-13548)

Mirteq Holdings Inc ....G 260 490-3706
Fort Wayne (G-4478)

Neosphere Energy Inc ....D 219 781-7893
Schererville (G-12339)

Omicron Biochemicals Inc ....F 574 287-6910
South Bend (G-12883)

Org Chem Group LLC ....D 812 464-4446
Evansville (G-3656)

Triangle Rubber Co LLC ....C 574 533-3118
Goshen (G-5340)

Vertellus Holdings LLC ....G 317 247-8141
Indianapolis (G-8153)

Vertellus LLC ....E 317 247-8141
Indianapolis (G-8155)

CHEMICALS: Phenol

Eco Services Operations Corp ....E 219 932-7651
Hammond (G-5874)

CHEMICALS: Reagent Grade, Refined From Technical Grade

Omicron Biochemicals Inc ....F 574 287-6910
South Bend (G-12883)

CHEMICALS: Soda Ash

Eco Services Operations Corp ....E 219 932-7651
Hammond (G-5874)

CHEMICALS: Sulfur, Incl Rcvrd/Refined, Fm Sour Natural Gas

Reagent Chemical & RES Inc ....F 574 772-7424
Knox (G-8578)

CHEMICALS: Tin, Stannic/Stannous, Compounds/Salts, Inorganic

Mason Corporation ....D 219 865-8040
Schererville (G-12333)

CHEMICALS: Water Treatment

Alpha Water Conditioning ....G 765 281-8820
Muncie (G-10429)

Astbury Water Technology Inc ....E 260 668-8900
Angola (G-194)

Craig Hydraulic Enterprises ....G 812 432-5108
Dillsboro (G-2464)

Driessen Water Inc ....G 765 529-4905
Muncie (G-10463)

Dumor Water Specialists Inc ....E 574 522-9500
Elkhart (G-2802)

Genchem International LLC ....G 317 574-4970
Carmel (G-1384)

Iron Out Inc ....E 800 654-0791
Fort Wayne (G-4383)

Kemira Water Solutions Inc ....E 219 397-2646
East Chicago (G-2542)

Summit Brands ....G 260 483-2519
Fort Wayne (G-4661)

Superior Manufacturing Div Mag ....G 260 456-3596
Fort Wayne (G-4668)

Watcon Inc ....F 574 287-3397
South Bend (G-12988)

Water Sciences ....G 260 485-4655
Fort Wayne (G-4737)

Weas Engineering Inc ....F 317 867-4477
Westfield (G-14200)

CHICKEN SLAUGHTERING & PROCESSING

Perdue Farms Inc ....D 765 436-7990
Thorntown (G-13377)

Tyson Foods Inc ....A 812 738-3219
Corydon (G-2114)

CHILD & YOUTH SVCS, NEC

New Hope Services Inc ....E 812 288-8248
Jeffersonville (G-8403)

New Hope Services Inc ....E 812 752-4892
Scottsburg (G-12377)

CHILDREN'S WEAR STORES

Aleo Inc ....G 317 324-8583
Fishers (G-3868)

CHINA & GLASS REPAIR SVCS

Broadway Auto Glass LLC ....F 219 884-5277
Merrillville (G-9704)

CHLORINE

Jci Jones Chemicals Inc ....F 317 787-8382
Beech Grove (G-599)

Ulrich Chemical Inc ....D 317 898-8632
Indianapolis (G-8125)

CHOCOLATE, EXC CANDY FROM BEANS: Chips, Powder, Block, Syrup

Abbotts Candy and Gifts Inc ....E 765 489-4442
Hagerstown (G-5801)

Candies Inc ....F 260 747-7514
Fort Wayne (G-4138)

Debrand Inc ....D 260 969-8333
Fort Wayne (G-4203)

Donaldsons Chocolates Inc ....F 765 482-3334
Lebanon (G-9181)

LLC Tipton Mills ....G 716 825-4422
Columbus (G-1964)

Lowerys Home Made Candies ....F 765 288-7300
Muncie (G-10513)

Olympia Candy Kitchen ....F 574 533-5040
Goshen (G-5301)

Stephen Libs Candy Co Inc ....F 812 473-0048
Evansville (G-3748)

Sweet Things Inc ....F 317 872-8720
Indianapolis (G-8028)

CHOCOLATE, EXC CANDY FROM PURCH CHOC: Chips, Powder, Block

Claeys Candy Inc ....F 574 287-1818
South Bend (G-12735)

Rabbit Lane LLC ....G 317 733-8380
Zionsville (G-14458)

South Bend Chocolate Co Inc ....F 574 233-2577
South Bend (G-12942)

CHROMATOGRAPHY EQPT

Inchromatics LLC ....G 317 872-7401
Indianapolis (G-7169)

CHUCKS

Chucks Stace-Allen Inc ....E 317 632-2401
Indianapolis (G-6604)

Rush Jaw Company The Inc ....G 317 729-5095
Shelbyville (G-12564)

CHURCHES

Fresh Start Inc ....F 812 254-3398
Washington (G-13982)

CIGAR & CIGARETTE HOLDERS

Cosmoprof ....G 317 897-0124
Indianapolis (G-6672)

CIGAR STORES

Black Swan Vapors LLC ....G 317 645-5210
Pendleton (G-11484)

CIGARETTE & CIGAR PRDTS & ACCESS

Churchill Cigars ....G 812 273-2249
Madison (G-9451)

Cigarettes Plus ....G 574 267-3166
Warsaw (G-13856)

Smoke Smoke Smoke ....G 219 942-3331
Hobart (G-6096)

CIGARETTE FILTERS

Industrial Utilities Inc ....G 812 346-4489
North Vernon (G-11265)

CIGARETTE STORES

Smoker Friendly ....G 812 556-0244
Jasper (G-8309)

(G-0000) Company's Geographic Section entry number

CIRCUIT BOARDS, PRINTED: Television & Radio

Bluering Stencils..................................E...... 260 203-5461
Fort Wayne **(G-4114)**
Cal-Comp USA (indiana) Inc ....B...... 956 342-5061
Logansport **(G-9326)**
Madison Electronics Inc.......................F...... 812 689-4204
Versailles **(G-13655)**
Tritech Manufacturing Inc ....E...... 260 747-9154
Fort Wayne **(G-4705)**

CIRCUITS: Electronic

Acterna LLC...E...... 317 788-9351
Indianapolis **(G-6320)**
Autosem Inc ....F...... 574 288-8866
South Bend **(G-12718)**
B Q Products Inc ....E...... 317 786-5500
Indianapolis **(G-6450)**
Carson Manufacturing Co Inc ....F...... 317 257-3191
Indianapolis **(G-6560)**
CTS Elctrnic Cmponents Cal Inc ....G...... 574 523-3800
Elkhart **(G-2781)**
Electronic Services LLC.......................E...... 765 457-3894
Kokomo **(G-8620)**
Heather Sound Amplification..................G...... 574 255-6100
Mishawaka **(G-10049)**
Indiana Integrated Circuits In ....G...... 574 217-4612
South Bend **(G-12810)**
Investwell Electronics Inc ....G...... 765 457-1911
Kokomo **(G-8648)**
Kendrion (mishawaka) LLC ....E...... 574 257-2422
Mishawaka **(G-10063)**
Key Electronics Inc ....C...... 812 206-2500
Jeffersonville **(G-8389)**
Kimball Electronics Mfg Inc ....A...... 812 482-1600
Jasper **(G-8274)**
Kimball Electronics Tampa Inc ....A...... 812 634-4000
Jasper **(G-8275)**
Mallory Sonalert Products Inc ....E...... 317 612-1000
Indianapolis **(G-7448)**
Marian Worldwide Inc ....D...... 317 638-6525
Indianapolis **(G-7454)**
Microform Inc ....G...... 574 522-9851
Elkhart **(G-3035)**
Mier Products Inc..................................E...... 765 457-0223
Kokomo **(G-8666)**
Orion Global Sourcing Inc ....G...... 812 332-3338
Bloomington **(G-792)**
Poly Electronics LLC.............................D...... 574 522-0246
Elkhart **(G-3101)**
Rogers Electro-Matics Inc.....................F...... 574 457-2305
Syracuse **(G-13143)**
Schumaker Technical Assembly ....G...... 765 742-7176
Lafayette **(G-8997)**
Techshot Inc ....E...... 812 923-9591
Greenville **(G-5655)**
Wilco Corporation ....F...... 317 228-9320
Indianapolis **(G-8196)**

CLAMPS & COUPLINGS: Hose

Guardian Ind Inc ....E...... 219 874-5248
Michigan City **(G-9799)**

CLAMPS: Metal

EJ Brooks Company ....D...... 260 624-4800
Angola **(G-210)**
Grrreat Creations ....E...... 574 773-5331
Nappanee **(G-10675)**
Indiana Custom Trucks LLC ....E...... 260 463-3244
Lagrange **(G-9046)**
Universal Consolidated Methods ....E...... 260 637-2575
Fort Wayne **(G-4719)**

CLAY PRDTS: Architectural

Stone Artisans Ltd ....G...... 317 362-0107
Indianapolis **(G-8008)**

CLAY: Ground Or Treated

American Art Clay Co Inc ....C...... 317 243-0066
Indianapolis **(G-6385)**

CLEANING & DESCALING SVC: Metal Prdts

Better Metal Systems LLC......................G...... 888 958-5945
Highland **(G-6038)**
Kadet Products Inc ....E...... 765 552-7341
Elwood **(G-3303)**

Professional Metal Refinishing..............G...... 260 436-2828
Fort Wayne **(G-4562)**

CLEANING & DYEING PLANTS, EXC RUGS

Chucks Cleaners ....G...... 260 488-3362
Hamilton **(G-5820)**

CLEANING COMPOUNDS: Rifle Bore

Wax Shield ....G...... 317 831-1349
Camby **(G-1270)**

CLEANING EQPT: Commercial

A&M Commercial Cleaning LLC ....G...... 765 720-3737
Greencastle **(G-5453)**
Industrial Services Group Inc ....F...... 317 334-0921
Indianapolis **(G-7210)**
Pats Cleaning Service Rob ....G...... 574 272-3067
South Bend **(G-12888)**

CLEANING EQPT: Floor Washing & Polishing, Commercial

Hawk Enterprises Elkhart Inc ....F...... 574 264-6772
Elkhart **(G-2911)**

CLEANING EQPT: High Pressure

Aqua Blast Corp ....F...... 260 728-4433
Decatur **(G-2368)**
Avon Mobile Wash ....G...... 317 517-1890
Avon **(G-431)**
Hanlon Solutions Resource Inc.............G...... 317 776-4880
Noblesville **(G-11118)**
Michrochem LLC....................................G...... 812 838-1832
Mount Vernon **(G-10401)**
Pressure Systems Inc............................F...... 317 755-3050
Indianapolis **(G-7743)**

CLEANING OR POLISHING PREPARATIONS, NEC

Arden Companies LLC ....D...... 260 747-1657
Fort Wayne **(G-4089)**
Astec Corp..G...... 317 872-7550
Indianapolis **(G-6432)**
Blue Ribbon Products Inc ....G...... 317 972-7970
Indianapolis **(G-6489)**
Brulin Holding Company Inc ....E...... 317 923-3211
Indianapolis **(G-6513)**
Brulin Holding Company Inc ....D...... 317 923-3211
Indianapolis **(G-6514)**
Danny Webb Plumbing...........................G...... 574 936-2746
Plymouth **(G-11679)**
Dennis Adams Inc ....G...... 260 493-4829
New Haven **(G-10938)**
F B C Inc ....E...... 574 848-5288
Bristol **(G-1059)**
Gillis Company ....G...... 574 273-9086
Granger **(G-5409)**
Holloway House Inc ....E...... 317 485-4272
Fortville **(G-4779)**
Kleen-Rite Supply Inc ....F...... 812 422-7483
Evansville **(G-3594)**
Parts Cleaning Tech LLC ....G...... 317 241-9379
Indianapolis **(G-7658)**
Servaas Laboratories Inc ....E...... 317 636-7760
Indianapolis **(G-7915)**
Tate Soaps & Surfactants Inc ....G...... 765 868-4488
Kokomo **(G-8707)**
W J Hagerty & Sons Ltd Inc ....E...... 574 288-4991
South Bend **(G-12985)**
Warsaw Chemical Company Inc ....D...... 574 267-3251
Warsaw **(G-13958)**

CLEANING PRDTS: Degreasing Solvent

Tgc Auto Care Products Inc...................G...... 765 962-7725
Richmond **(G-12064)**

CLEANING PRDTS: Disinfectants, Household Or Indl Plant

Aqua Utility Services LLC ....G...... 812 284-9243
New Albany **(G-10745)**

CLEANING PRDTS: Drain Pipe Solvents Or Cleaners

L&S Sanitation Service...........................G...... 765 932-5410
Rushville **(G-12227)**

CLEANING PRDTS: Drycleaning Preparations

Dry Inc ....F...... 503 977-9204
Fort Wayne **(G-4222)**
Reeders Cleaners ....F...... 812 945-4833
Clarksville **(G-1692)**

CLEANING PRDTS: Dusting Cloths, Chemically Treated

Ideal Inc ....G...... 765 457-6222
Kokomo **(G-8643)**

CLEANING PRDTS: Laundry Preparations

First Image ....G...... 219 791-9900
Merrillville **(G-9715)**

CLEANING PRDTS: Metal Polish

All Metal Polishing ....G...... 219 980-3011
Merrillville **(G-9695)**
Blitz Manufacturing Co Ind ....D...... 812 284-2548
Jeffersonville **(G-8330)**
Elkhart Metal Polishing Inc ....G...... 574 206-0666
Elkhart **(G-2826)**

CLEANING PRDTS: Polishing Preparations & Related Prdts

Elie Cleaning Services LLC....................F...... 317 983-3388
Indianapolis **(G-6837)**

CLEANING PRDTS: Sanitation Preparations

Carmel Process Solutions Inc ....G...... 317 705-0217
Carmel **(G-1331)**
Smart Systems ....G...... 800 348-0823
Mishawaka **(G-10126)**

CLEANING PRDTS: Sanitation Preps, Disinfectants/Deodorants

Altapure LLC ....G...... 574 485-2145
South Bend **(G-12698)**
Global Ozone Innovations LLC..............G...... 574 294-5797
Elkhart **(G-2886)**
Relevo Labs LLC ....G...... 317 900-6949
Carmel **(G-1466)**
Steritech-Usa Inc ....G...... 260 745-7272
Fort Wayne **(G-4647)**
Valley Sanitation ....G...... 574 893-7070
Akron **(G-9)**

CLEANING PRDTS: Specialty

Custom Bottling & Packg Inc.................E...... 877 401-7195
Ashley **(G-285)**
Kings-Qlity Rstrtion Svcs LLC................F...... 812 944-4347
New Albany **(G-10814)**
Opportunities ....G...... 574 518-0606
North Webster **(G-11298)**
Powerclean Inc ....E...... 260 483-1375
Fort Wayne **(G-4543)**
Rexford Rand Corp ....E...... 219 872-5561
Michigan City **(G-9834)**

CLEANING SVCS: Industrial Or Commercial

Elie Cleaning Services LLC....................F...... 317 983-3388
Indianapolis **(G-6837)**

CLOSURES: Closures, Stamped Metal

Charmaran Corporation ....F...... 260 347-3347
Kendallville **(G-8463)**
Rieke Corporation..................................B...... 260 925-3700
Auburn **(G-349)**

CLOSURES: Plastic

Kerr Group LLC......................................C...... 812 424-2904
Evansville **(G-3585)**
Poly-Seal LLC..A...... 812 306-2573
Evansville **(G-3678)**

PRODUCT

CLOTHING & ACCESS, WOMEN, CHILDREN & INFANT, WHOL: Handbags

Cinda B USA LLC ....G....... 260 469-0803
Fort Wayne (G-4150)

CLOTHING & ACCESS, WOMEN, CHILDREN & INFANT, WHOL: Uniforms

National Federation of ....E....... 317 972-6900
Indianapolis (G-7571)

CLOTHING & ACCESS, WOMENS, CHILDREN & INFANTS, WHOL: Hats

Mammoth Hats Inc ....F 812 849-2772
Mitchell (G-10166)

CLOTHING & ACCESS: Costumes, Lodge

Moose Lodge ....G....... 219 362-2446
La Porte (G-8798)

CLOTHING & ACCESS: Costumes, Masquerade

Death Studios ....G....... 219 362-4321
La Porte (G-8750)
Knotts and Frye Inc ....G....... 317 925-6406
Indianapolis (G-7362)

CLOTHING & ACCESS: Costumes, Theatrical

Rittenhouse Square ....G....... 260 824-4200
Bluffton (G-889)

CLOTHING & ACCESS: Handicapped

Nebo Ridge Enterprises LLC ....G....... 317 471-1089
Carmel (G-1441)

CLOTHING & ACCESS: Men's Miscellaneous Access

Him Gentlemans Boutique ....G....... 812 924-7441
New Albany (G-10793)
Regal Inc ....G....... 765 747-1155
Muncie (G-10557)
Troves ....G....... 260 672-0878
Roanoke (G-12108)

CLOTHING & APPAREL STORES: Custom

Celestial Designs LLC ....G....... 317 733-3110
Zionsville (G-14425)
Graphic Fx Inc ....F....... 812 234-0000
Terre Haute (G-13243)
Hoogies Sports House Inc ....G....... 574 533-9875
Goshen (G-5238)
Kennyleeholmescom ....G....... 574 612-2526
Elkhart (G-2961)
Motionwear LLC ....C....... 317 780-4182
Indianapolis (G-7547)
Ram Graphics Inc ....E....... 765 724-7783
Alexandria (G-48)
Select Embroidery/Top It Off ....F....... 812 337-8049
Bloomington (G-823)
Shirtails ....G....... 812 858-8605
Newburgh (G-11048)

CLOTHING & FURNISHINGS, MEN'S & BOYS', WHOLESALE: Shirts

Springhill Wholesale Inc ....E....... 812 299-2181
Terre Haute (G-13342)

CLOTHING & FURNISHINGS, MEN'S & BOYS', WHOLESALE: Uniforms

National Federation of ....E....... 317 972-6900
Indianapolis (G-7571)

CLOTHING & FURNISHINGS, MENS & BOYS, WHOL: Sportswear/Work

Meditation Company ....G....... 574 217-3157
South Bend (G-12859)

CLOTHING STORES, NEC

Hidinghilda LLC ....G....... 260 760-7093
Fort Wayne (G-4332)

Vera Bradley International LLC ....G....... 260 482-4673
Roanoke (G-12111)

CLOTHING STORES: Designer Apparel

Black Books Publishing Inc ....G....... 260 225-7479
Fort Wayne (G-4111)

CLOTHING STORES: Formal Wear

Formal Affairs Tuxedo Shop ....G....... 574 875-6654
Elkhart (G-2868)
Sugar Tree Incorporated ....G....... 260 417-3362
Fort Wayne (G-4660)

CLOTHING STORES: Leather

Hilltop Leather ....G....... 317 508-3404
Martinsville (G-9612)

CLOTHING STORES: Square Dance Apparel

Roses Square Dance Acc ....G....... 812 865-2821
Orleans (G-11369)

CLOTHING STORES: T-Shirts, Printed, Custom

Country Stitches Embroidery ....G....... 219 324-7625
La Porte (G-8746)
Custom Tees ....G....... 765 449-4893
Lafayette (G-8885)
Sportsmania Sales Inc ....G....... 317 873-5501
Zionsville (G-14465)
Springhill Wholesale Inc ....E....... 812 299-2181
Terre Haute (G-13342)

CLOTHING STORES: Uniforms & Work

Geckos ....G....... 765 762-0822
Attica (G-301)

CLOTHING: Access

Five Star Fabulous LLC ....G....... 260 579-3401
Fort Wayne (G-4264)
Golden Pride Hair Company LLC ....G....... 812 777-9604
Indianapolis (G-7020)
Pdb II Inc ....G....... 219 865-1888
Dyer (G-2507)
Precise Title Inc ....G....... 219 987-2286
Demotte (G-2445)
Revolver LLC ....G....... 317 418-1824
Noblesville (G-11175)
Urserys LLC ....G....... 619 206-1761
Gary (G-5113)

CLOTHING: Access, Women's & Misses'

Brighton Collectibles LLC ....E....... 317 580-0912
Indianapolis (G-6510)
CM Reed LLC ....G....... 517 546-4100
Greendale (G-5485)
Hidinghilda LLC ....G....... 260 760-7093
Fort Wayne (G-4332)

CLOTHING: Anklets & Socks

For Bare Feet Inc ....C....... 765 349-7474
Martinsville (G-9606)

CLOTHING: Athletic & Sportswear, Men's & Boys'

H3 Sportgear LLC ....G....... 317 595-7500
Fishers (G-3920)
Jcs Enterprises Inc ....G....... 812 284-4827
Clarksville (G-1688)
Sports Licensed Division ....A....... 317 895-7000
Indianapolis (G-7977)
Stallion Sportswear Inc ....E....... 765 584-5097
Winchester (G-14341)

CLOTHING: Athletic & Sportswear, Women's & Girls'

Best Friends Inc ....G....... 765 985-3872
Denver (G-2453)
H3 Sportgear LLC ....G....... 317 595-7500
Fishers (G-3920)
Maingate Inc ....D....... 317 243-2000
Indianapolis (G-7444)

Sports Licensed Division ....A....... 317 895-7000
Indianapolis (G-7977)

CLOTHING: Children's, Girls'

Indiana Knitwear Corporation ....E....... 317 462-4413
Greenfield (G-5540)
Rittenhouse Square ....G....... 260 824-4200
Bluffton (G-889)

CLOTHING: Clergy Vestments

Gary Muslim Center ....G....... 219 885-3018
Gary (G-5051)

CLOTHING: Coats, Hunting & Vests, Men's

Berne Apparel Company ....E....... 260 622-1500
Ossian (G-11397)

CLOTHING: Costumes

Celebration Creations Inc ....E....... 800 762-8286
Indianapolis (G-6573)
Ghost Forge L T D ....G....... 765 362-8654
Crawfordsville (G-2154)
Giggling Wenches Handcrafts ....G....... 765 482-9776
Lebanon (G-9183)
Higgins Dyan ....G....... 812 876-0754
Ellettsville (G-3281)
Rivars Inc ....E....... 765 789-6119
Indianapolis (G-7847)

CLOTHING: Dresses

Bcbg Max Azria Group LLC ....G....... 319 753-0437
Fort Wayne (G-4102)
Bcbg Max Azria Group LLC ....G....... 515 964-7355
Fishers (G-3875)
Bcbg Max Azria Group LLC ....G....... 515 993-4753
Evansville (G-3371)
Bcbg Max Azria Group LLC ....G....... 574 289-3937
Albion (G-16)
Bcbg Max Azria Group LLC ....G....... 620 694-4256
Petersburg (G-11561)
Bcbg Max Azria Group LLC ....G 620 442-1111
Monticello (G-10255)
Bcbg Max Azria Group LLC ....G....... 641 872-1842
Fort Wayne (G-4103)
Bcbg Max Azria Group LLC ....G....... 712 243-1965
Fort Wayne (G-4104)
Bcbg Max Azria Group LLC ....G....... 712 277-3937
Merrillville (G-9700)
Bcbg Max Azria Group LLC ....G....... 913 631-0090
Zionsville (G-14420)
Elysian Company LLC ....G....... 574 267-2259
Warsaw (G-13872)
Mark Heister Design Inc ....G....... 312 527-0422
La Porte (G-8789)

CLOTHING: Gowns & Dresses, Wedding

Simple To Elegant ....G....... 812 234-8700
Terre Haute (G-13328)
Spectacular Soirees ....G....... 812 841-4311
Terre Haute (G-13339)

CLOTHING: Gowns, Formal

Sugar Tree Incorporated ....G....... 260 417-3362
Fort Wayne (G-4660)

CLOTHING: Hats & Caps, NEC

Genesco Inc ....G....... 812 234-9722
Terre Haute (G-13239)
Lids Corporation ....G....... 260 471-4287
Fort Wayne (G-4434)

CLOTHING: Hats & Headwear, Knit

Mammoth Hats Inc ....F....... 812 849-2772
Mitchell (G-10166)

CLOTHING: Leather

Hilltop Leather ....G....... 317 508-3404
Martinsville (G-9612)

CLOTHING: Leather & Sheep-Lined

Clinton Harness Shop ....G....... 574 533-9797
Goshen (G-5189)

(G-0000) Company's Geographic Section entry number

CLOTHING: Maternity

Three Little Monkeys ....G...... 765 778-9370
Pendleton **(G-11508)**

CLOTHING: Men's & boy's clothing, nec

CJS Mens Wear ....G...... 260 436-4788
Fort Wayne **(G-4153)**
Image Concepts Inc ....G...... 317 408-5558
Noblesville **(G-11124)**

CLOTHING: Outerwear, Lthr, Wool/Down-Filled, Men, Youth/Boy

Vf Outdoor LLC ....F....... 317 843-9419
Indianapolis **(G-8159)**

CLOTHING: Outerwear, Women's & Misses' NEC

Berne Apparel Company ....E...... 260 622-1500
Ossian **(G-11397)**
Dance Sophisticates ....E...... 317 634-7728
Indianapolis **(G-6725)**
Hoogies Sports House Inc ....G...... 574 533-9875
Goshen **(G-5238)**
Pariah ....G...... 317 250-0612
Indianapolis **(G-7655)**

CLOTHING: Robes & Dressing Gowns

Wells Robe Sales & Rental.....................G...... 317 542-9062
Indianapolis **(G-8183)**

CLOTHING: Shirts

Hoogies Sports House Inc ....G...... 574 533-9875
Goshen **(G-5238)**
Stallion Sportswear Inc ....E...... 765 584-5097
Winchester **(G-14341)**

CLOTHING: Shirts, Dress, Men's & Boys'

European Concepts LLC ....G...... 888 797-9005
Fort Wayne **(G-4250)**
Him Gentlemans Boutique ....G...... 812 924-7441
New Albany **(G-10793)**

CLOTHING: Sleeping Garments, Men's & Boys'

Krazy Klothes Ltd ....G...... 317 687-8310
Indianapolis **(G-7368)**

CLOTHING: Socks

Fbf Originals Inc ....G...... 765 349-7474
Martinsville **(G-9603)**
Just Standout LLC ....G...... 317 531-6956
Indianapolis **(G-7325)**
Simply Socks Yarn Company ....G...... 260 416-2397
Fort Wayne **(G-4628)**
Socks For The Homeless Inc ....G...... 317 568-3942
Indianapolis **(G-7957)**
Standout Socks ....G...... 317 531-6950
Indianapolis **(G-7990)**

CLOTHING: Sportswear, Women's

Mgtc Inc ....G...... 317 786-1693
Indianapolis **(G-7494)**
Mgtc Inc ....E...... 317 780-0609
Zionsville **(G-14447)**
Stallion Sportswear Inc ....E...... 765 584-5097
Winchester **(G-14341)**

CLOTHING: Sweaters & Sweater Coats, Knit

She Lettered ....G...... 317 844-4555
Indianapolis **(G-7924)**

CLOTHING: T-Shirts & Tops, Knit

Dyer Signwerks Inc ....G...... 219 322-7722
Dyer **(G-2495)**
Professional Gifting Inc...........................F....... 317 257-3466
Indianapolis **(G-7771)**
Speechlesstees LLC ....G...... 260 417-9394
Fort Wayne **(G-4639)**
Zip-A-Tee Shirt Inc ....G...... 219 879-5556
Michigan City **(G-9863)**

CLOTHING: Tailored Suits & Formal Jackets

Hearts Rmned Lifestyle Cir LLC ....G...... 800 807-0485
Gary **(G-5061)**
Sugar Tree Incorporated ....G...... 260 417-3362
Fort Wayne **(G-4660)**

CLOTHING: Ties, Neck & Bow, Men's & Boys'

Sycamore Enterprises Inc ....G...... 812 491-0901
Evansville **(G-3756)**

CLOTHING: Trousers & Slacks, Men's & Boys'

Berne Apparel Company ....E...... 260 622-1500
Ossian **(G-11397)**

CLOTHING: Tuxedos, From Purchased Materials

Formal Affairs Tuxedo Shop ....G...... 574 875-6654
Elkhart **(G-2868)**
Jgr Enterprises LLC ....G...... 586 264-3400
Portage **(G-11771)**

CLOTHING: Uniforms & Vestments

Dance Sophisticates ....E...... 317 634-7728
Indianapolis **(G-6725)**
Designs 4 U Inc ....G...... 765 793-3026
Covington **(G-2118)**
Fall Creek Corporation ....G...... 765 482-1861
Lebanon **(G-9182)**

CLOTHING: Uniforms, Men's & Boys'

Ashley Worldwide Inc ....G...... 574 259-2481
Granger **(G-5390)**

CLOTHING: Uniforms, Military, Men/Youth, Purchased Materials

Raine Inc ....F....... 765 622-7687
Anderson **(G-157)**

CLOTHING: Uniforms, Team Athletic

Designs 4 U Inc ....G...... 765 793-3026
Covington **(G-2118)**
Official Sports Intl Inc ....F....... 574 269-1404
Warsaw **(G-13917)**

CLOTHING: Waterproof Outerwear

le Products Mad Dasher Inc....................E...... 260 747-0545
Fort Wayne **(G-4357)**
Nasco Industries Inc................................C...... 812 254-7393
Washington **(G-13992)**

CLOTHING: Work Apparel, Exc Uniforms

Berne Apparel Company ....E...... 260 622-1500
Ossian **(G-11397)**
Gohn Bros Manufacturing Co ....G...... 574 825-2400
Middlebury **(G-9889)**

CLOTHING: Work, Men's

Dance Sophisticates ....E...... 317 634-7728
Indianapolis **(G-6725)**
Steel Grip Inc ....D...... 765 397-3344
Kingman **(G-8533)**

COAL GASIFICATION

Sg Solutions LLC......................................E...... 812 535-6000
West Terre Haute **(G-14129)**

COAL MINING SERVICES

Al Perry Enterprises Inc ....G...... 812 867-7727
Evansville **(G-3347)**
Arrow Mining Inc......................................E...... 812 328-6154
Oakland City **(G-11308)**
B B Mining Inc..G...... 812 845-2717
Cynthiana **(G-2329)**
Black Panther Mining LLC ....G...... 812 745-2920
Oaktown **(G-11317)**
English Resources Inc ....G...... 812 423-6716
Evansville **(G-3479)**
Fretina Corp..F....... 812 547-6471
Tell City **(G-13163)**

Gibson County Coal LLC ....B...... 812 385-1816
Princeton **(G-11873)**
Kq Servicing LLC ....G...... 812 486-9244
Loogootee **(G-9388)**
Paringa Resources Limited......................G...... 314 422-4150
Evansville **(G-3663)**
Peabody Energy Corporation ....G...... 314 342-3400
Oakland City **(G-11311)**
Peabody Midwest Mining LLC ....C...... 812 743-9292
Vincennes **(G-13695)**
Peabody Midwest Mining LLC ....E...... 812 434-8500
Lynnville **(G-9436)**
Peabody Midwest Mining LLC ....G...... 812 795-0040
Oakland City **(G-11313)**
Rogers Group Inc.....................................E...... 812 333-6324
Bloomington **(G-816)**
Stone Coal Services LLC ....G...... 812 455-8215
Evansville **(G-3752)**
Sun Energy Group LLC ....F....... 812 683-1178
Huntingburg **(G-6180)**
Sycamore Coal Inc ....G...... 812 491-4000
Terre Haute **(G-13347)**
Triad Mining Inc..F....... 812 328-2117
Oakland City **(G-11316)**
Vectren Corporation ....A...... 812 491-4000
Evansville **(G-3794)**
Vectren Corporation ....E...... 812 424-6411
Evansville **(G-3795)**

COAL MINING SVCS: Bituminous, Contract Basis

Pittman Mine Service LLC.......................E...... 812 847-2340
Linton **(G-9311)**

COAL MINING: Bituminous & Lignite Surface

Gibson County Coal LLC ....B...... 812 385-1816
Princeton **(G-11873)**
Peabody Energy Corporation ....D...... 812 795-4026
Oakland City **(G-11312)**
Peabody Midwest Mining LLC ....C...... 812 743-2910
Wheatland **(G-14232)**
Peabody Midwest Mining LLC ....C...... 812 644-7323
Cannelburg **(G-1285)**
Peabody Midwest Mining LLC ....E...... 812 434-8500
Lynnville **(G-9436)**
Peabody Midwest Mining LLC ....G...... 812 254-7714
Washington **(G-13997)**
Peabody Midwest Mining LLC ....G...... 812 782-3209
Francisco **(G-4817)**

COAL MINING: Bituminous Coal & Lignite-Surface Mining

ANR Pipeline Company ....G...... 260 463-3342
Lagrange **(G-9031)**
Arrow Mining Inc......................................E...... 812 328-2117
Oakland City **(G-11307)**
Colony Bay Cond Owners.........................G...... 260 436-4764
Fort Wayne **(G-4167)**
Eagle River Coal LLC ....G...... 618 252-0490
Evansville **(G-3471)**
Mt Vernon Coal Transfer Co....................F....... 812 838-5531
Mount Vernon **(G-10403)**
Peabody Bear Run Mining LLC ....A...... 812 659-7126
Evansville **(G-3666)**
Peabody Midwest Mining LLC ....C...... 812 495-6070
Pimento **(G-11580)**
Peabody Midwest Mining LLC ....G...... 812 795-0040
Oakland City **(G-11313)**
Peabody Wild Boar Mining LLC................G...... 812 434-8500
Lynnville **(G-9437)**
Rogers Group Inc.....................................D...... 812 332-6341
Bloomington **(G-815)**
Sandy Little Coal Co Inc ....G...... 812 529-8216
Evanston **(G-3325)**

COAL MINING: Bituminous Underground

Peabody Midwest Mining LLC ....C...... 812 743-2910
Wheatland **(G-14232)**
Peabody Midwest Mining LLC ....E...... 812 434-8500
Lynnville **(G-9436)**
Solar Sources Underground LLC ....G...... 317 788-0084
Indianapolis **(G-7961)**
Sunrise Coal LLC ....C...... 812 299-2800
Terre Haute **(G-13346)**
Sunrise Coal LLC ....C...... 812 398-2200
Carlisle **(G-1297)**

Employee Codes: A=Over 500 employees, B=251-500
C=101-250, D=51-100, E=20-50, F=10-19, G=2-9

2018 Harris Indiana
Industrial Directory

933

PRODUCT

COAL MINING: Bituminous, Strip

Foertsch Construction Co Inc ....D...... 812 529-8211
Lamar (G-9099)
Solar Sources Inc ....F...... 317 788-0084
Indianapolis (G-7960)
Solar Sources Inc ....D...... 812 354-8776
Petersburg (G-11569)

COAL MINING: Bituminous, Surface, NEC

Arrow Mining Inc ....G...... 270 683-4186
Oakland City (G-11306)
Arrow Mining Inc ....E...... 812 328-6154
Oakland City (G-11308)
Vigo Coal Inc ....B...... 812 759-8446
Evansville (G-3800)
Vigo Coal Operating Co Inc ....C...... 812 759-8446
Evansville (G-3801)

COAL PREPARATION PLANT: Bituminous or Lignite

Hickman Williams & Company ....F...... 708 656-8818
La Porte (G-8764)

COAL, MINERALS & ORES, WHOLESALE: Coal

Al Perry Enterprises Inc ....G...... 812 867-7727
Evansville (G-3347)

COATING COMPOUNDS: Tar

Asphalt Cutbacks Inc ....F...... 219 398-4230
East Chicago (G-2521)

COATING OR WRAPPING SVC: Steel Pipe

Chemcoaters LLC ....E...... 219 977-1929
Gary (G-5036)

COATING SVC

Accent Coatings LLC ....G...... 317 712-0017
Fishers (G-3865)
Alliance Coating LLC ....G...... 574 772-3372
Knox (G-8562)
Blackfoot Powder Coating ....G...... 812 531-9315
Brazil (G-954)
Commercial Coatings Assoc LLC ....G...... 812 483-5130
Evansville (G-3425)
Dearborn Coatings LLC ....G...... 513 600-9580
Lawrenceburg (G-9136)
Elite Protective Coatings ....G...... 317 476-1712
Greenwood (G-5685)
Em Black Oxide ....G...... 574 233-4933
South Bend (G-12762)
Fasi Coatings LLC ....G...... 219 985-0788
Gary (G-5046)
Fremont Coatings Div ....G...... 260 495-4959
Fremont (G-4959)
French International Coatings ....G...... 574 505-0774
Akron (G-5)
Garrett Products ....G...... 260 357-5988
Garrett (G-5005)
Harmon Coatings LLC ....G 317 326-4298
Greenfield (G-5536)
Hoosier Powder Coating LLC ....G...... 574 253-7737
Nappanee (G-10684)
Ideal Coatings LLC ....G...... 574 358-0182
Middlebury (G-9891)
Jah Coatings LLC ....G...... 317 550-7169
Indianapolis (G-7296)
M S Powder Coating ....G...... 260 356-0300
Huntington (G-6227)
Make It Black Seal Coating ....G...... 219 629-6230
Hobart (G-6090)
Modern Powder Coating LLC ....G...... 765 342-7039
Martinsville (G-9627)
NC Coatings LLC ....G...... 574 213-4754
Nappanee (G-10698)
Nda Energized Coatings ....G...... 260 499-0307
Elkhart (G-3058)
Performance Coatings Spc LLC ....G...... 574 606-8153
Topeka (G-13427)
Premier Cstm Coatings LLC Ind ....G...... 317 557-7841
Greenwood (G-5253)
Specialty Coatings LLC ....G...... 812 431-3375
Evansville (G-3742)
Tri State Powder Coating LLC ....G...... 812 425-7010
Evansville (G-3771)

TW Performance Coatings LLC ....G...... 317 331-8664
Indianapolis (G-8115)
Twin Coatings & Finishes ....G...... 317 557-0633
Indianapolis (G-8117)
Universal Coatings LLC ....G...... 574 520-3403
Elkhart (G-3237)
Wright Coatings Corporation ....G...... 317 937-6768
Indianapolis (G-8218)

COATING SVC: Aluminum, Metal Prdts

Genesis Products Inc ....E...... 574 266-8293
Elkhart (G-2878)
Sp3 ....E...... 260 547-4150
Decatur (G-2406)

COATING SVC: Hot Dip, Metals Or Formed Prdts

AAA Galvanizing - Joliet Inc ....D...... 260 488-4477
Hamilton (G-5818)
AAA Galvanizing - Joliet Inc ....E...... 765 289-3427
Muncie (G-10421)
AAA Galvanizing - Joliet Inc ....E...... 574 935-4500
Plymouth (G-11661)
Indiana Galvanizing LLC ....E...... 574 822-9102
Middlebury (G-9892)
Witt Industries Inc ....E...... 765 289-3427
Muncie (G-10587)

COATING SVC: Metals & Formed Prdts

Alocit USA ....G...... 317 631-9111
Indianapolis (G-6377)
American Metal Coatings Inc ....F...... 765 608-2100
Anderson (G-61)
Angola Wire Products Inc ....C...... 260 665-9447
Angola (G-192)
Applied Metals & Mch Works Inc ....E...... 260 424-4834
Fort Wayne (G-4083)
Arrow Powder Coating LLC ....E...... 317 822-8002
Indianapolis (G-6422)
B-D Industries Inc ....F...... 574 295-1420
Elkhart (G-2712)
Commercial Finishing Corp ....E...... 317 267-0377
Indianapolis (G-6637)
Conforma Clad Inc ....C...... 812 948-2118
New Albany (G-10765)
Crown Group Co ....D...... 260 432-6900
Fort Wayne (G-4190)
Custom Coating Inc ....E...... 260 925-0623
Auburn (G-325)
DC Coaters Inc ....E...... 765 675-6006
Tipton (G-13390)
Diamond Manufacturing Company ......E...... 219 874-2374
Michigan City (G-9782)
Erler Industries Inc ....D...... 812 346-4421
North Vernon (G-11257)
Gale Enameling Co Inc ....G...... 317 839-7474
Indianapolis (G-6979)
Gammons Metal & Mfg Co Inc ....D...... 317 546-7091
Indianapolis (G-6982)
Group Dekko Inc ....D...... 260 357-3621
Garrett (G-5009)
IBC Coatings Technologies Ltd ....E...... 317 418-3725
Lebanon (G-9188)
IBC Materials & Tech LLC ....F...... 765 482-9802
Lebanon (G-9189)
Imagineering Enterprises Inc ....E...... 574 287-0642
South Bend (G-12808)
Imagineering Enterprises Inc ....C...... 574 287-2941
South Bend (G-12809)
Indy Powder Coatings LLC ....F...... 317 236-7177
Noblesville (G-11129)
Itsuwa Usa LLC ....F...... 812 375-0323
Columbus (G-1949)
Keco Engineered Coatings Inc ....F...... 317 356-7279
Indianapolis (G-7338)
Kennametal Stellite LP ....D...... 574 534-9532
Goshen (G-5253)
Kevin Kolish Corp ....G...... 574 946-3238
Winamac (G-14309)
Lansing Metallizing & Grinding ....G...... 219 931-1785
Hammond (G-5906)
Lein Corporation ....E...... 765 674-6950
Marion (G-9542)
Max Powder Coating Inc ....G...... 812 752-4200
Scottsburg (G-12373)
Metalized Coatings LLC ....G...... 219 851-0683
La Porte (G-8791)
Mills Custom Powder Coating ....G...... 812 766-0308
Winslow (G-14357)

Modern Materials Inc ....E...... 574 223-4509
Rochester (G-12139)
Natural Coating Systems ....G...... 765 642-2464
Anderson (G-143)
Powdercoil Technologies LLC ....G...... 708 634-2343
Crown Point (G-2288)
Praxair Surface Tech Inc ....C...... 317 240-2500
Indianapolis (G-7724)
Prince Manufacturing Corp ....E...... 260 357-4484
Garrett (G-5020)
Reed Contracting Company ....E...... 765 452-2638
Kokomo (G-8687)
Schafer Powder Coating Inc ....G...... 317 228-9987
Carmel (G-1475)
Seavac USA LLC ....E...... 260 747-7123
Fort Wayne (G-4614)
Secorp Inc ....G...... 219 874-5010
Michigan City (G-9842)
Sermatech Intl Canada Corp ....G...... 317 240-2500
Indianapolis (G-7913)
Specialty Coating Systems Inc ....F...... 317 451-8549
Indianapolis (G-7967)
T G R Inc ....F...... 765 452-8225
Kokomo (G-8705)
Unique Specialty Services LLC ....G...... 219 395-8898
Chesterton (G-1636)
Winona Powder Coating Inc ....D...... 574 267-8311
Etna Green (G-3324)
Winona Pvd Coatings LLC ....E...... 574 269-3255
Warsaw (G-13968)

COATING SVC: Metals, With Plastic Or Resins

Denver Stone ....E...... 317 244-5889
Indianapolis (G-6734)
Evansville Metal Products Inc ....D...... 812 423-5632
Evansville (G-3487)
Henkel ....D...... 765 284-5050
Muncie (G-10486)
Job Shop Coating Inc ....E...... 317 462-9714
Greenfield (G-5544)

COATING SVC: Rust Preventative

Electro-Coat Technologies ....E...... 574 266-7356
Elkhart (G-2815)
Mays+red Spot Coatings LLC ....G...... 317 558-2024
Indianapolis (G-7470)
Metal Improvement Company LLC ......E...... 260 495-4445
Fremont (G-4967)

COATING SVC: Silicon

Momentive Performance Mtls Inc ....D...... 260 357-2000
Garrett (G-5017)

COATINGS: Air Curing

Oerlikon Balzers Coating USA ....E...... 765 935-7424
Richmond (G-12025)
Pendry Coatings LLC ....G...... 574 268-2956
Warsaw (G-13925)
Tnemec Company Inc ....G...... 317 884-1806
Greenwood (G-5753)
Vitracoat America Inc ....E...... 574 262-2188
Elkhart (G-3249)
Winslow-Browning Inc ....E...... 765 458-5157
Liberty (G-9273)

COATINGS: Epoxy

Cornerstone Industries Corp ....D...... 317 852-6522
Brownsburg (G-1145)

COATINGS: Polyurethane

Pinder Polyurethane & Plas Inc ....G...... 219 397-8248
East Chicago (G-2559)
T&T Coatings Inc ....G...... 317 408-3752
Camby (G-1269)

COFFEE SVCS

Suncoast Coffee Inc ....E...... 317 251-3198
Indianapolis (G-8018)

COIL WINDING SVC

Qp Inc ....F...... 574 295-6884
Elkhart (G-3125)

(G-0000) Company's Geographic Section entry number

COILS & ROD: Extruded, Aluminum

Jupiter Aluminum Corporation............C...... 219 932-3322
Hammond (G-5903)

COILS & TRANSFORMERS

Andover Coils LLC.................................D...... 765 447-1157
Fishers (G-3871)
Coil Tran Corp..D...... 219 942-8511
Hobart (G-6076)
Custom Magnetics Inc..............................E...... 773 463-6500
North Manchester (G-11227)
Hermetic Coil Co Inc...............................E...... 812 735-2400
Bicknell (G-631)
Kendrion (mishawaka) LLC......................E...... 574 257-2422
Mishawaka (G-10063)
Midwest Coil LLC....................................F...... 765 807-5429
Lafayette (G-8969)
Performance Mstr Coil Proc Inc.............E...... 765 364-1300
Crawfordsville (G-2185)
R B Annis Instruments Inc......................G...... 765 848-1621
Greencastle (G-5476)
Southern Electric Coil LLC.....................E...... 219 931-5500
Hammond (G-5944)
Warsaw Coil Co Inc.................................D...... 574 267-6041
Warsaw (G-13959)

COILS: Electric Motors Or Generators

Red Barn Industries Inc..........................F...... 765 379-3197
Mulberry (G-10419)
Southern Electric Coil LLC......................E...... 219 931-5500
Hammond (G-5944)

COIN-OPERATED LAUNDRY

H & H Partnership Inc.............................G...... 765 513-4739
Kokomo (G-8634)

COIN-OPERATED MACHINES & MECHANISMS, WHOLESALE

C & P Distributing LLC............................E...... 574 256-1138
Mishawaka (G-10016)

COKE OVEN PRDTS: Beehive

Beta Steel Corp......................................G...... 219 787-0001
Portage (G-11751)

COLLECTION AGENCIES

Sentinel Services Inc..............................F...... 574 360-5279
Granger (G-5432)

COLOGNES

Di Cologne Group....................................G...... 260 616-0158
Fort Wayne (G-4209)

COLOR PIGMENTS

Cathay Industries (usa) Inc....................E...... 219 531-5359
Valparaiso (G-13520)
Kibbechem Inc...E...... 574 266-1234
Elkhart (G-2964)

COLORING & FINISHING SVC: Aluminum Or Formed Prdts

Saturn Wheel Company Inc....................D...... 260 375-4720
Warren (G-13833)

COLORS: Pigments, Inorganic

A Schulman Inc.......................................E...... 574 935-5131
Plymouth (G-11660)
Altair Nanotechnologies Inc...................A...... 317 333-7617
Anderson (G-60)
Hammond Group Inc................................E...... 219 933-1560
Hammond (G-5885)
United Minerals and Prpts Inc...............E...... 812 838-5236
Mount Vernon (G-10412)

COLORS: Pigments, Organic

Ampacet Corporation..............................C...... 812 466-5231
Terre Haute (G-13193)
Holland Colours Americas Inc................D...... 765 935-0329
Richmond (G-11998)
Kibbechem Inc...E...... 574 266-1234
Elkhart (G-2964)

COMBINATION UTILITIES, NEC

Ald Indy Inc...G...... 317 826-3833
Fishers (G-3867)

COMBINED ELEMENTARY & SECONDARY SCHOOLS, PRIVATE

Boeke Road Baptist Church Inc.............G...... 812 479-5342
Evansville (G-3389)

COMFORTERS & QUILTS, FROM MANMADE FIBER OR SILK

Joseph Fisher...G...... 765 435-7231
Waveland (G-14028)

COMMERCIAL & INDL SHELVING WHOLESALERS

Cottom Automated Bus Soluti.................G...... 317 853-6531
Carmel (G-1346)

COMMERCIAL & OFFICE BUILDINGS RENOVATION & REPAIR

DC Construction Services Inc...............E...... 317 577-0276
Indianapolis (G-6730)
Reed Contracting Company.....................F...... 765 452-2638
Kokomo (G-8687)

COMMERCIAL ART & GRAPHIC DESIGN SVCS

Chromasource Inc...................................C...... 260 420-3000
Columbia City (G-1772)
Classic Graphics Inc...............................F...... 260 482-3487
Fort Wayne (G-4156)
Classic Media LLC..................................G...... 260 482-3487
Fort Wayne (G-4157)
Cs Kern Inc...E...... 765 289-8600
Muncie (G-10451)
Deem & Loureiro Inc...............................G...... 770 652-9871
Indianapolis (G-6731)
Freckles Graphics Inc.............................F...... 765 448-4692
Lafayette (G-8900)
Game Face Graphix LLC.........................G...... 317 340-0973
Camby (G-1267)
Graphic Arts & Publ Svcs........................G...... 574 294-1770
Elkhart (G-2894)
Grayson Graphics....................................G...... 574 264-6466
Elkhart (G-2895)
Jam Printing Inc......................................G...... 765 649-9292
Anderson (G-125)
Karemar Productions..............................G...... 765 766-5117
Mooreland (G-10295)
Kennyleeholmescom................................G...... 574 612-2526
Elkhart (G-2961)
Marketing Services Group Inc................B...... 317 381-2268
Indianapolis (G-7456)
North Vernon Plain Dlr & Sun.................E...... 812 346-3973
North Vernon (G-11272)
Pheonix Inc...G...... 765 489-3030
Hagerstown (G-5811)
Schaffsteins Truck Clean LLC.................F...... 812 464-2424
Evansville (G-3715)
Sexton Melinda.......................................G...... 812 522-4059
Seymour (G-12484)
Thomas E Slade Inc................................F...... 812 471-7100
Evansville (G-3760)
World Graffix LLC....................................G...... 574 936-1927
Plymouth (G-11740)
Young & Kenady Incorporated................G...... 317 852-6300
Brownsburg (G-1178)

COMMERCIAL ART & ILLUSTRATION SVCS

Indianapolis Signworks Inc.....................E...... 317 872-8722
Indianapolis (G-7205)
Shadow Graphix Inc................................G...... 317 481-9710
Indianapolis (G-7922)

COMMERCIAL EQPT WHOLESALERS, NEC

Playfair Shuffleboard Company..............F...... 260 747-7288
Fort Wayne (G-4534)
Storageworks Inc....................................G...... 317 577-3511
Fishers (G-3971)
Thermodyne Food Service Pdts.............E...... 260 428-2535
Fort Wayne (G-4682)

COMMERCIAL EQPT, WHOLESALE: Comm Cooking & Food Svc Eqpt

Brand Sheet Metal Works Inc.................G...... 765 284-5594
Muncie (G-10443)

COMMERCIAL EQPT, WHOLESALE: Merchandising Machines

Premier Strctres Acqsition Inc...............D...... 574 522-4011
Elkhart (G-3113)

COMMERCIAL EQPT, WHOLESALE: Neon Signs

Delaplane & Son Neon & Sign.................G...... 574 859-3431
Camden (G-1273)

COMMERCIAL EQPT, WHOLESALE: Restaurant, NEC

M D Holdings LLC....................................G...... 317 831-7030
Mooresville (G-10319)
US Water Systems Inc............................F...... 317 209-0889
Indianapolis (G-8138)

COMMERCIAL EQPT, WHOLESALE: Scales, Exc Laboratory

Indiana Scale Company Inc....................F...... 812 232-0893
Terre Haute (G-13255)
Technical Weighing Svcs Inc..................E...... 219 924-3366
Griffith (G-5793)

COMMERCIAL EQPT, WHOLESALE: Store Fixtures & Display Eqpt

Markley Enterprise Inc............................D...... 574 295-4195
Elkhart (G-3018)
Wert Fixture & Display Inc.......................G...... 317 577-0905
Indianapolis (G-8184)
Wood Technologies LLC...........................E...... 260 627-8858
Grabill (G-5385)

COMMERCIAL EQPT, WHOLESALE: Vending Machines, Coin-Operated

Window Man Inc.......................................G...... 317 755-3207
Indianapolis (G-8203)

COMMERCIAL PRINTING & NEWSPAPER PUBLISHING COMBINED

411 Newspaper.......................................G...... 219 922-8846
Munster (G-10590)
Aim Media Indiana Oper LLC...................D...... 812 372-7811
Columbus (G-1852)
Aim Media Indiana Oper LLC...................F...... 812 522-4871
Seymour (G-12427)
Aim Media Indiana Oper LLC...................G...... 812 988-2221
Nashville (G-10712)
Aim Media Indiana Oper LLC...................G...... 812 358-2111
Brownstown (G-1179)
Aim Media Indiana Oper LLC...................G...... 765 778-2324
Pendleton (G-11482)
Aim Media Indiana Oper LLC...................G...... 317 462-5528
Greenfield (G-5498)
Aim Media Indiana Oper LLC...................G...... 812 736-7101
Franklin (G-4864)
Aim Media Indiana Oper LLC...................E...... 317 462-5528
Greenfield (G-5499)
Aim Media Indiana Oper LLC...................D...... 812 372-7811
Columbus (G-1851)
Ckmt Associates Inc...............................E...... 219 924-2820
Hammond (G-5863)
Cnhi LLC..E...... 574 936-3101
Plymouth (G-11674)
Colormax Digital Imaging Inc..................E...... 812 477-3805
Evansville (G-3422)
Delphos Herald of Indiana Inc................E...... 812 537-0063
Lawrenceburg (G-9138)
Elwood Publishing Co Inc........................E...... 765 552-3355
Elwood (G-3298)
George P Stewart Printing Co.................E...... 317 924-5143
Indianapolis (G-7002)
Graphic Printing Co Inc...........................G...... 765 768-6022
Dunkirk (G-2484)
Graphic Printing Co Inc...........................E...... 260 726-8141
Portland (G-11825)

Employee Codes: A=Over 500 employees, B=251-500
C=101-250, D=51-100, E=20-50, F=10-19, G=2-9

2018 Harris Indiana
Industrial Directory

PRODUCT

935

Indiana Newspapers LLC ....A 317 444-4000
Indianapolis (G-7186)
Indiana Newspapers LLC ....F 317 444-3800
Indianapolis (G-7187)
Journal Gazette Foundation ....G 260 424-5257
Fort Wayne (G-4400)
Journal Publishing Co Inc ....G 812 876-2254
Ellettsville (G-3282)
Kankakee Valley Publishing Co ....C 219 866-5111
Rensselaer (G-11930)
Kpc Media Group Inc ....C 260 347-0400
Kendallville (G-8488)
La Grange Publishing Co Inc ....F 260 463-3243
Lagrange (G-9052)
Life Path Numerology Center ....G 317 638-9752
Indianapolis (G-7404)
Manchester North News Journal ....G 260 982-6383
North Manchester (G-11233)
News Publishing Company LLC ....F 812 547-3424
Tell City (G-13169)
Paper of Montgomery County ....G 765 361-8888
Crawfordsville (G-2183)
Paper of Wabash County Inc ....E 260 563-8326
Wabash (G-13746)
Paxton Media Group LLC ....G 765 664-5111
Marion (G-9550)
Pierce Oil Co Inc ....F 812 268-6356
Sullivan (G-13090)
Pilcher Publishing Co Inc ....E 219 696-7711
Lowell (G-9419)
Princeton Publishing Inc ....G 812 385-2525
Princeton (G-11881)
Purdue Student Pubg Foundation ....F 765 743-1111
West Lafayette (G-14099)
R R Donnelley Inc ....F 317 631-2203
Indianapolis (G-7810)
Republic Inc ....E 812 342-8028
Columbus (G-2006)
Russ Publishing ....G 812 847-4487
Linton (G-9313)
Schurz Communications Inc ....B 574 235-6496
South Bend (G-12930)
Sentinel Inc ....G 574 223-2111
Rochester (G-12153)
Shelbyville Newspapers Inc ....D 317 398-6631
Shelbyville (G-12568)
South Bend Tribune Corp ....B 574 235-6161
South Bend (G-12946)
Southsider ....G 317 781-0023
Indianapolis (G-7964)
Spencer Evening World ....D 812 829-2255
Spencer (G-13037)
Teragraphics Ink LLC ....G 765 430-2863
West Lafayette (G-14112)
Triple Crown Media LLC ....D 574 533-2151
Goshen (G-5342)
Wabash Plain Dealer ....E 260 563-2131
Wabash (G-13764)
Warrick Publishing Co Inc ....E 812 897-2330
Boonville (G-924)

COMMODITY CONTRACTS BROKERS, DEALERS

Louis Dreyfus Co AG Inds LLC ....F 574 566-2100
Claypool (G-1706)

COMMON SAND MINING

Country Estates ....G 812 925-6443
Boonville (G-913)
Harrison Sand and Gravel Co ....F 812 663-2021
Greensburg (G-5606)
Hilltop Basic Resources Inc ....E 812 594-2293
Patriot (G-11468)
Shelby Gravel Inc ....E 317 398-4485
Shelbyville (G-12567)

COMMUNICATION HEADGEAR: Telephone

Byte Blue Technology Solutions ....G 574 903-5637
Elkhart (G-2741)

COMMUNICATIONS EQPT & SYSTEMS, NEC

A Plus Datacomm ....G 219 472-1644
Portage (G-11747)
Integratorcom Inc ....G 317 849-2250
Indianapolis (G-7250)
Port Services LLC ....G 317 840-7606
Indianapolis (G-7707)

COMMUNICATIONS EQPT WHOLESALERS

Emergency Radio Service LLC ....E 317 821-0422
Ligonier (G-9282)
Shf Microwave Parts Co ....G 219 785-2602
La Porte (G-8820)

COMMUNICATIONS EQPT: Microwave

Commtineo LLC ....F 219 476-3667
Wanatah (G-13822)

COMMUNICATIONS SVCS

Trilithic Inc ....C 317 895-3600
Indianapolis (G-8099)

COMMUNICATIONS SVCS, NEC

Mobile Communications Tech ....G 812 423-7322
Evansville (G-3631)

COMMUNICATIONS SVCS: Data

American Eagle Security Inc ....G 219 980-1177
Merrillville (G-9696)
Mesh Systems LLC ....E 317 661-4800
Carmel (G-1437)

COMMUNICATIONS SVCS: Internet Connectivity Svcs

Indy Web Inc ....G 317 356-3622
Indianapolis (G-7224)

COMMUNICATIONS SVCS: Internet Host Svcs

Dbisp LLC ....F 317 222-1671
Indianapolis (G-6729)

COMMUNICATIONS SVCS: Online Svc Providers

Data-Vision Inc ....F 574 243-8625
Mishawaka (G-10033)
Hoosier Times Inc ....C 812 331-4270
Bloomington (G-741)
Pretty Brilliant LLC ....G 765 277-2308
Richmond (G-12031)

COMMUNICATIONS SVCS: Proprietary Online Svcs Networks

Telamon Corporation ....C 317 818-6888
Carmel (G-1488)

COMMUNITY CENTER

Cyberia Ltd ....G 317 721-2582
Indianapolis (G-6719)

COMPACT DISC PLAYERS

Kauffman Enterprises Inc ....G 260 434-1590
Fort Wayne (G-4404)

COMPACT LASER DISCS: Prerecorded

Asahi TEC America Corporation ....G 765 962-8399
Richmond (G-11956)
Sony Dadc US Inc ....A 812 462-8100
Terre Haute (G-13334)

COMPOSITION STONE: Plastic

Tekmodo Structures LLC ....G 574 970-5800
Elkhart (G-3210)

COMPOST

City of Fort Wayne ....G 260 749-8040
Fort Wayne (G-4151)
Compost Bins Pro ....G 317 873-0555
Zionsville (G-14428)
Creative Ldscp & Compost Co ....G 317 776-2909
Noblesville (G-11087)
Earth Mama Compost ....G 317 759-4589
Indianapolis (G-6787)
Elvin L Nuest Sales and Servic ....G 219 863-5216
Francesville (G-4811)
Greencycle Inc ....G 317 773-3350
Noblesville (G-11114)

COMPRESSORS, AIR CONDITIONING: Wholesalers

Mobile Climate Control Corp ....D 574 534-1516
Goshen (G-5296)

COMPRESSORS: Air & Gas

ABB Flexible Automation Inc ....E 317 876-9090
Indianapolis (G-6307)
Abro Industries Inc ....E 574 232-8289
South Bend (G-12692)
Boss Industries LLC ....E 219 324-7776
La Porte (G-8740)
Brama Inc ....E 317 786-7770
Indianapolis (G-6502)
Cook Compression Inc ....A 502 515-6900
Jeffersonville (G-8345)
Custom Compressor Svcs Corp ....G 219 879-4966
Michigan City (G-9777)
Howden Roots LLC ....C 765 827-9200
Connersville (G-2052)
Midwest Finishing Systems Inc ....E 574 257-0099
Mishawaka (G-10087)
Precisionair LLC ....G 219 380-9267
La Porte (G-8806)
Systems Engineering and Sls Co ....G 260 422-1671
Fort Wayne (G-4671)
Three Rivers Comprsd AR Sstms ....G 260 248-8908
Columbia City (G-1841)
Ultra Elec Precsion Air & Land ....G 260 327-4112
Columbia City (G-1843)

COMPRESSORS: Air & Gas, Including Vacuum Pumps

Air Fixtures Inc ....F 260 982-2169
North Manchester (G-11224)
K Grimmer Industries Inc ....E 317 736-3800
Leo (G-9243)
Kobelco Cmpsr Mfg Ind Inc ....D 574 295-3145
Elkhart (G-2973)
Sullair LLC ....B 219 879-5451
Michigan City (G-9849)
Sullivan-Palatek Inc ....D 219 874-2497
Michigan City (G-9850)
Vanair Manufacturing Inc ....C 219 879-5100
Michigan City (G-9857)

COMPRESSORS: Refrigeration & Air Conditioning Eqpt

Griffen Plmbng-Heating-Cooling ....E 574 295-2440
Elkhart (G-2900)

COMPRESSORS: Repairing

Cook Compression Inc ....A 502 515-6900
Jeffersonville (G-8345)

COMPRESSORS: Wholesalers

Atlas Machine and Supply Inc ....F 812 423-7762
Evansville (G-3367)
Motorcraft Inc ....G 765 282-4272
Muncie (G-10525)

COMPUTER & COMPUTER SOFTWARE STORES

3btech Inc ....E 574 233-0508
South Bend (G-12688)
Byte Blue Technology Solutions ....G 574 903-5637
Elkhart (G-2741)
Country Club Computer ....G 317 271-4000
Indianapolis (G-6675)
Coy & Associates ....G 317 787-5089
Indianapolis (G-6682)
PC Max Inc ....G 812 337-0630
Bloomington (G-796)

COMPUTER & COMPUTER SOFTWARE STORES: Peripheral Eqpt

Alpha Prime Computers ....G 260 347-4800
Kendallville (G-8452)

(G-0000) Company's Geographic Section entry number

COMPUTER & COMPUTER SOFTWARE STORES: Software & Access

Riddell Technologies LLC ....G....... 219 213-9602
  Crown Point (G-2296)

COMPUTER & COMPUTER SOFTWARE STORES: Software, Bus/Non-Game

Intelligent Software Inc.......................G....... 219 923-6166
  Munster (G-10610)

COMPUTER & DATA PROCESSING EQPT REPAIR & MAINTENANCE

Bull Hn Info Systems Inc ....E....... 317 686-5500
  Indianapolis (G-6521)
C & P Distributing LLC ....E....... 574 256-1138
  Mishawaka (G-10016)

COMPUTER & OFFICE MACHINE MAINTENANCE & REPAIR

Compumark Industries Inc.....................G....... 219 365-0508
  Saint John (G-12261)
Lasertech Inc ....G....... 812 277-1321
  Bedford (G-559)
PC Max Inc ....G....... 812 337-0630
  Bloomington (G-796)
Riddell Technologies LLC ....G....... 219 213-9602
  Crown Point (G-2296)
Rob Nolley Inc ....G....... 317 825-5211
  Shelbyville (G-12563)
T n Z Technology LLC ....G....... 812 438-1205
  Dillsboro (G-2473)

COMPUTER & SFTWR STORE: Modem, Monitor, Terminal/Disk Drive

Computer Solutions Systems Co ....F....... 812 235-9008
  Terre Haute (G-13215)
Dbisp LLC ....F....... 317 222-1671
  Indianapolis (G-6729)
Johnco Corp ....G....... 317 576-4417
  Indianapolis (G-7308)

COMPUTER FACILITIES MANAGEMENT SVCS

Computer Solutions Systems Co ....F....... 812 235-9008
  Terre Haute (G-13215)
Rob Nolley Inc ....G....... 317 825-5211
  Shelbyville (G-12563)

COMPUTER FORMS

Iu East Business Office ....G....... 765 973-8218
  Richmond (G-12003)
Printegra Corp ....D....... 317 328-0022
  Indianapolis (G-7752)

COMPUTER GRAPHICS SVCS

Big Picture Data Imaging LLC ....G....... 812 235-0202
  Terre Haute (G-13202)
Blasted Works ....G....... 574 583-3211
  Monticello (G-10256)
Byte Blue Technology Solutions ....G....... 574 903-5637
  Elkhart (G-2741)
Cooperative Ventures Ind Corp ....G....... 317 259-7063
  Carmel (G-1343)
Long Tail Corporation ....G....... 260 918-0489
  Fort Wayne (G-4441)

COMPUTER HARDWARE REQUIREMENTS ANALYSIS

Technology MGT Group Inc ....F....... 765 606-1512
  Anderson (G-173)

COMPUTER INTERFACE EQPT: Indl Process

Agri-Tronix Corp ....F....... 317 738-4474
  Franklin (G-4862)
C & K Manufacturing Inc ....F....... 574 264-4063
  Elkhart (G-2743)
Hurco Companies Inc ....C....... 317 293-5309
  Indianapolis (G-7146)
Hurco Companies Inc ....G....... 317 347-6208
  Indianapolis (G-7147)

Milltronics Usa Inc ....E 317 293-5309
  Indianapolis (G-7523)

COMPUTER PAPER WHOLESALERS

Priority Press Inc ....E 317 241-4234
  Indianapolis (G-7759)
Priority Press Inc ....G....... 317 848-9695
  Indianapolis (G-6278)

COMPUTER PERIPHERAL EQPT REPAIR & MAINTENANCE

Diverse Tech Services Inc....................F....... 317 432-6444
  Indianapolis (G-6748)

COMPUTER PERIPHERAL EQPT, NEC

Bull Hn Info Systems Inc ....E....... 317 686-5500
  Indianapolis (G-6521)
C & G Labeling ....G....... 317 396-2953
  Indianapolis (G-6526)
Carson Manufacturing Co Inc ....F....... 317 257-3191
  Indianapolis (G-6560)
Clovis LLC ....G....... 812 944-4791
  Floyds Knobs (G-4009)
Environmental Technology Inc...............E....... 574 233-1202
  South Bend (G-12765)
Impact Cnc LLC ....C....... 260 244-5511
  Columbia City (G-1794)
La Zee Tek ....G....... 260 351-3274
  Hudson (G-6133)
Motorola Inc ....G....... 765 455-5100
  Kokomo (G-8673)
Paradise Ink Inc.................................G....... 812 402-4465
  Evansville (G-3662)
PC Max Inc ....G....... 812 337-0630
  Bloomington (G-796)
Record / Play Tek Inc ....G....... 574 848-5233
  Bristol (G-1078)
Scott Billman ....G....... 317 293-9921
  Indianapolis (G-7905)
Sony Dadc US Inc ....A....... 812 462-8100
  Terre Haute (G-13334)
T n Z Technology LLC ....G....... 812 438-1205
  Dillsboro (G-2473)
Whyte Haus ....G....... 260 484-5666
  Fort Wayne (G-4754)
Xerox Corporation ....G....... 765 778-6249
  Anderson (G-183)

COMPUTER PERIPHERAL EQPT, WHOLESALE

Osc Holdings LLC ....G....... 765 751-7000
  Muncie (G-10540)

COMPUTER PERIPHERAL EQPT: Graphic Displays, Exc Terminals

I E Signs & Graphics LLC ....G....... 574 936-4652
  Plymouth (G-11689)

COMPUTER PHOTOGRAPHY OR PORTRAIT SVC

Formal Affairs Tuxedo Shop ....G....... 574 875-6654
  Elkhart (G-2868)

COMPUTER PROGRAMMING SVCS

Blue Burro Inc ....G....... 904 825-9900
  Bloomington (G-689)
Daily Peru Tribune Pubg Co..................E....... 765 473-6641
  Peru (G-11523)
Envisio Design LLC ....G....... 574 274-4394
  Mishawaka (G-10042)
Fiserv Mrtg Servicing Systems..............C....... 574 282-3300
  South Bend (G-12779)
Ilab LLC ....D....... 317 218-3258
  Indianapolis (G-7158)
Jpe Consulting LLP ....G....... 574 675-9552
  Osceola (G-11379)
Rox Software Inc ....G....... 765 430-7616
  Brookston (G-1107)
Spotlight Cybersecurity LLC ....G....... 805 886-4456
  Lafayette (G-9001)
Spring Ventures Infovation LLC ....G 317 847-1117
  Greenwood (G-5750)
Sullivan Engineered Services................G....... 812 294-1724
  Henryville (G-6033)

Techknowledgey Inc ....G....... 574 971-4267
  Goshen (G-5339)
Via Development Corp.........................E....... 888 225-5842
  Marion (G-9570)

COMPUTER PROGRAMMING SVCS: Custom

Business Adventures Inc ....G....... 574 674-9996
  Osceola (G-11371)
Cyberia Ltd ....G....... 317 721-2582
  Indianapolis (G-6719)

COMPUTER RELATED MAINTENANCE SVCS

Computrain Learning Center Inc ....F....... 812 235-7419
  Terre Haute (G-13216)
Sim 2 K Inc.......................................F....... 317 251-7920
  Indianapolis (G-7947)

COMPUTER SOFTWARE DEVELOPMENT

39 Degrees North LLC ....F....... 855 447-3939
  Bloomington (G-650)
Advanced Designs Corp ....F....... 812 333-1922
  Bloomington (G-657)
App Press LLC ....G....... 317 661-4759
  Indianapolis (G-6408)
Leidos Inc ....E....... 812 863-3100
  Crane (G-2128)
Lhp Software LLC ....D....... 812 373-0870
  Columbus (G-1960)
Lord Fms Games ....G....... 317 710-2253
  Indianapolis (G-7419)
Policystat LLC ....D....... 317 644-1296
  Carmel (G-1452)
Regional Data Services Inc ....F....... 219 661-3200
  Crown Point (G-2295)
Riddell Technologies LLC ....G....... 219 213-9602
  Crown Point (G-2296)
Sahasra Technologies Corp..................E....... 317 845-5326
  Indianapolis (G-7887)
SBS Cybermetrix Inc ....G....... 812 378-7960
  Columbus (G-2011)
SGS Cybermetrix Inc ....G....... 800 713-1203
  Columbus (G-2013)
Technalysis Inc ....E....... 317 291-1985
  Indianapolis (G-8049)

COMPUTER SOFTWARE DEVELOPMENT & APPLICATIONS

Depth Plus Design LLC ....G....... 317 370-0532
  Westfield (G-14158)
Flat Electronics LLC ....G....... 765 414-6635
  Lafayette (G-8899)
Life Less Ordinary LLC ....G....... 317 727-4277
  Indianapolis (G-7403)
Paragon Medical Inc ....B....... 574 594-2140
  Pierceton (G-11576)
Peter Stone Company.........................E....... 260 768-9150
  Shipshewana (G-12643)
Pillar Innovations LLC ....G....... 812 474-9080
  Evansville (G-3670)
Smallwood Consulting LLC ....G....... 812 406-8040
  Sellersburg (G-12418)
Spensa Technologies Inc ....E....... 765 588-3592
  West Lafayette (G-14110)

COMPUTER SOFTWARE SYSTEMS ANALYSIS & DESIGN: Custom

Aunalytics Inc...................................G....... 574 307-9230
  South Bend (G-12716)
Baugh Enterprises Inc.........................F....... 812 334-8189
  Bloomington (G-674)
Diverse Tech Services Inc....................F....... 317 432-6444
  Indianapolis (G-6748)
Flynn Media LLC ....G....... 317 536-2972
  Indianapolis (G-6942)
Image Vault LLC ....G....... 812 948-8400
  New Albany (G-10802)
Infinite Ai Inc ....G....... 317 965-4850
  Carmel (G-1415)
Technology MGT Group Inc ....F....... 765 606-1512
  Anderson (G-173)
Thickstat Inc.....................................G....... 201 294-1896
  Indianapolis (G-8061)
Tipton Engrg Elc Mtr Svcs Inc ....G....... 765 963-3380
  Sharpsville (G-12507)
W T Boone Enterprises Inc ....G....... 317 738-0275
  Franklin (G-4939)

Web Software LLC .... F 765 452-3936
Kokomo (G-8716)

COMPUTER STORAGE DEVICES, NEC

EMC Corporation .... E 317 706-8600
Indianapolis (G-6849)
EMC Projects .... G 317 420-8005
Indianapolis (G-6850)
Emc2 .... G 317 435-8021
Indianapolis (G-6851)
Integrity Qntum Innvations LLC .... G 765 537-9037
Martinsville (G-9617)
Quantum 7 Group LLC .... G 812 824-9378
Bloomington (G-804)
Quantum Covers LLC .... G 219 307-0893
Valparaiso (G-13605)
Quantum Creative LLC .... G 812 381-2586
Bloomington (G-805)
Quantum Tech USA .... G 360 400-0905
Bloomington (G-806)
Quantumtech LLC .... G 786 512-0827
Indianapolis (G-7803)
R B Annis Instruments Inc .... G 765 848-1621
Greencastle (G-5476)
Scale Computing Inc .... E 317 856-9959
Indianapolis (G-7901)
Sony Dadc US Inc .... A 812 462-8100
Terre Haute (G-13334)
Techknowledgey Inc .... G 574 971-4267
Goshen (G-5339)

COMPUTER SYSTEMS ANALYSIS & DESIGN

Compumark Industries Inc .... G 219 365-0508
Saint John (G-12261)
Diverse Tech Services Inc .... F 317 432-6444
Indianapolis (G-6748)

COMPUTER TERMINALS

Server Partners LLC .... G 317 917-2000
Indianapolis (G-7916)

COMPUTER-AIDED ENGINEERING SYSTEMS SVCS

Future Wave Graphics Inc .... G 574 389-8803
Elkhart (G-2873)

COMPUTER-AIDED MANUFACTURING SYSTEMS SVCS

Shadow Graphix Inc .... G 317 481-9710
Indianapolis (G-7922)

COMPUTERS, NEC

3btech Inc .... E 574 233-0508
South Bend (G-12688)
Alpha Prime Computers .... G 260 347-4800
Kendallville (G-8452)
C & K Enterprises Inc .... E 260 624-3123
Angola (G-201)
Computer Solutions Systems Co ...... F 812 235-9008
Terre Haute (G-13215)
Country Club Computer .... G 317 271-4000
Indianapolis (G-6675)
Creative Logic Equipment Corp ...... G 317 271-1100
Indianapolis (G-6689)
Dcs Car Audio .... G 812 437-8488
Evansville (G-3454)
Ewireless LLC .... G 317 536-0400
Indianapolis (G-6887)
Futuretek .... G 317 631-0098
Indianapolis (G-6972)
Gary Devoss .... G 765 369-2492
Redkey (G-11898)
Hewlett-Packard Co .... G 765 534-4468
Lapel (G-9119)
Jacyl Technology Inc .... G 260 471-6067
Fort Wayne (G-4390)
Kimball Electronics Inc .... B 812 634-4200
Jasper (G-8272)
Kimball Electronics Group LLC ...... A 812 634-4000
Jasper (G-8273)
L5 Solutions LLC .... G 317 436-1044
Indianapolis (G-7371)
Milani Custom Homes LLC .... G 219 455-5804
Merrillville (G-9734)
Packetvac LLC .... G 317 414-6137
Indianapolis (G-7647)

PC Max Inc .... G 812 337-0630
Bloomington (G-796)
Prevail Design Systems LLC .... G 260 245-1245
Huntertown (G-6145)
Q-Edge Corporation .... E 317 203-6800
Plainfield (G-11638)

COMPUTERS, NEC, WHOLESALE

C & P Distributing LLC .... E 574 256-1138
Mishawaka (G-10016)

COMPUTERS, PERIPHERALS & SOFTWARE, WHOLESALE: Mainframe

Maddenco Inc .... F 812 474-6245
Evansville (G-3609)

COMPUTERS, PERIPHERALS & SOFTWARE, WHOLESALE: Software

Ilab LLC .... D 317 218-3258
Indianapolis (G-7158)
Tclogic LLC .... G 317 464-5152
Indianapolis (G-8042)

COMPUTERS: Mainframe

Bull Hn Info Systems Inc .... E 317 686-5500
Indianapolis (G-6521)

COMPUTERS: Mini

Oracle America Inc .... E 317 581-0078
Carmel (G-1447)

COMPUTERS: Personal

A Is For Apple Learning Center ...... G 219 629-3514
Hammond (G-5833)
Appel-Olson LLC .... G 219 926-6679
Westville (G-14213)
Apple American Group .... G 317 889-1167
Greenwood (G-5667)
Apple American Language Inst .... G 812 867-7239
Evansville (G-3359)
Apple Blossom Floral .... G 765 649-2480
Anderson (G-68)
Apple Cyber LLC .... G 812 822-1341
Bloomington (G-663)
Apple III LLC .... G 317 691-2869
Carmel (G-1313)
Apple Inc .... G 812 342-4225
Columbus (G-1855)
Apple Ly Ever After Inc .... G 219 838-9397
Highland (G-6035)
Apple Terrace LLC .... G 260 347-9400
Kendallville (G-8454)
Bad Apple Macs LLC .... G 812 274-0469
Madison (G-9445)
Fletchs Apple Lane .... F 317 489-2697
Indianapolis (G-6934)
Green Apple Active LLC .... G 910 585-1151
Westfield (G-14167)
Green Apple Active LLC .... G 317 698-1032
Carmel (G-1389)
Green Apple Utilities Llc .... G 440 278-0183
Zionsville (G-14436)
Greenfield Coffee Company .... G 317 498-9568
Greenfield (G-5533)
Gregory & Appel .... G 317 823-0131
Indianapolis (G-7047)
Happy Apple Educational Svcs .... G 765 338-9293
Connersville (G-2050)
HP Inc .... D 317 566-6200
Indianapolis (G-6268)
HP Inc .... A 317 334-3400
Indianapolis (G-7141)
Indy Web Inc .... G 317 356-3622
Indianapolis (G-7224)
Little Green Apple .... G 219 836-5025
Munster (G-10616)
Little Green Apple .... G 317 272-1168
Avon (G-454)
Little Green Apple .... G 812 853-8761
Newburgh (G-11036)
Little Green Apple Hallmark .... G 219 661-0420
Crown Point (G-2277)
P F Apple LLC .... G 317 773-8683
Noblesville (G-11163)
Road Apple Psychotherapy .... G 574 230-3449
Knox (G-8579)

CONCERT MANAGEMENT SVCS

Mid-America Sound Corporation ..... F 317 947-9880
Greenfield (G-5552)
Trinity Cmmnications Group Inc ..... G 260 484-1029
Fort Wayne (G-4704)

CONCRETE BUGGIES: Powered

Lindas Gone Buggie .... G 219 299-0174
Hobart (G-6089)

CONCRETE BUILDING PRDTS WHOLESALERS

CMa Supply Co Fort Wayne Inc ...... F 260 471-9000
Fort Wayne (G-4164)
Irving Materials Inc .... G 812 254-0820
Washington (G-13987)
Kuert Concrete Inc .... E 574 232-9911
South Bend (G-12831)
Kuert Concrete Inc .... F 574 293-0430
Goshen (G-5259)
Minnick Concrete Products Inc ...... E 260 432-5031
Fort Wayne (G-4477)

CONCRETE PRDTS

AK Industries Inc .... D 574 936-6022
Plymouth (G-11662)
Beaver Gravel Corporation .... D 317 773-0679
Noblesville (G-11065)
Cash Concrete Products Inc .... F 765 653-4007
Greencastle (G-5454)
Cheetah Building Products .... G 812 466-1234
Terre Haute (G-13210)
Concrete Supply LLC .... E 812 474-6715
Evansville (G-3427)
County Materials Corp .... G 317 262-4920
Indianapolis (G-6678)
E & B Paving Inc .... D 317 773-4132
Noblesville (G-11097)
Erie-Haven Inc .... D 260 478-1674
Fort Wayne (G-4241)
Hanson Aggregates East LLC .... F 260 490-9006
Fort Wayne (G-4319)
Hd Supply Construction Supply ...... F 260 471-7619
Fort Wayne (G-4325)
Hi-Tech Concrete Inc .... G 765 477-5550
Lafayette (G-8914)
Hog Slat Incorporated .... F 765 828-0828
Universal (G-13467)
Hydro Conduit of Texas LP .... G 317 769-2261
Whitestown (G-14254)
Illinois Tool Works Inc .... D 219 874-4217
Michigan City (G-9803)
Jones & Sons Inc .... E 812 882-2957
Vincennes (G-13687)
Kerr Concrete Pipe Co .... G 317 569-9949
Carmel (G-1422)
Lafarge North America Inc .... G 219 378-1193
East Chicago (G-2547)
Legacy Vulcan LLC .... E 219 987-3040
Demotte (G-2443)
Legacy Vulcan LLC .... F 574 293-1536
Elkhart (G-2993)
Legacy Vulcan LLC .... E 219 462-5832
Valparaiso (G-13576)
Maso Inc .... F 260 432-3568
Fort Wayne (G-4454)
Midwest Tile and Concrete Pdts ...... G 260 749-5173
Woodburn (G-14388)
Mjs Concrete .... G 260 341-5640
Woodburn (G-14389)
Oldcastle Apg Midwest Inc .... A 317 786-0971
Indianapolis (G-7615)
Plaster Shak .... G 317 881-6518
Greenwood (G-5733)
Precast Specialties Inc .... F 260 623-6131
Monroeville (G-10198)
Rinker Materials .... G 317 241-8237
Indianapolis (G-7845)
Rogers Group Inc .... G 765 342-6898
Martinsville (G-9635)
Scepter Steel Inc .... F 317 996-2103
Monrovia (G-10206)
Slon Inc .... F 765 884-1792
Fowler (G-4807)
St Regis Culvert Inc .... F 317 353-8065
Indianapolis (G-7982)
Western Green LLC .... E 812 963-3373
Poseyville (G-11862)

Wilbert Sexton Corporation ....G...... 812 882-3555
  Vincennes (G-13717)

CONCRETE PRDTS, PRECAST, NEC

Beaver Products Inc ....F...... 317 773-0679
  Noblesville (G-11066)
Concrete Lady Inc ....E...... 812 256-2765
  Otisco (G-11416)
Dyer Vault Company Inc ....F...... 219 865-2521
  Dyer (G-2496)
Edgewood Corporation Indiana............E...... 317 786-9208
  Carmel (G-1369)
Hessit Works Inc ....G...... 812 829-6246
  Freedom (G-4949)
Hoosier Precast LLC ....F...... 812 883-4665
  Salem (G-12292)
Jones & Sons Inc ....E...... 812 299-2287
  Terre Haute (G-13261)
L Thorn Company Inc ....E...... 812 246-4461
  New Albany (G-10815)
Lowell Concrete Products Inc ....E...... 219 696-3339
  Lowell (G-9415)
McCreary Concrete Products Inc ....G...... 765 932-3058
  Rushville (G-12229)
McCreary Concrete Products Inc ....G...... 317 844-5157
  Tipton (G-13399)
S & M Precast Inc ....G...... 812 294-3703
  Henryville (G-6032)
S & S Precast Inc ....E...... 574 946-4123
  Winamac (G-14320)
S S M Inc ....G...... 317 357-4552
  Indianapolis (G-7880)
Sanders Pre-Cast Concrete ....E...... 317 769-5503
  Whitestown (G-14261)
Trenwa Inc ....E...... 812 427-2217
  Florence (G-4005)

CONCRETE: Asphaltic, Not From Refineries

03 Corp ....G...... 812 597-0276
  Morgantown (G-10346)
Concrete & Asphalt Recycl Inc ....F...... 574 237-1928
  Mishawaka (G-10021)
Dynamic Landscapes LLC ....E...... 317 409-3487
  Indianapolis (G-6779)
Freds Driveways Inc ....G...... 317 770-6094
  Noblesville (G-11106)

CONCRETE: Ready-Mixed

A & T Concrete Supply Inc ....E...... 812 753-4252
  Fort Branch (G-4025)
Aggregate Industries - Mwr Inc ....E...... 260 665-2052
  Angola (G-189)
All-Rite Ready Mix Inc ....F...... 812 926-0920
  Aurora (G-369)
Attica Ready Mixed Concrete ....E...... 765 762-2424
  Attica (G-297)
Beaver Gravel Corporation ....D...... 317 773-0679
  Noblesville (G-11065)
Brim Concrete Inc ....G...... 765 564-4975
  Delphi (G-2415)
Busters Cement Products Inc...............F...... 765 529-0287
  New Castle (G-10894)
Cash Concrete Products Inc ....F...... 765 653-4007
  Greencastle (G-5454)
Cash Concrete Products Inc ....G...... 765 653-4887
  Greencastle (G-5455)
Cemex ....G...... 317 351-9912
  Indianapolis (G-6575)
Cemex Materials LLC..........................E...... 317 891-7500
  Greenfield (G-5512)
Cemex Materials LLC..........................E...... 317 891-3015
  Indianapolis (G-6576)
Cemex Materials LLC..........................E...... 317 891-3015
  Greenfield (G-5513)
Cemex Materials LLC..........................E...... 317 769-5801
  Whitestown (G-14250)
Center Concrete Inc...........................G...... 800 453-4224
  Butler (G-1224)
Central Concrete Supply LLC ....F...... 812 481-2331
  Jasper (G-8242)
Concrete Pumping Michiana LLC..........G...... 574 936-2140
  Plymouth (G-11677)
Concrete Supply LLC ....E...... 812 474-6715
  Evansville (G-3427)
Crawford County Concrete ....G...... 812 739-2707
  Leavenworth (G-9163)
E & B Paving Inc ....F...... 260 356-0828
  Huntington (G-6201)

E & B Paving Inc ....G...... 765 472-3626
  Peru (G-11525)
E & B Paving Inc ....F...... 317 781-1030
  Noblesville (G-11096)
E & B Paving Inc ....G...... 317 773-8216
  Noblesville (G-11098)
Eagle Ready-Mix Inc ....E...... 574 642-4455
  Goshen (G-5209)
Erie Haven Inc ....G...... 260 665-2052
  Angola (G-212)
Erie-Haven Inc ....D...... 260 478-1674
  Fort Wayne (G-4241)
Erie-Haven Inc ....E...... 260 353-1133
  Bluffton (G-874)
Erie-Haven Inc ....G...... 260 478-1674
  Auburn (G-330)
Ernest Enterprises Inc ....G...... 765 584-5700
  Winchester (G-14329)
Ernst Concrete ....G...... 260 726-8282
  Portland (G-11818)
Ernst Concrete Enterprises ....G...... 812 284-5205
  Sellersburg (G-12393)
Harrison Concrete...............................G...... 812 275-6682
  Bedford (G-547)
Hoosier Ready Mix LLC ....F...... 812 254-7625
  Washington (G-13986)
Hopkins Gravel Sand & Concrete..........G...... 317 831-2704
  Mooresville (G-10311)
Im Indiana Holdings Inc.......................G...... 260 478-1674
  Fort Wayne (G-4359)
IMI Bloomfield ....G...... 812 384-0045
  Bloomfield (G-639)
IMI South LLC ....E...... 812 945-6605
  New Albany (G-10803)
IMI South LLC ....G...... 812 273-1428
  Madison (G-9472)
IMI South LLC ....G...... 812 738-4173
  Corydon (G-2103)
IMI South LLC ....G...... 812 284-9732
  Clarksville (G-1686)
IMI Southwest Inc ....E...... 812 424-3554
  Evansville (G-3548)
Interstate Block Corporation ....G...... 812 273-1742
  Madison (G-9473)
Irving Materials Inc ....D...... 317 326-3101
  Greenfield (G-5542)
Irving Materials Inc ....F...... 812 424-3551
  Evansville (G-3567)
Irving Materials Inc ....G...... 765 825-2581
  Connersville (G-2056)
Irving Materials Inc ....G...... 765 644-8819
  Anderson (G-122)
Irving Materials Inc ....F...... 317 770-1745
  Noblesville (G-11132)
Irving Materials Inc ....E...... 317 773-3640
  Noblesville (G-11133)
Irving Materials Inc ....G...... 317 335-2121
  Fishers (G-3989)
Irving Materials Inc ....E...... 317 784-5433
  Indianapolis (G-7268)
Irving Materials Inc ....F...... 765 654-5333
  Frankfort (G-4838)
Irving Materials Inc ....G...... 765 482-5620
  Lebanon (G-9193)
Irving Materials Inc ....G...... 765 342-3369
  Martinsville (G-9618)
Irving Materials Inc ....G...... 812 254-0820
  Washington (G-13987)
Irving Materials Inc ....G...... 765 836-4007
  Muncie (G-10495)
Irving Materials Inc ....E...... 765 288-5566
  Muncie (G-10496)
Irving Materials Inc ....G...... 765 755-3447
  Springport (G-13059)
Irving Materials Inc ....F...... 260 824-3428
  Bluffton (G-880)
Irving Materials Inc ....F...... 765 288-0288
  Muncie (G-10497)
Irving Materials Inc ....G...... 765 478-4914
  Cambridge City (G-1257)
Irving Materials Inc ....F...... 574 946-3754
  Winamac (G-14308)
Irving Materials Inc ....G...... 812 883-4242
  Scottsburg (G-12368)
Irving Materials Inc ....F...... 812 683-4444
  Huntingburg (G-6172)
Irving Materials Inc ....G...... 765 362-6904
  Crawfordsville (G-2163)
Irving Materials Inc ....E...... 765 423-2533
  Lafayette (G-8926)

Irving Materials Inc ....E...... 765 743-3806
  West Lafayette (G-14078)
Irving Materials Inc ....G...... 219 261-2441
  Remington (G-11908)
Irving Materials Inc ....F...... 765 922-7991
  Swayzee (G-13124)
Irving Materials Inc ....G...... 765 552-5041
  Elwood (G-3300)
Irving Materials Inc ....G...... 765 728-5335
  Montpelier (G-10292)
Irving Materials Inc ....G...... 812 275-7450
  Bedford (G-554)
Irving Materials Inc ....G...... 765 452-4044
  Kokomo (G-8649)
Irving Materials Inc ....G...... 765 922-7931
  Swayzee (G-13125)
Irving Materials Inc ....G...... 317 888-0157
  Greenwood (G-5708)
Irving Materials Inc ....F...... 765 778-4760
  Anderson (G-123)
Irving Materials Inc ....G...... 765 472-5370
  Peru (G-11533)
Irving Materials Inc ....G...... 765 675-6327
  Tipton (G-13394)
Irving Materials Inc ....F...... 765 922-7285
  Marion (G-9534)
Irving Materials Inc ....F...... 765 674-2271
  Marion (G-9535)
Irving Materials Inc ....G...... 812 333-8530
  Bloomington (G-751)
Irving Materials Inc ....G...... 317 535-7566
  Whiteland (G-14241)
Irving Materials Inc ....F...... 317 872-0152
  Indianapolis (G-7269)
Irving Materials Inc ....G...... 317 843-2944
  Indianapolis (G-7270)
Irving Materials Inc ....F...... 317 783-3381
  Indianapolis (G-7271)
Irving Materials Inc ....G...... 574 722-3420
  Logansport (G-9342)
Irving Materials Inc ....F...... 317 243-7391
  Indianapolis (G-7272)
Irving Materials Inc ....F...... 317 831-0224
  Mooresville (G-10315)
Irving Materials Inc ....F...... 317 899-2187
  Indianapolis (G-7273)
Irving Materials Inc ....G...... 765 647-6533
  Brookville (G-1119)
Irving Materials Inc ....F...... 260 356-7214
  Huntington (G-6219)
Jack Mix ....G...... 812 923-8679
  Floyds Knobs (G-4014)
Jones & Sons Inc ....G...... 812 254-4731
  Washington (G-13988)
Jones & Sons Inc ....E...... 812 882-2957
  Vincennes (G-13687)
Jones & Sons Inc ....E...... 812 299-2287
  Terre Haute (G-13261)
Kentucky Concrete Indiana LLC............E...... 812 282-6671
  Jeffersonville (G-8388)
Keystone Concrete Inc ....E...... 260 693-6437
  Churubusco (G-1653)
Kuert Concrete Inc.............................E...... 574 232-9911
  South Bend (G-12831)
Kuert Concrete Inc.............................G...... 574 293-0430
  Goshen (G-5259)
Kuert Concrete Inc.............................G...... 574 223-2414
  Rochester (G-12131)
Kuert Concrete Inc.............................F...... 574 453-3993
  Warsaw (G-13899)
Lafarge North America Inc ....G...... 219 378-1193
  East Chicago (G-2547)
Lake George Material & Sup Co ....G...... 219 942-1912
  Hobart (G-6087)
Lees Ready-Mix & Trucking ....G...... 812 522-7270
  Seymour (G-12466)
Lees Ready-Mix & Trucking Inc............E...... 812 346-9767
  North Vernon (G-11267)
Lees Ready-Mix & Trucking Inc............F...... 812 372-1800
  Columbus (G-1958)
Lehigh Cement Company LLC...............C...... 812 849-2191
  Mitchell (G-10165)
Lehigh Cement Company LLC...............G...... 877 534-4442
  Logansport (G-9347)
Lewis Jerry Cnstr & Excvtg ....G...... 765 653-2800
  Greencastle (G-5467)
Lone Star Industries Inc......................D...... 317 706-3314
  Indianapolis (G-6271)
Ma-Ri-Al Corp ....D...... 317 773-0679
  Noblesville (G-11143)

PRODUCT

McIntire Concrete ....E..... 765 759-7111
Muncie (G-10519)

Mendoza Mexican Mix ....G... 219 791-9034
Merrillville (G-9731)

Mendozas Inc ....G... 219 791-9034
Merrillville (G-9732)

Meuth Construction Supply Inc ....F..... 812 424-8554
Evansville (G-3624)

Mulzer Crushed Stone Inc ....E..... 812 547-7921
Tell City (G-13167)

Mulzer Crushed Stone Inc ....E..... 812 547-3467
Tell City (G-13168)

N E W Interstate Concrete Inc ....F..... 812 234-5983
Terre Haute (G-13288)

Naas Inc ....F..... 812 385-3578
Princeton (G-11879)

Ohio Valley Ready Mix Inc ....E..... 812 282-6671
Jeffersonville (G-8407)

Orange County Concrete Inc ......G... 812 865-2425
Orleans (G-11365)

Ozinga Bros Inc ....G... 219 956-3418
Wheatfield (G-14228)

Ozinga Bros Inc ....E..... 574 546-2550
Bremen (G-1013)

Ozinga Bros Inc ....E..... 574 642-4455
Goshen (G-5303)

Ozinga Bros Inc ....D..... 574 971-8239
Goshen (G-5304)

Ozinga Bros Inc ....D..... 219 949-9800
Portage (G-11786)

Ozinga Bros Inc ....E..... 219 662-0925
Crown Point (G-2282)

Ozinga Indiana Rdymx Con Inc ....F..... 219 949-9800
Gary (G-5082)

Pepcon Concrete Inc ....G... 765 964-6572
Union City (G-13459)

Plymouth Ready Mart Inc ....G... 574 936-5251
Plymouth (G-11715)

Prairie Group ....E..... 812 877-9886
Terre Haute (G-13307)

Precast Solutions Inc ....F..... 317 545-6557
Whitestown (G-14259)

Primed & Ready LLC ....G... 317 694-2028
Indianapolis (G-7747)

Purdy Concrete Inc ....E..... 765 477-7687
Lafayette (G-8984)

Purdy Materials Inc ....F..... 765 474-8993
Lafayette (G-8985)

Quikrete Companies Inc ....E..... 317 251-2281
Indianapolis (G-7805)

Raver Ready Mix Concrete LLC ....G... 812 662-7900
Greensburg (G-5631)

Rosskovenski Concrete & Rdymx ....G... 765 832-6103
Clinton (G-1720)

Sagamore Ready Mix ....G... 317 573-5410
Indianapolis (G-6280)

Sagamore Ready-Mix LLC ....G... 317 783-3768
Indianapolis (G-7886)

Sagamore Ready-Mix LLC ....G... 317 570-6201
Fishers (G-3967)

Schmaltz Ready Mix Concrete ....G... 812 689-5140
Osgood (G-11394)

Shelby Gravel Inc ....E..... 317 398-4485
Shelbyville (G-12567)

Shelby Gravel Inc ....F..... 317 738-3445
Franklin (G-4929)

Shelby Gravel Inc ....E..... 317 784-6678
Indianapolis (G-7929)

Shelby Gravel Inc ....G... 765 932-3292
Rushville (G-12233)

Shelby Gravel Inc ....E..... 317 804-8100
Westfield (G-14188)

Shelby Gravel Inc ....F..... 317 216-7556
Indianapolis (G-7930)

Smith Ready Mix Inc ....F..... 219 462-3191
Valparaiso (G-13620)

Smith Ready Mix Inc ....G... 219 374-5581
Cedar Lake (G-1533)

Smith Ready Mix Inc ....F..... 219 874-6219
Michigan City (G-9844)

Smith Ready Mix Inc ....F..... 219 374-5581
Valparaiso (G-13621)

Southfield Corporation ....E..... 812 824-1355
Bloomington (G-829)

Southfield Corporation ....E..... 317 773-5340
Noblesville (G-11186)

Speedway Redi Mix Inc ....G... 260 496-8877
Fort Wayne (G-4641)

Speedway Redi Mix Inc ....G... 765 671-1020
Marion (G-9563)

Speedway Redi Mix Inc ....G... 260 244-7205
Columbia City (G-1836)

Speedway Redi Mix Inc ....F..... 260 356-5600
Huntington (G-6250)

Speedway Redi Mix Inc ....G... 260 665-5999
Angola (G-244)

Spurlino Mtls Indianapolis LLC ....E..... 765 339-4055
Linden (G-9305)

St Henry Tile Co Inc ....E..... 260 589-2880
Berne (G-626)

Sullivan IMI ....G... 812 268-3306
Sullivan (G-13096)

Van Keppel Redi-Mix Inc ....F..... 219 987-2811
Demotte (G-2450)

Wdmi Inc ....G... 574 291-7100
South Bend (G-12989)

Wdmi Inc ....F..... 765 868-9646
Kokomo (G-8715)

Zimco Materials Inc ....G... 219 883-0870
Gary (G-5117)

CONDENSERS: Heat Transfer Eqpt, Evaporative

Stewart Warner South Wind ....G... 812 547-7071
Indianapolis (G-8005)

CONDENSERS: Refrigeration

Emerson Climate Tech Inc ....G... 765 932-2956
Rushville (G-12219)

Emerson Climate Tech Inc ....G... 937 498-3671
Greenfield (G-5525)

Emerson Climate Tech Inc ....B..... 765 932-1902
Rushville (G-12220)

Emerson Climate Tech Inc ....C..... 317 968-4250
Greenfield (G-5526)

CONDUITS & FITTINGS: Electric

Appleton Grp LLC ....D..... 219 326-5936
La Porte (G-8734)

Regal Beloit America Inc ....C..... 574 583-9171
Monticello (G-10282)

CONFECTIONERY PRDTS WHOLESALERS

Poore Brothers - Bluffton LLC ....B..... 260 824-2800
Bluffton (G-885)

Sweet Things Inc ....F..... 317 872-8720
Indianapolis (G-8028)

CONFECTIONS & CANDY

Abbotts Candy and Gifts Inc ......E..... 765 489-4442
Hagerstown (G-5801)

Albanese Conf Group Inc ....C..... 219 942-1877
Merrillville (G-9693)

Albanese Conf Group Inc ....G... 219 738-2333
Merrillville (G-9694)

Brookes Candy Co ....G... 765 665-3646
Clinton (G-1715)

Candies Inc ....F..... 260 747-7514
Fort Wayne (G-4138)

Candy Dish Inc ....G... 317 269-6262
Nashville (G-10719)

CK Products LLC ....D..... 260 484-2517
Fort Wayne (G-4154)

Claeys Candy Inc ....F..... 574 287-1818
South Bend (G-12735)

Dulceria Garza Inc ....G... 219 397-1062
East Chicago (G-2525)

Goods Candies ....G... 765 785-6776
Kennard (G-8516)

Lowerys Home Made Candies ......E..... 765 288-7300
Muncie (G-10513)

Nestle Usa Inc ....C..... 765 778-6000
Anderson (G-144)

Olympia Candy Kitchen ....F..... 574 533-5040
Goshen (G-5301)

Schimpff Confectionery ....F..... 812 283-8367
Jeffersonville (G-8423)

Stephen Libs Candy Co Inc ....F..... 812 473-0048
Evansville (G-3748)

Sugar Creek Candies Inc ....F..... 765 681-1607
Peru (G-11550)

Sweet Properties LLC ....G... 812 283-8367
Jeffersonville (G-8431)

Ugo Bars LLC ....G... 812 322-3499
Bloomington (G-850)

Zachary Confections Inc ....C..... 765 659-4751
Frankfort (G-4861)

CONFINEMENT SURVEILLANCE SYS MAINTENANCE & MONITORING SVCS

Applied Technology Group Inc .....F..... 260 482-2844
Fort Wayne (G-4084)

CONNECTORS & TERMINALS: Electrical Device Uses

Outman Industries Inc ....G... 260 467-1576
Fort Wayne (G-4514)

CONNECTORS: Cord, Electric

E M F Corp ....E..... 260 665-9541
Angola (G-208)

CONNECTORS: Electrical

Connecta Corporation ....F..... 317 923-9282
Indianapolis (G-6651)

CONNECTORS: Electronic

Accu-Mold LLC ....E..... 269 323-0388
Mishawaka (G-9989)

Advanced Metal Etching Inc ....E..... 260 894-4189
Ligonier (G-9275)

Alexander Machine ....G... 812 879-4982
Gosport (G-5349)

Assembly Masters Inc ....G... 574 293-9026
Mishawaka (G-9999)

CTS Corporation ....E..... 574 293-7511
Elkhart (G-2780)

Edinburgh Connector Company .....E..... 812 526-8801
Edinburgh (G-2611)

Kirby Risk Corporation ....B..... 765 447-1402
Lafayette (G-8942)

Major League Electronics LLC .....E..... 812 670-4174
Jeffersonville (G-8394)

Molex LLC ....G... 317 770-4900
Noblesville (G-11154)

Molex LLC ....G... 317 834-5600
Mooresville (G-10323)

PMG Incorporated ....G... 574 291-3805
South Bend (G-12899)

Smith Ruth C Rn Prof Electrlg ....G... 812 423-4760
Evansville (G-3737)

Zh Brothers International Inc ......G... 313 718-6732
Mishawaka (G-10153)

CONSTRUCTION & MINING MACHINERY WHOLESALERS

Caterpillar Inc ....D..... 630 743-4094
Greenfield (G-5511)

Macallister Machinery Co Inc ......F..... 765 966-0759
Richmond (G-12012)

Paulus Plastic Company Inc ....G... 574 834-7663
North Webster (G-11299)

Square 1 Dsign Manufacture Inc ....F..... 866 647-7771
Shelbyville (G-12570)

CONSTRUCTION & ROAD MAINTENANCE EQPT: Drags, Road

Linkel Company ....G... 812 934-5190
Batesville (G-510)

CONSTRUCTION EQPT REPAIR SVCS

Cindon Inc ....F..... 812 853-5450
Newburgh (G-11024)

CONSTRUCTION EQPT: Airport

Ameribridge LLC ....D..... 317 826-2000
Indianapolis (G-6384)

Mears Machine Corp ....D..... 317 745-0656
Danville (G-2353)

CONSTRUCTION EQPT: Attachments

Coneqtec Corp ....F..... 812 446-4055
Carbon (G-1292)

Maximum Spndle Utilization Inc ....E..... 812 526-8250
Edinburgh (G-2618)

Premier Hydraulic Augers Inc ......E..... 260 456-8518
Fort Wayne (G-4555)

Tmf Center Inc ....C..... 765 762-3800
Williamsport (G-14298)

Tmf Center Inc.................................F 765 762-1000
  Williamsport (G-14299)

CONSTRUCTION EQPT: Backhoes, Tractors, Cranes & Similar Eqpt

Dyna-Fab Corporation.............................E 765 893-4423
  West Lebanon (G-14119)

CONSTRUCTION EQPT: Buckets, Excavating, Clamshell, Etc

A & T Construction and Excvtg ....G 219 314-2439
  Cedar Lake (G-1524)
Wag-Way Tool Incorporated..................F 812 886-0598
  Vincennes (G-13715)

CONSTRUCTION EQPT: Bulldozers

Joyce Consulting LLC............................G 317 577-8504
  Indianapolis (G-7315)

CONSTRUCTION EQPT: Catch Basin Cleaners

Mortar Net Usa Ltd ....G 800 664-6638
  Burns Harbor (G-1218)

CONSTRUCTION EQPT: Cranes

Konecranes Inc ....F 219 661-9602
  Crown Point (G-2272)
Marshall Companies Indiana ....G 317 769-2666
  Lebanon (G-9202)

CONSTRUCTION EQPT: Entrenching Machines

Hurricane Ditcher Company Inc ....F 812 886-9663
  Vincennes (G-13684)

CONSTRUCTION EQPT: Finishers & Spreaders

American Industrial Corp ....E 317 859-9900
  Greenwood (G-5665)

CONSTRUCTION EQPT: Hammer Mills, Port, Incl Rock/Ore Crush

Commercial Star Inc ....F 765 386-2800
  Coatesville (G-1747)

CONSTRUCTION EQPT: Spreaders, Aggregates

Wick - Fab Inc..E 260 897-3303
  Avilla (G-421)

CONSTRUCTION EQPT: Subgraders

Harrell Family LLC ....G 317 770-4550
  Noblesville (G-11119)

CONSTRUCTION EQPT: Tractors

Wakarusa Ag LLC ....G 574 862-1163
  Wakarusa (G-13797)

CONSTRUCTION EQPT: Wrecker Hoists, Automobile

Pro-Tote System Inc ....F 574 287-6006
  South Bend (G-12905)

CONSTRUCTION MATERIALS, WHOL: Concrete/Cinder Bldg Prdts

Irving Materials Inc ....G 765 478-4914
  Cambridge City (G-1257)
Larry Atwood..G 765 525-6851
  Waldron (G-13800)
Martinsville Vault Company ....G 765 342-4576
  Martinsville (G-9623)
Stephenson Block Inc ....G 574 264-6660
  Elkhart (G-3193)

CONSTRUCTION MATERIALS, WHOLESALE: Aggregate

Garrity Stone Inc ....G 317 546-0893
  Indianapolis (G-6985)
Hanson Agrigoods Midwest Inc ....F 317 635-9048
  Cloverdale (G-1727)
Irving Materials Inc ....F 765 288-0288
  Muncie (G-10497)
Lehigh Cement Company LLC...............G 877 534-4442
  Logansport (G-9347)
Marietta Martin Materials Inc................G 317 831-7391
  Martinsville (G-9622)

CONSTRUCTION MATERIALS, WHOLESALE: Air Ducts, Sheet Metal

River Valley Sheet Metal Inc..................E 574 259-2538
  Mishawaka (G-10118)

CONSTRUCTION MATERIALS, WHOLESALE: Architectural Metalwork

Johns Architectural Media ....G 630 450-7539
  Dyer (G-2502)

CONSTRUCTION MATERIALS, WHOLESALE: Asphalt Felts & coating

Monument Chemical LLC.......................F 317 223-2630
  Indianapolis (G-7539)

CONSTRUCTION MATERIALS, WHOLESALE: Awnings

Image One LLC......................................E 317 576-2700
  Fishers (G-3927)

CONSTRUCTION MATERIALS, WHOLESALE: Block, Concrete & Cinder

Slaters Concrete Products.....................G 260 347-0164
  Kendallville (G-8510)

CONSTRUCTION MATERIALS, WHOLESALE: Building, Exterior

Hunter Nutrition Inc ....G 765 563-1003
  Brookston (G-1105)
Kleptz Aluminum Inc ....G 812 238-2946
  Terre Haute (G-13266)
Patrick Industries Inc............................C 574 294-7511
  Elkhart (G-3080)

CONSTRUCTION MATERIALS, WHOLESALE: Building, Interior

Borkholder Corporation ....E 574 773-4083
  Nappanee (G-10654)
Faulkens Floorcover..............................F 574 300-4260
  South Bend (G-12773)

CONSTRUCTION MATERIALS, WHOLESALE: Concrete Mixtures

Shelby Gravel Inc..................................F 812 526-2731
  Edinburgh (G-2628)

CONSTRUCTION MATERIALS, WHOLESALE: Door Frames

Trim-A-Door..G 317 769-8746
  Whitestown (G-14264)

CONSTRUCTION MATERIALS, WHOLESALE: Drywall Materials

Edgewood Corporation Indiana.............E 317 786-9208
  Carmel (G-1369)
Plaster Shak ....G 317 881-6518
  Greenwood (G-5733)

CONSTRUCTION MATERIALS, WHOLESALE: Fiberglass Building Mat

Craft Metal Products Inc........................G 317 545-3252
  Indianapolis (G-6684)
Polygon..G 317 240-1130
  Indianapolis (G-7705)

CONSTRUCTION MATERIALS, WHOLESALE: Glass

Trivector Manufacturing Inc...................E 260 637-0141
  Fort Wayne (G-4706)

Hartford TEC Glass Co Inc....................E 765 348-1282
  Hartford City (G-5983)
Indy Glass Center Inc ....F 317 591-5000
  Indianapolis (G-7217)
Keusch Glass Inc ....F 812 482-2566
  Jasper (G-8271)

CONSTRUCTION MATERIALS, WHOLESALE: Gravel

Rogers Group Inc...................................F 765 893-4463
  Williamsport (G-14296)

CONSTRUCTION MATERIALS, WHOLESALE: Insulation, Mineral Wool

Insulation Fabricators Inc ....D 219 845-2008
  Hammond (G-5900)

CONSTRUCTION MATERIALS, WHOLESALE: Lime Building Prdts

Carmeuse Lime Inc................................D 773 221-9400
  Gary (G-5034)

CONSTRUCTION MATERIALS, WHOLESALE: Lime, Exc Agricultural

Majestic Block & Supply Inc ....G 317 842-6602
  Fishers (G-3943)

CONSTRUCTION MATERIALS, WHOLESALE: Limestone

Hanson Aggregates Midwest LLC.........G 419 399-4846
  Woodburn (G-14383)
Ionic Cut Stone Inc ....G 812 829-3416
  Spencer (G-13029)
U S Aggregates Inc ....E 765 564-2282
  Delphi (G-2430)

CONSTRUCTION MATERIALS, WHOLESALE: Millwork

Architectural Accents Inc.......................F 219 922-9333
  Munster (G-10596)

CONSTRUCTION MATERIALS, WHOLESALE: Molding, All Materials

AMS of Indiana Inc ....E 574 293-5526
  Elkhart (G-2689)
Phoenix Closures Inc ....D 765 658-1800
  Greencastle (G-5472)
Reeds Plastic Tops Inc ....G 765 282-1471
  Muncie (G-10556)

CONSTRUCTION MATERIALS, WHOLESALE: Pallets, Wood

Buckingham Pallets Inc..........................F 317 846-8601
  Carmel (G-1323)
Commercial Pallet Recycl Inc................F 260 829-1021
  Orland (G-11347)
D&G Timber Inc.....................................E 812 486-3356
  Odon (G-11324)
K & S Pallet Inc.....................................F 260 422-1264
  Fort Wayne (G-4402)

CONSTRUCTION MATERIALS, WHOLESALE: Particleboard

Kay Company Inc...................................E 765 659-3388
  Frankfort (G-4840)

CONSTRUCTION MATERIALS, WHOLESALE: Paving Materials

Scotts Grant County Asp Inc ....G 765 664-2754
  Marion (G-9561)

Employee Codes: A=Over 500 employees, B=251-500
C=101-250, D=51-100, E=20-50, F=10-19, G=2-9

2018 Harris Indiana
Industrial Directory

PRODUCT

941

CONSTRUCTION MATERIALS, WHOLESALE: Plywood

National Products Inc ....F 574 457-4565
Syracuse (G-13138)
Robert Weed Plywood Corp ....B 574 848-7631
Bristol (G-1081)

CONSTRUCTION MATERIALS, WHOLESALE: Prefabricated Structures

Bridgewell Resources LLC ....G 812 285-1811
Jeffersonville (G-8331)
Morton Buildings Inc ....F 260 563-2118
Wabash (G-13741)

CONSTRUCTION MATERIALS, WHOLESALE: Roofing & Siding Material

Patrick Industries Inc ....C 574 294-7511
Elkhart (G-3080)

CONSTRUCTION MATERIALS, WHOLESALE: Sand

Irving Materials Inc ....D 317 326-3101
Greenfield (G-5542)
Mulzer Crushed Stone Inc ....E 812 649-5055
Rockport (G-12170)
Old Dutch Sand Co Inc ....G 219 938-7020
Gary (G-5080)

CONSTRUCTION MATERIALS, WHOLESALE: Septic Tanks

Creed & Dyer Precast Inc ....G 574 784-3361
Lakeville (G-9095)

CONSTRUCTION MATERIALS, WHOLESALE: Sewer Pipe, Clay

Independent Concrete Pipe Co ....E 800 875-4920
Indianapolis (G-7171)
M & W Concrete Pipe & Supply ....E 812 426-2871
Evansville (G-3607)
Midwest Tile and Concrete Pdts ....G 260 749-5173
Woodburn (G-14387)

CONSTRUCTION MATERIALS, WHOLESALE: Siding, Exc Wood

C & K United Shtmtl & Mech ....E 812 423-5090
Evansville (G-3407)
Lasalle Bristol Corporation ....C 574 295-4400
Elkhart (G-2985)
Martin Spouting Inc ....G 260 485-5703
Fort Wayne (G-4453)

CONSTRUCTION MATERIALS, WHOLESALE: Stone, Crushed Or Broken

Aggrock Quarries Inc ....E 812 246-2582
Charlestown (G-1557)
Barrett Paving Materials Inc ....F 765 935-3060
Richmond (G-11960)
Crawford County Concrete ....G 812 739-2707
Leavenworth (G-9163)
Hanson Aggregates Midwest LLC ....F 765 653-7205
Cloverdale (G-1726)
Irving Materials Inc ....F 765 778-4760
Anderson (G-123)
Jones & Sons Inc ....E 812 882-2957
Vincennes (G-13687)
Mulzer Crushed Stone Inc ....E 812 547-3467
Tell City (G-13168)
Rogers Group Inc ....E 812 333-6324
Bloomington (G-816)
Rogers Group Inc ....E 812 333-8560
Bloomington (G-813)
Rogers Group Inc ....E 219 474-5125
Kentland (G-8523)
Rogers Group Inc ....D 812 332-6341
Bloomington (G-815)
Rogers Group Inc ....E 812 849-3530
Mitchell (G-10170)

CONSTRUCTION MATERIALS, WHOLESALE: Tile & Clay Prdts

Evansville Block Co Inc ....F 812 422-2864
Evansville (G-3484)

CONSTRUCTION MATERIALS, WHOLESALE: Trim, Sheet Metal

Pb Metal Works ....G 765 489-1311
Hagerstown (G-5810)

CONSTRUCTION MATERIALS, WHOLESALE: Veneer

Dimension Plywood Inc ....G 812 944-6491
New Albany (G-10768)
Heitink Veneers Incorporated ....E 812 336-6436
Bloomington (G-739)
Marwood Inc ....F 812 288-8344
Jeffersonville (G-8398)

CONSTRUCTION MATERIALS, WHOLESALE: Windows

Lansing Building Products Inc ....G 765 448-4363
Lafayette (G-8955)

CONSTRUCTION MATLS, WHOL: Composite Board Prdts, Woodboard

Gutter One Supply ....G 317 872-1257
Indianapolis (G-7060)
Wolfe Engineered Plastics LLC ....G 812 623-8403
Sunman (G-13122)

CONSTRUCTION MATLS, WHOL: Doors, Combination, Screen-Storm

All-Weather Products Inc ....G 812 867-6403
Evansville (G-3348)
Benthall Bros Inc ....E 800 488-5995
Evansville (G-3372)

CONSTRUCTION MATLS, WHOL: Lumber, Rough, Dressed/Finished

Chisholm Lumber & Sup Co Inc ....E 317 547-3535
Indianapolis (G-6601)
Forest Products Group Inc ....E 765 659-1807
Frankfort (G-4832)
Gordon Lumber Company ....G 219 924-0500
Griffith (G-5774)
Hollingsworth Sawmill Inc ....F 765 883-5836
Russiaville (G-12241)
J M McCormick ....G 317 874-4444
Indianapolis (G-7288)
Kinser Timber Products Inc ....E 812 876-4775
Gosport (G-5352)
Mitchell Veneers Inc ....G 812 941-9663
New Albany (G-10832)
MJB Wood Group Inc ....E 574 295-5228
Elkhart (G-3043)
Northside Machine & Tool Inc ....F 765 654-4538
Frankfort (G-4845)
Stock Building Supply LLC ....E 260 490-0616
Fort Wayne (G-4650)
Ufp Granger LLC ....E 574 277-7670
Granger (G-5445)
Waninger Knneth Sons Log Tmber ......F 812 357-5200
Fulda (G-4992)

CONSTRUCTION SAND MINING

Krafft Gravel Inc ....G 260 238-4653
Spencerville (G-13049)
Old Dutch Sand Co Inc ....G 219 938-7020
Gary (G-5080)
Utility Access Solutions Inc ....G 765 744-6528
Ridgeville (G-12083)

CONSTRUCTION: Agricultural Building

Cozy Cat Inc ....G 765 463-1254
Lafayette (G-8879)

CONSTRUCTION: Athletic & Recreation Facilities

Wallar Additions Inc ....E 574 262-1989
Elkhart (G-3253)

CONSTRUCTION: Bridge

Beer and Slabaugh Inc ....E 574 773-3413
Nappanee (G-10653)
Goh Con Inc ....E 812 282-1349
Clarksville (G-1682)
Milestone Contractors LP ....E 812 579-5248
Columbus (G-1975)

CONSTRUCTION: Commercial & Institutional Building

B & G Sales ....G 765 473-7668
Peru (G-11517)
Kammerer Inc ....G 260 349-9098
Kendallville (G-8484)
Milani Custom Homes LLC ....G 219 455-5804
Merrillville (G-9734)
Morgan Excavating ....G 812 385-6036
Oakland City (G-11310)
Structural Source ....G 260 489-0035
Fort Wayne (G-4657)

CONSTRUCTION: Commercial & Office Building, New

A L E Enterprises ....G 317 856-2981
Indianapolis (G-6297)
Burns Construction Inc ....G 574 382-2315
Macy (G-9440)
Cyclone Shop Inc ....G 812 683-2887
Huntingburg (G-6154)
J G Bowers Inc ....E 765 677-1000
Marion (G-9536)
North Webster Construction Inc ....E 574 834-4448
North Webster (G-11297)

CONSTRUCTION: Commercial & Office Buildings, Prefabricated

Classic Buildings Inc ....E 812 944-5821
Clarksville (G-1677)

CONSTRUCTION: Dams, Waterways, Docks & Other Marine

Hampton Equipment LLC ....G 260 740-8704
Fort Wayne (G-4316)

CONSTRUCTION: Drainage System

Park County Aggregates LLC ....G 765 245-2344
Rockville (G-12178)

CONSTRUCTION: Farm Building

Lowes Pellets and Grain Inc ....E 812 663-7863
Greensburg (G-5621)
Schlabach Window & Glass LLC ....G 765 628-2024
Kokomo (G-8691)

CONSTRUCTION: Food Prdts Manufacturing or Packing Plant

Dmp LLC ....G 812 699-0086
Worthington (G-14394)

CONSTRUCTION: Foundation & Retaining Wall

Thatcher Engineering Corp ....D 219 949-2084
Gary (G-5105)

CONSTRUCTION: Grain Elevator

Miles Farm Supply LLC ....F 812 359-4463
Boonville (G-917)

CONSTRUCTION: Heavy Highway & Street

Niblock Excavating Inc ....F 260 248-2100
Columbia City (G-1812)

CONSTRUCTION: Indl Building & Warehouse

All-Phase Construction Co LLC ....G 317 345-7057
Fishers (G-3869)
Egenolf Contg & Rigging II Inc ....D 317 787-5301
Indianapolis (G-6812)
Hale Industries Inc ....E 317 577-0337
Fortville (G-4778)

Hgmc Supply Inc.................................F........317 351-9500
Indianapolis (G-7101)

CONSTRUCTION: Indl Buildings, New, NEC

Industrial Contrs Skanska Inc ....E........812 423-7832
Evansville (G-3555)

Matrix Nac.......................................F........219 931-6600
Hammond (G-5914)

CONSTRUCTION: Multi-Family Housing

Miller Brothers Builders Inc..................E........574 533-8602
Goshen (G-5293)

CONSTRUCTION: Pharmaceutical Manufacturing Plant

Biologics Modular LLC.......................G........317 456-9191
Brownsburg (G-1137)

CONSTRUCTION: Pipeline, NEC

GI Properties Inc ....G........219 763-1177
Portage (G-11765)

CONSTRUCTION: Pond

Leistner Aquatic Services Inc...............G........317 535-6099
Whiteland (G-14242)

Sanco Industries Inc..........................G........260 467-1791
Fort Wayne (G-4603)

Sanco Industries Inc..........................E........260 426-6281
Fort Wayne (G-4604)

CONSTRUCTION: Residential, Nec

Kings-Qlity Rstrtion Svcs LLC..............F........812 944-4347
New Albany (G-10814)

CONSTRUCTION: Scaffolding

Top Lock Corporation.........................G........317 831-2000
Mooresville (G-10344)

CONSTRUCTION: Sewer Line

Beer and Slabaugh Inc.......................E........574 773-3413
Nappanee (G-10653)

CONSTRUCTION: Single-Family Housing

Abari Properties Development ....G........317 721-9230
Indianapolis (G-6306)

All American Group Inc ....E........574 262-0123
Elkhart (G-2674)

Expedition Log Homes ....G........219 663-5555
Crown Point (G-2252)

H & H Home Improvement Inc ....G........812 288-8700
Clarksville (G-1684)

Landmark Home & Land Co Inc............G........219 874-4065
Michigan City (G-9808)

CONSTRUCTION: Single-family Housing, New

E & L Construction Inc ....G........765 525-7081
Manilla (G-9503)

Ettensohn & Company LLC ....G........812 547-5491
Tell City (G-13160)

K Lash & Son Inc ....G........260 347-3660
Kendallville (G-8482)

Miller Brothers Builders Inc..................E........574 533-8602
Goshen (G-5293)

CONSTRUCTION: Steel Buildings

3c Coman Ltd ....G........317 650-5156
Fortville (G-4766)

CONSTRUCTION: Street Surfacing & Paving

E & B Paving Inc ....E........765 674-5848
Marion (G-9522)

E & B Paving Inc ....F........765 289-7131
Muncie (G-10465)

E & B Paving Inc ....D........317 773-4132
Noblesville (G-11097)

Huehls Seal Coating & Lawn Car ....G........317 782-4069
Indianapolis (G-7143)

Rieth-Riley Cnstr Co Inc.....................C........574 875-5183
Gary (G-5093)

S & S Industry & Manufacturing............F........219 963-0213
Lake Station (G-9076)

Scotts Grant County Asp Inc ....G........765 664-2754
Marion (G-9561)

Super Seal Inc ....F........765 639-4993
Summitville (G-13106)

Triangle Asphalt Paving Corp ....E........765 482-5701
Lebanon (G-9229)

Walsh & Kelly Inc ....D........219 924-5900
South Bend (G-12987)

CONSTRUCTION: Swimming Pools

Chester Pool Systems Inc ....E........812 949-7333
New Albany (G-10759)

Hagerstown Gravel & Cnstr ....G........765 489-4812
Hagerstown (G-5806)

Sparkle Pools Inc ....F........812 232-1292
Terre Haute (G-13337)

CONSTRUCTION: Transmitting Tower, Telecommunication

Commtineo LLC ....F........219 476-3667
Wanatah (G-13822)

Swager Communications Inc................E........260 495-2515
Fremont (G-4976)

CONSTRUCTION: Utility Line

Milestone Contractors LP ....E........812 579-5248
Columbus (G-1975)

Niblock Excavating Inc ....D........574 848-4437
Bristol (G-1074)

Phend and Brown Inc ....E........574 658-4166
Milford (G-9961)

Vectren Corporation ....A........812 491-4000
Evansville (G-3794)

CONSTRUCTION: Waste Water & Sewage Treatment Plant

Astbury Water Technology Inc ....D........317 328-7153
Indianapolis (G-6431)

CONSULTING SVC: Actuarial

Franklin Barry Gallery ....G........317 822-8455
Indianapolis (G-6959)

CONSULTING SVC: Business, NEC

Agi International Inc ....F........317 536-2415
Indianapolis (G-6352)

Aleo Inc ....G........317 324-8583
Fishers (G-3868)

Aunalytics Inc...................................G........574 307-9230
South Bend (G-12716)

Automobile Dealers Assn of Ind...........G........317 635-1441
Indianapolis (G-6446)

Cr Publications.................................G........219 931-6700
Hammond (G-5866)

Crown Training & Development.............E........219 947-0845
Merrillville (G-9708)

Enterprise MGT Solutions LLC.............G........219 545-8544
Merrillville (G-9713)

Environmental Test Systems ....F........574 262-2060
Elkhart (G-2835)

Indy Rapid 3d LLC ....G........812 243-4175
Indianapolis (G-7221)

Nebo Ridge Enterprises LLC ....G........317 471-1089
Carmel (G-1441)

Pyrotek Incorporated ....E........260 248-4141
Columbia City (G-1820)

RAD Cube LLC ....F........317 456-7560
Indianapolis (G-7813)

Rebound Project LLP ....G........765 621-5604
Anderson (G-158)

Samaron Corp ....E........574 970-7070
Elkhart (G-3154)

Sentinel Services Inc ....F........574 360-5279
Granger (G-5432)

Smallwood Consulting LLC ....G........812 406-8040
Sellersburg (G-12418)

Vigo Coal Operating Co Inc ....C........812 759-8446
Evansville (G-3801)

CONSULTING SVC: Chemical

Innovative Chemical Resources...........G........317 695-6001
Indianapolis (G-7235)

Robinson International Inc...................G........812 637-0678
West Harrison (G-14042)

CONSULTING SVC: Computer

Acterna LLC.....................................E........317 788-9351
Indianapolis (G-6320)

Aspen Solutions Group Inc..................G........317 839-9274
Avon (G-429)

Corporate Systems Engrg LLC.............D........317 322-7984
Indianapolis (G-6671)

Spring Ventures Infovation LLC ....G........317 847-1117
Greenwood (G-5750)

CONSULTING SVC: Data Processing

Big Picture Data Imaging LLC ....G........812 235-0202
Terre Haute (G-13202)

CONSULTING SVC: Educational

DMC Distribution LLC.........................G........219 926-6401
Porter (G-11805)

Solution Tree Inc ....C........812 336-7700
Bloomington (G-828)

Standard For Success LLC ....F........844 737-3825
Cloverdale (G-1739)

CONSULTING SVC: Engineering

Accucast Inc.....................................G........317 849-5521
Indianapolis (G-6314)

Hrezo Industrial Eqp & Engrg...............F........812 537-4700
Greendale (G-5489)

In Space LLC ....G........765 775-2107
West Lafayette (G-14076)

Leman Engrg & Consulting Inc ....G........574 870-7732
Brookston (G-1106)

SBS Cybermetrix Inc ....E........812 378-7960
Columbus (G-2011)

SGS Cybermetrix Inc ....G........800 713-1203
Columbus (G-2013)

Stratikore..G........574 807-0028
La Porte (G-8824)

Technalysis Inc ....E........317 291-1985
Indianapolis (G-8049)

CONSULTING SVC: Executive Placement & Search

Smallwood Consulting LLC ....G........812 406-8040
Sellersburg (G-12418)

CONSULTING SVC: Financial Management

Heritage Financial Group Inc...............D........574 522-8000
Elkhart (G-2914)

Sentinel Services Inc.........................F........574 360-5279
Granger (G-5432)

CONSULTING SVC: Management

Advanced Prtctive Slutions LLC ....G........765 720-9574
Coatesville (G-1746)

Agi International Inc ....F........317 536-2415
Indianapolis (G-6352)

American Veteran Group LLC...............G........317 600-4749
Westfield (G-14136)

Blue Burro Inc ....G........904 825-9900
Bloomington (G-689)

Destiny Solutions Inc ....G........502 384-0031
Georgetown (G-5142)

Enpak LLC ....G........574 268-7273
Warsaw (G-13873)

Enterprise MGT Solutions LLC.............G........219 545-8544
Merrillville (G-9713)

Global Isotopes Inc ....G........317 578-1251
Noblesville (G-11111)

Old Gary Inc.....................................G........941 755-0976
Merrillville (G-9742)

Pmw Holdings LLC ....G........317 339-4685
Indianapolis (G-7703)

Spring Ventures Infovation LLC ....G........317 847-1117
Greenwood (G-5750)

CONSULTING SVC: Marketing Management

Citizens By-Products Coal Co ....F........317 927-4738
Indianapolis (G-6613)

Emarsys North America Inc ....E........844 693-6277
Indianapolis (G-6846)

Growth Principals LLC ....G........812 320-1574
Bloomington (G-735)

Holic LLC ....F........765 444-8115
Middletown (G-9936)

PRODUCT

Humphrey Printing Company Inc ....F 765 452-0093
Crown Point (G-2259)

Ike Newton LLC ....G....... 317 902-1772
Greenwood (G-5705)

Jam Printing Inc ....G....... 765 649-9292
Anderson (G-125)

Kennyleeholmescom ....G....... 574 612-2526
Elkhart (G-2961)

Octiv Inc ....D....... 317 550-0148
Indianapolis (G-7609)

Pinnacle Oil Holdings LLC ....F 317 875-9465
Indianapolis (G-7695)

Pinnacle Oil Holdings LLC ....E 317 875-9465
Indianapolis (G-7696)

Recon Group LLP ....G....... 855 874-8741
Greenfield (G-5566)

Rogers Marketing & Printing ....G....... 317 838-7203
Avon (G-465)

Roi Marketing Company ....G....... 317 644-0797
Indianapolis (G-7855)

Smallwood Consulting LLC ....G....... 812 406-8040
Sellersburg (G-12418)

Spark Marketing LLC ....G....... 219 301-0071
Schererville (G-12346)

CONSULTING SVC: Online Technology

Byte Blue Technology Solutions ....G....... 574 903-5637
Elkhart (G-2741)

Depth Plus Design LLC ....G....... 317 370-0532
Westfield (G-14158)

General Cable Industries Inc ....E 317 271-8447
Indianapolis (G-6994)

Knowledge Diffusion Games LLC ....G....... 812 361-4424
Bloomington (G-759)

CONSULTING SVC: Telecommunications

Commtineo LLC ....F 219 476-3667
Wanatah (G-13822)

CONSULTING SVCS, BUSINESS: Energy Conservation

Al Perry Enterprises Inc ....G....... 812 867-7727
Evansville (G-3347)

CONSULTING SVCS, BUSINESS: Environmental

Boilers & More Inc ....G....... 317 873-2007
Zionsville (G-14423)

F D Deskins Company Inc ....F 317 284-4014
Fishers (G-3909)

US Water Systems Inc ....F 317 209-0889
Indianapolis (G-8138)

CONSULTING SVCS, BUSINESS: Publishing

Ingroup ....G....... 317 817-9997
Indianapolis (G-7232)

P J J T Distributors Inc ....E 812 254-2218
Washington (G-13996)

CONSULTING SVCS, BUSINESS: Safety Training Svcs

Asphalt Materials Inc ....G....... 317 875-4670
Indianapolis (G-6428)

Rescom Management Systems Inc ......E 812 254-5641
Washington (G-14002)

CONSULTING SVCS, BUSINESS: Sys Engnrg, Exc Computer/Prof

Corvano LLC ....G....... 317 403-0471
Fishers (G-3894)

Indy Web Inc ....G....... 317 356-3622
Indianapolis (G-7224)

CONSULTING SVCS, BUSINESS: Systems Analysis & Engineering

Ipheion Development Corp ....G....... 240 281-1619
Indianapolis (G-7265)

Spring Ventures Infovation LLC ....G....... 317 847-1117
Greenwood (G-5750)

CONSULTING SVCS, BUSINESS: Systems Analysis Or Design

Radian Research Inc ....D....... 765 449-5500
Lafayette (G-8988)

CONSULTING SVCS, BUSINESS: Testing, Educational Or Personnel

Industrial Research Inc ....G....... 812 401-2333
Evansville (G-3557)

CONSULTING SVCS: Oil

Payne George A Petroleum Engr ....G....... 812 853-3813
Newburgh (G-11040)

Pulse Energy ....G....... 812 268-6700
Sullivan (G-13091)

CONSULTING SVCS: Scientific

Ipheion Development Corp ....G....... 240 281-1619
Indianapolis (G-7265)

Telamon Entp Ventures LLC ....G....... 317 818-6888
Carmel (G-1489)

CONTACT LENSES

American Contact Lens Service ....G....... 317 347-2900
Indianapolis (G-6387)

CONTACTS: Electrical

Contact Fabricators Ind Inc ....G....... 765 779-4125
Shirley (G-12661)

CONTAINERS, GLASS: Food

Hearthmark LLC ....C....... 765 557-3000
Muncie (G-10485)

Hearthmark LLC ....C....... 765 557-3000
Fishers (G-3924)

CONTAINERS, GLASS: Packers' Ware

Anchor Glass Container Corp ....B....... 765 584-6101
Winchester (G-14325)

CONTAINERS: Air Cargo, Metal

Diversified Qulty Svcs Ind LLC ....G....... 765 644-7712
Anderson (G-97)

W & M Enterprises Inc ....E 812 537-4656
Lawrenceburg (G-9161)

CONTAINERS: Cargo, Wood

Bravo Trailers LLC ....D....... 574 848-7500
Bristol (G-1049)

Industrial Lumber Products Inc ....G....... 219 324-7697
La Porte (G-8770)

CONTAINERS: Cargo, Wood & Metal Combination

H & A Products Inc ....F 574 226-0079
Elkhart (G-2902)

H & M Bay Inc ....G....... 410 463-5430
Fort Wayne (G-4312)

Satco Inc ....E 317 856-0301
Indianapolis (G-7896)

CONTAINERS: Cargo, Wood & Wood With Metal

Chep (usa) Inc ....E 317 780-0700
Indianapolis (G-6598)

CONTAINERS: Corrugated

B&W Packaging Mfg LLC ....E 812 280-9578
New Albany (G-10749)

Buckeye Corrugated Inc ....D....... 330 576-0590
Wooster (G-6519)

Color-Box LLC ....D....... 765 983-7618
Richmond (G-11971)

Combined Technologies Inc ....E 574 251-4968
South Bend (G-12739)

Corrugated Packaging Systems ....G....... 317 848-0000
Westfield (G-14145)

Freedom Corrugated LLC ....G....... 317 290-1140
Indianapolis (G-6963)

Indiana Box Company ....E 260 356-9660
Huntington (G-6215)

Innovative Packaging Assoc Inc ....F 260 356-6577
Huntington (G-6217)

Midland Plastics Co Division ....F 317 352-7785
Indianapolis (G-7503)

Powell Systems Inc ....G....... 765 884-0613
Fowler (G-4804)

Royal Box Group LLC ....G....... 317 462-7743
Greenfield (G-5568)

Solid Rock Gbc ....G....... 260 723-4806
South Whitley (G-13003)

Temple-Inland Inc ....G....... 765 675-6732
Tipton (G-13408)

Tre Paper Co Inc ....E 765 649-2536
Anderson (G-178)

Welch Packaging Group Inc ....C....... 574 295-2460
Elkhart (G-3256)

Westrock CP LLC ....G....... 574 296-2817
Elkhart (G-3258)

CONTAINERS: Food & Beverage

Red Gold LP ....F 765 754-8750
Alexandria (G-49)

CONTAINERS: Food, Liquid Tight, Including Milk

International Paper Company ....C....... 317 510-6410
Indianapolis (G-7257)

International Paper Company ....E 800 643-7244
Terre Haute (G-13259)

CONTAINERS: Food, Metal

Silgan Containers Mfg Corp ....F 219 362-7002
La Porte (G-8822)

CONTAINERS: Glass

Anchor Glass Container Corp ....B....... 812 537-1655
Greendale (G-5482)

Ardagh Glass Inc ....F 765 651-1260
Marion (G-9508)

Ardagh Glass Inc ....E 765 768-7891
Dunkirk (G-2483)

Ardagh Glass Inc ....G....... 765 662-1172
Marion (G-9509)

Ardagh Glass Inc ....B....... 317 558-1002
Indianapolis (G-6418)

Verallia North America ....G....... 765 768-7891
Dunkirk (G-2490)

CONTAINERS: Metal

Anthony Wayne Rehabilitation C ....D....... 260 744-6145
Fort Wayne (G-4078)

Container Life Cycle MGT LLC ....D....... 317 357-9853
Indianapolis (G-6653)

Nova Packaging Group Inc ....E 765 651-2600
Marion (G-9548)

Packaging Corporation America ....E 812 522-3100
Seymour (G-12473)

Phoenix Drum Dryer Inc ....F 574 251-9040
South Bend (G-12894)

Powell Systems Inc ....G....... 765 884-0613
Fowler (G-4804)

Powell Systems Inc ....G....... 765 884-0980
Fowler (G-4805)

Tru-Form Steel & Wire Inc ....E 765 348-5001
Hartford City (G-5993)

CONTAINERS: Plastic

Amcor Rigid Plastics Usa LLC ....D....... 317 736-4313
Franklin (G-4867)

Assmann Corporation America ....E 260 357-3181
Garrett (G-4995)

Associated Materials LLC ....G....... 260 451-9072
Fort Wayne (G-4094)

Berry Film Products Co Inc ....E 812 306-2690
Evansville (G-3374)

Berry Global Inc ....C....... 812 424-2904
Bloomington (G-680)

Berry Global Inc ....G....... 812 558-3510
Odon (G-11320)

Berry Global Inc ....A....... 812 424-2904
Evansville (G-3376)

Berry Global Group Inc ....F 812 424-2904
Evansville (G-3377)

Bprex Closures LLC ....D....... 812 424-2904
Evansville (G-3398)

Bway Corporation ....F 317 297-4638
Indianapolis (G-6525)

(G-0000) Company's Geographic Section entry number

Captive Plastics Inc ....C 812 424-2904
Evansville *(G-3412)*

Central Packaging Inc ....C 260 436-7225
Fort Wayne *(G-4143)*

Com-Tech Plastics Inc .... D 812 421-3600
Evansville *(G-3423)*

D&W Fine Pack LLC .... B 260 432-3027
Fort Wayne *(G-4198)*

Elkhart Plastics Inc ....E 574 389-9911
Elkhart *(G-2827)*

Elkhart Plastics Inc .... D 574 232-8066
South Bend *(G-12760)*

Fibertech Inc..................................... D 812 983-2642
Elberfeld *(G-2635)*

Genesis Plastics Welding Inc ....E 317 485-7887
Fortville *(G-4776)*

Genpak LLC....................................... C 812 752-3111
Scottsburg *(G-12358)*

Grafco Industries Ltd Partnr ....E 812 424-2904
Evansville *(G-3522)*

Graham Packaging Company LP .... D 812 868-8012
Evansville *(G-3523)*

Ie Products Mad Dasher Inc ....E 260 747-0545
Fort Wayne *(G-4357)*

Jadcore LLC...................................... C 812 234-2724
Terre Haute *(G-13260)*

Letica Corporation .... C 248 652-0557
Fremont *(G-4966)*

Mullinix Packages Inc .... C 260 747-3149
Fort Wayne *(G-4483)*

Mytex Polymers US Corp ....E 812 280-2900
Jeffersonville *(G-8402)*

Norton Packaging Inc ....E 574 867-6002
Hamlet *(G-5831)*

Paragon Medical Inc .... G 574 594-2140
Pierceton *(G-11575)*

Paragon Medical Inc .... B 574 594-2140
Pierceton *(G-11576)*

Plastic Package LLC...........................F 916 921-3399
La Porte *(G-8804)*

Pliant Corp International .... G 812 424-2904
Evansville *(G-3675)*

Polycon Industries Inc .... C 219 738-1000
Merrillville *(G-9748)*

PRC - Desoto International Inc ....E 317 290-1600
Indianapolis *(G-7728)*

Primex Design Fabrication Corp .... D 765 935-2990
Richmond *(G-12033)*

Remco Products Corporation ....F 317 876-9856
Zionsville *(G-14460)*

Silgan Plastics Corporation .... G 812 522-0900
Seymour *(G-12489)*

Silgan Plastics LLC ....F 812 522-0900
Seymour *(G-12491)*

Tulox Plastics Corporation .... C 765 664-5155
Marion *(G-9568)*

Yanfeng US Automotive .... C 260 347-0500
Kendallville *(G-8515)*

CONTAINERS: Plywood & Veneer, Wood

Corr-Wood Manufacturing Inc ....E 812 867-0700
Evansville *(G-3431)*

CONTAINERS: Sanitary, Food

Affinis Group LLC............................... G 317 831-3830
Mooresville *(G-10301)*

Divine Grace Homecare....................... G 219 290-5911
Gary *(G-5041)*

Genpak LLC....................................... C 812 752-3111
Scottsburg *(G-12358)*

Huhtamaki Inc .... B 765 664-2330
Marion *(G-9532)*

CONTAINERS: Shipping & Mailing, Fiber

Cornerstone Expediting LLC .... G 317 893-2891
Indianapolis *(G-6670)*

CONTAINERS: Shipping, Bombs, Metal Plate

Manitex International Inc.................... C 574 772-5380
Knox *(G-8573)*

CONTAINERS: Shipping, Wood

Artisanz Fabrication Mch LLC .... G 317 708-0228
Plainfield *(G-11594)*

CH Ellis Co Inc ....E 317 636-3351
Indianapolis *(G-6592)*

CONTAINERS: Wood

A S M Inc.. G 260 724-8220
Decatur *(G-2363)*

A-1 Pallet Co Inc Clarksville................ G 812 288-6339
Clarksville *(G-1672)*

American Fibertech Corporation ....E 219 261-3586
Clarks Hill *(G-1670)*

Anthony Wayne Rehabilitation C .... D 260 744-6145
Fort Wayne *(G-4078)*

Bryant Products Inc ....F 812 522-5929
Seymour *(G-12435)*

Conner Sawmill Inc ....F 574 626-3227
Walton *(G-13815)*

F & F Contracting .... G 574 867-4471
Grovertown *(G-5795)*

Gordon Lumber Company ....E 219 924-0500
Griffith *(G-5774)*

Indiana Southern Hardwoods ....E 812 326-2053
Huntingburg *(G-6171)*

Industrial Woodkraft Inc.....................E 812 897-4893
Boonville *(G-914)*

Star Case Manufacturing Co LLC..........E 219 922-4440
Munster *(G-10630)*

W & M Enterprises Inc ....E 812 537-4656
Lawrenceburg *(G-9161)*

CONTRACTORS: Appliance Installation

Elliott-Williams Company Inc.............. D 317 453-2295
Indianapolis *(G-6843)*

CONTRACTORS: Asphalt

Asphalt Engineers Inc ....E 574 289-5557
South Bend *(G-12712)*

E & B Paving Inc ....F 765 289-7131
Muncie *(G-10465)*

Hughes Paving Company Inc ....F 812 678-2126
French Lick *(G-4986)*

Rieth-Riley Cnstr Co Inc.................... D 765 447-2324
Lafayette *(G-8993)*

Rogers Group Inc...............................E 812 882-3640
Vincennes *(G-13703)*

CONTRACTORS: Awning Installation

Shade By Design Inc .... G 317 602-3513
Indianapolis *(G-7920)*

CONTRACTORS: Banking Machine Installation & Svc

Corrquest Automation Inc................... G 812 596-0049
Crandall *(G-2124)*

CONTRACTORS: Blasting, Exc Building Demolition

Dyno Nobel Inc...................................F 260 731-4431
Pennville *(G-11513)*

CONTRACTORS: Boiler Maintenance Contractor

Allied Boiler & Welding Co.................. G 317 272-4820
Avon *(G-426)*

CONTRACTORS: Building Eqpt & Machinery Installation

Davis Tool and Gage Company .... G 317 852-5400
Brownsburg *(G-1148)*

Electro Corporation ....F 219 393-5571
Kingsbury *(G-8536)*

Indiana Industrial Svcs LLC................ C 317 769-6099
Whitestown *(G-14255)*

RPC Machinery Inc .... G 765 458-5655
Liberty *(G-9271)*

Triple J Ironworks Inc .... G 765 544-9152
Carthage *(G-1517)*

CONTRACTORS: Building Sign Installation & Mntnce

Alveys Sign Co Inc.............................E 812 867-2567
Evansville *(G-3350)*

Burkhart Advertising Inc.....................F 574 234-4444
South Bend *(G-12728)*

Clermont Neon Sign Company .... G 317 638-4123
Brownsburg *(G-1143)*

Federal Heath Sign Company LLC .... G 317 581-7790
Carmel *(G-1380)*

Hutchison Sign Co Inc.........................E 317 894-8787
Indianapolis *(G-7148)*

J W Signs Inc..................................... G 260 747-5168
Fort Wayne *(G-4388)*

Kinder Group Inc................................ C 765 457-5966
Kokomo *(G-8651)*

Lesh Advertising Inc .... G 574 859-2141
Camden *(G-1275)*

Pioneer Signs Inc...............................F 219 884-7587
Merrillville *(G-9746)*

Premiere Signs Co Inc........................F 574 533-8585
Goshen *(G-5312)*

Sign Group Inc ....F 317 875-6969
Indianapolis *(G-7941)*

Sign Write Signs LLC .... G 219 477-3840
Valparaiso *(G-13618)*

Signcenter Inc .... G 812 232-4994
Terre Haute *(G-13326)*

Signdoc Identity LLC .... G 317 247-9670
Indianapolis *(G-7946)*

US Signcrafters Inc.............................F 574 674-5055
Osceola *(G-11385)*

Whitehead Signs Inc...........................F 317 632-1800
Indianapolis *(G-8193)*

CONTRACTORS: Building Site Preparation

Landmark Home & Land Co Inc............ G 219 874-4065
Michigan City *(G-9808)*

CONTRACTORS: Carpentry Work

Continntal Crpntry Cmpnnts LLC.........E 219 369-4839
Wanatah *(G-13823)*

Dutch Country Woodworking Inc .... G 260 499-4847
Lagrange *(G-9038)*

Marquise Enterprises Ltd .... G 317 578-3400
Indianapolis *(G-7458)*

Master Piece Krafts LLC...................... G 260 768-4330
Shipshewana *(G-12632)*

Rodeswood LLC.................................. G 574 457-4496
Syracuse *(G-13142)*

CONTRACTORS: Carpentry, Cabinet & Finish Work

Academy Inc....................................... G 574 293-7113
Elkhart *(G-2663)*

Douglas Dye and Associates .... G 317 844-1709
Carmel *(G-1362)*

Ettensohn & Company LLC .... G 812 547-5491
Tell City *(G-13160)*

Four Woods Laminating Inc.................E 260 593-2246
Topeka *(G-13419)*

Freedom Valley Cabinets .... G 812 875-2509
Freedom *(G-4948)*

Indianian Woodcrafts .... G 574 586-3741
Walkerton *(G-13803)*

Innovative Corp.................................E 317 804-5977
Westfield *(G-14171)*

Kostyo Woodworking Inc .... G 812 466-7350
Terre Haute *(G-13267)*

M & H Woodworking LLC .... G 812 486-2570
Montgomery *(G-10233)*

Middlebury Hardwood Pdts Inc .... G 574 825-9524
Middlebury *(G-9907)*

CONTRACTORS: Carpentry, Cabinet Building & Installation

Campbell Cobert Woodcraft .... G 812 883-5399
Salem *(G-12285)*

Country Corner Woodworks LLC .... G 574 825-6782
Middlebury *(G-9878)*

Country Mill Cabinet Co Inc ....F 260 693-9289
Laotto *(G-9106)*

Delbert Kemp .... G 812 486-3325
Montgomery *(G-10222)*

John Pater Design Fabrication ....F 812 926-4845
Aurora *(G-381)*

Millwood Custom Cabinets .... G 574 646-3009
Etna Green *(G-3322)*

Tristate Plastic Tops .... G 812 853-7827
Newburgh *(G-11053)*

William A Kadar .... G 219 884-7404
Gary *(G-5116)*

P
R
O
D
U
C
T

CONTRACTORS: Carpet Laying

Eds Wood Craft .... G 812 768-6617
Haubstadt *(G-6000)*

CONTRACTORS: Chimney Construction & Maintenance

Oesterling Chimney Sweep Inc .... G 812 372-3512
Columbus *(G-1984)*

CONTRACTORS: Closed Circuit Television Installation

Vidicom Corporation .... F 219 923-7475
Hammond *(G-5956)*

CONTRACTORS: Closet Organizers, Installation & Design

All About Organizing .... G 513 238-8157
Lawrenceburg *(G-9130)*

CONTRACTORS: Coating, Caulking & Weather, Water & Fire

Midwest Pipecoating Inc .... D 219 322-4564
Schererville *(G-12335)*

CONTRACTORS: Commercial & Office Building

Hi-Tech Housing Inc .... D 574 848-5593
Bristol *(G-1062)*
Kq Servicing LLC .... G 812 486-9244
Loogootee *(G-9388)*
Marshall Companies Indiana .... G 317 769-2666
Lebanon *(G-9202)*
Miller Brothers Builders Inc .... E 574 533-8602
Goshen *(G-5293)*
Tri-Esco Inc .... G 765 446-7937
Colburn *(G-1755)*

CONTRACTORS: Communications Svcs

Trilithic Inc .... C 317 895-3600
Indianapolis *(G-8099)*

CONTRACTORS: Computerized Controls Installation

Custom Controls & Engineering .... G 812 663-0755
Greensburg *(G-5596)*

CONTRACTORS: Concrete

AAA Mudjackers .... G 317 574-1990
Sharpsville *(G-12503)*
E & B Paving Inc .... E 765 674-5848
Marion *(G-9522)*
Lewis Jerry Cnstr & Excvtg .... G 765 653-2800
Greencastle *(G-5467)*
Milestone Contractors LP .... E 812 579-5248
Columbus *(G-1975)*
Niblock Excavating Inc .... F 260 248-2100
Columbia City *(G-1812)*
Rex Alton & Companies Inc .... E 812 882-8519
Vincennes *(G-13701)*
Rieth-Riley Cnstr Co Inc .... E 574 288-8321
South Bend *(G-12915)*
Sagamore Ready Mix .... G 317 573-5410
Indianapolis *(G-6280)*
Tri-Esco Inc .... G 765 446-7937
Colburn *(G-1755)*
Walsh & Kelly Inc .... D 219 924-5900
South Bend *(G-12987)*

CONTRACTORS: Construction Site Cleanup

Complete Property Care LLC .... G 765 288-0890
Muncie *(G-10447)*
Dr Restorations Inc .... G 317 646-7150
Clermont *(G-1712)*
Onsite Construction Services .... E 312 723-8060
Chesterton *(G-1625)*

CONTRACTORS: Construction Site Metal Structure Coating

3c Coman Ltd .... G 317 650-5156
Fortville *(G-4766)*

Diversified Coating & Fabg Inc .... E 260 563-2858
Wabash *(G-13724)*

CONTRACTORS: Countertop Installation

Carmel Countertops Inc .... G 317 843-0331
Carmel *(G-1330)*
Centura Solid Surfacing Inc .... F 317 867-5555
Westfield *(G-14142)*
Custom Design Laminates Inc .... F 574 674-9174
Osceola *(G-11375)*
Just For Granite .... G 317 842-8255
Indianapolis *(G-7324)*
Kostyo Woodworking Inc .... G 812 466-7350
Terre Haute *(G-13267)*
Laminated Tops of Terre Haute .... G 812 235-2920
Terre Haute *(G-13271)*
Quality Surfaces Inc .... E 812 876-5838
Spencer *(G-13034)*
Tristate Plastic Tops .... G 812 853-7827
Newburgh *(G-11053)*

CONTRACTORS: Demolition, Building & Other Structures

Onsite Construction Services .... E 312 723-8060
Chesterton *(G-1625)*
Schrock Excavating Inc .... E 574 862-4167
Wakarusa *(G-13796)*

CONTRACTORS: Demountable Partition Installation

Perfection Kitchen & Bath Ctr .... G 765 289-7594
Selma *(G-12425)*

CONTRACTORS: Directional Oil & Gas Well Drilling Svc

Coy Oil Inc .... G 618 966-2126
Mount Vernon *(G-10390)*
Directional Business Intellige .... G 317 770-0805
Noblesville *(G-11094)*
Directional Drilling Co LLC .... G 812 208-3392
Farmersburg *(G-3837)*
G & B Directional Boring LLC .... G 574 538-8132
Shipshewana *(G-12615)*
Hoosier Drilling Contrs Inc .... F 812 689-1260
Madison *(G-9470)*
Hydro-Exc Inc .... E 219 922-9886
Griffith *(G-5778)*
US Oilfield Company LLC .... E 888 584-7565
Carmel *(G-1505)*

CONTRACTORS: Dock Eqpt Installation, Indl

M & J Shelton Enterprises Inc .... G 260 745-1616
Fort Wayne *(G-4446)*
Trivett Contracting Inc .... E 317 539-5150
Clayton *(G-1708)*

CONTRACTORS: Drapery Track Installation

Doris Drapery Boutique .... G 765 472-5850
Peru *(G-11524)*
M C L Window Coverings Inc .... F 317 577-2670
Fishers *(G-3942)*

CONTRACTORS: Drywall

All-Phase Construction Co LLC .... G 317 345-7057
Fishers *(G-3869)*
Dr Restorations Inc .... G 317 646-7150
Clermont *(G-1712)*

CONTRACTORS: Earthmoving

Vigo Coaf Inc .... B 812 759-8446
Evansville *(G-3800)*

CONTRACTORS: Electrical

Bull Hn Info Systems Inc .... E 317 686-5500
Indianapolis *(G-6521)*
Commtineo LLC .... F 219 476-3667
Wanatah *(G-13822)*
Electric Plus .... G 812 336-4992
Bloomington *(G-719)*
Expert Electric .... G 765 664-6642
Marion *(G-9523)*
Hubbard Inc .... G 317 535-1926
Whiteland *(G-14239)*

Lancon Electric Inc .... G 260 897-3285
Laotto *(G-9113)*
Lynn Bros Electric Inc .... G 219 762-6386
Portage *(G-11774)*
Martin Electric Inc .... G 765 288-3254
Eaton *(G-2585)*
North Vernon Electric Inc .... F 812 392-2985
North Vernon *(G-11271)*
Ohio Valley Electric .... G 812 532-5288
Lawrenceburg *(G-9149)*
PBM Industries Inc .... G 812 346-2648
North Vernon *(G-11277)*
Tank Construction & Service Co .... F 317 509-6294
Whitestown *(G-14263)*
Wills Electric Service Inc .... G 812 883-5653
Pekin *(G-11480)*

CONTRACTORS: Electronic Controls Installation

Complete Controls Inc .... G 260 489-0852
Fort Wayne *(G-4170)*
Rex Byers Htg & Coolg Systems .... F 765 459-8858
Kokomo *(G-8689)*

CONTRACTORS: Epoxy Application

Baril Coatings .... F 260 665-8431
Angola *(G-196)*

CONTRACTORS: Excavating

Circle R Industries Inc .... G 765 379-2768
Rossville *(G-12210)*
Durcholz Excavating & Cnstr Co .... G 812 634-1764
Huntingburg *(G-6161)*
E & B Paving Inc .... E 765 643-5358
Anderson *(G-101)*
Englert & Meyer Corporation .... G 812 683-3540
Huntingburg *(G-6163)*
Foertsch Construction Co Inc .... D 812 529-8211
Lamar *(G-9099)*
Globe Asphalt Paving Co Inc .... E 317 568-4344
Indianapolis *(G-7015)*
Hagerstown Gravel & Cnstr .... G 765 489-4812
Hagerstown *(G-5806)*
Hunts Maintenance Inc .... G 219 785-2333
Westville *(G-14218)*
Kellers Limestone Service .... F 219 326-1688
La Porte *(G-8776)*
Lewis Jerry Cnstr & Excvtg .... G 765 653-2800
Greencastle *(G-5467)*
LPI Paving & Excavating .... G 260 726-9564
Portland *(G-11834)*
Niblock Excavating Inc .... F 260 248-2100
Columbia City *(G-1812)*
Niblock Excavating Inc .... D 574 848-4437
Bristol *(G-1074)*
Phend and Brown Inc .... G 574 658-4166
Milford *(G-9961)*
Rogers Group Inc .... E 812 333-6324
Bloomington *(G-816)*
S & G Excavating Inc .... G 812 234-4848
Terre Haute *(G-13322)*
Schrock Excavating Inc .... E 574 862-4167
Wakarusa *(G-13796)*
Seiler Excavating Inc .... G 260 925-0507
Auburn *(G-355)*
Thatcher Engineering Corp .... D 219 949-2084
Gary *(G-5105)*
Tri-Esco Inc .... G 765 446-7937
Colburn *(G-1755)*

CONTRACTORS: Excavating Slush Pits & Cellars Svcs

Crossroads Services Inc .... G 219 972-3631
Munster *(G-10603)*
E Z Choice .... G 219 852-4281
Hammond *(G-5873)*
Filson Earthwork Company .... F 317 774-3180
Noblesville *(G-11104)*

CONTRACTORS: Fence Construction

K & K Fence Inc .... E 317 359-5425
Indianapolis *(G-7326)*
Merchants Metals LLC .... D 574 831-4060
New Paris *(G-10990)*
Mofab Inc .... G 765 649-1288
Anderson *(G-139)*

Quality Fence Ltd..........................G...... 260 768-4986
Shipshewana (G-12645)
S & S Industry & Manufacturing..........F....... 219 963-0213
Lake Station (G-9076)

CONTRACTORS: Fiberglass Work

Fiberglass Pdts Boat Repairing............G....... 260 337-5636
Saint Joe (G-12255)

CONTRACTORS: Fire Detection & Burglar Alarm Systems

American Fire Company..................G...... 219 840-0630
Valparaiso (G-13491)
Johnson Controls........................C...... 317 826-2130
Indianapolis (G-7309)
Phil & Son Inc..........................F....... 219 663-5757
Crown Point (G-2283)
Sentinel Alarm Inc......................G...... 219 874-6051
Trail Creek (G-13442)

CONTRACTORS: Fire Sprinkler System Installation Svcs

Hydro Fire Protection Inc................E....... 317 780-6980
Indianapolis (G-7151)
Johnson Controls........................C...... 317 826-2130
Indianapolis (G-7309)

CONTRACTORS: Floor Laying & Other Floor Work

Doris Drapery Boutique..................G...... 765 472-5850
Peru (G-11524)
Jeff Hury Hardwood Floors Pntg..........G...... 812 204-8650
Evansville (G-3574)
Santarossa Mosaic Tile Co Inc...........C...... 317 632-9494
Indianapolis (G-7895)

CONTRACTORS: Flooring

Jeff Hury Hardwood Floors Pntg..........G...... 812 204-8650
Evansville (G-3574)
Johnson Eh Construction LLC.............G...... 812 344-8450
Columbus (G-1952)
Santarossa Mosaic Tile Co Inc...........C...... 317 632-9494
Indianapolis (G-7895)
Vans TV & Appliance Inc.................F....... 260 927-8267
Auburn (G-366)

CONTRACTORS: Food Svcs Eqpt Installation

Carmel Engineering Inc..................F....... 765 279-8955
Kirklin (G-8547)
Conover Custom Fabrication Inc..........F....... 317 784-1904
Indianapolis (G-6652)

CONTRACTORS: Foundation & Footing

Niblock Excavating Inc..................D....... 574 848-4437
Bristol (G-1074)

CONTRACTORS: Gas Detection & Analysis Svcs

G E Kerr Companies Inc..................G...... 417 426-5504
Kokomo (G-8627)

CONTRACTORS: Gas Field Svcs, NEC

ARS Nebraska LLC.......................E...... 765 832-5210
Clinton (G-1713)
Pinnacle Oil Trading LLC................G...... 317 875-9465
Indianapolis (G-7697)

CONTRACTORS: Gas Leak Detection

Ald Indy Inc...........................G...... 317 826-3833
Fishers (G-3867)

CONTRACTORS: General Electric

B & D Electric Inc......................F....... 812 254-2122
Washington (G-13978)
Charm-Lite Inc.........................G...... 765 644-6876
Anderson (G-84)
Electronic Services LLC.................E...... 765 457-3894
Kokomo (G-8620)
Franklin Electric Co Inc................D....... 765 677-6900
Gas City (G-5124)
Gottman Electric Co Inc.................G...... 812 838-0037
Mount Vernon (G-10393)

Hoosier Industrial Electric..............F....... 812 346-2232
North Vernon (G-11262)
J V Crane & Engineering Inc.............E...... 219 942-8566
Hobart (G-6082)
Link Electrical Service..................G...... 812 288-8184
Jeffersonville (G-8391)
Nrk Inc................................E...... 812 232-1800
Terre Haute (G-13292)
Three Star Electric Inc..................G...... 574 272-3136
South Bend (G-12969)

CONTRACTORS: Glass Tinting, Architectural & Automotive

Broadway Auto Glass LLC................F....... 219 884-5277
Merrillville (G-9704)

CONTRACTORS: Glass, Glazing & Tinting

Bizik Masonry Corporation...............G...... 219 659-1348
Whiting (G-14270)
Hartford TEC Glass Co Inc...............E...... 765 348-1282
Hartford City (G-5983)
Helming Bros Inc.......................G...... 812 634-9797
Jasper (G-8254)
Horizon Terra Incorporated..............D....... 812 280-0000
Jeffersonville (G-8377)
Kaleidoscope Inc.......................G...... 765 423-1951
Lafayette (G-8936)
Moss L Glass Co Inc....................F....... 765 642-4946
Indianapolis (G-7546)
Stalter Glass Inc.......................G...... 574 825-2225
Middlebury (G-9920)
Syracuse Glass Inc.....................G...... 574 457-5516
Syracuse (G-13147)

CONTRACTORS: Grave Excavation

Wilson Burial Vault Inc..................G...... 260 356-5722
Huntington (G-6261)

CONTRACTORS: Gutters & Downspouts

Sure-Flo Seamless Gutters Inc...........G...... 260 622-4372
Ossian (G-11412)

CONTRACTORS: Heating & Air Conditioning

Fletcher Heating & Cooling..............G...... 812 865-2984
Paoli (G-11450)
Geo-Flo Products Corporation............F....... 812 275-8513
Bedford (G-546)
Hayward & Sams LLP....................G...... 260 351-4166
Stroh (G-13077)
Paniccia Heating & Cooling..............G...... 219 872-2198
Michigan City (G-9827)
T R Bulger Inc.........................G...... 219 879-8525
Trail Creek (G-13443)
Tri-State Mechanical Inc.................F....... 260 471-0345
Fort Wayne (G-4702)
Vindhurst Sheet Metal LLC...............F....... 812 422-0143
Evansville (G-3802)
Washburn Heating & AC..................G...... 574 825-7697
Middlebury (G-9924)

CONTRACTORS: Heating Systems Repair & Maintenance Svc

Economy Electric Htg & Coolg............G...... 219 923-4441
Highland (G-6044)
Vincent Aliano Elc Htg & Coolg..........G...... 812 332-3332
Bloomington (G-852)

CONTRACTORS: Highway & Street Construction, General

Goh Con Inc...........................E...... 812 282-1349
Clarksville (G-1682)
Rogers Group Inc.......................E...... 812 333-8550
Bloomington (G-817)
Sssi Inc..............................D....... 219 880-0818
Gary (G-5101)
Utility Access Solutions Inc.............G...... 765 744-6528
Ridgeville (G-12083)
Vans Industrial Inc.....................E...... 219 931-4881
Hammond (G-5954)

CONTRACTORS: Highway & Street Paving

E & B Paving Inc.......................E...... 765 643-5358
Anderson (G-101)

Hughes Paving Company Inc..............F....... 812 678-2126
French Lick (G-4986)
Milestone Contractors LP................C...... 765 772-7500
Lafayette (G-8970)
Milestone Contractors LP................E...... 812 579-5248
Columbus (G-1975)
Niblock Excavating Inc..................D....... 574 848-4437
Bristol (G-1074)
Phend and Brown Inc....................E...... 574 658-4166
Milford (G-9961)
Wallace Construction Inc................F....... 317 422-5356
Martinsville (G-9647)

CONTRACTORS: Highway & Street Resurfacing

Irving Materials Inc.....................F....... 765 922-7285
Marion (G-9534)

CONTRACTORS: Home & Office Intrs Finish, Furnish/Remodel

Aynes Upholstery LLC...................G...... 812 829-1321
Freedom (G-4947)

CONTRACTORS: Hydraulic Well Fracturing Svcs

Hellweg Holdings LLC...................G...... 317 909-6764
McCordsville (G-9669)

CONTRACTORS: Indl Building Renovation, Remodeling & Repair

Milani Custom Homes LLC................G...... 219 455-5804
Merrillville (G-9734)
Reed Contracting Company...............F....... 765 452-2638
Kokomo (G-8687)
Trifab & Construction Inc................G...... 219 845-1300
Hammond (G-5952)
Trivett Contracting Inc..................E...... 317 539-5150
Clayton (G-1708)

CONTRACTORS: Insulation Installation, Building

Installed Building Pdts LLC..............G...... 317 398-3216
Shelbyville (G-12539)

CONTRACTORS: Irrigation Land Leveling

Bullseye Technologies Inc................G...... 574 753-0102
Elkhart (G-2737)

CONTRACTORS: Kitchen Cabinet Installation

Johnny Graber Woodworking..............G...... 260 466-4957
Grabill (G-5376)

CONTRACTORS: Lighting Syst

Signdoc Identity LLC....................G...... 317 247-9670
Indianapolis (G-7946)
Uberlux Inc............................G...... 317 580-0111
Carmel (G-1501)

CONTRACTORS: Machine Rigging & Moving

Egenolf Contg & Rigging II Inc...........D....... 317 787-5301
Indianapolis (G-6812)
Egenolf Machine Inc.....................D....... 317 787-5301
Indianapolis (G-6814)
Padgett Inc............................C...... 812 945-2391
New Albany (G-10839)
Precision Surveillance Corp..............E...... 219 397-4295
East Chicago (G-2564)
Stahl Welding Inc.......................G...... 765 457-3386
Kokomo (G-8699)
Trivett Contracting Inc..................E...... 317 539-5150
Clayton (G-1708)

CONTRACTORS: Machinery Installation

Engineered Conveyors Inc................F....... 765 459-4545
Kokomo (G-8621)
M R S Printing Erectors Inc..............G...... 317 888-1314
Greenwood (G-5722)
Mid-State Automation Inc................G...... 765 795-5500
Cloverdale (G-1730)

PRODUCT

CONTRACTORS: Masonry & Stonework

Charles Coons ....G 765 362-6509
Crawfordsville *(G-2138)*

Patrick & Sharon Hoctor ....G 812 898-2678
Terre Haute *(G-13297)*

Tremain Ceramic Tile & Flr Cvg ....E 317 542-1491
Indianapolis *(G-8093)*

CONTRACTORS: Mechanical

C & K United Shtmtl & Mech ....E 812 423-5090
Evansville *(G-3407)*

Grunau Company Inc ....E 317 872-7360
Indianapolis *(G-7054)*

Slate Mechanical Inc ....F 765 452-9611
Kokomo *(G-8697)*

Sterling Boiler and Mech LLC ....A 812 479-5447
Evansville *(G-3750)*

Vans Industrial Inc ....E 219 931-4881
Hammond *(G-5954)*

CONTRACTORS: Millwrights

Centurion Industries Inc ....D 260 357-6665
Garrett *(G-4996)*

Wabash Welding Services Inc ....G 260 563-2363
Wabash *(G-13766)*

CONTRACTORS: Oil & Gas Aerial Geophysical Exploration Svcs

Countrymark Coop Holdg Corp ....E 800 808-3170
Indianapolis *(G-6676)*

Countrymark Ref Logistics LLC ....D 812 838-4341
Mount Vernon *(G-10388)*

CONTRACTORS: Oil & Gas Building, Repairing & Dismantling Svc

Helvie & Sons Inc ....G 765 674-1372
Marion *(G-9530)*

Specialized Services Inc ....G 317 485-8561
Fortville *(G-4782)*

Sunrise Energy LLC ....G 812 886-9990
Vincennes *(G-13708)*

CONTRACTORS: Oil & Gas Field Fire Fighting Svcs

Centre Township ....E 765 482-1729
Lebanon *(G-9173)*

CONTRACTORS: Oil & Gas Well Casing Cement Svcs

Gas City B & K Inc ....G 765 674-9651
Gas City *(G-5125)*

Indiana Petroleum Contractors ....G 812 477-1575
Evansville *(G-3552)*

CONTRACTORS: Oil & Gas Well Drilling Svc

Armstrong Drilling Inc ....G 765 455-2445
Burlington *(G-1209)*

Bkb Petroleum Inc ....G 574 389-8159
Elkhart *(G-2725)*

Countrymark Coop Holdg Corp ....E 812 759-6962
Evansville *(G-3433)*

Diamond III Inc ....G 812 882-6269
Vincennes *(G-13674)*

Energy Drilling LLC ....G 618 943-5314
Vincennes *(G-13676)*

Energy Inc ....G 765 948-3504
Alexandria *(G-41)*

Gagan Petroleum Inc ....G 765 254-1330
Muncie *(G-10475)*

Gallagher Drilling Inc ....E 812 477-6746
Evansville *(G-3514)*

Gwaltney Drilling Inc ....G 812 254-5085
Washington *(G-13985)*

Hindi Petroleum Group II Inc ....G 317 574-0619
Carmel *(G-1405)*

Hoover Well Drilling Inc ....G 574 831-4901
New Paris *(G-10984)*

Indiana Drilling Company Inc ....G 812 477-1575
Evansville *(G-3551)*

John Remmler Well Drilling ....G 812 663-8178
Greensburg *(G-5616)*

Magnum Drilling Svcs Inc ....F 812 985-3981
Evansville *(G-3611)*

Michael R Harris ....G 812 425-9411
Evansville *(G-3625)*

Midwest Energy Partners LLC ....G 317 600-3235
Indianapolis *(G-7505)*

Sr Petroleum Inc ....G 574 383-5879
Granger *(G-5439)*

Universal Operating Inc ....G 812 477-1584
Evansville *(G-3789)*

Vickery Drilling Co ....G 812 473-4671
Evansville *(G-3798)*

CONTRACTORS: Oil & Gas Well Spudding Svcs

Coy Oil Inc ....G 812 838-3146
Mount Vernon *(G-10389)*

CONTRACTORS: Oil & Gas Wells Pumping Svcs

K S Oil Corp ....G 812 453-3026
Evansville *(G-3581)*

CONTRACTORS: Oil & Gas Wells Svcs

Imperial Petroleum Inc ....G 812 867-1433
Evansville *(G-3549)*

Quick Well Service Inc ....G 812 426-1924
Evansville *(G-3692)*

CONTRACTORS: Oil Field Lease Tanks: Erectg, Clng/Rprg Svcs

Tradebe Environmental Svcs LLC ....G 800 388-7242
Merrillville *(G-9759)*

Tradebe GP ....G 800 388-7242
East Chicago *(G-2572)*

Tradebe Industrial Svcs LLC ....E 800 388-7242
East Chicago *(G-2573)*

CONTRACTORS: Oil Field Mud Drilling Svcs

AAA Mudjackers ....G 317 574-1990
Sharpsville *(G-12503)*

CONTRACTORS: Oil/Gas Well Construction, Rpr/Dismantling Svcs

Abari Properties Development ....G 317 721-9230
Indianapolis *(G-6306)*

All-Phase Construction Co LLC ....G 317 345-7057
Fishers *(G-3869)*

Apex AG Solutions LLC ....F 937 564-5421
Richmond *(G-11954)*

Complete Property Care LLC ....G 765 288-0890
Muncie *(G-10447)*

Field Construction ....G 574 664-2010
Twelve Mile *(G-13450)*

Johnson Eh Construction LLC ....G 812 344-8450
Columbus *(G-1952)*

Jtm Home & Building ....G 219 690-1445
Lowell *(G-9411)*

Lucas Oil Pro Plling Prmotions ....G 812 246-3350
Charlestown *(G-1572)*

Matrix Nac ....F 219 931-6600
Hammond *(G-5914)*

Onsite Construction Services ....E 312 723-8060
Chesterton *(G-1625)*

P & J Sectional Housing ....G 260 982-7231
North Manchester *(G-11240)*

RC Enterprise LLC ....G 317 225-6747
Indianapolis *(G-7823)*

Ricker Oil Company Inc ....E 317 780-1777
Indianapolis *(G-7841)*

Rodgers Enterprises LLC ....G 765 396-3143
Eaton *(G-2588)*

Wallys Construction ....G 812 254-4154
Washington *(G-14006)*

CONTRACTORS: On-Site Welding

Best Weld Inc ....F 765 641-7720
Anderson *(G-74)*

Carmichael Welding Inc ....G 812 825-5156
Bloomfield *(G-636)*

CD & Ws Bordner Entps Inc ....G 765 268-2120
Cutler *(G-2328)*

Christie Machine Works Co Inc ....G 317 638-8840
Indianapolis *(G-6603)*

City Welding & Fabrication ....G 765 569-5403
Rockville *(G-12175)*

Custom Blacksmith Shop ....G 765 292-2745
Atlanta *(G-293)*

Davern Machine Shop ....G 765 505-1051
Dana *(G-2342)*

E & R Fabricating Inc ....G 812 275-0388
Bedford *(G-539)*

F T Moore and Sons Inc ....G 812 466-3762
Terre Haute *(G-13233)*

General Sheet Metal Works Inc ....E 574 288-0611
South Bend *(G-12788)*

J & J Repair ....G 574 831-3075
Goshen *(G-5246)*

Johns Welding and Fabrication ....G 574 936-1702
Plymouth *(G-11697)*

Jomar Machining & Fabg Inc ....E 574 825-9837
Middlebury *(G-9897)*

Made Rite Manufacturing Inc ....G 812 967-2652
Salem *(G-12300)*

Moores Welding Service Inc ....G 260 627-2177
Leo *(G-9244)*

Pyramid Equipment ....F 219 778-2591
Rolling Prairie *(G-12193)*

R & M Welding & Fabricating Sp ....G 812 295-9130
Loogootee *(G-9392)*

R & S Welding & Fabricating ....G 574 946-6816
Winamac *(G-14319)*

Smart Manufacturing Inc ....G 765 482-7481
Lebanon *(G-9225)*

Southwest Welding ....G 574 862-4453
Goshen *(G-5325)*

SSd Control Technology Inc ....E 574 289-5942
South Bend *(G-12950)*

Yankee Steel Inc ....G 812 232-5353
Terre Haute *(G-13374)*

Zimmer Welding Co ....G 317 632-5212
Indianapolis *(G-8226)*

CONTRACTORS: Paint & Wallpaper Stripping

Bare Metal Inc ....F 812 948-1313
New Albany *(G-10750)*

CONTRACTORS: Painting & Wall Covering

DC Coaters Inc ....E 765 675-6006
Tipton *(G-13390)*

Dr Restorations Inc ....G 317 646-7150
Clermont *(G-1712)*

Plasfinco LLC ....E 812 346-3900
North Vernon *(G-11278)*

CONTRACTORS: Painting, Commercial

Helming Bros Inc ....G 812 634-9797
Jasper *(G-8254)*

Huber Brothers Inc ....G 317 392-1566
Shelbyville *(G-12537)*

Quality Pnt Prstned Fnshes Inc ....G 574 294-6944
Elkhart *(G-3129)*

Van Zandt Enterprises Inc ....E 812 423-3511
Evansville *(G-3792)*

CONTRACTORS: Painting, Commercial, Exterior

Mancor Indiana Inc ....E 765 779-4800
Anderson *(G-134)*

CONTRACTORS: Painting, Indl

Creative Liquid Coatings Inc ....A 260 349-1862
Fort Wayne *(G-4185)*

Northern Ind Indus Catings LLC ....G 574 893-4621
Akron *(G-6)*

Rex Alton & Companies Inc ....E 812 882-8519
Vincennes *(G-13701)*

CONTRACTORS: Parking Lot Maintenance

Super Seal Inc ....F 765 639-4993
Summitville *(G-13106)*

CONTRACTORS: Patio & Deck Construction & Repair

Powerclean Inc ....E 260 483-1375
Fort Wayne *(G-4543)*

CONTRACTORS: Pavement Marking

Super Seal Inc ....F 765 639-4993
Summitville *(G-13106)*

2018 Harris Indiana
Industrial Directory

(G-0000) Company's Geographic Section entry number

CONTRACTORS: Petroleum Storage Tanks, Pumping & Draining

Tank Construction & Service Co ....F 317 509-6294
Whitestown *(G-14263)*

CONTRACTORS: Pile Driving

Thatcher Engineering Corp....................D...... 219 949-2084
Gary *(G-5105)*

CONTRACTORS: Pipe Laying

Hd Mechanical Inc............................G....... 219 924-6050
Griffith *(G-5776)*

CONTRACTORS: Plaster & Drywall Work

Milani Custom Homes LLC ....G....... 219 455-5804
Merrillville *(G-9734)*

CONTRACTORS: Plumbing

Danny Webb Plumbing.......................G....... 574 936-2746
Plymouth *(G-11679)*
Griffen Plmbng-Heating-Cooling ....E....... 574 295-2440
Elkhart *(G-2900)*
Huntingburg Machine Works Inc..........F 812 683-3531
Huntingburg *(G-6169)*

CONTRACTORS: Power Generating Eqpt Installation

Discount Power Equipment ....G....... 765 642-0040
Anderson *(G-96)*

CONTRACTORS: Prefabricated Window & Door Installation

Concord Realstate Corp ....F 765 423-5555
Lafayette *(G-8876)*
H & H Home Improvement Inc ....G....... 812 288-8700
Clarksville *(G-1684)*

CONTRACTORS: Process Piping

Tron Mechanical Incorporated..............C...... 812 838-4715
Mount Vernon *(G-10410)*

CONTRACTORS: Refractory or Acid Brick Masonry

Pyro Industrial Services Inc.................E....... 219 787-5700
Portage *(G-11790)*

CONTRACTORS: Renovation, Aircraft Interiors

Indy Aerospace Inc ....G....... 817 521-6508
Indianapolis *(G-7212)*
Regent Aerospace Corporation............G....... 317 837-4000
Plainfield *(G-11640)*

CONTRACTORS: Roof Repair

V M Integrated ....G....... 877 296-0621
Indianapolis *(G-8143)*

CONTRACTORS: Roofing

Alpha Systems LLC ....F 574 295-5206
Elkhart *(G-2678)*
B & L Sheet Metal & Roofing ....F 812 332-4309
Bloomington *(G-670)*
Maher Supply Inc ....E....... 812 234-7699
Terre Haute *(G-13278)*
Osterholt Construction Inc ....G....... 260 672-3493
Roanoke *(G-12106)*
Roof Masters Plus.............................G....... 765 572-1321
Westpoint *(G-14207)*
Schmidt Contracting Inc ....F 812 482-3923
Jasper *(G-8303)*
Slatile Roofing and Shtmtl Co ....E....... 574 233-7485
South Bend *(G-12939)*
Webster Custom Canvas Inc ....G....... 574 834-4497
North Webster *(G-11302)*

CONTRACTORS: Safe Or Vault Installation

S C Pryor Inc ....E....... 317 352-1281
Indianapolis *(G-7878)*

CONTRACTORS: Sandblasting Svc, Building Exteriors

C & S Sandblasting & Wldg LLC ....G....... 317 867-6341
Westfield *(G-14140)*
Reed Contracting Company..................F 765 452-2638
Kokomo *(G-8687)*
Van Zandt Enterprises Inc ....E....... 812 423-3511
Evansville *(G-3792)*

CONTRACTORS: Seismograph Survey Svcs

Seismic Vision LLC............................G....... 219 548-8704
Valparaiso *(G-13613)*

CONTRACTORS: Septic System

Eaton Septic Tank Company.................G....... 765 396-3275
Eaton *(G-2582)*
Jones & Sons Inc ....E....... 812 299-2287
Terre Haute *(G-13261)*
Russells Excvtg & Septic Tanks...........G....... 812 838-2471
Mount Vernon *(G-10406)*

CONTRACTORS: Sheet Metal Work, NEC

Bright Sheet Metal Company Inc..........C...... 317 291-7600
Indianapolis *(G-6508)*
C & K United Shtmtl & Mech ....E....... 812 423-5090
Evansville *(G-3407)*
Cassini - D & D Mfg Inc......................G....... 765 449-7992
Lafayette *(G-8870)*
Clover Sheet Metal Company ....E....... 574 293-5912
Elkhart *(G-2761)*
F D Ramsey & Co Inc ....F 219 362-2452
La Porte *(G-8757)*
F R Sheet Metal Co Inc ....G....... 219 949-2290
Gary *(G-5045)*
Hartman Brothers Heat & AC ....F 260 493-4402
New Haven *(G-10942)*
Helming Bros Inc ....G....... 812 634-9797
Jasper *(G-8254)*
Icon Metal Forming LLC ....B....... 812 738-5900
Corydon *(G-2102)*
J Coffey Metal Masters Inc ....D...... 317 780-1864
Indianapolis *(G-7284)*
Pb Metal Works ....G....... 765 489-1311
Hagerstown *(G-5810)*
Seib Machine & Tool Co Inc ....G....... 812 453-6174
Evansville *(G-3721)*
Snyder & Co Inc ....G....... 765 447-3452
Lafayette *(G-9000)*
Vidimos Inc.......................................D...... 219 397-2728
East Chicago *(G-2579)*

CONTRACTORS: Sheet metal Work, Architectural

Artisan Sheet Metal Corp ....G....... 812 422-7393
Wadesville *(G-13770)*

CONTRACTORS: Ship Boiler & Tank Cleaning & Repair

Tradebe Environmental Svcs LLC........G....... 800 388-7242
Merrillville *(G-9759)*
Tradebe GP ....G....... 800 388-7242
East Chicago *(G-2572)*
Tradebe Industrial Svcs LLC................E....... 800 388-7242
East Chicago *(G-2573)*

CONTRACTORS: Siding

H & H Home Improvement Inc ....G....... 812 288-8700
Clarksville *(G-1684)*

CONTRACTORS: Single-family Home General Remodeling

A L E Enterprises ....G....... 317 856-2981
Indianapolis *(G-6297)*
Bee Window Incorporated....................C...... 317 283-8522
Fishers *(G-3876)*
Biggerstaff & Son Excavating..............G....... 317 784-6034
Indianapolis *(G-6474)*
Hudec Construction Company ....E....... 219 922-9811
Griffith *(G-5777)*
Leroy E Doty Cabinet Shop..................G....... 219 663-1139
Crown Point *(G-2275)*
Maher Supply Inc ....E....... 812 234-7699
Terre Haute *(G-13278)*

Styled Rite Company Inc ....G....... 219 931-9844
Gary *(G-5102)*

CONTRACTORS: Steeplejacks

Helming Bros Inc ....G....... 812 634-9797
Jasper *(G-8254)*

CONTRACTORS: Stone Masonry

Accent Limestone & Carving Inc..........G....... 812 876-7040
Bloomington *(G-655)*

CONTRACTORS: Storage Tank Erection, Metal

Hmt LLC..F 219 736-9901
Merrillville *(G-9720)*
Tank Construction & Service Co ....F 317 509-6294
Whitestown *(G-14263)*
Tj Maintenance LLC ....G....... 219 776-8427
Lake Village *(G-9088)*

CONTRACTORS: Structural Iron Work, Structural

Buhrt Engineering & Cnstr...................G....... 574 267-3720
Warsaw *(G-13852)*
Precision Surveillance Corp ....E....... 219 397-4295
East Chicago *(G-2564)*
Reese Forge Orna Ironwork ....G....... 219 775-1039
Lake Village *(G-9086)*

CONTRACTORS: Structural Steel Erection

Ambassador Steel Corporation ....E....... 317 834-3434
Mooresville *(G-10302)*
D & M Systems Inc ....G....... 812 327-2384
Owensburg *(G-11425)*
Harpring Steel Inc ....G....... 812 256-6326
Charlestown *(G-1568)*
Hgmc Supply Inc................................F 317 351-9500
Indianapolis *(G-7101)*
Padgett Inc.......................................C...... 812 945-2391
New Albany *(G-10839)*
Snyder & Co Inc ....G....... 765 447-3452
Lafayette *(G-9000)*
Stevens Ironworks Inc........................E....... 219 987-6332
Demotte *(G-2448)*
Triple J Ironworks Inc ....G....... 765 544-9152
Carthage *(G-1517)*

CONTRACTORS: Svc Well Drilling Svcs

Beechler Well Drlg & Pump Svc ....G....... 317 849-2535
Fishers *(G-3877)*
McGrews Well Drilling Inc ....G....... 574 857-3875
Rochester *(G-12137)*

CONTRACTORS: Terrazzo Work

Santarossa Mosaic Tile Co Inc ....C...... 317 632-9494
Indianapolis *(G-7895)*

CONTRACTORS: Tile Installation, Ceramic

Concepts In Stone & Tile Inc ....G....... 574 267-4712
Warsaw *(G-13859)*
Tremain Ceramic Tile & Flr Cvg............E....... 317 542-1491
Indianapolis *(G-8093)*

CONTRACTORS: Trenching

Hydro-Exc Inc....................................E....... 219 922-9886
Griffith *(G-5778)*

CONTRACTORS: Tuck Pointing & Restoration

Slatile Roofing and Shtmtl Co ....E....... 574 233-7485
South Bend *(G-12939)*

CONTRACTORS: Underground Utilities

LGS Plumbing Inc...............................E....... 219 663-2177
Crown Point *(G-2276)*

CONTRACTORS: Ventilation & Duct Work

ABC Industries Inc.............................D...... 800 426-0921
Winona Lake *(G-14349)*
Cor-A-Vent Inc...................................F 574 255-1910
Mishawaka *(G-10023)*

PRODUCT

Millenium Sheet Metal Inc ....F 574 935-9101
Plymouth (G-11706)
Superior Distribution ....G 618 242-5560
Indianapolis (G-8021)

CONTRACTORS: Vinyl Flooring Installation, Tile & Sheet

Coronado Stone Inc ....E 812 284-2845
Jeffersonville (G-8347)

CONTRACTORS: Warm Air Heating & Air Conditioning

Bowmans Tin Shop Inc ....G 574 936-3234
Plymouth (G-11671)
Brackett Heating & AC ....F 812 476-1138
Evansville (G-3400)
Brouillette Heating & Cooling ....G 765 884-0176
Fowler (G-4798)
Expert Electric ....G 765 664-6642
Marion (G-9523)
Frank H Monroe Htg & Coolg Inc ....F 812 945-2566
New Albany (G-10784)
Halsen Brothers Sheet Metal ....G 574 583-3358
Monticello (G-10264)
Hartman Brothers Heat & AC ....F 260 493-4402
New Haven (G-10942)
Jack Frost LLC ....E 812 477-7244
Evansville (G-3571)
Knox Inc ....F 260 665-6617
Angola (G-226)
Midwest Sheet Metal Inc ....G 574 223-3332
Rochester (G-12138)
Naas Inc ....F 812 385-3578
Princeton (G-11879)
Rex Byers Htg & Coolg Systems ....F 765 459-8858
Kokomo (G-8689)
Schmidt Contracting Inc ....F 812 482-3923
Jasper (G-8303)
Schneder Elc Bldngs Amrcas Inc ....G 317 894-6374
Greenfield (G-5571)
Shank Brothers Inc ....F 260 744-4802
Fort Wayne (G-4618)
Snyder & Co Inc ....G 765 447-3452
Lafayette (G-9000)

CONTRACTORS: Water Intake Well Drilling Svc

Hamilton Bros Inc ....F 317 241-2571
Indianapolis (G-7067)
Maurer Environmental Drilling ....G 574 272-7524
South Bend (G-12855)

CONTRACTORS: Water Well Drilling

Ald Indy Inc ....G 317 826-3833
Fishers (G-3867)
Armstrong Drilling Inc ....G 765 455-2445
Burlington (G-1209)
Bonar Inc ....G 260 636-7430
Albion (G-17)
Helvie & Sons Inc ....G 765 674-1372
Marion (G-9530)
Hoover Well Drilling Inc ....G 574 831-4901
New Paris (G-10984)
John Remmler Well Drilling ....G 812 663-8178
Greensburg (G-5616)
McGrews Well Drilling Inc ....G 574 857-3875
Rochester (G-12137)
Rose-Wall Mfg Inc ....G 317 894-4497
Greenfield (G-5567)

CONTRACTORS: Water Well Servicing

Dilden Bros Inc ....F 765 742-1717
Lafayette (G-8891)

CONTRACTORS: Window Treatment Installation

Sun Control Center LLC ....F 260 490-9902
Fort Wayne (G-4666)

CONTRACTORS: Windows & Doors

A-1 Door Specialties Inc ....G 260 749-1635
South Bend (G-12689)
R & A Goodman Enterprises ....G 765 296-3446
Lafayette (G-8987)

CONTRACTORS: Wood Floor Installation & Refinishing

Cornerstone Industries Corp ....D 317 852-6522
Brownsburg (G-1145)
Milani Custom Homes LLC ....G 219 455-5804
Merrillville (G-9734)

CONTRACTORS: Wrecking & Demolition

A & T Construction and Excvtg ....G 219 314-2439
Cedar Lake (G-1524)

CONTROL CIRCUIT DEVICES

Neo Magnequench Dist LLC ....G 765 778-7809
Pendleton (G-11496)

CONTROL EQPT: Electric

Advantage Electronics Inc ....F 317 888-1946
Greenwood (G-5659)
Control Consultants of America ....G 219 989-3311
Hammond (G-5865)
Doron Distribution Inc ....G 317 594-9259
Indianapolis (G-6759)
Enginring Cncpts Unlimited Inc ....G 317 826-1558
Fishers (G-3905)
Harris Corporation ....G 260 451-6000
Fort Wayne (G-4322)
ITT LLC ....G 260 451-6000
Fort Wayne (G-4385)
Kreuter Manufacturing Co Inc ....G 574 831-4626
New Paris (G-10989)
Rockwell Automation Inc ....E 219 924-3002
Munster (G-10626)
Touch Plate Technologies Inc ....F 260 426-1565
Fort Wayne (G-4695)
Touchplate Technologies Inc ....F 260 424-4323
Fort Wayne (G-4696)

CONTROL EQPT: Electric Buses & Locomotives

Illinois Tool Works Inc ....E 317 298-5000
Indianapolis (G-7160)

CONTROL EQPT: Noise

Enoise Control Inc ....G 317 774-1900
Westfield (G-14162)

CONTROL PANELS: Electrical

Advance MCS Electronics Inc ....F 574 642-3501
Goshen (G-5166)
Advanced Control Panels Inc ....F 219 763-4000
Portage (G-11748)
Blinkless Power Equipment LLC ....G 317 844-7328
Indianapolis (G-6484)
Bonner & Associates ....G 317 571-1911
Carmel (G-1321)
Caddo Connections Inc ....E 219 874-8119
La Porte (G-8744)
Control Consultants of America ....G 219 989-3311
Hammond (G-5865)
Controlled Automation Inc ....F 317 770-3870
Noblesville (G-11084)
Fabricated Specialties Inc ....G 219 996-4787
Hebron (G-6012)
Fabtration LLC ....F 812 989-6730
Georgetown (G-5144)
Integrated Tech Resources ....G 317 757-5432
Indianapolis (G-7249)
Proteus Solutions LLC ....G 317 222-1138
Indianapolis (G-7783)
Quality Industrial Supplies ....F 219 324-2654
La Porte (G-8808)
Sullivan Engineered Services ....G 812 294-1724
Henryville (G-6033)

CONTROLS & ACCESS: Indl, Electric

Aptiv Services Us LLC ....F 765 451-5011
Kokomo (G-8591)
Direct Control Systems Inc ....G 765 282-7474
Muncie (G-10460)
Duesenburg Inc ....G 260 496-9650
Fort Wayne (G-4223)
E C T Franklin Control Systems ....G 765 939-2531
Richmond (G-11979)
GM Components Holdings LLC ....G 765 451-9049
Kokomo (G-8629)

Horner Apg LLC ....D 317 916-4274
Indianapolis (G-7127)
Horner Industrial Services Inc ....G 317 916-4274
Indianapolis (G-7128)
Horner Industrial Services Inc ....G 812 466-5281
Terre Haute (G-13249)
Horner Industrial Services Inc ....G 260 434-1189
Fort Wayne (G-4348)
JMS Electronics Corporation ....E 574 522-0246
Elkhart (G-2949)
MRC Technology Inc ....F 574 232-9057
South Bend (G-12867)
Rs2 Technologies LLC ....F 877 682-3532
Munster (G-10628)

CONTROLS & ACCESS: Motor

Brenda Sue Ware Eaton LLC ....G 317 462-2058
Greenfield (G-5509)
Eaton & Hancock Associates ....G 317 291-6513
Indianapolis (G-6795)
Eaton Corporation ....C 574 283-5004
South Bend (G-12755)
Eaton Emts ....G 765 587-4910
Muncie (G-10467)
Eaton Hydraulics LLC ....G 260 248-5800
Columbia City (G-1782)
Eaton Partners LLC ....G 765 458-7896
Liberty (G-9260)
Kcma & Services LLC ....G 260 645-0885
Waterloo (G-14016)
Ron Eaton ....G 219 464-1607
Valparaiso (G-13610)
Tamara Eaton ....G 219 872-9151
Michigan City (G-9851)
Terry Eaton ....G 812 687-7579
Plainville (G-11655)

CONTROLS: Automatic Temperature

Abbott Controls Inc ....G 317 697-7102
Indianapolis (G-6308)
Advantage Engineering Inc ....D 317 887-0729
Greenwood (G-5660)
Automated Logic Corporation ....E 765 286-1993
Muncie (G-10436)
Building Temp Solutions LLC ....F 260 449-9201
Fort Wayne (G-4126)
Invensys Processs Systems Inc ....A 317 372-2839
Indianapolis (G-7264)
Open Control Systems LLC ....G 317 429-0627
Indianapolis (G-7626)
Pinder Instruments Company Inc ....E 219 924-7070
Munster (G-10624)
Temperature Control Svcs LLC ....G 765 325-2439
Fishers (G-3975)
Temptek Inc ....G 317 887-6352
Greenwood (G-5752)

CONTROLS: Electric Motor

Nidec Motor Corporation ....D 812 385-2564
Princeton (G-11880)
SBS Cybermetrix Inc ....G 812 378-7960
Columbus (G-2011)
SGS Cybermetrix Inc ....G 800 713-1203
Columbus (G-2013)

CONTROLS: Environmental

Caltherm Corporation ....C 812 372-0281
Columbus (G-1864)
Caltherm Corporation ....F 812 372-0281
Columbus (G-1865)
Hmmcopl LLC ....E 219 757-3575
Merrillville (G-9719)
Nidec Motor Corporation ....A 317 328-4079
Indianapolis (G-7587)
OMI Industries Inc ....G 812 438-9218
Rising Sun (G-12090)
Pyromation Inc ....C 260 484-2580
Fort Wayne (G-4566)
Redi/Controls Inc ....G 317 494-6600
Franklin (G-4926)
Rees Inc ....F 260 495-9811
Fremont (G-4972)
Thatcher Engineering Corp ....D 219 949-2084
Gary (G-5105)
United Technologies Electr ....A 260 359-3514
Huntington (G-6260)

CONTROLS: Marine & Navy, Auxiliary

Electromechanical RES Labs ....E 812 948-8484
New Albany *(G-10771)*

CONTROLS: Relay & Ind

ABB Flexible Automation Inc.................E 317 876-9090
Indianapolis *(G-6307)*
Advanced Control Tech Inc ....G 317 806-2750
Indianapolis *(G-6332)*
Automation & Control Svcs Inc ....F 219 558-2060
Scherertown *(G-12315)*
Borgwarner Pds Anderson LLC ....B 765 778-6499
Noblesville *(G-11068)*
Borgwarner Pds Anderson LLC ....C 765 778-6499
Anderson *(G-76)*
Carson Manufacturing Co Inc ....F 317 257-3191
Indianapolis *(G-6560)*
Control Solutions ....G 765 313-1984
West Lafayette *(G-14060)*
D & E Auto Electric Inc ....F 219 763-3892
Portage *(G-11759)*
Damping Technologies Inc ....E 574 258-7916
Mishawaka *(G-10031)*
Damping Technologies Inc ....E 574 258-7916
Mishawaka *(G-10032)*
Electro Corporation ....F 219 393-5571
Kingsbury *(G-8536)*
Environmental Technology Inc ....E 574 233-1202
South Bend *(G-12765)*
Frakes Engineering Inc ....E 317 577-3000
Indianapolis *(G-6956)*
Franklin Electric Co Inc ....D 765 677-6900
Gas City *(G-5124)*
General Automation Company ....F 317 849-7483
Indianapolis *(G-6992)*
Hitachi Automotive Systems ....B 859 734-9451
Ligonier *(G-9287)*
L H Controls Inc ....F 260 432-9020
Fort Wayne *(G-4420)*
Nidec Motor Corporation ....A 317 328-4079
Indianapolis *(G-7587)*
Pyromation Inc ....C 260 484-2580
Fort Wayne *(G-4566)*
Siemens Industry Inc ....D 219 763-7927
Portage *(G-11794)*
Teaco Inc ....F 219 874-6234
Michigan City *(G-9852)*
West Side Automation ....F 812 768-6878
Haubstadt *(G-6008)*
Western Consolidated Tech Inc ....D 260 495-9866
Fremont *(G-4982)*
Wolfe and Swickard Mch Co Inc ....D 317 241-2589
Indianapolis *(G-8210)*

CONTROLS: Thermostats

Advanced Control Tech Inc ....G 317 806-2750
Indianapolis *(G-6332)*

CONTROLS: Truck, Indl Battery

G W Enterprises ....G 260 868-2555
Butler *(G-1228)*
Innovative Battery Power Inc ....G 260 267-6582
Fort Wayne *(G-4372)*

CONTROLS: Water Heater

Suburban Manufacturing Company ......F 574 294-5681
Elkhart *(G-3196)*

CONVENIENCE STORES

Premier AG Co-Op Inc ....E 812 522-4911
Seymour *(G-12477)*

CONVERTERS: Data

Cisco Systems Inc ....E 317 816-5200
Carmel *(G-1339)*

CONVERTERS: Phase Or Rotary, Electrical

Kay Industries Inc ....F 574 236-6220
Plymouth *(G-11698)*
Kay Industries Inc ....F 574 236-6220
Plymouth *(G-11699)*

CONVERTERS: Torque, Exc Auto

Aisin Drivetrain Inc ....C 812 793-2427
Crothersville *(G-2214)*

Champ Torque Converters Inc................G 812 424-2602
Evansville *(G-3415)*

CONVEYOR SYSTEMS

Frontier Engineering ....G 317 823-6885
Indianapolis *(G-6965)*
General Material Handling Co ....G 317 888-5735
Indianapolis *(G-6998)*
Iron Bull Mfg LLC ....G 765 597-2480
Marshall *(G-9592)*
Martin Grgory Cnvyor Engrg LLC ....G 812 923-9814
Georgetown *(G-5149)*
Systec Corporation ....D 317 890-9230
Indianapolis *(G-8031)*

CONVEYOR SYSTEMS: Bulk Handling

C & S Family Inc ....E 812 886-5500
Vincennes *(G-13670)*
Summerlot Engineered Pdts Inc ....F 812 466-7266
Rosedale *(G-12206)*

CONVEYOR SYSTEMS: Pneumatic Tube

Air Equipment & Engrg Inc ....E 765 349-9259
Martinsville *(G-9594)*
Berendsen Inc ....G 812 423-6486
Evansville *(G-3373)*
Ctb Inc ....E 765 654-8517
Frankfort *(G-4825)*
CTB MN Investment Co Inc ....E 765 654-8517
Frankfort *(G-4826)*

CONVEYOR SYSTEMS: Robotic

Butterworth Industries Inc ....E 765 677-6725
Gas City *(G-5121)*
Koehler Welding Supply Inc ....F 812 574-4103
Madison *(G-9476)*
Pia Automation US Inc ....C 812 474-3126
Evansville *(G-3669)*

CONVEYORS & CONVEYING EQPT

1st Source Products Inc ....F 812 288-7466
Jeffersonville *(G-8315)*
Accu-Tech Automation Inc ....F 317 352-1490
Indianapolis *(G-6313)*
Advance Fabricators Inc ....E 812 944-6941
New Albany *(G-10741)*
Aggreate Systems ....F 260 854-4711
Rome City *(G-12197)*
Banks Machine & Engrg Inc ....D 317 642-4980
Shelbyville *(G-12519)*
C & P Engineering & Mfg ....E 765 825-4293
Connersville *(G-2042)*
C T C Corporation ....G 812 849-2500
Mitchell *(G-10156)*
C&M Conveyor Inc ....C 812 849-5647
Mitchell *(G-10157)*
Carman Industries Inc ....E 812 288-4710
Jeffersonville *(G-8335)*
CPM Conveyor LLC ....G 765 918-5190
Crawfordsville *(G-2143)*
Direct Conveyors LLC ....F 317 346-7777
Franklin *(G-4881)*
Fabricated Steel Corporation ....G 317 899-0012
Indianapolis *(G-6901)*
George Koch Sons LLC ....C 812 465-9600
Evansville *(G-3519)*
Gravel Conveyors Inc ....F 317 873-8686
Zionsville *(G-14435)*
H & H Design & Tool Inc ....G 765 886-6199
Economy *(G-2591)*
Halo LLC ....D 317 575-9992
Indianapolis *(G-6266)*
Hillenbrand Inc ....C 812 934-7500
Batesville *(G-504)*
Hirata Corporation of America ....E 317 856-8600
Indianapolis *(G-7109)*
Industrial Transmission Eqp ....E 574 936-3028
Plymouth *(G-11694)*
Keener Corporation ....F 765 825-2100
Connersville *(G-2058)*
Keener Corporation ....D 765 825-2711
Connersville *(G-2060)*
M Pro LLC ....G 765 459-4750
Kokomo *(G-8661)*
Mainline Conveyor Systems Inc ....F 317 831-2795
Mooresville *(G-10320)*
McClamroch AG LLC ....G 765 362-4495
Crawfordsville *(G-2171)*

McGinty Conveyors Inc ....G 317 240-4315
Indianapolis *(G-7472)*
Mid-State Automation Inc ....G 765 795-5500
Cloverdale *(G-1730)*
Omni-Tron Tooling & Engrg ....G 574 262-2083
Elkhart *(G-3069)*
Prime Conveyor Inc ....E 219 736-1994
Merrillville *(G-9749)*
Pro Epuipment Service ....G 317 322-7858
Indianapolis *(G-7765)*
Production Hdlg Systems Inc ....F 317 738-0485
Franklin *(G-4924)*
Rowe Conveyor LLC ....G 317 602-1024
Greenwood *(G-5743)*
Sager Metal Strip Company LLC ....E 219 874-3609
Michigan City *(G-9837)*
Screw Conveyor Corporation ....E 219 931-1450
Hammond *(G-5936)*
Screw Conveyor Pacific Corp ....E 219 931-1450
Hammond *(G-5937)*
Shuttleworth LLC ....D 260 356-8500
Huntington *(G-6248)*
Smock Material Handling Co ....F 317 890-3200
Indianapolis *(G-7954)*
Sparks Belting Company Inc ....G 800 451-4537
Hammond *(G-5945)*
Stahl Equipment Inc ....E 812 925-3341
Chandler *(G-1554)*
United Conveyor Corporation ....E 574 256-0991
Mishawaka *(G-10142)*
Vestil Manufacturing Corp ....B 260 665-7586
Angola *(G-258)*
Vibcon Corp ....F 317 984-3543
Arcadia *(G-271)*
W M Kelley Co Inc ....E 812 945-3529
New Albany *(G-10873)*
Webber Manufacturing Company ....G 317 357-8681
Indianapolis *(G-8181)*

COOKING & FOOD WARMING EQPT: Commercial

Accutemp Products Inc ....D 260 493-0415
Fort Wayne *(G-4039)*
Bottom Line Management Inc ....F 812 944-7388
Clarksville *(G-1674)*
Leslie-Fisher Engineering Inc ....G 765 457-7796
Kokomo *(G-8658)*
M D Holdings LLC ....G 317 831-7030
Mooresville *(G-10319)*
Thomas Green LLC ....G 317 337-0000
Indianapolis *(G-8064)*

COOKING & FOODWARMING EQPT: Commercial

Thermodyne Food Service Pdts ....E 260 428-2535
Fort Wayne *(G-4682)*

COOKING & FOODWARMING EQPT: Popcorn Machines, Commercial

Indiana Concession Supply LLC ....F 317 353-1667
Indianapolis *(G-7178)*

COOKING WARE: Cooking Ware, Porcelain Enameled

Columbian Home Products LLC ....E 812 238-5041
Terre Haute *(G-13214)*

COOKWARE, STONEWARE: Coarse Earthenware & Pottery

Molded Acstcal Pdts Easton Inc ....C 574 968-3124
Granger *(G-5424)*
Yellow Banks Clay Company Inc ....F 812 567-4703
Dale *(G-2336)*

COOLING TOWERS: Metal

Advantage Engineering Inc ....D 317 887-0729
Greenwood *(G-5660)*
SPX Corporation ....C 812 849-5647
Mitchell *(G-10171)*
SPX Corporation ....C 219 879-6561
Michigan City *(G-9846)*
SPX Corporation ....C 704 752-4400
Angola *(G-245)*

PRODUCT

COOLING TOWERS: Wood

Action Cooling Towers Inc ....G....... 219 285-2660
Morocco (G-10359)

COOPERAGE STOCK PRODUCTS

Premier AG Co-Op Inc ....E....... 812 522-4911
Seymour (G-12477)

COPPER PRDTS: Refined, Primary

Univertical LLC ....D....... 260 665-1500
Angola (G-255)

COPPER: Rolling & Drawing

Alconex Specialty Products ....D....... 260 744-3446
Fort Wayne (G-4056)
Brand Sheet Metal Works Inc ....G....... 765 284-5594
Muncie (G-10443)
Dereeltech LLC ....E....... 812 293-4786
Nabb (G-10639)

COPY MACHINES WHOLESALERS

Oce Copiers ....G....... 812 479-0000
Evansville (G-3652)

COPYRIGHT BUYING & LICENSING

Cliff A Ostermeyer ....G....... 615 361-7902
Indianapolis (G-6621)
Maingate Inc ....D....... 317 243-2000
Indianapolis (G-7444)

CORRUGATING MACHINES

Dovey Corporation ....F....... 765 649-2576
Anderson (G-99)
Haire Machine Corporation ....E....... 219 947-4545
Merrillville (G-9718)
Owens Machinery Inc ....G....... 812 968-3285
Palmyra (G-11437)

COSMETIC PREPARATIONS

Allen Industries Inc ....G....... 317 595-0730
Indianapolis (G-6368)
Energy Delivery Solutions LLC ....G....... 502 271-8753
Jeffersonville (G-8354)
Hair Associates LLC ....F....... 317 844-7207
Carmel (G-1392)
Kbshimmer Bath and Body Inc ....G....... 317 979-2307
Terre Haute (G-13264)
Relevo Inc ....G....... 317 644-0099
Carmel (G-1465)
Universal Packg Systems Inc ....B....... 260 829-6721
Orland (G-11359)

COSMETICS & TOILETRIES

Ambre Blends ....G....... 317 257-0202
Indianapolis (G-6381)
Bath & Body Works LLC ....E....... 219 531-2146
Valparaiso (G-13504)
Bath & Body Works LLC ....F....... 317 468-0834
Greenfield (G-5508)
Bath & Body Works LLC ....G....... 317 209-1517
Avon (G-432)
Century Pharmaceuticals Inc ....F....... 317 849-4210
Indianapolis (G-6586)
Conopco Inc ....C....... 219 659-3200
Hammond (G-5864)
Desirable Scents ....G....... 317 504-4976
Lafayette (G-8888)
Indiana Nanotech LLC ....G....... 317 385-1578
Indianapolis (G-7185)
Kims Scrub Connection LLC ....G....... 812 867-1237
Evansville (G-3590)
Komun Scents ....G....... 317 308-0714
Indianapolis (G-7365)
Mahogany Scents ....G....... 574 271-1364
South Bend (G-12849)
Mansfield - King LLC ....D....... 317 788-0750
Indianapolis (G-7450)
National Notification Ctr LLC ....G....... 317 613-6060
Indianapolis (G-7574)
North Coast Organics LLC ....G....... 260 246-0289
Fort Wayne (G-4505)
Pieniadze Inc ....G....... 888 226-6241
Zionsville (G-14456)
Prairie Scents LLC ....G....... 765 361-6908
Crawfordsville (G-2187)

Sincerely Different LLC ....G....... 574 292-1727
Granger (G-5435)
Soulful Scents LLC ....G....... 317 319-8001
Noblesville (G-11185)
Vera Bradley Inc ....B....... 877 708-8372
Roanoke (G-12110)
William Roam LLC ....G....... 317 356-2715
Indianapolis (G-8199)

COSTUME JEWELRY & NOVELTIES: Exc Semi & Precious

Annie Oakley Enterprises Inc ....F....... 260 894-7100
Ligonier (G-9276)
Ntr Metals LLC ....G....... 317 522-2891
Indianapolis (G-7603)
Sisson & Son Mfg Jewelers ....G....... 574 967-4331
Flora (G-4003)

COSTUME JEWELRY & NOVELTIES: Ornament, Exc Precious Mtl/Gem

Rhinestone Supply LLC ....G....... 260 484-2711
Fort Wayne (G-4591)

COSTUME JEWELRY & NOVELTIES: Rosaries & Sm Religious Items

Dicksons Inc ....C....... 812 522-1308
Seymour (G-12445)
Templeton Coal Company Inc ....G....... 812 232-7037
Terre Haute (G-13350)

COSTUMES & WIGS STORES

Higgins Dyan ....G....... 812 876-0754
Ellettsville (G-3281)

COUNTER & SINK TOPS

American Stonecast Pdts Inc ....F....... 574 206-0097
Elkhart (G-2686)
Double T Manufacturing Corp ....F....... 574 262-1340
Elkhart (G-2799)
Fisher Specialties Inc ....G....... 260 385-8251
Harlan (G-5971)
Keystone Designs Inc ....E....... 574 269-5531
Warsaw (G-13897)
Lami-Crafts Inc ....G....... 812 232-3012
Terre Haute (G-13270)
Precision Stone Works ....F....... 812 683-1102
Huntingburg (G-6178)
Premier Kitchen & Bath Inc ....G....... 574 294-6805
Elkhart (G-3111)
Premium Srfc Fbrication of Ind ....E....... 317 867-1013
Westfield (G-14181)
Quality Surfaces Inc ....G....... 812 876-5838
Spencer (G-13034)
Reeds Plastic Tops Inc ....G....... 765 282-1471
Muncie (G-10556)

COUNTERS & COUNTING DEVICES

Kendrion (mishawaka) LLC ....E....... 574 257-2422
Mishawaka (G-10063)
Memcor Inc ....F....... 260 356-4300
Huntington (G-6228)
Scalar Design Engrg & Dist LLC ....G....... 765 429-5545
Lafayette (G-8995)
Steiner Enterprises Inc ....F....... 765 429-6409
Lafayette (G-9004)

COUNTERS OR COUNTER DISPLAY CASES, EXC WOOD

Plastic Line Manufacturing ....E....... 219 769-8022
Merrillville (G-9747)
Solid Surface Craftsmen Inc ....G....... 317 535-2333
Whiteland (G-14246)

COUNTERS OR COUNTER DISPLAY CASES, WOOD

Carmel Countertops Inc ....G....... 317 843-0331
Carmel (G-1330)
Classic Cabinetry ....G....... 317 823-1853
Indianapolis (G-6617)
Custom Counters Inc ....G....... 812 546-0052
Columbus (G-1903)
Gotokiosk LLC ....G....... 800 206-0177
Monroe (G-10182)

Mica Shop Inc ....E....... 574 533-1102
Goshen (G-5287)
Mouron & Company Inc ....F....... 317 243-7955
Indianapolis (G-7551)

COUNTERS: Mechanical

Mechanical Parts & Svcs Inc ....G....... 219 670-1986
Valparaiso (G-13580)

COUNTING DEVICES: Controls, Revolution & Timing

Custom Controls & Engineering ....G....... 812 663-0755
Greensburg (G-5596)

COUNTING DEVICES: Gauges, Press Temp Corrections Computing

Prosperus LLC ....G....... 317 786-8990
Indianapolis (G-7782)

COUNTING DEVICES: Production

Parker Exploration & Productio ....G....... 812 673-4017
Wadesville (G-13774)

COUNTING DEVICES: Tachometer, Centrifugal

Phoenix America Inc ....E....... 260 432-9664
Fort Wayne (G-4529)

COUNTRY CLUBS

Country Club Computer ....G....... 317 271-4000
Indianapolis (G-6675)

COUPLINGS: Hose & Tube, Hydraulic Or Pneumatic

M & M Svc Stn Eqp Spcalist Inc ....G....... 317 347-8001
Indianapolis (G-7429)

COUPLINGS: Shaft

Guardian Ind Inc ....E....... 219 874-5248
Michigan City (G-9799)
Odin Corporation of Delaware ....G....... 317 849-3770
Indianapolis (G-7610)
Rexnord Industries LLC ....B....... 865 220-7700
Avon (G-463)
Rexnord Industries LLC ....D....... 317 273-5500
Avon (G-464)
Sanlo Inc ....D....... 219 879-0241
Michigan City (G-9841)

COURIER OR MESSENGER SVCS

P413 Corporation ....G....... 317 769-0679
Zionsville (G-14454)

COURIER SVCS: Ground

Cosner Ice Company Inc ....E....... 812 279-8930
Bedford (G-535)

COURIER SVCS: Package By Vehicle

UPS Store 5219 ....G....... 219 750-9597
Merrillville (G-9760)

COURIER SVCS: Parcel By Vehicle

Schwans Home Service Inc ....E....... 317 882-6624
Greenwood (G-5748)

COVERS: Automobile Seat

Summit Seating Inc ....F....... 574 264-9636
Elkhart (G-3198)
Wiseguys Seating & Accessry Co ....G....... 574 294-6030
Elkhart (G-3264)

COVERS: Automotive, Exc Seat & Tire

Carcapsule USA Inc ....G....... 219 945-9493
Hobart (G-6073)
Indiana Fabric Solutions Inc ....E....... 812 279-0255
Bedford (G-551)

COVERS: Canvas

J Ennis Fabrics Inc (usa)..................G...... 877 953-6647
   Plainfield *(G-11620)*

COVERS: Slip Made Of Fabric, Plastic, Etc.

Rhyne & Associates Inc ....F...... 317 786-4459
   Indianapolis *(G-7838)*

CRADLES: Drum

Phoenix Engineering & Mfg Inc.............G...... 574 251-9040
   South Bend *(G-12895)*

CRANE & AERIAL LIFT SVCS

Hoosier Crane Service Company ....E...... 574 523-2945
   Elkhart *(G-2920)*
T & M Equipment Company Inc ....F...... 317 293-9255
   Indianapolis *(G-8032)*

CRANES: Indl Plant

Royal ARC Welding Company ....E...... 260 587-3711
   Ashley *(G-290)*

CRANES: Indl Truck

Sto-Away Power Crane Inc ....G...... 219 942-9797
   Crown Point *(G-2310)*

CRANES: Overhead

Hoosier Crane Service Company ....E...... 574 523-2945
   Elkhart *(G-2920)*
Indiana Steel & Engrg Inc....................E...... 812 275-3363
   Bedford *(G-552)*
J V Crane & Engineering Inc................E...... 219 942-8566
   Hobart *(G-6082)*

CRANKSHAFTS & CAMSHAFTS: Machining

Goad Crankshaft Service Inc ....G...... 812 477-1127
   Evansville *(G-3521)*
Odyssey Machine Inc ....G...... 812 951-1160
   Georgetown *(G-5151)*

CRATES: Berry, Wood Wirebound

Timber Line Crating LP ....F...... 260 238-3075
   Spencerville *(G-13052)*

CREATIVE SVCS: Advertisers, Exc Writers

Hot Rod Car Care LLC ....G...... 317 660-2077
   Indianapolis *(G-7134)*
Ron Glasscock..................................G...... 812 986-2342
   Poland *(G-11743)*
Screen Art Advertising Co Inc ....G...... 260 483-6514
   Fort Wayne *(G-4611)*

CREDIT INST, SHORT-TERM BUSINESS: Financing Dealers

Ford Motor Company...........................D...... 317 837-2302
   Plainfield *(G-11610)*

CROWNS & CLOSURES

Drug Plastics Closures Inc ....D...... 812 526-0555
   Edinburgh *(G-2608)*

CRUDE PETROLEUM & NATURAL GAS PRODUCTION

C Modesitt Oil Production LLC..............G...... 812 249-0678
   Rosedale *(G-12203)*
Countrymark Coop Holdg Corp.............E...... 800 808-3170
   Indianapolis *(G-6676)*
Countrymark Ref Logistics LLC............D...... 812 838-4341
   Mount Vernon *(G-10388)*
Universal Operating Inc.......................G...... 812 477-1584
   Evansville *(G-3789)*

CRUDE PETROLEUM & NATURAL GAS PRODUCTION

ANR Pipeline Company ....G...... 260 463-3342
   Lagrange *(G-9031)*
Avon Carbon Capture RES Assoc.........G...... 317 753-8829
   Avon *(G-430)*
B N Oil LLC..G...... 859 816-2244
   Lawrenceburg *(G-9132)*

Briggs Exploration Prod Co LLC............G...... 812 249-0564
   Evansville *(G-3401)*
Carlton West Oil Company LLC.............G...... 812 375-9689
   Columbus *(G-1867)*
Ceres Solutions LLP...........................G...... 765 477-6542
   Lafayette *(G-8874)*
Common Sense Producing LLC.............G...... 317 622-1682
   Greenfield *(G-5515)*
Four Season Oil Inc ....G...... 317 215-1214
   Plainfield *(G-11611)*
Fred D McCrary ....G...... 812 354-6520
   Petersburg *(G-11564)*
Heflin Hflin Oil Gas Producers.............G...... 812 536-3464
   Stendal *(G-13074)*
Iam Petroleum Inc ....G...... 260 625-9951
   Columbia City *(G-1793)*
James Mobile Oil Change ....G...... 219 455-5321
   Crown Point *(G-2266)*
Lassus Bros Oil Inc ....E...... 260 625-4003
   Fort Wayne *(G-4424)*
Shell ....G...... 765 282-4635
   Muncie *(G-10561)*
Strategic Talent LLC ....G...... 317 489-4000
   Indianapolis *(G-8011)*
Tamarack Petroleum Company Inc ....G...... 812 567-4023
   Tennyson *(G-13181)*
Viannos Village Cretan Oil ....G...... 219 513-6720
   Highland *(G-6058)*

CRUDE PETROLEUM PRODUCTION

Barger Engineering Inc ....G...... 812 476-3077
   Evansville *(G-3370)*
Core Minerals Operating Co Inc ....G...... 812 759-6950
   Evansville *(G-3430)*
Coy Oil Inc ....G...... 812 838-3146
   Mount Vernon *(G-10389)*
Gallagher Drilling Inc..........................G...... 812 477-6746
   Evansville *(G-3514)*
Hux Oil Corp ....G...... 812 894-2096
   Terre Haute *(G-13251)*
K S Oil Corp ....G...... 812 453-3026
   Evansville *(G-3581)*
Mannon L Walters Inc ....F...... 812 867-5946
   Evansville *(G-3613)*
Mayhew Oil & Gas LLC ....G...... 812 985-9966
   Mount Vernon *(G-10399)*
Moore Engineering & Prod Co ....F...... 812 479-1051
   Evansville *(G-3636)*
Nickolick Development.........................G...... 812 422-8526
   Evansville *(G-3644)*
Paul E Potts ....G...... 812 354-3241
   Hazleton *(G-6010)*
Payne George A Petroleum Engr...........G...... 812 853-3813
   Newburgh *(G-11040)*
Robinson Engineering & Oil Co ....F...... 812 477-1575
   Evansville *(G-3707)*
Ryan Oil Co LLC.................................G...... 812 422-4168
   Evansville *(G-3713)*
Sater Enterprises ....G...... 812 477-1529
   Evansville *(G-3714)*
Speedway LLC ....F...... 765 827-0321
   Connersville *(G-2071)*
Speedway LLC ....F...... 317 867-3699
   Noblesville *(G-11188)*
Speedway LLC ....F...... 317 838-5479
   Plainfield *(G-11644)*
Speedway LLC ....F...... 219 929-1054
   Chesterton *(G-1631)*
Speedway LLC ....F...... 317 770-0225
   Noblesville *(G-11189)*
Speedway LLC ....F...... 317 783-6361
   Indianapolis *(G-7974)*
Trey Exploration Inc...........................G...... 812 858-3146
   Newburgh *(G-11052)*
Vickery Drilling Co ....G...... 812 473-4671
   Evansville *(G-3798)*

CRYOGENIC COOLING DEVICES: Infrared Detectors, Masers

Kadel Engineering Corporation.............E...... 317 745-2798
   Danville *(G-2350)*

CULTURE MEDIA

Culture Media LLC ....G...... 317 966-0847
   Carmel *(G-1350)*
Gul For Media Development ....G...... 317 726-9544
   Noblesville *(G-11115)*
Indycoast Partners LLC......................G...... 317 454-1050
   Carmel *(G-1414)*

Micrology Laboratories Llc ....G...... 574 533-3351
   Goshen *(G-5289)*
Quick Click Marketing Inc ....G...... 765 857-2167
   Ridgeville *(G-12081)*

CULVERTS: Metal Plate

Kuharic Enterprises............................G...... 574 288-9410
   South Bend *(G-12832)*

CULVERTS: Sheet Metal

Buschman Tank Cars Inc ....G...... 219 984-5444
   Reynolds *(G-11944)*
Park County Aggregates LLC ....G...... 765 245-2344
   Rockville *(G-12178)*

CUPOLAS: Metal Plate

Pb Metal Works ....G...... 765 489-1311
   Hagerstown *(G-5810)*

CUPS & PLATES: Foamed Plastics

Opflex Technologies LLC.....................G...... 317 731-6123
   Indianapolis *(G-7628)*
Sevenoks Inc ....G...... 800 523-8715
   La Porte *(G-8818)*
Tp/Elm Acquisition Sbusid Inc ....D...... 260 728-2161
   Decatur *(G-2408)*

CUPS: Plastic Exc Polystyrene Foam

Sterling Berry Corporation...................G...... 812 424-2904
   Evansville *(G-3749)*

CURBING: Granite Or Stone

Cassini - D & D Mfg Inc.......................G...... 765 449-7992
   Lafayette *(G-8870)*
Concepts In Stone & Tile Inc ....G...... 574 267-4712
   Warsaw *(G-13859)*
Interior Design Surfaces Inc ....G...... 317 829-3970
   Carmel *(G-1417)*
Selvins Marble & Gran Sp LLC ....G...... 317 370-4237
   Zionsville *(G-14461)*
Stone Artisans Ltd ....G...... 317 362-0107
   Indianapolis *(G-8008)*

CURTAIN & DRAPERY FIXTURES: Poles, Rods & Rollers

Ascot Enterprises Inc.........................D...... 574 773-3104
   Nappanee *(G-10650)*
Beauti Pleat Draperies Inc...................G...... 317 887-1728
   Greenwood *(G-5669)*
Custom Blind Co ....G...... 812 867-9280
   Evansville *(G-3449)*
Custom Draperies of Indiana ....G...... 219 924-2500
   Hammond *(G-5867)*
Draper Inc ....B...... 765 987-7999
   Spiceland *(G-13054)*
Greenwood Draperie Corp ....G...... 317 882-0130
   Greenwood *(G-5699)*
J P Whitt Inc ....G...... 765 759-0521
   Muncie *(G-10498)*
Mill End Drapery Inc ....G...... 317 257-4800
   Indianapolis *(G-7518)*

CURTAIN WALLS: Building, Steel

Sigma Steel Inc ....E...... 812 275-4489
   Bedford *(G-578)*

CURTAINS: Window, From Purchased Materials

Ascot Enterprises Inc.........................E...... 877 773-7751
   Nappanee *(G-10648)*
Ascot Enterprises Inc.........................D...... 574 773-7751
   Nappanee *(G-10649)*
Foremost Flexible Fabricating..............G...... 812 663-4756
   Greensburg *(G-5600)*
Mar-Co Packaging Inc ....G...... 765 564-3979
   Delphi *(G-2423)*

CUSHIONS & PILLOWS

Arden Companies LLC ....D...... 260 747-1657
   Fort Wayne *(G-4089)*
Barrett Manufacturing Inc ....G...... 812 753-5808
   Fort Branch *(G-4026)*
Bleu Rooster Designs..........................G...... 317 845-0889
   Fishers *(G-3880)*

PRODUCT

Jordan Manufacturing Co Inc ....C 800 328-6522
Monticello (G-10268)

CUSHIONS & PILLOWS: Boat

R&D Investment Holdings Inc ....E 260 749-1301
Fort Wayne (G-4575)

CUT STONE & STONE PRODUCTS

Absolute Stone Polsg Repr LLC ....G 317 709-9539
Westfield (G-14132)
Architectural Stone Sales Inc ....E 812 279-2421
Bedford (G-529)
Bsbw Cultured Marble Inc ....E 812 246-5619
Sellersburg (G-12389)
Centura Solid Surfacing Inc ....F 317 867-5555
Westfield (G-14142)
Ceramica Inc ....F 317 546-0087
Indianapolis (G-6589)
Dreamwork Stones LLC ....F 317 709-2202
Carmel (G-1363)
Edw C Levy Co ....E 765 364-9251
Crawfordsville (G-2151)
Glas-Col LLC ....D 812 235-6167
Terre Haute (G-13240)
Hanson Aggregates East LLC ....F 812 883-2191
Salem (G-12290)
Hanson Aggregates Midwest LLC ....F 812 889-2120
Lexington (G-9251)
Indiana Lmstone Acqisition LLC ....D 812 275-3341
Bloomington (G-745)
Indiana Stone Works ....E 812 279-0448
Bedford (G-553)
Ionic Cut Stone Inc ....G 812 829-3416
Spencer (G-13029)
J & N Stone Inc ....C 574 862-4251
Wakarusa (G-13779)
J & N Stone Inc ....F 260 627-2404
Grabill (G-5373)
John Ley Monument Sales Inc ....G 260 347-7346
Avilla (G-408)
Kopelov Cut Stone Inc ....E 812 675-0099
Bedford (G-558)
Liberty Cut Stone Inc ....E 812 935-5515
Gosport (G-5353)
Majestic Marble Imports Inc ....F 317 237-4400
Indianapolis (G-7445)
My Choice Recycling Inc ....G 219 313-1388
Schererville (G-12336)
Ohio River Trading Co ....G 765 653-4100
Cloverdale (G-1733)
Quality Surfaces Inc ....E 812 876-5838
Spencer (G-13034)
Rush County Stone Co Inc ....G 765 629-2211
Milroy (G-9985)
Stone Center of Indiana LLC ....E 317 849-9100
Indianapolis (G-8009)
Stone Street Quarries Inc ....E 260 639-6511
Hoagland (G-6067)
Texacon Cut Stone LLC ....G 812 824-3211
Bloomington (G-838)
Tremain Ceramic Tile & Flr Cvg ....E 317 542-1491
Indianapolis (G-8093)
Unimin Corporation ....G 812 683-2179
Huntingburg (G-6183)
Wearly Monuments Inc ....E 765 284-9796
Muncie (G-10581)

CUTLERY

Bemcor Inc ....F 219 937-1600
Hammond (G-5850)
Ceg & Supply LLC ....E 317 435-6398
Martinsville (G-9598)

CUTTING EQPT: Glass Cutters

Stalter Glass Inc ....G 574 825-2225
Middlebury (G-9920)

CYCLIC CRUDES & INTERMEDIATES

Hammond Group Inc ....E 219 933-1560
Hammond (G-5885)

CYLINDER & ACTUATORS: Fluid Power

Elevator Equipment Corporation ....D 765 966-7761
Richmond (G-11981)
Five Star Hydraulics Inc ....E 219 762-1619
Portage (G-11763)

Hook Industrial Sales Inc ....F 317 545-8100
Indianapolis (G-7119)
Logansport Machine Co Inc ....E 574 735-0225
Logansport (G-9350)
Micro-Precision Operations ....E 260 589-2136
Berne (G-620)
Micromatic LLC ....D 260 589-2136
Berne (G-621)
PHD Inc ....G 260 747-6151
Fort Wayne (G-4527)
R P S Hydraulics Sales & Svc ....E 219 845-5526
Hammond (G-5931)

CYLINDERS: Pressure

Manchester Tank & Equipment Co ....C 574 295-8200
Elkhart (G-3016)
Parker-Hannifin Corporation ....E 219 297-3182
Goodland (G-5160)
Twincorp Inc ....E 812 934-9226
Batesville (G-522)

CYLINDERS: Pump

Flickinger Industries Inc ....E 260 432-4527
Fort Wayne (G-4267)
PHD Inc ....G 260 356-0120
Huntington (G-6238)
R P S Hydraulics Sales & Svc ....E 219 845-5526
Hammond (G-5931)

DAIRY EQPT

Garver Manufacturing Inc ....G 765 964-5828
Union City (G-13456)

DAIRY PRDTS STORE: Cheese

Graham Cheese Corporation ....E 812 692-5237
Elnora (G-3289)

DAIRY PRDTS STORE: Ice Cream, Packaged

Ice Cream On Wheels Inc ....G 800 884-9793
Griffith (G-5779)
Mishawaka Frozen Custard ....E 574 255-8000
Mishawaka (G-10092)

DAIRY PRDTS WHOLESALERS: Fresh

Instantwhip-Indianapolis Inc ....F 317 899-1533
Indianapolis (G-7244)

DAIRY PRDTS: Butter

Conagra Brands Inc ....B 317 329-3700
Indianapolis (G-6646)
Dairy Farmers America Inc ....D 574 533-3141
Goshen (G-5196)
Dillman Farm Incorporated ....G 812 825-5525
Bloomington (G-713)
Tulip Tree Creamery LLC ....G 317 331-5469
Indianapolis (G-8112)

DAIRY PRDTS: Cheese

Foremost Farms USA Cooperative ....G 317 842-7755
Indianapolis (G-6949)

DAIRY PRDTS: Dairy Based Desserts, Frozen

Saniserv ....E 317 831-7030
Mooresville (G-10339)

DAIRY PRDTS: Dietary Supplements, Dairy & Non-Dairy Based

Vesta Pharmaceuticals Inc ....E 317 895-9000
Indianapolis (G-8158)
Vitamorph Labs LLC ....G 219 237-0174
Highland (G-6059)
Wholistic Gardens ....G 260 573-1088
Waterloo (G-14026)

DAIRY PRDTS: Dips & Spreads, Cheese Based

Middlebury Cheese Company LLC ....E 574 825-9511
Middlebury (G-9906)

DAIRY PRDTS: Evaporated Milk

Nestle Usa Inc ....C 765 778-6000
Anderson (G-144)

DAIRY PRDTS: Fermented & Cultured Milk Prdts

Jacobs & Brichford LLC ....G 765 692-0056
Connersville (G-2057)

DAIRY PRDTS: Frozen Desserts & Novelties

Cloverleaf Farms Dairy ....G 219 938-5140
Gary (G-5038)
Ice Cream Specialties Inc ....D 765 474-2989
Lafayette (G-8919)
Meyer Ice Cream LLC ....G 812 941-8267
New Albany (G-10829)
Mishawaka Frozen Custard ....E 574 255-8000
Mishawaka (G-10092)
National Ice Corp ....G 317 887-9446
Indianapolis (G-7572)
Penguin Enterprises LLC ....E 812 333-0475
Bloomington (G-797)

DAIRY PRDTS: Ice Cream & Ice Milk

Bonnie Doon Ice Cream Corp ....F 574 255-9841
Mishawaka (G-10011)
Suiza Dairy Group LLC ....C 260 724-2136
Decatur (G-2407)

DAIRY PRDTS: Ice Cream, Bulk

AJS Gyros To Go ....G 812 951-1715
New Salisbury (G-11007)
Brics ....G 317 257-5757
Indianapolis (G-6507)
Browns Dairy Inc ....F 219 464-4141
Valparaiso (G-13514)
Buckner Inc ....F 317 570-0533
Indianapolis (G-6520)
La Michoacana ....G 574 293-9799
Elkhart (G-2980)
Nestle Dreyers Ice Cream Co ....C 260 483-3102
Fort Wayne (G-4497)
Ritters Frozen Custard Inc ....G 317 859-1038
Greenwood (G-5739)

DAIRY PRDTS: Ice Cream, Packaged, Molded, On Sticks, Etc.

Ice Cream On Wheels Inc ....G 800 884-9793
Griffith (G-5779)

DAIRY PRDTS: Milk & Cream, Cultured & Flavored

Swissland Milk Company Inc ....G 260 589-2761
Berne (G-628)

DAIRY PRDTS: Milk, Condensed & Evaporated

Dairy Farmers America Inc ....D 574 533-3141
Goshen (G-5196)

DAIRY PRDTS: Milk, Fluid

Dean Foods Co ....G 214 303-3400
Plymouth (G-11680)
Suiza Dairy Group LLC ....D 260 355-2273
Huntington (G-6254)

DAIRY PRDTS: Milk, Processed, Pasteurized, Homogenized/Btld

Dairy Farmers America Inc ....D 574 533-3141
Goshen (G-5196)
Dean Foods Company ....C 574 223-2141
Rochester (G-12121)
East Side Jersey Dairy Inc ....G 812 536-2207
Holland (G-6105)
East Side Jersey Dairy Inc ....E 765 649-1261
Anderson (G-104)
Prairie Farms Dairy Inc ....D 765 649-1261
Anderson (G-154)
Smithfoods Richmond Inc ....C 330 683-8710
Richmond (G-12051)

DAIRY PRDTS: Natural Cheese

Capriole Inc ....G 812 923-9408
Greenville (G-5647)
Graham Cheese Corporation ....E 812 692-5237
Elnora (G-3289)

Huber Orchards Inc .... E 812 923-9463
Borden (G-930)
Kroger Limited Partnership II .... D 765 364-5200
Crawfordsville (G-2166)

DAIRY PRDTS: Powdered Baby Formula

Combustion and Systems Inc .... G 859 814-8847
Rising Sun (G-12086)

DAIRY PRDTS: Processed Cheese

Dream Kraft LLC .... G 317 545-2988
Indianapolis (G-6766)
Karens Kountry Krafts .... G 765 238-2873
New Castle (G-10908)
Kitchen Krafts .... G 765 458-6858
Liberty (G-9262)
Kraft N Kreations .... G 812 243-1754
West Terre Haute (G-14125)
Tulip Tree Creamery LLC .... G 317 331-5469
Indianapolis (G-8112)

DAIRY PRDTS: Sour Cream

Royal Food Products Inc .... D 317 782-2660
Indianapolis (G-7865)

DAIRY PRDTS: Whipped Topping, Exc Frozen Or Dry Mix

Conagra Dairy Foods Company .... B 317 329-3700
Indianapolis (G-6647)
Instantwhip-Indianapolis Inc .... F 317 899-1533
Indianapolis (G-7244)

DAIRY PRDTS: Yogurt, Exc Frozen

Jujuberry LLC .... G 765 673-0058
Marion (G-9539)
Urban Swirl .... G 574 387-4035
Granger (G-5448)
Yogurtz .... G 317 853-6600
Carmel (G-1511)

DATA PROCESSING & PREPARATION SVCS

Aunalytics Inc .... G 574 307-9230
South Bend (G-12716)
NP Converters Inc .... E 812 448-2555
Brazil (G-973)
Rob Nolley Inc .... G 317 825-5211
Shelbyville (G-12563)
Telamon Entp Ventures LLC .... G 317 818-6888
Carmel (G-1489)
Urschel Air Leasing LLC .... G 219 464-4811
Chesterton (G-1638)

DATA PROCESSING SVCS

Fiserv Mrtg Servicing Systems .... C 574 282-3300
South Bend (G-12779)
Kaplan Inc .... D 317 872-7220
Indianapolis (G-7333)
Whiteco Industries Inc .... A 219 769-6601
Merrillville (G-9761)

DECALS, WHOLESALE

Tc4llc .... G 317 709-5429
Fishers (G-3973)

DECORATIVE WOOD & WOODWORK

A S M Inc .... G 260 724-8220
Decatur (G-2363)
Acorn Woodworks .... G 317 867-4377
Westfield (G-14133)
Alpine Enterprises .... G 574 773-5475
Nappanee (G-10645)
Automated Routing Inc .... C 812 357-2429
Saint Meinrad (G-12274)
Champion Wood Products Inc .... D 812 282-9460
Sellersburg (G-12391)
County Line Woodworking .... G 574 935-7107
Bremen (G-994)
Custom Woodworks Inc .... G 317 867-2929
Westfield (G-14153)
Daed Toolworks .... G 317 861-7419
Greenfield (G-5518)
Dutch Country Woodworking Inc .... G 260 499-4847
Lagrange (G-9038)
Gessner Woodworking .... G 812 389-2594
Celestine (G-1535)

Hartley J Company Inc .... G 812 376-9708
Columbus (G-1938)
J M Woodworking Co Inc .... G 260 627-8362
Grabill (G-5374)
Jolar Enterprises .... G 574 875-8369
Elkhart (G-2950)
Koetter Woodworking .... F 812 923-8875
Borden (G-933)
L and D Custom Woodworking .... G 812 486-2958
Montgomery (G-10231)
M & H Woodworking LLC .... G 812 486-2570
Montgomery (G-10233)
Marc Woodworking Inc .... D 317 635-9663
Indianapolis (G-7451)
Master Piece Krafts LLC .... G 260 768-4330
Shipshewana (G-12632)
Millers Woodnthings Inc .... F 574 825-2996
Middlebury (G-9911)
Mj Finishing .... G 574 646-2080
Bremen (G-1011)
MJB Wood Group Inc .... G 574 295-5228
Elkhart (G-3043)
Moores Country Wood Crafting .... F 317 984-3326
Arcadia (G-266)
Omega National Products LLC .... C 574 295-5353
Elkhart (G-3068)
Patrick Industries Inc .... E 574 294-5758
Elkhart (G-3083)
Pumpkin Patch Market Inc .... G 574 825-3312
Middlebury (G-9915)
R & R Custom Woodworking Inc .... E 574 773-5436
Nappanee (G-10703)
Reising Son Originals .... G 812 437-1831
Evansville (G-3703)
Riegseckers Woodworks Inc .... G 574 642-3504
Goshen (G-5318)
Robert W Sheffer .... G 219 464-2095
Valparaiso (G-13609)
Roudebush Company Incorporated .... G 574 595-7115
Star City (G-13070)
Sac Acquisition LLC .... G 317 575-1795
Indianapolis (G-7883)
Schmuckers Wood Shop .... G 260 485-1434
Fort Wayne (G-4609)
Serie Hardwoods Inc .... G 765 275-2321
Attica (G-309)
Sharon Sperry .... G 219 736-0121
Merrillville (G-9753)
Ufp Nappanee LLC .... D 574 773-2505
Nappanee (G-10709)
Urban Logging Company LLC .... F 317 710-4070
Indianapolis (G-8133)
Vernon Sharp .... G 317 398-0631
Shelbyville (G-12582)
W & S Woodworking .... G 812 486-3673
Loogootee (G-9396)
Wittmer Distributors .... G 812 636-7786
Odon (G-11345)
Yb Normal Custom Wood Working .... G 260 338-2003
Huntertown (G-6149)

DEFENSE SYSTEMS & EQPT

Cypress Springs Enterprises .... G 812 743-8888
Wheatland (G-14231)
Harris Corporation .... G 812 202-5171
Crane (G-2126)
Raytheon Company .... E 317 306-4872
Indianapolis (G-7821)
Raytheon Company .... D 310 647-9438
Fort Wayne (G-4577)
Value Production Inc .... E 574 246-1913
South Bend (G-12983)
Xtreme ADS Limited .... E 765 644-7323
Anderson (G-184)

DEGREASING MACHINES

Federal-Mogul LLC .... G 260 497-5563
Fort Wayne (G-4261)
Federal-Mogul LLC .... G 574 271-0274
South Bend (G-12775)
Safety-Kleen Systems Inc .... F 219 397-1131
East Chicago (G-2568)

DEHYDRATION EQPT

Hinsdale Farms Ltd .... G 574 848-0344
Bristol (G-1063)

DEICING OR DEFROSTING FLUID

Andersons Agriculture Group LP .... E 574 626-2522
Galveston (G-4993)

DENTAL EQPT

American Medical & Dntl Eqp LL .... G 219 628-2928
Valparaiso (G-13492)

DENTAL EQPT & SPLYS

Adec .... G 503 538-7478
Carmel (G-1301)
Cooks Fabrication Inc .... G 317 782-1722
Indianapolis (G-6661)
Den-Craft Dental Laboratory .... G 219 663-7776
Crown Point (G-2245)
Dental Professional Labs .... E 219 769-6225
Merrillville (G-9710)
G & H Wire Company Inc .... D 317 346-6655
Franklin (G-4888)
Heraeus .... G 574 299-1862
South Bend (G-12796)
Heraeus Kulzer LLC (mitsui) .... D 574 299-5466
South Bend (G-12797)
Heraus Kulzer Inc .... F 574 291-0661
South Bend (G-12798)
J F Jelenko Co .... G 914 273-8600
South Bend (G-12820)
Lafayette Dental Laboratory .... E 765 447-9341
Lafayette (G-8947)
Lehi Prosthetics Dental Lab .... G 765 288-4613
Muncie (G-10511)
National Dentex LLC .... D 317 849-5143
Indianapolis (G-7570)
Panoramic Rental Corp .... E 800 654-2027
Fort Wayne (G-4519)
Pearl Custom Plastic Molding .... G 765 763-6961
Gwynneville (G-5800)
Somer Inc .... E 317 873-1111
Zionsville (G-14464)
Terrafina Inc .... E 317 346-6655
Franklin (G-4936)

DENTAL EQPT & SPLYS WHOLESALERS

Orthodontic Design and Prod .... E 760 734-3995
Franklin (G-4917)

DENTAL EQPT & SPLYS: Dental Hand Instruments, NEC

Hayes Enterprises LLC .... G 260 636-3262
Albion (G-28)

DENTAL EQPT & SPLYS: Dental Materials

Knitting Mill Specialties .... G 219 942-8031
Hobart (G-6085)

DENTAL EQPT & SPLYS: Enamels

ABC Dental of Goshen .... G 574 534-8777
Goshen (G-5164)
Gordon B Crawford DMD .... G 812 288-8560
Jeffersonville (G-8371)
Kathy Zuccarelli .... G 219 865-4095
Schererville (G-12328)
Michael J Meyer D M D P C .... G 812 275-7112
Bedford (G-563)
Ronald L Miller .... G 765 662-3881
Marion (G-9560)

DENTAL EQPT & SPLYS: Hand Pieces & Parts

Fidelity Dental Handpiece Svc .... G 317 254-0277
Indianapolis (G-6919)

DENTAL EQPT & SPLYS: Orthodontic Appliances

Exclusively Orthodontics Lab .... G 317 887-1076
Greenwood (G-5693)
Growing Smiles Inc .... G 317 787-6404
Indianapolis (G-7052)
Orthodontic Design and Prod .... E 760 734-3995
Franklin (G-4917)
Protero Corporation .... E 219 393-5591
Kingsford Heights (G-8546)

Employee Codes: A=Over 500 employees, B=251-500
C=101-250, D=51-100, E=20-50, F=10-19, G=2-9

2018 Harris Indiana
Industrial Directory

955

PRODUCT

DENTAL EQPT & SPLYS: Plaster

Plaster Shak ....G....... 317 881-6518
Greenwood *(G-5733)*

DENTAL EQPT & SPLYS: Teeth, Artificial, Exc In Dental Labs

William Wesley Professional ....F....... 317 635-1000
Indianapolis *(G-8200)*

DENTAL INSTRUMENT REPAIR SVCS

Fidelity Dental Handpiece Svc ....G....... 317 254-0277
Indianapolis *(G-6919)*

DENTISTS' OFFICES & CLINICS

National Dentex LLC ....D....... 317 849-5143
Indianapolis *(G-7570)*

Somer Inc ....E....... 317 873-1111
Zionsville *(G-14464)*

DEODORANTS: Personal

Relevo Labs LLC ....G....... 317 900-6949
Carmel *(G-1466)*

DERMATOLOGICALS

Birkat Adonai LLC ....G....... 219 221-9810
Elizabeth *(G-2643)*

Noah Worcester Derm Society ....G....... 317 257-5907
Indianapolis *(G-7588)*

DESIGN SVCS, NEC

Concept Prints Inc ....F....... 317 290-1222
Indianapolis *(G-6648)*

Jackson Systems LLC ....E....... 317 788-6800
Indianapolis *(G-7295)*

Menard Inc ....A....... 812 466-1234
Terre Haute *(G-13282)*

Specialty Process Eqp Ctrl Inc ....G....... 812 473-8528
Evansville *(G-3743)*

Travis Britton ....G....... 317 762-6018
Indianapolis *(G-8092)*

Westlund Concepts ....F....... 317 819-0611
Lapel *(G-9120)*

Yb Normal Custom Wood Working ....G....... 260 338-2003
Huntertown *(G-6149)*

Zojila LLC ....G....... 765 404-3767
Lafayette *(G-9029)*

DESIGN SVCS: Commercial & Indl

Expo Designers Co Inc ....E....... 317 784-5610
Indianapolis *(G-6896)*

K C Creations ....G....... 937 748-8181
Indianapolis *(G-7327)*

King Investments Inc ....F....... 812 752-6000
Scottsburg *(G-12371)*

Sampco Inc ....C....... 413 442-4043
South Bend *(G-12925)*

DESIGN SVCS: Computer Integrated Systems

Byte Blue Technology Solutions ....G....... 574 903-5637
Elkhart *(G-2741)*

Crown Training & Development ....E....... 219 947-0845
Merrillville *(G-9708)*

Determine Inc ....E....... 317 594-8600
Carmel *(G-1356)*

Determine Inc ....C....... 650 532-1500
Carmel *(G-1357)*

Determine Sourcing Inc ....C....... 408 570-9700
Carmel *(G-1358)*

Fiserv Mrtg Servicing Systems ....C....... 574 282-3300
South Bend *(G-12779)*

Flynn Media LLC ....G....... 317 536-2972
Indianapolis *(G-6942)*

Gta Enterprises Inc ....E....... 260 478-7800
Fort Wayne *(G-4309)*

Long Tail Corporation ....G....... 260 918-0489
Fort Wayne *(G-4441)*

Orion Global Sourcing Inc ....G....... 812 332-3338
Bloomington *(G-792)*

PC Max Inc ....G....... 812 337-0630
Bloomington *(G-796)*

Rob Nolley Inc ....G....... 317 825-5211
Shelbyville *(G-12563)*

DETECTORS: Water Leak

Ald Indy Inc ....G....... 317 826-3833
Fishers *(G-3867)*

DETINNING: Cans & Scrap

AMG Resources Corporation ....F....... 219 949-8150
Gary *(G-5028)*

DIAGNOSTIC SUBSTANCES

Archaeasolutions Inc ....G....... 770 487-5303
Evansville *(G-3362)*

Cardinal Health 414 LLC ....D....... 317 981-4100
Indianapolis *(G-6552)*

Companion Diagnostics Inc ....G....... 860 227-9028
Indianapolis *(G-6640)*

Intervention Diagnostics Inc ....G....... 317 432-6091
Indianapolis *(G-7263)*

Pragmatics Inc ....G....... 574 295-7908
Elkhart *(G-3106)*

R 2 Diagnostics Inc ....G....... 574 288-4377
South Bend *(G-12910)*

Roche Diagnostics Corporation ....A....... 800 428-5076
Indianapolis *(G-7851)*

Stanbio Laboratory LP ....F....... 830 249-0772
Elkhart *(G-3186)*

Strand Diagnostics LLC ....E....... 317 455-2100
Indianapolis *(G-8010)*

Uridynamics Inc ....F....... 317 915-7896
Indianapolis *(G-8135)*

DIAGNOSTIC SUBSTANCES OR AGENTS: Blood Derivative

Chematics Inc ....F....... 574 834-2406
North Webster *(G-11290)*

DIAGNOSTIC SUBSTANCES OR AGENTS: In Vitro

Savran Technologies LLC ....G....... 765 409-2050
West Lafayette *(G-14105)*

Synermed International Inc ....G....... 317 896-1565
Westfield *(G-14193)*

Sysgenomics LLC ....G....... 574 302-5396
Granger *(G-5442)*

DIAGNOSTIC SUBSTANCES OR AGENTS: Microbiology & Virology

Agdia Inc ....D....... 574 264-2014
Elkhart *(G-2671)*

Core Biologic LLC ....G....... 888 390-8838
Fort Wayne *(G-4177)*

Microworks Inc ....G....... 219 661-8620
Crown Point *(G-2278)*

Poly Group LLC ....G....... 812 590-4750
New Albany *(G-10846)*

DIAMONDS, GEMS, WHOLESALE

Downey Creations LLC ....D....... 317 248-9888
Indianapolis *(G-6764)*

DIAMONDS: Cutting & Polishing

Diamond Tools Technology Inc ....F....... 847 537-8686
Indianapolis *(G-6741)*

DICE & DICE CUPS

Chessex Manufacturing Co LLC ....F....... 260 471-9511
Fort Wayne *(G-4146)*

DIE CUTTING SVC: Paper

Bruce Payne ....G....... 260 492-2259
Fort Wayne *(G-4124)*

DIE SETS: Presses, Metal Stamping

Modern Die Systems Inc ....E....... 765 552-3145
Elwood *(G-3307)*

Standard Die Supply of Indiana ....E....... 317 236-6200
Indianapolis *(G-7989)*

DIES & TOOLS: Special

AAA Tool and Die Company Inc ....F....... 574 246-1222
South Bend *(G-12691)*

Ahaus Tool & Engineering Inc ....D....... 765 962-3573
Richmond *(G-11952)*

Ajax Tool Inc ....G....... 260 747-7482
Fort Wayne *(G-4052)*

Allegiance Tool & Die Inc ....G....... 574 277-1819
Granger *(G-5389)*

Ameri-Tek Manufacturing Inc ....F....... 574 753-8058
Logansport *(G-9320)*

Apex Tool and Manufacturing ....F....... 812 425-8121
Evansville *(G-3358)*

Ark Model and Stampings Inc ....F....... 317 549-3394
Indianapolis *(G-6420)*

Atkisson Enterprises Inc ....F....... 765 675-7593
Tipton *(G-13388)*

Aul In The Family Tool and Die ....G....... 765 759-5161
Yorktown *(G-14401)*

B & D Manufacturing Inc ....G....... 765 452-2761
Kokomo *(G-8595)*

B B & H Tool of Columbus Inc ....F....... 812 372-3707
Columbus *(G-1858)*

B&J Rocket America Inc ....E....... 574 825-5802
Middlebury *(G-9874)*

B/C Precision Tool Inc ....G....... 812 577-0642
Greendale *(G-5483)*

Batesville Tool & Die Inc ....C....... 812 934-5616
Batesville *(G-494)*

Beckys Die Cutting Inc ....G....... 260 467-1714
Fort Wayne *(G-4105)*

Bennett Tool & Die Inc ....G....... 317 422-5140
Bargersville *(G-478)*

Bettner Wire Coating Dyes Inc ....G....... 812 372-2732
Columbus *(G-1859)*

Blessing Tool & Die Inc ....G....... 574 875-1982
Elkhart *(G-2727)*

Boston Tool Company Inc ....F....... 765 935-6282
Richmond *(G-11967)*

Btd Manufacturing Inc ....G....... 812 934-5616
Batesville *(G-495)*

Budco Tool and Die ....G....... 574 522-4004
Elkhart *(G-2736)*

Butler Tool & Design Inc ....F....... 219 297-4531
Goodland *(G-5158)*

Century Tool & Engineering ....G....... 317 685-0942
Indianapolis *(G-6587)*

Classic Products Corp ....G....... 260 748-6907
Fort Wayne *(G-4158)*

Claymore Tools Inc ....G....... 574 255-6483
Mishawaka *(G-10018)*

Clifty Engineering and Tool Co ....C....... 812 273-3272
Madison *(G-9452)*

Collins Tool & Die Inc ....G....... 812 273-4765
Madison *(G-9453)*

Competition TI Engrg line Inc ....G....... 812 524-1991
Seymour *(G-12438)*

Corydon Machine & Tool Co Inc ....E....... 812 738-3107
Corydon *(G-2095)*

Covington Products Inc ....F....... 765 282-6626
Muncie *(G-10450)*

Custom Engineering Inc ....G....... 812 424-3879
Evansville *(G-3450)*

Custom Gage & Tool Co Inc ....G....... 317 547-8257
Indianapolis *(G-6713)*

D & E Machine Inc ....G....... 765 653-8919
Greencastle *(G-5457)*

D 1 Mold & Tool LLC ....F....... 765 378-0693
Alexandria *(G-39)*

D A Hochstetler & Sons LLP ....F....... 574 642-1144
Topeka *(G-13416)*

De Witt Tool & Die Inc ....G....... 765 998-7320
Upland *(G-13469)*

Dedrick Tool & Die Inc ....G....... 260 824-3334
Bluffton *(G-872)*

Defelice Engineering Inc ....G....... 317 834-2832
Mooresville *(G-10307)*

Delta Tool Manufacturing Inc ....G....... 574 223-4863
Rochester *(G-12122)*

Design & Mfg Solutions LLC ....F....... 765 478-9393
Cambridge City *(G-1255)*

Die Protection Tech LLC ....G....... 812 837-9507
Nashville *(G-10722)*

Die-Rite Machine and Tool Corp ....G....... 574 522-2366
Elkhart *(G-2797)*

Dieco of Indiana Inc ....F....... 765 825-4151
Connersville *(G-2046)*

Dietech Corporation ....G....... 260 724-8946
Decatur *(G-2375)*

E F M Corporation ....D....... 812 372-4421
Columbus *(G-1916)*

Elkhart Tool and Die Inc ....E....... 574 295-8500
Elkhart *(G-2832)*

Evansville Tool & Die Inc ....F....... 812 422-7101
Evansville *(G-3492)*

Evart Engineering Co Inc ....F 765 354-2232
   Middletown (G-9935)
Fayette Tool and Engineering ....D 765 825-7518
   Connersville (G-2048)
Franklin Stamping Inds Inc ....F 765 282-5138
   Muncie (G-10473)
Future Tool & Engineering Co ....F 812 376-8699
   Columbus (G-1932)
Granite Engineering & Tool Co ....F 812 375-9077
   Columbus (G-1933)
Grotrian Tool & Die ....G 260 894-3558
   Ligonier (G-9286)
Gvs Technologies LLC ....F 574 293-0974
   Elkhart (G-2901)
H & H Design & Tool Inc ....F 765 886-6199
   Economy (G-2591)
H & M Tool & Die Inc ....F 812 663-8252
   Greensburg (G-5605)
Hanover Machine & Tool Inc ....G 812 265-6265
   Hanover (G-5961)
Hermetic Coil Co Inc ....E 812 735-2400
   Bicknell (G-631)
Hipsher Tool & Die Inc ....F 260 563-4143
   Wabash (G-13730)
Humphrey Tool Coinc ....G 574 753-3853
   Logansport (G-9338)
Huntington Tool & Die Inc ....F 260 356-5940
   Huntington (G-6214)
IAm Aw Tl Die Makers LL 229 ....G 574 333-5955
   Elkhart (G-2927)
Industrial Tool & Die Corp ....F 812 424-9971
   Evansville (G-3559)
Injection Plastic & Mfg Co ....F 574 784-2070
   Lapaz (G-9117)
J B Tool Die & Engineering Co ....C 260 483-9586
   Fort Wayne (G-4386)
J O Wolf Tool & Die Inc ....G 260 672-2605
   Huntington (G-6220)
J P Corporation ....G 317 783-1000
   Beech Grove (G-598)
Jacobs Machine & Tool Co Inc ....F 317 831-2917
   Mooresville (G-10316)
Jam-Ko Engineering Company ....F 574 294-7684
   Elkhart (G-2944)
JD Norman Industries Inc ....E 765 584-6069
   Winchester (G-14334)
Jj Machine ....G 765 723-1511
   New Ross (G-11005)
K & K Inc ....F 574 266-8040
   Elkhart (G-2953)
Ken-Bar Tool & Engineering Inc ....E 765 284-4408
   Muncie (G-10503)
Kent Machine Inc ....E 765 778-7777
   Pendleton (G-11492)
King Industrial Corporation ....D 812 522-3261
   Seymour (G-12464)
Knox Tool & Die Inc ....G 574 255-1256
   Mishawaka (G-10064)
Krukemeier Machine and Tool Co ....F 317 784-7042
   Beech Grove (G-600)
L H Carbide Corporation ....C 260 432-5563
   Fort Wayne (G-4419)
Laff or Die Productions ....G 219 942-3790
   Hobart (G-6086)
Le Hue Machine & Tool Co Inc ....G 574 255-8404
   Mishawaka (G-10069)
Lone Star Tool & Die Weld ....G 812 346-9681
   Vernon (G-13651)
Mac Machine & Metal Works Inc ....E 765 825-5873
   Connersville (G-2062)
Madison Tool and Die Inc ....D 812 273-2250
   Madison (G-9482)
Manchester Tool and Die Plant ....G 260 982-0702
   North Manchester (G-11235)
Matrix Manufacturing Inc ....G 260 854-4659
   Wolcottville (G-14374)
McGinn Tool & Engineering Co ....F 317 736-5512
   Franklin (G-4905)
Mdl Mold Die Components Inc ....G 812 373-0021
   Columbus (G-1970)
Michiana Metal Fabrication ....G 574 256-9010
   Elkhart (G-3032)
Midwest Tool & Die Corp ....E 260 483-4282
   Fort Wayne (G-4474)
Millennium Tool Inc ....E 812 273-1566
   Madison (G-9488)
Modern Drop Forge Company LLC ....B 708 489-4208
   Merrillville (G-9737)
Mold Service Inc ....G 260 868-2920
   Butler (G-1233)

Northern Tool and Die ....G 260 495-7314
   Fremont (G-4971)
Northside Machine & Tool Inc ....F 765 654-4538
   Frankfort (G-4845)
O & R Precision Grinding Inc ....E 260 368-9394
   Geneva (G-5137)
Overton & Sons Tl & Die Co Inc ....E 317 831-4542
   Mooresville (G-10331)
Overton & Sons Tl & Die Co Inc ....F 317 831-4542
   Mooresville (G-10332)
Perfection Mold & Tool Inc ....G 574 292-0824
   South Bend (G-12891)
Perm Industries Inc ....E 219 365-5000
   Saint John (G-12267)
Ploog Engineering Co Inc ....G 219 663-2854
   Crown Point (G-2284)
Precision Tubes Inc ....G 317 783-2339
   Indianapolis (G-7738)
Progressive Tool & Machine ....G 812 346-1837
   Columbus (G-2001)
Proton Mold Tool Inc ....G 812 923-7263
   Floyds Knobs (G-4018)
Qualidie Corp ....F 317 632-6845
   Indianapolis (G-7796)
Quality Steel & Aluminium ....G 574 294-7221
   Elkhart (G-3131)
Quality Tool Co Inc ....F 260 484-0187
   Fort Wayne (G-4572)
R & L Die Co Inc ....G 765 759-6880
   Yorktown (G-14411)
R S E Tool and Die Inc ....G 574 848-7966
   Bristol (G-1077)
Ready Machine Tool & Die Corp ....F 765 825-3108
   Connersville (G-2070)
River Valley Plastics Inc ....E 574 262-5221
   Elkhart (G-3148)
Ross Engineering & Machine ....E 574 586-7791
   Walkerton (G-13810)
Specialty Engrg Tl & Die LLC ....G 260 356-2678
   Huntington (G-6249)
Specialty Tool & Die Company ....F 765 452-9209
   Kokomo (G-8698)
Specialty Tooling Inc ....F 812 464-8521
   Evansville (G-3744)
Stamina Metal Products Inc ....G 574 534-7410
   Goshen (G-5327)
Star Tool & Die Inc ....F 574 264-3815
   Elkhart (G-3189)
Stolle Tool Inc ....F 765 935-5185
   Richmond (G-12055)
T & L Tool & Die II Co Inc ....G 574 722-6246
   Logansport (G-9368)
Tmak Inc ....E 219 874-7661
   Michigan City (G-9853)
Toolcraft LLC ....E 260 749-0454
   Fort Wayne (G-4692)
Toolmasters Inc ....G 574 256-1881
   Mishawaka (G-10140)
W W G Inc ....G 317 783-6413
   Indianapolis (G-8172)
Walkerton Tool & Die Inc ....E 574 586-3162
   Walkerton (G-13813)

DIES: Cutting, Exc Metal

Atlas Die LLC ....D 574 295-0277
   Elkhart (G-2700)
Pro-Form Plastics Inc ....E 812 522-4433
   Crothersville (G-2220)

DIES: Diamond, Metalworking

C & A Tool Engineering Inc ....B 260 693-2167
   Churubusco (G-1644)
C & A Tool Engineering Inc ....C 260 693-2167
   Churubusco (G-1645)
C & A Tool Engineering Inc ....G 260 693-2167
   Churubusco (G-1646)
C & A Tool Engineering Inc ....G 260 693-2167
   Churubusco (G-1647)
C & A Tool Engineering Inc ....G 260 693-2167
   Churubusco (G-1648)
C & A Tool Engineering Inc ....E 260 693-2167
   Auburn (G-319)
Fort Wayne Wire Die Inc ....C 260 747-1681
   Fort Wayne (G-4281)
Heritage Wire Die Inc ....G 260 728-9300
   Decatur (G-2385)
Woodburn Diamond Die Co Inc ....D 260 632-4217
   Woodburn (G-14392)

DIES: Extrusion

Al-Ex Inc ....G 574 206-0100
   Elkhart (G-2673)

DIES: Paper Cutting

Dynamic Dies Inc ....E 317 247-4706
   Indianapolis (G-6778)

DIES: Plastic Forming

Grimm Mold & Die Co Inc ....F 219 778-4211
   Rolling Prairie (G-12186)
Herman Tool & Machine Inc ....F 574 594-5544
   Pierceton (G-11572)
Hermetic Coil Co Inc ....E 812 735-2401
   Bicknell (G-632)
Quality Machine & Tool Inc ....G 574 534-5664
   Goshen (G-5314)
Smith Machine and Tool ....G 574 223-2318
   Rochester (G-12155)
Wcm Tool & Machine Inc ....G 812 422-2315
   Evansville (G-3810)

DIES: Steel Rule

Allied Steel Rule Dies Inc ....F 317 634-9835
   Indianapolis (G-6369)
American Steel Rule Die Inc ....E 574 262-3437
   Elkhart (G-2685)
Atlas Die Inc ....E 574 295-0050
   Elkhart (G-2701)
Meck Die Inc ....G 574 262-5441
   Elkhart (G-3026)
Midwest Stl Rule Cutng Die Inc ....E 317 780-4600
   Indianapolis (G-7512)
Unique-Prescotech Inc ....E 479 646-2973
   Evansville (G-3783)

DIES: Wire Drawing & Straightening

Bell Machine Company Inc ....F 765 654-5225
   Frankfort (G-4819)
Dwd Industries LLC ....E 260 728-9272
   Decatur (G-2377)
Dwd Industries LLC ....G 260 639-3254
   Hoagland (G-6064)
Esteves-Dwd LLC ....D 260 728-9272
   Decatur (G-2378)
Precision Die Technologies ....E 260 482-5001
   Fort Wayne (G-4548)
Premier Consulting Inc ....F 260 496-9300
   Fort Wayne (G-4554)
Royer Enterprises Inc ....F 260 359-0689
   Huntington (G-6245)
Wynn Wire Die Services Inc ....E 260 471-1395
   Fort Wayne (G-4762)

DIFFERENTIAL ASSEMBLIES & PARTS

Auburn Gear LLC ....C 260 925-3200
   Auburn (G-313)
Fairfield Manufacturing Co Inc ....E 765 772-4547
   Lafayette (G-8895)
Northern Trans & Differential ....G 219 764-4009
   Portage (G-11785)

DIODES: Light Emitting

Amerlight LLC ....G 812 602-3452
   Evansville (G-3355)

DIRECT SELLING ESTABLISHMENTS, NEC

Big Red Liquors Inc ....G 812 339-9552
   Bloomington (G-683)

DIRECT SELLING ESTABLISHMENTS: Food Svc, Coffee-Cart

All Occasions Gift Shop LLC ....G 513 314-5693
   Metamora (G-9762)

DISC JOCKEYS

Entertainment Express ....F 219 763-3610
   Portage (G-11760)

DISCS & TAPE: Optical, Blank

Sony Dadc US Inc ....E 812 462-8116
   Terre Haute (G-13333)

Employee Codes: A=Over 500 employees, B=251-500
C=101-250, D=51-100, E=20-50, F=10-19, G=2-9

2018 Harris Indiana
Industrial Directory

957

PRODUCT

Sony Dadc US Inc ....A...... 812 462-8100
Terre Haute **(G-13334)**
Sony Dadc US Inc ....B...... 812 462-8784
Terre Haute **(G-13335)**

DISPENSING EQPT & PARTS, BEVERAGE: Beer

Grinon Industries LLC ....E...... 317 388-5100
Indianapolis **(G-7051)**

DISPENSING EQPT & PARTS, BEVERAGE: Cold, Exc Coin-Operated

Multiplex Company Inc ....G...... 812 246-7000
Sellersburg **(G-12409)**

DISPENSING EQPT & PARTS, BEVERAGE: Coolers, Milk/Water, Elec

Polar King International Inc ....E...... 260 428-2530
Fort Wayne **(G-4536)**

DISPENSING EQPT & PARTS, BEVERAGE: Fountain/Other Beverage

Manitowoc Beverage Systems Inc ....A...... 800 367-4233
Sellersburg **(G-12406)**

DISPLAY FIXTURES: Showcases, Wood, Exc Refrigerated

J G Bowers Inc ....E...... 765 677-1000
Marion **(G-9536)**

DISPLAY FIXTURES: Wood

Ell Enterprises Inc ....G...... 317 783-7838
Indianapolis **(G-6841)**

DISPLAY ITEMS: Corrugated, Made From Purchased Materials

Cox John ....G...... 765 463-6396
West Lafayette **(G-14061)**
Hamilton Exhibits LLC ....D...... 317 898-9300
Indianapolis **(G-7068)**

DISTILLATES: Hardwood

Wholesale Hrdwood Intriors Inc ....F 317 867-3660
Westfield **(G-14202)**

DISTILLERS DRIED GRAIN & SOLUBLES

Cardinal Ethanol LLC ....D...... 765 964-3137
Union City **(G-13454)**

DOCK EQPT & SPLYS, INDL

M & J Shelton Enterprises Inc ....G...... 260 745-1616
Fort Wayne **(G-4446)**
T & S Equipment Company ....C...... 260 665-9521
Angola **(G-249)**
Turnkey Instrument Solutions ....G...... 317 946-6354
Indianapolis **(G-8114)**
Vestil Manufacturing Corp ....B...... 260 665-7586
Angola **(G-258)**

DOCK OPERATION SVCS, INCL BLDGS, FACILITIES, OPERS & MAINT

Culvers Port Side Marina ....F 574 223-5090
Rochester **(G-12120)**

DOLLIES: Industrial

Landgrebe Manufacturing Inc ....G...... 219 462-9587
Valparaiso **(G-13570)**
Tk Sales and Marketing LLC ....G...... 812 430-5103
Evansville **(G-3766)**

DOOR FRAMES: Wood

Mishawaka Door LLC ....G...... 574 259-2822
Mishawaka **(G-10090)**

DOOR OPERATING SYSTEMS: Electric

American Door Controls Inc ....G...... 812 988-4853
Morgantown **(G-10349)**

DOORS & WINDOWS WHOLESALERS: All Materials

Dyna Technology Inc ....G...... 219 663-2920
Crown Point **(G-2247)**

DOORS & WINDOWS: Storm, Metal

All-Weather Products Inc ....G...... 812 867-6403
Evansville **(G-3348)**
Champion of Evansville LLC ....F 812 424-2456
Evansville **(G-3416)**
Champion Opco LLC ....E...... 260 271-4076
Fort Wayne **(G-4144)**
Kinro Manufacturing Inc ....C...... 574 535-1125
Elkhart **(G-2970)**
Maher Supply Inc ....E...... 812 234-7699
Terre Haute **(G-13278)**
Sun Control Center LLC ....F 260 490-9902
Fort Wayne **(G-4666)**
Trim-A-Seal of Indiana Inc ....F 219 883-2180
Gary **(G-5109)**

DOORS: Fiberglass

R3 Composites Corp ....D...... 260 627-0033
Grabill **(G-5383)**
Starquest Products LLC ....G...... 574 537-0486
Goshen **(G-5330)**

DOORS: Fire, Metal

A & A Sheet Metal Products ....D...... 219 326-1288
La Porte **(G-8725)**

DOORS: Folding, Plastic Or Plastic Coated Fabric

Irvine Shade & Door Inc ....D...... 574 522-1446
Elkhart **(G-2940)**

DOORS: Garage, Overhead, Metal

Hrh Door Corp ....G...... 812 479-5680
Evansville **(G-3544)**
Modern Door Corporation ....D...... 574 586-3117
Walkerton **(G-13806)**

DOORS: Garage, Overhead, Wood

Central Overhead Door ....G...... 219 696-1566
Lowell **(G-9402)**
Hrh Door Corp ....G...... 812 479-5680
Evansville **(G-3544)**

DOORS: Glass

Vernon Greyber ....G...... 812 636-7880
Odon **(G-11343)**

DOORS: Safe & Vault, Metal

Assa Abloy Door Group LLC ....F 800 826-2617
Elkhart **(G-2697)**

DOORS: Screen, Metal

Kinro Manufacturing Inc ....E...... 574 535-1125
Elkhart **(G-2971)**
Kinro Manufacturing Inc ....D...... 574 535-1125
Elkhart **(G-2972)**
Kitty Mac Inc ....G...... 888 549-0783
Indianapolis **(G-7356)**

DOORS: Wooden

Complete Lumber Inc ....F 812 473-6400
Evansville **(G-3426)**
Genesis Products Inc ....E...... 574 266-8293
Elkhart **(G-2878)**
Genesis Products LLC ....C...... 877 266-8292
Elkhart **(G-2879)**
Ideal Wood Products ....D...... 812 949-5181
New Albany **(G-10801)**
John Pater Design Fabrication ....F 812 926-4845
Aurora **(G-381)**
Miller Door & Trim Inc ....G...... 574 533-8141
Goshen **(G-5294)**
Nu-TEC Industries Inc ....E...... 219 844-1233
Schererville **(G-12340)**
Ohio Valley Door Corp ....G...... 812 945-5285
New Albany **(G-10836)**
Patrick Industries Inc ....C...... 574 293-1521
Elkhart **(G-3082)**

Pendleton Door Company ....G...... 765 778-4164
Pendleton **(G-11499)**

DOWELS & DOWEL RODS

Buckaroos Inc ....F 317 899-9100
Indianapolis **(G-6518)**

DOWNSPOUTS: Sheet Metal

Martin Spouting Inc ....G...... 260 485-5703
Fort Wayne **(G-4453)**

DRAINAGE PRDTS: Concrete

Stephenson Block Inc ....G...... 574 264-6660
Elkhart **(G-3193)**
Wholesale Drainage Supply Inc ....G...... 812 397-5100
Shelburn **(G-12513)**

DRAPERIES & CURTAINS

Ascot Enterprises Inc ....D...... 260 593-3733
Topeka **(G-13411)**
Ascot Enterprises Inc ....G...... 574 773-3104
Nappanee **(G-10650)**
F & R Draperies ....G...... 812 284-4682
Clarksville **(G-1680)**
Femyer Drapery Shop ....G...... 765 282-3398
Muncie **(G-10471)**
Greenwood Draperie Corp ....G...... 317 882-0130
Greenwood **(G-5699)**
Industrial Sewing Machine Co ....G...... 812 425-2255
Evansville **(G-3558)**
M & D Draperies ....G...... 812 886-4608
Vincennes **(G-13691)**
Majesty Enterprises Inc ....G...... 812 752-6446
Scottsburg **(G-12372)**
Merin Interiors Indianapolis ....G...... 317 251-6603
Indianapolis **(G-7482)**
Mill End Drapery Inc ....G...... 317 257-4800
Indianapolis **(G-7518)**
Mm Window Fashions ....G...... 317 585-4933
Fishers **(G-3947)**
Quality Drapery Corporation ....E...... 765 481-2370
Lebanon **(G-9218)**
Queen Ann Custom Drapies ....G...... 317 802-6130
Carmel **(G-1460)**

DRAPERIES & DRAPERY FABRICS, COTTON

Autumn Interiors ....G...... 317 894-1494
Indianapolis **(G-6447)**
Custom Qlting Pllow Cshion Svc ....G...... 219 464-7316
Valparaiso **(G-13526)**
Majestic Draperies ....G...... 574 259-3080
Mishawaka **(G-10073)**
Panel Solutions Inc ....F 574 295-0222
Elkhart **(G-3072)**
Ping Custom Drapery Workroom ....G...... 317 984-3251
Cicero **(G-1665)**

DRAPERIES: Plastic & Textile, From Purchased Materials

Artisan Interiors Inc ....E...... 574 825-9494
Middlebury **(G-9873)**
Custom Draperies of Indiana ....G...... 219 924-2500
Hammond **(G-5867)**
Custom Drapery Service Inc ....G...... 317 587-1518
Indianapolis **(G-6712)**
Doris Drapery Boutique ....G...... 765 472-5850
Peru **(G-11524)**
Lafayette Venetian Blind Inc ....A...... 765 464-2500
West Lafayette **(G-14082)**
Northwest Interiors Inc ....E...... 574 294-2326
Elkhart **(G-3067)**
Silk Mountain Creation ....G...... 317 815-1660
Carmel **(G-1481)**

DRAPERY & UPHOLSTERY STORES: Draperies

Beauti Pleat Draperies Inc ....G...... 317 887-1728
Greenwood **(G-5669)**
Custom Drapery Service Inc ....G...... 317 587-1518
Indianapolis **(G-6712)**
Custom Sewing Service ....G...... 812 428-7015
Evansville **(G-3451)**
Greenwood Draperie Corp ....G...... 317 882-0130
Greenwood **(G-5699)**

Shelby Westside Upholstering ....G 317 631-8911
   Indianapolis (G-7931)

DRILL BITS

Drake Corporation ....F 636 464-5070
   Indianapolis (G-6765)

DRILLING MACHINERY & EQPT: Oil & Gas

Evergreen Drilling LLC ....G 812 961-7701
   Evansville (G-3494)
Laibe Corporation ....D 317 231-2250
   Indianapolis (G-7374)
Mobile Drill Operating Co LLC ....E 317 260-8108
   Indianapolis (G-7531)

DRILLING MACHINERY & EQPT: Water Well

Dilden Bros Inc ....F 765 742-1717
   Lafayette (G-8891)
Rose-Wall Mfg Inc ....G 317 894-4497
   Greenfield (G-5567)

DRINK MIXES, NONALCOHOLIC: Cocktail

Boomerang Bay LLC ....G 812 236-2027
   Terre Haute (G-13204)

DRINKING PLACES: Alcoholic Beverages

Frickers Inc ....E 765 965-6655
   Richmond (G-11988)
Mishawaka Brewing Company ....E 574 256-9993
   Granger (G-5423)
Upland Brewing Company Inc ....E 812 330-7421
   Bloomington (G-851)

DRINKING PLACES: Bars & Lounges

Oaken Barrel Brewing Co Inc ....E 317 887-2287
   Greenwood (G-5730)

DRINKING PLACES: Tavern

Indiana City Brewing LLC ....F 317 643-1103
   Indianapolis (G-7177)

DRIVE SHAFTS

D & E Auto Electric Inc ....F 219 763-3892
   Portage (G-11759)
Lances Driveshaft & Components ....G 219 762-2531
   Portage (G-11772)
Patterson Driveshaft Inc ....G 317 481-0495
   Indianapolis (G-7663)

DRIVES: High Speed Indl, Exc Hydrostatic

Moore Machine & Gear Inc ....G 812 963-3074
   Evansville (G-3637)

DRIVES: Hydrostatic

Hydro-Gear Inc ....G 317 821-0477
   Indianapolis (G-7152)
Terra Drive Systems Inc ....C 219 279-2801
   Brookston (G-1108)

DROP CLOTHS: Fabric

R J Hanlon Company Inc ....E 317 867-2900
   Westfield (G-14182)

DRUG STORES

Kroger Co ....C 574 291-0740
   South Bend (G-12830)
Merrill Corporation ....F 574 255-2988
   Mishawaka (G-10078)
Williams Bros Health Care Pha ....E 812 335-0000
   Bloomington (G-856)

DRUG TESTING KITS: Blood & Urine

Business Health ....G 219 762-7105
   Portage (G-11752)
Workflow Solutions LLC ....G 502 627-0257
   New Albany (G-10875)

DRUGS & DRUG PROPRIETARIES, WHOLESALE

Defrukuscn LLC ....G 219 718-2128
   Highland (G-6042)

DRUGS & DRUG PROPRIETARIES, WHOLESALE: Pharmaceuticals

Komodo Pharmaceuticals Inc ....E 317 485-0023
   Fortville (G-4781)
Martin Ekwlor Phrmcuticals Inc ....F 765 962-4410
   Richmond (G-12014)

DRUGS: Parasitic & Infective Disease Affecting

Cretaceous Cures ....G 317 379-7744
   Westfield (G-14149)

DRUMS: Knockout Or Reflux, Metal Plate

Dennis Manufacturing Inc ....G 812 755-4891
   Campbellsburg (G-1276)

DRYCLEANING & LAUNDRY SVCS: Commercial & Family

Daniel Korb Laundry Company ....D 812 425-6121
   Evansville (G-3453)

DRYCLEANING PLANTS

Daniel Korb Laundry Company ....D 812 425-6121
   Evansville (G-3453)

DUCTING: Plastic

Anderson Products Incorporated ....D 574 293-5574
   Elkhart (G-2692)
Lasalle Bristol Corporation ....C 574 295-4400
   Elkhart (G-2985)

DUCTS: Sheet Metal

Ba Romines Sheet Metal Inc ....E 260 657-5500
   Harlan (G-5966)
H & H Sheet Metal Inc ....F 317 787-0883
   Beech Grove (G-595)
Nash Sheet Metal Co ....G 812 397-5306
   Shelburn (G-12508)
S & H Metal Products Inc ....E 260 593-2565
   Topeka (G-13428)
Southwark Metal Mfg Co ....C 317 823-5300
   Indianapolis (G-7965)

DUMPSTERS: Garbage

Dragon ESP Ltd ....D 574 893-1569
   Akron (G-4)
Estes Waste Solutions LLC ....G 812 283-6400
   Jeffersonville (G-8359)
Galfab LLC ....D 574 946-7767
   Winamac (G-14306)
Hunts Maintenance Inc ....G 219 785-2333
   Westville (G-14218)
M A C Corporation ....D 317 545-3341
   Indianapolis (G-7432)
Mvp Dumpsters Inc ....G 317 502-3155
   Pendleton (G-11495)
Par-Kan Company LLC ....D 260 352-2141
   Silver Lake (G-12677)

DURABLE GOODS WHOLESALERS, NEC

Caliente ....G 260 471-0700
   Fort Wayne (G-4136)
National Ice Corp ....G 317 887-9446
   Indianapolis (G-7572)
Shepherd Distributing ....G 317 991-3877
   Indianapolis (G-7932)

DUST OR FUME COLLECTING EQPT: Indl

Honeyville Metal Inc ....D 800 593-8377
   Topeka (G-13421)

DYES & PIGMENTS: Organic

Primex Color Compounding ....G 800 222-5116
   Richmond (G-12032)

EATING PLACES

Angelinas Cigars ....G 574 935-5544
   Plymouth (G-11667)
Barley Island Brewing Co ....F 317 770-5280
   Noblesville (G-11061)
Ed and Daves Wood Chips LLC ....G 574 699-1263
   Galveston (G-4994)

Frickers Inc ....E 765 965-6655
   Richmond (G-11988)
Harvey Hinklemeyers ....G 765 452-1942
   Kokomo (G-8636)
Jojos Pretzels ....F 260 768-7759
   Shipshewana (G-12623)
Kroger Co ....C 574 291-0740
   South Bend (G-12830)
Lanthier Winery & Restaurant ....F 812 273-2409
   Madison (G-9477)
MI Tierra ....G 812 376-0668
   Columbus (G-1973)
Mishawaka Brewing Company ....E 574 256-9993
   Granger (G-5423)
Mishawaka Frozen Custard ....E 574 255-8000
   Mishawaka (G-10092)
Olympia Candy Kitchen ....G 574 533-5040
   Goshen (G-5301)
Schnuck Markets Inc ....C 812 853-9505
   Newburgh (G-11046)
Tavistock Restaurants LLC ....D 317 488-1230
   Indianapolis (G-8040)
Turonis Forget ME Not Inn ....E 812 477-7500
   Evansville (G-3779)
Upland Brewing Company Inc ....E 812 330-7421
   Bloomington (G-851)
Wasser Brewing Company LLC ....G 765 653-3240
   Greencastle (G-5481)
Widows Walk ....G 812 285-8850
   Clarksville (G-1700)
Zels ....E 219 864-1011
   Schererville (G-12353)

EDITING SVCS

Precisely Write Inc ....G 317 585-7701
   Indianapolis (G-7730)

EDUCATIONAL SVCS

Friends of Third World Inc ....G 260 422-6821
   Fort Wayne (G-4288)
Kcma & Services LLC ....C 260 645-0885
   Waterloo (G-14016)
Spaceport Explrtion Centre Inc ....G 765 606-1512
   New Whiteland (G-11014)
Worth Tax and Financial Svc ....G 574 267-4687
   Warsaw (G-13969)

EDUCATIONAL SVCS, NONDEGREE GRANTING: Continuing Education

Wiley Publishing Inc ....B 317 842-2032
   Indianapolis (G-8198)

EGG WHOLESALERS

Lambrights Inc ....D 260 463-2178
   Lagrange (G-9056)

ELASTOMERS

Triangle Rubber Co LLC ....C 574 533-3118
   Goshen (G-5340)

ELECTRIC MOTOR REPAIR SVCS

Altek Inc ....G 812 385-2561
   Princeton (G-11863)
American Encoder Repair Servic ....D 219 872-2822
   Michigan City (G-9765)
B & D Electric Inc ....F 812 254-2122
   Washington (G-13978)
Bassett Electric Motor Repair ....G 260 925-0868
   Auburn (G-317)
C & L Electric Motor Repr Inc ....G 574 533-2643
   Goshen (G-5184)
Columbus Industrial Electric ....F 812 372-8414
   Columbus (G-1877)
Electric Motor Services Inc ....E 219 931-2850
   Hammond (G-5876)
Electric Power Service ....G 260 493-4913
   Fort Wayne (G-4234)
Electrical Motor Products Inc ....G 877 455-1599
   Fort Wayne (G-4235)
Electrik Connection Inc ....G 219 362-4581
   La Porte (G-8754)
Electro Corporation ....F 219 393-5571
   Kingsbury (G-8536)
Enyart Electric Motor Service ....G 574 288-4731
   South Bend (G-12766)
Flanders Electric Mtr Svc Inc ....E 812 867-4014
   Evansville (G-3509)

PRODUCT

Gary Electric Motor Service Co ....F 219 884-6555
Valparaiso (G-13546)
Gottman Electric Co Inc ....G 812 838-0037
Mount Vernon (G-10393)
Harrison Electric Inc ....F 219 879-0444
Michigan City (G-9801)
Hess Electric Motor Service ....G 812 926-0346
Aurora (G-378)
Hoosier Industrial Electric ....F 812 346-2232
North Vernon (G-11262)
Horner Apg LLC ....D 317 916-4274
Indianapolis (G-7127)
Horner Industrial Services Inc ....G 317 916-4274
Indianapolis (G-7128)
Horner Industrial Services Inc ....G 812 466-5281
Terre Haute (G-13249)
Horner Industrial Services Inc ....G 260 434-1189
Fort Wayne (G-4348)
Industrial Motor & Tool LLC ....G 574 534-8282
Goshen (G-5244)
Jasper Electric Motor Inc ....G 812 482-1660
Jasper (G-8258)
Jasper Electric Motor Inc ....F 812 482-1660
Jasper (G-8259)
Kesters Electric Motor Service ....G 574 269-2889
Warsaw (G-13896)
Kiemle-Hankins Company ....F 219 213-2643
Crown Point (G-2271)
Kirby Risk Corporation ....D 765 448-4567
Lafayette (G-8940)
Kirby Risk Corporation ....E 765 423-4205
Lafayette (G-8941)
Kirby Risk Corporation ....F 765 664-5185
Marion (G-9540)
Kochs Electric Inc ....F 317 639-5624
Indianapolis (G-7364)
Kw Maintenance Services LLC ....E 574 232-2051
South Bend (G-12833)
Magnetech Industrial Svc ....G 219 937-0100
Hammond (G-5911)
Motor Electric Inc ....G 574 294-7123
Elkhart (G-3051)
Motorcraft Inc ....G 765 282-4272
Muncie (G-10525)
North Vernon Electric Inc ....F 812 392-2985
North Vernon (G-11271)
P H C Industries Inc ....G 260 423-9461
Fort Wayne (G-4516)
Peter Austin Co ....G 765 288-6397
Muncie (G-10545)
Phase Three Electric Inc ....G 812 945-9922
New Albany (G-10842)
Phazpak Inc ....G 260 692-6416
Monroe (G-10184)
Precision Electric Inc ....E 574 256-1000
Mishawaka (G-10106)
Pres-Del Electric Inc ....G 219 884-3146
Gary (G-5086)
Quality Repair Services Inc ....F 317 881-0205
Greenwood (G-5738)
Robinson Industries Inc ....E 317 867-3214
Westfield (G-14185)
Ronald Holloway ....G 574 223-6825
Rochester (G-12151)
Three Star Electric Inc ....G 574 272-3136
South Bend (G-12969)
Tipton Engrg Elc Mtr Svcs Inc ....G 765 963-3380
Sharpsville (G-12507)
Truman Ritchie ....G 219 956-2211
Rensselaer (G-11943)
Wabash Valley Motor & Mch Inc ....G 812 466-7400
Terre Haute (G-13366)
Wagner Electric Fort Wayne Inc ....G 260 484-5532
Fort Wayne (G-4730)
Wills Electric Service Inc ....G 812 883-5653
Pekin (G-11480)
Wright Repairs Inc ....F 765 674-3300
Gas City (G-5128)

ELECTRIC SERVICES

ARS Nebraska LLC ....E 765 832-5210
Clinton (G-1713)
Vectren Corporation ....A 812 491-4000
Evansville (G-3794)
Vectren Corporation ....E 812 424-6411
Evansville (G-3795)

ELECTRIC TOOL REPAIR SVCS

Peter Austin Co ....G 765 288-6397
Muncie (G-10545)

ELECTRICAL APPARATUS & EQPT WHOLESALERS

Academy Energy Group LLC ....G 312 931-7443
Newburgh (G-11017)
Flanders Electric Mtr Svc Inc ....E 812 421-4300
Evansville (G-3510)
Gregory Thomas Inc ....G 219 324-3801
La Porte (G-8758)
Hoosier Fire Equipment Inc ....E 219 462-1707
Valparaiso (G-13557)
Horner Apg LLC ....D 317 916-4274
Indianapolis (G-7127)
Horner Industrial Services Inc ....D 317 639-4261
Indianapolis (G-7130)
Horner Industrial Services Inc ....G 260 434-1189
Fort Wayne (G-4348)
Horner Industrial Services Inc ....G 317 916-4274
Indianapolis (G-7128)
Logical Concepts ....D 317 885-6330
Greenwood (G-5721)
Robinson Industries Inc ....E 317 867-3214
Westfield (G-14186)
Schneider Electric Usa Inc ....F 260 356-2060
Huntington (G-6247)

ELECTRICAL CURRENT CARRYING WIRING DEVICES

Advanced Control Tech Inc ....G 317 806-2750
Indianapolis (G-6332)
An-Mar Wiring Systems Inc ....F 574 255-5523
Mishawaka (G-9996)
Bender Products Inc ....E 574 255-5350
Mishawaka (G-10009)
Bowmar LLC ....E 260 747-3121
Fort Wayne (G-4116)
Cme LLC ....B 260 623-3700
Monroeville (G-10192)
E M F Corp ....E 260 488-2479
Hamilton (G-5821)
Freudenberg-Nok General Partnr ....C 765 763-7246
Morristown (G-10369)
Functional Devices Inc ....G 765 883-5538
Sharpsville (G-12505)
Group Dekko Inc ....F 260 637-3964
Laotto (G-9109)
Group Dekko Inc ....D 260 357-3621
Garrett (G-5009)
Kendrion (mishawaka) LLC ....G 574 257-2422
Mishawaka (G-10063)
Kirby Risk Corporation ....B 765 447-1402
Lafayette (G-8942)
Lime City Manufacturing Co ....E 260 356-6826
Huntington (G-6224)
Nidec Motor Corporation ....A 317 328-4079
Indianapolis (G-7587)
Odyssian Technology LLC ....G 574 257-7555
South Bend (G-12882)
Pent Assemblies ....D 260 347-5828
Kendallville (G-8501)
REA Magnet Wire Company Inc ....B 765 477-8000
Lafayette (G-8989)
Rees Inc ....F 260 495-9811
Fremont (G-4972)
Thomas & Betts Corp ....G 901 252-8000
Westfield (G-14194)
Touchplate Technologies Inc ....F 260 424-4323
Fort Wayne (G-4696)
Ucom Inc ....F 260 829-1294
Orland (G-11358)
Western Consolidated Tech Inc ....D 260 495-9866
Fremont (G-4982)

ELECTRICAL DISCHARGE MACHINING, EDM

Clifty Engineering and Tool Co ....C 812 273-3272
Madison (G-9452)
Decatur Mold Tool and Engrg ....C 812 346-5188
North Vernon (G-11253)
Intri-Cut Tool Company LLC ....F 260 672-9602
Roanoke (G-12104)
Pinnacle Tool Inc ....G 812 336-5000
Bloomington (G-799)
Wirecut Technologies Inc ....F 317 885-9915
Indianapolis (G-8205)

ELECTRICAL EQPT & SPLYS

Academy Energy Group LLC ....G 312 931-7443
Newburgh (G-11017)

Adaptek Systems Inc ....E 260 637-8660
Fort Wayne (G-4041)
Advantage Cartridge Co Inc ....F 260 747-9941
Fort Wayne (G-4046)
Alliance Electric ....G 812 590-3500
Sellersburg (G-12387)
Automtion Ctrl Panl Sltons Inc ....F 219 961-8308
Munster (G-10597)
B & H Electric and Supply Inc ....G 812 333-7303
Bloomington (G-669)
Babsco Supply Inc ....G 574 267-8999
Warsaw (G-13841)
Becker Elec ....G 812 362-9000
Rockport (G-12166)
Broadwave Technologies Inc ....F 317 888-8316
Greenwood (G-5671)
Carmichael Electric LLC ....G 574 722-4028
Logansport (G-9327)
Chase Electric ....G 765 388-2183
New Castle (G-10896)
Connecticut Electric Inc ....F 800 730-2557
Anderson (G-89)
Copper Smith Electric ....G 260 849-4299
Berne (G-610)
Digiop Inc ....E 800 968-3606
Indianapolis (G-6742)
Don Moline Electric ....G 317 987-7606
Avon (G-438)
E M F Corp ....E 260 665-9541
Angola (G-208)
Eaton Electric Holdings LLC ....G 317 578-7724
Fishers (G-3900)
Economy Electric Htg & Coolg ....G 219 923-4441
Highland (G-6044)
Electric Motor Sales & Service ....G 812 574-3233
Madison (G-9460)
Electric Plus ....G 812 336-4992
Bloomington (G-719)
Energy Access Inc ....F 317 329-1676
Indianapolis (G-6864)
Esaote North America Inc ....D 317 813-6000
Fishers (G-3907)
Expert Electric ....G 765 664-6642
Marion (G-9523)
Flager Electric ....G 574 295-8007
Elkhart (G-2851)
Fortes Bros Electric ....G 219 472-0111
Merrillville (G-9716)
G & T Distribution ....G 765 759-8611
Yorktown (G-14404)
Gabbard and Son Electric ....G 812 747-7621
Lawrenceburg (G-9142)
Group Dekko Inc ....G 260 357-5988
Garrett (G-5010)
Group Dekko Inc ....D 260 635-2134
Wolflake (G-14379)
Hitachi Automotive Systems ....B 859 734-9451
Ligonier (G-9287)
Hubbell Incorporated Delaware ....B 574 234-7151
South Bend (G-12806)
Image Vault LLC ....E 812 948-8400
New Albany (G-10802)
Industrial Trning Unlmted Corp ....G 812 961-8801
Dugger (G-2480)
Indy Control Corp ....G 317 787-4639
Beech Grove (G-597)
Jason Incorporated ....C 847 215-1948
Richmond (G-12007)
Kelley Electric ....G 765 778-8203
Anderson (G-127)
Koester Metals Inc ....E 260 495-1818
Fremont (G-4964)
Lancon Electric Inc ....G 260 897-3285
Laotto (G-9113)
Lumen Cache Incorporated ....G 317 739-4218
McCordsville (G-9673)
Lynn Bros Electric Inc ....G 219 762-6386
Portage (G-11774)
Magnetic Instrumentation Inc ....E 317 842-9000
Indianapolis (G-7438)
Magnetic Instrumentation LLC ....E 317 842-7500
Indianapolis (G-7439)
Martin Electric Inc ....G 765 288-3254
Eaton (G-2585)
Master Electric Service LLC ....G 812 246-3707
Sellersburg (G-12407)
Meade Electric Co ....G 219 787-8317
Chesterton (G-1620)
Murphy Electric ....G 574 224-9473
Rochester (G-12141)

Nmm Electric .... G 219 864-9688
Dyer (G-2504)
Northwest Electric Connection .... G 219 465-5205
Carmel (G-1444)
Ohio Valley Electric .... G 812 532-5288
Lawrenceburg (G-9149)
Pioneer Electric .... G 765 762-2000
Williamsport (G-14294)
Qp Inc .... F 574 295-6884
Elkhart (G-3125)
Quality Hydraulic & Mch Svc .... G 317 892-2596
Danville (G-2355)
R C Electric .... E 317 600-3001
Indianapolis (G-7808)
Ryco Electric .... G 219 319-0934
Schererville (G-12344)
Samtec Inc .... G 812 517-6081
Scottsburg (G-12379)
Silent Witness Enterprises .... G 219 365-6660
Saint John (G-12270)
Stage Ninja LLC .... G 317 829-1507
Indianapolis (G-7985)
Sumitomo Electric Carbide Inc .... G 317 859-1601
Greenwood (G-5751)
Sun Power Technologies LLC .... G 317 399-8113
Westfield (G-14192)
Superior Electric Nwi LLC .... G 219 696-0717
Lowell (G-9423)
Tap-A-Lite Inc .... E 219 932-8067
Hammond (G-5948)
Thermo Cube Incorporated .... G 574 936-5096
Plymouth (G-11727)
Touchplate Technologies Inc .... F 260 424-4323
Fort Wayne (G-4696)
V The Electric Brew .... G 574 296-7785
Elkhart (G-3239)
Vincent Aliano Elc Htg & Coolg .... G 812 332-3332
Bloomington (G-852)
William D Darr .... G 574 518-0453
Syracuse (G-13154)
Xfmrs Holdings Inc .... G 317 834-1066
Camby (G-1271)

ELECTRICAL EQPT FOR ENGINES

Almega/Tru-Flex Inc .... E 574 546-2113
Bremen (G-982)
Ballantrae Inc .... B 800 372-3555
Pendleton (G-11483)
Borgwarner Pds Anderson LLC .... B 765 778-6499
Noblesville (G-11068)
Borgwarner Pds Anderson LLC .... C 765 778-6499
Anderson (G-76)
Caddo Connections Inc .... E 219 874-8119
La Porte (G-8744)
Cummins Inc .... B 812 377-5000
Columbus (G-1891)
Cummins Inc .... F 812 377-8601
Columbus (G-1894)
Cummins Inc .... E 812 377-2932
Columbus (G-1895)
Cummins Inc .... G 317 244-7251
Indianapolis (G-6709)
Cummins Inc .... G 317 610-2493
Indianapolis (G-6710)
Delco Electronics .... G 765 451-9325
Kokomo (G-8613)
Design Engineering .... F 219 926-2170
Chesterton (G-1602)
E M F Corp .... E 260 665-9541
Angola (G-208)
E M F Corp .... E 260 488-2479
Hamilton (G-5821)
Group Dekko Inc .... D 260 635-2134
Wolflake (G-14379)
Indiana Research Institute .... F 812 378-5363
Columbus (G-1948)
Kirby Risk Corporation .... B 765 447-1402
Lafayette (G-8942)
Motherson Sumi Systems Limited .... A 260 726-6501
Portland (G-11836)
Patrick Industries Inc .... D 260 665-6112
Angola (G-235)
United Starter Alternator LLC .... G 219 696-9095
Lowell (G-9424)

ELECTRICAL EQPT REPAIR & MAINTENANCE

Advantage Cartridge Co Inc .... F 260 747-9941
Fort Wayne (G-4046)

Allied Boiler & Welding Co .... G 317 272-4820
Avon (G-426)
Baseline Tool Co Inc .... F 260 761-4932
Wawaka (G-14030)
Columbus Signs .... G 812 376-7877
Columbus (G-1881)
Egenolf Machine Inc .... D 317 787-5301
Indianapolis (G-6814)
Johnson Bros S Whitley Sign Co .... F 260 723-5161
South Whitley (G-13000)
Northeast Machine & Tool Co .... G 317 823-6594
Indianapolis (G-7592)
Ohio Transmission Corporation .... G 812 466-2734
Terre Haute (G-13294)
United Machine Corporation .... E 219 548-8050
Valparaiso (G-13633)
Vandergriff & Associates Inc .... G 812 422-6033
Evansville (G-3793)

ELECTRICAL EQPT REPAIR SVCS

Agri-Tronix Corp .... F 317 738-4474
Franklin (G-4862)
Best Equipment Co Inc .... E 317 823-3050
Indianapolis (G-6469)
I E M C .... G 219 464-2890
Valparaiso (G-13558)
Raytheon Company .... C 317 306-8471
Indianapolis (G-7822)
Sign Group Inc .... F 317 875-6969
Indianapolis (G-7941)

ELECTRICAL EQPT REPAIR SVCS: High Voltage

Horner Industrial Services Inc .... G 317 916-4274
Indianapolis (G-7128)
Horner Industrial Services Inc .... G 812 466-5281
Terre Haute (G-13249)

ELECTRICAL EQPT: Automotive, NEC

Federal-Mogul LLC .... G 574 271-0274
South Bend (G-12775)
GM Components Holdings LLC .... G 765 451-5011
Kokomo (G-8630)
Noel-Smyser Engineering Corp .... F 317 293-2215
Indianapolis (G-7590)
Porter Systems Inc .... G 317 867-0234
Westfield (G-14178)
R & R Regulators Inc .... F 574 522-5846
Elkhart (G-3134)
Remy Logistics LLC .... G 765 683-3700
Anderson (G-160)

ELECTRICAL EQPT: Household

T & H Sweeper Co .... G 765 641-9800
Anderson (G-172)

ELECTRICAL GOODS, WHOLESALE: Batteries, Storage, Indl

B T Bttery Charger Systems Inc .... G 574 533-6030
Goshen (G-5176)

ELECTRICAL GOODS, WHOLESALE: Burglar Alarm Systems

Phil & Son Inc .... F 219 663-5757
Crown Point (G-2283)

ELECTRICAL GOODS, WHOLESALE: Connectors

Telamon International Corp .... E 317 818-6888
Carmel (G-1490)

ELECTRICAL GOODS, WHOLESALE: Electrical Appliances, Major

Long Item Development Corp .... G 317 844-9491
Carmel (G-1427)

ELECTRICAL GOODS, WHOLESALE: Electronic Parts

Avnet .... G 260 359-9513
Huntington (G-6189)

ELECTRICAL GOODS, WHOLESALE: Facsimile Or Fax Eqpt

Oce Copiers .... G 812 479-0000
Evansville (G-3652)

ELECTRICAL GOODS, WHOLESALE: Fire Alarm Systems

American Fire Company .... G 219 840-0630
Valparaiso (G-13491)

ELECTRICAL GOODS, WHOLESALE: Garbage Disposals

Pyramid Equipment .... F 219 778-2591
Rolling Prairie (G-12193)

ELECTRICAL GOODS, WHOLESALE: Generators

Cummins Crosspoint LLC .... E 812 867-4400
Evansville (G-3447)
Cummins Crosspoint LLC .... E 317 243-7979
Indianapolis (G-6706)
Lancon Electric Inc .... G 260 897-3285
Laotto (G-9113)

ELECTRICAL GOODS, WHOLESALE: Light Bulbs & Related Splys

Bonner & Associates .... G 317 571-1911
Carmel (G-1321)
Elkhart Supply Corp .... E 574 264-4156
Elkhart (G-2831)
National Handicapped Workshop .... D 765 287-8331
Muncie (G-10538)
Vivid Leds Inc .... F 800 974-3570
Sellersburg (G-12421)

ELECTRICAL GOODS, WHOLESALE: Lighting Fittings & Access

General Electric Company .... D 812 933-0700
Batesville (G-501)

ELECTRICAL GOODS, WHOLESALE: Lighting Fixtures, Comm & Indl

American Green Technology Inc .... F 269 340-9975
South Bend (G-12704)
Source Products Inc .... G 260 424-0864
Columbia City (G-1835)

ELECTRICAL GOODS, WHOLESALE: Mobile telephone Eqpt

Flat Electronics LLC .... G 765 414-6635
Lafayette (G-8899)

ELECTRICAL GOODS, WHOLESALE: Motors

Altek Inc .... G 812 385-2561
Princeton (G-11863)
B & H Electric and Supply Inc .... E 812 522-5607
Seymour (G-12431)
C & L Electric Motor Repr Inc .... G 574 533-2643
Goshen (G-5184)
Electric Power Service .... G 260 493-4913
Fort Wayne (G-4234)
Electrik Connection Inc .... G 219 362-4581
La Porte (G-8754)
Electro Corporation .... F 219 393-5571
Kingsbury (G-8536)
Enyart Electric Motor Service .... G 574 288-4731
South Bend (G-12766)
Harrison Electric Inc .... F 219 879-0444
Michigan City (G-9801)
Hess Electric Motor Service .... G 812 926-0346
Aurora (G-378)
Hoosier Industrial Electric .... F 812 346-2232
North Vernon (G-11262)
Jasper Electric Motor Inc .... G 812 482-1660
Jasper (G-8258)
Jasper Electric Motor Inc .... F 812 482-1660
Jasper (G-8259)
McBroom Electric Co Inc .... D 317 926-3451
Indianapolis (G-7471)
Motor Electric Inc .... G 574 294-7123
Elkhart (G-3051)

P
R
O
D
U
C
T

Motorcraft Inc ....G...... 765 282-4272
Muncie (G-10525)

Phase Three Electric Inc ....G...... 812 945-9922
New Albany (G-10842)

Phazpak Inc ....G...... 260 692-6416
Monroe (G-10184)

Regal-Beloit Corporation ....D...... 260 416-5400
Fort Wayne (G-4587)

Robinson Industries Inc ....E...... 317 867-3214
Westfield (G-14185)

Tipton Engrg Elc Mtr Svcs Inc ....G...... 765 963-3380
Sharpsville (G-12507)

Wabash Valley Motor & Mch Inc ....G...... 812 466-7400
Terre Haute (G-13366)

Wagner Electric Fort Wayne Inc ......G...... 260 484-5532
Fort Wayne (G-4730)

ELECTRICAL GOODS, WHOLESALE: Rectifiers

R & R Regulators Inc ....F...... 574 522-5846
Elkhart (G-3134)

ELECTRICAL GOODS, WHOLESALE: Security Control Eqpt & Systems

Allegion Public Ltd Company ....F...... 317 810-3700
Carmel (G-1307)

ELECTRICAL GOODS, WHOLESALE: Signaling, Eqpt

Doron Distribution Inc ....G...... 317 594-9259
Indianapolis (G-6759)

Dux Signal Kits LLC ....G...... 260 623-3017
Monroeville (G-10194)

ELECTRICAL GOODS, WHOLESALE: Switchgear

Power Components of Midwest ....C...... 574 256-6990
Mishawaka (G-10105)

ELECTRICAL GOODS, WHOLESALE: Video Eqpt

Motion Engineering Company Inc .....G...... 317 804-7990
Westfield (G-14177)

ELECTRICAL GOODS, WHOLESALE: Wire & Cable

Hessville Cable & Sling Co ....E...... 773 768-8181
Gary (G-5064)

Patrick Industries Inc ....D...... 574 293-2990
Elkhart (G-3089)

ELECTRICAL MEASURING INSTRUMENT REPAIR & CALIBRATION SVCS

Chance Indiana Standards Lab ....F...... 317 787-6578
Indianapolis (G-6593)

ELECTRICAL SPLYS

Babsco Supply Inc ....G...... 574 267-8999
Warsaw (G-13841)

Kirby Risk Corporation ....D...... 765 448-4567
Lafayette (G-8940)

Kirby Risk Corporation ....G...... 765 643-3384
Anderson (G-130)

Kirby Risk Corporation ....F...... 765 664-5185
Marion (G-9540)

Kirby Risk Corporation ....E...... 765 423-4205
Lafayette (G-8941)

Kirby Risk Corporation ....B...... 765 447-1402
Lafayette (G-8942)

Kirby Risk Corporation ....F...... 765 254-5460
Muncie (G-10505)

North Vernon Electric Inc ....F...... 812 392-2985
North Vernon (G-11271)

ELECTRICAL SUPPLIES: Porcelain

Insulation Specialties of Amer..........E...... 219 733-2502
Wanatah (G-13824)

Leco Corporation ....G...... 574 288-9017
South Bend (G-12838)

ELECTROLYZING SVC: Steel, Light Gauge

Arcelormittal Kote Inc ....G...... 574 654-1000
New Carlisle (G-10878)

ELECTROMEDICAL EQPT

B & J Specialty Inc ....F...... 260 636-2067
Kendallville (G-8458)

Biomet Inc ....A...... 574 267-6639
Warsaw (G-13845)

Global Isotopes LLC ....G...... 317 578-1251
Noblesville (G-11111)

Greenwald Surgical Co Inc ....E...... 219 962-1604
Lake Station (G-9075)

Guidant Intercontinental Corp ....E...... 317 218-7012
Carmel (G-1391)

Medishield ....G...... 502 939-9903
New Albany (G-10824)

Medtronic ....G...... 317 837-8664
Plainfield (G-11626)

Mr-Link LLC ....G...... 765 476-3185
West Lafayette (G-14088)

Plastic Assembly Tech Inc ....G...... 317 841-1202
Indianapolis (G-7700)

Telamon Entp Ventures LLC ....G...... 317 818-6888
Carmel (G-1489)

ELECTRONIC COMPONENTS

Avnet ....G...... 260 359-9513
Huntington (G-6189)

Broadwave Technologies Inc ....G...... 317 346-6101
Franklin (G-4873)

Cool-Shirts Inc ....G...... 317 826-1674
Indianapolis (G-6663)

George Marshall ....G...... 317 839-6563
Plainfield (G-11612)

K J S Associates ....G...... 317 842-7500
Indianapolis (G-7328)

K Ra International LLC ....G...... 574 258-7151
South Bend (G-12827)

Power Systems Innovations Inc ....G...... 812 480-4380
Newburgh (G-11043)

Signaling Solution Inc ....G...... 812 533-1345
Shelburn (G-12510)

Technology Dynamics ....G...... 317 524-6338
Indianapolis (G-8050)

Top Shelf Acoustics LLC ....G...... 317 512-4569
Indianapolis (G-8081)

Vista Worldwide LLC ....G...... 574 264-0711
Elkhart (G-3248)

ELECTRONIC DEVICES: Solid State, NEC

Paul Nelson ....G...... 765 352-0698
Martinsville (G-9632)

Payne-Sparkman Manufacturing ....F...... 812 944-4893
New Albany (G-10840)

Pursuit Defense Technology LLC ....G...... 630 687-3826
Indianapolis (G-7791)

ELECTRONIC EQPT REPAIR SVCS

Reeds RFI Inc ....G...... 812 659-2872
Switz City (G-13126)

Richard J Bagan Inc ....E...... 260 244-5115
Columbia City (G-1826)

Teaco Inc ....F...... 219 874-6234
Michigan City (G-9852)

ELECTRONIC LOADS & POWER SPLYS

Green Cubes Technology Corp ....E...... 502 416-1060
Kokomo (G-8633)

Wattre Inc ....G...... 260 657-3701
Woodburn (G-14391)

ELECTRONIC PARTS & EQPT WHOLESALERS

Acterna LLC ....E...... 317 788-9351
Indianapolis (G-6320)

Coil Tran Corp ....D...... 219 942-8511
Hobart (G-6076)

Elkhart Supply Corp ....E...... 574 264-4156
Elkhart (G-2831)

Harman Embedded Audio LLC ....E...... 317 849-8175
Indianapolis (G-7077)

Td Innovations ....G...... 530 477-9780
Bloomington (G-835)

Xfmrs Inc ....A...... 317 834-1066
Camby (G-1272)

ELECTRONIC TRAINING DEVICES

Allied Mfg Partners Inc ....G...... 260 428-2670
Fort Wayne (G-4062)

Automation Consultants Inc ....G...... 502 552-4995
Floyds Knobs (G-4007)

Innotek Inc ....C...... 800 826-5527
Auburn (G-337)

Lovetts Electronics ....G...... 812 446-1093
Brazil (G-967)

Moffitt Consulting Services ....G...... 317 773-5570
Noblesville (G-11153)

Targamite LLC ....G...... 260 489-0046
Fort Wayne (G-4674)

Terick Sales ....G...... 574 626-3173
Walton (G-13817)

ELECTROPLATING & PLATING SVC

Hgc Custom Chrome ....G...... 260 447-4731
Yoder (G-14398)

Industrial Research Inc ....G...... 812 401-2333
Evansville (G-3557)

Neo Industries (indiana) Inc ....C...... 219 762-6075
Portage (G-11782)

ELEMENTARY & SECONDARY SCHOOLS, SPECIAL EDUCATION

Solution Tree Inc ....C...... 812 336-7700
Bloomington (G-828)

ELEVATORS & EQPT

Elevator One LLC ....G...... 317 634-8001
Indianapolis (G-6821)

Otis Elevator Company ....E...... 812 471-9770
Evansville (G-3658)

ELEVATORS WHOLESALERS

Thyssenkrupp Elevator Corp ....E...... 317 595-1125
Indianapolis (G-8074)

ELEVATORS: Automobile

Otis Elevator Company ....G...... 812 331-5605
Bloomington (G-793)

ELEVATORS: Installation & Conversion

Michiana Lift Equipment Inc ....G...... 574 257-1665
Mishawaka (G-10082)

Thyssenkrupp Elevator Corp ....E...... 317 595-1125
Indianapolis (G-8074)

Zeller Elevator Co ....G...... 812 985-5888
Mount Vernon (G-10415)

ELEVATORS: Stair, Motor Powered

Convertastep LLC ....G...... 260 969-8645
Markle (G-9576)

EMBLEMS: Embroidered

Celestial Designs LLC ....G...... 317 733-3110
Zionsville (G-14425)

Sew Unique Inc ....G...... 317 257-0503
Indianapolis (G-7918)

Spectrum Marketing ....G...... 765 643-5566
Anderson (G-168)

Sportsmania Sales Inc ....G...... 317 873-5501
Zionsville (G-14465)

EMBOSSING SVC: Paper

Bruce Payne ....G...... 260 492-2259
Fort Wayne (G-4124)

Moeller Printing Co Inc ....E...... 317 353-2224
Indianapolis (G-7533)

EMBROIDERING & ART NEEDLEWORK FOR THE TRADE

2 Bears LLC ....G...... 317 375-1634
Indianapolis (G-6284)

A D I Screen Printing ....G...... 765 457-8580
Kokomo (G-8589)

A Time To Stitch Inc ....G...... 812 422-5968
Evansville (G-3330)

Advantage Embroidery Inc ....G...... 765 471-0188
Bringhurst (G-1037)

After Hours Embroidery ....G...... 812 926-9355
Aurora (G-368)

Apparel Promotions Inc ....G.... 574 294-7165
Elkhart (G-2694)
Apple Group Inc ....E.... 765 675-4777
Tipton (G-13387)
Baron Embroidery Corp ....G.... 260 484-8700
Auburn (G-316)
Bears Den EMB & More LLC ....G.... 260 724-4070
Decatur (G-2370)
Burston Marketing Inc ....F.... 574 262-4005
Elkhart (G-2739)
Classic Products Corp ....E.... 260 484-2695
Fort Wayne (G-4159)
Company Pride Shirts LLC ....G.... 812 526-5700
Edinburgh (G-2601)
Concept Prints Inc ....F.... 317 290-1222
Indianapolis (G-6648)
Corporate Shirts Direct Inc ....G.... 317 474-6033
Franklin (G-4877)
Country Stitches Embroidery ....G.... 219 324-7625
La Porte (G-8746)
Creative Embroidery Designs ....G.... 812 479-8280
Evansville (G-3438)
D & J Custom Embroidery ....G.... 219 874-9061
Michigan City (G-9779)
Digistitch ....G.... 574 538-3960
Goshen (G-5199)
Embroidery Nation ....G.... 574 967-3928
Flora (G-3994)
Embroidery Plus Inc ....G.... 317 243-3445
Indianapolis (G-6848)
Embroidery Solutions U S ....G.... 812 923-9152
Greenville (G-5649)
Favor It Promotions Inc ....F.... 317 733-1112
Carmel (G-1379)
Gettelfinger Holdings LLC ....G.... 812 923-9065
Floyds Knobs (G-4012)
Golden Threads ....G.... 765 557-7801
Elwood (G-3299)
HWH Embroidery Inc ....F.... 317 895-0201
Indianapolis (G-7149)
Imperial Designs ....G.... 765 985-2712
Denver (G-2454)
J N P Custom Designs Inc ....G.... 317 253-2198
Indianapolis (G-7289)
Just Monograms LLC ....G.... 812 827-3693
Jasper (G-8269)
Lloyd & Mona Sulivan ....G.... 812 522-9191
Seymour (G-12467)
Locoli Inc ....E.... 219 365-3125
Schererville (G-12332)
Maingate Inc ....D.... 317 243-2000
Indianapolis (G-7444)
Marie S Embroidery ....G.... 219 931-2561
Hammond (G-5912)
McBeth Designs Inc ....G.... 317 848-7313
Carmel (G-1435)
McKinneys Embroidery & Sup Co ....G.... 317 984-9039
Arcadia (G-265)
Outfitter ....G.... 765 289-6456
Muncie (G-10541)
P Js Custom Embroidering LLC ....G.... 219 787-9161
Chesterton (G-1627)
Precision Stitch Indiana Inc ....G.... 765 473-6734
Peru (G-11541)
Progressive Design Apparel Inc ....E.... 317 293-5888
Indianapolis (G-7775)
Real Image Llc ....G.... 765 675-7325
Tipton (G-13403)
Rensew Inc ....G.... 574 257-0665
Mishawaka (G-10116)
Robert Burkhart ....G.... 219 448-0365
Alexandria (G-52)
Rustic N Chic LLC ....G.... 219 987-4957
Wheatfield (G-14230)
Shirts N Things S N T Graphics ....G.... 317 271-3515
Indianapolis (G-7935)
T L E LLC ....G.... 317 257-1424
Noblesville (G-11191)
Topstitch Inc ....F.... 574 293-6633
Elkhart (G-3220)
Unique Graphic Designs Inc ....G.... 574 583-7119
Monticello (G-10287)
Vickers Graphics Inc ....G.... 765 868-4646
Kokomo (G-8712)
Village Custom Embroidery Inc ....G.... 317 733-3110
Zionsville (G-14470)
Wasu Inc ....G.... 765 448-4450
Lafayette (G-9022)
Wildman Corporate Apparel Ltd ....F.... 574 269-7266
Warsaw (G-13966)

Woods Enterprises ....G.... 574 232-7449
South Bend (G-12992)

EMBROIDERING SVC

A B C Embroidery Inc ....G.... 260 636-7311
Albion (G-14)
Abracadabra Graphics ....G.... 812 336-1971
Bloomington (G-654)
Avon Sports Apparel Corp ....G.... 317 887-2673
Greenwood (G-5668)
Barrett Manufacturing Inc ....G.... 812 753-5808
Fort Branch (G-4026)
Cindys In Stitches ....G.... 317 841-1408
Fishers (G-3890)
CLC Embroidery LLC ....G.... 219 395-9600
Chesterton (G-1600)
Columbus Embroidery ....G.... 812 273-0860
Madison (G-9454)
Cowpokes Inc ....E.... 765 642-3911
Anderson (G-91)
Creative Solutions ....G.... 219 778-4919
Rolling Prairie (G-12184)
Custom Imprint Corporation ....E.... 800 378-3397
Merrillville (G-9709)
Dkm Embroidery Inc ....G.... 260 471-4070
Fort Wayne (G-4215)
Dugout ....G.... 765 642-8528
Anderson (G-100)
Elegan Sportswear Inc ....E.... 219 464-8416
Valparaiso (G-13534)
Embroidery N Things Inc ....G.... 317 859-8963
Bargersville (G-482)
Four Season Sports Inc ....G.... 812 279-0384
Bedford (G-543)
Freckles Graphics Inc ....F.... 765 448-4692
Lafayette (G-8900)
Giraffe X Graphics Inc ....G.... 317 546-4944
Indianapolis (G-7007)
Graphic22 Inc ....G.... 219 921-5409
Chesterton (G-1608)
Jasper EMB & Screen Prtg ....G.... 812 482-4787
Jasper (G-8260)
Jer-Maur Corporation ....G.... 812 384-8290
Bloomfield (G-640)
Kellum Imprints Inc ....G.... 812 347-2546
Ramsey (G-11893)
Logo Boys Inc ....G.... 574 256-6844
Mishawaka (G-10070)
Mary Duncan ....F.... 812 238-3637
Terre Haute (G-13279)
National Athletic Sportswear ....F.... 260 436-2248
Fort Wayne (G-4490)
Paige Marschall ....G.... 574 277-1631
Granger (G-5428)
Perdue Printed Products Inc ....G.... 260 456-7575
Fort Wayne (G-4523)
Profit Finders Incorporated ....F.... 317 251-7792
Indianapolis (G-7773)
Raymond Truex ....G.... 574 858-2260
Warsaw (G-13933)
Select Embroidery/Top It Off ....F.... 812 337-8049
Bloomington (G-823)
Shirtails ....G.... 812 858-8605
Newburgh (G-11048)
Stogdill Sports ....G.... 812 524-7081
Seymour (G-12495)
Sues Custom Shirts ....G.... 812 535-4429
Sandford (G-12311)
Thread Creations Inc ....G.... 765 521-3886
New Castle (G-10919)
Vco Inc ....G.... 812 235-3540
Terre Haute (G-13361)
Wanda Harrington ....G.... 765 642-1628
Anderson (G-182)
Wildman Business Group LLC ....C.... 866 369-1552
Warsaw (G-13965)
Winning Edge of Rochester Inc ....F.... 574 223-6090
Rochester (G-12162)

EMBROIDERY ADVERTISING SVCS

Athletic Edge Inc ....F.... 260 489-6613
Fort Wayne (G-4095)
Dark Star Inc ....F.... 765 759-4764
Muncie (G-10453)
Gd Cox Inc ....G.... 317 398-0035
Shelbyville (G-12536)
High End Concepts Inc ....F.... 317 630-9901
Indianapolis (G-7106)
Rookies Unlimited Inc ....G.... 765 536-2726
Summitville (G-13104)

Spark Marketing LLC ....G.... 219 301-0071
Schererville (G-12346)
Spectrum Marketing ....G.... 765 643-5566
Anderson (G-168)
Stien Designs & Graphics Inc ....G.... 260 347-9136
Kendallville (G-8511)

EMBROIDERY KITS

Aus Embroidery Inc ....G.... 317 899-1225
Indianapolis (G-6440)

EMERGENCY ALARMS

American Eagle Security Inc ....G.... 219 980-1177
Merrillville (G-9696)
General Dynamics Mission ....C.... 260 434-9500
Fort Wayne (G-4296)
Johnson Controls ....G.... 812 423-9000
Evansville (G-3576)
Johnson Controls ....E.... 260 692-6666
Monroe (G-10183)
Johnson Controls ....G.... 812 423-9000
Evansville (G-3577)
Molex LLC ....E.... 317 834-5600
Mooresville (G-10323)

EMPLOYMENT AGENCY SVCS

Old Gary Inc ....G.... 941 755-0976
Merrillville (G-9742)

ENAMELING SVC: Metal Prdts, Including Porcelain

Advanced Finishing Corporation ....G.... 317 335-2210
McCordsville (G-9664)
Klinge Enameling Company Inc ....E.... 317 359-8291
Indianapolis (G-7359)

ENCLOSURES: Electronic

Koester Metals Inc ....E.... 260 495-1818
Fremont (G-4964)
Mier Products Inc ....E.... 765 457-0223
Kokomo (G-8666)

ENGINE PARTS & ACCESS: Internal Combustion

Cosworth LLC ....D.... 844 278-6941
Indianapolis (G-6673)
Ertl Enterprises Inc ....F.... 765 622-9900
Anderson (G-105)
Lingenfelter Prfmce Engrg Inc ....E.... 260 724-2552
Decatur (G-2390)
Power Investments Inc ....G.... 317 738-2117
Franklin (G-4921)
Rng Performance LLC ....G.... 260 602-5613
Monroeville (G-10199)
W A P LLC ....E.... 317 421-3180
Shelbyville (G-12583)
Wap Inc ....G.... 877 421-3187
Shelbyville (G-12584)

ENGINE REBUILDING: Diesel

Jolliff Diesel Service ....G.... 812 692-5725
Elnora (G-3290)

ENGINEERING SVCS

AM General Holdings LLC ....F.... 574 237-6222
South Bend (G-12699)
AM General LLC ....D.... 574 235-7326
South Bend (G-12700)
Apex AG Solutions LLC ....F.... 937 564-5421
Richmond (G-11954)
Butler Tool & Design Inc ....F.... 219 297-4531
Goodland (G-5158)
Crown Training & Development ....E.... 219 947-0845
Merrillville (G-9708)
Damping Technologies Inc ....E.... 574 258-7916
Mishawaka (G-10031)
Damping Technologies Inc ....E.... 574 258-7916
Mishawaka (G-10032)
Daylight Engineering Inc ....G.... 812 983-2518
Elberfeld (G-2633)
Design Engineering ....F.... 219 926-2170
Chesterton (G-1602)
Enginered Refr Shapes Svcs LLC ....G.... 765 778-8040
Pendleton (G-11488)

Employee Codes: A=Over 500 employees, B=251-500
C=101-250, D=51-100, E=20-50, F=10-19, G=2-9

2018 Harris Indiana
Industrial Directory

PRODUCT

963

Enterprise MGT Solutions LLC ....G 219 545-8544
  Merrillville (G-9713)
Future Mold Inc ....F 812 941-8661
  New Albany (G-10785)
Gmp Holdings LLC ....G 317 353-6580
  Indianapolis (G-7016)
Halo LLC ....D 317 575-9992
  Indianapolis (G-6266)
Hgl Dynamics Inc ....G 317 782-3500
  Indianapolis (G-7100)
Hirata Corporation of America ....E 317 856-8600
  Indianapolis (G-7109)
Imagineering Enterprises Inc ....E 574 287-0642
  South Bend (G-12808)
Imagineering Enterprises Inc ....C 574 287-2941
  South Bend (G-12809)
Imagineering Enterprises Inc ....F 317 635-8565
  Indianapolis (G-7162)
Industrial Conductor Products ......G 219 662-9477
  Crown Point (G-2262)
Indy Rapid 3d LLC ....G 812 243-4175
  Indianapolis (G-7221)
Ipheion Development Corp ....G 240 281-1619
  Indianapolis (G-7265)
KYB Americas Corporation ....B 317 736-7774
  Franklin (G-4903)
Lingenfelter Prfmce Engrg Inc ......E 260 724-2552
  Decatur (G-2390)
Modern Forge Companies LLC ......A 708 388-1806
  Merrillville (G-9738)
Odyssian Technology LLC ....G 574 257-7555
  South Bend (G-12882)
Paden Engineering Co Inc ....G 812 546-4447
  Hope (G-6117)
Pia Automation US Inc ....C 812 474-3126
  Evansville (G-3669)
Rd Rubber Products Inc ....G 260 357-3571
  Garrett (G-5021)
Rwb & Associates LLC ....G 317 219-6572
  Noblesville (G-11178)
Setco LLC ....B 812 424-2904
  Evansville (G-3724)
Stedman Machine Company ....B 812 926-0038
  Aurora (G-390)
Telamon Corporation ....C 317 818-6888
  Carmel (G-1488)
Webco Inc ....G 260 244-4233
  Columbia City (G-1847)
World Rdo Mssnary Fllwship Inc ....E 574 970-4252
  Elkhart (G-3268)
Xtreme ADS Limited ....E 765 644-7323
  Anderson (G-184)

ENGINEERING SVCS: Acoustical

Metal Technologies Inc Alabama ....D 260 925-4717
  Auburn (G-345)

ENGINEERING SVCS: Building Construction

JMS Engineered Plastics Inc ....D 574 277-3228
  South Bend (G-12823)
Royal Adhesives & Sealants LLC ....D 574 246-5000
  South Bend (G-12920)

ENGINEERING SVCS: Electrical Or Electronic

Carmel Process Solutions Inc ....G 317 705-0217
  Carmel (G-1331)
Computer Age Engineering Inc ....E 765 674-8551
  Marion (G-9518)
Crown Elec Svcs & Automtn Inc ....D 972 929-4700
  Portage (G-11758)
Direct Control Systems Inc ....G 765 282-7474
  Muncie (G-10460)
Duesenburg Inc ....G 260 496-9650
  Fort Wayne (G-4223)
Integratorcom Inc ....D 317 776-3500
  Noblesville (G-11130)
Llama Corporation ....G 888 701-7432
  Decatur (G-2391)
Mesh Systems LLC ....E 317 661-4800
  Carmel (G-1437)
Span Inc ....F 317 347-2646
  Lebanon (G-9226)

ENGINEERING SVCS: Energy conservation

Infrastructure and Energy ....F 765 828-2580
  Indianapolis (G-7228)

ENGINEERING SVCS: Heating & Ventilation

T R Bulger Inc ....G 219 879-8525
  Trail Creek (G-13443)

ENGINEERING SVCS: Industrial

Industrial Combustn Engineers ....E 219 949-5066
  Gary (G-5068)
Midwest Finishing Systems Inc ....E 574 257-0099
  Mishawaka (G-10087)
Selco Engineering Inc ....E 317 297-1888
  Shelbyville (G-12566)

ENGINEERING SVCS: Machine Tool Design

Lyntech Engineering Inc ....G 574 224-2300
  Rochester (G-12134)

ENGINEERING SVCS: Mechanical

Biosafe Engineering LLC ....G 317 858-8099
  Indianapolis (G-6477)
K&T Performance Engrg LLC ....G 765 437-0185
  Peru (G-11535)
Klinge Enameling Company Inc ....E 317 359-8291
  Indianapolis (G-7359)
Robert Perez ....G 317 291-7311
  Indianapolis (G-7849)
S-B Capable Concepts LLC ....G 812 420-2565
  Brazil (G-977)
Specialty Tooling Inc ....F 812 464-8521
  Evansville (G-3744)
Tomlinson Manufacturing ....G 317 209-9375
  Avon (G-470)
Wolf Technical Engineering LLC ....G 800 783-9653
  Indianapolis (G-8209)

ENGINEERING SVCS: Petroleum

Barger Engineering Inc ....G 812 476-3077
  Evansville (G-3370)
Moore Engineering & Prod Co ....F 812 479-1051
  Evansville (G-3636)
Oilfield Research Inc ....G 812 424-2907
  Evansville (G-3653)
Robinson Engineering & Oil Co ....F 812 477-1575
  Evansville (G-3707)

ENGINEERING SVCS: Structural

Precision Surveillance Corp ....E 219 397-4295
  East Chicago (G-2564)

ENGINES & ENGINE PARTS: Guided Missile, Research & Develpt

N Rolls-Royce Amercn Tech Inc ....C 317 230-4347
  Indianapolis (G-7567)

ENGINES: Diesel & Semi-Diesel Or Duel Fuel

Cummins Inc ....A 812 522-9366
  Seymour (G-12442)
Engler Machine & Tool Inc ....F 812 386-6254
  Princeton (G-11869)

ENGINES: Gasoline, NEC

Bes Racing Engines Inc ....F 812 576-2371
  Guilford (G-5797)
Michael Dargie ....G 765 935-2241
  Richmond (G-12017)
Ultra Tech Racing Engines ....G 574 674-6028
  Osceola (G-11384)

ENGINES: Internal Combustion, NEC

Carlson Motorsports ....G 765 339-4407
  Linden (G-9303)
Champion Racing Engines ....G 317 335-2491
  McCordsville (G-9665)
Cummins ....G 812 524-6381
  Seymour (G-12441)
Cummins - Allison Corp ....G 317 872-6244
  Indianapolis (G-6705)
Cummins Americas Inc ....G 812 377-5000
  Columbus (G-1886)
Cummins Crosspoint LLC ....E 317 244-7251
  Indianapolis (G-6707)
Cummins Crosspoint LLC ....G 574 252-2154
  Mishawaka (G-10026)
Cummins Crosspoint LLC ....G 317 484-2146
  Indianapolis (G-6708)

Cummins Crosspoint LLC ....E 260 482-3691
  Fort Wayne (G-4192)
Cummins Crosspoint LLC ....E 812 867-4400
  Evansville (G-3447)
Cummins Crosspoint LLC ....E 317 243-7979
  Indianapolis (G-6706)
Cummins Dist Holdco Inc ....E 812 377-5000
  Columbus (G-1888)
Cummins Emission Solutions Inc ....E 608 987-3206
  Columbus (G-1889)
Cummins Engine Service ....G 260 657-1436
  Woodburn (G-14382)
Cummins Inc ....B 812 377-5000
  Columbus (G-1891)
Cummins Inc ....B 812 377-0150
  Columbus (G-1892)
Cummins Inc ....B 812 377-6072
  Columbus (G-1893)
Cummins Inc ....F 812 377-8601
  Columbus (G-1894)
Cummins Inc ....G 812 377-2932
  Columbus (G-1895)
Cummins Inc ....G 812 374-4774
  Columbus (G-1897)
Cummins Inc ....G 317 244-7251
  Indianapolis (G-6709)
Cummins Inc ....G 317 610-2493
  Indianapolis (G-6710)
Cummins Inc ....B 812 377-7000
  Columbus (G-1899)
Cummins Inc ....G 812 524-6455
  Columbus (G-1896)
Cummins Power Generation Inc ....E 574 262-4611
  Elkhart (G-2783)
Cummins Power Generation Inc ....F 812 377-5000
  Columbus (G-1900)
Cummins Repair Inc ....G 260 632-4800
  Harlan (G-5969)
Cummins-Scania Xpi Mfg LLC ....G 812 377-5000
  Columbus (G-1901)
Engineered Machined Pdts Inc ....C 317 462-8894
  Greenfield (G-5528)
FCA US LLC ....A 765 454-0018
  Kokomo (G-8624)
Glidden Racing Engines ....G 317 535-5225
  Whiteland (G-14238)
Mitchell Smith Racing ....G 765 640-0237
  Anderson (G-137)
Powerhouse Engines LLC ....G 765 576-1418
  Lynn (G-9431)
Price Motor Sport Engineering ....G 812 546-4220
  Hope (G-6118)
Progress Rail Services Corp ....G 765 472-2002
  Peru (G-11542)
Stensland Engines Inc ....G 260 623-6859
  Monroeville (G-10200)

ENGINES: Steam

R W Machine Incorporated ....G 317 769-6798
  Whitestown (G-14260)

ENGRAVING SVC, NEC

B and R Engraving Inc ....G 317 894-3599
  Greenfield (G-5506)
Bills Industries LLC ....G 765 629-0227
  Milroy (G-9977)
Cedar Woodworking ....G 812 486-2765
  Montgomery (G-10216)
Classic Engraving ....G 765 523-3355
  Stockwell (G-13076)
Engraving and Stamp Center Inc ....G 812 336-0606
  Bloomington (G-720)
Gary Printing Inc ....G 219 886-1767
  Gary (G-5052)
Hunt and Sons Memorial LLC ....G 317 745-0940
  Danville (G-2348)
Riverside Printing Co ....G 812 275-1950
  Bedford (G-574)
Rock Garden Engraving ....G 765 647-3357
  Brookville (G-1125)
Shirley Engraving Co Inc ....F 317 634-4084
  Indianapolis (G-7934)

ENGRAVING SVC: Jewelry & Personal Goods

Asempac Inc ....E 812 945-6303
  New Albany (G-10747)
Custom TS & Trophies ....G 219 926-4174
  Porter (G-11804)

Khamis Fine Jewelers Inc ....G...... 317 841-8440
Indianapolis (G-7348)
Larry H Poole..................................G...... 812 466-9345
Terre Haute (G-13272)
Laser Graphx Inc ....G...... 574 834-4443
North Webster (G-11296)
Mains Enterprises Inc......................G...... 765 425-0162
Wilkinson (G-14279)
Professional Bowling Ball Svc ....G...... 317 786-4329
Indianapolis (G-7770)

ENGRAVING SVCS

A Mayes Ing Inc ....G...... 317 925-5777
Indianapolis (G-6298)
Dd Stoops Laser Engraving................G...... 765 868-4999
Kokomo (G-8611)
Edward ONeil Associates...................G...... 317 244-5400
Indianapolis (G-6810)
J P Corporation ....G...... 317 783-1000
Beech Grove (G-598)
J P Industries Inc ....F...... 574 293-8763
Elkhart (G-2942)
Laser Marking Technologies..............G...... 812 852-7999
Osgood (G-11392)
Mains Enterprises Inc......................G...... 765 425-0162
Wilkinson (G-14279)
Specialty Shoppe ....G...... 574 772-7873
Knox (G-8582)
Star Quality Awards Inc ....G...... 812 273-1740
Madison (G-9496)

ENGRAVING: Steel line, For The Printing Trade

C & J Corporation ....G...... 574 255-6793
Mishawaka (G-10015)

ENGRAVINGS: Plastic

A Mayes Ing Inc ....G...... 317 925-5777
Indianapolis (G-6298)
Allin Plastics Engraving....................G...... 219 972-2223
Hammond (G-5838)
Hoosier Badge & Trophies Inc............G...... 317 257-4441
Indianapolis (G-7120)
Stien Designs & Graphics Inc.............G...... 260 347-9136
Kendallville (G-8511)

ENTERTAINMENT SVCS

Tyler Truss Systems Inc....................F...... 765 221-5050
Pendleton (G-11509)

ENVELOPES

BSC Vntres Acquisition Sub LLC........D...... 260 665-7521
Angola (G-198)
Cenveo Inc....................................D...... 317 791-5250
Indianapolis (G-6588)
Double Envelope Corp ....G...... 260 434-0500
Fort Wayne (G-4219)
Envelope Service Inc ....E...... 260 432-6277
Fort Wayne (G-4237)
Westrock Mwv LLC.........................C...... 317 787-3361
Indianapolis (G-8187)

ENVELOPES WHOLESALERS

Double Envelope Corp ....G...... 260 434-0500
Fort Wayne (G-4219)
Millcraft Paper Company ....E...... 317 240-3500
Indianapolis (G-7519)

ENZYMES

Enzyme Solutions Inc ....G...... 800 523-1323
Fort Wayne (G-4239)
Midwest Bio-Products Inc ....G...... 765 793-3426
Covington (G-2119)

EPOXY RESINS

Leepoxy Plastics Inc........................G...... 260 747-7411
Fort Wayne (G-4430)
Royal Adhesives & Sealants LLC........E...... 574 246-5000
South Bend (G-12921)
Star Technology Inc.........................E...... 260 837-7833
Waterloo (G-14024)
V Global Holdings LLC......................A...... 317 247-8141
Indianapolis (G-8142)

EQUIPMENT: Pedestrian Traffic Control

Highway Safety Services Inc..............G...... 765 474-1000
Lafayette (G-8915)
J A Larr & Co ....G...... 317 627-3192
Indianapolis (G-7282)

EQUIPMENT: Rental & Leasing, NEC

Heat Wagons Inc.............................F...... 219 464-8818
Valparaiso (G-13555)
M C L Window Coverings Inc..............F...... 317 577-2670
Fishers (G-3942)
Macallister Machinery Co Inc.............F...... 765 966-0759
Richmond (G-12012)
Motion Engineering Company Inc........G...... 317 804-7990
Westfield (G-14177)
Standard Change-Makers Inc.............C...... 317 899-6955
Indianapolis (G-7987)
T S F Co Inc ....E...... 812 985-2630
Evansville (G-3757)

ETCHING & ENGRAVING SVC

Carmel Traphies Plus ....G...... 317 844-3770
Carmel (G-1332)
Dd Stoops Laser Engraving................G...... 765 868-4999
Kokomo (G-8611)
Golden Frame Inc............................G...... 812 232-0048
Terre Haute (G-13242)
Hoosier Badge & Trophies Inc............G...... 317 257-4441
Indianapolis (G-7120)
JM Christian LLC ....G...... 317 460-0984
Chesterton (G-1616)
Northern Ind Indus Catings LLC..........G...... 574 893-4621
Akron (G-6)
Parsing Laser Designs LLC................G...... 317 677-4316
Avon (G-460)
Star Quality Awards Inc ....G...... 812 273-1740
Madison (G-9496)

ETCHING SVC: Metal

Aceys Trophies & Awards..................G...... 574 267-1426
Warsaw (G-13835)
Johnson Engraving & Trophies............G...... 260 982-7868
North Manchester (G-11232)

ETHANOLAMINES

Aventine Renewable Energy...............G...... 812 838-9598
Mount Vernon (G-10385)
Poet Biorefining - Portland ....G...... 260 726-7154
Portland (G-11840)

ETHYLENE-PROPYLENE RUBBERS: EPDM Polymers

Fiber Technologies LLC ....G...... 812 569-4641
Bloomington (G-725)
ICO Polymers North America Inc ....G...... 219 392-3375
East Chicago (G-2536)

EXCAVATING EQPT

Biggerstaff & Son Excavating.............G...... 317 784-6034
Indianapolis (G-6474)
Kenn Feld Group LLC.......................F...... 260 632-4242
Woodburn (G-14385)

EXERCISE SALON

Worth Tax and Financial Svc ....G...... 574 267-4687
Warsaw (G-13969)

EXHAUST SYSTEMS: Eqpt & Parts

Arvin Sango Inc...............................A...... 812 265-2888
Madison (G-9444)
Cummins Emission Solutions Inc.........E...... 608 987-3206
Columbus (G-1889)
Elsa LLC..B...... 765 552-5200
Elwood (G-3296)
Elsa Corporation.............................B...... 765 552-5200
Elwood (G-3297)
Exhaust Productions Inc...................G...... 219 942-0069
Merrillville (G-9714)
Faurecia Emissions Contl Tech...........B...... 812 341-2620
Columbus (G-1923)
Faurecia Emissions Contl Tech...........D...... 248 758-8160
Fort Wayne (G-4259)
Faurecia Emissions Control ....G...... 937 823-5393
Columbus (G-1925)

Faurecia Emissions Control ....B...... 812 341-2000
Columbus (G-1926)
Faurecia Emissions Control TEC.........B...... 812 341-2000
Columbus (G-1928)
Faurecia Exhaust Systems LLC..........C...... 812 341-2079
Columbus (G-1929)
Heavy Duty Manufacturing Inc ....F...... 260 432-2480
Fort Wayne (G-4328)
Integrated Energy Technologies ....E...... 812 421-7810
Evansville (G-3563)
Viking Inc......................................E...... 260 244-6141
Columbia City (G-1845)

EXPLOSIVES

Adranos Rdx LLC............................G...... 208 539-2439
West Lafayette (G-14047)
Austin Powder Company ....G...... 812 536-2885
Stendal (G-13073)
Dyno Nobel Inc ....G...... 219 253-2525
Indianapolis (G-6780)
Dyno Nobel Inc ....F...... 260 731-4431
Pennville (G-11513)
Dyno Nobel Inc ....E...... 859 278-4770
Evansville (G-3467)
Ireco Metals Inc ....G...... 574 936-2146
Plymouth (G-11696)
Midland Powder LLC ....G...... 812 402-4070
Evansville (G-3627)
Orica USA Inc ....F...... 812 256-7800
Jeffersonville (G-8409)

EXPLOSIVES, EXC AMMO & FIREWORKS WHOLESALERS

Orica USA Inc ....F...... 812 256-7800
Jeffersonville (G-8409)

EXPLOSIVES, FUSES & DETONATORS: Primary explosives

Mine Equipment Mill Supply Co ....D...... 812 402-4070
Evansville (G-3630)

EXPLOSIVES: Black Powder

Austin Powder Company ....F...... 812 342-1237
Columbus (G-1857)

EXTERMINATING PRDTS: Household Or Indl Use

Alpha Systems LLC ....F...... 574 295-5206
Elkhart (G-2678)

EXTRACTS, FLAVORING

Callisons Inc..................................G...... 574 896-5074
North Judson (G-11208)
Dairychem Laboratories Inc...............F...... 317 849-8400
Fishers (G-3897)
William Leman Co...........................E...... 574 546-2371
Bremen (G-1033)

EXTRACTS: Dying Or Tanning, Natural

Artemis International Inc...................G...... 260 436-6899
Fort Wayne (G-4092)

EYEGLASSES

2020 Lab Inc ....G...... 219 756-8703
Merrillville (G-9690)
Armada Optical Services Inc ....F...... 812 476-6623
Evansville (G-3365)
Columbus Optical Service Inc.............G...... 812 372-2678
Columbus (G-1878)
Essilor Laboratories Amer Inc ....D...... 317 637-2391
Indianapolis (G-6878)
Frecker Optical Inc..........................F...... 260 747-9653
Fort Wayne (G-4287)
Jackson Vision Quest ....G...... 219 882-9397
Gary (G-5071)
Kokomo Optical Company Inc.............G...... 765 459-5137
Kokomo (G-8655)
Samco Group Inc ....G...... 219 872-4413
Michigan City (G-9838)

EYEGLASSES: Sunglasses

Fatheadz Inc..................................F...... 800 561-6640
Indianapolis (G-6906)

Employee Codes: A=Over 500 employees, B=251-500
C=101-250, D=51-100, E=20-50, F=10-19, G=2-9

2018 Harris Indiana
Industrial Directory

PRODUCT

965

Solar Bat Enterprises Inc ....G....... 812 986-3551
Brazil *(G-978)*

EYES: Artificial

Hetzler Ocular Prosthetics ....G....... 317 598-6298
Fishers *(G-3925)*

FABRIC STORES

Gohn Bros Manufacturing Co ....G....... 574 825-2400
Middlebury *(G-9889)*
Pumpkinvine Quilting Inc ....G....... 574 825-1151
Middlebury *(G-9916)*

FABRICATED METAL PRODUCTS, NEC

A & T Metal Fabricators LLC ....G....... 219 949-5066
Gary *(G-5025)*
Amrosia Metal Fabrication Inc ....G....... 812 425-5707
Evansville *(G-3356)*
Core Resources LLC ....G....... 812 829-2240
Spencer *(G-13021)*
Custom Metal Fabrication LLC ....G....... 574 257-8851
Mishawaka *(G-10027)*
Hg Metal Fabrication ....G....... 317 491-3381
Indianapolis *(G-7099)*
Huver Manufacturing Tech LLC ....G....... 317 460-8605
Noblesville *(G-11122)*
JC Metal Fabrication ....G....... 574 340-1109
Mishawaka *(G-10061)*
Michiana Metal Fabricatio ....G....... 574 256-9010
Mishawaka *(G-10083)*
Midwest Industrial Metal ....G....... 260 358-0373
Huntington *(G-6231)*
Orange Cnty Wldg & Fabrication ....G....... 812 653-5754
Orleans *(G-11364)*
Tungsten Company LLC ....G....... 317 788-6732
Indianapolis *(G-8113)*
Tusca 2 ....G....... 812 876-2857
Bloomington *(G-849)*
Twisted Mtal Fbrication Svcs I ....G....... 219 923-8045
Munster *(G-10635)*
Vet Signs LLC ....G....... 937 733-4727
Richmond *(G-12073)*

FABRICS & CLOTH: Quilted

Lavender Patch Fabr Quilts LLC ....G....... 574 848-0011
Bristol *(G-1066)*
Pumpkinvine Quilting Inc ....G....... 574 825-1151
Middlebury *(G-9916)*

FABRICS & YARN: Plastic Coated

Aoc LLC ....D....... 219 465-4384
Valparaiso *(G-13494)*

FABRICS: Acrylic, Broadwoven

Hard Surface Fabrications Inc ....G....... 574 259-4843
Mishawaka *(G-10048)*

FABRICS: Alpacas, Cotton

Onu Acre LLC ....G....... 765 565-1355
Carthage *(G-1515)*

FABRICS: Alpacas, Mohair, Woven

Alpaca Holler LLC ....G....... 513 544-6866
Guilford *(G-5796)*
Blumenau Alpacas ....G....... 219 713-6171
Lowell *(G-9400)*
Cornerstone Woods Alpaca LLC ....G....... 574 546-4179
Bremen *(G-993)*
Duneland Alpacas Ltd ....G....... 219 877-4417
Michigan City *(G-9784)*
Special K Alpacas ....G....... 260 638-4515
Ossian *(G-11408)*

FABRICS: Apparel & Outerwear, Broadwoven

RB Concepts ....G....... 317 735-2172
Bloomington *(G-808)*

FABRICS: Apparel & Outerwear, Cotton

Kleidoscope Quilting ....G....... 812 932-3264
Batesville *(G-507)*

FABRICS: Basket Weave, Cotton

Zig-Zag Crnr Qilts Baskets LLC ....G....... 317 326-3115
Greenfield *(G-5586)*

FABRICS: Bonded-Fiber, Exc Felt

Fiber Bond Corporation ....C....... 219 879-4541
Trail Creek *(G-13441)*

FABRICS: Broadwoven, Cotton

Covers of Indiana Inc ....G....... 317 244-0291
Indianapolis *(G-6680)*
Mpr Corporation ....E....... 574 848-5100
Bristol *(G-1073)*

FABRICS: Broadwoven, Synthetic Manmade Fiber & Silk

Raine Inc ....F....... 765 622-7687
Anderson *(G-157)*
Thorgren Tool & Molding Co ....D....... 219 462-1801
Valparaiso *(G-13628)*

FABRICS: Canvas

Artsy Canvas ....G....... 855 206-9045
Indianapolis *(G-6423)*
Columbus Canvas LLC ....G....... 812 376-9414
Columbus *(G-1874)*
Custom Cut Canvas LLC ....G....... 260 221-3000
Ligonier *(G-9280)*
Hamilton Canvas Inc ....G....... 219 763-1686
Portage *(G-11770)*
Millers Custom Care Candes ....G....... 574 658-4976
Milford *(G-9960)*
Open Canvas LLC ....G....... 317 908-6524
West Lafayette *(G-14091)*
Wine & Canvas South Bend LLC ....G....... 574 807-1562
Elkhart *(G-3263)*
Wine and Canvas Dev LLC ....F....... 317 345-1567
Indianapolis *(G-8204)*
Wnc of Dayton LLC ....G....... 937 999-8868
Indianapolis *(G-8207)*

FABRICS: Canvas & Heavy Coarse, Cotton

Pyro Shield Inc ....F....... 219 661-8600
Crown Point *(G-2290)*

FABRICS: Chemically Coated & Treated

Pmw Holdings LLC ....G....... 317 339-4685
Indianapolis *(G-7703)*

FABRICS: Coated Or Treated

Apparel Promotions Inc ....G....... 574 294-7165
Elkhart *(G-2694)*
C M I Enterprises Inc ....D....... 305 685-9651
Elkhart *(G-2744)*
Clear Edge Filtration Inc ....G....... 219 306-7339
Crown Point *(G-2235)*
Patrick Industries Inc ....C....... 574 255-9692
Mishawaka *(G-10100)*

FABRICS: Denims

House of Bluez ....G....... 812 401-2583
Evansville *(G-3543)*
Maloney Group Inc ....F....... 812 285-7400
Jeffersonville *(G-8395)*

FABRICS: Drills, Cotton

Whitetower Collection LLC ....G....... 847 826-0927
Lafayette *(G-9024)*

FABRICS: Fiberglass, Broadwoven

Altec Engineering Inc ....E....... 574 293-1965
Elkhart *(G-2679)*
Goldshield Fiber Glass Inc ....C....... 260 728-2476
Decatur *(G-2382)*
Kabert Industries Inc ....E....... 765 874-1300
Lynn *(G-9429)*
Sampson Fiberglass Inc ....E....... 574 255-4356
Mishawaka *(G-10120)*
Structural Composites Ind Inc ....D....... 260 894-4083
Ligonier *(G-9296)*

FABRICS: Furniture Denim

Dean Boslers ....G....... 812 476-8787
Evansville *(G-3455)*

FABRICS: Glass & Fiberglass, Broadwoven

Kabert Industries Inc ....D....... 765 874-2335
Lynn *(G-9428)*

FABRICS: Laminated

Mpr Corporation ....E....... 574 848-5100
Bristol *(G-1073)*

FABRICS: Metallized

D K Enterprises LLC ....G....... 260 356-9011
Huntington *(G-6200)*
Ferrill-Fisher Incorporated ....G....... 812 935-9000
Bloomington *(G-724)*

FABRICS: Nonwoven

Carver Non-Woven Tech LLC ....C....... 260 627-0033
Fremont *(G-4954)*
Midwest Nonwovens Indiana LLC ....E....... 317 241-8956
Indianapolis *(G-7508)*
Vita Nonwovens LLC ....E....... 260 747-0990
Fort Wayne *(G-4729)*

FABRICS: Print, Cotton

Scaggs Lrgent Scrnprinting LLC ....G....... 765 362-5477
Crawfordsville *(G-2195)*

FABRICS: Resin Or Plastic Coated

Elite Crete Systems Inc ....E....... 219 465-7671
Valparaiso *(G-13535)*
Sirmax North America Inc ....E....... 765 639-0300
Anderson *(G-167)*

FABRICS: Slip Cover, From Manmade Fiber Or Silk

Slipcover Xpress Inc ....G....... 260 482-7177
Fort Wayne *(G-4631)*

FABRICS: Stockinettes, Knit

McHenry Manufacturing Inc ....F....... 260 824-8146
Bluffton *(G-881)*

FABRICS: Trimmings

A New Company Inc ....F....... 574 293-9088
Elkhart *(G-2658)*
A-1 Awards Inc ....F....... 317 546-9000
Indianapolis *(G-6301)*
American Keeper Corporation ....E....... 765 521-2080
New Castle *(G-10891)*
Arizona Sport Shirts Inc ....G....... 317 481-2160
Indianapolis *(G-6419)*
Asempac Inc ....E....... 812 945-6303
New Albany *(G-10747)*
Berry Plastics Ik LLC ....D....... 641 648-5047
Evansville *(G-3379)*
Big Als Athletics ....G....... 765 836-5203
Mount Summit *(G-10378)*
Blythes Sport Shop Inc ....E....... 219 476-0026
Valparaiso *(G-13510)*
Charles Coons ....G....... 765 362-6509
Crawfordsville *(G-2138)*
Chicago Color Graphics ....G....... 312 856-1433
Hammond *(G-5860)*
Coaches Connection Inc ....G....... 260 356-0400
Huntington *(G-6198)*
Crescendo Inc ....G....... 812 829-4759
Spencer *(G-13022)*
D S E Inc ....G....... 812 376-0310
Columbus *(G-1904)*
Dave Turner ....G....... 765 674-3360
Gas City *(G-5122)*
East 40 Sports Apparel Inc ....G....... 812 877-3695
Terre Haute *(G-13229)*
F Robert Gardner Co Inc ....G....... 317 634-2333
Indianapolis *(G-6900)*
Futaba Indiana America Corp ....B....... 812 895-4700
Vincennes *(G-13683)*
Geckos ....G....... 765 762-0822
Attica *(G-301)*
Graphix Unlimited Inc ....E....... 574 546-3770
Bremen *(G-1000)*
Greensburg Printing Co Inc ....G....... 812 663-8265
Greensburg *(G-5604)*
Greenwood Models Inc ....G....... 317 859-2988
Greenwood *(G-5700)*

Imperial Trophy & Awards Co ....G...... 260 432-8161
   Fort Wayne (G-4361)
Indiana Ribbon Inc ....E...... 219 279-2112
   Wolcott (G-14365)
Kerham Inc ....E...... 260 483-5444
   Fort Wayne (G-4409)
Kewanna Screen Printing Inc ....G...... 574 653-2683
   Kewanna (G-8526)
Masco Corporation of Indiana ....D...... 317 848-1812
   Indianapolis (G-7463)
Mito-Craft Inc...................................G...... 574 287-4555
   South Bend (G-12864)
Modern Muscle Car Factory Inc...........G...... 574 329-6390
   Elkhart (G-3044)
New Hope Services Inc ....E...... 812 752-4892
   Scottsburg (G-12377)
New Hope Services Inc ....E...... 812 288-8248
   Jeffersonville (G-8403)
P J Marketing Services Inc ....G...... 574 259-9843
   South Bend (G-12886)
Safety Vehicle Emblem Inc ....F...... 317 885-7565
   Indianapolis (G-7884)
Select Embroidery/Top It Off..............F...... 812 337-8049
   Bloomington (G-823)
Sir Graphics Inc ....G...... 574 272-9330
   Granger (G-5436)
SPI Binding Co Inc ....E...... 765 794-4992
   Darlington (G-2361)
Spp Inc ....F...... 812 882-6203
   Vincennes (G-13707)
Stallion Sportswear Inc ....E...... 765 584-5097
   Winchester (G-14341)
Stines Printing ....G...... 260 356-5994
   Huntington (G-6253)
Tko Enterprises Inc...........................D...... 317 271-1398
   Plainfield (G-11647)
Winters Assoc Prmtnal Pdts Inc..........F...... 812 330-7000
   Bloomington (G-858)

FABRICS: Upholstery, Cotton

Perfect Seating LLC..........................F...... 317 733-1284
   Zionsville (G-14455)

FABRICS: Upholstery, Wool

Kds Industries LLC............................G...... 574 333-2720
   Elkhart (G-2957)

FABRICS: Wool, Broadwoven

Pendleton Woolen Mills Inc ....D...... 219 879-0326
   Michigan City (G-9828)

FACE PLATES

Touch Plate Technologies Inc.............F...... 260 426-1565
   Fort Wayne (G-4695)

FACILITIES SUPPORT SVCS

Fiserv Mrtg Servicing Systems............C...... 574 282-3300
   South Bend (G-12779)
Johnson Controls Inc ....F...... 812 868-1374
   Evansville (G-3578)
Johnson Controls Inc ....D...... 317 917-5043
   Pittsboro (G-11583)

FACILITY RENTAL & PARTY PLANNING SVCS

Country Moon Winery LLC...................G...... 317 773-7942
   Noblesville (G-11086)

FAMILY CLOTHING STORES

Cool Cayenne LLC.............................G...... 765 282-0977
   Muncie (G-10449)
Springhill Wholesale Inc ....E...... 812 299-2181
   Terre Haute (G-13342)

FANS, BLOWING: Indl Or Commercial

Gsi Group Inc ....E...... 317 787-3047
   Indianapolis (G-7056)
Horner Industrial Services Inc..............F...... 317 634-7165
   Indianapolis (G-7129)
Universal Blower Pac Inc ....E...... 317 773-7256
   Noblesville (G-11198)

FANS, VENTILATING: Indl Or Commercial

Airjet Inc..D...... 574 264-0123
   Elkhart (G-2672)

Lau Industries Inc ....D...... 574 223-3181
   Rochester (G-12132)
New York Blower Company ....C...... 217 347-3233
   La Porte (G-8799)
Thermo-Cycler Industries Inc..............G...... 219 767-2990
   Union Mills (G-13465)

FANS: Ceiling

Fanimation Inc..................................E...... 317 733-4113
   Zionsville (G-14431)

FARM & GARDEN MACHINERY WHOLESALERS

Bane-Welker Equipment LLC...............F...... 812 234-2627
   Terre Haute (G-13197)
Hahn Enterprises Inc ....G...... 574 862-4491
   Wakarusa (G-13778)

FARM MACHINERY REPAIR SVCS

Buffington Electric Motors...................G...... 574 935-5453
   Plymouth (G-11673)
Croy Machine & Fabrication ....G...... 260 565-3682
   Bluffton (G-871)
Fayette Welding Service Inc ....G...... 317 852-2929
   Brownsburg (G-1150)
Pauls Welding ....E...... 574 646-2015
   Nappanee (G-10702)

FARM PRDTS, RAW MATERIALS, WHOLESALE: Feathers

Maple Leaf Inc ....B...... 574 453-4455
   Leesburg (G-9238)

FARM SPLY STORES

Hunter Nutrition Inc ....G...... 765 563-1003
   Brookston (G-1105)

FARM SPLYS WHOLESALERS

Archer-Daniels-Midland Company ....D...... 260 824-0079
   Bluffton (G-864)
Blue River Farm Supply Inc ....G...... 812 364-6675
   Palmyra (G-11435)
Bristow Milling Co LLC.........................G...... 812 843-5176
   Bristow (G-1094)
Co-Alliance LLP ....G...... 765 659-2596
   Frankfort (G-4822)
Helena Agri-Enterprises LLC ....G...... 765 869-5518
   Ambia (G-55)
International A I Inc ....G...... 812 824-2473
   Bloomington (G-750)
Kuntry Lumber and Farm Sup Ltd.........E...... 260 463-3242
   Lagrange (G-9051)
Laughery Valley AG Co-Op Inc ....G...... 812 689-4401
   Osgood (G-11393)
Northwest Farm Fertilizers...................E...... 219 785-2331
   Westville (G-14220)
Premier AG Co-Op Inc ....E...... 812 522-4911
   Seymour (G-12477)
Sun Rise Metal Shop ....G...... 260 463-4026
   Topeka (G-13430)

FARM SPLYS, WHOLESALE: Equestrian Eqpt

Schutz Brothers Inc...........................F...... 260 982-8581
   North Manchester (G-11244)

FARM SPLYS, WHOLESALE: Feed

Archer-Daniels-Midland Company ....E...... 574 773-4131
   Nappanee (G-10647)
Bundy Bros & Sons Inc ....F...... 812 966-2551
   Medora (G-9681)
Co-Alliance LLP ....G...... 765 659-3420
   Frankfort (G-4823)
Co-Alliance LLP ....G...... 765 249-2233
   Michigantown (G-9864)
Co-Alliance Ltd Lblty Partnr ....D...... 317 745-4491
   Avon (G-435)
Hunter Nutrition Inc ....G...... 765 563-1003
   Brookston (G-1105)
Salamonie Mills Inc ....F...... 260 375-2200
   Warren (G-13832)
Wallace Grain Co Inc ....F...... 317 758-4434
   Sheridan (G-12601)

FARM SPLYS, WHOLESALE: Fertilizers & Agricultural Chemicals

AG Plus Inc.......................................G...... 260 623-6121
   Monroeville (G-10190)
Harvest Land Co-Op Inc ....F...... 765 489-4141
   Hagerstown (G-5807)
Kova Fertilizer Inc ....E...... 812 663-5081
   Greensburg (G-5620)
Superior AG Resources Coop Inc ....G...... 812 724-4455
   Owensville (G-11430)

FARM SPLYS, WHOLESALE: Garden Splys

Millburn Peat Company Inc..................E...... 219 362-7025
   La Porte (G-8794)

FARM SPLYS, WHOLESALE: Insecticides

Hub States Corporation.......................G...... 317 816-9955
   Carmel (G-1408)

FARM SPLYS, WHOLESALE: Limestone, Agricultural

Mulzer Crushed Stone Inc ....E...... 812 547-7921
   Tell City (G-13167)

FARM SPLYS, WHOLESALE: Saddlery

Judson Harness & Saddlery ....G...... 765 569-0918
   Rockville (G-12176)

FASTENERS: Brads, Alum, Brass/Other Nonferrous Metal/Wire

Intermetco Processing Inc ....G...... 812 423-5914
   Evansville (G-3564)

FASTENERS: Metal

Elgin Fastener Group LLC ....G...... 812 689-8917
   Versailles (G-13653)
TEC-Tool Inc ....E...... 812 526-3158
   Indianapolis (G-8044)

FASTENERS: Metal

Indiana U Bolts Inc.............................E...... 317 870-1940
   Waterloo (G-14015)

FASTENERS: Notions, NEC

Archimedes Inc ....G...... 260 347-3903
   Kendallville (G-8455)
B&H Industries Corporation ....G...... 765 794-4428
   Darlington (G-2360)
Bollhoff Inc ....E...... 260 347-3903
   Kendallville (G-8461)
Enterkin Manufacturing Co Inc.............E...... 317 462-4477
   Greenfield (G-5529)
Nicholson Group LLC..........................G...... 219 926-3528
   Chesterton (G-1624)
Rightway Fasteners Inc.......................C...... 812 342-2700
   Columbus (G-2009)
Scotts Fasteners & Supply LLC ....G...... 317 372-8743
   Danville (G-2357)
Smart Machine Inc ....G...... 219 922-0706
   Hammond (G-5942)

FASTENERS: Wire, Made From Purchased Wire

Dekko Acquisition Parent Inc ....G...... 260 347-0700
   Kendallville (G-8472)

FAUCETS & SPIGOTS: Metal & Plastic

Lasalle Bristol Corporation..................C...... 574 936-9894
   Plymouth (G-11701)

FEATHERS & FEATHER PRODUCTS

LSI Wallcovering Inc...........................D...... 502 458-1502
   New Albany (G-10820)

FENCES & FENCING MATERIALS

Indiana Wire Products Inc....................F...... 812 663-7441
   Greensburg (G-5615)

PRODUCT

FENCES OR POSTS: Ornamental Iron Or Steel

Decor Ironworks Inc ....G...... 219 865-1222
Dyer *(G-2493)*
Ironcraft Co Inc ....G...... 574 272-0866
South Bend *(G-12819)*
K & K Fence Inc ....E...... 317 359-5425
Indianapolis *(G-7326)*

FENCING DEALERS

Hunter Nutrition Inc ....G...... 765 563-1003
Brookston *(G-1105)*
K & K Fence Inc ....E...... 317 359-5425
Indianapolis *(G-7326)*
Wunder Co Inc ....F...... 219 962-8573
Lake Station *(G-9081)*

FENCING MATERIALS: Docks & Other Outdoor Prdts, Wood

Ecovantage LLC ....G...... 260 337-0338
Saint Joe *(G-12254)*
Jt-Fencing LLC ....G...... 765 323-8591
Lafayette *(G-8934)*

FENCING MATERIALS: Plastic

Mide Products LLC ....G...... 574 333-5906
Goshen *(G-5290)*
Wunder Co Inc ....F...... 219 962-8573
Lake Station *(G-9081)*

FENCING MATERIALS: Wood

Menard Inc ....A...... 812 466-1234
Terre Haute *(G-13282)*
Quality Fence Ltd ....G...... 260 768-4986
Shipshewana *(G-12645)*

FENCING: Chain Link

Ifc Fence LLC ....G...... 219 977-4000
Gary *(G-5067)*
Merchants Metals LLC ....D...... 574 831-4060
New Paris *(G-10990)*

FENDERS: Automobile, Stamped Or Pressed Metal

Body Panels Co ....F...... 812 962-6262
Evansville *(G-3388)*
Fenders Inc ....G...... 574 293-3717
Elkhart *(G-2847)*

FERTILIZER MINERAL MINING

Excel Co-Op Inc ....G...... 219 984-5950
Reynolds *(G-11945)*

FERTILIZER, AGRICULTURAL: Wholesalers

AG Plus Inc ....E...... 260 723-5141
South Whitley *(G-12996)*
Andersons Agriculture Group LP ....F...... 765 564-6135
Delphi *(G-2414)*
Andersons Agriculture Group LP ....E...... 574 626-2522
Galveston *(G-4993)*
Andersons Fertilizer Service ....G...... 765 538-3285
Romney *(G-12202)*
Clunette Elevator Co Inc ....F...... 574 858-2281
Leesburg *(G-9234)*
Don Hartman Oil Co Inc ....G...... 765 643-5026
Anderson *(G-98)*
Frick Services Inc ....E...... 260 761-3311
Wawaka *(G-14032)*
Roy Umbarger and Sons Inc ....F...... 317 422-5195
Bargersville *(G-486)*

FERTILIZERS: NEC

Agbest Cooperative Inc ....G...... 765 358-3388
Gaston *(G-5129)*
Andersons Agriculture Group LP ....F...... 574 753-4974
Logansport *(G-9321)*
Andersons Agriculture Group LP ....E...... 574 626-2522
Galveston *(G-4993)*
Andersons Fertilizer Service ....G...... 765 538-3285
Romney *(G-12202)*
Bundy Bros & Sons Inc ....F...... 812 966-2551
Medora *(G-9681)*

Ceres Solutions Coop Inc ....G...... 765 473-3922
Peru *(G-11521)*
Clunette Elevator Co Inc ....F...... 574 858-2281
Leesburg *(G-9234)*
Co-Alliance LLP ....G...... 765 249-2233
Michigantown *(G-9864)*
Co-Alliance LLP ....G...... 765 659-3420
Frankfort *(G-4823)*
Co-Alliance Ltd Lblty Partnr ....D...... 317 745-4491
Avon *(G-435)*
Harvest Land Co-Op Inc ....G...... 317 861-5080
Fountaintown *(G-4791)*
Harvest Land Co-Op Inc ....F...... 765 489-4141
Hagerstown *(G-5807)*
Kova Fertilizer Inc ....E...... 812 663-5081
Greensburg *(G-5620)*
Laughery Valley AG Co-Op Inc ....E...... 812 689-4401
Osgood *(G-11393)*
Lesco Inc ....G...... 317 876-7968
Indianapolis *(G-7398)*
Md/Lf Incorporated ....G...... 765 575-8130
New Castle *(G-10912)*
Miles Farm Supply LLC ....F...... 812 359-4463
Boonville *(G-917)*
Nachurs Alpine Solutions Corp ....G...... 812 738-1333
Corydon *(G-2106)*
Northwest Farm Fertilizers ....G...... 219 785-2331
Westville *(G-14220)*
Rogers Group Inc ....E...... 812 882-3640
Vincennes *(G-13703)*
Roy Umbarger and Sons Inc ....F...... 317 422-5195
Bargersville *(G-486)*
Superior AG Resources Coop Inc ....G...... 812 724-4455
Owensville *(G-11430)*
Wilson Fertilizer & Grain Inc ....G...... 574 223-3175
Rochester *(G-12161)*

FERTILIZERS: Nitrogenous

Andersons Agriculture Group LP ....F...... 574 753-4974
Logansport *(G-9321)*
Co-Alliance LLP ....G...... 765 659-2596
Frankfort *(G-4822)*
Knox Fertilizer Company Inc ....G...... 574 772-6275
Knox *(G-8570)*

FERTILIZERS: Phosphatic

Andersons Agriculture Group LP ....F...... 574 753-4974
Logansport *(G-9321)*
Wilson Fertilizer & Grain Inc ....G...... 574 223-3175
Rochester *(G-12161)*

FIBER & FIBER PRDTS: Organic, Noncellulose

Debra Schneider ....G...... 317 420-9360
Arcadia *(G-263)*
Indy Composite Works Inc ....E...... 317 280-9766
Indianapolis *(G-7214)*

FIBER & FIBER PRDTS: Protein

Butterfield Foods LLC ....C...... 317 776-4775
Noblesville *(G-11075)*

FIBER & FIBER PRDTS: Soybean

Energy Two Inc ....G...... 812 497-3113
Seymour *(G-12447)*

FIBER & FIBER PRDTS: Synthetic Cellulosic

Applied Composites Engrg Inc ....E...... 317 243-4225
Indianapolis *(G-6411)*
Huhtamaki Inc ....C...... 219 972-4264
Hammond *(G-5896)*

FIBER & FIBER PRDTS: Vinyl

Fdc Graphics Films Inc ....D...... 574 273-4400
South Bend *(G-12774)*

FIBERS: Carbon & Graphite

Applied Composites Engrg Inc ....E...... 317 243-4225
Indianapolis *(G-6411)*
Composite Specialties ....G...... 317 852-1408
Brownsburg *(G-1144)*

FILM & SHEET: Unsuppported Plastic

Avery Dennison Corporation ....D...... 219 696-7777
Lowell *(G-9399)*

Azimuth Custom Extrusions LLC ....E...... 812 423-6180
Evansville *(G-3368)*
B&F Plastics Inc ....D...... 765 962-6125
Richmond *(G-11959)*
Bcw Diversified Inc ....E...... 765 644-2033
Anderson *(G-73)*
Berry Global Inc ....G...... 812 334-7090
Bloomington *(G-679)*
Berry Global Inc ....G...... 812 386-1525
Princeton *(G-11865)*
Berry Global Inc ....G...... 765 966-1414
Richmond *(G-11964)*
Berry Global Inc ....E...... 812 867-6671
Evansville *(G-3375)*
Berry Global Inc ....B...... 765 962-4253
Richmond *(G-11965)*
Berry Global Inc ....A...... 812 424-2904
Evansville *(G-3376)*
D and M Enterprises LLC ....F...... 260 483-4008
Fort Wayne *(G-4197)*
Futurex Industries Inc ....E...... 765 498-8900
Bloomingdale *(G-648)*
Hoosier Fiberglass Industries ....F...... 812 232-5027
Terre Haute *(G-13248)*
Ie Products Mad Dasher Inc ....E...... 260 747-0545
Fort Wayne *(G-4357)*
Pactiv Corporation ....C...... 574 936-7065
Plymouth *(G-11709)*
Polymer Science Inc ....E...... 574 583-3751
Monticello *(G-10280)*
Sabic Innovative Plastics Mt V ....A...... 812 838-4385
Mount Vernon *(G-10407)*
Sonoco Products Company ....C...... 812 526-5511
Edinburgh *(G-2629)*
Specialty Adhesive Film Co ....G...... 812 926-0156
Aurora *(G-387)*

FILM DEVELOPING SVCS

Graphik Mechanix Inc ....G...... 260 426-7001
Fort Wayne *(G-4303)*

FILM PROCESSING & FINISHING LABORATORY

Budget Printing Centers Inc ....G...... 812 282-8832
Jeffersonville *(G-8334)*

FILM: Motion Picture

Heartland Film Inc ....G...... 317 464-9405
Indianapolis *(G-7085)*
Success Entrmt Group Intl Inc ....G...... 260 490-9990
Ossian *(G-11409)*
Success Holding Group Corp USA ....G...... 260 490-9990
Ossian *(G-11410)*

FILTER ELEMENTS: Fluid & Hydraulic Line

Hook Industrial Sales Inc ....D...... 260 432-9441
Fort Wayne *(G-4342)*
Hy-Pro Corporation ....D...... 317 849-3535
Anderson *(G-117)*
S&F Manufacturing Inc ....D...... 574 278-7865
Winamac *(G-14321)*

FILTERING MEDIA: Pottery

Daramic LLC ....C...... 812 738-8274
Corydon *(G-2097)*

FILTERS

Alpha-Pure Corporation ....G...... 877 645-7676
Trail Creek *(G-13440)*
Asl Technologies LLC ....G...... 219 733-2777
Wanatah *(G-13820)*
Burgess Enterprises LLC ....G...... 260 615-5194
Albion *(G-18)*
Clear Decision Filtration Inc ....F...... 219 567-2008
Francesville *(G-4809)*
Cpp Filter Corporation ....G...... 765 446-8416
Lafayette *(G-8881)*
Don Detzer LLC ....G...... 812 362-7599
Tennyson *(G-13179)*
Donaldson Company Inc ....G...... 952 887-3131
Monticello *(G-10260)*
Esco Technologies Inc ....G...... 317 346-0393
Franklin *(G-4884)*
F D Deskins Company Inc ....F...... 317 284-4014
Fishers *(G-3909)*
Filters Plus ....G...... 812 430-0347
Evansville *(G-3504)*

GLS Machining & Design LLC ....G...... 765 754-8248
  Alexandria *(G-44)*
Gvs Filter Technology Inc ....G...... 317 442-3925
  Zionsville *(G-14437)*
Heartland Filled Machine LLC...............G...... 574 223-6931
  Rochester *(G-12127)*
Rosedale Filters LLC ....G...... 219 879-4700
  Michigan City *(G-9835)*
Spencer Machine and TI Co Inc...........E...... 812 282-6300
  Jeffersonville *(G-8426)*
SRK Filters LLC ....G...... 765 647-9962
  Cedar Grove *(G-1523)*
T and T Hydraulics Inc.........................G...... 765 548-2355
  Rosedale *(G-12207)*
U S Filter ....G...... 317 280-4251
  Indianapolis *(G-8121)*
U S Filter Distribution ....G...... 317 271-1463
  Indianapolis *(G-8122)*
United States Filter ....G...... 812 471-0414
  Evansville *(G-3788)*

FILTERS & SOFTENERS: Water, Household

American Melt Blown Filtration ......E...... 219 866-3500
  Rensselaer *(G-11912)*
Astbury Water Technology Inc ....D...... 317 328-7153
  Indianapolis *(G-6431)*
H20 Factory ....G...... 812 858-1948
  Newburgh *(G-11030)*
Leach & Sons WaterCare ....G...... 317 248-8954
  Danville *(G-2351)*
New Aqua LLC ....D...... 317 272-3000
  Avon *(G-456)*
On The Go Portble Wtr Sftnr LL ....F...... 260 482-9614
  Bloomington *(G-788)*
Puritan Water Conditioning ....F...... 765 362-6340
  Crawfordsville *(G-2189)*

FILTERS: Air

American Air Filter Co Inc ....D...... 888 223-2003
  Lebanon *(G-9167)*
Blocksom & Co ....G...... 219 878-4455
  Michigan City *(G-9770)*
Purolator Pdts A Filtration Co...............C...... 866 925-2247
  Jeffersonville *(G-8418)*

FILTERS: Air Intake, Internal Combustion Engine, Exc Auto

Konal Automated Systems Inc ....D...... 616 659-4774
  Elkhart *(G-2974)*
Rayco Mch & Engrg Group Inc.............E...... 317 291-7848
  Indianapolis *(G-7819)*

FILTERS: General Line, Indl

Action Filtration Inc ....G...... 812 546-6262
  Hope *(G-6110)*
Bofrebo Industries Inc.........................E...... 219 322-1550
  Schererville *(G-12318)*
Enviro Filtration Inc ....G...... 815 469-2871
  Gary *(G-5044)*
Filtration Plus Inc ....E...... 219 879-0663
  Michigan City *(G-9793)*
Lesac Corporation ....E...... 219 879-3215
  Michigan City *(G-9810)*
Pittsfield Products Inc ....D...... 260 488-2124
  Hamilton *(G-5826)*
Sullair LLC ....B...... 219 879-5451
  Michigan City *(G-9849)*

FILTRATION DEVICES: Electronic

Andon Specialties Inc..........................G...... 317 983-1700
  Indianapolis *(G-6400)*
Arctic Clear Products Inc ....G...... 574 533-7671
  Goshen *(G-5172)*
Chemtrex LLC ....G...... 317 508-4223
  Noblesville *(G-11080)*
Separation Technologies Inc ....G...... 219 548-5814
  Valparaiso *(G-13614)*
Sonicu LLC ....G...... 317 468-2345
  Greenfield *(G-5576)*
Tetrasolv Inc ....F...... 765 643-3941
  Anderson *(G-176)*
Tri Star Filtration Inc ....G...... 317 337-0940
  Indianapolis *(G-8095)*

FINANCIAL INVESTMENT ADVICE

Horizon Publishing Company LLC.......E...... 219 852-3200
  Hammond *(G-5895)*

Worth Tax and Financial Svc ....G...... 574 267-4687
  Warsaw *(G-13969)*

FINANCIAL SVCS

Oxinas Partners LLC ....G...... 812 725-8649
  Jeffersonville *(G-8411)*
Sentinel Services Inc ....F...... 574 360-5279
  Granger *(G-5432)*

FINDINGS & TRIMMINGS: Fabric

Fiedeke Vinyl Coverings Inc ....F...... 574 534-3408
  Goshen *(G-5214)*
Quality Converters Inc.........................E...... 260 829-6541
  Orland *(G-11356)*

FINGERNAILS, ARTIFICIAL

Cali Nail ....G...... 574 674-4126
  Osceola *(G-11373)*
Lil Girls Glam LLC ....G...... 317 507-3443
  Indianapolis *(G-7406)*

FINGERPRINTING SVCS

Workflow Solutions LLC ....G...... 502 627-0257
  New Albany *(G-10875)*

FINISHING AGENTS

Restorco Inc ....F...... 812 882-3987
  Vincennes *(G-13700)*

FINISHING SVCS

Crossrads Rhbilitation Ctr Inc...............C...... 317 897-7320
  Indianapolis *(G-6697)*

FIRE ALARM MAINTENANCE & MONITORING SVCS

American Fire Company.........................G...... 219 840-0630
  Valparaiso *(G-13491)*

FIRE ARMS, SMALL: Guns Or Gun Parts, 30 mm & Below

Acme Sports Inc...................................G...... 812 522-4008
  Seymour *(G-12426)*
Blythes Sport Shop Inc ....F...... 219 924-4403
  Griffith *(G-5766)*
Eds Trading Post Inc ....G...... 317 933-4867
  Nineveh *(G-11057)*
Favres Gun Shop ....G...... 812 235-0198
  Terre Haute *(G-13234)*
Namacle LLC ....G...... 574 320-1436
  Elkhart *(G-3056)*
Patriot Arms ....G...... 812 859-4293
  Coal City *(G-1743)*
Rajo Guns Corp....................................G...... 812 422-6945
  Evansville *(G-3694)*
Red Bull Armory LLC ....G...... 757 287-7738
  Mitchell *(G-10169)*
Solotat Industries LLC ....G...... 574 320-1436
  Elkhart *(G-3180)*
Suppress TEC LLC ....G...... 812 453-5813
  Elberfeld *(G-2640)*
Wraith Arms Resolutions LLC ....G...... 812 380-1208
  Velpen *(G-13650)*

FIRE ARMS, SMALL: Pistols Or Pistol Parts, 30 mm & below

Headstamp Fine Brass LLC ....G...... 812 212-8326
  Batesville *(G-502)*

FIRE CONTROL EQPT REPAIR SVCS, MILITARY

Integrity Defense Services Inc..............F...... 812 675-4913
  Springville *(G-13064)*

FIRE CONTROL OR BOMBING EQPT: Electronic

T Shorter Manufacturing Inc ....G...... 574 264-4131
  Elkhart *(G-3203)*

FIRE DETECTION SYSTEMS

Grunau Company Inc.............................E...... 317 872-7360
  Indianapolis *(G-7054)*

FIRE EXTINGUISHER SVC

American Eagle Security Inc..................G...... 219 980-1177
  Merrillville *(G-9696)*

FIRE EXTINGUISHERS, WHOLESALE

Abro Industries Inc ....E...... 574 232-8289
  South Bend *(G-12692)*

FIRE OR BURGLARY RESISTIVE PRDTS

Davis Hezakih Corp ....F...... 260 768-7300
  Shipshewana *(G-12611)*
E & H Bridge & Grating Inc ....E...... 812 277-8343
  Bedford *(G-538)*
Fire King Security Pdts LLC ....C...... 812 948-8400
  New Albany *(G-10780)*
Midwest Indus Met Fbrction Inc ....E...... 260 356-5262
  Huntington *(G-6230)*
Rko Enterprises LLC ....G...... 812 273-8813
  Madison *(G-9492)*
S C Pryor Inc ....E...... 317 352-1281
  Indianapolis *(G-7878)*
Schafer Industries Inc ....D...... 574 234-4116
  South Bend *(G-12929)*
Tru-Flex LLC ....C...... 765 893-4403
  West Lebanon *(G-14122)*

FIRE PROTECTION EQPT

Task Force Tips Inc..............................C...... 219 462-6161
  Valparaiso *(G-13626)*
Thomas L Wehr ....G...... 317 835-7824
  Fairland *(G-3827)*
Tier 1 Medical LLC ....G...... 317 316-7871
  Carmel *(G-1497)*

FIREARMS & AMMUNITION, EXC SPORTING, WHOLESALE

A & W Firearms ....G...... 765 716-6856
  Yorktown *(G-14400)*
Blythes Sport Shop Inc ....F...... 219 924-4403
  Griffith *(G-5766)*
Leeps Supply Co ....G...... 219 696-9511
  Lowell *(G-9413)*
Solotat Industries LLC ....G...... 574 320-1436
  Elkhart *(G-3180)*

FIREARMS: Large, Greater Than 30mm

A & W Firearms ....G...... 765 716-6856
  Yorktown *(G-14400)*
J DS Big Boys Toys ....G...... 219 365-7807
  Saint John *(G-12264)*
Zr Tactical Solutions LLC ....G...... 317 721-9787
  Noblesville *(G-11201)*

FIREARMS: Small, 30mm or Less

BCI Defense LLC...................................G...... 574 546-2411
  Bremen *(G-983)*
CF Gunworks LLC..................................G...... 317 538-1122
  Frankfort *(G-4821)*
Enterprise MGT Solutions LLC...............G...... 219 545-8544
  Merrillville *(G-9713)*

FIREPLACE EQPT & ACCESS

American Flame Inc ....D...... 260 459-1703
  Fort Wayne *(G-4070)*
Bottom Line Management Inc ....F...... 812 944-7388
  Clarksville *(G-1674)*
Gibson Brothers Welding Inc ....F...... 765 948-5775
  Fairmount *(G-3832)*
Seymour Manufacturing Co Inc.............C...... 812 522-2900
  Seymour *(G-12485)*

FIREWORKS

Bada Boom Fireworks LLC ....G...... 219 472-6700
  Gary *(G-5029)*
Dannys Fireworks ....F...... 219 324-5757
  La Porte *(G-8748)*
Jackson Hewitt Tax Service ....C...... 574 255-2200
  Mishawaka *(G-10057)*
Johnny Lemas ....G...... 260 833-8850
  Angola *(G-222)*
Kaplan Enterprises Inc ....G...... 219 933-7993
  Hammond *(G-5904)*
Lynch Fireworks Display Inc ....G...... 812 537-1750
  Greendale *(G-5490)*

PRODUCT

Mark & Jessies Firework Shack ....G...... 812 372-3855
Columbus **(G-1968)**

Melrose Pyrotechnics Inc ....G...... 219 393-5522
Kingsbury **(G-8542)**

Millennial Fireworks..........................G...... 812 732-5126
Mauckport **(G-9657)**

Patriotic Fireworks Inc ....G...... 317 381-0529
Indianapolis **(G-7662)**

Pyrotechnic Productions Inc ....G...... 812 448-8196
Brazil **(G-976)**

Sky Fire Group LLC ....G...... 812 623-8980
Sunman **(G-13118)**

Sky King Unlimited Inc ....F...... 574 271-9170
South Bend **(G-12938)**

Vw Co ....G...... 812 397-0102
Shelburn **(G-12512)**

FIREWORKS DISPLAY SVCS

Pyrotechnic Productions Inc ....G...... 812 448-8196
Brazil **(G-976)**

FIRST AID SPLYS, WHOLESALE

Wildman Business Group LLC ....C...... 866 369-1552
Warsaw **(G-13965)**

Workflow Solutions LLC ....G...... 502 627-0257
New Albany **(G-10875)**

FISH & SEAFOOD PROCESSORS: Fresh Or Frozen

Bell Aquaculture LLC ....E...... 765 369-3100
Redkey **(G-11896)**

Ohio Valley Caviar ....G...... 812 338-4367
English **(G-3317)**

FISHING EQPT REPAIR SVCS

Robert J Matt..............................G...... 317 831-2400
Mooresville **(G-10337)**

FISHING EQPT: Lures

EMB Fishing LLC ....G...... 317 244-8741
Indianapolis **(G-6847)**

FITTINGS & ASSEMBLIES: Hose & Tube, Hydraulic Or Pneumatic

Cindon Inc ....F...... 812 853-5450
Newburgh **(G-11024)**

Dependable Rubber Industrial..............G...... 765 447-5654
Lafayette **(G-8887)**

Innovtive Hydrlic Slutions LLC............G...... 317 252-0120
Indianapolis **(G-7239)**

Kilgore Manufacturing Co Inc..............D...... 260 248-2002
Columbia City **(G-1804)**

Kobaltec LLC...............................G...... 219 462-1483
Valparaiso **(G-13567)**

Macallister Machinery Co Inc..............D...... 260 483-6469
Fort Wayne **(G-4447)**

Mary Jonas ....F...... 317 500-0600
Indianapolis **(G-7462)**

P H C Industries Inc.......................G...... 260 423-9461
Fort Wayne **(G-4516)**

Parker-Hannifin Corporation...............A...... 260 748-6000
New Haven **(G-10951)**

Techna-Fit Inc.............................G...... 317 350-2153
Brownsburg **(G-1174)**

Terry Liquidation III Inc..................D...... 219 362-9908
La Porte **(G-8828)**

FITTINGS: Pipe

Elkhart Products Corporation..............C...... 260 368-7246
Geneva **(G-5135)**

Indiana Seal ....G...... 317 841-3547
Indianapolis **(G-7190)**

JM Fittings LLC............................D...... 260 747-9200
Fort Wayne **(G-4396)**

FITTINGS: Pipe, Fabricated

Barry Company Inc..........................G...... 317 578-2486
Fishers **(G-3874)**

FIXTURES & EQPT: Kitchen, Metal, Exc Cast Aluminum

Premier Concepts Inc ....G...... 574 269-7570
Warsaw **(G-13929)**

Zojila LLC.................................G...... 765 404-3767
Lafayette **(G-9029)**

FIXTURES: Cut Stone

Imperial Marble Incorporated...............F...... 812 752-5384
Scottsburg **(G-12364)**

Roman Marblene Company Inc ....F...... 812 738-1367
Corydon **(G-2110)**

FLAGPOLES

Original Tractor Cab Co Inc ....E...... 765 663-2214
Arlington **(G-282)**

FLARES

Sharyls Hair With Flare....................G...... 765 885-5121
Fowler **(G-4806)**

FLAT GLASS: Sheet

Calumite Company LLC ....F...... 219 787-8667
Portage **(G-11753)**

FLAT GLASS: Tempered

Cleer Vision Tempered GL LLC ....E...... 574 262-0449
Elkhart **(G-2758)**

FLAT GLASS: Window, Clear & Colored

Graber Therm-O-Loc Windows...............G...... 812 486-3273
Montgomery **(G-10225)**

Mr Tintz ....G...... 219 844-5500
Hammond **(G-5919)**

Tint Unlimited ....G...... 812 402-6102
Evansville **(G-3764)**

FLOCKING METAL PRDTS

Decatur Plastic Products Inc ....D...... 812 352-6050
North Vernon **(G-11254)**

FLOOR COVERING STORES

Faulkens Floorcover........................F...... 574 300-4260
South Bend **(G-12773)**

Indiana Rug Company ....G...... 574 252-4653
Mishawaka **(G-10053)**

Jack Laurie Coml Floors Inc ....G...... 317 569-2095
Indianapolis **(G-7293)**

Stock Building Supply LLC ....E...... 260 490-0616
Fort Wayne **(G-4650)**

Todd K Hockemeyer Inc ....G...... 260 639-3591
Fort Wayne **(G-4689)**

FLOOR COVERING STORES: Carpets

Fashion Flooring and Ltg Inc...............G...... 219 531-5667
Valparaiso **(G-13540)**

Indiana Lumber Inc ....G...... 812 837-9493
Bloomington **(G-746)**

Shelby Westside Upholstering ....G...... 317 631-8911
Indianapolis **(G-7931)**

FLOOR COVERINGS WHOLESALERS

Faulkens Floorcover........................F...... 574 300-4260
South Bend **(G-12773)**

Lasalle Bristol Corporation................G...... 574 936-9894
Plymouth **(G-11701)**

Lasalle Bristol Corporation................E...... 574 295-4400
Bristol **(G-1065)**

Lasalle Bristol Corporation................C...... 574 295-4400
Elkhart **(G-2985)**

Todd K Hockemeyer Inc ....G...... 260 639-3591
Fort Wayne **(G-4689)**

FLOOR COVERINGS: Rubber

DSM Coating Resins Inc.....................F...... 765 659-4721
Frankfort **(G-4829)**

Excell Usa Inc.............................D...... 812 895-1687
Vincennes **(G-13678)**

Midwest Rubber Products Inc ....G...... 317 237-4037
Indianapolis **(G-7511)**

FLOOR COVERINGS: Textile Fiber

Faulkens Floorcover........................F...... 574 300-4260
South Bend **(G-12773)**

FLOOR COVERINGS: Tile, Support Plastic

Quick Walk Systems Inc.....................G...... 317 255-2247
Indianapolis **(G-7804)**

FLOOR COVERINGS: Twisted Paper, Grass, Reed, Coir, Etc

Recreation Insites LLC ....G...... 317 578-0588
Fishers **(G-3961)**

FLOORING & SIDING: Metal

Nicorr LLC ....G...... 574 353-1700
Tippecanoe **(G-13384)**

FLOORING: Baseboards, Wood

Ecojacks LLC...............................G...... 574 306-0414
South Whitley **(G-12998)**

FLOORING: Hard Surface

Eagle Flooring Brokers Inc ....G...... 260 422-6100
Fort Wayne **(G-4231)**

Sorbashock LLC ....G...... 574 520-9784
Fort Wayne **(G-4635)**

FLOORING: Hardwood

Cross Country Hardwoods LLC ....F...... 812 571-4226
Vevay **(G-13661)**

Floortech..................................G...... 317 887-6825
Indianapolis **(G-6939)**

Indiana Hardwood Specialists...............G...... 812 829-4866
Spencer **(G-13028)**

James A Andrew Inc ....G...... 765 269-9807
Lafayette **(G-8929)**

Jeff Hury Hardwood Floors Pntg............G...... 812 204-8650
Evansville **(G-3574)**

Kentucky Wood Floors LLC..................E...... 812 256-2164
Borden **(G-932)**

Knies Sawmill Inc ....G...... 812 683-3402
Huntingburg **(G-6173)**

Langfords Delivery Service..................G...... 317 996-3594
Monrovia **(G-10204)**

Santarossa Mosaic Tile Co Inc ....C...... 317 632-9494
Indianapolis **(G-7895)**

FLOORING: Rubber

Recreation Insites LLC ....G...... 317 578-0588
Fishers **(G-3961)**

FLORIST: Flowers, Fresh

Larry Flowers Wholesale....................G...... 765 747-5156
Muncie **(G-10509)**

FLORISTS

Kroger Co ....C...... 574 291-0740
South Bend **(G-12830)**

Schnuck Markets Inc ....C...... 812 853-9505
Newburgh **(G-11046)**

Sweet Art Inc ....G...... 317 787-3647
Indianapolis **(G-8026)**

FLORISTS' SPLYS, WHOLESALE

Candles By Dar Inc ....F...... 260 482-2099
Fort Wayne **(G-4139)**

FLOWERS & NURSERY STOCK, WHOLESALE

Salt Creek Harvest LLC ....G...... 708 927-5569
Valparaiso **(G-13611)**

FLOWERS, ARTIFICIAL, WHOLESALE

Floralcraft Distributors ....G...... 574 262-2639
Elkhart **(G-2859)**

Jadco Ltd ....F...... 219 661-2065
Crown Point **(G-2265)**

FLOWERS: Artificial & Preserved

Memories By Design Inc ....G...... 317 254-1708
Indianapolis **(G-7478)**

FLUES & PIPES: Stove Or Furnace

Kitchen Queen LLC..........................G...... 812 662-8399
Saint Paul **(G-12277)**

FLUID METERS & COUNTING DEVICES

Dwyer Instruments Inc ....D 260 723-5138
South Whitley (G-12997)

FLUID POWER PUMPS & MOTORS

American Gorwood Corporation ....E 765 948-3401
Fairmount (G-3829)
Camco Manufacturing Inc ....F 574 264-1491
Elkhart (G-2747)
Crown Elec Svcs & Automtn Inc ....D 972 929-4700
Portage (G-11758)
D A Hochstetler & Sons LLP ....F 574 642-1144
Topeka (G-13416)
Elevator Equipment Corporation..........D 765 966-7761
Richmond (G-11981)
Freudenberg-Nok General Partnr ....B 260 894-7183
Ligonier (G-9285)
Gravel Conveyors Inc ....F 317 873-8686
Zionsville (G-14435)
Hy-Matic Mfg Inc ....E 260 347-3651
Kendallville (G-8479)
Jomar Machining & Fabg Inc ....E 574 825-9837
Middlebury (G-9897)
Met-Pro Technologies LLC ....E 317 293-2930
Indianapolis (G-7485)
Murray Equipment Inc ....D 260 484-0382
Fort Wayne (G-4486)
Nidec Motor Corporation......................D 812 385-2564
Princeton (G-11880)
Parker-Hannifin Corporation ....F 219 736-0400
Merrillville (G-9744)
Parker-Hannifin Corporation ....D 812 547-4710
Tell City (G-13171)
Parker-Hannifin Corporation ....G 502 810-5823
Jeffersonville (G-8412)
Parker-Hannifin Corporation ....C 574 528-9400
Syracuse (G-13139)
R P S Hydraulics Sales & Svc ....E 219 845-5526
Hammond (G-5931)
Steel Parts Corporation ....B 765 675-2191
Tipton (G-13406)
Terry Liquidation III Inc ....E 219 362-3557
La Porte (G-8829)

FLUID POWER VALVES & HOSE FITTINGS

Coupled Products LLC ....B 260 248-3200
Columbia City (G-1776)
Hitachi Cble Auto Pdts USA Inc ....C 812 945-9011
New Albany (G-10796)
JM Fittings LLC ....D 260 747-9200
Fort Wayne (G-4396)
Proportion-Air Inc ....D 317 335-2602
McCordsville (G-9674)
R P S Hydraulics Sales & Svc ....E 219 845-5526
Hammond (G-5931)
Slb Corporation ....F 574 255-9774
Mishawaka (G-10125)
Tri-State Hydraulics Indus Sup ....G 812 537-3485
Greendale (G-5495)

FM & AM RADIO TUNERS

Continntal Broadcast Group LLC..........E 317 924-1071
Indianapolis (G-6657)
Mobile Communications Tech ....G 812 423-7322
Evansville (G-3631)

FOAM CHARGE MIXTURES

Crown Technology Inc ....E 317 845-0045
Indianapolis (G-6700)
Kibbechem Inc ....E 574 266-1234
Elkhart (G-2964)

FOAM RUBBER

Exemplary Foam Inc ....E 574 295-8888
Elkhart (G-2841)
Foamcraft Inc ....D 574 534-4343
Goshen (G-5216)
General Furniture & Bedg Pdts ....G 317 849-2670
Indianapolis (G-6997)
Hi-Tech Foam Products LLC ....E 270 684-8331
Indianapolis (G-7105)
Indiana Spray Foam ....G 219 696-6100
Lowell (G-9408)
Pactiv Corporation ....C 574 936-7065
Plymouth (G-11709)

FOAMS & RUBBER, WHOLESALE

Foam Rubber LLC ....C 765 521-2000
New Castle (G-10901)
Foamcraft Inc ....D 574 293-8569
Elkhart (G-2860)
Foamcraft Inc ....D 574 534-4343
Goshen (G-5216)
Vahala Foam Inc ....D 574 293-1287
Elkhart (G-3240)

FOIL & LEAF: Metal

API Americas Inc ....G 812 689-6502
Osgood (G-11388)
Avery Dennison Corporation ....D 219 696-7777
Lowell (G-9399)
Revere Industries LLC ....G 317 580-2420
Westfield (G-14184)

FOIL: Laminated To Paper Or Other Materials

Foil Laminating Inc ....E 574 935-3645
Plymouth (G-11686)

FOLIAGE: Artificial & Preserved

American Oak Preserving Co Inc ....E 574 896-2171
North Judson (G-11206)

FOOD COLORINGS

Sugarpaste ....G 574 276-8703
South Bend (G-12960)

FOOD PRDTS, CANNED OR FRESH PACK: Vegetable Juices

Caj Food Products Inc ....F 888 524-6882
Fishers (G-3884)

FOOD PRDTS, CANNED: Barbecue Sauce

Douglas K Gresham ....G 812 445-3174
Seymour (G-12446)

FOOD PRDTS, CANNED: Beans & Bean Sprouts

Eden Foods Inc ....E 765 396-3344
Eaton (G-2583)

FOOD PRDTS, CANNED: Broth, Chicken

H & H Partnership Inc ....G 765 513-4739
Kokomo (G-8634)

FOOD PRDTS, CANNED: Chili Sauce, Tomato

Holic LLC ....F 765 444-8115
Middletown (G-9936)

FOOD PRDTS, CANNED: Fruit Butters

Dillman Farm Incorporated ....G 812 825-5525
Bloomington (G-713)

FOOD PRDTS, CANNED: Fruits

Nestle Usa Inc ....C 765 778-6000
Anderson (G-144)

FOOD PRDTS, CANNED: Fruits

Bay Valley Foods LLC ....C 574 936-4061
Plymouth (G-11668)
Eden Foods Inc ....E 765 396-3344
Eaton (G-2583)
Millers Mill ....G 574 825-2010
Middlebury (G-9908)
New Business Corporation ....G 219 886-2700
Gary (G-5079)
Red Gold Inc ....C 260 368-9017
Geneva (G-5138)
Zentis North America LLC ....B 574 941-1100
Plymouth (G-11741)
Zentis Sweet Ovtions Holdg LLC ....C 574 941-1100
Plymouth (G-11742)

FOOD PRDTS, CANNED: Jams, Including Imitation

Candy Dish Inc ....G 317 269-6262
Nashville (G-10719)

Dutch Kettle LLC................................F 574 546-4033
Bremen (G-997)

FOOD PRDTS, CANNED: Jams, Jellies & Preserves

Kick Out Jams LLC ....G 765 763-0225
Morristown (G-10373)

FOOD PRDTS, CANNED: Mexican, NEC

Avarrotes Luliana ....G 574 232-6803
South Bend (G-12719)
El Popular Inc ....F 219 397-3728
East Chicago (G-2526)
Tyson Foods Inc ....B 260 726-3118
Portland (G-11854)

FOOD PRDTS, CANNED: Soups, Exc Seafood

Morgan Foods Inc ....A 812 794-1170
Austin (G-398)
Park 100 Foods Inc ....E 317 549-4545
Indianapolis (G-7656)
Park 100 Foods Inc ....D 765 675-3480
Tipton (G-13400)

FOOD PRDTS, CANNED: Spaghetti & Other Pasta Sauce

Sprigati LLC ....G 219 484-9455
Munster (G-10629)

FOOD PRDTS, CANNED: Tomatoes

Conagra Brands Inc ....F 765 563-3182
Brookston (G-1103)
Milroy Canning Company ....G 765 629-2221
Milroy (G-9983)
Ray Brothers Noble Canning Co ....G 765 552-9432
Tipton (G-13402)
Red Gold Inc ....G 260 726-8140
Portland (G-11845)

FOOD PRDTS, CONFECTIONERY, WHOLESALE: Snack Foods

Snax In Pax Inc ....E 260 593-3066
Topeka (G-13429)

FOOD PRDTS, CONFECTIONERY, WHOLESALE: Syrups, Fountain

Swanel Inc ....D 219 932-7676
Hammond (G-5947)

FOOD PRDTS, FISH & SEAFOOD: Caviar, Preserved

Midwest Caviar LLC............................G 812 338-3610
English (G-3315)

FOOD PRDTS, FISH & SEAFOOD: Prepared Cakes & Sticks

H & H Partnership Inc ....G 765 513-4739
Kokomo (G-8634)

FOOD PRDTS, FISH & SEAFOOD: Seafood, Frozen, Prepared

Collins Caviar Company ....G 269 231-5100
Michigan City (G-9775)

FOOD PRDTS, FROZEN: Fruits, Juices & Vegetables

Fox Smoothies LLC ....G 812 333-3051
Bloomington (G-726)
Frozen Garden LLC ....F 219 286-3578
Valparaiso (G-13544)
Hawaiian Smoothie LLC ....G 317 598-1730
Fishers (G-3923)
Hawaiian Smoothie LLC ....G 317 881-7290
Greenwood (G-5702)
Zentis Sweet Ovtions Holdg LLC ....C 574 941-1100
Plymouth (G-11742)

PRODUCT

FOOD PRDTS, FROZEN: NEC

Bimbo Bakeries Usa Inc ....E 812 678-3471
Dubois (G-2475)
Bounthanhs Egg Rolls ....G 574 546-4276
Nappanee (G-10656)
Conagra Brands Inc ....B 402 240-5000
Indianapolis (G-6645)
Crystal Lake LLC ....D 574 858-2514
Warsaw (G-13861)
Grabill Country Meat 1 Inc ....F 260 627-3691
Grabill (G-5369)

FOOD PRDTS, FROZEN: Pizza

Franklins Mercantile ....G 812 876-0426
Spencer (G-13027)
Schwans Home Service Inc ....E 317 882-6624
Greenwood (G-5748)

FOOD PRDTS, FROZEN: Snack Items

Snax In Pax Inc ....E 260 593-3066
Topeka (G-13429)

FOOD PRDTS, FROZEN: Soups

Butterfield Foods LLC ....C 317 776-4775
Noblesville (G-11075)

FOOD PRDTS, FRUITS & VEGETABLES, FRESH, WHOLESALE: Vegetable

Ready Pac Foods Inc ....B 574 935-9800
Plymouth (G-11720)

FOOD PRDTS, MEAT & MEAT PRDTS, WHOLESALE: Cured Or Smoked

Hobart Locker & Meat Pkg Co ....G 219 942-5952
Crown Point (G-2257)

FOOD PRDTS, MEAT & MEAT PRDTS, WHOLESALE: Fresh

Fisher Packing Company ....E 260 726-7355
Portland (G-11822)
Jemdd LLC ....E 260 768-4156
Lagrange (G-9049)
Merkley & Sons Inc ....E 812 482-7020
Jasper (G-8295)
Smithland Butchering Co Inc ....G 317 729-5398
Elizabethtown (G-2651)
Wolfs Bar B Q Inc ....D 812 424-8891
Evansville (G-3814)

FOOD PRDTS, WHOL: Canned Goods, Fruit, Veg, Seafood/Meats

Grabill Country Meat 1 Inc ....F 260 627-3691
Grabill (G-5369)

FOOD PRDTS, WHOLESALE: Beverages, Exc Coffee & Tea

Pepsi-Cola Metro Btlg Co Inc ....E 812 332-1200
Bloomington (G-798)
Shepherd Distributing ....G 317 991-3877
Indianapolis (G-7932)

FOOD PRDTS, WHOLESALE: Chocolate

South Bend Chocolate Co Inc ....F 574 233-2577
South Bend (G-12942)

FOOD PRDTS, WHOLESALE: Coffee & Tea

Buckner Inc ....F 317 570-0533
Indianapolis (G-6520)
Harvest Cafe Coffee & Tea LLC ....G 317 585-9162
Indianapolis (G-7079)

FOOD PRDTS, WHOLESALE: Coffee, Green Or Roasted

Suncoast Coffee Inc ....E 317 251-3198
Indianapolis (G-8018)

FOOD PRDTS, WHOLESALE: Cooking Oils & Shortenings

Pepsi Beverage Company ....G 574 271-0633
South Bend (G-12890)

FOOD PRDTS, WHOLESALE: Corn

Landec Ag Inc ....F 765 385-1000
Oxford (G-11433)

FOOD PRDTS, WHOLESALE: Flour

New Carbon Company LLC ....G 574 247-2270
South Bend (G-12873)

FOOD PRDTS, WHOLESALE: Grain Elevators

AG Plus Inc ....E 260 723-5141
South Whitley (G-12996)
AG Plus Inc ....G 260 623-6121
Monroeville (G-10190)
Bundy Bros & Sons Inc ....F 812 966-2551
Medora (G-9681)
Clunette Elevator Co Inc ....F 574 858-2281
Leesburg (G-9234)
Northwest Farm Fertilizers ....G 219 785-2331
Westville (G-14220)
Premier AG Co-Op Inc ....E 812 522-4911
Seymour (G-12477)
Roy Umbarger and Sons Inc ....F 317 422-5195
Bargersville (G-486)
Salamonie Mills Inc ....F 260 375-2200
Warren (G-13832)

FOOD PRDTS, WHOLESALE: Grains

Co-Alliance LLP ....G 765 249-2233
Michigantown (G-9864)
Co-Alliance LLP ....G 765 659-3420
Frankfort (G-4823)
Co-Alliance Ltd Lblty Partnr ....D 317 745-4491
Avon (G-435)
Frick Services Inc ....E 260 761-3311
Wawaka (G-14032)
Jbs United Inc ....F 800 382-9909
Sheridan (G-12591)
Laughery Valley AG Co-Op Inc ....G 812 689-4401
Osgood (G-11393)
Lowes Pellets and Grain Inc ....E 812 663-7863
Greensburg (G-5621)
United Animal Health Inc ....D 317 758-4495
Sheridan (G-12599)
United Animal Health Inc ....F 207 771-0965
Sheridan (G-12600)
Wallace Grain Co Inc ....F 317 758-4434
Sheridan (G-12601)
Wilson Fertilizer & Grain Inc ....G 574 223-3175
Rochester (G-12161)

FOOD PRDTS, WHOLESALE: Health

Natural Answers ....G 219 922-3663
Highland (G-6052)

FOOD PRDTS, WHOLESALE: Honey

R D Laney Family Honey Company ......G 574 656-8701
North Liberty (G-11219)

FOOD PRDTS, WHOLESALE: Organic & Diet

Lebermuth Company Inc ....D 574 259-7000
South Bend (G-12837)

FOOD PRDTS, WHOLESALE: Specialty

Darrins Coffee Company ....F 317 732-5037
Clermont (G-1711)

FOOD PRDTS, WHOLESALE: Spices & Seasonings

Reidco Inc ....E 812 358-3000
Brownstown (G-1191)
Yoli Inc ....E 812 945-8530
New Albany (G-10876)

FOOD PRDTS, WHOLESALE: Syrups, Exc Fountain Use

Flavor Burst Co LLP ....F 317 745-2952
Danville (G-2347)

FOOD PRDTS, WHOLESALE: Water, Distilled

New Aqua LLC ....D 317 272-3000
Avon (G-456)

FOOD PRDTS: Animal & marine fats & oils

Bunge North America Inc ....D 260 724-2101
Decatur (G-2372)
Darling Ingredients Inc ....E 317 784-4486
Indianapolis (G-6727)
Geo Pfaus Sons Company Inc ....E 800 732-8645
Jeffersonville (G-8369)
Griffin Industries LLC ....E 812 659-3399
Newberry (G-11015)
Hrr Enterprises Inc ....E 219 362-9050
La Porte (G-8768)
Nutritional Research Assoc ....F 260 723-4931
South Whitley (G-13002)

FOOD PRDTS: Baking Powder

Clabber Girl Corporation ....D 812 232-9446
Terre Haute (G-13211)
Hulman & Company ....C 812 232-9446
Terre Haute (G-13250)

FOOD PRDTS: Baking Powder, Soda, Yeast & Leavenings

Vivolac Cultures Corporation ....E 317 866-9528
Greenfield (G-5583)

FOOD PRDTS: Breakfast Bars

Bosphorus Breakfast Hookah Bar ......G 317 624-1700
Indianapolis (G-6497)

FOOD PRDTS: Cereals

General Mills Inc ....D 317 509-3709
Fishers (G-3916)
Kellogg Company ....A 812 877-1588
Seelyville (G-12386)
Loutsa Inc ....F 317 273-0123
Indianapolis (G-7420)

FOOD PRDTS: Chicken, Processed, Fresh

Perdue Farms Inc ....G 765 325-2997
Lebanon (G-9214)

FOOD PRDTS: Chili Pepper Or Powder

G and G Peppers LLC ....E 765 358-4519
Gaston (G-5132)
Global Packaging LLC ....E 317 896-2089
Westfield (G-14165)

FOOD PRDTS: Coconut Oil

Catchrs LLC ....G 310 902-9723
Indianapolis (G-6567)
Skinny and Company LLC ....F 888 865-4278
Indianapolis (G-7950)

FOOD PRDTS: Coffee

Blue River Roasters LLC ....G 317 392-9668
Shelbyville (G-12522)
Cold Craft Brewing LLC ....G 314 712-0883
North Judson (G-11210)
Darrins Coffee Company ....F 317 732-5037
Clermont (G-1711)
Harvest Cafe Coffee & Tea LLC ....G 317 585-9162
Indianapolis (G-7079)
Hoosier Roaster Llc ....G 574 257-1415
Mishawaka (G-10051)
Last Round Coffee LLC ....G 317 292-0500
Morgantown (G-10356)
Tjs Roaster ....G 812 985-9615
Evansville (G-3765)

FOOD PRDTS: Coffee Roasting, Exc Wholesale Grocers

Cadillac Coffee Company ....E 260 489-6281
Fort Wayne (G-4133)
Farmer Bros Co ....G 812 424-3309
Evansville (G-3499)
Java Roaster ....G 765 742-2037
Lafayette (G-8930)
Suncoast Coffee Inc ....E 317 251-3198
Indianapolis (G-8018)

FOOD PRDTS: Corn Chips & Other Corn-Based Snacks

Mike-Sells West Virginia Inc ....F ... 317 241-7422
Indianapolis *(G-7516)*

Monogram Comfort Foods LLC ....D 574 848-0344
Bristol *(G-1071)*

Specialty Food Group LLC ....F 219 531-2142
Valparaiso *(G-13623)*

FOOD PRDTS: Corn Flour

Bunge North America Inc ....E 812 875-3113
Worthington *(G-14393)*

FOOD PRDTS: Corn Meal

Cargill Dry Corn Ingrdents Inc ....D 317 632-1481
Indianapolis *(G-6555)*

FOOD PRDTS: Corn Oil, Crude

APM&co Inc ....G 317 409-5639
Lewisville *(G-9248)*

FOOD PRDTS: Corn Oil, Refined

Cargill Incorporated ....B 402 533-4227
Hammond *(G-5858)*

FOOD PRDTS: Cottonseed Oil, Cake & Meal

Albertson Seed Sales ....G 765 267-0680
Russellville *(G-12238)*

FOOD PRDTS: Dessert Mixes & Fillings

Vitality Bowls....................................G 317 581-9496
Carmel *(G-1506)*

FOOD PRDTS: Doughs & Batters

Kerry Inc ....C 812 464-9151
Evansville *(G-3586)*

Kerry Inc ....G 812 464-9151
Evansville *(G-3587)*

FOOD PRDTS: Dressings, Salad, Raw & Cooked Exc Dry Mixes

Food Specialties Inc ....G 317 271-0862
Indianapolis *(G-6945)*

Grafton Peek Incorporated...................E 317 557-8377
Greenwood *(G-5698)*

Richards Restaurant Inc ....F 260 997-6823
Bryant *(G-1201)*

FOOD PRDTS: Duck Slaughtering & Processing

Culver Duck Farms Inc ....C 574 825-9537
Middlebury *(G-9880)*

Maple Leaf Farms Inc ....G 574 658-4121
Milford *(G-9958)*

Maple Leaf Farms Inc ....A 574 453-4500
Milford *(G-9957)*

FOOD PRDTS: Ducks, Processed, NEC

Maple Leaf Inc ....B 574 453-4455
Leesburg *(G-9238)*

FOOD PRDTS: Edible Oil Prdts, Exc Corn Oil

Northern Indiana Oil LLC ....G 765 749-3791
Indianapolis *(G-7593)*

FOOD PRDTS: Edible fats & oils

Bunge North America Inc ....D 260 724-2101
Decatur *(G-2372)*

Cargill Incorporated ....E 765 423-4302
Lafayette *(G-8866)*

FOOD PRDTS: Eggs, Processed

Crystal Lake LLC ....D 574 858-2514
Warsaw *(G-13861)*

Egg Innovations LLC ....G 574 267-7545
Warsaw *(G-13868)*

Midwest Poultry Services LP ....F 574 353-7232
Mentone *(G-9689)*

P & R Farms LLC ....G 812 326-2010
Saint Anthony *(G-12248)*

FOOD PRDTS: Eggs, Processed, Frozen

Crystal Lake LLC ....G 574 267-3101
Warsaw *(G-13860)*

FOOD PRDTS: Flavored Ices, Frozen

Archibald Brothers Intl Inc...................G 812 941-8267
New Albany *(G-10746)*

FOOD PRDTS: Flour & Other Grain Mill Products

AG Plus Inc ....E 260 723-5141
South Whitley *(G-12996)*

AG Plus Inc ....G 260 623-6121
Monroeville *(G-10190)*

Agricor Inc ....D 765 662-0606
Marion *(G-9507)*

Archer-Daniels-Midland Company ....G 219 297-4582
Goodland *(G-5157)*

Archer-Daniels-Midland Company ....G 317 783-3321
Beech Grove *(G-592)*

Archer-Daniels-Midland Company ....E 574 773-4138
Nappanee *(G-10646)*

Archer-Daniels-Midland Company ....E 574 773-4131
Nappanee *(G-10647)*

Archer-Daniels-Midland Company ....G 260 824-0079
Bluffton *(G-864)*

Archer-Daniels-Midland Company ....F 317 784-2200
Indianapolis *(G-6415)*

Archer-Daniels-Midland Company ....G 219 866-2810
Rensselaer *(G-11913)*

Archer-Daniels-Midland Company ....E 260 728-8000
Decatur *(G-2369)*

Archer-Daniels-Midland Company ....E 812 424-3581
Evansville *(G-3363)*

Archer-Daniels-Midland Company ....G 765 762-6763
Attica *(G-296)*

Archer-Daniels-Midland Company ....G 219 866-3939
Rensselaer *(G-11914)*

Archer-Daniels-Midland Company ....G 765 793-2512
State Line *(G-13071)*

Archer-Daniels-Midland Company ....G 765 523-3286
Frankfort *(G-4818)*

Archer-Daniels-Midland Company ....C 765 362-2965
Crawfordsville *(G-2134)*

Archer-Daniels-Midland Company ....F 812 268-4334
Sullivan *(G-13079)*

Bundy Bros & Sons Inc ....F 812 966-2551
Medora *(G-9681)*

Cargill Incorporated ....G 574 353-7621
Mentone *(G-9685)*

Clunette Elevator Co Inc ....F 574 858-2281
Leesburg *(G-9234)*

Dillman Farm Incorporated ....G 812 825-5525
Bloomington *(G-713)*

Laughery Valley AG Co-Op Inc ....G 812 689-4401
Osgood *(G-11393)*

Martinsville Milling Co Inc ....G 317 253-2581
Indianapolis *(G-7461)*

New Carbon Company LLC...................G 574 247-2270
South Bend *(G-12873)*

Roy Umbarger and Sons Inc ....F 317 422-5195
Bargersville *(G-486)*

Salamonie Mills Inc............................F 260 375-2200
Warren *(G-13832)*

Wallace Grain Co Inc ....F 317 758-4434
Sheridan *(G-12601)*

FOOD PRDTS: Flour Mixes & Doughs

Clabber Girl Corporation......................D 812 232-9446
Terre Haute *(G-13211)*

Harlan Bakeries LLC ....G 317 272-3600
Avon *(G-443)*

Harlan Bakeries-Avon LLC ....B 317 272-3600
Avon *(G-444)*

Indybake Products LLC ....D 812 877-1588
Terre Haute *(G-13257)*

FOOD PRDTS: Flours & Flour Mixes, From Purchased Flour

Donuts N Coffee Inc............................G 812 376-2796
Columbus *(G-1908)*

FOOD PRDTS: Fruit Juices

Caj Food Products Inc ....F 888 524-6882
Fishers *(G-3884)*

FOOD PRDTS: Fruits & Vegetables, Pickled

Indiana Pickle Company LLC ....G 317 698-7292
Indianapolis *(G-7189)*

Pickle Bites ....G 219 902-6315
Hammond *(G-5927)*

Pickled Pedaler ....G 317 877-0624
Noblesville *(G-11165)*

FOOD PRDTS: Fruits, Dehydrated Or Dried

Zentis Sweet Ovtions Holdg LLC ....C 574 941-1100
Plymouth *(G-11742)*

FOOD PRDTS: Honey

Eiseles Honey LLC ....G 317 896-5830
Indianapolis *(G-6817)*

R D Laney Family Honey Company.......G 574 656-8701
North Liberty *(G-11219)*

FOOD PRDTS: Ice, Blocks

Home City Ice Company.......................E 317 926-2451
Indianapolis *(G-7114)*

United States Cold Storage Inc ....E 765 482-2653
Lebanon *(G-9231)*

FOOD PRDTS: Ice, Cubes

Bryant Ice Co Inc ....G 765 459-4543
Kokomo *(G-8602)*

Home City Ice Company.......................E 219 661-8369
Crown Point *(G-2258)*

FOOD PRDTS: Macaroni, Noodles, Spaghetti, Pasta, Etc

I Noodles...G 765 447-2288
West Lafayette *(G-14075)*

FOOD PRDTS: Meat Meal & Tankage, Inedible

Standard Fertilizer Company ....F 812 663-8391
Greensburg *(G-5634)*

FOOD PRDTS: Mixes, Pancake From Purchased Flour

New Carbon Company LLC...................G 574 247-2270
South Bend *(G-12873)*

FOOD PRDTS: Mixes, Pizza

Crust N More Inc ....F 317 890-7878
Indianapolis *(G-6701)*

Rico Aroma LLC ....G 765 471-1700
Lafayette *(G-8992)*

FOOD PRDTS: Nuts & Seeds

Diamond Foods LLC ....F 209 467-6000
Van Buren *(G-13639)*

Lgin LLC ....G 260 562-2233
Howe *(G-6127)*

Stephen Libs Candy Co Inc ....F 812 473-0048
Evansville *(G-3748)*

FOOD PRDTS: Oils & Fats, Animal

American Reusable Energy LLC ....G 317 965-2604
Greenwood *(G-5666)*

FOOD PRDTS: Olive Oil

Debbies Handmade Soap ....G 765 747-5090
Muncie *(G-10455)*

Olive Leaf LLC ....G 812 323-3073
Bloomington *(G-786)*

Olive Mill ....G 317 574-9200
Carmel *(G-1445)*

FOOD PRDTS: Onions, Pickled

Van Schouwen Farms ....G 219 696-0877
Hebron *(G-6023)*

FOOD PRDTS: Pasta, Rice/Potatoes, Uncooked, Pkgd

Big Brick House Bakery LLP ....G 260 563-1071
Fort Wayne *(G-4107)*

PRODUCT

FOOD PRDTS: Pasta, Uncooked, Packaged With Other Ingredients

C & G Salsa Company LLC ....G....... 317 569-9099
Noblesville **(G-11076)**

FOOD PRDTS: Peanut Butter

B Happy Peanut Butter LLC ....G....... 317 733-3831
Zionsville **(G-14419)**
Peanut Butter and Jelly ....G....... 317 205-9211
Indianapolis **(G-7667)**

FOOD PRDTS: Pickles, Vinegar

Rickles Pickles ....G....... 260 495-9024
Fremont **(G-4974)**
Sechlers Pickles Inc ....E....... 260 337-5461
Saint Joe **(G-12258)**

FOOD PRDTS: Popcorn, Unpopped

Amish Country Popcorn Inc ....E....... 260 589-8513
Berne **(G-607)**
Conagra Brands Inc ....C....... 740 387-2722
Rensselaer **(G-11918)**
Jones Popcorn Inc ....D....... 812 941-8810
New Albany **(G-10810)**
LLC Black Jewell ....G....... 800 948-2302
Columbus **(G-1963)**
Pop Tique Popcorn ....G....... 260 459-3767
Fort Wayne **(G-4539)**
Preferred Popcorn LLC ....F....... 308 850-6631
Palmyra **(G-11438)**
Ramsey Popcorn Co Inc ....E....... 812 347-2441
Ramsey **(G-11894)**
Select Gourmet Popcorn ....G....... 812 212-2202
Sunman **(G-13117)**

FOOD PRDTS: Potato & Corn Chips & Similar Prdts

Candy Cents Vending Inc ....G....... 317 378-9197
Indianapolis **(G-6546)**
Chester Inc ....E....... 574 896-5600
North Judson **(G-11209)**
Conagra Brands Inc ....C....... 219 866-3020
Rensselaer **(G-11919)**
Frito-Lay North America Inc ....B....... 765 659-1831
Frankfort **(G-4834)**
Frito-Lay North America Inc ....C....... 765 471-1833
Lafayette **(G-8901)**
Frito-Lay North America Inc ....C....... 812 877-2425
Terre Haute **(G-13236)**
Frito-Lay North America Inc ....E....... 765 659-4517
Frankfort **(G-4835)**
Grace Island Spcalty Foods Inc ....G....... 260 357-3336
Garrett **(G-5006)**
Inventure Foods Inc ....E....... 260 824-2800
Bluffton **(G-879)**
Poore Brothers - Bluffton LLC ....B....... 260 824-2800
Bluffton **(G-885)**
Tyson Foods Inc ....B....... 260 726-3118
Portland **(G-11854)**

FOOD PRDTS: Potato Chips & Other Potato-Based Snacks

Magic Company ....E....... 260 747-1502
Fort Wayne **(G-4449)**

FOOD PRDTS: Preparations

Atkins Nutritionals Inc ....G....... 317 622-4154
Greenfield **(G-5504)**
Ciderleaf Tea Company Inc ....G....... 812 375-1937
Columbus **(G-1870)**
Conagra Brands Inc ....C....... 317 329-3700
Indianapolis **(G-6644)**
Conagra Brands Inc ....B....... 402 240-5000
Indianapolis **(G-6645)**
Conagra Brands Inc ....C....... 219 866-3020
Rensselaer **(G-11919)**
Danisco USA Inc ....G....... 812 299-6700
Terre Haute **(G-13222)**
Deep Pockets Foods LLC ....G....... 317 815-4898
Carmel **(G-1354)**
Dole ....G....... 812 576-2186
Guilford **(G-5798)**
E I Du Pont De Nemours & Co ....G....... 812 299-6700
Terre Haute **(G-13226)**

Entree Vous Greenwood ....G....... 317 881-0800
Greenwood **(G-5691)**
Frito-Lay North America Inc ....B....... 765 659-1831
Frankfort **(G-4834)**
Frito-Lay North America Inc ....E....... 765 659-4517
Frankfort **(G-4835)**
Harvey Hinklemeyers ....G....... 765 452-1942
Kokomo **(G-8636)**
Kerry Inc ....C....... 812 464-9151
Evansville **(G-3586)**
Keywest LLC ....G....... 317 821-8419
Indianapolis **(G-7347)**
Magic Company ....E....... 260 747-1502
Fort Wayne **(G-4449)**
Mead Johnson & Company LLC ....B....... 812 429-5000
Evansville **(G-3620)**
Meyer Foods Inc ....G....... 317 773-6594
Noblesville **(G-11149)**
MI Tierra ....G....... 812 376-0668
Columbus **(G-1973)**
Mike-Sells West Virginia Inc ....F....... 317 241-7422
Indianapolis **(G-7516)**
Mishawaka Food Pantry Inc ....G....... 574 220-6213
Mishawaka **(G-10091)**
Natural Answers ....G....... 219 922-3663
Highland **(G-6052)**
Paytons Barbecue ....G....... 765 294-2716
Veedersburg **(G-13645)**
Pgp International Inc ....G....... 812 867-5129
Evansville **(G-3668)**
Poore Brothers - Bluffton LLC ....B....... 260 824-2800
Bluffton **(G-885)**
Preston Farms LLC ....G....... 812 364-6123
Palmyra **(G-11439)**
Pretzels Inc ....C....... 574 941-2201
Plymouth **(G-11717)**
Pretzels Inc ....C....... 260 824-4838
Bluffton **(G-886)**
Pro Foods America Inc ....G....... 317 826-8526
Indianapolis **(G-7766)**
Qbc Catering ....G....... 812 364-4293
Palmyra **(G-11440)**
Red Gold ....G....... 765 254-1705
Muncie **(G-10555)**
Reeves Feed & Grain LLC ....G....... 812 453-3313
Poseyville **(G-11861)**
Rolands Processing ....G....... 574 831-4301
New Paris **(G-10992)**
Skjodt-Brrett Cntract Pckg LLC ....B....... 765 482-6856
Lebanon **(G-9224)**
Thyme In Kitchen LLC ....G....... 812 624-0344
Evansville **(G-3763)**
Tipton Mills Foods LLC ....G....... 812 372-0900
Columbus **(G-2021)**
Todd Couch Regional Office ....F....... 312 863-2520
Fishers **(G-3977)**

FOOD PRDTS: Prepared Sauces, Exc Tomato Based

Royal Food Products Inc ....D....... 317 782-2660
Indianapolis **(G-7865)**

FOOD PRDTS: Prepared Seafood Sauces Exc Tomato & Dry

Kolossos Inc ....G....... 312 952-6991
Long Beach **(G-9377)**

FOOD PRDTS: Rabbit, Processed, Frozen

Graber ....G....... 812 636-7699
Odon **(G-11326)**

FOOD PRDTS: Salads

Calhoun St Soup Salad Spirits ....G....... 260 456-7005
Fort Wayne **(G-4134)**
Hoople Country Kitchens Inc ....E....... 812 649-2351
Rockport **(G-12168)**
I Love Salad LLC ....G....... 317 688-7512
Indianapolis **(G-7154)**
Ready Pac Foods Inc ....B....... 574 935-9800
Plymouth **(G-11720)**

FOOD PRDTS: Sandwiches

Butterfield Foods LLC ....C....... 317 776-4775
Noblesville **(G-11075)**
Tea Unwrapped LLC ....G....... 317 558-8550
Noblesville **(G-11192)**

FOOD PRDTS: Seasonings & Spices

McCormick & Company Inc ....D....... 574 234-8101
South Bend **(G-12858)**
Reidco Inc ....E....... 812 358-3000
Brownstown **(G-1191)**
Yoli Inc ....E....... 812 945-8530
New Albany **(G-10876)**

FOOD PRDTS: Soup Mixes, Dried

Williams West & Witts Pdts Co ....G....... 219 879-8236
Michigan City **(G-9860)**

FOOD PRDTS: Soybean Protein Concentrates & Isolates

Bunge North America Foundation ....E....... 219 261-2124
Remington **(G-11905)**
Mothersoy Inc ....G....... 812 424-5357
Evansville **(G-3639)**
Solae LLC ....D....... 219 261-2124
Remington **(G-11910)**

FOOD PRDTS: Starch, Corn

Clabber Girl Corporation ....D....... 812 232-9446
Terre Haute **(G-13211)**
Grain Processing Corporation ....F....... 812 257-0480
Washington **(G-13983)**
Ingredion Incorporated ....D....... 317 635-4455
Indianapolis **(G-7231)**

FOOD PRDTS: Starches

Pacmoore Products Inc ....E....... 317 831-2666
Mooresville **(G-10334)**

FOOD PRDTS: Sugar, Maple, Indl

Harris Sugar Bush LLC ....G....... 765 653-5108
Greencastle **(G-5460)**

FOOD PRDTS: Syrup, Maple

Kcma & Services LLC ....G....... 260 645-0885
Waterloo **(G-14016)**
Lm Sugarbush LLC ....G....... 812 967-4491
Borden **(G-935)**
Maple Acres ....G....... 260 636-2073
Avilla **(G-414)**
Treehugger Maple Syrup LLC ....G....... 765 698-3728
Laurel **(G-9129)**

FOOD PRDTS: Syrup, Sorghum, For Sweetening

Tc Heartland LLC ....C....... 317 876-7121
Indianapolis **(G-8041)**
Tc Heartland LLC ....B....... 317 566-9750
Carmel **(G-1487)**

FOOD PRDTS: Tea

Cold Craft Brewing LLC ....G....... 314 712-0883
North Judson **(G-11210)**

FOOD PRDTS: Tortillas

Gonzalez International Inc ....G....... 317 558-3700
Carmel **(G-1387)**
O-M Distributors Inc ....E....... 219 853-1900
Hammond **(G-5924)**
Red Tortilla Inc ....G....... 260 403-2681
Fort Wayne **(G-4584)**
Shirley Foods Inc ....F....... 765 738-6511
Shirley **(G-12662)**
Tordilleria Del Valle ....G....... 765 654-9590
Frankfort **(G-4857)**
Torti Products Inc ....G....... 219 730-2071
Highland **(G-6057)**

FOOD PRDTS: Turkey, Processed, NEC

Farbest Foods Inc ....A....... 812 683-4200
Huntingburg **(G-6165)**
Farbest Foods Intl Inc ....G....... 812 683-4200
Huntingburg **(G-6166)**

FOOD PRDTS: Vegetable Oil Mills, NEC

Solae LLC ....G....... 800 325-7108
Remington **(G-11909)**

(G-0000) Company's Geographic Section entry number

FOOD PRDTS: Wheat Flour

Big Brick House Bakery LLP ....G..... 260 563-1071
Fort Wayne *(G-4107)*
Nunn Milling Company Inc...................E...... 812 425-3303
Evansville *(G-3649)*
Prinova Solutions ....F...... 219 879-7356
Michigan City *(G-9829)*

FOOD PRDTS: Wheat gluten

Enjoy Life Natural Brands LLC ....F...... 773 632-2163
Jeffersonville *(G-8356)*

FOOD PRODUCTS MACHINERY

Carmel Engineering Inc....................F...... 765 279-8955
Kirklin *(G-8547)*
Carmel Process Solutions Inc ....G...... 317 705-0217
Carmel *(G-1331)*
CTB MN Investment Co Inc.................E...... 574 658-4191
Milford *(G-9955)*
Intek Manufacturing LLC.....................G...... 260 637-4100
Fort Wayne *(G-4378)*
Kitchen-Quip Inc ....E...... 260 837-8311
Kendallville *(G-8487)*
Mssh Inc...G...... 812 663-2180
Greensburg *(G-5624)*
Norris Thermal Tech Inc ....G...... 574 353-7855
Tippecanoe *(G-13385)*
Romculinary LLC ....G...... 630 235-3338
Indianapolis *(G-7859)*
Rota Skipper Corporation ....F...... 708 331-0660
Crown Point *(G-2298)*
Smithfield Foods ....G...... 765 473-3086
Peru *(G-11546)*
Urschel Air Leasing LLC ....G...... 219 464-4811
Chesterton *(G-1638)*
Your Window Washer LLC ....G...... 317 701-1710
Noblesville *(G-11200)*

FOOD STORES: Grocery, Chain

Lakeshore Foods Corp.......................C...... 219 362-8513
La Porte *(G-8785)*

FOOD STORES: Grocery, Independent

Babbs Supermarket Inc......................D...... 812 829-2231
Spencer *(G-13017)*
Rihm Inc..G...... 765 478-3426
Cambridge City *(G-1260)*
Yellow Banks Clay Company Inc..........F...... 812 567-4703
Dale *(G-2336)*

FOOD STORES: Supermarkets, Chain

Kroger Co ....D...... 574 294-6092
Elkhart *(G-2975)*
Kroger Co ....C...... 574 291-0740
South Bend *(G-12830)*
Schnuck Markets Inc ....C...... 812 853-9505
Newburgh *(G-11046)*

FOOD STORES: Supermarkets, Independent

Buehler Foods Inc.............................C...... 812 467-7255
Evansville *(G-3404)*

FOOD WARMING EQPT: Commercial

Meister Cook LLC ....G...... 260 399-6692
Fort Wayne *(G-4464)*

FOOTWEAR, WHOLESALE: Boots

Cowpokes Inc....................................E...... 765 642-3911
Anderson *(G-91)*

FORGINGS

Ashley F Ward Inc ....E...... 219 879-4177
Michigan City *(G-9767)*
Avis Industrial Corporation ....E...... 765 998-8100
Upland *(G-13468)*
Custom Blacksmith Shop ....G...... 765 292-2745
Atlanta *(G-293)*
Flexible Concepts Inc........................D...... 574 296-0941
Elkhart *(G-2854)*
Fountaintown Forge Inc ....E...... 317 861-5403
Fountaintown *(G-4790)*
General Products Corporation ....C...... 260 668-1440
Angola *(G-217)*

Impact Forge Group LLC....................G...... 812 342-4437
Columbus *(G-1944)*
Impact Forge Group LLC....................C...... 812 342-5527
Columbus *(G-1945)*
Impact Forge Group LLC....................C...... 219 261-2115
Remington *(G-11907)*
Joyce/Dayton Corp ....D...... 260 726-9361
Portland *(G-11831)*
Metaldyne Bsm LLC...........................D...... 260 495-4315
Fremont *(G-4968)*
Modern Drop Forge Company LLC......B...... 708 489-4208
Merrillville *(G-9737)*
Modern Forge Indiana LLC ....F...... 219 945-5945
Merrillville *(G-9739)*
Nagakura Engrg Works Co Inc ....C...... 812 375-1382
Columbus *(G-1978)*
Netshape Technologies LLC ....C...... 812 755-4501
Campbellsburg *(G-1278)*
Omnisource LLC ....C...... 260 422-5541
Fort Wayne *(G-4510)*
Onspot of North America Inc ....E...... 812 346-1719
North Vernon *(G-11275)*
Prox Company Inc ....F...... 812 232-4324
Terre Haute *(G-13311)*
Servaas Inc ....G...... 317 633-2020
Indianapolis *(G-7914)*
Tdy Industries LLC ....B...... 260 726-8121
Portland *(G-11849)*
Tecumseh Products Company ....B...... 812 883-3575
Salem *(G-12307)*
Thyssenkrupp Crankshaft Co LLC.......D...... 765 294-0045
Veedersburg *(G-13647)*
Union Electric Steel Corp ....C...... 219 464-1031
Valparaiso *(G-13632)*

FORGINGS: Anchors

Quality Connections of Indiana.............G...... 812 279-5852
Bedford *(G-568)*

FORGINGS: Armor Plate, Iron Or Steel

Patriot Products LLC ....F...... 317 736-8007
Franklin *(G-4919)*

FORGINGS: Automotive & Internal Combustion Engine

Federal-Mogul LLC ....G...... 574 271-0274
South Bend *(G-12775)*

FORGINGS: Bearing & Bearing Race, Nonferrous

Terrecorp Inc ....F...... 317 951-8325
Indianapolis *(G-8054)*

FORGINGS: Construction Or Mining Eqpt, Ferrous

Deister Concentrator LLC ....E...... 260 747-2700
Fort Wayne *(G-4204)*
Harrell Family LLC ....G...... 317 770-4550
Noblesville *(G-11119)*
Poseidon Barge Ltd ....D...... 260 422-8767
Fort Wayne *(G-4541)*

FORGINGS: Engine Or Turbine, Nonferrous

CMI Pgi Holdings LLC ....G...... 812 377-5000
Columbus *(G-1871)*

FORGINGS: Gear & Chain

Emco Gears Inc.................................G...... 317 243-3836
Indianapolis *(G-6852)*
Fairfield Manufacturing Co Inc ....A...... 765 772-4000
Lafayette *(G-8896)*
Indiana Tool & Mfg Co Inc ....D...... 574 936-5548
Plymouth *(G-11693)*

FORGINGS: Iron & Steel

Hoosier Metal Products Inc..................G...... 812 372-5151
Columbus *(G-1941)*
Krupp Gerlach Company......................G...... 765 294-0045
Veedersburg *(G-13644)*

FORGINGS: Machinery, Nonferrous

Fountaintown Forge Inc ....E...... 317 861-5403
Fountaintown *(G-4790)*

FORGINGS: Metal , Ornamental, Ferrous

Horneco Fabrication Inc......................G...... 260 672-2064
Fort Wayne *(G-4347)*

FORGINGS: Nonferrous

Impact Forge Group LLC....................G...... 812 342-4437
Columbus *(G-1944)*
JM Fittings LLC ....D...... 260 747-9200
Fort Wayne *(G-4396)*
Parker-Hannifin Corporation ....C...... 260 636-2104
Albion *(G-32)*
Symmetry Medical Mfg Inc.................D...... 574 371-2284
Warsaw *(G-13949)*
Tdy Industries LLC ....B...... 260 726-8121
Portland *(G-11849)*

FORGINGS: Nuclear Power Plant, Ferrous

Bwxt Nclear Oprtions Group Inc ....C...... 812 838-1200
Mount Vernon *(G-10387)*
Rolls-Royce Corporation.....................G...... 317 230-8515
West Lafayette *(G-14104)*
Rolls-Royce Corporation.....................A...... 317 230-2000
Indianapolis *(G-7858)*

FORGINGS: Pump & Compressor, Ferrous

H & H Manufacturing Inc ....G...... 812 664-3582
Patoka *(G-11466)*

FORMS HANDLING EQPT

Bastian Automation Engrg LLC............D...... 317 467-2583
Greenfield *(G-5507)*

FORMS: Concrete, Sheet Metal

Carroll Distrg & Cnstr Sup Inc ....G...... 317 984-2400
Noblesville *(G-11078)*
CMa Supply Co Fort Wayne Inc............F...... 260 471-9000
Fort Wayne *(G-4164)*
Larry Atwood.....................................G...... 765 525-6851
Waldron *(G-13800)*
Peri Formwork Systems Inc.................F...... 317 390-0062
Indianapolis *(G-7678)*

FOUNDRIES: Aluminum

Ashley Aluminum Foundry Inc ....G...... 812 793-2654
Crothersville *(G-2215)*
Batesville Products Inc ....D...... 812 926-4230
Aurora *(G-373)*
Ce Systems Inc ....E...... 812 372-8234
Columbus *(G-1868)*
Dualtech Inc......................................E...... 317 738-9043
Franklin *(G-4882)*
Enkei America Inc ....A...... 812 373-7000
Columbus *(G-1920)*
FCA US LLC.......................................A...... 765 454-0018
Kokomo *(G-8624)*
FCA US LLC.......................................A...... 765 454-1005
Kokomo *(G-8625)*
General Aluminum Mfg Company ....C...... 260 495-2600
Fremont *(G-4960)*
Global..G...... 317 494-6174
Franklin *(G-4889)*
Grandview Aluminum Products ....E...... 812 649-2569
Grandview *(G-5387)*
Indiana Refractories Inc ....E...... 260 426-3286
Fort Wayne *(G-4365)*
Madison Precision Products Inc ....B...... 812 273-4702
Madison *(G-9481)*
Metaldyne Bsm LLC...........................G...... 260 495-4315
Fremont *(G-4968)*
New Point Products Inc......................G...... 812 663-6311
New Point *(G-11003)*
Ryobi Die Casting (usa) Inc ....A...... 317 398-3398
Shelbyville *(G-12565)*
Shipston Aluminum Tech Ind Inc ....D...... 317 738-0282
Franklin *(G-4932)*
SUs Cast Products Inc ....D...... 574 753-4111
Logansport *(G-9367)*
Wabash Castings Inc ....C...... 260 563-8371
Wabash *(G-13761)*
Ward Corporation..............................C...... 260 426-8700
Fort Wayne *(G-4735)*

FOUNDRIES: Brass, Bronze & Copper

A Raymond Tinnerman Auto Inc ....C...... 574 722-5168
Logansport *(G-9319)*

P
R
O
D
U
C
T

Beckett Bronze Company Inc ....E 765 282-2261
Muncie **(G-10438)**

Crosbie Foundry Co Inc ....E 574 262-1502
Elkhart **(G-2777)**

Demotte Manufacturing Inc ....G 219 987-6196
Demotte **(G-2435)**

Grandview Aluminum Products ....E 812 649-2569
Grandview **(G-5387)**

Netshape Technologies LLC ....C 812 755-4501
Campbellsburg **(G-1278)**

New Point Products Inc ....G 812 663-6311
New Point **(G-11003)**

Parker-Hannifin Corporation ....C 260 636-2104
Albion **(G-32)**

Stalcop LLC ....D 765 436-7926
Thorntown **(G-13378)**

FOUNDRIES: Gray & Ductile Iron

Atlas Foundry Company Inc ....C 765 662-2525
Marion **(G-9510)**

Ce Systems Inc ....E 812 372-8234
Columbus **(G-1868)**

Grede LLC ....C 765 521-8000
New Castle **(G-10903)**

J A Smit Inc ....G 812 424-8141
Evansville **(G-3568)**

La Porte Technologies LLC ....F 219 362-1000
La Porte **(G-8784)**

Leons Fabrication Inc ....F 219 365-5272
Schererville **(G-12330)**

Metal Technologies Indiana Inc ....C 260 925-4717
Auburn **(G-346)**

United Mechanical Tech Inc ....G 219 608-0717
Schererville **(G-12350)**

Vernon North Industry Corp ....D 812 346-8772
North Vernon **(G-11285)**

West Allis Gray Iron ....D 260 925-4717
Auburn **(G-367)**

FOUNDRIES: Iron

Accurate Castings Inc ....D 219 393-3122
La Porte **(G-8726)**

Ce Systems Inc ....E 812 372-8234
Columbus **(G-1868)**

Ewing Light Metals Co Inc ....F 317 926-4591
Indianapolis **(G-6886)**

Grede LLC ....C 765 521-8000
New Castle **(G-10903)**

Mosey Manufacturing Co Inc ....D 765 983-8889
Richmond **(G-12022)**

Muncie Casting Corp ....E 765 288-2611
Muncie **(G-10528)**

Plymouth Foundry Inc ....E 574 936-2106
Plymouth **(G-11713)**

Wirco Inc ....C 260 897-3768
Avilla **(G-422)**

FOUNDRIES: Nonferrous

Accurate Castings Inc ....D 219 393-3122
La Porte **(G-8726)**

Aluminum Foundries Inc ....C 765 584-6501
Winchester **(G-14324)**

Batesville Products Inc ....D 812 926-4230
Aurora **(G-373)**

Batesville Products Inc ....D 513 381-2057
Lawrenceburg **(G-9133)**

Crosbie Foundry Co Inc ....E 574 262-1502
Elkhart **(G-2777)**

Ewing Light Metals Co Inc ....F 317 926-4591
Indianapolis **(G-6886)**

Excel Manufacturing Inc ....D 812 523-6764
Seymour **(G-12448)**

General Products Corporation ....C 260 668-1440
Angola **(G-217)**

Howmet Castings & Services Inc ....A 219 326-7400
La Porte **(G-8767)**

Kitchen-Quip Inc ....E 260 837-8311
Kendallville **(G-8487)**

New Point Products Inc ....G 812 663-6311
New Point **(G-11003)**

Nonferrous Products Inc ....E 317 738-2558
Franklin **(G-4914)**

Orthodontic Design and Prod ....E 760 734-3995
Franklin **(G-4917)**

Ward Corporation ....C 260 426-8700
Fort Wayne **(G-4735)**

FOUNDRIES: Steel

Bahr Bros Mfg Inc ....E 765 664-6235
Marion **(G-9512)**

CM Tech ....G 765 584-6501
Winchester **(G-14327)**

FCA US LLC ....A 765 454-0018
Kokomo **(G-8624)**

Hoosier Engineering Co Inc ....G 260 694-6887
Poneto **(G-11746)**

IBC US Holdings Inc ....G 317 738-2558
Franklin **(G-4898)**

Jec Steel Company ....G 574 326-3829
Elkhart **(G-2946)**

Metaldyne Bsm LLC ....D 260 495-4315
Fremont **(G-4968)**

Set Enterprises of Mi Inc ....F 812 346-1700
North Vernon **(G-11281)**

Southland Metals Inc ....G 574 252-4441
Mishawaka **(G-10134)**

Stanley Fastening Systems LP ....D 317 398-0761
Greenfield **(G-5578)**

Tupy American Foundry Corp ....G 317 859-0066
Greenwood **(G-5757)**

United States Steel Corp ....B 219 888-2000
Gary **(G-5111)**

United States Steel Corp ....B 219 391-2045
East Chicago **(G-2576)**

West Allis Gray Iron ....D 260 925-4717
Auburn **(G-367)**

Wrib Manufacturing Inc ....G 765 294-2841
Veedersburg **(G-13648)**

FOUNDRIES: Steel Investment

Howmet Castings & Services Inc ....A 219 326-7400
La Porte **(G-8767)**

Wegener Steel and Fabricating ....G 219 462-3911
Valparaiso **(G-13636)**

Winchester Steel ....G 812 591-2071
Westport **(G-14212)**

FOUNDRY MACHINERY & EQPT

Chuck Bivens Services Inc ....F 260 747-6195
Fort Wayne **(G-4149)**

E & S Metal Inc ....F 260 563-7714
Wabash **(G-13726)**

Summit Foundry Systems Inc ....F 260 749-7740
Fort Wayne **(G-4663)**

Wrib Manufacturing Inc ....G 765 294-2841
Veedersburg **(G-13648)**

FRACTIONATION PRDTS OF CRUDE PETROLEUM, HYDROCARBONS, NEC

HK Petroleum Ltd ....G 229 366-1313
Madison **(G-9469)**

FRAMES & FRAMING WHOLESALE

Editions Ltd Gallery Fine Arts ....G 317 466-9940
Indianapolis **(G-6806)**

FRAMES: Chair, Metal

Moyers Inc ....E 574 264-3119
Elkhart **(G-3052)**

FREIGHT TRANSPORTATION ARRANGEMENTS

Envista Concepts LLC ....E 317 208-9100
Carmel **(G-1373)**

Envista Freight Managment LLC ....F 317 208-9100
Carmel **(G-1375)**

Phoenix Assembly LLC ....D 317 884-3600
Greenwood **(G-5732)**

Phoenix Assembly Indiana LLC ....E 317 884-3600
Columbus **(G-1995)**

Tpg Mt Vernon Marine LLC ....C 317 631-0234
Indianapolis **(G-8087)**

FREON

Ambandash ....G 260 415-1709
Fort Wayne **(G-4067)**

FRICTION MATERIAL, MADE FROM POWDERED METAL

Aisin Chemical Indiana LLC ....E 812 793-2888
Crothersville **(G-2213)**

B6 Manufacturing LLC ....G 317 549-4290
Indianapolis **(G-6451)**

GKN Sinter Metals LLC ....C 812 883-3381
Salem **(G-12288)**

Hibbing International Friction ....F 765 529-7001
New Castle **(G-10904)**

Innovative 3d Mfg LLC ....G 317 560-5080
Franklin **(G-4901)**

Nst Campbellsburg Inc ....C 812 755-4501
Campbellsburg **(G-1279)**

FUEL ADDITIVES

Keil Chemical Corporation ....D 219 931-2630
Hammond **(G-5905)**

Petroleum Solutions Inc ....G 574 546-2133
Bremen **(G-1016)**

FUEL BRIQUETTES & WAXES

American Pellet Supply LLC ....F 812 398-2225
Carlisle **(G-1295)**

Calumet Superior LLC ....C 317 328-5660
Indianapolis **(G-6543)**

FUEL DEALERS: Coal

Carter Fuel Systems LLC ....B 574 722-6141
Logansport **(G-9328)**

FUEL DEALERS: Wood

Blackwood Solutions Inc ....G 812 824-6728
Bloomington **(G-684)**

FUEL OIL DEALERS

Calumet Superior LLC ....C 317 328-5660
Indianapolis **(G-6543)**

Spence/Banks Inc ....F 812 234-3538
Terre Haute **(G-13341)**

FUELS: Diesel

Emerald Cast Rnewable Fuel LLC ....G 765 942-5019
Ladoga **(G-8840)**

Imperial Petroleum Inc ....G 812 867-1433
Evansville **(G-3549)**

Integrity Bio-Fuels LLC ....F 765 763-6020
Morristown **(G-10371)**

FUELS: Ethanol

Alternative Fuel Solutions LLC ....G 260 224-1965
Huntington **(G-6185)**

AMP Americas LLC ....G 312 300-6700
Fair Oaks **(G-3817)**

Aviation Fuel Group LLC ....G 219 462-6081
Valparaiso **(G-13500)**

Brown & Brown Fuel ....G 219 984-5173
Chalmers **(G-1546)**

Cheli Fuel ....G 317 377-1480
Indianapolis **(G-6596)**

Countrymark Ref Logistics LLC ....G 800 808-3170
Indianapolis **(G-6677)**

Elwood Fuel and Cigs LLC ....G 317 244-5744
Indianapolis **(G-6845)**

Food & Fuel Upland ....G 765 998-0840
Upland **(G-13470)**

Fountain Food and Fueling ....G 765 847-5257
Fountain City **(G-4787)**

Fuel Prfmce Enhancement LLC ....G 317 979-2316
Indianapolis **(G-6966)**

Gary Vehicle Maintenance-Fuel ....G 219 881-0219
Gary **(G-5053)**

Harvest Fuels LLC ....G 832 895-6621
Carmel **(G-1396)**

Hucks Food Fuel ....G 812 683-5566
Huntingburg **(G-6168)**

Iroquois Bio-Energy Co LLC ....G 219 866-5990
Rensselaer **(G-11928)**

Jerry L Fuelling ....G 317 709-6978
Zionsville **(G-14441)**

Mr Fuel ....G 317 531-0891
Spiceland **(G-13056)**

Ohio Valley Fuel Injection ....G 812 987-5857
Charlestown **(G-1578)**

Owens Fuel Center ....G 260 358-1211
Huntington **(G-6234)**

Racing Fuel Ignite ....G 765 733-0833
Marion **(G-9558)**

Rudys Food & Fuel LLC ....G 812 547-2530
Tell City **(G-13173)**

Ryan Fuelling ....G...... 260 403-6450
  Fort Wayne (G-4599)
S Huck Food and Fuel ....G...... 812 886-4323
  Vincennes (G-13704)
Southern Fuel LLC ....G...... 219 689-3552
  Rensselaer (G-11939)
Super Hicksgas Fuel ....G...... 219 345-2656
  Demotte (G-2449)
Swift Fuels LLC ....G...... 765 464-8336
  West Lafayette (G-14111)
Tobacco Zone Inc ....G...... 317 268-6808
  Plainfield (G-11648)
Top Fuel Crossfit ....G...... 219 281-7001
  Crown Point (G-2315)
Warrior Oil Service Inc ....F...... 317 738-9777
  Franklin (G-4940)

FUELS: Nuclear

Central Indiana Ethanol LLC ....D...... 765 384-4001
  Marion (G-9517)

FUELS: Oil

Advance Energy LLC ....G...... 312 665-0022
  Hobart (G-6068)
Cdg Operation LLC ....F...... 812 682-3770
  New Harmony (G-10924)
Fuel Recovery Service Inc ....G...... 317 372-3029
  Indianapolis (G-6967)
Jpt Enterprises Inc ....G...... 260 672-1605
  Fort Wayne (G-4401)

FUNERAL HOMES & SVCS

Aurora Casket Company LLC ....B...... 800 457-1111
  Aurora (G-370)
Romark Industries Inc ....E...... 765 966-6211
  Richmond (G-12047)

FUNGICIDES OR HERBICIDES

Sepro Corporation ....E...... 317 580-8282
  Carmel (G-1478)

FUR APPAREL STORES

Yannis Furs Inc ....G...... 317 580-0914
  Indianapolis (G-8224)

FUR STRIPPING

Sentinel Services Inc ....F...... 574 360-5279
  Granger (G-5432)

FUR: Coats & Other Apparel

Yannis Furs Inc ....G...... 317 580-0914
  Indianapolis (G-8224)

FURNACE CASINGS: Sheet Metal

T R Bulger Inc ....G...... 219 879-8525
  Trail Creek (G-13443)

FURNACES & OVENS: Fuel-Fired

Furnace Design Technology LLC ....G...... 317 896-5506
  Westfield (G-14164)
Power Plant Service Inc ....E...... 260 432-6716
  Fort Wayne (G-4542)
Thermo Transfer Inc ....F...... 317 398-3503
  Shelbyville (G-12575)
W C Grant Company Incorporated ..F...... 260 484-6688
  Markle (G-9583)

FURNACES & OVENS: Indl

Al-Fe Systems Inc ....F...... 260 483-4411
  Columbia City (G-1763)
Austin-Westran LLC ....C...... 815 234-2811
  Indianapolis (G-6441)
Brouillette Heating & Cooling ....G...... 765 884-0176
  Fowler (G-4798)
E & S Metal Inc ....F...... 260 563-7714
  Wabash (G-13726)
George Koch Sons LLC ....C...... 812 465-9600
  Evansville (G-3519)
Green Fast Cure LLC ....G...... 812 486-2510
  Montgomery (G-10227)
Heat Wagons Inc ....F...... 219 464-8818
  Valparaiso (G-13555)
Industrial Combustn Engineers ....E...... 219 949-5066
  Gary (G-5068)

Light Beam Technologies Inc ....G...... 260 635-2195
  Kimmell (G-8530)
Midwest Finishing Systems Inc ....E...... 574 257-0099
  Mishawaka (G-10087)
Rogers Engineering and Mfg Co .....E...... 765 478-5444
  Cambridge City (G-1261)
Thermal Product Solutions ....G...... 708 758-6530
  Schererville (G-12348)
Universal Door Carrier Inc ....G...... 317 241-3447
  Indianapolis (G-8129)
Wax Connections Inc ....G...... 219 778-2325
  Rolling Prairie (G-12195)

FURNACES: Indl, Electric

Ajax Tocco Magnethermic Corp ....G...... 317 352-9880
  Indianapolis (G-6357)
Gillespie Mrrell Gen Contg LLC ....G...... 765 618-4084
  Marion (G-9526)

FURNACES: Warm Air, Electric

Thermo Products LLC ....D...... 574 896-2133
  North Judson (G-11214)

FURNITURE & CABINET STORES: Cabinets, Custom Work

Fehrenbacher Cabinets Inc ....E...... 812 963-3377
  Evansville (G-3502)
Lee Supply Corp ....G...... 812 333-4343
  Bloomington (G-764)
Real Wood Works ....G...... 812 277-1462
  Bedford (G-571)
Ronald Chileen Furniture ....G...... 574 542-4505
  Rochester (G-12150)
Vans Cabinet Shop ....G...... 574 658-9625
  Milford (G-9966)
Weaver Fine Cabinets Furniture ....G...... 812 342-4833
  Columbus (G-2031)

FURNITURE & CABINET STORES: Custom

Carriage House Woodworking ....G...... 317 406-3042
  Plainfield (G-11599)

FURNITURE & FIXTURES Factory

Bollock Interprises Inc ....F...... 765 448-6000
  Lafayette (G-8864)

FURNITURE COMPONENTS: Porcelain Enameled

Ffesar Inc ....G...... 812 378-4220
  McCordsville (G-9667)

FURNITURE PARTS: Metal

Ditto Sales Inc ....E...... 812 482-3043
  Jasper (G-8245)
Extreme Metal Fab Inc ....F...... 812 988-9353
  Nashville (G-10724)
Fabtron Corporation ....G...... 260 925-9553
  Auburn (G-331)
Shrock Manufacturing Inc ....E...... 574 264-4126
  Elkhart (G-3168)

FURNITURE REPAIR & MAINTENANCE SVCS

Douglas Dye and Associates ....G...... 317 844-1709
  Carmel (G-1362)

FURNITURE STOCK & PARTS: Carvings, Wood

Digital Carvings LLC ....G...... 812 269-6123
  Ellettsville (G-3278)
Rwh Woodworking ....G...... 317 714-5179
  Greenfield (G-5570)
Weberdings Carving Shop Inc ....F...... 812 934-3710
  Batesville (G-524)

FURNITURE STOCK & PARTS: Dimension Stock, Hardwood

A JS Furniture LLC ....G...... 574 642-1273
  Topeka (G-13410)
Burton Lumber Co Inc ....F...... 812 866-4438
  Lexington (G-9249)
Forest Products Mfg Co ....E...... 812 482-5625
  Jasper (G-8251)

Mo-Wood Products Inc ....G...... 812 482-5625
  Jasper (G-8296)
Olon Industries Inc (us) ....F...... 812 256-6400
  Jeffersonville (G-8408)
Tedrows Wood Products Inc ....F...... 812 247-2260
  Shoals (G-12670)

FURNITURE STOCK & PARTS: Frames, Upholstered Furniture, Wood

Miller Milling Inc ....G...... 260 768-9171
  Shipshewana (G-12634)

FURNITURE STOCK & PARTS: Hardwood

Graber Furniture ....G...... 812 295-4939
  Loogootee (G-9383)
R & R Custom Woodworking Inc ....E...... 574 773-5436
  Nappanee (G-10703)
Swartzndrber Hrdwood Creat LLC ....E...... 574 534-2502
  Goshen (G-5337)

FURNITURE STOCK & PARTS: Turnings, Wood

Brown Ridge Studio ....G...... 812 335-0643
  Bloomington (G-690)
Indiana Handle Company Inc ....D...... 812 723-3159
  Paoli (G-11453)
Prized Possession ....G...... 317 842-1498
  Indianapolis (G-7762)

FURNITURE STORES

American Natural Resources LLC .....F...... 219 922-6444
  Griffith (G-5762)
Best Chairs Incorporated ....E...... 812 367-1761
  Paoli (G-11445)
Bollock Interprises Inc ....F...... 765 448-6000
  Lafayette (G-8864)
Chris Schwartz ....G...... 260 615-9574
  Grabill (G-5360)
Classic Kitchen & Granite ....G...... 317 575-8883
  Carmel (G-1340)
Coffeys Custom Upholstery ....G...... 812 948-8611
  New Albany (G-10763)
Custom Cabinets & Furn LLC ....F...... 812 486-2503
  Montgomery (G-10220)
Graber Furniture ....G...... 812 295-4939
  Loogootee (G-9383)
Izzy Plus ....G...... 574 821-1200
  Middlebury (G-9895)
Johnny Bontrager ....G...... 260 463-8912
  Lagrange (G-9050)
Lambright Woodworking LLC ....E...... 260 593-2721
  Topeka (G-13423)
Oeding Corporation ....G...... 812 367-1271
  Ferdinand (G-3860)
REM Industries Inc ....E...... 574 862-2127
  Wakarusa (G-13792)
Roudebush Company Incorporated ...G...... 574 595-7115
  Star City (G-13070)
Sylvia Kay Hartley ....G...... 317 984-3424
  Arcadia (G-270)
Yb Normal Custom Wood Working .....G...... 260 338-2003
  Huntertown (G-6149)

FURNITURE STORES: Custom Made, Exc Cabinets

Martins Wood Works ....G...... 574 862-4080
  Goshen (G-5281)
Wooden Concept Inc ....G...... 317 293-3137
  Indianapolis (G-8213)

FURNITURE STORES: Office

A & H Enterprises LLC ....G...... 317 398-3070
  Shelbyville (G-12517)
Shearer Printing Service Inc ....E...... 765 457-3274
  Kokomo (G-8695)

FURNITURE STORES: Outdoor & Garden

De Vols Ornamental Iron ....G...... 765 482-1171
  Lebanon (G-9180)

FURNITURE WHOLESALERS

A JS Furniture LLC ....G...... 574 642-1273
  Topeka (G-13410)

PRODUCT

Affordable Furniture ....G...... 317 881-7726
Greenwood *(G-5662)*

American Natural Resources LLC ....F...... 219 922-6444
Griffith *(G-5762)*

Family Leisurecom Inc ....G...... 317 823-4448
Indianapolis *(G-6903)*

Ffesar Inc ....G...... 812 378-4220
McCordsville *(G-9667)*

Martins Wood Works ....G...... 574 862-4060
Goshen *(G-5281)*

Sac Acquisition LLC ....G...... 317 575-1795
Indianapolis *(G-7883)*

Spectrum Finishing LLC ....E...... 260 463-7300
Lagrange *(G-9066)*

FURNITURE, GARDEN: Concrete

Wicker Gallery ....G...... 219 942-0783
Hobart *(G-6100)*

FURNITURE, HOUSEHOLD: Wholesalers

Candles By Dar Inc ....F...... 260 482-2099
Fort Wayne *(G-4139)*

Johnny Bontrager ....G...... 260 463-8912
Lagrange *(G-9050)*

Lasalle Bristol Corporation ....C...... 574 295-4400
Elkhart *(G-2985)*

FURNITURE, MATTRESSES: Wholesalers

Crash Beds LLC ....G...... 317 601-4436
Greenwood *(G-5677)*

FURNITURE, OFFICE: Wholesalers

Altstadt Business Forms Inc ....F...... 812 425-3393
Evansville *(G-3349)*

Jofco Inc ....C...... 812 482-5154
Jasper *(G-8267)*

Jsj Furniture Corporation ....C...... 574 825-5871
Middlebury *(G-9899)*

Smith & Butterfield Co Inc ....F...... 812 422-3261
Evansville *(G-3735)*

FURNITURE, OUTDOOR & LAWN: Wholesalers

C & C Mailbox Products ....G...... 765 358-4880
Gaston *(G-5130)*

Jordan Manufacturing Co Inc ....C...... 800 328-6522
Monticello *(G-10268)*

FURNITURE, WHOLESALE: Beds & Bedding

Superior Mattress Inc ....G...... 812 422-5761
Evansville *(G-3754)*

FURNITURE, WHOLESALE: Dining Room

Country Woodshop LLC ....E...... 574 642-3681
Goshen *(G-5194)*

FURNITURE, WHOLESALE: Filing Units

Meilink Safe Company ....E...... 812 941-0024
New Albany *(G-10825)*

FURNITURE, WHOLESALE: Theater Seats

Preferred Seating Company LLC ....G...... 317 782-3323
Indianapolis *(G-7740)*

FURNITURE: Bar furniture

Longs Landing of Bedford ....G...... 812 278-8986
Bedford *(G-560)*

FURNITURE: Bedroom, Metal

Hoosier Wallbeds Inc ....G...... 812 926-0055
Aurora *(G-379)*

FURNITURE: Bedroom, Wood

Bedder Way Company Inc ....E...... 317 783-5105
Indianapolis *(G-6463)*

Borkholder Corporation ....E...... 574 773-4083
Nappanee *(G-10654)*

E & S Wood Creations LLC ....F...... 260 768-3033
Lagrange *(G-9040)*

J & J Woodcrafters ....G...... 765 436-2466
Thorntown *(G-13376)*

Mobel Incorporated ....C...... 812 367-1214
Ferdinand *(G-3859)*

Streamside Woodshop LLC ....G...... 260 768-7887
Shipshewana *(G-12654)*

FURNITURE: Bookcases & Partitions, Office, Exc Wood

Kramer Furn & Cab Makers Inc ....F...... 812 526-2711
Edinburgh *(G-2615)*

FURNITURE: Bookcases, Wood

Jds Pugh Cabinets Inc ....F...... 317 835-2910
Fairland *(G-3822)*

Ro Vic Wood Products Inc ....E...... 812 283-9199
Jeffersonville *(G-8420)*

Shamrock Cabinets Inc ....E...... 812 482-7969
Jasper *(G-8308)*

FURNITURE: Box Springs, Assembled

Leggett & Platt Incorporated ....B...... 219 866-7181
Rensselaer *(G-11931)*

FURNITURE: Chair & Couch Springs, Assembled

Loewenstein Furniture Inc ....G...... 800 521-5381
Huntingburg *(G-6174)*

FURNITURE: Chairs, Folding

Sauder Woodworking Co ....G...... 800 537-1530
Grabill *(G-5384)*

FURNITURE: Chairs, Household Upholstered

Best Chairs Incorporated ....A...... 812 367-1761
Ferdinand *(G-3846)*

Best Chairs Incorporated ....E...... 812 367-1761
Paoli *(G-11445)*

Best Chairs Incorporated ....D...... 812 367-1761
Cannelton *(G-1287)*

Custom Wood Products Inc ....D...... 574 522-3300
Elkhart *(G-2784)*

FURNITURE: Chairs, Household Wood

Edna Troyer ....G...... 260 894-4405
Ligonier *(G-9281)*

F & N Woodworking LLC ....F...... 260 463-8938
Lagrange *(G-9041)*

Middlebury Hardwood Pdts Inc ....C...... 574 825-9524
Middlebury *(G-9907)*

Ramer Chair Co ....G...... 574 862-4179
Goshen *(G-5316)*

FURNITURE: Chairs, Household, Metal

Pinnacle Seating Inc ....G...... 574 522-2636
Elkhart *(G-3096)*

FURNITURE: Chairs, Office Exc Wood

Environmental Products Inc ....F...... 219 393-3446
Kingsbury *(G-8537)*

FURNITURE: Chairs, Office Wood

Jasper Chair Company Inc ....D...... 812 482-5239
Jasper *(G-8255)*

Jasper Seating Company Inc ....D...... 812 936-9977
French Lick *(G-4987)*

Jasper Seating Company Inc ....D...... 812 326-2361
Saint Anthony *(G-12247)*

Jofco Inc ....C...... 812 482-5154
Jasper *(G-8268)*

Jofco Inc ....C...... 812 482-5154
Jasper *(G-8267)*

FURNITURE: Console Tables, Wood

Dorel Home Furnishings Inc ....B...... 812 372-0141
Columbus *(G-1909)*

FURNITURE: Cribs, Metal

Cosco Inc ....A...... 812 372-0141
Columbus *(G-1883)*

Dorel USA Inc ....D...... 812 372-0141
Columbus *(G-1914)*

FURNITURE: Cut Stone

Century Marble Co Inc ....E...... 317 867-5555
Westfield *(G-14143)*

Coronado Stone Inc ....E...... 812 284-2845
Jeffersonville *(G-8347)*

FURNITURE: Desks & Tables, Office, Exc Wood

Kimball Office Inc ....F...... 812 634-3220
Jasper *(G-8284)*

Kimball Office Inc ....B...... 812 482-1600
Jasper *(G-8285)*

FURNITURE: Desks & Tables, Office, Wood

Great American Desk Co Inc ....F...... 574 293-3591
Elkhart *(G-2896)*

FURNITURE: Desks, Household, Wood

Dmi Furniture Inc ....G...... 812 683-2123
Huntingburg *(G-6155)*

FURNITURE: Desks, Metal

Great American Desk Co Inc ....F...... 574 293-3591
Elkhart *(G-2896)*

FURNITURE: Desks, Wood

Dmi Furniture Inc ....G...... 812 683-2123
Huntingburg *(G-6155)*

J W Woodworking Inc ....G...... 574 831-3033
New Paris *(G-10987)*

Jasper Desk Company Inc ....F...... 812 482-4132
Jasper *(G-8256)*

Jasper Desk Company Inc ....D...... 812 482-6827
Jasper *(G-8257)*

FURNITURE: Dining Room, Wood

Custom Wood Products Inc ....D...... 574 522-3300
Elkhart *(G-2784)*

Prolam Products Inc ....D...... 812 867-1662
Evansville *(G-3687)*

FURNITURE: End Tables, Wood

Millers Woodnthings Inc ....F...... 574 825-2996
Middlebury *(G-9911)*

FURNITURE: Fiberglass & Plastic

Laminique Inc ....E...... 765 482-4222
Lebanon *(G-9197)*

Resin Partners Inc ....D...... 765 724-7761
Alexandria *(G-51)*

FURNITURE: Foundations & Platforms

Firesmoke Org ....G...... 317 690-2542
Indianapolis *(G-6923)*

FURNITURE: Garden, Exc Wood, Metal, Stone Or Concrete

Beachfront Furniture ....F...... 574 875-0817
Elkhart *(G-2719)*

FURNITURE: High Chairs, Children's, Wood

Cosco Inc ....A...... 812 372-0141
Columbus *(G-1883)*

Dorel USA Inc ....D...... 812 372-0141
Columbus *(G-1914)*

FURNITURE: Hospital

Kimball Hospitality Inc ....D...... 812 482-8090
Jasper *(G-8281)*

Knu LLC ....D...... 812 367-2068
Ferdinand *(G-3855)*

Ofs Brands Holdings Inc ....A...... 800 521-5381
Huntingburg *(G-6177)*

Wittrock Enterprises LLC ....E...... 812 222-0373
Greensburg *(G-5642)*

FURNITURE: Hotel

Kimball Hospitality Inc ....F...... 812 482-8090
Jasper *(G-8280)*

Troy Stuart ....G...... 812 887-0403
Washington *(G-14004)*

FURNITURE: Household, Metal

Best Chairs Incorporated ....D...... 812 367-1761
Cannelton (G-1287)
Bo-Mar Industries Inc ....E...... 317 899-1240
Indianapolis (G-6491)
Delta Excell Incorporated ....E...... 765 642-0288
Anderson (G-93)
Flambeau Inc ....C...... 812 372-4899
Columbus (G-1931)
Lakemaster Inc ....E...... 765 288-3718
Muncie (G-10507)
Mastercraft Inc ....C...... 260 463-8702
Lagrange (G-9060)
Mehringer Metal Design LLC ....G...... 812 634-6100
Jasper (G-8294)
Mouron & Company Inc ....F...... 317 243-7955
Indianapolis (G-7551)
Poly-Wood LLC ....D...... 574 457-3284
Syracuse (G-13140)

FURNITURE: Household, NEC

Ed and Daves Wood Chips LLC ....G...... 574 699-1263
Galveston (G-4994)

FURNITURE: Household, Upholstered On Metal Frames

Seating Technology Inc ....C...... 574 971-4100
Goshen (G-5322)
Valley Line Wood Products LLC ....G...... 260 768-7807
Shipshewana (G-12655)

FURNITURE: Household, Upholstered, Exc Wood Or Metal

Aristocrat Inc ....G...... 812 634-0460
Jasper (G-8236)
Columbus Cstm Cbinets Furn LLC ....G...... 812 379-9411
Columbus (G-1875)
Ditto Sales Inc ....G...... 812 424-4098
Evansville (G-3460)
Weaver Fine Cabinets Furniture ....G...... 812 342-4833
Columbus (G-2031)

FURNITURE: Household, Wood

A L E Enterprises ....G...... 317 856-2981
Indianapolis (G-6297)
Able Woodcrafters LLC ....G...... 317 915-1225
Indianapolis (G-6311)
Als Woodcraft Inc ....F...... 812 967-4458
Borden (G-927)
Antreasian Design Inc ....F...... 317 546-3234
Indianapolis (G-6404)
Barry A Wilcox ....G...... 260 495-3677
Fremont (G-4951)
Beebe Cabinet Co Inc ....F...... 574 293-3580
Elkhart (G-2720)
Best Chairs Incorporated ....D...... 812 367-1761
Cannelton (G-1287)
Cabinetmaker Inc ....G...... 812 723-3461
Paoli (G-11446)
Chromcraft Revington Inc ....E...... 662 562-8203
West Lafayette (G-14058)
Commercial Electric Co Inc ....E...... 260 726-9357
Portland (G-11813)
Coppes-Nappanee Company Inc ....F...... 574 773-0007
Nappanee (G-10663)
Country Cabinets ....G...... 260 694-6777
Poneto (G-11745)
Country View Furn Mfg & Uphl ....G...... 812 636-5024
Odon (G-11321)
Custom Millwork & Display LLC ....G...... 574 289-9772
South Bend (G-12749)
Dmi Furniture Inc ....F...... 812 683-4035
Huntingburg (G-6156)
Douglas Dye and Associates ....G...... 317 844-1709
Carmel (G-1362)
Eagle Nest Workshop ....G...... 812 876-3215
Spencer (G-13023)
Ecojacks LLC ....G...... 574 306-0414
South Whitley (G-12998)
Ed Lloyd Co ....G...... 812 342-2505
Columbus (G-1917)
Efurnituremax LLC ....G...... 317 697-9504
Indianapolis (G-6811)
Fehrenbacher Cabinets Inc ....E...... 812 963-3377
Evansville (G-3502)
Flat Rock Furniture Inc ....E...... 317 398-1501
Waldron (G-13798)

Gloria J Burnworth ....G...... 765 366-3950
Attica (G-302)
Graber Woodworks Inc ....G...... 812 486-2861
Montgomery (G-10226)
Grabill Cabinet Company Inc ....C...... 877 472-2782
Grabill (G-5368)
Haas Cabinet Co Inc ....C...... 812 246-4431
Sellersburg (G-12395)
Hackney Home Furnishings Inc ....E...... 317 895-4300
Indianapolis (G-7065)
Heartwood Manufacturing Inc ....E...... 812 933-0388
Batesville (G-503)
Hickory Furniture Designs Inc ....F...... 765 642-0700
Anderson (G-114)
Homestead Primitives Inc ....G...... 812 782-3521
Francisco (G-4816)
Hoosier Wood Creations Inc ....D...... 574 831-6330
New Paris (G-10983)
Indiana Architectural Plywood ....E...... 317 878-4822
Trafalgar (G-13436)
Indianan Woodcrafts ....G...... 574 586-3741
Walkerton (G-13803)
J Jesse Inc ....F...... 574 862-4538
Wakarusa (G-13780)
J Miller Cabinetry Inc ....G...... 260 691-2032
Columbia City (G-1800)
J W Woodworking Inc ....G...... 574 831-3033
New Paris (G-10987)
Jason Randall Designs ....G...... 317 319-6747
Kokomo (G-8650)
Jasper Chair Company Inc ....D...... 812 482-5239
Jasper (G-8255)
Johnny Bontrager ....G...... 260 463-8912
Lagrange (G-9050)
Kasnak Restorations Inc ....G...... 317 852-9770
Brownsburg (G-1159)
Kimball International Inc ....B...... 812 482-1600
Jasper (G-8282)
Kountry Kraft Wood Products ....G...... 574 831-6736
New Paris (G-10988)
Kramer Furn & Cab Makers Inc ....F...... 812 526-2711
Edinburgh (G-2615)
L R Nisley & Sons ....F...... 574 642-1245
Goshen (G-5261)
Lambright Woodworking LLC ....E...... 260 593-2721
Topeka (G-13423)
Leibering Dimension Inc ....E...... 812 367-2971
Ferdinand (G-3856)
Lockerbie Square Cab Co Inc ....G...... 317 635-1134
Indianapolis (G-7413)
Madison Cabinets Inc ....G...... 260 639-3915
Hoagland (G-6066)
Martins Wood Works ....G...... 574 862-4080
Goshen (G-5281)
Moores Country Wood Crafting ....F...... 317 984-3326
Arcadia (G-266)
Oeding Corporation ....G...... 812 367-1271
Ferdinand (G-3860)
Ofs Brands Holdings Inc ....A...... 800 521-5381
Huntingburg (G-6177)
Old Barn Creations LLC ....G...... 219 324-2553
La Porte (G-8801)
Old Guy Woodcrafters LLC ....G...... 574 527-9044
Winona Lake (G-14352)
Patrick Industries Inc ....E...... 574 293-1521
Elkhart (G-3084)
Philip Reinisch Company Llc ....C...... 812 326-2626
Saint Anthony (G-12249)
Progressive Woodcraft LLC ....G...... 574 546-9010
Bremen (G-1017)
Rbk Development Inc ....E...... 574 267-5879
Warsaw (G-13934)
REM Industries Inc ....E...... 574 862-2127
Wakarusa (G-13792)
Rentown Cabinets ....G...... 574 546-2569
Bremen (G-1020)
Rodeswood LLC ....G...... 574 457-4496
Syracuse (G-13142)
Roudebush Company Incorporated ......G...... 574 595-7115
Star City (G-13070)
Sampler Inc ....F...... 765 663-2233
Homer (G-6109)
Schmidt Cabinet Co Inc ....E...... 812 347-1031
New Salisbury (G-11011)
Stump Home Specialties Mfg Inc ....G...... 574 291-0050
South Bend (G-12959)
Superior Woodcrafts LLC ....G...... 260 357-3743
Garrett (G-5023)
Swartzndrber Hrdwood Creat LLC ....E...... 574 534-2502
Goshen (G-5337)

Swings N Things ....G...... 260 336-8811
Lagrange (G-9070)
Tdf of Indiana Inc ....E...... 812 597-4009
Morgantown (G-10358)
Thomasville Furniture Inds Inc ....G...... 336 476-2175
Hammond (G-5950)
Timber Creek Design Co Inc ....F...... 317 297-5336
Indianapolis (G-8075)
Walters Cabinet Shop ....G...... 765 452-9634
Kokomo (G-8714)
Weberdings Carving Shop Inc ....E...... 812 934-3710
Batesville (G-524)
William A Kadar ....G...... 219 884-7404
Gary (G-5116)
Woodcrafters LLC ....G...... 765 469-5103
Denver (G-2455)
Woodcrest Manufacturing Inc ....D...... 765 472-4471
Peru (G-11559)
Woodcrest Manufacturing Inc ....G...... 765 472-5361
Peru (G-11560)
Wooden Concept Inc ....G...... 317 293-3137
Indianapolis (G-8213)

FURNITURE: Hydraulic Barber & Beauty Shop Chairs

Pioneer Signs Inc ....F...... 219 884-7587
Merrillville (G-9746)

FURNITURE: Institutional, Exc Wood

Chromcraft Revington Inc ....E...... 662 562-8203
West Lafayette (G-14058)
Clayton Dant Corporation ....G...... 317 842-2420
Fishers (G-3891)
Custom Millwork & Display LLC ....G...... 574 289-9772
South Bend (G-12749)
Custom Wood Products Inc ....G...... 574 522-3300
Elkhart (G-2784)
Erl Properties Inc ....G...... 812 948-8484
New Albany (G-10772)
Finish Design Woodworking Inc ....F...... 812 284-9240
Jeffersonville (G-8360)
H John Enterprise Inc ....E...... 574 293-6008
Elkhart (G-2903)
Integrated Mfg & Assembly LLC ....B...... 260 244-1700
Columbia City (G-1797)
Lakemaster Inc ....E...... 765 288-3718
Muncie (G-10507)
Lear Corporation ....B...... 219 852-0014
Hammond (G-5907)
Norco Industries Inc ....C...... 574 262-3400
Elkhart (G-3065)
R&D Investment Holdings Inc ....E...... 260 749-1301
Fort Wayne (G-4575)
REM Industries Inc ....E...... 574 862-2127
Wakarusa (G-13792)
T F S Inc ....G...... 260 422-5896
Fort Wayne (G-4672)
Tls By Design ....F...... 765 683-1971
Indianapolis (G-8077)
Weberdings Carving Shop Inc ....E...... 812 934-3710
Batesville (G-524)

FURNITURE: Juvenile, Wood

Rwb & Associates LLC ....G...... 317 219-6572
Noblesville (G-11178)

FURNITURE: Kitchen & Dining Room

Country Woodshop LLC ....E...... 574 642-3681
Goshen (G-5194)

FURNITURE: Kitchen & Dining Room, Metal

Prolam Products Inc ....D...... 812 867-1662
Evansville (G-3687)

FURNITURE: Lawn & Garden, Except Wood & Metal

Keter North America LLC ....G...... 765 298-6800
Anderson (G-129)

FURNITURE: Lawn & Garden, Metal

Wabash Valley Manufacturing ....C...... 260 352-2102
Silver Lake (G-12682)

PRODUCT

FURNITURE: Lawn, Wood

Georges Custom Wood Working ....G 812 944-3344
New Albany *(G-10787)*

FURNITURE: Living Room, Upholstered On Wood Frames

Shelby Westside Upholstering ....G 317 631-8911
Indianapolis *(G-7931)*

FURNITURE: Mattresses & Foundations

Holder Bedding Inc ....G 765 447-7907
Lafayette *(G-8916)*
May and Co Inc ....E 317 236-6500
Greenwood *(G-5724)*
Vans TV & Appliance Inc ....F 260 927-8267
Auburn *(G-366)*
Williamsburg Furniture Inc ....G 574 387-5691
South Bend *(G-12991)*
Williamsburg Furniture Inc ....C 800 582-8183
Nappanee *(G-10710)*

FURNITURE: Mattresses, Box & Bedsprings

Futon Factory Inc ....F 317 549-8639
Indianapolis *(G-6971)*
Kimalco Inc ....G 812 463-3105
Evansville *(G-3589)*
KMC Corporation ....D 574 267-7033
Warsaw *(G-13898)*
Leggett & Platt Incorporated ....D 219 766-2261
Kouts *(G-8717)*
Leggett & Platt Incorporated ....C 260 347-2600
Kendallville *(G-8490)*
Sleepmadecom LLC ....E 662 350-0999
Evansville *(G-3734)*
Superior Mattress Inc ....G 812 422-5761
Evansville *(G-3754)*
Woodcrest Manufacturing Inc ....F 765 472-5361
Peru *(G-11560)*

FURNITURE: Mattresses, Innerspring Or Box Spring

Derby Inc ....D 574 233-4500
South Bend *(G-12751)*
Elkhart Bedding Co Inc ....F 574 293-6200
Elkhart *(G-2820)*
Mastercraft Inc ....C 260 463-8702
Lagrange *(G-9060)*
Wolf Corporation ....E 260 749-9393
Fort Wayne *(G-4760)*

FURNITURE: NEC

Affordable Furniture ....E 317 881-7726
Greenwood *(G-5662)*
No Sag ....F 260 347-2600
Kendallville *(G-8500)*
Zoom Seating ....G 574 825-3368
Middlebury *(G-9932)*

FURNITURE: Novelty, Wood

Dubois Wood Products Inc ....C 812 683-3613
Huntingburg *(G-6158)*

FURNITURE: Nursery, Wood

WC Redmon Co Inc ....F 765 473-6683
Peru *(G-11556)*

FURNITURE: Office Panel Systems, Exc Wood

Genesis Products Inc ....E 574 262-4054
Elkhart *(G-2877)*
Modernfold Inc ....C 800 869-9685
Greenfield *(G-5557)*
Trendway Corporation ....F 317 870-3269
Indianapolis *(G-8094)*

FURNITURE: Office, Exc Wood

F D Ramsey & Co Inc ....F 219 362-2452
La Porte *(G-8757)*
Fire King Security Pdts LLC ....C 812 948-8400
New Albany *(G-10780)*
Gjs Home and Office Furniture ....G 765 472-2478
Peru *(G-11528)*

Global ....G 317 494-6174
Franklin *(G-4889)*
Growth Principals LLC ....G 812 320-1574
Bloomington *(G-735)*
Jasper Chair Company Inc ....D 812 482-5239
Jasper *(G-8255)*
Jasper Seating Company Inc ....D 812 723-1323
Paoli *(G-11454)*
Jasper Seating Company Inc ....A 812 482-3204
Jasper *(G-8264)*
Jsj Furniture Corporation ....C 574 825-5871
Middlebury *(G-9899)*
Kimball Furniture Group LLC ....C 812 482-8517
Jasper *(G-8276)*
Kimball Furniture Group LLC ....B 812 634-3526
Jasper *(G-8277)*
Kimball Furniture Group LLC ....C 812 883-1850
Salem *(G-12297)*
Kimball Furniture Group LLC ....C 812 482-1600
Jasper *(G-8279)*
Kimball International Inc ....B 812 482-1600
Jasper *(G-8282)*
Kimball National Office F ....C 812 634-3356
Jasper *(G-8283)*
Lui Plus ....G 812 309-9350
Indianapolis *(G-7425)*
Office Furniture Warehouse Inc ....G 317 872-6477
Indianapolis *(G-7611)*
Ofs Brands Holdings Inc ....A 800 521-5381
Huntingburg *(G-6177)*
Pinnacle Seating Inc ....G 574 522-2636
Elkhart *(G-3096)*
Pulley-Kellam Co Inc ....E 260 356-6326
Huntington *(G-6240)*
Unique Global Solutions LLC ....G 765 779-5030
Anderson *(G-180)*

FURNITURE: Office, Wood

Antreasian Design Inc ....F 317 546-3234
Indianapolis *(G-6404)*
Aynes Upholstery LLC ....G 812 829-1321
Freedom *(G-4947)*
Beebe Cabinet Co Inc ....F 574 233-3580
Elkhart *(G-2720)*
Chromcraft Revington Inc ....E 662 562-8203
West Lafayette *(G-14058)*
Custom Millwork & Display LLC ....G 574 289-9772
South Bend *(G-12749)*
Custom Wood Products Inc ....D 574 522-3300
Elkhart *(G-2784)*
Dbisp LLC ....F 317 222-1671
Indianapolis *(G-6729)*
Double T Manufacturing Corp ....F 574 262-1340
Elkhart *(G-2799)*
Dubois Wood Realty Inc ....C 812 683-3613
Huntingburg *(G-6160)*
Ecojacks LLC ....G 574 306-0414
South Whitley *(G-12998)*
Environmental Products Inc ....F 219 393-3446
Kingsbury *(G-8537)*
Graber Cabinetry LLC ....E 260 627-2243
Grabill *(G-5366)*
Indiana Furniture Inds Inc ....C 812 678-2396
Dubois *(G-2476)*
Indiana Southern Millwork Inc ....E 812 346-6129
North Vernon *(G-11263)*
Izzy Plus ....G 574 821-1200
Middlebury *(G-9895)*
Jasper Seating Company Inc ....A 812 482-3204
Jasper *(G-8264)*
Jasper Seating Company Inc ....D 812 723-1323
Paoli *(G-11454)*
Johnco Corp ....G 317 576-4417
Indianapolis *(G-7308)*
Jsj Furniture Corporation ....C 574 825-5871
Middlebury *(G-9899)*
Kimball Furniture Group LLC ....C 812 482-1600
Jasper *(G-8279)*
Kimball International Inc ....B 812 482-1600
Jasper *(G-8282)*
Knox County Association ....D 812 886-4312
Vincennes *(G-13689)*
Millmade Inc ....G 812 424-7778
Evansville *(G-3629)*
National Office Furniture Inc ....C 812 482-1600
Jasper *(G-8298)*
Ofs Brands Holdings Inc ....A 800 521-5381
Huntingburg *(G-6177)*
Shamrock Cabinets Inc ....E 812 482-7969
Jasper *(G-8308)*

Swartzndrber Hrdwood Creat LLC ....E 574 534-2502
Goshen *(G-5337)*

FURNITURE: Outdoor, Wood

Custom Built Barns Inc ....G 765 457-9037
Kokomo *(G-8610)*
Fresh Start Inc ....F 812 254-3398
Washington *(G-13982)*
Home & Lawn Services ....G 260 633-9155
Fort Wayne *(G-4338)*
Numark Industries Company Ltd ....F 317 718-2502
Avon *(G-459)*
Wingards Sales LLC ....G 260 768-7961
Shipshewana *(G-12659)*

FURNITURE: Picnic Tables Or Benches, Park

County of Steuben ....G 260 833-2401
Angola *(G-205)*
Nvb Playgrounds Inc ....G 317 826-2777
Indianapolis *(G-7607)*
Recreation Insites LLC ....G 317 578-0588
Fishers *(G-3961)*

FURNITURE: Recliners, Upholstered On Wood Frames

Seating Technology Inc ....C 574 971-4100
Goshen *(G-5322)*

FURNITURE: Restaurant

Hanco Inc ....E 800 968-6655
Carmel *(G-1393)*
U B Klem Furniture Co Inc ....D 812 326-2236
Saint Anthony *(G-12250)*

FURNITURE: Rockers, Wood, Exc Upholstered

D & E Workshop ....G 260 593-0195
Topeka *(G-13415)*

FURNITURE: School

Jasper Chair Company Inc ....D 812 482-5239
Jasper *(G-8255)*
Jasper Seating Company Inc ....A 812 482-3204
Jasper *(G-8264)*

FURNITURE: Screens, privacy, Wood

Out of Sight Screen Co Inc ....G 317 430-1705
Indianapolis *(G-7638)*

FURNITURE: Silverware Chests, Wood

A S M Inc ....G 260 724-8220
Decatur *(G-2363)*

FURNITURE: Sofa Beds Or Convertible Sofas)

Seating Technology Inc ....C 574 971-4100
Goshen *(G-5322)*

FURNITURE: Storage Chests, Household, Wood

Graber Manufacturing LLC ....G 260 657-3400
Grabill *(G-5367)*
Mission Woodworking Inc ....E 574 848-5697
Bristol *(G-1069)*

FURNITURE: Table Tops, Marble

Marstone Products Ltd ....E 800 466-7465
Fairland *(G-3824)*

FURNITURE: Tables & Table Tops, Wood

Dubois Wood Products Inc ....E 812 683-5105
Huntingburg *(G-6159)*

FURNITURE: Tables, Household, Metal

Austin-Westran LLC ....C 815 234-2811
Indianapolis *(G-6441)*

FURNITURE: Tables, Office, Wood

Mouron & Company Inc ....F 317 243-7955
Indianapolis *(G-7551)*

FURNITURE: Theater

Cinematic Captioning Systems ....G....... 317 862-3418
Indianapolis (G-6606)

FURNITURE: Unfinished, Wood

Heritage Fine Furn & Cabinetry ....G...... 812 205-5437
Evansville (G-3538)

FURNITURE: Upholstered

Aaron Company Incorporated ....F 219 838-0852
Gary (G-5026)
Campbell Cobert Woodcraft ....G.... 812 883-5399
Salem (G-12285)
Chromcraft Revington Inc ....E 662 562-8203
West Lafayette (G-14058)
Coffeys Custom Upholstery ....G.... 812 948-8611
New Albany (G-10763)
Country View Furn Mfg & Uphl ....G.... 812 636-5024
Odon (G-11321)
Design Works Inc ....G.... 317 815-8619
Fishers (G-3899)
Furniture Sales & Marketing ....G.... 317 849-1508
Indianapolis (G-6970)
Home Reserve LLC ....F 260 969-6939
Fort Wayne (G-4339)
Jasper Chair Company Inc ....D.... 812 482-5239
Jasper (G-8255)
Kimball International Inc ....B 812 482-1600
Jasper (G-8282)
KMC Corporation ....D.... 574 267-7033
Warsaw (G-13898)
Mastercraft Inc ....C 260 463-8702
Lagrange (G-9060)
Peggy Williams ....G.... 765 724-3862
Alexandria (G-47)
Smith Brothers Berne Inc ....B 260 589-2131
Berne (G-623)
Sylvia Kay Hartley ....G.... 317 984-3424
Arcadia (G-270)
Transformations By Wieland Inc ....D.... 800 440-9337
Fort Wayne (G-4698)
Vans TV & Appliance Inc ....F 260 927-8267
Auburn (G-366)
Williamsburg Furniture Inc ....G.... 574 387-5691
South Bend (G-12991)
Williamsburg Furniture Inc ....C 800 582-8183
Nappanee (G-10710)

FURNITURE: Vehicle

Fbsa LLC..E 574 542-2001
Rochester (G-12123)
Fiberglass Engrg & Design Inc.............G.... 317 293-0002
Indianapolis (G-6918)
Lippert Components Inc ....F 574 534-8177
Goshen (G-5266)
Lippert Components Inc ....D.... 574 534-2163
Goshen (G-5270)
Lippert Components Inc ....E 574 295-8166
Elkhart (G-3001)
Transportation Tech Inds ....F 812 962-5000
Evansville (G-3769)
Veada Industries Inc ....A 574 831-4775
New Paris (G-11000)

FURNITURE: Waterbed Frames, Wood

Merrill Manufacturing Inc ....F 812 752-6688
Scottsburg (G-12374)

FURNITURE: Wicker & Rattan

Dimensions Furniture Inc.......................F 317 218-0025
Carmel (G-1361)

FUSES & FUSE EQPT

Hoffmaster Electric Inc..........................G.... 219 616-1313
Schererville (G-12323)

Furs

Fur Real Taxidermy LLC........................G.... 812 667-6365
Cross Plains (G-2212)

GAMES & TOYS: Baby Carriages & Restraint Seats

Dorel Juvenile Group Inc ....F 812 314-6629
Columbus (G-1910)

Snuggy Baby LLC...................................G.... 260 418-6795
Fort Wayne (G-4632)

GAMES & TOYS: Banks

Harris Bmo Bank National Assn............G.... 219 939-0164
Gary (G-5059)
PNC Bank National Association ....G.... 812 948-4490
New Albany (G-10845)

GAMES & TOYS: Bingo Boards

Continuum Games Incorporated ....G.... 877 405-2662
Indianapolis (G-6658)

GAMES & TOYS: Board Games, Children's & Adults'

Fundex Games Ltd ....D.... 317 248-1080
Indianapolis (G-6969)
Ludo Fact USA LLC ....D.... 765 588-9137
Lafayette (G-8962)

GAMES & TOYS: Books, Picture & Cutout

4 Kids Books ....F 317 733-8710
Zionsville (G-14414)

GAMES & TOYS: Child Restraint Seats, Automotive

EVS Ltd ....F 574 233-5707
South Bend (G-12767)
Merritt Manufacturing Inc......................G.... 317 409-0148
Indianapolis (G-7483)

GAMES & TOYS: Craft & Hobby Kits & Sets

Country Cabin LLC ....G.... 812 232-4635
Terre Haute (G-13218)
Country Woodcrafts Inc ....G.... 260 244-7578
Columbia City (G-1775)
K&D Crafts ....G.... 812 667-2575
Dillsboro (G-2469)
Old Lumber Yard Clay Factory ....F 260 627-3567
Grabill (G-5382)
Planet Mind LLC ....G.... 765 452-2341
Kokomo (G-8681)
Shepherds Loft ....G.... 812 486-2304
Montgomery (G-10241)

GAMES & TOYS: Darts & Dart Games

Kan Jam LLC ....F 317 804-9129
Westfield (G-14172)

GAMES & TOYS: Dolls & Doll Clothing

Kls Santas ....G.... 765 474-6951
Lafayette (G-8944)

GAMES & TOYS: Dolls, Exc Stuffed Toy Animals

Turner Dolls Inc ....G.... 812 834-5065
Heltonville (G-6029)
Virginias Very Own LLC ....G.... 812 834-5065
Heltonville (G-6030)

GAMES & TOYS: Electronic

Lightuptoyscom LLC ....E 812 246-1916
Sellersburg (G-12403)

GAMES & TOYS: Hobby Horses

Peter Stone Company ....E 260 768-9150
Shipshewana (G-12643)

GAMES & TOYS: Kits, Science, Incl Microscopes/Chemistry Sets

Eureka Science Corp ....G...... 317 821-0805
Camby (G-1266)
Scitt Inc ....G.... 574 208-6649
Mishawaka (G-10122)

GAMES & TOYS: Models, Airplane, Toy & Hobby

B & B Specialties Inc ....G.... 574 277-0499
Granger (G-5391)

Midwest Products Co Inc ....D....... 219 942-1134
Hobart (G-6092)

GAMES & TOYS: Models, Automobile & Truck, Toy & Hobby

Greenlight LLC ....F 317 287-0600
Indianapolis (G-7044)

GAMES & TOYS: Models, Railroad, Toy & Hobby

Rix Products Inc.....................................G.... 812 426-1749
Evansville (G-3706)

GAMES & TOYS: Puzzles

Claywood Creation ....G.... 260 244-7719
Columbia City (G-1774)
Jigsaw Creations ....G.... 260 691-2196
Columbia City (G-1802)
Lafayette Puzzle Factory LLC ....G.... 800 883-6408
Lafayette (G-8949)
Lpf Limited ....G.... 765 447-0939
Lafayette (G-8961)
Warren Industries Inc ....D.... 765 447-2151
Lafayette (G-9020)

GAMES & TOYS: Strollers, Baby, Vehicle

Cosco Inc..A 812 372-0141
Columbus (G-1883)
Dorel USA Inc ....D.... 812 372-0141
Columbus (G-1914)

GARBAGE CONTAINERS: Plastic

Ameri-Kart Corp ....C 574 848-7462
Bristol (G-1044)
Therma-Tru Corp ....F 260 868-5811
Butler (G-1245)
Waste 1 ....G.... 765 477-9138
Lafayette (G-9021)

GAS & OIL FIELD EXPLORATION SVCS

Barger Engineering Inc ....G.... 812 476-3077
Evansville (G-3370)
Breitburn Operating LP ....G.... 812 738-3338
Corydon (G-2091)
Enviropeel USA ....G.... 317 631-9100
Indianapolis (G-6873)
Gemini Oil LLC ....G.... 260 571-8388
Warren (G-13830)
Hansford Co ....G.... 317 255-4756
Indianapolis (G-7070)
Imperial Petroleum Inc ....G.... 812 867-1433
Evansville (G-3549)
Legacy Resources Co LP.......................G.... 317 328-5660
Indianapolis (G-7394)
Michael R Harris....................................G.... 812 425-9411
Evansville (G-3625)
Mid Central Land & Exploration ....G.... 812 476-9393
Carmel (G-1440)
Pioneer Oil Company Inc ....F 812 494-2800
Vincennes (G-13697)
Plymouth Oil and Gas Inc ....G.... 574 875-4808
Goshen (G-5311)
Silver Petroleum Corp ....G.... 260 824-2220
Bluffton (G-891)
Trey Exploration Inc...............................G.... 812 858-3146
Newburgh (G-11052)
Vickery Drilling Co ....G.... 812 473-4671
Evansville (G-3798)

GAS & OIL FIELD SVCS, NEC

Breitburn Operating LP ....G.... 812 738-3338
Corydon (G-2091)
Ken Tex Crude Producers Inc................G.... 812 723-2108
Lafayette (G-8938)
Rs Used Oil Services Inc........................F 866 778-7336
Carmel (G-1473)

GAS APPLIANCE REPAIR SVCS

American Flame Inc................................D.... 260 459-1703
Fort Wayne (G-4070)
Goudy Brothers Boiler Co Inc ....E 765 459-4416
Kokomo (G-8631)

GAS FIELD MACHINERY & EQPT

Daylight Engineering Inc ....G...... 812 983-2518
Elberfeld (G-2633)
Gesco Group LLC ....G...... 260 747-5088
Fort Wayne (G-4300)
Llama Corporation ....G...... 888 701-7432
Decatur (G-2391)

GAS PROCESSING SVC

Panhandle Eastrn Pipe Line LP ....E...... 317 873-2410
Indianapolis (G-7649)
Siswd Processing ....G...... 812 574-4080
Madison (G-9495)

GAS PRODUCTION & DISTRIBUTION: Coke Oven

Sssi Inc ....D...... 219 880-0818
Gary (G-5101)

GAS: Refinery

Shell Pipe Line Corporation ....G...... 765 962-1329
Richmond (G-12049)

GASES & LIQUIFIED PETROLEUM GASES

Hometown Energy ....G...... 812 663-3391
Greensburg (G-5611)
Williams Companies Inc ....G...... 765 886-6149
Williamsburg (G-14285)

GASES: Acetylene

Northern Gases and Sups Inc ....F...... 574 594-2551
Pierceton (G-11574)

GASES: Carbon Dioxide

Airgas Usa LLC ....G...... 812 537-4101
Moores Hill (G-10296)
Jt Composites LLC ....G...... 317 297-9520
Indianapolis (G-7320)

GASES: Flourinated Hydrocarbon

Eco Services Operations Corp ....E...... 219 932-7651
Hammond (G-5874)

GASES: Helium

Digital Helium LLC ....G...... 219 365-4038
Saint John (G-12262)

GASES: Indl

A G A Gas Inc ....E...... 317 783-2331
Indianapolis (G-6295)
Air Products and Chemicals Inc ....E...... 260 868-9145
Butler (G-1221)
Air Products and Chemicals Inc ....E...... 219 787-9551
Chesterton (G-1591)
Airgas Inc ....G...... 812 376-9155
Greenwood (G-5664)
Airgas Usa LLC ....E...... 812 838-8808
Mount Vernon (G-10382)
Airgas Usa LLC ....F...... 317 783-2331
Indianapolis (G-6356)
Airgas Usa LLC ....G...... 317 892-5221
Pittsboro (G-11582)
Airgas Usa LLC ....F...... 260 749-9576
Fort Wayne (G-4051)
Airgas Usa LLC ....F...... 317 248-8072
Indianapolis (G-6355)
Airgas Usa LLC ....E...... 812 474-0440
Evansville (G-3345)
Airgas Usa LLC ....G...... 812 362-7593
Rockport (G-12163)
Ferrellgas LP ....F...... 574 936-2725
Plymouth (G-11684)
Indiana Oxygen Company Inc ....D...... 317 290-0003
Indianapolis (G-7188)
Linde LLC ....G...... 574 234-4887
South Bend (G-12839)
Matheson Tri-Gas Inc ....F...... 812 838-5518
Mount Vernon (G-10398)
Matheson Tri-Gas Inc ....F...... 812 257-0470
Washington (G-13990)
Matheson Tri-Gas Inc ....G...... 317 892-5221
Pittsboro (G-11585)
Petrogas International Corp ....G...... 260 484-0859
Auburn (G-347)

Praxair Inc ....F...... 219 398-3777
Whiting (G-14274)
Praxair Inc ....E...... 765 456-1128
Kokomo (G-8683)
Praxair Inc ....F...... 219 949-8407
Gary (G-5085)
Praxair Inc ....G...... 317 240-2500
Indianapolis (G-7721)
Praxair Inc ....C...... 219 398-3700
East Chicago (G-2562)
Praxair Inc ....F...... 219 397-6940
East Chicago (G-2563)
Praxair Inc ....G...... 765 447-8171
Lafayette (G-8982)
Praxair Inc ....E...... 812 537-2898
Lawrenceburg (G-9153)
Praxair Distribution Inc ....G...... 317 481-4550
Indianapolis (G-7722)
Praxair Distribution Inc ....G...... 260 423-4468
Fort Wayne (G-4546)
Praxair Distribution Inc ....G...... 317 481-4550
Indianapolis (G-7723)
Weaver Air Products LLC ....G...... 317 848-4420
Carmel (G-1508)

GASES: Neon

Neon Bay ....G...... 574 583-6366
Monticello (G-10273)
Neon Glassworks LLC ....G...... 765 497-1135
West Lafayette (G-14090)
Neon Safety Group LLC ....G...... 317 774-5144
Noblesville (G-11157)

GASES: Nitrogen

Linde LLC ....D...... 219 324-0498
La Porte (G-8786)

GASES: Oxygen

Alig LLC ....G...... 812 362-7593
Rockport (G-12165)
Linde Gas North America LLC ....F...... 219 989-9304
Hammond (G-5908)
Praxair Inc ....E...... 219 326-7808
La Porte (G-8805)

GASKET MATERIALS

Tfco Incorporated ....G...... 219 324-4166
La Porte (G-8830)

GASKETS

Bonar Inc ....G...... 260 636-7430
Albion (G-17)
Breiner Company Inc ....F...... 317 272-2521
Avon (G-434)
Cannon Fabrication Company ....F...... 765 629-2277
Milroy (G-9978)
Freudenberg-Nok General Partnr ....C...... 765 763-7246
Morristown (G-10369)
Gaska Tape Inc ....D...... 574 294-5431
Elkhart (G-2875)
Gindor Inc ....G...... 574 642-4004
Goshen (G-5225)
Hoosier Gasket Corporation ....D...... 317 545-2000
Indianapolis (G-7121)
Ilpea Industries Inc ....D...... 812 752-2526
Scottsburg (G-12362)
Ilpea Industries Inc ....D...... 812 752-2526
Scottsburg (G-12363)
Jeans Extrusions Inc ....C...... 812 883-2581
Salem (G-12296)
Marian Worldwide Inc ....D...... 317 638-6525
Indianapolis (G-7454)
Metallic Seals Inc ....G...... 317 780-0773
Indianapolis (G-7489)
Midwest Gasket Corporation ....E...... 765 629-2221
Milroy (G-9982)
Parker-Hannifin Corporation ....D...... 574 533-1111
Goshen (G-5307)

GASKETS & SEALING DEVICES

EMT Industries Inc ....E...... 574 533-1273
Granger (G-5406)
Federal-Mogul Powertrain LLC ....B...... 574 271-5954
South Bend (G-12776)
Hi-Tech Foam Products LLC ....E...... 270 684-8331
Indianapolis (G-7105)

Triangle Rubber Co LLC ....C...... 574 533-3118
Goshen (G-5340)
Trifab & Construction Inc ....G...... 219 845-1300
Hammond (G-5952)

GASOLINE FILLING STATIONS

Fairfield Gas Way ....G...... 260 744-2186
Fort Wayne (G-4253)

GATES: Ornamental Metal

Reese Forge Orna Ironwork ....G...... 219 775-1039
Lake Village (G-9086)

GAUGE BLOCKS

Krukemeier Machine and Tool Co ....F...... 317 784-7042
Beech Grove (G-600)

GAUGES

A & A Machine Service Inc ....G...... 317 745-7367
Avon (G-423)
Chesterfield Tool & Engrg Inc ....E...... 765 378-5101
Daleville (G-2338)
Ken-Bar Tool & Engineering Inc ....E...... 765 284-4408
Muncie (G-10503)
Merit Tool & Manufacturing Inc ....F...... 765 396-9566
Eaton (G-2586)
Nixon Tool Co Inc ....E...... 765 966-6608
Richmond (G-12024)

GEARS

Kanoff Enterprises ....G...... 574 575-6787
Mishawaka (G-10062)
Mtr Machining Concept Inc ....G...... 260 587-3381
Ashley (G-288)
Schafer Industries Inc ....D...... 574 234-4116
South Bend (G-12929)

GEARS: Power Transmission, Exc Auto

United Precision Gear Co Inc ....G...... 317 784-4665
Indianapolis (G-8128)

GENEALOGICAL INVESTIGATION SVCS

Selby Publishing & Printing ....G...... 765 453-5417
Kokomo (G-8693)

GENERAL MERCHANDISE STORES, NEC

Motorola Inc ....G...... 765 455-5100
Kokomo (G-8673)

GENERAL MERCHANDISE, NONDURABLE, WHOLESALE

Sycamore Enterprises Inc ....G...... 812 491-0901
Evansville (G-3756)

GENERATING APPARATUS & PARTS: Electrical

Hendershot Service Center Inc ....F...... 765 653-2600
Greencastle (G-5464)
Liberty Green Renewables LLP ....G...... 812 951-3143
Georgetown (G-5148)
Summit/Ems Corporation ....E...... 574 722-1317
Logansport (G-9366)

GENERATION EQPT: Electronic

Amerawhip Inc ....G...... 317 639-5248
Indianapolis (G-6383)
Empro Manufacturing Co Inc ....E...... 317 823-3000
Indianapolis (G-6859)
Globalvue International LLC ....G...... 866 974-1968
Indianapolis (G-7014)
Motion & Control Entps LLC ....F...... 219 844-4224
Hammond (G-5918)
R B Annis Instruments Inc ....G...... 765 848-1621
Greencastle (G-5476)
Southwater Sourcing LLC ....G...... 219 809-7106
Michigan City (G-9845)

GENERATOR SETS: Motor

W W Williams Company LLC ....F...... 260 827-0553
Bluffton (G-896)

GENERATORS: Electric

Cummins Power Generation Inc..........E 574 262-4611
Elkhart (G-2783)

GENERATORS: Vehicles, Gas-Electric Or Oil-Electric

Go Electric Inc..........F 765 400-1347
Anderson (G-111)

GIFT SHOP

Abbotts Candy and Gifts Inc.................E 765 489-4442
Hagerstown (G-5801)
Alan W Long..........G 812 265-6717
Madison (G-9442)
All Occasions Gift Shop LLC ....G 513 314-5693
Metamora (G-9762)
Concrete Lady Inc..........E 812 256-2765
Otisco (G-11416)
Cowpokes Inc..........E 765 642-3911
Anderson (G-91)
Friends of Third World Inc ....G 260 422-6821
Fort Wayne (G-4288)
Mercantile Store..........G 812 988-6939
Nashville (G-10729)
Pgs LLC..........E 812 988-4030
Nashville (G-10732)

GIFT WRAP: Paper, Made From Purchased Materials

American Stationery Co ....G 765 473-4438
Peru (G-11515)

GIFT, NOVELTY & SOUVENIR STORES: Artcraft & carvings

Schuster Glass Studio..........G 812 988-7377
Nashville (G-10734)

GIFT, NOVELTY & SOUVENIR STORES: Gifts & Novelties

Bbs Celebration Center..........G 765 730-6575
Yorktown (G-14402)
Crystal Source..........G 812 988-7009
Nashville (G-10721)
Entertainment Express..........F 219 763-3610
Portage (G-11760)

GIFT, NOVELTY & SOUVENIR STORES: Trading Cards, Sports

Eds Trading Post Inc ....G 317 933-4867
Nineveh (G-11057)

GIFTS & NOVELTIES: Wholesalers

Bbs Celebration Center..........G 765 730-6575
Yorktown (G-14402)
Howe House Ltd Editions Inc ....G 765 742-6831
Lafayette (G-8918)

GLASS FABRICATORS

American Window and Glass Inc ....C 812 464-9400
Evansville (G-3352)
Bizik Masonry Corporation..........G 219 659-1348
Whiting (G-14270)
Cardinal Glass Industries Inc ....B 260 495-4105
Fremont (G-4953)
Carlex Glass America LLC..........B 260 894-7750
Ligonier (G-9279)
Crown Industries Inc..........E 219 791-9930
Crown Point (G-2239)
Etching Industries Corporation ....E 317 591-3500
Indianapolis (G-6882)
Fox Studios Inc..........F 317 253-0135
Indianapolis (G-6953)
Gardner Glass Products Inc ....F 317 464-0881
Indianapolis (G-6984)
Great Panes Glass Co ....G 260 426-0203
Fort Wayne (G-4306)
Indy Glass Center Inc ....F 317 591-5000
Indianapolis (G-7217)
International Steel Company ....D 812 425-3311
Evansville (G-3565)
JC Moag Corporation ....D 812 284-8400
Jeffersonville (G-8383)

Kinro Manufacturing Inc..........C 574 535-1125
Elkhart (G-2970)
Lippert Components Mfg Inc ....C 574 935-5122
Plymouth (G-11703)
Moores Country Wood Crafting..........F 317 984-3326
Arcadia (G-266)
Moss L Glass Co Inc..........F 765 642-4946
Indianapolis (G-7546)
Oldcastle Buildingenvelope Inc..........G 317 876-1155
Indianapolis (G-7616)
Pilkington North America Inc..........A 317 392-7000
Shelbyville (G-12557)
Rainbows Stained Glass..........G 812 265-0030
Madison (G-9491)
Recycling Center Inc..........D 765 966-8295
Richmond (G-12041)
Recycling Works Inc..........F 574 293-3751
Elkhart (G-3141)
Taylor Made Group Holdings Inc..........C 260 347-1368
Kendallville (G-8512)
Whitaker Glass & Mirror LLC..........G 765 482-1500
Lebanon (G-9232)
Winandy Greenhouse Company..........E 765 935-2111
Richmond (G-12076)

GLASS PRDTS, FROM PURCHASED GLASS: Glassware

Kokomo Opalescent Glass Co..........E 765 457-8136
Kokomo (G-8654)
Parsing Laser Designs LLC ....G 317 677-4316
Avon (G-460)

GLASS PRDTS, FROM PURCHASED GLASS: Mirrored

D & W Inc..........D 574 264-9674
Elkhart (G-2785)
Faries-Mcmeekan Inc..........E 574 293-3526
Elkhart (G-2845)
Omega National Products LLC..........C 574 295-5353
Elkhart (G-3068)

GLASS PRDTS, FROM PURCHASED GLASS: Mirrors, Framed

Floralcraft Distributors..........E 574 262-2639
Elkhart (G-2858)

GLASS PRDTS, FROM PURCHASED GLASS: Windshields

Carlex Glass America LLC..........B 260 925-5656
Auburn (G-320)
Dewilde Glass Inc..........G 765 742-0229
Lafayette (G-8890)
Glass Surgeons..........G 219 374-2500
Cedar Lake (G-1528)
Safelite Glass Corp..........G 260 423-2477
Fort Wayne (G-4601)

GLASS PRDTS, FROM PURCHD GLASS: Strengthened Or Reinforced

Cleer Vision Windows Inc..........F 574 262-0449
Elkhart (G-2759)
Cleer Vision Windows Inc..........F 574 262-0449
Elkhart (G-2760)
Creative Industries Inc..........F 317 248-1102
Indianapolis (G-6688)
Pittsburgh Glass Works LLC..........B 812 867-6601
Evansville (G-3673)
State Wide Aluminum Inc..........D 574 262-2594
Elkhart (G-3191)

GLASS PRDTS, PRESSED OR BLOWN: Blocks & Bricks

Colliers Glassblock Inc..........G 574 288-8682
South Bend (G-12738)

GLASS PRDTS, PRESSED OR BLOWN: Bulbs, Electric Lights

Dekker Lighting..........G 219 227-8520
Schererville (G-12320)
Vivid Leds Inc..........F 800 974-3570
Sellersburg (G-12421)

GLASS PRDTS, PRESSED OR BLOWN: Candlesticks

Cedar Shack..........G 219 682-5531
Cedar Lake (G-1527)

GLASS PRDTS, PRESSED OR BLOWN: Furnishings & Access

Hh Rellim Inc..........G 812 662-9944
Greensburg (G-5609)

GLASS PRDTS, PRESSED OR BLOWN: Glass Fibers, Textile

Global Composites Inc..........C 574 522-9956
Elkhart (G-2883)

GLASS PRDTS, PRESSED OR BLOWN: Glassware, Art Or Decorative

Inspired Fire Glass Studio & G..........G 765 474-1981
Lafayette (G-8925)
Zimmerman Art Glass Company..........G 812 738-2206
Corydon (G-2117)

GLASS PRDTS, PRESSED OR BLOWN: Glassware, Novelty

L D Barger Wholesale Neon Inc..........G 765 643-4506
Anderson (G-131)

GLASS PRDTS, PRESSED OR BLOWN: Reflector, Lighting Eqpt

General Signals Inc..........F 812 474-4256
Evansville (G-3518)

GLASS PRDTS, PURCHASED GLASS: Glassware, Scientific/Tech

Hector Engineering Co..........G 812 876-5274
Ellettsville (G-3280)

GLASS PRDTS, PURCHSD GLASS: Ornamental, Cut, Engraved/Décor

A New Company Inc..........F 574 293-9088
Elkhart (G-2658)
Middletown Enterprises Inc..........E 765 348-3100
Hartford City (G-5985)
Sherwood Industries Inc..........E 574 262-2639
Elkhart (G-3166)

GLASS STORE: Leaded Or Stained

Golden Frame Inc..........G 812 232-0048
Terre Haute (G-13242)
Indiana Bevel Inc..........G 317 596-0001
Fishers (G-3928)
Mominee Studios Inc..........G 812 473-1691
Evansville (G-3633)
Whitaker Glass & Mirror LLC..........G 765 482-1500
Lebanon (G-9232)

GLASS STORES

Dewilde Glass Inc..........G 765 742-0229
Lafayette (G-8890)
Great Panes Glass Co..........G 260 426-0203
Fort Wayne (G-4306)
Moss L Glass Co Inc..........F 765 642-4946
Indianapolis (G-7546)
Oldcastle Buildingenvelope Inc..........D 317 876-1155
Indianapolis (G-7617)

GLASS: Fiber

B Thystrup US Corporation..........G 574 834-2554
North Webster (G-11289)
Map of Easton..........G 574 293-0966
Elkhart (G-3017)
Palmetto Planters LLC..........G 765 396-4446
Eaton (G-2587)
Pyrotek Incorporated..........E 260 248-4141
Columbia City (G-1820)
Stability America Inc..........G 574 642-3029
Goshen (G-5326)
Talon Products LLC..........F 574 218-0100
Bristol (G-1089)

Employee Codes: A=Over 500 employees, B=251-500
C=101-250, D=51-100, E=20-50, F=10-19, G=2-9

2018 Harris Indiana
Industrial Directory

983

PRODUCT

V & H Fiberglass Repair ....G...... 574 772-4920
Knox *(G-8586)*

GLASS: Flat

Capitol City Glass Inc ....G...... 317 635-2556
Indianapolis *(G-6550)*
Carlex Glass America LLC ....B...... 260 925-5656
Auburn *(G-320)*
Carlex Indiana Assembly ....E...... 765 471-9399
Lafayette *(G-8867)*
Ceran Inc...................................G...... 812 882-2680
Vincennes *(G-13673)*
Fox Studios Inc ....F...... 317 253-0135
Indianapolis *(G-6953)*
Guardian Industries LLC ....G...... 812 422-6987
Evansville *(G-3525)*
Indiana Bevel Inc......................G...... 317 596-0001
Fishers *(G-3928)*
Lippert Components Mfg Inc ....C...... 574 935-5122
Plymouth *(G-11703)*
Pilkington North America Inc......E...... 317 346-0621
Franklin *(G-4920)*
Pilkington North America Inc......A...... 317 392-7000
Shelbyville *(G-12557)*
Wallar Additions Inc..................E...... 574 262-1989
Elkhart *(G-3253)*
Wilmes Window Mfg Co Inc ....E...... 812 275-7575
Ferdinand *(G-3864)*

GLASS: Insulating

Indy Glass Center Inc ....F...... 317 591-5000
Indianapolis *(G-7217)*

GLASS: Leaded

Larry Robertson Associates ....E...... 812 537-4090
Indianapolis *(G-7381)*
Schuster Glass Studio ....G...... 812 988-7377
Nashville *(G-10734)*

GLASS: Pressed & Blown, NEC

Anchor Glass Container Corp ......B...... 765 584-6101
Winchester *(G-14325)*
Apollo Design Technology Inc......D...... 260 497-9191
Fort Wayne *(G-4081)*
Creations In Glass ....G...... 219 326-7941
La Porte *(G-8747)*
Diversified Ophthalmics Inc.......F...... 317 780-1677
Indianapolis *(G-6750)*
G K Optical Company Inc ....E...... 317 881-2585
Indianapolis *(G-6975)*
Maul Technology Co ....G...... 765 584-2101
Winchester *(G-14337)*
Naptown Etching ....G...... 317 733-8776
Zionsville *(G-14450)*
Northern Indiana Manufacturing ....G...... 574 342-2105
Bourbon *(G-946)*
S & S Optical Co Inc ....F...... 260 749-9614
New Haven *(G-10955)*
Spectrum Brands Inc ....E...... 317 773-6627
Noblesville *(G-11187)*

GLASS: Stained

Amish Robs Tattoos LLC ....G...... 219 863-9727
Morocco *(G-10360)*
Bowman Art Glass Studio ....G...... 765 281-4527
Muncie *(G-10442)*
Hartford TEC Glass Co Inc ....E...... 765 348-1282
Hartford City *(G-5983)*
Kaleidoscope Inc ....G...... 765 423-1951
Lafayette *(G-8936)*
Mominee Studios Inc ....G...... 812 473-1691
Evansville *(G-3633)*

GLASS: Tempered

Oldcastle Buildingenvelope Inc....D...... 317 876-1155
Indianapolis *(G-7617)*
Schott Gemtron Corporation ....B...... 812 882-2680
Vincennes *(G-13705)*

GLASSWARE STORES

Warsaw Cut Glass Company Inc ....G...... 574 267-6581
Warsaw *(G-13961)*

GLASSWARE: Cut & Engraved

Warsaw Cut Glass Company Inc ....G...... 574 267-6581
Warsaw *(G-13961)*

GLOBAL POSITIONING SYSTEMS & EQPT

Abk Tracking Inc ....G...... 812 473-9554
Evansville *(G-3333)*
Orbital Installation Tech LLC ....G...... 317 774-3668
Noblesville *(G-11162)*

GLOVES: Fabric

Setser Fabricating LLC ....G...... 812 546-2169
Columbus *(G-2012)*
Steel Grip Inc ....D...... 765 397-3344
Kingman *(G-8533)*
Tmgg LLC ....G...... 812 687-7444
Plainville *(G-11656)*

GLOVES: Leather

Glove Corporation ....D...... 501 362-2437
Alexandria *(G-43)*

GLOVES: Woven Or Knit, From Purchased Materials

Glove Corporation ....D...... 501 362-2437
Alexandria *(G-43)*

GLYCERIN

Louis Dreyfus Co AG Inds LLC ....E...... 574 566-2100
Claypool *(G-1706)*

GO-CART DEALERS

Carlson Motorsports...................G...... 765 339-4407
Linden *(G-9303)*

GOLF CARTS: Wholesalers

Indian Creek Outdoor Power LLC ....G...... 812 597-3055
Morgantown *(G-10354)*
Mid America Powered Vehicles ....G...... 812 925-7745
Chandler *(G-1551)*

GOLF CLUB & EQPT REPAIR SVCS

Fairway Custom Golf ....G...... 317 842-0017
Fishers *(G-3910)*
Mid America Powered Vehicles ....G...... 812 925-7745
Chandler *(G-1551)*

GOLF COURSES: Public

Stone Quary..............................E...... 765 473-5578
Peru *(G-11549)*

GOLF EQPT

Triunity LLC ....G...... 317 703-1147
Noblesville *(G-11196)*
Uebelhors Golf ....G...... 317 881-4109
Indianapolis *(G-8124)*

GOLF GOODS & EQPT

Fairway Custom Golf ....G...... 317 842-0017
Fishers *(G-3910)*
Uebelhors Golf ....G...... 317 881-4109
Indianapolis *(G-8124)*

GOVERNMENT, LEGISLATIVE BODIES: Local

City of Anderson ....G...... 765 648-6715
Anderson *(G-86)*

GOVERNORS: Diesel Engine, Pump

Enhancement Power Products.............G...... 317 359-3461
Indianapolis *(G-6870)*

GRADING SVCS

Globe Asphalt Paving Co Inc ....E...... 317 568-4344
Indianapolis *(G-7015)*

GRAIN & FIELD BEANS WHOLESALERS

Bridgewell Resources LLC ....G...... 812 285-1811
Jeffersonville *(G-8331)*

GRANITE: Cut & Shaped

Classic Kitchen & Granite ....G...... 317 575-8883
Carmel *(G-1340)*
Granite Innovations Inc ....G...... 219 690-1081
Hebron *(G-6013)*

Granite Marble & More Inc ....G...... 765 939-4846
Richmond *(G-11991)*
Indianapolis Granite & MBL Inc ....G...... 317 259-4478
Indianapolis *(G-7200)*
Michael and Sons Incorporated ....F...... 812 876-4736
Bloomfield *(G-644)*

GRANITE: Dimension

M U Holdings Inc ....F...... 765 675-8054
Tipton *(G-13396)*

GRAPHIC ARTS & RELATED DESIGN SVCS

Accent Signs & Graphics ....G...... 866 769-7446
French Lick *(G-4983)*
Burston Marketing Inc ....F...... 574 262-4005
Elkhart *(G-2739)*
Business Art & Design Inc ....G...... 317 782-9108
Beech Grove *(G-593)*
Creative Concept Ventures Inc ....G...... 812 282-9442
Jeffersonville *(G-8348)*
Drs Graphix Group Inc ....G...... 317 569-1855
Indianapolis *(G-6768)*
Graphic Visions ....G...... 812 331-7446
Bloomington *(G-733)*
Graphicorp.................................G...... 317 867-3099
Indianapolis *(G-7036)*
Hetty Incorporated ....G...... 219 836-2517
Munster *(G-10605)*
Hetty Incorporated ....G...... 219 933-0833
Hammond *(G-5892)*
Indiana Dimensional Pdts LLC ....D...... 574 834-7681
North Webster *(G-11293)*
Mid West Digital Express Inc ....F...... 317 733-1214
Zionsville *(G-14449)*
Moose Lake Products Co ....G...... 260 432-2768
Fort Wayne *(G-4480)*
Prolam Products Inc ....D...... 812 867-1662
Evansville *(G-3687)*
Reinforcements Design ....G...... 219 866-8626
Rensselaer *(G-11935)*
Rlr Associates Inc ....G...... 317 632-1300
Indianapolis *(G-7848)*
Sig Media LLC ....G...... 317 858-7624
Indianapolis *(G-7938)*
Storm Graphics Inc ....G...... 812 402-5202
Evansville *(G-3753)*
Techcom Inc ....F...... 812 372-0960
Columbus *(G-2020)*
Techcom Inc ....E...... 317 865-2530
Indianapolis *(G-8048)*

GRAPHIC LAYOUT SVCS: Printed Circuitry

Orion Global Sourcing Inc ....G...... 812 332-3338
Bloomington *(G-792)*

GRATINGS: Open Steel Flooring

ABI Attachments Inc ....E...... 877 788-7253
Mishawaka *(G-9988)*

GRATINGS: Tread, Fabricated Metal

E & H Bridge & Grating Inc ....G...... 812 277-8343
Bedford *(G-538)*
Hilltop Metal Fabricating LLC ....G...... 574 773-4975
Nappanee *(G-10680)*

GRAVEL & PEBBLE MINING

Nugent Sand Company ....G...... 812 372-7508
Columbus *(G-1983)*
Phend and Brown Inc ....E...... 574 658-4166
Milford *(G-9961)*
Stafford Gravel Inc ....F...... 260 868-2503
Butler *(G-1243)*

GRAVEL MINING

Beaver Gravel Corporation ....D...... 317 773-0679
Noblesville *(G-11065)*
Cgs Services Inc ....G...... 765 763-6258
Morristown *(G-10367)*
Hagerstown Gravel & Cnstr ....G...... 765 489-4812
Hagerstown *(G-5806)*
Hopkins Gravel Sand & Concrete......G...... 317 831-2704
Mooresville *(G-10311)*
La Fontaine Gravel Inc ....G...... 765 981-4849
La Fontaine *(G-8724)*
Longhorn Sand and Gravel LLC ....G...... 574 656-3231
North Liberty *(G-11218)*

LPI Paving & Excavating ....G....... 260 726-9564
   Portland (G-11834)
Paddack Brothers Inc ....F....... 765 659-4777
   Frankfort (G-4849)
Rogers Group Inc ....F....... 812 275-7860
   Springville (G-13068)
Schrock Aggregate Company Inc ....G....... 574 862-4167
   Wakarusa (G-13795)
Schrock Excavating Inc ....E....... 574 862-4167
   Wakarusa (G-13796)
Shelby Gravel Inc ....F....... 812 526-2731
   Edinburgh (G-2628)
Spray Sand & Gravel Inc ....G....... 812 523-8081
   Seymour (G-12493)
U S Aggregates Inc ....G....... 317 872-6010
   Indianapolis (G-8120)
U S Aggregates Inc ....F....... 765 362-2500
   Crawfordsville (G-2202)
U S Aggregates Inc ....F....... 765 564-2580
   Delphi (G-2429)
U S Aggregates Inc ....G....... 765 564-2282
   Delphi (G-2430)
Van Duyne Block and Gravel ....G....... 574 223-6656
   Rochester (G-12159)
W & W Gravel Co Incorporated ....F....... 260 672-3591
   Roanoke (G-12112)
West Plains Distribution LLC ....G....... 260 563-9500
   Wabash (G-13767)
Wilhelm Gravel Co Inc ....E....... 260 837-6511
   Waterloo (G-14027)

GREASES & INEDIBLE FATS, RENDERED

Griffin Industries LLC ....E....... 812 379-9528
   Columbus (G-1935)

GREASES: Lubricating

Steelco Industrial Lubricants ....G....... 219 462-0333
   Valparaiso (G-13624)
Universal Services Inc ....G....... 219 397-4373
   East Chicago (G-2577)

GREENHOUSES: Prefabricated Metal

Winandy Greenhouse Company ....E....... 765 935-2111
   Richmond (G-12076)

GRILLS & GRILLWORK: Woven Wire, Made From Purchased Wire

Kewanna Metal Specialties Inc ....D....... 574 653-2554
   Kewanna (G-8525)

GRINDING SAND MINING

C & J Plating & Grinding LLC ....G....... 765 288-8728
   Muncie (G-10444)

GRINDING SVC: Precision, Commercial Or Indl

A & A Machine Service Inc ....G....... 317 745-7367
   Avon (G-423)
Beverly Industrial Service ....F....... 812 667-5047
   Dillsboro (G-2463)
Huth Tool ....G....... 260 749-9411
   Fort Wayne (G-4350)
Huth Tool & Machine Corp ....G....... 260 749-9411
   Fort Wayne (G-4351)
Illiana Grinding Machining Inc ....G....... 219 884-5828
   Merrillville (G-9722)
Midwest Accurate Grinding Svc ....F....... 219 696-4060
   Lowell (G-9417)
Muncie Precision Hard Chrome ....G....... 765 288-2489
   Muncie (G-10535)
Riverside Tool Corp ....E....... 574 522-6798
   Elkhart (G-3149)
Schuler Precision Tool LLC ....G....... 260 982-2704
   North Manchester (G-11243)

GRINDING SVCS: Ophthalmic Lens, Exc Prescription

City Optical Co Inc ....G....... 317 788-4243
   Indianapolis (G-6616)
Shimp Optical Corp ....G....... 317 636-4448
   Indianapolis (G-7933)

GRITS: Crushed & Broken

Johnson Materials ....G....... 812 373-9044
   Columbus (G-1953)
Mulzer Crushed Stone Inc ....C....... 812 739-4777
   Leavenworth (G-9165)

GROCERIES WHOLESALERS, NEC

American Beverage Marketers ....G....... 812 944-3585
   New Albany (G-10743)
American Bottling Company ....E....... 260 484-4177
   Fort Wayne (G-4068)
Calumet Breweries Inc ....E....... 219 845-2242
   Hammond (G-5856)
Central Coca-Cola Btlg Co Inc ....E....... 317 243-3771
   Indianapolis (G-6581)
Conagra Brands Inc ....C....... 219 866-3020
   Rensselaer (G-11919)
Grabers Kountry Korner ....E....... 812 636-4399
   Odon (G-11329)
Lewis Brothers Bakeries Inc ....C....... 812 425-4642
   Evansville (G-3600)
P-Americas LLC ....E....... 812 522-3421
   Seymour (G-12472)
P-Americas LLC ....C....... 317 876-6800
   Indianapolis (G-7644)

GROCERIES, GENERAL LINE WHOLESALERS

Albanese Conf Group Inc ....C....... 219 942-1877
   Merrillville (G-9693)
MI Tierra ....G....... 812 376-0668
   Columbus (G-1973)

GUARD PROTECTIVE SVCS

Advanced Prtctive Slutions LLC ....G....... 765 720-9574
   Coatesville (G-1746)

GUIDED MISSILES & SPACE VEHICLES

Cypress Springs Enterprises ....G....... 812 743-8888
   Wheatland (G-14231)

GUIDED MISSILES & SPACE VEHICLES: Research & Development

Raytheon Company ....D....... 310 647-9438
   Fort Wayne (G-4577)

GUIDED MISSILES/SPACE VEHICLE PARTS/AUX EQPT: Research/Devel

Cypress Springs Enterprises ....G....... 812 743-8888
   Wheatland (G-14231)

GUM & WOOD CHEMICALS

Arch Wood Protection Inc ....F....... 219 464-3949
   Valparaiso (G-13497)
Jefferson Homebuilders Inc ....E....... 317 398-0874
   Shelbyville (G-12541)
Pag Holdings Inc ....G....... 814 446-2525
   Brazil (G-974)
Pag Holdings Inc ....G....... 317 290-5006
   Indianapolis (G-7648)

GUN SVCS

Favres Gun Shop ....G....... 812 235-0198
   Terre Haute (G-13234)

GUTTERS

Patrick Industries Inc ....C....... 574 546-5222
   Bremen (G-1014)

GUTTERS: Sheet Metal

All N One ....G....... 219 226-9263
   Crown Point (G-2224)
Hallett Enterprises Inc ....G....... 317 495-7800
   Crawfordsville (G-2157)
Sure-Flo Seamless Gutters Inc ....G....... 260 622-4372
   Ossian (G-11412)

GYPSUM BOARD

Esco Industries Inc ....E....... 574 522-4500
   Elkhart (G-2837)

GYPSUM PRDTS

Georgia-Pacific LLC ....C....... 219 956-3100
   Wheatfield (G-14223)
New Ngc Inc ....D....... 219 866-7570
   Rensselaer (G-11933)
New Ngc Inc ....E....... 765 828-0898
   Clinton (G-1718)
Patrick Industries Inc ....C....... 574 294-7511
   Elkhart (G-3080)
Patrick Industries Inc ....C....... 574 534-5300
   Goshen (G-5308)
Patrick Industries Inc ....F....... 574 295-9660
   Elkhart (G-3090)
Patrick Industries Inc ....C....... 574 294-1975
   Elkhart (G-3091)
Precast Solutions Inc ....F....... 317 545-6557
   Whitestown (G-14259)
United States Gypsum Company ....C....... 812 247-2101
   Shoals (G-12671)
United States Gypsum Company ....C....... 812 388-6866
   Shoals (G-12672)
United States Gypsum Company ....C....... 219 392-4600
   East Chicago (G-2575)
Westech Building Products Inc ....E....... 812 985-3628
   Mount Vernon (G-10414)

HAIR & HAIR BASED PRDTS

Hair Necessities ....G....... 812 288-5887
   Clarksville (G-1685)
The Eminence Hair Collectn LLC ....G....... 317 222-5085
   Indianapolis (G-8057)

HAIR CARE PRDTS

Kenra Professional LLC ....F....... 317 356-6491
   Indianapolis (G-7343)
Malibu Wellness Inc ....E....... 317 624-7560
   Indianapolis (G-7447)
Maverick Packaging Inc ....E....... 574 264-2891
   Elkhart (G-3022)
Signature Formulations LLC ....G....... 317 878-4086
   Trafalgar (G-13438)

HAIR CARE PRDTS: Tonics

Magnolia Products LLC ....G....... 812 306-8638
   Evansville (G-3610)

HAIR DRESSING, FOR THE TRADE

Vickie Hildreth ....G....... 812 350-3575
   Columbus (G-2029)

HAIRDRESSERS

CD & Ws Bordner Entps Inc ....G....... 765 268-2120
   Cutler (G-2328)
Sharyls Hair With Flare ....G....... 765 885-5121
   Fowler (G-4806)

HAND TOOLS, NEC: Wholesalers

Buckaroos Inc ....F....... 317 899-9100
   Indianapolis (G-6518)
Tartan Properties LLC ....G....... 317 714-7337
   Indianapolis (G-8037)

HANDBAGS

Amanda Elizabeth LLC ....G....... 602 317-9633
   Fort Wayne (G-4066)
CM Reed LLC ....G....... 517 546-4100
   Greendale (G-5485)
Maloney Group Inc ....F....... 812 285-7400
   Jeffersonville (G-8395)
Vera Bradley Inc ....E....... 219 878-1093
   Michigan City (G-9858)
Vera Bradley Inc ....C....... 260 482-4673
   Roanoke (G-12109)
Vera Bradley Inc ....B....... 877 708-8372
   Roanoke (G-12110)
Vera Bradley International LLC ....G....... 260 482-4673
   Roanoke (G-12111)

HANDBAGS: Men's

Maloney Group Inc ....F....... 812 285-7400
   Jeffersonville (G-8395)

Employee Codes: A=Over 500 employees, B=251-500
C=101-250, D=51-100, E=20-50, F=10-19, G=2-9

2018 Harris Indiana
Industrial Directory

PRODUCT

985

HANDBAGS: Women's

Aubry Lane LLC ....G....... 317 644-6372
Indianapolis **(G-6439)**

HANDLES: Wood

American Wedge Company Inc ....G....... 812 883-1086
Salem **(G-12282)**
G & J 765 457-9889
Kokomo **(G-8626)**
Handle With Care Packaging 812 250-1920
Evansville **(G-3530)**
Handle With Kare LLC ....G....... 260 420-1698
Fort Wayne **(G-4317)**
Pioneer Cane & Handle Co ....G....... 812 859-4415
Clay City **(G-1705)**

HANDYMAN SVCS

Northern Indiana Ordnance Co ....G....... 574 289-5938
South Bend **(G-12879)**

HANGERS: Garment, Wire

Innovative Fabrication LLC ....D....... 317 215-5988
Indianapolis **(G-7237)**

HARDBOARD & FIBERBOARD PRDTS

Midwest Products Co Inc ....D....... 219 942-1134
Hobart **(G-6092)**

HARDWARE

A Raymond Tinnerman Auto Inc ....C....... 574 722-5168
Logansport **(G-9319)**
Assurance Locking Systems LLC ....G....... 317 786-8724
Indianapolis **(G-6430)**
Batesville Products Inc ....D....... 513 381-2057
Lawrenceburg **(G-9133)**
Budget Sales Inc ....G....... 260 657-5185
Woodburn **(G-14381)**
Crossroads Door & Hardware Inc ....G....... 812 234-9751
Terre Haute **(G-13219)**
Dorma ....G....... 317 468-6742
Greenfield **(G-5521)**
Fiedeke Vinyl Coverings Inc ....F....... 574 534-3408
Goshen **(G-5214)**
Frederick Tool Corp ....E....... 574 295-6700
Elkhart **(G-2870)**
Grace Manufacturing Inc ....F....... 574 267-8000
Warsaw **(G-13884)**
Hart Plastics Inc ....E....... 574 264-7060
Elkhart **(G-2909)**
Holland Metal Fab Inc ....F....... 574 522-1434
Elkhart **(G-2918)**
Illinois Tool Works Inc ....D....... 219 874-4217
Michigan City **(G-9803)**
Indiana Architectural Plywood ....E....... 317 878-4822
Trafalgar **(G-13436)**
JM Fittings LLC ....D....... 260 747-9200
Fort Wayne **(G-4396)**
Kautex Inc ....B....... 937 238-8096
Avilla **(G-409)**
L & W Engineering Inc ....D....... 574 825-5351
Middlebury **(G-9900)**
Modern Forge Companies LLC ....A....... 708 388-1806
Merrillville **(G-9738)**
Osr Inc ....F....... 812 342-7642
Columbus **(G-1987)**
Parker-Hannifin Corporation ....A....... 260 748-6000
New Haven **(G-10951)**
Pridgeon & Clay Inc ....C....... 317 738-4885
Franklin **(G-4923)**
Quality Converters Inc 260 829-6541
Orland **(G-11356)**
R & R Regulators Inc ....F....... 574 522-5846
Elkhart **(G-3134)**
R&D Investment Holdings Inc 260 749-1301
Fort Wayne **(G-4575)**
Reelcraft Industries Inc 855 634-9109
Columbia City **(G-1824)**
S C Pryor Inc ....E....... 317 352-1281
Indianapolis **(G-7878)**
Samaron Corp ....E....... 574 970-7070
Elkhart **(G-3154)**
Slb Corporation ....F....... 574 255-9774
Mishawaka **(G-10125)**
Sparks Belting Company Inc ....G....... 800 451-4537
Hammond **(G-5945)**
Standard Fusee Corporation ....E....... 765 472-4375
Peru **(G-11548)**

Steel Parts Corporation ....B....... 765 675-2191
Tipton **(G-13406)**
Sur-Loc Inc ....F....... 260 495-4065
Fremont **(G-4975)**
Terry Liquidation III Inc ....E....... 219 362-3557
La Porte **(G-8829)**
Tri-State Hydraulics Indus Sup ....G....... 812 537-3485
Greendale **(G-5495)**
Velko Hinge Inc ....E....... 219 924-6363
Munster **(G-10638)**
Viking Inc ....E....... 260 244-6141
Columbia City **(G-1845)**
Ward Industries Inc ....F....... 574 825-2548
Middlebury **(G-9923)**
Western Products Indiana Inc ....F....... 765 529-6230
New Castle **(G-10921)**

HARDWARE & BUILDING PRDTS: Plastic

Cor-A-Vent Inc ....E....... 574 258-6161
Mishawaka **(G-10024)**
Deflecto LLC ....B....... 317 849-9555
Indianapolis **(G-6732)**
Digger Specialties Inc ....D....... 574 546-5999
Bremen **(G-996)**
First Place Trophy Inc ....E....... 574 293-6147
Elkhart **(G-2850)**
General Fabricators Inc ....E....... 317 787-9354
Indianapolis **(G-6996)**
Hancor Inc ....E....... 812 443-2080
Brazil **(G-964)**
J Plus Products Inc ....G....... 317 660-1003
Carmel **(G-1418)**
Life Management Inc ....G....... 260 747-7408
Fort Wayne **(G-4435)**
Nibco Inc ....B....... 574 295-3000
Elkhart **(G-3062)**
Outsource Technologies Inc ....E....... 574 233-1303
South Bend **(G-12884)**
Permalatt Products Inc ....G....... 574 546-6311
Bremen **(G-1015)**
Royal Outdoor Products Inc ....C....... 574 658-9442
Milford **(G-9964)**
Topp Industries Incorporated ....D....... 574 223-3681
Rochester **(G-12157)**

HARDWARE & EQPT: Stage, Exc Lighting

Energy Saver Lights Inc ....F....... 202 544-7868
Indianapolis **(G-6866)**
Lhp Software LLC ....D....... 812 373-0870
Columbus **(G-1960)**

HARDWARE STORES

Attica Ready Mixed Concrete ....E....... 765 762-2424
Attica **(G-297)**
Barry Company Inc ....G....... 812 333-1850
Bloomington **(G-673)**
Dbisp LLC ....F....... 317 222-1671
Indianapolis **(G-6729)**
Dunham Rubber & Belting Corp ....E....... 317 888-3002
Greenwood **(G-5683)**
Dunham Rubber & Belting Corp ....G....... 800 876-5340
Fort Wayne **(G-4224)**
Englert & Meyer Corporation ....G....... 812 683-3540
Huntingburg **(G-6163)**
Johnco Corp ....G....... 317 576-4417
Indianapolis **(G-7308)**
Lansing Building Products Inc ....G....... 765 448-4363
Lafayette **(G-8955)**
Leeps Supply Co Inc ....D....... 219 756-5337
Merrillville **(G-9726)**
Neumayr Lumber Co Inc ....F....... 765 764-4148
Attica **(G-308)**
Robinson Industries Inc ....E....... 317 867-3214
Westfield **(G-14186)**
T K Sales & Service ....G....... 219 962-8982
Gary **(G-5104)**
Wright Brothers Implements LLC ....G....... 812 967-3029
Borden **(G-938)**

HARDWARE STORES: Builders'

Stock Building Supply LLC ....E....... 260 490-0616
Fort Wayne **(G-4650)**
Tartan Properties LLC ....G....... 317 714-7337
Indianapolis **(G-8037)**

HARDWARE STORES: Door Locks & Lock Sets

Allegion Public Ltd Company ....F....... 317 810-3700
Carmel **(G-1307)**

HARDWARE STORES: Pumps & Pumping Eqpt

McGrews Well Drilling Inc ....G....... 574 857-3875
Rochester **(G-12137)**
Progress Group Inc ....D....... 219 322-3700
Schererville **(G-12342)**
Robinson Industries Inc ....E....... 317 867-3214
Westfield **(G-14185)**

HARDWARE STORES: Tools

All-Rite Ready Mix Inc ....F....... 812 926-0920
Aurora **(G-369)**
Earth First Kentuckiana Inc ....G....... 812 923-1227
Greenville **(G-5648)**

HARDWARE WHOLESALERS

Ditto Sales Inc ....E....... 812 482-3043
Jasper **(G-8245)**
DL Schwartz Co LLC 260 692-1464
Berne **(G-612)**
Kentuckiana Wire Rope & Supply ....F....... 812 282-3667
Jeffersonville **(G-8386)**
Stanley Security Solutions Inc ....E....... 317 598-0421
Indianapolis **(G-7991)**

HARDWARE, WHOLESALE: Builders', NEC

Tamco Manufacturing Co ....G....... 574 294-1909
Elkhart **(G-3205)**

HARDWARE, WHOLESALE: Chains

Onspot of North America Inc ....G....... 203 377-0777
North Vernon **(G-11274)**

HARDWARE, WHOLESALE: Garden Tools, Hand

U-Nitt LLC ....G....... 812 251-9980
Carmel **(G-1499)**

HARDWARE, WHOLESALE: Rivets

Bender Wholesale Distributors ....F....... 574 264-4409
Elkhart **(G-2721)**

HARDWARE, WHOLESALE: Screws

Harry B Higley & Sons Inc ....G....... 219 558-8183
Dyer **(G-2501)**

HARDWARE, WHOLESALE: Security Devices, Locks

Standard Change-Makers Inc ....F....... 317 899-6955
Indianapolis **(G-7988)**
Stanley Security Solutions Inc ....E....... 678 533-3846
Indianapolis **(G-7992)**

HARDWARE: Builders'

Hingecraft Corporation ....F....... 574 293-6543
Elkhart **(G-2917)**
L & S Lumber ....G....... 765 886-1452
Greens Fork **(G-5587)**
Von Duprin LLC ....B....... 317 429-2866
Indianapolis **(G-8168)**
Von Duprin LLC ....G....... 317 899-2760
Indianapolis **(G-8169)**

HARDWARE: Cabinet

Houck Industries Inc ....G....... 812 663-5675
Greensburg **(G-5614)**
Yoder Woodworking Inc ....G....... 574 546-5100
Bremen **(G-1035)**

HARDWARE: Casket

Christopher Miller ....G....... 812 442-0949
Brazil **(G-956)**
Geneva Manufacturing Inc ....E....... 260 368-7555
Geneva **(G-5136)**
Schuler Products Co ....G....... 812 852-4419
Napoleon **(G-10642)**

HARDWARE: Door Opening & Closing Devices, Exc Electrical

Bloomfield Mfg Co Inc ....E 812 384-4441
Bloomfield (G-635)
L E Johnson Products Inc ....D 574 293-5664
Elkhart (G-2977)
L E Johnson Products Inc ....C 574 293-5664
Elkhart (G-2978)
Oak Security Group LLC ....F 317 585-9830
Indianapolis (G-7608)

HARDWARE: Furniture

Olon Industries Inc (us) ....F 812 254-0427
Washington (G-13994)
REM Industries Inc ....E 574 862-2127
Wakarusa (G-13792)

HARDWARE: Furniture, Builders' & Other Household

Elkhart Hinge Co Inc ....F 574 293-2841
Elkhart (G-2825)
J Game Ventures LLC ....G 812 241-7096
Brownsburg (G-1157)
Pk USA Inc ....B 317 395-5500
Shelbyville (G-12558)
Tubular Engrg & Sls Co Inc ....F 765 536-2225
Summitville (G-13108)

HARDWARE: Plastic

Mossberg Industries Inc ....D 260 357-5141
Garrett (G-5018)
Tecnoplast Usa LLC ....G 317 769-4929
Anderson (G-174)

HARDWARE: Saddlery

Fabri-Tech Inc ....E 317 849-7755
McCordsville (G-9666)

HARNESS ASSEMBLIES: Cable & Wire

A-1vet LLC ....G 317 498-1804
Indianapolis (G-6304)
Almega/Tru-Flex Inc ....E 574 546-2113
Bremen (G-982)
Assembly Masters Inc ....F 574 293-9026
Elkhart (G-2698)
C & G Wiring Inc ....F 574 333-3433
Elkhart (G-2742)
Caddo Connections Inc ....E 219 874-8119
La Porte (G-8744)
Electric-Tec LLC ....E 260 665-1252
Angola (G-211)
Electro Transfer Systems Inc ....D 574 234-0600
Mishawaka (G-10040)
Ets International Llc ....D 574 234-0700
Mishawaka (G-10043)
Freedom Wire Inc ....F 260 856-3059
Cromwell (G-2208)
Gartech Enterprises Inc ....E 812 794-4796
Austin (G-397)
HB Connect Inc ....D 260 422-1212
Fort Wayne (G-4324)
Hermac Incorporated ....E 260 925-0312
Auburn (G-335)
Hi-Pro Inc ....F 260 665-5038
Angola (G-218)
Jag Wire LLC ....F 260 463-8537
Lagrange (G-9048)
Kauffman Engineering Inc ....D 574 732-2154
Bremen (G-1007)
Kauffman Engineering Inc ....D 765 483-4919
Lebanon (G-9195)
Kauffman Engineering Inc ....D 765 482-5640
Lebanon (G-9196)
Kauffman Engineering Inc ....D 574 722-3800
Logansport (G-9344)
Kirby Risk Corporation ....D 765 448-4567
Lafayette (G-8940)
Kra International LLC ....D 574 259-3550
Mishawaka (G-10065)
Madison Electronics Inc ....F 812 689-4204
Versailles (G-13655)
Mssl Wiring System Inc ....E 260 726-6501
Portland (G-11837)
Mursix Corporation ....C 765 282-2221
Yorktown (G-14408)

Northwind Electronics LLC ....F 317 288-0787
Indianapolis (G-7596)
Patrick Industries Inc ....D 574 293-2990
Elkhart (G-3089)
Pent Assemblies ....D 260 347-5828
Kendallville (G-8501)
Pinder Instruments Company Inc ....E 219 924-7070
Munster (G-10624)
Precision Wire Assemblies Inc ....D 765 489-6302
Hagerstown (G-5812)
Precision Wire Inc ....G 574 834-7545
North Webster (G-11300)
Priority Electronics LLC ....G 260 749-0143
New Haven (G-10954)
Qualitronics Inc ....D 765 966-2039
Richmond (G-12039)
Quality Plastics and Engrg Inc ....E 574 262-2621
Elkhart (G-3128)
Tap-A-Lite Inc ....E 219 932-8067
Hammond (G-5948)
Tri TEC Systems Inc ....E 260 724-8874
Decatur (G-2409)
Walton Industrial Park Inc ....F 574 626-2929
Walton (G-13818)

HARNESS WIRING SETS: Internal Combustion Engines

Cpx Inc ....D 219 474-5280
Kentland (G-8519)
Qualtronics LLC ....E 812 375-8880
Columbus (G-2004)

HARNESSES, HALTERS, SADDLERY & STRAPS

Schutz Brothers Inc ....F 260 982-8581
North Manchester (G-11244)

HEADPHONES: Radio

Haven Technologies Inc ....G 317 490-7197
Carmel (G-1399)

HEALTH AIDS: Exercise Eqpt

C L Holdings LLC ....G 317 736-4414
Franklin (G-4874)
Duclas Fitness LLC ....G 812 217-8544
Evansville (G-3466)
Power Place Products Inc ....G 765 583-2333
West Lafayette (G-14095)
Powering Athletics ....G 260 672-1700
Fort Wayne (G-4544)

HEARING AIDS

Affordable Sounds Inc ....G 260 493-7742
New Haven (G-10926)
Audio Diagnostics Inc ....G 765 477-7016
Lafayette (G-8855)
D J Investments Inc ....G 260 726-7346
Portland (G-11814)
D J Investments Inc ....G 765 348-3558
Hartford City (G-5979)
Integrity Hearing ....G 317 882-9151
Noblesville (G-11131)
Spry-Clear Ear Inc ....G 219 934-9747
Griffith (G-5790)
Wilson Hearing Aid Center ....G 765 747-4131
Muncie (G-10585)

HEARING TESTING SVCS

Audio Diagnostics Inc ....G 765 477-7016
Lafayette (G-8855)

HEAT EXCHANGERS: After Or Inter Coolers Or Condensers, Etc

Hale Industries Inc ....E 317 577-0337
Fortville (G-4778)
Heat Exchanger Design Inc ....E 317 917-1566
Indianapolis (G-7086)

HEAT TREATING SALTS

Schindler Electric Inc ....G 317 858-8215
Brownsburg (G-1168)

HEAT TREATING: Metal

A Raymond Tinnerman Auto Inc ....C 574 722-5168
Logansport (G-9319)
Advanced Ntrding Solutions LLC ....F 812 932-1010
Batesville (G-489)
Al Fe Heat Treating-Ohio Inc ....F 260 747-9422
Fort Wayne (G-4053)
Al-Fe Heat Treating Inc ....D 260 747-9422
Fort Wayne (G-4054)
Al-Fe Heat Treating Inc ....F 888 747-2533
Fort Wayne (G-4055)
Al-Fe Heat Treating Inc ....E 260 563-8321
Wabash (G-13720)
Albany Metal Treating Inc ....D 765 789-6470
Albany (G-10)
Allegheny Ludlum LLC ....C 765 529-9570
New Castle (G-10890)
Applied Thermal Tech Inc ....E 574 269-7116
Warsaw (G-13839)
B&J Rocket America Inc ....E 574 825-5802
Middlebury (G-9874)
Bodycote Thermal Proc Inc ....E 812 662-0500
Greensburg (G-5591)
Bodycote Thermal Proc Inc ....D 260 423-1691
Fort Wayne (G-4115)
Bodycote Thermal Proc Inc ....D 574 295-2491
Elkhart (G-2730)
Bodycote Thermal Proc Inc ....D 317 924-4321
Indianapolis (G-6493)
Boyd Machine & Repair Co Inc ....E 260 635-2195
Kimmell (G-8529)
Bwt LLC ....E 574 232-3338
South Bend (G-12729)
Circle City Heat Treating Inc ....F 317 638-2252
Indianapolis (G-6607)
Dependable Metal Treating Inc ....F 260 347-5744
Kendallville (G-8473)
Exotic Metal Treating Inc ....F 317 784-8565
Indianapolis (G-6895)
Gerdau Macsteel Inc ....E 260 356-9520
Huntington (G-6207)
H & H Commercial Heat Treating ....G 765 288-3618
Muncie (G-10480)
Hartford Heat Treatment ....E 812 725-8272
New Albany (G-10792)
Honeycomb Products Inc ....E 317 787-9351
Indianapolis (G-7115)
HTI ....F 574 722-2814
Logansport (G-9337)
Indiana Metal Treating Inc ....F 317 636-2421
Indianapolis (G-7183)
Learman Electronic Tool Assoc ....G 574 226-0420
Elkhart (G-2991)
Leed Thermal Processing Inc ....G 317 637-5102
Indianapolis (G-7393)
McLaughlin Services LLC ....F 260 897-4328
Avilla (G-415)
Metal Improvement Company LLC ....G 317 875-6030
Indianapolis (G-7487)
Mp Steel Indiana LLC ....E 260 347-1203
Kendallville (G-8496)
Niagara Lasalle Corporation ....E 800 262-2558
Hammond (G-5921)
Nitrex Inc ....E 317 346-7700
Franklin (G-4913)
Northern Indiana Manufacturing ....E 574 342-2105
Bourbon (G-946)
Precision Heat Treating Corp ....E 260 749-5125
Fort Wayne (G-4550)
Quality Steel Treating Co Inc ....E 317 357-8691
Indianapolis (G-7799)
Rochester Heat Treating Co ....G 574 224-4328
Syracuse (G-13141)
Rogers Engineering and Mfg Co ....E 765 478-5444
Cambridge City (G-1261)
Saran Industries LLC ....D 317 897-2170
Kokomo (G-8690)
Saran Industries LLC ....D 317 897-2170
Bloomington (G-821)
Simpson Alloy Services Inc ....G 812 969-2766
Elizabeth (G-2646)
Sinden Racing Service Inc ....F 317 243-7171
Indianapolis (G-7949)
Steel Technologies LLC ....C 502 245-2110
Portage (G-11796)
Sturm Heat Treating Inc ....F 317 357-2368
Indianapolis (G-8014)
Tool Dynamics LLC ....E 812 379-4243
Columbus (G-2022)

Employee Codes: A=Over 500 employees, B=251-500
C=101-250, D=51-100, E=20-50, F=10-19, G=2-9

2018 Harris Indiana
Industrial Directory

987

PRODUCT

Tri-State Metals Inc ....E 219 397-0470
  East Chicago (G-2574)
Ward Corporation ....E 260 489-2281
  Fort Wayne (G-4736)

HEATER RADIANTS: Clay

Hale Industries Inc ....E 317 577-0337
  Fortville (G-4778)

HEATERS: Induction & Dielectric

IDI Fabrication Inc ....D 317 776-6577
  Noblesville (G-11123)

HEATERS: Room & Wall, Including Radiators

Hale Industries Inc ....E 317 577-0337
  Fortville (G-4778)

HEATERS: Space, Exc Electric

Heat Wagons Inc ....F 219 464-8818
  Valparaiso (G-13555)

HEATING & AIR CONDITIONING EQPT & SPLYS WHOLESALERS

Horner Industrial Services Inc ....F 317 634-7165
  Indianapolis (G-7129)
Mitsubishi Heavy Industries ....E 714 960-3785
  Franklin (G-4910)

HEATING & AIR CONDITIONING UNITS, COMBINATION

Fletcher Heating & Cooling ....G 812 865-2984
  Paoli (G-11450)
Grayson Thermal Systems Corp ....C 317 739-3290
  Franklin (G-4893)
MD Moxie LLC ....E 260 347-1203
  Kendallville (G-8494)
Mr Heat Inc ....G 219 345-5629
  Demotte (G-2444)
Thomas P Kasten ....G 574 806-4663
  Winamac (G-14322)
Validated Custom Solutions LLC ....G 317 259-7604
  Indianapolis (G-8145)
Washburn Heating & AC ....G 574 825-7697
  Middlebury (G-9924)

HEATING EQPT & SPLYS

Allied Boiler & Welding Co ....G 317 272-4820
  Avon (G-426)
Carrier Corporation ....D 317 243-0851
  Indianapolis (G-6559)
Fives N Amercn Combustn Inc ....G 219 662-9600
  Crown Point (G-2254)
Ngh Retail LLC ....G 219 476-0772
  Valparaiso (G-13589)
Purolator Pdts A Filtration Co ....C 866 925-2247
  Jeffersonville (G-8418)
Quanex Heat Treat ....E 260 356-9520
  Huntington (G-6241)
Schmidt Contracting Inc ....F 812 482-3923
  Jasper (G-8303)
Southwark Metal Mfg Co ....C 317 823-5300
  Indianapolis (G-7965)
Temptek Inc ....G 317 887-6352
  Greenwood (G-5752)
Thermo Products LLC ....D 574 896-2133
  North Judson (G-11214)
Troy Meggitt Inc ....D 812 547-7071
  Troy (G-13448)
Wrib Manufacturing Inc ....G 765 294-2841
  Veedersburg (G-13648)

HEATING EQPT: Complete

Air Tech Comfort Systems ....G 219 663-9778
  Cedar Lake (G-1525)
Caliente LLC ....E 260 426-3800
  Fort Wayne (G-4137)
Hrezo Industrial Eqp & Engrg ....F 812 537-4700
  Greendale (G-5489)
Lute Supply ....G 260 480-2441
  Fort Wayne (G-4444)
Madden Manufacturing Inc ....F 574 295-4292
  Elkhart (G-3013)
Superior Distribution ....G 618 242-5560
  Indianapolis (G-8021)

Templeton Coal Company Inc ....D 812 232-7037
  Terre Haute (G-13351)

HEATING EQPT: Induction

Thermal Tech & Temp Inc ....G 219 808-1258
  Crown Point (G-2313)

HEATING SYSTEMS: Radiant, Indl Process

Ndiana Warm Floors Inc ....G 260 668-8836
  Angola (G-232)

HEATING UNITS & DEVICES: Indl, Electric

Contour Hardening Inc ....E 888 867-2184
  Indianapolis (G-6660)
Reward Inc ....F 574 936-7196
  Plymouth (G-11721)
Sherwood-Templeton Coal Co Inc ....G 812 232-7037
  Terre Haute (G-13325)
Templeton Coal Company Inc ....G 812 232-7037
  Terre Haute (G-13350)

HELICOPTERS

Utilities Aviation Specialists ....G 219 662-8175
  Crown Point (G-2317)

HELMETS: Athletic

Cheercussion LLC ....F 317 762-4009
  Carmel (G-1336)
Hellbent Inc ....G 765 631-4934
  Indianapolis (G-7088)

HITCHES: Trailer

Hardins Speed Service Co ....G 219 962-8080
  Hobart (G-6079)
Southern Indiana Linings & Coa ....G 812 206-7250
  Charlestown (G-1580)
Trimas Corporation ....G 260 925-3700
  Auburn (G-364)

HOBBY GOODS, WHOLESALE

Ellwocks Auto Parts Restorat ....G 812 962-4942
  Newburgh (G-11027)

HOBBY, TOY & GAME STORES: Arts & Crafts & Splys

Old Lumber Yard Clay Factory ....F 260 627-3567
  Grabill (G-5382)
Stitch N Frame ....G 260 478-1301
  Fort Wayne (G-4649)

HOBBY, TOY & GAME STORES: Dolls & Access

Turner Dolls Inc ....G 812 834-5065
  Heltonville (G-6029)

HOBBY, TOY & GAME STORES: Toys & Games

Royal Pin Leisure Ctr ....G 317 247-4426
  Indianapolis (G-7866)

HOISTING SLINGS

TEC Hoist LLC ....F 708 598-2300
  Griffith (G-5791)

HOISTS

Cranewerks Inc ....E 765 663-2909
  Morristown (G-10368)
Lakemaster Inc ....E 765 288-3718
  Muncie (G-10507)
Mooresville Welding Inc ....G 317 831-2265
  Mooresville (G-10324)

HOLDING COMPANIES: Investment, Exc Banks

Countrymark Coop Holdg Corp ....E 800 808-3170
  Indianapolis (G-6676)
Navistar Cmponent Holdings LLC ....B 317 352-4500
  Indianapolis (G-7578)
V Global Holdings LLC ....A 317 247-8141
  Indianapolis (G-8142)

HOLDING COMPANIES: Personal, Exc Banks

Dallara USA Holding Inc ....G 317 388-5400
  Speedway (G-13014)

HOME ENTERTAINMENT EQPT: Electronic, NEC

Digital Evolution ....G 317 839-7963
  Plainfield (G-11604)
JP Technology Inc ....G 219 947-2525
  Crown Point (G-2270)
Kas Satellite & Cable Inc ....G 260 833-3941
  Angola (G-224)
Mark Murray ....G 812 372-8390
  Columbus (G-1969)

HOME FURNISHINGS WHOLESALERS

Candles By Dar Inc ....F 260 482-2099
  Fort Wayne (G-4139)
Onward Manufacturing Company ....D 260 358-4111
  Huntington (G-6233)

HOME HEALTH CARE SVCS

3M Indianapolis ....G 317 692-3000
  Indianapolis (G-6289)
Predictive Wear LLC ....F 765 464-4891
  West Lafayette (G-14096)

HOME MOVIES DEVELOPING & PROCESSING

Success Entrmt Group Intl Inc ....G 260 490-9990
  Ossian (G-11409)
Success Holding Group Corp USA ....G 260 490-9990
  Ossian (G-11410)

HOMEFURNISHING STORES: Metalware

Pb Metal Works ....G 765 489-1311
  Hagerstown (G-5810)

HOMEFURNISHING STORES: Pottery

Schmidt Marken Designs ....G 219 785-4238
  La Porte (G-8816)
Strawtown Pottery & Antiques ....G 317 984-5080
  Noblesville (G-11190)

HOMEFURNISHING STORES: Venetian Blinds

A-1 Shade Co ....G 317 247-6447
  Indianapolis (G-6303)
Doris Drapery Boutique ....G 765 472-5850
  Peru (G-11524)

HOMEFURNISHING STORES: Window Furnishings

Midwest Blind & Shade Co ....G 574 271-0770
  Mishawaka (G-10085)
Sun Control Center LLC ....F 260 490-9902
  Fort Wayne (G-4666)

HOMEFURNISHINGS & SPLYS, WHOLESALE: Decorative

Floralcraft Distributors ....E 574 262-2639
  Elkhart (G-2858)
Floralcraft Distributors ....G 574 262-2639
  Elkhart (G-2859)
Sac Acquisition LLC ....G 317 575-1795
  Indianapolis (G-7883)
WC Redmon Co Inc ....F 765 473-6683
  Peru (G-11556)

HOMEFURNISHINGS, WHOLESALE: Blinds, Vertical

Midwest Blind & Shade Co ....G 574 271-0770
  Mishawaka (G-10085)

HOMEFURNISHINGS, WHOLESALE: Carpets

Craft Metal Products Inc ....G 317 545-3252
  Indianapolis (G-6684)
Santarossa Mosaic Tile Co Inc ....C 317 632-9494
  Indianapolis (G-7895)

HOMEFURNISHINGS, WHOLESALE: Decorating Splys

Country Cabin LLC ....G....... 812 232-4635
　Terre Haute *(G-13218)*

HOMEFURNISHINGS, WHOLESALE: Draperies

Quality Drapery Corporation....................E....... 765 481-2370
　Lebanon *(G-9218)*

HOMEFURNISHINGS, WHOLESALE: Pottery

Strawtown Pottery & Antiques ....G....... 317 984-5080
　Noblesville *(G-11190)*

HOMEFURNISHINGS, WHOLESALE: Wood Flooring

Brenco LLC ....G....... 219 844-9570
　Hammond *(G-5854)*

HOMES, MODULAR: Wooden

All American Group Inc ....B....... 574 262-0123
　Elkhart *(G-2676)*
All American Group Inc ....E....... 574 262-0123
　Elkhart *(G-2674)*
All American Homes LLC ....E....... 574 266-3044
　Elkhart *(G-2677)*
All American Homes Indiana LLC ....B....... 260 724-9171
　Decatur *(G-2366)*
Craftech Building Systems Inc ....E....... 574 773-4167
　Nappanee *(G-10665)*
Cross Modular Set Inc ....G....... 765 836-1511
　New Castle *(G-10898)*
Delaware County Home Bldrs Inc ....G....... 765 289-6328
　Muncie *(G-10456)*
Hi-Tech Housing Inc ....D....... 574 848-5593
　Bristol *(G-1062)*
Homette Corporation ....G....... 574 294-6521
　Elkhart *(G-2919)*
Itera LLC ....G....... 574 538-3838
　New Paris *(G-10986)*
New Castle Modular Inc ....F....... 765 521-0788
　Indianapolis *(G-7584)*
Premier Strctres Acqsition Inc ....D....... 574 522-4011
　Elkhart *(G-3113)*
Rochester Homes Inc ....C....... 574 223-4321
　Rochester *(G-12146)*

HOMES: Log Cabins

Appalachian Log HMS Fultn Elc............G....... 260 356-5431
　Huntington *(G-6186)*
Appalachian Log Structures ....G....... 812 744-5711
　Moores Hill *(G-10297)*
Burnside Enterprises ....G....... 765 664-4032
　Marion *(G-9513)*
Colluci Construction-Log Homes.........G....... 812 843-5607
　English *(G-3312)*
Country Charm.......................................G....... 765 572-2588
　Attica *(G-299)*
E & L Construction Inc ....G....... 765 525-7081
　Manilla *(G-9503)*
Expedition Log Homes ....G....... 219 663-5555
　Crown Point *(G-2252)*
Hearthstone of Indiana ....G....... 812 988-2127
　Nashville *(G-10725)*
Heritage Log Homes ....G....... 812 427-2591
　Vevay *(G-13664)*
Heston Log Homes Inc ....G....... 219 778-4074
　La Porte *(G-8763)*
Lauer Log Homes......................................G....... 260 486-7010
　Fort Wayne *(G-4426)*
Napoleon Lumber Co.................................G....... 812 852-4545
　Napoleon *(G-10641)*
Sidney & Janice Bond ....G....... 812 366-8160
　Sellersburg *(G-12415)*
Wagler Mini Barn Products ....G....... 812 687-7372
　Plainville *(G-11657)*

HONES

G & S Super Abrasives Inc........................E....... 260 665-5562
　Angola *(G-215)*

HONING & LAPPING MACHINES

Miko-Hone Machine Co Inc ....G....... 574 642-4701
　Goshen *(G-5291)*

Rx Honing Machine Corp ....G....... 574 259-1606
　Mishawaka *(G-10119)*

HOOPS: Iron & Steel

Pizo Operating Company LLC ....E....... 317 243-0811
　Indianapolis *(G-7699)*

HOPPERS: Sheet Metal

Vibromatic Company Inc ....E....... 317 773-3885
　Noblesville *(G-11199)*

HORSE & PET ACCESSORIES: Textile

Fabri-Tech Inc...E....... 317 849-7755
　McCordsville *(G-9666)*
Lakestreet Enterprises LLC ....G....... 260 768-7991
　Lagrange *(G-9055)*
Smiths TAC Shack ....G....... 765 345-5590
　Knightstown *(G-8560)*

HORSE ACCESS: Harnesses & Riding Crops, Etc, Exc Leather

Frazier Products ....F....... 317 781-9781
　Indianapolis *(G-6961)*

HORSE DRAWN VEHICLE REPAIR SVCS

Hoosier Buggy Shop ....G....... 260 593-2192
　Topeka *(G-13422)*

HORSESHOEING SVCS

Beaver Mouldings LLC ....G....... 260 463-4822
　Lagrange *(G-9033)*

HORSESHOES

Hammer Time Forge ....G....... 812 448-2171
　Brazil *(G-963)*
Ty Bowells Farrier Service ....G....... 812 537-3990
　Greendale *(G-5496)*

HOSE: Flexible Metal

Engineered Industrial Products..................G....... 317 684-4280
　Indianapolis *(G-6868)*
Esco Enterprises Indiana Inc ....F....... 317 241-0318
　Indianapolis *(G-6876)*
Flexaust Company Inc...............................G....... 574 371-3248
　Warsaw *(G-13875)*
Hose Technology Inc ....E....... 765 762-5501
　Williamsport *(G-14291)*

HOSE: Plastic

Quadrant Epp Usa Inc ....D....... 260 479-4700
　Fort Wayne *(G-4568)*
Quadrant Epp Usa Inc ....C....... 260 479-4100
　Fort Wayne *(G-4569)*

HOSE: Pneumatic, Rubber Or Rubberized Fabric, NEC

Clean-Seal Inc ....E....... 574 299-1888
　South Bend *(G-12736)*

HOSE: Rubber

Flexible Technologies Inc ....E....... 574 936-2432
　Plymouth *(G-11685)*
Nova Flex Group ....F....... 317 334-1444
　Indianapolis *(G-7598)*
Radiator Specialty Company ....E....... 574 546-5606
　Bremen *(G-1018)*
S & R Welding Inc ....G....... 317 710-0360
　Indianapolis *(G-7877)*
Slb Corporation ....F....... 574 255-9774
　Mishawaka *(G-10125)*

HOSES & BELTING: Rubber & Plastic

Artisanz Fabrication Mch LLC ....G....... 317 708-0228
　Plainfield *(G-11594)*
Coupled Products LLC ....B....... 260 248-3200
　Columbia City *(G-1776)*
Dunham Rubber & Belting Corp ....E....... 317 888-3002
　Greenwood *(G-5683)*
Dunham Rubber & Belting Corp ....G....... 800 876-5340
　Fort Wayne *(G-4224)*
Dura-Vent Corp...G....... 574 936-2432
　Plymouth *(G-11681)*

Exactseal Inc ....G....... 317 559-2220
　Indianapolis *(G-6889)*
Flexaust Inc ....C....... 574 267-7909
　Warsaw *(G-13876)*
General Rbr Plas of Evansville ....E....... 812 464-5153
　Evansville *(G-3517)*
Hitachi Cable America Inc ....C....... 812 945-9011
　New Albany *(G-10794)*
Hitachi Cble Auto Pdts USA Inc ....C....... 812 945-9011
　New Albany *(G-10796)*
Kilgore Manufacturing Co Inc ....D....... 260 248-2002
　Columbia City *(G-1804)*
Mulhern Belting Inc...................................G....... 219 879-2385
　Michigan City *(G-9822)*
Rubber Shop Inc ....G....... 574 291-6440
　South Bend *(G-12924)*
Tri-State Hydraulics Indus Sup.................G....... 812 537-3485
　Greendale *(G-5495)*

HOT TUBS

Master Spas Inc ....C....... 260 436-9100
　Fort Wayne *(G-4456)*

HOTEL & MOTEL RESERVATION SVCS

Horizon Publishing Company LLC.......E....... 219 852-3200
　Hammond *(G-5895)*

HOTLINE

Mishawaka Frozen Custard........................E....... 574 255-8000
　Mishawaka *(G-10092)*

HOUSEHOLD APPLIANCE STORES

Duncan Supply Co Inc...............................G....... 765 446-0105
　Lafayette *(G-8892)*
Industrial Sewing Machine Co ....G....... 812 425-2255
　Evansville *(G-3558)*
Zinn Kitchens Inc......................................E....... 574 967-4179
　Bringhurst *(G-1039)*

HOUSEHOLD APPLIANCE STORES: Air Cond Rm Units, Self-Contnd

Lute Supply ....G....... 260 480-2441
　Fort Wayne *(G-4444)*

HOUSEHOLD APPLIANCE STORES: Electric Household, Major

Vans TV & Appliance Inc ....F....... 260 927-8267
　Auburn *(G-366)*

HOUSEHOLD ARTICLES, EXC KITCHEN: Pottery

Schmidt Marken Designs ....G....... 219 785-4238
　La Porte *(G-8816)*

HOUSEHOLD ARTICLES: Metal

Grace Manufacturing Inc ....F....... 574 267-8000
　Warsaw *(G-13884)*
Kimball Electronics Inc ....D....... 317 545-5383
　Indianapolis *(G-7351)*
Outsource Technologies Inc ....E....... 574 233-1303
　South Bend *(G-12884)*

HOUSEHOLD FURNISHINGS, NEC

Ascot Enterprises Inc ....D....... 574 773-3104
　Nappanee *(G-10650)*
Baird Home Corporation ....G....... 812 883-1141
　Salem *(G-12284)*
Inhabit Inc ....G....... 317 636-1699
　Indianapolis *(G-7233)*
Keter North America LLC ....G....... 765 298-6800
　Anderson *(G-129)*
Nice-Pak Products Inc ....A....... 845 365-1700
　Mooresville *(G-10328)*
Pgs LLC ....E....... 812 988-4030
　Nashville *(G-10732)*
Quilt Designs Inc.......................................G....... 574 534-2502
　Elkhart *(G-3132)*
Veada Industries Inc ....A....... 574 831-4775
　New Paris *(G-11000)*
Vera Bradley Inc ....B....... 877 708-8372
　Roanoke *(G-12110)*

P
R
O
D
U
C
T

HOUSEWARE STORES

Jolar Enterprises.................................G...... 574 875-8369
Elkhart *(G-2950)*

Meyer Mill Oak Woodcrafters..............G...... 317 462-1413
Greenfield *(G-5550)*

Sampler Inc...F...... 765 663-2233
Homer *(G-6109)*

HOUSEWARES, ELECTRIC: Appliances, Personal

Dometic Corporation ....E...... 574 389-3759
Goshen *(G-5202)*

Scott Fetzer Company ....D...... 260 488-3531
Hamilton *(G-5828)*

HOUSEWARES, ELECTRIC: Cooking Appliances

Hyndman Industrial Pdts Inc ....E...... 260 483-6042
Fort Wayne *(G-4354)*

HOUSEWARES, ELECTRIC: Heaters, Space

Ultra-Heat Inc....................................F...... 574 522-6594
Elkhart *(G-3232)*

HOUSEWARES, ELECTRIC: Lighters, Cigarette

Naptown Vapors LLC ....G...... 765 315-0554
Martinsville *(G-9629)*

HOUSEWARES, ELECTRIC: Roasters

Hoosier Roaster Llc.............................G...... 574 257-1415
Mishawaka *(G-10051)*

HOUSEWARES: Dishes, Plastic

Affinis Group LLC ....G...... 317 831-3830
Mooresville *(G-10301)*

Dorel Juvenile Group Inc ....G...... 812 372-0141
Columbus *(G-1911)*

Dorel Juvenile Group Inc ....C...... 812 372-0141
Columbus *(G-1913)*

H A P Industries Inc ....G...... 765 948-3385
Jonesboro *(G-8445)*

HOUSEWARES: Kettles & Skillets, Cast Iron

Precision Gage LLC..............................G...... 260 925-4717
Auburn *(G-348)*

HOUSING COMPONENTS: Prefabricated, Concrete

Alberding Woodworking Inc ....E...... 260 728-9526
Decatur *(G-2365)*

HOUSINGS: Motor

Ipfw Student Housing ....G...... 260 481-4180
Fort Wayne *(G-4382)*

HUMIDIFIERS & DEHUMIDIFIERS

Air Technology Inc...............................G...... 574 231-0579
South Bend *(G-12696)*

HYDRAULIC EQPT REPAIR SVC

B & C Machining Inc ....E...... 219 924-5411
Rensselaer *(G-11915)*

Dependable Rubber Industrial ....G...... 765 447-5654
Lafayette *(G-8887)*

Five Star Hydraulics Inc ....E...... 219 762-1619
Portage *(G-11763)*

Fourman Enterprises Inc.......................F...... 812 546-5734
Hope *(G-6113)*

Industrial Hydraulics Inc ....E...... 317 247-4421
Indianapolis *(G-7208)*

K M Specialty Pumps Inc ....F...... 812 925-3000
Chandler *(G-1550)*

Macallister Machinery Co Inc...............D...... 260 483-6469
Fort Wayne *(G-4447)*

Motion & Control Entps LLC ....F...... 219 844-4224
Hammond *(G-5918)*

Ottosons Industries Inc ....G...... 219 365-8330
Cedar Lake *(G-1532)*

T and T Hydraulics Inc.........................G...... 765 548-2355
Rosedale *(G-12207)*

Hard Rubber & Molded Rubber Prdts

Eis Fibercoating Inc ....E...... 574 722-5192
Logansport *(G-9334)*

Roembke Mfg & Design Inc..................E...... 260 622-4135
Ossian *(G-11406)*

Roembke Mfg & Design Inc..................E...... 260 622-4030
Ossian *(G-11407)*

ICE

Airgas Inc..E...... 317 632-7106
Indianapolis *(G-6354)*

Arctic Ice Express Inc...........................E...... 812 333-0423
Bloomington *(G-664)*

Celebration Ice LLC ....G...... 812 634-9801
Jasper *(G-8240)*

Cosner Ice Company Inc ....E...... 812 279-8930
Bedford *(G-535)*

Home City Ice Company ....E...... 317 638-0437
Indianapolis *(G-7112)*

Home City Ice Company ....E...... 317 926-2451
Indianapolis *(G-7113)*

Home City Ice Company ....E...... 765 762-6096
Attica *(G-305)*

Quikset Bollard Company ....G...... 502 648-6734
New Albany *(G-10852)*

Slip Harris Company LLC.......................G...... 812 923-5674
Greenville *(G-5654)*

Superior Ice Co Inc ....F...... 812 847-4312
Linton *(G-9314)*

ICE: Dry

Airgas Inc..E...... 317 632-7106
Indianapolis *(G-6354)*

Continental Carbonic Pdts Inc..............G...... 574 273-2800
South Bend *(G-12741)*

IGNEOUS ROCK: Crushed & Broken

Barrett Paving Materials Inc ....F...... 765 935-3060
Richmond *(G-11960)*

New Point Stone Co Inc ....F...... 812 663-2422
Greensburg *(G-5628)*

IGNITER GRAINS: Boron Potassium Nitrate

Scp Holdings Inc..................................G...... 260 925-2588
Auburn *(G-354)*

IGNITION SYSTEMS: Internal Combustion Engine

Standard Motor Products Inc................C...... 574 259-6253
Mishawaka *(G-10135)*

INCENSE

Beverlys Incense ....G...... 219 558-2461
Saint John *(G-12260)*

Incense Incense ....G...... 317 544-9444
Danville *(G-2349)*

Intense Incense ....G...... 765 457-3602
Kokomo *(G-8647)*

Kyles Incense LLC ....G...... 219 682-4278
Merrillville *(G-9724)*

Lebermuth Company Inc ....D...... 574 259-7000
South Bend *(G-12837)*

Magnifiscents ....G...... 317 549-3880
Indianapolis *(G-7440)*

INCINERATORS

R & K Incinerator Inc ....G...... 260 565-3214
Decatur *(G-2400)*

INDL & PERSONAL SVC PAPER WHOLESALERS

Central Packaging Inc ....C...... 260 436-7225
Fort Wayne *(G-4143)*

Farm Boy Meats of Evansville ....C...... 812 425-5231
Evansville *(G-3498)*

Millcraft Paper Company ....E...... 317 240-3500
Indianapolis *(G-7519)*

Servants Inc...D...... 812 634-2201
Jasper *(G-8306)*

INDL & PERSONAL SVC PAPER, WHOL: Bags, Paper/Disp Plastic

Viking Paper Company ....E...... 574 936-6300
Plymouth *(G-11734)*

INDL & PERSONAL SVC PAPER, WHOL: Boxes, Corrugtd/Solid Fiber

Servants Inc...G...... 812 634-2201
Jasper *(G-8307)*

Westrock Cp LLC ....C...... 574 256-0318
Mishawaka *(G-10151)*

Westrock CP LLC ....E...... 574 296-2817
Elkhart *(G-3258)*

INDL & PERSONAL SVC PAPER, WHOL: Paper, Wrap/Coarse/Prdts

Orora North America ....E...... 317 879-4628
Indianapolis *(G-7631)*

INDL & PERSONAL SVC PAPER, WHOLESALE: Boxes & Containers

Gta Containers Inc ....E...... 574 288-3459
South Bend *(G-12793)*

INDL & PERSONAL SVC PAPER, WHOLESALE: Patterns, Paper

Temple Inland ....G...... 765 362-1074
Crawfordsville *(G-2201)*

INDL & PERSONAL SVC PAPER, WHOLESALE: Sanitary Food

Acd Suppliers LLC.................................G...... 317 527-9715
Indianapolis *(G-6315)*

INDL & PERSONAL SVC PAPER, WHOLESALE: Shipping Splys

PSC Industries Inc ....E...... 812 425-9071
Evansville *(G-3688)*

INDL EQPT CLEANING SVCS

Whitlocks Pressure Wash ....F...... 765 825-5868
Connersville *(G-2078)*

INDL EQPT SVCS

3-T Corp ....G...... 812 424-7878
Evansville *(G-3326)*

Automation Consultants Inc ....G...... 502 552-4995
Floyds Knobs *(G-4007)*

B & H Electric and Supply Inc ....E...... 812 522-5607
Seymour *(G-12431)*

Bastian Automation Engrg LLC.............D...... 317 467-2583
Greenfield *(G-5507)*

Buhrt Engineering & Cnstr....................E...... 574 267-3720
Warsaw *(G-13852)*

Evansville Assn For The Blind ....C...... 812 422-1181
Evansville *(G-3482)*

Mtr Machining Concept Inc ....G...... 260 587-3381
Ashley *(G-288)*

Refractory Service Corporation.............E...... 219 397-7108
East Chicago *(G-2567)*

Saran Industries LLC............................D...... 317 897-2170
Kokomo *(G-8690)*

Saran Industries LLC............................D...... 317 897-2170
Bloomington *(G-821)*

Southlake Machine Corp ....G...... 219 285-6150
Morocco *(G-10364)*

Storageworks Inc..................................G...... 317 577-3511
Fishers *(G-3971)*

T & M Equipment Company Inc ....F...... 317 293-9255
Indianapolis *(G-8032)*

Tarpenning-Lafollette Co Inc ....E...... 317 780-1500
Indianapolis *(G-8036)*

INDL GASES WHOLESALERS

Airgas Usa LLC ....G...... 812 362-7593
Rockport *(G-12163)*

Indiana Oxygen Company Inc ....D...... 317 290-0003
Indianapolis *(G-7188)*

Indiana Oxygen Company Inc ....G...... 765 662-8700
Marion *(G-9533)*

Northern Gases and Sups Inc..............F 574 594-2551
Pierceton (G-11574)

INDL MACHINERY & EQPT WHOLESALERS

Aam-Equipco Inc..........................G 574 272-8886
Granger (G-5388)

American Veteran Group LLC...............G...... 317 600-4749
Westfield (G-14136)

Asphalt Equipment Company Inc........G...... 260 672-3004
Fort Wayne (G-4093)

Autoform Tool & Mfg LLC ....C...... 260 624-2014
Angola (G-195)

Banks Machine & Engrg Inc................D...... 317 642-4980
Shelbyville (G-12519)

Basiloid Products Corp ....E...... 812 692-5511
Elnora (G-3286)

Capital Adhesives & Packg Corp ....F...... 317 834-5415
Mooresville (G-10304)

Craft Laboratories Inc..........................F...... 260 432-9467
Fort Wayne (G-4183)

Hawkins Darryal..................................G...... 765 282-6021
Muncie (G-10482)

Hintz Equipment Inc............................G...... 765 362-6115
Thorntown (G-13375)

Hoffman Sls & Specialty Co Inc...........G...... 317 846-6428
Carmel (G-1406)

Hoosier Fire Equipment Inc ....E...... 219 462-1707
Valparaiso (G-13557)

Hoosier Metal Polish Inc ....F...... 219 474-6011
Kentland (G-8520)

Horner Industrial Services Inc ....F...... 317 634-7165
Indianapolis (G-7129)

Indco Inc ....G...... 812 945-4383
New Albany (G-10805)

Interstate Power Systems Inc ....E...... 952 854-2044
Gary (G-5070)

Koch Enterprises Inc...........................G...... 812 465-9800
Evansville (G-3596)

Landis Equipment & Tool Rental..........G...... 812 847-2582
Linton (G-9309)

Logansport Machine Co Inc ....E...... 574 735-0225
Logansport (G-9350)

Machine Tool Service Inc ....F...... 812 232-1912
Terre Haute (G-13277)

Mainline Conveyor Systems Inc ....F...... 317 831-2795
Mooresville (G-10320)

Mitsubishi Heavy Industries ....E...... 714 960-3785
Franklin (G-4910)

Murray Equipment Inc ....D...... 260 484-0382
Fort Wayne (G-4486)

Ogden Welding Systems Inc................E...... 219 322-5252
Schererville (G-12341)

Pyramid Equipment ....F...... 219 778-2591
Rolling Prairie (G-12193)

Robinson Industries Inc ....E...... 317 867-3214
Westfield (G-14186)

Rochester Cement Products ....G...... 574 223-3917
Rochester (G-12145)

Specialty Tool LLC...............................F...... 260 493-6351
Indianapolis (G-7969)

Steel Tank & Fabricating Corp ....E...... 260 248-8971
Columbia City (G-1838)

Storageworks Inc ....G...... 317 577-3511
Fishers (G-3971)

Systems Engineering and Sls Co.........G...... 260 422-1671
Fort Wayne (G-4671)

T & M Equipment Company Inc ....F...... 317 293-9255
Indianapolis (G-8032)

Technical Water Treatment Inc ....G...... 574 277-1949
Granger (G-5444)

Tsune America LLC...............................F...... 812 378-9875
Edinburgh (G-2631)

US Crane & Hoist Inc...........................G...... 219 963-1400
Lake Station (G-9080)

W M Kelley Co Inc................................E...... 812 945-3529
New Albany (G-10873)

Wiese Holding Company.......................E...... 317 241-8600
Indianapolis (G-8194)

INDL MACHINERY REPAIR & MAINTENANCE

Ajax Tocco Magnethermic Corp ....G...... 317 352-9880
Indianapolis (G-6357)

Aluminum Wldg & Mch Works Inc.........G...... 219 787-8066
Chesterton (G-1592)

American Machine Fabrication...............G...... 812 944-4136
New Albany (G-10744)

Applied Metals & Mch Works Inc..........E...... 260 424-4834
Fort Wayne (G-4083)

Boyd Machine & Repair Co Inc.............E...... 260 635-2195
Kimmell (G-8529)

Cummins Repair Inc ....G...... 260 632-4800
Harlan (G-5969)

D&D Automation Inc ....G...... 812 299-1045
Terre Haute (G-13221)

Decatur Mold Tool and Engrg ....C...... 812 346-5188
North Vernon (G-11253)

Flamespray Machine Service................G...... 260 726-6236
Portland (G-11823)

Gary Bridge and Iron Co Inc ....G...... 219 884-3792
Gary (G-5049)

Gravelton Machine Shop Inc.................G...... 574 773-3413
Nappanee (G-10674)

Heartland Filled Machine LLC...............G...... 574 223-6931
Rochester (G-12127)

Hook Industrial Sales Inc ....F...... 317 545-8100
Indianapolis (G-7119)

Jeda Equipment Services Inc ....G...... 317 842-9377
Fishers (G-3933)

Mantra Enterprise LLC ....G...... 201 428-8709
Fishers (G-3944)

Odyssey Machine Inc ....G...... 812 951-1160
Georgetown (G-5151)

Peerless Machinery Inc ....G...... 574 210-5990
South Bend (G-12889)

Reynolds & Co Inc ....E...... 812 232-5313
Terre Haute (G-13319)

Slabaugh Metal Fab ....E...... 574 546-2882
Bremen (G-1024)

T & M Equipment Company Inc ....E...... 219 942-2299
Merrillville (G-9755)

Wall Control Services Inc ....G...... 260 450-6411
Fort Wayne (G-4733)

INDL PATTERNS: Foundry Cores

Shells Inc ....D...... 574 342-2673
Bourbon (G-947)

INDL PATTERNS: Foundry Patternmaking

Baseline Tool Co Inc............................F...... 260 761-4932
Wawaka (G-14030)

Charles Bane ....G...... 765 855-5100
Centerville (G-1541)

Diversified Pattern & Engrg Co ....E...... 260 897-3771
Avilla (G-403)

Maxwell Engineering Inc ....G...... 260 745-4991
Fort Wayne (G-4458)

Nvsd LLC ....G...... 502 561-0007
New Albany (G-10834)

INDL PROCESS INSTRUMENTS: Absorp Analyzers, Infrared, X-Ray

Texmo Prcision Castings US Inc ....D...... 574 269-1368
Warsaw (G-13951)

INDL PROCESS INSTRUMENTS: Analyzers

Analyticalab Inc...................................G...... 219 473-9777
Whiting (G-14267)

Harman Professional Inc......................B...... 574 294-8000
Elkhart (G-2908)

INDL PROCESS INSTRUMENTS: Boiler Controls, Power & Marine

Advanced Boiler Ctrl Svcs Inc..............F...... 708 429-7066
Crown Point (G-2223)

INDL PROCESS INSTRUMENTS: Data Loggers

Cosworth Electronics LLC.....................G...... 317 808-3800
Indianapolis (G-6674)

INDL PROCESS INSTRUMENTS: Digital Display, Process Variables

Ovideon LLC...G...... 812 577-3274
Lawrenceburg (G-9151)

INDL PROCESS INSTRUMENTS: Fluidic Devices, Circuit & Systems

Mtcr Site Services LLC.........................G...... 812 598-6516
Newburgh (G-11039)

INDL PROCESS INSTRUMENTS: Indl Flow & Measuring

Maxim Pipette Service Inc....................G...... 877 536-2946
Plainfield (G-11625)

INDL PROCESS INSTRUMENTS: On-Stream Gas Or Liquid Analysis

Thermco Instrument Corporation..........F 219 362-6258
La Porte (G-8831)

INDL PROCESS INSTRUMENTS: Temperature

Pyromation Inc....................................C...... 260 484-2580
Fort Wayne (G-4566)

INDL PROCESS INSTRUMENTS: Water Quality Monitoring/Cntrl Sys

Monitoring Solutions Inc.......................E...... 317 856-9400
Indianapolis (G-7535)

Ray Kammer ....G...... 219 938-1708
Gary (G-5088)

INDL SPLYS WHOLESALERS

Airgas Usa LLC ....E...... 812 474-0440
Evansville (G-3345)

Ferguson...G...... 317 254-5965
Indianapolis (G-6916)

Freudenberg-Nok General Partnr ....C...... 765 763-7246
Morristown (G-10370)

Hogen Industries Inc Indiana...............E...... 317 591-5070
Indianapolis (G-7111)

Hoosier Industrial Supply ....G...... 574 535-0712
Goshen (G-5239)

Hoosier Industrial Supply Inc ....F...... 574 533-8565
Goshen (G-5240)

Jac Jmr Inc ....G...... 219 663-6700
Crown Point (G-2264)

Kaiser Tool Company Inc ....E...... 260 484-3620
Fort Wayne (G-4403)

Mulzer Crushed Stone Inc....................E...... 812 547-7921
Tell City (G-13167)

Northern Gases and Sups Inc..............F...... 574 594-2551
Pierceton (G-11574)

Polygon...G...... 317 240-1130
Indianapolis (G-7705)

Puck Supply & Machine LLC ....F...... 574 293-3333
Elkhart (G-3122)

Standard Die Supply of Indiana............E...... 317 236-6200
Indianapolis (G-7989)

Steelco Industrial Lubricants.................G...... 219 462-0333
Valparaiso (G-13624)

Terry Liquidation III Inc.........................D...... 219 362-9908
La Porte (G-8828)

Tri-State Power Supply LLC...................G...... 812 537-2500
Lawrenceburg (G-9160)

INDL SPLYS, WHOL: Fasteners, Incl Nuts, Bolts, Screws, Etc

Emhart Teknologies LLC.......................C...... 765 728-2433
Montpelier (G-10290)

INDL SPLYS, WHOLESALE: Abrasives

Daylight Engineering Inc.......................G...... 812 983-2518
Elberfeld (G-2633)

INDL SPLYS, WHOLESALE: Adhesives, Tape & Plasters

Abro Industries Inc ....E...... 574 232-8289
South Bend (G-12692)

Adhesive Solutions Company LLC ....G...... 260 691-0304
Columbia City (G-1760)

Capital Adhesives & Packg Corp ....F...... 317 834-5415
Mooresville (G-10304)

Custom Building Products Inc ....D...... 765 656-0234
Frankfort (G-4827)

INDL SPLYS, WHOLESALE: Barrels, New Or Reconditioned

OBryan Barrel Company Inc.................E...... 812 479-6741
Evansville (G-3651)

INDL SPLYS, WHOLESALE: Bearings

Hanwha Machinery America Corp ....B 574 546-2261
Bremen (G-1001)
Headco Industries Inc ....G 219 924-7758
Highland (G-6049)
NSK Corporation ....C 765 458-5000
Liberty (G-9267)

INDL SPLYS, WHOLESALE: Bins & Containers, Storage

Universal Package LLC ....F 812 937-3605
Dale (G-2335)

INDL SPLYS, WHOLESALE: Fasteners & Fastening Eqpt

Illinois Tool Works Inc ....D 219 874-4217
Michigan City (G-9803)

INDL SPLYS, WHOLESALE: Filters, Indl

Filtration Plus Inc ....E 219 879-0663
Michigan City (G-9793)

INDL SPLYS, WHOLESALE: Fittings

Rankin Pump and Supply Co Inc ....G 812 238-2535
Terre Haute (G-13315)

INDL SPLYS, WHOLESALE: Gaskets

Freudenberg-Nok General Partnr ....C 317 421-3400
Shelbyville (G-12534)

INDL SPLYS, WHOLESALE: Gaskets & Seals

Clean-Seal Inc ....E 574 299-1888
South Bend (G-12736)
Nitto Inc ....G 317 879-2840
Zionsville (G-14451)
Press-Seal Gasket Corporation ....C 260 436-0521
Fort Wayne (G-4557)

INDL SPLYS, WHOLESALE: Gears

Fairfield Manufacturing Co Inc ....A 765 772-4000
Lafayette (G-8896)

INDL SPLYS, WHOLESALE: Power Transmission, Eqpt & Apparatus

P H C Industries Inc ....G 260 423-9461
Fort Wayne (G-4516)

INDL SPLYS, WHOLESALE: Rope, Exc Wire

Tway Company Incorporated ....E 317 636-2591
Indianapolis (G-8116)

INDL SPLYS, WHOLESALE: Rubber Goods, Mechanical

Dunham Rubber & Belting Corp ....E 317 888-3002
Greenwood (G-5683)
Dunham Rubber & Belting Corp ....G 800 876-5340
Fort Wayne (G-4224)
Exactseal Inc ....G 317 559-2220
Indianapolis (G-6889)
General Rbr Plas of Evansville ....E 812 464-5153
Evansville (G-3517)

INDL SPLYS, WHOLESALE: Seals

Hook Industrial Sales Inc ....D 260 432-9441
Fort Wayne (G-4342)

INDL SPLYS, WHOLESALE: Sewing Thread

Kirby Risk Corporation ....F 765 664-5185
Marion (G-9540)

INDL SPLYS, WHOLESALE: Signmaker Eqpt & Splys

Commercial Signs ....G 260 745-2678
Fort Wayne (G-4168)

INDL SPLYS, WHOLESALE: Tools

Rusach International Inc ....F 317 638-0298
Hope (G-6119)

INDL SPLYS, WHOLESALE: Tools, NEC

Peter Austin Co ....G 765 288-6397
Muncie (G-10545)

INDL TOOL GRINDING SVCS

Pgc Mulch LLC ....G 812 455-0700
Evansville (G-3667)

INDL TRUCK REPAIR SVCS

Fire Aparatus Service Inc ....G 219 985-0788
Gary (G-5047)

INDUCTORS

REO-Usa Inc ....F 317 899-1395
Indianapolis (G-7834)

INDUSTRIAL & COMMERCIAL EQPT INSPECTION SVCS

Dearborn Crane and Engrg Co ....E 574 259-2444
Mishawaka (G-10035)
Hmt LLC ....F 219 736-9901
Merrillville (G-9720)

INFORMATION RETRIEVAL SERVICES

First Databank Inc ....G 317 571-7200
Indianapolis (G-6926)
Gannett Co Inc ....G 765 423-5511
Lafayette (G-8903)
Job Scholar LLC ....G 419 564-9574
Huntington (G-6221)
Kaplan Inc ....D 317 872-7220
Indianapolis (G-7333)
Smartgait LLC ....G 765 404-0726
West Lafayette (G-14107)
Xlibris Corporation ....D 812 671-9162
Bloomington (G-861)

INGOT, EXTRUSION: Extrusion ingot, aluminum: rolling mills

A/C Fabricating Corp ....E 574 534-1415
Goshen (G-5163)
Alconex Specialty Products ....D 260 744-3446
Fort Wayne (G-4056)
Postle Operating LLC ....E 574 389-0800
Elkhart (G-3105)

INGOTS: Steel

Valbruna Slater Stainless Inc ....C 260 434-2800
Fort Wayne (G-4722)

INK: Duplicating

Nor-Cote International Inc ....E 765 230-7252
Crawfordsville (G-2177)

INK: Letterpress Or Offset

Brand Prtg & Photo-Litho Co ....G 317 921-4095
Indianapolis (G-6503)
Craftsnmoregalore LLC ....G 574 303-2231
Logansport (G-9333)

INK: Printing

Braden Sutphin Ink Co ....G 317 352-8781
Indianapolis (G-6499)
Budget Inks LLC ....G 877 636-4657
Angola (G-199)
CP Group Inc ....G 765 551-7768
Lafayette (G-8880)
Enviro Ink ....G 260 748-0636
Fort Wayne (G-4238)
Flint Group US LLC ....E 317 471-8435
Indianapolis (G-6936)
Flint Group US LLC ....E 317 870-4422
Indianapolis (G-6937)
Flint Group US LLC ....E 574 269-4603
Warsaw (G-13877)
Industrial Organic Inks Inc ....G 219 878-0613
Chesterton (G-1614)
INX International Ink Co ....G 765 939-6625
Richmond (G-12002)
Nor-Cote International Inc ....G 800 488-9180
Crawfordsville (G-2176)
Nor-Cote International Inc ....E 765 362-9180
Crawfordsville (G-2178)

Peafield Products Inc ....F 317 839-8473
Plainfield (G-11634)
Stamp N Scrap Ink Corp ....G 219 440-7239
Dyer (G-2510)
Sun Chemical Corporation ....D 765 659-6000
Frankfort (G-4854)
Sun Chemical Corporation ....G 812 235-8031
Terre Haute (G-13345)

INSECTICIDES

Hub States Corporation ....G 317 816-9955
Carmel (G-1408)

INSECTICIDES & PESTICIDES

Midwest AG Fly Services Inc ....G 812 275-5579
Bedford (G-564)
Prime Source LLC ....G 812 867-8921
Evansville (G-3685)
V Global Holdings LLC ....A 317 247-8141
Indianapolis (G-8142)

INSPECTION & TESTING SVCS

Ald Indy Inc ....G 317 826-3833
Fishers (G-3867)
Red Bull Armory LLC ....G 757 287-7738
Mitchell (G-10169)
Teaco Inc ....F 219 874-6234
Michigan City (G-9852)
Watcon Inc ....F 574 287-3397
South Bend (G-12988)

INSPECTION SVCS, TRANSPORTATION

T K Sales & Service ....G 219 962-8982
Gary (G-5104)

INSTR, MEASURE & CONTROL: Gauge, Oil Pressure & Water Temp

Wbh Inc ....F 317 269-1510
Indianapolis (G-8180)

INSTRUMENTS, LAB: Spectroscopic/Optical Properties Measuring

Lk Technologies Inc ....G 812 332-4449
Bloomington (G-766)

INSTRUMENTS, LABORATORY: Spectrometers

Anasazi Instruments Inc ....F 317 861-7657
New Palestine (G-10967)

INSTRUMENTS, MEASURING & CNTRL: Radiation & Testing, Nuclear

Nuclear Measurements Corp ....G 317 546-2415
Indianapolis (G-7604)

INSTRUMENTS, MEASURING & CNTRL: Testing, Abrasion, Etc

Nrp Jones LLC ....D 219 362-4508
La Porte (G-8800)
Stout Plastic Weld ....F 219 926-7622
Chesterton (G-1634)

INSTRUMENTS, MEASURING & CNTRLG: Thermometers/Temp Sensors

Sensortec Inc ....E 260 497-8811
Fort Wayne (G-4616)

INSTRUMENTS, MEASURING & CONTROLLING: Breathalyzers

Linde Gas North America LLC ....G 888 345-0894
Terre Haute (G-13275)

INSTRUMENTS, MEASURING & CONTROLLING: Ion Chambers

Containment Tech Group Inc ....G 317 862-5945
Indianapolis (G-6654)

INSTRUMENTS, MEASURING & CONTROLLING: Leak Detection, Liquid

Automatic Tool Control ....E....... 317 328-8492
Indianapolis **(G-6445)**

INSTRUMENTS, MEASURING & CONTROLLING: Polygraph

Integrtive Plygraph Trning LLC ....G....... 812 595-2884
Scottsburg **(G-12367)**

INSTRUMENTS, MEASURING & CONTROLLING: Weather Tracking

Advanced Designs Corp ....F....... 812 333-1922
Bloomington **(G-657)**

INSTRUMENTS, MEASURING/CNTRLNG: Med Diagnostic Sys, Nuclear

Center For Diagnostic Imaging.............F....... 812 234-0555
Terre Haute **(G-13206)**
Dose Shield Corporation....................G....... 317 576-0183
Markleville **(G-9587)**
M RI Solutions ....E....... 317 218-3006
Indianapolis **(G-7433)**
RNS Imaging Inc ....G....... 812 523-2435
Seymour **(G-12480)**

INSTRUMENTS, OPTICAL: Aiming Circles, Fire Control

Better Visions PC............................G....... 260 627-2669
Leo **(G-9239)**
Better Visions PC............................G....... 260 244-7542
Columbia City **(G-1766)**

INSTRUMENTS, OPTICAL: Glasses, Field Or Opera

Union Optical Eyecare Ctr Inc ....G....... 812 279-3466
Bedford **(G-587)**

INSTRUMENTS, OPTICAL: Magnifying, NEC

Motion Engineering Company Inc........G....... 317 804-7990
Westfield **(G-14177)**

INSTRUMENTS, SURGICAL & MED: Needles & Syringes, Hypodermic

Becton Dickinson and Company........B....... 317 561-2900
Plainfield **(G-11595)**

INSTRUMENTS, SURGICAL & MEDICAL: Blood & Bone Work

Advanced Mbility Solutions LLC ....G....... 812 438-2338
Rising Sun **(G-12085)**
Arcamed LLC..................................E....... 317 375-7733
Indianapolis **(G-6413)**
Bd Medical Development Inc ....G....... 219 310-8551
Crown Point **(G-2227)**
Biomet Europe Ltd ....G....... 574 267-2038
Warsaw **(G-13847)**
Depuy Synthes Inc ....B....... 574 267-8143
Warsaw **(G-13865)**
Freudenberg Medical Mis Inc..............C....... 812 280-2400
Jeffersonville **(G-8364)**
Poyser Kelshaw Group LLC................G....... 317 571-8493
Carmel **(G-1453)**
Truarch Inc.....................................G....... 812 402-9511
Evansville **(G-3777)**

INSTRUMENTS, SURGICAL & MEDICAL: Blood Transfusion

Helmer Inc......................................C....... 317 773-9073
Noblesville **(G-11120)**

INSTRUMENTS, SURGICAL & MEDICAL: Catheters

Cook Incorporated ....A....... 812 339-2235
Bloomington **(G-705)**
Cook Incorporated ....C....... 812 339-2235
Ellettsville **(G-3277)**
Cook Incorporated ....C....... 812 876-7790
Bloomington **(G-706)**

T H S International Inc ....G....... 317 759-2869
Indianapolis **(G-8033)**

INSTRUMENTS, SURGICAL & MEDICAL: Inhalation Therapy

Ascensia Diabetes Care US Inc ....E....... 201 875-8066
Mishawaka **(G-9998)**
Cork Medical LLC............................G....... 317 361-4651
Indianapolis **(G-6667)**

INSTRUMENTS, SURGICAL & MEDICAL: Lasers, Ophthalmic

Lca-Vision Inc..................................G....... 317 818-3980
Indianapolis **(G-7387)**

INSTRUMENTS, SURGICAL & MEDICAL: Lasers, Surgical

AMD Group LLC...............................F....... 317 202-9530
Indianapolis **(G-6382)**

INSTRUMENTS, SURGICAL & MEDICAL: Muscle Exercise, Ophthalmic

Jemarkel Health-Tech LLC ....F....... 219 548-5881
Valparaiso **(G-13563)**
Vertical Power Co.............................G....... 574 276-8094
Osceola **(G-11387)**

INSTRUMENTS: Analytical

Animated Dynamics Inc ....G....... 765 418-5359
West Lafayette **(G-14050)**
Beckman Coulter Inc ....D....... 317 471-8029
Indianapolis **(G-6460)**
Beckman Coulter Inc ....D....... 317 808-4200
Indianapolis **(G-6461)**
Beckman Coulter Inc ....G....... 317 808-4200
Indianapolis **(G-6462)**
Environmental Test Systems ....F....... 574 262-2060
Elkhart **(G-2835)**
Griffin Analytical Tech LLC ....E....... 765 775-1701
West Lafayette **(G-14072)**
Hach Company.................................G....... 574 262-2060
Elkhart **(G-2904)**
Infrared Lab Systems LLC ....F....... 317 896-1565
Westfield **(G-14170)**
Ipheion Development Corp ....G....... 240 281-1619
Indianapolis **(G-7265)**
Labtest Equipment Company ....D....... 219 462-3300
Valparaiso **(G-13568)**
Leco Corporation ....G....... 574 288-9017
South Bend **(G-12838)**
Lloyd Jr Frank P and Assoc.................G....... 317 388-9225
Indianapolis **(G-7410)**
Prosolia Inc.....................................G....... 317 275-5794
Indianapolis **(G-7781)**
Roche Diagnostics Corporation ....G....... 317 521-2000
Indianapolis **(G-7852)**
Smartgait LLC ....G....... 765 404-0726
West Lafayette **(G-14107)**
Templeton Coal Company Inc.............D....... 812 232-7037
Terre Haute **(G-13351)**
Trilithic Inc ....C....... 317 895-3600
Indianapolis **(G-8099)**

INSTRUMENTS: Analyzers, Radio Apparatus, NEC

Jfw Industries Incorporated................C....... 317 887-1340
Indianapolis **(G-7304)**

INSTRUMENTS: Analyzers, Spectrum

Spectrum Industry ....G....... 812 231-8355
Terre Haute **(G-13340)**

INSTRUMENTS: Differential Pressure, Indl

Hsm Eagle Ltd ....G....... 812 491-9666
Evansville **(G-3545)**

INSTRUMENTS: Electronic, Analog-Digital Converters

SBS Cybermetrix Inc ....G....... 812 378-7960
Columbus **(G-2011)**
SGS Cybermetrix Inc ....G....... 800 713-1203
Columbus **(G-2013)**

INSTRUMENTS: Eye Examination

Lebanon Corp..................................G....... 765 482-7273
Lebanon **(G-9199)**

INSTRUMENTS: Flow, Indl Process

Ameriflo Inc ....E....... 317 844-2019
Indianapolis **(G-6394)**
AMG LLC...E....... 317 329-4004
Indianapolis **(G-6397)**
Endress + Huser Flowtec AG Inc..........C....... 317 535-7138
Greenwood **(G-5688)**

INSTRUMENTS: Frequency Meters, Electrical, Mech & Electronic

Matson Counsulting Engineers ....G....... 260 478-8813
Fort Wayne **(G-4457)**

INSTRUMENTS: Indl Process Control

Amatrol Inc ....C....... 812 288-8285
Jeffersonville **(G-8322)**
Cognex Corporation ....G....... 317 867-5079
Westfield **(G-14144)**
Covidien LP ....C....... 317 837-8199
Plainfield **(G-11602)**
Crown Elec Svcs & Automtn Inc ....D....... 972 929-4700
Portage **(G-11758)**
Damping Technologies Inc ....E....... 574 258-7916
Mishawaka **(G-10031)**
Dwyer Instruments Inc ....D....... 574 862-2590
Wakarusa **(G-13775)**
Dwyer Instruments Inc ....C....... 219 279-2031
Wolcott **(G-14363)**
Dwyer Instruments Inc ....C....... 219 879-8868
South Bend **(G-12754)**
Dwyer Instruments Inc ....C....... 219 879-8000
Michigan City **(G-9785)**
Dwyer Instruments Inc ....F....... 219 879-8000
Michigan City **(G-9786)**
Emerson Electric Co..........................G....... 219 465-2411
Valparaiso **(G-13537)**
Emerson Electric Co..........................G....... 317 322-2055
Indianapolis **(G-6853)**
Endress + Hauser Inc ....C....... 317 535-7138
Greenwood **(G-5686)**
Endress + Hauser Inc ....C....... 317 535-7138
Greenwood **(G-5687)**
Endress+hauser (usa) Automatio.........D....... 317 535-2121
Greenwood **(G-5689)**
Endress+hauser Wetzer USA Inc ....E....... 317 535-1362
Greenwood **(G-5690)**
Envirnmntal Ctrl Solutions LLC............G....... 317 358-5985
Indianapolis **(G-6872)**
Functional Devices Inc ....G....... 765 883-5538
Sharpsville **(G-12505)**
Harris Corporation ....C....... 812 202-5171
Crane **(G-2127)**
Harris Corporation ....B....... 260 451-5597
Fort Wayne **(G-4323)**
Integratorcom Inc.............................D....... 317 776-3500
Noblesville **(G-11130)**
Leco Corporation ....G....... 574 288-9017
South Bend **(G-12838)**
Norman Tool Inc ....G....... 812 867-3496
Evansville **(G-3646)**
Quality Industrial Supplies..................F....... 219 324-2654
La Porte **(G-8808)**
Siemens Industry Inc ....D....... 219 763-7927
Portage **(G-11794)**
Superior Oprting Solutions Inc.............G....... 765 993-4094
Richmond **(G-12056)**
Syscon International Inc ....C....... 574 232-3900
South Bend **(G-12964)**
Technidyne Corporation.....................E....... 812 948-2884
New Albany **(G-10870)**
Thermphyscal Prpts RES Lab Inc ....G....... 765 463-1581
West Lafayette **(G-14113)**
Zs Systems LLC ....G....... 765 586-2738
West Lafayette **(G-14118)**

INSTRUMENTS: Liquid Level, Indl Process

Gainescraft Inc ....G....... 765 932-3590
Rushville **(G-12222)**

INSTRUMENTS: Measuring & Controlling

Chapman Environmental Controls........G....... 574 674-8706
Osceola **(G-11374)**

PRODUCT

Chesterfield Tool & Engrg Inc ....E 765 378-5101
Daleville *(G-2338)*

Damping Technologies Inc ....E 574 258-7916
Mishawaka *(G-10031)*

Dyno One Inc ....E 812 526-0500
Edinburgh *(G-2609)*

Hoosier Industrial Supply Inc ....F 574 533-8565
Goshen *(G-5240)*

Ias Corp ....G 209 836-8610
Peru *(G-11531)*

Indiana Veco Manufacturing ....E 765 932-2858
Rushville *(G-12223)*

Lafayette Instrument Co Inc ....E 765 423-1505
Lafayette *(G-8948)*

Lomont Holdings Co Inc ....E 800 545-9023
Angola *(G-228)*

Matrix Technologies Inc ....G 765 284-3335
Muncie *(G-10518)*

Mattox & Moore Inc ....G 317 632-7534
Indianapolis *(G-7468)*

Micro-Precision Operations ....E 260 589-2136
Berne *(G-620)*

P C Communication Inc ....G 219 838-2546
Highland *(G-6053)*

Piezotech LLC ....G 317 876-4670
Indianapolis *(G-7690)*

Robco Engineered Rubber Pdts ....F 260 248-2888
Columbia City *(G-1829)*

Technical Controls Solutions ....G 260 416-0329
Churubusco *(G-1659)*

Therametric Technologies Inc ....F 317 565-8065
Noblesville *(G-11194)*

Vibromatic Company Inc ....E 317 773-3885
Noblesville *(G-11199)*

INSTRUMENTS: Measuring Electricity

Acterna LLC ....E 317 788-9351
Indianapolis *(G-6320)*

App Engineering Incorporated ....F 317 755-3422
Indianapolis *(G-6407)*

Dwyer Instruments Inc ....D 260 723-5138
South Whitley *(G-12997)*

Emnet LLC ....G 574 360-1093
Granger *(G-5405)*

Hgl Dynamics Inc ....G 317 782-3500
Indianapolis *(G-7100)*

K J S Associates ....G 317 842-7500
Indianapolis *(G-7328)*

Kirby Risk Corporation ....B 765 447-1402
Lafayette *(G-8942)*

Leco Corporation ....G 574 288-9017
South Bend *(G-12838)*

Nano Universe LLC ....G 765 457-5860
Kokomo *(G-8675)*

Pdma Inc ....G 317 844-7750
Indianapolis *(G-6275)*

R K C Instrument ....F 574 273-6099
South Bend *(G-12911)*

Rail Scale Inc ....G 317 339-6486
Wilkinson *(G-14280)*

INSTRUMENTS: Measuring, Electrical Energy

Technical Weighing Svcs Inc ....E 219 924-3366
Griffith *(G-5793)*

INSTRUMENTS: Medical & Surgical

Accu-Mold LLC ....E 269 323-0388
Mishawaka *(G-9989)*

Admiral Medical Center Inc ....G 317 924-3757
Indianapolis *(G-6328)*

Advanced Vscular Therapies Inc ....G 765 423-1720
Lafayette *(G-8847)*

Advantis Medical Inc ....C 317 859-2300
Greenwood *(G-5661)*

After Action Med Dntl Sup LLC ....G 317 831-2699
Indianapolis *(G-6351)*

Airgas Usa LLC ....G 317 248-8072
Indianapolis *(G-6355)*

Alli Medical LLC ....G 317 625-4535
Westfield *(G-14134)*

Alpha Manufacturing and Design ....E 574 267-2171
Warsaw *(G-13837)*

American Veteran Group LLC ....G 317 600-4749
Westfield *(G-14136)*

Ameriflo2 Inc ....F 317 844-2019
Indianapolis *(G-6395)*

Ash Access Technology Inc ....G 765 742-4813
Lafayette *(G-8854)*

Baxter Healthcare Corp ....G 847 948-2000
Hammond *(G-5845)*

Baxter Healthcare Corporation ....B 812 355-7167
Bloomington *(G-675)*

Baxter Healthcare Corporation ....E 317 291-0620
Indianapolis *(G-6459)*

Baxter Healthcare Corporation ....D 812 333-0887
Bloomington *(G-676)*

Bioanalytical Systems Inc ....C 765 463-4527
West Lafayette *(G-14053)*

Biomet Inc ....A 574 267-6639
Warsaw *(G-13845)*

Biomet Inc ....G 574 372-6999
Warsaw *(G-13848)*

Biomet Sports Medicine LLC ....D 574 267-6639
Warsaw *(G-13850)*

Boston Scientific Corporation ....A 812 829-4877
Spencer *(G-13018)*

C & K Enterprises Inc ....E 260 624-3123
Angola *(G-201)*

Carecycle LLC ....G 317 372-7444
Indianapolis *(G-6554)*

Catheter Research Inc ....C 317 872-0074
Indianapolis *(G-6568)*

Century Pharmaceuticals Inc ....G 317 849-4210
Indianapolis *(G-6586)*

Circle M Spring Inc ....E 574 267-2883
Warsaw *(G-13857)*

Circle Medical Products Inc ....G 317 271-2626
Indianapolis *(G-6611)*

Compassionate Procedures LLC ....G 317 259-4656
Indianapolis *(G-6641)*

Cook Biodevice LLC ....F 800 265-0945
Bloomington *(G-703)*

Cook Group Incorporated ....G 812 331-1025
Ellettsville *(G-3276)*

Cook Incorporated ....A 812 829-4891
Spencer *(G-13020)*

Cook Medical LLC ....G 812 339-2235
Bloomington *(G-707)*

Corbett Phrmceuticals Dvcs LLC ....E 765 513-0674
Indianapolis *(G-6666)*

Covidien LP ....C 317 837-8199
Plainfield *(G-11602)*

Cspine Inc ....G 574 936-7893
South Bend *(G-12743)*

Depuy Mitek LLC ....G 574 267-8143
Warsaw *(G-13863)*

Ed Boilini ....G 317 921-0155
Indianapolis *(G-6802)*

Eli Lilly International Corp ....F 317 276-2000
Indianapolis *(G-6836)*

Engineered Medical Systems ....D 317 246-5500
Indianapolis *(G-6869)*

Esaote North America Inc ....D 317 813-6000
Fishers *(G-3907)*

First Gear Inc ....F 260 490-3238
Fort Wayne *(G-4263)*

Greatbatch Ltd ....G 260 755-7300
Fort Wayne *(G-4307)*

Group Dekko Inc ....E 260 599-3405
Kendallville *(G-8477)*

Guidant Intercontinental Corp ....E 317 218-7012
Carmel *(G-1391)*

Hansa Medical Products Inc ....G 317 815-0708
Carmel *(G-1394)*

Hemocleanse Inc ....F 765 742-4813
Lafayette *(G-8913)*

Holgin Technologies LLC ....F 317 774-5181
Noblesville *(G-11121)*

Immunores-Therapeutics LLC ....G 860 514-0526
Indianapolis *(G-7166)*

Innovtive Surgical Designs Inc ....F 484 584-4230
Bloomington *(G-749)*

Inscope Medical Solutions Inc ....G 502 882-0183
Jeffersonville *(G-8381)*

Kilgore Manufacturing Co Inc ....D 260 248-2002
Columbia City *(G-1804)*

King Systems Corporation ....B 317 776-6823
Noblesville *(G-11137)*

Mattox & Moore Inc ....G 317 632-7534
Indianapolis *(G-7468)*

Mectra Labs Inc ....E 812 384-3521
Bloomfield *(G-641)*

Med Devices LLC ....G 317 508-1699
Indianapolis *(G-7474)*

Med-Cut Manufacturing ....D 574 269-1982
Warsaw *(G-13907)*

Med2950 LLC ....F 317 545-5383
Indianapolis *(G-7475)*

Micropulse Inc ....C 260 625-3304
Columbia City *(G-1810)*

Nanovis LLC ....G 260 625-1502
Columbia City *(G-1811)*

Nemco Medical Ltd ....D 260 484-1500
Fort Wayne *(G-4494)*

Nextremity Solutions Inc ....G 732 383-7901
Warsaw *(G-13914)*

Nexxt Spine LLC ....F 317 436-7801
Noblesville *(G-11159)*

Nginstruments Inc ....D 574 268-2112
Warsaw *(G-13915)*

Omnitech Systems Inc ....E 219 531-5532
Valparaiso *(G-13595)*

On Guard ....G 317 753-5312
Indianapolis *(G-7621)*

Opsys Ltd ....G 765 236-6331
Bloomington *(G-790)*

Paragon Medical Inc ....G 574 594-2140
Pierceton *(G-11575)*

Paragon Medical Inc ....B 574 594-2140
Pierceton *(G-11576)*

Point Medical Corporation ....A 219 663-1775
Crown Point *(G-2285)*

Point Medical Corporation ....A 219 663-1775
Crown Point *(G-2286)*

Predictive Wear LLC ....F 765 464-4891
West Lafayette *(G-14096)*

Promex Technologies LLC ....E 317 736-0128
Indianapolis *(G-7778)*

Prp Technologies LLC ....G 260 433-3769
Fort Wayne *(G-4564)*

Qig LLC ....E 260 244-3591
Columbia City *(G-1821)*

Rmi Holdings LLC ....E 317 214-7076
Warsaw *(G-13936)*

Roche Diabetes Care Inc ....D 317 521-2000
Indianapolis *(G-7850)*

Roche Health Solutions Inc ....C 317 570-5100
Indianapolis *(G-7853)*

Rx Help Centers LLC ....G 866 478-9593
Indianapolis *(G-7876)*

Smiths Medical Asd Inc ....C 219 365-2376
Saint John *(G-12272)*

Smiths Medical Asd Inc ....E 219 554-2196
Gary *(G-5098)*

Sophysa USA Inc ....G 219 663-7711
Crown Point *(G-2308)*

Symmetry Medical Inc ....G 574 268-2252
Warsaw *(G-13948)*

Symmetry New Bedford RE LLC ....G 574 268-2252
Warsaw *(G-13950)*

Tricounty Surgical and Assoc ....G 260 726-2890
Portland *(G-11853)*

Universal Precision Instrs Inc ....G 574 264-3997
Elkhart *(G-3238)*

Vance Products Incorporated ....B 812 829-4891
Spencer *(G-13041)*

Vasmo Inc ....F 317 549-3722
Indianapolis *(G-8149)*

Vicair America LLC ....G 317 281-0809
Westfield *(G-14198)*

INSTRUMENTS: Nautical

Undersea Sensor Systems Inc ....C 260 244-3500
Columbia City *(G-1844)*

INSTRUMENTS: Power Measuring, Electrical

Radian Research Inc ....D 765 449-5500
Lafayette *(G-8988)*

INSTRUMENTS: Pressure Measurement, Indl

Dwyer Instruments Inc ....D 260 723-5138
South Whitley *(G-12997)*

INSTRUMENTS: Refractometers, Indl Process

Enginered Refr Shapes Svcs LLC ....G 765 778-8040
Pendleton *(G-11488)*

INSTRUMENTS: Temperature Measurement, Indl

Capital Tech Solutions LLC ....G 812 303-4357
Evansville *(G-3409)*

Complete Controls Inc ....G 260 489-0852
Fort Wayne *(G-4170)*

Environmental Technology Inc.............E 574 233-1202
South Bend (G-12765)
Heraeus Electro-Nite Co LLC..............C 765 473-8275
Peru (G-11529)

INSTRUMENTS: Test, Electrical, Engine

Indiana Research Institute....................E 812 378-4221
Columbus (G-1947)
Indiana Research Institute....................F 812 378-5363
Columbus (G-1948)
Renk Systems Corporation...................F 317 455-1367
Camby (G-1268)

INSTRUMENTS: Test, Electronic & Electric Measurement

Advantage Electronics Inc....................F 317 888-1946
Greenwood (G-5659)
Chance Indiana Standards Lab ....F 317 787-6578
Indianapolis (G-6593)
Contact Products Inc............................E 219 838-1911
Munster (G-10602)
Magnetic Instrumentation Inc ....E 317 842-9000
Indianapolis (G-7438)
Noel-Smyser Engineering Corp.............F 317 293-2215
Indianapolis (G-7590)

INSTRUMENTS: Test, Electronic & Electrical Circuits

Ball Systems Inc..................................E 317 804-2330
Westfield (G-14138)
Doyle Manufacturing Inc.......................G 574 848-5624
Bristol (G-1056)
Empro Manufacturing Co Inc.................E 317 823-3000
Indianapolis (G-6859)
System Solutions Inc............................G 317 877-7572
Cicero (G-1668)
Teaco Inc...F 219 874-6234
Michigan City (G-9852)

INSTRUMENTS: Thermal Conductive, Indl

Fire Aparatus Service Inc.....................G 219 985-0788
Gary (G-5047)
Indiana Thermal Solutions LLC............F 317 570-5400
Indianapolis (G-7195)

INSTRUMENTS: Vibration

Fleming Assoc Calibration Inc ....G 317 631-4605
Indianapolis (G-6933)

INSULATION & CUSHIONING FOAM: Polystyrene

Carpenter Co ....B 574 522-2800
Elkhart (G-2750)
Carpenter Co ....E 812 367-2211
Ferdinand (G-3847)
Century Foam Inc..................................C 574 293-5547
Elkhart (G-2753)
Elliott Co of Indianapolis.......................F 317 291-1213
Indianapolis (G-6842)
Foam Rubber LLC.................................C 765 521-2000
New Castle (G-10901)
G & T Industries Inc..............................E 812 634-2252
Jasper (G-8252)
Gaska Tape Inc....................................D 574 294-5431
Elkhart (G-2875)

INSULATION & ROOFING MATERIALS: Wood, Reconstituted

Standard Industries Inc.........................C 812 838-4861
Mount Vernon (G-10409)
Standard Industries Inc.........................C 219 872-1111
Michigan City (G-9847)

INSULATION MATERIALS WHOLESALERS

Innovative Energy Inc............................E 219 696-3639
Lowell (G-9409)

INSULATION: Fiberglass

Anderson Products Incorporated.........D 574 293-5574
Elkhart (G-2692)
Hy-TEC Fiberglass Inc..........................G 260 489-6601
Fort Wayne (G-4352)

Insul-Coustic Corporation.....................E 260 420-1480
Fort Wayne (G-4376)
Insulation Fabricators Inc......................D 219 845-2008
Hammond (G-5900)
Johns Manville Corporation...................C 765 973-5200
Richmond (G-12010)
Knauf Insulation Inc..............................B 317 421-3341
Shelbyville (G-12545)
Knauf Insulation Inc..............................B 317 398-4434
Shelbyville (G-12546)
Knauf Insulation Inc..............................C 317 398-4434
Shelbyville (G-12547)
Owens Corning Sales LLC.....................G 260 563-2111
Wabash (G-13745)
Owens Corning Sales LLC.....................E 260 665-7318
Angola (G-233)
Thermafiber Inc....................................D 260 563-2111
Wabash (G-13758)

INSULATORS & INSULATION MATERIALS: Electrical

Bo-Witt Products Inc.............................E 812 526-5561
Edinburgh (G-2597)
Gund Company Inc................................E 219 374-9944
Cedar Lake (G-1529)
Napier & Napier....................................G 765 580-9116
Liberty (G-9266)
Winona Building Products LLC.............F 574 822-0100
Etna Green (G-3323)

INSURANCE AGENTS, NEC

Cook Group Incorporated ....F 812 339-2235
Bloomington (G-704)

INTEGRATED CIRCUITS, SEMICONDUCTOR NETWORKS, ETC

Leidos Inc..C 812 863-3100
Crane (G-2128)

INTERCOMMUNICATION EQPT REPAIR SVCS

Reeds RFI Inc.......................................G 812 659-2872
Switz City (G-13126)

INTERCOMMUNICATIONS SYSTEMS: Electric

Acterna LLC..E 317 788-9351
Indianapolis (G-6320)
Harris Corporation................................D 260 451-6180
Fort Wayne (G-4321)
Lyra LLC..G 260 452-4058
Fort Wayne (G-4445)
Messagenet Systems Inc ....G 317 566-1677
Carmel (G-1438)

INTERIOR DECORATING SVCS

Custom Interior Dynamics LLC............F 317 632-0477
Indianapolis (G-6714)

INTERIOR DESIGN SVCS, NEC

Color Glo...G 812 926-2639
Aurora (G-375)
Deem & Loureiro Inc.............................G 770 652-9871
Indianapolis (G-6731)
Rlr Associates Inc.................................G 317 632-1300
Indianapolis (G-7848)

INTRAVENOUS SOLUTIONS

Saint-Gobain Abrasives Inc ....C 317 837-0700
Plainfield (G-11642)

INVERTERS: Nonrotating Electrical

Delta Microinverter LLC........................G 317 274-5935
Zionsville (G-14430)
Xantrex Technology USA Inc ....F 574 522-9628
Elkhart (G-3270)

INVESTORS, NEC

Integrity Marketing Team Inc ....G 317 517-0012
Plainfield (G-11617)
Sater Enterprises ....G 812 477-1529
Evansville (G-3714)

IRON & STEEL PRDTS: Hot-Rolled

Elkhart Steel Service Inc ....E 574 262-2552
Elkhart (G-2830)
Gerdau Ameristeel US Inc.....................C 765 286-5454
Muncie (G-3834)
Kankakee Valley Steel Inc ....G 219 828-4011
Wheatfield (G-14227)
Nlmk Indiana LLC.................................B 219 787-8200
Portage (G-11784)

IRON ORES

Arcelormittal Holdings LLC ....D 219 399-1200
East Chicago (G-2516)

JANITORIAL EQPT & SPLYS WHOLESALERS

Central Packaging Inc ....C 260 436-7225
Fort Wayne (G-4143)
Evansville Assn For The Blind ....C 812 422-1181
Evansville (G-3482)
Ideal Inc...G 765 457-6222
Kokomo (G-8643)
Johnco Corp...G 317 576-4417
Indianapolis (G-7308)
Kleen-Rite Supply Inc...........................F 812 422-7483
Evansville (G-3594)
Kuhn & Sons Inc...................................E 812 424-8268
Evansville (G-3597)
Modrak Products Company Inc.............F 219 838-0308
Gary (G-5078)
Wildman Business Group LLC...............C 866 369-1552
Warsaw (G-13965)

JEWELERS' FINDINGS/MTRLS: Gem Prep, Settings, Real/Imitation

Aaland Gem Company Inc ....G 219 769-4492
Merrillville (G-9691)

JEWELRY & PRECIOUS STONES WHOLESALERS

Amore Forte LLC...................................G 702 763-2550
Hammond (G-5842)
Edward ONeil Associates......................G 317 244-5400
Indianapolis (G-6810)

JEWELRY APPAREL

Aaland Gem Company Inc ....G 219 769-4492
Merrillville (G-9691)
Alan W Long..G 812 265-6717
Madison (G-9442)
Brinker Mfg Jewelers Inc.......................F 812 476-0651
Evansville (G-3402)
Design Msa Inc.....................................G 317 817-9000
Carmel (G-1355)
Flawless Beauty LLC.............................G 317 914-7952
Indianapolis (G-6932)

JEWELRY FINDINGS & LAPIDARY WORK

Alex and Ani LLC..................................G 317 575-8449
Indianapolis (G-6361)
RC Enterprises.....................................G 812 279-2755
Bedford (G-570)
Woodburn Diamond Die Co Inc.............D 260 632-4217
Woodburn (G-14392)

JEWELRY FINDINGS WHOLESALERS

Gillis Company.....................................G 574 273-9086
Granger (G-5409)

JEWELRY REPAIR SVCS

Chownings Jewelers ....G 765 294-4476
Veedersburg (G-13642)
Ginas Creative Jewelry Inc ....G 317 272-0032
Avon (G-442)
Golden Lion Inc.....................................G 765 446-9557
Lafayette (G-8909)
Goldstone Jewelry Inc...........................G 765 742-1975
West Lafayette (G-14070)
Interntnal Damnd Gold Exch Ltd..........F 317 872-6666
Indianapolis (G-7262)
Khamis Fine Jewelers Inc ....G 317 841-8440
Indianapolis (G-7348)
Rogers Enterprises Inc..........................G 317 851-5500
Greenwood (G-5742)

PRODUCT

Sisson & Son Mfg Jewelers ....G....... 574 967-4331
Flora **(G-4003)**

JEWELRY STORES

Alan W Long ....G....... 812 265-6717
Madison **(G-9442)**

Collegiate Pride Inc ....G....... 260 726-7818
Portland **(G-11812)**

Crystal Source ....G....... 812 988-7009
Nashville **(G-10721)**

Dyer Charles B and Ratliff Co ....G....... 317 634-3381
Indianapolis **(G-6772)**

Ginas Creative Jewelry Inc ....G....... 317 272-0032
Avon **(G-442)**

Golden Lion Inc ....G....... 765 446-9557
Lafayette **(G-8909)**

Interntnal Damnd Gold Exch Ltd ....F....... 317 872-6666
Indianapolis **(G-7262)**

Jewelers Boutique Inc ....G....... 317 788-7679
Indianapolis **(G-7303)**

Rogers Enterprises Inc ....G....... 317 851-5500
Greenwood **(G-5742)**

JEWELRY STORES: Precious Stones & Precious Metals

Argentum Jewelry Inc ....G....... 812 336-3100
Bloomington **(G-665)**

Ashleys Jewelry By Design Ltd ....G....... 219 926-9039
Chesterton **(G-1596)**

Brinker Mfg Jewelers Inc ....F....... 812 476-0651
Evansville **(G-3402)**

David Gonzales ....G....... 765 284-6960
Muncie **(G-10454)**

Design Msa Inc ....G....... 317 817-9000
Carmel **(G-1355)**

Edward E Petri Company ....G....... 317 636-5007
Indianapolis **(G-6809)**

G Thrapp Jewelers Inc ....E....... 317 255-5555
Indianapolis **(G-6977)**

Goldstone Jewelry Inc ....G....... 765 742-1975
West Lafayette **(G-14070)**

J C Sipe Inc ....G....... 317 848-0215
Indianapolis **(G-7283)**

Khamis Fine Jewelers Inc ....G....... 317 841-8440
Indianapolis **(G-7348)**

Peter Franklin Jewelers Inc ....G....... 260 749-4315
New Haven **(G-10952)**

Ronaldo Designer Jewelry Inc ....D....... 812 972-7220
New Albany **(G-10859)**

Sisson & Son Mfg Jewelers ....G....... 574 967-4331
Flora **(G-4003)**

Surplus Store and Exchange ....F....... 765 447-0200
Lafayette **(G-9006)**

Welmer Jewelers Inc ....G....... 812 522-4082
Seymour **(G-12499)**

JEWELRY STORES: Watches

Stall & Kessler Inc ....G....... 765 742-1259
Lafayette **(G-9002)**

JEWELRY, PRECIOUS METAL: Cigar & Cigarette Access

Smokes - Berne ....G....... 260 849-4038
Berne **(G-624)**

JEWELRY, PRECIOUS METAL: Mountings & Trimmings

Rogers Enterprises Inc ....G....... 317 851-5500
Greenwood **(G-5742)**

JEWELRY, PRECIOUS METAL: Rings, Finger

Herff Jones LLC ....D....... 620 365-5181
Indianapolis **(G-7090)**

Herff Jones LLC ....C....... 800 419-5462
Indianapolis **(G-7092)**

J Lewis Small Co Inc ....D....... 765 552-5011
Elwood **(G-3301)**

Jostens Inc ....G....... 317 326-2782
Greenfield **(G-5545)**

Jostens Inc ....G....... 317 843-1958
Indianapolis **(G-6270)**

JEWELRY, PRECIOUS METAL: Settings & Mountings

Downey Creations LLC ....D....... 317 248-9888
Indianapolis **(G-6764)**

J C Sipe Inc ....G....... 317 848-0215
Indianapolis **(G-7283)**

Surplus Store and Exchange ....F....... 765 447-0200
Lafayette **(G-9006)**

Welmer Jewelers Inc ....G....... 812 522-4082
Seymour **(G-12499)**

JEWELRY, PRECIOUS METAL: Studs, Precious & Semi Metal/Stone

Verona LLC ....G....... 317 248-9888
Indianapolis **(G-8151)**

JEWELRY, WHOLESALE

Ronaldo Designer Jewelry Inc ....D....... 812 972-7220
New Albany **(G-10859)**

Surplus Store and Exchange ....F....... 765 447-0200
Lafayette **(G-9006)**

JEWELRY: Decorative, Fashion & Costume

Swarovski North America Ltd ....G....... 317 841-0037
Indianapolis **(G-8025)**

JEWELRY: Precious Metal

Amore Forte LLC ....G....... 702 763-2550
Hammond **(G-5842)**

Argentum Jewelry Inc ....G....... 812 336-3100
Bloomington **(G-665)**

Ashleys Jewelry By Design Ltd ....G....... 219 926-9039
Chesterton **(G-1596)**

Collegiate Pride Inc ....G....... 260 726-7818
Portland **(G-11812)**

Crystal Source ....G....... 812 988-7009
Nashville **(G-10721)**

David Gonzales ....G....... 765 284-6960
Muncie **(G-10454)**

Dyer Charles B and Ratliff Co ....G....... 317 634-3381
Indianapolis **(G-6772)**

Ed Stump Assembly Inc ....G....... 574 291-0058
South Bend **(G-12758)**

Edward E Petri Company ....G....... 317 636-5007
Indianapolis **(G-6809)**

G Thrapp Jewelers Inc ....E....... 317 255-5555
Indianapolis **(G-6977)**

Ginas Creative Jewelry Inc ....G....... 317 272-0032
Avon **(G-442)**

Gold N Gems ....G....... 317 895-6002
Indianapolis **(G-7018)**

Golden Lion Inc ....G....... 765 446-9557
Lafayette **(G-8909)**

Goldstone Jewelry Inc ....G....... 765 742-1975
West Lafayette **(G-14070)**

Herff Jones LLC ....G....... 800 837-4235
Indianapolis **(G-7091)**

Herff Jones Co Indiana - Inc ....G....... 317 297-3740
Indianapolis **(G-7093)**

Interntnal Damnd Gold Exch Ltd ....F....... 317 872-6666
Indianapolis **(G-7262)**

Janette Walker ....G....... 219 937-9160
Hammond **(G-5902)**

Jewelers Boutique Inc ....G....... 317 788-7679
Indianapolis **(G-7303)**

Peter Franklin Jewelers Inc ....G....... 260 749-4315
New Haven **(G-10952)**

Ronaldo Designer Jewelry Inc ....D....... 812 972-7220
New Albany **(G-10859)**

Stall & Kessler Inc ....G....... 765 742-1259
Lafayette **(G-9002)**

Terri Logan Studios ....G....... 765 966-7876
Richmond **(G-12062)**

JIGS & FIXTURES

H & P Tool Co Inc ....E....... 765 962-4504
Richmond **(G-11993)**

Jus Rite Engineering Inc ....E....... 574 522-9600
Elkhart **(G-2952)**

K C Machine Inc ....G....... 574 293-1822
Elkhart **(G-2954)**

Kain Tool Inc ....G....... 260 829-6569
Orland **(G-11351)**

Merit Tool & Manufacturing Inc ....F....... 765 396-9566
Eaton **(G-2586)**

Meyer Engineering Inc...........................F....... 812 663-6535
Greensburg **(G-5623)**

Nixon Tool Co Inc ....E....... 765 966-6608
Richmond **(G-12024)**

Reber Machine & Tool Co Inc ....E....... 765 288-0297
Muncie **(G-10554)**

Taurus Tech & Engrg LLC ....E....... 765 282-2090
Muncie **(G-10568)**

JOB PRINTING & NEWSPAPER PUBLISHING COMBINED

Courier Printing Co Allen Cnty ....G....... 260 627-2728
Grabill **(G-5362)**

Duboisspencer Counties Pubg...............F....... 812 367-2041
Ferdinand **(G-3848)**

Exchange Publishing Corp ....E....... 574 831-2138
New Paris **(G-10979)**

Indiana News Media LLC ....G....... 812 546-4940
Hope **(G-6116)**

Midcountry Media Inc ....D....... 765 345-5133
Knightstown **(G-8557)**

News-Gazette ....F....... 765 584-4501
Winchester **(G-14338)**

North Vernon Plain Dlr & Sun ....G....... 812 346-3973
North Vernon **(G-11272)**

Posey County News ....G....... 812 682-3950
New Harmony **(G-10925)**

Royal Center Record ....G....... 574 643-3165
Royal Center **(G-12214)**

Whitewater Publications Inc ....E....... 765 647-4221
Brookville **(G-1131)**

JOB TRAINING & VOCATIONAL REHABILITATION SVCS

Adec Inc ....C....... 574 848-7451
Bristol **(G-1040)**

ARC of Greater Boone Cnty Inc ....F....... 765 482-0051
Lebanon **(G-9169)**

Success Holding Group Intl Inc ....G....... 260 450-1982
Ossian **(G-11411)**

JOB TRAINING SVCS

Cardinal Services Inc Indiana ....D....... 574 267-3823
Warsaw **(G-13853)**

Rauch Inc ....C....... 812 945-4063
New Albany **(G-10854)**

JOINTS & COUPLINGS

Millennium Supply Inc ....G....... 765 764-7000
Attica **(G-307)**

JOINTS: Expansion

Hammond Group Inc ....E....... 219 845-0031
Hammond **(G-5886)**

Right Angle Stl & Fabrication ....G....... 574 862-2432
Wakarusa **(G-13794)**

JOISTS: Long-Span Series, Open Web Steel

New Mllennium Bldg Systems LLC ....G....... 260 969-3500
Fort Wayne **(G-4501)**

New Mllennium Bldg Systems LLC ....C....... 260 868-6000
Butler **(G-1236)**

KEYS: Machine

Machine Keys Inc...................................G....... 765 228-4208
Muncie **(G-10514)**

KILNS & FURNACES: Ceramic

Hoosier Metal Polish Inc ....F....... 219 474-6011
Kentland **(G-8520)**

KITCHEN & TABLE ARTICLES: Coarse Earthenware

Bastine Pottery Inc ....G....... 317 776-0210
Noblesville **(G-11062)**

KITCHEN CABINET STORES, EXC CUSTOM

Academy Inc...G....... 574 293-7113
Elkhart **(G-2663)**

Coppes-Nappanee Company Inc...........F....... 574 773-0007
Nappanee **(G-10663)**

Counterfitters Inc ....G....... 219 531-0848
Valparaiso **(G-13523)**

Douglas Dye and Associates ....G.....317 844-1709
  Carmel (G-1362)
Elko Inc ....E.....812 473-8400
  Evansville (G-3473)
Fergys Cabinets ....G.....765 529-0116
  New Castle (G-10900)
Graber Woodworks Inc ....G.....812 486-2861
  Montgomery (G-10226)
Johnny Bontrager ....G.....260 463-8912
  Lagrange (G-9050)
Kountry Wood Products LLC ....C.....574 773-5673
  Nappanee (G-10689)
Laminated Tops of Terre Haute ....G.....812 235-2920
  Terre Haute (G-13271)
Roanoke Woodworking Inc ....G.....260 672-8462
  Roanoke (G-12107)

KITCHEN CABINETS WHOLESALERS

Classic Cabinetry ....G.....317 823-1853
  Indianapolis (G-6617)
Country Woodshop LLC ....E.....574 642-3681
  Goshen (G-5194)
Elko Inc ....E.....812 473-8400
  Evansville (G-3473)
Johnny Bontrager ....G.....260 463-8912
  Lagrange (G-9050)
Kountry Wood Products LLC ....C.....574 773-5673
  Nappanee (G-10689)
Sims-Lohman Inc ....G.....317 467-0710
  Greenfield (G-5574)
Superior Laminating Co ....F.....574 361-7266
  Goshen (G-5331)

KITCHEN UTENSILS: Food Handling & Processing Prdts, Wood

Rpf Inc ....G.....317 727-6386
  Boggstown (G-902)

KITCHEN UTENSILS: Wooden

Detweilers Cabinet Shop ....G.....765 629-2698
  Milroy (G-9979)
Earl Chupp ....G.....574 372-8400
  Etna Green (G-3320)
Grabill Woodworking Specialty ....G.....260 627-5982
  Grabill (G-5371)
Lillsun Manufacturing Co Inc ....G.....260 356-6514
  Huntington (G-6223)
Meyer Mill Oak Woodcrafters ....G.....317 462-1413
  Greenfield (G-5550)
This & That Products ....G.....812 299-2688
  Terre Haute (G-13354)

KITCHENWARE STORES

Woodland Manufacturing & Sup ....F.....317 271-2266
  Avon (G-472)

KNIVES: Agricultural Or indl

Illiana Grinding Machining Inc ....G.....219 884-5828
  Merrillville (G-9722)

LABELS: Cotton, Printed

Graphic22 Inc ....G.....219 921-5409
  Chesterton (G-1608)
Tt2 LLC ....G.....260 438-4575
  Fort Wayne (G-4707)

LABELS: Paper, Made From Purchased Materials

Associated Label Inc ....G.....812 877-3682
  Terre Haute (G-13195)
Discount Labels LLC ....A.....812 945-2617
  New Albany (G-10769)
Enterprise Marking Products ....F.....317 867-7600
  Westfield (G-14163)
HI Tech Label Inc ....F.....765 659-1800
  Frankfort (G-4836)
Indilabel LLC ....F.....317 839-8814
  Plainfield (G-11616)
Label Tech Inc ....E.....765 747-1234
  Muncie (G-10506)

LABORATORIES, TESTING: Product Testing

Corbett Phrmceuticals Dvcs LLC ....E.....765 513-0674
  Indianapolis (G-6666)

Moseley Laboratories Inc ....E.....317 866-8460
  Greenfield (G-5560)

LABORATORIES, TESTING: Product Testing, Safety/Performance

Cortex Safety Technologies LLC ....G.....317 414-5607
  Carmel (G-1344)
Thermphyscal Prpts RES Lab Inc ....G.....765 463-1581
  West Lafayette (G-14113)

LABORATORIES: Biotechnology

Catalent Indiana LLC ....B.....812 355-6746
  Bloomington (G-697)

LABORATORIES: Commercial Nonphysical Research

Scitt Inc ....G.....574 208-6649
  Mishawaka (G-10122)
Sealcorpusa Inc ....E.....866 868-0791
  Evansville (G-3720)

LABORATORIES: Dental

Den-Craft Dental Laboratory ....G.....219 663-7776
  Crown Point (G-2245)
William Wesley Professional ....F.....317 635-1000
  Indianapolis (G-8200)

LABORATORIES: Dental & Medical X-Ray

Center For Diagnostic Imaging ....F.....812 234-0555
  Terre Haute (G-13206)

LABORATORIES: Dental, Crown & Bridge Production

Dental Professional Labs ....E.....219 769-6225
  Merrillville (G-9710)
Lafayette Dental Laboratory ....E.....765 447-9341
  Lafayette (G-8947)
National Dentex LLC ....D.....317 849-5143
  Indianapolis (G-7570)
Somer Inc ....E.....317 873-1111
  Zionsville (G-14464)

LABORATORIES: Electronic Research

Pynco Inc ....E.....812 275-0900
  Bedford (G-567)
Silicis Technologies Inc ....E.....317 896-5044
  Westfield (G-14189)

LABORATORIES: Noncommercial Research

Cyberia Ltd ....G.....317 721-2582
  Indianapolis (G-6719)

LABORATORIES: Physical Research, Commercial

AG Technologies Inc ....G.....574 224-8324
  Rochester (G-12114)
Ampacet Corporation ....E.....812 466-9828
  Terre Haute (G-13194)
Bangs Laboratories Inc ....F.....317 570-7020
  Fishers (G-3873)
Crown Bioscience Indiana Inc ....G.....317 872-6001
  Indianapolis (G-6699)
Eli Lilly International Corp ....F.....317 276-2000
  Indianapolis (G-6836)
Enerdel Inc ....C.....317 703-1800
  Indianapolis (G-6863)
Faztech LLC ....G.....812 327-0926
  Bloomington (G-723)
Kp Pharmaceutical Tech Inc ....E.....812 330-8121
  Bloomington (G-760)
Pfizer Inc ....A.....212 733-2323
  Terre Haute (G-13301)
Polymod Technologies Inc ....F.....260 436-1322
  Fort Wayne (G-4538)

LABORATORIES: Testing

Acterna LLC ....E.....317 788-9351
  Indianapolis (G-6320)
Divsys International LLC ....E.....317 405-9427
  Indianapolis (G-6752)
Goh Con Inc ....E.....812 282-1349
  Clarksville (G-1682)

Indiana Research Institute ....E.....812 378-4221
  Columbus (G-1947)
Integrated Instrument Services ....F.....317 248-1958
  Indianapolis (G-7248)
Northern Indiana Ordnance Co ....G.....574 289-5938
  South Bend (G-12879)
Odyssian Technology LLC ....G.....574 257-7555
  South Bend (G-12882)

LABORATORY APPARATUS & FURNITURE

Current Technologies Inc ....F.....765 364-0490
  Crawfordsville (G-2147)
Envigo Rms Inc ....C.....317 806-6080
  Indianapolis (G-6871)
Envigo Rms Inc ....G.....317 806-6080
  Greenfield (G-5530)
Fast Track Technologies LLC ....F.....317 229-6080
  Carmel (G-1378)
I2r ....G.....812 235-6167
  Terre Haute (G-13253)
Parker-Hannifin Corporation ....F.....608 824-0500
  Tell City (G-13172)
Poly-Wood LLC ....D.....574 457-3284
  Syracuse (G-13140)
Soil Dynamics Instruments Inc ....G.....765 497-0511
  West Lafayette (G-14108)
Templeton Coal Company Inc ....D.....812 232-7037
  Terre Haute (G-13351)

LABORATORY APPARATUS, EXC HEATING & MEASURING

Leco Corporation ....G.....574 288-9017
  South Bend (G-12838)

LABORATORY APPARATUS: Crushing & Grinding

Chryso Inc ....E.....812 256-4220
  Charlestown (G-1561)

LABORATORY APPARATUS: Physics, NEC

Wabash Instrument Corp ....F.....260 563-8406
  Wabash (G-13762)

LABORATORY APPARATUS: Pipettes, Hemocytometer

Cook Group Incorporated ....F.....812 339-2235
  Bloomington (G-704)

LABORATORY CHEMICALS: Organic

Als Enviromental ....G.....219 299-8127
  Valparaiso (G-13489)
Beckman Coulter Inc ....D.....317 471-8029
  Indianapolis (G-6460)
Defrukuscn LLC ....G.....219 718-2128
  Highland (G-6042)

LABORATORY EQPT: Chemical

Beckman Coulter Inc ....D.....317 471-8029
  Indianapolis (G-6460)

LABORATORY EQPT: Clinical Instruments Exc Medical

N-Ovations Inc ....G.....219 464-0441
  Valparaiso (G-13583)

LABORATORY EQPT: Sterilizers

Merss Corporation ....G.....317 632-7299
  Indianapolis (G-7484)

LADDERS: Metal

Briter Products Inc ....G.....574 386-8167
  South Bend (G-12725)
L & W Engineering Inc ....D.....574 825-5351
  Middlebury (G-9900)
Miller Mfg Corp ....E.....574 773-4136
  Nappanee (G-10695)

LADDERS: Permanent Installation, Metal

Evans Metal Products Co Inc ....F.....574 264-2166
  Elkhart (G-2838)

PRODUCT

LAMINATED PLASTICS: Plate, Sheet, Rod & Tubes

Ameri-Kart Corp ....D...... 225 642-7874
Bristol (G-1043)

Applied Composites Engrg Inc ....E...... 317 243-4225
Indianapolis (G-6411)

Berry Global Group Inc ....F...... 812 424-2904
Evansville (G-3377)

DSM Engineering Plastics Inc ....F...... 812 435-7500
Evansville (G-3463)

DSM Engineering Plastics Inc ....C...... 248 530-5500
Evansville (G-3465)

Elko Inc ....E...... 812 473-8400
Evansville (G-3473)

F Robert Gardner Co Inc ....G...... 317 634-2333
Indianapolis (G-6900)

Flexible Materials Inc ....D...... 812 280-9578
Jeffersonville (G-8362)

General Fabricators Inc ....E...... 317 787-9354
Indianapolis (G-6996)

Hancor Inc ....E...... 812 443-2080
Brazil (G-964)

Heywood Williams Inc ....G...... 574 295-8400
Elkhart (G-2915)

Jaeger-Ntek Sling Slutions Inc ....D...... 219 324-1111
La Porte (G-8774)

Lockerbie Square Cab Co Inc ....G...... 317 635-1134
Indianapolis (G-7413)

Marian Worldwide Inc ....C...... 317 638-6525
Indianapolis (G-7454)

Miller Waste Mills Inc ....E...... 507 454-6900
Indianapolis (G-7522)

Omni Plastics LLC ....D...... 812 422-0888
Evansville (G-3655)

Positron Corporation ....E...... 574 295-8777
Elkhart (G-3103)

Sabic Innovative Plas US LLC ....E...... 812 372-0197
Columbus (G-2010)

Sabin Corporation ....C...... 812 323-4500
Bloomington (G-820)

Sonoco Products Company ....C...... 812 526-5511
Edinburgh (G-2629)

Thrust Industries Inc ....F...... 812 437-3643
Evansville (G-3762)

Triangle Rubber Co LLC ....C...... 574 533-3118
Goshen (G-5340)

LAMINATING MATERIALS

Specialty Adhesive Film Co ....E...... 812 926-0156
Aurora (G-387)

LAMINATING SVCS

Genesis Products Inc ....E...... 574 266-8293
Elkhart (G-2878)

Genesis Products LLC ....C...... 877 266-8292
Elkhart (G-2879)

Jknk Ventures Inc ....F...... 812 246-0900
Sellersburg (G-12399)

Lamco Finishers Inc ....E...... 317 471-1010
Indianapolis (G-7379)

Laminating Specialties Inc Ind ....G...... 765 385-0023
Templeton (G-13178)

Patrick Industries Inc ....E...... 574 293-1521
Elkhart (G-3084)

LAMP & LIGHT BULBS & TUBES

Acuity Brands Lighting Inc ....B...... 765 362-1837
Crawfordsville (G-2132)

GE Lexington Lamp Plant ....G...... 859 277-1161
Fort Wayne (G-4294)

Lomont Holdings Co Inc ....E...... 800 545-9023
Angola (G-228)

Pent Plastics Inc ....C...... 260 897-3775
Kendallville (G-8502)

Tap-A-Lite Inc ....E...... 219 932-8067
Hammond (G-5948)

Valeo North America Inc ....A...... 248 619-8300
Seymour (G-12498)

LAMP BULBS & TUBES, ELECTRIC: Light, Complete

6605 E State LLC ....G...... 260 433-7007
Fort Wayne (G-4033)

Energy Saver Lights Inc ....F...... 202 544-7868
Indianapolis (G-6866)

LAMP BULBS & TUBES/PARTS, ELECTRIC: Generalized Applications

General Electric Company ....D...... 812 933-0700
Batesville (G-501)

LAMPS: Incandescent, Filament

Vista Manufacturing Inc ....E...... 574 264-0711
Elkhart (G-3247)

LAMPS: Ultraviolet

American Ultraviolet Company ....D...... 765 483-9514
Lebanon (G-9168)

LAND SUBDIVIDERS & DEVELOPERS: Commercial

R E Casebeer & Sons Inc ....G...... 812 829-3284
Spencer (G-13035)

Whiteco Industries Inc ....A...... 219 769-6601
Merrillville (G-9761)

LAND SUBDIVISION & DEVELOPMENT

C-L Building & Leasing Inc ....G...... 574 293-8959
Elkhart (G-2746)

Old Gary Inc ....G...... 941 755-0976
Merrillville (G-9742)

LANGUAGE SCHOOLS

Lakota Language Consortium ....F...... 888 525-6828
Bloomington (G-762)

LANTERNS

Ward Industries Inc ....F...... 574 825-2548
Middlebury (G-9923)

LAPIDARY WORK: Jewel Cut, Drill, Polish, Recut/Setting

Chownings Jewelers ....G...... 765 294-4476
Veedersburg (G-13642)

LASER SYSTEMS & EQPT

Automated Laser Corporation ....E...... 260 637-4140
Fort Wayne (G-4097)

Cnc Laser Inc ....G...... 260 562-3953
Shipshewana (G-12608)

Directed Photonics Inc ....G...... 317 877-3142
Noblesville (G-11093)

Fairway Laser Systems Inc ....G...... 219 462-6892
Valparaiso (G-13539)

X-Treme Lazer Tag ....G...... 812 238-8412
Terre Haute (G-13372)

LASERS: Welding, Drilling & Cutting Eqpt

Troyer Brothers Inc ....E...... 260 565-2244
Bluffton (G-895)

LAUNDRY & GARMENT SVCS, NEC: Garment Alteration & Repair

Country Sewing ....G...... 260 347-9733
Kendallville (G-8467)

LAUNDRY EQPT: Commercial

Hansford Prevent LLC ....G...... 317 985-2346
Indianapolis (G-7071)

Randolph Carpet-Tile Cleaning ....G...... 317 401-2300
Cicero (G-1666)

LAUNDRY EQPT: Household

Accra-Pac Inc ....D...... 574 295-0000
Elkhart (G-2665)

Accra-Pac Inc ....D...... 905 660-0444
Elkhart (G-2666)

LAUNDRY SVC: Treated Eqpt Sply, Mats, Rugs, Mops, Etc

Ideal Inc ....G...... 765 457-6222
Kokomo (G-8643)

LAWN & GARDEN EQPT

Brinly-Hardy Company ....D...... 812 218-7200
Jeffersonville (G-8332)

Deer Country Equipment LLC ....E...... 812 522-1922
Seymour (G-12444)

Discount Power Equipment ....G...... 765 642-0040
Anderson (G-96)

Forest Commodities Inc ....G...... 765 349-3291
Martinsville (G-9607)

Husqvrna Cnsmr Otdr Prod NA ....C...... 812 883-3575
Salem (G-12294)

Jacobsen Prof Lawn Care Inc ....F...... 765 246-7737
Coatesville (G-1750)

Mtd Products Inc ....B...... 317 986-2042
Indianapolis (G-7555)

Novae Corp ....E...... 260 982-7075
North Manchester (G-11239)

Rich Manufacturing Inc ....G...... 765 436-2744
Lebanon (G-9220)

S Phillippe Lawn & Landscape ....G...... 765 724-2020
Alexandria (G-53)

Shelby Products Corporation ....G...... 317 398-4870
West Harrison (G-14043)

Talon Terra LLC ....G...... 219 393-1400
La Porte (G-8826)

Wheel Horse Sales & Service ....F...... 574 272-4242
South Bend (G-12990)

Wright Implement I LLC ....E...... 812 522-1922
Seymour (G-12502)

LAWN & GARDEN EQPT STORES

Carmel Welding and Supply ....F...... 317 846-3493
Carmel (G-1333)

Deer Country Equipment LLC ....E...... 812 522-1922
Seymour (G-12444)

Hudson Concrete Products Inc ....G...... 812 825-2917
Solsberry (G-12685)

Jtn Services Inc ....G...... 765 653-7158
Greencastle (G-5465)

Lear Manufacturing ....G...... 765 282-6273
Muncie (G-10510)

Rettig Enterprises Inc ....G...... 765 567-2441
West Lafayette (G-14102)

Siteone Landscape Supply LLC ....G...... 219 769-2351
Merrillville (G-9754)

Wright Implement I LLC ....E...... 812 522-1922
Seymour (G-12502)

LAWN & GARDEN EQPT: Blowers & Vacuums

Palmor Products Inc ....E...... 800 872-2822
Lebanon (G-9210)

LAWN & GARDEN EQPT: Carts Or Wagons

Graber Manufacturing ....G...... 812 636-7725
Odon (G-11327)

LAWN & GARDEN EQPT: Grass Catchers, Lawn Mower

Bane-Welker Equipment LLC ....F...... 812 234-2627
Terre Haute (G-13197)

LAWN & GARDEN EQPT: Lawnmowers, Residential, Hand Or Power

Great States Corporation ....E...... 317 392-3615
Indianapolis (G-7040)

Huncilman Inc ....G...... 812 945-3544
New Albany (G-10800)

Magic Circle Corporation ....C...... 765 246-7737
Coatesville (G-1751)

Rochester Metal Products Corp ....D...... 765 288-6624
Muncie (G-10559)

LAWN & GARDEN EQPT: Tractors & Eqpt

Country Compact ....G...... 574 831-6682
New Paris (G-10976)

Egenolf Enterprise Inc ....G...... 317 501-5069
Indianapolis (G-6813)

Lafayette Marketing Inc ....E...... 765 474-5374
West Lafayette (G-14081)

Peters Enterprises ....G...... 260 493-6435
New Haven (G-10953)

LAWN MOWER REPAIR SHOP

Hayward & Sams LLP ....G 260 351-4166
  Stroh *(G-13077)*
Zionsville Towing Inc ....G 317 873-4550
  Zionsville *(G-14474)*

LEAD

Eco-Bat America LLC ....C 317 247-1303
  Indianapolis *(G-6801)*

LEAD & ZINC

E & S Metal Inc ....F 260 563-7714
  Wabash *(G-13726)*

LEASING & RENTAL SVCS: Cranes & Aerial Lift Eqpt

Stahl Welding Inc ....G 765 457-3386
  Kokomo *(G-8699)*

LEASING & RENTAL: Construction & Mining Eqpt

GI Properties Inc ....G 219 763-1177
  Portage *(G-11765)*
Hampton Equipment LLC ....G 260 740-8704
  Fort Wayne *(G-4316)*
Macallister Machinery Co Inc ....F 765 966-0759
  Richmond *(G-12012)*
Macallister Machinery Co Inc ....D 260 483-6469
  Fort Wayne *(G-4447)*
Pittman Mine Service LLC ....E 812 847-2340
  Linton *(G-9311)*
Poseidon Barge Ltd ....D 260 422-8767
  Fort Wayne *(G-4541)*
Randall Rents of Indiana Inc ....F 219 763-1155
  Portage *(G-11791)*
Shelby Products Corporation ....G 317 398-4870
  West Harrison *(G-14043)*

LEASING & RENTAL: Medical Machinery & Eqpt

Williams Bros Health Care Inc ....E 812 257-2505
  Washington *(G-14007)*
Williams Bros Health Care Pha ....E 812 335-0000
  Bloomington *(G-856)*
Williams Bros Health Care Pha ....C 812 254-2497
  Washington *(G-14008)*

LEASING & RENTAL: Mobile Home Sites

Charles Coons ....G 765 362-6509
  Crawfordsville *(G-2138)*
Heritage Financial Group Inc ....D 574 522-8000
  Elkhart *(G-2914)*
Paddack Brothers Inc ....F 765 659-4777
  Frankfort *(G-4849)*

LEASING & RENTAL: Modular Office Trailers

Mitsubishi Heavy Industries ....C 317 346-5000
  Franklin *(G-4911)*

LEASING & RENTAL: Other Real Estate Property

Complete Property Care LLC ....G 765 288-0890
  Muncie *(G-10447)*
Vickery Drilling Co ....G 812 473-4671
  Evansville *(G-3798)*

LEASING & RENTAL: Trucks, Without Drivers

Carmel Welding and Supply ....F 317 846-3493
  Carmel *(G-1333)*
Eds Trading Post Inc ....G 317 933-4867
  Nineveh *(G-11057)*
Landis Equipment & Tool Rental ....G 812 847-2582
  Linton *(G-9309)*
Stout Plastic Weld ....F 219 926-7622
  Chesterton *(G-1634)*

LEASING: Passenger Car

Ford Motor Company ....D 317 837-2302
  Plainfield *(G-11610)*

LEASING: Residential Buildings

Charles Coons ....G 765 362-6509
  Crawfordsville *(G-2138)*

LEATHER GOODS: Harnesses Or Harness Parts

Southern Indiana Collar Co ....G 812 486-3714
  Montgomery *(G-10242)*

LEATHER GOODS: Holsters

Daltech Enterprises Inc ....G 260 527-4590
  Fremont *(G-4957)*
Fast Holster LLC ....G 317 727-5243
  Indianapolis *(G-6264)*
Indy Holsters LLC ....G 317 370-7451
  Brownsburg *(G-1152)*

LEATHER GOODS: NEC

De Masqu Productions Ltd ....G 812 556-0061
  Jasper *(G-8244)*
Hilltop Leather ....G 317 831-4855
  Mooresville *(G-10310)*
Mad Hatters Unlimited ....G 219 852-6011
  Hammond *(G-5910)*
Midwest Leather & Vinyl ....G 574 266-1700
  Elkhart *(G-3039)*
Whisler Custom Leather Co ....G 765 212-8932
  Muncie *(G-10583)*

LEATHER GOODS: Personal

Long Leather Works LLC ....G 812 336-5309
  Bloomington *(G-767)*
Moonshine Leather Company Inc ....F 812 988-1326
  Nashville *(G-10730)*
Pit Bull Leather Company Inc ....G 812 988-6007
  Nashville *(G-10733)*
Sleepy Hollow Leather Inc ....G 219 926-1071
  Chesterton *(G-1630)*

LEATHER GOODS: Saddles Or Parts

Judson Harness & Saddlery ....G 765 569-0918
  Rockville *(G-12176)*

LEATHER GOODS: Straps

L M Products Inc ....E 765 643-3802
  Anderson *(G-132)*
Sand Designs Inc ....G 574 293-5791
  Elkhart *(G-3155)*

LEATHER GOODS: Wallets

Wallets Belts & Stuff LLC ....G 219 218-3576
  Whiting *(G-14276)*

LEATHER TANNING & FINISHING

Clinton Harness Shop ....G 574 533-9797
  Goshen *(G-5189)*
Color Glo ....G 812 926-2639
  Aurora *(G-375)*

LEATHER: Accessory Prdts

Fbf Originals Inc ....G 765 349-7474
  Martinsville *(G-9603)*
Vera Bradley Inc ....B 877 708-8372
  Roanoke *(G-12110)*

LEATHER: Bookbinders'

Liberty Book & Bb Manufactures ....E 317 633-1450
  Indianapolis *(G-7402)*

LEATHER: Bridal

Horse N Around Animal & Tack ....G 765 618-2032
  Upland *(G-13471)*

LEATHER: Equestrian Prdts

Royal Acres Equestrian Center ....G 219 874-7519
  Michigan City *(G-9836)*

LEGAL & TAX SVCS

Mellon Tax Service ....G 219 947-1660
  Hobart *(G-6091)*

LEGAL OFFICES & SVCS

Eaton Corporation ....F 317 704-2520
  Indianapolis *(G-6796)*
Enterprise MGT Solutions LLC ....G 219 545-8544
  Merrillville *(G-9713)*

LESSORS: Farm Land

Napoleon Lumber Co ....G 812 852-4545
  Napoleon *(G-10641)*

LICENSE TAGS: Automobile, Stamped Metal

Express Motor Vehicle ADM LLC ....G 812 909-0116
  Evansville *(G-3496)*
Irwin Hodson Group Indiana LLC ....G 260 482-8052
  Fort Wayne *(G-4384)*

LIGHT SENSITIVE DEVICES: Solid State

Millennia Technologies Inc ....G 574 830-5161
  Goshen *(G-5292)*

LIGHTING EQPT: Bicycle Lamps

Hokey Spokes ....G 219 938-7360
  Gary *(G-5065)*

LIGHTING EQPT: Flashlights

Cloud Defensive LLC ....G 812 760-5017
  Newburgh *(G-11025)*
Orka Technologies LLC ....G 812 378-9842
  Columbus *(G-1986)*

LIGHTING EQPT: Locomotive & Railroad Car Lights

New Vision Manufacturing Inc ....G 812 522-5585
  Seymour *(G-12471)*

LIGHTING EQPT: Miners' Lamps

Triad Warsh Plant Scale House ....G 812 385-0909
  Petersburg *(G-11571)*

LIGHTING EQPT: Motor Vehicle

Business Adventures Inc ....G 574 674-9996
  Osceola *(G-11371)*

LIGHTING EQPT: Motor Vehicle, Flasher Lights

Jtn Services Inc ....G 765 653-7158
  Greencastle *(G-5465)*

LIGHTING EQPT: Motor Vehicle, Headlights

Dajac Inc ....G 317 608-0500
  Westfield *(G-14155)*
Lund International Holding Co ....E 765 742-7200
  Lafayette *(G-8963)*

LIGHTING EQPT: Motor Vehicle, NEC

J J Lites ....G 765 966-3252
  Richmond *(G-12004)*
Patrick Industries Inc ....D 574 522-0871
  Elkhart *(G-3085)*

LIGHTING EQPT: Reflectors, Metal, For Lighting Eqpt

Metalite Corporation ....D 812 944-6600
  New Albany *(G-10828)*

LIGHTING EQPT: Searchlights

Searchlight Social LLC ....G 317 983-3802
  Kokomo *(G-8692)*

LIGHTING EQPT: Spotlights

Comcast Spotlight ....G 317 502-5098
  Indianapolis *(G-6636)*
Comcast Spotlight Muncie ....G 765 216-1728
  Muncie *(G-10446)*
In The Spotlight LLC ....G 260 519-1805
  North Manchester *(G-11231)*
Spotlight LLC ....G 219 616-4421
  Culver *(G-2326)*
Spotlight On Drama ....G 765 643-7170
  Anderson *(G-169)*

Employee Codes: A=Over 500 employees, B=251-500
C=101-250, D=51-100, E=20-50, F=10-19, G=2-9

2018 Harris Indiana
Industrial Directory

PRODUCT

999

LIGHTING FIXTURES WHOLESALERS

A Homestead Shoppe Inc ....E 574 784-2307
Lapaz *(G-9116)*

Amerlight LLC ....G 812 602-3452
Evansville *(G-3355)*

Professional Lighting Services ....F 317 844-4261
Carmel *(G-1456)*

Vista Manufacturing Inc ....E 574 264-0711
Elkhart *(G-3247)*

LIGHTING FIXTURES, NEC

Advanced Kinematics Inc ....G 574 533-8178
Goshen *(G-5167)*

B and D Lighting ....G 317 414-8056
Indianapolis *(G-6449)*

Badger Daylighting Corp ....G 219 762-9177
Portage *(G-11750)*

Charm-Lite Inc ....F 765 644-6876
Anderson *(G-84)*

Circle City Lighting Inc ....G 317 439-0824
Noblesville *(G-11081)*

Dekker Lighting ....G 219 227-8520
Schererville *(G-12320)*

General Manufacturing Inc ....E 260 824-3627
Bluffton *(G-875)*

Gmp Holdings LLC ....G 317 353-6580
Indianapolis *(G-7016)*

Ikio Led Lighting LLC ....F 765 414-0835
Indianapolis *(G-7157)*

J&L Lighting Solutions LLC ....G 317 413-8768
Indianapolis *(G-7291)*

Lake Effect Lighting LLC ....G 812 783-9482
Bloomington *(G-761)*

Logical Lighting and Controls ....G 317 244-8234
Indianapolis *(G-7415)*

Lumen Cache Inc ....G 317 222-1314
Indianapolis *(G-7426)*

Mag Instrument Inc ....G 574 262-1521
Elkhart *(G-3015)*

Mid-America Sound Corporation ....F 317 947-9880
Greenfield *(G-5552)*

Mobile Stadium Lighting LLC ....G 219 325-0000
La Porte *(G-8796)*

Natural Lighting LLC ....G 574 907-9457
Nappanee *(G-10697)*

Nu Led Lighting ....G 317 989-7352
Greenwood *(G-5729)*

Spectrum Brands Inc ....E 317 773-6627
Noblesville *(G-11187)*

Touch Plate Technologies Inc ....F 260 426-1565
Fort Wayne *(G-4695)*

Touchplate Technologies Inc ....F 260 424-4323
Fort Wayne *(G-4696)*

Vista Worldwide LLC ....G 574 264-0711
Elkhart *(G-3248)*

LIGHTING FIXTURES: Decorative Area

Around Campus LLC ....G 574 360-6571
South Bend *(G-12711)*

Lawncreations LLC ....G 574 536-1546
Millersburg *(G-9971)*

LIGHTING FIXTURES: Fluorescent, Commercial

B&D Lights LLC ....G 765 452-2761
Kokomo *(G-8596)*

Lomont Holdings Co Inc ....E 800 545-9023
Angola *(G-228)*

LIGHTING FIXTURES: Indl & Commercial

Acuity Brands Inc ....F 765 362-1837
Crawfordsville *(G-2131)*

Acuity Brands Lighting Inc ....B 765 362-1837
Crawfordsville *(G-2132)*

Acuity Brands Lighting Inc ....F 317 849-1233
Fishers *(G-3866)*

Amerlight LLC ....G 812 602-3452
Evansville *(G-3355)*

Craft Metal Products Inc. ....G 317 545-3252
Indianapolis *(G-6684)*

Digital Cmmnties Intiative Inc ....G 317 580-0111
Carmel *(G-1360)*

Dream Lighting Inc ....G 574 206-4888
Elkhart *(G-2800)*

Eco Lighting Solutions LLC ....F 866 897-1234
Indianapolis *(G-6800)*

Green Illuminating Systems Inc ....G 317 869-7430
Noblesville *(G-11113)*

Metalite Corporation ....D 812 944-6600
New Albany *(G-10828)*

Premiere Building Mtls Inc ....G 574 293-5800
Elkhart *(G-3114)*

Professional Grade Svcs LLC ....G 317 688-8898
Indianapolis *(G-7772)*

Semcor Inc ....F 219 362-0222
La Porte *(G-8817)*

Source Products Inc ....G 260 424-0864
Columbia City *(G-1835)*

Specified Lighting Fixs of Ind ....F 317 577-8100
Indianapolis *(G-7970)*

Specified Ltg Systems Ind Inc ....F 317 577-8100
Indianapolis *(G-7971)*

Ward Industries Inc ....F 574 825-2548
Middlebury *(G-9923)*

LIGHTING FIXTURES: Motor Vehicle

BTR Engineering ....G 812 360-9415
Bloomington *(G-691)*

Grote Industries Inc ....A 812 273-2121
Madison *(G-9463)*

Grote Industries LLC ....A 812 265-8273
Madison *(G-9464)*

North American Lighting Inc ....A 812 983-2663
Elberfeld *(G-2637)*

Tcb Enterprises LLC ....F 574 522-3971
Elkhart *(G-3207)*

Techshot Lighting LLC ....G 812 923-9591
Floyds Knobs *(G-4020)*

LIGHTING FIXTURES: Residential

Fashion Flooring and Ltg Inc ....G 219 531-5667
Valparaiso *(G-13540)*

Lasalle Bristol Corporation ....E 574 295-4400
Bristol *(G-1065)*

Lasalle Bristol Corporation ....C 574 295-4400
Elkhart *(G-2985)*

Metalite Corporation ....D 812 944-6600
New Albany *(G-10828)*

Professional Lighting Services ....F 317 844-4261
Carmel *(G-1456)*

Ward Industries Inc ....F 574 825-2548
Middlebury *(G-9923)*

LIGHTING FIXTURES: Residential, Electric

Uberlux Inc ....G 317 580-0111
Carmel *(G-1501)*

LIGHTING MAINTENANCE SVC

Ikio Led Lighting LLC ....F 765 414-0835
Indianapolis *(G-7157)*

LIME

Calcar Quarries Incorporated ....F 812 723-2109
Paoli *(G-11447)*

Carmeuse Lime Inc ....D 773 221-9400
Gary *(G-5034)*

Carmeuse Lime & Stone ....G 219 787-9190
Portage *(G-11755)*

Dotted Lime Resale LLC ....G 317 908-3905
Westfield *(G-14160)*

Hanson Aggregates Midwest LLC ....F 812 889-2120
Lexington *(G-9251)*

Harris Stone Service Inc ....F 765 522-6241
Bainbridge *(G-477)*

Jolene D Pavey ....G 765 473-6171
Peru *(G-11534)*

Meshberger Stone Inc ....G 812 579-5241
Columbus *(G-1971)*

Mulzer Crushed Stone Inc ....F 812 365-2145
English *(G-3316)*

New Point Stone Co Inc ....F 812 663-2422
Greensburg *(G-5628)*

Rogers Group Inc ....G 765 342-6898
Martinsville *(G-9635)*

Rogers Group Inc ....E 219 474-5125
Kentland *(G-8523)*

Rogers Group Inc ....G 812 882-3640
Vincennes *(G-13703)*

Rogers Group Inc ....E 812 849-3530
Mitchell *(G-10170)*

Rush County Stone Co Inc ....G 765 629-2211
Milroy *(G-9985)*

Twisted Lime Bartending ....G 317 607-6836
Indianapolis *(G-8118)*

LIMESTONE: Crushed & Broken

Aggrock Quarries Inc ....E 812 246-2582
Charlestown *(G-1557)*

Barrett Paving Materials Inc ....F 765 935-3060
Richmond *(G-11960)*

Carmeuse Lime Inc ....E 219 949-1450
Gary *(G-5033)*

Cave Quarries Inc ....E 812 936-7743
Paoli *(G-11448)*

Corydon Stone & Asphalt Inc ....E 812 738-2216
Corydon *(G-2096)*

Francesville Vulcan Materials ....G 219 567-9155
Francesville *(G-4812)*

Global Stone Portage LLC ....G 219 787-9190
Portage *(G-11766)*

Handson ....F 812 246-4481
Sellersburg *(G-12396)*

Hanson Aggregates Midwest LLC ....E 812 246-1942
Sellersburg *(G-12397)*

Harris Stone Service Inc ....F 765 522-6241
Bainbridge *(G-477)*

Indian Creek Quarries LLC ....G 812 388-5622
Williams *(G-14282)*

John S Davis Inc ....E 812 347-2707
Depauw *(G-2457)*

Kellers Limestone Service ....F 219 326-1688
La Porte *(G-8776)*

Legacy Vulcan LLC ....E 219 465-3066
Valparaiso *(G-13575)*

Marietta Martin Materials Inc ....F 765 459-3194
Kokomo *(G-8663)*

Marietta Martin Materials Inc ....F 317 789-4020
Indianapolis *(G-7455)*

Marietta Martin Materials Inc ....F 317 776-4460
Noblesville *(G-11145)*

Martin Marietta Materials Inc ....F 317 846-8540
Indianapolis *(G-6272)*

Meshberger Stone Inc ....G 765 525-6442
Flat Rock *(G-3991)*

Mulzer Crushed Stone Inc ....E 812 547-7921
Tell City *(G-13167)*

Mulzer Crushed Stone Inc ....E 812 723-4137
Paoli *(G-11456)*

Mulzer Crushed Stone Inc ....E 812 547-7921
Evansville *(G-3642)*

Mulzer Crushed Stone Inc ....G 812 937-2442
Dale *(G-2332)*

Mulzer Crushed Stone Inc ....E 812 256-3346
Charlestown *(G-1574)*

Mulzer Crushed Stone Inc ....E 812 649-5055
Rockport *(G-12170)*

Nalc LLC ....G 502 548-9590
Cloverdale *(G-1732)*

New Point Stone Co Inc ....F 812 663-2021
Greensburg *(G-5627)*

New Point Stone Co Inc ....F 812 852-4225
Batesville *(G-512)*

New Point Stone Co Inc ....F 765 698-2227
Laurel *(G-9128)*

New Point Stone Co Inc ....F 812 663-2422
Greensburg *(G-5628)*

Paul H Rohe Co Inc ....F 812 926-1471
Aurora *(G-384)*

Robertson Crushed Stone Inc ....F 812 633-4881
Milltown *(G-9976)*

Rogers Group Inc ....E 812 333-8560
Bloomington *(G-813)*

Stone Quary ....E 765 473-5578
Peru *(G-11549)*

U S Aggregates Inc ....G 765 436-7665
Thorntown *(G-13379)*

U S Aggregates Inc ....E 765 564-2282
Delphi *(G-2430)*

LIMESTONE: Cut & Shaped

3d Stone Purchaser Inc ....E 812 824-5805
Bloomington *(G-652)*

Accent Limestone & Carving Inc ....G 812 876-7040
Bloomington *(G-655)*

Bedford Limestone Suppliers ....E 812 279-9120
Bedford *(G-532)*

Bedford Stonecrafters Inc ....E 812 275-2646
Bedford *(G-534)*

Bybee Stone Company Inc ....D 812 876-2215
Ellettsville *(G-3272)*

C & H Stone Co Inc ....E 812 336-2560
Bloomington *(G-694)*

Elliott Stone Co Inc ....E 812 275-5556
Bedford *(G-540)*

2018 Harris Indiana
Industrial Directory

(G-0000) Company's Geographic Section entry number

Indiana Cut Stone Inc ....F 812 275-0264
  Bedford (G-550)
Justin Blackwell ....F 812 834-6350
  Norman (G-11203)
Midwest Calcium Carbonates LLC .....G 217 222-1800
  Cloverdale (G-1731)

LIMESTONE: Dimension

B G Hoadley Quarries Inc ....E 812 332-1447
  Bloomington (G-671)
B G Hoadley Quarries Inc ....E 812 332-1447
  Bloomington (G-672)
Elliott Stone Co Inc ....E 812 275-5556
  Bedford (G-540)
Independent Limestone Co LLC ....E 812 824-4951
  Bloomington (G-744)
Indiana Lmstone Acqisition LLC ....D 812 275-3341
  Bloomington (G-745)
Indiana Stone Works ....E 812 279-0448
  Bedford (G-553)
Martin Mretta Magnesia Spc LLC ....E 765 795-3536
  Cloverdale (G-1729)
Rush County Stone Co Inc ....G 765 629-2211
  Milroy (G-9985)

LIMESTONE: Ground

3d Stone Inc ....E 812 824-5805
  Bloomington (G-651)
Big Creek LLC ....F 812 876-0835
  Stinesville (G-13075)
Calcar Quarries Incorporated ....F 812 723-2109
  Paoli (G-11447)
Hanson Aggregates Midwest LLC ....G 419 399-4846
  Woodburn (G-14383)
Hanson Aggregates Midwest LLC ....E 812 689-5017
  Versailles (G-13654)
Hanson Aggregates Midwest LLC ....D 260 747-3105
  Fort Wayne (G-4320)
Hanson Aggregates Midwest LLC ....F 812 889-2120
  Lexington (G-9251)
Hanson Aggregates Midwest LLC ....F 812 346-6100
  North Vernon (G-11260)
Hanson Aggregates Midwest LLC ....F 765 653-7205
  Cloverdale (G-1726)
Hanson Aggrgates Southeast Inc ....D 317 788-4086
  Indianapolis (G-7072)
Meshberger Stone Inc ....F 812 579-5241
  Columbus (G-1971)
Mulzer Crushed Stone Inc ....F 812 365-2145
  English (G-3316)
Rogers Group Inc ....E 219 474-5125
  Kentland (G-8523)
Seminole Stone Inc ....F 812 634-7115
  Jasper (G-8305)
Stone Street Quarries Inc ....E 260 639-6511
  Hoagland (G-6067)
West Plains Mining LLC ....E 260 563-9500
  Wabash (G-13768)

LINEN SPLY SVC: Non-Clothing

Wildman Business Group LLC ....C 866 369-1552
  Warsaw (G-13965)

LINEN SPLY SVC: Uniform

Daniel Korb Laundry Company ....D 812 425-6121
  Evansville (G-3453)

LINERS & COVERS: Fabric

Transhield Inc ....E 574 742-4333
  Elkhart (G-3222)

LIPSTICK

Champagne Lipstick ....G 317 691-6045
  Carmel (G-1335)
Kissy Face Lipstick LLC ....G 260 797-5024
  Fort Wayne (G-4411)
Pink Lipstick and Company ....G 317 992-6818
  Indianapolis (G-7692)

LIQUEFIED PETROLEUM GAS DEALERS

Industrial Sewing Machine Co ....G 812 425-2255
  Evansville (G-3558)

LITHOGRAPHIC PLATES

Graphik Mechanix Inc ....G 260 426-7001
  Fort Wayne (G-4303)

LIVESTOCK WHOLESALERS, NEC

Patrick & Sharon Hoctor ....G 812 898-2678
  Terre Haute (G-13297)

LOCK & KEY SVCS

S C Pryor Inc ....E 317 352-1281
  Indianapolis (G-7878)
Sleepy Hollow Leather Inc ....G 219 926-1071
  Chesterton (G-1630)

LOCKERS

A & A Sheet Metal Products ....D 219 326-1288
  La Porte (G-8725)

LOCKS

Allegion S&S Holding Co Inc ....B 317 810-3700
  Carmel (G-1308)
Avis Industrial Corporation ....E 765 998-8100
  Upland (G-13468)
Fire King International LLC ....E 812 948-2795
  New Albany (G-10779)
Fki Security Group LLC ....B 812 948-8400
  New Albany (G-10781)
Stanley Security Solutions Inc ....E 317 598-0421
  Indianapolis (G-7991)
Stanley Security Solutions Inc ....E 678 533-3846
  Indianapolis (G-7992)
Stanley Security Solutions Inc ....D 317 849-2250
  Indianapolis (G-7993)
Top Lock Corporation ....G 317 831-2000
  Mooresville (G-10344)
Wallys Lockshop ....G 765 748-2282
  Muncie (G-10579)

LOCKS & LOCK SETS, WHOLESALE

S C Pryor Inc ....E 317 352-1281
  Indianapolis (G-7878)
Stanley Security Solutions Inc ....E 317 598-0421
  Indianapolis (G-7991)
Stanley Security Solutions Inc ....D 317 849-2250
  Indianapolis (G-7993)

LOCKS: Coin-Operated

Standard Change-Makers Inc ....C 317 899-6955
  Indianapolis (G-7987)

LOCKS: Safe & Vault, Metal

E&P Technologies LLC ....G 317 828-8482
  Carmel (G-1366)
Fire King International LLC ....E 812 948-8400
  New Albany (G-10778)

LOCKSMITHS

Customer 1st LLC ....G 812 967-6727
  Pekin (G-11471)
Phil & Son Inc ....F 219 663-5757
  Crown Point (G-2283)

LOCOMOTIVES & PARTS

Powerrail Holdings Inc ....F 765 827-4660
  Connersville (G-2068)

LOGGING

A & A Logging ....G 502 553-4132
  Henryville (G-6031)
A & S Logging Inc ....G 574 896-3136
  North Judson (G-11205)
Albert Ransom Logging Inc ....G 812 567-2012
  Dale (G-2330)
Anthony D Etienne Logging ....G 812 843-5872
  Magnet (G-9502)
Arboramerica Inc ....G 765 572-1212
  Westpoint (G-14204)
Artys Logging ....G 812 969-3124
  Elizabeth (G-2641)
B M P Logging LLC ....G 812 272-2149
  Williams (G-14281)
Baldwin Logging Inc ....G 812 834-1040
  Norman (G-11202)
Bill Graber Logging LLC ....G 812 486-2709
  Montgomery (G-10215)
Boondocks Logging LLC ....G 812 247-3363
  Shoals (G-12664)

Brocks Incorporated ....G 765 721-3068
  Bainbridge (G-473)
Burton Lumber Co Inc ....F 812 866-4438
  Lexington (G-9249)
Campbell Logging ....G 812 972-6280
  Birdseye (G-634)
Carr Logging ....G 812 863-7585
  Owensburg (G-11424)
Carvers Logging LLP ....G 812 732-4932
  Mauckport (G-9653)
Charles Kolb Sons Logging ....G 765 647-4309
  Brookville (G-1112)
Christman Logging ....G 502 525-2649
  Madison (G-9449)
CJ Logging LLC ....G 812 360-0163
  Morgantown (G-10350)
Dennis Etiennes Logging Inc ....G 812 843-4518
  Cannelton (G-1289)
Dennis K Marvell ....G 812 779-5107
  Patoka (G-11465)
Duncan Logging Inc ....G 812 564-2488
  Coalmont (G-1745)
Ebs Logging LLC ....G 812 346-9248
  North Vernon (G-11256)
Ferree Logging LLC ....G 812 786-1676
  Corydon (G-2098)
First Choice Forestry & Log ....G 574 271-9425
  Granger (G-5407)
George Voyles Sawmill Inc ....E 812 472-3968
  Salem (G-12287)
Graber Ronald D Yoder & ....G 574 268-9512
  Warsaw (G-13883)
Griffin Logging LLC ....G 765 592-5701
  Mecca (G-9678)
Grove Forest Products ....G 812 432-3312
  Rising Sun (G-12088)
Ice Logging LLC ....G 312 860-0897
  Chesterfield (G-1587)
Indiana Logging Company Corp ....G 765 523-2616
  Lafayette (G-8921)
J Robert Switzer ....G 765 474-1307
  Lafayette (G-8927)
Jim Graber Logging LLC ....G 812 636-7000
  Odon (G-11331)
Jim Rhodes Logging ....G 812 739-4221
  English (G-3313)
John M Wooley Lumber Company ....E 317 831-2700
  Mooresville (G-10317)
Keith Bixler ....G 812 866-1637
  Lexington (G-9252)
Keller Logging LLC ....G 219 309-0379
  Valparaiso (G-13565)
Log Lifestyles Inc ....G 574 850-6158
  Walkerton (G-13805)
Loggers Incorporated ....E 812 939-2797
  Clay City (G-1704)
Logging ....G 812 216-3544
  Seymour (G-12468)
Louanna Stilwell ....G 812 631-0647
  Velpen (G-13649)
Mark Morin Logging ....G 812 327-4917
  West Baden Springs (G-14034)
Maurice Lukens Jr ....G 765 345-2971
  Knightstown (G-8555)
Michael L Baker ....G 812 967-2160
  Salem (G-12301)
Michael Skaggs ....G 812 732-8809
  Mauckport (G-9656)
Mike Gross ....G 574 529-2201
  New Paris (G-10991)
Napoleon Hardwood Lbr Co Inc ....E 812 852-4090
  Greensburg (G-5626)
Newbury Farm & Logging LLC ....G 574 825-9969
  Shipshewana (G-12639)
Paul Marshall and Son Log ....G 260 724-2852
  Decatur (G-2398)
Pingleton Sawmill Inc ....E 765 653-2878
  Greencastle (G-5473)
Poplar Log Homes Inc ....G 765 342-9910
  Martinsville (G-9633)
R E Casebeer & Sons Inc ....G 812 829-3284
  Spencer (G-13035)
Ralph Ransom Veneers ....G 812 858-9956
  Newburgh (G-11044)
Robert L Young ....G 812 863-4475
  Springville (G-13067)
Ronald Lee Allen ....G 812 644-7649
  Loogootee (G-9394)
Ronald Wright Logging LLC ....G 812 338-2665
  English (G-3319)

PRODUCT

Rural Land Inc ....G........ 812 843-4518
  Cannelton (G-1291)
Spencer Logging ....G........ 812 595-0987
  Scottsburg (G-12382)
Tdc Logging LLC ....G........ 574 289-4243
  South Bend (G-12967)
Tri-State Forest Products Inc ....F........ 317 328-1850
  Indianapolis (G-8096)
Universal Forest Products Indi ....C........ 574 273-6326
  Granger (G-5447)
Walton Logging ....G........ 812 365-9635
  Marengo (G-9505)
Waninger Knneth Sons Log Tmber ....F........ 812 357-5200
  Fulda (G-4992)
Weaver Logging ....G........ 260 589-9985
  Berne (G-629)
Wilkerson Logging Inc ....G........ 812 988-4960
  Nashville (G-10738)

LOGGING CAMPS & CONTRACTORS

Andis Logging Inc ....F........ 812 723-2357
  Paoli (G-11442)
Bray Logging ....G........ 812 863-7947
  Owensburg (G-11423)
Buchan Logging Inc ....G........ 260 728-2136
  Decatur (G-2371)
Buchan Logging Inc ....F........ 260 749-4697
  New Haven (G-10932)
Cash Logging ....G........ 812 843-5335
  Mount Pleasant (G-10377)
Charles Kolb Logging ....G........ 765 458-7766
  Liberty (G-9258)
Coffman Logging ....G........ 812 732-4857
  Corydon (G-2094)
Daniel Griffin ....G........ 765 492-3257
  Cayuga (G-1518)
Daniel Skaggs & Company ....G........ 765 342-0071
  Martinsville (G-9600)
Delmar Knepp Logging ....G........ 812 486-2565
  Loogootee (G-9381)
Dwight Smith Logging ....G........ 812 834-5546
  Heltonville (G-6026)
Graber Lumber LP ....E........ 260 238-4124
  Spencerville (G-13047)
Hartman Logging ....G........ 765 653-3889
  Greencastle (G-5461)
Jeff Halls Logging Inc ....G........ 812 941-8020
  Floyds Knobs (G-4015)
Joseph M Schmidt ....G........ 260 223-3498
  Decatur (G-2387)
Kaho Brothers Inc ....G........ 812 659-2901
  Lyons (G-9439)
Kester Logging Inc ....G........ 765 672-8170
  Reelsville (G-11902)
Kinser Timber Products Inc ....G........ 812 876-4775
  Gosport (G-5352)
Knepps Logging Bandmilling ....G........ 812 486-7721
  Montgomery (G-10230)
Michael Deom Professional ....G........ 812 836-2206
  Tell City (G-13166)
Midwest Logging & Veneer ....G........ 765 342-2774
  Martinsville (G-9626)
Newman Logging Inc ....G........ 260 351-3550
  Wolcottville (G-14375)
NJ Logging LLC ....G........ 812 597-0782
  Morgantown (G-10357)
Northern Wood Products Inc ....G........ 574 586-3068
  Walkerton (G-13807)
Ohio River Veneer LLC ....F........ 812 824-7928
  Bloomington (G-784)
Rasche Bro Logging ....G........ 812 357-7782
  Ferdinand (G-3862)
Richard Greg Etienne Logging ....G........ 812 843-5132
  Derby (G-2462)
Rodney Sloan Logging ....G........ 812 934-5321
  Batesville (G-518)
Slabach Logging LLC ....G........ 260 768-4644
  Shipshewana (G-12650)
William Browning ....G........ 765 647-6397
  Brookville (G-1132)
Williams Bros Logging LLC ....G........ 270 547-0266
  Mauckport (G-9659)

LOGGING: Fuel Wood Harvesting

Blackwood Solutions Inc ....G........ 812 824-6728
  Bloomington (G-684)
Hearth Glow Inc ....G........ 260 839-3205
  North Manchester (G-11229)

LOGGING: Timber, Cut At Logging Camp

Blue River Timber LLC ....G........ 812 291-0411
  Evansville (G-3387)
Cannon Timber LLC ....G........ 219 754-1088
  La Crosse (G-8719)
D Timber Inc ....G........ 219 374-8085
  Crown Point (G-2242)
Knepp Logging ....G........ 812 486-3741
  Loogootee (G-9387)
White Oak Land & Timber LLC ....G........ 812 482-5102
  Jasper (G-8314)
William S Bane ....G........ 812 358-5790
  Brownstown (G-1193)

LOGGING: Veneer Logs

Lake States Veneer Inc ....G........ 260 244-4767
  Columbia City (G-1806)

LOGGING: Wood Chips, Produced In The Field

Wrights Timber Products ....G........ 812 383-7138
  Shelburn (G-12514)

LOOSELEAF BINDERS

No-Sail Splash Guard Co Inc ....G........ 765 522-2100
  Roachdale (G-12094)
Omni Looseleaf Inc ....G........ 219 253-8020
  Monticello (G-10275)

LOOSELEAF BINDERS: Forms & Fillers, Ruled Or Printed Only

Codybro LLC ....G........ 765 827-5441
  Connersville (G-2044)

LOTIONS OR CREAMS: Face

All Occasions Gift Shop LLC ....G........ 513 314-5693
  Metamora (G-9762)
Wholeaf Aloe Distributors ....G........ 219 322-7217
  Schererville (G-12352)

LOTIONS: SHAVING

Kin Naturals LLC ....G........ 219 213-9516
  Highland (G-6051)

LUBRICANTS: Corrosion Preventive

Gabriel Products Inc ....G........ 502 291-5388
  Jeffersonville (G-8366)

LUBRICATING EQPT: Indl

Leasenet Incorporated ....G........ 317 575-4098
  Indianapolis (G-7392)

LUBRICATING OIL & GREASE WHOLESALERS

Koehler Welding Supply Inc ....F........ 812 574-4103
  Madison (G-9476)
Petrochoice Holdings Inc ....E........ 317 634-7300
  Indianapolis (G-7680)
Petroleum Solutions Inc ....G........ 574 546-2133
  Bremen (G-1016)
Pinnacle Oil Holdings LLC ....F........ 317 875-9465
  Indianapolis (G-7695)
Pinnacle Oil Holdings LLC ....E........ 317 875-9465
  Indianapolis (G-7696)

LUBRICATING SYSTEMS: Centralized

Lube-Line Corporation ....G........ 260 637-3779
  Fort Wayne (G-4442)

LUBRICATION SYSTEMS & EQPT

Perma Lubrication ....G........ 219 531-9155
  Valparaiso (G-13597)
Perma Lubrication ....G........ 317 241-0797
  Indianapolis (G-7679)
Summit Manufacturing Corp ....G........ 317 823-2848
  Indianapolis (G-8016)
Systems Engineering and Sls Co ......G........ 260 422-1671
  Fort Wayne (G-4671)

LUGGAGE & BRIEFCASES

American Tourister ....G........ 812 526-0344
  Edinburgh (G-2594)
C H Ellis LLC ....E........ 317 636-3351
  Indianapolis (G-6528)
Carr Metal Products Inc ....C........ 317 542-0691
  Indianapolis (G-6558)
Leed Selling Tools Corp ....C........ 812 482-7888
  Ireland (G-8229)
Raine Inc ....F........ 765 622-7687
  Anderson (G-157)

LUGGAGE & LEATHER GOODS STORES

Sleepy Hollow Leather Inc ....G........ 219 926-1071
  Chesterton (G-1630)

LUGGAGE: Traveling Bags

Cinda B USA LLC ....G........ 260 469-0803
  Fort Wayne (G-4150)
One Stop Travel Shop Inc ....G........ 812 339-9496
  Bloomington (G-789)
Td Innovations ....G........ 530 477-9780
  Bloomington (G-835)

LUMBER & BLDG MATLS DEALER, RET: Electric Constructn Matls

Rees Inc ....F........ 260 495-9811
  Fremont (G-4972)

LUMBER & BLDG MATRLS DEALERS, RET: Bath Fixtures, Eqpt/Sply

United Home Supply Inc ....G........ 765 288-2737
  Muncie (G-10576)

LUMBER & BLDG MTRLS DEALERS, RET: Closets, Interiors/Access

Innovative Corp ....E........ 317 804-5977
  Westfield (G-14171)
Organized Living Inc ....C........ 812 334-8839
  Bloomington (G-791)

LUMBER & BLDG MTRLS DEALERS, RET: Doors, Storm, Wood/Metal

Kleptz Aluminum Inc ....G........ 812 238-2946
  Terre Haute (G-13266)

LUMBER & BLDG MTRLS DEALERS, RET: Planing Mill Prdts/Lumber

Pike Lumber Company Inc ....E........ 574 893-4511
  Carbon (G-1293)

LUMBER & BLDG MTRLS DEALERS, RET: Windows, Storm, Wood/Metal

Classee Vinyl Windows LLC ....G........ 574 825-7863
  Middlebury (G-9875)
Wilmes Window Mfg Co Inc ....E........ 812 275-7575
  Ferdinand (G-3864)

LUMBER & BUILDING MATERIAL DEALERS, RETAIL: Roofing Material

Gillespie Mrrell Gen Contg LLC ....G........ 765 618-4084
  Marion (G-9526)

LUMBER & BUILDING MATERIALS DEALER, RET: Door & Window Prdts

A-1 Door Specialties Inc ....G........ 260 749-1635
  South Bend (G-12689)
Concord Realstate Corp ....F........ 765 423-5555
  Lafayette (G-8876)
Hoosier Interior Doors Inc ....G........ 574 534-3072
  Goshen (G-5241)
Woodwright Door & Trim Inc ....G........ 574 522-1667
  Elkhart (G-3267)

LUMBER & BUILDING MATERIALS DEALER, RET: Masonry Matls/Splys

Independent Concrete Pipe Co ....E........ 317 262-4920
  Indianapolis (G-7172)

Lake George Material & Sup Co ....G...... 219 942-1912
  Hobart (G-6087)
Stone Center of Indiana LLC ....E...... 317 849-9100
  Indianapolis (G-8009)

LUMBER & BUILDING MATERIALS DEALERS, RET: Solar Heating Eqpt

Inovateus Solar LLC ....E...... 574 485-1400
  South Bend (G-12813)

LUMBER & BUILDING MATERIALS DEALERS, RETAIL: Brick

Carters Concrete Block Inc ....E...... 574 722-2644
  Logansport (G-9330)
Edgewood Corporation Indiana ....E...... 317 786-9208
  Carmel (G-1369)
L Thorn Company Inc ....E...... 812 246-4461
  New Albany (G-10815)
Prairie Group ....E...... 812 877-9886
  Terre Haute (G-13307)

LUMBER & BUILDING MATERIALS DEALERS, RETAIL: Cement

Sagamore Ready Mix ....G...... 317 573-5410
  Indianapolis (G-6280)
Shelby Gravel Inc ....E...... 317 804-8100
  Westfield (G-14188)
Shelby Gravel Inc ....F...... 317 216-7556
  Indianapolis (G-7930)
St Henry Tile Co Inc ....E...... 260 589-2880
  Berne (G-626)
Zimco Materials Inc ....E...... 219 883-0870
  Gary (G-5117)

LUMBER & BUILDING MATERIALS DEALERS, RETAIL: Countertops

Kline Cabinet Makers LLC ....F...... 317 326-3049
  Maxwell (G-9662)
Laminated Tops of Central Ind ....E...... 812 824-6299
  Bloomington (G-763)

LUMBER & BUILDING MATERIALS DEALERS, RETAIL: Lime & Plaster

Global Stone Portage LLC ....G...... 219 787-9190
  Portage (G-11766)

LUMBER & BUILDING MATERIALS DEALERS, RETAIL: Modular Homes

Light House Homes Center ....F...... 765 448-4502
  Lafayette (G-8957)

LUMBER & BUILDING MATERIALS DEALERS, RETAIL: Sand & Gravel

Merritt Sand and Gravel Inc ....F...... 260 665-2513
  Waterloo (G-14018)

LUMBER & BUILDING MATERIALS DEALERS, RETAIL: Siding

Lansing Building Products Inc ....G...... 765 448-4363
  Lafayette (G-8955)
Zimmer Metal Sales LLC ....G...... 574 862-1800
  Goshen (G-5348)

LUMBER & BUILDING MATERIALS RET DEALERS: Millwork & Lumber

John Gebhart Woodworkings ....G...... 765 492-3898
  Cayuga (G-1521)
Stock Building Supply LLC ....E...... 260 490-0616
  Fort Wayne (G-4650)

LUMBER & BUILDING MATLS DEALERS, RET: Concrete/Cinder Block

McIntire Concrete ....E...... 765 759-7111
  Muncie (G-10519)
Orange County Concrete Inc ....G...... 812 865-2425
  Orleans (G-11365)
Slaters Concrete Products ....G...... 260 347-0164
  Kendallville (G-8510)

LUMBER: Dimension, Hardwood

Als Woodcraft Inc ....F...... 812 967-4458
  Borden (G-927)
Midwest Cnstr Components ....G...... 765 654-8719
  Frankfort (G-4841)
Mould-Rite Inc ....E...... 812 967-3200
  Pekin (G-11477)

LUMBER: Fiberboard

Kay Company Inc ....E...... 765 659-3388
  Frankfort (G-4840)

LUMBER: Hardwood Dimension

Ecojacks LLC ....G...... 574 306-0414
  South Whitley (G-12998)
Holmes & Company Inc ....E...... 260 244-6149
  Columbia City (G-1790)
Indiana Wood Products Inc ....D...... 574 825-2129
  Middlebury (G-9893)
Kinsers Hardwood ....G...... 812 834-5568
  Heltonville (G-6027)
Pallet One of Indiana Inc ....D...... 260 768-4021
  Shipshewana (G-12641)
Salt Creek Harvest LLC ....G...... 708 927-5569
  Valparaiso (G-13611)

LUMBER: Hardwood Dimension & Flooring Mills

A New Covenant Woodwork LLC ....G...... 812 737-2929
  Laconia (G-8835)
Cabinetmaker Inc ....G...... 812 723-3461
  Paoli (G-11446)
Champion Wood Products Inc ....D...... 812 282-9460
  Sellersburg (G-12391)
Chisholm Lumber & Sup Co Inc ....E...... 317 547-3535
  Indianapolis (G-6601)
Custom Millwork & Display LLC ....G...... 574 289-9772
  South Bend (G-12749)
Dehart Pallet & Lumber Co ....F...... 812 794-2974
  Austin (G-396)
Dmi Furniture Inc ....F...... 812 683-4035
  Huntington (G-6156)
Dutch Made Inc ....G...... 260 657-3331
  Harlan (G-5970)
Enviro Finishing of Indiana ....F...... 765 966-8183
  Richmond (G-11983)
Ervins Millwork Shop LLC ....G...... 260 768-3222
  Shipshewana (G-12613)
Ford Sawmills Inc ....E...... 812 324-2134
  Vincennes (G-13682)
Forest Products Group Inc ....E...... 765 659-1807
  Frankfort (G-4832)
Frank Miller Lumber Co Inc ....C...... 800 345-2643
  Union City (G-13455)
George Voyles Sawmill Inc ....E...... 812 472-3968
  Salem (G-12287)
Helmsburg Sawmill Inc ....F...... 812 988-6161
  Nashville (G-10726)
Herbert S Sawmill ....F...... 812 663-9347
  Greensburg (G-5607)
Heritage Hardwoods KY Inc ....D...... 812 288-5855
  Jeffersonville (G-8372)
Homestead Properties Inc ....F...... 812 866-4415
  Deputy (G-2460)
Hoosier Hrdwood Rclamation LLC ....G...... 765 299-6507
  Crawfordsville (G-2159)
Jackson Brothers Lumber Co ....F...... 812 847-7812
  Linton (G-9308)
John M Wooley Lumber Company ....E...... 317 831-2700
  Mooresville (G-10317)
Kentucky-Indiana Lumber Co Inc ....E...... 812 464-2428
  Evansville (G-3584)
Maurice Lukens Jr ....G...... 765 345-2971
  Knightstown (G-8555)
Mikro Furniture ....G...... 812 877-9550
  Terre Haute (G-13286)
Napoleon Hardwood Lbr Co Inc ....E...... 812 852-4090
  Greensburg (G-5626)
Norstam Veneers Inc ....D...... 812 732-4391
  Mauckport (G-9658)
Olon Industries Inc (us) ....F...... 812 254-0427
  Washington (G-13994)
Phil Etiennes Timber Harvest ....E...... 812 843-5132
  Saint Croix (G-12251)
Pike Lumber Company Inc ....G...... 574 893-4511
  Carbon (G-1293)
Pingleton Sawmill Inc ....E...... 765 653-2878
  Greencastle (G-5473)

Quality Hardwood Products Inc ....F...... 260 982-2043
  North Manchester (G-11241)
R E Casebeer & Sons Inc ....G...... 812 829-3284
  Spencer (G-13035)
Randall Lowe & Sons Sawmill ....F...... 812 936-2254
  French Lick (G-4988)
Rice Flooring ....G...... 574 830-5147
  Elkhart (G-3145)
Rogers Group Inc ....E...... 812 333-6324
  Bloomington (G-816)
Stateline Woodturnings LLC ....G...... 260 768-4507
  Shipshewana (G-12652)
Stemwood Corp ....D...... 812 945-6646
  New Albany (G-10866)
Universal Forest Products Indi ....C...... 574 273-6326
  Granger (G-5447)
Vead Dodd Sawmill Inc ....E...... 812 268-4486
  Sullivan (G-13098)
Werner Sawmill Inc ....E...... 812 482-7565
  Jasper (G-8313)

LUMBER: Kiln Dried

C C Cook and Son Lbr Co Inc ....E...... 765 672-4235
  Reelsville (G-11900)
John M Wooley Lumber Company ....E...... 317 831-2700
  Mooresville (G-10317)
Stemwood Manufacturing LLC ....E...... 812 945-6646
  New Albany (G-10867)

LUMBER: Piles, Foundation & Marine Construction, Treated

Woodgrain Construction Inc ....G...... 317 873-5608
  Zionsville (G-14471)

LUMBER: Plywood, Hardwood

Besse Veneers Inc ....E...... 906 428-3113
  Trafalgar (G-13434)
Carlisle Veneers Inc ....E...... 812 398-2225
  Carlisle (G-1296)
Chisholm Lumber & Sup Co Inc ....E...... 317 547-3535
  Indianapolis (G-6601)
Danzer Services Inc ....G...... 812 526-2601
  Edinburgh (G-2603)
Danzer Veneer Americas Inc ....F...... 812 526-6789
  Edinburgh (G-2604)
David R Webb Company Inc ....B...... 812 526-2601
  Edinburgh (G-2605)
FBN Corporation ....D...... 765 728-2438
  Montpelier (G-10291)
Flexible Materials Inc ....D...... 812 280-7000
  Jeffersonville (G-8361)
Flexible Materials Inc ....D...... 812 280-9578
  Jeffersonville (G-8362)
Flexible Materials Inc ....G...... 812 948-7786
  Floyds Knobs (G-4010)
Ideal Wood Products ....D...... 812 949-5181
  New Albany (G-10801)
Kimball Furniture Group LLC ....D...... 812 482-8401
  Jasper (G-8278)
Midwest Veneer Products Co ....F...... 765 728-2950
  Montpelier (G-10293)
Miller Veneers Inc ....C...... 317 638-2326
  Indianapolis (G-7521)
Patrick Industries Inc ....D...... 574 522-7710
  Elkhart (G-3081)
Rwp West LLC ....G...... 208 549-2410
  Bristol (G-1083)
Sexton Plywood & Veneer Co ....G...... 812 454-0488
  Evansville (G-3725)
Sims-Lohman Inc ....G...... 317 467-0710
  Greenfield (G-5574)
Superior Veneer & Plywood LLC ....G...... 812 941-8850
  New Albany (G-10869)
Universal Forest Products Indi ....C...... 574 273-6326
  Granger (G-5447)
Veneer Curry Sales LLC ....F...... 812 945-6623
  New Albany (G-10871)
Wible Lumber Inc ....E...... 260 351-2441
  South Milford (G-12995)

LUMBER: Plywood, Hardwood or Hardwood Faced

Dimension Plywood Inc ....G...... 812 944-6491
  New Albany (G-10768)
Hoehn Hardwoods ....G...... 812 968-3242
  Corydon (G-2101)

P
R
O
D
U
C
T

Indiana Architectural Plywood ....E 317 878-4822
Trafalgar *(G-13436)*

Patrick Industries Inc ....C 574 294-7511
Elkhart *(G-3080)*

Wholesale Hrdwood Intriors Inc ....F 317 867-3660
Westfield *(G-14202)*

LUMBER: Plywood, Prefinished, Hardwood

Custom Plywood Inc ....D 812 944-7300
New Albany *(G-10766)*

Heritage Unlimited LLC ....F 574 538-8021
Goshen *(G-5237)*

LUMBER: Plywood, Softwood

JDC Veneers Inc ....D 812 284-9775
Jeffersonville *(G-8384)*

LUMBER: Plywood, Softwood

HI Tech Veneer LLC ....E 812 284-9775
Jeffersonville *(G-8373)*

Kimball Furniture Group LLC ....D 812 482-8401
Jasper *(G-8278)*

LUMBER: Rails, Fence, Round Or Split

Specialties Co LLC ....F 260 432-3973
Fort Wayne *(G-4638)*

LUMBER: Resawn, Small Dimension

Great Lakes Forest Pdts Inc ....E 574 389-9663
Elkhart *(G-2897)*

Great Lakes Forest Pdts Inc ....D 574 389-9663
Elkhart *(G-2898)*

LUMBER: Treated

Babb Lumber Company Inc ....F 812 886-0551
Vincennes *(G-13668)*

Kustom Kilms LLC ....G 317 512-5813
Columbus *(G-1956)*

Preserving Past ....G 574 835-0833
Elkhart *(G-3115)*

Railworks Wood Products Inc ....G 812 789-5331
Winslow *(G-14358)*

Stella-Jones Corporation ....F 812 789-5331
Winslow *(G-14360)*

Tangent Rail Products Inc ....E 412 325-0202
Terre Haute *(G-13348)*

Universal Forest Products Indi ....C 574 273-6326
Granger *(G-5447)*

Wood Medic Inc ....G 765 778-4544
Pendleton *(G-11512)*

LUMBER: Veneer, Hardwood

Amos-Hill Associates Inc ....C 812 526-2671
Edinburgh *(G-2595)*

E M Cummings Veneers Inc ....E 812 944-2269
New Albany *(G-10770)*

Form Wood Industries Inc ....E 812 284-3676
Jeffersonville *(G-8363)*

Heitink Veneers Incorporated ....E 812 336-6436
Bloomington *(G-739)*

Heritage Hardwoods KY Inc ....D 812 288-5855
Jeffersonville *(G-8372)*

Indiana Veneers Corp ....D 317 926-2458
Indianapolis *(G-7196)*

Jasper Veneer Inc ....E 812 482-4245
Jasper *(G-8265)*

Louisville Veneer Corp ....G 502 500-7176
New Albany *(G-10818)*

Marwood Inc ....F 812 288-8344
Jeffersonville *(G-8398)*

Mitchell Veneers Inc ....G 812 941-9663
New Albany *(G-10832)*

Norstam Veneers Inc ....D 812 732-4391
Mauckport *(G-9658)*

Stemwood Corp ....D 812 945-6646
New Albany *(G-10866)*

LUMBER: Veneer, Softwood

Douglas Dye and Associates ....G 317 844-1709
Carmel *(G-1362)*

MACHINE PARTS: Stamped Or Pressed Metal

Accu-Tool Inc ....G 260 248-4529
Columbia City *(G-1758)*

Bemr LLC ....G 812 385-8509
Princeton *(G-11864)*

Charmaran Corporation ....F 260 347-3347
Kendallville *(G-8463)*

Cnc Industries Inc ....D 260 490-5700
Fort Wayne *(G-4165)*

Computer Technology ....G 812 283-5094
Jeffersonville *(G-8344)*

Countryside Tool ....G 260 357-3839
Garrett *(G-4999)*

Haven Manufacturing Ind Inc ....E 260 622-4150
Ossian *(G-11400)*

J & K Associates ....G 317 255-3588
Indianapolis *(G-7279)*

JM Machine ....G 219 464-4477
Valparaiso *(G-13564)*

Kable Tool & Engineering ....G 260 726-9670
Portland *(G-11833)*

KMC Enterprises Inc ....G 765 584-1533
Winchester *(G-14335)*

Metalstamp Inc ....D 574 232-5997
South Bend *(G-12860)*

P & A Machine Inc ....G 317 634-3673
Indianapolis *(G-7641)*

Perfecto Tool & Engineering Co ....E 765 644-2821
Anderson *(G-150)*

Tube Processing Corp ....B 317 787-1321
Indianapolis *(G-8107)*

Tube Processing Corp ....C 317 264-7760
Indianapolis *(G-8109)*

Ultra Manufacturing Inc ....E 574 586-2320
Walkerton *(G-13812)*

MACHINE SHOPS

Acme Industrial Inc ....E 260 422-6518
Columbia City *(G-1759)*

American Fabricated Carbide Co ....D 317 773-5520
Noblesville *(G-11059)*

Aqua Nova ....G 812 941-8995
Floyds Knobs *(G-4006)*

Banks Machine & Engrg Inc ....D 317 642-4980
Shelbyville *(G-12519)*

Bristol Tool and Die Inc ....F 574 848-5354
Bristol *(G-1050)*

Burkholder Machine ....G 574 862-2004
Goshen *(G-5182)*

Cad & Machining Services Inc ....F 317 535-1067
Whiteland *(G-14234)*

Checkered Past Racing Pdts LLC ....G 317 852-6978
Brownsburg *(G-1142)*

Country Components Inc ....G 812 345-9594
Edinburgh *(G-2602)*

Crane Hill Machine Inc ....E 812 358-3534
Seymour *(G-12439)*

Custom Engineering Inc ....G 812 424-3879
Evansville *(G-3450)*

De Witt Tool & Die Inc ....G 765 998-7320
Upland *(G-13469)*

Eagle Cnc Machining Inc ....F 765 289-2816
Muncie *(G-10466)*

Ecm Photo Tooling Inc ....E 574 264-4433
Elkhart *(G-2813)*

Executive MGT Svcs Ind Inc ....G 317 594-6000
Indianapolis *(G-6892)*

Flenar Manufacturing LLC ....G 574 893-4070
Rochester *(G-12124)*

Harman Machine & Engineering ....G 574 266-5015
Elkhart *(G-2907)*

Illiana Grinding Machining Inc ....G 219 884-5828
Merrillville *(G-9722)*

Indiana Research Institute ....E 812 378-4221
Columbus *(G-1947)*

Industrial Control Service ....F 260 356-4698
Huntington *(G-6216)*

Innovative 3d Mfg LLC ....G 317 560-5080
Franklin *(G-4901)*

J & T Marine Specialists Inc ....G 317 890-9444
Indianapolis *(G-7280)*

K C Machine Inc ....G 574 293-1822
Elkhart *(G-2954)*

Kelly Metal Products Inc ....G 812 232-1221
Terre Haute *(G-13265)*

Ken Anliker ....G 219 984-5676
Chalmers *(G-1547)*

Kitterman Machine Co Inc ....G 317 773-2283
Noblesville *(G-11139)*

Leis Machine Shop Inc ....G 574 278-6000
Buffalo *(G-1204)*

Lycro Products Co Inc ....E 574 862-4981
Wakarusa *(G-13784)*

M G Products Inc ....E 574 293-0752
Elkhart *(G-3009)*

Major Tool and Machine Inc ....B 317 636-6433
Indianapolis *(G-7446)*

Maschino Industries Inc ....G 812 346-3083
North Vernon *(G-11270)*

Monticello Machine Co Inc ....G 574 583-9537
Monticello *(G-10270)*

Motsinger Auto Supply Inc ....G 317 782-8484
Indianapolis *(G-7549)*

Nector Machine & Fabricating ....G 219 322-6878
Schererville *(G-12338)*

Northern Indiana Manufacturing ....E 574 342-2105
Bourbon *(G-946)*

On Point Machining Inc ....G 219 393-5132
Kingsbury *(G-8544)*

P M Fabricating Incorporated ....G 219 362-9926
La Porte *(G-8802)*

Peerless Pattern & Machine Co ....G 765 477-7719
Lafayette *(G-8979)*

Reber Machine & Tool Co Inc ....E 765 288-0297
Muncie *(G-10554)*

S&C Machine LLC ....G 812 768-6731
Haubstadt *(G-6005)*

Shull Machine Service Inc ....G 260 925-4198
Butler *(G-1240)*

Stamina Metal Products Inc ....G 574 534-7410
Goshen *(G-5327)*

Standish Steel Inc ....F 812 834-5255
Bedford *(G-580)*

Stumlers Machine Inc ....G 812 944-2467
New Albany *(G-10868)*

Superior Tool & Die Company ....E 574 293-2591
Elkhart *(G-3201)*

T & S Engineering LLC ....G 812 969-3860
New Palestine *(G-10973)*

Tasco Industries Inc ....G 219 922-6100
Highland *(G-6056)*

TT Machining & Fabricating LLC ....G 219 878-0399
Michigan City *(G-9856)*

Versatile Fabrication LLC ....G 574 293-8504
Elkhart *(G-3244)*

MACHINE TOOL ACCESS: Boring Attachments

B & W Specialized Drilling ....G 219 746-9463
Highland *(G-6036)*

MACHINE TOOL ACCESS: Cams

Precision Cams Inc ....E 317 631-9100
Indianapolis *(G-7731)*

Precision Cams Inc ....G 317 780-0117
Indianapolis *(G-7732)*

MACHINE TOOL ACCESS: Collars

E-Collar Technologies Inc ....G 260 357-0051
Garrett *(G-5002)*

MACHINE TOOL ACCESS: Cutting

Astro Cutting Tools................................F 765 478-3662
Cambridge City *(G-1253)*

Ati Inc ....G 812 431-5409
Mount Vernon *(G-10384)*

Diamond Stone Technologies Inc ....F 812 276-6043
Bedford *(G-537)*

Drake Corporation ....E 812 683-2101
Jasper *(G-8246)*

Global Cutting Solutions ....F 812 683-5808
Huntingburg *(G-6167)*

Haven Manufacturing Ind Inc ....E 260 622-4150
Ossian *(G-11400)*

Kennametal Inc ....C 812 948-2118
New Albany *(G-10813)*

Kennametal Inc ....C 574 534-2585
Goshen *(G-5252)*

KTI Cutting Tools Inc ....G 260 749-1465
Fort Wayne *(G-4418)*

Nicholas Precision Works LLC ....G 260 306-3426
North Manchester *(G-11237)*

Rite Way Industries Inc ....E 812 206-8665
New Albany *(G-10856)*

Whitney Tool Company Inc ....E 812 275-4491
Bedford *(G-590)*

MACHINE TOOL ACCESS: Diamond Cutting, For Turning, Etc

Tascon Corp ....E...... 317 547-6127
  Indianapolis (G-8038)
W F Meyers Company Inc ....E...... 812 275-4485
  Bedford (G-589)

MACHINE TOOL ACCESS: End Mills

Frontier Additive Mfg LLC ....G...... 765 413-5568
  Crawfordsville (G-2153)

MACHINE TOOL ACCESS: Files

T & L Sharpening Inc ....E...... 574 583-3868
  Monticello (G-10285)

MACHINE TOOL ACCESS: Knives, Metalworking

Advanced Prtctive Slutions LLC ....G...... 765 720-9574
  Coatesville (G-1746)

MACHINE TOOL ACCESS: Machine Attachments & Access, Drilling

Drilling & Trenching Sup Inc ....F...... 317 825-0919
  Shelbyville (G-12530)

MACHINE TOOL ACCESS: Milling Machine Attachments

Sapp Inc ....F...... 317 512-8353
  Edinburgh (G-2627)
Zps America LLC ....E...... 317 452-4030
  Indianapolis (G-8228)

MACHINE TOOL ACCESS: Tools & Access

Bel-Mar Products Corporation ....G...... 317 769-3262
  Whitestown (G-14249)
Butler Tool & Design Inc ....F...... 219 297-4531
  Goodland (G-5158)
Continental Enterprises Inc ....E...... 260 447-7000
  Fort Wayne (G-4173)
General Crafts Corp ....G...... 574 533-1936
  Goshen (G-5223)
H & P Tool Co Inc ....E...... 765 962-4504
  Richmond (G-11993)
Nap Asset Holdings Ltd ....D...... 812 482-2000
  Jasper (G-8297)
Oak View Tooling Inc ....F...... 260 244-7677
  Columbia City (G-1814)
Riverside Tool Corp ....E...... 574 522-6798
  Elkhart (G-3149)
S-B Capable Concepts LLC ....G...... 812 420-2565
  Brazil (G-977)

MACHINE TOOL ACCESS: Wheel Turning Eqpt, Diamond Point, Etc

Bates Technologies LLC ....D...... 317 841-2400
  Noblesville (G-11063)

MACHINE TOOL ATTACHMENTS & ACCESS

Aeromet Industries Inc ....D...... 219 924-7442
  Griffith (G-5761)
Curtis Dyna-Fog Ltd ....D...... 317 896-2561
  Westfield (G-14151)
Custom Gage & Tool Co Inc ....G...... 317 547-8257
  Indianapolis (G-6713)
Dimensions In Tooling Inc ....F...... 574 273-1505
  Granger (G-5401)
Fastener Equipment Corporation ....G...... 708 957-5100
  Valparaiso (G-13541)
Hoosier Spline Broach Corp ....E...... 765 452-8273
  Kokomo (G-8639)
Indiana Tool & Mfg Co Inc ....D...... 574 936-5548
  Plymouth (G-11693)
Kaiser Tool Company Inc ....E...... 260 484-3620
  Fort Wayne (G-4403)
Logansport Machine Co Inc ....E...... 574 735-0225
  Logansport (G-9350)
Lotec Inc ....E...... 574 294-1506
  Elkhart (G-3008)
Rusach International Inc ....F...... 317 638-0298
  Hope (G-6119)
Scg Acquisition Company LLC ....E...... 574 294-1506
  Elkhart (G-3157)

Tri-State Industries Inc ....D...... 219 933-1710
  Hammond (G-5951)

MACHINE TOOLS & ACCESS

Berkey Machine Corporation ....G...... 260 761-4002
  Wawaka (G-14031)
Bristol Tool and Die Inc ....F...... 574 848-5354
  Bristol (G-1050)
C & A Tool Engineering Inc ....B...... 260 693-2167
  Churubusco (G-1644)
C & A Tool Engineering Inc ....E...... 260 693-2167
  Auburn (G-319)
C-Way Tool and Die Inc ....G...... 812 256-6341
  Charlestown (G-1559)
Capital Machine Company Inc ....F...... 317 638-6661
  Indianapolis (G-6548)
Century Tool & Engineering ....G...... 317 685-0942
  Indianapolis (G-6587)
Claymore Tools Inc ....G...... 574 255-6483
  Mishawaka (G-10018)
Dwyer Instruments Inc ....D...... 260 723-5138
  South Whitley (G-12997)
Fairfield Manufacturing Co Inc ....E...... 765 772-4547
  Lafayette (G-8895)
Feddema Industries Inc ....F...... 260 665-6463
  Angola (G-213)
Frederick Tool Corp ....E...... 574 295-6700
  Elkhart (G-2870)
G & S Super Abrasives Inc ....E...... 260 665-5562
  Angola (G-215)
General Aluminum Mfg Company ....C...... 260 495-2600
  Fremont (G-4960)
Grimm Mold & Die Co Inc ....F...... 219 778-4211
  Rolling Prairie (G-12186)
Herman Tool & Machine Inc ....F...... 574 594-5544
  Pierceton (G-11572)
Hoosier Tool & Die Co Inc ....D...... 812 376-8286
  Columbus (G-1942)
Indiana Precision Tooling Inc ....F...... 812 667-5141
  Dillsboro (G-2468)
Industrial Sales & Supply Inc ....F...... 317 240-0560
  Indianapolis (G-7209)
Jones Machine & Tool Inc ....E...... 812 364-4588
  Fredericksburg (G-4945)
K-K Tool and Design Inc ....E...... 260 758-2940
  Markle (G-9578)
Kennametal Inc ....C...... 317 696-8798
  Indianapolis (G-7341)
Kent Brenneke ....G...... 260 446-5383
  Harlan (G-5973)
Klueg Tool & Machine Inc ....G...... 812 867-5702
  Evansville (G-3595)
Liberty Tool and Engineering ....G...... 765 354-9550
  Middletown (G-9937)
Longbow Machining LLC ....G...... 812 599-6728
  Lexington (G-9253)
Loughmiller Mch Tl Design Inc ....E...... 812 295-3903
  Loogootee (G-9390)
Lowe Machine Tools LLC ....G...... 248 705-7562
  Noblesville (G-11142)
M4 Sciences LLC ....G...... 765 479-6215
  West Lafayette (G-14084)
Micro-Precision Operations ....E...... 260 589-2136
  Berne (G-620)
Morris Mold and Machine Co ....G...... 317 923-6653
  Indianapolis (G-7544)
Nachi America Inc ....C...... 317 535-5527
  Greenwood (G-5726)
Nachi Tool America Inc ....F...... 317 535-0320
  Greenwood (G-5728)
Netshape Technologies LLC ....C...... 812 755-4501
  Campbellsburg (G-1278)
Overton & Sons Tl & Die Co Inc ....E...... 317 736-7700
  Franklin (G-4918)
Overton & Sons Tl & Die Co Inc ....E...... 317 831-4542
  Mooresville (G-10331)
Pannell & Son Welding Inc ....G...... 765 948-3606
  Summitville (G-13100)
Plymouth Pdts Acquisition Inc ....G...... 574 936-4757
  Plymouth (G-11714)
Precision Tubes Inc ....G...... 317 783-2339
  Indianapolis (G-7738)
Progressive Tool & Machine ....E...... 812 346-1837
  Columbus (G-2001)
Qualtech Tool & Engrg Inc ....E...... 260 726-6572
  Portland (G-11844)
R B Tool & Machinery Co ....G...... 574 679-0082
  Osceola (G-11383)
Slick Engineering Industries ....G...... 765 354-2822
  Middletown (G-9941)

Specialty Tool LLC ....F...... 260 493-6351
  Indianapolis (G-7969)
Spectrum Services Inc ....G...... 574 272-7605
  Granger (G-5437)
Stapert Tool & Machine Co Inc ....G...... 317 787-2387
  Indianapolis (G-7995)
Superior Tool & Die Company ....E...... 574 293-2591
  Elkhart (G-3201)
Thomas L Wehr ....G...... 317 835-7824
  Fairland (G-3827)
Toolcraft LLC ....E...... 260 749-0454
  Fort Wayne (G-4692)
Tsune America LLC ....F...... 812 378-9875
  Edinburgh (G-2631)
Wbh Inc ....F...... 317 269-1510
  Indianapolis (G-8180)

MACHINE TOOLS, METAL CUTTING: Die Sinking

Wood Truss Systems Inc ....G...... 765 751-9990
  Muncie (G-10588)

MACHINE TOOLS, METAL CUTTING: Drilling & Boring

Station 21 American Drill ....G...... 219 661-0021
  Crown Point (G-2309)

MACHINE TOOLS, METAL CUTTING: Electron-Discharge

Bailey Tools & Supply Inc ....G...... 502 635-6348
  Evansville (G-3369)

MACHINE TOOLS, METAL CUTTING: Exotic, Including Explosive

Claymore Tools Inc ....G...... 574 255-6483
  Mishawaka (G-10018)

MACHINE TOOLS, METAL CUTTING: Facing, Flange

API International Inc ....F...... 317 894-1100
  Greenfield (G-5502)

MACHINE TOOLS, METAL CUTTING: Grind, Polish, Buff, Lapp

G & S Super Abrasives Inc ....E...... 260 665-5562
  Angola (G-215)

MACHINE TOOLS, METAL CUTTING: Home Workshop

Cyberia Ltd ....G...... 317 721-2582
  Indianapolis (G-6719)
Solomon M Eicher ....G...... 812 289-1252
  Marysville (G-9651)

MACHINE TOOLS, METAL CUTTING: Plasma Process

Ynot Metal Inc ....G...... 517 617-6039
  Angola (G-260)

MACHINE TOOLS, METAL CUTTING: Robot, Drilling, Cutting, Etc

Thermwood Corporation ....D...... 812 937-4476
  Dale (G-2334)

MACHINE TOOLS, METAL CUTTING: Saws, Power

Nap Asset Holdings Ltd ....D...... 812 482-2000
  Jasper (G-8297)

MACHINE TOOLS, METAL CUTTING: Tool Replacement & Rpr Parts

American Tool Service Inc ....E...... 260 493-6351
  Fort Wayne (G-4073)
American Tool Service Inc ....F...... 317 782-3551
  Indianapolis (G-6391)
Creative Tool Inc ....G...... 260 338-1222
  Huntertown (G-6136)
Eagle Precision Machining Inc ....G...... 260 637-4649
  Huntertown (G-6137)

Employee Codes: A=Over 500 employees, B=251-500
C=101-250, D=51-100, E=20-50, F=10-19, G=2-9

2018 Harris Indiana
Industrial Directory

PRODUCT

1005

G & G Millwright Service LLC ....G...... 260 571-4908
La Fontaine (G-8722)

Indiana Hand Piece Repair....................G...... 260 436-0765
Fort Wayne (G-4364)

Landrums Mch Tl Repr & Svcs ....G...... 574 256-0312
Mishawaka (G-10068)

Neuhaus Industrial Machining I..........G...... 260 710-2845
Fort Wayne (G-4498)

Pt Services Inc ....G...... 574 970-0512
Elkhart (G-3121)

S&S Machinery Repair LLC.................G...... 812 521-2368
Norman (G-11204)

MACHINE TOOLS, METAL CUTTING: Vertical Turning & Boring

Danubius Machine Inc.........................G...... 219 662-7787
Crown Point (G-2243)

Superior Precision Inc.........................F...... 260 229-3871
South Whitley (G-13007)

MACHINE TOOLS, METAL FORMING: Forging Machinery & Hammers

AAA-Gpc Holdings LLC.......................D...... 260 668-1468
Angola (G-187)

MACHINE TOOLS, METAL FORMING: Headers

A & M Systems Inc ....F...... 574 522-5000
Elkhart (G-2656)

A/C Fabricating Corp ....E...... 574 534-1415
Goshen (G-5163)

MACHINE TOOLS, METAL FORMING: Magnetic Forming

Mishawaka LLC ....G...... 574 259-1981
Mishawaka (G-10089)

MACHINE TOOLS, METAL FORMING: Mechanical, Pneumatic Or Hyd

Independent Rail Corporation ....E...... 317 780-8480
Indianapolis (G-7175)

Roadhog Inc ....E...... 317 858-7050
Brownsburg (G-1166)

MACHINE TOOLS, METAL FORMING: Nail Heading

Hkn International LLC..........................G...... 317 243-5959
Indianapolis (G-7110)

MACHINE TOOLS, METAL FORMING: Presses, Hyd & Pneumatic

Fred S Carver Inc ....G...... 260 563-7577
Wabash (G-13727)

Plant Engineering Services Inc ....G...... 260 281-2917
Corunna (G-2085)

Wabash Metal Products Inc ....D...... 260 563-1184
Wabash (G-13763)

MACHINE TOOLS, METAL FORMING: Pressing

Precision Industries Corp ....F...... 574 522-2626
Elkhart (G-3108)

MACHINE TOOLS, METAL FORMING: Punching & Shearing

Beatty International Inc ....E...... 219 931-3000
Hammond (G-5846)

Beatty Machine & Mfg Co ....D...... 219 931-3000
Hammond (G-5847)

MACHINE TOOLS, METAL FORMING: Rebuilt

Applied Metals & Mch Works Inc..........E...... 260 424-4834
Fort Wayne (G-4083)

Quality Die Set Corp ....E...... 574 967-4411
Logansport (G-9361)

MACHINE TOOLS, METAL FORMING: Spinning, Metal

G & G Metal Spinners Inc ....E...... 317 923-3225
Indianapolis (G-6974)

MACHINE TOOLS: Metal Cutting

Butler Tool & Design Inc ....F...... 219 297-4531
Goodland (G-5158)

Capital Machine Company Inc ....F...... 317 638-6661
Indianapolis (G-6548)

Charleston Metal Products Inc ....E...... 260 837-8211
Waterloo (G-14011)

Continental Diamond Tool Corp ....E...... 260 493-1294
New Haven (G-10935)

Cut-Pro Indexable Tooling LLC ....G...... 260 668-2400
Angola (G-207)

Dmg Mori Usa Inc...............................G...... 317 913-0978
Indianapolis (G-6755)

Drake Corporation ....E...... 812 683-2101
Jasper (G-8246)

EDM Specialties Inc ....E...... 317 856-4700
Indianapolis (G-6807)

Emhart Teknologies LLC ....C...... 765 728-2433
Montpelier (G-10290)

Epco Products Inc ....E...... 260 747-8888
Fort Wayne (G-4240)

Express Machine..................................G...... 812 719-5979
Cannelton (G-1290)

EZ Cut Tool LLC ....G...... 260 748-0732
New Haven (G-10939)

Grinding and Polsg McHy Corp ....F...... 317 898-0750
Indianapolis (G-7050)

Hoosier Spline Broach Corp ....E...... 765 452-8273
Kokomo (G-8639)

Indiana Oxygen Company Inc...............G...... 765 662-8700
Marion (G-9533)

Integrity Machine Systems...................E...... 317 897-3338
New Palestine (G-10972)

Kaiser Tool Company Inc ....E...... 260 484-3620
Fort Wayne (G-4403)

Kennedy Enterprises Inc.....................E...... 765 724-2225
Anderson (G-128)

Loughmiller Mch Tl Design Inc.............E...... 812 295-3903
Loogootee (G-9390)

Macallister Machinery Co Inc...............F...... 765 966-0759
Richmond (G-12012)

Micro Tool & Machine Co Inc...............G...... 574 272-9141
Granger (G-5421)

Micro-Precision Operations ....E...... 260 589-2136
Berne (G-620)

Midstates Tool & Die and Engrg ....E...... 574 264-3521
Elkhart (G-3037)

Midwest Mfg Resources Inc ....G...... 317 821-9872
Indianapolis (G-7507)

Modern Die Systems Inc ....E...... 765 552-3145
Elwood (G-3307)

Mosey Manufacturing Co Inc ....E...... 765 983-8800
Richmond (G-12019)

Mosey Manufacturing Co Inc ....D...... 765 768-7462
Dunkirk (G-2486)

Mosey Manufacturing Co Inc ....D...... 765 552-3504
Dunkirk (G-2487)

Mosey Manufacturing Co Inc ....G...... 765 983-8870
Richmond (G-12020)

Mosey Manufacturing Co Inc ....G...... 765 983-8870
Richmond (G-12021)

Mosey Manufacturing Co Inc ....D...... 765 983-8889
Richmond (G-12022)

Peerless Machinery Inc ....G...... 574 210-5990
South Bend (G-12889)

Prototype Baker Engineering ....G...... 574 266-7223
Elkhart (G-3120)

PSc Machining and Engrg Inc ....F...... 219 764-4270
Portage (G-11789)

Qig LLC ....E...... 260 244-3591
Columbia City (G-1821)

Qig LLC ....E...... 260 244-3591
Columbia City (G-1822)

Reeder & Kline Machine Co Inc ....E...... 317 846-6591
Sheridan (G-12596)

Roeder Industries ....G...... 812 654-3322
Milan (G-9946)

Specialty Tool LLC ....F...... 260 493-6351
Indianapolis (G-7969)

Spindle-Tech Inc ....G...... 812 926-1114
Aurora (G-388)

Standard Locknut LLC ....C...... 317 399-2230
Westfield (G-14190)

Stedman Machine Company ....D...... 812 926-0038
Aurora (G-390)

Tascon Corp ....E...... 317 547-6127
Indianapolis (G-8038)

Titus Inc ....F...... 574 936-3345
Plymouth (G-11728)

Versatile Metal Works LLC ....F...... 765 754-7470
Frankton (G-4944)

Whitesell Prcsion Cmpnents Inc ....C...... 812 282-4014
Jeffersonville (G-8442)

Wyrco LLC ....G...... 317 691-2832
Fishers (G-3986)

Zps America LLC ....E...... 317 452-4030
Indianapolis (G-8228)

Ztmt Inc ....E...... 502 296-4032
Georgetown (G-5155)

MACHINE TOOLS: Metal Forming

Bemcor Inc ....F...... 219 937-1600
Hammond (G-5850)

Beulah Inc...G...... 219 309-5635
Valparaiso (G-13508)

Black Equipment Company South ....G...... 812 477-6481
Evansville (G-3386)

Crosspower LLC ....G...... 812 591-2009
Westport (G-14209)

Davis Machine & Tool Inc ....F...... 812 526-2674
Edinburgh (G-2606)

Die-Mensional Metal Stamping ....F...... 812 265-3946
Madison (G-9456)

Egenolf Machine Inc ....D...... 317 787-5301
Indianapolis (G-6814)

Ferguson Equipment Inc ....F...... 574 234-4303
South Bend (G-12778)

Fortville Automotive Sup Inc ....G...... 317 485-5114
Fortville (G-4774)

Frech U S A Inc ....F...... 219 874-2812
Michigan City (G-9795)

Fulk Inc ....G...... 260 338-1012
Laotto (G-9107)

Klueg Tool & Machine Inc ....G...... 812 867-5702
Evansville (G-3595)

M R S Printing Erectors Inc.................G...... 317 888-1314
Greenwood (G-5722)

Nachi America Inc ....C...... 317 535-5527
Greenwood (G-5726)

Olympus Manufacturing Systems ....G...... 219 465-1520
Valparaiso (G-13594)

Smgf LLC ....D...... 812 354-8899
Petersburg (G-11568)

Sullivan Engineered Services ....G...... 812 294-1724
Henryville (G-6033)

Toolmasters Inc ....G...... 574 256-1881
Mishawaka (G-10140)

Tru-Cut Machine & Tool Inc..................G...... 260 569-1802
Wabash (G-13759)

United Machine Corporation ....E...... 219 548-8050
Valparaiso (G-13633)

Versatile Metal Works LLC ....F...... 765 754-7470
Frankton (G-4944)

MACHINERY & EQPT, AGRICULTURAL, WHOL: Grain Elev Eqpt/Splys

Buffington Electric Motors....................G...... 574 935-5453
Plymouth (G-11673)

MACHINERY & EQPT, AGRICULTURAL, WHOLESALE: Garden, NEC

Shelby Products Corporation................G...... 317 398-4870
West Harrison (G-14043)

MACHINERY & EQPT, AGRICULTURAL, WHOLESALE: Landscaping Eqpt

Jones & Sons Inc ....E...... 812 299-2287
Terre Haute (G-13261)

Langfords Delivery Service...................G...... 317 996-3594
Monrovia (G-10204)

MACHINERY & EQPT, AGRICULTURAL, WHOLESALE: Lawn & Garden

American Lawn Mower ....G...... 800 633-1501
Indianapolis (G-6389)

Dexter Axle Company ....C...... 574 294-6651
Elkhart (G-2794)

Siteone Landscape Supply LLC ....G...... 219 769-2351
Merrillville (G-9754)

MACHINERY & EQPT, AGRICULTURAL, WHOLESALE: Livestock Eqpt

Townsend Sales Inc ....G..... 317 736-4047
 Trafalgar **(G-13439)**

MACHINERY & EQPT, AGRICULTURAL, WHOLESALE: Poultry Eqpt

Dpc Inc ....E 765 564-3752
 Delphi **(G-2419)**

MACHINERY & EQPT, AGRICULTURAL, WHOLESALE: Tractors

Wakarusa Ag LLC ....G..... 574 862-1163
 Wakarusa **(G-13797)**

MACHINERY & EQPT, INDL, WHOL: Environ Pollution Cntrl, Air

Samco Inc...G..... 812 926-4282
 Sunman **(G-13116)**

MACHINERY & EQPT, INDL, WHOLESALE: Chemical Process

Industrial Water MGT Inc.....................G..... 317 889-0836
 Greenwood **(G-5706)**
Separation Technologies Inc ....G..... 219 548-5814
 Valparaiso **(G-13614)**

MACHINERY & EQPT, INDL, WHOLESALE: Compaction

Braun Motor Works Inc ....G..... 574 205-0102
 Winamac **(G-14303)**
Link Rental Company Inc ....G..... 574 946-7373
 Winamac **(G-14310)**

MACHINERY & EQPT, INDL, WHOLESALE: Conveyor Systems

C&M Conveyor Inc ....C..... 812 849-5647
 Mitchell **(G-10157)**
Omni-Tron Tooling & Engrg ....G..... 574 262-2083
 Elkhart **(G-3069)**
United Conveyor Corporation...............E 574 256-0991
 Mishawaka **(G-10142)**

MACHINERY & EQPT, INDL, WHOLESALE: Engines & Parts, Diesel

Ccts Technology Group Inc ....G..... 305 209-5743
 Indianapolis **(G-6570)**
Cummins Americas Inc ....G..... 812 377-5000
 Columbus **(G-1886)**
Cummins Crosspoint LLC.....................E 317 243-7979
 Indianapolis **(G-6706)**
Cummins Crosspoint LLC.....................E 812 867-4400
 Evansville **(G-3447)**
Cummins Crosspoint LLC.....................E 317 244-7251
 Indianapolis **(G-6707)**
Cummins Crosspoint LLC.....................E 574 252-2154
 Mishawaka **(G-10026)**
Cummins Crosspoint LLC.....................E 260 482-3691
 Fort Wayne **(G-4192)**
Macallister Machinery Co Inc...............D..... 260 483-6469
 Fort Wayne **(G-4447)**

MACHINERY & EQPT, INDL, WHOLESALE: Engs/Transportation Eqpt

Allied Enterprises Inc ....E 765 288-8849
 Muncie **(G-10428)**

MACHINERY & EQPT, INDL, WHOLESALE: Heat Exchange

Hale Industries Inc ....E 317 577-0337
 Fortville **(G-4778)**

MACHINERY & EQPT, INDL, WHOLESALE: Hoists

Tway Company Incorporated................E 317 636-2591
 Indianapolis **(G-8116)**

MACHINERY & EQPT, INDL, WHOLESALE: Hydraulic Systems

Berendsen Inc ....G..... 812 423-6468
 Evansville **(G-3373)**
Headco Industries Inc..........................G..... 219 924-7758
 Highland **(G-6049)**
Headco Industries Inc..........................G..... 574 288-4471
 South Bend **(G-12795)**
Motion & Control Entps LLC.................F 219 844-4224
 Hammond **(G-5918)**
National Consolidated Corp..................F 574 289-7885
 South Bend **(G-12868)**
Power Drives Inc ....G..... 812 344-4351
 Columbus **(G-1997)**
Terra Drive Systems Inc ....C..... 219 279-2801
 Brookston **(G-1108)**
Terry Liquidation III Inc........................E 219 362-3557
 La Porte **(G-8829)**
Troyer Brothers Inc.............................E 260 565-2244
 Bluffton **(G-895)**

MACHINERY & EQPT, INDL, WHOLESALE: Indl Machine Parts

Aqua Blast Corp..................................F 260 728-4433
 Decatur **(G-2368)**
Mantra Enterprise LLC ....G..... 201 428-8709
 Fishers **(G-3944)**
R B Tool & Machinery Co ....G..... 574 679-0082
 Osceola **(G-11383)**

MACHINERY & EQPT, INDL, WHOLESALE: Instruments & Cntrl Eqpt

Cast Products LP ....E 574 294-2684
 Elkhart **(G-2751)**
Cummins Power Generation Inc............F 812 377-5000
 Columbus **(G-1900)**
Dehco Inc..D..... 574 294-2684
 Elkhart **(G-2792)**
Richard J Bagan Inc ....E 260 244-5115
 Columbia City **(G-1826)**

MACHINERY & EQPT, INDL, WHOLESALE: Lift Trucks & Parts

Toyota Industries N Amer Inc ....B..... 812 341-3810
 Columbus **(G-2025)**

MACHINERY & EQPT, INDL, WHOLESALE: Machine Tools & Access

Macallister Machinery Co Inc...............F 765 966-0759
 Richmond **(G-12012)**
Roeder Industries ....G..... 812 654-3322
 Milan **(G-9946)**
SSd Control Technology Inc ....E 574 289-5942
 South Bend **(G-12950)**

MACHINERY & EQPT, INDL, WHOLESALE: Machine Tools & Metalwork

Fastener Equipment Corporation..........G..... 708 957-5100
 Valparaiso **(G-13541)**

MACHINERY & EQPT, INDL, WHOLESALE: Plastic Prdts Machinery

Jeda Equipment Services Inc ....G..... 317 842-9377
 Fishers **(G-3933)**

MACHINERY & EQPT, INDL, WHOLESALE: Processing & Packaging

Magnum Venus Products Inc................F 727 573-2955
 Goshen **(G-5277)**

MACHINERY & EQPT, INDL, WHOLESALE: Safety Eqpt

Western-Cullen-Hayes Inc....................E 765 962-0526
 Richmond **(G-12075)**

MACHINERY & EQPT, INDL, WHOLESALE: Sawmill

Square 1 Dsign Manufacture Inc ....F 866 647-7771
 Shelbyville **(G-12570)**

MACHINERY & EQPT, INDL, WHOLESALE: Sewing

Hope Hardwoods Inc ....F 812 546-4427
 Hope **(G-6114)**
Industrial Sewing Machine Co ....G..... 812 425-2255
 Evansville **(G-3558)**

MACHINERY & EQPT, INDL, WHOLESALE: Tool & Die Makers

Adept Tool and Engineering ....G..... 317 896-9250
 Carmel **(G-1302)**
Khorporate Holdings Inc ....C..... 260 357-3365
 Laotto **(G-9110)**
Pro-Tech Tool & Engineering ....G..... 765 258-3613
 Frankfort **(G-4851)**

MACHINERY & EQPT, INDL, WHOLESALE: Trailers, Indl

Novae Corp..D..... 260 758-9800
 Markle **(G-9581)**

MACHINERY & EQPT, INDL, WHOLESALE: Waste Compactors

Best Equipment Co Inc.........................E 317 823-3050
 Indianapolis **(G-6469)**

MACHINERY & EQPT, INDL, WHOLESALE: Water Pumps

3w Enterprises LLC ....G..... 847 366-6555
 Elkhart **(G-2654)**

MACHINERY & EQPT, INDL, WHOLESALE: Woodworking

Marquise Enterprises Ltd ....G..... 317 578-3400
 Indianapolis **(G-7458)**

MACHINERY & EQPT, WHOLESALE: Construction, General

AF Ohab Company Inc ....E 317 225-4740
 Indianapolis **(G-6350)**
Delphi Body Works ....F 765 564-2212
 Delphi **(G-2417)**
Poseidon Barge Ltd ....D..... 260 422-8767
 Fort Wayne **(G-4541)**
Schlatters Inc ....G..... 219 567-9158
 Francesville **(G-4815)**

MACHINERY & EQPT, WHOLESALE: Contractors Materials

Carroll Distrg & Cnstr Sup Inc ....G..... 317 984-2400
 Noblesville **(G-11078)**
Hoosier Industrial Supply Inc ....F 574 533-8565
 Goshen **(G-5240)**
Macallister Machinery Co Inc................D..... 260 483-6469
 Fort Wayne **(G-4447)**

MACHINERY & EQPT: Farm

Andersons Agriculture Group LP..........F 765 564-6135
 Delphi **(G-2414)**
AT Ferrell Company Inc........................E 260 824-3400
 Bluffton **(G-865)**
Azland Inc ....G..... 765 429-6200
 West Lafayette **(G-14051)**
California Pellet Mill Company ....G..... 765 362-2600
 Crawfordsville **(G-2137)**
Case and Quart Inc ....G..... 260 368-7808
 Geneva **(G-5134)**
Case New Holland LLC.........................F 765 482-5446
 Lebanon **(G-9172)**
Case Show Homes LLC.........................G..... 317 669-6202
 Carmel **(G-1334)**
Case Weinkauff ....G..... 219 733-9484
 Valparaiso **(G-13519)**
Chief Metal Works Inc..........................G..... 765 932-2134
 Rushville **(G-12217)**
City Welding & Fabrication ....G..... 765 569-5403
 Rockville **(G-12175)**
Cnh Industrial America LLC...................C..... 765 482-5409
 Lebanon **(G-9174)**
Cowco Inc ....G..... 812 346-8993
 North Vernon **(G-11250)**

Employee Codes: A=Over 500 employees, B=251-500
C=101-250, D=51-100, E=20-50, F=10-19, G=2-9

2018 Harris Indiana
Industrial Directory

1007

PRODUCT

Ctb Inc...E........574 658-4191
Milford (G-9951)

CTB MN Investment Co Inc.................E........574 658-4191
Milford (G-9955)

Custom Case Place LLC......................G........260 715-1413
Fort Wayne (G-4194)

D A Hochstetler & Sons LLP................574 642-1144
Topeka (G-13416)

Davern Machine Shop.........................G........765 505-1051
Dana (G-2342)

Delphi Products Co Inc........................F........800 382-7903
Delphi (G-2418)

Don Case...G........765 748-1325
Muncie (G-10462)

Dugherty Inc..F........260 375-2010
Warren (G-13828)

Earthway Products Inc..........................D........574 848-7491
Bristol (G-1058)

Farm Innovators Inc.............................E........574 936-5096
Plymouth (G-11683)

Fix & Sons Manufacturing Inc..............F........765 724-4041
Alexandria (G-42)

Frazier Products..................................F........317 781-9781
Indianapolis (G-6961)

Gator Cases Inc...................................F........260 627-8070
Columbia City (G-1787)

Hahn Enterprises Inc...........................G........574 862-4491
Wakarusa (G-13778)

Hampton Equipment LLC......................G........260 740-8704
Fort Wayne (G-4316)

Headsight Inc.......................................G........574 546-5022
Bremen (G-1003)

Honeyville Metal Inc.............................D........800 593-8377
Topeka (G-13421)

Hurricane Ditcher Company Inc............F........812 886-9663
Vincennes (G-13684)

Jacobs Mfg LLC...................................G........574 583-3883
Monticello (G-10267)

JI Manfcturing Fabrication Inc.............G........260 589-3723
Berne (G-618)

Kasco Mfg Co Inc.................................F........317 398-7973
Shelbyville (G-12542)

Land Enterprises..................................G........317 774-9475
Noblesville (G-11140)

Madison Manufacturing Inc..................E........574 633-4433
Bremen (G-1009)

Mooresville Welding Inc.......................G........317 831-2265
Mooresville (G-10324)

National Equipment Inc........................G........219 462-1205
Valparaiso (G-13586)

New Holland Richmond Inc...................G........765 962-7724
Richmond (G-12023)

Onyett Welding & Machine Inc.............G........812 582-2999
Petersburg (G-11565)

Oxbo International Corporation.............G........260 768-3217
Shipshewana (G-12640)

Red Case LLC.......................................G........317 250-5538
Beech Grove (G-603)

Spankys Paintball.................................G........812 752-7375
Scottsburg (G-12381)

Specialty Welding & Machine...............G........812 969-2139
Elizabeth (G-2649)

Superb Horticulture LLC.......................F........800 567-8264
Plymouth (G-11726)

Townsend Sales Inc..............................G........317 736-4047
Trafalgar (G-13439)

Wood Lighter Cases LLC.......................G........812 969-3908
Elizabeth (G-2650)

Writers of Vision...................................G........812 239-6347
Farmersburg (G-3839)

MACHINERY & EQPT: Gas Producers, Generators/Other Rltd Eqpt

Nichols Operating LLC..........................G........812 753-3600
Fort Branch (G-4028)

MACHINERY & EQPT: Liquid Automation

Duesenburg Inc....................................G........260 496-9650
Fort Wayne (G-4223)

Faztech LLC..G........812 327-0926
Bloomington (G-723)

Maxim Automation Inc..........................G........317 418-9561
Fishers (G-3945)

Melrose Group LLC...............................G........317 437-6784
Indianapolis (G-7477)

MACHINERY & EQPT: Metal Finishing, Plating Etc

Anodizing Technologies Inc..................G........317 253-5725
Indianapolis (G-6402)

Cardinal Metal Finishing LLC...............C........866 585-8024
Kokomo (G-8604)

Koch Enterprises Inc............................G........812 465-9800
Evansville (G-3596)

Plating Products Inc.............................G........775 241-0416
Kokomo (G-8682)

Union Tool Corp....................................E........574 267-3211
Warsaw (G-13956)

MACHINERY & EQPT: Metal Pickling

Pgp Corp..D........812 285-7700
Jeffersonville (G-8413)

MACHINERY & EQPT: Petroleum Refinery

Systems Engineering and Sls Co.........G........260 422-1671
Fort Wayne (G-4671)

MACHINERY & EQPT: Vibratory Parts Handling Eqpt

American Feeding Systems Inc.............E........317 773-5517
Noblesville (G-11060)

Feeding Concepts Inc..........................F........317 773-2040
Noblesville (G-11102)

Frontier Engineering.............................G........317 823-6885
Indianapolis (G-6965)

J & J Engineering Inc............................F........317 462-2309
Greenfield (G-5543)

Mid-State Automation Inc.....................G........765 795-5500
Cloverdale (G-1730)

Moorfeed Acquisition LLC.....................F........317 545-7171
Indianapolis (G-7542)

Vibcon Corp..F........317 984-3543
Arcadia (G-271)

Vibromatic Company Inc.......................E........317 773-3885
Noblesville (G-11199)

MACHINERY BASES

Barnett Industrial Inc............................F........219 814-7500
Valparaiso (G-13503)

Ms Manufacturing LLC..........................E........812 442-7468
Brazil (G-972)

Nector Machine & Fabricating...............G........219 322-6878
Schererville (G-12338)

Stulls Mch & Fabrication Inc.................G........765 942-2717
Ladoga (G-8843)

MACHINERY, COMM LAUNDRY: Rug Cleaning, Drying Or Napping

Moores Inc..G........574 533-6089
Goshen (G-5297)

MACHINERY, COMMERCIAL LAUNDRY & Drycleaning: Ironers

Chucks Cleaners...................................G........260 488-3362
Hamilton (G-5820)

MACHINERY, COMMERCIAL LAUNDRY & Drycleaning: Pressing

Steam Specialties Inc...........................G........317 849-5601
Fishers (G-3970)

MACHINERY, COMMERCIAL LAUNDRY: Dryers, Incl Coin-Operated

Commercial Laundry Equipment...........G........317 856-1234
Indianapolis (G-6638)

Upland Village Laundry LLC..................G........765 998-1260
Upland (G-13475)

MACHINERY, COMMERCIAL LAUNDRY: Washing, Incl Coin-Operated

Brian T Klem..G........812 342-4080
Columbus (G-1862)

Donald L Gard.......................................G........219 663-7945
Crown Point (G-2246)

W C Grant Company Incorporated........F........260 484-6688
Markle (G-9583)

MACHINERY, ENGRAVING TRADES: Blocks, Wood

Parsing Laser Designs LLC...................G........317 677-4316
Avon (G-460)

MACHINERY, EQPT & SUPPLIES: Parking Facility

City of Anderson...................................G........765 648-6715
Anderson (G-86)

MACHINERY, FOOD PRDTS: Cream Separators

Centrifuge Support & Sups LLC............G........317 830-6141
Camby (G-1264)

MACHINERY, FOOD PRDTS: Cutting, Chopping, Grinding, Mixing

Stutz Products Corp..............................G........765 348-2510
Hartford City (G-5992)

Urschel Laboratories Inc......................B........219 464-4811
Chesterton (G-1639)

Willow Way LLC....................................G........765 886-4640
Hagerstown (G-5817)

MACHINERY, FOOD PRDTS: Dairy & Milk

Kaeb Sales Inc......................................F........574 862-2777
Wakarusa (G-13781)

Metzger Dairy Inc.................................F........260 564-5445
Kimmell (G-8531)

MACHINERY, FOOD PRDTS: Ovens, Bakery

Roost...G........317 842-3735
Fishers (G-3964)

MACHINERY, FOOD PRDTS: Slicers, Commercial

Tgf Enterprises LLC..............................G........440 840-9704
Indianapolis (G-8056)

MACHINERY, MAILING: Canceling

Pitney Bowes Inc..................................G........317 769-8300
Whitestown (G-14257)

MACHINERY, MAILING: Postage Meters

Pitney Bowes Inc..................................E........260 436-7395
Indianapolis (G-7698)

Pitney Bowes Inc..................................D........317 769-8300
Whitestown (G-14258)

Vernon A Stevens.................................812 626-0010
Evansville (G-3796)

MACHINERY, METALWORKING: Assembly, Including Robotic

Banks Machine & Engrg Inc..................D........317 642-4980
Shelbyville (G-12519)

Da-Mar Industries Inc..........................F........260 347-1662
Kendallville (G-8471)

Hy-Tech Machining Systems LLC........F........765 649-6852
Anderson (G-118)

Illinois Tool Works Inc..........................E........317 298-5000
Indianapolis (G-7160)

Jcr Automation Inc...............................F........260 749-6606
New Haven (G-10945)

Micro-Precision Operations..................E........260 589-2136
Berne (G-620)

MACHINERY, METALWORKING: Coil Winding, For Springs

Wge Equipment Solutions LLC..............G........260 636-7218
Fort Wayne (G-4751)

MACHINERY, METALWORKING: Cutting & Slitting

Gary Machinery LLC..............................E........219 980-5700
Griffith (G-5773)

Larrys Tls Hydraulic Jack Svcs.............G........317 243-8666
Indianapolis (G-7382)

MACHINERY, OFFICE: Duplicating

Oce Copiers..................................G...... 812 479-0000
Evansville *(G-3652)*

MACHINERY, OFFICE: Shorthand

Glander ....G...... 317 889-1039
Greenwood *(G-5697)*

MACHINERY, PAPER INDUSTRY: Coating & Finishing

Custom Machining Inc...................E...... 317 392-2328
Shelbyville *(G-12529)*

MACHINERY, PAPER INDUSTRY: Converting, Die Cutting & Stampng

C & W Inkd ....F...... 317 352-1000
Indianapolis *(G-6527)*

MACHINERY, PAPER INDUSTRY: Cutting

Hoosier Shred ....G...... 317 915-7473
Indianapolis *(G-7123)*

MACHINERY, PRINTING TRADES: Copy Holders

Nea LLC ....G...... 574 295-0024
Elkhart *(G-3059)*

MACHINERY, PRINTING TRADES: Plates

Precision Rubber Plate Co Inc.........D...... 317 783-3226
Indianapolis *(G-7737)*

MACHINERY, SEWING: Sewing & Hat & Zipper Making

Illinois Tool Works Inc ....E...... 317 390-5940
Indianapolis *(G-7159)*

MACHINERY, TEXTILE: Embroidery

Leap Frogz Screanprinting EMB ....G...... 317 786-2441
Indianapolis *(G-7390)*

MACHINERY, TEXTILE: Silk Screens

Big Als Athletics..........................G...... 765 836-5203
Mount Summit *(G-10378)*
Custom Tees................................G...... 765 449-4893
Lafayette *(G-8885)*

MACHINERY, WOODWORKING: Bandsaws

Sp Holdings Inc ....F...... 765 284-9545
Muncie *(G-10564)*
Veneer Services LLC ....F...... 317 346-0711
Indianapolis *(G-8150)*

MACHINERY, WOODWORKING: Cabinet Makers'

Gr Huber Enterprises Inc ....G...... 574 293-7113
Elkhart *(G-2892)*

MACHINERY, WOODWORKING: Sanding, Exc Portable Floor Sanders

Sandman Products LLC...................G...... 574 264-7700
Elkhart *(G-3156)*

MACHINERY, WOODWORKING: Scarfing

Indiana Flame Service ....E...... 219 787-7129
Chesterton *(G-1613)*

MACHINERY, WOODWORKING: Veneer Mill

Capital Machine Company Inc...........F...... 317 638-6661
Indianapolis *(G-6548)*

MACHINERY/EQPT, INDL, WHOL: Machinist Precision Measrng Tool

Littler Diecast A Brahm Corp.............D...... 765 789-4456
Albany *(G-11)*

MACHINERY: Assembly, Exc Metalworking

Adaptek Systems Inc ....E...... 260 637-8660
Fort Wayne *(G-4041)*
Agi International Inc ....F...... 317 536-2415
Indianapolis *(G-6352)*
Best Machine Co Inc ....G...... 765 827-0250
Connersville *(G-2041)*
Boyer Machine & Tool Co Inc ....E...... 812 379-9581
Columbus *(G-1861)*
Cardinal Services Inc Indiana ....E...... 574 371-1305
Warsaw *(G-13854)*
Federal Assembly Inc ....E...... 812 386-7062
Princeton *(G-11871)*
Glaze Tool and Engineering Inc..........E...... 260 493-4557
New Haven *(G-10941)*
Hy-Tech Machining Systems LLC ....F...... 765 649-6852
Anderson *(G-118)*
Industrial Mint Wldg Machining...........E...... 219 393-5531
Kingsbury *(G-8539)*
Phoenix Assembly LLC ....D...... 317 884-3600
Greenwood *(G-5732)*
Phoenix Assembly Indiana LLC ....E...... 317 884-3600
Columbus *(G-1995)*
Shamrock Engineering Inc................E...... 812 867-0009
Oakland City *(G-11315)*

MACHINERY: Automotive Maintenance

Cox John......................................G...... 765 463-6396
West Lafayette *(G-14061)*

MACHINERY: Automotive Related

AMI Industries Inc ....E...... 989 786-3755
Angola *(G-190)*
Amt Parts International Corp ....E...... 260 490-0223
Fort Wayne *(G-4075)*
Automatic Fastner Tools ....G...... 317 784-4111
Indianapolis *(G-6444)*
Computer Age Engineering Inc ....E...... 765 674-8551
Marion *(G-9518)*
D W Stewart ....G...... 260 463-2607
Lagrange *(G-9036)*
Eagle Consulting Inc ....G...... 317 590-0485
Indianapolis *(G-6785)*
First Gear Inc...............................F...... 260 490-3238
Fort Wayne *(G-4263)*
Lyntech Engineering Inc ....G...... 574 224-2300
Rochester *(G-12134)*
Metal Technologies Inc...................D...... 812 384-9800
Bloomfield *(G-643)*
Mvo Usa Inc ....F...... 317 585-5785
Indianapolis *(G-7562)*
Reynoldsrussell Entps LLC ....G...... 317 431-5886
Anderson *(G-162)*
Sinden Racing Service Inc ....F...... 317 243-7171
Indianapolis *(G-7949)*
SMC Corporation of America ....B...... 317 899-3182
Noblesville *(G-11184)*
Trimax Machine LLC ....G...... 812 887-9281
Bruceville *(G-1198)*
Vauterbuilt Inc ....G...... 219 712-2384
Hebron *(G-6024)*
Vibracoustic North America L P ....C...... 260 894-7199
Ligonier *(G-9301)*
Wurk Metal Products Inc ....F...... 317 828-0170
Clayton *(G-1710)*

MACHINERY: Billing

Woundvision ....G...... 317 775-6054
Indianapolis *(G-8217)*

MACHINERY: Bottling & Canning

Whallon Machinery Inc ....E...... 574 643-9561
Royal Center *(G-12216)*

MACHINERY: Bridge Or Gate, Hydraulic

Beatty International Inc ....E...... 219 931-3000
Hammond *(G-5846)*
Bemcor Inc ....F...... 219 937-1600
Hammond *(G-5850)*

MACHINERY: Centrifugal

Centrifuge Chicago Corporation ....G...... 219 852-5200
Hammond *(G-5859)*
US Innovation Group Inc ....F...... 800 899-2040
Indianapolis *(G-8137)*

MACHINERY: Construction

AF Ohab Company Inc ....E...... 317 225-4740
Indianapolis *(G-6350)*
AMA Usa Inc ....G...... 317 329-6590
Indianapolis *(G-6380)*
Avis Industrial Corporation ....E...... 765 998-8100
Upland *(G-13468)*
Birdeye Inc..................................F...... 812 886-0598
Vincennes *(G-13669)*
Boarder Magic By J & A ....G...... 317 545-4401
Indianapolis *(G-6492)*
Caterpillar Inc..............................C...... 765 448-5000
Lafayette *(G-8871)*
Caterpillar Inc..............................D...... 630 743-4094
Greenfield *(G-5511)*
Colby L Stanger ....G...... 574 536-5835
Goshen *(G-5190)*
Custom Machine Mfr LLC ....E...... 574 251-0292
South Bend *(G-12748)*
Galfab LLC ....D...... 574 946-7767
Winamac *(G-14306)*
Highland Park Services Inc ....G...... 317 954-0456
Indianapolis *(G-7107)*
Indco Inc ....G...... 812 945-4383
New Albany *(G-10805)*
J & J Stables...............................G...... 812 279-2581
Bedford *(G-555)*
Kentuckiana Machine & Tool ....G...... 502 301-9005
Lanesville *(G-9102)*
Keystone Engrg & Mfg Corp ....G...... 317 271-6192
Avon *(G-453)*
Maddock Construction Eqp LLC ....E...... 812 349-3000
Bloomington *(G-768)*
Randall Rents of Indiana Inc.............F...... 219 763-1155
Portage *(G-11791)*
Smith Excavating ....G...... 812 636-0054
Odon *(G-11341)*
Speedway Cnstr Pdts Corp ....G...... 260 203-9806
Fort Wayne *(G-4640)*
Square 1 Dsign Manufacture Inc ....F...... 866 647-7771
Shelbyville *(G-12570)*
Stedman Machine Company ....D...... 812 926-0038
Aurora *(G-390)*
Summerlot Engineered Pdts Inc..........F...... 812 466-7266
Rosedale *(G-12206)*
Templeton Coal Company Inc ....D...... 812 232-7037
Terre Haute *(G-13351)*
Terex Corporation ....G...... 574 342-0086
Bourbon *(G-949)*
Terex Corporation ....C...... 260 497-0728
Fort Wayne *(G-4678)*

MACHINERY: Cryogenic, Industrial

International Cryogenics Inc...............F...... 317 297-4777
Indianapolis *(G-7253)*
Technifab Products Inc ....D...... 812 442-0520
Brazil *(G-979)*

MACHINERY: Custom

Advanced Machine & Tool Corp ....C...... 260 489-3572
Fort Wayne *(G-4044)*
Ahaus Tool & Engineering Inc ....D...... 765 962-3573
Richmond *(G-11952)*
American Industrial McHy Inc............F...... 219 755-4090
Merrillville *(G-9697)*
Bcd & Associates..........................G...... 317 873-5394
Zionsville *(G-14421)*
Carmel Engineering Inc ....F...... 765 279-8955
Kirklin *(G-8547)*
CL Tech Inc ....G...... 812 526-0995
Edinburgh *(G-2600)*
Davis Tool & Machine Inc ....F...... 317 896-9278
Westfield *(G-14157)*
Dial-X Acquisition Company Inc..........E...... 260 636-7588
Albion *(G-26)*
Echelbarger Machining Co LLC ....F...... 765 252-1965
Kokomo *(G-8619)*
Edge Technologies Inc ....G...... 317 408-0116
Indianapolis *(G-6805)*
Electro-Tech Inc ....G...... 219 937-0826
Hammond *(G-5877)*
Evart Engineering Co Inc ....G...... 765 354-2232
Middletown *(G-9935)*
Fortville Feeders Inc ....E...... 317 485-5095
Fortville *(G-4775)*
Fourman Enterprises Inc..................F...... 812 546-5734
Hope *(G-6113)*
Genuine Machine Design Inc ....G...... 219 866-8060
Rensselaer *(G-11926)*

Grimm Mold & Die Co Inc ....F 219 778-4211
  Rolling Prairie (G-12186)
Grindco Inc ....E 219 763-6130
  Chesterton (G-1610)
Guide Engineering LLC ....E 260 483-1153
  Fort Wayne (G-4310)
HI Tech Systems Inc ....G 317 704-1077
  Indianapolis (G-7103)
Industrial Hydraulics Inc ....E 317 247-4421
  Indianapolis (G-7208)
Injection Plastic & Mfg Co ....F 574 784-2070
  Lapaz (G-9117)
J M S Machine Inc ....E 260 244-0077
  Columbia City (G-1799)
Jennerjahn Machine Inc ....E 765 998-2733
  Matthews (G-9652)
Keller Machine & Welding Inc ....E 219 464-4915
  Valparaiso (G-13566)
King Investments Inc ....F 812 752-6000
  Scottsburg (G-12371)
Kokomo Metal Fabricators Inc ....G 765 459-8173
  Kokomo (G-8653)
Lynn Tool Company Inc ....G 765 874-2471
  Lynn (G-9430)
Mechanical Engineering Control .....F 574 294-7580
  Elkhart (G-3025)
Mesco Manufacturing LLC ....D 812 663-3870
  Greensburg (G-5622)
Metaltec Inc ....G 219 362-9811
  La Porte (G-8792)
Micromatic LLC ....D 260 589-2136
  Berne (G-621)
Midstate Manufacturing Corp ....F 317 738-0094
  Franklin (G-4908)
Miller Welding & Mechanic Svc ......G 812 923-3359
  Pekin (G-11476)
Mitchum-Schaefer Inc ....D 317 546-4081
  Indianapolis (G-7528)
Moran Engineering LLC ....G 574 266-6799
  Elkhart (G-3050)
Oakley Industries LLC ....G 812 246-2600
  Sellersburg (G-12410)
Perfecto Tool & Engineering Co .....E 765 644-2821
  Anderson (G-150)
Prodigy Mold & Tool Inc ....E 812 753-3029
  Haubstadt (G-6004)
Qig LLC ....E 260 244-3591
  Columbia City (G-1821)
Qig LLC ....E 260 244-3591
  Columbia City (G-1822)
Reynolds & Co Inc ....E 812 232-5313
  Terre Haute (G-13319)
Selco Engineering Inc ....E 317 297-1888
  Shelbyville (G-12566)
Square 1 Dsign Manufacture Inc ....F 866 647-7771
  Shelbyville (G-12570)
SSd Control Technology Inc ....E 574 289-5942
  South Bend (G-12950)
Stamping Specialty Co Inc ....G 812 829-0760
  Spencer (G-13038)
T & M Precision Inc ....G 812 689-5769
  Versailles (G-13659)
Titus Inc ....F 574 936-3345
  Plymouth (G-11728)
Tmak Inc ....E 219 874-7661
  Michigan City (G-9853)
Total Tote Inc ....F 260 982-8318
  North Manchester (G-11246)
Tree City Tool & Engrg Co Inc ....D 812 663-4196
  Greensburg (G-5639)
Trison Industries Inc ....G 812 945-7775
  Floyds Knobs (G-4022)
U S Valves Inc ....G 812 476-6662
  Evansville (G-3782)
Union Tool Corp ....F 574 267-3211
  Warsaw (G-13956)
Uway Extrusion LLC ....F 765 592-6089
  Marshall (G-9593)

MACHINERY: Deburring

Hautau Tube Cutoff Systems LLC ......F 765 647-1600
  Brookville (G-1116)

MACHINERY: Die Casting

Idra North America Inc ....G 765 459-0085
  Kokomo (G-8644)
Sapp Inc ....F 317 512-8353
  Edinburgh (G-2627)

MACHINERY: Electronic Component Making

Moorfeed Corporation ....E 317 545-7171
  Greenfield (G-5559)

MACHINERY: Electronic Teaching Aids

Indiana Instruments Inc ....G 317 875-8032
  Indianapolis (G-7180)
Seib Machine & Tool Co Inc ....G 812 453-6174
  Evansville (G-3721)

MACHINERY: Gas Separators

Separation By Design Inc ....G 812 424-1239
  Evansville (G-3722)

MACHINERY: Gear Cutting & Finishing

TSA America LLC ....G 317 915-1950
  Indianapolis (G-8105)

MACHINERY: General, Industrial, NEC

C&S Machinery Inc ....G 812 937-2160
  Dale (G-2331)
Donaldson Company Inc ....G 317 838-5568
  Plainfield (G-11606)
Homer Banes ....G 765 449-8551
  Lafayette (G-8917)
Horizon Atomtn Fabrication LLC ......G 765 896-9491
  Muncie (G-10492)
Jenco Engineering Inc ....G 574 267-4608
  Warsaw (G-13895)
Midwest Fabrication LLC ....G 574 276-5041
  Granger (G-5422)
Power Drives Inc ....G 812 344-4351
  Columbus (G-1997)

MACHINERY: Glassmaking

H C Schumacher Machine Co Inc ....E 317 787-9361
  Indianapolis (G-7062)
Vhc Ltd ....E 765 584-2101
  Winchester (G-14343)

MACHINERY: Grinding

Accutech Mold & Machine Inc ....C 260 471-6102
  Fort Wayne (G-4038)
Custom Machining Inc ....E 317 392-2328
  Shelbyville (G-12529)
Precision Abrasive Machinery ....G 765 378-3315
  Daleville (G-2341)

MACHINERY: Ice Cream

Flavor Burst Co LLP ....F 317 745-2952
  Danville (G-2347)
M D Holdings LLC ....G 317 831-7030
  Mooresville (G-10319)

MACHINERY: Ice Making

Manitowoc Beverage Eqp Inc ....C 812 246-7000
  Sellersburg (G-12405)

MACHINERY: Industrial, NEC

Absolute Custom Machine LLC ....G 812 724-2284
  Owensville (G-11426)
Centerline Manufacturing ....G 260 348-7400
  Churubusco (G-1651)
Custom Keepsakes Machine EMB ....G 317 894-5506
  Indianapolis (G-6715)
Donaldson Company Inc ....G 317 838-5568
  Plainfield (G-11606)
Eds Machine & Tool ....G 812 295-7264
  Loogootee (G-9382)
Filca LLC ....G 812 637-3559
  Lawrenceburg (G-9141)
Franks Industries ....G 765 647-2080
  Brookville (G-1114)
Gentec Inc ....G 260 436-7333
  Fort Wayne (G-4298)
Hitarth LLC ....G 812 372-1744
  Columbus (G-1939)
Hoosier Industrial Supply ....G 574 535-0712
  Goshen (G-5239)
Jenco Engineering Inc ....G 574 267-4608
  Warsaw (G-13895)
Joint & Clutch Service Inc ....G 317 264-5038
  Indianapolis (G-7310)

Lamb Machine & Tool Co ....G 317 780-9106
  Indianapolis (G-7376)
Larrys Machine ....G 574 596-4994
  Goshen (G-5263)
Lightbeam Technology ....G 219 397-1684
  East Chicago (G-2548)
Michfab Machinery ....G 260 244-6117
  Columbia City (G-1809)
Nathan Millis Tools LLC ....G 219 996-3305
  Hebron (G-6019)
Okaya USA ....G 317 362-0696
  Indianapolis (G-7614)
Ossenbeck Mach Co ....G 937 564-6092
  Lawrenceburg (G-9150)
Precision Agronomy ....G 219 552-0032
  Lowell (G-9420)
Precision Fiber Solutions LLC ....G 317 421-9642
  Franklin (G-4922)
R & Y Professional Tools LLC ....G 765 354-9076
  Middletown (G-9940)
San Mar ....G 574 286-6884
  South Bend (G-12926)
Teresa L Powell CPA ....G 765 962-1862
  Richmond (G-12061)
Thinking Machine LLC ....G 812 539-2968
  Lawrenceburg (G-9158)
Tri Don LLC ....G 765 966-7300
  Richmond (G-12069)

MACHINERY: Jack Screws

Joyce/Dayton Corp ....D 260 726-9361
  Portland (G-11831)

MACHINERY: Kilns

Custom Kiln Works ....G 812 535-3561
  West Terre Haute (G-14123)
Kustom Kilns 5 LLC ....G 260 820-3636
  Terre Haute (G-13268)
Shanxi-Indiana LLC ....G 219 885-2209
  Gary (G-5097)

MACHINERY: Kilns, Cement

Merriman Steel and Equipment ....G 812 849-2784
  Bedford (G-562)

MACHINERY: Labeling

Huhtamaki Inc ....B 765 664-2330
  Marion (G-9532)

MACHINERY: Metalworking

Aam-Equipco Inc ....G 574 272-8886
  Granger (G-5388)
Abell Tool Co Inc ....G 317 887-0021
  Greenwood (G-5658)
American Integrated Mfg Co ....S 317 445-2056
  Westfield (G-14135)
Brown Advanced Mfg LLC ....G 574 209-2003
  Bremen (G-989)
Dual Machine & Tool Co Inc ....G 812 256-2202
  Charlestown (G-1563)
Dubois Machine Co Inc ....E 812 482-3644
  Jasper (G-8249)
Finite Filtation Company ....G 219 789-8084
  Crown Point (G-2253)
George Koch Sons LLC ....C 812 465-9600
  Evansville (G-3519)
Glaze Tool and Engineering Inc ....E 260 493-4557
  New Haven (G-10941)
Grinding and Polsg McHy Corp ....F 317 898-0750
  Indianapolis (G-7050)
Innovative Mold & Machine Inc ....G 317 634-1177
  Indianapolis (G-7238)
Jpg Machine & Tool LLC ....G 812 265-4512
  Madison (G-9474)
McBroom Electric Co Inc ....D 317 926-3451
  Indianapolis (G-7471)
Meriwether Tool & Engineering ....F 260 744-6955
  Fort Wayne (G-4466)
Midwest Precision Machining ....G 260 459-6866
  Fort Wayne (G-4473)
Modern Die Systems Inc ....E 765 552-3145
  Elwood (G-3307)
Nix Equipment LLC ....E 812 874-2231
  Poseyville (G-11859)
Pia Automation US Inc ....C 812 474-3126
  Evansville (G-3669)
Precision Automation Co Inc ....E 812 283-7963
  Clarksville (G-1691)

Quality Industrial Supplies....................F 219 324-2654
La Porte (G-8808)
Tube Form Solutions LLC ....E 574 295-5041
Elkhart (G-3228)
Tube Form Solutions LLC ....E 574 266-5230
Elkhart (G-3229)
Walkerton Tool & Die Inc ....E 574 586-3162
Walkerton (G-13813)
Wastequip Mfg ....E 574 946-6631
Winamac (G-14323)

MACHINERY: Milling

Jones Fabrication & Machining............E 812 466-2237
Terre Haute (G-13262)
Maxwell Milling Indiana Inc ....G 765 489-3506
Hagerstown (G-5809)
Wood-Mizer LLC ....G 317 271-1542
Indianapolis (G-8211)

MACHINERY: Mining

Claymore Tools Inc ....G 574 255-6483
Mishawaka (G-10018)
Deister Machine Company Inc..............C 260 426-7495
Fort Wayne (G-4205)
Deister Machine Company Inc..............F 260 426-7495
Fort Wayne (G-4206)
Deister Machine Company Inc..............C 260 422-0354
Fort Wayne (G-4207)
Jones Trucking Inc ....G 765 537-2279
Paragon (G-11459)
Keystone Engrg & Mfg Corp ....G 317 271-6192
Avon (G-453)
Pillar Innovations LLC ....G 812 474-9080
Evansville (G-3670)
Prox Company Inc ....F 812 232-4324
Terre Haute (G-13311)
United Conveyor Corporation...............E 574 256-0991
Mishawaka (G-10142)

MACHINERY: Packaging

Chicago Automated Labeling ....F 219 531-0646
Valparaiso (G-13522)
Elf Machinery LLC................................C 219 393-5541
La Porte (G-8755)
Grrk Holdings Inc.................................E 317 872-0172
Indianapolis (G-7053)
Kwik Lok Corporation Indiana ....D 260 493-1220
New Haven (G-10947)
Lindal North America Inc ....D 812 657-7142
Columbus (G-1962)
Liquid Packaging Solutions Inc............E 219 393-3600
La Porte (G-8787)
Monosol LLC ....D 219 763-7589
Portage (G-11778)
Morgan Adhesives Company LLC........D 812 342-2004
Columbus (G-1976)
Patriot Packaging LLC.........................G 812 346-0700
North Vernon (G-11276)
Powell Systems Inc..............................E 765 884-0980
Fowler (G-4805)
Precision Automation Co Inc ....E 812 283-7963
Clarksville (G-1691)
Rethceif Enterprises LLC.....................F 260 622-7200
Ossian (G-11405)
Webber Manufacturing Company.........E 317 357-8681
Indianapolis (G-8181)

MACHINERY: Paint Making

Indco Inc..G 812 945-4383
New Albany (G-10805)
UFS Corporation ....F 219 464-2027
Valparaiso (G-13630)

MACHINERY: Paper Industry Miscellaneous

Bahr Bros Mfg Inc................................E 765 664-6235
Marion (G-9512)
Corrquest Automation Inc....................G 812 596-0049
Crandall (G-2124)
GTW Enterprises Inc............................E 219 362-2278
La Porte (G-8759)
Indiana Fiber Works.............................G 317 524-5711
Indianapolis (G-7179)
Jennerjahn Machine Inc ....E 765 998-2733
Matthews (G-9652)
Peerless Machine & Tool Corp ....D 765 662-2586
Marion (G-9552)
RPC Machinery Inc ....G 765 458-5655
Liberty (G-9271)

Stickle Steam Specialties Co ....F 317 636-6563
Indianapolis (G-8007)

MACHINERY: Pharmaciutical

Global Isotopes LLC............................G 317 578-1251
Noblesville (G-11111)
Hoosier Feeder Company Inc ....E 765 445-3333
Knightstown (G-8550)

MACHINERY: Plastic Working

Dubois Machine Co Inc ....E 812 482-3644
Jasper (G-8249)
Hermetic Coil Co Inc ....E 812 735-2400
Bicknell (G-631)
Honey Creek Machine Inc ....E 812 299-5255
Terre Haute (G-13247)
Kenco Plastics Inc ....F 219 324-6621
La Porte (G-8777)
Lindas ....G 812 265-0099
Hanover (G-5962)
Majestic Tool Inc ....G 812 426-0332
Evansville (G-3612)
Peerless Machine & Tool Corp ....D 765 662-2586
Marion (G-9552)
Summit Industrial Technologies...........G 260 494-3461
Fort Wayne (G-4664)
Tamco Manufacturing Co ....G 574 294-1909
Elkhart (G-3205)
Triplet Tool and Die Co Inc ....E 812 867-2494
Evansville (G-3775)

MACHINERY: Pottery Making

American Art Clay Co Inc ....C 317 243-0066
Indianapolis (G-6385)

MACHINERY: Printing Presses

Indiana Imprint LLC ....G 812 704-2773
Jeffersonville (G-8380)
Kbc Machine..G 317 446-6163
Greenfield (G-5546)

MACHINERY: Road Construction & Maintenance

County of Lagrange ....E 260 499-6353
Lagrange (G-9035)

MACHINERY: Robots, Molding & Forming Plastics

Roland International Co LLC ....G 319 400-1106
Carmel (G-1469)

MACHINERY: Semiconductor Manufacturing

Anatolia Group Ltd Partnership ....G 203 343-7808
Indianapolis (G-6398)
Applied Material Solutions LLC............G 317 769-3829
Zionsville (G-14418)
Sugarcube Systems Inc ....G 765 543-6709
Lafayette (G-9005)
Univertical LLC....................................E 260 665-1500
Angola (G-256)

MACHINERY: Service Industry, NEC

D K Tools & Engineering ....G 812 325-4532
Morgantown (G-10351)
Freije Treatment Systems Inc ....G 317 508-3848
Indianapolis (G-6964)

MACHINERY: Specialty

PSI Repair Services Inc ....G 812 485-5575
Evansville (G-3689)
Toco Inc ....G 317 627-8854
Greenwood (G-5754)
Vibration Control Tech LLC ....G 260 894-7199
Ligonier (G-9302)

MACHINERY: Stone Working

E & R Manufacturing Company.............G 765 279-8826
Kirklin (G-8548)

MACHINERY: Textile

Logo Zone Inc......................................G 574 753-7569
Logansport (G-9352)

Machining Solutions.............................G 574 292-3227
South Bend (G-12846)
Moores Inc ....G 574 533-6089
Goshen (G-5297)

MACHINERY: Thread Rolling

Rickie Allan Pease ....G 260 244-7579
Columbia City (G-1827)

MACHINERY: Tire Shredding

Gabriel Intl Group LLC.........................G 812 537-5400
Lawrenceburg (G-9143)
Hoosier Shred Llc ....G 317 989-9333
Indianapolis (G-7124)
Integra Certified Document ....G 574 295-4611
Elkhart (G-2936)

MACHINERY: Wire Drawing

HI Def Machining LLC ....G 812 493-9943
Madison (G-9465)
JI Manfcturing Fabrication Inc..............G 260 589-3723
Berne (G-618)
Millers Quick Production ....G 812 278-8374
Springville (G-13065)
Stulls Machining Center Inc.................G 765 942-2717
Ladoga (G-8842)

MACHINERY: Woodworking

Braun Witte Pattern Works Inc ....G 260 463-8210
Wolcottville (G-14369)
Core Wood Components LLC................G 574 370-4457
Elkhart (G-2774)
Dubois Machine Co Inc ....E 812 482-3644
Jasper (G-8249)
Grinding and Polsg McHy Corp............F 317 898-0750
Indianapolis (G-7050)
Hoosier Woodworking McHy LLC ....G 812 944-3302
New Albany (G-10798)
Lafree Enterprises ....G 574 674-5906
Osceola (G-11380)
Lozier Machinery Incorporated.............G 812 945-2558
New Albany (G-10819)
Nobbe Concrete Products Inc ....G 765 647-4017
Brookville (G-1121)
Northtech Machine LLC........................G 812 967-7400
Borden (G-936)
PDQ Workholding LLC ....E 260 244-2919
Columbia City (G-1817)
Scheumann Cabinet Co........................G 260 747-3509
Fort Wayne (G-4608)

MACHINES: Forming, Sheet Metal

Ten Point Trim Corp.............................E 317 875-5424
Zionsville (G-14468)

MACHINISTS' TOOLS & MACHINES: Measuring, Metalworking Type

Clarks Cnc LLC ....G 812 508-1773
Springville (G-13061)

MACHINISTS' TOOLS: Measuring, Precision

Harford Industries Inc..........................G 219 929-6455
Chesterton (G-1612)

MACHINISTS' TOOLS: Precision

Advent Precision Inc ....G 317 908-6937
Indianapolis (G-6340)
Beverly Industrial Service ....F 812 667-5047
Dillsboro (G-2463)
Davis Tool and Gage Company ....G 317 852-5400
Brownsburg (G-1148)
Fuhrman Precision Services.................G 260 728-9600
Decatur (G-2379)
Marion Tool & Die Inc ....D 812 533-9800
West Terre Haute (G-14126)
Scheidler Machine Incorporated ....G 812 662-6555
Greensburg (G-5633)
Swiss Labs Machine & Engrg Inc.........G 317 346-6190
Franklin (G-4935)
V I P Tooling Inc ....F 317 398-0753
Shelbyville (G-12581)
Yamaguchi Mfg Usa Inc ....G 765 973-9130
Richmond (G-12077)

PRODUCT

MAGAZINES, WHOLESALE

Great Deals Magazine.....................F...... 765 649-3302
  Anderson **(G-112)**
Magazine Fulfillment Corp................E...... 219 874-4245
  Michigan City **(G-9814)**

MAGNETIC SHIELDS, METAL

Ad-Vance Magnetics Inc...................E...... 574 223-3158
  Rochester **(G-12113)**

MAGNETIC TAPE, AUDIO: Prerecorded

Boeke Road Baptist Church Inc.........G...... 812 479-5342
  Evansville **(G-3389)**

MAGNETS: Ceramic

Ies Subsidiary Holdings Inc..............F...... 330 830-3500
  South Bend **(G-12807)**
Ies Subsidiary Holdings Inc..............D...... 219 937-0100
  Hammond **(G-5897)**
Thomas & Skinner Inc......................F...... 812 689-4811
  Osgood **(G-11396)**

MAGNETS: Permanent

Magnequench Inc...........................A...... 765 778-7809
  Pendleton **(G-11494)**
Magnets R US Inc...........................G...... 574 633-0061
  South Bend **(G-12848)**
Thomas & Skinner Inc......................B...... 317 923-2501
  Indianapolis **(G-8063)**

MAIL-ORDER HOUSE, NEC

Indiana Botanic Gardens Inc..............C...... 219 947-4040
  Hobart **(G-6081)**

MAIL-ORDER HOUSES: Clothing, Exc Women's

Favor It Promotions Inc....................F...... 317 733-1112
  Carmel **(G-1379)**
Tt2 LLC.....................................G...... 260 438-4575
  Fort Wayne **(G-4707)**

MAIL-ORDER HOUSES: Computer Eqpt & Electronics

Lovetts Electronics.........................G...... 812 446-1093
  Brazil **(G-967)**
Tempest Technical Sales Inc..............F...... 317 844-9236
  Carmel **(G-1492)**

MAIL-ORDER HOUSES: Educational Splys & Eqpt

DMC Distribution LLC.......................G...... 219 926-6401
  Porter **(G-11805)**

MAIL-ORDER HOUSES: Electronic Kits & Parts

Advance MCS Electronics Inc.............F...... 574 642-3501
  Goshen **(G-5166)**

MAIL-ORDER HOUSES: Fitness & Sporting Goods

Geist Bike and Hobby Company..........G...... 317 855-1346
  Indianapolis **(G-6990)**
Official Sports Intl Inc......................F...... 574 269-1404
  Warsaw **(G-13917)**

MAIL-ORDER HOUSES: Furniture & Furnishings

Roudebush Company Incorporated......G...... 574 595-7115
  Star City **(G-13070)**

MAIL-ORDER HOUSES: Gift Items

Youniquely Yours...........................G...... 219 942-1489
  Hobart **(G-6103)**

MAIL-ORDER HOUSES: Record & Tape, Music Or Video Club

Voice of God Recordings Inc...............D...... 812 246-2137
  Jeffersonville **(G-8439)**

MAILBOX RENTAL & RELATED SVCS

C&C Polo Enterprises Inc..................G...... 317 577-8266
  Indianapolis **(G-6529)**
Noblesville Pack & Ship....................G...... 317 776-6306
  Noblesville **(G-11161)**

MAILING SVCS, NEC

Anthony Wayne Rehabilitation C..........D...... 260 744-6145
  Fort Wayne **(G-4078)**
Anthony Wayne Rehabilitation C..........E...... 317 972-1000
  Indianapolis **(G-6403)**
Baugh Enterprises Inc......................F...... 812 334-8189
  Bloomington **(G-674)**
Cozy Cat Inc................................G...... 765 463-1254
  Lafayette **(G-8879)**
Delp Printing & Mailing Inc................E...... 317 872-9744
  Indianapolis **(G-6733)**
Faris Mailing Inc............................F...... 317 246-3315
  Indianapolis **(G-6905)**
Fineline Graphics Incorporated............D...... 317 872-4490
  Indianapolis **(G-6921)**
Printing Partners Inc........................E...... 317 635-2282
  Indianapolis **(G-7755)**
Q S I Inc....................................E...... 574 282-1200
  South Bend **(G-12908)**
Service Graphics Inc........................D...... 317 471-8246
  Indianapolis **(G-7917)**
Un Communications Group Inc..............E...... 317 844-8622
  Carmel **(G-1503)**

MANAGEMENT CONSULTING SVCS: Administrative

Moffitt Consulting Services................G...... 317 773-5570
  Noblesville **(G-11153)**

MANAGEMENT CONSULTING SVCS: Automation & Robotics

General Automation Company..............F...... 317 849-7483
  Indianapolis **(G-6992)**

MANAGEMENT CONSULTING SVCS: Banking & Finance

Envista LLC.................................D...... 317 208-9100
  Carmel **(G-1372)**
Envista Entp Solutions LLC................E...... 317 208-9100
  Carmel **(G-1374)**

MANAGEMENT CONSULTING SVCS: Business

Eli Lilly International Corp...................F...... 317 276-2000
  Indianapolis **(G-6836)**
Tgf Enterprises LLC.........................G...... 440 840-9704
  Indianapolis **(G-8056)**
Winfield Solutions LLC......................G...... 317 838-3733
  Plainfield **(G-11652)**

MANAGEMENT CONSULTING SVCS: Business Planning & Organizing

Paringa Resources Limited.................G...... 314 422-4150
  Evansville **(G-3663)**

MANAGEMENT CONSULTING SVCS: Distribution Channels

Georg Utz Inc..............................E...... 812 526-2240
  Edinburgh **(G-2612)**

MANAGEMENT CONSULTING SVCS: General

Digital Carvings LLC........................G...... 812 269-6123
  Ellettsville **(G-3278)**
Life Path Numerology Center..............G...... 317 638-9752
  Indianapolis **(G-7404)**

MANAGEMENT CONSULTING SVCS: Hospital & Health

Clinical Architecture LLC...................E...... 317 580-8400
  Carmel **(G-1341)**

MANAGEMENT CONSULTING SVCS: Industrial

McNeil Coatings Consultants..............G...... 317 885-1557
  Greenwood **(G-5725)**

MANAGEMENT CONSULTING SVCS: Industry Specialist

Northern Indiana Ordnance Co............G...... 574 289-5938
  South Bend **(G-12879)**

MANAGEMENT CONSULTING SVCS: Manufacturing

Ditech Inc..................................D...... 812 526-0850
  Edinburgh **(G-2607)**

MANAGEMENT CONSULTING SVCS: Planning

Utilities Aviation Specialists...............G...... 219 662-8175
  Crown Point **(G-2317)**

MANAGEMENT CONSULTING SVCS: Quality Assurance

Smith Consulting Inc.......................E...... 765 728-5980
  Montpelier **(G-10294)**

MANAGEMENT CONSULTING SVCS: Training & Development

Christian Sound & Song Inc................G...... 574 294-2893
  Elkhart **(G-2756)**
Leidos Inc..................................C...... 812 863-3100
  Crane **(G-2128)**

MANAGEMENT SERVICES

Abari Properties Development..............G...... 317 721-9230
  Indianapolis **(G-6306)**
Agi International Inc.........................F...... 317 536-2415
  Indianapolis **(G-6352)**
Automated Laser Corporation..............E...... 260 637-4140
  Fort Wayne **(G-4097)**
Borgwarner Pds Anderson LLC.............C...... 765 778-6499
  Anderson **(G-76)**
Central Coca-Cola Btlg Co Inc.............G...... 812 482-7475
  Jasper **(G-8241)**
Central Coca-Cola Btlg Co Inc.............G...... 800 241-2653
  Bloomington **(G-699)**
Central Coca-Cola Btlg Co Inc.............G...... 260 726-7126
  Portland **(G-11810)**
Central Coca-Cola Btlg Co Inc.............G...... 800 241-2653
  Shelbyville **(G-12526)**
Crown Training & Development.............E...... 219 947-0845
  Merrillville **(G-9708)**
Eaton Corporation..........................F...... 317 704-2520
  Indianapolis **(G-6796)**
Fretina Corp.................................F...... 812 547-6471
  Tell City **(G-13163)**
Indiana Scale Company Inc.................F...... 812 232-0893
  Terre Haute **(G-13255)**
LH Industries Corp..........................B...... 260 432-5563
  Fort Wayne **(G-4431)**
Patrick Industries Inc.......................C...... 574 293-1521
  Elkhart **(G-3082)**

MANAGEMENT SVCS: Business

Commtineo LLC.............................F...... 219 476-3667
  Wanatah **(G-13822)**

MANAGEMENT SVCS: Construction

Hgmc Supply Inc...........................F...... 317 351-9500
  Indianapolis **(G-7101)**
Pac Corporation............................G...... 260 637-8792
  Fort Wayne **(G-4517)**
Pittman Mine Service LLC..................E...... 812 847-2340
  Linton **(G-9311)**

MANAGEMENT SVCS: Industrial

Phoenix Assembly LLC.....................D...... 317 884-3600
  Greenwood **(G-5732)**
Phoenix Assembly Indiana LLC.............E...... 317 884-3600
  Columbus **(G-1995)**

MANHOLES & COVERS: Metal

Ej Usa Inc ....F...... 765 744-1184
Indianapolis **(G-6818)**
Jkr Inc ....F 260 665-1067
Angola **(G-221)**

MANICURE PREPARATIONS

Aqua Spa ....G...... 219 548-4772
Valparaiso **(G-13496)**
French Tips ....G...... 812 923-9055
Floyds Knobs **(G-4011)**
Nail Pro ....G...... 219 322-9220
Schererville **(G-12337)**
Star Nail ....G...... 765 453-0743
Kokomo **(G-8700)**
Wonder Nail LLC ....G...... 317 462-8404
Greenfield **(G-5585)**

MANPOWER TRAINING

Cooperative Ventures Ind Corp ....G...... 317 259-7063
Carmel **(G-1343)**

MANUFACTURED & MOBILE HOME DEALERS

Delaware County Home Bldrs Inc ....G...... 765 289-6328
Muncie **(G-10456)**
Fairmont Homes LLC ....G...... 574 773-2041
Nappanee **(G-10670)**
Light House Homes Center ....F 765 448-4502
Lafayette **(G-8957)**
Thornes Homes Inc ....G...... 812 275-4656
Bedford **(G-584)**

MANUFACTURING INDUSTRIES, NEC

ABS Mfg Rep Inc ....G...... 317 407-0406
Carmel **(G-1299)**
Accra Pac Holding Co LLC ....G...... 765 326-0005
Fort Wayne **(G-4035)**
Adec Industries ....G...... 574 522-7729
Elkhart **(G-2669)**
Advanced Manufacturing In ....G...... 260 273-9669
Geneva **(G-5133)**
Agile Mfg Inc ....G...... 417 845-6065
Milford **(G-9948)**
Aidan Industries Incorporated ....G...... 812 239-2803
Terre Haute **(G-13189)**
Air Way Mfg ....G...... 269 749-2161
Hamilton **(G-5819)**
Allergyfree Inc ....G...... 765 349-0006
Martinsville **(G-9595)**
America Corn Cutter ....G...... 219 733-0885
Wanatah **(G-13819)**
American Chemical Service ....G...... 219 613-4114
Crown Point **(G-2225)**
Anchor Industries ....G...... 812 664-0772
Owensville **(G-11427)**
Anglers Manufacturing ....G...... 812 988-8040
Nashville **(G-10713)**
ARC Industries ....G...... 812 471-1633
Evansville **(G-3361)**
Armor Contract Mfg Inc ....F 574 327-2962
Elkhart **(G-2695)**
Ashe Industries ....G...... 219 852-6040
Hammond **(G-5844)**
Aunt Netts Country Candles LLC ....G...... 765 557-2770
Elwood **(G-3294)**
Austins Metal Mafia Inc ....G...... 812 619-6115
Cannelton **(G-1286)**
B&R Manufacturing Inc ....G...... 574 293-5669
Elkhart **(G-2711)**
B2 Manufacturing LLC ....G...... 765 993-4519
Fountain City **(G-4784)**
Bantam Industries Inc ....G...... 714 561-6122
Indianapolis **(G-6456)**
Bawel Industries LP ....G...... 812 634-8004
Jasper **(G-8238)**
Bbs Celebration Center ....G...... 765 730-6575
Yorktown **(G-14402)**
Benchmark Consumer Industries ....G...... 317 576-0931
Fishers **(G-3878)**
Bkb Manufacturing Inc ....G...... 260 982-8524
North Manchester **(G-11225)**
Brothers Industries ....G...... 812 560-6224
Greensburg **(G-5592)**
Burkhart Manufacturing Inc ....G...... 260 316-0715
Angola **(G-200)**

Byers Scientific Mfg ....G...... 812 269-6218
Bloomington **(G-693)**
Byrd Industries ....G...... 812 867-5859
Evansville **(G-3406)**
C & B Industries LLC ....G...... 260 490-3000
Fort Wayne **(G-4128)**
C & C Industries ....G...... 260 804-6518
Fort Wayne **(G-4129)**
C & F Industries ....G...... 765 580-0378
Liberty **(G-9257)**
C & J K Industries Inc ....G...... 219 746-5760
Munster **(G-10600)**
C&B Industries LLC ....G...... 260 493-3288
Fort Wayne **(G-4132)**
Caliente ....G...... 260 471-0700
Fort Wayne **(G-4136)**
Carousel Industries ....G...... 317 674-8111
Fishers **(G-3885)**
Carter Enterprises Inc ....G...... 317 984-1497
Arcadia **(G-262)**
Carters Manufacturing & Weld ....G...... 630 464-1520
Knox **(G-8563)**
CCM Industries Inc ....G...... 765 545-0597
Winchester **(G-14326)**
Cde Industries LLC ....G...... 317 573-6790
Indianapolis **(G-6571)**
Clover Industries LLC ....G...... 574 892-5760
Argos **(G-273)**
Cobar Industries Inc ....G...... 317 691-7124
Indianapolis **(G-6627)**
Cobo Industries ....G...... 812 341-4318
Indianapolis **(G-6628)**
Coffman & Fairbanks Industries ....G...... 765 458-7896
Liberty **(G-9259)**
Commercial Technical Svcs Inc ....G...... 260 436-9898
Fort Wayne **(G-4169)**
Cottage Industries DBA ....G...... 765 617-8360
Alexandria **(G-38)**
Cottage Industries Inc ....G...... 260 482-1100
Fort Wayne **(G-4181)**
Csn Industries Inc ....G...... 317 697-6549
Bargersville **(G-479)**
CT Industries LLC ....G...... 574 675-9422
Granger **(G-5398)**
Custom Fitz LLC ....G...... 219 405-0896
Porter **(G-11803)**
Custom Mfg & Fabrication LLC ....G...... 260 908-1088
Auburn **(G-326)**
D & F Industries Inc ....G...... 219 865-2926
Schererville **(G-12319)**
D&A Industries Inc ....G...... 260 357-1830
Garrett **(G-5000)**
Damage Industries II LLC ....G...... 574 256-7006
Mishawaka **(G-10029)**
Darlage Investments LLC ....F 812 522-5929
Seymour **(G-12443)**
Davis Industries Inc ....G...... 317 871-0103
Indianapolis **(G-6728)**
Dmp Industries LLC ....G...... 260 413-6701
Warsaw **(G-13867)**
Door Tech Industries Inc ....G...... 219 322-3465
Dyer **(G-2494)**
Dragon Industries Incorporated ....G...... 574 772-3508
Knox **(G-8565)**
Drummond Industries ....F 260 348-5550
Fort Wayne **(G-4221)**
Dubois Manufacturing Inc ....G...... 574 674-6988
Elkhart **(G-2801)**
Earthy Industries LLC ....G...... 260 483-7588
Fort Wayne **(G-4232)**
Echo Manufacturing LLC ....G...... 574 333-3669
Elkhart **(G-2812)**
Edsal Inc ....G...... 219 427-1294
Gary **(G-5043)**
Eligius Industries LLC ....G...... 574 267-5313
Warsaw **(G-13869)**
Elite Industries LLC ....G...... 317 407-6869
Indianapolis **(G-6838)**
Elliott Manufacturing and Fabr ....G...... 812 865-0516
Paoli **(G-11449)**
English Industries LLC ....G...... 812 218-9882
Jeffersonville **(G-8355)**
Enhanced Mfg Solutions LLC ....G...... 812 932-1101
Batesville **(G-499)**
Excel Industries Inc ....G...... 574 264-2131
Elkhart **(G-2840)**
Fabcore Industries LLC ....G...... 260 438-3431
Fort Wayne **(G-4252)**
Fast Manufacturing LLC ....G...... 219 778-8123
Rolling Prairie **(G-12185)**

Fia-Indiana ....G...... 812 895-4700
Vincennes **(G-13681)**
Fillmanns Industries LLC ....G...... 765 744-4772
Daleville **(G-2339)**
Filmtec Fabrications LLC ....G...... 419 435-7504
Fort Wayne **(G-4262)**
Fire Star Industries LLC ....G...... 317 432-3212
Greenwood **(G-5695)**
Foy Industries ....G...... 317 727-3905
Indianapolis **(G-6954)**
Frankinstein Industries Inc ....G...... 217 918-4548
Indianapolis **(G-6958)**
Fruition Industries LLC ....G...... 260 854-2325
Rome City **(G-12199)**
Fuel Fabrication LLC ....G...... 219 390-7022
Crown Point **(G-2255)**
G F M S Industries ....G...... 219 464-1445
Valparaiso **(G-13545)**
Gdp Industries LLC ....G...... 260 414-4003
Fort Wayne **(G-4293)**
Gem Industries Inc ....G...... 574 773-4513
Nappanee **(G-10673)**
Geny Industries LLC ....G...... 574 536-0297
Bremen **(G-999)**
Gnome Industries Inc ....G...... 219 764-3337
Valparaiso **(G-13549)**
Goat Industries LLC ....G...... 770 940-0433
Indianapolis **(G-7017)**
Gold Standard Truss LLC ....G...... 219 987-7781
Demotte **(G-2438)**
Goodlife Industries Inc ....G...... 317 339-6341
Indianapolis **(G-7024)**
Goodwill Industries ....G...... 317 546-7251
Indianapolis **(G-7027)**
Goodwill Industries ....E 317 524-4293
Indianapolis **(G-7028)**
Graysville Mfg Inc ....G...... 812 382-4616
Sullivan **(G-13083)**
Great Lakes Waterjet Inc ....G...... 574 651-2158
Granger **(G-5411)**
Green Mountain Industries LLC ....G...... 812 585-1531
Centerpoint **(G-1538)**
Hager Industries Inc ....G...... 317 219-6622
Noblesville **(G-11117)**
Hangout At Flames LLC ....G...... 765 483-2009
Lebanon **(G-9186)**
Havoc Motor Company LLC ....G...... 973 407-9933
Elkhart **(G-2910)**
Hensley Composites LLC ....G...... 574 202-3840
Elkhart **(G-2913)**
Hentz Mfg LLC ....G...... 260 469-0800
Fort Wayne **(G-4331)**
Hestad Industries Inc ....G...... 574 271-7609
Granger **(G-5412)**
Hicks Mfg ....G...... 317 219-9891
Carmel **(G-1404)**
High Velocity Manufacturing ....G...... 260 413-8429
Fort Wayne **(G-4333)**
Highpoint Mfg LLC ....G...... 812 273-8987
Madison **(G-9466)**
HK Manufacturing Inc ....G...... 260 925-1680
Auburn **(G-336)**
Holiday House Inc ....E 574 773-9536
Nappanee **(G-10683)**
Hurst Enterprise ....G...... 812 853-0901
Newburgh **(G-11031)**
Imagine Industries LLC ....G...... 260 494-6530
Fort Wayne **(G-4360)**
Industries LLC ....G...... 765 759-5577
Yorktown **(G-14406)**
Integritech Mfg Inc ....G...... 574 656-3046
North Liberty **(G-11217)**
Irish Industries ....G...... 773 213-2422
McCordsville **(G-9672)**
Iron Men Industries Inc ....G...... 574 596-2251
Russiaville **(G-12242)**
Jacobs Mfg LLC ....G...... 765 490-6111
Lafayette **(G-8928)**
Jani Industries Inc ....G...... 317 985-3916
Avon **(G-449)**
JG and JG Industries LLC ....G...... 765 742-0260
Lafayette **(G-8932)**
Jlp Manufacturing LLC ....G...... 765 647-2991
Brookville **(G-1120)**
Joy MI Industries Inc ....G...... 317 876-3917
Indianapolis **(G-7314)**
Jrds Industries ....G...... 260 729-5037
Portland **(G-11832)**
Junoll Industries ....G...... 574 586-2719
Walkerton **(G-13804)**

PRODUCT

K&P Industries LLC ....G....... 317 881-9245
Greenwood *(G-5711)*

K-M Machine & Mfg ....G....... 765 886-5717
Economy *(G-2592)*

Karma Industries Inc ....G....... 765 742-9200
Lafayette *(G-8937)*

Keihin Ipt Mfg ....G....... 317 578-5260
Indianapolis *(G-7340)*

Kemco Manufacturing LLC ....G....... 574 546-2025
Bremen *(G-1008)*

Kt Industries LLC ....G....... 260 432-0027
Fort Wayne *(G-4417)*

Lafferty & Lafferty LLC ....G....... 574 935-4852
Plymouth *(G-11700)*

Lamarvis Industries LLC ....G....... 317 797-0483
Terre Haute *(G-13269)*

Lawrence Industries ....G....... 260 432-9693
Columbia City *(G-1807)*

Lee Mfg LLC ....G....... 260 403-2775
Fort Wayne *(G-4429)*

Leland Manufacturing ....G....... 812 367-2068
Ferdinand *(G-3857)*

Lennon Industries ....G....... 219 996-6024
Hebron *(G-6017)*

Licensed Eliquid Manufacturing ....G....... 260 687-9213
Fort Wayne *(G-4433)*

Lippert Extrusions ....G....... 574 312-6467
Elkhart *(G-3003)*

Little Mfg LLC ....G....... 812 453-8137
Boonville *(G-916)*

Lozano Wldg & Fabrication LLC ....G....... 812 858-1379
Newburgh *(G-11037)*

Luckmann Industries ....G....... 317 464-0323
Indianapolis *(G-7424)*

M & S Curtis LLC ....G....... 317 946-8440
Indianapolis *(G-7431)*

M2 Industries LLC ....G....... 812 246-0651
Jeffersonville *(G-8392)*

Madison River Industries LLC ....G....... 317 472-6375
Noblesville *(G-11144)*

Mainline Manufacturing Company ......G....... 219 237-0770
Griffith *(G-5782)*

Mamon Global Industries Inc ....G....... 317 721-1657
Fort Wayne *(G-4450)*

Martin Industries ....G....... 502 553-6599
New Albany *(G-10822)*

Medical Structures Mfg Corp ....G....... 574 612-0353
Elkhart *(G-3027)*

Merritt Manufacturing Inc ....G....... 317 422-1167
Bargersville *(G-485)*

Meteor Manufacturing LLC ....G....... 317 587-1414
Carmel *(G-1439)*

Miles Systems Manufacturing ....G....... 574 988-0067
New Carlisle *(G-10885)*

Mk Mfg LLC ....G....... 260 768-4678
Shipshewana *(G-12637)*

Mobile Dental Van Mfg ....G....... 812 626-3010
Evansville *(G-3632)*

Moosein Industries LLC ....G....... 219 406-7306
Portage *(G-11780)*

Navspar Industries LLC ....G....... 812 344-1476
Columbus *(G-1979)*

NM Industries LLC ....G....... 812 985-3608
Evansville *(G-3645)*

Norco Industries ....G....... 800 347-2232
Elkhart *(G-3064)*

Nova Manufacturing ....G....... 512 750-5165
Avon *(G-458)*

NPS Xofigo Mfg Plant 5889 ....G....... 317 981-4129
Indianapolis *(G-7602)*

Omega Co ....G....... 317 831-4471
Mooresville *(G-10330)*

Osterfeld Industries ....G....... 219 926-4646
Chesterton *(G-1626)*

Outdoor Industries ....G....... 574 551-5936
Warsaw *(G-13921)*

Ovr There Industries Inc ....G....... 317 946-8365
Indianapolis *(G-7639)*

P & M Fabrication ....G....... 812 232-7640
Terre Haute *(G-13295)*

Pangloss Industries Inc ....G....... 574 217-8505
Mishawaka *(G-10099)*

Papayan Industries ....G....... 765 387-7274
West Lafayette *(G-14092)*

Pbs Mfg LLC ....G....... 317 515-2875
Indianapolis *(G-7665)*

Pdk Industries Inc ....G....... 765 721-3085
Greencastle *(G-5471)*

Peerless Manufacturing ....G....... 260 897-3070
Laotto *(G-9114)*

Peerless Manufacturing LLC ....G....... 260 760-0880
Avilla *(G-417)*

Pgw Industries Inc ....G....... 317 322-3599
Indianapolis *(G-7682)*

Phantom Industries LLC ....G....... 812 276-5956
Jeffersonville *(G-8414)*

Pinnacle Manufacturing Group ....G....... 317 691-2460
Indianapolis *(G-7694)*

Platinum Industries LLC ....G....... 765 744-8323
Fishers *(G-3953)*

Pollution Control Industries ....E....... 219 391-7020
East Chicago *(G-2561)*

Predator Percussion LLC ....G....... 317 919-7659
New Whiteland *(G-11013)*

Prime Time Manufacturing ....G....... 574 862-3001
Wakarusa *(G-13790)*

Pro Series Products LLC ....G....... 812 793-3506
Crothersville *(G-2219)*

Procoat Products Inc ....G....... 812 352-6083
North Vernon *(G-11279)*

Prowler Industries LLC ....F....... 877 477-6953
Greensburg *(G-5630)*

R M Mfg Housing Svc ....G....... 574 288-5207
South Bend *(G-12912)*

R N A Industries Corp ....G....... 765 288-4413
Redkey *(G-11899)*

Rappid Mfg Inc ....G....... 317 440-8084
Indianapolis *(G-7816)*

Raw Design and Fabrication LLC ....G....... 708 466-5835
Saint John *(G-12269)*

Rbc Manufacturing Corp ....C....... 260 416-5400
Fort Wayne *(G-4579)*

RE Industries Inc. ....G....... 219 987-1764
Demotte *(G-2446)*

Redab Industries ....G....... 219 484-8382
Crown Point *(G-2293)*

Redman Industries LLC ....G....... 317 768-3004
Zionsville *(G-14459)*

Redstar Contract Manufacturing ....G....... 260 327-3145
Larwill *(G-9126)*

Reilly Industries Inc ....G....... 317 247-8141
Indianapolis *(G-7829)*

Resourcemfg ....G....... 574 206-1522
Elkhart *(G-3144)*

Ridge Iron LLC ....G....... 646 450-0092
Plymouth *(G-11722)*

Ring Industries Inc. ....G....... 219 204-1577
Lake Village *(G-9087)*

Ronlewhorn Industries LLC ....G....... 765 661-9343
Indianapolis *(G-7860)*

Rose Industries LLC ....G....... 260 348-2610
Fort Wayne *(G-4596)*

Rowan Industries LLC ....G....... 574 302-1203
South Bend *(G-12919)*

S & J Creative Design LLC ....G....... 765 251-0110
Wabash *(G-13754)*

Scaggs Moto Designs ....G....... 765 426-2526
West Lafayette *(G-14106)*

Schmigbob LLC ....G....... 219 781-7991
Crown Point *(G-2300)*

Sebasty Manufacturing Inc ....G....... 574 505-1511
Laketon *(G-9091)*

Shark-Co Mfg LLC. ....G....... 317 670-6397
Lebanon *(G-9223)*

Sherrcom Industries LLC ....G....... 574 266-7389
Elkhart *(G-3165)*

Shields Mech & Fabrication LLC ....G....... 219 863-3972
Demotte *(G-2447)*

SLM Industries LLC ....G....... 317 537-1090
Indianapolis *(G-7952)*

SM Industries LLC ....G....... 219 613-5295
Saint John *(G-12271)*

Smart Pergola ....G....... 317 987-7750
Carmel *(G-1482)*

Smokestack Industries LLC ....G....... 812 267-8646
Elizabeth *(G-2648)*

So Industries LLC ....G....... 765 606-7596
Pendleton *(G-11506)*

Sonner Industries LLC ....G....... 574 370-9387
Middlebury *(G-9919)*

Specialty Manufacturing ....G....... 317 587-4999
Carmel *(G-1484)*

Star Manufacturing LLC ....G....... 574 329-6042
Elkhart *(G-3188)*

Startracks Custom Lifts ....G....... 574 596-5331
Elkhart *(G-3190)*

Strategic Mfg & Sup Inc ....G....... 574 643-1050
South Bend *(G-12957)*

T S Manufacturing ....G....... 574 831-6647
New Paris *(G-10998)*

Tango Romeo Industries LLC ....G....... 765 623-1317
Pendleton *(G-11507)*

Terrapin Mfg ....G....... 717 339-6007
Fort Wayne *(G-4679)*

Thanatos Manufacturing LLC ....G....... 260 251-8498
Portland *(G-11850)*

Thermtron Mfg Inc ....G....... 260 622-6000
Ossian *(G-11413)*

Thomas Strickler ....G....... 574 457-2473
Syracuse *(G-13149)*

Thomson Industries Inc ....G....... 574 529-2496
Syracuse *(G-13150)*

Thoroughbred Industries Inc ....G....... 260 486-8343
Fort Wayne *(G-4683)*

Titus Mfg LLC ....G....... 574 286-1928
Plymouth *(G-11729)*

Tomlinson Manufacturing ....G....... 800 881-9769
Indianapolis *(G-8080)*

Tomlinson Manufacturing ....G....... 317 209-9375
Avon *(G-470)*

Topgard LLC ....G....... 317 525-0700
Indianapolis *(G-8082)*

Topps Industries ....G....... 574 892-5016
Argos *(G-279)*

Trans Industries Incorporated ....G....... 219 977-9190
Gary *(G-5108)*

Transformation Industries LLC ....G....... 574 457-9320
South Bend *(G-12977)*

Tri-State Shtmtl & Mfg LLC ....G....... 260 402-8831
Fort Wayne *(G-4703)*

Trv Industries ....C....... 765 413-2301
Lafayette *(G-9011)*

Ultimate Mfg ....G....... 765 517-1160
Marion *(G-9569)*

Vandelay Industries ....G....... 317 657-6205
Indianapolis *(G-8147)*

Victory Mfg ....G....... 317 731-5063
Indianapolis *(G-8162)*

Wabcoindustries LLC ....G....... 317 361-3653
Indianapolis *(G-8174)*

Wayne Manufacturing LLC ....G....... 260 432-2233
Fort Wayne *(G-4741)*

Whetstone Industries ....G....... 260 724-2461
Decatur *(G-2412)*

White Cap LLC ....G....... 812 425-6221
Evansville *(G-3812)*

Wiley Industries Inc ....G....... 317 574-1477
Carmel *(G-1510)*

Wimmer Mfg Inc ....F....... 765 465-9846
New Castle *(G-10922)*

Windsong K-9 Coach Inc ....G....... 574 971-6358
Elkhart *(G-3260)*

Yellow Cup LLC ....G....... 260 403-3489
Fort Wayne *(G-4763)*

Yes Feed & Supply LLC ....G....... 765 361-9821
Crawfordsville *(G-2206)*

York Tank and Mfg LLC ....F....... 765 401-0667
Kingman *(G-8534)*

MAPMAKING SVCS

Creative Computer Services ....G....... 317 729-5779
Franklin *(G-4880)*

Sepro Corporation ....E....... 317 580-8282
Carmel *(G-1478)*

MARBLE BOARD

Custom Marble Unlimited ....G....... 574 594-2948
Silver Lake *(G-12676)*

MARBLE, BUILDING: Cut & Shaped

Granitech ....E....... 574 674-6988
Elkhart *(G-2893)*

MARINAS

Culvers Port Side Marina ....F....... 574 223-5090
Rochester *(G-12120)*

West Lakes Marine Inc ....F....... 260 854-2525
Rome City *(G-12201)*

MARINE CARGO HANDLING SVCS: Marine Terminal

American Barge Line Company ....G....... 812 288-0100
Jeffersonville *(G-8323)*

American Coml Barge Line LLC ....C....... 812 288-0100
Jeffersonville *(G-8324)*

American Commercial Lines Inc ....C....... 812 288-0100
Jeffersonville *(G-8325)*

Commercial Barge Line Company ....F 812 288-0100
Jeffersonville (G-8341)

MARINE HARDWARE

Epco Products Inc ....E 260 747-8888
Fort Wayne (G-4240)

MARINE RELATED EQPT

Jeffboat LLC ....C 812 288-0200
Jeffersonville (G-8385)

MARINE SPLYS WHOLESALERS

Hoosier Industrial Supply Inc ....F 574 533-8565
Goshen (G-5240)

MARINE SVC STATIONS

West Lakes Marine Inc ....F 260 854-2525
Rome City (G-12201)

MARKETS: Meat & fish

Kroger Co ....C 574 291-0740
South Bend (G-12830)
Lengerich Meats Inc ....E 260 638-4123
Zanesville (G-14413)
Moody Meats ....G 317 272-4533
Avon (G-455)
Royal Center Locker Plant Inc ....F 574 643-3275
Royal Center (G-12213)

MARKING DEVICES

Arben Corp ....F 812 477-7763
Evansville (G-3360)
Bulldog Award Co Inc ....G 317 773-3379
Noblesville (G-11073)
Ehrgotts Signs & Stamps Inc ....G 317 353-2222
Indianapolis (G-6816)
Impressions That Count Inc ....G 317 423-0581
Indianapolis (G-7168)
Indianapolis Rubber Stamp Co ....F 317 263-9540
Indianapolis (G-7204)
J V C Rubber Stamp Company ....G 574 293-0113
Elkhart (G-2943)
Riverside Printing Co ....G 812 275-1950
Bedford (G-574)
S & T Fulfillment LLC ....F 812 466-4900
Terre Haute (G-13323)
Sign A Rama ....G 812 477-7763
Evansville (G-3727)

MARKING DEVICES: Canceling Stamps, Hand, Rubber Or Metal

Toomuchfun Rubberstamps Inc ....G 260 557-4808
Fort Wayne (G-4693)

MARKING DEVICES: Embossing Seals & Hand Stamps

A & M Rubber Stamps Inc ....G 219 836-0892
Munster (G-10591)
Indiana Stamp Co Inc ....E 260 424-8973
Fort Wayne (G-4366)
Plastimatic Arts Corp ....E 574 254-9000
Mishawaka (G-10104)
Stamp Works ....G 765 962-5201
Richmond (G-12054)

MARKING DEVICES: Embossing Seals, Corporate & Official

Seal Corp USA ....G 812 430-8441
Evansville (G-3719)

MARKING DEVICES: Figures, Metal

Tyden Group Holdings Corp ....F 740 420-6777
Angola (G-253)

MARKING DEVICES: Postmark Stamps, Hand, Rubber Or Metal

Stampcrafter ....G 574 892-5206
Argos (G-277)

MARKING DEVICES: Time Stamps, Hand, Rubber Or Metal

Heartfelt Creations Inc ....F 574 773-3088
Goshen (G-5236)

MASQUERADE OR THEATRICAL COSTUMES STORES

Rivars Inc ....E 765 789-6119
Indianapolis (G-7847)

MASSAGE MACHINES, ELECTRIC: Barber & Beauty Shops

Pure Image Laser and Spa LLC ....G 317 306-6603
Indianapolis (G-7790)

MATERIAL GRINDING & PULVERIZING SVCS NEC

Brunk Corp ....E 574 533-1109
Goshen (G-5180)
Walls Lawn & Garden Inc ....G 317 535-9059
Whiteland (G-14247)

MATERIALS HANDLING EQPT WHOLESALERS

B T Bttery Charger Systems Inc ....G 574 533-6030
Goshen (G-5176)
General Material Handling Co ....G 317 888-5735
Indianapolis (G-6998)
Industrial Transmission Eqp ....E 574 936-3028
Plymouth (G-11694)
McGinty Conveyors Inc ....G 317 240-4315
Indianapolis (G-7472)
Shelby Gravel Inc ....F 317 216-7556
Indianapolis (G-7930)
Smock Material Handling Co ....F 317 890-3200
Indianapolis (G-7954)
T & M Equipment Company Inc ....E 219 942-2299
Merrillville (G-9755)

MATS OR MATTING, NEC: Rubber

Jpc LLC ....F 574 293-8030
Elkhart (G-2951)
Pierceton Rubber Products Inc ....F 574 594-3002
Pierceton (G-11577)

MATS, MATTING & PADS: Nonwoven

Circle City Services Ltd ....G 317 770-6287
Noblesville (G-11082)
Mountville Mats ....G 574 753-8858
Logansport (G-9355)

MATS: Table, Plastic & Textile

Ohio Table Pad of Indiana ....E 260 463-2139
Lagrange (G-9062)

MATTRESS STORES

Affordable Furniture ....G 317 881-7726
Greenwood (G-5662)
Crash Beds LLC ....G 317 601-4436
Greenwood (G-5677)
Holder Bedding Inc ....G 765 447-7907
Lafayette (G-8916)
Holder Bedding Inc ....G 765 642-1256
Anderson (G-115)

MEAT & FISH MARKETS: Freezer Provisioners, Meat

Millers Locker Plant ....G 765 234-2381
Crawfordsville (G-2175)

MEAT & MEAT PRDTS WHOLESALERS

A L S Inc ....E 765 497-4750
West Lafayette (G-14045)
Uselman Packing Co ....G 765 832-2112
Clinton (G-1722)

MEAT CUTTING & PACKING

A L S Inc ....E 765 497-4750
West Lafayette (G-14045)

Bains Packing and Rfrgn ....F 260 244-5209
Columbia City (G-1765)
Berne Locker Storage ....G 260 589-2806
Berne (G-608)
Beutler Meat Processing Co ....F 765 742-7285
Lafayette (G-8860)
Brook Locker Plant ....G 219 275-2611
Brook (G-1098)
Butcher Block ....F 219 696-9111
Lowell (G-9401)
C&C Deer Processing ....G 812 836-2323
Tell City (G-13157)
Cannelburg Processing Plant ....G 812 486-3223
Cannelburg (G-1283)
Cargill Incorporated ....B 402 533-4227
Hammond (G-5858)
Dewig Bros Meats ....G 812 768-6208
Haubstadt (G-5998)
Drews Deer Processing ....G 812 279-6246
Mitchell (G-10162)
Fender 4 Star Meats Processing ....G 812 829-3240
Spencer (G-13025)
Ferdinand Processing Inc ....G 812 367-2073
Ferdinand (G-3850)
Foods Peer ....G 317 735-4283
Indianapolis (G-6946)
Griffin Industries LLC ....E 812 379-9528
Columbus (G-1935)
H P Schmitt Packing Co Inc ....G 260 724-3146
Decatur (G-2384)
Hilltop Processing Inc ....G 812 544-2174
Lamar (G-9100)
Hobart Locker & Meat Pkg Co ....G 219 942-5952
Crown Point (G-2257)
Hrr Enterprises Inc ....G 219 362-9050
La Porte (G-8768)
Johns Butcher Shop ....G 574 773-4632
Nappanee (G-10688)
K W Deer Processing ....G 812 824-2492
Bloomington (G-756)
Kenny Dewig Meats Sausage Inc ....G 812 724-2333
Owensville (G-11428)
Lengerich Meats Inc ....E 260 638-4123
Zanesville (G-14413)
Manley Meats Inc ....E 260 592-7313
Decatur (G-2392)
Mariah Foods Corp ....C 812 378-3366
Columbus (G-1967)
Merkley & Sons Inc ....E 812 482-7020
Jasper (G-8295)
Milan Food Bank ....G 812 654-3682
Milan (G-9945)
Monon Meat Packing Company ....G 219 253-6363
Monon (G-10177)
Moody Meats ....G 317 272-4533
Avon (G-455)
Mpi Holdings Inc ....C 765 473-3086
Peru (G-11538)
Orange County Processing ....F 812 865-2028
Orleans (G-11366)
Ortman Meat Processing Inc ....G 574 946-7113
Winamac (G-14313)
Parretts Meat Proc & Catrg ....F 574 967-3711
Flora (G-4001)
Pates Slaughtering & Proc ....G 812 866-4710
Hanover (G-5963)
Rihm Inc ....G 765 478-3426
Cambridge City (G-1260)
Royal Center Locker Plant Inc ....F 574 643-3275
Royal Center (G-12213)
Sander Processing ....E 812 481-0044
Celestine (G-1537)
Slabaughs Meat Processing ....G 574 773-0381
Nappanee (G-10706)
Smithfield Direct LLC ....G 812 867-6644
Evansville (G-3738)
Smithfield Direct LLC ....E 765 473-3086
Peru (G-11545)
Smithland Butchering Co Inc ....G 317 729-5398
Elizabethtown (G-2651)
Tyson Foods Inc ....A 574 753-6121
Logansport (G-9373)
Uselman Packing Co ....G 765 832-2112
Clinton (G-1722)
W & W Locker ....G 260 344-3400
Andrews (G-185)
Wilsons Locker & Proc Plant ....G 812 358-2632
Brownstown (G-1194)
Yoders Meats Inc ....G 260 768-4715
Shipshewana (G-12660)

MEAT MARKETS

Brook Locker Plant	G	219 275-2611
Brook (G-1098)		
Dewig Bros Packing Co Inc	E	812 768-6208
Haubstadt (G-5999)		
Fisher Packing Company	E	260 726-7355
Portland (G-11822)		
Jemdd LLC	E	260 768-4156
Lagrange (G-9049)		
Johns Butcher Shop	G	574 773-4632
Nappanee (G-10688)		
Klemms Meat Market	G	317 632-1963
Indianapolis (G-7357)		
Manley Meats Inc	E	260 592-7313
Decatur (G-2392)		
Merkley & Sons Inc	E	812 482-7020
Jasper (G-8295)		
Parretts Meat Proc & Catrg	F	574 967-3711
Flora (G-4001)		
Yoders Meats Inc	G	260 768-4715
Shipshewana (G-12660)		

MEAT PRDTS: Bacon, Side & Sliced, From Purchased Meat

Plumrose USA Inc	C	574 295-8190
Elkhart (G-3100)		

MEAT PRDTS: Canned

Big B Distributors Inc	F	812 425-5235
Evansville (G-3384)		
Manley Meats Inc	E	260 592-7313
Decatur (G-2392)		

MEAT PRDTS: Cured, From Slaughtered Meat

Myers Frozen Food Provisioners	G	765 525-6304
Saint Paul (G-12279)		

MEAT PRDTS: Dried Beef, From Purchased Meat

Farm Boy Meats of Evansville	C	812 425-5231
Evansville (G-3498)		

MEAT PRDTS: Frozen

Park 100 Foods Inc	E	317 549-4545
Indianapolis (G-7656)		
Park 100 Foods Inc	D	765 675-3480
Tipton (G-13400)		
Park 100 Foods Inc	D	765 763-6064
Morristown (G-10375)		

MEAT PRDTS: Lamb, From Slaughtered Meat

Onu Acre LLC	G	765 565-1355
Carthage (G-1515)		
Ruwaldt Packing Co Inc	E	219 942-2911
Hobart (G-6093)		

MEAT PRDTS: Meat By-Prdts, From Slaughtered Meat

Old Hoosier Meats	G	574 825-2940
Middlebury (G-9913)		

MEAT PRDTS: Pigs Feet, Cooked & Pickled, From Purchased Meat

Perfect Pig Inc	G	219 984-5355
Reynolds (G-11947)		

MEAT PRDTS: Pork, From Slaughtered Meat

Cherrytree Farms LLC	F	317 758-4495
Sheridan (G-12588)		
Dewig Bros Packing Co Inc	E	812 768-6208
Haubstadt (G-5999)		
H & B Pork Inc	G	219 261-3053
Wolcott (G-14364)		
Indiana Packers Corporation	A	765 564-3680
Delphi (G-2422)		
Kane-Miller Corp	E	219 362-9050
La Porte (G-8775)		
Tyson Fresh Meats Inc	B	574 753-6134
Logansport (G-9374)		

MEAT PRDTS: Prepared Pork Prdts, From Purchased Meat

Cottonwood Corp	G	260 820-0415
Ossian (G-11398)		
Grandma Hams Farm LLC	G	317 253-0635
Indianapolis (G-7035)		
Paytons Barbecue	G	765 294-2716
Veedersburg (G-13645)		

MEAT PRDTS: Roast Beef, From Purchased Meat

Zels	E	219 864-1011
Schererville (G-12353)		

MEAT PRDTS: Sausages & Related Prdts, From Purchased Meat

Saint Adrian Meats Sausage LLC	G	317 403-3305
Lebanon (G-9221)		

MEAT PRDTS: Sausages, From Purchased Meat

Klemms Meat Market	G	317 632-1963
Indianapolis (G-7357)		

MEAT PRDTS: Sausages, From Slaughtered Meat

Bob Evans Farms Inc	G	317 846-3261
Carmel (G-1319)		

MEAT PRDTS: Snack Sticks, Incl Jerky, From Purchased Meat

Cosmos Superior Foods LLC	G	317 975-2747
Carmel (G-1345)		

MEAT PROCESSED FROM PURCHASED CARCASSES

A L S Inc	E	765 497-4750
West Lafayette (G-14045)		
Butcher Block	F	219 696-9111
Lowell (G-9401)		
Conagra Brands Inc	B	402 240-5000
Indianapolis (G-6645)		
Cottonwood Corp	G	260 565-3185
Craigville (G-2121)		
El Popular Sausage Factory LLC	G	219 476-7040
Valparaiso (G-13532)		
Fisher Packing Company	E	260 726-7355
Portland (G-11822)		
Grabill Country Meat 1 Inc	F	260 627-3691
Grabill (G-5369)		
Hillshire Brands Company	G	260 456-4802
Fort Wayne (G-4335)		
Hilltop Processing Inc	G	812 544-2174
Lamar (G-9100)		
Indiana Packers Corporation	A	765 564-3680
Delphi (G-2422)		
Jemdd LLC	E	260 768-4156
Lagrange (G-9049)		
Merkley & Sons Inc	E	812 482-7020
Jasper (G-8295)		
Millers Locker Plant	G	765 234-2381
Crawfordsville (G-2175)		
Monogram Frozen Foods LLC	C	574 848-0344
Bristol (G-1072)		
Mpi Holdings Inc	C	765 473-3086
Peru (G-11538)		
Parretts Meat Proc & Catrg	F	574 967-3711
Flora (G-4001)		
Pates Slaughtering & Proc	G	812 866-4710
Hanover (G-5963)		
Rihm Inc	G	765 478-3426
Cambridge City (G-1260)		
Royal Center Locker Plant Inc	F	574 643-3275
Royal Center (G-12213)		
Rubicon Foods LLC	F	317 826-8793
Indianapolis (G-7872)		
Ruwaldt Packing Co Inc	E	219 942-2911
Hobart (G-6093)		
Sander Processing	E	812 481-0044
Celestine (G-1537)		
Tyson Foods Inc	A	574 753-6121
Logansport (G-9373)		
Tyson Fresh Meats Inc	E	812 486-2800
Washington (G-14005)		
Wilsons Locker & Proc Plant	G	812 358-2632
Brownstown (G-1194)		
Wolfs Bar B Q Inc	D	812 424-8891
Evansville (G-3814)		
Yoders Meats Inc	G	260 768-4715
Shipshewana (G-12660)		

MEATS, PACKAGED FROZEN: Wholesalers

Farm Boy Meats of Evansville	C	812 425-5231
Evansville (G-3498)		
Myers Frozen Food Provisioners	G	765 525-6304
Saint Paul (G-12279)		

MEDIA: Magnetic & Optical Recording

Optical Media Mfg Inc	E	317 822-1850
Indianapolis (G-7630)		
R B Annis Instruments Inc	G	765 848-1621
Greencastle (G-5476)		
Sony Corporation of America	G	812 462-8726
Terre Haute (G-13332)		

MEDICAL & HOSPITAL EQPT WHOLESALERS

All About Organizing	G	513 238-8157
Lawrenceburg (G-9130)		
Biomet Inc	G	574 372-6999
Warsaw (G-13848)		
Kilgore Manufacturing Co Inc	D	260 248-2002
Columbia City (G-1804)		
Merrill Corporation	F	574 255-2988
Mishawaka (G-10078)		
Standard Fusee Corporation	E	765 472-4375
Peru (G-11548)		
Tier 1 Medical LLC	G	317 316-7871
Carmel (G-1497)		

MEDICAL & SURGICAL SPLYS: Absorbent Cotton, Sterilized

Beltone Hearing Care	G	812 274-4116
Madison (G-9446)		

MEDICAL & SURGICAL SPLYS: Bandages & Dressings

3M Company	B	317 692-6666
Indianapolis (G-6288)		
Current Technologies Inc	F	765 364-0490
Crawfordsville (G-2147)		

MEDICAL & SURGICAL SPLYS: Belts, Linemen's Safety

Automated Weapon Security Inc	G	860 559-7176
Indianapolis (G-6443)		

MEDICAL & SURGICAL SPLYS: Braces, Orthopedic

Advanced Orthopro Inc	E	317 924-4444
Indianapolis (G-6334)		
Calumet Orthpd Prosthetics Co	G	219 942-2148
Hobart (G-6072)		
Central Brace & Limb Co Inc	G	812 232-2145
Terre Haute (G-13207)		
Central Brace & Limb Co Inc	G	317 872-1596
Indianapolis (G-6579)		
Circle City Medical Inc	E	317 228-1144
Carmel (G-1338)		
Midwest Orthotic Services LLC	E	219 736-9960
Merrillville (G-9733)		
Midwest Orthotic Services LLC	D	574 233-3352
South Bend (G-12863)		
Ultra Athlete LLC	G	317 520-9898
Carmel (G-1502)		

MEDICAL & SURGICAL SPLYS: Clothing, Fire Resistant & Protect

1st Choice Safety LLC	G	260 797-5338
Fort Wayne (G-4032)		

MEDICAL & SURGICAL SPLYS: Ear Plugs

Aearo Technologies LLC	A	317 692-6666
Indianapolis (G-6341)		

Custom Outfitted Protection..................G........ 317 373-2092
  Indianapolis *(G-6716)*

MEDICAL & SURGICAL SPLYS: *Foot Appliances, Orthopedic*

Positrax Inc....................................D....... 317 293-4858
  Indianapolis *(G-7708)*

MEDICAL & SURGICAL SPLYS: *Ligatures*

Alli Medical LLC..............................G...... 317 625-4535
  Westfield *(G-14134)*

MEDICAL & SURGICAL SPLYS: *Limbs, Artificial*

Advanced Limb Wound Care..............G....... 812 232-0957
  Terre Haute *(G-13187)*
American Limb & Orthopedic Co ....G....... 574 522-3643
  Elkhart *(G-2684)*
Central Brace & Limb Co Inc ....G....... 765 457-4868
  Kokomo *(G-8605)*
Hanger Prsthetcs & Ortho Inc............F....... 219 844-2021
  Hammond *(G-5889)*
Hanger Prsthetcs & Ortho Inc............G....... 765 966-5069
  Richmond *(G-11995)*
Mobile Limb & Brace Inc ....G....... 765 463-4100
  West Lafayette *(G-14087)*
Orthotic & Prosthetic Lab ....F....... 812 479-6298
  Evansville *(G-3657)*
Orthotic Prosthetic Specialist............G....... 219 836-8668
  Munster *(G-10620)*
Prevail Prsthtics Orthtics Inc.............G....... 260 969-0605
  Fort Wayne *(G-4560)*
Transmed Associates Inc ....G....... 317 293-9993
  Avon *(G-471)*

MEDICAL & SURGICAL SPLYS: *Orthopedic Appliances*

Biomet Inc......................................A....... 574 267-6639
  Warsaw *(G-13845)*
Biopoly LLC ....E....... 260 999-6135
  Fort Wayne *(G-4109)*
Central Brace & Limb Co Inc ....F....... 317 925-4296
  Indianapolis *(G-6578)*
Cooks Fabrication Inc ....G....... 317 782-1722
  Indianapolis *(G-6661)*
Crossroads Orthotics & Cnsltn ....G....... 765 359-0041
  Crawfordsville *(G-2145)*
Del Palma Orthopedics Llc ....G....... 260 625-3169
  Columbia City *(G-1778)*
Jatex Inc...F....... 574 773-5928
  Nappanee *(G-10687)*
M & A Orthotics Inc ....G....... 317 281-5253
  Fishers *(G-3941)*
Midwest Orthotic Services LLC ....G....... 317 334-1114
  Indianapolis *(G-7509)*
Neull Incorporated ....G....... 574 267-5575
  Warsaw *(G-13912)*
Northern Brace Co Inc.......................G....... 574 233-4221
  South Bend *(G-12878)*
Precision Medical Tech Inc ....E....... 574 267-6385
  Warsaw *(G-13928)*
Rayco Steel Process Inc ....F....... 574 267-7676
  Warsaw *(G-13932)*
Rmi Holdings LLC..............................E....... 317 214-7076
  Warsaw *(G-13936)*
Soley Orthotics LLC ....G....... 317 373-7395
  Indianapolis *(G-7962)*
Symmetry Medical Inc ....G....... 574 268-2252
  Warsaw *(G-13948)*
Triple Inc ....G....... 574 267-1450
  Warsaw *(G-13954)*
Zimmer Inc......................................B....... 330 343-8801
  Warsaw *(G-13971)*
Zimmer Inc......................................G....... 574 268-3100
  Warsaw *(G-13972)*
Zimmer Inc......................................G....... 574 371-1557
  Warsaw *(G-13973)*
Zimmer Inc......................................G....... 574 267-6131
  Warsaw *(G-13974)*
Zimmer Production Inc ....G....... 574 267-6131
  Warsaw *(G-13976)*
Zimmer Us Inc ....D....... 574 267-6131
  Warsaw *(G-13977)*

MEDICAL & SURGICAL SPLYS: *Personal Safety Eqpt*

Accra-Pac Inc ....D....... 574 295-0000
  Elkhart *(G-2665)*
Cortex Safety Technologies LLC...........G....... 317 414-5607
  Carmel *(G-1344)*
Infinity Products Inc ....G....... 317 272-3435
  Avon *(G-448)*
Patriot Safety Products LLC ....G....... 317 945-7023
  Fountaintown *(G-4792)*
Peyton Technical Services LLC ....F....... 812 738-2016
  Corydon *(G-2107)*
Safety Wear Fort Wayne ....E....... 260 456-3535
  Fort Wayne *(G-4602)*
Steel Grip Inc...................................D....... 765 793-3652
  Covington *(G-2120)*
Steel Grip Inc...................................D....... 765 397-3344
  Kingman *(G-8533)*
TW Enterprises LLC...........................G....... 513 520-8453
  Brookville *(G-1128)*

MEDICAL & SURGICAL SPLYS: *Prosthetic Appliances*

Action Brace and Prosthetics..............F....... 317 347-4222
  Indianapolis *(G-6321)*
Bionic Prosthetics and Ortho ....G....... 219 791-9200
  Merrillville *(G-9701)*
Bionic Prosthetics and Ortho ....G....... 219 221-6119
  Michigan City *(G-9769)*
Central Brace & Limb Co Inc ....G....... 812 334-2524
  Bloomington *(G-698)*
Hanger Prsthetcs & Ortho Inc ....G....... 317 818-1459
  Indianapolis *(G-6267)*
Hanger Prsthetcs & Ortho Inc ....G....... 317 923-2351
  Indianapolis *(G-7069)*
Hanger Prsthetcs & Ortho Inc ....F....... 260 456-5998
  Fort Wayne *(G-4318)*
Hanger Prsthetcs & Ortho Inc ....G....... 812 235-6451
  Terre Haute *(G-13244)*
Johnsons Orthotics Prosthetics ....G....... 317 272-9993
  Avon *(G-450)*
Magnolia ....G....... 317 831-3221
  Jasper *(G-8289)*
Maxcare Orthtics Prsthtics LLC ....G....... 574 267-5852
  Warsaw *(G-13905)*
Midwest Orthotic Services LLC ....G....... 574 233-3352
  Fort Wayne *(G-4472)*
Northern Prosthetics Inc ....G....... 574 233-2459
  South Bend *(G-12880)*
Prevail Prsthtics Orthtics Inc ....G....... 317 577-2273
  Indianapolis *(G-7745)*
Prevail Prsthtics Orthtics Inc ....G....... 765 668-0890
  Fort Wayne *(G-4558)*
Prevail Prsthtics Orthtics Inc ....E....... 260 483-5219
  Fort Wayne *(G-4559)*
Srt Prosthetics Orthotics LLC ....G....... 815 679-6900
  Butler *(G-1241)*
Srt Prosthetics Orthotics LLC ....G....... 847 855-0030
  Butler *(G-1242)*
Wiley Young & Associates ....G....... 574 269-7006
  Warsaw *(G-13967)*

MEDICAL & SURGICAL SPLYS: *Supports, Abdominal, Ankle, Etc*

Active Ankle Systems Inc ....F....... 812 258-0663
  Jeffersonville *(G-8320)*

MEDICAL & SURGICAL SPLYS: *Technical Aids, Handicapped*

Mobility Vehicles Indiana LLC ....G....... 317 471-7169
  Knightstown *(G-8558)*
Sensorycritterscom ....G....... 260 373-0900
  Fort Wayne *(G-4617)*

MEDICAL & SURGICAL SPLYS: *Trusses, Orthopedic & Surgical*

United Ortho ....F....... 260 422-5827
  Fort Wayne *(G-4717)*

MEDICAL & SURGICAL SPLYS: *Walkers*

Assistive Technology Inc ....G....... 574 522-7201
  Elkhart *(G-2699)*
Walker Information Inc ....F....... 317 843-3939
  Indianapolis *(G-8176)*

MEDICAL & SURGICAL SPLYS: *Welders' Hoods*

Brewer Machine & Mfg Inc ....E....... 317 398-3505
  Shelbyville *(G-12525)*

MEDICAL CENTERS

Advanced Mbility Solutions LLC ....G....... 812 438-2338
  Rising Sun *(G-12085)*

MEDICAL EQPT REPAIR SVCS, NON-ELECTRIC

Merss Corporation ....G....... 317 632-7299
  Indianapolis *(G-7484)*

MEDICAL EQPT: *Defibrillators*

Aeds & Safety Services LLC ....G....... 502 641-3118
  Jeffersonville *(G-8321)*

MEDICAL EQPT: *Diagnostic*

Bayer Healthcare LLC.........................E....... 574 262-6136
  Elkhart *(G-2716)*
Bbs Enterprises Inc ....E....... 574 255-3173
  Mishawaka *(G-10006)*
Bcd & Associates ....G....... 317 873-5394
  Zionsville *(G-14421)*
Community Diagnostic Center ....G....... 219 836-4599
  Munster *(G-10601)*
Fort Wyne Rdlgy Assn Fundation ....F....... 260 266-8120
  Fort Wayne *(G-4283)*
Integrated Biomedical Tech ....F....... 574 264-0025
  Elkhart *(G-2937)*
Magitek LLC......................................G....... 260 488-2226
  Hamilton *(G-5825)*
Miftek Corporation ....G....... 765 491-3848
  West Lafayette *(G-14085)*
Polymer Technology Systems Inc ....D....... 317 870-5610
  Indianapolis *(G-7706)*
R 2 Diagnostics Inc...........................G....... 574 288-4377
  South Bend *(G-12910)*
Reed Immunodiagnostics LLC ....G....... 317 446-3582
  Indianapolis *(G-7826)*
Restoration Med Polymers LLC............G....... 260 625-1573
  Columbia City *(G-1825)*
Sundance Enterprises Inc....................E....... 317 856-9780
  Indianapolis *(G-8019)*

MEDICAL EQPT: *Electromedical Apparatus*

Biomet Europe Ltd ....G....... 574 267-2038
  Warsaw *(G-13847)*
Covidien LP ....C....... 317 837-8199
  Plainfield *(G-11602)*
Innovtive Nurological Dvcs LLC ....G....... 317 674-2999
  Carmel *(G-1416)*
Morel Company Llc ....F....... 812 932-6100
  Batesville *(G-511)*
Philips Ultrasound Inc ....F....... 317 591-5242
  Indianapolis *(G-7684)*

MEDICAL EQPT: *Electrotherapeutic Apparatus*

Bionode LLC.....................................G....... 317 292-7686
  Indianapolis *(G-6476)*

MEDICAL EQPT: *Heart-Lung Machines, Exc Iron Lungs*

Indiana Laser Spine Center.................G....... 317 577-1800
  Indianapolis *(G-7181)*

MEDICAL EQPT: *Laser Systems*

C Laser Inc......................................G....... 317 641-5185
  Kokomo *(G-8603)*

MEDICAL EQPT: *Pacemakers*

Cook Group Incorporated ....F....... 812 339-2235
  Bloomington *(G-704)*

MEDICAL EQPT: *Patient Monitoring*

Cascade Metrix LLC...........................G....... 317 572-7094
  Fishers *(G-3886)*
Pda Solutions LLC ....G....... 219 629-4658
  Munster *(G-10622)*

PRODUCT

MEDICAL EQPT: Ultrasonic Scanning Devices

Nanosonics Inc ....E....... 844 876-7466
Indianapolis (G-7569)
Orthoconcepts Inc ....G....... 317 727-0100
Indianapolis (G-7632)
Radiation Physics Consulting ....G....... 317 251-0193
Indianapolis (G-7814)

MEDICAL EQPT: Ultrasonic, Exc Cleaning

Esaote North America Inc ....D....... 317 813-6000
Fishers (G-3907)
Focus Surgery Inc ....F....... 317 541-1580
Indianapolis (G-6944)
Point Care Ultrasound LP ....G....... 317 459-8113
Indianapolis (G-7704)
Sonacare Medical LLC ....E....... 888 874-4384
Indianapolis (G-7963)

MEDICAL FIELD ASSOCIATION

Indiana State Medical Assn ....E....... 317 261-2060
Indianapolis (G-7192)

MEDICAL RESCUE SQUAD

Tier 1 Medical LLC ....G....... 317 316-7871
Carmel (G-1497)

MEDICAL, DENTAL & HOSPITAL EQPT, WHOL: Hosptl Eqpt/Furniture

Williams Bros Health Care Inc ....E....... 812 257-2505
Washington (G-14007)
Williams Bros Health Care Pha ....E....... 812 335-0000
Bloomington (G-856)

MEDICAL, DENTAL & HOSPITAL EQPT, WHOLESALE: Med Eqpt & Splys

Active Ankle Systems Inc ....F....... 812 258-0663
Jeffersonville (G-8320)
Adaptive Mobility Inc ....F....... 317 347-6400
Indianapolis (G-6323)
After Action Med Dntl Sup LLC ....G....... 317 831-2699
Indianapolis (G-6351)
Bryton Corporation ....F....... 317 334-8700
Indianapolis (G-6516)
Cook Incorporated ....C....... 812 876-7790
Bloomington (G-706)
Indy Medical Supplies LLC ....G....... 866 744-9013
Zionsville (G-14439)
Med-Rep Inc ....F....... 317 574-0497
Carmel (G-1436)
Merss Corporation ....G....... 317 632-7299
Indianapolis (G-7484)
Plastic Assembly Tech Inc ....G....... 317 841-1202
Indianapolis (G-7700)
Roche Health Solutions Inc ....C....... 317 570-5100
Indianapolis (G-7853)
T H S International Inc ....G....... 317 759-2869
Indianapolis (G-8033)
Williams Bros Health Care Pha ....C....... 812 254-2497
Washington (G-14008)

MEDICAL, DENTAL & HOSPITAL EQPT, WHOLESALE: Orthopedic

LH Medical Corporation ....D....... 260 387-5194
Fort Wayne (G-4432)
Triple Inc ....G....... 574 267-1450
Warsaw (G-13954)

MEDICAL, DENTAL & HOSPITAL EQPT, WHOLESALE: Safety

Ascensia Diabetes Care US Inc ....E....... 201 875-8066
Mishawaka (G-9998)
TW Enterprises LLC.............................G....... 513 520-8453
Brookville (G-1128)

MEDICAL, DENTAL/HOSPITAL EQPT, WHOL: Veterinarian Eqpt/Sply

Campbell Pet Company ....G....... 812 692-5208
Elnora (G-3287)

MEMBERSHIP ORGANIZATIONS, LABOR UNIONS & SIMILAR: Trade

Dist Council 91 ....G....... 812 962-9191
Evansville (G-3459)

MEMBERSHIP ORGANIZATIONS, NEC: Charitable

Apartment Assn of Fort Wayne ....G....... 260 482-2916
Fort Wayne (G-4080)
Goodwill Inds of Centl Ind.....................E....... 317 587-0281
Carmel (G-1388)

MEMBERSHIP ORGANIZATIONS, NEC: Personal Interest

Academy of Mdel Aronautics Inc ....D....... 765 287-1256
Muncie (G-10422)
Fourth Freedom Forum Inc ....F....... 574 534-3402
Goshen (G-5221)

MEMBERSHIP ORGANIZATIONS, PROFESSIONAL: Health Association

American School Health Assn ....G....... 703 506-7675
Bloomington (G-660)

MEMBERSHIP ORGANIZATIONS, REL: Churches, Temples & Shrines

Wesleyan Church Corporation ....D....... 317 774-7900
Fishers (G-3984)

MEMBERSHIP ORGANIZATIONS, RELIGIOUS: Baptist Church

Boeke Road Baptist Church Inc ....G....... 812 479-5342
Evansville (G-3389)

MEMBERSHIP ORGANIZATIONS, RELIGIOUS: Nonchurch

Catholic Press of Evansville ....G....... 812 424-5536
Evansville (G-3414)
Old Paths Tract Society Inc ....F....... 812 247-2560
Shoals (G-12668)

MEMBERSHIP ORGS, RELIGIOUS: Non-Denominational Church

World Rdo Mssnary Fllwship Inc...........E....... 574 970-4252
Elkhart (G-3268)

MEMORIALS, MONUMENTS & MARKERS

Thomas Monuments Inc.......................G....... 317 244-6525
Indianapolis (G-8065)

MEN'S & BOYS' CLOTHING ACCESS STORES

Gohn Bros Manufacturing Co...............G....... 574 825-2400
Middlebury (G-9889)

MEN'S & BOYS' CLOTHING WHOLESALERS, NEC

Ram Graphics Inc ....E....... 765 724-7783
Alexandria (G-48)

MEN'S & BOYS' HATS STORES

Country Stitches Embroidery ....G....... 219 324-7625
La Porte (G-8746)
Mammoth Hats Inc ....F....... 812 849-2772
Mitchell (G-10166)

MEN'S & BOYS' SPORTSWEAR CLOTHING STORES

Goods On Target Sporting Inc ....G....... 812 623-2300
Sunman (G-13111)

MEN'S & BOYS' SPORTSWEAR WHOLESALERS

Arizona Sport Shirts Inc ....E....... 317 481-2160
Indianapolis (G-6419)

Locoli Inc ....E....... 219 365-3125
Schererville (G-12332)
Sport Form Inc ....G....... 260 589-2200
Berne (G-625)

MERCHANDISING MACHINE OPERATORS: Vending

Refreshment Services Inc ....E....... 812 466-0602
Terre Haute (G-13318)

MESH, REINFORCING: Plastic

ABC Industries Inc ....D....... 800 426-0921
Winona Lake (G-14349)

METAL & STEEL PRDTS: Abrasive

Hi-Perfrmnce Sperabrasives Inc...........G....... 317 899-1050
Indianapolis (G-7104)

METAL COMPONENTS: Prefabricated

Metal Resources Inc ....G....... 219 886-2710
Gary (G-5075)
Nci Group Inc ....E....... 317 392-3536
Shelbyville (G-12553)

METAL CUTTING SVCS

Ad-Vance Magnetics Inc......................E....... 574 223-3158
Rochester (G-12113)
Chicago Steel Ltd Partnership..............G....... 219 949-1111
Gary (G-5037)
Culver Tool & Engineering Inc ....D....... 574 935-9611
Plymouth (G-11678)
Gammons Metal & Mfg Co Inc ....D....... 317 546-7091
Indianapolis (G-6982)
Great Lakes Waterjet Inc ....G....... 574 651-2158
Granger (G-5411)
Progress Rail Services Corp.................C....... 219 397-5326
East Chicago (G-2565)
Tri-State Metals Inc ....E....... 219 397-0470
East Chicago (G-2574)

METAL DETECTORS

Discount Detector Sales Inc ....G....... 765 866-0320
Crawfordsville (G-2149)
Mikes Metal Dectors ....G....... 812 366-3558
Georgetown (G-5150)
New Concept Metal Detector ....G....... 765 447-2681
Lafayette (G-8976)

METAL FABRICATORS: Architechtural

American Stair Corporation Inc.............D....... 815 886-9600
Hammond (G-5841)
Artisan Sheet Metal Corp ....G....... 812 422-7393
Wadesville (G-13770)
B & L Sheet Metal & Roofing ....F....... 812 332-4309
Bloomington (G-670)
Builders Iron Works Inc.......................E....... 574 254-1553
Mishawaka (G-10014)
Coffee Lomont & Moyer Inc ....F....... 260 422-7825
Fort Wayne (G-4166)
Custom Interior Dynamics LLC ....F....... 317 632-0477
Indianapolis (G-6714)
De Vols Ornamental Iron ....G....... 765 482-1171
Lebanon (G-9180)
Dpc Inc ....E....... 765 564-3752
Delphi (G-2419)
Flag & Banner Company Inc ....F....... 317 299-4880
Indianapolis (G-6931)
G & N Fabrications LLC ....G....... 317 698-9539
Carmel (G-1383)
Gammons Metal & Mfg Co Inc ....D....... 317 546-7091
Indianapolis (G-6982)
General Crafts Corp ....G....... 574 533-1936
Goshen (G-5223)
Goudy Brothers Boiler Co Inc ....E....... 765 459-4416
Kokomo (G-8631)
Hampton Ironworks Inc ....G....... 219 929-6448
Chesterton (G-1611)
Imperial Stamping Corporation ....D....... 574 294-3780
Elkhart (G-2930)
Imperial Trophy & Awards Co ....G....... 260 432-8161
Fort Wayne (G-4361)
Independent Protection Co Inc ....C....... 574 533-4116
Goshen (G-5242)
Indiana Gratings Inc ....F....... 765 342-7191
Martinsville (G-9615)

(G-0000) Company's Geographic Section entry number

Industrial Contrs Skanska Inc ....E 812 423-7832
  Evansville *(G-3555)*
J A Smit Inc..................................G 812 424-8141
  Evansville *(G-3568)*
Jones & Sons Inc ....E 812 882-2957
  Vincennes *(G-13687)*
Kawneer Company Inc ....E 317 882-2314
  Greenwood *(G-5712)*
Leons Fabrication Inc ....F 219 365-5272
  Schererville *(G-12330)*
Metal Sales Manufacturing Corp ....E 812 941-0041
  New Albany *(G-10827)*
Mofab Inc.................................G 765 649-1288
  Anderson *(G-139)*
Parkers Custom Ironworks LLC ....G 812 897-3007
  Boonville *(G-920)*
Power Train Corp Fort Wayne ....F 317 241-9393
  Indianapolis *(G-7712)*
Refax Wear Products Inc ....G 219 977-0414
  Gary *(G-5091)*
Reiss Orna & Structurall Pdts ....E 317 925-2371
  Indianapolis *(G-7830)*
Rettig Enterprises Inc....................G 765 567-2441
  West Lafayette *(G-14102)*
Richardson Imaging Svcs Inc ....G 888 561-0007
  New Albany *(G-10855)*
Rock Run Industries LLC ....E 574 361-0848
  Millersburg *(G-9972)*
S S M Inc ....G 317 357-4552
  Indianapolis *(G-7880)*
San Jo Steel Inc ....F 317 888-6227
  Greenwood *(G-5747)*
Sharps Baton Mfg Corp ....G 574 214-9389
  Elkhart *(G-3164)*
Sigma Steel Inc ....E 812 275-4489
  Bedford *(G-578)*
Sisson Steel Inc ....F 812 354-8701
  Winslow *(G-14359)*
Stevens Ironworks Inc ....E 219 987-6332
  Demotte *(G-2448)*
Titus Inc ....F 574 936-3345
  Plymouth *(G-11728)*
Vans Iron Works ....G 219 934-1935
  Munster *(G-10636)*
Wiw Inc..................................E 219 663-7900
  Crown Point *(G-2321)*

METAL FABRICATORS: Plate

A & B Fabricating & Maint Inc..............F 574 353-1012
  Mentone *(G-9684)*
Ace Welding and Machine Inc ....G 812 379-9625
  Columbus *(G-1849)*
Aearo Technologies LLC ....C 317 692-6666
  Indianapolis *(G-6342)*
Allied Boiler & Welding Co.................G 317 272-4820
  Avon *(G-426)*
Aluminum Wldg & Mch Works Inc..........G 219 787-8066
  Chesterton *(G-1592)*
Asphalt Equipment Company Inc..........G 260 672-3004
  Fort Wayne *(G-4093)*
Banks Machine & Engrg Inc ....D 317 642-4980
  Shelbyville *(G-12519)*
Batesville Products Inc ....D 513 381-2057
  Lawrenceburg *(G-9133)*
Buhrt Engineering & Cnstr.................E 574 267-3720
  Warsaw *(G-13852)*
Carmel Engineering Inc ....F 765 279-8955
  Kirklin *(G-8547)*
Carr Metal Products Inc....................C 317 542-0691
  Indianapolis *(G-6558)*
Chegar Manufacturing Co Inc ....E 765 945-7444
  Windfall *(G-14347)*
Coffee Lomont & Moyer Inc ....F 260 422-7825
  Fort Wayne *(G-4166)*
Contech Engnered Solutions LLC........G 317 407-4914
  Fishers *(G-3893)*
Contech Engnered Solutions LLC........F 317 842-7766
  Indianapolis *(G-6655)*
Contech Engnered Solutions LLC........E 812 849-3933
  Mitchell *(G-10159)*
Contech Engnered Solutions LLC........E 812 849-3933
  Mitchell *(G-10160)*
Croy Machine & Fabrication ....G 260 565-3682
  Bluffton *(G-871)*
Dietrich Industries Inc ....C 219 931-3741
  Hammond *(G-5870)*
Don R Fruchey Inc ....E 260 493-3626
  Fort Wayne *(G-4218)*
Dpc Inc..................................E 765 564-3752
  Delphi *(G-2419)*

Dyna-Fab Corporation......................E 765 893-4423
  West Lebanon *(G-14119)*
Elsie Manufacturing Co Inc...............G 260 837-8841
  Waterloo *(G-14013)*
Erapsco ....G 260 248-3524
  Columbia City *(G-1783)*
F D Ramsey & Co Inc.......................F 219 362-2452
  La Porte *(G-8757)*
Four Star Fabricators Inc ....D 812 354-9995
  Petersburg *(G-11562)*
Galbreath LLC ....D 574 946-6631
  Winamac *(G-14305)*
Goudy Brothers Boiler Co Inc ....E 765 459-4416
  Kokomo *(G-8631)*
Grant County Steel Inc ....F 765 668-7547
  Marion *(G-9527)*
Greenfield Feeders Inc ....F 317 462-6363
  Greenfield *(G-5534)*
Industrial Contrs Skanska Inc ....E 812 423-7832
  Evansville *(G-3555)*
Industrial Metal-Fab Inc ....E 574 288-8368
  South Bend *(G-12812)*
Industrial Steel Cnstr Inc..................C 219 885-5610
  Gary *(G-5069)*
Industrial Transmission Eqp ....G 574 936-3028
  Plymouth *(G-11694)*
Ira Preservation Partners ....G 317 722-0710
  Indianapolis *(G-7267)*
J & J Welding Inc ....E 812 838-4391
  Mount Vernon *(G-10396)*
J A Smit Inc..................................G 812 424-8141
  Evansville *(G-3568)*
Kammerer Inc ....G 260 347-0389
  Kendallville *(G-8485)*
Kokomo Metal Fabricators Inc............G 765 459-8173
  Kokomo *(G-8653)*
Lakeview Engineered Pdts Inc ....G 260 432-3479
  Fort Wayne *(G-4422)*
Leons Fabrication Inc ....F 219 365-5272
  Schererville *(G-12330)*
Lippert Components Inc...................D 574 535-1125
  Goshen *(G-5268)*
M & S Steel Corp ....E 260 357-5184
  Garrett *(G-5015)*
Madden Manufacturing Inc ....F 574 295-4292
  Elkhart *(G-3013)*
Marion Steel Fabrication Inc ....E 765 664-1478
  Marion *(G-9545)*
Materials Processing Inc...................G 317 803-3010
  Indianapolis *(G-7466)*
Miller Mfg Corp ....E 574 773-4136
  Nappanee *(G-10695)*
Moon Fabricating Corp.....................E 765 459-4194
  Kokomo *(G-8670)*
Pruett Manufacturing Co Inc ....F 812 234-9497
  Terre Haute *(G-13312)*
Quikcut Incorporated......................G 260 447-3880
  Fort Wayne *(G-4574)*
Rogers Engineering and Mfg Co ....E 765 478-5444
  Cambridge City *(G-1261)*
Sigma Steel Inc ....E 812 275-4489
  Bedford *(G-578)*
Sisson Steel Inc ....F 812 354-8701
  Winslow *(G-14359)*
SMS Group Inc ....E 219 880-0256
  Gary *(G-5099)*
Snyder & Co Inc ....G 765 447-3452
  Lafayette *(G-9000)*
Spreuer & Son Inc.........................F 260 463-3513
  Lagrange *(G-9067)*
Stahl Equipment Inc ....E 812 925-3341
  Chandler *(G-1554)*
Steel Tank & Fabricating Corp ....E 260 248-8971
  Columbia City *(G-1838)*
Sterling Boiler and Mech LLC ....A 812 479-5447
  Evansville *(G-3750)*
Sun Engineering Inc ....E 219 962-1191
  Lake Station *(G-9078)*
T J B Inc..................................G 219 293-8030
  Elkhart *(G-3202)*
Tank Construction & Service Co ....F 317 509-6294
  Whitestown *(G-14263)*
Temptek Inc ....G 317 887-6352
  Greenwood *(G-5752)*
Tishler Industries Inc.....................G 765 286-5454
  Muncie *(G-10569)*
Varied Products Indiana Inc..............F 219 763-2526
  Chesterton *(G-1640)*
Wrib Manufacturing Inc...................G 765 294-2841
  Veedersburg *(G-13648)*

METAL FABRICATORS: *Sheet*

A & B Fabricating & Maint Inc..............F 574 353-1012
  Mentone *(G-9684)*
A S C Industries Inc ....E 574 264-1987
  Elkhart *(G-2659)*
Abell Engineering & Mfg ....F 317 687-1174
  Indianapolis *(G-6310)*
Abtrex Industries Inc......................E 574 234-7773
  South Bend *(G-12693)*
Ace Welding and Machine Inc ....G 812 379-9625
  Columbus *(G-1849)*
Ad-Vance Magnetics Inc ....E 574 223-3158
  Rochester *(G-12113)*
Advanced Mtlwrking Prctces LLC..........G 317 337-0441
  Carmel *(G-1303)*
Advantage Manufacturing ....G 317 237-4289
  Indianapolis *(G-6339)*
Aearo Technologies LLC ....C 317 692-6666
  Indianapolis *(G-6342)*
Alro Steel Corporation.....................E 317 781-3800
  Indianapolis *(G-6378)*
Ameri-Kart Corp ....D 225 642-7874
  Bristol *(G-1043)*
American Machine Fabrication ....G 812 944-4136
  New Albany *(G-10744)*
AMS of Indiana Inc.........................E 574 293-5526
  Elkhart *(G-2689)*
Applied Metals & Mch Works Inc..........E 260 424-4834
  Fort Wayne *(G-4083)*
Arconic Inc ....G 812 842-3300
  Newburgh *(G-11022)*
Artisan Sheet Metal Corp ....G 812 422-7393
  Wadesville *(G-13770)*
Atco-Gary Metal Tech LLC ....C 219 885-3232
  Griffith *(G-5763)*
Austin-Westran LLC ....C 815 234-2811
  Indianapolis *(G-6441)*
Auto Truck Group LLC ....F 260 356-1610
  Huntington *(G-6188)*
Avionics Mounts Inc ....G 812 988-2949
  Nashville *(G-10714)*
B&J Rocket America Inc ....E 574 825-5802
  Middlebury *(G-9874)*
Benthall Bros Inc ....E 800 488-5995
  Evansville *(G-3372)*
Blume Metal Sales LLC ....G 765 490-0600
  Brookston *(G-1101)*
Bon L Manufacturing Company ....G 815 351-6802
  Kentland *(G-8517)*
Bowmans Tin Shop Inc ....G 574 936-3234
  Plymouth *(G-11671)*
Brackett Heating & AC ....F 812 476-1138
  Evansville *(G-3400)*
Brazeway Inc ....D 317 392-2533
  Shelbyville *(G-12524)*
Bright Sheet Metal Company Inc..........C 317 291-7600
  Indianapolis *(G-6508)*
Buhrt Engineering & Cnstr.................E 574 267-3720
  Warsaw *(G-13852)*
Burkhart Advertising Inc ....E 574 234-4444
  South Bend *(G-12728)*
C & K United Shtmtl & Mech ....E 812 423-5090
  Evansville *(G-3407)*
C & L Sheet Metal LLC.....................G 812 449-9126
  Evansville *(G-3408)*
C & P Engineering & Mfg...................E 765 825-4293
  Connersville *(G-2042)*
C&F Fabricating LLC ....G 765 362-5922
  Crawfordsville *(G-2136)*
Campbell Ventilation Inc ....F 317 636-7211
  Indianapolis *(G-6545)*
Cardinal Manufacturing Co Inc............F 317 283-4175
  Indianapolis *(G-6553)*
Carr Metal Products Inc....................C 317 542-0691
  Indianapolis *(G-6558)*
Cartesian Corp ....E 765 742-0293
  Lafayette *(G-8868)*
Central States Mfg Inc ....D 219 879-4770
  Michigan City *(G-9773)*
Chisholm Lumber & Sup Co Inc..........E 317 547-3535
  Indianapolis *(G-6601)*
Citadel Architectural Pdts Inc ....E 317 894-9400
  Indianapolis *(G-6612)*
City Welding & Fabrication ....G 765 569-5403
  Rockville *(G-12175)*
Cline Brothers Welding ....G 812 738-3537
  Corydon *(G-2093)*
Clover Sheet Metal Company ....E 574 293-5912
  Elkhart *(G-2761)*

Employee Codes: A=Over 500 employees, B=251-500
C=101-250, D=51-100, E=20-50, F=10-19, G=2-9

2018 Harris Indiana
Industrial Directory

PRODUCT

1019

Cmg Inc .... G 317 890-1999
Indianapolis *(G-6626)*

Coffee Lomont & Moyer Inc .... F ... 260 422-7825
Fort Wayne *(G-4166)*

Columbus Engineering Inc .... E ... 812 342-1231
Columbus *(G-1876)*

Conover Custom Fabrication Inc .... F ... 317 784-1904
Indianapolis *(G-6652)*

Contech Engnered Solutions LLC .... E ... 812 849-3933
Mitchell *(G-10160)*

Continental Industries Inc .... D 574 262-4511
Elkhart *(G-2771)*

D A Hochstetler & Sons LLP .... F 574 642-1144
Topeka *(G-13416)*

Davids Inc .... F 812 376-6870
Columbus *(G-1905)*

Deister Machine Company Inc .... C 260 422-0354
Fort Wayne *(G-4207)*

Delbert M Dawson & Son Inc .... G 765 284-9711
Muncie *(G-10458)*

Dexter Axle Company .... E 574 295-7888
Bristol *(G-1054)*

Die-Mensional Metal Stamping .... F ... 812 265-3946
Madison *(G-9456)*

Dietrich Industries Inc .... C 219 931-3741
Hammond *(G-5870)*

Ditech Inc .... D 812 526-0850
Edinburgh *(G-2607)*

Dpc Inc .... E 765 564-3752
Delphi *(G-2419)*

Dyna-Fab Corporation .... E 765 893-4423
West Lebanon *(G-14119)*

E & B Paving Inc .... G 317 773-4132
Noblesville *(G-11097)*

E & R Fabricating Inc .... G 812 275-0388
Bedford *(G-539)*

E & S Metal Inc .... F 260 563-7714
Wabash *(G-13726)*

E Fab Incorporated .... G 317 786-9593
Indianapolis *(G-6782)*

Eagle Magnetic Company Inc .... E ... 317 297-1030
Indianapolis *(G-6786)*

Edwards Steel Inc .... G 317 462-9451
Greenfield *(G-5522)*

Elixir Industries .... D 574 294-5685
Elkhart *(G-2818)*

Erny Sheet Metal Inc .... F 812 482-1044
Jasper *(G-8250)*

Eta Fabrication Inc .... F 260 897-3711
Avilla *(G-404)*

Exact Sheet Metal & Skylights .... G ... 219 670-3520
Crown Point *(G-2251)*

F D Ramsey & Co Inc .... F 219 362-2452
La Porte *(G-8757)*

F R Sheet Metal Co Inc .... G 219 949-2290
Gary *(G-5045)*

Frank H Monroe Htg & Coolg Inc .... F ... 812 945-2566
New Albany *(G-10784)*

Freudenberg-Nok General Partnr .... B ... 260 894-7183
Ligonier *(G-9285)*

G & G Metal Spinners Inc .... E 317 923-3225
Indianapolis *(G-6974)*

G & N Warehouse & Packaging .... G ... 574 234-3717
South Bend *(G-12785)*

Gammons Metal & Mfg Co Inc .... D ... 317 546-7091
Indianapolis *(G-6982)*

General Crafts Corp .... G 574 533-1936
Goshen *(G-5223)*

General Motors LLC .... B 765 668-2000
Marion *(G-9525)*

General Sheet Metal Works Inc .... E ... 574 288-0611
South Bend *(G-12788)*

Gleason Corporation .... C 574 533-1141
Goshen *(G-5226)*

Goudy Brothers Boiler Co Inc .... E ... 765 459-4416
Kokomo *(G-8631)*

Grant County Steel Inc .... G 765 668-7547
Marion *(G-9527)*

Greenfield Feeders Inc .... G 317 462-6363
Greenfield *(G-5534)*

Greenwood Models Inc .... G 317 859-2988
Greenwood *(G-5700)*

Greg Moser Engineering Inc .... E ... 260 726-6689
Portland *(G-11827)*

Gross Roofing Sheet Metals .... G ... 765 965-0068
Richmond *(G-11992)*

Gsp-2700 LLC .... G 219 885-3232
Gary *(G-5056)*

Halsen Brothers Sheet Metal .... G ... 574 583-3358
Monticello *(G-10264)*

Hartman Brothers Heat & AC .... F ... 260 493-4402
New Haven *(G-10942)*

Heidtman Steel Products Inc .... C ... 419 691-4646
Butler *(G-1229)*

Helfin Sheet Metal Inc .... G 260 563-2417
Wabash *(G-13729)*

Helming Bros Inc .... G 812 634-9797
Jasper *(G-8254)*

Herman Tool & Machine Inc .... F ... 574 594-5544
Pierceton *(G-11572)*

Hogen Industries Inc Indiana .... E ... 317 591-5070
Indianapolis *(G-7111)*

Holbrook Manufacturing Inc .... E ... 317 736-9387
Franklin *(G-4896)*

Horner Industrial Services Inc .... F ... 317 634-7165
Indianapolis *(G-7129)*

Hub City Stl & Fabrication LLC .... G ... 260 760-0370
Union City *(G-13457)*

Hy-Flex Corporation .... E 765 571-5125
Knightstown *(G-8551)*

Hydro Extrusion North Amer LLC .... B ... 888 935-5757
North Liberty *(G-11216)*

Independent Protection Co Inc .... G ... 574 533-4116
Goshen *(G-5242)*

Indiana Gratings Inc .... E 765 342-7191
Martinsville *(G-9615)*

Indiana Model Company Inc .... D ... 317 787-6358
Indianapolis *(G-7184)*

Indiana Steel & Engrg Inc .... E 812 275-3363
Bedford *(G-552)*

Indiana U Bolts Inc .... E 317 870-1940
Waterloo *(G-14015)*

Industrial Contrs Skanska Inc .... E ... 812 423-7832
Evansville *(G-3555)*

Industrial Steel Cnstr Inc .... C 219 885-5610
Gary *(G-5069)*

Italmac USA Inc .... G 574 243-0217
Granger *(G-5416)*

J & J Repair .... G 574 831-3075
Goshen *(G-5246)*

J & J Welding Inc .... E 812 838-4391
Mount Vernon *(G-10396)*

Jack Frost LLC .... E 812 477-7244
Evansville *(G-3571)*

Jack Howard .... G 317 788-7643
Indianapolis *(G-7292)*

JO Mory Inc .... E 260 897-3541
Avilla *(G-407)*

Joe Tricker .... G 630 759-0251
Fishers *(G-3934)*

Josam Company .... D 219 872-5531
Michigan City *(G-9805)*

K-K Tool and Design Inc .... E 260 758-2940
Markle *(G-9578)*

Kairos Specialty Metals Corp .... E ... 765 836-5540
Mount Summit *(G-10379)*

Kammerer Inc .... G 260 347-0389
Kendallville *(G-8485)*

Knox Inc .... F 260 665-6617
Angola *(G-226)*

Koester Metals Inc .... E 260 495-1818
Fremont *(G-4964)*

Kokomo Metal Fabricators Inc .... G ... 765 459-8173
Kokomo *(G-8653)*

Koomler & Sons Inc .... F 260 482-7641
Fort Wayne *(G-4414)*

L & W Engineering Inc .... D 574 825-5351
Middlebury *(G-9900)*

L L Welding .... G 765 565-6006
Carthage *(G-1514)*

Lake Air Balance .... G 219 988-2449
Hebron *(G-6015)*

Lapis Services Inc .... G 219 464-9131
Valparaiso *(G-13572)*

Lenex Steel Company .... E 317 818-1622
Terre Haute *(G-13274)*

Leons Fabrication Inc .... F 219 365-5272
Schererville *(G-12330)*

M & S Indus Met Fbricators Inc .... D ... 260 356-0300
Huntington *(G-6226)*

M T M Machining Inc .... F 219 872-8677
Michigan City *(G-9813)*

Major Tool and Machine Inc .... B ... 317 636-6433
Indianapolis *(G-7446)*

Marion Steel Fabrication Inc .... E ... 765 664-1478
Marion *(G-9545)*

Maron Products Incorporated .... D ... 574 259-1971
Mishawaka *(G-10074)*

Mc Bride & Son Welding & Engrg .... G ... 260 724-3534
Decatur *(G-2393)*

McD Machine Incorporated .... G ... 812 339-1240
Bloomington *(G-770)*

Meese Inc .... D 812 273-1008
Madison *(G-9485)*

Mestek Inc .... E 317 831-5314
Mooresville *(G-10322)*

Metal Art Inc .... G 765 354-4571
Middletown *(G-9938)*

Metal Dynamics Ltd .... E 812 949-7998
New Albany *(G-10826)*

Metal Sales Manufacturing Corp .... E ... 812 246-1866
Sellersburg *(G-12408)*

Metal Sales Manufacturing Corp .... E ... 812 941-0041
New Albany *(G-10827)*

Micro Metl Corporation .... C 800 662-4822
Indianapolis *(G-7497)*

Microform Inc .... G 574 522-9851
Elkhart *(G-3035)*

Mid America Powered Vehicles .... G ... 812 925-7745
Chandler *(G-1551)*

Midwest Roll Forming & Mfg Inc .... C ... 574 594-2100
Pierceton *(G-11573)*

Midwest Sheet Metal Inc .... G 574 223-3332
Rochester *(G-12138)*

Millenium Sheet Metal Inc .... F ... 574 935-9101
Plymouth *(G-11706)*

Miller Mfg Corp .... E 574 773-4136
Nappanee *(G-10695)*

Models LLC .... E 765 676-6700
Lebanon *(G-9207)*

Modern Door Corporation .... D ... 574 586-3117
Walkerton *(G-13806)*

Moore Metal Works & A/C L L C .... E ... 812 422-9473
Evansville *(G-3638)*

Mooresville Welding Inc .... G 317 831-2265
Mooresville *(G-10324)*

Morin Corp .... G 219 465-8334
Valparaiso *(G-13581)*

Morse Metal Fab Inc .... E 574 674-6237
Granger *(G-5425)*

Mossman Metal Works .... G 765 676-6055
Lebanon *(G-9208)*

Moyers Inc .... E 574 264-3119
Elkhart *(G-3052)*

Mssh Inc .... G 812 663-2180
Greensburg *(G-5624)*

Napier & Napier .... G 765 580-9116
Liberty *(G-9266)*

Nector Machine & Fabricating .... G ... 219 322-6878
Schererville *(G-12338)*

New England Sheets LLC .... E ... 978 487-2500
Indianapolis *(G-7585)*

North American Manufacturing .... E ... 765 948-3337
Fairmount *(G-3833)*

Novelis Corporation .... C 812 462-2287
Terre Haute *(G-13291)*

Original Tractor Cab Co Inc .... E ... 765 663-2214
Arlington *(G-282)*

Ottenweller Co Inc .... C 260 484-3166
Fort Wayne *(G-4513)*

Owens Machine & Welding .... G 574 583-9566
Monticello *(G-10277)*

Padgett Inc .... C 812 945-2391
New Albany *(G-10839)*

Palmor Products Inc .... E 800 872-2822
Lebanon *(G-9210)*

Paniccia Heating & Cooling .... G ... 219 872-2198
Michigan City *(G-9827)*

Patrick Industries Inc .... D 574 294-5959
Elkhart *(G-3087)*

Pinnacle Equipment Company Inc .... G ... 317 259-1180
Indianapolis *(G-7693)*

Powell Systems Inc .... G 765 884-0613
Fowler *(G-4804)*

Poynter Sheet Metal Inc .... B ... 317 893-1193
Greenwood *(G-5735)*

Precision Racg Components LLC .... F ... 317 248-4764
Indianapolis *(G-7735)*

Precisn Fbrctn of Shlbyvle Inc .... G ... 765 544-2204
Shelbyville *(G-12560)*

Proaxis Inc .... E 765 742-4200
West Lafayette *(G-14097)*

Pulley-Kellam Co Inc .... E 260 356-6326
Huntington *(G-6240)*

Quality Galvanized Pdts Inc .... G ... 574 848-5151
Bristol *(G-1076)*

R & M Welding & Fabricating Sp .... G ... 812 295-9130
Loogootee *(G-9392)*

R & R Tool Manufacturing Inc .... E ... 219 362-1681
La Porte *(G-8810)*

R C Laser Inc ....G...... 812 923-1918
Pekin *(G-11478)*
R Concepts Industries Inc ....D...... 574 295-6641
Elkhart *(G-3135)*
Rance Aluminum Fabrication ....E...... 574 266-9028
Elkhart *(G-3137)*
Ricks Custom Sheet Metal LLC ....G...... 812 825-3959
Solsberry *(G-12687)*
Rite-Way Steel Inc ....F...... 574 262-3465
Elkhart *(G-3147)*
River Valley Sheet Metal Inc ....E...... 574 259-2538
Mishawaka *(G-10118)*
Rogers Engineering and Mfg Co ......E...... 765 478-5444
Cambridge City *(G-1261)*
Ryobi Die Casting (usa) Inc ....A...... 317 398-3398
Shelbyville *(G-12565)*
Sanbar of Indiana Inc ....G...... 317 375-6220
Indianapolis *(G-7890)*
Sheet Metal Services Inc ....F...... 219 924-1206
Highland *(G-6055)*
Sheet Mtl Wkrs Local No 20 ....F...... 317 541-0050
Indianapolis *(G-7926)*
Sigma Steel Inc ....E...... 812 275-4489
Bedford *(G-578)*
Sisson Steel Inc ....F...... 812 354-8701
Winslow *(G-14359)*
Slabaugh Metal Fab ....E...... 574 546-2882
Bremen *(G-1024)*
Slabaugh Metal Fab LLC ....G...... 574 342-0554
Bourbon *(G-948)*
Slate Mechanical Inc ....F...... 765 452-9611
Kokomo *(G-8697)*
Slatile Roofing and Shtmtl Co ....E...... 574 233-7485
South Bend *(G-12939)*
Snodgrass Sheet Metal ....F...... 317 783-3181
Indianapolis *(G-7955)*
Snyder & Co Inc ....G...... 765 447-3452
Lafayette *(G-9000)*
Spreuer & Son Inc ....F...... 260 463-3513
Lagrange *(G-9067)*
Stahl Equipment Inc ....E...... 812 925-3341
Chandler *(G-1554)*
Stalcop LLC ....D...... 765 436-7926
Thorntown *(G-13378)*
State Wide Aluminum Inc ....D...... 574 262-2594
Elkhart *(G-3191)*
Steel Tank & Fabricating Corp ....E...... 260 248-8971
Columbia City *(G-1838)*
Summit Manufacturing Corp ....E...... 260 428-2600
Fort Wayne *(G-4665)*
Sur-Loc Inc ....F...... 260 495-4065
Fremont *(G-4975)*
Tarpenning-Lafollette Co Inc ....E...... 317 780-1500
Indianapolis *(G-8036)*
Thomas Cubit Inc ....G...... 219 933-0566
Hammond *(G-5949)*
Thomco Inc ....G...... 317 359-3539
Indianapolis *(G-8067)*
Total Concepts Design Inc ....D...... 812 752-6534
Scottsburg *(G-12384)*
Trade Line Fabricating Inc ....E...... 812 637-1444
Lawrenceburg *(G-9159)*
Trim-A-Seal of Indiana Inc ....F...... 219 883-2180
Gary *(G-5109)*
Triple J Ironworks Inc ....G...... 765 544-9152
Carthage *(G-1517)*
Triumph Group Operations Inc ....G...... 317 392-5000
Shelbyville *(G-12579)*
Tube Processing Corp ....C...... 317 782-9486
Indianapolis *(G-8108)*
Tube Processing Corp ....B...... 317 787-1321
Indianapolis *(G-8107)*
Tube Processing Corp ....C...... 317 264-7760
Indianapolis *(G-8109)*
U S Sheet Metal and Roofing Co ......G...... 812 425-2428
Evansville *(G-3781)*
Universal Metalcraft Inc ....E...... 260 547-4457
Decatur *(G-2411)*
V N C Inc ....F...... 219 696-5031
Lowell *(G-9425)*
Vindhurst Sheet Metal LLC ....F...... 812 422-0143
Evansville *(G-3802)*
Vogler Copperworks LLC ....G...... 812 630-9010
Haubstadt *(G-6007)*
W & W Fabricating Inc ....G...... 765 362-2182
Crawfordsville *(G-2203)*
Wabash Valley Manufacturing ....C...... 260 352-2102
Silver Lake *(G-12682)*
Wait Industries LLC ....G...... 574 347-4320
Granger *(G-5451)*

Wick - Fab Inc ....E...... 260 897-3303
Avilla *(G-421)*
Wiley Metal Fabricating Inc ....C...... 765 671-7865
Marion *(G-9573)*
Wiley Metal Fabricating Inc ....D...... 765 674-9707
Marion *(G-9574)*
Williams Tool & Machine Corp ....F...... 765 676-5859
Jamestown *(G-8233)*
Wilmes Window Mfg Co Inc ....E...... 812 275-7575
Ferdinand *(G-3864)*
Zimmer Welding Co ....G...... 317 632-5212
Indianapolis *(G-8226)*

METAL FINISHING SVCS

Beemsterboer Slag Corp ....E...... 219 931-7462
Hammond *(G-5849)*
Best Metal Finishing Inc ....E...... 812 689-9950
Osgood *(G-11389)*
Crown Coatings LLC ....G...... 317 482-2766
Fortville *(G-4771)*
DOT America Inc ....F...... 260 244-5700
Columbia City *(G-1779)*
Lambert Metal Finishing Inc ....G...... 260 493-0529
Fort Wayne *(G-4423)*
Michiana Metal Finishing Inc ....G...... 574 206-0666
Elkhart *(G-3033)*
Mpp Inc ....E...... 260 422-5426
Fort Wayne *(G-4482)*
Pioneer Metal Finishing LLC ....D...... 574 287-7239
South Bend *(G-12896)*
Pro Tech Metal Finishing ....E...... 260 894-4011
Ligonier *(G-9293)*
Rhinehart Finishing LLC ....D...... 260 238-4442
Spencerville *(G-13051)*
Tk Finishing ....G...... 574 233-1617
South Bend *(G-12973)*
Wayne Black Oxide Inc ....G...... 260 484-0280
Fort Wayne *(G-4738)*

METAL MINING SVCS

Better Metal Systems LLC ....G...... 219 290-2539
Hammond *(G-5851)*
Diamond Mining Lead ....G...... 317 340-7760
Indianapolis *(G-6740)*
P M I LLC ....G...... 812 374-3856
Edinburgh *(G-2619)*
Postle Aluminum Company LLC ....E...... 574 389-0800
Elkhart *(G-3104)*
Turner Contracting Inc ....D...... 812 834-5954
Bedford *(G-586)*
Vibronics Inc ....G...... 812 853-2300
Newburgh *(G-11055)*

METAL ORES, NEC

General Steel ....G...... 317 251-9583
Indianapolis *(G-6999)*

METAL RESHAPING & REPLATING SVCS

JL Walter & Associates Inc ....E...... 317 524-3600
Indianapolis *(G-7306)*
Lime City Manufacturing Co ....E...... 260 356-6826
Huntington *(G-6224)*

METAL SERVICE CENTERS & OFFICES

Angola Wire Products Inc ....E...... 260 665-3061
Angola *(G-193)*
Calpipe Industries LLC ....G...... 219 844-6800
Hobart *(G-6071)*
Chicago Steel Ltd Partnership ....G...... 219 949-1111
Gary *(G-5037)*
Edcoat Limited Partnership ....E...... 574 654-9105
New Carlisle *(G-10881)*
Elkhart Steel Service Inc ....G...... 574 262-2552
Elkhart *(G-2830)*
Illiana Steel Inc ....E...... 219 397-3250
East Chicago *(G-2537)*
Keywest Metal ....G...... 219 654-4063
Hobart *(G-6084)*
National Material LP ....C...... 219 397-5088
East Chicago *(G-2554)*
Newco Metals Inc ....G...... 765 644-6649
Anderson *(G-145)*
Newco Metals Inc ....E...... 317 485-7721
Pendleton *(G-11497)*
Ryerson Tull Inc ....D...... 219 764-3500
Burns Harbor *(G-1219)*
Set Enterprises of Mi Inc ....F...... 812 346-1700
North Vernon *(G-11281)*

US Metals Inc ....G...... 219 398-1350
East Chicago *(G-2578)*

METAL SLITTING & SHEARING

Pgp Corp ....D...... 812 285-7700
Jeffersonville *(G-8413)*
Vicksmetal Armco Associates ....E...... 765 659-5555
Frankfort *(G-4858)*

METAL SPINNING FOR THE TRADE

B&J International LLC ....G...... 260 854-2215
Kendallville *(G-8459)*
Dixie Metal Spinning Corp ....G...... 317 541-1330
Indianapolis *(G-6753)*
Galloway Fabricating ....G...... 574 453-3802
Leesburg *(G-9236)*
Indianapolis Metal Spinning Co ....F...... 317 273-7440
Indianapolis *(G-7203)*
Jag Metal Spinning Inc ....G...... 812 533-5501
Sandford *(G-12310)*
Metal Spinners Inc ....F...... 260 665-2158
Angola *(G-229)*
Metal Spinners Inc ....E...... 260 665-7741
Angola *(G-230)*
Muncie Metal Spinning Inc ....F...... 765 288-1937
Muncie *(G-10530)*
Swiss Metal Spinning Co ....E...... 260 692-1401
Monroe *(G-10187)*
Wenzel Acquisition Inc ....E...... 260 495-9898
Fremont *(G-4979)*
Wenzel Metal Spinning Inc ....D...... 260 495-9898
Fremont *(G-4980)*
Wenzel Metal Spinning Inc Ind ....D...... 260 495-9898
Fremont *(G-4981)*

METAL STAMPING, FOR THE TRADE

Ameri-Tek Manufacturing Inc ....F...... 574 753-8058
Logansport *(G-9320)*
Ark Model and Stampings Inc ....F...... 317 549-3394
Indianapolis *(G-6420)*
ATI Products Inc ....G...... 260 358-9254
Huntington *(G-6187)*
Aul Brothers Tool & Die Inc ....F...... 765 759-5124
Muncie *(G-10434)*
Austin Tri-Hawk Automotive Inc ....C...... 812 794-0062
Austin *(G-395)*
B Walter & Company Inc ....E...... 260 563-2181
Wabash *(G-13721)*
B&J Rocket America Inc ....E...... 574 825-5802
Middlebury *(G-9874)*
Batesville Tool & Die Inc ....C...... 812 934-5616
Batesville *(G-494)*
Btd Manufacturing Inc ....G...... 812 934-5616
Batesville *(G-495)*
C E R Metal Marking Corp ....G...... 219 924-9710
Highland *(G-6039)*
Capco LLC ....D...... 812 375-1700
Columbus *(G-1866)*
Covington Products Inc ....F...... 765 282-6626
Muncie *(G-10450)*
Da-Mar Industries Inc ....F...... 260 347-1662
Kendallville *(G-8471)*
Domar Machine & Tool Inc ....G...... 574 295-8791
Elkhart *(G-2798)*
Evansville Metal Products Inc ....D...... 812 423-5632
Evansville *(G-3487)*
Franklin Stamping Inds Inc ....F...... 765 282-5138
Muncie *(G-10473)*
Gammons Metal & Mfg Co Inc ....D...... 317 546-7091
Indianapolis *(G-6982)*
Gt Stamping Inc ....D...... 574 533-4108
Goshen *(G-5231)*
Harold Precision Products Inc ....E...... 765 348-2710
Hartford City *(G-5981)*
Humphrey Tool Coinc ....G...... 574 753-3853
Logansport *(G-9338)*
Imh Fabrication Inc ....F...... 317 252-5566
Indianapolis *(G-7163)*
Imperial Stamping Corporation ....D...... 574 294-3780
Elkhart *(G-2930)*
Indiana Fine Blanking ....G...... 574 772-3850
Knox *(G-8568)*
Indiana Metal Stamping Co ....G...... 574 936-2964
Plymouth *(G-11691)*
Jam-Ko Engineering Company ....F...... 574 294-7684
Elkhart *(G-2944)*
L H Stamping Corporation ....D...... 260 432-5563
Fort Wayne *(G-4421)*

Employee Codes: A=Over 500 employees, B=251-500
C=101-250, D=51-100, E=20-50, F=10-19, G=2-9

2018 Harris Indiana
Industrial Directory

1021

PRODUCT

LH Industries Corp ....B 260 432-5563
Fort Wayne (G-4431)

Lime City Manufacturing Co ....E 260 356-6826
Huntington (G-6224)

Lippert Components Inc ....E 574 535-1125
Goshen (G-5272)

Lippert Components Inc ....C 800 551-9149
Elkhart (G-2999)

Lippert Components Inc ....D 574 535-1125
Goshen (G-5268)

Lippert Components Inc ....D 574 294-6852
Elkhart (G-3000)

Lippert Components Inc ....D 574 849-0869
Goshen (G-5273)

Lippert Components Inc ....C 574 971-4320
Goshen (G-5275)

Lippert Components Inc ....D 574 312-7445
Middlebury (G-9904)

Logan Stampings Inc ....E 574 722-3101
Logansport (G-9349)

MA Metal Co Inc ....E 812 526-2666
Columbus (G-1966)

Maron Products Incorporated ....D 574 259-1971
Mishawaka (G-10074)

Master Manufacturing Company ....E 812 425-1561
Evansville (G-3615)

Mc Metalcraft Inc ....G 574 259-8101
Mishawaka (G-10076)

Mc Metalcraft Inc ....G 574 259-8101
Mishawaka (G-10077)

Metal Fab Engineering Inc ....F 574 278-7150
Winamac (G-14312)

Mid-West Spring Mfg Co ....D 574 353-1409
Mentone (G-9688)

Mpi Products LLC ....B 574 772-3850
Knox (G-8575)

Mursix Corporation ....C 765 282-2221
Yorktown (G-14408)

New Process Steel LP ....E 260 868-1445
Butler (G-1237)

Precision Stamping Inc ....E 574 522-8987
Elkhart (G-3109)

Pruett Manufacturing Co Inc ....F 812 234-9497
Terre Haute (G-13312)

Quality Die Set Corp ....E 574 967-4411
Logansport (G-9361)

Ready Machine Tool & Die Corp ....E 765 825-3108
Connersville (G-2070)

Rhinehart Development Corp ....E 260 238-4442
Spencerville (G-13050)

Samco Inc ....E 812 279-8131
Bedford (G-576)

Stamina Metal Products Inc ....G 574 534-7410
Goshen (G-5327)

Steelmaster Machine & TI Corp ....F 574 825-7670
Middlebury (G-9922)

Stone City Products Inc ....D 812 275-3373
Bedford (G-582)

Titan Manufacturing Co ....G 219 662-7238
Crown Point (G-2314)

Valley Tool & Die Stampings ....E 574 722-4566
Logansport (G-9375)

METAL STAMPINGS: Perforated

Diamond Manufacturing Company ....E 219 874-2374
Michigan City (G-9782)

METAL TREATING COMPOUNDS

Blue Grass Chemical Spc LLC ....E 812 948-1115
New Albany (G-10753)

Univertical Semicdtr Pdts Inc ....G 260 665-1500
Angola (G-257)

METALS SVC CENTERS & WHOL: Structural Shapes, Iron Or Steel

Ridge Iron LLC ....G 646 450-0092
Plymouth (G-11722)

METALS SVC CENTERS & WHOLESALERS: Cable, Wire

Rankin Pump and Supply Co Inc ....G 812 238-2535
Terre Haute (G-13315)

Tway Company Incorporated ....E 317 636-2591
Indianapolis (G-8116)

METALS SVC CENTERS & WHOLESALERS: Concrete Reinforcing Bars

Zimco Materials Inc ....E 219 883-0870
Gary (G-5117)

METALS SVC CENTERS & WHOLESALERS: Ferrous Metals

Univertical Holdings Inc ....G 260 665-1500
Angola (G-254)

METALS SVC CENTERS & WHOLESALERS: Flat Prdts, Iron Or Steel

Feralloy Corporation ....D 219 787-9698
Portage (G-11762)

METALS SVC CENTERS & WHOLESALERS: Foundry Prdts

Hill & Griffith Company ....E 317 241-9233
Indianapolis (G-7108)

Sterling Sales and Engineering ....G 765 376-0454
Veedersburg (G-13646)

METALS SVC CENTERS & WHOLESALERS: Iron & Steel Prdt, Ferrous

Reeves Manufacturing Inc ....G 765 935-3875
Richmond (G-12042)

METALS SVC CENTERS & WHOLESALERS: Misc Nonferrous Prdts

Global ....G 317 494-6174
Franklin (G-4889)

METALS SVC CENTERS & WHOLESALERS: Pipe & Tubing, Steel

Hancor Inc ....E 812 443-2080
Brazil (G-964)

Independent Concrete Pipe Co ....E 317 262-4920
Indianapolis (G-7172)

METALS SVC CENTERS & WHOLESALERS: Plates, Metal

Gldn Rule Truss & Metal Sales ....G 812 866-1800
Lexington (G-9250)

METALS SVC CENTERS & WHOLESALERS: Rails & Access

Dynamic Composites LLC ....G 260 625-8686
Columbia City (G-1781)

METALS SVC CENTERS & WHOLESALERS: Rope, Wire, Exc Insulated

Kentuckiana Wire Rope & Supply ....F 812 282-3667
Jeffersonville (G-8386)

METALS SVC CENTERS & WHOLESALERS: Sheets, Metal

Flexco Products Inc ....C 574 294-2502
Elkhart (G-2852)

L L Welding ....G 765 565-5006
Carthage (G-1514)

New Process Steel LP ....E 260 868-1445
Butler (G-1237)

Preferred Metal Services Inc ....G 219 988-2386
Crown Point (G-2289)

METALS SVC CENTERS & WHOLESALERS: Stampings, Metal

Pro-Tech Tool & Engineering ....G 765 258-3613
Frankfort (G-4851)

METALS SVC CENTERS & WHOLESALERS: Steel

Alro Steel Corporation ....E 317 781-3800
Indianapolis (G-6378)

Alro Steel Corporation ....D 260 749-1829
Fort Wayne (G-4064)

Barks Welding Supplies ....G 812 732-4366
Corydon (G-2089)

Central Illinois Steel Company ....G 219 882-1026
Gary (G-5035)

Grant County Steel Inc ....F 765 668-7547
Marion (G-9527)

Kammerer Inc ....G 260 349-9098
Kendallville (G-8484)

Kelly Metal Products Inc ....G 812 232-1221
Terre Haute (G-13265)

Lenex Steel Company ....E 317 818-1622
Terre Haute (G-13274)

Mill Steel Co ....C 765 622-4545
Anderson (G-136)

Mofab Inc ....E 765 649-1288
Anderson (G-138)

Pgp Corp ....D 812 285-7700
Jeffersonville (G-8413)

Plateplus Inc ....D 219 392-3400
East Chicago (G-2560)

Quality Steel & Alum Pdts Inc ....E 574 295-8715
Elkhart (G-3130)

Stahl Welding Inc ....G 765 457-3386
Kokomo (G-8699)

Steel Storage Inc ....E 574 282-2618
South Bend (G-12955)

Summerlot Engineered Pdts Inc ....F 812 466-7266
Rosedale (G-12206)

W & W Fabricating Inc ....G 765 362-2182
Crawfordsville (G-2203)

Wegener Steel and Fabricating ....G 219 462-3911
Valparaiso (G-13636)

Westfield Steel Inc ....G 812 466-3500
Terre Haute (G-13368)

Winski Brothers Inc ....F 765 654-5323
Frankfort (G-4860)

METALS SVC CENTERS & WHOLESALERS: Tubing, Metal

Aluminum Wldg & Mch Works Inc ....G 219 787-8066
Chesterton (G-1592)

Fluid Handling Technology Inc ....G 317 216-9629
Indianapolis (G-6940)

G and P Enterprises Ind Inc ....G 812 723-3837
Paoli (G-11451)

METALS SVC CNTRS & WHOL: Metal Wires, Ties, Cables/Screening

Matrix Nac ....F 219 931-6600
Hammond (G-5914)

METALS SVC CTRS & WHOLESALERS: Aluminum Bars, Rods, Etc

Lasalle Bristol Corporation ....C 574 295-4400
Elkhart (G-2985)

Novelis Corporation ....C 812 462-2287
Terre Haute (G-13291)

Postle Operating LLC ....E 574 389-0800
Elkhart (G-3105)

Spectra Metal Sales Inc ....E 317 822-8291
Indianapolis (G-7973)

Superior Aluminum Alloys LLC ....C 260 749-7599
New Haven (G-10959)

METALS: Primary Nonferrous, NEC

Dallas Group of America Inc ....D 812 283-6675
Jeffersonville (G-8350)

Exide Technologies ....C 765 747-9980
Muncie (G-10470)

Expanded Metals Co Ind LLC ....E 574 287-6471
South Bend (G-12768)

Univertical Holdings Inc ....G 260 665-1500
Angola (G-254)

Whiting Metals LLC ....G 219 659-6955
Whiting (G-14278)

METALWORK: Miscellaneous

Alexander Screw Products Inc ....E 317 898-5313
Indianapolis (G-6362)

Aluminum Wldg & Mch Works Inc ....G 219 787-8066
Chesterton (G-1592)

Ambassador Steel Corporation ....E 317 834-3434
Mooresville (G-10302)

Coffee Lomont & Moyer Inc ....F 260 422-7825
Fort Wayne (G-4166)

Delta Tool Manufacturing Inc ....G...... 574 223-4863
  Rochester *(G-12122)*
Double E Enterprise Inc ....G...... 812 689-0671
  Osgood *(G-11390)*
Edge Manufacturing Inc ....E...... 260 827-0482
  Bluffton *(G-873)*
Engineered Rubber & Plastics...............F...... 574 254-1405
  Mishawaka *(G-10041)*
General Crafts Corp ....G...... 574 533-1936
  Goshen *(G-5223)*
Induction Iron Incorporated ....F...... 813 969-3300
  Evansville *(G-3554)*
Interstate Metals LLC...............F...... 765 893-4449
  West Lebanon *(G-14121)*
K and S Farm and Machine Shop.........F...... 812 663-8567
  Greensburg *(G-5617)*
Made Rite Manufacturing Inc ....G...... 812 967-2652
  Salem *(G-12300)*
McD Machine Incorporated ....G...... 812 339-1240
  Bloomington *(G-770)*
Metal Sales Manufacturing Corp ....E...... 812 941-0041
  New Albany *(G-10827)*
Metal Spinners Inc ....F...... 260 665-2158
  Angola *(G-229)*
Metal Technology of Indiana...............E...... 765 482-1100
  Lebanon *(G-9205)*
Performance Tool Inc ....F...... 260 726-6572
  Portland *(G-11838)*
Pier-Mac Plastics Inc ....E...... 260 726-9844
  Portland *(G-11839)*
Qfs Holdings LLC...............G...... 317 634-2543
  Indianapolis *(G-7792)*
Roll Forming Corporation ....D...... 812 284-0650
  Jeffersonville *(G-8421)*
Sellersburg Metals & Wldg Co ....F...... 812 248-0811
  Sellersburg *(G-12414)*
Ten Point Trim Corp ....E...... 317 875-5424
  Zionsville *(G-14468)*
Trulite GL Alum Solutions LLC ....D...... 317 273-0646
  Indianapolis *(G-8104)*
Vet Signs LLC...............G...... 937 733-4727
  Richmond *(G-12073)*
Voges Restoration and Wdwkg ....G...... 812 299-1546
  Terre Haute *(G-13364)*

METALWORK: Ornamental

All City Metal Craft Inc...............G...... 317 782-9340
  Indianapolis *(G-6366)*
Centrum Force Fabrication ....G...... 574 295-5367
  Goshen *(G-5186)*
Hamilton Iron Works Inc...............G...... 574 533-3784
  Goshen *(G-5234)*
Herman Tool & Machine Inc ....F...... 574 594-5544
  Pierceton *(G-11572)*
Hot Stone LLC...............G...... 812 949-4969
  New Albany *(G-10799)*
Mofab Inc ....E...... 765 649-1288
  Anderson *(G-138)*
Muncie Metal Spinning Inc...............F...... 765 288-1937
  Muncie *(G-10530)*
Schouten Metal Craft Inc...............G...... 317 546-2639
  Indianapolis *(G-7903)*
Signature Metals Inc...............G...... 317 335-2207
  McCordsville *(G-9676)*
Sugar Creek Fabricators Inc.................G...... 765 361-0891
  Crawfordsville *(G-2198)*
Upright Iron Works Inc ....G...... 219 922-1994
  Griffith *(G-5794)*

METALWORKING MACHINERY WHOLESALERS

Beatty International Inc ....E...... 219 931-3000
  Hammond *(G-5846)*
Bemcor Inc ....F...... 219 937-1600
  Hammond *(G-5850)*
Contour Hardening Inc ....E...... 888 867-2184
  Indianapolis *(G-6660)*

METEOROLOGIC TRACKING SYSTEMS

Ati Inc ....G...... 812 431-5409
  Mount Vernon *(G-10384)*

METERING DEVICES: Water Quality Monitoring & Control Systems

Bernard Hasten ....G...... 317 824-4544
  Indianapolis *(G-6467)*

Midwest Meter Inc ....G...... 574 967-0175
  Flora *(G-3999)*

METERS: Liquid

Madden Manufacturing Inc ....F...... 574 295-4292
  Elkhart *(G-3013)*
Micro Motion Inc ....G...... 317 334-1893
  Indianapolis *(G-7498)*

METERS: Magnetic Flow, Indl Process

Frew Process Group LLC.....................G...... 317 565-5000
  Noblesville *(G-11107)*

MGMT CONSULTING SVCS: Matls, Incl Purch, Handle & Invntry

Finvantage LLC ....F...... 317 500-4949
  Carmel *(G-1381)*

MICA PRDTS: Built-Up Or Sheet

Nf Friction Composites Inc ....G...... 414 365-1550
  Logansport *(G-9359)*

MICA: Built-Up

Double E Distributing Co Inc ....G...... 812 334-2220
  Bloomington *(G-715)*

MICROCIRCUITS, INTEGRATED: Semiconductor

Maxim Integrated Products Inc...............G...... 252 227-7202
  Westfield *(G-14175)*

MICROPROCESSORS

Intel Corporation ....G...... 317 336-5464
  Mccordsville *(G-9671)*

MICROWAVE COMPONENTS

Microwave Devices Inc...............G...... 317 736-8833
  Franklin *(G-4907)*
Polyphase Microwave Inc ....G...... 812 323-8708
  Bloomington *(G-800)*
Tempest Technical Sales Inc ....F...... 317 844-9236
  Carmel *(G-1492)*

MILITARY INSIGNIA, TEXTILE

Team Spirit...............G...... 219 924-6272
  Munster *(G-10631)*

MILL PRDTS: Structural & Rail

Midwest Metal Products Inc...............E...... 219 879-8595
  Michigan City *(G-9819)*
Progress Rail Services Corp...............C...... 219 397-5326
  East Chicago *(G-2565)*

MILLINERY SUPPLIES: Veils & Veiling, Bridal, Funeral, Etc

M A Studio Inc ....G...... 574 275-2200
  San Pierre *(G-12309)*

MILLING: Cereal Flour, Exc Rice

ADM Milling Co...............E...... 317 783-3321
  Beech Grove *(G-591)*
Pillsbury Company LLC ....E...... 812 944-8411
  New Albany *(G-10844)*

MILLING: Chemical

Advanced Metal Etching Inc ....E...... 260 894-4189
  Ligonier *(G-9275)*
Excel Machine ....G...... 317 467-0299
  Greenfield *(G-5531)*
Global Air Inc...............F...... 317 634-5300
  Indianapolis *(G-7008)*
Global Air Inc...............G...... 317 251-1251
  Indianapolis *(G-7009)*
Indiana Micro Met Etching Inc ....F...... 574 293-3342
  Elkhart *(G-2931)*

MILLING: Feed, Wheat

AG Processing A Cooperative ....G...... 574 831-2292
  Goshen *(G-5168)*

MILLING: Grains, Exc Rice

ADM Milling Co...............D...... 812 838-4445
  Mount Vernon *(G-10380)*
Prairie Mills Products LLC ....F...... 574 223-3177
  Rochester *(G-12143)*
Tribine Industries LLC ....G...... 316 282-8011
  Logansport *(G-9371)*

MILLING: Wheat Germ

Vitamins Inc ....E...... 219 879-7356
  Michigan City *(G-9859)*

MILLS: Ferrous & Nonferrous

Amerifab Inc ....D...... 317 231-0100
  Indianapolis *(G-6393)*

MILLWORK

A & M Woodworking ....G...... 574 642-4555
  Millersburg *(G-9968)*
A&J Woodworking LLC ....G...... 574 642-4551
  Goshen *(G-5162)*
AMC Acquisition Corporation ....D...... 215 572-0738
  Elkhart *(G-2681)*
Americas Best Millwrk Supplrs ....G...... 574 780-0066
  Plymouth *(G-11665)*
Amish Hills Woodworking and MA...............G...... 574 875-3558
  Goshen *(G-5170)*
Amish Woodworking LLC ....G...... 574 941-4439
  Plymouth *(G-11666)*
Antreasian Design Inc ....F...... 317 546-3234
  Indianapolis *(G-6404)*
Bittersweet LLC...............G...... 574 642-1184
  Wolcottville *(G-14368)*
Borkholder Wood Products ....G...... 574 546-2613
  Bremen *(G-984)*
Bratco Inc ....G...... 812 536-4071
  Holland *(G-6104)*
Bwt Custom Woodworking LLC ....G...... 812 634-1800
  Jasper *(G-8239)*
Byler Family Wood Working ....G...... 574 825-3339
  Goshen *(G-5183)*
C&A Woodworking Inc ....G...... 574 875-1273
  Elkhart *(G-2745)*
C&M Woodworking LLC ....G...... 260 403-4555
  Leo *(G-9240)*
Cash & Carry Lumber Co Inc ....F...... 765 378-7575
  Daleville *(G-2337)*
Center Line Wood Works Inc ....G...... 317 770-9486
  Fishers *(G-3887)*
Centerline Woodworking...............G...... 260 768-4116
  Lagrange *(G-9034)*
Central Ind Muldings Mllwk Inc ....F...... 317 568-1639
  Indianapolis *(G-6582)*
Central Indiana Woodworkers ....G...... 317 407-9228
  Indianapolis *(G-6584)*
Chase Manufacturing LLC ....C...... 574 546-4776
  Nappanee *(G-10660)*
Chisholm Lumber & Sup Co Inc ....E...... 317 547-3535
  Indianapolis *(G-6601)*
Circle City Woodworking ....G...... 765 637-6687
  Indianapolis *(G-6610)*
Clinton Custom Wood Turning ....G...... 574 535-0543
  Goshen *(G-5188)*
Cns Custom Woodworks Inc ....G...... 812 350-2431
  Columbus *(G-1872)*
Cornerstone Mill Work...............G...... 260 357-0754
  Garrett *(G-4998)*
Couden Woodworks Inc ....G...... 317 370-0835
  Noblesville *(G-11085)*
Country Craftsman Wdwkg LLC...........G...... 574 773-4911
  Nappanee *(G-10664)*
Country Woodworking LLC ....G...... 812 636-6004
  Odon *(G-11322)*
Crestview Woodworking LLC ....G...... 260 768-4707
  Shipshewana *(G-12609)*
Custom Draperies of Indiana ....G...... 219 924-2500
  Hammond *(G-5867)*
Custom Millwork & Display Inc...............F...... 574 289-4000
  South Bend *(G-12750)*
Custom Wood Finishing...............G...... 574 642-1213
  Millersburg *(G-9969)*
Custom Woodworking ....G...... 812 339-6601
  Bloomington *(G-709)*
Custom Woodworking...............G...... 812 422-6786
  Evansville *(G-3452)*
D L Miller Woodworking ....G...... 260 562-9329
  Shipshewana *(G-12610)*

PRODUCT

Diverse Woodworking LLC ....G....... 812 366-3000	John G Wagler.....................G....... 812 709-1681	PJmort Woodworking......................G....... 574 542-9680
Georgetown *(G-5143)*	Odon *(G-11332)*	Monterey *(G-10208)*
Dobbins Interior Woodworks...........G....... 812 221-0058	John Garrison Woodworking LLC.........G....... 765 795-4681	Power Plant Service Inc ....E....... 260 432-6716
Dillsboro *(G-2466)*	Quincy *(G-11891)*	Fort Wayne *(G-4542)*
Double L Woodworking L L C ......F....... 260 768-3155	K Lash & Son Inc ....G....... 260 347-3660	PTG Inc ....G....... 317 892-4625
Goshen *(G-5204)*	Kendallville *(G-8482)*	Brownsburg *(G-1165)*
Dovetail Woodworks.......................G....... 812 448-8832	Kentucky-Indiana Lumber Co Inc....E....... 812 464-2428	Redlin Custom Woodworking LLC.......G....... 317 578-1852
Brazil *(G-959)*	Evansville *(G-3584)*	Fishers *(G-3962)*
Dubois Wood Products Inc ....E....... 812 683-5105	Key Millwork Inc.........................G....... 260 426-6501	Riddle Ridge Woodworks...............G....... 812 596-4503
Huntingburg *(G-6159)*	Fort Wayne *(G-4410)*	English *(G-3318)*
Dutch Made Inc ....G....... 260 657-3331	Kh Woodworking ....G....... 317 702-5094	Ro Vic Wood Products Inc ....E....... 812 283-9199
Harlan *(G-5970)*	Greenfield *(G-5548)*	Jeffersonville *(G-8420)*
Dutchcraft Corporation ....G....... 260 463-8366	Kitchen Konnection Inc ....G....... 812 277-0393	Rockville Woodworks.....................G....... 765 569-6483
Lagrange *(G-9039)*	Bedford *(G-557)*	Rockville *(G-12179)*
E M Woodworking...........................G....... 812 486-2696	Knothole Woodworks LLC ....G....... 317 600-8151	Rockwell Diversified Woodworks.......G....... 317 758-4797
Montgomery *(G-10223)*	Sheridan *(G-12595)*	Sheridan *(G-12597)*
Earthwise Woodworks LLC.............G....... 317 887-0142	Kostyo Woodworking Inc ....G....... 812 466-7350	Rogers Group Inc...........................E....... 812 333-6324
Greenwood *(G-5684)*	Terre Haute *(G-13267)*	Bloomington *(G-816)*
Eleys Woodworking ....G....... 765 584-3531	Kraigs Custom Woodworking ....G....... 574 904-7501	Rst Custom Woodworking LL ....G....... 317 602-2490
Winchester *(G-14328)*	Mishawaka *(G-10066)*	Indianapolis *(G-7870)*
Englehardt Custom Woodworking.....G....... 812 425-9282	Kuntry Lumber and Farm Sup Ltd....E....... 260 463-3242	Rustic Acres Woodworks...............G....... 765 886-5699
Evansville *(G-3478)*	Lagrange *(G-9051)*	Williamsburg *(G-14284)*
Ettensohn & Company LLC ....G....... 812 547-5491	L & N Woodworking.......................G....... 260 768-7008	Salt Creek Woodworks.................G....... 219 730-7553
Tell City *(G-13160)*	Shipshewana *(G-12626)*	Valparaiso *(G-13612)*
Expert Woodworks ....G....... 219 345-2705	L A M B Woodworking.....................G....... 260 768-7992	Samswoodworking ....G....... 574 772-6482
Lake Village *(G-9082)*	Shipshewana *(G-12627)*	Knox *(G-8580)*
Fairview Woodworking ....G....... 260 768-3255	L W Woodworking LLC...................G....... 260 463-8938	Schindler Woodwork ....G....... 513 314-5943
Shipshewana *(G-12614)*	Wolcottville *(G-14373)*	Cedar Grove *(G-1522)*
Faske Wood Moulding Inc.............F....... 812 923-5601	Lakeside Woodworking ....G....... 812 687-7901	Schmucker Woodworking LLC ....G....... 260 413-9784
Borden *(G-929)*	Odon *(G-11333)*	New Haven *(G-10957)*
Ferry Street Woodworks ....G....... 812 427-9663	Lakeview Woodworking ....G....... 574 642-1335	Schwartz Woodworking ....G....... 260 593-3193
Vevay *(G-13663)*	Goshen *(G-5262)*	Millersburg *(G-9973)*
Finish Design Woodworking Inc .....E....... 812 284-9240	Larkin Woodworks ....G....... 765 795-5332	Schwartz Woodworking LLC ....G....... 260 854-9457
Jeffersonville *(G-8360)*	Cloverdale *(G-1728)*	Wolcottville *(G-14376)*
Flp Woodworks...............................G....... 260 424-3904	Legacy Wood Creations LLC ....G....... 574 773-4405	Scp Building Products LLC ....G....... 574 772-2955
Fort Wayne *(G-4268)*	Nappanee *(G-10691)*	Knox *(G-8581)*
Forest Products Group Inc ....E....... 765 659-1807	Light House Woodworking DBA ....G....... 260 704-0589	Shiloh Custom Woodworks ....G....... 812 636-0100
Frankfort *(G-4832)*	Saint Joe *(G-12256)*	Odon *(G-11340)*
Four Woods Laminating Inc............E....... 260 593-2246	Ligonier Woodworking ....G....... 260 894-9969	Sorg Millwork ....G....... 260 639-3223
Topeka *(G-13419)*	Ligonier *(G-9289)*	Fort Wayne *(G-4637)*
Franks Woodworking ....G....... 765 378-0424	Lockerbie Square Cab Co Inc ....G....... 317 635-1134	South Bend Woodworks LLC ....F....... 574 232-8875
Anderson *(G-107)*	Indianapolis *(G-7413)*	South Bend *(G-12947)*
G & R Woodworking LLC ....G....... 812 687-7701	Loggers Incorporated ....E....... 812 939-2797	Spectrum Finishing LLC ....E....... 260 463-7300
Montgomery *(G-10224)*	Clay City *(G-1704)*	Lagrange *(G-9066)*
G & S Rural Woodworking ....G....... 765 348-7781	Maple City Woodworking Corp ....D....... 574 642-3342	State Line Woodworking ....G....... 260 768-4577
Hartford City *(G-5980)*	Goshen *(G-5279)*	Shipshewana *(G-12651)*
Garyrae Inc ....F....... 574 255-7141	Maple Leaf Woodworking ....G....... 260 768-8166	Stephens Woodworking ....G....... 812 487-2818
Mishawaka *(G-10045)*	Lagrange *(G-9059)*	Guilford *(G-5799)*
Georgia-Pacific LLC.......................C....... 219 956-3100	Marquise Enterprises Ltd ....G....... 317 578-3400	Steven Block ....G....... 765 749-5394
Wheatfield *(G-14223)*	Indianapolis *(G-7458)*	Muncie *(G-10567)*
Gilpin Custom Woodworking ....G....... 260 413-6618	Marvelous Woodworking LLC ....G....... 317 679-5890	Stock Building Supply LLC ....E....... 260 490-0616
Roanoke *(G-12103)*	Lebanon *(G-9203)*	Fort Wayne *(G-4650)*
Guereca Woodworking ....G....... 260 724-3994	Maschino Woodworks ....G....... 812 230-7428	Stolls Woodworking LLC ....G....... 812 486-5117
Decatur *(G-2383)*	Terre Haute *(G-13280)*	Odon *(G-11342)*
Gutter One Supply ....G....... 317 872-1257	Mast Woodworking ....G....... 812 636-7938	Stoney Acres Woodworking LLC .....G....... 260 768-4367
Indianapolis *(G-7060)*	Odon *(G-11334)*	Shipshewana *(G-12653)*
Heidenreich Woodworking Inc ....G....... 317 861-9331	Mdl Woodworking LLC...................G....... 260 242-1824	Swiss Woodworking & Sales ....G....... 260 849-9669
New Palestine *(G-10970)*	Fort Wayne *(G-4463)*	Berne *(G-627)*
Hickory Valley Woodworking LLC ....G....... 812 486-2857	Menard Inc ....E....... 260 441-0406	Tarter Woodworking LLC ....G....... 765 349-4193
Loogootee *(G-9385)*	Fort Wayne *(G-4465)*	Martinsville *(G-9640)*
Hilltop Woodworking ....G....... 812 689-3462	Midwest Custom Woodworking ....G....... 574 349-1645	Timothy J Troyer...........................G....... 574 546-1115
Madison *(G-9468)*	Lagrange *(G-9061)*	Bremen *(G-1029)*
Hiltys Woodwork...........................G....... 260 627-2905	Mikes Creative Woodworks LLC ....G....... 502 649-3665	Tru-Cut Inc ....E....... 765 683-9920
Fort Wayne *(G-4336)*	Charlestown *(G-1573)*	Anderson *(G-179)*
Hoosier Custom Woodworking ....G....... 574 642-3764	Molargik Woodworking Inc ....G....... 260 357-6625	Universal Door Carrier Inc ....G....... 317 241-3447
Millersburg *(G-9970)*	Garrett *(G-5016)*	Indianapolis *(G-8129)*
Hoosier Daddy Woodworks ....G....... 812 949-2801	Monroe Wood Works ....G....... 317 979-0964	Universal Forest Products Indi ....C....... 574 273-6326
New Albany *(G-10797)*	Indianapolis *(G-7537)*	Granger *(G-5447)*
Hoosier Wood Works ....G....... 812 325-9823	Mountjoy Wooding ....G....... 317 897-6792	Verns Woodworking ....G....... 574 773-7930
Bloomington *(G-742)*	Indianapolis *(G-7550)*	Bremen *(G-1031)*
Hudec Construction Company ....E....... 219 922-9811	N & R Woodworking Llc ....G....... 812 787-0644	W & M Woodworking ....G....... 260 854-3126
Griffith *(G-5777)*	Odon *(G-11336)*	Lagrange *(G-9071)*
Indiana Dimension Inc ....D....... 574 739-2319	Nalleys Woodworking ....G....... 812 923-1299	Wagler Woodworking ....G....... 812 486-6357
Logansport *(G-9340)*	Greenville *(G-5651)*	Loogootee *(G-9397)*
Indiana Southern Millwork Inc ....E....... 812 346-6129	Napoleon Hardwood Lbr Co Inc ....E....... 812 852-4090	Walnut Lane Woodworking...............G....... 574 633-2114
North Vernon *(G-11263)*	Greensburg *(G-5626)*	Bremen *(G-1032)*
Indianapolis Wdwkg Intl LLC ....E....... 317 841-7800	Nov Oak Woodworking ....G....... 812 422-1973	Waynedale Mill Inc.........................F....... 260 436-7100
Fishers *(G-3929)*	Evansville *(G-3647)*	Fort Wayne *(G-4746)*
Integrity Woodcrafting ....G....... 260 562-2067	Olon Industries Inc (us) ....F....... 812 254-0427	Weaver Woodworking ....G....... 260 565-3647
Shipshewana *(G-12620)*	Washington *(G-13994)*	Bluffton *(G-897)*
Interior Fixs & Mllwk Co Inc ....G....... 812 446-0933	Omega National Products LLC ....C....... 574 295-5353	Weberdings Carving Shop Inc ....F....... 812 934-3710
Knightsville *(G-8561)*	Elkhart *(G-3068)*	Batesville *(G-524)*
Irvine Shade & Door Inc ....D....... 574 522-1446	Owen Woodworking ....G....... 317 331-6936	West Point Woodworking LLC ....G....... 260 768-4750
Elkhart *(G-2940)*	Danville *(G-2354)*	Shipshewana *(G-12658)*
Ivy Woodworks LLC.......................G....... 317 842-4085	Philip Konrad & Sons Inc ....F....... 574 772-3966	White Aspen Woodworking LLC ....G....... 765 471-4962
Indianapolis *(G-7278)*	Knox *(G-8576)*	Lafayette *(G-9023)*
Jackson Brothers Lumber Co ....F....... 812 847-7812	Pickslays Woodworking ....G....... 530 388-8697	Whites Woodworks ....G....... 765 341-6678
Linton *(G-9308)*	Winona Lake *(G-14353)*	Martinsville *(G-9648)*
James G Henager...........................G....... 812 795-2230	Pinnacle Woodworking LLC ....G....... 765 345-2301	Wible Lumber Inc...........................E....... 260 351-2441
Elberfeld *(G-2636)*	Knightstown *(G-8559)*	South Milford *(G-12995)*

2018 Harris Indiana
Industrial Directory

(G-0000) Company's Geographic Section entry number

Wichman Woodworking Inc ....G..... 812 522-8450
  Seymour (G-12500)
Wildwood Millwork LLC ....G..... 574 535-9104
  Goshen (G-5346)
Wilmes Window Mfg Co Inc ....E..... 812 275-7575
  Ferdinand (G-3864)
Wood Creations Inc ....G..... 574 522-7765
  Elkhart (G-3265)
Wood Specialists LLC ....G..... 219 779-9026
  Crown Point (G-2322)
Woodland Ridge Woodworking ....G..... 812 821-8032
  Ellettsville (G-3285)
Woodside Woodworks ....G..... 260 499-3220
  Wolcottville (G-14378)
Woodworking By Rich ....G..... 317 535-5750
  Whiteland (G-14248)
Wrights Woodworking ....G..... 765 723-1546
  New Ross (G-11006)
Yellow Dog Woodworking LLC ....G..... 502 817-9395
  Greenville (G-5656)
Yoder Woodworking ....G..... 574 825-0402
  Middlebury (G-9929)

MIMEOGRAPHING SVCS

Regal Printing Inc ....G..... 317 844-1723
  Carmel (G-1464)

MINE & QUARRY SVCS: Nonmetallic Minerals

243 Quarry ....G..... 765 653-4100
  Cloverdale (G-1723)

MINE DEVELOPMENT, METAL

James F Reilly 3 Ent ....G..... 574 277-8267
  Mishawaka (G-10058)

MINERAL ABRASIVES MINING SVCS

Peabody Midwest Mining LLC ....G..... 812 795-0040
  Oakland City (G-11313)

MINERAL PIGMENT MINING

Wild Boar Mine ....G..... 812 922-1015
  Lynnville (G-9438)

MINERAL WOOL

Aearo Technologies LLC ....C..... 317 692-6666
  Indianapolis (G-6342)
Global Composites Inc ....G..... 574 522-0475
  Elkhart (G-2884)
Insulation Specialties of Amer ....E..... 219 733-2502
  Wanatah (G-13824)
Johns Manville Corporation ....E..... 574 546-4666
  Bremen (G-1006)
Molded Acstcal Pdts Easton Inc ....E..... 610 253-7135
  Elkhart (G-3045)
Owens Corning Sales LLC ....C..... 765 647-4131
  Brookville (G-1122)
Owens Corning Sales LLC ....E..... 765 647-2857
  Brookville (G-1123)
Owens Corning Sales LLC ....D..... 219 465-4324
  Valparaiso (G-13596)
PSC Industries Inc ....E..... 317 547-5439
  Indianapolis (G-7785)
Unifrax I LLC ....C..... 574 654-7100
  New Carlisle (G-10889)
Unique-Prescotech Inc ....E..... 479 646-2973
  Evansville (G-3783)
United States Mineral Pdts Co ....D..... 260 356-2040
  Huntington (G-6259)

MINERALS: Ground Or Otherwise Treated

Calcean LLC ....G..... 812 672-4995
  Seymour (G-12437)
Performance Minerals Corp ....G..... 219 365-8356
  Saint John (G-12266)

MINERALS: Ground or Treated

Beemsterboer Slag Corp ....E..... 219 931-7462
  Hammond (G-5848)
Beemsterboer Slag Corp ....E..... 219 931-7462
  Hammond (G-5849)
Hydraulic Press Brick Company ....E..... 317 290-1140
  Mooresville (G-10313)
Irving Materials Inc ....F..... 765 922-7285
  Marion (G-9534)

Mid-Continent Coal and Coke Co ....E..... 219 787-8171
  Portage (G-11775)
Rogers Group Inc ....E..... 812 849-3530
  Mitchell (G-10170)
Suez Wts Usa Inc ....G..... 219 397-0554
  East Chicago (G-2569)
Unimin Corporation ....G..... 812 683-2179
  Huntingburg (G-6183)
United Minerals and Prpts Inc ....E..... 812 838-5236
  Mount Vernon (G-10412)

MINIATURES

Litko Aerosystems Inc ....G..... 219 462-9295
  Valparaiso (G-13577)
Mercs Miniatures LLC ....G..... 765 661-6724
  Westfield (G-14176)
Mid America Prototyping Inc ....G..... 765 643-3200
  Anderson (G-135)

MINING MACHINERY & EQPT WHOLESALERS

Mining Machine Parts Inc ....G..... 812 897-1256
  Boonville (G-918)
Vandergriff & Associates Inc ....G..... 812 422-6033
  Evansville (G-3793)

MINING MACHINES & EQPT: Feeders, Ore & Aggregate

Quality Systems LLC ....F..... 317 326-4660
  Indianapolis (G-7800)

MINING MACHINES & EQPT: Rock Crushing, Stationary

J W Jones Company LLC ....E..... 765 537-2279
  Paragon (G-11458)
Stedman Machine Company ....D..... 812 926-0038
  Aurora (G-390)

MINING SVCS, NEC: Anthracite

ERC Mining Indiana Corp ....G..... 812 665-9780
  Jasonville (G-8234)

MINING: Oil Shale

C Milligan Investments LLC ....G..... 219 241-5811
  Valparaiso (G-13518)

MINING: Tar Sand

Imperial Petroleum Inc ....G..... 812 867-1433
  Evansville (G-3549)

MIRRORS: Motor Vehicle

Grote Industries Inc ....A..... 812 273-2121
  Madison (G-9463)
Grote Industries LLC ....A..... 812 265-8273
  Madison (G-9464)
Ramco Engineering Inc ....E..... 574 266-1455
  Elkhart (G-3136)

MISCELLANEOUS FINANCIAL INVEST ACT: Mineral Leasing Dealers

Calcean LLC ....G..... 812 672-4995
  Seymour (G-12437)

MISCELLANEOUS FINANCIAL INVEST ACT: Oil/Gas Lease Brokers

United Minerals ....G..... 812 842-0978
  Newburgh (G-11054)

MISSILE GUIDANCE SYSTEMS & EQPT

Attco Machine Products Inc ....E..... 574 234-1063
  South Bend (G-12714)

MITTENS: Leather

5m Poultry LLC ....G..... 812 890-5558
  Carlisle (G-1294)

MITTENS: Rubber

Td Consulting LLC ....G..... 260 925-3089
  Auburn (G-360)

MIXING EQPT

Asphalt Drum Mixers Inc ....E..... 260 637-5729
  Huntertown (G-6134)
Asphalt Equipment Company Inc ....G..... 260 672-3004
  Fort Wayne (G-4093)

MIXTURES & BLOCKS: Asphalt Paving

Aaron Asphalt Maintenance Seal ....G..... 574 528-6370
  Syracuse (G-13128)
Allterrain Paving & Cnstr LLC ....E..... 502 265-4731
  New Albany (G-10742)
Asphalt Cutbacks Inc ....F..... 219 398-4230
  East Chicago (G-2521)
Asphalt Engineers Inc ....E..... 574 289-5557
  South Bend (G-12712)
Asphalt Materials Inc ....E..... 317 243-8304
  Indianapolis (G-6427)
Bowman Brothers Inc ....F..... 317 253-6043
  Indianapolis (G-6498)
Dave OMara Paving Inc ....G..... 812 346-1214
  North Vernon (G-11252)
DC Construction Services Inc ....E..... 317 577-0276
  Indianapolis (G-6730)
E & B Paving Inc ....E..... 765 674-5848
  Marion (G-9522)
E & B Paving Inc ....F..... 765 289-7131
  Muncie (G-10465)
F E Harding Paving Co Inc ....E..... 317 846-7401
  Indianapolis (G-6899)
Hco Holding I Corporation ....E..... 317 248-1344
  Indianapolis (G-7081)
Heritage Asphalt LLC ....G..... 317 872-6010
  Indianapolis (G-7095)
Lafarge North America Inc ....G..... 219 378-1193
  East Chicago (G-2547)
Laketon Refining Corporation ....E..... 260 982-0703
  Laketon (G-9090)
Milestone Contractors LP ....C..... 765 772-7500
  Lafayette (G-8970)
Milestone Contractors LP ....G..... 812 579-5248
  Columbus (G-1975)
Monument Chemical LLC ....F..... 317 223-2630
  Indianapolis (G-7539)
Niblock Excavating Inc ....F..... 260 248-2100
  Columbia City (G-1812)
Parsleys Seal Coating Inc ....G..... 812 876-5450
  Ellettsville (G-3283)
Rieth-Riley Cnstr Co Inc ....D..... 765 447-2324
  Lafayette (G-8993)
Rieth-Riley Cnstr Co Inc ....E..... 574 288-8321
  South Bend (G-12915)
Rieth-Riley Cnstr Co Inc ....C..... 574 875-5183
  Gary (G-5093)
Rogers Group Inc ....E..... 812 333-8550
  Bloomington (G-817)
Rogers Group Inc ....G..... 765 342-6898
  Martinsville (G-9635)
Scotts Grant County Asp Inc ....G..... 765 664-2754
  Marion (G-9561)
Semmaterials LP ....G..... 574 267-5076
  Warsaw (G-13937)
Super Seal Inc ....F..... 765 639-4993
  Summitville (G-13106)
Valley Asphalt Corporation ....E..... 812 926-1471
  Aurora (G-392)
Walters Development LLC ....G..... 260 747-7531
  Fort Wayne (G-4734)

MOBILE COMMUNICATIONS EQPT

At T ....G..... 765 649-5900
  Anderson (G-70)
Haven Technologies Inc ....G..... 317 490-7197
  Carmel (G-1399)

MOBILE HOME REPAIR SVCS

Thornes Homes Inc ....G..... 812 275-4656
  Bedford (G-584)

MOBILE HOMES

Accent Complex Inc ....G..... 574 522-2368
  Elkhart (G-2664)
Bayview Estates ....G..... 574 457-4136
  Syracuse (G-13129)
Champion Home Builders Inc ....B..... 260 593-2962
  Topeka (G-13412)
Clayton Homes Inc ....G..... 260 553-5500
  Garrett (G-4997)

Clayton Homes Inc ....G 812 423-4052
Evansville *(G-3419)*

Dutchtown Homes ....G 812 354-2197
Otwell *(G-11422)*

Fr Chinook LLC ....G 317 356-1666
Indianapolis *(G-6955)*

Gulf Stream Coach Inc ....C 574 773-7761
Nappanee *(G-10677)*

Heritage Financial Group Inc ....D 574 522-8000
Elkhart *(G-2914)*

Home Phone Inc ....G 812 280-3657
Jeffersonville *(G-8375)*

Kropf Industries Inc ....E 574 533-2171
Goshen *(G-5258)*

Lcf Enterprises LLC ....G 260 483-3248
Fort Wayne *(G-4428)*

Liberty Homes Inc ....D 574 533-0438
Goshen *(G-5265)*

Lippert Components Inc ....E 574 535-1125
Goshen *(G-5271)*

Lippert Components Inc ....D 574 535-1125
Goshen *(G-5268)*

Rev Recreation Group Inc ....E 260 728-9564
Decatur *(G-2401)*

Rev Recreation Group Inc ....C 260 724-4217
Decatur *(G-2403)*

Skyline Champion Corporation ......B 574 294-6521
Elkhart *(G-3175)*

Skyline Homes Inc ....C 574 294-6521
Elkhart *(G-3176)*

Thornes Homes Inc ....G 812 275-4656
Bedford *(G-584)*

Tyson Corporation ....E 317 241-8396
Indianapolis *(G-8119)*

Zieman Manufacturing Company ...G 574 522-5202
Goshen *(G-5347)*

MOBILE HOMES WHOLESALERS

Martin Spouting Inc ....G 260 485-5703
Fort Wayne *(G-4453)*

MOBILE HOMES, EXC RECREATIONAL

Commodore Corporation ....C 574 534-3067
Goshen *(G-5192)*

Fairmont Homes LLC ....C 574 773-7941
Nappanee *(G-10669)*

Fairmont Homes LLC ....G 574 773-2041
Nappanee *(G-10670)*

Hi-Tech Housing Inc ....D 574 848-5593
Bristol *(G-1062)*

Skyline Corporation ....C 574 848-7621
Bristol *(G-1087)*

MOBILE HOMES: Indl Or Commercial Use

Modular Builders Inc ....E 574 223-4934
Rochester *(G-12140)*

Rodeswood LLC ....G 574 457-4496
Syracuse *(G-13142)*

MOBILE HOMES: Personal Or Private Use

Jay Mobile Home Additions ....G 260 726-9274
Portland *(G-11830)*

Rochester Homes Inc ....C 574 223-4321
Rochester *(G-12146)*

Woodland Park Inc ....D 574 825-2104
Middlebury *(G-9927)*

MODELS

Taurus Tech & Engrg LLC ....E 765 282-2090
Muncie *(G-10568)*

MODELS: General, Exc Toy

Maxwell Engineering Inc ....G 260 745-4991
Fort Wayne *(G-4458)*

Realize Inc ....F 317 915-0295
Noblesville *(G-11172)*

Techcom Inc ....E 317 865-2530
Indianapolis *(G-8048)*

Techcom Inc ....F 812 372-0960
Columbus *(G-2020)*

MODULES: Computer Logic

Federal-Mogul LLC ....G 574 271-0274
South Bend *(G-12775)*

MOLDED RUBBER PRDTS

Acme Masking Company Inc ....E 317 272-6202
Avon *(G-425)*

BRC Rubber & Plastics Inc ....D 260 827-0871
Bluffton *(G-869)*

E Industries Inc ....G 574 522-7550
Elkhart *(G-2808)*

Field Rubber Products Inc ....F 317 773-3787
Noblesville *(G-11103)*

Gorilla Plastic Rbr Group LLC ....F 317 635-9616
Indianapolis *(G-7029)*

Griffith Rbr Mills of Garrett ....F 260 357-0876
Garrett *(G-5008)*

H A King Co Inc ....F 260 482-6376
Fort Wayne *(G-4313)*

Hawkins Darryal ....G 765 282-6021
Muncie *(G-10482)*

Iris Rubber Company Inc ....F 317 984-3561
Cicero *(G-1662)*

McCammon Engineering Corp ....G 812 356-4455
Sullivan *(G-13086)*

Phoenix Closures Inc ....D 765 658-1800
Greencastle *(G-5472)*

Protective Coatings Inc ....E 260 424-2900
Fort Wayne *(G-4563)*

Schachtpfister Inc ....G 260 356-9775
Huntington *(G-6246)*

Specialty Products & Polymers ....G 269 684-5931
South Bend *(G-12948)*

Ten Cate Enbi Inc (indiana) ....C 317 398-3267
Shelbyville *(G-12574)*

Vestil Manufacturing Corp ....B 260 665-7586
Angola *(G-258)*

MOLDING COMPOUNDS

A Schulman Inc ....G 812 253-5238
Evansville *(G-3329)*

Alterra Plastics LLC ....F 812 271-1890
Seymour *(G-12429)*

Bd Medical Development Inc ....G 219 310-8551
Crown Point *(G-2227)*

Best Formed Plastics LLC ....E 574 293-6128
Elkhart *(G-2722)*

Industrial Dielectrics Inc ....D 317 773-1766
Noblesville *(G-11127)*

Matrix Tool Inc ....F 574 259-3093
Mishawaka *(G-10075)*

Matrixx Group Incorporated ....C 812 423-5218
Evansville *(G-3618)*

Replas of Texas Inc ....G 812 421-3600
Evansville *(G-3704)*

Sabic Innovative Plas US LLC ....D 812 372-0197
Columbus *(G-2010)*

Stenidy Industries Inc ....G 317 873-5343
Zionsville *(G-14466)*

Venture Indus ....G 765 348-5780
Hartford City *(G-5995)*

Vidal Plastics LLC ....G 812 431-8075
Evansville *(G-3799)*

MOLDING SAND MINING

Warsaw Foundry Company Inc ....D 574 267-8772
Warsaw *(G-13962)*

MOLDINGS & TRIM: Metal, Exc Automobile

Oak-Rite Mfg Corp ....E 317 839-2301
Plainfield *(G-11632)*

MOLDINGS & TRIM: Wood

Alexandria Mw LLC ....G 219 324-9541
La Porte *(G-8729)*

Clark Millworks ....G 260 665-1270
Angola *(G-203)*

Eckhart Woodworking Inc ....E 260 692-6218
Monroe *(G-10181)*

Louisiana-Pacific Corporation ....D 574 825-5845
Middlebury *(G-9905)*

Robert Weed Plywood Corp ....B 574 848-7631
Bristol *(G-1081)*

Rodeswood LLC ....G 574 457-4496
Syracuse *(G-13142)*

Ufp Nappanee LLC ....D 574 773-2505
Nappanee *(G-10709)*

MOLDINGS OR TRIM: Automobile, Stamped Metal

Impressive Stamping & Mfg Co ....G 260 824-2610
Bluffton *(G-878)*

MOLDINGS: Picture Frame

Editions Ltd Gallery Fine Arts ....G 317 466-9940
Indianapolis *(G-6806)*

Gibbs Susie Framing & Art ....G 765 428-2434
Lafayette *(G-8907)*

Pfortune Art & Design Inc ....G 317 872-4123
Indianapolis *(G-7681)*

Radecki Galleries Inc ....G 574 287-0266
South Bend *(G-12913)*

MOLDS: Indl

Accurate Tool & Engineering ....G 812 963-6677
Evansville *(G-3335)*

Acme Masking Company Inc ....E 317 272-6202
Avon *(G-425)*

Admar Mold & Engineering Inc ....G 574 848-7085
Bristol *(G-1041)*

Advanced Mold & Engineering ....F 812 342-9000
Columbus *(G-1850)*

Aluminum Foundries Inc ....C 765 584-6501
Winchester *(G-14324)*

Applied Composites Engrg Inc ....E 317 243-4225
Indianapolis *(G-6411)*

AR Tee Enterprises Inc ....G 574 848-5543
Bristol *(G-1046)*

Artisan Tool & Die Inc ....G 765 288-6653
Muncie *(G-10433)*

Asbestos Abatement & Mold ....G 317 783-0350
Indianapolis *(G-6425)*

Atlas Die LLC ....D 574 295-0277
Elkhart *(G-2700)*

Axis Mold Inc ....G 574 292-8904
New Carlisle *(G-10879)*

Boe Knows Mold ....G 260 760-7136
New Haven *(G-10931)*

Broken Mold Customs Inc ....D 219 863-1008
Demotte *(G-2433)*

Constellation Mold Inc ....F 812 424-5338
Evansville *(G-3429)*

Davis Machine & Tool Inc ....G 812 526-2674
Edinburgh *(G-2606)*

Drp Mold Inc ....G 765 349-3355
Martinsville *(G-9602)*

Engrave Inc ....F 812 537-8693
Lawrenceburg *(G-9140)*

Epw LLC ....D 574 293-5090
Elkhart *(G-2836)*

Fort Wayne Mold & Engrg Inc ....E 260 747-9168
Fort Wayne *(G-4276)*

Glaze Tool and Engineering Inc ......E 260 493-4557
New Haven *(G-10941)*

Guardian Mold Prevent Corp ....G 708 878-5788
Dyer *(G-2499)*

Huth Tool & Machine Corp ....G 260 749-9411
Fort Wayne *(G-4351)*

Indiana Southern Mold Corp ....E 812 346-2622
North Vernon *(G-11264)*

Injection Mold Inc ....F 812 346-7002
North Vernon *(G-11266)*

JMS Mold & Engineering Co Inc ......F 574 272-0198
South Bend *(G-12824)*

Jones Machine & Tool Inc ....E 812 364-4588
Fredericksburg *(G-4945)*

Journeyman Tool & Mold Inc ....G 574 237-1880
South Bend *(G-12825)*

K Mold and Engineering Inc ....F 574 272-5858
Granger *(G-5417)*

Kitterman Machine Co Inc ....G 317 773-2283
Noblesville *(G-11139)*

Kruis Mold & Engineering Inc ....F 574 293-4613
Elkhart *(G-2976)*

Lb Mold Inc ....E 812 526-2030
Edinburgh *(G-2616)*

Lorentson Manufacturing Co ....E 765 452-4425
Kokomo *(G-8660)*

M & R Pattern Inc ....G 219 778-4675
La Porte *(G-8788)*

Matchless Machine & Tool Co ....E 765 342-4550
Martinsville *(G-9624)*

Maxwell Engineering Inc ....G 260 745-4991
Fort Wayne *(G-4458)*

Micro Tool & Machine Co Inc ....G 574 272-9141
Granger *(G-5421)*

(G-0000) Company's Geographic Section entry number

Midwest Mold Remediation...................G..... 502 386-6559
  Jeffersonville (G-8401)
Midwest Remediation.........................E..... 317 826-0940
  Indianapolis (G-7510)
Mold Busters LLC.............................G..... 812 989-0008
  Floyds Knobs (G-4016)
Mold Removal Team of Hammond ....G..... 219 554-9719
  Hammond (G-5917)
Mold Stoppers of Indiana...................G..... 812 325-1609
  Bloomington (G-774)
Moonlight Mold & Machine Inc ....G..... 765 868-9860
  Kokomo (G-8671)
Morris Mold and Machine Co..............G..... 317 923-6653
  Indianapolis (G-7544)
Msk Mold Inc.................................G..... 812 985-5457
  Wadesville (G-13773)
Muncie Mold & Engineering LLC..........G..... 765 282-0522
  Muncie (G-10531)
Omega Enterprises Inc.....................E..... 765 584-1990
  Winchester (G-14339)
Overton Mold Inc............................F..... 317 831-9595
  Mooresville (G-10333)
Pinnacle Tool Inc............................G..... 812 336-5000
  Bloomington (G-799)
Precise Tooling Solutions Inc ....D..... 812 378-0247
  Columbus (G-1999)
Precision Mold & Tool Inc ....F..... 765 284-4415
  Muncie (G-10547)
Precision Plastics Indiana Inc ....C..... 260 244-6114
  Columbia City (G-1819)
Premier Mold ....G..... 574 293-2846
  Elkhart (G-3112)
Pro Tool & Engineering Inc ....F..... 574 256-5911
  Mishawaka (G-10110)
Quality Mold & Engineering ....G..... 812 346-6577
  Vernon (G-13652)
R & D Mold & Engineering Inc ....G..... 574 257-1070
  Mishawaka (G-10113)
Richeys Mold and Tool Inc.................G..... 812 752-1059
  Scottsburg (G-12378)
Royal Tool & Molding Inc ....G..... 574 643-6800
  Royal Center (G-12215)
Shakour Industries Inc ....G..... 574 289-0100
  South Bend (G-12932)
Six Sigma Mold Inc ....G..... 219 285-6539
  Morocco (G-10363)
Tri State Mold ....G..... 859 240-7643
  Rising Sun (G-12092)
Triple H Tool Co ....G..... 812 567-4600
  Tennyson (G-13182)
Triplex Industries Inc ....F..... 574 256-9253
  Mishawaka (G-10141)
Wirco Inc.....................................C..... 260 897-3768
  Avilla (G-422)

MOLDS: Plastic Working & Foundry

Accu-Mold LLC..............................E..... 269 323-0388
  Mishawaka (G-9989)
Astar Inc.....................................E..... 574 234-2137
  South Bend (G-12713)
C & T Engineering Inc......................F..... 812 522-5854
  Seymour (G-12436)
Center Line Mold & Tool Inc...............F..... 812 526-0970
  Edinburgh (G-2598)
D & J Tool Co Inc ....G..... 260 636-2682
  Albion (G-22)
D&D Automation Inc ....G..... 812 299-1045
  Terre Haute (G-13221)
Future Mold Inc ....F..... 812 941-8661
  New Albany (G-10785)
Hopper Development Inc ....F..... 574 753-6621
  Logansport (G-9336)
Kc Engineering Inc ....G..... 317 352-9742
  Indianapolis (G-7337)
Michiana Global Mold Inc ....F..... 574 259-6262
  Mishawaka (G-10081)
Michiana Plastics Inc ....E..... 574 259-6262
  Mishawaka (G-10084)
Ruco Inc......................................E..... 574 262-4110
  Elkhart (G-3151)
Southern Mold and Tool Inc ....G..... 812 752-3333
  Scottsburg (G-12380)
Western Consolidated Tech Inc...........D..... 260 495-9866
  Fremont (G-4982)

MONOFILAMENTS: Nontextile

H and H 3d Plastics Inc ....G..... 812 699-0379
  Linton (G-9307)

MONUMENTS & GRAVE MARKERS, EXC TERRAZZO

55 Monument Cir Level Off LLC ....G..... 317 423-9472
  Indianapolis (G-6292)
Beyond Monumental.........................G..... 317 454-8519
  Indianapolis (G-6471)
Monument Lighthouse Chart ....G..... 317 657-0160
  Indianapolis (G-7541)
Tri State Monument Company ....G..... 812 386-7303
  Princeton (G-11888)
Vandivier Tudor Monuments ....G..... 317 736-5292
  Franklin (G-4938)
Wearlypocock Monuments ....G..... 574 223-2010
  Rochester (G-12160)
Yoders Monuments Inc ....G..... 260 768-7934
  Middlebury (G-9930)

MONUMENTS: Concrete

Monument Construction Inc ....G..... 317 472-0271
  Indianapolis (G-7540)
Rensselaer Eagle Vault Corp ....G..... 219 866-5123
  Rensselaer (G-11936)

MONUMENTS: Cut Stone, Exc Finishing Or Lettering Only

Terre Haute Wilbert Burial Vlt ....F..... 812 235-0339
  Terre Haute (G-13353)

MOPS: Floor & Dust

Evansville Assn For The Blind ....C..... 812 422-1181
  Evansville (G-3482)
Reit-Price Mfg Co Incorporated ....G..... 765 964-3252
  Union City (G-13460)

MOTEL: Franchised

Whiteco Industries Inc......................A..... 219 769-6601
  Merrillville (G-9761)

MOTION PICTURE & VIDEO PRODUCTION SVCS

Motion Engineering Company Inc.........G..... 317 804-7990
  Westfield (G-14177)

MOTION PICTURE PRODUCTION ALLIED SVCS

Creative Impressions Inc ....F..... 317 244-9842
  Indianapolis (G-6687)

MOTOR & GENERATOR PARTS: Electric

Hillside Motor Sales LLC....................G..... 219 322-7700
  Schererville (G-12322)
Matrix Nac....................................F..... 219 931-6600
  Hammond (G-5914)
MO Trailer Corporation......................F..... 574 533-0824
  Goshen (G-5295)

MOTOR HOMES

Aip/Fw Funding Inc..........................G..... 212 627-2360
  Decatur (G-2364)
All American Group Inc ....E..... 574 262-0123
  Elkhart (G-2674)
All American Group Inc ....F..... 574 262-9889
  Elkhart (G-2675)
All American Group Inc ....D..... 574 825-1720
  Middlebury (G-9869)
Bison Horse Trailers LLC....................G..... 574 658-4161
  Milford (G-9950)
Damon Corporation..........................F..... 574 262-2624
  Elkhart (G-2787)
Damon Corporation..........................B..... 574 262-2624
  Elkhart (G-2788)
Damon Corporation..........................F..... 574 264-2900
  Elkhart (G-2789)
Ds Corp.......................................C..... 260 593-3850
  Topeka (G-13417)
Fiber-Tron Corp...............................E..... 574 294-8545
  Elkhart (G-2848)
Fleetwood Motor Homes ....G..... 260 627-6800
  Spencerville (G-13046)
Forest River Inc..............................C..... 574 262-3474
  Elkhart (G-2862)
Forest River Inc..............................C..... 574 296-7700
  Elkhart (G-2866)

Gulf Stream Coach Inc ....A..... 574 773-7761
  Nappanee (G-10676)
Gulf Stream Coach Inc ....C..... 574 773-7761
  Nappanee (G-10677)
Jayco Inc.....................................A..... 574 825-5861
  Middlebury (G-9896)
Newmar Corporation........................A..... 574 773-7791
  Nappanee (G-10699)
Phoenix Usa Inc ....E..... 574 266-2020
  Elkhart (G-3095)
Rev Recreation Group Inc ....E..... 260 728-9564
  Decatur (G-2401)
Rev Recreation Group Inc ....C..... 260 728-2121
  Decatur (G-2402)
Rev Recreation Group Inc ....C..... 260 724-4217
  Decatur (G-2403)
Starcraft Corporation ....C..... 574 534-7827
  Goshen (G-5329)
Thor Motor Coach ....G..... 574 266-1111
  Elkhart (G-3215)
Thor Motor Coach Inc.......................B..... 574 266-1111
  Elkhart (G-3216)
Zoomers Rv of Indiana LLC ....G..... 260 414-1978
  Wabash (G-13769)

MOTOR REBUILDING SVCS, EXC AUTOMOTIVE

Kirby Risk Corporation......................F..... 765 254-5460
  Muncie (G-10505)
McBroom Electric Co Inc ....D..... 317 926-3451
  Indianapolis (G-7471)
Morgan Automotive...........................G..... 765 378-0593
  Chesterfield (G-1588)

MOTOR REPAIR SVCS

Horner Industrial Services Inc ....D..... 317 639-4261
  Indianapolis (G-7130)
Ies Subsidiary Holdings Inc ....D..... 219 937-0100
  Hammond (G-5897)
Indian Creek Outdoor Power LLC ....G..... 812 597-3055
  Morgantown (G-10354)

MOTOR SCOOTERS & PARTS

Dngco LLC....................................E..... 800 643-7332
  Fort Wayne (G-4216)

MOTOR VEHICLE ASSEMBLY, COMPLETE: Ambulances

Medix Specialty Vehicles LLC...............C..... 574 266-0911
  Elkhart (G-3028)
Medtec Ambulance Corporation...........C..... 574 534-2631
  Goshen (G-5284)
Medtec Ambulance Corporation...........G..... 574 533-2924
  Goshen (G-5285)
Valparaiso Fire Fighters ....D..... 219 462-5291
  Valparaiso (G-13634)

MOTOR VEHICLE ASSEMBLY, COMPLETE: Autos, Incl Specialty

Elringklinger Mfg Ind Inc ....G..... 734 788-1776
  Fort Wayne (G-4236)
Flexform Technologies LLC..................E..... 574 295-3777
  Elkhart (G-2853)
Ford Motor Company.........................D..... 317 837-2302
  Plainfield (G-11610)
Fred Sibley Sr.................................G..... 574 264-2237
  Elkhart (G-2869)
Global Trnsp Organization LLC ....G..... 574 226-6372
  Elkhart (G-2887)
Honda Manufacturing Ind LLC.............A..... 812 222-6000
  Greensburg (G-5612)
Hoosier Hot Rods Classics Inc.............G..... 812 768-5221
  Haubstadt (G-6003)
Jbm Race Cars LLC.........................G..... 812 305-3666
  Evansville (G-3572)
K & D Custom Coach Inc....................E..... 574 537-1716
  Goshen (G-5250)
Mastersbilt Chassis Inc.....................F..... 812 793-3666
  Crothersville (G-2218)
Midway Specialty Vehicles LLC............C..... 574 264-2530
  Elkhart (G-3038)
Mirrus Corporation Inc ....E..... 812 689-1411
  Versailles (G-13656)
Nemesis Race Cars...........................G..... 812 361-9743
  Bloomington (G-778)

PRODUCT

Olson Race Cars ....G...... 765 529-6933
New Castle (G-10914)
Race Cars USA LLC ....G...... 317 508-3500
Carmel (G-1462)
Race Engineering ....G...... 219 661-8904
Crown Point (G-2291)
Rayburn Automotive Inc ....G...... 317 535-8232
Whiteland (G-14244)
Schumacher Racing Corporation ....E...... 317 858-0356
Brownsburg (G-1169)
Spitzers Racing Enterprises ....F...... 317 894-9533
Greenfield (G-5577)
Team Green Inc ....D...... 317 872-2700
Indianapolis (G-8043)
Tony Stewart Racing Entps LLC ....G...... 317 858-8620
Brownsburg (G-1175)
Toyota Boshoku America Inc ....E...... 812 385-2040
Princeton (G-11885)
Vuteq Usa Inc ....G...... 812 385-2584
Princeton (G-11889)
Wgs Global Services LC ....C...... 812 548-4446
Tell City (G-13177)

MOTOR VEHICLE ASSEMBLY, COMPLETE: Bus/Large Spclty Vehicles

Coachmen Recrtl Vehicles Co ....G...... 574 825-5821
Middlebury (G-9876)

MOTOR VEHICLE ASSEMBLY, COMPLETE: Buses, All Types

Besi Manufacturing Inc ....F...... 812 427-4114
Vevay (G-13660)
Capital City Transit LLC ....G...... 317 813-5800
Indianapolis (G-6547)
Damon Corporation ....F...... 574 264-2900
Elkhart (G-2789)
Forest River Inc ....G...... 574 262-5466
Elkhart (G-2863)
Goshen Coach Inc ....C...... 574 970-6300
Elkhart (G-2891)
Independent Protection Co Inc ....C...... 574 533-4116
Goshen (G-5242)
Independent Protection Co Inc ....E...... 574 533-4116
Goshen (G-5243)
Jbh Manufacturing LLC ....G...... 574 612-1379
Goshen (G-5247)
Nix Bus Sales Inc ....E...... 812 464-2576
Poseyville (G-11858)
Thor Industries Inc ....C...... 574 970-7460
Elkhart (G-3214)
Turtle Top Mini Motor Homes ....G...... 574 831-4340
Goshen (G-5343)

MOTOR VEHICLE ASSEMBLY, COMPLETE: Fire Department Vehicles

1st Attack Engineering Inc ....G...... 260 837-2435
Waterloo (G-14009)
Fishers Fire Station 92 ....G...... 317 595-3292
Fishers (G-3912)
Mc Ginley Fire Apparatus ....G...... 765 482-3152
Lebanon (G-9204)
Renewed Performance Company ....F...... 765 675-7586
Tipton (G-13404)

MOTOR VEHICLE ASSEMBLY, COMPLETE: Military Motor Vehicle

AM General Holdings LLC ....F...... 574 237-6222
South Bend (G-12699)
AM General LLC ....A...... 574 258-7523
Mishawaka (G-9995)
AM General LLC ....B...... 574 258-6699
South Bend (G-12702)
U S O of Indiana Inc ....G...... 317 704-2400
Indianapolis (G-8123)

MOTOR VEHICLE ASSEMBLY, COMPLETE: Motor Homes, Self Contain

Royale Phoenix Inc ....G...... 574 206-1216
Elkhart (G-3150)

MOTOR VEHICLE ASSEMBLY, COMPLETE: Snow Plows

Discount Power Equipment ....G...... 765 642-0040
Anderson (G-96)

MOTOR VEHICLE ASSEMBLY, COMPLETE: Truck & Tractor Trucks

Ring-Co LLC ....G...... 317 641-7050
Trafalgar (G-13437)
Toyota Motor Mfg Ind Inc ....C...... 812 387-2266
Princeton (G-11887)

MOTOR VEHICLE ASSEMBLY, COMPLETE: Truck Tractors, Highway

Freightliner Cstm Chassis Corp ....G...... 260 517-9678
Wakarusa (G-13777)
Richard Sheets ....G...... 574 536-8247
Bristol (G-1080)

MOTOR VEHICLE ASSEMBLY, COMPLETE: Trucks, Pickup

Badlands Pick Up Van ACC Salv ....G...... 574 633-2156
Wyatt (G-14396)

MOTOR VEHICLE ASSEMBLY, COMPLETE: Wreckers, Tow Truck

B & B Industries Inc ....E...... 574 262-8551
Elkhart (G-2710)
Sparkling Clean Inc ....G...... 812 422-4871
Evansville (G-3741)

MOTOR VEHICLE DEALERS: Automobiles, New & Used

Sternberg Inc ....E...... 812 867-0077
Evansville (G-3751)

MOTOR VEHICLE DEALERS: Cars, Used Only

Coach Line Motors ....G...... 765 825-7893
Connersville (G-2043)
Motorama Auto Ctr Inc ....G...... 317 831-0036
Mooresville (G-10325)

MOTOR VEHICLE PARTS & ACCESS: Air Conditioner Parts

Keihin Aircon North America ....C...... 765 213-4915
Muncie (G-10502)
Mobile Climate Control Corp ....D...... 574 534-1516
Goshen (G-5296)

MOTOR VEHICLE PARTS & ACCESS: Axel Housings & Shafts

Dexter Axle Company ....D...... 260 495-5100
Fremont (G-4958)

MOTOR VEHICLE PARTS & ACCESS: Bearings

Hanwha Machinery America Corp ....B...... 574 546-2261
Bremen (G-1001)
Universal Bearings LLC ....C...... 574 546-2261
Bremen (G-1030)

MOTOR VEHICLE PARTS & ACCESS: Body Components & Frames

Camaco Portage Mfg LLC ....G...... 248 657-0246
Portage (G-11754)
CTA Acoustics Inc ....C...... 260 829-1030
Orland (G-11350)
Decker Sales Inc ....G...... 812 330-1580
Bloomington (G-711)
Dwyer Enterprises ....G...... 317 573-9628
Carmel (G-1364)
Flora Racing ....G...... 574 233-0642
South Bend (G-12781)
G E C O M Corp ....A...... 812 663-2270
Greensburg (G-5601)
Global Glass Inc ....G...... 574 294-7681
Elkhart (G-2885)
L & W Engineering Inc ....D...... 574 825-5351
Middlebury (G-9900)
Madison Manufacturing Inc ....E...... 574 633-4433
Bremen (G-1009)
Rance Aluminum Fabrication ....E...... 574 266-9028
Elkhart (G-3137)

S & H Metal Products Inc ....E...... 260 593-2565
Topeka (G-13428)
State Wide Aluminum Inc ....D...... 574 262-2594
Elkhart (G-3191)
Valley Distributing Inc ....E...... 574 266-4455
Elkhart (G-3241)

MOTOR VEHICLE PARTS & ACCESS: Brakes, Air

Advics Manufacturing Ind LLC ....B...... 812 298-1617
Terre Haute (G-13188)
Comhar LLC ....F...... 812 399-2123
New Albany (G-10764)
TOA (usa) LLC ....B...... 317 834-0522
Mooresville (G-10343)

MOTOR VEHICLE PARTS & ACCESS: Brakes, Vacuum

SMI Manufacturing Inc ....B...... 812 428-2794
Newburgh (G-11051)

MOTOR VEHICLE PARTS & ACCESS: Cleaners, air

Donaldson Company Inc ....B...... 765 659-4766
Frankfort (G-4828)
Roppel Industries Inc ....G...... 812 425-0267
Evansville (G-3709)

MOTOR VEHICLE PARTS & ACCESS: Clutches

Eaton Corporation ....C...... 260 925-3800
Auburn (G-328)
FCC (adams) LLC ....B...... 260 589-8555
Berne (G-614)
FCC (indiana) Inc ....A...... 260 726-8023
Portland (G-11819)
South Bend Clutch Inc ....E...... 574 256-5064
Mishawaka (G-10131)

MOTOR VEHICLE PARTS & ACCESS: Connecting Rods

Performance Rod & Custom Inc ....G...... 812 897-5805
Boonville (G-921)

MOTOR VEHICLE PARTS & ACCESS: Cylinder Heads

Indy Cylinder Head ....E...... 317 862-3724
Indianapolis (G-7216)
Tri State Cylinder Head ....E...... 812 421-0095
Evansville (G-3770)

MOTOR VEHICLE PARTS & ACCESS: Electrical Eqpt

Lear Corporation ....G...... 317 481-0530
Indianapolis (G-7391)
Trin Inc ....E...... 260 587-9282
Ashley (G-292)

MOTOR VEHICLE PARTS & ACCESS: Engines & Parts

3d Engineering Inc ....G...... 317 729-5430
Edinburgh (G-2593)
Aisin USA Mfg Inc ....B...... 812 523-1969
Seymour (G-12428)
Ballantrae Inc ....B...... 800 372-3555
Pendleton (G-11483)
Borgwarner Pds (indiana) Inc ....A...... 800 372-3555
Pendleton (G-11485)
Champion Racing Engines ....G...... 317 335-2491
McCordsville (G-9665)
D&D Motors ....G...... 765 358-3856
Gaston (G-5131)
Freudenberg-Nok General Partnr ....B...... 260 894-7183
Ligonier (G-9285)
Heads First ....G...... 219 785-4100
Westville (G-14217)
Mpt Muncie LLC ....E...... 765 587-1300
Muncie (G-10526)
Old Remco Holdings LLC ....C...... 765 778-6499
Pendleton (G-11498)
Performance Technology Inc ....G...... 574 862-2116
Wakarusa (G-13789)

Pk USA Inc ....B 317 395-5500
  Shelbyville (G-12558)
PMG Indiana LLC ....C 812 379-4606
  Columbus (G-1996)
Raybestos Powertrain LLC ....E 812 268-1211
  Sullivan (G-13093)
Rayburn Automotive Inc ....G 317 535-8232
  Whiteland (G-14244)
Reman Holdings LLC ....G 800 372-5131
  Pendleton (G-11502)
Robert Bosch LLC ....C 260 636-1005
  Albion (G-34)
Sterling Industries Inc ....E 812 376-6560
  Columbus (G-2016)
Tenneco Automotive Oper Co Inc ......D 574 296-9400
  Elkhart (G-3211)

MOTOR VEHICLE PARTS & ACCESS: Engs & Trans,Factory, Rebuilt

Caterpillar Remn Powrtrn Indna ....B 317 738-2117
  Franklin (G-4875)
Indiana Research Institute ....F 812 378-5363
  Columbus (G-1948)
Jasper Engine Exchange Inc ....A 812 482-1041
  Jasper (G-8261)
Jasper Engine Exchange Inc ....D 812 482-1041
  Leavenworth (G-9164)
Power Investments Inc ....F 317 738-2117
  Franklin (G-4921)
Townsend Transmissions LLC ....G 765 342-0042
  Martinsville (G-9643)
Western Reman Industrial Inc ....G 765 472-2002
  Peru (G-11557)

MOTOR VEHICLE PARTS & ACCESS: Fuel Pumps

Avis Industrial Corporation ....E 765 998-8100
  Upland (G-13468)
Carter Fuel Systems LLC ....B 574 722-6141
  Logansport (G-9328)

MOTOR VEHICLE PARTS & ACCESS: Fuel Systems & Parts

Keihin Ipt Mfg LLC ....A 317 462-3015
  Greenfield (G-5547)
Keihin North America Inc ....A 765 298-6030
  Anderson (G-126)
Smart Technologies LLC ....G 317 738-4338
  Franklin (G-4933)

MOTOR VEHICLE PARTS & ACCESS: Gas Tanks

Kautex Inc ....B 260 897-3250
  Avilla (G-410)

MOTOR VEHICLE PARTS & ACCESS: Gears

Dexter Axle Company ....C 574 294-6651
  Elkhart (G-2794)
Fairfield Manufacturing Co Inc ....A 765 772-4000
  Lafayette (G-8896)

MOTOR VEHICLE PARTS & ACCESS: Heaters

Ultra-Heat Inc ....F 574 522-6594
  Elkhart (G-3232)

MOTOR VEHICLE PARTS & ACCESS: Instrument Board Assemblies

Aptiv Services Us LLC ....F 765 451-5011
  Kokomo (G-8591)
GM Components Holdings LLC ....G 765 451-9049
  Kokomo (G-8629)
Killer Camaros Custom Camaro ....G 260 255-2425
  New Haven (G-10946)

MOTOR VEHICLE PARTS & ACCESS: Manifolds

General Products Angola Corp ....C 260 665-8441
  Angola (G-216)

MOTOR VEHICLE PARTS & ACCESS: Mufflers, Exhaust

Tenneco Automotive Oper Co Inc ....C 260 894-9214
  Ligonier (G-9299)

MOTOR VEHICLE PARTS & ACCESS: Oil Pumps

Engineered Machined Pdts Inc ....D 317 462-8894
  Greenfield (G-5527)
Precision Racg Components LLC ....F 317 248-4764
  Indianapolis (G-7735)

MOTOR VEHICLE PARTS & ACCESS: Pickup Truck Bed Liners

Advance Prtective Coatings Inc ....G 317 228-0123
  Indianapolis (G-6330)
Automated Products Intl LLC ....F 260 463-2515
  Lagrange (G-9032)

MOTOR VEHICLE PARTS & ACCESS: Propane Conversion Eqpt

Joe Wade Customs ....G 765 548-0333
  Rosedale (G-12204)
Woodys Hot Rodz LLc ....G 812 637-1933
  Lawrenceburg (G-9162)

MOTOR VEHICLE PARTS & ACCESS: Thermostats

Caltherm Corporation ....C 812 372-0281
  Columbus (G-1864)
Caltherm Corporation ....F 812 372-0281
  Columbus (G-1865)

MOTOR VEHICLE PARTS & ACCESS: Trailer Hitches

Cardinal Services Inc Indiana ....E 574 267-3823
  Warsaw (G-13855)
Pulliam Enterprises Inc ....E 574 259-1520
  Mishawaka (G-10112)

MOTOR VEHICLE PARTS & ACCESS: Transmission Housings Or Parts

JD Norman Industries Inc ....D 765 288-8098
  Muncie (G-10499)
JD Norman Industries Inc ....E 765 584-6069
  Winchester (G-14334)
Parker-Hannifin Corporation ....C 260 894-7125
  Ligonier (G-9292)
Ryobi Die Casting (usa) Inc ....A 317 398-3398
  Shelbyville (G-12565)

MOTOR VEHICLE PARTS & ACCESS: Transmissions

Aisin Drivetrain Inc ....C 812 793-2427
  Crothersville (G-2214)
Allison Transmission Inc ....A 317 242-5000
  Indianapolis (G-6373)
Allison Transmission Inc ....D 317 242-2080
  Indianapolis (G-6375)
AM General LLC ....D 574 235-7326
  South Bend (G-12700)
FCA US LLC ....A 765 854-4234
  Kokomo (G-8623)
FCC (north America) Inc ....E 260 726-8023
  Portland (G-11820)
Steel Parts Manufacturing Inc ....E 765 675-2191
  Tipton (G-13407)
Stephen G Morrow Inc ....E 812 876-7837
  Spencer (G-13040)
Stored Energy Solutions Inc ....G 574 457-2199
  Anderson (G-171)
Tsuda USA Corporation ....F 317 468-9177
  Greenfield (G-5582)

MOTOR VEHICLE PARTS & ACCESS: Universal Joints

Dana Driveshaft Products LLC ....B 260 432-2903
  Marion (G-9520)

MOTOR VEHICLE PARTS & ACCESS: Wheel rims

Americana Development Inc ....D 574 295-3535
  Elkhart (G-2688)
Armor Parent Corp ....F 812 962-5000
  Evansville (G-3366)
Wheel Group Holdings LLC ....G 317 780-1661
  Indianapolis (G-8189)

MOTOR VEHICLE PARTS & ACCESS: Wipers, Windshield

Taylor Made Group Holdings Inc ....C 260 347-1368
  Kendallville (G-8512)

MOTOR VEHICLE PARTS & ACCESS: Wiring Harness Sets

Gartech Enterprises Inc ....E 812 794-4796
  Austin (G-397)
Motherson Sumi Systems Limited ....A 260 726-6501
  Portland (G-11836)
Northwind Electronics LLC ....F 317 288-0787
  Indianapolis (G-7596)

MOTOR VEHICLE RACING & DRIVER SVCS

Team Green Inc ....D 317 872-2700
  Indianapolis (G-8043)

MOTOR VEHICLE SPLYS & PARTS WHOLESALERS: New

Abro Industries Inc ....E 574 232-8289
  South Bend (G-12692)
Aptiv Services Us LLC ....F 765 451-5011
  Kokomo (G-8591)
Cummins Inc ....E 812 524-6455
  Columbus (G-1896)
Frank Wiss Racg Components Inc ....E 317 248-4764
  Indianapolis (G-6957)
Hoosier Fire Equipment Inc ....E 219 462-1707
  Valparaiso (G-13557)
K-Motion Racing Engines ....G 765 742-8494
  Lafayette (G-8935)
Muncie Power Products Inc ....C 765 284-7721
  Muncie (G-10533)
Phoenix Assembly LLC ....D 317 884-3600
  Greenwood (G-5732)
T & M Equipment Company Inc ....F 317 293-9255
  Indianapolis (G-8032)

MOTOR VEHICLE SPLYS & PARTS WHOLESALERS: Used

A-Fab LLC ....D 812 897-0900
  Boonville (G-904)
KOI Enterprises Inc ....G 812 537-2335
  Lawrenceburg (G-9146)
Power Train Corp Fort Wayne ....F 317 241-9393
  Indianapolis (G-7712)

MOTOR VEHICLE: Hardware

Allegion Public Ltd Company ....F 317 810-3700
  Carmel (G-1307)
Creek Chassis Inc ....G 317 247-4480
  Indianapolis (G-6690)
Qmp Inc ....E 574 262-1575
  Elkhart (G-3124)
Ultra-Fab Products Inc ....F 574 294-7571
  Elkhart (G-3231)

MOTOR VEHICLE: Radiators

Indiana Heat Transfer Corp ....C 574 936-3171
  Plymouth (G-11690)
Saldana Racing Tanks Inc ....F 317 852-4193
  Indianapolis (G-7888)

MOTOR VEHICLE: Shock Absorbers

Advanced Racg Suspensions Inc ....F 317 896-3306
  Indianapolis (G-6335)
KYB Americas Corporation ....B 317 736-7774
  Franklin (G-4903)
KYB Americas Corporation ....E 630 620-5555
  Greenwood (G-5715)
Vibration Eliminator Co Inc ....E 765 932-2858
  Rushville (G-12237)

PRODUCT

MOTOR VEHICLE: Steering Mechanisms

Industrial Steering Pdts Inc ....E 260 488-1880
Hamilton (G-5824)

MOTOR VEHICLE: Wheels

Accuride Corporation ....C 812 962-5000
Evansville (G-3336)
Enkei America Inc ....A 812 373-7000
Columbus (G-1920)
Reliable Tool & Machine Co ....D 260 343-7150
Kendallville (G-8506)
Transwheel Corporation ....C 260 358-8660
Huntington (G-6256)

MOTOR VEHICLES & CAR BODIES

AM General LLC ....A 574 257-4268
South Bend (G-12701)
AM General LLC ....D 574 235-7326
South Bend (G-12700)
Android Industries LLC ....D 260 672-0112
Roanoke (G-12098)
Concept Cars Inc ....G 260 668-7553
Angola (G-204)
Daimler Trucks North Amer LLC ....G 317 769-8500
Whitestown (G-14252)
Damon Motor Coach ....E 574 536-3781
Elkhart (G-2790)
General Motors LLC..........................G 419 576-9472
Bloomington (G-730)
General Motors LLC..........................A 260 672-1224
Roanoke (G-12102)
General Motors LLC..........................B 765 668-2000
Marion (G-9525)
Hardins Speed Service Co ....G 219 962-8080
Hobart (G-6079)
Howerton Racecar Works Inc ....F 317 241-0868
Indianapolis (G-7140)
Independent Protection Co Inc ....D 574 831-5680
New Paris (G-10985)
NRC Modifications Inc ....F 574 825-3646
Middlebury (G-9912)
Rebel Devil Customs ....G 303 921-7131
Noblesville (G-11173)
Think North America Inc ....E 313 565-6781
Elkhart (G-3213)
Toyota ....G 317 755-4791
Nineveh (G-11058)
Travel Home Solutions ....G 260 592-7628
Pleasant Mills (G-11658)
Utilimaster Holdings Inc ....A 800 237-7806
Bristol (G-1093)
Wave Express ....G 574 642-0630
Goshen (G-5345)

MOTOR VEHICLES, WHOLESALE: Commercial

Sparkling Clean Inc..........................G 812 422-4871
Evansville (G-3741)

MOTOR VEHICLES, WHOLESALE: Fire Trucks

Fire Aparatus Service Inc ....G 219 985-0788
Gary (G-5047)

MOTOR VEHICLES, WHOLESALE: Truck tractors

Wakarusa Ag LLC ....G 574 862-1163
Wakarusa (G-13797)

MOTOR VEHICLES, WHOLESALE: Trucks, commercial

Bulk Truck & Transport Service...........E 812 866-2155
Hanover (G-5959)
Selking International Inc ....G 574 522-2001
Elkhart (G-3161)
Selking International Inc ....E 260 482-3000
Fort Wayne (G-4615)
Wee Engineer Inc ....F 765 449-4280
Dayton (G-2362)

MOTORCYCLE & BICYCLE PARTS: Gears

Sram LLC..G 317 481-1120
Indianapolis (G-7979)

MOTORCYCLE ACCESS

Ksm Enterprises ....G 317 773-7440
Fishers (G-3937)
Time Out Trailers Inc ....G 574 294-7671
Elkhart (G-3217)

MOTORCYCLE DEALERS

Graphics Lab Uv Printing Inc..............F 765 457-5784
Kokomo (G-8632)

MOTORCYCLE PARTS & ACCESS DEALERS

Evill Cycles ....G 812 401-2045
Evansville (G-3495)

MOTORCYCLE REPAIR SHOPS

Bike-N-Trikes ....G 317 835-4544
Boggstown (G-899)
Evill Cycles ....G 812 401-2045
Evansville (G-3495)

MOTORCYCLES & RELATED PARTS

B B Cycles LLC ....G 812 723-4265
Paoli (G-11443)
Cheetah Trikes Inc ....G 812 256-9199
Charlestown (G-1560)
Choppers Kickstand LLC ....G 260 739-6966
Fort Wayne (G-4148)
Evill Cycles ....G 812 401-2045
Evansville (G-3495)
Jrotten Chopper ....G 765 517-1779
Jonesboro (G-8446)
Outdoor Performance ....G 765 732-3335
Liberty (G-9268)
R Falcone Powersports Inc ....G 317 803-2432
Indianapolis (G-7809)
Reality Motor Sports Inc....................G 765 662-3000
Marion (G-9559)
Red Hawk Choppers Inc ....G 765 307-2269
Crawfordsville (G-2193)
Ss Custom Choppers LLC ....G 260 415-3793
Fort Wayne (G-4643)
Thugs Inc Choppers ....G 317 454-3762
Indianapolis (G-8072)

MOTORCYCLES: Wholesalers

Thorntons Mtrcycle Sls - Mdson ....G 812 574-6347
Madison (G-9498)

MOTORS: Electric

American Mitsuba Corporation ....C 989 779-4962
Monroeville (G-10191)
B & H Electric and Supply Inc............E 812 522-5607
Seymour (G-12431)
Bluffton Motor Works LLC ....C 800 579-8527
Bluffton (G-867)
Burt Products Inc.............................G 812 386-6890
Princeton (G-11867)
Electric Motors and Spc ....C 260 357-4141
Garrett (G-5003)
Franklin Electric Co Inc ....B 260 824-2900
Fort Wayne (G-4285)
Hansen Corporation ....B 812 385-3000
Princeton (G-11874)
Lynx Motion Technology Corp.............G 812 923-7474
Greenville (G-5650)
OH Hunt Lines Inc............................G 260 856-2126
Cromwell (G-2210)
Pete D Limkemann ....G 260 403-4297
Fort Wayne (G-4526)
Regal Beloit America Inc...................C 574 583-9171
Monticello (G-10282)
Remy Power Products LLC ....A 765 778-6499
Pendleton (G-11504)
Scottorsville Sales and Svc ....G 765 250-5245
Lafayette (G-8998)
Sterling Electric Inc ....G 317 872-0471
Indianapolis (G-8002)
Sterling Electric Inc ....E 317 872-0471
Indianapolis (G-8001)

MOTORS: Generators

An-Mar Wiring Systems Inc ....F 574 255-5523
Mishawaka (G-9996)
Blinkless Power Equipment LLC ....G 317 844-7328
Indianapolis (G-6484)

Borgwarner Pds Anderson LLC ....B 765 778-6499
Noblesville (G-11068)
Borgwarner Pds Anderson LLC ....C 765 778-6499
Anderson (G-76)
Coil Tran Corp ....D 219 942-8511
Hobart (G-6076)
Contour Hardening Inc ....G 317 876-1530
Indianapolis (G-6659)
Contour Hardening Inc ....E 888 867-2184
Indianapolis (G-6660)
Cummins Inc ....A 812 522-9366
Seymour (G-12442)
Custom Magnetics Inc ....E 773 463-6500
North Manchester (G-11227)
Electro Corporation ....F 219 393-5571
Kingsbury (G-8536)
Elevator Equipment Corporation.........D 765 966-7761
Richmond (G-11981)
Franklin Electric Intl..........................F 260 824-2900
Fort Wayne (G-4286)
G & M Rebuilders Inc ....G 812 858-9233
Newburgh (G-11029)
General Electric Company ....B 260 439-2000
Fort Wayne (G-4297)
Ies Subsidiary Holdings Inc ....F 330 830-3500
South Bend (G-12807)
JMS Electronics Corporation ....G 574 522-0246
Elkhart (G-2949)
Jones Engineering Inc ....G 812 254-6456
Washington (G-13989)
Kendrion (mishawaka) LLC ....G 574 257-2422
Mishawaka (G-10063)
Mighty-Quip Industries ....G 260 615-1899
Fort Wayne (G-4475)
Qp Inc...F 574 295-6884
Elkhart (G-3125)
Regal Beloit America Inc...................G 260 416-5400
Fort Wayne (G-4586)
Siemens Industry Inc ....D 219 763-7927
Portage (G-11794)
Vanair Manufacturing Inc ....C 219 879-5100
Michigan City (G-9857)
Warner Electric LLC..........................C 260 244-6183
Columbia City (G-1846)

MOUNTING SVC: Swatches & Samples

Leed Selling Tools Corp ....E 812 867-4340
Evansville (G-3599)
Superior Sample Co Inc ....E 260 894-3136
Ligonier (G-9297)

MOWERS & ACCESSORIES

American Gardenworks Inc ....F 765 869-4033
Boswell (G-939)
American Lawn Mower ....G 800 633-1501
Indianapolis (G-6389)
Lastec LLC.....................................F 317 892-4444
Lizton (G-9317)
Novae Corp ....D 260 758-9800
Markle (G-9581)
Schaefers Indiana Turf Corp ....G 260 489-3391
Fort Wayne (G-4607)
Trudel Family Ltd Partnership ....G 260 627-5626
Leo (G-9246)
Wood-Mizer Holdings Inc ....D 317 892-4444
Lizton (G-9318)
Wood-Mizer Holdings Inc ....C 317 271-1542
Indianapolis (G-8212)

MULTILITHING SVCS

Service Graphics Inc ....D 317 471-8246
Indianapolis (G-7917)

MUSEUMS & ART GALLERIES

Brush Strokes Inc ....G 800 272-2307
South Bend (G-12726)

MUSIC BROADCASTING SVCS

Cliff A Ostermeyer ....G 615 361-7902
Indianapolis (G-6621)

MUSIC DISTRIBUTION APPARATUS

Haven Technologies Inc ....G 317 490-7197
Carmel (G-1399)

(G-0000) Company's Geographic Section entry number

MUSIC LICENSING TO RADIO STATIONS

Rebound Project LLP ....G...... 765 621-5604
Anderson **(G-158)**

MUSICAL INSTRUMENT LESSONS

Loys Sales Inc...................................G...... 765 552-7250
Elwood **(G-3304)**

MUSICAL INSTRUMENT PARTS & ACCESS, WHOLESALE

American Way Marketing Inc ....F.... 574 295-7466
Elkhart **(G-2687)**

MUSICAL INSTRUMENT REPAIR

Markle Music ....G...... 812 847-2103
Linton **(G-9310)**

MUSICAL INSTRUMENTS & ACCESS: Carrying Cases

Ds Wood Products Inc........................G....574 642-3855
Goshen **(G-5205)**
Elkcases Inc ....E.... 574 295-7700
Elkhart **(G-2819)**
Humes & Berg Mfg Co Inc..................G...... 219 391-5880
East Chicago **(G-2534)**
L M Products Inc................................E.... 765 643-3802
Anderson **(G-132)**
MTS Products Corp ....F.... 574 295-3142
Elkhart **(G-3055)**

MUSICAL INSTRUMENTS & ACCESS: NEC

Conn-Selmer Inc ....D.... 574 522-1675
Elkhart **(G-2765)**
Conn-Selmer Inc ....E.... 574 522-1675
Elkhart **(G-2766)**
Main Music..G...... 812 295-2020
Loogootee **(G-9391)**
Mountain Made Music Inc ....G...... 812 988-8869
Nashville **(G-10731)**
Normal City Music Co........................G...... 765 289-2041
Muncie **(G-10539)**
Self Care LLC ....G...... 317 295-8279
Indianapolis **(G-7909)**
Stanbinger Flutes Inc ....G...... 317 784-3012
Indianapolis **(G-7986)**
T Shorter Manufacturing Inc ....G...... 574 264-4131
Elkhart **(G-3203)**
Uniflex Relay Systems LLC ....G...... 765 232-4675
Union City **(G-13462)**
Woodwind & Brasswind Inc ....F.... 574 251-3547
Indianapolis **(G-8214)**

MUSICAL INSTRUMENTS & ACCESS: Pianos

Piano Shop Llc...................................G...... 812 951-2462
Georgetown **(G-5152)**
Steinway Piano Company Inc ....D.... 574 522-1675
Elkhart **(G-3192)**
Walter Piano Company Inc..................F.... 574 266-0615
Elkhart **(G-3254)**

MUSICAL INSTRUMENTS & ACCESS: Pipe Organs

Goulding & Wood Inc ....F.... 317 637-5222
Indianapolis **(G-7031)**

MUSICAL INSTRUMENTS & ACCESS: Stands

Humes & Berg Mfg Co Inc...................G...... 219 391-5880
East Chicago **(G-2534)**

MUSICAL INSTRUMENTS & PARTS: Percussion

Stone Custom Drum LLC ....G...... 260 403-7519
Fort Wayne **(G-4651)**

MUSICAL INSTRUMENTS & PARTS: Woodwind

Conn-Selmer Inc ....A.... 574 295-0079
Elkhart **(G-2768)**

MUSICAL INSTRUMENTS & SPLYS STORES

Fox Products Corporation ....C.... 260 723-4888
South Whitley **(G-12999)**
Gemeinhardt Musical Instr LLC............E.... 574 295-5280
Elkhart **(G-2876)**
Music Store ....G...... 812 949-3004
Clarksville **(G-1689)**
Rees Harps Inc ....F.... 812 438-3032
Rising Sun **(G-12091)**

MUSICAL INSTRUMENTS & SPLYS STORES: Pianos

Conn-Selmer Inc ....D.... 574 522-1675
Elkhart **(G-2765)**
Walter Piano Company Inc..................F.... 574 266-0615
Elkhart **(G-3254)**

MUSICAL INSTRUMENTS & SPLYS STORES: String instruments

Markle Music ....G...... 812 847-2103
Linton **(G-9310)**

MUSICAL INSTRUMENTS WHOLESALERS

Conn-Selmer Inc ....B.... 574 295-6730
Elkhart **(G-2767)**
Rees Harps Inc ....F.... 812 438-3032
Rising Sun **(G-12091)**

MUSICAL INSTRUMENTS: Bassoons

Fox Products Corporation ....C.... 260 723-4888
South Whitley **(G-12999)**

MUSICAL INSTRUMENTS: Guitars & Parts, Electric & Acoustic

Conn-Selmer Inc ....B.... 574 295-6730
Elkhart **(G-2767)**
Eddie S Guitars ....G...... 219 689-7007
Dyer **(G-2497)**
Lucas Custom Instruments..................G...... 812 342-3093
Columbus **(G-1965)**

MUSICAL INSTRUMENTS: Harps & Parts

Jubilee Harps Inc ....G...... 812 426-2547
Evansville **(G-3580)**
Rees Harps Inc ....F.... 812 438-3032
Rising Sun **(G-12091)**

MUSICAL INSTRUMENTS: Mouthpieces

J J Babbitt Co....................................G...... 574 315-1639
Elkhart **(G-2941)**

MUSICAL INSTRUMENTS: Piccolos & Parts

Gemeinhardt Musical Instr LLC............E.... 574 295-5280
Elkhart **(G-2876)**

MUSICAL INSTRUMENTS: Reeds

Flavoreeds ....G...... 260 373-2233
Fort Wayne **(G-4266)**

NAIL SALONS

Cali Nail..G...... 574 674-4126
Osceola **(G-11373)**

NAILS: Steel, Wire Or Cut

Fuzion Products LLC...........................G...... 317 536-0745
Indianapolis **(G-6973)**

NAME PLATES: Engraved Or Etched

Crichlow Industries Inc ....G...... 317 925-5178
Indianapolis **(G-6692)**

NATIONAL SECURITY FORCES

Dla Document Services.......................G...... 812 854-1465
Crane **(G-2125)**
Spotlight Cybersecurity LLC ....G...... 805 886-4456
Lafayette **(G-9001)**

NATIONAL SECURITY, GOVERNMENT: Military Training Schools

Advanced Prtctive Slutions LLC ....G...... 765 720-9574
Coatesville **(G-1746)**

NATURAL GAS COMPRESSING SVC, On-Site

Gallagher Drilling Inc..........................E.... 812 477-6746
Evansville **(G-3514)**

NATURAL GAS DISTRIBUTION TO CONSUMERS

K Grimmer Industries Inc ....E.... 317 736-3800
Leo **(G-9243)**
Vectren Corporation ....A.... 812 491-4000
Evansville **(G-3794)**
Vectren Corporation ....E.... 812 424-6411
Evansville **(G-3795)**

NATURAL GAS LIQUIDS PRODUCTION

Daylight Engineering Inc.....................G...... 812 983-2518
Elberfeld **(G-2633)**

NATURAL GAS LIQUIDS PRODUCTION

Air Liquide Tom Utley.........................G...... 812 838-0599
Mount Vernon **(G-10381)**
Citizens By-Products Coal Co ....F.... 317 927-4738
Indianapolis **(G-6613)**
Nisource Inc......................................G...... 877 647-5990
Valparaiso **(G-13590)**

NATURAL GAS PRODUCTION

Atlas Energy Indiana LLC ....G...... 812 268-4900
Sullivan **(G-13080)**
Green Cow Power LLC ....G...... 219 984-5915
Goshen **(G-5229)**
South Bend Ethanol LLC.....................G...... 574 703-3360
South Bend **(G-12943)**

NATURAL LIQUEFIED PETROLEUM GAS PRODUCTION

Jackson-Jennings LLC........................G...... 812 522-4911
Seymour **(G-12461)**
Mid-West Oil Company Inc..................G...... 812 533-1227
West Terre Haute **(G-14127)**

NATURAL PROPANE PRODUCTION

Excel Co-Op Inc ....G...... 574 967-4166
Flora **(G-3995)**
Semstream LP...................................G...... 765 482-8105
Lebanon **(G-9222)**

NEWS DEALERS & NEWSSTANDS

Spencer Evening World.......................G...... 765 795-4438
Cloverdale **(G-1738)**

NEWSPAPER COLUMN WRITING SVCS

News Publishing Company LLC...........G...... 812 838-4811
Mount Vernon **(G-10404)**

NICKEL ALLOY

Ed Nickels..G...... 219 887-6128
Merrillville **(G-9712)**
Haynes International Inc ....C.... 219 326-8530
La Porte **(G-8762)**
Haynes International Inc ....A.... 765 456-6000
Kokomo **(G-8638)**
Patricia J Nickels Inc ....G...... 502 489-4358
Charlestown **(G-1579)**

NONFERROUS: Rolling & Drawing, NEC

Demotte Manufacturing Inc..................G...... 219 987-6196
Demotte **(G-2435)**
Eco-Bat America LLC ....C.... 317 247-1303
Indianapolis **(G-6801)**
Hammond Group Inc ....E.... 219 845-0031
Hammond **(G-5886)**
Indiana U Bolts Inc............................E.... 317 870-1940
Waterloo **(G-14015)**
Metals and Additives Corp Inc............E.... 812 446-2525
Brazil **(G-969)**
Rhon Inc..G...... 574 297-5217
Monticello **(G-10283)**

PRODUCT

Special Metals Corporation....................E   574 262-3451
  Elkhart (G-3183)
TI Group Auto Systems LLC C   260 587-6100
  Ashley (G-291)

NONMETALLIC MINERALS & CONCENTRATE WHOLESALERS

Calcean LLC ....G   812 672-4995
  Seymour (G-12437)

NONMETALLIC MINERALS: Support Activities, Exc Fuels

Imine Corporation ....G   877 464-6388
  Indianapolis (G-7165)
United Minerals ....G   812 842-0978
  Newburgh (G-11054)

NOTARIES PUBLIC

United Parcel Service Inc ....G   317 776-9494
  Noblesville (G-11197)

NOVELTIES

Buztronics Inc ....D   317 876-3413
  Brownsburg (G-1140)
Candles By Dar Inc ....F   260 482-2099
  Fort Wayne (G-4139)
Eastons Lettering Service ....G   219 942-5101
  Hobart (G-6078)
Ellwocks Auto Parts Restorat ....G   812 962-4942
  Newburgh (G-11027)
XYZ Model Works ....G   260 413-1873
  Decatur (G-2413)

NOVELTIES & SPECIALTIES: Metal

4board LLC ....G   317 997-3354
  Indianapolis (G-6291)
Metal Fab Engineering Inc ....F   574 278-7150
  Winamac (G-14312)

NOVELTIES, PAPER, WHOLESALE

Stump Printing Co Inc C   260 723-5171
  South Whitley (G-13006)

NOVELTIES: Paper, Made From Purchased Materials

Stump Printing Co Inc C   260 723-5171
  South Whitley (G-13006)

NOVELTIES: Plastic

Hot Stamping & Printing ....G   219 767-2429
  Union Mills (G-13463)
Royer Corporation ....D   800 457-8997
  Madison (G-9493)

NOZZLES & SPRINKLERS Lawn Hose

Cloudburst Lawn Sprinkler Syst ....F   260 492-8400
  Fort Wayne (G-4162)
Siteone Landscape Supply LLC ....G   219 769-2351
  Merrillville (G-9754)

NOZZLES: Fire Fighting

Task Force Tips Inc C   219 462-6161
  Valparaiso (G-13626)
Task Force Tips Inc ....F   219 462-6161
  Valparaiso (G-13627)
W S F Fire Store ....E   812 421-3826
  Evansville (G-3805)

NURSERIES & LAWN & GARDEN SPLY STORE, RET: Lawn/Garden Splys

Earth First Kentuckiana Inc ....G   812 248-0712
  Charlestown (G-1565)
Earth First Kentuckiana Inc ....G   812 923-1227
  Greenville (G-5648)
Greencycle Inc ....G   317 773-3350
  Noblesville (G-11114)

NURSERIES & LAWN & GARDEN SPLY STORES, RETAIL: Fertilizer

Agbest Cooperative Inc ....G   765 358-3388
  Gaston (G-5129)

Andersons Agriculture Group LP ....E   574 626-2522
  Galveston (G-4993)
Bristow Milling Co LLC ....G   812 843-5176
  Bristow (G-1094)
Frick Services Inc ....E   260 761-3311
  Wawaka (G-14032)
Harvest Land Co-Op Inc ....G   317 861-5080
  Fountaintown (G-4791)
Nachurs Alpine Solutions Corp ....G   812 738-1333
  Corydon (G-2106)
Wanafeed Corporation ....G   317 862-4032
  Indianapolis (G-8178)

NURSERIES & LAWN & GARDEN SPLY STORES, RETAIL: Lawn Ornament

U-Nitt LLC ....G   812 251-9980
  Carmel (G-1499)

NURSERIES & LAWN/GARDEN SPLY STORE, RET: Lawnmowers/Tractors

Beckler Power Equipment ....G   260 356-1188
  Huntington (G-6190)

NURSERIES/LAWN/GARDEN SPLY STORE, RET: Christmas Tree, Natrl

Sappers Market and Greenhouses ....G   219 942-4995
  Hobart (G-6094)

NURSERY & GARDEN CENTERS

Langfords Delivery Service ....G   317 996-3594
  Monrovia (G-10204)
Zionsville Towing Inc ....G   317 873-4550
  Zionsville (G-14474)

NYLON FIBERS

Quadrant Epp Usa Inc ....D   260 479-4700
  Fort Wayne (G-4568)
Quadrant Epp Usa Inc C   260 479-4100
  Fort Wayne (G-4569)

NYLON RESINS

Quadrant Epp Usa Inc ....D   260 479-4700
  Fort Wayne (G-4568)
Quadrant Epp Usa Inc C   260 479-4100
  Fort Wayne (G-4569)

OFFICE EQPT WHOLESALERS

Cummins - Allison Corp ....G   317 872-6244
  Indianapolis (G-6705)
Dbisp LLC ....F   317 222-1671
  Indianapolis (G-6729)
The Office Sup of Southern Ind ....G   812 283-5523
  Jeffersonville (G-8434)

OFFICE EQPT, WHOLESALE: Photocopy Machines

ASAP Identification SEC Inc ....G   317 488-1030
  Indianapolis (G-6424)
Classic Products Corp ....E   260 484-2695
  Fort Wayne (G-4159)

OFFICE MACHINES, NEC

Voter Registration ....G   219 755-3795
  Crown Point (G-2319)

OFFICE SPLY & STATIONERY STORES

Paper Tigers Inc ....G   317 573-9040
  Indianapolis (G-7651)

OFFICE SPLY & STATIONERY STORES: Office Forms & Splys

A & H Enterprises LLC ....G   317 398-3070
  Shelbyville (G-12517)
Automobile Dealers Assn of Ind ....G   317 635-1441
  Indianapolis (G-6446)
Bryant Printing ....G   765 521-3379
  New Castle (G-10893)
Cecils Printing & Office Sups ....G   812 683-4416
  Huntington (G-6153)
Coy & Associates ....G   317 787-5089
  Indianapolis (G-6682)

Journal and Chronicle Inc ....G   812 752-5060
  Scottsburg (G-12370)
Premier Print & Svcs Group Inc ....F   574 273-2525
  Granger (G-5429)
Professional Print Brokers ....G   260 824-2328
  Bluffton (G-888)
Q Graphics Inc ....F   765 564-2314
  Delphi (G-2426)
Scott Culbertson ....G   260 357-6430
  Garrett (G-5022)
Shearer Printing Service Inc ....E   765 457-3274
  Kokomo (G-8695)
Smith & Butterfield Co Inc ....F   812 422-3261
  Evansville (G-3735)
Tippecanoe Press Inc ....F   317 392-1207
  Shelbyville (G-12576)

OFFICE SPLYS, NEC, WHOLESALE

Dbisp LLC ....F   317 222-1671
  Indianapolis (G-6729)
Peerless Printing Corp ....F   765 664-8341
  Marion (G-9553)
Systems & Services of Michiana ....G   574 273-1111
  South Bend (G-12965)
Systems & Services of Michiana ....G   574 277-3355
  South Bend (G-12966)
The Office Sup of Southern Ind ....G   812 283-5523
  Jeffersonville (G-8434)

OFFICES & CLINICS OF DOCTORS OF MEDICINE: Radiologist

Fort Wyne Rdlgy Assn Fundation ....F   260 266-8120
  Fort Wayne (G-4283)

OFFICES & CLINICS OF DOCTORS OF MEDICINE: Surgeon, Plastic

Zollman Plastic Surgery PC ....G   317 328-1100
  Indianapolis (G-8227)

OFFICES & CLINICS OF HEALTH PRACTITIONERS: Nutritionist

Natural Answers....................................G   219 922-3663
  Highland (G-6052)

OFFICES & CLINICS OF HEALTH PRACTITIONERS: Physical Therapy

Sidney & Janice Bond ....G   812 366-8160
  Sellersburg (G-12415)

OFFICES & CLINICS OF OPTOMETRISTS: Specialist, Optometrists

Harmon Hrmon Uysugi Optmtrists........F   812 723-4752
  Paoli (G-11452)

OIL & GAS FIELD EQPT: Drill Rigs

Diedrich Drill Inc ....E   219 326-7788
  La Porte (G-8751)

OIL & GAS FIELD MACHINERY

Emquip Corporation ....G   317 849-3977
  Indianapolis (G-6860)
Systems Engineering and Sls Co ....G   260 422-1671
  Fort Wayne (G-4671)

OIL FIELD MACHINERY & EQPT

Lufkin Industries Inc............................G   765 472-2935
  Peru (G-11536)
National Oilwell Varco Inc ....G   317 897-3099
  Indianapolis (G-7575)
Nrp Jones LLC ....D   219 362-4508
  La Porte (G-8800)

OIL FIELD SVCS, NEC

Bst Corp ....G   812 925-7911
  Boonville (G-909)
Central Ind Oil Co.................................G   317 253-1131
  Indianapolis (G-6583)
Core Laboratories LP ....F   260 312-0455
  Fort Wayne (G-4178)
Jay Costas Companies Inc ....G   219 663-4364
  Crown Point (G-2267)

Morgan Excavating ....G...... 812 385-6036
Oakland City *(G-11310)*
Oilfield Research Inc ....G...... 812 424-2907
Evansville *(G-3653)*
Pioneer Oilfield Services LLC ....D...... 812 882-0999
Vincennes *(G-13698)*
United Oil Corp ....G...... 260 489-3511
Fort Wayne *(G-4716)*
US Oilfield Company LLC ....E...... 888 584-7565
Carmel *(G-1505)*

OIL TREATING COMPOUNDS

Consolidated Recycling Co Inc ....E...... 812 547-7951
Troy *(G-13446)*
Polyfreeze LLC ....F...... 812 547-7951
Troy *(G-13447)*

OILS & GREASES: Blended & Compounded

Crescent Oil Company Inc ....G...... 317 634-1415
Indianapolis *(G-6691)*
Linder Oil Co Inc ....F...... 260 622-4680
Ossian *(G-11403)*
Packaging Group Corp ....E...... 219 879-2500
Michigan City *(G-9826)*
Petrochoice Holdings Inc ....E...... 317 634-7300
Indianapolis *(G-7680)*

OILS & GREASES: Lubricating

Allegheny Petroleum Pdts Co ....E...... 812 897-0760
Boonville *(G-906)*
F B C Inc ....E...... 574 848-5288
Bristol *(G-1059)*
Hill & Griffith Company ....E...... 317 241-9233
Indianapolis *(G-7108)*
Idemitsu Lubricants Amer Corp ....D...... 812 284-3300
Jeffersonville *(G-8378)*
Illinois Lubricants LLC ....G...... 260 436-2444
Fort Wayne *(G-4358)*
J 2 Systems and Supply LLC ....G...... 317 602-3940
Indianapolis *(G-7281)*
Keil Chemical Corporation ....D...... 219 931-2630
Hammond *(G-5905)*
Klotz Special Formula Products ....F...... 260 490-0489
Fort Wayne *(G-4412)*
Lane Quick ....G...... 812 896-1890
Salem *(G-12298)*
Metalloid Corporation ....E...... 260 356-3200
Huntington *(G-6229)*
Permawick Company Inc ....F...... 812 376-0703
Columbus *(G-1993)*
Petroleum Solutions Inc ....G...... 574 546-2133
Bremen *(G-1016)*
Pinnacle Oil Holdings LLC ....F...... 317 875-9465
Indianapolis *(G-7695)*
Pinnacle Oil Holdings LLC ....E...... 317 875-9465
Indianapolis *(G-7696)*
Tj Performance LLC ....G...... 765 580-0481
Brownsville *(G-1196)*

OILS: Core Or Binders

Ncp Coatings Inc ....G...... 574 255-9678
Mishawaka *(G-10094)*

OILS: Cutting

Metalworking Lubricants Co ....E...... 317 269-2444
Indianapolis *(G-7491)*

OILS: Lubricating

Illinois Lubricants LLC ....G...... 260 436-2444
Fort Wayne *(G-4358)*

OILS: Lubricating

Calumet Operating LLC ....F...... 317 328-5660
Indianapolis *(G-6539)*
Golden Trngle Lbrcant Svcs LLC ....G...... 317 875-9465
Indianapolis *(G-7021)*
Michiana Elkhart Inc ....G...... 574 206-0620
Elkhart *(G-3030)*
Spence/Banks Inc ....F...... 812 234-3538
Terre Haute *(G-13341)*

OINTMENTS

Apothecarys Ointment LLC ....G...... 574 930-6662
South Bend *(G-12710)*
Bloom Pharmaceutical ....G...... 260 615-2633
Fort Wayne *(G-4113)*

Merrill Corporation ....F...... 574 255-2988
Mishawaka *(G-10078)*

ON-LINE DATABASE INFORMATION RETRIEVAL SVCS

Fiserv Mrtg Servicing Systems ....C...... 574 282-3300
South Bend *(G-12779)*

OPEN PIT IRON MINING, NEC

Arcelormittal Minorca Mine Inc ....G...... 219 399-1200
East Chicago *(G-2518)*

OPERATOR: Nonresidential Buildings

Erl Properties Inc ....G...... 812 948-8484
New Albany *(G-10772)*
Jasper Engine Exchange Inc ....A...... 812 482-1041
Jasper *(G-8261)*
Tartan Properties LLC ....G...... 317 714-7337
Indianapolis *(G-8037)*

OPHTHALMIC GOODS

City Optical Co Inc ....D...... 317 924-1300
Indianapolis *(G-6615)*
Diversified Ophthalmics Inc ....F...... 317 780-1677
Indianapolis *(G-6750)*
G K Optical Company Inc ....E...... 317 881-2585
Indianapolis *(G-6975)*
Jasper Optical Lab ....G...... 812 634-9020
Jasper *(G-8262)*
Luxottica Retail N Amer Inc ....E...... 219 736-0141
Merrillville *(G-9729)*
Luxottica Retail N Amer Inc ....E...... 317 293-9999
Indianapolis *(G-7428)*
Singer Optical Company Inc ....F...... 812 423-1179
Evansville *(G-3732)*
Tri State Optical Inc ....E...... 765 289-4475
Muncie *(G-10575)*
Vision Associates ....G...... 765 288-1575
Muncie *(G-10577)*

OPHTHALMIC GOODS WHOLESALERS

City Optical Co Inc ....D...... 317 924-1300
Indianapolis *(G-6615)*
Diversified Ophthalmics Inc ....F...... 317 780-1677
Indianapolis *(G-6750)*
Frecker Optical Inc ....F...... 260 747-9653
Fort Wayne *(G-4287)*
Kokomo Optical Company Inc ....G...... 765 459-5137
Kokomo *(G-8655)*
Singer Optical Company Inc ....F...... 812 423-1179
Evansville *(G-3732)*

OPHTHALMIC GOODS: Eyewear, Protective

Aearo Technologies LLC ....A...... 317 692-6666
Indianapolis *(G-6341)*

OPHTHALMIC GOODS: Frames & Parts, Eyeglass & Spectacle

Usv Optical Inc ....G...... 260 482-5033
Fort Wayne *(G-4721)*

OPHTHALMIC GOODS: Frames, Lenses & Parts, Eyeglasses

Lenstech Optical Lab Inc ....E...... 317 882-1249
Greenwood *(G-5718)*

OPHTHALMIC GOODS: Lenses, Ophthalmic

Harmon Hrmon Uysugi Optmtrists ....F...... 812 723-4752
Paoli *(G-11452)*

OPHTHALMIC GOODS: Spectacles

Spectacles of Carmel Inc ....G...... 317 848-9081
Carmel *(G-1485)*
Spectacles of Carmel Inc ....G...... 317 475-9011
Indianapolis *(G-7972)*

OPTICAL GOODS STORES

City Optical Co Inc ....D...... 317 924-1300
Indianapolis *(G-6615)*
Jackson Vision Quest ....G...... 219 882-9397
Gary *(G-5071)*

OPTICAL GOODS STORES: Contact Lenses, Prescription

Better Visions PC ....G...... 260 627-2669
Leo *(G-9239)*
Better Visions PC ....G...... 260 244-7542
Columbia City *(G-1766)*

OPTICAL GOODS STORES: Eyeglasses, Prescription

Columbus Optical Service Inc ....G...... 812 372-2678
Columbus *(G-1878)*
Jasper Optical Lab ....G...... 812 634-9020
Jasper *(G-8262)*
Kokomo Optical Company Inc ....G...... 765 459-5137
Kokomo *(G-8655)*
Luxottica Retail N Amer Inc ....E...... 317 293-9999
Indianapolis *(G-7428)*
Luxottica Retail N Amer Inc ....E...... 219 736-0141
Merrillville *(G-9729)*
Shimp Optical Corp ....G...... 317 636-4448
Indianapolis *(G-7933)*
Usv Optical Inc ....G...... 260 482-5033
Fort Wayne *(G-4721)*

OPTICAL GOODS STORES: Opticians

Tri State Optical Inc ....E...... 765 289-4475
Muncie *(G-10575)*

OPTICAL INSTRUMENTS & APPARATUS

Control Development Inc ....F...... 574 288-7338
South Bend *(G-12742)*
Dave Jones Machinists LLC ....G...... 574 256-5500
Mishawaka *(G-10034)*
Murrell Optical LLC ....G...... 317 280-0114
Indianapolis *(G-7561)*
Vision Aid Systems Inc ....G...... 317 888-0323
Greenwood *(G-5758)*

OPTICAL INSTRUMENTS & LENSES

Conmoto Enterprises Inc ....G...... 219 787-1622
Indianapolis *(G-6650)*
G K Optical Company Inc ....E...... 317 881-2585
Indianapolis *(G-6975)*
S & S Optical Co Inc ....F...... 260 749-9614
New Haven *(G-10955)*
Thomas Optical LLC ....G...... 502 548-2163
Charlestown *(G-1584)*

OPTICAL ISOLATORS

Jdsu Acterna Holdings LLC ....G...... 317 788-9351
Indianapolis *(G-7300)*
Viavi Solutions Inc ....B...... 317 788-9351
Indianapolis *(G-8161)*

OPTOMETRISTS' OFFICES

City Optical Co Inc ....D...... 317 924-1300
Indianapolis *(G-6615)*
Lca-Vision Inc ....G...... 317 818-3980
Indianapolis *(G-7387)*
Luxottica Retail N Amer Inc ....E...... 317 293-9999
Indianapolis *(G-7428)*
Union Optical Eyecare Ctr Inc ....G...... 812 279-3466
Bedford *(G-587)*

ORDNANCE

Allied Mfg Partners Inc ....G...... 260 428-2670
Fort Wayne *(G-4062)*
Indiana Ordnance Works Inc ....G...... 812 256-4478
Pekin *(G-11474)*
Prototech Enterprises Inc ....G...... 317 250-9644
Carmel *(G-1457)*
Raytheon Company ....A...... 260 429-6000
Fort Wayne *(G-4576)*

ORGAN TUNING & REPAIR SVCS

Goulding & Wood Inc ....F...... 317 637-5222
Indianapolis *(G-7031)*

ORGANIZATIONS: Medical Research

Ash Access Technology Inc ....G...... 765 742-4813
Lafayette *(G-8854)*
Crown Bioscience Indiana Inc ....G...... 317 872-6001
Indianapolis *(G-6699)*

PRODUCT

ORGANIZATIONS: Religious

Christian Sound & Song Inc ....G....... 574 294-2893
Elkhart (G-2756)
Gospel Echoes Team Association ....G....... 574 533-0221
Goshen (G-5228)

ORGANIZATIONS: Research Institute

Ampacet Corporation ....E....... 812 466-9828
Terre Haute (G-13194)
Spaceport Explrtion Centre Inc ....G....... 765 606-1512
New Whiteland (G-11014)

ORGANIZERS, CLOSET & DRAWER Plastic

Home Pdts Intl - N Amer Inc..............B....... 773 890-1010
Seymour (G-12456)
Innovative Corp..................................E....... 317 804-5977
Westfield (G-14171)

ORIENTED STRANDBOARD

Midwest Bc ....G....... 219 369-4839
La Porte (G-8793)

ORNAMENTS: Lawn

D A Merriman Inc ....G....... 260 636-3464
Albion (G-23)
Ingredion Incorporated......................E....... 317 635-4455
Indianapolis (G-7230)

OSCILLATORS

Innovative Rfid Inc............................G....... 260 433-5835
Huntertown (G-6141)

OUTBOARD MOTORS & PARTS

Brunswick Corporation ....C....... 260 459-8200
Fort Wayne (G-4125)

OVENS: Infrared

Blasdel Enterprises Inc ....F....... 812 663-3213
Greensburg (G-5590)
Infrared Technologies LLC ....G....... 317 326-2019
Greenfield (G-5541)

OVERSHOES: Plastic

Artisanz Fabrication Mch LLC ....G....... 317 708-0228
Plainfield (G-11594)

PACKAGE DESIGN SVCS

Queen City Candy LLC ....G....... 812 537-5203
Greendale (G-5494)

PACKAGING & LABELING SVCS

Adec Inc ....C....... 574 848-7451
Bristol (G-1040)
Ahf Industries Inc ....C....... 812 936-9988
French Lick (G-4984)
Asempac Inc ....E....... 812 945-6303
New Albany (G-10747)
Century Pharmaceuticals Inc ....F....... 317 849-4210
Indianapolis (G-6586)
Crider Holcomb Partnership LLC ....G....... 812 279-2200
Bedford (G-536)
Custom Bottling & Packg Inc ....E....... 877 401-7195
Ashley (G-285)
Custom Carton Inc ....F....... 260 563-7411
Wabash (G-13723)
Ditech Inc ....D....... 812 526-0850
Edinburgh (G-2607)
Fedex Office & Print Svcs Inc ....F....... 317 974-0378
Indianapolis (G-6909)
Fedex Office & Print Svcs Inc ....F....... 317 917-1529
Indianapolis (G-6910)
Handle With Care Packaging ....E....... 812 250-1920
Evansville (G-3530)
Insertec Inc ....D....... 800 556-1911
Indianapolis (G-7240)
Kik Custom Products Inc ....E....... 574 295-0000
Elkhart (G-2968)
National Products LLC ....E....... 219 393-5536
Kingsbury (G-8543)
Pathfinder Services Inc ....E....... 260 356-0500
Huntington (G-6236)
Rauch Inc ....C....... 812 945-4063
New Albany (G-10854)

Royal Adhesives & Sealants LLC ....D....... 574 246-5000
South Bend (G-12920)
Service Graphics Inc ....D....... 317 471-8246
Indianapolis (G-7917)
Universal Packg Systems Inc ....B....... 260 829-6721
Orland (G-11359)

PACKAGING MATERIALS, INDL: Wholesalers

Essential Sealing Products Inc............G....... 219 787-8711
Chesterton (G-1604)

PACKAGING MATERIALS, WHOLESALE

ABC Industries Inc ....D....... 800 426-0921
Winona Lake (G-14349)
Bethlehem Packg Die Cutng Inc..........F....... 812 282-8740
New Albany (G-10751)
ISI Inc ....F....... 317 631-7980
Indianapolis (G-7275)
Jamil Packaging Corporation ....C....... 574 256-2600
Mishawaka (G-10059)
Kelly Box and Packaging Corp ....D....... 260 432-4570
Fort Wayne (G-4407)

PACKAGING MATERIALS: Paper

3M Company ....B....... 765 348-3200
Hartford City (G-5976)
Accu-Label Inc ....E....... 260 482-5223
Fort Wayne (G-4036)
American Containers Inc ....D....... 574 936-4068
Plymouth (G-11664)
Bprex Closures LLC ....D....... 812 386-1525
Princeton (G-11866)
Crichlow Industries Inc ....G....... 317 925-5178
Indianapolis (G-6692)
Custom Packaging Inc ....F....... 317 876-9559
Indianapolis (G-6717)
Eagle Packaging Inc ....G....... 260 281-2333
Goshen (G-5208)
Flexible Materials Inc ....D....... 812 260-9578
Jeffersonville (G-8362)
G & T Industries of Indiana ....E....... 812 634-2252
Jasper (G-8253)
Hooven - Dayton Corp ....E....... 765 935-3999
Richmond (G-12000)
Huhtamaki Inc ....C....... 219 972-4264
Hammond (G-5896)
Innovative Energy Inc ....E....... 219 696-3639
Lowell (G-9409)
Label Tech Inc ....E....... 765 747-1234
Muncie (G-10506)
LDI Ltd LLC ....F....... 317 237-5400
Indianapolis (G-7388)
Multi-Color Corporation ....C....... 812 752-3187
Scottsburg (G-12376)
NP Converters Inc ....E....... 812 448-2555
Brazil (G-973)
Pactiv Corporation ....C....... 574 936-7065
Plymouth (G-11709)
PSC Industries Inc ....E....... 812 425-9071
Evansville (G-3688)
Sonoco Products Company ....C....... 812 526-5511
Edinburgh (G-2629)
Stoffel Seals Corporation ....E....... 845 353-3800
Angola (G-248)
Taghleef Industries Inc ....A....... 302 326-5500
Rosedale (G-12208)
Vti Packaging Specialties ....G....... 574 277-4119
Granger (G-5449)
Westrock Cp LLC ....G....... 574 936-2118
Plymouth (G-11735)

PACKAGING MATERIALS: Paper, Coated Or Laminated

Patty Processing Inc ....C....... 574 936-9901
Plymouth (G-11710)
Vista Grphic Cmmunications LLC ....F....... 317 898-2000
Indianapolis (G-8166)

PACKAGING MATERIALS: Plastic Film, Coated Or Laminated

Cpg - Ohio LLC ....F....... 260 829-6721
Orland (G-11348)
Interactive Surface Tech LLC..............G....... 812 246-0900
Sellersburg (G-12398)
Monosol LLC ....F....... 219 762-3165
Merrillville (G-9741)

Monosol LLC ....D....... 219 763-7589
Portage (G-11778)
Monosol LLC ....E....... 219 324-9459
La Porte (G-8797)
Monosol LLC ....D....... 219 762-3165
Portage (G-11779)
Poly Plastics Ltd ....F....... 260 569-9088
Wabash (G-13750)
Sabert Corporation ....G....... 260 747-3149
Fort Wayne (G-4600)
Universal Package LLC ....F....... 812 937-3605
Dale (G-2335)
Universal Packg Systems Inc ....B....... 260 829-6721
Orland (G-11359)

PACKAGING MATERIALS: Polystyrene Foam

Ace Extrusion LLC ....G....... 812 463-5230
Evansville (G-3338)
Ace Extrusion LLC ....D....... 812 463-5230
Evansville (G-3340)
B&W Packaging Mfg LLC ....E....... 812 280-9578
New Albany (G-10749)
Barger Packaging Corporation ....D....... 574 389-1860
Elkhart (G-2715)
Bremen Corporation ....A....... 574 546-4238
Bremen (G-987)
Createc Corporation ....E....... 317 566-0022
Indianapolis (G-6686)
Creative Foam Corporation ....E....... 574 546-4238
Bremen (G-995)
Cryovac Inc ....C....... 317 876-4100
Indianapolis (G-6702)
Fxi Inc ....C....... 260 747-7485
Fort Wayne (G-4291)
Hi-Tech Foam Products LLC ....E....... 270 684-8331
Indianapolis (G-7105)
Innovative Packaging Assoc Inc ....F....... 260 356-6577
Huntington (G-6217)
M & C LLC ....G....... 812 482-7447
Jasper (G-8288)
Pregis LLC ....G....... 574 936-7065
Plymouth (G-11716)
Pyramid Paper Products Inc ....E....... 812 372-0288
Columbus (G-2002)
Solotat Industries LLC ....G....... 574 320-1436
Elkhart (G-3180)
Total Concepts Design Inc ....D....... 812 752-6534
Scottsburg (G-12384)
Unique-Prescotech Inc ....E....... 479 646-2973
Evansville (G-3783)
US Foam Corporation ....G....... 260 456-4998
Fort Wayne (G-4720)
Useful Products LLC ....E....... 877 304-9036
Goodland (G-5161)
Worldwide Foam Ltd...........................G....... 574 968-8268
Elkhart (G-3269)

PACKING & CRATING SVC

Packaging Group Corp.........................E....... 219 879-2500
Michigan City (G-9826)

PACKING & CRATING SVCS: Containerized Goods For Shipping

Red Gold Inc ....G....... 260 726-8140
Portland (G-11845)

PACKING MATERIALS: Mechanical

Barger Packaging Inc ....G....... 888 525-2845
Elkhart (G-2714)
C&C Polo Enterprises Inc ....G....... 317 577-8266
Indianapolis (G-6529)
Uniform Hood Lace Inc.......................G....... 317 896-9555
Westfield (G-14196)

PACKING SVCS: Shipping

C&C Polo Enterprises Inc ....G....... 317 577-8266
Indianapolis (G-6529)

PACKING: Metallic

Apexx Enterprises LLC ....F....... 812 486-2443
Montgomery (G-10213)

PACKING: Rubber

Griffith Rbr Mills of Garrett ....F....... 260 357-0876
Garrett (G-5008)

PADDING: Foamed Plastics

Foamcraft Inc ....D 574 293-8569
Elkhart (G-2860)

Residue West Inc ....E 731 587-9596
Evansville (G-3705)

PADS: Mattress

Crash Beds LLC ....G 317 601-4436
Greenwood (G-5677)

Regency Pad Corp ....D 731 587-9596
Evansville (G-3702)

Virtus Inc ....E 812 932-0131
Batesville (G-523)

PADS: Permanent Waving

M M Converting Inc ....G 260 563-7411
Wabash (G-13735)

PAILS: Plastic

North America Packaging Corp ....C 219 462-8915
Valparaiso (G-13592)

PAINT STORE

Sun Rise Metal Shop ....G 260 463-4026
Topeka (G-13430)

PAINTING SVC: Metal Prdts

Carrara Industries Inc ....G 765 643-3430
Anderson (G-81)

Chief Metal Works Inc ....G 765 932-2134
Rushville (G-12217)

Craddock Finishing Corporation ....E 812 425-2691
Evansville (G-3436)

Cunningham Quality Painting ....G 317 925-8852
Indianapolis (G-6711)

D & S Industries Inc ....F 574 848-7144
Bristol (G-1053)

Edcoat Limited Partnership ....E 574 654-9105
New Carlisle (G-10881)

Holscher Products Inc ....E 765 884-8021
Fowler (G-4801)

Huber Brothers Inc ....G 317 392-1566
Shelbyville (G-12537)

Jupiter Aluminum Corporation ....E 219 932-3322
Fairland (G-3823)

Mestek Inc ....E 317 831-5314
Mooresville (G-10322)

Panacea Paints & Coatings Inc ....G 260 728-4222
Decatur (G-2397)

Precoat Metals Corp ....E 317 462-7761
Greenfield (G-5564)

Precoat Metals Corp ....D 219 393-3561
La Porte (G-8807)

Precoat Metals Corp ....C 317 462-7761
Greenfield (G-5565)

Steve Reiff Inc ....D 260 723-4360
South Whitley (G-13005)

Superior Metal Tech LLC ....D 317 897-9850
Indianapolis (G-8022)

PAINTS & ADDITIVES

A F Wolke Co Inc ....G 812 738-4141
Corydon (G-2086)

Advanced Protective Tech LLC ....G 877 548-9323
Valparaiso (G-13484)

Davies-Imperial Coatings Inc ....E 219 933-0877
Hammond (G-5869)

Nanochem Technologies LLC ....E 574 970-2436
Elkhart (G-3057)

Red Spot Paint & Varnish Co ....B 812 428-9100
Evansville (G-3699)

Silcotec Inc ....F 219 324-4411
La Porte (G-8821)

United Coatings Tech Inc ....F 574 287-4774
South Bend (G-12981)

PAINTS & ALLIED PRODUCTS

Ampacet Corporation ....C 812 466-5231
Terre Haute (G-13193)

Ampacet Corporation ....E 812 466-9828
Terre Haute (G-13194)

Aoc LLC ....D 219 465-4384
Valparaiso (G-13494)

B C C Products Inc ....F 317 494-6420
Franklin (G-4870)

Baril Coatings Usa LLC ....F 260 665-8431
Angola (G-197)

Bloomington Concret Surfaces ....G 812 345-0011
Bloomington (G-686)

Bondline Adhesives Inc ....F 812 423-4651
Evansville (G-3390)

Columbus Paint Supply ....G 812 375-1118
Columbus (G-1879)

Contego International Inc ....G 574 223-5989
Rochester (G-12119)

Cp Inc ....E 765 825-4111
Connersville (G-2045)

D S E Inc ....E 812 376-0310
Columbus (G-1904)

Hammond Group Inc ....E 219 933-1560
Hammond (G-5885)

IVc Industrial Coatings Inc ....C 812 442-5080
Brazil (G-966)

J D Petro and Associates Inc ....G 317 736-6566
Franklin (G-4902)

Liquid Technologies Elkhart ....G 574 596-1883
Wakarusa (G-13782)

Margco International LLC ....G 317 568-4274
Indianapolis (G-7452)

Mason Total Property Care ....G 260 385-3573
New Haven (G-10948)

Mautz Paint Factory ....G 574 289-2497
South Bend (G-12856)

Midwest Pipecoating Inc ....D 219 322-4564
Schererville (G-12335)

Ncp Coatings Inc ....G 574 255-9678
Mishawaka (G-10094)

PPG Industries ....G 812 867-6601
Evansville (G-3681)

PPG Industries Inc ....E 317 745-0427
Avon (G-462)

PPG Industries Inc ....E 317 849-2340
Indianapolis (G-7714)

PPG Industries Inc ....E 317 267-0511
Indianapolis (G-7715)

PPG Industries Inc ....E 812 424-4774
Evansville (G-3682)

PPG Industries Inc ....E 812 473-0339
Evansville (G-3683)

PPG Industries Inc ....E 317 897-3836
Indianapolis (G-7716)

PPG Industries Inc ....E 317 577-2344
Fishers (G-3956)

PPG Industries Inc ....E 260 373-2373
Fort Wayne (G-4545)

PPG Industries Inc ....G 317 598-9448
Fishers (G-3957)

PPG Industries Inc ....G 812 285-0546
Jeffersonville (G-8415)

PPG Industries Inc ....E 317 787-9393
Indianapolis (G-7717)

PPG Industries Inc ....E 317 870-0345
Carmel (G-1454)

PPG Industries Inc ....E 812 944-4164
New Albany (G-10847)

PPG Industries Inc ....E 317 251-9494
Indianapolis (G-7718)

PPG Industries Inc ....E 317 546-5714
Indianapolis (G-7719)

PPG Industries Inc ....E 812 232-0672
Terre Haute (G-13306)

PPG Industries Inc ....E 812 882-0440
Vincennes (G-13699)

PPG Industries Inc ....E 317 867-5934
Westfield (G-14180)

Redspot Paint and Varnish Co ....C 812 428-9100
Evansville (G-3700)

Sonoco Products Company ....C 812 526-5511
Edinburgh (G-2629)

Technicote Inc ....D 812 466-9844
Terre Haute (G-13349)

Testworth Laboratories Inc ....F 260 244-5137
Columbia City (G-1840)

Timber Ox Inc ....G 317 758-5942
Cicero (G-1669)

Transcendia Inc ....C 765 935-1520
Richmond (G-12068)

United Minerals and Prpts Inc ....E 812 838-5236
Mount Vernon (G-10412)

Van Zandt Enterprises Inc ....E 812 423-3511
Evansville (G-3792)

Wabash Valley Manufacturing ....C 260 352-2102
Silver Lake (G-12682)

Wayne Metal Protection Company ......E 260 492-2529
Fort Wayne (G-4742)

Woodys Paint Spot Ltd ....G 574 255-0348
Bremen (G-1034)

Worwag Coatings LLC ....E 765 447-2137
Lafayette (G-9026)

PAINTS & VARNISHES: Plastics Based

Red Spot Paint & Varnish Co ....B 812 428-9100
Evansville (G-3697)

Red Spot Paint & Varnish Co ....E 812 428-9100
Evansville (G-3698)

PAINTS, VARNISHES & SPLYS WHOLESALERS

Bender Wholesale Distributors ....F 574 264-4409
Elkhart (G-2721)

Jack Laurie Coml Floors Inc ....G 317 569-2095
Indianapolis (G-7293)

PAINTS, VARNISHES & SPLYS, WHOLESALE: Paints

Mautz Paint Factory ....G 574 289-2497
South Bend (G-12856)

PAINTS: Asphalt Or Bituminous

Aci Construction Company Inc ....F 317 549-1833
Indianapolis (G-6317)

PAINTS: Oil Or Alkyd Vehicle Or Water Thinned

Quality Coatings Inc ....F 812 925-3314
Chandler (G-1553)

PAINTS: Waterproof

Dist Council 91 ....G 812 962-9191
Evansville (G-3459)

PALLET REPAIR SVCS

American Pallet & Recycl Inc ....G 219 322-4391
Dyer (G-2492)

Clm Pallet Recycling Inc ....G 317 485-4080
Fortville (G-4770)

Green Stream Company ....D 574 293-1949
Elkhart (G-2899)

J & J Pallet Corp ....E 812 944-8670
New Albany (G-10809)

X-L Box Inc ....E 219 763-3736
Valparaiso (G-13638)

PALLET SPACERS: Fiber, Made From Purchased Materials

Logistick Inc ....G 800 758-5840
South Bend (G-12844)

PALLETS

A1 Pallet Liquidators ....G 765 356-4020
Anderson (G-57)

American Fibertech Corporation ....E 219 261-3586
Clarks Hill (G-1670)

B & B Pallet ....G ......
Clinton (G-1714)

Billy D Snider ....G 765 795-6426
Cloverdale (G-1724)

Bristol Pallet ....G 574 862-1862
Goshen (G-5179)

D and S Pallet ....G 765 866-7263
Crawfordsville (G-2148)

Evansville Pallets ....G 812 550-0199
Evansville (G-3489)

Garr Custom Pallets Inc ....G 812 352-8887
North Vernon (G-11258)

Graber Box & Pallet Fmly Lmt P ....E 260 657-5657
Grabill (G-5365)

Hoosier Pallet ....G 765 629-2899
Milroy (G-9981)

Industrial Pallet Corporation ....G 574 583-4800
Monticello (G-10266)

Indy Pallet Company Inc ....G 317 843-0452
Carmel (G-1413)

K J Pallets ....G 812 342-6476
Columbus (G-1954)

M M Paltech Inc ....G 219 932-5308
Hammond (G-5909)

PRODUCT

Millwood Box & Pallet ....G 765 628-7330
   Kokomo *(G-8667)*

Newport Pallet Inc ....G 217 497-8220
   Newport *(G-11056)*

Newport Pallet Inc ....E 765 505-9463
   Hillsdale *(G-6061)*

Owen County Pallet ....G 812 859-4617
   Worthington *(G-14395)*

Pallet Builder Inc ....F 765 948-3345
   Fairmount *(G-3834)*

Pallets Viveros LLC ....G 765 307-0112
   Crawfordsville *(G-2182)*

Phoenix Pallet Inc ....F 574 262-0458
   Elkhart *(G-3094)*

Pro Pallet LLC ....G 219 292-3389
   Gary *(G-5087)*

Quality Pallet ....E 765 348-4840
   Hartford City *(G-5989)*

Quality Pallet ....G 765 212-2215
   Muncie *(G-10551)*

R & E Pallet Inc ....G 219 873-9671
   Michigan City *(G-9833)*

Rs Pallet Inc ....G 574 596-8777
   Bristol *(G-1082)*

Schwartzville Pallet ....G 260 244-4144
   Columbia City *(G-1834)*

Steves Pallets Inc ....F 574 457-3620
   Syracuse *(G-13144)*

Vest Pallet Co ....G 812 839-6247
   Canaan *(G-1282)*

W & W Pallet Co LLC ....G 812 486-3548
   Montgomery *(G-10246)*

Yager Pallet ....G 219 365-2766
   Saint John *(G-12273)*

PALLETS & SKIDS: Wood

A S M Inc ....G 260 724-8220
   Decatur *(G-2363)*

A-1 Pallet Co Inc Clarksville ......E 812 288-6339
   Clarksville *(G-1671)*

A-1 Pallet Co Inc Clarksville ......G 812 288-6339
   Clarksville *(G-1672)*

Anthony Wayne Rehabilitation C ......D 260 744-6145
   Fort Wayne *(G-4078)*

Basiloid Products Corp ....E 812 692-5511
   Elnora *(G-3286)*

Danwood Industries ....G 219 369-1484
   La Porte *(G-8749)*

F & F Contracting ....G 574 867-4471
   Grovertown *(G-5795)*

Gonzalez Pallets ....G 317 644-1242
   Indianapolis *(G-7023)*

Integrity Pallet LLC ....G 574 612-2119
   Shipshewana *(G-12619)*

Lemler Pallet Inc ....G 574 646-2707
   Bourbon *(G-944)*

Myers Wood Products ....G 765 597-2147
   Bloomingdale *(G-649)*

Powell Systems Inc ....E 765 884-0980
   Fowler *(G-4805)*

Servants Inc ....G 812 634-2201
   Jasper *(G-8307)*

Servants Inc ....D 812 634-2201
   Jasper *(G-8306)*

Sparkman Mfg Inc ....G 812 873-6052
   Commiskey *(G-2037)*

Steves Pallets ....G 260 856-2047
   Cromwell *(G-2211)*

Trinity Cstm Built Pallets LLC ......G 260 466-4625
   New Haven *(G-10961)*

Ufp Granger LLC ....E 574 277-7670
   Granger *(G-5445)*

Waupaca Pallet ....G 812 547-1565
   Troy *(G-13449)*

Whitakerr Dalemon ....G 812 738-2396
   Corydon *(G-2116)*

PALLETS: Corrugated

F & F Contracting ....G 574 867-4471
   Grovertown *(G-5795)*

PALLETS: Plastic

Flambeau Inc ....C 812 372-4899
   Columbus *(G-1931)*

Paxxal Inc ....G 317 296-7724
   Noblesville *(G-11164)*

Perfect Manufacturing LLC ....G 317 924-5284
   Indianapolis *(G-7675)*

Perfect Pallets Inc ....D 888 553-5559
   Indianapolis *(G-7676)*

Richardson Molding LLC ....C 812 342-0139
   Columbus *(G-2008)*

PALLETS: Wooden

A Pallet Company ....G 317 687-9020
   Indianapolis *(G-6299)*

A1 Pallets Inc ....G 812 425-0381
   Evansville *(G-3331)*

Alsip Pallet Company Inc ....G 219 322-3288
   Schererville *(G-12314)*

American Fibertech Corporation ......D 219 261-3586
   Remington *(G-11904)*

American Pallet & Recycl Inc ......G 219 322-4391
   Dyer *(G-2492)*

Ash-Lin Inc ....F 317 861-1540
   Fountaintown *(G-4789)*

Axtrom Industries ....E 812 859-4873
   Freedom *(G-4946)*

Barks Lumber Co Inc ....G 812 732-4680
   Central *(G-1545)*

Buckingham Pallets Inc ....F 317 846-8601
   Carmel *(G-1323)*

Burton Lumber Co Inc ....F 812 866-4438
   Lexington *(G-9249)*

C & C Pallets and Lumber LLC ......G 765 524-3214
   New Castle *(G-10895)*

C C Cook and Son Lbr Co Inc ......E 765 672-4235
   Reelsville *(G-11900)*

C E Kersting & Sons ....G 574 896-2766
   North Judson *(G-11207)*

Calumet Pallet Company Inc ......D 219 932-4550
   Michigan City *(G-9772)*

Columbus Pallet Corporation ......G 812 372-7272
   Columbus *(G-1880)*

Commercial Pallet Recycl Inc ......F 260 829-1021
   Orland *(G-11347)*

Conner Sawmill Inc ....F 574 626-3227
   Walton *(G-13815)*

Coomer & Sons Sawmill & Pallet ......D 765 659-2846
   Frankfort *(G-4824)*

Corr-Wood Manufacturing Inc ......E 812 867-0700
   Evansville *(G-3431)*

D&G Timber Inc ....E 812 486-3356
   Odon *(G-11324)*

Dehart Pallet & Lumber Co ....F 812 794-2974
   Austin *(G-396)*

Dmi Distribution Inc ....E 765 287-0035
   Muncie *(G-10461)*

Dodd Saw Mills Inc ....E 812 268-4811
   Sullivan *(G-13081)*

Duro Inc ....G 574 293-6860
   Elkhart *(G-2804)*

Duro Recycling Inc ....G 574 522-2572
   Elkhart *(G-2805)*

Ernest A Cooper ....E 812 284-0436
   Jeffersonville *(G-8357)*

Findley Foster Corp ....E 812 524-7279
   Seymour *(G-12450)*

Ford Sawmills Inc ....E 812 324-2134
   Vincennes *(G-13682)*

Green Stream Company ....D 574 293-1949
   Elkhart *(G-2899)*

Greene County Pallet Inc ....F 812 384-8362
   Bloomfield *(G-638)*

Hagemier Products ....G 812 526-0377
   Franklin *(G-4894)*

Hillcrest Pallets ....G 812 883-3636
   Salem *(G-12291)*

Hoosier Box and Skid Inc ....G 574 256-2111
   Mishawaka *(G-10050)*

Indiana Pallet Co Inc ....E 219 398-4223
   East Chicago *(G-2539)*

Indiana Wood Products Inc ....D 574 825-2129
   Middlebury *(G-9893)*

Industrial Woodkraft Inc ....E 812 897-4893
   Boonville *(G-914)*

J & J Pallet Corp ....E 812 948-9382
   New Albany *(G-10808)*

J & J Pallet Corp ....E 812 944-8670
   New Albany *(G-10809)*

J & J Pallet Corp ....E 812 288-4487
   Clarksville *(G-1687)*

Jennings County Pallets Inc ....E 812 458-6288
   Butlerville *(G-1248)*

Jennings County Pallets Inc ....E 812 458-6288
   Butlerville *(G-1249)*

JR Grber Sons Fmly Ltd Prtnr ......G 260 657-1071
   Grabill *(G-5377)*

K & S Pallet Inc ....F 260 422-1264
   Fort Wayne *(G-4402)*

Kamps Inc ....E 317 634-8360
   Indianapolis *(G-7332)*

Kerst Pallet ....G 765 585-3026
   Attica *(G-306)*

Kevin Coomer Pallet Co ....G 765 324-2294
   Colfax *(G-1756)*

Leclere Manufacturing Inc ....G 812 683-5627
   Jasper *(G-8287)*

Lovett Pallet Recycling LLC ....D 317 638-4840
   Indianapolis *(G-7421)*

Meagan Inc ....F 574 267-8626
   Warsaw *(G-13906)*

Michiana Pallet Recycle Inc ....G 574 232-8566
   South Bend *(G-12861)*

Midwestern Pallet Service Inc ......G 260 563-1526
   Wabash *(G-13739)*

Milroy Pallet Inc ....G 765 629-2919
   Milroy *(G-9984)*

Monroeville Box Pallet & Wood ......E 260 623-3128
   Monroeville *(G-10197)*

Napoleon Hardwood Lbr Co Inc ......E 812 852-4090
   Greensburg *(G-5626)*

Neumayr Lumber Co Inc ....F 765 764-4148
   Attica *(G-308)*

North Central Pallets Inc ....E 574 892-6142
   Argos *(G-276)*

Oldenburg Pallet Inc ....G 812 933-0568
   Batesville *(G-513)*

Pallet One of Indiana Inc ....D 260 768-4021
   Shipshewana *(G-12641)*

Pallet Recyclers LLC ....G 812 402-0095
   Evansville *(G-3661)*

Palletone Indiana Trnsp LLC ....F 260 768-4021
   Shipshewana *(G-12642)*

Paul Knepp Sawmill Inc ....G 812 486-3773
   Montgomery *(G-10236)*

Peru Hardwood Products Inc ......F 765 473-4844
   Peru *(G-11539)*

Premier Lumber Company ....F 219 801-6018
   Chesterton *(G-1628)*

Quality Fence Ltd ....G 260 768-4986
   Shipshewana *(G-12645)*

Quality Pallets Inc ....G 812 873-6818
   Commiskey *(G-2036)*

Richard Squier Pallets Inc ....E 260 281-2434
   Waterloo *(G-14023)*

Ridg-U-Rak Inc ....G 574 273-8036
   Granger *(G-5431)*

Schneiders Wood Shop Inc ....G 812 522-4621
   Seymour *(G-12482)*

Skid Row Wood Products Inc ......F 812 828-0349
   Spencer *(G-13036)*

Tc Pallets & Peddler Sweet LLC ......G 812 283-1090
   Jeffersonville *(G-8433)*

Vision IV Inc ....E 812 423-0119
   Evansville *(G-3804)*

X-L Box Inc ....E 219 763-3736
   Valparaiso *(G-13638)*

Yoder & Sons Pallets ....G 260 625-2835
   Columbia City *(G-1848)*

PANEL & DISTRIBUTION BOARDS & OTHER RELATED APPARATUS

J & J Industrial Services Inc ....G 219 362-4973
   La Porte *(G-8772)*

Mechanical Engineering Control ......F 574 294-7580
   Elkhart *(G-3025)*

Pinder Instruments Company Inc ......E 219 924-7070
   Munster *(G-10624)*

Richard J Bagan Inc ....E 260 244-5115
   Columbia City *(G-1826)*

Semcor Inc ....F 219 362-0222
   La Porte *(G-8817)*

PANEL & DISTRIBUTION BOARDS: Electric

Leman Engrg & Consulting Inc ......G 574 870-7732
   Brookston *(G-1106)*

PANELS & SECTIONS: Prefabricated, Concrete

Ram North America Inc ....F 317 984-1971
   Arcadia *(G-268)*

PANELS, CORRUGATED: Plastic

MTA Technology LLC..................F 765 447-2221
Lafayette (G-8973)
Warnke Associates Inc ....G..... 574 586-3331
Walkerton (G-13814)

PANELS: Building, Metal

Central States Mfg Inc ....D..... 219 879-4770
Michigan City (G-9773)

PANELS: Building, Plastic, NEC

Crane Composites Inc ....D..... 815 467-8600
Goshen (G-5195)
Panolam Industries Inc ....G..... 574 264-0702
Elkhart (G-3073)
Ram North America Inc ....F..... 317 984-1971
Arcadia (G-268)

PANELS: Building, Wood

Edna Troyer ....G..... 260 894-4405
Ligonier (G-9281)
Omega National Products LLC ....C..... 574 295-5353
Elkhart (G-3068)
Ufp Nappanee LLC ....D..... 574 773-2505
Nappanee (G-10709)

PANELS: Electric Metering

Landis Gyr Utilities Svcs Inc.......E..... 765 742-1001
Lafayette (G-8953)

PANELS: Wood

Robert Weed Plywood Corp.........B..... 574 848-7631
Bristol (G-1081)

PAPER & BOARD: Die-cut

A-1 Graphics Inc ....G..... 765 289-1851
Muncie (G-10420)
AK Tool and Die ....G..... 574 286-9010
Mishawaka (G-9992)
American Steel Rule Die Inc ....G..... 574 262-3437
Elkhart (G-2685)
C & W Inkd ....F..... 317 352-1000
Indianapolis (G-6527)
Graphix Unlimited Inc................E..... 574 546-3770
Bremen (G-1000)
Harcourt Industries Inc..............E..... 765 629-2625
Milroy (G-9980)
Millcraft Paper Company ....E..... 317 240-3500
Indianapolis (G-7519)
Rink Printing Company Inc ....E..... 574 232-7935
South Bend (G-12916)
Ross-Gage Inc ....D..... 317 283-2323
Indianapolis (G-7863)
Shirley Engraving Co Inc ....F..... 317 634-4084
Indianapolis (G-7934)
Tre Paper Co Inc.......................E..... 765 649-2536
Anderson (G-178)
Triangle Printing Inc ....G..... 317 786-3488
Indianapolis (G-8098)
Westrock Rkt Company................C..... 812 372-8873
Columbus (G-2033)

PAPER CONVERTING

Applied Coating Converting LLC ....G..... 260 436-4455
Fort Wayne (G-4082)
Larry Flowers Wholesale.............G..... 765 747-5156
Muncie (G-10509)
Palacio Tropical ....G..... 574 289-0742
South Bend (G-12887)
Schwarz Partners LP ....E..... 317 290-1140
Indianapolis (G-7904)
Signode Industrial Group LLC.............E..... 574 266-6933
Elkhart (G-3171)
Web Industries Dallas Inc ....E..... 260 432-0027
Fort Wayne (G-4749)

PAPER MANUFACTURERS: Exc Newsprint

Alliance Sheets LLC ....E..... 574 622-6020
Bristol (G-1042)
C D Ventures Inc ....G..... 765 482-9179
Lebanon (G-9171)
International Paper Company ....E..... 317 871-6999
Indianapolis (G-7255)
International Paper Company ....F..... 317 481-4000
Indianapolis (G-7256)

International Paper Company ....C..... 317 510-6410
Indianapolis (G-7257)
International Paper Company ....C..... 765 675-6732
Tipton (G-13393)
International Paper Company ....F..... 317 715-9080
Indianapolis (G-7258)
International Paper Company ....C..... 260 747-9111
Fort Wayne (G-4380)
International Paper Company ....E..... 800 643-7244
Terre Haute (G-13259)
International Paper Company ....C..... 219 844-6509
Hammond (G-5901)
Pratt Paper (in) LLC ....E..... 219 477-1040
Valparaiso (G-13602)
Royal Imprints Inc ....E..... 800 894-3151
Ligonier (G-9294)
Space Kraft ....F..... 317 871-6999
Indianapolis (G-7966)
Supremex Midwest Inc ....E..... 317 253-4321
Indianapolis (G-8024)
Temple Inland ....G..... 765 362-1074
Crawfordsville (G-2201)

PAPER PRDTS: Feminine Hygiene Prdts

Johnson & Johnson ....G..... 732 524-0400
Fishers (G-3935)
Johnson & Johnson ....G..... 317 539-8300
Mooresville (G-10318)

PAPER PRDTS: Infant & Baby Prdts

Bobby Little Creations................G..... 219 313-5102
Crown Point (G-2229)

PAPER PRDTS: Molded Pulp Prdts

Huhtamaki Inc ....C..... 219 972-4264
Hammond (G-5896)

PAPER PRDTS: Sanitary Tissue Paper

Nice-Pak Products Inc ....B..... 317 839-0373
Plainfield (G-11630)

PAPER, WHOLESALE: Printing

Millcraft Paper Company ....E..... 317 240-3500
Indianapolis (G-7519)

PAPER: Adhesive

American Label Products Inc ....G..... 317 873-9850
Zionsville (G-14416)
Avery Dennison Corporation ....C..... 260 481-4500
Fort Wayne (G-4098)
Avery Dennison Corporation ....D..... 219 696-7777
Lowell (G-9399)
Quality Engineered Products.............E..... 574 294-6943
Elkhart (G-3127)
Standard Label Co ....E..... 574 522-3548
Elkhart (G-3187)

PAPER: Art

Twinrocker Hand Made Paper Inc.........G..... 765 563-3119
Brookston (G-1109)

PAPER: Bristols

Bristol Myers ....G..... 812 428-1927
Evansville (G-3403)

PAPER: Building, Insulating & Packaging

John Wallace Builder Inc ....G..... 765 447-3614
Lafayette (G-8933)

PAPER: Business Form

Roi Marketing Company...............G..... 317 644-0797
Indianapolis (G-7855)

PAPER: Carbon

Stenno Carbon Co ....F..... 317 890-8710
Indianapolis (G-8000)

PAPER: Cardboard

Guy Cardboard...........................G..... 812 989-4809
Elizabeth (G-2644)
Mill Creek Custom Deluxe Box............G..... 765 934-3901
Van Buren (G-13640)

PAPER: Catalog

Harper Direct LLC ....B..... 214 245-5026
Greendale (G-5488)

PAPER: Coated & Laminated, NEC

3M Company...............................B..... 765 348-3200
Hartford City (G-5976)
Abro Industries Inc ....E..... 574 232-8289
South Bend (G-12692)
Accu-Label Inc ....E..... 260 482-5223
Fort Wayne (G-4036)
Avery Dennison Corporation ....G..... 765 221-9277
Anderson (G-71)
Daubert Vci Inc ....E..... 574 772-9310
Knox (G-8564)
F Robert Gardner Co Inc ....G..... 317 634-2333
Indianapolis (G-6900)
Fedex Office & Print Svcs Inc ....E..... 317 337-2679
Indianapolis (G-6912)
Gindor Inc ....G..... 574 642-4004
Goshen (G-5225)
HI Tech Label Inc.......................F..... 765 659-1800
Frankfort (G-4836)
International Paper Company ....E..... 800 643-7244
Terre Haute (G-13259)
Jknk Ventures Inc ....F..... 812 246-0900
Sellersburg (G-12399)
L & L Press Inc ....F..... 765 664-3162
Marion (G-9541)
Label Tech Inc ....E..... 765 747-1234
Muncie (G-10506)
Lambel Corporation ....F..... 317 849-6828
Indianapolis (G-7377)
Lamco Finishers Inc ....E..... 317 471-1010
Indianapolis (G-7379)
Mito-Craft Inc ....G..... 574 287-4555
South Bend (G-12864)
Morgan Adhesives Company LLC........D..... 812 342-2004
Columbus (G-1976)
NP Converters Inc......................E..... 812 448-2555
Brazil (G-973)
R R Donnelley & Sons Company ....B..... 260 624-2350
Angola (G-242)
Tippecanoe Press Inc ....F..... 317 392-1207
Shelbyville (G-12576)
Westrock Cp LLC ....G..... 574 936-2118
Plymouth (G-11735)

PAPER: Coated, Exc Photographic, Carbon Or Abrasive

Covalnce Spcialty Coatings LLC..........E..... 812 424-2904
Evansville (G-3435)

PAPER: Corrugated

Cps Inc ....G..... 317 804-2300
Westfield (G-14147)
Flutes Inc ....D..... 317 870-6010
Indianapolis (G-6941)
Georgia-Pacific LLC ....G..... 219 776-0069
Wheatfield (G-14222)
Sheets LLC ....G..... 317 290-1140
Indianapolis (G-7927)
Sinflex Paper Co Inc ....E..... 765 789-6688
Muncie (G-10563)

PAPER: Milk Filter

American Melt Blown Filtration ....E..... 219 866-3500
Rensselaer (G-11912)

PAPER: Specialty Or Chemically Treated

Noblesville Pack & Ship ....G..... 317 776-6306
Noblesville (G-11161)

PAPER: Tissue

Mann Distribution Inc ....G..... 317 293-6785
Indianapolis (G-7449)

PAPER: Wallpaper

E&S Wallcovering ....G..... 812 256-6668
Charlestown (G-1564)
Panel Solutions Inc....................F..... 574 389-8494
Elkhart (G-3071)

PRODUCT

PAPER: Waxed, Made From Purchased Materials

Bomarko Inc ....C 574 936-9901
  Plymouth (G-11669)

PAPER: Wrapping & Packaging

Goodwill Inds of Centl Ind ....E 317 587-0281
  Carmel (G-1388)
Inland Paper Board & Packaging ....G 317 879-9710
  Indianapolis (G-7234)
New-Indy Hartford City LLC ....D 765 348-5440
  Hartford City (G-5986)
New-Indy Hartford City LLC ....F 260 347-4739
  Kendallville (G-8499)

PAPERBOARD

American Containers Inc ....D 574 936-4068
  Plymouth (G-11664)
Graphic Packaging Intl ....G 765 289-7391
  Muncie (G-10478)
Graphic Packaging Intl LLC ....B 260 347-7612
  Kendallville (G-8476)
Indiana Ribbon Inc ....E 219 279-2112
  Wolcott (G-14365)
International Paper Company ....G 765 359-0107
  Crawfordsville (G-2162)
Michigan City Paper Box Co ....D 219 872-8383
  Michigan City (G-9817)
Paperworks Industries Inc ....G 260 569-3352
  Wabash (G-13748)
PSC Industries Inc ....E 812 425-9071
  Evansville (G-3688)
Sonoco Products Company ....C 812 526-5511
  Edinburgh (G-2629)
Sonoco Products Company ....D 574 893-4521
  Akron (G-7)
Viking Paper Company ....E 574 936-6300
  Plymouth (G-11734)
Westrock Cp LLC ....G 574 936-2118
  Plymouth (G-11735)
Westrock CP LLC ....B 219 762-4855
  Portage (G-11801)
Westrock CP LLC ....E 574 296-2817
  Elkhart (G-3258)
Westrock Rkt Company ....C 812 372-8873
  Columbus (G-2033)

PAPERBOARD CONVERTING

Interpak Inc ....G 765 482-9179
  Lebanon (G-9192)
Mach 1 Paper and Poly Pdts Inc ....G 574 522-4500
  Elkhart (G-3012)
Manchester Industries Inc VA ....E 765 489-4521
  Hagerstown (G-5808)
Westrock Rkt Company ....E 812 372-8873
  Columbus (G-2033)

PAPERBOARD PRDTS: Container Board

Graphic Packaging Intl LLC ....D 219 762-4855
  Portage (G-11768)

PAPERBOARD PRDTS: Folding Boxboard

Artistic Carton Company ....E 260 925-6060
  Auburn (G-312)
Clondalkin Pharma & Healthcare ....C 812 464-2461
  Evansville (G-3420)
Paperworks Industries Inc ....C 260 563-3102
  Wabash (G-13747)

PAPERBOARD PRDTS: Packaging Board

Shell Packaging Corporation ....G 765 965-6861
  Richmond (G-12048)

PAPERBOARD: Boxboard

Arrow Container LLC ....D 317 882-6444
  Indianapolis (G-6421)

PAPERBOARD: Chipboard

Westrock Rkt Company ....D 765 396-3317
  Eaton (G-2590)

PARACHUTES

Indiana Skydiving Center ....E 765 659-5557
  Frankfort (G-4837)

PARTITIONS & FIXTURES: Except Wood

Burns Cabinets and Disp Inc ....G 260 897-2219
  Avilla (G-401)
Creative Industries Inc ....F 317 248-1102
  Indianapolis (G-6688)
Elkhart Brass Manufacturing Co ....F 800 346-0250
  Elkhart (G-2822)
Flambeau Inc ....C 812 372-4899
  Columbus (G-1931)
Organized Living Inc ....C 812 334-8839
  Bloomington (G-791)
Patrick Industries Inc ....E 574 293-1521
  Elkhart (G-3084)
R Concepts Industries Inc ....D 574 295-6641
  Elkhart (G-3135)
Shamrock Cabinets Inc ....E 812 482-7969
  Jasper (G-8308)
Tru-Form Steel & Wire Inc ....E 765 348-5001
  Hartford City (G-5993)
Wick - Fab Inc ....E 260 897-3303
  Avilla (G-421)
William A Kadar ....G 219 884-7404
  Gary (G-5116)

PARTITIONS: Nonwood, Floor Attached

Modernfold Inc ....C 800 869-9685
  Greenfield (G-5557)
Tamwall Inc ....F 317 546-5055
  Indianapolis (G-8034)

PARTITIONS: Solid Fiber, Made From Purchased Materials

Westrock Rkt Company ....F 574 936-2118
  Plymouth (G-11736)

PARTITIONS: Wood & Fixtures

Bright Ideas LLC ....G 574 295-5533
  Elkhart (G-2735)
Crown Cab & Counter Top Inc ....F 219 663-2725
  Crown Point (G-2238)
Eds Wood Craft ....G 812 768-6617
  Haubstadt (G-6000)
Elko Inc ....E 812 473-8400
  Evansville (G-3473)
Fehrenbacher Cabinets Inc ....E 812 963-3377
  Evansville (G-3502)
Garyrae Inc ....F 574 255-7141
  Mishawaka (G-10045)
Indiana Southern Millwork Inc ....E 812 346-6129
  North Vernon (G-11263)
Jurgen Associates Inc ....G 317 786-3513
  Indianapolis (G-7322)
Kline Cabinet Makers LLC ....F 317 326-3049
  Maxwell (G-9662)
Lambright Woodworking LLC ....E 260 593-2721
  Topeka (G-13423)
Laminated Tops of Central Ind ....E 812 824-6299
  Bloomington (G-763)
Laminique Inc ....E 765 482-4222
  Lebanon (G-9197)
Lawrence Shirks ....G 574 223-5118
  Rochester (G-12133)
Our Country Home Entps Inc ....D 260 657-5605
  Harlan (G-5974)
Patrick Industries Inc ....E 574 294-5758
  Elkhart (G-3083)
Patrick Industries Inc ....E 574 293-1521
  Elkhart (G-3084)
Perfection Kitchen & Bath Ctr ....G 765 289-7594
  Selma (G-12425)
Plastic Line Manufacturing ....E 219 769-8022
  Merrillville (G-9747)
Rabb & Howe Cabinet Top Co ....F 317 926-6442
  Indianapolis (G-7811)
Rbk Development Inc ....E 574 267-5879
  Warsaw (G-13934)
Sims Cabinet Co Inc ....E 317 634-1747
  Indianapolis (G-7948)
SJS Components LLC ....G 260 578-0192
  Warsaw (G-13941)
Solid Surface Craftsmen Inc ....G 317 535-2333
  Whiteland (G-14246)
Tremain Ceramic Tile & Flr Cvg ....E 317 542-1491
  Indianapolis (G-8093)
Tristate Plastic Tops ....E 812 853-7827
  Newburgh (G-11053)
Walters Cabinet Shop ....G 765 452-9634
  Kokomo (G-8714)

PARTS: Metal

Metal Technologies Indiana Inc ....C 260 925-4717
  Auburn (G-346)
Royal Stamping Inc ....F 260 925-3312
  Auburn (G-350)
Small Parts Inc ....B 574 753-6323
  Logansport (G-9364)
Steel Storage Inc ....E 574 282-2618
  South Bend (G-2955)
Summit Manufacturing Corp ....E 260 428-2600
  Fort Wayne (G-4665)
Versatile Metal Works LLC ....F 765 754-7470
  Frankton (G-4944)
Wayne Metals LLC ....C 260 758-3121
  Markle (G-9584)
Yardarm Marine Products Inc ....E 317 831-4950
  Mooresville (G-10345)

PATENT OWNERS & LESSORS

Odyssian Technology LLC ....G 574 257-7555
  South Bend (G-12882)

PATTERNS: Indl

Bidwhist Industries ....G 219 879-2508
  La Porte (G-8739)
Braun Witte Pattern Works Inc ....G 260 463-8210
  Wolcottville (G-14369)
Cindys Crossstitch & Patterns ....G 317 410-0764
  Indianapolis (G-6605)
Core-Tech Inc ....D 260 748-4477
  Fort Wayne (G-4179)
Cunningham Pattern & Engrg Inc ......F 812 379-9571
  Columbus (G-1902)
D R Pattern Inc ....G 260 868-5585
  Butler (G-1227)
Dillon Pattern Works Inc ....F 765 642-3549
  Anderson (G-95)
Foley Pattern Company Inc ....E 260 925-4113
  Auburn (G-332)
Hopper Development Inc ....F 574 753-6621
  Logansport (G-9336)
K & K Inc ....F 574 266-8040
  Elkhart (G-2953)
Muncie Casting Corp ....E 765 288-2611
  Muncie (G-10528)
New Point Products Inc ....G 812 663-6311
  New Point (G-11003)
Northbend Pattern Works Inc ....E 812 637-3000
  West Harrison (G-14041)
Northside Pattern Works Inc ....G 317 290-0501
  Indianapolis (G-7595)
Ooten Pattern Works ....G 317 244-7348
  Indianapolis (G-7625)
Owings Patterns Inc ....F 812 944-5577
  Sellersburg (G-12411)
Peerless Pattern & Machine Co ....G 765 477-7719
  Lafayette (G-8979)
Richmond Pattern ....G 765 935-7342
  Richmond (G-12046)
Standard Pattern Company Inc ....G 260 456-4870
  Fort Wayne (G-4644)
Weberdings Carving Shop Inc ....F 812 934-3710
  Batesville (G-524)

PAVERS

Paver Rescue Inc ....G 317 259-4880
  Indianapolis (G-7664)
Turner Paving Company ....G 765 962-4408
  Richmond (G-12070)

PAVING MATERIALS: Coal Tar, Not From Refineries

Pavement Coatings Inc ....F 812 424-3400
  Evansville (G-3665)

PAVING MATERIALS: Prefabricated, Concrete

Crenshaw Paving Inc ....G 765 249-2342
  Michigantown (G-9865)
Schrock Aggregate Company Inc ......G 574 862-4167
  Wakarusa (G-13795)

PAVING MIXTURES

Schrock Aggregate Company Inc ......G 574 862-4167
  Wakarusa (G-13795)

Schrock Excavating Inc................................E....... 574 862-4167
   Wakarusa (G-13796)
Wallace Construction Inc ....F....... 317 422-5356
   Martinsville (G-9647)

PAWN SHOPS

Golden Lion Inc..G....... 765 446-9557
   Lafayette (G-8909)

PEAT MINING & PROCESSING SVCS

Millburn Peat Company Inc.....................E....... 219 362-7025
   La Porte (G-8794)

PENCILS & PENS WHOLESALERS

Harcourt Industries Inc...........................E....... 765 629-2625
   Milroy (G-9980)

PERFUME: Perfumes, Natural Or Synthetic

Annie Oakley Enterprises Inc ....F....... 260 894-7100
   Ligonier (G-9276)

PERFUMES

Jeannine Stassen....................................G....... 765 289-3756
   Muncie (G-10500)
Oil Palace Limited ....G....... 317 679-9187
   Indianapolis (G-7613)
Perfumery ....G....... 812 777-0657
   New Albany (G-10841)

PERLITE: Processed

Metal Services LLC ....G....... 219 787-1514
   Burns Harbor (G-1217)
Phoenix Services LLC ....E....... 219 397-0650
   East Chicago (G-2557)

PERSONAL CREDIT INSTITUTIONS: Consumer Finance Companies

Heritage Financial Group Inc ....D....... 574 522-8000
   Elkhart (G-2914)

PERSONAL CREDIT INSTITUTIONS: Financing, Autos, Furniture

Ford Motor Company...............................D....... 317 837-2302
   Plainfield (G-11610)

PERSONAL SVCS

Hot Shot Multimedia Entps LLC ....G....... 317 537-7527
   South Bend (G-12805)

PERSONAL SVCS, NEC

Simple To Elegant ....G....... 812 234-8700
   Terre Haute (G-13328)

PET & PET SPLYS STORES

Birds Nest Inc...G....... 574 247-0201
   Granger (G-5394)

PET COLLARS, LEASHES, MUZZLES & HARNESSES: Leather

Campbell Pet Company ....G....... 812 692-5208
   Elnora (G-3287)
Scott Pet Products Inc............................C....... 765 569-4636
   Rockville (G-12180)

PET FOOD WHOLESALERS

Bhj Usa Inc ....E....... 574 722-3933
   Logansport (G-9324)

PET SPLYS

Becks Bird Feeders ....G....... 765 874-1496
   Markleville (G-9586)
Goose Bumps LLC..................................G....... 765 491-2142
   West Lafayette (G-14071)
Green Dog..G....... 260 483-1267
   Fort Wayne (G-4308)
MBC Cereal Fines Inc ....G....... 812 299-2191
   Terre Haute (G-13281)
Nick-Em Builders LLC ....G....... 574 516-1060
   Logansport (G-9360)

Planet Pets..G....... 812 539-7316
   Lawrenceburg (G-9152)
Sittin Pretty LLC ....G....... 219 947-4121
   Crown Point (G-2306)

PET SPLYS WHOLESALERS

Innovative Concepts Group ....G....... 317 408-0292
   Indianapolis (G-7236)
Scott Pet Products Inc............................C....... 765 569-4636
   Rockville (G-12180)

PETROLEUM & PETROLEUM PRDTS, WHOLESALE Crude Oil

Lucas Oil Products Inc ....G....... 317 569-0039
   Carmel (G-1428)

PETROLEUM & PETROLEUM PRDTS, WHOLESALE Engine Fuels & Oils

Advance Energy LLC...............................G....... 312 665-0022
   Hobart (G-6068)

PETROLEUM & PETROLEUM PRDTS, WHOLESALE Fuel Oil

Swift Fuels LLC ....G....... 765 464-8336
   West Lafayette (G-14111)

PETROLEUM & PETROLEUM PRDTS, WHOLESALE Petroleum Brokers

Countrymark Coop Holdg Corp..............E....... 800 808-3170
   Indianapolis (G-6676)
Premier AG Co-Op Inc ....E....... 812 522-4911
   Seymour (G-12477)

PETROLEUM & PETROLEUM PRDTS, WHOLESALE Petroleum Terminals

Laketon Refining Corporation ....E....... 260 982-0703
   Laketon (G-9090)

PETROLEUM & PETROLEUM PRDTS, WHOLESALE: Bulk Stations

AMP Americas LLC ....G....... 312 300-6700
   Fair Oaks (G-3817)
Hoosier Penn Oil Co Inc ....G....... 812 284-9433
   Jeffersonville (G-8376)

PETROLEUM BULK STATIONS & TERMINALS

Co-Alliance LLP ....G....... 765 249-2233
   Michigantown (G-9864)
Co-Alliance LLP ....G....... 765 659-3420
   Frankfort (G-4823)
Co-Alliance Ltd Lblty Partnr ....D....... 317 745-4491
   Avon (G-435)

PETROLEUM PRDTS WHOLESALERS

J 2 Systems and Supply LLC..................G....... 317 602-3940
   Indianapolis (G-7281)
Laughery Valley AG Co-Op Inc ....G....... 812 689-4401
   Osgood (G-11393)
Spence/Banks Inc ....F....... 812 234-3538
   Terre Haute (G-13341)
Wannemuehler Distribution Inc.............F....... 812 422-3251
   Evansville (G-3809)

PHARMACEUTICAL PREPARATIONS: Druggists' Preparations

Global Isotopes LLC...............................G....... 317 578-1251
   Noblesville (G-11111)
Vesta Ingredients Inc.............................G....... 317 895-9000
   Indianapolis (G-8157)

PHARMACEUTICAL PREPARATIONS: Medicines, Capsule Or Ampule

Windsor Wartcare ....G....... 574 266-6555
   Elkhart (G-3262)

PHARMACEUTICAL PREPARATIONS: Proprietary Drug PRDTS

Naturegenic Inc......................................G....... 765 807-5525
   West Lafayette (G-14089)

PHARMACEUTICAL PREPARATIONS: Solutions

Crown Bioscience Indiana Inc ....G....... 317 872-6001
   Indianapolis (G-6699)
Ips-Integrated Prj Svcs LLC ....G....... 317 247-1200
   Indianapolis (G-7266)
Lodos Theranostics LLC ....G....... 765 427-2492
   West Lafayette (G-14083)

PHARMACEUTICAL PREPARATIONS: Tablets

Biokorf LLC ....G....... 765 727-0782
   West Lafayette (G-14054)
Kremers Urban Phrmcuticals Inc ....C....... 812 523-5347
   Seymour (G-12465)

PHARMACEUTICALS

Accra-Pac Inc ....D....... 574 295-0000
   Elkhart (G-2665)
Accra-Pac Inc ....D....... 905 660-0444
   Elkhart (G-2666)
Acura Pharmaceutical Tech ....D....... 574 842-3305
   Culver (G-2324)
Akina Inc ....F....... 765 464-0501
   West Lafayette (G-14048)
Amri Ssci LLC ....D....... 765 463-0112
   West Lafayette (G-14049)
Applied Laboratories Inc ....D....... 812 372-2607
   Columbus (G-1856)
Aquestive Therapeutics ....C....... 219 762-4143
   Portage (G-11749)
Areva Pharmaceuticals Inc ....F....... 855 853-4760
   Georgetown (G-5141)
Assembly Biosciences Inc......................D....... 317 210-9311
   Carmel (G-1316)
Astrazeneca Pharmaceuticals LP..........E....... 812 429-5000
   Mount Vernon (G-10383)
Baxter Phrm Solutions ....G....... 812 355-5289
   Bloomington (G-677)
Baxter Phrm Solutions LLC.....................D....... 812 333-0887
   Bloomington (G-678)
Bayer Healthcare LLC.............................F....... 574 252-4734
   Mishawaka (G-10004)
Bayer Healthcare LLC.............................C....... 574 252-4735
   Mishawaka (G-10005)
Bayer Healthcare LLC.............................D....... 574 255-3327
   Elkhart (G-2717)
Briovarx ....F....... 812 256-8600
   Jeffersonville (G-8333)
Bristol-Myers Squibb Company ....D....... 260 432-2764
   Fort Wayne (G-4121)
Bristol-Myers Squibb Company ....C....... 812 307-2000
   Mount Vernon (G-10386)
Brogan Pharmaceuticals LLC.................F....... 219 644-3693
   Crown Point (G-2231)
Cardinal Health 414 LLC.........................D....... 317 981-4100
   Indianapolis (G-6552)
Catalent Indiana LLC ....B....... 812 355-6746
   Bloomington (G-697)
Century Pharmaceuticals Inc..................F....... 317 849-4210
   Indianapolis (G-6586)
Chemigen Inc ....G....... 317 902-6630
   Zionsville (G-14426)
Chyall Pharmaceutical............................G....... 765 237-3391
   West Lafayette (G-14059)
Colorcon Inc ....E....... 317 545-6211
   Indianapolis (G-6633)
Colorcon Inc ....G....... 317 545-6211
   Indianapolis (G-6634)
Colorcon Inc ....G....... 317 545-6211
   Indianapolis (G-6635)
Crosswind Pharmaceuticals LLC ....G....... 317 436-8522
   Indianapolis (G-6698)
Diabco Life Sciences LLC ....G....... 317 697-9988
   Carmel (G-1359)
Elan Corp PLC ....G....... 317 442-1502
   Fishers (G-3901)
Elanco US Inc ....C....... 877 352-6261
   Greenfield (G-5523)
Eli Lilly ....G....... 812 242-5900
   Terre Haute (G-13231)
Eli Lilly and Co ....G....... 317 433-1244
   Noblesville (G-11099)

Employee Codes: A=Over 500 employees, B=251-500
C=101-250, D=51-100, E=20-50, F=10-19, G=2-9

2018 Harris Indiana
Industrial Directory

1039

PRODUCT

Eli Lilly and Company.................A..... 317 276-2000
Indianapolis **(G-6822)**
Eli Lilly and Company.................F..... 317 276-2000
Indianapolis **(G-6823)**
Eli Lilly and Company.................C..... 317 748-1622
Fishers **(G-3903)**
Eli Lilly and Company.................F..... 317 276-2000
Indianapolis **(G-6824)**
Eli Lilly and Company.................F..... 317 277-1079
Indianapolis **(G-6825)**
Eli Lilly and Company.................F..... 317 276-7907
Indianapolis **(G-6826)**
Eli Lilly and Company.................G..... 317 276-2000
Indianapolis **(G-6827)**
Eli Lilly and Company.................F..... 317 651-7790
Indianapolis **(G-6828)**
Eli Lilly and Company.................F..... 317 276-2000
Indianapolis **(G-6829)**
Eli Lilly and Company.................E..... 317 277-0147
Indianapolis **(G-6830)**
Eli Lilly and Company.................F..... 317 276-2000
Greenfield **(G-5524)**
Eli Lilly and Company.................F..... 317 433-3624
Plainfield **(G-11608)**
Eli Lilly and Company.................F..... 317 276-7907
Indianapolis **(G-6831)**
Eli Lilly and Company.................F..... 317 276-5925
Indianapolis **(G-6832)**
Eli Lilly and Company.................F..... 317 276-2000
Indianapolis **(G-6833)**
Eli Lilly and Company.................G..... 317 276-2118
Indianapolis **(G-6834)**
Eli Lilly and Company.................F..... 317 276-2000
Indianapolis **(G-6835)**
Eli Lilly International Corp.................F..... 317 276-2000
Indianapolis **(G-6836)**
Emphymab Biotech LLC.................G..... 317 274-5935
Indianapolis **(G-6858)**
Endocyte Inc.................D..... 765 463-7175
West Lafayette **(G-14066)**
Energy Delivery Solutions LLC.................G..... 502 271-8753
Jeffersonville **(G-8354)**
Exelead Inc.................C..... 317 347-2800
Indianapolis **(G-6893)**
Fenwick Pharma LLC.................G..... 765 296-7443
Lafayette **(G-8898)**
Fisher Clinical Services Inc.................D..... 317 277-0337
Indianapolis **(G-6930)**
Genoa Healthcare LLC.................G..... 219 427-1837
Gary **(G-5054)**
Giles Manufacturing Company.................G..... 812 537-4852
Greendale **(G-5487)**
Horizon Biotechnologies LLC.................G..... 317 534-2540
Greenwood **(G-5703)**
Jbs United Animal Hlth II LLC.................F..... 317 758-2616
Sheridan **(G-12593)**
Komodo Pharmaceuticals Inc.................E..... 317 485-0023
Fortville **(G-4781)**
Kp Pharmaceutical Tech Inc.................E..... 812 330-8121
Bloomington **(G-760)**
Kylin Therapeutics Inc.................G..... 765 412-6661
West Lafayette **(G-14079)**
Lexington Pharmaceuticals.................G..... 317 870-0370
Indianapolis **(G-7400)**
Loaded Pharmaceuticals Inc.................G..... 300 300-1996
Indianapolis **(G-7412)**
Martin Ekwlor Phrmcuticals Inc.................F..... 765 962-4410
Richmond **(G-12014)**
Mead Johnson & Company LLC.................G..... 812 429-5000
Mount Vernon **(G-10400)**
Mead Johnson & Company LLC.................B..... 812 429-5000
Evansville **(G-3620)**
Med-Rep Inc.................F..... 317 574-0497
Carmel **(G-1436)**
Merck Sharp & Dohme Corp.................F..... 317 286-3038
Indianapolis **(G-7481)**
Muroplex Therapeutics Inc.................G..... 317 502-0545
Indianapolis **(G-7560)**
Northwind Pharmaceuticals LLC.................G..... 800 722-0772
Indianapolis **(G-7597)**
Novartis Corporation.................G..... 317 852-3839
Brownsburg **(G-1161)**
Nutritional Research Assoc.................F..... 260 723-4931
South Whitley **(G-13002)**
OH Pharmaceutical Co Ltd.................G..... 219 644-3239
Crown Point **(G-2281)**
Pd Sub LLC.................E..... 812 524-0534
Seymour **(G-12474)**
Pfizer Inc.................F..... 574 232-9927
South Bend **(G-12892)**

Pfizer Inc.................A..... 212 733-2323
Terre Haute **(G-13301)**
Pharma Form Finders LLC.................G..... 317 362-1191
Fishers **(G-3950)**
Phytoption LLC.................G..... 765 490-7738
West Lafayette **(G-14094)**
Procyon Pharmaceuticals Inc.................G..... 765 778-9710
Pendleton **(G-11501)**
Purdue Gmp Center LLC.................F..... 765 464-8414
West Lafayette **(G-14098)**
R2 Pharma LLC.................G..... 317 810-6205
Carmel **(G-1461)**
Relevo Inc.................G..... 317 644-0099
Carmel **(G-1465)**
Rph On Call LLC.................E..... 317 622-4800
Greenfield **(G-5569)**
Sanofi US Services Inc.................E..... 317 228-5750
Indianapolis **(G-7894)**
Schwarz Pharma.................G..... 812 523-3457
Seymour **(G-12483)**
Somersaults LLC.................G..... 317 747-7496
Fishers **(G-3990)**
Sysgenomics LLC.................G..... 574 302-5396
Granger **(G-5442)**
Vitamins Inc.................E..... 219 879-7356
Michigan City **(G-9859)**

PHARMACEUTICALS: Medicinal & Botanical Prdts

Acell Inc.................F..... 765 464-8198
Lafayette **(G-8845)**
Dickey Consumer Products Inc.................F..... 317 773-8330
Noblesville **(G-11092)**
Medtric LLC.................G..... 765 586-8228
Lafayette **(G-8965)**
Nuaxon Bioscience Inc.................G..... 812 762-4400
Bloomington **(G-782)**
Pfizer Inc.................A..... 212 733-2323
Terre Haute **(G-13301)**
Pragmatics Inc.................G..... 574 295-7908
Elkhart **(G-3106)**

PHARMACIES & DRUG STORES

Buehler Foods Inc.................C..... 812 467-7255
Evansville **(G-3404)**
Genoa Healthcare LLC.................G..... 219 427-1837
Gary **(G-5054)**
Lakeshore Foods Corp.................C..... 219 362-8513
La Porte **(G-8785)**
Schnuck Markets Inc.................C..... 812 853-9505
Newburgh **(G-11046)**
Williams Bros Health Care Inc.................E..... 812 257-2505
Washington **(G-14007)**

PHOTOCOPYING & DUPLICATING SVCS

Blue River Printing Inc.................G..... 317 392-3676
Shelbyville **(G-12521)**
Commercial Print Shop Inc.................G..... 260 724-3722
Decatur **(G-2373)**
Copy-Print Shop Inc.................E..... 765 447-6868
Lafayette **(G-8877)**
Copymat Service Inc.................E..... 765 743-5995
Lafayette **(G-8878)**
Creative Concept Ventures Inc.................G..... 812 282-9442
Jeffersonville **(G-8348)**
Dynamark Graphics Group Inc.................E..... 317 328-2555
Indianapolis **(G-6775)**
Ed Sons Inc.................F..... 317 897-8821
Indianapolis **(G-6803)**
Express Impressions Prtg LLC.................G..... 765 966-2679
Richmond **(G-11985)**
Fedex Office & Print Svcs Inc.................E..... 317 631-6862
Indianapolis **(G-6908)**
Fedex Office & Print Svcs Inc.................E..... 317 849-9683
Indianapolis **(G-6911)**
Fedex Office & Print Svcs Inc.................E..... 574 271-0398
South Bend **(G-12777)**
Fedex Office & Print Svcs Inc.................E..... 317 337-2679
Indianapolis **(G-6912)**
Fedex Office & Print Svcs Inc.................G..... 317 295-1063
Indianapolis **(G-6913)**
Fedex Office & Print Svcs Inc.................F..... 765 449-4950
Lafayette **(G-8897)**
Fedex Office & Print Svcs Inc.................F..... 317 251-2406
Indianapolis **(G-6914)**
Fedex Office & Print Svcs Inc.................F..... 317 885-6480
Indianapolis **(G-6915)**
Fedex Office & Print Svcs Inc.................F..... 317 974-0378
Indianapolis **(G-6909)**

Fedex Office & Print Svcs Inc.................F..... 317 917-1529
Indianapolis **(G-6910)**
Fedex Office & Print Svcs Inc.................G..... 219 462-6270
Valparaiso **(G-13542)**
Fedex Office & Print Svcs Inc.................G..... 317 839-3896
Plainfield **(G-11609)**
Hiatt Enterprises Inc.................E..... 765 289-7756
Muncie **(G-10487)**
Hiatt Enterprises Inc.................G..... 765 289-2700
Muncie **(G-10488)**
Kays Graphics Inc.................G..... 317 236-9755
Indianapolis **(G-7335)**
Mar Kel Inc.................G..... 812 853-6133
Newburgh **(G-11038)**
MPS Printing Inc.................G..... 812 273-4446
Madison **(G-9489)**
Mr Copy Inc.................G..... 812 334-2679
Bloomington **(G-776)**
Nova Graphics Inc.................F..... 317 577-6682
Indianapolis **(G-7599)**
Ovation Communications Inc.................G..... 812 401-9100
Evansville **(G-3659)**
Perfect Impressions Printing.................G..... 317 923-1756
Indianapolis **(G-7674)**
Printing Partners East Inc.................G..... 317 356-2522
Indianapolis **(G-7756)**
Priority Press Inc.................G..... 317 240-0103
Indianapolis **(G-7760)**
Qsp Printing Inc.................G..... 317 773-0864
Noblesville **(G-11168)**
Randall Corp.................G..... 812 425-7122
Evansville **(G-3695)**
Rhr Corporation.................G..... 317 788-1504
Indianapolis **(G-7837)**
Rrc Corporation.................F..... 317 687-8325
Indianapolis **(G-7869)**
Sharp Printing Services Inc.................G..... 317 842-5159
Fishers **(G-3969)**
Stamprint Inc.................G..... 574 233-3900
South Bend **(G-12953)**
Tdk Graphics Inc.................F..... 219 663-7799
Crown Point **(G-2312)**
Thomas E Slade Inc.................F..... 812 471-7100
Evansville **(G-3760)**

PHOTOFINISHING LABORATORIES

Galaxy Arts.................G..... 219 836-6033
Munster **(G-10604)**

PHOTOGRAPHIC & OPTICAL GOODS EQPT REPAIR SVCS

Blasted Works.................G..... 574 583-3211
Monticello **(G-10256)**

PHOTOGRAPHIC EQPT & SPLYS

Aerial Imaging Resources LLC.................G..... 317 550-5970
Indianapolis **(G-6344)**
Draper Inc.................B..... 765 987-7999
Spiceland **(G-13054)**
Xerox Corporation.................G..... 317 471-4220
Zionsville **(G-14472)**

PHOTOGRAPHIC EQPT & SPLYS, WHOLESALE: Motion Picture Camera

Motion Engineering Company Inc.................G..... 317 804-7990
Westfield **(G-14177)**

PHOTOGRAPHIC EQPT & SPLYS: Diazotype Or Whiteprint Reprod

Gs Sales Inc.................G..... 317 595-6750
Westfield **(G-14168)**

PHOTOGRAPHIC EQPT & SPLYS: Film, Cloth & Paper, Sensitized

Printing Technologies Inc.................E..... 800 428-3786
Indianapolis **(G-7758)**

PHOTOGRAPHIC EQPT & SPLYS: Printing Eqpt

Able Printing & Bus Svcs LLC.................G..... 574 834-7006
North Webster **(G-11288)**
Image Inks Company.................G..... 317 432-5041
Indianapolis **(G-7161)**

(G-0000) Company's Geographic Section entry number

PHOTOGRAPHIC EQPT & SPLYS: Toners, Prprd, Not Chem Plnts

Laser Systems ....G 219 465-1155
  Valparaiso (G-13573)
Lasertone Inc ....F 812 473-5945
  Evansville (G-3598)
Mid-America Environmental LLC ....F 812 475-1644
  Evansville (G-3626)

PHOTOGRAPHIC SVCS

Stewart Graphics Inc ....E 812 283-0455
  Jeffersonville (G-8430)

PHOTOGRAPHY SVCS: Portrait Studios

Kennyleeholmescom ....G 574 612-2526
  Elkhart (G-2961)

PHOTOGRAPHY SVCS: Still Or Video

Stands Photography ....G 812 723-3922
  Paoli (G-11457)
TEC Photography ....G 812 332-9847
  Bloomington (G-836)

PHOTOTYPESETTING SVC

A-1 Graphics Inc ....G 765 289-1851
  Muncie (G-10420)

PHYSICAL EXAMINATION & TESTING SVCS

Workflow Solutions LLC ....G 502 627-0257
  New Albany (G-10875)

PHYSICIANS' OFFICES & CLINICS: Medical doctors

Advanced Orthopro Inc ....E 317 924-4444
  Indianapolis (G-6334)

PIANO TUNING & REPAIR SVCS

Walter Piano Company Inc....................F 574 266-0615
  Elkhart (G-3254)

PICTURE FRAMES: Wood

Hjj Inc ....G 219 362-4421
  La Porte (G-8765)
Stitch N Frame ....G 260 478-1301
  Fort Wayne (G-4649)

PICTURE FRAMING SVCS, CUSTOM

Golden Frame Inc ....G 812 232-0048
  Terre Haute (G-13242)
Randall Corp ....G 812 425-7122
  Evansville (G-3695)

PICTURE TUBE REPROCESSING

Applied Biomedical Techno ....G 219 465-2079
  Valparaiso (G-13495)

PIECE GOODS & NOTIONS WHOLESALERS

Custom Sewing Service ....G 812 428-7015
  Evansville (G-3451)
J Ennis Fabrics Inc (usa) ....G 877 953-6647
  Plainfield (G-11620)
Samaron Corp ....E 574 970-7070
  Elkhart (G-3154)

PIECE GOODS, NOTIONS & DRY GOODS, WHOL: Jute Piece Goods

Anokhi International Inc ....G 260 750-0418
  Fort Wayne (G-4077)

PIECE GOODS, NOTIONS & DRY GOODS, WHOL: Textiles, Woven

Georg Utz Inc..E 812 526-2240
  Edinburgh (G-2612)

PIECE GOODS, NOTIONS & DRY GOODS, WHOL: Trimmings, Apparel

Rhinestone Supply LLC ....G 260 484-2711
  Fort Wayne (G-4591)

PIECE GOODS, NOTIONS & DRY GOODS, WHOLESALE: Fabrics

Mpr Corporation ....E 574 848-5100
  Bristol (G-1073)

PIECE GOODS, NOTIONS & DRY GOODS, WHOLESALE: Fabrics, Knit

C M I Enterprises Inc ....D 305 685-9651
  Elkhart (G-2744)

PIECE GOODS, NOTIONS & OTHER DRY GOODS, WHOL: Flags/Banners

Flag & Banner Company Inc ....F 317 299-4880
  Indianapolis (G-6931)

PIECE GOODS, NOTIONS & OTHER DRY GOODS, WHOLESALE: Fabrics

Tiedemann-Bevs Industries LLC ....E 765 962-4914
  Richmond (G-12067)

PIECE GOODS, NOTIONS/DRY GOODS, WHOL: Drapery Mtrl, Woven

Mitchell Fabrics Inc..............................E 309 674-8631
  Lafayette (G-8971)

PIECE GOODS, NOTIONS/DRY GOODS, WHOL: Nylon Piece, Woven

Raine Inc ....F 765 622-7687
  Anderson (G-157)

PIGMENTS, INORGANIC: Chrome Green, Chrome Yellow, Zinc Yellw

Old Jim Customs LLC ....G 812 431-1460
  Evansville (G-3654)

PIGMENTS, INORGANIC: Metallic & Mineral, NEC

Silberline Mfg Co Inc ....C 260 728-2111
  Decatur (G-2404)

PILE DRIVING EQPT

Jinnings Equipment LLC........................G 260 447-4343
  Fort Wayne (G-4395)

PINS

Blush & Bobby Pins..............................G 317 789-5166
  Carmel (G-1318)
Mr Pin Shi Peter Lee ....G 574 264-9754
  Elkhart (G-3053)
Philip Pins ....G 219 769-1059
  Merrillville (G-9745)
Pin Point Av LLC ....G 317 750-3120
  Indianapolis (G-7691)
Pin-Up Curls LLC ....G 260 241-5871
  Fort Wayne (G-4530)
Pinup Curls Salon ....G 260 267-9659
  Fort Wayne (G-4531)
Royal Pin Leisure Centers Inc ....E 317 881-8686
  Greenwood (G-5744)

PINS: Dowel

Rbc Prcision Pdts - Bremen Inc ....F 574 546-4455
  Bremen (G-1019)

PIPE & FITTING: Fabrication

Allied Tube & Conduit Corp ....E 765 459-8811
  Kokomo (G-8590)
Allied Tube & Conduit Corp ....C 812 265-9255
  Madison (G-9443)
Big Inch Fabricators Cnstr Inc..............D 765 245-9353
  Montezuma (G-10209)
Cal Pipe Manufacturing Inc..................F 219 844-6800
  Hobart (G-6070)
Calpipe Industries LLC ....G 219 844-6800
  Hobart (G-6071)
Curtis Products Inc..............................C 574 289-4891
  South Bend (G-12746)
Green Leaf Inc ....C 812 877-1546
  Fontanet (G-4024)

Hd Mechanical Inc................................G 219 924-6050
  Griffith (G-5776)
JM Fittings LLC ....D 260 747-9200
  Fort Wayne (G-4396)
Johnson Controls ....C 317 826-2130
  Indianapolis (G-7309)
Kautex Inc ....B 937 238-8096
  Avilla (G-409)
Klene Pipe Structures Inc ....G 812 663-6445
  Greensburg (G-5619)
L & W Engineering Inc ....D 574 825-5351
  Middlebury (G-9900)
Parker-Hannifin Corporation..................E 260 587-9102
  Ashley (G-289)
Plymouth Tube Company ....C 574 946-6191
  Winamac (G-14314)
Porter County Fabricators ....G 219 663-4665
  Crown Point (G-2287)
Precision Products Group Inc ....E 260 484-4111
  Fort Wayne (G-4552)
Scot Industries Inc ....F 608 778-2251
  Auburn (G-353)
Southwark Metal Mfg Co ....C 317 823-5300
  Indianapolis (G-7965)
St Regis Culvert Inc ....F 317 353-8065
  Indianapolis (G-7982)
Staples Pipe & Muffler ....G 812 522-3569
  Butlerville (G-1251)
Steuben Fabg & Engrg Inc ....G 260 665-3001
  Angola (G-247)
Tb Plastic Extrusions Michiana ....E 574 266-7409
  Elkhart (G-3206)
Technifab Products Inc ....D 812 442-0520
  Brazil (G-979)
Thormax Enterprises LLC ....G 812 530-7744
  Seymour (G-12496)
Tube Processing Corp ....C 317 787-5747
  Indianapolis (G-8106)
Tube Processing Corp ....B 317 787-1321
  Indianapolis (G-8107)
Tube Processing Corp ....C 317 264-7760
  Indianapolis (G-8109)
Tube Processing Corp ....C 317 787-1321
  Indianapolis (G-8110)
Uniseal Inc ....G 812 425-1361
  Evansville (G-3785)

PIPE & TUBES: Copper & Copper Alloy

Essex Group Inc....................................B 260 461-4000
  Fort Wayne (G-4244)

PIPE & TUBES: Seamless

37 Pipe & Supply LLC..........................G 812 275-5676
  Bedford (G-526)
Moyers Inc ....E 574 264-3119
  Elkhart (G-3052)

PIPE CLEANERS

Forterra Concrete Inds Inc ....G 812 426-5353
  Evansville (G-3512)

PIPE FITTINGS: Plastic

Fairview Fittings & Mfg ....G 574 206-8884
  Elkhart (G-2843)
Filtration Parts Incorporated..................F 704 661-8135
  Rensselaer (G-11923)
Green Leaf Inc ....C 812 877-1546
  Fontanet (G-4024)
Nibco Inc ....C 812 256-8500
  Charlestown (G-1576)
Nibco Inc ....C 574 296-1240
  Goshen (G-5298)
Nibco Inc ....F 812 256-8500
  Charlestown (G-1577)
Rieke Corporation ....B 260 925-3700
  Auburn (G-349)

PIPE, CULVERT: Concrete

Independent Concrete Pipe Co..............F 317 262-4920
  Indianapolis (G-7173)

PIPE, SEWER: Concrete

Terrys Sewer Service ....G 219 756-5238
  Merrillville (G-9758)

Employee Codes: A=Over 500 employees, B=251-500
C=101-250, D=51-100, E=20-50, F=10-19, G=2-9

2018 Harris Indiana
Industrial Directory

PRODUCT

1041

PIPE: Concrete

Ace Extrusion LLC ....E 812 436-4840
Evansville (G-3341)
County Materials Corp ....E 317 323-6000
Maxwell (G-9660)
Fred Weber Inc ....F 317 262-4920
Indianapolis (G-6962)
Independent Concrete Pipe Co ....E 419 841-3361
Indianapolis (G-7170)
Independent Concrete Pipe Co ....E 800 875-4920
Indianapolis (G-7171)
Independent Concrete Pipe Co ....E 317 262-4920
Indianapolis (G-7172)
Independent Concrete Pipe Co ....E 317 262-4920
Indianapolis (G-7174)
Independent Concrete Pipe Co ....E 317 326-2600
Maxwell (G-9661)
M & W Concrete Pipe & Supply ....E 812 426-2871
Evansville (G-3607)

PIPE: Plastic

Ace Extrusion LLC ....G 812 463-5230
Evansville (G-3338)
Ace Extrusion LLC ....D 812 463-5230
Evansville (G-3340)
Advanced Drainage Systems Inc ....F 812 443-2080
Brazil (G-953)
Corrosion Technologies Inc ....G 317 894-0627
Greenfield (G-5516)
Cresline Plastic Pipe Co Inc ....E 812 428-9300
Evansville (G-3442)
Cresline-Northwest LLC ....E 812 428-9300
Evansville (G-3443)
Cresline-West Inc ....E 812 428-9300
Evansville (G-3444)
Diamond Plastics Corporation ....D 765 287-9234
Muncie (G-10459)
Genova Products Inc ....D 219 866-5136
Rensselaer (G-11925)
Hancor Inc ....E 812 443-2080
Brazil (G-964)
Kuri TEC Manufacturing Inc ....E 765 764-6000
Williamsport (G-14293)
Liner Products LLC ....F 812 723-0244
Paoli (G-11455)
Nibco Inc ....C 812 256-8500
Charlestown (G-1576)
Pipeconx ....G 800 443-9081
Evansville (G-3672)
Uniseal Inc ....G 812 425-1361
Evansville (G-3785)

PIPE: Sheet Metal

37 Pipe & Supply LLC ....G 812 275-5676
Bedford (G-526)
J T D Spiral Inc ....G 260 497-1300
Fort Wayne (G-4387)
Kalenborn Abresist Corporation ....E 800 348-0717
Urbana (G-13477)

PIPE: Water, Cast Iron

37 Pipe & Supply LLC ....G 812 275-5676
Bedford (G-526)

PIPELINES: Natural Gas

ANR Pipeline Company ....G 260 463-3342
Lagrange (G-9031)

PIPES & TUBES

Interntional Pipe Cons Sls LLC ....F 765 388-2222
New Castle (G-10907)
Kanoff Enterprises ....G 574 575-6787
Mishawaka (G-10062)
Norres North America Inc ....G 855 667-7370
South Bend (G-12876)

PIPES & TUBES: Steel

Advanced Drainage Systems ....G 317 917-7960
Indianapolis (G-6333)
AK Tube LLC ....G 317 736-8888
Franklin (G-4866)
AK Tube LLC ....F 812 341-3200
Columbus (G-1853)
Century Tube LLC ....C 812 265-9255
Madison (G-9448)

E & H Tubing Inc ....E 812 358-3894
Brownstown (G-1186)
E & H Tubing Inc ....E 812 358-3894
Brownstown (G-1187)
Hd Mechanical Inc ....G 219 924-6050
Griffith (G-5776)
Indiana Tube Corporation ....B 812 467-7155
Evansville (G-3553)
Kalenborn Abresist Corporation ....E 800 348-0717
Urbana (G-13477)
Martinrea Industries Inc ....E 812 346-5750
North Vernon (G-11269)
Midwest Steel & Tube LLC ....E 219 398-2200
East Chicago (G-2552)
Napier & Napier ....G 765 580-9116
Liberty (G-9266)
Paragon Tube Corporation ....E 260 424-1266
Fort Wayne (G-4520)
Perch Tree Inc ....G 630 450-4591
Fishers (G-3949)
Plymouth Tube Company ....G 574 946-6191
Winamac (G-14314)
Plymouth Tube Company ....G 574 653-2575
Kewanna (G-8527)
Ptc Alliance Corporation ....E 765 259-3334
Richmond (G-12036)
Ptc Tubular Products LLC ....D 765 259-3334
Richmond (G-12037)
Tejas Tubular Products Inc ....D 574 249-0623
New Carlisle (G-10888)
Thormax Enterprises LLC ....G 812 530-7744
Seymour (G-12496)
Tube Processing Corp ....C 317 782-9486
Indianapolis (G-8108)

PIPES & TUBES: Welded

Allied Tube & Conduit Corp ....C 812 265-9255
Madison (G-9443)
Applegate Livestock Eqp Inc ....D 765 964-3715
Union City (G-13452)
Expanded Metals Co Ind LLC ....E 574 287-6471
South Bend (G-12768)
Lock Joint Tube LLC ....C 574 299-5326
South Bend (G-12843)
Phoenix Specialities Ltd ....G 219 345-5812
Lake Village (G-9084)
Steuben Fabg & Engrg Inc ....G 260 665-3001
Angola (G-247)

PIPES OR FITTINGS: Sewer, Clay

Can-Clay Corp ....E 812 547-3461
Cannelton (G-1288)

PISTONS & PISTON RINGS

Federal-Mogul Powertrain LLC ....B 574 271-5954
South Bend (G-12776)
Precision Rings Incorporated ....E 317 247-4786
Indianapolis (G-7736)

PLANING MILL, NEC

Millwork Specialties Co Inc ....G 219 362-2960
La Porte (G-8795)

PLANING MILLS: Millwork

Schlabach Hardwoods ....G 574 642-1157
Goshen (G-5320)

PLANTS: Artificial & Preserved

Chapdells Tree & Plant Design ....G 317 845-9980
Fishers (G-3888)

PLAQUES: Clay, Plaster/Papier-Mache, Factory Production

Plaster Shak ....G 317 881-6518
Greenwood (G-5733)

PLAQUES: Picture, Laminated

Awards America ....E 219 462-7903
Valparaiso (G-13501)
Floralcraft Distributors ....G 574 262-2639
Elkhart (G-2859)
Lamco Finishers Inc ....E 317 471-1010
Indianapolis (G-7379)
Lloyds of Indiana Inc ....G 317 251-5430
Indianapolis (G-7411)

Plaquemaker Plus Inc ....G 317 594-5556
Fishers (G-3952)
Plastimatic Arts Corp ....E 574 254-9000
Mishawaka (G-10104)

PLASMAS

Baxter Heathcare Plasma Center ....G 260 451-8119
Fort Wayne (G-4101)
Biolife Plasma Services LP ....G 574 264-7204
Elkhart (G-2724)
Csl Plasma Inc ....G 260 454-5083
Fort Wayne (G-4191)
Csl Plasma Inc ....G 317 688-5852
Indianapolis (G-6703)
Octapharma Plasma Inc ....G 574 234-9568
South Bend (G-12881)

PLASTERING ACCESS: Metal

Superior Coatings Inc ....G 574 546-0591
Bremen (G-1027)

PLASTIC COLORING & FINISHING

Color Master Inc ....D 260 868-2320
Butler (G-1226)
Craddock Finishing Corporation ....E 812 425-2691
Evansville (G-3436)

PLASTIC PRDTS

Beemak Plastics Inc ....G 317 841-4398
Indianapolis (G-6464)
Berry Plastics Group Inc ....G 812 424-2904
Evansville (G-3378)
Crane Composites ....G 574 295-9391
Elkhart (G-2775)
Deep Three Inc ....G 260 705-2283
Spencerville (G-13045)
Elkhart Plastics Inc ....G 574 370-1079
Michigan City (G-9788)
H W Molders ....G 812 423-3552
Evansville (G-3528)
Madillion Plastics Inc ....G 574 293-4434
Elkhart (G-3014)
Mike H Inc ....G 574 262-0518
Elkhart (G-3041)
Msca LLC ....G 574 583-6220
Monticello (G-10272)
R R Forrest Company Inc ....G 317 502-3286
Noblesville (G-11169)

PLASTIC PRDTS REPAIR SVCS

C & T Engineering Inc ....F 812 522-5854
Seymour (G-12436)
Morris Mold and Machine Co ....G 317 923-6653
Indianapolis (G-7544)
Polymod Technologies Inc ....F 260 436-1322
Fort Wayne (G-4538)

PLASTIC WOOD

Earthwise Plastics Inc ....E 765 673-0308
Gas City (G-5123)

PLASTICS FILM & SHEET

American Renolit Corporation ....C 219 324-6886
La Porte (G-8733)
Berry Global Group Inc ....F 812 424-2904
Evansville (G-3377)
Foil Laminating Inc ....E 574 935-3645
Plymouth (G-11686)
Futurex Industries Inc ....D 812 299-5708
Terre Haute (G-13237)
Futurex Industries Inc ....E 765 597-2221
Marshall (G-9591)
Futurex Industries Inc ....C 765 498-3900
Bloomingdale (G-647)
Piedmont Plastics Inc ....G 317 947-4500
Indianapolis (G-7689)
Primex Plastics Corporation ....B 765 966-7774
Richmond (G-12034)
Printpack Inc ....B 812 663-5091
Greensburg (G-5629)

PLASTICS FILM & SHEET: Polyethylene

Bemis Company Inc ....D 812 466-2213
Terre Haute (G-13198)
Petoskey Plastics Inc ....C 765 348-9808
Hartford City (G-5987)

Tredegar Corporation .... D 812 466-0266
Terre Haute *(G-13356)*

PLASTICS FILM & SHEET: Polypropylene

Mirwec Film Incorporated .... F 812 331-7194
Bloomington *(G-773)*

Taghleef Industries Inc .... A 302 326-5500
Rosedale *(G-12208)*

PLASTICS FILM & SHEET: Polyvinyl

Seymour Midwest LLC .... G 574 269-2782
Warsaw *(G-13939)*

Transcendia Inc .... C 765 935-1520
Richmond *(G-12068)*

PLASTICS FILM & SHEET: Vinyl

Rustic N Chic LLC .... G 219 987-4957
Wheatfield *(G-14230)*

PLASTICS FINISHED PRDTS: Laminated

American Art Clay Co Inc .... C 317 243-0066
Indianapolis *(G-6385)*

Brownsburg Custom Cabinets .... G 317 271-1887
Indianapolis *(G-6512)*

Eichstedt Manufacturing Inc .... G 574 288-8881
South Bend *(G-12759)*

Hartson-Kennedy Cabinet Top Co .... B 765 668-8144
Marion *(G-9529)*

Pioneer Plastics Corporation .... D 574 264-0702
Elkhart *(G-3097)*

Plasticraft-Complete Acrylics .... G 765 610-9502
Anderson *(G-153)*

Sims Cabinet Co Inc .... E 317 634-1747
Indianapolis *(G-7948)*

PLASTICS MATERIAL & RESINS

Advance Prtective Coatings Inc .... G 317 228-0123
Indianapolis *(G-6330)*

Aearo Technologies LLC .... C 317 692-6666
Indianapolis *(G-6342)*

Akzo Nobel Coatings Inc .... F 574 372-2000
Warsaw *(G-13836)*

Ameri-Kart Corp .... D 225 642-7874
Bristol *(G-1043)*

Ameri-Kart Corp .... C 574 848-7462
Bristol *(G-1044)*

Ampacet Corporation .... C 812 466-5231
Terre Haute *(G-13193)*

Aoc LLC .... D 219 465-4384
Valparaiso *(G-13494)*

Atc Plastics LLC .... G 317 469-7552
Indianapolis *(G-6435)*

B C C Products Inc .... F 317 494-6420
Franklin *(G-4870)*

Bpc Manufacturing Operation .... E 574 936-9894
Plymouth *(G-11672)*

Cabinets & Counters Inc .... E 812 858-3300
Newburgh *(G-11023)*

Cellofoam North America Inc .... F 317 535-0826
Greenwood *(G-5674)*

Com-Tech Plastics Inc .... F 812 423-8270
Evansville *(G-3424)*

Createc Corporation .... E 317 566-0022
Indianapolis *(G-6686)*

Crossroads Sourcing Group Ltd .... F 847 940-4123
Carmel *(G-1348)*

Double H Manufacturing Corp .... D 765 664-9090
Marion *(G-9521)*

DSM Engineering Plastics Inc .... G 812 435-7638
Evansville *(G-3464)*

Echo Engrg & Prod Sups Inc .... E 317 876-8848
Indianapolis *(G-6798)*

Efficient Plastics Solutions .... G 574 965-4690
Delphi *(G-2420)*

Evoqua Water Technologies LLC .... E 317 280-4251
Indianapolis *(G-6885)*

Foamcraft Inc .... D 574 534-4343
Goshen *(G-5216)*

Freudenberg-Nok General Partnr .... E 734 354-5504
Shelbyville *(G-12535)*

G & T Industries of Indiana .... E 812 634-2252
Jasper *(G-8253)*

Graber Cabinetry LLC .... E 260 627-2243
Grabill *(G-5366)*

Grace W R & Co-Co .... G 317 876-4100
Indianapolis *(G-7033)*

Green Plus Plastics LLC .... G 931 510-0525
Indianapolis *(G-7042)*

Green Tree Plastics LLC .... F 812 402-4127
Evansville *(G-3524)*

Henry Holsters LLC .... G 812 369-2266
Solsberry *(G-12684)*

Hoehn Plastics Inc .... D 812 874-3646
Poseyville *(G-11856)*

ICI Americas Inc .... G 317 535-5626
Whiteland *(G-14240)*

ICO Polymers North America Inc .... G 219 392-3375
East Chicago *(G-2535)*

Imperial Marble Incorporated .... F 812 752-5384
Scottsburg *(G-12364)*

Industrial Dlctrics Hldngs Inc .... A 317 773-1766
Noblesville *(G-11128)*

Industrial Plastics Group LLC .... E 812 831-4053
Evansville *(G-3556)*

Indy Rapid 3d LLC .... G 812 243-4175
Indianapolis *(G-7221)*

Innovative Composites Ltd .... F 574 857-2224
Rochester *(G-12129)*

Integral Technologies Inc .... G 812 550-1770
Evansville *(G-3562)*

Interplastic Corporation .... E 574 234-1105
South Bend *(G-12818)*

Interplastic Corporation .... F 574 259-1505
Mishawaka *(G-10054)*

Ip Moulding Inc .... D 574 825-5845
Middlebury *(G-9894)*

J Jesse Inc .... F 574 862-4538
Wakarusa *(G-13780)*

Jp Incorporated - Indiana .... B 574 457-2062
Syracuse *(G-13136)*

Kvk US Technologies Inc .... G 765 529-1100
New Castle *(G-10909)*

Lucent Polymers Inc .... G 812 492-7214
Evansville *(G-3606)*

Makuta Technics Inc .... F 317 642-0001
Shelbyville *(G-12550)*

Martin Holding Company LLC .... D 812 401-9988
Evansville *(G-3614)*

Matrixx Group Incorporated .... G 812 421-3600
Evansville *(G-3616)*

Nova Polymers Incorporated .... E 812 476-0339
Evansville *(G-3648)*

Omni Plastics LLC .... D 812 422-0888
Evansville *(G-3655)*

Pactiv Corporation .... C 574 936-7065
Plymouth *(G-11709)*

Polyfusion LLC .... G 260 624-7659
Angola *(G-237)*

Polymod Technologies Inc .... F 260 436-1322
Fort Wayne *(G-4538)*

Polyone Corporation .... C 574 267-1100
Warsaw *(G-13927)*

Precision Colors LLC .... F 260 969-6402
Fort Wayne *(G-4547)*

Process Systems & Services .... G 812 427-2331
Florence *(G-4004)*

Rim Molding and Engrg Inc .... F 574 294-1932
Elkhart *(G-3146)*

Sabic Innovative Plastics Mt V .... A 812 838-4385
Mount Vernon *(G-10407)*

Schulman .... G 812 253-5238
Evansville *(G-3716)*

Shaw Polymers LLC .... F 219 779-9450
Crown Point *(G-2303)*

Solid Surface Craftsmen Inc .... G 317 535-2333
Whiteland *(G-14246)*

Spartech LLC .... C 765 281-5100
Muncie *(G-10565)*

Teknor Apex Co .... G 812 246-3357
Charlestown *(G-1583)*

Toray Resin Company .... D 317 398-7833
Shelbyville *(G-12577)*

Triangle Rubber Co LLC .... E 574 533-3118
Goshen *(G-5341)*

Vahala Foam Inc .... D 574 293-1287
Elkhart *(G-3240)*

PLASTICS MATERIALS, BASIC FORMS & SHAPES WHOLESALERS

Arrowhead Plastic Engineering .... F 765 396-9113
Eaton *(G-2581)*

Brunk Corp .... E 574 533-1109
Goshen *(G-5180)*

C-L Building & Leasing Inc .... G 574 293-8959
Elkhart *(G-2746)*

Dunham Rubber & Belting Corp .... E 317 888-3002
Greenwood *(G-5683)*

Dunham Rubber & Belting Corp .... G 800 876-5340
Fort Wayne *(G-4224)*

Jadcore LLC .... C 812 234-2724
Terre Haute *(G-13260)*

Johnson Plastics & Sup Co Inc .... E 812 424-5554
Evansville *(G-3579)*

Meyer Plastics Inc .... G 765 447-2195
Lafayette *(G-8967)*

Meyer Plastics Inc .... D 317 259-4131
Indianapolis *(G-7493)*

Shaw Polymers LLC .... F 219 779-9450
Crown Point *(G-2303)*

PLASTICS PROCESSING

Accelerated Curing Inc .... F 260 726-3202
Portland *(G-11807)*

Apr Plastic Fabricating Inc .... E 206 482-8523
Fort Wayne *(G-4085)*

Arrowhead Plastic Engineering .... E 765 286-0533
Muncie *(G-10432)*

B D Custom Manufacturing Inc .... F 574 848-0925
Bristol *(G-1047)*

Butler-Macdonald Inc .... D 317 872-5115
Indianapolis *(G-6523)*

CMS Technologies Inc .... G 219 395-8272
Chesterton *(G-1601)*

Continental Strl Plas Inc .... C 260 355-4011
Huntington *(G-6199)*

CT Phoenix of Indiana Inc .... F 812 838-2414
Mount Vernon *(G-10391)*

DA Inc .... E 812 503-2302
Charlestown *(G-1562)*

Diamond Manufacturing Company .... E 219 874-2374
Michigan City *(G-9782)*

Display Craft .... G 260 726-4535
Portland *(G-11816)*

Eis Fibercoating Inc .... E 574 722-5192
Logansport *(G-9334)*

Elkcases Inc .... E 574 295-7700
Elkhart *(G-2819)*

Elkhart Plastics Inc .... D 574 232-8066
South Bend *(G-12761)*

Elkhart Plastics Inc .... E 574 825-9797
Middlebury *(G-9884)*

Fiberglas & Plastic Fabg .... E 317 549-1779
Indianapolis *(G-6917)*

First Metals & Plastics Inc .... E 812 379-4400
Columbus *(G-1930)*

Form/TEC Plastics Incorporated .... E 765 342-2300
Martinsville *(G-9608)*

Genova Products Inc .... D 219 866-5136
Rensselaer *(G-11925)*

Green Plus Plastics LLC .... G 317 672-2410
Indianapolis *(G-7041)*

Inside Systems .... G 317 831-3772
Mooresville *(G-10314)*

Kendrion (mishawaka) LLC .... E 574 257-2422
Mishawaka *(G-10063)*

Makuta Technics Inc .... F 317 642-0001
Shelbyville *(G-12550)*

Mayco International LLC .... E 765 348-5780
Hartford City *(G-5984)*

Meyer Plastics Inc .... G 765 447-2195
Lafayette *(G-8967)*

Omni Plastics Incorporated .... D 812 537-4102
Greendale *(G-5492)*

Patrick Industries Inc .... C 574 294-8828
Elkhart *(G-3088)*

Penz Products Inc .... E 574 255-4736
Mishawaka *(G-10103)*

Polygon .... G 317 240-1130
Indianapolis *(G-7705)*

Precision Products Group Inc .... C 301 474-3100
Indianapolis *(G-6277)*

Reschcor Inc .... G 574 295-2413
Elkhart *(G-3143)*

Splendor Boats LLC .... F 260 352-2835
Silver Lake *(G-12681)*

Taghleef Industries Inc .... A 302 326-5500
Rosedale *(G-12208)*

Tredegar Corporation .... D 812 466-0266
Terre Haute *(G-13356)*

Trellborg Sling Sltions US Inc .... E 260 749-9631
Fort Wayne *(G-4700)*

Trivalence Technologies LLC .... G 800 209-2517
Evansville *(G-3776)*

Tru-Form Steel & Wire Inc .... E 765 348-5001
Hartford City *(G-5993)*

Tru-Form Steel & Wire Inc .... E 765 348-5001
Hartford City *(G-5994)*

Western Consolidated Tech Inc .... D 260 495-9866
Fremont *(G-4982)*
ZF North America Inc .... B 765 429-1984
Lafayette *(G-9028)*

PLASTICS SHEET: Packing Materials

Artisanz Fabrication Mch LLC .... G 317 708-0228
Plainfield *(G-11594)*

PLASTICS: Blow Molded

Fort Wayne Plastics Inc .... C 260 432-2520
Fort Wayne *(G-4278)*
Kn Platech America Corporation .... G 317 392-7707
Shelbyville *(G-12544)*

PLASTICS: Cast

Thrust Industries Inc .... F 812 437-3643
Evansville *(G-3762)*

PLASTICS: Extruded

Cor-A-Vent Inc .... F 574 255-1910
Mishawaka *(G-10023)*
Flexseals Manufacturing LLC .... G 574 293-0333
Elkhart *(G-2856)*
Kibbechem Inc .... E 574 266-1234
Elkhart *(G-2964)*
North American Extrusn & Assem .... E 260 636-3336
Albion *(G-30)*
Plastic Extrusions Company .... G 812 479-3232
Evansville *(G-3674)*
Plastic Processors Inc .... F 260 488-3999
Hamilton *(G-5827)*
Reschcor Inc .... F 574 295-2413
Bristol *(G-1079)*
Vytec Inc .... E 574 277-4295
Granger *(G-5450)*

PLASTICS: Finished Injection Molded

Akka Plastics Inc .... E 812 849-9256
Mitchell *(G-10155)*
AR Tee Enterprises Inc .... G 574 848-5543
Bristol *(G-1046)*
Artek Inc .... E 260 484-4222
Fort Wayne *(G-4091)*
Burco Molding Inc .... D 317 773-5699
Noblesville *(G-11074)*
Challenge Plastic Products Inc .... F 812 526-0582
Edinburgh *(G-2599)*
Ckc Tool Inc .... G 219 285-6415
Morocco *(G-10361)*
Custom Urethanes Inc .... G 219 924-1644
Highland *(G-6041)*
Decatur Mold Tool and Engrg .... C 812 346-5188
North Vernon *(G-11253)*
Exton Inc .... D 574 533-0447
Goshen *(G-5212)*
Genesis Molding Inc .... D 574 256-9271
Mishawaka *(G-10046)*
Genesis Plastics and Engrg LLC .... C 812 752-6742
Scottsburg *(G-12357)*
Genesis Plastics Solutions LLC .... G 812 283-4435
Jeffersonville *(G-8368)*
Greenville Technology Inc .... F 765 221-7576
Anderson *(G-113)*
Hartland Products Inc .... E 219 778-9034
Rolling Prairie *(G-12187)*
Helfrich Engineering Inc .... G 812 985-3118
Evansville *(G-3537)*
Hoosier Custom Plastics LLC .... E 574 772-2120
Knox *(G-8567)*
Illinois Tool Works Inc .... C 260 347-8040
Kendallville *(G-8480)*
Interactive Engineering Inc .... G 574 272-5851
Granger *(G-5415)*
Jones Machine & Tool Inc .... E 812 364-4588
Fredericksburg *(G-4945)*
Kenco Plastics Inc .... F 219 324-6621
La Porte *(G-8777)*
Kenco Plastics Inc .... F 219 362-7565
La Porte *(G-8778)*
Kenco Plastics Inc .... F 219 326-5501
La Porte *(G-8779)*
Kimball Electronics Inc .... D 317 357-3175
Indianapolis *(G-7350)*
Kimball Electronics Inc .... D 317 545-5383
Indianapolis *(G-7351)*
Mary Jonas .... F 317 500-0600
Indianapolis *(G-7462)*
New Market Plastics Inc .... F 317 758-5494
Ladoga *(G-8841)*
Nexgen Mold & Tool Inc .... E 812 945-3375
New Albany *(G-10833)*
Plastics Research and Dev Inc .... E 812 279-8885
Springville *(G-13066)*
Precision Plastics Indiana Inc .... C 260 244-6114
Columbia City *(G-1819)*
Spin-Cast Plastics Inc .... D 574 232-8066
South Bend *(G-12949)*
Srg Global Trim Inc .... A 812 473-6200
Evansville *(G-3745)*
Standard Plastic Corp .... F 260 824-0214
Bluffton *(G-893)*
TEC-Air LLC .... D 219 301-7084
Munster *(G-10632)*
Templeton Coal Company Inc .... G 812 232-7037
Terre Haute *(G-13350)*
Vee Engineering Inc .... G 765 778-7895
Anderson *(G-181)*
Vee Engineering Inc .... D 260 424-6635
Fort Wayne *(G-4725)*
Wabash Plastics Inc .... B 812 428-9300
Evansville *(G-3806)*
York Group Inc .... G 765 966-0077
Richmond *(G-12079)*

PLASTICS: Injection Molded

ABI Plastics LLC .... G 574 294-1700
Elkhart *(G-2662)*
Accu-Mold LLC .... E 269 323-0388
Mishawaka *(G-9989)*
American Plastic Molding Corp .... C 812 752-2292
Scottsburg *(G-12355)*
Anderson Products .... G 765 794-4242
Darlington *(G-2359)*
Apr Plastic Fabricating Inc .... E 260 482-8523
Fort Wayne *(G-4086)*
Aptimise Composites LLC .... E 260 484-3139
Fort Wayne *(G-4088)*
Astar Inc .... E 574 234-2137
South Bend *(G-12713)*
Aucilla Incorporated .... E 574 234-9036
South Bend *(G-12715)*
B&B Molders LLC .... D 574 259-7838
Mishawaka *(G-10003)*
B&J International LLC .... G 260 854-2215
Kendallville *(G-8459)*
Bamar Plastics Inc .... E 574 234-4066
South Bend *(G-12720)*
Beach Mold & Tool Inc .... G 502 649-9915
Jeffersonville *(G-8328)*
Bender Mold & Machine Inc .... F 574 255-5176
Mishawaka *(G-10008)*
Bender Products Inc .... E 574 255-5350
Mishawaka *(G-10009)*
Berry Plastics Ik LLC .... D 641 648-5047
Evansville *(G-3379)*
Bhar Incorporated .... G 260 749-5168
Fort Wayne *(G-4106)*
Carrera Manufacturing Inc .... F 260 726-9800
Portland *(G-11809)*
Cedar Creek Studios Inc .... G 260 627-7320
Leo *(G-9241)*
Concept Tool & Engineering .... G 812 352-0055
North Vernon *(G-11249)*
Crawford Industries LLC .... C 800 428-0840
Crawfordsville *(G-2144)*
Crescent-Cresline-Wabash Plast .... G 812 428-9300
Evansville *(G-3441)*
Custom Plastics LLC .... F 574 259-2340
Mishawaka *(G-10028)*
D & M Tool Corporation .... E 812 279-8882
Springville *(G-13062)*
Decatur Plastic Products Inc .... C 812 346-5159
North Vernon *(G-11255)*
Dexterous Mold and Tool Inc .... E 812 422-8046
Evansville *(G-3457)*
Eckco Inc .... G 574 257-0299
Mishawaka *(G-10039)*
Elkhart Cases Inc .... E 574 295-7700
Elkhart *(G-2823)*
Exhibit A Plastics LLC .... E 765 386-6702
Coatesville *(G-1749)*
Exo-S US LLC .... B 260 562-4131
Howe *(G-6123)*
Exo-S US LLC .... C 260 562-4100
Howe *(G-6124)*
Exo-S US LLC .... C 260 562-4100
Howe *(G-6125)*
Fas Plastic Enterprises Inc .... D 812 265-2928
Hanover *(G-5960)*
Flair Molded Plastics Inc .... D 812 425-6155
Evansville *(G-3508)*
Flw Plastics Inc .... E 812 546-0050
Hope *(G-6112)*
Focus Mold & Machine Inc .... G 812 422-9627
Evansville *(G-3511)*
Future Mold Inc .... F 812 941-8661
New Albany *(G-10785)*
Global Plastics Inc .... D 317 299-2345
Indianapolis *(G-7012)*
Grrk Holdings Inc .... E 317 872-0172
Indianapolis *(G-7053)*
H & W Molders Inc .... G 812 423-9340
Evansville *(G-3527)*
Hagerstown Plastics Inc .... G 765 939-3849
Richmond *(G-11994)*
Holzmeyer Die & Mold Mfg Corp .... E 812 386-6015
Princeton *(G-11876)*
Hoosier Pride Plastics Inc .... E 260 497-7080
Fort Wayne *(G-4345)*
Hopper Development Inc .... F 574 753-6621
Logansport *(G-9336)*
Indiana Plastics Inc .... E 574 294-3253
Elkhart *(G-2932)*
Indiana Precision Plastics Inc .... F 765 762-2452
Williamsport *(G-14292)*
Injection Plastic & Mfg Co .... F 574 784-2070
Lapaz *(G-9117)*
Innovative Mold & Machine Inc .... G 317 634-1177
Indianapolis *(G-7238)*
J H J Inc .... E 574 256-6966
Mishawaka *(G-10055)*
Jet Technologies Inc .... E 574 264-3613
Elkhart *(G-2948)*
Kautex Inc .... B 937 238-8096
Avilla *(G-409)*
Khorporate Holdings Inc .... C 260 357-3365
Laotto *(G-9110)*
Lepark Mold & Tool .... C 574 262-0518
Elkhart *(G-2995)*
Lighthouse Industries Inc .... E 219 879-1550
Michigan City *(G-9811)*
Lincoln Industries Inc .... E 812 897-0715
Boonville *(G-915)*
Link Engineering LLC .... G 765 457-1166
Kokomo *(G-8659)*
Lorentson Manufacturing Co .... E 765 452-4425
Kokomo *(G-8660)*
Lukemeier Indus Mold & Mch Co .... E 812 945-3375
New Albany *(G-10821)*
Manar Inc .... E 812 346-2858
North Vernon *(G-11268)*
Marco Plastics Inc .... F 812 333-0062
Bloomington *(G-769)*
Metro Plastics Tech Inc .... D 317 776-0860
Noblesville *(G-11148)*
Midwest-Tek Inc .... G 812 981-3551
New Albany *(G-10830)*
Models LLC .... E 765 676-6700
Lebanon *(G-9207)*
Nyloncraft Inc .... B 574 256-1521
Mishawaka *(G-10098)*
OTech Corporation .... D 219 778-8001
Rolling Prairie *(G-12190)*
Paramount Plastics Inc .... E 574 264-2143
Elkhart *(G-3074)*
Paul Tirotta .... F 574 255-4101
Mishawaka *(G-10102)*
Pent Assemblies .... D 260 347-5828
Kendallville *(G-8501)*
Phoenix Closures Inc .... D 765 658-1800
Greencastle *(G-5472)*
Pier-Mac Plastics Inc .... E 260 726-9844
Portland *(G-11839)*
Pk USA Inc .... B 317 395-5500
Shelbyville *(G-12558)*
Plas-Tech Molding & Design Inc .... F 260 761-3006
Brimfield *(G-1036)*
Plastic Components Inc .... E 574 264-7514
Elkhart *(G-3099)*
Plastic Molding Mfg Inc .... E 574 234-9036
South Bend *(G-12897)*
Plastic Moldings Company Llc .... C 317 392-4139
Shelbyville *(G-12559)*
Plastics Fabg & Distrg LLC .... G 574 233-7527
South Bend *(G-12898)*
Poly Hl Solidur Inc .... B 260 479-4100
Fort Wayne *(G-4537)*

Polymer Equipment Co Inc ....G...... 765 855-3448
  Centerville (G-1543)
Premier Fiberglass Co Inc ....E...... 574 264-5457
  Elkhart (G-3110)
Prodigy Mold & Tool Inc ....E...... 812 753-3029
  Haubstadt (G-6004)
Production Plastic Molding ....G...... 317 872-4669
  Indianapolis (G-7769)
Progressive Plastics Inc ....F...... 765 552-2004
  Elwood (G-3310)
Prolon Inc ....E...... 574 522-8900
  Elkhart (G-3119)
PSI Molded Plastics Ind Inc ....C...... 574 288-2100
  South Bend (G-12907)
PTG Silicones Inc ....G...... 812 948-8719
  New Albany (G-10850)
Puck Supply & Machine LLC ....F...... 574 293-3333
  Elkhart (G-3122)
Pyramid Plastic Group Inc ....G...... 260 327-3145
  Larwill (G-9124)
Quad 4 Plastics Inc ....E...... 574 293-8660
  Elkhart (G-3126)
Quality Molded Products Inc ....D...... 574 272-3733
  South Bend (G-12909)
Quality Plastics and Engrg Inc ....E...... 574 262-2621
  Elkhart (G-3128)
R & R Plastics Inc ....D...... 219 393-5505
  Kingsbury (G-8545)
R & R Technologies LLC ....E...... 812 526-2655
  Edinburgh (G-2623)
Revere Industries LLC ....G...... 317 580-2420
  Westfield (G-14184)
Revere Plastics Systems LLC ....G...... 812 670-2240
  Jeffersonville (G-8419)
River Valley Plastics Inc ....E...... 574 262-5221
  Elkhart (G-3148)
Rix Products Inc ....G...... 812 426-1749
  Evansville (G-3706)
Sanko Gosei Tech USA Inc ....E...... 260 749-5168
  Fort Wayne (G-4605)
Southern Indiana Plastics Inc ....E...... 812 280-7474
  Jeffersonville (G-8425)
Syndicate Sales Inc ....B...... 765 457-7277
  Kokomo (G-8704)
Tasus Corporation ....C...... 812 333-6500
  Bloomington (G-834)
Tech Group North America Inc ....C...... 765 650-2300
  Frankfort (G-4855)
Tedco Inc ....G...... 765 489-5807
  Hagerstown (G-5815)
Thorgren Tool & Molding Co ....D...... 219 462-1801
  Valparaiso (G-13628)
Tomken Plastic Tech Inc ....E...... 765 284-2472
  Muncie (G-10572)
Wabash Plastics Inc ....E...... 812 867-2447
  Evansville (G-3807)
Williams Plastics LLC ....C...... 317 398-1630
  Shelbyville (G-12585)

PLASTICS: Molded

Adkev Inc ....F...... 574 583-4420
  Monticello (G-10251)
Altec Engineering Inc ....E...... 574 293-1965
  Elkhart (G-2679)
Ashley Industrial Molding Inc ....C...... 260 587-9155
  Ashley (G-283)
Ashley Industrial Molding Inc ....G...... 260 349-1982
  Kendallville (G-8456)
Auburn Hardwood Molding ....G...... 260 925-5959
  Auburn (G-314)
B Plus Enterprises Inc ....G...... 219 733-9404
  Wanatah (G-13821)
Beechys Molding Plus ....G...... 260 768-7030
  Shipshewana (G-12606)
Buckhorn Inc ....D...... 260 824-0997
  Bluffton (G-870)
Co-Tronics Inc ....F...... 574 722-3850
  Peru (G-11522)
Cpx Inc ....D...... 219 474-5280
  Kentland (G-8519)
Electro Transfer Systems Inc ....D...... 574 234-0600
  Mishawaka (G-10040)
Engineered Rubber & Plastics ....F...... 574 254-1405
  Mishawaka (G-10041)
Engrave Inc ....F...... 812 537-8693
  Lawrenceburg (G-9140)
Futurex Industries Inc ....E...... 765 498-8900
  Bloomingdale (G-648)
Group Dekko Inc ....D...... 260 357-3621
  Garrett (G-5009)

Indus LLC ....G...... 502 553-1770
  New Albany (G-10806)
Integrity Molding Inc ....G...... 812 524-1243
  Seymour (G-12459)
Integrity Rttional Molding LLC ....E...... 317 837-1101
  Plainfield (G-11618)
Jeco Plastic Products LLC ....F...... 317 839-4943
  Plainfield (G-11621)
Kyle Machine & Tool Inc ....G...... 317 736-4743
  Franklin (G-4904)
Manar Inc ....C...... 812 526-2891
  Edinburgh (G-2617)
Midwest Rotational Molding LLC ....F...... 574 294-6891
  Elkhart (G-3040)
Neptune Flotation LLC ....F...... 317 588-3600
  Indianapolis (G-6274)
Pent Plastics Inc ....C...... 260 897-3775
  Kendallville (G-8502)
Red Star Contract Mfg Inc ....G...... 260 327-3145
  Larwill (G-9125)
Richardson Molding LLC ....E...... 317 787-9463
  Indianapolis (G-7839)
Rochester Rttional Molding Inc ....F...... 574 223-8844
  Rochester (G-12149)
Rotational Molding Tech Inc ....D...... 574 831-6450
  New Paris (G-10993)
Sabin Corporation ....C...... 812 323-4500
  Bloomington (G-820)
Smiths Enterprises Inc ....E...... 765 378-6267
  Chesterfield (G-1589)
Sonoco Prtective Solutions Inc ....D...... 260 726-9333
  Portland (G-11847)
Trim-Lok Inc ....G...... 574 227-1143
  Elkhart (G-3223)
US Molders Inc ....E...... 219 984-5058
  Reynolds (G-11949)
Webco Inc ....G...... 260 244-4233
  Columbia City (G-1847)

PLASTICS: Polystyrene Foam

Abbp LLC ....G...... 812 402-5966
  Evansville (G-3332)
Aearo Technologies LLC ....C...... 317 692-6666
  Indianapolis (G-6342)
American Whitetail Inc ....F...... 812 937-7185
  Ferdinand (G-3845)
Cellofoam North America Inc ....D...... 317 535-9008
  Whiteland (G-14235)
Display Craft ....G...... 260 726-4535
  Portland (G-11816)
Efp LLC ....D...... 574 295-4690
  Elkhart (G-2814)
Foam Fabricators Inc ....E...... 812 948-1696
  New Albany (G-10783)
Foamcraft Inc ....C...... 317 545-3626
  Indianapolis (G-6943)
Foamcraft Inc ....E...... 812 849-3350
  Mitchell (G-10163)
Foamcraft Inc ....D...... 574 534-4343
  Goshen (G-5216)
Fostek ....F...... 540 587-5870
  Mishawaka (G-10044)
Fxi Inc ....C...... 260 925-1073
  Auburn (G-333)
Gdc Inc ....C...... 574 533-3128
  Goshen (G-5222)
Johnson Plastics & Sup Co Inc ....E...... 812 424-5554
  Evansville (G-3579)
Kibbechem Inc ....E...... 574 266-1234
  Elkhart (G-2964)
Knox Enterprises Inc ....G...... 317 714-3073
  Indianapolis (G-7363)
Latham Manufacturing Corp ....C...... 260 459-4115
  Fort Wayne (G-4425)
Lifoam Industries LLC ....G...... 410 889-1023
  Fishers (G-3939)
Molded Foam LLC ....D...... 574 848-1500
  Bristol (G-1070)
Mossberg Industries Inc ....D...... 260 357-5141
  Garrett (G-5018)
Opflex Solutions Inc ....D...... 800 568-7036
  Indianapolis (G-7627)
Opflex Technologies LLC ....E...... 518 568-7036
  Indianapolis (G-7629)
Perry Foam Products Inc ....E...... 765 474-3404
  Lafayette (G-8980)
PSC Industries Inc ....E...... 812 425-9071
  Evansville (G-3688)
Rau Creations ....G...... 317 774-8789
  Carmel (G-1463)

Security Paks Intl LLC ....F...... 317 536-2662
  Carmel (G-1477)
Sonoco Prtective Solutions Inc ....G...... 260 726-9333
  Portland (G-11846)
Teach Enterprises Inc ....E...... 574 773-3108
  Nappanee (G-10708)
Vahala Foam Inc ....E...... 574 293-1287
  Elkhart (G-3240)

PLASTICS: Thermoformed

Arrowhead Plastic Engineering ....F...... 765 396-9113
  Eaton (G-2581)
Carr Metal Products Inc ....C...... 317 542-0691
  Indianapolis (G-6558)
Crescent Plastics Inc ....D...... 812 428-9305
  Evansville (G-3439)
Crescent Plastics Inc ....D...... 812 428-9300
  Evansville (G-3440)
D M Sales & Engineering Inc ....E...... 317 783-5493
  Indianapolis (G-6722)
Hart Plastics Inc ....E...... 574 264-7060
  Elkhart (G-2909)
Hoosier Fiberglass Industries ....E...... 812 232-5027
  Terre Haute (G-13248)
Indiana Vac-Form ....F...... 574 269-1725
  Warsaw (G-13892)
Meyer Plastics Inc ....D...... 317 259-4131
  Indianapolis (G-7493)
Osborn Manufacturing Corp ....F...... 574 267-6156
  Warsaw (G-13920)
Patrick Industries Inc ....D...... 260 665-6112
  Angola (G-235)
Pro-Form Plastics Inc ....E...... 812 522-4433
  Crothersville (G-2220)
Special Product Services Inc ....F...... 260 632-1302
  Woodburn (G-14390)
Spencer Industries Inc ....C...... 812 937-4561
  Dale (G-2333)
Thermform Engineered Qulty LLC ....F...... 260 495-9842
  Fremont (G-4977)

PLATEMAKING SVC: Color Separations, For The Printing Trade

Accucraft Imaging Inc ....G...... 219 933-3007
  Hammond (G-5834)

PLATEMAKING SVC: Embossing, For The Printing Trade

Crichlow Industries Inc ....G...... 317 925-5178
  Indianapolis (G-6692)

PLATES

Bottcher America Corporation ....E...... 765 675-4449
  Tipton (G-13389)
Cecils Printing & Office Sups ....G...... 812 683-4416
  Huntingburg (G-6153)
Dynamic Dies Inc ....E...... 317 247-4706
  Indianapolis (G-6778)
Evantek Manufacturing Inds LLC ....E...... 812 437-9100
  Evansville (G-3493)
Ewing Printing Company Inc ....F...... 812 882-2415
  Vincennes (G-13677)
Excell Color Graphics Inc ....E...... 260 482-2720
  Fort Wayne (G-4251)
Express Press Indiana Inc ....E...... 574 277-3355
  South Bend (G-12769)
Fedex Office & Print Svcs Inc ....F...... 765 449-4950
  Lafayette (G-8897)
Gary Printing Inc ....G...... 219 886-1767
  Gary (G-5052)
Grandview Aluminum Products ....E...... 812 649-2569
  Grandview (G-5387)
Ludwick Graphics Inc ....F...... 574 233-2165
  South Bend (G-12845)
M Nelson & Associates Inc ....G...... 317 228-1422
  Carmel (G-1430)
Maury Boyd & Associates Inc ....F...... 317 849-6110
  Indianapolis (G-7469)
Multi-Color Corporation ....E...... 812 752-0586
  Scottsburg (G-12375)
Peafield Products Inc ....F...... 317 839-8473
  Plainfield (G-11634)
Pengad/West Inc ....E...... 765 286-3000
  Muncie (G-10544)
Rotation Dynamics Corporation ....E...... 219 325-8808
  La Porte (G-8813)

PRODUCT

Shirley Engraving Co Inc ....F 317 634-4084
Indianapolis (G-7934)

PLATES: Aluminum

Taylor Made Enterprises ....G 765 653-8481
Greencastle (G-5479)

PLATES: Sheet & Strip, Exc Coated Prdts

Dynamic Holdings LLC ....G 260 969-3500
Fort Wayne (G-4230)
Omnisource Holdings LLC ....G 260 969-3500
Fort Wayne (G-4511)
Resource Ventures LLC ....G 260 432-9177
Fort Wayne (G-4589)
Resource Ventures II LLC ....G 260 969-3500
Fort Wayne (G-4590)
Steel Dynamics Inc ....A 260 248-2600
Columbia City (G-1837)
Steel Dynamics Inc ....A 260 868-8000
Butler (G-1244)
Steel Dynamics Inc ....D 812 218-1490
Jeffersonville (G-8428)
Steel Dynamics Inc ....B 317 892-7000
Pittsboro (G-11588)

PLATES: Steel

McCombs and Son Company ....G 765 825-4581
Connersville (G-2063)

PLATES: Truss, Metal

Gldn Rule Truss & Metal Sales ....G 812 866-1800
Lexington (G-9250)
Grabill Truss Incorporated ....G 260 627-0933
Grabill (G-5370)
Mitek Usa Inc ....D 219 924-3835
Griffith (G-5786)

PLATING & FINISHING SVC: Decorative, Formed Prdts

Justin Mollo ....G 812 361-7694
Morgantown (G-10355)

PLATING & POLISHING SVC

A Raymond Tinnerman Auto Inc ....C 574 722-5168
Logansport (G-9319)
Albany Metal Treating Inc ....D 765 789-6470
Albany (G-10)
Allegheny Ludlum LLC ....C 765 529-9570
New Castle (G-10890)
Bare Metal Inc ....F 812 948-1313
New Albany (G-10750)
Batesville Products Inc ....D 513 381-2057
Lawrenceburg (G-9133)
Bon L Manufacturing Company ....C 815 351-6802
Kentland (G-8517)
C & J Plating & Grinding LLC ....G 765 288-8728
Muncie (G-10444)
Ceramica Inc ....F 317 546-0087
Indianapolis (G-6589)
Circle City Heat Treating Inc ....F 317 638-2252
Indianapolis (G-6607)
Commercial Finishing Corp ....G 317 267-0377
Indianapolis (G-6637)
Heidtman Steel Products Inc ....C 419 691-4646
Butler (G-1229)
Hydro Extrusion North Amer LLC ....B 888 935-5757
North Liberty (G-11216)
Industrial Contrs Skanska Inc ....E 812 423-7832
Evansville (G-3555)
J & J Welding Inc ....E 812 838-4391
Mount Vernon (G-10396)
Linden Machine Shop LLC ....G 765 339-7244
Linden (G-9304)
Napier & Napier ....G 765 580-9116
Liberty (G-9266)
National Material LP ....C 219 397-5088
East Chicago (G-2554)
Neo Industries LLC ....G 219 762-6075
Portage (G-11781)
Praxair Surface Tech Inc ....G 317 240-2544
Indianapolis (G-7726)
Precoat Metals Corp ....C 317 462-7761
Greenfield (G-5565)
Pruett Manufacturing Co Inc ....F 812 234-9497
Terre Haute (G-13312)
Roll Coater Inc ....G 317 652-1102
Indianapolis (G-7856)

Ternet Metal Finishing Inc ....G 260 897-3903
Avilla (G-419)
Thorntons Welding ....G 812 332-8564
Bloomington (G-841)
United States Steel Corp ....D 219 762-3131
Portage (G-11799)
Whitlocks Pressure Wash ....F 765 825-5868
Connersville (G-2078)
Worthington Steel Company ....C 219 929-4000
Porter (G-11806)

PLATING COMPOUNDS

Warsaw Black Oxide Inc ....E 574 491-2975
Burket (G-1208)

PLATING SVC: Chromium, Metals Or Formed Prdts

Chrome Deposit Corporation ....E 219 763-1571
Portage (G-11756)
G and P Enterprises Ind Inc ....G 812 723-3837
Paoli (G-11451)
Muncie Precision Hard Chrome ....G 765 288-2489
Muncie (G-10535)
P & J Industries Inc ....E 260 894-7143
Ligonier (G-9291)
Wrr Inc ....C 317 577-1149
Indianapolis (G-8221)

PLATING SVC: Electro

Anderson Silver Plating Co ....F 574 294-6447
Elkhart (G-2693)
C & R Plating Corp ....E 586 755-4900
Columbia City (G-1770)
Deuxfreres LLC ....D 317 241-7600
Indianapolis (G-6736)
Electro-Spec Inc ....D 317 738-9199
Franklin (G-4883)
Elkhart Plating Corp ....F 574 294-1800
Elkhart (G-2828)
Emi LLC ....E 812 437-9100
Evansville (G-3475)
K & I Hard Chrome Inc ....E 812 948-1166
New Albany (G-10811)
Kromet America Inc ....E 812 346-5117
Lafayette (G-8946)
Madison Plating Inc ....F 812 273-2211
Madison (G-9480)
Metal Finishing Co Inc ....G 317 546-9004
Indianapolis (G-7486)
Mid-City Plating Company Inc ....E 765 289-2374
Muncie (G-10520)
Progressive Plating Company ....E 317 923-2413
Indianapolis (G-7776)
Sumco LLC ....D 317 241-7600
Indianapolis (G-8015)
T & J Plating Inc ....G 765 664-9669
Marion (G-9566)
Tfx Plating Company LLC ....G 765 289-2436
Yorktown (G-14412)
Transportation Tech Inds ....F 812 962-5000
Evansville (G-3769)
Triplex Plating Inc ....E 219 874-3209
Michigan City (G-9855)
Wayne Metal Protection Company ....E 260 492-2529
Fort Wayne (G-4742)

PLATING SVC: Gold

Reckon Plating Inc ....E 260 744-4339
Fort Wayne (G-4582)

PLATING SVC: NEC

Dekalb Metal Finishing Inc ....E 260 925-1820
Auburn (G-327)
Franke Plating Works Inc ....D 260 422-8477
Fort Wayne (G-4284)
Huthone LLC ....G 260 248-2384
Columbia City (G-1792)
Industrial Plating Inc ....D 765 447-5036
Lafayette (G-8924)
J & P Custom Plating Inc ....E 260 726-9696
Portland (G-11829)
Keystone Automotive Inds Inc ....G 574 206-1421
Elkhart (G-2963)
McDowell Enterprises Inc ....E 574 293-1042
Elkhart (G-3024)
Miller Plating & Metal Finishi ....G 812 424-3837
Evansville (G-3628)

Neo Industries LLC ....F 574 217-4078
South Bend (G-12871)
R & S Plating Inc ....G 317 925-2396
Indianapolis (G-7807)
Seleco Inc ....E 317 872-4148
Indianapolis (G-7908)
Southside Plating Works Inc ....G 219 293-5508
Elkhart (G-3182)
W & M Manufacturing Inc ....C 260 726-9800
Portland (G-11855)

PLAYGROUND EQPT

American Playground Corp ....G 765 642-0288
Anderson (G-62)
American Playground Corp ....G 765 642-0288
Anderson (G-63)
AP Acquisition LLC ....F 765 642-0288
Anderson (G-67)
Delta Excell Incorporated ....G 765 642-0288
Anderson (G-93)
Kidstuff Playsystems Inc ....E 219 938-3331
Gary (G-5072)
Lester Recreation Designs LLC ....G 317 888-2071
Greenwood (G-5719)
Recreation Insites LLC ....G 317 578-0588
Fishers (G-3961)
S & W Swing Sets ....G 260 414-6200
New Haven (G-10956)
Sb Finishing ....G 317 598-0965
Indianapolis (G-7899)

PLEATING & STITCHING SVC

A-1 Awards Inc ....F 317 546-9000
Indianapolis (G-6301)
Arizona Sport Shirts Inc ....E 317 481-2160
Indianapolis (G-6419)
Charles Coons ....G 765 362-6509
Crawfordsville (G-2138)
Coaches Connection Inc ....G 260 356-0400
Huntington (G-6198)
Connies Satin Stitch ....G 219 942-1887
Hobart (G-6077)
Crescendo Inc ....G 812 829-4759
Spencer (G-13022)
Dave Turner ....G 765 674-3360
Gas City (G-5122)
Imperial Trophy & Awards Co ....G 260 432-8161
Fort Wayne (G-4361)
Kerham Inc ....E 260 483-5444
Fort Wayne (G-4409)
P J Marketing Services Inc ....G 574 259-8843
South Bend (G-12886)
Ram Graphics Inc ....E 765 724-7783
Alexandria (G-48)
Safety Vehicle Emblem Inc ....F 317 885-7565
Indianapolis (G-7884)
Shilling Sales Inc ....E 260 426-2626
Fort Wayne (G-4621)
Spp Inc ....F 812 882-6203
Vincennes (G-13707)
Stoffel Seals Corporation ....E 845 353-3800
Angola (G-248)
Winters Assoc Prmtnal Pdts Inc ....F 812 330-7000
Bloomington (G-858)

PLUGS: Electric

Aearo Technologies LLC ....A 317 692-6666
Indianapolis (G-6341)
Tap-A-Lite Inc ....E 219 932-8067
Hammond (G-5948)

PLUMBING & HEATING EQPT & SPLY, WHOL: Htg Eqpt/Panels, Solar

Cummins Power Generation Inc ....F 812 377-5000
Columbus (G-1900)
Our Country Home Entps Inc ....D 260 657-5605
Harlan (G-5974)

PLUMBING & HEATING EQPT & SPLY, WHOLESALE: Hydronic Htg Eqpt

Frew Process Group LLC ....G 317 565-5000
Noblesville (G-11107)

(G-0000) Company's Geographic Section entry number

PLUMBING & HEATING EQPT & SPLYS WHOLESALERS

Barry Company Inc ....G....... 812 333-1850
  Bloomington (G-673)
Huntingburg Machine Works Inc...........F....... 812 683-3531
  Huntingburg (G-6169)
Lee Supply Corp ....G....... 812 333-4343
  Bloomington (G-764)
Power Plant Service Inc ....E....... 260 432-6716
  Fort Wayne (G-4542)
Sun Rise Metal Shop ....G....... 260 463-4026
  Topeka (G-13430)

PLUMBING & HEATING EQPT & SPLYS, WHOL: Pipe/Fitting, Plastic

David Indus Process PDT Co..................G....... 317 577-0351
  Fishers (G-3898)
Fred Weber Inc ....F....... 317 262-4920
  Indianapolis (G-6962)

PLUMBING & HEATING EQPT & SPLYS, WHOL: Plumbing Fitting/Sply

Barry Company Inc ....G....... 317 578-2486
  Fishers (G-3874)
Bath Gallery Showroom ....G....... 219 531-2150
  Valparaiso (G-13505)
Cast Products LP ....E....... 574 294-2684
  Elkhart (G-2751)
Dehco Inc...D....... 574 294-2684
  Elkhart (G-2792)
Elkhart Supply Corp ....E....... 574 264-4156
  Elkhart (G-2831)
Ferguson..G....... 317 254-5965
  Indianapolis (G-6916)
Forsyth Brothers Concrete Pdts ....G....... 812 466-4080
  Terre Haute (G-13235)
Leeps Supply Co Inc...............................D....... 219 756-5337
  Merrillville (G-9726)
Templeton Coal Company Inc................G....... 812 232-7037
  Terre Haute (G-13350)

PLUMBING & HEATING EQPT & SPLYS, WHOL: Water Purif Eqpt

New Aqua LLC...D....... 317 272-3000
  Avon (G-456)
US Water Systems Inc ....F....... 317 209-0889
  Indianapolis (G-8138)

PLUMBING & HEATING EQPT & SPLYS, WHOLESALE: Convectors

Hrezo Industrial Eqp & Engrg................F....... 812 537-4700
  Greendale (G-5489)

PLUMBING & HEATING EQPT & SPLYS, WHOLESALE: Steam Fittings

Flosource Inc...E....... 765 342-1360
  Martinsville (G-9605)
Hoffman Sls & Specialty Co Inc.............G....... 317 846-6428
  Carmel (G-1406)

PLUMBING & HEATING EQPT & SPLYS, WHOLESALE: Wood Burn Stove

Patrick & Sharon Hoctor ....G....... 812 898-2678
  Terre Haute (G-13297)

PLUMBING & HEATING EQPT, WHOLESALE: Water Heaters/Purif

Evoqua Water Technologies LLC ....E....... 317 280-4251
  Indianapolis (G-6885)

PLUMBING FIXTURES

Ashley F Ward Inc ....E....... 574 294-1502
  Elkhart (G-2696)
Ashley F Ward Inc ....E....... 219 879-4177
  Michigan City (G-9767)
Barry Company Inc ....G....... 812 333-1850
  Bloomington (G-673)
Bath Gallery Showroom ....G....... 219 531-2150
  Valparaiso (G-13505)
Bootz Manufacturing Company...............D....... 812 425-4646
  Evansville (G-3393)

Delta Faucet Company ....G....... 812 663-4433
  Greensburg (G-5599)
Ferguson..G....... 317 254-5965
  Indianapolis (G-6916)
Ferguson Waterworks ....G....... 219 440-5254
  Schererville (G-12321)
Geberit Manufacturing Inc ....E....... 219 879-4466
  Michigan City (G-9797)
Josam Company ....D....... 219 872-5531
  Michigan City (G-9805)
Lee Supply Corp ....G....... 812 333-4343
  Bloomington (G-764)
Masco Corporation of Indiana ....B....... 317 848-1812
  Indianapolis (G-6273)
Nibco Inc...C....... 574 296-1240
  Goshen (G-5298)
Parker-Hannifin Corporation...................C....... 260 636-2104
  Albion (G-32)
Rex Byers Htg & Coolg Systems...........F....... 765 459-8858
  Kokomo (G-8689)
Schmidt Contracting Inc ....F....... 812 482-3923
  Jasper (G-8303)
St Regis Culvert Inc ....F....... 317 353-8065
  Indianapolis (G-7982)
Stanley Oliver Products LLC ....G....... 260 499-3506
  Lagrange (G-9068)
US Metals ....G....... 219 515-2756
  Schererville (G-12351)

PLUMBING FIXTURES: Plastic

Altec Engineering Inc ....E....... 574 293-1965
  Elkhart (G-2679)
Frontline Mfg Inc ....D....... 574 269-6751
  Warsaw (G-13878)
Geberit Manufacturing Inc ....E....... 219 879-4466
  Michigan City (G-9797)
Imperial Marble Incorporated..................F....... 812 752-5384
  Scottsburg (G-12364)
Nibco Inc...C....... 574 296-1240
  Goshen (G-5298)
Royal Spa Corporation ....D....... 317 781-0828
  Indianapolis (G-7867)

PLUMBING FIXTURES: Vitreous

Bootz Manufacturing Company...............D....... 812 425-4646
  Evansville (G-3393)
E-Z Sweep & Rake LLC..........................G....... 574 533-2083
  Goshen (G-5207)
Josam Company ....D....... 219 872-5531
  Michigan City (G-9805)
Leeps Supply Co Inc...............................D....... 219 756-5337
  Merrillville (G-9726)
Patriot Porcelain LLC ....G....... 574 583-5128
  Monticello (G-10278)

POINT OF SALE DEVICES

Front End Digital Inc...............................G....... 317 652-6134
  Fishers (G-3914)

POLISHING SVC: Metals Or Formed Prdts

502 Mold Polishing LLC ....G....... 502 436-0239
  Greenville (G-5646)
Custom Polish & Chrome.........................G....... 260 665-7448
  Angola (G-206)
Db Polishing ....G....... 574 518-2443
  Nappanee (G-10666)
Doug Wilcox ....G....... 812 476-1957
  Lynnville (G-9434)
Precision Buffing and Polsg...................G....... 574 262-3430
  Elkhart (G-3107)
Reliable Polishing Co ....G....... 765 744-7824
  Parker City (G-11464)
Surface Enhancement ....G....... 574 269-1366
  Warsaw (G-13945)

POLYETHYLENE RESINS

Sun Polymers International Inc ....G....... 317 834-6410
  Mooresville (G-10342)

POLYSTYRENE RESINS

Apexx Enterprises LLC ....F....... 812 486-2443
  Montgomery (G-10213)
Cellofoam North America Inc..................D....... 317 535-9008
  Whiteland (G-14235)
Foam Fabricators Inc ....E....... 812 948-1696
  New Albany (G-10783)

Sonoco Prtective Solutions Inc.............D....... 260 726-9333
  Portland (G-11847)

POLYVINYL CHLORIDE RESINS

AM Stabilizers Corporation ....G....... 219 844-3980
  Valparaiso (G-13490)
Integrity Custom Concepts LLC.............G....... 574 252-2366
  South Bend (G-12815)

PONTOONS: Rubber

Indiana Factory Outlet Marine ....G....... 260 799-4764
  Larwill (G-9122)

POPCORN & SUPPLIES WHOLESALERS

Amish Country Popcorn Inc ....E....... 260 589-8513
  Berne (G-607)
Ramsey Popcorn Co Inc..........................E....... 812 347-2441
  Ramsey (G-11894)

POSTERS

Phantom Neon LLC..................................G....... 765 362-2221
  Crawfordsville (G-2186)

POSTS: Lamp, Metal

Ward Industries Inc.................................F....... 574 825-2548
  Middlebury (G-9923)

POTTERY

Ohio Valley Creative Enrgy Inc ....G....... 502 468-9787
  New Albany (G-10835)
Pigeon Switch Pottery ....G....... 812 567-4124
  Tennyson (G-13180)
Reiberg Ceramics ....G....... 317 283-8441
  Indianapolis (G-7828)
Sissys Ceramics ....G....... 951 550-7728
  Elkhart (G-3173)
Tinas Ceramics & Things ....G....... 812 917-4190
  Terre Haute (G-13355)

POTTING SOILS

Green Thumb of Indiana Inc ....G....... 260 897-2319
  Avilla (G-405)
Millburn Peat Company Inc.....................E....... 219 362-7025
  La Porte (G-8794)
Ostler Enterprises Inc............................G....... 765 656-1275
  Frankfort (G-4847)

POULTRY & POULTRY PRDTS WHOLESALERS

Farbest Foods ....G....... 812 886-2125
  Vincennes (G-13680)

POULTRY & SMALL GAME SLAUGHTERING & PROCESSING

Cargill Incorporated................................B....... 402 533-4227
  Hammond (G-5858)
Crystal Valley Farms LLC.......................A....... 260 829-6550
  Orland (G-11349)
Farbest Farms Inc ....F....... 812 481-1034
  Huntingburg (G-6164)
Farbest Foods ....G....... 812 886-2125
  Vincennes (G-13680)
Hollands Deer Processing LLC ....F....... 765 472-5876
  Peru (G-11530)
Hy-Line North America LLC ....E....... 260 375-3041
  Warren (G-13831)
Lambrights Inc ....D....... 260 463-2178
  Lagrange (G-9056)
Perdue Farms Inc ....E....... 812 886-0593
  Vincennes (G-13696)
Perdue Farms Inc ....C....... 757 787-5210
  Washington (G-13999)
Pletchers Poultry Processing ....G....... 574 831-2329
  Goshen (G-5310)
Rose Acre Farms Inc ....D....... 219 253-6681
  Monon (G-10178)
Tyson Foods Inc......................................E....... 812 347-2452
  Ramsey (G-11895)

POULTRY SLAUGHTERING & PROCESSING

Perdue Farms Inc ....D....... 812 254-8500
  Washington (G-13998)
Pine Manor Inc ....B....... 800 532-4186
  Orland (G-11355)

PRODUCT

POWDER: Aluminum Atomized

Algalco LLC ....G...... 317 361-2787
  Indianapolis (G-6365)
Revere Industries LLC....................G...... 317 580-2420
  Westfield (G-14184)

POWDER: Iron

Powdertech Corp ....D...... 219 462-4141
  Valparaiso (G-13600)
Ssw International Inc......................E...... 219 763-1199
  Burns Harbor (G-1220)

POWDER: Metal

Creative Powder Coatings LLC ....D...... 260 489-3580
  Fort Wayne (G-4186)
Hawk Precision Components Inc ....G...... 812 755-4501
  Campbellsburg (G-1277)
Hope Powder Coat Inc ....G...... 812 546-5555
  Hope (G-6115)
Imerys Steelcasting Usa Inc ....G...... 219 921-1012
  Westville (G-14219)
ITW Gema ....G...... 317 298-5000
  Indianapolis (G-7277)
Jbs Powder Coating LLC ....G...... 812 952-1204
  Lanesville (G-9101)
Netshape Technologies LLC..............C...... 812 755-4501
  Campbellsburg (G-1278)
Powder Processing & Tech LLC.........E...... 219 462-4141
  Valparaiso (G-13599)
Shelton Powder Coating LLC ....G...... 574 323-8369
  Granger (G-5433)

POWDER: Silver

Pro-Kote Indy ....G...... 317 872-0001
  Indianapolis (G-7767)

POWER GENERATORS

Engenaire......................................G...... 574 264-0391
  Elkhart (G-2834)
Ipower Technologies Inc ....E...... 317 574-0103
  Anderson (G-121)

POWER OUTLETS & SOCKETS

Energypoint LLC ....G...... 317 275-7979
  Carmel (G-1371)

POWER SPLY CONVERTERS: Static, Electronic Applications

Gimme Charge LLC ....G...... 317 759-4067
  Indianapolis (G-7006)

POWER SUPPLIES: Transformer, Electronic Type

Vista Worldwide LLC ....G...... 574 264-0711
  Elkhart (G-3248)

POWER TOOL REPAIR SVCS

Servsteel Inc ....E...... 219 736-6030
  Gary (G-5096)

POWER TOOLS, HAND: Drill Attachments, Portable

Illinois Tool Works Inc ....D...... 219 874-4217
  Michigan City (G-9803)

POWER TOOLS, HAND: Drills & Drilling Tools

Diedrich Drill Inc ....E...... 219 326-7788
  La Porte (G-8751)
Key Sheet Metal Inc ....G...... 317 546-7151
  Indianapolis (G-7345)

POWER TOOLS, HAND: Guns, Pneumatic, Chip Removal

Tippmann Sports LLC ....D...... 800 533-4831
  Fort Wayne (G-4686)
Tippmann Sports LLC ....F...... 260 749-6022
  Fort Wayne (G-4687)

POWER TRANSMISSION EQPT WHOLESALERS

Cummins Power Generation Inc...........F...... 812 377-5000
  Columbus (G-1900)

POWER TRANSMISSION EQPT: Aircraft

Allison Transmission Inc...................A...... 317 280-6206
  Indianapolis (G-6372)

POWER TRANSMISSION EQPT: Mechanical

Aisin Drivetrain Inc ....C...... 812 793-2427
  Crothersville (G-2214)
Allied Enterprises Inc ....E...... 765 288-8849
  Muncie (G-10428)
Auburn Gear LLC ....C...... 260 925-3200
  Auburn (G-313)
Bearing Service Company PA..............G...... 773 734-5132
  Griffith (G-5765)
Bludot Inc ....G...... 574 277-2306
  South Bend (G-12723)
Cablecraft Motion Controls LLC ....B...... 260 749-5105
  New Haven (G-10933)
Drake Corporation ....E...... 812 683-2101
  Jasper (G-8246)
Eaton Corporation ....C...... 260 925-3800
  Auburn (G-328)
Eaton Corporation ....D...... 574 288-4446
  South Bend (G-12756)
Eaton Corporation ....F...... 317 704-2520
  Indianapolis (G-6796)
Fairfield Manufacturing Co Inc ....E...... 765 772-4547
  Lafayette (G-8895)
Fort Wayne Clutch Inc ....F...... 260 484-8505
  Fort Wayne (G-4271)
Friskney Gear & Machine Corp............G...... 260 281-2200
  Corunna (G-2084)
Guardian Couplings LLC...................G...... 219 874-5248
  Michigan City (G-9798)
Ktr Corporation ....E...... 219 872-9100
  Michigan City (G-9807)
NSK Corporation ....C...... 765 458-5000
  Liberty (G-9267)
NSK Precision America Inc ....C...... 317 738-5000
  Franklin (G-4916)
Parker-Hannifin Corporation..............C...... 260 894-7125
  Ligonier (G-9292)
Prox Company Inc ....F...... 812 232-4324
  Terre Haute (G-13311)
Pruett Manufacturing Co Inc..............F...... 812 234-9497
  Terre Haute (G-13312)
Siemens Industry Inc......................D...... 219 763-7927
  Portage (G-11794)
Sparks Belting Company Inc ....G...... 800 451-4537
  Hammond (G-5945)
Star Engineering & Mch Co Inc ....E...... 260 824-4825
  Bluffton (G-894)
Steel Parts Corporation ....B...... 765 675-2191
  Tipton (G-13406)
Tecumseh Products Company ....B...... 812 883-3575
  Salem (G-12307)
Tesla Wireless Company LLC..............G...... 219 363-7922
  Wanatah (G-13826)
Uniseal Inc ....G...... 812 425-1361
  Evansville (G-3785)

POWER TRANSMISSION EQPT: Vehicle

Discount Power Equipment ....G...... 765 642-0040
  Anderson (G-96)
Griner Engineering ....G...... 765 296-2955
  Mulberry (G-10417)
Miasa Automotive LLC ....E...... 765 751-9967
  Yorktown (G-14407)

POWERED GOLF CART DEALERS

Mid America Powered Vehicles ....G...... 812 925-7745
  Chandler (G-1551)

PRECAST TERRAZZO OR CONCRETE PRDTS

Hanson Pipe Precast ....G...... 219 873-9509
  Michigan City (G-9800)
Horn Pre-Cast Inc..........................F...... 812 372-4458
  Columbus (G-1943)
Indiana Precast Inc ....E...... 812 372-7771
  Columbus (G-1946)

PRECIOUS METALS

Dnm Converters & Cores ....G...... 502 599-5225
  Clarksville (G-1679)

PRECIOUS STONE MINING SVCS, NEC

Classic Rock Face Block Inc ....G...... 260 704-3113
  Fort Wayne (G-4160)

PRECISION INSTRUMENT REPAIR SVCS

Lievore Custom Machine Inc ....G...... 574 848-0150
  Bristol (G-1067)

PRERECORDED TAPE, CD & RECORD STORE: Record, Disc/Tape

Mountain Made Music Inc ....G...... 812 988-8869
  Nashville (G-10731)

PRERECORDED TAPE, COMPACT DISC & RECORD STORES: Records

Praise Gathering Music Group ....F...... 765 640-4428
  Anderson (G-155)

PRESSED FIBER & MOLDED PULP PRDTS, EXC FOOD PRDTS

Avery Dennison Corporation ....D...... 219 696-7777
  Lowell (G-9399)
Urban Forest Products Llc ....G...... 219 697-2900
  Brook (G-1100)

PRESSES

A & M Tool Inc ....G...... 812 934-6533
  Batesville (G-488)
Roeder Industries ....G...... 812 654-3322
  Milan (G-9946)

PRESTRESSED CONCRETE PRDTS

Prestress Services Inc.....................C...... 260 724-7117
  Decatur (G-2399)
Strescore Inc ....E...... 574 233-1117
  South Bend (G-12958)

PRIMARY FINISHED OR SEMIFINISHED SHAPES

General Mch & Saw Co of Ind..............F...... 574 232-6077
  South Bend (G-12787)

PRIMARY METAL PRODUCTS

Jag Metal Solutions Inc ....G...... 765 445-4459
  Knightstown (G-8552)
Keywest Metal ....G...... 219 513-8429
  Griffith (G-5781)
Keywest Metal ....G...... 219 654-4063
  Hobart (G-6084)
Sit Can Happen LLC ....G...... 812 346-4188
  North Vernon (G-11282)
Wendell Denton.............................G...... 317 736-8397
  Franklin (G-4941)

PRINT CARTRIDGES: Laser & Other Computer Printers

Cartridge Specialist Inc ....G...... 317 257-4465
  Indianapolis (G-6562)
Lasertech Inc................................G...... 812 277-1321
  Bedford (G-559)

PRINTED CIRCUIT BOARDS

Active Sensors Incorporated ....G...... 317 713-2973
  Indianapolis (G-6322)
Carrier Corporation.........................A...... 260 358-0888
  Huntington (G-6196)
David Kechel ....G...... 260 627-2749
  Leo (G-9242)
Divsys International LLC....................E...... 317 405-9427
  Indianapolis (G-6752)
Hamby ....G...... 765 664-4045
  Marion (G-9528)
Illinois Tool Works Inc ....C...... 260 347-8040
  Kendallville (G-8480)
Jtd Enterprises Inc.........................F...... 574 533-9438
  Goshen (G-5249)

Kimball Elec Indianapolis.................D...... 812 634-4000
   Indianapolis *(G-7349)*
Kimball Electronics Inc.....................B...... 812 634-4200
   Jasper *(G-8272)*
Kimball Electronics Tampa Inc...........A...... 812 634-4000
   Jasper *(G-8275)*
Pinder Instruments Company Inc.........E...... 219 924-7070
   Munster *(G-10624)*
Teaco Inc....................................F...... 219 874-6234
   Michigan City *(G-9852)*

PRINTERS & PLOTTERS

Printmaster LLC..............................G...... 260 459-1900
   Fort Wayne *(G-4561)*

PRINTERS' SVCS: Folding, Collating, Etc

Ao Inc *(G-427)*.............................G...... 317 280-3000
   Avon
Precise Printing Plus Signs................G...... 317 545-5117
   Indianapolis *(G-7729)*
Tdk Graphics Inc.............................F...... 219 663-7799
   Crown Point *(G-2312)*

PRINTERS: Computer

Laser Plus....................................G...... 574 269-1246
   Warsaw *(G-13901)*

PRINTERS: Magnetic Ink, Bar Code

Marteck Inc...................................E...... 317 824-0240
   Indianapolis *(G-7459)*
Syntag Rfld...................................G...... 317 685-5292
   Indianapolis *(G-8030)*

PRINTING & BINDING: Books

Biblical Enterprises LLC...................G...... 812 391-0071
   Bloomington *(G-682)*
Codybro LLC..................................G...... 765 827-5441
   Connersville *(G-2044)*
Solema USA Inc.............................G...... 765 361-0806
   Crawfordsville *(G-2196)*
Traveling Bookbinder Inc...................G...... 317 441-4901
   Noblesville *(G-11195)*
W Robbins & Sons Inc......................G...... 765 522-1736
   Roachdale *(G-12096)*

PRINTING & BINDING: Pamphlets

Burkert-Walton Inc..........................G...... 812 425-7157
   Evansville *(G-3405)*
Franklin Publishing Inc.....................G...... 800 634-1993
   Greenwood *(G-5696)*

PRINTING & EMBOSSING: Plastic Fabric Articles

Precision Multi Media.......................G...... 765 359-0466
   Crawfordsville *(G-2188)*
Printing Plus Inc.............................G...... 317 574-1313
   Carmel *(G-1455)*

PRINTING & ENGRAVING: Card, Exc Greeting

Hiatt Enterprises Inc.......................E...... 765 289-7756
   Muncie *(G-10487)*

PRINTING & ENGRAVING: Invitation & Stationery

Entertainment Express......................F...... 219 763-3610
   Portage *(G-11760)*
Formal Affairs Tuxedo Shop................G...... 574 875-6654
   Elkhart *(G-2868)*
Newton Business Forms.....................G...... 812 256-5399
   Charlestown *(G-1575)*
Paper Tigers Inc.............................G...... 317 573-9040
   Indianapolis *(G-7651)*

PRINTING & STAMPING: Fabric Articles

Apple Group Inc.............................E...... 765 675-4777
   Tipton *(G-13387)*
Diverse Sales Solutions LLC................G...... 317 514-2403
   Indianapolis *(G-6747)*
Lomont Holdings Co Inc....................E...... 800 545-9023
   Angola *(G-228)*
Specialty Shoppe............................G...... 574 772-7873
   Knox *(G-8582)*

Sport Form Inc...............................G...... 260 589-2200
   Berne *(G-625)*

PRINTING & WRITING PAPER WHOLESALERS

Reprocomm Inc...............................E...... 765 472-5700
   Peru *(G-11544)*

PRINTING MACHINERY

Acutech LLC..................................F...... 574 262-8228
   Elkhart *(G-2667)*
Blue Grass Chemical Spc LLC..............E...... 812 948-1115
   New Albany *(G-10753)*
Egenolf Machine Inc.........................D...... 317 787-5301
   Indianapolis *(G-6814)*
Numerical Concepts Inc....................D...... 812 466-5261
   Terre Haute *(G-13293)*
Perfecta USA.................................E...... 317 862-7371
   Indianapolis *(G-7677)*
Rotation Dynamics Corporation.............E...... 219 325-8808
   La Porte *(G-8813)*
Scheffer International Inc...................F...... 219 736-6200
   Crown Point *(G-2299)*

PRINTING MACHINERY, EQPT & SPLYS: Wholesalers

Bottcher America Corporation..............E...... 765 675-4449
   Tipton *(G-13389)*
Jac Jmr Inc...................................G...... 219 663-6700
   Crown Point *(G-2264)*
Paradise Ink Inc.............................G...... 812 402-4465
   Evansville *(G-3662)*

PRINTING PLATES: Stereotyping

Kik Custom Products Inc....................E...... 574 295-0000
   Elkhart *(G-2968)*

PRINTING TRADES MACHINERY & EQPT REPAIR SVCS

M R S Printing Erectors Inc................G...... 317 888-1314
   Greenwood *(G-5722)*
Whiffen Machine and Press Repr...........G...... 812 876-1257
   Gosport *(G-5357)*

PRINTING, COMMERCIAL: Announcements, NEC

Mission Announcement Co...................E...... 626 332-4084
   Peru *(G-11537)*

PRINTING, COMMERCIAL: Business Forms, NEC

Evansville Bindery Inc.......................G...... 812 423-2222
   Evansville *(G-3483)*
In Business For Life Inc.....................G...... 317 691-6169
   Carmel *(G-1411)*
Premier Print & Svcs Group Inc............F...... 574 273-2525
   Granger *(G-5429)*
Taylor Communications Inc.................D...... 317 392-3235
   Shelbyville *(G-12573)*

PRINTING, COMMERCIAL: Cards, Visiting, Incl Business, NEC

David Indus Process PDT Co...............G...... 317 577-0351
   Fishers *(G-3898)*
James Wafford...............................G...... 317 773-7200
   Noblesville *(G-11135)*
Karemar Productions........................G...... 765 766-5117
   Mooreland *(G-10295)*

PRINTING, COMMERCIAL: Decals, NEC

Graphix Unlimited Inc.......................E...... 574 546-3770
   Bremen *(G-1000)*
Mandala Screen Printing Inc................G...... 574 946-6290
   Winamac *(G-14311)*
Maple-Hunter Decals........................G...... 812 894-9759
   Riley *(G-12084)*
Panther Graphics LLC.......................G...... 317 223-3845
   Indianapolis *(G-7650)*
Williams Plastics LLC........................C...... 317 398-1630
   Shelbyville *(G-12585)*

PRINTING, COMMERCIAL: Envelopes, NEC

Stines Printing...............................G...... 260 356-5994
   Huntington *(G-6253)*

PRINTING, COMMERCIAL: Imprinting

Terz Design and Imprinting LLC............G...... 765 965-9762
   Richmond *(G-12063)*

PRINTING, COMMERCIAL: Invitations, NEC

American Stationery Co.....................G...... 765 473-4438
   Peru *(G-11515)*
Cozy Cat Inc.................................G...... 765 463-1254
   Lafayette *(G-8879)*
Phillips Diversified Services................G...... 260 248-2975
   Columbia City *(G-1818)*
Stands Photography.........................G...... 812 723-3922
   Paoli *(G-11457)*

PRINTING, COMMERCIAL: Labels & Seals, NEC

Headlands Ltd...............................G...... 260 426-9884
   Wolcottville *(G-14371)*
Hooven - Dayton Corp.......................E...... 765 935-3999
   Richmond *(G-12000)*
International Label Mfg LLC.................F...... 812 235-5071
   Terre Haute *(G-13258)*
Label Logic Inc..............................E...... 574 266-6007
   Elkhart *(G-2981)*
Label Tech Inc...............................G...... 765 747-1234
   Muncie *(G-10506)*
Lambel Corporation.........................F...... 317 849-6828
   Indianapolis *(G-7377)*
Liberty Book & Bb Manufactures............E...... 317 633-1450
   Indianapolis *(G-7402)*
Matrix Label Systems Inc...................E...... 317 839-1973
   Plainfield *(G-11624)*
Multi-Color Corporation.....................E...... 812 752-0586
   Scottsburg *(G-12375)*
Stranco Inc...................................F...... 219 874-5221
   Michigan City *(G-9848)*

PRINTING, COMMERCIAL: Letterpress & Screen

Graphic22 Inc................................G...... 219 921-5409
   Chesterton *(G-1608)*
Just Ink LLC..................................G...... 800 948-7671
   South Bend *(G-12826)*
Spark Marketing LLC.........................G...... 219 301-0071
   Schererville *(G-12346)*

PRINTING, COMMERCIAL: Literature, Advertising, NEC

Game Face Graphix LLC.....................G...... 317 340-0973
   Camby *(G-1267)*
MPS Indianapolis Inc........................C...... 317 241-2020
   Indianapolis *(G-7552)*
Printwerk Graphics & Design................G...... 219 322-7722
   Dyer *(G-2508)*

PRINTING, COMMERCIAL: Magazines, NEC

Rubenstein LLC..............................G...... 317 946-2752
   Indianapolis *(G-7871)*

PRINTING, COMMERCIAL: Promotional

B-Hive Printing...............................G...... 812 897-3905
   Boonville *(G-908)*
Brenmeer LLC................................G...... 260 267-0249
   Fort Wayne *(G-4120)*
Dimensional Imprinting Inc..................G...... 260 417-0202
   Milton *(G-9987)*
Distinct Images Inc..........................F...... 317 613-4413
   Indianapolis *(G-6744)*
Graphic Fx Inc................................F...... 812 234-0000
   Terre Haute *(G-13243)*
Masco Corporation of Indiana..............D...... 317 848-1812
   Indianapolis *(G-7463)*
Moose Lake Products Co....................F...... 260 432-2768
   Fort Wayne *(G-4480)*
Nielsen Enterprises Inc......................G...... 574 277-3748
   Granger *(G-5427)*
Thoughts Are Things.........................G...... 317 585-8053
   Indianapolis *(G-8069)*
XI Graphics Inc...............................F...... 317 738-3434
   Franklin *(G-4942)*

P
R
O
D
U
C
T

PRINTING, COMMERCIAL: Publications

5 Diamond X..................G....... 574 601-8056
Monticello *(G-10250)*
Achievers Institute LLC..................G....... 812 278-8785
Bedford *(G-527)*
Docutech Document Service..................G....... 219 690-3038
Lowell *(G-9404)*
Gen Enterprises..................G....... 574 498-6777
Tippecanoe *(G-13381)*
Herff Jones Yearbooks..................G....... 717 334-9123
Indianapolis *(G-7094)*
Hoosier Horse Review LLC..................G....... 765 212-1320
Muncie *(G-10491)*
Kelley Pagels Enterprises LLC..................F....... 219 872-8552
Michigan City *(G-9806)*
Offset House Inc..................F....... 317 849-5155
Indianapolis *(G-7612)*
Regal Publications LLC..................G....... 260 693-0698
Churubusco *(G-1656)*
Walkerton Tool & Die Inc..................E....... 574 586-3162
Walkerton *(G-13813)*

PRINTING, COMMERCIAL: Screen

A & M Innovations LLC..................G....... 317 306-6118
Whiteland *(G-14233)*
A Mayes Ing Inc..................G....... 317 925-5777
Indianapolis *(G-6298)*
A Plus Images I N C..................G....... 317 405-8955
Indianapolis *(G-6300)*
Aardvark Graphics..................G....... 574 267-4799
Warsaw *(G-13834)*
Abracadabra Graphics..................G....... 812 336-1971
Bloomington *(G-654)*
Advantex Inc..................G....... 812 339-6479
Bloomington *(G-658)*
After Hours Embroidery..................G....... 812 926-9355
Aurora *(G-368)*
Allsports..................G....... 812 883-3561
Salem *(G-12281)*
Almost Famous Printing..................G....... 219 793-6388
Whiting *(G-14266)*
Andresen Graphic Processors..................F....... 317 291-7071
Brownsburg *(G-1133)*
Apparel Design Group..................G....... 812 339-3355
Bloomington *(G-662)*
Baxter Printing Inc..................G....... 219 923-1999
Highland *(G-6037)*
Big Picture Data Imaging LLC..................G....... 812 235-0202
Terre Haute *(G-13202)*
Bill Baldwins Screenprinting..................G....... 317 881-2712
Greenwood *(G-5670)*
Blue Octopus Printing Company..................G....... 317 247-1997
Indianapolis *(G-6487)*
Blue River Services Inc..................C....... 812 738-2437
Corydon *(G-2090)*
BT Management Inc..................G....... 219 794-9546
Merrillville *(G-9705)*
Business Adventures Inc..................G....... 574 674-9996
Osceola *(G-11371)*
C R Graphics..................G....... 317 881-6192
Greenwood *(G-5673)*
Cause Printing Company..................G....... 765 573-3330
Marion *(G-9516)*
CD Grafix LLC..................G....... 812 945-4443
Clarksville *(G-1675)*
Cdb Screen Printing Inc..................G....... 765 472-4404
Peru *(G-11520)*
Celestial Designs LLC..................G....... 317 733-3110
Zionsville *(G-14425)*
Company Pride Shirts LLC..................G....... 812 526-5700
Edinburgh *(G-2601)*
Cool Cayenne LLC..................G....... 765 282-0977
Muncie *(G-10449)*
Countryside Printing..................G....... 812 486-2454
Montgomery *(G-10218)*
County West Sports..................G....... 317 839-4076
Plainfield *(G-11601)*
Craigs Printing Co..................G....... 812 358-5010
Brownstown *(G-1185)*
Crossing Creations..................G....... 812 587-0212
Columbus *(G-1885)*
Custom Art Screen Printing..................F....... 260 456-3909
Fort Wayne *(G-4193)*
D S E Inc..................E....... 812 376-0310
Columbus *(G-1904)*
Daniel Korb Laundry Company..................D....... 812 425-6121
Evansville *(G-3453)*
Dec-O-Art Inc..................E....... 574 294-6451
Elkhart *(G-2791)*
El Shaddai Inc..................G....... 260 359-9080
Huntington *(G-6203)*
Elegan Graphics..................G....... 219 462-9921
Valparaiso *(G-13533)*
Elengas Customwear..................G....... 317 577-1677
Fishers *(G-3902)*
Embroidme..................G....... 219 465-1400
Valparaiso *(G-13536)*
Evansville Print Specialist..................G....... 812 423-5831
Evansville *(G-3490)*
Excell Color Graphics Inc..................E....... 260 482-2720
Fort Wayne *(G-4251)*
Faith Walkers..................G....... 219 873-1900
Michigan City *(G-9791)*
Freckles Graphics Inc..................F....... 765 448-4692
Lafayette *(G-8900)*
Gd Cox Inc..................G....... 317 398-0035
Shelbyville *(G-12536)*
Gettelfinger Holdings LLC..................G....... 812 923-9065
Floyds Knobs *(G-4012)*
Giraffe X Graphics Inc..................G....... 317 546-4944
Indianapolis *(G-7007)*
Golden Corporation..................F....... 765 423-4366
Lafayette *(G-8908)*
Goose Graphics L L C..................G....... 260 563-4516
Fort Wayne *(G-4301)*
Graphic Visions..................G....... 812 331-7446
Bloomington *(G-733)*
Graphics Lab Uv Printing Inc..................F....... 765 457-5784
Kokomo *(G-8632)*
H M C Screen Printing Inc..................F....... 317 773-8532
Noblesville *(G-11116)*
High End Concepts Inc..................F....... 317 630-9901
Indianapolis *(G-7106)*
Hinen Printing Co..................G....... 260 248-8984
Columbia City *(G-1789)*
Hot Cake..................G....... 317 889-2253
Indianapolis *(G-7132)*
Idenitee..................G....... 317 462-4606
Greenfield *(G-5537)*
IM Impressed..................G....... 219 838-7959
Munster *(G-10609)*
Imagination Graphics..................G....... 812 423-6503
Evansville *(G-3547)*
Imprint It All..................G....... 812 234-0024
Terre Haute *(G-13254)*
Industrial Graphic Design..................G....... 260 856-2110
Cromwell *(G-2209)*
Inner City Sports TS..................G....... 812 402-4143
Evansville *(G-3561)*
J N P Custom Designs Inc..................G....... 317 253-2198
Indianapolis *(G-7289)*
J Tees..................G....... 812 524-9292
Seymour *(G-12460)*
Jer-Maur Corporation..................G....... 812 384-8290
Bloomfield *(G-640)*
Jeremy Parker..................G....... 765 284-5414
Muncie *(G-10501)*
Joans T-Shirt Printing LLC..................G....... 812 934-2616
Batesville *(G-506)*
Keen Screen..................G....... 812 945-5336
New Albany *(G-10812)*
Kennyleeholmescom..................G....... 574 612-2526
Elkhart *(G-2961)*
Kewanna Screen Printing Inc..................G....... 574 653-2683
Kewanna *(G-8526)*
Kirchoff Custom Sports..................G....... 812 434-0355
Evansville *(G-3592)*
Knoy Apparel..................G....... 765 448-1031
Lafayette *(G-8945)*
Leap Frogz Screanprinting EMB..................G....... 317 786-2441
Indianapolis *(G-7390)*
McCormick Printing Impressions..................G....... 765 675-9556
Tipton *(G-13398)*
Midnite Grafix..................G....... 812 386-9430
Princeton *(G-11878)*
Minds Eye Graphics Inc..................F....... 260 724-2050
Decatur *(G-2396)*
Mito-Craft Inc..................G....... 574 287-4555
South Bend *(G-12864)*
Mr BS Sports & Design..................G....... 260 347-4830
Kendallville *(G-8497)*
New Haven Trophies & Shirts..................G....... 260 749-0269
New Haven *(G-10949)*
New Process Graphics LLC..................E....... 260 489-1700
Fort Wayne *(G-4502)*
Nickprint Inc..................G....... 317 489-3033
Carmel *(G-1442)*
Notables..................G....... 765 649-1648
Anderson *(G-146)*
Ooshirts Inc..................G....... 317 246-9083
Indianapolis *(G-7624)*
Outfitter..................G....... 765 289-6456
Muncie *(G-10541)*
Parlor City Trophy & Apparel..................G....... 260 824-0216
Bluffton *(G-884)*
Perdue Printed Products Inc..................G....... 260 456-7575
Fort Wayne *(G-4523)*
Perrys Country Store..................G....... 260 693-0084
Churubusco *(G-1655)*
Pheonix Inc..................G....... 765 489-3030
Hagerstown *(G-5811)*
Phil Irwin Advertising Inc..................F....... 317 547-5117
Indianapolis *(G-7683)*
Photo Screen Service Inc..................G....... 317 636-7712
Indianapolis *(G-7688)*
Photo Specialties..................G....... 812 944-5111
New Albany *(G-10843)*
Plastimatic Arts Corp..................E....... 574 254-9000
Mishawaka *(G-10104)*
Play 2 Win Screenprinting LLC..................G....... 765 426-0679
Oxford *(G-11434)*
Portage Custom Wear LLC..................G....... 219 841-9070
Portage *(G-11788)*
Ppi Acquisition LLC..................F....... 765 674-8627
Marion *(G-9555)*
Printers Express Inc..................G....... 765 348-0069
Hartford City *(G-5988)*
Prn Graphics LLC..................G....... 317 426-3545
Indianapolis *(G-7763)*
Prn Incorporated..................G....... 317 624-4401
Indianapolis *(G-7764)*
Rivera Screenprinting..................G....... 812 663-0816
Burney *(G-1213)*
Romanart Inc..................G....... 219 736-9150
Merrillville *(G-9751)*
Rookies Unlimited Inc..................G....... 765 536-2726
Summitville *(G-13104)*
Sampan Screen Print New Image..................G....... 812 282-8499
Jeffersonville *(G-8422)*
Screen Art Advertising Co Inc..................G....... 260 483-6514
Fort Wayne *(G-4611)*
Screen Print Express Inc..................G....... 765 521-2727
New Castle *(G-10917)*
Screen Printing Super Store..................G....... 317 804-9904
Westfield *(G-14187)*
Screenprint Special Tees LLC..................G....... 317 396-0349
Indianapolis *(G-7906)*
Shirt Shack..................G....... 812 550-0158
Evansville *(G-3726)*
Shirtails..................G....... 812 858-8605
Newburgh *(G-11048)*
Sideline Graphix..................G....... 765 520-9042
New Castle *(G-10918)*
Sir Graphics Inc..................G....... 574 272-9330
Granger *(G-5436)*
South Bend Screen Process Inc..................G....... 574 254-9000
Mishawaka *(G-10133)*
Southwest Grafix and AP Inc..................F....... 812 425-5104
Evansville *(G-3740)*
Sports Screen Impact..................G....... 812 926-9355
Aurora *(G-389)*
Sports Unlimited Printed AP..................G....... 574 772-4239
Knox *(G-8583)*
Spp Inc..................F....... 812 882-6203
Vincennes *(G-13707)*
T Productions Inc..................F....... 574 257-8610
Mishawaka *(G-10139)*
Team Image LLC..................E....... 317 468-0802
Greenfield *(G-5579)*
Team Image LLC..................E....... 317 477-7468
Greenfield *(G-5580)*
Team Pride Athletic AP Corp..................G....... 574 224-8326
Rochester *(G-12156)*
Teeki Hut Custom Tees Inc..................G....... 317 205-3589
Indianapolis *(G-8052)*
Tma Enterprises Inc..................G....... 317 272-0694
Avon *(G-469)*
To a Tee Inc..................F....... 317 757-8842
Indianapolis *(G-8078)*
Topstitch Inc..................F....... 574 293-6633
Elkhart *(G-3220)*
Travis Britton..................G....... 317 762-6018
Indianapolis *(G-8092)*
Unique Graphic Designs Inc..................G....... 574 583-7119
Monticello *(G-10287)*
Valley Screen Process Co Inc..................D....... 574 256-0901
Mishawaka *(G-10144)*
Varsity Sports Inc..................G....... 219 987-7200
Demotte *(G-2451)*

Vickers Graphics Inc ....G...... 765 868-4646
  Kokomo (G-8712)
Warren Printing Services LLC ....F 812 738-6508
  Corydon (G-2115)
Wildman Business Group LLC ....C...... 866 369-1552
  Warsaw (G-13965)
Williams Printing Inc ....G...... 765 468-6033
  Farmland (G-3844)
Wilson Enterprises Inc ....G...... 765 362-1089
  Crawfordsville (G-2205)
X Printwear Inc ....F 812 336-0700
  Bloomington (G-860)
Xtreme Graphics ....G...... 812 989-6948
  Jeffersonville (G-8443)

PRINTING, COMMERCIAL: Stationery, NEC

Behning Inc ....G...... 260 672-2663
  Roanoke (G-12099)

PRINTING, COMMERCIAL: Tickets, NEC

Trinity Cmmnications Group Inc ....G...... 260 484-1029
  Fort Wayne (G-4704)

PRINTING, COMMERCIAL: Wrappers, NEC

Custom Candy Wrappers Company ......G...... 574 247-0756
  Granger (G-5399)
Shadow Graphix Inc ....G...... 317 481-9710
  Indianapolis (G-7922)

PRINTING, LITHOGRAPHIC: Advertising Posters

Advanced Print Solutions LLC ....G...... 513 405-3452
  Brookville (G-1110)
Franklin Barry Gallery ....G...... 317 822-8455
  Indianapolis (G-6959)

PRINTING, LITHOGRAPHIC: Calendars

Kellmark Corporation ....E 574 264-9695
  Elkhart (G-2958)

PRINTING, LITHOGRAPHIC: Calendars & Cards

Tfi Inc ....F 317 290-1333
  Indianapolis (G-8055)
UPS Store 5219 ....G...... 219 750-9597
  Merrillville (G-9760)

PRINTING, LITHOGRAPHIC: Color

Jam Printing Inc ....G...... 765 649-9292
  Anderson (G-125)
Schutte Lithography Inc ....E 812 469-3500
  Evansville (G-3717)
Sycamore Services Inc ....F 317 745-5456
  Avon (G-468)

PRINTING, LITHOGRAPHIC: Decals

Duramark Technologies Inc ....D....... 317 867-5700
  Westfield (G-14161)

PRINTING, LITHOGRAPHIC: Forms & Cards, Business

Almighty Business Cards LLC ....G...... 260 615-4663
  Fort Wayne (G-4063)
Drs Graphix Group Inc ....G...... 317 569-1855
  Indianapolis (G-6768)
Envelope Service Inc ....E 260 432-6277
  Fort Wayne (G-4237)

PRINTING, LITHOGRAPHIC: Forms, Business

Altstadt Business Forms Inc ....F 812 425-3393
  Evansville (G-3349)

PRINTING, LITHOGRAPHIC: Maps

Blue Creek Trail Map Co ....G...... 765 455-9867
  Kokomo (G-8599)
Creative Computer Services ....G....... 317 729-5779
  Franklin (G-4880)

PRINTING, LITHOGRAPHIC: Menus

Graphic Menus Inc ....F 765 396-3003
  Eaton (G-2584)

PRINTING, LITHOGRAPHIC: Offset & photolithographic printing

B-Hive Printing ....G...... 812 897-3905
  Boonville (G-908)
Creative Concept Ventures Inc ....G...... 812 282-9442
  Jeffersonville (G-8348)
Humphrey Printing Company Inc ....F 765 452-0093
  Crown Point (G-2259)
Image Group Inc ....E 574 457-3111
  Syracuse (G-13135)
Rink Printing Company Inc ....E 574 232-7935
  South Bend (G-12916)

PRINTING, LITHOGRAPHIC: On Metal

Bowen Printing Inc ....G...... 574 936-3924
  Plymouth (G-11670)
Brand Prtg & Photo-Litho Co ....G...... 317 921-4095
  Indianapolis (G-6503)
Printing Emporium Inc ....G...... 574 256-0059
  Mishawaka (G-10109)
Service Graphics Inc ....D...... 317 471-8246
  Indianapolis (G-7917)

PRINTING, LITHOGRAPHIC: Post Cards, Picture

Charles E Watts ....G...... 812 547-8516
  Tell City (G-13158)

PRINTING, LITHOGRAPHIC: Posters & Decals

Image House Inc ....F 219 947-0800
  Crown Point (G-2260)
Moan Racing Products LLC ....G...... 317 644-3100
  Greenfield (G-5556)

PRINTING, LITHOGRAPHIC: Transfers, Decalcomania Or Dry

Business Art & Design Inc ....G...... 317 782-9108
  Beech Grove (G-593)
Springhill Wholesale Inc ....E 812 299-2181
  Terre Haute (G-13342)

PRINTING: Books

Augustin Prtg & Design Svcs ....G...... 765 966-7130
  Richmond (G-11957)
RR Donnelley & Sons Company ....A...... 765 362-1300
  Crawfordsville (G-2194)
Wayseeker LLC ....G...... 574 529-0199
  Syracuse (G-13153)

PRINTING: Books

Collier Pubg & Consulting ....E 317 513-8176
  Indianapolis (G-6632)
Courier Kendallville Inc ....E 260 347-3044
  Kendallville (G-8469)
Graessle-Mercer Co ....E 812 522-5478
  Seymour (G-12451)
Herff Jones LLC ....E 317 612-3400
  Indianapolis (G-7089)
Lsc Communications Inc ....G...... 812 234-1585
  Terre Haute (G-13276)
Lsc Communications Us LLC ....G...... 765 362-1300
  Crawfordsville (G-2169)
Mitchell-Fleming Printing Inc ....F 317 462-5467
  Greenfield (G-5554)
Priority Printing LLC ....G...... 317 241-4234
  Indianapolis (G-7761)

PRINTING: Broadwoven Fabrics. Cotton

Graphic22 Inc ....G...... 219 921-5409
  Chesterton (G-1608)

PRINTING: Checkbooks

Clarke American Checks Inc ....C...... 812 283-9598
  Jeffersonville (G-8338)
Deluxe Homes ....G...... 219 256-1701
  Westville (G-14215)

Writeguard Business Systems ....G...... 317 849-7292
  Indianapolis (G-8219)

PRINTING: Commercial, NEC

A & E Screen Printing ....G...... 574 875-4488
  Elkhart (G-2655)
Acclaim Graphics Inc ....G...... 812 424-5035
  Evansville (G-3334)
Accuprint of Kentuckiana Inc ....G...... 812 944-8603
  New Albany (G-10740)
Adams Smith ....G...... 219 661-2812
  Crown Point (G-2222)
Altstadt Business Forms Inc ....F 812 425-3393
  Evansville (G-3349)
American Printing Indiana LLC ....E 765 825-7600
  Anderson (G-64)
American Reprographics Co LLC ....G...... 574 287-2944
  South Bend (G-12705)
American Veteran Group LLC ....G...... 317 600-4749
  Westfield (G-14136)
Anthony Wayne Rehabilitation C ....E 317 972-1000
  Indianapolis (G-6403)
Bartel Printing Company Inc ....G...... 574 267-7421
  Warsaw (G-13842)
Bell Graphics and Design LLC ....G...... 765 827-5441
  Connersville (G-2040)
Bennett Printing ....G...... 812 966-2917
  Medora (G-9680)
Bev Can Printers Llc ....G...... 219 617-6181
  La Porte (G-8738)
Bex Screen Printing Inc ....G...... 317 791-0375
  Indianapolis (G-6470)
Bloomington Discount Prtg Inc ....G...... 812 332-9789
  Bloomington (G-688)
Blue River Printing Inc ....G...... 317 392-3676
  Shelbyville (G-12521)
Bm Creations Inc ....G...... 219 922-8935
  Griffith (G-5767)
Brand Prtg & Photo-Litho Co ....G...... 317 921-4095
  Indianapolis (G-6503)
Bredensteiner & Assoc Inc ....G...... 317 921-2226
  Indianapolis (G-6505)
C E M Printing & Specialities ....G...... 269 684-6898
  South Bend (G-12730)
Ccmp Inc ....E 219 922-8935
  Griffith (G-5769)
Clarke American Checks Inc ....G...... 812 283-9598
  Jeffersonville (G-8340)
Clarke American Checks Inc ....C...... 812 283-9598
  Jeffersonville (G-8339)
Classic Graphics Inc ....F 260 482-3487
  Fort Wayne (G-4156)
Clondalkin Pharma & Healthcare ....C...... 317 328-7355
  Indianapolis (G-6623)
Clover Printing LLC ....G...... 260 657-3003
  Harlan (G-5968)
Coaches Connection Inc ....G...... 260 356-0400
  Huntington (G-6198)
Consolidated Printing Svcs Inc ....F 765 468-6033
  Farmland (G-3841)
Courier Printing Co Allen Cnty ....G...... 260 627-2728
  Grabill (G-5362)
Courier-Times Inc ....D...... 765 529-1111
  New Castle (G-10897)
Crider Holcomb Partnership LLC ....G...... 812 279-2200
  Bedford (G-536)
Criterion Press Inc ....F 317 236-1570
  Indianapolis (G-6693)
Cs Kern Inc ....E 765 289-8600
  Muncie (G-10451)
Custom Packaging Inc ....F 317 876-9559
  Indianapolis (G-6717)
D-J Printing Specialists Inc ....G...... 219 465-1164
  Valparaiso (G-13527)
Dance World Bazaar Corporation ....G...... 812 663-7679
  Greensburg (G-5598)
Design Media Connections LLC ....G...... 317 819-2022
  Indianapolis (G-6735)
Doerr Printing Co ....G...... 317 568-0135
  Indianapolis (G-6756)
Dog Ear Publishing ....G...... 317 228-3656
  Indianapolis (G-6757)
Douglas P Terrell ....G...... 812 254-1976
  Washington (G-13981)
E James Dant ....G...... 812 476-2271
  Evansville (G-3468)
E James Dant ....G...... 812 476-2271
  Evansville (G-3469)
Ed Sons Inc ....F 317 897-8821
  Indianapolis (G-6803)

PRODUCT

Ewing Printing Company Inc ....F 812 882-2415
  Vincennes (G-13677)
F Robert Gardner Co Inc ....G 317 634-2333
  Indianapolis (G-6900)
Faulkenberg Printing Co Inc ....F 317 638-1359
  Franklin (G-4886)
Fedex Office & Print Svcs Inc ....G 219 462-6270
  Valparaiso (G-13542)
Fedex Office & Print Svcs Inc ....G 317 839-3896
  Plainfield (G-11609)
Fedex Office & Print Svcs Inc ....F 317 251-2406
  Indianapolis (G-6914)
First Class Printing ....G 317 808-2222
  Indianapolis (G-6925)
Fiserv Inc ....B 317 576-6700
  Indianapolis (G-6929)
Fort Wayne Newspapers Inc ....B 260 461-8444
  Fort Wayne (G-4277)
Full Color Direct LLC ....G 317 538-4500
  Indianapolis (G-6968)
Goldleaf Promotional Products ....G 317 202-2754
  Indianapolis (G-7022)
Graphic Menus Inc ....F 765 396-3003
  Eaton (G-2584)
Graphic Ventures Inc ....G 812 288-6093
  Clarksville (G-1683)
Greensburg Printing Co Inc ....G 812 663-8265
  Greensburg (G-5604)
Harcourt Industries Inc ....E 765 629-2625
  Milroy (G-9980)
HI Tech Label Inc ....F 765 659-1800
  Frankfort (G-4836)
Hiatt Enterprises Inc ....G 765 289-2700
  Muncie (G-10488)
Hoosier Printing Co Inc ....G 219 836-8877
  Munster (G-10606)
Hot Off Press ....G 317 253-5987
  Indianapolis (G-7133)
J Y Design & Print Inc ....G 260 357-3759
  Garrett (G-5014)
Jac Jmr Inc ....G 219 663-6700
  Crown Point (G-2264)
Jam Graphics Inc ....G 317 896-5662
  Noblesville (G-11134)
JB Graphics Inc. ....G 317 819-0008
  Carmel (G-1419)
JC Printing & Mailing ....G 765 742-6829
  Colburn (G-1752)
Jones & Webb Associates Inc ....G 317 236-9755
  Indianapolis (G-7311)
Journal and Chronicle Inc ....G 812 752-5060
  Scottsburg (G-12370)
Jt Printing LLC ....G 317 271-7700
  Avon (G-451)
Kays Graphics Inc. ....G 317 236-9755
  Indianapolis (G-7335)
Keefer Graphic Imaging Inc ....G 260 426-7500
  Columbia City (G-1803)
Kingery Group Inc. ....E 317 823-9585
  Indianapolis (G-7354)
L & L Press Inc ....G 765 664-3162
  Marion (G-9541)
L C Typesetting Company Inc ....G 574 232-4700
  South Bend (G-12834)
La Grange Publishing Co Inc ....F 260 463-3243
  Lagrange (G-9052)
Laconia Laser Engraving ....G 812 786-3641
  Laconia (G-8837)
Languell Printing Inc ....G 317 889-3545
  Greenwood (G-5717)
Largus Speedy Print Corp ....E 219 922-8414
  Munster (G-10612)
Leader Publishing Co of Salem ....E 812 883-4446
  Salem (G-12299)
Lee Publications Inc ....D 219 933-9251
  Munster (G-10614)
Light & Ink Corp ....G 812 421-1400
  Evansville (G-3602)
Lightning Printing ....G 765 362-5999
  Crawfordsville (G-2168)
Lincoln Printing Corporation ....E 260 424-5200
  Fort Wayne (G-4437)
M Nelson & Associates Inc ....G 317 228-1422
  Carmel (G-1430)
Marie S Embroidery ....G 219 931-2561
  Hammond (G-5912)
Marketing Services Group Inc ....B 317 381-2268
  Indianapolis (G-7456)
Matrix Photo Laboratories Inc ....F 317 635-4756
  Indianapolis (G-7467)

Midwest Graphics Inc ....E 317 780-4600
  Indianapolis (G-7506)
Minuteman Press ....G 317 209-1677
  Indianapolis (G-7525)
MPS Printing Inc ....G 812 273-4446
  Madison (G-9489)
Multi Packaging Solutions Inc ....B 317 241-2020
  Indianapolis (G-7558)
Multi-Color Corporation ....C 812 752-3187
  Scottsburg (G-12376)
News Publishing Company LLC ....G 812 838-4811
  Mount Vernon (G-10404)
Nicholls Printing ....G 574 233-1388
  South Bend (G-12875)
Npp Packaging Graphics ....G 317 522-2010
  Zionsville (G-14453)
Nussmeier Engraving Co ....E 812 425-1339
  Evansville (G-3650)
Offset One Inc ....F 260 456-8828
  Fort Wayne (G-4509)
Omnisource Marketing Group Inc ....E 317 575-3300
  Indianapolis (G-7620)
P413 Corporation ....G 317 769-0679
  Zionsville (G-14454)
Pengad/West Inc ....E 765 286-3000
  Muncie (G-10544)
Pentzer Printing Inc ....F 812 372-2896
  Columbus (G-1992)
Perfect Plastic Printing Corp ....G 317 888-9447
  Greenwood (G-5731)
Pierce Oil Co Inc ....F 812 268-6356
  Sullivan (G-13090)
Planks Printing Service Inc ....G 574 533-1739
  Goshen (G-5309)
Pratt Visual Solutions Company ....E 800 428-7728
  Indianapolis (G-7720)
Precision Label Incorporated ....F 812 877-3811
  Terre Haute (G-13308)
Preferred Enterprises Inc ....G 765 457-0637
  Kokomo (G-8684)
Premier Printing ....G 765 459-8339
  Kokomo (G-8685)
Premiere Advertising ....G 317 722-2400
  Indianapolis (G-7742)
Presstime Graphics Inc ....E 812 234-3815
  Terre Haute (G-13309)
Prince Manufacturing Corp ....E 260 357-4484
  Garrett (G-5020)
Printing Place Inc-Photos Plus ....F 260 665-8444
  Angola (G-239)
Printing Services Inc ....G 317 300-0363
  Indianapolis (G-7757)
Printpack Inc ....B 812 663-5091
  Greensburg (G-5629)
Priority Press Inc ....E 317 241-4234
  Indianapolis (G-7759)
Priority Press Inc ....G 317 240-0103
  Indianapolis (G-7760)
Priority Press Inc ....G 317 848-9695
  Indianapolis (G-6278)
Professional Print Brokers ....E 260 824-2328
  Bluffton (G-888)
Progressive Printing Co Inc ....G 765 653-3814
  Greencastle (G-5475)
Quality Imagination Corp ....G 317 753-0042
  Indianapolis (G-7797)
Quality Printing of NW Ind ....G 219 322-6677
  Schererville (G-12343)
R & B Fine Printing Inc ....G 219 365-9490
  Saint John (G-12268)
R R Donnelley & Sons Company ....A 574 267-7101
  Warsaw (G-13931)
R R Donnelley & Sons Company ....G 812 523-1800
  Seymour (G-12478)
Rayco Marketing ....G 574 293-8416
  Elkhart (G-3139)
Raymond Little Print Shop ....G 317 246-9083
  Indianapolis (G-7820)
Reprocomm Inc ....E 765 472-5700
  Peru (G-11544)
Republic Etching Carving ....G 812 366-8111
  New Salisbury (G-11010)
Rogers Marketing & Printing ....G 317 838-7203
  Avon (G-465)
Rowland Printing Co Inc ....F 317 773-1829
  Noblesville (G-11177)
Schutte Lithography Inc ....G 812 469-3500
  Evansville (G-3717)
Selby Publishing & Printing ....G 765 453-5417
  Kokomo (G-8693)

Service Graphics Inc ....D 317 471-8246
  Indianapolis (G-7917)
Shadow Custom Graphics ....G 317 481-9710
  Indianapolis (G-7921)
Shaughnessy-Kniep-Hawe-paper ....E 317 837-7041
  Plainfield (G-11643)
Sonoco Products Company ....C 812 526-5511
  Edinburgh (G-2629)
Spectrum ....G 812 923-7830
  Georgetown (G-5153)
Spectrum ....G 812 941-6899
  New Albany (G-10865)
Spencer Evening World ....G 765 795-4438
  Cloverdale (G-1738)
Stafford Construction Inc ....G 574 287-9696
  South Bend (G-12952)
Stage Door Graphics ....G 317 398-9011
  Shelbyville (G-12571)
Stamprint Inc ....G 574 233-3900
  South Bend (G-12953)
Standout Creations LLC ....G 765 203-9110
  Anderson (G-170)
Stoffel Seals Corporation ....E 845 353-3800
  Angola (G-248)
Storm Graphics Inc ....G 812 402-5202
  Evansville (G-3753)
Studio Printers ....G 574 772-0900
  Knox (G-8585)
Stump Printing Co Inc ....C 260 723-5171
  South Whitley (G-13006)
Syzygy Media Inc ....G 317 509-8987
  McCordsville (G-9677)
T N D Printing ....G 260 493-4949
  New Haven (G-10960)
Tabco Business Forms Inc ....G 812 882-2836
  Vincennes (G-13709)
Tc Printing & More LLC ....G 812 936-3069
  West Baden Springs (G-14036)
Thomas E Slade Inc ....F 812 471-7100
  Evansville (G-3760)
Tko Enterprises Inc. ....D 317 271-1398
  Plainfield (G-11647)
Trademark Screen Printing ....G 317 885-3258
  Greenwood (G-5755)
Trident Engraving Inc ....G 812 282-2098
  Jeffersonville (G-8435)
Triple Crown Media LLC ....D 574 533-2151
  Goshen (G-5342)
Un Communications Group Inc ....E 317 844-8622
  Carmel (G-1503)
V & P Printing ....G 260 495-3741
  Fremont (G-4978)
Vinyl Creator ....G 260 318-5133
  Wolcottville (G-14377)
W Robbins & Sons Inc ....G 765 522-1736
  Roachdale (G-12096)
WAr - LLC- Westville Prtg ....G 219 785-2821
  Westville (G-14221)
Whitewater Publications Inc ....E 765 647-4221
  Brookville (G-1131)
Wise Business Forms Inc ....C 260 489-1561
  Fort Wayne (G-4759)
Woodburn Graphics Inc ....E 812 232-0323
  Terre Haute (G-13371)
Woodfield Printing Inc. ....G 317 848-2000
  Indianapolis (G-6283)
Writeguard Business Systems ....G 317 849-7292
  Indianapolis (G-8219)

PRINTING: Engraving & Plate

Its Personal Laser Engraving ....G 812 934-6657
  Batesville (G-505)
Shakour Industries Inc ....G 574 289-0100
  South Bend (G-12932)

PRINTING: Flexographic

Accu-Label Inc ....E 260 482-5223
  Fort Wayne (G-4036)
Premier Label Company Inc ....F 765 289-5000
  Muncie (G-10548)
Tranter Graphics Inc ....D 574 834-2626
  Syracuse (G-13151)
Useful Products LLC ....E 877 304-9036
  Goodland (G-5161)
Waterloo Press Inc ....G 260 837-3781
  Waterloo (G-14025)

PRINTING: Gravure, Business Form & Card

A & H Enterprises LLC ....G..... 317 398-3070
Shelbyville (G-12517)

Mid America Coop Education ....G..... 317 726-6910
Indianapolis (G-7502)

PRINTING: Gravure, Forms, Business

Viking Business Products Inc ....G..... 260 489-7787
Fort Wayne (G-4727)

PRINTING: Gravure, Imprinting

Goon Jonn ....G..... 574 306-2927
Warsaw (G-13882)

PRINTING: Gravure, Job

Acclaim Graphics Inc ....G..... 812 424-5035
Evansville (G-3334)

PRINTING: Gravure, Labels

Data Label Inc ....C..... 812 232-0408
Terre Haute (G-13223)

Gary Printing Inc ....G..... 219 886-1767
Gary (G-5052)

PRINTING: Gravure, Rotogravure

Classic Media LLC ....G..... 260 482-3487
Fort Wayne (G-4157)

Edward ONeil Associates ....G..... 317 244-5400
Indianapolis (G-6810)

Gulsad Inc ....G..... 317 541-1940
Indianapolis (G-7059)

Multi-Color Corporation ....C..... 812 752-3187
Scottsburg (G-12376)

Multi-Color Corporation ....E..... 812 752-0586
Scottsburg (G-12375)

Proedge Inc ....E..... 219 552-9550
Shelby (G-12515)

Stien Designs & Graphics Inc ....G..... 260 347-9136
Kendallville (G-8511)

PRINTING: Gravure, Stationery & Invitation

Nussmeier Engraving Co ....E..... 812 425-1339
Evansville (G-3650)

Scott Culbertson ....G..... 260 357-6430
Garrett (G-5022)

Westwood Paper Co ....G..... 317 843-1212
Carmel (G-1509)

PRINTING: Intaglio

Enterprise Marking Pdts Inc ....E..... 317 867-7600
Fishers (G-3906)

PRINTING: Laser

Lamco Finishers Inc ....E..... 317 471-1010
Indianapolis (G-7379)

Laser Marking Technologies ....G..... 812 852-7999
Osgood (G-11392)

Prototype Systems Inc ....E..... 317 634-3040
Carmel (G-1458)

Shakour Industries Inc ....G..... 574 289-0100
South Bend (G-12932)

Simplified Imaging LLC ....G..... 219 663-5122
Crown Point (G-2305)

PRINTING: Letterpress

Anchor Enterprises ....G..... 812 282-7220
Jeffersonville (G-8326)

Apollo Prtg & Graphics Ctr Inc ....E..... 574 287-3707
South Bend (G-12709)

Burkert-Walton Inc ....G..... 812 425-7157
Evansville (G-3405)

Campbell Printing Co Inc ....G..... 219 866-5913
Rensselaer (G-11916)

Cecils Printing & Office Sups ....G..... 812 683-4416
Huntingburg (G-6153)

Commercial Print Shop Inc ....G..... 260 724-3722
Decatur (G-2373)

Fehring F N & Son Printers ....G..... 219 933-0439
Hammond (G-5879)

Harmony Press Inc ....E..... 800 525-3742
Bourbon (G-943)

Hartley J Company Inc ....G..... 812 376-9708
Columbus (G-1938)

Haywood Printing Co Inc ....E..... 765 742-4085
Lafayette (G-8912)

Highway Press Inc ....G..... 812 283-6462
Jeffersonville (G-8374)

Hoosier Jiffy Print ....G..... 260 563-8715
Wabash (G-13731)

Indiana Letterpress LLC ....G..... 574 967-0154
Flora (G-3997)

Keefer Printing Company Inc ....E..... 260 424-4543
Fort Wayne (G-4405)

Kissel Printers Inc ....G..... 812 424-5333
Evansville (G-3593)

Kozs Quality Printing Inc ....G..... 219 696-6711
Lowell (G-9412)

Little Cricket Letterpress ....G..... 317 762-2044
Winona Lake (G-14351)

Maco Press Inc ....G..... 317 846-5754
Carmel (G-1432)

Mooney Copy Service Inc ....G..... 812 423-6626
Evansville (G-3635)

Mossberg & Company Inc ....C..... 574 289-9253
South Bend (G-12865)

Overgaards Artcraft Printers ....G..... 574 234-8464
South Bend (G-12885)

Paragon Printing Center Inc ....G..... 574 533-5835
Goshen (G-5306)

Paramount Printing Ltd Inc ....G..... 219 980-0445
Gary (G-5083)

Pearson Printing Company ....G..... 765 664-8769
Marion (G-9551)

Printcrafters Inc ....G..... 812 838-4106
Mount Vernon (G-10405)

Printing Partners Inc ....D..... 317 635-2282
Indianapolis (G-7755)

Rink Printing Company Inc ....E..... 574 232-7935
South Bend (G-12916)

Tatman Inc ....E..... 765 825-2164
Connersville (G-2075)

TEC Photography ....G..... 812 332-9847
Bloomington (G-836)

Tippecanoe Press Inc ....F..... 317 392-1207
Shelbyville (G-12576)

Town & Country Press Inc ....F..... 574 936-9505
Plymouth (G-11730)

Tribune Showprint Inc ....G..... 574 943-3281
Earl Park (G-2513)

Wayne Press Incorporated ....G..... 260 744-3022
Fort Wayne (G-4743)

Wilson Printing ....G..... 317 745-5868
Danville (G-2358)

PRINTING: Lithographic

2fresh Prints LLC ....G..... 317 947-7164
Indianapolis (G-6286)

2sweet Printing Service LLC ....G..... 317 476-4402
Indianapolis (G-6287)

3d Printing & Prototyping LLC ....G..... 317 319-8515
Greenwood (G-5657)

A&A Screen Printing ....G..... 765 473-8783
Peru (G-11514)

Accent Complex Inc ....G..... 574 522-2368
Elkhart (G-2664)

Acclaim Graphics Inc ....G..... 812 424-5035
Evansville (G-3334)

Accu-Label Inc ....E..... 260 482-5223
Fort Wayne (G-4036)

Ace Screen Printing LLC ....G..... 317 861-7477
New Palestine (G-10965)

Ad Craft Printers Incorporated ....G..... 219 942-9799
Merrillville (G-9692)

Ad Plex-Rhodes Inc ....G..... 812 256-3396
Charlestown (G-1556)

Affordable Footwear & T-Shrt ....G..... 260 702-5134
Fort Wayne (G-4049)

Affordable Screen Printing EMB ......G..... 574 278-7885
Monticello (G-10252)

Ah Printing Service ....G..... 219 933-7686
Hammond (G-5837)

Aim Media Indiana Oper LLC ....E..... 317 736-7101
Franklin (G-4863)

Aim Media Indiana Oper LLC ....E..... 317 462-5528
Greenfield (G-5497)

Aleph Bet Document Centre ....G..... 260 749-2288
New Haven (G-10927)

All American Screen Prtg LLC ....G..... 765 914-7600
Hagerstown (G-5802)

All Printing and Publications ....E..... 260 636-2727
Albion (G-15)

American Express Travel ....C..... 812 523-0106
Seymour (G-12430)

American Intl Mfg Slutions LLP ....G..... 317 443-5778
Carmel (G-1310)

Anchor Enterprises ....G..... 812 282-7220
Jeffersonville (G-8326)

Angies Printing LLC ....G..... 765 966-6237
Richmond (G-11953)

Anyprint LLC ....G..... 317 402-5979
Zionsville (G-14417)

Apparel Design Group ....G..... 812 339-3355
Bloomington (G-662)

Apple Press Inc ....G..... 317 253-7752
Indianapolis (G-6409)

Avalon Enterprises Inc ....G..... 317 894-8666
Indianapolis (G-6448)

Beast Custom Athletic Printing ....G..... 765 610-6802
Fairmount (G-3830)

Benitos Printing ....G..... 812 282-4855
Jeffersonville (G-8329)

Biela Printing ....G..... 219 874-8094
Michigan City (G-9768)

Bills Printing ....G..... 765 962-7674
Richmond (G-11966)

Bizcard ....G..... 317 436-8649
Indianapolis (G-6480)

Bloomington Discount Prtg Inc ....G..... 812 332-9789
Bloomington (G-688)

Blue Print Specialties Inc ....G..... 765 742-6976
Lafayette (G-8862)

Brand Wave Inc ....G..... 661 414-2115
Noblesville (G-11069)

Bright Corp ....G..... 765 642-3114
Anderson (G-77)

Browns Simply Printings ....G..... 317 490-7493
Mooresville (G-10303)

Bryson C Toothaker ....G..... 219 462-9179
Valparaiso (G-13516)

C B Printing ....G..... 765 569-0900
Rockville (G-12174)

Casino Printing For Less ....G..... 765 742-0000
Lafayette (G-8869)

Cause Printing Company ....G..... 260 224-3515
Huntington (G-6197)

Cave Company Printing Inc ....G..... 812 863-4333
Bloomfield (G-637)

Chameleon Lifestyles LLC ....G..... 317 468-3246
Greenfield (G-5514)

Chicago Color Graphics ....G..... 312 856-1433
Hammond (G-5860)

Ckmt Associates Inc ....E..... 219 924-2820
Hammond (G-5863)

Clarke American Checks Inc ....C..... 812 283-9598
Jeffersonville (G-8339)

Cnhi LLC ....E..... 812 944-6481
New Albany (G-10762)

Coaches Connection Inc ....G..... 260 356-0400
Huntington (G-6198)

Colormax Digital Imaging Inc ....E..... 812 477-3805
Evansville (G-3422)

Community Holdings Indiana Inc .....F..... 574 722-5000
Logansport (G-9332)

Community Holdings Indiana Inc .....G..... 765 482-4650
Lebanon (G-9175)

Community Holdings Indiana Inc .....F..... 765 459-3121
Kokomo (G-8608)

Community Holdings Indiana Inc .....E..... 812 663-3111
Greensburg (G-5594)

Copy Solutions Inc ....G..... 260 436-2679
Fort Wayne (G-4175)

Cornerstone Business Prtg LLC ....G..... 574 642-4060
Middlebury (G-9877)

Courier Communications LLC ....B..... 260 347-3044
Kendallville (G-8468)

Courier Printing Co Allen Cnty ....G..... 260 627-2728
Grabill (G-5362)

Craigs Printing Co ....G..... 812 358-5010
Brownstown (G-1185)

Creative Impressions Inc ....F..... 317 244-9842
Indianapolis (G-6687)

Crescendo Inc ....G..... 812 829-4759
Spencer (G-13022)

Crossroads Imprints Inc ....G..... 765 482-2931
Lebanon (G-9177)

Damalak Printing Inc ....G..... 317 896-5337
Westfield (G-14156)

Delp Printing & Mailing Inc ....E..... 317 872-9744
Indianapolis (G-6733)

Delphos Herald of Indiana Inc ....E..... 812 537-0063
Lawrenceburg (G-9138)

Digital Reprographics Inc ....G..... 260 483-8066
Fort Wayne (G-4210)

Employee Codes: A=Over 500 employees, B=251-500
C=101-250, D=51-100, E=20-50, F=10-19, G=2-9

2018 Harris Indiana
Industrial Directory

1053

PRODUCT

Dirty Squeegee Screen Prtg LLC	G	574 358-0003	
Middlebury (G-9882)			
Dla Document Services	G	812 854-1465	
Crane (G-2125)			
Don Michiel Prints LLC	G	812 550-7767	
Evansville (G-3461)			
Dove Printing Services	G	317 843-8222	
Indianapolis (G-6761)			
Duneland Specialties Inc	G	219 464-1616	
Valparaiso (G-13530)			
E James Dant	G	812 476-2271	
Evansville (G-3469)			
Em Printing & Embroidery LLC	G	812 373-0082	
Columbus (G-1919)			
Et Printing	G	317 219-7966	
Noblesville (G-11101)			
Evansville Print Specialist	G	812 423-5831	
Evansville (G-3490)			
Excel Business Printing Inc	G	317 259-1075	
Indianapolis (G-6891)			
Excell Color Graphics Inc	E	260 482-2720	
Fort Wayne (G-4251)			
Express Impressions Prtg LLC	G	765 966-2679	
Richmond (G-11985)			
Extreme Quality Prints	G	812 987-7617	
New Albany (G-10774)			
Fanstand Prints	G	317 579-9413	
Fishers (G-3911)			
Faris Mailing Inc	F	317 246-3315	
Indianapolis (G-6905)			
Fedex Office & Print Svcs Inc	E	317 631-6862	
Indianapolis (G-6908)			
Fedex Office & Print Svcs Inc	F	317 974-0378	
Indianapolis (G-6909)			
Fedex Office & Print Svcs Inc	F	317 917-1529	
Indianapolis (G-6910)			
Fedex Office & Print Svcs Inc	F	765 449-4950	
Lafayette (G-8897)			
Firehouse Printing LLC	G	812 547-3109	
Tell City (G-13162)			
Fiserv Inc	B	317 576-6700	
Indianapolis (G-6929)			
Forget ME Not Printing Ltd	G	317 508-7401	
Indianapolis (G-6950)			
Four Star Printing	G	765 620-9728	
Frankton (G-4943)			
Four Star Screen Printing LLC	G	765 533-3006	
New Castle (G-10902)			
Friends of Third World Inc	G	260 422-6821	
Fort Wayne (G-4288)			
Froggy Print LLC	G	317 965-7954	
Bloomington (G-728)			
Gannett Co Inc	C	765 423-5512	
Lafayette (G-8902)			
Giles Agency Incorporated	G	317 842-5546	
Indianapolis (G-7005)			
Go Print LLC	G	765 778-1111	
Pendleton (G-11490)			
Goatee Shirt Printing	G	219 916-2443	
Valparaiso (G-13550)			
Goodprint LLC	G	201 926-0133	
Indianapolis (G-7025)			
Grace Amazing Graphics	G	812 737-2841	
Laconia (G-8836)			
Grace Digital Printing	G	317 903-6172	
Indianapolis (G-7032)			
Gracies Paw Prints	G	317 910-9969	
Fishers (G-3918)			
Granger Gazette	G	574 277-2679	
Granger (G-5410)			
Graphic Expressions	G	219 663-2085	
Merrillville (G-9717)			
Graphic Expressions Inc	G	317 577-9622	
Fishers (G-3919)			
Graphic Packaging Intl Inc	E	812 948-1608	
New Albany (G-10790)			
Gryphon Print Studio	G	574 514-1644	
South Bend (G-12791)			
Hatch Prints	G	312 952-1908	
South Bend (G-12794)			
Hennessey Montage Prints	G	317 841-7562	
Carmel (G-1402)			
Herff Jones LLC	E	317 612-3400	
Indianapolis (G-7089)			
Hiatt Enterprises Inc	G	765 289-2700	
Muncie (G-10488)			
Hiatt Enterprises Inc	E	765 289-7756	
Muncie (G-10487)			
Hinen Printing Co	G	260 248-8984	
Columbia City (G-1789)			
Hoffman Quality Graphics	G	574 223-5738	
Rochester (G-12128)			
Home News Enterprises LLC	E	812 342-1056	
Columbus (G-1940)			
Hoosier Times Inc	E	812 275-3372	
Bedford (G-548)			
Hoosier Times Inc	C	812 331-4270	
Bloomington (G-741)			
Humphrey Printing Co	G	317 241-6049	
Indianapolis (G-7144)			
Ijs Custom Printing LLC	G	219 769-2050	
Merrillville (G-9721)			
Impressions LLC	G	765 490-2575	
Lafayette (G-8920)			
Impressive Printing	G	812 913-1101	
New Albany (G-10804)			
In-Print	G	219 956-3001	
Wheatfield (G-14225)			
Indiana Newspapers LLC	A	317 444-4000	
Indianapolis (G-7186)			
Indiana Newspapers LLC	D	812 886-9955	
Vincennes (G-13685)			
Indy Color Printing LLC	G	317 371-8829	
Indianapolis (G-7213)			
Infinity Printing Promoti	G	317 332-4811	
Fishers (G-3930)			
Ink Well Business Center	G	812 476-9147	
Evansville (G-3560)			
Inkme LLC	G	574 520-1203	
Osceola (G-11378)			
Inline Shirt Printing LLC	G	765 647-6356	
Brookville (G-1118)			
Innerprint Inc	G	317 509-6511	
McCordsville (G-9670)			
Instant Auto Finance Inc	G	260 483-9000	
Fort Wayne (G-4374)			
Instant Memorabilia Inc	G	219 661-8942	
Crown Point (G-2263)			
Instant Rain Irrigation LLC	G	260 336-1237	
Shipshewana (G-12618)			
Instant Refund Tax Service	G	317 536-1689	
Indianapolis (G-7243)			
Instant Warehouse	G	765 342-3430	
Martinsville (G-9616)			
Insty-Prints	G	317 788-1504	
Indianapolis (G-7245)			
J&J Sprts Screen Prtg Sprit Wr	G	812 909-2686	
Evansville (G-3570)			
J4 Printing LLC	G	260 417-5382	
Fort Wayne (G-4389)			
Jackson Group Inc	C	317 791-9000	
Indianapolis (G-7294)			
James J Maginot Printing	G	219 836-5692	
Munster (G-10611)			
JC Printing	G	574 721-9000	
Logansport (G-9343)			
Jk Graphics Inc	G	219 374-5930	
Cedar Lake (G-1531)			
Journal and Chronicle Inc	G	812 752-5060	
Scottsburg (G-12370)			
K Irpcheadstart Program	G	219 345-2011	
Demotte (G-2440)			
K2m Printing	G	812 623-3040	
Sunman (G-13113)			
Kankakee Valley Publishing Co	C	219 866-5111	
Rensselaer (G-11930)			
Kasting Printing Service	G	317 881-9411	
Indianapolis (G-7334)			
Kc Designs	G	812 876-4020	
Bloomington (G-757)			
Kile Enterprises Inc	F	317 844-6629	
Carmel (G-1423)			
Kinkos Inc	G	765 449-4950	
Lafayette (G-8939)			
Kpc Media Group Inc	C	260 347-0400	
Kendallville (G-8488)			
Kpc Media Group Inc	E	260 426-2640	
Fort Wayne (G-4415)			
La Grange Publishing Co Inc	F	260 463-3243	
Lagrange (G-9052)			
Lagwana Printing Inc	E	260 463-4901	
Lagrange (G-9054)			
Langley Fine Art Prints	G	219 872-0087	
Long Beach (G-9378)			
LAp Cstm EMB Grment Prtg LLC	G	260 782-0762	
Wabash (G-13733)			
Legacy Screen Printing Promoti	G	219 262-4000	
Chesterton (G-1618)			
Legacy Screen Prtg Prmtons LLC	G	219 262-4000	
Michigan City (G-9809)			
Link Printing Services LLC	G	317 826-9852	
Indianapolis (G-7408)			
Lsc Communications Us LLC	G	574 267-7101	
Warsaw (G-13902)			
M M Printing Plus	G	574 658-9345	
Milford (G-9956)			
Madison Courier	E	812 265-3641	
Madison (G-9479)			
Margins Printing LLC	G	773 981-4251	
Gary (G-5074)			
Masco Corporation of Indiana	D	317 848-1812	
Indianapolis (G-7463)			
Maury Boyd & Associates Inc	F	317 849-6110	
Indianapolis (G-7469)			
Maximum Screen Printing	G	502 802-4652	
Jeffersonville (G-8399)			
Messenger LLC	E	260 925-1700	
Auburn (G-343)			
Mf Printing LLC	G	317 462-6895	
Greenfield (G-5551)			
Mid America Print Council	G	765 463-3971	
Lafayette (G-8968)			
Midwest Printing	G	812 238-1641	
Terre Haute (G-13285)			
Mik Mocha Prints LLC	G	812 376-8891	
Columbus (G-1974)			
Mike Mugler	G	812 945-4266	
New Albany (G-10831)			
Minuteman Press	G	317 316-0566	
Noblesville (G-11151)			
Mito-Craft Inc	G	574 287-4555	
South Bend (G-12864)			
Mo3d Printing LLC	G	317 345-0061	
Noblesville (G-11152)			
Mossberg & Company Inc	G	574 236-1094	
South Bend (G-12866)			
Movie Poster Print	G	812 679-7301	
Columbus (G-1977)			
Multi Packaging Solutions Inc	B	317 241-2020	
Indianapolis (G-7558)			
Muncie Novelty Company Inc	D	765 288-8301	
Muncie (G-10532)			
Nai Print Solutions	G	317 392-1207	
Shelbyville (G-12552)			
ND Prints	G		
Indianapolis (G-7581)			
Newcomb Printing Services Inc	G	219 874-3201	
Michigan City (G-9763)			
News Banner Publications Inc	E	260 824-0224	
Bluffton (G-883)			
Newsletter Express Ltd	G	317 876-8916	
Indianapolis (G-7586)			
Nicholls Printing	G	574 233-1388	
South Bend (G-12875)			
Nielsen Company	G	812 889-3493	
Lexington (G-9254)			
North Vernon Plain Dlr & Sun	E	812 346-3973	
North Vernon (G-11272)			
Nussmeier Engraving Co	E	812 425-1339	
Evansville (G-3650)			
Nwi Print & Mail LLC	G	219 916-1358	
Dyer (G-2505)			
Oce Corporate Printing Div	G	260 436-7395	
Fort Wayne (G-4507)			
Old Capital Printing LLC	G	812 946-9444	
New Albany (G-10837)			
Optimum System Products Inc	F	812 289-1905	
Marysville (G-9650)			
Pack Printing	G	317 437-9779	
Indianapolis (G-7645)			
Panda Prints	G	574 322-1050	
Bristol (G-1075)			
Pandora Printing	G	574 551-9624	
Warsaw (G-13922)			
Pats Custom Printing and EMB	G	765 456-1532	
Kokomo (G-8678)			
PC Imprints	G	812 622-0855	
Poseyville (G-11860)			
Pengad/West Inc	E	765 286-3000	
Muncie (G-10544)			
Pickle Prints LLC	G	317 344-2495	
Carmel (G-1450)			
Picture Perfect Printing	G	765 482-4241	
Lebanon (G-9217)			
Pinpoint Printer	G	812 577-0630	
Aurora (G-385)			
Plastic Cardz	G	260 440-1964	
Fort Wayne (G-4532)			
Plastic Cardz LLC	G	260 431-6380	
Fort Wayne (G-4533)			

Posters 2 Prints LLC...G... 317 769-3784
Zionsville (G-14457)
Posters 2 Prints LLC...F... 800 598-5837
Indianapolis (G-7709)
Posters2prints LLC...G... 317 414-8972
Indianapolis (G-7710)
Precision Print LLC...G... 765 789-8799
Albany (G-12)
Preferred Print...G... 317 371-8829
Indianapolis (G-7739)
Premier Prints...G... 812 987-1129
Jeffersonville (G-8416)
Pretty In Prints LLC...G... 317 252-3672
Indianapolis (G-7744)
Princeton Publishing Inc...E... 812 385-2525
Princeton (G-11881)
Print and Save LLP...G... 317 567-1459
Indianapolis (G-7748)
Print Center Inc...G... 219 874-9683
Long Beach (G-9379)
Print It Wear It Inc...G... 317 946-1456
Shelbyville (G-12561)
Print Management Solutions...G... 574 234-7269
South Bend (G-12903)
Print My Merch LLC...G... 574 323-5541
South Bend (G-12904)
Print My Merch LLC...G... 765 269-6772
Mishawaka (G-10108)
Print Sharp Enterprises Inc...G... 317 899-2754
Indianapolis (G-7750)
Print Works of Lafayette Inc...G... 765 446-9735
Lafayette (G-8983)
Print2promo Group Inc...G... 219 778-4649
Rolling Prairie (G-12192)
Printec Solutions Inc...G... 317 289-6510
Indianapolis (G-7751)
Printed By Erik Inc...G... 574 295-1203
Elkhart (G-3116)
Printing Company LLC...G... 812 367-2668
Ferdinand (G-3861)
Printing In Time Inc...G... 502 807-3545
Elizabeth (G-2645)
Printing Partners East Inc...G... 317 356-2522
Indianapolis (G-7756)
Printing Phantom...G... 765 719-2097
Greencastle (G-5474)
Printing Plus Inc...G... 317 574-1313
Carmel (G-1455)
Printing Solutions...G... 812 923-0756
Floyds Knobs (G-4017)
Printpack Inc...G... 812 334-5500
Bloomington (G-802)
Pro Prints...G... 812 932-3800
Batesville (G-515)
Proforma Premier Printing...G... 317 842-9181
Indianapolis (G-7774)
Proforma Print Promo Group...G... 574 931-2941
South Bend (G-12906)
Pubco Inc...F... 219 874-4245
Michigan City (G-9830)
Publishers Consulting Corp...E... 219 874-4245
Michigan City (G-9831)
Pussob Apparel & Printing LLC...G... 574 229-5795
Elkhart (G-3123)
Quality Graphics Corp...G... 219 845-7084
Hammond (G-5929)
Quantumgraphix LLC...G... 317 819-0009
Indianapolis (G-6279)
Rasure Prints...G... 812 454-6222
Evansville (G-3696)
Rewright Printing...G... 219 513-8133
Highland (G-6054)
Rigdon Incorporated...G... 765 393-2283
Anderson (G-163)
Rock Hard Stones Custom...G... 219 613-0112
Merrillville (G-9750)
Ronnie Elmore Jr...G... 765 719-1681
Cloverdale (G-1736)
Row Printing...G... 317 796-3289
Brownsburg (G-1167)
Row Printing Inc...G... 317 441-4301
Pittsboro (G-11586)
Scott Printing LLC...G... 812 306-7477
Evansville (G-3718)
Sharp Shirt Printing LLC...G... 260 413-9346
Fort Wayne (G-4620)
Sherry Print Solutions Inc...G... 708 255-5457
Valparaiso (G-13615)
Shirley Engraving Co Inc...F... 317 634-4084
Indianapolis (G-7934)
Shopping Guide News Inc...F... 574 223-5417
Rochester (G-12154)
Sledgehammer Printing...G... 812 629-2160
Newburgh (G-11050)
Small Town Printers LLC...G... 812 596-1536
Elizabeth (G-2647)
Smith & Butterfield Co Inc...F... 812 422-3261
Evansville (G-3735)
Smith & Butterfield Co Inc...E... 812 422-3261
Evansville (G-3736)
Solutions For Print LLC...G... 812 584-2701
Fountaintown (G-4793)
Sommers Graphics Inc...F... 574 282-2000
South Bend (G-12940)
Sound & Graphics...G... 219 963-7293
Lake Station (G-9077)
Springs Valley Publishing Co...G... 812 936-9630
French Lick (G-4989)
St Clair Press...G... 317 612-9100
Indianapolis (G-7980)
St Meinrad Archabbey...C... 812 357-6611
Saint Meinrad (G-12276)
Starlight Printing...G... 812 486-3905
Montgomery (G-10243)
Stines Printing...G... 260 356-5994
Huntington (G-6253)
T-Flyerz Printing and Prom LLC...G... 260 729-7392
Bryant (G-1202)
Tc Printing...G... 812 865-5127
French Lick (G-4990)
Tdk Graphics Inc...F... 219 663-7799
Crown Point (G-2312)
Team Gear Printing LLC...G... 765 935-4748
Richmond (G-12059)
Team Gear Printing LLC...G... 765 977-2995
Richmond (G-12060)
Templeton Myers Inc...E... 317 898-6688
Indianapolis (G-8053)
This That EMB Screen Prtg LLC...G... 317 541-8548
Indianapolis (G-8062)
Thomas E Slade Inc...F... 812 471-7100
Evansville (G-3760)
Times...E... 765 296-3622
Frankfort (G-4856)
Tints & Prints By Tierney LLC...G... 317 769-5895
Zionsville (G-14469)
Tko Enterprises Inc...D... 317 271-1398
Plainfield (G-11647)
Tonya Gerhardt...G... 260 434-1370
Fort Wayne (G-4691)
Town & Country Industries Inc...E... 219 712-0893
Crown Point (G-2316)
Town Country Printing...G... 765 452-0093
Kokomo (G-8709)
Tri State Printing & Embroider...G... 812 316-0094
Vincennes (G-13710)
Tri-State Printing & EMB LLC...G... 812 743-2825
Monroe City (G-10189)
Triple Crown Media LLC...D... 574 533-2151
Goshen (G-5342)
Truth Publishing Company Inc...E... 765 653-5151
Greencastle (G-5480)
United Hero Apparel Printing...G... 812 306-1998
Evansville (G-3787)
United Parcel Service Inc...G... 317 776-9494
Noblesville (G-11197)
Unlimited Ink Custom Screen...G... 765 889-3212
Russiaville (G-12244)
Upside Prints Corporation...F... 812 319-4883
Evansville (G-3791)
Upside Prints Corporation...G... 812 205-7374
Bedford (G-588)
V & P Printing...G... 260 495-3741
Fremont (G-4978)
Vdk Printing LLC...G... 260 602-8212
Fort Wayne (G-4724)
Visions Printing LLC...G... 317 960-2322
Indianapolis (G-8165)
Voice of God Recordings Inc...D... 812 246-2137
Jeffersonville (G-8439)
Vomela...G... 574 522-6016
Elkhart (G-3251)
W Robbins & Sons Inc...G... 765 522-1736
Roachdale (G-12096)
W/S Packaging Group Inc...G... 317 578-4454
Indianapolis (G-8173)
Wabash Plain Dealer...E... 260 563-2131
Wabash (G-13764)
Wabash Printing Company...G... 765 650-1701
West Lafayette (G-14116)
WAr - LLC- Westville Prtg...G... 219 785-2821
Westville (G-14221)
Well Ink...G... 765 743-3413
West Lafayette (G-14117)
Whitewater Publications Inc...E... 765 647-4221
Brookville (G-1131)
Wilkes Printing Inc...G... 812 847-0005
Linton (G-9315)
Willis Curtis Genie Jr...G... 317 377-4711
Indianapolis (G-8202)
Wise Business Forms Inc...C... 260 489-1561
Fort Wayne (G-4759)
Wise Printing Inc...G... 317 861-6220
New Palestine (G-10974)
Writeguard Business Systems...G... 317 849-7292
Indianapolis (G-8219)
Xl Graphics Inc...F... 317 738-3434
Franklin (G-4942)
Yahweh Design and Printing...G... 765 874-1003
Lynn (G-9433)
Your Face Our Place Print Shop...G... 812 567-4510
Tennyson (G-13183)

PRINTING: Manmade Fiber & Silk, Broadwoven Fabric

Graphic22 Inc...G... 219 921-5409
Chesterton (G-1608)

PRINTING: Offset

323ink LLC...G... 812 282-3620
Jeffersonville (G-8316)
A-1 Graphics Inc...G... 765 289-1851
Muncie (G-10420)
A-1 Letter Shop Inc...G... 317 632-7212
Indianapolis (G-6302)
AC Printing Inc...G... 708 418-9100
Highland (G-6034)
Advantage Direct365 Corp...E... 260 490-1961
Fort Wayne (G-4047)
AG Apparel and Screen Prtg LLC...G... 260 483-3817
Fort Wayne (G-4050)
AG Printing Specialists LLC...G... 866 445-6824
Lafayette (G-8848)
All 4u Printing LLC...G... 317 845-2955
Morgantown (G-10347)
Allen C Terhune & Associates...G... 765 948-4164
Fairmount (G-3828)
Allison Payment Systems LLC...C... 317 808-2400
Indianapolis (G-6370)
American Printing...G... 219 836-5600
Munster (G-10595)
American Printing Company...F... 574 533-5399
Goshen (G-5169)
Athena Arts & Graphics Inc...G... 317 876-8916
Indianapolis (G-6436)
Augustin Prtg & Design Svcs...G... 765 966-7130
Richmond (G-11957)
Ave Maria Press Inc...D... 574 287-2831
Notre Dame (G-11303)
Aztec Printing Inc...G... 812 422-1462
Wadesville (G-13771)
Bartel Printing Company Inc...G... 574 267-7421
Warsaw (G-13842)
Baugh Enterprises Inc...F... 812 334-8189
Bloomington (G-674)
Baxter Printing Inc...G... 219 923-1999
Highland (G-6037)
Bhar Printing Inc...G... 317 899-1020
Indianapolis (G-6472)
Blasted Works...G... 574 583-3211
Monticello (G-10256)
Bobs Quick Copy Shop...G... 765 457-9160
Kokomo (G-8601)
Boy-Conn Printers Inc...G... 219 462-2665
Valparaiso (G-13512)
Brainstorm Print LLC...G... 317 466-1600
Indianapolis (G-6500)
Brinkman Press Inc...G... 317 722-0305
Indianapolis (G-6511)
Broadway Press...G... 765 644-8813
Anderson (G-78)
Brq Quickprint Inc...G... 219 464-1070
Valparaiso (G-13515)
Bryant Printing...G... 765 521-3379
New Castle (G-10893)
Budget Printing Centers Inc...G... 812 282-8832
Jeffersonville (G-8334)
Buis Enterprises Inc...E... 317 839-7394
Plainfield (G-11598)

Employee Codes: A=Over 500 employees, B=251-500
C=101-250, D=51-100, E=20-50, F=10-19, G=2-9
2018 Harris Indiana
Industrial Directory
1055

Bumblebee Quick Print Inc ....G....... 765 962-0368
Richmond (G-11968)

Burkert-Walton Inc ....G....... 812 425-7157
Evansville (G-3405)

C J P Corporation ....G....... 219 924-1685
Highland (G-6040)

Campbell Printing Co Inc ....G....... 219 866-5913
Rensselaer (G-11916)

Carlton Ventures Inc ....G....... 317 637-2590
Indianapolis (G-6556)

Cave & Company Printing ....G....... 317 896-5337
Westfield (G-14141)

Cecils Printing & Office Sups ....G....... 812 683-4416
Huntingburg (G-6153)

Chromasource Inc ....C....... 260 420-3000
Columbia City (G-1772)

Circle Printing LLC ....G....... 812 663-7367
Greensburg (G-5593)

CJ Printing ....G....... 219 924-1685
Hammond (G-5862)

Classic Graphics Inc ....F....... 260 482-3487
Fort Wayne (G-4156)

Clondalkin Pharma & Healthcare ....C....... 317 328-7355
Indianapolis (G-6623)

Clondalkin Pharma & Healthcare ....C....... 812 464-2461
Evansville (G-3420)

Commercial Print Shop Inc ....G....... 260 724-3722
Decatur (G-2373)

Commercial Printing of Lagro ....G....... 260 782-2421
Lagro (G-9072)

Complete Printer Inc ....G....... 574 936-9505
Plymouth (G-11676)

Complete Prtg Solutions Inc ....G....... 812 285-9200
Jeffersonville (G-8343)

Consolidated Printing Svcs Inc ....F....... 765 468-6033
Farmland (G-3841)

Copy-Print Shop Inc ....E....... 765 447-6868
Lafayette (G-8877)

Copymat Service Inc ....G....... 765 743-5995
Lafayette (G-8878)

Country Pines Inc ....F....... 812 247-3315
Shoals (G-12665)

CPC ....G....... 812 358-5010
Brownstown (G-1184)

Crystal Graphics Inc ....G....... 317 535-9202
Whiteland (G-14237)

Cunningham Printing Inc ....G....... 812 347-2438
New Salisbury (G-11008)

Custom Forms Inc ....G....... 765 463-6162
Lafayette (G-8884)

D & E Printing Company Inc ....G....... 317 852-9048
Brownsburg (G-1147)

D & M Printing Inc ....G....... 812 847-4837
Linton (G-9306)

Data Print Initiatives LLC ....G....... 260 489-2665
Fort Wayne (G-4200)

Digital Printing Incorporated ....F....... 812 265-2205
Madison (G-9457)

Diverse Sales Solutions LLC ....G....... 317 514-2403
Indianapolis (G-6747)

Diversfied Cmmunications Group ....F....... 317 755-3191
Indianapolis (G-6749)

Diversity Press LLC ....G....... 317 241-4234
Indianapolis (G-6751)

Doerr Printing Co ....G....... 317 568-0135
Indianapolis (G-6756)

Dps Printing ....G....... 260 503-9681
Columbia City (G-1780)

Duley Press Inc ....E....... 574 259-5203
Mishawaka (G-10037)

Dynamark Graphics Group Inc ....G....... 317 569-1855
Indianapolis (G-6774)

Dynamark Graphics Group Inc ....G....... 317 328-2565
Indianapolis (G-6776)

Dynamark Graphics Group Inc ....G....... 317 634-2963
Indianapolis (G-6777)

Dynamark Graphics Group Inc ....E....... 317 328-2555
Indianapolis (G-6775)

Economy Offset Printers Inc ....G....... 574 534-6270
Goshen (G-5210)

Ed Sons Inc ....F....... 317 897-8821
Indianapolis (G-6803)

Elite Printing Inc ....G....... 317 781-9701
Indianapolis (G-6839)

Elite Printing Inc ....G....... 317 257-2744
Indianapolis (G-6840)

Envision Graphics Inc ....G....... 260 925-2266
Auburn (G-329)

EP Graphics Inc ....C....... 877 589-2145
Berne (G-613)

Epi Printers Inc ....D....... 317 579-4870
Indianapolis (G-6875)

Espich Printing Inc ....G....... 260 244-0132
Columbia City (G-1784)

Evansville Bindery Inc ....G....... 812 423-2222
Evansville (G-3483)

Evansville Lithograph Co Inc ....G....... 812 477-0506
Evansville (G-3486)

Ewing Printing Company Inc ....F....... 812 882-2415
Vincennes (G-13677)

Express Press Indiana Inc ....E....... 574 277-3355
South Bend (G-12769)

Express Press Indiana Inc ....G....... 219 874-2223
South Bend (G-12770)

Express Printing & Copying ....G....... 219 762-3508
Portage (G-11761)

F Robert Gardner Co Inc ....G....... 317 634-2333
Indianapolis (G-6900)

Falls Cities Printing Inc ....F....... 812 949-9051
New Albany (G-10775)

Fast Print Incorporated ....G....... 260 484-5487
Fort Wayne (G-4257)

Faulkenberg Printing Co Inc ....F....... 317 638-1359
Franklin (G-4886)

Fehring F N & Son Printers ....G....... 219 933-0439
Hammond (G-5879)

Fineline Graphics Incorporated ....D....... 317 872-4490
Indianapolis (G-6921)

First Quality Printing Inc ....F....... 317 506-8633
Indianapolis (G-6927)

First Quality Printing Center ....G....... 317 546-5531
Indianapolis (G-6928)

Fort Wayne Printing Co Inc ....F....... 260 471-7744
Fort Wayne (G-4280)

Four Part Inc ....G....... 219 926-7777
Chesterton (G-1607)

Garrett Printing & Graphics ....G....... 812 422-6005
Evansville (G-3515)

Gary Printing Inc ....G....... 219 886-1767
Gary (G-5052)

Get Printing Inc ....G....... 574 533-6827
Goshen (G-5224)

Goetz Printing ....F....... 812 243-2086
Terre Haute (G-13241)

Good Impressions Printing Inc ....G....... 317 873-6809
Zionsville (G-14434)

Gospel Echoes Team Association ....G....... 574 533-0221
Goshen (G-5228)

Graessle-Mercer Co ....E....... 812 522-5478
Seymour (G-12451)

Grafcor Inc ....E....... 765 966-7030
Richmond (G-11990)

Graphic Arts & Publ Svcs ....G....... 574 294-1770
Elkhart (G-2894)

Graphicorp ....G....... 317 867-3099
Indianapolis (G-7036)

Green Banner Publications Inc ....E....... 812 967-3176
Pekin (G-11473)

Greencastle Offset Inc ....G....... 765 653-4026
Greencastle (G-5458)

Greenline Screen Printing ....G....... 317 572-1155
Indianapolis (G-7045)

Greensburg Printing Co Inc ....G....... 812 663-8265
Greensburg (G-5604)

Hager Inc ....G....... 260 483-7075
Fort Wayne (G-4314)

Hardesty Printing Co Inc ....F....... 574 223-4553
Rochester (G-12126)

Hardesty Printing Co Inc ....F....... 574 267-7591
Warsaw (G-13889)

Hardingpoorman Inc ....C....... 317 876-3355
Indianapolis (G-7074)

Hardingpoorman Group Inc ....G....... 317 876-3355
Indianapolis (G-7075)

Harmony Press Inc ....E....... 800 525-3742
Bourbon (G-943)

Hartford City News Times ....C....... 765 348-0110
Hartford City (G-5982)

Haywood Printing Co Inc ....E....... 765 742-4085
Lafayette (G-8912)

Heckley Printing ....G....... 260 434-1370
Fort Wayne (G-4330)

Heron Printing Co Inc ....G....... 317 865-0007
Indianapolis (G-7097)

Hetty Incorporated ....G....... 219 836-2517
Munster (G-10605)

Hetty Incorporated ....G....... 219 933-0833
Hammond (G-5892)

Highway Press Inc ....G....... 812 283-6462
Jeffersonville (G-8374)

Hoosier Jiffy Print ....G....... 260 563-8715
Wabash (G-13731)

Hoosier Press Inc ....G....... 765 649-3716
Anderson (G-116)

Hoosier Reproduction Services ....G....... 765 664-3162
Marion (G-9531)

Horoho Printing Company Inc ....G....... 765 452-8862
Kokomo (G-8640)

Howard Print Shop ....G....... 765 453-6161
Kokomo (G-8641)

Huelseman Printing Co ....G....... 765 647-3947
Brookville (G-1117)

Hugh K Eagan ....G....... 574 269-5411
Warsaw (G-13891)

Impression Printing ....G....... 765 342-6977
Martinsville (G-9614)

Indigo Printing & Graphics ....G....... 260 432-1320
Huntertown (G-6140)

Ink Spot ....G....... 260 482-4492
Fort Wayne (G-4370)

Ink Spot Tattoo ....G....... 260 244-0025
Columbia City (G-1796)

Insty-Prints of South Bend ....G....... 574 289-6977
South Bend (G-12814)

International Label Mfg LLC ....F....... 812 235-5071
Terre Haute (G-13258)

J & J Printing Co ....G....... 765 642-6642
Anderson (G-124)

James David Inc ....G....... 260 744-0579
Roanoke (G-12105)

Jem Printing Inc ....G....... 812 376-9264
Columbus (G-1951)

Jkp Printing Inc ....G....... 574 246-1650
South Bend (G-12822)

JP Ownership Group Inc ....D....... 317 791-1122
Indianapolis (G-7317)

K V S Inc ....G....... 260 925-0525
Auburn (G-338)

Kalems Enterprises Inc ....G....... 317 399-1645
Indianapolis (G-7330)

Kelley Pagels Enterprises LLC ....F....... 219 872-8552
Michigan City (G-9806)

Kill-N-Em Inc ....G....... 574 233-6655
South Bend (G-12828)

Kozs Quality Printing Inc ....G....... 219 696-6711
Lowell (G-9412)

L & L Press Inc ....F....... 765 664-3162
Marion (G-9541)

Lagnaippe LLC ....G....... 812 288-9291
New Albany (G-10816)

Largus Speedy Print Corp ....E....... 219 922-8414
Munster (G-10612)

Leader Publishing Co of Salem ....E....... 812 883-4446
Salem (G-12299)

Lincoln Printing Corporation ....E....... 260 424-5200
Fort Wayne (G-4437)

Litho Press Inc ....E....... 317 634-6468
Indianapolis (G-7409)

Lithogrphic Communications LLC ....E....... 219 924-9779
Munster (G-10615)

Lithotone Inc ....E....... 574 294-5521
Elkhart (G-3004)

Livings Graphics Inc ....G....... 574 264-4114
Elkhart (G-3006)

Loudon Printing Co Inc ....G....... 574 967-3944
Flora (G-3998)

Lsc Communications Us LLC ....C....... 812 256-3396
Charlestown (G-1571)

Lucas Bus Forms & Swift Prtg ....G....... 260 482-7644
Fort Wayne (G-4443)

Ludwick Graphics Inc ....F....... 574 233-2165
South Bend (G-12845)

Maco Press Inc ....G....... 317 846-5754
Carmel (G-1432)

Maco Reprograhics LLC ....G....... 812 464-8108
Evansville (G-3608)

Maple Leaf Graphics Inc ....G....... 317 410-0321
Carmel (G-1434)

Mapleleaf Printing Co Inc ....G....... 574 534-7790
Goshen (G-5280)

Mar Kel Inc ....G....... 812 853-6133
Newburgh (G-11038)

MD Laird Inc ....G....... 317 842-6338
Indianapolis (G-7473)

Metropolitan Printing Svcs LLC ....E....... 812 332-7279
Bloomington (G-771)

Mid West Digital Express Inc ....F....... 317 733-1214
Zionsville (G-14449)

Midwest Color Printing LLC ....G....... 812 822-2947
Bloomington (G-772)

Midwest Empire LLC....G.... 317 786-7446
Indianapolis *(G-7504)*
Miles Printing Corporation....F.... 317 870-6115
Indianapolis *(G-7517)*
Miller Rainbow Printing Inc....E.... 812 275-3355
Bedford *(G-565)*
Milliner Printing Company Inc....G.... 260 563-5717
Wabash *(G-13740)*
Minute Print It Inc....G.... 765 482-9019
Lebanon *(G-9206)*
Minuteman Press....G.... 317 209-1677
Indianapolis *(G-7525)*
Mitchell-Fleming Printing Inc....F.... 317 462-5467
Greenfield *(G-5554)*
Modern Printing Co....G.... 260 347-1679
Kendallville *(G-8495)*
Moeller Printing Co Inc....E.... 317 353-2224
Indianapolis *(G-7533)*
Montgomery & Associates Inc....F.... 219 879-0088
Michigan City *(G-9821)*
Mooney Copy Service Inc....G.... 812 423-6626
Evansville *(G-3635)*
Moreton Printing Co....G.... 812 926-1692
Aurora *(G-383)*
Morris Printing Company Inc....G.... 317 639-5553
Indianapolis *(G-7545)*
Mossberg & Company Inc....C.... 574 289-9253
South Bend *(G-12865)*
MPS Printing Inc....G.... 812 273-4446
Madison *(G-9489)*
Mr Copy Inc....G.... 812 334-2679
Bloomington *(G-776)*
Mr Copyrite....G.... 219 462-1108
Valparaiso *(G-13582)*
Multi-Color Corporation....C.... 812 752-3187
Scottsburg *(G-12376)*
Nea LLC....G.... 574 295-0024
Elkhart *(G-3059)*
New Image Prtg & Design Inc....F.... 260 969-0410
Fort Wayne *(G-4500)*
Nicholson & Sons Printing Inc....F.... 812 283-1200
Jeffersonville *(G-8405)*
Nova Graphics Inc....F.... 317 577-6682
Indianapolis *(G-7599)*
Offset House Inc....F.... 317 849-5155
Indianapolis *(G-7612)*
Offset One Inc....F.... 260 456-8828
Fort Wayne *(G-4509)*
Oswalt Menu Company Inc....G.... 317 257-8039
Indianapolis *(G-7636)*
Ovation Communications Inc....G.... 812 401-9100
Evansville *(G-3659)*
Overgaards Artcraft Printers....G.... 574 234-8464
South Bend *(G-12885)*
Par Digital Imaging....G.... 317 787-3330
Indianapolis *(G-7652)*
Paust Inc....F.... 765 962-1507
Richmond *(G-12027)*
Peerless Printing Corp....F.... 765 664-8341
Marion *(G-9553)*
Pentzer Printing Inc....F.... 812 372-2896
Columbus *(G-1992)*
Perdue Printed Products Inc....G.... 260 456-7575
Fort Wayne *(G-4523)*
Perfect Impressions Printing....G.... 317 923-1756
Indianapolis *(G-7674)*
Pettit Printing Inc....G.... 260 563-2346
Wabash *(G-13749)*
Phoenix Color Corp....D.... 812 234-1585
Terre Haute *(G-13302)*
Phoenix Color Corp....F.... 812 238-1551
Terre Haute *(G-13303)*
PIP Printing....G.... 317 843-5755
Carmel *(G-1451)*
Prairie Creek Prtg & Bk Str....G.... 812 636-7243
Montgomery *(G-10238)*
Presstime Graphics Inc....E.... 812 234-3815
Terre Haute *(G-13309)*
Prestige Printing Inc....F.... 812 372-2500
Columbus *(G-2000)*
Print Ideas....G.... 317 299-8766
Indianapolis *(G-7749)*
Print Place Inc....G.... 260 768-7878
Shipshewana *(G-12644)*
Print Source Corporation....G.... 260 589-2842
Bluffton *(G-887)*
Printcraft Press Inc....G.... 765 457-2141
Kokomo *(G-8686)*
Printcrafters Inc....G.... 812 838-4106
Mount Vernon *(G-10405)*
Printer Plus....G.... 812 945-5955
New Albany *(G-10848)*
Printer Zink Inc....D.... 765 644-3959
Anderson *(G-156)*
Printing All Stars....G.... 812 288-9291
New Albany *(G-10849)*
Printing Center Inc....G.... 317 545-8518
Indianapolis *(G-7753)*
Printing Concepts Inc....G.... 317 899-2754
Indianapolis *(G-7754)*
Printing Creations Inc....G.... 765 759-9679
Yorktown *(G-14410)*
Printing Inc Louisville KY....E.... 502 368-6555
Jeffersonville *(G-8417)*
Printing Partners Inc....D.... 317 635-2282
Indianapolis *(G-7755)*
Printing Place Inc-Photos Plus....F.... 260 665-8444
Angola *(G-239)*
Printworks Inc....G.... 317 535-1250
Whiteland *(G-14243)*
Priority Press Inc....G.... 317 240-0103
Indianapolis *(G-7760)*
Priority Printing LLC....G.... 317 241-4234
Indianapolis *(G-7761)*
Progressive Printing Co Inc....G.... 765 653-3814
Greencastle *(G-5475)*
Pulaski County Press Inc....G.... 574 946-6628
Winamac *(G-14317)*
Q Graphics Inc....F.... 765 564-2314
Delphi *(G-2426)*
Q S I Inc....E.... 574 282-1200
South Bend *(G-12908)*
Qsp Printing Inc....G.... 317 773-0864
Noblesville *(G-11168)*
Quad/Graphics Inc....B.... 260 748-5300
Fort Wayne *(G-4567)*
Quality Printing of NW Ind....G.... 219 322-6677
Schererville *(G-12343)*
Rainbow Printing LLC....F.... 812 275-3372
Bedford *(G-569)*
Randall Corp....G.... 812 425-7122
Evansville *(G-3695)*
Red Line Graphics Incorporated....E.... 317 591-9400
Indianapolis *(G-7825)*
Regal Printing Inc....G.... 317 844-1723
Carmel *(G-1464)*
Rensselaer Print Co....G.... 219 866-5000
Rensselaer *(G-11937)*
Reprocomm Inc....F.... 765 423-2578
Lafayette *(G-8990)*
Reprocomm Inc....E.... 765 472-5700
Peru *(G-11544)*
Rhr Corporation....G.... 317 788-1504
Indianapolis *(G-7837)*
Richards Printery....G.... 812 406-0295
Greenville *(G-5652)*
Riden Inc....G.... 219 362-5511
La Porte *(G-8812)*
Riverside Printing Co....G.... 812 275-1950
Bedford *(G-574)*
Rowland Printing Co Inc....F.... 317 773-1829
Noblesville *(G-11177)*
Royal Center Record....G.... 574 643-3165
Royal Center *(G-12214)*
Rrc Corporation....F.... 317 687-8325
Indianapolis *(G-7869)*
Running Around Screen Printing....G.... 260 248-1216
Columbia City *(G-1832)*
Russ Print Shop....F.... 219 996-3142
Hebron *(G-6022)*
Service Printers Inc....E.... 574 266-6710
Elkhart *(G-3162)*
Shackelford Graphics....G.... 317 783-3582
Indianapolis *(G-7919)*
Sharp Printing Services Inc....G.... 317 842-5159
Fishers *(G-3969)*
Shearer Printing Service Inc....E.... 765 457-3274
Kokomo *(G-8695)*
Shelbyville Newspapers Inc....D.... 317 398-6631
Shelbyville *(G-12568)*
Smith Business Supply Inc....G.... 765 654-4442
Frankfort *(G-4853)*
Smitson Cmmnications Group LLC....G.... 317 876-8916
Indianapolis *(G-7953)*
Spectrum Press Inc....E.... 812 335-1945
Bloomington *(G-831)*
Spencer Evening World....D.... 812 829-2255
Spencer *(G-13037)*
Spencer Evening World....G.... 765 795-4438
Cloverdale *(G-1738)*
Spencer Printing Inc....G.... 765 288-6111
Muncie *(G-10566)*
Stage Door Graphics....G.... 317 398-9011
Shelbyville *(G-12571)*
Stamprint Inc....G.... 574 233-3900
South Bend *(G-12953)*
Starken Printing Co Inc....G.... 317 839-6852
Plainfield *(G-11645)*
Summit LLC....G.... 574 287-7468
South Bend *(G-12961)*
Superior Print Inc....E.... 812 246-6311
Sellersburg *(G-12420)*
Swiss Alps Printing Inc....G.... 812 427-3844
Vevay *(G-13666)*
Systems & Services of Michiana....G.... 574 273-1111
South Bend *(G-12965)*
Systems & Services of Michiana....G.... 574 277-3355
South Bend *(G-12966)*
Tabco Business Forms Inc....G.... 812 882-2836
Vincennes *(G-13709)*
Target Printing Inc....G.... 260 744-6038
Fort Wayne *(G-4675)*
Tatman Inc....E.... 765 825-2164
Connersville *(G-2075)*
Tek Print LLC....G.... 812 336-2525
Bedford *(G-583)*
The Office Sup of Southern Ind....G.... 812 283-5523
Jeffersonville *(G-8434)*
Thompson Printing Service Inc....G.... 317 783-7448
Indianapolis *(G-8068)*
Tippecanoe Press Inc....F.... 317 392-1207
Shelbyville *(G-12576)*
Town & Country Press Inc....F.... 574 936-9505
Plymouth *(G-11730)*
Triangle Printing Inc....G.... 317 786-3488
Indianapolis *(G-8098)*
Twin Prints Inc....G.... 765 742-8656
Lafayette *(G-9014)*
Two B Enterprises Inc....F.... 260 245-0119
Fort Wayne *(G-4711)*
Un Communications Group Inc....E.... 317 844-8622
Carmel *(G-1503)*
Valley Press Tc....F.... 812 234-8030
Terre Haute *(G-13360)*
Wayne Press Incorporated....G.... 260 744-3022
Fort Wayne *(G-4743)*
Williams Plastics LLC....C.... 317 398-1630
Shelbyville *(G-12585)*
Wise Printing Inc....G.... 317 351-9477
Indianapolis *(G-8206)*
Wolf Printing LLC....G.... 317 577-1771
Indianapolis *(G-8208)*
Woodburn Graphics Inc....E.... 812 232-0323
Terre Haute *(G-13371)*
Woodfield Printing Inc....G.... 317 848-2000
Indianapolis *(G-6283)*
Woods Printing Company Inc....F.... 812 536-2261
Holland *(G-6106)*
Wraco Enterprises Inc....G.... 812 339-3987
Bloomington *(G-859)*
Zogman Enterprises Inc....G.... 317 873-6809
Zionsville *(G-14475)*

PRINTING: Screen, Broadwoven Fabrics, Cotton

A D I Screen Printing....G.... 765 457-8580
Kokomo *(G-8589)*
Action Embroidery Inc....G.... 850 626-1796
Jeffersonville *(G-8319)*
Concept Prints Inc....F.... 317 290-1222
Indianapolis *(G-6648)*
Gad-A-Bout Screenprinting Inc....G.... 765 855-5681
Centerville *(G-1542)*
OHara Sports Inc....G.... 219 836-5554
Munster *(G-10618)*
Sullivan Group Inc....F.... 574 773-2108
Nappanee *(G-10707)*
UC Ink LLC....G.... 765 220-5502
West College Corner *(G-14038)*

PRINTING: Screen, Fabric

Ad Vision Graphics Inc....G.... 812 476-4932
Evansville *(G-3343)*
Athletic Edge Inc....F.... 260 489-6613
Fort Wayne *(G-4095)*
Burston Marketing Inc....F.... 574 262-4005
Elkhart *(G-2739)*
Codybro LLC....G.... 765 827-5441
Connersville *(G-2044)*

Cross Printwear Inc ....F 317 293-1776
Indianapolis (G-6694)

Custom Imprint Corporation ....E 800 378-3397
Merrillville (G-9709)

Dance World Bazaar Corporation ....G 812 663-7679
Greensburg (G-5598)

Dark Star Inc ....F 765 759-4764
Muncie (G-10453)

Elegan Sportswear Inc ....F 219 464-8416
Valparaiso (G-13534)

Flag & Banner Company Inc ....F 317 299-4880
Indianapolis (G-6931)

Game Plan Graphics LLC ....G 812 663-3238
Greensburg (G-5602)

Jasper EMB & Screen Prtg ....G 812 482-4787
Jasper (G-8260)

JAT Inc LLC ....G 317 201-3684
Indianapolis (G-7298)

Jer-Maur Corporation ....G 812 384-8290
Bloomfield (G-640)

Kennyleeholmescom ....G 574 612-2526
Elkhart (G-2961)

Locoli Inc ....G 219 365-3125
Schererville (G-12332)

Logo Designs Inc ....G 812 293-4750
New Washington (G-11012)

Logo USA Corporation ....F 317 867-8518
Westfield (G-14174)

Logos Express Inc ....G 317 272-1200
Lebanon (G-9201)

Mac Designs ....G 317 580-9390
Carmel (G-1431)

Maingate Inc ....D 317 243-2000
Indianapolis (G-7444)

Plastimatic Arts Corp ....E 574 254-9000
Mishawaka (G-10104)

Progressive Design Apparel Inc ....G 317 293-5888
Indianapolis (G-7775)

Ram Graphics Inc ....E 765 724-7783
Alexandria (G-48)

Rbs Tees Co ....G 812 522-8675
Seymour (G-12479)

Robert Burkhart ....G 219 448-0365
Alexandria (G-52)

Shirts N Things S N T Graphics ....G 317 271-3515
Indianapolis (G-7935)

Spectrum Marketing ....G 765 643-5566
Anderson (G-168)

Sportscenter Inc ....G 260 436-6198
Fort Wayne (G-4642)

Star Quality Awards Inc ....G 812 273-1740
Madison (G-9496)

Sycamore Enterprises Inc ....G 812 491 0901
Evansville (G-3756)

Thread Creations Inc ....G 765 521-3886
New Castle (G-10919)

Travis Britton ....G 317 762-6018
Indianapolis (G-8092)

Winning Edge of Rochester Inc ....F 574 223-6090
Rochester (G-12162)

Woods Enterprises ....G 574 232-7449
South Bend (G-12992)

PRINTING: Screen, Manmade Fiber & Silk, Broadwoven Fabric

Apparel Promotions Inc ....G 574 294-7165
Elkhart (G-2694)

Classic Products Corp ....E 260 484-2695
Fort Wayne (G-4159)

Main Event Mdsg Group LLC ....F 317 570-8900
Indianapolis (G-7442)

PRINTING: Thermography

North Enterprises Inc ....G 765 362-4410
Crawfordsville (G-2179)

Thermography Indianapolis LLC ....G 317 370-5111
Indianapolis (G-8059)

Thermovision Thermography ....G 317 306-6622
Indianapolis (G-8060)

PROFESSIONAL EQPT & SPLYS, WHOLESALE: Analytical Instruments

Lazar Scientific Incorporated ....G 574 271-7020
Granger (G-5418)

PROFESSIONAL EQPT & SPLYS, WHOLESALE: Engineers', NEC

Blue Print Specialties Inc ....G 765 742-6976
Lafayette (G-8862)

Maco Reprograhics LLC ....G 812 464-8108
Evansville (G-3608)

Priority Press Inc ....E 317 241-4234
Indianapolis (G-7759)

Priority Press Inc ....G 317 848-9695
Indianapolis (G-6278)

PROFESSIONAL EQPT & SPLYS, WHOLESALE: Optical Goods

City Optical Co Inc ....G 317 788-4243
Indianapolis (G-6616)

City Optical Co Inc ....D 317 924-1300
Indianapolis (G-6615)

PROFESSIONAL INSTRUMENT REPAIR SVCS

Heads First ....G 219 785-4100
Westville (G-14217)

Indiana Hand Piece Repair ....G 260 436-0765
Fort Wayne (G-4364)

Metal Technology of Indiana ....E 765 482-1100
Lebanon (G-9205)

T & L Sharpening Inc ....E 574 583-3868
Monticello (G-10285)

Uncle Alberts Amplifier Inc ....G 317 845-3037
Indianapolis (G-8126)

PROFILE SHAPES: Unsupported Plastics

3d Parts Mfg LLC ....G 317 860-6941
Anderson (G-56)

Polygon Company ....C 574 586-3145
Walkerton (G-13808)

Polygon Company ....D 574 586-3145
Walkerton (G-13809)

Precision Products Group Inc ....C 301 474-3100
Indianapolis (G-6277)

Prolon Inc ....E 574 522-8900
Elkhart (G-3119)

Quadrant Epp Usa Inc ....D 260 479-4700
Fort Wayne (G-4568)

Quadrant Epp Usa Inc ....C 260 479-4100
Fort Wayne (G-4569)

Specialty Manufacturing of Ind ....E 812 256-4633
Charlestown (G-1581)

PROMOTION SVCS

High End Concepts Inc ....F 317 630-9901
Indianapolis (G-7106)

PROPELLERS: Boat & Ship, Cast

Yamaha Marine Precision Propel ....E 317 545-9080
Indianapolis (G-8223)

PROPELLERS: Boat & Ship, Machined

Hoverstream LLC ....G 317 489-0075
Indianapolis (G-7139)

PROTECTION EQPT: Lightning

Independent Protection Co Inc ....C 574 533-4116
Goshen (G-5242)

Independent Protection Co Inc ....E 574 533-4116
Goshen (G-5243)

Independent Protection Co Inc ....D 574 831-5680
New Paris (G-10985)

Llama Corporation ....G 888 701-7432
Decatur (G-2391)

PROTECTIVE FOOTWEAR: Rubber Or Plastic

Wise Industries Inc (del) ....G 219 947-5333
Hobart (G-6101)

PUBLIC ORDER & SAFETY OFFICES, GOVERNMENT: Level Of Govt

Cortex Safety Technologies LLC ....G 317 414-5607
Carmel (G-1344)

PUBLIC RELATIONS & PUBLICITY SVCS

Kamrex Inc ....E 317 204-3779
Avon (G-452)

PUBLIC RELATIONS SVCS

Annual Reports Inc ....E 317 736-8838
Franklin (G-4868)

Printing Creations Inc ....G 765 759-9679
Yorktown (G-14410)

PUBLISHERS: Art Copy & Poster

Brush Strokes Inc ....G 800 272-2307
South Bend (G-12726)

PUBLISHERS: Book

Bibles For Blind & Visually ....G 812 466-3134
Terre Haute (G-13201)

Bird Publishing Company ....G 219 462-6330
Valparaiso (G-13509)

Black Books Publishing Inc ....G 260 225-7479
Fort Wayne (G-4111)

Clinical Drug Information LLC ....G 317 735-5300
Indianapolis (G-6622)

Corby Publishing LP ....G 574 229-1107
Lakeville (G-9094)

Cr Publications ....G 219 931-6700
Hammond (G-5866)

Distance Learning Systems Ind ....E 888 955-3276
Greenwood (G-5681)

Freight Trnsp RES Assoc Inc ....F 888 988-1699
Bloomington (G-727)

Frugal Times ....G 317 326-4165
Greenfield (G-5532)

Get Published Inc ....B 812 334-5279
Bloomington (G-731)

Gingerbread House Publications ....G 260 622-4868
Ossian (G-11399)

Glue + Paper Workshop LLC ....G 773 275-8935
Beverly Shores (G-630)

Hackett Publishing Company ....F 317 635-9250
Indianapolis (G-7064)

Herff Jones LLC ....E 317 612-3400
Indianapolis (G-7089)

Herff Jones Yearbooks ....G 717 334-9123
Indianapolis (G-7094)

Horizon Publishing Company LLC ....E 219 852-3200
Hammond (G-5895)

Houghton Mifflin Harcourt Co ....G 317 359-5585
Indianapolis (G-7137)

Houghton Mifflin Harcourt Pubg ....C 317 359-5585
Indianapolis (G-7138)

Iuniverse Inc ....D 812 330-2909
Bloomington (G-752)

Kamrex Inc ....E 317 204-3779
Avon (G-452)

Kaplan Inc ....D 317 872-7220
Indianapolis (G-7333)

Kids World Productions Inc ....G 317 674-6090
Zionsville (G-14444)

Lakota Language Consortium ....F 888 525-6828
Bloomington (G-762)

Our Little Books LLC ....G 812 987-2475
Jeffersonville (G-8410)

Palibrio ....G 812 671-9757
Bloomington (G-795)

Princeton Publishing Inc ....E 812 385-2525
Princeton (G-11881)

Regulations Update Svcs LLC ....G 812 334-4020
Bloomington (G-809)

Solution Tree Inc ....C 812 336-7700
Bloomington (G-828)

St Meinrad Archabbey ....D 812 357-6611
Saint Meinrad (G-12275)

Studio Indiana ....G 812 332-5073
Bloomington (G-833)

Tom Doherty Company Inc ....G 317 352-8200
Indianapolis (G-8079)

Trustees Indiana University ....B 812 855-0763
Bloomington (G-846)

University Notre Dame Du Lac ....F 574 631-6346
Notre Dame (G-11305)

University of Evansville ....G 812 479-2963
Evansville (G-3790)

Voice of God Recordings Inc ....D 812 246-2137
Jeffersonville (G-8439)

W Robbins & Sons Inc ....G 765 522-1736
Roachdale (G-12096)

Whitman Publications Inc ....G..... 574 268-2062
Winona Lake *(G-14355)*
William H Sadlier Inc ....G..... 219 465-0453
Valparaiso *(G-13637)*
Xlibris Corporation ....D..... 812 671-9162
Bloomington *(G-861)*

PUBLISHERS: Books, No Printing

Athentic Inc ....F..... 219 362-8508
La Porte *(G-8735)*
Author Solutions LLC ....B..... 812 339-6000
Bloomington *(G-667)*
Bright Corp ....E..... 765 642-3114
Anderson *(G-77)*
Hachette Book Group Inc ....C..... 765 483-9900
Lebanon *(G-9185)*
Harpercollins Publishers LLC ....D..... 219 324-4880
La Porte *(G-8760)*
Hawthorne Publishing ....G..... 317 867-5183
Carmel *(G-1400)*
National Federation of ....E..... 317 972-6900
Indianapolis *(G-7571)*
Norlightspresscom ....G..... 812 675-8054
Bedford *(G-566)*
Pearson Education Inc ....E..... 317 715-2150
Indianapolis *(G-7669)*
Penguin Random House LLC ....G..... 800 672-7836
Lebanon *(G-9213)*
Penguin Random House LLC ....C..... 765 362-5125
Crawfordsville *(G-2184)*
Random House Inc ....G..... 410 386-7717
Crawfordsville *(G-2191)*
Sewing Connection L L C ....G..... 317 745-1501
Avon *(G-466)*
St Augustines Press Inc ....G..... 574 291-3500
South Bend *(G-12951)*
Three Cups LLC ....G..... 317 633-8082
Indianapolis *(G-8070)*
Trafford Holdings Ltd ....G..... 888 232-4444
Bloomington *(G-843)*
Worth Tax and Financial Svc ....G..... 574 267-4687
Warsaw *(G-13969)*

PUBLISHERS: Comic Books, No Printing

Compucomics ....G..... 812 876-1480
Ellettsville *(G-3275)*

PUBLISHERS: Directories, NEC

Criterion Press Inc ....F..... 317 236-1570
Indianapolis *(G-6693)*
International Code Council Inc ....G..... 317 879-1677
Indianapolis *(G-7252)*
Riebel Roque Inc ....G..... 317 849-3680
Indianapolis *(G-7844)*

PUBLISHERS: Globe Cover Maps

Round World Products Inc ....F..... 317 257-7352
Carmel *(G-1472)*

PUBLISHERS: Guides

College Network Inc ....G..... 800 395-3276
Indianapolis *(G-6631)*
United Media Group Inc ....G..... 260 436-7417
Fort Wayne *(G-4715)*

PUBLISHERS: Magazines, No Printing

American Chiropractor Mag Inc ....E..... 260 471-4090
Fort Wayne *(G-4069)*
American Graphics Group ....G..... 260 589-3117
Berne *(G-606)*
Ameriforce Media LLC ....G..... 812 961-9478
Bloomington *(G-661)*
Connection LLC ....G..... 260 593-3999
Topeka *(G-13413)*
Cr Publications ....G..... 219 931-6700
Hammond *(G-5866)*
Dennis Polk & Associates Inc ....G..... 574 831-3555
New Paris *(G-10977)*
Emmis Operating Company ....E..... 317 266-0100
Indianapolis *(G-6855)*
Emmis Publishing LP ....E..... 317 266-0100
Indianapolis *(G-6856)*
Inari Information Services ....G..... 812 331-2298
Bloomington *(G-743)*
Indy Sports Preview Program ....E..... 317 259-0570
Indianapolis *(G-7222)*

Informa Business Media Inc ....E..... 317 233-1310
New Palestine *(G-10971)*
Linear Publishing Corp ....G..... 317 722-8500
Indianapolis *(G-7407)*
Michiana Business Publications ....G..... 260 497-0433
Fort Wayne *(G-4470)*
P J J T Distributors Inc ....F..... 812 254-2218
Washington *(G-13996)*
Rick Singleton ....E..... 574 259-5555
Mishawaka *(G-10117)*
Roann Publishers ....G..... 574 831-2795
Goshen *(G-5319)*
Rough Notes Company Inc ....E..... 800 428-4384
Carmel *(G-1470)*
Saturday Evening Post Soc Inc ....D..... 317 634-1100
Indianapolis *(G-7898)*
Servaas Inc ....G..... 317 633-2020
Indianapolis *(G-7914)*
St Meinrad Archabbey ....C..... 812 357-6611
Saint Meinrad *(G-12276)*
Towne Post Network Inc ....G..... 317 288-7101
Indianapolis *(G-8084)*
Trustees Indiana University ....G..... 812 855-3439
Bloomington *(G-847)*
Tucker Publishing Group Inc ....F..... 812 426-2115
Evansville *(G-3778)*
Ultra Montane Associates Inc ....G..... 574 289-9786
South Bend *(G-12980)*
United Media Group Inc ....G..... 260 436-7417
Fort Wayne *(G-4715)*
USA Travel Magazine ....G..... 317 834-3683
Martinsville *(G-9646)*

PUBLISHERS: Miscellaneous

124 Publishing LLC ....G..... 574 784-0046
Lakeville *(G-9092)*
200 Express ....G..... 260 833-2125
Angola *(G-186)*
Academy of Mdel Aronautics Inc ....D..... 765 287-1256
Muncie *(G-10422)*
Accurate Publishing Co ....G..... 219 836-1397
Munster *(G-10593)*
Advertising Communications Gro ....E..... 317 843-2523
Carmel *(G-1304)*
Afterimage Gis ....G..... 765 744-1346
Muncie *(G-10425)*
Aim Media Indiana Oper LLC ....D..... 812 372-7811
Columbus *(G-1851)*
Aj Express Broker Service ....G..... 812 866-1380
Madison *(G-9441)*
Alacheri Publishing LLC ....G..... 317 755-6670
Indianapolis *(G-6359)*
American Classifieds ....E..... 317 782-8111
Indianapolis *(G-6386)*
Ancient Faith Ministries ....G..... 219 728-6786
Chesterton *(G-1593)*
Annabella Publications LLC ....G..... 219 663-4244
Crown Point *(G-2226)*
Arson Press ....G..... 812 345-3527
Bloomington *(G-666)*
Artistic Expressions Pubg ....G..... 317 502-6213
Gas City *(G-5119)*
AT&T Corp ....C..... 317 347-2163
Indianapolis *(G-6434)*
Athena Arts & Graphics Inc ....G..... 317 876-8916
Indianapolis *(G-6436)*
Athentic Inc ....F..... 219 362-8508
La Porte *(G-8735)*
Barr None Music Publishers/Lea ....G..... 502 413-5443
Borden *(G-928)*
Batch Small Press LLC ....G..... 317 410-8923
Indianapolis *(G-6457)*
Bc Publications Inc ....G..... 765 334-8277
Carthage *(G-1512)*
Bittersweet Publishing ....G..... 317 640-3943
Fishers *(G-3879)*
Blue Guardian Publishing Co ....G..... 317 506-0763
Indianapolis *(G-6485)*
Bradford Press ....G..... 574 876-3601
Mishawaka *(G-10013)*
Brallan Press LLC ....G..... 317 525-4335
Westfield *(G-14139)*
Brallan Press LLC ....G..... 765 337-7909
Indianapolis *(G-6501)*
Brasilia Press Inc ....G..... 574 262-9700
Elkhart *(G-2732)*
Bright Corp ....E..... 765 642-3114
Anderson *(G-77)*
Brighter Dayz Publishing LLC ....G..... 317 793-1364
Indianapolis *(G-6509)*

Broccoli Press LLC ....G..... 317 815-4687
Fishers *(G-3882)*
Buchanan Publishing ....G..... 317 546-4524
Indianapolis *(G-6517)*
Buddy Eugene Publishing LLC ....G..... 574 223-6048
Akron *(G-3)*
Caine Publishing LLC ....G..... 312 215-5253
Long Beach *(G-9376)*
Card Calendar Publishing LLC ....G..... 812 234-5999
Terre Haute *(G-13205)*
Cardinal Publishers Group ....G..... 317 846-8190
Carmel *(G-1329)*
Carl Hugness Publishing ....G..... 812 273-2472
Madison *(G-9447)*
Cheyenne Enterprises LLC ....G..... 317 253-7795
Indianapolis *(G-6599)*
Collective Press Inc ....G..... 812 325-1385
Bloomington *(G-701)*
Creative Publishing Concep ....G..... 317 844-3549
Carmel *(G-1347)*
Crown Training & Development ....E..... 219 947-0845
Merrillville *(G-9708)*
Current Publishing LLC ....G..... 317 489-4444
Carmel *(G-1351)*
D&G Publishing Inc ....G..... 317 531-8678
Westfield *(G-14154)*
East Fork Studio & Press Inc ....G..... 765 458-6103
Brownsville *(G-1195)*
Echo Publications ....G..... 219 696-3756
Lowell *(G-9405)*
Education Connection Pubg LLC ....G..... 317 876-3355
Indianapolis *(G-6808)*
El Mexicano Inc ....G..... 260 456-6843
Fort Wayne *(G-4233)*
El Puente LLC ....G..... 574 533-9082
Goshen *(G-5211)*
Endowment Development Services ......F..... 317 542-9829
Indianapolis *(G-6861)*
Exploding Brain Press......................G..... 219 393-0796
Michigan City *(G-9789)*
Express Motors ....G..... 812 437-9495
Evansville *(G-3497)*
Fairylan LLC ....G..... 219 866-3077
Rensselaer *(G-11922)*
Fish Factory..................................G..... 219 929-9375
Chesterton *(G-1606)*
Flying Turtle Publishing LLC ....G..... 219 221-8488
Hammond *(G-5881)*
Full Press LLC ....G..... 260 433-7731
Fort Wayne *(G-4290)*
Gaunt Family LLC ....G..... 812 473-3167
Evansville *(G-3516)*
Gingerbread House Publications ....G..... 260 622-4868
Ossian *(G-11399)*
Gourmet Express ....G..... 219 921-9927
Valparaiso *(G-13551)*
Gypsum Express Ltd ....D..... 219 987-2181
Demotte *(G-2439)*
Gyrewide Publications & Bad ....G..... 765 721-7676
Greencastle *(G-5459)*
Harrison Macdonald & Sons ....F..... 765 742-9012
Lafayette *(G-8911)*
Harry B Higley & Sons Inc ....G..... 219 558-8183
Dyer *(G-2501)*
Hart Publishers Inc ....G..... 260 672-8978
Huntington *(G-6208)*
Harvard Business Publishing ....G..... 317 815-8232
Carmel *(G-1395)*
Hatfield Publications LLC ....G..... 317 581-9804
Carmel *(G-1398)*
Heron Blue Publications LLC ....G..... 317 696-0674
Carmel *(G-1403)*
High Note Publishing ....G..... 765 313-1699
Swayzee *(G-13123)*
Hot Off Press ....G..... 260 591-8331
Wabash *(G-13732)*
Imagination Publications LLC ....G..... 574 256-6666
Mishawaka *(G-10052)*
Indiana Town Planner LLC ....G..... 219 384-3555
Schererville *(G-12324)*
Jensen Publications Inc ....G..... 317 514-8864
Zionsville *(G-14440)*
Jossey-Bass Publishers ....G..... 877 762-2974
Indianapolis *(G-7313)*
Journeymann Precision Press ....G..... 260 724-6934
Decatur *(G-2388)*
Joyful Noise Recordings LLC ....G..... 317 632-3220
Indianapolis *(G-7316)*
Kelk Publishing LLC ....G..... 812 268-6356
Sullivan *(G-13084)*

PRODUCT

Ketch Publishing...................................G......812 327-0072
   Bloomington (G-758)

Kids At Heart Publishing LLC...........G......765 478-5773
   Cambridge City (G-1259)

Kiel Media LLC.....................................G......219 544-2060
   La Crosse (G-8720)

Kokomo Press LLC...............................G......317 575-9903
   Carmel (G-1424)

Laptop Publishing LLC.........................G......317 379-5716
   Carmel (G-1426)

Lcas Inc...G......541 219-0229
   Hobart (G-6088)

Leader Publishing Co of Salem...........E......812 883-4446
   Salem (G-12299)

Leslie Webber Media & Pubg LLC.......G......317 774-0598
   Noblesville (G-11141)

Lighthouse Publ Ministries.................G......260 209-6948
   Fort Wayne (G-4436)

Lime City Press LLC.............................G......260 344-3435
   Huntington (G-6225)

Little I Publications LLC......................G......317 467-9297
   Greenfield (G-5549)

Logansport Pharos Press.....................G......574 753-4169
   Logansport (G-9351)

Luna Press Productions LLC................G......317 398-8895
   Shelbyville (G-12549)

Macs Express Inc.................................G......765 865-9700
   Kokomo (G-8662)

Martin Brown Publishers LLC...........G......765 459-8258
   Kokomo (G-8664)

McCrory Publishing.............................G......260 485-1812
   Fort Wayne (G-4460)

McMillan Express................................G......260 447-7648
   Fort Wayne (G-4461)

Measure Press Inc...............................G......812 473-0361
   Evansville (G-3621)

Mining Media Inc.................................G......317 802-7116
   Indianapolis (G-7524)

Momaki Publishing LLC.......................G......847 454-4641
   Merrillville (G-9740)

MT Publishing Company Inc..............G......812 468-8022
   Evansville (G-3640)

Mud Creek Publishing Inc...................G......317 577-9659
   Indianapolis (G-7556)

My County Publishing LLC.................G......765 630-8221
   Greencastle (G-5469)

Narrow Gate Publishing LLC................G......219 464-8579
   Valparaiso (G-13585)

New Philosopher Prss..........................G......406 992-5791
   Bloomington (G-780)

New Readers Press...............................G......317 514-6515
   Avon (G-457)

News Banner Publications Inc.............E......260 824-0224
   Bluffton (G-883)

Novels By Nellotie..............................G......812 583-1196
   Mitchell (G-10168)

Paper Street Press...............................G......765 894-0027
   West Lafayette (G-14093)

PCA Publishing Inc.............................G......317 658-2055
   Indianapolis (G-7666)

Penlines Publishing LLC....................G......219 884-2632
   Gary (G-5084)

Pentera Group Inc...............................F......317 543-2055
   Indianapolis (G-7670)

Pike Publishing..................................G......812 354-4701
   Petersburg (G-11567)

Portals of Light Inc............................G......765 981-2651
   Marion (G-9554)

Praiseworthy Press LLC.......................G......765 536-2077
   Summitville (G-13101)

Press Control Systems........................G......317 887-1369
   Greenwood (G-5737)

Provision Publishing LLC....................G......765 282-3928
   Muncie (G-10550)

Pubco Inc..F......219 874-4245
   Michigan City (G-9830)

Publishers Consulting Corp................E......219 874-4245
   Michigan City (G-9831)

Publishers Sovereign Grace...............G......765 296-5538
   Mulberry (G-10418)

Purple Door Press...............................G......219 690-1046
   Lowell (G-9421)

Rabboni Book Publishing Co LLC.......G......765 254-9969
   Muncie (G-10552)

Red Lark Press Inc..............................G......260 224-7974
   Huntington (G-6243)

Richard E Leonard LLC.......................G......812 882-7343
   Vincennes (G-13702)

Rol Publications.................................G......812 366-4154
   Greenville (G-5653)

Rosswyvern Press LLC.........................G......859 421-0864
   Clarksville (G-1694)

Rust Publishing In LLC.......................G......765 653-5151
   Greencastle (G-5477)

Rutkowski & Associates Inc...............G......812 476-4520
   Evansville (G-3712)

Ryobi Press Parts...............................G......800 901-3304
   Carmel (G-1474)

Sand Dune Publishing Compa............G......219 938-7118
   Gary (G-5095)

Scalable Press...................................G......510 396-5226
   Indianapolis (G-7900)

Schatzi Press.....................................G......317 335-2335
   McCordsville (G-9675)

Scher Maihem Publishing Ltd.............G......260 897-2697
   Auburn (G-352)

Scribe Publications Inc.......................G......219 791-9254
   Merrillville (G-9752)

Scurvy Palace Publishing LLC.............G......317 809-4591
   Martinsville (G-9637)

Service Publication Inc.......................G......219 845-4445
   Hammond (G-5938)

Sitesuccess Inc..................................G......219 808-4076
   Schererville (G-12345)

Skyward Publishing LLC.....................G......317 791-2212
   Indianapolis (G-7951)

Spiritbuilding Publishing....................G......765 623-2238
   Summitville (G-13105)

Tacair Publications............................G......260 429-7975
   Churubusco (G-1658)

Tale Chaser Publishing Inc.................G......765 962-4309
   Richmond (G-12057)

Tanglewood Publishing Inc.................G......812 877-9488
   Indianapolis (G-8035)

Tendre Press LLC................................G......812 606-9563
   Bloomington (G-837)

Testimony Publications LLC................G......812 602-3031
   Evansville (G-3758)

Thinkshortcut Publishing LLC...........G......765 935-1127
   Richmond (G-12065)

Thm Publishing Sacramento LLC........G......317 810-1340
   Carmel (G-1495)

Thomson Reuters Corporation............G......317 570-9387
   Fishers (G-3976)

Thrify Nickel Wnt ADS Evansvil.........E......812 428-8484
   Evansville (G-3761)

Thunder Rolls Express.........................G......812 667-5111
   Canaan (G-1281)

Timothy Reed Carry ME Mus Pubg......G......812 322-7187
   Bloomington (G-842)

Triangle Publishing............................G......765 677-2544
   Marion (G-9567)

True Stories Publishing Co LLC...........G......765 425-8224
   Indianapolis (G-8103)

Trustees Indiana University................E......812 855-4848
   Bloomington (G-848)

Un Communications Group Inc..........E......317 844-8622
   Carmel (G-1503)

Un Seen Press Co................................G......317 867-5594
   Westfield (G-14195)

Valvoline Express................................G......765 473-4891
   Peru (G-11554)

Vintage Publishing LLC.......................G......812 719-7200
   Evansville (G-3803)

Wamingo Publishing LLP.....................G......317 443-1326
   Indianapolis (G-8177)

Washington 2 Mount Publi..................G......812 332-1600
   Bloomington (G-853)

Wiggins Press LLC..............................G......574 273-1769
   Granger (G-5452)

Williams Woods Pubg Svcs LLC..........G......317 270-0976
   Indianapolis (G-8201)

Willowgreen Inc................................G......260 490-2222
   Fort Wayne (G-4756)

Woodsong Publishing.........................G......812 528-0875
   Seymour (G-12501)

Worth Publications LLC.......................G......219 808-4001
   Crown Point (G-2323)

Wth Publications Inc..........................G......574 646-2007
   Bourbon (G-951)

X Press Storage LLC...........................G......219 942-1227
   Hobart (G-6102)

Yellow Door Publishing LLC................G......574 256-5797
   Mishawaka (G-10152)

Zeppelin Commander Press Inc...........G......317 839-9025
   Plainfield (G-11653)

PUBLISHERS: Music Book

Sacred Selections..............................G......260 347-3758
   Kendallville (G-8509)

PUBLISHERS: Music Book & Sheet Music

Cola Voce Music Inc...........................G......317 466-0624
   Indianapolis (G-6630)

Praise Gathering Music Group.............F......765 640-4428
   Anderson (G-155)

Rewind...G......812 361-0411
   Bloomington (G-810)

PUBLISHERS: Newsletter

Fourth Freedom Forum Inc..................F......574 534-3402
   Goshen (G-5221)

Ingroup...G......317 817-9997
   Indianapolis (G-7232)

Russ Print Shop.................................F......219 996-3142
   Hebron (G-6022)

PUBLISHERS: Newspaper

Allen C Terhune & Associates.............G......765 948-4164
   Fairmount (G-3828)

Alymat Publishing LLC........................G......812 933-9940
   Batesville (G-490)

American Classifieds...........................E......317 782-8111
   Indianapolis (G-6386)

Aurora Services Inc...........................G......260 463-4901
   Shipshewana (G-12604)

Ball State University...........................G......765 285-8218
   Muncie (G-10437)

Benton Review Newspaper...................G......765 884-1902
   Fowler (G-4795)

Beverly G Inc.....................................G......812 401-1819
   Evansville (G-3383)

Big E Publications Inc.........................G......317 485-4097
   Fortville (G-4768)

Catholic Moment.................................G......765 742-2050
   Lafayette (G-8872)

Chicken Scratch LLC...........................G......260 486-9800
   Fort Wayne (G-4147)

Ecom Publishing Inc...........................G......574 862-2179
   Wakarusa (G-13776)

El Mexicano Inc..................................G......260 456-6843
   Fort Wayne (G-4233)

Elephant Enterprises...........................G......248 366-5383
   Hammond (G-5878)

Frankfort Newspaper...........................G......859 254-2385
   Frankfort (G-4833)

Franklin Township Civic League...........G......317 862-1774
   Indianapolis (G-6960)

Ginger Oliviae Publishing LLC.............G......765 762-3132
   Williamsport (G-14290)

Granger Gazette.................................G......574 277-2679
   Granger (G-5410)

Green Banner Publications Inc.............G......812 883-5555
   Salem (G-12289)

Guide Book Publishing.........................G......317 259-0599
   Indianapolis (G-7057)

Hamilton News Inc..............................G......260 488-3780
   Fort Wayne (G-4315)

Hendricks County Flyer.......................G......317 272-5800
   Avon (G-447)

Hielo Services LLC..............................G......219 973-1952
   Hobart (G-6080)

Hoosier Times Inc..............................F......812 332-4401
   Beech Grove (G-596)

Horizon Publications Inc.....................E......260 244-5153
   Columbia City (G-1791)

How Pubs USA....................................G......219 933-9251
   Munster (G-10607)

IBJ Book Publishing LLC.....................G......317 564-9924
   Carmel (G-1409)

Info Publishing Impact LLC.................G......317 912-3642
   Fishers (G-3931)

J Aime Music Publishing LLC.............G......574 772-2934
   Knox (G-8569)

Janis Buhl..G......765 478-5448
   Cambridge City (G-1258)

Kaiser Press LLC................................G......317 619-7092
   Indianapolis (G-7329)

Kaspar Broadcasting Co Inc................E......765 659-3338
   Frankfort (G-4839)

Kendallville Mall................................G......260 897-2697
   Avilla (G-411)

King Tut Inc.......................................G......317 938-9907
   Zionsville (G-14445)

La Ola Latino Americana.....................F......317 822-0345
   Indianapolis (G-7372)

Lebanon Reporter...............................F......765 482-4650
   Lebanon (G-9200)

Mexicano Newsletter..........................G......260 704-0682
   Fort Wayne (G-4469)

Monster House Press .... G..... 440 364-4548
  Bloomington *(G-775)*
News and Tribune .... G..... 812 206-2168
  Jeffersonville *(G-8404)*
News Publishing Company Inc .... G..... 260 461-8444
  Fort Wayne *(G-4503)*
Northwest News & Printing .... G..... 260 637-9003
  Fort Wayne *(G-4506)*
Printers Group .... G..... 317 835-7720
  Fairland *(G-3826)*
Rapt Pen LLC .... G..... 317 547-8113
  Indianapolis *(G-7817)*
Rowland Printing Co Inc .... F..... 317 773-1829
  Noblesville *(G-11177)*
Russ Print Shop .... F..... 219 996-3142
  Hebron *(G-6022)*
Snark Publishing LLC .... G..... 574 256-1027
  Mishawaka *(G-10129)*
Sommer Letter Company LLC .... G..... 260 414-6686
  Huntertown *(G-6147)*
South Bend Tribune .... G..... 574 971-5651
  Goshen *(G-5324)*
South Whtly Trbne Prctn News .... G..... 260 723-4771
  South Whitley *(G-13004)*
Southern Indiana Bus Source .... G..... 812 206-6397
  New Albany *(G-10863)*
Special Ideas Incorporated .... G..... 812 834-5691
  Heltonville *(G-6028)*
Spencer Evening World .... G..... 765 795-4438
  Cloverdale *(G-1738)*
The Findlay Publishing Co .... G..... 812 222-8000
  Batesville *(G-519)*
Thrify Nickel Wnt ADS Evansvil .... E..... 812 428-8484
  Evansville *(G-3761)*
Trading Post .... G..... 574 935-5460
  Plymouth *(G-11731)*
Turkey Roost Publishing LLC .... G..... 402 972-6388
  Hardinsburg *(G-5965)*
Twin Sparrow Press .... G..... 917 331-5247
  Munster *(G-10634)*
University Notre Dame Du Lac .... F..... 574 631-6346
  Notre Dame *(G-11305)*
USA Today .... G..... 212 715-2188
  Fishers *(G-3982)*
Vincennes Sun Commercial .... D..... 812 886-9955
  Vincennes *(G-13711)*
Wabash Valley Publishing LLC .... G..... 812 494-2152
  Vincennes *(G-13714)*

PUBLISHERS: Newspapers, No Printing

Berne Tri Weekly News Inc .... G..... 260 589-2101
  Berne *(G-609)*
Brown County Democrat Inc .... G..... 812 988-2221
  Nashville *(G-10717)*
Carroll Papers Inc .... G..... 574 967-4135
  Flora *(G-3993)*
Carroll Papers Inc .... G..... 765 564-2222
  Delphi *(G-2416)*
Catholic Press of Evansville .... G..... 812 424-5536
  Evansville *(G-3414)*
Chesterton Tribune Inc .... F..... 219 926-1131
  Chesterton *(G-1599)*
Cliff A Ostermeyer .... G..... 615 361-7902
  Indianapolis *(G-6621)*
Community Holdings Indiana Inc ...... E..... 765 482-4650
  Lebanon *(G-9175)*
Community Holdings Indiana Inc ...... F..... 765 459-3121
  Kokomo *(G-8608)*
Community Papers Inc .... G..... 317 241-7363
  Noblesville *(G-6639)*
Criterion Press Inc .... F..... 317 236-1570
  Indianapolis *(G-6693)*
Delphos Herald of Indiana .... E..... 812 537-0063
  Lawrenceburg *(G-9137)*
Delphos Herald of Indiana Inc .... G..... 812 438-2011
  Rising Sun *(G-12087)*
Dubois County Free Press LLC .... G..... 812 639-9651
  Huntingburg *(G-6157)*
Elwood Publishing Co Inc .... G..... 765 724-4469
  Alexandria *(G-40)*
Federated Publications Inc .... C..... 765 962-1575
  Richmond *(G-11987)*
Gannett Co Inc .... C..... 765 423-5512
  Lafayette *(G-8902)*
Green Banner Publications Inc .... G..... 812 752-3171
  Scottsburg *(G-12359)*
Green Banner Publications Inc .... G..... 812 752-3171
  Scottsburg *(G-12360)*
Hoosier Times Inc .... C..... 812 331-4270
  Bloomington *(G-741)*

Hoosier Times Inc .... E..... 812 275-3372
  Bedford *(G-548)*
Horse Circuit News Inc .... G..... 800 537-3958
  New Castle *(G-10906)*
Huntington County Tab Inc .... F..... 260 356-1107
  Huntington *(G-6211)*
IBJ Corporation .... D..... 317 634-6200
  Indianapolis *(G-7156)*
Jackson County Banner .... F..... 812 358-2111
  Brownstown *(G-1189)*
Kankakee Valley Post News .... G..... 219 987-5111
  Demotte *(G-2441)*
Kentuckiana Publishing .... G..... 812 273-2259
  Madison *(G-9475)*
Knightstown Banner LLC .... E..... 765 345-2292
  Knightstown *(G-8554)*
Kpc Media Group Inc .... E..... 260 925-2611
  Auburn *(G-339)*
Lagrange Publishing Co Inc .... F..... 260 463-2166
  Lagrange *(G-9053)*
Loogootee Tribune Inc .... G..... 812 295-2500
  Loogootee *(G-9389)*
Madison Courier .... E..... 812 265-3641
  Madison *(G-9479)*
New Wolcott Enterprise .... G..... 219 279-2167
  Wolcott *(G-14367)*
News Banner Publications Inc .... E..... 260 824-0224
  Bluffton *(G-883)*
News Dispatch .... C..... 219 874-7211
  Michigan City *(G-9823)*
News Publishing Company LLC .... G..... 502 633-4334
  Tell City *(G-13170)*
News Publishing Company LLC .... G..... 812 649-4440
  Rockport *(G-12171)*
Newspaper Holding Inc .... D..... 812 231-4200
  Terre Haute *(G-13290)*
Newspaper Holding Inc .... E..... 812 254-0480
  Washington *(G-13993)*
Nuvo Inc .... E..... 317 254-2400
  Indianapolis *(G-7605)*
Owen Leader Inc .... G..... 812 829-3936
  Spencer *(G-13031)*
Papers Inc .... G..... 574 534-2591
  Goshen *(G-5305)*
Papers Inc .... G..... 574 269-2932
  Warsaw *(G-13923)*
Pathfinder Communications Corp ..... E..... 574 295-2500
  Elkhart *(G-3077)*
Pike County Publishing Corp .... F..... 812 354-8500
  Petersburg *(G-11566)*
Pulaski County Press Inc .... G..... 574 946-6628
  Winamac *(G-14317)*
Region Communications Inc .... G..... 219 662-8888
  Crown Point *(G-2294)*
Republican .... G..... 317 745-2777
  Danville *(G-2356)*
Ripley Publishing Co Inc .... F..... 812 689-6364
  Versailles *(G-13657)*
Service Publication Inc .... G..... 219 845-4445
  Hammond *(G-5938)*
Shoals News .... G..... 812 247-2828
  Shoals *(G-12669)*
Sports Hotline .... G..... 765 664-8732
  Marion *(G-9564)*
Torch Newspapers Inc .... G..... 765 569-2033
  Rockville *(G-12182)*
Trustees Indiana University .... B..... 812 855-0763
  Bloomington *(G-846)*
Truth Publishing Company Inc .... E..... 765 653-5151
  Greencastle *(G-5480)*
Twin City Journal Reporter .... G..... 765 674-0070
  Gas City *(G-5127)*
Vevay Newspapers Inc .... G..... 812 427-2311
  Vevay *(G-13667)*
Waynedale News Inc .... G..... 260 747-4535
  Fort Wayne *(G-4747)*
Western Wayne News .... G..... 765 478-5448
  Cambridge City *(G-1262)*

PUBLISHERS: Periodical, With Printing

Emmis Communications Corp .... D..... 317 266-0100
  Indianapolis *(G-6854)*
Emmis Publishing Corporation .... G..... 317 266-0100
  Indianapolis *(G-6857)*
Midcountry Media Inc .... D..... 765 345-5133
  Knightstown *(G-8557)*
Stork News Northwest Indiana .... G..... 219 405-0499
  Chesterton *(G-1633)*
Stork News Northwest Indiana .... G..... 219 808-5221
  Hobart *(G-6097)*

PUBLISHERS: Periodicals, Magazines

Apartment Assn of Fort Wayne .... G..... 260 482-2916
  Fort Wayne *(G-4080)*
B E A LI Inc .... G..... 219 322-5158
  Schererville *(G-12316)*
Baxter Design & Advertising .... G..... 219 464-9237
  Valparaiso *(G-13507)*
Bonnier Corporation .... G..... 317 231-5862
  Indianapolis *(G-6495)*
Diamond Hoosier .... G..... 317 773-1411
  Noblesville *(G-11091)*
Donnie Michaels Kicks .... G..... 765 457-4083
  Kokomo *(G-8617)*
Endowment Development Services ... F..... 317 542-9829
  Indianapolis *(G-6861)*
Greencastle Offset Inc .... G..... 765 653-4026
  Greencastle *(G-5458)*
Herff Jones LLC .... C..... 800 419-5462
  Indianapolis *(G-7092)*
Hoosier All-Stars Inc .... G..... 317 408-0513
  Portland *(G-11828)*
Horizon Publishing Company LLC ..... E..... 219 852-3200
  Hammond *(G-5895)*
Indiana Business Magazine .... G..... 317 692-1200
  Indianapolis *(G-7176)*
Indiana State Medical Assn .... E..... 317 261-2060
  Indianapolis *(G-7192)*
International English Inc .... G..... 260 868-2670
  Butler *(G-1231)*
It Factor Publications Inc .... E..... 219 228-8424
  Highland *(G-6050)*
Limelight Publishing .... G..... 765 448-4461
  Lafayette *(G-8958)*
Magazine Fulfillment Corp .... E..... 219 874-4245
  Michigan City *(G-9814)*
Mappa Mundi Magazine .... G..... 574 896-4952
  North Judson *(G-11213)*
Pearson Education Inc .... C..... 765 483-6500
  Lebanon *(G-9211)*
Pearson Education Inc .... C..... 765 483-6738
  Lebanon *(G-9212)*
Quarterly Group .... G..... 812 526-5600
  Columbus *(G-2005)*
Senior Pathways Magazine LLC .... G..... 812 697-1750
  New Albany *(G-10861)*
TI Enterprises LLC .... F..... 574 262-4706
  Elkhart *(G-3218)*
Un Communications Group Inc .... E..... 317 844-8622
  Carmel *(G-1503)*
United Brethren In Christ .... F..... 260 356-2312
  Huntington *(G-6258)*
University Notre Dame Du Lac .... F..... 574 631-6346
  Notre Dame *(G-11305)*
Wabash Valley Magazine .... G..... 812 231-4294
  Terre Haute *(G-13365)*

PUBLISHERS: Periodicals, No Printing

Brian Bex Report Inc .... G..... 765 489-5566
  Hagerstown *(G-5804)*
Eco Partners Inc .... G..... 317 450-3346
  Carmel *(G-1367)*
Growing Child .... G..... 765 464-0920
  West Lafayette *(G-14073)*
Muzfeed Inc .... G..... 815 252-7676
  Fort Wayne *(G-4487)*
Prairie Gold Rush .... G..... 812 342-3608
  Seymour *(G-12476)*
Society For Ethnmusicology Inc ...... G..... 812 855-6672
  Bloomington *(G-827)*
Whitetail Heartbeat .... G..... 260 336-1052
  Middlebury *(G-9925)*

PUBLISHERS: Posters

Noel Studio Inc .... F..... 317 297-1117
  Zionsville *(G-14452)*

PUBLISHERS: Shopping News

Advertiser Inc .... G..... 260 824-4770
  Bluffton *(G-862)*
Journal Publishing Co Inc .... G..... 812 876-2254
  Ellettsville *(G-3282)*

PUBLISHERS: Technical Manuals

First Databank Inc .... G..... 317 571-7200
  Indianapolis *(G-6926)*

PUBLISHERS: Technical Manuals & Papers

Precisely Write Inc ....G....... 317 585-7701
Indianapolis *(G-7730)*

Sams Technical Publishing LLC ....F....... 317 396-9850
Indianapolis *(G-7889)*

PUBLISHERS: Telephone & Other Directory

Nationwide Publishing Company ....G....... 260 312-3924
Fort Wayne *(G-4492)*

PUBLISHERS: Textbooks, No Printing

Aom Bookshop ....G....... 317 493-8095
Indianapolis *(G-6405)*

Beeman Jorgensen Inc ....G....... 317 841-7677
Indianapolis *(G-6465)*

Bittinger Writings Inc ....G....... 317 846-9136
Carmel *(G-1317)*

Hackett Publishing Company ....E....... 317 635-9250
Indianapolis *(G-7063)*

PUBLISHERS: Trade journals, No Printing

American School Health Assn ....G....... 703 506-7675
Bloomington *(G-660)*

Creative Construction Pubg ....G....... 765 743-9704
West Lafayette *(G-14062)*

Don R Kill Publishing Inc ....G....... 574 271-9381
Granger *(G-5402)*

Homes & Lifestyles Magazine ....E....... 574 674-6639
Osceola *(G-11377)*

Kamrex Inc ....E....... 317 204-3779
Avon *(G-452)*

Raven Communications Inc ....G....... 317 576-9889
Indianapolis *(G-7818)*

PUBLISHING & BROADCASTING: Internet Only

App Factor ....G....... 219 229-1039
Chesterton *(G-1594)*

Dungan Aerial Services Inc ....G....... 765 827-1355
Connersville *(G-2047)*

Job Scholar LLC ....G....... 419 564-9574
Huntington *(G-6221)*

Porchlight Group Inc ....G....... 317 804-1166
Fishers *(G-3954)*

Pretty Brilliant LLC ....G....... 765 277-2308
Richmond *(G-12031)*

Smallwood Consulting LLC ....G....... 812 406-8040
Sellersburg *(G-12418)*

Taught It LLC ....G....... 317 469-4120
Indianapolis *(G-8039)*

PUBLISHING & PRINTING: Art Copy

Rough Notes Company Inc ....E....... 317 582-1600
Carmel *(G-1471)*

PUBLISHING & PRINTING: Book Music

Russel Warfield Inc ....G....... 317 243-7650
Indianapolis *(G-7873)*

PUBLISHING & PRINTING: Books

AM Publishing Inc ....G....... 317 806-0001
Fishers *(G-3870)*

Ave Maria Press Inc ....D....... 574 287-2831
Notre Dame *(G-11303)*

Beacon House ....G....... 219 756-2131
Schererville *(G-12317)*

Brethren In Christ Media Minis ....G....... 574 773-3164
Nappanee *(G-10657)*

Fideli Publishing ....G....... 888 343-3542
Martinsville *(G-9604)*

No-Load Fund Investor Inc ....G....... 317 571-1471
Carmel *(G-1443)*

Pearson Education Inc ....E....... 317 428-3049
Indianapolis *(G-7668)*

United Methodist Pubg Hse ....C....... 812 654-1325
Milan *(G-9947)*

Wesleyan Church Corporation ....D....... 317 774-7900
Fishers *(G-3984)*

Wiley Publishing Inc ....B....... 317 842-2032
Indianapolis *(G-8198)*

World Missionary Press Inc ....E....... 574 831-2111
New Paris *(G-11001)*

PUBLISHING & PRINTING: Catalogs

Degler Mktg & Mailing Svcs ....E....... 317 873-5550
Zionsville *(G-14429)*

Oleta Publishing Co Inc ....G....... 765 730-7195
Yorktown *(G-14409)*

PUBLISHING & PRINTING: Guides

Pelican Bay Solutions LLC ....G....... 574 268-4456
Warsaw *(G-13924)*

PUBLISHING & PRINTING: Magazines: publishing & printing

1632 Inc ....G....... 219 398-4155
East Chicago *(G-2514)*

Athletes Management & Service ....G....... 317 925-8200
Indianapolis *(G-6437)*

Bloom Magazine ....G....... 812 323-8959
Bloomington *(G-685)*

Brent Croxton Inc ....G....... 317 846-7591
Carmel *(G-1322)*

Christian Sound & Song Inc ....G....... 574 294-2893
Elkhart *(G-2756)*

Emp of Evansville ....F....... 812 962-1309
Evansville *(G-3476)*

Fort Wayne Newspapers Inc ....B....... 260 461-8444
Fort Wayne *(G-4277)*

Galbe Magazine LLC ....G....... 248 742-5231
Indianapolis *(G-6265)*

Indy Metro Woman Magazine ....G....... 317 843-1344
Indianapolis *(G-7218)*

Literature Sales ....G....... 219 873-3093
Michigan City *(G-9812)*

Lsc Communications Us LLC ....G....... 765 362-1300
Crawfordsville *(G-2169)*

Market Place Publications ....G....... 219 769-7733
Merrillville *(G-9730)*

Mennonite Inc Inc ....G....... 574 535-6050
Goshen *(G-5286)*

National Retail Hardware Assn ....E....... 317 290-0338
Indianapolis *(G-7576)*

Omega One Connect Inc ....G....... 317 626-3445
Indianapolis *(G-7618)*

Pages Editorial Services Inc ....F....... 765 674-4212
Marion *(G-9549)*

PUBLISHING & PRINTING: Music, Book

Home News Enterprises LLC ....E....... 574 583-5121
Monticello *(G-10265)*

Tom Doherty Company Inc ....G....... 317 352-8200
Indianapolis *(G-8079)*

PUBLISHING & PRINTING: Newsletters, Business Svc

Automobile Dealers Assn of Ind ....G....... 317 635-1441
Indianapolis *(G-6446)*

Cupprint LLC ....G....... 574 323-5250
South Bend *(G-12744)*

Dow Theory Forecasts Inc ....E....... 219 931-6480
Hammond *(G-5872)*

Horizon Management Services ....E....... 219 852-3200
Hammond *(G-5894)*

PUBLISHING & PRINTING: Newspapers

Aim Media Indiana Oper LLC ....E....... 317 462-5528
Greenfield *(G-5497)*

Aim Media Indiana Oper LLC ....E....... 317 736-7101
Franklin *(G-4863)*

Alan Daily ....G....... 574 595-6253
Star City *(G-13069)*

All Printing and Publications ....E....... 260 636-2727
Albion *(G-15)*

American Senior Homecare ....F....... 317 849-4968
Indianapolis *(G-6390)*

Beacon Publishing Co Inc ....G....... 812 637-0660
Lawrenceburg *(G-9134)*

Cnhi LLC ....E....... 812 944-6481
New Albany *(G-10762)*

Community Holdings Indiana Inc ....F....... 765 622-1212
Anderson *(G-88)*

Community Holdings Indiana Inc ....F....... 574 722-5000
Logansport *(G-9332)*

Community Holdings Indiana Inc ....F....... 317 272-5800
Avon *(G-436)*

Community Holdings Indiana Inc ....G....... 812 934-4343
Batesville *(G-497)*

Community Holdings Indiana Inc ....E....... 765 932-2222
Rushville *(G-12218)*

Community Holdings Indiana Inc ....G....... 317 873-6397
Lebanon *(G-9176)*

Community Holdings Indiana Inc ....E....... 812 663-3111
Greensburg *(G-5594)*

Courier-Times Inc ....D....... 765 529-1111
New Castle *(G-10897)*

Daily Peru Tribune Pubg Co ....E....... 765 473-6641
Peru *(G-11523)*

Decatur Publishing Co Inc ....E....... 260 724-2121
Decatur *(G-2374)*

Evansville Courier Co ....B....... 812 464-7500
Evansville *(G-3485)*

Fairmount News ....G....... 765 948-4164
Fairmount *(G-3831)*

Fort Wayne Newspapers Inc ....B....... 260 461-8444
Fort Wayne *(G-4277)*

Fountain County Neighbor ....G....... 765 762-2411
Attica *(G-300)*

Ft Wayne Reader ....G....... 260 420-8580
Fort Wayne *(G-4289)*

Gannett Co Inc ....C....... 765 962-1575
Richmond *(G-11989)*

Gannett Co Inc ....G....... 765 423-5511
Lafayette *(G-8903)*

Green Banner Publications Inc ....E....... 812 967-3176
Pekin *(G-11473)*

Growing Child ....G....... 765 464-0920
West Lafayette *(G-14073)*

Harrison Cnty Democrate ....G....... 812 734-0560
Corydon *(G-2100)*

Hartford City News Times ....C....... 765 348-0110
Hartford City *(G-5982)*

Home News Enterprises LLC ....E....... 812 342-1056
Columbus *(G-1940)*

Home News Enterprises LLC ....E....... 574 583-5121
Monticello *(G-10265)*

Hoosier Times Inc ....E....... 765 342-3311
Martinsville *(G-9613)*

Indiana Newspapers LLC ....D....... 812 886-9955
Vincennes *(G-13685)*

Indiana Newspapers LLC ....E....... 765 213-5700
Muncie *(G-10494)*

Indiana University Bloomington ....F....... 812 855-2816
Bloomington *(G-748)*

Kpc Media Group Inc ....G....... 678 645-0000
Angola *(G-227)*

Kpc Media Group Inc ....E....... 260 426-2640
Fort Wayne *(G-4415)*

La Voz De Indiana Inc ....G....... 317 423-0957
Indianapolis *(G-7373)*

Leader Publishing Co of Salem ....E....... 812 883-4446
Salem *(G-12299)*

Lee Enterprises Inc Times ....E....... 219 933-3200
Munster *(G-10613)*

Lee Publications Inc ....E....... 219 462-5151
Valparaiso *(G-13574)*

Lee Publications Inc ....D....... 219 933-9251
Munster *(G-10614)*

Liberty Herald ....G....... 765 458-5114
Liberty *(G-9264)*

Mayhill Publications Inc ....E....... 765 345-5133
Knightstown *(G-8556)*

Montgomery & Associates Inc ....F....... 219 879-0088
Michigan City *(G-9821)*

My Daily Wedding Deals LLC ....G....... 812 603-6149
Indianapolis *(G-7563)*

Myers Enterprises Inc ....E....... 812 636-7350
Odon *(G-11335)*

News Examiner Circulation Dept ....G....... 765 825-2914
Connersville *(G-2066)*

News Reminder ....F....... 574 583-5121
Monticello *(G-10274)*

Newton County Enterprises Inc ....G....... 219 474-5532
Kentland *(G-8522)*

Nwitimescom ....F....... 219 933-3200
Munster *(G-10617)*

Odb Inc ....G....... 260 673-0062
Fort Wayne *(G-4508)*

Patrick & Sharon Hoctor ....G....... 812 898-2678
Terre Haute *(G-13297)*

Pendleton Times ....G....... 765 778-2324
Pendleton *(G-11500)*

Progress Examiner ....G....... 812 865-3242
Orleans *(G-11368)*

Schurz Communications Inc ....E....... 317 773-9960
Noblesville *(G-11180)*

Schurz Communications Inc ....F....... 574 247-7237
Mishawaka *(G-10121)*

Seymour Trbune A Cal Ltd Prtnr ....E 812 522-4871
  Seymour (G-12487)
South Gibson Star-Times Inc.................F 812 753-3553
  Fort Branch (G-4029)
Spectrum Print & Marketing.................G 317 908-7471
  Avon (G-467)
Sports Chronicle LLC.............................G 317 353-9365
  Indianapolis (G-7975)
Springs Valley Publishing Co ....G 812 936-9630
  French Lick (G-4989)
Times..E 765 296-3622
  Frankfort (G-4856)
Times Leader Publications LLC ....F 317 300-8782
  Indianapolis (G-8076)
Topics Newspapers Inc ....D 888 357-7827
  Fishers (G-3978)
Towneost LLC ....G 317 288-7101
  Indianapolis (G-8085)
Truth Publishing Company Inc ....C 574 294-1661
  Elkhart (G-3227)
Twice Daily LLC...................................G 812 484-5417
  Evansville (G-3780)
University Notre Dame Du Lac ....D 574 631-7471
  Notre Dame (G-11304)

PUBLISHING & PRINTING: Pamphlets

Ilf Industries......................................G 260 749-1931
  New Haven (G-10944)
Main1media LLC..................................G 317 841-7000
  Indianapolis (G-7443)
Old Paths Tract Society Inc.................F 812 247-2560
  Shoals (G-12668)

PUBLISHING & PRINTING: Periodical Statistical Reports

Americas Coml Trnsp RES Co LLC....F 812 379-2085
  Columbus (G-1854)

PUBLISHING & PRINTING: Posters

Image House Inc ....F 219 947-0800
  Crown Point (G-2260)

PUBLISHING & PRINTING: Shopping News

Crown Point Shopping News................G 219 663-4212
  Crown Point (G-2241)

PUBLISHING & PRINTING: Trade Journals

Michiana Executive Journal..................E 574 256-6666
  Mishawaka (G-10080)
Rough Notes Company Inc ....E 317 582-1600
  Carmel (G-1471)
Trustees Indiana University ....G 812 856-4186
  Bloomington (G-845)

PUBLISHING & PRINTING: Yearbooks

Herff Jones LLC ....E 317 612-3400
  Indianapolis (G-7089)
Herff Jones LLC ....C 800 419-5462
  Indianapolis (G-7092)

PULP MILLS

International Paper Company ....E 800 643-7244
  Terre Haute (G-13259)
International Paper Company ....C 317 510-6410
  Indianapolis (G-7257)
Qrs Inc...G 812 948-1323
  New Albany (G-10851)
Recycling Center Inc ....D 765 966-8295
  Richmond (G-12041)
Recycling Works Inc ....F 574 293-3751
  Elkhart (G-3141)

PULP MILLS: Chemical & Semichemical Processing

Mafcote Wabash Paper Coating ....G 260 563-4181
  Wabash (G-13736)

PULP MILLS: Mechanical & Recycling Processing

Exeon Processors LLC........................E 765 674-2266
  Jonesboro (G-8444)
Jeda Equipment Services Inc ....G 317 842-9377
  Fishers (G-3933)

PUMPS

All-Pro Pump & Repair Inc ....G 317 738-4203
  Morgantown (G-10348)
Automatic Pool Covers Inc ....E 317 579-2000
  Westfield (G-14137)
Bradley Innovation Group LLC.............G 765 942-7127
  Ladoga (G-8838)
Dura Products Inc ....F 855 502-3872
  Arcadia (G-264)
E C Schleyer Pump Co Inc ....G 765 643-3334
  Anderson (G-102)
FL Smidth ....G 812 402-9210
  Evansville (G-3507)
Flowserve Corporation........................G 219 763-1000
  Portage (G-11764)
Franklin Electric Co Inc ....B 260 824-2900
  Fort Wayne (G-4285)
Grundfos Pumps Mfg Corp ....F 317 925-9661
  Indianapolis (G-7055)
Hayward Tyler Inc ....G 812 867-2848
  Evansville (G-3536)
Hoosier Fire Equipment Inc ....G 219 462-1707
  Valparaiso (G-13557)
Met-Pro Technologies LLC...................E 317 293-2930
  Indianapolis (G-7485)
Netshape Technologies LLC.................C 812 755-4501
  Campbellsburg (G-1278)
Ohio Transmission Corporation ....G 812 466-2734
  Terre Haute (G-13294)
Parker-Hannifin Corporation ....C 260 636-2104
  Albion (G-32)
Parker-Hannifin Corporation.................F 608 824-0500
  Tell City (G-13172)
R B Tool & Machinery Co ....G 574 679-0082
  Osceola (G-11383)
Rankin Pump and Supply Co Inc..........G 812 238-2535
  Terre Haute (G-13315)
Shoemaker Welding Co ....G 574 656-4412
  North Liberty (G-11221)
Specialty Manufacturing of Ind............E 812 256-4633
  Charlestown (G-1581)
Tbk America Inc ....E 765 962-0147
  Richmond (G-12058)
Thrush Co Inc ....E 765 472-3351
  Peru (G-11551)
Tuthill Corporation ....C 260 747-7529
  Fort Wayne (G-4709)
Tuthill Corporation ....G 260 747-7529
  Fort Wayne (G-4710)

PUMPS & PARTS: Indl

Autoform Tool & Mfg LLC ....C 260 624-2014
  Angola (G-195)
Flint & Walling Inc ....C 260 347-1781
  Kendallville (G-8475)
Hy-Flex Corporation ....E 765 571-5125
  Knightstown (G-8551)
Madden Manufacturing Inc ....F 574 295-4292
  Elkhart (G-3013)
Mantra Enterprise LLC ....G 201 428-8709
  Fishers (G-3944)
Pump Meter Solutions ....G 317 984-7867
  Arcadia (G-267)
Roland International Co LLC ....G 319 400-1106
  Carmel (G-1469)
Sterling Fluid Systems USA LLC..........C 317 925-9661
  Indianapolis (G-8003)
Wee Engineer Inc ....F 765 449-4280
  Dayton (G-2362)

PUMPS & PUMPING EQPT REPAIR SVCS

Altek Inc ....G 812 385-2561
  Princeton (G-11863)
Hamilton Bros Inc ....F 317 241-2571
  Indianapolis (G-7067)
Horner Industrial Services Inc ....G 317 916-4274
  Indianapolis (G-7128)
Horner Industrial Services Inc ....G 812 466-5281
  Terre Haute (G-13249)
Horner Industrial Services Inc ....G 260 434-1189
  Fort Wayne (G-4348)
Kochs Electric Inc...............................F 317 639-5624
  Indianapolis (G-7364)
Progress Group Inc ....D 219 322-3700
  Schererville (G-12342)
Rankin Pump and Supply Co Inc...........G 812 238-2535
  Terre Haute (G-13315)
T M E Inc ....G 219 769-6627
  Merrillville (G-9756)

Wills Electric Service Inc......................G 812 883-5653
  Pekin (G-11480)

PUMPS & PUMPING EQPT WHOLESALERS

Dekker Vacuum Technologies Inc ....E 219 861-0661
  Michigan City (G-9781)
Hrezo Industrial Eqp & Engrg ....F 812 537-4700
  Greendale (G-5489)
Mills Electric Co Inc ....G 219 931-3114
  Hammond (G-5916)
Power Investments Inc ....F 317 738-2117
  Franklin (G-4921)
Rankin Pump and Supply Co Inc...........G 812 238-2535
  Terre Haute (G-13315)
Robinson Industries Inc ....E 317 867-3214
  Westfield (G-14185)

PUMPS: Domestic, Water Or Sump

3w Enterprises LLC ....G 847 366-6555
  Elkhart (G-2654)
Hayward & Sams LLP ....G 260 351-4166
  Stroh (G-13077)

PUMPS: Measuring & Dispensing

Chemical Control Systems Inc ....G 219 465-5103
  Griffith (G-5770)
Cortex Safety Technologies LLC...........G 317 414-5607
  Carmel (G-1344)
Dispensit...G 317 776-8740
  Noblesville (G-11095)
Indco Inc ....G 812 945-4383
  New Albany (G-10805)
Madden Manufacturing Inc ....F 574 295-4292
  Elkhart (G-3013)
Royal Adhesives & Sealants LLC ....E 574 246-5000
  South Bend (G-12921)
Separation By Design Inc......................G 812 424-1239
  Evansville (G-3722)

PUMPS: Oil, Measuring Or Dispensing

Rj Fuel Services Inc.............................G 812 350-2897
  Edinburgh (G-2625)

PUNCHES: Forming & Stamping

Dayton Progress Corporation................E 260 726-6861
  Portland (G-11815)

PURCHASING SVCS

Finvantage LLC....................................F 317 500-4949
  Carmel (G-1381)

PURIFICATION & DUST COLLECTION EQPT

Electro Painters Inc ....G 317 875-8816
  Carmel (G-1370)
U S Air Filtration Inc ....G 260 486-7399
  Fort Wayne (G-4712)

PURIFIERS: Centrifugal

US Centrifuge Systems LLC ....F 317 299-2020
  Indianapolis (G-8136)

QUICKLIME

Mississippi Lime Company....................G 800 437-5463
  Portage (G-11777)

QUILTING SVC

Quilt Designs Inc.................................G 574 534-2502
  Elkhart (G-3132)
Zig-Zag Crnr Qilts Baskets LLC............G 317 326-3115
  Greenfield (G-5586)

QUILTING SVC & SPLYS, FOR THE TRADE

Quilt Expressions ....G 317 913-1916
  Fishers (G-3960)
Quilters Garden ....G 812 539-4939
  Lawrenceburg (G-9154)

QUILTING: Individuals

Zig-Zag Crnr Qilts Baskets LLC............G 317 326-3115
  Greenfield (G-5586)

P
R
O
D
U
C
T

RACETRACKS

Royal Acres Equestrian Center ....G....... 219 874-7519
Michigan City **(G-9836)**

RACEWAYS

E Squared Motorsports LLC ....G....... 317 626-2937
Avon **(G-439)**

Fastlane Raceway ....G....... 812 430-8818
Evansville **(G-3501)**

Juncos Racing ....G....... 317 640-2348
Indianapolis **(G-7321)**

Lucas Oil Raceway ....F....... 317 291-4090
Indianapolis **(G-7423)**

Miller Raceway ....G....... 219 939-9688
Gary **(G-5076)**

Raceway Commons ....G....... 303 503-4333
Indianapolis **(G-7812)**

Raceway Distributing Inc ....G....... 574 850-8191
Mishawaka **(G-10115)**

Raceway Hand Car Wash LLC ....G....... 260 242-9866
Kendallville **(G-8505)**

RACKS & SHELVING: Household, Wood

Oak Lief ....G....... 765 642-9010
Anderson **(G-147)**

RACKS: Bicycle, Automotive

Sportcrafters Inc ....G....... 574 243-4994
Granger **(G-5438)**

RACKS: Display

Hitzer Inc ....E....... 260 589-8536
Berne **(G-617)**

Star Nova US LLC ....G....... 269 830-5802
South Bend **(G-12954)**

Title Ten Manufacturing LLC ....G....... 765 388-2482
Muncie **(G-10570)**

RACKS: Railroad Car, Vehicle Transportation, Steel

Ftr Trnsportation Intelligence ....G....... 888 988-1699
Bloomington **(G-729)**

RACKS: Trash, Metal Rack

Creative Craftsmen Inc ....E....... 812 423-2844
Evansville **(G-3437)**

RADAR SYSTEMS & EQPT

Radar Assoc Corp ....G....... 219 838-8030
Munster **(G-10625)**

RADIO & TELEVISION COMMUNICATIONS EQUIPMENT

Acoustical Audio Designs LLC ....F....... 812 282-7522
Jeffersonville **(G-8318)**

Broadcast Connection Inc ....G....... 765 847-2519
Williamsburg **(G-14283)**

Corporate Systems Engrg LLC ....D....... 317 322-7984
Indianapolis **(G-6671)**

Destiny Solutions Inc ....G....... 502 384-0031
Georgetown **(G-5142)**

Ejl Tech ....G....... 812 374-8808
Columbus **(G-1918)**

Furrion LLC ....F....... 574 327-6571
Elkhart **(G-2871)**

GH Products Inc ....G....... 619 208-4823
West Lafayette **(G-14068)**

I E M C ....G....... 219 464-2890
Valparaiso **(G-13558)**

Llama Corporation ....G....... 888 701-7432
Decatur **(G-2391)**

Microwave Devices Inc ....G....... 317 736-8833
Franklin **(G-4907)**

Motorola Solutions Inc ....G....... 317 716-8064
Indianapolis **(G-7548)**

Raytheon Company ....E....... 317 306-4872
Indianapolis **(G-7821)**

Shf Microwave Parts Co ....G....... 219 785-2602
La Porte **(G-8820)**

RADIO BROADCASTING & COMMUNICATIONS EQPT

B JS Electronics ....G....... 812 482-3484
Jasper **(G-8237)**

Telectro-Mek Inc ....G....... 260 747-0586
Fort Wayne **(G-4677)**

RADIO BROADCASTING STATIONS

Continnntal Broadcast Group LLC ....E....... 317 924-1071
Indianapolis **(G-6657)**

Emmis Communications Corp ....D....... 317 266-0100
Indianapolis **(G-6854)**

Emmis Operating Company ....E....... 317 266-0100
Indianapolis **(G-6855)**

Kaspar Broadcasting Co Inc ....E....... 765 659-3338
Frankfort **(G-4839)**

The Findlay Publishing Co ....G....... 812 222-8000
Batesville **(G-519)**

World Rdo Mssnary Fllwship Inc ....E....... 574 970-4252
Elkhart **(G-3268)**

RADIO COMMUNICATIONS: Airborne Eqpt

Gwin Enterprises ....G....... 317 881-6401
Indianapolis **(G-7061)**

Managed Cmmunications Svcs LLC .....F....... 260 480-7885
Huntertown **(G-6142)**

Nello Capital Inc ....G....... 574 288-3632
South Bend **(G-12869)**

RADIO RECEIVER NETWORKS

W Ay-FM Media Group Inc ....G....... 812 945-1043
New Albany **(G-10872)**

RADIO, TELEVISION & CONSUMER ELECTRONICS STORES: Antennas

Tempest Technical Sales Inc ....F....... 317 844-9236
Carmel **(G-1492)**

RADIO, TELEVISION & CONSUMER ELECTRONICS STORES: Eqpt, NEC

3M Indianapolis ....G....... 317 692-3000
Indianapolis **(G-6289)**

RADIO, TELEVISION & CONSUMER ELECTRONICS STORES: TV Sets

Vans TV & Appliance Inc ....F....... 260 927-8267
Auburn **(G-366)**

RAIL & STRUCTURAL SHAPES: Aluminum rail & structural shapes

Highmark Technologies LLC ....E....... 260 483-0012
Fort Wayne **(G-4334)**

RAILINGS: Prefabricated, Metal

Colbin Tool Company Inc ....E....... 574 457-3183
Syracuse **(G-13130)**

RAILROAD CAR RENTING & LEASING SVCS

Transportation Tech Inds ....F....... 812 962-5000
Evansville **(G-3769)**

RAILROAD CAR REPAIR SVCS

ARS Nebraska LLC ....E....... 765 832-5210
Clinton **(G-1713)**

RAILROAD CROSSINGS: Steel Or Iron

L B Foster Company ....G....... 260 244-2887
Columbia City **(G-1805)**

RAILROAD EQPT

Amsted Rail Company Inc ....D....... 219 931-1900
Hammond **(G-5843)**

Cai Rail ....G....... 317 669-2555
Carmel **(G-1325)**

General Signals Inc ....F....... 812 474-4256
Evansville **(G-3518)**

J P Industries Inc ....F....... 574 293-8763
Elkhart **(G-2942)**

Stella Jones ....G....... 812 232-2316
Terre Haute **(G-13344)**

Tangent Rail Products Inc ....E....... 412 325-0202
Terre Haute **(G-13348)**

Transco Railway Products Inc ....D....... 574 753-6227
Logansport **(G-9370)**

Western-Cullen-Hayes Inc ....E....... 765 962-0526
Richmond **(G-12075)**

RAILROAD EQPT & SPLYS WHOLESALERS

General Signals Inc ....F....... 812 474-4256
Evansville **(G-3518)**

RAILROAD EQPT: Brakes, Air & Vacuum

Hadady Corporation ....C....... 219 322-7417
Dyer **(G-2500)**

RAILROAD EQPT: Cars & Eqpt, Train, Freight Or Passenger

Adams & Westlake Ltd ....E....... 574 264-1141
Elkhart **(G-2668)**

Kiel NA LLC ....F....... 574 293-3600
Elkhart **(G-2965)**

Mark Hedge ....G....... 812 288-8037
Jeffersonville **(G-8397)**

RAILROAD EQPT: Locomotives & Parts, Electric Or Nonelectric

Rolls-Royce Corporation ....G....... 317 230-8515
West Lafayette **(G-14104)**

Rolls-Royce Corporation ....A....... 317 230-2000
Indianapolis **(G-7858)**

RAILROAD EQPT: Locomotives & Parts, Indl

Western Reman Industrial LLC ....D....... 765 472-2002
Peru **(G-11558)**

RAILROAD EQPT: Tenders, Locomotive

Locomotive S Professional ....G....... 219 398-9123
East Chicago **(G-2549)**

RAILROAD EQPT: Trackless Trolley Buses

Tcb Enterprises LLC ....F....... 574 522-3971
Elkhart **(G-3207)**

Tcb Industries Inc ....F....... 574 522-3971
Elkhart **(G-3208)**

RAILROAD MAINTENANCE & REPAIR SVCS

Progress Rail Services Corp ....C....... 219 397-5326
East Chicago **(G-2565)**

RAILROAD TIES: Concrete

Dynamic Composites LLC ....G....... 260 625-8686
Columbia City **(G-1781)**

RAMPS: Prefabricated Metal

Full Metal Solutions LLC ....G....... 812 725-9660
Jeffersonville **(G-8365)**

Pathfinder Amramp LLC ....G....... 260 356-0500
Huntington **(G-6235)**

T & S Equipment Company ....C....... 260 665-9521
Angola **(G-249)**

REAL ESTATE AGENCIES & BROKERS

Complete Property Care LLC ....G....... 765 288-0890
Muncie **(G-10447)**

REAL ESTATE AGENTS & MANAGERS

Brockwood Farm ....G....... 812 837-9607
Nashville **(G-10716)**

Vectren Corporation ....A....... 812 491-4000
Evansville **(G-3794)**

REAL ESTATE BROKERS: Manufactured Homes, On-Site

Thornes Homes Inc ....G....... 812 275-4656
Bedford **(G-584)**

REAL ESTATE MANAGERS: Cemetery

Anderson Memorial Park ....F....... 765 643-3211
Anderson **(G-65)**

REAL ESTATE OPERATORS, EXC DEVEL: Theater Bldg, Owner & Op

Kendalville Mall ....G..... 260 897-2697
Avilla (G-411)

REAL ESTATE OPERATORS, EXC DEVELOPERS: Commercial/Indl Bldg

Accent Complex Inc..........................G..... 574 522-2368
Elkhart (G-2664)
Cook Group Incorporated ....F..... 812 339-2235
Bloomington (G-704)
Nickolick Development.......................G..... 812 422-8526
Evansville (G-3644)

REAL ESTATE OPS, EXC DEVELOPER: Residential Bldg, 4 Or Less

Milani Custom Homes LLC ....G..... 219 455-5804
Merrillville (G-9734)

RECORDING HEADS: Speech & Musical Eqpt

Music Store.......................................G..... 812 949-3004
Clarksville (G-1689)

RECORDS & TAPES: Prerecorded

Cliff A Ostermeyer.............................G..... 615 361-7902
Indianapolis (G-6621)
Rhi US Ltd...G..... 219 237-2420
Hammond (G-5934)
Voice of God Recordings Inc ....D..... 812 246-2137
Jeffersonville (G-8439)
World Media Group Inc ....C..... 317 549-8484
Indianapolis (G-8216)

RECOVERY SVC: Iron Ore, From Open Hearth Slag

Golden Beam Metals LLC...................G..... 317 806-2750
Indianapolis (G-7019)
Newjac Inc ....D..... 765 483-2190
Lebanon (G-9209)

RECREATIONAL & SPORTING CAMPS

Knox County Association ....D..... 812 886-4312
Vincennes (G-13689)

RECREATIONAL CAMPS

Yellow Banks Clay Company Inc..........F..... 812 567-4703
Dale (G-2336)

RECREATIONAL DEALERS: Campers/Pickup Coaches Truck Mounted

Highland Ridge Rv Inc........................B..... 260 768-7771
Shipshewana (G-12616)

RECREATIONAL SPORTING EQPT REPAIR SVCS

Geist Bike and Hobby Company ....G..... 317 855-1346
Indianapolis (G-6990)

RECREATIONAL VEHICLE DEALERS

Forest River Inc.................................E..... 574 389-4600
Elkhart (G-2865)

RECREATIONAL VEHICLE PARTS & ACCESS STORES

Camco Manufacturing Inc ....F..... 574 264-1491
Elkhart (G-2747)
Eash LLC...F..... 574 295-4450
Elkhart (G-2811)
Jpc LLC..F..... 574 293-8030
Elkhart (G-2951)
Kentuckiana Yacht Services LLC ....G..... 812 282-2660
Jeffersonville (G-8387)
Kinro Manufacturing Inc......................C..... 574 533-8337
Goshen (G-5257)
Ranch Fiberglass Inc..........................D..... 574 294-7550
Elkhart (G-3138)
Ultra-Heat Inc.....................................F..... 574 522-6594
Elkhart (G-3232)

RECREATIONAL VEHICLE: Wholesalers

All American Group Inc ....B..... 574 825-8555
Middlebury (G-9868)
Damon Corporation ....B..... 574 262-2624
Elkhart (G-2788)
Dmi Holding Corp ....C..... 574 534-1224
Goshen (G-5200)
Dna Enterprises Inc ....E..... 574 534-0034
Goshen (G-5201)
Forest River Inc ....C..... 574 533-5934
Goshen (G-5217)
Forest River Inc ....C..... 574 296-7700
Elkhart (G-2866)
Suburban Manufacturing Company ......F..... 574 294-5681
Elkhart (G-3196)

RECYCLING: Paper

Midwest Plastics Company Inc.............G..... 574 674-0161
Osceola (G-11382)
Parrish of Indiana Inc ....G..... 317 859-0934
Indianapolis (G-7657)
Starke County Recycling Inc ....F..... 574 772-2594
Knox (G-8584)

REELS: Cable, Metal

Hosetract Industries Ltd......................F..... 260 489-8828
Fort Wayne (G-4349)
Mossberg Industries Inc.....................D..... 260 357-5141
Garrett (G-5018)
Murpac of Fort Wayne LLC ....G..... 260 424-2299
Fort Wayne (G-4485)
Reelcraft Industries Inc ....C..... 855 634-9109
Columbia City (G-1824)

REELS: Fiber, Textile, Made From Purchased Materials

Elder Group Inc ....D..... 765 966-7676
Richmond (G-11980)

REELS: Wood

Corr-Wood Manufacturing Inc ....E..... 812 867-0700
Evansville (G-3431)

REFINERS & SMELTERS: Aluminum

Joe W Morgan Inc..............................D..... 812 423-5914
Evansville (G-3575)
Koch Enterprises Inc ....G..... 812 465-9800
Evansville (G-3596)
Nanshn Amrc Adv Alum Tech LLC ....C..... 765 838-8645
Lafayette (G-8974)
Real Alloy Recycling LLC....................E..... 260 563-2409
Wabash (G-13753)
Recycling Services Indiana Inc ....E..... 812 279-8114
Bedford (G-572)
Superior Aluminum Alloys LLC ....C..... 260 749-7599
New Haven (G-10959)
Transmetco Corporation ....F..... 260 355-0089
Huntington (G-6255)

REFINERS & SMELTERS: Antimony, Primary

Netshape Technologies LLC................E..... 812 248-9273
Noblesville (G-11158)

REFINERS & SMELTERS: Nonferrous Metal

Ad-Vance Magnetics Inc.....................E..... 574 223-3158
Rochester (G-12113)
Advanced Magnesium Alloys Corp......E..... 765 643-5873
Anderson (G-59)
All Pro Shearing Inc ....F..... 317 691-1005
Indianapolis (G-6367)
Aluminum Conversion Inc ....G..... 260 856-2180
Cromwell (G-2207)
American Scrap Processing Inc............D..... 219 398-1444
East Chicago (G-2515)
Eco-Bat America LLC ....C..... 317 247-1303
Indianapolis (G-6801)
Exide Technologies ....C..... 765 747-9980
Muncie (G-10470)
Haynes International Inc......................C..... 219 326-8530
La Porte (G-8762)
Howmet Castings & Services Inc ....A..... 219 326-7400
La Porte (G-8767)
Induction Iron Incorporated ....F..... 813 969-3300
Evansville (G-3554)

J Trockman & Sons Inc ....E..... 812 425-5271
Evansville (G-3569)
Kendallville Iron & Metal Inc ....E..... 260 347-1958
Kendallville (G-8486)
Loeb-Lorman Metals Inc.....................G..... 574 892-5063
Argos (G-275)
Mervis Industries Inc ....F..... 812 232-1251
Terre Haute (G-13284)
Mervis Industries Inc ....D..... 765 454-5800
Kokomo (G-8665)
Metal Spinners Inc ....F..... 260 665-2158
Angola (G-229)
Newco Metals Inc ....G..... 765 644-6649
Anderson (G-145)
Newco Metals Inc ....E..... 317 485-7721
Pendleton (G-11497)
P & H Iron & Supply Inc ....F..... 219 853-0240
Hammond (G-5925)
Plymouth Tube Company ....C..... 574 946-6191
Winamac (G-14314)
Porter County Ir & Met Recycle ....F..... 219 996-7630
Hebron (G-6020)
Qrs Inc..G..... 812 948-1323
New Albany (G-10851)
Real Alloy Recycling LLC....................E..... 262 637-9858
Wabash (G-13752)
Recovery Technologies LLC ....E..... 260 745-3902
Fort Wayne (G-4583)
Recycling Center Inc ....D..... 765 966-8295
Richmond (G-12041)
Recycling Works Inc ....F..... 574 293-3751
Elkhart (G-3141)
S W Industries Inc..............................F..... 317 788-4221
Indianapolis (G-7882)
Scepter Inc...D..... 812 735-2500
Bicknell (G-633)
Special Metals Corporation..................E..... 574 262-3451
Elkhart (G-3183)
Versatile Processing Group Inc............G..... 317 577-8930
Indianapolis (G-8152)
Winski Brothers Inc ....F..... 765 654-5323
Frankfort (G-4860)

REFINING LUBRICATING OILS & GREASES, NEC

Hartland Distillations Inc.....................F..... 812 464-4446
Evansville (G-3534)
Oil Technology Inc..............................E..... 219 322-2724
Dyer (G-2506)
Warrior Oil Service Inc ....F..... 317 738-9777
Franklin (G-4940)

REFINING: Petroleum

Admiral Petroleum Company................G..... 574 272-2051
South Bend (G-12695)
Airgas Inc...E..... 317 632-7106
Indianapolis (G-6354)
American Petroleum ....G..... 269 223-4135
Middlebury (G-9870)
B P Security ....G..... 219 473-3700
Whiting (G-14268)
Calumet Finance Corp ....G..... 317 328-5660
Indianapolis (G-6534)
Calumet Gp LLC.................................F..... 317 328-5660
Indianapolis (G-6535)
Calumet International Inc.....................G..... 317 328-5660
Indianapolis (G-6536)
Calumet Karns City Ref LLC................D..... 317 328-5660
Indianapolis (G-6537)
Calumet Refining LLC ....G..... 317 328-5660
Indianapolis (G-6540)
Calumet Shreveport Llc.......................D..... 317 328-5660
Indianapolis (G-6541)
Cjs Stop N Go ....G..... 317 877-0681
Noblesville (G-11083)
Countrymark Coop Holdg Corp............E..... 800 808-3170
Indianapolis (G-6676)
Countrymark Ref Logistics LLC ....D..... 812 838-4341
Mount Vernon (G-10388)
Don Hartman Oil Co Inc......................G..... 765 643-5026
Anderson (G-98)
Mid-Town Petro Acquisition LLC ....E..... 219 728-4110
Chesterton (G-1621)
Oxbow Carbon & Minerals ....G..... 219 473-0359
Whiting (G-14272)
Superior Oil Company Inc....................E..... 574 264-0161
Elkhart (G-3199)
Upland Stop & Go LLC ....G..... 765 998-0840
Upland (G-13474)

PRODUCT

REFLECTIVE ROAD MARKERS, WHOLESALE

Mgi Traffic Control Pdts Inc ....G........ 317 835-9212
Fairland *(G-3825)*

REFRACTORIES: Brick

Thermal Ceramics Inc ....E 574 296-3500
Elkhart *(G-3212)*

REFRACTORIES: Clay

Can-Clay Corp ....E 812 547-3461
Cannelton *(G-1288)*

Champion Target ....E 765 966-7745
Richmond *(G-11969)*

Dvs Refractories LLC ....G 219 886-2004
Gary *(G-5042)*

Grefco Minerals Inc ....F 765 362-6000
Crawfordsville *(G-2155)*

Harbisonwalker Intl Inc ....G 219 881-4440
Gary *(G-5057)*

Harbisonwalker Intl Inc ....D 219 883-3335
Gary *(G-5058)*

Quikrete Companies Inc ....E 317 251-2281
Indianapolis *(G-7805)*

REFRACTORIES: Foundry, Clay

Veitsch-Radex America LLC ....E 219 237-2420
Munster *(G-10637)*

Wb Refractory Service Inc ....G 317 450-7386
Speedway *(G-13016)*

REFRACTORIES: Glasshouse

Bmi Refractory Services Inc ....G 219 885-2209
Gary *(G-5030)*

Refractory Specialists LLC ....G 260 969-1099
Fort Wayne *(G-4585)*

REFRACTORIES: Nonclay

E J Bognar Inc ....F 412 344-9900
Schneider *(G-12354)*

Harbisonwalker Intl Inc ....D 219 883-3335
Gary *(G-5058)*

Hill & Griffith Company ....E 317 241-9233
Indianapolis *(G-7108)*

Insulation Specialties of Amer ....E 219 733-2502
Wanatah *(G-13824)*

Magneco/Metrel Inc ....F 219 885-4190
Gary *(G-5073)*

Minteq International Inc ....E 219 397-5978
East Chicago *(G-2553)*

Minteq International Inc ....C 219 886-9555
Gary *(G-5077)*

Minteq Shapes and Services Inc ....F 219 762-4863
Portage *(G-11776)*

One Eight Seven Incorporated ....G 219 886-2060
Gary *(G-5081)*

Pyro Industrial Services Inc ....E 219 787-5700
Portage *(G-11790)*

Refractory Service Corporation ....E 219 853-0885
Hammond *(G-5932)*

Resco Products Inc ....D 219 844-7830
Hammond *(G-5933)*

Servsteel Inc ....E 219 736-6030
Gary *(G-5096)*

Simko Sons Indus Refractories ....F 219 933-9100
Hammond *(G-5941)*

REFRACTORIES: Tile & Brick, Exc Plastic

Ht Enterprises Inc ....G 765 794-4174
Crawfordsville *(G-2160)*

REFRACTORY CASTABLES

J W Hicks Inc ....E 219 736-2212
Merrillville *(G-9723)*

Refractory Service Corporation ....E 219 397-7108
East Chicago *(G-2567)*

REFRACTORY MATERIALS WHOLESALERS

Magneco/Metrel Inc ....F 219 885-4190
Gary *(G-5073)*

Pyro Industrial Services Inc ....E 219 787-5700
Portage *(G-11790)*

Refractory Service Corporation ....E 219 853-0885
Hammond *(G-5932)*

REFRIGERATION & HEATING EQUIPMENT

Air Systems Compents LP ....G 765 483-5841
Lebanon *(G-9166)*

Carrier Corporation ....D 317 243-0851
Indianapolis *(G-6559)*

Continental Carbonic Pdts Inc ....G 317 784-3311
Indianapolis *(G-6656)*

Crosspoint Power and Rfrgn LLC ....E 317 240-1967
Indianapolis *(G-6695)*

Crown Products & Services Inc ....G 317 564-4799
Carmel *(G-1349)*

Delivery Concepts Inc ....E 574 522-3981
Elkhart *(G-2793)*

Evansville Metal Products Inc ....E 812 421-6589
Evansville *(G-3488)*

Evansville Metal Products Inc ....D 812 423-5632
Evansville *(G-3487)*

Flex-Tech Inc ....F 317 546-0183
Indianapolis *(G-6935)*

Flow Center Products Inc ....G 765 364-9460
Crawfordsville *(G-2152)*

Geo-Flo Products Corporation ....F 812 275-8513
Bedford *(G-546)*

Ilpea Industries Inc ....D 812 752-2526
Scottsburg *(G-12363)*

Industrial Combustn Engineers ....E 219 949-5066
Gary *(G-5068)*

Jlb Industrial LLC ....G 765 561-1751
Rushville *(G-12225)*

Lennox Ind Production Lxud 240 ....G 317 253-0353
Indianapolis *(G-7395)*

Lennox Lir Lennox Inds Intl ....G 317 334-1339
Indianapolis *(G-7396)*

Mitsubishi Heavy Industries ....E 714 960-3785
Franklin *(G-4910)*

Parker-Hannifin Corporation ....A 260 748-6000
New Haven *(G-10951)*

Qsens Equipment Solutions LLC ....G 317 443-6167
Indianapolis *(G-7793)*

Ram Services Rfrgn & Mech ....G 317 679-8541
Indianapolis *(G-7815)*

Redi/Controls Inc ....E 317 494-6600
Franklin *(G-4926)*

Rheem Sales Company Inc ....G 479 648-4900
Indianapolis *(G-7836)*

Supreme Corporation ....A 574 642-4888
Goshen *(G-5332)*

Supreme Corporation ....B 260 894-9191
Ligonier *(G-9298)*

Trane US Inc ....D 812 421-8725
Evansville *(G-3768)*

Trane US Inc ....D 317 255-8777
Indianapolis *(G-8090)*

Trane US Inc ....E 574 282-4880
South Bend *(G-12976)*

Trane US Inc ....E 260 489-0884
Fort Wayne *(G-4697)*

Trane US Inc ....D 765 932-7200
Rushville *(G-12236)*

Webber Manufacturing Company ....E 317 357-8681
Indianapolis *(G-8181)*

REFRIGERATION EQPT & SPLYS WHOLESALERS

Elliott-Williams Company Inc ....D 317 453-2295
Indianapolis *(G-6843)*

Stanton & Associates Inc ....G 574 247-5522
Granger *(G-5441)*

REFRIGERATION EQPT & SPLYS, WHOLESALE: Beverage Coolers

Swanel Inc ....D 219 932-7676
Hammond *(G-5947)*

REFRIGERATION EQPT & SPLYS, WHOLESALE: Commercial Eqpt

Duncan Supply Co Inc ....G 765 446-0105
Lafayette *(G-8892)*

REFRIGERATION EQPT: Complete

Advantage Engineering Inc ....D 317 887-0729
Greenwood *(G-5660)*

Duncan Supply Co Inc ....G 765 446-0105
Lafayette *(G-8892)*

Elliott-Williams Company Inc ....D 317 453-2295
Indianapolis *(G-6843)*

REFRIGERATION & HEATING EQUIPMENT (cont.)

Refrigeration Package Corp ....G 812 867-0900
Evansville *(G-3701)*

Stanton & Associates Inc ....G 574 247-5522
Granger *(G-5441)*

Whirlpool Corporation ....C 812 426-4000
Evansville *(G-3811)*

REFRIGERATION SVC & REPAIR

Expert Electric ....G 765 664-6642
Marion *(G-9523)*

REFRIGERATOR REPAIR SVCS

JC Refrigeration LLC ....G 260 768-4067
Shipshewana *(G-12622)*

REFUSE SYSTEMS

Harsco Corporation ....E 219 397-0200
East Chicago *(G-2532)*

Hartland Distillations Inc ....F 812 464-4446
Evansville *(G-3534)*

K & S Pallet Inc ....F 260 422-1264
Fort Wayne *(G-4402)*

Loeb-Lorman Metals Inc ....G 574 892-5063
Argos *(G-275)*

Recycling Works Inc ....F 574 293-3751
Elkhart *(G-3141)*

REGISTERS: Air, Metal

Continental Industries Inc ....D 574 262-4511
Elkhart *(G-2771)*

REGULATORS: Generator Voltage

Gasco LLC ....G 317 565-5000
Noblesville *(G-11109)*

REGULATORS: Transmission & Distribution Voltage

General Transmission Pdts LLC ....F 574 284-2917
South Bend *(G-12789)*

REGULATORS: Voltage, Automotive

R & R Regulators Inc ....G 574 522-5846
Elkhart *(G-3133)*

REHABILITATION CTR, RESIDENTIAL WITH HEALTH CARE INCIDENTAL

Cardinal Services Inc Indiana ....D 574 267-3823
Warsaw *(G-13853)*

REHABILITATION SVCS

ARC of Greater Boone Cnty Inc ....F 765 482-0051
Lebanon *(G-9169)*

RELAYS & SWITCHES: Indl, Electric

Riverside Mfg LLC ....B 260 637-4470
Fort Wayne *(G-4595)*

RELAYS: Electronic Usage

American Elctrnic Cmpnents Inc ....E 574 295-6330
Elkhart *(G-2682)*

Functional Devices Inc ....G 765 883-5538
Sharpsville *(G-12505)*

RELIGIOUS SPLYS WHOLESALERS

Dicksons Inc ....C 812 522-1308
Seymour *(G-12445)*

Templeton Coal Company Inc ....G 812 232-7037
Terre Haute *(G-13350)*

RELOCATION SVCS

Owens Machinery Inc ....G 812 968-3285
Palmyra *(G-11437)*

REMOVERS & CLEANERS

Chad Simons ....G 219 405-1620
Chesterton *(G-1598)*

Lambert Asphlting Slcating Inc ....G 317 985-8061
Indianapolis *(G-7378)*

Phaze One LLC ....G 812 634-9545
Jasper *(G-8301)*

Randy Gehlhausen ....G...... 812 327-4454
Bloomington (G-807)
Snow Management Group....................G...... 574 252-5253
Mishawaka (G-10130)

REMOVERS: Paint

Chemicals Solvents & Lubr ....G...... 260 484-2000
Fort Wayne (G-4145)
Sansher Corporation ....G...... 260 484-2000
Fort Wayne (G-4606)

RENTAL CENTERS: Party & Banquet Eqpt & Splys

Beverly Tent & Awning Co ....G...... 219 931-3723
Hammond (G-5852)

RENTAL SVCS: Business Machine & Electronic Eqpt

Pitney Bowes Inc ....E...... 260 436-7395
Indianapolis (G-7698)
Pitney Bowes Inc ....D...... 317 769-8300
Whitestown (G-14258)

RENTAL SVCS: Costume

Higgins Dyan......................................G...... 812 876-0754
Ellettsville (G-3281)
Knotts and Frye Inc ....G...... 317 925-6406
Indianapolis (G-7362)

RENTAL SVCS: Golf Cart, Power

Mid America Powered Vehicles ....G...... 812 925-7745
Chandler (G-1551)

RENTAL SVCS: Lawn & Garden Eqpt

J & J Repair ....G...... 574 831-3075
Goshen (G-5246)

RENTAL SVCS: Oil Eqpt

Gesco Group LLC ....G...... 260 747-5088
Fort Wayne (G-4300)

RENTAL SVCS: Recreational Vehicle

Grand Design Rv LLC..........................A...... 574 825-8000
Middlebury (G-9890)

RENTAL SVCS: Sporting Goods, NEC

Global Ozone Innovations LLC............G...... 574 294-5797
Elkhart (G-2886)

RENTAL SVCS: Stores & Yards Eqpt

Chappys Rent To Own LLC..................G...... 765 622-9500
Anderson (G-83)

RENTAL SVCS: Tent & Tarpaulin

All American Tent & Awning Inc ....F...... 812 232-4220
Terre Haute (G-13190)
Phil Irwin Advertising Inc ....F...... 317 547-5117
Indianapolis (G-7683)

RENTAL: Passenger Car

Perma Lubrication ....G...... 317 241-0797
Indianapolis (G-7679)

RENTAL: Portable Toilet

Nix Sanitary Service ....G...... 812 475-9774
Boonville (G-919)

RENTAL: Video Tape & Disc

Eds Trading Post Inc ....G...... 317 933-4867
Nineveh (G-11057)
Royal Inc ....F...... 812 424-4925
Evansville (G-3711)

RESEARCH, DEV & TESTING SVCS, COMM: Chem Lab, Exc Testing

Chemtura Corporation.........................C...... 765 497-6782
West Lafayette (G-14057)

RESEARCH, DEVELOPMENT & TEST SVCS, COMM: Cmptr Hardware Dev

La Zee Tek...G...... 260 351-3274
Hudson (G-6133)
Spensa Technologies Inc ....E...... 765 588-3592
West Lafayette (G-14110)
Tab Technologies ....G...... 765 482-7561
Lebanon (G-9227)

RESEARCH, DEVELOPMENT & TESTING SVCS, COMM: Agricultural

Agdia Inc ....D...... 574 264-2014
Elkhart (G-2671)
Dow Agrosciences LLC ....A...... 317 337-3000
Indianapolis (G-6763)
Mycogen Corporation ....F...... 317 337-3000
Indianapolis (G-7565)
Naturegenic Inc ....G...... 765 807-5525
West Lafayette (G-14089)

RESEARCH, DEVELOPMENT & TESTING SVCS, COMM: Research Lab

Terronics Development Corp................G...... 765 552-0808
Elwood (G-3311)

RESEARCH, DEVELOPMENT & TESTING SVCS, COMMERCIAL: Economic

Americas Coml Trnsp RES Co LLC......F...... 812 379-2085
Columbus (G-1854)

RESEARCH, DEVELOPMENT & TESTING SVCS, COMMERCIAL: Medical

Bioanalytical Systems Inc ....C...... 765 463-4527
West Lafayette (G-14053)
Biokorf LLC ....G...... 765 727-0782
West Lafayette (G-14054)
Biopoly LLC ....E...... 260 999-6135
Fort Wayne (G-4109)
Nextremity Solutions Inc.....................G...... 732 383-7901
Warsaw (G-13914)

RESEARCH, DEVELOPMENT & TESTING SVCS, COMMERCIAL: Physical

Contour Hardening Inc ....E...... 888 867-2184
Indianapolis (G-6660)
Leidos Inc ....C...... 812 863-3100
Crane (G-2128)

RESEARCH, DVLPMT & TESTING SVCS, COMM: Merger, Acq & Reorg

Tgf Enterprises LLC............................G...... 440 840-9704
Indianapolis (G-8056)

RESEARCH, DVLPT & TEST SVCS, COMM: Mkt Analysis or Research

Trinity Cmmnications Group Inc ....G...... 260 484-1029
Fort Wayne (G-4704)

RESEARCH, DVLPT & TESTING SVCS, COMM: Mkt, Bus & Economic

Growth Principals LLC ....G...... 812 320-1574
Bloomington (G-735)

RESIDENTIAL MENTAL HEALTH & SUBSTANCE ABUSE FACILITIES

Fresh Start Inc....................................F...... 812 254-3398
Washington (G-13982)

RESIDENTIAL REMODELERS

Concord Realstate Corp.......................F...... 765 423-5555
Lafayette (G-8876)

RESIDUES

Residual Pays Daily ....G...... 260 267-1617
Fort Wayne (G-4588)

RESINS: Custom Compound Purchased

B C C Products Inc ....F 317 494-6420
Franklin (G-4870)
Chase Plastic Services Inc...................F...... 574 239-4090
South Bend (G-12734)
Color Master Inc ....D...... 260 868-2320
Butler (G-1226)
Com-Tech Plastics Inc ....F...... 812 423-8270
Evansville (G-3424)
Crosspoint Polymer Tech LLC...............D...... 812 426-1350
Evansville (G-3445)
DSM Engineering Plastics Inc ....F...... 812 435-7500
Evansville (G-3463)
DSM Engineering Plastics Inc ....C...... 248 530-5500
Evansville (G-3465)
Enviroplas Inc ....G...... 812 868-0808
Evansville (G-3480)
Matrixx-Qtr Inc ....D...... 812 429-0901
Evansville (G-3619)
McCammon Engineering Corp ....G...... 812 356-4455
Sullivan (G-13086)
Miller Waste Mills Inc..........................E...... 507 454-6900
Indianapolis (G-7522)
Mwf LLC ....G...... 812 936-5303
West Baden Springs (G-14035)
Pmw Holdings LLC ....G...... 317 339-4685
Indianapolis (G-7703)
Polyone Corporation ....G...... 812 466-5116
Terre Haute (G-13305)
Polyram Compounds LLC.....................G...... 703 439-7945
Evansville (G-3679)
Sabic Innovative Plastics Mt V ....A...... 812 838-4385
Mount Vernon (G-10407)
Testworth Laboratories Inc...................F...... 260 244-5137
Columbia City (G-1840)

RESISTORS

Dayton-Phoenix Group Inc...................D...... 765 742-4410
West Lafayette (G-14063)
Khorporate Holdings Inc ....G...... 260 357-3365
Laotto (G-9110)
Vishay Americas Inc ....G...... 765 778-4878
Pendleton (G-11510)

RESISTORS & RESISTOR UNITS

Dayton-Phoenix Group Inc...................D...... 765 742-4410
West Lafayette (G-14063)

RESPIRATORS

Airgas Usa LLC ....F...... 317 248-8072
Indianapolis (G-6355)

RESTAURANT EQPT: Food Wagons

S & R Concessions LLC ....F 260 570-3247
Auburn (G-351)

RESTAURANT RESERVATION SVCS

Roost...G...... 317 842-3735
Fishers (G-3964)

RESTAURANTS: Fast Food

All Occasions Gift Shop LLC ....G...... 513 314-5693
Metamora (G-9762)

RESTAURANTS:Full Svc, American

Clancys of Portage ....F 219 764-4995
Portage (G-11757)

RESTAURANTS:Full Svc, Barbecue

Wolfs Bar B Q Inc................................D...... 812 424-8891
Evansville (G-3814)

RESTAURANTS:Full Svc, Family, Chain

Richards Restaurant Inc.......................F 260 997-6823
Bryant (G-1201)

RESTAURANTS:Full Svc, Family, Independent

Buckner Inc ....F 317 570-0533
Indianapolis (G-6520)
Essenhaus Inc ....B...... 574 825-6790
Middlebury (G-9885)

PRODUCT

Yoders Meats Inc...........................G........ 260 768-4715
Shipshewana (G-12660)

RESTAURANTS:Full Svc, Mexican

Las Perlas Tapatias Inc ....G........ 765 447-0601
Lafayette (G-8956)

RESTAURANTS:Limited Svc, Chicken

Lennies Inc ....D........ 812 323-2112
Bloomington (G-765)

RESTAURANTS:Limited Svc, Coffee Shop

Java Roaster...G........ 765 742-2037
Lafayette (G-8930)

RESTAURANTS:Limited Svc, Ice Cream Stands Or Dairy Bars

Bonnie Doon Ice Cream Corp ....F........ 574 255-9841
Mishawaka (G-10011)
Browns Dairy Inc...................................F........ 219 464-4141
Valparaiso (G-13514)

RESTAURANTS:Limited Svc, Lunch Counter

Schimpff Confectionery ....F........ 812 283-8367
Jeffersonville (G-8423)

RESTAURANTS:Limited Svc, Pizza

Royal Pin Leisure Ctr............................G........ 317 247-4426
Indianapolis (G-7866)

RESTAURANTS:Limited Svc, Pizzeria, Chain

Rico Aroma LLC ....G........ 765 471-1700
Lafayette (G-8992)

RESUME WRITING SVCS

Cozy Cat Inc ....G........ 765 463-1254
Lafayette (G-8879)

RETAIL BAKERY: Bread

Ganal Corporation ....G........ 260 749-2161
New Haven (G-10940)
Shipshewana Bread Box Corp...............E........ 260 768-4629
Shipshewana (G-12649)

RETAIL BAKERY: Cakes

Almiras Bakery.....................................E........ 219 844-4334
Hammond (G-5839)
Concannons Pastry Shop ....E........ 765 288-8551
Muncie (G-10448)
Fingerhut Bakery Inc.............................F........ 574 896-5937
North Judson (G-11212)

RETAIL BAKERY: Cookies

Blondies Cookies Inc.............................F........ 765 628-3978
Greentown (G-5644)

RETAIL BAKERY: Doughnuts

Square Donuts Inc ....G........ 812 232-6463
Terre Haute (G-13343)
Westfield Donuts ....G........ 317 896-5856
Westfield (G-14201)

RETAIL BAKERY: Pretzels

Auntie Annes..F........ 765 288-8077
Muncie (G-10435)
Auntie Annes..G........ 574 271-8740
Mishawaka (G-10001)
Pretzels Inc ....C........ 574 941-2201
Plymouth (G-11717)

RETAIL LUMBER YARDS

Blue River Farm Supply Inc ....G........ 812 364-6675
Palmyra (G-11435)
C & C Pallets and Lumber LLC ....G........ 765 524-3214
New Castle (G-10895)
Gross & Sons Lumber and Veneer........G........ 574 457-5214
Syracuse (G-13132)
Grove Forest Products ....G........ 812 432-3312
Rising Sun (G-12088)
Hollingsworth Sawmill Inc ....F........ 765 883-5836
Russiaville (G-12241)

Kinser Timber Products Inc ....G........ 812 876-4775
Gosport (G-5352)
New Castle Saw Mill..............................G........ 765 529-6635
New Castle (G-10913)
Ramco Builder and Supply LLC ....E........ 574 223-7802
Rochester (G-12144)
Serie Hardwoods Inc ....G........ 765 275-2321
Attica (G-309)

RETAIL STORES, NEC

Ridge Iron LLC.....................................G........ 646 450-0092
Plymouth (G-11722)
Vitamorph Labs LLC ....G........ 219 237-0174
Highland (G-6059)

RETAIL STORES: Alarm Signal Systems

Sign Craft Industries Inc ....E........ 317 842-8664
Indianapolis (G-7940)

RETAIL STORES: Artificial Limbs

American Orthpdics Prosthetics ....G........ 765 447-0111
Lafayette (G-8851)
Northern Prosthetics Inc ....G........ 574 233-2459
South Bend (G-12880)

RETAIL STORES: Audio-Visual Eqpt & Splys

Technology Cons Group LLC ....G........ 219 525-4064
Merrillville (G-9757)

RETAIL STORES: Awnings

Mofab Inc ....G........ 765 649-1288
Anderson (G-139)
Ruby Enterprises Inc ....G........ 765 649-2060
Anderson (G-164)

RETAIL STORES: Business Machines & Eqpt

Gesco Group LLC ....G........ 260 747-5088
Fort Wayne (G-4300)
Hines Bindery Systems Service ....G........ 317 839-6432
Plainfield (G-11615)

RETAIL STORES: Canvas Prdts

Hare Canvas Products...........................G........ 260 758-8800
Markle (G-9577)

RETAIL STORES: Christmas Lights & Decorations

Candles By Dar Inc ....F........ 260 482-2099
Fort Wayne (G-4139)
Herman Tool & Machine Inc ....F........ 574 594-5544
Pierceton (G-11572)
Pgs LLC ....E........ 812 988-4030
Nashville (G-10732)

RETAIL STORES: Cleaning Eqpt & Splys

Modrak Products Company Inc ....F........ 219 838-0308
Gary (G-5078)

RETAIL STORES: Cosmetics

Flawless Beauty LLC.............................G........ 317 314-7952
Indianapolis (G-6932)

RETAIL STORES: Decals

Pyramid Sign & Design Inc ....G........ 765 447-4174
Lafayette (G-8986)

RETAIL STORES: Drafting Eqpt & Splys

Digital Reprographics Inc ....G........ 260 483-8066
Fort Wayne (G-4210)

RETAIL STORES: Electronic Parts & Eqpt

Northwind Electronics LLC.....................F........ 317 288-0787
Indianapolis (G-7596)

RETAIL STORES: Engines & Parts, Air-Cooled

Ngh Retail LLC ....G........ 219 476-0772
Valparaiso (G-13588)

RETAIL STORES: Fire Extinguishers

Johnson Controls ....C........ 317 826-2130
Indianapolis (G-7309)

RETAIL STORES: Flags

Flag & Banner Company Inc ....F........ 317 299-4880
Indianapolis (G-6931)

RETAIL STORES: Hair Care Prdts

Magnolia Products LLC..........................G........ 812 306-8638
Evansville (G-3610)

RETAIL STORES: Hearing Aids

D J Investments Inc ....G........ 765 348-3558
Hartford City (G-5979)
Integrity Hearing ....G........ 317 882-9151
Noblesville (G-11131)
Wilson Hearing Aid Center ....G........ 765 747-4131
Muncie (G-10585)

RETAIL STORES: Ice

Home City Ice Company.........................E........ 317 926-2451
Indianapolis (G-7113)
Superior Ice Co Inc ....F........ 812 847-4312
Linton (G-9314)

RETAIL STORES: Infant Furnishings & Eqpt

Wasu Inc ....G........ 765 448-4450
Lafayette (G-9022)

RETAIL STORES: Medical Apparatus & Splys

Mathes Home Care................................G........ 812 944-2211
New Albany (G-10823)
Roche Health Solutions Inc ....C........ 317 570-5100
Indianapolis (G-7853)
Sundance Enterprises Inc.....................E........ 317 856-9780
Indianapolis (G-8019)
Vintage Chemical Enterprises ....G........ 260 745-7272
Fort Wayne (G-4728)

RETAIL STORES: Monuments, Finished To Custom Order

Billman Monument & Sign Co................G........ 574 753-2394
Logansport (G-9325)
Dwyer-Wilbert Inc..................................G........ 765 962-3605
Richmond (G-11978)
Harris Pre Cast Inc...............................G........ 219 362-2457
La Porte (G-8761)
John Ley Monument Sales Inc ....G........ 260 347-7346
Avilla (G-408)
Mark Concrete Products Inc ....G........ 317 398-8616
Shelbyville (G-12551)
Thomas Monuments Inc.........................G........ 317 244-6525
Indianapolis (G-8065)
Wearly Monuments Inc..........................E........ 765 284-9796
Muncie (G-10581)
Wilhoite Monuments Inc.........................G........ 765 286-7423
Muncie (G-10584)

RETAIL STORES: Motors, Electric

Flanders Electric Mtr Svc Inc................E........ 812 421-4300
Evansville (G-3510)
Jasper Electric Motor Inc ....G........ 812 482-1660
Jasper (G-8258)
Pres-Del Electric Inc ....G........ 219 884-3146
Gary (G-5086)
Robinson Industries Inc ....E........ 317 867-3214
Westfield (G-14185)
Three Star Electric Inc ....G........ 574 272-3136
South Bend (G-12969)

RETAIL STORES: Orthopedic & Prosthesis Applications

American Limb & Orthopedic Co ....G........ 574 522-3643
Elkhart (G-2684)
Central Brace & Limb Co Inc ....F........ 317 925-4296
Indianapolis (G-6578)
Central Brace & Limb Co Inc ....G........ 812 232-2145
Terre Haute (G-13207)
Central Brace & Limb Co Inc ....G........ 317 872-1596
Indianapolis (G-6579)
Hanger Prsthetcs & Ortho Inc...............F........ 219 844-2021
Hammond (G-5889)

Hanger Prsthetcs & Ortho Inc..............G...... 765 966-5069
   Richmond *(G-11995)*
Northern Brace Co Inc.....................G...... 574 233-4221
   South Bend *(G-12878)*
Orthopediatrics Corp.........................D...... 574 268-6379
   Warsaw *(G-13918)*
Tornier Inc.......................................G...... 574 268-0861
   Warsaw *(G-13953)*

RETAIL STORES: Perfumes & Colognes

Bath & Body Works LLC ....E...... 219 531-2146
   Valparaiso *(G-13504)*
Bath & Body Works LLC ....F...... 317 468-0834
   Greenfield *(G-5508)*
Bath & Body Works LLC ....E...... 317 209-1517
   Avon *(G-432)*

RETAIL STORES: Pet Splys

Bench & Field Pet Foods LLC............G...... 800 525-4802
   Mishawaka *(G-10007)*
Scott Pet Products Inc.....................C...... 765 569-4636
   Rockville *(G-12180)*

RETAIL STORES: Plumbing & Heating Splys

Barry Company Inc..........................G...... 812 333-1850
   Bloomington *(G-673)*

RETAIL STORES: Rubber Stamps

Crystal Source.................................G...... 812 988-7009
   Nashville *(G-10721)*
Precise Printing Plus Signs ....G...... 317 545-5117
   Indianapolis *(G-7729)*

RETAIL STORES: Spas & Hot Tubs

Master Spas Inc................................C...... 260 436-9100
   Fort Wayne *(G-4456)*

RETAIL STORES: Technical Aids For The Handicapped

Mobility Vehicles Indiana LLC ....G...... 317 471-7169
   Knightstown *(G-8558)*

RETAIL STORES: Telephone & Communication Eqpt

Williams Bros Health Care Inc............E...... 812 257-2505
   Washington *(G-14007)*
Williams Bros Health Care Pha...........E...... 812 335-0000
   Bloomington *(G-856)*
Williams Bros Health Care Pha...........C...... 812 254-2497
   Washington *(G-14008)*

RETAIL STORES: Tents

Lafayette Tent & Awning Co.................E...... 765 742-4277
   Lafayette *(G-8951)*
Montgomery Tent & Awning Co............F...... 317 357-9759
   Indianapolis *(G-7538)*

RETAIL STORES: Vaults & Safes

Johnson Safe Company ....G...... 317 876-7233
   Zionsville *(G-14443)*

RETAIL STORES: Water Purification Eqpt

Driessen Water Inc............................G...... 765 529-4905
   Muncie *(G-10463)*
Markle Water Treatment Plant...............G...... 260 758-3482
   Markle *(G-9580)*
New Aqua LLC ....D...... 317 272-3000
   Avon *(G-456)*
Puritan Water Conditioning ....F...... 765 362-6340
   Crawfordsville *(G-2189)*
US Water Systems Inc.........................F...... 317 209-0889
   Indianapolis *(G-8138)*

RETAIL STORES: Welding Splys

Koehler Welding Supply Inc ....F...... 812 574-4103
   Madison *(G-9476)*
Northern Gases and Sups Inc..............F...... 574 594-2551
   Pierceton *(G-11574)*
Praxair Distribution Inc ....G...... 317 481-4550
   Indianapolis *(G-7722)*
Praxair Distribution Inc ....G...... 260 423-4468
   Fort Wayne *(G-4546)*

RETAIL STORES: Wheelchair Lifts

Trinity Cmmnications Group Inc ....G...... 260 484-1029
   Fort Wayne *(G-4704)*

REUPHOLSTERY & FURNITURE REPAIR

Spectrum Marketing ....G...... 765 643-5566
   Anderson *(G-168)*

REUPHOLSTERY SVCS

Aaron Company Incorporated ....F...... 219 838-0852
   Gary *(G-5026)*
Coffeys Custom Upholstery..................G...... 812 948-8611
   New Albany *(G-10763)*
Covers of Indiana Inc.........................G...... 317 244-0291
   Indianapolis *(G-6680)*
Rhyne & Associates Inc ....F...... 317 786-4459
   Indianapolis *(G-7838)*
Shelby Westside Upholstering ....G...... 317 631-8911
   Indianapolis *(G-7931)*

REWINDING SVCS

Eemsco Inc.......................................E...... 812 426-2224
   Evansville *(G-3472)*
Mills Electric Co Inc...........................G...... 219 931-3114
   Hammond *(G-5916)*

RIBBONS, NEC

Indiana Ribbon Inc............................E...... 219 279-2112
   Wolcott *(G-14365)*
Tower Advertising Products Inc ....D...... 260 593-2103
   Topeka *(G-13431)*

RINGS: Angle

Ward Forging Co Inc..........................G...... 812 923-7463
   Floyds Knobs *(G-4023)*

ROBOTS: Assembly Line

ABB Flexible Automation Inc................E...... 317 876-9090
   Indianapolis *(G-6307)*
Amatrol Inc.......................................C...... 812 288-8285
   Jeffersonville *(G-8322)*
Arbuckle Industries Inc ....G...... 317 835-7489
   Fairland *(G-3819)*
Banks Machine & Engrg Inc.................D...... 317 642-4980
   Shelbyville *(G-12519)*
Enpak LLC ....G...... 574 268-7273
   Warsaw *(G-13873)*
J-I-T Distributing Inc ....D...... 574 251-0292
   South Bend *(G-12821)*
Nachi America Inc..............................C...... 317 535-5527
   Greenwood *(G-5726)*
Star Automation Inc ....G...... 812 475-9947
   Evansville *(G-3747)*
Via Development Corp.........................E...... 888 225-5842
   Marion *(G-9570)*
Wall Control Services Inc ....G...... 260 450-6411
   Fort Wayne *(G-4733)*

RODS: Extruded, Aluminum

Hydro Extrusion North Amer LLC ....B...... 888 935-5757
   North Liberty *(G-11216)*

RODS: Plastic

Stratikore ....G...... 574 807-0028
   La Porte *(G-8824)*

ROLL COVERINGS: Rubber

Finzer Roller Inc................................E...... 812 829-1455
   Spencer *(G-13026)*

ROLL FORMED SHAPES: Custom

Hoosier Trim Products LLC ....E...... 317 271-4007
   Indianapolis *(G-7125)*
United Roll Forming Corp ....E...... 574 294-2800
   Elkhart *(G-3235)*

ROLLING MACHINERY: Steel

AAA-Gpc Holdings LLC.........................D...... 260 668-1468
   Angola *(G-187)*
Premier Components LLC......................G...... 219 776-9372
   Hebron *(G-6021)*
Southlake Machine Corp ....G...... 219 285-6150
   Morocco *(G-10364)*

ROLLING MILL EQPT: Galvanizing Lines

Witt Industries Inc...............................E...... 765 289-3427
   Muncie *(G-10587)*

ROLLING MILL MACHINERY

Enbi Global Inc...................................F...... 317 395-7324
   Shelbyville *(G-12532)*
Hoosier Roll Shop Services LLC ....F...... 219 844-8077
   Hammond *(G-5893)*
Overton & Sons TI & Die Co Inc ....E...... 317 736-7700
   Franklin *(G-4918)*

ROLLING MILL ROLLS: Cast Steel

Arcelormittal USA LLC ....D...... 219 787-2120
   Chesterton *(G-1595)*
Union Electric Steel Corp......................C...... 219 464-1031
   Valparaiso *(G-13632)*

ROLLS & BLANKETS, PRINTERS': Rubber Or Rubberized Fabric

Enbi Indiana Inc.................................C...... 317 398-3267
   Shelbyville *(G-12533)*

ROLLS & ROLL COVERINGS: Rubber

American Roller Company LLC.............E...... 574 586-3101
   Walkerton *(G-13801)*

ROOF DECKS

Daviess County Metal Sales ....D...... 812 486-4299
   Cannelburg *(G-1284)*
Menard Inc..A...... 812 466-1234
   Terre Haute *(G-13282)*

ROOFING GRANULES

Harsco Corporation ....F...... 219 944-6250
   Gary *(G-5060)*

ROOFING MATERIALS: Asphalt

Architectural Metal Roofg Sup ....G...... 812 423-5257
   Evansville *(G-3364)*
Polar Seal Inc ....G...... 260 356-2369
   Huntington *(G-6239)*
Pro-Mark Bldg Solutions LLC ....F...... 812 798-1178
   Linton *(G-9312)*

ROOFING MATERIALS: Sheet Metal

3c Coman Ltd ....G...... 317 650-5156
   Fortville *(G-4766)*
H & H Metal Products Inc ....F...... 812 256-0444
   Charlestown *(G-1567)*
Lippert Components Inc.......................C...... 800 551-9149
   Elkhart *(G-2999)*
Lippert Components Inc.......................D...... 574 535-1125
   Goshen *(G-5268)*
Lippert Components Inc.......................D...... 574 294-6852
   Elkhart *(G-3000)*
Lippert Components Inc.......................E...... 574 535-1125
   Goshen *(G-5272)*
Lippert Components Inc.......................D...... 574 849-0869
   Goshen *(G-5273)*
Lippert Components Inc.......................C...... 574 971-4320
   Goshen *(G-5275)*
Lippert Components Inc.......................D...... 574 312-7445
   Middlebury *(G-9904)*
Nci Group Inc ....E...... 317 392-3536
   Shelbyville *(G-12553)*
Ramco Builder and Supply LLC ....E...... 574 223-7802
   Rochester *(G-12144)*
Roof Masters Plus...............................G...... 765 572-1321
   Westpoint *(G-14207)*

ROOFING MEMBRANE: Rubber

Daramic LLC......................................C...... 812 738-8274
   Corydon *(G-2097)*

ROPE

Kentuckiana Wire Rope & Supply ....F...... 812 282-3667
   Jeffersonville *(G-8386)*

RUBBER

BRC Rubber & Plastics Inc ....E...... 765 728-8510
   Montpelier *(G-10289)*

PRODUCT

RUBBER (continued)

Coleman Cable LLC ....C 765 449-7227
Lafayette (G-8875)

Gdc Inc ....C 574 533-3128
Goshen (G-5222)

Iris Rubber Company Inc ....F 317 984-3561
Cicero (G-1662)

Parker-Hannifin Corporation ....D 574 533-1111
Goshen (G-5307)

Royal Adhesives & Sealants LLC ....E 574 246-5000
South Bend (G-12921)

Sealwrap Systems LLC ....G 317 462-3310
Greenfield (G-5572)

T & M Rubber Inc ....E 574 533-3173
Goshen (G-5338)

Triangle Rubber Co LLC ....C 574 533-3118
Goshen (G-5340)

United Minerals and Prpts Inc ....E 812 838-5236
Mount Vernon (G-10412)

RUBBER PRDTS

Knox Enterprises Inc ....G 317 714-3073
Indianapolis (G-7363)

Medegen Holdings LLC ....G 219 473-1674
Whiting (G-14271)

RUBBER PRDTS REPAIR SVCS

S & R Welding Inc ....G 317 710-0360
Indianapolis (G-7877)

RUBBER PRDTS: Automotive, Mechanical

Ati Inc ....G 812 431-5409
Mount Vernon (G-10384)

BRC Rubber & Plastics Inc ....D 260 827-0871
Bluffton (G-869)

BRC Rubber & Plastics Inc ....C 260 693-2171
Fort Wayne (G-4118)

BRC Rubber & Plastics Inc ....D 260 203-5300
Fort Wayne (G-4119)

BRC Rubber & Plastics Inc ....C 260 693-2171
Hartford City (G-5978)

Fellwocks Automotive ....G 812 867-3658
Evansville (G-3503)

RUBBER PRDTS: Mechanical

Ace Extrusion LLC ....E 812 868-8640
Evansville (G-3339)

Bluffton Rubber ....G 260 824-4501
Bluffton (G-868)

BRC Rubber & Plastics Inc ....C 260 693-2171
Churubusco (G-1643)

BRC Rubber & Plastics Inc ....C 260 894-4121
Ligonier (G-9278)

BRC Rubber & Plastics Inc ....E 765 728-8510
Montpelier (G-10289)

Coleman Cable LLC ....C 765 449-7227
Lafayette (G-8875)

Cooper-Standard Automotive Inc ....B 260 925-0700
Auburn (G-322)

Cooper-Standard Automotive Inc ....B 260 925-0700
Auburn (G-324)

EMT Industries Inc ....E 574 533-1273
Granger (G-5406)

Engineered Rubber & Plastics ....F 574 254-1405
Mishawaka (G-10041)

Envirotech Extrusion Inc ....E 765 966-8068
Richmond (G-11984)

Finzer Roller Inc ....E 812 829-1455
Spencer (G-13026)

Freudenberg-Nok General Partnr ....E 734 354-5504
Shelbyville (G-12535)

Freudenberg-Nok General Partnr ....C 765 763-7246
Morristown (G-10369)

Griffith Rbr Mills of Garrett ....E 260 357-3125
Garrett (G-5007)

Iris Rubber Company Inc ....F 317 984-3561
Cicero (G-1662)

Jasper Rubber Products Inc ....A 812 482-3242
Jasper (G-8263)

Lear Manufacturing ....G 765 282-6273
Muncie (G-10510)

Parker-Hannifin Corporation ....C 574 528-9400
Syracuse (G-13139)

Parker-Hannifin Corporation ....D 574 533-1111
Goshen (G-5307)

Rd Rubber Products Inc ....G 260 357-3571
Garrett (G-5021)

Rubber Shop Inc ....G 574 291-6440
South Bend (G-12924)

South Bend Modern Molding Inc ....D 574 255-0711
Mishawaka (G-10132)

T & M Rubber Inc ....E 574 533-3173
Goshen (G-5338)

Triangle Rubber Co LLC ....C 574 533-3118
Goshen (G-5340)

Viking Inc ....E 260 244-6141
Columbia City (G-1845)

Western Consolidated Tech Inc ....D 260 495-9866
Fremont (G-4982)

RUBBER PRDTS: Silicone

Exactseal Inc ....G 317 559-2220
Indianapolis (G-6889)

PTG Silicones Inc ....G 812 948-8719
New Albany (G-10850)

RUBBER PRDTS: Sponge

Seymour Midwest LLC ....G 574 269-2782
Warsaw (G-13939)

RUBBER STAMP, WHOLESALE

Bulldog Award Co Inc ....G 317 773-3379
Noblesville (G-11073)

RUBBER STRUCTURES: Air-Supported

Indianapolis Industrial Pdts ....G 317 359-3078
Indianapolis (G-7201)

RULERS: Metal

Rapid Rule Co Inc ....G 574 784-2273
North Liberty (G-11220)

RUST ARRESTING COMPOUNDS: Animal Or Vegetable Oil Based

Shalee Oils LLC ....G 765 329-4057
Hartford City (G-5990)

Yushiro Manufacturing Amer Inc ....E 317 398-9862
Shelbyville (G-12586)

RUST PROOFING SVC: Hot Dipping, Metals & Formed Prdts

Quick Turn Anodizing LLC ....G 877 716-1150
Edinburgh (G-2622)

RUST REMOVERS

American Hydro Systems Inc ....F 866 357-5063
Fort Wayne (G-4071)

SADDLERY STORES

Cowpokes Inc ....E 765 642-3911
Anderson (G-91)

Judson Harness & Saddlery ....G 765 569-0918
Rockville (G-12176)

Southern Indiana Collar Co ....G 812 486-3714
Montgomery (G-10242)

SAFE DEPOSIT BOXES

Phoenix Safe International LLC ....G 765 483-0954
Lebanon (G-9216)

Risco Products Inc ....G 317 392-6150
Shelbyville (G-12562)

SAFES & VAULTS: Metal

Customer 1st LLC ....G 812 967-6727
Pekin (G-11471)

Fire King International LLC ....E 812 948-2795
New Albany (G-10779)

Fki Security Group LLC ....B 812 948-8400
New Albany (G-10781)

Johnson Safe Company ....G 317 876-7233
Zionsville (G-14443)

Meilink Safe Company ....E 812 941-0024
New Albany (G-10825)

Tuff Stuff Sales and Svc Inc ....G 765 354-4151
Middletown (G-9943)

SAFETY EQPT & SPLYS WHOLESALERS

Asphalt Materials Inc ....G 317 875-4670
Indianapolis (G-6428)

Region Signs Inc ....F 219 473-1616
Whiting (G-14275)

SAFETY INSPECTION SVCS

Wise Industries Inc (del) ....G 219 947-5333
Hobart (G-6101)

SALES PROMOTION SVCS

Gs Sales Inc ....G 317 595-6750
Westfield (G-14168)

Plaquemaker Plus Inc ....G 317 594-5556
Fishers (G-3952)

SALT

Alebro LLC ....G 317 876-9212
Indianapolis (G-6360)

Es Deicing ....G 260 422-2020
Fort Wayne (G-4242)

Giles Chemical Corporation ....G 812 537-4852
Greendale (G-5486)

SAMPLE BOOKS

Leed Selling Tools Corp ....E 812 867-4340
Evansville (G-3599)

SAND & GRAVEL

Access Solutions ....G 812 490-6026
Newburgh (G-11018)

Beer and Slabaugh Inc ....E 574 773-3413
Nappanee (G-10653)

Bob Belcher ....G 317 996-3712
Monrovia (G-10202)

Corydon Stone & Asphalt Inc ....E 812 738-2216
Corydon (G-2096)

Country Stone ....E 260 837-7134
Waterloo (G-14012)

D H Gravel Company ....G 765 893-4914
Williamsport (G-14289)

Flynn Sons Sand & Gravel ....G 812 636-4400
Odon (G-11325)

Fred Jay Stewart ....F 765 284-1386
Muncie (G-10474)

Gibson County Sand & Grav Inc ....G 812 851-5800
Haubstadt (G-6001)

Gravel Doctor Indianapolis LLC ....G 317 399-4585
Indianapolis (G-7037)

Handson ....F 812 246-4481
Sellersburg (G-12396)

Happy Valley Sand & Gravel Inc ....G 317 839-6800
Plainfield (G-11613)

Harrison Hauling Inc ....G 574 862-3196
Goshen (G-5235)

Henschen Sand and Gravel ....G 260 367-2636
Howe (G-6126)

Hydraulic Press Brick Company ....E 317 290-1140
Mooresville (G-10313)

Irving Materials Inc ....F 765 922-7285
Marion (G-9534)

Irving Materials Inc ....F 765 778-4760
Anderson (G-123)

Lafarge North America Inc ....G 219 378-1193
East Chicago (G-2547)

Lake County Sand & Gravel LLC ....G 219 988-4540
Merrillville (G-9725)

Lees Ready-Mix & Trucking Inc ....F 812 372-1800
Columbus (G-1958)

Legacy Vulcan LLC ....F 219 567-9155
Francesville (G-4814)

Legacy Vulcan LLC ....F 219 253-6686
Monon (G-10176)

Longhorn Sand and Gravel LLC ....G 574 532-2788
Mishawaka (G-10071)

M and G Dirt and Gravel LLC ....G 219 778-9341
Rolling Prairie (G-12189)

Marietta Martin Materials Inc ....F 317 776-4460
Noblesville (G-11145)

Marietta Martin Materials Inc ....G 317 831-7391
Martinsville (G-9622)

Mauckport Sand & Gravel ....G 812 732-8800
Mauckport (G-9655)

Michele L Gravel ....G 317 889-0521
Indianapolis (G-7496)

Mulzer Crushed Stone Inc ....E 812 649-5055
Rockport (G-12170)

Muncie Sand & Gravel Inc ....G 765 282-6422
Muncie (G-10536)

Paul H Rohe Co Inc ....F 812 926-1471
Aurora (G-384)

Quikrete Companies Inc ....E 317 251-2281
Indianapolis (G-7805)

Rex Alton & Companies Inc ....E 812 882-8519
  Vincennes (G-13701)
Rinker Materials Corp ....G 317 353-2118
  Indianapolis (G-7846)
Rogers Group Inc ....G 765 342-9655
  Martinsville (G-9634)
Rogers Group Inc ....G 765 342-6898
  Martinsville (G-9635)
Rogers Group Inc ....E 812 824-8565
  Bloomington (G-814)
Rogers Group Inc ....E 812 849-3530
  Mitchell (G-10170)
Rogers Group Inc ....F 765 893-4463
  Williamsport (G-14296)
Rogers Group Inc ....E 812 882-3640
  Vincennes (G-13703)
Rogers Group Inc ....E 812 333-6324
  Bloomington (G-816)
Roskovenski Sand & Gravel Inc ....G 765 832-6748
  Clinton (G-1719)
S & G Excavating Inc ....D 812 234-4848
  Terre Haute (G-13322)
Shelby Gravel Inc ....F 317 738-3445
  Franklin (G-4929)
Southfield Corporation ....E 812 824-1355
  Bloomington (G-829)
Speedway Sand & Gravel Inc ....G 574 893-7355
  Silver Lake (G-12680)
Spray Sand & Gravel Inc ....G 812 522-5417
  Seymour (G-12494)
Stone Quary ....G 574 936-2975
  Plymouth (G-11725)
Stonehenge Concrete & Gravel ....G 260 726-8282
  Portland (G-11848)
Sugar Creek Gravel & Stone ....G 765 362-1646
  Crawfordsville (G-2199)
Todd L Wise ....G 260 799-4828
  Albion (G-36)
U S Aggregates Inc ....G 765 966-8155
  Richmond (G-12071)
Wallace Construction Inc ....F 317 422-5356
  Martinsville (G-9647)
White River Gravel Company Inc ....G 317 834-6818
  Indianapolis (G-8192)
Zimmerman-Newcomer Gravel ....G 574 658-4063
  Milford (G-9967)

SAND MINING

Asphalt Materials Inc ....B 317 872-6010
  Indianapolis (G-6426)
Asphalt Materials Inc ....G 317 875-4670
  Indianapolis (G-6428)
Brookfield Sand & Gravel Inc ....E 317 835-2235
  Fairland (G-3821)
Crisman Sand Co Inc ....G 219 762-2619
  Valparaiso (G-13524)
Elkhart County Gravel Inc ....F 574 831-2815
  New Paris (G-10978)
Elkhart County Gravel Inc ....G 574 831-2815
  Warsaw (G-13870)
Elkhart County Gravel Inc ....G 574 825-7913
  Middlebury (G-9883)
Hanson Aggrgates Southeast Inc ....D 317 788-4086
  Indianapolis (G-7072)
Illiana Remedial Action Inc ....G 219 844-4862
  Hammond (G-5898)
Irving Materials Inc ....F 574 653-2749
  Huntington (G-6218)
Merritt Sand and Gravel Inc ....F 260 665-2513
  Waterloo (G-14018)
Rogers Group Inc ....F 765 762-2660
  Williamsport (G-14297)
Schmaltz Ready Mix Concrete ....G 812 689-5140
  Osgood (G-11394)
Stone Quary ....E 765 473-5578
  Peru (G-11549)

SAND: Hygrade

3M Indianapolis ....G 317 692-3000
  Indianapolis (G-6289)
Millburn Peat Company Inc ....E 219 362-7025
  La Porte (G-8794)

SANDBLASTING EQPT

Forecast Sales Inc ....G 317 829-0147
  Indianapolis (G-6948)
Hoosier Truck & Trailer Srv ....G 317 887-4887
  Indianapolis (G-7126)

Taggarts Custom Sndblst LLC ....G 765 825-4584
  Connersville (G-2074)

SANDBLASTING SVC: Building Exterior

Powerclean Inc ....E 260 483-1375
  Fort Wayne (G-4543)
Rex Alton & Companies Inc ....E 812 882-8519
  Vincennes (G-13701)

SANITARY SVCS: Hazardous Waste, Collection & Disposal

Tradebe Environmental Svcs LLC ....G 800 388-7242
  Merrillville (G-9759)
Tradebe GP ....G 800 388-7242
  East Chicago (G-2572)
Winski Brothers Inc ....F 765 654-5323
  Frankfort (G-4860)

SANITARY SVCS: Medical Waste Disposal

Circle Medical Products Inc ....G 317 271-2626
  Indianapolis (G-6611)

SANITARY SVCS: Nonhazardous Waste Disposal Sites

Creative Ldscp & Compost Co ....G 317 776-2909
  Noblesville (G-11087)

SANITARY SVCS: Refuse Collection & Disposal Svcs

Recycling Center Inc ....D 765 966-8295
  Richmond (G-12041)

SANITARY SVCS: Rubbish Collection & Disposal

Hunts Maintenance Inc ....G 219 785-2333
  Westville (G-14218)

SANITARY SVCS: Sanitary Landfill, Operation Of

Cgs Services Inc ....G 765 763-6258
  Morristown (G-10367)
Greencycle Inc ....G 317 773-3350
  Noblesville (G-11114)

SANITARY SVCS: Sewage Treatment Facility

Aqua Utility Services LLC ....G 812 284-9243
  New Albany (G-10745)

SANITARY SVCS: Waste Materials, Recycling

Blackwood Solutions Inc ....G 812 824-6728
  Bloomington (G-684)
Concrete & Asphalt Recycl Inc ....F 574 237-1928
  Mishawaka (G-10021)
Green Stream Company ....D 574 293-1949
  Elkhart (G-2899)
Mervis Industries Inc ....F 812 232-1251
  Terre Haute (G-13284)
Qrs Inc ....G 812 948-1323
  New Albany (G-10851)
Recovery Technologies LLC ....E 260 745-3902
  Fort Wayne (G-4583)

SANITARY WARE: Metal

Bootz Manufacturing Company ....D 812 425-4646
  Evansville (G-3393)
H A P Industries Inc ....G 765 948-3385
  Jonesboro (G-8445)
Maax Inc ....E 574 936-3838
  Plymouth (G-11704)
Olympic Fiberglass Industries ....D 574 223-3101
  Rochester (G-12142)
Shank Brothers Inc ....F 260 744-4802
  Fort Wayne (G-4618)

SANITATION CHEMICALS & CLEANING AGENTS

3M Company ....B 317 692-6666
  Indianapolis (G-6288)
Abro Industries Inc ....E 574 232-8289
  South Bend (G-12692)

Andersons Agriculture Group LP ....F 765 564-6135
  Delphi (G-2414)
B & S Products Corp ....G 574 537-0770
  Goshen (G-5175)
Bane-Clene Corp ....E 317 546-5448
  Indianapolis (G-6455)
Camco Manufacturing Inc ....F 574 264-1491
  Elkhart (G-2747)
Carestone Inc ....G 219 853-0600
  Hammond (G-5857)
Craft Laboratories Inc ....F 260 432-9467
  Fort Wayne (G-4183)
Dynaloy LLC ....F 317 788-5694
  Indianapolis (G-6773)
Ecolab Inc ....D 260 359-3280
  Huntington (G-6202)
Iron Out Inc ....E 800 654-0791
  Fort Wayne (G-4383)
J 2 Systems and Supply LLC ....G 317 602-3940
  Indianapolis (G-7281)
Kik Custom Products ....C 574 294-8695
  Elkhart (G-2967)
Kuhn & Sons Inc ....E 812 424-8268
  Evansville (G-3597)
Metalworking Lubricants Co ....E 317 269-2444
  Indianapolis (G-7491)
Modrak Products Company Inc ....F 219 838-0308
  Gary (G-5078)
National Handicapped Workshop ....D 765 287-8331
  Muncie (G-10538)
National Products LLC ....C 219 393-5536
  Kingsbury (G-8543)
NCH Corporation ....E 317 899-3660
  Indianapolis (G-7579)
Online Packaging Incorporated ....E 219 872-0925
  Michigan City (G-9825)
Prosco Inc ....G 317 353-2920
  Indianapolis (G-7779)
Servaas Inc ....G 317 633-2020
  Indianapolis (G-7914)
Wayne Chemical Inc ....E 260 432-1120
  Fort Wayne (G-4739)
Yushiro Manufacturing Amer Inc ....E 317 398-9862
  Shelbyville (G-12586)

SASHES: Door Or Window, Metal

Southeastern Aluminum Pdts Inc ....F 904 781-8200
  Carmel (G-1483)
Wilmes Window Mfg Co Inc ....E 812 275-7575
  Ferdinand (G-3864)

SATCHELS

Seed & Satchel LLC ....G 317 892-2557
  Pittsboro (G-11587)
Skirt & Satchel ....G 812 727-0292
  Bloomington (G-824)
Traveling Satchel LLC ....G 317 502-3241
  Indianapolis (G-8091)

SATELLITE COMMUNICATIONS EQPT

AAA Satellite Link ....G 765 642-7000
  Anderson (G-58)
Digital Solutions ....G 812 257-0333
  Washington (G-13980)
Directv Inc ....G 260 471-3474
  Fort Wayne (G-4211)
Echostar Corporation ....E 574 271-0595
  South Bend (G-12757)
Raytheon Company ....D 310 647-9438
  Fort Wayne (G-4577)
Satellite Oasis ....G 317 375-1097
  Indianapolis (G-7897)
Spaceport Exprtion Centre Inc ....G 765 606-1512
  New Whiteland (G-11014)

SATELLITES: Communications

Dish Express ....G 812 962-3982
  Evansville (G-3458)

SAW BLADES

Archer Products Inc ....G 317 899-0700
  Indianapolis (G-6414)
Drake Corporation ....E 812 683-2101
  Jasper (G-8246)
Tsb LLC ....G 812 314-8331
  Edinburgh (G-2630)
Wood-Mizer Holdings Inc ....C 317 271-1542
  Indianapolis (G-8212)

PRODUCT

SAWDUST & SHAVINGS

North Central Ind Shavings LLC..........G...... 765 395-3875
Converse *(G-2080)*

SAWING & PLANING MILLS

Adkins Sawmill Inc ....G...... 812 849-4036
Mitchell *(G-10154)*

B & B Sawmill Inc ....G...... 812 834-5072
Bedford *(G-530)*

Benham Sawmill LLC ....G...... 812 723-2644
Paoli *(G-11444)*

Burton Lumber Co Inc ....F...... 812 866-4438
Lexington *(G-9249)*

Byler Sawmill ....G...... 812 577-5761
Bennington *(G-605)*

C & L Lumber Inc ....G...... 812 536-2171
Huntingburg *(G-6152)*

Campbell Road Sawmill ....G...... 260 238-4252
Spencerville *(G-13044)*

Cedar Creek Sawmill LLC ....E...... 260 627-3985
Grabill *(G-5359)*

Chisholm Lumber & Sup Co Inc ....E...... 317 547-3535
Indianapolis *(G-6601)*

Coomer & Sons Sawmill & Pallet ....D...... 765 659-2846
Frankfort *(G-4824)*

Countryside Sawmill....................G...... 812 486-2991
Montgomery *(G-10219)*

Crookedstick Sawmill LLC ....G...... 317 714-8930
Coatesville *(G-1748)*

Deer Run Sawmill LLC ....G...... 812 732-4608
Mauckport *(G-9654)*

Dehart Pallet & Lumber Co ....F...... 812 794-2974
Austin *(G-396)*

Dodd Wood Products Inc ....E...... 812 268-0798
Sullivan *(G-13082)*

Eastern Red Cedar Products LLC ....E...... 812 365-2495
Marengo *(G-9504)*

Fleenor Sawmill Inc ....G...... 812 752-3594
Scottsburg *(G-12356)*

Flodders Sawmill ....G...... 765 628-0280
Greentown *(G-5645)*

Forest Products Group Inc ....E...... 765 659-1807
Frankfort *(G-4832)*

Forest Products Mfg Co ....E...... 812 482-5625
Jasper *(G-8251)*

George Voyles Sawmill Inc ....E...... 812 472-3968
Salem *(G-12287)*

Grabers Portable Band Mill ....G...... 812 636-4158
Odon *(G-11330)*

Green Forest Sawmill LLC ....F...... 812 745-3335
Oaktown *(G-11318)*

Gross & Sons Lumber and Veneer........G...... 574 457-5214
Syracuse *(G-13132)*

Herbert S Sawmill ....F...... 812 663-9347
Greensburg *(G-5607)*

Hites Hardwood Lumber Corp ......F...... 574 278-7783
Buffalo *(G-1203)*

Homestead Properties Inc ....F...... 812 866-4415
Deputy *(G-2460)*

Hope Hardwoods Inc ....F...... 812 546-4427
Hope *(G-6114)*

Indiana Wood Products Inc..........D...... 574 825-2129
Middlebury *(G-9893)*

International Wood Inc ....E...... 812 883-5778
Salem *(G-12295)*

J M McCormick..........................G...... 317 874-4444
Indianapolis *(G-7288)*

Kinser Timber Products Inc ....G...... 812 876-4775
Gosport *(G-5352)*

Kinsers Hardwood ....G...... 812 834-5568
Heltonville *(G-6027)*

Koetter Woodworking ....F...... 812 923-8875
Borden *(G-933)*

Lasher Lumber Inc......................G...... 812 836-2618
Tell City *(G-13165)*

Loggers Incorporated ....E...... 812 939-2797
Clay City *(G-1704)*

Mann Road Sawmill Inc ....G...... 765 342-2700
Martinsville *(G-9621)*

Manuwal Sawmill Inc ....G...... 574 936-8187
Plymouth *(G-11705)*

Mark Middleton..........................G...... 812 967-2853
Pekin *(G-11475)*

Maurice Lukens Jr ....G...... 765 345-2971
Knightstown *(G-8555)*

Michael O Baird ....G...... 765 569-6721
Rockville *(G-12177)*

Miller Custom Forest Products..........G...... 765 478-3057
Connersville *(G-2064)*

Miller Hardwoods LLC ....G...... 574 773-9371
Nappanee *(G-10693)*

Millers Saw Mill ....G...... 812 883-5246
Salem *(G-12302)*

Napoleon Hardwood Lbr Co Inc ....E...... 812 852-4090
Greensburg *(G-5626)*

New Castle Saw Mill ....G...... 765 529-6635
New Castle *(G-10913)*

ONeal Wood Products Inc ....G...... 765 342-2709
Martinsville *(G-9631)*

Pike Lumber Company Inc ....E...... 574 893-4511
Carbon *(G-1293)*

Pingleton Sawmill Inc ....E...... 765 653-2878
Greencastle *(G-5473)*

PLM Holdings Inc ....E...... 812 232-0624
Terre Haute *(G-13304)*

R Booe & Son Hardwoods Inc ......E...... 812 835-2663
Centerpoint *(G-1540)*

R E Casebeer & Sons Inc ....G...... 812 829-3284
Spencer *(G-13035)*

Randall Lowe & Sons Sawmill ......F...... 812 936-2254
French Lick *(G-4988)*

Robinson Lumber Company Inc ......E...... 812 944-8020
New Albany *(G-10858)*

Rodney Sloan Logging ....G...... 812 934-5321
Batesville *(G-518)*

Ronald Wright Logging LLC ....E...... 812 338-2665
English *(G-3319)*

Salesman Sawmill Inc ....E...... 812 382-9154
Sullivan *(G-13094)*

Sanders Saw Mill Inc ....F...... 812 738-4793
Corydon *(G-2111)*

Shouse Sawmill ....G...... 812 743-2017
Monroe City *(G-10188)*

Speer Ron Sawmill & Lumber Co ....G...... 812 834-5515
Bedford *(G-579)*

Swartzentruber Sawmill ....G...... 812 486-3350
Montgomery *(G-10244)*

Terry L Ray ....G...... 765 342-3180
Martinsville *(G-9641)*

Timberland Resources Inc ....E...... 765 245-2634
Montezuma *(G-10211)*

Tree City Saw Mill ....G...... 812 663-6363
Greensburg *(G-5638)*

Tri-State Hardwood Company..........E...... 260 351-3111
South Milford *(G-12994)*

Universal Forest Products Indi..........C...... 574 273-6326
Granger *(G-5447)*

W & J Sawmill Llc ....G...... 812 486-2719
Montgomery *(G-10245)*

Wakelam John ....G...... 812 752-5243
Scottsburg *(G-12385)*

Walnut Acres Sawmill LLC ....G...... 765 344-0027
Rockville *(G-12183)*

Walnut Street Hardwoods ....E...... 574 287-1023
South Bend *(G-12986)*

Werner Sawmill Inc ....E...... 812 482-7565
Jasper *(G-8313)*

Wilkerson Sawmill ....G...... 812 988-7436
Nashville *(G-10739)*

Woodparts International Corp ....F...... 574 293-0566
Elkhart *(G-3266)*

SAWING & PLANING MILLS: Custom

Arbor Industries Inc....................E...... 574 825-2375
Middlebury *(G-9872)*

Conner Sawmill Inc......................F...... 574 626-3227
Walton *(G-13815)*

Frank Miller Lumber Co Inc..........C...... 800 345-2643
Union City *(G-13455)*

Hollingsworth Sawmill Inc ....F...... 765 883-5836
Russiaville *(G-12241)*

National Products Inc....................F...... 574 457-4565
Syracuse *(G-13138)*

Quality Hardwood Products Inc ....F...... 260 982-2043
North Manchester *(G-11241)*

R & M Enterprises ....G...... 765 795-6395
Indianapolis *(G-7806)*

Scrapwood Sawmill ....G...... 574 223-2725
Rochester *(G-12152)*

SAWMILL MACHINES

Wood-Mizer Holdings Inc ....C...... 317 271-1542
Indianapolis *(G-8212)*

SAWS & SAWING EQPT

Beckler Power Equipment..........G...... 260 356-1188
Huntington *(G-6190)*

Drake Corporation ....F...... 636 464-5070
Indianapolis *(G-6765)*

SAWS: Hand, Metalworking Or Woodworking

Valley Sharpening Inc..................G...... 574 674-9077
Osceola *(G-11386)*

SCAFFOLDS: Mobile Or Stationary, Metal

Sonny Scaffolds Inc....................F...... 317 831-3900
Mooresville *(G-10341)*

SCALE REPAIR SVCS

Technical Weighing Svcs Inc..........E...... 219 924-3366
Griffith *(G-5793)*

Valley Scale Company LLC ....F...... 812 282-5269
Clarksville *(G-1699)*

SCALES & BALANCES, EXC LABORATORY

Powell Systems Inc....................E...... 765 884-0980
Fowler *(G-4805)*

Raco Industries LLC ....G...... 812 232-3676
Terre Haute *(G-13314)*

Sinden Racing Service Inc ....F...... 317 243-7171
Indianapolis *(G-7949)*

SCALES: Indl

A H Emery Company ....E...... 812 466-5265
Terre Haute *(G-13184)*

Indiana Scale Company Inc ....F...... 812 232-0893
Terre Haute *(G-13255)*

Indianapolis Scale Company ....G...... 317 856-6606
Lafayette *(G-8923)*

Richards Scale Company ....G...... 812 246-3354
Sellersburg *(G-12412)*

Winslow Scale Company..................D...... 812 466-5265
Terre Haute *(G-13370)*

SCALES: Railroad Track

Valley Scale Company LLC ....F...... 812 282-5269
Clarksville *(G-1699)*

SCANNING DEVICES: Optical

Ncs Pearson Inc ....D...... 317 297-0259
Indianapolis *(G-7580)*

SCHOOL BUS SVC

Kuharic Enterprises....................G...... 574 288-9410
South Bend *(G-12832)*

SCHOOLS: Vocational, NEC

Crown Training & Development..........E...... 219 947-0845
Merrillville *(G-9708)*

SCIENTIFIC INSTRUMENTS WHOLESALERS

Lk Technologies Inc....................E...... 812 332-4449
Bloomington *(G-766)*

SCISSORS: Hand

Allen-Davis Enterprises Inc ....G...... 574 303-2173
Mishawaka *(G-9993)*

SCRAP & WASTE MATERIALS, WHOLESALE: Ferrous Metal

J Trockman & Sons Inc ....E...... 812 425-5271
Evansville *(G-3569)*

Joe W Morgan Inc ....D...... 812 423-5914
Evansville *(G-3575)*

Omnisource LLC..........................C...... 260 422-5541
Fort Wayne *(G-4510)*

Porter County Ir & Met Recycle ....F...... 219 996-7630
Hebron *(G-6020)*

Recycling Center Inc ....D...... 765 966-8295
Richmond *(G-12041)*

S W Industries Inc......................F...... 317 788-4221
Indianapolis *(G-7882)*

SCRAP & WASTE MATERIALS, WHOLESALE: Metal

American Scrap Processing Inc..........D...... 219 398-1444
East Chicago *(G-2515)*

Kendallville Iron & Metal Inc ....E...... 260 347-1958
Kendallville *(G-8486)*

(G-0000) Company's Geographic Section entry number

Loeb-Lorman Metals Inc...................G...... 574 892-5063
Argos (G-275)

Mervis Industries Inc...................F...... 812 232-1251
Terre Haute (G-13284)

Mervis Industries Inc...................D...... 765 454-5800
Kokomo (G-8665)

P & H Iron & Supply Inc...................F...... 219 853-0240
Hammond (G-5925)

Remedium Services Group LLC...........F...... 317 660-6868
Carmel (G-1467)

Winski Brothers Inc...................F...... 765 654-5323
Frankfort (G-4860)

SCRAP & WASTE MATERIALS, WHOLESALE: Nonferrous Metals Scrap

Newco Metals Inc...................G...... 765 644-6649
Anderson (G-145)

Newco Metals Inc...................E...... 317 485-7721
Pendleton (G-11497)

SCRAP & WASTE MATERIALS, WHOLESALE: Paper

Recycling Works Inc...................F...... 574 293-3751
Elkhart (G-3141)

SCRAP STEEL CUTTING

Steel Dynamics Inc...................B...... 260 969-3500
Fort Wayne (G-4646)

SCREENS: Projection

Milestone AV Technologies LLC...........B...... 574 267-8101
Warsaw (G-13911)

SCREENS: Window, Metal

Lansing Building Products Inc..............G...... 765 448-4363
Lafayette (G-8955)

SCREW MACHINE PRDTS

Aegis Sales & Engineering Inc............F...... 260 483-4160
Fort Wayne (G-4048)

Alexander Screw Products Inc...........E...... 317 898-5313
Indianapolis (G-6362)

Ashley F Ward Inc...................E...... 574 294-1502
Elkhart (G-2696)

Ashley F Ward Inc...................E...... 219 879-4177
Michigan City (G-9767)

Auburn Manufacturing Inc...........F...... 260 925-8651
Auburn (G-315)

Auspro Manufacturing Co Inc...........G...... 574 264-3705
Elkhart (G-2707)

Beckett Bronze Company Inc...........E...... 765 282-2261
Muncie (G-10438)

Charleston Metal Products Inc...........C...... 260 837-8211
Waterloo (G-14010)

Charleston Metal Products Inc...........E...... 260 837-8211
Waterloo (G-14011)

Demotte Manufacturing Inc...................G...... 219 987-6196
Demotte (G-2435)

Ds Products Inc...................D...... 260 563-9030
Wabash (G-13725)

Dual Machine Corporation...................F...... 317 921-9850
Indianapolis (G-6769)

Ebert Machine Company Inc...........E...... 765 473-3728
Peru (G-11526)

EMC Precision Machining II LLC...........D...... 317 758-4451
Sheridan (G-12589)

Epco Products Inc...................E...... 260 747-8888
Fort Wayne (G-4240)

Exactifab...................G...... 812 420-2723
Brazil (G-961)

F & F Screw Machine Products............E...... 574 293-0362
Elkhart (G-2842)

Fitech Inc...................E...... 513 398-1414
Michigan City (G-9794)

Gapco Inc...................G...... 317 787-6440
Indianapolis (G-6983)

Guardian Tech Group Ind LLC...........G...... 765 364-0863
Crawfordsville (G-2156)

H & E Machined Specialties...........F...... 260 424-2527
Fort Wayne (G-4311)

Ham Enterprises Machine Co...........G...... 765 342-7966
Martinsville (G-9611)

Hy-Matic Mfg Inc...................E...... 260 347-3651
Kendallville (G-8479)

Jerden Industries Inc...................E...... 812 332-1762
Bloomington (G-754)

Jessen Manufacturing Co Inc...........D...... 574 295-3836
Elkhart (G-2947)

Jrp Machine Co...................G...... 317 955-1905
Indianapolis (G-7318)

Kent Brenneke...................G...... 260 446-5383
Harlan (G-5973)

Madison Tool and Die Inc...................D...... 812 273-2250
Madison (G-9482)

Mid America Screw Products...........F...... 574 294-6905
Elkhart (G-3036)

Mitchel & Scott Machine Co...........B...... 317 639-5331
Indianapolis (G-7526)

Mitchel Group Incorporated...................C...... 317 639-5331
Indianapolis (G-7527)

Ms & J Quality Screw Mch Pdts...........F...... 812 623-3002
Sunman (G-13115)

Multitech Swiss Machining LLC...........D...... 260 894-4180
Ligonier (G-9290)

National Consolidated Corp...........F...... 574 289-7885
South Bend (G-12868)

Newsom Industries Inc...................F...... 812 372-2844
Columbus (G-1980)

Northern Indiana Manufacturing...........E...... 574 342-2105
Bourbon (G-946)

Precision Piece Parts Inc...................D...... 574 255-3185
Mishawaka (G-10107)

Prodigy Mold & Tool Inc...................E...... 812 753-3029
Haubstadt (G-6004)

Production Machining Company...........G...... 812 466-2885
Terre Haute (G-13310)

RCO-Reed Corporation...................E...... 317 736-8014
Franklin (G-4925)

RD Smith Manufacturing Inc...........G...... 260 829-6709
Orland (G-11357)

RTC...................G...... 260 503-9770
Columbia City (G-1831)

S H Leggitt Company...................G...... 574 264-0230
Elkhart (G-3152)

Sierra Machine...................G...... 574 232-5694
South Bend (G-12934)

Standard Locknut LLC...................C...... 317 399-2230
Westfield (G-14190)

Terry Liquidation III Inc...................E...... 219 362-3557
La Porte (G-8829)

Tri Aerospace LLC...................E...... 812 872-2400
Terre Haute (G-13358)

Whitcraft Enterprises Inc...................F...... 260 422-6518
Fort Wayne (G-4753)

Winn Machine Inc...................G...... 219 324-2978
La Porte (G-8833)

SCREWS: Metal

Indiana Automotive Fas Inc...................B...... 317 467-0100
Greenfield (G-5538)

SEALANTS

Ace Extrusion LLC...................G...... 812 463-5230
Evansville (G-3338)

Ace Extrusion LLC...................D...... 812 463-5230
Evansville (G-3340)

Koch Enterprises Inc...................G...... 812 465-9800
Evansville (G-3596)

Multiseal Inc...................C...... 812 428-3422
Evansville (G-3641)

Tyden Group Holdings Corp...........F...... 740 420-6777
Angola (G-253)

Uniseal Inc...................C...... 812 425-1361
Evansville (G-3784)

Uniseal Inc...................G...... 812 425-1361
Evansville (G-3785)

SEALING COMPOUNDS: Sealing, synthetic rubber or plastic

Franco Corporation...................G...... 765 675-6691
Tipton (G-13391)

PRC - Desoto International Inc...........E...... 317 290-1600
Indianapolis (G-7728)

Trellborg Sling Sltions US Inc...........C...... 260 748-5895
Fort Wayne (G-4699)

SEALS: Hermetic

EJ Brooks Company...................D...... 800 348-4777
Angola (G-209)

SEALS: Oil, Rubber

Freudenberg-Nok General Partnr...........C...... 317 421-3400
Shelbyville (G-12534)

Press-Seal Gasket Corporation...........C...... 260 436-0521
Fort Wayne (G-4557)

T & M Rubber Inc...................E...... 574 533-3173
Goshen (G-5338)

SEARCH & DETECTION SYSTEMS, EXC RADAR

Flir Detection Inc...................F...... 765 775-1701
West Lafayette (G-14067)

SEARCH & NAVIGATION SYSTEMS

Bae Systems Controls Inc...................A...... 260 434-5195
Fort Wayne (G-4100)

Harris Corporation...................B...... 260 451-5597
Fort Wayne (G-4323)

Harris Corporation...................C...... 812 202-5171
Crane (G-2127)

Pyromation Inc...................C...... 260 484-2580
Fort Wayne (G-4566)

Raytheon Company...................A...... 310 647-9438
Fort Wayne (G-4578)

Raytheon Company...................C...... 317 306-8471
Indianapolis (G-7822)

SEAT BELTS: Automobile & Aircraft

Gerardot Performance Products...........G...... 260 623-3048
Monroeville (G-10195)

Jack House LLC...................G...... 251 990-5960
Converse (G-2079)

Shield Restraint Systems Inc...................C...... 574 266-8330
Elkhart (G-3167)

Wolf Technical Engineering LLC...........G...... 800 783-9653
Indianapolis (G-8209)

SEATING: Bleacher, Portable

National Rcreation Systems Inc...........E...... 260 482-6023
Fort Wayne (G-4491)

SEATING: Stadium

Jsj Furniture Corporation...................C...... 256 768-2871
Middlebury (G-9898)

Preferred Seating Company LLC...........G...... 317 782-3323
Indianapolis (G-7740)

SECURITIES DEALING

General Electric Company...................D...... 812 933-0700
Batesville (G-501)

SECURITY CONTROL EQPT & SYSTEMS

Data Technologies Inc...................G...... 317 580-9161
Carmel (G-1352)

Instellus Inc...................G...... 734 415-3013
Griffith (G-5780)

Nrk Inc...................E...... 812 232-1800
Terre Haute (G-13292)

Phil & Son Inc...................F...... 219 663-5757
Crown Point (G-2283)

USA Vision Systems Inc...................G...... 949 583-1519
Fishers (G-3983)

SECURITY DEVICES

Applied Technology Group Inc...........F...... 260 482-2844
Fort Wayne (G-4084)

Conzer Security Inc...................G...... 317 580-9460
Carmel (G-1342)

PBM Industries Inc...................E...... 812 346-2648
North Vernon (G-11277)

Quick Panic Release LLC...................G...... 812 841-5733
Terre Haute (G-13313)

Reese Forge Orna Ironwork...........G...... 219 775-1039
Lake Village (G-9086)

Sentinel Alarm Systems Inc...................F...... 317 842-6482
Indianapolis (G-7912)

SECURITY GUARD SVCS

AM General LLC...................A...... 574 258-7523
Mishawaka (G-9995)

SECURITY SYSTEMS SERVICES

American Eagle Security Inc...................G...... 219 980-1177
Merrillville (G-9696)

Phil & Son Inc...................F...... 219 663-5757
Crown Point (G-2283)

Roi Marketing Company ....G...... 317 644-0797
Indianapolis (G-7855)

SEEDS & BULBS WHOLESALERS

Dow Agrosciences LLC ....A...... 317 337-3000
Indianapolis (G-6763)

Mycogen Corporation ....F...... 317 337-3000
Indianapolis (G-7565)

SELF-DEFENSE & ATHLETIC INSTRUCTION SVCS

Advanced Prtctive Slutions LLC ....G...... 765 720-9574
Coatesville (G-1746)

SEMICONDUCTORS & RELATED DEVICES

Advanced Control Tech Inc ....G...... 317 806-2750
Indianapolis (G-6332)

Allegro Microsystems LLC ....G...... 765 854-2263
Carmel (G-1309)

Autosem Inc ....F...... 574 288-8866
South Bend (G-12718)

Bowmar LLC ....E...... 260 747-3121
Fort Wayne (G-4116)

E-Certa Incorporated ....E...... 812 323-7824
Bloomington (G-717)

Environmental Technology Inc ....E...... 574 233-1202
South Bend (G-12765)

Fairchild Semiconductor Corp ....G...... 317 616-3641
Carmel (G-1377)

Heraeus Electro-Nite Co LLC ....C...... 765 473-8275
Peru (G-11529)

Indiana Intgrated Circuits LLC ....G...... 724 244-4560
Granger (G-5414)

Infineon Tech Americas Corp ....G...... 765 454-2144
Kokomo (G-8646)

Microchip Technology Inc ....G...... 317 773-8323
Noblesville (G-11150)

Microscreen LLC ....E...... 574 232-4358
South Bend (G-12862)

Nxp Usa Inc ....E...... 765 455-5100
Kokomo (G-8677)

Perfection Products Inc ....G...... 765 482-7786
Lebanon (G-9215)

Power Components of Midwest ....C...... 574 256-6990
Mishawaka (G-10105)

Pyromation Inc ....C...... 260 484-2580
Fort Wayne (G-4566)

Raytheon Company ....E...... 317 306-4872
Indianapolis (G-7821)

Semicndctor Cmponents Inds LLC ....G...... 765 868-5015
Kokomo (G-8694)

Texas Instruments Incorporated ....F...... 317 574-2611
Carmel (G-1493)

SENSORS: Radiation

Mark Lamaster......................................G...... 765 534-4185
Noblesville (G-11146)

SENSORS: Temperature, Exc Indl Process

Pyromation Inc ....C...... 260 484-2580
Fort Wayne (G-4566)

SENSORS: Ultraviolet, Solid State

American Ultraviolet Company..............D...... 765 483-9514
Lebanon (G-9168)

Rapid Sensors Inc ....G...... 260 562-3614
Howe (G-6131)

SEPTIC TANKS: Concrete

Carter Septic Tank Inc ....G...... 574 583-5796
Monticello (G-10257)

Creed & Dyer Precast Inc ....G...... 574 784-3361
Lakeville (G-9095)

Eaton Septic Tank Company ....G...... 765 396-3275
Eaton (G-2582)

Farmer Tank Incorporated....................G...... 574 264-4625
Elkhart (G-2846)

Holman Septic Tank Sls Redymix ....F...... 812 689-1913
Holton (G-6108)

Hudson Concrete Products Inc ....G...... 812 825-2917
Solsberry (G-12685)

Midwest Tile and Concrete Pdts...........G...... 260 749-5173
Woodburn (G-14387)

Quality Tank Trucks & Eqp Inc ....G...... 317 635-0000
Indianapolis (G-7801)

Rochester Cement Products..................G...... 574 223-3917
Rochester (G-12145)

Russells Excvtg & Septic Tanks...........G...... 812 838-2471
Mount Vernon (G-10406)

SERVICES, NEC

Jpt Enterprises Inc ....G...... 260 672-1605
Fort Wayne (G-4401)

Lapis Services Inc................................G...... 219 464-9131
Valparaiso (G-13572)

SEWAGE & WATER TREATMENT EQPT

American Hydro Systems Inc ....F...... 866 357-5063
Fort Wayne (G-4071)

Aqseptence Group Inc ....D...... 574 223-3980
Rochester (G-12116)

Canature Watergroup Usa Inc ....G...... 877 771-6789
Carmel (G-1327)

Clute Enterprises Inc ....G...... 260 413-0810
Huntertown (G-6135)

Davis Water Services Inc ....G...... 219 394-2270
Rensselaer (G-11920)

Evoqua Water Technologies LLC ....G...... 317 280-4255
Indianapolis (G-6884)

Jatech Scientific Inc ....G...... 765 345-2085
Knightstown (G-8553)

Kessco Water LLC ....G...... 765 362-3890
Crawfordsville (G-2165)

Leistner Aquatic Services Inc ....G...... 317 535-6099
Whiteland (G-14242)

Mohawk Laboratories ....G...... 317 899-3660
Indianapolis (G-7534)

Technical Water Treatment Inc ....G...... 574 277-1949
Granger (G-5444)

Western Wyne Rgonal Sewage Dst.......G...... 765 478-3788
Cambridge City (G-1263)

SEWER CLEANING & RODDING SVC

Hintz Equipment Inc ....G...... 765 362-6115
Thorntown (G-13375)

SEWER CLEANING EQPT: Power

Brockwood Farm ....G...... 812 837-9607
Nashville (G-10716)

Hintz Equipment Inc ....G...... 765 362-6115
Thorntown (G-13375)

SDP Manufacturing Inc.........................F...... 765 768-5000
Dunkirk (G-2488)

SEWING CONTRACTORS

Celestial Designs LLC ....G...... 317 733-3110
Zionsville (G-14425)

Connies Satin Stitch ....G...... 219 942-1887
Hobart (G-6077)

Freckles Graphics Inc..........................F...... 765 448-4692
Lafayette (G-8900)

SEWING MACHINE REPAIR SHOP

Spectrum Services Inc ....G...... 574 272-7605
Granger (G-5437)

SEWING MACHINES & PARTS: Indl

Globaltech Manufacturing L ....G...... 317 571-1910
Carmel (G-1386)

SEWING, NEEDLEWORK & PIECE GOODS STORES: Notions, Incl Trim

Indiana Ribbon Inc...............................E...... 219 279-2112
Wolcott (G-14365)

Sharps Baton Mfg Corp........................G...... 574 214-9389
Elkhart (G-3164)

SEWING, NEEDLEWORK & PIECE GOODS STORES: Sewing & Needlework

Hot Cake ....G...... 317 889-2253
Indianapolis (G-7132)

SHADES: Lamp & Light, Residential

A Homestead Shoppe Inc......................E...... 574 784-2307
Lapaz (G-9116)

SHADES: Window

A-1 Shade Co ....G...... 317 247-6447
Indianapolis (G-6303)

Ascot Enterprises Inc ....E...... 877 773-7751
Nappanee (G-10648)

Ascot Enterprises Inc ....D...... 574 773-7751
Nappanee (G-10649)

Continental Express ....G...... 574 294-5684
Elkhart (G-2770)

United Shade LLC ....G...... 574 262-0954
Elkhart (G-3236)

SHALE: Expanded

Hydraulic Press Brick Company ....E...... 317 290-1140
Indianapolis (G-7150)

SHAPES & PILINGS, STRUCTURAL: Steel

Indiana Steel Fabricating Inc ....F...... 765 742-1031
Lafayette (G-8922)

Proaxis Inc ....E...... 765 742-4200
West Lafayette (G-14097)

Steel Structural Products LLC ....F...... 812 670-4195
Jeffersonville (G-8429)

SHAPES: Extruded, Aluminum, NEC

80/20 Inc ....B...... 260 248-8030
Columbia City (G-1757)

Alexandria Extrusion Company.............E...... 317 545-1221
Indianapolis (G-6363)

Hoosier Trim Products LLC ....G...... 317 271-4007
Indianapolis (G-7125)

SHAVING PREPARATIONS

103 Collection LLC...............................G...... 800 896-2945
Schererville (G-12312)

SHEET METAL SPECIALTIES, EXC STAMPED

Bearcat Corp ....E...... 574 533-0448
Goshen (G-5177)

Bo-Mar Industries Inc ....E...... 317 899-1240
Indianapolis (G-6491)

Brand Sheet Metal Works Inc ....G...... 765 284-5594
Muncie (G-10443)

Creative Craftsmen Inc ....E...... 812 423-2844
Evansville (G-3437)

Cyclone Manufacturing Co Inc ....F...... 260 774-3311
Urbana (G-13476)

D & V Precision Sheetmetal ....E...... 317 462-2601
Greenfield (G-5517)

E H Baare Corporation ....G...... 765 778-7895
Anderson (G-103)

Estes Design and Manufacturing ....D...... 317 899-2203
Indianapolis (G-6880)

Flexco Products Inc ....C...... 574 294-2502
Elkhart (G-2852)

Fort Wayne Fabrication ....G...... 260 459-8848
Fort Wayne (G-4272)

Gary Metal Mfg LLC ....C...... 219 885-3232
Gary (G-5050)

Girtz Industries Inc ....D...... 844 464-4789
Monticello (G-10263)

Huntington Sheet Metal Inc...................D...... 260 356-9011
Huntington (G-6213)

Imh Fabrication Inc ....F...... 317 252-5566
Indianapolis (G-7163)

Imh Fabrication Inc ....F...... 317 252-5566
Indianapolis (G-7164)

Lauck Manufacturing Co Inc.................F...... 317 787-6269
Indianapolis (G-7385)

Loyal Mfg Corp ....F...... 317 359-3185
Indianapolis (G-7422)

Matrix Manufacturing Inc ....G...... 260 854-4659
Wolcottville (G-14374)

Noble Industries Inc ....E...... 317 773-1926
Noblesville (G-11160)

Omnimax International Inc....................E...... 574 294-8576
Elkhart (G-3070)

Professional Fabricators Inc.................G...... 260 665-2555
Angola (G-240)

Sam Mouron Equipment Co Inc............F...... 317 776-1799
Noblesville (G-11179)

Schuster Sheet Metal Inc ....G...... 574 293-4802
Elkhart (G-3159)

Sheet Metal Models Inc ....F...... 317 783-1303
Indianapolis (G-7925)

SHEETING: Laminated Plastic

Midwest Cabinet Solutions Inc ....F 765 664-3938
Marion (G-9547)
Olon Industries Inc (us) ....G 812 254-6718
Washington (G-13995)

SHEETING: Window, Plastic

Shade Techniques LLC ....G 765 396-9903
Eaton (G-2589)

SHEETS & STRIPS: Aluminum

Alcoa Inc ....C 765 447-1707
Lafayette (G-8849)
Arconic Inc ....G 812 842-3300
Newburgh (G-11022)
Arconic Inc ....C 317 241-9393
Indianapolis (G-6416)
Arconic Inc ....B 412 553-4545
Newburgh (G-11021)
Closure Systems Intl Inc ....G 765 364-6300
Crawfordsville (G-2139)
Novelis Corporation ....C 812 462-2287
Terre Haute (G-13291)

SHEETS: Solid Fiber, Made From Purchased Materials

Csc-Indiana LLC ....E 708 625-3255
New Haven (G-10936)

SHELLAC

Armor Clad Inc ....G 812 883-8734
Salem (G-12283)

SHELTERED WORKSHOPS

Cyberia Ltd ....G 317 721-2582
Indianapolis (G-6719)
New Hope Services Inc ....E 812 288-8248
Jeffersonville (G-8403)
New Hope Services Inc ....E 812 752-4892
Scottsburg (G-12377)
Rise Inc ....E 260 665-9408
Angola (G-243)

SHELVING, MADE FROM PURCHASED WIRE

Lafayette Wire Products Inc ....D 765 474-7896
Lafayette (G-8952)
Organized Living Inc ....C 812 334-8839
Bloomington (G-791)

SHELVING: Office & Store, Exc Wood

Cottom Automated Bus Soluti ....G 317 853-6531
Carmel (G-1346)

SHIELDS OR ENCLOSURES: Radiator, Sheet Metal

Mary Jonas ....F 317 500-0600
Indianapolis (G-7462)

SHIMS: Metal

Agi International Inc ....F 317 536-2415
Indianapolis (G-6352)

SHIP BLDG & RPRG: Drilling & Production Platforms, Oil/Gas

Harvest Petroleum Inc ....G 219 924-8236
Hammond (G-5890)

SHIP BUILDING & REPAIRING: Cargo, Commercial

Cargo Skiff Corporation ....G 812 873-6349
Butlerville (G-1247)

SHIP BUILDING & REPAIRING: Ferryboats

Smoker Craft Inc ....B 574 831-2103
New Paris (G-10994)

SHIP BUILDING & REPAIRING: Lighters, Marine

Lake Lite Inc ....G 260 918-2758
Laotto (G-9112)

SHIP BUILDING & REPAIRING: Military

Integrity Defense Services Inc ....F 812 675-4913
Springville (G-13064)

SHIP BUILDING & REPAIRING: Towboats

Marine Builders Inc ....D 812 283-7932
Jeffersonville (G-8396)

SHIPBUILDING & REPAIR

Acl Professional Services Inc ....B 812 288-0100
Jeffersonville (G-8317)
General Dynamics Corporation ....G 260 637-4773
Fort Wayne (G-4295)
Innovations By ....G 260 413-1869
Fort Wayne (G-4371)
Nsa Crane ....G 812 854-4723
Crane (G-2130)
Nswc Crane Division ....G 812 854-2865
Bloomington (G-781)
Tpg Mt Vernon Marine LLC ....C 317 631-0234
Indianapolis (G-8087)
Waterways Equipment Exchange ....G 812 925-8104
Chandler (G-1555)

SHOE & BOOT ACCESS

Karran USA ....G 410 975-0128
Vincennes (G-13688)

SHOE MATERIALS: Counters

Suke Inc ....G 219 689-0321
Crown Point (G-2311)
Top Design Cnc Inc ....G 219 662-2915
Valparaiso (G-13629)

SHOE MATERIALS: Inner Parts

Air Feet LLC ....G 317 441-1817
Greenwood (G-5663)

SHOE MATERIALS: Quarters

Comfort Quarters Conversions ....G 574 262-3701
Elkhart (G-2763)
Fat Quarter Annies Qui ....G 317 918-1481
Monrovia (G-10203)
Indiana KY III Interstate Qua ....G 812 985-9966
Mount Vernon (G-10395)
Pfrank Quarter Horses ....G 765 220-0257
Richmond (G-12029)
Simple Quarters LLC ....G 812 216-8602
Cicero (G-1667)

SHOE MATERIALS: Uppers

Upper Level Networks ....G 317 863-0955
Westfield (G-14197)
Upper Level Sports LLC ....G 317 681-3754
Indianapolis (G-8132)

SHOE STORES

Amos D Graber & Sons ....F 260 749-0526
New Haven (G-10929)

SHOE STORES: Athletic

Game Plan Graphics LLC ....G 812 663-3238
Greensburg (G-5602)

SHOE STORES: Custom & Orthopedic

Integrated Orthotic Lab Inc ....G 317 852-4640
Brownsburg (G-1156)

SHOES & BOOTS WHOLESALERS

Fbf Originals Inc ....G 765 349-7474
Martinsville (G-9603)

SHOES: Athletic, Exc Rubber Or Plastic

Marios Athletic Zone ....G 219 845-1800
Hammond (G-5913)

Onfield Apparel Group LLC ....G 317 895-7249
Indianapolis (G-7622)

SHOES: Canvas, Rubber Soled

Adidas Group ....G 317 895-7000
Indianapolis (G-6326)

SHOES: Infants' & Children's

Integrated Orthotic Lab Inc ....G 317 852-4640
Brownsburg (G-1156)

SHOES: Men's

Red Wing Shoe Company Inc ....G 317 219-6777
Noblesville (G-11174)

SHOES: Men's, Dress

Him Gentlemans Boutique ....G 812 924-7441
New Albany (G-10793)

SHOES: Moccasins

Carl Dyers Original Moccasins ....G 812 667-5442
Friendship (G-4991)

SHOES: Plastic Or Rubber

Nike Inc ....E 219 879-1320
Michigan City (G-9824)
Piro Shoes LLC ....F 888 849-0916
Fishers (G-3951)

SHOPPING CENTERS & MALLS

Coach Line Motors ....G 765 825-7893
Connersville (G-2043)

SHOT PEENING SVC

Toyo Seiko North America Inc ....G 574 288-2000
South Bend (G-12975)

SHOWCASES & DISPLAY FIXTURES: Office & Store

Deflecto LLC ....B 317 849-9555
Indianapolis (G-6732)
Idx Corporation ....C 812 280-0000
Jeffersonville (G-8379)

SHOWER STALLS: Metal

LCI Industries ....D 574 535-1125
Elkhart (G-2989)

SHOWER STALLS: Plastic & Fiberglass

Frontline Mfg Inc ....D 574 453-2902
Warsaw (G-13879)
Oasis Lifestyle LLC ....E 574 948-0004
Plymouth (G-11708)
Ultra/Glas of Lakeville Inc ....F 574 784-8958
Lakeville (G-9098)

SHREDDERS: Indl & Commercial

Commercial Star Inc ....F 765 386-2800
Coatesville (G-1747)
East Chicago Machine Tool Sls ....D 219 663-4525
Crown Point (G-2248)
Olympia Business Systems Inc ....F 800 225-5644
Wabash (G-13744)
Proshred Indianapolis Inc ....F 317 578-3650
Indianapolis (G-7780)
SSP Technologies Inc ....G 888 548-4668
Chesterton (G-1632)
Stop & Shred ....G 260 483-6200
Fort Wayne (G-4653)

SHUTTERS, DOOR & WINDOW: Metal

Challenger Door Llc ....D 574 773-0470
Nappanee (G-10658)
Kinro Manufacturing Inc ....C 574 535-1125
Elkhart (G-2969)

SHUTTERS, DOOR & WINDOW: Plastic

All Amrcan Shtter Cmpnents LLC ....G 260 639-0112
Hoagland (G-6062)
Bk International LLC ....G 260 639-0112
Hoagland (G-6063)

P
R
O
D
U
C
T

V N C Inc ....F 219 696-5031
Lowell **(G-9425)**

SIDING & STRUCTURAL MATERIALS: Wood

D and E Surplus LLC ....G 260 351-3200
Wolcottville **(G-14370)**
Menard Inc ....A 812 466-1234
Terre Haute **(G-13282)**
Ufp Granger LLC ....E 574 277-7670
Granger **(G-5445)**
Universal Forest Products Inc ....E 574 277-7670
Granger **(G-5446)**

SIDING MATERIALS

American Wholesalers Inc ....E 812 464-8781
Evansville **(G-3351)**

SIDING: Sheet Metal

Johns Architectural Media ....G 630 450-7539
Dyer **(G-2502)**
Zimmer Metal Sales LLC ....G 574 862-1800
Goshen **(G-5348)**

SIGN LETTERING & PAINTING SVCS

Doell Designs ....G 260 486-4504
Fort Wayne **(G-4217)**

SIGN PAINTING & LETTERING SHOP

Alveys Sign Co Inc ....E 812 867-2567
Evansville **(G-3350)**
Christys Design & Sign Co ....G 317 882-5444
Greenwood **(G-5675)**
Pioneer Signs Inc ....F 219 884-7587
Merrillville **(G-9746)**
Reed Sign Service Inc ....G 765 459-4033
Kokomo **(G-8688)**
Wagner Signs Inc ....E 317 788-0202
Indianapolis **(G-8175)**
Whitehead Signs Inc ....F 317 632-1800
Indianapolis **(G-8193)**

SIGNALING APPARATUS: Electric

Dux Signal Kits LLC ....G 260 623-3017
Monroeville **(G-10194)**
Pumpalarmcom LLC ....G 888 454-5051
Indianapolis **(G-7789)**

SIGNALS: Traffic Control, Electric

Mgi Traffic Control Pdts Inc ....G 317 835-9212
Fairland **(G-3825)**
SC Supply Company LLC ....G 574 287-0252
South Bend **(G-12928)**

SIGNS & ADVERTISING SPECIALTIES

1global Ds LLC ....F 765 413-2211
Westfield **(G-14131)**
20 Minute Signs Plus ....G 765 413-1046
Lafayette **(G-8844)**
A Harris Verl Inc ....G 317 736-4680
Indianapolis **(G-6296)**
A Plus Sign Area Ltg Spcalists ......G 765 966-4857
Richmond **(G-11951)**
A S P Parrott Signs ....G 812 325-9102
Bloomington **(G-653)**
A Sign Above ....G 317 392-2144
Laurel **(G-9127)**
A Sign Odyssey LLC ....G 219 962-1247
Lake Station **(G-9074)**
A To Z Sign Shop ....G 219 462-7489
Valparaiso **(G-13481)**
Aardvark Vinyl Signs ....G 260 833-0800
Angola **(G-188)**
Absograph Sign Co ....G 630 940-4093
Valparaiso **(G-13483)**
Accent Signs & Graphics ....G 866 769-7446
French Lick **(G-4983)**
Ace Sign Company Inc ....G 812 232-4206
Terre Haute **(G-13186)**
ACS Sign Solution ....G 317 201-4838
Indianapolis **(G-6319)**
ADM Custom Creations LLC ....G 765 499-0584
Hartford City **(G-5977)**
Advanced Sign & Graphics Inc ......F 765 284-8360
Muncie **(G-10424)**
Advanced Sign & Lighting Svc ....G 812 430-2817
Evansville **(G-3344)**

Advantage Signs & Graphics Inc ....G 219 853-1427
Hammond **(G-5835)**
Aerial Sign Co ....G 317 258-9696
Indianapolis **(G-6345)**
Affordable Sign & Neon Inc ....G 219 853-1855
Hammond **(G-5836)**
Affordable Signs ....G 260 349-1710
Kendallville **(G-8451)**
All American Tent & Awning Inc ......F 812 232-4220
Terre Haute **(G-13190)**
AMS Embroidery & Signs LLC ....G 513 313-1613
Brookville **(G-1111)**
Anderson Enterprises LLC ....G 317 569-1099
Carmel **(G-1311)**
Anderson Sign Pro ....G 765 642-0281
Anderson **(G-66)**
Any Reason Signs ....G 260 450-6756
Fort Wayne **(G-4079)**
Apex Electric & Sign Inc ....G 317 326-1325
Greenfield **(G-5501)**
Apex Electric & Sign Inc ....G 317 326-1325
Morristown **(G-10365)**
Arizona Sport Shirts Inc ....E 317 481-2160
Indianapolis **(G-6419)**
ASAP Sign & Lighting Maint ....G 219 464-8865
Valparaiso **(G-13499)**
Asempac Inc ....E 812 945-6303
New Albany **(G-10747)**
Athletic Avenue & More Inc ....G 812 547-7655
Tell City **(G-13155)**
Auto & Sign Specialties Inc ....G 260 824-1987
Bluffton **(G-866)**
Auto Art & Signs ....G 765 448-6800
Lafayette **(G-8856)**
Awards Unlimited Inc ....G 765 447-9413
Lafayette **(G-8858)**
B & B Signs ....G 812 282-5366
Floyds Knobs **(G-4008)**
Baugh Enterprises Inc ....F 812 334-8189
Bloomington **(G-674)**
Bc Awards Inc ....G 317 852-3240
Brownsburg **(G-1136)**
Beacon Sign Company LLC ....G 317 272-2388
Avon **(G-433)**
Bill Banner Signs ....G 765 209-2642
Falmouth **(G-3836)**
Biltz Signs ....G 574 594-2703
Warsaw **(G-13844)**
Bloomington Design Inc ....G 812 332-2033
Bloomington **(G-687)**
Bo-Mar Industries Inc ....E 317 899-1240
Indianapolis **(G-6491)**
Bob Prescott ....G 219 736-7804
Merrillville **(G-9703)**
Boezeman Enterprises Inc ....G 219 345-2732
Demotte **(G-2432)**
Booth Signs Inc ....G 812 376-7446
Columbus **(G-1860)**
Brand Wave LLC ....G 661 414-2115
Noblesville **(G-11070)**
Brick Street Embroidery ....G 574 453-3729
Leesburg **(G-9233)**
Broadway Auto Glass LLC ....F 219 884-5277
Merrillville **(G-9704)**
Brownsburg Signs & Graphics ....G 317 858-1907
Brownsburg **(G-1138)**
Built By Bill ....G 317 745-2666
Danville **(G-2345)**
Bulldog Award Co Inc ....G 317 773-3379
Noblesville **(G-11073)**
Burkhart Advertising Inc ....G 574 522-4421
Elkhart **(G-2738)**
Business Art & Design Inc ....G 317 782-9108
Beech Grove **(G-593)**
Buttons Galore Inc ....F 800 626-8168
Brownsburg **(G-1139)**
Buy Bulk Displays LLC ....G 574 222-4378
Osceola **(G-11372)**
C & H Signs Inc ....G 765 642-7777
Anderson **(G-79)**
Capital Custom Signs ....G 765 689-7170
Peru **(G-11519)**
Castleton Village Center Inc ....F 260 434-2600
Fort Wayne **(G-4140)**
Castleton Village Center Inc ....G 317 577-1995
Indianapolis **(G-6565)**
Ces Company Llc ....G 317 290-0491
Indianapolis **(G-6590)**
CJ Developers Inc ....G 219 942-5051
Hobart **(G-6075)**

Classic City Signs Inc ....G 260 927-8438
Auburn **(G-321)**
Classic Trophy Co ....F 260 483-1161
Fort Wayne **(G-4161)**
Clear Channel Outdoor Inc ....E 317 686-2350
Indianapolis **(G-6619)**
Cockerhams Signs & Graphics ....G 812 358-3737
Brownstown **(G-1183)**
Connections Sign Language Inte .....G 812 491-6036
Evansville **(G-3428)**
Corsair Graphics ....G 219 938-8317
Gary **(G-5040)**
Courtney Signs & Graphics Inc ....G 317 841-3297
Indianapolis **(G-6679)**
Creative Inc ....G 765 447-3500
Lafayette **(G-8882)**
Cumulus Intrmdate Holdings Inc .....G 765 452-5704
Kokomo **(G-8609)**
Designs 4 U Inc ....G 765 793-3026
Covington **(G-2118)**
Dezigns By Cindy Ziese ....G 219 819-8786
Rensselaer **(G-11921)**
Dg Graphics LLC ....G 765 349-9500
Martinsville **(G-9601)**
Don Anderson ....G 574 278-7243
Monticello **(G-10259)**
Dxd Signs ....G 219 588-4403
Highland **(G-6043)**
Earl R Hamilton ....G 317 838-9386
Plainfield **(G-11607)**
Economy Signs Inc ....G 219 932-1233
Hammond **(G-5875)**
Ej Schmidt Inc ....G 317 290-0491
Avon **(G-440)**
Everywhere Signs LLC ....G 812 323-1471
Bloomington **(G-721)**
Fast Signs ....G 574 254-0545
South Bend **(G-12772)**
Fastsigns ....G 260 373-0911
Fort Wayne **(G-4258)**
Fine Guys Inc ....G 812 547-8630
Tell City **(G-13161)**
Fine Signs and Graphics ....G 812 944-7446
New Albany **(G-10777)**
First Place Trophies ....G 812 385-3279
Princeton **(G-11872)**
Flag & Banner Company Inc ....F 317 299-4880
Indianapolis **(G-6931)**
French Lick Auto Signs ....G 812 936-7777
French Lick **(G-4985)**
Future Signs Sales & Service ....G 765 749-5180
Winchester **(G-14330)**
Future Wave Graphics Inc ....G 574 389-8803
Elkhart **(G-2873)**
Gast Sign Co ....G 219 759-4336
Valparaiso **(G-13547)**
Gc Solutions Inc ....G 317 334-1149
Indianapolis **(G-6987)**
Geckos ....G 765 762-0822
Attica **(G-301)**
Get Noticed Portable Signs ....G 765 649-6645
Anderson **(G-110)**
Gindor Inc ....G 574 642-4004
Goshen **(G-5225)**
Good Signs ....G 317 738-4663
Franklin **(G-4891)**
Grandview Aluminum Products ....E 812 649-2569
Grandview **(G-5387)**
Granite Tee Signs LLC ....G 317 670-4967
Fort Branch **(G-4027)**
Graphex International ....G 219 696-4849
Lowell **(G-9406)**
Graphic Visions ....G 812 331-7446
Bloomington **(G-733)**
Graphically Speaking ....G 219 921-1572
Chesterton **(G-1609)**
Graphics Systems Inc ....G 260 485-9667
Fort Wayne **(G-4302)**
Graycraft Signs Plus Inc ....G 574 269-3780
Warsaw **(G-13885)**
Grayson Graphics ....G 574 264-6466
Elkhart **(G-2895)**
Greenwood Light & Sign Service ......G 317 840-5729
Boggstown **(G-900)**
H L Signworks ....G 812 325-5750
Ellettsville **(G-3279)**
Heres Your Sign Diy Workshop & .....G 574 238-6369
New Paris **(G-10981)**
Hernandez Signs LLC ....G 317 500-1303
Indianapolis **(G-7096)**

Hi-Rise Sign & Lighting LLC	G	812 825-4448
Bloomington (G-740)		
Holloway Vinyl Signs Grap	G	765 717-1581
Yorktown (G-14405)		
Hot Rod Car Care LLC	G	317 660-2077
Indianapolis (G-7134)		
Hubbard Services Inc	G	317 881-2828
Greenwood (G-5704)		
Hydrojet Signs	G	765 584-2125
Winchester (G-14331)		
I F S Corp	G	317 898-6118
Indianapolis (G-7153)		
Icon International Inc	D	260 482-8700
Fort Wayne (G-4356)		
Ideal Sign Corp	G	219 406-2092
Valparaiso (G-13559)		
Image Group Inc	E	574 457-3111
Syracuse (G-13135)		
Imperial Trophy & Awards Co	G	260 432-8161
Fort Wayne (G-4361)		
Indiana Logo Sign Group	G	800 950-1093
Indianapolis (G-7182)		
Indiana Sign & Barricade Inc	E	317 377-8000
Indianapolis (G-7191)		
Indiana Stamp Co Inc	E	260 424-8973
Fort Wayne (G-4366)		
Indianapolis Signworks Inc	E	317 872-8722
Indianapolis (G-7205)		
Indys Sign Source Inc	G	317 372-2260
Indianapolis (G-7225)		
Insign Inc	G	317 251-0131
Indianapolis (G-7241)		
Insignia Sign Shop LLC	G	317 356-4639
Indianapolis (G-7242)		
Integrity Sign Solutions Inc	G	502 233-8755
New Albany (G-10807)		
J W P Vinyl Designs	G	812 873-8744
Dupont (G-2491)		
Jabra Signs & Graphics	G	765 584-7100
Winchester (G-14333)		
James Wafford	G	317 773-7200
Noblesville (G-11135)		
Jef Enterprises Inc	F	812 425-0628
Evansville (G-3573)		
Johnson Engraving & Trophies	G	260 982-7868
North Manchester (G-11232)		
Jsn Advertising Inc	G	317 888-7591
Indianapolis (G-7319)		
Karbach Holdings Corporation	F	219 924-2454
Hobart (G-6083)		
Kellmark Corporation	E	574 264-9695
Elkhart (G-2958)		
Kerham Inc	E	260 483-5444
Fort Wayne (G-4409)		
Konrady Graphics Inc	G	219 662-0436
Crown Point (G-2273)		
Link Electrical Service	G	812 288-8184
Jeffersonville (G-8391)		
Lotus Design Group	G	812 206-7281
Charlestown (G-1570)		
M F Y Designs Inc	G	260 563-6662
Wabash (G-13734)		
Magic Light Neon Sign Company	G	765 361-5887
Crawfordsville (G-2170)		
Markle Music	G	812 847-2103
Linton (G-9310)		
Marshall Signs	G	260 350-1492
Auburn (G-342)		
Masco Corporation of Indiana	D	317 848-1812
Indianapolis (G-7463)		
McCaffery Sign Designs	G	574 232-9991
South Bend (G-12857)		
Midwest Graphix LLC	G	812 649-2522
Rockport (G-12169)		
Midwest Sign Company Inc	G	317 931-9535
Seymour (G-12470)		
Mjs Businesses LLC	G	317 845-1932
Indianapolis (G-7530)		
MO Signs LLC	G	574 780-4075
Plymouth (G-11707)		
Morgan Commercial Lettering	G	260 482-6430
Fort Wayne (G-4481)		
Mullin Sign Studio	G	219 926-8937
Chesterton (G-1623)		
New Hope Services Inc	E	812 288-8248
Jeffersonville (G-8403)		
New Hope Services Inc	E	812 752-4892
Scottsburg (G-12377)		
Next Day Signs	G	574 259-7446
Mishawaka (G-10095)		

Next Products LLC	F	317 392-4701
Shelbyville (G-12554)		
No-Sail Splash Guard Co Inc	G	765 522-2100
Roachdale (G-12094)		
North Star Signs Inc	G	219 365-5935
Crown Point (G-2279)		
Northwest Indus Specialist	F	219 397-7446
East Chicago (G-2555)		
Ovation Communications Inc	G	812 401-9100
Evansville (G-3659)		
Over Hill & Dale Sign Studio	G	812 867-1664
Evansville (G-3660)		
Paint The Town Graphics Inc	E	260 422-9152
Fort Wayne (G-4518)		
Pathfinder Communications Corp	E	574 295-2500
Elkhart (G-3077)		
Pathfinder Communications Corp	G	574 266-5115
Elkhart (G-3078)		
Perfect Sign LLC	G	812 518-6459
Newburgh (G-11041)		
Phantom Neon LLC	G	765 362-2221
Crawfordsville (G-2186)		
Pjw Inc	G	574 295-1203
Elkhart (G-3098)		
Plainfield Sign Graphic Design	G	317 839-9499
Plainfield (G-11636)		
Plastimatic Arts Corp	E	574 254-9000
Mishawaka (G-10104)		
Precise Printing Plus Signs	G	317 545-5117
Indianapolis (G-7729)		
Prentice Products Holdings LLC	E	260 747-3195
Fort Wayne (G-4556)		
Printec Solutions Inc	G	317 289-6510
Indianapolis (G-7751)		
Professional Permits	G	574 257-2954
Mishawaka (G-10111)		
Progressive Design Apparel Inc	E	317 293-5888
Indianapolis (G-7775)		
Pts Signs & Wraps	G	317 653-1807
Indianapolis (G-7788)		
Pyramid Sign & Design Inc	G	765 447-4174
Lafayette (G-8986)		
R&S Sign Design	G	765 520-5594
New Castle (G-10916)		
Radical Graphics & Sign Sp LLC	G	574 870-8873
Monticello (G-10281)		
Raeco/Promo-Sports LLC	E	574 537-9387
Goshen (G-5315)		
Recognition Plus	G	812 232-2372
Terre Haute (G-13316)		
Reddington Design Inc	G	574 272-0790
South Bend (G-12914)		
Redneck Monshiners Signs T-Shi	G	812 844-0694
Salem (G-12304)		
Reed Sign Service Inc	G	765 459-4033
Kokomo (G-8688)		
Reinforcements Design	G	219 866-8626
Rensselaer (G-11935)		
Richardson Entps Blmington LLC	G	812 287-8179
Bloomington (G-811)		
Rlr Associates Inc	G	317 632-1300
Indianapolis (G-7848)		
Ron Glasscock	G	812 986-2342
Poland (G-11743)		
Rookies Unlimited Inc	G	765 536-2726
Summitville (G-13104)		
Sampco Inc	C	413 442-4043
South Bend (G-12925)		
Seaton Springs Inc	G	812 282-2440
Clarksville (G-1696)		
Sexton Melinda	G	812 522-4059
Seymour (G-12484)		
Sig Media LLC	G	317 858-7624
Indianapolis (G-7938)		
Sign	G	260 422-7446
Fort Wayne (G-4623)		
Sign A Rama	G	812 477-7763
Evansville (G-3727)		
Sign A Rama	G	812 537-5516
Lawrenceburg (G-9157)		
Sign Age Inc	G	765 778-5254
Pendleton (G-11505)		
Sign Arama	G	812 657-7449
Columbus (G-2014)		
Sign Creations LLC	G	574 855-1246
South Bend (G-12935)		
Sign Deals Delivered	G	574 276-7404
South Bend (G-12936)		
Sign Factory	G	574 255-7446
Mishawaka (G-10123)		

Sign For It LLC	G	317 834-4636
Mooresville (G-10340)		
Sign Graphics	G	574 834-7100
North Webster (G-11301)		
Sign Guys Inc	G	317 875-7446
Indianapolis (G-7943)		
Sign Here Ltd	G	317 487-8001
Indianapolis (G-7944)		
Sign Pros	G	765 289-2177
Muncie (G-10562)		
Sign Pros Inc	G	765 642-1175
Anderson (G-166)		
Sign Pros of Marion	G	765 677-1234
Marion (G-9562)		
Sign Ser Homes	G	317 214-8005
Noblesville (G-11183)		
Sign Services	G	317 546-1111
Indianapolis (G-7945)		
Sign Write Signs LLC	G	219 477-3840
Valparaiso (G-13618)		
Sign-A-Rama	G	317 477-2400
Greenfield (G-5573)		
Signplex LLC	G	765 795-7446
Cloverdale (G-1737)		
Signs By Sulane Inc	G	765 565-6773
Carthage (G-1516)		
Signs In Time By Greg Inc	G	260 749-7446
Fort Wayne (G-4626)		
Signs Magic LLC	G	812 473-5155
Evansville (G-3730)		
Signs of Life LLC	G	317 575-1049
Carmel (G-1480)		
Signs of Seasons	G	219 866-4507
Rensselaer (G-11938)		
Signs of Times Llc	G	812 981-3000
New Albany (G-10862)		
Signs On Time Inc	F	219 661-4488
Crown Point (G-2304)		
Signs Unlimited	G	574 255-0500
Mishawaka (G-10124)		
Signs Xp Inc	G	765 453-4812
Kokomo (G-8696)		
Signtech Sign Services Inc	G	574 537-8080
Goshen (G-5323)		
Skyline Signs Inc	G	765 564-4422
Delphi (G-2427)		
Snykin Inc	G	317 818-0618
Indianapolis (G-7956)		
Spark Marketing LLC	G	219 301-0071
Schererville (G-12346)		
Speckin Sign Service Inc	G	317 539-5133
Greencastle (G-5478)		
Spp Inc	F	812 882-6203
Vincennes (G-13707)		
Stingel Enterprises Inc	F	812 883-0054
Salem (G-12306)		
Stoffel Seals Corporation	E	845 353-3800
Angola (G-248)		
Supreme Signs	G	219 384-0198
Valparaiso (G-13625)		
T G R Inc	F	765 452-8225
Kokomo (G-8705)		
T&S Signs	G	317 996-3027
Martinsville (G-9639)		
Tc4llc	G	317 709-5429
Fishers (G-3973)		
Team Hillman LLC	F	260 426-2626
Fort Wayne (G-4676)		
Thousand One Inc	G	765 962-3636
Richmond (G-12066)		
Tko Enterprises Inc	D	317 271-1398
Plainfield (G-11647)		
Todays Signs and Graphics	G	765 288-4771
Muncie (G-10571)		
Tomlin Enterprises Inc	G	866 994-9200
Fort Wayne (G-4690)		
Tower Advertising Products Inc	D	260 593-2103
Topeka (G-13431)		
Town & Country Industries Inc	E	219 712-0893
Crown Point (G-2316)		
Traffic Sign Company Inc	G	317 845-9305
Indianapolis (G-8089)		
Trulinesigns LLC	G	219 644-7231
Dyer (G-2511)		
Unique Signs	G	812 384-4967
Bloomfield (G-646)		
Universal Sign Group Inc	G	317 697-1165
Plainfield (G-11649)		
Van Der Weele Jon D	G	574 892-5005
Argos (G-280)		

Vart Grafix ....G....... 317 513-5522
Indianapolis *(G-8148)*
Vince Rogers Signs Inc ....G....... 574 264-0542
Elkhart *(G-3245)*
Vital Signs Marketing LLC ....G....... 765 453-5088
Kokomo *(G-8713)*
Vkf Renzel Usa Corp ....F....... 219 661-6300
Crown Point *(G-2318)*
Wagner Signs Inc ....E....... 317 788-0202
Indianapolis *(G-8175)*
Ward Industries Inc ....F....... 574 825-2548
Middlebury *(G-9923)*
Westlund Concepts ....F....... 317 819-0611
Lapel *(G-9120)*
Whiteco Industries Inc ....A....... 219 769-6601
Merrillville *(G-9761)*
Wildside Signs ....G....... 812 358-3849
Vallonia *(G-13478)*
Williams Signs Inc ....G....... 765 448-6725
Lafayette *(G-9025)*
Winters Assoc Prmtnal Pdts Inc ....F....... 812 330-7000
Bloomington *(G-858)*
World Graffix LLC ....G....... 574 936-1927
Plymouth *(G-11740)*
Xl Graphics Inc ....F....... 317 738-3434
Franklin *(G-4942)*
Ya-Nvr-No ....G....... 260 833-8883
Orland *(G-11360)*
Young & Kenady Incorporated ....G....... 317 852-6300
Brownsburg *(G-1178)*

SIGNS & ADVERTISING SPECIALTIES: Artwork, Advertising

Clients Choice Ltd ....G....... 812 853-2911
Boonville *(G-912)*
Image One LLC ....E....... 317 576-2700
Fishers *(G-3927)*

SIGNS & ADVERTISING SPECIALTIES: Novelties

Athletic Edge Inc ....F....... 260 489-6613
Fort Wayne *(G-4095)*
Business & Industrial Pdts Co ....G....... 812 376-6149
Columbus *(G-1863)*
Indiana Dimensional Pdts LLC ....D....... 574 834-7681
North Webster *(G-11293)*
Indiana Metal Craft Inc ....D....... 812 336-2362
Bloomington *(G-747)*

SIGNS & ADVERTISING SPECIALTIES: Scoreboards, Electric

Sign Group Inc ....G....... 317 228-8049
Indianapolis *(G-7942)*

SIGNS & ADVERTISING SPECIALTIES: Signs

Aarvee Associates LLC ....G....... 312 222-5665
Indianapolis *(G-6305)*
Ace Sign Systems Inc ....G....... 765 288-1000
Muncie *(G-10423)*
Aplus Signs ....G....... 765 966-4857
Richmond *(G-11955)*
Arben Corp ....F....... 812 477-7763
Evansville *(G-3360)*
Art Works Sign Co Inc ....G....... 574 360-9290
Mishawaka *(G-9997)*
B B & H Signs Incorporated ....G....... 812 235-1340
Terre Haute *(G-13196)*
Bandit Signs ....G....... 574 370-7067
Elkhart *(G-2713)*
Big Guy Signs LLC ....G....... 317 780-6000
Indianapolis *(G-6473)*
Billman Monument & Sign Co ....G....... 574 753-2394
Logansport *(G-9325)*
Blumling Design and Graphics ....G....... 765 477-7446
Lafayette *(G-8863)*
Burkhart Advertising Inc ....F....... 574 234-4444
South Bend *(G-12728)*
Cardinal Manufacturing Co Inc ....F....... 317 283-4175
Indianapolis *(G-6553)*
Castleton Village Center Inc ....F....... 260 471-5959
Fort Wayne *(G-4141)*
Christys Design & Sign Co ....G....... 317 882-5444
Greenwood *(G-5675)*
Commercial Signs ....G....... 260 745-2678
Fort Wayne *(G-4168)*
Crichlow Industries Inc ....G....... 317 925-5178
Indianapolis *(G-6692)*
D D McKay and Associates ....G....... 317 546-7446
Indianapolis *(G-6721)*
Diskey Architectural Signage ....F....... 260 424-0233
Fort Wayne *(G-4212)*
Doell Designs ....G....... 260 486-4504
Fort Wayne *(G-4217)*
Federal Heath Sign Company LLC ....G....... 317 581-7790
Carmel *(G-1380)*
Four Points Development Corp ....F....... 317 357-3275
Indianapolis *(G-6951)*
Graycraft Signs Plus Inc ....G....... 260 432-3760
Fort Wayne *(G-4305)*
Hall Signs Inc ....D....... 812 332-9355
Bloomington *(G-737)*
J W Signs Inc ....G....... 260 747-5168
Fort Wayne *(G-4388)*
Legendary Designs Inc ....G....... 260 768-9170
Shipshewana *(G-12630)*
Lesh Advertising Inc ....G....... 574 859-2141
Camden *(G-1275)*
Margison Graphics LLC ....G....... 765 529-8250
New Castle *(G-10911)*
Mid America Sign Corporation ....F....... 260 744-2200
Fort Wayne *(G-4471)*
Neon Accents ....G....... 812 537-0102
Lawrenceburg *(G-9148)*
Olive Branch Etc Inc ....G....... 765 449-1884
Lafayette *(G-8977)*
Region Signs Inc ....F....... 219 473-1616
Whiting *(G-14275)*
Sabco Sign Co Inc ....G....... 317 882-3380
Greenwood *(G-5746)*
Safety Vehicle Emblem Inc ....F....... 317 885-7565
Indianapolis *(G-7884)*
Sign Graphics Evansville Inc ....G....... 812 476-9151
Evansville *(G-3729)*
Sign Masters ....G....... 765 525-7446
Saint Paul *(G-12280)*
Sign Pro of Fort Wayne Inc ....G....... 260 497-8484
Fort Wayne *(G-4624)*
Sign Shoppe ....G....... 260 483-1922
Fort Wayne *(G-4625)*
Signs By Design ....G....... 812 853-7784
Newburgh *(G-11049)*
Signs More ....G....... 317 392-9184
Shelbyville *(G-12569)*
Signs of Times ....G....... 574 296-7464
Elkhart *(G-3172)*
Signworks ....G....... 219 462-5353
Valparaiso *(G-13619)*
Sjg Enterprises Inc ....G....... 574 269-4806
Warsaw *(G-13940)*
Smith Signs Inc ....G....... 574 255-6446
Mishawaka *(G-10128)*
Stans Sign Design ....G....... 317 251-3838
Indianapolis *(G-7994)*
Stello Products Inc ....F....... 812 829-2246
Spencer *(G-13039)*
Stritto Sign Art Company ....G....... 317 356-2126
Indianapolis *(G-8012)*
Travis Britton ....G....... 317 762-6018
Indianapolis *(G-8092)*
Vital Signs ....G....... 219 548-1605
Valparaiso *(G-13635)*
Weber Sign Service Inc ....G....... 219 872-5060
Trail Creek *(G-13444)*

SIGNS & ADVERTSG SPECIALTIES: Displays/Cutouts Window/Lobby

Kay Company Inc ....E....... 765 659-3388
Frankfort *(G-4840)*
L R Green Co Inc ....D....... 317 781-4200
Indianapolis *(G-7370)*
Lillich Sign Co Inc ....F....... 260 463-3930
Lagrange *(G-9058)*

SIGNS, ELECTRICAL: Wholesalers

Sign Craft Industries Inc ....E....... 317 842-8664
Indianapolis *(G-7940)*
Signdoc Identity LLC ....G....... 317 247-9670
Indianapolis *(G-7946)*

SIGNS, EXC ELECTRIC, WHOLESALE

Economy Signs Inc ....G....... 219 932-1233
Hammond *(G-5875)*
Fedex Office & Print Svcs Inc ....G....... 219 462-6270
Valparaiso *(G-13542)*
Fedex Office & Print Svcs Inc ....G....... 317 839-3896
Plainfield *(G-11609)*
Fedex Office & Print Svcs Inc ....F....... 317 974-0378
Indianapolis *(G-6909)*
Fedex Office & Print Svcs Inc ....F....... 317 917-1529
Indianapolis *(G-6910)*
Graphic22 Inc ....G....... 219 921-5409
Chesterton *(G-1608)*
Link Electrical Service ....G....... 812 288-8184
Jeffersonville *(G-8391)*
Northwest Indus Specialist ....F....... 219 397-7446
East Chicago *(G-2555)*
Over Hill & Dale Sign Studio ....G....... 812 867-1664
Evansville *(G-3660)*
Traffic Sign Company Inc ....G....... 317 845-9305
Indianapolis *(G-8089)*

SIGNS: Electrical

A Sign-By-Design Inc ....E....... 317 876-7900
Zionsville *(G-14415)*
ACS Sign Solution ....F....... 317 925-2835
Indianapolis *(G-6318)*
Alveys Sign Co Inc ....E....... 812 867-2567
Evansville *(G-3350)*
AP Sign Group LLC ....E....... 317 257-1869
Indianapolis *(G-6406)*
Begley Sign Painting Inc ....G....... 317 835-2027
Fairland *(G-3820)*
Burkhart Advertising Inc ....F....... 574 233-2101
South Bend *(G-12727)*
Chads Signs Installations Inc ....E....... 317 867-2737
Noblesville *(G-11079)*
Clermont Neon Sign Company ....G....... 317 638-4123
Brownsburg *(G-1143)*
Clover Signs Co ....F....... 812 442-7446
Brazil *(G-958)*
Custom Sign & Engineeri ....G....... 812 401-1550
Newburgh *(G-11026)*
Custom Signs Unlimited Co ....G....... 260 483-4444
Fort Wayne *(G-4196)*
Green Sign Co Inc ....F....... 812 663-2550
Greensburg *(G-5603)*
Greenfield Signs Inc ....G....... 317 469-3095
Greenfield *(G-5535)*
Hutchison Sign Co Inc ....E....... 317 894-8787
Indianapolis *(G-7148)*
Isf Inc ....E....... 317 251-1219
Indianapolis *(G-7274)*
Johnson Bros S Whitley Sign Co ....F....... 260 723-5161
South Whitley *(G-13000)*
Jrowe Signs ....G....... 260 668-7100
Angola *(G-223)*
Kinder Group Inc ....C....... 765 457-5966
Kokomo *(G-8651)*
Landmark Signs Inc ....D....... 219 762-9577
Chesterton *(G-1617)*
Martin Signs & Crane Services ....G....... 317 908-9708
Indianapolis *(G-7460)*
North American Signs Inc ....D....... 574 234-5252
South Bend *(G-12877)*
Phoenix Sign Works Inc ....G....... 317 432-4027
Indianapolis *(G-7687)*
Pioneer Signs Inc ....F....... 219 884-7587
Merrillville *(G-9746)*
Premier Sign Group Inc ....G....... 317 613-4411
Indianapolis *(G-7741)*
Premiere Signs Co Inc ....F....... 574 533-8585
Goshen *(G-5312)*
Sign Craft Industries Inc ....E....... 317 842-8664
Indianapolis *(G-7940)*
Sign Crafters Inc ....E....... 812 424-9011
Evansville *(G-3728)*
Sign Group Inc ....F....... 317 875-6969
Indianapolis *(G-7941)*
Sign Solutions Inc ....F....... 317 881-1818
Greenwood *(G-5749)*
Sign Source One I Group Inc ....G....... 219 736-5865
Hobart *(G-6095)*
Signcenter Inc ....G....... 812 232-4994
Terre Haute *(G-13326)*
Signdoc Identity LLC ....G....... 317 247-9670
Indianapolis *(G-7946)*
Signs Unlimited ....G....... 260 484-5769
Fort Wayne *(G-4627)*
Sojane Technologies Inc ....G....... 317 915-1059
Indianapolis *(G-7958)*
Square 1 Designs & Signs ....G....... 219 552-0079
Shelby *(G-12516)*
Stackman Signs/Graphics Inc ....E....... 317 784-6120
Indianapolis *(G-7984)*
Steindler Signs ....G....... 219 733-2551
Wanatah *(G-13825)*

The Baldus Company Inc ....G... 260 424-2366
Fort Wayne (G-4680)
US Signcrafters Inc ....F ... 574 674-5055
Osceola (G-11385)
Wendell Conger ....G... 812 282-2564
Jeffersonville (G-8441)

SIGNS: Neon

Burkhart Advertising Inc ....G... 260 482-9566
Fort Wayne (G-4127)
Columbus Signs ....G... 812 376-7877
Columbus (G-1881)
Delaplane & Son Neon & Sign ....G... 574 859-3431
Camden (G-1273)
Express Sign & Neon Llc ....G... 812 882-0104
Vincennes (G-13679)
Hanks Neon & Plastic Service ....G... 812 423-7447
Evansville (G-3532)
L D Barger Wholesale Neon Inc ....G... 765 643-4506
Anderson (G-131)
Military Neon Signs ....G... 574 258-9804
Mishawaka (G-10088)
Neon Cactus ....G... 765 743-6081
Lafayette (G-8975)
Whitehead Signs Inc ....F ... 317 632-1800
Indianapolis (G-8193)

SILICONES

Dow Silicones Corporation ....F ... 260 347-5813
Kendallville (G-8474)
Momentive Performance Mtls Inc ....D... 260 357-2000
Garrett (G-5017)

SILK SCREEN DESIGN SVCS

Asempac Inc ....E ... 812 945-6303
New Albany (G-10747)
Custom TS & Trophies ....G... 219 926-4174
Porter (G-11804)
Dave Turner ....G... 765 674-3360
Gas City (G-5122)
East 40 Sports Apparel Inc ....G... 812 877-3695
Terre Haute (G-13229)
Logo Boys Inc ....G... 574 256-6844
Mishawaka (G-10070)
Main Event Mdsg Group LLC ....F ... 317 570-8900
Indianapolis (G-7442)
Stien Designs & Graphics Inc ....G... 260 347-9136
Kendallville (G-8511)
Tranter Graphics Inc ....D... 574 834-2626
Syracuse (G-13151)
United Media Group Inc ....G... 260 436-7417
Fort Wayne (G-4715)
Wagner Signs Inc ....E ... 317 788-0202
Indianapolis (G-8175)

SILVERWARE

Simply Silver ....G... 260 824-4667
Bluffton (G-892)

SIMULATORS: Flight

Flight Integrity LLC ....G... 812 455-6642
Newburgh (G-11028)
Xwind LLC ....G... 317 350-2080
Brownsburg (G-1177)

SINK TOPS, PLASTIC LAMINATED

Mishawaka Whse & Distrg LLC ....G... 574 259-6011
Mishawaka (G-10093)

SINKS: Vitreous China

Interglobal Way Network LLC ....G... 574 971-4490
Elkhart (G-2938)
Karran USA ....G... 410 975-0128
Vincennes (G-13688)

SIRENS: Vehicle, Marine, Indl & Warning

Carson Manufacturing Co Inc ....F ... 317 257-3191
Indianapolis (G-6560)

SKIDS: Wood

Fowler Ridge IV Wind Farm LLC ....G... 765 884-1029
Fowler (G-4800)
Megan Inc ....F ... 574 267-8626
Warsaw (G-13910)

Powell Systems Inc ....G... 765 884-0613
Fowler (G-4804)
W-M Lumber and Wood Pdts Inc ....E ... 812 944-6711
New Albany (G-10874)

SKILL TRAINING CENTER

Cabinetmaker Inc ....G... 812 723-3461
Paoli (G-11446)

SLAB & TILE: Precast Concrete, Floor

Brim Concrete Inc ....G... 765 564-4975
Delphi (G-2415)
Envision Epoxy ....G... 317 448-3400
Noblesville (G-11100)

SLABS: Steel

Steel Avenue Inc ....G... 517 238-2220
Mishawaka (G-10136)

SLAG: Crushed Or Ground

Beemsterboer Slag Corp ....D... 219 392-1930
East Chicago (G-2522)
Butler Mill Service Company ....E ... 260 625-4930
Columbia City (G-1769)
Butler Mill Service Company ....E ... 260 868-5123
Butler (G-1223)
Edw C Levy Co ....E ... 765 364-9251
Crawfordsville (G-2151)
South Shore Slag LLC ....F ... 219 881-6544
Hammond (G-5943)
Tms International LLC ....C... 219 307 6550
East Chicago (G-2571)

SLAUGHTERING & MEAT PACKING

Jemdd LLC ....E ... 260 768-4156
Lagrange (G-9049)

SLIDES & EXHIBITS: Prepared

Searle Exhibit Tech Inc ....F ... 317 787-3012
Indianapolis (G-7907)

SMOKE DETECTORS

St Louis Group LLC ....E ... 317 975-3121
Indianapolis (G-7981)

SNOW REMOVAL EQPT: Residential

Brian J Spilman ....G... 765 663-2860
Arlington (G-281)
Original Tractor Cab Co Inc ....E ... 765 663-2214
Arlington (G-282)

SNOWMOBILES

Dorel Juvenile Group Inc ....C... 800 457-5276
Columbus (G-1912)

SOAPS & DETERGENTS

Aperion Care ....G... 219 874-5211
Michigan City (G-9766)
Craft Laboratories Inc ....F ... 260 432-9467
Fort Wayne (G-4183)
Ecolab Inc ....E ... 317 816-0983
Carmel (G-1368)
Ecolab Inc ....F ... 260 375-4710
Warren (G-13829)
Ecolab Inc ....D... 260 359-3280
Huntington (G-6202)
Ginas Essentials ....G... 812 406-3276
Nabb (G-10640)
Holloway House Inc ....E ... 317 485-4272
Fortville (G-4779)
J 2 Systems and Supply LLC ....G... 317 602-3940
Indianapolis (G-7281)
Lather Up LLC ....G... 260 638-4978
Markle (G-9579)
Lush ....G... 317 842-5874
Indianapolis (G-7427)
Metalworking Lubricants Co ....E ... 317 269-2444
Indianapolis (G-7491)
National Handicapped Workshop ....D... 765 287-8331
Muncie (G-10538)
Paradigm Industries Inc ....G... 317 574-8590
Carmel (G-1448)
Phoenix Brands LLC ....F ... 203 975-0319
Indianapolis (G-7685)

Phoenix Brands LLC ....D... 317 231-8044
Indianapolis (G-7686)
Soapy Soap Company ....G... 812 575-0005
Bloomington (G-826)
Unilever United States Inc ....E ... 219 659-3200
Hammond (G-5953)
Vintage Chemical Enterprises ....G... 260 745-7272
Fort Wayne (G-4728)
Warsaw Chemical Company Inc ....D... 574 267-3251
Warsaw (G-13958)
Yushiro Manufacturing Amer Inc ....E ... 317 398-9862
Shelbyville (G-12586)

SOAPS & DETERGENTS: Textile

Harts Handmade Naturals LLC ....G... 317 407-9988
Greenwood (G-5701)
Wills-Stockton Acres LLC ....G... 765 366-7307
Crawfordsville (G-2204)

SOCIAL SVCS, HANDICAPPED

Adec Inc ....C... 574 848-7451
Bristol (G-1040)

SOCKETS & RECEPTACLES: Lamp, Electric Wiring Devices

Bb Wiring LLC ....G... 765 376-0190
Crawfordsville (G-2135)

SOFT DRINKS WHOLESALERS

American Bottling Company ....E ... 574 291-9000
South Bend (G-12703)
Central Coca-Cola Btlg Co Inc ....G... 812 482-7475
Jasper (G-8241)
Central Coca-Cola Btlg Co Inc ....G... 800 241-2653
Bloomington (G-699)
Central Coca-Cola Btlg Co Inc ....G... 260 726-7126
Portland (G-11810)
Central Coca-Cola Btlg Co Inc ....G... 800 241-2653
Shelbyville (G-12526)
Clark Foods Inc ....D... 812 949-3075
New Albany (G-10761)
P-Americas LLC ....E ... 765 289-0270
Muncie (G-10542)

SOFTWARE PUBLISHERS: Application

Anabaptist Mennonite Biblical ....D... 574 295-3726
Elkhart (G-2691)
Black Ember LLC ....G... 317 840-5523
Indianapolis (G-6482)
Blue Pillar Inc ....E ... 317 723-6601
Indianapolis (G-6488)
Blue Sun Ventures Ltd ....G... 317 426-0001
Indianapolis (G-6490)
Boomstick Interactive LLC ....G... 812 528-4875
Indianapolis (G-6496)
Bronze Bow Software Inc ....G... 260 672-9516
Roanoke (G-12100)
Clinical Architecture LLC ....E ... 317 580-8400
Carmel (G-1341)
Computrain Learning Center Inc ....F ... 812 235-7419
Terre Haute (G-13216)
Crowdpixie LLC ....G... 317 578-3137
Fishers (G-3895)
Depth Plus Design LLC ....G... 317 370-0532
Westfield (G-14158)
Eat Here Indy LLC ....G... 317 502-4419
Indianapolis (G-6794)
Emplify LLC ....E ... 800 580-5344
Fishers (G-3904)
Envisio Design LLC ....G... 574 274-4394
Mishawaka (G-10042)
Envista LLC ....D... 317 208-9100
Carmel (G-1372)
Envista Concepts LLC ....E ... 317 208-9100
Carmel (G-1373)
Envista Entp Solutions LLC ....E ... 317 208-9100
Carmel (G-1374)
Envista Freight Managment LLC ....F ... 317 208-9100
Carmel (G-1375)
Eon Performance LLC ....E ... 847 997-8619
Indianapolis (G-6874)
Helios LLC ....E ... 317 554-9911
Indianapolis (G-7087)
Help Help LLC ....G... 317 910-6631
Avon (G-446)
Ike Newton LLC ....G... 317 902-1772
Greenwood (G-5705)

PRODUCT

Indy Mobile Apps LLC ....G....... 508 685-5240
Greenwood *(G-5707)*
Infinite Ai Inc ....G....... 317 965-4850
Carmel *(G-1415)*
Innovtive Nurological Dvcs LLC ....G....... 317 674-2999
Carmel *(G-1416)*
Intelligent Software Inc ....G....... 219 923-6166
Munster *(G-10610)*
Knowledge Diffusion Games LLC ....G....... 812 361-4424
Bloomington *(G-759)*
Lactor LLC ....G....... 765 496-6838
West Lafayette *(G-14080)*
Lh Software Concepts LLC ....G....... 317 222-1779
Indianapolis *(G-7401)*
Long Tail Corporation ....G....... 260 918-0489
Fort Wayne *(G-4441)*
Luxly LLC ....G....... 617 415-8031
Carmel *(G-1429)*
Mag Software Inc ....G....... 317 755-4080
Zionsville *(G-14446)*
Mesh Systems LLC ....E....... 317 661-4800
Carmel *(G-1437)*
Microsoft Corporation ....F....... 317 705-6900
Indianapolis *(G-7501)*
Mobile Enerlytics LLC ....G....... 765 464-6909
West Lafayette *(G-14086)*
No Pass LLC ....G....... 516 713-6885
Kokomo *(G-8676)*
Novacove LLC ....G....... 219 775-2966
Indianapolis *(G-7600)*
Oxinas Partners LLC ....G....... 812 725-8649
Jeffersonville *(G-8411)*
RAD Cube LLC ....F....... 317 456-7560
Indianapolis *(G-7813)*
Rebound Project LLP ....G....... 765 621-5604
Anderson *(G-158)*
Registration System LLC ....G....... 317 548-4090
Fishers *(G-3963)*
Simeoc LLC ....G....... 240 210-5685
South Bend *(G-12937)*
Tab Software ....G....... 260 490-7132
Fort Wayne *(G-4673)*
Tech Innovation LLC ....G....... 317 506-8343
Indianapolis *(G-8046)*
Tk Software Inc ....G....... 317 569-8887
Carmel *(G-1498)*
Trackahead LLC ....G....... 800 780-3519
Fishers *(G-3979)*
Trill Machine LLC ....G....... 219 730-0744
Kentland *(G-8524)*

SOFTWARE PUBLISHERS: Business & Professional

250ok LLC ....G....... 855 250-6529
Indianapolis *(G-6285)*
A Dine Tech Inc ....G....... 219 464-4764
Valparaiso *(G-13480)*
Accent Software Inc ....G....... 317 846-6025
Carmel *(G-1300)*
Adaptasoft Inc ....F....... 219 567-2547
Francesville *(G-4808)*
App Press LLC ....G....... 317 661-4759
Indianapolis *(G-6408)*
Application Software Inc ....G....... 317 823-3525
Indianapolis *(G-6410)*
Aptera Software Inc ....G....... 260 969-1410
Fort Wayne *(G-4087)*
Aunalytics Inc ....G....... 574 307-9230
South Bend *(G-12716)*
Blue Burro Inc ....G....... 904 825-9900
Bloomington *(G-689)*
Bolstra LLC ....G....... 317 660-9131
Carmel *(G-1320)*
Brangene LLC ....G....... 317 203-9172
Plainfield *(G-11597)*
Captivated LLC ....G....... 317 554-7400
Carmel *(G-1328)*
Clear Software LLC ....G....... 317 732-8831
Zionsville *(G-14427)*
Corvano LLC ....G....... 317 403-0471
Fishers *(G-3894)*
Createit Hlthcare Slutions Inc ....G....... 765 993-0988
Richmond *(G-11974)*
Cummins Digital Ventures Inc ....E....... 812 377-5000
Columbus *(G-1887)*
Curvo Labs Inc ....G....... 619 316-1202
Evansville *(G-3448)*
Diverse Tech Services Inc ....F....... 317 432-6444
Indianapolis *(G-6748)*
Enghouse Networks (us) Inc ....D....... 317 262-4666
Indianapolis *(G-6867)*
Everything Underground Inc ....G....... 317 491-8148
Indianapolis *(G-6883)*
Fiserv Mrtg Servicing Systems ....C....... 574 282-3300
South Bend *(G-12779)*
Flynn Media LLC ....G....... 317 536-2972
Indianapolis *(G-6942)*
Gale Force Software Corp ....F....... 317 570-4900
Fishers *(G-3915)*
Genesys Telecom Labs Inc ....G....... 317 715-8545
Indianapolis *(G-7000)*
Genesys Telecom Labs Inc ....A....... 317 872-3000
Indianapolis *(G-7001)*
Getsaydo LLC ....G....... 317 800-8319
Indianapolis *(G-7003)*
Glidepath Com LLC ....G....... 317 288-4459
Fishers *(G-3917)*
Holli Helms ....G....... 574 253-8923
Warsaw *(G-13890)*
Hyperbole Software Unltd ....G....... 812 839-6635
Madison *(G-9471)*
Identity Logix LLC ....G....... 219 379-5560
Munster *(G-10608)*
JKL Software ....G....... 765 778-3032
Pendleton *(G-11491)*
Maddenco Inc ....F....... 812 474-6245
Evansville *(G-3609)*
Nechanna One Productions Corp ....G....... 317 400-8908
Indianapolis *(G-7582)*
Patriot Software Solutions Inc ....G....... 317 573-5431
Indianapolis *(G-7661)*
Renaissnce Electronic Svcs LLC ....E....... 317 786-2235
Indianapolis *(G-7833)*
Rics Software Inc ....E....... 317 455-5338
Indianapolis *(G-7843)*
S & S Programming Inc ....G....... 765 423-4472
Lafayette *(G-8994)*
School Doctor Notes LLC ....G....... 317 660-1552
Carmel *(G-1476)*
Sedona Inc ....G....... 219 764-9675
Portage *(G-11793)*
Simma Software Inc ....G....... 812 418-0526
Terre Haute *(G-13327)*
Snappy Minds Llc ....G....... 812 661-8506
Jasper *(G-8310)*
Software Informatics Group LLC ....G....... 317 326-2598
Greenfield *(G-5575)*
Spotlight Cybersecurity LLC ....G....... 805 886-4456
Lafayette *(G-9001)*
Structural LLC ....G....... 317 713-7500
Indianapolis *(G-8013)*
Tgx Medical Systems LLC ....F....... 317 575-0300
Carmel *(G-1494)*

SOFTWARE PUBLISHERS: Computer Utilities

Compumark Industries Inc ....G....... 219 365-0508
Saint John *(G-12261)*
Steady Demand LLC ....G....... 765 404-1763
Lafayette *(G-9003)*

SOFTWARE PUBLISHERS: Education

Cooperative Ventures Ind Corp ....G....... 317 259-7063
Carmel *(G-1343)*
Edtechzone LLC ....G....... 317 902-7594
Cloverdale *(G-1725)*
Express Study LLC ....G....... 812 272-2247
Bloomington *(G-722)*
Lessonly Inc ....D....... 317 469-9194
Indianapolis *(G-7399)*
Rough Notes Company Inc ....E....... 800 428-4384
Carmel *(G-1470)*
Speak Modalities LLC ....G....... 765 742-4252
West Lafayette *(G-14109)*
Standard For Success LLC ....F....... 844 737-3825
Cloverdale *(G-1739)*
Wolfe Diversified Inds LLC ....E....... 765 683-9374
Pendleton *(G-11511)*

SOFTWARE PUBLISHERS: Home Entertainment

Freehold Games LLC ....G....... 574 656-9031
Walkerton *(G-13802)*
Lord Fms Games ....G....... 317 710-2253
Indianapolis *(G-7419)*
Uber Dragon Studios Inc ....G....... 317 520-2837
Carmel *(G-1500)*
Voidteam Studios ....G....... 765 414-9777
Lafayette *(G-9016)*

SOFTWARE PUBLISHERS: NEC

Aging Parent Software ....G....... 317 848-9548
Carmel *(G-1305)*
Akori Software ....G....... 574 595-5413
Rochester *(G-12115)*
Application Software ....G....... 317 814-8010
Greenfield *(G-5503)*
Application Software ....G....... 317 843-9775
Carmel *(G-1314)*
Ark Software LLC ....G....... 317 835-7912
Fountaintown *(G-4788)*
Artemis Intl Solutions Corp ....G....... 708 665-3155
Valparaiso *(G-13498)*
Articode Inc ....G....... 317 569-8357
Carmel *(G-1315)*
Aspen Solutions Group Inc ....G....... 317 839-9274
Avon *(G-429)*
Awave Software LLC ....G....... 219 285-1852
Munster *(G-10598)*
Blackboxit Inc ....G....... 260 489-8014
Fort Wayne *(G-4112)*
Bluefin Software LLC ....G....... 574 643-1091
South Bend *(G-12724)*
C&S Solutions ....G....... 812 895-0048
Vincennes *(G-13671)*
Cad/CAM Technologies Inc ....G....... 765 778-2020
Pendleton *(G-11487)*
Catalyst Inc ....G....... 317 227-3499
Indianapolis *(G-6566)*
Cheddar Stacks Inc ....G....... 317 566-0425
Indianapolis *(G-6595)*
Cornerstone Communications LLC ....F....... 317 802-0107
Indianapolis *(G-6669)*
Crusaderbit Software LLC ....G....... 317 773-2317
Noblesville *(G-11088)*
D X Systems ....G....... 812 332-4699
Bloomington *(G-710)*
Dallara Research Center LLC ....G....... 317 388-5416
Speedway *(G-13013)*
Dallara USA Holding Inc ....G....... 317 388-5400
Speedway *(G-13014)*
Data-Vision Inc ....F....... 574 243-8625
Mishawaka *(G-10033)*
Dedicated Software ....G....... 260 341-4166
Yoder *(G-14397)*
Determine Inc ....E....... 317 594-8600
Carmel *(G-1356)*
Determine Inc ....C....... 650 532-1500
Carmel *(G-1357)*
Determine Sourcing Inc ....G....... 408 570-9700
Carmel *(G-1358)*
Do Technologies LLC ....G....... 812 272-2306
Bloomington *(G-714)*
Dotstaff LLC ....E....... 317 806-6100
Indianapolis *(G-6760)*
Emarsys North America Inc ....E....... 844 693-6277
Indianapolis *(G-6846)*
Exacttarget Inc ....C....... 317 423-3928
Indianapolis *(G-6890)*
Finvantage LLC ....F....... 317 500-4949
Carmel *(G-1381)*
Frank R Komar CPA ....G....... 812 477-9110
Evansville *(G-3513)*
Glio Software Inc ....G....... 314 856-5855
Carmel *(G-1385)*
Greenwell Software LLC ....G....... 812 295-4665
Loogootee *(G-9384)*
Guide Technologies LLC ....G....... 317 844-3162
Indianapolis *(G-7058)*
Healthcare Data Inc ....F....... 812 342-9947
Morgantown *(G-10352)*
Hot Shot Multimedia Entps LLC ....G....... 317 537-7527
South Bend *(G-12805)*
Hurco Companies Inc ....C....... 317 293-5309
Indianapolis *(G-7146)*
Ilab LLC ....D....... 317 218-3258
Indianapolis *(G-7158)*
Imminent Software Inc ....G....... 317 340-4562
Carmel *(G-1410)*
Indigo Bioautomation Inc ....E....... 317 493-2400
Carmel *(G-1412)*
Industrial Software LLC ....G....... 317 862-0650
Indianapolis *(G-7211)*
Infront Software LLC ....G....... 317 501-1871
Fishers *(G-3988)*
Insertec Inc ....D....... 800 556-1911
Indianapolis *(G-7240)*

Intempo Software Inc..............G....800 950-2221
Indianapolis (G-7251)
Intuitive Software LLC..............G....574 268-8239
Warsaw (G-13894)
Ip Software Inc..............G....317 569-1313
Indianapolis (G-6269)
Jem Software Development LLC..........G....812 339-2970
Bloomington (G-753)
Jim Couch..............G....574 533-5107
Goshen (G-5248)
Jpe Consulting LLP..............G....574 675-9552
Osceola (G-11379)
Kaplan Inc..............D....317 872-7220
Indianapolis (G-7333)
Keystone Consulting Services..........G....260 693-0250
Churubusco (G-1654)
Kgn Software LLC..............G....812 618-4723
Evansville (G-3588)
Laney Software Co..............G....260 312-0759
South Bend (G-12835)
Leadtrack Software..............G....317 823-0748
Indianapolis (G-7389)
Leaf Hut Software LLC..............G....317 770-3632
Fishers (G-3938)
Lhp Software LLC..............C....812 373-0870
Columbus (G-1959)
Lincs Software Corp..............G....812 204-3619
Evansville (G-3603)
Lots of Software LLC..............G....317 578-8120
Fishers (G-3940)
M2m Holdings Inc..............A....317 249-1700
Indianapolis (G-7434)
Marshall & Poe LLC..............E....574 266-5244
Elkhart (G-3019)
Mellon Tax Service..............G....219 947-1660
Hobart (G-6091)
Mental Rehabilitation..............G....765 414-5590
Lafayette (G-8966)
Metakite Software LLC..............G....317 441-7385
Fishers (G-3946)
Micro Businessware Inc..............G....502 424-6613
Jeffersonville (G-8400)
Middletowne Software LLC..............G....765 760-5007
Muncie (G-10524)
Mike Burroughs Sftwr Dev LLC..........G....317 927-7195
Indianapolis (G-7514)
Mike Jones Software..............G....317 845-7479
Indianapolis (G-7515)
Millstone Specialties Inc..............G....765 653-7382
Greencastle (G-5468)
Milltronics Usa Inc..............E....317 293-5309
Indianapolis (G-7523)
Nolan Brubaker Software LLC..............G....574 238-0676
Goshen (G-5300)
Octiv Inc..............D....317 550-0148
Indianapolis (G-7609)
Old Gary Inc..............G....941 755-0976
Merrillville (G-9742)
Oprato Software LLC..............G....317 573-0168
Carmel (G-1446)
Osc Holdings LLC..............G....765 751-7000
Muncie (G-10540)
Paradigm Software Corp..............G....317 770-7862
Cicero (G-1664)
Pathology Computer Systems..........G....812 265-3264
Madison (G-9490)
Pineapple Software Inc..............G....812 987-8277
Borden (G-937)
Policystat LLC..............D....317 644-1296
Carmel (G-1452)
Propellerheads..............G....317 219-0408
Muncie (G-10549)
Quality Data Products Inc..............G....317 595-0700
Fishers (G-3959)
Recon Group LLP..............G....855 874-8741
Greenfield (G-5566)
Regional Data Services Inc..............F....219 661-3200
Crown Point (G-2295)
Relational Gravity Inc..............G....317 855-7685
Indianapolis (G-7831)
Relational Intelligence LLC..............G....317 669-8900
Westfield (G-14183)
Rightrez..............G....812 219-1893
Bloomington (G-812)
Rob Nolley Inc..............G....317 825-5211
Shelbyville (G-12563)
Rox Software Inc..............G....765 430-7616
Brookston (G-1107)
Rs2 Technologies LLC..............F....877 682-3532
Munster (G-10628)

Rt Software..............G....317 578-8518
Fishers (G-3965)
Sanborn Software Systems LLC..........G....317 283-7735
Indianapolis (G-7891)
Satellite Software..............G....574 842-3370
Plymouth (G-11724)
Seasoned Software LLC..............G....260 431-5666
Fort Wayne (G-4613)
Sharpen Technologies Inc..............D....855 249-3357
Indianapolis (G-7923)
Sigma Micro Corp..............G....317 631-6580
Indianapolis (G-7939)
Sim 2 K Inc..............F....317 251-7920
Indianapolis (G-7947)
Sleepy Owl Software LLC..............G....765 299-2862
Bloomington (G-825)
Software Pub LLC..............G....260 486-7839
Fort Wayne (G-4633)
Software Sales Incorporated..............G....317 258-7442
Whitestown (G-14262)
Software Sneak..............G....219 510-5894
Valparaiso (G-13622)
Sports Software Inc..............G....812 738-2735
Corydon (G-2113)
Spring Ventures Infovation LLC..........G....317 847-1117
Greenwood (G-5750)
SS&c Technologies Inc..............G....812 266-2000
Evansville (G-3746)
Sugar Coded Software LLC..............G....858 652-0797
Westfield (G-14191)
Sunyata Software LLC..............G....310 923-1821
Indianapolis (G-8020)
Swifttrip LLC..............G....812 206-5200
Jeffersonville (G-8432)
Symantec Corporation..............G....317 575-4010
Indianapolis (G-8029)
Synergy Software Group Inc..............G....765 229-4003
Union City (G-13461)
Tag Software..............G....219 866-3100
Rensselaer (G-11941)
Technalysis Inc..............E....317 291-1985
Indianapolis (G-8049)
Thickstat Inc..............G....201 294-1896
Indianapolis (G-8061)
Three Dog Software Inc..............G....317 823-7080
Indianapolis (G-8071)
Trh Software Inc..............G....812 264-2428
Terre Haute (G-13357)
Trivaeo LLC..............G....765 387-4451
Montezuma (G-10212)
User Wise Software Ltd..............G....317 894-1385
Indianapolis (G-8141)
Vizai LLC..............G....630 677-6583
Indianapolis (G-8167)
Web Software LLC..............F....765 452-3936
Kokomo (G-8716)
Wolfgang Software..............G....317 443-5147
Fishers (G-3985)
Yoder Software Inc..............G....574 302-6232
South Bend (G-12993)

SOFTWARE PUBLISHERS: Publisher's

Casper Inc..............G....660 221-5906
Indianapolis (G-6564)
Quality Council of Indiana..............G....812 533-4215
West Terre Haute (G-14128)
Sahasra Technologies Corp..............E....317 845-5326
Indianapolis (G-7887)
Two El Exito..............G....574 830-5104
Goshen (G-5344)

SOFTWARE TRAINING, COMPUTER

Cad/CAM Technologies Inc..............G....765 778-2020
Pendleton (G-11487)
Computrain Learning Center Inc..........F....812 235-7419
Terre Haute (G-13216)

SOIL TESTING KITS

Ploog Engineering Co Inc..............G....219 663-2854
Crown Point (G-2284)

SOLAR CELLS

Benson Solar Enterprises LLC..........G....855 533-7467
Huntington (G-6193)

SOLAR HEATING EQPT

Gmp Holdings LLC..............G....317 353-6580
Indianapolis (G-7016)

Inovateus Solar LLC..............E....574 485-1400
South Bend (G-12813)
Our Country Home Entps Inc..........D....260 657-5605
Harlan (G-5974)
Solar America Solutions LLC..............G....317 688-8581
Indianapolis (G-7959)

SOLID CONTAINING UNITS: Concrete

Martinsville Vault Company..............G....765 342-4576
Martinsville (G-9623)

SOLVENTS

Calumet Missouri LLC..............E....318 795-3800
Indianapolis (G-6538)
Calumet Spclty Pdts Prtners LP..........B....317 328-5660
Indianapolis (G-6542)

SOLVENTS: Organic

Hoosier Penn Oil Co Inc..............G....812 284-9433
Jeffersonville (G-8376)

SONAR SYSTEMS & EQPT

Raytheon Company..............A....260 429-6000
Fort Wayne (G-4576)

SOUND EQPT: Electric

Chappys Rent To Own LLC..............G....765 622-9500
Anderson (G-83)
Projected Sound Inc..............E....317 839-4111
Plainfield (G-11637)
Top In Sound Inc..............G....765 649-8111
Anderson (G-177)

SOUVENIR SHOPS

Goldden Corporation..............F....765 423-4366
Lafayette (G-8908)

SOYBEAN PRDTS

Bunge North America Inc..............D....260 724-2101
Decatur (G-2372)
Bunge North America Foundation........D....765 763-7500
Morristown (G-10366)
Cargill Incorporated..............E....765 423-4302
Lafayette (G-8866)
Dupont..............D....219 261-2124
Remington (G-11906)
Solae..............G....260 724-2101
Decatur (G-2405)
Solae LLC..............G....800 325-7108
Remington (G-11909)

SPACE PROPULSION UNITS & PARTS

Adranos Energetics LLC..............G....208 539-2439
West Lafayette (G-14046)
In Space LLC..............G....765 775-2107
West Lafayette (G-14076)

SPACE VEHICLE EQPT

Attco Machine Products Inc..............E....574 234-1063
South Bend (G-12714)
Major Tool and Machine Inc..............B....317 636-6433
Indianapolis (G-7446)
Thermal Ceramics Inc..............E....574 296-3500
Elkhart (G-3212)

SPEAKER SYSTEMS

Kelley Global Brands LLC..............G....833 554-8326
Noblesville (G-11136)
MTS Products Corp..............E....574 295-3142
Elkhart (G-3054)
MTS Products Corp..............F....574 295-3142
Elkhart (G-3055)

SPECIAL PRODUCT SAWMILLS, NEC

L M Woodworking..............G....574 534-9177
Goshen (G-5260)

SPECIALTY FOOD STORES: Vitamin

Oza Compound Products..............G....260 483-0406
Fort Wayne (G-4515)

Employee Codes: A=Over 500 employees, B=251-500
C=101-250, D=51-100, E=20-50, F=10-19, G=2-9

2018 Harris Indiana
Industrial Directory

PRODUCT

1081

SPEED CHANGERS

Mitsubsh Trbchrgr & Engn AM In ....E 317 346-5291
Franklin *(G-4912)*

SPICE & HERB STORES

G & W Herbs ....G 574 646-2134
Nappanee *(G-10671)*

Reidco Inc ....E 812 358-3000
Brownstown *(G-1191)*

SPONGES: Bleached & Dyed

Lsm Manufacturing LLC ....G 260 409-4030
Grabill *(G-5379)*

SPOOLS: Fiber, Made From Purchased Materials

Indiana Ribbon Inc ....E 219 279-2112
Wolcott *(G-14365)*

Indiana Ribbon Inc ....E 219 279-2112
Wolcott *(G-14366)*

SPOOLS: Indl

Mossberg Industries Inc ....D 260 357-5141
Garrett *(G-5018)*

SPORTING & ATHLETIC GOODS: Arrows, Archery

Easton Technical Products Inc ....E 574 583-5131
Monticello *(G-10261)*

Pieniadze Inc ....G 888 226-6241
Zionsville *(G-14456)*

Send A Scent Arrow Co Inc ....G 317 297-5232
Indianapolis *(G-7910)*

SPORTING & ATHLETIC GOODS: Bags, Golf

Touchdown Fishing Lures LLC ....G 812 873-8355
Paris Crossing *(G-11461)*

SPORTING & ATHLETIC GOODS: Bags, Rosin

Side Kick Lure Retriever ....G 812 329-9068
Bedford *(G-577)*

SPORTING & ATHLETIC GOODS: Basketball Eqpt & Splys, NEC

Dick Baumgartners Basket ....E 765 220-1767
Richmond *(G-11977)*

SPORTING & ATHLETIC GOODS: Batons

Flo Realty LLC ....G 317 636-6481
Indianapolis *(G-6938)*

Indiana Baton Twirling Assoc ....G 317 769-6826
Lebanon *(G-9191)*

Sharps Baton Mfg Corp ....G 574 214-9389
Elkhart *(G-3164)*

SPORTING & ATHLETIC GOODS: Boomerangs

Boomerang Ventures LLC ....G 317 852-7786
Danville *(G-2344)*

SPORTING & ATHLETIC GOODS: Bowling Balls

Rbg Inc ....G 812 866-3983
Lexington *(G-9255)*

SPORTING & ATHLETIC GOODS: Bowling Pins

Royal Pin Leisure Ctr ....G 317 247-4426
Indianapolis *(G-7866)*

SPORTING & ATHLETIC GOODS: Bows, Archery

David W Miller Miller Longbow ....G 765 482-3234
Lebanon *(G-9179)*

Thundrbird Traditional Archery ....G 812 699-1099
Culver *(G-2327)*

SPORTING & ATHLETIC GOODS: Buckets, Fish & Bait

Sevier Manufacturing ....G 317 892-2784
Brownsburg *(G-1171)*

SPORTING & ATHLETIC GOODS: Camping Eqpt & Splys

Pathfinder School LLC ....F 317 791-8777
Indianapolis *(G-7660)*

Westfield Outdoor Inc ....C 317 334-0364
Indianapolis *(G-8186)*

SPORTING & ATHLETIC GOODS: Crossbows

Crossbow Group Inc ....G 317 603-0406
Westfield *(G-14150)*

Native Crossbows LLC ....G 765 641-2224
Anderson *(G-142)*

SPORTING & ATHLETIC GOODS: Decoys, Duck & Other Game Birds

Braniff Game Birds ....G 574 784-3919
Lakeville *(G-9093)*

Flambeau Inc ....C 812 372-4899
Columbus *(G-1931)*

SPORTING & ATHLETIC GOODS: Fish & Bait Baskets Or Creels

Team Supreme Bait Company ....G 812 366-3200
Georgetown *(G-5154)*

SPORTING & ATHLETIC GOODS: Fishing Eqpt

B & M Products ....G 574 238-7468
Goshen *(G-5174)*

Hubs Chub Inc ....F 317 758-5494
Sheridan *(G-12590)*

Speedhook Specialists Inc ....G 877 773-4665
Schererville *(G-12347)*

SPORTING & ATHLETIC GOODS: Fishing Tackle, General

Fisherman S Lurecraft Shop Inc ....G 260 829-1274
Lagrange *(G-9042)*

SPORTING & ATHLETIC GOODS: Game Calls

Totschlager Game Calls LLC ....G 574 354-1620
Bourbon *(G-950)*

SPORTING & ATHLETIC GOODS: Gymnasium Eqpt

Midwest Gym Supply Inc ....F 812 265-4099
Madison *(G-9486)*

SPORTING & ATHLETIC GOODS: Lacrosse Eqpt & Splys, NEC

Empire Lacrosse & Sports Inc ....G 317 574-4529
Indianapolis *(G-6263)*

SPORTING & ATHLETIC GOODS: Ping-Pong Tables

Indian Industries Inc ....D 812 467-1200
Evansville *(G-3550)*

SPORTING & ATHLETIC GOODS: Pools, Swimming, Exc Plastic

Chester Pool Systems Inc ....E 812 949-7333
New Albany *(G-10758)*

Chester Pool Systems Inc ....E 812 949-7333
New Albany *(G-10759)*

Keesling Custom Pools & Patios ....G 317 823-3526
Indianapolis *(G-7339)*

SPORTING & ATHLETIC GOODS: Pools, Swimming, Plastic

Aquatic Renovation Systems Inc ....E 317 251-0207
Indianapolis *(G-6412)*

Cover Care LLC ....G 513 297-4094
Westfield *(G-14146)*

Fort Wayne Pools ....C 260 459-4100
Fort Wayne *(G-4279)*

Sparkle Pools Inc ....F 812 232-1292
Terre Haute *(G-13337)*

SPORTING & ATHLETIC GOODS: Shafts, Golf Club

Brickyard Crossing ....G 317 492-6573
Indianapolis *(G-6506)*

Delilah Club Covers ....G 812 401-0012
Evansville *(G-3456)*

Fairway Custom Golf ....G 317 842-0017
Fishers *(G-3910)*

Indiana Section of Pga of Amer ....G 317 738-9696
Franklin *(G-4899)*

SPORTING & ATHLETIC GOODS: Shooting Eqpt & Splys, General

Cloud Defensive LLC ....G 812 760-5017
Newburgh *(G-11025)*

L&N Supply LLC ....G 219 397-9500
East Chicago *(G-2546)*

SPORTING & ATHLETIC GOODS: Shuffleboards & Shuffleboard Eqpt

Playfair Shuffleboard Company ....F 260 747-7288
Fort Wayne *(G-4534)*

SPORTING & ATHLETIC GOODS: Soccer Eqpt & Splys

Official Sports Intl Inc ....F 574 269-1404
Warsaw *(G-13917)*

SPORTING & ATHLETIC GOODS: Target Shooting Eqpt

Prt South LLC ....G 708 354-3786
East Chicago *(G-2566)*

SPORTING & ATHLETIC GOODS: Targets, Archery & Rifle Shooting

Deer Track Archery ....G 765 643-6847
Anderson *(G-92)*

Reagent Chemical & RES Inc ....F 574 772-7424
Knox *(G-8578)*

White Flyer Targets ....G 574 772-3271
Knox *(G-8588)*

SPORTING & ATHLETIC GOODS: Team Sports Eqpt

Dmp LLC ....G 812 699-0086
Worthington *(G-14394)*

Graphic Fx Inc ....F 812 234-0000
Terre Haute *(G-13243)*

Tarver Wolff LLC ....G 765 265-7416
Brookville *(G-1127)*

SPORTING & ATHLETIC GOODS: Tennis Eqpt & Splys

Master Corporation ....F 260 471-0001
Fort Wayne *(G-4455)*

SPORTING & ATHLETIC GOODS: Trap Racks, Clay Targets

Federal Cartridge Company ....G 765 966-7745
Richmond *(G-11986)*

SPORTING & ATHLETIC GOODS: Water Sports Eqpt

Destro Machines LLC ....G 412 999-1619
Lafayette *(G-8889)*

Dunn-Rite Products Inc ....E 765 552-9433
Elwood *(G-3295)*

Hudson Aquatic Systems LLC ....F 260 665-1635
Angola *(G-220)*

Leisure Pool & Spa ....G 812 537-0071
Lawrenceburg *(G-9147)*

SPORTING & REC GOODS, WHOLESALE: Boats, Canoes, Etc/Eqpt

B Thystrup US Corporation ....G...... 574 834-2554
North Webster (G-11289)
Leistner Aquatic Services Inc..............G...... 317 535-6099
Whiteland (G-14242)

SPORTING & RECREATIONAL GOODS & SPLYS WHOLESALERS

Coaches Connection Inc ....G...... 260 356-0400
Huntington (G-6198)
Crescendo Inc ....G...... 812 829-4759
Spencer (G-13022)
Cummins Dist Holdco Inc ....F...... 812 377-5000
Columbus (G-1888)
Global Ozone Innovations LLC...........G...... 574 294-5797
Elkhart (G-2886)
Meditation Company ....G...... 574 217-3157
South Bend (G-12859)
Procoat Inc ....G...... 317 263-5071
Indianapolis (G-7768)
Team & Club Sporting Goods ....G...... 219 762-5477
Portage (G-11797)

SPORTING & RECREATIONAL GOODS, WHOLESALE: Athletic Goods

Midwest Gym Supply Inc.....................F...... 812 265-4099
Madison (G-9486)
Ppi Acquisition LLC ....F...... 765 674-8627
Marion (G-9555)

SPORTING & RECREATIONAL GOODS, WHOLESALE: Bicycle

Sportcrafters Inc ....G...... 574 243-4994
Granger (G-5438)

SPORTING & RECREATIONAL GOODS, WHOLESALE: Bowling

Classic Products Corp ....E...... 260 484-2695
Fort Wayne (G-4159)
Kerham Inc ....E...... 260 483-5444
Fort Wayne (G-4409)

SPORTING & RECREATIONAL GOODS, WHOLESALE: Fishing Tackle

Robert J Matt....................................G...... 317 831-2400
Mooresville (G-10337)

SPORTING & RECREATIONAL GOODS, WHOLESALE: Golf

Uebelhors Golf ....G...... 317 881-4109
Indianapolis (G-8124)

SPORTING & RECREATIONAL GOODS, WHOLESALE: Hunting

Cloud Defensive LLC..........................G...... 812 760-5017
Newburgh (G-11025)

SPORTING & RECREATIONAL GOODS, WHOLESALE: Outboard Motors

Power Investments Inc ....F....... 317 738-2117
Franklin (G-4921)

SPORTING CAMPS

Dick Baumgartners Basket ....E...... 765 220-1767
Richmond (G-11977)

SPORTING GOODS

Active Trading International..................G...... 260 637-1990
Fort Wayne (G-4040)
AJS Belts ....G...... 219 628-0074
Valparaiso (G-13488)
American Whitetail Inc ....F...... 812 937-7185
Ferdinand (G-3845)
Battle Creek Equipment Co..................E...... 260 495-3472
Fremont (G-4952)
Chicago Case Company ....G...... 317 636-3351
Indianapolis (G-6600)
Compositech Inc ....E...... 800 231-6755
Indianapolis (G-6643)

Escalade Incorporated ....D...... 812 467-4449
Evansville (G-3481)
Fallen Timber Bats LLC ....G...... 260 387-5841
Fort Wayne (G-4254)
Fields Outdoor Adventures LLP ....G...... 765 932-3964
Rushville (G-12221)
Fishing Abilities Inc ....G...... 574 273-0842
South Bend (G-12780)
Foot Locker Retail Inc ....G...... 317 578-1892
Indianapolis (G-6947)
G & S Johnson Outdoors LLC..............G...... 574 267-3891
Warsaw (G-13880)
Gameface Inc....................................G...... 317 363-8855
Zionsville (G-14433)
Gared Holdings LLC ....C...... 317 774-9840
Noblesville (G-11108)
Global Ozone Innovations LLC...........G...... 574 294-5797
Elkhart (G-2886)
Global USA Inc ....G...... 317 219-5647
Noblesville (G-11112)
Harvard Sports Inc.............................G...... 812 467-4449
Evansville (G-3535)
Hinton Keith & Hinton Tammy ....G...... 260 749-4867
New Haven (G-10943)
Hook & Arrow ....G...... 260 739-6661
Fort Wayne (G-4340)
Hooker Deer Drag Co LLC...................G...... 812 623-2706
Sunman (G-13112)
Impact Safety Inc ....G...... 317 852-3067
Indianapolis (G-7167)
Imperial Marble Incorporated..............F...... 812 752-5384
Scottsburg (G-12364)
Jns Sports ....G...... 317 852-8314
Brownsburg (G-1158)
Life Less Ordinary LLC ....G...... 317 727-4277
Indianapolis (G-7403)
Meditation Company ....G...... 574 217-3157
South Bend (G-12859)
Mid America Powered Vehicles ....G...... 812 925-7745
Chandler (G-1551)
Mulry Manufacturing LLC....................G...... 317 253-2756
Indianapolis (G-7557)
Patriot Range Technologies.................G...... 708 354-3150
East Chicago (G-2556)
Peranis Hockey World ....G...... 317 288-5183
Indianapolis (G-7673)
Proteq Custom Gear LLC ....G...... 812 201-6002
Brazil (G-975)
Robert J Matt....................................G...... 317 831-2400
Mooresville (G-10337)
Royal Spa Corporation ....D...... 317 781-0828
Indianapolis (G-7867)
Running Company LLC ....G...... 317 887-0606
Greenwood (G-5745)
S P R Athletics LLC............................G...... 419 308-2732
Winchester (G-14340)
Screwy Lewy Lures Inc ....G...... 812 786-7369
Corydon (G-2112)
Sea Quest Lures Inc ....G...... 219 762-4362
Portage (G-11792)
Sg Helmets ....G...... 317 286-3616
Brownsburg (G-1172)
Sinden Racing Service Inc ....F...... 317 243-7171
Indianapolis (G-7949)
Sports Licensed Division ....F...... 508 758-6101
Indianapolis (G-7976)
Standard Fusee Corporation ....E...... 765 472-4375
Peru (G-11548)
Team & Club Sporting Goods ....G...... 219 762-5477
Portage (G-11797)
Tippmann Sports LLC ....F...... 260 749-6022
Fort Wayne (G-4687)
Unique Outdoor Products LLC ....G...... 260 486-4955
Fort Wayne (G-4714)
Urban-Ert Slings LLC ....G...... 317 223-6509
Clayton (G-1709)
White River Outfitters LLC ....G...... 812 787-0921
Shoals (G-12673)
Wildman Enterprise ....G...... 317 985-0924
Greenfield (G-5584)

SPORTING GOODS STORES, NEC

Athletic Avenue & More Inc..................G...... 812 547-7655
Tell City (G-13155)
Coaches Connection Inc ....G...... 260 356-0400
Huntington (G-6198)
Crescendo Inc ....G...... 812 829-4759
Spencer (G-13022)
East 40 Sports Apparel Inc ....G...... 812 877-3695
Terre Haute (G-13229)

Eds Trading Post Inc ....G...... 317 933-4867
Nineveh (G-11057)
Four Season Sports Inc. ....G...... 812 279-0384
Bedford (G-543)
G & S Johnson Outdoors LLC..............G...... 574 267-3891
Warsaw (G-13880)
Game Plan Graphics LLC ....G...... 812 663-3238
Greensburg (G-5602)
Geist Bike and Hobby Company ....G...... 317 855-1346
Indianapolis (G-6990)
Global Ozone Innovations LLC............G...... 574 294-5797
Elkhart (G-2886)
Goods On Target Sporting Inc..............G...... 812 623-2300
Sunman (G-13111)
Jer-Maur Corporation ....G...... 812 384-8290
Bloomfield (G-640)
Knoy Apparel......................................G...... 765 448-1031
Lafayette (G-8945)
Nebo Ridge Enterprises LLC ....G...... 317 471-1089
Carmel (G-1441)
Rajo Guns Corp..................................G...... 812 422-6945
Evansville (G-3694)
Varsity Sports Inc..............................G...... 219 987-7200
Demotte (G-2451)
Winning Edge of Rochester Inc............F...... 574 223-6090
Rochester (G-12162)
Xtreme Graphics ....G...... 812 989-6948
Jeffersonville (G-8443)

SPORTING GOODS STORES: Archery Splys

Deer Track Archery ....G...... 765 643-6847
Anderson (G-92)

SPORTING GOODS STORES: Bait & Tackle

B & M Products ....G...... 574 238-7468
Goshen (G-5174)
Robert J Matt ....G...... 317 831-2400
Mooresville (G-10337)
Schwartz Manufacturing Inc ....G...... 260 589-3865
Berne (G-622)

SPORTING GOODS STORES: Camping & Backpacking Eqpt

Montgomery Tent & Awning Co.............F...... 317 357-9759
Indianapolis (G-7538)

SPORTING GOODS STORES: Firearms

A & W Firearms ....G...... 765 716-6856
Yorktown (G-14400)
Blythes Sport Shop Inc ....E...... 219 476-0026
Valparaiso (G-13510)

SPORTING GOODS STORES: Fishing Eqpt

Websters Sporting Goods Inc ....F...... 317 255-4855
Indianapolis (G-8182)

SPORTING GOODS STORES: Football Eqpt

OHara Sports Inc...............................G...... 219 836-5554
Munster (G-10618)

SPORTING GOODS STORES: Playground Eqpt

Kidstuff Playsystems Inc ....E...... 219 938-3331
Gary (G-5072)
Nvb Playgrounds Inc ....G...... 317 826-2777
Indianapolis (G-7607)

SPORTING GOODS STORES: Soccer Splys

Avon Sports Apparel Corp....................G...... 317 887-2673
Greenwood (G-5668)

SPORTING GOODS STORES: Specialty Sport Splys, NEC

Rookies Unlimited Inc ....G...... 765 536-2726
Summitville (G-13104)

SPORTING GOODS STORES: Team sports Eqpt

Sportscenter Inc...............................G...... 260 436-6198
Fort Wayne (G-4642)

P
R
O
D
U
C
T

SPORTING GOODS: Archery

Proline Bowstrings ....G..... 513 259-3738
Liberty **(G-9270)**

SPORTING GOODS: Hammocks & Other Net Prdts

American Orthpdics Prosthetics ....G..... 765 447-0111
Lafayette **(G-8851)**
Widows Walk ....G..... 812 285-8850
Clarksville **(G-1700)**

SPORTING GOODS: Skin Diving Eqpt

Divers Supply Company Inc ....D..... 317 923-4523
Indianapolis **(G-6745)**
G L D Inc ....G..... 317 924-7981
Indianapolis **(G-6976)**

SPORTING GOODS: Surfboards

Lake House ....G..... 574 265-6945
Winona Lake **(G-14350)**

SPORTS APPAREL STORES

Dugout ....G..... 765 642-8528
Anderson **(G-100)**
Four Season Sports Inc ....G..... 812 279-0384
Bedford **(G-543)**
Goldden Corporation ....F..... 765 423-4366
Lafayette **(G-8908)**
Hoosier Racing Tire Corp ....D..... 574 784-3409
Lakeville **(G-9096)**
Locoli Inc ....E..... 219 365-3125
Schererville **(G-12332)**
Mercantile Store ....G..... 812 988-6939
Nashville **(G-10729)**
Shirts N Things S N T Graphics ....G..... 317 271-3515
Indianapolis **(G-7935)**
Stallion Sportswear Inc ....E..... 765 584-5097
Winchester **(G-14341)**
Websters Sporting Goods Inc ....F..... 317 255-4855
Indianapolis **(G-8182)**
Xtreme Graphics ....G..... 812 989-6948
Jeffersonville **(G-8443)**

SPORTS CLUBS, MANAGERS & PROMOTERS

Athletes Management & Service ....G..... 317 925-8200
Indianapolis **(G-6437)**

SPORTS PROMOTION SVCS

Diamond Hoosier ....G..... 317 773-1411
Noblesville **(G-11091)**

SPRAYING EQPT: Agricultural

Equipment Technologies Inc ....E..... 800 861-2142
Mooresville **(G-10308)**
Et Works LLC ....E..... 317 834-4500
Mooresville **(G-10309)**
Nichols Mfg Co Inc ....F..... 219 696-8577
Lowell **(G-9418)**
Robertson Machine Co Inc ....G..... 317 881-9405
Greenwood **(G-5741)**
Stan Clamme ....G..... 765 348-0008
Hartford City **(G-5991)**

SPRINGS: Coiled Flat

Kokomo Spring Company Inc ....F..... 765 459-5156
Kokomo **(G-8656)**

SPRINGS: Gun, Precision

Integrated Systems Management ....G..... 765 565-6108
Carthage **(G-1513)**

SPRINGS: Mechanical, Precision

Leggett & Platt Incorporated ....C..... 260 347-2600
Kendallville **(G-8490)**
Myers Spring Co Inc ....E..... 574 753-5105
Logansport **(G-9357)**
Winamac Coil Spring Inc ....C..... 574 653-2186
Kewanna **(G-8528)**

SPRINGS: Precision

Hoosier Spring Co Inc ....C..... 574 291-7550
South Bend **(G-12802)**
Pepka Spring Company Inc ....F..... 765 459-3114
Kokomo **(G-8679)**
Suzuki Garphyttan Corp ....D..... 574 232-8800
South Bend **(G-12963)**
Walton Industrial Park Inc ....F..... 574 626-2929
Walton **(G-13818)**

SPRINGS: Sash Balances

United Air Works Inc ....G..... 317 576-0040
Indianapolis **(G-8127)**

SPRINGS: Steel

Ferguson Equipment Inc ....F..... 574 234-4303
South Bend **(G-12778)**
Matthew Warren Inc ....F..... 574 722-8200
Logansport **(G-9354)**
Muehlhausen Spring Company ....G..... 574 626-2351
Walton **(G-13816)**
Muehlhausen Spring Company ....G..... 574 859-2481
Flora **(G-4000)**
Myers Spring Co Inc ....E..... 574 753-5105
Logansport **(G-9357)**
Pepka Spring Company Inc ....F..... 765 459-3114
Kokomo **(G-8679)**
Precision Products Group Inc ....B..... 330 698-4711
Indianapolis **(G-6276)**
Preferred Metal Services Inc ....G..... 219 988-2386
Crown Point **(G-2289)**
Valley Tool & Die Stampings ....E..... 574 722-4566
Logansport **(G-9375)**
Wellspring Components LLC ....G..... 260 768-7336
Shipshewana **(G-12657)**
Winamac Coil Spring Inc ....C..... 574 653-2186
Kewanna **(G-8528)**

SPRINGS: Torsion Bar

Cargo Systems Inc ....G..... 574 264-1600
Elkhart **(G-2749)**
M-3 and Associates Inc ....E..... 574 294-3988
Elkhart **(G-3010)**

SPRINGS: Upholstery, Unassembled

Barber Manufacturing Co Inc ....D..... 765 643-6905
Anderson **(G-72)**

SPRINGS: Wire

A J Coil Inc ....G..... 574 353-7174
Tippecanoe **(G-13380)**
A Raymond Tinnerman Auto Inc ....C..... 574 722-5168
Logansport **(G-9319)**
Circle M Spring Inc ....E..... 574 267-2883
Warsaw **(G-13857)**
Mid-West Spring Mfg Co ....D..... 574 353-1409
Mentone **(G-9688)**
Pimmler Holdings Inc ....G..... 574 583-8090
Monticello **(G-10279)**
Precision Products Group Inc ....B..... 330 698-4711
Indianapolis **(G-6276)**
Valley Tool & Die Stampings ....E..... 574 722-4566
Logansport **(G-9375)**

SPRINKLING SYSTEMS: Fire Control

Guardian Fire Systems Inc ....F..... 317 752-2768
Fortville **(G-4777)**
Hydro Fire Protection Inc ....E..... 317 780-6980
Indianapolis **(G-7151)**
Pillar Innovations LLC ....G..... 812 474-9080
Evansville **(G-3670)**

STACKING MACHINES: Automatic

Rowe Conveyor LLC ....G..... 317 602-1024
Greenwood **(G-5743)**

STAGE LIGHTING SYSTEMS

Ao Inc ....G..... 317 280-3000
Avon **(G-427)**

STAINLESS STEEL

3d Parts Mfg LLC ....G..... 317 860-6941
Anderson **(G-56)**

AK Steel Corporation ....C..... 812 362-7317
Rockport **(G-12164)**
Allegheny Ludlum LLC ....C..... 765 529-9570
New Castle **(G-10890)**
ATI ....G..... 317 238-3073
Indianapolis **(G-6438)**
Bahr Bros Mfg Inc ....E..... 765 664-6235
Marion **(G-9512)**
Endurance Metals LLC ....G..... 765 960-5834
Richmond **(G-11982)**
Hebron Ventures North America ....G..... 260 437-7733
Fort Wayne **(G-4329)**
Hynes Kokomo LLC ....G..... 330 799-3221
Kokomo **(G-8642)**
Nachi America Inc ....C..... 317 535-5527
Greenwood **(G-5726)**
Shetlers Famous Staineless ....G..... 260 368-9069
Geneva **(G-5139)**
Specialty Stainless ....G..... 317 337-9800
Indianapolis **(G-7968)**
Swi ....G..... 812 342-2409
Columbus **(G-2019)**

STAINS: Biological

Pfizer Inc ....A..... 212 733-2323
Terre Haute **(G-13301)**

STAINS: Wood

Weatherall Indiana Inc ....F..... 812 256-3378
Charlestown **(G-1585)**

STAIRCASES & STAIRS, WOOD

J W Woodworking Inc ....G..... 574 831-3033
New Paris **(G-10987)**
Shinabargar Custom Stairs ....G..... 219 462-1735
Valparaiso **(G-13616)**

STAMPING: Fabric Articles

Mercantile Store ....G..... 812 988-6939
Nashville **(G-10729)**

STAMPINGS: Automotive

Benteler Automotive Corp ....C..... 574 534-1499
Goshen **(G-5178)**
Blue River Stamping Inc ....D..... 317 395-5600
Shelbyville **(G-12523)**
Flex-N-Gate Corporation ....C..... 260 665-8288
Angola **(G-214)**
Fogwell Technologies ....G..... 260 410-1898
Roanoke **(G-12101)**
General Motors LLC ....B..... 765 668-2000
Marion **(G-9525)**
Lakepark Industries Ind Inc ....D..... 260 768-7411
Shipshewana **(G-12628)**
Lcm Realty IV LLC ....G..... 574 312-6182
Goshen **(G-5264)**
Lime City Manufacturing Co ....E..... 260 356-6826
Huntington **(G-6224)**
Mpi Products LLC ....B..... 574 772-3850
Knox **(G-8575)**
Nasg Indiana LLC ....E..... 765 381-4310
Muncie **(G-10537)**
Pridgeon & Clay Inc ....C..... 317 738-4885
Franklin **(G-4923)**
Pro-Tech Tool & Engineering ....G..... 765 258-3613
Frankfort **(G-4851)**
Robert Atkins ....G..... 765 536-4164
Summitville **(G-13103)**
Sacoma International Llc ....D..... 812 526-5600
Edinburgh **(G-2626)**
Sermershiems Fiberglass Inc ....G..... 812 424-4701
Evansville **(G-3723)**
Shiloh Industries Inc ....F..... 574 594-9681
Pierceton **(G-11579)**
Steel Parts Corporation ....B..... 765 675-2191
Tipton **(G-13406)**
The Pro Shear Corporation Corp ....G..... 260 408-1010
Fort Wayne **(G-4681)**
TOA Winchester LLC ....B..... 765 584-7639
Winchester **(G-14342)**
Tower Automotive Operations ....C..... 260 925-5113
Auburn **(G-363)**
Tru-Form Metal Products Inc ....F..... 574 266-8020
Elkhart **(G-3225)**
Twin Maple Tool Inc ....F..... 574 586-7500
Walkerton **(G-13811)**

STAMPINGS: Metal

A Raymond Tinnerman Auto Inc ....C 574 722-5168
Logansport *(G-9319)*

Advanced Metal Fabricators Inc...........F 574 259-1263
Mishawaka *(G-9991)*

Atkisson Enterprises Inc.....................F 765 675-7593
Tipton *(G-13388)*

Carr Metal Products Inc......................C 317 542-0691
Indianapolis *(G-6558)*

Colbin Tool Company Inc ....E 574 457-3183
Syracuse *(G-13130)*

Crichlow Industries Inc ....G 317 925-5178
Indianapolis *(G-6692)*

Crossrads Rhbilitation Ctr Inc ....C 317 897-7320
Indianapolis *(G-6697)*

Die-Mensional Metal Stamping ....F 812 265-3946
Madison *(G-9456)*

Dietech Corporation ....G 260 724-8946
Decatur *(G-2375)*

Dwyer Instruments Inc ....E 219 393-5250
La Porte *(G-8752)*

Eaton Corporation ....C 260 925-3800
Auburn *(G-328)*

Elixir Industries ....E 574 294-5685
Elkhart *(G-2816)*

Elixir Industries ....E 574 294-5685
Elkhart *(G-2817)*

Elixir Industries ....D 574 294-5685
Elkhart *(G-2818)*

Epco Products Inc ....E 260 747-8888
Fort Wayne *(G-4240)*

Flambeau Inc ....C 812 372-4899
Columbus *(G-1931)*

General Devices Co Inc ....E 317 897-7000
Indianapolis *(G-6995)*

General Motors LLC ....B 765 668-2000
Marion *(G-9525)*

General Sheet Metal Works Inc ....E 574 288-0611
South Bend *(G-12788)*

Group Dekko Inc ....D 260 357-3621
Garrett *(G-5009)*

H D Williams Co ....G 812 372-6476
Columbus *(G-1936)*

H P Products Corporation ....G 812 331-8793
Bloomington *(G-736)*

Hasser Enterprises Inc ....G 765 583-1444
West Lafayette *(G-14074)*

Hoosier Stamping LLC ....G 812 993-2040
Chandler *(G-1549)*

Hoosier Stamping & Mfg Corp ....E 812 426-2778
Evansville *(G-3540)*

Hoosier Tank and Mfg Inc ....D 574 232-8368
South Bend *(G-12803)*

Hoosier Trim Products LLC ....E 317 271-4007
Indianapolis *(G-7125)*

Hopper Development Inc......................F 574 753-6621
Logansport *(G-9336)*

Imh Fabrication Inc ....F 317 252-5566
Indianapolis *(G-7164)*

Impressive Stamping & Mfg Co ....G 260 824-2610
Bluffton *(G-878)*

Jason Incorporated.............................C 847 215-1948
Richmond *(G-12007)*

JM Hutton & Co Inc ....D 765 962-3591
Richmond *(G-12008)*

Johnson Controls Inc ....D 260 489-6104
Fort Wayne *(G-4397)*

Kimball Electronics Inc ....D 317 545-5383
Indianapolis *(G-7351)*

Krukemeier Machine and Tool Co ....F 317 784-7042
Beech Grove *(G-600)*

Lakepark Industries Ind Inc ....D 260 768-7411
Shipshewana *(G-12628)*

Lauck Manufacturing Co Inc ....F 317 787-6269
Indianapolis *(G-7385)*

Lynn Tool Company Inc.......................G 765 874-2471
Lynn *(G-9430)*

Mac Machine & Metal Works Inc...........E 765 825-5873
Connersville *(G-2062)*

Miller Mfg Corp ....E 574 773-4136
Nappanee *(G-10695)*

Oak-Rite Mfg Corp ....E 317 839-2301
Plainfield *(G-11632)*

Pent Plastics Inc ....C 260 897-3775
Kendallville *(G-8502)*

Qmp Inc..E 574 262-1575
Elkhart *(G-3124)*

R & R Tool Manufacturing Inc...............E 219 362-1681
La Porte *(G-8810)*

RBM Manufacturing Inc.......................G 765 364-6933
Crawfordsville *(G-2192)*

Reeves Manufacturing Inc ....G 765 935-3875
Richmond *(G-12042)*

Rotam Tool Corporation ....F 260 982-8318
North Manchester *(G-11242)*

Royal Stamping Inc............................F 260 925-3312
Auburn *(G-350)*

Sha-Do Corp ....G 574 848-9296
Bristol *(G-1085)*

Shakour Industries Inc ....G 574 289-0100
South Bend *(G-12932)*

Small Parts Inc ....B 574 739-6236
Logansport *(G-9365)*

Smith Small Engine Service.................G 812 232-1318
Terre Haute *(G-13329)*

Steel Parts Corporation......................B 765 675-2191
Tipton *(G-13406)*

Symmetry Medical Mfg Inc ....E 574 371-2284
Warsaw *(G-13949)*

TEC-Air LLC ....D 219 301-7084
Munster *(G-10632)*

Trivector Manufacturing Inc.................E 260 637-0141
Fort Wayne *(G-4706)*

Twin Maple Tool Inc ....F 574 586-7500
Walkerton *(G-13811)*

Wayne Manufacturing Corp ....E 260 637-5586
Laotto *(G-9115)*

Webber Manufacturing Company..........E 317 357-8681
Indianapolis *(G-8181)*

York Group Inc ....D 765 966-1576
Richmond *(G-12078)*

ZF North America Inc.........................G 765 429-1678
Lafayette *(G-9027)*

ZF North America Inc.........................B 765 429-1984
Lafayette *(G-9028)*

STANDS: Ground Servicing, Aircraft

Par-Kan Company LLC........................D 260 352-2141
Silver Lake *(G-12677)*

STAPLES, MADE FROM PURCHASED WIRE

Stanley Fastening Systems LP.............D 317 398-0761
Greenfield *(G-5578)*

STARTERS & CONTROLLERS: Motor, Electric

Benshaw Inc ....G 412 487-8235
Noblesville *(G-11067)*

Remy Power Products LLC..................A 765 778-6499
Pendleton *(G-11504)*

STARTERS: Electric Motor

Amt Parts International Corp.................E 260 490-0223
Fort Wayne *(G-4075)*

B & M Electrical Co Inc ....F 765 448-4532
Lafayette *(G-8859)*

STARTERS: Motor

D & E Auto Electric Inc ....F 219 763-3892
Portage *(G-11759)*

Jeannie and Rachel Heidenreich...........G 260 244-4583
Columbia City *(G-1801)*

MRC Technology Inc...........................F 574 232-9057
South Bend *(G-12867)*

Remy Electric Motors LLC ....E 765 778-6466
Pendleton *(G-11503)*

STATIC ELIMINATORS: Ind

Gregory Thomas Inc ....G 219 324-3801
La Porte *(G-8758)*

STATIONARY & OFFICE SPLYS, WHOL: Computer/Photocopying Splys

Lasertone Inc.....................................F 812 473-5945
Evansville *(G-3598)*

STATIONER'S SUNDRIES: Rubber

Discount Labels LLC ....A 812 945-2617
New Albany *(G-10769)*

Engraving and Stamp Center Inc ....G 812 336-0606
Bloomington *(G-720)*

STATIONERY & OFFICE SPLYS WHOLESALERS

Edward ONeil Associates.....................G 317 244-5400
Indianapolis *(G-6810)*

Johnco Corp......................................G 317 576-4417
Indianapolis *(G-7308)*

Label Tech Inc ....E 765 747-1234
Muncie *(G-10506)*

Smith & Butterfield Co Inc ....F 812 422-3261
Evansville *(G-3735)*

Smith & Butterfield Co Inc ....E 812 422-3261
Evansville *(G-3736)*

STATIONERY PRDTS

Altstadt Business Forms Inc ....F 812 425-3393
Evansville *(G-3349)*

Asc Inc ....D 765 472-5331
Peru *(G-11516)*

Avery Dennison Corporation ....D 219 696-7777
Lowell *(G-9399)*

STATORS REWINDING SVCS

Buffington Electric Motors....................G 574 935-5453
Plymouth *(G-11673)*

Kirby Risk Corporation........................G 765 643-3384
Anderson *(G-130)*

STEEL & ALLOYS: Tool & Die

Brownstown Qlty TI Automtn LLC........F 812 358-9059
Brownstown *(G-1180)*

Indiana Tool Inc.................................F 765 825-7117
Connersville *(G-2055)*

Kretler Tool & Engineering ....G 260 897-2662
Avilla *(G-412)*

Qualtech Tool & Engrg Inc ....E 260 726-6572
Portland *(G-11844)*

STEEL FABRICATORS

99 Nufab Rebar LLC...........................D 260 572-1315
Auburn *(G-311)*

A & B Fabricating & Maint Inc ....F 574 353-1012
Mentone *(G-9684)*

A & D Constructors Inc ....C 812 428-3708
Evansville *(G-3328)*

A-1 Welding & Repair ....G 812 853-9701
Newburgh *(G-11016)*

Accuburn Williamsport Inc ....F 765 762-1100
Williamsport *(G-14286)*

Advance Aero Inc...............................E 317 513-6071
Mooresville *(G-10300)*

Advance Fabricators Inc ....E 812 944-6941
New Albany *(G-10741)*

Advanced Systems Intgrtion LLC ....F 260 447-5555
Fort Wayne *(G-4045)*

Aeromotive Mfg Inc............................G 765 552-0668
Elwood *(G-3293)*

Afc Industries Inc...............................E 574 264-1987
Elkhart *(G-2670)*

Ajem Welding ....G 812 595-3541
Austin *(G-394)*

All City Metal Craft Inc........................G 317 782-9340
Indianapolis *(G-6366)*

Allen Fabricators Inc ....F 260 458-0008
Fort Wayne *(G-4059)*

Aluminum Wldg & Mch Works Inc........G 219 787-8066
Chesterton *(G-1592)*

Ambassador Steel Corporation ....E 317 834-3434
Mooresville *(G-10302)*

American Fabricating ....G 812 897-0900
Boonville *(G-907)*

American Fabricators Inc......................E 219 844-4744
Hammond *(G-5840)*

American Machine Fabrication ....G 812 944-4136
New Albany *(G-10744)*

Amerimax Fabricated Products............G 574 389-8960
Bristol *(G-1045)*

Anthony Wayne Rehabilitation C ....D 260 744-6145
Fort Wayne *(G-4078)*

Avenue Industries Inc..........................G 574 674-6971
Osceola *(G-11370)*

Awol Metal Contorsion LLC ....G 260 909-0411
Kendallville *(G-8457)*

B & M Steel & Welding Inc ....G 765 964-5868
Union City *(G-13453)*

B C Welding Inc..................................G 574 272-9008
Granger *(G-5392)*

Employee Codes: A=Over 500 employees, B=251-500
C=101-250, D=51-100, E=20-50, F=10-19, G=2-9

2018 Harris Indiana
Industrial Directory

PRODUCT

1085

Baker Metalworks ....G........ 260 572-9353
Saint Joe **(G-12252)**

Blackhawk Millwright & Rigging ....G........ 765 662-7922
Kokomo **(G-8598)**

Bralin Laser Services Inc ....E 260 357-6511
Auburn **(G-318)**

Buchanan Iron Works Inc ....G........ 219 785-4480
Westville **(G-14214)**

Buhrt Engineering & Cnstr ....E 574 267-3720
Warsaw **(G-13852)**

Builders Iron Works Inc ....E 574 254-1553
Mishawaka **(G-10014)**

C & P Engineering & Mfg ....E 765 825-4293
Connersville **(G-2042)**

C F Slattery Steel Fabrication ....G........ 812 948-9167
New Albany **(G-10756)**

C Fabco/L Inc ....E 219 785-4181
La Porte **(G-8743)**

CAM Metal Fabrication LLC ....G........ 260 982-6280
North Manchester **(G-11226)**

Centerline Studio ....G........ 317 423-3220
Indianapolis **(G-6577)**

Central Illinois Steel Company ....G........ 219 882-1026
Gary **(G-5035)**

Central States Fabricating ....F 574 288-5607
South Bend **(G-12733)**

Central States Mfg Inc ....D........ 219 879-4770
Michigan City **(G-9773)**

Century Steel Fabricating Inc ....F 317 834-1295
Camby **(G-1265)**

Chicago Specialty Steel Corp ....E 219 922-8888
Griffith **(G-5771)**

Chief Industries Inc ....G........ 219 866-4121
Rensselaer **(G-11917)**

Circle R Industries Inc ....G........ 765 379-2768
Rossville **(G-12210)**

CJ Automotive Indiana LLC ....G........ 260 868-2147
Butler **(G-1225)**

Coffee Lomont & Moyer Inc ....F 260 422-7825
Fort Wayne **(G-4166)**

Craig Welding and Mfg Inc ....G........ 574 353-7912
Mentone **(G-9687)**

Crossrads Rhbilitation Ctr Inc ....G........ 317 897-7320
Indianapolis **(G-6697)**

Crown Mtal Fbricators Erectors ....G........ 219 661-8277
Crown Point **(G-2240)**

Cryogenic Support Systems Inc ....G........ 765 764-4961
Williamsport **(G-14288)**

Crystal Industries Inc ....E 574 264-6166
Elkhart **(G-2779)**

Cutting Edge Craftsmen LLC ....G........ 317 757-6975
Indianapolis **(G-6718)**

Cyclone Shop Inc ....G........ 812 683-2887
Huntingburg **(G-6154)**

D & M Systems Inc ....G........ 812 327-2384
Owensburg **(G-11425)**

D A Hochstetler & Sons LLP ....F 574 642-1144
Topeka **(G-13416)**

Deco Corporation ....E 812 342-4767
Columbus **(G-1906)**

Deister Machine Company Inc ....C........ 260 422-0354
Fort Wayne **(G-4207)**

Delbert M Dawson & Son Inc ....G........ 765 284-9711
Muncie **(G-10458)**

Delphi Body Works ....F 765 564-2212
Delphi **(G-2417)**

DH Machine Inc ....D........ 574 773-9211
Nappanee **(G-10667)**

Die-Mensional Metal Stamping ....F 812 265-3946
Madison **(G-9456)**

Diversified Coating & Fabg Inc ....E 260 563-2858
Wabash **(G-13922)**

DL Schwartz Co LLC ....G........ 260 692-1464
Berne **(G-612)**

Dpc Inc ....E 765 564-3752
Delphi **(G-2419)**

Dx 4 LLC ....F 260 410-3749
Fort Wayne **(G-4229)**

Dynamic Industrial Group LLC ....G........ 574 295-5525
Elkhart **(G-2806)**

Dynamic Metals LLC ....D........ 574 262-2497
Elkhart **(G-2807)**

Ebc LLC ....G........ 812 234-4111
Terre Haute **(G-13230)**

Edgewood Metal Fab LLC ....G........ 574 546-5947
Bremen **(G-998)**

Electric Metal Fab Inc ....F 812 988-9353
Nashville **(G-10723)**

Elevator Equipment Corporation ....D........ 765 966-7761
Richmond **(G-11981)**

Elixir Industries ....E 574 294-5685
Elkhart **(G-2817)**

Elixir Industries ....D........ 574 294-5685
Elkhart **(G-2818)**

Engineered Conveyors Inc ....F 765 459-4545
Kokomo **(G-8621)**

Ernstberger Enterprises Inc ....D........ 812 282-0488
Jeffersonville **(G-8358)**

Eta Fabrication Inc ....F 260 897-3711
Avilla **(G-404)**

Euclid Machine & Tool Inc ....E 219 397-1374
East Chicago **(G-2528)**

Fab-Tech Industries ....G........ 765 478-4191
Cambridge City **(G-1256)**

Fabricated Metals Corp ....F 219 734-6896
Chesterton **(G-1605)**

Fabricated Metals Corp ....F 219 871-0230
Michigan City **(G-9790)**

Fabricated Steel Corporation ....G........ 317 899-0012
Indianapolis **(G-6901)**

Farm Fab ....G........ 574 862-4775
Goshen **(G-5213)**

Fasttimes Fabrication Cus ....G........ 574 858-9222
Etna Green **(G-3321)**

First Metals & Plastics Inc ....E 812 379-4400
Columbus **(G-1930)**

Gannon Mtal Fbrcators Erectors ....G........ 219 398-0299
East Chicago **(G-2529)**

Gary Earl ....G........ 812 279-6780
Bedford **(G-544)**

Gary Ratcliff ....G........ 765 538-3170
Lafayette **(G-8905)**

Gem-Rose Corp ....G........ 317 773-6400
Noblesville **(G-11110)**

General Fabr ....G........ 260 593-3858
Topeka **(G-13420)**

GI Properties Inc ....G........ 219 763-1177
Portage **(G-11765)**

Graber Steel & Fab LLC ....E 812 636-8418
Odon **(G-11328)**

Grant County Steel Inc ....F 765 668-7547
Marion **(G-9527)**

Greensgroomer Worldwide Inc ....G........ 317 388-0695
Indianapolis **(G-7046)**

Griffith Machine & Fabricating ....G........ 219 980-8855
Gary **(G-5055)**

Halo Metalworks Inc ....F 317 481-0100
Indianapolis **(G-7066)**

Hamilton Iron Works Inc ....G........ 574 533-3784
Goshen **(G-5234)**

Harris Rebar Nufab LLC ....D........ 260 925-5440
Auburn **(G-334)**

Heidtman Steel Products Inc ....C........ 419 691-4646
Butler **(G-1229)**

Horner Industrial Services Inc ....F 317 634-7165
Indianapolis **(G-7129)**

Huntington Sheet Metal Inc ....F 260 356-9011
Huntington **(G-6212)**

Igh Steel Fabrication Inc ....G........ 765 482-7534
Lebanon **(G-9190)**

Imperial Stamping Corporation ....D........ 574 294-3780
Elkhart **(G-2930)**

In-Fab Inc ....G........ 812 279-8144
Bedford **(G-549)**

Indiana Bridge-Midwest Stl Inc ....D........ 765 288-1985
Muncie **(G-10493)**

Indiana Gratings Inc ....F 765 342-7191
Martinsville **(G-9615)**

Indiana Steel Fabricating Inc ....E 317 247-4545
Indianapolis **(G-7193)**

Indiana Steel Fabricating Inc ....F 765 742-1031
Lafayette **(G-8922)**

Indianapolis Fabrications LLC ....F 317 600-3522
Indianapolis **(G-7198)**

Industrial Contrs Skanska Inc ....E 812 423-7832
Evansville **(G-3555)**

Industrial Metal-Fab Inc ....E 574 288-8368
South Bend **(G-12812)**

Industrial Steel Cnstr Inc ....C........ 219 885-5610
Gary **(G-5069)**

Industrial Transmission Eqp ....E 574 936-3028
Plymouth **(G-11694)**

International Metals Proc Inc ....E 317 895-4141
Indianapolis **(G-7254)**

J A Smit Inc ....G........ 812 424-8141
Evansville **(G-3568)**

J Coffey Metal Masters Inc ....D........ 317 780-1864
Indianapolis **(G-7284)**

J L Squared Inc ....G........ 317 354-1513
Indianapolis **(G-7287)**

JD Metal Concepts Inc ....G........ 812 342-9111
Columbus **(G-1950)**

Jerico Metal Specialties Inc ....F 812 339-3182
Bloomington **(G-755)**

Jezroc Metalworks LLC ....G........ 317 417-1132
Zionsville **(G-14442)**

JL Walter & Associates Inc ....G........ 317 524-3600
Indianapolis **(G-7306)**

Just For Granite ....G........ 317 842-8255
Indianapolis **(G-7324)**

K-K Tool and Design Inc ....E 260 758-2940
Markle **(G-9578)**

Kammerer Dynamics Inc ....F 260 349-9098
Kendallville **(G-8483)**

Kammerer Inc ....G........ 260 347-0389
Kendallville **(G-8485)**

Keller Machine & Welding Inc ....E 219 464-4915
Valparaiso **(G-13566)**

Kenley Corporation ....G........ 765 825-7150
Connersville **(G-2061)**

Kennedy Metal Products Inc ....F 219 322-9388
Schererville **(G-12329)**

Keppler Steel and Fabricating ....F 765 289-1529
Muncie **(G-10504)**

Kirby Tool and Die Inc ....G........ 812 369-7779
Solsberry **(G-12686)**

Kokomo Metal Fabricators Inc ....G........ 765 459-8173
Kokomo **(G-8653)**

L & W Engineering Inc ....D........ 574 825-5351
Middlebury **(G-9900)**

Lacay Fabrication and Mfg Inc ....E 574 288-4678
Elkhart **(G-2982)**

Lakemaster Inc ....E 765 288-3718
Muncie **(G-10507)**

Lawrence Cnty Fabrication Corp ....E 812 849-0124
Mitchell **(G-10164)**

Lawrenco Steel Inc ....G........ 812 466-7115
Terre Haute **(G-13273)**

Leons Fabrication Inc ....F 219 365-5272
Schererville **(G-12330)**

Liberty Industries LC ....G........ 812 853-0595
Newburgh **(G-11035)**

Lippert Components Inc ....G........ 574 537-8900
Goshen **(G-5269)**

M and B Fabricating LLC ....F 219 762-5032
Valparaiso **(G-13578)**

Marcums Welding & Stl Proc Inc ....G........ 765 763-7279
Morristown **(G-10374)**

Marine Builders Inc ....D........ 812 283-7932
Jeffersonville **(G-8396)**

Marson International LLC ....E 574 295-4222
Elkhart **(G-3020)**

Metal Dynamics Ltd ....E 812 949-7998
New Albany **(G-10826)**

Metal Masters Inc ....G........ 812 421-9162
Evansville **(G-3623)**

Metal Solutions Inc ....F 317 781-6734
Indianapolis **(G-7488)**

Metal Technologies Inc ....G........ 812 384-9800
Bloomfield **(G-642)**

Metal Technologies Inc ....D........ 812 384-9800
Bloomfield **(G-643)**

Metaltec Inc ....G........ 219 362-9811
La Porte **(G-8792)**

Metfab Inc ....G........ 317 322-0385
Indianapolis **(G-7492)**

Micrometl Indianapolis ....G........ 317 524-5400
Indianapolis **(G-7499)**

Miller Mfg Corp ....E 574 773-4136
Nappanee **(G-10695)**

Miller Steel Fabricators ....G........ 260 768-7321
Shipshewana **(G-12635)**

Modern Welding & Boiler Works ....G........ 812 232-5039
Terre Haute **(G-13287)**

Mofab Inc ....E 765 649-1288
Anderson **(G-138)**

Morse Metal Fab Inc ....E 574 674-6237
Granger **(G-5425)**

Nello Inc ....F 574 288-3632
South Bend **(G-12870)**

New Nello Operating Co LLC ....C........ 574 288-3632
South Bend **(G-12874)**

Noble County Welding Inc ....F 260 897-4082
Avilla **(G-416)**

Northwest Alum Fabricators Inc ....G........ 219 844-4354
Hammond **(G-5923)**

Omnimax International Inc ....C........ 574 773-7981
Nappanee **(G-10701)**

Ottenweller Co Inc ....C........ 260 484-3166
Fort Wayne **(G-4513)**

P & E Products ....G.... 765 969-2644
Connersville (G-2067)
Paden Engineering Co Inc ....G.... 812 546-4447
Hope (G-6117)
Pauls Welding ....E.... 574 646-2015
Nappanee (G-10702)
Penz Products Inc ....E.... 574 255-4736
Mishawaka (G-10103)
Phoenix Specialties Ltd ....G.... 219 345-5812
Lake Village (G-9085)
Porter Systems Inc ....E.... 317 867-0234
Westfield (G-14179)
Precision Fabrication Inc ....F.... 260 422-4448
Fort Wayne (G-4549)
Precision Surveillance Corp ....E.... 219 397-4295
East Chicago (G-2564)
Prestress Services Inc ....C.... 260 724-7117
Decatur (G-2399)
Profab Custom Metal Works Inc ....G.... 812 865-3999
Orleans (G-11367)
Prokuma Incorporated ....G.... 812 461-1681
Evansville (G-3686)
Quality Fabrication Ind Inc ....F.... 765 529-9776
New Castle (G-10915)
Quikcut Incorporated ....E.... 260 447-8090
Fort Wayne (G-4573)
R Concepts Industries Inc ....D.... 574 295-6641
Elkhart (G-3135)
Rcr Metal Fab LLC ....G.... 219 923-9104
Griffith (G-5788)
Reeves Manufacturing Inc ....G.... 765 935-3875
Richmond (G-12042)
Refax Inc ....C.... 219 977-0414
Gary (G-5090)
Refax Wear Products Inc ....G.... 219 977-0414
Gary (G-5091)
Rf Manufacturing Inc ....G.... 317 773-8610
Noblesville (G-11176)
Robert D Meadows ....G.... 812 797-8294
Bedford (G-575)
San Jo Steel Inc ....F.... 317 888-6227
Greenwood (G-5747)
Sanbar of Indiana Inc ....G.... 317 375-6220
Indianapolis (G-7890)
Schmidt Contracting Inc ....F.... 812 482-3923
Jasper (G-8303)
Schuler Precision Tool LLC ....G.... 260 982-2704
North Manchester (G-11243)
Scott Steel Services Inc ....G.... 219 663-4740
Crown Point (G-2301)
Seiler & Sons ....G.... 812 858-9598
Newburgh (G-11047)
Simko Industrial Fabricators ....E.... 219 933-9100
Hammond (G-5940)
Sinden Racing Service Inc ....F.... 317 243-7171
Indianapolis (G-7949)
Smco Inc ....E.... 574 295-1482
Elkhart (G-3178)
Smgf LLC ....D.... 812 354-8899
Petersburg (G-11568)
SMS Group Inc ....E.... 219 880-0256
Gary (G-5099)
Snyder & Co Inc ....G.... 765 447-3452
Lafayette (G-9000)
Special Fabrication Services ....G.... 812 384-5384
Elnora (G-3292)
Specialty Process Eqp Ctrl Inc ....G.... 812 473-8528
Evansville (G-3743)
Spreuer & Son Inc ....F.... 260 463-3513
Lagrange (G-9067)
Staab Sheet Metal Inc ....G.... 317 241-2553
Indianapolis (G-7983)
Steel Services Inc ....G.... 317 783-5255
Indianapolis (G-7999)
Steel Tank & Fabricating Corp ....E.... 260 248-8971
Columbia City (G-1838)
Steeltech Partners LLC ....G.... 812 849-0124
Mitchell (G-10172)
Stephens Fabrication Inc ....E.... 765 459-9770
Kokomo (G-8701)
Stevens Ironworks Inc ....E.... 219 987-6332
Demotte (G-2448)
Stone City Ironworks Inc ....E.... 812 279-3023
Bedford (G-581)
Structural Iron & Fab Inc ....G.... 260 758-2273
Markle (G-9582)
Superior Equipment & Mfg ....G.... 260 925-0152
Auburn (G-359)
Superior Fabrication Inc ....F.... 812 649-2630
Rockport (G-12173)
Superior Layout ....G.... 812 371-1709
Columbus (G-2018)
Swan Real Estate Mgmt Inc ....G.... 765 664-1478
Marion (G-9565)
Tank Construction & Service Co ....F.... 317 509-6294
Whitestown (G-14263)
TC Burton Enterprises LLC ....G.... 317 446-8776
Fishers (G-3972)
Thomas Cubit Inc ....G.... 219 933-0566
Hammond (G-5949)
Titan Metal Spinning Inc ....G.... 260 665-1067
Angola (G-251)
Titus Inc ....F.... 574 936-3345
Plymouth (G-11728)
Trade Line Fabricating Inc ....E.... 812 637-1444
Lawrenceburg (G-9159)
Tri-State Mechanical Inc ....F.... 260 471-0345
Fort Wayne (G-4702)
Triton Metal Products Inc ....E.... 260 488-1800
Hamilton (G-5830)
Tron Mechanical Incorporated ....C.... 812 838-4715
Mount Vernon (G-10410)
Tru-Form Steel & Wire Inc ....E.... 765 348-5001
Hartford City (G-5994)
Tru-Form Steel & Wire Inc ....E.... 765 348-5001
Hartford City (G-5993)
Tube Processing Corp ....C.... 317 782-9486
Indianapolis (G-8108)
Tuttle Aluminum Intl Inc ....E.... 317 842-2420
Fishers (G-3980)
United States Steel Corp ....B.... 219 888-2000
Gary (G-5111)
Universal Door Carrier Inc ....G.... 317 241-3447
Indianapolis (G-8129)
Usw Lu 6103-07 ....G.... 219 762-4433
Portage (G-11800)
Valmont Industries Inc ....G.... 574 935-3058
Plymouth (G-11733)
Valmont Industries Inc ....D.... 574 295-6942
Elkhart (G-3242)
Vandergriff & Associates Inc ....G.... 812 422-6033
Evansville (G-3793)
Vans Industrial Inc ....E.... 219 931-4881
Hammond (G-5954)
Varied Products Indiana Inc ....F.... 219 763-2526
Chesterton (G-1640)
Vidimos Inc ....D.... 219 397-2728
East Chicago (G-2579)
Vincennes Welding Co Inc ....F.... 812 882-9682
Vincennes (G-13712)
Wabash Valley Manufacturing ....C.... 260 352-2102
Silver Lake (G-12682)
Wabash Welding Services Inc ....E.... 260 563-2363
Wabash (G-13766)
Westfield Steel Inc ....E.... 812 466-3500
Terre Haute (G-13368)
Westlund Concepts ....F.... 317 819-0611
Lapel (G-9120)
Wick - Fab Inc ....E.... 260 897-3303
Avilla (G-421)
Wings N Things Fabrication ....G.... 260 432-2992
Fort Wayne (G-4757)
Wiw Inc ....E.... 219 663-7900
Crown Point (G-2321)
Wrib Manufacturing Inc ....G.... 765 294-2841
Veedersburg (G-13648)
Yankee Steel Inc ....G.... 812 232-5353
Terre Haute (G-13374)
Zieman Manufacturing Company ....G.... 574 522-5202
Goshen (G-5347)

STEEL MILLS

Allegheny Ludlum Corp ....G.... 412 394-2800
Portland (G-11808)
Alro Steel Corporation ....D.... 260 749-1829
Fort Wayne (G-4064)
Arcelormittal Burns Harbor LLC ....A.... 219 787-2120
Burns Harbor (G-1214)
Arcelormittal Holdings LLC ....D.... 219 399-1200
East Chicago (G-2516)
Arcelormittal Indiana Hbr LLC ....A.... 219 399-1200
East Chicago (G-2517)
Arcelormittal USA LLC ....D.... 219 787-2120
Chesterton (G-1595)
Arcelormittal USA LLC ....A.... 312 899-3400
East Chicago (G-2519)
Arcelormittal USA LLC ....C.... 219 399-6500
East Chicago (G-2520)
Armco ....G.... 219 981-8864
Merrillville (G-9698)
Barsteel Corporation ....G.... 219 650-7100
Merrillville (G-9699)
Chicago Flame Hardening Co ....E.... 773 768-3608
East Chicago (G-2524)
Chicago Steel Ltd Partnership ....G.... 219 949-1111
Gary (G-5037)
CPM Acquisition Corp ....D.... 765 362-2600
Crawfordsville (G-2142)
Dietrich Industries Inc ....C.... 219 931-3741
Hammond (G-5870)
Heidtman Steel Products Inc ....C.... 419 691-4646
Butler (G-1229)
Indiana Harbor Coke Company LP ....C.... 219 397-5769
East Chicago (G-2538)
Industrial Steel Cnstr Inc ....C.... 219 885-5610
Gary (G-5069)
Isg Burns Harbor Services LLC ....F.... 219 787-2120
Burns Harbor (G-1215)
Kammerer Inc ....G.... 260 349-9098
Kendallville (G-8484)
Leed Thermal Processing Inc ....G.... 317 637-5102
Indianapolis (G-7393)
Liberation ....G.... 219 736-7329
Schererville (G-12331)
LTV Steel Co ....G.... 219 391-2076
East Chicago (G-2550)
Mid-Continent Coal and Coke Co ....E.... 219 787-8171
Portage (G-11775)
Mitchell Industries Inc ....F.... 812 849-4931
Mitchell (G-10167)
Mittal Steel USA ....C.... 219 787-2113
Chesterton (G-1622)
National Material LP ....C.... 219 397-5088
East Chicago (G-2554)
Niagara Lasalle Corporation ....E.... 800 262-2558
Hammond (G-5921)
Nicks Automotive Inc ....F.... 765 964-6843
Union City (G-13458)
Nonferrous Products Inc ....E.... 317 738-2558
Franklin (G-4914)
Nucor Cold Finish ....G.... 219 937-1442
Crown Point (G-2280)
Nucor Corporation ....D.... 260 337-1800
Saint Joe (G-12257)
Nucor Corporation ....D.... 260 837-7891
Waterloo (G-14019)
Nucor Corporation ....A.... 765 364-1323
Crawfordsville (G-2180)
Nucor Corporation ....C.... 260 837-7891
Waterloo (G-14020)
Nucor Steel Corp ....E.... 765 364-1323
Crawfordsville (G-2181)
Parker-Hannifin Corporation ....E.... 260 587-9102
Ashley (G-289)
Parker-Hannifin Corporation ....C.... 260 636-2104
Albion (G-32)
Phoenix Services LLC ....D.... 219 399-7808
East Chicago (G-2558)
Plymouth Tube Company ....C.... 574 946-6191
Winamac (G-14314)
Prox Company Inc ....F.... 812 232-4324
Terre Haute (G-13311)
Rbc Prcsion Pdts - Plymuth Inc ....D.... 574 935-3027
Plymouth (G-11719)
Ryerson Tull Inc ....D.... 219 764-3500
Burns Harbor (G-1219)
S W Industries Inc ....F.... 317 788-4221
Indianapolis (G-7882)
Schwartz Wheel Co ....G.... 574 546-0101
Bremen (G-1022)
Set Enterprises of Mi Inc ....F.... 812 346-1700
North Vernon (G-11281)
Sssi Inc ....D.... 219 880-0818
Gary (G-5101)
Steel Dynamics Inc ....B.... 260 969-3500
Fort Wayne (G-4646)
Steel Technologies LLC ....C.... 502 245-2110
Portage (G-11796)
Structural Source ....G.... 260 489-0035
Fort Wayne (G-4657)
Ten Cate Enbi Inc (indiana) ....C.... 317 398-3267
Shelbyville (G-12574)
Tms International LLC ....G.... 219 881-0266
Gary (G-5106)
Tms International LLC ....G.... 219 762-2176
Portage (G-11798)
Tms International LLC ....G.... 219 864-0044
Schererville (G-12349)
Tms International LLC ....G.... 219 885-7491
Gary (G-5107)

Employee Codes: A=Over 500 employees, B=251-500
C=101-250, D=51-100, E=20-50, F=10-19, G=2-9
2018 Harris Indiana
Industrial Directory
1087

Tms International LLC ....G....... 219 881-0155
East Chicago **(G-2570)**

Union Electric Steel Corp ....C....... 219 464-1031
Valparaiso **(G-13632)**

United States Steel Corp ....B....... 219 391-2045
East Chicago **(G-2576)**

United States Steel Corp ....B....... 219 888-2000
Gary **(G-5111)**

Vicksmetal Armco Associates ....E....... 765 659-5555
Frankfort **(G-4858)**

Western-Cullen-Hayes Inc ....E....... 765 962-0526
Richmond **(G-12075)**

Wheels In Sky ....G....... 812 249-8233
Terre Haute **(G-13369)**

Windsor Steel Inc ....E....... 574 294-1060
Elkhart **(G-3261)**

STEEL SHEET: Cold-Rolled

Plateplus Inc ....D....... 219 392-3400
East Chicago **(G-2560)**

STEEL WOOL

Hilltop Specialties LLC ....G....... 574 773-4975
Nappanee **(G-10681)**

STEEL, COLD-ROLLED: Sheet Or Strip, From Own Hot-Rolled

Insight Equity Holdings LLC ....A....... 219 378-1930
East Chicago **(G-2540)**

STEEL, COLD-ROLLED: Strip NEC, From Purchased Hot-Rolled

I/N Tek LP ....C....... 574 654-1000
New Carlisle **(G-10883)**

STEEL, COLD-ROLLED: Strip Or Wire

Heartland Steel Processing LLC ....C....... 812 299-4157
Terre Haute **(G-13246)**

Illiana Steel Inc ....E....... 219 397-3250
East Chicago **(G-2537)**

Mill Steel Co. ....C....... 765 622-4545
Anderson **(G-136)**

Ohio River Metal Services Inc ....C....... 812 282-4770
Jeffersonville **(G-8406)**

Steel Technologies LLC ....C....... 765 362-3110
Crawfordsville **(G-2197)**

STEEL, HOT-ROLLED: Sheet Or Strip

Daechang Seat Co Ltd USA ....F....... 317 755-3663
Indianapolis **(G-6723)**

Lana Hudelson ....G....... 812 865-3951
Orleans **(G-11363)**

Steel Technologies LLC ....C....... 765 362-3110
Crawfordsville **(G-2197)**

United States Steel Corp ....D....... 219 762-3131
Portage **(G-11799)**

STEEL: Cold-Rolled

Allegheny Ludlum LLC ....C....... 765 529-9570
New Castle **(G-10890)**

Arcelormittal USA LLC ....D....... 219 787-2120
Chesterton **(G-1595)**

Chief Industries Inc ....C....... 219 866-4121
Rensselaer **(G-11917)**

Dietrich Industries Inc ....C....... 219 931-3741
Hammond **(G-5870)**

Feralloy Corporation ....D....... 219 787-9698
Portage **(G-11762)**

Heidtman Steel Products Inc ....C....... 419 691-4646
Butler **(G-1229)**

Nucor Corporation ....A....... 765 364-1323
Crawfordsville **(G-2180)**

Plymouth Tube Company ....C....... 574 946-6191
Winamac **(G-14314)**

Quanex Corp Lasalle Steel Div ....G....... 219 853-6202
Hammond **(G-5930)**

Ryerson Tull Inc ....D....... 219 764-3500
Burns Harbor **(G-1219)**

Set Enterprises of Mi Inc ....F....... 812 346-1700
North Vernon **(G-11281)**

Stalcop LLC ....D....... 765 436-7926
Thorntown **(G-13378)**

Steel Dynamics Inc ....B....... 260 969-3500
Fort Wayne **(G-4646)**

Steel Technologies LLC ....C....... 502 245-2110
Portage **(G-11796)**

Ten Point Trim Corp ....E....... 317 875-5424
Zionsville **(G-14468)**

United States Steel Corp ....D....... 219 762-3131
Portage **(G-11799)**

Worthington Steel Company ....C....... 219 929-4000
Porter **(G-11806)**

STEEL: Galvanized

Heartland Steel Processing LLC ....C....... 812 299-4157
Terre Haute **(G-13246)**

STENCILS & LETTERING MATERIALS: Die-Cut

Rcs Contractor Supplies Inc ....G....... 317 773-6279
Noblesville **(G-11171)**

STERILIZERS, BARBER & BEAUTY SHOP

E-Beam Services Inc ....G....... 765 447-6755
Lafayette **(G-8893)**

STITCHING SVCS

Action Embroidery Inc ....G....... 850 626-1796
Jeffersonville **(G-8319)**

Dave Turner ....G....... 765 674-3360
Gas City **(G-5122)**

Queen Ann Custom Drapies ....G....... 317 802-6130
Carmel **(G-1460)**

STOCK: Vehicle, Hardwood

Auto Wood Restoration ....G....... 219 797-3775
Hanna **(G-5958)**

STONE: Cast Concrete

Accucast Industries ....F....... 219 929-1137
Chesterton **(G-1590)**

STONE: Crushed & Broken, NEC

Pipe Creek Jr ....G....... 765 922-7991
Sims **(G-12683)**

STONE: Dimension, NEC

Demotte Decorative Stone Inc ....G....... 219 987-5461
Demotte **(G-2434)**

Garrity Stone Inc ....G....... 317 546-0893
Indianapolis **(G-6985)**

Indiana Quarriers & Carvers ....F....... 812 935-8383
Gosport **(G-5351)**

Legacy Vulcan LLC ....F....... 219 696-5467
Lowell **(G-9414)**

Marietta Martin Materials Inc ....F....... 317 776-4460
Noblesville **(G-11145)**

Stone Center of Indiana LLC ....E....... 317 849-9100
Indianapolis **(G-8009)**

Tremain Ceramic Tile & Flr Cvg ....E....... 317 542-1491
Indianapolis **(G-8093)**

STONE: Quarrying & Processing, Own Stone Prdts

Evans Limestone Co. ....E....... 812 279-9744
Bedford **(G-541)**

New Point Stone Co Inc ....F....... 765 698-2227
Laurel **(G-9128)**

Slon Inc ....F....... 765 884-1792
Fowler **(G-4807)**

STONEWARE PRDTS: Pottery

Davis Vachon Artworks ....G....... 260 489-9160
Fort Wayne **(G-4201)**

Stoneware 3 ....G....... 812 696-2679
Farmersburg **(G-3838)**

STORE FIXTURES, EXC REFRIGERATED: Wholesalers

Ell Enterprises Inc ....G....... 317 783-7838
Indianapolis **(G-6841)**

STORE FIXTURES: Exc Wood

Precision Millwork & Plas Inc ....E....... 574 243-8720
South Bend **(G-12902)**

STORE FIXTURES: Wood

Franks Wood Shop ....G....... 317 738-2039
Franklin **(G-4887)**

JC Moag Corporation ....D....... 812 284-8400
Jeffersonville **(G-8383)**

Platinum Display Group ....G....... 317 731-5026
Indianapolis **(G-7701)**

Precision Millwork & Plas Inc ....E....... 574 243-8720
South Bend **(G-12902)**

STORES: Auto & Home Supply

C & P Machine Service Inc ....E....... 260 484-7723
Fort Wayne **(G-4131)**

J & P Custom Plating Inc ....G....... 260 726-9696
Portland **(G-11829)**

Metaldyne Bsm LLC ....D....... 260 495-4315
Fremont **(G-4968)**

U B Machine Inc ....G....... 260 493-3381
New Haven **(G-10962)**

STORES: Drapery & Upholstery

M C L Window Coverings Inc ....F....... 317 577-2670
Fishers **(G-3942)**

Mill End Drapery Inc ....G....... 317 257-4800
Indianapolis **(G-7518)**

STOVES: Wood & Coal Burning

Hitzer Inc ....E....... 260 589-8536
Berne **(G-617)**

Oesterling Chimney Sweep Inc ....G....... 812 372-3512
Columbus **(G-1984)**

STRAIGHTENERS

Mae of America Inc ....G....... 765 561-4539
Indianapolis **(G-7436)**

STRAIN GAGES: Solid State

Qualitex Inc ....F....... 260 244-7839
Fort Wayne **(G-4571)**

STRAPPING

Dubose Strapping Inc ....G....... 765 361-0000
Crawfordsville **(G-2150)**

Illinois Tool Works Inc ....C....... 260 347-8040
Kendallville **(G-8480)**

Rowe Conveyor LLC ....G....... 317 602-1024
Greenwood **(G-5743)**

STRAPS: Bindings, Textile

Round Two Begins Corporation ....G....... 574 825-9800
Middlebury **(G-9917)**

STRAPS: Cotton Webbing

Masson M Ross Co Inc ....F....... 317 632-8021
Indianapolis **(G-7464)**

STRAWS: Drinking, Made From Purchased Materials

Lucky Straw Inc ....E....... 219 397-9910
East Chicago **(G-2551)**

STRUCTURAL SUPPORT & BUILDING MATERIAL: Concrete

Carters Concrete Block Inc ....E....... 574 722-2644
Logansport **(G-9330)**

Roofing & Insulation Sup Inc ....G....... 317 547-4373
Indianapolis **(G-7861)**

Tom Spencer Concrete Products ....F....... 812 659-2318
Switz City **(G-13127)**

Vertex Building Materials LLC ....G....... 765 547-1883
Brookville **(G-1129)**

STUCCO

C & E Exteriors Inc ....G....... 317 984-5463
Arcadia **(G-261)**

STUDIOS: Artist

Fabcreation ....G....... 812 246-6222
Sellersburg **(G-12394)**

Gibbs Susie Framing & Art ....G....... 765 428-2434
Lafayette **(G-8907)**

STUDIOS: Artists & Artists' Studios

Playn2win LLC ....G.....317 345-4653
Indianapolis *(G-7702)*

STUDIOS: Sculptor's

Magaws of Boston ....G......765 935-6170
Richmond *(G-12013)*

STYRENE

Futurex Industries Inc ....C......765 498-3900
Bloomingdale *(G-647)*
Futurex Industries Inc ....D......812 299-5708
Terre Haute *(G-13237)*
Styrene Solutions LLC ....G......574 876-4610
Elkhart *(G-3195)*

SUBMARINE BUILDING & REPAIR

Rolls-Royce Corporation..................G......317 230-8515
West Lafayette *(G-14104)*
Rolls-Royce Corporation..................A......317 230-2000
Indianapolis *(G-7858)*

SUNDRIES & RELATED PRDTS: Medical & Laboratory, Rubber

Gdc Inc ....C......574 533-3128
Goshen *(G-5222)*
Ink Angel Inc ....G......574 534-4415
Goshen *(G-5245)*
Midwest Rubber Sales Inc................G......765 468-7105
Farmland *(G-3842)*
North American Latex Corp ....D......812 268-6608
Sullivan *(G-13089)*
Sperry & Rice LLC ....E......765 647-4141
Brookville *(G-1126)*

SUPERMARKETS & OTHER GROCERY STORES

Franklins Mercantile ....G......812 876-0426
Spencer *(G-13027)*
Market Place Publications................G......219 769-7733
Merrillville *(G-9730)*
MI Tierra ....G......812 376-0668
Columbus *(G-1973)*
Plymouth Ready Mart Inc ....G......574 936-5251
Plymouth *(G-11715)*

SURFACE ACTIVE AGENTS

Classic Chemical Corp ....G......812 934-3289
Indianapolis *(G-6618)*
D S E Inc ....E......812 376-0310
Columbus *(G-1904)*

SURGICAL & MEDICAL INSTRUMENTS WHOLESALERS

Alli Medical LLC ....G......317 625-4535
Westfield *(G-14134)*

SURGICAL APPLIANCES & SPLYS

Bryton Corporation..........................F......317 334-8700
Indianapolis *(G-6516)*

SURGICAL APPLIANCES & SPLYS

Accra-Pac Inc ....D......905 660-0444
Elkhart *(G-2666)*
American Veteran Group LLC............G......317 600-4749
Westfield *(G-14136)*
Battle Creek Equipment Co...............E......260 495-3472
Fremont *(G-4952)*
Biomet Biologics LLC ....E......574 267-2038
Warsaw *(G-13846)*
Bionic Prosth & Orthos Grp LLC ......G......765 838-8222
Lafayette *(G-8861)*
Bleys Prosthetics & Orthotics ....G......812 704-3894
Seymour *(G-12434)*
Braun Corporation............................B......574 946-7413
Winamac *(G-14302)*
Cook Medical LLC............................G......812 339-2235
Bloomington *(G-707)*
Depuy Products Inc ....E......574 267-8143
Warsaw *(G-13864)*
Depuy Synthes Sales Inc ....F......574 267-8143
Warsaw *(G-13866)*

Ehob Inc ....C......317 972-4600
Indianapolis *(G-6815)*
Fort Wayne Metals Res Pdts ....E......260 747-4154
Fort Wayne *(G-4273)*
Glove Corporation ....D......501 362-2437
Alexandria *(G-43)*
Hanger Prosthetics & ....G......812 479-1121
Evansville *(G-3531)*
Health Equipment Manufacturers........E......260 495-3472
Fremont *(G-4961)*
Howmedica Osteonics Corp ....G......317 587-2008
Carmel *(G-1407)*
Invacare Corporation........................F......317 838-5500
Plainfield *(G-11619)*
Kenney Orthopedics Carmel LLC......G......317 993-3664
Carmel *(G-1421)*
Kenney Orthopedics Seymour LLC ......F......812 271-1627
Seymour *(G-12462)*
Kenney Orthpdics Indnpolis LLC ....G......317 300-0814
Greenwood *(G-5713)*
Lafayette Dental Laboratory ....E......765 447-9341
Lafayette *(G-8947)*
Medical Device Bus Svcs Inc ....G......317 596-3320
Indianapolis *(G-7476)*
Medical Device Bus Svcs Inc ....A......574 267-8143
Warsaw *(G-13908)*
National Dentex LLC ....D......317 849-5143
Indianapolis *(G-7570)*
Nemcomed Instrs & Implants ....G......800 255-4576
Fort Wayne *(G-4496)*
Orthopediatrics Corp ....D......574 268-6379
Warsaw *(G-13918)*
Orthopediatrics US Dist ....D......574 268-6379
Warsaw *(G-13919)*
Orthotic & Prosthetic Designs............G......317 882-9002
Indianapolis *(G-7633)*
OSI Specialties Inc ....E......317 293-4858
Indianapolis *(G-7635)*
Paragon Medical Inc ....G......317 570-5830
Indianapolis *(G-7654)*
Point Medical Corporation..................A......219 663-1775
Crown Point *(G-2285)*
Precision Piece Parts Inc ....D......574 255-3185
Mishawaka *(G-10107)*
Somer Inc ....E......317 873-1111
Zionsville *(G-14464)*
Standard Fusee Corporation ....E......765 472-4375
Peru *(G-11548)*
Surestep LLC ....E......574 233-3352
South Bend *(G-12962)*
United Surgical Inc ....G......260 422-5827
Fort Wayne *(G-4718)*
USA Medical Suppliers Ltd ....G......608 782-1855
Indianapolis *(G-8139)*
Zimmer Biomet Holdings Inc ....B......574 267-6131
Warsaw *(G-13975)*

SURGICAL EQPT: See Also Instruments

3M Company......................................B......317 692-6666
Indianapolis *(G-6288)*
3M Company......................................B......574 948-8103
Plymouth *(G-11659)*
Cook Group Incorporated ....F......812 339-2235
Bloomington *(G-704)*
Greenwald Surgical Co Inc ....E......219 962-1604
Lake Station *(G-9075)*
LH Medical Corporation ....D......260 387-5194
Fort Wayne *(G-4432)*
Life Dme LLC....................................G......219 795-1296
Merrillville *(G-9727)*
Symmetry Medical Inc ....C......574 267-8700
Warsaw *(G-13947)*

SURGICAL IMPLANTS

Biomet Europe Ltd............................G......574 267-2038
Warsaw *(G-13847)*
Biomet Orthopedics LLC....................A......574 267-6639
Warsaw *(G-13849)*
Golden-Helvey Holdings Inc ....D......574 266-4500
Elkhart *(G-2890)*
Maitland Engineering Inc ....E......574 287-0155
South Bend *(G-12850)*
Medtrnic Sofamor Danek USA Inc ......G......574 267-6826
Warsaw *(G-13909)*
Nemcomed Fw LLC............................C......260 480-5226
Fort Wayne *(G-4495)*
Tornier Inc ....G......574 268-0861
Warsaw *(G-13953)*
Warsaw Orthopedic Inc ....C......901 396-3133
Warsaw *(G-13963)*

Zollman Plastic Surgery PC ....G......317 328-1100
Indianapolis *(G-8227)*

SURVEYING SVCS: Photogrammetric Engineering

Indy Rapid 3d LLC ....G......812 243-4175
Indianapolis *(G-7221)*

SUSPENSION SYSTEMS: Acoustical, Metal

Liquidspring LLC ....G......765 474-7816
Lafayette *(G-8959)*

SVC ESTABLISH EQPT, WHOLESALE: Carpet/Rug Clean Eqpt & Sply

Bane-Clene Corp ....E......317 546-5448
Indianapolis *(G-6455)*

SVC ESTABLISHMENT EQPT, WHOL: Concrete Burial Vaults & Boxes

Lebanon Berg Vault Co Inc ....G......765 482-0302
Lebanon *(G-9198)*
Meyer Industries Inc ....G......317 769-3497
Whitestown *(G-14256)*
Quality Vault Company......................F......812 336-8127
Bloomington *(G-803)*
Rensselaer Eagle Vault Corp ....G......219 866-5123
Rensselaer *(G-11936)*

SVC ESTABLISHMENT EQPT, WHOLESALE: Beauty Parlor Eqpt & Sply

State Beauty Supply ....G......260 755-6361
Fort Wayne *(G-4645)*

SVC ESTABLISHMENT EQPT, WHOLESALE: Electrolysis Eqpt & Splys

Cosmoprof..G......317 897-0124
Indianapolis *(G-6672)*

SVC ESTABLISHMENT EQPT, WHOLESALE: Firefighting Eqpt

Elkhart Brass Manufacturing Co ....F......800 346-0250
Elkhart *(G-2822)*
Hoosier Fire Equipment Inc ....E......219 462-1707
Valparaiso *(G-13557)*

SWIMMING POOL EQPT: Filters & Water Conditioning Systems

Canature USA Inc.............................G......877 771-6789
Carmel *(G-1326)*

SWIMMING POOL SPLY STORES

Automatic Pool Covers Inc ....E......317 579-2000
Westfield *(G-14137)*
Leisure Pool & Spa ....G......812 537-0071
Lawrenceburg *(G-9147)*
Sparkle Pools Inc..............................F......812 232-1292
Terre Haute *(G-13337)*

SWIMMING POOLS, EQPT & SPLYS: Wholesalers

Automatic Pool Covers Inc ....E......317 579-2000
Westfield *(G-14137)*
Dunn-Rite Products Inc ....E......765 552-9433
Elwood *(G-3295)*
Fort Wayne Pools..............................C......260 459-4100
Fort Wayne *(G-4279)*
Leisure Pool & Spa ....G......812 537-0071
Lawrenceburg *(G-9147)*
Sparkle Pools Inc..............................F......812 232-1292
Terre Haute *(G-13337)*
Team Supreme Bait Company ....G......812 366-3200
Georgetown *(G-5154)*

SWITCHBOARD APPARATUS, EXC INSTRUMENTS

Custom Magnetics Inc.......................E......773 463-6500
North Manchester *(G-11227)*

SWITCHES

Cloud Defensive LLC................................G....... 812 760-5017
Newburgh **(G-11025)**

Elkhart Supply Corp..............................E....... 574 264-4156
Elkhart **(G-2831)**

SWITCHES: Electric Power

Power Components of Midwest.............C....... 574 256-6990
Mishawaka **(G-10105)**

Sigma Switches Plus Inc......................E....... 574 294-5776
Elkhart **(G-3170)**

SWITCHES: Electric Power, Exc Snap, Push Button, Etc

Burt Products Inc................................G....... 812 386-6890
Princeton **(G-11867)**

SWITCHES: Electronic

Dwyer Instruments Inc........................E....... 219 393-5250
La Porte **(G-8752)**

Infinias LLC..G....... 317 348-1249
Indianapolis **(G-7226)**

Intelliray Inc.......................................G....... 260 547-4399
Decatur **(G-2386)**

Regency Technologies Inc.....................G....... 317 543-9740
Indianapolis **(G-7827)**

Stuart Manufacturing Inc.....................F....... 260 403-2003
Fort Wayne **(G-4658)**

ZF North America Inc...........................B....... 765 429-1984
Lafayette **(G-9028)**

SWITCHES: Electronic Applications

AEL/Span LLC.....................................E....... 317 203-4602
Plainfield **(G-11591)**

Touchtronics Inc.................................F....... 574 294-2570
Elkhart **(G-3221)**

SWITCHES: Thermostatic

Green Air LLC.....................................G....... 317 335-1706
Fishers **(G-3987)**

SWITCHGEAR & SWITCHBOARD APPARATUS

Breakers Unlimited Inc.........................G....... 317 474-9431
Noblesville **(G-11072)**

Circuit Breaker Sales Co Inc.................G....... 219 575-5420
Crown Point **(G-2234)**

CTS Corporation.................................G....... 574 293-7511
Berne **(G-611)**

Direct Control Systems Inc...................G....... 765 282-7474
Muncie **(G-10460)**

Hubbell Incorporated Delaware.............B....... 574 234-7151
South Bend **(G-12806)**

Integratorcom Inc...............................D....... 317 776-3500
Noblesville **(G-11130)**

Janco Engineered Products LLC............C....... 574 255-3169
Mishawaka **(G-10060)**

Schneder Elc Bldngs Amrcas Inc.........G....... 317 894-6374
Greenfield **(G-5571)**

Schneider Electric..............................G....... 574 293-0877
Elkhart **(G-3158)**

Sigma Switches Plus Inc......................E....... 574 294-5776
Elkhart **(G-3170)**

Standard Fusee Corporation.................E....... 765 472-4375
Peru **(G-11548)**

Teaco Inc...F....... 219 874-6234
Michigan City **(G-9852)**

Touchplate Technologies Inc.................F....... 260 424-4323
Fort Wayne **(G-4696)**

Western Consolidated Tech Inc.............D....... 260 495-9866
Fremont **(G-4982)**

SWITCHGEAR & SWITCHGEAR ACCESS, NEC

Integrity Marketing Team Inc................G....... 317 517-0012
Plainfield **(G-11617)**

Siemens Industry Inc...........................D....... 219 763-7927
Portage **(G-11794)**

SYNCHROS

Shooting Stars Synchro Inc..................G....... 317 710-1462
Noblesville **(G-11182)**

SYNTHETIC RESIN FINISHED PRDTS, NEC

Calico Precision Molding LLC...............E....... 260 484-4500
Fort Wayne **(G-4135)**

SYSTEMS ENGINEERING: Computer Related

Leidos Inc..C....... 812 863-3100
Crane **(G-2128)**

SYSTEMS INTEGRATION SVCS

Bull Hn Info Systems Inc......................E....... 317 686-5500
Indianapolis **(G-6521)**

Drs Graphix Group Inc..........................G....... 317 569-1855
Indianapolis **(G-6768)**

Frakes Engineering Inc........................E....... 317 577-3000
Indianapolis **(G-6956)**

SYSTEMS INTEGRATION SVCS: Office Computer Automation

Lumen Cache Incorporated...................G....... 317 739-4218
McCordsville **(G-9673)**

SYSTEMS SOFTWARE DEVELOPMENT SVCS

Smartgait LLC.....................................G....... 765 404-0726
West Lafayette **(G-14107)**

TABLE OR COUNTERTOPS, PLASTIC LAMINATED

Boardworks Inc...................................G....... 219 464-8111
Valparaiso **(G-13511)**

Cabinets & Counters Inc.......................E....... 812 858-3300
Newburgh **(G-11023)**

Counter Design Co Inc..........................E....... 812 477-1243
Evansville **(G-3432)**

Countertop Connections Inc..................G....... 317 822-9858
Franklin **(G-4878)**

Crown Supply Co Inc............................F....... 812 522-6987
Seymour **(G-12440)**

Custom Design Laminates Inc...............F....... 574 674-9174
Osceola **(G-11375)**

Eash LLC..F....... 574 295-4450
Elkhart **(G-2811)**

H & S Custom Countertops Inc...............G....... 812 422-6314
Evansville **(G-3526)**

Interior Design Surfaces Inc.................G....... 317 829-3970
Carmel **(G-1417)**

Lue Manufacturing Inc..........................F....... 574 862-4249
Wakarusa **(G-13783)**

Michiana Laminated Products................F....... 260 562-2871
Howe **(G-6129)**

Mission Woodworking Inc......................E....... 574 848-5697
Bristol **(G-1069)**

Molargik Woodworking Inc....................G....... 260 357-6625
Garrett **(G-5016)**

Newlett Inc..D....... 574 294-8899
Elkhart **(G-3061)**

Prolam Products Inc.............................D....... 812 867-1662
Evansville **(G-3687)**

Ptf Cabinets & Tops LLC.......................G....... 317 786-4367
Indianapolis **(G-7787)**

TABLES: Lift, Hydraulic

Ameri-Kart Corp..................................C....... 574 848-7462
Bristol **(G-1044)**

TACKS: Nonferrous Metal Or Wire

Trinity Metals LLC...............................G....... 317 358-8265
Indianapolis **(G-8101)**

Trinity Metals LLC...............................G....... 317 358-8265
Indianapolis **(G-8102)**

TAGS & LABELS: Paper

Chronotrack Systems Corp....................G....... 314 406-7243
Evansville **(G-3417)**

G M S I Inc..G....... 574 457-4646
Syracuse **(G-13131)**

Gl Tape & Label...................................G....... 574 269-2836
Warsaw **(G-13881)**

Hooven - Dayton Corp...........................E....... 765 935-3999
Richmond **(G-12000)**

Patriot Label Inc..................................G....... 812 877-1611
Terre Haute **(G-13298)**

Shelf Tag Supply Corporation................G....... 317 580-4030
Carmel **(G-1479)**

TALLOW: Animal

Kane-Miller Corp.................................E....... 219 362-9050
La Porte **(G-8775)**

TANK REPAIR SVCS

Bulk Truck & Transport Service.............E....... 812 866-2155
Hanover **(G-5959)**

Hmt LLC...F....... 219 736-9901
Merrillville **(G-9720)**

Tank Construction & Service Co.............F....... 317 509-6294
Whitestown **(G-14263)**

Trifab & Construction Inc......................G....... 219 845-1300
Hammond **(G-5952)**

TANKS & OTHER TRACKED VEHICLE CMPNTS

AM General LLC...................................A....... 574 258-7523
Mishawaka **(G-9995)**

Ceramix 101..G....... 219 531-6536
Valparaiso **(G-13521)**

Nix Sanitary Service.............................G....... 812 475-9774
Boonville **(G-919)**

TANKS: Cryogenic, Metal

Alloy Custom Products LLC...................D....... 765 564-4684
Lafayette **(G-8850)**

Precision Cryogenic Systems................F....... 317 273-2800
Indianapolis **(G-7733)**

TANKS: Fuel, Including Oil & Gas, Metal Plate

Hmt LLC...F....... 219 736-9901
Merrillville **(G-9720)**

Jiffy Lube..F....... 317 882-5823
Greenwood **(G-5709)**

McWane Inc...G....... 574 534-9328
Goshen **(G-5283)**

TANKS: Lined, Metal

Abtrex Industries Inc...........................E....... 574 234-7773
South Bend **(G-12693)**

Axis Unlimited LLC..............................G....... 574 370-8923
Elkhart **(G-2708)**

Lagrange Products Inc..........................C....... 260 495-3025
Fremont **(G-4965)**

TANKS: Plastic & Fiberglass

AK Industries Inc.................................D....... 574 936-6022
Plymouth **(G-11662)**

Apexx Enterprises LLC.........................F....... 812 486-2443
Montgomery **(G-10213)**

Composites Syndicate LLC....................E....... 260 484-3139
Fort Wayne **(G-4172)**

Tj Maintenance LLC.............................G....... 219 776-8427
Lake Village **(G-9088)**

TANKS: Standard Or Custom Fabricated, Metal Plate

Bulk Truck & Transport Service.............E....... 812 866-2155
Hanover **(G-5959)**

Hensley Fabricating & Eqp Co...............E....... 574 498-6514
Tippecanoe **(G-13382)**

Hoosier Tank and Mfg Inc.....................D....... 574 232-8368
South Bend **(G-12803)**

Kennedy Tank & Mfg Co........................C....... 317 787-1311
Indianapolis **(G-7342)**

Manchester Tank & Equipment Co..........D....... 812 275-5931
Bedford **(G-561)**

Manitex Sabre Inc................................D....... 574 772-5380
Knox **(G-8574)**

Norman Stein & Associates...................F....... 260 749-5468
New Haven **(G-10950)**

Ottenweller Co Inc...............................C....... 260 484-3166
Fort Wayne **(G-4513)**

Penway Inc..E....... 812 526-2645
Edinburgh **(G-2621)**

Quick Tanks Inc...................................E....... 260 347-3850
Kendallville **(G-8503)**

Quick Tanks Inc...................................G....... 260 347-3850
Kendallville **(G-8504)**

Wessels Company................................D....... 317 888-9800
Greenwood **(G-5759)**

TANKS: Storage, Farm, Metal Plate

CTB MN Investment Co Inc ....E 574 658-4191
Milford (G-9955)

TANKS: Water, Metal Plate

Phoenix Fbrcators Erectors LLC ....C 317 271-7002
Avon (G-461)

TANNING SALONS

Always Sun Tanning Center ....G 812 238-2786
Terre Haute (G-13192)
Hot Cake ....G 317 889-2253
Indianapolis (G-7132)

TAPE SLITTING SVCS

Web Industries Fort Wayne Inc ....E 260 432-0027
Fort Wayne (G-4750)

TAPE STORAGE UNITS: Computer

Leroy R Sollars ....G 765 284-9417
Selma (G-12424)

TAPE: Rubber

Unique Tape Manufacturing LLC ....G 219 617-4204
Chesterton (G-1637)

TAPES, ADHESIVE: MedicaL

Djo LLC ....G 317 406-2000
Plainfield (G-11605)

TAPES: Coated Fiberglass, Pipe Sealing Or Insulating

American Elkhart LLC ....G 574 293-0333
Elkhart (G-2683)

TAPES: Fabric

Leap Frogz Screanprinting EMB ....G 317 786-2441
Indianapolis (G-7390)

TAPES: Insulating

Web Industries Fort Wayne Inc ....E 260 432-0027
Fort Wayne (G-4750)

TAPES: Plastic Coated

ISI Inc ....F 317 631-7980
Indianapolis (G-7275)

TAPES: Pressure Sensitive

3M Company ....B 317 692-6666
Indianapolis (G-6288)
Hooven - Dayton Corp ....E 765 935-3999
Richmond (G-12000)
Marian Worldwide Inc ....D 317 638-6525
Indianapolis (G-7454)
Vickery Tape & Label Co Inc ....F 765 472-1974
Peru (G-11555)

TARPAULINS

Gosport Manufacturing Co Inc ....E 812 879-4224
Gosport (G-5350)
Gta Containers Inc ....E 574 288-3459
South Bend (G-12793)
Indianapolis Marine Co ....F 317 545-4646
Indianapolis (G-7202)
Mosiers Tarps ....G 260 563-3332
Wabash (G-13742)
T K Sales & Service ....G 219 962-8982
Gary (G-5104)

TARPAULINS, WHOLESALE

T K Sales & Service ....G 219 962-8982
Gary (G-5104)

TATTOO PARLORS

Amish Robs Tattoos LLC ....G 219 863-9727
Morocco (G-10360)

TAX RETURN PREPARATION SVCS

Jackson Hewitt Tax Service ....C 574 255-2200
Mishawaka (G-10057)

P C Communication Inc ....G 219 838-2546
Highland (G-6053)
Worth Tax and Financial Svc ....G 574 267-4687
Warsaw (G-13969)

TAXIDERMISTS

American Natural Resources LLC ....F 219 922-6444
Griffith (G-5762)

TECHNICAL MANUAL PREPARATION SVCS

Inari Information Services ....G 812 331-2298
Bloomington (G-743)
Rough Notes Company Inc ....E 800 428-4384
Carmel (G-1470)

TECHNICAL WRITING SVCS

Precisely Write Inc ....G 317 585-7701
Indianapolis (G-7730)

TELECOMMUNICATION SYSTEMS & EQPT

C&D Technologies Inc ....C 765 762-2461
Attica (G-298)
GE Power Electronics Inc ....G 317 259-9264
Indianapolis (G-6988)
Lyra LLC ....G 260 452-4058
Fort Wayne (G-4445)

TELECOMMUNICATIONS CARRIERS & SVCS: Wired

Mobile Communications Tech ....G 812 423-7322
Evansville (G-3631)
Tuthill Corporation ....C 260 747-7529
Fort Wayne (G-4709)
Vectren Corporation ....E 812 424-6411
Evansville (G-3795)

TELECOMMUNICATIONS CARRIERS & SVCS: Wireless

Commtineo LLC ....F 219 476-3667
Wanatah (G-13822)

TELEMARKETING BUREAUS

National Handicapped Workshop ....D 765 287-8331
Muncie (G-10538)

TELEPHONE ANSWERING MACHINES

Telecom LLC ....G 317 805-1090
Indianapolis (G-6282)

TELEPHONE CENTRAL OFFICE EQPT: Dial Or Manual

Acd Suppliers LLC ....G 317 527-9715
Indianapolis (G-6315)

TELEPHONE EQPT: Modems

American Cmnty Bnk Ind Modem 2 ....G 219 627-3381
Saint John (G-12259)
Great Deals Magazine ....F 765 649-3302
Anderson (G-112)

TELEPHONE EQPT: NEC

Coriant Operations Inc ....D 219 785-1737
La Porte (G-8745)
International Resources Inc ....G 317 813-5300
Indianapolis (G-7261)
Siemens AG ....G 574 522-6807
Elkhart (G-3169)
Telamon Technologies Corp ....A 317 818-6888
Carmel (G-1491)

TELEPHONE SVCS

Accent Complex Inc ....G 574 522-2368
Elkhart (G-2664)

TELEPHONE: Fiber Optic Systems

Telamon International Corp ....E 317 818-6888
Carmel (G-1490)

TELEPHONE: Sets, Exc Cellular Radio

Smart Choice Mobile Inc ....F 574 830-5727
Elkhart (G-3177)
Sprint Spectrum LP ....G 765 983-6991
Richmond (G-12053)

TELEVISION BROADCASTING STATIONS

Emmis Operating Company ....E 317 266-0100
Indianapolis (G-6855)
Schurz Communications Inc ....F 574 247-7237
Mishawaka (G-10121)

TELEVISION SETS

Vidicom Corporation ....F 219 923-7475
Hammond (G-5956)

TEMPERING: Metal

Gerdau Macsteel Atmosphere Ann ....E 812 346-1275
North Vernon (G-11259)

TEMPLES, RELIGIOUS

Temple-Inland Inc ....G 765 675-6732
Tipton (G-13408)

TENTS: All Materials

Montgomery Tent & Awning Co ....F 317 357-9759
Indianapolis (G-7538)

TEST BORING SVC: Anthracite Mining

R D-N-P Drilling Inc ....G 219 956-3481
Wheatfield (G-14229)

TESTERS: Battery

Advance Stores Company Inc ....G 317 253-5034
Indianapolis (G-6331)

TESTERS: Environmental

Webber Manufacturing Company ....E 317 357-8681
Indianapolis (G-8181)

TESTERS: Gas, Exc Indl Process

R F Express Corp ....G 219 510-5193
Valparaiso (G-13606)
Sentech Corporation ....G 317 596-1988
Indianapolis (G-7911)

TESTERS: Hardness

Accu-Chek Qulty Solutions LLC ....E 812 704-5491
Corydon (G-2087)

TESTERS: Physical Property

Adaptek Systems Inc ....E 260 637-8660
Fort Wayne (G-4041)
Magwerks Corporation ....F 317 241-8011
Danville (G-2352)
Moyer Process & Controls Co ....G 260 495-2405
Fremont (G-4969)
Power Place Products Inc ....G
Boswell (G-941)
Sonam Technologies LLC ....G 844 887-6626
Crown Point (G-2307)

TESTERS: Water, Exc Indl Process

Astbury Water Technology Inc ....E 260 668-8900
Angola (G-194)

TEXTILE & APPAREL SVCS

Paige Marschall ....G 574 277-1631
Granger (G-5428)

TEXTILE FABRICATORS

Country Sewing ....G 260 347-9733
Kendallville (G-8467)
Edna B LLC ....G 574 271-4300
Granger (G-5403)
Kathys Sewing Inc ....G 260 623-6387
Monroeville (G-10196)
Workroom Inc ....G 574 269-6624
Winona Lake (G-14356)
Wt Products Inc ....G 765 216-7998
Muncie (G-10589)

PRODUCT

TEXTILE: Finishing, Cotton Broadwoven

Chattin Walter R Cotton ....G....... 812 254-5031
Columbus (G-1869)

TEXTILE: Goods, NEC

Tippmann Products LLC ....G....... 260 438-7946
Fort Wayne (G-4685)

TEXTILES: Bagging, Jute

Anokhi International Inc ....G....... 260 750-0418
Fort Wayne (G-4077)

TEXTILES: Jute & Flax Prdts

Blush Salon Boutique ....G....... 317 523-1635
Fishers (G-3881)

TEXTILES: Padding & Wadding

Ruby Enterprises Inc ....G....... 765 649-2060
Anderson (G-164)
Wolf Corporation ....E....... 260 749-9393
Fort Wayne (G-4760)

TEXTILES: Wool Waste, Processes

East Heat Wood Pellets LLC ....G....... 317 638-4840
Indianapolis (G-6790)

THEATRICAL PRODUCTION SVCS

Whiteco Industries Inc.........................A....... 219 769-6601
Merrillville (G-9761)

THEOLOGICAL SEMINARIES

Anabaptist Mennonite Biblical.................D....... 574 295-3726
Elkhart (G-2691)
St Meinrad Archabbey ....D....... 812 357-6611
Saint Meinrad (G-12275)

THERMOCOUPLES

Intech Automation Systems Corp ....G....... 209 836-8610
Peru (G-11532)

THERMOPLASTIC MATERIALS

Chemtrusion Inc.........................D....... 812 280-2910
Jeffersonville (G-8336)
Encom Inc.........................G....... 812 421-7700
Evansville (G-3477)
Gaska Tape Inc ....G....... 574 294-5431
Elkhart (G-2875)
Jamplast Inc ....G....... 812 838-8562
Mount Vernon (G-10397)
Matrixx Group Incorporated.................G....... 812 421-3600
Evansville (G-3617)
Monument Chemical LLC ....F....... 317 223-2630
Indianapolis (G-7539)
Polyone Corporation ....G....... 812 466-5116
Terre Haute (G-13305)
Primex Plastics Corporation.................B....... 765 966-7774
Richmond (G-12034)

THERMOSTAT REPAIR SVCS

Grayson Thermal Systems Corp ....C....... 317 739-3290
Franklin (G-4893)

THERMOSTATS: Refrigeration

Digi International Inc ....G....... 877 272-3111
Mishawaka (G-10036)
Smart Temps LLC ....G....... 574 217-8847
Mishawaka (G-10127)

THREAD WHOLESALERS

Sew Creative Threads LLC.................G....... 574 266-7397
Elkhart (G-3163)

THREAD: Embroidery

Groovemade LLC.........................G....... 574 834-1138
North Webster (G-11292)

THREAD: Needle & Handicraft

Elegant Needleworks Inc.........................G....... 765 284-9427
Muncie (G-10468)

TIES, FORM: Metal

Midwest Bale Ties Inc ....E....... 765 364-0113
Crawfordsville (G-2173)

TILE: Brick & Structural, Clay

Meridian Brick LLC ....E....... 812 894-2454
Terre Haute (G-13283)

TILE: Clay, Drain & Structural

Marv Kahlig & Sons Inc ....G....... 260 335-2212
Portland (G-11835)

TILE: Rubber

Valley Tile Corporation ....G....... 812 268-3328
Sullivan (G-13097)

TIMBER PRDTS WHOLESALERS

Shelby Products Corporation.................G....... 317 398-4870
West Harrison (G-14043)

TIMERS: Indl, Clockwork Mechanism Only

Montgomery Manufacturing Co.................G....... 812 724-2505
Owensville (G-11429)

TIN

Arcelormittal USA LLC ....D....... 219 787-2120
Chesterton (G-1595)
Murrays Tin Cup ....G....... 260 349-1002
Kendallville (G-8498)

TIRE & INNER TUBE MATERIALS & RELATED PRDTS

Simon and Sons ....G....... 812 852-3636
Osgood (G-11395)

TIRE DEALERS

Hoosier Racing Tire Corp.........................D....... 574 784-3409
Lakeville (G-9096)
Midwest Auto Repair Inc ....E....... 219 322-0364
Schererville (G-12334)

TIRE INFLATORS: Hand Or Compressor Operated

Wee Engineer Inc ....F....... 765 449-4280
Dayton (G-2362)

TIRE INNER-TUBES

Goodyear Tire & Rubber Company ....G....... 219 762-0651
Portage (G-11767)

TIRES & INNER TUBES

BF Shaffer Co ....G....... 812 949-8356
New Albany (G-10752)
Hoosier Racing Tire Corp.........................D....... 574 784-3409
Lakeville (G-9096)
Rubber Shop Inc ....G....... 574 291-6440
South Bend (G-12924)
Williamsport Tire Mart LLC ....G....... 765 762-6315
Williamsport (G-14300)

TIRES & TUBES WHOLESALERS

Cast Products LP ....E....... 574 294-2684
Elkhart (G-2751)
Dehco Inc ....D....... 574 294-2684
Elkhart (G-2792)
Goodyear Tire & Rubber Company ....G....... 219 762-0651
Portage (G-11767)
Midwest Auto Repair Inc ....E....... 219 322-0364
Schererville (G-12334)

TIRES & TUBES, WHOLESALE: Automotive

BF Goodrich Tire Manufacturing.................G....... 260 493-8100
Woodburn (G-14380)
Hoosier Racing Tire Corp.........................D....... 574 784-3409
Lakeville (G-9096)
Tire Rack Inc ....B....... 888 541-1777
South Bend (G-12972)

TIRES: Auto

Michelin North America Inc.........................A....... 260 493-8100
Woodburn (G-14386)

TIRES: Cushion Or Solid Rubber

Hammer Industries Inc ....F....... 812 422-6953
Evansville (G-3529)

TIRES: Motorcycle, Pneumatic

Enovapremier LLC.........................D....... 812 385-0576
Princeton (G-11870)

TITANIUM MILL PRDTS

GKN Aerospace Muncie Inc ....E....... 765 747-7147
Muncie (G-10477)
Titanium Eagles Nutrition ....G....... 219 781-6018
Lake Station (G-9079)
Titanium LLC.........................G....... 765 236-6906
Kokomo (G-8708)
Titanium Rails Nutrition LLC ....G....... 219 940-3704
Hobart (G-6099)

TOBACCO & PRDTS, WHOLESALE: Smokeless

Black Swan Vapors LLC.........................G....... 317 645-5210
Pendleton (G-11484)

TOBACCO & PRDTS, WHOLESALE: Smoking

Smoker Friendly.........................G....... 812 556-0244
Jasper (G-8309)

TOBACCO LEAF PROCESSING

Kraft Heinz Foods Company.................E....... 260 347-1300
Kendallville (G-8489)

TOBACCO STORES & STANDS

Big Red Liquors Inc.........................G....... 812 339-9552
Bloomington (G-683)

TOBACCO: Chewing

Black Swan Vapors LLC.........................G....... 317 645-5210
Pendleton (G-11484)

TOBACCO: Cigarettes

Big Red Liquors Inc.........................G....... 812 339-9552
Bloomington (G-683)
Fast Lane Foods Inc.........................F....... 219 879-3300
Michigan City (G-9792)
Smoker Friendly.........................G....... 812 556-0244
Jasper (G-8309)
Smokers Host 307.........................G....... 765 938-1877
Rushville (G-12234)
South Bend Smoke Time Inc ....G....... 574 318-4837
South Bend (G-12945)

TOBACCO: Cigars

Angelinas Cigars.........................G....... 574 935-5544
Plymouth (G-11667)
Bob Low Discount Tobacco.................G....... 765 868-9713
Kokomo (G-8600)
Link Rental Company Inc ....G....... 574 946-7373
Winamac (G-14310)
National Cigar Corporation.................E....... 765 659-3326
Frankfort (G-4842)

TOBACCO: Smoking

La Porte Smokes and Beverages ....G....... 219 575-7754
La Porte (G-8783)

TOILETRIES, COSMETICS & PERFUME STORES

Kids World Productions Inc.................G....... 317 674-6090
Zionsville (G-14444)
North Coast Organics LLC.................G....... 260 246-0289
Fort Wayne (G-4505)
Relevo Labs LLC.........................G....... 317 900-6949
Carmel (G-1466)

TOILETRIES, WHOLESALE: Toilet Soap

Tall Cotton Marketing LLC ....G....... 312 320-5862
La Porte (G-8825)

TOILETRIES, WHOLESALE: Toiletries

North Coast Organics LLC ....G..... 260 246-0289
Fort Wayne **(G-4505)**

Past & Present Soap & Snd LLC ....G..... 812 852-4328
Batesville **(G-514)**

TOILETS, PORTABLE, WHOLESALE

Satellite Shelters ....E..... 574 350-2150
Bristol **(G-1084)**

TOILETS: Metal

T S F Co Inc ....E..... 812 985-2630
Evansville **(G-3757)**

TOILETS: Portable Chemical, Plastics

Olympic Fiberglass Industries...............D..... 574 223-3101
Rochester **(G-12142)**

Polyjohn Enterprises Corp.....................D..... 219 659-1152
Whiting **(G-14273)**

TOOL & DIE STEEL

101 Tool & Die LLC ....G..... 260 203-2981
Fort Wayne **(G-4031)**

Advanced Engineering Inc.....................F..... 260 356-8077
Huntington **(G-6184)**

C & G Tool Inc ....G..... 812 524-7061
Jonesville **(G-8448)**

Classic Industries Inc..........................G..... 812 421-4006
Evansville **(G-3418)**

Delaware Dynamics LLC ....D..... 765 284-3335
Muncie **(G-10457)**

Gregs Tool & Machine ....G..... 812 373-9329
Columbus **(G-1934)**

Kirby Machine Company LLC ....F..... 317 773-6700
Noblesville **(G-11138)**

Mc Metalcraft Inc.................................G..... 574 259-8101
Mishawaka **(G-10076)**

Meriwether Tool & Engineering ....F..... 260 744-6955
Fort Wayne **(G-4466)**

Pace Tool and Engineering Inc..............G..... 812 373-9885
Columbus **(G-1988)**

United Machine & Design Inc.................E..... 812 442-7468
Brazil **(G-980)**

TOOL REPAIR SVCS

Perry Products Inc...............................G..... 260 668-7860
Angola **(G-236)**

TOOLS: Carpenters', Including Levels & Chisels, Exc Saws

Airodapt LLC ....G..... 559 331-0156
Rensselaer **(G-11911)**

Carpenter Co Inc ....E..... 317 297-2900
Indianapolis **(G-6557)**

TOOLS: Hand

AK Tool and Die ....G..... 574 286-9010
Mishawaka **(G-9992)**

Brinly-Hardy Company ....D..... 812 218-7200
Jeffersonville **(G-8332)**

BT&f LLC ....G..... 574 272-6128
Granger **(G-5395)**

C-L Building & Leasing Inc ....G..... 574 293-8959
Elkhart **(G-2746)**

Frederick Tool Corp ....E..... 574 295-6700
Elkhart **(G-2870)**

Hogen Industries Inc Indiana.................E..... 317 591-5070
Indianapolis **(G-7111)**

Ideal Pro Cnc Inc.................................F..... 260 693-1954
Churubusco **(G-1652)**

Indiana Precision Tooling Inc ....F..... 812 667-5141
Dillsboro **(G-2468)**

J Porter Mfg Co ....G..... 812 853-9395
Newburgh **(G-11034)**

James W Hager ....G..... 765 643-0188
Alexandria **(G-46)**

Josam Company ....D..... 219 872-5531
Michigan City **(G-9805)**

Kaiser Tool Company Inc ....E..... 260 484-3620
Fort Wayne **(G-4403)**

Laidig Inc ....E..... 574 256-0204
Mishawaka **(G-10067)**

Mid-West Spring Mfg Co ....D..... 574 353-1409
Mentone **(G-9688)**

Nestor Sales LLC ....G..... 574 295-5535
Elkhart **(G-3060)**

Osborn Manufacturing Corp ....F..... 574 267-6156
Warsaw **(G-13920)**

Perry Products Inc...............................G..... 260 668-7860
Angola **(G-236)**

Rich Manufacturing Inc ....G..... 765 436-2744
Lebanon **(G-9220)**

TOOLS: Hand, Carpet Layers

D & D Manufacturing Inc ....G..... 812 432-3294
Dillsboro **(G-2465)**

TOOLS: Hand, Ironworkers'

Indy Stud Welding.................................G..... 317 416-3617
Indianapolis **(G-7223)**

Master Manufacturing Company ....E..... 812 425-1561
Evansville **(G-3615)**

TOOLS: Hand, Power

Black & Decker (us) Inc ....G..... 317 241-1200
Indianapolis **(G-6481)**

Bolttech Mannings Inc..........................F..... 219 310-8389
Crown Point **(G-2230)**

Claymore Tools Inc ....G..... 574 255-6483
Mishawaka **(G-10018)**

Frederick Tool Corp ....E..... 574 295-6700
Elkhart **(G-2870)**

Innovative Rescue Systems Inc ....G..... 219 548-1028
Valparaiso **(G-13560)**

James W Hager ....G..... 765 643-0188
Alexandria **(G-46)**

Stanley Fastening Systems LP...............D..... 317 398-0761
Greenfield **(G-5578)**

Steam Specialties Inc ....G..... 317 849-5601
Fishers **(G-3970)**

TOOLS: Hand, Stonecutters'

Stone Artisans Ltd ....G..... 317 362-0107
Indianapolis **(G-8008)**

TOOTHPASTES, GELS & TOOTHPOWDERS

Dentisse Inc...G..... 260 444-3046
Fort Wayne **(G-4208)**

TOWELS: Indl

Anippe..G..... 317 979-1110
Fishers **(G-3872)**

TOWERS, SECTIONS: Transmission, Radio & Television

Emergency Radio Service LLC...........E..... 317 821-0422
Ligonier **(G-9282)**

Ers Holding Company Inc ....E..... 260 894-4145
Ligonier **(G-9283)**

Ers Tower LLC ....E..... 260 894-4145
Ligonier **(G-9284)**

Ph Inc ....E..... 877 467-4763
Plymouth **(G-11711)**

Pirod Inc..F..... 574 936-7221
Plymouth **(G-11712)**

Swager Communications Inc.................E..... 260 495-2515
Fremont **(G-4976)**

TOWING BARS & SYSTEMS

Landgrebe Manufacturing Inc................G..... 219 462-9587
Valparaiso **(G-13570)**

TOYS

Chelseas Model Horses........................G..... 765 366-1082
Ladoga **(G-8839)**

Christopher Engle ....G..... 812 876-3540
Ellettsville **(G-3274)**

Flambeau Inc ....C..... 812 372-4899
Columbus **(G-1931)**

Gameoto LLC ....G..... 317 883-9322
Indianapolis **(G-6981)**

Geist Bike and Hobby Company ....G..... 317 855-1346
Indianapolis **(G-6990)**

Gener8 LLC ....G..... 317 253-8737
Indianapolis **(G-6991)**

Gigglicious LLC ....G..... 317 272-4064
Avon **(G-441)**

Honey and ME ....G..... 317 668-3924
Franklin **(G-4897)**

Marquette Council 3631 Kn..................G..... 219 864-3255
Griffith **(G-5784)**

Milam Toys Inc ....G..... 765 362-2826
Crawfordsville **(G-2174)**

Purrfectplay ....G..... 219 926-7604
Chesterton **(G-1629)**

Red Wagon ....G..... 260 768-3090
Shipshewana **(G-12646)**

T & G Games Inc ....G..... 574 297-5455
Monticello **(G-10284)**

Tedco Inc ....F..... 765 489-4527
Hagerstown **(G-5814)**

Timberline Scenery LLC ....G..... 260 244-5588
Columbia City **(G-1842)**

Wagon Train Ventures LLC ....G..... 260 625-5301
Fort Wayne **(G-4732)**

TOYS & HOBBY GOODS & SPLYS, WHOLESALE: Arts/Crafts Eqpt/Sply

Honey and ME ....G..... 317 668-3924
Franklin **(G-4897)**

TOYS & HOBBY GOODS & SPLYS, WHOLESALE: Board Games

Continuum Games Incorporated ....G..... 877 405-2662
Indianapolis **(G-6658)**

TOYS & HOBBY GOODS & SPLYS, WHOLESALE: Model Kits

Brasilia Press Inc ....G..... 574 262-9700
Elkhart **(G-2732)**

TOYS & HOBBY GOODS & SPLYS, WHOLESALE: Toys & Games

Gener8 LLC ....G..... 317 253-8737
Indianapolis **(G-6991)**

TOYS & HOBBY GOODS & SPLYS, WHOLESALE: Video Games

Depth Plus Design LLC ....G..... 317 370-0532
Westfield **(G-14158)**

TOYS, HOBBY GOODS & SPLYS WHOLESALERS

American Art Clay Co Inc ....C..... 317 243-0066
Indianapolis **(G-6385)**

Red Wagon ....G..... 260 768-3090
Shipshewana **(G-12646)**

TOYS: Dolls, Stuffed Animals & Parts

Red Wagon ....G..... 260 768-3090
Shipshewana **(G-12646)**

TOYS: Electronic

RC Fun Parks LLC ....G..... 574 217-7715
Granger **(G-5430)**

TOYS: Kites

Kite & Key LLC ....G..... 317 654-7703
Indianapolis **(G-7355)**

TRADING STAMP PROMOTION & REDEMPTION

Tasus Corporation ....C..... 812 333-6500
Bloomington **(G-834)**

TRAFFIC CONTROL FLAGGING SVCS

Highway Safety Services Inc ....G..... 765 474-1000
Lafayette **(G-8915)**

TRAILER COACHES: Automobile

Kzrv LP ....B..... 260 768-4016
Shipshewana **(G-12624)**

New Image Travel LLC...........................E..... 812 426-1423
Evansville **(G-3643)**

TRAILERS & CHASSIS: Camping

Highland Ridge Rv Inc...........................B..... 260 768-7771
Shipshewana **(G-12616)**

Wolfpack Chassis LLC ....E 260 349-1887
Kendallville (G-8514)

TRAILERS & PARTS: Boat

CC Manufacturing Inc ....F 574 293-1696
Elkhart (G-2752)

E Z Loader Boat Trailers Inc ....G 574 266-0092
Elkhart (G-2810)

J Q Tex Inc ....E 574 259-0329
Mishawaka (G-10056)

Spreuer & Son Inc ....G 260 463-3513
Lagrange (G-9067)

T I B Inc ....E 574 892-5151
Argos (G-278)

TRAILERS & PARTS: Horse

Heritage Convertion LLC ....G 574 773-0750
Nappanee (G-10679)

Miller Carriage Co ....G 260 768-4553
Shipshewana (G-12633)

Sierra Motor Corp ....D 574 848-1300
Bristol (G-1086)

TRAILERS & PARTS: Truck & Semi's

Agritraders Mfg Inc ....G 260 238-4225
Spencerville (G-13043)

Aluminum Cargo Trailers Inc ....F 260 463-0185
Lagrange (G-9030)

Alvin J Nix ....G 812 347-2510
Ramsey (G-11892)

Angels Wings Expedited ....F 574 339-3038
South Bend (G-12707)

Atc Trailers Holdings Inc ....C 574 773-2440
Nappanee (G-10651)

Brindle Products Inc ....E 260 627-2156
Grabill (G-5358)

BSB Trans Inc ....G 317 919-8778
Greenwood (G-5672)

Bull Manufacturing LLC ....G 812 530-1064
Brownstown (G-1182)

Bullseye Technologies Inc ....G 574 753-0102
Elkhart (G-2737)

C & J Services & Supplies Inc ....E 317 569-7222
Fort Wayne (G-4130)

Diamonds Componets Inc ....E 574 358-0452
Middlebury (G-9881)

Eaton Corporation ....D 574 288-4446
South Bend (G-12756)

Great Dane LLC ....A 812 443-4711
Brazil (G-962)

Hendrickson International Corp ....C 765 483-5350
Lebanon (G-9187)

Impact Trailers ....G 574 322-4369
Elkhart (G-2929)

Kruz Inc ....E 574 772-6673
Knox (G-8571)

Kuckuck Transport LLC ....G 260 609-0316
South Whitley (G-13001)

Lakota Corp ....E 574 848-1636
Bristol (G-1064)

Quality Steel & Alum Pdts Inc ....E 574 295-8715
Elkhart (G-3130)

Schwartzs Trailer Sales Inc ....G 317 773-2608
Noblesville (G-11181)

Sternberg Inc ....E 812 867-0077
Evansville (G-3751)

Strick Corporation ....B 260 692-6121
Monroe (G-10185)

Superior Mfg Inc ....F 812 983-9900
Elberfeld (G-2639)

Tail Wind Transport ....F 574 343-2157
Elkhart (G-3204)

Talbert Manufacturing Inc ....C 219 866-7141
Rensselaer (G-11942)

Team Spirit Trlrs Elkhart Inc ....E 574 266-2966
Elkhart (G-3209)

TEC Transport LLC ....G 765 534-3253
Noblesville (G-11193)

Travel Lite Inc ....G 574 831-3000
New Paris (G-10999)

Truck Life LLC ....F 219 655-0018
Gary (G-5110)

United Trailers Inc ....G 574 848-7088
Bristol (G-1091)

Vanguard National Trailer Corp ....B 219 253-2000
Monon (G-10179)

Wabash National LP ....D 765 771-5300
Lafayette (G-9017)

Wabash National Corporation ....C 765 659-3856
Frankfort (G-4859)

Wabash National Corporation ....B 765 771-5300
Lafayette (G-9018)

Wabash National Mfg LP ....D 765 771-5310
Lafayette (G-9019)

Whitewater Valley Rvs Inc ....G 765 458-5171
Liberty (G-9272)

TRAILERS & TRAILER EQPT

Chubbs Steel Sales Inc ....E 574 295-3166
Elkhart (G-2757)

Collins Trailers Inc ....G 574 294-2561
Elkhart (G-2762)

Flj Transport LLC ....G 574 642-0200
Goshen (G-5215)

Hadley Products Corporation ....F 574 266-3700
Elkhart (G-2905)

Iea Management Services Inc ....G 765 832-8526
Clinton (G-1716)

Logistick Inc ....G 800 758-5840
South Bend (G-12844)

MO Trailer Corporation ....F 574 533-0824
Goshen (G-5295)

Nomanco Trailers ....G 765 833-6711
Roann (G-12097)

Olympic Fiberglass Industries ....D 574 223-3101
Rochester (G-12142)

P R F ....G 219 477-8660
Portage (G-11787)

Rapsure Inc ....G 574 773-2995
Nappanee (G-10704)

Ridge Trailers ....G 260 244-5443
Columbia City (G-1828)

Saladin Trailer Sales Inc ....F 812 692-5288
Elnora (G-3291)

Supreme Industries Inc ....D 574 642-3070
Goshen (G-5336)

Vintage Trailers Ltd ....E 574 522-2261
Elkhart (G-3246)

Zieman Manufacturing Company ....G 574 522-5202
Goshen (G-5347)

TRAILERS OR VANS: Horse Transportation, Fifth-Wheel Type

Heartcare LLC ....G 260 432-7000
Fort Wayne (G-4327)

TRAILERS: Bodies

Agri - Traders & Repair LLC ....G 260 238-4225
Spencerville (G-13042)

Delphi Body Works ....F 765 564-2212
Delphi (G-2417)

Durcholz Excavating & Cnstr Co ....G 812 634-1764
Huntingburg (G-6161)

Fontaine Trailer Company ....G 574 772-6673
Knox (G-8566)

H & H Sales Company Inc ....F 260 637-3177
Huntertown (G-6139)

Intech Trailers Inc ....D 574 773-9536
Nappanee (G-10685)

LCI Industries ....D 574 535-1125
Elkhart (G-2989)

Strick Trailers LLC ....G 260 692-6121
Monroe (G-10186)

TRAILERS: Camping, Tent-Type

Forest River Inc ....C 574 264-5179
Elkhart (G-2861)

Forest River Inc ....C 574 264-2513
Goshen (G-5218)

Forest River Inc ....C 574 642-3112
Goshen (G-5219)

Forest River Inc ....C 574 262-2212
Elkhart (G-2864)

Forest River Inc ....C 574 848-1335
Bristol (G-1060)

Yurts of America Inc ....G 317 377-9878
Indianapolis (G-8225)

TRAILERS: Demountable Cargo Containers

Forest River Inc ....C 574 848-1335
Bristol (G-1060)

H John Enterprise Inc ....E 574 293-6008
Elkhart (G-2903)

Millers Superior Entps Inc ....F 877 475-5665
Middlebury (G-9909)

Pace American Enterprises Inc ....E 800 247-5767
Middlebury (G-9914)

Universal Trlr Crgo Group Inc ....B 574 264-9661
Bristol (G-1092)

Wellco Holdings Inc ....C 574 264-9661
Elkhart (G-3257)

TRAILERS: House, Exc Permanent Dwellings

Jayco Inc ....A 574 825-5861
Middlebury (G-9896)

Kropf Industries Inc ....E 574 533-2171
Goshen (G-5258)

TRAILERS: Semitrailers, Truck Tractors

Rail Protection Plus LLC ....G 812 399-1084
New Albany (G-10853)

TRAILERS: Truck, Chassis

Lantzs Coachworks Inc ....G 317 487-1111
Indianapolis (G-7380)

Zieman Manufacturing Company ....G 574 522-5202
Goshen (G-5347)

TRANSDUCERS: Electrical Properties

Mark Russell ....G 812 386-8069
Princeton (G-11877)

TRANSFORMERS: Distribution

Hoffmaster Electric Inc ....G 219 616-1313
Schererville (G-12323)

Powers Energy America Inc ....G 812 473-5500
Evansville (G-3680)

TRANSFORMERS: Electronic

Custom Magnetics Inc ....E 773 463-6500
North Manchester (G-11228)

Xfmrs Inc ....A 317 834-1066
Camby (G-1272)

TRANSFORMERS: Furnace, Electric

Ajax Tocco Magnethermic Corp ....G 317 352-9880
Indianapolis (G-6357)

TRANSFORMERS: Power Related

Ball Systems Inc ....E 317 804-2330
Westfield (G-14138)

Coil Tran Corp ....D 219 942-8511
Hobart (G-6076)

Kay Industries Inc ....F 574 236-6220
Plymouth (G-11698)

R & R Regulators Inc ....F 574 522-5846
Elkhart (G-3134)

R B Annis Instruments Inc ....G 765 848-1621
Greencastle (G-5476)

Schneider Electric Usa Inc ....F 260 356-2060
Huntington (G-6247)

Whiting Clean Energy Inc ....E 219 473-0653
Whiting (G-14277)

Xfmrs Inc ....A 317 834-1066
Camby (G-1272)

TRANSFORMERS: Specialty

Custom Magnetics Inc ....E 773 463-6500
North Manchester (G-11227)

TRANSLATION & INTERPRETATION SVCS

Inari Information Services ....G 812 331-2298
Bloomington (G-743)

TRANSMISSIONS: Motor Vehicle

Allied Enterprises Inc ....E 765 288-8849
Muncie (G-10428)

Allomatic Products Company ....C 800 686-4729
Sullivan (G-13078)

American Gorwood Corporation ....E 765 948-3401
Fairmount (G-3829)

Borgwarner Pds Anderson LLC ....C 765 778-6499
Anderson (G-76)

FCA US LLC ....A 765 454-1705
Kokomo (G-8622)

Mor/Ryde Inc ....C 574 293-1581
Elkhart (G-3046)

Mor/Ryde International Inc ....E 574 293-1581
Elkhart (G-3049)

Morris Holding Company LLC ....C...... 812 446-6141
Brazil (G-970)

Morris Mfg & Sls Corp ....C...... 812 446-6141
Brazil (G-971)

Mosey Manufacturing Co Inc ....C...... 765 983-8870
Richmond (G-12020)

Nagakura Engrg Works Co Inc ....C...... 812 375-1382
Columbus (G-1978)

Pullman Company...............B...... 260 667-2200
Angola (G-241)

Teal Automotive Inc ....E...... 765 768-7726
Dunkirk (G-2489)

TRANSPORTATION EPQT & SPLYS, WHOL: Aircraft Engs/Eng Parts

Troy Meggitt Inc ....D...... 812 547-7071
Troy (G-13448)

TRANSPORTATION EPQT & SPLYS, WHOLESALE: Acft/Space Vehicle

Indiana Aircraft Hardware Co ....G...... 317 485-6500
Fortville (G-4780)

TRANSPORTATION EPQT & SPLYS, WHOLESALE: Combat Vehicles

Wbh Inc ....F...... 317 269-1510
Indianapolis (G-8180)

TRANSPORTATION EPQT & SPLYS, WHOLESALE: Pulleys

R & R Regulators Inc ....F...... 574 522-5846
Elkhart (G-3134)

TRANSPORTATION EPQT & SPLYS, WHOLESALE: Tanks & Tank Compnts

Norman Stein & Associates ....F...... 260 749-5468
New Haven (G-10950)

TRANSPORTATION EPQT/SPLYS, WHOL: Marine Propulsn Mach/Eqpt

Allied Enterprises Inc ....E...... 765 288-8849
Muncie (G-10428)

TRANSPORTATION EQPT & SPLYS WHOLESALERS, NEC

Turbines Inc...............E...... 812 877-2587
Terre Haute (G-13359)

TRANSPORTATION EQUIPMENT, NEC

Innovative Equipment Inc ....G...... 765 572-2367
Westpoint (G-14206)

Mighty Transport LLC...............G...... 812 401-7433
Chandler (G-1552)

Professional Comp Naskart Inc...............G...... 765 552-9745
Elwood (G-3309)

TRANSPORTATION SVCS, WATER: Canal Barge Operations

American Barge Line Company...............G...... 812 288-0100
Jeffersonville (G-8323)

American Coml Barge Line LLC ....C...... 812 288-0100
Jeffersonville (G-8324)

American Commercial Lines Inc ....C...... 812 288-0100
Jeffersonville (G-8325)

Commercial Barge Line Company ....F...... 812 288-0100
Jeffersonville (G-8341)

TRANSPORTATION: Bus Transit Systems

Cardinal Services Inc Indiana ....D...... 574 267-3823
Warsaw (G-13853)

TRANSPORTATION: Water Freight, NEC

Acl Professional Services Inc...............B...... 812 288-0100
Jeffersonville (G-8317)

TRAP ROCK: Crushed & Broken

S & G Excavating Inc...............D...... 812 234-4848
Terre Haute (G-13322)

TRAPS: Stem

Hoffman Sls & Specialty Co Inc...............G...... 317 846-6428
Carmel (G-1406)

TRAVEL AGENCIES

American Express Travel ....C...... 812 523-0106
Seymour (G-12430)

New Image Travel LLC...............E...... 812 426-1423
Evansville (G-3643)

R Drew & Co Inc ....F...... 765 420-7232
West Lafayette (G-14100)

TRAVEL TRAILER DEALERS

Bullseye Technologies Inc...............G...... 574 753-0102
Elkhart (G-2737)

TRAVEL TRAILERS & CAMPERS

All American Group Inc ....B...... 574 825-8555
Middlebury (G-9868)

All American Group Inc ....E...... 574 262-0123
Elkhart (G-2674)

Bison Coach LLC ....E...... 574 658-4161
Milford (G-9949)

Damon Corporation ....F...... 574 262-2624
Elkhart (G-2787)

Dmi Holding Corp ....C...... 574 534-1224
Goshen (G-5200)

Dna Enterprises Inc ....E...... 574 534-0034
Goshen (G-5201)

Ds Corp ....C...... 260 593-3850
Topeka (G-13417)

Evergreen Recrtl Vehicles LLC ....F...... 574 825-4298
Middlebury (G-9886)

Forest River Inc ....F...... 574 389-4636
Middlebury (G-9887)

Forest River Inc ....C...... 574 296-7700
Elkhart (G-2866)

Forest River Inc ....C...... 574 533-5934
Goshen (G-5217)

Forest River Inc ....C...... 574 262-3474
Elkhart (G-2862)

Forest River Cherokee Inc ....G...... 260 593-2566
Topeka (G-13418)

Forest River Custom Extrusions ....G...... 574 975-0206
Goshen (G-5220)

Forest River Vibe ....G...... 574 296-2084
Elkhart (G-2867)

Gulf Stream Coach Inc ....C...... 574 773-7761
Nappanee (G-10677)

Homette Corporation ....G...... 574 294-6521
Elkhart (G-2919)

Hy-Line Enterprises Intl Inc ....D...... 574 294-1112
Elkhart (G-2924)

Independent Protection Co Inc...............D...... 574 831-5680
New Paris (G-10985)

Keystone Rv Company ....C...... 574 535-2100
Goshen (G-5254)

Keystone Rv Company ....D...... 574 534-9430
Goshen (G-5255)

Keystone Rv Company ....C...... 574 535-2100
Goshen (G-5256)

L S R Conversions LLC ....F...... 574 206-9610
Elkhart (G-2979)

Layton Homes Corporation ....G...... 574 294-6521
Elkhart (G-2987)

Layton Homes Corporation ....D...... 574 294-6521
Elkhart (G-2988)

LGS Pace International Inc ....G...... 574 848-5665
Middlebury (G-9903)

Lippert Components Inc...............C...... 574 971-4320
Goshen (G-5275)

Livin Lite Corp ....E...... 574 862-2228
Shipshewana (G-12631)

Newmar Corporation ....A...... 574 773-7791
Nappanee (G-10699)

Rance Aluminum Fabrication ....E...... 574 266-9028
Elkhart (G-3137)

Recreation By Design LLC...............D...... 574 294-2117
Elkhart (G-3140)

Skyline Champion Corporation ....B...... 574 294-6521
Elkhart (G-3175)

Skyline Homes Inc ....C...... 574 294-6521
Elkhart (G-3176)

Spectrum Rv LLC...............G...... 574 970-5554
Elkhart (G-3184)

Starcraft Corporation...............E...... 574 534-7827
Goshen (G-5329)

Starcraft Rv Inc ....B...... 800 945-4787
Middlebury (G-9921)

Supreme Corporation ....A...... 574 642-4888
Goshen (G-5332)

Supreme Corporation ....B...... 260 894-9191
Ligonier (G-9298)

Thor Motor Coach Inc ....B...... 574 266-1111
Elkhart (G-3216)

Thorntons Welding ....G...... 812 332-8564
Bloomington (G-841)

TI Industries Inc ....E...... 419 666-8144
Elkhart (G-3219)

Two Rivers Camping Club I...............G...... 812 838-3687
Mount Vernon (G-10411)

Wabash National LP ....D...... 765 771-5300
Lafayette (G-9017)

Winnebago of Indiana LLC ....C...... 574 825-5250
Middlebury (G-9926)

TRAVELER ACCOMMODATIONS, NEC

All Occasions Gift Shop LLC ....G...... 513 314-5693
Metamora (G-9762)

Colluci Construction-Log Homes ....G...... 812 843-5607
English (G-3312)

TROPHIES, NEC

Bruce Fox Inc ....C...... 812 945-3511
New Albany (G-10754)

TROPHIES, SILVER

A-1 Awards Inc ....F...... 317 546-9000
Indianapolis (G-6301)

TROPHIES, WHOLESALE

Bruce Fox Inc ....C...... 812 945-3511
New Albany (G-10754)

First Place Trophy Inc...............G...... 574 293-6147
Elkhart (G-2850)

Imperial Trophy & Awards Co ....G...... 260 432-8161
Fort Wayne (G-4361)

Ram Graphics Inc ....E...... 765 724-7783
Alexandria (G-48)

Tower Advertising Products Inc ....D...... 260 593-2103
Topeka (G-13431)

TROPHIES: Metal, Exc Silver

Classic Trophy Co...............F...... 260 483-1161
Fort Wayne (G-4161)

Professional Bowling Ball Svc ....G...... 317 786-4329
Indianapolis (G-7770)

Tic Toc Trophy Shop Inc ....G...... 574 893-4234
Akron (G-8)

Trophies & Awards Inc ....G...... 260 925-4672
Auburn (G-365)

TROPHY & PLAQUE STORES

Aceys Trophies & Awards ....G...... 574 267-1426
Warsaw (G-13835)

Awards Unlimited Inc ....G...... 765 447-9413
Lafayette (G-8858)

Bc Awards Inc ....G...... 317 852-3240
Brownsburg (G-1136)

Carmel Traphies Plus ....G...... 317 844-3770
Carmel (G-1332)

Classic Trophy Co...............F...... 260 483-1161
Fort Wayne (G-4161)

First Place Trophies ....G...... 812 385-3279
Princeton (G-11872)

First Place Trophy Inc...............G...... 574 293-6147
Elkhart (G-2850)

Game Plan Graphics LLC ....G...... 812 663-3238
Greensburg (G-5602)

Golden Frame Inc...............G...... 812 232-0048
Terre Haute (G-13242)

Hoosier Badge & Trophies Inc...............G...... 317 257-4441
Indianapolis (G-7120)

Imperial Trophy & Awards Co ....G...... 260 432-8161
Fort Wayne (G-4361)

Jef Enterprises Inc ....F...... 812 425-0628
Evansville (G-3573)

Jer-Maur Corporation ....G...... 812 384-8290
Bloomfield (G-640)

Johnson Engraving & Trophies...............G...... 260 982-7868
North Manchester (G-11232)

Larry H Poole...............G...... 812 466-9345
Terre Haute (G-13272)

P
R
O
D
U
C
T

New Haven Trophies & Shirts .... G 260 749-0269
New Haven (G-10949)

Parlor City Trophy & Apparel .... G 260 824-0216
Bluffton (G-884)

Parsing Laser Designs LLC .... G 317 677-4316
Avon (G-460)

Recognition Plus .... G 812 232-2372
Terre Haute (G-13316)

Regal Inc .... G 765 747-1155
Muncie (G-10557)

Schug Awards LLC .... G 765 447-0002
Lafayette (G-8996)

Specialty Shoppe .... G 574 772-7873
Knox (G-8582)

Tic Toc Trophy Shop Inc .... G 574 893-4234
Akron (G-8)

Trophies & Awards Inc .... G 260 925-4672
Auburn (G-365)

Van Der Weele Jon D .... G 574 892-5005
Argos (G-280)

Varsity Sports Inc .... G 219 987-7200
Demotte (G-2451)

Wanda Harrington .... G 765 642-1628
Anderson (G-182)

Winning Edge of Rochester Inc .... F 574 223-6090
Rochester (G-12162)

TRUCK & BUS BODIES: Ambulance

Sjc Industries Corp .... C 574 264-7511
Elkhart (G-3174)

TRUCK & BUS BODIES: Automobile Wrecker Truck

Chads LLC .... G 812 323-7377
Ellettsville (G-3273)

Grahams Wrecker Service Inc .... G 317 736-4355
Franklin (G-4892)

TRUCK & BUS BODIES: Beverage Truck

Cowan Systems LLC .... G 317 241-4158
Indianapolis (G-6681)

TRUCK & BUS BODIES: Cement Mixer

Indiana Phoenix Inc .... D 260 897-4397
Avilla (G-406)

McNeilus Truck and Mfg Inc .... G 260 489-3031
Fort Wayne (G-4462)

TRUCK & BUS BODIES: Dump Truck

Gea Inc .... G 812 944-1401
New Albany (G-10786)

Gerald S Zins .... G 812 623-4980
Milan (G-9944)

Kruz Inc .... E 574 772-6673
Knox (G-8571)

S CJ Incorporated .... F 317 822-3477
Indianapolis (G-7879)

Wimmer Lime Service Inc .... G 765 948-4001
Fairmount (G-3835)

TRUCK & BUS BODIES: Garbage Or Refuse Truck

Autocar LLC .... C 765 489-5499
Hagerstown (G-5803)

Roys Disposal .... G 812 721-3443
Oakland City (G-11314)

TRUCK & BUS BODIES: Motor Vehicle, Specialty

Delivery Concepts Inc .... E 574 522-3981
Elkhart (G-2793)

Mavron Inc .... F 574 267-3044
Warsaw (G-13904)

Monroe Custom Utility Bodies .... D 317 894-8684
Greenfield (G-5558)

Sharp Wraps LLC .... G 317 989-8447
Zionsville (G-14462)

TRUCK & BUS BODIES: Tank Truck

Wannemuehler Distribution Inc .... F 812 422-3251
Evansville (G-3809)

TRUCK & BUS BODIES: Truck Beds

Mooresville Welding Inc .... G 317 831-2265
Mooresville (G-10324)

Rowe Truck Equipment Inc .... D 765 583-4461
Otterbein (G-11421)

TRUCK & BUS BODIES: Truck Cabs, Motor Vehicles

American Reliance Inds Co .... E 260 768-4704
Shipshewana (G-12603)

Indiana Custom Trucks LLC .... E 260 463-3244
Lagrange (G-9046)

Supreme Corporation .... B 574 642-4888
Goshen (G-5333)

TRUCK & BUS BODIES: Truck Tops

Leer Midwest .... F 574 522-5337
Elkhart (G-2992)

TRUCK & BUS BODIES: Truck, Motor Vehicle

B & G Truck Conversions Inc .... F 574 892-6666
Argos (G-272)

Bay Bridge Manufacturing Inc .... E 574 848-7477
Bristol (G-1048)

Brindle Products Inc .... E 260 627-2156
Grabill (G-5358)

Delphi Body Works .... F 765 564-2212
Delphi (G-2417)

H & H Sales Company Inc .... F 260 637-3177
Huntertown (G-6139)

M H EBY Inc .... F 574 753-4000
Logansport (G-9353)

Manasek Acquisition Co LLC .... E 765 551-1600
Elwood (G-3305)

Morgan Olson LLC .... G 269 659-0243
Angola (G-231)

NRC Modifications Inc .... F 574 825-3646
Middlebury (G-9912)

Supreme Corporation .... A 574 642-4888
Goshen (G-5332)

Supreme Corporation .... B 260 894-9191
Ligonier (G-9298)

Wiers Fleet Partners Inc .... F 574 936-4076
Plymouth (G-11737)

TRUCK & BUS BODIES: Van Bodies

Herberts Truck & Van .... G 812 663-6970
Greensburg (G-5608)

Independent Protection Co Inc .... G 574 533-4116
Goshen (G-5243)

TRUCK BODIES: Body Parts

Accuride Corporation .... C 812 962-5000
Evansville (G-3336)

Armor Parent Corp .... F 812 962-5000
Evansville (G-3366)

Bentz Transport Products Inc .... F 260 622-9100
Zionsville (G-14422)

Double Eagle Industries Inc .... E 260 768-4121
Shipshewana (G-12612)

Hausers Reclamation & REM .... G 812 663-6378
Burney (G-1212)

Kneppers Inc .... F 260 636-2180
Albion (G-29)

Mantra Enterprise LLC .... G 201 428-8709
Fishers (G-3944)

R & B Associates Inc .... G 812 471-1550
Evansville (G-3693)

Vanguard National Trailer Corp .... B 219 253-2000
Monon (G-10179)

TRUCK BODY SHOP

Harmon Boats Inc .... G 765 963-5358
Sharpsville (G-12506)

TRUCK DRIVER SVCS

Majesty Enterprises Inc .... G 812 752-6446
Scottsburg (G-12372)

R & A Goodman Enterprises .... G 765 296-3446
Lafayette (G-8987)

TRUCK GENERAL REPAIR SVC

CD & Ws Bordner Entps Inc .... G 765 268-2120
Cutler (G-2328)

TRUCK PAINTING & LETTERING SVCS

Alveys Sign Co Inc .... E 812 867-2567
Evansville (G-3350)

B B & H Signs Incorporated .... G 812 235-1340
Terre Haute (G-13196)

Martin Signs & Crane Services .... G 317 908-9708
Indianapolis (G-7460)

Schaffsteins Truck Clean LLC .... F 812 464-2424
Evansville (G-3715)

Steve Reiff Inc .... D 260 723-4360
South Whitley (G-13005)

TRUCK PARTS & ACCESSORIES: Wholesalers

Switzerland Hills Inc .... E 812 594-2810
Patriot (G-11469)

TRUCKING & HAULING SVCS: Contract Basis

Haas Cabinet Co Inc .... C 812 246-4431
Sellersburg (G-12395)

TRUCKING & HAULING SVCS: Haulage & Cartage, Light, Local

Lees Ready-Mix & Trucking Inc .... F 812 372-1800
Columbus (G-1958)

TRUCKING & HAULING SVCS: Heavy Machinery, Local

Industrial Mint Wldg Machining .... E 219 393-5531
Kingsbury (G-8539)

TRUCKING & HAULING SVCS: Lumber & Log, Local

Blackwood Solutions Inc .... G 812 824-6728
Bloomington (G-684)

TRUCKING & HAULING SVCS: Steel, Local

Jec Steel Company .... G 574 326-3829
Elkhart (G-2946)

TRUCKING, DUMP

Gravel Conveyors Inc .... F 317 873-8686
Zionsville (G-14435)

Kellers Limestone Service .... F 219 326-1688
La Porte (G-8776)

LPI Paving & Excavating .... G 260 726-9564
Portland (G-11834)

Van Duyne Block and Gravel .... G 574 223-6656
Rochester (G-12159)

TRUCKING: Except Local

Frick Services Inc .... E 260 761-3311
Wawaka (G-14032)

Jennings County Pallets Inc .... E 812 458-6288
Butlerville (G-1249)

Southlake Lift Truck .... G 219 962-4695
Gary (G-5100)

TRUCKING: Local, With Storage

Blackwood Solutions Inc .... G 812 824-6728
Bloomington (G-684)

Ruben Martinez .... G 574 735-0803
Logansport (G-9363)

TRUCKING: Local, Without Storage

C & C Pallets and Lumber LLC .... G 765 524-3214
New Castle (G-10895)

Circle R Industries Inc .... G 765 379-2768
Rossville (G-12210)

Fred Jay Stewart .... F 765 284-1386
Muncie (G-10474)

Goh Con Inc .... E 812 282-1349
Clarksville (G-1682)

Jadcore LLC .... C 812 234-2724
Terre Haute (G-13260)

Kendallville Iron & Metal Inc .... E 260 347-1958
Kendallville (G-8486)

Krafft Gravel Inc .... G 260 238-4653
Spencerville (G-13049)

Lees Ready-Mix & Trucking ....G.... 812 522-7270
Seymour (G-12466)

Lees Ready-Mix & Trucking Inc ....E.... 812 346-9767
North Vernon (G-11267)

Paddack Brothers Inc ....F.... 765 659-4777
Frankfort (G-4849)

Rex Alton & Companies Inc ....E.... 812 882-8519
Vincennes (G-13701)

TRUCKS & TRACTORS: Industrial

AM General LLC ....A.... 574 258-7523
Mishawaka (G-9995)

American Truck Company LLC ....F.... 260 969-4510
Fort Wayne (G-4074)

Bemcor Inc ....F.... 219 937-1600
Hammond (G-5850)

Buhrt Engineering & Cnstr..................E.... 574 267-3720
Warsaw (G-13852)

Eaton Corporation ....C.... 260 925-3800
Auburn (G-328)

Eaton Corporation ....D.... 574 288-4446
South Bend (G-12756)

Elpers Truck Equipment LLC ....F.... 812 423-5787
Evansville (G-3474)

Galfab LLC ....D.... 574 946-7767
Winamac (G-14306)

Gleason Industrial Pdts Inc ....C.... 574 533-1141
Goshen (G-5227)

Great Dane LLC ....A.... 812 443-4711
Brazil (G-962)

Hirata Corporation of America.............E.... 317 856-8600
Indianapolis (G-7109)

Hy-TEC Fiberglass Inc.........................G.... 260 489-6601
Fort Wayne (G-4352)

Industrial Transmission Eqp ....E.... 574 936-3028
Plymouth (G-11694)

JD Materials..G.... 219 662-1418
Crown Point (G-2268)

Joyce/Dayton Corp..............................D.... 260 726-9361
Portland (G-11831)

Lafayette Wire Products Inc ....D.... 765 474-7896
Lafayette (G-8952)

Laidig Inc ....E.... 574 256-0204
Mishawaka (G-10067)

Major Tool and Machine Inc ....B.... 317 636-6433
Indianapolis (G-7446)

Mooresville Welding Inc ....G.... 317 831-2265
Mooresville (G-10324)

Nelson J Hochstetler ....G.... 260 499-0315
Howe (G-6130)

Nomanco Trailers.................................G.... 765 833-6711
Roann (G-12097)

Ogden Welding Systems Inc ....E.... 219 322-5252
Schererville (G-12341)

Pierce Tracy..G.... 765 748-2361
Anderson (G-152)

Rance Aluminum Fabrication ....E.... 574 266-9028
Elkhart (G-3137)

Selking International Inc ....G.... 574 522-2001
Elkhart (G-3161)

Selking International Inc ....E.... 260 482-3000
Fort Wayne (G-4615)

Stahl Equipment Inc ....E.... 812 925-3341
Chandler (G-1554)

Storageworks Inc ....G.... 317 577-3511
Fishers (G-3971)

Supreme Corporation Georgia ....G.... 574 228-4130
Goshen (G-5335)

Supreme Industries Inc ....D.... 574 642-3070
Goshen (G-5336)

Wiese Holding Company ....E.... 317 241-8600
Indianapolis (G-8194)

TRUCKS: Forklift

Basiloid Products Corp ....E.... 812 692-5511
Elnora (G-3286)

Hoist Liftruck Mfg LLC ....B.... 708 552-2722
East Chicago (G-2533)

Michiana Forklift Inc ....F.... 574 326-3702
Elkhart (G-3031)

Southlake Lift Truck ....G.... 219 962-4695
Gary (G-5100)

Toyota Industrial Eqp Mfg Inc ....B.... 812 342-0060
Columbus (G-2024)

TRUCKS: Indl

All Borders Expediting LLC ....G.... 260 459-1434
Fort Wayne (G-4058)

Arctrans LLC ....F.... 317 231-1620
Indianapolis (G-6417)

Clp Towne Inc ....G.... 574 233-3183
South Bend (G-12737)

Extreme Trailer Service LLC ....G.... 812 406-1984
Charlestown (G-1566)

Fuentes Distributing ....G.... 219 808-2147
Hammond (G-5882)

Gypsum Express Ltd ....G.... 812 247-2648
Shoals (G-12666)

Ruben Martinez ....G.... 574 735-0803
Logansport (G-9363)

Two Sticks Inc ....G.... 219 926-7910
Chesterton (G-1635)

TRUSSES & FRAMING: Prefabricated Metal

B & A Cnstr & Design Inc ....F.... 812 683-4600
Huntingburg (G-6150)

Carter-Lee Building Components..........E.... 317 639-5431
Indianapolis (G-6561)

TRUSSES: Wood, Floor

Beachwood Lumber Co Inc...................F.... 574 858-9325
Warsaw (G-13843)

Georgetown Truss Company Inc..........E.... 812 951-2647
Georgetown (G-5145)

Kerkhoff Associates Inc ....E.... 765 583-4491
Otterbein (G-11419)

White Water Truss Llc ....G.... 765 489-6261
Hagerstown (G-5816)

TRUSSES: Wood, Roof

Bryant Products Inc.............................F.... 812 522-5929
Seymour (G-12435)

Carter Lee Building Component............D.... 317 834-5380
Mooresville (G-10305)

Carter-Lee Building Components..........E.... 317 639-5431
Indianapolis (G-6561)

Classic Truss WD Cmponents Inc........E.... 812 944-5821
Clarksville (G-1678)

Custom Moulding..................................G.... 812 636-7110
Odon (G-11323)

Daviess County Metal Sales ....D.... 812 486-4299
Cannelburg (G-1284)

K & K Industries Inc............................D.... 812 486-3281
Montgomery (G-10229)

Martin Truss Manufacturing.................G.... 574 862-4457
Elkhart (G-3021)

Meadors & Assoc Inc ....G.... 317 736-6944
Franklin (G-4906)

Michiana Column & Truss LLC.............F.... 574 862-2828
Wakarusa (G-13788)

North Webster Construction Inc...........E.... 574 834-4448
North Webster (G-11297)

Premier Truss & Lumber Company.......F.... 574 498-6022
Tippecanoe (G-13386)

Stark Truss Company Inc.....................D.... 219 866-2772
Rensselaer (G-11940)

Superior Truss & Panel Inc ....E.... 708 339-1200
Gary (G-5103)

Truss Partners LLC ....D.... 765 675-5700
Tipton (G-13409)

Truss Systems Inc ....F.... 812 897-3064
Boonville (G-923)

Wagner Truss Manufacturing ....F.... 812 852-2206
Napoleon (G-10643)

TUB CONTAINERS: Plastic

Meese Inc...D.... 812 273-1008
Madison (G-9485)

Priority Plastics Inc..............................D.... 260 726-7000
Portland (G-11843)

TUBE & PIPE MILL EQPT

Fab-Tech Industries ....G.... 765 478-4191
Cambridge City (G-1256)

Systems Contracting Corp....................F.... 765 361-2991
Crawfordsville (G-2200)

TUBE & TUBING FABRICATORS

A S C Industries Inc ....E.... 574 264-1987
Elkhart (G-2659)

A/C Fabricating Corp ....E.... 574 534-1415
Goshen (G-5163)

B&J Rocket America Inc ....E.... 574 825-5802
Middlebury (G-9874)

Curtis Products Inc ....E.... 574 289-4891
South Bend (G-12745)

Elkhart Products Corporation ....B.... 574 264-3181
Elkhart (G-2829)

Fabshop ....G.... 317 549-1681
Reelsville (G-11901)

Globe Mechanical Inc ....D.... 812 949-2001
New Albany (G-10788)

Green Lake Tube LLC ....E.... 219 397-0495
East Chicago (G-2531)

Industrial Tube Components Inc ....G.... 317 431-2188
Lizton (G-9316)

Indy Tube Fabrication LLC ....G.... 317 883-2000
Franklin (G-4900)

Jae Enterprises Inc ....E.... 260 747-0568
Fort Wayne (G-4391)

Jae Enterprises Inc ....G.... 260 489-6249
Fort Wayne (G-4392)

Nelson Global Products Inc ....D.... 608 719-1752
Fort Wayne (G-4493)

Quality Hydraulic & Mch Svc ....G.... 317 892-2596
Danville (G-2355)

Russells Tube Forming Inc ....E.... 317 241-4072
Indianapolis (G-7874)

Tcb Enterprises LLC ....F.... 574 522-3971
Elkhart (G-3207)

Tube Processing Corp ....C.... 317 782-9486
Indianapolis (G-8108)

Whipp In Holdings LLC ....C.... 260 478-2363
Fort Wayne (G-4752)

TUBES: Extruded Or Drawn, Aluminum

Alconex Specialty Products..................D.... 260 744-3446
Fort Wayne (G-4056)

Arconic Inc ....A.... 765 771-3600
Lafayette (G-8852)

TUBES: Finned, For Heat Transfer

Stewart Warner South Wind.................G.... 812 547-7071
Indianapolis (G-8005)

TUBES: Gas Or Vapor

Vapourflow LLC....................................G.... 812 284-5204
Jeffersonville (G-8438)

TUBES: Generator, Electron Beam, Beta Ray

Iotron Industries USA Inc ....E.... 260 212-1722
Columbia City (G-1798)

TUBES: Light Sensing & Emitting

HB Connect Inc ....D.... 260 422-1212
Fort Wayne (G-4324)

TUBES: Mailing

Precision Products Group Inc ....B.... 330 698-4711
Indianapolis (G-6276)

TUBES: Paper

Mach 1 Paper and Poly Pdts Inc..........G.... 574 522-4500
Elkhart (G-3012)

Phenix Tube Corp.................................G.... 260 424-3734
Fort Wayne (G-4528)

Precision Products Group Inc ....C.... 301 474-3100
Indianapolis (G-6277)

Stone Industrial Inc..............................C.... 301 474-3100
Fort Wayne (G-4652)

TUBES: Steel & Iron

Allied Tube & Conduit Corp ....E.... 765 459-8811
Kokomo (G-8590)

Avis Industrial Corporation...................E.... 765 998-8100
Upland (G-13468)

Midwest Tube Mills Inc ....D.... 812 265-1553
Madison (G-9487)

Nelson Acquisition LLC ....D.... 574 753-6377
Logansport (G-9358)

Seymour Tubing Inc..............................B.... 812 523-0842
Seymour (G-12488)

Steel Warehouse of Ohio LLC ....G.... 574 236-5100
South Bend (G-12956)

TUBES: Television

J&L Uebelhor Enterprises LLC ....B.... 812 367-1591
Ferdinand (G-3854)

PRODUCT

TUBES: Welded, Aluminum

Overton & Sons TI & Die Co Inc ....E 317 736-7700
Franklin **(G-4918)**

TUBES: Wrought, Welded Or Lock Joint

Bock Industries Inc ....D 574 295-8070
Elkhart **(G-2729)**
Ljt Texas LLC ....E 800 257-6859
South Bend **(G-12842)**
Plymouth Tube Company ....C 574 946-6657
Winamac **(G-14316)**

TUBING, COLD-DRAWN: Mech Or Hypodermic Sizes, Stainless

American Hydroformers Inc ....F 260 428-2660
Fort Wayne **(G-4072)**
Schuyler Corp ....F 574 533-2597
Goshen **(G-5321)**

TUBING: Flexible, Metallic

OHM Enterprise LLC ....G 812 879-5455
Gosport **(G-5354)**
Parker-Hannifin Corporation ....E 260 587-9102
Ashley **(G-289)**

TUBING: Plastic

Filtration Parts Incorporated ....F 704 661-8135
Rensselaer **(G-11923)**
Precision Products Group Inc ....B 330 698-4711
Indianapolis **(G-6276)**
S H Leggitt Company ....G 574 264-0230
Elkhart **(G-3152)**
Sabin Corporation ....C 812 323-4500
Bloomington **(G-820)**
Stone Industrial Inc ....C 301 474-3100
Fort Wayne **(G-4652)**

TUBING: Rubber

Fluid Handling Technology Inc ....G 317 216-9629
Indianapolis **(G-6940)**

TUBING: Seamless

Plymouth Tube Company ....D 574 946-3125
Winamac **(G-14315)**
Specialty Steel Works Inc ....G 877 289-2277
Hammond **(G-5946)**

TUNGSTEN CARBIDE

Kennametal Inc ....G 219 362-1000
La Porte **(G-8780)**

TUNGSTEN MILL PRDTS

Mi-Tech Tungsten Metals LLC ....D 317 549-4290
Indianapolis **(G-7495)**

TURBINES & TURBINE GENERATOR SET UNITS, COMPLETE

Windstream Technologies Inc ....E 812 953-1481
North Vernon **(G-11287)**

TURBINES & TURBINE GENERATOR SET UNITS: Gas, Complete

Siemens Energy Inc ....E 317 677-1340
Indianapolis **(G-7936)**

TURBINES & TURBINE GENERATOR SETS

Allison Transmission Inc ....C 317 821-5104
Indianapolis **(G-6376)**
Auxilius Heavy Industries LLC ....E 765 885-5099
Fowler **(G-4794)**
Clayhill Wind & Solar LLC ....G 765 437-2395
Sharpsville **(G-12504)**
Cummins Inc ....A 812 522-9366
Seymour **(G-12442)**
Design Engineering ....F 219 926-2170
Chesterton **(G-1602)**
Drive Process Services Inc ....G 765 741-9717
Muncie **(G-10464)**
Falcon Manufacturing LLC ....F 317 884-3600
Columbus **(G-1922)**
Glenwood M Brown Co LLC ....G 260 710-4428
Laotto **(G-9108)**

Mantech Manifold ....G 260 479-2383
Fort Wayne **(G-4452)**
Power Wall Systems LLC ....G 317 348-1260
Fishers **(G-3955)**
Prime Tech Inc ....G 317 715-1162
Indianapolis **(G-7746)**
Rolls-Royce PLC ....G 317 306-2441
Martinsville **(G-9636)**
Tosmo America Inc ....F 812 953-1481
North Vernon **(G-11284)**
Tri Aerospace LLC ....G 812 872-2400
Terre Haute **(G-13358)**

TURBINES & TURBINE GENERATOR SETS & PARTS

Integrated Energy Technologies ....E 812 421-7810
Evansville **(G-3563)**

TURBINES: Steam

General Electric Company ....D 812 933-0700
Batesville **(G-501)**

TURBO-GENERATORS

Tab Technologies ....G 765 482-7561
Lebanon **(G-9227)**

TYPESETTING SVC

Acclaim Graphics Inc ....G 812 424-5035
Evansville **(G-3334)**
Aim Media Indiana Oper LLC ....E 317 462-5528
Greenfield **(G-5497)**
Athena Arts & Graphics Inc ....G 317 876-8916
Indianapolis **(G-6436)**
Brand Prtg & Photo-Litho Co ....G 317 921-4095
Indianapolis **(G-6503)**
BSC Vntres Acquisition Sub LLC ....D 260 665-7521
Angola **(G-198)**
C J P Corporation ....G 219 924-1685
Highland **(G-6040)**
Cecils Printing & Office Sups ....G 812 683-4416
Huntingburg **(G-6153)**
Ckmt Associates Inc ....E 219 924-2820
Hammond **(G-5863)**
Clarke American Checks Inc ....C 812 283-9598
Jeffersonville **(G-8339)**
Classic Graphics Inc ....F 260 482-3487
Fort Wayne **(G-4156)**
Clondalkin Pharma & Healthcare ....C 317 328-7355
Indianapolis **(G-6623)**
Cnhi LLC ....E 812 944-6481
New Albany **(G-10762)**
Community Holdings Indiana Inc ....E 765 482-4650
Lebanon **(G-9175)**
Community Holdings Indiana Inc ....F 765 459-3121
Kokomo **(G-8608)**
Community Holdings Indiana Inc ....E 812 663-3111
Greensburg **(G-5594)**
Community Papers Inc ....G 317 241-7363
Indianapolis **(G-6639)**
Composition LLC ....G 317 979-7214
Fishers **(G-3892)**
Consolidated Printing Svcs Inc ....F 765 468-6033
Farmland **(G-3841)**
Copyfire Typesetting Inc ....G 317 894-0408
Indianapolis **(G-6665)**
Copymat Service Inc ....G 765 743-5995
Lafayette **(G-8878)**
Country Pines Inc ....F 812 247-3315
Shoals **(G-12665)**
Courier Printing Co Allen Cnty ....G 260 627-2728
Grabill **(G-5362)**
Courier-Times Inc ....D 765 529-1111
New Castle **(G-10897)**
Coy & Associates ....G 317 787-5089
Indianapolis **(G-6682)**
Creative Concept Ventures Inc ....G 812 282-9442
Jeffersonville **(G-8348)**
Crescendo Inc ....G 812 829-4759
Spencer **(G-13022)**
D & M Printing Inc ....G 812 847-4837
Linton **(G-9306)**
Digital Printing Incorporated ....F 812 265-2205
Madison **(G-9457)**
Doerr Printing Co ....G 317 568-0135
Indianapolis **(G-6756)**
Dynamark Graphics Group Inc ....G 317 634-2963
Indianapolis **(G-6777)**

Dynamark Graphics Group Inc ....E 317 328-2555
Indianapolis **(G-6775)**
Ed Sons Inc ....F 317 897-8821
Indianapolis **(G-6803)**
Evansville Bindery Inc ....G 812 423-2222
Evansville **(G-3483)**
Evansville Courier Co ....B 812 464-7500
Evansville **(G-3485)**
Ewing Printing Company Inc ....F 812 882-2415
Vincennes **(G-13677)**
Excell Color Graphics Inc ....E 260 482-2720
Fort Wayne **(G-4251)**
Express Press Indiana Inc ....E 574 277-3355
South Bend **(G-12769)**
Fedex Office & Print Svcs Inc ....E 317 631-6862
Indianapolis **(G-6908)**
Fedex Office & Print Svcs Inc ....E 317 849-9683
Indianapolis **(G-6911)**
Fedex Office & Print Svcs Inc ....E 574 271-0398
South Bend **(G-12777)**
Fedex Office & Print Svcs Inc ....E 317 337-2679
Indianapolis **(G-6912)**
Fedex Office & Print Svcs Inc ....G 317 295-1063
Indianapolis **(G-6913)**
Fedex Office & Print Svcs Inc ....E 317 251-2406
Indianapolis **(G-6914)**
Fedex Office & Print Svcs Inc ....E 317 885-6480
Indianapolis **(G-6915)**
Fedex Office & Print Svcs Inc ....F 765 449-4950
Lafayette **(G-8897)**
Fineline Digital Group Inc ....E 317 872-4490
Indianapolis **(G-6920)**
Fineline Graphics Incorporated ....D 317 872-4490
Indianapolis **(G-6921)**
First Quality Printing Inc ....G 317 506-8633
Indianapolis **(G-6927)**
Fort Wayne Printing Co Inc ....G 260 471-7744
Fort Wayne **(G-4280)**
Gary Printing Inc ....G 219 886-1767
Gary **(G-5052)**
Goetz Printing ....F 812 243-2086
Terre Haute **(G-13241)**
Graessle-Mercer Co ....E 812 522-5478
Seymour **(G-12451)**
Granger Gazette ....G 574 277-2679
Granger **(G-5410)**
Graphics Unlimited ....G 765 288-6816
Muncie **(G-10479)**
Green Banner Publications Inc ....E 812 967-3176
Pekin **(G-11473)**
Greensburg Printing Co Inc ....G 812 663-8265
Greensburg **(G-5604)**
Hager Inc ....G 260 483-7075
Fort Wayne **(G-4314)**
Hardesty Printing Co Inc ....F 574 223-4553
Rochester **(G-12126)**
Hardesty Printing Co Inc ....F 574 267-7591
Warsaw **(G-13889)**
Hetty Incorporated ....G 219 836-2517
Munster **(G-10605)**
Hetty Incorporated ....G 219 933-0833
Hammond **(G-5892)**
Hiatt Enterprises Inc ....G 765 289-2700
Muncie **(G-10488)**
Hiatt Enterprises Inc ....E 765 289-7756
Muncie **(G-10487)**
Hinen Printing Co ....G 260 248-8984
Columbia City **(G-1789)**
Home News Enterprises LLC ....E 574 583-5121
Monticello **(G-10265)**
Hoosier Printing Co Inc ....G 219 836-8877
Munster **(G-10606)**
Hoosier Times Inc ....C 812 331-4270
Bloomington **(G-741)**
Howard Print Shop ....G 765 453-6161
Kokomo **(G-8641)**
Indiana Newspapers LLC ....D 812 886-9955
Vincennes **(G-13685)**
Journal and Chronicle Inc ....G 812 752-5060
Scottsburg **(G-12370)**
Kpc Media Group Inc ....C 260 347-0400
Kendallville **(G-8488)**
Kpc Media Group Inc ....E 260 426-2640
Fort Wayne **(G-4415)**
L & L Press Inc ....F 765 664-3162
Marion **(G-9541)**
L C Typesetting Company Inc ....G 574 232-4700
South Bend **(G-12834)**
La Grange Publishing Co Inc ....F 260 463-3243
Lagrange **(G-9052)**

Largus Speedy Print Corp ......E 219 922-8414
Munster (G-10612)
Leader Publishing Co of Salem ......E 812 883-4446
Salem (G-12299)
Lee Publications Inc ......D 219 933-9251
Munster (G-10614)
Lincoln Printing Corporation ......E 260 424-5200
Fort Wayne (G-4437)
Ludwick Graphics Inc ......F 574 233-2165
South Bend (G-12845)
M Nelson & Associates Inc ......G 317 228-1422
Carmel (G-1430)
Maury Boyd & Associates Inc ......F 317 849-6110
Indianapolis (G-7469)
Miller Rainbow Printing Inc ......E 812 275-3355
Bedford (G-565)
Minute Print It Inc ......G 765 482-9019
Lebanon (G-9206)
Muncie Novelty Company Inc ......D 765 288-8301
Muncie (G-10532)
News Publishing Company LLC ......G 812 649-4440
Rockport (G-12171)
North Vernon Plain Dlr & Sun ......E 812 346-3973
North Vernon (G-11272)
Nussmeier Engraving Co ......E 812 425-1339
Evansville (G-3650)
Offset House Inc ......F 317 849-5155
Indianapolis (G-7612)
Offset One Inc ......F 260 456-8828
Fort Wayne (G-4509)
Overgaards Artcraft Printers ......G 574 234-8464
South Bend (G-12885)
Pierce Oil Co Inc ......F 812 268-6356
Sullivan (G-13090)
PIP Printing ......G 317 843-5755
Carmel (G-1451)
Presstime Graphics Inc ......E 812 234-3815
Terre Haute (G-13309)
Printing Emporium Inc ......G 574 256-0059
Mishawaka (G-10109)
Printing Place Inc-Photos Plus ......F 260 665-8444
Angola (G-239)
Progressive Printing Co Inc ......G 765 653-3814
Greencastle (G-5475)
Pubco Inc ......F 219 874-4245
Michigan City (G-9830)
Publishers Consulting Corp ......E 219 874-4245
Michigan City (G-9831)
Q Graphics Inc ......G 574 967-3733
Flora (G-4002)
Q S I Inc ......E 574 282-1200
South Bend (G-12908)
Quality Printing of NW Ind ......G 219 322-6677
Schererville (G-12343)
Quality Typesetting ......G 317 787-4466
Indianapolis (G-7802)
Regal Printing Inc ......G 317 844-1723
Carmel (G-1464)
Reprocomm Inc ......E 765 472-5700
Peru (G-11544)
Rhr Corporation ......G 317 788-1504
Indianapolis (G-7837)
Riden Inc ......G 219 362-5511
La Porte (G-8812)
Rink Printing Company Inc ......E 574 232-7935
South Bend (G-12916)
Rrc Corporation ......F 317 687-8325
Indianapolis (G-7869)
Russ Print Shop ......F 219 996-3142
Hebron (G-6022)
Service Printers Inc ......E 574 266-6710
Elkhart (G-3162)
Shirley Engraving Co Inc ......F 317 634-4084
Indianapolis (G-7934)
Spectrum Press Inc ......E 812 335-1945
Bloomington (G-831)
Spencer Evening World ......D 812 829-2255
Spencer (G-13037)
Stamprint Inc ......G 574 233-3900
South Bend (G-12953)
Stines Printing ......G 260 356-5994
Huntington (G-6253)
Tabco Business Forms Inc ......G 812 882-2836
Vincennes (G-13709)
Tatman Inc ......E 765 825-2164
Connersville (G-2075)
Thomas E Slade Inc ......F 812 471-7100
Evansville (G-3760)
Times ......E 765 296-3622
Frankfort (G-4856)

Town & Country Press Inc ......F 574 936-9505
Plymouth (G-11730)
Triple Crown Media LLC ......D 574 533-2151
Goshen (G-5342)
Truth Publishing Company Inc ......E 765 653-5151
Greencastle (G-5480)
Voice of God Recordings Inc ......D 812 246-2137
Jeffersonville (G-8439)
WAr - LLC- Westville Prtg ......G 219 785-2821
Westville (G-14221)
Woodburn Graphics Inc ......E 812 232-0323
Terre Haute (G-13371)
Writeguard Business Systems ......G 317 849-7292
Indianapolis (G-8219)

TYPESETTING SVC: Computer

Annual Reports Inc ......E 317 736-8838
Franklin (G-4868)
Rowland Printing Co Inc ......F 317 773-1829
Noblesville (G-11177)

TYPESETTING SVC: Linotype Composition, For Printing Trade

Priority Printing LLC ......G 317 241-4234
Indianapolis (G-7761)

TYPOGRAPHY

XI Graphics Inc ......F 317 738-3434
Franklin (G-4942)

ULTRASONIC EQPT: Cleaning, Exc Med & Dental

Global Sonics LLC ......G 765 522-5548
Roachdale (G-12093)

UNIFORM SPLY SVCS: Indl

Wildman Business Group LLC ......C 866 369-1552
Warsaw (G-13965)

UNIFORM STORES

OHara Sports Inc ......G 219 836-5554
Munster (G-10618)
Winning Edge of Rochester Inc ......F 574 223-6090
Rochester (G-12162)

UNISEX HAIR SALONS

Best Electric Motor Service ......G 765 583-2408
Otterbein (G-11417)
Classique Hair Style ......G 317 738-2104
Franklin (G-4876)

UNIVERSITY

Ball State University ......G 765 285-8218
Muncie (G-10437)
Indiana University Bloomington ......F 812 855-2816
Bloomington (G-748)
Trustees Indiana University ......G 812 856-4186
Bloomington (G-845)
Trustees Indiana University ......G 812 855-3439
Bloomington (G-847)
Trustees Indiana University ......E 812 855-4848
Bloomington (G-848)
University Notre Dame Du Lac ......D 574 631-7471
Notre Dame (G-11304)
University Notre Dame Du Lac ......F 574 631-6346
Notre Dame (G-11305)
University of Evansville ......G 812 479-2963
Evansville (G-3790)

UNSUPPORTED PLASTICS: Floor Or Wall Covering

Custom Covers Inc ......G 765 481-7800
Lebanon (G-9178)
Jack Laurie Coml Floors Inc ......G 317 569-2095
Indianapolis (G-7293)

UPHOLSTERERS' EQPT & SPLYS WHOLESALERS

G & T Industries of Indiana ......E 812 634-2252
Jasper (G-8253)
General Furniture & Bedg Pdts ......G 317 849-2670
Indianapolis (G-6997)

UPHOLSTERY WORK SVCS

Autumn Interiors ......G 317 894-1494
Indianapolis (G-6447)
Industrial Sewing Machine Co ......G 812 425-2255
Evansville (G-3558)

UREA

Ureas Music Group LLC ......G 317 426-3103
Indianapolis (G-8134)

URNS: Cut Stone

Aurora Casket Company LLC ......B 800 457-1111
Aurora (G-370)
Poyser Kelshaw Group LLC ......G 317 571-8493
Carmel (G-1453)

USED CAR DEALERS

Futurex Industries Inc ......E 765 597-2221
Marshall (G-9591)
Heritage Financial Group Inc ......D 574 522-8000
Elkhart (G-2914)
Oxford House Incorporated ......D 765 884-3265
Fowler (G-4803)
Transwheel Corporation ......C 260 358-8660
Huntington (G-6256)

USED MERCHANDISE STORES

Fall Creek Corporation ......G 765 482-1861
Lebanon (G-9182)
Goodwill Inds of Centl Ind ......E 317 587-0281
Carmel (G-1388)

UTENSILS: Household, Cooking & Kitchen, Metal

Fayette Tool and Engineering ......D 765 825-7518
Connersville (G-2048)

UTILITY TRAILER DEALERS

Chief Metal Works Inc ......G 765 932-2134
Rushville (G-12217)
Collins Trailers Inc ......G 574 294-2561
Elkhart (G-2762)
Ridge Trailers ......G 260 244-5443
Columbia City (G-1828)
Saladin Trailer Sales Inc ......F 812 692-5288
Elnora (G-3291)
Schwartzs Trailer Sales Inc ......G 317 773-2608
Noblesville (G-11181)

VACUUM CLEANERS: Household

Arden Companies LLC ......D 260 747-1657
Fort Wayne (G-4089)

VACUUM CLEANERS: Indl Type

Clover Industrial Services LLC ......E 317 879-5001
Indianapolis (G-6625)

VACUUM PUMPS & EQPT: Laboratory

Integrated Instrument Services ......F 317 248-1958
Indianapolis (G-7248)

VACUUM SYSTEMS: Air Extraction, Indl

Dekker Vacuum Technologies Inc ......E 219 861-0661
Michigan City (G-9781)

VALUE-ADDED RESELLERS: Computer Systems

Knowledge Diffusion Games LLC ......G 812 361-4424
Bloomington (G-759)

VALVES

Consolidated Pipe & Valve ......G 574 262-3758
Elkhart (G-2769)
Stfrancis Mdwest Hart Vlve Ctr ......G 877 788-2583
Indianapolis (G-8006)
Tri State Valve Instrument Co ......G 812 434-0141
Evansville (G-3772)
Valve Serve LLC ......G 260 421-1927
Fort Wayne (G-4723)

PRODUCT

VALVES & PARTS: Gas, Indl

S H Leggitt Company ....G...... 574 264-0230
Elkhart *(G-3152)*

Specilzed Cmpnent Prts Ltd LLC ....C...... 260 925-2588
Auburn *(G-357)*

VALVES & PIPE FITTINGS

Air Fixtures Inc ....F...... 260 982-2169
North Manchester *(G-11224)*

Ashley F Ward Inc ....E...... 574 294-1502
Elkhart *(G-2696)*

Ashley F Ward Inc ....E...... 219 879-4177
Michigan City *(G-9767)*

Coupled Products LLC ....B...... 260 248-3200
Columbia City *(G-1776)*

Epco Products Inc ....E...... 260 747-8888
Fort Wayne *(G-4240)*

Green Pipe & Supply Inc ....G...... 219 762-1077
Portage *(G-11769)*

Hancor Inc ....E...... 812 443-2080
Brazil *(G-964)*

Honeywell International Inc ....G...... 574 231-2000
South Bend *(G-12799)*

Hy-Matic Mfg Inc ....E...... 260 347-3651
Kendallville *(G-8479)*

Madden Manufacturing Inc ....F...... 574 295-4292
Elkhart *(G-3013)*

Nibco Inc ....B...... 574 295-3000
Elkhart *(G-3062)*

Parker-Hannifin Corporation ....A...... 260 748-6000
New Haven *(G-10951)*

PHD Inc ....C...... 260 356-0120
Huntington *(G-6238)*

R P S Hydraulics Sales & Svc ....E...... 219 845-5526
Hammond *(G-5931)*

Strahman Holdings Inc ....G...... 317 818-5030
Indianapolis *(G-6281)*

Strataflo Products Inc ....F...... 260 482-4366
Fort Wayne *(G-4655)*

VALVES & REGULATORS: Pressure, Indl

SMC Corporation of America ....B...... 317 899-3182
Noblesville *(G-11184)*

VALVES Solenoid

Gould Solenoid Valve Co ....F...... 317 547-5289
Indianapolis *(G-7030)*

J D Gould Company Inc ....F...... 317 542-1876
Indianapolis *(G-7285)*

VALVES: Aerosol, Metal

H & H Sales Company Inc ....F...... 260 637-3177
Huntertown *(G-6139)*

Indy Aerospace Inc ....G...... 817 521-6508
Indianapolis *(G-7212)*

Keener Corporation ....E...... 765 825-2100
Connersville *(G-2059)*

Sssi Inc ....G...... 219 762-8901
Portage *(G-11795)*

VALVES: Aircraft

Victor Reinz Valve Seals LLC ....D...... 260 897-2827
Avilla *(G-420)*

VALVES: Aircraft, Control, Hydraulic & Pneumatic

Nrp Jones LLC ....D...... 219 362-4508
La Porte *(G-8800)*

VALVES: Control, Automatic

Shoemaker Inc ....F...... 260 625-4321
Fort Wayne *(G-4622)*

U S Valves Inc ....G...... 812 476-6662
Evansville *(G-3782)*

VALVES: Fluid Power, Control, Hydraulic & pneumatic

Daman Products Company Inc ....D...... 574 259-7841
Mishawaka *(G-10030)*

Hydro Systems Mfg Inc ....G...... 260 436-4476
Fort Wayne *(G-4353)*

Noble Composites Inc ....C...... 574 533-1462
Goshen *(G-5299)*

SMC Corporation of America ....B...... 317 899-3182
Noblesville *(G-11184)*

VALVES: Indl

AMG LLC ....E...... 317 329-4004
Indianapolis *(G-6397)*

Fitch Inc ....G...... 260 637-0835
Huntington *(G-6138)*

Flosource Inc ....E...... 765 342-1360
Martinsville *(G-9605)*

Frew Process Group LLC ....G...... 317 565-5000
Noblesville *(G-11107)*

Henry Pratt Company LLC ....F...... 219 931-0405
Hammond *(G-5891)*

Nexus Valve Inc ....E...... 317 257-6050
Fishers *(G-3948)*

Nibco Inc ....B...... 574 295-3000
Elkhart *(G-3062)*

Parker-Hannifin Corporation ....C...... 260 636-2104
Albion *(G-32)*

Proportion-Air Inc ....D...... 317 335-2602
McCordsville *(G-9674)*

TEC Inc ....E...... 765 827-3868
Connersville *(G-2076)*

VAN CONVERSIONS

ADM Mobility Solutions Inc ....G...... 317 481-8707
Indianapolis *(G-6327)*

C M I Enterprises Inc ....D...... 305 685-9651
Elkhart *(G-2744)*

Fiedeke Vinyl Coverings Inc ....F...... 574 534-3408
Goshen *(G-5214)*

Forest River Inc ....E...... 574 533-5934
Goshen *(G-5217)*

Independent Protection Co Inc ....C...... 574 533-4116
Goshen *(G-5242)*

Independent Protection Co Inc ....D...... 574 831-5680
New Paris *(G-10985)*

Twin Air Products Inc ....G...... 574 295-1129
Elkhart *(G-3230)*

VAN CONVERSIONS

Chariot Vans Inc ....E...... 574 264-7577
Elkhart *(G-2755)*

Coach Line Motors ....G...... 765 825-7893
Connersville *(G-2043)*

Independent Protection Co Inc ....D...... 574 831-5680
New Paris *(G-10985)*

Southside Mini Storage ....G...... 574 293-3270
Elkhart *(G-3181)*

Sportsmobile Inc ....F...... 260 356-5435
Huntington *(G-6251)*

Van Explorer Company Inc ....E...... 574 267-7666
Warsaw *(G-13957)*

VARIETY STORES

Circle Printing LLC ....G...... 812 663-7367
Greensburg *(G-5593)*

Gohn Bros Manufacturing Co ....G...... 574 825-2400
Middlebury *(G-9889)*

VAULTS & SAFES WHOLESALERS

Fire King International LLC ....E...... 812 948-8400
New Albany *(G-10778)*

Fire King International LLC ....E...... 812 948-2795
New Albany *(G-10779)*

Fire King Security Pdts LLC ....C...... 812 948-8400
New Albany *(G-10780)*

Fki Security Group LLC ....B...... 812 948-8400
New Albany *(G-10781)*

Meilink Safe Company ....E...... 812 941-0024
New Albany *(G-10825)*

S C Pryor Inc ....E...... 317 352-1281
Indianapolis *(G-7878)*

VEGETABLE OILS: Medicinal Grade, Refined Or Concentrated

Nutritional Research Assoc ....F...... 260 723-4931
South Whitley *(G-13002)*

VEHICLES: All Terrain

Dutch Park Homes Inc ....E...... 574 642-0150
Goshen *(G-5206)*

Goods On Target Sporting Inc ....G...... 812 623-2300
Sunman *(G-13111)*

Perkinsville Power Sports ....G...... 765 734-1314
Anderson *(G-151)*

Sx4 ....G...... 812 967-2502
Palmyra *(G-11441)*

Thorntons Mtrcycle Sls - Mdson ....G...... 812 574-6347
Madison *(G-9498)*

VEHICLES: Recreational

Asw LLC ....G...... 260 432-1596
Columbia City *(G-1764)*

BBC Distribution LLC ....G...... 574 266-3601
Elkhart *(G-2718)*

Bridgeview Manufacturing LLC ....E...... 574 970-0116
Elkhart *(G-2734)*

Competitive Designs Inc ....G...... 574 223-9406
Rochester *(G-12118)*

Creative Manufacturing Rv LLC ....F...... 574 333-3302
Elkhart *(G-2776)*

D Rv Luxury Suites LLC ....D...... 260 562-1075
Howe *(G-6121)*

Drv Llc ....E...... 260 562-1075
Howe *(G-6122)*

E T & T Powder Coat ....G...... 574 293-2725
Elkhart *(G-2809)*

Fiber-Tron Corp ....E...... 574 294-8545
Elkhart *(G-2848)*

Forest River Inc ....E...... 574 389-4600
Elkhart *(G-2865)*

Gardiner Rentals Bill ....G...... 765 447-5111
Lafayette *(G-8904)*

Grand Design Rv LLC ....A...... 574 825-8000
Middlebury *(G-9890)*

Highland Ridge Rv Inc ....B...... 260 768-7771
Shipshewana *(G-12616)*

IKON Group ....G...... 574 326-3661
Elkhart *(G-2928)*

Landjet International ....F...... 574 970-7805
Elkhart *(G-2984)*

Little Trailer Co Inc ....F...... 877 545-4897
Elkhart *(G-3005)*

Mudd-Ox Inc ....F...... 260 768-7221
Shipshewana *(G-12638)*

Parallax Group Inc ....G...... 800 443-4859
Anderson *(G-149)*

Recreational Customs Inc ....G...... 574 642-0632
Goshen *(G-5317)*

Showhaulers Trucks Inc ....E...... 574 825-6764
Middlebury *(G-9918)*

Slicers ....G...... 812 255-0655
Vincennes *(G-13706)*

Structural Composites Ind Inc ....D...... 260 894-4083
Ligonier *(G-9296)*

Thor Industries Inc ....C...... 574 970-7460
Elkhart *(G-3214)*

TRC Mfg Inc ....E...... 574 262-9299
South Bend *(G-12978)*

Use What Youve Got Ministry ....G...... 317 924-4124
Indianapolis *(G-8140)*

VENDING MACHINE REPAIR SVCS

C & P Distributing LLC ....E...... 574 256-1138
Mishawaka *(G-10016)*

Standard Change-Makers Inc ....F...... 317 899-6955
Indianapolis *(G-7988)*

VENDING MACHINES & PARTS

Brashear ....G...... 219 778-2422
La Porte *(G-8741)*

Diane Dixon ....G...... 812 836-4179
Rome *(G-12196)*

VENETIAN BLINDS & SHADES

Leeps Supply Co ....G...... 219 696-9511
Lowell *(G-9413)*

VETERINARY PHARMACEUTICAL PREPARATIONS

Hawthorne Products Inc ....G...... 765 768-6585
Dunkirk *(G-2485)*

Mattox & Moore Inc ....G...... 317 632-7534
Indianapolis *(G-7468)*

Vita Vet Laboratories Inc ....G...... 765 662-9398
Marion *(G-9571)*

VETERINARY PRDTS: Instruments & Apparatus

Thompson................................G....... 219 942-8133
Hobart *(G-6098)*

VIALS: Glass

Amcor Phrm Packg USA Inc ....C....... 812 591-2332
Westport *(G-14208)*

Nipro Phrmpckging Amricas Corp ....G....... 812 591-2332
Westport *(G-14210)*

VIDEO & AUDIO EQPT, WHOLESALE

Csd Group Inc ....E....... 260 918-3500
New Haven *(G-10937)*

VIDEO CAMERA-AUDIO RECORDERS: Household Use

Itech Holdings LLC ....E....... 317 567-5160
Indianapolis *(G-7276)*

U-Nitt LLC ....G....... 812 251-9980
Carmel *(G-1499)*

VIDEO EQPT

Dage-MTI Michigan City Inc ....G....... 219 872-5514
Michigan City *(G-9780)*

Oscar Telecom Inc ....G....... 317 359-7000
Indianapolis *(G-7634)*

VIDEO TAPE PRODUCTION SVCS

Bird Publishing Company ....G....... 219 462-6330
Valparaiso *(G-13509)*

National Federation of ....E....... 317 972-6900
Indianapolis *(G-7571)*

VIDEO TRIGGERS EXC REMOTE CONTROL TV DEVICES

Skytech II Inc ....G....... 260 459-1703
Fort Wayne *(G-4629)*

Skytech-Systems Inc ....F....... 260 459-1703
Fort Wayne *(G-4630)*

VIDEO TRIGGERS: Remote Control TV Devices

Skytech II Inc ....G....... 260 459-1703
Fort Wayne *(G-4629)*

Skytech-Systems Inc ....F....... 260 459-1703
Fort Wayne *(G-4630)*

VINYL RESINS, NEC

Pmw Holdings LLC ....G....... 317 339-4685
Indianapolis *(G-7703)*

VISUAL COMMUNICATIONS SYSTEMS

Tct Technologies LLC ....G....... 317 833-6730
Fishers *(G-3974)*

VITAMINS: Natural Or Synthetic, Uncompounded, Bulk

G & W Herbs ....G....... 574 646-2134
Nappanee *(G-10671)*

Oza Compound Products ....G....... 260 483-0406
Fort Wayne *(G-4515)*

Vitamins Inc ....E....... 219 879-7356
Michigan City *(G-9859)*

VOCATIONAL REHABILITATION AGENCY

Anthony Wayne Rehabilitation C ....D....... 260 744-6145
Fort Wayne *(G-4078)*

Goodwill Inds of Centl Ind....................E....... 317 587-0281
Carmel *(G-1388)*

Pathfinder Services Inc ....E....... 260 356-0500
Huntington *(G-6236)*

WALL & CEILING SQUARES: Concrete

Indiana Barrier Wall LLC ....G....... 260 747-5777
Fort Wayne *(G-4363)*

WALL COVERINGS WHOLESALERS

Blumling Design and Graphics............G....... 765 477-7446
Lafayette *(G-8863)*

WALLBOARD: Decorated, Made From Purchased Materials

Hoosier Wallbeds Incorporated ....G....... 812 747-7154
Lawrenceburg *(G-9145)*

WALLBOARD: Gypsum

New Ngc Inc ....C....... 812 247-2424
Shoals *(G-12667)*

WALLPAPER STORE

Doris Drapery Boutique......................G....... 765 472-5850
Peru *(G-11524)*

WALLS: Curtain, Metal

Ertl Fabricating Inc ....F....... 765 393-1376
Anderson *(G-106)*

WAREHOUSING & STORAGE FACILITIES, NEC

P-Americas LLC ....E....... 812 522-3421
Seymour *(G-12472)*

Wire America Inc ....E....... 260 969-1700
Fort Wayne *(G-4758)*

WAREHOUSING & STORAGE, REFRIGERATED: Cold Storage Or Refrig

United States Cold Storage Inc ....E....... 765 482-2653
Lebanon *(G-9231)*

WAREHOUSING & STORAGE, REFRIGERATED: Frozen Or Refrig Goods

Johns Butcher Shop..........................G....... 574 773-4632
Nappanee *(G-10688)*

WAREHOUSING & STORAGE: Bulk St & Termnls, Hire, Petro/Chem

Quaker Chemical Corp ....G....... 765 668-2441
Marion *(G-9557)*

WAREHOUSING & STORAGE: Farm Prdts

Frick Services Inc ....E....... 260 761-3311
Wawaka *(G-14032)*

WAREHOUSING & STORAGE: General

Dmi Distribution Inc..........................E....... 765 287-0035
Muncie *(G-10461)*

Gary Bridge and Iron Co Inc ....G....... 219 884-3792
Gary *(G-5049)*

Haas Cabinet Co Inc ....C....... 812 246-4431
Sellersburg *(G-12395)*

Hickman Williams & Company ....F....... 708 656-8818
La Porte *(G-8764)*

Jadcore LLC ....C....... 812 234-2724
Terre Haute *(G-13260)*

Mahomed Sales & Whsng LLC ....D....... 317 472-5800
Indianapolis *(G-7441)*

Matrix Nac ....F....... 219 931-6600
Hammond *(G-5914)*

P-Americas LLC ....E....... 765 289-0270
Muncie *(G-10542)*

Phoenix Assembly Indiana LLC ....E....... 317 884-3600
Columbus *(G-1995)*

Suburban Manufacturing Company ......F....... 574 294-5681
Elkhart *(G-3196)*

Tfi Inc ....F....... 317 290-1333
Indianapolis *(G-8055)*

WAREHOUSING & STORAGE: General

AEL/Span LLC ....E....... 317 203-4602
Plainfield *(G-11591)*

Agi International Inc ....F....... 317 536-2415
Indianapolis *(G-6352)*

Alpha Baking Co Inc ....F....... 574 234-0188
South Bend *(G-12697)*

Bendix Coml Vhcl Systems LLC...........B....... 260 356-9720
Huntington *(G-6191)*

Bootz Manufacturing Company............D....... 812 425-4646
Evansville *(G-3393)*

Indiana Research Institute ....F....... 812 378-5363
Columbus *(G-1948)*

Indiana Ribbon Inc ....E....... 219 279-2112
Wolcott *(G-14366)*

Pridgeon & Clay Inc ....E....... 317 738-4885
Franklin *(G-4923)*

Proedge Inc ....E....... 219 552-9550
Shelby *(G-12515)*

Quick Tanks Inc ....C....... 260 347-3850
Kendallville *(G-8504)*

Reeds RFI Inc ....G....... 812 659-2872
Switz City *(G-13126)*

Saran Industries LLC ....D....... 317 897-2170
Kokomo *(G-8690)*

Saran Industries LLC ....D....... 317 897-2170
Bloomington *(G-821)*

Westrock Cp LLC ....E....... 574 936-2118
Plymouth *(G-11735)*

WAREHOUSING & STORAGE: Miniwarehouse

Thormax Enterprises LLC....................G....... 812 530-7744
Seymour *(G-12496)*

WAREHOUSING & STORAGE: Self Storage

Georg Utz Inc..................................E....... 812 526-2240
Edinburgh *(G-2612)*

Mark Concrete Products Inc ....G....... 317 398-8616
Shelbyville *(G-12551)*

WARM AIR HEAT & AC EQPT & SPLYS, WHOLESALE Fan, Heat & Vent

Poynter Sheet Metal Inc ....B....... 317 893-1193
Greenwood *(G-5735)*

WARM AIR HEATING & AC EQPT & SPLYS, WHOLESALE Air Filters

American Melt Blown Filtration ....E....... 219 866-3500
Rensselaer *(G-11912)*

Wicks Air Filter Service Inc..................G....... 260 426-1782
Fort Wayne *(G-4755)*

WARM AIR HEATING/AC EQPT/SPLYS, WHOL Warm Air Htg Eqpt/Splys

Air Energy Systems Inc......................G....... 317 290-8500
Indianapolis *(G-6353)*

AMS of Indiana Inc ....E....... 574 293-5526
Elkhart *(G-2689)*

D & W Inc ....D....... 574 264-9674
Elkhart *(G-2785)*

Lute Supply ....G....... 260 480-2441
Fort Wayne *(G-4444)*

Superior Distribution ....G....... 618 242-5560
Indianapolis *(G-8021)*

Thermo-Cycler Industries Inc ....G....... 219 767-2990
Union Mills *(G-13465)*

WARRANTY INSURANCE: Automobile

Creative Manufacturing Rv LLC ....F....... 574 333-3302
Elkhart *(G-2776)*

WASHERS

Crystal Clear Inc..............................G....... 317 753-5393
Greenwood *(G-5678)*

Hoosier Gasket Corporation ....D....... 317 545-2000
Indianapolis *(G-7121)*

WASHERS: Lock

Rose Engineering Co Inc ....G....... 317 788-4446
Indianapolis *(G-7862)*

WASHERS: Rubber

Larry G Byrd ....F....... 765 458-7285
Liberty *(G-9263)*

WASHING MACHINES: Household

Souder Power Washing LLC ....G....... 812 894-2544
Terre Haute *(G-13336)*

PRODUCT

WATCH REPAIR SVCS

Welmer Jewelers Inc ....G....... 812 522-4082
Seymour (G-12499)

WATER HEATERS

Ebert Machine Company Inc................E....... 765 473-3728
Peru (G-11526)

WATER PURIFICATION EQPT: Household

Kendle Custom Inc ....G....... 812 985-5917
Evansville (G-3583)
Lonn Manufacturing Inc ....G....... 317 897-1440
Indianapolis (G-7417)
Samco Inc ....G....... 812 926-4282
Sunman (G-13116)
True Chem Inc ....G....... 317 769-2701
Greenwood (G-5756)
US Water Systems Inc ....F....... 317 209-0889
Indianapolis (G-8138)

WATER PURIFICATION PRDTS: Chlorination Tablets & Kits

Kemiron Great Lakes LLC ....E....... 219 397-2646
East Chicago (G-2543)

WATER SOFTENER SVCS

Driessen Water Inc ....G....... 765 529-4905
Muncie (G-10463)
Leach & Sons WaterCare ....G....... 317 248-8954
Danville (G-2351)
Leistner Aquatic Services Inc ....G....... 317 535-6099
Whiteland (G-14242)
Markle Water Treatment Plant............G....... 260 758-3482
Markle (G-9580)
New Aqua LLC ....D....... 317 272-3000
Avon (G-456)
On The Go Portble Wtr Sftnr LL ....F....... 260 482-9614
Bloomington (G-788)
Puritan Water Conditioning ....F....... 765 362-6340
Crawfordsville (G-2189)

WATER TREATMENT EQPT: Indl

Algaewheel Inc ....G....... 317 582-1400
Indianapolis (G-6364)
Bio-Response Solutions Inc ....F....... 317 386-3500
Danville (G-2343)
Chem-Aqua ....G....... 317 899-3660
Indianapolis (G-6597)
Chemical Control Systems Inc ....G....... 219 465-5103
Griffith (G-5770)
City of Anderson ....D....... 765 648-6560
Anderson (G-85)
City of Columbia City.........................G....... 260 248-5118
Columbia City (G-1773)
Crestwood Equity Partners LP ....G....... 812 265-3313
Madison (G-9455)
Eco Water of Southern Indiana...........G....... 812 734-1407
New Salisbury (G-11009)
Environmental Management & Dev ......G....... 765 874-1539
Lynn (G-9426)
Ferguson Waterworks ....G....... 219 440-5254
Schererville (G-12321)
Flora Wastewater Treatment ....G....... 574 967-3005
Flora (G-3996)
Freije Treatment Systems Inc ....E....... 888 766-7258
Fishers (G-3913)
Global Water Technologies Inc...........G....... 317 452-4488
Indianapolis (G-7013)
Kemtune Inc ....G....... 260 745-0722
Fort Wayne (G-4408)
Kirklin Waste Water Treatment ....G....... 765 279-5251
Kirklin (G-8549)
Markle Water Treatment Plant............G....... 260 758-3482
Markle (G-9580)
Mid State Water Treatment ....G....... 765 884-1220
Fowler (G-4802)
Onion Enterprises Inc........................G....... 317 762-6007
Indianapolis (G-7623)
Precision Chemical LLC ....G....... 317 570-1538
Fishers (G-3958)
Watcon Inc ....F....... 574 287-3397
South Bend (G-12988)
Water Energizers Inc ....F....... 812 288-6900
Jeffersonville (G-8440)
Water Tec LLC ....G....... 219 554-1790
Hammond (G-5957)

WATER: Mineral, Carbonated, Canned & Bottled, Etc

American Water Works Co Inc............G....... 765 362-3940
Crawfordsville (G-2133)
Ice River Springs Kentland LLC ....E....... 219 474-6300
Kentland (G-8521)

WATER: Pasteurized, Canned & Bottled, Etc

Angel Falls Water Company ....G....... 812 939-9107
Clay City (G-1701)
Glacier Bottling Company LLC............G....... 574 293-0357
Elkhart (G-2880)
Niagara Bottling LLC ....G....... 909 758-5313
Plainfield (G-11629)

WATERPROOFING COMPOUNDS

Merediths Inc ....E....... 765 966-5084
Richmond (G-12016)

WAX Sealing wax

Mt Olive Manufacturing Inc ....D....... 317 834-8525
Mooresville (G-10326)

WAXES: Mineral, Natural

Paralogics LLC ....G....... 765 587-4618
Muncie (G-10543)

WAXES: Petroleum, Not Produced In Petroleum Refineries

Paralogics LLC ....G....... 765 587-4618
Muncie (G-10543)

WEATHER STRIP: Sponge Rubber

Ilpea Industries Inc ....D....... 812 752-2526
Scottsburg (G-12363)
Nishikawa Cooper LLC ....C....... 260 593-2156
Fort Wayne (G-4504)
Nishikawa Cooper LLC ....B....... 260 593-2156
Topeka (G-13425)
Nishikawa Cooper LLC ....A....... 574 546-5938
Bremen (G-1012)
Nishikawa of America Inc ....G....... 260 593-2156
Topeka (G-13426)

WEB SEARCH PORTALS: Internet

Smallwood Consulting LLC ....G....... 812 406-8040
Sellersburg (G-12418)

WEIGHING MACHINERY & APPARATUS

Cullman Casting Corporation..............G....... 256 735-0900
North Vernon (G-11251)
Technical Weighing Svcs Inc..............E....... 219 924-3366
Griffith (G-5793)

WELDING & CUTTING APPARATUS & ACCESS, NEC

Star Metal Products ....E....... 317 631-5902
Indianapolis (G-7996)

WELDING EQPT

Best Equipment & Welding Co ....E....... 317 271-8652
Indianapolis (G-6468)
Bryant Machining & Welding LLC ....G....... 260 997-6059
Bryant (G-1199)
Coleman Cable LLC ....C....... 765 449-7227
Lafayette (G-8875)
GC Fuller Mfg Co Inc ....F....... 812 539-2831
Lawrenceburg (G-9144)
Ken Anliker ....G....... 219 984-5676
Chalmers (G-1547)
Kennametal Inc ....C....... 574 534-2585
Goshen (G-5252)
Manufacturing Technology Inc ....C....... 574 230-0258
South Bend (G-12851)
Manufacturing Technology Inc ....E....... 574 233-9490
South Bend (G-12852)
Ogden Welding Systems Inc ....E....... 219 322-5252
Schererville (G-12341)
Tri-State Industries Inc ....D....... 219 933-1710
Hammond (G-5951)
United Industrial & Wldg LLC ....G....... 812 526-4050
Columbus (G-2028)

WELDING EQPT & SPLYS WHOLESALERS

Airgas Usa LLC ....G....... 812 362-7593
Rockport (G-12163)
Aluminum Wldg & Mch Works Inc.......G....... 219 787-8066
Chesterton (G-1592)
Indiana Oxygen Company Inc..............D....... 317 290-0003
Indianapolis (G-7188)
Indiana Oxygen Company Inc..............G....... 765 662-8700
Marion (G-9533)
Matheson Tri-Gas Inc ....F....... 812 838-5518
Mount Vernon (G-10398)
Matheson Tri-Gas Inc ....G....... 812 257-0470
Washington (G-13990)
Matheson Tri-Gas Inc ....G....... 317 892-5221
Pittsboro (G-11585)
Northern Gases and Sups Inc.............F....... 574 594-2551
Pierceton (G-11574)
Praxair Distribution Inc ....G....... 317 481-4550
Indianapolis (G-7722)
Praxair Distribution Inc ....G....... 260 423-4468
Fort Wayne (G-4546)

WELDING EQPT & SPLYS: Resistance, Electric

Topspeed ....G....... 260 665-8889
Angola (G-252)

WELDING EQPT & SPLYS: Wire, Bare & Coated

Schmucker Welding ....G....... 574 773-0456
Bremen (G-1021)

WELDING EQPT REPAIR SVCS

Flanders Electric Mtr Svc Inc.............E....... 812 421-4300
Evansville (G-3510)

WELDING EQPT: Electric

Praxair Surface Tech Inc ....C....... 317 240-2500
Indianapolis (G-7725)
S T Praxair Technology Inc ....G....... 317 240-2500
Indianapolis (G-7881)

WELDING EQPT: Electrical

Marian Inc ....A....... 317 638-6525
Indianapolis (G-7453)
Ogden Welding Systems Inc ....E....... 219 322-5252
Schererville (G-12341)

WELDING MACHINES & EQPT: Ultrasonic

B Y M Electronics Inc ....G....... 574 674-5096
Granger (G-5393)
Best Equipment Co Inc.......................E....... 317 823-3050
Indianapolis (G-6469)

WELDING REPAIR SVC

ABF Welding & Pipe LLC ....G....... 765 977-7349
Cambridge City (G-1252)
Absolute Welding Inc ....G....... 812 923-8001
Borden (G-926)
Accurate Tool & Engineering ....G....... 812 963-6677
Evansville (G-3335)
Ace Welding and Machine Inc ....G....... 812 379-9625
Columbus (G-1849)
Acro Engineering Inc.........................E....... 812 663-6236
Greensburg (G-5588)
Allied Boiler & Welding Co..................G....... 317 272-4820
Avon (G-426)
American Machine Fabrication.............G....... 812 944-4136
New Albany (G-10744)
Amos D Graber & Sons ....F....... 260 749-0526
New Haven (G-10929)
Annette Balfour ....G....... 765 286-1910
Muncie (G-10431)
Atp Welding Inc.................................G....... 765 483-9273
Lebanon (G-9170)
Auto Truck Group LLC ....F....... 260 356-1610
Huntington (G-6188)
B&M Millwright Inc............................G....... 765 883-8177
Russiaville (G-12240)
Barks Welding Supplies ....G....... 812 732-4366
Corydon (G-2089)
Bel-Mar Products Corporation.............G....... 317 769-3262
Whitestown (G-14249)
Best Equipment & Welding Co ....E....... 317 271-8652
Indianapolis (G-6468)

Bobs Welding Repair ...... G ...... 765 744-4192 Farmland *(G-3840)*	Four Star Welding ...... G ...... 574 825-3856 Middlebury *(G-9888)*	K & B Trailer Sales Mfg ...... G ...... 574 946-4382 Monterey *(G-10207)*
Brand Sheet Metal Works Inc ...... G ...... 765 284-5594 Muncie *(G-10443)*	Fullenkamp Machine & Mfg Inc ...... F ...... 260 726-8345 Portland *(G-11824)*	K Fab Inc ...... G ...... 812 663-6299 Greensburg *(G-5618)*
Buchanan Iron Works Inc ...... G ...... 219 785-4480 Westville *(G-14214)*	G & N Warehouse & Packaging ...... G ...... 574 234-3717 South Bend *(G-12785)*	K-K Tool and Design Inc ...... E ...... 260 758-2940 Markle *(G-9578)*
C & S Sandblasting & Wldg LLC ...... G ...... 317 867-6341 Westfield *(G-14140)*	Gary Earl ...... G ...... 812 279-6780 Bedford *(G-544)*	Kammerer Inc ...... G ...... 260 349-9098 Kendallville *(G-8484)*
C M Welding Inc ...... G ...... 765 258-4024 Frankfort *(G-4820)*	General Sheet Metal Works Inc ...... E ...... 574 288-0611 South Bend *(G-12788)*	Kammerer Inc ...... G ...... 260 347-0389 Kendallville *(G-8485)*
C-Way Tool and Die Inc ...... G ...... 812 256-6341 Charlestown *(G-1559)*	Gerke Welding Inc ...... G ...... 260 724-7701 Decatur *(G-2380)*	Knepps Custom Welding ...... G ...... 765 525-5130 Saint Paul *(G-12278)*
Campbells Welding & Machine ...... G ...... 574 643-6705 Royal Center *(G-12212)*	Gibson Brothers Welding Inc ...... F ...... 765 948-5775 Fairmount *(G-3832)*	Knip Welding ...... G ...... 219 987-5123 Demotte *(G-2442)*
Carmel Welding and Supply ...... F ...... 317 846-3493 Carmel *(G-1333)*	Gillum Machine & Tool Inc ...... F ...... 765 893-4426 West Lebanon *(G-14120)*	Kocsis Brothers Machine Co ...... E ...... 219 397-8400 East Chicago *(G-2545)*
Carmichael Welding Inc ...... G ...... 812 825-5156 Bloomfield *(G-636)*	Gravelton Machine Shop Inc ...... G ...... 574 773-3413 Nappanee *(G-10674)*	Kortzendorf Machine & Tool ...... F ...... 317 783-5449 Indianapolis *(G-7367)*
Central Welding Inc ...... G ...... 317 784-7730 Indianapolis *(G-6585)*	Greenwood Models Inc ...... G ...... 317 859-2988 Greenwood *(G-5700)*	L & C Welding LLC ...... G ...... 260 593-3410 Shipshewana *(G-12625)*
Century Tool & Engineering ...... G ...... 317 685-0942 Indianapolis *(G-6587)*	H & H Design & Tool Inc ...... G ...... 765 886-6199 Economy *(G-2591)*	L & L Engineering Co Inc ...... G ...... 317 786-6886 Beech Grove *(G-601)*
Certified Welding Co Inc ...... G ...... 765 522-3238 Bainbridge *(G-475)*	H W Hasty Welding Inc ...... G ...... 765 482-8925 Lebanon *(G-9184)*	L & R Machine Company Inc ...... G ...... 317 787-7251 Beech Grove *(G-602)*
Chesterfield Tool & Engrg Inc ...... E ...... 765 378-5101 Daleville *(G-2338)*	Halcomb Welding LLC ...... G ...... 765 345-7156 Spiceland *(G-13055)*	Lane Shady Welding ...... G ...... 574 825-5553 Middlebury *(G-9901)*
Chief Metal Works Inc ...... G ...... 765 932-2134 Rushville *(G-12217)*	Helfin Sheet Metal Inc ...... G ...... 260 563-2417 Wabash *(G-13729)*	Lauck Manufacturing Co Inc ...... F ...... 317 787-6269 Indianapolis *(G-7385)*
Circle R Industries Inc ...... G ...... 765 379-2768 Rossville *(G-12210)*	Hepton Welding LLC ...... G ...... 800 570-4238 Nappanee *(G-10678)*	Lawson Welding Shop ...... G ...... 812 448-8984 Harmony *(G-5975)*
City Welding & Fabrication ...... G ...... 765 569-5403 Rockville *(G-12175)*	Herman Tool & Machine Inc ...... F ...... 574 594-5544 Pierceton *(G-11572)*	Ldn Welding Corp ...... G ...... 219 996-5643 Hebron *(G-6016)*
Cline Brothers Welding ...... G ...... 812 738-3537 Corydon *(G-2093)*	Highland Machine Tool Inc ...... E ...... 812 923-8884 Floyds Knobs *(G-4013)*	Leons Fabrication Inc ...... F ...... 219 365-5272 Schererville *(G-12330)*
Collins Tool & Die Inc ...... G ...... 812 273-4765 Madison *(G-9453)*	Hill Top Welding LLC ...... G ...... 765 585-2549 Attica *(G-304)*	Lievore Custom Machine Inc ...... G ...... 574 848-0150 Bristol *(G-1067)*
Conley Welding Specialties Inc ...... G ...... 260 343-9051 Kendallville *(G-8466)*	Hite Welding & Chassis ...... G ...... 765 741-0046 Muncie *(G-10489)*	Linden Machine Shop LLC ...... G ...... 765 339-7244 Linden *(G-9304)*
Country Welding LLC ...... G ...... 260 352-2938 Silver Lake *(G-12675)*	Hively Welding Co Inc ...... G ...... 219 843-5111 Medaryville *(G-9679)*	Lloyds Machine Co ...... G ...... 812 422-7064 Evansville *(G-3605)*
Craig Welding and Mfg Inc ...... E ...... 574 353-7912 Mentone *(G-9687)*	Hochstetler Welding ...... G ...... 574 773-0600 Nappanee *(G-10682)*	Loading Dock Maintenance LLC ...... G ...... 260 424-3635 Fort Wayne *(G-4439)*
Custom Gage & Tool Co Inc ...... G ...... 317 547-8257 Indianapolis *(G-6713)*	Hochstetler Welding ...... G ...... 260 463-2793 Lagrange *(G-9044)*	Lockwood Welding Inc ...... G ...... 260 925-2086 Waterloo *(G-14017)*
Custom Machining Services Inc ...... E ...... 219 462-6128 Valparaiso *(G-13525)*	Hoosier Machine & Welding Inc ...... F ...... 317 638-6286 Indianapolis *(G-7122)*	Loughmiller Mch TI Design Inc ...... E ...... 812 295-3903 Loogootee *(G-9390)*
Da-Mar Industries Inc ...... F ...... 260 347-1662 Kendallville *(G-8471)*	Hoosier Spline Broach Corp ...... E ...... 765 452-8273 Kokomo *(G-8639)*	M T M Machining Inc ...... F ...... 219 872-8677 Michigan City *(G-9813)*
Davids Inc ...... F ...... 812 376-6870 Columbus *(G-1905)*	Hoosier Welding ...... G ...... 765 521-4539 New Castle *(G-10905)*	Major Tool and Machine Inc ...... B ...... 317 636-6433 Indianapolis *(G-7446)*
Davis Tool & Machine Inc ...... F ...... 317 896-9278 Westfield *(G-14157)*	Hs Machine Welding ...... G ...... 812 752-2825 Scottsburg *(G-12361)*	Manier Welding & Fabrications ...... G ...... 765 675-6078 Tipton *(G-13397)*
Davron Fabricating ...... G ...... 765 339-7303 New Richmond *(G-11004)*	Hubbard Welding ...... G ...... 317 539-2758 Clayton *(G-1707)*	Manufacturing Technology Inc ...... C ...... 574 230-0258 South Bend *(G-12851)*
Denver Stone ...... E ...... 317 244-5889 Indianapolis *(G-6734)*	Huehls Seal Coating & Lawn Car ...... G ...... 317 782-4069 Indianapolis *(G-7143)*	Martin Welding Shop ...... G ...... 574 862-2578 Wakarusa *(G-13785)*
Diverse Fabrication Services ...... G ...... 317 781-8800 Indianapolis *(G-6746)*	Humphreys Welding Service ...... G ...... 317 881-9024 Indianapolis *(G-7145)*	Matts Repair Inc ...... F ...... 219 696-6765 Lowell *(G-9416)*
Dougs Welding Shop ...... G ...... 765 689-8396 Bunker Hill *(G-1205)*	Huntington Sheet Metal Inc ...... D ...... 260 356-9011 Huntington *(G-6213)*	Mc Bride & Son Welding & Engrg ...... G ...... 260 724-3534 Decatur *(G-2393)*
E & H Industrial Services LLC ...... F ...... 317 569-8819 Carmel *(G-1365)*	Imperial Stamping Corporation ...... D ...... 574 294-3780 Elkhart *(G-2930)*	McGinn Tool & Engineering Co ...... F ...... 317 736-5512 Franklin *(G-4905)*
E & S Metal Inc ...... F ...... 260 563-7714 Wabash *(G-13726)*	Indiana Industrial Svcs LLC ...... C ...... 317 769-6099 Whitestown *(G-14255)*	Melching Machine Inc ...... E ...... 260 622-4315 Ossian *(G-11404)*
East Side Welding Inc ...... G ...... 317 823-4065 Indianapolis *(G-6792)*	Innovative Metalworks LLC ...... G ...... 260 839-0295 Sidney *(G-12674)*	Mervin M Burkholder ...... G ...... 574 862-4144 Wakarusa *(G-13786)*
Ebwa Industries Inc ...... F ...... 317 637-5860 Indianapolis *(G-6797)*	Instate Welding Service Inc ...... G ...... 260 483-0461 Fort Wayne *(G-4375)*	Metcalf Engineering Inc ...... G ...... 765 342-6792 Martinsville *(G-9625)*
Eckstein Welding & Fabrication ...... G ...... 812 934-2059 Batesville *(G-498)*	J & J Repair ...... G ...... 574 831-3075 Goshen *(G-5246)*	Midwest Machining & Fabg ...... F ...... 219 924-0206 Griffith *(G-5785)*
Edco Welding and Hydraulic Inc ...... F ...... 317 783-2323 Indianapolis *(G-6804)*	J & J Welding ...... G ...... 219 872-7282 Michigan City *(G-9804)*	Miller Machine & Welding ...... G ...... 812 882-7566 Vincennes *(G-13693)*
Egenolf Machine Inc ...... D ...... 317 787-5301 Indianapolis *(G-6814)*	J & J Welding Inc ...... E ...... 812 838-4391 Mount Vernon *(G-10396)*	Miller Welding & Mechanic Svc ...... G ...... 812 923-3359 Pekin *(G-11476)*
Englert & Meyer Corporation ...... G ...... 812 683-3540 Huntington *(G-6163)*	J A Smit Inc ...... G ...... 812 424-8141 Evansville *(G-3568)*	Misner Welding & Construction ...... G ...... 812 648-2980 Dugger *(G-2481)*
Ernstberger Enterprises Inc ...... D ...... 812 282-0488 Jeffersonville *(G-8358)*	Jar Welding & Machine Inc ...... G ...... 812 752-6253 Scottsburg *(G-12369)*	Mitchum-Schaefer Inc ...... D ...... 317 546-4081 Indianapolis *(G-7528)*
F T Moore and Sons Inc ...... G ...... 812 466-3762 Terre Haute *(G-13233)*	Jarrod Zachary Weld ...... G ...... 765 230-6424 Crawfordsville *(G-2164)*	Moores Welding Service Inc ...... G ...... 260 627-2177 Leo *(G-9244)*
Fabcreation ...... G ...... 812 246-6222 Sellersburg *(G-12394)*	Jerry Lambert ...... G ...... 765 378-7599 Daleville *(G-2340)*	Morris Machine & Tool ...... G ...... 219 866-3018 Rensselaer *(G-11932)*
Fancil Robert Welding Svc LLC ...... G ...... 574 267-8627 Warsaw *(G-13874)*	Joe Woodrow ...... G ...... 765 866-0436 New Market *(G-10963)*	Motsinger Auto Supply Inc ...... G ...... 317 782-8484 Indianapolis *(G-7549)*
Faulkner Fabricating Inc ...... F ...... 574 342-0022 Bourbon *(G-942)*	Johns Welding and Fabrication ...... G ...... 574 936-1702 Plymouth *(G-11697)*	N K Welding Products Inc ...... G ...... 260 424-1901 Fort Wayne *(G-4488)*
Fayette Welding Service Inc ...... G ...... 317 852-2929 Brownsburg *(G-1150)*	Johnsons Welding Service ...... G ...... 317 835-2438 Boggstown *(G-901)*	Nector Machine & Fabricating ...... G ...... 219 322-6878 Schererville *(G-12338)*
Flare Inc ...... G ...... 260 490-1101 Fort Wayne *(G-4265)*	Jomar Machining & Fabg Inc ...... E ...... 574 825-9837 Middlebury *(G-9897)*	Newlins Welding & Tank Maint ...... G ...... 765 245-2741 Montezuma *(G-10210)*

P
R
O
D
U
C
T

Nichols Mfg Co Inc .... F 219 696-8577
  Lowell *(G-9418)*

Noble County Welding Inc .... F 260 897-4082
  Avilla *(G-416)*

Northeast Machine & Tool Co .... G 317 823-6594
  Indianapolis *(G-7592)*

Northside Machining Inc .... G 812 683-3500
  Huntingburg *(G-6176)*

O & R Precision Grinding Inc .... E 260 368-9394
  Geneva *(G-5137)*

OBrien Jack & Pat Enterprises ...... G 765 653-5070
  Greencastle *(G-5470)*

OHM Automotive LLC .... G 812 879-5455
  Bloomington *(G-785)*

On Site Welding & Maintenance ..... G 812 755-4184
  Campbellsburg *(G-1280)*

Onyett Welding & Machine Inc ...... G 812 582-2999
  Petersburg *(G-11565)*

Overton & Sons TI & Die Co Inc .... E 317 831-4542
  Mooresville *(G-10331)*

Owens Machine & Welding .... G 574 583-9566
  Monticello *(G-10277)*

P & H Engineering Inc .... G 765 676-6323
  Jamestown *(G-8232)*

Pannell & Son Welding Inc .... G 765 948-3606
  Summitville *(G-13100)*

Peerless Pattern & Machine Co ..... G 765 477-7719
  Lafayette *(G-8979)*

Pierceton Welding & Fabg .... G 260 352-0106
  Silver Lake *(G-12678)*

Precision Pulse LLP .... G 765 472-6002
  Peru *(G-11540)*

Precision Tubes Inc .... G 317 783-2339
  Indianapolis *(G-7738)*

Precision Welding Corporation ...... G 260 637-5514
  Huntertown *(G-6144)*

Pro-Weld LLC .... G 219 922-8861
  Griffith *(G-5787)*

Pruett Manufacturing Co Inc .... F 812 234-9497
  Terre Haute *(G-13312)*

PSc Machining and Engrg Inc .... F 219 764-4270
  Portage *(G-11789)*

Pyramid Equipment .... F 219 778-2591
  Rolling Prairie *(G-12193)*

Pyramid Equipment .... G 219 778-4253
  Rolling Prairie *(G-12194)*

Quality Die Set Corp .... E 574 967-4411
  Logansport *(G-9361)*

Quints Welding .... G 574 936-9138
  Plymouth *(G-11718)*

R & A Goodman Enterprises .... G 765 296-3446
  Lafayette *(G-8987)*

R & M Welding & Fabricating Sp .... G 812 295-9130
  Loogootee *(G-9392)*

R & R Tool Manufacturing Inc .... E 219 362-1681
  La Porte *(G-8810)*

R & S Welding & Fabricating .... G 574 946-6816
  Winamac *(G-14319)*

Rabers Buggy Shop LLC .... G 812 486-3789
  Montgomery *(G-10239)*

Ready Machine Tool & Die Corp ..... E 765 825-3108
  Connersville *(G-2070)*

Red Forge Inc .... G 812 934-9641
  Batesville *(G-516)*

Rescom Management Systems Inc ... E 812 254-5641
  Washington *(G-14002)*

Richard Myers Mllwrght .... G 765 883-8177
  Russiaville *(G-12243)*

Robert L Wehr .... G 812 482-2673
  Jasper *(G-8302)*

Rods Welding Shop .... G 812 859-4250
  Coal City *(G-1744)*

Roembke Mfg & Design Inc .... E 260 622-4030
  Ossian *(G-11407)*

Rogers Engineering and Mfg Co ..... E 765 478-5444
  Cambridge City *(G-1261)*

Rons General Repair .... G 765 732-3805
  West College Corner *(G-14037)*

Rota Skipper Corporation .... F 708 331-0660
  Crown Point *(G-2298)*

S & S Service .... G 812 952-2306
  Lanesville *(G-9103)*

S-Tech Inc .... G 812 793-3506
  Crothersville *(G-2221)*

Saliwanchik & Sons Welding & F ... G 219 362-9009
  La Porte *(G-8815)*

Schenk Sons Wldg & Tree Svc In ... G 812 985-3954
  Mount Vernon *(G-10408)*

Schmucker Welding .... G 574 773-0456
  Bremen *(G-1021)*

Schuler Precision Tool LLC .... G 260 982-2704
  North Manchester *(G-11243)*

Seib Machine & Tool Co Inc .... G 812 453-6174
  Evansville *(G-3721)*

Seiler Excavating Inc .... G 260 925-0507
  Auburn *(G-355)*

Shoemaker Welding Co .... G 574 656-4412
  North Liberty *(G-11221)*

Six Mile Welding .... G 260 768-3126
  Lagrange *(G-9065)*

Slabaugh Welding LLC .... G 574 773-5410
  Milford *(G-9965)*

Smith Welding & Repair Service ..... G 260 563-0710
  Wabash *(G-13756)*

Southwest Welding .... G 574 862-4453
  Goshen *(G-5325)*

Specialty Welding & Machine .... G 812 969-2139
  Elizabeth *(G-2649)*

Stahl Welding Inc .... G 765 457-3386
  Kokomo *(G-8699)*

Star Engineering & Mch Co Inc ..... E 260 824-4825
  Bluffton *(G-894)*

Starkey Welding Inc .... G 765 932-2005
  Rushville *(G-12235)*

Steel Works Welding Inc .... F 812 268-0334
  Sullivan *(G-13095)*

Stolle Tool Inc .... F 765 935-5185
  Richmond *(G-12055)*

Stout Plastic Weld .... F 219 926-7622
  Chesterton *(G-1634)*

Summerlot Engineered Pdts Inc ..... F 812 466-7266
  Rosedale *(G-12206)*

Sun Engineering Inc .... E 219 962-1191
  Lake Station *(G-9078)*

Swags Welding Services LLC .... G 260 417-7510
  Churubusco *(G-1657)*

T & E Welding Inc .... F 812 324-0140
  Petersburg *(G-11570)*

TAS Welding & Gran Services LL .... G 765 210-4274
  Wabash *(G-13757)*

Technical Weighing Svcs Inc .... G 219 924-3433
  Griffith *(G-5792)*

Terrys Welding Inc .... G 765 742-4191
  Lafayette *(G-9009)*

Terrys Welding Inc .... G 765 564-3331
  Delphi *(G-2428)*

Thomas Cubit Inc .... G 219 933-0566
  Hammond *(G-5949)*

Thorntons Welding .... G 812 332-8564
  Bloomington *(G-841)*

Thrasher Welding and Mch Sp ...... G 260 475-5550
  Angola *(G-250)*

Titus Inc .... F 574 936-3345
  Plymouth *(G-11728)*

Toolcraft LLC .... E 260 749-0454
  Fort Wayne *(G-4692)*

Total Concepts Design Inc .... D 812 752-6534
  Scottsburg *(G-12384)*

Trade Line Fabricating Inc .... E 812 637-1444
  Lawrenceburg *(G-9159)*

Tri-Esco Inc .... G 765 446-7937
  Colburn *(G-1755)*

Tri-State Machine Co Inc .... F 812 479-3159
  Evansville *(G-3774)*

Tyco Welding .... G 812 988-8770
  Nashville *(G-10736)*

United Tool Company Inc .... F 260 563-3143
  Wabash *(G-13760)*

Vincennes Welding Co Inc .... F 812 882-9682
  Vincennes *(G-13712)*

Vision Machine Works Inc .... F 574 259-6500
  Mishawaka *(G-10148)*

Wagner Welding Incorporated ...... G 812 985-9929
  Evansville *(G-3808)*

Walts Welding & Fabricating .... G 812 637-5338
  West Harrison *(G-14044)*

Weld Done .... G 260 597-7237
  Ossian *(G-11415)*

Weldors Inc .... G 765 289-9074
  Muncie *(G-10582)*

Whitley Welding & Fabg & Repr ..... G 260 723-5111
  South Whitley *(G-13010)*

William F Shirley .... G 812 426-2599
  Evansville *(G-3813)*

Wilson Machine Shop Inc .... G 812 392-2774
  Elizabethtown *(G-2652)*

Wrib Manufacturing Inc .... G 765 294-2841
  Veedersburg *(G-13648)*

Yoders & Sons Repair Shop .... G 260 593-2727
  Topeka *(G-13433)*

Zimmer Welding Co .... G 317 632-5212
  Indianapolis *(G-8226)*

Zionsville Towing Inc .... G 317 873-4550
  Zionsville *(G-14474)*

WELDING SPLYS, EXC GASES: *Wholesalers*

Airgas Usa LLC .... F 260 749-9576
  Fort Wayne *(G-4051)*

Airgas Usa LLC .... G 812 362-7593
  Rockport *(G-12163)*

C F Slattery Steel Fabrication .... G 812 948-9167
  New Albany *(G-10756)*

Jar Welding & Machine Inc .... G 812 752-6253
  Scottsburg *(G-12369)*

Koehler Welding Supply Inc .... F 812 574-4103
  Madison *(G-9476)*

WELDMENTS

Lynn Tool Company Inc .... G 765 874-2471
  Lynn *(G-9430)*

WELL LOGGING EQPT

Lucas Oil Racing Inc .... F 812 738-1147
  Corydon *(G-2104)*

WESTERN APPAREL STORES

Cowpokes Inc .... E 765 642-3911
  Anderson *(G-91)*

WET CORN MILLING

Colorcon Inc .... E 317 545-6211
  Indianapolis *(G-6633)*

Ingredion Incorporated .... F 317 295-4122
  Indianapolis *(G-7229)*

Tate Lyle Ingrdnts Amricas LLC ..... B 765 474-5474
  Lafayette *(G-9007)*

Tate Lyle Ingrdnts Amricas LLC ..... D 765 448-7123
  Lafayette *(G-9008)*

WHEELCHAIR LIFTS

Adaptive Mobility Inc .... F 317 347-6400
  Indianapolis *(G-6323)*

Braun Corporation .... B 574 946-6153
  Winamac *(G-14301)*

Covidien LP .... C 317 837-8199
  Plainfield *(G-11602)*

Michiana Lift Equipment Inc .... G 574 257-1665
  Mishawaka *(G-10082)*

Portable Left Foot Accelerator ...... G 260 637-4447
  Fort Wayne *(G-4540)*

Thyssenkrupp Elevator Corp .... E 317 595-1125
  Indianapolis *(G-8074)*

Williams Bros Health Care Inc ...... E 812 257-2505
  Washington *(G-14007)*

Williams Bros Health Care Pha ...... B 812 254-2497
  Washington *(G-14008)*

Williams Bros Health Care Pha ...... E 812 335-0000
  Bloomington *(G-856)*

WHEELCHAIRS

Equippe Advanced Mobility .... G 317 807-6789
  Greenwood *(G-5692)*

Loving Care Ptnt/Wheelchair Tr ..... G 219 427-1137
  Merrillville *(G-9728)*

Mathes Home Care .... G 812 944-2211
  New Albany *(G-10823)*

Ms Wheelchair Indiana Inc .... G 317 408-0947
  Indianapolis *(G-7554)*

Rising Improvements LLC .... G 608 295-8301
  South Bend *(G-12917)*

Wheelchair Help LLC .... G 574 295-2220
  Elkhart *(G-3259)*

Wheelchair of Indiana .... G 317 627-6560
  Indianapolis *(G-8190)*

WHEELS

Act Systems International LLC .... F 812 437-4609
  Evansville *(G-3342)*

Best Tires & Wheels .... G 317 306-3379
  Franklin *(G-4872)*

Hoosier Wheel LLC .... G 812 421-6900
  Evansville *(G-3541)*

WHEELS & GRINDSTONES, EXC ARTIFICIAL: Abrasive

Calumet Abrasives Co Inc.................E....... 219 844-2695
  Hammond (G-5855)

WHEELS & PARTS

FTC Products Corp.....................G....... 219 567-2441
  Francesville (G-4813)
Miller Mfg Corp...............................E....... 574 773-4136
  Nappanee (G-10695)
Tire Rack Inc..................................B....... 888 541-1777
  South Bend (G-12972)
Transportation Tech Inds...................F....... 812 962-5000
  Evansville (G-3769)
Wheels 4 Tots Inc..........................G....... 219 987-6812
  Demotte (G-2452)

WHEELS: Abrasive

Sandusky Abrasive Wheel Co ....E....... 219 879-6601
  Michigan City (G-9840)

WHEELS: Buffing & Polishing

Osborn Intl......................................G....... 765 965-3722
  Richmond (G-12026)

WHEELS: Disc, Wheelbarrow, Stroller, Etc, Stamped Metal

Gleason Corporation ....C....... 574 533-1141
  Goshen (G-5226)
Hammer Industries Inc ....F....... 812 422-6953
  Evansville (G-3529)

WHIRLPOOL BATHS: Hydrotherapy

Kaldewei USA Inc ....G....... 866 822-2527
  Fishers (G-3936)
Oasis Lifestyle LLC.........................E....... 574 948-0004
  Plymouth (G-11708)

WHISTLES

Whistle Stop ....G....... 219 253-4100
  Monon (G-10180)

WICKING

Permawick Company Inc...................F....... 812 376-0703
  Columbus (G-1993)

WINCHES

Chads LLC......................................G....... 812 323-7377
  Ellettsville (G-3273)
My-Te Products Inc ....F....... 317 897-9880
  Indianapolis (G-7564)

WIND CHIMES

Lambright Country Chimes L L C.......G....... 260 768-9138
  Shipshewana (G-12629)

WINDINGS: Coil, Electronic

G G B Inc..G....... 219 733-2897
  Westville (G-14216)
Qp Inc...F....... 574 295-6884
  Elkhart (G-3125)
Warner Electric LLC.........................C....... 260 244-6183
  Columbia City (G-1846)

WINDMILLS: Electric Power Generation

Fowler Ridge II Wind Farm LLC...........E....... 713 354-2100
  Fowler (G-4799)
Infrastructure and Energy ....F....... 765 828-2580
  Indianapolis (G-7228)

WINDMILLS: Farm Type

BP Alternative Energy NA Inc ....G....... 765 884-1000
  Fowler (G-4796)
Millers Windmill Service...................G....... 574 825-2877
  Middlebury (G-9910)

WINDOW & DOOR FRAMES

Door Service Supply.........................G....... 317 496-0391
  Greenwood (G-5682)
Global Building Products LLC...........E....... 574 296-6868
  Elkhart (G-2882)

Imperial Products LLC......................D....... 765 966-0322
  Richmond (G-12001)
LCI Industries ....D....... 574 535-1125
  Elkhart (G-2989)
Quanex Homeshield LLC...................D....... 765 966-0322
  Richmond (G-12040)

WINDOW CLEANING SVCS

Crystal Clear Inc.............................G....... 317 753-5393
  Greenwood (G-5678)

WINDOW FRAMES & SASHES: Plastic

Graber Manufacturing LLC ....G....... 260 657-3400
  Grabill (G-5367)
Ilpea Industries Inc ....D....... 812 752-2526
  Scottsburg (G-12362)
Schlabach Window & Glass LLC.........G....... 765 628-2024
  Kokomo (G-8691)

WINDOW FRAMES, MOLDING & TRIM: Vinyl

Bee Window Incorporated..................C....... 317 283-8522
  Fishers (G-3876)
Home Guard Industries Inc.................D....... 260 627-6060
  Grabill (G-5372)
Keusch Glass Inc ....F....... 812 482-2566
  Jasper (G-8271)
Laird Plastics Inc ....G....... 317 890-1808
  Indianapolis (G-7375)
Wilmes Window Mfg Co Inc ....E....... 812 275-7575
  Ferdinand (G-3864)

WINDOWS, LOUVER: Metal

Classee Vinyl Windows LLC ....G....... 574 825-7863
  Middlebury (G-9875)

WINDOWS: Frames, Wood

Clear View Cstm Windows Doors.........G....... 812 877-1000
  Terre Haute (G-13212)
Dr Restorations Inc..........................G....... 317 646-7150
  Clermont (G-1712)

WINDOWS: Storm, Wood

Toms Interior Windows LLC ....G....... 574 233-0799
  South Bend (G-12974)

WINDOWS: Wood

Andersen Corporation.......................A....... 260 694-6861
  Poneto (G-11744)

WINE CELLARS, BONDED: Wine, Blended

Easley Enterprises Inc......................E....... 317 636-4516
  Indianapolis (G-6789)
Huber Orchards Inc..........................E....... 812 923-9463
  Borden (G-930)
Kenneth Fiekert...............................G....... 812 551-5122
  Rising Sun (G-12089)
Rain Song Farms LLC.......................G....... 317 640-4534
  Noblesville (G-11170)
Wine N Vine ....G....... 765 282-3300
  Muncie (G-10586)

WIRE

Group Dekko Inc ....D....... 260 357-3621
  Garrett (G-5009)
S & J Manufacturing LLC...................G....... 812 662-6640
  Greensburg (G-5632)
Tru-Form Steel & Wire Inc ....E....... 765 348-5001
  Hartford City (G-5993)

WIRE & CABLE: Nonferrous, Building

Belden Inc.......................................A....... 765 962-7561
  Richmond (G-11962)
Essex Group Inc..............................B....... 260 461-4000
  Fort Wayne (G-4244)
Essex Group Inc..............................D....... 260 248-5500
  Columbia City (G-1785)

WIRE & WIRE PRDTS

Abz Corp...G....... 317 758-2699
  Sheridan (G-12587)
Accel International ....F....... 260 897-9990
  Avilla (G-400)
Accent Wire Products........................G....... 765 628-3587
  Greentown (G-5643)

American Wire Rope & Sling of...........G....... 877 634-2545
  Indianapolis (G-6392)
Angola Wire Products Inc...................C....... 260 665-9447
  Angola (G-192)
Angola Wire Products Inc...................E....... 260 665-3061
  Angola (G-193)
Belden Inc.......................................A....... 765 962-7561
  Richmond (G-11962)
Bender Products Inc..........................E....... 574 255-5350
  Mishawaka (G-10009)
Benthall Bros Inc.............................E....... 800 488-5995
  Evansville (G-3372)
Breyden Products Inc........................E....... 260 244-2995
  Columbia City (G-1767)
Cmj & Associates Corporation............G....... 765 962-1947
  Richmond (G-11970)
Commercial Group Lifting Pdts...........G....... 219 944-7200
  Gary (G-5039)
Elevator Equipment Corporation..........D....... 765 966-7761
  Richmond (G-11981)
Essex Group Inc..............................D....... 260 248-5500
  Columbia City (G-1785)
F D Ramsey & Co Inc........................F....... 219 362-2452
  La Porte (G-8757)
Fab Solutions LLC............................G....... 765 744-2671
  Redkey (G-11897)
Group Dekko Holdings Inc..................G....... 260 347-0700
  Garrett (G-5011)
Hessville Cable & Sling Co ....E....... 773 768-8181
  Gary (G-5064)
Hewitt Manufacturing Company...........F....... 765 525-9829
  Waldron (G-13799)
Kingsford Products Inc......................G....... 740 862-4450
  Decatur (G-2389)
Lake Cable of Indiana LLC.................C....... 847 238-3000
  Valparaiso (G-13569)
Lauck Manufacturing Co Inc...............F....... 317 787-6269
  Indianapolis (G-7385)
Macpactor Inc..................................G....... 502 643-7845
  Jeffersonville (G-8393)
Meese Inc..D....... 812 273-1008
  Madison (G-9485)
Mid-West Metal Products Co Inc ....E....... 888 741-1044
  Muncie (G-10521)
Mid-West Spring Mfg Co ....D....... 574 353-1409
  Mentone (G-9688)
Myers Spring Co Inc.........................E....... 574 753-5105
  Logansport (G-9357)
Noble Wire Products Inc....................G....... 317 773-1926
  Orland (G-11354)
Outtadaway LLC...............................G....... 219 866-8885
  Rensselaer (G-11934)
Precision Products Group Inc ....B....... 330 698-4711
  Indianapolis (G-6276)
Pwt Group LLC.................................E....... 260 490-6477
  Fort Wayne (G-4565)
R & R Engineering Co Inc...................E....... 765 536-2331
  Summitville (G-13102)
Reelcraft Industries Inc.....................C....... 855 634-9109
  Columbia City (G-1824)
S & S Industry & Manufacturing...........F....... 219 963-0213
  Lake Station (G-9076)
Sanlo Inc...D....... 219 879-0241
  Michigan City (G-9841)
Tubular Engrg & Sls Co Inc.................F....... 765 536-2225
  Summitville (G-13108)
Valley Tool & Die Stampings..............E....... 574 722-4566
  Logansport (G-9375)
Vans Iron Works...............................G....... 219 934-1935
  Munster (G-10636)
Winamac Coil Spring Inc....................C....... 574 653-2186
  Kewanna (G-8528)
Wire-Tek Inc....................................G....... 812 623-8300
  Sunman (G-13121)

WIRE FABRIC: Welded Steel

Four Star Field Services.....................G....... 812 354-9995
  Petersburg (G-11563)
Warren Power Attachments ....G....... 317 892-4737
  Pittsboro (G-11589)

WIRE MATERIALS: Copper

Cerro Wire LLC.................................D....... 812 793-2929
  Crothersville (G-2217)
E M F Corp......................................E....... 260 488-2479
  Hamilton (G-5821)
International Wire Group Inc.................D....... 574 546-4680
  Bremen (G-1005)
Lake Copper Conductors LLC.............F....... 847 238-3000
  Elkhart (G-2983)

PRODUCT

REA Magnet Wire Company Inc...........B...... 765 477-8000
Lafayette (G-8989)

WIRE MATERIALS: Steel

Accel International..................F...... 260 897-9990
Avilla (G-400)
Belden Inc.............................A...... 765 962-7561
Richmond (G-11962)
Best Weld Inc........................F...... 765 641-7720
Anderson (G-74)
Cablecraft Motion Controls LLC...........B...... 260 749-5105
New Haven (G-10933)
Essex Group Inc......................C...... 260 424-1708
Fort Wayne (G-4248)
Essex Group Inc......................D...... 260 248-5500
Columbia City (G-1785)
Fort Wayne Metals RES Pdts...........F...... 260 747-4154
Fort Wayne (G-4275)
Hammond Steel Components LLC.......G...... 630 816-1343
Hammond (G-5888)
Kingsford Products Inc................G...... 740 862-4450
Decatur (G-2389)
Madsen Wire LLC.....................E...... 260 829-6561
Orland (G-11353)
Mayfield-Glenn Group Inc.............F...... 219 393-7117
Kingsbury (G-8541)
Merchants Metals Inc.................F...... 317 783-7678
Indianapolis (G-7480)
Metal Technologies Auburn LLC........G...... 260 925-4717
Auburn (G-344)
Nippon Steel & Sumikin...............G...... 219 228-0110
Shelbyville (G-12555)
Precision Battery Fabricat.............G...... 260 563-5138
Wabash (G-13751)
Pwt Group LLC........................E...... 260 490-6477
Fort Wayne (G-4565)
REA Magnet Wire Company Inc...........B...... 765 477-8000
Lafayette (G-8989)
Shivom Jay Steels Intl LLC............G...... 574 271-7222
Granger (G-5434)
Suggs Custom Design Solutions.........G...... 574 549-2174
Elkhart (G-3197)
Truckpro LLC.........................F...... 765 482-6525
Lebanon (G-9230)
Wolfpack Chassis LLC.................E...... 260 349-1887
Kendallville (G-8514)

WIRE PRDTS: Ferrous Or Iron, Made In Wiredrawing Plants

A-1 Wire Tech Inc....................D...... 815 226-0477
Elkhart (G-2660)
E H Baare Corporation................G...... 765 778-7895
Anderson (G-103)

WIRE PRDTS: Steel & Iron

Spiral-Fab Inc........................G...... 812 427-3006
Vevay (G-13665)

WIRE ROPE CENTERS

Sandin Mfg Inc.......................D...... 219 872-2253
Michigan City (G-9839)

WIRE: Communication

Belden Wire & Cable Co LLC...........B...... 606 348-8433
Richmond (G-11963)
Essex Group Inc......................C...... 260 461-4000
Fort Wayne (G-4243)
General Cable Industries Inc..........B...... 765 664-2321
Marion (G-9524)
General Cable Industries Inc..........E...... 317 271-8447
Indianapolis (G-6994)
Telamon Corporation.................C...... 317 818-6888
Carmel (G-1488)
Wire America Inc.....................E...... 260 969-1700
Fort Wayne (G-4758)

WIRE: Magnet

Alconex Specialty Products...........D...... 260 744-3446
Fort Wayne (G-4056)
Elektrisola Incorporated..............G...... 317 375-8192
Indianapolis (G-6819)
Essex Group Inc......................C...... 260 461-4183
Fort Wayne (G-4245)
Essex Group Inc......................G...... 704 598-0222
Fort Wayne (G-4247)
Essex Group Inc......................E...... 317 738-4365
Franklin (G-4885)

WIRE: Mesh

Spaceguard Inc.......................E...... 812 523-3044
Seymour (G-12492)

WIRE: Nonferrous

Accel International..................F...... 260 897-9990
Avilla (G-400)
Almega/Tru-Flex Inc.................E...... 574 546-2113
Bremen (G-982)
Belden 1993 LLC.....................C...... 606 348-8433
Richmond (G-11961)
Belden Inc...........................C...... 317 818-6300
Indianapolis (G-6262)
Cerro Wire LLC.......................D...... 812 793-2929
Crothersville (G-2217)
Essex Group Inc......................G...... 260 461-4994
Fort Wayne (G-4246)
Essex Group Inc......................D...... 260 248-5500
Columbia City (G-1786)
General Cable Industries Inc..........E...... 317 271-8447
Indianapolis (G-6993)
Installed Building Pdts LLC............G...... 317 398-3216
Shelbyville (G-12539)
International Wire Group Inc...........D...... 574 546-4680
Bremen (G-1005)
Latch Gard Co Inc....................G...... 574 862-2373
Elkhart (G-2986)
REA Magnet Wire Company Inc...........B...... 260 421-5400
Fort Wayne (G-4580)
REA Magnet Wire Company Inc...........B...... 765 477-8000
Lafayette (G-8989)
Sanlo Inc............................D...... 219 879-0241
Michigan City (G-9841)

WIRE: Nonferrous, Appliance Fixture

Indy Wiring Services LLC.............G...... 317 371-7044
Brownsburg (G-1155)

WIRE: Steel, Insulated Or Armored

Fort Wayne Metals Res Pdts...........E...... 260 747-4154
Fort Wayne (G-4273)
Fort Wayne Metals Res Pdts...........C...... 260 747-4154
Fort Wayne (G-4274)
Kokoku Wire Industries Corp...........E...... 574 287-5610
South Bend (G-12829)
Mid-West Metal Products Co Inc.......F...... 765 741-3140
Muncie (G-10522)
Midwest Bale Ties Inc................F...... 765 364-0113
Crawfordsville (G-2172)

WOMEN'S & CHILDREN'S CLOTHING WHOLESALERS, NEC

Hoogies Sports House Inc.............G...... 574 533-9875
Goshen (G-5238)
Ram Graphics Inc....................E...... 765 724-7783
Alexandria (G-48)
Springhill Wholesale Inc..............E...... 812 299-2181
Terre Haute (G-13342)

WOMEN'S & GIRLS' SPORTSWEAR WHOLESALERS

Arizona Sport Shirts Inc..............E...... 317 481-2160
Indianapolis (G-6419)
Locoli Inc...........................E...... 219 365-3125
Schererville (G-12332)
Meditation Company.................G...... 574 217-3157
South Bend (G-12859)
Sport Form Inc.......................G...... 260 589-2200
Berne (G-625)

WOMEN'S CLOTHING STORES

CM Reed LLC.........................G...... 517 546-4100
Greendale (G-5485)

WOOD & WOOD BY-PRDTS, WHOLESALE

Core Wood Components LLC............G...... 574 370-4457
Elkhart (G-2774)
Serie Hardwoods Inc.................G...... 765 275-2321
Attica (G-309)

WOOD PRDTS

Esarey Hardwood Creations LLC.........G...... 419 610-6486
New Albany (G-10773)

FDS Northwood LLC...................G...... 765 289-2481
Selma (G-12423)
Hardwoods By Bill LLC................G...... 219 465-5346
Valparaiso (G-13554)
J R Newby............................G...... 765 664-3501
Marion (G-9537)
North Woods Village.................G...... 574 247-1866
Mishawaka (G-10097)
Southern Indiana Sawmill LLC..........G...... 502 664-5723
Salem (G-12305)
Touchwood Trans Inc.................C...... 317 941-0009
Indianapolis (G-8083)
Wildwood Floral Co LLC...............G...... 916 220-4900
Indianapolis (G-8197)
Woodhollow LLC.....................G...... 219 384-2802
Highland (G-6060)
Woodland Lbor Rltons Cnsulting........G...... 219 879-6095
Michigan City (G-9861)
Woodland Restoration LLC.............G...... 219 509-3078
Hebron (G-6025)

WOOD PRDTS: Applicators

Fort Wayne Box & Pallet LLC..........G...... 260 409-4067
Fort Wayne (G-4270)
Hilltop Wood Working.................F...... 270 604-1962
Madison (G-9467)
Natures Woodshop LLC...............G...... 317 691-1462
Indianapolis (G-7577)
Voges Restoration and Wdwkg.........G...... 812 299-1546
Terre Haute (G-13364)

WOOD PRDTS: Battery Separators

Daramic LLC.........................C...... 812 738-8274
Corydon (G-2097)

WOOD PRDTS: Brackets

Lana Hudelson.......................E...... 812 865-3951
Orleans (G-11363)

WOOD PRDTS: Bungs

Patrick Industries Inc................D...... 574 522-6100
Elkhart (G-3086)

WOOD PRDTS: Hampers, Laundry

WC Redmon Co Inc...................F...... 765 473-6683
Peru (G-11556)

WOOD PRDTS: Letters

Display Craft........................G...... 260 726-4535
Portland (G-11816)

WOOD PRDTS: Mantels

Architectural Accents Inc.............F...... 219 922-9333
Munster (G-10596)
R P Wakefield Company Inc............E...... 260 837-8841
Waterloo (G-14022)
Shamrock Cabinets Inc...............E...... 812 482-7969
Jasper (G-8308)

WOOD PRDTS: Moldings, Unfinished & Prefinished

Barkman Custom Woodworking.........F...... 574 773-9212
Nappanee (G-10652)
Beaver Mouldings LLC................G...... 260 463-4822
Lagrange (G-9033)
Branik Inc...........................G...... 260 467-1808
Fort Wayne (G-4117)
By-Pass Paint Shop Inc...............F...... 574 264-5334
Elkhart (G-2740)
Champion Wood Products Inc..........D...... 812 282-9460
Sellersburg (G-12391)
Cornerstone Moulding Inc.............E...... 574 546-4249
Bremen (G-992)
Indiana Lumber Inc...................G...... 812 837-9493
Bloomington (G-746)
Knapke & Sons Inc...................E...... 260 639-0112
Hoagland (G-6065)
Mervin Knepps Molding...............G...... 812 486-2971
Montgomery (G-10235)
Mullet Custom Interiors LLC...........F...... 574 773-9442
Nappanee (G-10696)
New Style of Crossroads LLC..........F...... 260 593-3800
Topeka (G-13424)
Nickell Moulding Company Inc..........C...... 574 295-5223
Elkhart (G-3063)

Ubelhor Construction Inc ....F 812 357-2220
Bristow (G-1095)
Warsaw Foundry Company Inc ....D..... 574 267-8772
Warsaw (G-13962)
Woodwright Door & Trim Inc ....G..... 574 522-1667
Elkhart (G-3267)

WOOD PRDTS: Mulch Or Sawdust

Earth First Kentuckiana Inc ....G..... 812 248-0712
Charlestown (G-1565)
Earth First Kentuckiana Inc ....G..... 812 923-1227
Greenville (G-5648)
Greencycle of Indiana Inc ....G..... 317 780-8175
Indianapolis (G-7043)
Greencycle of Indiana Inc ....G..... 317 769-5668
Whitestown (G-14253)

WOOD PRDTS: Mulch, Wood & Bark

Clm Pallet Recycling Inc ....G..... 317 485-4080
Fortville (G-4770)
Green Thumb of Indiana Inc ....G..... 260 897-2319
Avilla (G-405)
Ostler Enterprises Inc...............G..... 765 656-1275
Frankfort (G-4847)
Pgc Mulch LLC ....G..... 812 455-0700
Evansville (G-3667)

WOOD PRDTS: Outdoor, Structural

Better Built Barns Inc ....G..... 812 477-2001
Evansville (G-3382)
Classic Baluster LLC ....F..... 765 344-1619
Brazil (G-957)
Modular Green Systems LLC...............G..... 260 547-4121
Craigville (G-2123)
Tangent Rail Products Inc ....E..... 812 789-5331
Winslow (G-14361)

WOOD PRDTS: Panel Work

Cac Wall Panels LP ....G..... 260 437-4003
Harlan (G-5967)
Grabill Cabinet Company Inc...............C..... 877 472-2782
Grabill (G-5368)
Kerkhoff Associates Inc ....E..... 765 583-4491
Otterbein (G-11419)

WOOD PRDTS: Porch Work

Burkes Garden Wood Pdts LLC ....F..... 765 344-1724
Brazil (G-955)

WOOD PRDTS: Shoe & Boot Prdts

Bendix Mc II ....G..... 260 356-9720
Huntington (G-6192)

WOOD PRDTS: Signboards

Cin-Nan Treasures ....G..... 574 533-6593
Goshen (G-5187)

WOOD PRDTS: Spokes

Rabers Whl Works & Buggy Works ......G..... 812 486-2786
Montgomery (G-10240)

WOOD PRDTS: Trim

Daniel Bontrager ....G..... 574 825-5656
Goshen (G-5198)
Jrs Wood Shop...............G..... 765 498-2663
Kingman (G-8532)
Pro-Form Plastics Inc ....E..... 812 522-4433
Crothersville (G-2220)
Tartan Properties LLC ....G..... 317 714-7337
Indianapolis (G-8037)

WOOD PRDTS: Trophy Bases

Deer Ridgewood Craft LLC...............G..... 812 535-3744
West Terre Haute (G-14124)
Dynamic Designs Scottys ....G..... 219 809-7268
Michigan City (G-9787)
Schug Awards LLC ....G..... 765 447-0002
Lafayette (G-8996)

WOOD PRODUCTS: Reconstituted

Good Earth Compost LLC...............G..... 812 824-7928
Bloomington (G-732)
Greif Inc ....G..... 219 746-3753
Lowell (G-9407)
Michiana Column & Truss LLC ....G..... 574 862-2828
Wakarusa (G-13787)
Patrick Industries Inc...............C..... 574 294-7511
Elkhart (G-3080)
Patrick Industries Inc...............E..... 574 294-5758
Elkhart (G-3083)

WOOD TREATING: Creosoting

Steinkamp Warehouses Inc ....E..... 812 683-3860
Huntingburg (G-6179)

WOOD TREATING: Structural Lumber & Timber

Birch Wood ....G..... 260 432-0011
Fort Wayne (G-4110)
Chinet Company ....G..... 219 989-7040
Hammond (G-5861)
Jefferson Homebuilders Inc...............E..... 317 398-0874
Shelbyville (G-12541)
Rodeghero Enterprise ....G..... 574 935-0568
Plymouth (G-11723)

WOOD TREATING: Vehicle Lumber

Madelyn Harwood Inc ....G..... 317 839-7890
Plainfield (G-11622)

WOOD TREATING: Wood Prdts, Creosoted

Bridgewell Resources LLC ....G..... 812 285-1811
Jeffersonville (G-8331)
Frederick Tool Corp ....E..... 574 295-6700
Elkhart (G-2870)
Hampels Woodland Products ....G..... 574 293-2124
Elkhart (G-2906)
Pumpkin Patch Market Inc ....G..... 574 825-3312
Middlebury (G-9915)

WOODWORK & TRIM: Interior & Ornamental

Custom Interior Dynamics LLC ....F..... 317 632-0477
Indianapolis (G-6714)
Ed Lloyd Co ....G..... 812 342-2505
Columbus (G-1917)
L & L Woodworking LLC ....G..... 574 535-4613
Nappanee (G-10690)
M & M Trim Inc...............G..... 317 791-7009
Indianapolis (G-7430)
Miter Craft Inc...............G..... 317 462-3621
Greenfield (G-5555)
Real Wood Works ....G..... 812 277-1462
Bedford (G-571)
Woods Enterprises ....G..... 574 232-7449
South Bend (G-12992)

WOODWORK: Carved & Turned

Weberdings Carving Shop Inc...............F..... 812 934-3710
Batesville (G-524)
Woods of Amber ....G..... 765 763-6926
Morristown (G-10376)

WOODWORK: Interior & Ornamental, NEC

Borkholder Lavon ....G..... 574 773-3714
Nappanee (G-10655)
Burks Door & Sash Inc ....F..... 317 844-2484
Carmel (G-1324)
Chris Schwartz ....G..... 260 615-9574
Grabill (G-5360)
Custom Millwork & Display LLC...............G..... 574 289-9772
South Bend (G-12749)
Fischer Woodcraft Inc ....G..... 317 627-6035
Beech Grove (G-594)
Fischer Woodworking Inc ....G..... 812 985-9488
Mount Vernon (G-10392)
Guys Wood N Things...............G..... 812 689-0433
Holton (G-6107)
Hurst Jeff Custom Woodworking...............G..... 812 367-1430
Ferdinand (G-3853)
JC Treeations Inc ....G..... 219 322-2911
Schererville (G-12325)
John Gebhart Woodworkings...............G..... 765 492-3898
Cayuga (G-1521)
Kleeman Cabinetry ....G..... 812 926-0428
Aurora (G-382)
Tinchers Creative Woodworks ....G..... 765 344-0062
Rockville (G-12181)
Van Go Inc ....G..... 574 862-2807
Shipshewana (G-12656)
Wittmer Woodworking LLC ....G..... 812 486-3115
Montgomery (G-10248)

WOVEN WIRE PRDTS, NEC

Beal Systems Inc ....G..... 260 693-0772
Laotto (G-9104)
Bridon-American Corporation ....E..... 812 749-3115
Oakland City (G-11309)
Wirco Inc...............C..... 260 897-3768
Avilla (G-422)

WREATHS: Artificial

Dj Wreath Creations LLC...............G..... 317 723-3268
Indianapolis (G-6754)
Jadco Ltd ....F..... 219 661-2065
Crown Point (G-2265)

X-RAY EQPT & TUBES

CXR Company Inc...............F..... 574 269-6020
Warsaw (G-13862)

X-RAY EQPT REPAIR SVCS

CXR Company Inc...............F..... 574 269-6020
Warsaw (G-13862)

YARN MILLS: Texturizing, Throwing & Twisting

BP Wind Energy North Amer Inc ....G..... 765 884-1000
Fowler (G-4797)

YARN WHOLESALERS

U-Nitt LLC ....G..... 812 251-9980
Carmel (G-1499)

YARN: Animal Fiber, Spun

Three Points Alpaca Farm LLC...............G..... 812 363-3876
Batesville (G-520)

PRODUCT